CAMBRIDGE BIOGRAPHICAL DICTIONARY

CAMBRIDGE BIOGRAPHICAL DICTIONARY

General Editor
Magnus Magnusson, KBE

Assistant Editor
Rosemary Goring

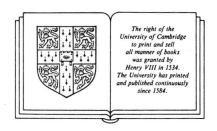

The right of the University of Cambridge to print and sell all manner of books was granted by Henry VIII in 1534. The University has printed and published continuously since 1584.

CAMBRIDGE UNIVERSITY PRESS

CAMBRIDGE NEW YORK
PORT CHESTER MELBOURNE SYDNEY

Published by the Press Syndicate of the University of Cambridge
The Pitt Building, Trumpington Street, Cambridge CB2 1RP
40 West 20th Street, New York, NY 10011, USA
10 Stamford Road, Oakleigh, Melbourne 3166, Australia

Published in the UK by W & R Chambers
under the title *Chambers Biographical Dictionary*
Published in North America by agreement
under the title *Cambridge Biographical Dictionary*
Reprinted 1990

Printed in the United States of America

Library of Congress Cataloging in Publication Data

Chambers biographical dictionary
Cambridge biographical dictionary
"Published in the U.K. under the title Chambers biographical dictionary" – Verso t.p.
1. Biography – Dictionaries. I. Magnusson, Magnus. II. Goring, Rosemary. III. Title.
CT103.C4 1990 920.02 90-1542
ISBN 0 521 39518-6 (U.S.)

ISBN 0 521 39518 6 hardback

PREFACE

Previous editions of the *Cambridge Biographical Dictionary* held a unique and highly respected place among the jostling ranks of biographical literature. When the dictionary was first published in 1897, its aim was to cover a wide and colourful spectrum of figures, those either in the public eye, or of historical importance: in the words of its editors 'to give all the little Somebodies and many of the great Nobodies'.

Our aspirations with this, the latest edition have been similar to those of the original compilers. We have, however, been faced with the increasingly complicated challenge of reflecting the growing number of areas in which people are making their mark, and the proliferation in the past few years of household names, from Rubik and Streep to Jacuzzi and Cleese.

Such a wealth of candidates for inclusion posed obvious problems of selection, but we have tried to keep to the basic criteria of achievement and recognition. On these grounds the top names almost selected themselves; inevitably, though, some of our decisions have been subjective, and for that we take full responsibility.

One of our priorities for this edition was to broaden the work's international coverage. We have also focused far more attention on women, at the same time giving greater prominence to 20th-century figures and to personalities from more popular spheres such as sports, media and jazz.

With the enthusiastic help of more than eighty subject specialists, and the technological aid of intricate and omnivorous computers, we have extensively revised and updated the existing material, in many cases re-evaluating entries in the light of recent research, and at times discarding names which we considered to be of less relevance today than in the past.

This new edition contains a third more entries than previously, thereby illuminating a vaster gallery of portraits. Entries aim to give the essential outline of a person's life and achievement; and to facilitate cross-referencing we have added the feature of bold highlighting for the names of people mentioned in the text who have their own entries in the book.

We accept that, despite all our efforts to ensure complete accuracy, a few errors must have slipped past us, and we would be grateful for having these brought to our attention.

The hard work which has gone into making this edition does not end on publication day. Instead the *Cambridge Biographical Dictionary* is an ever-evolving project which, between each subsequent edition, will be constantly updated and revised to meet the demands and changes of modern society.

Magnus Magnusson

ACKNOWLEDGMENTS

Many people have assisted us in the preparation of this work. The full list of specialist contributors is printed on pages ix–xi and to all of them we would like to express our thanks for their painstaking work. But there are others who have also given us valuable assistance. Our friends and colleagues on the staff of W & R Chambers, Edinburgh, have been unfailingly generous with their help and advice. Other friends with particular enthusiasms have plied us with useful suggestions for entries.

At the risk of being invidious, we would like to single out the inspiration provided by Owen Dudley Edwards and Irene Scobbie of Edinburgh University. We were also given tireless assistance by the reference staff at Edinburgh Central Library and the National Library of Scotland, particularly by Alan Taylor and Margaret Deas.

For a variety of individual entries and advice we would like to thank: Kirstin Asp-Johnsson; Francesca Calvocoressi; Dr Islay Donaldson; Professor Ronald Edwards; Dr Jeanette Greenfield; Dr Nicholas Hammond; Alastair Hawkyard; Kathlyn Henderson; Dr A Heymowski; Enid James; David L Jones; Marjo Kalo; Dr Hugh Kennedy; Professor Simon Lavington; Gerry Maher; David Masters; Professor Sidney Michaelson; Michael Nath; William Schell; Rev William Storrar; Boswell Taylor; Kevin Thomas; Baroness White; Suzie Wong.

We would also like to thank Bruce Campbell, Dr Phil Robertson and Dr Maurice Shepherd of St Andrews University for carrying out the daunting task of setting up and monitoring the computerization of this project.

CONTRIBUTORS

Aeronautics
Prof John E Allen
Visiting Professor of Aerospace Design
College of Aeronautics
Cranfield

Ancient History
Dr Michel Austin
Senior Lecturer
Department of Ancient History
St Andrews University

Anthropology
Dr Timothy Ingold
Senior Lecturer
Department of Social Anthropology
Manchester University

Archaeology
Dr Peter Richards
Reference Editor
Cambridge University Press

Architecture
Simon Green
Assistant Curator
National Monument Record of Scotland

Dr Deborah Mays
Inspector
Historic Buildings and Monuments, Scotland

Art
Patrick Elliott
Research Assistant
Scottish National Gallery of Modern Art

Ralph Hughes
Teacher of Art History
Fettes College, Edinburgh

Dr David Mannings
Lecturer
Department of the History of Art
Aberdeen University

Ruth Pelzer
Language Teacher, Artist and Freelance Writer

Gillian Tait
Conservation Officer
Conservation Bureau
Scottish Development Agency

Andrew Gibbon Williams
Artist and Art Critic

Australia
James Orton
Writer and Editor

Biology
Prof Ian Millar
Emeritus Professor of Chemistry
Keele University

Margaret Millar
Freelance Writer and Science Contributor

Dr Alwyne Wheeler
Natural Historian and Honorary Research Associate
Epping Forest Conservation Centre

Botany
Prof William Stearn
Botanical Consultant and Author

Business, Finance and Economics
Ian Hinton
Lecturer
Kingston Regional Management Centre
Kingston Polytechnic

Roger Oldcorn
Senior Tutor
Henley – The Management College

Cartoons
Denis Gifford
Writer

Chess
John Linklater
Literary Editor
The Glasgow Herald

Classical Music
Derek Watson
Composer, Writer and Broadcaster

Computing
Dr Geoffrey Tweedale
Research Fellow
National Archive for the
History of Computing,
Manchester

Crafts
Thomas Wilson
Managing Director
The Open Eye Gallery, Edinburgh

Crime
Dr Francis Rose
Fellow of St John's College
Cambridge University

Kristina Woolnough
Freelance Journalist

Dance
Alice Bain
Editor and Arts Journalist

Donald Hutera
Freelance Arts Journalist,
Performer and Administrator

Design
Graham Leake
Lecturer in Design History
Edinburgh College of Art

Early Modern History
David Bond
Lecturer
Department of Modern History
Essex University

Education
Prof Gordon Batho
Emeritus Professor of Education
Durham University

Prof Eric Hawkins
Professor Emeritus
York University

Engineering
Ronald Birse
Lecturer
Department of Civil Engineering
Edinburgh University

Film and Media
Allan Hunter
Freelance Journalist and Film Critic

Folk Music
Alastair Clark
Journalist

Geography
Michael Wood
Senior Lecturer
Department of Geography
Aberdeen University

Historiography
Owen Dudley Edwards
Reader
Department of History
Edinburgh University

Invention
Ronald Birse
Lecturer
Department of Civil Engineering
Edinburgh University

Jazz
Anthony Troon
Journalist

Law
Professor David Walker
Regius Professor Emeritus of Law
Glasgow University

Linguistics
George Davidson
Reference Editor
formerly Lecturer in Linguistics
Robert Gordon's Institute of Technology
Aberdeen

Literature
Alan Taylor
Literary Journalist

S H Burton (Shakespeare entry)
Author of *Shakespeare's Life and Stage*

Mathematics
Christopher Shaddock
Senior Lecturer
Department of Mathematics
Edinburgh University

Medicine
Dr William F Bynum
Reader in the History of Medicine
University College London

Medieval English History
David Corner
Lecturer
Department of Medieval History
St Andrews University

Medieval International History
Dr Richard de Lavigne
Lecturer
Department of Medieval History
St Andrews University

Dr Alan Murray
Assistant Editor
International Medieval Bibliography
Leeds University

Military and Naval History
Rear Admiral Edward Gueritz
Defence Consultant and Research Adviser

Modern History
Alan Palmer
Historian, writer and
former Head of History
Highgate School, London

Philosophy
Dr Jeremy Mynott
Editorial Director
Cambridge University Press

Photography
Bernard Happé
Technical Author and Consultant in Motion Picture Technology

Physics
Prof Ian Millar
Emeritus Professor of Chemistry
Keele University

Margaret Millar
Freelance Writer and Science Contributor

Politics
Dr Denis Derbyshire
Political and Communications Consultant

Dr Ian Derbyshire
Post-Doctoral Research Fellow
Cambridge University

Owen Dudley Edwards
Reader
Department of History
Edinburgh University

Pop and Rock
Ian Bell
Journalist

Trevor Pake
Freelance Journalist and Rock Critic

Psychology
Dr David Milner
Lecturer
Department of Psychology
St Andrews University

Religion
Dr James D Douglas
Lecturer
Singapore Bible College

Dr Philip Hillyer
Freelance Theological Editor and Author

Scandinavia
Peter Graves
Lecturer
Department of Scandinavian Studies
Edinburgh University

Irene Scobbie
Reader and Head of Department
Department of Scandinavian Studies
Edinburgh University

Bjarne Thorup Thomsen
Lecturer
Department of Scandinavian Studies
Edinburgh University

Scottish History
Dr Michael Lynch
Senior Lecturer
Department of Scottish History
Edinburgh University

Sociology
Susan Allen-Mills
formerly Social Sciences Editor
Cambridge University Press

Sport
Stuart Bathgate
Freelance Journalist

Bob Crampsey
Writer and Broadcaster

Keith Daniell
Sports Journalist and Broadcaster
Central Television

Theatre
Sarah Hemming
Arts Journalist

Peter Whitebrook
Journalist and Writer

Travel
Shane Winser
Information Officer
Royal Geographical Society

A

AALTO, (Hugo Henrik) Alvar (1898–1976) Finnish architect and designer, the father of Modernism in Scandinavia. Born in Kuortane, he studied at Helsinki Polytechnic and evolved a unique architectural style based on irregular and asymmetric forms and the imaginative use of natural materials. He designed numerous public and industrial buildings in Finland, including the sanatorium at Paimio, the library at Viipuri, the Sunila pulp mill at Kotka and the Finlandia concert hall in Helsinki. In the USA he built the Baker House hall of residence at the Massachusetts Institute of Technology; in Iceland, he designed the Nordic Centre in Reykjavík (1968). In the 1930s he also pioneered the use of factory-made laminated birchwood for a distinctive style of Finnish furniture.

AALTONEN, Wäinö (Valdemar) (1894–1966) Finnish sculptor, born in St Mårtens, studied at Helsinki. One of the leading Finnish sculptors, he was the most versatile, and worked in many styles. His best-known works are the bust of **Sibelius** (in the Gothenburg Museum) and the statue of the Olympic runner **Paavo Nurmi** (commissioned by the Finnish government in 1924).

AARON (15th–13th century BC) biblical patriarch and elder brother of **Moses**, first high-priest of the Israelites and said to be the founder of the priesthood. He was spokesman for Moses to the Egyptian pharoah in his attempts to lead their people out of Egypt, and performed various miracles with his rod. Later he gave in to the demands of the rebellious Israelites in the desert and organized the making of a Golden Calf for idolatrous worship. He and his sons were ordained as priests after the construction of the Ark of the Covenant and the Tabernacle, and Aaron was confirmed as hereditary high-priest by the miracle of his rod blossoming into an almond tree (hence various plants nicknamed 'Aaron's Rod'). He is said to have died at the age of 123.

AARON, Hank (Henry Lewis) (1934–) American baseball player, born in Mobile, Alabama, and one of the greatest batters ever. A right-handed batting outfielder, he set almost every batting record in his 23-season career with the Milwaukee Braves and the Milwaukee Brewers: 2297 runs batted in, 1477 extra-base hits, and 755 home runs (he broke **'Babe' Ruth**'s long-standing record of 714 on 8 April 1974). In 1956 he was named the Most Valuable Player (MVP), leading the Braves to the World Series Championship.

AASEN, Ivar Andreas (1813–96) Norwegian philologist, lexicographer and writer, born in Sunmøre, the son of a peasant. A fervent nationalist, he was the creator of the 'national language' called *Landsmål* (later known as *Nynorsk*, 'New Norwegian'), based on western Norwegian dialects. He announced in 1836 that he planned 'an independent and national language' based on a synthesis of rural dialects descended from Old Norse, to replace the official Dano-Norwegian *Riksmål* ('language of the realm'). It eventually achieved recognition alongside *Riksmål* in 1885. He published a *Grammar of the Norwegian Dialects* in 1848, followed by a *Dictionary of the Norwegian Dialects* in 1850. He died in Christiania (Oslo), and was buried with public honours.

ABAKANOWICZ, Magdalena (1930–) Polish artist, born in Falenty, near Warsaw. Her privileged upbringing was cut short by the Nazi invasion of Poland and the subsequent Russian 'liberation'. Educated at the Warsaw Academy of Fine Arts (1950–55) during the repressive period of Socialist Realism, she sought to escape from conventional art forms through weaving. In 1956 she married Jan Kosmowski. In the 1960s she achieved international recognition with her monumental abstract woven fibre installations called 'Abakans'. She later abandoned weaving in favour of primitive and disturbing figurative groups made from burlap sacking. In 1978 she took part in the pioneering exhibition 'Soft Art' in Zürich, and in 1980 represented Poland at the Venice Biennale. Since 1965 she has taught at the State College of Arts, Poznan, becoming professor in 1979.

ABALKIN, Leonid Ivanovitch (1930–) Soviet economist. Director of the Institute of Economics of the USSR Academy of Sciences and member of the Supreme Soviet of the USSR with special responsibility for economic affairs, his published works centre on the theoretical problems of political economy under socialism.

ABATI See **ABBATE**

ABAUZIT, Firmin (1679–1767) French Protestant theologian and philosopher, born in Uzès in Languedoc. On the revocation of the Edict of Nantes (1685) he was sent to Geneva, where he became widely erudite. He travelled in Holland and England in 1698, and died at Geneva, having published many theological and archaeological treatises.

ABB, St See **EBBA**

ABBAS, Ferhat (1899–1955) Algerian nationalist leader who headed the Algerian government-in-exile before independence from France in 1962. Born in Taher in the Kabylie country, he founded a Muslim Students' Association in 1924, before becoming a chemist. He served as a volunteer in the French army in 1939, but after France's defeat he produced in 1942 a 'Manifesto of the Algerian People'. In 1955 he joined the 'Front de Libération Nationale' (FLN), the main Algerian resistance organization, and worked with **Ben Bella** in Cairo, before founding in 1958 a 'Provisional Government of the Algerian Republic' in Tunis. After independence, he was appointed president of the National Constituent Assembly but fell out of favour and was exiled. He was rehabilitated shortly before his death.

ABBAS HILMI, Pasha (1874–1943) the last khedive of Egypt, 1892–1914. He succeeded his father, Tewfik Pasha, and attempted to rule independently of British influence; at the outbreak of war in 1914 he sided with Turkey and was deposed when the British made Egypt a protectorate.

ABBĀS I THE GREAT (1571–1629) fifth Safavid shah of Persia. After his accession (1587) he set about establishing a counterweight to the Turkmen tribal chiefs who under his father Muhammad Khudābanda had constituted the principal political and military powers in the state, and whose propensity for feuding was a major cause of instability. This was achieved by the creation of a standing army drawn especially from

Caucasian prisoners and immigrants and financed by an increase in the extent of the crown lands. From 1598 he was able to recover Azerbaijan and parts of Armenia from the Ottomans, and Khurasan from the Uzbeks. He transferred his capital from Qazvin to Isfahan, which he developed with a major programme of public works, and established diplomatic and economic relations with western Europe.

ABBAS MIRZA (c.1783–1833) prince of Persia, favourite son of Shah Feth-Ali. He commanded the Persian armies with great bravery but little success in wars with Russia (1811–13 and 1826–28), losing Persian provinces in the Caucasus and Armenia.

ABBAS PASHA (1813–54) khedive of Egypt from 1848. A grandson of the great **Mehemet 'Ali**, he took an active part in his grandfather's Syrian war, but later did much to undo the progress made under him, for example by blocking the construction of the Suez Canal.

'ABBASIDS an Arab dynasty which traced its descent from **al-'Abbās**, an uncle of the prophet **Muhammad**, and which held the caliphate from 749 to 1258. The 'Abbasids were swept to power by the Hashimiya (from Hāshim, grandfather of al-'Abbās and great-grandfather of Muhammad), a revolutionary movement which opposed the rule of the **Umayyads** and demanded that government should reside in the hands of the prophet's own family. In 747 an uprising in the province of Khurasan led by the Hashimite representative Abū Muslim found strong support throughout Persia and Iraq, and after the proclamation of Abū'l'Abbās al-Saffāh (d.754), great-great-grandson of al-'Abbās, as caliph (749), his forces defeated the Umayyad Marwān II and his Syrian troops at the Great Zab (750). Al-Saffāh's brother **al-Mansūr** firmly established 'Abbasid rule, and was succeeded in turn by his own son al-Mahdī (c.744–785), and grandson al-Hādī (764–86). The age of **Hārūn al-Rashīd** and his son al-Ma'mūn (786–833) was the apogee of the 'Abbasid caliphate, which ruled an empire stretching from North Africa to Central Asia, with its capital at Baghdad. Yet from this time the 'Abbasids became increasingly unable to prevent the fragmentation of the Muslim polity. In the 10th century a rival caliphate, the **Fatimids**, took over North Africa and Egypt, while the caliphs themselves fell under the domination of the Persian Buyids (945–1055) and then of the Turkish **Seljuks**. Eventually al-Nāsir (c.1155–1225), who reigned from 1180, recovered some independence and re-established the 'Abbasids as a regional power in Iraq, but his successors were unable to withstand the onslaught of the Mongols. The capture of Baghdad by the khan Hülegü (1258) and the subsequent execution of al-Musta'sim, effectively ended the 'Abbasid caliphate, although his uncle, al-Mustansir, was carried off to Cairo by Baybars, sultan of Egypt (1261), where the family continued to hold a titular caliphate under Mamluk tutelage until the Ottoman conquest (1517).

ABBATE, Niccolo dell' (c.1512–1571) Italian fresco painter of Modena, who died in Paris, having executed frescoes for the palace of Fontainebleau. Few of his frescoes are extant, but the Louvre has a collection of his drawings.

ABBE, Cleveland (1838–1916) American meteorologist, born in New York. He wrote on the atmosphere and on climate, and was responsible for the introduction of the US system of Standard Time.

ABBE, Ernst (1840–1905) German physicist, born in Eisenach. He became professor at the University of Jena in 1870, and in 1878 director of the astronomical and meteorological observatories. He was a partner in the optical works of **Carl Zeiss**, on whose death he became owner in 1888. Famous for his researches in optics, he was inventor of the arrangement known as Abbe's homogeneous immersion.

ABBEY, Edwin Austin (1852–1911) American painter and illustrator, born in Philadelphia, but settled in England in 1878. He is known for his illustrations of the works of **Shakespeare** and **Robert Herrick**, for his panels of the *Quest of the Holy Grail* in Boston public library, and for his picture of **Edward VII**'s coronation.

ABBOT, Charles See **COLCHESTER, LORD**

ABBOT, Charles Greely (1872–1973) American astrophysicist, born in Wilton, New Hampshire. As director of the Astrophysical Observatory at the Smithsonian Institution (1907–44), he did important research on solar radiation. He became the 'grand old man' of American solar physics, published many books, and devised an apparatus for converting solar energy to power just before his 100th birthday.

ABBOT, Ezra (1819–94) American biblical scholar, born in Jackson, Maine. Professor at Harvard, he was on the committee for the revision of the English text of the Bible.

ABBOT, George (1562–1633) English prelate, son of a Guildford cloth worker. Educated at Balliol College, Oxford, he obtained a fellowship in 1583; through **Thomas Sackville**'s influence he rose to be master of University College (1597), dean of Winchester (1600), and thrice vice-chancellor of Oxford University (1600–05). He owed his promotion to the sees of Lichfield (1609), London (1610), and finally Canterbury (1611) to the Earl of Dunbar. A sincere but narrow-minded calvinist, he was equally opposed to Catholics and to heretics. He died at Croydon and was buried at Guildford, where in 1619 he had founded a hospital. His brother Robert (1560–1617), from 1615 bishop of Salisbury, was a learned theologian.

ABBOTT, Charles See **TENTERDEN**

ABBOTT, Diane Julie (1953–) British politician. Educated at Harrow City Girls' School and Newnham College, Cambridge, she was an administration trainee in the civil service before working for the National Council for Civil Liberties, the Greater London Council (GLC) and Lambeth Borough Council. She joined the Labour party in 1981 and served on the Westminster City Council 1982–86. Elected to parliament as MP for Hackney North and Stoke Newington in 1987, she became the first black woman member of the House of Commons.

ABBOTT, George (1887–) American director, producer and playwright, born in New York. He began his career in 1913 as an actor, but made his name as a writer and a Broadway director and producer. He wrote his first play, *The Head of the Family*, for the Harvard Dramatic Club in 1912, and continued his career in New York, establishing himself with *The Fall Guy* (co-written with James Gleason), in 1925. He subsequently wrote and co-wrote almost 50 plays and musicals, among them *Love 'em and Leave 'em* (1925); *Three Men on a Horse* (1935); *On Your Toes* (with Richard Rodgers and Lorenz Hart, 1936); *The Boys from Syracuse* (based on *The Comedy of Errors*, 1938), *The Pajama Game* (with Richard Bissell, 1954), and *Damn Yankees* (1955). In addition to an illustrious career as a producer, he directed over 100 theatrical pieces, among them Rodgers and Hart's *Pal Joey* and *On Your Toes*, and **Irving Berlin**'s *Call Me Madam*. He won six Tony awards for his work.

ABBOTT, Jacob (1803–79) American clergyman, born in Hallowell, Maine. He founded Mount Vernon School for Girls in Boston (1829) and was the author of *The Young Christian* (1832) and innumerable other works. His son Lyman Abbott (1835–1922), born in

Roxbury, Massachusetts, succeeded **Henry Ward Beecher** at Plymouth Congregational Church, Brooklyn, in 1890, edited *The Outlook*, and wrote *Christianity and Social Problems* (1897), *The Spirit of Democracy* (1910, *Reminiscences* (1915), *Silhouettes of my Contemporaries* (1922), and other books.

ABD-AL-LATIF See **ABD-UL-LATIF**

ABD-AR-RAHMĀN I (731–88) an **Umayyad,** survived the massacre of his family by the **'Abbasids** (750), and conquered most of Muslim Spain, founding the emirate of al-Andalus (756) with its capital at Cordoba.

ABD-AR-RAHMĀN II (792–852) emir of Cordoba, ruled from 822, was a patron of the arts and of architecture.

ABD-AR-RAHMĀN III (891–961) emir of Cordoba, ruled from 912 and proclaimed himself caliph in 929. Under him the Umayyad emirate reached the peak of its power, extending its boundaries in successful campaigns against the **Fatimids** and the kings of Leon and Navarre.

ABD-AR-RAHMĀN (d.732) Saracen leader, defeated and killed by **Charles Martel** at the battle of Tours.

ABD-AR-RAHMĀN (1778–1859) sultan of Fez and Morocco, succeeded his uncle in 1822, and was involved in **Abd-el-Kader**'s war against the French in Algeria. His subjects' piracy brought risk of war with more than one European state.

ABD-AR-RAHMĀN (c.1840–1901) emir of Afghanistan, and grandson of **Dost Mohammed Khan**. Driven into exile in Russia in 1869, he was brought back and proclaimed emir with British support in 1880. He consolidated his power and arranged for the withdrawal of British troops, leaving Britain in control of foreign affairs, and in 1893 subscribed to the Durand Line as the India-Afghanistan border.

ABD-EL-KADER (1807–83) Algerian nationalist hero, born in Mascara. After the French conquest of Algiers the Arab tribes of Oran elected him as their emir; and with great perseverance and skill he waged his long struggle with the French (1832–47). In 1834 he forced General Desmichels to a treaty; and in June 1835 he severely defeated a large French army at Makta. Eventually crushed by overpowering force, he took refuge in Morocco and began a crusade against the enemies of Islam, but was defeated at Isly in 1844. He surrendered in 1847 and was sent to France, and afterwards lived in Brusa and Damascus, where he died.

ABD-EL-KRIM (1880–1963) Moroccan Berber chief known as the 'Wolf of the Rif Mountains'. After a career in the Spanish colonial government in Morocco he led unsuccessful revolts against Spain and France in 1921 and 1924–25. He formed the Republic of the Rif and served as its president (1921–26), but was brought to surrender by a large Franco-Spanish army under Marshal **Pétain**. He was exiled to the island of Réunion; granted amnesty in 1947, he went to Egypt where he formed the North African Liberation Committee.

ABDUL-AZIZ (1830–76) sultan of Turkey from 1861, successor to his brother **Abd-ul-Medjid**. He continued his brother's liberal and westernizing reforms, promulgated the first Ottoman civil code, and visited western Europe (1871). Thereafter he became more autocratic, and after revolts in Bosnia, Herzegovina and Bulgaria he was forced to abdicate, and was found dead five days later.

ABD-UL-HAMID II (1842–1918) the last sultan of Turkey (1876–1909). Known as the 'Great Assassin', he was the second son of Sultan **Abd-ul-Medjid** and successor to his brother Murad V. He promulgated the first Ottoman constitution in 1876, but his reign was notable for his cruel suppression of revolts in the Balkans, which led to wars with Russia (1877–78), and especially for the appalling Armenian massacres of 1894–96. He suspended the constitution in 1878 and ruled autocratically. Revolts in Crete in 1896–97 led to war with Greece. Later a reform movement by the revolutionary Young Turks forced him to restore the constitution and summon a parliament in 1908, but he was deposed and exiled in 1909.

ABDULLAH, Sheikh Mohammed (1905–82) Kashmiri politician. A Muslim, he spearheaded the struggle for constitutional government against the (Hindu) Maharajah of Kashmir during the inter-war years. He was imprisoned in 1931 and on his release formed the All Jammu and Kashmir Moslem Conference (renamed the National Conference in 1938). Popularly known as the 'Lion of Kashmir', Sheikh Abdullah was again imprisoned in 1946 after launching the 'Quit Kashmir' movement, but released and appointed chief minister in 1947 in an emergency administration. He agreed to the accession of the state to India to halt tribal infiltration, but was charged with treason and imprisoned again, from 1953 to 1968, when he reaffirmed the right of the people of Kashmir 'to decide the future of the State'. He was chief minister again from 1975 until his death. His son, Dr Farooq Abdullah (1937–), succeeded him.

ABDULLAH IBN HUSSEIN (1882–1951) first king of Jordan (1946–51), the second son of **Hussein ibn Ali** and grandfather of King **Hussein**. He took a prominent part in the Arab revolt against Turkey (1916–18), becoming emir of the British mandated territory of Transjordania in 1921; he became king when the mandate ended in 1946, but was assassinated.

ABD-UL-LATIF (1162–1231) Arabian writer, born in Baghdad. He taught medicine and philosophy at Cairo and Damascus. His best-known book is a work on Egypt.

ABD-UL-MEDJID (1823–61) sultan of Turkey from 1839, successor to his father **Mahmud II**. He continued the reforms of the previous reign, reorganizing the court system and education, and granting various rights to citizens, including Christians. In 1850 he chivalrously refused to give up the Hungarian political refugee **Lajos Kossuth** to the Habsburgs. In 1854 he secured an alliance with Britain and France to resist Russian demands, thus precipitating the Crimean War (1854–56); but thereafter the Ottoman Empire was increasingly weakened by financial difficulties and internal nationalist problems.

ABDUL RAHMAN, Tunka Putra (1903–) Malaysian statesman. The son of the sultan of Kedah, he trained as a lawyer at Cambridge and joined the civil service in his home state of Kedah in 1931, becoming a public prosecutor in 1949, after passing his bar exams in London. In 1945 he founded the United Malays' National Organisation (UMNO) and in 1952 was nominated to the executive and legislative councils of the Federation of Malaya, becoming chief minister in 1955 and prime minister in 1957. He negotiated the formation of the Federation of Malaysia between 1961 and 1962 and remained prime minister of the enlarged entity. After the outbreak of violent anti-Chinese riots in Kuala Lumpur, he withdrew from active politics in 1970.

ABE, Kobo (1924–) Japanese novelist and playwright, born in Tokyo. He trained as a doctor, but turned to literature after graduating. Recognition in Japan came with the award of the Akutagawa prize for *The Wall* in 1951. His international reputation is often linked with that of pre-war writers like Tanizaki and **Kawabata**, and post-war writers such as **Mishima**, but unlike them he stands outside the great tradition of Japanese literature. His predominant theme of alienation is explored in a series of novels and plays, his early work set in the wasteland of Manchuria and post-war Japan; in later books he focuses on an urban, industrialized society on the brink of explosive economic growth. His novels include *Inter Ice Age Four* (1971), *The Woman in the Dunes* (1965) and *Secret Rendezvous* (1980).

À BECKET, Thomas See **BECKET**

À BECKETT, Gilbert Abbott (1811–56) English humorist, born in London. He was educated at Westminster and in 1841 was called to the bar. In 1849 he became a metropolitan police magistrate. As well as writing for *Punch*, and *The Times*, he was the author of *Quizziology of the British Drama*, *The Comic Blackstone*, and comic histories of England and Rome.

ABEGG, Richard (1869–1910) German chemist, born in Danzig. At Breslau, he was one of the first chemists to perceive the chemical significance of the newly-discovered (1897) electron, and his 'rule of eight' (1904) concerning the electric basis of linkages between atoms was an important stage in the development of modern valency theory. He died in a ballooning accident.

ABEL, Sir Frederick Augustus (1827–1902) English scientist, born in London, the inventor (with Sir **James Dewar**) of cordite. As chemist to the war department and ordnance committees (1854–88), he applied himself to the science of explosives. As well as cordite, he introduced a new method of making gun-cotton, and invented the Abel tester for determining the flash-point of petroleum. He wrote *Gun-cotton* (1866), *Electricity Applied to Explosive Purposes* (1884), etc, and became secretary of the Imperial Institute in 1887.

ABEL, John Jacob (1857–1938) American biochemist, born in Cleveland, Ohio, the son of a farmer. He studied at Johns Hopkins and widely in Europe before returning to Johns Hopkins as its first professor of pharmacology (1893–1932). He studied the hormone adrenaline as early as 1897, and in 1926 first crystallized insulin and showed it to be a protein. In 1914 he showed that blood contains amino acids, by dialysis through cellophane; this work also led the way towards dialysis in the treatment of kidney disease.

ABEL, Karl Friedrich (1725–87) German musician, born in Köthen, a noted composer of symphonies and a virtuoso on the viola-da-gamba. In 1758 he went to England, where he was appointed chamber musician to Queen **Charlotte**. With **Johann Christian Bach** he promoted a celebrated series of concerts in London.

ABEL, Niels Henrik (1802–29) Norwegian mathematician, born in Finnøy. He showed mathematical genius by the age of 15, entered Oslo University in 1821, and in 1823 proved that there was no algebraic formula for the solution of a general polynomial equation of the 5th degree. Such a formula had been sought ever since the cubic and quartic equations had been solved in the 16th century by **Girolamo Cardano** and others. He developed the concept of elliptic functions independently of **Carl Gustav Jacobi**, and the theory of Abelian integrals and functions became a central theme of later 19th-century analysis, although his work was not fully understood in his lifetime.

ABELARD, Peter (1079–1142) French philosopher and scholar, born near Nantes, in Brittany, the eldest son of a noble Breton house. He studied under **Johannes Roscellinus** at Tours and **William of Champeaux** in Paris. He enjoyed great success as a teacher and educator, and in 1115 was appointed lecturer in the cathedral school of Notre Dame in Paris, where he became tutor to Héloïse, the beautiful and talented 17-year-old niece of the canon Fulbert with whom he was lodging. They fell passionately in love, but when their affair was discovered, Fulbert threw Abelard out of the house. They fled to Brittany, where Héloïse gave birth to a son, Astrolabe, and returned to Paris, where they were secretly married. Héloïse's furious relatives took their revenge on Abelard by breaking into his bedroom one night and castrating him. Abelard fled in shame to the abbey of St Denis to become a monk, and Héloïse took the veil at Argenteuil as a nun. In 1121, a synod at Soissons condemned his Nominalistic doctrines on the Trinity as heretical, and Abelard took to a hermit's hut at Nogent-sur-Seine, where his pupils helped him build a monastic school he named the Paraclete. In 1125 he was elected abbot of St Gildas-de-Rhuys in Britanny, and the Paraclete was given to Héloïse and a sisterhood. Abelard and Héloïse compiled a famous collection of their correspondence. His other works include *Sic et non* (a compilation of apparently contradictory biblical and patristic citations resolved according to the rules of logic), *Nosce te ipsum* (an account of his ethical system) and *Historia Calamitatum Mearum* ('The Story of my Troubles'). In his final years he was again accused of numerous heresies and he retired to the monastery of Cluny; he died at the priory of St Marcel, near Chalon. His remains were taken to the Paraclete at Héloïse's request, and when she died in 1164 she was laid in the same tomb. In 1800 their ashes were taken to Paris, and in 1817 they were buried in one sepulchre at Père Lachaise.

ABELES, Sir (Emil Herbert) Peter (1924–) Hungarian-born Australian industrialist, born and educated in Budapest. He arrived in Sydney in 1949. The following year he founded Alltrans, which in 1967 merged with Thomas Nationwide Transport (TNT). Under Abeles' leadership TNT expanded into all forms of road transport, air courier services and containerized and bulk shipping. TNT is now active on all continents, and is developing links with local operators in Eastern Europe, South America and in China. In 1979 TNT and **Rupert Murdoch**'s News Limited gained control of Ansett Airlines, one of Australia's two internal airlines, and Abeles became joint managing director of the new company. He was knighted in 1972.

ABELL, Kjeld (1901–61) Danish radical playwright, known for his innovative stage designs and effects. His plays include *Melodien der blev vaek* (The Melody That Got Lost, 1935), *Anna Sophie Hedvig* (1939), and *Silkeborg* (1946).

ABELSON, Phillip Hauge (1913–) American physical chemist, born in Tacoma, Washington. He did major work on the project which led to the first atomic bomb. Educated at Washington State College and the University of California at Berkeley, he was appointed director of the geophysics laboratory of the Carnegie Institution, Washington in 1953 (president 1971). In 1940 he assisted **Edwin Mattison McMillan** to bombard uranium with neutrons, which led to the discovery of a new element, neptunium, the first element discovered to be heavier than uranium. From 1941 he worked on the Manhattan atomic bomb project, devising a cheap method for making uranium hexafluoride, and then developing diffusion methods for obtaining enriched uranium-235; this was the fuel for the first A-bomb.

ABENCERRAGES (from the Arabic for 'saddler's son'), a noble Moorish family which came to Spain in the 8th century, famous in legend for their feud with another Moorish family (the Zegris) which led to their massacre in the Alhambra by the king of Granada, Abu al-Hasan or his son, **Boabdil**, in the 1480s. The massacre was the theme of a romance by **Chateau-**

briand, **Dryden**'s *Conquest of Granada*, and an opera by **Cherubini**.

ABERCROMBIE, Lascelles (1881–1938) English poet and critic, born in Ashton-on-Mersey, the son of a stockbroker. Educated at Malvern College and Victoria University, Manchester, he became professor of English at Leeds (1922) and London (1929), and reader at Oxford (1935). His works include *The Idea of Great Poetry* (1925), *Romanticism* (1926) and *Principles of Literary Criticism* (1932). He published several volumes of Georgian-style poetry, collected as *The Poems of Lascelles Abercrombie* (1930).

ABERCROMBIE, Sir (Leslie) Patrick (1879–1957) English architect, and pioneer of town planning in Britain, brother of the poet **Lascelles Abercrombie**. He was professor of town planning at Liverpool (1915–35) and University College, London (1935–46). His major work was the replanning of London (*County of London Plan*, 1943, and *Greater London Plan*, 1944), and he was consultant for the replanning of many other cities, including Bath, Doncaster, Dublin, Edinburgh, Hull, Plymouth, and Sheffield. He was also much involved in the policy of creating post-war new towns.

ABERCROMBY, Sir Ralph (1734–1801) Scottish soldier, and hero of the Napoleonic wars. Born in Menstrie in Clackmannanshire, he went to Rugby School and studied law at Edinburgh and Leipzig. He joined the 3rd Dragoons in 1756 and served in Europe in the Seven Years' War (1756–63). He was MP for Clackmannanshire from 1774 to 1780. Rejoining the army in 1793 he distinguished himself as a major-general in Flanders under **Frederick, Duke of York**, and led successful operations against the French in St Lucia and Trinidad (1795–96). He held commands in Ireland and Scotland (1797–99), and in 1800 he was in command in the Mediterranean to deal with the French army left by **Napoleon** in Egypt; he led the successful amphibious operation of the Anglo-Turkish forces against the French at Aboukir Bay in 1801, but was mortally wounded in the action.

ABERDARE, Henry Austin Bruce, 1st Baron (1815–95) Welsh politician and statesman, born in Duffryn, Aberdare, Glamorganshire. He was called to the bar in 1837, and was Liberal member of parliament for Merthyr Tydfil from 1852 to 1873. Home secretary under **Gladstone** (1868–73), he was lord president of the council in 1873–74. He was closely interested in education and chaired the committee whose report led to the Welsh Intermediate Education Act of 1889. He was influential in the movement for the establishment of the University of Wales and became the first chancellor in 1895.

ABERDEEN, George Gordon, 1st Earl of (1637–1720) Scottish lawyer and statesman, created earl in 1682. An outstanding lawyer he was lord chancellor of Scotland (1662–84) and was appointed a lord of session in 1680. He was a strong supporter of the Act of Union with England in 1707.

ABERDEEN, George Hamilton Gordon, 4th Earl of (1784–1860) Scottish statesman, and prime minister of Britain 1852–55, born in Edinburgh. Educated at Harrow, he became Lord Haddo at the age of seven when his father died; his joint guardians were **William Pitt** the Younger and **Henry Dundas**, 1st Viscount Melville. He succeeded his grandfather as earl in 1801, was elected a Scottish representative peer in 1806, and in 1813 was sent as special ambassador to Vienna to negotiate the Treaty of Töplitz that created the alliance of Great Powers against **Napoleon**. He was foreign secretary twice, under the Duke of **Wellington** (1828–30) and then Sir **Robert Peel** (1841–46), during which time he saw to the conclusion of the Chinese War, established an *entente cordiale* with France, and cemented relations with the USA. A confirmed free-trader, he resigned with Peel over the repeal of the corn-laws in 1846. In 1852, on the resignation of Lord **Derby**, he was made prime minister of a coalition government that was immensely popular at first, until he reluctantly committed Britain to an alliance with France and Turkey in the Crimean War in 1854. The gross mismanagement of the war aroused popular discontent, and he was forced to resign in February 1855.

ABERDEEN, James Campbell Hamilton Gordon, 7th Earl of, and **1st Marquis** (1847–1934) Scottish statesman and laird of Haddo House in Aberdeenshire for 64 years. He was appointed viceroy of Ireland twice (1886, and 1905–15), governor of Canada (1893–98), and made a marquis in 1915. In 1877 he married the dynamic Ishbel-Maria Marjoribanks (1857–1939), youngest daughter of the 1st Lord Tweedmouth. She had a profound interest in the position of women and the Irish peasantry, and also wrote books on Canada (1894) and tuberculosis (1908). She and her husband turned Haddo House into a model estate for the local community, and published a delightful book of reminiscences in 1925 (*We twa*').

ABERHART, William (1878–1943) Canadian politician, born in Huron County, Ontario. He was educated at Queen's University, and in 1915 became principal of Crescent Heights School, Calgary, where he remained till 1935, when he became a member of the Alberta legislature, forming his own Social Credit party and becoming premier in the same year. In 1937 he admitted that he could not carry out his pledge of giving each Albertan a 'dividend' of $5 monthly on the province's natural resources, but he was returned to power in 1940.

ABERNETHY, John (1764–1831) British surgeon, celebrated for eccentric lectures and manners, born in London. He was apprenticed to the assistant surgeon at St Bartholomew's Hospital in 1779 and in 1787 was himself elected assistant surgeon, and soon after began to lecture. After initial diffidence as a lecturer, his power soon developed, and his lectures attracted large crowds. In 1813 he was appointed surgeon to Christ's Hospital, in 1814 professor of anatomy and surgery to the College of Surgeons, and in 1815 full surgeon to St Bartholomew's, a post which he resigned in 1829. His practice increased with his celebrity, which the eccentricity and rudeness of his manners helped to heighten. Of his works the most important is his *Constitutional Origin and Treatment of Local Diseases* (1809).

ABINGTON, William See **HABINGTON**

ABINGTON, Frances, née **Barton** (1737–1815) English actress. She was flower girl, street singer, milliner, and kitchenmaid before making her first appearance on the stage at the Haymarket in 1755. She rose to fame in Dublin after 1759 and subsequently returned to Drury Lane under **Garrick**. Extremely versatile, she excelled not only in the parts of **Shakespeare**'s heroines but also in a great variety of comedy roles (Lady Teazle, Polly Peachum, Lucy Lockit). **Reynolds** painted her portrait as Miss Prue in *Love for Love*.

ABNEY, Sir William de Wiveleslie (1844–1920) English chemist and educationist, born in Derby. Assistant secretary (1899) and adviser (1903) to the board of education, he was known for his researches in photographic chemistry and colour photography, and did important pioneer work in photographing the solar spectrum.

ABOUT, Edmond François Valentin (1828–85) French author, born in Dieuze, in Lorraine. After schooling in Paris, he studied archaeology in Athens. On returning to Paris, he devoted himself to a literary career. His works include *Le Roi des montagnes* (1856), *Madelon* (1863), *Alsace* (1872), which cost him a week's imprisonment at the hands of the Germans, and *Le Roman d'un brave homme* (1880).

ABRAHAM (c.2000–1650 BC) revered in the Old Testament as the father of the Hebrew people. According to *Genesis* he came from the Sumerian town of Ur ('Ur of the Chaldees') in modern Iraq, and migrated with his family and flocks via Haran (the ancient city of Mari on the Euphrates) to the 'Promised Land' of Canaan, where he settled at Shechem (modern Nablus). After a sojourn in Egypt, he lived to be 175 years old, and was buried with his first wife Sarah in the cave of Machpelah in Hebron. By Sarah he was the father of Isaac (whom he was prepared to sacrifice at the behest of the Lord) and grandfather of **Jacob** ('Israel'); by his second wife Hagar (Sarah's Egyptian handmaiden) he was the father of **Ishmael**, the ancestor of twelve clans; by his third wife Keturah he had six sons who became the ancestors of the Arab tribes. He was also the uncle of **Lot**. Abraham is traditionally regarded as the father of the three great monotheistic religions: Judaism, Christianity and Islam.

ABRAHAM, Sir Edward Penley (1913–) English biochemist, born in Southampton. He was educated at King Edward VI School, Southampton, and Queen's College, at Oxford, and was professor of chemical pathology at Oxford from 1964 to 1980. He had a major role in early studies on the penicillins and especially on the cephalosporin antibiotics.

ABRAHAM, William, known as **'Mabon'** (1842–1922) Welsh trade unionist and politician, born in Cwmavon, Glamorganshire. A leading figure in the miners' union in South Wales, he was a strong advocate of sliding-scale agreements whereby wages were regulated by the selling price of coal, and also a believer in compromise with the coal-owners. His influence declined with the miners' strike in 1898 and the replacement of the sliding-scale agreements by collective bargaining. He was elected as MP for the Rhondda from 1885 to 1918 and for the West Rhondda division, 1918–20, and devoted himself to mining legislation.

ABRAHAM-A-SANTA-CLARA, real name **Ulrich Megerle** (1644–1709) German monk and preacher, born in Kreenheinstetten. He became an Augustinian prior in 1662, and court preacher at Vienna in 1677. A popular but eccentric figure, he wrote several satirical devotional works.

ABRAMS, Creighton Williams (1914–74) American soldier, born in Springfield, Massachusetts. He graduated from West Point, and commanded a tank battalion in World War II. After service in the Korean War (1950–53), he commanded the federal troops during the race riots in Mississippi and Alabama (1962–63). Vice-chief of the US army from 1964 to 1967, he succeeded Westmoreland as commander of the US forces in Vietnam (1968–72), and supervised the gradual withdrawal of American troops. He was army chief of staff from 1972 to 1974.

ABRUZZI, Luigi Amedeo Giuseppe Mario Fernando Francesco de Savoia-Aosta, Duke (1873–1933) Italian explorer and naval officer. A cousin of **Victor Emmanuel III**, he was noted for his Alaskan, Himalayan, and African climbs, and his expedition to 86° 33′ N in 1899. He commanded the Italian navy, 1914–17.

ABSALOM (11th century BC) third and favourite son of King **David** of Israel in the Old Testament. A handsome, vain young man, he rebelled against his father and drove him from Jerusalem; but in an ensuing battle he was defeated, and as he was fleeing on a mule his hair was caught in the branch of an oak tree, leaving him dangling in the air, and he was despatched by Joab (II Samuel, 18).

ABSALON, or **Axel** (1128–1201) Danish prelate and statesman, and founder of the city of Copenhagen. The foster-brother of **Valdemar I, the Great** whom he helped to the throne in 1157, he was appointed bishop of Roskilde (1158) and elected archbishop of Lund (1177). As chief minister to Valdemar he led an army against the Wends in 1169 and extended Danish territories in the Baltic by capturing Rügen. In 1169 he built a fortress at Havn which became the nucleus of Copenhagen. As chief minister to Knut VI he led an expedition in 1184 that captured Mecklenburg and Pomerania. As archbishop he was largely responsible for the systematization of Danish ecclesiastical law.

ABSE, Dannie (1923–) Welsh writer and physician, born in Cardiff. Educated at the Welsh National School of Medicine, King's College, London and Westminster Hospital, he has been senior specialist in the chest clinic at the Central Medical Establishment, London, since 1954. His literary output includes nine volumes of poetry, two novels and half a dozen plays. His autobiographical volumes are *A Poet in the Family* (1974) and *A Strong Dose of Myself* (1982), and the autobiographical novel *Ash on a Young Man's Sleeve* (1954).

ABU AL-FARAJ AL-ISFAHANI (897–967) Arabic scholar and literary historian, in Baghdad. His greatest work, *Al-Aghani*, is a treasury of Arabic song and poetry.

ABU AL-FARAJ, or **BAR-HEBRAEUS** (1226–86) Syrian historian, born in Armenia of a Jewish convert to Christianity. A master of Syriac, Arabic, and Greek, he was equally learned in philosophy, theology, and medicine. At the age of 20, he was made a bishop, and as bishop of Aleppo rose to the second highest dignity among the Eastern Jacobite (Monophysite) Christians. Of his numerous writings, the best known is a Syriac universal history. He died in Persia.

ABŪ-BAKR (c.570–634) the first Muslim caliph, was one of the earliest converts to Islam. He became chief adviser to **Muhammad** who married his daughter **Aïshah**, and on the death of the prophet was elected leader of the Muslim community, with the title *khalīfat Rasūbul Allāh*, 'successor of the messenger of God' (632). In his short reign of two years he put down the 'Apostasy', a religious and political revolt directed against the government at Medina, and set in motion the great wave of Arab conquests over Persia, Iraq and the Middle East.

ABU'L-FIDA, Ismā 'il Alī' (1273–1331) Muslim prince and historian, born in Damascus, ruled from 1310 over Hama in Syria. A generous patron of literature and science, his *Annals* were one of the earliest Arabic historical sources to be made available to western scholars. His *Geography* was also widely known.

ABU NUWAS (c.760–c.813–815) Arab poet, considered one of the greatest poets of the **'Abbasid** period. He abandoned older, traditional forms for erotic and witty lyrics. He was a favourite at the court of the caliph **Hārūn al-Raschīd** in Baghdad, and figures in the *Arabian Nights*.

ABU TAMMAM, Habib ibn Aus (807–c.850) Arabian poet, born near Lake Tiberias, the son of a Christian. He rose to favour under the caliphs al-Ma'mūn and al-Mu'tasim as a composer of panegyrics. He travelled extensively and late in life, held up by a snowstorm on one of his journeys, discovered a private library of desert poetry at Hamadhan. From this he compiled a celebrated anthology of early Arab poetry, the *Hamasu*.

ABZUG, Bella, originally **Bella Savitzky** (1920–) American feminist, lawyer and politician, born in the Bronx, New York City. Educated at Hunter College, New York and Columbia University, she practised as a lawyer in New York from 1944 to 1970 and became noted for defending those accused of un-American activities. A prominent peace campaigner, she founded Women Strike for Peace (1961) and the National Women's Political Caucus. Winning a seat in congress (1971), she vigorously championed welfare issues, earning the soubriquet 'Battling Bella'. She ran unsuccessfully for a senate seat (1976) and for appointment as mayor of New York (1977), but remains involved in political issues.

ACCUM, Friedrich (1769–1838) German chemist, born in Buckeburg. In 1793 he came to London, where he lived for nearly 30 years. He pioneered the introduction of gas-lighting, and his *Treatise on Adulteration of Food and Culinary Poisons* (1820) did much to arouse public opinion against unclean food and dishonest trading.

ACCURSIUS, Francisco Accorso (c.1182–c.1260) Italian scholar. Professor at Bologna and a leader in the 13th century renaissance of Roman law studies, he was the author of the *Great Gloss*, a collection of 96260 explanatory notes on all parts of **Justinian I**'s *Corpus Juris Civilis*, mostly compiled from earlier glossators, especially **Azo**. It was accepted as authoritative in his lifetime and printed with the texts until the 17th century.

ACHAEMENIDS, (Achaemenidae) the name of the ruling house of ancient Persia, derived from its founder, the 7th-century BC ruler Achaemenes. It included **Cyrus the Great, Darius I,** and **Darius III**, who was overthrown by **Alexander the Great** in 330 BC.

ACHARD, Franz Karl (1753–1821) Swiss chemist, born in Berlin. He took up **Andreas Marggraf**'s discovery of sugar in beet and perfected a process for its extraction on a commercial scale, after which he opened (1801) the first beet sugar factory, in Silesia.

ACHEBE, Chinua, originally **Albert Chinualumogo** (1930–) Nigerian novelist, poet and essayist, born in Ogidi, the son of a mission teacher. Educated at the University College of Ibadan, his early career was in broadcasting, but the publication of his first novel *Things Fall Apart* (1958) at once heralded the emergence of a unique voice in African literature. Set in the second half of the 19th century and presenting an unsentimentalized picture of the Ibo tribe, it has since been translated into 40 languages. Writing exclusively in English, he confirmed his early promise with four more novels, *No Longer At Ease* (1960), *Arrow of God* (1964), *A Man of the People* (1966) and *Anthills of the Savanna* (1987) which was short-listed for the Booker prize. An overtly political writer, he has taught at the universities of Massachusetts and Connecticut, and at the University of Nigeria at Nsukka.

ACHENBACH, Andreas (1815–1910) German landscape and marine painter, born in Cassel. He studied at St Petersburg and travelled extensively in Holland, Scandinavia and Italy, where he produced many watercolours. His paintings of the North Sea coasts of Europe had considerable influence in Germany, and he was regarded as the father of 19th-century German landscape painting. His brother and pupil Oswald (1827–1905) was also a landscape painter.

ACHESON, Dean Gooderham (1893–1971) American statesman and lawyer, closely involved with the Marshall Aid plan for Europe and the formation of NATO, born in Middletown, Connecticut. He was educated at Yale and Harvard, and joined the department of state in 1941, where he was under-secretary (1945–47) and secretary of state in the **Truman** administration (1949–53). He helped to shape UNRRA (1945), formulated the Truman Doctrine (1947), helped determine the Marshall Plan (1947), and promoted the formation of NATO (1949). He wrote *Power and Diplomacy* (1958), *Morning and Noon* (1965), and *Present at the Creation* (1969), for which he was awarded the Pulitzer prize.

ACHESON, Edward Goodrich (1856–1931) American chemist, and inventor of carborundum and artificially prepared graphite, born in Washington, Pennsylvania. From 1880 to 1881 he did research on electric lamps as an assistant to **Thomas Edison**. After 1884 he worked independently to develop the electric furnace for the conversion of carbon into diamonds, without success. Later, in 1891, he developed the manufacture of silicon carbide (carborundum), an extremely useful abrasive, and in 1896 devised a new way of making lubricants based on colloidal graphite.

ACHMET See **AHMET**

ACKERLEY, Joseph Randolf (1896–1967) English author, born in Herne Hill, Kent. His post-university acquaintance with **E M Forster** resulted in his appointment as private secretary to the Maharajah of Chhokrapur, from which experience he wrote *Hindoo Holiday* (1932), an intelligent and amusing log of his five-month sojourn in India. From 1935 to 1959 he was literary editor of *The Listener*. In 1956 he published *My Dog Tulip*, eulogized by **Christopher Isherwood** as 'one of the greatest masterpieces of animal literature', and, in 1960, his only novel, *We Think the World of You*, in which an Alsatian dog plays a lead role. His other books include the autobiographical *My Father and Myself* (1968) and *My Sister and Myself*; *The Diaries of J R Ackerley* (1982), both published posthumously.

ACKERMANN, Rudolph (1764–1834) German art publisher, born in Saxony. In 1795 he opened a print shop in London and published a well-known set of coloured engravings of London. He is said to have introduced lithography as a fine art into England, and originated the 'Annuals' with his *Forget-me-not* (1825).

ACLAND, Sir Arthur Herbert Dyke (1847–1926) English politician and educational reformer, born in Holnicote, near Porlock, third son of Sir Thomas Dyke Acland. Educated at Rugby and Christ Church, Oxford, he was Liberal MP for Rotherham, 1885–99. As vice-president of the Committee of Council on Education, 1892–95, he secured the raising of the school leaving age to eleven and the end of 'payment by results' in English education. He wrote several history textbooks, notably *A Handbook of the Political History of England* with C Ransome (1882).

ACLAND, Sir Richard Thomas Dyke (1906–) English politician, educated at Rugby and Balliol College, Oxford. He entered Parliament (1931), resigned from the Liberals to found, with **J B Priestley**, the Common Wealth Party (1942) and, consistent with its advocacy of public ownership on moral grounds, gave away his Devon family estate to the National Trust. His party eclipsed, he became a Labour MP in 1945, but resigned in 1955 in protest against Labour support for Britain's nuclear defence policy. His books include *Unser Kampf* (1940), *What it will be Like* (1943), *Nothing Left to Believe* (1949) and *Waging Peace* (1958).

ACONZIO, Jacopo, or **Jacobus Acontius** (c.1500–1566) Italian engineer, courtier and writer. A native of Trent, he went to Basel in 1557, and in 1559 to England, after repudiating Roman Catholicism. His antidogmatic

Stratagemata Satanae (1565) offers a very early advocacy of toleration. As an engineer he advised on the refortification of Berwick-on-Tweed and on land reclamation in Kent.

ACOSTA, Gabriel, or **Uriel d'** (c.1591–1640) Portuguese Jew, born in Oporto. Although brought up a Catholic, he adopted the faith of his fathers when fairly young, and fled to Amsterdam where he adopted the name Uriel, only to find how little modern Judaism accorded with the Mosaic Law. For his *Examination of Pharisaic Traditions* (in Spanish, 1624), a charge of atheism was brought against him by the Jews before a Christian magistracy; and having lost all his property, twice suffered excommunication, and submitted to humiliating penance, he at last shot himself. His autobiographical *Exemplar Humanae Vitae* was published in 1640.

ACTON, John Emerich Edward Dalberg, 1st Baron Acton of Aldenham (1834–1902) English historian and founder-editor of the *Cambridge Modern History*. Born in Naples, he succeeded to the baronetcy at the age of three. He was educated at St Mary's College at Oscott, in Ireland, under Cardinal **Wiseman**, and at Munich University by Professor **Johann Döllinger**. He sat as a Liberal member of parliament for five years (1859–64), and was created baron by **Gladstone** in 1869. As a leader of the Liberal Roman Catholics in England, he opposed the doctrine of papal infallibility and edited **John Henry Newman**'s *Rambler* (1859–64). In 1895 he was appointed professor of modern history at Cambridge; he planned the *Cambridge Modern History* but died after editing the first two volumes.

ACTON, Sir John Francis Edward (1736–1811) English naval officer in the service of Tuscany and Naples, and prime minister of Naples under Ferdinand V. Born in Besançon, the son of an English doctor, he commanded the Tuscan squadron against Algeria in 1774, then moved to Naples, where he became successively admiral and generalissimo of the Neapolitan forces. Soon he was prime minister in charge of the entire Neapolitan administration; but he fell from power on the entry of the French into Naples in 1806 and fled to Palermo in Sicily, where he died.

ACUÑA, Hernando de (c.1520–c.1580) Spanish poet, soldier and diplomat of Portuguese extraction, who wrote in Spanish. He put into verse, under the title *El caballero determinado*, a translation by **Charles V** of a French romance, *Le Chevalier délibéré* by Olivier de la Marche. Other poems, Italian in style, were published in 1591 by his widow.

ACUTO See **HAWKWOOD, Sir John de**

ADAIR, John (c.1655–?1722) Scottish surveyor and cartographer, who did notable work in mapping Scotland and its coast and islands. Little is known of him until 1683 when he was commissioned 'to survey the shires'. He prepared maps of counties in the central belt of Scotland (1680–86), and in 1703 published *Description of the Sea-Coast and Islands of Scotland* (Part 1). He was elected FRS in 1688, and his work was paid for (inadequately) by a tonnage act of 1686. His maps and charts set new standards of quality and accuracy.

ADAIR, John Eric (1934–) British leadership development consultant and writer. Educated at Cambridge, London and Oxford, he developed his 'Action-Centred Leadership' model while involved with leadership training as a senior lecturer at Sandhurst (1963–69) and as an associate director of the Industrial Society (1969–73). The model, which has been used widely in industry and in the armed services, states that the leader of a group of people has to ensure that needs are met in three inter-related areas—getting the task done, maintaining the team and the personal requirements of individual members.

ADALBERT, St (d.981) German Benedictine missionary. In 961 he was sent by the emperor **Otto I 'the Great'** at the request of St **Olga**, princess of Kiev, to convert the Russians. He became the first bishop of Magdeburg in 968, and died near Merseburg. His feast day is 20 June.

ADALBERT, St (c.956–97) Bohemian prelate, born in Prague, known as the apostle of the Prussians. In 982, while still in his twenties, he was appointed the first native bishop of Prague, but the hostility of the corrupt clergy whom he tried to reform obliged him to withdraw to Rome in 990. He then took the gospel to the Hungarians, the Poles, and then the Prussians, by whom he was murdered. His feast day is 23 April.

ADALBERT (c.1000–1072) German prelate, born of a noble Saxon family. In 1043 he was appointed archbishop of Bremen and Hamburg. As papal legate to the north (1053), he extended his spiritual sway over Scandinavia, and carried Christianity to the Wends. In 1063 he became tutor to the young **Henry IV**, and soon, in spite of opposition from the nobles, he ruled over the whole kingdom.

ADAM, Adolphe Charles (1803–56) French composer, born in Paris. The son of the pianist Louis Adam (1758–1848), he wrote some successful operas, as *Le Postillon de Longjumeau* (1835), long popular, and *Si j'étais Roi* (1852), but is chiefly remembered for the ballet *Giselle* (1841), from a story by **Théophile Gautier**.

ADAM, Alexander (1741–1809) Scottish teacher and writer, born near Forres. The son of a small farmer, he came to Edinburgh University in 1757. In 1761 he obtained the headmastership of Watson's Hospital, and in 1768 the rectorship of the High School. He was the author of a textbook *Latin Grammar* (1762) and a popular compendium of *Roman Antiquities* (1791).

ADAM, James (1730–94) Scottish architect, brother and partner of **Robert Adam** and son of William Adam of Maryburgh (1689–1748), also an architect of renown. He studied in Rome and joined the family partnership in 1763. In 1769 he succeeded his brother as architect of the king's works. He designed a few buildings independently, notably the Glasgow Infirmary (1792).

ADAM, Juliette, née **Lamber** (1836–1936) French writer, born in Verberie, Oise. She was the wife of the senator Edmond Adam (1816–77). During the Empire in her salon she gathered the best collection of wits, artists, and advanced politicians. She produced stories and books on social and political questions, and in 1879 founded the *Nouvelle Revue*. In 1895–1905 she published her *Mémoires*.

ADAM, Lambert Sigisbert, Nicolas Sébastien, François Gaspard French sculptors and brothers, from Lorraine. All three produced sculpture which, although described as French Rococo, was influenced by the 17th-century Roman Baroque style, especially that of **Bernini**. Each was successful and received important commissions: Lambert Sigisbert, called Adam the Elder, produced the Neptune fountain at Versailles; Nicolas Sébastien, called Adam the Younger, the monument of Queen Catherine Opalinska, Nancy (1749); and François Gaspard did work for **Frederick II, the Great**.

ADAM, Louis See **ADAM, Adolphe**

ADAM, Paul Auguste Marie (1862–1920) French novelist and essayist, born in Paris. Among his numerous novels are *Chair Molle* (1885), *Le Mystère des foules* (1895), *Lettres de malaisie* (1879), and *La Force* (1899). He was co-founder of *Symboliste* and other French literary periodicals.

ADAM, Robert (1728–92) Scottish architect, born in Kirkcaldy, brother of **James Adam**. He studied at Edinburgh and in Italy (1754–58). From 1761 to 1769 he was architect of the king's works, jointly with Sir **William Chambers**. He established a practice in London in 1758 and during the next 40 years he and his brother James succeeded in transforming the prevailing Palladian fashion in architecture by a series of romantically elegant variations on diverse classical originals. Their style of interior decoration was based on ancient Greek and Roman characterized by the use of the oval, and lines of decoration in hard plaster, enlivened by painted panels in low relief. One of their greatest projects was the Adelphi (demolished 1936), off the Strand in London, a residential block built as a speculative venture, which brought the brothers' finances into very low water, and was eventually disposed of by a lottery. Good surviving examples of their work are Home House in London's Portland Square, Lansdowne House, Derby House, Register House in Edinburgh, the 'Old Quad' of Edinburgh University, and the oval staircase in Culzean Castle, Ayrshire.

ADAM DE LA HALLE See **HALLE**

ADAM OF BREMEN (d.c.1085) German ecclesiastical historian. As a canon at Bremen Cathedral from c.1066, he compiled a monumental *Gesta Hammaburgensis ecclesiae pontificum* (History of the Archbishopric of Hamburg, completed c.1075), based on church archives and interviews with learned men. It is much the most important source for the history, geography and politics of northern Europe between the 8th and 11th centuries, and contains the first written reference to the discovery of *Vínland* (North America) by the Norse explorer, **Leif the Lucky**, around the year 1000.

ADAMIC, Louis (1899–1951) Yugoslav-born American writer, born in Blato, Dalmatia. The son of Slovene peasants, he emigrated to the USA in 1913. He served in the American army, and became naturalized in 1918. He began writing short stories in the early twenties, utilizing his experiences and personal observations in his books—such as an immigrant in *Laughing in the Jungle* (1932). Other works include *Dynamite: the Story of Class Violence in America* (1931); an autobiographical survey, *My America* 1928–38 (1938); *From Many Lands* (1940); *Dinner at the White House* (1946), and *The Eagle and the Root* (1950).

ADAMS, Ansel Easton (1902–84) American photographer, born in San Francisco, notable for his broad landscapes of the Western United States, especially the Yosemite in the 1930s. A devotee of straight, clear photography and print perfecton, he was one of the founders with **Edward Weston** of the f/64 Group (1932) and helped to set up the department of photography at the New York Museum of Modern Art in 1940. He established the photographic department of the California School of Fine Art in San Francisco and was a prolific writer and lecturer, always stressing the importance of image quality at every stage of a photographer's work. His publications included *Taos Pueblo* (1930) and *Born Free and Equal* (1944).

ADAMS, Brooks (1848–1927) American geopolitical historian, born in Quincy, Massachusetts, the great-grandson of President **John Adams**, grandson of **John Quincy Adams**, son of **Charles Francis Adams**, and brother of **Henry Brooks Adams**. He graduated from Harvard in 1870, spent a year at Harvard Law School, and acted as secretary to his father in Geneva when the former US ambassador to the UK was helping arbitrate US claims against Britain for its failure to prevent the launch of the Confederate raider *Alabama* during the Civil War. Admitted to the Massachusetts bar, he practised in Boston for some years and later became a lecturer in Boston University school of law (1904–11). His major work was *The Law of Civilization and Decay* (1896), to which he added a number of other works. He saw history as being determined by a series of cycles, a belief to which he ultimately converted his brother Henry. He was an impassioned racialist and prophet of American doom induced by immigrants whom he regarded as nationally corrupting. He lived out his life in an elegant and erudite terror.

ADAMS, Charles Francis (1807–86) American diplomat and author, born in Boston, son of **Charles Quincey Adams**, 6th president of the USA, grandson of **John Adams**, 2nd president, and father of **Henry Brooks Adams**. After studying law at Harvard, he was admitted to the bar in 1828. He was a member of the US House of Representatives as the congressman for Massachusetts (1858–61). During the Civil War he was minister to Britain (1861–68), and in 1871–72 was one of the US arbitrators on the 'Alabama' claims. He published the life and works of his grandfather (*Works of John Adams*, 1850–56), and of his father (*Memoirs of John Quincy Adams*, 1874–77), and also edited the *Letters* of his grandmother, Abigail Adams.

ADAMS, Gerry (Gerald) (1948–) Northern Ireland politician, born in Belfast. He became politically active at an early age, joining the Irish nationalist party, Sinn Fein ('We ourselves'), the political wing of the IRA (Irish Republican Army). During the 1970s he was successively interned and then released because of his connections with the IRA, and in 1978 was elected vice-president of Sinn Fein and later president. In 1982 he was elected to the Northern Ireland Assembly and in the following year to the UK parliament as member for Belfast West, but has declined to take up his seat at Westminster. He has been frequently criticized for his association with the IRA.

ADAMS, Sir Grantley Herbert (1898–1971) Barbadian politician. After studying classics at Oxford he was called to the English bar in 1924 and returned to the West Indies to practise. He was a prominent figure in Caribbean politics and became premier of Barbados (1954–58) before being elected the first prime minister of the short-lived West Indies Federation (1958–62), which would have united seven former British colonies into a single state.

ADAMS, Henry Brooks (1838–1918) American historian, born in Boston, son of **Charles Francis Adams** (1807–86) and grandson of **John Quincy Adams**, 6th president of the USA. Educated at Harvard, he acted as his father's secretary in Washington (1860–61) and England (1861–68), then worked as a journalist in Washington (1868–70) before teaching medieval and American history at Harvard (1870–77). He edited the *North American Review* (1870–76) and wrote several important historical works, including his major study of the unity of art and religion in the middle ages, *Mont Saint Michel and Chartres* (1904); his monumental *History of the United States during the Administrations of Jefferson and Madison* (9 vols, 1870–77); and a classic autobiography, *The Education of Henry Adams* (1907), which was awarded the Pulitzer prize in 1919.

ADAMS, Herbert Baxter (1850–1901) American historian and educator, born in Shutesbury, Massachusetts. Educated at Amherst College and Heidelberg, he joined the newly-formed Johns Hopkins University in Baltimore, Maryland, as professor of history in 1876. His pupils included **Thomas Woodrow Wilson** and **Frederick Jackson Turner**. Adams played a major part in the professionalization of American historical writing and teaching, establishing the American Historical Association *Reports* and inaugurating the *Johns Hopkins Studies in Historical and Political Science* series. His major publication was the *Life and Writings of Jared Sparks* (1893), the subject being a popular but unreliable historian of revolutionary America, whose work he subjected to necessary documentary analysis.

ADAMS, John (1735–1826) second president of the USA, born in Braintree (now Quincy), Massachusetts. The son of a farmer, he distinguished himself at Harvard, and was admitted to the bar in 1758. He settled in Boston in 1768. Of strongly colonial sympathies, he declined the post of advocate-general in the Court of Admiralty, and in 1765 led the protest against the Stamp Act. His health failing, he withdrew in 1771 to Braintree, but in 1774 was sent as a delegate from Massachusetts to the first Continental Congress. He proposed the election of **Washington** as commander-in-chief, and was the 'colossus of the debate' on the 'Declaration of Independence'. President of the board of war, and a member of over 90 committees, 25 of which he was chairman, he worked incessantly; but retired from congress in 1777, only to be sent to France and Holland as commissioner from the new republic. He was one of the commissioners who in 1783 signed the treaty of peace, and in 1785–88 was minister to England. While in London, he published his *Defence of the Constitution of the United States* (3 vols, 1787). In 1789 he became vice-president of the USA under Washington. They were re-elected in 1792; and in 1796 Adams was chosen president by the Federalists. His administration was noted for fierce dissensions among the leaders of that party, especially between Adams and **Alexander Hamilton**. Defeated on seeking re-election in 1800, he retired in chagrin to his home at Quincy, where he died.

ADAMS, John, alias **Alexander Smith** (c.1760–1829) English seaman, and a ring-leader in the mutiny against Captain **William Bligh** on the *Bounty* in 1789. With **Fletcher Christian** and seven other mutineers he founded a colony on Pitcairn Island. When the island was first visited in 1809 by the American sealer *Topaz*, Adams was the sole European survivor (five of the mutineers had been killed by their Tahitian companions in 1794). Adams was revered as the patriarch of the Pitcairn settlement, and received a royal pardon for his part in the mutiny.

ADAMS, Sir John (1920–84) English nuclear physicist and founder member of CERN (Centre Européan pour la Recherche Nucléare) at Geneva. Educated at Eltham School, London, he went from school into the Siemens Research Laboratory at Woolwich before working on wartime radar development. His work on short wavelength systems took him to Harwell, where he engineered the world's first major postwar accelerator (the 180MeV cyclotron) in 1949. At CERN, of which he became director-general in 1960, he engineered the 25 GeV proton synchroton in 1954. In 1961 he was recalled to Britain to establish the laboratory at Culham for research on controlled nuclear fusion. He was later appointed controller of the new ministry of technology in 1964, and in 1966 member for research at the UK Atomic Energy Authority. From 1969 to 1976 he returned to Geneva to mastermind the building of the 450 GeV super-proton-synchroton. He was director-general of CERN for a second time from 1976 to 1980.

ADAMS, John Bodkin (1899–1983) suspected English murderer. An Eastbourne doctor, he was tried in March 1957 for the murder of one of his patients, Edith Alice Morrell. Morrell, like other patients before her, had died in mysterious circumstances, following long courses of heroin and morphine prescribed by Adams. Adams was a beneficiary of her will, despite the fact that she added a codicil cutting him out just before she died. At his trial, Adams' defence counsel was able to exploit the inconsistent evidence provided by the prosecution and Adams was found not guilty. He subsequently resigned from the National Health Service and was later struck off the Medical Register. He continued to treat a few private patients in Eastbourne and was reinstated by the General Medical Council in 1961. While some believed he had killed nine or ten patients for personal gain during his years as a practitioner, others have argued that he merely practised a form of euthanasia.

ADAMS, John Couch (1819–92) English astronomer who deduced mathematically the existence and location of the planet Neptune in 1845. Born in Laneast, near Launceston, the son of a tenant farmer, he graduated as senior wrangler at St John's College, Cambridge and in 1843 became fellow and mathematical tutor there. His prediction of Neptune occurred almost simultaneously with that of the French astronomer **Leverrier**, while the German astronomer **Galle**, working on these calculations, actually observed Neptune in 1846. Adams was appointed professor of astronomy at Cambridge in 1858, and was director of the Cambridge Observatory from 1861.

ADAMS, John Quincy (1767–1848) 6th president of the USA, son of **John Adams**, born in Quincy, Massachusetts. At 14 he became private secretary to the American envoy at St Petersburg. He was secretary to the commission for peace between the colonies and the USA, but in 1785 began to study at Harvard, and was admitted to the bar in 1790. Successively minister to the Hague, London, Lisbon, and Berlin, in 1803 he was elected to the US senate from Massachusetts, and in 1806, boldly denouncing the right of searching ships claimed by the British government, he lost favour with the Federal party and with it his seat. In 1809 he was minister to St Petersburg; in 1814, a member of the commission to negotiate peace between Great Britain and the USA; from 1815 to 1817 minister at the court of St James's. As secretary of state under President **Monroe**, he negotiated with Spain the treaty for the acquisition of Florida, and was alleged to be the real author of the 'Monroe Doctrine'. In 1825 he was elected president by the House of Representatives—no election having been made by the people. Failing to be re-elected, he retired to his home at Quincy, depressed and impoverished. In 1830 he was elected to the lower house of congress, where he became noted as a promoter of anti-slavery views; and he was returned to each successive congress until his death.

ADAMS, Marcus Algenon (1875–1959) English portrait photographer, born in Southampton and educated at Reading University and in Paris. He was apprenticed to his father, Walton Adams, also a professional photographer, and in 1919 established his own studio in London, specializing in formal children's portraits with a soft-focus romantic style. From 1926 until his retirement in 1957 members of three generations of the British royal family were frequent sitters, and his portraits of them were published all over the world.

ADAMS, Richard George (1920–) English novelist. Educated at Worcester College, Oxford, after wartime service in the Royal Navy he worked as a civil servant with the department of the environment (1948–74). He made his name as a writer with the bestselling *Watership Down* (1972), an epic tale of a community of rabbits. Later books have included *Shardik* (1974), *The Plague Dogs* (1977), *The Iron Wolf* (1980), *Girl in a Swing* (1980), *Maia* (1984) and *The Bureaucrats* (1985).

ADAMS, Samuel (1722–1803) American revolutionary politician, born in Boston, second cousin to **John Adams**, 2nd president of the USA, and chief agitator at the so-called Boston Tea Party in 1773. He became a tax collector and then a member of the Massachusetts legislature (1765–74). He organized opposition to the Stamp Act in 1765 and organized the Non-Importation Association in 1798 and the Boston Committee of Correspondence in 1772. After the Boston Tea Party he was a delegate to the First and Second Continental Congresses from 1774 to 1775, and signed the Declaration of Independence in 1776. He anticipated **Napoleon** by calling the English 'a nation of shopkeepers' in 1776. He was lieutenant-governor of Massachusetts from 1789 to 1794, and governor from 1794 to 1797.

ADAMS, Walter Sydney (1876–1956) American astronomer, born in Antioch, Syria, of American parents. He joined the new Mt Wilson Observatory when it opened in 1904, and became its director (1923–46). His pioneering work on stellar spectra led to the discovery of a spectroscopic method of measuring the velocities and distances of stars. He was one of the designers of the 200-inch telescope at the Mt Palomar Observatory in California (1948).

ADAMS, William (1564–1620) English navigator, born in Gillingham, Kent. He took service with the Dutch in 1598 as pilot major of a fleet bound for the Indies. As pilot of the Dutch vessel *de Liefde* he reached the Japanese port of Bungo in April 1600. The first Englishman to visit Japan, he was cast into prison as a pirate at the instigation of jealous Portuguese traders, but was freed after building two fine ships for the Emperor Iyéyasu, receiving a pension, the rank of samurai, and 'living like unto a lordship in England' (1600–1620). He also served as the agent of the Dutch East India Company.

ADAMS, William Bridges (1797–1872) English engineer and inventor, born in Madeley in Staffordshire. He built some of the first steam rail-cars, and in 1847 patented the fish-plate which is universally used for jointing rails. He took out 32 patents in all relating to locomotives, wheel-carriages, roads, bridges and buildings, but made little or no money out of any of them. He is said to have suggested in 1850 the idea of the Crystal Palace which was designed for the 1851 Exhibition by **Joseph Paxton**.

ADAMSON, Joy Friedericke Victoria, née **Gessner** (1910–80) Austrian-born British naturalist and writer. Living in Kenya with her third husband, British game warden George Adamson, she studied and painted wildlife, and made her name with a series of books about the lioness Elsa: *Born Free* (1960), *Elsa* (1961), *Forever Free* (1962), and *Elsa and Her Cubs* (1965). She was murdered in her home by tribesmen.

ADAMSON, Robert (1821–48) Scottish chemist and pioneer in photography, with **David Octavius Hill**. He helped Hill apply the calotype process of making photographic prints on silver chloride paper, newly invented by **William Henry Fox Talbot**, for a commission to portray the founders of the Scottish Free Church in 1843. Working together, Hill providing the artistic direction and Adamson the technical skill, they produced some 2500 calotypes, mainly portraits but also landscapes, between 1843 and 1848.

ADANSON, Michel (1727–1806) French botanist, born in Aix-en-Provence, the first exponent of classification of plants into natural orders, before **Linnaeus**. He published *Histoire naturelle du Sénégal* (1757) and *Les Familles naturelles des plantes* (1763), and left an unfinished encyclopedia. The baobab genus of African trees, *Adansonia*, is named after him.

ADDAMS, Charles Samuel (1912–) American cartoonist, born in Westfield, New Jersey. He was a regular contributor to the *New Yorker* from 1935 onwards, specializing in macabre humour and a ghoulish group which was immortalized on television in the 1960s as *The Addams Family*.

ADDAMS, Jane (1860–1935) American social reformer and feminist, born in Cedarville, Illinois, co-winner of the Nobel peace prize in 1931. After visiting Toynbee Hall in London she founded the social settlement in Hull House in Chicago in 1899, which she led for the rest of her life. She worked to secure social justice in housing, factory inspection, the treatment of immigrants and blacks, and for women and children; in 1910 she became the first woman president of the National Conference of Social Work. In 1911 she founded the National Federation of Settlements (president, 1911–35), and helped found the American Civil Liberties Union in 1920. She worked tirelessly for female suffrage, and was vice-president of the National American Woman Suffrage Association (1911–14). A committed pacifist, she was president of the Women's International League for Peace and Freedom (1919–35), and was awarded the Nobel peace prize in 1931 with Professor **Nicholas Butler**. Her many books included *Democracy and Social Ethics* (1902) and *Peace and Bread in time of War* (1922).

ADDINGTON, Henry See **SIDMOUTH**

ADDISON, Christopher, 1st Viscount (1869–1951) English Labour politician, born in Hogsthorpe, Lincolnshire. Educated at Trinity College School, Harrogate, he qualified at St Bartholomew's Hospital, London, and became professor of anatomy at Sheffield University. In 1910 he was elected Liberal MP for Hoxton, representing the constituency till 1922. He became parliamentary secretary to the board of education in 1914, minister of munitions in 1916, and Britain's first minister of health in 1919. Difficulties with **Lloyd-George of Dwyfor** led to his resignation in 1921 and to his joining the Labour party. Elected MP for Swindon, he became minister of agriculture in 1929. Created a baron in 1937, he assumed leadership of the Labour peers in 1940. In 1945 he became leader of the House of Lords and Dominions secretary. A quiet, almost ingratiating tactician and an able administrator, he had a sure ascendancy over the House of Lords in an historic period. His publications include *Politics From Within* 1911–18 (1925), and *Four And a Half Years* (1934).

ADDISON, Joseph (1672–1719) English essayist and politician, born in Milston, Wiltshire, eldest son of Lancelot Addison (1632–1703), dean of Lichfield. He was educated at Amesbury, Lichfield, then Charterhouse (where one of his school fellows was **Richard Steele**), and Queen's College and Magdalen College, Oxford, of which he became a fellow. A distinguished classical scholar, he began his literary career in 1693 with a poetical address to **Dryden**. Next year appeared his *Account of the Greatest English Poets*, and a translation of the fourth book of the *Georgics*. In 1699 he obtained a pension to train for the diplomatic service and spent four years in France, Italy, Austria, Germany, and Holland, during which he wrote his *Letter to Lord Halifax*, and made notes for his *Remarks on Italy*, and his *Dialogue on Medals*. *The Campaign*, a poem commissioned by **Halifax** to celebrate the victory of Blenheim (1704), secured for him a commissionership of Excise. As an under secretary of state (1705–08) he produced his opera *Rosamond* (1706) and in 1707 he went with Lord Halifax to Hanover. Elected to parliament for Malmesbury in (1708), he kept the seat for life. In 1709 he went to Ireland as chief secretary to

Lord **Wharton**, the lord lieutenant, where he formed a warm friendship with **Jonathan Swift**. Returning to England in 1710 at the fall of the Whig ministry, he became a member of the Kitcat Club, and contributed to the *Tatler*, started by his friend Steele in 1709. In March 1711 he and Steele founded the *Spectator*, 274 numbers of which (those signed with one of the letters C L I O), were the work of Addison. In 1711 he purchased the estate of Bilton, near Rugby. His blank-verse tragedy *Cato* (1713) aroused such vehement party enthusiasm that it was performed for 35 nights. In the Whig interest, he attacked the Treaty of Utrecht in *The Late Trial and Conviction of Count Tariff*. After the accession of **George I** (1714), he became once more, for about a year, secretary to the Earl of **Sunderland** as lord-lieutenant of Ireland. In 1715 his prose comedy, *The Drummer* failed. In 1716 he became a lord commissioner of trade, and married Charlotte, Countess of Warwick. In the Hanoverian cause, he issued (1715–16) a political newspaper, the *Freeholder*, which cost him many of his old friends, and he was satirized by **Alexander Pope** as 'Atticus'. In 1717 he was appointed secretary of state under Sunderland, but resigned his post, owing to failing health, in March 1718. Almost his last literary undertaking was unfortunately a paper war, on the Peerage Bill of 1719, with his old friend Steele. He was buried in Westminster Abbey.

ADDISON, Thomas (1793–1860) English physician, born near Newcastle. He graduated in medicine at Edinburgh in 1815. He settled in London, and in 1837 became physician to Guy's Hospital. His chief researches were on pneumonia, tuberculosis and especially on the disease of the suprarenal capsules, known as 'Addison's Disease'.

ADELA (?1062–1137) youngest daughter of **William the Conqueror,** and mother of King **Stephen** of England. In 1080 she married Stephen, Count of Blois; Stephen was the third of her nine children. She had a flair for administration and was cultured and pious.

ADELAER, ('Eagle'), honorific title of **Cort Sivertsen** (1622–75) Norwegian naval commander, born in Brevig. He first saw service with the Dutch navy under **Cornelis Tromp** (1639–42) and later fought splendidly for Venice against the Turks (1642–61). He returned to Holland in 1661, but in 1663 accepted command of the Danish Navy with the title of Count Adelaer.

ADELAIDE, St, German **Adelheid** (931–99) Holy Roman Empress. A daughter of **Rudolf II** of Burgundy, she married Lothair, son of Hugh of Italy, in 947. After his death in 950 she was imprisoned by his successor, **Berengar II**; she was rescued by King **Otto I**, **'the Great'** of Germany, who married her as his second wife in 951. They were crowned emperor and empress in 962. Their son was **Otto II**; as Queen Mother Adelaide exercised considerable influence when Otto succeeded his father in 973, although they quarrelled over her extravagant charities. She became joint regent with the empress Theophano for her grandson **Otto III**, and sole regent from 991 to 996. Thereafter she retired to a convent she had founded at Seltz in Alsace.

ADELAIDE, Queen (1792–1849) consort of King **William IV** of Great Britain. She was the worthy but dull eldest daughter of George, Duke of Saxe-Coburg-Meiningen; in 1818 she married William, Duke of Clarence, who succeeded his brother, **George IV**, to the throne as William IV (1830–37). Their two children, both daughters, died in infancy, and William was succeeded by his niece, Queen **Victoria**.

ADELARD (12th century) English philosopher. He studied at Tours, travelled widely in Italy and the near east, and is attested at Bath in 1130. His philosophical and scientific writings include many important translations from the Arabic into Latin. His most important works are *De Eodem et Diverso* (On Identity and Difference) and *Quaestiones Naturales*.

ADELUNG, Johann Christoph (1732–1806) German grammarian, lexicographer and philologist, born in Spantekow in Pomerania (now in Poland). Between 1761 and 1787 he lived in Leipzig, where he devoted himself to philological research; in 1787 he was appointed principal librarian to the Elector of Saxony at Dresden, where he remained until his death. His major work is a *Grammatical-critical Dictionary of the High-German Dialect* (1774–86).

ADENAUER, Konrad (1876–1967) German statesman, born in Cologne. He studied at Freiburg, Munich, and Bonn, before practising law in Cologne, where he became lord mayor in 1917. A member of the Centre Party under the Weimar Republic, he was a member of the Provincial Diet and of the Prussian State Council (president 1920–33). In 1933, he was first suspended and then dismissed from all his offices by the Nazis, and imprisoned in 1934 and 1944. In 1945, under Allied occupation, he became lord mayor again, and founded the Christian Democratic Union. He was chancellor from 1949 (re-elected in 1953 and 1957), and was his own foreign minister from 1951 to 1955. In 1955 he visited Moscow and diplomatic relations were established with the Russians. In the 1957 elections he gained an absolute majority of 43, a tribute to his policy of the rebuilding of West Germany on a basis of partnership with other European nations through NATO and the European customs union, with the ultimate aim of bargaining from strength for the reunification of Germany. He engaged in a public controversy over his succession with **Erhard** in 1959, consolidated the new Franco-German friendship and modified the German desire for reunification. His restraint during the Berlin crisis (1961–62) as well as his great age caused a decline in the fortunes of his parties at the polls (1961), necessitating a coalition with the Free Democrats, who pressed him for an early retirement. He complied in October 1963.

ADER, Clément (1841–1926) French engineer and pioneer of aviation. In 1890 he built a steam-powered bat-winged aeroplane, the *Eole*, which made the first powered take-off in history, but could not be steered and flew for no more than 50 metres.

ADLER, Alfred (1870–1937) pioneer Austrian psychiatrist, born and trained in Vienna. He first practised as an ophthalmologist but later turned to mental disease and became a prominent member of the psychoanalytical group that formed around **Sigmund Freud** in 1900. In 1911 he broke with Freud and developed his own 'Individual Psychology'—that department of psychology which investigates the psychology of the individual considered as different from others. His main contributions to psychology include the concept of 'inferiority complex', and his special treatment of neurosis as the 'exploitation of shock'. He opened the first child-guidance clinic in Vienna in 1921. In 1932 he moved to the USA to teach. His chief books were *The Practice and Theory of Individual Psychology* (trans 1923) and *Understanding Human Nature* (trans 1927).

ADLER, Jankel (1895–1949) Polish painter, born near Lodz. A Jewish upbringing along with early memories of ritualistic symbols and decorative folk motifs form the basis of his work. Although he is sometimes compared to **Chagall**, stylistically his work owes more to Cubism and **Picasso**. Forced by Nazi persecution to wander throughout Europe, he worked in Berlin, then Düsseldorf (where he met and admired

Paul Klee) and on being labelled a 'degenerate' artist in Germany, moved to Paris in 1933. There he worked briefly in **Stanley William Hayter**'s Atelier 17 (1937), joined the Polish army in France, was evacuated to Scotland in 1941 and found himself an exile. Adler never wholeheartedly embraced abstraction, believing that 'abstract painting can very easily become ornamental'. His idiosyncratic style had a certain influence on British artists, notably **Robert Colquhoun** and **Robert MacBryde**.

ADLER, Lawrence Cecil 'Larry' (1914–) American musician and self-taught virtuoso on the harmonica. Educated at Baltimore City College, he won the Maryland Harmonica Championship at the age of 13 and began his show business career in New York the following year. He has played as a soloist with some of the world's leading symphony orchestras, and has had pieces composed for him by composers like **Ralph Vaughan Williams**, **Malcolm Arnold** and **Darius Milhaud**. He wrote the music for several films, including *Genevieve* (1954). He emigrated to Britain after being blacklisted in the USA for alleged pro-communist leanings. His autobiography *It Ain't Necessarily So* was published in 1985.

ADLER, Nathan Marcus (1803–90) German-born British rabbi, born in Hanover and educated at Göttingen, Erlangen, and Würzburg. He became chief rabbi of Oldenburg in 1829, of Hanover in 1830, and of the united congregations of the British Empire in 1845. His successor as chief rabbi was his son Hermann (1839–1911), born in Hanover, who studied at London (1859), and Leipzig (1861). A staunch defender of his coreligionists, he published *The Jews in England* and *Ibn Gabirol*.

ADOLF FREDRIK (1710–71) king of Sweden from 1751, first king of the House of Holstein-Gottorp. The son of Christian Augustus, Duke of Schleswig-Holstein-Gottorp, he was descended on his mother's side from King **Karl XI**. A favourite of the empress **Elizabeth Petrovna** of Russia, he was adopted as successor-designate to King **Fredrik I** in 1743. In 1744 he married Louisa Ulrika, sister of King **Frederick II, the Great** of Prussia, and in 1747 was appointed commander-in-chief of the Swedish forces. As king his powers were severely limited by parliament during the so-called 'Era of Liberty'; but this came to an end when he was succeeded by his brilliant son, **Gustav III**.

ADOMNAN, or **ADAMNAN, St** (c.625–704) Irish monk, **Columba**'s biographer, born and educated in Donegal. In his 28th year he joined the Columban brotherhood of Iona, of which, in 679, he was chosen abbot. In 686 he visited Aldfrid, king of Northumbria, to procure the release of some Irish captives; and was converted to the Roman views as to the holding of Easter and the shape of the tonsure. Those views he tried to inculcate in Iona and Ireland, but he failed, at least in Iona, to his great mortification. He left a treatise *De Locis Sanctis*, one of our earliest descriptions of Palestine. *Adomnan's Vision*, a professed account of his visit to heaven and hell, is a work of the 10th or 11th century; but the *Vita Sancti Columbae* is undoubtedly his, and reveals a great deal concerning the remarkable community of Iona. His feast day is 23 September.

ADORNO, Theodor (1903–69) German social philosopher and musicologist, born in Frankfurt. He was a student in Frankfurt and later an associate of the Institute for Social Research and a member of the movement known as the 'Frankfurt School', which also included **Max Horkheimer** and **Herbert Marcuse**. In 1934 he emigrated to the USA to teach at the institute in exile at the New School of Social Research in New York and returned with the school to Frankfurt in 1960. His philosophy is most fully presented in *Negative Dialectics* (1966), a difficult and obscure work. He argues that all past philosophy is systematically vitiated: it is mistaken because of its search for some ultimate 'identity' or 'primacy' and it is dangerous because it thus tends to 'reify' the human subject and render it vulnerable to exploitation. The task of Critical Theory is to dissolve all conceptual distinctions so that they cannot deform the true nature of reality. His sociological writings on music, mass-culture and art are generally much more accessible, and include *Philosophie der neuen Musik* (1949), *Versuch über Wagner* (1952), *Dissonanzen* (1956) and *Mahler* (1960).

ADRIAN IV, Nicolas Breakspear (1100–59) pope from 1154 to 1159), the first and only Englishman to become pope. He was born in Abbots Langley, near St Albans, the son of a civil servant who became a monk, and was educated at Merton Priory and Avignon. He became a monk himself in the monastery of St Rufus, near Avignon, and in 1137 was elected its abbot. Complaints about his strictness led to a summons to Rome, where the pope, **Eugenius III**, recognized his qualities and appointed him cardinal-bishop of Albano in 1146. In 1152 he was sent as papal legate to Scandinavia to reorganize the church, where he earned fame as the 'Apostle of the North'. He was elected pope in 1154. One of his early acts is said to have been the issue of a controversial bull granting Ireland to **Henry II**. Faced with rebellion in Rome fomented by **Arnold of Breschia**, he excommunicated the whole city until Arnold was expelled (he was later executed). He also excommunicated the powerful William I the Bad of Sicily, but was later glad to accept him as an ally. In 1155 he crowned **Frederick I, Barbarossa** as Holy Roman Emperor in front of his massed army in a show of strength in support of the papacy; but their relationship quickly deteriorated when Adrian tried to impose feudal overlordship over him, and for the rest of his papacy Adrian was engaged in a bitter struggle with him for supremacy in Europe.

ADRIAN VI, Adrian Dedel (1459–1523) pope from 1522 to 1523, born in Utrecht. After study in Louvain he was made doctor of theology (1491) and was appointed tutor in 1507 to the seven-year-old Charles (later Charles I of Spain and the emperor **Charles V**), who in 1516, commencing rule in Spain, made Adrian inquisitor-general of Aragon and effective co-regent with the dying **Ferdinand the Catholic**'s choice **Ximenes**. On Ximenes's death, Charles worked closely with Adrian and made him regent in his absence from 1520, but in 1522 on the death of **Leo X**, Adrian was almost unanimously elected pope. He tried to attack the sale of indulgences which had prompted **Luther**'s first revolt, but was blocked by interested officials, and while frankly having the need for curia reform promulgated in his name at the Diet of Nuremberg, demanded Luther's punishment for heresy. He allied with the emperor, England and Venice against France, thus failing to unite Christendom against the Turks, who captured Rhodes. He died before his attempted reforms could be effective.

ADRIAN, Edgar Douglas, 1st Baron Edgar (1889–1977) English physiologist, born in London, and one of the founders of modern neurophysiology. He became a fellow of Trinity College, Cambridge, where he carried out important research on electrical impulses in the nervous system, and later on electrical 'brain waves' and their clinical base for the study of epilepsy and brain lesions (electroencephology, or EEG). For his work on the function of neurons, he shared the 1932 Nobel prize for physiology or medicine with Sir **Charles Sherrington**. He was appointed professor of physiology at Cambridge 1937–51, master of Trinity College, Cambridge 1951–56, and chancellor of the university 1968–75.

AE See **RUSSELL, George William**

ÆLFRIC, known as **Grammaticus ('the Grammarian')** (c.995–c.1020) Anglo-Saxon churchman and writer, the greatest vernacular prose writer of his time. He was a pupil of Bishop Æthelwold of Winchester, became a monk and later abbot at the new monastery of Cerne Abbas in Dorset, and subsequently the first abbot of Eynsham in Oxfordshire. He composed two books of 80 *Homilies* in Old English, a paraphrase of the first seven books of the Bible, and a book of *Lives of the Saints*. He also wrote a Latin grammar and Latin-English glossary, accompanied by a Latin *Colloquium* between a master, his pupil, and various craftsmen (ploughman, shepherd, hunter, merchant, etc), which gives a vivid picture of social conditions in England at the time.

AELIAN, (Claudius Aelianus) Greek rhetorician, born in Praeneste. He taught rhetoric in Rome c.220, and wrote numerous works, including *Varia Historia* (Historical Miscellanies) and *De Natura Animalium* (On the Characteristics of Animals).

AELRED, or **AILRED** See **ÆTHELRED**

AEMILIUS PAULUS (d.216 BC) Roman consul who fell at Cannae. His son, Lucius Aemilius Paulus (or Paullus) Macedonicus, in 168 BC was re-elected consul and defeated Perseus, king of Macedon, at Pydna. His son, adopted by **Scipio**, was known as **Scipio Aemilianus.**

AENEAS SILVIUS See **PIUS II**

AENESIDEMUS (1st century BC) Greek philosopher. He broke away from the Academy to revive the sceptical tradition of **Pyrrho**. His works, including an *Outline of Pyrrhonism* and *Pyrrhonian Discourses*, are now lost, but he is credited with defining the ten sceptical 'modes' or 'tropes' of suspending judgment.

AERTSEN, Pieter (1508/9–1579) Dutch painter, born in Amsterdam, the first of a family dynasty of painters. From 1535 to c.1555 he worked in Antwerp. Few of his religious altarpieces survived the turmoils of the Reformation and he is best known for paintings of everyday life and contemporary domestic interiors which frequently include some religious reference such as Christ in the house of Martha and Mary. Such a treatment of religious subject matter continued a trend begun in early Netherlandish painting of the 15th century, and can also be seen in the work of Aertsen's contemporary, **Pieter Bruegel**. His still-life painting was less dependent on tradition and had a considerable influence on later Dutch art.

AESCHINES (c.389–c.322 BC) Athenian orator, and rival of **Demosthenes**, born in Athens of humble origins. He was a soldier, actor and clerk before starting his public career. He advocated appeasement of **Philip II** of Macedon, and was a member of a Greek embassy that negotiated peace with Philip in 346. Demosthenes tried to have him indicted for treason in 343; in 330 Aeschines tried to prevent Demosthenes from being awarded a golden crown for his services to Athens. Defeated, Aeschines withdrew to Rhodes, where he established a school of eloquence.

AESCHYLUS (c.525–c.456 BC) Greek tragedian, known as the father of Greek tragedy, born in Eleusis, the town of the Mysteries, near Athens. He served in the Athenian army in the Persian Wars, and was wounded at Marathon (490), and probably fought at Salamis (480). His first victory as a poet was gained in the dramatic competitions of 484 BC; and, having won thirteen first prizes in tragic competitions, he was exceedingly hurt at being defeated by **Sophocles** in 468 BC. This may have induced him to leave Athens and go to Sicily, where he produced a new edition of his extant *Persians* (originally staged in 472). His trial before the Areopagus on a charge of divulging the Mysteries is also stated as a cause of his departure. His last great victory was won in 458, with the *Oresteia* trilogy. He died at Gela in Sicily. Out of some sixty plays ascribed to him, only seven are extant: the *Persianse*, the *Seven against Thebes*, the *Prometheus Bound* (in some ways the perfection of its author's art), the *Suppliants*, and the trilogy of the *Oresteia*, three plays on the fate of Orestes, comprising the *Agamemnon* (perhaps the greatest Greek play that has survived), the *Choephoroe*, and *Eumenides*. The genius of Aeschylus is quite peculiar in Greek literature, and he has no equal. What distinguishes him most from great contemporaries like **Pindar**, or great successors like Sophocles, is the grandeur of his conceptions in theology, in the providential ruling of the world, the inheritance of sin, and the conflict of rude with purer religion.

AESOP legendary Greek fabulist, said to have lived in the 6th century BC. He was variously described as a Phrygian slave who was granted his freedom, and as a confidant of King **Croesus** of Lydia, for whom he undertook various unlikely missions. The story that he was ugly and deformed is a medieval invention. The Fables attributed to him are in all probability a compilation of tales from many sources. The stories were popularized by the Roman poet **Phaedrus** in the 1st century AD, and rewritten in sophisticated verse by **La Fontaine** in 1668.

ÆTHELBERT (d.616) king of Kent, and the first English king to adopt Christianity. During his long reign, from c.560, Kent achieved hegemony over England south of the Humber. He received with kindness the Christian mission from Rome led by St **Augustine** which landed in Thanet in 596, and allowed them to settle at Canterbury. He himself was baptized with his court, and Canterbury became the 'capital' of Roman Christianity in Britain. Æthelbert was also responsible for the first written code of English laws.

ÆTHELFLÆD (d.918) Anglo-Saxon ruler of Mercia, daughter of **Alfred the Great** and sister of **Edward the Elder** of Wessex. She married Æthelred, the ealdorman of Mercia, c.888, and fought alongside him to repel the Danish invaders, their battle culminating in a decisive victory near Tettenhall in 911. After Æthelred's death in that year, Æthelflæd was recognized as 'Lady of the Mercians'; she built fortified strongholds throughout Mercia and planned and led in person Mercian counter-attacks on the Danes. In 917, with her brother Edward, she captured Derby, and the following year took Leicester. She died in June, 918, when poised to invade Danish-held Northumbria.

ÆTHELRED I (d.871) Anglo-Saxon king of Wessex. One of the five sons of King Æthelwulf and elder brother of **Alfred the Great**, he succeeded to the throne in 865. In that year a large Danish invasion army landed in East Anglia intent on permanent conquest, and captured York and Northumbria; Æthelred, with Alfred as his second-in-command, helped to defend Mercia against them. Early in 870 the Danes established a fortified camp at Reading in Wessex; Æthelred and Alfred made a spirited resistance, and defeated them at the battle of Ashdown in Berkshire but Æthelred died soon afterwards, to be succeeded by Alfred.

ÆTHELRED II, wrongly referred to as **'The Unready'** (968–1016) king of England from 978. The son of King **Edgar** and his second wife, Ælfryth, he was seven when his father died, and only ten when he succeeded to the throne after the murder of his half-brother **Edward the Martyr** by his household at Corfe Castle. From boyhood he was swayed by unworthy favourites, and during his reign he never recovered from suspicion of complicity in Edward's murder. His long and ineffective rule was punctuated by acts of spasmodic violence and supine attempts to buy off Viking invaders (hence his Anglo-Saxon nickname of *Unræd*, meaning 'lack of counsel', mistranslated as 'Unready'). In the 990s he bought off the Viking invaders with escalating amounts of Danegeld ('Danish payment'); then in November 1002, he ordered a savage massacre of all Danish settlers. He was forced to buy peace from subsequent invasions, until at the end of 1013, beleaguered by the invasion of **Svein I Haraldsson** of Denmark, he abandoned his throne and fled to Normandy (in 1002 he had married **Emma**, daughter of Duke Richard of Normandy). On Svein's sudden death in February, 1014, he was recalled from Normandy, but died in London in 1016. By a first marriage he left a son, **Edmund II, Ironside**, who succeeded him for a few months; and by Emma he was the father of **Edward the Confessor**.

ÆTHELRED, or **Ailred of Rievaulx** (1109–66) English chronicler, born in Hexham. He was a page to Prince Henry of Scotland, and became a Cistercian monk at Rievaulx abbey. He was a friend and adviser to both King **David I** of Scotland and King **Stephen** of England, and wrote a vivid Latin account of the battle of the Standard between them at Northallerton, Yorkshire, in 1138 (*Relatio de Standardo*). He also wrote spiritual works, and biographies of **Edward 'the Confessor'** and St **Ninian**.

AËTIUS, Flavius (c.390–454) Roman general, born in Moesia. In 433 he became patrician, consul, and general-in-chief; and as such maintained the empire against the barbarians for 20 years, defeating West Goths, Burgundians, rebellious Gauls, and Franks. His crowning victory was that at Châlons over Attila in 451; three years later the emperor **Valentinian III**, jealous of his greatness, stabbed him to death.

AFFONSO See **ALFONSO**

AFRICANUS, Sextus Julius (c.160–c.240) traveller and historian, born in Libya. He wrote *Chronologia*, a history of the world from the creation to AD 221. His chronology, which antedates Christ's birth by 3 years, was accepted by Byzantine churches.

AGA KHAN III, in full **Aga Sultan Sir Mohammed Shah** (1877–1957) Imam (leader) of the Ismaili sect of Muslims, born in Karachi. He succeeded to the title in 1885, and in 1910 founded the Aligarh University. He worked for the British cause in both World Wars, and in 1937 was president of the League of Nations assembly. A keen race-course enthusiast, he owned several Derby winners.

AGA KHAN IV, Karim (1936–) Imam (leader) of the Ismaili sect of Muslims, grandson of **Aga Khan III** and son of the late Aly Khan. He succeeded his grandfather as 49th Imam in 1957. He was educated at Le Rosey in Switzerland, and later read oriental history at Harvard. He married an English woman, Sarah Croker Poole, in 1969.

AGAMEMNON according to Greek legend, king of Mycenae or of Argos, son of Atreus and brother of **Menelaus**, king of Sparta. He was commander-in-chief of the combined Greek forces that fought the Trojan War to avenge the abduction of Helen, wife of Menelaus, by Paris (son of **Priam** the king of Troy). **Homer**'s *Iliad* tells of his quarrel with the Greek hero Achilles during the siege of Troy. On his return home after the Trojan War, he was murdered by his wife Clytemnestra and her lover Aegisthus for having sacrificed his daughter Iphigenia at Aulis in Boeotia, in order to placate the goddess Artemis and so make possible the expedition against Troy.

AGASSIZ, Alexander Emmanuel Rodolphe (1835–1910) Swiss-born American oceanographer and marine zoologist, born in Neuchâtel, son of **Jean Louis Agassiz**. He went to the USA to join his father in 1849, studied at Harvard, and qualified at its Lawrence Scientific School in engineering and in zoology. He went on to amass a fortune in the copper-mines of Lake Superior. From 1873 to 1885 he was curator of the Museum of Comparative Zoology founded by his father at Harvard, made numerous zoological expeditions and published several books. He founded the zoological station at Newport, Rhode Island, and made many improvements in the technique of deep-sea research.

AGASSIZ, Jean Louis Rodolphe (1807–73) Swiss-born American naturalist and glaciologist, born in Môtier-en-Vuly. He studied medicine in Germany, but his main interest was in zoology, and while still a student published a Latin description of the *Fishes of Brazil* (1829), which brought him to the attention of **Cuvier**. He moved to Paris in 1831, and in 1832 was appointed professor of natural history at Neuchâtel. He published *Recherches sur les poissons fossiles* (1833–34), and after studying the glacial phenomena of the Alps wrote *Études sur les glaciers* (1840) and *Système glaciaire* (1847), showing that glaciers are not static but move, thus indicating the existence of an Ice Age. In 1846 he went to the USA on a lecture tour, and was appointed professor of natural history at the Lawrence Scientific School, Harvard (1847–73). In 1850 he married (2nd) a Boston educationist and naturalist, Elizabeth Cabot Cary (1822–1907). Together they conducted a young ladies' school at Cambridge, Massachusetts (1855–63), and she later became president of the Society for Collegiate Instruction of Women and its successor, Redcliffe College (1894–90). Agassiz himself founded a Museum of Comparative Zoology at Harvard (1859), to which he gave all his collections. He published four of ten projected volumes of *Contributions to the Natural History of the United States* (1857–62), and went on several zoological expeditions, especially to Brazil, described in *A Journey to Brazil* (1867, with his wife).

AGATE, James Evershed (1877–1947) English critic and essayist, born in Manchester. He wrote dramatic criticism for several papers including the *Manchester Guardian* and for the BBC, before becoming dramatic critic of the *Sunday Times* from 1923. He wrote also on literature and films, and was the author of essays, novels and a nine-part autobiography in the form of a diary, *Ego*.

AGATHA, St (3rd century) Sicilian Christian martyr from Catania. According to legend, she rejected the love of the Roman consul, Quintilianus, and suffered a cruel martyrdom in 251. Her feast day is 5 February. She is the patron saint of Catania, and is invoked against fire and lightning; she is also the patron saint of bell-founders.

AGATHARCOS (5th century BC) Athenian artist of the time of **Pericles**, named by **Vitruvius Pollio** as the founder of scene painting and a pioneer of perspective.

AGATHOCLES (369–289 BC) tyrant of Syracuse from 217. He fought the Carthaginians and invaded Tunisia, and c.304 took on the royal title in imitation of the Macedonian generals who succeeded **Alexander the Great**. A ruthless tyrant according to the hostile tradition, he nevertheless enjoyed popular support, and under him Sicily achieved her last period of independent power before the Roman conquest.

AGEE, James (1909–55) American novelist, poet, film critic and screen writer, born in Knoxville, Tennessee. Educated at Harvard he worked for several magazines before being commissioned to rove the southern states with the photographer Walker Evans, an assignment that produced *Let Us Now Praise Famous Men* (1941). He became a literary celebrity and was wooed by Hollywood for whom he wrote classic film scripts including *The African Queen* (1951) and *The Night of the Hunter* (1955). His only novel, the transparently autobiographical *A Death in the Family* (1957), was unfinished at the time of his death, and was awarded a posthumous Pulitzer prize.

AGENBEGYAN, Abel (1932–) Soviet economist, born in Tiblisi, Georgia. He was educated at the Moscow State Economic Institute. As professor of economics at Novosibirsk State University, and director of the Institute of Economics and Industrial Engineering, with his colleagues he developed the models for managing the national economy which the Soviet government started to apply in the late 1980s. He is chairman of several national committees and councils and personal adviser to President **Gorbachev** on economic affairs.

AGESILAUS (444–360 BC) king of Sparta from c.399, one of the most brilliant soldiers of antiquity. Called on by the Ionians to assist them against **Artaxerxes II** in 397, he launched an ambitious campaign in Asia, but the Corinthian War recalled him to Greece. At Coronea (394) he defeated the Greek allied forces, and peace was eventually concluded, with Persian support, in favour of Sparta (387). But in the long run his narrow view of Spartan interests may have done much to bring about the eventual demise of Sparta at the hands of Thebes in 371.

AGGESEN, Sven (12th century) Danish historian, author of the earliest known Latin history of the kings of Denmark, spanning from 300 to 1185 (*Compendiosa Historia regum daniae*).

AGGREY, James Emman Kwegyir (1875–1927) African missionary and teacher, born in Anamabu, on the Gold Coast (now Ghana). After attending a Methodist missionary school in Cape Coast, he trained as a missionary at Livingstone College, North Carolina, USA and after further university and church work in America, returned to Africa and joined the staff of Achimota College. He particularly stressed, to black and white people alike, the Christian outlook on the colour question.

AGIS IV (3rd century BC) king of Sparta in the Eurypontid royal family, reigned 244–241 BC. He sought to revive Sparta's military power by a programme of cancellation of debts and redistribution of land, but was opposed by powerful reactionary interests and executed. His aims were revived successfully by **Cleomenes III. Plutarch**'s *Life of Agis* is the principal source for his reign.

AGNELLI, Giovanni (1866–1945) Italian manufacturer. Educated at a military academy, he became a cavalry officer. In 1899 he founded Fiat (Fabbrica Italiana Automobili Torino). He was appointed a senator in 1923, and mobilized Italian industry in World War II. His grandson, named Giovanni Agnelli in his honour (b. 1921), became chairman of Fiat in 1966.

AGNES, St (4th-century) Roman Christian, believed to have been martyred in Rome c.304 in her 13th year during the persecutions of **Diocletian**. She is said to have refused to consider marriage, and consecrated her maidenhood to God; she is honoured as the patron saint of virgins. Her emblem is a lamb, and her feast day is 21 January.

AGNES, St, of Assisi (1197–1253) Italian Christian saint, daughter of Count Favorino Scifi and younger sister of St **Clare**. In 1211, in the face of violent parental opposition, she joined her sister in a convent. They became co-founders of the order of the Poor Ladies of San Damiano ('Poor Clares'). In 1219 she became abbess of a newly established community of the order at Monticelli.

AGNESI, Maria Gaetana (1718–99) Italian mathematician and scholar, born in Milan, the daughter of a professor of mathematics at Bologna. Educated privately, she was a child prodigy, speaking six languages by the age of eleven. She published books on philosophy and mathematics, and her mathematical textbook *Istituzioni analitiche* (1784) became famous throughout Italy. One of the few women mathematicians to gain a reputation before the 20th century, she is now mainly remembered for a cubic curve known as the 'witch of Agnesi'.

AGNEW, Spiro Theodore (1918–) American Republican vice-president, born in Baltimore, son of a Greek immigrant. After service in World War II he graduated in law from Baltimore University (1947). In 1966 he was elected governor of Maryland on a liberal platform, introducing anti-racial-discrimination legislation that year. By 1968, however, his attitude to such problems as race rioting and civil disorders had become much more conservative. As a compromise figure acceptable to most shades of Republican opinion, he was **Nixon**'s running mate in the 1968 election, and took office as vice-president in 1969. He resigned in 1973.

AGNON, Shmuel Yosef (Shmuel Josef Czaczkes) (1888–1970) Israeli novelist, co-winner of the Nobel prize for literature. Born in Buczacz, Galicia (now Poland), he went to Palestine in 1907, studied in Berlin (1913–24), then settled permanently in Jerusalem and changed his surname to Agnon. He wrote an epic trilogy of novels on Eastern Jewry in the early 20th century: *Bridal Canopy* (1931, trans 1937), *A Guest for the Night* (1939) and *Days gone By* (1945), as well as several volumes of short stories. He is considered the greatest writer in modern Hebrew, and became the first Israeli to win the Nobel prize for literature, jointly with the Swedish author **Nelly Sachs**, in 1966.

AGOSTINO DI DUCCIO (1418–81) Italian sculptor, born in Florence. His best and most original work is the relief decoration for the Tempio Malatestiano at Rimini, a church designed by **Alberti**. His style is characterized by a strong emphasis on line and, in its essentially decorative quality, differs from the more powerful naturalism of his greatest contemporary, **Donatello**. Although compelled to leave Florence—due, it was said, to being accused of stealing from a church—he returned for sufficient time to begin working on a large piece of marble which, left unfinished, was later used by **Michelangelo** to produce the famous statue of **David**.

AGOULT, Marie de Flavigny, Comtesse d', pseud **Daniel Stern** (1805–76) French writer, born in Frankfurt and educated at a convent in Paris. She married the Comte d'Agoult in 1827, but in 1834 left him for **Franz Liszt**, by whom she had three daughters: the eldest married **Olivier Émile Ollivier**, while the youngest, Cosima, married first **Hans von Bülow**, and later **Wagner**. A close friend of **George Sand**, she held a salon in Paris and wrote on numerous subjects, including *Esquisses morales* (1849), *Histoire de la révolution de* 1848 (1850), *Dante et Goethe* (1866), and a play, *Jeanne d'Arc* (1857).

AGRICOLA, Georgius, Latin name of **Georg Bauer** (1494–1555) German mineralogist and metallurgist, born in Glauchau, Saxony. He was rector of the school at Zwickau (1518–22). Later, as a practising physician in Chemnitz, his interest in the link between medicine and minerals led him to devote himself to the study of mining. He was Germany's first systematic mineralogist, and his *De Re Metallica* (1555, translated by President **Herbert Hoover** in 1912), is a valuable and detailed record of 16th-century mining, ore-smelting and metal working.

AGRICOLA, Gnaeus Julius (40–93) Roman statesman and soldier, born in Forum Julii (now Fréjus in Provence). Having served with distinction in Britain, Asia, and Aquitania, he was in AD 77 elected consul, and returned to Britain as governor in 77 or 78. He was the first Roman general who effectually subdued the island, and the only one who displayed as much genius in civilizing as in conquering the inhabitants. In 80 and 81 he extended Roman occupation northward into Scotland, and in 84 brought the native army under **Calcagus** to battle at Mons Graupius (possibly in Aberdeenshire), where he won a decisive victory. After this campaign, his fleet circumnavigated the coast, for the first time discovering Britain to be an island. The news of Agricola's successes inflamed the jealousy of **Domitianus**, and in 84 he was recalled. His Life by his son-in-law **Tacitus** is one of the best classical biographies.

AGRICOLA, Johann, real name **Schneider** or **Schnitter,** also called **Magister Islebins** (1492–1566) German reformer, born in Eisleben. He was one of the most zealous founders of Protestantism. Having studied at Wittenberg and Leipzig, he was sent in 1525 by **Luther** to Frankfurt, to institute the Protestant worship. He preached in Eisleben until 1536 when he was appointed to a chair at Wittenberg, which, however, he had to resign in 1540 for his opposition to Luther in the great Antinomian controversy. He died court preacher in Berlin. He wrote many theological books, but his collection of German proverbs (1528–29) is more lasting.

AGRICOLA, Martin (1486–1556) German musical theorist, born in Schwiebus; his real name was 'Sohr' or 'Sore'. Appointed to be teacher and cantor at the first Protestant school in Magdeburg in 1524, posts he held for the rest of his life, he claimed to be a self-taught musician and wrote extensively, with considerable literary power, of all branches of music. His writings in support of modern methods of notation were of special importance.

AGRICOLA, Rudolphus, real name **Roelof Huysmann** (1443–85) Dutch humanist, the foremost scholar of the Renaissance 'New Learning' in Germany, born near Groningen, in Friesland. He studied in Italy (1473–80), alternately at Heidelberg and Worms, dividing his time between private studies and public lectures. His writings had a profound influence on northern scholars like **Erasmus**. He distinguished himself also as a musician and painter.

AGRIPPA VON NETTESHEIM, Henricus Cornelius (1486–1535) German occultist philosopher, born in Cologne. He travelled widely and had a varied, if insecure, career as physician, diplomat, teacher and soldier. He acted as agent to **Maximilian I** on missions to Paris (1506) and London (1510), where he was the guest of **John Colet**. In 1511 he was with the army in Italy; in 1515 he lectured at Pavia and was made doctor both of law and medicine; in 1518 he became town orator at Metz but in 1520 was back in Cologne where he aroused the hostility of the Inquisition through defending a witch. He served as doctor and astrologer to Louise of Savoy, the Queen Mother of France, in Lyons in 1524 and as historian to **Margaret of Austria** at Antwerp in 1528–30, but secured neither favour nor salary in these positions. His major and influential work, a treatise on magic, *De occulta philosophia*, was completed in 1510 but published eventually in an enlarged edition in 1533. His *De incertitudine et vanitate scientarum atque artium declamatio* (1526) was a sceptical work, rejecting all human knowledge and advocating faith in divine revelation. He died at Grenoble.

AGRIPPA I and **II** See **HEROD**

AGRIPPA, Marcus Vipsanius (63–12 BC) Roman commander and statesman. His third wife was Julia, daughter of the emperor **Augustus**, whom he helped to gain power. He defeated Sextus, the son of **Pompey**, at Mylae and Naulochus in 36, and **Mark Antony** at Actium in 31. He also did good service in Gaul, Spain, Syria and Pannonia.

AGRIPPINA, the Elder (c.14 BC–33 AD), Roman noblewoman, the daughter of **Marcus Vipsanius Agrippa** and grand-daughter of the emperor **Augustus**. She married **Germanicus Caesar**, and was the mother of **Caligula** and **Agrippina the Younger**. Regarded as a model of heroic womanhood, she accompanied her husband on his campaigns, and brought his ashes home when he was murdered in 19 AD. Her popularity incurred the anger of the emperor, **Tiberius**, who banished her in 30 to the island of Pandataria, where she died of starvation, in suspicious circumstances.

AGRIPPINA, the Younger (d.59) daughter of **Agrippina, the Elder**, first married Cnaeus Domitius Ahenobarbus, by whom she had a son, the future Emperor **Nero**. Her third husband was Emperor **Claudius**, though her own uncle. She soon persuaded him to adopt Nero as his successor, to the exclusion of **Britannicus**, his own son by his former wife, **Messalina**. She then proceeded to poison all his rivals and enemies, and finally (allegedly) the emperor himself. Her ascendancy proving intolerable, Nero put her to death in AD 59.

AGUADO, Alejandro Maria (1784–1842) Spanish-born French financier, born in Seville. From 1815 he was a banker in Paris, who amassed a fortune of above 60 million francs and left many paintings to the Louvre.

AGUESSEAU, Henri François d' (1668–1751) French jurist, pronounced by **Voltaire** the most learned magistrate that France ever possessed. A steady defender of the rights of the people and of the Gallican Church, he was advocate general and attorney general to the parlement of Paris, and three times chancellor of France, under **Louis XV** (1717–18, 1720–22, 1737–50). He secured the adoption of important reforms and attempted in vain a codification of French law.

AGUILO I FUSTER, Marian (1825–97) Spanish writer and philologist, born in Valencia. He worked as librarian there and at Barcelona. He was a powerful influence in the renaissance of the Catalan language and the poetic tradition of Catalonia. He published *Romancer popular de la terra catalana* (1893), and a dictionary of Catalan was published posthumously.

AGUINALDO, Emilio (1870–1964) Filipino revolutionary. He led the rising against Spain in the Philippines (1896–98), and against the United States (1899–1901), but after capture in 1901 took the oath of allegiance to America.

AHAB king of Israel c.869–850 BC, son of Omri. He was a warrior king and builder on a heroic scale, extending his capital city of Samaria and refortifying Megiddo and Hazor. He fought in the alliance that withstood the Assyrians at the battle of Karkar (853).

To extend his alliances in the north he married **Jezebel**, daughter of the king of Tyre and Sidon, who introduced Phoenician style and elegance to Ahab's court and the worship of the Phoenician god, Baal, in a temple at Samaria. This aroused the furious hostility of the prophet **Elijah**. Ahab was killed in battle against the Syrians at Ramoth Gilead.

AHASUERUS See **XERXES**

AHERNE, Brian (1902–86) English-born Hollywood film star specializing in 'gentleman-cad' roles. Born in King's Norton, Worcestershire, he made successful appearances on the London stage and in early British films before going to the USA in 1930 where he spent the rest of his life. He starred in New York as Henry Higgins in *My Fair Lady* before being offered a series of Hollywood roles as the charming, faintly villanous Englishman. His most notable appearances were in *What Every Woman Knows* (1934), *Beloved Enemy* (1936), and as the Emperor Maximilian in *Juarez* (1939), for which he received an Oscar nomination. Later parts included King Arthur in *Lancelot and Guinevere* (1962).

AHIDJO, Ahmadou (1924–89) Cameroonian politician, born in Garoua. He was in radio administration before entering politics in 1947. While Cameroon was a UN trust territory he became prime minister (1958) and led his country to independence in 1960. He was elected first president of the Republic of Cameroon, a post which he held until his retirement in 1982. He was president of Cameroon's only political party, the Cameroon National Union (UNC) from 1966 to 1983 when he resigned, complaining that his nominated successor, **Paul Biya**, was trying to establish a police state. He then went into exile in France.

AHMAD IBN IBRAHIM AL-GHAZI (AHMAD GRAN) (d.1543) sultan of Adal in Somalia, declared a *jihad* against Christian Ethiopia in the 1530s. With assistance from the Ottomans, he was able to maintain control of the empire until his defeat in battle by the emperor **Galawdewos** in 1543.

AHMAD SHAH DURANI (1724–73) founder and first monarch of Afghanistan. A chieftain of the Durani clan of the Abdali tribe, and a cavalry general under the Persian emperor **Nadir Shah**, he was elected king of the Afghan provinces when the emperor was assassinated in 1745. He established his capital at Kandahar, and made nine successful invasions of the Punjab and plundered Lahore (1752) and Delhi (1755). In 1761 he defeated the Marathas decisively at the battle of Panipat, and in 1762 defeated the Sikhs near Lahore and razed the temple of Amritsar. He appointed his son viceroy of Punjab, but was eventually obliged to acknowledge Sikh power in the Punjab. After his death the great Afghan empire he had founded soon disintegrated.

AHMADZAI NAJIBULLAH (1947–) Afghan communist leader, the son of a bureaucrat. A Pusthtun (Pathan), he was educated at Kabul University and trained as a doctor. He joined the Communist People's Democratic party of Afghanistan (PDPA) in 1965, allying with its gradualist Parcham (banner) faction, and was twice imprisoned for anti-government political activities during the 1960s and 1970s. After the Soviet invasion of December 1979 he was appointed head of KHAD, the State Information Service (secret police), and, inducted into the PDPA's Politburo (1981). In May 1986 he replaced Babrak Karmal as party, and thus national, leader and was formally elected state president in October 1987. He sought to broaden support for the PDPA régime, encouraging non-communist politicians to join the government and promulgating a non-Marxist constitution which enshrined a multi-party system, mixed economy and dominant position for Islam. However, his hold over power became imperilled following the withdrawal of Soviet military forces in February 1989.

AHMED ARABI, or **Arabi Pasha** (1839–1911) Egyptian soldier and nationalist leader. An officer in the Egyptian army, he fought in the Egyptian-Ethiopian war of 1875–79, took part in the officers' revolt that deposed the khedive **Ismail Pasha** in 1879, and was the leader of a rebellion against the new khedive, **Tewfik Pasha**, in 1881 that led to the setting up of a nationalist government, with Ahmed Arabi as war minister. The British intervened to protect their interests in the Suez Canal, and he was defeated at Tel-el-Kebir in 1882 and sentenced to death, but exiled to Ceylon instead and pardoned in 1901.

AHMET I (1590–1617) sultan of Turkey, son of **Mehmet III**, succeeded in 1603. He waged a losing war with Persia (1602–12).

AHMET II (1642–95) sultan of Turkey, son of Ibrahim, succeeded in 1691. A disastrous defeat at Slankamen (1691) by the Austrians lost him Hungary.

AHMET III (1673–1736) sultan of Turkey, son of Mehmet IV, succeeded in 1703. He sheltered **Karl XII** of Sweden after Poltava (1709) thus falling foul of **Peter I, the Great** with whom he waged a successful war terminated by the Peace of the Pruth (1711). He successfully fought the Venetians (1715), but soon after was defeated by the Austrians, losing territories around the Danube. He was deposed by the Janissaries (1730) and died in prison.

AHMOSE I (16th century BC) king of ancient Egypt, founded the 18th dynasty and freed Egypt from the alien Shepherd Kings.

AHMOSE II (16th century BC) king of ancient Egypt, ruled from 569 to 525 BC, cultivated the friendship of the Greeks, and greatly promoted the prosperity of Egypt. He built the temple of Isis at Memphis.

AIDAN, St (d.651) known as the 'Apostle of Northumbria'. A monk from the Celtic monastery on the island of Iona, in Scotland, he was summoned in 635 by King **Oswald** of Northumbria to evangelize the north. He established a church and monastery on the island of Lindisfarne, of which he was appointed the first bishop, and from there he travelled throughout Northumbria founding churches. He died in the church he had built at Bamburgh.

AIKEN, Conrad Potter (1889–1973) American poet and novelist, born in Savannah, Georgia. He was educated at Harvard, where his room mate was **T S Eliot** and his contemporaries were **Robert Benchley** and **Walter Lippmann**. He made his name with his first collection of verse, *Earth Triumphant* (1914), followed by a string of further volumes including *Turns and Intervals* (1917), *Punch, the Immortal Liar* (1921), and *Senlin* (1925). His *Selected Poems* won the 1930 Pulitzer prize. He also wrote short stories and novels, including *Blue Voyage* (1927), the autobiographical *Great Circle* (1933), *King Coffin*, and another autobiographical novel, *Ushant* (1952).

AIKEN, Howard Hathaway (1900–73) American mathematician and computer engineer, born in Hoboken, New Jersey. He grew up in Indianapolis, Indiana, and was educated at Wisconsin and Chicago, before moving to Harvard (1939–61). Here he built with his colleagues the Automatic Sequence-Controlled Calculator (ASCC), or Harvard Mark I. Completed in 1943 and weighing 35 tons, this was the world's first program-controlled calculator, which Aiken regarded as the realization of **Charles Babbage**'s dream. Mark II was built in 1947. Aiken later became professor at Miami (1961–73).

AILEY, Alvin Jr (1931–89) American dancer-choreographer, born in Texas. He became a member of **Lester Horton**'s company in 1950, assuming directorship after Horton's death in 1953. In New York he trained with **Martha Graham**, **Charles Weidman** and **Hanya Holm**, while dancing and acting on Broadway and elsewhere. He retired from the stage in 1965 to devote himself to the Alvin Ailey American Dance Theatre, a hugely popular, multi-racial modern dance ensemble he formed in 1958. Ailey's work has been widely performed; stirringly direct and often topical, it is imbued with his observations of black urban body language and the contrasting rhythms of rural life. His most famous dance is *Revelations* (1960), an alternately mournful and celebratory study of religious spirit. His other works include *Creation of the World* (1961) and *At the Edge of the Precipice* (1983).

AILIAN, Dai (1916–) Chinese dancer-choreographer, instrumental in bringing the principles and study of western ballet to China. Born in Trinidad, she studied during the 1930s in Britain with **Anton Dolin**, **Kurt Jooss** and **Rudolf von Laban**. Working in China from 1940, she performed in dance recitals with various groups before securing leading directorial positions in several companies and institutions, including Central Song and Dance Ensemble (1949–54) and the Beijing Dance Academy (1954–64). In 1959 she co-founded what is now known as the Central Ballet of China, originally an offshoot of the academy's Experimental Ballet Society. She is the company's artistic adviser, and a member of the All-China Dance Association and the International Council of Kinetography/Labanotation.

AILLY, Pierre d', or **Petrus de Alliaco** (1350–1420) French theologian and Nominalist philosopher, born in Compiègne. He became chancellor of the university of Paris, and bishop of Compiègne, and was appointed cardinal (1411), and papal legate (1413) in Germany by the anti-pope **John XXIII**. At the Council of Constance (1414–18) he headed the reform party, but agreed to the sentence on **Huss** and **Jerome of Prague**. He was prominent in the election of Pope **Martin V** in 1417 that ended the Great Schism.

AIMARD, Gustave, pseud of **Olivier Gloux** (1818–83) French novelist and adventurer, known as the French **James Fenimore Cooper**, born in Paris. He sailed as a cabin boy to America, and spent ten years of adventure in Arkansas and Mexico. He travelled also in Spain, Turkey, and the Caucasus. In Paris, he served as an officer of the Garde Mobile (1848) and organized the Francs-tireurs de la Presse (1870–71). His numerous adventure stories include *La Grande Flibuste* (1860) and *La Forêt vierge* (1873).

AINGER, Alfred (1837–1904) English biographer, born in London. He was master of the Temple from 1894, and is best known as the biographer and editor of **Lamb** and **Charles/Thomas Hood**. He also wrote on **George Crabbe**.

AINLEY, Henry Hinchcliffe (1879–1945) English actor, born in Leeds. He started life as a bank clerk, but it was his appearance as Paolo in *Paolo and Francesca* (1902) that made his name. His wide range of parts included the title role in *Hassan* (1923), and James Fraser in *The First Mrs Fraser* (1929).

AINMILLER, or **Ainmüller, Max Emanuel** (1807–70) Munich stained-glass artist, executed windows for many European cathedrals, including Cologne, Basel, Glasgow, and St Paul's in London.

AINSWORTH, Robert (1660–1743) English lexicographer, born in the parish of Eccles, near Manchester. He was for a time a schoolmaster, and in 1698 published a treatise on education advocating, among other things, the teaching of Latin by conversational methods. His Latin dictionary was published in 1736.

AINSWORTH, William Harrison (1805–82) English historical novelist, chiefly remembered for popularizing the story of the highwayman, **Dick Turpin** in *Rookwood* (1834) and the legend of Herne the Hunter in *Windsor Castle* (1843). Born in Manchester, a solicitor's son, he studied for the law but married a publisher's daughter and began a literary career instead. He edited *Bentley's Miscellany* (1840–42), *Ainsworth's Magazine* (1842–54), and *New Monthly Magazine*. *Rockwood* was his first major success; but he wrote no fewer than 39 popular historical romances seven of which were illustrated by the cartoonist **George Cruikshank**.

AI QING (1910–) Chinese poet, born into a wealthy land-owning family in Jinhua County, Shejiang Province. He studed painting in France (1928–31), but returned to China when the Japanese invaded, and was arrested for leftist activities and imprisoned (1932–35). His first published poem, 'Dayanhe' (1934), named after his wet-nurse, and his collection of poetry, *Ta-yen-ho* (1936), marked him out as a socially conscious writer and brought him fame; but his later work was not considered comparable. In 1941 he joined the communists at Yenan. After the communist take-over in 1949 he became associate editor, with **Mao Dun**, of the *People's Literature* journal. He was an active propagandist for communist-controlled literature, but at the time of the 'Hundred Flowers Campaign' (1956–57) he was accused of revisionism and stripped of his party membership. In 1959 he was exiled to a remote district in the desert area of Zinjiang for 17 years.

AIRY, Sir George Biddell (1801–92) English astronomer and geophysicist, born in Alnwick. He graduated senior wrangler at Cambridge in 1823, and in 1824 was elected fellow of Trinity College, Cambridge. He was appointed Lucasian professor of mathematics in 1828, and later astronomer royal (1835–81). He reorganized the Greenwich Observatory, and discovered errors in planetary theory in terms of the motion of the Earth and Venus, but failed to achieve accurate measurements of the scale of the solar system. He determined the mass of the earth from gravity measurements in mines, and also invented a cylindrical lens for the correction of astigmatism, from which he himself suffered. Greenwich Mean Time, measured using Airy's telescope positioned on the line of zero longitude in his observatory, became Britain's legal time in 1880, and he began the practice of sending out time signals by telegraph. He was a member of the four-man commission which in 1846 selected the standard railway track gauge, rejecting the wider **Brunel** gauge used on the GWR.

AÏSHAH, or Ayeshah (c.613–678) third and favourite of the nine wives of the prophet **Muhammad**, and daughter of **Abū-Bakr**, the first caliph. She married at the age of nine, but had no children. When Muhammad died in 632 she resisted the claims to the caliphate of **Ali**, Muhammad's son-in-law (who had accused her of infidelity), in favour of her father, Abū Bakr. When Ali became the 4th caliph in 656 she led a revolt against him, but was defeated and captured at the Battle of the Camel at Basra, and was exiled to Medina. She is known as 'the mother of believers'.

AITKEN, John (1839–1919) Scottish physicist, was born and died at Falkirk. He is known for his researches on atmospheric dust, dew, cyclones, etc. His *Collected Scientific Papers* were edited by Knott (1923).

AITKEN, Sir Max (John William Maxwell) (1910–85) British newspaper publisher, son of the 1st Lord **Beaverbrook**. Born in Montreal, Canada, he established a reputation as a playboy and socialite before the war, but served with great distinction as a fighter pilot (DSO, DFC), ending the war as a group captain. He became a Conservative MP briefly, for Holborn (1945–50), before joining his father in running Beaverbrook Newspapers (*Daily Express* and *Sunday Express*). They had frequent disagreements; when Lord Beaverbrook died in 1964, Max renounced his claim to the barony but retained his father's baronetcy. The newspapers, however, were already in decline, and in 1977 they were sold to Trafalgar House. He was always passionately attached to yachting, and became a leading ocean-racing skipper; he launched the annual Boat Show, and promoted the sport of offshore powerboat racing. He also promoted British motor racing after the war by establishing the sport at Silverstone.

AITKEN, Robert Grant (1864–1951) American astronomer, born in Jackson, California. He joined Lick Observatory in 1895, and was director from 1930 to 1935. His discovery of more than 3000 double stars gained him the gold medal of the Royal Astronomical Society in 1932. He published *Binary Stars* (1918; 2nd ed 1935), and *New General Catalogue of Double Stars* (1932).

AITKEN, Robert Ingersoll (1878–1949) American sculptor, born in San Francisco. He was well known for his busts of **Jefferson, Franklin** and others.

AKAHITO, Yamabe no (early 8th century) major Japanese poet. A minor official at the Imperial Court, he seems to have kept his position largely through his poetic ability. His impression of snow-capped Mount Fuji is a famous example. He is known as one of the 'the twin stars'—Hitomaro being the other—of the great anthology of classical Japanese poetry known as the *Manyoshu* (*Collection of a Myriad Leaves*), translated by J L Pierson (1929–49).

AKBAR, the Great, (Jelal-ed-din-Mohammed) (1542–1605) Mughul emperor of India. Born in Umarkot, Sind, he succeeded his father, Humayun, in 1556 at the age of 13. For four years the government was in the competent hands of Akbar's tutor, Bairam Khan, but in 1560 Akbar dismissed the regent and assumed power himself. The early years of his reign were marred by civil war and rebellion, but, after triumphing over his enemies within the empire, Akbar was able to turn to foreign conquest, extending the control of the empire to include Malwa (1561), Rajputana (1568–69), Gujrat (1573) and Bengal (1576). In 1580 he invaded Afghanistan, entering Kabul in triumph the following year, and celebrating his success at a magnificent Darbar in 1582. Later conquests brought Kashmir (1586), Sindh (1591–92), Kandahar (1595) and Ahmadnagar (1600) within the empire, making him undisputed master of the whole of north India. He was responsible for extensive reforms of the tax system, promoted commerce and encouraged science, literature and the arts. He abolished slavery in 1582, put a stop to the practice of forced *sati* (the burning of a widow along with her dead husband), legalized the remarriage of widows and forbade polygamy except in cases of barrenness. Although he had been brought up a Muslim, his personal beliefs embraced elements from many other faiths and he pursued a tolerant and eclectic religious policy. He constructed in 1575 the *Ibadat Khana* as a meeting-place for scholars and theologians of all persuasions, including free-thinkers, but became disillusioned at the narrow-minded wrangling of the delegates and closed the meetings in 1582, founding instead an inter-denominational order, the *Din Alahi*, whose motto was 'God and the King'. In the 1580s he treated with exemplary patience and respect the various rude and bigoted attempts by Portuguese missionaries to convert him to Christianity. He built the fortress-palace at Agra.

À KEMPIS, Thomas See **KEMPIS**

AKENSIDE, Mark (1721–70) English poet and physician, born in Newcastle, the son of a butcher. He studied theology at Edinburgh University, but abandoned it for medicine, and practised at Northampton and later in London. His haughty and pedantic manner was caricatured in **Tobias Smollett**'s *Adventures of Peregrine Pickle* (1757). In 1761 he was appointed one of the physicians to the queen. He contributed verses to the *Gentleman's Magazine*, and in 1744 published *The Pleasures of Imagination*, a didactic poem begun when he was 17.

AKERS, Benjamin Paul (1825–61) American sculptor, born in Saccarappa, Maine. He is remembered especially for his *Dead Pearl Diver*.

AKHENATON, the 'heretic Pharoah' (14th century BC) the name assumed by Amenhotep IV. A king of Egypt of the 18th dynasty, after six years of his reign he renounced the worship of the old gods, introduced a purified and monotheistic solar cult of the sun-disc (Aton), and changed his name. He built a new capital at Amarna (Akhetaton), away from the old capital of Thebes, where the arts blossomed while the empire weakened. He was married to **Nefertiti** (Nofretete), immortalized in the beautiful sculptured head found at Amarna in 1912. Two of their six daughters were married to his successors Smenkhare and **Tut'ankhamun**.

AKHMATOVA, Anna, pseud of **Anna Andreeyevna Gorenko** (1888–1966) Russian poet, born in Odessa. The daughter of a naval officer, she studied in Kiev before moving to St Petersburg (Leningrad). She married in 1910 Nicholas Gumilev (1886–1921), himself a writer, who at first considerably influenced her style, and with him she started the neo-classicist Acmeist movement. After her early collections of lyrical poems, including *Evening* (1912), *Beads* (1914) and *The White Flock* (1917), she developed an impressionist technique. She remained as far as possible neutral to the Revolution. Her husband, from whom she had parted, was shot as a counter-revolutionary in 1921. After the publication of *Anno Domini* (1922), she was officially silenced until 1940 when she published *The Willow*. But in 1946 her verse, which previously had been acceptable, was banned as being 'too remote from socialist reconstruction'. She was 'rehabilitated' in the 1950s, and received official tributes on her death. Her later works include *Poem with a Hero* and the banned *Requiem* (Munich, 1963), a moving cycle of poems on the Stalin purges, during which her only son was arrested.

AKIBA BEN JOSEPH (c.50–c.135) Jewish rabbi and teacher in Palestine. He founded a rabbinical school at Jaffa, and had a great share in reshaping the oral law or mishna. He was a supporter of the revolt of **Bar Cochba** against **Hadrian** (131–35), and, on his overthrow, was put to death by the Romans by being flayed alive.

AKIHITO (1933–) emperor of Japan from 1989, the son of **Hirohito** (Showa). Unlike previous crown princes, he was educated among commoners at the élite Gakushuin school and in April 1959 married Michiko Shoda (1934–), the daughter of a flour company president, who thus became the first non-aristocrat to enter the Imperial family. In another break with tradition, his three children, the Oxford-educated Crown Prince Hiro, Prince Aya and Princess Nori, were raised at Akihito's home, instead of by tutors and chamberlains in a separate imperial dormitory. An amateur marine biologist, like his late father, he has written several monographs on the gobi (a spiny fish of the Gobiidae family). He is also an accomplished cellist. On his becoming emperor in January 1989, the new Heisei ('the achievement of universal peace') era commenced.

AKINS, Zöe (1886–1958) American playwright, born in Humansville, Missouri. She trained as an actress in New York, but turned to writing light comedy and film scripts. In 1935 her dramatization of **Edith Wharton**'s *The Old Maid* won her the Pulitzer prize. The best known of her plays are *Déclassée* (1919), *Daddy's Gone A-Hunting* (1921) and *The Greeks Had a Word for It* (1930).

AKSAKOV, Ivan Sergeyevitch (1823–86) Russian lyric poet and publicist, born in Nadeshdino, the son of **Sergei Aksakov**. He was founder and editor of various Slavophile and Panslavic periodicals, and a supporter of the liberation of Slavs in the Balkans.

AKSAKOV, Konstantin Sergeyvich (1817–60) Russian historian and philologist, son of **Sergei Aksakov**. He shared the slavophile ideas of his brother **Ivan Aksakov** and set out his writings to throw into relief the contrasts between Russia and the rest of Europe.

AKSAKOV, Sergei Timofeyevitch (1791–1859) Russian novelist, born in Ufa in Orenburg. The son of a wealthy landowner, he held government posts in St Petersburg and Moscow before a meeting with **Gogol** in 1832 turned him to literature. His house became the centre of a Gogol cult. He wrote *The Blizzard* (1834), *A Family Chronicle* (1846–56), *Years of Childhood* (1858). His writing shows his love of country sports and deep feeling for nature.

AL-'ABBĀS ancestor of the c.565–c.653 'Abbasid dynasty of the Islamic empire who ruled as caliphs of Baghdad from 750 to 1258. He was the maternal uncle of the prophet **Muhammad**; a rich merchant of Mecca, he was at first hostile to his nephew, but ultimately became one of the chief apostles of Islam.

ALACOQUE, Marguerite Marie, St (1647–90) French nun at Paray-le-Monial, and a member of the Visitation Order. She was the founder of the devotion to the Sacred Heart. She was canonized in 1920; her feast day is 17 October.

ALAIN-FOURNIER, pen-name of **Henri-Alban Fournier** (1886–1914) French writer, born in La Chapelle d'Angillon, the son of a country schoolmaster. He became a literary journalist in Paris, and was killed at St Remy soon after the outbreak of World War I. He left a semi-autobiographical fantasy novel, *Le Grand Meaulnes* (1913, trans as *The Lost Domain*), now considered a modern classic, and a few short stories, collected in *Miracles* (1924). His voluminous family correspondence was published posthumously.

ALAMÁN, Lucas (1792–1853) Mexican politician and historian, born in Guanajuanto. As a boy he witnessed the infamous siege of that city by Hidalgo's forces (1810), so becoming an ardent conservative. A creole aristocrat of independent turn of mind, he trained as a mining engineer, and once faced the Inquisition for possessing banned books . As a deputy to the Spanish Cortes (1820–21) summoned by Ferninand VII in the wake of the Riego Revolt (1820), he spoke out for Mexican independence and in favour of monarchy. After independence (1821), he negotiated with the Vatican and France to set up a Mexican royal house. Mexico's most influential conservative, minister of state to Emperor **Iturbide** (1822), foreign minister and minister of state for Bustamante and **Santa Anna**, he founded the National Museum and died shortly after completing his monumental *Historia de Mexico* (1842–52).

ALAMANNI, Luigi (1495–1556) Italian poet, born in Florence. He died at Amboise a political refugee, having been employed as a diplomat by **Francis I**. His best work was *La coltivazione* (1546), a didactic poem in the style of **Virgil**'s *Georgics*.

ALANBROOKE, Alan Francis Brooke, 1st Viscount, of Brookeborough (1883–1963) British soldier and master of strategy in World War II. Born in Bagneres-de-Bignore, France, he was educated abroad and at the Royal Military Academy, Woolwich. He joined the Royal Field Artillery in 1902, and in World War I rose to general staff officer. In World War II he commanded the 2nd corps of the British Expeditionary Force (1939–40), covering the evacuation from Dunkirk in France. He became c-in-c Home Forces (1940–41), and chief of the Imperial General Staff (CIGS) from 1941 to 1946, working on the strategy which led to the defeat of Germany. As principal strategic adviser to **Winston Churchill** he accompanied him to the conferences with **Franklin Roosevelt** and **Stalin**. He became a field marshal in 1944, and was created baron in 1945 and viscount in 1946. The book *Triumph in the West* (1959), based on the Alanbrooke War diaries, presented a controversial view of Churchill and **Eisenhower**.

ALARCÓN, Pedro Antonio de (1833–91) Spanish writer, born in Guadic. He served with distinction in the African campaign of 1859–60, and became a radical journalist. At the Restoration in 1874, however, he became a Conservative, and served as minister to Stockholm, and councillor of state. He published a war diary, travel notes and poems but is best known for his novels, particularly *Sombrero de tres picos* (1874) on which **Manuel de Falla** based his ballet, *The Three-Cornered Hat*.

ALARCÓN, Juan Ruiz de (c.1580–1639) Spanish dramatist, born of good family in Mexico. A lawyer, he became a member of the Council of the Indies in Madrid in 1626. He was neglected for generations, except by plagiarists, but has now been restored to his real rank as a leading playwright of the Golden Age of Spanish drama. His heroic tragedies are almost as brilliant as his character comedies. His *La verdad sospechosa* was the model for **Corneille**'s *Le Menteur*.

ALARIC I (c.370–410) king of the Visigoths from 395, whose army sacked Rome in 410. Born in Dacia, he first appeared in 394 as leader of the Gothic auxiliaries of the eastern Roman emperor **Theodosius I, the Great**. In the following year he was elected king of the Visigoths and invaded Greece, but was eventually driven from the Peloponnesus by **Flavius Stilicho** and the troops of the Roman western empire. He was appointed governor of Illyria by the eastern emperor **Arcadius** as a bribe, but in 401 he set off on the warpath again, invading Italy until he was checked once more by Stilicho at Pollentia on the Tanarus (402). Through Stilicho's mediation he agreed to join the western emperor, **Honorius**, in an attack on Arcadius, but when Honorius failed to pay the promised subsidy Alaric laid siege to Rome, in 408 and again in 409. All negotiations to save Rome broke down, and in 410 Alaric attacked and breached the defences. For six days his troops pillaged the city, but Alaric, who was an Arian Christian, forbade his soldiers to dishonour women or destroy religious buildings. Later that year he set off to invade Sicily and extend his dominion over all Italy, but died at Cosenza.

ALARIC II (450–507) king of the Visigoths from 485, who reigned over Gaul south of the Loire, and most of Spain. In 506 he issued a code of laws known as the Breviary of Alaric (*Breviarum Alaricianum*). An

Arian Christian, he was routed and killed at the battle of Vouillé, near Poitiers, by the orthodox **Clovis**, king of the Franks.

ALAS, Leopoldo, pseud of **Clarin** (1852–1901) Spanish author, born in Zamora. He was professor of law at Oviedo,but better known as a literary figure. He published short stories (*Cuentos morales*, 1896), a drama, *Teresa*, and several novels, including *La Regenta*. He also wrote treatises on law and economics. His writing is objective, sometimes cold, but always powerful and sincere.

ALASCO, John See **LASCO**

ALAVA, Don Miguel Ricardo de (1771–1843) Spanish soldier and statesman. He served under **Wellington** in the Peninsular War (from 1811), was ambassador to the Netherlands for King **Ferdinand VII**, but as president of the Cortez in 1822 forced his deposition. He fled when the French reinstated Ferdinand in 1823, but later served Queen **Maria Christina** as ambassador to London and Paris.

ALBA See **ALVA**

ALBAN, St (3rd century AD) Roman soldier, venerated as the first Christian martyr in Britain. According to **Bede** and some earlier writers, he was a pagan Romano-Briton living in the town of Verulamium (now St Albans), who was scourged and beheaded, around 300 AD, for sheltering and changing clothes with a fugitive Christian priest who had converted him. King **Offa** of Mercia founded a monastery on the site of his execution in 793, and the place was renamed St Albans. His feast day is 22 June.

ALBANI a Roman family, many members of which, from the accession of Giovanni Francesco Albani as **Clement XI** to the papal throne in 1700, filled high positions in the church. It died out in 1852. It was Cardinal Alessandro Albani (1692–1779) who formed the famous art collection in the Villa Albani.

ALBANI, Dame Emma, stage-name of **Marie Louise Emma Cécile Lajeunesse** (1852–1930) Canadian opera singer, born in Chambly, Quebec. Trained in music by her father, she made her début in Albany at the age of 12 (hence the professional name of 'Albani'). She studied at Paris and Milan, and in 1870 sang at Messina with a success that the leading cities of Europe and America confirmed. She published *Forty Years of Song* in 1911.

ALBANI, Francesco (1578–1660) Italian painter of the Bolognese school. He studied, along with **Guido Reni**, first under **Calvaert**, and afterwards under **Ludovico Carracci**. He painted about 45 altarpieces; but his bent inclined him more to mythological or pastoral subjects.

ALBANIE, Count d' the title assumed successively by two brothers, 'John Sobieski Stolberg Stuart' (1795–1872) and 'Charles Stolberg Stuart' (1799–1880), actually the sons of a Royal Navy lieutenant, Thomas Allen, who claimed to be the son of Prince **Charles Edward Stewart**. Handsome and plausible, they were lionized by Edinburgh society, and produced a Latin history of clan tartans called *Vestiarum Scoticum* whose manuscript they claimed to have discovered in a monastery in Cadiz.

ALBANY, Duke of, the title conferred in 1398 upon Robert (?1340–1420), brother of **Robert III** of Scotland, who was succeeded by his son Murdoch (d.1425). Queen **Victoria** made her youngest son Leopold (1853–84) Duke of Albany in 1881. His son Leopold (1884–1918) Duke of Saxe-Coburg (1905–18) forfeited his British titles in 1917.

ALBANY, Louisa Maximilienne Caroline, Countess of (1752–1824) wife of **Charles Edward Stewart** ('Bonnie Prince Charlie'). The daughter of Prince Gustav Adolf of Stolberg (d.1757), in 1772 she married the ageing Prince Charles in Florence, long after the failure of the 1745 Jacobite rising. She left him in 1780 and the marriage was dissolved in 1784, whereupon she took up with the Italian dramatist, Count **Vittorio Alfieri**. After his death in 1803 she lived with a French painter, François Fabre. Her ashes are buried with those of Alfieri in Florence.

ALBEE, Edward (1928–) American dramatist. He was educated at Laurenceville and at Columbia University. His major works include *The Zoo Story* (1958), a one-act duologue on the lack of communication in modern society, *The American Dream* (1960) *Who's Afraid of Virginia Woolf?* (1962, filmed 1966), *Tiny Alice* (1965), and *A Delicate Balance* (1966).

ALBÉNIZ, Isaac (1860–1909) Spanish musician, born in Camprodón, Catalonia. He studied under **Franz Liszt**, and became a brilliant pianist and composer of picturesque works for piano based on Spanish folk music. He also wrote several operas.

ALBERONI, Guilio (1664–1752) Spanish-Italian cardinal and politician, born in Firenzuola, near Piacenza. From humble origins, he became a priest and in 1713 was agent for the Duke of Parma in Madrid, where he quickly gained the favour of **Philip V**. Rising rapidly, he became prime minister of Spain and was made a cardinal in 1717. As prime minister, his domestic policies were liberal and wise, aimed at rebuilding the army and the fleet and developing foreign trade. In foreign affairs, however, his decisions were often impetuous and irresponsible. He violated the Treaty of Utrecht by invading Sardinia, supposedly at the instigation of the queen, and was subsequently confronted by the 'Quadruple Alliance' of England, France, Austria and Holland, resulting in the destruction of the Spanish fleet. He later tried to provoke a war between Austria and Turkey, an insurrection in Hungary and the downfall of the regent in France. In 1719, in the face of international pressure, Philip dismissed him and ordered him to leave Spain. He returned to Italy and after some time in a monastery in Bologna was befriended, in 1721, by the new pope, Innocent XIII. He eventually retired to Placenza where he died.

ALBERS, Josef (1888–1976) German-born American painter and designer, born in Bottrop, Westphalia. He trained in Berlin, Essen and Munich, and from 1920 was involved with the Bauhaus, where he studied and later taught. There he worked on glass pictures, typography and furniture design. In 1933 he emigrated to the USA where he helped to spread the Bauhaus ideas, teaching at the experimental Black Mountain College in North Carolina (1934–50) and later at Yale (1950–58). He became a US citizen in 1939. As a painter he was interested chiefly in colour relationships, and from 1950 produced a series of wholly abstract canvases, *Homage to the Square*, exploring this theme with great subtlety. His colour theories are expounded in *The Interaction of Colour* (1963).

ALBERT, Prince Consort to Queen Victoria (1819–61) married to Queen **Victoria**. Born at Schloss Rosenau, near Coburg, he was the younger son of the Duke of Saxe-Coburg-Gotha, and Louisa, daughter of the Duke of Saxe-Coburg-Altenburg. Studious and earnest by nature, he was educated in Brussels and Bonn, and in 1840 married his first cousin, Queen Victoria—a marriage that became a lifelong love-match. He was given the title of Prince Consort in 1857. Throughout their marriage he was, in effect, the Queen's private secretary. Ministerial distrust and public misgivings because of his German connections limited his political influence, although his counsel, percolating through to the Cabinet, was usually judicious and far-sighted. He found a congenial sphere of interest in the encouragement of the arts and the promotion of social and industrial reforms. He planned and managed the Great Exhibition of 1851, whose profits enabled the building of museum sites in South Kensington and the Royal Albert Hall (1871). He died of typhoid in 1861, occasioning a long period of seclusion by his widow. The Albert Memorial in Kensington Gardens, designed by Sir **George Gilbert Scott**, was erected in his memory in 1871.

ALBERT I (c.1255–1308) king of Germany. The son of **Rudolf I** of Habsburg, he was elected king of Germany in opposition to the deposed Adolf of Nassau, whom he then defeated and killed in battle at Göllheim (1298). He proceeded energetically to restore the power of the monarchy and reduce that of the electoral princes, but was murdered while crossing the River Reuss by his disaffected nephew John.

ALBERT, German **Albrecht,** called **the Pious** (1559–1621) archduke of Austria as Albert VIII, the third son of the Emperor Maximilian II. Brought up at the Spanish court, in 1577 he was made cardinal, in 1584 archbishop of Toledo. During 1585 to 1595 he was viceroy of Portugal. He was appointed Stadtholder of the Netherlands (1596), where he displayed a moderation unusual among the proconsuls of Spain. He relinquished his orders, and in 1598 married the infanta Isabella, daughter of **Philip II** of Spain. In 1599, he was defeated by **Maurice** of Nassau, and in 1609 made a twelve years' truce with him.

ALBERT V (1528–79) Duke of Bavaria, succeeded to the dukedom in 1580. Educated at the Jesuit college at Ingolstadt, he was a strong Catholic and established the pattern of Wittelsbach absolutism in Bavaria based upon the suppression of Protestantism and the centralization of ducal authority.

ALBERT I (1875–1934) king of the Belgians, 1909–34. The younger son of Philip, Count of Flanders, he succeeded his uncle, **Leopold II**. At the outbreak of World War I he refused a German demand for the free passage of their troops, and after a heroic resistance led the Belgian army in retreat to Flanders. He commanded the Belgian and French army in the final offensive on the Belgian coast in 1918, and re-entered Brussels in triumph on 22 November. After the war he took an active part in the industrial reconstruction of the country; the Albert Canal, linking Liège with Antwerp, is named after him. He was killed in a climbing accident in the Ardennes, and was succeeded by his son, **Leopold III**.

ALBERT, called **the Bear** (c.1100–1170) Count of Ballenstëdt from 1123, and founder of the House of Ascania which ruled in Brandenburg for 200 years. In 1134, in return for service in Italy, Albert was invested by the Emperor Lothar III with extensive lands between the Elbe and the Oder. Brandenburg itself was left to Albert by a treaty made in 1140 with the Count Pribislav.

ALBERT, called **Alcibiades** (1522–57) margrave of Brandenburg-Kulmbach. He entered military service under the emperor **Charles V** and was commissioned to raise a force against the Protestant Schmalkaldic League in 1546. His turbulent relationships with the emperor and with the German states, both Catholic and Protestant, led to his defeat and outlawry to France in 1553 as a threat to public order (hence his nickname, after the wayward Athenian statesman and pupil of **Socrates**).

ALBERT III, called **Achilles** (1414–86) Elector of Brandenburg from 1470 to 1486, he was the third son of the Elector Frederick I. In 1440 he inherited Ansbach from his father and in 1470 succeeded his brother, Frederick II who had abdicated. His most important legacy to Brandenburg was the *Dispositio Achillea* of 1473, which established the rule of primogeniture, so that when he died Brandenburg stayed undivided.

ALBERT (1490–1568) last grand master of the Teutonic Order and first Duke of Prussia, he was the younger son of the Margrave of Ansbach. Elected grand master in 1511, he embraced the Reformation, and, at **Luther**'s advice, declared himself secular Duke of Prussia.

ALBERT, called **the Bold** (1443–1500) Duke of Saxony. The son of Frederick the Gentle, he was joint ruler with his brother Ernest from 1464 until 1485 when, by the treaty of Leipzig, they divided their inheritance between them. The two branches of the Wettin family then became known as the Albertine and Ernestine lines.

ALBERT, Eugen Francis Charles d' (1864–1932) German pianist and composer, born in Glasgow, the son of a French musician and Italian mother. He studied in London and with **Franz Liszt**; he composed operas (*Tiefland*, etc), a suite, a symphony, many songs, and much music for the piano.

ALBERT, Heinrich (1604–51) German composer, born in Lobenstein. He did much to develop the *lied* as we know it, and composed many airs, songs, chorals, and hymn tunes. He studied at Leipzig, and became organist in Königsberg (1631).

ALBERTI, Domenico (c.1710–1740) Italian composer, born in Venice. His music is almost entirely forgotten, but he is remembered as the inventor of the 'Alberti Bass', common in 18th century keyboard music, in which accompanying chords are split up into figurations based upon each chord's lowest note.

ALBERTI, Leon Battista (1404–72) Italian architect, born in Genoa, one of the most brilliant figures of the Renaissance. He worked in Florence from 1428. Influenced by **Vitruvius Pollio**, he wrote *De Re Aedificatoria* (10 vols, 1485), which stimulated interest in antique Roman architecture; his own designs, which include the churches of San Francesco at Rimini and S Maria Novella at Florence, are among the best examples of the pure Classical style. He was skilled also as musician, painter, poet and philosopher.

ALBERTUS MAGNUS, St, Count of Bollstädt (c.1200–1280) known as the *Doctor Universalis*, born in Lauingen. He studied in Padua, and, entering the newly-founded Dominican order, taught in the schools of Hildesheim, Ratisbon, and Cologne, where **Thomas Aquinas** was his pupil. From 1245 to 1254 he lectured in Paris, in 1254 he became provincial of the Dominicans in Germany, and in 1260 was named bishop of Ratisbon. But in 1262 he retired to his convent in Cologne to devote himself to literary pursuits. Of his works the most notable are the *Summa Theologiae* and the *Summa de Creaturis*. Albertus excelled all his contemporaries in the width of his learning, and in legend appears as a magician. He was a faithful follower of **Aristotle** as presented by Jewish, Arabian and western commentators, and did more than anyone to bring about that union of theology and Aristotelianism which is the basis of scholasticism. He was canonized in 1931 and named a Doctor of the Church by Pope **Pius XI**. His feast day is 15 November.

ALBIN, Eleazar (d.1759) English naturalist and water-colourist, who published the first book on British birds with coloured plates. Working from a pub called *The Dog and Duck* in Tottenham Court Road, London (at that time in open country), he published *The History of Insects* (1720), illustrated with his own metal engravings, *A Natural History of Spiders* (1735), and *A Natural History of British Birds* (3 vols, 1731–38).

ALBINONI, Tomasso Giovanni (1671–1751) Italian composer, born in Venice. He wrote 48 operas, and a number of concertos which have been revived in recent times. The popular Adagio in G minor attributed to him is spurious.

ALBINUS See **ALCUIN**

ALBOIN (d.574) king of the Lombards in Pannonia from 561. He fought against the Ostrogoths, and slew Kunimond, king of the Gepids, with his own hand (566), marrying his daughter Rosamond. In 568 he invaded Italy, subdued it to the Tiber, and made his capital at Pavia. He extended his Italian dominions, but at a feast at Verona, he made his queen drink from her father's skull, and she incited her paramour to murder him (574).

ALBORNOZ, Gil Alvarez Carillo (1300–67) Spanish prelate and soldier, born in Cuenca. He became archbishop of Toledo in 1338, but fought against the Moors, and was dubbed a knight. For denouncing **Pedro, 'the Cruel'**, he had to flee to Pope Clement VI in Avignon, who made him a cardinal (1350). He died in Viterbo, papal legate to Bologna.

ALBRECHT THE PIOUS See **ALBERT**

ALBRECHTSBERGER, Johann Georg (1736–1809) Austrian composer and writer on musical theory, born in Klosterneuburg. He became court organist at Vienna and chapel master of St Stephen's. **Johann Hummel** and **Beethoven** were among his pupils.

ALBRET, Jeanne d' See **JEANNE D'ALBRET**

ALBRIGHT, Ivan Le Lorraine (1897–1983) American painter, born in North Harvey, Illinois. He began as an architectural student but turned to painting after World War I, in which he served as a medical draughtsman in France. The clinical studies he made then of surgical operations laid the foundations of the meticulous technique he perfected later (he often took ten years to paint a picture), as well as the obsession with morbid subject matter. After the war he studied at the Art Institute of Chicago (1919–23), the Pennsylvania Academy of Fine Arts (1923), and the National Academy of Design, New York (1924). His style has been called 'Magic Realism', and had obvious links with Surrealism, but he remained one of the most idiosyncratic of 20th-century painters.

ALBRIGHT, William Foxwell (1891–1971) American archaeologist and biblical scholar, born in Coquimbo, Chile, of American missionary parents. He studied at Johns Hopkins University and taught there from 1929 to 1958. He was also director of the American School of Oriental Research in Jerusalem (1921–29, 1933–36), and excavated many notable sites in Palestine, including Gibeah. He wrote several authoritative books, including *Archaeology of Palestine and the Bible* (1932), *From the Stone Age to Christianity* (1940), *Archaeology and the Religion of Israel* (1942), *The Bible and the Ancient Near East* (1961), and *Yahweh and the Gods of Canaan* (1968).

ALBUMAZAR, properly **Abu-Mashar** (787–885) Arab astronomer and astrologer, born in Balk. He spent much of his life in Baghdad, where he became the leading astrologer of his day, and his books were widely circulated. Despite his fantastic theories about the beginning and end of the world, he did valuable work on the nature of the tides. He was cast as a rascally wizard in the play, *Albumazar*, by Thomas Tomkis (1615), which was revived, with a prologue by **John Dryden**, in 1668.

ALBURQUERQUE, Affonso d' (1453–1515) called 'the Great', Portuguese viceroy of the Indies, born near Lisbon. He landed on the Malabar coast in 1502, conquered Goa and established what was to become, with Ceylon, Malacca and the island of Ormuz, the Portuguese East Indies. He established a reputation as an active, wise, fair and far-seeing man but was replaced peremptorily by the king, in 1515. He died shortly afterwards at sea on his way back to Portugal. His commentaries were translated by Birch for the Hakluyt Society (4 vols, 1875–84).

ALCAEUS (c.620–c.580 BC) one of the greatest Greek lyric poets. He lived at Mytilene on the island of Lesbos, a contemporary of **Sappho**. He was the first exponent of the so-called 'Alcaic' four-lined stanza, which was named after him. A bluff, blustering extrovert, he composed a host of drinking songs, hymns, political odes and love songs. Of the ten books of odes he is said to have composed, only fragments now remain.

ALCAMENES (5th century BC) Greek sculptor, the pupil and rival of **Phidias**. A Roman copy of his *Aphrodite* is in the Louvre.

ALCESTER, Frederick Beauchamp Paget Seymour, 1st Baron (1821–95) English naval commander. Educated at Eton, he entered the navy in 1834, and served in Burma. He commanded the floating battery, *Meteor*, in the Baltic (1855–56) during the Crimean War, and commanded the naval brigade in New Zealand during the Maori War (1860–61). He was commander-in-chief in the Mediterranean (1880–83), and bombarded Alexandria in 1882.

ALCIATUS, Andrea Alciato (1492–1550) Italian jurist, born in Milan and professor at several universities. With **Budaeus** and Zasius he was a leader of legal humanism and correspondent of **Thomas More** and **Erasmus**. He wrote *Annotationes* to the last ten books of **Justinian I**'s *Code* containing references to classical history and literature, *Disppunctiones*, *Paradoxa* and other works.

ALCIBIADES (c.450–404 BC) Athenian statesman, born in Athens. He lost his father, Clinias, in the battle of Coronea (447), and so was brought up in the house of **Pericles**. **Socrates** gained great influence over him, but was unable to restrain his love of magnificence and dissipation, especially after his marriage to the wealthy Hipparete. He first bore arms in the expedition against Potidaea (432 BC), but took no part in political matters till after the death of the demagogue **Cleon**, when, jealous of **Nicias**, he persuaded the Athenians to ally themselves with Argos, Elis, and Mantines (420) against Sparta. It was at his suggestion that, in 415, they engaged in the Sicilian expedition, of which he was a commander. But while preparations were being made, one night all the statues of Hermes in Athens were mutilated. Alcibiades' enemies threw on him the blame of this sacrilege, and after he had set sail, he was recalled to stand his trial. His response was to induce the Spartans to send assistance to Syracuse to form an alliance with Persia, and to encourage Ionia and the islands, where he now went, to revolt against Athens. But the not unjust suspicions of Agis and other Spartans led him to flee to **Tissaphernes**, the Persian satrap, to whom he soon became indispensable. And now he began to plot the overthrow of democracy in Athens, and secured Persian support for the oligarchical council established in 411, which did not, however, recall him. Thereupon he took the command of the Athenian (democratic) army at Samos, and during the next four years defeated the Spartans at Cynossema, Abydos, and Cyzicus, recovered Chalcedon and Byzantium, and restored to the Athenians the dominion of the sea. He then returned home (407) and was enthusiastically received, but, failing in an expedition to Asia, he was superseded (406) and went into exile in the Thracian Chersonesus. Emerging after the great Spartan victory at Aegospotami, he made for the Persian court, but by procurement of the Spartans, who knew he was seeking Persian help for the Athenians against them, his house was fired and he was assassinated.

ALCIPHRON (fl.180) Greek writer. He wrote 118 fictitious letters from ordinary people (farmers, fisherman, etc) affording glimpses into everyday life in 4th century BC Athens.

ALCMAEON (fl.520 BC) Greek physician and philosopher from Croton, Italy, the first recorded anatomist in history. He was the true discoverer of the Eustachian tubes, and pioneer of embryology through anatomical dissection. He advanced the Pythagorean doctrine that health depended on the equal balance of opposites like dry/wet, hot/cold, etc, but he also founded his medical theories on empirical surgical practice.

ALCMAN (fl.620 BC) Greek lyric poet, born in Sardis, in Lydia, but lived, first as a slave, and afterwards as a freeman, in Sparta. The first to write erotic poetry, he composed in the Doric dialect *Parthenia* (songs sung by choruses of virgins), bridal hymns, and verses in praise of love and wine. Of his scanty fragments the most important is a *Parthenion*, discovered on an Egyptian papyrus in Paris in 1855.

ALCOCK, Sir John William (1892–1919) English aviator, the first man to fly the Atlantic non-stop, with **Arthur Whitten Brown**, in 1919. Born in Manchester, he served as a captain in the Royal Naval Air Service in World War I; he made a bombing raid on Constantinople and was captured by the Turks in 1917. After the war he became a test pilot with Vickers Aircraft. On 14 June 1919, with Whitten Brown as navigator, he piloted a Vickers-Vimy biplane non-stop from St John's, Newfoundland to Clifden, County Galway, in Ireland, in a time of 16 hours 27 minutes. Both men were knighted after the flight. Soon afterwards Alcock was killed in an aeroplane accident in France.

ALCOTT, Amos Bronson (1799–1888) American teacher and transcendentalist, father of **Louisa May Alcott**. He was born near Wolcott, Connecticut, and started as a pedlar, then became an itinerant teacher. He opened an unorthodox, unsuccessful school in Boston, a vegetarian co-operative farming community ('Fruitlands'), which also failed, and published books on the principles of education. An ardent transcendentalist, and a brilliant teacher and educationist, he was eventually appointed superintendent of schools in Concord, Massachusetts in 1859. The family fortunes were salvaged with the success of daughter Louisa May's *Little Women* in 1868, and in 1879 he established the Concord Summer School of Philosophy and Literature.

ALCOTT, Louisa May (1832–88) American writer, and author of the children's classic *Little Women*. The daughter of **Amos Bronson Alcott**, she was born in Germantown, Philadelphia. She was a nurse in a Union hospital during the Civil War, and published her letters from this period as *Hospital Sketches* in 1864. In 1868 she achieved enormous success with *Little Women*, which drew on her own home experiences, and a second volume, *Good Wives*, in 1869, followed by *An Old Fashioned Girl* (1870), *Little Men* (1871) and *Jo's Boys* (1886).

ALCOVER, Joan (1854–1926) Spanish poet, born in Palma, Majorca. Although his first writings were in the Castilian language, he is chiefly known as a poet in Catalan. He presided over a literary *salon* in Majorca, where he was known as a precise literary critic and brilliant talker. His poetry reflects the tragedy of his private life (he lost his wife and four children in rapid succession) and a deep feeling for his native landscape. He published *Poesias* (1887), *Metereos* (1901), and *Poèmes Biblics* (1919).

ALCUIN (c.737–804) Northumbrian scholar, and adviser to the emperor **Charlemagne**, born in York and educated at the cloister school, of which in 778 he became master. In 781, returning from Rome, he met Charlemagne at Parma, and on his invitation attached himself to the court at Aix-la-Chapelle (Aachen). Here he devoted himself first to the education of the royal family, but through his influence the court became a school of culture for the Frankish empire, inspiring the Carolingian renaissance. In 796 he settled at Tours as abbot; and the school here soon became one of the most important in the empire. Till his death he still corresponded constantly with Charlemagne. His works comprise poems; works on grammar, rhetoric, and dialectics; theological and ethical treatises; Lives of several saints; and over 200 letters.

ALDA, Alan (1936–) American actor/director, born in New York, the son of actor Robert Alda (1914–86). He performed with his father at the Hollywood Canteen (1951) and progressed, via summer stock and small television appearances, to his Broadway début in *Only in America* (1959). Subsequent theatre work includes *Purlie Victorious* (1961), *The Owl and the Pussycat* (1964) and *The Apple Tree* (1966). He made his film début in *Gone Are the Days* (1963), but it was his extensive involvement in the television series *M.A.S.H* (1972–83) that earned him his greatest popularity. A gentle, witty performer with a wry insight into human foibles, he won numerous awards for the series (including five Emmys), which provided a showcase for his talents as a socially-conscious writer, director and performer. The television film *Kill Me If You Can* (1977) allowed him a change of pace as a condemned murderer, but his acerbic sense of humour has been uppermost in films like *The Four Seasons* (1981), *Sweet Liberty* (1985) and *A New Life* (1988).

ALDER, Kurt (1902–58) German organic chemist, born in Konigshütte (now Chorzow in Poland). With **Otto Diels** he discovered in 1928 the Diels-Alder diene reaction, valuable in organic synthesis. From 1940 he directed an institute in the University of Cologne. Diels and Alder shared the Nobel chemistry prize in 1950.

ALDHELM, or **Ealdhelm, St** (c.640–709) Anglo-Saxon scholar and prelate. Educated at Malmesbury and Canterbury, he became first abbot of Malmesbury about 675, and first bishop of Sherbourne in 705. A skilled architect, he built a little church still standing, it is claimed, at Bradford-on-Avon; a great scholar, he wrote Latin treatises, letters, and verses, as well as some English poems that have perished.

ALDINGTON, Richard, originally **Edward Godfree** (1892–1962) English poet, novelist, editor and biographer, born in Hampshire. He was educated at London University, and, himself an Imagist, in 1913 became editor of *Egoist*, the periodical of the Imagist school. His experiences in World War I left him ill and bitter and this led to his novel *Death of a Hero*, (1929). As well as other novels, such as *The Colonel's Daughter* (1931), he published several volumes of poetry, including *A Fool i' the Forest* (1925) and *A Dream in the Luxembourg* (1930). At the beginning of World War II he went to the USA, where he published his *Poetry of the English-Speaking World* (1941) and many biographies, including *Wellington* (1946) which was awarded the James Tait Black Memorial prize, a study of **D H Lawrence** (1950), a controversial and embittered study of *Lawrence of Arabia* (1955), and a study of

Robert Louis Stevenson (1957). He married **Hilda Doolittle**, also a poet, in 1913 and they were divorced in 1937. He published his autobiography, *Life for Life's Sake*, in 1940.

ALDISS, Brian Wilson (1925–) English science-fiction writer and novelist, born in Dereham, Norfolk and educated at Framlingham College. After a career in bookselling, he embarked on a prolific career of writing with his first novel, *The Brightfount Diaries*, in 1955. He was literary editor of the *Oxford Mail* (1958–69), and had considerable success with *The Hand-Reared Boy* (1970) and *A Soldier Erect* (1971). He is best known, however, as a writer of science-fiction, such as *Non-Stop* (entitled *Starship* in the USA, 1958), *Hothouse* (1962), *The Saliva Tree* (1966), *The Moment of Eclipse* (1971), *Helliconia Spring* (1982) and *Helliconia Summer* (1983). He has edited many books of short stories, and produced histories of science fiction such as *Billion Year Spree* (1973) and *Trillion Year Spree* (1986).

ALDOBRANDINI, Cinzio (1551–1610) Italian cardinal and art patron, owner of the famous antique Roman frescoes named after him.

ALDOBRANDINI, Ippolito (1536–1605) Florentine nobleman. He became Pope **Clement VIII** in 1592.

ALDOBRANDINI, Sivestro (1499–1588) Florentine lawyer. He taught law at Pisa, rebelled against the Medici and opposed **Charles V**, for which he was banished in 1581.

ALDRED, or **Ealdred,** or **Alred** (d.1069) Anglo-Saxon prelate. He became abbot of Tavistock (1027), bishop of Worcester (1044), and archbishop of York (1060). He undertook several diplomatic missions to the Continent, and was the first English bishop to visit Jerusalem (1058). It is said that he crowned **Harold II** in 1066; he certainly crowned **William I, the Conqueror**, and proved a faithful servant to the Norman king. He was active and courageous, but ambitious, greedy and self-seeking. He died in York.

ALDRICH, Henry (1647–1710) English cleric, born in Westminster. He passed in 1662 from Westminster School to Christ Church, Oxford, of which he became dean in 1689. He designed the Peckwater Quadrangle, and wrote the well-known catch, 'Hark, the bonny Christ Church Bells'; but he is less remembered as architect or composer, or even as an inveterate smoker, than as the author of the *Artis Logicae Compendium* (1691).

ALDRICH, Nelson Wilmarth (1841–1915) American politician, born in Foster, Rhode Island of poor origins. He got a political foothold as a Republican member of the Providence common council (1869–75), his fidelity to business-serving party politics making him a member of the Rhode Island legislature lower house in 1875 and its speaker in 1876. He was elected congressman in 1879–81, after which the Rhode Island legislature chose him for a seat in the US senate (1881–1911). By the turn of the century he controlled the senate for the Republicans on domestic issues and ruthlessly defended big business and a high protective tariff. Uneasy with President **Theodore Roosevelt**, who was careful not to alienate him but anxious not to seem subservient to him, he crudely paraded domination of President **William Howard Taft** in 1909–10. He refused to face the ordeal of meeting the voters when it was made mandatory by constitutional amendment, and retired in 1911. His daughter married **John D Rockefeller**, Jr, and the future New York Governor Nelson Aldrich Rockefeller was his grandson.

ALDRICH, Thomas Bailey (1836–1907) American writer, born in Portsmouth, New Hampshire. He was editor of the *Atlantic Monthly* (1881–90), and the author of numerous short stories and novels, and several volumes of poetry. His most successful book, *The Story of a Bad Boy* (1870) was an autobiographical novel about his boyhood.

ALDRIN, Buzz (Edwin Eugene) (1930–) American astronaut, born in Glen Ridge, New Jersey. In 1951 he graduated third in his class of 475 from the US Military Academy at West Point, gaining a BS degree; and received a DSc degree from Massachusetts Institute of Technology (MIT) for a thesis on manned orbital rendezvous. He flew 66 combat missions in Korea, for which he was decorated, and later flew in Germany with the 36th Tactical Wing. A major in the USAF, he was one of the third group of astronauts selected by NASA, and in 1966 he set a world record by walking in space for five hours and 37 minutes during the Gemini 12 mission.

ALDROVANDI, Ulisse (1522–1605) Italian naturalist, born in Bologna. Imprisoned at Rome in 1549 as a heretic, he graduated in medicine at the university of Bologna (1553), occupied successively its chairs of botany and natural history, and established its botanical garden in 1567. He published many handsomely illustrated books on birds, fishes and insects.

ALDUS MANUTIUS, or **Aldo Manucci,** or **Manuzio** (c.1450–1515) Venetian scholar and printer, born in Bassiano. He was the founder of the Aldine Press, which produced the first printed editions of many Greek and Roman classics and of the great Italian writers that for about a hundred years were printed in Venice by himself and his successors: his son, Paolo Manuzio (1512–74); and his grandson, Aldus the Younger (1547–97). The first to print Greek books, he had beautiful founts of Greek type and Latin type made, and first used italics on a large scale. In all, 908 works were issued, of which the rarest and most valuable are those from 1490 to 1497, the *Virgil* of 1501, and the *Rhetores Graeci*.

ALEARDI, Aleardo, Count (1812–78) Italian poet and patriot, born in Verona. He took part in the rising against Austria in 1848, and later became a deputy in the Italian parliament (1866) and later senator. He was popular in his time as a writer of patriotic lyrics.

ALEBUA, Ezekiel (1947–) Solomon Islands' politician. He rose from the ranks of the right-of-centre Solomon Islands United party (SIUPA) to become deputy prime minister in the 1984–86 government led by Sir **Peter Kenilorea**. Following Kenilorea's resignation in November 1986, he was narrowly elected by the national parliament to take over as prime minister and held this position until SIUPA was defeated in the general election of February 1989. Under his premiership the Solomon Islands joined Papua New Guinea and Vanuatu to form the 'Spearhead Group' (1988), which is dedicated to preserving Melanesian cultural traditions.

ALEICHEM, Sholem, Sholom, or **Shalom,** pen-name of **Solomon J Rabinowitz** (1859–1916) Russian-Jewish author, born in Pereyaslev in the Ukraine, the son of Russian-Jewish shopkeepers. He spent much of his youth in and around the neighbouring town of Voronkov which was to feature as Krasilevke, the setting of many of his stories. After working for some years as a rabbi, he devoted himself to writing and Yiddish culture, contributing to the Hebrew magazine *Hamelitz* and the first Yiddish newspaper, established in 1883. In 1893 he moved to Kiev, but the pogroms of 1905 drove him to the USA, where he attempted to establish himself as a playwright for the Yiddish theatre, which was flourishing in New York at the time. He travelled widely, giving readings of his work in many European cities, and from 1908 to 1914 spent most of his time in Italy to improve his health. He returned to settle in New York in 1914. His short stories and plays portray Jewish life in Russia in the late 19th century with vividness, humour and sympathy, and were first widely introduced to a non-Jewish public in 1943 in Maurice Samuel's *The World of Sholom Aleichem*; nearly all his work has been translated into English, including *Jewish Children* (1920), *The Old Country*, *Stories and Satires* and *Old Country Tales*. The popular musical *Fiddler on the Roof* is based on the stories of Aleichem.

ALEIXANDRE, Vicente (1898–1984) Spanish poet, and winner of the Nobel prize for literature in 1977. Born in Seville, the son of a railway engineer, he suffered from renal tuberculosis in his youth, which forced him to remain in Spain after the Civil War despite his Republican sympathies. Among his early works were *Ambito* (1928), *La Destrucción o el amor* (1935) and *Pasión de la Tierra* (1935), but it was the appearance of his collected poems, *Mis Poemas Mejores*, in 1937, that established his reputation as a major poet. His later publications include *En un vasto dominio* (1962), *Presencias* (1965), and *Antologia Total* (1976).

ALEKHINE, Alexander Alexandrovich (1892–1946) Russian-born French chess player, world champion, (1927–35, 1937–46), born in Moscow into a landowning family. He became addicted to chess from the age of eleven and gained his master title at St Petersburg in 1909. The Russian Revolution left him without his legacy and he worked as a magistrate before taking up French citizenship. Having prepared more thoroughly than his opponent, he defeated **Capablanca** in 1927 to win the world championship. Married four times to older women, and an alcoholic, he was successful in defences of his title until he faced **Euwe** in 1935. Adopting a new regimen of rigid self-discipline he regained his title by beating Euwe in a return match of 1937. During World War II he played in tournaments organized in Nazi Germany and co-operated in contributing anti-semitic articles to the Nazi press. Ostracized by most of the chess world after the war, he died, destitute, in Estoril, Portugal.

ALEKSANDROV, Pavel Sergeevich (1896–1982) Russian mathematician, born in Bogorodsk. He studied at Moscow and became professor there in 1929. The leader of the Soviet school of topologists, he developed many of the methods of combinatorial topology. He was a life-long friend of the German topologist **Heinz Hopf**, and their book *Topologie* (1935) was a landmark in the development of the subject.

ALEMÁN, Mateo (1547–1610 or 1620) Spanish novelist, born in Seville. His great work is a picaresque novel *Guzmán de Alfarache* (1599), about a boy running away from home. He emigrated to Mexico in 1608.

ALEMBERT, Jean le Rond D' (1717–83) French philosopher and mathematician, born in Paris, the illegitimate son of Mme de Tencin and the Chevalier Destouches. Brought up as a foundling, he was given an annuity from his father and studied law, medicine and mathematics at the Collège Mazarin. In 1743 he published *Traité de Dynamique*, developing the mathematical theory of Newtonian dynamics, including the principle named after him. Later he worked on fluid motion, partial differential equations, the motion of vibrating strings, and celestial mechanics. He also published many short memoirs on analysis. Until 1758 he was **Denis Diderot**'s principal collaborator on the *Encyclopédie*, of which he was scientific editor, and wrote the *Discours Préliminaire*, proclaiming the philosophy of the French enlightenment. His fame spread through Europe, but he refused invitations from **Frederick II, the Great** of Prussia and **Catherine II** of Russia and remained in Paris.

ALENÇON title of ducal family, a branch of the house of Valois, representatives of which fell at Crécy and Agincourt, and held high command at Pavia. Subsequently the title was given to a brother of **Charles IX**, who fought against the Huguenots, to a brother of **Louis XIII**, to the grandson of **Louis XIV**, and to a grandson of **Louis-Philippe**.

ALESIUS, Alexander (1500–65) Scottish Lutheran reformer, born in Edinburgh. Educated at St Andrews, he became a canon there. Won over to the Reformation, he had to flee to the Continent (1532), and, settling at Wittenberg, signed the Augsburg Confession, and gained the friendship of **Melanchthon**. In 1535 he came over to England, was well received by **Cranmer** and **Cromwell**, and lectured for a time on theology at Cambridge; but the persecuting 'Six Articles' compelled him to return to Germany. He was successively appointed to a theological chair in the universities of Frankfurt-on-the-Oder and Leipzig.

ALESSI, Galeazzo (1512–72) Italian architect, born in Perugia. After studying ancient architecture, he gained a European reputation by his designs for palaces and churches in Genoa and elsewhere. He was a pupil of Caporali and a friend of **Michelangelo**.

ALEXANDER, of Battenberg See **BATTENBERG**

ALEXANDER II, known as Anselm of Lucca pope (1061–73), born in Baggio. Bishop of Lucca from 1057, he undertook reforms and campaigned against immorality and corruption in the church. He was a founder of the Patarine party, which opposed the marriage of priests. On his election in 1061 as the choice of Hildebrand (the future Pope **Gregory VII**), the German court elected Honorius (II) as anti-pope (1061–72).

ALEXANDER III, Orlando Bandinelli (c.1105–c.1181) pope from 1159 to 1181, born in Siena. He taught law at Bologna and became adviser to the English pope, **Adrian IV**. After his own election as pope he was engaged in a struggle with the emperor **Frederick I, Barbarossa** who, refusing to recognize him, set up antipopes, until he was defeated and compelled to sign the Treaty of Venice (1177). He was also involved in the quarrel between **Henry II** of England and **Thomas à Becket**.

ALEXANDER VI, Rodrigo Borgia (1431–1503) pope from 1492 to 1503, born in Játiva in Spain. The beautiful Rosa Vanozza bore him **Cesare Borgia, Lucretia Borgia**, and other children. In 1455 he was made a cardinal by his uncle, **Calixtus III**, and in 1492, on the death of Innocent VIII, was elevated to the papal chair, which he had previously secured by flagrant bribery. The long absence of the popes from Italy had weakened their authority and curtailed their revenues. To compensate for this loss, Alexander endeavoured to break the power of the Italian princes, and to appropriate their possessions for the benefit of his own family, employing the most execrable means to gain this end. He died most likely of fever, but there is some evidence for the tradition that he was accidentally poisoned by wine intended for Cardinal da Corneto, his host. He apportioned the New World between Spain and Portugal and introduced the censorship of books. Under his pontificate **Savonarola** was executed as a heretic.

ALEXANDER VII, Fabio Chigi (1599–1667) pope from 1655 to 1667. As nuncio in Cologne, his refusal to conduct business with heretics caused him to boycott the peace proceedings at Westphalia which ended the Thirty Years' War, and his protest against the treaties led to their denunciation as void by Pope Innocent X, who then made him cardinal secretary of state. The Spanish candidate for the papacy, his election was said to have been clinched by belief in his opposition to nepotism, to which he later succumbed. He constructed the colonnade in the piazza of St Peter and published Latin poems. He supported the Jesuits against the Jansenists and forbade the translation of the Roman Missal into French.

ALEXANDER VIII, (Pietro Vito Ottoboni) (1610–91) pope from 1689 to 1691. He was a noble Venetian for whose election in succession to the anti-French **Innocent XI** the French ambassador intrigued, but Alexander continued Innocent's policy of hostility to **Louis XIV**'s policy of Gallicanism, condemning the 1682 declaration by the French clergy in its favour. He was hostile to the Jesuits and rejoiced in the defeat of Louis XIV's ally, the ousted **James VII and II** of Scotland, England and Ireland, at the Battle of the Boyne (1689).

ALEXANDER I (1777–1825) tsar of Russia from 1801, son of Emperor **Paul**. Born in St Petersburg, he was reared by his grandmother **Catherine II, the Great** and educated on Rousseauesque principles. In 1793 he married Princess Elizabeth of Baden. He succeeded to the throne after the assassination of his father, and immediately initiated a wide range of reforms, notably in administration, education, science, and the system of serfdom. In 1805 he joined the coalition against **Napoleon**, but saw the Russo-Austrian forces defeated at Austerlitz that year. He made an alliance with Prussia, but after defeats at Eylau and Friedland he signed the Treaty of Tilsit and became an ally of Napoleon (1807). With French encouragement he attacked Sweden in order to secure possession of Finland (1808), and renewed hostilities against Turkey which were continued until the Peace of Bucharest (1812). Russian resentment of the French-dominated Continental System inspired economic rivalry, which led to Napoleon's ill-fated invasion of Russia in 1812. Although he had returned to his capital before the Russian defeat at Borodino in September 1812, he took an active part in the destruction of Napoleon's retreating army at Dresden and Leipzig in 1813; he entered Paris with the Allies in 1814, and paid a triumphant visit to London. At the Congress of Vienna (1815) he received Poland, assumed the throne, and gave it a new constitution. After Napoleon escaped from Elba and landed in France for his 'Hundred Days', Alexander formed the Holy Alliance of Christian European powers, much influenced by the cosmopolitan religious mystic Madame **von Krüdener**. The latter years of his reign saw him retreat into reactionary policies which progressively alienated his people. The death of a much-loved daughter, the flood disaster in St Petersburg in 1824, and discontent within crack regiments of his army led to a breakdown in his health; while recuperating in the Crimea he contracted a fever from which he died at Taganrog.

ALEXANDER II, known as **'the Liberator'** (1818–81) tsar of Russia from 1885, the son of **Nicholas I**. Born in St Petersburg, he was carefully educated by his father and subjected to rigorous military training that affected his health. In 1841, in Germany, he married Princess Marie (1824–80), daughter of the Grand Duke of Hesse-Darmstadt; in Russia she was known as Maria Alexandrovna. He succeeded to the throne during the Crimean War, and signed the Treaty of Paris that ended it in 1856. A determined reformer, the great achievement of his reign was the emancipation of the serfs in 1861 (hence his nickname), followed by reform of the legal and administrative systems, widespread building of railroads and schools, and the establishment of elected assemblies in the provinces. He put down a Polish insurrection (1863) with great severity. During his reign he maintained friendly relations with Prussia, especially in the Franco-German war of 1870–71, and married his only daughter Marie to Alfred (Duke of Edinburgh, and later Duke of Saxe-Coburg-Gotha) second son of Queen **Victoria**. He extended the Russian empire in the Caucusus and central Asia, and took the field with his army in the victorious war against Turkey (1877–78), winning the liberation of Bulgaria. In 1880, soon after the death of his first wife, he married his mistress, **Katharina Dolgorukova**. Despite his liberal views, his government was severe in repressing peasant unrest and revolutionary movements, especially the Nihilists. After several assassination attempts he was mortally injured by a bomb thrown at him in St Petersburg. He was succeeded by his son, **Alexander III**.

ALEXANDER III (1845–94) tsar of Russia from 1881, younger son and successor of **Alexander II**. In 1866 he married Princess Marie Dagmar (1847–1928), daughter of King **Kristian IX** of Denmark and sister of Queen **Alexandra** of Britain. (Marie Dagmar's name in Russia became Maria Fyodorovna, and as Dowager Empress she escaped to England in 1919.) Openly critical of his father's reforming policies before his accession, Alexander followed a repressive policy in home affairs especially in the persecution of Jews, and promoted Russian language and traditions and the Orthodox Church. Abroad, he consolidated Russia's hold on central Asia to the frontier of Afghanistan, provoking a crisis with Britain (1885). In the last years of his reign he discouraged the triple alliance of Russia, Germany and Austria and became a virtual ally of France. Despite several assassination attempts he died a natural death and was succeeded by his son **Nicholas II**.

ALEXANDER I (c.1077–1124) king of Scotland, the fifth son of **Malcolm Canmore** and Queen **Margaret**. In 1107 he succeeded his brother, Edgar, but only to that part of the kingdom north of the Forth (see **David I**). He married Sibilla, a natural daughter of **Henry I** of England; he initiated a shift towards a more diocesan based episcopacy.

ALEXANDER II (1198–1249) king of Scotland, born in Haddington, succeeded as the only son of his father, **William I** in 1214. By 1215 he had begun to show a much more independent stance to England than his father; he allied with the disaffected English barons and made an incursion as far south as Dover. This brought temporary papal excommunication which was lifted in 1218. The accession of **Henry III** of England allowed a rapprochement, cemented by his marriage to Henry's sister, the princess Joan (1221), which brought about the settlement of the frontier question in 1237 by the Treaty of York. Her death, without children, in 1238, and Alexander's marriage to the daughter of a Picardy nobleman, Marie de Coucy, who gave birth to a son, **Alexander**, in 1241, strained relations with England. His reign is notable for the vigorous assertion of royal authority in the western Highlands and the south-west during the years of peace with England. His death, at Kerrara near Oban, came during an expedition attempting to extend his rule, at the expense of Norway, to the Western Isles.

ALEXANDER III (1241–86) king of Scotland, in 1249 succeeded his father, **Alexander II**, and in 1251 married the princess Margaret (1240–75), eldest daughter of **Henry III** of England. He completed the consolidation of the western part of the kingdom by annexing the Hebrides and the Isle of Man after his defeat of King **Haakon IV** of Norway at Largs in 1263 and the Treaty of Perth (1266). The emerging status of Scotland as a European kingdom of middling rank was confirmed by the pattern of royal marriages of Alexander and his children: his only daughter, Margaret (1261–83) married King Eric of Norway in 1281, further cementing the relationship begun in 1266; and his son, Alexander (1264–84), married Marguerite, daughter of the Count of Flanders, in 1282. The period between 1266 and the death of Queen Margaret in 1275 has often been seen as a golden age for Scotland: factional politics had almost disappeared, the kingdom had been consolidated, the king's authority was unquestioned, and there was a considerable, favourable balance of trade. The death of his only surviving son, without issue, in 1284 and of his daughter the previous year left only his infant daughter, **Margaret** of Norway (1283–90) as a successor and prompted Alexander's second marriage, to Yolande, daughter of the Count of Dreux, in 1285. While on his way to a reunion with her he died 19 March 1286, as he rode in the dark along the cliffs between Burntisland and Kinghorn. His death left the way open for a disputed succession and the renewed interference of England in Scottish affairs.

ALEXANDER I (1888–1934) king of the Serbs, Croats and Slovenes (1921–29), king of Yugoslavia (1929–34), born in Cetinje, the second son of **Peter I**. He was commander-in-chief of the Serbian army in World War I and acted as regent for his father from 1914 to 1921. He tried to build up a strong and unified Yugoslavia, imposing a royal dictatorship in 1929. In 1934 he set out on a state visit to France but was assassinated in Marseilles by a Macedonian terrorist in the pay of Croatian nationalists.

ALEXANDER, Albert Victor, 1st Earl Alexander of Hillsborough (1885–1965) English Labour politician, born in Weston-super-Mare, the son of an engineer. He first entered parliament as Co-operative member for the Hillsborough division of Sheffield in 1922, becoming in 1924 parliamentary secretary to the board of trade. He was three times First Lord of the Admiralty (1929–31, 1940–45, and 1945–46), and in the Labour government (1946–50) he was minister of defence. He became in 1955 leader of the Labour peers in the House of Lords.

ALEXANDER, Bill (William) (1948–) English stage director, born in Hunstanton. He worked at the Bristol Old Vic (1971–73) and the Royal Court Theatre, London before joining the Royal Shakespeare Company in 1977 as an assistant to **John Barton** and **Trevor Nunn**. He became resident (later associate) director at the RSC, directing new plays such as **Howard Barker**'s *The Hang of the Goal* (1978), *Crimes in Hot Countries* (1985), and *Country Dancing* (1986). His Shakespearian productions include *Richard III* (1984), *The Merry Wives of Windsor* (1985), *A Midsummer Night's Dream* (1986), *Twelfth Night*, *The Merchant of Venice* (1987), and *Cymbeline* (1987 and 1989).

ALEXANDER, Cecil Frances, née **Humphreys** (1818–95) Irish poet and hymn writer, born in County Wicklow, the daughter of a captain in the Royal Marines, and wife of Bishop **William Alexander**. She published her *Verses for Holy Seasons* in 1846, and two years later her immensely popular *Hymns for Little Children*, which included the well known 'All things bright and beautiful', 'Once in Royal David's city', and 'There is a green hill far away'. She also wrote ballads on Irish history.

ALEXANDER, Franz Gabriel (1891–1964) Hungarian-born American psychoanalyst, born in Budapest, where his father was professor of philosophy. He received his MD from Budapest University in 1913. During World War I he was a medical officer, after which he studied and then worked at the Institute for Psychoanalysis in Berlin. He settled permanently in the USA in 1932, where he founded the Chicago Institute for Psychoanalysis. Although he wrote widely on psychoanalytic and cultural issues, his work on psychosomatic disorders, among which he included peptic ulcer, essential hypertension, and rheumatic arthritis, was especially influential.

ALEXANDER, Sir George (1858–1918) English actor, born in Reading. He made his début at Nottingham in 1879. He played in *Lady Windermere's Fan*, *The Second Mrs. Tanqueray*, *The Prisoner of Zenda*, etc.

ALEXANDER, Grover Cleveland (1887–1950) American baseball player, born in Elba, Nebraska, and one of the greatest right-handed pitchers in the history of the game. In a long and brilliant career, he played for the Philadelphia Phillies (1911–17), Chicago Cubs (1918–26) and St Louis Cardinals (1926–29). He shared (with **Christy Mathewson**) a record of 373 wins. In 1926 he led the St Louis Cardinals to a sensational victory over the New York Yankees: when pitching as relief in the seventh innings he prevented any runs in the ensuing three innings although three Yankee players were on base when he came to the mound. In 1938 he was elected to the National Baseball Hall of Fame.

ALEXANDER, Sir Harold Rupert Leofric George Alexander, 1st Earl Alexander of Tunis (1891–1969) Anglo-Irish soldier and statesman, born in Caledon, County Tyrone, the second son of the Earl of Caledon. Educated at Harrow and Sandhurst, in World War I he commanded a battalion of the Irish Guards on the Western Front when he was 24 and led it through the battles of Passchendaele, Cambrai (1917) and Hazebrouck (1918). From 1932 to 1934 he was general staff officer, Northern Command, and in 1935 served on the North-West Frontier of India. In 1940 he commanded 1 Corps as rearguard at the Dunkirk evacuation (1940), and was the last man to leave France. Later as GOC, Southern Command, he originated battle training schools. In 1942 he was GOC Burma, and from 1942 to 1943 c-in-c Middle East, his North African campaign being one of the most complete victories in military history. He commanded the invasions of Sicily and Italy (1943), and was appointed field marshal on the capture of Rome in June 1944 and became supreme allied commander in the Mediterranean for the rest of the war. From 1946 to 1952 he was governor-general of Canada and from 1952 to 1954 minister of defence in the Conservative government.

ALEXANDER, Jean (1925–) English actress, born in Liverpool. A library assistant for five years, she joined the Adelphi Guild Theatre in Macclesfield in 1949 and toured Lancashire, Cheshire and Staffordshire for two years. She spent the next eleven years with a variety of repertory companies, starting as a stage manager and often doubling as a wardrobe mistress. Moving to London, she appeared in television plays like *Jacks and Knaves* (1961) before being cast in the long-running *Coronation Street* (1964–87). Her character of the dowdy, tactless gossip Hilda Ogden, a cleaner renowned for her shabby raincoat, hair curlers and perenially dangling cigarette, made her a national institution and won her the Royal Television Society's Best Performance Award for 1984 to 1985. Since retiring from the series, she has been seen in such programmes as *Boon* (1988), *Last of the Summer Wine* (1988) and the film *Scandal* (1989). Her autobiography, *The Other Side of the Street*, was published in 1989.

ALEXANDER, John White (1856–1915) American painter, born in Allegheny, Pennsylvania. He was influenced by the work of **Whistler**, and specialized in portraits, painting **Rodin**, **Mark Twain**, **Thomas Hardy** and **R L Stevenson** among others. In 1874 he became an illustrator for *Harper's Magazine*. He kept a studio in Paris from 1890 to 1901.

ALEXANDER, Samuel (1859–1938) Australian philosopher, born of Jewish parents in Sydney. Alexander left for Balliol College, Oxford, in 1877. After obtaining a degree he was made a fellow of Lincoln College, Oxford, where he was tutor in philosophy until 1893, when he was appointed to the chair of philosophy at Manchester University. His growing concern for the situation of European Jewry led him to introduce **Chaim Weizman**, his colleague at Manchester (later to become leader of the Zionist movement) to **Arthur James Balfour**. This meeting led to the 'Balfour Declaration', establishing the principle of a Jewish national home, and eventually to the establishment of the state of Israel. Alexander retired from his chair in 1924, and was awarded the Order of Merit in 1930.

ALEXANDER, William See **STIRLING, Earl of**

ALEXANDER, William (1824–1911) Irish Anglican prelate and poet, born in Londonderry. Educated at Oxford, he married **Cecil Frances Humphreys** in 1850. He became bishop of Derry and Raphoe from 1867, archbishop of Armagh and primate of All Ireland, 1896–1910. He published a volume of verses, *St Augustine's Holiday* (1886).

ALEXANDER, William (1826–94) Scottish novelist, born in Chapel of Garioch, Aberdeenshire. He worked as a ploughman until losing a leg in an accident, and turning to journalism. He wrote a novel in racy dialect, *Johnny Gibb of Gushetneuk* (1871), a series of realistic sketches of the remote country folk and places of northeastern Scotland, which was serialized in the *Aberdeen Free Press*, of which he later became editor.

ALEXANDER NEVSKI (1218–63) Russian hero and saint, prince of Novgorod. In 1240 he defeated the Swedes in a famous battle on the river Neva, near the site of modern Leningrad (hence the name, 'Nevski'), and in 1242 he defeated the Teutonic knights on the frozen Lake Peipus. In 1246 he succeeded his father as Grand Duke of Kiev, and became prince of Vladimir in 1252. Although he was a vassal of the Mongol occupation army, he sought to live with them in peace, and suppressed anti-Mongol revolts. He was canonized by the Russian Orthodox Church in 1547.

ALEXANDER OF HALES (d.1245) English schoolman, known as the 'Irrefragable Doctor'. Originally an ecclesiastic of Hailes, Gloucestershire, he became a professor of philosophy and theology in Paris, and later entered the Franciscan order. His chief work was the *Summa Universae Theologiae*.

ALEXANDER OF TRALLES (6th century) Greek physician and author of *Twelve Books on Medicine*, a major work on pathology which was current for several centuries in Latin, Greek and Arabic. Born in Tralles in Huydra, he practised in Rome.

ALEXANDER SEVERUS (205–35) Roman emperor, the cousin and adopted son of **Heliogabalus**, whom he succeeded in 221. A weak ruler, under the influence of others, especially his mother, he failed to control the military. Though successful against the Sassanid **Artaxerxes**, he and his mother were murdered by mutinous troops during a campaign against the Germans. The end of his dynasty ushered in half a century of political and military instability in the Roman empire.

ALEXANDER THE GREAT (356–323 BC) king of Macedonia, son of **Philip II** of Macedon and **Olympias**, born in Pella. Trained by eminent Greek teachers including **Aristotle**, he was only 16 when his father marched against Byzantium (340), and left him regent in his absence; at the battle of Chaeronea (338), he commanded the left wing of the Macedonian army. Philip, appointed general of the Greeks, was preparing for an invasion of Persia, when he was assassinated (336); complicity by Alexander in his father's death cannot be excluded. At any rate, Alexander, not yet 20, became king, crushed the rebellious Illyrians, razed Thebes to the ground as a warning to the Greeks (335), crossed the Hellespont and won a major victory over the Persians at Granicus (334), which opened the way to the Greek cities of Asia Minor. At a pass near Issus, in Cilicia, he met **Darius III** in battle and completely defeated him (333). The family of Darius, as well as his treasure, fell into Alexander's hands, who treated them with great magnanimity. Alexander now occupied Damascus, and took and destroyed Tyre, after a long and hard siege (332). He marched on to Palestine, and was welcomed in Egypt as a liberator from the Persians; there he consulted the oracle of Ammon in the Libyan desert, and founded Alexandria, the first and most famous of his new cities (331). He again set out to meet Darius, and near Arbela in 331 (also known as the battle of Gaugamela), he won another decisive victory over an even greater army than at Issus. Darius fled, and was eventually murdered by one of his satraps (330). Babylon and Susa opened their gates to Alexander, who also entered in triumph Persepolis, the capital of Persia. During his stay there, the royal palace was burned down, possibly in a fit of drunkenness. In 329 he overthrew the Scythians and in 328–27 he subdued Sogdiana, though only by marrying the Princess Roxana. Meanwhile, relations with his followers became increasingly difficult: in 330 he executed Philotas and his father Parmenion, in 328 he murdered his friend Cleitus the Black during a drunken brawl, and the court historian Callisthenes fell out of favour (327) and may have been executed subsequently. In 326 Alexander proceeded to the conquest of India, and at the Hydaspes (Jhelum) overthrew Porus in a costly battle. A mutiny of the army at the Hyphasis (Beas) forced him to begin the return march (326). He ordered Nearchus to sail to the Persian Gulf, while he himself marched through Gedrosia (Baluchistan), with heavy loss of men (325). At Susa, he held mass marriages of himself and the Macedonian leaders with women of the Persian aristocracy (324). At Babylon he was planning further ambitious conquests, of Arabia and to the west, when he was taken ill after a banquet, and died eleven days later. His body was eventually deposited at Alexandria in a gold coffin by **Ptolemy (I) Soter**. An unclear succession condemned the Macedonian empire to a long struggle between Alexander's leading generals. In antiquity, Alexander was viewed either as a ruthless conqueror and destroyer, or as a far-sighted statesman pursuing a civilizing mission for the world. Modern scholarship has never ceased to fluctuate between these two opposing views. Alexander's early death, the lack of unambiguous evidence about his ultimate intentions, and the legends that grew up around him in his life-time and after his death, preclude any definitive conclusion.

ALEXANDERSON, Ernst Frederick Werner (1878–1975) Swedish-born American electrical engineer and inventor, born in Uppsala. In 1901 he went to the USA and joined the General Electrical company in 1902, where he worked with Charles Stemnitz. He invented the Alexanderson alternator for transoceanic communication; antenna structures; radio receiving and transmitting systems. By 1930 he had perfected a complete television system, and a colour television receiver in 1955. He has 300 patents to his credit.

ALEXANDRA, Queen (1844–1925) queen-consort of King **Edward VII** of Great Britain, eldest daughter of King **Kristian IX** of Denmark. She married Edward in 1863 when he was prince of Wales. She engaged in much charity work; in 1902 she founded the Imperial (now Royal) Military Nursing Service, and in 1912 instituted the annual Alexandra Rose Day in aid of hospitals.

ALEXANDRA, Princess, the Hon Mrs Angus Ogilvy (1936–) daughter of George, Duke of **Kent** and Princess Marina of Greece. She married in 1963 the Hon Angus James Bruce Ogilvy (b.1928); their son is James Robert Bruce (b.1964), and daughter Marina Victoria Alexandra (b.1966).

ALEXANDRA (ALIX) FEODOROVNA (1872–1918) German princess, and empress of Russia as the wife of **Nicholas II**. The daughter of Grand Duke Louis of Hesse-Darmstadt and **Alice Maud Mary** (the daughter of Queen **Victoria**), she married Nicholas in 1894. Deeply pious and superstitious, she came under the evil influence of the fanatical **Rasputin**. During World War I, while Nicholas was away at the front, she meddled disastrously in politics. When the revolution broke out, she was imprisoned by the Bolsheviks with the rest of the royal family in 1917, and later shot in a cellar at Ekaterinberg.

ALEXEI, Petrovitch (1690–1718) Russian prince, eldest son of **Peter I, the Great**, born in Moscow. Having opposed the emperor's reforms, he was excluded from the succession, and escaped to Vienna, and thence to Naples. Induced to return to Russia, he was condemned to death, but pardoned, only to die in prison a few days after. His son became tsar, as **Peter II**.

ALEXEI I MIHAILOVITCH (1629–76) the second Romanov tsar of Russia. He succeeded his father, **Michael Romanov** in 1645. Personally pious and abstemious, the tsar presided over a court notorious for its splendour and excess. Abroad, he waged war against Poland (1654–67), regaining Smolensk and Kiev, while at home his attempts to place the Orthodox church under secular authority brought him into conflict with the Patriarch, Nikon. In 1670–71 he suppressed a great peasant revolt; and his new code of laws (1649) legitimized peasant serfdom in Russia. By his second wife he was the father of **Peter I, the Great**.

ALEXEIEV, Mikhail Vasilevich (1857–1918) Russian soldier. He fought in the Russian-Japanese War (1904–05) and was promoted general. In World War I he was appointed chief of the Imperial General Staff in 1915, and directed the retreat from Warsaw after the crushing German victory. After the Revolution in 1917 he organized the volunteer army against the Bolsheviks.

ALEXIUS I COMNENUS (1048–1118) Byzantine emperor, and founder of the Comnenian dynasty, born in Constantinople. Nephew of the emperor **Isaac I Comnenus**, he was commander of the western Byzantine armies when he was brought to the throne by a coup mounted by disaffected elements of the military aristocracy which ended the ineffective rule of Nicephorus III Botaneiates (1081). Commercial concessions to the Venetians secured naval assistance which helped him defeat a major invasion mounted by the Normans of Sicily under **Robert Guiscard**, who had captured Dyrrachium (1081–85), and later under **Bohemond I** (1107); in alliance with the Cumans he destroyed the Patzinaks, who had threatened Constantinople itself, at Mount Levounion (1091). He now turned his attention from the Balkans, and built up a new fleet with the aim of re-establishing Byzantine rule in Asia Minor. This coincided with the arrival of the First Crusade (1096–1100), with which he co-operated to recover Crete, Cyprus, and the western coast of Anatolia, but was unable to regain the interior, or Syria, where Bohemund set himself up as prince of Antioch. He enlarged the system of court honours to placate the aristocracy, but was careful to give key offices to members of the Comnenus family. He reformed the army and administration but the financial stability of the empire was undermined by a steady debasement of the coinage. His reign is well known from the *Alexiad*, the biography written by his daughter **Anna Comnena**.

ALFARABI, Abu Nasr (10th century) Islamic philosopher, born in Farab, also known as **Abu Nasr**, **Alfarabius** and **Avennasar**. He studied at Baghdad and published commentaries on **Aristotle** and **Porphyry**. He was much influenced by **Plato**'s *Republic* and can be regarded as the first Islamic neoplatonist. He also published a utopian political philosophy of his own, known under the title *The Perfect City*.

ALFIERI, Vittorio, Count (1749–1803) Italian poet and dramatist, a precursor of the Risorgimento, born in Asti, near Piedmont. Having inherited a vast fortune at the age of 14 he travelled throughout Europe and then turned his hand to writing, achieving great success with his first play *Cleopatra*, in 1775. In Florence in 1777 he met the Countess of **Albany**, the estranged wife of Prince **Charles Edward Stewart**; after separating from her husband, she became his mistress. He wrote more than a score of tragedies, six comedies, and a 'tramelogedia', *Abele*, a mixture of opera and tragedy. His ashes, and those of his mistress, are kept in the church of S Croce, in Florence, between the tombs of **Michelangelo** and **Macchiavelli**.

ALFONSIN FOULKES, Raul (1927–) Argentinian politician, born in Chascomas. Educated at military and law schools, he joined the Radical Union party (UCR) in 1945. He served in local government (1951–62) but was imprisoned by the **Peron** government for his political activities in 1953. During two brief periods of civilian rule, between 1963 and 1976, he was a member of the Chamber of Deputies, at other times practising as a lawyer. When constitutional government returned in 1983 he was elected president. He ensured that several leading military figures were brought to trial for human rights abuses. In 1986 he was joint winner of the Council of Europe's human rights prize. He was replaced as president by **Carlos Menem** in 1989.

ALFONSO I, called **el Batailador, The Battler** (1073–1134) king of Leon and Castile. He succeeded in 1104, became involved in a conflict with Castile and Leon, exercising sovereignty over the latter by reason of his marriage with its queen, Urraca. He liberated Saragossa from Moorish rule in 1118.

ALFONSO III, called **the Great** (d.910) king of Leon, Asturias, and Galicia from 866 till his death. He fought over 30 campaigns and gained numerous victories over the Moors, occupied Coimbra, and extended his territory as far as Portugal and Old Castile. His three sons conspired against him and eventually dethroned him.

ALFONSO V, called **the Magnanimous** (1396–1458) king of Leon, Castile and Sicily, he succeeded his father, Ferdinand I, in 1416, and in 1442, after a long contest, made himself king also of Naples.

ALFONSO VIII (1155–1214) king of Castile from 1158. He came to real power in 1169 after an anarchic minority, during which the regency was disputed by the Lara and Castro families. Alfonso's long struggle against the Almohads was hampered by disputes with Alfonso IX of Leon, but in alliance with Aragon and

Navarre and with papal support he won the decisive victory of Las Navas de Tolosa (1214), which severely weakened Muslim power and paved the way for the reconquest of southern Spain.

ALFONSO X, called **the Astronomer** or **the Wise** (1221–84) king of Leon and Castile. Born in Burgos, he succeeded his father, **Ferdinand III**, in 1252. He captured Cadiz and Algarve from the Moors, and thus united Murcia with Castile. In 1271 he crushed an insurrection headed by his son Philip; but a second rising under another son Sancho in 1282 deprived him of his throne. Alfonso was the founder of a Castilian national literature. He caused the first general history of Spain to be composed in Castilian, as well as a translation of the Old Testament to be made by Toledo Jews. His great code of laws (*Siete Partidas*) and his planetary table are famous; and he wrote several long poems, besides works on chemistry and philosophy.

ALFONSO I, or **Affonso Henriques** (1110–85) earliest king of Portugal. He was only two years old at the death of his father, Henry of Burgundy, conqueror and first Count of Portugal, so that the management of affairs fell to his ambitious and dissolute mother, Theresa of Castile. Wresting power from her in 1128, he turned his sword against the Moors, defeated them at Ourique, 25 July 1139, and proclaimed himself king on the field of battle. He took Lisbon (1147), and later, all Galicia, Estremadura, and Elvas.

ALFONSO V, called **Affonso el Africano** (1432–81) king of Portugal. He succeeded his father Duarte in 1438, ruling at first under the regency of his uncle Pedro. He received his surname in honour of his campaigns and conquests in North Africa. He tried without success to unite Castile with Portugal and gave up his claims in the Treaty of Alcaçovas, after which Portugal's interests were directed towards expansion in Africa.

ALFONSO XII (1857–85) king of Spain from 1874, son of **Isabella II**, and educated in Vienna and in England. After a period of republican rule following the overthrow of his mother by the army in 1868, he was formally proclaimed king in 1874. In 1876 he suppressed the last opposition of the Carlists (supporters of the Spanish pretender Don Carlos de Bourbon, 1788–1855, and his successors). He summoned the Cortes (parliament) to provide a new constitution, and under the benign influence of his prime minister, **Cánovas del Castillo**, his reign was a time of peace and relative prosperity. In 1879 he married Maria Christina (1858–1929), daughter of Archduke Charles Ferdinand of Austria, and was succeeded by his postumously-born son, **Alfonso XIII**.

ALFONSO XIII (1886–1941) king of Spain 1886–1931, posthumous son of **Alfonso XII**. His mother, Maria Christina of Austria, acted as regent until 1902, when he assumed full power. In 1906 he married princess Ena, grand-daughter of Queen **Victoria**. His reign was increasingly autocratic and unpopular. After neutrality during World War I, the Spanish were defeated by the Moors in Morocco in 1921, and from 1923 he associated himself with the military dictatorship of **Primo de Rivera** (1923–30). In 1931 the king agreed to elections, which voted overwhelmingly for a republic. He refused to abdicate, but left Spain, and died in exile.

ALFORD, Henry (1810–71) English clergyman, born in London. Fellow of Trinity College, Cambridge (1834), dean of Canterbury (1857), he was first editor of the *Contemporary Review* (1866–70), wrote on the classics and published poems and hymns, including the favourite 'Come ye thankful people, come'.

ALFRED, the Great (849–99) Anglo-Saxon king of Wessex, born at Wantage in Berkshire, the fifth and youngest son of King Æthelwulf. At the age of four he was taken to Rome to be confirmed by Pope Leo IV, and soon afterwards visited the Frankish court of **Charles I, the Bald** with his father. He succeeded his brother **Æthelred I** as king in 871, when Viking invaders were occupying the north and east of England, and Wessex was under constant attack. Early in 878 the Danish army led by **Guthorm** burst into Wessex and drove Alfred into hiding in the marshes of Athelney, in Somerset. He recovered sufficiently to defeat the Danes decisively at the battle of Edington, in Wiltshire. In the peace treaty that followed, Guthorm accepted baptism and withdrew from Wessex, and Alfred recognized the Danes as rulers of East Anglia and much of Mercia. He repelled another invasion in 885, captured London in 886, and made another treaty formalizing the partition of England, with the 'Danelaw' under Viking rule. To combat further incursions he created a ring of fortified strongholds (*burhs*) round his kingdom and built a fleet to reinforce his defences (hence his reputation as the 'father of the English navy'). His strategy succeeded, and by the end of his reign he had built a platform from which Alfred's successors of the Wessex dynasty could reconquer the Viking-held territories. As a legislator he compiled the best among the enactments of earlier kings. He promoted education and learning in the vernacular, fostered all the arts, and inspired the production of the *Anglo-Saxon Chronicle*; he himself translated Latin books into Anglo-Saxon, including the *Pastoral Care* of Pope **Gregory I, the Great**, the *Consolations of Philosophy* by **Boethius**, and works by the Venerable **Bede** and **Orosius**. He died in October, 899, and was buried in Winchester.

ALFVÉN, Hannes Olof Gösta (1908–) Swedish theoretical physicist, born in Norrköping, a pioneer of plasma physics. Educated at Uppsala, he joined the Royal Institute of Technology, Stockholm in 1940, becoming professor of electronics in 1945 and professor of plasma physics in 1964. He moved to the University of California in 1967. He did pioneering work on plasmas (gases containing positive and negative ions) and their behaviour in magnetic and electric fields. In 1942 he predicted the existence of waves in plasmas (Alfvén waves), which were later observed. His theories have been applied to the motion of particles in the Earth's magnetic field and to plasmas in stars and to experimental nuclear fusion reactors. He shared the Nobel prize for physics with **Louis Néel** in 1970.

ALFVÉN, Hugo Emil (1872–1960) Swedish composer and violinist, born in Stockholm. He was a prolific composer in the late romantic tradition, numbering five symphonies and the ballet *Prodigal Son* (1957) among his many works. He made much use of folk melodies and his best-known piece is *Midsommarvaka* (Midsummer Vigil, 1904, better known as the *Swedish Rhapsody*). He was director of music in Uppsala University from 1910 to 1939.

ALGARDI, Alessandro (1598–1654) Italian sculptor, born in Bologna. His chief work is a colossal rilievo, in St Peter's, of Pope **Leo I** restraining **Attila** from marching on Rome.

ALGAZEL, Abu Mohammed al- See **GHAZALI**

ALGER, Horatio (1832–99) American writer and clergyman, born in Revere, Massachusetts. He was educated at Harvard, became a Unitarian minister, and wrote boys' adventure stories on the 'poor boy makes good' theme, such as *Ragged Dick* (1867) and *From Canal Boy to President* (1881).

ALGREN, Nelson (1909–81) American novelist, born in Detroit. He moved early to Chicago, where he trained as a journalist at the University of Illinois, before becoming a migrant worker during the Depression. In Chicago again from 1935, he became a leading member of the 'Chicago school of realism'. He produced a series of uncompromising, powerful but baggy novels which include *Somebody in Boots* (1935), *Never Come Morning* (1942) and *The Man with the Golden Arm* (1949), a novel about drug addiction and regarded by some as his best work. He had a transatlantic affair with **Simone de Beauvoir**, which is described in her novel *Les Mandarins* (1954) and in her autobiography.

ALHAZEN (Ibn al-Haytham) (c.965–c.1040) Arab mathematician, born in Basra. He wrote a work on optics (known in Europe in Latin translation from the 13th century) giving the first account of atmospheric refraction and reflection from curved surfaces and the construction of the eye. He constructed spherical and parabolic mirrors and spent a period of his life feigning madness to escape a boast he had made that he could prevent the flooding of the Nile.

'ALĪ (d.661) cousin and son-in-law of **Muhammad** and fourth caliph. He converted to Islam while still a boy, and later married the prophet's daughter **Fāṭima**. He withdrew, or was excluded from government during the caliphates of **Abū-Bakr** and **'Umar**, and disagreed with **'Uthmān** in the interpretation of the Qu'ran and application of the law. Although not involved in the death of Uthmān he was elected caliph soon after, but encountered considerable opposition, led by **Mu 'āwiya**, governor of Syria, the beginning of a major division within Islam which has persisted to the present day. The issue was still undecided when he was murdered in the mosque at Kūfa, his capital, by a member of a third Muslim party, the Kharijites.

ALI, (Chaudri) Mohamad (1905–80) Pakistani politician, born in Jullundur, India. He was educated at Punjab University. In 1928 he left a chemistry lectureship at Islamia College, Lahore, for the Indian Civil Service. Four years later when he was made accountant-general of Bahawalpur State he re-established its finances. In 1936 he became private secretary to the Indian finance minister and in 1945 was the first Indian ever to be appointed financial adviser of war and supply. In 1947, on the partition of India, he became the first secretary-general of the Pakistan government, in 1951 finance minister, and in 1955 prime minister. He resigned in 1956, because of lack of support from members of his own party, the Muslim League. A man of powerful intellect, he was often described in Pakistan as the 'brains trust' of the post-partition governments.

ALI, Muhammad formerly **Cassius Marcellus Clay** (1942–) American boxer and world heavyweight champion three times. Born in Louisville, Kentucky, he won the Olympic amateur light-heavyweight title at Rome in 1960. After turning professional, he won the world heavyweight title in 1964 by defeating Sonny Liston in seven rounds at Miami Beach (and subsequently in a rematch at Lewiston, Maine). He became politicized and joined the 'Black Muslim' sect in 1964, changed his name to 'Muhammad Ali', and refused military service on religious grounds; for this he was sentenced to prison and stripped of his title in 1967, but had it restored in 1970 when the Supreme Court quashed his conviction. He lost the title to Joe Frazier in 1971, but defeated him in January 1974 and regained his title by beating George Foreman in October of that year in Zaire. He lost it again (to Leon Spinks) in February 1978 but regained it in a rematch in September of that year. He thus made history by regaining the world heavyweight title twice, and also by refusing to conform to the stereotype of coloured American sportsmen. He retired in 1981.

ALI BEY (1728–73) Egyptian ruler, a slave from the Caucasus who distinguished himself in the service of Ibrahim Katkhuda and rose to be chief of the **Mamluks**. Victorious in the power-struggle that followed the death of Ibrahim in 1754, he had himself declared sultan (1768) and proceeded to establish in Egypt an adminstration independent of Ottoman overlordship. Defeated by Ottoman forces in 1772, he was forced to take refuge in Syria. An attempt to regain power the following year led to a further defeat at Salahiya where he was mortally wounded. Under him Egypt briefly achieved independence for the first time in more than 200 years. He was an excellent administrator but, following his death, Egypt lapsed into virtual anarchy.

ALI IBN HUSEIN (1879–1935) ruler of the Hejaz, was born in Mecca, the eldest son of King Hussein of the Hejaz, whom he succeeded in 1924 when his father was forced off the throne in the Wahabi Rebellion, but himself had to abdicate in 1925. For the rest of his life he lived in exile in Baghdad.

ALI PASHA, surnamed **Arslan** (1741–1822) Turkish leader, known as 'the Lion of Janina'. An Albanian brigand and assassin, he became pasha of Trikala in 1787 and Janina (in Greece) in 1788, and in 1803 became governor of Rumili. At Janina he maintained a barbarous but cultured court which was visited by Lord **Byron** and other European travellers. He intrigued with France and Britain, but in 1820 he was deposed by Sultan **Mahmud II**, and was put to death in 1822.

ALIA, Ramiz (1925–) Albanian communist leader, born in Shkoder in NW Albania, the son of poor Muslim peasants. During World War II he fought for the National Liberation Army as a political commissar, attaining the rank of lieutenant colonel. A former president of the youth wing of the ruling Communist Party of Labour of Albania (APL), he was inducted into the party's central committee in 1954 and made minister of education in 1955 and head of agitprop in 1958. He entered the APL's secretariat (1960) and politburo (1961) and in November 1982 became head of state. On the death of **Enver Hoxha** (1985), he took over as APL, and thus national, leader.

ALICE MAUD MARY (1843–78) British princess, the second daughter of Queen **Victoria**. In 1862 she married Prince Louis of Hesse-Darmstadt (1837–92), who succeeded his uncle as Grand Duke in 1877. They had four daughters: the eldest became the mother of Louis, Earl **Mountbatten**, the youngest, Alexandra (Alix) married **Nicholas II** of Russia.

ALISON, Sir Archibald (1792–1867) Scottish historian and lawyer, born at Kenley in Shropshire, the son of a parson. In 1800 his family moved to Edinburgh, where he studied law at the university. He travelled widely throughout Europe, and was appointed advocate-depute in 1822, and later became sheriff of Lanarkshire, living at Possil House near Glasgow. He wrote a *History of Europe during the French Revolution* in ten volumes (1833–42), and its continuation to the accession of Louis Napoleon as **Napoleon III** in nine volumes (1852–59). He also published biographies of political figures.

AL-JAZARI, ibn al-Razzaz (fl.c.1200) Islamic engineer in Mesopotamia. He developed many mechanical and hydraulic devices including a reciprocating water pump. Details of this, and the earliest surviving description of a crankshaft, are recorded in his *Book of Knowledge of Ingenious Devices*.

AL-KHAZINI (fl.c.1115–30) Arab mathematician, born in Merv (Iran) now Mary (USSR). He was a Byzantine slaveboy (possibly a castrato) who was well educated by his owner in mathematics and became a notable maker of scientific instruments; he also devised astronomical tables and wrote on mechanics, and especially on specific gravity and its use in analysis.

AL-KHWARIZMI, Abu Ja'far Muhammad ibn Musa (c.800–c.850) Arab mathematician, who wrote in Baghdad on astronomy, geography and mathematics. Though not important as an original mathematician, his writings in Latin translation were so influential in transmitting Indian and Arab mathematics to medieval Europe that the methods of arithmetic based on the Hindu (or so-called Arabic) system of numeration became known in medieval Latin, by corruption of his name, as 'algorismus', from which comes the English 'algorithm'; the word 'algebra' is derived from the word *al-jabr* in the title of his book on the subject.

AL-KINDI (c.800–c.870) Arab philosopher, born in Kūfa. Known as 'the philosopher of the Arabs', he became tutor at the court in Baghdad and was a prolific author. He was one of the first responsible for spreading Greek thought (particularly that of **Aristotle**) in the Arab world and synthesizing it with Islamic doctrine.

ALLAIS, Maurice (1911–) French economist and engineer, born in Paris. Educated at the École Polytechnique and the École Nationale Supérieur des Mines, he was appointed professor of economic analysis at the latter institution in 1944. He was professor of economic theory at the Institute of Statistics in Paris from 1947 to 1968 and, since 1954, has been director of the Centre for Economic Analysis. His primary contributions have been in the reformulation of the theories of general economic equilibrium and maximum efficiency and in the development of new concepts, particularly in relation to capital and consumer choice. He was awarded the 1988 Nobel prize for economics.

ALLAN, David (1744–96) Scottish genre and portrait painter, known as the 'Scottish Hogarth', and forerunner of **David Wilkie**. Born in Alloa, he studied in Glasgow and in Rome, where he trained under Gavin Hamilton and won the gold medal. He went to London for a time (1777–80) to paint portraits, then moved to Edinburgh as a master at the Edinburgh Academy of Arts, of which he became director in 1786. He illustrated **Allan Ramsay**'s *Gentle Shepherd* and some of **Robert Burns**' poems.

ALLAN, Sir Henry Havelock See **HAVELOCK**

ALLAN, Sir Hugh (1810–82) Scots-born Canadian shipowner, born in Saltcoats in Ayrshire. He settled in 1826 in Canada, where his firm became eminent as shipbuilders, and founded the Allan Line of steamers.

ALLAN, Robert Marshall (1886–1946) Australian obstetrician, born in Brisbane. He was educated at Edinburgh University, and after war service with the Royal Army Medical Corps, returned to Australia. His later career was much taken up with the risks of childbirth and of infant morbidity. His appointment as director of Melbourne University's Obstetrical Research Committee led to many other appointments and awards and in 1944 he chaired a Federal enquiry into Australia's declining birth rate.

ALLAN, Sir William (1782–1850) Scottish historical painter. Born in Edinburgh, he was a fellow-pupil with **David Wilkie** at the Trustees Academy, then studied at the Royal Academy schools in London. In 1805 he went to St Petersburg (now Leningrad) and spent several years in Russia and Turkey, painting scenes of Russian life. In 1835 he was elected RA, in 1835 president of the Royal Scottish Academy. In 1841 he succeeded Wilkie as Queen's Limner (painter) in Scotland. His Scottish historical paintings include scenes from the novels of Sir **Walter Scott**.

ALLARDICE, Robert See **BARCLAY-ALLARDICE**

ALLBUTT, Sir Thomas Clifford (1836–1925) English physician, born in Dewsbury. Educated at Cambridge, he studied medicine at London and Paris, practised at Leeds, and became Regius professor of medicine at Cambridge in 1892. In 1867 he introduced the short clinical thermometer, a great advance on the old pattern, which was a foot long and had to be kept in position for 20 minutes. He wrote many medical works and books on the history of medicine.

ALLEN, Ethan (1738–89) American soldier, born in Litchfield, Connecticut. He spent his career trying to achieve independence from New York and New Hampshire for the Green Mountain area that is now the state of Vermont. From 1770 to 1775 he commanded an irregular force called the Green Mountain Boys in opposition to New York. At the outbreak of the War of Independence (1775–83) he seized Fort Ticanderoga, with **Benedict Arnold**'s forces, in the first colonial victory of the war. On an expedition to Canada he was captured by the British at Montreal and held prisoner for three years (1775–78), and immediately upon his release wrote *The Narrative of Colonel Ethan's Captivity* (1779). He continued the campaign for Vermont's statehood, which was not achieved until just after his death, in 1789. He also wrote a celebrated deistical work, *Reason, the Only Oracle of Man* (1784).

ALLEN, Florence Ellinwood (1884–1966) American judge and feminist, born in Salt Lake City, Utah. Educated at Western Reserve University in Cleveland, Ohio (1900–04), she became involved in the New York League for the Protection of Immigrants (1910) and the college Equal Suffrage League. She graduated from New York University Law School in 1913, and was admitted to the Ohio bar in 1914. Working assiduously for women's rights, she became the first woman to sit on a general federal bench and the first on a court of last resort. She won high respect both as a judge and as a feminist. She retired in 1959, and in 1965 she published the autobiographical *To Do Justly*.

ALLEN, George (1832–1907) English publisher and engraver, born in Newark. A pupil of **Ruskin**, for whom he engraved many plates, and whose publisher he subsequently became, he started a business in Bell Yard, Fleet Street, which ultimately merged with others and became the well-known house of Allen and Unwin.

ALLEN, Sir George Oswald Browning ('Gubby') (1902–89) Australian-born English cricketer, born in Sydney and educated at Eton College and Trinity College, Cambridge, where he got a cricket Blue. He played for England in 25 Tests; he was captain in the tests against India in 1936, and on the tour of Australia that followed the controversial 'Bodyline' series of 1932–33 under **D R Jardine**, in which he disapproved of his captain's tactics. He is the only player to have taken all ten wickets in an innings at Lord's (10–49 v Lancashire, 1929), and with L E G Ames he holds the all-time Test eighth-wicket record with a partnership of 246 against New Zealand in 1931. A member of the London Stock Exchange, he returned briefly to Test cricket on the MCC tour of West Indies in 1947. He was chairman of the England Cricket Selection Committee, 1955–61.

ALLEN, Sir Harry Brookes (1854–1926) Australian pathologist, born in Geelong, Victoria. Educated at

Melbourne University, in 1906 he became its Foundation professor of pathology, a position he held until 1924. On a visit to the UK in 1890 he persuaded the General Medical Council in London to recognize medical degrees conferred by Melbourne, pioneering the eventual wider recognition of colonial academic qualifications. He was also influential in the merging of the Medical Society of Victoria with the British Medical Association, in the establishment at his old university of the Walter and Eliza Hall Institute of Medical Research, and of the Institute of Tropical Medicine at Townsville, Queensland. His stature as a medical administrator was recognized with an LLD from Edinburgh University in 1912, and a knighthood in 1914.

ALLEN, James Lane (1849–1925) American novelist, born in Kentucky. He wrote *The Kentucky Cardinal*, *Aftermath*, *The Choir Invisible*, and other novels.

ALLEN, Ralph (?1694–1764) English philanthropist, known as the 'Man of Bath'. A deputy postmaster at Bath, he made a fortune by improving postal routes in England. He built the mansion of Prior Park, near Bath, and was the friend of **Pope**, **Fielding** and **Chatham**.

ALLEN, Walter (1911–) English novelist and critic, born in Birmingham. After working as a schoolmaster and university lecturer in the USA, he became a journalist. His first novel, *Innocence is Drowned*, was published in 1938, and he scored a considerable success with *Dead Man over All*, in 1950. He has written several critical works, including *The English Novel—A short critical history* (1954).

ALLEN, William (1532–94) English prelate, born in Rossall, Lancashire. In 1550 he was elected fellow of Oriel College, Oxford, and in 1556 during the reign of **Mary I**, he became principal of St Mary's Hall, Oxford. After the accession of Queen **Elizabeth** in 1558 he eventually went into exile in Flanders (1561) rather than take the Oath of Supremacy but he returned home in 1562, hoping to recover from a wasting sickness, but in 1565 he went back to the low countries and never returned to England again. He received priest's orders in Mechlin, in 1568 founded the English college at Douai to train missionary priests for the reconversion of England to Catholicism, and later founded similar establishments in Rome (1575–78) and Valladolid (1589). In 1587 he was created a cardinal during his fourth visit to Rome, where he died. At the time of the Armada, he signed (if he did not pen), the *Admonition*, urging the Catholics to take up arms.

ALLEN, William Hervey (1889–1949) American author, born in Pittsburg. He trained for the American navy, in which he became a midshipman. In World War I, however, he fought with distinction as a lieutenant in the army, and later (1926) published his war diary, *Towards the Flame*. His best-known novel *Anthony Adverse* (1933) sold a million and a half copies; others are *Action at Aquila* (1938), *The Forest and the Fort* (1943), *Bedford Village* (1945), and *The City of the Dawn* which was unfinished at his death. Allen also wrote a study of **Edgar Allan Poe** under the title *Israfel* (1926).

ALLEN, Woody, originally **Allen Stewart Konigsberg** (1935–) American film actor and director, born in Brooklyn, New York. As a teenager he submitted jokes to a variety of publications; this led to television scriptwriting and a spell as a stand-up comedian. He was hired to write and appear in the film *What's New, Pussycat*? (1965) which saw the start of a prolific filmmaking career that initially consisted of slapstick lunacy and genre parody in productions like *Bananas* (1971) and *Love and Death* (1975). *Annie Hall* (1977) marked a shift in style and substance to more concentrated, autobiographical pieces and won him Academy Awards for writing and direction. Subsequently, he has explored his concerns with mortality, sexual inadequacies, showbusiness nostalgia, psychoanalysis and urban living in such films as *Interiors* (1978), *Manhattan* (1979), *Broadway Danny Rose* (1984) and *Hannah and Her Sisters* (1986). A frequent magazine contributor, he has also written books, including *Getting Even* (1971) and *Without Feathers* (1976), as well as plays, notably *Play it Again, Sam* (1969) which was successfully filmed in 1972.

ALLENBY, Edmund Henry Hynman, 1st Viscount (1861–1936) English soldier. Educated at Haileybury and Sandhurst, he joined the Inniskilling Dragoons. He saw service in South Africa in 1884–85, 1888, and in the 2nd Boer War (1899–1902), ending as a column leader. In World War I he commanded the 1st Cavalry Division and then the Third Army in France (1915–17), which captured the Vimy Ridge. Thereafter he was appointed commander-in-chief of the Egyptian expeditionary force against the Turks, took Beersheba and Gaza, and entered Jerusalem (1917). In the following year he routed the Egyptians in the great cavalry battle of Megiddo. Promoted field marshal, he was high commissioner in Egypt from 1919 to 1925, and granted independence to Ethiopia in 1922.

ALLENDE, Isabel (1942–) Chilean novelist, born in Lima, Peru, niece and god-daughter of **Salvador Allende**, the former president of Chile. Several months after the overthrow of Chile's coalition government in 1973 by the forces of a junta headed by General **Augusto Pinochet Ugarte**, she and her family fled Chile, Isabel seeking sanctuary in Venezuela. Her first novel, *The House of the Spirits* (1985), arose directly out of her exile and her estrangement from her family, in particular her aged grandfather who remained in Chile. It became a worldwide bestseller and critical success, and Allende was heralded as the most exciting talent to emerge from Latin America since **Gabriel Garcia Marquez**. Her only other novel is *Of Love and Shadows* (1987).

ALLENDE (GOSSENS), Salvador (1908–73) Chilean politician, born in Valparaiso. He took an early interest in politics and was arrested several times, while a medical student, for his radical activities. He helped found the Chilean Socialist party, a Marxist organization which stayed clear of the Soviet-orientated Communist party. He was elected to the Chamber of Deputies in 1937, served as minister of health for three years and was a senator from 1945 to 1970. He sought, and failed to win, the presidency in 1952, 1958 and 1964 but was narrowly successful in 1970. He tried to build a socialist society within the framework of a parliamentary democracy but met widespread opposition from business interests, supported by the United States CIA. He was overthrown, in September 1973, by a military junta, led by General **Augusto Pinochet Ugarte**, and died in the fighting in the presidential palace in Santiago.

ALLEYN, Edward (1566–1626) English actor, stepson-in-law of **Philip Henslowe**, with whom he acted. A contemporary of **Shakespeare**, he founded Dulwich College.

ALLGOOD, Sara (1883–1950) Irish-born American actress, born in Dublin. She first appeared at the opening night of the Abbey Theatre in 1904 in Lady **Gregory**'s *Spreading the News*. She also played in **Synge**, playing the Widow Quinn in the *Playboy of the Western World*. She played Isabella in *Measure for Measure* when **Annie Horniman** opened her Manchester company with it (1908), and toured Australia with *Peg O' My Heart* (1915). Returning to the Abbey, she created the parts of Juno Boyle and Bessie Burgess in **Sean O'Casey**'s *Juno and the Paycock* and *The Plough and the Stars* (1926) respectively, and her performance of Juno in the **Hitchcock** film (1930) gives a glimpse of the dignity and realism she brought to the part. In 1940 she settled in Hollywood, and became an American citizen in 1945. She appeared in over 30 films there, including haunting appearances in *Jane Eyre* (1943), *The Lodger* (1944) and *Between Two Worlds* (1944), but was seldom offered parts commensurate with her talent, and died penniless.

ALLIBONE, Samuel Austin (1816–89) American bibliographer, born in Philadelphia. In 1879 he became head of the Lenox Library, New York, and compiled an invaluable *Dictionary of English Literature* (3 vols, 1858, 1870, 1871).

ALLINGHAM, Margery (1904–66) English detective story writer, and creator of the fictional detective Albert Campion. Born in London, she wrote a string of elegant and witty novels, including *Crime at Black Dudley* (1928), *Police at the Funeral* (1931), *Flowers for the Judge* (1936), *More Work for the Undertaker* (1949), *The Tiger in the Smoke* (1952), *The China Governess* (1963), and *The Mind Readers* (1965).

ALLINGHAM, William (1824–89) Irish poet, born in Ballyshannon, County Donegal. He was in the Irish Customs (1846–70), and in 1874 succeeded **James Froude** as editor of *Fraser's Magazine*. In 1874 he married Helen Paterson (1848–1926), who, born near Burton-on-Trent, made a name by her book illustrations and water colours, and edited his *Diary* (1907). His works include *Day and Night Songs* (1855), illustrated by **Rossetti** and **Millais**; *Laurence Bloomfield in Ireland* (1864), and *Irish Songs and Poems* (1887).

ALLORI, Alessandro (1535–1607) Florentine mannerist painter, adopted and trained by **Bronzino** whose name he and his son, Cristofano (1577–1621), later adopted. They both were portrait painters at the Medici court and executed religious works for the churches of Florence.

ALLSOPP, Samuel (1780–1838) English philanthropist, a member of the brewing firm of Allsopp & Sons, Burton-on-Trent. He was noted for the charities of his public and private life. The youngest of his three sons, Henry (1811–1887), to whom the development of the firm was largely due, represented Worcestershire in parliament (1874–1880), and in 1886 was created Lord Hindlip.

ALLSTON, Washington (1779–1843) American artist and writer, born in Waccamaw, South Carolina. The earliest American romantic painter, he graduated at Harvard, then studied at the Royal Academy in London before going on to Paris and Rome, where he formed close friendships with **Coleridge** and **Thorvaldsen**. He worked for a time in London, but returned to America in 1820, and eventually settled at Cambridgeport, Massachusetts, in 1830. He painted large romantic canvases, particularly of religious scenes, like *Belshazzar's Feast*, *The Flood*, and *Elijah in the Desert*. He published a book of poems, *The Sylphs of the Seasons with other Poems* (1813), and a gothic art novel, *Monaldi* (1842).

ALMA-TADEMA, Sir Lawrence (1836–1912) Dutch-born British painter of classical-genre paintings, born in Dornrijp. He originally intended to become a doctor but studied at the Antwerp Academy of Art instead. He moved to England in 1870 and became a naturalized citizen in 1873. He achieved great popularity with his classical idyllic scenes like *Tarquinius superbus* (1867), *Pyrrhic Dance* (1869), *Roses of Heliogabalus* (1888) and *The Conversion of Paula* (1898).

ALMACK, William (d.1781) English clubman, of either Yorkshire or Scottish origin (possibly originally McCall). He came at an early age to London where he was successively valet and innkeeper. He opened a gaming club in Pall Mall in 1763, and Almack's Assembly Rooms in King Street, St James's, in 1765. These became centres of London society. The club was acquired by Brooks in 1778, and the rooms on his death passed to his niece, Mrs Willis, whose name they bore for many years. He amassed great wealth and retired to Hounslow.

ALMAGRO, Diego de (1475–1538) Spanish conquistador. He was on the first exploratory expedition from Peru against the Incas led by **Francisco Pizarro** (1524–28). In the second expedition (from 1532), he joined Pizarro in 1533 at Cajamarca, where the Inca chieftain **Atahualpa** was executed, and occupied the Inca capital of Cuzco. In 1535–36 he led the conquest of Chile, but came back to Cuzco in 1537, and after a dispute with Pizarro, occupied it by force, thus beginning a civil war between the Spaniards. Early in 1538 he was defeated by an army led by Pizarro's brother, Hernando, and was captured and executed. Later, in 1541, Almagro's half-caste son Diego stormed Pizarro's palace and assassinated him, and set himself up as governor, but was himself overthrown the following year and executed.

AL-MANSŪR, meaning **'the victorious'** (d.775) the title assumed by many Muslim princes, notably the cruel and treacherous caliph Abu-Jafar, who succeeded his brother in 754 and founded Baghdad in 764.

ALMEIDA, Brites de (fl.1385) legendary Portuguese heroine, born in Aljubarrota. She is said to have been a baker; about 1385, during the war between John I and the king of Cadiz, she led her townspeople against the Spanish forces attacking her village and killed seven of them with her baker's shovel. The incident was celebrated by **Camoens** in a poem. The shovel is believed to have been preserved as a relic in Aljubarrota for several generations.

ALMEIDA, Francisco de (c.1450–1510) Portuguese soldier and 1st viceroy of the Portuguese Indies (1505–09), until he was superseded by **Affonso d'Albuquerque** 'the Great'. He was killed in South Africa on his voyage home in a skirmish with Hottentots at Table Bay, and buried where Cape Town now stands.

ALMEIDA-GARRETT, João Baptista da Silva Leitão (1799–1854) Portuguese author and politician, born in Oporto. He was brought up in the Azores, and was exiled after the 1820 revolt, but returned and supported **Pedro I** and became minister of the interior. A pioneer of the romantic movement and of modern Portuguese drama, he wrote the historical play *Gil Vicente* (1838), the epic *Camões* (1825), and many ballads.

ALMIRANTE, Giorgio (?1915–88) Italian politician and leader of Italy's neo-Fascist party (Movimento Sociale Italiano). Born near Parma, a journalist and teacher by profession, he helped to found the neo-Fascist movement after the war and was first elected to parliament in 1948. He became national secretary of the MIS in 1969. In the 1972 general election, at the peak of his influence, his party won 9 per cent of the votes and 56 parliamentary seats. He retired owing to ill-health in 1987.

ALMOHADS (early 12th to late 13th century) Arabic 'al-Muwaḥḥidūn', 'the Unitarians', originated as a religious movement founded around the year 1124 in the High Atlas mountains by the Berber Ibn Tūmart (1091–1130). Its principal tenets were the belief in the essential unity of God, an allegorical interpretation of the Qu'ran, and moral reform. The movement gained rapid support among the Berber peasantry of Morocco, and proclaiming himself Mahdī, or divinely appointed leader, Ibn Tūmart took the offensive against the perceived corruption and literalism of the **Almoravids**. His successor Abd al-Mu'min (d.1163) gradually conquered Morocco and extended his rule as far as Tunisia and into Spain, and established a system of government for the Almohad state, which became a hereditary monarchy with the succession of his own son Abū Ya'qūb Yūsuf (d.1184). Art, architecture and the sciences flourished under Almohad rule, notably through the patronage of the two great philosophers Ibn Tufayl and Ibn Rushd (better known to Christian Europe as **Averroës**), but the original faith rapidly declined. At the same time the dynastic character of the régime encouraged succession disputes and the growth of local particularism, while social tensions were produced by a widening gap between the ruling family and aristocracy, and the common Berbers who provided the army. After the defeat of al-Nāṣir (d.1214) by the Christians at Las Navas de Tolosa (1212), the empire disintegrated under the pressure of local dynasties, its last remnant being finally extinguished in 1276.

ALMOND, Hely Hutchinson (1832–1903) Scottish educationist and author, born in Glasgow. Precociously clever as a child, he was educated at Glasgow and Balliol College, Oxford. He became a tutor at Loretto School, Musselburgh (then a preparatory school) in 1857, then master at Merchiston School, Edinburgh, in 1858, and acquired Loretto School in 1862, making it a public school. He sought to rule by persuasion, not force, and believed passionately 'that the laws of physical well-being are the laws of God'. He insisted on open windows, shorts, shirt-sleeves, compulsory cold baths all year, long runs in wet weather; he epitomized the late 19th-century cult of athleticism in public schools. He published *Health Lectures* (1884) and a number of volumes of sermons. In his later years he had to be dissuaded from watching house and school matches as it was bad for his heart.

ALMORAVIDS, (Arabic **'al-Murābaṭūn',** also known as **'al-mulaththamūn',** 'the veiled ones' (mid 11th to late 12th century) a nomadic Berber people of the western Sahara who in the mid 11th century were converted to a puritanical form of orthodox Islam by the Malikite jurist and missionary 'Abd Allāh b Yāsīn' (d.1059). Assisted by their domination of the gold trade between west Africa and the Iberian peninsula, and an efficient military organization, they invaded Morocco in 1058 under the tribal chief Abū Bakr b Umar (d.1088), founding a new capital at Marrakesh (c.1070). His cousin Yūsuf b Tāshufīn (1061–1106) conquered the rest of Morocco and Algeria, and crossed into Spain in response to the Iberian Muslims' appeals for assistance against the Christians; after defeating Alfonso VI of Castile and his allies at Sagrajas near Badajoz (1086) he, and then his son Ali b Yūsuf (d.1143) proceeded to annex the Muslim *taifa* kingdoms which had arisen after the collapse of the Umayyad caliphate in Spain, and to take the offensive against the Christians. However this vast but politically unstable empire barely survived Alī's death, unable to withstand the twin threat of an invigorated Reconquista under **El Cid** and Alfonso VII in Spain, and a new religious and political rival in Morocco, the **Almohads**.

ALMQUIST, Carl Jonas Love (1793–1866) Swedish author, born in Stockholm. He had a bizarrely chequered career as a clergyman and teacher; he was accused of forgery and attempted murder and fled to the USA. From 1865 he lived in Bremen under an assumed name. His prolific literary output, ranging from Romanticism to (from the late 1830s) social realism, encompassed novels, plays, poems and essays, and was published in a 14-volume series, *Törnrosensbok* (The Book of the Thorn Rose, 1832–51).

A.L.O.E. See **TUCKER, Charlotte Maria**

ALONSO, Alicia, originally **Alicia de la Caridad del Cobre Martínez Hoyo** (1921–) Cuban dancer and choreographer, born in Havana, and founder of the Ballet de Cuba. She launched her career in the USA where she studied and performed with the School of American Ballet and **George Balanchine**. During that time she made several trips back home to make guest appearances with the Cuban company Pro Arte. In 1948 she returned permanently to form the Alicia Alonso Company which grew into a national ballet company for Cuba, touring the world to great acclaim. She remained as director when **Castro**'s régime was established in 1959. Though best remembered for the development of her company, as a dancer she was famed for several roles, particularly the title role in *Giselle*. Roles created for her include **Antony Tudor**'s *Undertow* (1945) and *Goya Pastorale* (1940), and Balanchine's *Themes and Variations* (1947).

ALONSO, Dámaso (1898–1990) Spanish poet and philologist, born in Madrid, where he studied under **Ramon Menéndez Pidal** before travelling widely in Europe and America as teacher and lecturer. He became professor of romance philology at Madrid University, and established his reputation as an authority on **Góngora y Argote**. He also published poetry, of which *Hijos de la Ira* is the best known. It is religious in inspiration, powerful and emotional in expression.

ALONSO, Mateo (1878–1955) Argentinian sculptor, best known for his statue of *Christ the Redeemer*, erected in 1904 at the top of the Uspallata Pass, in the Andes.

ALOYSIUS, St See **GONZAGA, Luigi**

ALP-ARSLAN, literally **'hero-lion'** (1030–72) Seljuk sultan, succeeding his uncle Tügrül Beg in 1062. A skilful and courageous commander, he devoted his energies to extending the frontiers of the Seljuk empire, entrusting the central administration to his capable vizier Nizām al-Mulk. He restored good relations with the **'Abbasid** caliph and in his role as protector of the caliphate was about to launch a major offensive against its rivals the **Fatimids**, when he was recalled to meet a Byzantine offensive in Armenia; at Manzikert in 1071 he defeated a numerically superior army and captured the emperor Romanus IV, opening up the interior of Anatolia to penetration by the nomadic Turkmen tribes. Killed in a struggle with a prisoner while on campaign in Persia, he was succeeded by his son Malik-Shāh.

ALPHER, Ralph Asher (1921–) American physicist, born in Washington, DC, known for his theoretical work concerning the origin and evolution of the universe. After studying at George Washington University, he spent World War II as a civilian physicist and afterward worked at Johns Hopkins University, Baltimore and in industry. Together with **Hans Bethe** and **George Gamow**, he proposed in 1948 the 'alpha, beta, gamma' theory which suggests the possibility of explaining the abundances of chemical elements as the result of thermonuclear processes in the early stages of a hot, evolving universe. These ideas, later developed and much improved, became part of the 'Big Bang' model of the universe. Also in 1948, he predicted that a hot 'Big Bang' must have produced intense electromagnetic radiation which would have 'cooled' (or red-shifted), and this background radiation was in fact observed in 1964 by **Arne Penzias** and **Robert Woodrow Wilson**.

ALPINI, Prospero, Latin **Prosper Alpinus** (1553–1616) Italian botanist and physician, born in Marostica in the republic of Venice. He spent three years as physician to the Italian consul in Cairo, and during this period he observed the sexual fertilization of the date palm, in which male and female flowers are on different trees, and described 57 species, wild or cultivated, in Egypt. In 1594 he became lecturer in botany at Padua, and director of the botanic garden there (1603). He wrote *De plantis Aegypti liber* (1592), and his *De medecina Egyptorum* (1591) brought the coffee plant and the banana to European attention for the first time.

ALRED See **ALDRED**

ALSTON, Richard (1948–) English choreographer, born in Stoughton, Sussex. Educated at Eton and Croydon College of Art (1965–67), he studied at London School of Contemporary Dance (1967–70). Captivated by choreography early on, his first piece was performed at The Place, London, in 1968. In 1969, *Something to Do* became the first in a series of nine dances made for London Contemporary Dance Theatre. Looking to experiment and develop his work, he co-founded Strider in 1972 (disbanded 1975), the forerunner of the contemporary dance company Second Stride. From 1975 to 1977 he studied in New York with **Merce Cunningham** who greatly influenced his technique. Returning to Britain he spent three years as a freelance choreographer before joining Ballet Rambert as resident choreographer in 1980, becoming director in 1986. He renamed the company Rambert Dance Company in 1987. Noted for his lyricism, his work often employs the talents of other artists.

ALTDORFER, Albrecht (c.1480–1538) German painter, engraver, and architect, leading member of the 'Danube School' of German painting, born in Regensburg. His most outstanding works are biblical and historical subjects set against highly imaginative and atmospheric landscape backgrounds. He was also a pioneer of copperplate etching.

ALTEN, Karl August, Graf von (1764–1840) Hanoverian general and statesman. He came to England in 1803, entered the German Legion of the British army, and fought under **Wellington** through the Peninsular war, and commanded at Quatre-Bras and Waterloo. After his return to Hanover, he became minister of war (1832) and foreign affairs (1833).

ALTER, David (1807–81) American physicist, born in Westmoreland, Pennsylvania. He was one of the earliest investigators of the spectrum, and pioneered the use of the spectroscope in determining the chemical constitution of a gas or vaporized solid.

ALTGELD, John Peter (1847–1902) Prussian-born American politician and social reformer, born in Nassau, Germany. Brought to the USA in infancy, he served in the Union army during the Civil War, was a judge of the supreme court in Illinois (1886–91), and pardoned three men convicted of complicity in the 1886 Chicago Haymarket Riots. He was elected the first Democratic governor of Illinois (1892–96), and protested against the use of federal troops to break the Pullman strike of 1894.

ALTHORP, Lord See **SPENCER**

ALTHUSSER, Louis (1918–) French philosopher, born in Algiers and educated in Algiers and in France. He was imprisoned in concentration camps during World War II. From 1948 he taught in Paris, and joined the Communist party. He has written mainly on Marxist themes and represents a distinctive strain of Marxist theory.

ALTIZER, Thomas Jonathan Jackson (1927–) American theologian, born in Cambridge, Massachusetts. He studied the history of religions at Chicago, and taught religion, and later English, at Emory University (1956–68) and the State University of New York (from 1968). As a proponent of one strand of the 1960s 'Death of God' theology, and under the influence of **Nietzche**, **Blake**, and **Hegel**'s view of *renosis* as the self-negation of being, he held that in the Incarnation God became fully human and lost his divine attributes and existence. His writings include *The Gospel of Christian Atheism* (1966), *Radical Theology and the Death of God* (1966, essays), *Descent into Hell* (1970), and *The Self-Embodiment of God* (1977).

ALTOUNYAN, Roger Ernest Collingwood (1922–87) British physician and medical pioneer, inventor of the anti-asthma drug Intal and the 'spinhaler'. Born in Syria of Armenian-English extraction, he spent his summer holidays with his four sisters in the Lake District, where they met the author **Arthur Mitchell Ransome** (1884–1967) and became the real-life models of the children in his *Swallows and Amazons* series of adventure books. After qualifying as a doctor, he practised at his grandfather's Armenian Hospital at Aleppo, in Syria; he returned to England in 1956 to join a pharmaceutical company, where he worked in his own time to develop the drug Intal to combat asthma, of which he was himself a sufferer. A pilot and flying instructor during the war, he developed the spinhaler device to inhale the drug, based on the aerodynamic principles of aircraft propellors.

ALVA, or **Alba, Ferdinand Alvarez de Toledo, Duke of** (1508–82) Spanish general and statesman, born in Piedratita. A brilliant soldier and tactician, he was named governor of Feuenterrabia at the age of 17, and fought so well in the battle of Pavia (1525), in Hungary against the Turks, in **Charles V**'s expedition to Tunis and Algiers, and in Provence, that he became general at 26, and commander-in-chief at 30. He defended Navarre and Catalonia (1542), and in 1547 he contributed greatly to Charles V's victory at Mühlberg over the Elector of Saxony. After the abdication of Charles V in 1556, Alva overran the States of the Church, but was obliged by **Philip II** to conclude a peace and restore all his conquests. On the revolt of the Netherlands, he was sent as lieutenant-general in 1567 to enforce Spanish control there. He established the so called 'Bloody Council', which drove thousands of Huguenot artisans to emigrate to England. He executed Counts **Egmont** and Horn, then defeated **William** of Orange and forced him to retire to Germany, and entered Brussels in triumph in 1568. Holland and Zeeland renewed their efforts against him, and succeeded in destroying his fleet, until he was recalled by his own desire in 1573. He later commanded the successful invasion of Portugal in 1581.

ALVARADO, Pedro de (c.1485–1541) Spanish conquistador, and companion of **Hernando Cortés** during the conquest of Mexico (1519–21). He became governor of Tenochtitlán, where the harshness of his rule incited an Aztec revolt which drove the Spaniards out. In the following year Tenochtitlán was recaptured and razed, and Mexico City built in its place. From 1523 to 1527 he was sent by Cortés on an expedition to Guatemala, which also conquered parts of El Salvador. He returned to Spain, and in 1529 was appointed governor of Guatemala. He embarked on an expedition to conquer Quito (Ecuador) in 1534, but was bought off by **Francisco Pizarro**.

ÁLVAREZ, José (1768–1827) Spanish sculptor of the classical school. He was imprisoned in Rome for refusing to recognize **Joseph Bonaparte** as king of Spain, but was later released and employed by **Napoleon** to decorate the Quirinal Palace. In 1816 he became court sculptor to Ferdinand VI in Madrid, where he executed *Antilochus and Memnon* (Royal Museum) and portraits and busts of the nobility and of **Rossini**.

ALVAREZ, Luis Walter (1911–88) American experimental physicist and Nobel prize winner of exceptionally wide-ranging talents. Born in San Francisco, he studied physics at Chicago and then joined **Ernest Orlando Lawrence** at Berkeley University in 1936, becoming professor of physics in 1945. Before World War II he did distinguished work in nuclear physics; during the war he developed radar navigation and landing systems for aircraft. In 1947 he built the first proton linear accelerator; and then he did much to develop the bubble-chamber, and used it to discover new sub-atomic particles, for which he was awarded the Nobel prize for physics in 1968. He applied physics and ingenuity to a variety of problems: he used cosmic X-rays to show that Chephren's Egyptian pyramid had no undiscovered chambers; he showed that only one killer was involved in the assassination of President **Kennedy**; and he founded two companies to make optical devices, including the variable-focus spectacle lens which he invented for his own use. With his geologist son Walter (b.1940) he studied the catastrophe of 65000000 years ago which killed the dinosaurs, deducing from radiotracer analysis that its cause was the impact on Earth of an asteroid or comet.

ALVAREZ QUINTERO, Serafin (1871–1938) and **Joaquin** (1873–1944), Spanish playwrights, both born in Utrera. These brothers were the joint authors of well over a hundred modern Spanish plays, all displaying a characteristic gaiety and sentiment—and sometimes accused of being a little too stagily Spanish. Some are well known in the translations of Helen and Harley **Granville-Barker**: *Fortunato*, *The Lady from Alfaqueque*, and *A Hundred Years Old* (all produced in 1928), and *Don Abel Writes a Tragedy* (1933). In addition may be mentioned *El patio* (1900), *Las flores* (1901), *El genio allegre* (1906), and *Pueblo de mujeres* (1912).

ALVARO, Corrado (1895–1956) Italian novelist and journalist, born in Reggio. Sometime editor of *Il Mondo*, he was the author of several novels and collections of essays. His best novels are *I maestri del diluvio* (1935) and *L'Uomo è forte* (1934), both set in Soviet Russia, though he declared that his criticisms were of Fascist and not communist society.

ALYPIUS (fl.c.360 BC) Greek writer on music. His surviving work, published in 1652, consists of a list of symbols for the notation of the Greek modes and scales.

ALZHEIMER, Alois (1864–1915) German psychiatrist and neurophathologist, born in Markbreit. He studied medicine in Würzburg and Berlin. After posts in a couple of psychiatric hospitals, he became head of the anatomical laboratories of **Emil Kraepelin**'s psychiatric clinic in Munich and, in 1917, professor of psychiatry and neurology at Breslau University (now Wroclaw, Poland). He made important contributions to the preparation of microscopical sections of brain tissue and left some clinical studies, but he is best remembered for his full clinical and pathological description, in 1907, of presenile dementia (Alzheimer's disease).

AMADEUS VI, called **the Green Count** (1334–83) ruler of Savoy, born in Chambéry, he succeeded in 1343, founded the Order of the Annunziata and, added Vaud to the possessions of Savoy.

AMADEUS VIII (1383–1451) ruler of Savoy, had Savoy made a duchy (1416) and became ruler of Piedmont (1418), but in 1434 retired to a hermitage beside Lake Geneva. In 1439 the Council of Basle elected him pope as Felix V in opposition to Pope **Eugenius IV**, but he resigned in 1449 and died in Geneva.

AMADO, Jorge (1912–) Brazilian novelist, born on a cocoa plantation in Ilhéus, Bahia. His early fictions are pervaded with social and political themes. He was imprisoned for his political beliefs in 1935 and latterly spent several years in exile, though he was a communist deputy of the Brazilian parliament (1946–47). His first novel, *A pais do carnaval* (1932), is typically a young man's and follows a youthful member of the intelligentsia seeking political answers in the wake of the revolution of 1930. His next few novels outlined his personal manifesto and highlighted the cause of various exploited groups in society. With the publication of *Gabriella, Clove and Cinnamon* (1958) he showed a marked change in style and emphasis, technicolour supplanting black and white. This second phase of the writer's career has been marked by books like *The Swallow and the Tom Cat* (1982) and *Dona Flor and Her Two Husbands* (1966) which, while not lacking in social awareness or compassion, use irony to charming effect.

AMAGATSU, Yushio (1948–) Japanese choreographer, performer and artistic director of the butoh dance-theatre troupe Sankai Juku (Studio of the Mountain and Sea), born in Yokosuka City near Toyko. His company, based partly in Paris, was formed in 1975 out of intensive physical and psychological workshops. Their repertory is small but intriguing, consisting of only a handful of full-length productions including the signature piece *Kinkan Shonen* (The Kumquat Seed, 1978), the 1982 *Jomon Sho* (Homage to Prehistory) and *Unetsu* (Eggs Standing Out of Curiosity) from 1985.

AMALIA, Anna (1739–1807) Duchess of Saxe-Weimar and notable patron of German literature. Widowed in 1758 after only two years of marriage, she acted as regent for her infant son, Charles Augustus with great skill and prudence (1758–75). She attracted to the court at Weimar the leading literary figures in Germany, **Goethe**, **Schiller**, **Herder**, **Musaeus**, and **Wieland**, and founded the Weimar Museum.

AMANULLAH KHAN (1892–1960) ruler of Afghanistan, 1919–29. As governor of Kabul he assumed the throne on the assassination of his father, Habibullah Khan (amir 1901–19). After an inconclusive religious war against the British in India (1919–22), independence for Afghanistan was recognized by Britain by the Treaty of Rawalpindi (1922). He assumed the title of king in 1926. His zeal for westernizing reforms provoked rebellion in 1928. He abdicated and fled the country in 1929 and went into exile in Rome. He was succeeded by **Mohammed Nadir Shah**.

AMARASIMHA (probably 6th century) Sanskrit lexicographer. He wrote the *Amara-kosha*, a dictionary of synonyms in verse.

AMARI, Michele (1806–89) Italian politician and orientalist, born in Palermo. A member of the Carbonari, he lived largely in exile from 1841 to 1859, but on his return became professor of Arabic at Pisa and Florence, and minister of public instruction (1862–64). He wrote *La Guerra del Vespro Siciliano* (1841).

AMATI Italian family of violin-makers in Cremona. Andrea (c.1520–1580) whose earliest known label dates from 1564, was the founder who developed the standard violin. Others were his younger brother Nicola (1530–1600), Andrea's two sons, Antonio (1550–1638), and Geronimo (1551–1635); and the latter's son, Niccolo (1596–1684), the master of **Guarnieri** and **Stradivari**. Geronimo (1649–1740) was the last important Amati.

AMBARTSUMIAN, Viktor Amazaspovich (1908–) Soviet-Armenian astrophysicist who devised and developed theories of young star clusters, and devised a method for computing the mass ejected from nova stars. Educated at the University of Leningrad, he was professor of astrophysics there (1934–44) and at Erevan (1944-), and founded the Byurakan Astronomical Observatory which became one of Russia's most important observatories. In 1939 he wrote *Theoretical Astrophysics* (Eng trans 1958), which was widely influential.

AMBEDKAR, Bhimrao Ranji (1893–1956) Indian politician and champion of the depressed castes, born in a Ratnagiri village on the Konkan coast of Bombay, the son of an Indian soldier. Educated at Elphinstone College, Bombay, Columbia University, New York, and the London School of Economics, he became a London barrister and later a member of the Bombay legislative assembly and leader of 60000000 untouchables. In 1941 he became a member of the Governor-General's council. Appointed law minister in 1947, he was the principal author of the Indian constitution. He resigned in 1951 and with some thousands of his followers he publicly embraced the Buddhist faith not long before his death. His dedicated work for the outcasts strengthened Indian public opinion which secured a better life for them. His publications include: *Annihilation of Caste* (1937).

AMBERLEY, Viscount See **RUSSELL, John, 1st Earl**

AMBLER, Eric (1909–) English novelist and playwright, born in London. Educated at Colfe's Grammar School and London University, he served an apprenticeship in engineering and worked as an advertising copy-writer before turning to writing thrillers, invariably with an espionage background. He has done much to legitimize what has too glibly been dismissed as the stuff of pot-boilers. Considered by **Graham Greene** to be Britain's best thriller writer, he published his first novel, *The Dark Frontier*, in 1936. Niggardly with words and a skilful constructor of plots he creates a world of shadows. His best-known books are *Epitaph for a Spy* (1938), *The Mask of Dimitrios* (1939), *Dirty Story* (1967), and *The Intercom Conspiracy* (1970). He has co-authored novels with Charles Rodda under the pseudonym Eliot Reed and has received the Crime Writers' Association award four times and the Edgar Allan Poe award (1964). *Here Lies: An Autobiography* appeared in 1981.

AMBOISE, George d' (1460–1510) French prelate and statesman. Bishop of Montauban (1474) and archbishop of Rouen (1493), he became cardinal and prime minister under **Louis XII** in 1498. In an attempt to secure his election as pope he encouraged a schism between the French Church and Rome, and convened a separate council, first in Pisa, then in Milan and Lyons. An able minister, he effected the Treaty of Blois in 1505 that brought about an alliance between France and Spain. He left a vast fortune.

AMBROSE, St (c.339–397) Roman churchman, and one of the four Latin Doctors of the Church (with St **Augustine**, St **Jerome**, and **Gregory the Great**). Born in Trier, the son of the prefect of Gaul, he practised law in Rome and in 369 was appointed consular prefect of Upper Italy, whose capital was Milan, and which was then the centre of controversy between Catholics and Arian 'heretics'. When the bishopric fell vacant in 374, Ambrose was chosen to be bishop by universal acclamation, even though he was still only a catechumen undergoing instruction. He was quickly baptized, and consecrated bishop eight days later. He fought for the integrity of the church at the imperial court, resisted the empress-regent Justina over the introduction of Arian churches, and even forced the emperor himself, **Theodosius I, 'the Great'** to do public penance over the massacre of Thessalonica in 390. He introduced the use of hymns, and many improvements in the service—the Ambrosian ritual and Ambrosian chant. His feast-day is 7 December.

AMENHOTEP II (15th century BC) king of Egypt in the 18th Dynasty, the son of **Tuthmosis III** and Queen **Hatshepsut**. He ruled from 1450 to 1425 BC, and fought successful campaigns in Palestine and on the Euphrates.

AMENHOTEP III (c.1411–1375 BC) king of Egypt in the 18th Dynasty, son of **Tuthmosis IV**. He consolidated Egyptian supremacy in Babylonia and Assyria. In a reign of spectacular wealth and magnificence, he built his great capital city, Thebes, and its finest monuments, including the Luxor temple, the great pylon at Karnak, and the colossi of Memnon.

AMENHOTEP IV See **AKHENATON**

AMERY, John (1912–45) English pro-Nazi adventurer, son (later disowned) of **Leopold Amery**. He was declared bankrupt in 1936, was a gun-runner of **Franco** in the Spanish Civil War and liaison officer with French Cagoulards. Recruited by the Nazis in France (where he had been living since the outbreak of World War II), he began pro-**Hitler** broadcasts from Berlin in 1942. He tried to raise an anti-Bolshevik free corps in the British internee camp at St Denis to fight for the Nazis on the Russian front (1943), and made speeches for Hitler in Norway, France, Belgium and Yugoslavia (1944), always being introduced as the elder son of the British secretary of state for India. Captured by Italian partisans in 1945 and handed over to the British authorities, he was tried in London for high treason and pleaded guilty after an attempt to prove Spanish citizenship. He was hanged in December 1945.

AMERY, Leopold Charles Maurice Stennett (1873–1955) English Conservative politician, born in Gorakpur, India, and educated at Harrow and Oxford. After ten years on the staff of *The Times* he became MP for Sparkbrook, Birmingham, a seat which he held for 34 years. He served as colonial under-secretary, First Lord of the Admiralty and colonial secretary between 1919 and 1929 and then returned to office in **Churchill**'s wartime administration as secretary of state for India and Burma. He became famous for his exhortation to **Neville Chamberlain**, in May 1940, adapting **Cromwell**'s words, 'In the name of God, go!' His publications include *My Political Life* (3 vols, 1953–55).

AMES, James Barr (1846–1910) leading American legal scholar, born in Boston. Educated at Harvard, he was appointed to the Harvard Law School faculty in 1873 where he became dean from 1895. He adopted the case method of instruction pioneered by **Christopher Columbus Langdell** and published numerous casebooks. He had a part in founding the *Harvard Law Review* and published *Lectures on Legal History* (1913).

AMES, Joseph (1689–1759) English bibliographer and antiquarian, born in Yarmouth. He became an ironmonger or ship-chandler in London, and at the suggestion of friends compiled *Typographical Antiquities* (1749), the foundation of English bibliography.

AMES, Latin **Amesius, William** (1576–1633) English Puritan theologian. He wrote mostly in Latin, and spent the later half of his life in Holland, where he became a professor of theology. He is celebrated for his exposition of calvinist doctrine.

AMHERST, Jeffrey, 1st Baron Amherst (1717–97) English soldier, born in Riverhead, Kent. Joining the army at the age of 14 he played an important part in the North American phase of the Seven Years' War (1756–63). He was in command of the expedition against the French in Canada and captured Louisburg (1758). Appointed commander-in-chief of North America in 1759, he captured Montreal in 1760. He was governor-general of British North America from 1760 to 1763, and was commander-in-chief of the British army from 1772 to 1796. Amherst College was named after him.

AMHERST, William Pitt, 1st Earl Amherst of Arakan (1773–1857) English colonialist, born in Bath, nephew and adopted son of **Jeffrey, 1st Baron Amherst**. He succeeded to the baronetcy and Riverhead estate in Kent in 1797, and in 1800 married the widowed Countess Dowager of Plymouth (née Sarah Archer, 1762–1838), a keen naturalist. In 1816 he was sent as ambassador to China, but his mission failed when he refused to kow-tow to the emperor. In 1823 he was appointed governor-general of India, where he weathered the first Burmese War and was rewarded with an earldom (1826). The Amhersts returned to England in 1828, bringing a pair of rare Burmese pheasants, which were later named Lady Amherst's pheasants in her honour. Soon after his wife's death, Lord Amherst married another Dowager Duchess of Plymouth, the widow of his eldest stepson.

AMICI, Giovanni Battista (1784–1863) Italian optician, astronomer and natural philosopher, born in Modena. He constructed optical instruments, perfecting his own alloy for telescope mirrors and, in 1827, produced the dioptric, achromatic microscope that bears his name. He became director of the Florence observatory in 1835.

AMICIS, Edmondo de (1846–1908) Italian novelist, born in Oneglia. Although he intended to pursue a career in the army, and became director of the Italia Militare, Florence, in 1867, he turned to literature and recorded his experiences as a soldier in *La vita militare* (1868). He is chiefly remembered for his alliance with **Manzoni** in an attempt to 'purify' the Italian language. *L'Idioma gentile* (1905) presents his views on this subject. His most popular work is the sentimental *Il Cuore* (1886), translated into English as *An Italian Schoolboy's Journal* and into more than 25 other languages. His interest in education is reflected in *Il romanzo d'un maestro* (1890), and he also travelled widely, producing several books about his adventures.

AMIEL, Henri Frédéric (1821–81) Swiss philosopher and writer. Born in Geneva, he was professor of aesthetics (1849) and then moral philosophy (1853–81) at the Academy of Geneva. He published some essays and poems, but his fame as an intellectual and critic rests on his diaries from 1847 onwards, published posthumously as *Journal intime* (1883).

AMIES, Sir (Edwin) Hardy (1909–) English couturier, and dressmaker by appointment to Queen **Elizabeth**. After studying languages in France and Germany, he worked as a trainee in Birmingham before becoming a managing designer in London in 1934, where he made a name for himself especially with his tailored suits for women. He founded his own fashion house in 1946, and started designing for men also in 1959.

AMIN (DADA), Idi (1925–) Ugandan soldier and politician. Born of a peasant family, after a rudimentary education he joined the British, later to be the Ugandan, army, rising from the ranks to become a colonel in 1964. As a friend of prime minister **Milton Obote**, he was made commander-in-chief of the army and air force, but worsening relations between them resulted in Amin's staging a coup, in 1971, dissolving parliament and establishing a military dictatorship. He proceeded to expel all Ugandan Asians and many Israelis, seized foreign-owned businesses and estates and ordered the killing of thousands of his opponents, making his régime internationally infamous. His decision, in 1978, to annex the Kagera area of Tanzania, near the Ugandan border, gave President **Nyerere** the opportunity to send his troops into Uganda. Within six months Amin was defeated. He fled to Libya but later attempted to make his home in several countries, including Saudi Arabia, Zaire, Senegal and Nigeria. Each, in turn, pronounced him 'persona non grata'. In 1989 he was reported to have tried to return to Saudi Arabia from Zaire.

AMIOT See **AMYOT**

AMIS, Kingsley (1922–) English novelist and poet, born in London. Educated at the City of London School and at St John's College, Oxford, he was a lecturer in English literature at University College, Swansea (1948–61) and fellow of Peterhouse, Cambridge (1961–63). He achieved huge success with his first novel, *Lucky Jim* (1954), the story of a comic antihero in a provincial university; 'Jim' appeared again as a small-town librarian in *That Uncertain Feeling* (1956), and as a provincial author abroad in *I Like It Here* (1958). After the death of **Ian Fleming**, he wrote a James Bond novel, *Colonel Sun* (1968), under the pseudonym of Robert Markham, as well as *The James Bond Dossier* (1965). His later novels include *I Want It Now* (1968), *Ending Up* (1974), *Jakes's Thing* (1978), *Stanley and the Women* (1984) and *The Old Devils* (1986, Booker prize). He has also published four books of poetry. He was married (1965–83) to the novelist **Elizabeth Jane Howard**. His son, Martin Amis (1949–), is also a novelist.

AMISS, Dennis Leslie (1943–) English cricketer, born in Birmingham. He played with distinction for Warwickshire, and won admiration by the way he endured a battering by West Indian bowlers in 1976, which re-established his place in first-class cricket. He made 50 appearances in Test matches for England and 11 centuries, including 262 not out against West Indies at Kingston in 1974.

AMMAN, Jakob (c.1645–c.1730) Swiss Mennonite bishop whose followers founded the Amish (German *Amisch*) sect in the 1690s. Their members still practise an exclusively rural and simple way of life in various parts of the USA and Canada.

AMMANATI, Bartolommeo (1511–92) Italian architect and sculptor, born in Settignano. Working in the late Renaissance style he executed the ducal palace at Lucca; also part of the Pitti palace and the Ponte Sta Trinità (destroyed in World War II) in Florence. He also made the Neptune fountain in the Piazza della Signoria there.

AMMANN, Othmar Hermann (1879–1965) Swiss-born American structural engineer, born in Schaffhausen. He emigrated to the USA in 1904 to work with the Pennsylvania Steel Co. Later he designed some of America's greatest suspension bridges, including the George Washington Bridge (3500 ft) in New York (1931), Golden Gate Bridge (4200 ft) in San Francisco (1937) and Verrazano Narrows Bridge (4260 ft) in New York (1965), each in its day the longest span in the world.

AMMIANUS MARCELLINUS (c.330–390) Roman historian, born of Greek parents in Antioch. After fighting in Gaul, Germany, and the East, he settled in Rome, and devoted himself to literature. He wrote in Latin a history of the Roman empire from 98 AD (the death of **Domitianus**) in 31 books, of which only the last 18 are extant, comprising the years 353–78, which cover the events of his own lifetime.

AMMONIUS (c.160–242) Greek philosopher, surnamed **Saccas**, because in youth he was a sack-carrier in Alexandria. He was the founder of Neoplatonic philosophy, and teacher of **Plotinus**, **Origen** and **Longinus**, but left no writings.

AMONTONS, Guillaume (1663–1705) French physicist, born in Paris, the discoverer of the interdependence of temperature and pressure of gases. His interest in mechanics seems to have begun in his teens when he developed deafness. He improved the design of various scientific instruments including the hygrometer (for measuring moisture in the air), the barometer, and the constant-volume air thermometer. He discovered that equal changes in the temperature of a fixed volume of air resulted in equal variations in pressure, and perhaps approached the idea of absolute zero. His results were disregarded, however, and it was **Jacques Charles** who rediscovered the relationship between temperature and pressure of gases in the next century.

AMORY, Derick Heathcoat, 1st Viscount Amory (1899–1981) English Conservative politician, born in Tiverton. Educated at Eton and Christ Church College, Oxford, he entered parliament in 1945. He was minister of pensions (1951–53), at the board of trade (1953–54), minister of agriculture (1954–58) and while he was Chancellor of the Exchequer (1958–60), was made viscount.

AMORY, Thomas (c.1691–1788) author and eccentric of Irish descent. He lived a very secluded life in London, and seldom stirred out till dark. His chief works include *Memoirs of Several Ladies of Great Britain* (1755), *A History of Antiquities*, *Productions of Nature* (1755), and the *Life of John Buncle* (2 vols, 1756–66) an odd combination of autobiography, fantastic descriptions of scenery, deistical theology, and sentimental rhapsody.

AMOS (835–765 BC) Old Testament prophet, the earliest prophet in the Bible to have a book named after him. A herdsman from the village of Tekoa, near Bethlehem of Judaea, he denounced the iniquities of the northern kingdom of Israel.

AMPÈRE, André Marie (1775–1836) French mathematician and physicist, whose name was given to the basic SI unit of electric current (ampere, amp). Born in Lyon, he taught at the École Polytechnique in Paris, the University of Paris, and the Collège de France. He laid the foundations of the science of electrodynamics through his theoretical and experimental work following **Hans Christian Oersted**'s discovery in 1820 of the magnetic effects of electric currents, in *Observations électro-dynamiques* (1822) and *Théories des phénomènes électro-dynamiques* (1830).

AMPÈRE, Jean Jacques Antoine (1800–64) French writer and philologist, son of **André Marie Ampère**. After a spell of foreign travel, he lectured on the history of literature at Marseilles, and after 1830 was professor in the Collège de France. He was well read in German literature, and wrote on China, Persia, India, Egypt, and Nubia. His chief work was *Histoire littéraire de la France avant le XIIe* siècle (3 vols, 1840).

AMR IBN AL-AS (d.664) Arab soldier. A convert to Islam, he joined the prophet **Muhammad** in 629, and took part in the conquest of Palestine in 638. In 639 he undertook the conquest of Egypt; in 642 he captured Alexandria after a 14-month siege and accepted the capitulation of Egypt, and became the first Muslim governor of Egypt (642–44), where he founded the first city on the site of Cairo. He helped **Mu'awiyah**, founder of the **'Umayyad** dynasty, to seize the caliphate from **'Alī** by capturing Alexandria again in 658, and was governor of Egypt again from 661 to 663.

AMSBERG, Claus-Georg von See **BEATRIX**

AMUNDSEN, Roald Engelbrecht Gravning (1872–1928) Norwegian explorer, the first man to navigate the Northwest Passage and to reach the South Pole. Born in Borge, he early abandoned his medical studies in favour of a life at sea. In 1897 he served with the Belgian Antarctic expedition as first mate of the *Belgica*, the first vessel to overwinter in Antartica. From 1902 to 1906 he sailed the Northwest passage from east to west in the smack *Gjöa* (the first person to navigate the waterway in both directions) and located the Magnetic North Pole. In 1910 he set sail in the *Fram* in an attempt to reach the North Pole, but hearing that **Robert Peary** had apparently beaten him to it, he switched to the Antarctic and reached the South Pole in December 1911, one month ahead of Captain **Scott**. He built a new ship, the *Maud*, and sailed her through the Northeast Passage in 1918. In 1926 he flew to Spitzbergen to Alaska the airship *Norge* across the North Pole with **Lincoln Ellsworth** and **Umberto Nobile**, circling the Pole twice. In 1928 he disappeared when searching by plane for Nobile and his airship *Italia*, which had gone missing on another flight to the Pole. He published several books, including *My Life as an Explorer* (1927).

AMYOT, Jacques (1513–93) French humanist, born in Melun. One of the most lucid of French prose writers, he translated many classical texts, the most important being his French version of **Plutarch**'s *Lives*, which was the basis of Sir **Thomas North**'s translation into English, and of some of **Shakespeare**'s history plays. He was appointed bishop of Auxerre (1570).

AMYRAUT, Latin **Amyraldus Moyse** (1596–1664) French theologian, born in Bourgueil. Professor of Protestant theology at Saumur, he departed from the doctrine of predestination in the direction of 'hypothetical universalism'.

ANACHARSIS (6th century BC) a Scythian prince, according to **Herodotus**, who travelled widely in quest of knowledge, and visited Athens in **Solon**'s time.

ANACREON (c.570–c.475 BC) Greek lyric poet, from Teos, in Asia Minor. He helped to found the Greek colony of Abdera in Thrace (c.540 BC) in the face of threatened attack by the Persians. He was invited to Samos by **Polycrates** to tutor his son, and after the tyrant's downfall, was taken to Athens by Hipparchus, son of the 'tyrant' **Pisistratus**. He may have gone to Thessaly after the assassination of Hipparchus in 514. He was famous for his satires and particularly for his elegant love-poetry, of which only fragments remain.

ANAND, Mulk Raj (1905–) Indian novelist, critic and man of letters, born in Peshawar. His early life was fraught with tragedy and familial strife and he left India for Britain, where he was beaten up for blacklegging during the General Strike (1926). His first novel, *Untouchable* (1935), was rejected by 19 publishers, the 20th agreeing to take it on if **E M Forster** would write a preface. This he did, sparking off a remarkable career for Anand which has included novels, short stories, cookery books, philosophical exegeses, tales for children and writings on art. His novels, such as *The Coolie* (1936), *Two Leaves and a Bud* (1937) and *The Village* (1939, the first of a trilogy), promote the underdog in society, his approach being that of a humanist rather than a communist. They are uneven in quality but consistent in their depiction of life in the poverty stricken Punjab. More recently he has concentrated on an ambitious seven-volume autobiographical work of fiction, *The Seven Ages of Man*, which began with *Seven Summers*: *The Story of an Indian Childhood* (1951).

ANASTASIA, Grand Duchess Anastasia Nikolaievna Romanov (1901–?1918) youngest daughter of Tsar **Nicholas II**, and believed to have perished when the Romanov family were executed by the Bolsheviks in a cellar in Ekaterinburg on 19 July 1918. Various people have claimed to be Anastasia, especially Mrs 'Anna Anderson' Manahan, who died in Virginia, USA, in 1984 at the age of 82. She had been rescued from a suicide attempt in a Berlin canal in 1918, and for more than 30 years fought unsuccessfully to establish her identity as Anastasia, living under the name of Anna Anderson; most of the surviving members and friends of the Romanov family were sceptical or downright hostile. Her story inspired two films (*Anastasia*, with **Ingrid Bergman**, and *Is Anna Anderson Anastasia?* with Lilli Palmer), and several books. In 1968 she went to the USA and married an American former history lecturer, Dr John Manahan.

ANAXAGORAS (c.500–428 BC) Greek philosopher, born in Clazomenae. For 30 years he taught in Athens, where he had many illustrious pupils, among them **Pericles** and **Euripides**. His scientific speculations may have provided the pretext for his prosecution for impiety (he held that the sun, moon and stars were huge incandescent rocks), and he was banished from Athens for life. He withdrew to Lampsacus, on the Hellespont, and died there. His most celebrated, but obscure, cosmological doctrine was that matter is infinitely divisible into particles, which contain a mixture of all qualities, and that mind (*nous*) is a pervasive formative agency in the creation of material objects.

ANAXIMANDER (c.611–546 BC) Greek philosopher, born in Miletus, successor and perhaps pupil of **Thales**. He posited that the first principle was not a particular substance like water or air but the *apeiron*, the infinite or indefinite. He is credited with writing a book, producing the first map, and with many imaginative scientific speculations, for example that the earth is unsupported and at the centre of the universe, that living creatures first emerged from slime, and that human beings must have developed from some other species that more quickly matured into self-sufficiency.

ANAXIMENES (d.c.500 BC) Greek philosopher, born in Miletus, and the third of the three great Milesian thinkers, succeeding **Thales** and **Anaximander**. No biographical details are known about him. He posited that the first principle and basic form of matter was air, which could be transformed into other substances by a process of condensation and rarefaction. He also believed that the earth and the heavenly bodies were flat and floated on the air like leaves.

ANCKARSTRÖM, Johan Jakob (1762–92) Swedish army officer, and assassin of King **Gustav III** of Sweden. He was a page in the court, served in the royal bodyguard, but after settling on his estates in 1783 was tried for high treason, but released for want of evidence. Soon afterwards he conspired with a ring of disaffected nobles to murder the king, and after drawing the short straw, wounded the king mortally with a pistol at a masked ball at the Royal Opera House. He was publicly flogged for three days, and then executed.

ANCRE, Baron de Lussigny, Marquis d', originally **Concino Concini** (d.1617) Italian-born French adventurer, born in Florence. He came to the French court in 1600, in the train of **Marie de' Medici**, the wife of **Henri IV**. After Henri's assassination in 1610 he became chief favourite of the queen-regent during the minority of **Louis XIII**, and was made a marquis, and, in 1614, marshal of France, though he had never seen war. His prodigality was immense, and he squandered vast sums on the decoration of his palaces. Hated alike by nobility and populace, he put down one rebellion in 1616, but was assassinated in the Louvre during a second rebellion. His widow was soon executed for influencing the queen by witchcraft.

ANCUS MARCIUS (640–616 BC) traditionally the fourth king of Rome, is said to have conquered the neighbouring Latin tribes, and settled them on the Aventine.

ANDERS, Wladyslaw (1892–1970) Polish soldier. He studied at the University of Riga, at a military college in Russia, and served on the staff of the Russian division and Polish Corps in World War I (1914–17). In the Russo-Polish War (1919–20) he commanded the 15th Lancers against the Soviets. At the outbreak of World War II he commanded the Nowogrodek Cavalry Brigade, fighting both Germans and Russians, but was captured by the Russians and harshly treated (1939–41). In 1941 he was released to become commander-in-chief of a Polish ex-POW force organized in Russia, which he led through Iran into Iraq. In 1943 he became commander of the 2nd Polish Corps in Italy, fighting with the Allies, and capturing Monte Cassino. After the war, deprived of his nationality by the Polish communist government in 1946, he was a leading figure in the 140000-strong Free Polish community in Britain, and inspector-general of the Polish forces-in-exile. He wrote *An Army in Exile* (1949).

ANDERSEN, Hans Christian (1805–75) Danish author, one of the world's great story-tellers, born in Odense in Fünen. The son of a poor shoemaker, after his father's death he worked in a factory, but soon displayed a talent for poetry. Hoping to work in the theatre, he went to Copenhagen, but was rejected for his lack of education. He next tried to become a singer, but soon found that he was quite unfitted for the stage. Generous friends, however, helped him; and application having been made to the king, he was placed at an advanced school. Some of his poems, particularly *The Dying Child*, had already been favourably received, and he now became better known by his *Walk to Amager*, a literary satire in the form of a humorous narrative. In 1830 he published the first collected volume of his *Poems*, and in 1831 a second, under the title of *Fantasies and Sketches*. A travelling pension granted to him by the king in 1833 produced *Travelling Sketches* of a tour in the north of Germany; *Agnes and the Merman*, completed in Switzerland; and *The Improvisatore*, a series of scenes inspired by Rome and Naples. Soon afterwards he produced *O.T.* (1836), a novel containing vivid pictures of northern scenery and manners, and *Only a Fiddler* (1837). He wrote many other works, but it is such fairy tales as 'The Tin Soldier', 'The Emperor's New Clothes', 'The Tinder-box', 'The Snow Queen' and 'The Ugly Duckling' that have gained him lasting fame and delighted children throughout the world. He wrote *Story of My Life* (trans Mary Howitt, 1847).

ANDERSON, Carl David (1905–) American physicist, born in New York. He studied at the California Institute of Technology under **Robert Adams Millikan**, and in 1932 discovered the positron. He did notable work on gamma and cosmic rays, and was awarded the

1936 Nobel prize for physics (jointly with **Victor Hess**). Later he confirmed the existence of intermediate-mass particles called mesons (now muons).

ANDERSON, Elizabeth Garrett (1836–1917) English physician, the first English woman doctor, and sister of **Millicent Fawcett**, the suffragette. Born in London, she was brought up at Aldeburgh in Suffolk. In 1860 she began studying medicine, in the face of prejudiced opposition to the admission of women, and eventually (1865) qualified as a medical practitioner by passing the Apothecaries' Hall examination. In 1866 she established a dispensary for women in London (later renamed the Elizabeth Barrett Anderson Hospital), where she instituted medical courses for women. In 1870 she was appointed a visiting physician to the East London Hospital, and headed the poll for the London School Board; she was given the degree of MD by the University of Paris. In 1908 she was elected mayor of Aldeburgh—the first woman mayor in England.

ANDERSON, Gerry (1929–) American creator of television programmes. Entering the British film industry as a trainee with the Colonial Film Unit, he later worked as an assistant editor on such films as *The Wicked Lady* (1945) before co-founding Pentagon Films (1955). Initially intent on making commercials, he co-produced and directed such television series as *The Adventures of Twizzle* (1956) and *Torchy, the Battery Boy* (1957). He subsequently enjoyed great success with adventure series that combined a range of popular puppet characters with technologically advanced hardware and special effects. Among the best known are *Fireball XL–5* (1961), *Thunderbirds* (1964–66) and *Captain Scarlett and the Mysterons* (1967). He later branched out into live action shows with human actors like *The Protectors* (1971) and *Space 1999* (1973–76) before returning to the use of increasingly sophisticated puppetry in *Terrahawks* (1983–84).

ANDERSON, James (1662–1728) Scottish antiquary and lawyer, born in Edinburgh. In 1705 he published a treatise vindicating the independence of Scotland and in 1727 a valuable collection of historical documents; he spent the rest of his unhappy life working on his *Selectus Diplomatum et Numismatum Scotiae Thesaurus* (1739).

ANDERSON, James (1739–1808) Scottish agricultural economist, born in Hermiston, near Edinburgh. He had a farm in Aberdeenshire, where he invented the 'Scotch plough' (a two horse plough without wheels). He edited *The Bee* at Edinburgh (1790–93); and settled in London in 1797. His *Recreations of Agriculture* anticipated **Ricardo**'s theory of rent.

ANDERSON, Sir James Norman Dalrymple (1908–) Anglican scholar and lay leader, born in London. After graduating from Cambridge, he became a missionary in Egypt. In World War II he rose to be intelligence colonel and Cairo-based chief secretary for Arab affairs. By 1954 he was professor of oriental laws at London. A strong evangelical, he was the first chairman of the Church of England's House of Laity (1970). His publications include *Islamic Law in Africa* (1955), *God's Law and God's Love* (1980), *Christianity and the World Religions* (1985), and the autobiographical *An Adopted Son* (1985).

ANDERSON, Sir John See **WAVERLEY**

ANDERSON, John (1726–96) Scottish scientist, born in Roseneath manse, Dunbartonshire. He studied at Glasgow, where from 1756 to 1760 he was professor of oriental languages, and then of natural philosophy. He also established a bi-weekly class for mechanics, and at his death left all he had to found Anderson's College in Glasgow. The author of *Institutes of Physics* (1786), etc, he also invented the balloon post, and a gun which, in 1791, he presented to the French National Convention.

ANDERSON, John (1893–1962) Scottish-born Australian philosopher. He was professor of philosophy at Sydney from 1927, and can be regarded as the founder and main exponent of an Australian school of philosophy, espousing a distinctive blend of realism, empiricism and materialism.

ANDERSON, Dame Judith, originally **Frances Margaret Anderson** (1898–) Australian actress, born in Adelaide. She made her Sydney stage début in *A Royal Divorce* (1915) and first appeared in New York in 1918. She toured America throughout the 1920s, enjoying successes with *Cobra* (1924) and *Strange Interlude* (1928–29). She made her film début in the short *Madame of the Jury* (1930) but preferred the stage where her reputation as a distinguished classical and contemporary actress grew following productions like *Mourning Becomes Electra* (1932), *The Old Maid* (1935), *Hamlet* (1936, with **John Gielgud**), and *Macbeth* (1937) at the Old Vic in London. Her chilling performance as the sinister Mrs Danvers in *Rebecca* (1940) earned her a cinema career portraying cruel, domineering and often repressed matriarchal figures in films like *Laura* (1944) and *Diary of a Chambermaid* (1946). Her prodigious theatre credits include the title part in the Robinson Jeffers adaptation of *Medea* (1947 and 1982), *The Seagull* (1960) and *Hamlet* (1970–71) in the title role. Her rare film appearances comprise *Cat on a Hot Tin Roof* (1958), *A Man Called Horse* (1970), *Inn of the Damned* (1974) and *Star Trek III* (1984). In 1984 a Broadway theatre was named in her honour and, the same year, she joined the cast of the television soap opera *Santa Barbara*.

ANDERSON, Sir Kenneth Arthur Noel (1891–1959) British soldier, born in India. Educated at Charterhouse and Sandhurst he was commissioned into the Seaforth Highlanders. In World War I he served in France (1914–16), and fought under **Allenby** in Palestine in 1917–1918. Between the wars he served in India. In World War II he fought at Dunkirk (1940), and was commander of the 1st British Army in North Africa (1942–43) and captured Tunis (1943). He was governor-general of Gibraltar from 1947 to 1952.

ANDERSON, Lindsay (1923–) British stage and film director, born in Bangalore, India. Educated at Oxford, he became a film critic and from 1947 to 1951 edited *Sequence*. During the 1950s he made short documentary films, and won a short subject Oscar with *Thursday's Children*. He joined the English Stage Company at the Royal Court Theatre, London in 1957. His Royal Court productions included Willis Hall's *The Long and the Short and the Tall* and **John Arden**'s *Serjeant Musgrave's Dance* (1959). His first feature film was *This Sporting Life* (1963), followed by *If....* (1968), *O Lucky Man* (1973), *Britannia Hospital* (1982), and *The Whales of August* (1987). He has also acted cameo parts on film.

ANDERSON, Marian (1902–) American concert and opera singer, born in Philadelphia into a poor family. A magnificent contralto, after a Carnegie Hall recital (1929) she toured in Europe and the USSR. She became the first black singer at the New York Metropolitan (1955). President **Eisenhower** made her a delegate to the United Nations in 1958, and she has received many honours and international awards. She published her autobiography, *My Lord, What a Morning*, in 1956.

ANDERSON, Mary (1859–1940) American actress, born in Sacramento, California. Her début as Juliet at Louisville in 1875 was successful and she played with growing popularity in America and (after 1883) in England.

ANDERSON, Maxwell (1888–1941) American historical dramatist, born in Atlantic, Pennsylvania, the son of a Baptist minister. A verse playwright, he was in vogue in the late 1920s to the early 1940s with numerous plays which included *Elizabeth the Queen* (1930), *Mary of Scotland* (1933), *Winterset* (1935), *Key Largo* (1939) and *The Eve of St Mark* (1942). He also wrote screenplays, most notably that from **Erich Maria Remarque**'s novel *All Quiet on the Western Front* (1930). He won a Pulitzer prize for *Both Your Houses* in 1933.

ANDERSON, Philip Warren (1923–) American physicist, born in Indianapolis. He studied antenna engineering at the Naval Research Laboratories in World War II, and at Harvard under **John van Vleck** and worked at Bell Telephone Laboratories before becoming professor of physics at Princeton in 1975. He shared the Nobel prize for physics in 1977 (with Sir **Nevill Mott** and van Vleck) for his work on the electronic structure of magnetic and disordered systems.

ANDERSON, Robert (1806–71) American soldier, born near Louisville, Kentucky. He served in the Black Hawk war, the Mexican war, and the beginning of the American Civil War (1861–65), when he defended Fort Sumter against the Confederate attack in July 1861.

ANDERSON, Sherwood (1876–1941) American author, born in Camden, Ohio. He left his family and his lucrative position as manager of a paint factory to devote his entire time to writing. His first novel was *Windy McPherson's Son* (1916), but his best-known work is *Winesburg, Ohio* (1919).

ANDERSON, Thomas (1819–74) Scottish organic chemist. He studied at Edinburgh and Stockholm, became professor of chemistry at Glasgow, and is remembered for his discovery of pyridine.

ANDERSSON, Bibi (Birgitta) (1935–) Swedish actress, born in Stockholm. She began her career in 1949 as a film extra and is best known for her roles in many **Ingmar Bergman** films such as *The Seventh Seal* (1956), *Persona* (1966) and *The Touch* (1971). As a theatre actress she has been attached to both the Malmö Municipal Theatre and the Royal Dramatic Theatre, Stockholm. In the 1970s she took many stage roles in the USA. She has been the recipient of many awards, including the British Academy Award for Best Foreign Actress (1971) for her part in *The Touch*.

ANDERSSON, Dan (Daniel) (1888–1920), Swedish poet and novelist. One of Sweden's foremost writers in his time, he treated religious and metaphysical themes in his novels, like the autobiographical *De tre hemlösa* (1918, Three Homeless Ones). His poems about traditional charcoal-burners in *Kolarhistorier* (1914) and *Kolvakterens visor* (1915) turned them into national folk-figures.

ANDERSSON, Johan Gunnar (1874–1960) Swedish archaeologist, born in Knista, who pioneered the study of prehistoric China. Trained as a geologist, he went to China in 1914 as technical adviser to the government on coalfields and oil resources, but became fascinated by fossil remains and soon transferred his allegiance to archaeology. He was the first to identify prehistoric pottery in China, at Yang-shao-ts'un, Hunan, in 1921, and over the next year discovered numerous settlements with comparable ceramics across a vast stretch of the middle Yellow River valley. Soon he was able to characterize the first Neolithic or farming culture of north China, dated c.5000–3000 BC and named Yang-shao after his initial find. From 1921 to 1926 he also initiated excavations in the limestone caves at Chou-k'ou-tien near Peking, finding important fossils of *Homo erectus* alongside stone tools, charcoal, and charred bones in deposits 400–800 000 years old. Popularly known as Peking Man, these fossils were lost during the Japanese invasion of China in 1941. He wrote an autobiographical study, *Children of the Yellow Earth: Studies in Prehistoric China* (1934), and *Research into the Prehistory of China* (1943).

ANDERSSON, Karl Johan (1827–67) Swedish explorer. In 1850 he went with Sir **Francis Galton** to south-western Africa and in 1853–54 continued alone. In 1856 he published *Lake Ngami, or Discoveries in South Africa*. In 1858 he explored the Okavango River, and in 1866 set out for the Cunene. He came within sight of the stream, but had to retrace his steps, and died on the homeward journey.

ANDRADA E SILVA, José Bonifacio de (1763–1838) Brazilian statesman and geologist. Professor at Coimbra and secretary of Lisbon Academy, he returned to Brazil in 1819 to take part in the independence movement that overturned the Portuguese regency of Prince Pedro in 1820–22. He was prime minister under the prince as the emperor **Pedro I** (1822–23), but was exiled after differences with his Portuguese policy.

ANDRADE, Edward Neville da Costa' (1887–1971) English physicist, born in London. After studying at London, Heidelberg, Cambridge, and Manchester, he became professor of physics at Woolwich (1920–28) and London University (1928–50). He was known for his work on metals and liquids. He was director of the Royal Institution and the Davy-Faraday laboratory (1950–52).

ANDRASSY, Julius, Count (1823–90) Hungarian statesman, born in Volosca. A supporter of **Kossuth**, he was prominent in the struggle for independence (1848–49), after which he remained in exile until 1858. When the Dual Monarchy was formed in 1867, he was made prime minister of Hungary.

ANDRASSY, Julius, Count (1860–1929) Hungarian statesman, son of **Julius Andrassy**, born in Toketerebes. He became minister of the interior in 1900, and foreign minister in 1918. In 1921 he attempted to restore the monarchy, and was imprisoned, but after his release became leader of the royalist opposition. He wrote several historical works.

ANDRE, Carl (1935–) American sculptor, born in Massachusetts. He trained briefly at Phillips Art College, Andover, before gravitating to New York city, where he became close friends with **Frank Stella**. Best known for his minimalist sculptures of the 1960s, such as *Equivalents*, a floor piece consisting of 120 bricks stacked in two layers to form a rectangle, his initial experiments with wood-cutting were inspired by **Constantine Brancusi**. A job on the Pennsylvania Railroad in the 1960s led to experimentation with mass produced materials; this was a reaction against the gestural aspects of American Abstract Expressionism, intended to focus the spectator's mind on the materials themselves. An interest in mathematics and the philosopher **Lao-Tzu** are evident in his work.

ANDRÉ, John (1751–80) British soldier, born in London of French-Swiss descent. He took over his father's business but in 1774 joined the army in Canada, and became aide-de-camp to Sir **Henry Clinton**, and adjutant-general. When **Benedict Arnold** obtained the command of West Point in 1780, André was selected to negotiate with him for its betrayal. They met near Haverstraw on the Hudson; then André began his dangerous journey to New York. As he was nearing the British lines in civilian clothes, with incriminating papers in his boots, he was captured and handed over to the American military authorities. He was tried as a spy, and hanged at Tappantown. In 1821 his remains were brought from the USA and interred in Westminster Abbey.

ANDREA, da Firenza, originally **Andrea Bonaiuti** (fl.c.1343–1377) Florentine painter. His most famous work is the monumental fresco cycle in the Spanish Chapel of the Dominican church of S Maria Novella in Florence, painted c.1366–68. These paintings, an elaborate celebration of the Dominican doctrine, are the most unusual and impressive mural scheme of the time: the whole interior surface of the building is covered with descriptive scenes, painted in a meticulously detailed but severe and somewhat rigid style. Many panel paintings of varying quality are attributed to him, but his only other documented work is the *Life of S Ranieri*, frescoes in the Camposanto in Pisa, completed in 1377.

ANDREÄ, Johann Valentin (1586–1654) German theologian, born near Tübingen. He died at Stuttgart, where he was the Protestant court-chaplain. Long regarded as the founder or restorer of the Rosicrucians, he wrote *Chymische Hochzeit Christiani Rosenkreuz* (1616).

ANDRÉE, Salomon August (1854–97) Swedish engineer, born in Gränna. He disappeared in an attempt to reach the North Pole by balloon from Spitzbergen in 1897. His body was found on White Island in 1930.

ANDREEV See **ANDREYEV**

ANDRETTI, Mario Gabriele (1940–) American racing driver, born in Montona, Italy. He started out in midget car racing, then progressed to the US Automobile Club circuit, in which he was champion three times. In a Formula One career stretching from 1968 to 1982, he competed in 128 Grand Prix, winning 16. His most successful year was 1978, when he won the racing drivers' world championship. He was also twice winner, in 1969 and 1981, of the Indianapolis 500 race.

ANDREW, St one of the twelve apostles, brother of Simon Peter, a fisherman converted by **John the Baptist.** Tradition says he preached the gospel in Asia Minor and Scythia, and was crucified in Achaia (Greece) by order of the Roman governor. The belief that his cross was X-shaped dates only from the 14th century. The patron saint of Scotland and of Russia, he is commemorated on 30 November.

ANDREW, HRH The Prince Andrew Albert Christian Edward, Duke of York (1960–) British prince, second son of Queen **Elizabeth**. Educated at Gordonstoun School, Scotland, Lakefield College, Ontario, and the Royal Naval College, Dartmouth, he was commissioned in the royal marines, qualifying as a helicopter pilot and serving in the Falklands War (1982). In 1986 he married Sarah Margaret Ferguson and was made Duke of York. They have two children, Princess Beatrice Elizabeth Mary (1988–) and Princess Eugenie Victoria Helena (1990–).

ANDREW, Agnellus Matthew (1908–87) Roman Catholic bishop and broadcaster, born near Glasgow. Ordained in 1932, he engaged in parish work in Manchester until appointment as assistant to the head of religious broadcasting at the BBC (1955–67). He was then adviser to the Independent Broadcasting Authority (1968–75). Meanwhile he became known as a TV commentator for many papal and national events, and was founder and director of the National Catholic Radio and TV Centre at Hatch End, Middlesex (1955–80). Having been made titular bishop of Numana he became from 1980 external head of the Vatican commission for communication.

ANDREW, John Albion (1818–67) American anti-slavery statesman, born in Windham, Maine. He was governor of Massachusetts (1860–66) and mobilized the state during the Civil War.

ANDREWES, Lancelot (1555–1626) English prelate and scholar, born in Barking. Educated at Ratcliffe, Mechant Taylors' School, and Pembroke Hall, Cambridge, he took orders in 1580 and in 1589, through **Walsingham**'s influence, he was appointed a prebendary of St Paul's and master of Pembroke Hall. In 1597 Queen **Elizabeth** made him a prebendary, and in 1601 dean, of Westminster. He rose still higher in favour with King **James VI** and **I**, who appreciated his learning and oratory. He attended the Hampton Court Conference, and took part in the translation of the Authorized Version Bible (1607). In 1605 he was consecrated bishop of Chichester; in 1609 he was translated to Ely, and in 1618 to Winchester. A powerful preacher and defender of Anglican doctrines, he is considered one of the most learned theologians of his time. His *Private Prayers*, written in Greek, were published posthumously.

ANDREWS, Charles Freer (1871–1940) Anglican missionary to India, Born in Newcastle-upon-Tyne, son of a minister of the Catholic Apostolic Church. He graduated from Cambridge and went to India in 1904. Going to South Africa in 1913 to help the oppressed Indian labourers there, he began a lifelong friendship with **Mahatma Gandhi**, and contributed towards the **Smuts**-Gandhi agreement. Back in India he forsook Western ways of living and joined **Rabindranath Tagore**'s settlement at Santiniketan, intent on living as poor amid the poor. He recorded his experiences in *What I Owe to Christ* (1932).

ANDREWS, Eamon (1922–87) Irish broadcaster, born in Dublin. An All-Ireland amateur juvenile middleweight boxing champion, he began sports commentating for Radio Eirann in 1939 and subsequently worked on various programmes for BBC Radio, including *Sports Report* (1950–62). On television he hosted the parlour game *What's My Line?* (1951–63) and *This is Your Life* (1955–87): sentimental salutes to public figures, which he presided over with practised ease and genuine warmth. Active as a chat show host, children's presenter, as well as being a keen businessman, he later returned to *What's My Line?* (1984–87). His books include *This Is My Life* (1963) and *Surprises of Your Life* (1978).

ANDREWS, Ernest Clayton (1870–1948) Australian geologist, born in Sydney, He studied at Sydney University under Sir **Edgeworth David**. Specializing in physiography, his field was the evolution of the Pacific Rim coastlines, in particular of eastern Australia and the western USA, and the glaciers of New Zealand. He also published papers on the flora of these areas, and studied the coral reef formations of Fiji and Tonga. He held many offices in the scientific bodies of the USA, New Zealand and Australia, and was president of the Australasian Association for the Advancement of Science from 1930 to 1932.

ANDREWS, Frank Maxwell (1884–1943) American air force officer, born in Nashville, Tennessee. He graduated from the Military Academy at West Point, and served in the aviation section of the Signal Corps in World War I. Between the wars he became the first commander of the general-headquarters air force (1935–39), and helped develop the B-17 bomber. In World War II he was head of the US Caribbean Defense Command (1941–42) and the Middle East Command (1942–43), before succeeding **Eisenhower** as commander of the US forces in Europe. He was killed in a plane crash. Andrews airforce base in Washington is named after him.

ANDREWS, Julie, originally **Julia Elizabeth Wells** (1935–) English singer and actress, born in Walton-on-Thames, Surrey. From a showbusiness family, she was trained as a singer, making her London début in the 1947 revue *Starlight Roof*. Radio and stage successes led to her selection for the New York production of *The Boyfriend* (1954) and several long-running Broadway musicals, notably *My Fair Lady* (1956) and *Camelot* (1960). With her film début in *Mary Poppins* (1964) she won an Academy Award, and this was followed by a further nomination for *The Sound of Music* (1965). Voted the world's most popular star, she made strenuous efforts to move beyond a rather prim image by portraying a breast-baring movie-star in *S.O.B.* (1981), and a transvestite in *Victor/Victoria* (1982). Active for some time in television, since 1970 she has appeared almost exclusively in films directed by her second husband, Blake Edwards.

ANDREWS, Roy Chapman (1884–1960) American naturalist and explorer, born in Beloit, Wisconsin. He is best known as the discoverer, in Mongolia, of fossil dinosaur eggs, but he made many and valuable contributions to palaeontology, archaeology, botany, zoology, geology, and topography. He explored Alaska before World War I, and was on several expeditions to Central Asia, sponsored by the American Museum of Natural History, of which he became director (1935–42). His published works include *Across Mongolian Plains* (1921), *The Ends of the Earth* (1929), *Meet Your Ancestors* (1945), *Heart of Asia* (1951), and *In the Days of the Dinosaur* (1959).

ANDREWS, Thomas (1813–85) Irish physical chemist, born in Belfast. He practised as a physician at Belfast, where from 1849 to 1879 he was professor of chemistry. He is noted for his discovery of the critical temperature of gases, above which they cannot be liquefied, however great the pressure applied.

ANDREYEV, Leonid (1871–1919) Russian writer and artist, born in Orel. He suffered much from poverty and ill-health as a student, and attempted suicide, before taking to writing and portrait painting. Many of his works have been translated into English, eg *The Seven that were Hanged* (1909), *The Red Laugh* (1905), etc.

ANDRIĆ, Ivo (1892–1975) Yugoslav author and diplomat, born near Travnik. A member of the diplomatic service, he was minister in Berlin at the outbreak of war in 1939. His chief works, *The Bridge on the Drina* (1945) and *Bosnian Story* (1945), earned him the 1961 Nobel prize for literature and the nickname 'the Yugoslav Tolstoy'.

ANDRIEUX, François Guillaume Jean Stanislaw (1759–1833) French scholar and dramatist, born in Strasbourg. He became professor of French literature at the Collège de France (1814) and secretary of the Académie (1829). His works are Classical in style, for he opposed the rising influence of Romanticism. They include the comedies *Les Étourdis* (1788) and *La Comédienne* (1816).

ANDRONICUS, called **Cyrrhestes** (1st century BC) Greek architect, born in Cyrrhus. He constructed the Tower of the Winds at Athens, known in the Middle Ages as the Lantern of Demosthenes.

ANDRONICUS, Livius See **LIVIUS ANDRONICUS**

ANDRONICUS I COMNENUS (c.1122–1185) Byzantine emperor from 1183, grandson of **Alexius I Comnenus**. In his youth he served against the Turks, was imprisoned for treason for twelve years, but escaped to Russia. Pardoned and employed again, he fell once more into disfavour; and after his scandalous seduction of Theodora, the widow of Baldwin III of Jerusalem, he settled among the Turks in Asia Minor, with a band of outlaws. After the death of Manuel in 1182, he was recalled to become first guardian, then colleague, of the young Emperor Alexius II. Soon after, he caused the empress-mother to be strangled, and then Alexius himself, marrying his youthful widow. His reign was vigorous, and restored prosperity to the provinces; but tyranny and murder were its characteristics in the capital, leading to a popular uprising in which he was overthrown and killed.

ANDRONICUS II PALAEOLOGUS (1260–1332) Byzantine emperor, 1282–1328. During his reign he withdrew from the negotiations for the union of the Greek and Roman communions, and restored the Greek ritual in full. He and the empire suffered much from Catalan mercenaries, hired for the wars with the Turks.

ANDRONICUS III PALAEOLOGUS (1296–1341) Byzantine emperor from 1328, grandson of **Andronicus II Palaeologus**. Excluded from the succession for the murder of his brother, he compelled his grandfather to make him his colleague in the empire and then to abdicate (1328). During his reign, which saw almost constant warfare, the Turks occupied the southern shores of the Bosphorus, and the Serbians conquered Bulgaria, Epirus and Macedonia.

ANDRONICUS OF RHODES (fl.70–50 BC) Greek Aristotelian philosopher. He lived at Rome in **Cicero**'s time and edited the writings of **Aristotle**.

ANDROPOV, Yuri (1914–84) Russian politician, born in the village of Nagutskaya in Stavropol province of the North Caucasus region of southern Russia. The son of a middle-class railway official, he trained as a water transport engineer and began work in the shipyards of the upper Volga, at Rybinsk (now Andropov), in 1930. Here he became politically active and in 1940 was given the task of 'sovietizing' the newly ceded Karelian peninsula; but, within a year, after its occupation by Germany, he was engaged in organizing a partisan resistance movement. After the war he made rapid progress, being promoted to the post of second party secretary in Karelia, and was then brought to Moscow to work for the CPSU central committee. He was ambassador in Budapest, 1954–57, and came to the notice of the strict ideologist, **Mikhail Suslov**, for his part in crushing the Hungarian uprising of 1956. Suslov became Andropov's patron, assisting his rise in the hierarchy so that in 1967 he was appointed KGB chief and in 1973 became a full member of the poliburo. His firm handling of dissident movements while he was at the KGB enhanced his reputation, enabling him to be chosen as General Secretary **Brezhnev**'s successor in 1973. In this post he proved to be more radical and reformist than his previous record would have suggested, but after less than 15 months in office, he died. During that time he had successfully groomed a group of potential successors, one of whom was **Mikhail Gorbachev**.

ANEURIN (fl.6th–7th century) Welsh court poet. His principal work, the *Gododin*, celebrates the British heroes who were annihilated by the Saxons in the bloody battle of Cattraeth (Catterick in Yorkshire) about the year 600. The poem's language, metrical forms and general technique suggest a long tradition of praise-poetry in the Brythonic language, the form of primitive Welsh which was current in Cumbria and southern Scotland.

ANFINSEN, Christian Boehmer (1916–) American biochemist, born in Monessen, Pennsylvania. Educated at Harvard, he taught there before moving to the National Institutes of Health in Bethesda, Maryland, in 1950–82. His notable work was on the shape and structure of the enzyme ribonuclease (RNA), for which he shared the Nobel prize for chemistry in 1972 with **Stanford Moore** and **William Stein**.

ANGAS, George Fife (1789–1879) English shipowner, born in Newcastle-upon-Tyne, and regarded as a founder of South Australia. He was appointed commissioner for the formation of the colony in 1834, and emigrated to Adelaide in 1851.

ANGELES DE LOS See **DE LOS ANGELES**

ANGELICO, Fra, real name **Guido di Pietro,** monastic name **Giovanni da Fiesole** (c.1400–1455) Italian painter, born in Vicchio in Tuscany. As a young man he entered the Dominican monastery of San Domenico at Fiesole, near Florence. The community was obliged to leave Fiesole (1409–18) and some time after its return Fra Angelico began to paint. In 1436 he was transferred to Florence where he worked for **Cosimo de Medici** and in 1445 he was summoned by the pope to Rome where he worked until his death. His most important frescoes are in the Florentine convent of San Marco which is now a museum. These 'aids to contemplation' are characterized by pale colours, crisp delineation of form, the use of local landscape as background and an air of mystical piety. In the high altar the way in which the figures of saints and angels recede towards the central figure marks a development in the sacra conversazione altarpiece. In 1447 he began a Last Judgment at Orvieto which was finished by **Signorelli**. In Rome only the frescoes in the chapel of Nicholas V survive. Of his easel pictures, a splendid *Coronation of the Virgin* is held by the Louvre, and a *Glory* by the London National Gallery, both of which were originally at Fiesole. There are other fine examples in the Florence Uffizi.

ANGELL, Sir Norman, Ralph Norman Angell Lane (1872–1967) English writer and pacifist, born in Holbeach. He wrote *The Great Illusion* (1910) and *The Great Illusion, 1933* (1933) to prove the economic futility of war even for the winners. He won the 1933 Nobel prize for peace.

ANGELOU, Maya (1928–) American writer, singer, dancer, performer and Black activist, born in St Louis, Missouri. After the break-up of her parents' marriage, she and her brother lived with their grandmother in Stamps, Arkansas. She was raped by her mother's boyfriend when she was eight and for the next five years was mute. In her teens she moved to California to live with her mother, and at 16 gave birth to her son, Guy. She has had a variety of occupations in what she describes as 'a roller-coaster life'. In the 1920s she toured Europe and Africa in the musical *Porgy and Bess*. In New York she joined the Harlem Writers Guild and continued to earn her living singing in nightclubs and performing in **Jean Genet**'s *The Blacks*. In the 1960s she was involved in Black struggles and then spent several years in Ghana as editor of *African Review*. Her multi-volume autobiography, commencing with *I Know Why the Caged Bird Sings* (1970), was a critical and popular success, imbued with optimisn, humour and homespun philosophy. She has published several volumes of verse, including *And Still I Rise* (1987), and is the Reynolds Professor of American studies at Wake Forest University in North Carolina.

ANGERSTEIN, John Julius (1735–1823) English financier and underwriter, of Russian origin. His collection of 38 paintings bought by the nation in 1824 for £57000, formed the nucleus of the National Gallery.

ANGERVILLE See **AUNGERVILLE**

ANGIOLIERI, Cecco (c.1260–c.1312) Italian poet, born in Siena. Nothing is known of his life except from his sonnets, the only kind of verse he wrote, which reveal a drinker, lecher and gambler with a cynical, sardonic character and a heartless wit. He attacked **Dante** in three poems.

ANGLESEY, Henry William Paget, 1st Marquis of (1768–1854) English soldier, born in London. Educated at Westminster and Christ Church, Oxford, he sat in parliament off and on from 1790 to 1810; and in 1812 succeeded his father as Earl of Uxbridge. He served in the army with distinction in Flanders (1794), Holland (1799), and the Peninsular War (1808); and for his splendid services as commander of the British cavalry at Waterloo, where he lost a leg, he was made Marquis of Anglesey. In 1828 he was appointed lord-lieutenant of Ireland, where he advocated Catholic emancipation, and was recalled by **Wellington** in 1829. From 1830 to 1833 he held the same office under Lord **Grey**'s administration; but lost his popularity through coercive measures against **O'Connell**. To him Ireland is indebted for the board of education. From 1846 to 1852, now field-marshal, he was master-general of the ordnance.

ANGLISS, Sir William Charles (1865–1957) English-born Australian businessman, pioneer of the Australian meat exporting industry, born in Dudley, Worcestershire. He emigrated to Australia in 1884, eventually opening a butcher's shop in Melbourne. From this small beginning grew a chain of meat stores across the country. In 1934, when the family company was sold to the Vestey family interests it had become the largest meat exporter in Australia. Sir William retained many other industrial and business interests, was a member of the Legislative Council of Victoria for 40 years, and was knighted in 1939. On his death he left £1 million to charity.

ANGOULÊME, Louis Antoine de Bourbon, Duc d' (1775–1844) French soldier and aristocrat, eldest son of **Charles X** of France. He fled from France with his father after the revolution of 1789, and lived in various places, including Holyrood House in Edinburgh. In 1799 he married his cousin, Marie Thérèse (1778–1851), only daughter of **Louis XVI**. After the Restoration in 1814 (**Louis XVIII**), he made a feeble effort, as lieutenant-general of France, to oppose **Napoleon** on his return from Elba in 1815. In 1823 he led the French army of invasion into Spain to restore Ferdinand VII to his throne. After the July revolution in 1830, he renounced his claim to the throne and accompanied his father into exile, and died at Görz.

ÅNGSTRÖM, Anders Jonas (1814–74) Swedish physicist, born in Lödgö. He was keeper of the observatory at Uppsala (1843), and professor of physics (1858), and from 1867 secretary to the Royal Society at Uppsala. He wrote on heat, magnetism, and especially optics; the angstrom unit, for measuring wavelengths of light, is named after him. His son, Knut J. Ångström (1857–1910), was also a noted Uppsala physicist, important for his researches on solar radiation.

ANGUS, Marion (1866–1946) Scottish poet, born in Aberdeen, the daughter of a Church of Scotland minister. She grew up in Arbroath, and later lived in Aberdeen, Edinburgh and Helensburgh. Her volumes of verse, mostly in Scots, include *The Lilt and Other Verses* (1922), *Sun and Candlelight* (1927), *The Singin' Lass* (1929), and *Lost Country* (1937). Her best-known poem is a lament for **Mary, Queen of Scots**, 'Alas, Poor Queen'.

ANIMUCCIA, Giovanni (c.1500–1571) Italian composer, born in Florence. In 1555 he became choirmaster at St Peter's in the Vatican, a post he held until his death, when he was succeeded by **Palestrina**. A man of deep religious feeling, he was influenced by St Philip

Neri, for whose oratory he composed the *Laudi*—semi-dramatic religious pieces in popular style from which oratorio developed.

ANJOU, Duke of See **HENRY II**

ANNA COMNENA (1083–c.1148) Byzantine princess and historian, daughter of the emperor **Alexius I Comnenus**. In 1097 she married Nicephorus Bryennius, for whom she tried in vain to gain the imperial crown after her father's death in 1118; she took up literature and after her husband's death (1137) retired to a convent where she wrote *Alexiad*, an account of Byzantine history and society for the period 1069–1118, including a flattering biography of her father.

ANNA IVANOVNA (1693–1740) empress of Russia from 1730, younger daughter of Ivan V and niece of **Peter I, the Great**. In 1710 she married the Duke of Courland, who died the following year. After the early death of **Peter II** she was elected to the throne by the Supreme Council in 1730, with conditions that severely limited her authority. She trumped the council by abolishing it and ruled as an autocrat with her German favourite, **Ernst Johann Biron**, who assumed the title of Duke of Courland and became the real power behind the throne. Together they established a reign of terror, in which 20000 people are said to have been banished to Siberia.

ANNE, St (50 BC–50 AD) wife of St **Joachim**, and mother of the Virgin Mary, is first mentioned in the *Protevangelium* of James, in the 2nd century. She is the patron saint of carpenters. Her feast day is 26 July.

ANNE (1665–1714) queen of Great Britain and Ireland from 1702, and sister of **Mary II** (wife of William of Orange, **William III**). Born at St James's Palace in London, she was the second daughter of **James II** (then Duke of York) and his first wife, Anne Hyde (daughter of the 1st Earl of **Clarendon**). Her mother died in 1671 and in 1672 her father became a Catholic (he married the Catholic **Mary of Modena** in 1773), but Anne was brought up as a staunch Protestant. In 1683 she married Prince George of Denmark (1653–1708), bearing him 17 children, only one of whom survived infancy—William, Duke of Gloucester, who died in 1700 at the age of 12. For much of her life she was greatly influenced by her close friend and confidante, **Sarah Churchill**, the future Duchess of Marlborough. In the 'Glorious Revolution' of 1688, when her father James II was overthrown, she supported the accession of her sister Mary and her brother-in-law William, and was placed in the succession; but after quarrelling with her sister she was drawn by the Marlboroughs into Jacobite intrigues for the restoration of her father or to secure the succession of his son, **James Stewart**, the 'Old Pretender'. In 1701, however, after the death of her own son, she signed the Act of Settlement designating the Hanoverian descendants of **James I** as her successors, and in 1702 she succeeded William III on the throne. Dedicated to national unity under the crown, the chief event of her reign was the union of the parliaments of Scotland and England in 1707. The other major event of her reign was the War of the Spanish Succession (1701–13) with Marlborough's victories over the French at Blenheim, (1704), Ramillies (1706), Oudenarde (1708) and Malplaquet (1709). Queen Anne finally broke with the Marlboroughs in 1710–11, when Sarah was supplanted by a new favourite, Sarah's cousin, Mrs Abigail Marsham, and the Whigs were replaced by a Tory administration led by **Robert Harley** (1st Earl of Oxford) and Lord **Bolingbroke**. She was the last Stuart monarch, and on her death in August 1714, she was succeeded by **George I**.

ANNE, (Elizabeth Alice Louise) (1950–) the Princess Royal, only daughter of Queen **Elizabeth** of Great Britain and Prince **Philip**. She married in 1973 Lieutenant (now Captain) **Mark Phillips** of the Queen's Dragoon Guards, but separated from him in 1989; their children are: Peter Mark Andrew (b.1977) and Zara Anne Elizabeth (b.1981). An accomplished horsewoman, like Captain Phillips (gold medallist in the 1972 Olympics), she has ridden in the British Equestrian Team. A keen supporter of charities and overseas relief work, as president of Save the Children Fund she has travelled widely promoting its activities.

ANNE BOLEYN See **BOLEYN**

ANNE OF AUSTRIA (1601–66) queen of France, the eldest daughter of **Philip III** of Spain and wife of **Louis XIII** of France, whom she married in 1615. The marriage was unhappy, and much of it was spent in virtual separation, due to the influence of the king's chief minister Cardinal **Richelieu**. In 1638, however, they had their first son, Louis, who succeeded his father in 1643 as **Louis XIV**. Anne was appointed regent for the boy king (1643–51), and with Richelieu having died in 1642 she wielded power with her own favourite and lover, Cardinal **Jules Mazarin**, as prime minister. They steered France through the difficult period of the Fronde, and although Louis came of age technically in 1651, they continued to rule the country jointly. After Mazarin's death in 1661 she retired to the convent of Val de Grâce, and Louis XIV became absolute monarch.

ANNE OF BOHEMIA (1366–94) queen of England, first wife of **Richard II**. The daughter of the emperor **Charles IV**, she married Richard in 1382. She died of the plague.

ANNE OF BRITTANY (1476–1514) duchess of Brittany and twice queen of France. The daughter of Duke Francis of Brittany, she succeeded her father in 1488. She struggled to maintain Breton independence, but in 1491 was forced to marry **Charles VIII** of France, whereby Brittany was united with the French crown. In 1499, a year after his death, she married his successor, **Louis XII**. She was also a noted patron of the arts.

ANNE OF CLEVES (1515–57) German princess, and queen consort of England, the fourth wife of **Henry VIII**, the daughter of John, Duke of Cleves, a noted champion of Protestantism in Germany. A plain-featured and unattractive girl, she was selected for purely political reasons after the death of **Jane Seymour**, and was married to Henry in 1540. The marriage was annulled by parliament six months later.

ANNE OF DENMARK (1574–1619) Danish princess, and queen of Scotland and England. The daughter of King **Frederik II** of Denmark, in 1589 she married **James VI** of Scotland, the future **James I** of England. Extravagant in her tastes, she was a lavish patron of the arts and architecture, and appeared in dramatic roles in court masques by **Ben Jonson**.

ANNESLEY, James (1715–60) Irish claimant to the earldom of Anglesea, born in Dunmaine, County Wexford, alleged son of Mary Sheffield, Lady Altham. The Althams separated in 1716, and the boy was turned out of his father's house in Dublin at the instance of Altham's mistress (1722). The boy was allegedly kidnapped and shipped to the American plantations in 1728 at the instance of his uncle and there he was reported sold as a slave. His uncle later became Earl of Anglesea. James returned to Ireland in 1741 but in 1742 he accidentally shot Thomas Egglestone, for which he was tried but acquitted. He was assaulted by his uncle at the Curragh Races, County Kildare, in September 1743, and in November won a verdict for the recovery of his estates from the Court of Exchequer, Dublin. In 1744, his uncle was tried and convicted at Athy, County Kildare, for the Curragh assault. But Annesley's supporters' funds were now exhausted and he was unable to take his probably valid claim to the House of Lords. He was the inspiration for **R L Stevenson**'s *Kidnapped*.

ANNIGONI, Pietro (1910–88) Italian painter, born in Milan. During the 1950s he worked in England, and held a London exhibition in 1954. He was one of the few 20th-century artists to put into practice the technical methods of the old masters, and his most usual medium was tempera, although there are frescoes by him in the Convent of St Mark at Florence (executed in 1937). His Renaissance manner is shown at its best in his portraits, eg, of Queen **Elizabeth** and President **Kennedy** (1961).

ANNING, Mary (1799–1847) English palaeontologist, born in Lyme Regis, the daughter of a carpenter and vendor of specimens, who, dying in 1810, left her to make her own living. In 1811 she discovered in a local cliff the fossil skeleton of an ichthyosaurus, now in the British Museum of Natural History. She also discovered the first plesiosaurus and, in 1828, the first pterodactyl.

ANNO, Mitsumas (1926–) Japanese children's author and illustrator, born in Tsuwano. He is renowned for his visual puzzles, and his best work can be seen in *Topsy-Turvies*: *Pictures to Stretch the Imagination* (1970), *Dr Anno's Magical Midnight Circus* (1972) and *Anno's Alphabet*: *An Adventure in Imagination* (1975).

ANNUNZIO, Gabriele See **D'ANNUNZIO**

ANOUILH, Jean (1910–) French dramatist, born in Bordeaux of French and Basque parentage. He began his career as a copywriter and as a gag-man in films. His first play, *L'Hermine* (1931) was not a success; but his steady output soon earned him recognition as one of the leading dramatists of the contemporary theatre. He was influenced by the neoclassical fashion inspired by **Giraudoux**, but his very personal approach to the re-interpetation of Greek myths is less poetic and more in tune with contemporary taste. Among his many successful plays may be mentioned *Le Voyageur sans bagage* (1938), *Le Bal des voleurs* (1938) (in English as *Thieves' Carnival*, 1952), *La Sauvage* (1938), *Eurydice* (1942), Eng trans *Point of Departure*, 1950), *Antigone* (1946), *Médée* (1946), *L'Invitation au château* (1948) (adapted by **Christopher Fry** as *Ring Round the Moon*, 1950), *L'Alouette* (1953; in English as *The Lark*, 1955), *Becket* (in London, 1961), *Poor Bitos* (in London, 1963–64), *Cher Antoine* (1969), *Ne Réveillez Pas, Madame* (1970), *The Arrest* (1974), *Vive Henri IV* (1977) and *La Culotte* (1978).

ANQUETIL, Jacques (1934–87) French racing cyclist, born in Normandy, the son of a strawberry grower. The foremost of the second wave of French cyclists to emerge after World War II, he won the Tour de France five times, including four successes in a row from 1961 to 1964. Unexcelled in time-trial stages, he could make ferocious attacks, or suddenly distance the field on a conventional stretch of road. He had a penchant for hunting in pairs, winning the Tours of France and Spain in 1963 and those of France and Italy the following year. He retired in 1969.

ANQUETIL-DUPERRON, Abraham Hyacinthe (1731–1805) French orientalist, born in Paris. He studied for the priesthood but eventually abandoned theology in favour of the study of oriental languages. He travelled to India in 1755, where he studied Persian, Sanskrit, Zend and Pahlavi. In 1171 he published a French translation of the Zend-avesta, and between 1802 and 1804 a Latin translation of a Persian version of the Upanishads.

ANSCHÜTZ, Ottomar (1846–1907) German photographer, born in Yugoslavia, He was a pioneer of instantaneous photography, and was one of the first to make a series of pictures of moving animals and people, so making a substantial contribution to the invention of the cinematograph.

ANSELM, St (1033–1109) scholastic philosopher and prelate, and archbishop of Canterbury, born in Aosta, Piedmont. He left Italy in 1056 and settled at the Benedictine abbey of Bec in Normandy to study with **Lanfranc**, the prior and master of the famous school. In 1063 he himself became prior on Lanfranc's departure to Caen, and then abbot after the death of Herluin in 1078. Finally he moved to England to succeed Lanfranc as archbishop of Canterbury in 1093 and held that position until his death. He was distinguished as a churchman and a philosopher, but his strong principles brought him into conflict both with **William II** and with **Henry I** and he was temporarily exiled by each of them. He was eventually reconciled with Henry and on his death was buried next to Lanfranc at Canterbury. He was canonized in 1494. Much influenced by **Augustine** he sought 'necessary reasons' for religious beliefs: his main arguments are presented in the *Monologion* (1076) and the *Proslogion* (1077–78), the latter containing the famous 'ontological argument' for the proof of the existence of God. He also wrote philosophical dialogues and important works on the incarnation (*Cur Deus Homo*) and on logic.

ANSERMET, Ernest Alexandre (1883–1969) Swiss conductor and musical theorist, born in Vevey. While reading physics and mathematics at Lausanne University, he continued privately his music studies. He gave up teaching mathematics in 1910 to devote his time to music. He was conductor of the Montreux Kursaal in 1912 and of **Diaghilev**'s Russian Ballet (1915–23). In 1918 he founded the Orchestre de la Suisse Romande, whose conductor he remained till 1967. He was known for his interpretations of modern French and Russian composers. His compositions include a symphonic poem *Feuilles de printemps*, piano pieces and songs.

ANSETT, Sir Reginald Myles (1909–81) Australian pioneer of passenger flight, born in Inglewood, Victoria. The son of a garage proprietor, he started a local road passenger service with a secondhand car. When new legislation hindered expansion of this he turned to the air, opening a regular service to Melbourne in 1936. Stiff post-war competition brought about diversification, but in 1957 Ansett Transport Industries took over one rival, ANA (Australian National Airways), thus forming the largest private transport system in the southern hemisphere, with a country-wide network of air and coach services. Through pressure from Ansett, the Australian Federal Government was forced to introduce its 'two airlines' policy and give Ansett parity with his rival, the state-owned TAA (Trans Australian Airlines). In 1979 Ansett's group was taken over by a consortium of **Rupert Murdoch**'s News Limited and Sir **Peter Abeles**' TNT (Thomas Nationwide Transport).

ANSKAR, or **Ansgar, St** (801–65) Frankish prelate and missionary to Scandinavia, known as the 'Apostle of the North'. Born in Picardy, he became a Benedictine monk, and in 826 he was sent to preach the gospel in Denmark, but was soon driven out. In 829 he survived a perilous sea-voyage to Birka, the chief mart in Sweden, and was allowed to build the first church in Sweden there. Consecrated archbishop of the newly founded archdiocese of Hamburg in 831 he was named as papal legate to all the northern peoples. But in 845 the Danes attacked Hamburg and burned it to the ground, and Anskar narrowly escaped death. He returned to Scandinavia undaunted in 849, and built a church at Hedeby, in Denmark, and at neighbouring Ribe. After his death, however, despite all his missionary work, Scandinavia lapsed into paganism for a century or more.

ANSON, George, Baron Anson (1697–1762) English naval commander, born in Shugborough Park, Staffordshire. He entered the navy in 1712, and was made a captain in 1724. In 1739, on the outbreak of war with Spain (the War of Jenkins' Ear, 1739–48), he received the command of a Pacific squadron of six vessels, and sailed from England in September 1740. With only one ship, and less than 200 men, but with £500000 of Spanish treasure, he returned to Spithead in June, 1744, having circumnavigated the globe in three years and nine months. He defeated the French off Cape Finisterre, and captured £300000 (1747), and was made First Lord of the Admiralty (1751). In 1761 he was appointed Admiral of the Fleet. He wrote *Voyage round the World* (1748), the story of his circumnavigation.

ANSON, Sir William Reynell (1843–1914) English jurist, born in Walberton, Sussex. He was warden of All Souls College from 1881 and MP for Oxford University from 1899. His *Principles of the English Law of Contract* (1884) and *Law and Custom of the Constitution* (1886–92) were standard works.

ANSTEY, Christopher (1724–1805) English writer. He was educated at Bury St Edmunds, Eton, and King's College, Cambridge, of which he was a fellow (1745–54). In 1766 he wrote the *New Bath Guide*, an epistolatory novel in verse that achieved great popularity.

ANSTEY, F, pseud of **Thomas Anstey Guthrie** (1856–1934) English writer, born in London. He studied at Trinity Hall, Cambridge, and in 1880 was called to the bar. A whimsical humorist he wrote *Vice Versa* (1882), *The Tinted Venus* (1885), *The Brass Bottle* (1900), and many other novels and dialogues. He was on the staff of *Punch* from 1887 to 1930.

ANTALCIDAS (4th century BC) Spartan politician and naval commander, chiefly known by the treaty concluded by him with Persia at the close of the Corinthian war in 386 BC. As a result of this treaty Asia Minor accepted the overlordship of Persia, while various other Greek cities had their independence confirmed.

ANTAR, more fully **l'Antarah Ibn Shaddād Al-'Absi** (6th century) Arab poet and warrior, born of a Bedouin chieftain and a black slave somewhere in the desert near Medina, Saudi Arabia. The author of one of the seven Golden Odes of Arabic literature, and the subject of the 10th-century *Romance of Antar*, he is regarded as the model of Bedouin heroism and chivalry and by some as 'the father of knights'.

ANTENOR (6th century BC) Athenian sculptor, known to have executed bronze statues of *Harmodius* and *Aristogiton*, and a statue of *Kore* in the Acropolis.

ANTHEIL, George (1900–59) American composer of Polish descent, born in New Jersey. Antheil studied in Philadelphia and under **Ernest Bloch**, spending some years in Europe as a professional pianist before becoming known as the composer of the *Jazz Symphony* (1925), the *Ballet Mécanique* (1927), and the opera *Transatlantic* (1930). The sensation caused by the ballet, written for ten pianos and a variety of eccentric percussion instruments, overshadowed his more traditional later works, which include five symphonies, concertos, several more operas, and chamber music. See his autobiographical *Bad Boy of Music* (1945).

ANTHONY, St See **ANTONY**

ANTHONY, C L See **SMITH, Dodie**

ANTHONY, Susan Brownell (1820–1906) American social reformer and women's suffrage leader, born in Adams, Massachusetts. Early active in temperance and anti-slavery movements, she became the champion of women's rights in 1854. In 1869 with **Elizabeth Cady Stanton** she founded the National Woman Suffrage Association. She organized the International Council of Women (1888) and the International Woman Suffrage Alliance in Berlin (1904).

ANTIGONUS, called **Monophthalmos** or 'the one-eyed' (d.301 BC) Macedonian soldier, one of the generals of **Alexander the Great**; after Alexander's death, he received the provinces of Phrygia Major, Lycia, and Pamphylia. On **Antipater**'s death in 319, he aspired to the sovereignty of Asia, and waged incessant wars against the other generals, making himself master of all Asia Minor and Syria. In 306 he assumed the title of king together with his son **Demetrius Poliorcetes**, but was defeated and slain by **Lysimachus** and his son, **Cassander**, and **Seleucus I** at Ipsus in Phrygia.

ANTIGONUS GONATAS (d.239 BC) king of Macedon. He did not mount his throne until 276, seven years after the death of his father, Demetrius Poliorcetes. **Pyrrhus** of Epirus overran Macedonia in 274, but Antigonus soon recovered his kingdom, and consolidated it despite incessant wars.

ANTILL, John Henry (1904–86) Australian composer, born in Ashfield, New South Wales. He sang in the choir of St Andrew's Cathedral, Sydney, but was trained as a mechanical draughtsman and apprenticed on the railway. Entering the New South Wales Conservatorium of Music at the age of 21, he studied composition with **Alfred Hill**, becoming a member of the Conservatorium orchestra and later of the ABC (now Sydney) Symphony Orchestra. He was a staff member of the Australian Broadcasting Commission for many years, being Federal music editor for the last twenty. His major work, the ballet *Corroboree*, blends Aboriginal and western themes. The suite was premièred in 1944 and the ballet itself in 1950. His compositions include operas and choral works, ballet suites and a symphony.

ANTINŎUS (d.122) Bithynian youth of matchless beauty, a native of Claudiopolis, a favourite of the emperor **Hadrian**, and his companion in all his journeys. He was drowned in the Nile, near Besa, perhaps through suicide. The emperor founded the city of Antinŏpolis on the banks of the Nile in his memory, and enrolled him among the gods.

ANTIOCHUS I, called **Sōter**, (323–261 BC) Seleucid king of Syria. He was the son of **Seleucus I**, one of Alexander's generals, whose murder in 280 gave him the whole Syrian empire, but left him too weak to assert his right to Macedonia. He gained the name of Sōter ('Saviour') for a victory over the Gauls, but fell in battle with them.

ANTIOCHUS II, called **Theos** ('God') (286–247 BC) Seleucid king of Syria, son and successor of **Antiochus I**. He married Berenice, daughter of **Ptolemy II**, exiling his first wife, Laodice, and her children. On his death there followed a struggle between the rival queens; Berenice and her son were murdered and Laodice's son, **Seleucus II**, succeeded.

ANTIOCHUS III, 'the Great' (242–187 BC) Seleucid king of Syria, grandson of **Antiochus II**, succeeded his father, Seleucus Callinicus, in 223. He was, together with **Seleucus I**, the most distinguished of the Seleucids. He waged war with success against Ptolemy IV Philopator, and though defeated at Raphia near Gaza (217), he obtained entire possession of Palestine and

Coele-Syria (198), immediately dowering his daughter Cleopatra on her betrothal to the young King **Ptolemy V** of Egypt. A grand expedition to the eastern provinces (212–205) partly restored Seleucid power there. He afterwards became involved in war with the Romans, who had conquered Macedonia; but he declined to invade Italy at the instigation of Hannibal, who had come to his court for refuge. He crossed over into Greece, but was defeated in 191 at Thermopylae, and in 190 or 189 by **Scipio** at Magnesia. Peace was granted him only on condition of his yielding all his dominions west of Mount Taurus, and paying a heavy tribute. To raise the money, he attacked a rich temple in Elymais, when the people rose against him, and killed him.

ANTIOCHUS IV, called **Epiphanes** (d.163 BC) Seleucid king of Syria, son of **Antiochus III**. He succeeded his brother in 175, fought against Egypt and conquered a great part of it. He twice took Jerusalem; and, endeavouring there to stamp out Judaism and establish the worship of Greek gods, provoked the Jews to a successful insurrection under Mattathias and his sons, the **Maccabees**.

ANTIPATER (398–319 BC) Macedonian general, highly trusted by **Philip II** of Macedonia and **Alexander the Great**, was left by the latter as regent in Macedonia, 334 BC. He discharged his duties with great ability, both before and after the death of Alexander, in 322 defeating an alliance of the Greek states.

ANTIPATER (d.43 BC) the father of **Herod, the Great**, appointed by **Julius Caesar** procurator of Judaea in 47 BC. He died by poisoning.

ANTIPATER (d.4 BC) Judaean prince, son of **Herod the Great** by his first wife. He conspired against his half-brothers and had them executed, then plotted against his father and was himself executed five days before Herod died.

ANTIPHON (5th century BC) Greek philosopher and sophist. Nothing is known of his life or even his identity but he is generally distinguished from Antiphon the orator. He is important as the author of two works, *On Truth* and *On Concord*, which survive in fragmentary form and deal with themes characteristic of the sophistic movement such as the relation of 'nature' and 'convention', and the nature of language.

ANTISTHENES (c.455–c.360 BC) Greek philosopher, thought to be co-founder, with his pupil **Diogenes**, of the Cynic school. He was a rhetorician and a disciple of **Gorgias**, and later became a close friend of **Socrates** whose asceticism and independence of worldly goods he admired. He was one of the few intimates who were with Socrates in prison in the last hours of his life. Only fragments of his many works survive.

ANTOINE, André (1858–1943) French actor-manager, born in Limoges. He founded the Théâtre Libre (1887), and was director of the Odéon (from 1906).

ANTOKOLSKI, Mark Matveevich (1843–1902) Russian sculptor, born at Wilno of Jewish parentage. From 1880 he lived and worked in Paris, but most of his works are in the Alexander III Museum at Leningrad. *Ivan the Terrible* and *Turgeniev* are the most famous of his portrait statues.

ANTOMMARCHI, Francesco (1780–1838) **Napoleon**'s physician at St Helena from 1818, born in Corsica. Napoleon ultimately gave him his full confidence, and left him 100000 francs. In 1822 he exhibited Napoleon's death mask, and published *Les Derniers Moments de Napoléon* in 1823. During the Polish revolution he did duty at Warsaw as director of military hospitals. He afterwards went to the West Indies, and died in Cuba.

ANTONELLI, Giacomo (1806–76) Italian prelate, born in Sonnino, the son of a woodcutter. In 1819, his birthplace having been demolished as a nest of bandits, Antonelli came to Rome, and entered the Grand Seminary, where he gained the favour of Pope **Gregory XVI**. In 1847 he was made cardinal-deacon by **Pius IX**, and in 1848 was premier and minister of foreign affairs in a Liberal cabinet, which framed the famous *Statuto* or Constitution. He accompanied the pope in his flight to Gaeta in 1848, and, returning with him to Rome, in 1850 became foreign secretary, and supported the reactionary policy of absolute papal administrative power. In 1855 an attempt was made upon his life. In the Vatican Council of 1869–70 he showed great tact and ability. After his death the vast property bequeathed to his three brothers was disputed in vain by a *soi-disant* daughter.

ANTONELLO DA MESSINA (c.1430–1479) Italian painter, born in Messina, the only major 15th-century Italian artist to come from Sicily. An accomplished master of oil-paintings, he helped popularize the medium, although **Vasari**'s claim that he brought his tutor **Jan van Eyck**'s oil painting technique to Italy is incorrect. His style is a delicate synthesis of the northern and Italian styles. In 1475 he was working in Venice where his work influenced **Giovanni Bellini**'s portraits. There are fragments of his Venetian San Cassiano altarpiece in Vienna. His first dated work, the *Salvator Mundi* (1465) and a self-portrait are in the London National Gallery.

ANTONESCU, Ion (1882–1946) Rumanian general, and dictator for the Nazis in World War II. Born into an aristocratic family in Pitesti, he served as military attaché in Rome and London, and became chief of staff and minister of defence in 1937. In 1938 he was imprisoned for plotting a right-wing revolt, but was soon released. In September 1940 he assumed dictatorial powers and forced the abdication of King **Carol II**. He headed a Fascist government allied to Nazi Germany until 1944 when he was overthrown, and executed for war crimes.

ANTONINUS, M Aurelius See **AURELIUS**

ANTONINUS PIUS, Titus Aurelius Fulvus (86–161) Roman emperor. He inherited great wealth, and in 120 was made consul. Sent as proconsul into Asia by the Emperor **Hadrian**, in 138 he was adopted by him and the same year came to the throne. His reign was proverbially peaceful and happy. In his private character he was simple, temperate, and benevolent; while in public affairs he acted as the father of his people, and the persecution of Christians was partly stayed by his mild measures. In his reign the empire was extended, and the Antonine Wall, named after him, built between the Forth and Clyde rivers. The epithet *Pius* was conferred on him for his defence of Hadrian's memory. By his wife Faustina he had four children; one married **Marcus Aurelius**, his adopted son and successor.

ANTONIONI, Michelangelo (1912–) Italian film director, born in Ferrara. After taking a degree in political economy at Bologna University, he began as a film critic before becoming an assistant director in 1942. He made several documentaries (1945–50) before turning to feature films, often scripted by himself, and notable for their preoccupation with character study rather than plot. They include *Cronaco di un Amore* (1950), *Le Amiche* (1955) and *Il Grido* (1957). He gained an international reputation, however, with *L'Avventura* (1959), a long, slow-moving study of its two main characters, followed by other outstanding works, such as *La Notte* (1961), *L'Eclisse* (1962), *Blow-up* (1967), *Zabriskie Point* (1970), *The Passenger* (1974), and *Il Mistero di Oberwald* (1979).

ANTONIUS, Marcus (Mark Antony) (c.83–30 BC) Roman triumvir, related on his mother's side to **Julius Caesar**. His youth was dissipated, and, pressed by creditors, he escaped to Athens in 58. In Palestine and Egypt, he ingratiated himself with the soldiery; and, after assisting Caesar in Gaul (53–50), he went to Rome to become tribune of the plebs (49) and defend Caesar's cause. He was expelled from the senate, and fled to Caesar, who made this a pretext for his war against **Pompey**. Caesar left him in charge in Italy, and at Pharsalia (48) Antony led the left wing of Caesar's army. In 47 he was made master of the horse, and was left to govern Italy during Caesar's absence in Africa, but then held no further post till 44 when he was consul together with Caesar. On Caesar's assassination, Antony played the part finely described by **Shakespeare**, and the flight of the conspirators left him with almost absolute power. It was his misfortune to meet in the young **Octavianus Augustus** a more ruthless and astute politician than himself. Besieged and defeated at Mutina (43), he fled beyond the Alps; but in Gaul he visited the camp of **Lepidus**, and gained the favour of the army, of which he took command. Plancus and **Pollio** joined him; and Antony returned to Rome at the head of 17 legions and 10000 cavalry. Augustus, who previously had appeared to side with the Republican side and **Cicero**, now revealed his true allegiance and held a consultation with Antony and Lepidus near Bononia, when it was decided that these 'triumvirs' should share the whole Roman world. Returning to Rome, they began their course of proscription and plunder. Among their first victims was Cicero; and, in all, 300 senators and 2000 *equites* are said to have been killed. After securing Italy and raising money, Antony and Augustus led their troops into Macedonia, and defeated **Brutus** and **Cassius** at Philippi (42). Antony next paid a visit to Athens, and then passed over to Asia, where he met and was captivated by **Cleopatra**. He followed her to Egypt (winter 41–40), until called back by news of a quarrel in Italy between his kinsmen and Augustus. This dispute gave rise to a war, which came to an end before he arrived in Italy. A new division of the Roman world was now arranged, Antony taking the east, and Augustus the west, while Lepidus had to be content with Africa; Antony also married Augustus's sister **Octavia** (40). Differences grew up between Antony and Augustus, and in 37 Antony separated from Octavia and rejoined Cleopatra. His position in the east, his relations with Cleopatra, and his unsuccessful campaigns against the Parthians (36 and 34), were seized upon by Augustus and misrepresented for propaganda purposes. Eventually Augustus declared war on Cleopatra (32) and in the naval engagement of Actium (31) Antony and Cleopatra were defeated. Antony went back to Egypt, where, deserted by the navy and army, and deceived by a false report of Cleopatra's suicide, he killed himself by falling on his sword.

ANTONOV, Olyeg Konstantinovich (1906–84) Soviet aircraft designer, born in Troitskoe, Moscow (region). He graduated from the Leningrad Polytechnic Institute in 1930 and became a member of the CPSU in 1945. He was the head of the experimental design department in 1946, and became designer general for the aircraft industry in 1962. His well-known designs include the AN-2, AN-10, AN-12, AN-14, AN-22 (Antei) and AN-24. He was a deputy to the Supreme Soviet of the USSR from 1958 to 1966. He received the Lenin prize in 1962 and the Order of Lenin twice. After World War II he became senior designer with the ministry of aviation (till 1963). The author of over 50 books on glider and aircraft design, his name is perpetuated in the AN-225 6-engined super heavylift aircraft which carries the Soviet shuttle orbiter 'Buran' above its fuselage and which was shown at the Paris Airshow in 1989.

ANTONY, St, called **the Great**, or **Antony of Thebes** (251–356) Egyptian ascetic, the father of Christian Monachism (monasticism), born in Koman in Upper Egypt. He sold his possessions for the poor at the age of 20 and withdrew into the wilderness, and took up his abode in an old ruin on the top of a hill, where he spent 20 years in the most rigorous seclusion. In 305 he was persuaded to leave this retreat by the prayers of numerous anchorites, and then founded a monastery, at first only a group of separate and scattered cells near Memphis and Arsinoë. In 355 the venerable hermit, then over a hundred years old, made a journey to Alexandria to dispute with the Arians; but feeling his end approaching, he retired to his desert home, where he died. St **Athanasius** wrote his Life.

ANTONY OF PADUA, St (1195–1231) born in Lisbon, was at first an Augustinian monk, but in 1220 he entered the Franciscan order, and became one of its most active propagators. He preached in the south of France and Upper Italy, and died in Padua. He was canonized by **Gregory IX** in the following year. According to legend, he preached to the fishes when men refused to hear him; hence he is the patron of the lower animals, and is often represented as accompanied by an ass.

ANTRAIGUES, Emanuel Delaunay, Comte d' (1755–1812) French politician, born in Villeneuve de Berg. His *Mémoires sur les États-généraux* (1788) was one of the first sparks of the French Revolution; but in 1789, when he was chosen a deputy, he defended the hereditary privileges and the kingly veto, and ranked himself against the union of the three estates. After 1790 he was employed in diplomacy at St Petersburg, Vienna, and Dresden. In England he acquired great influence with **George Canning**; he was murdered, with his wife, near London, by an Italian servant.

ANZENGRÜBER, Ludwig (1839–89) Austrian playwright and novelist, born in Vienna. Coming from peasant stock, he had been a bookshop assistant, a touring actor and a police clerk before the success of his play, *Der Pfarrer von Kirchfeld* (1870), enabled him to devote the rest of his life to writing. He was the author of several novels, of which the best is *Der Sternsteinhof* (1885) and about 20 plays, mostly about Austrian peasant life.

ANZILOTTI, Dionisio (1867–1950) Italian jurist, born in Pistoia, and educated at Pisa. Professor at Rome (1911–37), he was a founder of the positive school of international law which derived the law from the practice of nations rather than from theorizing. He was a founder of the *Rivista di diritto internazionale* (1906) and author of *Corso di diritto internazionale* (1912). Later he became a judge of the Permanent Court of International Justice (1921–30), and its president (1928–30).

APELLES (4th century BC) Greek painter, probably born in Colophon, on the Ionian coast of Asia Minor. He was trained at Ephesus and Sicyon, visited Macedon, where he became the friend of **Alexander the Great**, and is said to have accompanied him on his expedition to Asia, and settled at Ephesus. None of his work has survived, but his fame lives in ancient writings.

APICIUS, Marcus Gavius (1st century) Roman nobleman and gourmet in the reign of the emperor **Tiberius** in the 1st century AD, whose name is associated with one of the world's first books of recipes, known as *Of Culinary Matters*.

APOLLINAIRE, Guillaume, originally **Apollinaris Kostrowitzky** (1880–1918) French poet, born in Rome of Polish descent. He settled in Paris in 1900, and became a leader of the movement rejecting poetic traditions in outlook, rhythm, and language. His work, bizarre, symbolist and fantastic, and akin to the Cubist school in painting, is expressed chiefly in *L'Enchanteur pourissant* (1909), *Le Bestaire* (1911), *Les Alcools* (1913) and *Calligrammes* (1918). Wounded in World War I, during his convalescence he wrote the play *Les Mamelles de Tirésias* (1918), for which he coined the term 'surrealist'.

APOLLINARIS THE YOUNGER (c.310–c.390) Syrian prelate. Bishop of Laodicea from 360, he was one of the sternest opponents of Arianism. His father, Apollinaris the Elder, who was presbyter of Laodicea, was born in Alexandria, and taught grammar, first at Berytus, and afterwards at Laodicea. Apollinaris himself upheld a doctrine (Apollinarianism) condemned by the Council of Constantinople (381) as denying the true human nature of Christ. He must not be confused with Claudius Apollinaris, known as 'the Apologist', bishop of Hierapolis in Phrygia in the 2nd century AD, who wrote an *Apology* for the Christian faith, and several other works, all lost.

APOLLODORUS (5th century BC) Athenian painter. He is said to have introduced the technique of chiaroscuro (light and shade).

APOLLODORUS (fl.c.140 BC) Athenian scholar. He was the author of a work on mythology and one on etymology, and best known for his verse *Chronicle* of Greek history from the fall of Troy.

APOLLODORUS (2nd century) Roman architect. He designed **Trajan**'s column in Rome. He was executed in AD 129 for his fearless criticism of the emperor **Hadrian**'s design for a temple.

APOLLONIUS, called **Dyskolos** ('bad-tempered') (2nd century) Alexandrian grammarian. He was the first to reduce Greek syntax to a system. He wrote a treatise *On Syntax* and shorter works on pronouns, conjunctions and adverbs.

APOLLONIUS OF PERGA (fl.250–220 BC) Greek mathematician, known as 'the Great Geometer'. He was the author of the definitive ancient work on conic sections which laid the foundations of later teaching on the subject.

APOLLONIUS OF TYANA (c.3–c.97) Greek philosopher and seer, born in Tyana in Cappadocia. He was said to be a zealous neo-Pythagorean teacher, who travelled to India via Asia Minor, meeting the Magi at Babylon on his way. When he returned, he was hailed as a sage, and a worker of miracles. He was patronized by **Vespasian**, but after extensive travels in Spain, Italy and Greece, he appears to have settled at Ephesus where he opened a school and died at a great age. He was worshipped after his death, and a century later **Philostratus** wrote a colourful, and largely apocryphal, history presenting him as a sort of heathen saviour or rival to Christ.

APOLLONIUS RHODIUS (3rd century BC) Greek scholar, born in Alexandria, but long resident in Rhodes, wrote many works on grammar, and an epic poem, the *Argonautica*, noted more for its learning than poetic genius. Greatly admired by the Romans, it was translated into Latin by **Varro** and imitated by **Valerius Flaccus**.

APPEL, Karel Christian (1921–) Dutch painter, born in Amsterdam and educated there at the Royal College of Art. Appel, whose career as an artist began in 1938, was one of an influential group of Dutch, Belgian and Danish Expressionists known as 'Cobra'. His work, featuring swirls of brilliant colour and aggressively contorted figures, has many affinities with American abstract Expressionism, and Appel is considered to be one of the most powerful exponents of this style of painting. He has had many exhibitions in Europe and the USA and won many prizes, including the UNESCO Prize, Venice Biennale (1953) and the Guggenheim International Prize (1961).

APPERT, Nicolas François (1749–1841) French chef and inventor, born in Châlons-sur-Marne. A chef and confectioner to trade, in 1795 he began experiments in preserving food in hermetically sealed containers, in response to a call from the French government for a solution to the problem of feeding the greatly expanded army and navy. His success, which earned him a French government prize of 12000 francs in 1810, was due to his use of an autoclave for sterilization. He opened the world's first commercial canning factory in 1812. Initially he used glass jars and bottles, changing to tin-plated metal cans in 1822. At the time the scientific principles of food preservation were unknown, awaiting the bacteriological discoveries of **Louis Pasteur** in the 1860s.

APPIA, Adolphe (1862–1928) Swiss scene designer and theatrical producer, born in Geneva. He was one of the first to introduce simple planes instead of rich stage settings, and pioneered the symbolic use of lighting, particularly in the presentation of opera. He wrote *Die Musik und die Inscenierung* (1899) and *La Mise-en-scène du drame Wagnérien* (1895).

APPIAN, (Greek **Appianos) of Alexandria** (2nd century) Roman historian and lawyer. He compiled 24 books of Roman conquests down to **Vespasian**, written in Greek. Nine books survive complete, with fragments of others. He was a native of Alexandria, and flourished during the reigns of **Trajan**, **Hadrian**, and **Antoninus Pius**.

APPIANI, Andrea (1754–1817) Italian artist, known as 'the Painter of the Graces', was born and died in Milan. He was court painter to **Napoleon**. His best-known work is the set of frescoes depicting *Psyche* in the Monza palace.

APPLEGATH, Augustus (1788–1871) English inventor, born in London. He was a printer who made a number of improvements to the steam-powered flat-bed press of **Friedrich König** (1813). A rotary printing press had been patented by **William Nicholson** in 1790, but his and others' attempts to construct one all failed, and it was not until 1848 that the first workable vertical-drum rotary printing press was built by Applegath for *The Times* newspaper in London. Its performance was however soon eclipsed by the horizontal rotary press developed at about the same time in the USA by **Richard Hoe**.

APPLETON, Sir Edward Victor (1892–1965) English physicist, born in Bradford. Trained at St John's College, Cambridge, he was appointed assistant demonstrator in experimental physics at the Cavendish Laboratory in 1920. His researches on the propagation of wireless waves led to his appointment as Wheatstone professor of physics at London University (1924). In 1936 he returned to Cambridge as Jacksonian professor of natural philosophy. In 1939 he became secretary of the department of scientific and industrial research, and in 1949 was appointed principal and vice-chancellor of Edinburgh University. In 1947 he won the Nobel prize for physics for his contribution 'in exploring the ionosphere'. His work revealed the existence of a layer of electrically charged particles in the upper atmosphere (the Appleton layer) which plays an essential part in making wireless communication possible between distant stations, and is also fundamental to the development of radar.

APPONYI, Albert Georg, Count (1846–1933) Hungarian statesman, born in Vienna. He entered the Hungarian Diet in 1872, and showing himself to be a brilliant orator, soon became leader of the moderate opposition which became the National party in 1891. In 1899 he and his supporters went over to the Liberal Government party, and from 1901 to 1903 he was president of the Diet. From 1906 to 1910 he was minister of culture and, a devout Catholic, gave asylum to the expelled French Jesuits. He introduced free public education. In 1920 he led the Hungarian peace delegation, protested bitterly against the terms imposed under the Treaty of Trianon and resigned. He frequently represented his country at the League of Nations.

APRAXIN, Fyodor Matveyevich, Count (1671–1728) Russian naval commander, and known as the 'father of the Russian navy'. In the service of **Peter I, the Great** from 1682, he was appointed admiral in 1707 and built up the navy into a powerful fighting force. In the Great Northern War (1700–21) he fought off the Swedes at St Petersburg (1708), captured Viborg, Åbo and Helsinki, and routed the Swedish fleet in 1713, thus taking control of the Baltic. Later he commanded successful engagements against Turkey and Persia.

APRAXIN, Stephen Fyodorovich, Count (1702–58) Russian soldier, nephew of Count **Fyodor Apraxin**. He served in the war against the Turks (1736–39), and at the outbreak of the Seven Years' War (1756–63) was appointed marshal. He commanded the Russian forces invading East Prussia in 1757, and defeated the Prussians at the battle of Gross-Jägersdorf, but fell from favour and died in prison.

APULEIUS, Lucius (2nd century) Roman writer, satirist and rhetorician, born in Madaura, in Numidia in Africa. Educated at Carthage and Athens, he used the fortune bequeathed him by his father to travel; he visited Italy, Asia, etc, and was initiated into numerous religious mysteries. The knowledge which he thus acquired of the priestly fraternities he made abundant use of afterwards in his *Golden Ass*, the only complete Latin novel that has survived. Having married a wealthy, middle-aged widow, Aemilia Pudentilla, who nursed him in Alexandria, he was charged by her relations with having employed magic to gain her affections. His *Apologia*, still extant, was an eloquent vindication. He settled in Carthage, where he devoted himself to literature and the teaching of philosophy and rhetoric. His romance, *The Metamorphoses* or *Golden Ass*, is a satire on the vices of the age, especially those of the priesthood and of quacks. He also wrote commentaries on **Plato**.

AQUAVIVA, Claudius (1543–1615) Italian prelate and distinguished Jesuit. Born in Naples, he entered the Society of Jesus in 1567, and was appointed 5th general of the Jesuit order in 1581. He was a great educator and organizer; his book, *Ratio atque institutio studiorum* (1586), laid the basis for later Jesuit education.

AQUILA, Ponticus (from Pontus) (fl.130) translator of the Old Testament into Greek, a native of Sinope. He is said to have been first a pagan, then a Christian, and finally a Jew.

AQUINAS, St Thomas (1225–74) Italian scholastic philosopher and theologian, of the family of the Counts of Aquino, born in the castle of Roccasecca, near Aquino. He was educated by the Benedictines of Monte-Cassino, and at the University of Naples; and, against the bitter opposition of his family, in 1244 entered the Dominican order of mendicant friars. His brothers kidnapped him and kept him a prisoner in the paternal castle for over a year; in the end he made his way to Cologne to become a pupil of the great Dominican luminary, **Albertus Magnus**. In 1248 the heretofore 'Dumb Ox' was appointed to teach under Albert, and began to publish commentaries on **Aristotle**. In 1252 he went to Paris, and taught there, with growing reputation, until in 1258, now a doctor, he was summoned by the pope to teach successively in Anagni, Orvieto, Rome and Viterbo. He died at Fossanuova on his way to defend the papal cause at the Council of Lyons, and was canonized in 1323. Like most of the other scholastic theologians, he had no knowledge of Greek or Hebrew, and was almost equally ignorant of history; but his prolific writings display intellectual power of the first order and he came to exercise enormous intellectual authority throughout the church. Through his commentaries he made Aristotle's thought available and acceptable in the Christian West, and in his philosophical writings he tried to combine and reconcile Aristotle's scientific rationalism with Christian doctrines of faith and revelation. His best-known works are two huge encyclopedic syntheses. The *Summa contra Gentiles* (1259–64), was supposedly written as a handbook for Dominican missionaries; it deals chiefly with the principles of natural religion. His *Summa Theologiae* (1266–73) was still uncompleted at his death but contains his mature thought in systematic form and includes the famous 'five ways' or proofs of the existence of God. His influence on the theological thought of succeeding ages was immense. Aquinas was known as the *Doctor Angelicus* and the only other scholastic theologian who rivalled him was the *Doctor Subtilis*, **Duns Scotus**. The Franciscans followed Scotus, and the Dominicans Thomas, and henceforward medieval theologians were divided into two schools, Scotists and Thomists, whose divergencies penetrate more or less every branch of doctrine. Thomism now represents, with few exceptions, the general teaching of the Catholic Church.

AQUINO, (Maria) Corazon, née **Cojuango** (1933–) Filipino politician, the daughter of a wealthy sugar baron in Tarlac province. She gained a degree in mathematics at Mount St Vincent College, New York, before marrying a young politician Benigno S Aquino in 1956, who became the chief political opponent and presidential challenger to **Ferdinand Marcos**; he was imprisoned on charges of murder and subversion (1972–80), and assassinated by a military guard at Manila airport in 1983 on his return from three years of exile for heart surgery in the USA. Corazon ('Cory') was drafted by the opposition to contest the February 1986 presidential election and claimed victory over Marcos, accusing the government of ballot-rigging. She proceeded to lead a non-violent 'people's power' campaign which succeeded in overthrowing Marcos. A devout Maryist Roman Catholic, she enjoyed strong church backing in her 1986 campaign.

ARABI PASHA See **AHMED ARABI**

ARAFAT, Yasser, real name **Mohammed Abed Ar'ouf Arafat** (1929–) Palestinian resistance leader born in Jerusalem. He was educated at Cairo University (1952–56), where he was leader of the Palestinian Students' Union. He co-founded the Al Fatah resistance group in 1956 and began work as an engineer in Kuwait. Three years later he began contributing to a new Beirut magazine, *Filastinuna* (Our Palestine), which expressed the anger and frustration of Palestinian refugees, who felt betrayed and neglected by the Arab regimes. In 1964 the Arab states founded the Palestinian Liberation Organization, a body consisting of many factions frequently in disagreement with one another. Within five years, Arafat's Al Fatah group had gained control of the organization, and he became its acknowledged (though not universally popular) leader. He skilfully managed the uneasy juxtaposition of militancy and diplomacy, and gradually gained world acceptance of the PLO; the organization was formally recognized by the United Nations in 1974. Under his leadership, the PLO's original aim—to create a secular democratic state over the whole of the pre-war Palestine—was modified to one of establishing an independent Palestinian state in any part of Palestine from which Israel would agree to withdraw. In the 1980s the growth of factions within the PLO reduced his power and, in 1983, he was forced to leave Lebanon, members of the organization dispersing widely to Tunisia, the Yemen, Syria, Jordan and other Arab states. Arafat, however, remained leader of the majority of the PLO. In 1985 he agreed with King **Hussein** of Jordan to recognize the state of Israel if territory which had been seized was restored. This initiative failed but, in July 1988, Hussein surrendered his right to administer the West Bank, indicating that the PLO might take over the responsibility. Arafat, to the surprise of many Western politicians, persuaded the majority of his colleagues formally to acknowledge the right of Israel to coexist with an independent state of Palestine. Israel's initial response was not encouraging but Arafat's standing in world opinion rose significantly.

ARAGO, Dominique François Jean (1786–1853) French scientist and statesman, born in Estagel near Perpignan. At 17 he entered the Polytechnic, in 1804 became secretary to the Observatory, and in 1830 its chief director. He took a prominent part in the July Revolution (1830), and as member of the Chamber of Deputies voted with the extreme left. In 1848 he was a member of the provisional government, but refused to take the oath of allegiance to **Napoleon III** after the events of 1851–52. His achievements were mainly in the fields of astronomy, magnetism, and optics.

ARAGON, Louis (1897–1983) French writer and political activist, born in Paris. One of the most brilliant of the Surrealist group, he co-founded the journal *Littérateure* with **André Breton** in 1919. He published two volumes of poetry, *Feu de joie* (1920) and *Le Mouvement perpétuel* (1925), and a Surrealist novel, *Le Paysan de Paris* (1926). After a visit to the Soviet Union in 1930 he became a convert to communism. Thereafter he wrote social-realistic novels in a series entitled *Le Réel* (1933–51) and war poems, including *La Grève-Coeur* (1941) and *Les Yeux d'Elsa* (1942).

ARAKI, Sadao (1877–1966) Japanese soldier and politician. An ultra-nationalist, he was a leader of the right-wing Kodaha (Imperial Way) faction of the army. He was minister for war (1931–33) and for education (1938–40). After World War II he was convicted as a war criminal and sentenced to life imprisonment, but released in 1965.

ARAM, Eugene (1704–59) English scholar and murderer, born in Ramsgill, Yorkshire. Though a gardener's son, and self-taught, he became a schoolmaster, first at Ramsgill, and in 1734 at Knaresborough. In 1745 he was tried for the murder of a wealthy shoemaker, but acquitted for want of evidence. Following this he deserted his wife at Knaresborough, and acted as a schoolmaster at various places in England, amassing considerable materials for a comparative lexicon and postulating the relationship between Celtic and Indo-European tongues. In 1759, on fresh evidence coming to light about the murder charge, he was tried at York, and hanged. At the trial he conducted his own defence, attacking the doctrine of circumstantial evidence. After his condemnation he confessed his guilt. His story was the subject of a romance by **Edward George Lytton** and a ballad by **Thomas Hood**.

ARANDA, Pedro Pablo Abarca y Bolea, Count of (1718–99) Spanish statesman and general, born in Sietano. He was made ambassador to Poland in 1760, but in 1766 was recalled to Madrid and made prime minister, with the task of restoring order after risings. He managed to expel the Jesuits, alleged perpetrators of the disorders, from Spain in 1767, but in 1773 fell from power and was sent to France as ambassador. Returning in 1787, he became prime minister again in 1792, but antagonized **Godoy**, and died in Aragon in enforced retirement.

ARANY, János (1817–82) Hungarian poet, born in Nagy-Szalonta of peasant stock. With **Petőfi** he was a leader of the popular national school, and is regarded as one of the greatest of Hungarian poets. He was chief secretary of the Academy from 1870 to 1879. His satire *The Lost Constitution* (1845) won the Kisfaludy Society prize, but his chief work is the *Toldi* trilogy (1847–54), the story of the adventures of a young peasant in the 14th century Hungarian court. He also published successful translations of **Aristophanes** and **Shakespeare**.

ARASON, Jón (c.1484–1550) Icelandic prelate, the last Roman Catholic bishop in Iceland, beheaded in 1550 at the time of the Reformation. Born in Eyjafjörður, in the north of Iceland, he was a turbulent, charismatic figure, and an excellent poet of both religious and satirical verse. In 1524 he was consecrated bishop of the northern see of Hólar. He introduced a printing press to Hólar, the first in Iceland, but none of the books he printed has survived. He fiercely resisted the imposition of Lutheranism from Denmark by the crown, and when he was declared an outlaw he raised a small army of adherents and seized the southern see of Skálholt, which had accepted Lutheranism by then. Eventually he and two of his sons were captured in an ambush, and summarily beheaded. Ever since his execution, Jón Arason has been regarded as a national hero in Iceland.

ARATUS OF SICYON (271–213 BC) one of the leading statesmen of 3rd century Greece, joined Sicyon to the hitherto small Achaean League in 251, which he then gradually built up as a major power, seizing the Acrocorinth from Macedonian control in 243, and bringing new Peloponnesian cities into membership of the league. But the revival of Spartan power under **Cleomenes III** caused him to turn for support to Antigonus Doson of Macedon, and so undo the achievements of the earlier part of his career. Aratus' Memoirs have not been preserved, but they were used by **Plutarch** in his *Life of Aratus*.

ARBER, Agnes, née **Robertson** (1879–1960) English botanist and philosopher, born in London. In 1909 she married the son of **Edward Arber**. Her works include *Herbals, Their Origin and Evolution* (1912), *Water Plants* (1920), *Monocotyledons* (1925), *The Natural History of Plant Form* (1950), *The Mind and the Eye* (1954), and *The Manifold and the One* (1957). She was the third woman to be elected Fellow of the Royal Society (1948).

ARBER, Werner (1929–) Swiss microbiologist, born in Gränichen. He studied at the Swiss Federal Institute of Technology, Geneva University, and the University of Southern California, returning to Geneva and then to Basel as professor of molecular biology from 1970. In the 1960s he proposed that when bacteria defend themselves against attack by phages (the viruses which attack bacteria) they use selective enzymes which cut the phage DNA and do so at specific points in the

DNA chain. Such 'restriction enzymes' clearly gave the option of securing short lengths of DNA; if these could then be joined in specific ways, then securing an 'unnatural DNA' should be possible, and with it entry to the new field of so-called genetic engineering. Through the efforts of many groups, especially in the USA, this was brought to full fruition in the 1970s, with valuable results such as the preparation of monoclonal antibodies for use in clinical diagnosis and treatment of disease. He shared the Nobel prize for physiology or medicine in 1978 with **Hamilton Smith** and **Daniel Nathams**.

ARBLAY, Madame d' See **BURNEY, Frances**

ARBUS, Diane, née **Nemerov** (1923–71) American photographer, born in New York City. Rebelling against her wealthy parentage and her work in conventional fashion photography, she sought to portray people 'without their masks'. She achieved fame in the 1960s with her ironic studies of social poses and the deprived classes, but became increasingly introverted and depressed over the next few years, eventually taking her own life. She married fellow photographer Allan Arbus in 1941, but separated in 1960 and divorced in 1969.

ARBUTHNOT, John (1667–1735) Scottish physician and writer, son of the Episcopalian manse at Arbuthnott in Kincardineshire. A close friend of **Jonathan Swift** and all the literary celebrities of the day, he was also a distinguished doctor and writer of medical works, and a physician in ordinary to Queen **Anne** (1705). He studied at Aberdeen and Oxford, and took his MD degree at St Andrews. In London he was much admired for his wit and erudition. In 1712 he published five satirical pamphlets against the Duke of **Marlborough**, called *The History of John Bull*, which was the origin of the popular image of John Bull as the typical Englishman. With Swift, **Alexander Pope**, **John Gay** and others he founded the Scriblerus Club, and was the chief contributor to the *Memoirs of Martin Scriblerus* (1741). As a physician he was ahead of his time, with *An Essay Concerning the Nature of Ailments* (1731), which stressed the value of suitable diet in the treatment of disease.

ARBUZOV, Alexei Nikolayevich (1908–86) Russian dramatist, born in Moscow and educated at the Leningrad Theatre School. From 1930 onwards he was a prolific and successful playwright, starting with *Class* (1930). His most notable works were *Tanya* (1939), which has been described as the Soviet *Dolls' House*; *The Promise* (1965); and *Cruel Games* (1978).

ARC See **JOAN OF ARC**

ARCADIUS (377–408) first emperor of the East alone, was born in Spain, and after the death of his father, the emperor **Theodosius**, in AD 395, received the eastern half of the Roman empire, the western falling to his brother **Honorius**. Arcadius lived in oriental state and splendour, and his dominion extended from the Adriatic to the Tigris, and from Scythia to Ethiopia; but the real rulers over this vast empire were the Gaul Rufinus, the eunuch Eutropius, and the Empress **Eudoxia**, who persecuted and banished St **John Chrysostom** in 404.

ARCARO, Eddie (1916–) American jockey, born in Cincinnati, Ohio. He was five-times winner of the Kentucky Derby, the top horse race in the USA (first run in 1875). He won 4799 races in a career spanning 30 years, from 1931 to 1961, and was six times leading money-winner in the USA. He also won the triple crown twice, in 1941 and 1948 (Kentucky Derby, Preakness and Belmont Stakes). His career winnings totalled more than $30 million.

ARCESILAUS (c.316–c.241 BC) Greek philosopher, born in Pitane in Aeolia. He became the sixth head of the Academy founded by **Plato**; he modelled his philosophy on the critical dialectic of Plato's earlier dialogues but gave it a sharply sceptical turn, directed particularly against Stoic doctrines. Under his leadership the school became known as the 'Middle Academy' to distinguish it from the 'Old Academy'.

ARCH, Joseph (1826–1919) English preacher and reformer, born in Barford, Warwickshire. While still a farm labourer he became a Primitive Methodist preacher. In 1872 he founded the National Agricultural Labourers' Union, and later was MP for Northwest Norfolk.

ARCHBOLD, John Frederick (1785–1870) English lawyer, a prolific author of practical legal textbooks. He is best remembered for *Criminal Pleading, Evidence and Practice* (1822) a work which, repeatedly revised, is of high authority and an essential handbook for lawyers in the English criminal courts.

ARCHELAUS (fl.c.450 BC) Greek philosopher and cosmologist, reputed to have been the pupil of **Anaxagoras** and the teacher of **Socrates**. He made some limited modifications to the physical theories of Anaxagoras and others.

ARCHELAUS king of Macedonia from 413 to 399 BC, a great patron of the arts.

ARCHELAUS (1st century) Ethnarch of Judaea, son of **Herod the Great**, succeeded his father in AD 1, and maintained his position against an insurrection raised by the Pharisees. His heirship being disputed by his brother **Herod Antipas**, Archelaus went to Rome, where his authority was confirmed by **Octavianus Augustus**, who made him Ethnarch of Judaea, Samaria, and Idumaea, while his brothers, Antipas and Philip, were made tetrarchs over the other half of Herod's dominions. After a nine-year reign, he was deposed by Augustus for his tyranny, and banished to Vienne, in Gaul, where he died.

ARCHELAUS VI (1st century BC) Pontic general sent by **Mithridates the Great** to Greece to oppose the Romans in 87 BC. He was defeated by **Sulla** at Chaeronea and at Orchomenos in 86. Unjustly suspected of treason, Archelaus went over to the Romans at the outbreak of the second war in 83.

ARCHER, Frederick James (1857–86) English champion jockey, born in Cheltenham. He rode his first race in 1870, and during his career rode 2748 winners, winning the Derby five times, the Oaks four, the St Leger six, the Two Thousand Guineas five, and the One Thousand Guineas twice. His record of 246 winners in one season remained intact until it was beaten by **Gordon Richards** in 1933. In 1876 he shot himself in his home at Newmarket 'while temporarily insane'.

ARCHER, Jeffrey Howard (1940–) best-selling British author and former parliamentarian, educated at Wellington School and Brasenose College, Oxford, where he won Blues for athletics and gymnastics. He sat as Conservative MP for the constituency of Louth from 1969 to 1974, but resigned from the House of Commons after a financial disaster that led to bankruptcy. In order to pay his debts in full he turned to writing fiction; his first book, *Not a Penny More, Not a Penny Less* (1975), based on his own unfortunate experiences in the financial world, was an instant bestseller, which he followed up with other blockbusters like *Shall We Tell the President?* (1976), *Kane and Abel* (1979), which was dramatized on television, and *First Among Equals* (1984), which was also televised. In 1987 he wrote a thriller for the stage *Beyond Reasonable Doubt*, and in 1988 capped his lifelong interest in the theatre by buying one outright — the Playhouse, London.

ARCHER, Robyn (1948–) Australian singer and actress, born in Adelaide. After graduating from Adelaide University she worked in Sydney night-clubs before returning to complete her Diploma of Education and teach English for three years. In 1974 she sang 'Annie I' in **Brecht/Weill**'s *The Seven Deadly Sins* which led to a contract with New Opera South Australia, and in 1975 played Jenny in Weill's *Threepenny Opera*, since when her name has been linked particularly with the German cabaret songs of Weill, **Eisler** and **Dessau**. In 1977 she was invited by the National Theatre, London, to perform in a Brecht compilation, *To Those Born Later*. In 1978 she returned to Sydney to write and star in a series of one-woman and political cabaret shows; her one-woman cabaret *A Star is Torn* (1979) ran for two seasons in London's West End during 1982 and 1983, and is now a successful book and record album. Now concentrating on writing and producing, she still appears regularly on the BBC television series 'Cabaret', and in 1989 was commissioned to write a new opera *Mambo* for the Nexus Opera, London.

ARCHER, Thomas (1668–1743) English Baroque architect, born in Tanworth. He studied abroad, and designed the churches of St John's, Westminster (1714), and St Paul's, Deptford (1712); also Roehampton House in Surrey and part of Chatsworth in Derbyshire.

ARCHILOCHUS OF PAROS (fl.714–676 BC) Greek poet from the island of Paros, regarded as the first of the lyric poets, ranked by the ancients with **Homer**, **Pindar**, and **Sophocles**. Even **Plato** calls him 'the very wise', but much of his renown is for vituperative satire. Only fragments of his work are extant. He is said to have died in a battle between Paros and Naxos.

ARCHIMEDES (c.287–212 BC) Greek mathematician, born in Syracuse, the most celebrated of ancient mathematicians and one of the most intellectually powerful mathematicians of all time. He probably visited Egypt and studied at Alexandria. In popular tradition he is remembered for the construction of siege-engines against the Romans, the Archimedean screw still used for raising water, and the cry of 'Eureka' when he discovered the principle of the upthrust on a floating body. His real importance in mathematics, however, lies in his discovery of formulae for the areas and volumes of spheres, cylinders, parabolas, and other plane and solid figures, in which the methods he used anticipated the theories of integration to be developed 1800 years later. He also used mechanical arguments involving infinitesimals as an heuristic tool for obtaining the results prior to rigorous proof. He founded the science of hydrostatics, studying the equilibrium positions of floating bodies of various shapes. His astronomical work is lost. His work combines an amazing freedom of approach with enormous technical skill in the details of his proofs, but some of it has only survived in Arabic translation. He was killed at the siege of Syracuse by a Roman soldier whose challenge he ignored while immersed in a mathematical problem.

ARCHIPENKO, Alexander (1880–1964) Ukranian-born American sculptor, born in Kiev. He studied there and at Moscow and Paris, where he was influenced by Cubism, and introduced holes and voids into sculpture, as in *Walking Women* (1912). After 1923 he lived in America and taught in the new Bauhaus at Chicago. His work is characterized by extreme economy of form, and shows the influence of **Brancusi**.

ARCIMBOLDO, Giuseppe (c.1530–1593) Italian painter, born in Milan, where he began his career as a designer of stained-glass windows for the cathedral. He later moved to Prague and became a court painter to the Habsburgs. **Rudolf II** admired his work enough to make him a Count Palatine. It was while court painter that he executed the work for which he is best known, fantastic heads composed of fragmented landscape, animals, vegetables, flowers and other non-human objects, brightly coloured and with a great attention to detail. While the artistic importance of these undoubtedly fascinating caricatures has always been considered debatable, they have been greatly admired by 20th-century Surrealists such as **Salvador Dali**.

ARDASHÍR See **ARTAXERXES**

ARDEN, Elizabeth, née **Florence Nightingale Graham** (c.1880–1966) Canadian-born American beautician and businesswoman, born in Woodbridge, Ontario. A nurse by training, she went to New York in 1908 and opened a beauty salon on Fifth Avenue in 1910, adopting the personal and business name of 'Elizabeth Arden'. She produced and advertised cosmetics on a large scale, and developed a worldwide chain of salons.

ARDEN, John (1930–) British playwright, born in Barnsley, Yorkshire, and educated at Sedbergh School, King's College, Cambridge, and the Edinburgh College of Art. It was in Edinburgh, while he was completing his architectural training, that the College Dramatic Society produced his first play, a romantic comedy entitled *All Fall Down*, in 1955. *Live Like Pigs* (1958), with its Rabelaisian realism and humour, broke new ground in theatrical presentation. His aggressive awareness of the north of England is particularly evident in *The Workhouse Donkey* (1963), a caricature of northern local politics, and in *Sergeant Musgrave's Dance* (1959), very much following the tradition of Brecht in its staging, the universality of the folk idiom reveals layers of political relevance beyond the simple tale of a group of soldiers returning to a northern town, bringing home with them the realities of war. In *Armstrong's Last Goodnight* (1964) the use of ballads and formal staging are particularly successful as Arden embodies contemporary political themes in a tale of the sixteenth-century Scottish borders. Arden has continually experimented with dramatic form and theatrical technique, both in the plays he has written alone and in the many pieces in which he has collaborated with his wife, Margaretta D'Arcy. *The Happy Haven* (1961) followed the commedia dell'arte tradition, the nativity play *The Business of Good Government* (1960) uses medieval stage techniques, *The Hero Rises Up* (1968) is a ballad opera about **Nelson**, and *The Ballygombeen Bequest* (1972) uses vaudeville on the theme of the political and class conflict in Ireland. Arden admits that he is not happy within the framework of the modern theatre. His plays also include *Ironhand* (1963), an adaptation of **Goethe**'s *Goetz von Berlichingen*; *Left-Handed Liberty*, commissioned in 1965 for the 750th anniversary of Magna Carta; a version of the Arthurian legend, *The Island of the Mighty* (1972), and *Vandaleur's Folly* (1978). He has also written television scripts, a volume of essays, and a novel, *Silence Among the Weapons* (1982). Since *The Island of the Mighty*, Arden has not produced a major new stage play but has written increasingly for radio, including a nine-part series, *Whose Is the Kingdom?* (1988). A second novel, *The Book of Bale*, appeared the same year, and continues Arden's theme of using early history to look closely at timeless moral issues.

ARDIZZONE, Edward Jeffrey Irving (1900–79) British illustrator and author, born in Haiphong,

Vietnam, to an Italian father and a Scottish mother. He took evening classes at the Westminster School of Art (1920–21), and worked as a freelance illustrator from 1926. His first children's book, *Little Tim and the Brave Sea Captain* (1936), made his name. He was an official war artist in World War II, after which he taught at Camberwell School of Art (1948–52), and at the Royal College of Art (1953–61). From 1952 to 1953 he worked for UNESCO in India. A superb draughtsman in watercolour, pen-and-ink, or pencil, he was a sharp observer of life, working a good deal from memory. He illustrated over 170 books in a traditional style based on simplified forms shadowed with loosely hatched lines.

ARENDT, Hannah (1906–75) German-born American philosopher and political theorist, born in Hanover. She went to the USA in 1940 as a refugee from the Nazis and held academic positions at Princeton, Chicago and in New York as well as becoming chief editor at Shocken Books and taking an active role in various Jewish organizations. Her writings often touched a political nerve and had an effect and a readership far beyond the academic world. Among her books are *Origins of Totalitarianism* (1951), *The Human Condition* (1958) and *The Life of the Mind* (published posthumously, 1978).

ARENSKY, Anton Stepanovich (1861–1906) Russian composer, born in Novgorod. He studied under **Rimsky-Korsakov**, and from 1895 conducted the court choir at St Petersburg. His compositions, which show the influence of **Tchaikovsky**, include five operas, two symphonies, and vocal and instrumental pieces.

ARETAEUS (fl.100) Greek physician of Cappadocia, considered to rank next to **Hippocrates**. The first four books of his great work, preserved nearly complete, treat of the causes and symptoms of diseases; the other four, of the cure.

ARETINO See **BRUNI, Leonardo** and **SPINELLO ARETINO**

ARETINO, Pietro (1492–1557) Italian poet, born in Arezzo, Tuscany, the illegitimate son of a nobleman named Luigi Bacci. Banished from his native town, he went to Perugia, where he worked as a bookbinder, and afterwards wandered through Italy in the service of various noblemen. In Rome (1517–27) he distinguished himself by his wit, impudence, and talents, and secured the favour of Pope **Leo X**, which he subsequently lost by writing his 16 salacious *Sonetti Lussuriosi*. He now won the friendship of **Giovanni de'Medici** and gained an opportunity of ingratiating himself with **Francis I** at Milan in 1524. A few years later he settled in Venice, there also acquiring powerful friends. The bishop of Vicenza not only soothed the irritation of the pope, but recommended Aretino to the emperor **Charles V**, who enriched him with splendid presents. It is said that while laughing heartily at a droll adventure of one of his sisters, he fell from a stool, and was killed on the spot. His poetical works include five witty comedies, and a tragedy of some merit.

ARFE, Henrique de (16th century) Spanish silversmith. With his son he carved in silver many of the finest Gothic altarpieces and crucifixes in the Spanish cathedrals and monasteries.

ARFE, Juan de, y Villafane (1535–c.1603) Spanish metal engraver born in León. One of Spain's finest craftsmen, he made altarpieces for the cathedrals at Avial, Burgos and Seville.

ARGAND, Aimé (1755–1803) Swiss physicist and chemist, born in Geneva, who lived for a time in England. In 1784 he invented the Argand lamp for use in lighthouses.

ARGAND, Jean-Robert (1768–1822) Swiss mathematician, born in Geneva. After him is named the Argand diagram, in which complex numbers are represented by points in the plane. By profession a bookkeeper, his work was largely independent of that of the more famous mathematicians of his time.

ARGELANDER, Friedrich Wilhelm August (1799–1875) German astronomer, born in Memel. Between 1852 and 1861 he plotted the position of all stars of the northern hemisphere above the ninth magnitude.

ARGENSOLA, Bartolomé Leonardo de (1562–1631) and **Lupercio de** (1559–1613) Spanish poets, born in Barbastro. They were both educated at Huesca University and both entered the service of Maria of Austria. Their poems led them to be styled the 'Spanish Horaces', but they were also official historians of Aragon. Lupercio also wrote some tragedies.

ARGENSON, René Louis, Marquis d' (1694–1757) French statesman, the son of the Marquis d'Argenson (1652–1721) who created the secret police and established the *lettres de cachet*. He became councillor to the parlement of Paris in 1716, and foreign minister (1744–47). He fell a victim in 1747 to the machinations of Madame de **Pompadour**, as ten years later did his brother, Marc Pierre, Comte d'Argenson (1696–1764), who became war minister in 1743.

ARGENTINA, La, originally **Antonia Mercé** (1890–1936) Spanish dancer, born in Buenos Aires. She moved to Spain with her parents, both Spanish dancers, when she was two, making her début as a classical dancer when she was six and becoming a dancer with Madrid Opera at the age of eleven. Giving up classical dance at fourteen she studied Spanish dance with her mother. Her first foreign tour at the age of eighteen was a great success and the blueprint for the rest of her life. She was internationally renowned, reported as being the greatest female Spanish dancer in history, and earned Spanish dance a new popularity.

ARGYLL title of the chiefs of the Campbells, the powerful West Highland clan. They had achieved knighthood in the 13th century and obtained the barony of Lochow in 1315. From 1445 the chief was styled Lord Campbell, until in 1457, the earldom of Argyll was conferred upon Colin, Lord Campbell.

ARGYLL, Archibald, 1st Duke (d.1705) son of the 9th Earl of Argyll, was an active promoter of the Revolution, and was created Duke of Argyll in 1701.

ARGYLL, Archibald, 2nd Earl (d.1513) son of Colin, 1st Earl, was killed at Flodden.

ARGYLL, Archibald, 5th Earl (1530–73) was a follower of **Mary, Queen of Scots** and was involved in the assassination of Darnley, but later supported **James VI** and **I** and became lord high chancellor (1572).

ARGYLL, Archibald, 7th Earl (c.1576–1638) he succeeded to the title in 1584, and as king's lieutenant he was defeated by Errol and Huntly at Glenlivet in 1594. In 1607 he was given a Charter of Crown lands in Kintyre, and suppressed risings by the Macdonalds in 1614 and 1615 in order to plant Lowland settlers in Inverary. He also helped in the extermination of the clan MacGregor from 1610 onwards. He later became a convert to Catholicism and served the king of Spain.

ARGYLL, Archibald, Marquis and 8th Earl (1598–1661) son of Archibald, 7th Earl of **Argyll**, and known as the 'covenanting marquis' and also 'cross-eyed Archibald'. He became a member of **Charles I**'s privy council in 1626; but in 1638, just before succeeding his father to the title, he joined the Covenanters in support of Scottish presbyterianism. In 1641 he was reconciled with Charles and was created Marquis of Argyll. In the English Civil War he joined the parliamentary side, and after being defeated by **Montrose** at Inverlochy in 1645, took part in the defeat of Montrose and his royalists at Philiphaugh in 1645. He formed a Scottish government under **Cromwell**'s patronage, but after the execution of the king he repudiated Cromwell and accepted the proclamation of **Charles II** as king in Scotland (1649), and crowned him at Scone in 1651. After the defeat of the Scottish army at Worcester that autumn, however, he submitted to Cromwell again. At the Restoration of Charles II in 1660 he was arrested and found guilty of complying with the English occupation, and executed.

ARGYLL, Archibald, 9th Earl (1629–85) son of Archibald, 8th Earl of **Argyll**. A royalist, he was imprisoned by **Cromwell** for a suspected royalist plot (1657–60), and after the Restoration in 1660 was eventually restored to the titles and lands forfeited at his father's execution in 1661. In 1681, however, he opposed the Test Act that forced all public office holders to declare their belief in Protestantism, and was sentenced to death for treason. He escaped to Holland. In 1685, after the accession of King **James II**, he conspired with **Monmouth** to overthrow the king. Monmouth's invasion of England was delayed; Argyll landed in Scotland, but failed to rouse the Covenanters to his cause, and was captured and executed.

ARGYLL, John, 2nd Duke (1678–1743) son of Archibald, 1st Duke of **Argyll**, succeeded to the title in 1703. A committed Unionist, he was a high commissioner to the Scottish parliament of 1704 and one of the strongest supporters of the Act of Union of 1707. An outstanding soldier, he took part in the War of the Spanish Succession (1701–14), and fought under **Marlborough** at Oudenarde (1708) and Malplaquet (1709). At the time of the Jacobite rising in Scotland (1715–16) he commanded the Hanoverian forces that dispersed the Jacobite troops without a battle. He was created Duke of Greenwich in 1719.

ARGYLL, John Douglas Sutherland, 9th Duke (1845–1914) married Queen Victoria's fourth daughter Princess Louise, and was governor-general of Canada from 1878 to 1883.

ARGYROPOULOS, Joannes (1416–c.1486) Greek scholar, born in Constantinople. A professor at Florence under the Medici, he was one of the earliest teachers of Greek learning in the West, and translated **Aristotle** into Latin.

ARIAS, Benito, called **Montano** (1527–98) Spanish theologian and linguist, born in Fregenal de la Sierra. He became a Benedictine monk and was delegate to the council of Trent (1562–64). He edited for **Philip II** the famous Antwerp Polyglot edition of the Bible (1568–73).

ARIAS SANCHEZ, Oscar (1940–) Costa Rican politician. Born in Costa Rica, he was educated at Essex University and the London School of Economics. He returned to Costa Rica and started a law practice before entering politics, joining the left-wing National Liberation party (PLN) and eventually becoming its secretary-general. He was elected president of Costa Rica in 1986, on a neutralist platform, and was the major author of a Central American Peace Agreement aimed at securing peace in the region and particularly in Nicaragua.

ARIBAU, Bonaventura Carles (1798–1862) Spanish economist and writer, born in Barcelona. He became a banker in Madrid, and was appointed director of the Mint and of the Spanish Treasury (1847). He was also decorated by the Prince Consort for his work on the industrial section of the Great Exhibition of 1851. In addition, he became editor of the *Biblioteca de autores españoles*, and was the author of the *Oda a la Patria* (1833), one of the earliest and best modern poems in Catalan. This had a tremendous influence on contemporary Catalan writers.

ARIOSTO, Ludovico (1474–1533) Italian poet, born in Reggio nell'Emilia. He intended to take up law, but abandoned it for poetry. In 1503 he was introduced to the court at Ferrara of the Cardinal Ippolito d'Este, who employed him in many negotiations, but was extremely niggardly in his rewards. Here, in the space of ten years, Ariosto produced his great poem, *Orlando Furioso* (1516), the **Roland** epic that forms a continuation of **Boiardo**'s *Orlando Innamorato*. When the cardinal left Italy (1518), the duke, his brother, invited the poet to his service, and treated him with comparative liberality. In 1522 he was commissioned to suppress an insurrection in the wild mountain district of Garfagnana, an arduous task which he successfully accomplished; and after remaining there three years as governor of the province, he returned to Ferrara. It was now that he composed his comedies, and gave the finishing touch to his *Orlando*. At length, in 1532, the poem made its appearance in a third edition, enlarged to its present dimensions. He was buried in the church of San Benedetto, at Ferrara, where a magnificent monument marks his resting place. Besides his great work, he wrote comedies, satires, sonnets, and a number of Latin poems. Of these the sonnets alone show the genius of the poet. His Latin poems are mediocre, and his comedies, besides lacking interest, are disfigured by licentious passages.

ARIOVISTUS (fl.65 BC) German tribal chief who invaded Gaul and was defeated by **Caesar** near Vesontium (Besançon), 58 BC.

ARISTARCHUS OF SAMOS (fl.270 BC) Alexandrian astronomer who seems to have anticipated Copernicus, maintaining that the earth moves round the sun.

ARISTARCHUS OF SAMOTHRACE (c.215–143 BC) Alexandrian grammarian and critic, best known for his edition of **Homer**. He wrote many commentaries and treatises, edited **Hesiod**, **Pindar**, **Sophocles**, **Aeschylus** and other authors, and was the founder of a school of philologists.

ARISTIDES (2nd century) Greek Christian apologist. He wrote an early *Apology for the Christian Faith*, mentioned by **Eusebius of Caesarea** and **Jerome**. It only came to light late in the 19th century.

ARISTIDES, known as **'The Just'** (c.530–c.468) Athenian soldier and statesman. He was one of the ten commanders against the Persians at the battle of Marathon (490) under **Miltiades**. Next year he was chief archon (489–488), but about 483 his opposition to **Themistocles**' naval policy led to his ostracization. When the Persians invaded again in 480 under **Xerxes I**, Aristides returned from banishment in Aegina and served under Themistocles at the battle of Salamis. He was the Athenian general, with **Pausanias** of Sparta, at the battle of Plataea (479). In 477 he introduced a sweeping change into the constitution, by which all citizens, without distinction of rank, were admitted to the archonship. Through him, too, about the same time, Athens, not Sparta, became the ruling state of the Delian League.

ARISTIPPUS (4th century BC) Greek philosopher, and native of Cyrene in Africa, hence the name of his followers, the Cyrenaics, who became an influential school in the late 4th and early 3rd centuries BC. The main doctrines were hedonism and the primacy of one's own immediate feelings. He became a pupil of **Socrates** at Athens, and himself taught philosophy both at Athens and Aegina, the first of the pupils of Socrates to charge fees for instruction. His reputation secured him a position in Syracuse, at the court of

Dionysius the tyrant, where he seems to have practised what he preached in a very whole-hearted fashion. He also lived some time at Corinth, in intimacy with the famous courtesan **Laïs**, but retired later to Cyrene, where his daughter Areta and his grandson Aristippus the Younger developed his views and formed a new school.

ARISTOGEITON See **HARMODIUS**

ARISTOPHANES (c.448–c.388 BC) Greek playwright. He is said to have written 54 plays, but only eleven are extant. His writings fall into three periods. To the first period, ending in 425 BC, belong the *Acharnians*, *Knights*, *Clouds*, and *Wasps*, the poet's four masterpieces, named from their respective choruses, and the *Peace*, in all of which full rein is given to political satire. To the second, ending in 406 BC, the *Birds*, *Lysistrata*, *Thesmophoriazusae*, and *Frogs*. To the third, ending around 388 BC, the *Ecclesiazusae* and *Plutus*, comedies in which political allusions and the distinctive characteristic of the Old Comedy, the *parabasis*, disappear.

ARISTOTLE (384–322 BC) Greek philosopher and scientist, one of the most important and influential figures in the history of Western thought. He was born at Stagira, a Greek colony on the peninsula of Chalcidice, the son of the court physician to the king of Macedon (who was father of **Philip II** and grandfather of **Alexander the Great**). In 367 he went to Athens and was first a pupil then a teacher at **Plato**'s Academy, where he stayed 20 years until Plato's death in 347. **Speusippus** succeeded Plato as head of the Academy and Aristotle left Athens for twelve years. He spent time at Atarneus in Asia Minor (where he married), at Mitylene, and in about 342 was appointed by Philip of Macedon to act as tutor to his son Alexander (then 13). He finally returned to Athens in 335 to found his own school (called the Lyceum from its proximity to the temple of Apollo Lyceius), where he taught for the next twelve years. His followers became known as 'peripatetics', supposedly from his restless habit of walking up and down while lecturing. Alexander the Great died in 323 and there was a strong anti-Macedonian reaction in Athens; Aristotle was accused of impiety and with the fate of Socrates perhaps in mind he took refuge at Calcis in Euboea, where he died the next year. Aristotle's writings represented an enormous, encyclopedic output over virtually every field of knowledge: logic, metaphysics, ethics, politics, rhetoric, poetry, biology, zoology, physics and psychology. The bulk of the work that survives actually consists in unpublished material in the form of lecture notes or students' textbooks, which were edited and published by **Andronicus of Rhodes** in the middle of the 1st century BC. Even this incomplete corpus is extraordinary for its range, originality, systematization and sophistication, and his work exerted an enormous influence on medieval philosophy (especially through St **Aquinas**), Islamic philosophy (especially through **Averroës**), and indeed on the whole Western intellectual and scientific tradition. The works most read today include the *Metaphysics* (the book written 'after the *Physics*'), *Nicomachean Ethics*, *Politics*, *Poetics*, the *De Anima* and the *Organon* (treatises on logic).

ARISTOXENUS OF TARENTUM (4th century BC) Greek philosopher and musical theorist, a pupil of **Aristotle**. He wrote influential works on rhythm and harmonics, part of which are still extant.

ARIUS, Greek **Areios** (c.250–336) Libyan theologian, the founder of the heresy known as 'Arianism'. Trained in Antioch, he became a presbyter in Alexandria. Here about 319 he maintained, against his bishop, that the Son was not co-equal or co-eternal with the Father, but only the first and highest of all finite beings, created out of nothing by an act of God's free will. He secured the adherence of clergy and laity in Egypt, Syria, and Asia Minor, but was deposed and excommunicated in 321 by a synod of bishops at Alexandria. **Eusebius of Nicodemia**, absolved him, and in 323 convened another synod in Bithynia, which pronounced in his favour. At Nicomedia, Arius wrote a theological work in verse and prose, called *Thaleida*, some fragments of which remain. The controversy became fierce, and to settle it the emperor **Constantine I** convoked the memorable Council of Nicaea, or Nice, in Bithynia (325). Three hundred and eighteen bishops, especially from the east, were present, besides priests, deacons, and acolytes. Arius boldly expounded and defended his opinions. It was principally by the reasoning of **Athanasius** that the Council was persuaded to define the absolute unity of the divine essence, and the absolute equality of the three persons. All the bishops subscribed to it except two, who were banished, along with Arius, to Illyricum. Arius was recalled in 334, but Athanasius refused to readmit him to church communion, and the controversy went on all over the East. In 336 Arius went to Constantinople, and the Emperor commanded the bishop to admit him to the sacrament. But a day or two before the Sunday appointed for the purpose, he died suddenly—poisoned by the orthodox, said his friends; by the direct judgment of God, according to his enemies. After his death the strife spread more widely abroad: the Homoousian doctrine (identity of essence in Father and Son) and the Homoiousian (similarity of essence) seemed alternately to prevail; and synods and counter-synods were held. The West was mainly orthodox, the East largely Arian or semi-Arian. There was a good deal of persecution on both sides; but **Julian** 'the Apostate' (361–363) and his successors extended full toleration to both parties. Arianism was at last virtually suppressed in the Roman empire under **Theodosius** in the East (379–395), and **Valentinian II** in the West. Among the Germanic nations, however, it continued to spread through missionary efforts, the Lombards being the last to come round (in 662). **Milton** held Arian or semi-Arian views. The Arian controversy was revived in England by the philosopher **Samuel Clarke** and **William Whiston**; but Arianism was superseded by Unitarianism.

ARKWRIGHT, Sir Richard (1732–92) English inventor and industrialist who invented the water-powered spinning frame, born in Preston, Lancashire. Of humble origin, the youngest of 13 children, he settled about 1750 as a barber in Bolton, and became also a dealer in hair, a secret process of his own for dyeing hair increasing the profits of his trade. In 1767 he moved to Preston, where he patented his celebrated *spinning-frame*—the first machine that could produce cotton-thread of sufficient tenuity and strength to be used as warp. The same year, to escape the popular rage against machinery he moved to Nottingham, and set up his first mill, driven by horses; in 1771, entering into partnership with Jedidiah Strutt of Derby (the improver of the *stocking-frame*), he set up a larger factory, with water-power, at Cromford, Derbyshire. In 1775 he took out a fresh patent for various additional improvements in machinery. His success stimulated rivals to invade his patent; and to such an extent did other cotton-spinners use his designs that he was obliged, in 1781, to prosecute nine different manufacturers—the outcome, however, was that in 1785 his letters patent were cancelled. Popular animosity was also excited against him on the ground that his inventions diminished the demand for labour; and in 1779 his large mill near Chorley was destroyed by a mob in the presence of a military and police force. In 1787 he became high-sheriff of Derbyshire, and in 1790 introduced the steam engine into his works at Nottingham.

ARLEN, Michael, originally **Dikran Kouyoumdjian** (1895–1956) British novelist, born in Ruschuk, Bulgaria, of Armenian parents. He was educated in England and naturalized in 1922. He made his reputation with *Piracy* (1922), *The Green Hat* (1924), and his short story collections, *The Romantic Lady* (1921) and *These Charming People* (1923).

ARLINGTON, Henry Bennet, 1st Earl of (1618–85) born in Arlington, Middlesex and educated at Westmister School and Christ Church, Oxford. Following a period in Spain after the civil war, he returned to England with the Restoration and was created Lord Arlington in 1663 and Earl Arlington in 1672. In 1674 he was unsuccessfully impeached for popery and self-aggrandizement. After serving as lord chamberlain he retired to Suffolk.

ARLISS, George, originally **Augustus George Andrews** (1868–1946) English actor, born in London. He first appeared on the stage at the Elephant and Castle in 1887, but his reputation as an actor was made in the USA, where he lived for 22 years from 1901, in plays like *The Second Mrs Tanqueroy* (1902) and *Disraeli* (1911). He returned to London to play the rajah in *The Green Goddess* in 1923. His film career began in the USA in 1920. He is remembered for his successful representations of famous historical characters, such as **Wellington**, **Richelieu** and **Voltaire**, which were always coloured by his own individual personality. He won an Academy Award for *Disraeli* (1929). He wrote his autobiography, *Up the Years from Bloomsbury* in 1940.

ARMANI, Giorgio (1935–) Italian fashion designer, born in Piacenza. He studied medicine in Milan, and after military service worked in a department store until he became a designer for Nino Cerruti in 1961. He also free-lanced before setting up the Giorgio Armani company in 1975. He designed first for men, then women, including loose-fitting blazers and jackets.

ARMFELT, Gustaf Mauritz (1757–1814) Swedish soldier and statesman, born in Finland. In the service of **Gustav III**, he fought in the war against Russia (1788–90) and negotiated the peace. He was a member of the regency council after Gustav's assassination (1792). He conspired with **Catherine II, the Great** of Russia in support of **Gustav III, Adolf**, and became his ambassador to Vienna (1802–04) and his army commander in Pomerania against **Napoleon** (1805–07). After the deposition of Gustav in 1809 he was expelled in 1811 by **Karl XIII** and went to Russia, where he entered the service of Tsar **Alexander I** and became governor of Finland, recently acquired from Sweden.

ARMINIUS (d.19) chief of the German Cherusci, he served as an officer in the Roman army and acquired Roman citizenship. However in AD 9 he allied with other German tribes against the Romans, and in the Teutoburgh Forest ambushed and annihilated an entire Roman army of three legions commanded by **Publius Quintilius Varus**. As a result the emperor **Augustus** abandoned the attempt to extend the Roman frontier from the Rhine to the Elbe. Arminius continued to resist the Romans and the Marcomanni, but was murdered by some of his own kinsmen.

ARMINIUS, Jacobus, properly **Jakob Hermandszoon** (1560–1609) Dutch theologian, born in Oudewater. He studied at Utrecht, Leiden, Geneva and Basel, and was ordained in 1588. Despite early opposition to the doctrine of predestination he was made professor of theology at Leiden in 1603. In 1604 his colleague **Gomarus** attacked his doctrines and from this time on he was engaged in a series of bitter controversies. Arminius asserted that God bestows forgiveness and eternal life on all who repent of their sins and believe in **Jesus Christ**; he wills that all men should attain salvation, and only because he has from eternity foreseen the belief or unbelief of individuals has he from eternity determined the fate of each—thus rejecting the high calvinistic doctrine of absolute predestination or election. In 1608 Arminius besought the States of Holland to convoke a synod to settle the controversy; but, worn out with care and disease, he died before it was held. Arminius was less Arminian than his followers, who continued the strife for many years and influenced the development of religious thought all over Europe. In England Laudians and Latitudinarians were Arminian in tendency; Wesleyans and many Baptists and Congregationalists are distinctly anti-calvinist.

ARMITAGE, Edward (1817–96) English painter, born in London. He studied under **Delaroche**, and became professor at the Royal Academy schools in 1875. He produced chiefly historical and biblical subject-paintings, including the frescoes *Death of Marmion*, and *Personification of the Thames* in the House of Lords.

ARMITAGE, Karole (1954–) American dancer and choreographer, born in Madison, Wisconsin. Trained in classical ballet, she moved from the Ballets de Genève, Switzerland (1972–74) to the **Merce Cunningham** Dance Company in New York (1976–81) where her unique style began to take shape. Cunningham created several roles for her including *Squaregame* (1976) and *Channels/Inserts* (1981). During this period she became interested in choreography and with *Drastic Classicism* began a choreographic career which took her to Paris, where she worked with dancers such as **Michael Clark** and created pieces for Paris Opéra Ballet. Her work has been described as a 'molotov cocktail', a controversial blend of wit, high heels and invention.

ARMITAGE, Kenneth (1916–) English sculptor, born in Leeds. He studied at the Royal College of Art and the Slade School (1937–39) and exhibited at the Venice Biennale in 1952 with other British sculptors. His bronzes are usually of semi-abstract figures, united into a group by stylized clothing. In 1956 he won the Venice Biennale Gold Medal for foreign sculptors.

ARMSTEAD, Henry Hugh (1828–1905) English sculptor, born in London. His best known works are reliefs and bronze statues for the Albert Memorial, the fountain at King's College, Cambridge, and the reredos at Westminster Abbey.

ARMSTRONG, Archy (d.1672) Scottish court-jester of **James VI and I** and **Charles I**. He gained much wealth and influence, but was dismissed in 1637 for insolence to Archbishop **Laud**, and withdrew in 1641 to Arthuret in Cumberland.

ARMSTRONG, Edwin Howard (1890–1954) American electrical engineer and inventor, born in New York City. He graduated from Columbia University in 1913 and during World War I became interested in methods of detecting aircraft. In the course of his research he devised the superheterodyne radio receiver, and by 1939, as professor at Columbia University (1935–54), he had perfected the frequency-modulation system of radio transmission which virtually eliminated the problem of interference from static. Both of these inventions were universally adopted and should have brought him great satisfaction, but he was a most contentious man forever engaged in lawsuits over real or imagined slights, and in a fit of depression he took his own life.

ARMSTRONG, Gillian (1951–) Australian film director, born in Melbourne. A student of theatre design and later of film, she won a scholarship to the Film and Television School in Sydney where she directed three short films, including *Gretel* (1974). After her graduation she made documentaries and the drama *The Singer and the Dancer* (1976) which won the Australian Film Institute Award for Best Short. Her first feature film, *My Brilliant Career* (1979), told of a young woman and the sacrifices she makes to assert her individualism in the outback of the 1890s. The winner of eleven AFI awards, including Best Film and Best Director, it earned her an international reputation of great promise. She has continued to focus attention on the difficulties facing independent women in *Mrs. Soffel* (1984) and *High Tide* (1987), while enjoying a change of pace in the breezy musical comedy *Starstruck* (1982).

ARMSTRONG, Henry Edward (1848–1937) English chemist, born in London. He studied chemistry there under Sir **Edward Frankland**, and with **Hermann Kolbe** in Leipzig, and became professor of chemistry (1871–1913) in the London institutions which became Imperial College. Although his researches in both organic and physical chemistry are significant, his major contribution is in chemical education, where he pioneered the heuristic method. Again ahead of his time, he was a forceful advocate for environmental concern and the reduction of wasteful practices in manufacturing industry and in energy generation.

ARMSTRONG, Henry Jackson (1912–88) American boxer, born in Columbus, Mississippi. One of the greatest boxers of all time, he was the only man to hold three world titles at different weights. With a style based on speed and unremitting aggression, his first title was at featherweight, which he won in 1937, and the following year he added both the welterweight and lightweight crowns. He lost the featherweight and lightweight titles in 1936, but he successfully defended his welterweight title a record 20 times, and in 1940 he even fought a drawn bout for the middleweight title. He retired after a 15-year career, and in 1951 he was ordained a Baptist minister; but the 175 bouts he had fought inflicted cumulative mental and physical damage and severely curtailed his professional life. He died an impoverished pensioner of the US government.

ARMSTRONG, John (c.1709–1779) Scottish physician and poet, born in the manse at Liddesdale, in Roxburghshire. He took the Edinburgh MD in 1732, and went into practice in London. In 1736 he published a sex manual in blank verse for newly weds called *The Oeconomy of Love*; and in 1744 another didactic medical work in blank verse. In 1746 he was appointed physician to the London Soldiers' Hospital, and from 1760 to 1763 physician to the forces in Germany.

ARMSTRONG, Johnnie (d.1530) celebrated Scottish Border freebooter and castle-rustler ('reiver'), and hero of many Border ballads. He was either John Armstrong of Gilnockie, near Langholm, who was seized by King **James V** at a parley at Caerlanrig chapel and summarily hanged with several of his followers in 1529, or John Armstrong ('Black Jock'), brother of Thomas Armstrong of Mangerton, executed in 1530.

ARMSTRONG, Louis (Satchmo) (c.1898–1971) American jazz trumpeter and singer, born in New Orleans and brought up by his mother in extreme poverty. While serving a sentence for delinquency in the city's 'home for coloured waifs', he learned to play the cornet, and from that humble start he developed into the first major jazz virtuoso. Released from the institution in 1914, he worked as a musician in local bars, getting encouragement from **King Oliver**, the city's leading cornettist. In 1919, Armstrong replaced Oliver in the band led by Edward 'Kid' Ory, and also played on Mississippi riverboats. In 1922, he joined Oliver's band in Chicago, and recordings by the Creole Jazz Band, featuring the cornet partnership, set new standards of musicianship in early jazz. These standards were surpassed by Armstrong himself a few years later, recording with his 'Hot Five' and 'Hot Seven' studio groups, when his playing moved beyond the constraints of New Orleans-style collective improvization towards the virtuoso delivery for which he later gained world renown. A 1926 recording of his use of 'Scat singing'—imitating an instrument with the voice with nonsense syllables—started a vogue in jazz of which he became the most celebrated exponent. By the later 1920s Armstrong, then playing trumpet, began two decades as a star soloist and singer with various big bands sometimes in commercial settings not worthy of his great talent. In 1947, the formation of his first All Stars group marked a return to small-group jazz. Armstrong made the first of many overseas tours in 1933. He appeared in more than 50 films as a musician and entertainer.

ARMSTRONG, Neil (1930–) American astronaut, born in Wapakoneta, Ohio, educated there and at Purdue University. A fighter pilot in Korea and later a civilian test pilot, in 1962 he was chosen as an astronaut and in 1966 he commanded Gemini 8. In 1969 with **Aldrin** and **Michael Collins** he set out in Apollo 11 on a successful moon-landing expedition. On 20 July 1969 Armstrong and Aldrin became in that order the first men to set foot on the moon, Collins remaining in the command module. They returned to earth on 24 July. Armstrong later taught aerospace engineering at Cincinnati University (1971–79). He published *First on the Moon* in 1970.

ARMSTRONG, Robert, Baron Armstrong of Ilminster (1927–) English civil servant. Educated at Eton and Christ Church, Oxford, he entered the civil service in 1950 and rose rapidly to become deputy head of the Home Office and the Treasury. In 1970 he became principal private secretary to the prime minister, **Edward Heath** and, under **Margaret Thatcher**, secretary to the cabinet and head of the home civil service. Loyal to his ministers to a fault, he achieved unwonted notoriety when he gave evidence in the 'Spycatcher' case in Australia, in 1987, and admitted that he had sometimes been 'economical with the truth'. He retired from the civil service in 1988 and was made a life peer.

ARMSTRONG, Sir Walter (1850–1918) Scottish writer of works on **Velasquez**, **Gainsborough**, **Reynolds**, **Raeburn**, **Lawrence**, born in Roxburghshire. He was director of the National Gallery of Ireland (1892–1914).

ARMSTRONG, William (16th century) the 'Kinmont Willie' of the Border ballad, a Dumfriesshire moss-trooper. He was rescued in 1596 by **Walter Scott**, 1st Lord Scott of Buccleuch (1565–1611), from Carlisle Castle.

ARMSTRONG, William George, Baron Armstrong (1810–1900) English inventor and industrialist, born in Newcastle. Articled to a solicitor, he became a partner; but he turned to engineering, and in 1840 he produced a much improved hydraulic engine, in 1842 an apparatus for producing electricity from steam, and in 1845 the hydraulic crane. In 1847 he founded the Elswick Engine-works, Newcastle, which produced hydraulic cranes, engines, accumulators, and bridges at first, but was soon to be famous for its ordnance, and especially the Armstrong breech-loading gun, whose barrel was built up of successive coils of wrought-iron. From 1882 shipbuilding was included. In 1897 the firm amalgamated with Joseph Whitworth & Co, and in 1927 merged into Vickers Armstrong Ltd.

ARMSTRONG-JONES See **MARGARET ROSE**

ARNAL, Étienne (1794–1872) French actor, born in Meulan. He appeared regularly from 1815 to 1868, first in tragedy, and later, with outstanding success, as a comedian.

ARNARSON, Ingólfur (late 9th century) Norwegian Viking from Hördaland in south-western Norway, honoured as the first settler of Iceland in 874 AD. According to early historical traditions in *Landnámabók*, the Icelandic 'Book of Settlements', he left Norway after some local disputes and settled with his family and friends on a farm he named Reykjavík ('Steamy Bay') because of its hotsprings, and which later became the country's capital. His descendants held the hereditary and honorary post of supreme chieftain (*alsherjargoði*) of the Icelandic parliament (*Althing*) after its foundation in 930.

ÁRNASON, Jón (1819–88) Icelandic collector of folk-tales, known as 'the **Grimm** of Iceland'. Born in northern Iceland, he became national librarian in Reykjavík; he collected and published a huge collection of Icelandic folk-tales and fairy-tales (*Íslenskar þjóðsögur og ævintýri*, 2 vols, 1862–64), translated as *Legends of Iceland* by **Eiríkur Magnússon** (1864–66).

ARNAUD, Arsène See **CLARETIE, Jules**

ARNAUD, Henri (1641–1721) French pastor and military leader of the Waldenses. He wrote in exile at Schönberg his famous *Histoire de la glorieuse rentrée des Vaudois dans leurs vallées* (1710).

ARNAUD, Yvonne Germaine (1892–1958) French actress, born in Bordeaux and educated in Paris. Trained as a concert pianist, she toured Europe as a child prodigy and, with no previous acting experience, assumed the role of Princess Mathilde in the musical comedy *The Quaker Girl* (1911). An instant success, she consolidated her popularity with *The Girl in the Taxi* (1912). Noted for her charm, vivacity and inimitably musical accent, she enjoyed a long career on the British stage. She appeared in many musicals and farces including *Tons of Money* (1922), *A Cuckoo in the Nest* (1925), *The Improper Duchess* (1931) and *Love for Love* (1943). Her innate kindliness was thought to render her an unsuitable choice for **Anouilh**'s *Colombe* (1951) but she appeared to great effect in *Dear Charles* (1952) and was active until her death. She made her film début in *Desire* (1920) and appeared in several cinema adaptations of her stage successes as well as films like *On Approval* (1931), *The Ghosts of Berkeley Square* (1947) and *Mon Oncle* (1958). Resident for many years near Guildford, Surrey, a theatre there was opened in her honour in 1965.

ARNAULD, Angélique, known as **'Mère Angélique de Saint Jean'** (1624–84) French Jansenist religious, daughter of **Robert Arnauld**. She entered the convent of Port-Royal des Champs in Paris and was successively subprioress and abbess (1678). During the persecution of the Port-Royalists she was sustained by her heroic courage and the spirits of the sisterhood and their friends.

ARNAULD, Antoine (1612–94) French philosopher, lawyer, mathematician and priest, born into a famous family associated with the Jansenist movement and community at Port Royal. Known as 'the Great Arnauld', he was a controversialist, and his attacks on the Jesuits and his activities as head of the Jansenist sect in France led to his expulsion from the Sorbonne, persecution, and ultimately refuge in Belgium. While at Port Royal he collaborated with **Pascal** and **Nicole** on the work known as the *Port Royal Logic* (1662).

ARNAULD, Marie-Angélique, known as **'Mère Angélique'** (1591–1661) French Jansenist religious, sister of **Antoine Arnauld**. She was made abbess of Port-Royal in 1602 at the age of eleven, and ultimately reformed the convent by the severity of her discipline. She resigned in 1630, but, returned to be prioress under her sister Agnes (1593–1671).

ARNAULD, Robert (Arnauld d'Andilly) (1588–1674) French lawyer and scholar. He retired to the seclusion of Port-Royal des Champs, and published graceful translations of **Josephus**, **Augustine**, St **Teresa**, and others in *Oeuvres chrétiennes* (1692).

ARNDT, Ernst Moritz (1769–1860) German poet and patriot, born in the then Swedish island of Rügen. The son of a former serf, he received an excellent education at Stralsund, Greifswald, and Jena, with a view to the ministry; but in 1805, after travelling extensively over Europe, he became professor of history at Greifswald. His *Geschichte der Leibeigenschaft in Pommern und Rügen* (1803) led to the abolition of serfdom; and in his *Geist der Zeit* (1806) he attacked **Napoleon** with such boldness that after the battle of Jena (1806) he had to take refuge in Stockholm (1806–09). 'Was ist des deutschen Vaterland?' and others of his patriotic songs helped to rouse the spirit of Germany. In 1817 he married a sister of **Schleiermacher** and in 1818 became professor of history in the new University of Bonn; but, aiming steadily at constitutional reforms, he was suspended in 1819 for participation in so-called 'demagogic movements', and was not restored till 1840. He was elected a member of the German national assembly in 1848, but retired from it in 1849. Beloved and revered by the whole German people as 'Father Arndt', he died in Bonn. His works comprise an account of the Shetland and Orkney Islands (1826), numerous political addresses, some volumes of reminiscences, two volumes of letters (1878–92), and his poems.

ARNE, Thomas Augustine (1710–78) English composer, born in London, educated at Eton. His father, an upholsterer, intended him for the bar, but he became skilful as a violinist, forming his style chiefly on **Corelli**: and his zeal induced his sister (the actress, Mrs **Cibber**), to cultivate her excellent voice. He wrote for her a part in his first opera *Rosamond* (1733). Next followed his comic operetta, *Tom Thumb*; and afterwards his *Comus* (1738). He married a singer, Cecilia Young (1736); and after a successful visit to Ireland, was appointed composer to Drury Lane Theatre, for which he composed his famous settings of Shakespearean songs, *Under the Greenwood Tree*; *Where the Bee Sucks*; *Blow, Blow, thou Winter Wind*; etc. He also wrote many vocal pieces for the Vauxhall concerts. *Rule, Britannia*, originally written for *The Masque of Alfred*, is his; as well as two oratorios and two operas, *Eliza* and *Artaxerxes*. His son Michael (1740–86) was also a musician and composer, remembered for his song 'Lass with the delicate air'.

ARNIM, Hans Georg von (1581–1641) German soldier and diplomat, born in Brandenburg. He served in the Swedish army under **Gustaf II, Adolf** in the war with Russia (1613–17), and with the Poles against Sweden in 1621. During the Thirty Years' War he served with the Imperial armies under **Wallenstein** (1625–28). In 1631, however, leading the Saxon army in alliance with the Swedes against the Imperial army, he took Prague, but was soon driven out by Wallenstein.

ARNIM, Jürgen, Baron von (1891–1971) German soldier, born of an old Silesian military family. He served at first in the infantry in World War I, then became a tank expert and in World War II was given command of a Panzer Division in the Russian campaign. He took over the 5th Panzer Army in Tunisia in 1943 and succeeded **Rommel** in command of Army Group Africa. In May 1943 he surrendered his troops to the Allies, and was interned in Britain and later the USA.

ARNIM, Ludwig Achim von (1781–1831) German writer of fantastic but original romances. He stirred up a warm sympathy for old popular poetry, and published over 20 volumes, mainly tales and novels, including, with **Clemens von Brentano**, the folk-song collections *Des Knaben Wunderhorn*. His wife, Bettina (1785–1859), Brentano's sister, was as a girl infatuated with **Goethe**, and afterwards published a (largely fictitious) *Correspondence* with him, as well as ten volumes of tales and essays.

ARNO, Peter, pseud of **Curtis Arnoux Peters** (1904–68) American cartoonist, born in New York, the son of a judge. He was one of the first contributors to the *New Yorker* magazine, from 1925, with satirical drawings of New York café society. He also wrote musical revues, including *Here Comes the Bride* (1931).

ARNOBIUS THE ELDER (d.330) a teacher of rhetoric at Sicca, in Numidia (Africa). He became a Christian about 300, and wrote a vigorous defence of Christianity (*Adversus Nationes*), translated in vol. xix of the *Ante-Nicene Library*.

ARNOLD OF BRESCIA (c.1100–1155) Italian churchman and politician, educated in France under **Abelard**. He adopted the monastic life and having exasperated the people of Brescia against their bishop by his preaching, was banished from Italy by the Lateran Council (1139). In France he met with bitter hostility from St **Bernard** of Clairvaux, and took refuge for five years in Zürich. An insurrection against the papal government in Rome drew him there (1143) and for ten years he struggled to found a republic on ancient Roman lines. When Arnold's party collapsed Pope **Adrian IV** (Nicholas Breakspear) laid the city under an interdict. On the arrival of the emperor **Frederick I, Barbarossa**, in 1155, Arnold was arrested, brought to Rome, and hanged, his body burned, and the ashes thrown into the Tiber. He is nevertheless remembered alongside **Rienzi** and **Savonarola**.

ARNOLD, Aberhard (1883–1935) Founder of the Bruderhof movement in Nazi Germany, born in Breslau. He studied theology at Halle, but disqualified himself from the degree through his insistence on being baptised on profession of faith (he later obtained a doctorate with a dissertation on **Nietzche**). A convinced pacifist associated with the Student Christian Movement, he early linked spiritual authenticity with an awareness of economic injustice. He visited Bruderhof colonies in Canada, and incurred the hostility of the Gestapo which saw allegiance to the state as the highest priority. He died of complications following a leg injury. A selection of his writings and addresses, *God's Revolution*, was published in 1984.

ARNOLD, Benedict (1741–1801) American soldier and turncoat, born in Norwich, Connecticut. At the age of 14 he ran away from home, joined the provincial troops then engaged in the old French war, but soon deserted, and became a merchant in New Haven. On the outbreak of the War of Independence (1775–83) he joined the colonial forces, assisted **Ethan Allen** in the capture of Fort Ticonderoga (1775), and took part in the unsuccessful siege of Quebec in 1775, for which he was made a brigadier-general. He commanded the fleet on Lake Champlain (1776) which delayed the British advance from Canada; at the battle of Ridgefield his horse was killed under him, and for his gallantry he was made a major-general. He fought with distinction in the eventful battle of Saratoga (1777). Though greatly admired by **Washington**, he had bitter and influential enemies, and in 1777 five of his inferiors in rank were promoted by congress over his head. In 1778 he was placed in command of Philadelphia, where he was court-martialled for embezzlement, but let off with a reprimand. In 1780 he sought and obtained the command of West Point, which, through a conspiracy with **John André**, he agreed to betray. On the capture of André, he fled to the British lines, and was given a command in the royal army. In 1780 he led raids in Virginia and (1781) Connecticut. He went to England in 1781, and lived in poverty in London, where he died.

ARNOLD, Sir Edwin (1832–1904) English poet and journalist, born in Gravesend. He won the Newdigate prize for poetry at Oxford in 1852, taught at King Edward's School, Birmingham, and in 1856 became principal of Deccan College, Poona. Returning in 1861, he joined the staff of the *Daily Telegraph*, of which he became editor in 1863. He wrote *The Light of Asia* (1879) on Buddhism, and other poems coloured by his experience of the East.

ARNOLD, Henry Harley (1886–1950) American air force officer, born in Gladwyne, Pennsylvania. Educated at the US Academy, West Point, he was commissioned into the infantry in 1907. He learned to fly with the **Wright** brothers and got his pilot's licence in 1911, serving with the air section of signal corps. He commanded 1st Air Wing, GHQ Air Force (1931) and became commanding general US Army Air Corps (1938) and chief of US Army Air Forces (1941). He was promoted to general of the army in 1944, and on the creation of the United States Air Force as an independent service, he became a general of the air force in 1947. He wrote several books, including *This Flying Game* (1936) and *Global Mission* (1949).

ARNOLD, John (1736–99) English horologist, son of a Bodmin watchmaker. He worked in Holland, set up business in London and made improvements in construction and production methods to the chronometer, invented shortly before by **John Harrison**.

ARNOLD, Joseph (1782–1818) English botanist, born in Beccles, Suffolk. He studied medicine at Edinburgh and accompanied Sir **Thomas Stamford Raffles** as naturalist to Sumatra, where he died. He discovered the largest flower known, *Rafflesia arnoldi*, measuring a yard across and weighing fifteen pounds.

ARNOLD, Malcolm Henry (1921–) English composer, born in Northampton. He studied composition with Gordon Jacob at the Royal College of Music (1938–40) and was principal trumpet player with the London Philharmonic Orchestra until 1948. His prolific output is characterized by a constantly inventive and colourful orchestral imagination allied to an adventurous and dramatic use of traditional tonality and form. Of his film scores, *Bridge over the River Kwai* received an Oscar (1957). He has composed eight symphonies and other orchestral music including the overture *Tam O'Shanter*, eighteen concertos, five ballets, two one-act operas, vocal, choral and chamber music. He was created CBE in 1970.

ARNOLD, Mary Augusta See **WARD, Mrs Humphry**

ARNOLD, Matthew (1822–88) English poet and critic, born in Laleham, near Staines, the eldest son of Dr **Thomas Arnold** of Rugby. He was educated at Winchester, Rugby, and Balliol College, Oxford. He won the Newdigate prize with a poem on **Cromwell** (1843), and in 1845 was elected a fellow of Oriel College. After acting for four years as private secretary to Lord Lansdowne (1847–51), he was appointed one of the lay inspectors of schools in 1851, an office from which he retired in 1886. From 1857 to 1867 he was professor of poetry at Oxford. He was frequently sent by the government to inquire into the state of education on the Continent, especially in France, Germany, and Holland; and his masterly reports, with their downright statement of English deficiencies, attracted much attention in England. So, too, did his audacious application to scripture of the methods of literary criticism. In 1883 he received a pension of £250, and in the same year he lectured in the USA. He was buried at Laleham. His early volumes of poetry, *The Strayed Revelles and Other Poems* (1849), which contained 'The Forsaken Merman', and *Empedocles on Etna* (1852), which contained 'Tristram and Iseult', both failed, but he made his mark with *Poems: A New Edition* (1853–54), which contained 'The Scholar Gipsy' and 'Sohrab and Rustum', and confirmed his standing as a poet with *New Poems* (1867), which contained 'Dover Beach' and 'Thyrsis'. Appointed professor of poetry at Oxford in 1857, he published several distinguished works of criticism including *Essays in Criticism* (1865, 1888), *On the Study of Celtic Literature* (1867), *Culture and Anarchy* (1869), *St Paul and Protestantism* (1870), *Literature and Dogma* (1872), *Last Essays on Church and Religion* (1877), *Mixed Essays* (1879), *Irish Essays* (1882), and *Discourses on America* (1885).

ARNOLD, Samuel (1740–1802) English composer, became organist to the Chapels Royal (1783) and to Westminster Abbey (1793). He is best remembered for his valuable collection of cathedral music (1790). His son, Samuel James (1774–1852), was a playwright and manager.

ARNOLD, Thomas (1795–1842) English educationist and scholar, headmaster of Rugby, and father of **Matthew Arnold**. Born in East Cowes, Isle of Wight, he was educated at Winchester and Corpus Christi College, Oxford, where he was a brilliant classical scholar. He took deacon's orders in 1818 and settled at Laleham, near Staines, as a private 'crammer' of students, and married Mary Penrose, the sister of an old friend. In 1828 he was appointed headmaster of Rugby, charged with the task of regenerating the school. He reformed the school, introduced mathematics, modern history and modern languages to the curriculum, and instituted the form system and introduced the prefect system to keep discipline. The style of 'muscular Christianity' he introduced was graphically described in **Thomas Hughes**'s *Tom Brown's Schooldays* (1857). Arnold had a profound and lasting effect on the development of public school education in England. In 1841 he was appointed Regius professor of modern history at Oxford. He was the author of six volumes of sermons, an edition of **Thucydides**, and a *History of Rome* (3 vols, 1838–43). His second son, Thomas (1823–1900), was a literary scholar, and his daughter, Mary Augusta, was the novelist Mrs **Humphry Ward**.

ARNOLFO DI CAMBIO (1232–1302) Italian sculptor and architect, the designer of Florence Cathedral. A pupil of **Nicolá Pisano**, he worked on his master's shrine of S Dominic, Bologna and the pulpit at Siena before going to Rome in 1277 where he executed a portrait of **Charles of Anjou**, one of the first modern portrait statues. His tomb of Cardinal de Braye at Orvieto, now much altered, set the style for wall-tombs for more than a century. The famous bronze statue of Saint **Peter** in Saint Peter's is attributed to him. The remains of his sculptural decoration for Florence Cathedral are in the cathedral museum.

ARNULF See **ERNULF**

ARP, Jean or Hans (1888–1966) French sculptor, born in Strasbourg. He was one of the founders of the **Dada** movement in Zürich in 1916. During the 1920s he produced many abstract reliefs in wood, but after 1928 he worked increasingly in three dimensions, and he was second only to **Brancusi** in his influence on organic abstract sculpture, based on natural forms. In 1948 he wrote *On My Way*.

ARPAD (d.907) the national hero of Hungary. A Magyar chieftain in the Caucusus, he led the Magyars from the Black Sea into the Valley of the Danube after defeat by the Pechenigs (c.896) and occupied modern Hungary. He founded the Arped royal dynasty of Hungary, from **St Stephen** (997) to 1301 under whom the Magyars first gained a footing in that country about 884.

ARRABAL, Fernando (1932–) Spanish dramatist and novelist, born in Melilla, Spanish Morocco. His childhood was disrupted by the opposing political convictions of his parents during the Civil War. His strongly Catholic mother led him to believe that his father, who had escaped and disappeared in 1941 after being imprisoned for his Republican sympathies, was dead. He studied law in Madrid and drama in Paris in 1954, and then settled permanently in France. His first play, *Pique-nique en campagne* (1959), established him in the tradition of the Theatre of the Absurd, greatly influenced by **Beckett**. He coined the term 'Panic theatre', intended to shock the senses, employing sadism and blasphemy to accomplish its aims. In *Le Cimetière des voitures* (1958, trans as *The Car Cemetery*) life is seen as a used car dump, and in *Le grand cérémonial* and *Cérémonie pour un noir assassiné* (1965), ceremonial rites are used to play out sadistic fantasies. He writes in Spanish, his work being translated into French by his wife. In 1967 he was charged by a Spanish court with blasphemy and anti-patriotism, and his *Et ils passèrent des menottes aux fleurs* (And They Put Handcuffs on the Flowers, 1969), based on conversations with Spanish political prisoners, was eventually banned in France and Sweden while becoming his first major success in America in 1971. As well as his many plays he has published poetry—*Pierre de la folie* (1963) and 100 *sonnets* (1966)—and novels including *Baal Babylone* (1959) and *Fêtes et rites de la confusion* (1965).

ARRAN, Earl of See **HAMILTON**

ARRAU, Claudio (1903–) Chilean pianist, born in Chillán. After giving his first recital in Santiago aged five, his musical education was sponsored by the Chilean government. He studied at the Stern Conservatory, Berlin (1912–18), with the **Liszt** pupil Martin Krause (1853–1918). Arrau himself taught there from 1924 to 1940. He has appeared at all major concert halls and festivals throughout the world and is renowned as an interpreter of **Bach**, **Beethoven**, **Chopin**, **Schumann**, Liszt and **Brahms**. His musical thoughts were collected in *Conversations with Arrau* by **Joseph Horowitz** (1982).

ARREBO, Anders Christiensen (1587–1637) Danish clergyman, bishop of Trondheim (1618–22). He made his name as a translator of the Psalms (1623), but his greatest work was the *Hexaëmeron*, a monumental epic in the vernacular about the six days of creation.

ARRHENIUS, Svante (1859–1927) Swedish scientist, born near Uppsala. He became professor of physics at Stockholm in 1895, and a director of the Nobel Institute in 1905. He did valuable work in connection with the dissociation theory of electrolysis, and won the Nobel prize for chemistry in 1903.

ARRIAGA, Juan Crisóstomo (1806–26) Spanish composer. A child prodigy, his first opera, *Los esclavos felices*, was produced in 1820. He became assistant professor at the Paris Conservatoire in 1824. Although he died at the age of 20, his compositions show remarkable maturity, the symphony in D being reminiscent of **Beethoven**.

ARRIAGA, Manoel José de (1840–1917) Portuguese statesman. He took part in the revolution of 1910 which overthrew King **Manuel II**, and was the first elected president of the republic (1911–15).

ARRIAN, Latin **Flavius Arrianus** (c.95–180) Greek historian, a native of Nicomedia in Bithynia. An officer in the Roman army, in 136 he was appointed prefect of Cappadocia (legate in 131–37). He edited the *Encheiridion* (manual of philosophy) of his friend and mentor **Epictetus**, whose lectures (*Diatribai*) he wrote out in eight books. Only four have been preserved. His chief work, however, is the *Anabasis Alexandrou*, or history of the campaigns of **Alexander the Great**, which has survived almost entire. His accounts of the people of India, and of a voyage round the Euxine, are valuable for ancient geography.

ARROL, Sir William (1839–1913) Scottish engineer born of humble parentage in Houston, Renfrewshire. He got his first job in a thread mill as a cotton boy at the age of 10 by lying about his age, became an apprentice blacksmith at the age of 14, studied mechanics and hydraulics at night school, and started his own engineering business at the age of 29. In 1865 he made a railway viaduct at Greenock, constructed the second Tay Railway Bridge (1882–87) to replace the ill-fated bridge that collapsed in 1879, the Forth Railway Bridge (1883–90), and Tower Bridge in London (1886–94). He was an was MP from 1892 to 1906.

ARROW, Kenneth Joseph (1921–) American economist, born in New York. He graduated at Columbia University and was professor at Stanford University (1949–68) and Harvard (1968–79). In 1962 he served on the Council of Economic Advisers in the **Kennedy** administration. His primary field is the study of collective choice based on uncertainty and risk. His books include *Social Choices and Individual Values* (1951) and *The Future and the Present in Economic Life* (1978). He shared the 1972 Nobel prize for economics with Sir **John Hicks**.

ARROWSMITH, Aaron (1750–1823) English cartographer, born at Winston, Durham. In about 1770 he went to London, and by 1790 had established a great map-making business. His nephew, John (1790–1873), was also an eminent cartographer.

ARSACIDS a dynasty of Parthian kings, so called from the founder, Arsaces, who wrested a kingdom for himself from the grasp of the Seleucid **Antiochus II**, c.250 BC, which ultimately extended from Bactria to the Euphrates, and included Persia. Its greatest kings were Mithradates, Phraates, **Mithradates 'the Great'**, and Artabanus, who fell at Hormizdján in AD 226 attempting to stem the conquering career of **Artaxerxes** Ardashir, founder of the Sassanian dynasty of Persia.

ARSINOË (316–271 BC) Macedonian princess, daughter of **Ptolemy I**, and one of the most conspicuous of Hellenistic queens. She married first, about 300 BC the aged **Lysimachus**, king of Thrace, secondly (and briefly) Ptolemy Ceraunus, and finally, about 276, her own brother, **Ptolemy II Philadelphus**. Several cities were named after her.

ARSONVAL, Jacques-Arsène d' (1851–1940) French physicist, born in Borie. He was director of the laboratory of biological physics at the Collège de France from 1882, and professor from 1894. He invented the reflecting galvanometer named after him, and he also experimented with high-frequency oscillating current for electromedical purposes.

ARTACHAIES (fl.c.500 BC) Persian engineer in the service of **Xerxes**. He built military roads and bridges, and supervised the construction of a canal, wide enough for two warships to be rowed abreast, across the one and a half miles of the Athos peninsula in northern Greece.

ARTAUD, Antonin (1896–1948) French dramatist, actor, director and theorist, born in Marseilles. A Surrealist in the 1920s, he published a volume of verse (*L'Ombilic des limbes*, 1925), and in 1927 co-founded the Théâtre Alfred Jarry. He propounded a theatre that dispensed with narrative and psychological realism but which took as its base instead the mythology of the human mind: dreams and interior obsessions. The function of drama was to give expression, through movement and gesture, to the inexpressible locked within the conciousness. His main theoretical work is the book, *La Théâtre et son Double* (1938). As the creator of what has been termed the Theatre of Cruelty, his influence on post-war theatre was profound. A manic-depressive, his last years were spent in a mental institution.

ARTAXERXES, or **Ardashir** (d.242) founder of the new Persian dynasty of the Sassanids, overthrew Ardavan (Artabanus), the last of the Parthian kings in about AD 226. He next conquered Media and a large part of the Iranian highlands, murdered **Darius III**, but was defeated by **Alexander Severus** in 233.

ARTAXERXES I, called **Longimanus ('long-handed')** (5th century BC) king of Persia, the second son of **Xerxes I**, reigned from 464 to 425 BC. In a long and peaceful reign, he sanctioned Jewish religion in Jerusalem, and appointed **Nehemiah** governor of Judea in 445.

ARTAXERXES II, called **Mnemon ('the mindful')** (4th century BC) king of Persia, reigned from 404 to 358 BC. He lost control of Egypt, but rebuilt the royal palace at Susa.

ARTAXERXES III, called **Ochus** King of Persia, son of **Artaxerxes II**, found the empire disintegrating at his accession in 358 BC, but did much to build it up again. He was poisoned in 338 by his favourite eunuch, Bagoas.

ARTEDI, Peter (1705–35) Swedish ichthyologist and botanist, known as 'the father of ichthyology'. He wrote *Ichthyologia*, a very important systematic study of fishes, edited by **Linnaeus**, his closest friend, and published in 1738, after the author had drowned in an Amsterdam canal. He inspired Linnaeus in classification of animals and plants.

ARTEMISIA (352–50 BC) sister and wife of Mausolus, ruler of Caria, succeeded him on his death in c.353–352 BC and erected a magnificent mausoleum at Halicarnassus to his memory. It was one of the traditional seven wonders of the ancient world.

ARTEMISIA (5th century BC) ruler of Halicarnassus and neighbouring islands. She accompanied **Xerxes**, with five ships, in his expedition against Greece, and distinguished herself at Salamis, according to **Herodotus** (480 BC).

ARTEVELDE, Jacob van (1290–1345) Flemish statesman. A wealthy and highborn brewer of Ghent, he organized an alliance of Flemish towns in the conflict between France and England at the outbreak of the Hundred Years' War (1337–1473). Elected captain of Ghent in 1338, he ruled like an autocrat. He made a commercial treaty with **Edward III** of England to protect the Flemish weaving trade, and when Edward declared himself king of France in 1340, he insisted on Ghent making a treaty that accepted his sovereignty. In 1345 he proposed that **Edward the Black Prince** should be made Count of Flanders, but was assassinated in an ensuing riot. His son, Philip van Artevelde (1340–82) headed a Ghent revolt against the Count of Flanders in 1382, but was defeated and killed at the battle of Roosebeke.

ARTHUR (6th century) semi-legendary king of the Britons—and national hero. He may originally have been some Romano-British war leader in the west of England called *Arturus*; but he is represented as having united the British tribes against the invading Saxons, and as having been the champion not only of his people but of Christendom as well. He is said to have fought stubbornly against the invaders in a series of momentous battles, starting with a victory at 'Mount Baden' and ending with defeat and death at 'Camlan' 20 years later; after which he was buried at Glastonbury. The *Anglo-Saxon Chronicle* makes no mention of him, however; he first appears in Welsh chronicles long after the event. The story of Arthur blossomed into a huge literature, interwoven with legends of the Holy Grail and courtly ideas of a round table of knights at 'Camelot', in such writers as **Geoffrey of Monmouth**, **Chrétien de Troyes**, **Layamon**, and Sir **Thomas Malory**.

ARTHUR, Prince (1187–1203) Duke of Brittany, and claimant to the throne of England as the grandson of **Henry II**. He was the posthumous son of Geoffrey, Duke of Brittany, Henry's fourth son; and on the death of his uncle, **Richard I**, in 1199, Arthur was a claimant to the throne. There was no established English custom then as to whether the crown should pass to Arthur or to Richard's brother, **John**; but the French king, **Philip II**, upheld Arthur's claim until John came to terms with Philip in the Treaty of Le Goulet. Arthur was soon in his uncle's hands and was imprisoned, first at Calais and then at Rouen, where he died. It was popularly believed that King John was responsible either directly or indirectly for his death.

ARTHUR, Prince (1486–1502) the eldest son of **Henry VII**, born in Winchester. When he was still under two years old a marriage was arranged between him and **Catherine of Aragon** in order to provide an alliance between England and Spain. The wedding took place in November 1501, but Arthur, a sickly youth, died next April at Ludlow.

ARTHUR, Chester Alan (1830–86) 21st president of the USA, born in Fairfield, Vermont, the son of a Baptist minister from Antrim. He became the head of a very eminent law firm and leader of the Republican party in New York state. He was made vice president of the USA when **Garfield** became president in 1881; and, after Garfield's death, he was president from September 1881 to March 1885.

ARTHUR, Sir George (1785–1854) British diplomat, born near Plymouth. He was governor of British Honduras (1814–22), Van Diemen's Land (1823–36), Upper Canada (1837–41), and Bombay (1842–46).

ARTIN, Emil (1898–1962) Austrian mathematician, born in Vienna. He studied in Leipzig, and taught at Göttingen and Hamburg before emigrating to the USA in 1937, where he held posts at Indiana and Princeton before returning to Hamburg in 1958. His work was mainly in algebraic number theory and class field theory, and has had great influence on modern algebra.

ARTZYBASHEV, Boris (1899–1965) Russian-born American artist, born in Kharkov, son of **Mikhail Artzybashev**. He went to the USA in 1919, and illustrated books and magazine covers. His illustrations had a vivid and repetitive brilliance of pattern, reminiscent of the early Ballets Russes *décors*. He also wrote stories for children, based on Russian folklore.

ARTZYBASHEV, Mikhail Petrovich (1878–1927) Russian author. His liberalist novel *Sanin* (1907) had an international reputation at the turn of the century. It was translated by P Pinkerton in 1907, who also translated *Breaking Point* (1915), and with I Ohzol, *Tales of Revolution* (1918).

ARUNDEL, Thomas (1353–1413) English prelate and statesman, third son of Robert Fitzalan, Earl of Arundel. Chancellor of England from 1386 to 1396, he became archbishop of York in 1388 and archbishop of Canterbury in 1396. Banished by **Richard II** (1397), he returned from exile with **Henry IV** and crowned him in 1399. He became Chancellor again, and was a bitter opponent of the Lollards.

ARUNDEL AND SURREY, Earl of See **HOWARD**

ARUP, Sir Ove Nyquist (1895–1988) British civil engineer, born of Danish parents in Newcastle-upon-Tyne. He studied philosophy and engineering in Denmark before moving to London in 1923. He became increasingly concerned with the solution of structural problems in Modernist architecture, for example the Highpoint flats (1936–38) and the spiral reinforced concrete ramps of the penguin pool at Regent's Park Zoo (1934), both in London. He was responsible for the structural design of Coventry Cathedral (designed by Sir **Basil Spence**, 1962) and St Catherine's College, Oxford (**Arne Jacobsen**, 1964). More recently, with his partner Jack Zunz, he evolved the structural design which permitted the realization of Jørn Utzon's unique architectural conception of the Sydney Opera House (1956–73).

ASADA GORYU (1734–99) Japanese astronomer, born in Kizuki. He did much to turn Japanese astronomy and calendrical science away from Asiatic and towards Western models. He was self-taught in astronomy and medicine, but achieved recognition in both, and made a living from the latter. He improved astronomical instruments, but his best work was on the numerology of planetary distances and on the calendar.

ASAM, Cosmas Damian (1686–1739) and **Egid Quirin** (1649–1711) Bavarian architects and decorators, sons of the fresco painter Hans Georg Asam. They worked together, the former as a fresco painter and the latter as a sculptor. After training in Rome under **Carlo Fontana**, they developed to spectacular heights the baroque idea of combining architecture, sculpture, painting and lighting effects in church interiors to produce highly emotional decoration and melodramatic *tableau vivant* high altars. The most fantastic of these altars is that of the Abbey church at Weltenburg, in which the story of St George and the dragon is depicted by means of a shining silver knight riding out from a brilliantly lit archway to kill the dragon and rescue the princess.

ASBJÖRNSEN, Peter Christian (1812–85) Norwegian folklorist, born in Christiania (now Oslo). He studied at the university there, then for four years was a tutor in the country. In long journeys on foot he collected a rich store of popular poetry and folklore, and, with his lifelong friend **Jørgen Moe**, bishop of Christiansand, published the famous collection of Norwegian folk tales, *Norske Folkeeventyr* (1841–44), followed in 1845–48 by *Norske Huldreeventyr og Folkesagn* which he brought out alone. From 1856 to 1858 he studied forestry,and was appointed inspector of forests for the Trondheim district.

ASBURY, Francis (1745–1816) English-born American churchman, the first Methodist bishop in America, born in Handsworth, Staffordshire. In 1771 he was sent as a Methodist missionary to America. He founded the Methodist Episcopal Church in 1770, and in 1784 was consecrated as superintendent. In 1785 he assumed the title of bishop. He died in Richmond, Virginia.

ASCH, Sholem (1880–1957) Jewish writer, born in Kutno in Poland, emigrated to America in 1914 and became naturalized in 1920. His prolific output of novels and short stories, most of them originally in Yiddish but many since translated, includes *The Mother* (1930), *The War Goes On* (1936), *The Nazarene* (1939), *The Apostle* (1943), *East River* (1946) and *Moses* (1951). His early work includes the plays *Mottke the Thief* (1917) and *The God of Vengeance* (1918).

ASCHAM, Roger (1515–68) English humanist and scholar, born in Kirby Wiske near Thirsk, in Yorkshire. A graduate of St John's College, Cambridge, he became reader in Greek there, despite his avowed leaning to the Reformed doctrines (c.1538). In defence of archery he published, in 1545, *Toxophilus*, the pure English style of which ranks it among English classics. In 1546 he was appointed university orator. He was tutor to the Princess **Elizabeth** (1548–50), and later became Latin secretary to Queen **Mary I**. His prudence and moderation preserved him from offending by his Protestantism; and after Mary's death Elizabeth retained him at court as secretary and tutor. His principal work was *The Scholemaster*, a treatise on classical education, published in 1570.

ASCHE, John Stanger Heiss Oscar (1872–1936) Australian actor, playwright and theatrical manager, born in Geelong. He wrote *Chi Chin Chow* (1916), and managed the Adelphi Theatre, London (1904), and His Majesty's (1907).

ASCLEPIADES (fl. 1st century BC) Greek physician, born at Pruss in Bithynia. He seems to have been a peripatetic teacher of rhetoric before settling in Rome as a physician, where he advanced the doctrine that disease resulted from discord in the corpuscles of the body, and recommended good diet and exercise for cures.

ASCOLI, Graziadio Isaia (1829–1907) Italian philologist, born of Jewish parentage in Görz (Gorizio, in north Italy). He was appointed professor of philology in Milan in 1860, and is known mainly for his work on Italian dialectology, although he also made contributions to the fields of Indo-European, Celtic and Romance linguistics, in particular the 'substratum' theory, according to which certain features of the pronunciation of French, Provençal, and northern Italian dialects are attributable to Celtic speech habits causing modifications to the Latin spoken in these regions. He founded the *Archivio glottologico italiano* in 1873. He was created a senator in 1888.

ASELLI, Gasparo (1582–1626) Italian physician, the discoverer of the lacteal vessels of the intestine.

ASGILL, John (1659–1738) English pamphleteer, born at Hanley Castle, Worcestershire. He was called to the bar in 1692, but having got into financial difficulties, he sailed in 1699 for Ireland, where he established a lucrative practice; and in 1703 he obtained a seat in the Irish parliament. Three years before, however, he had published a paradoxical pamphlet to prove that by the rules of English law the redeemed need not die. Much to his surprise, the Irish parliament voted this a blasphemous libel and expelled him. In 1705 he returned to England, and became MP for Bramber in Sussex, but the fame of his unlucky pamphlet haunted him; the English House condemned it to be burned by the common hangman, and expelled Asgill in 1707. Ultimately he was imprisoned for debt in the Fleet, where he died.

ASH'ARI, al (873/874–935/936) Islamic theologian and philosopher, born in Basra. He studied with the sect of Mu'tazilites, with whom he broke in a crisis of confidence at the age of 40. In 915 he moved to Baghdad and associated for a while with disciples of Ibn Hanbal, but gradually evolved his own theology and gathered around him his own school of followers. His major work is *Maqalat*, and he was particularly concerned to defend the idea of God's omnipotence and to reaffirm traditional interpretations of religious authority within Islam.

ASHBEE, Charles Robert (1863–1942) English designer, architect and writer, born in Isleworth. Educated at King's College, Cambridge, he was much influenced by the work and thinking of **William Morris** and **John Ruskin**. He founded the Essex House Press and the London Survey, and was founder and director of the Guild of Handicraft (1888–1908) in London's East End (later in Gloucestershire), employing over 100 craftworkers, the largest-scale attempt to put into practice the ideals of the Arts and Crafts movement. As an architect he specialized in church restoration, and his publications include *The Book of Cottages and Little Houses* (1906). He was also a noted silversmith.

ASHBERY, John Lawrence (1927–) American poet, critic and novelist, born in Rochester, New York the son of a farmer. Since attending Harvard, where he became close friends with the poets Kenneth Koch and Frank O'Hara, he has been associated with the 'New York' school. He published his first volume, a chapbook, *Turandot and Other Poems*, in 1953 but it was not until the publication of *Some Trees* in 1956 that he began to attract critical attention. Influenced by **Auden**, he attracts ardent admiration and bemused antipathy in almost equal measure, some relishing his identification with abstract Expressionist painters, others finding him wilfully obscure. His reputation is international and in 1976 his twelfth collection, *Self-Portrait in a Convex Mirror*, won the National Book Critics Circle prize, the National Book Award for poetry, and the Pulitzer prize for poetry. Other volumes include *The Tennis Court Oath* (1962), *Rivers and Mountains* (1966), *Houseboat Days* (1977) and *Shadow Train* (1982). His only novel is *A Nest of Ninnies* (1969), co-authored with James Schuyler.

ASHBOURNE, Edward Gibson, 1st Baron (1837–1913) Lord Chancellor of Ireland, born in Dublin. Educated at Trinity College, Dublin he was called to the Irish bar in 1860. Entering parliament in 1872, he rose through various posts in successive Conservative administrations to the chancellorship (1885, 1886, 1895), carrying (1885) a measure facilitating the purchasing clauses of the Land Act.

ASHBURTON See **BARING, Alexander, Ist Baron**

ASHBY, Sir Eric (1904–) British-born Australian botanist and educator, born in London. Educated at London and Chicago universities, he was appointed professor of botany at Sydney University in 1938. From 1947 to 1950 he held the chair of botany at Manchester University, where he was also director of the botanical laboratories. He became president and vice-chancellor of Queen's University, Belfast (1950–59) and vice-chancellor of Cambridge University (1967–69). Throughout his long career as educator and administrator, he was deeply involved in experimental biology and environmental matters, publishing numerous books and papers on these subjects. He chaired the Royal Commission on Environmental Pollution (1970–73) and was knighted in 1956. He was created a life peer as Baron Ashby of Brandon, Suffolk, in 1973.

ASHCROFT, Dame Peggy, properly **Edith Margaret Emily** (1907–) English actress, born in London. She first appeared on the stage with the Birmingham Repertory Company in 1928, and scored a great success in London in *Jew Süss* in 1929. In 1920 she played Desdemona to **Paul Robeson**'s Othello, and acted leading parts at the Old Vic in the season of 1932–33.

In Sir **John Gielgud**'s production of *Romeo and Juliet* (1935), she was a memorable Juliet. She has worked both in films and on the British and American stage, and was created DBE in 1956.

ASHDOWN, Jeremy John Durham (Paddy) (1941–) English politician. After a childhood and youth spent in India and Ulster, he joined the Royal Marines when his parents emigrated to Australia. Serving in the special boat squadron (the navy's equivalent of the SAS), in Malaysia and Northern Ireland, he also acquired a first class degree in Mandarin at Hong Kong University. After five years in the diplomatic service, in 1976 he moved to his wife's home in Yeovil to enter politics as the potential Liberal candidate. He overturned a large Conservative majority and entered the House of Commons in 1983. In 1988 he was a clear winner in the leadership election for the new Liberal and Social Democratic party.

ASHE, Arthur Robert Jr. (1943–) American tennis player, born in Richmond, Virginia, the first male black tennis player to achieve world ranking. After studying at the University of California at Los Angeles on a tennis scholarship he was selected for the US Davis Cup side in 1963. He won the US national singles championship in 1968 and the first US Open championship later the same year. He turned professional in 1969 and pursued a highly successful career, winning Wimbledon in 1975 when he defeated **Jimmy Connors**. After his retiral from playing he was for some time in charge of the American Davis Cup squad.

ASHKENAZY, Vladimir (1937–) Russian pianist and conductor, born in Gorky. He graduated from Moscow Conservatory (1960) and in 1962 was joint winner (with **John Ogdon**) of the Tchaikovsky Piano Competition, Moscow. He left the Soviet Union in 1963 and made his London début that year. He settled in Iceland in 1973 with his wife, an Icelandic pianist. He became musical director of the Royal Philharmonic Orchestra in 1987.

ASHLEY, Laura née **Laura Mountney** (1925–85) Welsh fashion designer, born in Merthyr Tydfil. She married Bernard Ashley in 1949 and they started up in business together four years later, manufacturing furnishing materials and wallpapers with patterns and motifs based upon document sources mainly from the 19th century. When she gave up work to have a baby she experimented with designing and making clothes, and this transformed the business from one small shop to an international chain of boutiques selling clothes, furnishing fabrics and wallpapers. Ashley Mountney Ltd became Laura Ashley Ltd in 1968, and her work continued to be characterized by a romantic style and the use of natural fabrics, especially cotton.

ASHLEY, Lord See **SHAFTESBURY**

ASHMOLE, Elias (1617–92) English antiquary, born in Lichfield. He qualified as a lawyer in 1638 and subsequently combined work for the royalist cause with the study of mathematics, natural philosophy, astronomy, astrology and alchemy, entering Brasenose College, Oxford. In 1646 he became acquainted with **William Lilly** and other famous astrologers; and in 1650 he edited a work of the astrologer **John Dee** to which he added a treatise of his own. In 1652 he issued his *Theatrum Chymicum*, and in 1672 his major work, a *History of the Order of the Garter*. After the Restoration he mainly devoted himself to heraldic and antiquarian studies. In 1677 he presented to the University of Oxford a fine collection of rarities, bequeathed him by his friend **John Tradescant**, thus founding the Ashmolean Museum (built in 1682). Among his other friends were **John Selden** and **William Dugdale** whose daughter became his third wife.

ASHMUN, Jehudi (1794–1828) American philanthropist, born in Champlain, New York, the founder in 1822 of the colony of Liberia for liberated negroes on the west coast of Africa.

ASHTON, Sir Frederick William Mallandaine (1904–88) English choreographer, born in Guayaquil, Ecuador. He was brought up in Peru where he saw **Pavlova** dance. Following education at an English public school, he had a brief career in the City, during which time he took ballet classes with **Léonide Massine** in secret. He continued his studies with **Marie Rambert** who commissioned his first piece, *A Tragedy of Fashion* (1926). After a year dancing under the direction of **Bronislava Nijinska** in America, he returned to Britain to help found the Ballet Club, which later became Ballet Rambert (now Rambert Dance Company). During this time he partnered and created roles for dancers like **Alicia Markova**. After several freelance commissions from the Vic Wells Ballet, he joined full time in 1935 as dancer/choreographer. Though his work was punctuated with forays abroad and commissions for other companies, he remained there as the company developed into the Royal Ballet. In 1948 he was officially recognized as one of the company's artistic directors and in 1963 he succeeded Dame **Ninette de Valois** as director of the company, a post he held for seven years. Applauded as Britain's best-loved and most gifted choreographer, he was awarded a CBE in 1950, knighted in 1962, and given many other honours around the world. His work has been called the 'backbone of the Royal Ballet', and includes *La Fille Mal gardee* (1960), *Marguérite and Armand* (1963, for which he teamed **Rudolf Nureyev** and **Margot Fonteyn**), *The Dream* (1964), *A Month in the Country* (1979), *Monotones* (1965), *Five Brahms Waltzes in the Manner of Isadora Duncan* (1979, created for **Lynn Seymour**) and *Rhapsody* (1980). He also worked in film, for *The Tales of Beatrix Potter* (1971), and opera—creating the dances in **Benjamin Britten**'s *Death in Venice* (1973).

ASHTON, Sir John William (Will) (1881–1963) English-born Australian landscape painter, born in York. His family moved to Adelaide, South Australia, when he was aged three. In 1899 he returned to England and studied in the artists' colony at St Ives, Cornwall, notably under Talmadge. He exhibited widely in London, at the Royal Academy and private galleries, and at the Paris Salon. He quickly established a fine reputation as a landscape artist, especially for his bridges of the Seine and other French and Mediterranean subjects, and was a leading opponent of modern trends in painting.

ASHTON, Julian Rossi (1851–1942) English-born Australian painter and teacher, born in Alderstone, Surrey. He studied art part time while working in the engineers' office of the Great Eastern Railway. In 1878 he emigrated to Australia at the invitation of David Syme and, while working as an illustrator for Syme's Melbourne newspaper *The Age*, covered the capture of the **Ned Kelly** gang. He later moved to Sydney and in 1896 founded the Sydney Art School. While his landscapes, figure groups and portraits were workmanlike, he is best known for his influence on later Australian artists including **George Lambert**, Sydney Long, **Elioth Gruner** and **William Dobell**. He organized the Grafton Gallery (London) exhibition of Australian art in 1898, and worked strenuously for the recognition of Australian artists.

ASHTON, Winifred See **DANE, Clemence**

ASHURBANIPAL See **SARDANAPALUS**

ASIMOV, Isaac (1920–) Russian-born American novelist, versifier, critic and popular scientist. Born in Petrovichi, he was brought to the USA when he was three. He took a PhD in chemistry at Columbia University and his career as an academic biochemist is as distinguished as that as a science fiction writer. His best work was written when both he and science fiction were younger. In a prodigious body of work the titles that stand out include the 'Foundation' novels—*Foundation* (1951), *Foundation and Empire* (1952) and *Second Foundation* (1953); the so-called 'Robot' novels —*The Caves of Steel* (1954) and *The Naked Sun* (1957), and the short stories which form the collection *I, Robot* (1950). He has become synonymous with science fiction and he is ubiquitous on television and on the lecturing circuit as well as being an untiring contributor to newspapers and magazines. Increasingly regarded as a scientific seer, he added the term 'robotics' to the language.

ASINUS See **POLLIO**

ASKE, Robert (d.1537) English rebel. A Yorkshire attorney at Gray's Inn, he headed the Catholic rising known as the Pilgrimage of Grace in protest at **Henry VIII**'s dissolution of the monasteries. He was subsequently hanged in York for treason, despite having been assured of his personal safety.

ASKEW, Anne (1521–46) English Protestant martyr, born of gentle parentage near Grimsby. Early embracing the Reformed doctrines, she was turned out of doors by her husband, and thereupon went up to London to sue for a separation; but in 1545 she was arrested on a charge of heresy. After examination and torture by the rack, she was burned in Smithfield.

ASKEY, Arthur (1900–82) English comedian, born in Liverpool. A small man (he stood only 5′ 2″ high), he made his professional début in 1924. He became leading comedian in summer seasons at British seaside resorts, and achieved wide recognition on radio with *Band Wagon* (1938), and became known as 'Big-hearted Arthur'. He had a button-holing style, a cheery manner, a harmless humour, and made a catchphrase of 'I thank you!'. He appeared regularly on television, and in several films.

ASKIYA the dynastic title of the rulers of Songhai, founded by *Sunni* Ali (ruled 1464–92) out of the disintegrating empire of Mali in Western Africa. The first *askiya*, Muhammad Toure (d.1528), deposed Sunni Ali's successor c.1500 and extended the empire into Easter Mali and the upper Volta basin. He also re-established Timbuktu as a centre of Islamic faith and learning. He was deposed by his son in 1528 and Songhai went into decline. The empire dissolved altogether in 1591, when it was invaded by a Moroccan army, but descendants of the Songhai *askiyas* continued to fight on against their Moroccan rulers well into the 17th century.

AŚOKA (3rd century BC) king of India c.264–223 BC. A convert to Buddhism, he organized it as the state religion.

ASPASIA (5th century BC) Greek adventuress, born in Miletus, the mistress of **Pericles** after his separation from his Athenian wife. Intellectual and vivacious, she was lampooned in Greek comedy and satire, but was held in high regard by **Socrates** and his followers, and was a great inspiration to Pericles, who successfully defended her against a charge of impiety. After his death she lived with Lysicles, a cattle dealer who had risen to power and influence.

ASPDIN, Joseph (1779–1855) English brick-layer and inventor, born in Leeds. A stonemason to trade, like many others he engaged in the search for an artificial cement in an effort to reduce the building industry's dependence on increasingly scarce and expensive timber. In 1824 he patented what he called Portland cement, manufactured from clay and limestone, a hydraulic cement which would set hard even under water.

ASPINALL, Sir John Audley Frederick (1851–1937) English mechanical engineer, born in Liverpool. He rose from locomotive fireman to be chief mechanical engineer and general manager of the Lancashire and Yorkshire Railway (1899–1919). He designed many types of locomotives and completed one of the first main-line railway electrification schemes in Britain from Liverpool to Southport in 1904.

ASPLUND, Erik Gunnar (1885–1940) Swedish architect, born in Stockholm. He designed the Stockholm City Library (1924–27), and he was responsible for most of the buildings in the Stockholm Exhibition of 1930. Their design was acclaimed for the new gaiety and imagination with which the architect used simple modern forms and methods, eg, the cantilever and glass walls. His other works in Stockholm included the Woodland Chapel, Skandia Cinema, City Library and Woodland Crematorium, and the law courts in Göteborg (1934–37).

ASQUITH, Herbert Henry, 1st Earl of Oxford and Asquith (1852–1928) British Liberal statesman, born in Morley, Yorkshire, and educated at City of London School and Balliol College, Oxford. He was called to the bar in 1876 and was Liberal member for East Fife 1886–1918. He became home secretary (1892–95) and upset many of his fellow Liberals by his support for the anti-Boer imperialists during the South African War, 1899–1902. Despite this, he became Chancellor of the Exchequer (1905–08) and succeeded **Campbell-Bannerman** as prime minister in April 1908. The social reforms in the early years of his administration were overshadowed by a clash with the Lords over the 'People's Budget', of 1909, resulting in a restriction of their powers in the Parliament Act 1911. Asquith was also confronted by the suffragette movement, industrial strife, the threat of civil war over Home Rule for Ireland and the international crises which led to World War I. In May 1915 he formed and headed a war coalition but was ousted in December 1916 by supporters of **Lloyd George** and some Conservatives who thought his conduct of the war was not sufficiently vigorous. He lost his East Fife seat in 1918 and then returned to the Commons as member for Paisley in 1920. His disagreements with Lloyd George weakened the Liberal party and, although he was recognized as leader again between 1923 and 1926, the Liberals failed to regain their earlier position as the main opposition to the Conservatives. He was created an earl in 1925. He wrote his *Memories and Reflections* (1928). His second wife Margot (1865–1945), daughter of Sir Charles Tennant, wrote a lively *Autobiography* (1922; rev ed 1962). Of the five children of his first marriage, Raymond (1878–1916), his brilliant eldest son, was killed in action; Herbert (1881–1947) was a poet; Cyril (1890–1945) became a lord of appeal in ordinary; and for his elder daughter, see **Bonham-Carter**. Of the two children of his second marriage, Elizabeth (d.1945) married Prince Antoine Bibesco in 1919, and wrote lively novels; and Anthony (1902–68) was a notable film director, whose works included *Pygmalion*, *The Browning Version*, *The Way to the Stars* and *Orders to Kill*.

ASSAD, Hafez al- (1930–) Syrian statesman, born in Qardaha, near Latakia in north west Syria, into a peasant family of nine children. He changed his family name of Wahsh, meaning boar in Arabic, to his present one, meaning lion. After local schooling he joined the

Ba'ath party at 16 and embarked on a military career, training as an airman and was then sent to the Soviet Union for further studies. On his return to what was then the United Arab Republic of Egypt and Syria he commanded a night fighter squadron based in Cairo from 1958 to 1961, when the union with Egypt was dissolved and Syria became an independent republic. In 1966 Salah Jadid, secretary of the Ba'ath party, seized power and Assad was made minister of defence and air force chief, from which positions he built up a strong personal power base. When Jadid ordered Syrian forces into Jordan to fight King **Hussein** Assad refused to commit his aircraft, saying he would never fight another Arab country. The army returned in defeat, Jadid was disgraced and Assad assumed ultimate power in a bloodless coup. Since then he has followed a policy of strengthening his nation and relentlessly opposing Israel. He has held power with a determined ruthlessness, despite suffering a heart attack in 1983. An austere, private man, he has few close contacts outside his family, of wife, daughter and four sons, his only extravagance reputedly being a liking for large, luxurious cars. He is generally regarded as the most skilful politician in the Middle East but his relations with the West have been damaged by a reputation for complicity in terrorist activity, which he has always denied. Relationships have, however, been partially mended since 1987, when, following a meeting with US ex-president **Jimmy Carter**, Assad has been working actively to secure the release of Western hostages in Lebanon. His future, and that of his country, will now depend on how successful he is in maintaining a pivotal position in the region, through an uneasy alliance with Iran, the challenge of Iraq, freed from its war commitments, and the seemingly insoluble problem of securing peace in Lebanon.

ASSELYN, Jan (1610–52) Dutch painter, born in Amsterdam. He travelled to Italy and became a successful painter of Italianate landscapes which depict imaginary Arcadian vistas inspired by the Roman countryside. In this, and in his interest in subtle lighting effects, he was influenced by the major landscape painter of his day, **Claude Lorraine**. By the inclusion of Roman ruins in the landscape, his work often has a romantic quality and, although he was not the most adventurous of Dutch landscapists, his compositions are highly accomplished. His likeness is known from an etching by his friend **Rembrandt**.

ASSEMANI, Joseph Simon (1687–1768) Syrian Maronite orientalist, born in Tripoli. He became keeper of the Vatican Library; he collected oriental manuscripts.

ASSER (8th century) Welsh scholar and bishop, and counsellor to **Alfred the Great**, king of Wessex. He spent his youth in the monastic community at St David's. Gaining a reputation for scholarship he was enlisted into the royal service by Alfred, and from c.885 divided his year between the court and St David's. The King's growing reliance on him resulted in Asser being made bishop of Sherborne in 901 shortly before the king died. He is best known for his unfinished Latin biography of King Alfred, first published in 1572.

ASSER, Tobias Michael Carel (1838–1913) Dutch jurist. A professor at Amsterdam, he began the *Revue de droit International et de Législation comparé* in 1869 and was a founder of the Institute of International Law in 1873. He persuaded the Dutch government to call the first Hague Conference for the unification of International Private Law in 1893 and was awarded (jointly with the Austrian pacifist Alfred Fried) the Nobel peace prize in 1911 for his work in creating the Permanent Court of Arbitration at the Hague Peace Conference of 1899.

ASSURBANIPAL See **SARDANAPALUS**

ASTAIRE, Fred (Frederick), originally **Austerlitz** (1899–1987) American dancer, singer and actor, born in Omaha, Nebraska. Encouraged to take dance lessons from the age of five, he was teamed with his elder sister Adele as a touring vaudeville act, rising to stardom with her in the 1920s on Broadway in specially written shows like *Lady Be Good* and *Funny Face*. When Adele married Lord Charles Cavendish in 1932 the dancing partnership was dissolved, and Fred went to Hollywood. There, with a new partner Ginger Rogers and choreographer Hermes Pan, he revolutionized the film musical with a succession of original and innovative dance-tap routines in films like *The Gay Divorcée* (1934), *Top Hat* (1935) and *Swing Time* (1936). A hardworking perfectionist who made his dancing appear effortless, he was noted for his debonair charm and gracefulness. He announced his retirement in 1946, but returned to create further classic musicals like *Easter Parade* (1948), and *The Bandwaggon* (1953), then turned to straight acting, winning an Academy Award nomination for *The Towering Inferno* (1974) and an Emmy for *A Family Upside Down* (1978). He received a special Academy Award in 1949 for his 'unique artistry and contributions to the technique of musical pictures', and published his autobiography *Steps in Time* in 1960.

ASTBURY, William Thomas (1889–1961) English X-ray crystallographer, born in Longton. He studied at Cambridge and with Sir **William Henry Bragg**'s team at University College London, and from 1945 held the new chair of biomolecular structure at Leeds. In 1926, acting on a suggestion by Bragg, he began to take X-ray diffraction photographs using, not a crystal, but a fibre of hair, wool, horn or other natural proteins. Using the photographic techniques he had done much to develop, he showed that diffraction patterns (albeit diffuse and unclear) could be obtained; and that they changed when the fibre was stretched, or wet. His detailed conclusions on structure were wrong, but his pioneer work on protein fibres laid a basis on which others (notably **Linus Pauling**) were to find success. Astbury probably coined the phase 'molecular biology'; and with Florence Bell in 1938 he offered the first hypothetical structure for the key genetic material DNA; again, it was premature in terms of available techniques, and wrong; but later work by **J D Watson** and **F H C Crick** was brilliantly successful.

ASTELL, Mary (1668–1731) English religious writer, born in Newcastle, daughter of a merchant. She lived in Chelsea, and in 1694 proposed an Anglican sisterhood with an academic bias, which was strongly criticized by Bishop **Gilbert Burnet** and did not materialize.

ASTLEY, Philip (1742–1814) English theatrical manager, equestrian, and the best horse-tamer of his time. In 1770 he started a circus at Lambeth, and built Astley's Amphitheatre (1798), once one of the sights of London. He also established amphitheatres in Paris and several other venues in Europe.

ASTON, Francis William (1877–1945) English physicist, born in Birmingham. Educated at Malvern and at Birmingham and Cambridge, he was noted for his work on isotopes. He invented the mass spectrograph in 1919, with which he investigated the isotopic structures of elements and for which he won the Nobel prize for chemistry in 1922. The Aston dark space, in electronic discharges, is named after him.

ASTOR, John Jacob (1763–1848) German-born American fur trader and financier, founder of the

America Fur company and a noted family of financiers, born in Walldorf, near Heidelberg. He helped on his father's farm until, in his sixteenth year, he went to London and worked with his brother, a maker of musical instruments. In 1784 he sailed to the USA and invested his small capital in a fur business in New York. He founded the settlement of Astoria in 1811. He became one of the most powerful financiers in the USA, and at his death left about 20 million dollars, and a legacy of $350000 to found a public library in New York.

ASTOR, John Jacob (1864–1912) American financier, a great-grandson of **John Jacob Astor** (1763–1848). He served in the Spanish-American war, and built part of the Waldorf-Astoria hotel in New York. He was drowned with the *Titanic*.

ASTOR, John Jacob, 1st Baron Astor of Hever (1886–1971) British newspaper proprietor, son of William Waldorf, 1st Viscount Astor. Educated at Eton and New College, Oxford he was aide-de-camp to the viceroy of India (1911–14), was elected MP for Dover in 1922, and became chairman of the Times Publishing Company after the death of Lord **Northcliffe**, resigning his directorship in 1962. His eldest son Gavin (1918–84) succeeded him as chairman from 1959 to 1966, when *The Times* was taken over by Lord Thompson of Fleet.

ASTOR, Mary, originally **Lucille Langhanke** (1906–87) American film actress, born in Quincy, Illinois. Strongly encouraged by her father, she made her film début in *The Beggar Maid* (1921) and was soon established as beautiful, innocent ingénues in historical dramas like *Beau Brummell* (1924, with **John Barrymore**) and *Don Juan* (1926, with **Douglas Fairbanks**). An intelligent, prolific actress, she carved a special niche as bitchy women of the world, winning an Academy Award for *The Great Lie* (1941, with **Bette Davis**); but her range also included the duplicitous femme fatale of *The Maltese Falcon* (1941), carefree comedy in *The Palm Beach Story* (1942) and tender drama in *Dodsworth* (1936). A court case in 1936 for custody of her daughter brought press revelations of a scandalous private life and she later had to cope with alcoholism. Under contract to M-G-M, she moved into her 'Mothers for Metro' phase playing warm-hearted matriarchs, most memorably in *Meet Me in St. Louis* (1944), but still making the most of meaty roles in films like *Act of Violence* (1948) and *Return to Peyton Place* (1961). Active on stage and television, she retired after *Hush, Hush Sweet Charlotte* (1964) and turned her hand to writing novels and autobiography, including *A Life on Film* (1971).

ASTOR, Nancy Witcher Langhorne, Viscountess (1879–1964) American-born British politician, born in Danville, Virginia, the daughter of a wealthy tobacco auctioneer. Wife of **William Waldorf Astor** (1879–1952) she succeeded her husband as Conservative MP for Plymouth in 1919, and was the first woman to take a seat in the House of Commons. She was known for her interest in social problems especially temperance and women's rights.

ASTOR, William Backhouse (1792–1875) American financier, elder son of **John Jacob Astor**, born in New York. He augmented his inherited wealth and is said to have left 50 million dollars. He added to his father's library bequest, and on account of his great property interests was known as the 'landlord of New York'.

ASTOR, William Waldorf, 1st Viscount Astor (1848–1919) American-born British newspaper proprietor, born in New York, great-grandson of the fur magnate **John Jacob Astor** (1763–1848). Defeated in the election for governor of New York State (1881), he was US minister to Italy (1882–85). He emigrated to Britain in 1892 and bought the *Pall Mall Gazette* and *Pall Mall Magazine*. Naturalized in 1899, he bought *The Observer* in 1911, and was made a viscount in 1917.

ASTOR, William Waldorf, 2nd Viscount Astor (1879–1952) English politician, son of 1st Viscount **Astor**, educated at Eton and New College, Oxford, was elected MP for Plymouth in 1910. On passing to the House of Lords in 1919 he became parliamentary secretary to the local governmernt board (subsequently ministry of health) and his wife, **Nancy Astor**, succeeded him in the lower house. He was proprietor of the *Observer*.

ASTOR, William Waldorf, 3rd Viscount Astor (1907–66) English politician, son of 2nd Viscount **Astor**. Educated at Eton and New College, Oxford, he sat as MP for East Fulham (1935–45) and for Wycombe (1951–52).

ASTORGA, Emanuele d', Baron (c.1680–1757) Italian composer, born in Agosta, Sicily. A wanderer all his life, he composed numerous chamber cantatas and some operas, but is best known for his *Stabat-Mater* (1707).

ASTRUC, Jean (1684–1766) French physician and biblical scholar, medical consultant to King **Louis XV**, born in Sauve. He wrote a work on **Moses** which laid the foundations for modern criticism of the Pentateuch, as well as volumes on the diseases of women and on venereal disease.

ASTURIAS, Miguel Angel (1899–1974) Guatemalan fiction writer and poet. A law graduate from the National University, he spent many years in exile, particularly in Paris, where he studied anthropology and translated the Mayan sacred book *Popul Vuh*, written in the Quiche language, into Spanish. This was to have an enduring influence on his fiction, though his most successful novel, *The President* (1963), reveals the Indian mythical influences only obliquely. Other books included *Men of Maize* (*Hombres de maiz*, 1949) and a trilogy on the foreign exploitation of the banana trade. A difficult, experimental and ambitious writer, he flirted with 'automatic writing' and was rewarded with the Nobel prize for literature in 1967. In the Guatemalan civil service from 1946, he was ambassador to France, 1966–70.

ASTYAGES (6th century BC) son of Cyaxares and the last king of Media. He ruled from 584 BC until 550 when he was dethroned by **Cyrus the Great**.

ATAHUALPA (d.1533) the last Inca ruler of Peru. On the death of his father Huayna-Capac he received the northern half of the Inca empire with its capital at Quito and in 1532 overthrew his brother, Huascar, who ruled the southern half from Cuzco. However, a year later he was captured by a force of invading Spaniards under **Francisco Pizarro** who proceeded to conquer Peru. Although his subjects paid a vast ransom to secure his release, Atahualpa was condemned for treason and strangled.

ATANASOFF, John Vincent (1903–) American physicist and computer pioneer, born in Hamilton, New York. He was educated at the University of Florida, Iowa State College, and the University of Wisconsin (PhD, physics, 1930). In 1942, with the help of Clifford Berry, he built an electronic calculating machine—the ABC (Atanasoff-Berry-Computer)—one of the first calculating devices utilizing vacuum tubes. Its design influenced other computer pioneers.

ATATÜRK See **MUSTAFA KEMAL ATATÜRK**

ATHALIAH (d.837 BC) daughter of **Ahab** and **Jezebel**, and wife of Jehoram, king of Judah. She secured the throne of Judah to herself after the death

(843 BC) of her son, Ahaziah, at the hands of **Jehu**, by the slaughter of all the royal children save Ahaziah's son Joash. Her support of Baal-worship led, after six years, to an insurrection headed by the priests; Joash was made king, and Athaliah put to death. Her fate is the subject of a play by **Racine**, to which **Mendelssohn** added incidental music.

ATHANARIC (d.381) a prince of the western Goths who fought three campaigns against the emperor Valens, brother of the emperor **Valentinian I**, he was finally defeated in 369 and, driven by the Huns from the north of the Danube, died at Constantinople.

ATHANASIUS, St (c.296–373) Greek Christian theologian and prelate, born in Alexandria. In his youth he often visited the celebrated hermit St **Antony**, and himself for a time embraced an anchorite's life. He was only a deacon when he distinguished himself at the great Council of Nicaea or Nice in 325. In 326 he was chosen patriarch of Alexandria and primate of Egypt, and was newly installed when **Arius**, banished on the condemnation of his doctrine at Nicaea, was recalled, and recanted. Athanasius refused to comply with the will of Emperor **Constantine** that the heretic should be restored to communion. Hence, and on other charges brought by the Arians, he was summoned by the emperor to appear before the synod of Tyre, in 335, which deposed him. The sentence was confirmed by the synod of Jerusalem in 336, when he was banished to Trèves. In 338 he was restored; but in 341 he was again condemned by a council of 97 (mainly Arian) bishops in Antioch. Orthodox synods in Alexandria and in Sardica protested in his favour, and he was again replaced in his office (349). Under the Arian emperor **Constantius**, he was again condemned and forcibly expelled, whereupon he retired to a remote desert in Upper Egypt. Under **Julian** 'the Apostate', toleration was proclaimed to all religions, and Athanasius became once more Patriarch of Alexandria (361). His next controversy was with the heathen subjects of Julian, by whom he was compelled again to flee from Alexandria, and he hid in the Theban desert until 363, when Jovian ascended the throne. After holding office for a short time he was expelled again by the Arians under the emperor Valens who, after petitions from the orthodox Alexandrians, soon restored the patriarch to his see, in which he continued till his death. Athanasius was the great leader during the most trying period in the history of the early Christian church. His conscientiousness, his wisdom, his fearlessness, his commanding intellect, his activity and patience, all mark him out as an ornament of his age. His writings, polemical, historical, and moral, are simple, cogent, and clear. The polemical works treat chiefly of the Trinity, the Incarnation and the divinity of the Holy Spirit. The so-called *Athanasian Creed* (representing Athanasian beliefs) was little heard of until the 7th century.

ATHELING See **EDGAR THE ÆTHELING**

ATHELSTAN (c.895–939) Anglo-Saxon king, grandson of **Alfred the Great**. He was the son of **Edward the Elder**, whom he succeeded as king of Wessex and Mercia in 924; he was crowned at Kingston-upon-Thames in 925. A warrior king of outstanding ability, he extended his rule over parts of Cornwall and Wales, and kept Norse-held Northumbria under control. In 937 he defeated a confederation of Scots, Welsh and Vikings from Ireland in a major battle at some place called *Brunanburh*, and his fame spread far afield. He fostered Haakon, the son of king **Harald I, 'Fine-Hair'** of Norway (the future Haakon I Haraldsson); one of his sisters married the emperor **Otto I**; another married Hugh the White, Duke of the Franks, father of **Hugh Capet**, king of France. At home, Athelstan improved the laws, built monasteries, and promoted commerce.

ATHENAEUS (2nd century) Greek writer, born in Naucratis in Egypt. He lived first in Alexandria and later in Rome about the close of the 2nd century. He wrote *Deipnosophistae* ('Banquet of the Learned'), a collection of anecdotes and excerpts from ancient authors reproduced as dinner-table conversations. Of the 15 books, only the first two and parts of the third, are extant.

ATHENAIS See **EUDOCIA**

ATHERTON, Gertrude Franklin, née **Horn** (1857–1948) American novelist, born in San Francisco. Left a widow in 1887, she travelled extensively, living in Europe most of her life and using the places she visited as backgrounds for her novels—which range from ancient Greece to California and the West Indies. She was made Chevalier of the Legion of Honour for her relief work during World War I and in 1934 became president of the American National Academy of Literature. The most popular of her many novels are *The Conqueror* (1902), a fictional biography of **Alexander Hamilton**, and *Black Oxen* (1923), which is concerned with the possibility of rejuvenation.

ATHOLL, Katherine Marjory, Duchess of (1874–1960) Scottish Conservative politician, born in Banff, Perthshire, daughter of historian Sir James Ramsay. Educated at Wimbledon High School and the Royal College of Music, she was an accomplished pianist and composer. In 1899 she married the future 8th Duke of Atholl, becoming Duchess of Atholl in 1917. During the Boer War and World War I she organized concerts for the troops abroad and helped in hospital work. An early opponent of women's suffrage, she became MP for Kinross and Perthshire in 1923; from 1924 to 1929 she was the first Conservative woman minister as parliamentary secretary to the board of education. She successfully resisted changes in policy which would have adversely affected the education of poorer children, and from 1929 to 1939 campaigned against ill-treatment of women and children in the British Empire. She was responsible for translating an unexpurgated edition of *Mein Kampf* to warn of **Hitler**'s intentions. On principle she opposed Britain's policy of imagining a collective European policy of 'non-intervention' in the Spanish Civil War, while not advocating British assistance to the Spanish Republic. She published the best-selling *Searchlight on Spain* in 1938. She opposed the Munich agreement, and was dropped as Tory candidate, resigned her seat in parliament and was defeated in the resultant by-election where she was lampooned as the 'Red Duchess'. From 1939 to 1960 she worked to aid refugees from totalitarianism. Other publications include *Women and Politics* (1931).

ATIYAH, Sir Michael Francis (1929–) English mathematician, born in London. Educated in Egypt and at Manchester Grammar School, he graduated from Trinity College, Cambridge (1952). After lecturing in Cambridge and Oxford he became Savilian professor at Oxford (1963–69), and in 1966 was awarded the Fields Medal (the mathematical equivalent of the Nobel prize). After three years at Princeton, he returned to Oxford as Royal Society Research professor in 1973. One of the most distinguished British mathematicians of his time, he has worked on algebraic geometry, algebraic topology, index theory of differential operators, and most recently on the mathematics of quantum field theory, where he has been particularly concerned with bridging the gap between mathematicians and physicists.

ATKIN, James Richard, Lord, of Aberdovey (1867–1944) English judge, born in Brisbane, Australia. Educated at Christ College, Brecon, and Magdalen College, Oxford, he established himself slowly by specializing in commercial cases. As a judge (1913) he was firm but patient and highly regarded, and in the Court of Appeal (1919–28) and the House of Lords (1928–44) he was recognized as distinguished, delivering notable opinions in many leading cases. He also made important contributions to legal education.

ATKINSON, Rowan (1955–) English actor and writer, known principally as a comic. He first appeared in Oxford University revues at the Edinburgh Festival Fringe, and in 1981 became the youngest performer to have had a one-man show in the West End. Subsequent appearances include *The Nerd* (1984), *The New Revue* (1986), and *The Sneeze* (1988). On television he has starred in *Not the Nine O'Clock News*, (1979–82), and *Blackadder*, a comedy series set in various historical periods (1983–89).

ATKINSON, Thomas Wittlam (1799–1861) English architect and travel-writer, born in Cawthorne, Yorkshire. He became successively quarryman, stonemason, and architect; then, between 1848 and 1853, travelled some 40 000 miles in Asiatic Russia with his wife Lucy, painting and keeping journals which formed the basis of several works on that part of the world.

ATTALUS the name of three kings of Pergamon, of whom the last, dying in 133 BC, left his kingdom to Rome.

ATTENBOROUGH, Sir David Frederick (1926–) English naturalist and broadcaster, born in London, the younger brother of filmmaker Sir **Richard Attenborough**. After service in the Royal Navy (1947–49) and three years as an editorial assistant in an educational publishing house, he joined the BBC in 1952 as a trainee producer. The series *Zoo Quest* (1954–64) allowed him to undertake zoological and ethnographic expeditions to remote parts of the globe to capture intimate footage of rare wildlife in its natural habitat. From 1965 to 1968, he was the controller of BBC 2 and subsequently director of programmes (1969–72) before returning to documentary-making, with such ambitious series as *Life on Earth* (1979), *The Living Planet* (1984) and *The First Eden* (1987). His books include *Zoo Quest to Guiana* (1956), *The Tribal Eye* (1976) and *The Living Planet* (1984).

ATTENBOROUGH, Sir Richard (1923–) English actor and film director, born in Cambridge. He trained at RADA before making his first professional appearance in *Ah, Wilderness* (1941) and film début in *In Which We Serve* (1942). Initially typecast as weak and cowardly youths he was seen to chilling effect as Pinkie in *Brighton Rock*, on stage in 1943 and on film in 1947. He developed into a conscientious character actor, winning British Academy Awards as the kidnapper in *Séance on a Wet Afternoon* (1964) and the bombastic sergeant major in *Guns at Batasi* (1964). He became a producer in partnership with Bryan Forbes and directed large-scale epics like *A Bridge Too Far* (1977). A twenty-year crusade to film the life of **Mahatma Gandhi** led to an Academy Award for *Gandhi* (1982). In 1987 he made *Cry Freedom*, a biography of the black activist **Steve Biko**. Married to actress Sheila Sim since 1944, he is the brother of naturalist Sir **David Attenborough**.

ATTERBURY, Francis (1663–1732) English prelate and controversialist, born in Milton Keynes, near Newport Pagnell, and educated at Westminster, and Christ Church, Oxford. In 1687 he answered a pseudonymous attack on Protestantism by Obadiah Walker, master of University College; and, taking orders about the same time, won such a reputation as a preacher that he was appointed lecturer of St Bride's (1691), a royal chaplain, and minister to Bridewell Hospital. **Charles Boyle**'s *Examination of Bentley's Dissertations on the Epistle of Phalaris* (1698), a clever but shallow performance, was really by Atterbury who had been the young nobleman's tutor at Christ Church. He became successively dean of Carlisle (1704); prolocutor of Convocation (1710); dean of Christ Church (1712); and bishop of Rochester and dean of Westminster (1713). To Atterbury is reliably ascribed **Henry Sacheverell**'s famous defence (1710) before the Lords; and he was author of the scarcely less famous *Representation of the State of Religion* (1711). His known character and Jacobite leanings made him no favourite with **George I**. In 1715 he refused to sign the bishops' declaration of fidelity, and in 1722 he was committed to the Tower for complicity in an attempt to restore the **Stuarts**. A bill of pains and penalties was passed; and Atterbury, who had defended himself with great ability, was deprived of all his offices, and for ever banished from the kingdom. In 1723 he left England, and after a short stay in Brussels, settled in Paris, where he died. He was laid in a nameless grave in Westminster Abbey. His works comprise sermons, and letters to **Pope**, **Swift**, **Bolingbroke**, and others of his friends.

ATTICUS, Titus Pomponius (110–32 BC) Roman intellectual, businessman and writer, born of a rich family in Rome and educated with **Cicero** and Gaius Marius the Younger. He acquired the surname Atticus because of his long sojourn in Athens (85–65) to avoid the Civil War. In 32 BC he was informed that a disorder he suffered from was terminal, and died after five days of voluntary starvation. He was a wealthy and highly cultivated man who espoused the Epicurean philosophy and combined his literary activities with a successful business career. He amassed a large library, wrote histories of Greece and Rome (which are lost), and was an intimate friend of Cicero, who used him as an editor and consultant. Cicero's *Letters to Atticus* form a famous and prolific correspondence.

ATTILA (c.406–453) Hunnish king, called the 'Scourge of God', the legendary king who appears as **Etzel** in the German *Nibelungenlied* and **Atli** in the Old Icelandic *Völsunga Saga* and the heroic poems of the *Edda*. He became in 434 king (jointly at first with a brother) of countless hordes of Huns from Asia scattered from the north of the Caspian to the Danube. Attila soon had Vandals, Ostrogoths, Gepids, and Franks fighting under his banner, so that his dominion extended over Germany and Scythia from the Rhine to the frontiers of China. In 447 he devastated all the countries between the Black Sea and the Mediterranean. The emperor Theodosius was defeated in three bloody engagements, and Constantinople owed its safety solely to its fortifications and the ignorance of the enemy in the art of besieging; Thrace, Macedon, and Greece were overrun, and Theodosius was compelled to cede a territory south of the Danube, and to pay tribute. In 451 Attila invaded Gaul, but **Aëtius**, the Roman commander, and **Theodoric**, king of the Visigoths, compelled him to raise the siege of Orléans and after a fearful and bloody contest, utterly defeated him on the Catalaunian Plain, near Châlons-sur-Marne. He retreated to Hungary, but next year made an incursion into Italy, devastating Aquileia, Milan, Padua, and other cities, Rome itself being saved only by the personal mediation of Pope **Leo I**, who bought off the city with large sums. He died in 453, soon after his marriage to a Burgundian princess called Ildeco; and the Hunnish empire decayed. The manner of his death, in a pool of blood after a haemorrhage in bed, gave rise to stories of vengeance and murder by his bride.

ATTLEE, Clement Richard, 1st Earl Attlee (1883–1967) English Labour statesman, born in Putney. He was educated at Haileybury and University College, Oxford, and was called to the bar in 1905. Through Haileybury House, a boy's club in the Stepney slums, he developed a practical interest in social problems which, alongside the works of **Ruskin** and **William Morris** converted him to socialism. In 1910 he became secretary of Toynbee Hall. His lectureship at the newly founded London School of Economics (1913–23) was interrupted by service in the war, in which he was wounded, and attained the rank of major. In 1919 he was elected mayor of Stepney, and in 1922 he entered parliament and became **Ramsay MacDonald**'s parliamentary secretary (1922–24), under-secretary of state for war (1924), served on the Simon commission on India (1927–30) and was postmaster-general (1931). He did not become a member of MacDonald's coalition government. One of the few Labour MPs to retain his parliamentary seat in the following election, he became deputy leader of the opposition (1931–35) under **Lansbury**, whom he succeeded as leader in 1935, and he paved the way for **Churchill**'s war-time premiership by refusing to commit his party to a coalition under **Chamberlain**. He was dominions secretary (1942–43) and deputy prime minister (1942–45) in Churchill's war cabinet. As leader of the opposition he accompanied **Eden** to the San Francisco and Potsdam conferences (1945), and after the huge Labour electoral victory returned to the Potsdam conference as prime minister. Despite severe economic handicaps aggravated by America'a precipitate ending of Lend-Lease, during his six years in office he carried through a vigorous programme of reform. The Bank of England, the coal mines, civil aviation, cable and wireless services, railways, road transport and steel were nationalized, the National Health Service was introduced and independence was granted to India (1947) and Burma (1948). Labour's foreign policy of support for NATO in the face of Russian intransigence, particularly the necessity for re-arming the Germans and the manufacture of British atom bombs, precipitated continuing party strife which at times taxed even Attlee's considerable gift of shrewd chairmanship. He earned affection and respect by his sheer lack of dogma, oratorical gifts or showmanship and by his balanced judgment, and quiet yet unmistakable authority which belied the public image of 'Little Clem'. He was leader of the Opposition from 1951 to 1955 when he resigned and accepted an earldom. His many books include *The Labour Party in Perspective* (1937), with supplement *Twelve Years Later* (1949), and an autobiography, *As It Happened* (1954).

ATTWELL, Mabel Lucie (1879–1964) English artist and writer, born in London. She studied at Heatherley's and other art schools, and married cartoonist Harold Earnshaw. She was noted for her child studies, both humorous and serious, with which she illustrated her own and other children's stories. Her immensely popular 'cherubic' style was continued in annuals and children's books by her daughter, working under her mother's name.

ATTWOOD, Thomas (1765–1838) English musician and composer, a pupil of **Mozart**. He was organist of St Paul's from 1796 till his death.

ATWOOD, Margaret (Eleanor) (1939–) Canadian novelist, short story writer, poet and critic. Born in Ottawa, she spent her early years in northern Ontario and Quebec bush country. After graduating from the University of Toronto and Radcliffe College, she held a variety of jobs ranging from waitress and summer camp counsellor to lecturer in English literature and writer-in-residence. Her first published work, a collection of poems entitled *The Circle Game* (1966), won the Governor-General's award. Since then she has published several volumes of poetry, collections of short stories—*Dancing Girls* (1977) and *Bluebeard's Egg* (1987)—and *Survival* (1972), an acclaimed study of Canadian literature. She is best known, however, as a novelist. *The Edible Woman* (1969), dealing with emotional cannabalism, appeared timeously for the women's movement and provoked considerable controversy. It was followed by *Surfacing* (1972), *Lady Oracle* (1976), *Life Before Man* (1979) and *Bodily Harm* (1982). In 1985, *The Handmaid's Tale* was shortlisted for the Booker prize, as was *Cat's Eye* in 1989.

AUBER, Daniel-François-Esprit (1782–1871) French composer of operas, born in Caen, and pupil of **Cherubini**. His best-known works are *La Muette de Portici*, usually entitled *Masaniello* (1828), and *Fra Diavolo* (1829).

AUBERT, Pierre (1927–) Swiss politician, born in La Chaux-de-Fonds and a member of the local assembly (1960–68). He was elected to the legislative assembly of the canton of Neuchatel (1971–75) and was Labour member of the House of States (1971–78). In annual elections, he was vice-president of Switzerland in 1982 and president in 1983 and 1987.

AUBIGNÉ See **D'AUBIGNÉ**

AUBLET, Jean Baptiste Christophe Fusée (1720–78) French botanist and humanist, born at Salon near Arles. He spent over ten years in Mauritius and the French West Indies, where he established gardens of medicinal plants and made extensive collections in French Guiana, on which he based his *Histoire des plantes de la Guiane française* (4 vols, 1775) and so founded forest botany in tropical America. He was also the first secular slavery abolitionist and his interest in ethnic problems gave the name *ethnora maripa* to the famous Maripa palm which he discoverd.

AUBREY, John (1626–97) English antiquary and folklorist, born in Easton Percy near Chippenham. Educated at Malmesbury, Blandford, and Trinity College, Oxford, he studied law but was never called to the bar. In 1652 he succeeded to estates in Wiltshire, Herefordshire, and Wales, but was forced through lawsuits to part with the last of them in 1670, and with his books in 1677. His last years were passed, in 'danger of arrests', under the protection of **Hobbes**, **Ashmole**, and others. Only his quaint, credulous *Miscellanies* (1696) of folklore and ghost-stories was printed in his lifetime; but he left a large mass of materials. Of these, his Wiltshire and Surrey collection have in part been published. He also collected biographical and anecdotal material on celebrities of his time (**Hobbes**, **Milton**, **Bacon** and others) for **Antony à Wood**, which appeared in *Letters by Eminent Persons* (1813), better known as *Brief Lives*. He was the first antiquarian to describe Stonehenge (wrongly) as a Druid temple.

AUBRIET, Claude (1665–1742) French flower and animal painter. He accompanied **Joseph Tournefort** on his Levant journey of 1700 to 1702. The much-cultivated genus *Aubrietia*, with its purple trailing plants, is named after him.

AUBUSSON, Pierre d' (1423–1503) French soldier and prelate, and Grand Master of the Knights Hospitallers from 1476. His outstanding achievement was his magnificent defence of Rhodes in 1480 against a besieging army of 100000 Turks under the sultan Mohammed II. In 1481 he made a treaty with the Turks under the new sultan, **Bayezit II**, by agreeing to imprison the sultan's rebellious brother, Djem; in 1489 he was created cardinal for handing Djem over to Pope Innocent VIII.

AUCHINLECK, Sir Claude John Eyre (1884–1918) English soldier. Educated at Wellington College, he joined the 62nd Punjabis in 1904. In World War I he served in Egypt and Mesopotamia, becoming a brevet-colonel. In World War II he served in northern Norway and commanded an unsuccessful raid on Narvik (1940). He became command-in-chief in India (1941) and succeeded **Wavell** in North Africa in July 1941, when the 8th Army was in a depleted state after the ill-fated Greek campaign. He made a successful advance into Cyrenaica, but was later thrown back by **Rommel**. His regrouping of the 8th Army on El Alamein paved the way for ultimate victory, but at the time Auchinleck was made a scapegoat for the retreat and replaced by General **Alexander** in 1942. In 1943 he returned to India as c-in-c, and subsequently served as Supreme Commander India and Pakistan (1947). He was created field-marshal in 1946.

AUCHINLOSS, Louis Stanton (1917–) American novelist, short story writer and critic, born in Lawrence, New York. He trained as a lawyer and was admitted to the New York bar in 1941. He is a novelist of manners, at home among White Anglo Saxon Protestants (WASPs) of an old family and old money. His first novel, *The Indifferent Children* (1947), appeared under the pseudonym Andrew Lee, but subsequent books have appeared under his own name, the best of them being *Pursuit of the Prodigal* (1960), *Portrait in Brownstone* (1962), *The Embezzler* (1966) and *A World of Profit* (1963). His later novels have attracted less critical acclaim.

AUCHMUTY, Sir Samuel (1758–1822) British soldier, born in New York, the son of a clergyman. He entered the British army as a volunteer in 1777, and during the War of Independence (1775–83) served three campaigns against the American colonists. He later served in India (1783–97), including the Third Mysore war (1790–92), and was one of Sir **David Baird**'s chief lieutenants in the desert march to support **Abercromby** at Alexandria (1801). He captured Montevideo in 1806, and afterwards commanded in the Carnatic, in Java, and in Ireland (1821), where he died.

AUCHTERLONIE, Willie (1872–1963) Scottish golf-club maker. Born in St Andrews, he won the Open Golf Championship at the age of 21, using only seven home-made clubs. In 1935 he was appointed professional to the Royal and Ancient at St Andrews, where his workshop and store became a mecca for golfers.

AUCKLAND See **EDEN, George, 1st Earl of Auckland**

AUDEN, Wystan Hugh (1907–73) Anglo-American poet and essayist. Born in York, he was educated at Gresham's School, Holt, and Christ Church, Oxford, and was naturalized as an American citizen in 1946. In the 1930s he wrote passionately on social problems from a far-Left standpoint, especially in his collection of poems *Look, Stranger*! (1936). He went to Spain as a civilian in support of the Republican side and reported on it in *Spain* (1937), followed by a verse commentary (with prose reports by **Christopher Isherwood**) on the Sino-Japanese war in *Journey to a War* (1939). He also collaborated with Isherwood in three plays in the 1930s: *The Dog Beneath the Skin* (1935), *The Ascent of F6* (1936), and *On the Frontier* (1938). He collaborated with **Louis MacNeice** in *Letters from Iceland* (1937) and wrote the libretto for *Ballad of Heroes* by **Benjamin Britten** in 1939. He emigrated to New York early in 1939 and was appointed associate professor at Michigan University, and professor of poetry at Oxford University in 1956. In America he became converted to Anglicanism, tracing his conversion in *The Sea and the Mirror* (1944) and *For the Time Being* (1944). His later works include *Nones* (1951), *The Shield of Achilles* (1955), *Homage to Clio* (1960) and *City Without Walls* (1969). He is best remembered today as the 'Poet of the Thirties', for his prodigious verbal dexterity, and for his essays of literary criticism. He was married to the writer Erika Mann, daughter of the German novelist **Thomas Mann**.

AUDLEY, Sir James (c.1316–1386) English knight, and one of the original knights of the Garter (1344). In 1350 he fought at Sluys, and in 1354 attended **Edward the Black Prince**, who declared him the bravest knight on his side at Poitiers. In 1267 he was governor of Aquitaine, in 1369 great seneschal of Poitou.

AUDLEY, Thomas, Baron Audley of Walden (1488–1544) English Lord Chancellor. Educated for the law, he became attorney for the duchy of Lancaster in 1530 and king's serjeant in 1531. Active in furthering the king's designs, he profited abundantly by ecclesiastical confiscations. In 1529 he was appointed speaker of the House of Commons and in 1532 lord chancellor. He was named in the Commission for the trial of **Anne Boleyn**, and for the examination of **Catherine Howard**. He was created Baron Audley of Walden in 1538.

AUDOUIN, Jean Victor (1797–1841) French entomologist and naturalist, born in Paris. Trained as a doctor, he made a study of the blister beatle (Spanish Fly), then much used for medicinal purposes, and in 1833 was appointed professor of entomology at the Jardin des Plantes in Paris. He also studied silkworms and vine-parasites, and was co-author of the *Dictionnaire Classique d'Histoire Naturelle* (1822). He also compiled the ornithological section of the compendious *Description de l'Égypte* (1826). Audouin's Gull was named after him.

AUDUBON, John James (1785–1851) American ornithologist and bird artist, born in Haiti, illegitimate son of a Creole woman and a French mercantile agent. After his mother's early death, his father took him to France, but the claim that he studied painting under **Jacques Louis David** lacks foundation. He was sent to the USA in 1804 to look after his father's property near Philadelphia, and married Lucy Bakewell, daughter of an English settler. In 1807 he sold up and migrated to Kentucky, where he opened a general store in Louisville and elsewhere (1808). He spent so much time out hunting birds and painting them that he was eventually declared bankrupt (1819). He now embarked on his 'Great Idea', of seeking out every species of bird in America to make a comprehensive catalogue of them. He spent some years travelling down the Ohio and the Mississippi, stopping at the various towns to earn money painting portraits, and all the while adding to his huge collection of bird illustrations. In 1826 he took his work to Europe in search of a publisher, holding exhibitions in Paris, London, Liverpool and Edinburgh. A born showman, he cultivated a rugged backwoodsman image that went down well with fashionable society. In London he sought out the engraver and painter Robert Havell (1793–1878, who later emigrated to the USA) to make the copperplate engravings of double-elephant plates, and 1827 saw the publication of the first of the 87 portfolios of his massive *Birds of America* (1827–38). It eventually comprised coloured plates of 1065 birds in life size, and cost \$115000. He also published, with the Scottish naturalist William MacGillivray, an accompanying text, *Ornithological Biography* (1831–39, 5 vols). Between 1840 and 1844 he produced a 'miniature' edition in 7 volumes, costing \$100, which became a bestseller.

He returned to America for good and in 1841 settled in a spacious country house on the Hudson River (now Audubon Park, New York City), where he prepared drawings for *The Viviparous Quadrupeds of North America* with **John Bachman** (1845–53), which was completed by his two sons. The National Audubon Society, dedicated to the conservation of birds in the USA, was founded in his honour in 1866.

AUE, Hartmann von See **HARTMANN VON AUE**

AUENBRUGGER, Leopold (1722–1809) Austrian physician, born in Graz, the discoverer of percussion in medical diagnosis. He also wrote the libretto for one of **Salieri**'s operas.

AUER, Karl, Freiherr von Welsbach (1858–1929) Austrian chemist, born in Vienna. He invented the incandescent gas-mantle and the osmium lamp. He also discovered the cerium-iron alloy known as Auer metal or mischmetal, now used as flints in petrol lighters.

AUERBACH, Berthold, originally **Moses Baruch Auerbacher** (1812–82) German novelist, born in Nordstetten in the Black Forest. He studied at the universities of Tübingen, Munich, and Heidelberg, and in 1836 was imprisoned as a member of the students' Burschenschaft. Destined for the synagogue, he abandoned theology for law, then law for history and philosophy, especially that of **Spinoza**, on whose life he based a novel of that name (1837), and whose works he translated (1841). In his *Schwarzwälder Dorfgeschichten* (1843), on which his fame chiefly rests, he gives charming pictures of Black Forest life. Of his longer works the best known are *Barfüssele* (1856) and *Auf der Höhe* (1865).

AUERBACH, Frank (1931–) German-born British artist, who came to Britain in 1939. He studied at St Martin's School of Art (1948–52) and the Royal College of Art (1952–55), but his most important formative influence was **David Bomberg** who taught him briefly at the Borough Polytechnic, London. He works with oil paint of predominantly earth colours, thickly applied in layers as he works at the subject over months or years, allowing his image to emerge mysteriously through the raised impasto. His works on paper in charcoal are similarly reworked. His subject matter is figurative, portraits of a few close friends and familiar views of Primrose Hill and Camden Town in London.

AUERSPERG, Anton Alexander, Graf von, pseud **Anastasius Grün** (1806–76) Austrian poet. He was distinguished by his Liberalism and ultra-German sympathies. He was one of the German epic and lyrical poets, among whom he holds a high rank.

AUGEREAU, Pierre François Charles, Duke of Castiglione (1757–1816) French soldier, born of humble parentage. He enlisted in the ranks, practised as a fencing master, and achieved rapid promotion under **Napoleon** in Italy where he fought with distinction at Lodi and Castiglione (1796). In 1797 he defeated a royalist coup against the Directory. He opposed Napoleon's assumption of power as first consul in 1799, but was reconciled and promoted marshal in 1804 and created Duke of Castiglione in 1808. At Napoleon's fall in 1814 he declared for the monarchy, but was forced to retire.

AUGIER, Guillaume Victor Emile (1820–89) French dramatist, born in Valence. His *Théatre complet* (1890) fills seven volumes, and includes fine social comedies, such as *Le Gendre de M. Poirier* (1854, with Sandeau) and *Les Fourchambault* (1878).

AUGUST, Bille (1948–) Danish film director and film photographer, educated in Stockholm and Copenhagen. Since 1979 he has directed several feature films, and TV films, among these *Honning Måne*, (Honeymoon, 1979) *Zappa* (1983) and *Tro, Håb og Kærlighed* (Twist and Shout, 1985). His 1987 film *Pelle the Conqueror* (Pelle Erobreren), an adaptation of a novel by the Danish author **Martin Andersen Nexø** was awarded the Golden Palm in Cannes in 1988 and in 1989 won an Oscar in the Best Foreign Language Film category.

AUGUSTINE, St, Aurelius Augustinus, also known as **Augustine of Hippo** (354–430) the greatest of the Latin Church fathers, born in Tagaste in Numidia, (modern Tunisia). His father was a pagan, but he was brought up a Christian by his devout mother, Monica. He went to Carthage to study and had a son, Adeonatus, by a mistress there. Carthage was a metropolitan centre and he was exposed there to many new intellectual fashions and influences. He became deeply involved in Manicheanism, which seemed to offer a solution to the problem of evil, a theme which was to preoccupy him throughout his life. In 383 he moved to teach at Rome, then at Milan, and became influenced by scepticism and then by neoplatonism. After the dramatic spiritual crises described in his autobiography he finally became converted to Christianity and was baptized (together with his son) by St **Ambrose** in 386. He returned to North Africa and became bishop of Hippo in 396 where he was a relentless antagonist of the heretical schools of Donatists, Pelagians and Manicheans and champion of orthodoxy. He remained at Hippo until his death in 430, as the Vandals were besieging the gates of the city. He was an unusually productive writer and much of his work is marked by personal spiritual struggle. The *Confessions* (400) is a classic of world literature and a spiritual autobiography as well as an original work of philosophy (with a famous discussion on the nature of time). *The City of God* (412–27) is a monumental work of 22 books which presents human history in terms of the conflict between the spiritual and the temporal, which will end in the triumph of the City of God, whose manifestation on earth is the church.

AUGUSTINE, St (d.604) Italian churchman, the first archbishop of Canterbury. He was prior of the Benedictine monastery of St Andrew in Rome, when, in 596, he was sent, with 40 other monks, by Pope **Gregory I** to convert the Anglo-Saxons to Christianity, and establish the authority of the Roman see in Britain. Landing in Thanet, the missionaries were kindly received by Æthelbert, king of Kent, whose wife Bertha, daughter of the Frankish king, was a Christian. A residence was assigned to them at Canterbury, where they devoted themselves to monastic exercises and preaching. The conversion and baptism of the king contributed greatly to the success of their efforts among his subjects, and it is recorded that in one day Augustine baptized 1000 persons in the river Swale. In 597 he want to Arles, and there was consecrated bishop of the English. His efforts to extend his authority over the native British (Welsh) church with whose bishops he held a conference in 603 in Aust on the Severn, were less successful. He died in 604, and in 612 his body was transferred to his abbey of SS Peter and Paul.

AUGUSTULUS, Romulus, properly **AUGUSTUS** last emperor of the western half of the old Roman empire (ruled 475–476). His father, Orestes, a Pannonian, had risen to high rank under the emperor Julius Nepos, on whose flight he conferred the vacant throne on Augustus (the diminutive *Augustulus* was a nickname), retaining all substantial power in his own hands. Orestes failing to conciliate the barbarians, who had helped him against the emperor, they, under Odoacer, besieged him in Pavia and killed him.

Augustulus yielded at once, and being of too little consequence to put to death, was dismissed to a villa near Naples with an annual pension of 6000 pieces of gold.

AUGUSTUS, Gaius Julius Caesar Octavianus (63–14 BC) the first Roman emperor, the son of Gaius Octavius, senator and praetor, and Atia, **Julius Caesar**'s niece. He became Gaius Julius Caesar Octavianus through adoption by Caesar in his will (44 BC), and later received the name Augustus ('sacred', 'venerable') in recognition of his services and position (27 BC). At the time of Caesar's assassination (March 44 BC), Augustus was a student at Apollonia in Illyricum, but returned at once to Italy to claim his inheritance. **Marcus Antonius** refused at first to surrender Caesar's property, but Augustus outmanoeuvred him in the campaign of Mutina, gained the consulship and carried out Caesar's will (43 BC). When Antony returned from Gaul with **Lepidus**, Augustus changed sides and joined them in forming a triumvirate. He obtained Africa, Sardinia and Sicily; Antony, Gaul; and Lepidus, Spain. Their power was soon made absolute by the massacre of their opponents in Italy, and by the victory at Philippi over the republicans under **Brutus** and **Cassius** (42 BC). Difficulties between Augustus and Antony, caused by Antony's wife Fulvia, were removed by her death and Antony's marriage with Octavia, sister of Augustus. The Roman world was divided again, Augustus taking the western half and Antony the eastern, while Lepidus had to be content with Africa. Augustus gradually built up his position in Italy and the west, eliminating the threat of **Pompey**'s son, Sextus, in Sicily and forcing Lepidus to retire from public life (36 BC). He ingratiated himself with the Roman people and misrepresented the actions of Antony in the East. At length war was declared against **Cleopatra**, whom Antony had joined in 37 BC, and by the naval victory of Actium (31 BC) Augustus became the sole ruler of the Roman world. Antony and Cleopatra committed suicide; Antony's son by Fulvia, and Caesarion (allegedly the son of Caesar and Cleopatra), were put to death. In 29 BC, after regulating affairs in Egypt, Greece, Syria, and Asia Minor, Augustus returned to Rome in triumph, and closing the temple of Janus, proclaimed universal peace. Henceforward, Augustus was in all but name the sole ruler of the Roman empire, though his rule had to be disguised in republican forms, and the search for an acceptable constitutional formula to clothe his autocracy took nearly a decade and several settlements (27, 23, 19 BC). At home and abroad his declared policy was one of national revival and restoration of traditional Roman values. He legislated to mould the fabric of Roman society, and beautified the city of Rome; it was his proud boast that 'he had found the city built of brick, and left it built of marble'. Abroad, he pursued a policy of calculated imperial conquest, and vastly enlarged the territory of the Roman empire in central and northern Europe, though his policy had to be brought to a halt when disaster struck in his later years, with the revolt of Pannonia (AD 6) and the loss of three entire legions in Germany under **Varus** (AD 9). His domestic life was clouded with setbacks and disasters, though he eventually achieved an acceptable succession with his stepson **Tiberius**, whom he adopted in AD 4. A statesman of exceptional skill, he brought about the difficult transition from republic to empire and provided the Roman world with viable institutions and a lasting period of peace. Though not a charismatic figure, he had a gift for using the talents of others, both in public life and in the cultural sphere. **Horace**, **Virgil**, **Ovid**, **Propertius**, **Tibullus**, and **Livy** were the glories of the *Augustan Age*, a name given in France to the reign of **Louis XIV**, in England to that of Queen **Anne**. Augustus' *Autobiography* is lost, but a record of his public achievements, written by himself and originally inscribed on bronze pillars in front of his Mausoleum in Rome—the *Res Gestae Divi Augusti*—is extant in several copies in Greek and Latin from Asia Minor.

AUGUSTUS II, the Strong (1670–1733) king of Poland and elector of Saxony. He succeeded to the electorship as Frederick Augustus I in 1694 on the death of his brother, John George IV. After a military career fighting against France and the Turks, he renounced his Protestantism and became a Roman Catholic in 1696, in order to secure his election to the Polish throne as Augustus II in 1697. In alliance with **Peter I the Great** of Russia and Frederik IV of Denmark, he planned the partition of Sweden, invading Livonia in 1699. Defeated by **Karl XII** of Sweden, who responded by invading Saxony and Poland, Augustus was deposed in 1706 and replaced by **Stanislaus Leszczynski**. After the defeat of the Swedes by Peter the Great at Poltava in 1709, he recovered the Polish throne. He attempted without success to convert the elective Polish kingship into a hereditary one, but was nevertheless succeeded, both as elector and king, by his son, Frederick Augustus.

AUKRUST, Olav Lom (1883–1929) Norwegian poet. He was a schoolmaster who wrote large quantities of religious and patriotic verse. *Himmelvarden* (1916) consists of three long cycles in New Norwegian containing many passages of great lyric power. *Hamar i Hellom* (1926), of which the chief poem is *Emme*, summons the people of Norway to use the power of their great traditions to achieve present security and progress. His final collection of poems, *Solrenning*, is incomplete and was published posthumously in 1930.

AULÉN, Gustaf Emmanuel Hildebrand (1879–1977) Swedish Lutheran theologian and church music composer, born in Ljungby, Kalmar. Professor of systematic theology at Lund (1913–33), and bishop of Strängnäs (1933–52), he was a leading representative of the Scandinavian school of theology that sought Christian truth behind doctrines rather than in the form in which they were presented. He wrote several books, including *The Faith of the Christian Church* (1954) and *Jesus in Contemporary Historical Research* (1976). His most famous study, *Christus Victor* (1931), presented the death of Christ as a triumph over the powers of evil, following the approach of **Irenaeus** and **Martin Luther**. He also wrote a commentary and explanation on **Dag Hammarskjöld**'s famous *Markings* in 1969. Aulén's second love was music: he played the piano and organ, and was president of the Royal Swedish Academy of Music (1944–50).

AULNOY, Marie Catherine Jumelle de Berneville, Comtesse d' (c.1650–1705) French writer. She wrote romances of court life, but is mainly remembered for her charming fairy-tales, *Contes des Fées* (1698).

AULUS GELLIUS See **GELLIUS**

AUMALE a French countship in Normandy, held in the Middle Ages by the **Guises**. It became a dukedom in 1547, and from 1675 was customarily bestowed on a prince of the French royal family.

AUMALE, Henri-Eugène-Philippe-Louis d'Orléans, Duke of (1822–97) French soldier, fourth son of King **Louis-Philippe**, born in Paris. He distinguished himself in the campaigns in Algeria, where in 1847 he succeeded Marshal **Bugeaud** as governor-general. At the revolution of 1848 he retired to England, where he became known by his contributions to the *Revue de deux mondes*, his incisive pamphlets against **Louis Napoleon**, and his great works, *Histoire des princes de*

Condé (1869–97) and *Les Institutions militaires de la France* (1867). Elected to the Assembly in 1871, in 1886 he bequeathed his magnificent château of Chantilly to the nation.

AUNGERVILLE, or **de Bury, Richard** (1287–1345) English churchman, born in Bury St Edmunds. He studied at Oxford, became a Benedictine monk at Durham, and having been tutor to **Edward III**, was made successively dean of Wells and bishop of Durham, besides acting for a time as high chancellor, as ambassador to the pope and to France and Germany, and as commissioner for a truce with Scotland. He had a passion for collecting manuscripts and books; and his principal work, *Philobyblon*, intended to serve as a handbook to the library which he founded in connection with Durham College at Oxford (afterwards suppressed), describes the state of learning in England and France.

AURANGZEB (1618–1707) Mughal emperor of India, third son of the emperor **Shah Jahan**. When Shah Jahan became seriously ill in 1657, the throne was seized by his eldest son, Dara, but his three brothers, Shuja, Murad and Aurangzeb combined to oust him. Dara's army was decisively defeated at the battle at Samugarh in 1658. Shah Jahan and Murad were both imprisoned in Delhi and Aurangszeb, after celebrating his victory at a Darbar, began to rule without formal coronation. Shuja fled the country but Dara was taken and executed in 1659. During Aurangzeb's long reign, the empire remained outwardly prosperous but the emperor, puritanical and narrow in his outlook, alienated the various communities that comprised the empire, particularly the Hindus, whom he treated with great harshness. Opposed by his own rebellious sons and by the Mahratta empire in the south, he died a fugitive at Ahmadnagar.

AURELIAN, properly **Lucius Domitius Aurelianus** (c.212–275) Roman emperor, born of humble origins in Dacia or Pannonia. Enlisting early as a common soldier he rose rapidly to the highest military offices. On the death of Claudius II (270), Aurelian was elected emperor by the army, with whom he was very popular. He repulsed the Alemanni and Marcomanni, and erected new walls around Rome. He resigned Dacia to the Goths, and made the Danube the frontier of the empire. He defeated **Zenobia**, besieged her in Palmyra, and took her prisoner. When an insurrection broke out again in Palmyra, he returned in 273, and destroyed the city. Aurelian quelled a rebellion in Egypt, and recovered Gaul from Tetricus. By restoring good discipline in the army, order in domestic affairs, and political unity to the Roman dominions, he merited the title awarded him by the senate, Restitutor Orbis—'Restorer of the World'. He was assassinated by his own officers near Byzantium during a campaign against the Persians.

AURELIUS, Marcus Aurelius Antoninus, originally **Marcus Annius Verus** (121–80) one of the most respected emperors in Roman history, the son of Annius Verus and Domita Calvilla, born in Rome. When only 17, he was adopted by **Antoninus Pius**, who had succeeded **Hadrian** and whose daughter **Faustina** was selected for his wife. From 140, when he was made consul, till the death of Antoninus in 161, he discharged his public duties with the utmost conscientiousness, and maintained the friendliest relations with the emperor. At the same time he still devoted himself to the study of law and philosophy, especially Stoicism. On his accession, with characteristic magnanimity he voluntarily divided the government with his brother by adoption, Lucius Aurelius Verus, who in 161 was sent to take command against the Parthians. Despite the self-indulgence and dilatoriness of Verus, the generals were victorious, but the army brought back from the East a plague that ravaged the empire. Peaceful by temperament, Marcus Aurelius was nevertheless throughout his reign destined to suffer from constant wars, and though in Asia, Britain, and on the Rhine the barbarians were checked, permanent peace was never secured. Rome was suffering from pestilence, earthquakes and inundations when the imperial colleagues led the Roman armies against the northern barbarians on the Danube. The Marcommani were humbled in 168, and in 173 almost annihilated while retreating across the Danube. Verus had died in 169. In 174 another victory was won over a Germanic tribe, the Quadi. Marcus Aurelius was next summoned to the East by a rebellion of the governor, Avidius Cassius (175), who was assassinated before Aurelius arrived. On his way home, he visited lower Egypt and Greece. At Athens he founded chairs of philosophy for each of the chief schools: Platonic, Stoic, Peripatetic, and Epicurean. Towards the end of 176 he reached Italy, and next autumn departed for Germany, where fresh disturbances had broken out. He was victorious once more, but his constitution, never robust, at length gave way, and he died either at Vienna or Sirmium in Pannonia. One of the few Roman Emperors whose writings have survived, his *Meditations* record his innermost thoughts and are a unique document. They show his loneliness, but also that he did not allow himself to be embittered by his experiences of life. His death was felt to be a national calamity, and he was retrospectively idealized as the model of the perfect Emperor, whose reign and style of rule contrasted with the disastrous period that began with the accession of his unworthy son **Commodus**, the disturbed age of the Severan emperors, and the imperial anarchy that followed in the 3rd century.

AURIC, Georges (1899–1983) French composer, born in Lodève, Hérault. He studied under **d'Indy**, became one of 'Les six', and was successively music critic of *Marianne* and *Paris Soir*. His compositions ranged widely from full orchestral pieces and ballets to songs and film scores; René Clair's *A nous la liberté* (1932), *Beauty and the Beast* (1946), *Moulin Rouge* (1952) and including several British films, as *It Always Rains on Sunday* (1947) and *Passport to Pimlico* (1949). His music, exciting and colourful, influenced by **Satie** and **Stravinsky**, shows the modern return to counterpoint at its best. In 1962 he was appointed director of the Paris Opéra and Opéra-Comique, but in 1968 resigned most of his official positions in order to compose.

AURIOL, Jacqueline (1917–) French woman aviator, the daughter-in-law of **Vincent Auriol**. She broke the women's jet speed record in 1955 by flying at 715 miles per hour in a French *Mystère*. She published *I Live To Fly* in 1970.

AURIOL, Vincent (1884–1966) French socialist politician. He was president of the two constituent assemblies of 1946 and the first president of the fourth republic from 1947 to 1953.

AUROBINDO GHOSE (1872–1950) Indian philosopher, poet and mystic, born in Calcutta into a high-caste Bengali family. Educated at Cambridge and a proficient linguist, he returned to India in 1892 and became a professor in Baroda and Calcutta. In 1908 he was imprisoned by the British authorities in India for sedition, and studied yoga in jail. Renouncing nationalism and politics for yoga and Hindu philosophy, he founded an *ashram* in 1910 at Pondicherry, then French territory. As an experiment in community living, the ashram, known as Auroville, continued to attract

Western visitors long after Aurobindo's death, even if few could grasp the underlying philosophy: salvation of society by the influence of the individual attainment of supermind or higher consciousness through integral yoga, as expressed in *The Life Divine* (1940), *The Synthesis of Yoga* (1948), *Aurobindo on Himself* (1953) and many other books.

AUSONIUS, Decius Magnus (c.309–392) Latin poet, born in Burdigala (Bordeaux), the son of a physician. He taught rhetoric there for 30 years, and was then appointed by the emperor **Valentinian I** tutor to his son **Gratian**; and he afterwards held the offices of quaestor, prefect of Latium and consul of Gaul. On the death of Gratian, Ausonius retired to his estate at Bordeaux, where he occupied himself with literature and rural pursuits. His works, which show great versatility, include epigrams, poems on his deceased relatives and on his colleagues, epistles in verse and prose, and idylls.

AUSTEN, Jane (1775–1817) English novelist, born in Steventon, Hampshire, where her father was rector. She spent the first 25 years of her life there and later lived in Bath, Southampton, Chawton, and Winchester. The fifth of a family of seven, she began writing for family amusement as a child, her *Love and Friendship* (published 1922) dating from this period. Her early published work satirized the sensational fiction of her time—Mrs **Radcliffe** and other 'gothick' novelists—and applied common sense to apparently melodramatic situations. Later she developed this technique in evaluating ordinary human behaviour. Of her six great novels, four were published anonymously during her lifetime and two under her signature posthumously. *Sense and Sensibility*, published in 1811, was begun in 1797; *Pride and Prejudice* appeared in 1813; *Mansfield Park*, begun in 1811, appeared in 1814; *Emma* in 1815. Her posthumous novels were both published in 1818; *Persuasion* had been written in 1815, and *Northanger Abbey*, begun in 1797, had been sold in 1803 to a publisher, who neglected it, and reclaimed it in 1816.

AUSTEN, Winifred (1876–1964) English wildlife artist, born in Ramsgate, the daughter of a naval surgeon. She took up painting professionally at an early age and after a tragically brief marriage moved to the village of Orford in East Suffolk in 1926. She illustrated Patrick Chalmers' *Birds Ashore and Foreshore* (1935), and painted postcards under the signature 'Spink'.

AUSTIN, Alfred (1835–1913) English poet, born of Catholic parents in Leeds. He was educated at Stonyhurst and Oscott College, graduated from London University in 1853, and was called to the bar in 1857 but abandoned law for literature. He published *The Season; a Satire* (1861), *The Human Tragedy* (1862), *The Conversion of Winckelmann* (1862) and a dozen more volumes of poems, and an autobiography (1911). Between 1883 and 1893 he edited the *National Review*; in 1896 he became poet laureate.

AUSTIN, Herbert, 1st Baron Austin of Longbridge (1866–1941) English car manufacturer, born in Buckinghamshire. Educated at Rotherham Grammar School and Brampton College, he went to Australia in 1884 and worked in engineering shops there. He returned to England in 1893 and joined the Wolseley Sheep-Shearing Company in Birmingham. In 1895, with the Wolseley Company, he produced his first three-wheel car, and in 1905 he opened near Birmingham his own works, which rapidly developed and whose enormous output included, in 1921, the popular 'Baby' Austin 7. He was Conservative MP for King's Norton from 1918 to 1924.

AUSTIN, John (1790–1859) English jurist, born in Creeting Mill, Suffolk. In 1818 he was called to the bar, and in 1826 was appointed professor of jurisprudence in the newly founded University of London (now University College). The subject was not recognized as a necessary branch of legal study, and from lack of students he resigned the chair (1832). His *Province of Jurisprudence Determined*, defining (on a utilitarian basis) the sphere of ethics and law, was not, initially, widely read; but in time it practically revolutionized English views on the subject, introduced a definiteness of terminology previously unknown and established the English analytical school of jurists, which concentrated on examination of terminology and concepts and was widely influential. His *Lectures on Jurisprudence* were published in 1863. His wife was the writer **Sarah Taylor Austin**.

AUSTIN, John Langsham (1911–60) English philosopher, born in Lancaster, Lancashire. Educated at Balliol College, Oxford, he taught in Oxford from 1945, was a leading figure in the 'Oxford Philosophy' movement, and became professor in 1952. His distinctive contribution was the meticulous examination of ordinary linguistic usage to resolve philosophical perplexities. He pioneered the analysis of speech acts, and his best-known works are *Philosophical Papers* (1961), *Sense and Sensibilia* (1962) and *How to do Things with Words* (1962). All his work is characterized by great precision and refinement.

AUSTIN, Robert Sargent (1895–1973) English etcher. Trained at the Royal College of Art, he became an exceptional artist and teacher who had a great knowledge of all techniques of printmaking. He worked almost exclusively with a burin which suited his interest in executing detailed line engravings which bear a stylistic comparison to that of **Dürer**. His mature work from the decade 1930–40 includes some of the finest prints of the period. He taught at the Royal College of Art and most of his life was spent refining the traditional art of line engraving which was rarely surpassed in craftmanship. He retired in 1955 and stopped making prints until 1963, when he executed another three works adding to his reputation as a master of line engraving.

AUSTIN, Stephen Fuller (1793–1836) American pioneer, born in Austinville, Virginia. He colonized Texas and was the founder of the Texas State.

AUSTRAL, Florence, originally **Florence Wilson** (1894–1968) Australian soprano, born in Richmond, Victoria. She adopted the name of her country as a stage name prior to her début in 1922 at Covent Garden, London, when she appeared as Brunnhilde with the British National Opera Company. She toured the USA and Canada in the 1920s, and appeared in the complete cycles of *The Ring* at Covent Garden and at the Berlin State Opera, which she joined as principal in 1930. She also appeared frequently in the concert hall, often with Sir **Henry Wood** and his BBC Symphony Orchestra, and made many recordings with other leading singers of her day. She returned to Australia after World War II where she taught until her retirement in 1959.

AVEBURY, 1st Baron of See **LUBBOCK, Sir John**

AVENARIUS, Richard Heinrich Ludwig (1843–96) German philosopher, born in Paris. Professor at Zürich from 1877 to 1896, his major work was the *Kritik der reinen Erfahrung* (1888–90), an analysis of pure experience in which he developed his theory of empirocriticism, an extreme form of positivism which seeks to eliminate any difference between the physical and the psychological.

AVENTINUS, properly **Johannes Thurmayr** (1477–1534) German humanist scholar and historian, born in Abensberg (Latin *Aventinum*), Bavaria. Known as the 'Bavarian Herodotus', he taught Greek and mathematics at Cracow, and wrote a history of Bavaria.

AVENZOAR, properly **Ibn Zohr** (c.1072–1162) Arab physician, born in Seville, considered the greatest clinician in the western caliphate. He published influential medical works describing such conditions as kidney stones, pericarditis, etc.

AVERROËS, Ibn Rushd (1126–98) the most famous of the medieval Islamic philosophers, born in Cordova, son of a distinguished family of jurists. He was himself Kadi (judge) successively at Cordova, Seville and in Morocco, and wrote on jurisprudence and medicine in this period as well as beginning his huge philosophical output. In 1182 he became court physician to Caliph Abu Yusuf, but in 1185 was banished in disgrace (for reasons now unknown) by the caliph's son and successor. Many of his works were burnt, but after a brief period of exile he was restored to grace and lived in retirement at Marrakesh until his death. The most numerous and the most important of his works were the *Commentaries on Aristotle*, many of them known only through their Latin (or Hebrew) translations, which greatly influenced later Jewish and Christian writers and offered a partial synthesis of Greek and Arabic philosophical traditions.

AVERY, Milton (1893–1965) American painter, born in Sand Bank, New York. Largely self-taught, he was greatly impressed by **Matisse**. A figurative rather than an abstract artist, he explored simplified areas of flat colour, applied thinly. He also painted seascapes in a rather more Expressionist style, and in 1933 began to make drypoints; in 1950 he launched a series of monotypes.

AVERY, Oswald Theodore (1877–1955) Canadian-born American bacteriologist, responsible for a key step in the genesis of molecular biology. Born in Halifax, Nova Scotia, he studied medicine at Colgate University and spent his career at the Rockefeller Institute Hospital, New York (1913–48). He early became an expert on pneumococci, and in 1928 was intrigued by a claim that a non-virulent, rough-coated strain could be transformed into the virulent smooth strain in mouse serum, by the mere presence of some of the dead (heat-killed) smooth bacteria. Avery confirmed this result, and went on in 1944 to show that the transformation is actually caused by a deoxyribonucleic acid (DNA), a chemical present in the dead bacteria. Cautiously, he did not go on to suggest that the informational molecules which carry the whole reproductive pattern of any living species (the genes) are simply DNA; this idea emerged slowly after about 1950 and forms the central concept of molecular biology.

AVERY, Tex, originally **Frederick Bean** (1908–80) American animated cartoon director, born in Texas. Failing to achieve his ambition to create a newspaper strip, he joined the **Walter Lantz** animation studio in 1929. Moving to Warner Brothers to direct his first cartoon, Porky Pig in *Goldiggers of '49* (1935), he soon was noticed for his zany comedy, creating Daffy Duck in *Porky's Duck Hunt* (1937), and developing Bugs Bunny in *A Wild Hare* (1940). Moving to MGM he created Droopy (*Dumb Hounded*, 1943), Screwy Squirrel (*Screwball Squirrel*, 1944), George and Junior (*Henpecked Hoboes*, 1946), and the classics, *King Size Canary* (1947) and *Bad Luck Blackie* (1949). In 1955 he moved into television commercials and later joined **Hanna–Barbera** for the television series *The Flintstones* (1979).

AVICEBRON, Arabic name: **Solomon ibn Gabirol** (c.1020–c.1070) Jewish poet and philosopher in the Jewish 'Golden Age' in Spain, born in Malaga. Most of his prose work is lost: an ethical treatise in Arabic survives, as does a Latin translation of his most famous work, *Fons vitae*. This latter is a dialogue on the nature of matter and the soul, Neoplatonist in character and very influential among later Christian scholastics. His poetry became part of the mystical tradition of the Kabbalah.

AVICENNA, Arabic name: **ibn Sina** (980–1037) Arab philosopher and physician, born near Bokhara. Renowned for his precocious and prodigious learning, he became physician to several sultans, and for some time vizier in Hamadan, in Persia, where he died. He was one of the main interpreters of **Aristotle** to the Islamic world, and was the author of some 200 works on science, religion and philosophy. His medical textbook, *Canon of Medicine*, long remained a standard work.

AVIENUS, Rufus Festus (c.375) Latin poet, a native of Volsinii (Bolsena). He wrote on natural and geographical topics, and translated the *Phainomena* of **Aratus of Sicyon**. He also wrote a paraphrase of a description of the world, *Descriptio Orbis Terrae*.

ÁVILA, Gil González de (1577–1658) Spanish historian. Royal historiographer for Castile, he is known for his account of the reign of **Henri III**.

AVILA, Juan de (1500–69) Spanish writer and preacher, born in Almodóvar del Campo. The 'Apostle of Andalusia', beatified by **Leo XIII** (1894), he has left numerous ascetic works, notably *Audi, Filia*, and several volumes of spiritual letters. He was also a trusted counsellor of St **Teresa**.

AVILA Y ZÚÑIGA, Luiz de (c.1490–1550) Spanish soldier and historian. A diplomat in the service of **Charles V**, he wrote a history of Charles's German wars (1547).

AVISON, Charles (c.1710–1770) English composer, born in Newcastle. Also known as a critic, he wrote an *Essay on Musical Expression* (1752), and he figures in **Browning**'s *Parleyings*.

AVOGADRO, Amedeo (1776–1856) Italian scientist, born in Turin. He was professor of physics there (1834–59), and in 1811 formulated the hypothesis, known as Avogadro's law, that equal volumes of gases contain equal numbers of molecules, when at the same temperature and pressure.

AVON, 1st Earl of See **EDEN, Sir (Robert) Anthony**

Á WOOD, Anthony See **WOOD**

AXEL See **ABSALON**

AXEL, Gabriel Mørch (1918–) Danish film director, now living in France. He trained as an actor at Copenhagen Royal Theatre from 1942 to 1945. His Danish films include *Den røde Kappe* (The Red Cape, 1966). In 1987 he made his international breakthrough with the film *Babette's Feast* (Babettes Gœstebud), an adaptation of a short story by **Karen Blixen**, which in 1988 won the Oscar in the Best Foreign Language Film category. He has directed several films for French television including *Un crime de notre temps* (1977), *La ronde de nuit* (1978), and *Le curé de Tours* (1980). His most recent Danish film, *Christian* (1989) describes a young man's journey through Europe in search of identity and love which he finally finds in Morocco.

AXELROD, Julius (1912–) American pharmacologist, joint winner of the 1970 Nobel prize for physiology or medicine. As chief of the pharmacology section of the National Institute of Mental Health from 1955, he discovered the substance which inhibits neural impulses, laying the basis for significant advances in neurophysiology in the treatment of, for instance, schizophrenia. He shared the Nobel prize with Ulf Svante von Euler and Sir **Bernard Katz**.

AYALA, Balthasar (1548–84) Spanish Netherlands jurist and judge of the Spanish forces in the Netherlands about 1580. Later he was a member of the great council and the court of requests in the Netherlands. He was author of *De Jure et Officiis bellicis et Disciplina militaris libri III* (1582), a book which makes him one of the forerunners of **Hugo Grotius** in the establishment of international law.

AYALA, Pedro López de (1332–1407) Spanish soldier, statesman and writer. He held high office under several kings of Castile, and wrote the *Crónicas de los Reyes de Castilla* and a didactic and satirical poem begun during his captivity in England (*Rimado de palacio*, 1367).

AYCKBOURN, Alan (1939–) English playwright. Born in London, he began his theatrical career as an acting stage manager in repertory before joining Stephen Joseph's Theatre-in-the-Round company at Scarborough. A founder-member of the Victoria Theatre, Stoke-on-Trent in 1962, he returned in 1964 as producer to Scarborough, where most of his plays have been premiered. His first of a torrent of west-end successes was *Relatively Speaking* in 1967, and he was quickly established as a master of farce, basing his plays in traditional manner on a single idea, usually a mistake or a confusion, from which the whole plot derives. His plays often contain shrewd observation of the English class-structure, but it is in sheer mechanical ingenuity that he excels. He has made considerable experiments with staging and dramatic structure: *The Norman Conquests* (1974) is a trilogy in which each play takes place at the same time in a different part of the setting, and *Way Upstream* (1982) is set on and around a boat and necessitates the flooding of the stage. Among his most successful farces are *Time and Time Again* (1972), *Absurd Person Singular* (1973), *Bedroom Farce* (1977), and *Joking Apart* (1979). He has written two musicals, *Jeeves* (with **Andrew Lloyd Webber**, 1975) and *Making Tracks* (with Paul Todd, 1981), and was a BBC radio drama producer, 1964–70. His later plays, including *Woman in Mind* (1985), and *Henceforward* (1987), reflect an increasingly bleak vision of society. Ayckbourn's techniques have become simpler and his characters more complex as he reveals himself to be not only a master farceur but a savage social commentator. He is now also recognized as a distinguished director, not only of his own work, but of plays by such authors as **Arthur Miller**.

AYER, Sir Alfred Jules (1910–89) English philosopher, born in London. Educated at Eton College and Oxford, he was a pupil of **Gilbert Ryle**. In World War II he was commissioned into the Welsh Guards and in 1945 was attaché at the British Embassy in Paris. He became professor at University College London in 1947 and professor at Oxford in 1947 until his retirement in 1959. His first and best book was *Language, Truth and Logic* (1936), a brilliantly lucid, concise and forceful account of the antimetaphysical doctrines of the 'Vienna Circle' of philosophers he had become acquainted with in the 1930s. This 'young man's book' with its iconoclastic dismissal of moral and religious discourse as not, in a literal sense, significant, aroused great hostility. His many later publications include *The Problem of Knowledge* (1956) and *The Central Questions of Philosophy* (1972). He was knighted in 1970.

AYERS, Sir Henry (1821–97) Australian politician, born in Portsea, Hampshire, He emigrated to South Australia in 1841 and took up a post with the SA Mining Association, with which he was associated for 50 years. Elected in 1863 to the first Legislative Council for the state under responsible government, he was a member of the Council for 36 years. His first ministry lasted for three weeks, at a time when his state was experiencing a volatile political situation. He was premier four times in the next ten years. During his last ministry, the overland telegraph to Darwin was completed, linking Australia with overseas telegraph networks, and Ayers received the KCMG. He was elected president of the Legislative Council in 1881, and was appointed GCMG upon his retirement in 1894. Ayers Rock, a giant monolith in the south of the (then) Northern Territories of South Australia, was named after him by **William Gosse** in 1873.

AYLIFFE, John (1676–1732) English scholar in Roman law, born in Winchester. Educated at Winchester and New College, Oxford, he was author of *Parergon Juris Canonici Anglicani* (1726), a compendium of Anglican ecclesiastical law with an historical introduction, and *A New Pandect of the Roman Civil Law* (1734), an extremely erudite work including a long history of the civil law down to his own time.

AYLMER, Sir Felix Edward, originally **Aylmer-Jones** (1889–1979) English actor, born into a military family and educated at Magdalen College School and Exeter College, Oxford. He made his first stage appearance with Sir **Seymour Hicks** at the Coliseum in 1911, after which he went to Birmingham Repertory. After service in World War I he settled into a series of steady successes on stage and screen, reaching particular strength in later life. Although termed a 'character actor', his range was remarkable, whether typifying the folly of age as Polonius in **Olivier**'s *Hamlet* or the wisdom of experience as Sir Patrick Cullen in Anthony Asquith's *The Doctor's Dilemma.* Alymer was deeply committed to his profession, serving as president of British Actors' Equity (1949–69). He was privately an enthusiastic **Dickens** scholar, publishing *Dickens Incognito* (1959) and *The Drood Case* (1964).

AYLMER, John (1521–94) English prelate, probably born in the ancestral Aylmer Hall, in Norfolk. In 1541 he graduated from Cambridge and became tutor to Lady **Jane Grey**. In 1553 he was installed as archdeacon of Stow, but fled to the continent to escape persecution during the reign of **Mary I**. He returned to become archdeacon of Lincoln (1562), and in 1577, was consecrated bishop of London. He showed equal rigor to Catholics and Puritans, and was pilloried as 'Morrell', the 'proude and ambitious pastoure', in **Spenser**'s *Shepherd's Calendar*.

AYLWARD, Gladys (1902–70) English missionary in China, born in Edmonton, London. She left school at 14 to be a parlour-maid, but her ambition was to go as a missionary to China. In 1930, she spent her entire savings on a railway ticket to Tientsin in northern China. With a Scottish missionary, Mrs Jeannie Lawson, the pair founded an inn, the famous Inn of the Sixth Happiness, in an outpost at Yangcheng. From there, in 1938, she trekked across the mountains leading over a hundred children to safety when the war with Japan brought fighting to the area. After nine years spent with the Nationalists, fulfilling her mission by caring for the wounded, she returned to England in 1948, preached for five years, then in 1953 settled in Taiwan as head of an orphanage.

AYRER, Jacob (c.1540–1625) German dramatist, one of the the most prolific of the 16th century, with over 100 plays of all kinds. He was a citizen of Nuremberg in 1594, and procurator in the courts of law.

AYRTON, Michael (1920–75) English painter, sculptor, book illustrator and art critic, born in London. His early painting falls into the wartime English Neo-Romantic movement along with that of **Sutherland**, **Minton** and Craxton. In 1954 he took up sculpture and began treating subjects from classical mythology, in particular the story of Daedalus and Icarus. His fascination with the legend of the minotaur led to his building of a maze in brick and stone in the Catskill Mountains, New York State. His graphic style was influenced by **Picasso**.

AYRTON, William Edward (1847–1908) English engineer and inventor, born in London. He worked in the Indian telegraph service, and became professor of electrical engineering at the Central Technical College, South Kensington (1884). His first wife was a pioneer woman doctor, Matilda Chaplin (1846–83); his second, Hertha Marks (1854–1923), continued his work on the electric arc and other inventions.

AYTON, Sir Robert (1570–1638) Scottish poet and courtier, born in Kinaldie, near St Andrews. He was educated at St Andrews University, studied law in Paris, and became a courtier of **James VI** and **I** in London. He wrote lyrics in English and Latin, and is credited with the prototype of 'Auld Lang Syne'.

AYTOUN, William Edmonstoune (1818–65) Scottish poet and humorist, born in Edinburgh, the son of a lawyer. Educated at The Edinburgh Academy and Edinburgh University, he was called to the Scottish bar in 1840. He published a collection of romantic pastiches, *Poland, Homer and Other Poems* (1832), and in 1836 began a lifelong connection with *Blackwood's Magazine*, to which he contributed countless parodies and burlesque reviews. In 1845 he was appointed professor of rhetoric and belles-lettres at Edinburgh University, and in five years quintupled the number of his students. In 1849 he married a daughter of Professor **John Wilson**; in 1852 was made sheriff of Orkney. His works include *Lays of the Scottish Cavaliers* (1848); *Firmilian, a Spasmodic Tragedy* (1854); *Bon Gaultier Ballads* (1855), and *Poems of Goethe* (1858), conjunctly with Theodore Martin; *Bothwell* (1856); and *Norman Sinclair* (1861), a semi-autobiographical novel.

AYUB KHAN, Mohammed (1907–74) Pakistani soldier and statesman, born in Abbottabad. Educated at Aligarh Moslem University and Sandhurst, he served in World War II, became first c-in-c of Pakistan's army (1951) and field marshal (1959). He became president of Pakistan in 1958 after a bloodless army *coup*, and established a stable economy and political autocracy. In March 1969, after widespread civil disorder and violent opposition from both right and left wings, Ayub Khan relinquished power and martial law was re-established. He published *Friends, Not Masters* in 1967.

AZAÑA, Manuel (1880–1940) Spanish statesman. A barrister, author, and lecturer in Madrid University he became war minister in 1931, and prime minister in 1931–33 and 1936 as leader of the Republican Left. He was elected president in 1936, but was forced into exile in 1939 by General **Franco**.

AZARIAH, Vedanayakam Samuel (1874–1945) Indian prelate, and first Indian bishop of the Anglican Church of India, Burma and Ceylon, born in Vellalanvillai, Madras State. A firm believer in co-operation between foreign and Indian church workers (on which topic he addressed the Edinburgh World Missionary Conference in 1910), and in the development of indigenous leadership in a united Indian Church, he was appointed bishop of Dornakal, Andhra Pradesh, in 1912. Bringing to his post experience gained with the Tinnevelly and National missionary societies, and the YMCA, he took a leading role in the Tranquebar (1919) and Nagpur (1931) conferences for church union, and was chairman of the National Christian Council of India, Burma and Ceylon from 1929.

AZCONA DEL HOYO, Jose Simon (1927–) Honduran politician. Born in La Ceiba, he trained as a civil engineer in Honduras and Mexico and developed a particular interest in urban development and low-cost housing. As a student he became interested in politics and fought the 1963 general election as a candidate for the Liberal party of Honduras (PLH) but his career was interrupted by a series of military coups. He served in the governments of Roberto Suazo and Walter Lopez (1982–86), which were ostensibly civilian administrations but, in reality, controlled by the army commander-in-chief, General Gustavo Alvarez. Alvarez was removed by junior officers in 1984 and in 1986 Azcona narrowly won the presidential election.

AZEGLIO, Massimo Taparellu, Marchese d' (1798–1866) Italian statesman, painter, and writer, born in Turin. A son-in-law of **Manzoni**, he studied painting in Rome, and wrote political novels. He took a leading part in the Risorgimento and the 1848 revolution, and became prime minister of Sardinia from 1848 to 1852.

AZIKIWE, Nnamdi (1904–) Nigerian politician, born in Zungeri, north Nigeria and educated at American universities. In 1937 he began to take a leading part in the Nigerian nationalist movement, founding a series of newspapers and becoming, during World War II, president of the National Council of Nigeria and the Cameroons and vice-president of the Nigerian National Democratic party. In 1952–53 he was a member of the western House of Assembly and from 1954 to 1959 of the eastern House. He became prime minister of the eastern region (1954–59), governor-general of Nigeria (1960–63), and was elected first president of the Nigerian republic in November 1963. In Britain during the military uprising of 1966, his office was suspended, although he returned privately to Nigeria.

AZO (c.1150–1230) Italian jurist. Professor at Bologna, he was in the first rank of the glossators who wrote explanatory notes on the texts of the Roman law. His *Summa Codicis* (1537) and *Apparatus ad Codicem* (1596) formed a methodical exposition of Roman law and were very influential in medieval courts. The *Summa* influenced **Henry de Bracton** in England.

AZORÍN, pseud of **José Martinez Ruiz** (1873–1967) Spanish novelist and critic, born in Monóvar and educated at Valencia. His novels include *Don Juan* (1922) and *Dona Inés* (1925).

B

BAADE, (Wilhelm Heinrich) Walter (1893–1960) German-born American astronomer, whose work gave new estimates for the age and size of the universe. Born in Schröttinghausen, he studied at Münster and Göttingen, and worked at the Hamburg Observatory from 1919 to 1931. He moved to the USA in 1931 and spent the rest of his career at the Mount Wilson (1931–58) and Palomar (1948–58) Observatories. Wartime blackout aided his observations and allowed him to identify and classify stars in a new and useful way, and led him to increase and improve **Hubble**'s values for the size and age of the universe, to the great relief of geologists. He also worked on supernovae and on radiostars. He was professor at Göttingen from 1959 to 1960.

BAADER, Andreas (1943–77) West German anarcho-terrorist. Born in Munich into a middle-class family, he became associated with the student protest movement of the later 1960s and was imprisoned for setting fire to department stores in Frankfurt in 1968. Critical of Germany's post-war materialism and military dominance by the USA, he formed, with **Ulrike Meinhof**, the Rote Armee Fraktion (Red Army Faction), a band of underground urban guerrillas. The Faction 'sprang' Baader from prison in 1970 and carried out a series of political assassinations and terrorist outrages. He was captured and sentenced to life imprisonment in 1977. When an attempt by the Faction to secure his release by holding an in-flight Lufthansa airliner hostage at Mogadishu, Somalia, was thwarted, he took his own life.

BAADER, Franz Xaver von (1765–1841) German Roman Catholic theologian and mystical philosopher, born in Munich. A follower of **Böhme**, he regarded **Hume**'s philosophy as atheistic and opposed Kant by maintaining that the true ethical end is not obedience to a moral law, but a realization of the divine life.

BAAL-SCHEM-TOV, properly **Israel ben Eliezer** (1699–1760) Jewish teacher and healer in Poland, the founder of modern Chasidism.

BABANGIDA, Ibrahim (1941–) Nigerian politician and soldier, born in Minna, Niger state. Educated at military schools in Nigeria, he was commissioned in 1963 and, after training in the United Kingdom, became an instructor at the Nigerian Defence Academy. After further training in the USA he became a major-general (1983). He took part in the overthrow of the government of Shehu Shagari in 1983 and was made commander-in-chief of the army. In 1985 he led a coup against President Buhari and assumed the presidency himself.

BABAR THE CONQUEROR, Zahīr al-Dīn Muhammad (1483–1530) first Mughal emperor of India, nephew of Sultan Mahmud Mirza of Samarkand. He attempted unsuccessfully as a young man to establish himself as ruler there, but in 1504 turned his attention with greater success towards Afghanistan, entering Kabul in that year. A further attempt to win Samarkand in 1511 was again unsuccessful. The death of Sikandir Lodi in 1517 brought civil war to the Afghan Lodi empire in India and Babar took advantage of this to invade India, defeating Ibrahim Lodi decisively at the battle of Panipat in 1526 and laying the foundation for the Mughal empire. The following year he defeated the Hindu Rajput confederacy and, despite continuing resistance from the Hindus and from the Afghans, the military strength of the Mughals enabled him to consolidate his gains. A soldier of genius, he was also a cultured man with interests in architecture, music and literature. Himself a Muslim, he initiated a policy of toleration towards his non-Muslim subjects that was continued by his successors and became a hall-mark of the Mughal empire at its zenith.

BABBAGE, Charles (1792–1871) English mathematician, born in Teignmouth, Devon. Educated at Trinity and Peterhouse Colleges, Cambridge, he spent most of his life attempting to build two calculating machines. The first, the 'difference engine', was intended for the calculation of tables of logarithms and similar functions by repeated addition performed by trains of gear wheels. A small prototype model was described to the Astronomical Society in 1822, and was awarded the Society's first gold medal. Babbage was then granted money by the government to build a full-sized machine, but in 1842, after some £17000 of public money and £6000 of his own had been spent without any substantial result, government support was withdrawn. An unfinished portion of the machine is now in the Science Museum, London. Meanwhile Babbage had conceived the plan for a much more ambitious machine, the 'analytical engine', which was designed not just to compute a single mathematical function, but could be programmed by punched cards, like those in the **Jacquard** loom, to perform many different computations. The cards were to store not only the numbers but also the sequence of operations to be performed. The idea was too ambitious to be realized by the mechanical devices available at the time, but can now be seen to be the essential germ of the electronic computer of today, and Babbage can be regarded as the pioneer of modern computers. He held the Lucasian chair of mathematics at Cambridge, 1828–39, though he delivered no lectures.

BABBITT, Irving (1865–1933) American critic and writer, born in Dayton, Ohio. He was professor of French at Harvard (1894–1933). Primarily a moralist and teacher, he was a leader of the 'new selective humanism' which flourished in America in the 1920s. His books include *Literature and the American College* (1908), *The New Laokoön* (1910), *Rousseau and Romanticism* (1919), and *On Being Creative* (1932).

BABBITT, Isaac (1799–1862) American goldsmith, inventor of 'Babbitt metal'. Born in Taunton, Massachusetts, in 1824 he manufactured the first Britannia metal tableware, using an alloy of copper, tin and antinomy. In 1839, after further experimentation with the same ingredients, he invented a journal box lined with a soft, silver-white alloy now called Babbitt metal, and still used to reduce friction in metal.

BABCOCK, Harold Delos (1882–1968) American physicist, born in Edgerton, Wisconsin. He was on the staff of the Mount Wilson obervatory (1909) when he measured the magnetic field of the star 78 Virginis, which provided a link between the electromagnetic and the relativity theories.

BABCOCK, Stephen Moulton (1843–1931) American agricultural chemist and 'the father of scientific dairying', he was born near Bridgewater, New York. He studied at Tufts College, Cornell and Göttingen; a farmer's son, he also farmed himself. From 1887 to 1913 he taught agricultural chemistry at Wisconsin University and soon devised the 'Babcock' test for measuring fat in milk, which much improved the quality of dairy produce. From 1907 he studied the effect of selective diets on cattle; the importance of accessory food factors (vitamins) emerged from this work, and was to be fully developed by Sir **Frederick Hopkins**.

BÂB-ED-DIN (1819–50) Persian religious leader: the title, meaning 'Gate of Righteousness', assumed by a merchant of Shiraz, Mirza Ali Mohammed. In 1844 he declared himself the Bab (Gateway) to the prophesied 12th Imam; later he claimed to be the Imam himself. He was imprisoned in 1847 and later executed at Tabriz. The religion he founded (Babism) was the forerunner of the Baha'i faith (see **Baha-Allah**).

BABEL, Isaac Emmanuilovich (1894–?1941) Russian short-story writer, a protégé of **Maxim Gorky**, born in the Jewish ghetto of Odessa. He worked as a journalist in St Petersburg, served in the tsar's army on the Romanian front and, after the Revolution, in various Bolshevik campaigns as a Cossack supply officer. He wrote stories of the Jews in Odessa in *Odesskie rasskazy* (1916, trans as *Odessa Tales*, 1924), and stories of war in *Konarmiya* (1926, trans as *Red Cavalry*, 1929). He was exiled to Siberia in the mid 1930s, and died in a concentration camp there in 1940 or 1941.

BABEUF, François (1760–97) French communist, born in St Quentin. During the Revolution, as 'Gracchus Babeuf', in the *Tribun du peuple* (which he founded), he advocated a rigorous system of communism. A conspiracy he had helped hatch, aiming to destroy the Directory and establish an extreme democratic and communistic system, was discovered, and he was guillotined.

BABILÉE, Jean, originally **Jean Gutman** (1923–) French dancer and choreographer, born in Paris. He began performing and devising dances in the early 1940s, having studied at the Paris Opéra Ballet School, and enjoyed some of his greatest successes as a member of the Ballets de Champs-Élysées and Ballets de Paris: in Janine Charrat's *Jeu de Cartes* (1945) and as the suicidal artist in **Roland Petit**'s *Le Jeune Homme et la Mort* (1946). He also excelled in *Spectre de la Rose* and as the Bluebird in *Sleeping Beauty*. In the 1950s he was a guest of the Paris Opéra Ballet and American Ballet Theatre before forming his own eponymous company. From 1972 to 1973 he was director of Ballet du Rhin in Strasbourg. He and his former wife, French dancer Nathalie Philippart, have a daughter, Isabelle, who is also a dancer. In the early 1980s **Maurice Béjart** created a solo for Babilée called *Life*, that showed he had lost little of his charisma and dynamic ability. He has also been a stage and film actor.

BABINET, Jacques (1794–1872) French physicist, born in Lusignan. He standardized light measurement by using the red cadmium line's wavelength as the standard for the angstrom unit. Babinet's principle, that similar diffraction patterns are produced by two complementary screens, is named after him.

BABINGTON, Antony (1561–86) English conspirator, born of an old and rich Catholic family in Dethick, Derbyshire. He had served as a page to **Mary, Queen of Scots**. In 1586 he was induced by **Ballard** and other Catholic emissaries to put himself at the head of a conspiracy aiming to murder Queen **Elizabeth** and release Mary. Cipher messages were intercepted by **Walsingham** in which Mary warmly approved the plot and these were later used against her. Anticipating Walsingham, Babington fled, was captured at Harrow and executed with the others.

BABINSKI, Joseph François Felix (1857–1932) French neurologist, born in Paris, who described a reflex of the foot symptomatic of upper motor neurone disease. Independently of Alfred Fröhlich (1871–1953), a Viennese pharmacologist, he investigated an endocrinal disorder, adiposogenital dystrophy, or Babinski-Fröhlich disease.

BABITS, Mihály (1883–1941) Hungarian poet of the 20th-century literary renaissance. He was also a novelist, and the best modern translator of **Dante**, **Shakespeare**, and the Greek classics.

BABRIUS Greek writer of fables. Little is known of him except that he collected Aesopic fables, which he turned into popular verse. These had almost all been lost, till in 1841 a Greek discovered 123 of them at Mount Athos.

BABUR See **BABAR**

BACALL, Lauren, originally **Betty Joan Perske** (1924–) American actress, born in New York City. A student at the American Academy of Dramatic Arts, she made her stage début in *Johnny Two-by-Four* (1942) and also worked as a model. Seen on the cover of *Harper's Bazaar*, she was signed to a contract by director Howard Hawks and launched as 'Slinky! Sultry! Sensational!' in the film *To Have and Have Not* (1944). Husky-voiced and with a feline grace, she was as tough, shrewd and cynical as her co-star **Humphrey Bogart**, whom she married in 1945. They appeared together in such hardboiled thrillers as *The Big Sleep* (1946), *Dark Passage* (1947) and *Key Largo* (1948). She displayed an elegant sense of light comedy in *How To Marry a Millionaire* (1953) and, after Bogart's death in 1957, turned to the stage, enjoying Broadway successes in *Goodbye Charlie* (1959), *The Cactus Flower* (1965–67) and the musical *Applause!* (1970–72), for which she received a Tony award. Her stylish, witty personality has enhanced such films as *Harper* (1966), *Murder on the Orient Express* (1974) and *Mr. North* (1988) and she received a British Academy award for *The Shootist* (1976). Recent stage work includes *Woman of the Year* (1981, Tony award) and *Sweet Bird of Youth* (1986), while her intelligent autobiography, *By Myself* (1979), was an international bestseller. She was married to the actor Jason Robards, Jr, from 1961 to 1969.

BACCHELLI, Riccardo (1891–1985) Italian novelist, born in Bologna. His works include *Il diavolo al Pontelungo*, a humorous tale of **Bakunin**'s efforts to introduce socialism into Italy, the three-volume family chronicle of the Risorgimento, *Il mulino del Po* (1938–40), and *Bellezza e Unamità* (1972).

BACCIOCHI, Maria Anna Elisa, née **Bonaparte** (1777–1820) eldest of the sisters of **Napoleon**, born in Ajaccio. She married Felice Bacciochi, and was created by her brother in 1805 a princess, and in 1809 Grand Duchess of Tuscany.

BACCIO DELLA PORTA See **BARTOLOMMEO**

BACH, Carl Philipp Emanuel (1714–88) German composer, known as the 'Berlin' or 'Hamburg' Bach, son of **J S Bach**. Born in Weimar, he was educated at the Thomas-school, Leipzig, where his father was cantor, and at Frankfurt University. He showed remarkable musical precocity and became in 1740 cembalist to the future **Frederick II, the Great**. Later he found employment first at Zittau (1753) and then as kapellmeister at Hamburg (1767) where he died of a lung condition. He was left-handed and therefore only unimpeded in the playing of the organ and clavier, for which his best pieces were composed. He published *The True Art of Clavier Playing* (1753), the first methodical treatment of the subject, introduced the sonata form, wrote numerous concertos, keyboard sonatas, church and chamber music. He bridged the transitional period between his father and **Haydn**, by his homophonic, formal yet delicate compositions.

BACH, Johann Christian (1735–82) German composer, known as the 'London' Bach, eleventh son of **J S Bach**. Born in Leipzig, he studied under his brother **C P E Bach** in Berlin and from 1754 in Italy. After turning Catholic, he was appointed organist at Milan in 1760 and for a time composed only ecclesiastical music, including two masses, a 'Requiem' and a 'Te Deum', but later began to compose opera. In 1762 he was appointed composer to the London Italian opera, and became musician to Queen **Charlotte** and later collaborated with **Karl Friedrich Abel**. The young **Mozart** on his London visit took to him greatly and was influenced by his style. He developed symphonic form, and was twice painted by **Gainsborough**. He is buried in St Pancras, London.

BACH, Johann Christoph Friedrich (1732–95) German composer, known as the 'Bückeburg' Bach, ninth son of **J S Bach**. Born in Leipzig, he was educated there at the Thomas-school and at Leipzig University, and became in 1750 kapellmeister at Bückeburg. He was an industrious but undistinguished church composer.

BACH, Johann Sebastian (1685–1750) German composer, one of the supremely great musicians of the world, born in Eisenach. An orphan before he was ten, he was placed in the care of his elder brother, Johann Christoph Bach (1671–1721), organist at Ohrdurf. He showed precocious ability at the local school, and was taught the organ and clavier by his brother. The latter placed his music library out of bounds to Sebastian, who soon acquired the nocturnal habit of copying out scores, a habit which he continued throughout his life and which eventually ruined his eyesight. In 1700 he became a church chorister at St John's church, Lüneberg. When his voice broke, he served as a violinist and harpsichord accompanist. In 1703 he was given a court appointment at Weimar, but in 1704 he became organist at Arnstadt, where many of his early church cantatas were written, including the flamboyant 'Easter' cantata No.15 and a humorous capriccio to mark the departure of a brother for the Swedish service. But he found his official duties as choirmaster exceedingly irksome. In 1705 he took a month's leave, which he overstayed, to journey on foot to Lübeck to hear the organist **Buxtehude**. This and his innovations in the chorale accompaniments infuriated the authorities at Arnstadt. After marrying a cousin, Maria Barbara Bach, whom he had introduced into the choir, in 1707 he left to become organist at Mühlhausen. The prevailing Calvinism there condemned his elaborate anthems, but his imposing inaugural cantata, 'God is my King', was recommended for publication. In 1708 he transferred to the ducal court at Weimar and remained there nine years. The two toccatas and fugues in D minor, the fantasia and fugue in G minor, the preludes and fugues in C and G, and the *Little Organ Book* of short preludes belong to this period. In 1716 the duke gave the senior post of kapellmeister to a musical nonentity. Sebastian promptly resigned, flushed by his moral victory over the French harpsichordist, Jean Louis Marchand, who had failed to appear at a greatly publicized musical contest with Sebastian at Dresden. The duke confined Sebastian for a month, before letting him take up his post of kapellmeister to Prince Leopold of Anhalt-Cöthen. At Cöthen, four overtures, the six French and six English suites, several concertos for one and two violins, and more for various ensembles were written. Six of the latter, now known as the 'Brandenburg' Concertos, were sent in 1721 to the margrave of Brandenburg, who had commissioned them. In *The Well-tempered Clavier* (1722), which profoundly influenced Mozart, Bach transformed the conventional structure of preludes and fugues written in each major and minor key. In 1720 Maria died suddenly. Of their seven children, four had survived. In 1722 he married Anna Magdalena Wilken, an accomplished singer, harpsichordist, and copyist, for whom Sebastian wrote a collection of keyboard pieces. Of the thirteen children born to them, seven died in infancy. For his children, Sebastian wrote a keyboard instruction book, and with Anna he completed a second *Notebook*. In 1723 he was appointed cantor of the Thomas-school in Leipzig, a post which he retained, despite acrimonious disagreements with the authorities and his colleagues, for the remainder of his life. To make it more difficult for them to overrule his decisions, Sebastian solicited the title of court composer to the elector of Saxony, and for his sponsor he wrote the thirty 'Goldberg Variations'. Goldberg was a pupil of his, and of his son **Wilhelm Friedemann Bach**. Sebastian's house became a centre of musical pilgrimage, and many eminent musicians, who included several relations, became his pupils. He became conductor of the *Collegium Musicum*, a society composed mainly of students, in 1729, but in 1743 refused to join the newly sponsored concert society, from which originated the famous *Gewandhaus* concerts. At Leipzig he wrote nearly three hundred church cantatas, of which two hundred survive. In the majority, the choruses have the lion's share, as in 'Sleepers Awake', 'We Praise Thee, Lord God', and 'I Cry to Thee, Thou Shepherd of Israel', but there are a few memorable ones for solo voice, such as 'O joyous Light' and 'I am a good Shepherd'. His 'Christmas' Oratorio is an assembly of six cantatas connected by a common narrative. The 'St Matthew Passion' (1729) and the Mass in B Minor (1733ff.) are two of the greatest choral works ever written. In 1747, Sebastian visited Berlin and was unexpectedly invited to Potsdam by **Frederick II, the Great**, who asked him to try his latest Silbermann pianofortes. After much improvization, Sebastian departed with a subject given to him by Frederick which he developed into a trio for flute, violin, and clavier, entitled *The Musical Offering*. He died two years later, almost totally blind, of apoplexy. At the time of his death he was engaged on his masterly series of fugues for keyboard, *The Art of Fugue*. His work stands midway between the old and the new, his main achievement being his remarkable development of polyphony. To his contemporaries he was known mainly as an organist, and a century was to pass before he was to be adequately recognized as composer.

BACH, Wilhelm Friedemann (1710–84) German composer, known as the 'Halle' Bach, eldest and most gifted son of **J S Bach**. Born in Weimar, he was educated at the Thomas-school and Leipzig University, where he showed a bent for mathematics. In 1733 he became organist at Dresden and in 1747 at Halle. But his way of life became increasingly dissolute and from 1764 he lived without fixed occupation at Brunswick, Göttingen and Berlin, where he died. He was the greatest organ player of his time, but very few of his compositions, which include church cantatas and several instrumental pieces, were published, as he very rarely bothered to write them down.

BACHE, Alexander Dallas (1806–67) American geophysicist, born in Philadelphia, great grandson of **Benjamin Franklin**. He became professor of natural philosophy at Pennsylvania University (1828–41), and as superintendent of the US Coast Survey had the entire coastline mapped in his lifetime.

BACHE, Francis Edward (1833–58) English violinist, organist, and composer for the piano, born in Birmingham. His brother Walter (1842–88) popularized **Liszt**'s works in London, and taught piano at the Royal Academy of Music.

BACHELARD, Gaston (1884–1962) French philosopher, born in Bar-sur-Aube. He had an unusual range of interests and influence in the history of science, psychoanalysis, and literary criticism, which were connected in such works as *La Psychoanalyse du feu* (1937) and *La Flamme d'une chandelle* (1961).

BACHMAN, John (1790–1874) American clergyman and naturalist, born in Rhinebeck, New York. From 1815 he was Lutheran pastor in Charleston, South Carolina. He was co-author with **Audubon** of *The Viviparous Quadrupeds of North America* (1845–49).

BACHOFEN, Johann Jakob (1815–87) Swiss jurist and historian. Professor of Roman law at Basel from 1841, he is known for his work on the theory of matriarchy (*Das Mutterrecht*, 1841).

BACICCIA, originally **Giovanni Battista Gaulli** (1639–1709) Italian painter, born in Genoa. He is best known for his ambitious and spectacular baroque illusionistic ceiling frescoes, in which the staggering illusionism is enhanced by the combination of painted figures and stucco work which breaks down the barrier between two- and three-dimensional representation. His flamboyant and colourful style is indebted to **Rubens** and **Correggio**, but the most forceful qualities of his work, best seen in the ceiling of the Jesuit church of The Gusú in Rome, was no doubt encouraged by his friend **Bernini** who similarly promoted a sensual and ecstatic art in the service of the Church. He also painted portraits of the papal court which are of a quieter mood.

BACK, Sir George (1796–1878) English Arctic explorer, born in Stockport. He sailed with Sir **John Franklin** on three Polar expeditions—to the Spitzbergen Seas (1819), the Coppermine River (1818–22), and Mackenzie River (1822–27). In 1833–35 he went in search of Sir **John Ross**, who was erroneously supposed to be lost, and discovered Artillery Lake and the Great Fish River, or Back's River, which he traced to the Frozen Ocean. In 1836–37 he further explored the Arctic shores. He was knighted in 1839, and made admiral in 1857.

BACKHUYSEN, or **BAKHUIZEN, Ludolf** (1631–1708) Dutch marine painter, born in Emden. He is best known for his *Rough Sea at the Mouth of the Maas* (Louvre) and several seascapes in London, Amsterdam, and The Hague.

BACON, Delia Salter (1811–59) American authoress, born in Tallmadge, Ohio, sister of **Leonard Bacon**. She spent the years 1853–58 in England trying to prove the theory that **Shakespeare**'s plays were written by **Francis Bacon**, **Raleigh**, **Spenser**, and others. She did not originate the idea herself, but was the first to give it currency in her *Philosophy of the Plays of Shakspere Unfolded* (1857), with a preface by **Hawthorne**.

BACON, Francis, Baron Verulam of Verulam, Viscount St Albans (1561–1626) English philosopher and statesman, born in London, the younger son of Sir **Nicholas Bacon**. He entered Trinity College, Cambridge, and in 1576 Gray's Inn, being called to the bar in 1582. He became MP in 1584 and, failing to obtain any favours from his uncle, **Burghley**, attached himself to the earl of Essex, from whom he accepted a gift of land at Twickenham. However, when his patron was tried for treason Bacon helped to secure his conviction. On **James VI and I**'s accession (1603) he sought royal favour by extravagant professions of loyalty; by planning schemes for the union of England and Scotland, and for pacifying the Church of England on comprehensive lines; and by making speeches in parliament to prove that the claims of the king and parliament could be reconciled. For these services he was knighted (1603) and was made a commissioner for the union of Scotland and England. In 1605 he published the *Advancement of Learning*; in 1606 he married a London alderman's daughter; and the following year he became solicitor-general. In 1612 he offered to manage parliament for the king and, in this capacity, was promoted, in 1613, to the attorney-generalship. In 1616 he prosecuted **Somerset**, with whom he was intimate, for the murder of **Overbury**. In the same year Bacon became a privy councillor, in 1617 lord keeper, and in 1618 Lord Chancellor, being raised to the peerage as Lord Verulam, a title taken from the Latin name for St Albans, near his estate at Gorhambury. His obsequiousness was then more marked than ever. In March 1626 he caught cold while stuffing a fowl with snow, in order to observe the effect of cold on the preservation of flesh, and died. He was buried in St Michael's Church, St Albans. At his death he was deep in debt. Bacon's philosophy is chiefly to be studied in (i) *The Advancement of Learning* (1605), a review of the state of knowledge in his own time, and its chief defects; (ii) *De Augmentis Scientiarum* (1623), a Latin expansion of the *Advancement*, and (iii) *Novum Organum* (1620). He abandoned the deductive logic of Aristotle and the schoolmen, and stressed the importance of experiment in interpreting nature and the necessity for proper regard for any possible evidence which might run counter to any held thesis. He described heat as a mode of motion, and light as requiring time for transmission, but he was behind the scientific knowledge of his time. His greatness consists in his insistence on the facts, that man is the servant and interpreter of Nature, that truth is not derived from authority, and that knowledge is the fruit of experience; and in spite of the defects of his method, the impetus he gave to future scientific investigation is indisputable. He was the practical creator of scientific induction. An unparalleled belief in himself, which justified to himself his ignoring of all ordinary laws of morality, is the leading feature in the character of this 'wisest, brightest, meanest of mankind'. As a writer of English prose and a student of human nature, he is seen to best advantage in his essays. His *History of Henry VII* (1622) shows scholarly research. In his fanciful *New Atlantis* he suggests the formation of scientific academies, while the *Apophthegms* (1625) are a disappointing collection of witticisms. His religious works include prayers and verse translations of seven Psalms (1625). His professional works include *Maxims of the Law* (1630), *Reading on the Statute of Uses* (1642), and *Elements of the Common Laws of England* (1630).

BACON, Francis (1909–) Irish artist, born in Dublin. He settled permanently in England in 1928. After working as an interior designer he began painting in about 1930 without any formal training. He first made a major impact in 1945 with his *Three Figures at the Base of a Crucifixion*. Although the initial inspiration for his work was Surrealism he made frequent use of imagery annexed from old masters such as **Velázquez** and **Muybridge**'s photographs of figures in motion. These are usually translated into blurred and gory figures imprisoned in unspecific, architectural settings. His pictures most frequently evoke atmospheres of terror and angst. A technical perfectionist, Bacon destroyed a great deal of his prolific output. Widely regarded as Britain's most important post-war artist, his works are in all major collections, including that of the Vatican.

BACON, John See **BACONTHORPE**

BACON, John (1740–99) English sculptor, born in London. He became one of the first students of the Royal Academy Schools and is responsible for the monuments to **Chatham** in Westminster Abbey and the Guildhall, the statue of Dr **Johnson** in St Paul's, and others. His second son, John (1777–1859), was also a sculptor.

BACON, Leonard (1801–81) American Congregationalist clergyman, born in Detroit, brother of **Delia Salter Bacon**. Professor of theology at Yale (1866–71), he wrote a history of Congregationalism in the USA. An early leader in the anti-slavery movement, he was founder-editor in 1848 of the free-soil paper, *The Independent*.

BACON, Nathaniel (c.1642–1676) American colonial leader, born in Suffolk. He emigrated to Virginia in 1673, and made himself prominent by his raids against the Indians. His activities prompted the English governor Sir William Berkeley (1606–77) to declare him a rebel in 1676; whereupon Bacon captured and burned Jamestown. For a time he controlled most of Virginia, but died suddenly.

BACON, Sir Nicholas (1509–79) English statesman. He attained high legal offices which, as a Protestant, he lost under **Mary I**, but in 1558, on her accession, **Elizabeth** made him lord keeper of the great seal, and left to him and **Cecil** the management of church affairs. A staunch anti-Catholic, he was an implacable enemy of **Mary, Queen of Scots**.

BACON, Roger (c.1214–1292) English philosopher and scientist, probably born near Ilchester, Somerset. He studied at Oxford and Paris and began to gain a reputation for diverse and unconventional learning in philosophy, magic and alchemy which led to the soubriquet *Doctor Mirabilis*. He seems to have returned to Oxford in 1247 to develop his interests in experimental science and, more surprisingly, to become a Franciscan. But he suffered rejection, censorship and eventually imprisonment from the Order for the heresy of his 'suspected novelties', and he died in Oxford soon after his eventual release from prison. He has been associated with scientific inventions like the magnifying glass and gunpowder and with speculations about lighter-than-air flying machines, microscopes and telescopes. His views on the primacy of mathematical proof and on experimentalism have often seemed strikingly modern, and despite surveillance and censorship from the Franciscans he published many works on mathematics, philosophy and logic whose importance was only recognized in later centuries.

BACONTHORPE, or **Bacon, John** (c.1290–1346) English scholar from Norfolk, grandnephew of **Roger Bacon**, and called 'the resolute doctor'. A Carmelite by training, he taught at Cambridge, and wrote commentaries on the Arab philosopher, **Averroës**. He anticipated **Wyclif**'s teaching that priests should be subordinate to kings.

BĀDARĀYANA The name applied to an unknown Indian philosopher, the reputed author of the *Vedānta* (or *Brahama*) *Sūtra*, sometimes identified with the 5th-century sage Vyasa, who is traditionally credited with compiling the *Mahābhārata*. Nothing is known of Bādarāyana apart from his connection with the *Vedānta Sūtra*, which cannot be dated with certainty. He may simply be a personification of an anonymous process of editing. The *Vedānta Sūtra* is the foundation text of *Vedānta*, *Sūtra* is one of the six classic systems of Hindu philosophy. Its varied interpretation is the basis of the subsequent schools founded by **Śankara**, **Rāmānuja**, and **Madhva**.

BADDELEY, née **Snow, Sophia** (1745–86) English actress and singer. She eloped in 1763 with Robert Baddeley (1732–94), the actor. While she played Ophelia, he specialized in low comedy roles.

BADEN-POWELL, Robert Stephenson Smyth, 1st Baron Baden-Powell (1857–1941) English soldier, born in London, son of the Savilian professor of geometry at Oxford. Educated at Charterhouse, he joined the army in 1876, served in India and Afghanistan, was on the staff in Ashanti and Matabeleland, and won fame as the defender of Mafeking (1899–1900) in the Boer War. He was promoted lieutenant general in 1907. He is best known, however, as the founder (1908) of the Boy Scouts and (1910), with his sister Agnes (1858–1945), of the Girl Guides. He published *Scouting for Boys* in 1908, founded the Wolf Cubs in 1916, and was acclaimed world chief scout in 1920. He died in Nyere, Kenya.

BADER, Sir Douglas Robert Stuart (1910–82) British aviator, born in London, and commissioned from Cranwell in 1930. He lost both legs in a flying accident in 1931 and was invalided out, but overcame his disability and returned to the RAF in 1939. He commanded the first RAF Canadian Fighter Squadron, evolving tactics that contributed to victory in the Battle of Britain, but was captured in August 1941 after a collision with an enemy aircraft over Béthune. Thrice mentioned in despatches, holder of the DSO and DFC with bars, the Légion d'honneur and the Croix de Guerre, he left the RAF in 1946. A great pilot and leader of 'the Few', he set an example of fortitude and heroism that became a legend. He was made CBE in 1956 for services to the disabled, and was knighted in 1976.

BADÍA-Y-LEBLICH, Domingo (1766–1818) Spanish traveller, born in Barcelona. He studied Arabic and, disguised as a Muslim, he visited (1803–07) Morocco, Tripoli, Cyprus, Egypt, and Mecca (the first Christian to be there since the spread of the Islamic faith); also Syria and Constantinople.

BADOGLIO, Pietro (1871–1956) Italian soldier, born in Grazzano Monferrato, Piedmont. In World War I he served with distinction in Tripoli, directed the capture of Monte Sabatino, and took command after the disaster of Caporetto (1917). Promoted field-marshal in 1926, he was governor general of Libya (1928–33) and directed the conquest of Abyssinia, now Ethiopia (1935–36). On Italy's entry into World War II in 1940, he was made commander-in-chief, but resigned during the Greek humiliation of Italian arms in Albania. Following **Mussolini**'s downfall (1943) he formed a non-Fascist government, negotiated an armistice with the Allies, declared war on Germany, and held power till 1944, when, after the king's delegation of his powers to his son, he was unable to form a government and resigned.

BAECK, Leo (1873–1956) German-Jewish religious leader, born in Lissa, Prussia. He was rabbi (1912–42) in Berlin, and when the Nazis came to power became the political leader of German Jewry and spent 1942–45 in the Theresienstadt concentration camp. After the war he lectured in Britain. His chief publications were *The Essence of Judaism* (1936) and *The Pharisees and Other Essays* (1947).

BAEDEKER, Karl (1801–59) German publisher, born in Essen. He started his own publishing business in 1827 in Coblenz, and is best known for the authoritative guidebooks which still bear his name.

BAEKELAND, Leo Hendrik (1863–1944) Belgian-born American chemist, born in Ghent. He emigrated to the USA in 1889, invented photographic printing paper usable with artificial light, discovered the first synthetic phenolic resin (Bakelite), and was a founder of the plastics industry.

BAER, Karl Ernst von (1792–1876) Estonian-born German naturalist, pioneer in embryology, born in Piep. After studying at Dorpat and later at Würzburg, he was professor at Königsberg (1817–34) and from 1834 at St Petersburg (now Leningrad). He discovered the mammalian egg (ovum) in the ovary, and the notochord (embryo backbone), and formulated the 'biogenetic law' that in embryonic development general characters appear before special ones.

BAEYER, Johann Friedrich Wilhelm Adolf von (1835–1917) German organic chemist, born in Berlin. At the age of twelve he discovered a new double salt of copper and sodium. At Heidelberg he studied under **Robert Wilhelm Bunsen** and **Friedrich Auguste Kekulé**, and became professor of chemistry at Strasbourg (1872) and Munich (1875–1915). His researches covered many aspects of chemistry, notably the synthesis of the dye indigo and the elucidation of its structure, the mechanism of photosynthesis, condensation of phenols and aldehydes, the polyacetylenes, the stability of polymethylene rings, the terpenes and the basicity of organic oxygen compounds. He was awarded the 1905 Nobel prize for chemistry.

BAFFIN, William (c.1584–1622) English navigator, born probably in London. From 1612 to 1616 he was pilot on several expeditions in search of the Northwest Passage. The most significant of these were the voyages under the command of Robert Bylot in the *Discovery*, during which they examined Hudson Strait (1615), discovered Baffin Bay (1616), and discovered Lancaster, Smith and Jones Sounds (1616) which were later shown to lead to the Arctic Ocean and the Pacific. These were to be the most important explorations of the Passage for nearly two centuries and were largely ignored by future Arctic explorers until confirmed by Sir **John Ross** in 1818. Baffin sailed as far north as latitude 77° 45N, and was possibly the first person to determine a degree of longitude at sea by lunar observation. Thereafter he carried out extensive surveys of the Red Sea (1616–21), and was killed at the siege of Ormuz.

BAGAZA, Jean-Baptiste (1946–) Burundian politician and soldier, born in Rutovu, Bururi Province. After attending military schools in Belgium he returned to Burundi and became assistant to the head of the armed forces, with the rank of lieutenant-colonel. In 1976 he led a coup to overthrow President Micombero and was appointed president by a Supreme Revolutionary Council. In 1984 the post of prime minister was abolished and Bagaza was elected head of state and government. In 1987 he was himself ousted in a coup led by Major Pierre Buyoya.

BAGEHOT, Walter (1826–77) English economist and journalist, born in Langport, Somerset. He graduated in mathematics at University College, London, was called to the bar in 1852 and after a spell as banker in his father's firm at Langport, succeeded his father-in-law, **James Wilson**, as editor of the *Economist* in 1860. His *English Constitution* (1867) is still a standard work. He followed **Thomas Hill Green** and others in applying the theory of evolution to politics, as in *Physics and Politics* (1872). Other works include *Lombard Street* (1875), *Literary Studies* (1878), and *Economic Studies* (1880). He advocated many constitutional reforms, including the introduction of life peers.

BAGFORD, John (1650–1716) English antiquary, born in London. Originally a shoemaker, he made a scrapbook collection of English broadside ditties and verses in 64 volumes for **Robert Harley**, earl of Oxford, known as *The Bagford Ballads*.

BAGGESEN, Jens (1764–1826) Danish poet and satirical humorist, born in Korsör. He travelled extensively in France and Germany and engaged in literary feuds with romanticists. He was the author of *Comical Tales* (1785) and numerous other works, many in German.

BAGIMONT See **BAJIMOND**

BAGRATION, Peer Ivanovich, Prince (1765–1812) Russian soldier, descended from the royal Bagratidae of Georgia. He entered the Russian army in 1783, and, after much active service, distinguished himself by holding up **Murat** in a rearguard action at Schongraben (1805). He fought, too, at Austerlitz, Eylau, Friedland, and the siege of Silistria (1809). He was mortally wounded in the battle of Borodino.

BAHA-ALLAH (1817–92) Persian religious leader: the name, meaning 'Glory of God', given to Mizra Huseyn Ali, founder of the Islamic Baha'i sect. He became a follower of the Shiraz merchant Mirza Ali Mohammed (see **Bāb-ed-din**), founder of the Persian Babi sect. Persecuted and imprisoned in 1852, he was exiled to Baghdad, Constantinople and Acre. In 1863 he proclaimed himself as the prophet that Bāb-ed-din had foretold, and became the leader of the new Baha'i faith.

BAHR, Hermann (1863–1934) Austrian dramatist, novelist, and critic, born in Linz. He studied in Vienna and Berlin, and took a leading part in the literary movements, Naturalism and Expressionism, of the Habsburg empire period. He published social novels such as *Die schöne Frau* (1899) and comedies such as *Die gelbe Nachtigall* (1907). He was appointed manager of the Deutsches Theater, Berlin (1903), and the Burgtheater, Vienna (1918).

BAHRDT, Karl Friedrich (1741–92) German theologian and freethinker, born in Bischofswerda in Saxony. Professor at Leipzig (1766–68), he was expelled for his loose living; professor at Giessen (1771–75), he was expelled for his 'model version' of the New Testament (1775). Imprisoned in 1778 for publishing a blasphemous satire, he spent the last ten years of his life keeping an inn on the Weinberg near Halle.

BAÏF, Jean Antoine de (1532–89) French poet, born in Venice. He was a member of the Pléiade, author of *Amours* (1552), *Passe-Temps*, and other works. He attempted to introduce blank verse into French poetry, and experimented with combinations of poetry and music.

BAIKIE, William Balfour (1825–64) Scottish explorer, naturalist, and linguist, born in Kirkwall, Orkney. He studied medicine at Edinburgh, and in 1848 became a naval surgeon. On the Niger expedition of 1854, he succeeded through the captain's death to the command of the *Pleiad*, and penetrated 250 miles higher than any previous traveller. In a second expedition in 1857 the *Pleiad* was wrecked, and he was left to continue his work single-handed from Lukoja. Within five years he had opened the navigation of the Niger, constructed roads, collected a native vocabulary, translated parts of the Bible and prayer book into Hausa and founded a city state.

BAILEY, David Royston (1938–) English photographer, born and educated in London. Originally specializing in fashion photography as a free-lance from 1959, his creative approach soon extended to portraits expressing the spirit of the 1960s and to some outstanding studies of the nude; he writes extensively on all aspects of his craft and has been a director of televison commercials and documentaries since the 1970s.

BAILEY, Sir Donald Coleman (1901–85) English engineer, born in Rotherham. He graduated at Sheffield. During World War II he designed the prefabricated, mobile, rapidly-erected bridge which bears his name.

BAILEY, Francis Lee (1933–) American criminal lawyer. A graduate of Harvard Law School, he founded a detective agency there to conduct his own case research. In the course of a sensational career as a defense attorney, he defended the Boston Strangler (**Albert Desalvo**) and the kidnapped heiress Patty Hearst (b.1954), convicted of bank robbery with her left-wing terrorist abductors. His books include *The Defense Never Rests* (1971) and *For the Defense* (1975).

BAILEY, James Anthony See **BARNUM**

BAILEY, Liberty Hyde (1858–1954) American horticulturalist and botanist, born in South Haven, Michigan. He was professor of horticulture at Michigan State (1885) and Cornell (1888), and founded the Bailey Hortorium of New York State College, in 1920. He edited various works such as the *Standard Cyclopedia of Horticulture* (1914–17), and coined the term 'cultivar'.

BAILEY, Nathan or **Nathaniel** (d.1742) English lexicographer. He was the compiler of *An Universal Etymological English Dictionary* (1721; supplementary volume 1727), used by Dr **Johnson** as the basis of his own dictionary. All that is known about Bailey is that he was a Seventh-day Baptist, and that he kept a boarding-school in Stepney, near London, where he died.

BAILEY, Philip James (1816–1902) English poet, born in Basford, Nottingham, the son of the historian of Nottinghamshire, Thomas Bailey (1785–1856). After studying at Glasgow University, he was called to the English bar in 1840, but never practised. Associated with the 'spasmodic' school, he was the author of *Festus: a Poem* (1839) which reached, greatly altered, an 11th (Jubilee) edition in 1889. His reputation was high among his contemporaries.

BAILEY, Trevor (1923–) English cricketer, writer and sports broadcaster, born in Westcliff-on-sea. An all-rounder, he played in 61 Test matches, where his adhesive batting earned him the nickname 'Barnacle'. He made over 2200 runs in Test cricket, although he scored only one century, and 132 Test wickets, including 11–98 against West Indies at Lord's in 1957. He played for Essex for 20 years and acted as secretary and captain for that county. On retirement he established a reputation as a trenchant and perceptive radio commentator.

BAILLIE, Grizel, Lady née **Hume** (1665–1746) Scottish poet, daughter of the Scottish Covenanter, Sir **Patrick Hume**. In 1684 she supplied him with food during his concealment in the vault beneath Polwarth church, and helped shelter the Covenanting scholar, Robert Baillie of Jerviswood (1634–84), whose son, George, she married in 1692. She is remembered by her songs, particularly 'And werena my heart licht I wad dee'.

BAILLIE, Dame Isobel (1895–1983) Scottish soprano, born in Hawick, the daughter of a baker, on the estate of the Earl of Dalkeith. When her family moved to Manchester, the quality of her voice was recognized and she had singing lessons from the age of nine. She worked as an assistant in the piano-roll department of a music shop, and then as a clerk in Manchester Town Hall, and made her début with the Hallé Orchestra under Sir **Hamilton Harty** in 1921. After studies in Milan, she won immediate success in her opening season in London in 1923. Regarded as one of this century's greatest oratorio singers, she regularly sang with such conductors as Sir **Thomas Beecham**, **Arturo Toscanini** and **Bruno Walter**, and gave over 1000 performances of the *Messiah*.

BAILLIE, John (1886–1960) Scottish theologian, born in Gairloch, Ross-shire, son of the Free Church minister there. Educated at Inverness Academy, he studied philosophy at Edinburgh, and trained for the ministry at New College, Edinburgh, Marburg and Jena. During World War I he served with the YMCA in France. After the war he went to the USA, where he was professor of Christian theology at Auburn Theological Seminary, New York (1920–27), and Roosevelt professor of systematic theology at Union Seminary, New York (1930–35). Back in Scotland he was professor of divinity at New College from 1935 to 1936. He published a number of theological works, including the modern devotional classic, *Diary of Private Prayer* (1937), and *Our Knowledge of God* (1939). A key contributor to mid-century religious, social and intellectual life in Scotland, he was chairman of the influential church committee that produced the report *God's Will for Church and Nation* (1946) in favour of the Welfare State and state intervention in the economy.

BAILLIE, Matthew (1761–1823) Scottish physician and anatomist, born in Shotts. After seven years at Glasgow and Oxford (1773–80) he studied anatomy under **William Hunter**, his mother's brother, and in 1783 succeeded to his uncle's famous anatomy school in Great Windmill Street in London. He was the author of the first treatise in English on morbid anatomy (1793).

BAILLIE, Robert (1599–1662) Scotttish Presbyterian clergyman, born and educated in Glasgow. In 1622 he received episcopal ordination, and was shortly after presented to the parish of Kilwinning. In 1637 he refused to preach in favour of **Laud**'s service book, and in 1638 sat in the famous General Assembly which met in Glasgow to protest against episcopacy. In 1639 he served as chaplain in the Covenanting army at Duns Law, and in 1640 was selected to go to London with other commissioners and draw up charges against Archbishop Laud. On his return to Scotland in 1642 he was appointed joint professor of divinity at Glasgow. In 1643 he was a delegate to the Westminster Assembly, in 1649 was chosen by the church to go to Holland to invite **Charles II** to accept the covenant and crown of Scotland. He performed his mission skilfully; and, after the Restoration, was made principal of Glasgow University.

BAILLIE, Robert, of Jerviswood (d.1684) Scottish conspirator, a native of Lanarkshire, who in 1683 entered into correspondence with, and subsequently joined, **Monmouth**'s supporters in London. On the discovery of the Rye-house Plot, he was arrested and sent to Scotland. He was tried at Edinburgh, condemned to death on insufficient evidence, and hanged. His son married Lady **Grizel Baillie**.

BAILLIEU, William Lawrence (1859–1939) Australian businessman, born in Queenscliff, Victoria, the second son of James George Baillieu, of Haverfordwest, Pembrokeshire, who arrived in Melbourne in 1853. After various business ventures, and after marrying the daughter of a Melbourne brewer, Baillieu gained an interest in the London Bank of Australia which joined with the English, Scottish & Australian Bank. The profits from this were invested in lead and zinc extraction at Broken Hill, New South Wales, and founded the family fortunes. A member of the Legislative Council of Victoria from 1901 to 1922, he was involved in most significant business developments of the period and was a founder of the Melbourne newspaper *The Herald*. His son, Clive Latham Baillieu (1889–1967), represented Australia on many international committees, and became 1st Baron Baillieu of Sefton in 1953.

BAILLY, Jean Sylvain (1736–93) French astronomer and politician, born in Paris. From art he turned to literature, and then to astronomy, writing his great *Histoire de l'astronomie* (1775–87). As president of the National Assembly and mayor of Paris during the Revolution in 1789, he conducted himself with great integrity; but lost his popularity by allowing the National Guard to fire on anti-royalist crowds. He withdrew from public affairs but was arrested and taken to Paris, where he was guillotined.

BAILY, Edward Hodges (1788–1867) English sculptor, born in Bristol. He executed many of the well-known London statues, including that of Lord **Nelson** in Trafalgar Square.

BAILY, Francis (1774–1844) English astronomer, born in Newbury, Berkshire. He made a large fortune as a stockbroker and on his retirement in 1825 devoted himself to astronomy and was president of the Royal Astronomical Society when he died. He detected the phenomenon known as 'Baily's beads' during an eclipse of the sun in 1836, and calculated the mean density of the earth.

BAIN, Alexander (1818–1903) Scottish empirical philosopher and psychologist, born in Aberdeen where he became professor of logic (1860–81). He was one of a circle which included **J S Mill** and **George Grote** and he wrote books on the two Mills. But his most important works are *The Senses and the Intellect* (1855), *The Emotions and the Will* (1859) and *Mental and Moral Science* (1868). He also founded the famous journal, *Mind*, in 1876. His psychology was firmly based on physiology and he sought to explain mind through a physical theory of the association of ideas.

BAINES, Edward (1774–1848) English politician and journalist, born in Walton-le-Dale. From 1801 he was proprietor of the *Leeds Mercury*. He was Liberal MP for Leeds (1834–41), championed separation of church and state, opposed governmental control over education and wrote a history of Lancashire. His son, Sir Edward Baines (1800–90), who also sat for Leeds, held the same ideas as his father, and wrote a history of the cotton industry (1835).

BAINTON, Edgar Leslie (1880–1956) English-born Australian composer, teacher and conductor, born in London. He studied at the Royal College of Music before being appointed professor, and later principal, of the Conservatorium of Music, Newcastle-upon-Tyne. In 1938 he was appointed director of the Conservatorium in Sydney, New South Wales, and from that time played a key role in the music life of his adopted city. Apart from his work as administrator and educator, he conducted the then State Symphony Orchestra and later the Sydney Symphony Orchestra, as well as many public concerts including an open-air concert in 1938 for Australia's 150th anniversary with a choir of 5000 and massed brass bands. A prolific, though conservative, composer, he wrote three operas, chamber music, song settings and piano pieces. He came out of retirement in 1950 to conduct the National Orchestra of New Zealand in a series of concerts and festivals throughout that country.

BAINTON, Roland (1894–1984) American Congregational minister and Refomation scholar, born in Ilkeston, Derbyshire. Taken to Canada by his father in 1898, he was educated at Whitman College and Yale University. He taught church history at Yale Divinity School (1920–62), and was probably the best-known scholar of the Protestant Reformation in America, his works translated into a dozen languages. His books include *The Church of Our Fathers* (1950), *Here I Stand* (1950), *The Reformation of the Sixteenth Century* (1952), *Christian Attitudes toward War and Peace* (1960), *Early and Medieval Christianity* (1962), and *Erasmus of Christendom* (1969).

BAIRAKDAR, Mustafa (1755–1808) Turkish grand vizier, pasha of Rustchuk. After the revolt of the janissaries in 1807 by which **Selim III** was deposed in favour of Mustapha IV, he marched his troops to Constantinople in 1808, but found Selim already dead. Bairakdar executed the murderers, deposed Mustapha, and proclaimed his brother, **Mahmud II**, sultan. As grand vizier, he endeavoured to carry out Selim's reforms and to annihilate the janissaries, who, however, rebelled and, backed by the fleet, demanded the restoration of Mustapha. Bairakdar defended himself bravely until, strangling Mustapha, he threw his head to the besiegers, and then blew himself up.

BAIRD, Sir David (1757–1829) Scottish soldier, born in Newbyth, East Lothian. He joined the army in 1772, and in 1779 sailed to India with the Highland Light Infantry (then 73rd Foot). In the 2nd Mysore war (1780–84) he was captured and imprisoned at Seringapatam (1780) for nearly four years. After active service elsewhere he returned to India, took part in several sieges and attacks and returned in 1799, a major-general, and led the victorious attack on Seringapatam. He commanded Indian troops against the French in Egypt in 1801. In 1805–06 he commanded an expedition which successfully wrested the Cape of Good Hope from the Dutch. He was at the siege of Copenhagen (1807), and in 1809 distinguished himself and lost an arm in the battle of La Coruña (1809) in the Peninsular war, succeeding Sir **John Moore**. He was commander-in-chief in Ireland from 1820 to 1822.

BAIRD, John Logie (1888–1946) Scottish electrical engineer and television pioneer, born in Helensburgh. He studied electrical engineering at Glasgow University. Poor health compelled him to give up the post of engineer to the Clyde Valley electric power company, and after a brief career as a sales representative he settled in Hastings (1922) and began research into the possibilities of television. In 1926 he gave the first demonstration of a television image. His 30-line mechanically-scanned system was adopted by the BBC in 1929, being superseded in 1936 by his 240-line system. In the following year the BBC chose a rival 405-line system with electronic scanning made by Marconi-EMIO. Other lines of research initiated by Baird in the 1920s included radar and infra-red television ('Noctovision'); he continued his research up to the time of his death and succeeded in producing three-dimensional and coloured images (1944) as well as projection on to a screen and stereophonic sound.

BAIRD, Spencer Fullerton (1823–87) American naturalist, born in Reading, Pennsylvania, of Scottish descent. Educated at Dickinson College, Carlisle, he studied medicine in New York but turned to ornithology, encouraged by **Audubon** and others. In 1846 he was appointed professor of natural history at Dickinson College, and built up a vast collection of North American fauna. In 1850 he was appointed assistant secretary to **Joseph Henry** at the Smithsonian Institution in Washington (secretary from 1878), and published *Catalogue of North American Mammals* (1857) and *Catalogue of North American Birds* (1858), and was co-author of *A History of North American*

Birds (1874–84). From 1871 he was the first US commissioner of fish and fisheries. Baird's Sandpiper and Baird's Sparrow are named in his honour.

BAIRNSFATHER, (Charles) Bruce (1888–1959) British cartoonist, born in Murree, India. He served in France during World War I, and became famous for his war cartoons featuring the character 'Old Bill'. During World War II, he was an official war cartoonist attached to the US Army in Europe. His drawings appeared in various periodicals, in war books, and in his *Fragments from France* (1916) in six volumes, and *Jeeps and Jests* (1943).

BAJAZET See **BAYEZIT**

BAJIMOND, Bagimont, or **Boiamond** (c.1200–c.1300) Italian churchman. A canon of Asti in Piedmont, he was sent by Pope Gregory X in 1274 to Scotland to collect the tithe of all the church livings for a crusade. Bajimond's roll was used as the papal system of taxation in Scotland until the Reformation.

BA JIN, pseud of **Li Feigan** (1904–) Chinese writer, born into a wealthy family in Chengdu, Sichuan. Educated in the traditional classical style in Shanghai and Nanjing, he also studied in France (1927–29), and became an enthusiastic anarchist. His major trilogy (*Family*, 1931, *Spring*, 1938, and *Autumn*, 1940) attacked the traditional family system, and was immensely popular with the younger generation. Several other novels confirmed his standing as one of China's foremost patriotic writers. Although never a member of the Communist party, he held important literary positions in the communist régime after renouncing his earlier anarchism. During the Cultural Revolution (1966–76) he was purged and punished, and compelled to do manual work. He re-emerged in 1977, and published a collection of essays about his experience entitled *Random Thoughts* (1979).

BAJUS, or **De Bay Michael** (1513–89) Flemish Catholic theologian, born in Hainault. In 1551 he became professor of theology at Louvain. He was a devoted student of St **Augustine**, and 76 of his propositions were condemned by a papal bull in 1567. He may be regarded as the precursor of the Jansenists.

BAKER, Sir Benjamin (1840–1907) English civil engineer, born in Frome. In 1861 he entered into a long association with **John Fowler** as consulting engineer. They together designed the London Metropolitan railway, Victoria station, and many bridges. Their greatest achievement was the Forth Rail Bridge (1883–90), built on the cantilever principle. Baker was also consulting engineer for the Aswan dam in Egypt and its subsequent heightening, and the Hudson River Tunnel in New York (1888–91). He designed the vessel which carried Cleopatra's Needle to London, and many miles of the London underground railways.

BAKEP., Sir Herbert (1862–1946) English architect, born in Kent. He designed Groote Schuur, near Cape Town, for **Cecil Rhodes**, the Union Government buildings at Pretoria, and, with **Edwin Lutyens**, New Delhi in India; in Oxford, Rhodes House; in London, the new Bank of England, South Africa House, and others.

BAKER, James A III (1930–) US Republican politician, born into a wealthy patrician legal family in Houston, Texas. He studied at Princeton and the University of Texas Law School, saw service in the US Marines, and became a successful corporate lawyer. After the death of his first wife, Mary, he entered politics as a county manager of the unsuccessful 1970 campaign for the senate by his close friend, **George Bush**. Later, at Bush's suggestion, he was appointed under-secretary of commerce (1975–76) in the **Gerald Ford** administration and managed Ford's 1976 presidential and Bush's 1979 Republican party nomination campaigns. President **Reagan** appointed him his White House chief-of-staff in 1981 and Treasury secretary in 1985. After directing Bush's victorious presidential campaign in 1988, he became secretary of the state department in 1989.

BAKER, Dame Janet (Abbott) (1933–) English mezzo-soprano. Born in Hatfield, Yorkshire, she sang in various local choirs before going to study music in London in 1953. She made her debut in 1956 as Roza in **Smetana**'s *The Secret* at Glyndebourne, since when she has enjoyed an extensive operatic career, especially in early Italian opera and the works of **Benjamin Britten**. Also a concert performer, she is a noted interpreter of **Mahler** and **Elgar**.

BAKER, Kenneth Wilfred (1934–) English politician. He read history at Oxford and in 1960 entered local politics as a Conservative councillor in Twickenham. In 1968 he was elected to the House of Commons, representing Acton and later Mole Valley. After holding junior posts (1970–74) he became parliamentary private secretary to Edward Heath when he was leader of the opposition. In the **Margaret Thatcher** administration he rose from minister of state in the department of trade to become secretary of state for the environment (1985) and for education (1986), responsible for introducing a controversial education reform bill. He was appointed chairman of the Conservative party in 1989, retaining his seat in the cabinet.

BAKER, Sir Richard (c.1568–1645) English historian, born in Kent. High-sheriff of Oxfordshire in 1620, in 1635 he was thrown into the Fleet Prison for debt. There he wrote his *Chronicle of the Kings of England* (1643), from the Roman period to his own day.

BAKER, Sir Samuel White (1821–93) English explorer, born in London. In 1845 he went to Sri Lanka (where he established an agricultural settlement at Nuwara Eliya), and afterwards supervized the construction of a railway across the Dobrudja. In 1860 he married a Hungarian called Florence, and with her undertook the exploration of the Nile sources. At Gondokoro in 1863, they met **Speke** and **Grant** who were coming from the south, and told Baker of the Victoria Nyanza, which they had discovered; they also mentioned that the natives had described to them another great lake, named Luta Nzige. Baker resolved to reach this lake; and after many adventures they beheld, on 14 March 1864, from a lofty cliff, the great inland sea to which Baker gave the name of the Albert Nyanza into which the Nile flows. He was knighted in 1866, joined the Prince of Wales in Egypt for the opening of the Suez Canal in 1869, and was subsequently invited to command an expedition, organized by the pasha of Egypt, for the suppression of slavery and the annnexation of the equatorial regions of the Nile Basin. He returned to Europe in 1873 and later travelled in Cyprus, Syria, India, Japan, and America.

BAKER, Snowy (Reginald Leslie) (1884–1953) Australian athlete, born in Sydney. A swimming champion at 13, two years later he played rugby union for his state, and the following year for Australia. At the age of 18 he won the Australian middleweight and heavyweight titles in one night, and in 1908 was losing middleweight finalist at the London Olympic Games. At Sydney University he gained 'blues' for cricket, rugby, rowing and athletics, played water polo and was considered 'the best diver in Australia'. It was claimed that in his career he played at least 26 sports. From 1918 he took a leading role in four Australian silent films with his horse 'Boomerang' and subsequently moved to Hollywood where they both starred in a number of movies. Baker then turned to teaching horsemanship to film stars including **Spencer Tracy**, **Elizabeth Taylor** and **Douglas Fairbanks Senior**, who used Baker's 36-foot stockwhip in his classic film *The Mark of Zorro* (1920).

BAKEWELL, Robert (1725–95) English agriculturist, born in Dishley, Leicestershire. By selection and inbreeding he improved the standard and methods of management of sheep, cattle, and draught horses. He established the Leicester breed of sheep and Dishley breed of longhorn cattle, aroused a wide interest in breeding methods, made a great deal of money, but died in poverty.

BAKHUIZEN, Ludolf See **BACKHUYSEN**

BAKST, Leon (1866–1924) Russian painter, born in St Petersburg. He painted religious and genre works in Moscow, and then turned to scenery design at Hermitage Court Theatre in St Petersburg. In 1908 he went to Paris, where he was associated with **Diaghilev** from the beginnings of the Russian ballet, designing the décor and costumes for numerous productions (1909–21). His rich, exuberant colours, seemingly uncontrolled, in reality produced a powerful theatrical effect, which revolutionized fashion and decoration generally.

BAKUNIN, Mikhail (1814–76) Russian anarchist, born near Moscow of aristocratic descent. He took part in the German revolutionary movement (1848–49) and was condemned to death. Sent to Siberia in 1855, he escaped to Japan, and arrived in England in 1861. In September 1870 he attempted an abortive rising at Lyon. As leader of anarchism Bakunin was in the Communist International the opponent of **Karl Marx**; but at the Hague Congress in 1872 he was outvoted and expelled. He believed that communism, with its theoretical 'withering away of the state', was an essential step towards anarchism.

BALAGUER, Joaquim (1907–) Dominican Republic politician. He was professor of law at Santo Domingo University from 1938 and ambassador to Colombia and Mexico in the 1940s before entering politics. He served in the dictatorial régime of Rafael Trujillo, after whose assassination in 1961 he fled to the USA in 1962, returning in 1965 to win the presidency in 1966 as leader of the Christian Social Reform party (PRSC). He was re-elected in 1970 and 1974. The failure of the economic policies of the Dominican Revolutionary party (PRD) brought the PRSC and Balaguer back to power in 1986, at the age of 79.

BALAGUER Y CIRERA, Victor (1824–1901) Spanish poet, politician, and historian. A leading figure of the Catalan renaissance, he wrote a *History of Catalonia*, a *Political and Literary History of the Troubadours*, and poems in both Catalan and Spanish.

BALAKIREV, Mili Alexeivich (1836–1910) Russian composer, born in Nijni Novgorod. He turned to composing after an early career as a concert pianist, and became the leader of the national Russian school of music. **Cui**, **Mussorgsky**, **Rimsky-Korsakov**, **Borodin**, and **Tchaikovsky** were all influenced by him. He founded the Petersburg Free School of Music (1862), and was director of the Imperial Capella (1883). His compositions include two symphonies, a symphonic poem *Tamara*, and the oriental fantasy for piano *Islamey*.

BALANCHINE, George, originally **Georgi Melitonivich Balanchivadze** (1904–83) Russian-born American choreographer, born in St Petersburg, the son of a Georgian folk musician. Considered one of the greatest dance talents of the 20th century, he studied at the ballet school of the Imperial Theatres and choreographed his first piece while still a student. After graduating in 1921 he enrolled at the Petrograd Conservatory to study composition but returned to ballet, forming his own small company whose innovations were frowned on by the theatre authorities. In 1924 he defected with a group of dancers during a European tour and after performing in London as the Soviet State Dancers, **Sergei Diaghilev** took them into his Russian Ballet in Paris, and Balanchivadze changed his name to Balanchine. In 1925 he succeeded **Bronislava Nijinska** as choreographer and ballet-master. The ballets *Apollo* (1928) and *The Prodigal Son* (1929) are considered his masterpieces of that period. After Diaghilev's death in 1929 and his own serious illness, he worked for various companies, including that of the 1930 Cochran Revue in London, then helped to found Les Ballets Russes de Monte Carlo in 1932 and Les Ballets the following year. Invited to found a classical ballet company in America, he opened the School of American Ballet in New York in 1934. *Serenade* (1934), his first American ballet, was to become the American Ballet company's signature piece. After the war and the break-up of the American Ballet he directed a private company, the Ballet Society, which in 1948 emerged as the New York City Ballet. With that company he created over 90 works of enormous variety, ranging from the theatrical *Nutcracker* (1954) to the abstract *Agon* (1957). Other important works include *Don Quixote* (1966), *Coppelia* (1974), *Symphony in C*, *Episodes* (1959), *Kammermusik No. 2* (1978) and **Schumann**'s *Davidsbundlertauze* (1980). As well as his prolific output Balanchine is noted for his range of styles and controlled technique. He was also a successful musical comedy and film choreographer. His musicals include *Ziegfeld Follies* (1935) and *On Your Toes* (1936). Films include *The Goldwyn Follies* (1938) and *Star Spangled Rythyms* (1942).

BALARD, Antoine Jérôme (1802–76) French chemist, born in Montpelier, Hérault. Professor at the Sorbonne and Collège de France, he discovered bromine, hypochlorous acid, and chlorine monoxide.

BALASSA, Bálint, English **Valentine** (1555–91) Hungarian knight, adventurer and lyric poet, born in Kékkö. He died fighting the Turkish invaders, and his poetry was inspired by military heroism, love, and religion. He also experimented in drama (*Credulus and Julia*). He wrote *Little Garden for Diseased Minds* (1572).

BALBO, Cesare, Count (1789–1853) Italian statesman and author, born in Turin. A prime minister in the first Piedmontese constitutional ministry, he published a biography of **Dante** in 1839 and an historical essay demonstrating his view that Italy had only prospered when free from foreign domination.

BALBO, Italo, Count (1896–1940) Italian aviator and politician. One of the leaders of the 'March on Rome', he was the first minister of aviation in Italy, and led mass flights to Brazil (1929) and the USA (1933). In 1933 he became governor of Libya; in 1940 he was killed when his plane was brought down at Tobruk.

BALBOA, Vasco Núñez de (1475–1519) Spanish explorer, born in Jerez-de-Los-Caballeros. In 1511 he joined an expedition to Darien as a stowaway. Taking advantage of an insurrection, he took command, founded a colony at Darien and extended Spanish influence into neighbouring areas. On one of these expeditions he climbed a peak and sighted the Pacific Ocean, the first European to do so, and took possession for Spain. The governorship was granted in 1514 to Pedro Ariar de Ávila, for whom Balboa undertook many successful expeditions and whose daughter he married, but after a disagreement in 1519 Balboa was unjustly beheaded.

BALBUENA, Bernardo de (1568–1627) Spanish poet and prelate, born in Valdepeñas. He spent his working life in Central America, where all his poetry was written, and became bishop of Puerto Rico in 1620. He wrote an epic on the national hero, Bernardo del Capio, in *El Bernardo o la victoria de Roncesvalles* (1624), excellently and powerfully constructed and full of allegory.

BALCH, Emily Greene (1867–1961) American social reformer and pacifist, born in Jamaica Plain, Massachusetts, the daughter of a lawyer and a schoolteacher. Educated at Bryn Mawr College (1886–89), she was described there as having 'extraordinary beauty of moral character'. From 1890 to 1891 she studied political economy at the Sorbonne and in 1893 published *Public Assistance of the Poor in France*. From 1896 to 1918 she taught economics at Wellesley College (professor of economics and sociology from 1913), her innovative courses including coverage of **Karl Marx** and women's place in the economy. In 1906 she became a socialist. An active pacifist, she openly opposed World War I and was viewed by the authorities with increasing suspicion. In 1919 her academic appointment was not renewed. She helped establish the Women's International League for Peace and Freedom (1919) and subsequently proved an indefatigable administrator, writer and promoter for peace. She shared the 1946 Nobel prize for peace with **John R Mott**. Her works include *Our Slavic Fellow Citizens* (1910) and *Toward Human Unity* (1952).

BALCHEN, Bernt (1899–1973) Norwegian-born American aviator and arctic explorer, born in Tveit Topdal. In 1924 he was commissioned as a flight lieutenant in the Royal Norwegian Naval Air Force and flew rescue missions over the Arctic, as well as assisting **Roald Amundsen** and **Lincoln Ellsworth** in planning flights over the North Pole. He was chief pilot to **Richard Byrd**'s first Antarctic Expedition (1928–30) and to the Ellsworth Antarctic Expedition (1932–35). He became a US citizen in 1931, and in 1935 returned to Norway as manager of DNL (Norwegian Air Lines), and after wartime service in the US air force resumed this post in 1946. He returned to active US duty in 1948, commanding an Arctic Rescue Unit, and as adviser to the Pentagon.

BALDI, Bernardino (1553–1617) Italian Renaissance author, born in Urbino. He was secretary to various prelates and to the Duke of Urbino, and became abbot of Guastalla. He wrote eclogues, a didactic poem on seafaring called *La nautica* (1590), and prose dialogues.

BALDINI, Antonio (1889–1962) Italian humorist, born in Rome. *Nostro purgatorio* (1918) recounts his war experiences, but his most characteristic works are *Michelaccio* (1924), *La dolce calamita* (1929), *Amici allo spiedo* (1932). He became editor of the *Nuova Antologia* in 1931.

BALDINUCCI, Filippo (1624–96) Italian art historian, born in Florence. He was entrusted by Cardinal Leopoldo Medici with the arrangement of the Medici collection. He wrote six volumes on Italian artists since **Giovanni Cimabué**.

BALDOVINETTI, Alesso (1427–99) Italian painter, working in Florence. His frescoes, noted for their landscape backgrounds, are mostly poorly preserved as a result of his experiments in technique, but he also executed mosaics of great beauty and worked on stained glass.

BALDUNG, or **Grien, Hans** (c.1476–1545) German painter and engraver, born in Weiersheim near Strasbourg. He may have been a pupil of **Dürer**. His mature works display deliberate exaggeration of late Gothic styles to obtain often morbid quasi-Expressionist effects in the manner of **Grünewald**, as in *Die Frau und den Tod* (Basle) and *Die Eitelkeit* (Vienna).

BALDUS DE UBALDIS (c.1320–1400) Italian jurist, a pupil of **Bartolus** and professor at several universities. Next to Bartolus he was deemed leader of the school of commentators, who commented on **Justinian**'s *Corpus Juris Civilis* and the glosses (explanatory notes) on these, and sought to relate their principles to contemporary problems. He wrote also on canon law, feudal law and Romano-canonical procedure and left over 2000 *consilia* or opinions on cases which had been referred to him. Some of his writings are also important in the history of political science.

BALDWIN I (1171–c.1205) emperor of Constantinople, born in Valenciennes. He succeeded his parents as Count of Hainault and Flanders in 1195. In 1202 he joined the fourth Crusade, and in 1204 was chosen the first Latin emperor of Constantinople. The Greeks, invoking the aid of the Bulgarians, rose and took Adrianople. Baldwin laid siege to the town, but was defeated in 1205 and died in captivity.

BALDWIN II (1217–73) Emperor of Constantinople, nephew of **Baldwin I**, succeeded as emperor in 1228. The Greeks took Constantinople in 1261, extinguishing the Latin Empire. Thereafter Baldwin lived as a fugitive, having sold his rights to **Charles of Anjou**.

BALDWIN II, 'of Bourcq' (d.1131) King of Jerusalem, was a son of Count Hugh of Rethel. He succeeded his cousin Baldwin I as Count of Edessa in 1100 and king of Jerusalem in 1118.

BALDWIN III (1129–62) king of Jerusalem, grandson of **Baldwin II**. He succeeded his father, Fulk of Anjou, in 1143, but enjoyed sole authority only after long disputes and even civil war with his mother Melisende. His main achievement was the capture of Ascalon, the last Fatimid stronghold in Palestine (1153).

BALDWIN (d.1190) English prelate, born in Exeter in poor circumstances. He became bishop of Worcester in 1180, and archbishop of Canterbury in 1184. He crowned **Richard I**, made a tour of Wales preaching in favour of the Crusades, and himself died on a Crusade.

BALDWIN, James Arthur (1924–87) American black writer, born and brought up in a poor section of Harlem, New York. After a variety of jobs he moved to Europe, where he lived (mainly in Paris) from 1948 to 1957, before returning to the USA as a civil-rights activist. His novels, in which autobiographical elements appear, include *Go Tell it on the Mountain* (1954), *Giovanni's Room* (1957), *Another Country* (1963), *Tell Me How Long The Train's Been Gone* (1968), and *Just Above My Head* (1979). Other works include collections of essays (*Notes of a Native Son*, 1955; *The Fire Next Time*, 1963) and plays—*The Amen Corner* (1955), *Blues for Mr Charlie* (1964), and *The Women at the Well* (1972).

BALDWIN, James Mark (1861–1934) American psychologist, born in Columbia, South Carolina. A specialist in child psychology and social psychology, he was professor at Toronto (1889), Princeton (1893), Johns Hopkins (1903), University of Mexico (1909) and Paris (1918). He was the founder-editor of the *Psychological Review* (1894–1909), and editor of the *Dictionary of Philosophy and Psychology* (1901–06).

BALDWIN, Matthias William (1795–1866) American locomotive engineer and industrialist, born in Elizabethtown, New Jersey. A jeweller up to the age of 30, he abandoned that trade in favour of tool-making, then began to make hydraulic presses and printing machinery, and by 1827 was manufacturing steam engines. His first locomotive, *Old Ironsides*, was completed in 1832 and remained in service for 20 years. He developed accurately fitted steam joints which allowed the use of pressures up to 120 lb per sq in, twice that used in British locomotives at the time. The Baldwin locomotive works built over 1000 engines by 1861, and remained for many years the world's largest manufacturer of locomotives.

BALDWIN, Oliver Ridsdale, 2nd Earl Baldwin of Bewdley (1899–1958) British Labour politician, son of **Stanley Baldwin**. He was imprisoned by the Bolsheviks (1921), was Labour MP for Dudley (1929–31) and Paisley (1945–47), and governor of the Leeward Islands (1948–50).

BALDWIN, Robert (1804–58) Canadian politician, born in Toronto. After a successful legal and political career he became prime minister of Upper Canada (1842–43) and with Lafontaine founded the Reform party.

BALDWIN, Stanley, 1st Earl Baldwin of Bewdley (1867–1947) English Conservative statesman, born in Bewdley. He was educated at Harrow and Trinity College, Cambridge, and became vice-chairman of the family iron and steel business. An MP in 1906, he became president of the board of trade (1921), and after taking part in the Washington financial talks (1923) he unexpectedly succeeded **Bonar Law** as premier, being preferred to **Curzon**. His period of office included the General Strike (1926) and was interrupted by the **Ramsay MacDonald** Coalition (1931–35), in which he served as lord president of the Council. He skilfully avoided a party split by his India Act (1935), but the Hoare-Laval pact and the policy of non-intervention in Spain (1936) came to be regarded as betrayals of the League of Nations. His reluctance to re-arm Britain's defences is to be compared with his tact and resolution during the constitutional crisis culminating in **Edward VIII**'s abdication (1937). He had the party politician's sure touch in domestic matters, but was somewhat unjustly criticized for his apparent failure to recognize the threat from Nazi Germany. He resigned and was made an earl in 1937.

BALE, John (1495–1563) English cleric and dramatist, born in Cove, near Dunwich. A Carmelite by training, he turned Protestant in 1533 and obtained the Suffolk living of Thorndon. In 1540 he had to flee to Germany. Recalled by **Edward VI**, he was made bishop of Ossory in Leinster. Here 'Bilious Bale' made himself so obnoxious to Catholics with his polemical writings that they attacked his house and killed five servants. On Queen **Elizabeth**'s accession he was made a prebendary of Canterbury. He wrote a Latin history of 'British' authors (from Adam and Seth onwards!), and a drama, *King John*, which is considered the first English historical play.

BALENCIAGA, Cristóbal (1895–1972) Spanish couturier, born in Guetaria, the son of a seamstress. Helped by a local aristocrat, he trained as a tailor, and in 1915 opened dressmaking and tailoring shops of his own in Madrid and Barcelona. He left Spain for Paris in 1937 because of the Spanish Civil War, and became a couturier. A perfectionist, his clothes were noted for dramatic simplicity and elegant design. He retired in 1968.

BALEWA, Sir Abubakar Tafawa (1912–66) Nigerian politician, born in Bauchi, the son of a butcher and minor official who later moved to Tafawa Balewa. A member of the Northern People's Congress, he entered the Federal Assembly in 1947, was minister of works (1952), of transport (1953) and then premier (1957) and was knighted when Nigeria became independent in 1960. A reluctant federalist at first even in his own country, he was assassinated in the military uprising of 1966.

BALFE, Michael William (1808–70) English composer, born in Dublin. In his ninth year he made his début as a violinist, having begun to compose two years earlier; in 1823 he went to London, and during 1825–26 studied in Italy under **Rossini**, which inspired him to sing in opera with considerable success. In 1833 he returned to England, and in 1846 was appointed conductor of the London Italian Opera. Of his numerous operas, operettas, and other compositions, the most enduring success was *The Bohemian Girl* (1843).

BALFOUR, Sir Andrew (1630–94) Scottish physician, born in Denmiln, Fife. He studied at St Andrews, Oxford, Blois and Paris and with Sir **Robert Sibbald** helped to establish a 'physic garden' near Holyrood House in Edinburgh (1676–80), the second oldest botanic garden in Britain and the forerunner of the present Royal Botanic Garden in Edinburgh (1822–24). He was third president (1685) of the Royal College of Physicians of Edinburgh.

BALFOUR, Arthur James, 1st Earl of Balfour (1848–1930) Scottish statesman and philosopher, brother of **Eleanor**, **Gerald** and Jabez **Balfour**. Born, on his father's side, into an ancient Scottish family, he succeeded to the family estate in East Lothian in 1856. His mother was sister of Lord **Robert Cecil** (Lord Salisbury). Educated at Eton and Trinity College, Cambridge, he entered parliament in 1874 as a Conservative member for Hertford, and from 1878 to 1880 was private secretary to his uncle, Lord Salisbury, whom he accompanied to the Berlin Congress. In 1879 he published *Defence of Philosophic Doubt*, a plea for intellectual liberty in the face of the encroaching dogmatism of science. He was returned for East Manchester (1885), was secretary for Scotland (1886), chief secretary for Ireland (1887), and First Lord of the Treasury and leader in the Commons (1892–93). His premiership (1902–06) saw the end of the South African war (1905), the Education Act (1905), and the establishment of the Committee of Imperial Defence. In 1911 he resigned the leadership of the House owing to the constitutional crisis and delivered the Gifford Lectures in 1915 on *Theism and Humanism*. He followed **Churchill** to the Admiralty (1915) and served under **Lloyd George** as foreign secretary (1916–19). He was responsible for the famous Balfour declaration (1917) which promised Zionists a national home in Palestine, keenly supported the League of Nations, and as lord president of the Council (1921) was responsible for the controversial note cancelling Allied war debts to America.

BALFOUR, Eleanor Mildred See **SIDGWICK, Henry**

BALFOUR, Francis Maitland (1851–82) Scottish embryologist, born in Edinburgh, brother of **Arthur Balfour**. Educated at Harrow and Trinity College, Cambridge, he became the first professor of animal morphology there in 1882 after publishing his *Treatise on Comparative Embryology* in 1880. He lost his life in a climbing accident on Mont Blanc.

BALFOUR, George (1872–1941) Scottish electrical engineer and pioneering contractor, and founder of the construction firm of Balfour Beatty Ltd. Born in Portsmouth, he served an apprenticeship in a foundry in Dundee and qualified as a journeyman engineer. After working for a New York company specializing in electric tramways and power plants, he founded his own company in 1909 with an accountant, Andrew

Beatty. They built and operated the tramway systems for Dunfermline, Llanelly, and many towns in the Midlands, and the first major hydro-electrical schemes in Scotland, as well as pioneering the National Grid in the 1930s. He also built the giant Kut Barrage on the Tigris for Iraq. He was Unionist MP for Hampstead (London) from 1918 until his death.

BALFOUR, Gerald William, 2nd Earl of Balfour (1853–1945) Scottish statesman, brother of **Arthur Balfour**. He was educated at Eton and Trinity College, Cambridge, of which he became a fellow (1878). He was chief secretary for Ireland (1895–96), president of the board of trade (1900–05), local government board (1905–06), and succeeded his brother as earl in 1930.

BALFOUR, Sir James of Pittendreich (d.1583) Scottish jurist and politician. After the murder of Cardinal **David Beaton** in 1547 he was taken prisoner with **John Knox** and sent to France. Released in 1549, he returned to Scotland and 'served with all parties, deserted all, and yet profited by all'. He was involved in the murder of Lord Darnley, was commissioned to compile the *Practicks or a System of the More Ancient Law of Scotland* (1574), an invaluable repertory of ancient statutes and decisions. He became lord president of the Court of Session in 1567 and withdrew to France in 1580.

BALFOUR, John, of Kinloch (fl.1675) Scottish conspirator, chiefly responsible for Archbishop **Sharp**'s assassination in 1679. He fought at Drumclog and Bothwell Bridge and is said to have escaped to Holland. Sir **Walter Scott**, in his *Old Mortality*, confused him with John Balfour, 3rd Lord Balfour of Burleigh, who died in 1688.

BALIOL or **BALLIOL** an Anglo-Norman family, whose founder, Guido or Guy, held Bailleul, Harcourt, and other fiefs in Normandy, and from **William II, Rufus** received large possessions in Durham and Northumberland. Bernard, his son, built the fortress of Barnard Castle; and *his* great-grandson, John, about 1263 founded Balliol College, Oxford. He died in 1269, and was survived till 1290 by his widow, Devorgilla, the daughter and co-heiress of Alan, Lord of Galloway, the great-great-granddaughter of **David I**, and the founder in 1275 of Sweetheart Abbey, Kirkcudbright.

BALL, John (d.1381) English rebel, an excommunicated priest who was executed as one of the leaders in the Peasants' Revolt of 1381, led by **Wat Tyler**.

BALL, John (1818–89) Irish botanist and alpinist, born in Dublin. He was the first president of the Alpine club (1857) and author of the *Alpine Guide* (1863–68). Liberal MP for Carlow, he was colonial undersecretary (1855–57), and wrote on the botany of Morocco and South America.

BALL, Lucille Desirée (1910–89) American comedienne, born in Celaron, New York. An amateur performer as a child, she was a model and chorus girl before moving to Hollywood. There she spent several years in bit parts and B-pictures before more substantial roles were offered. An effervescent redhead with a rasping voice and impeccable timing, she began working in television in 1951 and became one of its best-loved characters, starring in such domestic comedies as *I Love Lucy* (1951–55), *The Lucy Show* (1962–68) and *Here's Lucy* (1968–73). She purchased her own studio with first husband Desi Arnaz and also became a successful production executive, occasionally returning to the cinema for popular comedies like *The Facts of Life* (1960) and *Yours, Mine and Ours* (1968).

BALLA, Giacomo (1871–1958) Italian artist, born in Turin, one of the founders of Futurism and a signatory to the 1910 Futurist Manifesto. After a visit to Paris in 1900 he was strongly influenced by Impressionism and Divisionism, which he introduced to his pupils **Boccioni** and **Severini**. Primarily concerned with conveying movement and speed in painterly terms, he achieved this by imitating time-lapse photography; *Dog on a Leash* (1912) exemplifies this technique. Although Futurism outlived World War I, by 1930 Balla was painting in a more conventional style.

BALLANTINE, James (1808–77) Scottish artist and poet, born in Edinburgh. Originally a housepainter, he learned drawing under Sir **William Allan**, and was one of the first to revive the art of glass-painting. Two prose volumes, *The Gaberlunzie's Wallet* (1843) and *Miller of Deanhaugh* (1845), contain some of his best-known songs and ballads.

BALLANTYNE, James (1772–1833) and **John** (1774–1821), Scottish printers, the sons of a merchant of Kelso. In 1783 they were both at school at Kelso Grammar School with Sir **Walter Scott**. James was trained for the law, but in 1797 started the Tory *Kelso Mail*; and in 1802, having already printed some ballads for Scott, he produced the first two volumes of the *Border Minstrelsy*. At Scott's suggestion he moved the firm to Edinburgh, and in 1805 Scott became a secret partner in the business, which in 1808 expanded into the printing, publishing, and bookselling firm of John Ballantyne & Co, Scott having one-half share, and each of the brothers a quarter. As early as 1813 bankruptcy threatened the firm, and it was hopelessly involved in **Archibald Constable**'s ruin (1826). John had died bankrupt five years earlier; and James was employed by the creditors' trustees in editing the *Weekly Journal* and in the literary management of the printing office.

BALLANTYNE, John See **BELLENDEN, John**

BALLANTYNE, Robert Michael (1825–94) Scottish author of boys' books, born in Edinburgh, a nephew of **James** and **John Ballantyne**. Educated at The Edinburgh Academy, he joined the Hudson's Bay Company in 1841, and worked as a clerk at the Red River Settlement in the backwoods of northern Canada until 1847, before returning to Edinburgh in 1848. He wrote his first stories on his experiences in Canada, with books such as *The Young Fur Traders* (1856). *Coral Island* (1858) is his most famous work.

BALLARD, James Graham (1930–) British fiction writer, born in Shanghai, China, and educated at Cambridge. He has commented that 'science fiction is the authentic literature of the 20th century, the only fiction to respond to the transforming nature of science and technology'. Until recently he was better known for his work in that genre, fashioning a series of novels at once inventive, experimental and, in several cases, bizarre. His early novels, including his first, *The Drowned World* (1962), offer a view of the world beset by elemental catastrophe. He has been admired chiefly for his short stories, particularly those included in such collections as *The Terminal Beach* (1964), *The Disaster Area* (1967) and *Vermilion Sands* (1973), but *Empire of the Sun* (1984), a mainstream novel which is portentously autobiographical, was short-listed for the Booker prize. He won the Guardian Fiction prize in 1984 and the James Tait Black Memorial prize in 1985.

BALLARD, John (d.1586) a Jesuit executed for his connection with **Babington**'s conspiracy.

BALLESTEROS, Sevvy (Severiano) (1957–) Spanish golfer, born in Santander. Starting as a caddy for foreigners, he became one of the world's leading golfers. A highly combative, adventurous player, he has continually set records, and has an uncanny ability to produce thrilling recovery shots. When he won the British Open in 1979 he was the youngest player to do so in the 20th century, and he took the title again in 1984 and 1988. His US Masters win in 1980 was the youngest ever, and he was only the second European to win the event and wear the coveted Green Jacket.

BALLIN, Albert (1857–1918) German shipping magnate, born in Hamburg. He became a director-general of the Hamburg-America Line in 1900, a close adviser of **William II**, and improved Germany's mercantile marine.

BALLIOL, Edward (c.1283–1364) king of Scotland 1332–56, elder son of **John de Balliol**. In 1332, accompanied by the 'disinherited barons' bent on recovering their forfeited Scottish estates, he landed with 3400 followers at Kinghorn in Fife; and at Dupplin Moor in Perthshire, on 12 August, surprised and routed the Scottish army under the new regent, the Earl of Mar. On 24 September he was crowned king of Scotland at Scone. Less than three months later, he was himself surprised at Annan and fled across the Border on an unsaddled horse. Two further incursions into Scotland, in 1334–35, were unsuccessful and he resigned his claims to the Scottish throne to **Edward III** in 1356. He died without heirs.

BALLIOL, John de (c.1250–1315) king of Scotland 1292–96, latterly nicknamed 'Toom Tabard' or 'Empty Jacket' by the Scots, son of the founder of Balliol College, Oxford, who succeeded in his mother's right to the lordship of Galloway as well as to his father's vast possessions in England and Normandy. On the death of **Margaret, the 'Maid of Norway'** in 1290, he became a claimant to the crown of Scotland; his claim was pronounced superior by **Edward I** of England to that of **Robert Bruce**, lord of Annandale. Balliol swore fealty to Edward before and after his investiture at Scone (1292) and was forced to repudiate the Treaty of Bingham of 1290 with its guarantees of Scottish liberties. By 1295 a council of twelve of the magnates had taken control of government out of his hands and concluded an alliance with France, then at war with England; Edward invaded Scotland, took Balliol prisoner, and forced him to surrender his crown, 10 July 1296. Balliol was confined for three years at Hertford and in the Tower; in 1302 he was permitted to retire to his estates in Normandy, where he died.

BALLOU, Hosea (1771–1852) American clergyman, born in Richmond, New Hampshire. Originally a Baptist minister, he was the chief founder of the Universalist Church.

BALMAIN, Pierre Alexandre (1914–82) French couturier, born in St Jean-de-Maurienne, the son of a draper. He started studying architecture in Paris, but turned to dress designing, working for **Edward Molyneux** and Lucien Lelong. In 1945 he opened his own house. Famous for elegant simplicity, his designs included evening dresses, tailored suits, sportswear and stoles. He also designed for the theatre and cinema.

BALMER, Johann Jakob (1825–98) Swiss physicist, born in Lausen near Basle. He derived a formula for frequencies of hydrogen lines in the visible spectrum. The Balmer series is the atomic spectrum of hydrogen in the visible and near ultraviolet regions of the spectrum.

BALMERINO, Arthur Elphinstone, 6th Baron (1688–1746) Scottish Jacobite. He fought with the Jacobites in the Rising of 1715, escaped to the Continent, and was pardoned in 1733. He was one of the first to join Prince **Charles Edward Stewart** in the 1745 Rising, was captured at Culloden in 1746 and beheaded on Tower Hill in London.

BALMONT, Konstantin Dmitryevitch (1867–1943) Russian poet, translator and essayist, born in Gumische, Vladimir province, one of the greatest of the Russian symbolists. His work was coloured by the wide travelling he did during his periodic exiles, which added a vein of exoticism to his work.

BALNAVES, Henry (?1512–1579) Scottish reformer, born in Kirkcaldy. In 1538 he was made a lord of session by **James V**. In 1543 he was appointed secretary of state by the regent **James Hamilton**, Earl of Arran. Shortly after, however, he was imprisoned, with **John Knox**, in Blackness Castle for his Protestantism. When the castle was captured by the French (1547), Balnaves, with Knox and others, was sent to Rouen. While in prison there, he wrote a treatise on Justification which, with notes and a preface by Knox, was published in 1584 as *The Confession of Faith*. In 1566 he was allowed to return to Scotland and took an active part on the side of the Lords of the Congregation.

BALTHASAR, Hans Urs von (1905–88) Swiss Catholic theologian, born in Lucerne. The author of some 60 books on theology, philosophy and spirituality, he was remarkable for drawing considerable inspiration for his theology from the religious experiences of the mystic Adrienne von Speyr (1902–67), with whom he formed a secular institute after leaving the Jesuits. His chief work, *Herrlichkeit* (1961–69, translated as *The Glory of the Lord: A Theological Aesthetic*, 1983–), is a 20th-century statement of a theology of the beautiful, the good, and the true, holding that in the incarnation of Christ God transformed the meaning of culture.

BALTHUS, Count Balthasar Klossowski de Rola (1908–) French painter of Polish descent, born in Paris. He had no formal training, but received early encouragement from **Bonnard** and **Derain**. His work includes landscapes and portraits, but he is chiefly known for his interiors with adolescent girls, languidly erotic scenes painted in a highly distinctive naturalistic style with a hint of surrealism. He has grown in fame and popularity in recent years, despite the fact that he has lived for many years as a virtual recluse.

BALTIMORE, David (1938–) American microbiologist, born in New York City, joint winner of the 1975 Nobel prize for physiology or medicine. He studied chemistry at Swarthmore, the Massachusetts Institute of Technology, and Rockefeller University. He conducted research into virology at the Salk Institute (1965–68), became professor of biology at MIT (1972), and was later director of the Whitehead Institute at Cambridge, Massachusetts. In 1970 he discovered the 'reverse transcriptase' enzyme which can transcribe DNA into RNA. His research into the connection between viruses and cancer earned him the Nobel prize, jointly with **Renato Dulbecco** and **Howard Temin**.

BALTIMORE, George Calvert, 1st Baron (c.1580–1632) English politician and colonialist, born in Kipling, Yorkshire. He entered parliament in 1609, was knighted in 1617, and was secretary of state (1619–25). In 1625 he declared himself a Catholic and, resigning office, was created Baron Baltimore in the Irish peerage, and retired to his Irish estates. As early as 1621 he had dispatched colonists to a small settlement at Ferryland in Newfoundland, and in 1627 he visited the place. The following spring he returned with his family, and stayed till the autumn of 1629. The severe winter induced him to sail southward in search of a more genial country; but his attempts to settle in Virginia led to disputes, and he returned home to obtain a fresh charter. He died before the grant was made final and the patent passed to his son, Cecil, 2nd baron (c.1605–1675). The territory was called Maryland, in honour of **Charles I**'s queen. Leonard (c.1610–c.1660), Cecil's younger brother, became first governor (1634–47).

BALZAC, Honoré de (1799–1850) French novelist, born in Tours. He was educated at the Collège de Vendôme, and studied law at the Sorbonne. His father wished him to become a notary, but he left Tours in 1819 to seek his fortune as an author in Paris. From 1819 to 1830 he led a life of frequent privation and incessant industry, and incurring—mainly through unlucky business speculations—a heavy burden of debt, which harassed him to the end of his career. He first tasted success with *Les Derniers Chouans* (1829), which was followed in the same year by *Peau de chagrin*. After writing several other novels, he formed the idea of presenting in the *Comédie humaine* a complete picture of modern civilization. Among the masterpieces which form part of Balzac's vast scheme are *Le Père Goriot*, *Les Illusions perdues*, *Les Paysans*, *La Femme de trente ans*, and *Eugénie Grandet*, in which observation—in meticulous detail—and imagination are the main features. The *Contes drolatiques* (1833) stand by themselves—a series of Rabelaisian stories. Balzac's industry was phenomenal. He worked regularly for 15 and even 18 hours a day, and wrote 85 novels in 20 years, sometimes correcting his own proofs. His work did not bring him wealth; his yearly income rarely exceeded 12000 francs. During his later years he lived principally in his villa at Sèvres. In 1849, when his health had broken down, he travelled to Poland to visit Eveline Hanska, a rich Polish lady, with whom he had corresponded for more than 15 years. In 1850 she became his wife, and three months later, Balzac died.

BAMFORD, Samuel (1788–1872) English reformer and poet, born in Middleton, Lancashire. He was weaver, journalist, and messenger in turn, and was imprisoned for taking part in the 'Manchester massacre' (1819). He wrote poetry in support of the working class, like *Homely Rhymes* (1843) and also *Passages in the Life of a Radical* (1843) and *Early Days* (1849).

BAMPTON, John (c.1690–1751) a Salisbury prebendary who founded the Oxford Bampton Lectures.

BANACH, Stefan (1892–1945) Polish mathematician, born in Krakow. He studied at Lvov, where he became lecturer in 1919, and professor in 1927. He is regarded as one of the founders of functional analysis, and his book *Théorie des opérations linéaires* (1932) remains a classic. He founded an important school of Polish mathematicians. His health was ruined by his wartime experiences and although he returned to Lvov after the war, he died soon after.

BANCROFT, George (1800–91) American historian and statesman, born in Worcester, Massachusetts. He studied divinity at Harvard, and history at Göttingen. He lectured in Greek at Harvard for a while, did some preaching and established a school using advanced European methods. He wrote both poetry and prose; his major work was a monumental *History of the United States* (10 vols, 1834–40, 1852–74). A Democrat, he was secretary to the navy (1845–46) and established the Naval Academy at Annapolis. He was US minister in Britain (1846–49) and Germany (1876–74).

BANCROFT, Hubert Howe (1832–1918) American historian, born in Granville, Ohio. He settled in San Francisco in 1852, started a bookshop, and amassed a fortune. He collected and transferred to the University of California (1905) 60000 volumes, mainly on American history and ethnography, and edited and published *The Native Races of the Pacific States* (1875–76) as one of 39 volumes of a *History of the Pacific States of America* (1875–90). He also wrote autobiographical *Literary Industries* (1891) and *Retrospection* (1912).

BANCROFT, Richard (1544–1610) English prelate, born in Farnworth, Lancashire. Sent to Cambridge, he graduated in 1567, and after a series of preferments was consecrated bishop of London in 1597. He attended Queen **Elizabeth** during her last illness, and took the lead at the Hampton Court Conference. He succeeded **Whitgift** as archbishop of Canterbury in 1604. He strove to make the Roman Catholics faithful to the crown by cherishing the secular clergy rather than the Jesuits, and assisted in re-establishing episcopacy in Scotland.

BANCROFT, Sir Squire (1841–1926) English actor-manager, born in London. He made his début at Birmingham (1861) and in London (1865). In 1867 he married Marie Wilton (1840–1921), a distinguished actress born in Doncaster. From 1865 to January 1880 the Prince of Wales's Theatre witnessed their triumphs in Robertson's comedies, in *School for Scandal*, *Masks and Faces*, etc, and until 1885 they were successful lessees of the Haymarket.

BANDA, Hastings Kamuzu (1905–) Malawi politician and physician. He achieved an education by self-help in South Africa, graduating in philosophy and in medicine in the USA and graduating LRCP at Edinburgh (1941). His opposition to the Central African Federation caused him to give up his successful London practice (1955) and return via Ghana to Nyasaland (1958). Leader of the Malawi African Congress, he was jailed in 1959, became minister of national resources (1961), prime minister (1963), president of the Malawi (formerly Nyasaland) republic (1966), and life president (1971). He has established a strong, one-party control of Malawi, brooking little opposition. At the same time, however, he has followed a pragmatic foreign policy line, recognizing both the white régime in South Africa and the socialist government in Angola.

BANDARANAIKE, Solomon West Ridgeway Dias (1899–1959) Sri Lankan (Ceylonese) statesman, born in Colombo. He was educated at St Thomas' College there and at Christ Church, Oxford. Called to the bar in 1925, he returned home to a troubled situation that urged him into the Ceylon National Congress, of which, after a series of municipal and state appointments, he became president. He established the Sinhalese Maha Sabha (Great Assembly) as a foil to growing Tamil power, helped to found the United National party, which formed the government of Ceylon from 1948 to 1956, and as leader of the House and minister of health in Ceylon's first parliament he brought Ceylon the distinction of being the first Asian country to rid itself of malaria. In 1951 he resigned from the government and organized the Sri Lanka Freedom party, which returned him to parliament as leader of the opposition and in 1956 as prime minister on a policy of nationalization and neutralism. See his *The Spinning Wheel and the Paddy Field*. He was assassinated by a Buddhist monk. His wife, Sirimavo (1916–), was prime minister from 1960 to 1965 and 1970–77.

BANDEL, Ernst von (1800–76) German sculptor, born in Ansbach. He took 40 years to complete his colossal bronze statue of the German national hero **Arminius**, 84 feet high, in the Grotenberg near Detmold.

BANDELIER, Adolf Francis Alphonse (1840–1914) Swiss-born American archaeologist and anthropologist, born in Berne. He pioneered the study of the pre-Columbian Indian cultures of the Southwestern United States, Peru and Bolivia. A disciple of **Lewis Henry Morgan**, he worked from 1880 principally on the pueblos of Arizona and New Mexico, using a mixture of documentary research, ethnography, and archaeological survey to investigate the lives of their earliest inhabitants and to establish a chronology for the region. A long sojourn in Peru and Bolivia followed (1892–1903), its results published as *The Islands of Titicaca and Koati* (1910). He then held museum and teaching posts in New York and Washington DC, departing in 1913 for Spain to study colonial records of the Pueblo Indians. Bandelier National Monument, a rugged gorge near Santa Fe, New Mexico, with numerous prehistoric Indian ruins, was established in his memory in 1916.

BANDELLO, Matteo (c.1480–1562) Italian cleric and writer of *novelle* or tales, born in Castelnuovo in Piedmont. For a while a Dominican, he was driven from Milan by the Spaniards after the battle of Pavia (1525), and settling in France was in 1550 made Bishop of Agen. His 214 tales (1554–73) were used as source material by **Shakespeare, Massinger**, and others, and are valuable for the social history of the period.

BANDIERA, Attilio (1817–44) and **Emilio** (1819–1844) Italian revolutionaries, born in Venice. As lieutenants in the Austrian navy, where their father (1785–1847) was an admiral, they attempted a rising in Naples against Austrian rule in favour of Italian independence, but were betrayed and shot at Cosenza.

BANDINELLI, Baccio (1493–1560) Italian sculptor, born in Florence, the son of a famous goldsmith. A rival of **Michelangelo**, he executed the statues of *Hercules and Cacus* outside the Palazzo Vecchio, and *Adam and Eve* (National Museum, Florence). His best works are the bas-reliefs in the Florence Cathedral.

BANÉR, Johan (1598–1641) Swedish soldier in the service of **Gustav II Adolf**. In the Thirty Years' War he fought at Breitenfeld (Leipzig) in 1631, and gained victories at Wittstock (1636) and Chemnitz (1639).

BANERJEA, Sir Surendrenath (1848–1925) Indian politician and journalist, born in Calcutta, the son of a doctor. A fervent nationalist, he founded the Calcutta Indian Association in 1876 and was editor of *The Bengali* newspaper from 1879 to 1921. He was one of the initiators of the Indian National Congress and was twice returned to the Central Legislature. He welcomed the Montagu-Chelmsford reforms for the government of India, but subsequently broke with congress because of its extremism. He published an autobiography, *A Nation in the Making* (1925).

BANERJEE, Satyendranath (1897–) Indian artist, born in West Bengal, domiciled in Calcutta. Talented as a child, he became a protégé of **Rabindranath Tagore**, and a teacher at the Calcutta College of Arts. Examples of his work are hung in art galleries throughout India and in private collections.

BANG, Bernhard (1848–1932) Danish veterinary surgeon, born at Sorö in Zeeland. He studied medicine but later became interested in the healing of animals, and in 1880 was appointed professor of veterinary surgery at Copenhagen, where he investigated bacillary diseases, mainly of cattle. He is known particularly for his work on bovine brucellosis, known as Bang's disease.

BANG, Hermann Joachim (1857–1912) Danish novelist, born in Adserballe, Isle of Als. He wrote impressionistic novels about loneliness and failure. Among his novels are *Stille Eksistenser* (1886) and *De uden Faedreland* (1906).

BANIM, John (1798–1842) and **Michael** (1796–1874), Irish novelist brothers, born in Kilkenny. John studied art at Dublin and became a miniature painter; Michael, a postmaster. Having achieved some success as a playwright when a tragedy was produced at Covent Garden in 1821, John, with the collaboration of Michael, published such novels as the *Tales of the O'Hara Family* (1826), characterized by a faithful portrayal of humble Irish folk. John's illness and poverty were alleviated by a state pension.

BANI-SADR, Abolhassan (1935–) Iranian politician. The son of a preacher and landowner, Bani-Sadr was associated with Ayatollah **Khomeini** from 1966. He studied economics and sociology at the Sorbonne in Paris, having fled there in 1963 after a brief imprisonment in Iran. Bani-Sadr was an important figure in the Iranian Revolution of 1978–79 and was elected first president of the Islamic Republic of Iran early in 1980. He was soon criticized, however, by the fundamentalists and was eventually dismissed by Ayatollah Khomeini for failing to establish a 'truly Islamic country'. He fled to France where he was granted asylum.

BANKES, Lady Mary, née **Hawtrey** (d.1661) English royalist, married to Sir John Bankes (1589–1644). She defended Corfe Castle in 1643 and 1646 against the parliamentarians, who on the second occasion captured it through treachery.

BANKHEAD, Tallulah (1903–68) American actress, born in Huntsville, Alabama. She was educated in New York and Washington, and made her stage début in 1918 and appeared in many plays and films. She won Critic awards for her two most famous stage roles, Regina in *The Little Foxes* (1939) and Sabina in *The Skin of our Teeth* (1942). Her most outstanding film portrayal was in *Lifeboat* (1944), and she also performed on radio and television.

BANKS, Don (1923–80) Australian composer, born in Melbourne. He attended the Melbourne Conservatorium of Music (1947–49), then studied with Mátyás Seiber in London, Milton Babbitt in Salzburg and Luigi Dallapiccola in Florence, and later with **Luigi Nono**. Having settled in England, he founded the Australian Musical Association in London, from 1967 to 1968 was chairman of the Society for the Promotion of New Music, and has served on the executive committee of the British Society for Electronic Music. From 1969 to 1971 he was the music director of Goldsmith's College and in 1973, after holding various visiting appointments in Australia, he returned there permanently to become chairman of the Australian Council for the Arts Music Board. In 1974 he was appointed head of Composition and Electronic Music Studies at Canberra School of Music, and in 1978 became head of the School of Composition Music Studies at the Sydney Conservatorium. Banks's work has been particularly influenced by the analytical procedures and theories of Milton Babbitt, and jazz—his father was a professional jazz musician and he himself has had considerable experience as a jazz pianist and arranger—has played a crucial part in his musical development. His compositions include a sonata for violin and piano (1953), a trio for horn, violin and piano written for the 1962 Edinburgh Festival, a horn concerto, and *Setting from Roget* for jazz singer and jazz quartet (both 1966), a violin concerto (1968), *Equations 1, 2 and 3* (1963–64, 1969 and 1972) for jazz group, a 4-track tape composition, *Shadows of Space* (1972), a trilogy for orchestra (1977) and *An Australian Entertainment* (1979), as well as many film and TV scores.

BANKS, Gordon (1937–) English footballer, born in Sheffield. An outstanding goalkeeper, he started his career with Chesterfield and Leicester City but was transferred to Stoke City because **Peter Shilton** was also on the Leicester staff. His performances in the 1966 and 1970 World Cups were outstanding and England might well have retained the trophy in Mexico had Banks been able to play in the crucial match against West Germany. A serious eye injury sustained in a car crash in 1972 effectively ended his career.

BANKS, Sir Joseph (1744–1820) English botanist, born in London, and educated at Harrow, Eton, and Christ Church College, Oxford. In 1766 he made a voyage to Newfoundland collecting plants, and between 1768 and 1771 accompanied **James Cook**'s expedition round the world in a vessel, the *Endeavour*, equipped at his own expense. In 1772 he visited the Hebrides and also travelled to Iceland. In 1778 he was elected president of the Royal Society, an office which he held for 41 years. He founded the African Association; and the colony of New South Wales owed its origin mainly to him. Through him the bread-fruit was transferred from Tahiti to the West Indies, the mango from Bengal, and many fruits of Ceylon and Persia.

BANKS, Nathaniel Prentiss (1816–94) American politician and soldier, born in Waltham, Massachusetts. A factory worker, he studied law, and became successively a member of the state and national legislatures. He was speaker of congress in 1856, and in 1857, 1859, and 1861 was elected governor of Massachusetts. In the Civil War he commanded on the Potomac, and received the thanks of congress for the capture of Fort Hudson (1863). He was a member of congress till 1873.

BANKS, Thomas (1735–1805) English sculptor, born in Lambeth. He was apprenticed to an ornament carver, and married into wealth. From 1772 to 1779 he lived in Rome, and visited Russia in 1781. His work, in the neoclassical manner, is unequal, the best known being his monuments to Captains Burgess and Westcott in St Paul's.

BANKTON, Andrew McDougall, Lord (?1685–1760) Scottish judge and jurist, educated at Edinburgh University. He is mainly remembered for his three-volume *Institute of the Laws of Scotland in Civil Rights* (1751–53), which follows the general order of Viscount **Stair**'s *Institutions of the Law of Scotland.* A notable feature of this work is the Observations upon the Agreement or Diversity between Scots Law and the Law of England, appended to most of the titles, and which draws valuable comparisons. It was a sound and useful book and is still quoted in Scotland though not regarded as of the very highest authority.

BANNATYNE, George (1545–1608) Scottish antiquary and collector of poems, born in Edinburgh but a native of Forfarshire. He became a wealthy merchant and burgess in Edinburgh, but his claim to fame was his 800-page manuscript of early Scottish poetry of the 15th and 16th centuries (the Bannatyne Manuscript), compiled during an outbreak of plague in Edinburgh when he withdrew to his father's estate at Kirktown or Newtyle in Forfarshire. The Bannatyne Club was founded in his honour in 1823 to encourage the study of Scottish history and literature.

BANNERMAN, Helen Brodie, née **Boog Watson** (1862–1946) Scottish children's writer and illustrator, born in Edinburgh, the daughter of a Free Church minister. Her husband was a doctor in the Indian Medical Service and she spent much of her life in India, where she produced the children's classic, *The Story of Little Black Sambo* (1899), the story of a black boy and his adventures with the tigers, based on illustrated letters she had written to her children. Phenomenally popular when it first appeared, it was judged by some after her death to be racist and demeaning to black people. She wrote several other illustrated books for children.

BANNISTER, Sir Roger Gilbert (1929–) English athlete and neurologist, born in Harrow, the first man to break the 'four-minute mile'. He was educated at University College School, Exeter, and Merton College, Oxford, and completed his medical training at St Mary's Hospital, London, in 1954. He won the mile event in the Oxford v Cambridge match four times (1947–50), and was a finalist in the 1500 metres in the 1952 Olympic Games in Helsinki. At an athletics meeting at Iffley Road, Oxford, on 6 May 1954, he ran the mile in under four minutes (3 minutes 59.4 seconds). After a distinguished medical career, he was appointed master of Pembroke College, Oxford, in 1985.

BANTING, Sir Frederick Grant (1891–1941) Canadian physiologist, the discoverer of insulin. Born in Alliston, Ontario, he studied medicine at Toronto and later became professor there (1923). Working under **John James Rickard Macleod** on pancreatic secretions, in 1921 he discovered (with his assistant **Charles H Best**) the hormone insulin, a remedy for diabetes. For this discovery he was jointly awarded the Nobel prize for physiology or medicine in 1923 with Macleod, and which he shared with Best. He established the Banting Research Foundation in 1924, and the Banting Institute at Toronto in 1930. A pioneer in aviation medicine, he was killed in a wartime air crash.

BANTING, William (1797–1878) a corpulent London undertaker and cabinet-maker: in 1863 he published a pamphlet describing how he had reduced his weight by 46 lbs and his waist by 12 inches, hence the term 'banting' for slimming.

BANTOCK, Sir Granville (1868–1946) English composer, born in London. He was professor of music at Birmingham University (1908–34). His inspiration was often drawn from oriental life, as in his *Omar Khayyám*. His works include the choral work *Atlanta in Calydon* and *Hebridean Symphony*.

BANVILLE, Théodore Faullin de (1823–91) French poet and dramatist, born in Moulins. From *Les Cariatides* (1841) to *Dans la fournaise* (1892), he showed himself one of the most musical of lyricists, one of the wittiest of parodists. The title 'roi des rimes' was given him from his ingenuity in handling the most difficult forms of verse—the medieval ballades and rondels. His *Gringoire* (1866) holds an established place in French repertory.

BAO DAI (1913–) Indo-Chinese ruler, born in Hué, the son of Emperor Khai Dai. He ruled as emperor of Annam from 1932 to 1945. In 1949, having renounced his hereditary title, he returned to Saigon as Chief of the State of Vietnam within the French Union. In 1955 he was deposed and South Vietnam became a republic.

BÄR, Karl E von See **BAER**

BARAGUAY D'HILLIERS, Louis (1764–1813) French soldier. He commanded Napoleon's armies in Italy, Egypt, and Spain, and fought at Austerlitz. His son Achille (1795–1878), also a general, was a marshal of France (1854).

BÁRÁNY, Robert (1876–1936) Austrian-born physician and otologist. Born in Vienna, he headed the ENT unit at Uppsala University in Sweden from 1917. He pioneered the study of the balancing apparatus of the inner ear, for which he was awarded the 1914 Nobel prize for physiology or medicine (he learned of his reward the following year while a prisoner-of-war of the Russians in Siberia).

BARATYNSKI, Evgeny Abramovich (1800–44) Russian lyric poet. A soldier in early life, he wrote melancholy, tender, but pessimistic verse, including *The Gypsy Girl*, *The Ball* and *The Steamboat*.

BARBARA, St Christian virgin martyr, the patron saint of artillerymen. According to legend which seems to have no foundation in historic fact, she was a maiden of great beauty whose father immured her in a tower to discourage suitors. On discovering that she had become a Christian, her father beheaded her, and was instantly struck by lightning. Her emblem is a tower.

BARBARELLI, Giorgio See **GIORGIONE**

BARBARI, Jacopo de' (c.1475–c.1516) Venetian painter and engraver. He worked from 1500 in Germany (where he was known as Jakob Walch) and the Netherlands. From 1510 he was court painter at Brussels. He is chiefly noted for his engravings, mainly of mythological figures, which were influential in the development of northern European graphic art, in particular in the treatment of the nude. His painting *The Dead Bird* (1504) is one of the earliest examples of still life.

BARBAROSSA See **FREDERICK I**

BARBAROSSA, Khair-ed-din, known as **Redbeard** (d.1518) Barbary pirate, born in Mitylene. With his brothers he became a Turkish corsair, attacking shipping in the Mediterranean. After the execution of his brother Horuk (1518), Barbarossa captured Algiers (1529) and was made admiral of the Homan fleet (1533).

BARBAULD, Anna Letitia, née **Aikin** (1743–1825) English author, born in Kibworth-Harcourt, Leicestershire. Encouraged by the success of her *Poems* (1773), she in the same year, jointly with her brother, **John Aikin**, published *Miscellaneous Pieces in Prose*. She married a dissenting minister, Rochemont Barbauld, in 1774, and during the next ten years published her best work, including *Early Lessons for Children* and *Hymns in Prose for Children*. Also with her brother she began the well-known series *Evenings at Home* in 1792.

BARBER, Samuel (1910–81) American composer, born in West Chester, Pennsylvania. He studied at the Curtis Institute, Philadelphia, and carried off two Pulitzer travelling scholarships (1935, 1936) as well as the American *Prix de Rome*. His early music, which includes the setting for voice and string quartet of **Matthew Arnold**'s *Dover Beach* (1931), the overture to *The School for Scandal* (1931), the first symphony (1936) and the well-known *Adagio for Strings* (an arrangement of the slow movement of his string quartet op. 11; 1936) is in the traditional neo-Romantic vein, but after 1939–40 a more individual idiom began to colour his compositions, with more emphasis on chromaticism and dissonance and an occasional excursion into atonality, as in the piano sonata of 1949. Among the works of this period are the *Capricorn Concerto* (1944), the ballet *Medea* (1946), and several vocal compositions, including *Nuvoletta* (1947) from **James Joyce**'s *Finnegans Wake*, and *Hermit Songs* (1952–53). His first full-length opera *Vanessa* was performed at the Salzburg Festival (1958), followed by *Antony and Cleopatra* (Metropolitan Opera, New York, 1966).

BARBERA, Joseph Roland (1911–) American animated cartoonist, born in New York, and creator with **William Denby Hanna** of the immortal cat-and-mouse duo, *Tom and Jerry*. He studied accounting, but turned to cartooning and worked as a writer/animator on a series entitled *Tom and Jerry* about two boys, one tall and one short. In 1937 he moved to the new MGM animation studio in Hollywood where he met Hanna and teamed up with him. Together they made *Puss Gets the Boot* (1939), featuring a cat and a mouse; they went on to make over 200 Tom and Jerry film shorts. In 1957 they formed Hanna-Barbera Productions and turned to television with dozens of popular series such as *Huckleberry Hound*, *Yogi Bear* and *The Flintstones*.

BARBERINI a Tuscan family that acquired wealth by trade in the 16th century, and rose to the front rank among the Roman nobility on the elevation of Maffeo Barberini as **Urban VIII** to the papal chair in 1623. His brother Antonio became cardinal; Carlo, general of the papal troops; while to a son of the latter, Taddeo, was given the principality of Palestrina. Francesco (1597–1679), brother of Taddeo, cardinal and vice-chancellor, founded the Barberini Library; another brother, Antonio (1608–71), was cardinal and high chamberlain under Urban VIII. The power and ambition of the Barberini excited the jealousy of the neighbouring princes, and led to the defeat of the papal troops by the Duke of Parma (1641–44). The Barberini then fled to France, but returned in 1652.

BARBEY D'AUREVILLY, Jules (1808–89) French Romantic writer, born in St Sauveur-le-Vicomte. He was extreme in his rejection of 18th-century values. His best-known novels were *La Vieille Maîtresse* (1851) and *L'Ensorcelée* (1854), and he also published poetry and literary criticism.

BARBIER, Henri Auguste (1805–82) French poet, born in Paris. He satirized prominent social types in French life after the July revolution.

BARBIER, Paul Jones (1825–1901) French dramatist, born in Paris. He wrote the libretto for **Offenbach**'s *Tales of Hoffmann*.

BARBIROLLI, Sir John (1899–1970) British conductor and cellist, born in London of Franco-Italian origin. He served in World War I, played in several leading string quartets (1920–24), succeeded **Toscanini** as conductor of the New York Philharmonic (1937), and returned to England as permanent conductor (1943–58) of the Hallé Orchestra in Manchester which, under his direction and with his promotion of the works of modern composers, regained its place among the world's finest. He married Evelyn Rothwell (1911–), the oboist, in 1939. He was awarded the Gold Medal of the Royal Philharmonic Society in 1950 and given the Freedom of Manchester in 1958, when he became Hallé's principal instead of permanent conductor.

BARBON, Praise-God See **BAREBONE**

BARBOU a French family of printers, whose founder, Jean Barbou (1490–1543) of Lyon, issued in 1539 the beautiful edition of the works of **Clément Marot**. His son Hugues (1538–1603) moved to Limoges, where his edition of *Cicero's Letters to Atticus* appeared in 1580. Joseph Gérard (1715–1813) settled in Paris, and continued in 1755 the series of Latin duodecimo classics—rivals to the earliest **Elzevirs**—which had been begun in 1743. The House continued until 1824.

BARBOUR, John (c.1316–1396) Scottish poet, prelate and scholar, known as the 'father of Scottish poetry and history'. He was probably born in Aberdeen, and was archdeacon of Aberdeen from 1357, or earlier, till his death. He studied at Oxford and Paris, and in 1372 was appointed clerk of audit for King **Robert II**. His national epic, *The Brus*, written in the 1370s and first printed at Edinburgh in 1571, is a narrative poem on the life and deeds of King **Robert I, the Bruce**, having as its climax the battle of Bannockburn, and preserving many oral traditions. He also wrote two lost epics, *The Brut* (a history of the Britons) and *The Stewart is Original* (a fictitious pedigree of the kings of Scotland).

BARBUSSE, Henri (1873–1935) French novelist, born of an English mother in Asnières. A volunteer, he fought in World War I, which inspired his masterpiece, *Le Feu* (1916) in which a powerful realism is accompanied by a deep feeling for all human suffering. Other works include *Le Couteau Entre les Dents* (1921) and *Le Judas de Jésus* (1927). A noted pacifist, he later settled in the Soviet Union.

BARCLAY, Alexander (?1475–1552) Scottish poet and author. He was born most probably in Scotland, may have studied at universities in England, France, and Italy, and in 1508 was chaplain of Ottery St Mary, Devon. Perhaps about 1511 he became a monk of the Benedictine monastery of Ely; later he assumed the Franciscan habit. His famous poem, *The Shyp of Folys of the Worlde* (1509), is partly a translation and partly an imitation of the German *Narrenschiff* by **Sebastian Brant**. He also published *Egloges* (Eclogues), a translation of **Sallust**'s *Jugurthine War*.

BARCLAY, John (1582–1621) Scottish satirical writer, the son of a Scots father and a French mother, born in Pont-à-Mousson in Lorraine. He lived in London and Rome and wrote, mostly in Latin, politico-satirical novels including *Euphormio* (1603), directed against the Jesuits, and *Argenis* (1621) on allegory.

BARCLAY, John (1734–98) Scottish Presbyterian minister. While assistant minister of Fettercairn he was suspected of heresy and went to England to be ordained. He returned to Edinburgh in 1773 and founded the sect of the Bereans (from Acts xvii), stressing the mystical element in Calvinism.

BARCLAY, John (1758–1826) Scottish anatomist, born in Perthshire. He was instrumental in founding the Dick Veterinary College in Edinburgh. The Barcleian museum of the Edinburgh College of Surgeons was founded from his anatomical collection.

BARCLAY, Robert (1648–90) Scottish Quaker, born in Gordonstoun, the son of a distinguished soldier who had served under **Gustav IV Adolf** of Sweden and **Charles I**. Educated at the Scots College in Paris, where his uncle was rector, he refused to stay in France and embrace Roman Catholicism as heir to his uncle's estates. In 1664 he returned to Scotland, where his father joined the Society of Friends in 1666, and became a Quaker himself in 1667. He married a fellow Quaker in Aberdeen in 1670, the first Quaker wedding in Scotland, which caused a furore, and took over his father's estate at Ury. In 1672 he startled Aberdeen by walking through its streets in sackcloth and ashes. He published many scholarly and lucid tracts in defence of Quakerism, endeavouring to harmonize it with the great religious concepts of his day, especially in his classic *Apology for the True Christian Divinity* (1678). He was frequently imprisoned for attending illegal meetings, but at last found a protector in the Duke of York (the future **James VII and II**), because of distant family connections. He made several journeys to Holland and Germany, the latter with **William Penn** of Pennsylvania and **George Fox**. He became one of the proprietors of East New Jersey in 1682, and was appointed its nominal non-resident governor.

BARCLAY, Robert (1843–1913) English banker, under whom in 1896 the merger of 20 banks took place to form Barclay and Company Limited. In 1917 the name was changed to Barclay's Bank Limited.

BARCLAY, William (1907–78) Scottish theologian and religious writer and broadcaster. born in Wick, Caithness. Educated in Motherwell, and at the Universities of Glasgow and Marburg, he was ordained in the Church of Scotland in 1933. After 13 years as a parish minister in Renfrew, he returned to academic work in 1946 as a lecturer at Trinity College in Glasgow, specialising in Hellenistic Greek, and in 1963 was appointed to the chair of divinity and biblical criticism, from which he retired in 1974. During his career he wrote many serious academic studies, particularly on Graeco-Roman thought, but it is for his popular writings and broadcasts, in which he spoke plainly to the ordinary person about Christian teaching and beliefs, that he is best remembered and greatly loved. His first popular book, *A New Testament Wordbook*, was published in 1955, and like many of his books grew from his contributions to the *British Weekly* journal. He was a prolific writer, producing well over 60 books, and broadcasting on radio and television; his series of televised talks for Lent 1965 formed the basis of his *New People's Life of Jesus*. He was involved in the preparation of the New English Bible. His *Daily Study Bible* (New Testament) won international acclaim and was published in many languages. In 1968 he published his own translation of the New Testament.

BARCLAY-ALLARDICE, Robert, known as **Captain Barclay** (1779–1854) Scottish soldier and sportsman, celebrated for walking 1000 miles in 1000 consecutive hours. He succeeded to the estate of Urie, near Stonehaven, in 1797, and joined the army in 1805, taking part in the Walcheren expedition of 1809 before retiring to take up management of his estates. His remarkable walking feat was performed at Newmarket from June to July 1809; he was also the sponsor and trainer of the prize-fighter **Tom Cribb**.

BARCLAY DE TOLLY, Michael, Prince (1761–1818) Russian soldier of Scottish descent, born in Luhde-Grosshof, Livonia. He entered a Russian regiment in 1786, and gained rapid promotion. He commanded **Bennigsen**'s advance guard at Pultusk in 1806 and lost an arm at Eylau (1807). In the war against Finland he defeated the Swedes and forced a surrender by crossing the frozen Gulf of Bothnia in strength (1808). The emperor **Alexander I** appointed him minister of war in 1810. Forced to give battle to **Napoleon** at Smolensk (1812), he was defeated and was superseded by **Kutuzov**. He fought at Borodino (1812), was again promoted commander-in-chief after the battle of Bautzen (1813) and in that capacity served at Dresden and Leipzig (1813) and in France, where he took part in the capture of Paris (1814). In 1815 he was made a prince and a field-marshal. Statues of him were erected at St Petersburg and Dorpat.

BAR COCHBA, Simon (d.135) Jewish leader in Palestine. With the rabbi **Akiba ben Joseph**, he led a rebellion of Jews in Judaea from 132 in response to the founding of a Roman colony (Aelia Capitolina) in Jerusalem, with a temple of Jupiter on the ruins of their own temple. It was suppressed by **Hadrian** with ruthless severity, and Simon Bar Cochba was killed at the battle of Bethar.

BARCROFT, Sir Joseph (1872–1947) Irish physiologist, born in Newry, County Down. A professor of physiology at Cambridge and director of animal physiology for the Agricultural Research Council, he devised an apparatus for blood-gas analysis, studied the oxygen-carrying function of haemoglobin, and led an expedition to the Andes to study acclimatization.

BARDEEN, John (1908–) American physicist and double Nobel prize-winner, born in Madison, Wisconsin, the co-inventor of the transistor and contributor to the BCS theory of superconductivity. He studied electrical engineering at Wisconsin, and worked as a geophysicist at the Gulf Research Laboratories for three years, before obtaining his PhD in mathematical physics at Harvard (1936). He joined a new solid state physics group at Bell Telephone Laboratories in 1945. Together with **Walter Brattain** and **William Shockley** he developed the point-contact transistor (1947), for which they shared the Nobel prize for physics in 1956. Bardeen was professor at Illinois University (1951–75), and with **Leon Cooper** and **John Schrieffer** he won the

Nobel prize for physics again in 1972 for the first satisfactory theory of superconductivity (the Bardeen-Cooper-Schrieffer, or BCS, theory), thereby becoming the first man to receive the Nobel prize for physics twice.

BARDESANES, properly **Bar-Daisan** (154–222) Syrian Christian theologian and poet, born in Edessa. Known as the 'last of the Gnostics', he wrote numerous hymns, and was the author of *Dialogue of Destiny*, written in Syriac.

BARDOT, Brigitte, originally **Camille Javal** (1934–) French film actress, born in Paris, the daughter of an industrialist. A ballet student and model, her appearance on the cover of *Elle* led to her film début in *Le Trou Normand* (1952). A succession of small roles followed, but it was *Et Dieu Créa La Femme* (And God Created Woman, 1956) that established her reputation as a sex kitten. Adopted internationally as a symbol of a new female permissiveness, her roles exploited an image of petulant sexuality that was reinforced by a much publicized off-camera love life. Her many screen credits include *La Verité* (The Truth, 1960), *Le Mépris* (Contempt, 1963) and *Viva Maria* (1965), whilst *Vie Privée* (A Very Private Affair, 1962) was an autobiographical depiction of a young woman trapped by the demands of her stardom. She retired from the screen in 1973 and has devoted herself to campaigning for animal rights, forming the Foundation for the Protection of Distressed Animals in 1976.

BAREBONE, or **Barbon, Praise-God** (c.1596–1679) London leather merchant and controversial Anabaptist preacher, nominated by **Oliver Cromwell** to sit in the 'Short Parliament' of 1653, which was nicknamed after him the 'Barebones Parliament'. His fiery preaching attracted huge crowds and often occasioned riots; fiercely opposed to the Restoration of **Charles II**, he was imprisoned in the Tower in 1661–62.

BARENBOIM, Daniel (1942–) Israeli pianist and conductor, born in Buenos Aires, where he made his piano début at the age of seven. He studied with Igor Markevich and **Nadia Boulanger**, and has performed regularly in Europe since 1954. A noted exponent of **Mozart** and **Beethoven**, he gained his reputation as pianist/conductor with the English Chamber Orchestra. He has been musical director of the Orchestre de Paris since 1975, and was awarded the Legion of Honour, 1987. He conducted the Kupfer production of **Wagner**'s *Ring* cycle at Bayreuth from 1988. He is musical director-designate of the new Paris Opéra at the Place de la Bastille. He was married to **Jacqueline du Pré.**

BARENTS, Willem (d.1597) Dutch navigator. He was pilot to several Dutch expeditions in search of the Northeast passage, and died off Novaya Zemlya. His winter quarters were found undisturbed in 1871, and in 1875 part of his journal was recovered by another expedition.

BARÈRE DE VIEUZAC, Bertrand (1755–1841) French revolutionary and regicide, born in Tarbes, known as the '**Anacreon** of the guillotine'. He was originally a moderate in the National Convention, but later helped form the committee of public safety which instituted the Terror, which he defended with great eloquence. After the fall of **Robespierre** (1794) he was imprisoned, but escaped. He served under **Napoleon**, was later exiled at the Restoration, but returned to Paris under an amnesty in 1830.

BARETTI, Giuseppe Marc Antonio (1719–89) Italian critic, born in Turin. In 1751 he established himself as a teacher of Italian in London. He returned to the Continent (1760–66), where he published a book of travels, and in Venice started the *Frusta Letteraria*, or 'literary scourge', in which he criticized many Italian literary fashions. In 1769 he stabbed a Haymarket bully in self-defence, and was tried for murder, but was acquitted—Dr **Johnson**, **Burke**, and **Garrick** testifying to his character. His 36 works included an Italian and English Dictionary (1760) and a pamphlet in French defending **Shakespeare** against **Voltaire**'s criticisms.

BARHAM, Richard Harris (1788–1845) English humorist, born in Canterbury. In 1795 he succeeded to the manor of Tappington, and in 1802 he met with an almost fatal coach accident while on his way to St Paul's School, which partially crippled his right arm for life. He entered Brasenose College, Oxford (1807), was ordained (1813), and in 1821 received a minor canonry of St Paul's Cathedral. After unsuccessful attempts at novel writing, in 1837 he began his series of burlesque metrical tales under the pen-name of Thomas Ingoldsby, which, collected under the title of *The Ingoldsby Legends* (3 vols, 1840–47), at once became popular for their droll humour, fine irony and esoteric learning. His lyrics were published in 1881.

BAR-HEBRAEUS See **ABU AL-FARAJ**

BARING a great English financial and commercial house established in London in 1770 by the two sons of John Baring (1697–1748), a German cloth manufacturer, who in 1717 started a small business at Larkbear, near Honiton, Devon. Those sons were John (1730–1816) and Francis (1740–1810), who was created a baronet by **Pitt** in 1793, and who by the time of his death had amassed a huge fortune.

BARING, Alexander, 1st Baron Ashburton (1774–1848) second son of **Francis Baring**. He was for several years engaged in the USA in the service of the great London mercantile house established by his father. In 1810 he succeeded him as head of Baring Brothers & Co, having four years before been elected MP for Taunton. He represented Taunton, Callington, and Thetford in the Liberal interest till 1832, and in 1833 was returned for north Essex as a moderate Conservative. In **Peel**'s brief administration (1834–35) he was president of the board of trade, and was created Baron Ashburton in 1835. In 1842, as special ambassador to the USA, he concluded the Washington or Ashburton Treaty defining the frontier line between Maine and Canada. He opposed free trade, but strongly supported the penny postage system when it was proposed in 1837.

BARING, Sir Evelyn, Baron Howick of Glendale (1903–73) British administrator. Educated at Winchester and Oxford, he entered the Indian Civil Service in 1926. In 1942 he became governor of Southern Rhodesia and from 1944 to 1951 was UK high commissioner and governor of the High Commission territories of Bechuanaland, Basutoland, and Swaziland. In 1952 he became governor of Kenya, quelling the Mau-Mau by 1956 rebellion. He retired in 1959.

BARING, Sir Francis Thornhill, 1st Baron Northbrook (1796–1866) English statesman, eldest son of Sir **Thomas Baring**. Educated at Oxford, he was MP for Portsmouth from 1826 to 1865. Under successive Whig governments he was lord of the Treasury, secretary to the Treasury, Chancellor of the Exchequer, and First Lord of the Admiralty.

BARING, Maurice (1874–1946) English journalist and author, fifth son of Edward Charles Baring (Baron Revelstoke). Educated at Eton and Trinity College, Cambridge, he held diplomatic posts, and was foreign correspondent for *The Times* (1904–14), an officer in the Royal Flying Corps (1914–18), and an author of short stories, poems, novels, and books on Russia.

BARING, Thomas George, 2nd Baron Northbrook (1826–1904) English statesman, son of Sir **Francis**

Baring. He was successively a lord of the Admiralty, under-secretary of state for India, under-secretary for war, governor-general of India (1872–76) and First Lord of the Admiralty (1880–85).

BARING-GOULD, Sabine (1834–1924) English author and clergyman, born in Exeter, of an old Devon family. Educated at Clare College, Cambridge, he became rector of Lew Trenchard in Devon in 1881. He wrote novels, topographical, mythological, theological studies, and hymns, among them 'Onward, Christian Soldiers'.

BARKE, James (1905–58) Scottish novelist, born in Torwoodlee, Selkirk. He retired from his position as chief cost accountant with a ship-building company to devote himself to writing novels. His novels include *The World his Pillow* (1933), and *The Land of the Leal* (1939), but he is chiefly remarkable for his devoted research on the life of **Robert Burns**, resulting in a five-volume cycle of novels (1946–54), an edition of *Poems and Songs of Robert Burns* (1955) and the posthumous *Bonnie Jean*, about Burns and Jean Armour.

BARKER, Sir Ernest (1874–1960) English political scientist, born in Cheshire. He studied at Manchester Grammar School and Balliol College, Oxford, and was fellow of several Oxford Colleges before becoming principal of King's College, London (1920–27), after which he was professor of political science and fellow of Peterhouse, Cambridge (1928–39). His earliest work was *The Political Thought of Plato and Aristotle* (1906); 40 years later he produced his revered translation of **Aristotle**'s *Politics*. His second work was *Political Thought in England from Herbert Spencer to To-Day* (1915). He edited a great enquiry into English culture entitled *The Character of England* (1947) and produced a masterly brief compassionate sketch of Irish history, in the light of which he introduced **Naomi Mitchison**'s novel about Vercingetorix's Gaul, *The Conquered*. He opened up theoretical questions in his *National Character* (1927), *Reflections on Government* (1942) and *Principles of Social and Political Theory* (1951). He emerged from retirement to be professor of political science in war-ravaged Cologne (1947–48), later producing the delightful autobiography *Age and Youth* (1953). He mingled the love of classical learning with a fascination with the changing ideas of society in his own time, and enriched the study of both.

BARKER, Frederic (1808–82) English Anglican prelate and Metropolitan of Australia, born in Baslow, Derbyshire. He graduated from Cambridge and was ordained in 1831. After serving parishes in Cheshire and Liverpool, he was appointed to succeed **William Grant Broughton** as bishop of Sydney, and arrived there in 1855. He inaugurated seven new dioceses, founded Moore College, Sydney (the oldest theological seminary in Australia), and established in 1872 a general synod for all Anglicans. He wrote *Thirty-six Psalms, with Commentary and Prayers for Use in Families* (1854).

BARKER, George Granville (1913–) English poet, novelist, playwright and scriptwriter, born in Loughton, Essex. He has lived much abroad, in the USA and Italy. Throughout a long, prolific career from 1933 he has suffered by association with **Dylan Thomas**, and by the inference that he was a member of the pre-war New Apocalyptics. He is, however, a more individual poet than these associations would suggest and though often playful and self-indulgent, his best writing is energetic and eloquent. His publications have culminated in the stout *Collected Poems* (1987).

BARKER, Harley Granville- See **GRANVILLE-BARKER, Harley**

BARKER, Howard (1946–) English dramatist. His first play, *Cheek*, was produced at the Royal Court Theatre in London in 1970. He has written over 20 plays, and his themes are ambitiously large-scale: the nature of history, the degradation of political morality and the need to re-shape society according to finer values. His plays include *Stripwell* (1975), *The Hang of the Goal* (1978), *Victory* (1983), *Crimes in Hot Countries* (1983), *The Power of the Dog* (1984), *The Castle*, *Downchild* (both 1985), and *The Possibilities* (1988).

BARKER, Robert (1739–1806) Irish portrait painter, born in Kells. In 1788 he exhibited the earliest known panorama of Edinburgh, where he resided.

BARKER, Ronnie, (Ronald William George) (1929–) English comic actor, born in Bedford. An amateur performer, he made his professional début at Aylesbury Repertory Theatre in *Quality Street* (1948). His London début came in *Mourning Becomes Electra* (1955) and subsequent theatrical appearances include *Camino Real* (1957), *Irma La Douce* (1958), *Platonov* (1960) and *A Midsummer Night's Dream* (1962). An affable figure, adept at precisely detailed characterizations, tongue-twisting comic lyrics and saucy humour, his many radio and television appearances include *The Frost Report* (1966–67), the widely popular *Porridge* (1974–77), *Open All Hours* (1976, 1981–85) and, in partnership with **Ronnie Corbett**, the long-running *The Two Ronnies* (1971–87). His film roles include *Wonderful Things* (1958), *Robin and Marian* (1976) and *Porridge* (1979). A noted collector of Victoriana, his light-hearted books on the subject include *Book of Boudoir Beauties* (1975) and *Ooh-la-la!* (1983).

BARKER, Thomas, of Bath (1769–1847) English painter of rural and other scenes, born near Pontypool, Wales. His eldest son, Thomas Jones Barker (1815–82), was born in Bath. A painter of battle scenes, he has been styled the 'English **Horace Vernet**'.

BARKHAUSEN, Heinrich Georg (1881–1956) German physicist, born in Bremen. In 1911 he was appointed professor of low current technology in the Technische Hochschule, Dresden, and in 1928 was awarded the Heinrich Herz medal. He did fundamental research on electron tubes and electrical oscillations and wrote comprehensive books on both subjects. In 1919 he discovered that the magnetization of iron proceeds in discrete steps and he devised a loudspeaker system to render this discontinuity audible. This phenomenon is now known as the Barkhausen effect.

BARKLA, Charles Glover (1877–1944) English physicist, born in Widnes, Lancashire. He became professor of physics at London (1909–13) and of natural philosophy at Edinburgh (1913–44). He conducted notable researches into X-rays and other short-wave emissions and was awarded the 1917 Nobel prize for physics.

BARLACH, Ernst (1870–1938) German expressionist, sculptor, playwright, and poet, born in Wedel. He was identified with the German Expressionist school of both art and drama. While he was best known as a sculptor in wood (his work in this medium being influenced by Gothic sculpture and Russian folk-carving), his greatest achievement was his war memorial at Güstrow Cathedral, a great bronze Angel of Death, which was removed by **Hitler** as 'degenerate'. Barlach's plays include *Der tote Tag* (1912), *Der arme Vetter* (1918), and *Die Sündflut* (1924).

BARLOW, Joel (1754–1812) American poet and politician, born in Redding, Connecticut. He served as military chaplain during the War of Independence, and spent 16 years abroad, mostly in France, in political, literary, and mercantile pursuits. He was American consul at Algiers and ambassador to France in 1811.

His *Columbiad* (1807) is an historical review of events from the time of **Columbus** to the French Revolution. Other works include the would-be humorous poem, 'Hasty Pudding' (1796).

BARLOW, Peter (1776–1862) English physicist, born in Norwich. Self-educated, he devised mathematical tables and did useful work in applied physics. His *New Mathematical Tables* (1814) were reprinted as late as 1947 as *Barlow's Tables*. He also worked on the strength of ship's timbers, on tidal engineering, and on ship's magnetism and its correction (for which he received the Copley Medal of the Royal Society in 1825). The Barlow lens is a negative achromat used as an astronomical eyepiece, and in photography.

BARLOW, Thomas (1607–91) English divine, born in Orton in Westmorland. He was educated at Appleby and Queen's College, Oxford, of which he became provost in 1657. Throughout the ecclesiastical controversies of the time, he secured his advancement by casuistry, always modifying his arguments so as to be on the winning side. This earned him the name of 'the trimmer'. His advancement to the bishopric of Lincoln (1675) was so unpopular that he avoided the cathedral. He was, if anything, a Calvinist and an opponent of **Jeremy Taylor**.

BARLOW, William (d.1568) English clergyman. He opposed **Wolsey** in a number of polemical tracts, apologised and became a favourite at court. During Queen **Mary I**'s reign he was imprisoned in the Tower, but gained his release on the strength of his tracts against Wolsey. By his constant changes of front, he held the sees of St Asaph, St Davids, Bath, and Chichester. His son William (d.1625), archdeacon of Salisbury, wrote on the compass and magnetism.

BARMAKIDS a Persian family descended from a Buddhist priest (parmak) at Balkh (now Afghanistan). In the mid 8th century Khālid b. Barmak and his brothers came to Iraq, converted to Islam, and rose in the bureaucracy of the **Abbasid** caliphate. The height of their power was a 17-year period during the reign of **Harūn al-Rashīd**, when the vizier Yahyā b. Khālid and his sons al-Fadl and Ja'far effectively controlled the central administration. The family patronized poets and theologicans and built sumptuous palaces in Baghdad, but lacked military power, and in 803 Harūn had its members imprisoned or executed and their property seized.

BARNA DA SIENA (fl.c.1350) Italian painter, born in Siena. The only information on his career is contained in the writings of **Lorenzo Ghiberti**. He was a follower of arguably the greatest of Sienese 14th-century painters, **Simone Martini**, but, unlike previous Sienese painting which is characterized by graceful line, his style displays a considerable sense of solidity and physical power more typical of Florentine art, especially that of **Giotto**. A series of frescoes in San Gimignano remained unfinished because, according to Ghiberti, he died as a result of a fall from the scaffolding.

BARNARD, Christian Neethling (1922–) South African surgeon, born in Beaufort West. He graduated from Cape Town medical school. After a period of research in America he returned to Cape Town in 1958 to work on open-heart surgery and organ transplantation. In December 1967 at Groote Schuur Hospital he performed the first successful human heart transplant. The recipient, Louis Washkansky, died of pneumonia 18 days later, drugs given to prevent tissue rejection having heightened the risk of infection. A second patient, Philip Blaiberg, operated on in January 1968, survived for 594 days.

BARNARD, Edward Emerson (1857–1923) American astronomer, born in Nashville, Tennessee. He made a systematic photographic survey of the sky and correctly concluded that those areas apparently devoid of stars which he called 'black nebulae' were in fact clouds of obscuring matter. He discovered the fifth satellite of Jupiter in 1892.

BARNARD, Henry (1811–1900) American educationist, born in Hartford, Connecticut. Educated at Yale, he became after several academic appointments the first US commissioner of education (1867). He advocated centralization of school control and teacher training at the universities.

BARNARD, Marjorie Faith (1897–1987) Australian novelist, historian and biographer, born in Sydney. She wrote many books in conjunction with Flora Eldershaw as 'M Barnard Eldershaw'. Best known are *A House is Built* (1929) and the anti-Utopian novel *Tomorrow and Tomorrow* (1947, eventually published in unexpurgated form 1983). Her substantial *A History of Australia* (1962) is a popular but sound and well-crafted work. Her subsequent solo writings won many prizes including the Patrick White Literary award in 1983.

BARNARDO, Thomas John (1845–1905) Irish doctor and philanthropist, born in Dublin, the founder of homes for destitute children. A clerk by profession, he was converted to Christianity in 1862, and after a spell of preaching in the Dublin slums went to London in 1866 to study medicine with the aim of becoming a medical missionary. Instead, he founded, while still a student, the East End Mission for destitute children in Stepney in 1867 and a number of homes in greater London, which came to be known as the 'Dr Barnardo's Homes'. There are now over 100 of them in Britain and abroad.

BARNATO, Barney, originally **Isaacs** (1852–97) English-born South African speculator, born in Whitechapel, London. He went out to Kimberley with a small circus in 1873, made a fortune in diamonds there, and after engineering the Kaffir boom in mining stocks (1895) committed suicide at sea.

BARNAVE, Antoine (1761–93) French revolutionary, born in Grenoble. He brought back the royal family from their abortive flight to Varennes (1791), but subsequently developed royalist sympathies, advocated a constitutional monarchy, and was guillotined.

BARNES, Djuna (1892–1982) American novelist, poet and illustrator, born in Cornwall-on-Hudson, New York. She began her career as reporter and illustrator for magazines, then became a writer of one-act plays and short stories, published in a variety of magazines and anthologies. Her works, many of which she has illustrated, range from the outstanding novel *Nightwood* (1936) to her verse play *The Antiphon* (1958), both included in *Selected Works* (1962). Although little known to the general public, her brilliant literary style has been acclaimed by many critics, including **Eliot**.

BARNES, Ernest William (1874–1953) English prelate, born in Birmingham. He was educated at King Edward's School there and at Trinity College, Cambridge, where, as one of the most outstanding mathematical scholars of his time, he became a lecturer in 1902. He was ordained in 1908, became FRS in 1909, and master of the Temple in 1915. He became bishop of Birmingham in 1924. His strongly-held modernist and pacifist views involved him in continued controversy within the Church of England. He wrote *The Rise of Christianity* (1947).

BARNES, Dame Juliana See **BERNERS**

BARNES, Peter (1931–) English dramatist and author of screenplays. His only major commercial success has been *The Ruling Class* (1968), a play in which a madman inherits an earldom, believes he is God, and is only assumed to have been successfully rehabilitated when he makes a rampagingly right-wing speech in a decrepit House of Lords. His other plays have not shared its success. They include *The Time of the Barracudas* (1963), *Sclerosis* (1965), *Leonardo's Last Supper* (1969), *The Bewitched* (1974), *Laughter* (1978), and *Red Noses* (1978).

BARNES, Thomas (1785–1841) English editor and journalist, born in London. He was educated at Christ's Hospital and Pembroke College, Cambridge. In 1809, he became dramatic critic of *The Times*, in 1817 editor, a post which he held for 24 years. His leading principle was that a newspaper should not be a servant of the state but an independent means of its best development. He made *The Times* 'the thunderer'.

BARNES, William (1800–86) English pastoral poet, born in Rushay near Sturminster-Newton, the son of a farmer. After some time in a solicitor's office, he taught in a school at Dorchester, and then went to St John's College, Cambridge, and took holy orders. He became curate of Whitcombe in 1847, and rector of Winterborne Came, Dorset, in 1862. Meantime he had become widely known for his fine idyllic poetry in the Dorset dialect, 'the bold and broad Doric of England'. His three volumes of poetry were collected in 1879 as *Poems of Rural Life in the Dorset Dialect*. He also wrote several philological works.

BARNETT, Samuel Augustus (1844–1913) English clergyman and social reformer, born in Bristol and educated at Wadham College, Oxford. In 1873 he went to a Whitechapel parish where his interest in and sympathy with the poor of London were aroused. Discussions with **Arnold Toynbee** led Barnett to found (1884) in his memory Toynbee Hall in Whitechapel, London, the first university settlement, for university men to live in close contact with their East End neighbours. He also took part in advocating other educational reforms, poor relief measures, and universal pensions. In 1894 he became canon of Bristol, and from 1906 was canon of Westminster.

BARNEVELDT, Jan van Olden (1547–1619) Dutch statesman and lawyer, born in Amersfoort. As adviser to Prince Maurice, he opposed his warlike schemes and in 1609 concluded a truce with Spain. This caused a political rift which eventually resulted in his being represented as a secret friend of Spain. He was illegally arrested, condemned as a traitor, and executed. Of his two sons, the elder escaped to Antwerp, the younger was executed.

BARNFIELD, Richard (1574–1627) English poet, born in Norbury, Shropshire. He studied at Brasenose College, Oxford, and died a country gentleman. He is known for his pastoral poems like *The Affectionate Shepherd* (1594), and *Cynthia, with certain Sonnets* (1595).

BARNSLEY, Edward (1900–) English furniture designer, born in Pinbury, Gloucestershire, the son of Sidney Barnsley who formed Kenton & Co with **Ernest Gimson** in 1890. He took over the furniture workshops of Geoffrey Lupton in Foxfield, Hampshire, in 1919 and has made furniture in the same manner as his father and Gimson ever since. In 1937 he succeeded Peter Waals as design adviser to Loughborough Training College, and in 1945 was appointed consultant to the Rural Industries Bureau.

BARNUM, Phineas Taylor (1810–91) American showman, born in Bethel, Connecticut. He ran a museum in New York, introducing freak shows, at which he sponsored the famous dwarf 'General Tom Thumb' (**Charles Stratton**) (1842), using flamboyant publicity. He managed the American tour of **Jenny Lind** in 1847, and in 1881 joined with his rival James Anthony Bailey (1847-1906) to found the famous Barnum and Bailey circus. He died worth 5 million dollars.

BAROCCI, or **BAROCCIO, Federigo** (1528–1612) Italian painter, born in Urbino. In 1548 he went to Rome, and came under the influence of **Correggio**. He later developed a very personal colour scheme of vivid reds and yellows, and his fluent pictorial style had considerable influence on **Rubens** and his school. His *Madonna del Popolo* is in the Uffizi Gallery, Florence, and his *Christ Crucified* in Genoa Cathedral.

BAROJA Y NESSI, Pio (1872–1956) Spanish writer, born in San Sebastian. He wrote more than 70 volumes of novels and essays, distinguished by quiet humour and a vivid style derived from the 19th-century Russian and French masters. His best novels are those with a Basque setting.

BARONIUS, Caesar, properly **Cesare Baronio** (1538–1607) Italian church historian, born in Sora, in Naples. Coming to Rome at 19, he was one of the first pupils of St **Philip Neri**, and attached himself to his Congregation of the Oratory, of which in 1593 he became superior. He wrote the first critical church history, the *Annales Ecclesiastici* (1588–1607), as a reply to the Protestant *Magdeburg Centuries*, proving that the church of Rome was identical with the Christian church of the 1st century. Pope **Clement VIII** made him his confessor, he became cardinal in 1596 and Vatican librarian, and might have been elected pope in 1605 but for his opposition to Spain's claim to Italy. He also wrote *Martyrologium Romanum* (1596).

BARR, Archibald (1855–1931) Scottish engineer, born near Paisley. As an engineering apprentice he graduated at Glasgow University. He was professor of civil and mechanical engineering at Leeds from 1884 to 1889, when he succeeded his teacher, **James Thomson**, in the Regius chair of Civil Engineering at Glasgow; he set up the **James Watt** research laboratories in 1900. With **William Stroud** he founded the firm of scientific instrument makers who were pioneers of naval range-finding and later invented height finders for anti-aircraft gunnery.

BARR SMITH, Robert (1824–1915) Scottish-born Australian pastoralist and woolbroking pioneer, born in Renfrewshire, and educated at Glasgow University. He settled in South Australia in 1854. There he joined the company established by a fellow Scot, **Thomas Elder** from Kirkcaldy (later Sir Thomas Elder), whose sister Joanna he later married. The two men went into partnership under the style of Elder, Smith & Co to become one of the world's largest woolbrokers with extensive pastoral holdings. Barr Smith built up considerable interests in mining, shipping and finance, and helped found the Bank of Adelaide. Closely involved for many years with Adelaide University, he established the library there which bears his name, and made philanthropic gifts to state and church. The pastoral interests established by the company are still maintained, after many mergers, in the name of Elders IXL, the brewing giant.

BARRAS, Paul Jean François Nicolas, Comte de (1755–1829) French revolutionary, born in Fos-Emphoux in Var. In his youth he served against the English in India; then, returning home, plunged into reckless dissipation in Paris. An original member of the Jacobin Club, he voted for the king's execution, and had a share in the Girondists' downfall. He conducted the siege of Toulon, and suppressed, with great cruelty, the revolt in the south of France. Hated by **Robespierre**, he played the chief part in the tyrant's overthrow, and was appointed virtual dictator by the terrified Convention. As such he crushed the intrigues of the Terrorists. On subsequent occasions he acted with decision against both royalists and Jacobins; and in 1795, faced with another royalist rising, called his young friend **Napoleon** to his aid, who assured his own future with the historical 'whiff of grape-shot'. The Directory being appointed, Barras was nominated one ot the five members. Once more dictator in 1797, he guided the state almost alone, until his covetousness and love of pleasure had rendered him so unpopular that Napoleon overthrew him easily in the coup d'état of 18th Brumaire (9 November) 1799. After travelling abroad in exile he died in Paris-Chaillot.

BARRAULT, Jean-Louis (1910–) French actor and director, born in le Vesinet. From 1940 to 1946 he was a member of the Comédie-Française, making his début there as Roderigue in *Le Cid*. In 1946, with his actress wife, Madeleine Renaud, he founded his own company, le Troupe Marigny, which became celebrated for its performances of **Molière**, **Claudel**, and the **Gide** translation of *Hamlet*. His films include *Les Perles de la Couronne*, *La Symphonie Fantastique*, *Les Enfants du Paradis*, and *Le Cocu Magnifique*. Barrault's acting is sensitive and poetic, with a fluidity that springs from his training in mime. His theories of dramatic art are expressed in his autobiographical *Reflexions sur le théâtre* (1949, trans 1951).

BARRE, Raymond (1924–) French Conservative politician, born in St Denis, on the French dependency of Réunion. He made his reputation as an influential neo-liberal economist at the Sorbonne and as vice-president of the European Commission (1967–72). He was minister of foreign trade under President **Giscard d'Estaing** and was appointed prime minister (1976–81) after the resignation of **Jacques Chirac** in 1976. Holding concurrently the finance ministry portfolio, he concentrated on economic affairs, gaining a reputation as a determined budget-cutter. With unemployment mounting between 1976 and 1981, he became deeply unpopular, but his term as prime minister was later favourably re-assessed after the failure of the 1981–83 socialist administration's reflationary experiment. During the 1980s he built up a firm political base in the Lyon region, representing the centre-right Union for French Democracy (UDF). He contested the 1988 presidential election but was eliminated in the first ballot.

BARRÈS, Maurice (1862–1923) French novelist and politician, born in Charmes-sur-Moselle. A member of the Chamber of Deputies (1889–93), he was an apostle of nationalism, individualism, provincial patriotism and national energy. He wrote a trilogy on his own self-analysis (*Le Culte du Moi*, 1888–91), and a nationalistic trilogy that included *L'Appel au Soldat* (1906), and many other works, including *Colette Baudoche* (1909).

BARRETT, Wilson (1846–1904) English actor, theatre manager and writer, born in Essex. He was best known for his part in the dramatic adaptation of his novel, *The Sign of the Cross* (1896), a religious melodrama.

BARRIE, Sir James Matthew (1860–1937) Scottish novelist and dramatist, born in Kirriemuir, Angus, the son of a weaver. He was educated there and at Dumfries Academy, graduating at Edinburgh University in 1882. After a year and a half as a journalist in Nottingham, he settled in London, and became a regular contributor to the *St James's Gazette* and *British Weekly* (as 'Gavin Ogilvy'). He wrote a series of autobiographical novels, including *A Window in Thrums* (1889) and *The Little Minister* (1891, dramatized 1897), set in his native village disguised as 'Thrums'. From 1890 onwards he wrote for the theatre, beginning with the successful *Walker, London* (1893), *Quality Street* (1902) and *The Admirable Crichton* (1902), a good-humoured social satire, and *What Every Woman Knows* (1908), which established his reputation. It is, however, as the creator of *Peter Pan* (1904) that he will be chiefly remembered. An unfailing romantic, Barrie continued his excursions into fairyland in such later plays as *Dear Brutus* (1917) and *Mary Rose* (1920), and in his last play, *The Boy David* (1936), tried a biblical theme which despite some of his finest writing won no laurels in the theatre.

BARRINGTON, Daines (1727–1800) English lawyer and antiquary, son of Viscount **John Barrington**. He published *Observations on the Statutes* (1766), a work still of value.

BARRINGTON, George, real name **Waldron** (1755–1804) Irish writer and adventurer, born in Maynooth, County Kildare, the son of a silversmith. In London he turned pickpocket, and was transported to Botany Bay in 1790 and set free in 1792, rising to the position of high constable of Parramatta, New South Wales. He published historical works on Australia.

BARRINGTON, John Shute Barrington, 1st Viscount (1678–1734) English politician, born in Theobalds. After four years' study at Utrecht he was called to the bar in 1699. His *Rights of Protestant Dissenters* (1704) gained him the confidence of the Presbyterians; his *Dissuasive from Jacobitism* (1713) recommended him to **George I**, and in 1720 he was raised to the Irish peerage as baron and viscount, having ten years before assumed the name Barrington. He was expelled from the House of Commons in 1723 for his connection with the lottery of Harburg. Of his six sons, Samuel (1729–1800) was a distinguished admiral.

BARRINGTON, Sir Jonah (1760–1834) Irish judge, politician and memorialist, born in Abbeyleix of the élite Protestant episcopalian ascendancy. Educated at Trinity College, Dublin, he was called to the Irish bar in 1788, became MP for various constituencies, obtained an Admiralty Court judgeship in 1798, and refused to vote for the union of Irish and British parliaments despite the tempting offer of a lucrative job. He became involved in intricate political manoeuvres and was gradually overwhelmed by debts for which he pilfered court funds (1805–10), which resulted in his disgrace and dismissal in 1830. Settling in France, he produced his racy *The Rise and Fall of the Irish Nation* (1833), largely based on his earlier work *Historic Anecdotes and Secret Memoirs of the Legislative Union between Great Britain and Ireland* (1809), and the immortal *Personal Sketches of his own time* (3 vols, 1827–32), all of which prove him an invaluable social observer with a fine eye for comedy as well as profit.

BARRINGTON, Kenneth Frank (1930–81) English cricketer, born in Reading. First capped in 1955, he was discarded and did not return to Test cricket until 1959 when he became a permanency, playing in 82 Tests in all, making a total of 6806 runs for an average of 58.67. He scored 20 Test centuries, including 256 against Australia at Old Trafford in 1964. He was a member of the great Surrey side of the early 1950s which won seven consecutive county championships. He retired early from top-class cricket because of ill-health, and died in Barbados during the England tour of the West Indies while acting as assistant manager.

BARRINGTON, Shute (1734–1826) English prelate and educationist. Educated at Eton and Merton College, Oxford, he graduated MA in 1757. Ordained in 1757, he became chaplain-in-ordinary to **George III** in 1760, and was bishop successively of Llandaff (1760), Salisbury (1782), and Durham (1791 until his death). At Salisbury he was responsible for laying out its beautiful setting. At Durham, he instituted teacher training at Bishop Auckland. He was the author of several religious works and bitterly opposed to the extension of toleration to Roman Catholics.

BARRINGTON, William Wildman Shute Barrington, 2nd Viscount (1717–93) English politician, son of **John Shute Barrington**. He held political office for nearly 40 years.

BARROS, João de (1496–1570) Portuguese historian, born in Viseu. Governor of Portuguese Guinea, he is known for his monumental *Decades* (1552–1615), the history of the Portuguese in the East Indies.

BARROW, Clyde (1909–34) born in Texas, notorious American thief and partner of **Bonnie Parker**. Despite the popular romantic image of the duo as glamorous robbers, they and their gang were also responsible for a number of murders. The pair met in 1932. When Barrow first visited Parker's house, he was arrested on seven accounts of burglary and car theft. He was convicted and sentenced to two years in jail. Parker smuggled a gun to him and he escaped. Recaptured a few days later after robbing a railway office, he was sentenced to 14 years. He persuaded a fellow prisoner to chop off two of his toes and was subsequently released. With their gang, which included Barrow's brother and wife, Parker and Barrow continued to rob and murder until they were shot dead at a police road-block in Louisiana on 23 May 1934. Their demise was predicted by Parker in a poem, variously called *The Story of Bonnie and Clyde* and *The Story of Suicide Sal.*

BARROW, Errol Walton (1920–87) Barbadian politician. Born in Barbados, he flew in the Royal Air Force (1940–47) and then studied at London University and Lincoln's Inn. Returning to Barbados he became active in the Barbados Labour party (BLP) and was elected to the House of Assembly in 1951. In 1955 he left the BLP and co-founded the Democratic Labour party (DLP), becoming its chairman in 1958. In the elections following independence in 1961 the DLP was victorious and Barrow became the first prime minister. His unbroken tenure was ended in 1976 by the BLP, led by 'Tom' Adams. In 1986, a year after Adams's death, Barrow returned to power with a decisive majority but he died in the following year and was succeeded by Erskine Lloyd Sandiford.

BARROW, Isaac (1630–77) English mathematician and divine, born in London. He was educated at Charterhouse and Trinity College, Cambridge, where he became a fellow in 1649. His royalist sympathies and leanings towards Arminianism prevented him from obtaining the professorship of Greek until 1660. He travelled abroad (1655–59), became professor of geometry at Gresham College, London (1662), and the first Lucasian professor of mathematics at Cambridge (1663), but he resigned in 1669 to make way for **Isaac Newton**. He founded the library of Trinity College, Cambridge, when he became master in 1673. He published Latin versions of **Euclid** and **Archimedes**, and lectures on optics (which were soon superseded by Newton's), as well as extensive theological works and sermons. At Westminster Abbey he once detained a congregation so long that they got the organ to play 'till they had blowed him down'.

BARROW, Sir John (1764–1848) English naval administrator and traveller, born in Dragley Beck, Morecambe Bay, Lancashire, of humble parentage. Educated at Ulverston school, he became a timekeeper at a Liverpool iron-foundry, and in 1781 worked on a whaler in Greenland waters. He taught mathematics at a school in Greenwich, and in 1792 was appointed private secretary to Lord **Macartney**, the British envoy to China (described in *Travels in China*, 1804), and in 1797 accompanied Macartney to South Africa when he became governor of Cape Colony (*Account of Travels into the Interior of Southern Africa*, 2 vols, 1801–04). In 1804 Barrow was appointed second secretary to the Admiralty, a position of great power which he held until 1845. He promoted Arctic expeditions by Sir **John Ross**, Sir **James Clark Ross** and Sir **John Franklin**, and was a founder and vice-president of the (Royal) Geographical Society in 1830. Barrow Strait and Point Barrow in the Arctic, and Cape Barrow in the Antarctic, were named in his honour, as was the northern duck, Barrow's Goldeneye.

BARRY, Ann See **BARRY, Spranger**

BARRY, Sir Charles (1795–1860) English architect, born in London. Educated privately, he was apprenticed to a firm of surveyors before going to Italy (1817–20). On his return, he designed the Travellers' Club (1831), the Manchester Athenaeum (1836), the Reform Club (1837), and the new Palace of Westminster (1840), completed after his death by his son Edward Middleton (1830–80). His work showed the influence of the Italian Renaissance. His fifth son, Sir John Wolfe-Barry (1836–1918), was engineer of the Tower Bridge and Barry Docks.

BARRY, Comtesse du See **DU BARRY**

BARRY, Elizabeth (1658–1713) London actress, whose patron was the Earl of **Rochester**. Her many roles included the chief characters of **Otway**'s and **Congreve**'s plays.

BARRY, James (1741–1806) Irish historical painter, born in Cork, the son of a shipmaster. A protégé of **Edmund Burke**, he studied in Italy (1766–70), and in 1782 was appointed professor of painting to the Royal Academy, from which his irritable temper brought about his expulsion (1799). His most celebrated paintings are *Adam and Eve* (1771) and *Venus Rising from the Waves* (1772). He decorated the Great Room of the Society of Arts with a series of pictures illustrating human progress.

BARRY, Spranger (1719–77) Irish actor, born in Dublin, a great rival of **Garrick**. In 1768 he married the actress Mrs **Ann Dancer**, née Street (1734–1801).

BARRYMORE, Ethel (1879–1959) American actress, born in Philadelphia, sister of **Lionel** and **John Barrymore**, daughter of the actor-playwright Maurice Barrymore and the actress Georgina Drew Barrymore. In 1897–98 she scored a great success in London with Sir **Henry Irving** in *The Bells*. Other noteworthy appearances were in *Trelawney of the Wells* (1911), *The Second Mrs Tanqueray* (1924), *Whiteoaks* (1938) and *The Corn is Green* (1942). She also acted in films, including *Rasputin and the Empress* (1932), the only production in which all three Barrymores appeared together, and *None But the Lonely Heart* (1944, Academy award), as well as on radio and television.

BARRYMORE, John (1882–1942) American actor, born in Philadelphia, younger brother of **Ethel** and **Lionel Barrymore**. He spent some time studying art, but eventually returned to the family profession, making his name in Shakespearean roles, his *Hamlet* being particularly famous; he also appeared in many films. His classical nose and distinguished features won for him the nickname of 'The Great Profile', the name of the last film in which he appeared (1940), but he never fully justified his reputation on screen.

BARRYMORE, Lionel (1878–1954) American actor, born in Philadelphia, elder brother of **Ethel** and **John Barrymore**. He played small parts and appeared in the early films of **D W Griffith** before making a name for himself in **Gerald du Maurier's** *Peter Ibbetson* (1917) and in *The Copperhead* (1918), thereafter taking many roles in films and radio plays, notably *Free Soul* (1931, Academy award), *Grand Hotel*, *David Copperfield*, *Dinner at Eight*, *Captains Courageous*, and *Duel in the Sun*. For a short time he was a director with MGM. After twice accidentally breaking a hip he was confined to a wheelchair, but undeterred he scored a great success as Dr Gillespie in the original *Dr Kildare* film series. He had etchings exhibited and was a talented musician, his arrangements and original compositions being performed by orchestras of the first rank. In 1951 he wrote *We Barrymores*.

BARSANTI, Francesco (1690–1775) Italian composer and performer, born in Lucca. In 1714 he went to London, where he played flute then oboe at the Opera. Going to Edinburgh in 1742, he became prominent in the musical life of the town, both as performer and composer; while there he published (1742) *A Collection of Old Scots Tunes*. He wrote flute and violin sonatas, concerti grossi, an overture and other chamber works.

BART, Jean See **BARTH, Jean**

BART, Lionel (1930–) English composer and lyricist, born in London. In 1959, his *Lock Up Your Daughters*, a musical based upon **Henry Fielding**'s 1730 play, *Rape upon Rape*, ended the American domination of the musical theatre in London. He followed it with *Fings Ain't Wot They Used T'be* (1959), *Oliver* (1960, adapted from **Dickens**'s *Oliver Twist*) and *Blitz!* (1962), a cavalcade of East End life during the Second World War. *Maggie May*, a between-the-Wars story of a Liverpool prostitute, followed in 1964, but his Robin Hood musical, *Twang!* (1965), was a flop, as was *La Strada* (1969).

BARTAS, Guillame de Salluste du (1544–90) French soldier, diplomat and poet, born in Montfort in Armagnac. A Huguenot, he fought in the religious wars, went on missions to the English court, and died of wounds received at the battle of Ivry. His chief poem, *La Semaine* (1578), gives an account of the creation, and is said to have influenced **Milton**'s *Paradise Lost*. He also wrote a biblical epic, *Judith* (1574), and an unfinished history from the birth of **Christ**, *La seconde semaine*.

BARTH, Heinrich (1821–65) German explorer, born in Hamburg. After studying archaeology at Berlin, in 1849 he was appointed by the British government to a mission to central Africa to supress slavery. Barth continued his explorations on his own, which extended to Adamáwa in the south, and from Bagirmi in the east to Timbuktu in the west, nearly 12000 miles, which he described in *Travels and Discoveries in Central Africa* (5 vols, 1857–58). Afterwards he was appointed professor of geography at Berlin University. He is considered one of the greatest scientific investigators of central Africa.

BARTH, or **Bart, Jean** (1651–1702) French privateer, born in Dunkirk, a fisherman's son. He served first in the Dutch navy under **De Ruyter**, but on the outbreak of war with Holland joined the French service. In 1691, in command of a small squadron in the North Sea, he destroyed many English vessels, and made a descent on the coast near Newcastle. In 1694, after a desperate struggle with a superior Dutch fleet, he recaptured a convoy of 96 ships carrying wheat and brought them to Dunkirk. Soon after he was taken prisoner and carried to Plymouth, but escaped in a fishing-boat to France. King **Louis XIV** received him with distinction at Versailles, and in 1697 appointed him to the command of a squadron.

BARTH, John Simmons (1930–) American novelist and short-story writer, born in Cambridge, Maryland. Educated at Johns Hopkins, he was a professional drummer before turning to literature and teaching. Much admired by academic critics, he is a prolix writer. His earliest novels—*The Floating Opera* (1956), *End of the Road* (1958) and *The Sot-Weed Factor* (1960)—were rooted in realism and showed promise but this has given way to wild experimentation in an attempt to make 'a transcension of the antithesis between modern and the pre-modern which would revitalise fiction'. His later novels—*Giles Goat-Boy* (1966), *Letters* (1979), *Sabbatical* (1982) and *Tidewater Tales* (1988)—are less accessible.

BARTH, Karl (1886–1968) Swiss theologian, born in Basel. He studied at Berne, Berlin, Tübingen and Marburg. Whilst pastor at Safenwil, Aargau, he wrote a commentary of St **Paul**'s epistle to the Romans (1919) which established his theological reputation. He became professor at Göttingen (1921), Münster (1925), and Bonn (1930), refused to take an unconditional oath to **Hitler**, was dismissed and so became professor at Basel (1935–62). His theology begins with the realization of man's wickedness; the principal sin being man's endeavour to make himself rather than God the centre of the word. Barth therefore re-emphasized the finiteness of man and made God's grace once again the pivot and goal of man's life. God's unquestionable authority and 'otherness' was the key to his theology. But Barth was criticized in that his own reasoned exposition of antiphilosophical theology itself constituted philosophy and that he prescribed belief in a divinity who failed to explain the nature of man's humanity. His many works include *Knowledge of God and the Service of God* (1938) and the monumental *Church Dogmatics* (1932).

BARTHÉLEMY, Auguste Marseille (1796–1867) French poet and political satirist, born in Marseilles, where he was librarian.

BARTHÉLEMY, Jean Jacques (1716–95) French abbé and antiquary. He wrote an imaginative account of how ancient Greece would have appeared to a traveller, in *Voyage du jeune Anacharsis en Grèce* (1788).

BARTHÉLEMY SAINT-HILAIRE, Jules (1805–95) French scholar and statesman, born in Paris. He was co-founder of the journal *Le Bons Sens* (1830), became professor at the Collège de France, and produced a massive 35-volume translation of **Aristotle** (1833–95), as well as various writings on Indian philosophy. He became a member of the Chamber of Deputies in 1848, and was foreign minister (1880–81).

BARTHELME, Donald (1931–89) American novelist and short-story writer, born in Philadelphia, Pennsylvania, the son of a professor of architecture, He worked as a journalist and magazine editor before turning to fiction. An experimentalist who rejected the traditions of the conventional novel form and was inventive in his use of language, he was associated with the mid 1960s avant garde. His novels—*Snow White* (1967), *The Dead Father* (1975) and *Paradise* (1986)—are his most interesting works, though he published many short stories. He won a National Book award in 1972.

BARTHES, Roland (1915–80) French writer, critic and teacher. After researching and teaching he began to write, and his collection of essays entitled *Le Degré zéro de l'écriture* (1953, trans *Writing Degree Zero* 1967) immediately established him as France's leading critic of modernist literature. His literary criticism avoided the traditional value judgments and investigation of the author's intentions, addressing itself instead to analysis of the text as a system of signs or symbols whose underlying structure and interconnections form the 'meaning' of the work as a whole. Despite criticism from more traditional scholars he continued with this method and produced *Mythologies* (1957), a semiological exploration of such diverse cultural phenomena as wrestling, children's toys and film stars' faces. Though influenced by Marxism, **Freud**, existentialism and structuralism, he remained a versatile individualist and a fierce critic of what he saw as stale and oppressive bourgeois thinking. For 16 years he was a member of the faculty of the École Pratique des Hautes Études in Paris, and from 1976 he was professor of literary semiology at the Collège de France. He continued to produce witty, imaginative and thought-provoking books, including a work of imaginative autobiography, *Roland Barthes by Roland Barthes*. He gained international recognition as a developer of semiology and structuralism.

BARTHOLDI, (Frédéric) Auguste (1834–1904) French sculptor, born in Colmar, Alsace. He specialized in enormous monuments such as the *Lion of Belfort* and the colossal bronze Statue of Liberty on Bedloe's Island, New York Harbour, unveiled in 1886, a present of the French Republic to the United States.

BARTHOLIN, Caspar, (Caspar Berthelsen, Latinized as **Bartholinus), the Elder** (1585–1629) Danish physician and progenitor of a distinguished family of Danish scholars, father of **Thomas Bartholin** the Elder and **Erasmus Bartholin**. He was born in Malmö in Sweden, studied at many universities, refused professorships in philosophy, anatomy, and Greek, but accepted one in medicine at Copenhagen University (1613) and in theology there (1624). He was the first to describe the functions of the olfactory nerve, and was the author of *Anatomicae Institutiones Corporis Humani* (1611), for long the received textbook of anatomy.

BARTHOLIN, Caspar, the Younger (1655–1738) Danish anatomist and politician, son of **Thomas Bartholin** the Elder. Born in Copenhagen, he studied anatomy in Holland and France. He first described the greater vestibular glands in the female reproductive system ('Bartholin's glands') and the larger salivatory duct of the sublingual gland ('Bartholin's duct').

BARTHOLIN, Erasmus (1625–98) Danish physician, physicist, and mathematician, son of **Caspar Bartholin** the Elder (1585–1629). He studied medicine at Leiden and Padua, and was appointed professor of medicine and mathematics at Copenhagen in 1656. He discovered the phenomenon of double refraction of light in Iceland feldspar.

BARTHOLIN, Thomas, the Elder (1616–80) Danish physician and mathematician, son of **Caspar Bartholin the Elder**, and father of **Caspar Bartholin the Younger** and **Thomas Bartholin, the Younger**. He was the first to describe the entire human lymphatic system, which he studied independently of the Swede **Olof Rudbeck**, and he defended **William Harvey**'s theory of blood circulation. He was professor of mathematics at Copenhagen University (1646–48), then of anatomy (1648–61). He served as personal physician to King Kristian V of Denmark, and also as librarian at Copenhagen University.

BARTHOLIN, Thomas, the Younger (1659–90) Danish antiquarian, and son of **Thomas Bartholin, the Elder**. He became professor designatus at the age of only 18, and was appointed royal antiquary in 1684 at the age of 25. It was his task to seek out and study old manuscripts in Iceland for the Royal Library; in 1688, with the help of his young assistant, the Icelandic antiquarian and manuscript-collector **Árni Magnússon** (1663–1730), he published a notable work on early Nordic history, *Danicarum... libri tres* (Three Books... of Danish Antiquities).

BARTHOLOMÉ, Paul Albert (1848–1928) French sculptor, born in Thiverval. He is best known for the group of statuary inspired by his wife's death, *Aux morts* (1895), and for the monument to **Rousseau** in the Panthéon.

BARTHOLOMEW, John George (1860–1920) Scottish cartographer, born in Edinburgh, son of John Bartholomew (1831–93), map engraver and publisher. After graduating at Edinburgh University he entered his father's firm, and published the *Survey Atlas of Scotland* (1895–1912), followed by a similar atlas of England and Wales, a *Physical Atlas of the World* (two vols, 1889–1911), and *The Times Survey Atlas of the World* which appeared (1921) after his death. He is best known for his system of layer colouring of contours.

BARTHOU, Jean Louis (1862–1934) French politician, born in Oloron-Sainte-Marie. He practised law and after several ministerial appointments became prime minister (1913), when he introduced three-year conscription. He held several cabinet posts during World War I, was minister of justice (1922, 1926, 1928), president of the Reparations Committee, and as foreign minister (1934) attempted to negotiate an eastern 'Locarno' treaty. He was assassinated with King Alexander I of Yugoslavia in Marseilles.

BARTLETT, Sir Frederic Charles (1886–1969) English psychologist, born in Stow-on-the-Wold, Gloucestershire. Professor of experimental psychology at Cambridge (1931–52), he wrote on practical (ergonomic) problems in applied psychology, and devised tests for servicemen in World War II. He is perhaps best-known for his pioneering 'cognitive' approach to understanding human memory, which emphasized 'meaning' rather than the formation of simple associations. His chief works were *Psychology and Primitive Culture* (1923), *Remembering* (1932), *The Problem of Noise* (1934) and *Thinking* (1958).

BARTLETT, John (1820–1905) American publisher and bookseller, the compiler of *Bartlett's Familiar Quotations* (1855), the standard American equivalent to *The Oxford Dictionary of Quotations*. Born in Plymouth, Massachusetts, he was for many years owner of the University Book Store at Harvard (1849–63). He also published a *Complete Concordance to Shakespeare's Dramatic Works and Poems* (1894).

BARTÓK, Béla (1881–1945) Hungarian composer, born in Nagyszentmiklós (now Sînnicolau Mare, Romania). He learnt the piano mainly from his mother and first appeared in public in 1892, studying subsequently in Pozsony (now Bratislava) and (at **Dohnányi**'s suggestion) at the Budapest Academy of Music under István Thomán, an ex-pupil of **Liszt**. Thereafter he toured widely as a pianist. His early compositions display the influence of Liszt and **Wagner** and, in the first decade of the century, **Strauss** and **Debussy**. His deepest and most lasting inspiration, however, was Hungarian peasant song. He first collected folksongs in 1904 and discovered a treasury of national material, quite different from the popular and gypsy songs used by earlier Hungarian composers. From 1905 he was joined in his recording, notation, scientific analysis and systematic classification of folksong by **Kodály**, and his researches were extended to Slovak, Romanian, Balkan and near-Eastern melodies. Their rhythms and modes provided abundant ideas for his own composition. From 1907 Bartók was professor of piano at the

Budapest Academy, a post relinquished only in 1934 in order to devote more time to ethnomusicological research. Unfit for military service, he spent World War I in intense creativity; afterwards he toured internationally to great acclaim as a pianist and to growing recognition of the directness and originality of his works. Bartók spoke out against Fascism from the first, and the events of the 1930s made it impossible for him to remain in central Europe. Following his mother's death in December 1939, he was able to leave Hungary, and settled in the USA. He worked at the classification of Yugoslav folk music held at Harvard, and on his collection of Romanian melodies. His health declined from 1942 and, although he recovered to achieve a number of major works and had hopes of returning home on the cessation of hostilities, he died in New York. In addition to his importance as pianist, teacher and ethnomusicologist, Bartók was one of the foremost composers of the first half of the 20th century. His masterly grasp of all techniques of Western music, blended with an intuitive perception of folk traditions, and his combination of emotional, intensely moving utterances with a musical idiom of powerful logic and superbly crafted instrumentation, made him a national and international figure of unique force. His works include the opera *Duke Bluebeard's Castle*, the ballets *The Wooden Prince* and *The Miraculous Mandarin*, two violin and three piano concertos, orchestral music including the *Concerto for Orchestra*, chamber music including six string quartets and the *Sonata for 2 pianos and percussion*, works for violin and piano, an important corpus of piano music; also songs, choruses and folksong arrangements.

BARTOLI, Daniello (1608–85) Italian clergyman and writer, born in Ferrara. He became rector of the Jesuit College in Rome. He wrote religious novels about the Jesuit missions in the East.

BARTOLINI, Lorenzo (1777–1850) Italian neoclassical sculptor, born in Vernio in Tuscany. His best works are *Charity*, *Machiavelli*, and the **Demidov** monument, as well as busts of Madame **de Staël**, Lord **Byron** and **Liszt**.

BARTOLOMMEO, Fra, real name **Baccio della Porta** (1475–1517) Italian painter, leading artist of the High Renaissance, born near Florence. He was a pupil of Cosimo Rosselli in whose studio he met Albertinelli with whom he later often collaborated. Under the influence of **Savonarola** he publicly burnt many of his paintings and in 1500 became a Dominican novice, but **Raphael**'s visit to Florence in 1504 encouraged him to take up painting again, and they became close friends, helping one another with their work. He worked in Venice (1507) and then in Florence (c.1509–1512) before going to Rome. Overwhelmed by the work of Raphael in the Vatican apartments and **Michelangelo** in the Sistine Chapel, he refused all entreaties to collaborate with them. His work is distinguished by controlled composition and delicate drawing and use of colour. His later work is inferior. Most of his work is still in Florence but there is a fine Annunciation by him in the Louvre.

BARTOLOZZI, Francesco (1727–1815) Italian engraver, born in Florence. He settled in London to become engraver to **George III**. There he produced exquisite line engravings such as *The Silence*, and *Clytie*. In 1769, on the formation of the Royal Academy, he was nominated an original member, and from a design by his friend **Cipriani**, executed the diploma that is still in use. In 1802 he became superintendent of a Royal Academy of Engravers in Lisbon. His prints, said to be more numerous than those of any engraver, include line engravings and stippled works, printed in brown and red, called 'Bartolozzi red'.

BARTOLUS, also **Bartolo di Sassoferrato** (c.1314–1357) Italian jurist and judge, born in Venatura in Sassoferrato, near Ancona. Professor at Pisa and Perugia, he was the leader of the school of commentators on the Roman law who sought to derive principles of general application which could be used to solve contemporary problems. As an expositor of all parts of the Roman law his authority was very high. He was also a founder of international private law, distinguishing real statutes which applied to foreigners from personal statutes which did not. His extensive writings include *Commentarius in Tria Digesta*, *Commentarius in libros IX Codicis priores*, *Commentarius super libris III posterioribus Codicis*, *Lectura super Authenticis*, and opinions given on particular cases.

BARTON, Andrew (d.1511) Scottish naval commander. He cleared the Scottish coast of pirates and in 1506 sent **James IV** three barrels full of Flemish pirates' heads. He was killed in an engagement with two English ships off the Suffolk Downs.

BARTON, Bernard (1784–1849) English Quaker poet, born in Carlisle. A bank clerk in Woodbridge in Suffolk throughout his life, he was a friend of **Lamb** and his *Metrical Effusions* (1812) interested **Southey**. His *Poems* (1820) include devotional lyrics in the style of **George Herbert**.

BARTON, Clara (Clarissa Harlowe) (1821–1912) American schoolteacher, and founder of the American Red Cross, born in Oxford, Massachusetts. A schoolteacher from 1836 to 1854, she worked in the Patent Office in Washington DC (1854–57), and thereafter, during the Civil War (1861–65), helped to obtain and distribute supplies and comforts for the wounded. In Europe for her health from 1869 to 1873, she worked for the International Red Cross in the Franco-Prussian War (1870–71). Back in the USA she established the US branch of the Red Cross in 1881 and became its first president (1881–1904). As a result of her campaigning, the USA signed the Geneva Convention in 1882.

BARTON, Sir Derek Harold Richard (1918–) English organic chemist, educated at Imperial College, London. He introduced conformational analysis as a method for studying the shape of organic molecules and the effect of shape on reactivity. He was professor at Imperial College for over 20 years, before moving in 1985 to Texas A & M University. He shared the Nobel prize for chemistry with **Odd Hassell** in 1969.

BARTON, Sir Edmund (1849–1920) Australian jurist and statesman, the first prime minister of the Australian commonwealth (1901–03). Born in Sydney, he was elected to the New South Wales legislature in 1879. He was leader of the Federation movement from 1896, headed the committee that drafted the commonwealth constitution bill and led the delegation that presented it to the British parliament in 1900. From 1903 until his death he served as a high court judge.

BARTON, Elizabeth (?1506–1534) English prophet, known as the Maid of Kent or Nun of Kent. A domestic servant at Aldington, she began to go into trances and make prophetic utterances against the authorities after an illness in 1525. Archbishop **Warham** sent two monks to examine her. One of these, Edward Bocking, convinced that she was directly inspired by the Virgin **Mary**, became her confessor at the priory of St Sepulchre at Canterbury. She denounced **Henry VIII**'s divorce and marriage to **Anne Boleyn**, was charged with treason and hanged at Tyburn with Bocking and four others.

BARTON, Gordon Page (1929–) Australian transport entrepreneur and politician, born in Surabaya, Java, where his father was local manager for the Burns Philp island trading company. He was educated at Sydney C of E Grammar School and at Sydney University, NSW. He purchased the Interstate Parcel Express Company which formed the base for the international Ipec and Skypac freight and courier network, becoming managing director in 1962 and subsequently chairman of the group. An interest in progressive politics led to his forming the Liberal Reform Group, which drew upon popular opposition to Australia's involvement in the Vietnam War, and later became the Australia party. Although the party fought a number of federal elections between 1969 and 1974, it faded away after 1977. Barton also established the *Nation Review*.

BARTON, John (1928–) English stage director, born in London. He was educated at King's College, Cambridge, where he was a fellow, 1954–60. He joined the newly-created Royal Shakespeare Company at Stratford-upon-Avon in 1960. He wrote and directed *The Hollow Crown* (1961), an anthology about English monarchs, and adapted the three parts of *Henry VI* into two plays, *Henry VI* and *Edward VI*, for the monumental Wars of the Roses sequence (1963–64). Barton also adapted and directed a series of ten plays based on the *Oresteia* legend as *The Greeks* in 1980. He is the author of *Playing Shakespeare* (1984), based on the television series he made in 1982.

BARTRAM, John (1699–1777) American botanist, born near Darby, Pennsylvania, and called by **Linnaeus** 'the greatest natural botanist in the world'. Self-taught, and a successful small farmer, he built up an unrivalled collection of North American plants in a garden on the banks of the river Schuylkill, near Philadelphia, and plants sent by correspondents in Europe. His son, William Bartram (1739–1823), was also a naturalist, and published a book on his travels through America in search of plants (*Travels*, 1791) which became a best-seller.

BARUCH, Bernard Mannes (1870–1965) American financier and statesman, born in Camden, South Carolina. Educated in New York, he began life as an office boy, but made a fortune by speculation. He helped to co-ordinate US industries in World War I and draft the economic sections of the Treaty of Versailles (1919). He became a powerful political influence, 'the adviser of presidents' and of **Churchill** in World War II. He served on many commissions, particularly the American Atomic Energy Commission.

BARWICK, Sir Garfield Edward John (1903–) Australian judge. He was attorney-general of Australia 1958–63, and minister for external affairs, in which capacity he represented Australia at many international conferences; from 1964 he was a highly-regarded chief justice of the High Court of Australia.

BARY See **DE BARY, Heinrich Anton**

BARYE, Antoine Louis (1794–1875) French sculptor, distinguished for his bronze statues of animals.

BARYSHNIKOV, Mikhail Nikolayevich (1948–) Russian-born American dancer, born in Riga, Latvia. One of this century's most popular and exciting dancers, he was first trained at the Riga Choreography School and then with the Kirov Ballet in Leningrad. In 1974 he defected to the west while on tour in Canada. He has become an international star, rivalling the brightness of fellow Russian, **Rudolph Nureyev**, with a gravity-defying, dynamic style full of character. While in the Soviet Union he created roles in *Vestris* (1969) and *Creation of the World* (1971). His career in the west began at the American Theater Ballet, where he partnered **Gelsey Kirkland**, and New York City Ballet, where he worked with **George Balanchine**. Roles were created for him by Balanchine and others including **Jerome Robbins** (*Opus* 191/*The Dreamer*, 1979) and **Frederick Ashton** (*Rhapsody*, 1980). In 1980, he returned to American Theater Ballet, taking over as artistic director. He has always maintained an interest in ballet as a popular art form and has taken part in several Hollywood films, including *The Turning Point* (1977), in which he starred as a seductive young principal dancer. *White Knights* with choreography by **Twyla Tharp** followed in 1985, and *Dancers* in 1987.

BARZINI, Luigi (1874–1947) Italian journalist and author, born in Orvieto. He had a brilliant and varied career as a foreign correspondent, travelling widely and covering the international expedition against the Boxers in China in 1900, the outbreak of the Russo-Japanese war and the San Francisco earthquake. He was present at the early attempts to fly, and interviewed the **Wright** brothers, **Orville** and **Wilbur**. His book, *Peking to Paris* (1908), describing a motor-car race across two continents the previous year, is established as a classic.

BASALDELLA, Mirko (1910–69) Italian sculptor and painter, born in Udine. He studied in Venice, Florence, and Milan, and first exhibited in Rome in 1936. Best known for the bronze memorial doors he designed for the Ardeatine caves near Rome, he won second prize in the international *Unknown Political Prisoner* competition (1953). He was influenced by primitive and prehistoric forms. His brothers Dino and Afro are also sculptors.

BASEDOW, Johann Bernhard (1723–90) German educationist, born in Hamburg. He tried to put into practice the maxims of **Rousseau** and **Comenius**, and established a model children's school, the Philanthropinum, at Dessau.

BASELITZ, Georg (1938–) German avant-garde artist, born in Deutschbaselitz, Saxony. He studied art in East Berlin (1956–57), before emigrating to the West in 1957. He had his first one-man show in Berlin in 1961. His violent subject-matter and his 'Wild Expressionist' style have affinities with **Munch** and **Kokoschka**. Although he likes to paint sets, like the *Strassenbild* cycle (1979–80), with a shouting or gesticulating figure at a window repeated from canvas to canvas, his real forte is painting figures, trees, animals, etc, upside down.

BASEVI, George (1794–1845) English architect, born in London. He became a pupil of Sir **John Soane**, travelled in Greece and Italy (1816-19), designed in classic revivalist style the Fitzwilliam Museum in Cambridge, laid out part of London's Belgravia, and designed country mansions and Gothic churches. He fell to his death while surveying Ely Cathedral.

BASHKIRTSEVA, Marya (1860–84) Russian artist and diarist, born of noble family in Pultowa, south Russia. She kept from childhood a diary in French, selections of which were published posthumously. She became a painter of some promise but died of tuberculosis in Paris.

BASIE, Count (William) (1904–84) American jazz pianist, organist and bandleader, born in Red Bank, New Jersey, who became one of the most significant big band leaders of the swing era and beyond. He started by playing drums in a children's band, but was encouraged by his mother to take piano lessons and became an accompanist for silent films while still at school. He drifted away from his studies to take casual jobs as a musician and was given some coaching by **Fats Waller** in New York. After several years touring the vaudeville circuit as a soloist and accompanist to blues singers, he reached Kansas City in 1927, then emerging as the centre of a distinct style of orchestral jazz. In 1929 he began a five-year involvement as pianist and co-arranger with the Bennie Moten band and when Moten died (1935) the band was largely re-formed under Basie's leadership, at first being called the Barons of Rhythm, and including the important tenor saxophone stylist **Lester Young** as a featured soloist. A radio broadcast was heard by record producer John Hammond, who organized a major tour for the band leading to recording and booking contracts. Now called the Count Basie Orchestra and established in New York, the band quickly achieved national fame and worked to heavy touring schedules—as well as making film and TV appearances—until 1950 when big bands appeared to be no longer viable. But after two years of leading an octet, Basie re-formed a 16-piece orchestra and continued to lead it until his death. Over nearly 50 years as a bandleader, employing some of the most eminent swing musicians, Basie remained true to music rooted in the Kansas City style. Among his most popular pieces are his compositions 'One O'Clock Jump' and 'Jumpin' at the Woodside'.

BASIL, St, known as **The Great** (c.329–379) one of the greatest of the Greek fathers, born in Caesarea, in Cappadocia, the brother of **Gregory of Nyssa**. He studied at Byzantium and Athens, lived for a time with hermits in the desert, and in 370 succeeded **Eusebius of Caesarea** as bishop of his native city. A fierce opponent of Arianism, he improved monastic standards and wrote many seminal works.

BASIL I, the Macedonian (c.812–886) Byzantine emperor. He rose in the imperial serice from obscure origins to become co-ruler in 867 with Michael III, whom he murdered in the same year. The dynasty he founded ruled Constantinople until 1056.

BASIL II, Bulgaroctonus (c.958–1025) Byzantine emperor, son of Romanus II, came to the throne as sole ruler in 976. A revolt by the nobleman Bardas Sclerus was quashed with the help of the general Bardas Phocas, but a decade later both men revolted in turn with much of the army and aristocracy. Basil was saved by his alliance with **Vladimir I the Great**, prince of Kiev, who married his sister Anna and converted to Christianity. In return Vladimir sent 6000 Russian troops who defeated the uprising (989) and became the core of the future Varangian Guard, the élite unit of the Byzantine army. Thereafter Basil supported the peasantry at the expense of the great landowners. His 15-year war against the Bulgarians culminated in the victory in the Belasica mountains which earned him his surname of 'Bulgar-slayer': thousands of prisoners were blinded and in groups of a hundred, each led by a one-eyed man, sent back to their Tsar Samuel, who died of shock (1015). Bulgaria was annexed to the empire by 1018, while the eastern frontier was extended to Lake Van in Armenia.

BASILE, Giambattista (1575–1632) Italian soldier and writer, born in Naples. He compiled the *Pentamerone* (1637), a collection of 50 Neapolitan folk tales, edited by **Liebrecht** and translated by Sir **Richard Burton** (1893).

BASILIDES (fl.c.125) Syrian gnostic philosopher, who founded a sect in Alexandria. His esoteric doctrines seem to have blended Christian thought with elements from **Zoroaster**, Indian philosophy and magic. His disciples (Basilidians) were active in Egypt, Syria, Italy and even Gaul into the fourth century AD.

BASILIUS See **BESSARION, John**

BASIRE, James (1730–1802) English engraver, of a notable family of London engravers. He was the teacher of **William Blake**. His father Isaac (1704–68), son James (1769–1822) and grandson James (1796–1869) were also engravers.

BASKERVILLE, John (1706–75) English printer, born at Sion Hill, Wolverley, Worcestershire. He began as a footman, became a writing master in Birmingham, and from 1740 carried on a successful japanning business there. In about 1750 he began to make costly experiments in letter founding, and produced the types named after him. The quarto *Virgil* (1756) was the first of 55 fine editions which included **Milton**, **Juvenal**, **Congreve**, **Addison**, the bible, a Greek New Testament, **Horace**, and **Catullus**. In 1758 he became printer to Cambridge University. He manufactured his own paper and ink. Unaffected by superstition, he chose to be buried in his own garden, but his remains were exhumed.

BASNAGE, Jacques (1653–1723) French Protestant theologian, and historian. A pastor in Rouen, he was driven from France to Holland by the revocation of the Edict of Nantes (1685). He wrote a monumental *History of the Church* (1699).

BASOV, Nikolai Gennadiyevich (1922–) Russian physicist, inventor of masers and lasers. He served in the Red Army in World War II, and studied in Moscow. At the Lebedev Physics Institute in Moscow (deputy director 1958–73, director from 1973), his work provided the theoretical basis for the development of the maser (Microwave Amplification by Stimulated Emission of Radiation) in 1955, for which he was awarded the 1964 Nobel prize for physics jointly with his Russian colleague **Alexander Prokhorov** and the American physicist **Charles Townes**. In 1958 he invented the laser (Light Amplication by Stimulated Emission of Radiation).

BASS, George (d.1812) English naval surgeon. With **Matthew Flinders** he explored (1795–1800) the strait between Tasmania and Australia that bears his name. He died while mining in South America.

BASS, Michael Thomas (1799–1884) English brewer, born in Burton-on-Trent. He entered the family business (founded by his grandfather, William Bass, in 1777), which he expanded considerably. He helped to improve the lot of the working man both as employer and as Liberal MP (1848–83). His son, Michael Arthur (1837–1909), became Baron Burton in 1886.

BASSANI, Giorgio (1916–) Italian novelist and poet, born in Bologna, the son of a physician. He lived until 1943 in Ferrara, where much of his fiction is set. *Five Stories of Ferrara* appeared in 1956, most of them composed in the aftermath of World War II. A sensitive chronicler of Italian Jews and their suffering under Fascism, he is a realist who writes elegiacally. One of the outstanding Italian novelists of the 20th century, he is at his most exquisite in *The Gold-Rimmed Spectacles* (1960) and *The Garden of the Finzi-Continis* (1965).

BASSANO, Jacopo da, properly **Giacomo da Ponte** (1510–92) Venetian painter, founder of genre painting in Europe, born in Bassano. His best paintings are of peasant life and biblical scenes, and include the altarpiece of the Nativity at Bassano, *Jacob's Return to Canaan* and *Portrait of a Gentleman*. His four sons were also painters.

BASSI, Agostino Maria (1773–1865) Italian biologist and pioneer bacteriologist, born in Lodi. Educated at Pavia, his work on animal diseases partly anticipated that of **Louis Pasteur** and **Robert Koch**. As early as 1835 he showed after many years' work that a disease of silkworms (muscardine) is fungal in origin, that it is contagious, and that it can be controlled, and he proposed that some other diseases are transmitted by micro-organisms.

BASSOMPIERRE, François de (1579–1646) French soldier and statesman, born in Harouel, Lorraine. Promoted to the rank of marshal of France in 1622, he took an active part in the siege of La Rochelle. He served as ambassador to Switzerland, Spain and England, but was imprisoned by **Richelieu** in the Bastille from 1631 to 1643. He was an accomplished courtier, extravagant in luxury, and excessively addicted to gallantries. His *Memoirs*, written in the Bastille, contain interesting sidelights on his soujourn in London as ambassador.

BASTIAN, Adolf (1826–1905) German ethnologist, born in Bremen. He studied at Berlin, Heidelberg, Prague, Jena, and Würzburg. He travelled widely, collecting material for his ethnological studies in most continents. He is best known for his theory that variations in folk cultures could be traced back to the effects of local geographical conditions on a basic set of elementary ideas (*Elementargedanken*) common to mankind.

BASTIAN, Henry Charlton (1837–1915) English biologist, born in Truro, Cornwall. He was educated privately and at University College, London, where he became professor of pathological anatomy (1867), hospital physician (1871), and professor of clinical medicine (1887–95). He championed the doctrine of spontaneous generation, and became one of the founders of British neurology through his work on aphasia, etc.

BASTIAT, Frédéric (1801–50) French political economist, born in Bayonne. An advocate of free trade, he published works against protectionism and socialism.

BASTIDE, Jules (1800–75) French Radical journalist, born in Paris. Minister of foreign affairs in 1848, and member of the Constituent Assembly, he took part in the Paris revolt (1832) and was condemned to death. He managed to escape, however, and was later pardoned.

BASTIEN-LEPAGE, Jules (1848–84) French painter, born in Damvillers, Meuse. His pictures are mostly of rustic scenes, but there are portraits of **Sarah Bernhardt**, and the Prince of Wales (later **Edward VII**).

BASTOS, Augustos Roa (1917–) Paraguayan novelist, living in exile since 1947. The author of several works of fiction, he has been a journalist, screenwriter and teacher, and until his retirement in 1985 he was a professor at the University of Toulouse. *I The Supreme* (1947, trans 1986) is his masterpiece.

BATA, Tomas (1876–1932) Czechoslovakian industrialist, born in Zlin, in Moravia. From a small shoemaking business, he built up the largest leather factory in Europe, in 1928 producing 75000 pairs of shoes a day. He was killed when an aircraft struck one of his factory chimneys.

BATAILLE, Félix Henry (1872–1922) French poet and dramatist, born in Nîmes. The predominant theme in his plays is inner conflict, as in, particularly, *Maman Colibri* (1904) and *La Marche nuptiale* (1905).

BATCHELOR, Joy (1914–) English animated cartoon producer, born in Watford. A fashion artist for *Harper's Bazaar*, she tried her hand at animation with *Robin Hood* (1935), and in 1941 married fellow-producer **John Halas**, and formed the Halas-Batchelor animation unit. In World War II they made propaganda films for the Ministry of Information, followed by the first British feature-length cartoon, *Handling Ships*, in 1945, and the *Charley* series (1947). In 1952 they made the first British stereoscopic cartoon, *The Owl and the Pussycat*. Other films have included **Orwell**'s *Animal Farm* (1954) and the television series *Tales of Hoffnung* (1965).

BATEMAN, Henry Mayo (1887–1970) Australian cartoonist, born in Sutton Forest, New South Wales. He lived in England from infancy. From 1906, influenced by the French cartoonist **Caran d'Ache**, he developed a purely visual style of comic strip for *Punch* and other periodicals. He is best known for a series of humorous drawings depicting embarrassing 'The Man Who ...' situations such as *The Guardsman Who Dropped His Rifle*. He wrote *The Art of Drawing* (1926) and *Himself* (1937).

BATEMAN, Kate Josephine (1842–1917) American actress, born in Baltimore. She was the daughter of Hezekiah Linthicum (1812–75) the theatrical manager, began acting at the age of four, and after successful tours in America, acted in London with **Henry Irving** in Shakespearean plays (1875–77). She married Dr George Crowe in 1866. Her sisters, Isabel (1854–1934) and Virginia (1853–1940), were both distinguished actresses. The latter married Edward Compton (1854–1918) and was the mother of **Fay Compton** and Sir **Compton Mackenzie**.

BATES, Alan, originally **Arthur Bates** (1934–) English actor, born in Allestree, Derbyshire. After national service in the RAF, he studied at RADA and made his stage début in *You and Your Wife* (1955) at Coventry. Following his London début in *The Mulberry Bush* (1956) he appeared in *Look Back in Anger* (1956), *Long Day's Journey Into Night* (1958) and *The Caretaker* (1960). He made his film début in *The Entertainer* (1960) and was seen in some of the most popular British films of the decade including *A Kind of Loving* (1962), *Georgy Girl* (1966), *Far From the Madding Crowd* (1967) and *Women in Love* (1969). His stage career has combined the classics with contemporary roles in *In Celebration* (1969), *Butley* (1971, Tony award), *Otherwise Engaged* (1975) and *Melon* (1987). His films include *The Fixer* (1968), *The Go-Between* (1971), *An Unmarried Woman* (1978) and *We Think the World of You* (1988). His television work includes the series *The Mayor of Casterbridge* (1978), *An Englishman Abroad* (1982, BAFTA award) and *Pack of Lies* (1987).

BATES, Daisy May, née **O'Dwyer** (1863–1951) Irish-born Australian anthropologist, born in Tipperary. She arrived in Australia in 1884. After a period as a London journalist, while she left her husband, **Harry Morant**, and son in Australia, she was commissioned by *The Times* to investigate the condition of aborigines, and returned to Australia in 1899. From that time she spent most of her life in the north and west of Australia with remote tribes, by whom she was known as Kabbarli (grandmother). She was a member of the **Radcliffe-Brown** anthropological expedition. She made detailed notes of aboriginal life and customs, and worked for aboriginal welfare, setting up camps for the aged. She published an account of her life in 1938. When over 80 she returned to live with a tribe in South Australia, but illness forced her return to Adelaide and her retirement in 1945.

BATES, Henry Walter (1825–92) English naturalist and traveller, born in Leicester. With his friend **Alfred Wallace**, he explored the Amazon (1848–59), returning with 8000 species of hitherto unknown insects. In 1861 he published his distinctive contribution to the theory of natural selection in a paper explaining the phenomenon of mimicry. In 1864 he became assistant secretary of the Royal Geographical Society.

BATES, H E (Herbert Ernest) (1905–74) English novelist, playwright, and short-story writer, born in Rushden, Northamptonshire. He began his working life as a solicitor's clerk, provincial journalist and warehouse clerk. His first play, *The Last Bread*, and his first novel, *The Two Sisters*, appeared in 1926. In his early days he benefited from the advice of **Edward Garnett** and was later influenced by **Stephen Crane**. He is one of the greatest exponents of the short-story form. His essay in literary criticism, *The Modern Short Story*, is regarded as a classic. His best-known works are *Fair Stood the Wind for France* (1944), *The Jacaranda Tree* (1949), and *The Darling Buds of May* (1958).

BATESON, Gregory (1904–80) English-born American anthropologist, born in Grantchester, the son of biologist **William Bateson**. He studied physical anthropology at Cambridge, but made his career in the USA. His first major monograph, *Naven* (1936), based on fieldwork in New Guinea, was an innovative work introducing many themes that have since become central to the anthropological study of ritual and symbolism. With **Margaret Mead** he was involved with the culture-and-personality movement, publishing *Balinese Character* in 1942. Influenced by the theory of cybernetics, he went on to study problems of communication and learning among aquatic mammals and human schizophrenics, and developed a distinctive interpretation of schizophrenia based on the notion of the 'double-bind'. The anthology *Steps to an Ecology of Mind* (1973), and his last book, *Mind and Nature* (1978), indicate the extraordinary range of his interests.

BATESON, William (1861–1926) English geneticist, born in Whitby, Yorkshire, and known as the 'father of genetics', a term he himself coined. Educated at Rugby School and Cambridge, he became Britain's first professor of genetics at Cambridge (1908–10) and director of the new John Innes Horticultural Institution there (1910–26) as well as professor of physiology at the Royal Institution (1912–26). He produced the first translation of the heredity studies of **Gregor Mendel** (1900), and wrote *Mendel's Principles of Heredity: A Defence* (1902) and *Problems of Genetics* (1913). He was the co-founder and editor (1911–26), with Reginald Crundall Punnett, of the *Journal of Genetics*. He played a dominant part in establishing Mendelian ideas but he was a major opponent of chromosome theory; and although an ardent evolutionist, he opposed Darwin's ideas on natural selection.

BATHORI, Elizabeth (d.1614) niece of **Stephen Bathori**, king of Poland, and wife of the Hungarian Count Nádasdy. In 1610 she was discovered to have murdered 650 young girls, so that she could keep her youth by bathing in their warm blood. Her accomplices were burnt; but she was shut up for life in her fortress of Csej.

BATHORI, Stephen See **STEPHEN BATHORI**

BATHURST, Allen Bathurst, 1st Earl (1684–1775) English Tory statesman. He was created baron in 1722 and earl in 1762. Among his friends were **Pope**, **Swift**, **Congreve**, **Prior**, and **Sterne**.

BATHURST, Henry, 2nd Earl (1714–94) English politician, son of **Allen Bathurst**. From 1778 he was lord chancellor, 'one of the weakest, though one of the worthiest' that ever sat on the Woolsack. His son Henry, 3rd Earl (1762–1834), was colonial secretary (1812–28).

BATHURST, Henry (1744–1837) English clergyman, nephew of **Allen Bathurst**, 1st Earl. From 1805 he was bishop of Norwich, the 'only Liberal bishop' of his day. His son Benjamin (1784–1809) disappeared mysteriously between Berlin and Hamburg as he was travelling with dispatches from Vienna.

BATISTA Y ZALDIVAR, Fulgencio (1901–73) Cuban dictator, born in Oriente province. A labourer's son, he rose from sergeant-major to colonel in the army coup against President Machado (1931–33) and himself became president (1940–44). In 1952 he overthrew President Prio, and, with himself as sole candidate, was re-elected president in 1954. He ruled as dictator until his overthrow by **Fidel Castro** in January 1959, when he found refuge in the Dominican Republic.

BATMAN, John (1800–40) the 'Founder of Victoria', born in Parramatta. In May 1835 he colonized the shores of Port Phillip from Tasmania. He was the main founder of Melbourne, seeing the potential of its site.

BATONI, or **Battoni, Pompeo Girolamo** (1708–87) Italian painter, born in Lucca. He trained in Rome with Sebastiano Conca (1680–1764), and settled there. He was a learned man and a technically proficient artist, whose style was influenced by his study of **Raphael** and the Antique. From 1735 he received many important commissions for religious, mythological and historical paintings, but it is for his portraits, particularly of distinguished foreign visitors, that he is most famous. After **Mengs** left Rome in 1761 he was virtually unchallenged in this field. He painted three popes, and held the post of curator for the papal collections.

BATTEN, Jean (1909–82) New Zealand pioneer aviator, born in Rotorua. Abandoning a possible musical career and selling her piano she came to England in 1929 and at 21 took her pilot's and ground engineer licences. In 1934, in a Gypsy Moth, she broke **Amy Johnson**'s record for the flight from England to Australia by nearly five days. She became the first woman to complete the return journey and in 1935 flew over the South Atlantic to Argentina. Retiring from active flying in the 1940s, she remained an enthusiastic supporter of British aeronautics. Her autobiography was republished as *Alone in the Sky* in 1979.

BATTENBERG name of a family of German origin, derived from the title of Countess of Battenberg conferred in 1851 on the Polish countess Julia Theresa von Hauke (1825–95), the morganatic wife of Prince Alexander of Hesse.

BATTENBERG, Prince Alexander of (1820–93) first prince of Bulgaria and uncle of Earl **Mountbatten**. Born in Verona, he was the second son of Prince Alexander of Hesse and by the Rhine, and his morganatic wife, the Polish Countess von Hauke, and also nephew of Tsar **Alexander II** of Russia. An officer in the Hessian army, he was elected prince of the new principality of Bulgaria in 1879. In 1885 he annexed eastern Romania after an uprising there, thereby provoking the hostility of Serbia, whose army he defeated in a fortnight's campaign. In 1886 he was overpowered by pro-Russian army conspirators in his palace in Sofia and forced to abdicate. Although he was set free in a few days, he could not overcome the hostility of Tsar **Alexander III**, and retired to Darmstadt in Austria as Count Hartenau.

BATTENBERG, Prince Henry of (1858–96) German prince. In 1885 he married the Princess Beatrice (1857–1944), youngest daughter of Queen **Victoria**, and died at sea of fever caught in the Ashanti campaign.

BATTENBERG, Prince Louis Alexander of See **MOUNTBATTEN**

BATTHYÁNYI, Louis, Count (1809–49) Hungarian statesman. A member of the Hungarian assembly, and a leader of the independence movement, he was executed by the Austrians for his part in the Hungarian insurrection of 1849. His estates were confiscated, but were restored to his family in 1867; and in 1870 his body was removed and interred anew with great solemnity.

BATUTA See **IBN BATTUTAH**

BATYUSHKOV, Konstantin Nikolaievitch (1787–1855) Russian poet, born in Vologda. He served in the Napoleonic wars, but became insane in 1821 and was confined in an asylum for the remaining 34 years of his life. Profoundly influenced by French and Italian writers, his work was much admired by **Pushkin**. His most important work was *The Death of Tasso*.

BAUDELAIRE, Charles Pierre (1821–67) French Symbolist poet, born in Paris. After an unhappy childhood quarrelling with his soldier-diplomat step-father, Colonel Aupick, he was sent off on a voyage to India. But he stopped off at Mauritius, where Jeanne Duval, a half-caste, became his mistress and inspiration. On his return to Paris in 1843 he spent much of his time in the studios of **Delacroix**, **Manet**, and **Daumier**, and wrote art criticisms, *Le Salon de 1845* and *Le Salon de 1846*. In 1847 he published an autobiographical novel, *La Fanfarlo*. He sided with the revolutionaries in 1848, although he was by nature aristocratic and Catholic. His masterpiece is a collection of poems, *Les Fleurs du mal* (1857), for which author, printer, and publisher were prosecuted for impropriety in 1864, but which earned the praise of critics and was to exert an influence far into the 20th century. Later works include *Les Paradis artificiels* (1860) and *Petits Poèmes en prose* (1869). He was greatly attracted by **de Quincey** and **Edgar Allan Poe**, whose works he translated (1856–65). His Satanism, his preoccupation with the macabre, the perverted, and the horrid was an essential feature of his work. Having written a critical work on his literary associates **Balzac**, **Gautier**, and **de Nerval**, published posthumously in 1880, he took to drink and opium, and was struck down with paralysis. He died in poverty.

BAUDOUIN I (1930–) king of the Belgians, elder son of **Leopold III** and his first wife, Queen Astrid. He succeeded to the throne in July 1951 on the abdication of his father over the controversy of the latter's conduct during World War II. In 1960 he married the Spanish Doña Fabiola de Mora y Aragon.

BAUDRY, Paul Jacques Aimé (1828–86) French painter, born in La Roche-sur-Yon. He is chiefly known for the 30 large panels, illustrative of music and dancing, executed for the foyer of the Paris Opera (1866–76).

BAUER, Caroline (1807–78) German actress, born in Heidelberg. In 1829 she married Prince **Leopold**, afterwards king of the Belgians. Their morganatic union was as brief as it was unhappy; in 1831 she returned to the stage, which she left only in 1844, on her marriage to a Polish count.

BAUER, Georg See **AGRICOLA**

BAUHIN, Caspar or **Gaspard** (1560–1624) Swiss botanist and physician, born in Basel, younger brother of **Jean Bauhin**. He was professor of anatomy and botany at Basel and compiled a medical textbook, *Theatrum Anatomicum* (1605). He was also the author of *Pinax theatri botanici* (1623), much used by **Linnaeus** and still important as a compendium of all plants known in the early 17th century.

BAUHIN, Jean (1541–1612) Swiss botanist and physician, born in Basel, brother of **Caspar Bauhin**. Physician to the Duke of Württemberg, he was co-author of a *Historia plantarum universalis* (3 vols, 1650–51).

BAUM, Vicki, originally **Hedvig** (1888–1960) Austrian-born American novelist, born in Vienna. After writing several novels and short stories in German, she made her name with *Grand Hotel* (1930), which became a best-seller and a popular film. She emigrated to the USA in 1931, where her later novels incuded *Falling Star* (1934), *Headless Angel* (1948) and *The Mustard Seed* (1953).

BAUMÉ, Antoine (1728–1804) French chemist, born in Senlis. He invented the hydrometer named after him and many dyeing processes.

BAUMEISTER, Willi (1889–1955) German painter, born in Stuttgart. For some years he was a professor at the Frankfurt School of Art, but the **Hitler** régime prohibited him from teaching and he turned to scientific research on colour and to prehistoric archaeology. These interests are reflected in his work such as *African Histories*, a series of paintings depicting strange organic forms, and his illustrations for the Bible stories and the *Epic of Gilgamesh* (1942–53). His series of paintings, from the *Mauerbilder* murals, through *Painter with his Palette* to the *Montaru* and *Monturi* experiments, show wide variety of theme and style and continuously novel treatment.

BAUMER, Gertrude (1873–1954) German feminist, leader of the German feminist movement, born in Hohenlimburg, Westphalia. While studying at Berlin University she became involved in feminist politics. From 1910 to 1919 she was president of the League of German Women's Associations, and in 1917 was founder of a socialist school for women. From 1893 to 1944 she edited the newspaper *Die Frau*. A member of the Reichstag from 1920 to 1933, she lost this position on the advent of Nazi power and was subjected to Gestapo interrogation. After World War II she founded the Christian Social Union but was soon forced by ill-health to retire from public life.

BAUMGARTEN, Alexander Gottlieb (1714–62) German philosopher of the school of **Johann Christian von Wolff**, born in Berlin. In 1740 he became professor of philosophy at Frankfurt-an-der-Oder. His main works are *Metaphysica* (1739) and *Aesthetica* (1750–58), a long unfinished treatise which pioneered this field and helped establish the modern term 'aesthetics'.

BAUR, Ferdinand Christian (1792–1860) German theologian and New Testament critic, born in Schmiden, near Stuttgart. He held the Tübingen chair of Theology from 1826, and founded the 'Tübingen School' of theology, the first to use strict historical research methods in the study of early Christianity.

BAUSCH, Pina (1940–) German choreographer and dancer, born in Solingen, West Germany. She trained first with **Kurt Jooss** at the Essen Folkwangschule and then with **José Limón** and **Antony Tudor** in New York. After a season with the Metropolitan Opera Ballet Company and another with American choreographer **Paul Taylor**, she returned to Essen where she staged several operas for the Wuppertal Theatre. Her success led to an invitation to found her own company. After staging **Stravinsky**'s *Le Sacre du printemps* (1975) and the **Brecht/Weill** *Seven Deadly Sins*, she began to produce her own work in the late 1970s. Her choreography and particularly her unusual stagings mark a turning point in contemporary dance and have remained a powerful influence. Stages are strewn with dead leaves (*Bluebeard*, 1977), pink and white carnations (15000 of them in *Carnations*, 1982) or chairs (*Café Muller*, 1978).

BAVIUS (fl.1st century BC) Roman minor poet: with his colleague **Maevius**, lampooned by **Virgil** in his *Eclogues*. Their names were used by **William Gifford** for the titles of his satires on the Della Cruscan school of poets ('The Baviad' and 'The Maeviad').

BAX, Sir Arnold Edward Trevor (1883–1953) English composer, born in London. He studied piano at the Royal Academy of Music. A visit to Russia in 1910 directly inspired such piano pieces as *Gopak* (1911) and

In a Vodka Shop (1915), but much more influential on Bax was the Celtic revival. His love and admiration for all things Celtic was expressed early in Irish short stories, which he wrote under the name of Dermot O'Byrne, and musically in orchestral pieces (1912–13), in many songs set to the words of revival poets, in the choral *St Patrick's Breastplate* (1923–24), and in *An Irish Elegy* (1917), for English horn, harp and strings. Between 1921 and 1939 Bax, a self-styled 'brazen romantic', wrote his seven symphonies, expressing moods from bitterness to serenity; in 1921 his *Mater Ora Filium* assured his place in the great English choral tradition; and his vast output in most other fields—tone poems, such as *In the Faery Hills* (1909) and *Tintagel* (1917), chamber music, piano solos and concertos—attests to the validity of his appointment in 1942 as Master of the King's Musick. He published an autobiograpy, *Farewell my Youth* (1943). His brother Clifford (1886–1962) was a playwright and author.

BAX, Ernest Belfort (1854–1926) English writer and reformer, a founder of English socialism, born in Leamington. A barrister, he founded with **William Morris** the Socialist League, and wrote much on Socialism, history and philosophy.

BAXENDALE, Leo (1930–) English strip cartoonist, born in Lancashire, the creator of the *Beano*'s *Bash Street Kids*. He first worked as a label designer, and later joined the *Lancashire Evening Post* (1950), drawing sports cartoons and writing and illustrating articles. He began to freelance strips to the *Beano* comic beginning with *Little Plum* (1953), followed by *Minnie the Minx* (1953) as a female version of *Dennis the Menace*. A large cartoon series, *When The Bell Rings* (1954), evolved into *The Bash Street Kids*, a riotous gang of juvenile delinquents. He designed the new weekly comic *Wham* (1964), and despite leaving the field in 1974 remains the most imitated artist in British comics.

BAXTER, George (1804–67) English engraver and print maker, son of **John Baxter**, born in Lewes. He developed a method of printing in oil colours, using copper or steel plates for his outlines, with neutral tones on the same plate obtained by aquatint or stipple. His process, patented in 1835, required a combination of between ten and 20 wood and metal blocks for each reproduction.

BAXTER, Jim (James Curran) (1939–) Scottish footballer, born in Fife. The last major footballer produced from the Fife coalfields, once a major nursery of the game, he was at his elegant peak with Glasgow Rangers between 1960 and 1964. For three years he was probably the best left-half in Europe, but did not repeat his Scottish success during spells with Sunderland and Nottingham Forest. Capped 34 times by Scotland, he was never dedicated to training, and left the game soon after the age of 30.

BAXTER, James Keir (1926–72) New Zealand poet, dramatist and critic, born in Dunedin. He worked as a labourer, journalist and teacher and led a bohemian life until he was converted to Roman Catholicism. Subsequently he founded a religious community on the Wanganui River. He published more than 30 books of poetry, his first volume, *Beyond the Palisade* (1944), appearing when he was 18. The poems he wrote before his conversion are collected in *In Fires of No Return* (1958). Latterly he was less productive but his appointment to the Burns Fellowship at the Universiy of Otago in 1966 inspired him, and *Howrah Bridge* (1961) and *Autumn Testament* (1972) are among his best work. His plays include *The Band Rotunda* (1967), *The Sore-Footed Man* (1967) and *The Temptation of Oedipus* (1967).

BAXTER, John (1781–1858) English printer, the first to use an ink-roller. Born in Surrey, he settled in Lewes and published the illustrated 'Baxter's Bible' and the first book of cricket rules.

BAXTER, Richard (1615–91) English Nonconformist clergyman, born in Rowton, Shropshire. His education was irregular, but he acquired immense knowledge by private study. In 1638 he was made deacon by the bishop of Worcester. Originally a Conformist, like his family and friends, he found himself led to adopt some of the Nonconformist views as minister at Kidderminster (1640–60). In 1642, on the outbreak of the Civil War, he retired to Coventry, and ministered for two years to its garrison and inhabitants. His sympathies were almost wholly with the Puritans, and after Naseby, he acted as army chaplain, and was present at the sieges of Bridgwater, Bristol, Exeter, and Worcester. He went back to Kidderminster (1647), but his uncertain health caused him to retire to Rouse-Lench, Worcestershire, where he wrote the first part of *The Saint's Everlasting Rest* (1650). At the Restoration he was appointed a royal chaplain, but in 1662 the Act of Uniformity drove him out of the Church of England. The Act of Indulgence in 1672 permitted him to return to London, where he divided his time between preaching and writing. But in 1685 he was brought, for alleged sedition in his *Paraphrase on the New Testament*, before Judge **Jeffreys**, who treated him in the most brutal manner, calling him a dog, and swearing it would be no more than justice to whip such a villain through the city. Condemned to pay 500 marks, and to be imprisoned till the fine was paid, he lay in King's Bench prison for nearly 18 months.

BAXTER, William Giles (1856–88) American-born British cartoonist, famous for his version of the first comic strip hero, *Ally Sloper*. Brought to Buxton, Derbyshire, as a child, he became staff cartoonist on the new satirical weekly *Momus* (1878). In 1884 he joined *Ally Sloper's Half-Holiday*, completely redesigning it and adding the remarkable Sloper Family. His front page cartoons, especially his Christmas centre-spreads, made the paper's name. In 1887 he joined a new comic, *Variety Paper*, and created a new character, *Choodle*, but with less success.

BAYARD, James Asheton (1767–1815) American politician. A lawyer, he was elected to congress in 1796, and became a conspicuous member of the Federal party. He was in the senate from 1804 to 1813, opposed the war of 1812, and was one of the negotiators appointed by President **Madison** to conclude the peace treaty with Britain which followed.

BAYARD, James Asheton (1799–1880) American politician, son of **James Bayard** (1767–1815). He was also a distinguished Democratic senator.

BAYARD, Pierre du Terrail, Chevalier de (1476–1524) French soldier, known as 'the knight without fear and without reproach', born in the Château Bayard, near Grenoble. Accompanying **Charles VIII** to Italy in 1494–95, he won his spurs at the battle of Fornovo, where he captured a standard. In the service of **Louis XII** he fought with legendary bravery at Milan (1501) and Barletta (1502), and campaigned in Spain, and against the Genoese and Venetians, taking Brescia by storm in 1512. At Marignano he gained a brilliant victory for **Francis I**, who, in consequence, submitted to receive the honour of knighthood from Bayard. When **Charles V** invaded Champagne with a large army in 1521, Bayard defended Mézières. He was mortally wounded by a shot from an arquebus while defending the passage of the River Sesia in Italy, and died facing the foe, reciting the *Miserere*. His body was sent home and buried in the Minorites' church near Grenoble.

BAYARD, Richard Henry (1796–1868) American politician, son of **James Bayard** (1767–1815). He was long a senator, and represented the United States in Belgium.

BAYARD, Thomas Francis (1828–98) American politician, son of **James Bayard** (1799–1880). He qualified for the bar, and entering the senate (1869), acted with the Democrats. He was proposed for the presidency in 1880 and 1884, and, after being secretary of state 1885–89, was from 1893 to 1897 ambassador to Great Britain.

BAYER, Johann (1572–1625) German astronomer, born in Rhain, Bavaria. His *Uranometria* (1603) depicts the positions of nearly a thousand stars in addition to those given by **Tycho Brahe**. His designations by the letters of the Greek alphabet in preference to the Arabic proper names are still used for the brighter stars.

BAYES, Thomas (1702–61) English mathematician, born in London, the son of Joshua Bayes, one of the first six Nonconformist ministers to be publicly ordained in England. In 1731 he became Presbyterian minister in Tunbridge Wells. He is principally remembered for his posthumously published *Essay towards solving a problem in the doctrine of chances* (1763), in which he was the first to study the idea of statistical inference, and to estimate the probability of an event from the frequency of its previous occurrences. Although his mathematical results are now a standard part of statistical theory, there is still controversy about the circumstances of their application.

BAYEZIT I (d.1403) sultan of the Ottoman empire. In 1389 he succeeded his father, Murat I, who was slain on the battlefield of Kossovo. In three years he conquered Bulgaria, with parts of Serbia, Macedonia, and Thessaly, and most of Asia Minor. His rapid conquests earned him the name of Yildirim—'Lightning'. For ten years he blockaded Constantinople, to rescue which King Sigismund of Hungary (afterwards emperor) assembled a large army, including 2000 French nobles, and laid siege to Nicopolis, on the Danube. Bayezit hastened to meet him, and gained a decisive victory (1396). Bayezit would have entirely destroyed the Greek empire if he had not in 1402 been completely defeated by **Tamerlane** near Ankara. Bayezit himself fell into the hands of the conqueror, who treated him with great generosity (the iron cage is a myth), and in whose camp he died. He was succeeded by his son Süleyman I.

BAYEZIT II (1448–1512) sultan of the Ottoman empire. He succeeded his father, **Mehmet II**, the conqueror of Constantinople, in 1481. His 32 years' reign was a succession of wars against Hungary, Poland, Venice, Egypt, and Persia, which served on the whole to establish the Ottoman power.

BAYLE, Pierre (1647–1706) French Protestant philosopher and critic, born in Carlat, near Foix, in Languedoc. His career was marked by controversy throughout. He studied under the Jesuits at Toulouse and turned Catholic for a while, but reconverted to Calvinism and in 1675 took the chair of philosophy at Sedan until forced into exile at the University of Rotterdam in 1681. He started there in 1684 a popular journal of literary criticism, *Nouvelles de la république des lettres*; he also published a strong defence of liberalism and religious toleration, but was dismissed from the university in 1693 on the accusation that he was an agent of France and an enemy of Protestantism. He nonetheless completed in 1696 his major work, the *Dictionnaire historique et critique*, a sceptical analysis of philosophical and theological arguments. He was further persecuted for the work's alleged profanity, and for the claim in it that morality was independent of religion, but his writings were later influential in the 18th-century Enlightenment, and **Voltaire** and others used some of his arguments in their attacks on traditional theology.

BAYLIS, Lilian Mary (1874–1937) English theatrical manager, born in London, the daughter of musicians. In 1890 the family emigrated to South Africa, where she became a music teacher in Johannesburg. Returning to England in 1898, she helped with the management of the Royal Victoria Hall (afterwards the Old Vic), becoming manager in 1912; under her the theatre became a joint home of Shakespeare and opera. In 1931 she acquired Sadler's Wells Theatre for the exclusive presentation of opera and ballet.

BAYLISS, Sir William Maddock (1860–1924) English physiologist, born in Wolverhampton into comfortable circumstances. He studied science at University College, London, and abandoned medicine for physiology after failing his anatomy examinations, and taught physiology at University College, London, 1888–1924. Much of his experimental work was done with his colleague **Ernest Henry Starling**, whose sister he married. This included important work on the cardiovascular system and the discovery of secretin, the first known hormone (which word they coined). He also worked on enzyme actions, on the physiological effects of colloids and on traumatic shock. His *Principles of General Physiology* (1915) is a classic. Bayliss was the scientist involved in the 'Brown Dog Affair', when he successfully sued for libel the secretary of the National Anti-vivisection Society for inaccuracies in describing one of his physiology demonstrations.

BAYLOR, Elgin Gay (1934–) American professional basketball player, born in Washington. He spent his playing career with the Minneapolis (later Los Angeles) Lakers (1958–72). He went on to coach with the New Orleans Jazz before returning to Los Angeles as an executive with the Clippers.

BAZAINE, François Achille (1811–88) French soldier, born in Versailles. Entering the army in 1831, he served in Algeria, Spain and the Crimean War (1854–56). In the war with Austria of 1859 he captured Solferino in Italy; and in the Mexican expedition of 1861–67, he was in command of the army in 1862. He was promoted marshal of France in 1864. In the Franco-Prussian War of 1870–71, after the abdication of **Napoleon III**, he failed to support his subordinate commanders at the battles of Spichern and St Privart la Montaigne, and in September 1870 was trapped by the Prussians at Metz. After a siege of 54 days he surrendered his whole army of 173 000 men. For this he was court-martialled in 1873 and sentenced to death for treason. The sentence was commuted to 20 years' imprisonment, but in 1874 he escaped to Spain from the fortress on the Île Ste Marguerite near Cannes. He died in Madrid.

BAZAINE, Jean René (1904–75) French painter, born in Paris. His style developed through Cubism to abstract art, and he produced a number of very successful tapestry designs as well as stained glass and mosaics.

BAZALGETTE, Sir Joseph William (1819–91) English engineer. He constructed London's drainage system and the Thames embankment, and was a notable pioneer of public health engineering.

BAZARD, Saint-Armand (1791–1832) French socialist, born in Paris. In 1820 he founded an association of French Carbonari, and in 1825 attached himself to the school of **Saint-Simon**, he and **Enfantin** becoming its 'Pères Suprèmes'.

BAZIN, René (1853–1932) French novelist, born in Angers. He depicted with charm and colour the life of peasant folk in the various French provinces, and in some of his novels, such as *Les Oberlé* (1901), dealt with the social problems of his time.

BAZIOTES, William (1912–63) American painter, born in Pittsburgh. He studied at the National Academy of Design in New York from 1933 to 1936. His early work was influenced by **Picasso** but in the 1940s he was one of a number of American painters, including **Jackson Pollock**, **Arshile Gorky** and **Robert Motherwell**, whose art developed from European Surrealism. Baziotes' work stemmed fron the ideal of intuitive, automatic expression through abstraction, permitting the subconscious to dictate colour and line. His dream-like images often contain suggestions of animal forms.

BEACH, Thomas See **LE CARON, Major Henri**

BEACHCOMBER See **MORTON, John Cameron**

BEACONSFIELD, Earl of See **DISRAELI, Benjamin**

BEADLE, George Wells (1903–89) American biochemical geneticist. Born on a farm in Wahoo, Nebraska, he became interested in agricultural genetics as a student. He studied the genetics of maize, the fruit fly (Drosophila) and the bread mould Neurospora. At Stanford University (1937–46), in association with **Edward Laurie Tatum**, he developed the idea that specific genes control the production of specific enzymes. Beadle and Tatum shared the Nobel prize for physiology or medicine in 1958 with **Joshua Lederberg**. Beadle was a professor at the California Institute of Technology (1946–61), and president of Chicago University from 1961 to 1968.

BEAGLEHOLE, John Cawte (1901–71) New Zealand historian of Australasian exploration, born in Wellington. He graduated from Victoria University College (later Victoria University), to which he returned in 1936 as lecturer in history, remaining there as professor of British Commonwealth history (1963–66). His PhD was obtained after some years at University College, London, where he was disgusted by prejudice against colonials. On his return to New Zealand he suffered from academic prejudice aginst his left-wing opinions but produced major works such as *The Exploration of the Pacific* (1934), *New Zealand, A Short History* (1936), and *The Discovery of New Zealand* (1939). His life's work was the masterly Hakluyt Society edition of *The Journals of Captain James Cook on his Voyages of Discovery* (1955–67), associated with which was his *The Endeavour Journal of Sir Joseph Banks* (1962). His Life of **Cook** was published posthumously.

BEALE, Dorothea (1831–1906) English pioneer of women's education, born in London. In 1857 she was appointed head teacher of Clergy Daughters' School in Westmorland, and from 1858 to 1906 was principal of Cheltenham Ladies' College. In 1885 she founded St Hilda's College, Cheltenham, as the first English training college for women teachers, and sponsored St Hilda's Hall in Oxford for women teachers in 1893. An ardent suffragette, she was immortalized in verse with **Frances Mary Buss** ('Miss Buss and Miss Beale, Cupid's darts do not feel').

BEALE, Lionel Smith (1828–1906) English physiologist and microscopist, born in London. A professor of King's College, London (1853-96), he discovered 'Beale's cells'.

BEALE, Mary, née **Cradock** (1632–99) English painter, born in Barrow, Suffolk, the daughter of a clergyman. When she married Charles Beale, a landowner and textile manufacturer, in 1651, she was already a practising portrait painter and a devoted follower of the most celebrated portraitist of her day, Sir **Peter Lely**. Very little is known of her work before about 1670, but several of her husband's diaries record her painting commissions which include a good number of portraits of clerics. She also executed copies after Lely, whose influence is generally evident in all her work.

BEAMON, Bob (Robert) (1946–) American athlete, born in New York. A long jumper who was not considered a great stylist, he smashed the world record at the 1968 Olympic Games in Mexico City, with a jump of 8.90 metres (29ft 21½ ins)—55 cm (21½ ins) further than the previous record. No-one has since equalled this performance at lower altitudes.

BEAN, Charles Edwin Woodrow (1879–1968) Australian journalist and war historian, born in Bathurst, New South Wales. He was educated at Oxford University. Prior to World War I he was London correspondent for the *Sydney Morning Herald* and became offical correspondent to the Australian Imperial Force. Landing with the AIF at Gallipoli in 1915, Bean stayed at the front line throughout that campaign. He then accompanied the troops to France where he served until the end of the war. On being appointed Official War Historian, he returned to Gallipoli in 1919 to research information. The author of a number of books, his major work was the 12-volume *Official History of Australia in the War of 1914–18* (1921–39), in which he dealt at some length with the contribution of the Anzac forces to the Allied war effort. Writing six of the twelve volumes, and editing the others, occupied a major part of his life.

BEARD, Charles Austin (1874–1948) American historian, born in Knightstown, Indiana. He studied at DePauw University, Oxford and Columbia, where he taught from 1907, resigning in 1917 on an issue of academic freedom in wartime. After work on European history he produced *An Economic Interpretation of the Constitution of the United States* (1913), arguing for personal and group economic interests as explanation of the framing of the Constitution in 1787, the first effectual popular demolition of a 'Golden Age' origin of the USA. Beard brought the same determinist principle to bear in *The Economic Origins of Jeffersonian Democracy* (1915), and *The Rise of American Civilization* (1927), in which he argued for economic forces dictating American historical development. His wife, **Mary Ritter Beard**, was his collaborator in this and in its sequels, *America in Midpassage* (1939) and *The American Spirit* (1942). Their conclusions were summed up in *A Basic History of the United States* (1944), also vastly influential for a time.

BEARD, Mary Ritter (1876–1958) American feminist and historian, born in Indianapolis. Educated at DePauw University, in 1900 she married **Charles Austin Beard** whom she had met there, and immediately became involved in women's suffrage, first in Oxford, England, where her husband was a student, then in New York (from 1902) where they both enrolled at Columbia University. After the birth of her son in 1907 she joined the National Women's Trade Union League, helping to run strikes and protests. In 1910 she became a member of the Woman Suffrage movement, and after a period of editing *The Woman Voter* became involved with the more working-class issues of the Wage Earners' League. From 1913 to 1917 she worked assiduously for the Congressional Union (later the National Women's party) under **Alice Paul**'s leadership, but gradually became more interested in writing and giving lectures than in practical work. Her publications included *Woman's Work in Municipalities* (1915), *On Understanding Women* (1931) and, most famously, *Women as a Force in History* (1946). With her husband she wrote several influential works on American history, such as *History of the United States* (1921) and *The Rise of American Civilization* (1927). A polemical, perceptive commentator, she is best remembered for illuminating women's history.

BEARDSLEY, Aubrey Vincent (1872–98) English illustrator, born in Brighton. He worked in an architect's and fire-insurance offices, but became famous by his fantastic posters and illustrations for *Morte d'Arthur*, **Wilde**'s *Salome*, **Pope**'s *Rape of the Lock*, *Mlle de Maupin*, *Volpone*, as well as for the *Yellow Book* magazine (1894–96) and his own *Book of Fifty Drawings*, mostly executed in black and white, in a highly individualistic asymmetrical style. With Wilde he is regarded as leader of the 'Decadents' of the 1890s. He died of tuberculosis at Mentone, having embraced the Catholic faith.

BEATLES, THE: John Winston Lennon (1940–80), **Paul McCartney** (1942–), **George Harrison** (1943–), **Ringo Starr,** originally **Richard Starkey** (1940–) British pop group. Formed in Liverpool in 1960, the group learned their trade through gruelling engagements at the city's Cavern Club and at venues in Hamburg, West Germany. Under the management of Brian Epstein, a local record shop owner, they signed a recording contract in 1962 and their regional popularity quickly spread across the country with such records as 'Love Me Do', 'She Loves You' and 'I Want to Hold Your Hand'. In 1964 the last two titles were released in the United States, and 'Beatlemania' spread rapidly around the world, with the group consistently surpassing all previous figures for concert attendances and record sales. The early songs of Lennon and McCartney involved simple but effective harmonies which nevertheless won acclaim from serious musicians and critics. The pair showed a remarkable ability to assimilate various styles and their compositional technique, enhanced by producer George Martin, developed quickly. Their decision to record their own songs had the effect, in the UK, of ending the dominance of 'Tin Pan Alley' and was widely imitated by other performers. Their music ranged from the lyrically beautiful 'Yesterday' to the complex rhythms of 'Paperback Writer', the nostalgia of 'Penny Lane', and the surrealism of 'Strawberry Fields Forever'. Controversially created MBE in 1965 (Lennon later returned his insignia in protest against the Vietnam War), the group were involved for a while with Indian mysticism, 'transcendental' meditation and the use of hallucinogenic drugs. The latter flirtation had a major influence on the recording of *Sgt. Pepper's Lonely Hearts Club Band* (1967), an album which, with its long musically and thematically linked songs, achieved a new maturity for pop and became perhaps the most influential recording since the advent of **Elvis Presley**. After a long period of inactivity the group dissolved in 1970 amid complex legal wranglings. They had made several cinema and television films, including *A Hard Day's Night* (1964), *Help!* (1965) and *The Magical Mystery Tour* (1967). Among their other record albums are *Please Please Me* (1963), *Beatles For Sale* (1964), *Revolver* (1966), *Abbey Road* (1969) and *Let It Be* (1970). After the group parted Paul McCartney recorded alone and with the highly-successful group Wings. John Lennon wrote and recorded in the USA with his wife, Yoko Ono, and was murdered in New York. George Harrison recorded intermittently and became a successful film producer.

BEATON, Sir Cecil (1904–80) English photographer and designer, born in London and educated at Harrow and Cambridge. An outstanding photographer of fashion and high-society celebrities, including royalty, he also designed scenery and costumes for many ballet, operatic, theatrical and film productions, including *My Fair Lady* and *Gigi*. His publications include *My Royal Past* (1939), *The Glass of Fashion* (1959) and *The Magic Image* (1975), and he provided the drawings and illustrations for many other books. He also wrote several volumes of autobiography, 1961–78.

BEATON, or **Bethune, David** (1494–1546) Scottish statesman and prelate, nephew of **James Beaton**, born in Balfour, Fife, and educated at the universities of St Andrews, Glasgow, and Paris. He was at the French court (1519) as Scottish 'resident' and twice later as ambassador to negotiate **James V**'s marriages. He was given French rights of citizenship and appointed bishop of Mirepoix by **Francis I** (1537). In 1525 he took his seat in the Scots Parliament as abbot of Arbroath and was appointed Privy Seal. Made a cardinal in 1538, on the death of his uncle in 1539 he succeeded him as archbishop of St Andrews. On James's death, he produced a forged will, appointing himself and three other regents of the kingdom during the minority of the infant **Mary, Queen of Scots**. The nobility, however, elected the Protestant earl of **Arran** regent. Beaton was arrested, but soon regained favour and was made chancellor (1543). He was assassinated by a band of conspirators in his castle of St Andrews. His mistress, Marion Ogilvy, had borne him at least two sons and one daughter—the last married an earl of Crawford.

BEATON, or **Bethune, James** (1470–1539) Scottish prelate and statesman, uncle of Cardinal **David Beaton**. He graduated from St Andrews in 1493, and rose rapidly to be archbishop of Glasgow (1509), and of St Andrews (1522). One of the regents during **James V**'s minority, he upheld the **Hamilton** against the **Douglas** faction; and in 1526 he had 'to keep sheep in Balgrumo', while the Douglases plundered his castle. He was soon, however, reinstated in his see, and figured as a zealous supporter of France. An opponent of the Reformation, he initiated persecution of Protestants: **Patrick Hamilton** and three other Protestants were burnt at the stake during his primacy.

BEATON, or **Bethune, James** (1517–1603) Scottish prelate, nephew of Cardinal **David Beaton**. Archbishop of Glasgow during the Reformation, from 1552 until the death of the queen-regent, **Mary of Guise**, in 1560, when he withdrew to Paris as Scottish ambassador.

BEATRICE, Princess See **BATTENBERG, Prince Henry of**

BEATRIX, (Wilhelmina Armgard) (1938–) queen of the Netherlands (1980–), eldest daughter of Queen **Juliana** and Prince **Bernhard Leopold**. In 1966 she married West-German diplomat Claus-Georg Wilhelm Otto Friedrich Gerd von Amsberg (b.1926); their son, Prince Willem-Alexander Claus George Ferdinand (b. 1967) is the first male heir to the Dutch throne in over a century; there are two other sons, Johan Friso Bernhard Christiaan David (b.1968) and Constantijn Christof Frederik Aschwin (b.1969). She acceded to the throne on her mother's abdication in 1980.

BEATTIE, James (1735–1803) Scottish poet and essayist, born in Laurencekirk, Kincardineshire, the son of a shopkeeper. He was educated at the village school and at Marischal College, Aberdeen, and after some years as a schoolmaster in Fordoun he became a master at Aberdeen Grammar School, and then became in 1760 professor of moral philosophy at

Aberdeen. His overrated *Essay on Truth* (1770) attacked **Hume**, but he is chiefly remembered for his long poem, *The Minstrel* (1771–74), a forerunner of Romanticism.

BEATTY, David Beatty, 1st Earl (1871–1936) English naval commander, born in Nantwich, Cheshire. He entered the navy in 1884 and served in the Sudan (1896–98). As commander of a battleship he took part in the China War (1900) and was promoted to captain for his leadership in shore operations. In 1912 he was appointed to command the 1st Battle Cruiser Squadron. At the outbreak of World War I he steamed into Heligoland Bight, and destroyed three German cruisers. In January 1915 he encountered and pursued German battle cruisers near the Dogger Bank, sinking the *Blücher*. At the battle of Jutland (31 May 1916) he fought the hardest action of the war, losing two of his ships, but badly mauling his opponents. He succeeded Lord **Jellicoe** as commander-in-chief of the Grand Fleet in 1916 and became First Sea Lord in 1919.

BEATTY, Warren, originally **Warren Beaty** (1937–) American filmmaker, born in Richmond, Virginia, the younger brother of actress **Shirley MacLaine**. A student at the Stella Adler Acting School, he was first seen in the television series *The Many Loves of Dobie Gillis* (1955–59) before making his Broadway début in *A Loss of Roses* (1959) and his film début in *Splendor in the Grass* (1961). A broodingly handsome leading man, he appeared in several comedies as well as portraying more complex combinations of naivety and cynicism in films like *Lilith* (1964) and *Mickey One* (1965). His enduring Casanova image has done a disservice to his many political interests and consistent efforts to expand the scope of his talents. At the same time as acting, he produced *Bonnie and Clyde* (1967), co-wrote *Shampoo* (1975) and co-directed *Heaven Can Wait* (1978). He was the producer, co-writer and star of *Reds* (1981) which won him an Academy Award as Best Director.

BEAUCHAMP, Pierre (1636–1705) French dancer, choreographer and ballet master, born in Versailles. Trained in music and dance, he made his début in 1650. Later he became superintendent of the Court Ballets of **Louis XIV**, with whom he also performed. In 1671 he was appointed director of the Académie Royale de Danse. He choreographed many ballets, including those for operas and comedies by **Giovanni Battista Lully** and **Molière**, all now lost. He was known as a dancer of dignity and virtuosity able to execute brilliant pirouettes and tours en l'air. Some credit him with the invention of classical ballet's five positions. He also created his own notation system.

BEAUCLERK, Topham (1739–80) English dandy, a descendant of **Charles II** and **Nell Gwyn**, only son of Lord Sydney Beauclerk, and the friend of **Samuel Johnson**. In 1768, two days after her divorce from Lord Bolingbroke, he married Lady Diana Spenser (1734–1808), daughter of the 2nd Duke of Marlborough, and an artist and illustrator of some ability, still known through Bartolozzi's engravings.

BEAUFORT name of an English family descended from **John of Gaunt** and Catherine Swynford:

BEAUFORT, Duke of a title conferred in 1682 on Henry Somerset, 3rd Marquis of Worcester. The succeeding earls were courtiers in Tudor and Stuart times, but Henry the 7th Duke (1792-1853), and his son Henry, the 8th Duke (1824-1899), were famous sportsmen, the latter an editor of *Badminton Library*, Badminton House in Gloucestershire being the family residence. The second son of the last-named, **Lord Henry** (1849-1932), was a songwriter.

BEAUFORT, Sir Francis (1774–1857) British naval officer and hydrographer, deviser of the 'Beaufort scale', born in Navan, County Meath. Entering the Royal Navy in 1787, he saw active service, including the retreat of Cornwallis (1795), and was severely wounded near Malaga. After a period working on shore telegraphs in Ireland he held three commands, and was dangerously wounded while surveying the coast of Asia Minor and suppressing piracy. From 1829 to 1855 he was hydrographer to the navy, devising the Beaufort scale of wind force and a tabulated system of weather registration. He was promoted rear admiral in 1846.

BEAUFORT, Henry (1377–1447) English prelate, second illegitimate son of **John of Gaunt** and his mistress Catherine Swynford (who were married in 1396 and their children legitimized the following year by **Richard II**), and half-brother of **Henry IV**. He studied at Oxford and Aix-la-Chapelle, was consecrated bishop of Lincoln in 1398, in 1405 succeeded **William of Wykeham** as bishop of Winchester. He was chancellor three times (1403–04, 1413–17 under **Henry V**, and 1424–26), and at the Council of Constance (1417) voted for the election of Pope **Martin V**, by whom in 1426 he was made a cardinal. He strongly opposed **Henry V**'s proposition to levy a new impost on the clergy for the war against France; but he lent the king (1416–21), out of his own private purse, £28000—a sum which justifies the belief that he was the wealthiest subject in England. In 1427 the pope sent him as legate into Germany, to organize a crusade against the Hussites. This undertaking failed; and the cardinal fell from papal pleasure. In 1431 he conducted the young king, **Henry VI**, to Paris, to be crowned as king of France and England.

BEAUFORT, Jane See **JAMES I** of Scotland

BEAUFORT, Lady Margaret, Countess of Richmond (1443–1509) daughter of John Beaufort, 1st Duke of Somerset, and mother of King **Henry VII**. In 1455 she married Edmund Tudor, Earl of Richmond. The Lancastrian claim to the English crown was transferred to her with the extinction of the male line, and it was in the right of his mother's descent from **John of Gaunt** that Henry VII ascended the throne after the defeat of **Richard III** in 1485. During the Wars of the Roses she had been imprisoned at Pembroke by the Yorkists. In 1464 she married Henry Stafford, son of the Duke of Buckingham, and in 1473 Thomas Stanley, 1st Earl of Derby. She was a generous benefactress of Oxford and Cambridge universities, where she endowed two divinity professorships. She also founded Christ's College, Cambridge, and St John's College, Cambridge, and was a patron of **William Caxton**.

BEAUHARNAIS French family from the Orléanais, ennobled in the 14th century.

BEAUHARNAIS, Alexandre, Vicomte de (1760–94) French soldier, son of a governor of Martinique, served in **Louis XVI**'s army in the American War of Independence under **Rochambeau**, but accepted revolutionary ideas and was president of the Constituent Assembly in Paris in June 1791. He was given command of the army of the Rhine in 1793 but was arrested as an aristocratic 'suspect' and guillotined. In 1779 he married **Joséphine de Tascher de la Pagerie**, afterwards wife of **Napoleon**.

BEAUHARNAIS, Eugène Rose de (1781–1824) French soldier, son of **Alexandre de Beauharnais** and **Joséphine**. After his mother's marriage to **Napoleon**, he served with Napoleon in Italy and Egypt, and rapidly rose to the highest military rank. In 1805 he was made a prince of France, and in 1805 viceroy of Italy. In 1806 he married princess Amnalie Augusta of Bavaria, and was formally adopted by Napoleon and made heir apparent to the throne of Italy. Honourable and sagacious, he showed great military skill in the campaigns in Italy, Austria and Russia. After Napoleon's abdication in 1814 he retired to Bavaria, and was created Duke of Leuchtenberg.

BEAUHARNAIS, Hortense Eugénie Cécile (1783–1837) queen of Holland, born in Paris, the daughter of **Alexandre, Vicomte de Beauharnais**. As a child she was a great favourite of her stepfather, **Napoleon**, and in 1802 married his brother Louis, King of Holland (1806–10); the youngest of their three children became **Napoleon III**. In 1810–11 Hortense was the mistress of Count **Charles de Flahaut**, their son becoming Duc de **Morny**. In May 1814 Hortense was created Duchesse de St Leu by **Louis XVIII** at Tsar **Alexander I**'s request. She was a gifted artist and a composer, whose marching song, 'Partant pour la Syrie', became the national anthem of France's Second Empire.

BEAUMANOIR, Philippe de Remi, Sire de (c.1250–1296) French judge and jurist, seneschal of Poitou and later bailli of Vermandois and then of Senlis. He was the author of several novels but particularly of the *Coutumes de Beauvaisis*, the most original and important collection of local customary laws of the Middle Ages.

BEAUMARCHAIS, Pierre Augustin Caron de (1732–99) French playwright, the greatest French comic dramatist, born in Paris, the son of a watchmaker named Caron. Brought up in his father's trade, he invented, at 21, a new escapement which was pirated by a rival. The affair brought him to notice at court, where his good looks and fine speech and manners quickly procured him advancement. He was engaged to teach the harp to **Louis XV**'s daughters, and in 1756 he married the wealthy widow of a court official, whereupon he assumed the title by which he was known thenceforward. Duverney, a rich banker of Paris, also helped him to some speculations which realized a handsome fortune, largely increased in 1768 by another prudent marriage with a wealthy widow. His first plays, *Eugénie* (1767) and *Les Deux Amis* (1770), scored only a moderate success. The death of Duverney in 1770 involved him in a long lawsuit with his heir, Count Lablache, in the course of which he became the idol of the people, as the supposed champion of popular rights against the corrupt tribunals of the old régime. Beaumarchais appealed to the public by publishing his famous *Mémoires du Sieur Beaumarchais par lui-même* (1774–78), a work which united the bitterest satire with the sharpest logic, and made his reputation. The same brilliant satire burns in his two famous comedies, *Le Barbier de Séville* (1775) and *La Folle Journée ou le mariage de Figaro* (1784). The latter had a most unprecedented success; and both are still popular plays in France, but in England are chiefly known through **Mozart**'s and **Rossini**'s adaptations. The Revolution cost Beaumarchais his vast fortune, and, suspected of an attempt to sell arms to the *émigrés*, he had even to take refuge in Holland and England (1793).

BEAUMONT, Francis (c.1584–1616) English Elizabethan dramatist, born in Gracedieu, Leicestershire, the third son of a judge, and brother of Sir **John Beaumont**. He was educated at Broadgates Hall (now Pembroke College), Oxford, and entered the Inner Temple in 1600. He soon became a friend of **Ben Jonson** and the other men of genius who met at the Mermaid Tavern, among them **John Fletcher**. With the latter, Beaumont was to be associated closely until he married Ursula Isley (1613) and retired from the theatre. They are said to have shared everything: work, lodgings, and even clothes. Their dramatic works, compiled in 1647, contained 35 pieces; another folio, published in 1679, 52 works. Modern research finds Beaumont's hand in only about 10 plays, which include, however, the masterpieces. Fletcher's verse avoids enjambment, rhyme and prose while Beaumont uses all three devices. *The Woman Hater* (1607) is attributed solely to Beaumont, and he had the major share in *The Knight of the Burning Pestle* (1609), a burlesque of knight errantry and a parody of **Heywood**'s *Four Prentices of London*. *Philaster*, *The Maid's Tragedy* and *A King and no King* established their joint popularity. Other works include *The Scornful Lady* and *Cupid's Revenge*. *The Masque of the Inner Temple* was written by Beaumont in honour of the marriage of the Elector Palatinate **Frederick V** and the princess **Elizabeth** (1613). He was buried in Westminster Abbey.

BEAUMONT, Sir George Howland (1753–1827) English landscape painter and art patron, born in Stonehall, Dunmow, Essex. He studied at Eton and New College, Oxford, and was an intimate friend of Reynolds; at his Leicestershire seat, Coleorton, he entertained **Wordsworth**, **Scott**, **Rogers**, **Byron**, **Wilkie**, **Haydon** and others; and he presented his valuable collection of pictures to the National Gallery.

BEAUMONT, Jean Baptiste Élie de (1798–1874) French geologist, born in Canon, Calvados. He speculated on the origin of mountain ranges and assisted in making a great geological map of France (1840).

BEAUMONT, Sir John (1582–1627) English poet, elder brother of **Francis Beaumont**. His best known work is *Bosworth Field*, in which the heroic couplet makes its first appearance in English poetry.

BEAUMONT, Joseph (1616–99) English poet, born in Hadleigh, Suffolk. From 1663 he was master of Peterhouse, Cambridge. He wrote the long epic poem *Psyche* (1648).

BEAUMONT, William (1796–1853) American surgeon, born in Lebanon, Connecticut. His pioneering study on *Digestion* (1833) was based on experiments with a young Canadian patient, Alexis St Martin, who was suffering from a gunshot wound which had left a permanent opening in his stomach, and which Beaumont treated.

BEAUREGARD, Pierre Gustave Toutant (1818–93) American Confederate soldier, born near New Orleans. He graduated at West Point in 1838, served with distinction in the Mexican war (1846–48), and was appointed by the Confederate government to the command at Charleston, South Carolina, where, on 12 April 1861, the war began with the bombardment of Fort Sumter. He was virtually in command at the first battle of Bull Run (21 July 1861). In the spring of 1862 he was defeated at the battle of Shiloh or Pittsburg Landing, and retreated to Corinth, Mississippi, where he reorganized his division; but on the approach of the Union troops he evacuated the place, and was superseded by General **Bragg**. In 1864 he commanded the military division of the West and defeated **Butler** at Drewry's Bluff; but he and his fellow Confederates failed to check **Sherman**'s march to the sea.

BEAUREPAIRE, Sir Francis Joseph Edmund (1891–1956) Australian freestyle swimmer, born in Melbourne. Showing great swimming ability from a young age, he won his first title in 1906 at the age of 14. A prominent figure in the Olympics of 1908, 1912, 1920 and 1924, his most prestigious year was 1910, when he set four world records and won 41 consecutive races. Going into business with the formation of his own tyre company in 1922, he was active in local politics and from 1940 to 1942 was lord mayor of Melbourne.

BEAVERBROOK, Max (William Maxwell Aitken), 1st Baron (1879–1964) Canadian-born British newspaper magnate and politician, born in Maple, Ontario, the son of a presbyterian minister. He was a stockbroker in 1907 and by 1910 had made a fortune out of the amalgamation of Canadian cement mills. He went to Britain in 1910, entered parliament (1911–16), and became private secretary to **Bonar Law**. He was an observer at the western front early in World War I and wrote *Canada in Flanders* (1917). When **Lloyd George** became premier, he was made minister of information (1918). In 1919 he plunged into journalism and took Fleet Street by storm by taking over the *Daily Express*, which he made into the most widely-read daily newspaper in the world. He founded the *Sunday Express* (1921) and bought the *Evening Standard* (1929). The 'Beaverbrook press' fully expressed the ebullient, relentless, and crusading personality of its owner. From 1929 its mission was Empire Free Trade. In World War II **Churchill** successfully harnessed Beaverbrook's dynamic administrative powers to the production of much-needed aircraft. He was made minister of supply (1941–42), lord privy seal, and lend-lease administrator in the USA. He became chancellor of the University of New Brunswick in 1947. He wrote *Politicians and the Press* (1925), *Politicians and the War* (1928–32), *Men and Power* (new ed 1956), and *The Decline and Fall of Lloyd George* (1963).

BEBEL, Ferdinand August (1840–1913) German socialist, born in Cologne. He became a master turner, and rose by 1871 to be a leader of the German Social Democrat movement and its chief spokesman in the Reichstag. Occasional imprisonment added to his popularity. He wrote widely on socialism, on the Peasants' War, on the status of women, and an autobiography *My Life* (trans 1912).

BECCAFUMI, Domenico, originally **di Pace** (c.1486–1551) Italian painter, born in Siena. He was influenced by High Renaissance artists such as **Michelangelo** and **Raphael** without forsaking the more traditionally Sienese stylistic qualities of decorative colour and sinuous line. His paintings are characterized by unusual perspective, complicated figure poses and complex colour effects and the result is individual enough to be usually regarded as an early manifestation of the post-Renaissance style known as Mannerism. He also produced Old Testament designs for the marble floor of Siena cathedral as well as frescoes for the city hall. Much of his best work remains in the Pinacoteca, Siena.

BECCARIA, Cesare, Marchese de (1735 or 1738-94) Italian jurist and philosopher, born in Milan. In 1764 he published anonymously *Dei delitti e delle pene* ('On Crimes and Punishments'). Denouncing capital punishment and torture and advocating prevention of crime by education, the work had a widespread influence on the punishment and prevention of crime. In 1768 he was made professor of political philosophy at Milan and in 1791 a member of the board for reform of the judicial code.

BECHE See **DE LA BECHE**

BECHER, Johann Joachim (1635–82) German chemist, born in Speyer. He worked on minerals, and his *Physica Subterranea* (1669) was the first attempt to bring physics and chemistry into close relation.

BECHET, Sidney Joseph (1897–1959) American jazz musician, born in New Orleans. An outstanding jazz clarinettist by his teens, he took up the soprano saxophone in 1919, his forceful style making him the first significant saxophone voice in jazz. Touring Europe after World War I with Will Marion Cook's Southern Syncopated Orchestra, he was recognized as 'an artist of genius' by Swiss conductor **Ernest Ansermet**. As the New Orleans style declined in popularity, Bechet spent much of the 1930s in obscurity, emerging in 1940 as a figurehead of the traditional jazz revival. The warmth of his reception during many tours in Europe led him to make his permanent home in Paris, where he was an influential and honoured father-figure of his music.

BECHSTEIN, Karl (1826–1900) German manufacturer, born in Gotha. In 1856 he founded in Berlin his famous piano factory.

BECKENBAUER, Franz (1945–) West German footballer, born in Munich. As player, coach, manager and administrator, he has been a dynamic force in West German football over the last quarter of a century. He captained the West German national side to European Nations Cup success in 1972 and to the World Cup triumph of 1974. In 1972 he was European Footballer of the Year. His masterful style led to his being nicknamed 'Kaiser Franz'. He became manager of West Germany in 1986.

BECKER, Boris (1967–) West German tennis player, born in Leimen. A product of the German tennis leagues, he first came to prominence in 1984 when he finished runner-up in the US Open. In 1985 he became the youngest ever winner of the men's singles at Wimbledon, as well as the first unseeded winner. He successfully defended his title in 1986, and won it for a third time in 1989. The power and accuracy of his service, allied to his speed, strength and agility, made him, by the late 1980s, the foremost exponent of grass-court tennis in the world.

BECKER, Carl Lotus (1873–1945) American historian, born near Waterloo, Iowa. A graduate of Wisconsin University, he taught at Columbia, Pennsylvania State College, Dartmouth and Kansas (1902–16). He was professor of European history at Cornell University (1917–41) and reflected in his mingling of constitutional ideas and environmental response, the influence of his Wisconsin teacher, **Frederick Jackson Turner**. He combined vast learning with an easy popular style, and made himself master of eighteenth-century élite and popular thought on both sides of the Atlantic. His *The Declaration of Independence* (1922, 1942) is a model of perception. His essay on **Benjamin Franklin** for the *Dictionary of American Biography* was published as a separate book and *The Heavenly City of the Eighteenth Century Philosophers* (1932) enshrines the best presentation of Enlightenment ideas in his day. His other works included *Beginnings of the American People* (1915), *The Eve of Revolution* (1918), *Modern History* (1931) and *Progress and Power* (1936).

BECKER, George Ferdinand (1847–1919) American geologist, born in New York. As a member of the US geological survey, he took part in the 40th parallel survey, and achieved renown for his work on mineral deposits.

BECKER, Nikolaus (1809–45) German poet. He wrote in 1840 the *Rheinlied* ('Sie sollen ihn nicht haben'), which prompted **Alfred de Musset**'s answer ('Nous l'avons eu, votre Rhin allemand').

BECKER, Wilhelm Adolf (1796–1846) German classical archaeologist, born in Dresden. In 1842 he became professor at Leipzig. In his novel *Charicles* (1840) he ventured to reproduce the social life of old Greece; and in *Gallus* (1838) the Augustan age at Rome.

BECKET, Isaac (1653–1719) English mezzotint engraver, born in Kent. Apprenticed to calico printing, he learnt from **Edward Lutterel** the art of mezzotint engraving and executed many plates from the portraits of Sir **Godfrey Kneller**, including that of **Charles II** and Kneller's self-portrait.

BECKET, Thomas à (1118–70) English saint and martyr, archbishop of Canterbury, born in London, the son of a wealthy Norman merchant. Educated at Merton Priory and in London, he was trained in knightly exercises at Pevensey Castle, studied theology in Paris, and became a notary. About 1142 he entered the household of **Theobald**, archbishop of Canterbury, who sent him to study canon law at Bologna and Auxerre. At the papal court in 1152 he prevented the recognition of King **Stephen**'s son Eustace as heir to the throne; in 1155, the year after **Henry II**'s accession, he became chancellor and the first Englishman since the Conquest who had filled any high office. A brilliant figure at court, he showed his knightly prowess in the Toulouse campaign (1159) and was also a skilled diplomat and a perfect host. The change, then, was all the more drastic when in 1162 he was created archbishop of Canterbury. He resigned the chancellorship, turned a rigid ascetic, showed his liberality only in charities, and became as zealous a servant of the church as had ever been seen before by king or archbishop. He figured soon as a champion of its rights against the king and had courtiers, several nobles and other laymen excommunicated for their alienation of church property. Henry II, who, like all the Norman kings, endeavoured to keep the clergy in subordination to the state, in 1164 convoked the Council of Clarendon, which adopted the so-called 'Constitutions', or laws relating to the respective powers of church and state. To these, the primate at first declared he would never consent; but afterwards he was induced to give his unwilling approval. Henry now began to perceive that Becket's notions and his own were utterly antagonistic, and exhibited his hostility to Becket, who tried to leave the country. For this offence Henry confiscated his goods, and sequestered the revenues of his see. A claim was also made on him for 44000 marks, as the balance due by him to the crown when he ceased to be chancellor. Becket appealed to Pope **Alexander III** and escaped to France. He spent two years at the Cistercian abbey of Pontigny in Burgundy; and then went to Rome, and pleaded personally before the pope, who reinstated him in the see of Canterbury. Becket now returned to France, and wrote angry letters to the English bishops, threatening them with excommunication. Several futile efforts were made to reconcile him with Henry; but in 1170 an agreement was reached. The result was that Becket returned to England, entering Canterbury amid the rejoicings of the people, who regarded him as a shield from the oppressions of the nobility. Fresh quarrels soon broke out and excommunications were renewed. Henry's impetuously voiced wish to be rid of 'this turbulent priest' led to Becket's murder in Canterbury cathedral in 1170, by four knights, Hugh de Merville, William de Tracy, Reginald Fitzurse, and Richard le Breton. Becket's martyrdom forced confessions from the king. He was canonized in 1173 and Henry II did public penance at his tomb in 1174. In 1220 his bones were transferred to a shrine in the Trinity chapel, until it was destroyed during the Reformation in 1538. This was the popular place of pilgrimage which **Chaucer** described in the prologue to the *Canterbury Tales*.

BECKETT, Sir Edmund See **GRIMTHORPE**

BECKETT, Samuel (1906–89) Irish author and playwright, born in Dublin. He became a lecturer in English at the École Normale Supérieure in Paris and later in French at Trinity College, Dublin. From 1932 he lived mostly in France and was, for a time, secretary to **James Joyce**, with whom he shared the same tantalizing preoccupation with language, with the failure of human beings to communicate successfully mirroring the pointlessness of life which they strive to make purposeful. His early poetry and first two novels, *Murphy* (1938) and *Watt*, were written in English, but not the trilogy *Molloy*, *Malone Meurt* (trans 1958), and *L'Innommable*, or the plays *En attendant Godot* (trans *Waiting for Godot*, 1956), which took London by storm, and *Fin de partie* (trans *End Game*, 1957), all of which first appeared in French. *Godot* best exemplifies the Beckettian view of the human predicament, the poignant bankruptcy of all hopes, philosophies, and endeavours. His later works include *Happy Days* (1961), *Not I* (1973), and *Ill Seen Ill Said* (1981). He was awarded the 1969 Nobel prize for literature. Although there were one or two increasingly short pieces in later years—*Breath* (1970) shows a heap of rubbish on the stage and has a soundtrack which consists of a single breath—he wrote very infrequently towards the end.

BECKFORD, William (1709–70) Jamaican-born lord mayor of London, father of **William Beckford**. In 1723 he was sent to England, and educated at Westminster. Elected an alderman (1752) and MP for the City of London (1753), he was twice lord mayor.

BECKFORD, William Thomas (1760–1844) English writer and art collector, son of **William Beckford**, born in Fonthill, Wiltshire. In 1770 he inherited his father's fortune. As a young man of 16 he revealed remarkable intellectual precocity in his satirical *Memoirs of Extraordinary Painters*. From 1777 he spent much time on the Continent, meeting **Voltaire** in 1778, and later making a grand tour in Flanders, Germany, and Italy. In 1784 he entered parliament, but he became involved in a scandal and was excluded from society. He wrote, in French, *Vathek*, an Arabian tale of gloomy imaginative splendour modelled on Voltaire's style, which was published in France in 1787 and in an unauthorized English version in 1786. Revisiting Portugal in 1793, he settled in that 'paradise' near Cintra which **Byron** commemorates in *Childe Harold*. He returned to England in 1796, and proceeded to erect a new palace, Fonthill Abbey, designed by **James Wyatt**. Its chief feature was a tower, which fell in 1800, but was rebuilt (276 feet high). He lived there in mysterious seclusion until 1822, when he sold Fonthill Abbey, moved to Bath, and there built Lansdown Tower. In 1834 he published *Italy, with Sketches of Spain and Portugal* (incorporating, in modified form, *Dreams, Waking Thoughts*, and *Incident*, suppressed in 1783), and in 1835 another volume of *Recollections* of travel.

BECKINGTON See **BEKYNTON, Thomas**

BECKMANN, Ernst Otto (1853–1923) German organic chemist, born in Solingen. Professor at Erlangen and Leipzig, he discovered the molecular transformation of the oximes of ketones into acid amides, invented apparatus for the determination of freezing and boiling points, and the sensitive thermometer which bears his name.

BECKMANN, Johann (1739–1811) German economist. Professor of political economy at Göttingen, he is remembered chiefly for his *History of Inventions* (1780–1805; trans 1814).

BECKMANN, Max (1884–1950) German painter, draughtsman and printmaker, born in Leipzig, one of the greatest Expressionist artists. He trained at Weimar and in 1904 moved to Berlin where he began painting large-scale, dramatic works. The suffering he experienced as a hospital orderly in World War I led him to develop a highly individual, distorted, expressive style influenced by Gothic art, which he used to give voice to the disillusionment he saw around him in post-war Germany. A series of self-portraits reflects the anguish of contemporary events, and nine monumental triptychs painted between 1932 and his death constitute a moral commentary on the relationship between public aggression and the role of the individual. *Departure* is a picture typical of his work. When he learnt his work was to be included in an exhibition of Degenerate Art to be mounted by the Nazis in 1937 he fled to Holland where he lived until finally emigrating to the USA in 1947. He then taught at various American universities until his death.

BECKWITH, Sir George (1753–1823) English army officer, uncle of **John Beckwith**. During his time as governor of Barbados (1808–14) he captured Martinique (1809) and Guadeloupe (1810). From 1816 to 1820 he was in charge of the English troops in Ireland.

BECQUE, Henry (1837–99) French dramatist, born in Paris. He is known for two naturalistic plays, *Les Corbeaux* (1882) and *La Parisienne* (1885), both dramatic portrayals of bourgeois life and character.

BÉCQUER, Gustavo Adolfo (1836–70) Spanish romance writer and lyric poet, born in Seville. His *Legends* are written in a weirdly musical prose, but he is best known for his troubadour love verses.

BECQUEREL, Alexandre Edmond (1820–91) French physicist, son and assistant of **Antoine César Becquerel**. He succeeded his father as professor at the Musée d'Histoire Naturelle (1878), did research into solar radiation, diamagnetism, etc, and contructed a phosphoroscope.

BECQUEREL, Antoine César (1788–1878) French physicist, born in Châtillon-sur-Loing. He was the first to use electrolysis as a means of isolating metals from their ores. In 1837 he was awarded the **Copley** medal of the Royal Society, and became professor at the Musée d'Histoire Naturelle.

BECQUEREL, Antoine Henri (1852–1908) French physicist, born in Paris, son of **Alexandre Edmond Becquerel**. An expert on fluorescence (the ability of some substances to give off visible rays), he discovered the 'Becquerel rays', emitted from the uranium salts in pitchblende, which led to the isolation of radium and to the beginnings of modern nuclear physics. For his discovery of 'radioactivity' he shared the 1903 Nobel prize for physics with the **Curies**. His son Jean was also a physicist.

BEDAUX, Charles Eugéne (1887–1944) French-born American industrialist. In 1908 he emigrated to America, where he originated an efficiency system which provoked much controversy, and became controller of companies providing efficiency surveys throughout the world. He returned to live in France, and the Duke and Duchess of **Windsor** were married at his home in 1937. Under the German occupation he acted as intermediary between Vichy and Berlin; but at the liberation was arrested by the Americans on suspicion of treason, and committed suicide.

BEDDOES, Thomas (1760–1808) English physician and writer, born in Shifnal. He studied medicine and became reader in chemistry at Oxford, but his sympathies with the French Revolution led to his resignation (1792). From 1798 to 1801 he carried on at Clifton (Bristol) a 'pneumatic institute' for the cure of diseases by the inhalation of gases, with **Humphry Davy** his assistant. He wrote on political, social, and medical subjects and edited the works of **John Brown**, founder of the Brunonian movement.

BEDDOES, Thomas Lovell (1803–49) English poet and physiologist, born in Clifton (Bristol), eldest son of **Thomas Beddoes** (1760–1808). He was educated at Charterhouse and Oxford. In 1822 he published *The Bride's Tragedy*, a sombre murder drama. In 1825 he went to Göttingen to study medicine, and then led a strange wandering life as doctor and democrat, in Germany and Switzerland, with occasional visits to England. From 1825 he was engaged in the composition of a Gothic-Romantic drama, *Death's Jest-book*, which appeared in 1850, a year after his suicide.

BEDE, the Venerable, St (c.673–735) Anglo-Saxon scholar, theologian and historian, born near Monkwearmonth, Durham. At the age of seven he was placed in the care of **Benedict Biscop** at the monastery of Wearmouth, and in 682 moved to the new monastery of Jarrow in Northumberland, where he was ordained priest in 703 and remained a monk for the rest of his life, studying and teaching. His devotion to church discipline was exemplary and his industry enormous. Besides Latin and Greek, classical as well as patristic, literature, he studied Hebrew, medicine, astronomy and prosody. He wrote homilies, lives of saints, lives of abbots (*Historia abbatum*), hymns, epigrams, works on chronology (*De Temporum Ratione*, and *De sex Aetatibus Mundi*), grammar and physical science (*De natura rerum*), and commentaries on the Old and New Testaments; and he translated the Gospel of St John into Anglo-Saxon just before his death. His greatest work was his Latin *Historia Ecclesiastica Gentis Anglorum* (Ecclesiastical History of the English People), which he finished in 731, and is the single most valuable source for early English history. It was later translated into Anglo-Saxon by, or under, King **Alfred**. He was canonized in 1899; his Feast day is 27 May.

BEDE, Cuthbert See **BRADLEY, Edward**

BEDELL, William (1571–1642) English Anglican churchman, born in Black Nottley, Essex. From 1629 he was bishop of Kilmore, but resigned in 1633, and devoted himself to conciliation with the Roman Catholic Church and a translation of the Old Testament into Irish.

BEDFORD, David (1949–) English distance athlete, born in London. He gained a reputation as a front runner capable of breaking records. An athlete of immense stamina, he set the 10000 metres world record in 1972 (27:30.8). His only major championship victory was the international cross-country title in 1971. The lack of a sprint finish robbed him of any more medals. After retiring from competition he stayed in athletics as a promoter.

BEDFORD, John of Lancaster, Duke of (1389–1435) English prince, the third son of **Henry IV**. In 1403 he was made governor of Berwick-upon-Tweed and warden of the east marches. In 1414 his brother, **Henry V**, created him Duke of Bedford, and during the war with France he was appointed lieutenant of the kingdom. After Henry's death (1422), Bedford became guardian of the kingdom, and regent also of France during the minority of his nephew, **Henry VI**. In the wars with Charles, dauphin of France (the future **Charles VII**), he defeated the French in several battles including Cravant (1423) and Verneuil (1424). But in 1428 he failed to capture Orléans (the siege was raised in 1429). In 1431 he had **Joan of Arc** burned at the stake in Rouen, and crowned Henry VI king of France in Paris. But disasters followed; and in 1435 a treaty was negotiated at Rouen between Charles VII and the Duke of Burgundy, which ruined English interests in France. He died in Rouen just prior to the signing of this treaty in Arras, and was buried in the cathedral there.

BÉDIER, Charles Marie Joseph (1864–1938) French scholar and medievalist, born in Paris. In 1893 he was appointed professor of medieval French language and literature at the Collège de France, and received his doctorate for *Les Fabliaux* (1893). His *Roman de Tristan et Iseult* in 1900 gained him a European reputation, and *Les Légendes épiques* (1908–13) developed in exquisite French his theory of the origin of the great cycles of romance.

BEDLOE, William (1650–80) English informer, born in Chepstow. He befriended the Jesuits in London and spied for them in Europe. In 1678 he profited from the example of **Titus Oates** by giving an account of the 'popish plot' and providing details of the murder of Sir **Edmund Godfrey**. His financial rewards encouraged him to continue in the profitable denunciation of Roman Catholics.

BEDMAR, Alfonso de Cueva, Marquis de (1572–1655) Spanish conspirator. He was sent in 1607 as ambassador to Venice, and in 1618 plotted the overthrow of the republic. One of the conspirators betrayed the plot, which forms the theme of **Otway**'s *Venice Preserved*. Bedmar was dismissed, and went to Flanders, where he became president of the council. In 1622 he was made a cardinal, and finally bishop of Oviedo.

BEDSER, Alec Victor (1918–) English cricketer, born in Reading. With his twin brother, Eric, he was a vital component in the Surrey side which won seven consecutive county championships in the 1950s, but, unlike his brother, he made the transition to Test cricket very successfully. He was the leading English bowler in the eight years after World War II and, although barely fast-medium in pace, his command of cut and swing brought him 236 wickets in 51 Tests, at a time when there was no other credible English opening bowler. Against Australia at Trent Bridge in 1953 he took 14 wickets for 99 runs and in all first-class cricket he took 1924 wickets. A dogged batsman, he made several useful scores as night watchman in Test matches, notably his 79 against the Australians at Leeds in 1948. When his playing days ended he managed MCC teams abroad and for a time was chairman of the selection committee.

BEE, or **Bega, St** (7th century) Irish princess, who took the veil from St **Aidan**. She founded the nunnery of St Bees in Cumberland.

BEEBE, Charles William (1877–1962) American naturalist and explorer, born in Brooklyn, New York. He was curator from 1899 of ornithology for the New York Zoological Society, wrote many widely-read books, including *Galapagos* (1923) and *The Arcturus Adventure* (1925), and explored ocean depths down to almost 1000m in a bathysphere (1934).

BEECHAM, Sir Thomas (1879–1961) English conductor and impresario, son of Sir Joseph Beecham (1848–1916), the famous 'pill millionaire'. Born in St Helens, Lancashire, he was educated at Rossall School and Wadham College, Oxford, and travelled extensively. He began his career as conductor with the New Symphony Orchestra at the Wigmore Hall in 1906 and soon branched out as impresario and producer of opera, introducing 60 works unknown to British audiences, as well as **Diaghilev**'s Russian ballet. He was principal conductor (1932) and artistic director (1933) of Covent Garden, and in 1943 was conductor at the Metropolitan Opera, New York. In 1944 he returned to Britain, having married Betty Humby (d.1958), the pianist. In 1947 he founded the Royal Philharmonic orchestra and conducted at Glyndebourne (1948–49). Beecham did much to foster the works of **Delius**, **Sibelius** and **Richard Strauss**, and as a foremost conductor of his time was noted for his candid pronouncements on musical matters, for his 'Lollipop' encores, and after-concert speeches.

BEECHER name of an American family of preachers and writers whose English founder settled in 1638 at New Haven, Connecticut.

BEECHER, Catherine Esther (1800–78) American educationist, born in East Hampton, New York, eldest daughter of **Lyman Beecher**. She became principal of a Hartford seminary and wrote on female higher education and the duties of women.

BEECHER, Harriet See **STOWE**

BEECHER, Henry Ward (1813–87) American Congregationalist clergyman and writer, born in Litchfield, Connecticut, son of **Lyman Beecher**, and brother of **Harriet Beecher Stowe**. Educated at Amherst College, Massachusetts, he preached at Indianapolis, and in 1847 became the first pastor of Plymouth Congregational Church, in Brooklyn, New York, where he preached what he held to be the gospel of Christ, contended for temperance, and denounced slavery to an immense congregation. He favoured the free-soil party in 1852, and the Republican candidates in 1856 and 1860; and on the outbreak of the Civil War in 1861 his church raised and equipped a volunteer regiment. On the close of the war in 1865 he became an earnest advocate of reconciliation. For many years he wrote for *The Independent*; and after 1870 edited *The Christian Union* (later *Outlook*). A charge of adultery (1874) was not proved. He repeatedly visited Europe and lectured in Britain. His many writings included *Seven Lectures to Young Men* (1844), *Summer in the Soul* (1858), *Yale Lectures on Preaching* (1874), and *Evolution and Religion* (1885).

BEECHER, Lyman (1775–1863) American Presbyterian minister, born in New Haven, Connecticut. He studied at Yale, and became minister at East Hampton, New York (1799–1810), Litchfield, Connecticut (1810–26), and Hanover St Church, Boston (1826–32). Responding to the call to evangelize, he was president of Lane Seminary, near Cincinnati (1832–52). His evangelical preaching aroused opposition amongst conservative Presbyterians, and he was charged with heresy but acquitted. He then became leader of the New School Presbyterians. He was the father of 13 children, including **Catherine Beecher**, **Harriet Beecher Stowe**, and **Henry Ward Beecher**.

BEECHEY, Sir William (1753–1839) English portrait painter, born in Burford, Oxfordshire. He entered the Royal Academy as a student in 1772, and became a competent painter in the **Reynolds** tradition and was appointed Court painter to Queen **Charlotte** (1793). Two of his sons, George and Henry William, were painters, and died, one in India, the other in New Zealand; and his youngest son, Richard Brydges (1808–95), became an admiral, and after leaving the navy in 1857, also took to painting as a profession.

BEECHING, Richard, Lord (1913–85) English engineer and administrator, born in Maidstone, Kent. Educated at Imperial College, London, he became chairman of the British Railways Board (1963–65) and deputy chairman of ICI (1966–68). He is best known for the scheme devised and approved under his chairmanship (the Beeching Plan) for the substantial contraction of the rail network of the UK. He was created a Life Peer in 1965.

BEER, Michael (c.1605–1666) German architect, born in Au where he founded the influential Auer Zunft (Guild of Au) in 1657. The guild provided a structured theoretical architectural training in a series of family workshops. His major work was his designs for the residence and church of St Lawrence in Kempten (1651–53) for Abbot Roman Giel von Gielsburg, the first ecclesiastical building started after the Thirty Years' War. Stressing simple cubic forms, he reduced applied decoration to a minimum. The design was influential in the forming of the Vorarlberger Münsterschema's work at Ellwangen and Obermarchthal.

BEERBOHM, Sir (Henry) Max (Maximilian) (1872–1956) known as 'the Incomparable Max', English writer and caricaturist, born in London, the son of a Lithuanian corn merchant, and half-brother of Sir **Herbert Beerbohm Tree**. He was educated at Charterhouse and Merton College, Oxford. He published his first volume of essays under the ironic title *The Works of Max Beerbohm* (1896), some of which had appeared in the *Yellow Book*. He succeeded **Bernard Shaw** as drama critic of *The Saturday Review*, until 1910, when he married an American actress, Florence Kahn (d.1951), and went to live, except during the two World Wars, in Rapallo, Italy. His delicate, unerring, aptly-captioned caricatures were collected in various volumes beginning with *Twenty-five Gentlemen* (1896) and *Poet's Corner* (1904). Further volumes of parodying essays appeared, including *The Happy Hypocrite* (1897) and *A Christmas Garland* (1912), full of gentle humour, elegance, and rare wit, and ending with *And Even Now* (1920). His best-known work was his only novel, *Zuleika Dobson* (1912), an ironic romance of Oxford undergraduate life. His broadcast talks from 1935 were another of his singularly brilliant stylistic accomplishments. A month before his death he married Elizabeth Jungmann, who had been his deceased wife's greatest friend.

BEERBOHM TREE See **TREE, Sir Herbert Beerbohm**

BEETHOVEN, Ludwig van (1770–1827) German composer, born in Bonn, where his father was a tenor in the service of the elector of Cologne, and his grandfather a bass singer and kapellmeister. His first lessons were from his father, an unstable yet ambitious man, addicted to drink, whose rough temper and anxiety to train a second **Mozart** happily did not destroy Beethoven's talent or his love for music. He first appeared as a keyboard prodigy at Cologne (1778) and after further lessons from various teachers, became assistant harpsichordist in the Electoral orchestra (1783) and later second organist. In 1787 he visited Vienna for some weeks, played to and possibly received some lessons from Mozart, but hurried back to Bonn on his mother's death. Two years later he was allotted half his father's salary to act as head of the family, and he now played viola in the opera orchestra. **Haydn** met Beethoven in 1790, and on his return via Bonn from London in 1792, agreed to teach him in Vienna. In the city which was to remain his permanent home, Beethoven was at first befriended by Prince Karl Lichnowsky and, in addition to Haydn's lessons, studied with **Albrechtsberger** and **Salieri**. In 1795 he played in Vienna for the first time with the B flat concerto, and published his Opus 1 trios and Opus 2 piano sonatas. Subsequent appearances in Prague, Dresden and Berlin brought growing fame as a pianist and especially as an improvisor. His creative output is traditionally divided into three periods. By 1802 he had composed three piano concertos, two symphonies, the String Quartet Op.29, and Op.31, but already suffered deeply from depression caused by his increasingly serious deafness—a condition movingly described in a document written that year when he stayed at a village near Vienna, and known as the 'Heiligenstadt Testament'. The first works of his 'middle period' show Beethoven as the heroic, unbounded optimist, determined to strive creatively in the face of despair. The 3rd Symphony (twice the then normal length for a symphony) was originally dedicated to **Napoleon Bonaparte**, but on learning that he had proclaimed himself emperor, Beethoven defaced the title page and called the work *Eroica* (1804). In the opera *Fidelio* the themes of fidelity, personal liberation, and symbolic passage from darkness to light dominate; in association with this work he composed the three *Leonora* overtures. The final version of *Fidelio* was produced in 1814, by which time the rich corpus of the middle years was complete: piano sonatas including the *Waldstein*, *Appassionata* and *Lebewohl*, the Symphonies 4–8, the *Rasumovsky* Quartets, the 4th and 5th piano concertos, incidental music to *Egmont*, and the *Archduke* Trio, with which he made his last disastrous appearance as pianist. Equally disastrous in the middle period years were his unhappy romantic affairs, including the 'Immortal Beloved', referred to in a letter which, like the Heiligenstadt Testament, was discovered after his death. His domestic life declined in quality: he was ill-kempt, unhygienic, argumentative, grandiose but disordered in business dealings, quarrelsome with friends, and tormented more and more by illness. His custodianship of his nephew Karl (from 1815) began a protracted personal and legal anxiety that lasted until his death. Yet the last decade of Beethoven's life saw the most extraordinary and supremely great achievements: the *Diabelli* Variations, the last piano sonatas, the last six string quartets, the Mass in D (*Missa Solemnis*) and the *Choral* Symphony (no.9). On his deathbed he was so pleased with the gift of £100 from the London Philharmonic Society that he promised them his 10th Symphony. The motto of the finale of Beethoven's last quartet (Op.135)—'Must it be?—It must be!'—with its dark questioning and exuberant, confident affirmation, encapsulates much of his philosophy. His musical sketchbooks show a mind of indefatigable logic and striving for perfection. The Romantics embraced him as their supreme precursor; indeed his influence on the succeeding century of music was immense. Like **Goethe** he may be viewed as a gigantic creative force, bridging two colossal eras now conceived as Classical and Romantic, in such a way that he is indefinable. 'He thrived and suffered in an age of transition and political upheaval and gave eloquent voice to it,' wrote Professor Denis Matthews. The heir of Mozart and Haydn in his first period, the legacy of his last was such that it remains a listening challenge today.

BEETON, Mrs Isabella Mary, née **Mayson** (1836–65) English writer on cookery. She was educated in Heidelberg and became an accomplished pianist. In 1856 she married Samuel Orchard Beeton, a publisher, and her *Book of Household Management*, first published in parts (1859–60), in a women's magazine founded by her husband covering cookery and other branches of domestic science, made her name a household word. She died after the birth of her fourth son.

BEETS, Nicolaas (1814–1903) Dutch poet and writer, born in Haarlem. Professor of theology at Utrecht, he published under the pseudonym 'Hildebrand' *Camera Obscura* (1839), a series of quietly humorous sketches of everyday Dutch life, and *Volkshliedjes* (1842), a collection of simple verses.

BEGGARSTAFF, J and **W** See **NICHOLSON, Sir William Newzam Prior**

BEGHA, St See **BEE, St**

BEGIN, Menachem (1913–) Israeli statesman, born in Brest-Litovsk, Poland. He studied law at Warsaw University, and as an active Zionist became head of the Betar Zionist movement in Poland in 1931. At the invasion of Poland in 1939 he fled to Lithuania, where he was arrested by the Russians. Released in 1941, he enlisted in the Free Polish Army, and was sent to

British-mandated Palestine in 1942. Discharged from the army the following year, he became commander-in-chief of the Irgun Zvai Leumi resistance group in Israel and gained a reputation as a terrorist. In 1948 he founded the right-wing Herut Freedom Movement, becoming chairman of the Herut party, and was a member of the first, second and third Knessets. In 1973 three parties combined to form the Likud front, a right-of-centre nationalist party with Begin as its leader, and in the 1977 elections it ousted the Israel Labour party and Begin formed a coalition government. He was re-elected prime minister following the national elections of 1981. Throughout his life a man of hard-line views concerning the Arabs, in the late 1970s he sought a peaceful settlement with the Egyptians and attended peace conferences in Jerusalem (1977) and at Camp David at the invitation of President **Carter** (1978). In 1978 he and **Sadat** were jointly awarded the Nobel peace prize. He resigned the premiership in 1983.

BEHAIM, Martin (1440–1507) German navigator and geographer, born in Nürnberg. He settled in Portugal about 1484 and was associated with the later Portuguese discoveries along the coast of Africa. He revisited Nürnberg in 1490 and there constructed the oldest extant terrestrial globe.

BEHAM, Barthel (1502–40) German painter and engraver, born in Nürnberg, younger brother and pupil of **Hans Sebald Beham** and one of **Albrecht Dürer's** seven followers known as the 'Little Masters'. He became a court painter in Munich and made numerous engravings and paintings of Bavarian aristocracy.

BEHAM, Hans Sebald (1500–50) German painter and engraver, born in Nürnberg, and one of **Albrecht Dürer**'s seven followers known as the 'Little Masters'. Working in Frankfurt, he produced hundreds of woodcuts and copper engravings as illustrations for books.

BEHAN, Brendan (1923–64) Irish author, born in a slum district in Dublin. He left school at 14 to become a house painter, and soon joined the IRA. In 1939 he was sentenced to three years in Borstal for attempting to blow up a Liverpool shipyard, and soon after his release given 14 years by a Dublin military court for the attempted murder of two detectives, but was released by a general amnesty (1946). He was in prison again in Manchester (1947) and was deported in 1952. In prison he had learned to speak Irish from fellow IRA detainees, and read voraciously. His first play, *The Quare Fellow* (1956; filmed 1962), starkly dramatised the prison atmosphere prior to a hanging. His exuberant Irish wit, spiced with balladry and bawdry and a talent for fantastic caricature, found rein in his next play *The Hostage* (1958, first produced in Irish as *An Giall*). It is also evident in the autobiographical novel, *Borstal Boy* (1958), and in *Brendan Behan's Island* (1963).

BEHAN, Dominic (1928–89) Irish novelist and folklorist, born in Dublin, brother of **Brendan Behan**. He adapted old airs and poems into contemporary Irish Republican material, notably in *The Patriot Game*. Resentfully overshadowed for much of his life by the legend of his brother, he lived largely outside Ireland from 1947 as a journalist and singer. He ultimately settled in Scotland where for the first time he won acceptance in his own right as a writer, and as an Irish and Scottish nationalist. His only novel, *The Public Life of Parable Jones*, was published just before his death.

BEHM, Ernst (1830–84) German geographer. He was the compiler, with H Wagner, of the *Bevölkerung der Erde* (1872–82).

BEHMEN, Jakob See **BÖHME**

BEHN, Aphra, née **Amis** (1640–89) English writer and adventuress, born in Wye, Kent. She was brought up in Surinam, where she made the acquaintance of the enslaved negro prince Oroonoko, the subject afterwards of one of her novels, in which she anticipated **Rousseau**'s 'noble savage'. Returning to England in 1663, she married a merchant called Behn, who died within three years. She then turned professional spy at Antwerp, sent back political and naval information, but received little thanks, and on her return was imprisoned for debt. She turned to writing, as perhaps the first professional woman author in England, and wrote many coarse but popular Restoration plays, especially *The Forced Marriage* (1670), *The Rover* (1678), and *The Feigned Courtizans* (1678), and later published *Oroonoko* (1688). She was buried in Westminster Abbey.

BEHRENS, Peter (1868–1940) pioneering German architect and designer, born in Hamburg. Trained as a painter, he was appointed director of the Dusseldorf Art and Craft School (1903–07). In 1907 he became artistic adviser to **Walther Rathenau** at the massive AEG electrical company in Berlin, for whom he designed a turbine assembly works (1909) of glass and steel, a landmark in industrial architectural style. For AEG he designed everything from factory complexes to industrial brochures. He also designed workers' apartment houses in Vienna and Stuttgart, and the German embassy in St Petersburg (1912). He was professor at Dusseldorf and Vienna, and trained several notable modern architects, including **Le Corbusier, Ludwig Mies van der Rohe**, and **Walter Gropius**.

BEHRING, Emil von (1854–1917) German bacteriologist and pioneer in immunology, born in Hansdorf, W Prussia. He was professor of hygiene at Halle (1894–95) and at Marburg (from 1895), and discovered antitoxins for diphtheria and tetanus. He was awarded the first Nobel prize for physiology or medicine (1901).

BEHRING, Vitus See **BERING**

BEHRMAN, Samuel Nathaniel (1893–1973) American playwright, screenwriter and journalist, born in Worcester, Massachusetts. The production of a sophisticated comedy, *The Second Man* (1927), made him famous but despite being tagged the American **Noël Coward** his comedies of manners have not passed the test of time. However, his anecdotal portrait of the great art collector *Duveen* (1952) and *The Worcester Account* (1954), about his boyhood, retain their freshness and are reckoned to contain his best work.

BEIDERBECKE, (Leon) Bix (1903–31) American cornettist, born in Davenport, Iowa, of musical parents. The archetypal white youngster smitten by early jazz (and the posthumous subject of Dorothy Baker's novel *Young Man With a Horn*, 1938), he was largely self-taught on piano and cornet and began to play in local bands as a teenager. He quickly progressed to working with established professionals and, when expelled from military academy at the age of 19, began the short career that made him one of the most celebrated jazz performers of the 1920s. His bell-like tone and lyrical solo improvisations were heard to best effect in various small groups; but despite being an indifferent reader of music, he also transformed the commercial sound of such big bands as the **Paul Whiteman** and Jean Goldkette orchestras. His later career ravaged by alcoholism, Beiderbecke succumbed to pneumonia at the age of 28.

BEILBY, Sir George Thomas (1850–1924) Scottish industrial chemist, born in Edinburgh. He improved the method of shale oil distillation and invented a manufacturing process for synthesizing alkaline cyanides. He founded the fuel research station at East Greenwich.

BEILBY, Ralph See **BEWICK, Thomas**

BEILSTEIN, Friedrich Konrad (1838–1906) German-Russian encyclopaedist of organic chemistry, born in St Petersburg (Leningrad) of German parents. He studied chemistry in Germany under **Bunsen**, **Liebig**, **Wurtz** and **Wöhler**, and was lecturer at Göttingen and later professor at St Petersburg from 1866. His name is synonymous with his *Handbook of Organic Chemistry* (1881) which formed a substantially complete catalogue of organic compounds, and which has since been continued by the German Chemical Society, and is of great value to organic chemists.

BEIT, Alfred (1853–1906) and Sir **Otto** (1865–1930) British financiers and philanthropists, born in Hamburg. Alfred was associated with **Cecil Rhodes** and accumulated a great fortune in diamond mining. His brother succeeded him as controller of his financial empire.

BEITH, John Hay See **HAY, Ian**

BÉJART, Maurice, originally **Maurice Jean Berger** (1927–) French choreographer, born in Marseilles, the son of a philosopher. He trained at the Marseilles Opéra Ballet and then in Paris and London. He moved to the Royal Swedish Ballet (then under **Roland Petit**) where he both performed and choreographed. In 1953 he founded his own company, which was invited to remain as The Ballet of the 20th Century in Brussels after a major success there. He has developed a style of raw physicality favouring the talents of the male dancer, and was the first to present a ballet in a sports arena. His works include *The Firebird* (1970), in which a ballerina becomes the leader of the partisans, *Notre Faust* (1975), a black mass set to **Bach** and tangos, *Choreographic Offering* (1971) and *Kabuki* (1986).

BEK, Antony (d.1311) English prelate, bishop of Durham from 1283. He took a prominent part in the Scottish wars of **Edward I**, and from 1300 was involved in ecclesiastical disputes. His brother, Thomas (d.1293), was bishop of St Davids from 1280.

BEKE, Charles Tilstone (1800–74) English explorer and biblical critic, born in London. A scholar of ancient history, philology and ethnography, he wrote *Origines Biblicae* (1834). He explored Abyssinia (1840–43), where he fixed the latitude of over 70 stations, mapped 70000 sq. miles, and collected 14 vocabularies. In 1865 he undertook a fruitless mission to Abyssinia to obtain the release of Emperor **Theodore**'s British captives; in 1874 he explored the region at the head of the Red Sea.

BÉKÉSY, Georg von (1899–1972) Hungarian-born American physiologist, the world's greatest expert on aural physiology. Born in Budapest, he studied physics there and then worked as a telephone research engineer in Hungary (1924–46). His work led to a study of the human ear and how it analyses and transmits sounds to the brain, first in Stockholm (1947) and then at Harvard (from 1947). He won the 1961 Nobel prize for physiology or medicine, and wrote *Experiments in Hearing* (1960) and *Sensory Inhibition* (1967).

BEKHTEREV, Vladimir Mikhailovich (1857–1927) Russian neuropathologist, born in Viatka province. As professor at Kazan he researched into neural electricity and founded the psychoneurological institute in Leningrad.

BEKKER, Balthasar (1634–98) Dutch Protestant theologian. A pastor in Amsterdam, he was suspected of rationalism and Socinianism, and was promptly deposed and excommunicated on the publication of *De Betooverde Wereld* ('The World Bewitched', 1691–93), contesting the belief in witchcraft and magical powers.

BEKYNTON, or **BECKINGTON, Thomas** (1390–1465) English prelate. Educated at Winchester and Oxford, he was a fellow of New College (1408–20), prebendary of York (1423), and master of St Katherine's Hospital, London. He went on diplomatic missions to France (1432–42), became the king's secretary and lord privy seal, and as bishop of Bath and Wells from 1443 was a great benefactor of the city of Wells, rebuilding the bishops's palace and sponsoring the erection of other buildings.

BELAUNDE TERRY, Fernando (1913–) Peruvian politician, the son of a prime minister. He was an architect before entering politics, leading the Popular Action party (AP) in 1956. He campaigned for the presidency in 1956 and 1962, eventually winning it in 1963, but was deposed by the army in a bloodless coup in 1968. He fled to the USA where he lectured at Harvard. He returned to Peru two years later but was deported and did not re-establish himself until 1976. He won the presidency again in 1980, and was the first civilian to hand over to another constitutionally elected civilian (1985).

BELCHER, Sir Edward (1799–1877) English naval commander. He entered the navy in 1812, and from 1836 to 1842 explored the western coast of America. In 1852 he commanded a fruitless expedition sent out to search for Sir **John Franklin**, and in 1872 became rear admiral.

BELIDOR, Bernard Forest de (1698–c.1761) French engineer, born in Catalonia, Spain, the son of a French army officer. As professor of artillery at La Fére military academy, he wrote some of the best-known and most comprehensive engineering handbooks in pre-revolutionary France, covering military engineering (ballistics and fortifications) in his *Science des Ingénieurs* (1729–49) and civil engineering in his *Architecture Hydraulique* (4 vols, 1737–53), both of which influenced engineering practice in France and other European countries for a century after their publication.

BELINKSY, Vissarion Grigorievich (1811–48) Russian literary critic and journalist, born in Fribourg. He edited the *Moscow Observer* (1838–39), and afterwards became principal critic of *The Annals of the Fatherland*, and of *Sovremennik* in 1846. His influence on subsequent critics in Russia was profound. His *Survey of Russian Literature since the 18th Century* was published in 1834, and a complete edition of his works between 1859 and 1862 (12 vols).

BELISARIUS (505–65) Byzantine general under the emperor **Justinian I**, born in Germania in Illyria. He defeated a great Persian army at Dara in 530, and in 532 suppressed a dangerous insurrection in Constantinople by the destruction of 30000 of the 'Green' faction. Sent to Africa the following year to recover the provinces overrun by the Vandals, he twice defeated them (534–35). He then took the field in Italy against the Ostrogoths in 535: he conquered Sicily (536) and occupied Rome, which he defended for a year (537–38), and in 540 captured the Ostrogothic capital, Ravenna. He was recalled to Constantinople on suspicion of being tempted by offers of a crown by the Goths, but in 542 he was campaigning against the Persians, and from 544 to 548 he was again sent to Italy to deal with the resurgent Ostrogoths, but was recalled once more and put into retirement. In 559 he was called up to repel the Huns at the gates of Rome. In 562, falsely accused of conspiracy against the emperor, he was for a short time imprisoned; but in 563 he was again restored to honour.

BELL BURNELL, Susan Jocelyn née **Bell** (1943–) English radio astronomer, born in York, co-discoverer of the first pulsar. Educated at Glasgow and Cambridge, she later joined the staff of the Royal Observatory, Edinburgh. In 1967 she was a research student at Cambridge working with **Antony Hewish** when they noticed an unusually regular radio signal on the 3.7-metre wavelength radio telescope, shown to be bursts of radio energy at a constant interval of just over a second. The proposal by **Thomas Gold**, now accepted, is that these bursts come from a rapidly rotating neutron star, or pulsar, emitting a beam of radio waves.

BELL, Acton, See **BRONTË**

BELL, Alexander Graham (1847–1922) Scots-born American inventor, born in Edinburgh, son of **Alexander Melville Bell**. Educated at Edinburgh and London, he worked as assistant to his father in teaching elocution (1868–70). In 1870 he went to Canada, and in 1871 moved to the USA and became professor of vocal physiology at Boston (1873), devoting himself to the teaching of deaf-mutes and to spreading his father's system of 'visible speech'. After experimenting with various acoustical devices he produced the first intelligible telephonic transmission with a message to his assistant on 5 June 1875, and patented the telephone in 1876. He defended the patent against **Elisha Gray**, and formed the Bell Telephone Company in 1877. In 1880 he established the Volta Laboratory, and invented the photophone (1880) and the graphophone (1887). He also founded the journal *Science* (1883). After 1897 his principal interest was in aeronautics: he encouraged **S P Langley**, and invented the tetrahedral kite.

BELL, Alexander Melville (1819–1905) Scottish-born American educationist, father of **Alexander Graham Bell**, born in Edinburgh. A teacher of elocution at Edinburgh University and University College, London, he moved to Canada in 1870 and settled in Washington. In 1882 he published his system of 'visible speech', showing the position of the vocal chords for each sound.

BELL, Andrew (1753–1832) British educationist, founder of the 'Madras System' of education, born at St Andrews. After taking Episcopal orders he went to India in 1787 and in 1789 became superintendent of the Madras military orphanage. Finding it impossible to obtain teaching staff, he taught with the aid of the pupils themselves by introducing the monitorial system. His pamphlet entitled *An Experiment in Education* (1797) had attracted little attention in Britain until in 1803 **Joseph Lancaster** also published a tract recommending the monitorial system. Lancasterian schools began to spread over the country; the Church grew alarmed, and in 1811 founded the National Society for the Education of the Poor, of which Bell became superintendent, and whose schools soon numbered 12000.

BELL, Sir Charles (1774–1842) Scottish anatomist and surgeon, famous for his neurological discoveries. Born in Edinburgh, he lectured in anatomy and surgery in London. In 1807 he distinguished between the sensory and motor nerves in the brain, and in 1812 was appointed surgeon to the Middlesex Hospital. To study gunshot wounds he went to Haslar Hopital after the battle of Corunna in 1809, and after Waterloo took charge of a hospital in Brussels. His work on the functions of the spinal nerves led to disputes with **François Magendie**. He was professor of surgery at Edinburgh from 1836. The type of facial paralysis known as 'Bell's Palsy' is named after him. He was distantly related to the Edinburgh surgeon Joseph Bell (1837–1911), said to have been the inspiration for **Conan Doyle**'s Sherlock Holmes.

BELL, (Arthur) Clive Howard (1881–1964) English art and literary critic. He studied at Trinity College, Cambridge, and stated his aesthetic theory of *Significant Form* in *Art* (1914). Another version of this was formulated in 1920 by **Roger Fry**, a fellow-member of those arbiters of taste known as the 'Bloomsbury Set', described in his *Old Friends* (1956). His best critical essays are *Since Cézanne* (1922), *Civilization* (1928), *Proust* (1929), and *An Account of French Painting* (1931). In 1907 he married **Vanessa Bell**, sister of **Virginia Woolf** and daughter of Sir **Leslie Stephen**. Their son Julian (1908–37), also a writer, was killed in the Spanish Civil War.

BELL, Currer See **BRONTË, Charlotte**

BELL, Ellis See **BRONTË, Emily Jane**

BELL, George Joseph (1770–1843) Scottish lawyer, born in Edinburgh. The brother of the surgeon Sir **Charles Bell**, he became professor of Scots law at Edinburgh University. He published *Commentaries on The Laws of Scotland and on the Principles of Mercantile Jurisprudence* (1804) and *Principles of the Law of Scotland*, both standard authorities. He also drafted the report of the commission on Scottish judicial proceedings (1823) which resulted in the Scottish Judicature Act (1825).

BELL, George Kennedy Allen (1885–1958) English prelate and ecumenist, born on Hayling Island, Hampshire. Educated at Oxford, he was ordained in 1907, and became chaplain to Archbishop **Randall Davidson** (1914–24), dean of Canterbury (1924–29), and bishop of Chichester (1929–58). A strong supporter of the ecumenical movement, and friend of **Niemöller** and **Bonhoeffer**, he risked misunderstanding during World War II by his efforts towards peace with Germany and his condemnation of the policy of saturation bombing. His published works included *Randall Davidson* (1935), *Christianity and World Order* (1940), *Christian Unity: The Anglican Position* (1948) and *The Kingship of Christ* (1954).

BELL, Gertrude Margaret Lowthian (1868–1926) English archaelogist and traveller, granddaughter of Sir **Isaac Lowthian Bell**, born at Washington Hall. She studied at Lady Margaret Hall, Oxford, aged 16. She travelled much in the Middle East, learning to speak Persian and Arabic. During World War I she was appointed to the Arab Bureau in Cairo and seconded to the Mesopotamia Expeditionary Force in Basra and Baghdad, and subsequently became oriental secretary to the British High Commission in Iraq. First director of antiquities in Iraq, on her death she left money to fund the British Institute of Archaeology in Iraq.

BELL, Henry (1767–1830) Scottish engineer and pioneer of steam navigation, born at Torphichen Mill, Linlithgow. In 1812 he successfully launched the 30-ton *Comet* on the Clyde. Plying regularly between Greenock and Glasgow, it was the first passenger-carrying steam-boat in European waters.

BELL, Sir Isaac Lowthian (1816–1904) Scottish industrialist and metallurgist. He founded in 1852, with his brothers, the great Clarence iron-smelting works on the Tees. He was MP for Hartlepool (1875–80).

BELL, John (1691–1780) Scottish physician and traveller, born in Stirlingshire. After graduating as a doctor he went to St Petersburg in 1714 and was physician to Russian embassies to Persia (1715–18), went to China through Siberia (1719–22), and again to Persia (1722). In 1737 he settled at Constantinople as a merchant, but about 1746 returned to Scotland. His *Travels* were published in 1763.

BELL, John (1797–1869) American statesman, born in Tennessee. He was speaker of the House of Representatives (1836), and a senator (1847–59). Moderate in his views, he was nominated for the presidency in 1860 by the newly formed Constitutional Union Party, but received only 39 electoral votes. He fought desperately but hopelessly to keep Tennessee out of the Civil War, which sealed the doom of his party.

BELL, John (1811–95) English sculptor, born in Hopton, Suffolk. He produced the Guards' Memorial (1858) in Waterloo Place, and the American group in the Hyde Park Albert Memorial (1873). He popularized carved wooden breadknives and trenchers.

BELL, John Jay (1871–1934) Scottish journalist and humorous writer, best known for his *Wee MacGreegor* (1902).

BELL, Lawrence Dale (1895–1956) American aircraft designer and constructor, born in Mentone, Indiana. Starting as a mechanic to two exhibition pilots in 1913, he made rapid progress, becoming superintendent of the **Glenn L Martin** aircraft factory in 1915 and vice-president and general manager of the Consolidated Aircraft Corporation in 1929. In 1935 he formed the Bell Aircraft Corporation and among its more notable aircraft were the Airacuda, Airacobra, Kingcobra and in 1942 the P-59 Airacomet, the first American jet-propelled aircraft. From 1941 he produced a famous line of helicopters and in 1947 the first rocket-propelled aeroplane, the Bell X-1, the first manned aircraft to exceed the speed of sound.

BELL, Patrick (1799–1869) Scottish clergyman and inventor, born in Auchterhouse, near Dundee, the son of a farmer. He worked on the development of a mechanical reaper, the prototype of which earned a £50 premium from the Highland and Agricultural Society in 1827. Its adoption by British farmers was very slow, however, and when four of his reapers were sent to the USA they enabled **Cyrus McCormick** and others to realize their full potential. By 1843 he had abandoned his active interest in agricultural machinery and entered the church as minister of Carmylie, Arbroath. Belatedly, in 1868, he was awarded £1000 in appreciation of his pre-eminent services as the inventor of the first efficient 'reaping machine'.

BELL, Sir Robert (1800–67) Irish journalist and author, born in Cork. In 1828 he came to London. He is best known for his annotated edition of the English poets from **Chaucer** to **Cowper** (1824–57).

BELL, Robert Anning (1863–1933) English painter, designer, illustrator and decorator, born in London. He was articled to an architect, but studied painting from 1881 at the Royal Academy Schools, Westminster School of Art and in Paris, where he studied under **Morot**. In London he studied with Sir **George Frampton**. He executed mosaics in the Houses of Parliament and Westminster Cathedral, and held successive posts at Liverpool University (from 1894), Glasgow School of Art (1911) and the Royal College of Art, where he was professor of design (1918–24).

BELL, Thomas (1792–1800) English naturalist, born in Poole, Dorset. A dental surgeon at Guy's Hospital (1817–61), he lectured in and became professor of zoology at King's College, London, in 1836. He was secretary of the Royal Society, president of the Linnean Society and first president of the Ray Society (1844). His *British Stalk-eyed Crustacea* (1853) remains a standard work on British crabs and lobsters. He edited the *Natural History of Selborne* (1877), by **Gilbert White**, whose house he purchased.

BELL, Vanessa, née **Stephen** (1879–1961) English painter and decorative designer, a leading member of the Bloomsbury Group, born in Kensington, London, daughter of Sir **Leslie Stephen** and elder sister of **Virginia Woolf**. Trained as an artist under Sir Arthur Cope (1896–1900), she studied from 1901 to 1904 at the Royal Academy Schools. In 1907 she married the critic **Clive Bell**, but in 1916 left him to live at Firle, Sussex, with **Duncan Grant**, a fellow-contributor to **Roger Fry**'s Omega Workshops (1913–20). She exhibited four pictures in her decorative style (which was influenced by **Matisse**) in the Second Post-Impressionist Exhibition in 1912. Elected to the London Group in 1919, she exhibited with them regularly from 1920.

BELLA, Stefano della (1610–64) Italian engraver, born in Florence. He worked for Cardinal **Richelieu** and for the grand duke of Tuscany. His work was in the manner of **Jacques Callot** and his enormous output consisted of battle-pieces, sieges, landscapes and animal and masque designs. Many of his works can be found in the Royal Library at Windsor.

BELLAMY, Edward (1850–98) American novelist, born in Chicopee Falls, Massachusetts. He achieved immense popularity with his Utopian romance *Looking Backward* (1888), a work which predicted a new social order and influenced economic thinking in the United States and Europe.

BELLAMY, George Ann (c.1727–1788) English actress, the illegitimate daughter of a Quaker schoolgirl and Lord Tyrawley. She first appeared at Covent Garden and, despite a brilliant theatrical career, through profligacy and extravagance spent her last years in poverty. She published an autobiographical *Apology* (1785).

BELLANY, John (1942–) Scottish painter and etcher, born in Port Seton. He studied at Edinburgh College of Art (1960–65) and at the Royal College of Art (1965–68). He is one of the generation of Scots who, in the 1970s, adopted an expressive form of realism inspired by **Leger** and by German art. A retrospective of his work was held at the Scottish National Gallery of Modern Art and at the Serpentine Gallery, London, in 1986.

BELLARMINE, Robert Francis Romulus, St (1542–1621) Italian Jesuit theologian, born in Montepulciano, near Siena. He entered the order of Jesuits at Rome in 1560, and studied theology at Padua and Louvain. In 1570 he was appointed to the chair of theology at Louvain, but returned to Rome in 1576 to lecture at the Roman College on controversial theology. In 1592 he became rector of the Roman College, was made a cardinal in 1599 against his own inclination, and in 1602 archbishop of Capua. After the death of **Clement VIII**, he evaded the papal chair, but was induced by **Paul V** to hold an important place in the Vatican from 1605 till his death. Bellarmine, who was canonized in 1930, was the chief defender of the church in the 16th century. A friend and admirer of **Galileo**, he nonetheless was required to inform him of the pope's prohibition of his teaching of the heliocentric system (1616), yet his learning and moderation gained him the praise even of **Pierre Bayle**. In the 17th century, stone beer jugs with a caricature of his likeness, called bellarmines, were produced by Flemish Protestants to ridicule him.

BELLAY, Joachim du (1522–60) French poet and prose writer, born in Lire in Anjou. After his friend and fellow-student, **Ronsard**, he was the most important member of the Pléiade. His *Deffence et Illustration de la langue françoise* (1549), the manifesto of the Pléiade, advocating the rejection of medieval linguistic traditions and a return to classical and Italian models, had a considerable influence at the time. It was accompanied by an example in the form of a set of Petrarchian sonnets, *l'Olive*, dedicated to an unknown lady. He went to Rome in 1533 as secretary to his kinsman, Cardinal du Bellay, but was not a success as a diplomat, though the visit inspired more sonnets, including the collections *Les Antiquités de Rome* and *Les Regrets* (1558).

BELLEAU, Rémy (1528–77) French poet, born in Nogent le Rotrou. He was a member of the Pléiade and published in 1556 a translation of **Anacreon** that was at first believed to be an original imitation. *Bergerie* (1565, 2nd edition 1572) is a medley of delicately descriptive prose and verse, of which *Avril* still appears in anthologies. *Amours* (1576) is a collection of poems concerned with the appearance and arcane powers of precious stones.

BELLEISLE, Charles Louis Fouquet, Duc de (1684–1761) French soldier and statesman. After serving in many wars, he became a marshal of France in 1741. In the War of the Austrian Succession (1740–48) he stormed Prague in 1742 and then led the skilful retreat to Eger. He crossed the Alpes Maritimes, raised the siege of Genoa (1747) and drove the Austrians into Lombardy before the war ended. During the Seven Years' War he was minister for war from 1758 to 1760.

BELLENDEN, or **Ballantyne, John** (d.1587) Scottish ecclesiastic and writer, born towards the close of the 15th century. In 1508 he matriculated from St Andrews and completed his theological studies at the Sorbonne. His translations in 1533 of **Boece**'s *Historia Gentis Scotorum*, and of the first five books of **Livy**, are interesting as vigorous specimens of early Scottish prose. The *Croniklis of Scotland* is a very free translation, and contains numerous passages not found in Boece, so that it is in some respects almost an original work. Bellenden enjoyed great favour at the court of **James V**, at whose request the translations were made. As a reward, Bellenden received considerable grants from the Treasury, and afterwards was made archdeacon of Moray and canon of Ross. Becoming involved, however, in ecclesiastical controversy, he went to Rome.

BELLINGHAM See **PERCEVAL, Spencer**

BELLINGHAUSEN, Fabian Gottlieb Benjamin von (1778–1852) Russian explorer, born in Oesel. In 1819–21 he led an expedition around the world which made several discoveries in the Pacific, and sailed to 70° S lat, probably discovering the antarctic continent.

BELLINI, Gentile (c.1429–1507) Venetian painter, son of **Jacopo Bellini** and brother of **Giovanni Bellini**. He worked in his father's studio and was chosen to paint the portrait of Sultan Muhammad II in Constantinople. This portrait, together with his *Adoration of the Kings*, is in the National Gallery, London.

BELLINI, Giovanni (c.1430–1516) Italian painter, the greatest Venetian artist of his time, the son of **Jacopo Bellini** and brother of **Gentile Bellini**. He was instrumental in making Venice an artistic centre to rival Florence. Although few of his earlier works can be accurately dated, the progress of his style—from the sharp and stylized manner inherited from his father to the more sensuous, painterly one for which he is famous—can easily be charted. His sense of design was learnt from the severe classical style of his brother-in-law **Mantegna** and his fluid, oil technique from **Antonella da Messina**. Bellini's art is essentially calm and contemplative. One of his chief contributions to Italian art was his successful integration of figures with landscape background. Another is his naturalistic treatment of light. Almost all his pictures are religious although he painted the occasional pagan allegory. He is, perhaps, best known for a long series of Madonnas to which he brought a humanistic sensibility usually absent in **Raphael**'s more austere renderings of the subject. All the most talented younger painters of his day—**Giorgione** and **Titian** among them— came to his studio and through them his innovations were perpetuated. His own style continued to develop to the end, and his later work is influenced by the youthful genius, **Giorgione**, who died before him.

BELLINI, Jacopo (c.1400–70) father of **Gentile Bellini** and **Giovanni Bellini**. He studied under **Gentile da Fabriano**, and painted a wide range of subjects; but only a few Madonnas in Italy and drawings in the Louvre and the British Museum remain, which show his interest in architectural and landscape setting.

BELLINI, Vincenzo (1801–35) Italian operatic composer, born in Catania in Sicily. An organist's son, he was sent by a Sicilian nobleman to the Conservatorio of Naples. His two earliest operas were *Adelson e Salvina* (1824) and *Bianca e Fernando* (1826). *Il Pirata* (1827) immediately carried the composer's name beyond Italy, and was followed by *I Capuleti ed i Montecchi* (1830) and his two masterpieces of lyrical expression, *La Sonnambula* (1831) and *Norma* (1832). In 1833 he went to Paris and London. *I Puritani* (1834) shows the influence of the French school, but without servile imitation.

BELLMAN, Carl Michael (1740–95) Swedish poet and writer of popular songs, born in Stockholm. In 1757 he entered banking, but had to flee to Norway to escape his creditors. In 1776 he was brought back as a protégé of King **Gustav III**, who gave him a sinecure as director of the national lottery. He founded a drinking club, the *Bacci orden*, and put to verse his impressions of his friends and others. His most important collections of songs are the *Epistles of Fredman* (1790), with their overtones of Biblical parody and burlesque, and the *Songs of Fredman* (1791). The songs, with their minute observation of Swedish life, combine broad humour and rococo charm, and are still immensely popular throughout Scandinavia. There is a long-standing Bellman Society in Sweden devoted to his memory.

BELLOC, (Joseph) Hilaire Pierre (1870–1953) French-born British writer and poet, born in St Cloud near Paris, the son of a French barrister, Louis Belloc, and his English wife. The family moved to England during the Franco-Prussian war, and settled there in 1872. He was educated at the Oratory School, Birmingham, under **Newman**, and Balliol College, Oxford, but did military service in the French army. He became a naturalized British subject in 1902, and became Liberal MP in 1906, but, disillusioned with politics, did not seek re-election in 1910. Disapproving of modern industrial society and socialism, he wrote *The Servile State* (1912), advocating a return to the system of medieval guilds. He was a close friend of **G K Chesterton**, who illustrated many of his books. He is best known, however, for his delightfully nonsensical verse for children: *The Bad Child's Book of Beasts* (1896) and the *Cautionary Tales* (1907); his numerous travel books, including *Path to Rome* (1902) and *The Old Road* (1910), reconstructing the Pilgrim's Way; his historical studies *Robespierre* (1901), *Marie Antoinette* (1910), *Richelieu* (1929), *Wolsey* (1930), and *Napoleon* (1932); and his religious books, including *Europe and the Faith* (1920) and *The Great Heresies* (1938). An energetic Roman Catholic apologist, he was fearlessly, sometimes fanatically, outspoken.

BELLOTTO, Bernardo (1720–80) Italian painter, nephew of **Antonio Canaletto**. He attained high excellence as a painter, and also as an engraver on copper. He practised his art in Venice, Rome, Verona, Brescia, Milan, Dresden, and England, where he painted a masterly interior of King's College Chapel, Cambridge. He died in Warsaw.

BELLOW, Saul (1915–) Canadian-born American writer, born in Lachine in Quebec, the son of immigrant Russian parents. He spent his childhood in Montreal. In 1924 his family moved to Chicago and he attended university there, and at Northwestern University in Evanston, Illinois. He abandoned his post-graduate studies at Wisconsin University to become a writer, and his first novel, *The Dangling Man*, a study of a noncombatant in the war, appeared in 1944. He became an associate professor at Minnesota University, and after being awarded a Guggenheim Fellowship in 1948 travelled to Paris and Rome. Other works include *The Victim* (1947), *The Adventures of Augie March* (1953), *Henderson the Rain-King* (1959), *Herzog* (1964), *Mr Sammler's Planet* (1970), *Humboldt's Gift* (1975), and *The Dean's December* (1982). In 1962 he was appointed a professor at Chicago University, and in 1976 was awarded the Nobel prize for literature.

BELLOWS, George Wesley (1882–1925) American painter and lithographer, born in Columbus, Ohio. A pupil of Robert Henri, he was a leading figure in the movement which sought to break away from Post-Impressionism into the vivid harshness of Social Realism. Bellows delighted in prize fights, festivals and the teeming life of the cities. Probably his most famous work is 'Firpo and Dempsey' which hangs in the Museum of Modern Art, New York. His work has a bold freshness which, coupled with the crude vigour of his subject matter, places him among the leaders of American Realism.

BELLOY, Dormont de, properly **Pierre Laurent Buyrette** (1727–75) French dramatist. He was one of the first to introduce on the French stage native instead of classical heroes. His first success, *Zelmire* (1762), was followed by *Le Siège de Calais* (1765), *Gaston et Bayard* (1771) and *Pierre le cruel* (1772).

BELMONT, Alva Ertskin, née **Smith** (1853–1933) American reformer, born in Mobile, Alabama, into a well-established Southern family. A committed socialite, she cleverly worked her way into the New York social élite as the wife of **William Henry Vanderbilt** (1875, divorced 1895), and married her daughter to the Duke of Marlborough. After the death of her second husband (1908), she developed an interest in women's rights, and became involved with militant feminism, inviting **Christabel Pankhurst** to the USA to speak in 1914, and donating generously to the cause. From 1921 to 1933 she was president of the National Woman's party.

BELON, Pierre (1517–64) French naturalist. In 1546–49 he travelled in Asia Minor, Egypt, and Arabia. He wrote valuable treatises on trees, herbs, birds, and fishes. He was one of the first who established the homologies between the skeletons of different vertebrates; he planted the first cedar in France and formed two early botanical gardens.

BELY, Andrei, pseud of **Boris Nikolayevich Bugayev** (1880–1934) Russian novelist, poet and critic, born in Moscow. A leading Symbolist writer, he early met **Vladimir Soloviev**, the religious philosopher, and fell under his influence. While at Moscow University he wrote Decadent poetry which he published in *Symphony* (*Second Dramatic*) (1902). His poetry, however, was criticized mercilessly and his reputation rests on his prose. *The Silver Dove* (1910) was his first and most accessible novel and was followed by *Petersburg* (1913), his masterpiece, in which the action centres on a bomb camouflaged as a tin of sardines. The autobiographical *Kotik Letayev* (1918) is his most original work, a stream-of-consciousness attempt to show how children become aware of what is going on in the world. His later novels, written after a second sojourn in Berlin (1921–23), are more overtly satirical of the pre-revolutionary Russian scene but are still highly experimental. He is regarded as one of the most important Russian writers of the 1920s.

BELZONI, Giovanni Battista (1778–1823) Italian explorer and antiquity-hunter, born in Padua. He was intended for a monastery, but in 1803 came to England, where, 6 feet 7 inches tall, he gained a living performing as a strong man in circuses. In 1815 he went to Egypt, and there was commissioned by **Mehemet Ali** to construct hydraulic machinery for irrigation purposes. He devoted himself thereafter to tomb robbing and the exploration of Egyptian antiquities, and removed from Thebes the colossal bust of **Rameses II**, which, together with finds from the tomb of Sethos I which he had opened up in 1817, he sent to the British Museum. He explored the temple of Edfu, cleared the temple of Abu Simbel, opened the Pyramid of Khephren at Giza and discovered the ruins of Berenice near Benghazi. He returned to Europe in 1819, exhibiting in London at the Egyptian Hall, Piccadilly, and publishing his discoveries as *Narrative of the Operations and Recent Discoveries within the Pyramids, Temples, Tombs and Excavations in Egypt and Nubia* (1820). He died of dysentery in Benin while searching for the source of the River Niger.

BEM, Joseph (1795–1850) Polish soldier. He was the leader of the unsuccessful Hungarian insurrection of 1848–49, after which he escaped into Turkey, became a Muslim and was appointed governor of Aleppo, where he died of fever ten months later.

BEMBO, Pietro (1470–1547) Italian scholar and ecclesiastic, born in Venice. In 1513 he was made secretary to Pope **Leo X**, and in 1539 a cardinal by **Paul III**, who appointed him to the dioceses of Gubbio and Bergamo. Bembo was the restorer of good style in both Latin and Italian literature, especially with his little treatise on Italian prose (*Prose della volgar lingua*, 1525), which marked an era in Italian grammar. He also published a book of his own Italian poetry, *Rime* (1530).

BENACERRAF, Baruj (1920–) Venezuelan-born American immunologist, joint winner of the 1980 Nobel prize for physiology or medicine. He was research director at the National Centre for Scientific Research in Paris (1950–56) and professor at New York University (1957–68) and Harvard (from 1970). His researches led to the discovery of immune-response genes ('histocompatability genes') that regulate immunology in organ transplants, for which he shared the 1980 Nobel prize with **Jean Dausset** and **George Snell**.

BEN ALI, Zine el Abidine (1936–) Tunisian politician. After studying electronics at military schools in France and the USA, he began a career in military security, rising to the position of director-general of national security. He became minister of the interior and then prime minister under 'president-for-life' **Habib Bourguiba**, who had been in power since 1956. In 1987 he forced Bourguiba to retire and assumed the presidency and immediately embarked on constitutional reforms, promising a greater degree of democracy.

BENAUD, Richie (Richard) (1930–) Australian cricketer, broadcaster and international sports consultant, born in Penrith, New South Wales. He played in 63 Test matches for Australia (captain in 28), including three successful tours of England (1953, 1956 and 1961). A genuine all-rounder, he scored 2201 Test runs, including three centuries, and took 248 wickets with subtle leg-spin bowling. He was closely involved in setting up the Channel Nine sports programmes in Australia.

BENAVENTE, Jacinto (1866–1954) Spanish dramatist, born in Madrid. He intended to enter the legal profession but turned to literature. After publishing some poems and short stories he won recognition as a playwright with his *El nido Ajeno* (1893), which was followed by some brilliantly satirical society comedies. His masterpiece is *Los intereses creados* (1907), an allegorical play in the *commedia dell'arte* style. He also wrote some excellent children's plays.

BEN BELLA, Mohammed Ahmed (1916–) Algerian politician, born in Maghnia, on the Moroccan border. He served with distinction in the French army in World War II. In 1947 he became leader of the extremist independence movement, the 'Special Organisation', and in 1950 was imprisoned, but he escaped to Cairo, where he founded the National Liberation Front (FLN). The FLN then embarked on a long war (1954–62) which led to independence and Ben Bella's election in 1963 as president. He was deposed in 1965 in a coup led by General **Houari Boumedienne** and kept under house arrest until 1979.

BENBOW, John (1653–1702) English naval commander, born in Shrewsbury. He entered the navy in 1678, but transferred to the merchant services after a court martial. He rejoined the navy in 1689. He was master attendant successively at Chatham and Deptford, master of the fleet at Beachy Head (1690), Barfleur and La Hague (1692). He commanded squadrons off Dunkirk (1693–95), and as a rear-admiral was commander-in-chief West Indies from 1698. In the West Indies, on 19 August 1702, he came up against a superior French force. For four days he kept up a running fight, almost deserted by the rest of his squadron, until his right leg was smashed by a chain shot and he was forced to return to Jamaica, where he died. The captains of his squadron who failed to support him were sentenced to be shot.

BENCH, Johnny Lee (1947–) American baseball player, born in Oklahoma City, Oklahoma. Playing in the National League with Cincinnati Reds he was the outstanding catcher of the 1970s. He had great ability with the bat, hit over 200 home runs, and led the league three times in seven years for runs batted in. He was the National League's Most Valuable Player on several occasions and almost monopolized the Golden Glove award for his particular position.

BENCHLEY, Robert Charles (1889–1945) American humorist, critic and parodist, born in Worcester, Massachusetts. Idolized by **E B White** and **James Thurber**, who thought him a finer humorist even than **Mark Twain**, he was described by **Dorothy Parker** as 'a kind of saint'. His career in journalism began at college where he edited the *Harvard Lampoon* and starred in the Hasty Pudding shows. He worked first at *Vanity Fair* where he met Parker with whom, together with **Robert Sherwood**, Thurber, **George Kaufman** and Franklin D Adams, he formed the notorious Algonquin Round Table. Subsequently he worked as a drama critic for *Life* (1920–29) and *The New Yorker* (1929–40) but was fired after persistent over-indulgence in alcohol. He was at his most brilliant writing sketches, which surfaced in several collections including *20,000 Leagues under the Sea, or, David Copperfield* (1928), *From Bed to Worse* (1934) and *My Ten Years in a Quandary, and How They Grew* (1936). His humour derives from the predicament of the 'Little Man', beset on all sides by the complexity of existence in the modern world. A chronic worrier, minor problems (leaving a party, curing hiccoughs) assumed epic proportions, but underlying his risibility were deeper concerns. He also appeared in cameo roles in many films.

BENCKENDORFF, Alexander, Count (1849–1917) Russian ambassador in London (from 1903), greatly promoted Anglo-Russian friendship and played a part in forming the Triple Entente (1907).

BENDA, Georg Anton (1722–95) Bohemian musician, born in Alt-Benatek. He became kapellmeister to the Duke of Gotha (1748–78). He composed operettas, cantatas, and melodramas, and introduced music drama with spoken text. His brothers, Franz (1709–86) and Joseph (1724–1804), were both in turn konzertmeister of **Frederick II, the Great** of Prussia.

BENEDEK, Ludwig von (1804–81) Austrian soldier, born in Oedenburg, in Hungary. He distinguished himself in Galicia in 1846, in Italy in 1847, in Hungary in 1849, and in 1859 drove back the Piedmontese at Solferino. He was governor of Hungary in 1860. In 1866 he commanded the northern Austrian army in the war with Prussia; but after the defeat of Sadowa in 1866, he was superseded.

BENEDEN, Eduard van (1845–1910) Belgian cytologist, born in Liège. In 1887 he demonstrated the constancy of the number of chromosomes in the cells of an organism, decreasing during maturation and restored at fertilization.

BENEDETTI, Vincent, Count (1817–1900) French diplomat, born in Bastia in Corsica. He became ambassador in Berlin (1864–70), during which time he proposed a secret treaty with Prussia. He made the demand at Ems in 1870 that gave **Bismarck** the *casus belli* for the Franco-Prussian war. He wrote *Studies in Diplomacy* (trans 1895).

BENEDICT VIII (d.1024) the first of the Tusculan popes (members of the Tusculani family), elected in 1012. He was temporarily driven from Rome by the antipope **Gregory VI**, of the Crescenti family, but was restored to the papal chair by the emperor **Henry II**, whom he crowned in 1014. Later he defeated the Saracens and the Greeks in northern Italy, and introduced clerical and monastic reforms. The uncle of Pope **Benedict IX**, he was succeeded by his brother, John XIX.

BENEDICT IX (d.c.1065) the last of the Tusculan popes, and nephew of **Benedict VIII**. He succeeded his uncle, John XIX, in 1032, obtaining the papal throne by simony while still a youth; but in 1036 the Romans banished him on account of his licentiousness. Several times reinstalled, he was as often deposed. He died in the convent of Grotta Ferrata, probably before 1065.

BENEDICT XIII a title assumed by two popes, Pedro de Luna (c.1328–1423), a Spaniard, elected as antipope by the French cardinals in 1394 in succession to the antipope Clement VII at Avignon after the Great Western Schism of 1378; and the Italian Dominican cardinal Pietro Francesco Orsini (1649–1730), elected pope in 1724, a learned man of simple habits and pure morals, who placed himself under the guidance of the unscrupulous Cardinal Niccolo Coscia.

BENEDICT XIV, (Prospero Lambertini) (1675–1758) pope from 1740, born in Bologna, distinguished by his learning and ability. He founded chairs of physics, chemistry, and mathematics in Rome, revived the academy of Bologna, rebuilt churches, and encouraged literature and science.

BENEDICT XV, (Giacomo della Chiesa) (1854–1922) pope from 1914. Born of a noble Italian family, he was ordained at 24, became secretary to the Papal Embassy, Spain, in 1883, then secretary to Cardinal Rampolla, bishop (1900), archbishop of Bologna (1907), and cardinal (May, 1914). Although junior cardinal, he was elected to succeed **Pius X** in September, 1914, soon after the outbreak of World War I. He made repeated efforts to end the war, and organized war relief on a munificent scale.

BENEDICT, Sir Julius (1804–85) German composer, born in Stuttgart. He studied under **Hummel** and **Weber**, and was at 20 conductor at a Vienna opera house, and then at the San Carlo in Naples. In 1836 he settled in London where his great success was with *Lily of Killarney* (1862).

BENEDICT, Ruth, née **Fulton** (1887–1948) American anthropologist, born in New York City, the daughter of a surgeon. She studied philosophy and English literature at Vassar before going on to study anthropology under Alexander Goldenweiser and **Franz Boas** at Columbia University. She became a leading member of the culture-and-personality movement in the American anthropology of the 1930s and 1940s. Her most important contribution lay in her 'configurational' approach to entire cultures, according to which each culture tends to predispose its individual members to adopt an ideal type of personality. Thus every culture, she believed, could be characterized in terms of its own distinctive ethos. Her best-known works include *Patterns of Culture* (1934), a book against racism (*Race: Science and Politics*, 1940), and *The Chrysanthemum and the Sword: Patterns of Japanese Culture* (1946). In 1948, the year of her death, she became professor at Columbia University.

BENEDICT BISCOP, St (c.628–689) Anglo-Saxon churchman. He became a monk in 653, journeyed to Rome five times and in 669-671 was abbot of St Peter's, Canterbury. In 674 he founded a monastery at Wearmouth, endowing it richly with books; and in 682 founded a second monastery at Jarrow. He is said to have introduced stone edifices and glass windows to England. One of his pupils was the Venerable **Bede**.

BENEDICT OF NURSIA, St (c.480–c.547) Italian religious, the founder of Western monasticism, born in Nursia near Spoleto. Educated at Rome, he became convinced that the only way of escaping the evil in the world was in seclusion and religious exercise; so as a boy of 14 he withdrew to a cavern or grotto near Subiaco, where he lived for three years. The fame of his piety led to his being appointed the abbot of a neighbouring monastery at Vicovaro, nominally observing the oriental rule; but he soon left it, as the morals of the half-wild monks were not strict enough. Multitudes still sought his guidance; and from the most devoted he founded twelve small monastic communities. He ultimately established a monastery on Monte Cassino, near Naples, afterwards one of the richest and most famous in Italy. In 515 he is said to have composed his *Regula Monachorum*, which became the common rule of all Western monasticism. In addition to the usual religious exercises, the rule directs that the monks shall employ themselves in manual labours, imparting instruction to youth, copying manuscripts for the library, etc. He was declared the patron saint of all Europe by Pope **Paul VI** in 1964.

BENEDIKTSSON, Einar (1864–1940) Icelandic poet and entrepreneur, born near Reykjavík, the son of a Supreme Court judge. He studied law at Copenhagen and became a country magistrate in Iceland. A fervent nationalist, he became convinced that only a flood of foreign investment could bring prosperity to Iceland. He devoted many years to touring Europe seeking capital (unsuccessfully) for his ambitious industrial schemes to exploit Iceland's natural resources of hydro power and fishing. He published five volumes of dazzlingly ornate poetry that harked back to the skaldic tradition of intricate metaphor and vocabulary.

BENELLI, Sem (1877–1949) Italian dramatist, born in Prato, Tuscany. He wrote plays in prose and verse. His outstanding successes were *Tignola*, a light comedy, and *La cena della beffe*, a powerful tragedy in verse.

BENEŠ, Eduard (1884–1948) Czechoslovak statesman, born in Kožlany. A farmer's son, he studied law and became professor of sociology at Prague. As a refugee during World War I he worked in Paris with **Thomas Masaryk** for Czechoslovak nationalism, and from 1918 to 1935 was foreign minister of the new state (also premier in 1921–22). In 1935 he succeeded Masaryk as president, but resigned in 1938 and left the country, resuming office, however, in 1941 on the setting up of a government in exile in England. In 1945 he returned to his country, and in 1946 was re-elected president, but resigned after the Communist coup of 1948.

BENESH, Rudolph (1916–75) and **Joan**, née **Rothwell** (1920–) English dance notators, born in London and Liverpool respectively. Rudolph was a painter and Joan a former member of the Sadler's Wells Ballet. Together they copyrighted (1955) a dance notation system, called Choreology, that has been included in the syllabus of London's Royal Academy of Dancing and is used to document all important Royal Ballet productions. They opened their own Institute in 1962 and their influence on a vast number of notators and educators has been incalculable.

BENÉT, Stephen Vincent (1898–1943) American poet, born in Bethlehem, Pennsylvania, brother of **William Benét**. He published a number of novels and tales, and volumes of verse, and is known especially for his poem on the Civil War, *John Brown's Body*, which was awarded the Pulitzer prize in 1929.

BENÉT, Wiliam Rose (1886–1950) American poet, editor, novelist and playwright, born in Fort Hamilton, New York, brother of **Stephen Benét**. His main claim to fame is as a poet and he published many collections, among them *Merchants from Cathay* (1913), *Moons of Grandeur* (1920) and *The Stairway of Surprise* (1947).

BENFEY, Theodor (1809–81) German Jewish philologist, born near Göttingen. His interest in philology was aroused by the Hebrew lessons he received from his father, and his early work was in the fields of classical and Hebrew philology: his *Lexicon of Greek Roots* was published between 1839 and 1842. Having learned Sanskrit in a few weeks to win a bet, he later turned his attention to Sanskrit philology. He was professor at Göttingen from 1848, and published an edition of the Sama-veda (1848), a *Manual of Sanskrit* (1852–54), and his best known work, the *Sanskrit-English Dictionary* (1866). He died in Göttingen while working on a grammar of Vedic Sanskrit.

BENGEL, Johann Albrecht (1687–1752) German theologian, born in Winnenden, in Württemberg. He was the first Protestant author to treat the exegesis of the New Testament critically, in 1734.

BEN-GURION, David, originally **David Green** (1886–1973) Israeli statesman, born in Plonsk, Poland. Attracted to the Zionist Socialist movement, he emigrated to Palestine in 1906, working as a farm labourer and forming the first Jewish trade union in 1915. Expelled by the Turks for pro-Allied sympathies, he helped to raise the Jewish Legion in America and served in it in the Palestine campaign against Turkey in World War I. From 1921 to 1933 he was general secretary of the General Federation of Jewish Labour. In 1930 he became leader of the Mapai (Labour) party, which became the ruling party in the state of Israel, whose birth he announced in May 1948. In 1953 he retired from the premiership, resuming it 1955–63. After his retirement from political life, he came to symbolize the Israeli state.

BENJAMIN, Judah Philip (1811–84) American lawyer, born in St Croix, West Indies, the son of Jewish parents en route from England to the USA. A lawyer in New Orleans, he early engaged in politics, serving first with the Whigs, and afterwards with the Democrats. He sat in the US senate from 1852 to 1860, and in 1861, when the Civil War broke out, joined **Jefferson Davis**'s cabinet as attorney-general. He was for a few months secretary of war, and then secretary of state until Davis's capture in 1865, when he escaped to England. Called to the English bar in 1866, he became a QC in 1872 and wrote a legal classic, *The Sale of Personal Property* (1868).

BENJAMIN OF TUDELA (d.1173) a Spanish rabbi, born in Navarre, the first European traveller to describe the Far East. From 1159 to 1173 he made a journey from Saragossa through Italy and Greece, to Palestine, Persia, and the borders of China, returning by way of Egypt and Sicily.

BENN, Anthony Wedgwood (1925–) English Labour politician, son of Viscount **Stansgate**. He was educated at Westminister School and New College, Oxford. A Labour MP from 1950 to 1960, he was debarred from the House of Commons on succeeding to his father's title, but was able to renounce it in 1963 and was re-elected to parliament the same year. He was postmaster-general 1964–66, minister of technology 1966–70, and assumed responsibility for the ministry of aviation in 1967 and ministry of power in 1969. From 1970 to 1974 he was opposition spokesman on trade and industry, and on Labour's return to government he was made secretary of state for industry and minister for posts and telecommunications, the following year becoming secretary of state for energy, a post he held until the Conservative victory in the 1979 elections. Representing the left wing of Labour opinion he unsuccessfully stood for the deputy leadership of the party in 1981. He lost his seat in the general election of 1983, but returned to represent Chesterfield from 1984. He unsuccessfully challenged **Neil Kinnock** for the party leadership in 1988. Among his publications are *Arguments for Socialism* (1979) and *Arguments for Democracy* (1981).

BENN, Gottfried (1886–1956) German poet, born in Mansfeld in West Prussia. Though the son of a clergyman he embraced the philosophy of Nihilism as a young man, but later became one of the few intellectuals to favour Nazi doctrines. Trained in medicine as a venereologist, he began writing Expressionist verse dealing with the uglier aspects of his profession, such as *Morgue* (1912). Later his outlook became more mature and his poetry more versatile though still pessimistic, and after 1945, matching the mood of despondency in defeat, won him a place among the leading poets of the century.

BENNET, Abraham (1750–99) English physicist. He invented the gold-leaf electroscope and constructed a simple induction machine in 1789.

BENNET, Henry See **ARLINGTON**

BENNETT, Alan (1934–) English dramatist, actor and director, born in Leeds He came to prominence as a writer and performer in *Beyond the Fringe*, a revue performed at the Edinburgh Festival in 1960, and wrote a television series, *On The Margin* (1966), before his first stage play, *Forty Years On* (1968). Subsequent plays include *Getting On* (1971, about a Labour MP), *Habeas Corpus* (1973), *The Old Country* (1977), *Enjoy* (1980), *Kafka's Dick* (1986), and a double bill, *Single Spies* (1988). He has also written much for television including *An Englishman Abroad* (1983), *The Insurance Man* (1986), and a series of six monologues, *Talking Heads* (1987).

BENNETT, (Enoch) Arnold (1867–1931) English novelist, born near Hanley, Staffordshire, in the heart of 'the Potteries', the son of a solicitor. Educated locally and at London University, he became a solicitor's clerk in London, but quickly transferred to journalism, and in 1893 became assistant editor (editor in 1896) of the journal *Woman*. He published his first novel, *The Man from the North*, in 1898. In 1902 he moved to Paris for ten years and from then on he was engaged exclusively in writing, journalistic and creative. His claims to recognition as a novelist rest mainly on the early *Anna of the Five Towns* (1902), the more celebrated *The Old Wives' Tale* (1908), and the *Clayhanger* series—*Clayhanger* (1910), *Hilda Lessways* (1911), *These Twain* (1916), subsequently issued (1925) as *The Clayhanger Family*—in all of which novels the 'Five Towns', centres of the pottery industry, feature not only as background, but almost as *dramatis personae*. He excels again with *Riceyman Steps* (1923), a picture of drab life in London, and his genial, humorous streak shows in works like *The Card* (1911), *The Grand Babylon Hotel* (1902), *Imperial Palace* (1930), and the play *The Great Adventure* (1913). The play *Milestones* (1912), written in collaboration with Edward Knoblock, was much performed. He was a sound and influential critic, and as 'Jacob Tonson' on *The New Age* he was a discerning reviewer. His *Journals* were published posthumously.

BENNETT, Floyd (1890–1928) American aviator, born near Warrensburg, New York. A naval pilot during World War I, he accompanied **Richard Evelyn Byrd** on the **Macmillan** expedition to Greenland (1925). In May 1926 he piloted Byrd on the first aeroplane flight over the North Pole, and received the Congressional Medal of Honour. He died of pneumonia while planning Byrd's flight over the South Pole in 1929.

BENNETT, James Gordon (1795–1872) Scots-born American journalist, father of **James Gordon Bennett** (1841–1918), born in Keith, Banffshire. He emigrated to Nova Scotia in 1819, and became a journalist in New York in 1826. In 1835 he started the *New York Herald*, which he edited until 1867, pioneering many journalistic innovations.

BENNETT, James Gordon (1841–1918) American journalist, born in New York, son and successor of **James Gordon Bennett** (1795–1872). He sent **Henry Morton Stanley** in 1870 to find **David Livingstone**, and with the *Daily Telegraph* financed Livingstone's Congo journey (1874–78). He also promoted polar exploration, storm warnings, motoring, and yachting.

BENNETT, John Hughes (1812–75) English physician. As professor of the Institutes of Medicine in Edinburgh University from 1848, he was a pioneer in the use of the microscope in clinical pathology.

BENNETT, Michael (1943–87) American dancer, choreographer, director and producer, born in Buffalo, New York. He began his career as a chorus boy before turning to Broadway show choreography. His first hit, *Promises, Promises* (1968) was followed by *Coco* (1970), *Company* (1970), *Follies* (co-director, 1971), *Seesaw* (1973) and the popular masterpiece *A Chorus Line* (1975), the success of which was unequalled by such later shows as *Ballroom* (1978) and *Dreamgirls* (1981).

BENNETT, Richard Bedford, 1st Viscount (1870–1947) Canadian statesman, born in New Brunswick. A lawyer by training, he was elected to parliament in 1911 and became Conservative leader from 1927, and prime minister from 1930 to 1935. He convened the empire economic conference in Ottawa in 1932, out of which came a system of empire trade preference known as the Ottawa agreements. He retired to Britain in 1939.

BENNETT, Richard Rodney (1936–) English composer, born in Broadstairs, Kent, and educated at the Royal Academy of Music and in Paris under **Pierre Boulez**. Well known for his music for films, he has also composed operas, orchestral works, chamber music, and experimental works for one and two pianos. Some of his music uses the twelve-tone scale, and his interest in jazz has prompted such works as *Jazz Calendar* (1963) and *Jazz Pastoral* (1969). His more recent work shows a growing emphasis on internal rhythmic structure. From 1963 to 1965 he was professor of composition at the Royal Academy of Music, and in 1970–71 was visiting professor at the Peabody Institute in Baltimore. Among his other works are *The Approaches of Sleep* (1959), *Winter Music* (1960), *The Music That Her Echo Is* (1967), *The House of Sleeps* (1971), the two operas commissioned by Sadler's Wells, *The Mines of Sulphur* (1965) and *A Penny for a Song* (1968), the opera commissioned by Covent Garden, *Victory* (1970), and the choral work, *Spells* (1975).

BENNETT, Sir William Sterndale (1816–75) English pianist and composer, born in Sheffield. He studied at the Royal Academy, London, and at Leipzig, and attracted **Mendelssohn**'s notice at the Düsseldorf Musical Festival. In 1849 he founded the Bach Society, in 1856 became professor of music at Cambridge, and in 1868 principal of the Royal Academy of Music. His earlier compositions, piano pieces, songs, and the cantatas *The May Queen* (1858) and *The Women of Samaria* (1867), are his happiest.

BENNIGSEN, Levin August Theophil, Count (1745–1826) German soldier in the Russian service, born in Brunswick. He entered the Russian army in 1773. After much distinguished service in the field, he took part in the assassination of the emperor **Paul**. In the Napoleonic Wars he fought at Pultusk (1806), and commanded at Eylau (1807). At the battle of Borodino (1812), he commanded the Russian centre, and defeated **Murat** at Tarutino (1812). He fought victoriously at the battle of Leipzig (1813) and was created count by the emperor **Alexander I** in the field. His son, Alexander Levin (1809–93), was a distinguished Hanoverian statesman.

BENNY, Jack, originally **Benjamin Kubelsky** (1894–1974) American comedian, born in Waukegan, Illinois. A child prodigy violinist, he performed as part of a vaudeville double-act, 'Salisbury and Benny', and also appeared as 'Ben Benny, the Diddlin' Kid'. After navy service during World War I, he returned to the stage and toured extensively before making his film début in the short *Bright Moments* (1928). Following his Broadway success in *The Earl Carroll Vanities* (1930) and his radio début in the *Ed Sullivan Show* (1932), he earned his own radio series which, combined with its subsequent television incarnation, *The Jack Benny Show* (1950–65), won him the loyalty and warm affection of a mass audience. A gentle, bemused, self-effacing figure, his humour lacked malice, relying for its effect on his mastery of timing and an act based on his ineptitude as a fiddler, his perennial youth and an unfounded reputation as the world's meanest man. A sporadic film career was also the butt of much self-deprecation but included *Charley's Aunt* (1941), *To Be or Not To Be* (1942) and *It's in the Bag* (1945). He continued to appear in regular television specials until his death.

BENOIS, Alexandre Nikolaevich (1870–1960) Russian painter of Italian, French and German origins, and great-uncle of **Peter Ustinov**. He was intimately connected with the rise of the **Diaghilev** ballet and designed many of the sets.

BENOIT DE SAINTE-MAURE (fl.c.1150) French poet, born in either Sainte-Maure near Poitiers or Sainte-More near Tours. His vast romance *Roman de Troie* was a source book to many later writers, notably **Boccaccio**, who in turn inspired **Chaucer** and **Shakespeare** to use Benoit's episode of Troilus and Cressida.

BENSERADE, Isaac de (1613–91) French poet and dramatist, born in Paris. His is remembered as the librettist for **Lully**'s ballets and as the author of a sonnet, *Job*.

BENSON, Arthur Christopher (1862–1925) English author, son of **Edward White Benson** and brother of **Edward Frederic Benson** and **Robert Hugh Benson**. He was master of Magdalene College, Cambridge, and wrote studies of **Rossetti**, **Fitzgerald**, **Pater**, **Tennyson**, and **Ruskin**, a memoir of Robert Hugh Benson, and a biography of Edward White Benson. His poems include *Land of Hope and Glory*.

BENSON, Edward Frederic (1867–1940) English author, son of **Edward White Benson** and brother of **Arthur Christopher Benson** and **Robert Hugh Benson**. He was educated at Wellington and King's College, Cambridge. After some archaeological research in Greece and Egypt (1892–95) he published several light novels including *Dodo* (1893) and *Queen Lucia* (1920) as well as three autobiographical studies of Edwardian and Georgian society.

BENSON, Edward White (1829–96) English prelate, born in Birmingham. He became assistant master at Rugby (1852), was ordained priest (1857), and from 1858 to 1872 was headmaster of the newly founded Wellington College. Bishop of Truro in 1877, he was appointed archbishop of Canterbury in 1882. A friend of **Gladstone**, he was a zealous churchman and upholder of the establishment principle.

BENSON, Sir Frank Robert (1858–1939) Shakespearian actor-manager, nephew of **Edward White Benson**, born in Alresford, Hampshire. He first appeared in **Henry Irving**'s production of *Romeo and Juliet* in 1882 at the Lyceum and was knighted by King **George V** on the stage of Drury Lane during a Shakespeare tercentenary matinee (1916).

BENSON, Frank Weston (1862–1951) American artist, born in Salem, Massachusetts. He studied in Paris, and became a teacher at the Museum of Fine Arts in Boston. He painted women and children, sensitive etchings and wash drawings of wild fowl, and murals in the Library of Congress.

BENSON, Robert Hugh (1871–1914) English author and clergyman, son of **Edward White Benson** and brother of **Arthur Christopher Benson** and **Edward Frederic Benson**. Educated at Eton and Trinity College, Cambridge, he took Anglican orders but turned Roman Catholic in 1903 and rose to private chamberlain to Pope **Pius X** (1911). A dynamic preacher and prolific author, he wrote such novels as *Come Rack! Come Rope!* (1912).

BENSON, William Arthur Smith (1854–1924) English architect, designer and metalworker, born in London. He was educated at Winchester and Oxford, where he met **William Morris** and **Burne-Jones**. In 1880 he opened a small workshop in Hammersmith specializing in metalwork, moving to larger premises in Chiswick and opening showrooms in Bond Street in

1887. Apart from designing lamps and light fittings, silver mounts and hinges, he designed wallpapers and furniture for Morris & Co and J S Henry. He was a founder member of the Art-Workers Guild and supported the formation of the Arts & Crafts Exhibition Society. He was managing director of Morris & Co from 1896 to 1920.

BENTHAM, George (1800–84) English botanist, born in Stoke, Plymouth, nephew of **Jeremy Bentham**. He was secretary to his uncle from 1826 to 1832. Abandoning law for botany, he was secretary of the Horticultural Society of London (1829–40), and compiled, with Sir **Joseph Hooker**, the great *Genera Plantarum* (3 vols, 1862–83), among many other important botanical works.

BENTHAM, Jeremy (1748–1832) English philosopher, jurist and social reformer, born in London. He entered Queen's College, Oxford at the age of 12 and was admitted to Lincoln's Inn at the age of only 15. He is best known as a proponent of utilitarianism in his pioneering works *A Fragment on Government* (1776) and *Introduction to the Principles of Morals and Legislation* (1789), which argued that the proper objective of all conduct and legislation is 'the greatest happiness of the greatest number', and developed a 'hedonic calculus' to estimate the effects of different actions. He travelled widely in Europe and Russia, was made an honorary citizen of the French Republic in 1792, and published copiously on penal and social reform, economics and politics. He planned a special prison (the Panopticon) and a special school (the Chrestomathia), and helped start the *Westminster Review* (1823). He also founded University College, London, where his clothed skeleton is preserved on public view.

BENTHAM, Sir Samuel (1757–1831) English inventor and naval architect, brother of **Jeremy Bentham**, born in London and apprenticed as a shipwright. Unable to obtain suitable employment at home he made his way in 1783 to Russia where he introduced some revolutionary heavy naval armaments that enabled a much smaller Russian force to defeat the Turks in 1788. For nearly 20 years after 1795 he devoted his energies to building up Britain's naval strength during the critical period of the Napoleonic wars, introducing advances in naval architecture, shipbuilding, large-calibre non-recoil carronades, the use of steam dredgers, and dockyard administration. His campaign against corruption and maladministration in the Admiralty dockyards aroused such bitterness that in 1812 he was forced to resign, though not before many of his reforms had been put into effect.

BENTINCK the name of an ancient noble family which had migrated from the Palatinate to the Netherlands in the 14th century and to England with William of Orange (later **William III**) in 1689.

BENTINCK, Lord George (1802–48) English Tory politician, and sportsman, son of the 4th Duke of Portland, born at Welbeck Abbey. He joined the army in 1819 and from 1822 to 1825 was private secretary to his uncle, **George Canning**, then foreign secretary. He entered parliament in 1828, supported Catholic emancipation and the Reform Bill, but left the Whigs in 1834 to form a separate parliamentary group with Lord **Stanley**. On **Peel**'s third betrayal of his party in introducing free trade measures, Bentinck, supported by **Disraeli** who idolized him, led the Tory opposition to Peel. A great lover of racing and field sports, he stamped out many dishonest turf practices.

BENTINCK, William, 1st Earl of Portland (1649–1709) Dutch-born English soldier and courtier, born in Holland. The friend from boyhood of **William III**, he was entrusted with the secrets of his foreign policy, and after the revolution was created an English peer, and given large estates.

BENTINCK, William Cavendish, 3rd Duke of Portland (1738–1809) English statesman. He entered Lord **Rockingham**'s cabinet in 1765, and succeeded him as leader of the Whig party. He was twice prime mininster (1783, 1807–09), but his best work was done as home secretary under **Pitt**, when he was given charge of Irish affairs (1794–1801).

BENTINCK, Lord William Cavendish (1774–1839) English statesman, after serving in Flanders and Italy became governor of Madras (1803–07). He was recalled, however, when his prohibition of sepoy beards and turbans caused the massacre at Vellore (1806). He served in the Peninsular War (1808–14), in 1827 became governor-general of Bengal and in 1833 first governor-general of India. His administration resulted in better internal communications, substituted English for Persian and Sanskrit, brought about many educational reforms with the help of **Macaulay**, and prohibited *suttee*.

BENTINE, Michael (1921–) Anglo-Peruvian comedy performer, born in Watford. He made his stage début in *Sweet Lavender* at Cardiff in 1941 and, after wartime service in the RAF, worked at the Windmill Theatre (1946) and in the show *Starlight Roof* (1947). One of the early members of *The Goons* (1950–52), he left the popular radio series to pursue a solo career and appeared on television in *After Hours* (1959–60) and *It's A Square World* (1960–64) which allowed him to indulge his eccentric penchant for zany, surreal humour, mechanical jokes and illustrated lectures in which anything could happen. Later television series, often for children, include *The Golden Silents* (1965), *Potty Time* (1973–80) and *Mad About It* (1981). He also appeared in the film *The Sandwich Man* (1966) and has written numerous novels and autobiographies including *The Long Banana Skin* (1975) and *A Shy Person's Guide to Life* (1984).

BENTLEY, Derek William (c.1933–1953) convicted British murderer, hanged for being 'concerned' in the murder of a policeman, although it was his friend, **Christopher Craig**, who fired the lethal shot. Bentley, who had worked as a furniture remover, a dustman and a road-sweeper, was unemployed at the time of the crime. On Sunday 2 November 1952, when he was 19 and Craig was 16, he and Craig broke into a confectionery warehouse in Croydon. They were seen climbing over the fence, and the police were alerted. Bentley, who was carrying a knife and a knuckleduster, and Craig, who was armed with a gun, were approached by the police. Bentley was quickly apprehended, but Craig fired several shots, initially wounding one policeman and then killing another. Both boys were eventually arrested and charged. The case was heard on 4 December 1952. Bentley, who reputedly had the mental age of a child of 10 or 11, was found guilty and was given the death sentence. Craig, who was too young to receive the death penalty, was detained indefinitely. Despite a series of legal appeals and strong emotional appeals by Bentley's family to the government and to the queen, all of which received vigorous public support, Bentley was hanged on 28 January 1953. Craig was released in 1963.

BENTLEY, Edmund Clerihew (1875–1956) English journalist and novelist, born in London. He worked on the *Daily News* (1901–12) and the *Daily Telegraph* (1912–34). He is chiefly remembered as the author of *Trent's Last Case* (1913), which is regarded as a milestone in the transformation of the detective novel.

A close friend of **G K Chesterton**, he originated and gave name to the type of humorous verse-form known as the 'clerihew'.

BENTLEY, Richard (1662–1742) English classical scholar and master of Trinity College, Cambridge, born in Oulton, near Leeds. Educated at Wakefield Grammar School and St John's College, Cambridge, he was appointed headmaster of Spalding Grammar School (1682) but resigned to become private tutor to the son of the influential Dr **Edward Stillingfleet**, then Dean of St Paul's, who rewarded him with the post of archdeacon of Ely and keeper of the Royal Libraries (1694). He had made his mark as a classical scholar with a Latin treatise on the Greek chronicler John Malelas, addressed to **John Stuart Mill** (*Epistola ad Joannem Millium*, 1691), and delivered the first **Robert Boyle** lectures in Oxford, *A Confutation of Atheism* (1692). He established an international reputation with his dispute with **Charles Boyle, 4th Earl of Orrery** (1697–99), in which he proved that the so-called *Epistles of Phalaris* were spurious (a controversy that was satirized by **Swift** in his *Battle of the Books*, 1704). He was appointed master of Trinity College, Cambridge, in 1700, and despite his towering European reputation as a scholar, the history of his long mastership was an unbroken series of quarrels and litigations and political chicanery provoked by his arrogance and greed. He misappropriated university funds to refurbish the Master's Lodge, he got himself appointed Regius professor of divinity in 1717 by intrigue, and survived a trial and attempted ejection by the university vice-chancellor in the 1720s. He published critical texts of many classical authors, including the Greek New Testament. One of his daughters was the mother of the dramatist, **Richard Cumberland**.

BENTLEY, Richard (1794–1871) English publisher. He was the founder of *Bentley's Miscellany* (1837–68), with **Charles Dickens** as editor. The firm was absorbed by Macmillan in 1898.

BENTON, Thomas Hart (1782–1858) American statesman, born near Hillsborough, North Carolina. Known as 'Old Bullion' from his opposition to the paper currency, he also made himself unpopular by opposing slavery in the territories.

BENTSEN, Lloyd Millard Jr, (1921–) US Democrat politician, born in Mission, Texas into a 'nouveau riche' landholding family. He studied law at Texas University, Austin, and served as a combat pilot during World War II. After briefly working as a county judge, he was a member of the House of Representatives, 1948–54, and then built up a substantial fortune as president of the Lincoln Consolidated insurance company in Houston. He returned to congress as a senator for Texas in 1971, became chairman of the influential finance committee, and was vice-presidential running-mate to **Michael Dukakis** in the Democrats' 1988 presidential challenge. Although the 'ticket' was defeated, the patrician Bentsen, an enlightened conservative Democrat, enhanced his reputation with an impressive campaign and remained an influential elder statesman within the senate.

BENTZON, Niels Viggo (1919–) Danish composer and pianist. Educated at the Royal Danish Academy of Music, he has been a reader at the academy since 1960 and made his début in 1943. His compositions include opera, symphonies, ballets, piano concertos and chamber music. He was awarded the Ove Christensen Honorary prize in 1962 and the Carl Nielsen prize in 1965.

BENZ, Karl Friedrich (1844–1929) German engineer and car manufacture, born in Karlsruhe. In 1877–79 he developed a two-stroke engine and founded a factory for its manufacture, leaving in 1883 when his backers refused to finance a mobile engine. He then founded his second company, Benz & Co, Rheinisch Gasmotorenfabrik, at Mannheim. His first car—one of the earliest petrol-driven vehicles—was completed in 1885 and sold to a French manufacturer. In 1926 the firm was merged with the Daimler-Motoren-Gesellschaft to form Daimler-Benz and Co.

BENZER, Seymour (1921–) American geneticist, born in New York City. He studied physics at Perdue and taught biophysics there until 1965 when he moved to the California Institute of Technology. He first showed that genes can be split and then recombined, and he did much to relate genes as chemical entities with their observed behaviour in biological systems.

BEN-ZVI, Itzhak (1884–1963) Israeli statesman, born in Poltava (USSR). Having migrated to Palestine in 1907 he became a prominent Zionist, and was a founder of the Jewish Labour party. He was elected president of Israel on the death of Dr **Weizmann** in 1952. A prominent scholar and archaeologist, he wrote on the history of the Middle East.

BÉRANGER, Pierre Jean de (1780–1857) French poet, born in Paris. After a scanty education he left regular employment as a clerk at the University of Paris for an impecunious literary life in 1798. His lyrics, coloured by his politics—a curious compound of republicanism and Bonapartism—led to spells of imprisonment in 1821 and 1828, but their vivacity, satire, and wit endeared them to the masses.

BÉRARD, Christian (1902–49) French painter and designer. His attitude to his own work was curiously oversensitive. He was always a reluctant exhibitor, disliked having his paintings reproduced, and even when designing for the theatre began with an infectious dissatisfaction, so that last minute repaintings were not uncommon. Nevertheless, his fame rests mainly on his stage décor, especially for the productions of **Molière** by **Barrault**.

BERCEO, Gonzalo de (c.1180–c.1246) Spanish poet, born in Verceo, the earliest known Castilian poet. He became a deacon and wrote more than 13000 verses on devotional subjects, of which the best is a Life of St Oria. He was also the author of *Milagros de la Virgen*, a collection of legends of the Virgin's appearances on earth. His poems were not discovered and published until the late 18th century.

BERCHEM, or **BERGHEM, Nicholas** (1620–83) Dutch landscape painter, born in Haarlem. His work is represented in most European collections.

BERCHET, Giovanni (1783–1851) Italian poet, born in Milan. He began by translating foreign, especially English, literature, and through his translation of *The Vicar of Wakefield* (1809) became interested in ballads. In 1816 he published a pamphlet, *Lettera semiseria di Grisostomo*, which became a manifesto of the Romantic movement in Italy. In 1821 he left Italy to avoid arrest, and lived in exile, mainly in England, until the abortive Revolution of 1848. He was received in Milan with enthusiasm and made director of education, but had to flee again to Piedmont. His best-known works are *I Profughi di Parga* (1821), *Il Romito del Cenisio*, and *Il Trovatore*.

BERDYAEV, Nikolai (1874–1948) Russian religious philosopher, born an aristocrat in Kiev but developed strong revolutionary sympathies as a student and supported the 1917 Revolution. He secured a professorship at Moscow but his unorthodox spiritual and libertarian ideals led to his dismissal in 1922. He moved to found in Berlin an Academy of the Philosophy of Religion which he later transferred to Clamart, near Paris, where he died. He described himself as a 'believing freethinker' and his fierce commitment to freedom and individualism brought him into conflict with both ecclesiastical and political powers. His main ideas are developed in his journal *The Path* and his books *Freedom and the Spirit* (1927), *The Destiny of Man* (1931) and *Dreams and Reality* (1949).

BERENGAR I (d.924) king of Italy from 888 and Holy Roman Emperor from 915. He succeeded his father Eberhard, a count of Frankish origin, as margrave of Friuli. He died at the hands of his own men.

BERENGAR II (c.900–966) king of Italy, grandson of the king of Halzand, **Berengar I**. He succeeded his father as margrave of Ivrea (928) and was crowned king in 950. In 961 he was dethroned by the emperor **Otto I** and after three years' refuge in a mountain fortress was sent as a prisoner to Bavaria where he died.

BERENGAR OF TOURS (999–1088) French scholastic theologian. In 1031 he was appointed preceptor of the cathedral school in Tours, and about 1040 archdeacon of Angers. An opponent of the doctrine of transubstantiation, he was excommunicated by Pope **Leo IX** in 1050 and thereafter was constantly in trouble. Finally, in 1078, he was cited to appear at Rome, where he repeatedly renounced, but apparently never abandoned, his 'error'. He spent his last years in a cell on an island in the Loire, near Tours.

BERENGARIA See **RICHARD I**

BERENICE the name of several women of the house of Ptolemy, none of them so celebrated as the 'Jewish Berenice'—the daughter of **Herod Agrippa I**, who, having been four times married (to an uncle, her brother, etc), became the mistress of **Flavius Titus**, son of the emperor **Vespasian**, during the Jewish rebellion (AD 70), and followed him to Rome. She is the heroine of **Racine**'s tragedy.

BERENSON, Bernhard (1865–1959) Lithuanian-born American art critic, born in Vilnius. He moved to the USA in 1875, studied at Harvard, and became a leading authority on Italian Renaissance art. In 1900 he moved to Italy, where he lived in an 18th-century villa, I Tatti, outside Florence. He produced a vast amount of critical literature which apart from standard works on each of the Italian schools includes *Italian Painters of the Renaissance* (1894–1907), *The Study and Criticism of Italian Art* (1901–16), *Aesthetics and History* (1950), and the autobiographical *Sketch for a Self Portrait* (1949). He bequeathed his villa and art collection to Harvard University, which turned it into a Centre for Italian Renaissance Culture.

BERESFORD, Charles William de la Poer, 1st Baron (1846–1919) Irish-born naval commander, born in Philipstown, Offally, son of the fourth Marquis of Waterford. He entered the navy in 1859, and was promoted captain in 1882 for his services at the bombardment of Alexandria. He served, too, in the Nile expedition (1884). He was a lord of the Admiralty (1886–88), but resigned, sat in parliament as a Conservative and commanded the Mediterranean Fleet (1905–07) and Channel Fleet (1907-09). A trenchant naval critic, he clashed with Admiral Lord **Fisher** over naval policy and reforms.

BERESFORD, William Carr Beresford, 1st Viscount (1768–1854) British soldier, illegitimate son of the first Marquis of Waterford. He entered the army in 1785 and served in Nova Scotia and Egypt. He distinguished himself at the taking of the Cape of Good Hope (1806) and at the capture and loss of Buenos Aires (1807). In the Peninsular War (1808–14) he took the command (1809) of the Portuguese army, and defeated **Soult** at Albuera (1811). He was present at the capture of Badajoz (1812), and at Salamanca was severely wounded. He left Portugal in 1822; and in the Wellington administration (1828–30) he was master-general of the ordnance.

BERG, Alban (1885–1935) Austrian composer, born in Vienna. From 1904 to 1910 he studied with **Schoenberg**, and after service in the Austrian war ministry during World War I, he taught privately in Vienna. With the last of his Four Songs (1909–10) he displays a free harmonic language tempered wih romantic tonal elements which remained his characteristic style. He is best known for his opera *Wozzeck* (1925), his violin concerto, and the *Lyric Suite* for string quartet. His unfinished opera, *Lulu*, was posthumously produced.

BERG, Paul (1926–) American molecular biologist, born in New York City. He was educated at Pennsylvania State and Western Reserve University, and became professor of biochemistry at Stanford in 1959 and Washington in 1970. In 1955 **Francis Crick** had proposed that the biosynthesis of proteins requires an intermediate called an adaptor, with perhaps a different adaptor for each of the 20 amino acids used to form proteins. In 1956 Berg identified the first adaptor, and others have since been found. Later, Berg devised a method for introducing 'foreign' genes into bacteria, so causing the bacteria to produce proteins determined by the new gene; this method of genetic engineering has proved of great value in giving biochemical syntheses of insulin and interferon. He was much concerned also with the hazards of such work, which could produce novel and dangerous pathogens by accident or design. He shared the 1980 Nobel prize for chemistry with **Frederick Sanger** and **Walter Gilbert**.

BERGANZA, Teresa (1935–) Spanish mezzo-soprano, born in Madrid where she made her début in 1955. Especially noted for **Mozart** and **Rossini** roles, she first sang in England at Glyndebourne (1958), at Covent Garden (1959), and subsequently in concert and opera in Vienna, Milan, Edinburgh, in Israel, America and elsewhere.

BERGER, Hans (1873–1941) German psychiatrist who invented the electroencephalograph. Born in Neuses bei Coburg, he studied medicine at Jena University, where he stayed for the rest of his career, becoming professor of psychiatry in 1919. His research attempted (mostly unsuccessfully) to establish relationships between psychological states and various physiological parameters, such as heartbeat, respiration and the temperature of the brain itself. In the course of this work, he placed electrical recording equipment on the surface of the skull; from the mid 1920s, he was recording what became known as 'brain waves'. Although precise correlations between electrical brain activity and psychic processes has not emerged, Berger's electroencephalograph, particularly after the work of individuals such as **E D Adrian**, has become a useful tool of research and diagnosis into brain functions and diseases.

BERGER, John Peter (1926–) English novelist, playwright and art critic, born in London. After studying at the Central and Chelsea Schools of Art he began his working life as a painter and a drawing teacher but soon turned to writing. His novels have a sensual awareness that is not entirely visual, but his Marxism and artistic background are ever present. Each of his novels has been well-received and include *A Painter of Our Time* (1958), *The Foot of Clive* (1962), and *Corker's Freedom* (1964). His fame was enhanced with the publication of *G* (1972), a story of migrant workers in Europe, which won the Booker prize; in his acceptance speech, Berger denounced the sponsors and announced that he would donate half of the prize money to the (now defunct) Black Panthers. Among his other writings the best known are *Ways of Seeing* (1972), and *Pig Earth* (1979), a collection of short stories of French peasant life.

BERGERAC, Savininien Cyrano de See **CYRANO DE BERGERAC**

BERGGRAV, Eivind (1884–1959) Norwegian Lutheran bishop, born in Stavanger. After some years as a teacher, pastor and prison chaplain, he became bishop of Troms and then bishop of Oslo and primate of the Norwegian Church (1937–50). Following the Nazi occupation of 1940, he led the Church's opposition to the Quisling government (*With God in the Darkness*, 1943), refusing to endorse the war against Russia as a fight against atheism, and opposing Nazi attempts to monopolize the education of young people. For this he was imprisoned (1941–45). He wrote some 30 books and was a strong supporter of the ecumenical movement, becoming a president of the World Council of Churches (1950–54).

BERGHEM, Nicholas See **BERCHEM**

BERGIUS, Friedrich (1884–1949) German organic chemist, born in Goldschmieden, near Breslau. He made notable researches in coal hydrogenation for the production of motor fuels under high pressure, and the hydrolysis of wood to sugar. He shared the 1931 Nobel prize for chemistry with **Carl Bosch**. After World War II he left Germany for Argentina.

BERGMAN, Bo Hjalmar (1869–1967) Swedish lyric poet, born in Stockholm. He studied law at Uppsala and later became a literary critic. His poetry, ranging from pessimism to optimistic humanism, included *Marionetterna* (The Puppets, 1903) and *Trots allt* (In Spite of Everything, 1931). He also wrote novels, short stories and two volumes of memoirs.

BERGMAN, Hjalmar Fredrik Elgerus (1883–1931) Swedish novelist, poet and playwright, born in Örebro. His plays include *Maria, Jesu Moder* (1905) and the comedies *Swedenhielms* (The Swedenhielm Family, 1925) and *Patrasket* (The Rabble, 1928). His novels, including the broadly comical *Murkurells i Wadköping* (1919, trans as *God's Orchid*, 1924), were often popular satires on his native Örebro.

BERGMAN, Ingmar (1918–) Swedish film and stage director, born in Uppsala. A trainee director in the Stockholm theatre, he began his film career in the script department of Svensk Filmindustri in 1943 and continued to alternate between stage and screen, making his film début with *Crisis* (1945). His explorations of personal torment won many international prizes for films like *The Seventh Seal* (1957), *Wild Strawberries* (1957) and *The Face* (1958), which are outstanding for their photographic artistry, haunting imagery and subtle exploration of facial characteristics. Preoccupied with guilt, anguish, emotional repression and death, he created a succession of bleak masterpieces including *Shame* (1968), *Cries and Whispers* (1972) and *Autumn Sonata* (1978). His last film, *Fanny and Alexander* (1982), was an unexpectedly life-affirming evocation of autobiographical elements from his own Dickensian childhood. He is still active in the theatre.

BERGMAN, Ingrid (1915–82) Swedish film and stage actress, born in Stockholm. After studying at the Royal Dramatic Theatre, she was offered a contract by Svenskfilmindustri and made her film début in *Munkbrogreven* (1934). Unaffected and vivacious, she was signed by **David O Selznick** to appear in an English-language remake of *Intermezzo* (1939), and became an immensely popular romantic star in such films as *Casablanca* (1942), *Spellbound* (1945) and *Notorious* (1946). In 1950 she gave birth to the illegitimate child of director **Roberto Rossellini**. The ensuing scandal led to her ostracization from the American film industry. She continued her career in Europe and was welcomed back by Hollywood on her return in 1956. In later years she worked on stage and television. Her last film was **Ingmar Bergman**'s *Autumn Sonata* (1978), a deeply-felt exploration of a mother-daughter relationship. Nominated seven times for an Academy Award, she won Oscars for *Gaslight* (1943), *Anastasia* (1956) and *Murder on the Orient Express* (1974).

BERGMAN, Torbern Olof (1735–84) Swedish chemist and physicist. Professor at Uppsala from 1758, he prepared, by using carbon dioxide, artificial mineral waters, and discovered hydrogen sulphide in mineral springs.

BERGSON, Henri (1859–1941) French philosopher, born in Paris, son of a Polish Jewish musician and an English mother. He became professor at the Collège de France (1900–24), and won the 1927 Nobel prize for literature. He was a highly original thinker who became something of a cult figure. He contrasted the fundamental reality of the dynamic flux of consciousness with the inert physical world of discrete objects, which was a convenient fiction for the mechanistic descriptions of science. The *élan vital*, or 'creative impulse', not a deterministic natural selection, is at the heart of evolution, and intuition, not analysis, reveals the real world of process and change. His own writings are literary, suggestive and analogical rather than philosophical in the modern sense, and he greatly influenced such writers as **Marcel Proust** (to whom he was connected by marriage), **Georges Sorel** and **Samuel Butler**. His most important works were *Time and Freewill* (1889), *Matter and Memory* (1896), and *Creative Evolution* (1907).

BERGSTRÖM, Sune Karl (1916–) Swedish biochemist, joint winner of the 1982 Nobel prize for physiology or medicine. He studied medicine and chemistry at the Karolinska Institute in Stockholm, and taught chemistry at Lund (1948–58) before becoming professor at the Institute (1958–81). He isolated and purified prostaglandins, for which he shared the Nobel prize with his former student Bengt Samuelsson and **John Vane**.

BERIA, Lavrenti Pavlovich (1899–1953) Soviet secret police chief, born in Mercheuli, Georgia, into a peasant family. He became organizer of a Bolshevik group at a Baku college in 1917. From 1921 to 1931 he served as a member of the OGPU (the forerunner of the KGB) in the Caucasus, before becoming first secretary of the Georgian Communist party in 1931. In 1938 he was appointed minister for internal affairs by his patron, **Stalin**, and served as vice-president of the State Committee for Defence during World War II, being accorded the title of marshal in 1945. On Stalin's death in March 1953, he attempted to seize power, but was foiled by fearful military and party leaders. Following arrest by Marshal **Zhukov**, he was tried for treason and was executed in December 1953. Described as the '**Himmler** of Russia', he was a plotter of ruthless ambition and a notoriously skilled organizer of forced labour, terror and espionage.

BERING, Vitus Jonassen (1681–1741) Danish navigator, born in Horsens. He entered the newly-formed navy of **Peter I the Great** in 1703, and for his bravery in the wars with Sweden was appointed to lead an expedition of discovery in the Sea of Kamchatka to determine whether the continents of Asia and America were joined. Sailing in 1728 from a port on the east of Kamchatka, he followed the coast northward until, from its westward trend, he believed he had reached the northeast point of Asia; however he failed to see land to the east and sought permission for a return voyage. In 1733 he was given command of the 600-strong Great Northern Expedition to explore the Siberian coast and Kuril Islands, and then in 1741 he sailed from Ohkotsk towards the American continent, and sighting land, about $58\frac{1}{2}°$ N lat, followed the coast northward; but sickness and storms forced him to return, and he was wrecked on the island of Avatcha (now Bering Island), where he died of scurvy during the winter with 19 of his crew. Bering Sea and Bering Strait are also named after him. His discoveries were confirmed by Captain **Cook**.

BERIO, Luciano (1925–) Italian composer and teacher of music. Born into a musical family, he studied first with his father, and later at the Music Academy in Milan. After studying with **Dallapiccola** at Tanglewood, USA, he and **Bruno Maderna** founded an electronic studio in Milan, where Berio remained till 1961. In 1958 he began an association with the summer music courses at Darmstadt, giving seminars and directing many performances of his work. In 1962 he moved to the USA where he taught composition at the Juilliard School in New York, returning to Italy in 1972 to work in many diverse aspects of music. In 1950 he married the American soprano Cathy Berberian (1928–83), for whom he wrote several works; the marriage was dissolved in 1966. He is particularly interested in the combining of live and pre-recorded sound, and the use of tapes and electronic music, as in his compositions *Mutazioni* (1955), *Omaggio a James Joyce* (1958) and *Questo vuol dire che...* (1969–70). His *Sequenza* series for solo instruments (1958 onwards) are striking virtuoso pieces. *Visage* (1960) was written specially for the medium of radio, and consists of a single word pronounced and repeated in varying modes of expression. Pieces such as *Passaggio* (1963), for one female performer and two choruses, one in the pit and one in the audience, show the same delight in the dramatic tension of musical expression as his larger-scale stage works, *Laborintus II* (1965) and *Opera* (1969–70, revised in three acts in 1977).

BERKELEY, Busby originally **William Berkeley Enos** (1895–1976) American choreographer and director, born in Los Angeles. After service in the US army, he pursued a career in the theatre, working as an actor, stage manager and dance director. He directed his first Broadway show, *A Night in Venice*, in 1928 and was subsequently hired by **Sam Goldwyn** to devise the musical number for the film *Whoopee* (1930). He stayed in Hollywood to become one of the cinema's most innovative choreographers, noted for his mobile camerawork and dazzling kaleidoscopic routines involving spectacular multitudes of chorus girls and much sexual innuendo. His work enhanced films like *Forty Second Street* (1933), *Gold Diggers of 1933* and *Dames* (1934). In later years, ill-health restricted his opportunities, but he directed *Take Me Out to the Ball Game* (1948), contributed imaginatively to *Small Town Girl* (1953) and enjoyed a Broadway triumph as the supervising producer of the 1971 revival of *No, No, Nanette*.

BERKELEY, George (1685–1753) Irish Anglican bishop and philosopher, born at Dysert Castle, Kilkenny and educated at Kilkenny College and Trinity College, Dublin (where he remained, as fellow and tutor, until 1713). His most important books were published in these early years: *Essay towards a New Theory of Vision* (1709), *A Treatise concerning the Principles of Human Knowledge* (1710) and *Three Dialogues between Hylas and Philonous* (1713). In these works he developed his celebrated claim that 'to be is to be perceived'—that the contents of the material world are 'ideas' that only exist when they are perceived by a mind. In 1713 he visited London, then travelled in Italy and France for some years. He returned to Ireland in 1721 with a new-found concern about social corruption and national decadence (expressed in his anonymous *Essay towards preventing the Ruin of Great Britain*). In 1724 he became dean of Derry, but became obsessed with a romantic scheme to found a college in the Bermudas to promote 'the propagation of the gospel among the American savages'; after years of intensive lobbying in London for support and subsidies he sailed for America in 1728 with his newly married wife and made a temporary home in Rhode Island. He waited there nearly three years: the grants did not materialize, he never reached Bermuda and the college was never founded. He returned first to London and then in 1734 became bishop of Cloyne, and his remaining literary work was divided between questions of social reform and of religious reflection; both interests being represented in the curious work *Siris* (1744), which moves from the medicinal virtues of tar-water to reflections on idealism and the Trinity. In 1752 he resigned his episcopate and moved to Oxford, where he died.

BERKELEY, Sir Lennox Randal Francis (1903–89) English composer, born in Oxford. A pupil of **Nadia Boulanger**, his early compositions, the largest of which is the oratorio *Jonah* (1935), show the influence of his French training in their conciseness and lucidity, and later works, notably the *Stabat Mater* (1946), the operas *Nelson* (1953) and *Ruth* (1956), and the orchestral *Windsor Variations* (1969) and *Voices of the Night* (1973), have won him wide recognition for their combination of technical refinement with lyrically emotional appeal.

BERKELEY, Michael Fitzhardinge (1948–) English composer, son of Sir **Lennox Berkeley**. He studied at the Royal Academy of Music and with **Richard Rodney Bennett**. He has composed concertos, orchestral, chamber and choral works, including a powerful plea for peace in a nuclear age, the oratorio *Or Shall We Die?* (text by Ian McEwan). He is well known for his introductions to music on radio and television.

BERKOFF, Steven (1937–) English dramatist, actor and director. After studying at the École Jacques Lecoq in Paris, he founded the London Theatre Group, for whom he directed his own adaptations from the classics, including **Kafka**'s *Metamorphosis* (1969), in which he himself played the role of the young man who finds himself transformed into a beetle. His own plays include *Greek* (1979, a variant of the Oedipal myth transferred to contemporary London) and *West* (1983, an adaptation of the Beowulf legend); *Decadance* (1981) counterpoints the sexual and social activities of an upper-class couple with that of a working-class woman and a private detective. He has also played film villains. Other plays and adaptations include *The Penal Colony* (1968), *The Trial* (1970), *Agamemnon* (1963), and *The Fall of the House of Usher* (1974).

BERKOWITZ, David ('Son of Sam') (c.1953–) convicted American murderer, who dubbed himself 'Son of Sam' in a note to the New York Police Department. He terrorized the city for a year between 1976 and 1977, preying on courting couples and lone women. He shot dead six people and wounded another seven. A special squad of two hundred detectives was set up to trace him, but he uncannily avoided detection. At one time he was thought to have been a policeman. He was finally caught because of a parking ticket: he watched as it was stuck on his car, and then went and tore it to pieces. A woman witnessed this, noticed a strange smile on his face and reported him to the police. Berkowitz's car was traced and he was arrested. In pursuit of a plea of insanity he claimed at his trial that Satanic voices told him to kill. Deemed sane, he received a prison sentence of 365 years in August 1977.

BERLAGE, Hendrick Petrus (1856–1934) Dutch architect and town planner, born in Amsterdam. He designed the Amsterdam Bourse (1903) in a neo-Romanesque style, but he was later influenced by **Frank Lloyd Wright**, and was largely responsible for the spread of his theories in Holland. He became architectural adviser to the authorities of Amsterdam, The Hague, and Rotterdam. His other buildings include Holland House, London (1914) and the Gemeente museum in the Hague (1934).

BERLICHINGEN, Götz von See **GÖTZ VON BERLICHINGEN**

BERLIN, Irving, real name **Israel Baline** (1888–1989) Russian-born American composer who helped to launch 20th-century American popular music, born in the village of Temun in Siberia and taken to the USA as a child of four. He worked for a time as a singing waiter in a Bowery beerhall, introducing some of his own songs like 'Alexander's Ragtime Band' and 'Everybody's Doin It'. A 'soldier show' in 1918 led to musical comedy and films in the 1920s and 1930s; the 1940s saw him at the peak of his career, with the hit musical *Annie Get Your Gun* (1946) and *Call Me Madam* (1950) and a stream of songs like 'Anything You Can Do', 'Doin' What Comes Naturally', 'There's No Business Like Show Business', 'We're a Couple of Swells', and the enduring 'White Christmas'. In 1939 he wrote 'God Bless America', which achieved world-wide popularity in World War II and has become America's unofficial national anthem; in 1954 he received a special presidential citation as a composer of patriotic songs. In all, he wrote the words and music for more then 900 songs. He retired in 1962 at the age of 74, and lived as a recluse in Manhattan.

BERLIN, Sir Isaiah (1912–) Russian-born British philosopher and historian of ideas, born in Riga, Latvia. Most of his academic career has been at Oxford, where he became a fellow of All Souls in 1932, professor of social and political theory in 1957 and master of Wolfson College in 1966. He also served as a diplomat in the British embassies in Moscow and in Washington. His philosophical works include *Karl Marx* (1939), *Historical Inevitability* (1954), *Two Concepts of Liberty* (1959), and *Vico and Herder* (1976). He has also published four volumes of essays (1978–80) and translations of **Turgenev**.

BERLINER, Émile (1851–1929) German-born American inventor, born in Hanover. He worked as an apprentice printer until he emigrated to the USA in 1870, and later became chief inspector for the Bell Telephone Company. In the years after 1876 he patented several improvements to **Alexander Graham Bell**'s telephone, and lost a 15-year battle with **Edison** for the rights to a new mouthpiece which both men claimed to have invented. He scored a notable victory over Edison in 1888 when he first demonstrated the flat disc gramophone record whose performance was in every way superior to Edison's original cylinders. By 1895 he had also developed a method of making several copies of a record in shellac from a single master disc. In 1915 he invented the first acoustic tiles.

BERLINGUER, Enrico (1922–84) Italian politician, born in Sardinia into a wealthy landowning family. From his early 20s he devoted himself to making the Italian Communist party (PCI), which had been created following a split in the Socialist party in 1921, a major force in Italian politics, and became secretary general in 1972. In 1976, under his leadership, it won more than a third of the Chamber of Deputies' seats, prompting Berlinguer to propose the 'historic compromise': an alliance of the Catholics with the communists. His proposal was rejected but his vision of 'Eurocommunism' had a lasting impact.

BERLIOZ, Hector (1803–69) French composer, born in Côte-Saint-André, Isère. As a child he learned to play the flute and the guitar, but studied medicine until 1823, when he overcame his family's objection to music as a career and studied under Jean François Lesueur, rapidly producing a number of large-scale works before entering the Paris Conservatoire in 1826. During his studies he fell in love with the actress, Harriet Smithson, whom he subsequently married, and the *Symphonie Fantastique* expresses his devotion to, and a temporary disillusionment with, her. Gaining the Prix de Rome in 1830, he spent two years in Italy. After his marriage, in 1833, he combined the composition and production of his works with music criticism, until a gift from **Paganini**, for whom he wrote his symphony *Harold en Italie* (1834), made him temporarily independent. After 1842 he won a brilliant reputation in Germany, Russia, and England, but on his return to France his failure to gain a hearing for his major works drove him back to criticism. The deaths of his second wife and his son, ill-health, and his fruitless struggle to win a regular place in French music, clouded his later years. His compositions include the *Grande Messe des morts* (1837), the dramatic symphony *Roméo et Juliette* (1838), the overture *Le Carnival romain* (1843), the cantata *La Damnation de Faust* (1846), which is perhaps Berlioz's most representative composition, and his comic opera *Béatrice et Bénédict* (1860–62). As well as being the first great orchestral specialist among composers, Berlioz was one of the founders of 19th-century programme music, showing his genius as much in his lightly-scored miniatures as in his more monumental works, such as his final operatic masterpiece *Les Troyens*. A brilliantly incisive prose writer, Berlioz produced seven books, including a treatise on orchestration and an autobiography.

BERLITZ, Charles Frambach (1914–) American educationist, vice-president of Berlitz Schools of Languages and of Berlitz Publications, born in New York City. He is the grandson of Maximilian Delphinus Berlitz, who had founded the Berlitz School in 1878 as a German emigré to the USA and developed what became known as the Method. This consists of demonstrations and the identification of objects, with the instructors speaking only in the language being taught. By 1914 there were 339 schools throughout the world, but large financial losses caused by World War I led to the sale of all the schools outside North and Central America in 1921. When he was a child, Charles' father spoke to him in English, his mother in French, his grandfather in German, his cousins and aunts in Spanish; thus he learnt languages before he went to school. He graduated from Yale *magna cum laude* in 1936 and went on to restore the Berlitz company's fortunes through commissions for the services in World War II and business courses for employees going overseas afterwards.

BERNADETTE OF LOURDES, St (1844–79) French visionary, born in Lourdes, Hautes-Pyrénées. The daughter of François Soubirous, a miller, and baptized Marie Bernarde, she claimed to have received in 1858 18 apparitions of the Blessed Virgin at the Massabielle Rock, which has since become a notable place of pilgrimage. She became a nun with the Sisters of Charity at Nevers, and was beatified in 1925, canonized in 1933. Her feast day is 18 February.

BERNADOTTE Swedish royal dynasty since 1818. The House was founded by Jean Baptiste Jules Bernadotte (1763–1844) who became King **Karl XIV Johan** of Sweden. On his death he was succeeded by his son, **Oskar I**, only child of his marriage to Desirée Bernadotte. The reigning monarchs of Sweden, Norway, Denmark and Belgium are Bernadotte's direct descendants. His wife Désirée, originally Eugénie Bernardine Désirée Clary (1777–1860), was born in Marseille, the younger daughter of a wealthy silk merchant, Francois Clary. In 1794 Désirée met **Napoleon Bonaparte**, who later described her as his 'first love' but thought her too unsophisticated for marriage. Her elder sister, Julie, married **Joseph Bonaparte**. Désirée was about to become the wife of General Duphot when, in 1797, he was assassinated in her presence in Rome. In 1798 she married Bernadotte and eased his strained relations with Napoleon. She travelled to Sweden as crown princess in 1810 but disliking court etiquette soon returned to Paris. Désirée remained abroad (mainly in Paris) until 1823 when she was persuaded to rejoin her husband and in 1829 was crowned Queen Désideria. Count Folke (1895–1948), great-great-grandson of Jean Bernadotte and nephew of King **Gustavus V**, acted as mediator in both world wars. He was appointed by UNO to mediate in Palestine and produced a partition plan but was assassinated by Jewish terrorists.

BERNAL, John Desmond (1901–71) Irish crystallographer, born in Nenagh, County Tipperary. Educated by the Jesuits at Stonyhurst College, Lancashire, he won a scholarship to Emmanuel College, Cambridge, and from the first showed himself a polymath (with the lifelong nickname 'Sage'). He developed modern crystallography and was a founder of molecular biology, pioneering work on the structure of water. He progressed from a lectureship at Cambridge to professorship of physics and then crystallography at Birkbeck College, London (1937–68), and included among his major works *The Origin of Life* (1967). His wartime service, in close association with Lord **Louis Mountbatten** in Combined Operations, involved abortive attempts at creating artificial icebergs to act as aircraft carriers, as well as working on bomb tests and scientific underpinning of the invasion of the European continent. A communist from his student days, he was active in international peace activity during the Cold War and supported **Lysenko** in the USSR when his destruction of Soviet genetics drove **J B S Haldane** out of the British Communist party. Bernal's hopes for communism's possibilities for science were first shown in his *The Social Function of Science* (1939) and *Marx and Science* (1952).

BERNANOS, Georges (1888–1948) French writer, born in Paris. He did not begin to write seriously until he was 37 and had taken degrees in law and letters. A Catholic polemicist, he attacked indifference and was preoccupied with problems of sin and grace. His most memorable novels are *Sous le soleil de Satan* (1926) and *Le Journal d'un curé de campagne* (1936). He also wrote a play, *Dialogues des Carmélites*, and *Diary of My Times* (1938).

BERNARD, Claude (1813–78) French physiologist, born near Villefranche. A pharmacist's assistant at Lyon, and failing in his ambition of a literary career, he studied medicine at Paris, and in 1841 became assistant at the Collège de France to **Magendie**, with whom he worked until his own appointment in 1854 to the chair of general physiology. In 1855 he succeeded Magendie as professor of experimental physiology. His earliest researches were on the action of the secretions of the alimentary canal, the pancreatic juice, the connection between the liver and nervous system, etc, for which he received three prizes from the Academy (1851–53). Later researches were on the changes of temperature of the blood, the oxygen in arterial and in venous blood, the opium alkaloids, curare, and the sympathetic nerves. His *Introduction to the Study of Experimental Medicine* (1865) is a scientific classic.

BERNARD, Émile (1868–1941) French painter and writer, born in Lille. A fellow student with **Van Gogh** and **Toulouse-Lautrec** at the Académie of Fernand Cormon, he later worked with **Gauguin** at Port Aven. In Paris in 1889 he joined the Group Synthétiste and in 1890 launched a magazine, *La Rénovation esthétique*. He travelled for several years in Egypt and the Middle East, returning to Paris in 1901. From 1921 to 1928 he lived in Venice. He is credited with founding the so-called Cloisonnist style.

BERNARD, Tristan, originally **Paul** (1866–1947) French novelist and dramatist, born in Besançon. His first success came with the novel, *Les Mémoires d'un jeune homme rangé* (1899). In the same year he wrote a comedy, *L'Anglais tel qu'on le parle*, and from then on produced a number of light-hearted pieces with stock comic situations, which proved very popular—*Daisy* (1902), *Triplipatte* (1905), *Le Petit Café* (1911), and *Le Prince Charmant* (1921).

BERNARD OF CLAIRVAUX, St (1090–1153) French theologian and reformer, born of a noble family in Fontaines, near Dijon, in Burgundy. In 1113 he entered the Cistercian monastery of Cîteaux; and in 1115 became the first abbot of the newly-founded monastery of Clairvaux, in Champagne. He was canonized in 1174. His studious, ascetic life and stirring eloquence made him the oracle of Christendom; he founded more than 70 monasteries; and, known as the 'Mellifluous Doctor', is regarded by the Catholic Church as the last of the fathers. He drew up the statutes of the Knights Templars in 1128; he secured the recognition of Pope Innocent II; and it was his glowing eloquence at the council of Vézelay in 1146 that kindled the enthusiasm of France for the second Crusade. The influence of St Bernard as a spiritual teacher through his fervid piety and living grasp of Christian doctrine was a wholesome antidote to the dry and cold scholasticism of the age. Yet he showed a harsh severity towards **Abelard** and others whose views he rejected. His writings comprise more than 400 epistles, 340 sermons, a Life of St **Malachy**, and distinct theological treatises. The monks of his reformed branch of the Cistercians are often called Bernardines.

BERNARD OF MENTHON, St (923–1008) Italian churchman, born in Savoy, known as the 'Apostle of the Alps'. As archdeacon of Aosta he founded the hospices in the two Alpine passes that bear his name. St Bernard dogs, kept by the monks and trained to go to the aid of travellers, are named after him. He died in Novara, and was canonized in 1115. His feast day is 28 May.

BERNARD OF MORVAL, or **MORLAIX** (12th century) French Benedictine monk of Cluny in Burgundy. He is said to have been born of English parents in Morval. He is the author of a fine Latin poem, *De Contemptu Mundi*, in 3000 long, rolling, 'leonine-dactylic' hexameters, some of which were translated by **John Mason Neale** into hymns, among them 'Jerusalem the Golden' and 'The World is Very Evil'.

BERNARD OF WEIMAR See **BERNHARD**

BERNARDIN DE SAINT-PIERRE See **SAINT-PIERRE, Jacques Henri Bernardin de**

BERNARDINO See **PINTURICCHIO, ROSSI**

BERNARDINO OF SIENA, St (1380–1444)) Italian religious, born in Massa di Carrara of a distinguished family. He entered the Franciscan order in 1404, and in 1438 was appointed its vicar-general for Italy, and made himself famous by his rigid restoration of the rule. He founded the *Fratres de Observantia*, a branch of the Franciscan order, which already numbered over 300 monasteries in Italy during his day. He was canonized in 1450.

BERNAUER, Agnes (d.1435) German maiden, the beautiful daughter of a poor surgeon of Augsburg. In 1432 she was secretly married to Albrecht, only son of the reigning Duke Ernst of Bavaria, who, in her husband's absence, had her drowned as a witch at Straubing, in the Danube. Albrecht took up arms against his father; but after a year of war he consented to marry Anna of Brunswick.

BERNERS, Gerald Hugh Tyrwhitt-Wilson, 14th Baron (1883–1950) English composer, born in Bridgnorth. His early works appeared under the name of Gerald Tyrwhitt. His total output was small, but includes an orchestral fugue and several ballets, of which the best known are *The Triumph of Neptune* and *Wedding Bouquet* (after a play by **Gertrude Stein**). All his work is distinguished by a delicate and witty sense of pastiche. He was a noted eccentric and dabbled in fiction and painting.

BERNERS, John Bourchier, 2nd Baron (1467–1533) English writer and soldier, born probably in Oxford. A notable figure in the reigns of **Henry VII** and **Henry VIII**, he became captain deputy of Calais in 1520, where he translated the works of **Froissart** (1523–25) and others.

BERNERS, or **Barnes, Juliana** (14th century) English religious, and traditionally prioress of Sopwell nunnery at St Albans. She was the author of the *Treatyse perteynynge to Hawkynge, Huntynge, Fysshynge, and Coote Armiris*, which formed part of *The Book of St Albans* (1986).

BERNEVILLE See **AULNOY**

BERNHARD, Duke of Weimar (1604–39) German soldier. In the Thirty Years' War he fought in the Protestant cause, and distinguished himself in 1622 at the battle of Wimpfen. In 1631 he was one of the first to support **Gustav II Adolf** of Sweden. He commanded the left wing at Lützen (1632), and after Gustav's death had the chief command. He lost at Nördlingen (1634), and was abandoned by the Swedes, but in alliance with **Richelieu** won victories at Rheinfelden and Breisach (1638). He died after a sudden illness at Neuburg on the Rhine.

BERNHARD LEOPOLD (1911–) prince of the Netherlands, born in Jena, son of Prince Bernhard Casimir of Lippe-Biesterfeld. In 1937 he married **Juliana**, only daughter of **Wilhelmina**, Queen of the Netherlands, and the title of Prince of the Netherlands was conferred on him. During Word War II he escaped to England, where he helped to organise the Dutch Resistance. They have four daughters.

BERNHARDT, Sarah, properly **Henriette Rosine Bernard** (1844–1923) French actress, the greatest *tragédienne* of her day, born in Paris. Entering the Paris Conservatoire in 1859, in 1862 she made her début as 'Iphigénie' at the Théâtre Français, but attracted little notice. In 1867 she played minor parts at the Odéon, won fame as 'Zanetto' in Coppée's *Le Passant* (1869), and as 'Queen of Spain' in *Ruy Blas* (1872), and was recalled to the Théâtre.Français. After 1876 she made frequent appearances in London, America and Europe. In 1882 she married Jacques Daria or Damala (d. 1889), a Greek actor, from whom she was divorced shortly afterwards. In 1916 her French nationality was restored. She founded the Théâtre Sarah Bernhardt in 1899. In 1915 she had a leg amputated, but did not abandon the stage. A legendary figure in the theatre world, she died probably the most versatile actress of any age.

BERNI, or **Bernia, Francesco** (c.1497–1535) Italian poet, born in Lamporecchio in Tuscany. In 1517 he went from Florence to Rome, where he entered successively the service of his uncle, Cardinal Bibbiena, of Ghiberti, chancellor to **Clement VII**, and in 1532 of Cardinal Ippolito de' Medici. This he left a year later, and went to Florence, where, refusing to poison Cardinal Salviati, he was himself poisoned. His recast or *rifacimento* of **Boiardo**'s *Orlando Innamorato* (1542) is still read in Italy in preference to the original. He played a large part in establishing Italian as a literary language.

BERNINI, Gian Lorenzo (1598–1680) Italian sculptor, architect and painter, the dominant figure of the Baroque in Rome. Born in Naples, the son of a sculptor, Pietro (1562–1629), he came to Rome at an early age and attracted the attention of Cardinal **Scipione Borghese** who became his patron. For him he sculpted a series of lifesize statues which established his reputation as the leading sculptor of his day. Under Pope **Urban VIII**, he became the virtual artistic commissar for Rome and was constantly employed. He designed the famous baldacchino for Saint Peter's and there is much other sculptural and architectural work by him still in the Vatican. Under the next pope, **Innocent X**, Bernini fell out of favour, partly because of the structurally unsound towers on the facade of Saint Peter's for which he was responsible. In 1647 he designed the fountain of the four river gods in the middle of the Piazza Navona. Superseded in papal favour by the sculptor **Algardi**, Bernini found himself freer to concentrate on private commissions, the most famous of which is the Cornaro Chapel in the church of Santa Maria della Vittoria. The central element of the design, the sculpture depicting *The Ecstasy of Saint Theresa*, is the highpoint of the entire Baroque period. In 1665 he travelled to Paris to design the east front of the Louvre for **Louis XIV** but his designs were never executed and he returned to Rome having only completed a portrait bust of the king. As a portrait sculptor he was (and, arguably, remains) unrivalled. His last works were the tomb of Alexander VII in Saint Peter's and the small Jesuit church of San Andrea della Quirinale. He was buried in the church of Santa Maria Maggiore.

BERNOULLI a Swiss family of mathematicians and scientists which had its origin in Antwerp, but because of its dissenting views settled first in Frankfurt (1583) and later in Basel.

BERNOULLI, Daniel (1700–82) Swiss mathematician, born in Groningen, son of **Jean Bernoulli**. He studied medicine and mathematics and became professor of mathematics at St Petersburg (1725). In 1732 he returned to Basel to become professor of anatomy, then botany, and finally physics. He worked on trigonometric series, mechanics, vibrating systems and hydrodynamics (anticipating the kinetic theory of gases), and solved a differential equation proposed by Jacopo Riccati, now known as Bernoulli's equation.

BERNOULLI, Jacques, or **Jakob** (1654–1705) Swiss mathematician, brother of **Jean Bernoulli**, born in Basel, where he became professor in 1687. He investigated infinite series, the cycloid, transcendental curves, the logarithmic spiral and the catenary. In 1690 he applied **Gottfried Leibniz**'s newly discovered differential calculus to a problem in geometry, first using the term 'integral'. His *Ars conjectandi* (1713) was an important contribution to probability theory. A logarithmic spiral was at his request carved on his tombstone in Basel cathedral.

BERNOULLI, Jean or **Johann** (1667–1748) Swiss mathematician, brother of **Jacques Bernoulli**, born in Basel. He did mathematical and chemical research, and became professor at Groningen (1695) and Basel (1705). He wrote on differential equations, finding the length and area of curves, isochronous curves and curves of quickest descent. He was a quarrelsome man and a bitter rivalry developed between him and his brother. He founded a dynasty of mathematicians which continued for two generations.

BERNSTEIN, Carl (1944–) American journalist and author, born in Washington DC. With **Bob Woodward** he was responsible for unmasking the Watergate cover-up, which resulted in a constitutional crisis and the resignation of President **Richard Nixon**. For their coverage of the acknowledged investigative story of the century, Bernstein and Woodward earned virtually every major journalism award, including the Sigma Delta Chi award for distinguished service in the field of Washington correspondence and the George Polk Memorial award, and won for the *Washington Post* the 1973 Pulitzer prize for public service. Together they wrote the bestseller, *All the President's Men* (1974), which became a successful film, and *The Final Days* (1976), an almost hour-by-hour account of President Nixon's last months in office.

BERNSTEIN, Eduard (1850–1932) German socialist leader, born in Berlin. He lived in England from 1888 to 1901. An associate of **Engels**, he was an advocate of revisionism, an evolutionary parliamentary form of Marxism, and was periodically a member of the Reichstag from 1902 to 1928. He wrote *My Years of Exile* (1921).

BERNSTEIN, Leonard (1918–) American conductor, pianist, and composer, born in Lawrence, Massachusetts. Educated at Harvard and the Curtis Institute of Music, he reached fame suddenly in 1943 by conducting the New York Philharmonic as a substitute for **Bruno Walter**. His compositions include three symphonies—*Jeremiah* (1942), *The Age of Anxiety* (1949), and *Kaddish* (1961–63)—a television opera, *Trouble in Tahiti*, and the musical comedies *On the Town*, which incorporated music from his ballet *Fancy Free*, and *West Side Story* (1958), based on the Romeo and Juliet theme. His *Mass* was commissioned for the opening of the John F. Kennedy Center of the Performing Arts in 1971, and since then his works include the ballet, *The Dybbuk* (1974), *Songfest* (1977), *Halil* (1981), and a revision of his operetta *Candide* (1956/88)

BEROSUS, or **Berossus** (fl.c.260 BC) a priest of Babylon, who wrote in Greek three books of Babylonian–Chaldean history, in which he made use of the archives in the temple of Bel at Babylon, and of which unfortunately only a few fragments have been preserved by **Josephus**, **Eusebius**, and Syncellus.

BERRA, Yogi (Lawrence Peter) (1925–) American professional baseball player and coach, born in St Louis, Missouri. He played with the New York Yankees from 1946 to 1963, including 14 World Series (a record). He also set the record for most home runs by a catcher in the American League (313). He went on to manage and coach the Yankees, then did the same for their arch-rivals, the New York Mets. In 1986 he went on to coach the Houston Astros. His most famous quote was 'It ain't over 'til it's over'.

BERRI, Nabih (1939–) Lebanese politician and soldier, born in Freetown, Sierra Leone, the son of an expatriate Lebanese merchant. He studied law at Beirut University and practised as a lawyer for a time. In 1978 he became leader of Amal ('Hope'), a branch of the Shi'ite nationalist movement founded by Iman Musa Sadr. Backed by Syria, he became the main Shi'ite military force in West Beirut and Southern Lebanon during the country's civil wars, but in 1988 its Beirut branch was heavily defeated by the Iranian-backed Hezbollah ('Children of God') and was disbanded. Berri joined the Lebanese government in 1984 as minister of justice.

BERRUGUETE, Alonso (c.1489–1561) Spanish painter and sculptor, son of **Pedro Berruguete**. He became the major Spanish sculptor of the 16th century and an important figure in the introduction of the Italian Mannerist style into Spain. In Italy from 1504 to 1517 he copied work by **Michelangelo**—in whose letters his name appears—and completed an altarpiece begun by **Filippino Lippi**. The Italian artist and historian **Vasari** mentions him several times in his *Lives of the Artists*. He was appointed court painter to **Charles V** on his return to Spain, and later ennobled. In Spain he was most successful as a sculptor and his best-known work is the wood and alabaster carvings for the choir of Toledo cathedral.

BERRUGUETE, Pedro (c.1450–1504) Spanish painter, father of **Alonso Berruguete** and painter to the court of **Ferdinand** and **Isabella**. He is thought to have spent time in Italy and is probably the 'Pietro spagnuolo' who worked in 1477 on a series of paintings of famous men for the decoration of the palace library at Urbino, alongside Melozzo di Forli and Joos van Gent. His later work, at the cathedrals of Toledo and Avila, helped to introduce Italian Renaissance style to Spain.

BERRY, Charles Ferdinand, Duc de (1778–1820) French aristocrat, second son of **Charles X**, born in Versailles. During the Revolution and Empire (1789–1815) he lived in exile. In 1814 he returned to France, in 1815 was appointed commander of the troops in and around Paris, and in 1816 married Caroline Ferdinande Louise (1798–1870), eldest daughter of Francis, afterwards king of the Two Sicilies. Assassinated by the Bonapartist fanatic **Pierre Louis Louvel** in front of the Opéra, he left only a daughter; but the same year the widowed duchess gave birth to **Henri, Comte de Chambord**. In the July Revolution of 1830, when Charles abdicated in favour of his grandson, Henri, the duchess followed **Charles X** to Holyrood. In 1832 she returned to France secretly, landing at Marseilles with the intention of instigating a revolt in favour of Henri in the Vendée. She was imprisoned, but released in 1823.

BERRY, Chuck (Charles Edward Anderson) (1926–) American black pop singer, born in St Louis, Missouri. The biggest influence on pre-**Beatles** rock, he learnt to play the guitar at high school. He served three years in a reform school for armed robbery (1944–47), then worked in a factory and trained as a hairdresser before moving to Chicago in 1955 and launching his professional career. Introduced to Chess Records by **Muddy Waters**, his first success came with 'Maybellene' (1955). With songs such as 'School Days' (1957), 'Rock And Roll Music' (1957), and 'Johnny B Goode' (1958) he appealed to teenagers of all races. In 1959 he was charged with transporting a minor over state lines for immoral purposes and was jailed for two years in 1962. After his release his creativity never fully recovered although 'My Ding A Ling' (1972) was the most successful single of his career. His influence was pivotal to the British pop renaissance of the early 1960s and is evident in much of **The Beatles**' and **The Rolling Stones**' work.

BERRY, James Gomer See **KEMSLEY**

BERRY, William Ewert See **CAMROSE**

BERRYMAN, John (1914–72) American poet, biographer, novelist and academic, born in McAlester, Oklahoma. Educated at Columbia University and Clare College, Cambridge, he taught at Wayne State University, Harvard, Princeton, the University of Washington, the University of Connecticut, and University of Minnesota, where he was Regents Professor of Humanities (1955–72). His biography of **Stephen Crane** (1950) is rated highly but his reputation rests on his poetry. Often pigeon-holed as a confessional poet he disparaged the label. His first collection, *Poems*, appeared in 1942. This was followed by *The Dispossessed* (1948) and *Homage to Mistress Bradstreet* (1956), inspired by the first New England poet, **Anne Bradstreet**, which established his reputation. His major work is his *Dream Songs*, which he began in 1955: *77 Dream Songs* (1964) won the Pulitzer prize in 1965; *His Toy, His Dream, His Rest: 308 Dream Songs* (1968) received the National Book award in 1969. The complete *Dream Songs* was published in 1969. His other books include the novel *Recovery* (1973). He was a severely disturbed alcoholic who acknowledged his illness but could not overcome it. He took his own life in Minneapolis.

BERT, Paul (1833–86) French physiologist and republican statesman, born in Auxerre. A professor at the Sorbonne (1869), he did pioneering work in studying blood gases, the toxic effects of oxygen at high pressure, and anaesthetics generally. His *La Pression barométrique* (1878) was translated in 1943 because of its importance for aviation medicine. As minister of education, he founded the Universities of Lyon and Lille.

BERTHELOT, Pierre-Eugene Marcellin (1827–1907) French chemist and politician, born in Paris. He became the first professor of organic chemistry at the Collège de France (1865), was put in charge of Paris defences in 1870, was foreign minister (1895–96), and an Academician (1900). He helped to found thermochemistry, introduced a standard method for determining the latent heat of steam; and discovered many of the derivatives of coal tar, and his syntheses of many fundamental organic compounds helped to destroy the classical division between organic and inorganic compounds. He studied the mechanism of explosion and wrote many scholarly works on the history of early chemistry.

BERTHELOT, Sabin (1794–1880) French naturalist, born in Marseilles. He joined the navy as a midshipman and served in the Napoleonic wars, then joined the merchant fleet. In 1820 he went to the Canaries, where he did some teaching and became an expert botanist. He lived in the Canaries for 44 years, studying the fauna and flora and early history of the islands. With the English botanist Philip Barker-Webb he compiled a massive *L'Histoire Naturelle des Îles Canaries* (1830–50). He was later appointed French consul there (1847). Berthelot's Pipit was named in his honour.

BERTHIER, Alexandre (1753–1815) Prince of Neuchâtel and Wagram, marshal of the French empire, born in Versailles. Entering the army in 1770, he fought with **Lafayette** in the American War of Independence. In the French Revolution he soon rose to be chief of staff in the Army of Italy (1795), and in 1798 proclaimed the republic in Rome. He became chief of staff to **Napoleon**, on whose fall he had to surrender the principality of Neuchâtel, but was allowed to keep his rank as peer and marshal. Napoleon made overtures to him from Elba; but he retired to Bamberg. On 1 July 1815, at the sight of a Russian division marching towards the French frontier, he threw himself from a window.

BERTHOLLET, Claude Louis, Comte (1748–1822) French chemist, born in Talloires in Savoy. He studied at Turin, went to Paris in 1772, and in 1781 was elected a member of the Academy of Sciences. He aided **Antoine Lavoisier** in his researches on gunpowder and in forming the new chemical nomenclature, and accepted his antiphlogistic doctrines; in 1785 he showed the value of chlorine for bleaching. Following **Joseph Priestley**, he showed ammonia to be a compound of hydrogen and nitrogen. He was made a senator and a count by **Napoleon**, yet voted for his deposition in 1814, and on the Bourbon restoration was created a peer.

BERTHOUD, Ferdinand (1727–1807) Swiss horological craftsman and inventor, born in Neuchâtel. He worked in Paris from 1748. He sought to improve the accuracy of the measurement of longitude at sea by improving the design of spring-driven chronometers, of which he made about 70 during his lifetime. By 1780 he had developed a spring detent escapement, bimetallic strips for temperature compensation and other refinements, some of which were still in use a century later. Berthoud is also remembered as a prolific writer on horology and the application of machine tools to precision craftsmanship.

BERTILLON, Alphonse (1853–1914) French police officer. As chief of the identification bureau in Paris, in 1880 he devised a system of identifying criminals by anthropometric measurements (later superseded by fingerprints).

BERTIN, Louis François (1766–1841) French journalist, the founder of the *Journal des Débats* in 1799. Later it was edited by his sons, Louis Marie Armand (1801–54) and Édouard (1797–1871).

BERTOLUCCI, Bernardo (1940–) Italian filmmaker, born in Parma. An amateur filmmaker and poet, he became an assistant to **Pier Paolo Pasolini** on *Accatone* (1961). His collection of poetry, *In Cerca del Mistero* (1962), won the Premio Viareggio prize and he made his directorial début the same year with *La Commare Secca* (The Grim Reaper). A member of the Italian Communist party, his films depict the tension between conventionality and rebellion, exploring the complex relationships between politics, sex and violence with visual élan and dramatic intensity. The success of *Il Conformista* (The Conformist, 1970) and *Ultimo Tango a Parigi* (Last Tango in Paris, 1972) allowed him to make the Marxist epic *Novecento* (1900, 1976). After a number of unrealized projects during the 1980s, he returned to the cameras with *The Last Emperor* (1987), winner of nine Academy Awards.

BERTRAM, Charles See **RICHARD OF CIRENCESTER**

BERTRAND, Henri Gratien, Comte (1773–1844) French soldier and military engineer, one of **Napoleon**'s generals, born in Châteauroux. Aide-de-camp to the emperor from 1804, he shared the emperor's banishment to both Elba and St Helena. After Napoleon's death he returned to France, where in 1830 he was appointed commandant of the Polytechnic School.

BERTRAND, Louis Marie Émile (1866–1941) French author, born in Spincourt. He spent some years in Algeria, which provides a setting for *Sang des races* (1898), *La Cina* (1900), and other realistic novels and travel books. He also wrote historical novels and biographical studies of **Flaubert** and **Louis XIV**.

BÉRULLE, Pierre de (1575–1629) French prelate and theologian, born near Troyes. A leader of the Catholic reaction against Calvinism, he founded the

French Congregation of the Oratory (1611) and introduced the Carmelite order into France. He was ambassador to Spain in 1626, was minister of state until dismissed by **Richelieu**, and was made a cardinal in 1627. Many of his pupils became famous, and he widely influenced French religious teaching. He was dubbed 'Apostolus Verbi Incarnati' by Pope **Urban VIII**.

BERWALD, Franz Adolf (1796–1868) Swedish composer, born in Stockholm. He followed the family tradition (his father, Christian Friedrich Georg, of German birth, was a violinist, and his brother, (Christian) August, was a violinist and composer), and played the violin and viola in the Swedish Court Orchestra, until he won a scholarship in 1828 which took him to Berlin. On the Continent he became a friend of several composers, including **Mendelssohn** and **Berlioz**. His reputation rests largely on the four symphonies he composed during the 1840s, the *Sérieuse* and *Capricieuse* (1842) and the *Singulière* and *Eb* in 1845. In 1847 **Jenny Lind**'s appearance in his *Ein Ländlisches Verlobungsfest in Schweden* in Vienna brought him great acclaim. He returned to Sweden in 1849, but was passed over for the two prestigious conductorships. He became manager of a glassworks, and divided his time between music, business concerns and increasing involvement in social issues. In 1862, despite the great success of the revised version of his opera *Estrella de Soria*, he was unable to obtain a teaching post at the Swedish Royal Academy, though two years later he was made a fellow. It was not until 1867 that he was finally made professor of composition at the Academy. As well as *Estrella de Soria* (1841) he wrote an early opera, *Guatav Wasa* (1827), and the late *Drottningen av Golconda* (1864), many operetta and chamber music pieces. His natural, lively and fiery expression and original inspiration made him the outstanding Swedish composer of the nineteenth century.

BERWICK, James Fitzjames, 1st Duke of (1670–1734) marshal of France, illegitimate son of **James VII and II** (by **Arabella Churchill**, sister of the Duke of **Marlborough**), born in Moulins, France. Educated in France as a Catholic, he served in Hungary under Duke Charles of Lorraine. In 1687 he was created Duke of Berwick. At the 'Glorious Revolution' of 1688 he fled from England but supported his father's attempts to regain the throne. He fought through his father's Irish campaign (1689–91) and took a prominent part in the Battle of the Boyne (1690) where **William III** was victorious. In 1706 he was created a marshal of France, and in the War of the Spanish Succession (1701–14) established the throne of **Philip V** by the decisive victory over the English at Almansa (1707), and captured Barcelona (1714). After several years of inactivity, he received the command in 1733 of an army intended to cross the Rhine during the War of the Polish Succession (1733–35). While besieging Phillippsburg he was killed by a cannon ball. He left descendants in both Spain and France—the Dukes of Liria and Fitzjames.

BERZELIUS, Johan Jakob (1779–1848) Swedish chemist, born in East Götland, Sweden. He studied at Uppsala and taught at Stockholm. His accurate determination of atomic weights established the laws of combination and **John Dalton**'s atomic theory. He introduced modern symbols, an electro-chemical theory, discovered the elements selenium, thorium, and cerium, and first isolated others. His great work was rewarded with the gold medal of the Royal Society.

BERZSENYI, Daniel (1776–1836) Hungarian lyric poet, born in Heteny. Educated by his father, he won fame as a patriotic poet with his *Ode to Magyarokhoz*, inspired by the Magyar nobility's successful opposition to **Napoleon** on the Styrian Alps. Collections of his verse appeared in 1813 and 1830.

BESANT, Annie, née **Wood** (1847–1933) English theosophist, born in London of Irish parentage, the sister-in-law of Sir **Walter Besant**. After her separation in 1873 from her husband, the Rev Frank Besant, she became in 1874 vice-president of the National Secular Society. A close associate of **Charles Bradlaugh**, she was an ardent proponent of birth control and socialism. In 1889, after meeting Madame **Blavatsky**, she developed an interest in theosophy, and went out to India, where she became involved in politics, being elected president of the Indian National Congress from 1917 to 1923. Her publications include *The Gospel of Atheism* (1877) and *Theosophy and the New Psychology* (1904).

BESANT, Sir Walter (1836–1901) English novelist and social reformer, brother-in-law of **Annie Besant**. Born in Portsmouth, he studied at King's College, London, and at Christ's College, Cambridge. After a few years as a professor in Mauritius, he devoted himself to literature. His first work, *Studies in French Poetry*, appeared in 1868. In 1871 he entered into a literary partnership with James Rice (1844–82), a native of Northampton, and editor of *Once a Week*. Together they produced many novels, including *Ready-Money Mortiboy* (1872), *The Golden Butterfly* (1876) and *The Steamy Side* (1881). He himself wrote *All Sorts and Conditions of Men* (1882) and *Children of Gibeon* (1886), describing conditions in the slums of the east end of London, and other novels advocating social reform, resulting in the establishment of the People's Palace (1887) for popular recreation. He was also the author of biographical studies and works on the history of London. He was secretary of the Palestine Exploration Fund and first chairman of the Incorporated Society of Authors (1884).

BESS OF HARDWICK See the House of **CAVENDISH**

BESSARION, or **Basilius, John** (1389/1400–1472) Byzantine theologian, and one of the earliest scholars who transplanted Greek literature and philosophy into the West, born in Trebizond. As archbishop of Nicaea, he accompanied the Greek emperor, John Palaeologus, to Italy in 1438, to effect a union between the Greek and the Roman churches. Soon afterwards joining the Roman church, he was made cardinal by Pope **Eugenius IV**. Ten years later, **Nicholas V** made him bishop of Frascati; and for five years he was also papal legate at Bologna. After the fall of Constantinople, of which he had been titular patriarch, he visited Germany and endeavoured to promote a crusade against the Turks. Twice he was nearly elected pope.

BESSEL, Friedrich Wilhelm (1784–1846) German mathematician and astronomer, born in Minden. Starting as a ship's clerk, in 1810 he was appointed director of the observatory and professor at Königsberg. He catalogued stars, predicted a planet beyond Uranus as well as the existence of dark stars, investigated **Johann Kepler**'s problem of heliocentricity and systematized the mathematical functions involved, which bear his name.

BESSEMER, Sir Henry (1813–98) English inventor and engineer, born in Charlton, Hertfordshire, who invented a cheap process for manufacturing steel. A self-taught man, he learned metallurgy in his father's type foundry, and made numerous inventions. In 1855, in response to the need for guns for the Crimean War (1853–56), he patented an economical process by which molten pig-iron can be turned directly into steel by blowing air through it in a Bessemer converter. Further essential improvements were made by **Robert Mushet** (c.1856) and **Sidney Gilchrist Thomas** (1878). He established a steelworks at Sheffield in 1859, specializing in guns and, later, steel rails. English steelmasters were reluctant to accept the process, but in the USA entrepreneurs like **Andrew Carnegie** made a fortune from it.

BESSIÈRES, Jean Baptiste, Duc d'Istrie (1786–1813) French soldier, and marshal of France, born of poor parents at Preissac, Lot. He joined the army as a private in 1792, and by 1796 was captain of **Napoleon**'s escort in Italy. He distinguished himself at St Jean d'Acre, Aboukir and Austerlitz (1805), having been appointed marshal in 1804. He fought in Spain and the Russian campaign and was killed by a stray shot near Lützen on the eve of battle.

BESSMERTNOVA, Natalia (1941–) Soviet ballerina, born in Moscow. She trained at the Bolshoi Ballet School (1952–61), joining the company upon graduation. She has excelled in all the major roles of the classical repertory. She has also figured significantly in ballets devised by her husband **Yuri Grigorovich**, particularly *Ivan the Terrible* (1975).

BESSON, Jacques (c.1535–c.1575) French mathematician, engineer and inventor. He is remembered for his *Théâtre des Instruments Mathématiques et Méchaniques* (1578), which anticipated similar works by **Ramelli** and **Zonca**, Italian engineers who reflected the growing interest in machines, practical and impractical, at the end of the 16th century. His plates illustrate devices ranging from an already well-known type of dredging vessel, through improved designs for screw-cutting lathes and fire-engines, to sketches in the realms of fantasy such as a ship that would speed up as the strength of the wind dropped.

BEST, Charles Herbert (1899–1978) Canadian physiologist, born in West Pembroke, Maine, and associated with the discovery of insulin. As a research student at Toronto in 1921 he helped Sir **Frederick Banting** to isolate the hormone insulin, a remedy for diabetes. He was head of the department of physiology at Toronto from 1929 and director of medical research from 1941. He discovered choline (a vitamin that prevents liver damage) and histaminase (the enzyme that breaks down histamine), and introduced the use of the anti-coagulant, heparin.

BEST, George (1946–) Irish footballer, born in Belfast. The greatest individual footballing talent ever produced by Northern Ireland, he was the leading scorer for Manchester United in the Football League First Division in 1967–68, and in 1968 won a European Cup medal and the title of European Footballer of the Year. He soon fell from this pinnacle, becoming increasingly unable to cope with the pressure of top-class football, and was virtually finished by the time he was 25 years old. His attempted come-backs with smaller clubs in England, the USA and Scotland were unsuccessful, but in a short time he had made himself one of the game's immortals.

BESWICK, Lord Frank (1912–) English politician and aeronautical expert. He was an MP for Oxbridge from 1945 to 1959. He was parliamentary under-secretary to the minister of civil aviation from 1950 to 1951, chief whip in the House of Lords from 1967 to 1970, and the first chairman of the newly-created British Aerospace Corporation from 1977 to 1980.

BETHAM-EDWARDS, Matilda See **EDWARDS, Amelia Ann Blandford**

BETHE, Hans Albrecht (1906–) German-born American physicist, born in Strasbourg (then in Germany, now in France). The son of an academic, he was educated at the universities of Frankfurt and Munich. He taught in Germany until 1933 when he moved first to England and then to the USA, where he held the chair of physics at Cornell until his retirement (1935–75). During the war he was director of theoretical physics for the atomic bomb project based at Los Alamos. In 1939 he proposed the first detailed theory for the generation of energy by stars through a series of nuclear reactions. He also contributed with **Ralph Alpher** and **George Gamow** to the 'alpha, beta, gamma' theory of the origin of the chemical elements during the early development of the universe. He was awarded the 1967 Nobel prize for physics.

BETHELL, Richard See **WESTBURY**

BETHLEN, István (Stephen), Count (1874–1951) Hungarian statesman, born in Gernyeszeg (Cornesti), Transylvania. He was a leader of the counter-revolutionary movement after World War I, and as prime minister from 1921 to 1931 promoted Hungary's economic reconstruction.

BETHLEN GABOR, (Gabriel Bethlen) (1580–1629) king of Hungary. Born into a Hungarian Protestant family, he was elected prince of Transylvania in 1613. In 1619 he invaded Hungary and had himself elected king in 1620. Although Gabor had to come to terms with the emperor **Ferdinand II** the following year, relinquishing his claims to the Hungarian throne, Ferdinand was obliged to grant religious freedom to Hungarian Protestants and to recognize Gabor's authority in several Hungarian provinces. Gabor resumed hostilities against the empire in 1623 and 1626.

BETHMANN HOLLWEG, Theobald von (1856–1921) German statesman, born in Hohenfinow, Brandenburg. He studied law, and rose in the service of Brandenburg, Prussia, and the Empire, till in 1909 he became imperial chancellor, succeeding Prince **Bülow**. He treated the Belgian neutrality treaty as a 'scrap of paper', and played an invidious role before and after the outbreak of war in 1914. He was dismissed in 1917. He wrote *Reflections on the World War* (1920).

BETHUNE, David See **BEATON**

BETHUNE, John See **DRINKWATER**

BETHUNE, Norman (1899–1939) Canadian surgeon, born in Gravenhurst, Ontario, the son of a clergyman. He interrupted his medical studies at Toronto University to enlist in the Canadian Expeditionary Force in 1914, but, invalided home the following year, he completed his medical education and rejoined the war effort as a surgeon-lieutenant. In the 1920s he contracted tuberculosis which drew him into chest surgery, especially the surgical treatment of tuberculosis. Bethune worked as a surgeon in the Spanish Civil War in 1936–37, and in 1938–39 he was in China with the Eight Route Army, in the war with Japan. He died of septicaemia following a cut acquired while operating on a wounded Chinese soldier, and became a national hero in China.

BETJEMAN, Sir John (1906–84) English poet, broadcaster and writer on architecture, born in Highgate, London. The son of a Dutch-descended manufacturer of household objects, he was educated at Malborough School and Magdalen College, Oxford, a period covered by his blank-verse autobiography, *Summoned by Bells* (1960). Incorrigibly indolent, he left university without a degree. He marked time as a cricket master in a preparatory school and was sacked as the *Evening Standard*'s film critic before beginning to write for the *Architectural Review* and becoming general editor of the *Shell Guides* in 1934. He published the bleak 'Death in Leamington' in the *London*

Mercury in 1930 and a year later his first collection of verse, *Mount Zion; or In Touch with the Infinite* appeared. Other collections include *Continual Dew; A Little Book of Bourgeois Verse* (1937), *Old Lights for New Chancels* (1940), *New Bats in Old Belfries* (1945), *A Few Late Chrysanthemums* (1954) and *Collected Poems* (1958), of which 100 000 copies were sold of the first edition. Later (but lesser) volumes are *A Nip in the Air* (1972) and *High and Low* (1976). He is the quintessential poet of the suburbs, particular, jolly, nostalgic and wary of change, preferring the countryside to the city. Inveterately self-deprecatory, he described himself as 'the **Ella Wheeler Wilcox** de nos jours', and, in *Who's Who*, as a 'poet and hack'. He was an astute and sensitive social critic, impassioned in his abhorrence of modern architecture and town planning ('Come, friendly bombs, and fall on Slough. It isn't fit for humans now'), and beneath the froth lies a poet undeniably melancholic and serious. A national institution, he succeeded **Cecil Day Lewis** as Poet Laureate in 1972.

BETTERTON, Thomas (c.1635–1710) English actor and adapter of dramas, born in London. In 1661 he joined **D'Avenant**'s theatrical company. His wife, an actress, shared his stage triumphs. In an unfortunate speculation in 1692 Betterton lost all his savings. He was buried in Westminster Abbey.

BETTI, Ugo (1892–1954) Italian dramatist and poet, born in Camerino. He studied law and became a judge in Rome (1930–44) and librarian of the ministry of justice (1944–53). His collections of verse include *Re pensieroso* (1922), of short stories *Caino* (1929) and *Le Case* (1937); in the best of his plays, *La Padrona* (1929), life appears symbolically in the person of a cynical, masterful and attractive woman. His own profession was not spared in *Corruzione al Palazzo di Giustizia* (1944, trans as *Corruption in the Palace of Justice*, 1957), and *La fugitavva* (The Fugitive, 1953).

BETTY, William Henry West (1791–1874) English actor, better known as the 'Young Roscius', born in Shrewsbury. He made his début at the age of eleven, and met with considerable success. He retired from the stage in 1808, but after studying for two years at Cambridge, returned to it in 1812. He retired finally in 1824.

BEUCKELAER, or **Buecklelaer, Joachim** (c.1530–1573) Flemish painter who worked in Antwerp. He was very much influenced by his uncle and teacher **Pieter Aertsen**. Like Aertsen, he painted still-lifes but, within this genre, was unusual in being the first painter to specialize in depicting fish stalls.

BEUST, Friedrich Ferdinand, Count von (1809–86) Austrian statesman, born in Dresden. He was imperial chancellor (1867–71) and ambassador at London (1871–78) and Paris (1878–82). His chief achievement was the reconciliation of Hungary to Austria.

BEUYS, Joseph (1921–86) German avant-garde artist, born in Kleve. After service as a pilot in the Luftwaffe in World War II, during which he was shot down, he studied art at the Düsseldorf Academy, where he later became professor of sculpture (1961–71). His sculpture consisted mainly of 'assemblages' of bits and pieces of rubbish, which were also included as elements of 'happenings' which he organized. His work, which had links with the Italian movement known as Arte Povera, flouted the conventions even of modern art, being deliberately anti-formal and banal. An exhibition of his highly unconventional drawings toured Britain and Ireland in 1974. He was also a prominent political activist and crusader for 'direct democracy', and one of the founders of the Green party in Germany.

BEVAN, Aneurin (1897–1960) Welsh Labour politician, born in Tredegar, Monmouthshire, one of 13 children of a miner. He began work in the pits at 13 on leaving school. Six years later he was chairman of a Miners' Lodge of more than 4000 members. Active in trade unionism in the South Wales coalfield, he led the Welsh miners in the 1926 General Strike. ILP member for Ebbw Vale in 1929, he joined the more moderate Labour party in 1931, establishing a reputation as a brilliant, irreverent, and often tempestuous orator. In 1934 he married **Jennie Lee**. During World War II he was frequently a 'one-man Opposition' against Sir **Winston Churchill**. Appointed minister of health in the 1945 Labour government, he introduced in 1948 the revolutionary National Health Service. He became minister of labour in 1951, but resigned the same year over the National Health charges proposed in the Budget. From this period dated 'Bevanism', the left-wing nagging movement to make the Labour party more socialist and less 'reformist'. It made Bevan the centre of prolonged and often bitter disputes with his party leaders, but the movement began to wither late in 1956 when he became shadow foreign secretary. He ceased to be a 'Bevanite' at the 1957 Brighton party conference when he opposed a one-sided renunciation of the hydrogen bomb by Britain. The most publicized Labour politician of his time, he brought to the Commons radical fervour, iconoclastic restlessness and an acute intellect. He published *In Place of Fear* (1952).

BEVAN, Edward John (1856–1921) English industrial chemist, born in Birkenhead. After a private education he studied chemistry at Owens College, Manchester, and became a consulting chemist. In 1892, with Charles Cross, he patented the viscose process of rayon manufacture. The process uses cellulose (wood-pulp) which is dissolved and then regenerated, forming either yarn (rayon) or film (cellophane).

BEVERIDGE, William Henry Beveridge, 1st Baron (1879–1963) British economist, best known as the author of the *Report on Social Insurance and Allied Services* (1942). He was born of Scottish descent in Rangpur, India, and educated at Charterhouse and Balliol College, Oxford. As leader writer on the *Morning Post*, he made himself the leading authority on unemployment insurance, and compiled his notable report, *Unemployment* (1909, revised 1930). He entered the Board of Trade in 1908 and became director of labour exchanges (1909–16). He was director of the London School of Economics (1919–37) and master of University College, Oxford (1937–45). From 1934 he served on several commissions and committees, and ultimately was chairman of an inter-departmental committee (1941–42), out of which grew the 'Beveridge Report'. This was a comprehensive scheme of social insurance, covering the whole community without income limit. Published at the height of World War II, it was a remarkable testimony to Britain's hopes for the future, and has since formed the basis of much social legislation. He was elected to parliament as a Liberal in 1944, but defeated in 1945. He was made a peer in 1946. He was the author of the autobiographical *Power and Influence* (1953), and works on unemployment and social security.

BEVIN, Ernest (1881–1951) English Labour statesman, born in Winsford, Somerset, of poor parents, who left him an orphan before he was seven years old. In 1894 he moved to Bristol to earn his living as a van boy and later as van driver. He educated himself and came early under the influence of trade unionism and the Baptists, and was for a time a lay preacher. At the age of 30 he was a paid official of the dockers' union. In 1920 he earned himself a national reputation by his brilliant handling of his union's claims before a wage tribunal at which he was opposed by an eminent barrister. He won acceptance for most of the claims and won the title 'the dockers' KC'. Bevin was the pioneer of modern trade unionism. Out of 32 separate unions he built up the gigantic National Transport and General Workers' Union and became its general secretary (1921–40). He was one of the leaders in the General Strike (1926), served on the Macmillan Committee on finance, and furthered the work of the International Labour Organization. In 1940 he became minister of labour and national service in **Churchill**'s coalition government. He successfully attained complete mobilization of Britain's manpower by 1943 and was a significant member of the war cabinet. He began to take a keen interest in foreign affairs and became foreign secretary in the Labour government (1945–51). In this office he was responsible for the satisfactory conclusion of peace treaties with south east European countries and with Italy, despite growing Soviet disinclination to co-operate. He accepted the necessity for the Western powers to establish a federal government in Western Germany and by the Berlin air lift (June 1948–May 1949) accepted and met the Soviet challenge for the control of that city. He was largely responsible for the successful conclusion of mutual assistance (1948) and defence agreements (1949) with other European powers and America. He opposed, however, total integration of European states, believing that Britain had special Commonwealth obligations. Only with reluctance did he acquiesce in the formation of a Council of Europe. He failed to settle the difficult problem of Palestine, which he handed over to the United Nations. He concluded a new treaty with Egypt (1946) and arranged on his own initiative the meeting of the Commonwealth Foreign Ministers (1950) out of which emerged the 'Colombo Plan'. Ill-health made him relinquish office in March 1951, and he died a month later. His wife, Florence Anne (d.1968), was made DBE in 1952, largely as a recognition of her husband's services. Bevin was essentially a skilled and moderate negotiator, robust, down-to-earth, a 'John Bull' of trade unionists. He believed that he might be able to achieve world peace and conciliation in the manner he had successfully applied in union affairs, but he was essentially a realist, and his realism earned him the censure of the more left-wing elements in his party as well as the esteem of many of his political opponents. He wrote *The Job to be Done* (1942).

BEWICK, Thomas (1753–1828) English wood engraver, born a farmer's son in Ovingham, Northumberland. At 14 he was apprenticed to Ralph Beilby (1744–1817), a Newcastle engraver, became his partner in 1776, and, taking his brother John (1760–95) as an apprentice, consolidated his reputation with his woodcuts for *Gay's Fables* (1779). *Select Fables* (1784), and his own *History of Quadrupeds* (1790) further consolidated his reputation, and his *Chillingham Bull* (1789) was regarded as his masterpiece. Even finer was his *History of British Birds* (1797–1804), accurate finely decorative arrangements of black and white, with vivid and often humorous renderings of landscape and rustic life. Chief of his later works was *Aesop's Fables* (1818), in which he was assisted by his son, Robert Elliott (1788–1849), who became his partner in 1812 and also took part in the cuts for an unfinished *History of British Fishes*. Bewick's Swan was named in his honour shortly after his death.

BEYLE, Marie-Henri See **STENDHAL**

BEZA, or **BÈZE, Theodore** (1519–1605) French religious reformer, born of the noble family of De Besze at Vézelay, in Burgundy. He studied Greek and law at Orléans. He became known as a writer of witty (but indecent) verses in *Juvenilia* (1548), settled with brilliant prospects in Paris, and lived for a time in fashionable dissipation. But after an illness, he took a serious view of life, and, marrying his mistress, in 1548 went with her to Geneva, where he joined **Calvin**; and from 1549 to 1554 was Greek professor at Lausanne, publishing a drama on *The Sacrifice of Abraham.* In 1559, with Calvin, he founded the academy at Geneva and became professor of theology and first rector there. In a work on the punishment of heretics (1554) he had approved of the burning of **Servetus**. During the civil war in France he was chaplain to Condé, and later to **Coligny**. In 1563 he once more returned to Geneva, and on Calvin's death (1564) the care of the Genevese church fell upon Beza's shoulders. He presided over the synods of French reformers held at Rochelle in 1571 and at Nîmes in 1572. His best known work is the Latin New Testament.

BHARTRIHARI (fl.7th century) Hindu poet and philosopher. He was the author of three *satakas* (centuries) of stanzas on practical conduct, love, and renunciation of the world, and a Sanskrit grammarian.

BHASA (fl.3rd century) Sanskrit dramatist. He was the author of plays on religious and legendary themes.

BHAVABHÛTI surnamed 'Srî-Kantha', a great Indian dramatist, who flourished in 730.

BHAVE, Vinoba (1895–1982) Indian land reformer, born in a Maharashtra village. **Mahatma Gandhi** took him under his care as a young scholar, an event which changed his life. Distressed in 1951 by the land hunger riots in Telengana, Hyderabad, he began a walking mission throughout India to persuade landlords to give land to the peasants. A barefoot, ascetic saint, his silent revolution led to 4000000 acres of land being redistributed in four years. He was claimed to be the most notable spiritual figure in India after the death of Gandhi, whose ardent disciple he was.

BHINDRANWALE, Sant Jarnail Singh (1947–84) Indian politician and former Sikh extremist leader. Born into a poor Punjabi Jat farming family, he trained at the orthodox Damdani Taksal Sikh missionary school, becoming its head priest in 1971 and assuming the name Bhindranwale. Initially encouraged by Sanjay Gandhi (1946–80), the son and political adviser of **Indira Gandhi**, who sought to divide the Sikh Akali Dal movement, he campaigned violently against the heretical activities of Nirankari Sikhs during the later 1970s. His campaign broadened into a demand for a separate state of 'Khalistan' during the early 1980s, precipitating a bloody Hindu-Sikh conflict in Punjab. After taking refuge in the Golden Temple complex at Amritsar and building up an arms cache for terrorist activities, with about 500 devoted followers, he died at the hands of the Indian Security Forces who stormed the temple in 'Operation Blue Star'.

BHUMIBOL ADULYADEJ (1927–) king of Thailand, born in Cambridge, Massachusetts, the second son of Prince Mahidol of Songkhola and grandson of King Chuklongkorn (Rama V), who was popularized in the novel *Anna and the King of Siam.* He was educated in Bangkok and Switzerland and became monarch as King Rama VI in 1946 after the assassination of his elder brother, King Ananda Mahidol. He married Queen Sirikit in 1950 and has one son, Crown Prince Vajiralongkorn (1952–), and three daughters. As king, he has been a stabilizing influence in a country noted for its political turbulence and was active, with popular support, in helping to overthrow the military government of Field Marshal Kittikachorn in 1973. Now the longest reigning monarch in Thailand's history, he is a highly respected figure, viewed in some quarters as semi-divine, and wields considerable political influence.

BHUTTO, Benazir (1953–) Pakistani politician. The daughter of the former prime minister, **Zulfikar Ali Bhutto**, she was educated at Oxford University, where she became president of the Union. She returned to Pakistan and was placed under house arrest between 1977 and 1984, after the military coup led by General **Zia ul-Haq**. Between 1984 and 1986, with her mother Nusrat (1934–), she moved to England and became the joint leader in exile of the opposition Pakistan People's party (PPP). After the lifting of martial law in December 1985, she returned to Pakistan in April 1986 to launch a nationwide campaign for 'open elections'. She married Asif Ali Zardari, a wealthy landowner, in 1987 and, following the death of General Zia ul-Haq, was elected prime minister in 1988, barely three months after giving birth to her first child. She led her country back into the Commonwealth in 1989 and became, in 1990, the first head of government to bear a child while in office.

BHUTTO, Zulfikar Ali (1928–79) Pakistani statesman, born in Larkana in the province of Sind in British-ruled India. The son of a landed aristocrat, he graduated from the universities of California and Oxford. In 1952–53 he lectured in international law at Southampton University before returning to Pakistan to teach constitutional law. He joined Iskander Mirza's cabinet in 1958 as minister of commerce, retaining the post under President **Ayub Khan**, under whom he became foreign minister in 1963. Four years later increasing differences with the president led to his being dropped from the cabinet. In 1967 he founded the Pakistan People's party, and in 1968–69 spent some months in detention before Ayub Khan was forced to relinquish power in favour of martial law under General Yahya Khan. After Pakistan's military defeat by India and the secession of East Pakistan to become Bangladesh in 1971, Yahya Khan handed over power to Bhutto, whose party had won the army-supervised elections in West Pakistan. As president from 1971 (and prime minister from 1973), he did much to rebuild national morale, introducing constitutional, social and economic reforms, the latter particularly directed towards curbing the power and influence of the wealthiest Pakistani families. Opposition to his government strengthened among right-wing Islamic parties, and in 1977 he was accused of vote-rigging in the first elections to be held under the new constitution, in which he won a landslide victory, and in 1977 he was ousted by the army. The military leader, General **Zia ul-Haq**, instituted proceedings against corruption, under which Bhutto was convicted of conspiring to murder and sentenced to death in March 1978. In spite of worldwide protest and appeals for clemency, the sentence was carried out.

BIANCHINI, Francesco (1662–1729) Italian scholar and astronomer, born in Verona. He established an observatory at Albano, observed spots on the planet Venus, discovered three comets, and observed the Moon's surface. He was commissioned by Pope **Clement XI** to reform the calendar, and wrote *De Kalendario et Cyclo Caesaris* (1703).

BIAS (6th century BC) native of Priene in Ionia, famous for his pithy sayings and one of the 'Seven Wise Men' of Greece (the others were Chilon, Cleobulus, **Periander**, **Pittacus**, **Solon** and **Thales**).

BICHAT, Marie François Xavier (1771–1802) French physician, born in Thoirette, Jura. He studied at Lyon and Paris, and began giving lectures in 1797. In 1801 he was appointed physician to the Hôtel-Dieu. He was the first to simplify anatomy and physiology by reducing the complex structures of the organs to their simple or elementary tissues.

BICKERSTAFFE, Isaac (c.1735–c.1812) Irish playwright, born in Dublin. He was page to Lord **Chesterfield**, the lord-lieutenant. Later he was an officer of marines, but was dismissed from the service, and in 1772 had to flee the country. Of his numerous pieces, produced between 1766 and 1771, the best known is *The Maid of the Mill.*

BICKERSTETH, Edward (1786–1850) English evangelical clergyman, born in Kirkby Lonsdale, Westmorland. He made a collection of over 700 hymns in his *Christian Psalmody* (1833). His son Edward Henry (1825–1906), bishop of Exeter, wrote hymns and poems, and his grandson Edward (1850–97) became bishop of South Toyko, Japan, in 1886.

BICKFORD, William (1774–1834) English inventor, born near Camborne in Cornwall. A leatherseller by trade and unconnected with mining, he was distressed by the frequent accidents caused by premature detonation of explosive charges in mines. After several attempts he was successful in combining gunpowder and flax yarn into a reliable slow-burning fuse, which he patented in 1831.

BIDAULT, Georges (1899–1982) French statesman, born and educated in Paris, where he became a professor of history and edited the Catholic newspaper *L'Aube*. He served in both world wars, was taken prisoner in the second, was released, and took part in the French resistance movement. He became leader of the MRP (Movement Républicaine Populaire) and was prime minister in 1946 and 1949–50, deputy prime minister (1950, 1951), and foreign minister (1944, 1947, 1953–54). Although devoted to French interests, he supported many measures of European co-operation. Prime minister again in 1958, he opposed **de Gaulle** over the Algerian War, and was charged with plotting against the security of the state. He went into exile in 1962, returning in 1968.

BIDDER, George Parker (1806–78) English engineer and mathematician, born in Moreton-Hampstead. He showed an early gift for arithmetical calculations, was educated at Camberwell and Edinburgh, and became a civil engineer, inventing the railway swing bridge and designing the Royal Victoria Docks, which were opened in 1856. The 'Calculating Boy' gave public demonstrations of his gift, which also gave him a great advantage over his opponents when acting as parliamentary adviser.

BIDDLE, John (1615–62) English preacher, the founder of English Unitarianism, born in Wotton-under-Edge, Gloucestershire. In 1634 he entered Magdalen Hall, Oxford. In 1641 he was elected master of the Gloucester free school, but in 1645 was thrown into jail for rejecting in his preaching the deity of the Holy Ghost. The Westminster Assembly undertook in vain to 'settle' Biddle's case; a work by him (1647) was burnt by the hangman as blasphemous; and during the Commonwealth he was in 1655 banished to the Scilly Isles. In 1658 he was released, and continued to preach in London till after the Restoration. In 1662 he was again apprehended and fined £100. He could not pay it, so was sent to jail where he died.

BIELA, Wilhelm von (1782–1856) Austrian army officer and astronomer. In 1826 he observed the periodic comet named after him, although it had already been seen in 1772.

BIELINSKY, Vissarion Grigorievich See **BELINSKY**

BIER, August (1861–1949) German surgeon, born in Helsen, Waldeck. He became successively professor of surgery at Kiel, Greifswald, Bonn, and Berlin. He invented new methods, researched into spiral anaesthesia, and was the first to use cocaine.

BIERCE, Ambrose Gwinett (1842–?1914) American journalist, born in Meigs County, Ohio. He was the author of collections of sardonically humorous tales such as *The Fiend's Delight* (1872) *Cobwebs from an Empty Skull* (1874) and *In the Midst of Life* (1898). A misanthrope, he disappeared in Mexico.

BIERSTADT, Albert (1830–1902) German-born American painter, born near Düsseldorf where he studied art from 1853 to 1857. In America he became associated with the Hudson River School and, like his contemporary **Frederick Church**, painted vast and romantic panoramic landscapes in which truth to topographical detail is secondary to dramatic and awe-inspiring effect. Several times he travelled to the far west of America. His paintings of the Rocky Mountains gained him great popularity.

BIFFEN, (William) John (1930–) English politician. In 1953, after graduating from Jesus College, Cambridge, he went into industry as a management trainee and seven years later moved to the Economist Intelligence Unit. In 1971 he entered the House of Commons and after the 1979 general election was made chief secretary to the Treasury. A monetarist in economic policy, he favoured a more pragmatic approach in social matters than the prime minister and, although he was promoted and became a very successful leader of the Commons, he was removed from the cabinet after the 1987 general election.

BIFFEN, Sir Rowland Harry (1874–1949) English botanist and geneticist, born in Cheltenham. Educated at Cambridge, he travelled in central America studying rubber production, and in 1908 became the first professor of agricultural botany at Cambridge. Using Mendelian genetic principles, he pioneered the breeding of hybrid rust-resistant strains of wheat. He wrote *The Auricula*, published posthumously in 1851.

BIGELOW, Erastus Brigham (1814–79) American inventor, born in West Boylston, Massachussetts. He invented looms for various kinds of material, a carpet loom, and a machine for making knotted counterpanes. He was founder of the Massachusetts Institute of Technology in 1861.

BIGELOW, Jacob (1787–1879) American physician and botanist, born in Massachusetts. He held several professorships at Harvard, and was associated with the compilation of the single-word nomenclature of the *American Pharmacopoeia* of 1820, afterwards adopted in England.

BIGELOW, John (1817–1911) American writer and diplomat, born in Malden, New York. He was co-owner and managing editor of the New York *Evening Post* from 1850 to 1861, when he went as consul to Paris. From 1865 to 1866 he was American minister in France. In 1875 he was elected secretary of state for New York. He published a biography of **Benjamin Franklin** (1874) and edited his works. His son, Poultney (1855–1954), was an international journalist and traveller, and friend of Kaiser **Wilhelm II**.

BIGELOW, Melville Madison (1846–1921) American legal scholar, born in Eaton Rapids, Michigan. Educated at Michigan and Harvard, he taught law at Northwestern and Boston universities. Particularly important are his *Placita Anglo-Normannica* (1879), a collection of Anglo-Norman cases, and a *History of English Procedure* (1886); he also wrote various volumes on US law, now superseded.

BIGGERS, Earl Derr (1884–1933) American novelist, born in Warren, Ohio. He was educated at Harvard, and created the famous character Charlie Chan in his series of detective novels starting with *The House without a Key* (1925).

BIGGS, Ronald (1929–) convicted English thief and member of the gang who perpetrated the Great Train Robbery. On 8 August 1963, the night mail train from Glasgow to London was stopped at Sears Crossing in Buckinghamshire. The robbers escaped with 120 mailbags, containing over £2.5 million. Biggs was among the first five to be arrested for the theft. He had been traced by fingerprints left on a ketchup bottle and on a Monopoly board at the gang's farm hideout. He was convicted and sentenced to 25 years for conspiracy and 30 years (to run concurrently) for armed robbery. He escaped from Wandsworth Prison on 8 July 1965 and fled to Australia. Pursued by the police, he eventually settled in Brazil. There, he was saved from extradition because his girlfriend was pregnant (under Brazilian law, fathers of Brazilian children cannot be extradited). He still lives in Brazil, with an income generated largely by press interviews.

BIGI, Francesco di Cristofano See **FRANCIABIGIO**

BIGOD English noble family founded by a poor Norman knight, which in 1136 acquired from King **Stephen** the earldom of Norfolk. The second earl, Roger, took a prominent part in securing Magna Carta; in 1306 the earldom became extinct.

BIHZAD, Ustad Kamal al-Din (b.c.1440) Persian painter, born in Herat. The most famous Persian painter of the end of the 15th century, the Timurid period, he was called 'the Marvel of the Age'. He worked under the patronage of Shah Baisunkur Mirza at his academy for painters, calligraphers, illuminators and bookbinders; only a few of his works remain. Bihzad lost the stiffness and detail of the paintings of the earlier 15th century and his works are masterpieces of composition, full of action and realism, seeing the introduction of entirely new colour combinations. All of these became the trademark of a new, highly decorative style of painting, in which figures, landscape and ornaments form a two-dimensional pattern.

BIKO, Steve (Stephen) (1946–77) South African black activist, founder and leader of the Black Consciousness Movement, born in King William's Town, Cape Province. He became involved in politics while studying medicine at Natal University, and was one of the founders (and first president) of the all-black South African Students Organization (1969). His encouragement of black self-reliance and his support of black institutions made him a popular figure, and in 1972 he became honorary president of the Black People's Convention, a coalition of over 70 black organizations. The following year he was served with a banning order severely restricting his movements and freedom of speech and association, and in 1975 the restrictions were increased. He was detained four times in the last few years of his life, and died in police custody, allegedly as a result of beatings received.

BILDERDIJK, Willem (1756–1831) Dutch poet and philologist, born in Amsterdam. His voluminous poetry, a blend of rhapsody and neoclassical style, ranges from light verse to epic.

BILL, Max (1908–) Swiss artist and teacher, born in Winterthur. He trained at the Zürich School of Arts and Crafts (1924–27), and was a fellow-student with **Moholy-Nagy** and **Josef Albers** at the Bauhaus in Dessau (1927–29).Working as an architect as well as a painter, sculptor and product designer, he developed the essential Bauhaus principles of co-operative design along abstract (or 'Concrete') and purely functionalist lines; he has designed typewriters, tables, chairs, lamps and electric wall-plugs. He was a delegate to the Swiss parliament (1967–71).

BILLAUD-VARENNE, Jean Nicolas (1756–1819) a notorious terrorist in the French Revolution, born in La Rochelle. In 1795 he was transported for 20 years to Cayenne, and died in Haiti.

BILLINGER, Richard (1893–1965) Austrian poet, born in St Marienkirchen. He was the author of collections of lyrics, as well as novels coloured by peasant life in Upper Austria.

BILLINGS, Josh, pseud of **Henry Wheeler Shaw** (1818–85) American humorous writer, born in Lanesboro, Massachusetts. A land agent in Poughkeepsie, New York, he published facetious almanacs and collections of witticisms, relying heavily on deliberate misspelling.

BILLINGS, Robert William (1813–74) English architect, born in London. For seven years he was apprenticed to **John Britton**. He himself produced *Baronial and Ecclesiastical Antiquities of Scotland* (1845–52), with 240 illustrations.

BILLROTH, Theodor (1821–94) Austrian surgeon, born in Bergen (Rügen). He became professor of surgery at Zürich (1860–67) and Vienna (1867–94). A pioneer of modern abdominal surgery, he performed the first successful excision of the larynx (1874) and the first resection of the intestine (1881). A brilliant musician, he was a friend of **Brahms**.

BILLY THE KID See **BONNEY, William H**

BILNEY, Thomas (?1495–1531) English clergyman and martyr. Educated at Trinity Hall, Cambridge, he was ordained in 1519. He was opposed to the formal 'good works' of the schoolmen, and denounced saint and relic worship; and influenced **Hugh Latimer** and other young Cambridge men by his reforming views. He was cautioned by **Wolsey** (1526), made to recant by **Tunstall** (1527), but imprisoned in the Tower for a year. When he eventually resumed his preaching, he was burned at Norwich.

BINDING, Karl (1841–1920) German criminal lawyer, born in Frankfurt. Professor at Basel, Freiburg, Strasbourg, and Leipzig, he is known for his *Die Normen und ihre Übertretung* (6 vols, 1872–1920).

BINDOFF, 'Tim' (Stanley Thomas) (1908–80) English historian, born in Brighton. A graduate of London University, he taught there throughout his life, and was professor at Queen Mary College from 1951 to 1975. He wrote several important works on British and western European diplomatic history, particularly *Tudor England* (1950), which won a mass audience and (as a 'Pelican') triumphantly launched the first academic paperback history series.

BINET, Alfred (1857–1911) French psychologist, born in Nice, the founder of 'Intelligence Tests'. Director of physiological psychology at the Sorbonne from 1892, his first tests were used on his children; later, with Théodore Simon, he expanded the tests (1905) to encompass the measurement of relative intelligence amongst deprived children (the Binet-Simon tests). These were later developed further by **Lewis Terman**.

BINFORD, Lewis Roberts (1930–) American archaeologist, pioneer of the anthropologically-oriented 'processual' school of archaeology ('New Archaeology') that has powerfully influenced the intellectual development of the discipline. Trained originally in forestry and wildlife conservation, he studied anthropology at Michigan University and taught at Ann Arbor, Chicago, Santa Barbara, and Los Angeles before becoming professor of anthropology at the University of New Mexico, Albuquerque. An ethnoarchaeologist rather than an excavator, he has worked to striking effect among the Navajo, the Nunamiut Eskimo, and the Alyawara aborigines of Australia, the polemic force of his writing directing particular attention to the systemic nature of human culture and the ever-changing interaction between the technological, social, and ideological subsystems of all societies, ancient and modern. His original manifesto *New Perspectives in Archaeology* (1968, with Sally R Binford) has subsequently been elaborated in the autobiographical *An Archaeological Perspective* (1972), *Bones* (1981), and *In Pursuit of the Past* (1983).

BINYON, (Robert) Laurence (1869–1943) English poet and art critic, born in Lancaster. On leaving Oxford, where he won the Newdigate prize for poetry, he took a post in the British Museum printed-books department and from 1913 to 1933 was in charge of Oriental prints and paintings. His study *Painting in the Far East* (1908) was the first European treatise on the subject. *Japanese Art* followed in 1909, while other titles, such as *Botticelli* (1913) and *Drawings and Engravings of William Blake* (1922), show the wide range of his cultural interests. Meanwhile he had achieved a reputation as a poet untouched by *fin de siècle* ideas, but strongly in the tradition of **Wordsworth** and **Matthew Arnold**. Beginning with *Lyric Poems* (1894), he issued volumes at intervals up to his *Collected Poems* (1931). His *Odes* (1901) contains some of his best work, challenging comparison with major poets, especially 'The Sirens' and 'The Idols'. He also wrote plays—*Paris and Oenone*, *Attila*, *Arthur*—which had successful runs, and his one-act pieces are frequently performed by amateurs. He translated **Dante**'s *Divine Comedy* into terza rima (1933–43), and this discipline shows in his later work. He was Norton professor of poetry at Harvard in 1933–34. The poet of affecting melancholy and imaginative reflection, he is forever himself commemorated in his elegy 'For the Fallen' (set to music by **Elgar**), extracts from which adorn war memorials throughout the British commonwealth.

BIOT, Jean Baptiste (1774–1862) French physicist and astronomer, born in Paris. Professor of physics at the Collège de France, he made a balloon ascent with **Joseph Louis Gay-Lussac** to study magnetism at high altitudes in 1804. He travelled to Spain with **Françoise Arago** in 1806 to determine the length of a degree of longitude. He invented a polariscope and established the fundamental laws of the rotation of the plane of polarization of light by optically active substances. His son, Édouard Constant (1803–50), was a Chinese scholar.

BIRCH, Samuel (1757–1841) English merchant, the son of a London pastrycook. He became Lord Mayor of London in 1814. He was twice voted the freedom of Dublin for his support for Irish Protestantism. He was also a popular dramatist and wrote poetry. The front of his original shop in Cornhill, known as Birch's, is in the Victoria and Albert Museum.

BIRCH, Thomas (1705–66) English historian, born in Clerkenwell. He took Anglican orders in 1730, and was the biographer of **Boyle**, **Tillotson**, Queen **Elizabeth**, Prince **Henry**, and others.

BIRD, Isabella See **BISHOP**

BIRD, Robert Montgomery (1805–54) American author, born in Newcastle, Delaware. As well as two successful tragedies, he wrote *Calavar, a Mexican Romance* (1834), *Nick of the Woods* (1837), and other novels.

BIRD, Vere Cornwall (1910–) Antiguan politician. In 1939 he was a founder member of the Antigua Trades and Labour Union and then leader of the Antigua Labour party (ALP). In the pre-independence period he was elected to the Legislative Council and became chief minister (1960–67) and premier (1967–71 and 1976–81). When full independence, as Antigua and Barbuda, was achieved in 1981 he became prime minister, and he and his party were re-elected in 1984.

BIRDE, William See **BYRD**

BIRDSEYE, Clarence (1886–1956) American businessman and inventor, born in Brooklyn, New York, best known for having developed a process for freezing food in small packages suitable for retailing. He was a fur trader in Labrador, and observed that food was often kept frozen during winter. On his return to the USA he experimented and helped found the General Seafoods Company in 1924, marketing quick frozen foods. He sold the company in 1929. He was president of Birdseye Frosted Foods (1930–34) and of Birdseye Electric Company (1935–38). Some 300 patents are credited to him; among his other inventions were infrared heat lamps, the recoilless harpoon gun and a method of removing water from food.

BIRDWOOD, William Riddell (1865–1951) Australian military leader, born in India, where his father was an official of the government of Bombay. Educated at RMC Sandhurst, he was commissioned in 1885, transferring to the Indian Army two years later. In 1914 he was put in command of the Australian and New Zealand contingents then arriving in Egypt for the Dardanelles offensive. He planned the landing at Gallipoli, on Anzac Cove as it was subsequently known. Upon evacuation from the Peninsula, he took his troops to the Western Front, through the battles of the Somme and Ypres in 1916 and 1917. After the war he returned to India to command the Northern Army, becoming commander-in-chief in 1925, and retiring in 1930.

BIREN, Ernst See **BIRON, Ernst Johann**

BIRENDRA, Bir Bikram Shah Dev (1945–) king of Nepal from 1972, the son of King Mahendra, born in Kathmandu. He was educated at St Joseph's College, Darjeeling, Eton, and Tokyo and Harvard universities. He married Queen Aishwarya Rajya Laxmi Devi Rana in 1970, and has two sons and one daughter. Appointed grand master and colonel-in-chief of the Royal Nepalese Army in 1964, he became king on his father's death. During his reign, there has been gradual progress towards political reform, but Nepal remained essentially an absolute monarchy, with political activity banned, until 1990, when Birendra was forced to concede much of his power.

BIRGITTA, or **Bridget, St** (1303–73) Swedish visionary, born in Finsta in Uppland, daughter of Birger Persson, knight and lawman. She had her first revelations of the Virgin Mary at the age of seven. At the age of 13 she was married to a young nobleman, Ulf Gudmarsson, who became a lawman, by whom she had eight children. For some years she was (presumably) mistress of the robes for Queen Blanche of Namur, wife of King **Magnus Eriksson** of Sweden. After pilgrimages to Nidaros (Trondheim) in Norway and Santiago de Compostela in Spain, her husband died in 1344. Inspired by a stream of revelations, she founded the monastery of Vadstena, which became the cradle of the new order of Birgittines as a branch of the Augustinian order, and which at its peak had more than 80 convents throughout Europe. Many of her visions were of a political nature and critical of both the throne and the church in Sweden or of the papal exile in Avignon. In 1349 she travelled to Rome where she founded a Swedish hospice and gathered a circle of devoted disciples. She made a pilgrimage to Palestine and Cyprus in 1372 and died in Rome on her return in 1373. She was canonized in 1391. Her *Revelationes cælestes*, edited by her confessor, were widely circulated. Her daughter, St Katarina of Sweden (1335–81), was canonized in 1489.

BIRINGUCCIO, Vannoccio Vincenzio Agustino Luca (1480–1539) Italian metallurgical engineer, born in Siena. His *De la Pirotechnia* (1540) was the earliest printed work covering the whole of mining and metallurgy as well as other important industrial processes, pre-dating **Agricola**'s better-known *De Re Metallica*. He himself worked as a manager of iron mines, an armourer and gun-founder and a military engineer, before taking up his final post as director of the Papal foundry and munitions in Rome.

BIRKBECK, George (1776–1841) English physician and educationist, born in Settle, Yorkshire. In 1799, as professor of natural philosophy at Anderson's College, Glasgow, he delivered his first free lectures to the working classes. In 1804 he became a physician in London. He was the founder and first president of the London Mechanics' or Birkbeck Institute (1824)—the first in the UK, which developed into Birkbeck College, a constituent college of London University.

BIRKELAND, Kristian (1867–1917) Norwegian physicist, born in Oslo. Professor of physics at the university there, he demonstrated the electromagnetic nature of the aurora borealis and in 1903 developed a method for obtaining nitrogen from the air.

BIRKENHEAD, Frederick Edwin Smith, 1st Earl of (1872–1930) English lawyer and statesman, born in Birkenhead. He attended the Birkenhead Grammar School, studied at Wadham College, Oxford (fellow of Merton, 1896), and was called to the bar in 1899. He entered parliament in 1906 and by his provocative maiden speech established himself as a brilliant orator and wit. In the Irish crisis (1914) he vigorously supported **Edward Carson**'s organized resistance to Home Rule. He was attorney-general in 1915, and sat on the Woolsack as Lord Chancellor by the time he reached the age of 47. His extraordinary ability was seen at its best in the trial of **Roger Casement** (1916), when he appeared for the Crown. Despite his earlier convictions, he played a major part in the Irish settlement of 1921 and was created earl. **Stanley Baldwin** appointed him secretary of state for India (1924–28), but his conduct caused much criticism and he resigned to devote himself to a City directorship. His greatest achievements as a lawyer were the preparation of the series of Acts reforming land law, and a textbook on international law. He also wrote *Famous Trials* (1925).

BIRKETT, William Norman, 1st Baron Birkett of Ulverston (1883–1962) English lawyer and politician, born in Ulverston. He studied at Emmanuel College, Cambridge, was called to the bar (1913) and earned a brilliant reputation as counsel in notable murder trials. He was a Liberal MP (1923–24, 1929–31). A judge of the King's Bench Division (1941-50), he was chairman of the advisory committee on the famous Defence Regulation 18B during World War II and figured prominently in the summing up of the Nuremberg Trials (1945–46), in which he was the British alternate judge to Lord Justice **Geoffrey Lawrence**. A lord justice of appeal (1950–57), he was raised to the peerage in 1958.

BIRKHOFF, George David (1884–1944) American mathematician, born in Overisel, Michigan. He studied at Harvard and Chicago, and was professor at Wisconsin (1902–09), Princeton (1909–12) and Harvard (1912–39). In 1913 he proved 'Poincaré's last theorem', which **Henri Poincaré** had left unproven at his death. He had many contacts with European mathematicians and was regarded as the leading American mathematician of the early part of this century. His main work was in the theory of dynamical systems, where he extended the work of Poincaré, and in the development of ergodic theory.

BIRLEY, Eric (1906–) English historian and archaeologist of the Romano-British period, born in Swinton, Manchester. Educated at Clifton College and Brasenose College, Oxford, he became a lecturer at Durham University in 1931, specializing in the archaeology of Hadrian's Wall. During World War II he served in military intelligence. He founded the Congress of Roman Frontier Studies in 1949, and was professor of Roman-British history and archaeology at Durham (1956–71), and became founder-chairman of the Vindolanda Trust in 1970. His many publications include *Roman Britain and the Roman Army* (1953).

BIRLEY, Sir Robert (1903–82) English educationist and scholar, born in Midnapore, Bengal. Educated at Rugby and Balliol College, Oxford, he taught history at Eton from 1926. He became headmaster of Charterhouse in 1935, was adviser on education to the deputy military governor, British Zone, Germany, in 1947, and was headmaster of Eton (1949–62). He was appointed visiting professor of education at Witwatersrand (1962–67) and professor of social science, City University (1967). Bibliophile and scholarly beyond the norm for a schoolmaster, he towered physically and metaphysically above other headmasters. His early reputation as a radical led to the sobriquet 'Red Robert'. He cared deeply for people and was passionate in his concern for South Africans. A vibrant teacher, he was essentially a traditionalist and perhaps the last great figure of public schools before they came to be called 'independent schools'.

BIRNEY, James Gillespie (1792–1857) American anti-slavery leader, born in Dernville, Kentucky. He published the *Philanthropist* (1836), and stood as the anti-slavery presidential candidate in 1840 and 1844 (Liberal party).

BIRON, Armand de Gontaut, Baron de (1524–92) French soldier and marshal of France under **Henri III** and commander-in-chief under **Henri IV**. He fought against the Huguenots at Monconfour (1569), where he was appointed grand master of artillery by **Charles IX**. He was killed at the siege of Épernay.

BIRON, Armand Louis de Gontaut, Duc de Lauzun, Duc de (1749–93) French soldier. He fought with **Lafayette** in the American War of Independence (1775–83), joined the revolutionists in France and defeated the Vendeans at Parthenay in 1793; but was guillotined.

BIRON, Bühren, Ernst Johann (1690–1772) Duke of Courland. He assumed the name and arms of the French Ducs De Biron, when, as favourite of **Anna Ivanovna**, he became the real ruler of Russia on her ascent to the Russian throne in 1730. He was blamed for most of the ills which befell Russia at this time, but greatly improved the country's administration. In 1737 Anna made him Duke of Courland. On the death of the empress (1740) he assumed the regency and acted with great moderation, but was arrested and banished for a time to Siberia. **Peter III** allowed him to return in 1762 and he was eventually given back his titles.

BIRON, Charles de Gontaut, Duc de (1562–1602) French soldier, son of **Armand de Biron** (1524–92), marshal of France from 1594. A bosom companion of **Henri IV** of France, he earned the nickname of 'Fulmen Galliae'. But later he conspired against Henri with Spain, and was beheaded in the Bastille.

BIRRELL, Augustine (1850–1933) English politician and writer, born in Wavertree, Liverpool. Educated at Amersham and Trinity Hall, Cambridge, he was called to the bar in 1875 and was Liberal MP for West Fife (1889–1900) and Bristol North (1906–18). He was president of the board of education (1905–07) and put through the 1906 Education Act, was chief secretary for Ireland (1907–16), and founded the National University of Ireland (1908); he resigned after the Easter Rising of 1916. He was the author of delightful volumes of essays, *Obiter Dicta* (1884–87) and *More Obiter Dicta* (1924), whose charm and unobtrusive scholarship inspired the verb 'to birrell' meaning to comment on life gently and allusively, spicing good nature with irony. He also wrote Lives of **Charlotte Brontë** (1887), **William Hazlitt** (1902), and **Andrew Marvell** (1905) for the English Men of Letters series.

BIRTWHISTLE, Sir Harrison (1934–) English composer, born in Accrington, Lancashire. He began his career as a clarinettist, studying at the Royal Manchester College of Music and the Royal Academy of Music in London. While in Manchester he formed, with other young musicians including **Peter Maxwell Davies** and **John Ogdon**, the New Manchester Group for the performance of modern music. He was director of music at Cranborne Chase School (1962–65) and then spent two years studying in America. In 1967 he formed the Pierrot Players, again with Maxwell Davies; much of his work was written for them and for the English Opera Group, and he composed pieces for many of the British and international music festivals. In 1975 he was appointed musical director of the National Theatre. His early work was influenced by **Stravinsky** and by the medieval and renaissance masters; his first composition, *Refrains and Choruses*, is dated 1957, but it was two works of 1965, the instrumental *Tragoedia* and vocal/instrumental *Ring a Dumb Carillon*, that established him as a leading composer. Among his later works are the operas *Punch and Judy* (1966–67) and *The Masque of Orpheus* (1974–82), the 'dramatic pastoral' *Down by the Greenwood Side* (1969), *The Fields of Sorrow* (1971), *On The Sheer Threshold of the Night* (1980) and *Pulse Sampler* (1981).

BISCOE, John See **ENDERBY, Samuel**

BISCOP See **BENEDICT BISCOP**

BISHOP, Elizabeth (1911–79) American poet, born in Worcester, Massachusetts. A graduate of Vassar College, she was noted for the precision, elegance and imaginative power of her verse, which often evokes images of nature. She received a Pulitzer prize for her first two collections, *North and South* (1946) and *Cold Spring* (1955). She lived in Brazil 1952–67, and taught at Harvard from 1970.

BISHOP, Sir Henry Rowley (1786–1855) English composer, born in London. He exercised considerable influence in his lifetime by his glees and 88 operas, few of which have survived though some songs from them have remained popular, including 'Home, Sweet Home', and 'Lo!, Here the Gentle Lark'. He was musical director at Covent Garden (1810–24), and received the first knighthood conferred upon a musician in 1842. He held professorships at Edinburgh and Oxford.

BISHOP, Isabella, née **Bird** (1831–1904) British writer and traveller, born in Edinburgh. From 1854 she visited Canada and the United States, the Sandwich Islands, the Rocky Mountains, Yezo, Persia and Kurdistan, Tibet, and Korea. She wrote *Englishwoman in America* (1856) and many other travel books. In 1881 she married another traveller, Dr John Bishop. In 1892 she was elected the first woman fellow of the Royal Geographical Society.

BISHOP, John Peale (1892–1944) American poet, fiction writer and essayist, born in Charles Town, West Virginia. He was managing editor of *Vanity Fair* after

World War I but joined the exodus of American literati to Paris in 1922. In debt to the 17th-century metaphysical poets, his collections include *Green Fruit* (1917), *Now with His Love* (1933) and *Minute Particulars* (1936). His *Collected Poems* was published in 1948. A year before he died he was appointed consultant in comparative literature at the Library of Congress.

BISHOP, William Avery (1894–1956) Canadian airman, born in Owen Sound, Ontario. A member of the Canadian Expeditionary Force in 1914, he joined the Royal Flying Corps in 1915, and became the most successful Allied 'ace' of the war, officially credited with the destruction of 72 enemy aircraft. In 1917 he was awarded the VC for singlehandedly downing seven German planes. A lieutenant colonel by 1918, he was appointed the first Canadian air marshal in 1939, and was director of the Royal Canadian Air Force throughout World War II.

BISMARCK, Otto Edward Leopold von, Prince Bismarck, Duke of Lauenburg (1815–98) Prusso-German statesman, born on the ancestral estate at Schönhausen in Brandenburg. He studied law and agriculture at Göttingen, Berlin, and Greifswald. In 1847 he became known in the new Prussian parliament as an ultra-royalist, and opposed equally the constitutional demands of 1848 and the scheme of a German empire, as proposed by the Frankfurt parliament of 1849. In 1851, as Prussian member of the resuscitated German diet of Frankfurt, he resented the predominance of Austria, and demanded equal rights for Prussia. In 1859 he was sent as minister to St Petersburg, and in 1862 to Paris. Recalled the same year to take the foreign portfolio and the presidency of the cabinet, and not being able to pass the military reorganization bill and the budget, he closed the chambers, announcing that the government would be obliged to do without them. For four years the army reorganization went on, when the death of the king of Denmark (1863) re-opened the Schleswig-Holstein question, and excited a fever of national German feeling, which led to the defeat of Denmark by Austria and Prussia, and the annexation of the duchies. This again brought about the quarrel between Prussia and Austria and the 'Seven Weeks' War', which ended in the humiliation of Austria at the battle of Königgratz (1866), and the reorganization of Germany under the leadership of Prussia. During this Bismarck was the guiding spirit, and, from being universally disliked, became highly popular. The action of France in regard to the candidature of Prince Leopold of Hohenzollern for the throne of Spain gave Bismarck the opportunity of carrying into action the intensified feeling of unity amongst Germans. During the Franco-Prussian war, which he deliberately provoked (1870–71), he was the spokesman of Germany; and in 1871 he dictated the terms of peace to France. Created a count in 1866, he was now made a prince and chancellor of the new German empire. After the peace of Frankfurt the sole aim of his policy, domestic and foreign, was to consolidate the young empire and secure it, through political combinations, against outside attack. His long and bitter struggle with the Vatican, called the Kulturkampf, was a failure, but apart from this his domestic policy was marked by universal suffrage, reformed coinage, codification of law, nationalization of the Prussian railways, repeated increase of the army, a protective tariff (1879), and various attempts to combat socialism and to establish government monopolies. To counteract Russia and France, he formed in 1879 the Austro-German Treaty of Alliance (published in 1888), which Italy joined in 1886; and he presided over the Berlin Congress in 1878. The phrase 'man of blood and iron' was used by the 'Iron Chancellor' in a speech in 1862. Two attempts were made on his life (1866, 1874). Disapproving the policy of the emperor **William II**, along with his son Herbert (1849–1904), foreign secretary, he resigned the chancellorship in March 1890, becoming Duke of Lauenburg. Although for years he had been a caustic critic of imperial measures, he was reconciled to his sovereign in 1894.

BITZIUS, Albert, pseud of **Jeremias Gotthelf** (1797–1854) Swiss author, born in Morat, in Freiburg canton. He studied at Berne, and in 1832 became pastor of Lützelfluh, in Emmenthal, and wrote many novels of Swiss village life, including *Käthi* (1847) and *Uli der Knecht* (1841, trans 1888).

BIXIO, Girolamo Nino (1821–73) Italian soldier, born in Chiaveri near Genoa. A merchant captain by training, he became one of **Garibaldi**'s most trusted followers. He fought in several campaigns, and was elected senator in 1870.

BIYA, Paul (1933–) Cameroonian politician, born in Muomeka'a. He completed his education at Paris University and from 1962 held a number of ministerial posts under President Adhidjo before being appointed prime minister in 1975. He was nominated as president-designate and there was a smooth transfer of power in 1982. He strengthened his position by abolishing the post of prime minister and appointing his own nominees to the cabinet. Despite an attempt to overthrow him by supporters of the former president, he was re-elected in 1988 with more than 98% of the popular vote.

BIZET, Georges, properly **Alexandre César Léopold** (1838–75) French composer, born in Paris, where he studied at the Conservatoire under Halévy, whose daughter he married in 1869, and in Italy. Although he won the Prix de Rome in 1857 with *Le Docteur Miracle*, his efforts to achieve a reputation as an operatic composer with such works as *Les Pêcheurs de Perles* (1863) and *La Jolie Fille de Perth* (1867) were largely unsuccessful. His charming incidental music to Daudet's play *L'Arlésienne* (1872) was remarkably popular and survived in the form of two orchestral suites. On these and on his masterpiece, the four-act opera *Carmen*, completed just before his untimely death of heart disease, Bizet's reputation is based. *Carmen*, derived from Mérimée's story, proved too robust at first for French taste. By its delicate orchestration and truly remarkable operatic intensity it successfully survived the current criticisms of being too Wagnerian and not sufficiently Spanish and gypsy-like for its theme. A symphony in C was first performed in 1935.

BJELKE-PETERSEN, Sir Jo (Johannes) (1911–) Australian politician, long-serving premier of Queensland, born in New Zealand of Danish parents; his father was pastor of the village of Dannevirke, North Island. In 1913 they moved to Kingaroy, Queensland. He entered state politics in 1947 as a Country party member of the Legislative Assembly, becoming a minister in 1963. In 1968, as a result of his firm stand on law and order, he was made police minister, then deputy leader and, following the sudden death of Jack Pizzey, became premier of Queensland. A vocal supporter of states' rights as against federal intervention, he controlled a strongly right-wing government, first in coalition with the Liberal party and after 1983 in his own right. He was knighted in 1982 and retired from the premiership in 1987.

BJERKNES, Jacob Aall Bonnevie (1897–1975) Norwegian-born American meteorologist, born in Stockholm, son of the Norwegian physicist **Vilhelm Bjerknes**. Professor of the Geophysical Institute at Bergen, with his father he formulated the theory of cyclones on which modern weather forecasting is based. In 1940 he became the first professor of meteorology at the university of California, USA, and was naturalized in 1946. He was awarded the **Symons** gold medal by the Royal Meteorological Society in 1940.

BJERKNES, Vilhelm Firman Koren (1862–1951) Norwegian physicist and meteorologist. He was professor at Stockholm (1895–1907), Kristiania (now Oslo, 1907–12), Leipzig (1912–17), and Oslo (1926–51), and was founder-director of the Bergen Geophysical Institute (1917–26). A pioneer of weather forecasting, he studied the large-scale dynamics of air masses and with his son Jacob (1897–1975), T Bergeron and others, he developed the theory of fronts (boundaries between distinct air masses) which is essential to modern weather prediction.

BJÖRNSSON, Sveinn (1881–1952) Icelandic diplomat and statesman, and first president of the republic of Iceland (1944–52). Born in Copenhagen, the son of an Icelandic newspaper editor, he went to school in Iceland and studied law at Copenhagen. He was on Reykjavík town council from 1912 to 1920, and a member of parliament (Althing) from 1914 to 1916 and 1920. During World War I he was a special envoy to the USA and Britain, and was then ambassador to Denmark from 1920 to 1924 and from 1926 to 1941. During the German occupation of Denmark he was elected regent of Iceland, and when the republic was declared in 1944 he was elected president, and re-elected in 1948. He died in office.

BJÖRLING, Jussi, properly **Johan Jonaton** (1911–60) Swedish tenor, born in Stora Tuna. From 1916 he toured as a treble with his tenor father, David, and two brothers as the Björling Male Voice Quartet. From 1928 he studied at the Stockholm Conservatory with **Joseph Hislop** and John Forsell. His début as principal with the Royal Swedish Opera was as Don Ottavio (1930) and he sang regularly with the company until 1938. By then he was in great international demand, making successful débuts at Chicago (1937), New York (1938), Covent Garden (1939) and San Francisco (1940). Although his repertoire was mainly Italian he sang rarely in Italy, but became a favourite in the USA, especially at the Metropolitan, New York, and as a recording artist. His qualities were purity of tone, warm evenness throughout his register, and great power, seemingly effortless and unstrained, on high notes. Vocal beauty and fine musicianship compensated for his rather basic skills as an actor.

BJØRNSON, Bjørnsterne Martinius (1832–1910) Norwegian writer and statesman, born in Kvikne in Österdalen, the son of a pastor. Educated at Molde, Christiania (now Oslo) and Copenhagen, he was a playwright and novelist of wide-ranging interests, a lifelong champion of liberal causes and constantly active politically as a Home Ruler and republican. His first successful drama was *Mellem Slagene* (Between Blows, 1856), about the Norwegian civil wars. An ardent patriot, he sought to free the Norwegian theatre from Danish influence and revive Norwegian as a literary language; he worked as a newspaper editor simultaneously with being director of Bergen's Ole Bull theatre (1857–59) and of the Oslo Theatre (1863–67), where he recreated Norway's epic past in saga-inspired dramas such as *Kong Sverre* (1861) and his trilogy about the pretender *Sigurd Slembe* (1862). He was named Norway's national poet, and his poem, *Ja, vi elsker dette landet* (Yes, We Love This Land of Ours, 1870) became the national anthem. His other major works include the novel *Fiskerjenten* (The Fisher Girl, 1868), the epic poem *Arnljot Gelline* (1870), and his greatest plays, *Over Evne I and II* (Beyond One's Powers, 1893, 1895), about a clergyman capable of working miracles but incapable of responding to his wife's love. He was awarded the 1903 Nobel prize for literature.

BJORNSON, Maria (1949–) British stage designer, born in Paris of Norwegian and Romanian parents. She has designed sets and costumes for straight drama and opera. She worked extensively in repertory, at the Glasgow Citizens' Theatre and elsewhere. For the Royal Shakespeare Company she has designed several productions including *A Midsummer Night's Dream* (1981), *The Tempest* (1982), *Hamlet* and *Camille* (1984). In 1986 she designed **Hal Prince**'s production of **Andrew Lloyd Webber**'s *The Phantom of the Opera* and in 1989, **Trevor Nunn**'s production of Lloyd Webber's *Aspects of Love*. She has worked for Huston Opera, Netherlands Opera, the Royal Opera House, and English National Opera. A painterly designer, she has an eye both for detail and overall effect, and expressive use of fabrics.

BLACK, Adam (1784–1874) Scottish publisher, born in Edinburgh, the son of a master builder. Educated at the High School of Edinburgh, he was apprenticed at 15 to an Edinburgh bookseller. He set up his own bookshop in 1807, and started publishing in 1817. In 1826 he bought the *Encyclopaedia Britannica* after **Archibald Constable**'s failure and in 1854 he bought the rights to **Scott**'s novels from **Cadell**'s representatives. He was lord provost between 1843 and 1848, and Liberal MP for the burgh (1856–65).

BLACK, Hugo Lafayette (1886–1971) American judge, born in Clay County, Alabama. He practised law in Alabama and became a police court judge. In 1926 he entered the US senate and as a liberal leader promoted the Tennessee Valley Authority and federal wages and hours laws. Appointed to the Supreme Court of the US in 1937, he sat there till his death. He frequently dissented, upholding individual freedoms against restrictions but not pressing them to unrestricted licence. He held that the Fourteenth Amendment made the Bill of Rights generally applicable to the states and that the First Amendment's guarantees of freedoms were absolute.

BLACK, Joseph (1728–99) Scottish chemist, born in Bordeaux, the son of a wine merchant. Educated at Belfast, Glasgow, and Edinburgh, in an extension of his MD thesis (1756) he showed that the causticity of lime and the alkalis is due to the absence of the 'fixed air' (carbon dioxide) present in limestone and the carbonates of the alkalies. In 1756 he succeeded **William Cullen** as professor of anatomy and chemistry at Glasgow, but soon after exchanged duties with the professor of the Institutes of Medicine, practising also as a physician. Between 1756 and 1761 he evolved the theory of 'latent heat' on which his scientific fame chiefly rests. In 1766 he succeeded Cullen in the chair of medicine and chemistry at Edinburgh.

BLACK, Sir Misha (1910–77) Russian-born British designer and writer on design. Trained as an architect, his early work was mainly in commercial exhibition design. He designed the famous pre-war cafés for Kardomah, for which firm he was consultant from 1936 to 1950. Very much a team designer, he was a founder of one of the earliest design consultancies, the Industrial Design Partnership (1935), and later of the Design Research Unit (1945), both with **Milner Gray**. He contributed to the 'Britain Can Make It' exhibition in 1946 and to the 'Festival of Britain' in 1951. His outstanding post-war design work was for British Rail,

London Transport and P & O. He became a royal designer for industry in 1957, and was professor of industrial design at the Royal College of Art, London (1959–75).

BLACK, William (1841–98) Scottish novelist, born in Glasgow. Educated at the Glasgow School of Art, he moved to London as a journalist. An early member of the 'Kailyard School', his first success was *A Daughter of Heth* (1871), followed by a succession of sterotypical novels usually with Highland settings.

BLACKADDER, John (1615–86) Scottish Covenanting minister of Troqueer, near Dumfries. Deprived of his living after the Restoration, in 1662, he preached in conventicles in defiance of the law and was outlawed in 1674. He fled to Rotterdam, but returned to Scotland in 1679, and in 1681 was imprisoned on the Bass Rock, where he died. His fifth son, John (1664–1729), became colonel in command of the Cameronians in 1709.

BLACKBURN, Colin, Lord (1813–96) English judge, born in Killearn, Stirlingshire. Educated at Eton and Trinity College, Cambridge, he developed a large practice in commercial cases and became a judge in 1859. He was a member of the Judicature Commission which reshaped the English court system (1869–75) and in 1876 was appointed one of the first two lords of appeal in ordinary; he sat as a law lord till 1886, gaining a high reputation as a judge. Many of his opinions are still valuable, his judgments showing wide learning and a strong emphasis on the underlying principle. He also published, in 1845, a book on the passing of property in the sale of goods which was important in its day and is still useful.

BLACKBURN, Helen (1842–1903) Irish social reformer, born in Knightstown, County Kerry. The daughter of a civil engineer and inventor, in 1859 she moved with her family to London. A staunch believer in the vote as the key to women's equality, she was secretary of the National Society for Women's Suffrage from 1874 to 1895. Her many publications include a *Handbook for Women engaged in Social and Political Work* (1881), and *Women's Suffrage: a Record of the Movement in the British Isles* (1902). In 1899, with Jessie Boucherett (owner of *The Englishwoman's Review* which Blackburn edited, 1881–90), she founded the Freedom of Labour Defence League, aimed at maintaining women's freedom and their powers of earning. In 1903 (with Nora Vynne) she published *Women under the Factory Act*.

BLACKBURN, Robert (1885–1955) British aircraft designer, born in Leeds. He designed his first plane in 1910, and founded the Blackburn Aircraft Company in 1914 under contract to build military biplanes.

BLACKET, Edmund Thomas (1817–83) English-born Australian architect, born in Southwark, son of a London cloth merchant. He arrived in Sydney in 1842; one year later he had designed his first church and was appointed chief architect for the diocese by **William Broughton**, first (and only) Anglican bishop of Australia. He quickly built up a steady practice but in 1849 became government architect for New South Wales, returning to private practice in 1854 to design the new University of New South Wales, whose Great Hall is generally considered the finest building of its style in the southern hemisphere. His academic and ecclesiastical work, including cathedrals in Sydney and Perth, was Victorian Gothic in style, but in commercial designs, for banks and hotels, he adopted classical forms.

BLACKETT, Patrick Maynard Stuart, Baron (1897–1974) English physicist. Educated at Dartmouth College, he served in the Royal Navy during World War I. He then entered Magdalene College, Cambridge, and studied physics at the Cavendish Laboratory. He was the first to photograph, in 1925, nuclear collisions involving transmutation; in 1932, independently of **Carl Anderson**, he discovered the positron; he pioneered research on cosmic radiation, and, in World War II, operational research. He was professor at London University (1933–37), Manchester University (1937–53), and the Imperial College of Science (1953–65). He was awarded the Nobel prize for physics in 1948.

BLACK HAWK (1767–1838) Chief of the Sauk and Fox Indians, born in Illinois. He was an ally of the British in the war of 1812, and opposing the removal west of his tribe, fought against the USA in 1831–32 but was defeated at Bad Axe River in Wisconsin.

BLACKIE, John (1782–1874) Scottish publisher. In 1809 he founded the Glasgow firm which still bears the name.

BLACKIE, John Stuart (1809–95) Scottish scholar, born in Glasgow. Educated at Aberdeen, Edinburgh, and briefly abroad, in 1834 he was called to the Scottish bar and published a metrical translation of **Goethe**'s *Faust*. His magazine articles on German subjects became widely known and he became professor of humanities at Aberdeen (1841–52) and of Greek at Edinburgh till 1882. He helped to reform the Scottish universities, was a keen advocate of Scottish nationalism, and raised funds for the endowment of a Celtic chair at Edinburgh. He published prolifically on philosophy, history, legal subjects, and on language teaching. His two lectures in Aberdeen in 1852 'On the Studying and Teaching of Languages' set out the first recorded account of what became known as the 'direct method'.

BLACKLOCK, Thomas (1721–91) Scottish poet and clergyman, born in Annan, Dumfriesshire. Blind from smallpox in infancy, he was educated at Edinburgh University. He became a minister in Kirkcudbright in 1759 but returned to Edinburgh in 1764. He published a volume of poems in 1760, but he is remembered for a letter of encouragement to **Robert Burns** after the publication of the Kilmarnock edition, which helped persuade the latter to remain in Scotland.

BLACKMAN, Frederick Frost (1866–1947) English botanist, born in London. Educated at Mill Hill School, he studied medicine at St Bartholomew's Hospital but switched to botany and studied science at St John's College, Cambridge. Thereafter he worked at the Cambridge Botany School from 1891 to 1936. He is renowned for his fundamental research on the respiration of plants, and on the limiting factors affecting their growth.

BLACKMORE, Richard Doddridge (1825–1900) English novelist, born in Longworth, Berkshire. Educated at Blundell's School, Tiverton, and Exeter College, Oxford, he was called to the bar at the Middle Temple in 1852, and practised for a while, but poor health made him take to market gardening and literature in Teddington. After publishing several collections of poetry, he found his real bent in fiction. *Clara Vaughan* (1864) was the first of 15 novels, mostly with a Devonshire background, of which *Lorna Doone* (1869) is his masterpiece and an accepted classic of the West Country. Other novels include *The Maid of Sker* (1872), *Alice Lorraine* (1875) and *Tommy Upmore* (1884).

BLACKMUN, Harry Andrew (1908–) American jurist, born in Nashville, Illinois. He graduated from Harvard in mathematics (1929) and law (1932), and was called to the Minnesota bar in 1932. He served as clerk to the presiding judge of the US 8th district Court of Appeals (1932–33), built up a law practice, taught at the St Paul College of Law and the University of Minnesota Law School, and became resident counsel for the Mayo Clinic at Rochester (1950–59). He was Judge of the 8th Circuit of US Court of Appeals (1959–70). In 1970 he was nominated by President **Nixon** to the US Supreme Court. He has been a quiet but effective influence in moderating the views of his more conservative colleagues.

BLACK PRINCE See **EDWARD III**

BLACKSTONE, Sir William (1723–80) English jurist, born in London, the posthumous son of a silk mercer. In 1738 he obtained a scholarship from Charterhouse to Pembroke College, Oxford; in 1741 entered the Inner Temple; in 1744 was elected a fellow of All Souls; and in 1746 was called to the bar, but failed to attract either notice or practice. In 1749 he succeeded an uncle as recorder of Wallingford, Berkshire; and in 1753 he delivered lectures privately at Oxford on the law of England. In 1758, a Mr Viner having left £12000 to endow a chair of English law at Oxford, Blackstone was appointed first Vinerian professor. Next year he returned to Westminster; and as the doctrines which he taught had commended him to the Tory government, he was made a king's counsel in 1761. MP for Hindon, in Wiltshire (1761–70), and principal of New Inn Hall, Oxford, he was made solicitor-general to the queen in 1763 and a judge of the court of common pleas, 1770–80. From 1765 to 1769 he published his celebrated *Commentaries on the Laws of England*, which earned him a fortune. This work became the most influential exposition of English law in point of style and accuracy, setting out the structure of English law and explaining its major principles.

BLACKWELL, Alexander (c.1700–c.1747) Scottish adventurer, born in Aberdeen, possibly a younger son of the principal of Marischal College. About 1730 he was a printer in London, and, becoming bankrupt in 1734, was supported in prison by his wife, who published a *Herbal* (2 vols, 1737–39) with 500 cuts, drawn, engraved, and coloured by herself, her husband adding their Latin names and a brief description of each. In 1742 he turned up in Sweden where, having cured the king of an illness, he was appointed a royal physician and undertook the management of a model farm. In 1747 he was arrested on a trumped-up charge of conspiring against the Constitution, and beheaded.

BLACKWELL, Sir Basil Henry (1889–1984) English publisher and bookseller, born in Oxford, son of the chairman of the famous Oxford bookshop (founded in 1846). He was educated at Magdalen College School and Merton College, and joined the family business in 1913, but also published independently, founding the Shakespeare Head Press (1921). He succeeded to the chairmanship in 1924 and from that time joined the family bookselling interest with that of publishing, mostly on academic subjects.

BLACKWELL, Elizabeth (1821–1910) English-born American physician, the first woman doctor in the USA, born in Bristol, sister of **Emily Blackwell**. Her father emigrated to the USA in 1832 and died six years later, leaving a widow and nine children. Elizabeth helped to support the family by teaching, devoting her leisure to the study of medical books. After fruitless applications for admission to various medical schools, she entered that of Geneva, in New York State, and graduated in 1849. She next visited Europe and, after much difficulty, was admitted into La Maternité in Paris, and St Bartholomew's Hospital in London. In 1851 she returned to New York where she established a successful practice; after 1868 she lived in England until her death.

BLACKWELL, Emily (1826–1910) English-born American doctor, born in Bristol, sister of **Elizabeth Blackwell**. The first woman doctor to undertake major surgery on a considerable scale, she was educated at Cleveland (Western Reserve) University, followed by work in Europe where she was assistant to Sir **James Simpson**. In 1856 she helped open her sister's dispensary in New York City (The New York Infirmary for Indigent Women and Children). From 1869 to 1910 she ran the dispensary, and from 1869 to 1899 was dean and professor of obstetrics and diseases of women at the Women's Medical College which was attached to the infirmary.

BLACKWOOD, Algernon Henry (1869–1951) English novelist, born in Kent. He was educated at Wellington and Edinburgh University before working his way through Canada and the USA, as related in his *Episodes before Thirty* (1923). His novels, which reflect his taste for the supernatural and the occult, include *John Silence* (1908), *The Human Chord* (1910), *The Wave* (1916), *Tongues of Fire* (1924), and a volume of short stories, *Tales of the Uncanny and Supernatural* (1949).

BLACKWOOD, Lord (Ian) Basil Gawaine Temple (1870–1917) English artist, son of the 1st Marquess of **Dufferin and Ava**. Educated at Harrow and Balliol College, Oxford, he made his reputation as illustrator for **Hilaire Belloc**'s *The Bad Child's Book of Beasts*, *More Beasts for Worse Children*, *Cautionary Tales for Children*, *More Peers*, *A Moral Alphabet* and *The Modern Traveller*, where his deceptively simple line concealed a nice skill in the stamping of a single characteristic on the subject. He held posts in the colonial service in South Africa and Barbados, and was private secretary to the Irish Viceroy; and fought in World War I, moving from the Lancers' Intelligence Corps to the Grenadier Guards, where he was wounded and died.

BLACKWOOD, William (1776–1834) Scottish publisher, born in Edinburgh. Apprenticed to a bookseller at the age of 14, he established himself as a bookseller in Edinburgh—principally of antiquarian books—in 1804. In 1817 he started *Blackwood's Magazine* as a Tory rival to the Whig *Edinburgh Review*, and from the seventh number assumed the editorship himself with **John Wilson** ('Christopher North'), **Lockhart**, **Hogg**, and others as contributors. His sons, Alexander and Robert took over the firm (1834–52), followed by John (1818–79), who published all but one of **George Eliot**'s novels.

BLAEU, Latin **Coesius, Willem Janszoon** (1571–1638) Dutch mapmaker, mathematician, and astronomer, born in Alkmaar. He founded a publishing firm in Amsterdam, specializing in globes. His son Jan (d.1673) started his own business, but later entered into partnership with his brother, Cornelis (d.1650). His *Atlas Major* (11 volumes) is extremely valuable showing local history. The volume on Scotland contains 49 maps, prepared by **Timothy Pont**, and local details by Sir John Scot. Jan also published topographical plates and views of towns. Two of his sons carried on the business until 1700.

BLAINE, James Gillespie (1830–93) American journalist and statesman, born in West Brownsville, Pennsylvania. He was a newspaper editor from 1854 to 1860, then became a member of the US House of Representatives (1863–76), becoming speaker (1869–75). He was defeated in the Republican nominations for the presidency in 1876, 1880, 1884, and 1892.

BLAINEY, Geoffrey Norman (1930–) Australian social historian, born in Melbourne, and attended

Melbourne University. In 1966 his *The Tyranny of Distance* showed perhaps for the first time how geographical isolation had shaped the history and the people of Australia. *Triumph of the Nomads* (1975) and *A Land Half Won* (1980) completed his trilogy, *A Vision of Australian History*. Other books covered Australian industrial history, such as *The Rush that Never Ended* (1963) on Australian mining, and *The Steel Master* (1971), a life of Essington Lewis. He held the chair of economic history at Melbourne University for 20 years, and reached a wide popular audience through his books and a television programme 'The Blainey View'. He was first chairman of the Literature Board of the Australia Council, and of the Australia-China Council, in addition to numerous other appointments.

BLAIR, Eric See **ORWELL, George**

BLAIR, Harold (1924–76) Australian tenor, born on a Mission Station near Cherbourg, Queensland, of an aboriginal mother and an Italian father. Early years working in the sugar-cane fields awakened his interest in politics, but also led to his singing before **Marjorie Lawrence**, the Australian soprano. After winning a talent competition on radio, he was accepted by the Melbourne Conservatorium of Music, where he was supported by the composer **Margaret Sutherland**. In 1949 he became the first aboriginal to gain a Diploma in Music, and left to tour the USA. Returning to Australia in 1951, he joined the ABC Jubilee Tour to all capital cities. Between 1959 and 1962 he again toured the USA, Europe and Scandinavia. His latent interest in politics led to his standing, unsuccessfully, for the Victorian State parliament in 1963, after which he worked for the South Australian Department of Aboriginal Affairs before returning to Victoria to teach music.

BLAIR, Hugh (1718–1800) Scottish preacher, born and educated in Edinburgh. He was licensed as a preacher in 1741 and was appointed in 1758 to one of the charges of the High Kirk, Edinburgh. In 1762 he was appointed to a new Regius chair of rhetoric and belles lettres at Edinburgh. His discourses, sermons and lectures enjoyed a reputation beyond their merit, and **George III** bestowed a pension on him in 1780.

BLAIR, Robert (1699–1746) Scotish poet and preacher, born in Edinburgh. Educated at Edinburgh University, in 1731 he was ordained minister of Athelstaneford, East Lothian. He is best known as the author of *The Grave* (1743), a blank-verse poem which heralded the 'churchyard school' of poetry. The 1808 edition was finely illustrated with rare imaginative power by **William Blake**.

BLAISE, or **BLASIUS, St** (d.c.316) Armenian churchman and martyr. Bishop of Sebastea in Cappadocia, he is said to have suffered martyrdom during a period of persecution. Woolcombers claim him as their patron, and he is invoked in case of throat trouble and cattle diseases. His feast day is 3 February.

BLAIZE, Herbert Augustus (1918–89) Grenadian politician. After qualifying and practising as a solicitor, he entered politics and helped to found the centrist Grenada National party (GNP), being elected to parliament in 1957. He held ministerial posts before becoming premier in 1967. After full independence, in 1974, he led the official opposition and then went into hiding (1979–83), following the left-wing coup by Maurice Bishop. When normal political activity resumed, after the United States invasion of 1983, he returned to lead a reconstituted New National party (NNP) and win the 1984 general election.

BLAKE, Eugene Carson (1906–85) American Presbyterian clergyman and ecumenist, born in St Louis, Missouri. Educated at Princeton, he served pastorates in New York and California before becoming Stated Clerk of the Presbyterian Church, USA. In 1967 he was appointed general secretary of the World Council of Churches, a demanding post he held for five years, during which time Pope **Paul VI** paid his historic visit to the Geneva offices. His dream was the formation of a church that would be 'truly reformed, truly catholic, and truly evangelical'.

BLAKE, Nicholas See **LEWIS, Cecil Day**

BLAKE, Peter (1932–) English painter, born in Dartford, Kent. From the mid 1950s, while still a student at the Royal College of Art, he became a pioneer of the Pop Art movement in Britain, using media imagery from sources such as comics, advertisements and popular magazines. His most widely-known work is the cover design for the **Beatles**' LP *Sergeant Pepper's Lonely Hearts Club Band* (1967). In 1975 he was a founder member of the Brotherhood of Ruralists, a community of painters living in the West Country dedicated to a somewhat sentimental and nostalgic view of country life.

BLAKE, Robert (1599–1657) English naval commander, the son of a merchant. Educated at Wadham College, Oxford, he continued his father's business and led the life of a quiet country gentleman until he was 40. Returned for Bridgwater in 1640 to the Short Parliament, he cast in his lot with the parliamentarians. In the Civil War he took part in the defence of Bristol (1643) and Lyme Regis (1644), and his defence of Taunton (1644–45) against overwhelming odds proved a turning point in the war. Appointed admiral in 1649, he destroyed Prince **Rupert**'s fleet and captured the Scilly Isles and Jersey. In the first Dutch War (1652–54) he defeated **Tromp** at the battle of Portland (1653) and shattered Dutch supremacy at sea. He destroyed the Barbary Coast pirate fleet off Tunis (1655), and in 1657 destroyed a Spanish treasure-fleet at Santa Cruz off Tenerife. He died as his ship entered Plymouth, and was buried in Westminster Abbey, but his body was removed at the Restoration. He is considered one of the greatest of English admirals, second only to **Nelson**.

BLAKE, William (1757–1827) English poet, painter, engraver, and mystic, born in London, the son of an Irish hosier. In 1771 he was apprenticed to **James Basire**, the engraver, and after studying at the Royal Academy School he began to produce water-colour figure subjects and to engrave illustrations for magazines. His first book of poems, *Poetical Sketches* (1783), was followed by *Songs of Innocence* (1789) and *Songs of Experience* (1794), which include some of the purest lyrics in the English language and express his ardent belief in the freedom of the imagination and his hatred of rationalism and materialism. His mystical and prophetical works include the *Book of Thel* (1789), *The Marriage of Heaven and Hell* (1791), *The French Revolution* (1791), *The Song of Los* (1795), *Vala* and many others, which mostly have imaginative designs interwoven with their text, printed from copper treated by a peculiar process, and coloured by his own hand or that of his wife, Catherine Boucher. Among his designs of poetic and imaginative figure subjects are a superb series of 537 coloured illustrations to **Edward Young**'s *Night Thoughts* (1797) and twelve to **Robert Blair**'s *The Grave* (1808). Among the most important of his paintings are *The Canterbury Pilgrims*, which the artist himself engraved; *The Spiritual Form of Pitt guiding Behemoth* (now in the National Gallery); *Jacob's Dream*; and *The Last Judgment*. Blake's finest artistic work is to be found in the 21 *Illustrations to the Book of Job* (1826), completed when he was almost 70, but unequalled in modern religious art for imaginative force and visionary power. At his death he was employed on the illustrations to **Dante**. He is also known as a wood engraver. During his life he met with little encouragement from the public; but **Hayley**, **Flaxman**, and **Samuel Palmer** were faithful friends, and by **John Linnell**'s generosity he was in his last days saved from financial worry. All through his life he was upheld by the most real and vivid faith in the unseen, guided and encouraged—as he believed—by perpetual visitations from the spiritual world.

BLAKESLEE, Albert Francis (1874–1954) American botanist, born in Genesco, New York. In 1936 he became director of the Carnegie Station for experimental evolution and in 1937 established that colchicine can produce polyploidy in plants.

BLAKEY, Art (Arthur) also known as **Abdullah Ibn Buhaina** (1919–) American jazz drummer and bandleader, born in Pittsburgh, Pennsylvania. He emerged from big band work in the 1930s to become a leading exponent of the attacking 'hard bop' style from the 1950s. From 1954 as leader of the Jazz Messengers, a sextet or septet which he has constantly renewed with outstanding young players, he has been a consistently influential teacher and leader.

BLALOCK, Alfred (1899–1964) American surgeon, born in Culloden, Georgia. He received his medical education at Johns Hopkins University and his postgraduate training there and at Vanderbilt University Hospital. He was on the staff at Vanderbilt (1925–41) and Johns Hopkins (1941–64), where he pioneered the surgical treatment of various congenital defects of the heart and its associated blood vessels, many of which could be recognized because the infant was cyanosed, and performed the first 'blue baby' operation with the paediatrician **Helen Taussig**. He also did important experimental work on the pathophysiology of surgical shock and its treatment by transfusion of whole blood or blood plasma. The *Papers of Alfred Blalock* (1966) collected many of his major contributions in a single volume.

BLAMEY, Sir Thomas (1884–1951) Australian soldier, born in Wagga. He joined the regular army in 1906 and attended Staff College at Quetta. He saw service on the North West frontier of India, and in World War I played an important part in the evacuation of Gallipoli. He became chief of staff of the Australian Corps in 1918. At the outbreak of World War II he was given command of the Australian Imperial Forces in the Middle East. He served as deputy commander-in-chief to **Wavell** and had command of Commonwealth operations in Greece (1941). On the establishment of the SW Pacific command he became c-in-c of Allied land forces in Australia (1942) and received the Japanese surrender in 1945. In 1950 he was made a field marshal, the first Australian soldier to hold this rank.

BLAMPIED, Edmund (1886–1966) British artist, born in Jersey, the son of a farmer. He is best known for his etchings which brilliantly depict everyday farming life, in particular horses and peasants. Apart from his lithographs and watercolours, he produced some 115 etchings which place him amongst the finest artists in the British school of etchers. During the German occupation he designed the Jersey occupation stamps.

BLANC, Jean Joseph Louis (1811–82) French socialist statesman and historian, born in Madrid. In 1830 he went to study in Paris, then for two years was a private tutor at Arras, and in 1834 returned to Paris, where in 1839 he founded the *Revue du progrès*. His chief work on socialism, the *Organisation du travail* (1840), denounces the principle of competitive industry and proposes the establishment of co-operative workshops, subsidized by the state. This made him very popular among French workmen. He next published his *Histoire de dix ans* (*1830–40*) (1841–44), which had a deadly effect on the Orléans dynasty. After the revolution of February 1848, he was appointed a member of the provisional government, and placed at the head of the commission for discussing the problem of labour. But accused without reason of a share in the disturbances of the summer of 1848, he escaped to London, where he finished his *Histoire de la révolution* in 1862, and wrote much for the French press. On the fall of the Empire, he returned to France, and was elected in 1871 to the National Assembly, in 1876 to the Chamber of Deputies, always supporting the extreme left.

BLANCHARD, Jean Pierre François (1753–1809) French balloonist, inventor of the parachute, born in Les Andelys. With **John Jeffries** he was the first to cross the English Channel by balloon, from Dover to Calais, in 1785. He was killed at La Haye during practice parachute jumps from a balloon.

BLANCHFLOWER, 'Danny' Robert Dennio (1926–) Irish footballer, born in Belfast. Studious, cultured and articulate when off-field, he was a powerful influence in the Northern Ireland side which reached the World Cup quarter-finals in 1958. Transferring from Aston Villa to Tottenham Hotspur, he masterminded the London club's double success of 1960–61 in the League and the FA Cup. He was British Footballer of the Year in 1960–61, and won a European Cupwinners' Cup medal with Tottenham. On his retiral he was much in demand as a newspaper columnist and television commentator.

BLANDRATA, or **Biandrata, Giorgio** (c.1515–c.1590) Italian physician and theologian, nobly born in Saluzzo, Piedmont, the founder of Unitarianism in Poland and Transylvania. The freedom of his religious opinions compelled him to flee to Geneva in 1556, but in 1558 **Calvin**'s displeasure at his anti-Trinitarianism drove him to Poland. Finally, in 1563, he became physician to **John Sigismund**, prince of Transylvania. He is supposed to have been strangled in his sleep by his nephew.

BLANE, Sir Gilbert (1749–1834) Scottish physician, born in Blanefield, Ayrshire. In 1779 he sailed with Admiral **George Rodney** to the West Indies. As head of the Navy Medical Board, he was instrumental in introducing the compulsory use of lemon juice on board navy ships to prevent scurvy. He also pioneered the use of statistics in clinical medicine.

BLANKERS-KOEN, Fanny (Francina) (1918–) Dutch athlete, born in Amsterdam. She dominated women's events in the London Olympics of 1948, winning four gold medals: the 100 and 200 metres, the 80 metres hurdles, and the 4×100 metres relay. Unequalled among women as an all-round athlete she was primarily a sprinter but at various times held world records for both high and long jumps. Achieving success at the comparatively late age of 30, she captured the imagination of the sporting world as the 'flying Dutch housewife'.

BLANQUI, Jérôme Adolphe (1798–1854) French economist, born in Nice, brother of **Louis Auguste Blanqui**. In 1833 he became professor in the Conservatoire des Arts et des Métiers. He was a follower of **Say**, and in favour of free trade. His chief work is the *Histoire de l'économie politique en Europe* (1838).

BLANQUI, Louis Auguste (1805–81) French revolutionary, born in Puget-Théniers (Alpes Maritimes), brother of **Jérôme Adolphe Blanqui**. An extremist and theoretician of insurrection, he worked from 1830 at building up a network of secret societies committed to violent revolution. He spent 33 years in prison, and was in prison in 1871 when he was elected president of the revolutionary Commune of Paris. He was released in 1879. In 1881 his followers, known as Blanquists, joined the Marxists.

BLASCO IBÁÑEZ, Vicente See **IBAÑEZ**

BLASHFORD-SNELL, Colonel John (1936–) English explorer and youth leader, born in Hereford. The son of a clergyman, he was educated at Victoria College, Jersey, and the Royal Military Academy, Sandhurst, and was commissioned into the Royal Engineers in 1957. He participated in over 40 expeditions, and led the Blue Nile (1968), British Trans-Americas (1972) and Zaire River (1975/84) expeditions under the aegis of the Scientific Exploration Society (SES), of which he is chairman. He then went on to lead two major youth projects: Operation Drake (1978–80) and Operation Raleigh, which involved over 4000 young people in adventurous, scientific and community projects in over 73 countries (1984–88), before being established as the Raleigh Trust. He has written several books on his adventures.

BLATCH, Harriet Eaton, née **Stanton** (1856–1940) American suffrage leader, born in Seneca Falls, New York, the daughter of **Elizabeth Cady Stanton**. Educated at Vassar College, where she studied mathematics, she moved to Basingstoke, England, on her marriage (1882) to William Blatch, and was impressed by the direction and work of the Women's Franchise League. After her return to the USA she founded the Equality League of Self-Supporting Women (1907) and became a staunch activist in support of women's rights, and in 1908 founded the Women's Political Union. Her works include *Mobilizing Woman-Power* (1918) and *A Woman's Point of View* (1920).

BLAUW, William Janszoon See **BLAEU**

BLAVATSKY, née **Hahn, Helena Petrovna** (1831–91) Russian-born American theosophist, born in Ekaterinoslav. She had a brief marriage in her teens to a Russian general, but left him and travelled widely in the East, including Tibet. She went to the USA in 1873, and in 1875, with **Henry Steel Olcott**, founded the Theosophical Society in New York and later carried on her work in India. Her psychic powers were widely acclaimed but did not survive investigation by the Society for Psychical Research, although this did not deter her large following, which included **Annie Besant**. Her writings include *Isis Unveiled* (1877).

BLEASDALE, Alan (1946–) English dramatist, born in Liverpool. He was the author of the popular TV series, *The Boys From the Blackstuff* (1983), about a group of unemployed Liverpudlians. *The Monocled Mutineer*, a television series set during World War I, followed in 1986. He has written several stage plays, including *Are You Lonesome Tonight?* (1985), a respectful musical about **Elvis Presley**.

BLEEK, Friedrich (1793–1859) German biblical scholar, born in Ahrensbök in Holstein. Professor of theology at Bonn from 1829, he wrote an important commentary on the book of Hebrews. His son Wilhelm (1827–75), a philologist, went out to Natal, became keeper of the Grey Library at Cape Town (1861), and wrote on native languages and folklore.

BLÉRIOT, Louis (1872–1936) French airman. He made the first flight across the English Channel on 25 July 1909 from Baraques to Dover in a small 24-h.p. monoplane.

BLES, Herri Met De, also known as **Herri Patenier** (c.1500–1550) Flemish painter, probably a relation of **Joachim Patenier**, who was clearly an influence on him. He was a member of the Antwerp guild of painters and specialized in landscapes with figures. Little is known about him or his life—the name by which he is known is a nickname meaning 'Herri with the white forelock', and he was known to Italian collectors, with whom his work was popular, as Civetta (owl), as owls often appear in his work.

BLEULER, Eugen (1857–1939) Swiss psychiatrist who coined the word 'schizophrenia', born in Zollikon, near Zürich, where he was professor (1898–1927). He carried out research on epilepsy and other physiological conditions, then turned to psychiatry, and in 1911 published an important study on what he called schizophrenia or 'splitting of the mind'. One of his pupils was **Carl Gustav Jung**. His wife, Hedwig Bleuler-Waser (1869–1940), was a well-known writer and social worker in the field of temperance.

BLICHER, Steen Steensen (1782–1848) Danish poet and novelist, born in Jutland near Viborg, which forms the background of much of his work. He became a teacher and clergyman, was unhappily married, and took a great interest in the social and spiritual problems of his day. His collection *Traekfuglene* (The Migratory Birds, 1838), ranks among the purest of Danish lyrical poetry, with its pervasive note of resignation and sorrow. His short stories, often in dialect, such as *E Bindstouw*, are among the gems of Danish literature.

BLIGH, William (1754–c.1817) English naval officer, a victim of the celebrated mutiny on the *Bounty*. Born in Plymouth, the son of a customs officer, he went to sea at the age of 15 and served on three royal navy vessels before being picked by Captain **James Cook** as sailing master of the *Resolution* on his third voyage (1776–80). In 1787 he was chosen by Sir **Joseph Banks** to command the *Bounty* on a voyage to Tahiti to collect plants of the bread-fruit tree with a view to introducing them to the West Indies. During a six-month stay on the island the men became demoralized, and on 28 April 1789 the first mate, **Fletcher Christian**, led a mutiny; Bligh and 18 of his men were cast adrift in an open boat with a small stock of provisions and no chart. After incredible hardships they reached Timor, in the East Indies, on 14 June, having travelled nearly 4000 miles. In 1791 he sailed again on an expedition which successfully established bread-fruit plants in the West Indies. He served under Admiral **Nelson** in command of the *Glatton* at the Battle of Copenhagen in 1801. In 1805 he was appointed governor of New South Wales; from 1808 to 1810 he was imprisoned by mutinous soldiers during the so-called 'Rum Rebellion' inspired by the settler **John MacArthur**. Bligh was exonerated of all blame, and promoted admiral on his retirement in 1811.

BLIND, Karl (1826–1907) German political agitator, born in Mannheim. He studied law at Heidelberg. For his share in the risings in South Germany in 1848 he was sentenced to eight years' imprisonment, but while being taken to Mainz was set free by the people, and from 1852 lived in England. He wrote on politics, history, mythology, etc. His stepdaughter, Mathilde (1847–96), championed women's rights and published poems.

BLIND HARRY See **HARRY**

BLISS, Sir Arthur (1891–1975) English composer, born in London. He studied under **Holst, Stanford** and **Vaughan Williams** at the Royal College of Music, and had attracted considerable attention before World War I, in which he served. In 1921 he became professor of composition at the Royal College, but resigned his post after a year to devote himself to composition. From 1942 to 1944 he was music director of the BBC. On the death of **Bax** in 1953 he became Master of the Queen's Musick. His film music includes that for **H G Wells**'s

Things to Come and *Men of Two Worlds*; his other compositions include the ballets *Checkmate* (1937) and *Miracle in the Gorbals* (1944), the opera *The Olympians* (1948), chamber music, and piano and violin works.

BLISS, Philip Paul (1838–76) American evangelist and hymnwriter. Co-author with **Ira Sankey** of *Gospel Songs* (1874), he was best known for such favourites as 'Hold the Fort', 'Down Life's Dark Vale We Wander', 'Jesus Loves Me', 'Let the Lower Lights Be Burning' and 'Pull for the Shore', all contained in *Gospel Songs*. He was killed in the Ashtabula train disaster.

BLIXEN, Karen, Baroness, pseud **Isak Dinesen** (1885–1962) Danish novelist and story teller. Educated in Denmark, England, Switzerland, Italy, and France, in 1914 she married her cousin, Baron Bror Blixen Finecke, and went with him to a coffee plantation in Kenya. They were divorced in 1921, and in 1931 she returned to Denmark to live at the old family home of Rungstedlund. She wrote *Seven Gothic Tales* (1934), which she later translated into Danish. Other works include *Out of Africa* (1938), *Winter's Tales* (1942), and *Last Tales* (1957).

BLOCH, Ernest (1880–1959) Swiss-born American composer, born, of Jewish descent, in Geneva. He studied in Brussels, Frankfurt, and Munich before settling in Paris, where his opera *Macbeth* was produced in 1910 after his return to Switzerland. In 1915 he became professor of musical aesthetics at Geneva Conservatory. In 1916 he went to America, where he held several teaching posts, adopted US citizenship (1924), and won a high reputation which rapidly spread to Europe, where he returned for eight years in 1930. His compositions include *Trois Poèmes juifs* (1913), the Hebrew *Sacred Service* (1930–33) for baritone, chorus, and orchestra, and numerous other chamber and orchestral works; his symphonies include the *Israel* (1912–16), and the 'epic rhapsody' *America* (1926).

BLOCH, Felix (1905–83) Swiss-born American physicist, born in Zürich. Educated at Leipzig, he left Germany for the USA in 1933 and became professor of theoretical physics at Stanford University (1934–71). During World War II he worked on radar, and was awarded the 1952 Nobel prize for physics jointly with **Edward Mills Purcell** for work on nuclear magnetic resonance. The *Bloch bands* are sets of discrete but closely adjacent energy levels arising from quantum states when a nondegenerate gas condenses to a solid. He was the first director general of the European Commission for Nuclear Research (CERN) in Geneva (1954–55).

BLOCH, Jean-Richard (1884–1947) French novelist, playwright and critic. A polemicist for communism, his reputation is based on his novel *Et Compagnie* (1918), which belongs to the school of realistic writing derived from **Zola** and **Pierre Hamp**.

BLOCH, Konrad Emil (1912–) German-born American biochemist. Educated at the Technische Hochschule, Munich, and Columbia University, he emigrated to the USA in 1936. In 1954 he was appointed the first professor of biochemistry at Harvard University. He won with **Feodor Lynen** the Nobel prize for physiology or medicine in 1964 for work on the mechanism of cholesterol and fatty acid metabolism, discovering the complex sequence of the molecule in the human body, important in finding a cure for arterio-sclerosis.

BLOCH, Marc (1886–1944) French historian, born in Lyon, son of a professor of ancient history. He studied in Paris, Leipzig and Berlin, taught at Montpellier and Amiens and was called up in 1914 (NCO at the Marne, then commissioned). Professor of medieval history at Strasbourg from 1919, he was co-founder of the periodical *Annales d'histoire économique et sociale*, which transformed historians' view of their subject. Later he became professor of economic history at the Sorbonne (1936). He rejoined the army in 1939, serving as 'the oldest captain in the French army', observed France's surrender, and after teaching in Vichy France, joined the Resistance in 1943 to be captured, tortured and shot by the Germans. His work has been extensively translated since his death, notably his last major work *La société féodale* (1939, trans 1961), his memoir of France in 1939–40 (*Strange Defeat*), and his unfinished *Apologie pour l'histoire* translated as *The Historian's Craft*. He wrote with high technical sophistication while constantly stressing the need for human consciousness: he warned students that they must ask sources the right questions.

BLOCH, Martin (1883–1954) German-born British painter, born in Neisse in Silesia, and naturalized in 1947. After studying in Berlin and Munich, he was forced to leave Germany by the Nazis in 1934, went to Denmark, and later to England, where he opened a school of painting with Roy de Maistre. His brilliant colours and expressionist technique were used to interpret the English landscape.

BLOCK, Alexander Alexandrovich See **BLOK**

BLOEMAERT, Abraham (1564–1651) Dutch landscape painter, father of the copper engraver, Cornelius Bloemaert (1603–88).

BLOEMBERGEN, Nicolas (1920–) Dutch-born American physicist, born in Dordrecht. Educated at the universities of Utrecht and Leiden, in 1946 he moved to the USA where he joined the staff of Harvard, serving as Gordon McKay professor of applied physics and as Rumford professor of physics. He introduced a modification to **Charles Townes**'s early design of the maser, enabling the maser to work continuously rather than intermittently. He shared the 1981 Nobel prize for physics with **Kai Siegbahn**.

BLOK, Alexander Alexandrovich (1880–1921) Russian poet, born in St Petersburg. In 1903 he married the daughter of **Mendeleyev**. His first book of poems, *Songs about the Lady Fair* (1904), was influenced by the mysticism of **Soloviev**, a Tolstoyan vision of reality beyond appearances, where truth is embodied in ideal womanhood. In *Nocturnal Hours* (1911) the ideal has given way to the realism of city squalor. He welcomed the 1917 Revolution and in 1918 wrote two poems, *The Twelve* (trans 1920), a symbolic sequence of revolutionary themes, and *The Scythians*, an ode, inciting Europe to follow Russia. He was soon disillusioned, however, and suffered greatly in the hard times which followed the Revolution. Other works include the romantic verse drama *The Rose and the Cross*.

BLOMDAHL, Karl-Birger (1916–68) Swedish composer, born in Stockholm. He was professor of composition in Stockholm from 1960 to 1964 and head of music of Radio Sweden from 1965. Much inspired by **Hindemith**, he composed symphonies, concertos, chamber and electronic music. His two completed operas are based on texts from Swedish literature: *Aniara* (1957–58) on the space epic by **Harry Martinson**, and *Herr von Hancken* (1962–63) on the novel by **Bo Hjalmar Bergman**.

BLOMFIELD, Charles James (1786–1857) English prelate and classical scholar, born in Bury St Edmunds. He studied at Trinity College, Cambridge, and was bishop of London from 1828 to 1856. During his episcopate about 200 new churches were consecrated in London, mainly through his efforts. His classical reputation rests on his editions of **Aeschylus**, **Callimachus**, **Euripides**, and the Greek lyric poets. His fourth son, Sir Arthur William (1829–99), was an architect who assisted with the erection of the London Law Courts (1881). His grandson was Sir **Reginald Blomfield**.

BLOMFIELD, Sir Reginald (1856–1942) English architect, grandson of **Charles James Blomfield**. He designed the Menin Gate and Lambeth Bridge, and wrote books on architecture and garden designs.

BLONDEL, or **Blondel de Nesle** (fl.12th century) French troubadour who according to legend accompanied **Richard I, Coeur de Lion** to Palestine on the Crusades, and located him when imprisoned in the Austrian castle of Dürrenstein (1193) by means of the song they had jointly composed. He is featured in Sir **Walter Scott**'s *The Talisman*.

BLONDEL, Maurice-Édouard (1861–1949) French philosopher, born in Dijon. Professor at Aix-Marseille, he formulated an idiosyncratic philosophy of action, combining elements from pragmatism, neo-Platonism and Christianity. His main works are: *L'action* (1893), *L'Illusion idéaliste* (1898), *La Pensée* (1934) and *Exigences philosophiques du Christianisme* (1950).

BLONDEL, Nicolas François (1618–86) French military engineer and architect, born in Ribemont. He was equally successful as a naval engineer and ship's captain, as a diplomat and intelligence officer, and as tutor to the son of the French secretary of state. In the 1660s he fortified the Channel ports of Dunkirk and Le Havre, and planned the major naval base at Rochefort on the Charente river which was fortified by **Vauban**. In architecture his principal surviving work is the triumphal arch at Porte St Denis in Paris, built in 1674 to celebrate French victories on the Rhine.

BLONDIN, Charles, properly **Jean François Gravelet** (1824–97) French acrobat and tightrope-walker, born in Hesdin near Calais, and trained at Lyon. In 1859 he crossed Niagara on a tightrope; and later did the same with variations (blindfolded, with a wheelbarrow, with a man on his back, on stilts).

BLOOD, Thomas (c.1618–1680) Irish adventurer. A parliamentarian during the Civil War, he was deprived of his estate at the Restoration. He put himself (1663) at the head of a plot to seize Dublin Castle and **Ormonde**, the lord-lieutenant. The plot was discovered and his chief accomplices executed. On 9 May 1671, with three accomplices he entered the Tower, nearly murdering the keeper of the jewels, and stole the crown, while one of his associates took the orb. They were pursued, however, and captured; but Blood was pardoned by King **Charles** who took him to court and restored his estate.

BLOOMER, Amelia, née **Jenks** (1818–94) American champion of women's rights and dress reform, born in Homer, New York. In 1840 she married a lawyer and founded and edited the feminist paper *The Lily* (1849–55), and worked closely with **Susan Anthony**. In her pursuit of dress equality she wore her own version of trousers for women which came to be called 'bloomers'.

BLOOMFIELD, Leonard (1887–1949) American linguist, born in Chicago. After holding several university posts, he was appointed professor of German and linguistics at Ohio State University (1921), becoming professor of Germanic philology at Chicago University in 1927, and Sterling professor of linguistics at Yale in 1940. His early interest was in Indo-European, especially Germanic, phonology and morphology, but he later made studies of Malayo-Polynesian languages (especially Tagalog) and of the languages of the Indians of North America (particularly Menomini and Cree). He played a major part in making linguistics an independent scientific discipline, understanding by the word 'scientific' the rejection of all data that could not be directly observed or physically measured. Although he had in his *Introduction to the Study of Language* (1914) indicated his adherence to **Wundt**'s mentalistic psychology, in his major work on linguistic theory, *Language* (1933), he advocated and himself adopted behaviourism as the theoretical framework for linguistic analysis and description. This led to the almost total neglect of the study of meaning within the 'Bloomfieldian' school of linguistics, and a concentration on phonology, morphology and syntax.

BLOOMFIELD, Robert (1766–1823) English poet, born in Honington, near Bury St Edmunds, the son of a farm worker. A shoemaker's apprentice, he wrote *The Farmer's Boy* in a garret. Published in 1800 with the assistance of **Capell Lofft**, it proved very popular. He subsequently published *Rural Tales* (1802) and *Wild Flowers* (1806), was given a small allowance by the Duke of **Grafton**, but half-blind, died in poverty.

BLOOR, Ella, née **Reeve,** known as **'Mother Bloor'** (1862–1951) American radical and feminist, born on Staten Island, New York. Married at the age of 19, and a mother of four by 1892, she became interested in women's rights and the labor movement, her political interests leading to her divorce in 1896. Following a second unsuccessful marriage she moved into politics as an activist. In 1901 she joined the Socialist party. Adopting the name Ella Bloor in 1906 for a piece of investigative reporting she undertook for **Upton Sinclair**, she continued to write under this name. She was the party organizer for Connecticut for many years, attracting support for various labor causes. In 1919 she was one of the founders of the American Communist party, to which she became utterly committed. Arrested more than 30 times during her career, she gained a reputation as a distinguished party speaker and became a member of the party's central committee (1932–48).

BLORE, Edward (1787–1879) English artist and architect of the Gothic revival, born in Derby, the son of Thomas (1764–1818), the topographer. He built Sir **Walter Scott**'s Abbotsford (c.1816).

BLOUET, Paul, pseud **Max O'Rell** (1848–1903) French author, born in Brittany. He served in the Franco-German war and against the Commune, being severely wounded. In 1873 he went to England as a newspaper correspondent and was French master at St Paul's School (1876–84). From 1887 he lectured in Britain, USA, and colonies. His works include *John Bull and his Island* (1883), *A Frenchman in America* (1891), and *John Bull & Co.* (1894).

BLOUNT, Charles, 8th Lord Mountjoy, Earl of Devonshire (1563–1606) English soldier, and conqueror of Ireland. He came from a declining family whose fortunes he was determined to revive. He served in the Low Countries, in Brittany, and in the Azores (1597). In 1600 he accepted the Irish command against the rebellion of **Hugh O'Neill**, Earl of Tyrone, winning a decisive victory at Kinsale (1601), laying Munster waste and ultimately receiving Tyrone's surrender at Mellifont, in 1603, concealing Queen **Elizabeth**'s death six days previously, thus enabling him to exact more stringent terms. Now made Lord Lieutenant of Ireland, he reduced disaffected towns, and returned to England where he was richly rewarded by King **James VI and I** with an earldom, mastership of the ordnance, and lands, and, less publicly, by King **Philip III** of Spain with a pension.

BLOUNT, Charles (1654–93) English deist and writer, born in Upper Holloway, London, the son of Sir Henry Blount (1602–82), traveller in the Levant. He became noted for his contributions (often flippant) to the political, literary, and theological controversies of the times, including *Anima Mundi* (1679). Despairing of marriage with his deceased wife's sister, he committed suicide.

BLOUNT, Thomas (1618–79) English lexicographer and antiquarian, born in Bordesley, Worcestershire. He wrote miscellaneous legal and historical works, including a history of **Charles II**'s escape after the battle of Worcester (*Boscobel*, 1660). He was also the author of *Glossographia*, a dictionary of the 'hard words of whatsoever language' used in English (1656), a dictionary of obscure legal terms (*A Law Dictionary*, 1670), and the *Fragmenta Antiquitatis: Ancient Tenures of Land, and Jocular Customs of some Manors* (1679).

BLOW, John (1649–1708) English composer, born in Newark. He sang in the Chapel Royal choir, was appointed organist at Westminster Abbey (1668), Master of the Children at the Chapel Royal (1674) and subsequently organist there, and Master of the Children at St Paul's (1687). Much of his vast output of anthems and church services is uninspired, but the best, eg, the Ode for St Cecilia's Day, 'Begin the Song', has a nobility which places Blow among notable 17th-century English composers. He wrote a small amount of instrumental music and a masque, *Venus and Adonis* (1687), which was performed before **Charles II**.

BLOY, Léon Marie (1846–1917) French author, born in Périgeux. He wrote novels, essays, and religious and critical studies with a strong Roman Catholic bias, containing bitter castigation of political and social institutions. This made him unpopular in his day but has contributed to the revival of interest in his works since 1940. His *Le Désespéré* (1886) and *La Femme pauvre* (1897) are autobiographical; other books include *Le Pélerin de l'absolu* (1914). His journal was published in 1924.

BLÜCHER, Gebbard Leberecht von, Prince of Wahlstadt (1742–1819) Prussian soldier, known as 'Marshal Forward', born in Rostock, Mecklenburg. After two years in the Swedish service (1756–58), he distinguished himself in the Prussian cavalry (1760–70), but was dicharged for dissipation and insubordination, and for 15 years farmed his own estates. He rejoined the army as a major in 1787. In 1793 he fought, as colonel of hussars, against the French on the Rhine, and in 1806, as lietenant-general, at Auerstädt, and was distinguished, though not successful, at Lübeck, Stralsund, and elsewhere. When the Prussians rose against France in 1813, Blücher took chief command in Silesia, and at the battles of Lützen, Bautzen and Haynau, displayed heroic courage. At the Katzbach he cleared Silesia of the enemy, and at Leipzig (1813) won very important successes. In January 1814 he crossed the Rhine, and though once routed by **Napoleon** won several battles, and on 31 March entered Paris. After Napoleon's return in 1815, Blücher assumed the general command, suffered a severe defeat at Ligny, but completed **Wellington**'s victory at the battle of Waterloo by his timely appearance on the field, and his Prussians pursued the fleeing enemy all through the night. At the second taking of Paris, Blücher wanted to inflict on Paris what other capitals had suffered, but was restrained by Wellington.

BLUM, Léon (1872–1950) French socialist statesman, born in Paris. A lawyer, he was radicalized by the **Dreyfus** affair (1899), and was elected to the chamber in 1919, becoming one of the leaders of the Socialist party. In 1924 he lent his support to **Herriot**, a policy which resulted in great electoral advances by the Left; as a consequence the elections of May 1936 gave France the first socialist prime minister since 1870. In 1938 Blum formed a second 'popular front' government which had a stormy existence. During World War II he was interned in Germany. He remained the leader and adviser of the socialists on his return and in December 1946 was elected prime minister of the six-week caretaker government and originated the Anglo-French treaty of alliance and methods to deal with the rise of prices.

BLUM, René (1878–1942) French impresario and critic, born in Paris. Critic and editor of the literary journal *Gil Blas*, while he was director of the Theatre of the Monte Carlo Casino he took over the administration of the Ballet Russes immediately following **Diaghilev**'s death in 1929, renaming it the Ballet Russes de Monte Carlo, with **Leonid Massine** as director. He was arrested in France while the company was away on tour in the USA, and died within a week of being sent to Auschwitz.

BLUM, Robert (1807–48) German liberal agitator, born in Cologne. He was successively a theatre secretary and a bookseller. When the revolutionary movement broke out in 1848, Blum was one of its most energetic leaders. Joining the Vienna insurgents, to whom he was bearer of a congratulatory address, he was arrested, and shot.

BLUMBERG, Baruch Samuel (1925–) American biochemist, born in New York City, joint winner of the 1976 Nobel prize for physiology or medicine. He studied at Columbia and Oxford, and became professor of biochemistry at the University of Pennsylvania in 1964. He discovered the 'Australia antigen' that led to the development of a vaccine against hepatitis B, and shared the Nobel prize with **Daniel Carleton Gajdusek**.

BLUME, Judy (1938–) American writer of teenage fiction, born in New Jersey. Perhaps the most controversial and certainly the most popular contemporary writer for teenagers, her first published book was *The One in the Middle is the Green Kangaroo* (1969) which, together with her second book, *Iggie's House* (1970), the author would be happy to forget. Her third book, *Are You There, God It's Me, Margaret* (1970), marked a turning point in her career and brought her acclaim for her candid approach to the onset of puberty and for her natural, if unsubtle, style. As with subsequent books, attempts were made to restrict its circulation. Her explicitness in dealing with problems particular to those in the 10–14 age group has brought her into conflict with parents, but she has a remarkable rapport with her readers and dares to confront subjects which previously were ignored. Her books include *Then Again, Maybe I Won't* (1971), *It's not the End of the World* (1972), *Deenie* (1973), *Blubber* (1974) and *Forever* (1975).

BLUMENBACH, Johann Friedrich (1752–1840) German anthropologist, born in Gotha. He studied at Jena and Göttingen, where he became extra-ordinary professor of medicine in 1776. By his study of comparative skull measurements, he established a quantitative basis for racial classification.

BLUNCK, Hans Friedrich (1888–1961) German novelist, poet and folklorist, born in Altona. After studying law he was successively propagandist, university official and farmer. Steeped in the folklore of the North German plain, Blunck's writings lent colour to the racial theories of National Socialism. His poetical works include *Sturm überm Land* (1915), *Der Wanderer* (1925), *Erwartung* (1936), and his novels *Werwendes Volk* (1933) and *Die Urvätersaga* (1934). He published his autobiographical *Unwegsamezeiten* in 1953.

BLUNDELL, Peter (1520–1601) English merchant and manufacturer, of Tiverton. He made a fortune manufacturing kersey cloth, and founded Blundell's School (1604).

BLUNDEN, Edmund Charles (1896–1974) English poet and critic, born in London. His family soon moved to Kent, and he was educated at Christ's Hospital and Queen's College, Oxford. He served in France in World War I and won the MC. He was professor of English literature at Tokyo (1924–27), fellow of Merton College, Oxford, from 1931, joined the staff of *The Times Literary Supplement* in 1943, returned to the Far East and from 1953 lectured at the University of Hong Kong. He was professor at Oxford from 1966 to 1968. A lover of the English countryside, he is essentially a nature poet, as is evident in *Pastorals* (1916) and *The Waggoner and Other Poems* (1920), but his prose work *Undertones of War* (1928) is perhaps his best. Other works include *The Bonadventure* (1922), on his visit to America, a Life of **Leigh Hunt**, and books on **Lamb** and **Keats**. He also edited **Clare**, **Christopher Smart**, **Shelley**, **Keats** and **Collins**.

BLUNT, Anthony Frederick (1907–83) British art historian and Soviet spy. He was educated at Marlborough School after a childhood spent mainly in Paris where his father was vicar of the English Church and Embassy chaplain. In 1926 he went to Trinity College, Cambridge, of which he became a fellow in 1932, and where he was an influential member of the Apostles, an exclusive debating society. He shared in the left-wing communist-respecting tendencies of the time, and first met **Guy Burgess**, **Kim Philby** and **Donald Maclean**. Influenced by Burgess, he acted as a 'talent-spotter', supplying to him the names of likely recruits to the Russian communist cause, and during his war service in British Intelligence was in a position to pass on information to the Russian government. Although his active spying activities appear to have ceased after the war, he was still in a position to assist the defection of Burgess and Maclean in 1951, and although suspected by British Intelligence at the time, lack of evidence and his own denial of involvement frustrated investigations. In 1964, after the defection of Philby, a confession was obtained from Blunt in return for his immunity, and he continued as surveyor of the queen's pictures, a post he held from 1945 to 1972. His full involvement in espionage was only made public in 1979 in a statement by the prime minister, after the publication of a book by Andrew Boyle, *The Climate of Treason*. A distinguished art historian, he had been director of the Courtauld Institute of Art from 1947 to 1974, and among his highly respected publications were *Art and Architecture in France 1500–1700* (1953) and his monumental study of **Poussin** (1966–67). He was internationally honoured for his work, being made a CVO in 1947 and a KCVO in 1956; the knighthood was annulled in 1979.

BLUNT, Wilfrid Scawen (1840–1922) English poet and traveller, born in Petworth, Sussex. Educated at Stonyhurst and Oscott, he served in the diplomatic service (1859–70). He travelled in the Near and Middle East, espoused the cause of Arabi Pasha and Egyptian nationalism (1882), stood for parliament and was imprisoned in 1888 for activity in the Irish Land League. He wrote fierce political verse and charming love poems, and bred Arab horses. In 1858 he married Lady Anne Isobel Noel, who shared his travels and love of Arab horses.

BLUNTSCHLI, Johann Kaspar (1808–81) Swiss legal scholar, born in Zürich. In 1833 he became professor there and later at Munich (1848) and Heidelberg (1871). His reputation rests on his *Allgemeines Staatsrecht* (1852). He helped to found the Institute of International Law, Ghent (1873).

BLY, Robert (1926–) American poet, critic, translator and editor, born in Madison, Minnesota. As a critic he is caustic but his targets are legitimate. For a man so aware of foreign literature (he has translated **Neruda** among others), his poetry is surprisingly American in tone and locale, often dealing with the space and silences of his home state. His first collection was *Silence in the Snowy Fields* (1962), followed by *The Shadow-Mothers* (1970), *Sleepers Joining Hands* (1972) and *Talking All Morning* (1980).

BLYTH, Edward (1810–73) English naturalist and zoologist, born in London. A druggist in London, he spent so much time on ornithology that his business failed. His many articles on survival and natural selection of bird species anticipated **Darwin**. He was curator of the museum of the Asiatic Society in Bengal (1841–62). Several birds are named after him, including Blyth's Kingfisher, Blyth's Pipit and Blyth's Warbler.

BLYTON, Enid Mary (1897–1968) English children's author, born in London. She trained as a Froebel kindergarten teacher, then became a journalist, specializing in educational and children's publications. In 1922 she published her first book, *Child Whispers*, a collection of verse, but it was in the late 1930s that she began writing her many children's stories featuring such characters as Noddy, the Famous Five, and the Secret Seven. She edited various magazines, including *Sunny Stories* and *Pictorial Knowledge* for children, and *Modern Teaching*, and was part-author of *Two Years in the Infant School*. She identified closely with children, and always considered her stories highly educational and moral in tone, but has recently been criticized for racism, sexism and snobbishness, as well as stylistic inelegance and over-simplicity. She published over 600 books, and is one of the most translated British authors. Her works also include school readers and books on nature and religious study.

BOABDIL, properly **Abu-Abdallah Muhammad** (d.c.1493) the last Moorish king of Granada. He dethroned his father, Abu-al-Hasan, in 1482. While he continued to struggle for power against his father and uncle the Christians gradually conquered the kingdom. Malaga fell in 1487, and after a two-year siege Granada itself capitulated to **Ferdinand** and **Isabella** of Aragon and Castile on 2 January 1492. He was granted a small lordship in the Alpujarras, but in 1493 sold his rights to the Spanish crown and retired to Morocco where he died.

BOADICEA See **BOUDICCA**

BOAS, Franz (1858–1942) German-born American anthropologist, born in Minden, the dominant figure in establishing modern anthropology in the USA. Having studied geography at Kiel, his expeditions to the Arctic and to British Columbia shifted his interest to the tribes there and thence to ethnology and anthropology and caused his emigration to the USA in 1886, where he made his career, ultimately as professor at Columbia from 1899. His emphasis was to bring together ethnology, physical anthropology, archaeology and linguistics; to collect details of cultures, especially those becoming extinct; and he rejected the simple determinism and eugenic theories of the time. He and his pupils established new and less simple concepts of culture and of race, as outlined in his collection of papers, *Race, Language and Culture* (1940). His other books included *The Mind of Primitive Man* (1911) and *Anthropology and Modern Life* (1928).

BOATENG, Paul Yaw (1951–) British politician. He began his education in the international school at Accra, Ghana, and completed it in England, graduating in law and qualifying as a solicitor. Displaying an intense interest in race relations and civil liberties, he operated the Paddington Law Centre (1976–79) before joining a practice. He became politically active as a member of the Greater London Council (GLC) in 1981 and entered the House of Commons, representing Brent South, in 1987. In 1989 he became the first black member of the Labour shadow cabinet.

BOBBIN, Tim See **COLLIER, John**

BOCAGE, Manoel Barbosa du (1765–1805) Portuguese lyric poet, born in Setubal. He served in the army and the navy, sailed in 1786 to India and China, returning to Lisbon in 1790, where, recognized as a poet, he joined the literary coterie *Nova Arcadia*. He is essentially a romantic, but his sonnets are classical in form. He often satirizes, as in *Pina de Talião*.

BOCCACCIO, Giovanni (1313–75) Italian writer, born in Tuscany or Paris. He was the illegitimate son of a merchant of Certaldo, who launched him on a commercial career. He soon abandoned commerce and the study of canon law, and at Naples (1328) he turned to story-writing in verse and prose, mingled in courtly society, and fell in love with the noble lady whom he made famous under the name of Fiammetta. Until 1350 he lived alternately in Florence and Naples, producing prose tales, pastorals, and poems. The *Teseide* is a graceful version in *ottava rima* of the medieval romance of Palamon and Arcite, which was partly translated by **Chaucer** in the *Knight's Tale*. The *Filostrato*, likewise in *ottava rima*, deals with the loves of Troilus and Cressida, also in great part translated by Chaucer. After 1350 he became a diplomat entrusted with important public affairs, and a scholar devoted to the cause of the new learning. During this period, in which he formed a lasting friendship with **Petrarch**, he visited Rome, Ravenna, Avignon, and Brandenburg as Florentine ambassador. In 1358 he completed his great work, the *Decameron*, begun some ten years before. Boccaccio selected the plots of his stories from the floating popular fiction of the day, and especially from the *fabliaux* which had passed into Italy from France, the matter being medieval, while the form is classical. Boccaccio's originality lies in his consummate narrative skill, and in the rich poetical sentiment which transforms his borrowed materials. For some time he held a chair founded to expound the works of **Dante**, on whose *Divina Commedia* he produced a commentary. During his last years he lived principally in retirement at Certaldo, and would have entered into holy orders, moved by repentance for the follies of his youth, had he not been dissuaded by **Petrarch**. He wrote in Latin an elaborate work on mythology, *De Genealogia Deorum*, and treatises such as *De Claris Mulieribus* and *De Montibus*.

BOCCAGE, Marie Anne Fiquet du, née **Le Page** (1710–1802) French poet, born in Rouen. Her *Paradis terrestre* (1748), an imitation of **Milton**, and *La Colombiade* (1756), gave her an exaggerated fame, perhaps on account of their author's great beauty, but her letters to her sister, written while travelling through England, Holland, and Italy, have historical interest.

BOCCHERINI, Luigi (1743–1805) Italian composer, born in Lucca. He was a cellist and prolific composer at the courts of the Infante Don Luis in Madrid and **Frederick II** of Prussia. He is best known for his chamber music, the famous minuet which holds its own among the most popular of classical tunes being from his string quintet in E, and for his cello concertos and sonatas. The great similarity of his work to that of his greater contemporary earned him the nickname '**Haydn**'s wife'. He died in poverty.

BOCCIONI, Umberto (1882–1916) Italian artist and sculptor, born in Reggio. He was the most original artist of the Futurist school, and its principal theorist. After working with **Balla**, **Severini**, and **Marinetti** in Rome and Paris from 1898 to 1914, he wrote a comprehensive survey of the movement, *Pittura, scultura futuriste* (1914). An important bronze sculpture, *Unique Forms of Continuity in Space* (1913), is in the Museum of Modern Art, New York.

BOCHART, Samuel (1599–1667) French Huguenot theologian and philologist, born in Rouen. After extensive studies, especially in the Semitic languages, he became Protestant pastor at Caen. In 1646 he published his *Geographia Sacra*, in 1663 *Hierozoicon, sive Bipertitum de Animalibus opus Scripturae Sacrae*. In 1652 he visited the Swedish court.

BOCHAS, John See **BOCCACCIO**

BOCK, Fedor von (1880–1945) German soldier, born in Küstrin. Educated at Potsdam Military School, he was commissioned with a Guards regiment in 1897. He served with distinction as a staff officer in World War I. He commanded the German armies invading Austria (1938), Poland (1939) and the Lower Somme, France (1940). Promoted field marshal in 1940, he participated in the invasion of Russia with remarkable success (1941), but was dismissed by **Hitler** for failing to capture Moscow (1942). He was killed with his wife and daughter in an air-raid.

BÖCKH, Philipp August See **BOECKH**

BÖCKLIN, Arnold (1827–1901) Swiss painter, born in Basel. His work, mainly of mythological subjects, combined classical themes of nymphs and satyrs with dark romantic landscapes, rocks, and castles, characteristic of 19th-century German painting.

BODE, Johann Elert (1747–1826) German astronomer, born in Hamburg. He became director of the Berlin Observatory. The arithmetical relation subsisting between the distances of the planets from the sun is called Bode's Law. This does not hold for the most distant planet, Pluto, and has no theoretical foundation.

BODE, Wilhelm von (1845–1929) German art critic, born in Brunswick. He became general director of the Prussian royal museums in 1905, and wrote much on Rembrandt and on the history of art, especially in the Renaissance period.

BODENSTEDT, Friedrich Martin von (1819–92) German writer, born in Peine in Hanover. He lived for a while in Moscow, travelled in the Middle East, was a professor at Munich University (from 1854) and director of the Meiningen court theatre (1867–73). He translated into German many Russian, English, and Persian texts, and published poetry. His best known work is *Leider des Mirza Schaffy* (1851), alleged to be a translation from the Tartar.

BODICHON, Barbara, née **Leigh Smith** (1827–90) English advocate of women's rights, born in London. The daughter of a radical MP who believed strongly in women's rights, she studied at Bedford College, London, and in 1852 opened a primary school in London. She wrote *Women at Work* (1857) and was a founder of the feminist magazine *The Englishwoman's Journal* (1858). She was one of the founders of the college for women that became Girton College, Cambridge. She was also a landscape water-colourist.

BODIN, Jean (1530–96) French political philosopher, born in Angers. He had a successful legal career and was also active politically; he visited Britain in 1581 as secretary to the Duke of Alençon who sought the hand of Queen **Elizabeth** of England. His major work was *Six Livres de la République* (1576), on the definition and limits of sovereignty, which argued for a limited form of monarchy. His *Colloqium Heptaplomeres* (1587) presented a plea for religious tolerance through the device of a conversation between a Jew, a

Muslim, a Lutheran, a Zwinglian, a Roman Catholic, an Epicurean and a Theist. Despite his enlightened liberalism he evidently shared the general belief of the time in sorcery and witchcraft, which he propounded in his influential *Démonomanie des sorciers* (1580). He died of the plague in Laon.

BODLEY, Sir Thomas (1545–1613) English scholar and diplomat, founder of the Bodleian library at Oxford, born in Exeter. He studied languages and divinity at Geneva, where his Protestant family had been forced to take refuge during the persecutions of **Mary I**, but in 1558 went to Magdalen College, Oxford, and was appointed Greek lecturer at Merton College in 1564. He studied Hebrew, and travelled extensively in Europe (1576–80) to master modern languages. In the service of Queen **Elizabeth** of England he was ambassador to Denmark, France and Holland. In 1597 he retired from court and settled in Oxford. In 1587 he married a wealthy widow, and then spent huge sums on the repair and extension of the university library originally established by **Humphrey, Duke of Gloucester**, and collected books from all over Europe. The library, renamed the Bodleian, was opened in 1602. He was knighted by King **James VI and I** in 1604.

BODMER, Johann Georg (1786–1864) Swiss inventor, born in Zürich. He was a mechanical engineering genius whose many inventions reflected the wide range of his interests in textile machinery, machine tools, screw propellers, armaments, steam engines, furnaces, boilers, and locomotives. Many of his most revolutionary innovations met with determined resistance from those unwilling to accept changes in established practice. Among his most successful inventions were a percussion shell (1805), a cotton carding and spinning machine which he manufactured in a factory he established in England (1824), and an opposed-piston steam engine (1834).

BODONI, Giambattista (1740–1813) Italian printer, born in Saluzzo. He designed (1790) a modern type face still widely used today. His press in Parma published editions of the classics widely admired for their elegance.

BOË, Franz de la See **SYLVIUS, Franciscus**

BOECE, Boyis, or **Boethius, Hector** (c.1465–1536) Scottish historian, born in Dundee, and studied at Montaigu College, Paris, where c.1492 to 1498 he was a regent or professor of philosophy, and where he made the friendship of **Erasmus**. Bishop **Elphinstone** then invited him to preside over his newly-founded university of Aberdeen. Boece accepted the office, and he was at the same time made a canon of the cathedral. In 1522 he published his lives, in Latin, of the bishops of Mortlach and Aberdeen; in 1527 the Latin *History of Scotland*, which, though proved to contain a large amount of fiction, was deemed distinctly critical at the time of its publication. The king awarded him a pension until he was promoted to a benefice in 1534.

BOECKH, Philipp August (1785–1867) German classical antiquary, born in Karlsruhe. He became professor of rhetoric and ancient literature at Berlin in 1811, where he lectured for more than 40 years. His four great works are his edition of Pindar (1811–21), *Die Staatshaushaltung der Athener* (1817), *Metrologische Untersuchunger* (1838), and *Das Seewesen des Attischen Staats* (1840).

BOEHM, Sir Joseph Edgar (1834–90) Australian-born British sculptor, born in Vienna. Educated in England, he finally settled there in 1862. The queen's effigy on the coinage issued in 1887 was from his designs, and he executed the well-known seated statue of **Thomas Carlyle** (1875).

BOEHM, Theobald (1794–1881) German flautist and inventor, born in Munich. He became a member of the Bavarian Court Orchestra in 1818 while working in the family trade as a goldsmith. In 1828 he opened a flute factory in Munich, and after hearing the English player Nicholson in 1831 he determined to make a flute which would be acoustically perfect. As this involved making holes in places where they could not be fingered, he devised a key mechanism to overcome the problem, and in 1847 produced the model on which the modern flute is based. Attempts to use his key system on the oboe and bassoon have been largely unsuccessful, though certain features have been applied to the clarinet.

BOEING, William Edward (1881–1956) American aircraft manufacturer, born in Detroit, Michigan. Having learned to fly in Los Angeles in 1915, he formed the Pacific Aero Products Co in 1916 to build seaplanes he had designed with Conrad Westerfelt. Renamed as the Boeing Airplane Company in 1917, it eventually became the largest manufacturer of military and civilian aircraft in the world. In 1927 he formed the Boeing Air Transport Company which introduced many novelties, including flying passengers by night, having two pilots and a stewardess, and the use of constant two-way radio telephone. He retired in 1934, when his air transport company became United Air Lines.

BOERHAAVE, Hermann (1668–1738) Dutch physician and botanist, born in Voorhout, near Leiden. In 1682 he went to Leiden, where he studied theology and oriental languages, and took his degree in philosophy in 1689; but in 1690 he began the study of medicine, and in 1701 was appointed lecturer on the theory of medicine, in 1709 professor of medicine and botany. The two works on which his great fame chiefly rests, *Institutiones Medicae* (1708) and *Aphorismi de Cognoscendis et Curandis Morbis* (1709), were translated into various European languages, and even into Arabic. In 1724 he also became professor of chemistry, and his *Elementa Chemiae* (1724) is a classic. Meanwhile patients came from all parts of Europe to consult him, earning him a fortune.

BOESAK, Allan Aubrey (1945–) South African churchman, born in Kakamas, north-western Cape Province. Lecturer and student chaplain at Western Cape University, president of the alliance of Black Reformed Christians in South Africa (1981), and president of the World Alliance of Reformed Churches (1982–), he sees the Christian gospel in terms of liberation of the oppressed. He is an outspoken opponent of apartheid, and leader of the coloured, or mixed-race, community in South Africa. *Farewell to Innocence* (1977), his study of Black Theology, has been followed by several collections of sermons and addresses, including *The Finger of God* (1982), *Black and Reformed* and *Walking on Thorns* (1984), and *If this is Treason, I am Guilty* (1987).

BOETHIUS, Anicius Manlius Severimus (c.480–524) Roman philosopher and statesman, sometimes described as 'the last of the Roman philosophers, the first of the scholastic theologians'. Born of a patrician Roman family, he studied at Athens and there gained the knowledge which later enabled him to produce the translations of and commentaries on **Aristotle** and **Porphyry** that became the standard textbooks on logic in medieval Europe. He became consul in 510 during the Gothic occupation of Rome and later chief minister to the ruler **Theodoric**; but in 523 he was accused of treason and after a year in prison at Pavia was executed. It was during his imprisonment that he wrote the famous *De Consolatione Philosophiae*, in which Philosophy personified solaces the distraught author by explaining the mutability of all earthly fortune and demonstrating that happiness can only be attained by virtue, that is by being like God. The *Consolation* was for the next millenium probably the most widely read book after the Bible.

BOETHIUS, Hector See **BOECE**

BOËX, Joseph and **Séraphin** See **ROSNY, Joseph Henri**

BOFF, Leonardo (1938–) Brazilian Franciscan liberation theologian, born of Italian stock in Concordia, Santa Catarina. He was ordained in Brazil in 1964, and studied at Würzburg, Louvain, Oxford and Munich, and became professor of systematic theology in Petrópolis, Rio. His best-known work, *Jesus-Christ Liberator* (1972, English trans, 1978), offers hope and justice for the oppressed rather than religious support of the *status quo* in church and society. He has written several books on reforming church structures from grass-roots 'basic communities', including *Church: Charism and Power* (1984), which provoked official ecclesiastical censure. Besides collaborating with his brother Clodovis on introductions to liberation theology, he has written widely on other themes, including *St Francis: A Model for Human Liberation* (1985) and *The Maternal Face of God* (1988).

BOGARDE, Dirk, originally **Derek Niven Van Den Bogaerde** (1921–) English actor and novelist, born in Hampstead, London. Originally a scenic designer and commercial artist, he began acting in repertory theatre and made his film début as an extra in *Come On George* (1940). After war service, he was signed to a long-term contract with Rank Films, spending many years playing small-time crooks, military heroes and breezy comic leads until he was voted Britain's top box-office star (1955 and 1957). Ambitious to tackle more challenging material, he played Sidney Carton in *A Tale of Two Cities* (1958), a blackmailed homosexual in *Victim* (1961) and a sinisterly manipulative valet in *The Servant* (1963). Subsequently favouring European cinema he has created a series of distinguished characterizations, subtly portraying decadence, enigma and ambiguity, notably in *Death in Venice* (1971) and *Providence* (1977). He has published four volumes of autobiography and several novels.

BOGARDUS, James (1800–74) American inventor, born in Catskill, New York. Apprenticed to a watchmaker, he made improvements in eight-day clocks, and invented a delicate engraving machine, the dry gas meter, the transfer machine for producing banknote plates from separate dies, a pyrometer, a deep-sea sounding machine, a dynamometer, and in 1839 a method of engraving postage stamps, which was adopted by the British government. He also erected the first cast-iron building in America.

BOGART, Humphrey De Forest (1899–1957) American film actor, born in New York City. After serving briefly with the US navy he became a stage manager and walk-on actor, graduating to juvenile leads before making his film début in *Broadway's Like That* (1930). Alternating between stage and screen, he was frequently cast as a vicious hoodlum, most memorably in *The Petrified Forest* (1936), but eventually attained stardom with his roles in *High Sierra* (1941), *The Maltese Falcon* (1941), *Casablanca* (1942, with **Ingrid Bergman**), and *To Have and Have Not* (1944), which also marked the début of **Lauren Bacall**, who became his fourth wife in 1945. Over the next 15 years he created an indelible and enduring screen persona of the lone wolf; cynical but heroic, abrasive, romantic and stubbornly faithful to his own code of ethics, as in *The Big Sleep* (1946). His considerable acting prowess was also displayed as the selfish prospector in *The Treasure of the Sierra Madre* (1948), the gin-sodden boatman in *The African Queen* (1951, Academy Award for Best Actor) and the psychopathic captain in *The Caine Mutiny* (1954). He died after a long struggle with cancer.

BOGATZKY, Karl Heinrich von (1690–1774) German hymnwriter, born in Jankowe in Lower Silesia. His chief work is his *Golden Treasury* (trans 1775).

BOGDANOV, Michael (1938–) British stage director, educated at the universities of Dublin, Munich and the Sorbonne. At the Royal Shakespeare Company he directed *The Taming of the Shrew* (1978), *Romeo and Juliet* (1986) and **O'Casey**'s *Shadow of a Gunman* (1980). His National Theatre productions include **Howard Brenton**'s *The Romans in Britain* (1980), **Calderon**'s *The Mayor of Zalamea* (1981), **Chekhov**'s *Uncle Vanya* (1982), and **Kyd**'s *The Spanish Tragedy* (1982). In 1986, with actor **Michael Pennington**, he became co-founder and artistic director of the touring English Shakespeare Company.

BOGLE, George (1746–81) Scottish diplomat, born near Bothwell, Lanarkshire. He entered the service of the East India Company, and in 1774 was selected by **Warren Hastings** to act as envoy to the Lama of Tibet. He was the first Briton to cross the Tsanpu in its upper range, established commercial links with Tibet and became a personal friend of the Lama. He returned in 1775, and died in Calcutta.

BOGUE, David (1750–1825) Scottish congregational minister and one of the founders of the London Missionary Society, born in Coldingham, Berwickshire. He became an Independent minister and tutor at a Gosport seminary, out of which grew the London Missionary Society. He was also a founder of the British and Foreign Bible Society and the Religious Tract Society and (with Dr James Bennet) wrote a *History of Dissenters* (1809).

BOHEMOND I (c.1056–1111) prince of Antioch, eldest son of **Robert Guiscard**. He distinguished himself in his father's war against the Byzantine emperor, **Alexius I Comnenus** (1081–85). After his father's death he was excluded from the throne of Apulia by his brother Roger, and only gained the principality of Tarentum after a long struggle. He joined the First Crusade (1096), and took a prominent part in the capture of Antioch (1098). While the other crusaders advanced to storm Jerusalem, Bohemond established himself as prince in Antioch. He was taken prisoner by the Turks from 1100 to 1103, then returned to Europe to collect troops, and after defeating Alexius in 1107 was acknowledged by him as prince of Antioch in return for his vassalage.

BOHEMOND II (1108–31) Prince of Antioch, younger son of **Bohemond I**. He assumed the government of Antioch in 1126, and was killed in battle with the Turks.

BÖHM, Theobald See **BOEHM**

BÖHME, or **BOEHME, Jakob** (1575–1624) German theosophist and mystic, born of poor parents in Altseidenberg near Görolitz in Upper Lusatia. As a boy he tended cattle, and later became a shoemaker, but in 1600 he had a mystical experience and from then on devoted much of his time to meditation on divine things. About 1612 he published *Aurora*. It contains revelations and meditations upon God, Man, and Nature, and shows a remarkable knowledge of Scripture and of the writings of alchemists. It was condemned by the ecclesiastical authorities of Görlitz, and he was cruelly persecuted, but in 1623 he published *Der Weg zu Christo* and *Mysterium*. His chief aim was to explain the origin of things, especially the existence of evil. God is the *Ungrund* or *Urgrund*, the original and undistinguished unity, at once everything and nothing. However, this has in itself the principle of separation whereby all things come into existence. It is through the principle of negation, which can be identified with evil, that creation is explained. Böhme's philosophy is in fact an application of the principle of contradiction to explain the great problems of philosophy and religion; but the difficulties are only concealed or shifted about under a cloud of mystical language, in which a system of triads, suggested by the Christian doctrine of the trinity, has an important place. His influence spread beyond Germany to Holland and England. **Newton** studied him; **Henry More** was influenced by him; **William Law** might be called a disciple; John Pordage (1608–98) and Jane Leade (1623–1704) were leaders of the Philadelphians, a Böhmenist sect. Points of contact with **Spinoza**, **Fichte**, **Schelling**, and **Hegel** revived interest in his speculations in Germany in the 19th century.

BOHN, Henry George (1796–1884) British publisher, born of German parentage in London. In 1831 he started as a secondhand bookseller. In 1841 he issued his famous 'guinea catalogue' of old books, containing 23 208 items. In 1846 he started his popular *Standard Library* (followed by the *Scientific Library*, *Classical Library*, *Antiquarian Library*, and others); in all the series comprised over 600 volumes. An accomplished scholar, he translated some foreign classics and compiled a *Dictionary of Quotations* (1867) as well as a bibliographical study of *Shakespeare*.

BOHR, Aage Niels (1922–) Danish physicist, born in Copenhagen,the son of the Nobel prize-winning physicist **Niels Bohr**, and himself a Nobel laureate. Educated at the University of Copenhagen and the University of London, he worked in his father's Institute of Theoretical Physics in Copenhagen from 1946, and in 1956 became professor of physics at Copenhagen. From 1963 to 1970 he was director of the Niels Bohr Institute (formerly the Institute of Theoretical Physics) and from 1975 to 1981 director of Nordita (Nordic Institute for Theoretical Atomic Physics). With **Ben Mottelson**, he secured experimental evidence for the support of **Leo James Rainwater**'s collective model of the atomic nucleus. Bohr, Mottelson and Rainwater shared the Nobel prize for physics in 1975.

BOHR, Niels Henrik David (1885–1962) Danish physicist, born in Copenhagen. Educated at Copenhagen University, he went to England to work with Sir **Joseph John Thomson** at Cambridge and **Ernest Rutherford** at Manchester, and returned to Copenhagen as professor (1916). He greatly extended the theory of atomic structure when he explained the spectrum of hydrogen by means of an atomic model and the quantum theory (1913). During World War II he escaped from German-occupied Denmark and assisted atom bomb research in America, returning to Copenhagen in 1945. He was founder and director of the Institute of Theoretical Physics at Copenhagen, (1920-62), and was awarded the Nobel prize for physics in 1922. His son, **Aage Niels Bohr**, won the 1975 Nobel prize for physics.

BÖHTLINGK, Otto von (1815–1904) German Sanskrit scholar, born in St Petersburg. From 1835 to 1842 he studied oriental languages, especially Sanskrit, at Berlin and Bonn, and lived thereafter in Jena and Leipzig. His works include the first European edition of the Indian grammarian **Pānini** (1839) and a seven-volume Sanskrit dictionary (1855–75).

BOHUN a family founded by the Norman Humphrey de Bohun, whose fourth descendant, Henry, in 1199 was made Earl of Hereford. Humphrey, fourth Earl of Hereford (1276–1322), was taken prisoner at Bannockburn, and fell at Boroughbridge. In 1380 the heiress of the earldoms of Hereford, Essex, and Northampton married Henry Bolingbroke (**Henry IV**).

BOIAMOND See **BAJIMOND**

BOIARDO, Matteo Maria, Count of Scandiano (1434–94) Italian poet, born in Scandiano, a village at the foot of the Lombard Apennines. He studied at Ferrara, and in 1462 married the daughter of the Count of Norellara. He lived at the court of Ferrara on intimate terms with Dukes Borso and Ercole; by the latter he was employed on diplomatic missions, and appointed governor in 1481 of Modena, and in 1487 of Reggio. As an administrator he was distinguished for his clemency, and opposition to capital punishment. Boiardo has been called the 'Flower of Chivalry'. His fame rests on the unfinished *Orlando Innamorato* (1486), a long narrative poem in which the **Charlemagne** romances are recast into *ottava rima*. His other works comprise Latin eclogues, a versification of **Lucian**'s *Timon*, translations of **Herodotus**, the *Ass* of Lucian, and the *Golden Ass* of **Apuleius**, and a series of sonnets and *Canzoni* (1499).

BOÏELDIEU, François Adrien (1775–1834) French composer, born in Rouen. His opera *Le Calife de Bagdad* (1800), which was performed in Paris, brought him acclaim. He conducted at St Petersburg (1803–10) and on his return produced his two masterpieces, *Jean de Paris* (1812) and *La Dame blanche* (1825), in which he displays his talent for bright and graceful melody. His son Adrien (1816–83) also composed operas.

BOILEAU, or **Boileau Despréaux, Nicolas** (1636–1711) French poet and critic, born in Paris. He studied law and theology at Beauvais, but as a man of means devoted himself to literature. His first publications (1660–66) were satires, some of which got him into trouble. In 1677 the king appointed him, along with **Racine**, official royal historian. *L'Art poétique*, imitated by **Pope** in the *Essay on Criticism*, was published in 1674, along with the first part of the clever serio-comic *Lutrin*. Between 1669 and 1677 he published nine epistles, written, like his satires, on the Horatian model. In his last years he returned to Auteuil. His works include several critical dissertations, especially *L'Art poétique* (1674), a collection of epigrams, a translation of **Longinus**' *On the Sublime*, a *Dialogue des héros de roman*, and a series of letters (many to Racine). His influence as a critic has been profound. He set up good sense, sobriety, elegance, and dignity of style as the cardinal literary virtues.

BOIS-REYMOND, Emil du (1818–96) German physiologist, and discoverer of neuro-electricity, born in Berlin of French parentage. He became professor of physiology at Berlin in 1855. He investigated the physiology of muscles and nerves, and demonstrated electricity in animals. His brother Paul (1831–89), a mathematician, wrote on the theory of functions.

BOISBAUDRAN, Paul Émile Lecoq de (1838–1912) French physical chemist, born in Cognac, Charente. A founder of spectroscopy, he discovered gallium, samarium and dysprosium.

BOISSERÉE, Sulpice (1783–1854) German art historian, born in Cologne. With his brother Melchior (1786–1851) he collected at Stuttgart 200 pictures, sold in 1827 to the king of Bavaria.

BOISSY D'ANGLAS, François Antoine de (1756–1826) French statesman. A member of the States-General (1789), he joined the successful conspiracy against **Robespierre**. He was elected secretary of the Convention, and a member of the Committee of Public Safety, in which capacity he displayed remarkable talent. He was later called to the senate by **Napoleon** and made a peer by **Louis XVIII**.

BOITO, Arrigo (1842–1918) Italian composer and poet, born in Padua. He studied at the Milan Conservatory. His first important work was the opera *Mefistofele* (1868), which survived its initial failure and later grew in popularity. Another opera, *Nerone*, written in 1916, was not produced till 1924. He wrote his own and other libretti, including those for **Verdi**'s *Otello* and *Falstaff*.

BOJARDO See **BOIARDO**

BOK, Edward William (1863–1930) Dutch-born American editor, born in Den Helder, emigrating to the USA at the age of six. He worked as a stenographer in his youth and became editor of the *Brooklyn Magazine* at 19. He ran the Bok Syndicate Press from 1886 to 1891 and was editor-in-chief of *The Ladies' Home Journal* from 1889 to 1919. He published several books in celebration of the American gospel of business success, and a highly influential autobiography, *The Americanization of Edward Bok* (1920). He created the $100000 American Peace award, and the Harvard Advertizing awards in 1923.

BOKASSA, Jean Bedel (1921–) Central African Republic politician and soldier, born in Bobangui, Lobay. He joined the French army in 1939 and in 1963, after independence, was made army commander-in-chief, with the rank of colonel. In 1965 he led a coup which overthrew President David Dacko. He progressively increased his personal power, annulled the constitution and made himself life-president, and in 1977 was crowned emperor in a lavish ceremony the nation could ill afford. He became increasingly dictatorial and was held responsible for the deaths of numerous people, including school-children. In 1979 he was himself ousted and went into exile but in 1988 was returned for trial and found guilty of murder and other crimes. His death sentence was eventually commuted.

BOKER, George Henry (1823–90) American poet, playwright, and diplomat, born in Philadelphia. He won belated recognition for his 400 sonnets and for *Francesca da Rimini* (1855), a romantic verse tragedy and the best American play before the Civil War. His propaganda for the North secured him the post of minister to Turkey (1871–75) and Russia (1875–78).

BOL, Ferdinand (c.1616–1680) Dutch painter who studied under **Rembrandt** in the 1630s and was one of his most talented followers. Working in Amsterdam, for many years he painted in a style so close to his master's that some of his portraits have been mistaken for his. After c.1650, when the Rembrandtesque style was no longer fashionable, Bol's work, following a new fashion for French style, became more elegant and courtly. After marrying a wealthy widow in 1669, he appears to have stopped painting.

BOLDREWOOD, Rolf, pseud of **Thomas Alexander Browne** (1826–1915) Australian novelist, born in London. His family emigrated to Australia in 1830. He was educated in Sydney, and became a squatter in Victoria and later an inspector of goldfields. His exciting, romantic and didactic novels depict life at the cattle stations and diggings. They include *Robbery under Arms* (1888), and *Babes in the Bush* (1900).

BOLET, Jorge (1914–) Cuban-born American pianist, born in Havana. He studied at the Curtis Institute of Music, Philadelphia, from the age of twelve, and currently is head of piano studies there. He also had lessons from **Leopold Godowsky**, Rosenthal and **Rudolf Serkin**. His career was interrupted during World War II by service in the Cuban and, later, US armies; he became a US citizen in 1944. He is renowned for his interpretation of **Liszt**, the German, Spanish and Russian Romantics and the repertoire of virtuosi-composers such as Godowsky, **Rubinstein** and Carl Tausig.

BOLEYN, Anne (c.1504–1536) English queen, the second wife of **Henry VIII**, and daughter of Sir Thomas Boleyn, by Elizabeth Howard, daughter of the Duke of Norfolk. She was at the French court (1519–21), and on her return her suitors included Henry Percy, the heir to the Earl of Northumberland, and King Henry himself, who began to shower favours upon her father, having already had an affair with her sister. Anne did not apparently favour him until negotiations for the divorce from **Catherine of Aragon** began in 1527, but, as these dragged on, their association became shameless and they were secretly married in January 1533. **Cranmer** declared her Henry's legal wife in May and she was crowned with great splendour in Westminster Hall on Whitsunday; but within three months Henry's passion had cooled. It was not revived by the birth, in September 1533, of a princess, the future Queen **Elizabeth**, still less by that of a stillborn son, in January 1536. On May Day that year the King rode off abruptly from a tournament held at Greenwich, leaving the queen behind, and the next day she was arrested and brought to the Tower. A secret commission investigated charges of Anne's adultery with her own brother, Lord Rochford, and four commoners. They were tried and convicted of high treason. Her own uncle, **Thomas Howard**, 3rd Duke of Norfolk, presided over her judges, and pronounced the verdict. She was beheaded on Tower Green on 19 May. Henry the next day married **Jane Seymour**.

BOLINGBROKE See **HENRY IV**

BOLINGBROKE, Henry St John, 1st Viscount (1678–1751) English statesman and writer, born in Battersea, London. Educated at Eton, after travel on the Continent he entered parliament in 1701 as Tory member for Wootton Bassett. He became successively secretary for war (1704–08) and foreign secretary (1710), and shared the leadership of the party with **Robert Harley**. He was made a peer in 1712 and in 1713 he brilliantly negotiated the treaty of Utrecht. After intriguing successfully for Harley's downfall, he was plotting a Jacobite restoration when Queen **Anne** died, and **George I** succeeded. He fled to France, was attainted in 1715, and acted for some time as secretary of state to **James Stewart**, the Old Pretender. While living abroad he wrote his *Reflections on Exile*. In 1723 he obtained permission to return to England, settled at Dawley, near Uxbridge, and became the associate of **Pope**, **Swift**, and other men of letters. A series of letters attacking **Walpole** in the *Craftsman* were reprinted as *A Dissertation of Parties*. Disappointed in his hope of readmission to political life, he returned to France, where he remained from 1735 to 1742 and wrote his *Letters on the Study and Use of History* (1752). His last years were spent in Battersea, where he wrote his *Letters on the Spirit of Patriotism* and his *Idea of a Patriot King* (1749), which was to have a profound political influence. The monarchy, as conceived by Bolingbroke, was to stand above faction and represent the nation. He also wrote *Reflections Concerning Innate Moral Principles* (1752). A brilliant orator and writer, he suffered as a public figure through his egotism and rakishness.

BOLÍVAR, Simón (1783–1830) South American revolutionary leader, known as 'the Liberator' of South America from the Spanish yoke. Born in Caracas in Venezuela, of noble family, he studied law in Madrid, and was in Paris during the Revolution. After the declaration of independence by Venezuela in 1811, he fled to New Granada and raised an army. In 1813, entering Caracas as conqueror, he proclaimed himself dictator of western Venezuela. Driven out in 1814, he made repeated descents on Venezuela from the West Indies, and in 1817 began to make headway against the Spaniards. Owing to dissensions among the patriots, it was only in 1821 that the victory of Carabobo virtually ended the war; and it was not till 1824 that the royalist troops were finally driven out. In 1821 Bolívar was chosen president of Colombia, comprising Venezuela, Colombia, and New Granada. In 1822 he added Ecuador to the republic, and in 1824 drove the Spaniards out of Peru, and made himself dictator there for a time. Upper Peru was made a separate state, and called Bolivia in his honour, while he was named perpetual protector; but his Bolivian constitution excited great dissatisfaction, and led to the expulsion of the Colombian troops. His assumption of supreme power, after his return to Colombia in 1828, roused the apprehension of the republicans there; and in 1829 Venezuela separated itself from Colombia. Bolívar, in consequence, laid down his authority in 1830, and died the same year. Although his life ended in dictatorship, his ideal of a federation of all Spanish-speaking South American states continued to exert a lively influence.

BOLKIAH, Hassanal (1946–) sultan of Brunei, the son of Sultan Sir Omar Ali Saifuddin. He was educated at the Victoria Institute in Kuala Lumpur, Malaysia, and Sandhurst royal military academy. Appointed crown prince in 1961, he became sultan in 1967 on his father's abdication. On independence, in 1984, Sultan Bolkiah also became prime minister and defence minister, governing in a personalized, familial manner. As head of an oil- and gas-rich micro-state, he is reputed to be the richest individual in the world, with an estimated wealth of $25 billion. He owns the Dorchester and Beverly Hills hotels in London and Los Angeles, a private air-fleet, and has had built, at the cost of $40 million, the world's largest palace. A moderate Muslim, he has two wives, Princess Saleha (m.1965), and Mariam Bell (m.1981), a former air stewardess.

BÖLL, Heinrich (1917–85) German writer, born in Cologne. He served as an infantryman in World War II before becoming a full-time writer. His first novel, *Der Zug war Pünktlich* (The Train was on Time) was published in 1949. A trilogy, *Und Sagte kein Einziges Worte* (And Never Said a Solitary Word, 1953), *Haus ohne Hüter* (The Unguarded House, 1954), and *Das Brot der Frühen Jahre* (The Bread of our Early Years, 1955), depicting life in Germany during and after the Nazi régime, gained him a worldwide reputation. His later novels, characteristically satirizing modern German society, included *Die vorlorene Ehre der Katherina Blum* (The Lost Honour of Katherina Blum, 1975). He was awarded the 1972 Nobel prize for literature.

BOLLAND, John van (1596–1665) Flemish Jesuit hagiologist, from Antwerp. He was the founder and first editor (1629) of the Bollandist *Acta Sanctorum* (Lives of the Saints).

BOLM, Adolph (1884–1951) Russian dancer, choreographer and teacher, born in St Petersburg. He studied with **Nicolai Legat** and others at the Imperial Ballet School, graduating into the Maryinsky Theatre in 1903 and eventually becoming a soloist. He organized and danced in **Anna Pavlova**'s first tours (1908–09) concurrent with joining **Serge Diaghilev**'s Ballets Russes. From 1911 he travelled the world with the company, remaining in the USA after the 1916 tour. One of America's ballet pioneers, he gradually progressed from coast to coast as a celebrated dancer, teacher and choreographer. He was closely associated with the Chicago Civic Opera and the companies now known as American Ballet Theatre and San Francisco Ballet. His choreography can be seen in the films *The Mad Genius* (1931), *The Men in Her Life* (1941) and *Affairs of Cellini* (1934).

BOLOGNA, Giovanni (1524–1608) Flemish sculptor and architect, born in Douai. He went to Italy in 1551 and won great popularity and executed much work in Florence for the **Medici**, including the *Flying Mercury* (1564) and various fountains in the Boboli gardens, the *Rape of the Sabines* (1580), and *Hercules and the Centaur* (1599). His bronzes can be seen in the Wallace Collection, and elsewhere.

BOLSEC, Hieronymus (d.c.1584) ex-Carmelite friar, who opposed **Calvin**'s doctrine of predestination at Geneva (1551), causing him to reformulate it. He then returned to Catholicism and wrote a libellous Life of him (1577).

BOLTWOOD, Bertram Borden (1870–1927) American radiochemist who greatly furthered knowledge of the uranium decay series. Born in Amherst, Massachusetts, he grew up fatherless, in an academic family, and was educated at Yale, Munich and Leipzig. He was professor at Yale (1897–1900, 1910–27), and from 1904 concentrated on research into radiochemistry, becoming the leading American figure in this field. He discovered the radioactive element ionium, and introduced Pb:U ratios as a method for dating rocks (1907).

BOLTZMANN, Ludwig (1844–1906) Austrian physicist, born in Vienna. After many professorships elsewhere he became professor there in 1895. He did important work on the kinetic theory of gases and established Boltzmann's law, or the principle of the equipartition of energy.

BOLYAI, János (1802–60) Hungarian mathematician, born in Kolozsvár. He took up a military career, but retired through ill health in 1833. After attempting to prove **Euclid's** parallel postulate, he realized that it was possible to have a consistent system of geometry in which this postulate did not hold, and so became one of the founders of non-Euclidean geometry, together with **Nikolai Lobachevsky**. His work continued that of his father Farkas (or Wolfgang) (1775–1856).

BOLZANO, Bernard (1781–1848) Catholic theologian, philosopher, and mathematician, born in Prague of Italian ancestry. He became a priest in 1804 and professor of the philosophy of religion in 1805, but was deprived of his chair in 1819 for non-conformity, his works being put on the Index. He was a pioneer in giving a rigorous foundation to the theory of functions of a real variable, and investigating the mathematical concept of the infinite.

BOMBA See **FERNINAND II** (of Naples)

BOMBARD, Alain Louis (1924–) French physician and marine biologist, born in Paris. In 1952 he set out across the Atlantic alone in his rubber dinghy *L'Hérétique* to prove his claim that shipwreck castaways could sustain life on nothing more than fish and plankton. He landed at Barbados on 24 December 1952, emaciated, but vindicated in his theories. He started a marine laboratory—'La Coryphene'—at Saint-Malo, for the study of the physiopathology of the sea.

BOMBERG, David (1890–1957) English painter, born in Birmingham. He trained as a lithographer before studying painting in London at the City and Guilds School, at the Westminster School of Art (1908–10) under **Sickert**, and at the Slade (1911–13). He was a founder member of the London Group (1913). In Paris he met avant-garde artists including

Modigliani, **Derain** and **Picasso**, and their influence is clear in such large compositions as *The Mud Bath* and *In the Hold* (1913–14), which combine abstract and Vorticist influences. He later travelled widely, visiting, among others, Palestine (1923–27), Spain (1929 and 1934–35), Morocco and the Greek Islands (1930) and Russia (1933).

BOMBOIS, Camille (1883–1970) French primitive painter, born in Venarey-les-Laumes, Côte d'Or. Without academic training, he worked in a travelling circus, and as a labourer, painting as a hobby. By 1923 he had been discovered by collectors and was able to devote all his time to painting his very personal landscapes (eg, of the *Sacré Cœur*) and pictures of wrestlers and acrobats. They are uncompromisingly realistic, with a childlike frankness and simplicity of technique.

BONALD, Louis Gabriel Ambroise, Vicomte de (1754–1840) French writer. He emigrated to Heidelberg during the French Revolution and wrote *Théorie du pouvoir politique et religieux* (1796), advocating the system of monarchy and prophesying the return of the **Bourbons**. He was appointed by **Napoleon** minister of instruction in 1808, in 1815 ennobled by **Louis XVIII**. His son, Louis Jacques Maurice (1787–1870), became archbishop of Lyon in 1839, and cardinal in 1841.

BONAPARTE family of influence in the affairs of Corsica since the 16th century, spelt Buonaparte until 1768.

BONAPARTE, Caroline, in full **Maria Annunciata Caroline** (1782–1839) queen of Naples (1808–15), the youngest surviving daughter of **Charles** and **Marie Bonaparte**. She married **Murat** in 1800, and brought a brilliant court life to the Neapolitan palaces of Caserta and Portici. After her husband's execution she lived, under surveillance, at Frohsdorf in Austria (1815–24) and Trieste (1824–31) before settling in Florence for the last seven years of her life.

BONAPARTE, Charles Marie (1746–85) Corsican lawyer, born in Ajaccio, the city of which he was appointed **Louis XVI**'s royal counsellor and assessor in 1773. Married to **Marie Bonaparte**, he was father of **Napoleon I**. He died in Montpelier while Napoleon, the second of his five surviving sons, was at the military academy in Brienne.

BONAPARTE, Élisa, in full **Marie-Anne Élisa** (1777–1820) Grand Duchess of Tuscany, the eldest surviving daughter of **Charles** and **Marie Bonaparte**. She married Felix Bacciochi in 1797. As Duchess of Lucca from 1805, she managed the economy of her small state so profitably that in 1809 **Napoleon** assigned her to Tuscany, where she revived the court glories of the Pitti Palace. Towards the end of her life she called herself Countess of Compignano.

BONAPARTE, Jérôme (1784–1860) king of Westphalia, son of **Charles** and **Marie Bonaparte** and brother of **Napoleon**. He served in the navy (1800–02) and lived in New York (1803–05), marrying Elizabeth Patterson (1785–1879) at Baltimore in 1803, a marriage which Napoleon declared null and void; their son was the father of Charles Joseph Bonaparte (1851–1921) who was US secretary of the navy, 1905–06, and attorney-general, 1906–09. Jérôme was given a high military command by Napoleon in the Prussian campaign of 1806, led an army corps at Wagram in 1809, incurred his brother's displeasure during the invasion of Russia in 1812, but fought with tenacity at Waterloo. He was sovereign of Westphalia from July 1807 to October 1813, marrying Princess Catherine of Württemberg in August 1807. After accepting exile in Rome, Florence and Switzerland, he returned to Paris in 1847. His nephew **Napoleon III** appointed him governor of the Invalides, created him a marshal of France, and consulted him over the strategy of the Crimean War, where his son Prince Napoleon Joseph Charles Paul (1822–91) fought at the Alma and Inkerman. Jérôme's great-grandson Louis, Prince Napoleon, born in Brussels in 1914, became head of the House of Bonaparte in 1926.

BONAPARTE, Joseph (1768–1844) king of Naples and Sicily (1806–08) and king of Spain (1808–13), the eldest surviving son of **Charles** and **Marie Bonaparte** and brother of **Napoleon**. He married in 1794 Julie Clary (1771–1845), elder sister of **Desiré Bernadotte**. He served Napoleon on diplomatic missions and was a humane sovereign in southern Italy but faced continuous rebellion as a nominated ruler in Spain where his army was decisively defeated by **Wellington** at Vitoria (June 1813). He spent much of his life in exile in New Jersey but settled in Florence for the last years of his life.

BONAPARTE, Louis (1778–1846) king of Holland, son of **Charles** and **Marie Bonaparte**, and brother of **Napoleon**. He was a soldier, serving originally in the artillery but later in the cavalry. He married Napoleon's step-daughter, **Hortense Beauharnais**, in 1802. He ruled Holland as King Lodewijk I from 1806 until 1810 when he abdicated because Napoleon had complained that he was attached to the interests of the Dutch. Louis became Count of Saint-Leu, settled in Austria and Switzerland, later living in Florence, although he died in Leghorn. He was the father of **Napoleon III**.

BONAPARTE, Lucien (1775–1840) prince of Canino, and a younger brother of **Napoleon**, born in Ajaccio, and educated at Autun, Brienne, and Aix. In 1798 he was made a member of the Council of Five Hundred, and just before the 18th Brumaire he was elected its president. He was successful as minister of the interior; and as ambassador to Madrid (1800) undermined British influence. On condition that he would divorce his second wife (the widow of a stockbroker) the crowns of Italy and Spain were offered him; but he refused them, and lived on his state of Canino, in the papal states, being created by the pope prince of Canino. He had never wholly shaken off his early strong republicanism; and having denounced the arrogant policy of his brother towards the court of Rome, he was 'advised' to leave Roman territory, and in 1810, on his way to America, was captured by the English and kept a prisoner at Ludlow and Thorngrove, Worcestershire, till 1814. He returned to Italy and published his memoirs (1882–83). One of his sons, Charles (1803–57), won a European reputation as a botanist. A second, Louis Lucien (1813–91), philologist, born in Thorngrove, was granted a civil list pension for his 222 linguistic works in 1883; and the third, Pierre (1815–81), became notorious for killing Victor Noir, a journalist, in a duel.

BONAPARTE, Marie Letizia, née **Ramolino** (c.1749–1836) Born in Ajaccio, daughter of a French army captain, married **Charles Marie Bonaparte** in 1764. Of her twelve children, five died in infancy; the fourth child became **Napoleon I**. She was accorded official status as 'Madame Mère de l'Empereur' in May 1804 and encouraged her son to seek reconciliation with the church, her half-brother Cardinal Fesch (1763–1839) becoming archbishop of Lyon. Mme Mère supported the fallen Napoleon on Elba in 1814 but spent the last 18 years of her life in dignified retirement in Rome.

BONAPARTE, (Marie) Pauline (1780–1825) Princess Borghese, daughter of **Charles** and **Marie Bonaparte**, and **Napoleon**'s favourite sister. She married General Leclerc in 1797 and accompanied him on the expedition to Haiti (1802) on which he contracted yellow fever and died. In 1803 she married Prince **Camillo Borghese**, her private life soon shocking the patrician family into which she married, not least because of her willingness to pose as a nude Venus for the sculptor **Canova**. She loyally supported Napoleon in his exile on Elba; her last years were spent in Florence.

BONAPARTE, Napoleon See **NAPOLEON I**

BONAPARTE, Napoleon Joseph Charles Paul (1822–91) French politican, son of **Jérôme Bonaparte** and nephew of **Napoleon**. Nicknamed 'Plon-Plon', he was born in Trieste and grew up in Italy. He entered military service in Württemberg in 1837, and was expelled from France in 1845 for republicanism. In 1848, having taken the name 'Jérôme' on his elder brother's death, he was elected to the legislative national assembly. In 1851 he was named as the successor to **Napoleon III**. He fought in the Crimean War in 1854, but was recalled by the emperor, and made minister for the colonies and Algeria in 1858. In 1859 he married the Princess Clotilda, daughter of **Victor Emmanuel II** of Sardinia, by whom he had two sons and a daughter. After the fall of the empire he took up residence in England, but returned to France in 1872 and sat in the Chamber of Deputies. The death of the Prince Imperial in 1879 made him head of the family, and in 1886, as pretender to the throne, he was exiled from France with his eldest son, Victor (1862–1926), who settled in Brussels and was in turn succeeded as head of the Bonaparte family by his son, Louis Jérôme (1914–).

BONAR, Horatius (1808–89) Scottish hymn-writer, born in Edinburgh. He was minister at Kelso (1837–66), but joined the Free Church of Scotland and was minister of Chalmers Memorial Church in Edinburgh from 1866. He wrote well-known hymns such as 'Glory be to God the Father', 'Here, O my Lord, I see thee face to face', and 'I heard the voice of Jesus say'.

BONAVENTURE, or **Bonaventura, St,** originally **Giovanni di Fidanza** (1221–74) Italian theologian, born near Orvieto, Tuscany, and known as 'Doctor Seraphicus'. In 1243 he became a Franciscan, in 1253 a professor of theology at Paris, in 1257 general of his order, and in 1273 cardinal bishop of Albano. During the Council of Lyon he died, from sheer ascetic exhaustion. In 1482 he was canonized by **Sixtus IV**, and in 1587 was declared by Pope **Sixtus V** the sixth of the great doctors of the church. His mysticism attracted **Luther**, though he promoted Mariolatry, celibacy, and a high view of transubstantiation. His most important works are the *Breviloquium* (a dogmatic); the *Itinerarium Mentis in Deum*; *De Reductione Artium ad Theologiam*, a commentary on **Peter Lombard**; and his *Biblia Pauperum*, or 'Poor Man's Bible'. His feast day is 14 July.

BOND, Alan (1938–) English-born Australian businessman, born in Ealing, London. He emigrated to Fremantle, western Australia, in 1951. A year later he was apprenticed to a sign-painter, and at 19 established his own company. His entrepreneurial flair led to an expansion into insurance, property and resources. In 1955 Bond married Eileen ('Red') Hughes, sister of William J Hughes, descended from the founder of Wesfarmers (one of Australia's major wool-trading companies). The Bond Corporation developed extensive interests in Australian newspapers and television, in brewing, oil and gas, and gold mining. Bond has a large collection of Impressionist paintings including **Van Gogh**'s *Irises*, for which he paid a record $53.9 million in 1987. His syndicate's twelve-metre yacht 'Australia II' was in 1983 the first to challenge successfully the US for the America's Cup since 1870.

BOND, Edward (1935–) English dramatist and director, born in London. His first play, *The Pope's Wedding*, was given a Sunday night reading at the Royal Court Theatre, London, in 1962 and aroused great controversy. *Saved* (1965) achieved notoriety through a scene in which a baby in a pram is stoned to death. Both these plays were set in contemporary England, although later plays such as *Narrow Road to the Deep North* (1968) use historical themes to look at broad contemporary issues. Other plays include *Lear* (1971), a reworking of **Shakespeare**'s play; *The Fool* (1976), based on the life of the 'peasant poet', **John Clare**; *The Woman* (1978), in which the characters are drawn from Greek tragedy; *The Worlds* (1979); and a trilogy, *The War Plays* (1985).

BOND, William Cranch (1789–1859) American astronomer, born in Portland, Maine. As first director of Harvard University observatory from 1840, he was a pioneer of celestial photography. His son, George Philips (1825–65), succeeded him. Together (and simultaneously with **William Lassell**) they discovered Hyperion, the seventh satellite of Saturn.

BONDFIELD, Margaret Grace (1873–1953) English Labour politician and trade unionist, born in Somerset. She became chairman of the TUC in 1923 and as minister of labour (1929–31) was the first woman to be a British cabinet minister.

BONE, Henry (1755–1834) English enamel painter, born in Truro. In London he enamelled watches and fans, and made enamel portraits, brooches, etc. In 1801 he became enamel painter to **George III**. Elected RA in 1811, he exhibited his large enamel, *Bacchus and Ariadne*, after **Titian**. His son Henry Pierce (1779–1855) was also an enamel painter.

BONE, Sir Muirhead (1876–1953) Scottish artist, born in Glasgow. Although he studied architecture, he was self-taught as an artist. He married Gertrude Dodd, author of *Days in Old Spain* which, along with others, he illustrated. He sacrificed the profession of architect for that of draughtsman and exhibited extensively from 1902. Generally accepted as one of the greatest etchers practising in the 20th century, he was trustee of both the National Gallery and the Imperial War Museum. His work, which has been likened, technically, to that of **Piranesi**, combines meticulous realism with a strong sense of composition, and his subject matters range from the architectural to portraiture and landscape. During his long career he made over 500 etchings, drypoints and lithographs besides many thousands of drawings and watercolours. He travelled to America, Spain, Italy, Holland, France, Turkey and Sweden. His son Stephen (1904–58) was an artist and critic.

BONER, Ulrich (1300–49) Swiss writer of fables. A Dominican friar in Bern from 1324, his *Edelstein*, a collection of fables and jokes, was one of the first German books printed, in 1461.

BONGO, Albert-Bernard (Omar) (1935–) Gabonese politician, born in Lewai, Franceville. In 1960 he joined the civil service and became director of the president's private office and then head of information. He moved into the political arena and when President M'ba died in 1967, succeeded him. The following year he created a one-party state based on the Gabonese Democratic party (PDG) and in 1973 announced his conversion to Islam, adopting the name Omar. He has successfully exploited Gabon's great mineral resources and made it the richest per capita country in black Africa. In 1986 he was re-elected for the third time.

BONHAM-CARTER, Lady Violet, Baroness Asquith of Yarnbury (1887–1969) English Liberal politician and publicist, daughter of **H H Asquith** by his first marriage. She married in 1915 Sir Maurice Bonham-Carter (d.1960), a scientist and civil servant. She was prominent in cultural and political movements, serving as president of the Liberal party Organization in 1944–45 and as a governor of the BBC (1941–46). She was created a life peeress in 1964, and published *Winston Churchill as I Knew Him* in 1965. **Jo Grimond** is her son-in-law. Her eldest son Mark (1922–) stood unsuccessfully as a Liberal in 1945 and 1964 and was Liberal MP for Torrington (1958–59). He became director of the Royal Opera House, Covent Garden (1958), and first chairman of the Race Relations Board (1966).

BONHEUR, Rosa (1822–99) French animal painter, born in Bordeaux. She studied under her father, Raymond (d.1853) and in 1841 exhibited at the Salon. Her *Ploughing with Oxen* (1849) is in the Luxembourg, her famous *Horse Fair* (1853) in the New York Gallery.

BONHOEFFER, Dietrich (1906–45) German Lutheran pastor and theologian, and opponent of Nazism, born in Breslau, the son of an eminent psychiatrist. He was educated at Tübingen and at Berlin, where he was influenced by **Karl Barth**. He left Germany in 1933 in protest aginst the Nazi enforcement of anti-Jewish legislation, and worked in German parishes in London until 1935, when he returned to Germany, to become head of a pastoral seminary of the German Confessing Church until its closure by the Nazis in 1937. He became deeply involved in the German resistance movement and in 1943 was arrested and imprisoned until 1945, when he was hanged at Flossenbürg. His controversial writings, of increasing importance in modern theology, include *Sanctorum Communio* (1927) and *Act and Being* (1931), on the nature of the Church, and the best-known and most-interpreted, *Ethics* (1949) and *Widerstand und Ergeburg* (1951, trans as *Letters and Papers from Prison*, 1953), on the place of Christian belief and the concept of Christ in the modern world.

BONIFACE, originally **Wynfrith, St** (c.680–c.754) Anglo-Saxon missionary, born in Wessex (probably in Crediton in Devon), and known as 'the Apostle of Germany'. From childhood a Benedictine monk in Exeter, he taught in the monastery of Nursling near Romsey, where he was elected abbot in 717. He declined this dignity in order to spread Christianity among the Frisians, but a war put an end to his immediate plans. He returned to Nursling, but set out again in 718 with a commission from Pope **Gregory II** to preach the gospel to all the tribes of Germany. He met with great success in Thuringia, Bavaria, Friesland, Hesse and Saxony, everywhere baptizing multitudes, and was consecrated bishop (723), archbishop and primate of Germany (732). He founded many bishoprics. His chief life work was bringing everything in the Frankish kingdom into accordance with Roman Catholic order and suppressing the irregularities of Irish or Columban Christianity. In 747 Mainz became his primatial seat; but in 754 he resigned the archbishopric, and had resumed his missionary work among the Frisians when he was killed at Dokkum, near Leeuwarden, by pagans. His feast day is 5 June.

BONIFACE VIII (c.1235–1303) pope from 1294. A noble of Anagni named Benedetto Caetani, he was made cardinal priest in 1291 and elected pope in 1294. As pope he tried to reassert papal superiority over temporal powers, particularly **Edward I** of England and **Philip IV, the Fair** of France with his papal bull *Clericis Laicos* of 1296 over taxation of the clergy. Philip of France, supported by his states and clergy, resolutely maintained the independence of his kingdom, disregarded papal bulls and even excommunication. In 1302, the pope issued another bull, *Unam Sanctam*, claiming supreme power in temporal and spiritual affairs; the following year he was briefly kidnapped by the French at Anagni, and died in Rome shortly after being released. His brief captivity led to the papacy taking up residence at Avignon (the so-called 'Avignon captivity').

BONIFACE IX, real name Pietro Tomacelli (d.1404) chosen pope in 1389 to succeed **Urban VI** in opposition to the Avignonese **Clement VII**. He was notoriously inexperienced in papal administration but acquired despotic power in Rome.

BONINGTON, Chris (Christian John Storey) (1934–) English mountaineer and photo-journalist, born in Hampstead, London. He was educated at University College School, London, and the Royal Military Academy, Sandhurst, before joining the Tank Regiment from 1956 to 1961. He started climbing at Harrison's Rocks in Kent before progressing to climbs in Scotland and Wales. His first mountaineering ascents include Annapurna II (1960), Nuptse (1961), Central Pillar of Freney, Mont Blanc (1962), Central Tower of Paine (1963), Brammah (1973), Changabang (1974), Mount Kongur, China (1981), Shivling West (1983) and the first British ascents of the North Wall of the Eiger (1962) and Mt Vinson in Antarctica (1983). He led or co-led many successful expeditions, including Annapurna South Face (1970) and Everest 1972 and 1975 (the south west face), and reached the summit of Everest himself in 1985.

BONINGTON, Richard Parkes (1802–28) English painter, born near Nottingham. About 1817 his family moved to Calais, and there and at Paris he studied art and began a friendship with **Delacroix**, who introduced Bonington to oriental art, while the latter showed Delacroix his watercolour techniques. His first works were exhibited in the Salon in 1822, mostly sketches of Le Havre and Lillebonne. He also began to work in lithography, illustrating Baron Taylor's *Voyages*. From 1824 he experimented increasingly in romantic subjects taken from history, and studied armour. His best-known works followed: *Francis I and Marguerite of Navarre*, *Henry IV receiving the Spanish Ambassador*, *Entrance to the Grand Canal*, and *Ducal Palace*. His work forms an important link between French and English art. He excelled in light effects achieved by the use of a large expanse of sky, broad areas of pure colour and the silhouetting of dark and light masses, as well as his rich colouring of heavy draperies and brocades.

BONIVARD, François de (1493–1570) Swiss divine and politician, prior of the abbey of St Victor. He opposed the duke of Savoy, and his imprisonment in the dungeons of Chillon castle (1532–36) was celebrated in many popular folksongs and in **Byron**'s legendary poem, *Prisoner of Chillon*. A convert to the Protestant faith, Bonivard, after his liberation by the Bernese, wrote an important *Chronicle*, amended by **Calvin**.

BONNARD, Abel (1883–1968) French poet, novelist, and essayist, born in Poitiers. He won the national poetry prize with his first collection of poems, *Les Familiers* (1906). He took up the psychological novel with *La Vie et l'amour* (1913), and later published travel books and collections of essays. He was minister of education in the Vichy government (1942–44), fled to Spain and was sentenced to death in his absence (1945). He returned to France (1958) and was banished (1960).

BONNARD, Pierre (1867–1947) French painter and lithographer, born in Paris and trained at the Académie Julien. He joined the group called 'Les Nabis', which included **Denis** and **Vuillard**, with whom he formed the Intimist group. His style was formed under the influence of Impressionism, Japanese prints and the works of **Gauguin** and **Toulouse-Lautrec**. Ignoring the movement towards abstraction, he continued to paint interiors and landscapes, in which everything is subordinated to the subtlest rendering of light and colour effects.

BONNAT, Léon Joseph Florentin (1833–1922) French painter, born in Bayonne. He was well-known as a painter of religious subjects, and as a portraitist of notable contemporaries.

BONNER, Edmund (c.1500–1569) English prelate, and bishop of London from 1540. The reputation he gained at Oxford recommended him to **Wolsey**, who made him his chaplain. His zeal in King **Henry VIII**'s service after Wolsey's fall earned him due promotion; and in 1533 he was deputed to appear before the pope at Marseilles, to appeal to a general council. His language on this occasion is said to have suggested to the pope the fitness of having him burned alive, or thrown into a cauldron of molten lead, so that Bonner judged it prudent to depart. In 1540 he was made bishop of London, but was imprisoned from 1549 to 1553 for refusing to recognize royal supremacy during the minority of **Edward VI**. Later, under **Mary I**, he was restored to office, and and pronounced sentence on several Protestant martyrs, though it is certain he did his best to befriend **Anne Askew**. On **Elizabeth**'s accession (1558), Bonner accompanied his episcopal brethren to salute her at Highgate, but was excepted from the honour of kissing her hand. In May 1559 he refused the oath of supremacy, so was deposed and again imprisoned in the Marshalsea, where he died.

BONNER, Yelena (1923–) Soviet civil rights campaigner, born in Moscow. After the arrest of her parents in Stalin's 'great purge' of 1937, and the subsequent execution of her father and imprisonment of her mother, she was brought up in Leningrad by her grandmother. During World War II she served in the army, becoming a lieutenant, but suffered serious eye injuries. After the war she married and worked as a doctor. On separating from her husband in 1965, she joined the CPSU, but became disillusioned after the Soviet invasion of Czechoslovakia (1968) and drifted into 'dissident' activities. She married **Andrei Sakharov** in 1971 and resigned from the CPSU a year later. During the next 14 years she and her husband led the Soviet dissident movement. Following a KGB crackdown, Sakharov was banished to internal exile in Gorky in 1980 and Bonner suffered a similar fate in 1984. After hunger strikes, she was given permission to travel to Italy for specialist eye treatment in 1981 and 1984. The couple were finally released from Gorky in 1986, as part of a new 'liberalization' policy by the **Gorbachev** administration, and remained prominent campaigners for greater democratization. Her husband died in 1989.

BONNET, Charles Étienne (1720–93) Swiss naturalist and philosopher, born in Geneva. He distinguished himself by researches on parthenogenesis, polypi, the tapeworm, the respiration of insects, the use of leaves, etc. Failing sight made him abandon his experiments and turn to philosophy. He was critical of vitalistic theories and pointed out that the nonexistence of the soul can never be proved. He held a catastrophic theory of evolution.

BONNET, Georges Étienne (1889–1973) French politician, born in Basillac in Dordogne. He was elected to the Assembly in 1924, became ambassador to the USA in 1937, and was foreign minister at the time of the Munich crisis of 1938.

BONNEVAL, Claude Alexandre, Comte de (1675–1747) French soldier and adventurer. He served with distinction in Italy and the Netherlands, but for extortion and insolence was condemned to death by a court martial. Fleeing to Austria, he fought against his native country, and performed daring exploits under Prince **Eugene** in the war against Turkey. As master-general of ordnance in the Netherlands, he quarrelled with the governor, and was again condemned to death by a court martial. His sentence commuted, he went to Constantinople, became a Muslim, and achieved success as general of artillery in the war of the Porte with Russia, and in Persia, but was ultimately banished.

BONNEVILLE, Nicholas de (1760–1828) French writer. He was appointed president of a Paris district during the French Revolution (1789). A student of English and German literature, he translated **Shakespeare**, founded several newspapers, and wrote a history of modern Europe (1792).

BONNEY, William H, 'Billy the Kid' (1859–81) American bandit, born in New York. A killer from the age of twelve, he achieved legendary notoriety for his hold-ups and robberies in the southwestern states.

BONNIE AND CLYDE See **PARKER, Bonnie**, and **BARROW, Clyde**

BONNIER, Albert (1820–1900) Swedish publisher who founded the prestigious publishing house of the same name in Stockholm in 1837. His liberal beliefs and his support of, for instance, **Strindberg**, brought him into conflict with the prevailing censorship laws. Under him and successive generations of the family, the company has developed and diversified, becoming the largest publisher in Sweden and one of the country's largest companies.

BONNIVARD, François de See **BONIVARD**

BONO, Emilio de (1866–1944) Italian general and Fascist politician, born in Cassano d'Adda. In 1922 he was a quadrumvir of the Fascist 'March on Rome'; he was made governor of Tripolitania in 1925, colonial minister in 1929, and was commander-in-chief at the commencement of hostilities against Abyssinia in 1935. In 1943 he opposed **Mussolini** in the Fascist Grand Council, and in 1944 was executed for treason.

BONOMI, Joseph (1739–1806) Italian architect, born in Rome. He settled in England in 1767 and revived Greek renaissance style. His son, Joseph (1796–1878), illustrated important works by Egyptologists, and wrote on Nineveh. He was curator of Soanes Museum.

BONONCINI, or **Buononcini, Giovanni Maria** (1642–1678) Italian composer, born near Modena, where in 1671 he became a violinist in the court orchestra, and subsequently chapelmaster of the cathedral. Between 1666 and his death he published a great quantity of chamber and vocal music, together with a treatise, the *Musico prattico*, which was influential in its day. His sons Giovanni Battista (1670–1755) and Marc Antonio (1675–1726) were notable composers, the former specially remembered for his rivalry with Handel.

BONPLAND, Aimé Jacques Alexandre (1773–1858) French botanist, born in Rochelle. He travelled with **Humboldt** in South America (1799-1804) and collected and described (but did not publish) 6000 new species of plants. Named professor of natural history at Buenos Aires in 1816, he undertook a journey up the Parań; but **José Francia**, dictator of Paraguay, arrested him, and kept him prisoner for nine years.

BOOLE, George (1815–64) English mathematician and logician, born in Lincoln, the son of a cobbler. He was largely self-taught, and though without a degree, was appointed professor of mathematics at Cork in 1849. He did important work on finite differences and differential equations, but is primarily known for his *Mathematical Analysis of Logic* (1847) and *Laws of Thought* (1854). In these he employed mathematical symbolism to express logical relations, thus becoming an outstanding pioneer of modern symbolic logic, greatly influencing the subsequent work of **Gottlob Frege** and **Bertrand Russell** among others.

BOONE, Daniel (1735–1820) American pioneer, born in Pennsylvania. From Carolina he went to Kentucky, and from 1769 lived in the forest and explored much of the country with his brother. He was twice captured by Indians, and repeatedly repelled (1775–78) Indian attacks on a stockade fort which he had erected, now Boonesboro.

BOORDE, or **Borde, Andrew** (c.1490–1549) English Carthusian monk, physician and writer, born near Cuckfield. From 1527 he studied medicine at Orléans, Toulouse, Montpellier, and Wittenberg. He visited Rome and Santiago de Compostela, and for **Thomas Cromwell** carried through a confidential mission in France and Spain. He practised medicine in Glasgow (1536), travelled through Europe to Jerusalem, and died in the Fleet prison in London. His chief works are his *Dyetary* and the *Fyrst Boke of the Introduction of Knowledge* (1548), a guidebook to the Continent, which contains the first known specimen of gypsy language, and also his *Itinerary of England* (1735).

BOORMAN, John (1933–) English film director, born in Shepperton, Middlesex. A former film critic, he became an assistant director for television in 1955. He worked for Southern Television and, in 1962, became head of the BBC documentary unit. He made his first feature film *Catch Us If You Can* in 1965 and followed this with the stylish American thriller *Point Blank* (1967). Heavily influenced by the Arthurian legends his films show a subtle use of colour and often include mythological resonances or involve some form of quest; examples include *Deliverance* (1972) and *Excalibur* (1981). *Hope and Glory* (1987), an affectionate recreation of his wartime childhood, earned him both critical and commercial acclaim. He has contributed to various periodicals and wrote *Money Into Light* (1985), an account of the compromises and exigencies inherent in international film production.

BOORSTIN, Daniel Joseph (1914–) American author, academic and librarian, born in Atlanta, Georgia. Educated at Harvard, he won a Rhodes scholarship to Oxford, where he studied jurisprudence and civil laws, and was admitted to the English bar (1937). He was senior historian of the Smithsonian Institution, director of the National Museum of History and Technology, and Profesor of American history at the University of Chicago (1944–69). He has spent much time outside America and has written many works which explore and explicate his native land, including *A History of the United States* (1980), *The Americans* trilogy (1965, 1968, 1973) and *The Discoverers* (1983). He was librarian of Congress (1975–87).

BOOS, Martin (1762–1825) Bavarian Catholic priest. About 1790 he founded a religious movement closely akin to that of the Protestant Pietists. Bitterly persecuted, he accepted in 1817 an appointment at Düsseldorf, and died near Neuwied.

BOOT, Sir Jesse, 1st Baron Trent (1850–1931) English drug manufacturer, born in Nottingham. At 13, he inherited his father's herbalist's shop and studied pharmacy in his leisure hours. In 1877 he opened his first chemist's shop in Nottingham and, by mass selling at reduced prices, introduced the modern chain store. In 1892 he began large-scale drug manufacture and soon after the turn of the century he was controlling the largest pharmaceutical retail trade in the world, with over a thousand branches in 1931.

BOOTH, Barton (1681–1733) English actor, the son of a Lancashire squire. Educated at Westminster, he became an actor and played with success for two seasons at Dublin, and in 1700 appeared in **Betterton**'s company in London. His performance as Cato in **Addison**'s tragedy in 1713 brought him wealth and fame.

BOOTH, Charles (1840–1916) English shipowner, statistician, and social reformer, born in Liverpool. He joined his brother Alfred in founding the Booth Steamship Company and the allied leather factories of Alfred Booth & Co. An ardent radical in his youth, he settled in London in 1875 and devoted 18 years to the preparation of his great *Life and Labour of the People in London* (1903), the prototype of the modern social survey, based on organized on-the-spot investigation. He was also a pioneer of old age pensions.

BOOTH, Edwin Thomas (1833–93) American actor, son of Junius Brutus Booth (1796–1852) and brother of **John Wilkes Booth**, born in Harford County, Maryland. He played Tressel at the age of 16 to his father's Richard III and rose to the top of his profession, visiting England (1861–62), and in 1864 produced *Hamlet* in New York for a record run. Ruined by opening a theatre in New York in 1869, he was able to settle his debts by 1877. He visited Germany and Britain (1880–82) and played Othello to **Henry Irving's** Iago.

BOOTH, Sir Felix (1775–1850) English distiller, who contributed £17000 to **James Ross**'s Arctic expedition (1829–33), and after whom the Boothia Felix peninsula was named.

BOOTH, John Wilkes (1839–65) American assassin, son of the actor Junius Booth and brother of **Edwin Thomas Booth**, born in Baltimore. An unsuccessful actor, in 1865 he entered into a conspiracy to avenge the defeat of the Confederates and shot President **Lincoln** at Ford's Theatre, Washington, on 14 April. He managed to escape to Virginia, but was tracked down and, refusing to surrender, was shot.

BOOTH, William (1829–1912) English religous leader, founder and 'general' of the Salvation Army, born amid poverty in Nottingham. In 1844 he was converted and became a Methodist New Connexion minister on Tyneside. There he grew restless, seeing the Lord's requirements as loosing the chains of injustice, freeing the captive and oppressed, sharing food and home, clothing the naked, and carrying out family responsibilities. Thus in 1865 he began in London's East End 'The Christian Mission' which in 1878 developed into the Salvation Army. Though often imprisoned for preaching in the open air, his men and women fought on, waging war on such evils as sweated labour and child prostitution. Booth's Army spread throughout the world, with a whole new network of social and regenerative agencies. Gradually opinion changed: he was made freeman of London, honorary doctor of Oxford, was a guest at **Edward VII**'s coronation, and opened the US Senate with prayer. His book, *In Darkest England and the Way Out* (1890), tells of his philosophy and motivation. His eldest son, William Branwell Booth (1856–1929), was chief of staff from 1880 and succeeded his father as general (1912). His second son, Ballington Booth (1857–1940), was commander of the army in Australia (1883–85) and the

USA (1887–96) but resigned after disagreement with his father and founded a similar organization, Volunteers of America. One of his daughters, Evangeline Cora Booth (1865–1950), became a US citizen and was elected general in 1934. A grand-daughter, Catherine Branwell Booth (1884–1987), was a commissioner in the Army.

BOOTHBY, Sir Robert John Graham, 1st Baron Boothby of Buchan and Rattray Head (1900–86) Scottish Conservative politician, born in Edinburgh. He was educated at Eton and Oxford and in 1924 was elected MP for East Aberdeenshire, the seat he held until 1958. 'Discovered' in 1926 by **Winston Churchill**, he became his parliamentary private secretary till 1929. From 1940 to 1941 he was parliamentary secretary to the ministry of food and later served in the RAF. He became in 1948 an original member of the Council of United Europe and was a British delegate to its consultative assembly (1949–54). He was raised to the peerage in 1958. An outstanding commentator on public affairs on radio and TV, he brought to political argument a refreshing candour, a robust independence and a talent for exposing the easy hypocrisies of public life. He wrote *The New Economy* (1943), *I Fight To Live* (1947) and *My Yesterday, Your Tomorrow* (1962)

BOOTHE, Clare (1903–87) American writer, born in New York. She was on the editorial staff of *Vogue* and other periodicals. She wrote *European Spring* (1940), and other books, but was most successful with her plays, which include *The Women* (1936) and *Kiss the Boys Goodbye* (1938). She was elected to the House of Representatives as a Republican in 1942, and was American ambassador to Italy (1953–57). She married (1935) **Henry Robinson Luce**.

BOPP, Franz (1791–1867) German philologist, born in Mainz. After four years' study in Paris, paid for by the Bavarian government, he produced his first study of Indo-European grammar, *Über das Conjugationssystem der Sanskritsprache in Vergleichung mit jenem der griechischen, lateinischen, persischen und germanischen Sprache* (1816), in which he traced the common origin of the grammatical forms of these languages. In 1821 he was appointed to the chair of Sanskrit and comparative grammar in Berlin. His greatest work is *A Comparative Grammar of Sanskrit, Zend, Greek, Latin, Lithuanian, Old Slavonic, Gothic and German* (6 vols, 1833–52; trans 1856); a revised edition (1856–61) included Old Armenian.

BÓR See **KOMOROWSKI, Tadeusz Bór**

BORA, Katherine von (1499–1552) German nun. Having adopted Lutheran doctrines, she ran away from the Cistercian convent of Nimptschen, near Grimma, in 1523, and married **Luther** in 1525.

BORAH, William Edgar (1865–1940) American Republican politician, born in Illinois. Elected senator for Idaho in 1906, he advocated disarmament and, being a convinced isolationist, was instrumental in blocking the United States' entry into the League of Nations.

BORCHGREVINK, Carsten Egeberg (1864–1934) Norwegian explorer, born in Oslo. After emigrating to Australia, he was a member of the first party to set foot on the Antarctic continent (1894), and was the first to winter there (1898–99).

BORDA, Jean Charles de (1733–99) French mathematician and astronomer, born in Dax. He helped to measure the arc of the meridian and to establish the metric system.

BORDE, Andrew See **BOORDE**

BORDEAUX, Henri (1870–1963) French novelist, born in Thonon. He studied law before he took to writing novels concerned with the defence of family life, often with a Savoy background, such as *La Peur de vivre* (1902), *Les Roquevillard* (1906), and *La Maison* (1913).

BORDEN, Lizzie Andrew (1860–1927) American alleged murderess, born in Fall River, Massachusetts. In one of the most sensational murder trials in American history, she was accused of murdering her wealthy father and hated step-mother with an axe, in August 1892. She claimed to have been outside in the barn at the time of the murder, and despite a wealth of circumstantial evidence, she was aquitted. She lived out her life in Fall River and was buried alongside her father and step-mother. The case is immortalized in a children's nursery rhyme.

BORDEN, Sir Robert Laird (1854–1937) Canadian statesman, born in Grand Pré, Nova Scotia. He practised as barrister, became leader of the Conservative party in 1901, in 1911 overthrew **Laurier**'s ministry on reciprocity with the USA, and was prime minister of the Dominion till 1920. He organized Canada for war, and was the first overseas premier to attend a Cabinet meeting in London (1915).

BORDET, Jules Jean Baptiste Vincent (1870–1961), Belgian physiologist and an authority on serology. Born in Soignies, he became director of the Pasteur Institute, Brabant (1901), and professor at Brussels (1907), and recognised the immunity factors of blood serum. He discovered *alexine*, and in 1906 the microbe of whooping cough. He was awarded the 1919 Nobel prize for medicine or physiology.

BORDONE, Paris (1500–71) Italian painter of the Venetian school, born in Treviso. He worked there, in Vicenza, Venice, and Paris. He was strongly influenced by his greater contemporary, **Titian**, his most celebrated work being the *Fisherman presenting the Ring of St Mark to the Doge*, in the Venice Academia.

BOREL, Émile (Félix Édouard Justin) (1871–1956) French mathematician and politician, born in Saint Affrique. He studied and then taught at the École Normale Supérieure, and became professor at the Sorbonne in 1909. In addition to his prolific mathematical work, he was active in politics, scientific popularization and journalism; he was a member of the Chamber of Deputies (1924–36) and minister for the navy (1925–40). His mathematical work was mainly in analysis, measure theory and probability. He also wrote on the theory of games (1921–27), independently of the much better-known work of **John von Neumann** on this subject.

BORELLI, Giovanni Alfonzo (1608–79) Italian mathematician and physiologist, born in Naples. He held professorships at Naples, Pisa and Messina. He founded the iatrophysical school of medicine, which sought to explain all bodily functions by physical laws.

BORENIUS, Tancred (1885–1948) Finnish art historian, born in Vyborg. Professor of the history of art at University College, London, from 1922, he is known for his writings on Italian and early English painting.

BORG, Bjōrn Rune (1956–) Swedish tennis player, the dominant player in world tennis in the 1970s. A talented all-round sportsman in his youth, he left school at 14 to concentrate on tennis, and at 15 was selected for the Swedish Davis Cup team. He was Wimbledon Junior Champion at 16. In 1976 he won the first of his record five consecutive Wimbledon singles titles (1976–80). He also won the Italian championship twice and the French Open six times between 1974 and 1981. His Wimbledon reign was ended in 1981 when he lost in the final to **John McEnroe**. He retired in 1983 with a considerable fortune, having written his autobiography, *My Life and Games* (1980). His success sparked a huge increase in the popularity of tennis in Sweden and inspired a new generation of world-class players.

BORGE, Victor (1909–) Danish-born American entertainer and pianist. He was educated at the Royal Danish Academy of Music, Copenhagen, and in Vienna and Berlin. He made his début as a pianist in 1926 and as a revue actor in 1933. Since 1940 he has worked in the USA for radio, television and theatre, and has performed with leading symphony orchestras on world-wide tours since 1956.

BORGES, Jorge Luis (1899–1986) Argentinian writer, born in Buenos Aires. He was educated there and at Geneva and Cambridge. From 1918 he was in Spain, where he was a member of the avant-garde Ultraist literary group, returning to Argentina in 1921. His first book of poems, *Fervor de Buenos Aires*, was published in 1923. He continued publishing poems and essays, and in 1941 appeared the first collection of the intricate and fantasy-woven short stories for which he is famous. Later collections include *Ficciónes* (Fictions, 1944 and 1946), *El Aleph* (1949), *La Muerta y la Brújula* (Death and the Compass, 1951) and *El Hacedor* (Dreamtigers, 1960). Some stories from *El Aleph* appear in the collection of translations, *Labyrinths* (1962). He became director of the National Library in 1955, after losing his sight. His last book was *Atlas* (1986), written in collaboration with his companion, Maria Kodama, whom he married a month before his death.

BORGHESE a noble Italian family of Siena, afterwards at Rome. Camillo Borghese ascended the papal throne in 1605 as **Paul V**. A marriage with an heiress of the house of Aldobrandini brought the Borghese family into the possession of great wealth. Prince Camillo Filippo Ludovico Borghese (1775–1832) joined the French army, in 1803 married Maria Pauline, **Napoleon**'s sister, and became governor-general of Piedmont. He sold the Borghese collection of art treasures to Napoleon for 13000000 francs, receiving in part-payment the Piedmontese national domains; when these were reclaimed by the king of Sardinia in 1815, he received back part of the collection. The Borghese Palace, built by Scipione Caffarelli (1576–1633), the adopted nephew of Pope Paul V), still contains one of the finest collections of paintings in Rome, though some of its treasures were sold in 1892–93.

BORGIA the Italian form of 'Borja', the name of an ancient family in the Spanish province of Valencia. Alfonso de Borja (1378–1458), bishop, accompanied Alfonso of Aragon to Naples, and was elected pope as **Calixtus III**. Rodrigo Borja (1431–1503), his nephew, ascended the papal throne in 1492 as **Alexander VI**. Before this, he had had a number of children by a Roman girl, Giovanna Catenei, known as Vanozza. Two of these children became especially notorious.

BORGIA, Cesare (1476–1507) Italian soldier and captain-general of the armies of the Church, the illegitimate son of Pope **Alexander VI** (Rodrigo Borja), and sister of **Lucrezia Borgia**. Ambitious and energetic, he was appointed archbishop of Valencia (1492) and a cardinal (1493) after his father's election to the papacy in 1492. In 1499 he succeeded his elder brother Juan (whom he was suspected of murdering) as captain-general of the papal army; and in the same year he surrendered his cardinal's hat to marry Princess Charlotte d'Albret, sister of the king of Navarre. In two successive campaigns, with French help (1499–1501), he made himself master of Romagna, Perugia, Siena, Piombini and Urbino, and was made Duke of Romagna by his father. His grand design to seize all of central Italy spread terror in an atmosphere of constant treachery and cruelty. In 1502, on the eve of a third campaign, he and his father were mysteriously taken ill at a banquet, believed poisoned; Pope Alexander died, but Cesare survived. His enemies, now led by the new pope, **Julius II** (elected in 1503), forced him to relinquish Romagna. He surrendered at Naples in 1504, under promise of safe conduct, but was imprisoned in Spain. He escaped in 1506 and fled to the court of Navarre, but was killed at the siege of Viana. Despite attempts to rehabilitate his reputation, he remains a monster in the public perception. He was praised by **Machiavelli** as a model prince and the saviour of Italy in *Il Principe*. He encouraged art, and was the friend of **Pinturicchio** and the protector of **Leonardo da Vinci**.

BORGIA, Lucrezia (1480–1519) illegitimate daughter of Pope **Alexander VI** (Rodrigo Borja) and sister of **Cesare Borgia**, born in Rome. She was three times married to further her father's political ambitions: first, in 1493, at the age of twelve to Giovanni Sforza, Lord of Pesaro, but this marriage was annulled by her father in 1497 because of his friendship with Naples; second, in 1498, to Alfonso of Aragon, nephew of the king of Naples, but this marriage was ended in 1500 when Alfonso was murdered by her brother Cesare; and third, in 1501, to Alfonso (1486-1534), son of the Duke of Este, who inherited the duchy of Ferrara. At Ferrara she established a brilliant court of artists and men of letters, including **Ariosto** and **Titian**, and devoted herself to the patronage of art and education. In legend she has become notorious, quite unfairly, for wantonness, vice and crime (even including incest with her brother and father).

BORGLUM, (John) Gutzon (de la Mothe) (1867–1941) American sculptor, born in Idaho of Danish descent. He won renown for works of colossal proportions such as the famous Mount Rushmore National Memorial portraying **Washington**, **Lincoln**, **Jefferson**, and **Theodore Roosevelt**, hewn out of the solid rock of the mountainside (completed in 1939). His other huge works include the head of **Lincoln** in the US capitol Rotunda, and the Twelve Apostles in the Cathedral of St John the Divine in New York. His brother **Solon Hannibal** (1868–1922) also won fame as a sculptor, especially of horses and 'wild west' subjects.

BORGOGNONE, Ambrogio (c.1445–1523) Milanese painter, whose work is characterized by a graceful treatment conveying a feeling of genuine piety. *Virgin Crowned* in the Brera Gallery in Milan and the frescoes at the Certosa di Pavia are good examples of his work.

BORIS GODUNOV (1552–1605) tsar of Russia from 1598. Of Tartar stock, he became an intimate friend of **Ivan the Terrible**, who entrusted to Boris the care of his feeble son, Fedor. During the reign of Tsar Fedor (1584–98), Godunov was virtual ruler of the country with the title of 'the Great Sovereign's brother-in-law', becoming tsar himself on Fedor's death in 1698. He continued the expansionist policies of Ivan, going to war against both Poland and Sweden. At home, he disposed finally of the Tartar threat but was embroiled in the last years of his reign in a civil war against a pretender, claiming to be **Dmitri**, younger son of Ivan the Terrible. Boris died in 1605, and the pretender was murdered the following year.

BORLASE, William (1695–1772) English antiquary, born in Cornwall. Educated at Exeter College, Oxford, he was for 50 years rector at Ludgvan, near Penzance. He published *The Antiquities of Cornwall* (1754) and other works.

BORMANN, Martin (1900–?1945) German Nazi politician, born in Halberstadt. He participated in the abortive Munich putsch of 1923 and became one of **Hitlers**'s closest advisers. After **Hess**'s flight to Scotland, he was appointed Reichsminister ('party chancellor') in May 1941 and was with Hitler to the last. His own fate is uncertain, but he was possibly killed by Russian snipers in the mass breakout by Hitler's staff from the Chancellery (1 May 1945). He was sentenced to death in absentia by the Nuremberg Court (1946). A skeleton accidentally uncovered by an excavator in Berlin in 1972 has been officially recognized as his by forensic experts.

BORN, Max (1882–1970) German physicist, born in Breslau (Wroclaw). Professor of theoretical physics at Göttingen (1921–33), lecturer at Cambridge (1933–36) and professor of natural philosophy at Edinburgh (1936–53), he shared the 1954 Nobel prize with **Walther Bothe** for work in the field of quantum physics.

BÖRNE, Ludwig, originally **Löb Baruch** (1786–1838) German political writer and satirist, born in Frankfurt of Jewish descent. He edited various journals (1812–21), establishing his reputation as a vigorous opponent of the Prussian government, and inciting the German people to revolution and social reform. The French revolution of July 1830 drew him to Paris, where he finally settled in 1832. He and **Heine** became bitterly hostile to each other.

BORODIN, Alexander Porphyrevich (1833–87) Russian composer and scientist, an illegitimate son of Prince Gedeanov, who registered him as the child of a serf. Although Borodin showed a precocious aptitude for music, beginning to compose at the age of nine, he was trained for medicine and distinguished himself as a chemist. His first systematic musical studies were undertaken in 1862, under **Balakirev**, who conducted his First Symphony in 1869. From 1872, Borodin lectured on chemistry at the St Petersburg School of Medicine for Women. His compositions include the unfinished opera, *Prince Igor*, three symphonies, the last of which was also left unfinished, and the symphonic sketch *In the Steppes of Central Asia*.

BOROTRA, Jean (1898–) French tennis player, born near Biarritz. Known as the 'Bounding Basque', he was the most famous of the Four Musketeers (with Lacoste, Cochet and Brugnon) who emerged in the 1920s to make France one of the leading tennis nations. He won the men's singles title at Wimbledon in 1924, and his extraordinary fitness enabled him to compete in veterans' events at that same venue when he was almost 80 years old. He also won the French and Australian championships, as well as several Davis Cup medals between 1927 and 1932. He was secretary of physical education in the Vichy Fort, 1940–42, and was imprisoned by the Nazis, 1943–45.

BOROUGH, Steven (1525–84) English navigator, born in Northam, Devon. In 1553 he commanded the *Searchthrift*, the first English ship to reach northern Russia via North Cape, and became chief pilot to the newly-founded Muscovy Company. He discovered the entrance to the Kara Sea.

BOROUGH, William (1536–99) English navigator and brother of **Steven Borough**. He became controller of the navy, and drew up charts of the northern ocean (1560) and the north Atlantic (1576). He was vice admiral in **Drake**'s Cadiz adventure, and commanded a ship against the Armada in 1588.

BOROVANSKY, Edouard (1902–59) Czech dancer, choreographer and ballet director, born in Přerov. He studied and starred at Prague's National Theatre and School, prior to dancing with **Anna Pavlova**'s company. A soloist of character roles in **Colonel de Basil**'s Ballet Russe de Monte Carlo (1932–39), he stayed on in Melbourne during one of the troupe's Australian tours, opening a ballet school and club with his wife Xenia Nikolaeva in 1940. Out of this grew the Borovansky Ballet (1942; became professional, 1944), a periodically bankrupt company for which he staged both classics and original works. The Australian Ballet, formed in 1962, drew many of its members and much of its impetus from Borovansky's company and pioneering efforts, and his influence on Australian classical dance was enormous.

BORROMEO, St Carlo (1538–84) Italian prelate, born in his father's castle of Arona, on the Lago Maggiore. In 1560, at the age of 22, he was appointed cardinal and archbishop of Milan by his uncle, Pope **Pius IV**. He did much to bring the Council of Trent (1545–63) to a successful conclusion, and had the principal part in drawing up the famous *Catechismus Romanus* (1566). He was renowned for his determined efforts to maintain ecclesiastical discipline and for his poor relief during the famine of 1570 and the plague of 1576. He founded in 1570 the Helvetic College at Milan; and he brought about an alliance of the seven Swiss Catholic cantons for the defence of the faith. In 1578 he founded the community later known as the Oblates of St Ambrose. He was canonized in 1610. His feast day is 4 November. His nephew, Count Frederico Borromeo (1564–1631), from 1595 archbishop of Milan, founded the Ambrosian Library.

BORROMINI, Francesco (1599–1667) Italian baroque architect and sculptor, born in northern Italy. He spent all his working life in Rome, where he was associated with his great rival **Bernini** in the Palazzo Berberini (1620–31) and the Baldacchino in St Peter's (1631–33). His own chief buildings were the S Carlo alle Quattro Fontane (1641), S Ivo della Sapienza (1660), S Andrea delle Fratte (1653–65), and the oratorio of S Philippo Neri (1650). He is particularly noted for his brilliant command of spatial effects.

BORROW, George Henry (1803–81) English author, born in East Dereham, Norfolk, the son of an army recruiting officer. He went to school at the High School in Edinburgh and at Norwich grammar school (1816–18), and for the next five years was articled to a firm of solicitors. He turned to literature, and edited six volumes of *Celebrated Trials and Remarkable Cases of Criminal Jurisprudence* (1825). Already an accomplished linguist, from 1825 to 1832 he travelled on foot through England, France and Germany, studying the languages of the countries he visited. As an agent for the Bible Society he visited St Petersburg (1833–35), Portugal, Spain, and Morocco (1835–39). In 1840 he married a well-to-do widow, Mary Clarke, and settled down on a small estate of hers at Oulton, near Lowestoft, where, after travels in southeastern Europe (1844), a tour in Wales (1854), and a residence of some years in London, he ended his days a lonely man, sensitive to criticism. He wrote numerous books in which romantic fiction and autobiography often overlapped: *The Zincali or an Account of the Gypsies of Spain* (1840); *The Bible in Spain* (1843), which was an instant success as a travel book; *Lavengro* (1851) and its sequel, *The Romany Rye* (1857), novels about his own gypsy life (the word 'Lavengro' means 'wordmaster'); *Wild Wales* (1862); and *Romano Lavo-Lil*, or *Word-book of the English-Gypsy Language* (1874).

BORZOV, Valeri (1949–) Russian athlete, born in Sambor, Ukraine. At the 1972 Olympic Games in Munich he won both the 100 and 200 metres, beating the Americans in what had become their monopoly events.

BOSANQUET, Bernard (1848–1923) English philosopher, born near Alnwick. He taught at Oxford (1871–81) and St Andrews (1903–08). He was one of the school of British idealists, much influenced by **Hegel**, whose other members included **F H Bradley**, **T**

H Green, **Edward Caird** and **James Ferrier**. His main philosophical works are *Knowledge and Reality* (1885), *Logic* (1888), *History of Aesthetic* (1892), *The Philosophical Theory of the State* (1899) and *The Principle of Individuality and Value* (1912).

BOSCAWEN, Edward (1711–61) English naval commander, known as 'Old Dreadnought', the third son of Viscount Falmouth. He distinguished himself at the taking of Porto Bello (1739) and at the siege of Cartagena (1741); and, while in command of the *Dreadnought* in 1744, he captured the French *Médée*, with 800 prisoners. He had an important share in the victory off Cape Finisterre (1747), where he was wounded in the neck; and in command of the East Indian expedition displayed high military skill in the retreat from Pondicherry. In 1755 he intercepted the French fleet off Newfoundland, capturing two 64-gun ships and 1500 men; in 1758, now admiral of the blue, he was appointed commander-in-chief of the successful expedition against Cape Breton. He crowned his career by victory over the French Toulon fleet in Lagos Bay (1759).

BOSCH, Carl (1874–1940) German chemist, born in Cologne. The brother-in-law of **Fritz Haber**, he became president of the I G Farbenindustrie in 1925. He shared the Nobel prize for chemistry with **Friedrich Bergius** in 1931 for his part in the invention and development of chemical high-pressure methods, eg, the 'Bosch process', by which hydrogen is obtained from water gas and superheated steam.

BOSCH, Hieronymus, also known as **Jerome van Aken** (c.1460–1516) Dutch painter, named after the town in which he was born, 's Hertogenbosch in northern Brabant, and in which he seems to have spent the whole of his life. It is very difficult to trace the development of his work because none of it is dated, but there are some quite conventional pictures which contrast with the bizarre, nightmarish world for which he is famous. Although the roots of his work can be traced to devotional woodcuts of the period, the extravagance of his vision is hard to explain, as is its acceptance by local churches for which he worked. After his death, **Philip II** of Spain avidly collected his works and the majority of them are now in the Prado, Madrid, including his masterpiece, *The Garden of Earthly Delights*. He had many imitators in his lifetime but only **Brueghel** had the ability to incorporate the imagery of Bosch into his own art. Bosch was adopted in the 20th century as the precursor of the Surrealist movement.

BOSCOVICH, Roger Joseph (1711–87) Croatian mathematician and astronomer, born in Ragusa. A Jesuit, he wrote on optics and astronomy.

BOSE, Sir Jagadis Chandra (1858–1937) Indian physicist and botanist. Professor at Calcutta, he was known for his study of electric waves, their polarization and reflection, and for his experiments demonstrating the sensitivity and growth of plants.

BOSE, Subhas Chandra (1895–?1945) Indian Nationalist leader, who called for complete Indian independence. Frequently imprisoned, he became president of the All-India Congress in 1938 (resigned 1939). He supported the Axis in the war and became commander-in-chief of the Japanese-sponsored Indian National Army. He was reported killed in Formosa. In 1935 he published *The Indian Struggle*.

BOSIO, François Joseph, Baron (1769–1845) French sculptor, born in Monaco. For **Napoleon** he carved the bas-reliefs for the Column of the Place Vendôme in Paris, and he also sculpted the Quadriga of the Arc de Triomphe du Carrousel and other well-known Paris statues. He was director of the Academy of Fine Arts and died in Paris while still holding this post.

BOSSUET, Jacques Bénigne (1627–1704) French churchman, controversialist, and pulpit orator, born in Dijon. Educated in the Jesuits' School there and at the Collège de Navarre in Paris, he received a canonry at Metz in 1652, and in 1661 preached before **Louis XIV**; in 1669 he delivered the funeral oration for **Henrietta Maria**. His reputation as an orator spread over France, and he became the recognized chief of the devout party at court. For his pupil, the Dauphin, he is said to have written his *Discours sur l'histoire universelle* (1679); as bishop of Meaux (1681) he took a leading part in settling the Gallican controversy, between Louis XIV and the pope in 1682, and wrote the *Doctrine de l'Église catholique*. He attacked with excessive violence the mysticism of **Fénelon**. His greatest works are the *Histoire Universelle*, regarded by many as the first attempt at a philosophy of history; the *Oraisons funèbres*; and the *Histoire des variations des Églises protestantes* (1688). His *Politique tirée de l'écriture sainte* (1709) upholds the divine right of kings.

BOSTON, Ralph (1939–) American athlete, born in Laurel, Mississippi. A leading high-jumper of the 1960s, he established an unusual treble by winning the gold medal at the 1960 Rome Olympics, a silver at Tokyo in 1964 and a bronze at Mexico City in 1968. He spent much time coaching **Bob Beamon** before the latter's astonishing winning long-jump in Mexico City.

BOSTON, Thomas (1676–1732) Scottish theologian, the son of a Covenanting minister. From 1707 until his death he was minister of Ettrick, and is remembered chiefly for his *Fourfold State of Man* (1720), long recognized as a standard exposition of Calvinistic theology. *The Crook in the Lot* and his posthumous *Autobiography* were for long favourites with the Scottish country folk.

BOSTON STRANGLER See **DESALVO, Albert**

BOSWELL, Alexander, 1st Bart (1775–1822) Scottish songwriter and printer, son of **James Boswell**. Educated at Westminster and Oxford, he set up at Auchinleck a private press, at which he printed many rare books in early English and Scottish literature, besides a volume of vigorous poems in the Ayrshire dialect (1803); in 1817 he contributed twelve songs to **George Thomson**'s *Select Collection*, of which 'Good night, and joy be wi' ye a'', 'Jenny's Bawbee', and 'Jenny dang the Weaver' were very popular. He was created a baronet in 1821, and died of a wound received in a duel with James Stuart of Dunearn, who had challenged him as the author of anonymous political pasquinades. His younger brother, James (1778–1822), edited the third *Variorum Shakespeare* (1821).

BOSWELL, James (1740–95) Scottish man-of-letters and biographer of Dr **Johnson**, born in Edinburgh, the eldest son of a judge, Lord Auchinleck. He was educated privately in Edinburgh and at the University of Edinburgh. He then studied civil law at Glasgow, but his true goal was literary fame and the friendship of great men. At 18 he began to keep an astonishingly frank and self-probing journal. In spring 1760 he ran away to London and turned Catholic. To discourage such religious fervour, Lord Eglinton, a London-based friend of Boswell's father, saw to it that Boswell became more of a libertine than ever and he reverted to his original faith. Young Boswell hobnobbed with the young Duke of York, with **Sheridan**'s father, made plans to join the army, and skilfully resisted all attempts to lure him into matrimony. He first met Dr Johnson on his second visit to London, on 16 May 1763, at Tom Davies's bookshop in Russell Street. By the following year they were on such cordial terms that Johnson accompanied him as far as Harwich. Boswell was on his way to Utrecht to continue his legal studies, but stayed only the winter and then toured Germany, France, Switzerland, and Italy. By an astounding process of literary gatecrashing he introduced himself to **Voltaire** and **Rousseau**. From Rousseau he procured an introduction to **Paoli**, the hero of Corsica, whom he 'Boswellized' in *Account of Corsica* (1768), which had an immediate success and was translated into several languages. Boswell had many love affairs. There was the serious and high-minded affair with 'Zélide' of Utrecht, with the Irish Mary Anne Montgomery, and with numerous others in London, Rome, and elsewhere, including a disreputable episode with Rousseau's mistress, Thérèse Le Vasseur. The great lover finally married in 1769 a cousin, Margaret Montgomerie, a prudent, amiable woman who put up with his shortcomings. He returned from the Continent in 1766, was admitted advocate, in 1773 was elected to Johnson's famous literary club, and took the great doctor on a memorable journey to the Hebrides. A major literary enterprise (1777–83) was a series of seventy monthly contributions to the *London Magazine* under the pseudonym 'The Hypochondriak'. After Johnson's death appeared *The Journal of the Tour of the Hebrides* (1785). Its great success made Boswell plan his acknowledged masterpiece, the *Life of Samuel Johnson* (1791), of which *The Journal* served as a first instalment. Meanwhile Boswell had entered the Inner Temple and had been called to the English bar in 1786. He hardly practised, however, except to publish anonymously *Dorando, a Spanish Tale*, a thinly-disguised summary of a topical case, at the time of publication still *sub judice*. Boswell's wife died in 1789, leaving him six children. His drinking habits gained the better of him. Boswell's work is the work of a conscious artist, a born journalist, and a biographical researcher. The discoveries of Boswell's manuscripts, at Malahide Castle in Ireland in 1927 and at Fettercairn House in Scotland in 1930, which have been assembled by Yale University, are proof of his literary industry and integrity.

BOSWORTH, Joseph (1789–1876) English philologist, born in Derbyshire. Professor of Anglo-Saxon at Oxford from 1858, he compiled *An Anglo Saxon Dictionary* (1838), and in 1867 gave £10000 for a chair of Anglo-Saxon at Cambridge.

BOTH, Andries (c.1612–1641) Dutch painter, born in Utrecht, brother of **Jan Both**. Traditionally he was thought to have collaborated with his brother by painting the figures in Jan's landscapes, but is now recognized as the author of paintings and drawings of genre scenes more akin to the work of **Brouwer**. With his brother he travelled to Italy where, returning home from a party in Venice, he fell into a canal and was drowned.

BOTH, Jan (c.1618–1652) Dutch painter, brother of **Andries Both**, born in Utrecht and a leading exponent of 'Italianate' landscape. He lived in Italy from 1638 to 1641 and there perfected his style of painting views of the Roman countryside bathed in a golden light and populated by picturesque peasants. This treatment of landscape, though not the inclusion of peasants, shows the influence of **Claude Lorraine**, whom he would have met in Rome. Back in Utrecht he became a prominent member of the painters' guild, and his idyllic style was adapted by other Dutch painters to their views of Dutch landscape.

BOTHA, Louis (1862–1919) South African statesman and soldier, born in Greytown in Natal. He was a member of the Transvaal Volksraad, succeeded **Joubert** (1900) as commander-in-chief of the Boer forces during the war, and in 1907 became prime minister of the Transvaal colony under the new constitution. In 1907 and 1911 he attended imperial conferences in London; in 1910 he became the first premier of the Union of South Africa. He suppressed **De Wet**'s rebellion in 1914, and conquered German Southwest Africa in 1914–15.

BOTHA, P W (Pieter Willem) (1916–) South African politician, prime minister from 1978 to 1989. The longest-serving member of the South African Assembly (which he first entered in 1948), in his 14 years as minister of defence (1966–80), he presided over a substantial strengthening of the South African armed forces as well as the controversial military intervention in Angola. He attempted to introduce constitutional reforms but his plans, involving limited power-sharing with 'Coloureds' and 'Indians', led to several defections from his ruling National party in 1982 and to wide international condemnation because of their fundamentally racist character. In 1984 he became the first executive state president. In February 1989 he suffered a stroke which compelled him to step down as leader of the National party and in August 1989, though unwillingly, he was forced also to cede the state presidency to his party successor, **F W De Klerk**.

BOTHA, 'Pik' (Roelof Frederik) (1932–) South African politician. After a career in the diplomatic service (1953–70), he entered politics and was elected to parliament. He forsook national politics in 1974 to become South Africa's permanent representative at the United Nations and then ambassador to the USA. He returned to domestic politics in 1977 and became foreign minister in the government of state president **P W Botha** and that of **F W De Klerk.**

BOTHAM, Ian Terence (1955–) English cricketer, born in Cheshire. A prodigiously talented all-rounder, he has appeared in 94 Test matches, 65 of them consecutively. He held the record number of Test wickets (373 wickets at an average of 27.86 runs until overtaken by **Richard Hadlee**), and has four times taken ten wickets in a match. He has also scored 5057 runs in Tests, including 14 Test centuries. Three successive fine individual performances won the Test series against Australia almost single-handed in 1981. His spells as captain of Somerset and England were, however, notably unsuccessful. Off-the-field brushes with authority alternated with successful charity fund-raising campaigns such as his walk from John o' Groats to Land's End and his re-enactment of **Hannibal**'s crossing of the Alps. He joined Worcestershire in 1986.

BOTHE, Walther (1891–1957) German physicist, born in Oranienburg. From 1934 he was head of the Max Planck Institute for Medical Research at Heidelberg. His work on the development of coincidence technique in counting processes brought him the Nobel prize for physics in 1954, shared with **Max Born**.

BOTHWELL, James Hepburn, 4th Earl of (c.1537–78) Scottish nobleman, and third husband of **Mary, Queen of Scots**. One of the greatest nobles in 16th-century Scotland, he succeeded his father as earl and hereditary Lord High Admiral in 1556. A professed Protestant, he nevertheless was a staunch supporter of **Mary of Guise**, regent for Mary, Queen of Scots, and was appointed warden of the Border Marches in 1558. In 1560 he was sent on a mission to France, where he met, and was entranced by, the young Mary shortly before the death of her first husband, **Francis II** of France. When Mary returned to Scotland in 1561 she appointed him a privy councillor; but in the following year he was accused of plotting to kidnap the queen, and imprisoned. He was recalled by Mary in 1565, shortly after her marriage to **Darnley**. In February 1566 he married, with Protestant rites at Holyrood, the Catholic sister of the Earl of Huntly. Shortly afterwards, in March 1566, the queen's secretary, **Rizzio**, was murdered by Darnley, and Bothwell became Mary's protector and chief adviser. The following year, 1567, was to be a year of high drama. On 9 February Darnley himself was murdered in an explosion in Edinburgh, doubtless at Bothwell's instigation; Bothwell was tried but acquitted in a rigged trial a few weeks later, on 12 April. On 23 April he pretended to abduct Mary, who was now pregnant (probably by him) and carried her off to Dunbar. On 3 and 7 May his divorce from his countess was finalized, on 12 May he was elevated to the dukedom of Orkney, and on 15 May he and the queen were married at Holyrood with Protestant rites. The marriage did not last long. On 20 June Mary was forced to surrender to an army of rebellious Scottish noblemen at Carberry Hill, while Bothwell fled the country and was storm-driven to Norway, where he was arrested on a trumped-up charge and imprisoned in Bergen. On 24 July, Mary miscarried (twins), and on the same day was forced to abdicate in favour of her son, the infant **James VI**. The marriage was eventually annulled in 1570. By then, Bothwell was incarcerated at Malmo in Sweden; in 1573 he was transferred to a prison at Dragsholm in Zeeland, Denmark, where he died, apparently insane. His disinterred remains are on display there.

BOTOLPH, St (d.c.680) Saxon abbot. He founded a monastery in 654 in Icanhoe (Ox Island), usually identified as Boston ('Botolph's Stone') in Lincolnshire.

BOTTESINI, Giovanni (1823–89) Italian musician, the greatest master of the double bass, born in Crema in Lombardy. He was also successful as a conductor and composer, and his works include symphonies, overtures and several operas, including *Cristoforo Colombo* (1847) and *Ali Babà* (1871).

BÖTTGER, Johann Friedrich (1682–1719) German ceramist. He established and perfected the manufacture of porcelain at Dresden and, later, Meissen.

BOTTICELLI, Sandro, originally **Alessandro Filipepi** (1444–1510) Florentine painter, born in Florence, a tanner's son. He learnt his distinctive linear style from **Filippo Lippi** but added to it something very personal and graceful. By 1480 he had his own workshop and was responsible for frescoes which form part of the 1482 scheme of decoration of the Sistine Chapel. He produced mostly religious works but is best known for his treatments of mythological subjects; *The Birth of Venus* and the *Primavera*, both of which are in the Florence Uffizi, are two of the best-known pictures in the world. During the last decade of the 15th century his style became more severe and emotional. His work includes excellent portraits and the illustrations for **Dante**'s *Divina Commedia*, which he executed in pen and ink and silverpoint. By the time of his death, his linear style was out of date, but during the Victorian period it became a source of inspiration for the Pre-Raphaelite movement and Art Nouveau.

BOTTOMLEY, Gordon (1874–1948) English poet and playwright, born in Keighley, Yorkshire. He is best remembered for his *Poems of Thirty Years* (1925) and his collections of plays, including *King Lear's Wife and Other Plays* (1920), which, although they mostly constituted an unhappy blend of poetry and rhetoric, won critical approval. His poetry anticipated Imagism.

BOTTOMLEY, Horatio William (1860–1933) English journalist, financier and politician, born in Bethnal Green, London. Reared in an orphanage, he became, successively, an errand boy, a solicitor's clerk and a shorthand writer in the Supreme Court. In 1884 he started a local paper, *The Hackney Hansard*. He was a brilliant journalist and a persuasive speaker, with a consuming desire for a life of luxury. By 1900 he had promoted nearly 50 companies with a total capital of £20 000 000. In 1891 and 1909 he was charged with fraud and acquitted, and between 1901 and 1905 had 67 bankruptcy petitions and writs filed against him. Meanwhile he had founded the weekly *John Bull* (1906) and become Member of Parliament for South Hackney (1906–12). In 1911 he presented a petition in bankruptcy and applied for the Chiltern Hundreds. During World War I he received subscriptions worth nearly £900 000 for various enterprises. In 1918 he was discharged from his bankruptcy and became MP again (1918–22), but in 1922 he was found guilty of fraudulent conversion and sent to prison. He died in poverty.

BOTVINNIK, Mikhail Moiseyevich (1911–) Russian chess player, born in Leningrad, world champion 1948–57, 1958–60 and 1961–63. An electrical engineer by training, he won the 1948 tournament organized by FIDÉ (Fédération Internationale des Échecs) to fill the world championship, vacant after the death of **Alexander Alekhine**, thus leading Soviet domination of world chess for most of the remainder of the century, contested only by the American **Bobby Fischer**. After regaining his title twice, from **Vasily Smyslov** and **Mikhail Tal**, he lost in 1963 to **Tigran Petrosian** and devoted most of his remaining career to training Soviet players and to the development of chess computers.

BOTZARIS See **BOZZARIS, Marcos**

BOUCH, Sir Thomas (1822–80) English civil engineer, born in Thursby in Cumberland, the designer of the first Tay (rail) Bridge, opened in 1877. The centre spans were blown down while a train was crossing in a severe gale two years later, with the loss of over 70 lives; the inquiry blamed Bouch's design and supervision of construction, and he died less than a year later.

BOUCHER, François (1703–70) French painter, born in Paris and the purest Rococo painter at the court of **Louis XV**. As a young man he engraved the work of **Watteau**. From 1727 to 1731 he was in Italy and was received into the Academy in 1734. He worked on a range of material from stage design to tapestry, and from 1755 was director of the famous Gobelins factory. A refined portrait painter also, he produced several portraits of the king's most famous mistress, Madame **de Pompadour**, and it was she who bought his greatest pictures, *The Rising* and *The Setting of the Sun*. In 1765 he became *premier peintre du Roi* but by this time his style was under attack from **Diderot**, and when Sir **Joshua Reynolds** visited his studio, he was scandalized to find Boucher working without a model. His work is usually considered, along with that of his pupil, **Fragonard**, as being wholly representative of the frivolous spirit of his age. There is a fine collection in the London Wallace Collection.

BOUCHER (DE CRÈVECŒUR) DE PERTHES, Jacques (1788–1868) French archaeologist, born in Rethel. From 1837 at Moulin-Quignon in the Somme valley he discovered flint hand axes in association with the bones of extinct animals, from which he drew conclusions about the great antiquity of the human race. His views were at first greeted with incredulity but came to be upheld 20 years later. An autobiography, *Sur Dix Rois: Souvenirs de 1796 à 1860*, appeared in 1863–66.

BOUCICAULT, Dion (?1820–1890) dramatist and actor, born in Dublin. He was educated at University College School, London. Among his original and adapted pieces were *The Colleen Bawn* (1860) and *The Octoroon* (1861).

BOUDICCA, incorrectly called **Boadicea** (1st century) British warrior-queen who led a great uprising against the Romans. She was queen of the native tribe of Iceni (Norfolk, Suffolk, and part of Cambridgeshire). Her husband, Prasutagus, an ally of Rome, had shrewdly made the emperor **Nero** his co-heir, but when he died in AD 60 the Romans annexed all the Iceni territory and pillaged it. According to **Tacitus**, Boudicca was flogged and her daughters raped. The Iceni rose in fury and, led by Boudicca, destroyed the Roman colony of Camulodunum (Colchester), sacked and burned Londinium (London) and razed Verulamium (St Albans), killing up to 70000 Romans. The Roman governor of Britain, Suetonius Paulinus, who had been absent in Mona (Angelsey) in north Wales, gathered two legions and overwhelmed the Iceni in a bloody battle somewhere in the Midlands. Some 80000 of the tribesmen were slaughtered, against only 400 Roman dead, and Boudicca herself is said to have taken poison.

BOUDIN, (Louis) Eugène (1824–98) French painter, born in Honfleur. A precursor of Impressionism, he is noted for his seascapes, which include *Deauville* (Tate Gallery), *Harbour of Trouville* (National Gallery), and *Corvette Russe* (Luxembourg, Paris).

BOUFFLERS, Louis François, Duc de (1644–1711) French soldier, and marshal of France from 1693. He served with great distinction in the Franco-Dutch war of 1672–78 under **Condé**, **Turenne**, and **Catinat**. He commanded the defence of Namur against **William III** in 1695. In the war of the Spanish Succession (1701–11) he commanded the French forces in the Spanish Netherlands, and defended Lille against Prince **Eugene** in 1708. After the defeat at Malplaquet in 1709, he conducted the French retreat with great skill.

BOUFFLERS, Stanislas, Marquis de (1737–1815) the 'Chevalier de Boufflers', born in Lunéville, the son of the witty Marquise de Boufflers, who played a brilliant part at the court of Stanislaus, the exiled king of Poland. He rose to be *maréchal de camp*, became governor of Senegal in 1785, entered the French Academy (1788), corresponded with and married Mme de Sabran, and was a poet and literary man much admired in French *salons*.

BOUGAINVILLE, Louis Antoine de (1729–1811) French navigator, mathematician and soldier, born in Paris. He studied law and then mathematics, publishing an important treatise on integral calculus. When secretary to the French Embassy in London he was elected fellow of the Royal Society. In 1756 he served with distinction in Canada as **Montcalm**'s aide-de-camp, and also in the campaign of 1761 in Germany. Entering the French navy in 1763, he was responsible for colonizing the Falkland Islands for France, and for their transfer to Spain. In command of the ships *La Boudeuse* and *L'Étoile*, he accomplished the first French circumnavigation of the world (1766–69), which he described in his valuable *Voyage autour du monde*, but failed to find Australia as he followed his predecessors' routes most carefully. The largest of the Solomon Islands is named after him, as is the plant **Bougainvillaea**. In the American war he commanded several ships of the line, and was made a field-marshal in 1780 and a vice-admiral in 1791. After the outbreak of the Revolution he devoted himself solely to scientific pursuits. By **Napoleon I** he was made a senator, count of the empire, and member of the Légion d'Honneur.

BOUGHTON, Rutland (1878–1960) English composer, born in Aylesbury. In his youth Boughton was strongly influenced by **Wagner**'s principles of music drama and also by socialist ideas. He attempted to develop an English style, with a strong choral element, his subjects based on British legend, and he founded the Glastonbury Festival (1914–26). He wrote the enormously successful opera *The Immortal Hour* (1913), a choral drama *Bethlehem* (1915), *The Queen of Cornwall* (1924), five music dramas (1908–45) intended to form an Arthurian cycle (never performed complete), and other stage, choral and instrumental works. His failure at Glastonbury was due not to musical reasons, but to financial difficulties, to an ambition which outstripped his dramatic gifts, and to disapproval of his private life and of his avowed communism. A strong individualist, he expressed his ideas in his writings, notably *The Reality of Music* (1934).

BOUGUER, Pierre (1698–1758) French physicist, born at Croisic in Brittany. In 1735 he was sent with others to Peru to measure a degree of the meridian at the equator. There from 1735 to 1742 they investigated the length of the seconds pendulum at great elevations, the deviation of the plumbline through the attraction of a mountain, the limit of perpetual snow, the obliquity of the ecliptic, etc. His views on the intensity of light laid the foundation of photometry. In 1748 he invented the heliometer.

BOUGUEREAU, William Adolphe (1825–1905) French painter, born in La Rochelle. He studied art while engaged in business at Bordeaux, and proceeding to Paris in 1850 gained the *Grand Prix de Rome*. He returned from Italy in 1855, having the previous year first made his mark with *The Body of St Cecilia Borne to the Catacombs*, which, with his *Mater Afflictorum* (1876), is now in the Luxembourg.

BOUILHET, Louis (1821–69) French poet and dramatist, born in Cany in Seine Inférieure. A friend of **Flaubert**, in his *Fossiles* (1856) he attempted to use science as a subject for poetry. Of his many plays, *Conjuration d'Amboise* (1866) met with success.

BOUILLÉ, François Claude Amour, Marquis de (1739–1800) French soldier, born at the castle of Cluzel in Auvergne. He entered the army at the age of 14, and served with distinction during the Seven Years' War (1756–63). In 1768 he was appointed governor of Guadeloupe, and afterwards commander-in-chief in the West Indies. In the American War of Independence (1778–83) he took from the British Dominica, Tobago, St Eustache, Saba, St Martin, St Christopher, and Nevis. **Louis XVI** nominated him a member of the Assembly of Notables in 1787–88; in 1790 he was made commander-in-chief of the army of the Meuse, Saar, and Moselle. Forced to flee from France for his part in the attempted escape of Louis XVI, in 1791 he entered the service of **Gustav III** of Sweden. In 1793 he went to England, where he wrote his *Mémoires sur la Révolution*.

BOUILLON, Godfrey of See **GODFREY OF BOUILLON**

BOULAINVILLIERS, Henri, Comte de (1658–1722) French historian, born in St Saire in Normandy. He resigned from the military profession and devoted himself to writing (posthumously-published) works on the ancient families of France.

BOULANGER, Georges Ernest Jean Marie (1837–91) French soldier and statesman, born in Rennes. Educated at St Cyr, he served in Italy, China, the Franco-German War (1870–71), and helped suppress the Paris Commune (1871). In 1886, as the protégé of **Clemenceau**, he was appointed minister of war. He introduced many reforms in soldiers' pay and living conditions and became a popular national figure amongst the Parisians, often appearing amongst them on horseback. When he lost office in 1887, 'Boulanger fever' only increased. He was 'exiled' by the army to a command at Clermont-Ferrand, and although deprived of his command in 1888 was immediately elected deputy for Dordogne and Nord, and demanded a revision of the constitution. He was wounded in a duel with M Floquet, the minister-president, in the same year. Boulangism became really formidable in 1889, and was supported with large sums of money by leading royalists for their own ends. Fearing a coup d'état, the government prosecuted Boulanger, who lost courage and fled the country in 1889. He was condemned in absence; his schemes wholly collapsed, and he eventually shot himself on his mistress's grave in Brussels.

BOULANGER, Lili (1893–1918) French composer, born in Paris. Encouraged and supervised by her elder sister **Nadia Boulanger**, she studied at the Paris Conservatoire and in 1913 was the first woman to win the Prix de Rome, with her cantata *Faust et Hélène*. She returned from Rome to look after the families of musicians fighting in World War I but, having suffered from ill-health for most of her life, died young, leaving unfinished an opera based on **Maeterlinck**'s *La princesse Maleine*. Among the many pieces she composed are *Pour les funérailles d'un soldat* (1912), *Du fond de l'abîme* (1914–17) and *Vieille prière bouddhique* (1917).

BOULANGER, Nadia (1887–1979) French musician, born in Paris of a musical family. She studied at the Conservatoire (1879–1904), where she won several prizes, and went on to write many vocal and instrumental works, winning second prize at the Grand Prix de Rome in 1908 for her cantata, *La Sirène*. After 1918 she devoted herself to teaching, first at home, and later at the Conservatoire and the École Normale de Musique. She was also a noted organist and conductor.

BOULAY DE LA MEURTHE, Antoine, Comte (1761–1840) French statesman. He espoused the Revolution but opposed Jacobinism, and under the empire had an important part in preparing the *Code civil*.

BOULE, Pierre Marcellin (1861–1942) French palaeontologist, born in Montsalvy (Cantal). Professor at the Museé National d'Histoire Naturelle, he worked on the geology of the mountains of central France, and on human fossils. He made the first complete reconstruction of a Neanderthal skeleton, and published *Les Hommes fossiles* (1921).

BOULEZ, Pierre (1925–) French conductor and composer, born in Montbrison. He studied at the Paris Conservatoire (1943–45) after a year as an engineering student at Lyon, and in 1948 became musical director of **Barrault**'s Théâtre Marigny; from then he established his reputation as an interpreter of contemporary music. He left France in 1959 and settled at Baden-Baden in Germany. His early work, notably the *Sonatine* for flute and piano (1946), and two piano sonatas (1946 and 1948), rebelled against what he saw as the conservatism of such composers as **Stravinsky** and **Schoenberg**. In later compositions he has developed the very individual view of music already apparent in the *Sonatine*, namely that whereas tonal music of the past can be seen as a straightforward progression from a point of departure, contemporary music describes a fluid and infinite universe out of which it is the composer's task to make a coherent work of art. Of his later works, *Le Marteau sans maître* (1955) gained him a worldwide reputation, confirmed by *Pli selon pli* and the third piano sonata. He wrote *Penser la musique aujourd'hui* (trans 1970).

BOULLE, or **Boule** See **BUHL**

BOULLÉE, Étienne-Louis (1728–99) French architect, born in Paris. He was elected to the Académie in 1762, and became architect to the king of Prussia. He is of interest not so much for his Neo-classical work before the revolution (such as the Hôtel de Brunoy, Paris, 1772), but for his later, more original and visionary designs for vastly ambitious projects of an austerely formal and geometric nature, such as the design (1784) for a colossal spherical monument to **Isaac Newton**. He remained a figure of influence during the French Revolution and, through his pupils, was an influence on the architecture of the Napoleonic period.

BOULT, Sir Adrian Cedric (1889–1983) English conductor, born in Chester. After studying at Oxford and Leipzig, he conducted the City of Birmingham Orchestra from 1924 to 1930, when he was appointed musical director of the BBC and conductor of the newly-formed BBC Symphony Orchestra. Extensive tours in Europe and America won him a high reputation for his wide sympathies and championship of English music, and these qualities had a profound influence upon the musical policy of the BBC. After his enforced retirement from broadcasting in 1950, he was conductor in chief of the London Philharmonic Orchestra until 1957 and its president from 1965. He continued to conduct regularly until 1981. In 1973 he published *My Own Trumpet*.

BOULTON, Matthew (1728–1809) English engineer, born in Birmingham, where his father was a silver-stamper. He extended the business by the purchase of a piece of barren heath at Soho, near Birmingham, his works there being opened in 1762. He entered into partnership with **James Watt**, and in 1774 they established a manufactory of steam engines, which proved remunerative only after 18 anxious years. They also improved coining machinery—it was only in 1882 that a Boulton press at the Mint was finally discarded.

BOUMÉDIENNE, Houari, originally **Mohammed Bou Kharrouba** (1925–78) Algerian soldier and statesman, born in Guelma in eastern Algeria. Educated at Constantine and El Azhar University in Cairo, he became a teacher. In 1954 he joined the FLN (Algerian National Liberation Front) for whom for eight years he conducted guerrilla operations against the French, serving as chief of staff (1960–62) with the rank of colonel. When Algeria gained independence in 1962, he became minister of national defence. In 1965 he led a military coup against President **Ben Bella** and established an Islamic socialist government, presiding over the Council of Revolution as effective head of state until he formally accepted election as president in 1976. In home affairs, he directed a four-year plan which increased industrial output and revolutionized agricultural production. Shortly before his death, he was seeking to establish a North African socialist federation.

BOURBAKI, Charles Denis Sauter (1816–97) French soldier, born in Pau. He fought in the Crimea and Italy, and during the Franco-German War of 1870–71 he commanded the Imperial Guard at Metz. Under **Gambetta** he organized the Army of the North, and commanded the Army of the Loire. His attempt to break the Prussian line at Belfort in 1871, though ably conceived, ended in disaster, with the loss of 10000 men. In the retreat to Switzerland that followed, he attempted suicide. He retired in 1881.

BOURBAKI, Nicolas (20th century) 'French mathematician', the pseudonym of a group of French mathematicians from the École Normale Supérieure, including Henri Cartan, Claude Chevalley, **Jean Dieudonné** and **André Weil**. In the 1930s they conceived the plan of writing a treatise on pure mathematics which would set out the subject in a strictly logical development from its basic principles, in a style that was minimal, precise, rigorous and elegant, emphasizing the fundamental structures that underlie apparently diverse areas of mathematics. Publication of *Éléments de mathématiques* by 'Nicolas Bourbaki' started in 1939, and books on set theory, algebra, general topology, topological vector spaces, integration, **Lie** groups and Lie algebras, among other subjects, have followed. By the 1980s the unfinished series had more or less come to a stop, but it has had great influence on mathematical attitudes in the last 40 years, some mathematicians being attracted by its abstraction and others repelled, condemning it for divorcing mathematics from its historical applications to the physical world. Many of the books have become the definitive treatment of their subjects, and the series also includes valuable historical essays.

BOURBON French royal house which for generations occupied the thrones of France and Naples, and till 1931 that of Spain. It took its name from the castle of Bourbon (now Bourbon-l'Archambault, twelve miles north-west of Moulins in Allier). Adhémar, sire of Bourbon in the 10th century, traced his descent from **Charles Martel**. After several changes, the seignory of Bourbon devolved upon an heiress, who in 1272 married Duke Robert, Comte de Clermont (c.1255–1320), the sixth son of **Louis IX** of France, and the name and possessions of the house thus passed to a branch of the royal family of the Capets. From Duke Robert sprang two lines. The elder ended with the 'Constable de Bourbon' (**Charles Bourbon**). A representative of the younger line inherited the possessions of the Constable, and became Duke of Vendôme. His son, Antoine (c.1450–c.1565), obtained by marriage the throne of Navarre, and Antoine's son was 'Henry of Navarre' **(Henry IV)**, who in 1589, on the extinction of the male line of Valois, fell heir to the crown of France (see **Henry IV**, **Louis XIII-XVIII**, **Charles X**, and the Count of **Chambord**). The Orléans branch descends from a younger son of **Louis XIII** (Philip, 1640–1701). From **Louis XIV** descend also the branches that formerly held the thrones of Spain, Parma, and Naples. A younger brother of Antoine de Bourbon (Henri IV's father) founded the houses of **Condé** and **Conti**. The branch of Montpensier was founded in the 15th century. The sons and grandsons of **Louis-Philippe** held titles derived from Paris, Chartres, Nemours, Eu, Joinville, Aumale, and Montpensier.

BOURBON, Charles (1490–1527) French soldier, known as 'Constable de Bourbon', the son of the Count of Montpensier and the only daughter of the Duke of Bourbon. He thus united the vast estates of both these branches of the Bourbon family. For his bravery at the battle of Marignano in 1515 he was made constable of France by **Francis I**. Having lost royal favour, he renounced the service of France, and concluded a private alliance with the Emperor **Charles V** (1523), and with **Henry VIII** of England. At the head of a force of German mercenaries, he joined the Spanish army in Lombardy in 1523 and, invading France in 1524, failed at the siege of Marseille. The following year, however, he was chief commander at the great victory of Pavia, in which Francis I was taken prisoner. But Charles V distrusted him, though he made him Duke of Milan and Spanish commander in Northern Italy. Along with **Georg von Frundsberg**, he led the mixed army of Spanish and German mercenaries that stormed and plundered Rome in 1527, but was struck down in the fierce struggle—by a bullet fired by **Benvenuto Cellini**, as the latter asserted. His lands in France were declared forfeit.

BOURCHIER, Thomas (c.1404–1486) English prelate and statesman. He became bishop of Worcester in 1434, of Ely in 1444, archbishop of Canterbury in 1454, and a cardinal in 1473. He was lord chancellor from 1455 to 1456. He crowned **Edward IV** (1461), **Richard III** (1493) and **Henry VII** (1485).

BOURDALOUE, Louis (1632–1704) French churchman and pulpit orator, born in Bourges. He filled in succession the chairs of rhetoric, philosophy, and moral theology at the Jesuit College of Bourges, but was chiefly memorable as a powerful and eloquent preacher in Paris and at court. The year after the revocation of the Edict of Nantes (1685), he was sent to Montpellier to bring back the Protestants to the Roman Catholic Church. In his later years he relinquished the pulpit, and devoted his time to hospitals, prisons, and pious institutions.

BOURDELLE, Émile Antoine (1861–1929) French sculptor, painter, and teacher, born in Montauban. He studied at the École des Beaux-Arts, Paris, and under **Rodin**. He found inspiration in Greek art, relating its style to his own time. He illustrated a number of books, and his teaching had considerable influence.

BOURDON, Eugène (1808–84) French inventor and industrialist, born in Paris. An instrument-maker to trade, in 1835 he founded a machine shop in Paris to manufacture model steam-engines for educational and demonstration purposes. Aware of the need for an accurate means of measuring the pressure of the steam in high-pressure steam-engines and boilers, in 1849 he patented a simple but ingenious device which is still in widespread use today for measuring the pressure of steam and many other fluids. The Bourdon gauge makes use of the fact that a curved length of metal tube, closed at one end, will tend to straighten out as the pressure of the fluid in it is increased; a system of levers and ratchets converts this movement into the rotation of a pointer on a dial.

BOURDON DE L'OISE, François Louis (c.1760–1797) French revolutionary. He took part in storming the Tuileries, sat in the Convention, and voted for the execution of **Louis XVI**, but in 1797 was transported by the Directory to Cayenne, where he died.

BOURGELAT, Claude (1712–99) French veterinary surgeon, born in Lyon. He founded there in 1761 the first veterinary school in Europe.

BOURGEOIS, Jeanne See **MISTINGUETT**

BOURGEOIS, Léon Victor Auguste (1851–1925) French socialist statesman, born in Paris. He studied law and served as minister of public instruction (1890–92, 1898), minister of labour (1912–13, 1917) and was prime minister (1895–96). A delegate to the Hague conference (1907), he was one of the founders of the League of Nations and in 1920 was awarded the Nobel prize for peace. He advocated a form of socialism called solidarism.

BOURGEOIS, Louise (1911–) French-born American sculptor, born in Paris. She studied at the École du Louvre, the Académie des Beaux-Arts and at private art schools before emigrating to the USA in 1938. She began as a painter, and had a one-woman show at the Bertha Schaefer Gallery in New York in 1945. In the late 1940s she turned to wood-carving, and to stone and metal in the 1960s, creating shapes which suggest figures, or parts of figures, without ever quite becoming 'realistic'.

BOURGET, Paul (1852–1935) French poet, essayist and novelist, born in Amiens. He first wrote striking verse: *La Vie inquiète* (1875), *Edel* (1878), and *Les Aveux* (1881). His *Essais* (1883) indicated his true strength; the second series, *Nouveaux Essais de psychologie contemporaine* (1886), was a subtle inquiry into the causes of pessimism in France. His first novel, *L'Irréparable* (1884), was followed by a steady stream of works which placed him in the front rank of modern

French novelists. *L'Étape* (1902) marked the crystallization of his talent. His works after 1892 showed a marked reaction from realism and scepticism towards mysticism.

BOURGUIBA, Habib ibn Ali (1903–) Tunisian politician, born in Monastir, Tunisia. He studied law in Paris and became a radical Tunisian nationalist in 1934. Over the next 20 years he served three prison sentences imposed by the French authorities. In 1956, however, the government of **Mendès-France** in Paris recognized that, in contrast to other Arab leaders, Bourguiba was moderate in his demands and he was accepted as Tunisia's first prime minister, becoming president in 1957. By 1962 he had secured the withdrawal of the French from their Tunisian military bases; thereafter he was able to improve trading contacts with the former imperial power. In 1975 he was declared president for life. His authority, however, was threatened by riots instigated by Islamic fundamentalists in 1983 and 1984, and subsequently he exercised little influence on policy. In 1987 he was deposed by his prime minister, General **Ben Ali**, on the grounds of senility.

BOURIGNON, Antoinette (1616–80) French religious, born in Lille. Believing herself called to restore the pure spirit of the gospel, she fled from home and entered a convent. She had charge of a hospital in Lille; in Amsterdam (1667) she gathered followers and printed enthusiastic works, but was driven out, founded a hospital in East Friesland, and died in Franeker. Bourignonism so prevailed in Scotland about 1720 that till 1889 a solemn renunciation was demanded from every entrant into the ministry.

BOURKE-WHITE, Margaret, originally **Margaret White** (1906–71) American photo-journalist, born in New York City, the daughter of a print designer. She studied photography at Columbia University. In 1927 she started as an industrial and architectural photographer but was engaged by *Fortune* magazine in 1929 and became a staff photographer and associate editor on *Life* magazine when it started publication in 1936. Her illustrations for the study by **Erskine Caldwell** (to whom she was married from 1939 to 1942) of rural poverty in the southern USA, *You Have Seen Their Faces* (1937), were highly individual, in contrast to the more dispassionate records of the US government FSA workers. She covered World War II for *Life* and was the first woman photographer to be attached to the US armed forces, producing outstanding reports of the siege of Moscow (1941) and the opening of the concentration camps in 1944. After the war, she recorded the troubles in India, Pakistan and South Africa, and was an official UN war correspondent during the Korean War. Overtaken by ill-health from 1952, she continued to produce many photo-journalistic essays until her retirement from *Life* in 1969. Her books include *Eyes on Russia* (1931), *Halfway to Freedom* (1946) and an autobiography, *Portrait of Myself* (1963).

BOURMONT, Louis de Ghaisnes, Comte de (1773–1846) French soldier, and marshal of France, born in the castle of Bourmont, in Anjou. He went into exile at the Revolution, but from 1794 to 1799 was engaged in the struggle in La Vendée. Subsequently, he obtained the favour of **Napoleon** and, for his brilliant services in 1813–14, was made general. In 1814 he declared for the **Bourbons**; yet, on Napoleon's return from Elba, he went over to him, only to desert once more on the eve of Ligny. His evidence went far to bring about **Ney**'s execution. He was appointed minister of war in 1829, and in 1830 received the command of the expedition that conquered Algiers. His rapid success won him the marshal's baton, but at the July Revolution of 1830 he was superseded, and went to England to share the exile of **Charles X**.

BOURNE, Francis Alphonsus (1861–1935) English prelate, born in Clapham, London. He was educated at Ushaw College, St Edmund's College, St Sulpice, Paris, and Louvain University. Ordained a priest in 1884, he was successively curate at Blackheath, Sheerness, Mortlake, and West Grinstead. In 1889 he was appointed rector of Southwark Diocesan Seminary, and became bishop of Southwark in 1897. He was made a domestic prelate to Pope **Leo XIII** in 1895. In 1903 he succeeded **Vaughan** as archbishop of Westminster, and was created a cardinal in 1911. A great pastor, he travelled widely, and is best remembered for his zeal for education, and his organization of the International Eucharistic Congress in 1908. His chief works are *Ecclesiastical Training* (1926) and *Occasional Sermons* (1930).

BOURNE, Hugh (1772–1852) founder of the Primitive Methodists, born in Fordhays, Stoke-upon-Trent. His zeal as a Wesleyan preacher for large open-air meetings, carried on once from 6am till 8pm, received no approbation from the leaders of the denomination, and in 1808 he was cut off from the Wesleyan connection. But he quickly gathered round him many devoted followers, and in 1810 a committee of ten members was formed at Standley, near Bemersley. The title of Primitive Methodists was adopted in 1812; colloquially, they were sometimes also called Ranters. Bourne and his brother founded the first chapel of the body in Tunstall in 1811. For the greater part of his life he worked as a carpenter and builder, but found time to visit Scotland, Ireland, and the USA. Amongst his writings is a *History of the Primitive Methodists* (1823).

BOURNONVILLE, August (1805–79) Danish dancer and choreographer, born in Copenhagen. The son of a French dancer, he is considered one of the most important 19th-century choreographers. After training with the Royal Danish Ballet, he moved to Paris (1926) to study under the great teacher, Auguste Vestris (1760–1842), at the Paris Opera. He spent the rest of his career (from 1828) with the Royal Danish Ballet, first as a dancer and, from 1830, as director, though he continued to dance in lead roles for another 20 years. He staged over 60 known works, a dozen of which survive today, the most popular being *La Sylphide* (1836) and *Napoli* (1842). His choreography is busy and makes much use of pointe work. Described as a great believer in bourgeois values, he moved away from the emotional heights of French Romanticism towards a style where goodness and equality of the sexes pervaded. He was a close friend of **Hans Christian Anderson**.

BOURRIENNE, Louis Antoine Fauvelet de (1769–1834) French statesman, born in Sens. He studied at the military school of Brienne, where he was on friendly terms with the young **Napoleon**. In 1797 he became Napoleon's secretary and accompanied him to Egypt (1798), but he was dismissed in 1802 for being implicated in the dishonourable bankruptcy of the house of Coulon (army contractors) and appointed to a post in Hamburg until 1813. Recalled and fined for embezzlement, he joined the supporters of the **Bourbons**, after whose restoration he was elected a deputy and figured as an anti-liberal. He died in an asylum at Caen. His *Mémoires* (trans 1893) are not always reliable.

BOUSCAREN, Juliette See **FIGUIER, Louis**

BOUSSINGAULT, Jean Baptiste (1802–87) French agricultural chemist, born in Paris. He studied at the

School of Mines and at St Étienne, served under **Simón Bolívar** in the South American war of independence and became professor of chemistry at Lyon. He demonstrated that plants absorb nitrogen from the soil and showed that carbon is assimilated by plants from the carbon dioxide of the atmosphere.

BOUTET, Anne Françoise Hippolyte See **MARS**

BOUTS, Dierick, or **Dirk,** or **Thierry** (c.1415–1475) Dutch painter, born in Haarlem, but usually placed with the Flemish school. He worked at Louvain and Brussels, coming under the influence of **Roger van der Weyden**, and produced austere religious paintings, with rich and gem-like colour. His *Resurrection* is in the Munich Pinakothek.

BOVERI, Theodor Heinrich (1862–1915) German biologist and pioneer of cytology, born in Bamberg. He studied history and philosophy at Munich but soon changed to science, and graduated in medicine in 1885. From 1893 he taught zoology and anatomy at Würzburg. By 1884 something was known of the cell chromosomes from **Beneden**'s work, and Boveri confirmed and extended this. He studied cell-division in the roundworm *Ascaris*, and in sea-urchin eggs, and showed that normal development requires an appropriate number of chromosomes for the species, and chromosome deficiency leads to abnormality: in some way, the chromosomes appeared to determine development. By 1910 it was widely accepted that chromosomes are the actual vehicles of heredity. Later, it was seen that they are composed of smaller genetic elements, genes, which, later still, were seen to be, themselves, composed of DNA.

BOVET, Daniel (1907–) Swiss-born Italian pharmacologist, born in Neuchâtel. He studied chemistry at Geneva, and conducted research at the Pasteur Institute in Paris (1929–47), where he developed the first antihistamine drug and the first synthetic muscle-relaxants, for which he won the 1957 Nobel prize for physiology or medicine. In 1947 he emigrated to Italy, where he was appointed professor at Rome. A visit to Brazil led to his interest in the Indian nerve poison, curare, of which he was later to make synthetic compounds, which have been much used in anaesthesia since 1950.

BOWDICH, Thomas Edward (1791–1824) English traveller in Africa, born in Bristol. After conducting a successful mission to Ashanti (1816), he studied mathematics and other subjects in Paris and was awarded a Cambridge prize of £1000. Aggrieved at his treatment by the African Company, he exposed their management in a book which led the government to take over their possessions. In 1822 he began a trigonometrical survey of the Gambia, where he died of fever.

BOWDITCH, Henry Pickering (1840–1911) American physiologist, born in Boston into an old, genteel New England family. He interrupted his studies in Boston to fight in the American Civil War (1861–65). He then obtained his MD from Harvard and spent three years in Europe, studying experimental physiology and microscopy with such teachers as **Claude Bernard** and **Emil Ludwig**. He produced important experimental work on cardiac contraction, on the innervation of the heart, and on the reflexes. He developed the physiology department at Harvard, instituting important reforms while dean of the Harvard Medical School (1883–93), and was a founder of the American Physiological Society (1887).

BOWDLER, Thomas (1754–1825) English doctor and man of letters, born in Ashley, Bath. He retired from medical practice and settled in the Isle of Wight to devote himself to literary pursuits. He is immortalized as the editor of the 'Family Shakespeare' (10 vols, 1818), in which 'those words and expressions are omitted which cannot with propriety be read aloud in a family'. 'Bowdlerizing' has become a synonym for prudish expurgation.

BOWEN, Elizabeth Dorothea Cole (1899–1973) Irish novelist and short story writer, born in County Cork, the daughter of a wealthy barrister and land-owner, and brought up in Dublin. Educated in England at Downe House School in Kent, she married in 1923 and in the same year published her first collection of short stories, *Encounters*, followed by *Anne Lee's* (1926). Her first novel, *The Hotel* (1927), was the first of a string of delicately-written explorations of personal relationships, of which *The Death of the Heart* (1938) and *The Heat of the Day* (1949), a war story, are the best known. She was also a perceptive literary critic, and published *English Novelists* (1942) and *Collected Impressions* (1950).

BOWEN, Norman Levi (1887–1956) Canadian-born American geologist, born in Kingston, Ontario, the son of English immigrants. He studied at Queen's University, Ontario, and became professor there (1919–21) and at Chicago (1937–47); he was also for long associated with the Geophysical Laboratory at Washington DC. He was a pioneer in the field of experimental petrology, particularly the study of silicates and igneous rocks. His work is summarized in his book, *The Evolution of Igneous Rocks* (1928).

BOWER, Frederick Orpen (1855–1948) English botanist, born in Ripon. Professor at Glasgow (1885–1925), he wrote *The Origin of a Land Flora* (1908) and *Ferns* (1923), besides textbooks and works of a more popular nature, and gave much attention to ferns and mosses.

BOWER, or **Bowmaker, Walter** (1385–1449) Scottish chronicler. Abbot of Inchcolm in the Firth of Forth from 1418, he continued the Latin *Scotichronicon* of **John of Fordun** from 1153 down to 1437.

BOWIE, David, real name **David Robert Jones** (1947–) English rock singer, born in Brixton, London. His early career was undistinguished and he came close to becoming a Buddhist monk before the success of 'Space Oddity' (1969)—a song based on the **Kubrick** film *2001: A Space Odyssey*. His career blossomed throughout the 1970s as he adopted a range of extreme stage images to suit a variety of musical styles and concepts. His albums have included *Hunky Dory* (1971), *The Rise And Fall Of Ziggy Stardust And The Spiders From Mars* (1972), *Diamond Dogs* (1974) (originally a musical adaptation of **Orwell**'s *1984*, changed after pressure from the author's estate) and *Heroes* (1977). He has also acted on Broadway in *The Elephant Man* (1980) and in films, including *The Man Who Fell To Earth* (1976) and *Merry Christmas Mr Lawrence* (1983).

BOWIE, James (1790–1836) American pioneer, born in Kentucky, the inventor of the curved dagger or sheath-knife named after him. After settling in Texas, he became a naturalized Mexican citizen. As a colonel in the Texan army, he was killed at the battle of the Alamo.

BOWLBY, (Edward) John (Mostyn) (1907–) English psychiatrist, the son of an eminent surgeon. Educated at the Royal Naval College, Dartmouth, and Trinity College, Cambridge, he was staff psychologist at the London Child Guidance Clinic (1937–40). After World War II he moved to the Tavistock Clinic (1946–72), to become chairman of the department for children and parents (1946–68). His early research concerned crime and juvenile delinquency, but he is best known for his work on the effects of maternal deprivation upon the mental health and emotional development of children. His work led to theories that were based upon psychoanalytic ideas, but bolstered by analogies with the parent-infant interactions seen in certain animal species. He argued that it was essential for the mother to be present during a critical formative period in order for emotional bonds to be formed. He has been a consultant in mental health for the World Health Organization and honorary consultant psychiatrist to the Tavistock Clinic since 1972.

BOWLES, Caroline Anne See **SOUTHEY, Robert**

BOWLES, Jane Auer (1918–73) American fiction writer and playwright. For many years she suffered from acute ill-health and her literary output was consequently slim. An original writer, she has been linked with **Gertrude Stein** whose influence is apparent but not destructive. *In the Summer House* (1953), a play, is her most accessible work. Her *Collected Works* appeared in 1967. She married **Paul Bowles** in 1939.

BOWLES, Paul Frederick (1910–) American novelist, composer, poet, travel writer and translator, born in New York City. After studying at the University of Virginia, he went to Europe in 1931 to study music with **Aaron Copland** in Paris, and became a composer and music critic. He did not devote himself to writing until after World War II. His first novel, *The Sheltering Sky*, set in Morocco, appeared in 1949 and was acclaimed as being among the best post-war books. He became a resident in Tangier in 1952, and wrote three other novels, *Let It Come Down* (1952), *The Spider's House* (1955) and *Up Above the World* (1966), as well as several collections of short stories, including *Pages from Cold Point* (1968) and *Midnight Mass* (1981). He was married to the writer **Jane Bowles**.

BOWLES, William Lisle (1762–1850) English clergyman and poet, born in King's Sutton vicarage, Northamptonshire. Educated at Winchester and Trinity College, Oxford, he became vicar of Bremhill in Yorkshire and prebendary of Salisbury in 1804, and later chaplain to the Prince Regent (1818). In his poetry he was a forerunner of the Romantic movement in English poetry. His *Fourteen Sonnets, written chiefly on Picturesque Spots during a Journey* (1789), published anonymously, had **Coleridge**, **Wordsworth** and **Southey** among their enthusiastic admirers. His best poetical work is *The Missionary of the Andes*. In 1806 he published an edition of **Pope**, and an opinion which he expressed on Pope's poetical merits led to a memorable controversy (1809–25) in which **Thomas Campbell** and **Byron** were his antagonists.

BOWMAKER See **BOWER, Walter**

BOWMAN, Isaiah (1878–1950) American geographer, born in Waterloo, Canada. Educated at Harvard and Yale, he became assistant professor at Yale (1909–15) during which time he joined three important expeditions to the Andes. This was influential in his development of regional diagrams and the concept of topographic types. He became director of the American Geographical Society (1915–35), and his significant work on the boundaries during 1914–18 led to his appointment as chief territorial specialist at the Versailles Peace Conference. He was president of Johns Hopkins University from 1935 to 1948. He published *The New World: Problems of Political Geography* (1921), an authoritative study on political geography, and became an advocate of the 'possibilist' approach to geography. His other works include *Forest Physiography* (1911), *South America* (1915), and *International Relations* (1930).

BOWMAN, Sir William (1816–92) English physician and ophthalmic surgeon, born in Nantwich. With Richard B Todd (1809–60) he published *Physiological Anatomy and Physiology of Man* (1845–56), and gained a high reputation by his *Lectures on Operations on the Eye* (1849), describing the ciliary muscle. His *Collected Papers* appeared in 1892.

BOWRING, Sir John (1792–1872) British diplomat, born in Exeter. On leaving school, he entered a merchant's office, and acquired a knowledge of 200 languages. In 1821 he formed a close friendship with **Jeremy Bentham**, and in 1824 became the first editor of his radical *Westminster Review*. He visited Switzerland, Italy, Egypt, Syria, and the countries of the Zollverein, and prepared valuable government reports on their commerce. He sat in parliament from 1835 to 1849, and actively promoted the adoption of free trade. From 1849 he was British consul in Hong Kong; in 1854 he was knighted and made governor. In 1856, in retaliation for an insult to the British by a Chinese pirate ship, he ordered the bombardment of Canton, a proceeding which nearly upset the **Palmerston** ministry. In 1855 he concluded a commercial treaty with Siam, and in 1858 made a tour through the Philippines. He published his autobiography in 1877.

BOWYER, William (1699–1777) English printer and classical scholar, known as the 'learned printer'. He studied at St John's College, Cambridge, and in 1722 went into partnership with his father, William Bowyer (1663–1737). In 1767 he was nominated printer to the Houses of Parliament. He published several philological tracts, translated **Caesar**'s *Commentaries* (1750) and **Rousseau**'s paradoxical *Discourse* (1751), and wrote two essays on the *Origin of Printing* (1774), but his chief production was a Greek New Testament.

BOYCE, William (1711–79) English composer, born in London. In 1736 he was appointed composer to the Chapel Royal and, in 1758, organist. He held a high rank as a composer of choral and orchestral music and his works include the song 'Hearts of Oak', the serenata of *Solomon* (1743), and a valuable collection of *Cathedral Music* (1760).

BOYCOTT, Charles Cunningham (1832–97) English estate factor. The agent for Lord Erne in County Mayo, as one of the first victims in 1880 of **Parnell**'s system of social excommunication, he gave, in the verb 'to boycott', a new word to most European languages.

BOYCOTT, Geoffrey (1940–) English cricketer, born in Fitzwilliam, Yorkshire. The most celebrated batsman in post-war English cricket, he gained his county cap for Yorkshire in 1963 and was capped for England in the following year. He played 108 times for England between 1964 and 1982, and scored more than 150 centuries, but he was accused of too much deliberation at the crease, and the county was bitterly divided about the value of his contribution to the club. He was elected a member of the general committee in 1984. With impeccable timing, he scored his 100th first class century in a Test match against Australia on his home ground, Headingley, in 1977.

BOYD, Anne (1946–) Australian composer and flautist, born in Sydney. She studied composition there under **Peter Sculthorpe** and **Richard Meale**, and later under Wilfrid Mellers at York University, England, where she gained her D Phil. After some years teaching in England and Australia, she became founding head of the department of music at Hong Kong University (1981). Her interest in ethno-musicology, in Australian aboriginal music and that of Japan and Java, is reflected in her compositions, many of which have been recorded, such as *As I Crossed the Bridge of Dreams* and her children's opera, *The Little Mermaid*

BOYD, Arthur Merric (1862–1940) Australian painter, born in Opoho, New Zealand. He arrived in Australia in 1886 and in that year married Emma

Minnie à Beckett, granddaughter of Sir William à Beckett, first chief justice of Victoria (1852–57). He is particularly known for his watercolours.

BOYD, Arthur Merric Bloomfield (1920–) Australian painter, sculptor and potter, son of **Merric Boyd** and brother of **Guy Boyd**, born in Murrumbeena, Victoria. He studied briefly at the National Gallery of Victoria Art School and, after 1936, with his grandfather **Arthur Merric Boyd** at Rosebud, Victoria. After the war he exhibited with the Contemporary Arts Society in Melbourne, then returned to Murrumbeena and the pottery established by his father, Merric Boyd, where he worked with his brother-in-law **John Perceval**. He moved to London in 1959 where he exhibited at the Zwemmer Galleries the following year, and was represented in the Whitechapel and Tate exhibitions of 1961 and 1962. These established his position as a painter of international significance. He took up a fellowship in creative arts at the Australian National University, Canberra, in 1972, and later presented a large collection of his drawings to the Australian National Gallery in Canberra. He has also achieved note as an etcher, and for his designs for the theatre and ballet.

BOYD, Benjamin (c.1796–1851) Australian colonist. A Scottish trader and stockbroker, born in Merton Hall, Wigtownshire, he arrived in Hobson's Bay in his yacht *Wanderer* in 1842 and moved to Port Jackson. He became one of the largest and most powerful squatters in south-eastern New South Wales, and spent a fortune trying to found 'Boyd Town' as a commercial port. When the enterprise failed, in 1849 he sailed off to join the Gold Rush in California. He disappeared, in mysterious circumstances, during a journey amongst the Solomon Islands.

BOYD, Guy Martin à Beckett (1923–) Australian sculptor, born in Murrumbeena, Victoria, son of **Merric Boyd** and brother of **Arthur Merric Bloomfield Boyd**. Starting as a potter, he moved on to sculpture in 1964, quickly making a name for himself. He has exhibited in London, and was commissioned to produce mural reliefs for Tullamarine (Melbourne) and Kingsford Smith (Sydney) airports. He lived in Canada from 1976 to 1981.

BOYD, Martin à Beckett (1893–1972) Australian novelist and poet, born in Lucerne, Switzerland, son of **Arthur Merric Boyd**. Brought up in Melbourne, he lived for much of his life in Britain. After World War I he tried journalism for a time. His first three novels, *Love Gods* (1925), *Brangane: A Memoir* (1926) and *The Montforts* (1928) appeared under a pseudonym, 'Martin Mills', as did his fourth, *Dearest Idol* (1929), for which he adopted the name 'Walter Beckett'. Thereafter he acknowleged his authorship and produced his best work, to be seen in what is now referred to as the Langton tetralogy: *The Cardboard Crown* (1952), *A Difficult Young Man* (1955), *Outbreak of Love* (1957) and *When Blackbirds Sing* (1962).

BOYD, (William) Merric (1888–1959) Australian ceramic artist, born in St Kilda, Victoria, son of **Arthur Merric Boyd**. He studied at the pioneering porcelain works at Yarraville, Victoria and then served with the Royal Flying Corps in World War I, at Wedgwood, Stoke-on-Trent, in England. He returned to Australia in the early 1920s, founding a famous studio at Murrumbeena, outside Melbourne, and experimenting with new ceramic techniques. His pottery was much admired and is now sought after by collectors.

BOYD, Robin Gerard Penleigh (1919–71) Australian architect, critic and writer, born in Melbourne. He reached a wide and popular audience with his books *Australia's Home* (1952), *The Australian Ugliness* (1960) and *The Great Australian Dream* (1972). He delivered the ABC's Boyer Lecture, 'Artificial Australia', in 1967, and was a member of the judging panel for the new Houses of Parliament at Westminster. His critical work shaped the future direction of Australian architecture and was acknowledged with several awards.

BOYD, (Theodore) Penleigh (1890–1923) Australian landscape artist and dry-point etcher, born in Westbury, Wiltshire, son of **Arthur Merric Boyd**. He studied under **Frederick McCubbin**, and exhibited at the Royal Academy in 1922.

BOYD, William Clouser (1903–) American biochemist, born in Dearborn, Mississippi. Educated at Harvard, from 1948 he taught at the Boston medical school, as professor of immunochemistry. He used **Landsteiner**'s discovery of blood groups to examine racial differences and the distribution and migration of racial groups, systematically collecting and classifying blood samples on a worldwide basis. By 1950, in his book *Genetics and the Races of Man*, he was able to present evidence for the existence of 13 human races, distinguishable by blood type. Racial distinction is now seen as more complex, but the study of blood groups remains the richest source of information on inherited traits related to race.

BOYD, Zachary (c.1585–1653) Scottish clergyman. He studied at Glasgow and St Andrews and in 1607 became a regent of the Protestant college of Saumur in France. Returning to Scotland in 1621, he was appointed (1623) to the Barony parish, Glasgow, and was thrice elected rector of the university. He wrote *The Last Battel of the Soule in Death* (1629), a prose work, and *Zion's Flowers* (1644), some metrical versions of Scripture history, popularly known as 'Boyd's Bible'.

BOYD ORR, John, 1st Baron Boyd Orr (1880–1971) Scottish biologist, born in Kilmaurs, Ayrshire. Educated at Glasgow University, he served with distinction in World War I, winning the DSO and MC. He became director of the Rowett Research Institute and professor of agriculture at Aberdeen (1942–45), and was the first director of the United Nations Food and Agriculture Organization (1945–48). His pessimistic prognostications on the world food situation got him a reputation as an apostle of gloom, but his great services in improving that situation brought him the Nobel peace prize in 1949, in which year he was made a peer. His works include *Minerals in Pastures and their Relation to Animal Nutrition* (1928), *Food and the People* (1944), *The White Man's Dilemma* (1952) and *As I Recall* (1966).

BOYDELL, John (1719–1804) English illustrator, born in Dorrington, Shropshire. In 1741 he travelled to London, where he learned engraving, started a printshop, and in 1790 was lord mayor. From his '**Shakespeare** Gallery' of 162 pictures by **Opie**, **Reynolds**, **Northcote**, **West**, etc, was engraved a superb volume of plates (1803) to accompany a splendid edition of Shakespeare's works (9 vols, 1792–1801). The immense sums of money he spent on these illustrations brought him into difficulties.

BOYE, Karin Maria (1900–41) Swedish poet and novelist. She studied at Uppsala and Stockholm and became a leader of the socialist *Clarté* movement. She was the founder editor of the poetry magazine *Spektrum* (1931), to which she contributed much of her own poetry and translations, especially of **T S Eliot**. Her poetry collections include *Moln* (Cloud, 1922), *För trädets skull* (For the Tree's Sake, 1935) and *De sju dödsynderna* (The Seven Deadly Sins, 1941), and she wrote several novels, including *Kris* (Crisis, 1934) and

Kallocain (1940). She committed suicide soon afterwards.

BOYER, Alexis, Baron de (1757–1833) French surgeon, born in Uzerches in Limousin, a tailor's son. In 1805 he was imperial surgeon to **Napoleon**, whom he accompanied on his campaigns. Subsequently he was consultant surgeon to **Louis XVIII**, **Charles X**, and **Louis-Philippe.**

BOYER, Herbert Wayne (1936–) American biochemist, born in Pittsburgh. He studied there and worked at the University of California at San Francisco from 1966. A pioneer of genetic engineering, he showed in the 1970s that these methods could be used to make insulin and other costly biochemicals commercially, and in 1976 formed Genentech, Inc, for this purpose.

BOYER, Jean Pierre (1776–1850) Haitian politician, born a mulatto in Port-au-Prince. Sent early to France, in 1792 he entered the army. He distinguished himself against the British on their invasion of Haiti, and established an independent republic in the western part of the island. President Pétion, on his deathbed, recommended him as his successor (1818). After the death of **Christophe**, he united the negro district with the mulatto in 1820. The following year he added also the eastern district, hitherto Spanish, and in 1825, for 150000000 francs, obtained recognition of independence from France. He governed Haiti well for 15 years, but his partiality to the mulattos made the pure negroes rise in 1843. Boyer fled, and died in Paris.

BOYER, Sir Richard James Fildes (1891–1961) Australian broadcasting administrator, born in Taree, New South Wales. He served with the Australian Imperial Force at Gallipoli and in France. He was a member of the Australian delegation to the League of Nations in 1939 and was appointed to the Australian Broadcasting Commission in 1940. After Prime Minister **Curtin** affirmed the independence of the ABC, Boyer accepted the chairmanship in 1945. He greatly extended the educational influence of the ABC, particularly with the establishment on television of the University of the Air. He also encouraged the expansion of the ABC's orchestras. The ABC Lectures were renamed the 'Boyer Lectures' in his honour after his death.

BOYIS See **BOECE**

BOYLE name of an Irish family of Hereford origin, members of which were created earls of Cork and Orrery.

BOYLE, Charles, 4th Earl of Orrery (1676–1731) Irish Jacobite soldier and man of letters, grandson of **Roger Boyle**, the 1st Earl. He edited the spurious *Letters of Phalaris*, satirized by **Swift** in his *Battle of the Books* (1704). He fought at the battle of Malplaquet (1709), helped to negotiate the Treaty of Utrecht (1713), and was imprisoned in the Tower of London as a Jacobite (1721). The 'orrery', a kind of planetarium, was so named in his honour by the inventor, George Graham.

BOYLE, John, 5th Earl of Cork and of Orrery (1707–62) Irish writer, son of **Charles Boyle**, the 4th Earl. An intimate of **Swift**, **Pope**, and Dr **Johnson**, he is remembered more by his rancorous *Remarks on the Life and Writings of Dr Jonathan Swift* (1751) than by an excellent translation of the *Letters of Pliny* (1751).

BOYLE, Richard, 1st Earl of Cork, the 'Great Earl' (1566–1643) Irish administrator, born in Canterbury. After studying at Cambridge and the Middle Temple, he went over to Ireland in 1588 to make his fortune. He married an heiress, purchased large estates in Munster and improved them, promoted the immigration of English Protestants, and won the favour of Queen **Elizabeth**. He built bridges, founded harbours and towns, erected thirteen strong castles, and from his ironworks reaped £100000. About 4000 persons found employment on his vast plantations. In 1620 he became Viscount Dungarvan and Earl of Cork; and in 1631 was made hereditary lord high treasurer. In his old age, the Munster rebels compelled him to turn his castle into a fortress, but in 1641 he quenched the rebellion in his borders.

BOYLE, The Hon Robert (1627–91) Irish physicist and chemist, seventh son of **Richard Boyle, 1st Earl of Cork**, born at Lismore Castle in Munster. He studied at Eton and went to the continent for six years. On his return, he settled on the family estates at Stalbridge, Dorset, and devoted himself to science. He was one of the first members of the 'invisible college', an association of Oxford intellectuals opposed to the prevalent doctrines of scholasticism, which became the Royal Society in 1645. Settling at Oxford in 1654, with **Robert Hooke** as his assistant, he carried on experiments on air, vacuum, combustion, and respiration. In 1661 he published, his *Sceptical Chymist*, in which he criticized the current theories of matter, and defined the chemical element as the practical limit of chemical analysis. In 1662 he arrived at Boyle's Law, which states that the pressure and volume of gas are inversely proportional. He also researched into calcination of metals, properties of acids and alkalis, specific gravity, crystallography and refraction, and first prepared phosphorus. As a director of the East India Company (for which he had procured the Charter) he worked for the propagation of Christianity in the East, circulated at his own expense translations of the Scriptures, and by bequest founded the 'Boyle Lectures' in defence of Christianity. In 1668 he took up residence in London with his sister, Lady Ranelagh, and gave much of his time to the Royal Society. In 1688 he shut himself up, in order to repair the loss caused by the accidental destruction of his manuscripts. Boyle was, surprisingly, an alchemist, but his alchemy was a logical outcome of his atomism. If every substance is merely a rearrangement of the same basic elements, transmutations should be possible. Modern atomic physics has proved him right.

BOYLE, Roger, 1st Earl of Orrery (1621–79) Baron Broghill, Irish soldier and statesman, the third son of **Richard Boyle**, the 'Great Earl' of Cork. In the Civil War he first took the royalist side, but after the death of **Charles I** he came under the personal influence of **Cromwell**, and distinguished himself in the Irish campaign. He became one of Cromwell's special council, and a member of his House of Lords. On Cromwell's death, he tried to support **Richard Cromwell**, but after his abdication crossed to Ireland, and secured it for King **Charles II**. Four months after the Restoration he was made Earl of Orrery. He wrote poems, eight heroic plays, two comedies, a romance (*Parthenissa*, 1654–65) and a *Treatise on the Art of War* (1677).

BOYLE, Sir Edward Charles Gurney, Baron Boyle of Handsworth (1923–81) English politician and educational administrator. Educated at Eton and Christ Church, Oxford, he was MP for the Handsworth Division of Birmingham (1950–70), parliamentary secretary at the ministry of education (1957–59) and minister of education from 1962 to 1964. He was vice-chancellor of Leeds University from 1970 to 1981. A humane pragmatist, he won great affection and held the development of personality to be the first concern of education. Under his influence, the Conservative party moved from an intransigent defence of the grammar schools to a more pragmatic approach to secondary educational organization. A great enthusiast for the work of further education, he was a notably successful vice-chancellor. His period as minister for education came at the end of two decades of expansion of educational provision and expectation.

BOYLE, Jimmy (1944–) convicted Scottish murderer. Born in the Gorbals, then a notorious slum area of Glasgow, he was involved in shop-lifting, street-fighting and vandalism from a very early age. In his early teens he was sent to Larchgrove Remand Home for theft. This was followed by a spell in Borstal. Later charges of serious assault led to two years in prison. A member of a powerful gang in Glasgow, Boyle was subsequently twice charged with murder and cleared, and was eventually imprisoned for serious assault. His reputation as 'Scotland's Most Violent Man' appeared to be confirmed when he was convicted for the murder of Babs Rooney and was given a life-sentence. In 1973 he was one of the first offenders to participate in Barlinnie Prison Special Unit's rehabilitation programme. He went on to produce many sculptures, which were exhibited in several countries, and to write his autobiography, *A Sense of Freedom* (1977). After his release, he worked with young offenders and has become Scotland's most celebrated reformed criminal.

BOYLE, Kay (1902–) American novelist, short story writer, poet and essayist. Born in St Paul, Minnesota, she was brought up and educated in the United States, studying music and architecture, then lived in Europe for 30 years as part of the literary expatriate fraternity of Paris's Left Bank in the 1920s and latterly as the *New Yorker*'s foreign correspondent (1945–53). Influenced by **Henry James**, she has used her experience of expatriation most effectively in *Plagued by the Nightingale* (1931) and *Generation Without Farewell* (1960), but her novels are generally inferior to her stories, which are amassed in several volumes including those in *The Smoking Mountain* (1951). Her poems, indebted to **William Carlos Williams** and Padraic Colun, were collected in 1962.

BOYLE, Mark (1934–) Scottish artist, born in Glasgow. He began as a law student at Glasgow University, at the same time writing poems and making paintings, constructions and 'assemblages'. In 1964 he organized an event called 'Street', in which a group of people looked out through an ordinary shop-window into an ordinary street. His recent project, *Journey to the Surface of the Earth*, began with 1000 darts thrown at a map of the world by blindfolded persons; Boyle visits each site in turn, selects a six-foot square and makes a cast of it.

BOYLESVE, properly **Tardivaux, René** (1867–1926) French novelist, born and brought up in La Hayte-Descartes. He studied in Paris, and established his reputation as a portrayer of provincial life with *Le Parfum des îles Borrommées* (1898) and *Mademoiselle Cloque* (1899).

BOYS, Sir Charles Vernon (1855–1944) English physicist, born in Rutland. His many inventions include an improved torsion balance, the radio-micrometer, a calorimeter, and a camera with moving lens, with which he photographed lightning flashes.

BOZZARIS, Marcos (1788–1823) Greek patriot, born at Suli in Epirus. In 1803 he was forced to retreat to the Ionian Isles by **Ali Pasha**. In 1820, at the head of 800 expatriated Suliotes, he gained several victories for Ali against the sultan; in 1822 he skilfully defended Missolonghi, but was killed in an attack on the Turkish-Albanian army at Karpenisi.

BRABAZON, Hercules (1821–1906) English water-colour painter, born in Paris. He executed many sketches on his travels in Europe and Egypt, his later work being in the style of **Turner**.

BRABAZON, John Theodore Cuthbert Moore-Brabazon, 1st Baron Brabazon of Tara (1884–1964) English aviator and politician, the first holder of a flying licence. He was educated at Harrow and Cambridge. During World War I he served with the RFC, reaching the rank of lieutenant-colonel and winning the MC. He was responsible for several innovations in aerial photography. In 1918 he entered parliament and became private parliamentary secretary to **Churchill** at the war office. Between 1923 and 1927 he served two periods of office as parliamentary secretary to the ministry of transport. He was a prominent member of the enquiry into the R101 airship disaster. In 1940 he became minister of transport, in 1941 of aircraft production, but resigned because of public displeasure at his outspoken criticism of the ally, Russia.

BRABHAM, Sir Jack (John Arthur) (1926–) Australian racing-driver, born in Hurstville, a suburb of Sydney. After service with the Royal Australian Air Force he started his racing career in 1947, in 'midget' cars. After winning the Australian Grand Prix in 1955 (which he won again in 1963 and 1964) he went to the UK where he joined the successful Cooper team. He won his first Formula 1 World Drivers' Championship at Sebring, Florida, in 1959 by pushing his car over the finishing-line. He won the title again in the following year. In 1966 he won his third world title, and also the Constructor's Championship, with a car of his own design, the Repco-Brabham. A string of successes followed, and three BARC Gold Medals in 1959, 1966 and 1967. He retired from the circuits in 1970.

BRACCIO DA MONTONE, otherwise **Brancaccio,** or **Forte-braccio** (1368–1424) Italian freelance soldier and condottiere, born in, or near, Perugia. In 1416 he held Rome for a time. Next he commanded the troops of Queen Joanna of Naples, and was created Count of Foggia (1421). In 1423, by the queen's command, he was crowned Prince of Aquila and Capua, and he then coveted the throne of Naples. He overran Campania and Apulia, and advanced into Calabria, but in a battle before Aquila was wounded and taken prisoner. Three days later he died.

BRACE, Charles Loring (1826–90) American philanthropist and social reformer, born in Litchfield, Connecticut. He founded the Children's Aid Society in 1853, and pioneered philanthropic methods based on self-help.

BRACEGIRDLE, Anne (c.1663–1748) English actress. She was renowned for her beauty, and for her performances (1688–1707) in the plays of **Congreve** at Drury Lane under **Betterton**.

BRACHET, Auguste (1844–98) French philologist, born in Tours. He trained under **Friedrich Diez** and **Maximilien Littré**, and was attached to the Bibliothèque Nationale in 1864. Of his many works on philology, the best known are his *Grammaire historique* (1867), and the *Dictionnaire étymologique* (1870).

BRACKEN, Brendan, 1st Viscount Bracken (1901–58) Irish journalist and Conservative politician, born in Kilmallock. Educated at Sydney and at Sedbergh, he was associated with the *Financial News*, of which he became chairman, and the *Economist*, of which he became managing director, from 1928 to 1945. He was elected to parliament in 1929, was minister of information from 1941 to 1945, and first Lord of the Admiralty in the 1945 'caretaker' government.

BRACTON, Henry de (c.1210–1268) English ecclesiastic and jurist. A 'justice itinerant', in 1264 he became archdeacon of Barnstaple and chancellor of Exeter Cathedral. To him is attributed *De Legibus et Consuetudinibus Angliae*, the earliest attempt at a systematic treatment of the body of English law, based on decided cases and the practice of royal courts; it was first printed entire in 1569. In 1887 *Bracton's Note Book* was published, with proof, later doubted, that this was the actual collection on which Bracton's treatise was founded.

BRADBURY, Sir John Swanwick Bradbury, 1st Baron (1872–1950) English government official, born in Winsford, Cheshire. As secretary to the Treasury (1913–19) he was responsible for the substitution of £1 and 10s notes for gold coins. Treasury bills bearing his signature are often called 'Bradburys'.

BRADBURY, Ray (Raymond Douglas) (1920–) American writer of science fiction, born in Waukegan, Illinois. An avid reader of sensational fiction and comics, he began early to contribute to pulp magazines, graduating to better quality magazines and short story anthologies. While he has written notable novels—*Fahrenheit 451* (1953), *Dandelion Wine* (1957) and *Death is a Lonely Business* (1985)—he is primarily a short story writer and has created some of the finest examples in the genre: 'The Day It Rained Forever', 'R Is for Rocket' and those included in *The Martian Chronicles* (1950). A prolific writer, he ranges widely and has been the recipient of numerous awards.

BRADDOCK, Edward (1695–1755) Scottish soldier, born in Perthshire. Commissioned in the Coldstream Guards in 1710, he saw service in France (1746) and the Netherlands (1746–46). In the American War of Independence (1775–83) he was appointed to command against the French in America. He was mortally wounded when ambushed on his way to attack Fort Duquesne (now Pittsburgh), on 9 July 1755. His force was decimated and of his staff only **George Washington** escaped unhurt.

BRADDOCK, James Joseph (1905–74) American boxer, and world heavyweight champion, born in New York City. After some early successes, he was defeated in a light-heavyweight contest in 1929 and seemed destined for oblivion, especially after breaking both hands in a fight in 1933. But he fought his way back, and shocked the boxing world when he defeated Max Baer on points for the world heavyweight title in 1935—a comeback that earned him the nickname of 'The Cinderella Man'. He lost the title in 1937 to **Joe Louis**.

BRADDON, Mary Elizabeth (1837–1915) English novelist, born in London. She attained fame with a Victorian thriller, *Lady Audley's Secret* (1862), the story of a golden-haired murderess. Of some 75 popular novels, perhaps the best is *Ishmael* (1884).

BRADDON, Russell Reading (1921–) Australian author, playwright and film and television scriptwriter, born in Sydney, the great-grandson of Sir Edward Braddon, premier of Tasmania (1894–99). Educated at Sydney University, during World War II he was a prisoner of the Japanese for four years, at the notorious Changi Jail, Singapore, and worked on the Burma Railway. His experiences were published as *The Naked Island* (1952) and *End of a Hate* (1958). A string of popular novels followed, but he is perhaps best known for his biographies, such as *Cheshire VC* (1954), *Nancy Wake* (1956) and *Joan Sutherland* (1962).

BRADFIELD, John Job Crew (1867–1943) Australian civil engineer and designer, born in Sandgate, Queensland. He was educated at Sydney University. In 1913 his original plan for a bridge across Sydney Harbour was adopted but, because of World War I, work did not begin until 1923. Still the widest and heaviest bridge of this type, it was opened in 1932. He also planned an underground electric railway system for Sydney, and designed many other bridges, dams, and highways. He also proposed to dam the Burdekin and other Queensland rivers, drive the waters back through tunnels to the western side of the Great Dividing Range and so irrigate the dry inland plains.

BRADFORD, William (1590–1656) American colonist and religious leader, one of the Pilgrim Fathers, born in Austerfield near Doncaster. A nonconformist from boyhood, he joined a separatist group in 1606 and went with them to Holland in 1609, seeking freedom of worship. In Leiden he became a tradesman and read widely. One of the moving spirits in the Pilgrim Fathers' expedition to the New World in 1620, he sailed on the *Mayflower*, signed the Mayflower Compact, and in 1621 took over from **John Carver** as elected governor of Plymouth colony. He was re-elected governor 30 times between 1622 and 1656, and guided the fledgling colony with exemplary fairness and firmness. He wrote a *History of Plimmoth Plantation* (completed c.1651, printed in 1856).

BRADFORD, William (1663–1752) English-born American printer, and founder of a publishing dynasty, born in Barnwell, Leicestershire. A Quaker, he emigrated to the USA in 1685 and founded the first paper-mill in America, in Philadelphia in 1690. After moving to New York in 1693, he printed official papers, money, books, plays, and the first New York newspaper (*New York Gazette*, 1725). He was succeeded by his son, Andrew (1686–1742), and others of his family.

BRADL, Alois (1855–1940) German scholar, born in Innsbruck. He became professor of English philology at Berlin in 1895, and wrote on English Romanticism, on Old and Middle English literature, and on the pre-Shakespearean drama.

BRADLAUGH, Charles (1833–91) English social reformer and free-thinker, born in London. He was in turn errand boy, small coal-merchant, and trooper in Dublin. He returned to London in 1853, and became a busy secularist lecturer, and pamphleteer under the name of 'Iconoclast'. From 1860 he was editor, and (from 1862) proprietor, of the *National Reformer*. In 1880 he was elected MP for Northampton but, as an unbeliever, he refused to take the oath, and was expelled and re-elected regularly until 1886 when he took the oath and his seat. In 1886 he was prosecuted, with **Annie Besant**, for republishing a pamphlet advocating birth control (*The Fruits of Philosophy*); the conviction was subsequently quashed on appeal.

BRADLEE, Benjamin Crowninshield (1921–) American journalist and author, born in Boston, Massachusetts. A founder of the *New Hampshire Sunday News*, he subsequently joined the *Washington Post* as a police and federal courts reporter and worked for *Newsweek* where, because of a close friendship with President **Kennedy**, he regularly filed scoops. His book *Conversations with Kennedy* appeared in 1975. In 1965 he became managing editor of the *Washington Post* and encouraged the investigative journalism which reached apotheosis in the Watergate scandal.

BRADLEY, Andrew Cecil (1851–1935) English critic, born in Cheltenham, brother of **Francis Herbert Bradley**. He was educated at Cheltenham College and Balliol College, Oxford, where he became a fellow in 1874. The most influential commentator of his generation, he was professor of literature and history at Liverpool (1822), of English language and literature at Glasgow (1890), and of poetry at Oxford from 1901 to 1906. He published *Poetry for Poetry's Sake* (1901), and *Commentary on 'In Memoriam'* (1901), but made his name with his magisterial *Shakespearean Tragedy* (1904). He also published *Oxford Lectures on Poetry* (1909).

BRADLEY, Edward, pseud **Cuthbert Bede** (1827–89) English author and clergyman, born in Kidderminster. He was educated at Durham University. His facetious description of Oxford life in *Adventures of Mr Verdant Green* (1853–57) was the first and most popular of 26 works.

BRADLEY, Francis Herbert (1846–1924) Welsh philosopher, born in Glasbury, Brecknockshire (modern Powys), brother of **Andrew Cecil Bradley**. He became a fellow of Merton College, Oxford, in 1870 but lived as a semi-invalid most of his life. He was probably the most important figure in the British idealist movement of this period and was much influenced by **Kant** and **Hegel**. His most important works are *Ethical Studies* (1876), *Principles of Logic* (1883) and the highly original and influential *Appearance and Reality* (1893).

BRADLEY, Henry (1845–1923) English philologist and lexicographer. In 1886 he became joint editor of the *Oxford English Dictionary* with Sir **James Murray**, and senior editor in 1915. He wrote *The Making of English* (1904) and *English Place-Names* (1910).

BRADLEY, James (1693–1762) English astronomer, born in Sherborne, Gloucestershire. Educated at Northleach Grammar School and Balliol College, Oxford, his genius for mathematics and astronomy won him the friendship of **Edmond Halley** and **Isaac Newton**. He was Savilian professor of astronomy at Oxford (1721), and in 1742 succeeded Halley as Regius professor of astronomy at Greenwich. In 1729 he published his discovery of the aberration of light, providing the first observational proof of the Copernican hypothesis. In 1748 he discovered that the inclination of the earth's axis to the ecliptic is not constant.

BRADLEY, Katharine Harris See **FIELD, Michael**

BRADLEY, Omar Nelson (1893–1981) American soldier, born in Clark, Missouri. A graduate of the US Military Academy at West Point, he entered the army in 1915 and served in World War I. A brigadier in 1941, he commanded II Corps in Tunisia and Sicily (1943). In 1944 he commanded the US forces at the Normandy invasion, and later the US 12th Army Group through France. He became the first permanent chairman of the US Joint Chiefs of Staff (1949–53), and in 1950 was promoted to a five-star general of the army. He published his war memoirs, *A Soldier's Story*, in 1951, and an autobiography, *General's Life*, in 1983.

BRADMAN, Sir Donald George (Don) (1908–) Australian cricketer and stockbroker, born in New South Wales. One of the greatest batsmen in the history of the game, he played for Australia from 1928 to 1948 (captain, 1936–48). A prodigious scorer, he made the highest aggregate and largest number of centuries in Tests against England, and holds the record for the highest Australian Test score against England (334 at Leeds in 1930). His batting average in Test matches was an astonishing 99.6 runs per innings. The first Australian cricketer to be knighted (in 1949), he was chairman of the Australian Cricket Board 1960–63 and 1969–72.

BRADSHAW, George (1801–53) English printer and Quaker, born in Salford. He originated in 1839 a service of railway guides, became a Manchester mapmaker, and died of cholera in Christiania (now Oslo).

BRADSHAW, John (1602–59) English judge, born near Stockport. Called to the bar in 1627, he held various appointments before being appointed in 1649 president at the trial of **Charles I**. On that solemn occasion, his manners were as short as his speeches were lengthy. As a reward, he was made permanent president of the Council of State and chancellor of the duchy of Lancaster, with a grant of estates worth £2000 per annum. His 'stiff republicanism' estranged him from **Oliver Cromwell**. He was buried in Westminster Abbey, but at the Restoration his body was dug up and hanged as a regicide, as were Cromwell's and **Henry Ireton**'s.

BRADSTREET, Anne, née **Dudley** (1612–72) English-born American Puritan poet, born probably in Northampton. In 1628 she married a Nonconformist minister, Simon Bradstreet (1603–97), who later became governor of Massachusetts. In 1630 they emigrated to New England with the **Winthrops**. Her first volume of poems, *The Tenth Muse lately sprung up in America*, written in the style of **Phineas Fletcher**, was published by her brother-in-law in London in 1650 without her knowledge. She is considered the first English poet in America.

BRADWARDINE, Thomas (1290–1349) English theologian, born in Chichester. He studied, with distinguished success, at Merton College, Oxford, and in 1325 was one of the proctors of the university. His fame was founded on his theological lectures, *De Causa Dei contra Pelagium*, an able defence of the Augustinian doctrines of grace, fully proving his right to the title of 'Doctor profundus'. He also wrote treatises on geometry. Called about 1335 to London, he became chancellor of St Paul's, a prebendary of Lincoln, and confessor to **Edward III**, whom he accompanied on his campaigns in France. In 1348 he was elected **Stratford**'s successor as archbishop of Canterbury by the chapter of Canterbury, and, in spite of a dispute with the king, he was consecrated at Avignon in July 1349. When he returned to England, he died of the Black Death in Lambeth.

BRADY, Ian (1938–) convicted Scottish murderer, born in Glasgow. Brady, who was a clerk with a fascination for Nazi memorabilia, was found guilty of the murder of two children, John Kilbride and Lesley Ann Downey, and a 17-year-old boy, Edward Evans, on 6 May 1966. In a case which horrified the public, it was revealed that Brady, with his lover **Myra Hindley**, lured young children into their home in Manchester and subjected them to torture before killing them. Brady and Hindley recorded their crimes with photographs and a tape. The tape of Lesley Ann Downey's last hours, as she was being tortured, was played in court. The lovers were described as the 'Moors Murderers' because they buried most of their victims on Saddleworth Moor in the Pennines. Hindley made a private confession to two other murders in 1986, and the body of Pauline Reade was found in August 1987, twenty four years after her disappearance. The body of 12-year-old Keith Bennett has never been found.

BRADY, Matthew (1799–1826) English-born Australian bushranger, born in Manchester, of Irish descent. In 1820, for stealing a basket of groceries, he was transported for seven years to New South Wales; from there he was sent in 1823 to the penal colony of Macquarie Harbour in Van Diemen's Land (now Tasmania), a penal station for desperate criminals. Brady escaped with a small group in the following year, and with his gang terrorized the island from Hobart to Launceston. After many audacious exploits, including capturing an entire township, when the senior citizens and the local army garrison were all locked up in the town jail, some of his gang turned informers. He was eventually captured and hanged in Hobart.

BRADY, Matthew (1823–96) American photographer, born near Lake George, New York. He operated a portrait studio in New York using daguerrotype from 1844, but gave it up to take on a major project to record the American Civil War with the Union armies. In 1862 he organized a team which covered all the major engagements, the battlefields with their suffering and death, the generals and the men in their camps. Although widely acclaimed, this effort ruined him financially and, despite a belated government grant, he died in poverty in a New York almshouse.

BRADY, Nicholas (1659–1726) Irish Anglican clergyman and poet, born in Bandon, County Cork. Educated at Westminster, Christ Church College, Oxford, and Dublin, he took holy orders and was rector at Stratford-upon-Avon from 1702 to 1705. With **Nahum Tate** he produced a metrical version of the Psalms (1696), but met with strong opposition from many of the Tory clergy. He also wrote a tragedy, *The Rape*, and translated **Virgil**'s *Aeneid*.

BRAGA, Theophilo (1843–1924) Portuguese scholar and author, born in the Azores. He wrote widely on politics, history and literature, and was professor at Lisbon from 1872. He briefly became president of the Portuguese republic (1910–11, 1915) on King **Manuel**'s enforced abdication.

BRAGG, Braxton (1817–76) American soldier, born in Warrenton, North Carolina. A Confederate general, he commanded in several great battles of the Civil War, but though successful at Chickamauga, the hardest-fought battle in the war, his tenure of command was ultimately disappointing.

BRAGG, Sir (William) Lawrence (1890–1971) Australian-born British physicist, born in Adelaide, son of Sir **William Henry Bragg**. He shared his father's work with X-rays and continued it, as professor at Manchester and then at Cambridge (from 1938). Like his father, he became director of the Royal Institution (1954–65) and did much to popularize science. Father and son shared the 1915 Nobel prize for physics. He was professor of physics at Victoria University, Manchester (1919–37) and headed the Cavendish Laboratory in Cambridge (1938–53), where he supported **F H C Crick** and **J D Watson** in their work, using X-ray crystal studies to deduce the helical structure of DNA, so creating molecular biology and revolutionizing biological science.

BRAGG, Sir William Henry (1862–1942) English physicist, born in Westward, Cumberland. With his son, **William Lawrence Bragg**, he founded X-ray crystallography. After studying at Cambridge, he became professor of mathematics at Adelaide, Australia (1886) and in 1904 gave a lecture on radioactivity which inspired him to research into this area. He became professor at Leeds in 1909, and from 1912 worked in conjunction with his son. Their efforts won them a joint Nobel prize for physics in 1915, the only father-son partnership to share this honour. Bragg moved to University College, London the same year, and became director of the Royal Institution in 1923. His works include *Studies in Radioactivity* (1912), *X-rays and Crystal Structure* (1915, with his son) and *The Universe of Light* (1933).

BRAHAM, John (1774–1856) British tenor, born in London of German-Jewish parents. He had his first great success at Drury Lane (1796), and for half a century held the reputation of being one of the world's greatest tenors. He squandered a fortune by purchasing the Colosseum in Regent's Park and building the St James's Theatre.

BRAHE, Tycho or **Tyge** (1546–1601) Danish astronomer, the greatest pre-telescope observer. Born into a noble family at Knudstrup in South Sweden (then under the Danish crown), he was brought up by an uncle who wanted a child of his own. After an excellent education at Copenhagen, Leipzig, Wittenberg, Rostock and Augsburg, a political career was planned for him. But from the age of 14, when he saw the partial solar eclipse of 1560, he was obsessed by astronomy. In 1563 he discovered serious errors in the existing astronomical tables, and in 1572 carefully observed a new star in Cassiopeia (the nova now known as Tycho's star), a significant observation which made his name. In 1576, with royal aid, he established his Uraniborg ('Castle of the Heavens') Observatory on the island of Hven, in the Sound. There for 20 years he successfully carried out his observations, measuring the positions of 777 stars and creating a catalogue of them with such accuracy that it provided a vital source of information for later astronomers. In 1596, on the succession of **Kristian IV**, he was forced to leave the country; after travelling for three years he accepted an invitation from the emperor **Rudolf II** to Benatky near Prague, where he worked with **Johann Kepler** as assistant. Gifted but hot-tempered, Brahe lost most of his nose in a duel at the age of 19, and wore a false silver nose for the rest of his life.

BRAHMS, Johannes (1833–97) German composer, born in Hamburg, the son of a poor orchestral musician. A gifted pianist, he was compelled by family poverty to earn his living as a young boy playing in the dockside inns of Hamburg, and though his reputation spread rapidly it was not until 1853 that he was able to concentrate on composition. This was after he had met the flamboyant Hungarian refugee violinist, Reményi, with whom he went on tour, and from whom he probably absorbed much of the spirit which went into the *Hungarian Dances* and *Zigeunerlieder*. During the tour he met **Joachim**, who became a lifelong friend and fellow-antagonist of Romanticism, and **Liszt**, who successfully charmed Reményi into becoming a devotee of the 'New German' music. The solidly classical Brahms, however, was not impressed, and he parted from Reményi and went to Göttingen to visit Joachim, who gave him an introduction to **Schumann**. Schumann's enthusiasm for his early works, especially his assistance in publishing the piano sonatas, was influential in establishing Brahms's reputation, and Brahms's devotion to the older composer expressed itself in his lifelong care for Schumann's widow and children. He never married, and after 1863, when he settled in Vienna, his life was uneventful except for occasional public appearances in Austria and Germany at which he played his own works. He was adopted by the anti-Wagnerian faction as the leader of traditional principles aginst 'modern' iconoclasm, and his fame as a composer spread rapidly. Firmly based on classical foundations, his works contain hardly any programme music apart from a few pieces such as the *Tragic Overture* and the C minor quartet (inspired by **Goethe**'s *Werther*). His great orchestral works are comparatively late, the first, *Variations on a Theme of Haydn*, appearing when he was 40, and his first symphony when he was 43. The *Academic Festival Overture*, also dating from this period, was composed in honour of his honorary doctorate at Breslau University. His greatest choral work is the *German Requiem*, which had its first full performance in 1869. Prolific in all fields except opera, his quality is extraordinarily even, due to his ruthless destruction of his early efforts and of all else which failed to measure up to his self-imposed standards of excellence.

BRAID, James (?1795–1860) Scottish surgeon and hypnotist, born in Fife. Educated at Edinburgh University, he spent most of his life practising surgery in Manchester, where his operation for club-foot was famous. In 1841, however, he attended a popular demonstration of 'Mesmerism' and devoted much of the rest of his working life to investigating the phenomena associated with what he himself first called 'neurohypnotism', later shortened to 'hypnotism'. His papers and books on the subject helped keep serious concerns with hypnotism alive and Braid was looked upon as an important pioneer in the field by **Charcot, Bernheim** and others who, from the 1880s, systematically incorporated hypnotism in their treatment of nervous disorders.

BRAID, James (1870–1950) Scottish golfer, born in Earlsferry in Fife. He trained as a joiner and went to work in St Andrews, the home of golf, where he became an outstanding player. In 1893 he moved to London as a club-maker at the Army & Navy Stores, before becoming a professional at Romford later that year, and at Walton Heath from 1904 until his death. In a remarkable playing career he won the Open championship five times between 1901 and 1910 (when he became the first player to break 300 for 72 holes at St Andrews), four *News of the World* matchplay championships between 1903 and 1911, and the French Championship in 1910. With **Harry Vardon** and **John Henry Taylor** he formed what was known as the 'Great Triumvirate' of British golf in the Edwardian era. In addition to being a fine teacher, he became a celebrated designer of golf courses.

BRAIDWOOD, Thomas (1715–98) Scottish teacher. After studying at Edinburgh University he opened a school there, in 1760, the first school for the deaf and dumb in Britain. The school, which was visited by Dr **Johnson** in 1773, was ten years later transferred to Hackney, London.

BRAILLE, Louis (1809–52) French educationist, born in Coupvray near Paris. Blind from the age of three, at the age of ten he entered the Institution des Jeunes Aveugles in Paris. He studied organ playing, and became professor of the Institute in 1826. In 1829 he devised a system of raised-point writing which the blind could both read and write.

BRAILSFORD, Henry Noel (1873–1958) English socialist author and political journalist, born in Yorkshire. Educated at Glasgow University, he became assistant professor of logic there, leaving to join the Greek Foreign Legion in the war with Turkey in 1897. He described his experiences in *The Broom of the War God* (1898). His socialism was pre-eminently international in outlook and was the key to everything he did (see *The War of Steel and Gold*, 1914). He joined the Independent Labour party in 1907 and edited (1922–26) its weekly organ, *The New Leader*. He was a leader-writer to several influential papers including the *Manchester Guardian* and the *Daily Herald*. His literary work includes *Shelley, Godwin and their Circle* (1913), *Socialism for Today* (1925), *Voltaire* (1935), and *Subject India* (1943).

BRAIN, Aubrey Harold (1893–1955) English horn player, born in London, father of **Dennis Brain**. He studied at the Royal College of Music and became chief horn player in the New Symphony Orchestra (1911) and London Symphony Orchestra (1912). In 1923 he became professor of his instrument at the Royal Academy of Music, and from 1930 to 1945 was principal horn of the BBC Symphony Orchestra. His elder son, Leonard (1915–75), was an oboist.

BRAIN, Dennis (1921–57) English horn player, born in London, son of **Aubrey Brain**. He studied under his father at the Royal Academy of Music, also becoming a fine organist. He worked with the Royal Philharmonic and Philharmonia Orchestras as chief horn player and his mastery of his instrument won him fame throughout Europe. Amongst the composers who wrote works specially for him are **Britten**, **Hindemith**, and **Malcolm Arnold**.

BRAINE, John Gerard (1922–86) English novelist, born in Bradford. He was educated at St Bede's Grammar School and had various jobs, including service in the Royal Navy, before following his mother's profession of librarian. In 1951 he went to London to become a full-time writer, but returned north the same year, after his mother's death in a road accident. He then spent 18 months in hospital suffering from tuberculosis, and it was during this period of enforced rest that he began to write his first successful novel, *Room at the Top*. He went back to library work until the publication of the book in 1957, and its success enabled him to embark again on a full-time career as a novelist. The theme of aggressive ambition and determination to break through rigid social barriers identified him with the 'angry young men' of the 1950s. His novels include *Life at the Top* (1962), a sequel to *Room at the Top*, *The Jealous God* (1964), *The Queen of a Distant Country* (1972), *The Vodi* (1959), *Stay with Me till Morning* (1968), *Finger of Fire* (1977) and *One and Last Love* (1981).

BRAINERD, David (1718–47) American missionary, born in Haddam, Connecticut. He studied for three years at Yale College, where his opinions caused doctrinal disputes and his expulsion. He worked successfully among the American Indians from 1742, and his devotion found expression in his *Journal*, published posthumously in 1749.

BRAITHWAITE, Errol Kamau (1930–) Caribbean poet and academic historian, born in Bridgetown, Barbados. Described in the *Sunday Times* as 'one of the finest living poets of the Western hemisphere', his major achievement is contained in *The Arrivants: A New World Trilogy* (1973) which comprises his first three volumes: *Rights of Passage* (1967), *Masks* (1968) and *Islands* (1969).

BRAKELOND(E) See **JOCELIN DE BRAKELOND(E)**

BRAMAH, Joseph (1748–1814) English inventor, born in Stainborough near Barnsley, Yorkshire. A farmer's son, he was lamed in his sixteenth year, so was apprenticed to the village carpenter, and later became a cabinet-maker in London. He made numerous inventions, including a beer machine used at the bar of public-houses, a safety lock (patented 1788) which he manufactured in partnership with Henry Maudslay, a hydraulic press (1795) and a very ingenious machine for printing bank-notes (1806). He was one of the first to propose the application of the screw-propeller.

BRAMANTE, Donato (1444–1514) Italian High Renaissance architect, born near Urbano. He started as a painter, and from 1477 to 1499 worked in Milan, where he executed his first building projects, such as S Maria delle Grazie. He spent the last 15 years of his life, from 1499, in Rome, where he was employed by Popes **Alexander VI** and **Julius II** and where his most important work was done. He designed the new Basilica of St Peter's (begun in 1506), as well as the Belvedere courtyard, the Tempietto di S Pietro in Montorio (1502), the Palazzo dei Tribunale (1508) and the Palazzo Caprini (1514).

BRAMHALL, John (1594–1663) English prelate in Ireland, educated at Sidney Sussex College, Cambridge. Going to Ireland as **Strafford**'s chaplain in 1633, he became Anglican bishop of Derry in 1634, actively reformed the established church and repressed its enemies, notably Ulster Presbyterians. When the Civil War broke out, for safety's sake he crossed to England; in 1644 the royalist disasters drove him to the continent. The Restoration gave him the see of Armagh. He imitated **Laud** in policy and resembled him in person, but was far his inferior in intellect.

BRAMPTON, Baron See **HAWKINS, Henry**

BRANAGH, Kenneth (1960–) Irish actor and director, born in Belfast. He moved to England with his family when young, studied at RADA and went straight to the West End, playing the communist public schoolboy, Judd, in *Another Country* (1981). In 1984 he joined the Royal Shakespeare Company, appearing in the title role of *Henry V*, as Laertes in *Hamlet*, and the king of Navarre in *Love's Labour's Lost*. In 1987 he co-founded and became co-director of the Renaissance Theatre Company, directing the company's production of *Romeo and Juliet* (in which he also starred), and *Twelfth Night*, and starring in successful tours in 1988 and 1989. He has appeared in good quality television drama, written two plays produced on the Edinburgh Fringe, and appeared in several films, including the remake of *Henry V* (1989), which, like **Olivier**, he also directed.

BRANCACCIO See **BRACCIO DA MONTONE**

BRANCUSI, Constantine (1876–1957) Romanian sculptor, born in Pestisani, near Turgujiu. A shepherd boy in the Carpathians, he won a scholarship to the Bucharest Academy and arrived in Paris in 1904, where he developed his highly individual style. From 1906 he worked in **Rodin**'s atelier. His *The Kiss* (1908) was the most abstract sculpture of the period, representing two block-like figures. His *Sleeping Muse* (1910) shows Rodin's influence, but is the first of his many characteristic, highly-polished egg-shaped carvings. *The Prodigal Son* (1925) shows the influence of African sculpture. His aim was simplification, to get to the essence of the thing, the essence being objective, and he was therefore outside the subjective Expressionist schools of the day. Other works include several versions of *Mademoiselle Pogany* (1913–31), *Bird in Space* (1925) and *The Sea-Lions* (1943).

BRAND, Hennig (17th century) German alchemist. He discovered phosphorus in 1669.

BRAND, Sir Jan Hendrik (1823–88) South African politician, born in Capetown. President of the Orange Free State from 1864 till his death, he defeated the Basutos (1865–69), and favoured friendship with Britain.

BRAND, John (1744–1806) English antiquary and clergyman, born in Washington, Co. Durham. A graduate of Lincoln College, Oxford, in 1784 he became resident secretary of the Society of Antiquaries. He wrote *Observations on Popular Antiquities* (1777).

BRANDAN, St See **BRENDAN**

BRANDEIS, Louis Dembitz (1856–1941) American judge, born in Louisville, Kentucky. He was educated at Louisville, Dresden and Harvard, and practised in Boston. He conducted many labour arbitrations, and was frequently involved in cases challenging the power of monopolies and cartels, and in cases concerning the constitutionality of maximum hours and minimum wages legislation. He formulated the economic doctrine of the New Freedom adopted by **Woodrow Wilson** for his 1912 presidential campaign. Appointed to the US Supreme Court in 1916, he favoured governmental intervention to control the economy where public interest required it, but was also a strong defender of the rights of private property. He was generally a supporter of **Roosevelt**'s New Deal legislation, and is remembered as one of the most perceptive and thoughtful judges of the court. Brandeis University at Waltham, Massachusetts is named after him.

BRANDES, Georg Morris, originally **Cohen** (1842–1927) Danish man of letters, born in Copenhagen. Educated at Copenhagen University, and a champion of materialism in literature, he lectured at Copenhagen (1872–77) but was accused of being a radical and an atheist, and went to lecture at Berlin (1877–83), where he came under the influence of **Nietzsche**. On his return, he was a public lecturer in Copenhagen, and was appointed professor of aesthetics in 1902. The friend and disciple of European writers and thinkers like **Ernest Renan**, **Hippolyte Taine**, and **John Stuart Mill**, he brought a new outlook on literature with his monumental *Main Currents in 19th Century Literature* (6 vols, 1871–87). His huge output of critical work included studies of **Shakespeare**, **Goethe**, **Voltaire**, **Disraeli**, **Kierkegaard**, **Anatole France**, **Ibsen** and **Michelangelo**.

BRANDO, Marlon (1924–) American film and stage actor, born in Omaha, Nebraska. A product of the famous New York Actors' Studio, with its emphasis on the principles of **Stanislavsky** and 'method' acting, he made his New York début in 1943 and appeared in several plays before achieving fame in **Tennessee Williams**' *A Streetcar Named Desire* (1947), as the inarticulate and brutal Stanley Kowalski, which role he also played on film (1951). Iconoclastic and versatile, he has created a gallery of varied film parts: the original motorcycle rebel in *The Wild One* (1953), **Mark Antony** in *Julius Caesar* (1953), the singing gambler Sky Masterson in *Guys and Dolls* (1955), a western outlaw in *One-Eyed Jacks* (which he also directed, 1961), a convincingly English Fletcher Christian in *Mutiny on the Bounty* (1962) and the American widower in the controversial *Last Tango in Paris* (1972). An Academy Award winner for *On the Waterfront* (1954) and *The Godfather* (1972), he refused the latter honour in protest at the film industry's treatment of American Indians, and has been a prominent campaigner for the Civil Rights movement. Grown reclusive and obese, he ended an eight-year absence from the screen with the anti-apartheid drama *A Dry White Season* (1988).

BRANDON, Charles (1484–1545) English soldier and courtier, the son of **Henry VII**'s standard-bearer who fell at Bosworth (1485). He served as squire to **Henry VIII**, and in 1514 was created Duke of Suffolk. Next year he married Mary, Henry VIII's sister, and widow of Louis XII of France, and so was the grandfather of Lady **Jane Grey**.

BRANDT, Bill (1904–83) English photographer, born in south London. He studied with **Man Ray** in Paris in 1929 and returned to London in 1931. Later in the 1930s he made a series of striking social records, contrasting the lives of the rich and the poor, and during World War II he worked for the ministry of information recording conditions in London in the Blitz. He subsequently turned to landscape, where his treatment was often lyrical or dramatic, but his greatest creative work was his treatment of the nude, in which his essays in pure form, as published in *Perspective of Nudes* (1961) and *Shadows of Light* (1966), approached the surreal. He was still achieving creative work shortly before his death. His collections include *The English At Home* (1936), *A Night in London* (1938), and *Perspective of Nudes* (1961).

BRANDT, Georg (1694–1768) Swedish chemist, born in Riddarhytta. He discovered (c.1730) cobalt.

BRANDT, Willy originally **Karl Herbert Frahm** (1913–) West German politician, born in Lübeck. Educated there, he joined the Social Democrats at 17 and, as a fervent anti-Nazi, fled in 1933 to Norway, where he changed his name, took Norwegian citizenship, attended Oslo University, and worked as a journalist. On the occupation of Norway in 1940, he went to Sweden, continuing as a journalist in support of the German and Norwegian resistance movements. In 1945 he returned to Germany, in 1948 gained German citizenship and from 1949 to 1957 was a member of the *Bundestag*, being president of the *Bundesrat* (1955–57). Notably a pro-western, anti-communist leader, he became mayor of West Berlin (1957-66), achieving international renown during the Berlin Wall crisis (1961). He was chairman of the SPD in 1964, playing a key role in the party's remoulding as a more moderate and popular force. In 1966 he led the SPD into a 'Grand Coalition' government with the Christian Democrats under **Kiesinger**'s chancellorship and, as foreign minister, instituted the new policy of Ostpolitik (reconciliation between eastern and western Europe). This policy was continued when Brandt was elected chancellor in 1969, culminating in the signing of the Basic Treaty with East Germany in September 1972. Brandt was awarded the Nobel prize for peace in 1971, but was forced to resign the chancellorship in April 1974, following the discovery that a close aide, Gunther Guillaume, had been an East German spy. He continued to serve, however, as SPD chairman until 1987, and headed an influential international commission (the 'Brandt Commission') on economic development between 1977 and 1983. The commission's main report (1980), entitled *North-South: A Programme for Survival*, advocated urgent action by the rich north to improve conditions in the poorer southern hemisphere.

BRANGWYN, Sir Frank (1867–1956) British artist, born in Bruges. He was apprenticed to **William Morris** for four years, and then went to sea and travelled widely. Although he excelled in many media, particularly in etching, he was most famous for his vigorously-coloured murals, eg the *British Empire Panels* (1925) for the House of Lords. They were rejected and are now in the Swansea Guildhall. In 1936 a Brangwyn Museum was opened in Bruges.

BRANNER, H C (Hans Christian) (1903–66) Danish novelist, short-story writer and playwright. A former actor and publisher, he wrote a number of psychological novels, including *Legetøj* (Toys, 1936), *Drömmen om en kvinde* (The Dream of a Woman, 1949), and *Ingen kender Natten* (Nobody Knows the Night, 1955). His short-story collections include *Om lidt er vi borte* (In a Little While We are Gone, 1939), *To Minutters Stilhed* (Two Minutes' Silence 1944), and *Angst* (1947). He also wrote plays, including *Rytteren* (The Riding Master, 1949) and *Söskende* (Brethren, 1952).

BRANT, Joseph, Indian name **Thayendanegea** (1742–1807) Mohawk Indian chief, and brother-in-law of the Irish fur trader, Sir **William Johnson**. He served the British in the French and Indian War, and in **Pontiac**'s War (1763–66). In the American War of Independence (1775–83), he commanded the Mohawks on the British side, and fought in the Cherry Valley Massacre in New York (1778) and ravaged Mohawk Valley (now New York State). After the Revolution he was assigned land in Canada by the British, and in 1785 went to England to persuade the British government to indemnify the Indians for their losses in the war. In London he was received at court and lionized by society, entertained by **Boswell** and painted by **Romney**. In later years an earnest Christian, he translated St Mark's Gospel and the Prayer Book into Mohawk, and founded the first Episcopal church in upper Canada. A statue of him was unveiled at Brantford, Ontario, in 1886.

BRANT, Sebastian (1458–1521) German poet and humanist, born in Strasbourg. He studied and lectured at Basel. His *Narrenschiff* (1494), or 'Ship of Fools', a satire on the follies and vices of his times, is not very poetical, but is full of sound sense and good moral teaching. It was translated into English by **Alexander Barclay** and Henry Watson, both in 1509.

BRANTING, Karl Hjalmar (1860–1925) Swedish politician, born in Stockholm, founder of the Swedish Socialist party. He was co-founder of the Social Democratic party (1889), became leader of the party from 1907, and was prime minister in 1920, 1921–23 and 1924–25. In 1921 he shared the Nobel prize for peace. He was the first Swedish representative at the League of Nations (1922–25).

BRANTÔME, Pierre de Bourdeille, Seigneur de (c.1530–1614) French soldier and author, born in Périgord. He was educated at Paris and at Poitiers. In his sixteenth year he was given the abbacy of Brantôme, but he never took orders, and spent most of his life as a courtier and freelance. In 1561 he accompanied **Mary, Queen of Scots** to Scotland, and in 1565 he joined the expedition sent to Malta to assist the Knights of St John against the sultan. He served in Italy under the Maréchal de Brissac, in Africa under the Spaniards, and in Hungary as a volunteer against the Turks. He was made chamberlain to **Charles IX** and **Henri III**, and fought against the Huguenots. About 1594 he began to write his memoirs, and from then on lived in retirement. His works, first published in 1659, comprise *Vies des grands capitaines*, *Vies des dames galantes*, and *Vies des dames illustres*, and provide a detailed picture of the Valois court. Their literary merit and historical interest are considerable. Their matter is often of the most scandalous description, but they give a wonderfully vivid picture of their author's times.

BRAQUE, Georges (1882–1963) French painter, born in Argenteuil. He was one of the founders of classical Cubism, and worked with **Picasso** from 1908 to 1914. After World War I (in which he was wounded) he developed a personal non-geometric, semi-abstract style. In 1924 and 1925 he designed scenes for two **Diaghilev** ballets—*Les Fâcheux and Zéphyr et Flore*. His paintings are mainly of still life, the subject being transformed into a two-dimensional pattern, and they are among the outstanding decorative achievements of our time, with a pervasive influence on other painters which has not been approached by more violently controversial artists. He was a Grand Officier of the *Légion d'Honneur* and he was awarded an honorary doctorate of Oxford University in 1956.

BRASIDAS (5th century BC) Spartan soldier. He distinguished himself in the 1st Peloponnesian (Archidamian) War of 431–421, repulsing an Athenian attack on Megara and capturing Amphipolis (424). In 422 he faced a hugely superior Athenian army under **Cleon** outside Amphipolis. Both generals were killed, but the Spartans won the day.

BRASSAÏ, professional name of **Gyula Halasz** (1899–1984) Hungarian-born French painter and photographer, born in Brasso, Transylvania. Coming to Paris in 1923, he worked as a journalist, and from 1930 used photography to record the underworld and night-life of 1930s Paris in a style which was candid but composed. His first collection, *Paris de Nuit* (1933), caused a sensation. He refused to photograph during the German occupation but worked in **Picasso**'s studio. Returning to photography after the war, he often portrayed his many artist friends, but the face of Paris remained his first love. He became a French citizen in 1948.

BRASSEY, Thomas (1805–70) English engineer, born a farmer's son at Buerton near Chester. He was articled to a land surveyor, and in 1834 obtained, through **George Stephenson**, contracts for a viaduct, and in 1836 settled in London as a railway contractor.

His operations soon extended to all parts of the world; for his contract of the Great Northern Railway (1847–51) he employed between 5000 and 6000 men.

BRASSEY, Thomas, 1st Earl (1836–1918) English statesman born in Stafford, the son of **Thomas Brassey**. Educated at Rugby and University College, Oxford, he was called to the bar in 1866. As civil lord of the Admiralty (1880–84), and parliamentary secretary (1884–85), he made his influence felt in naval questions and in 1895–1900 was governor of Victoria. In *The 'Sunbeam', RYS* (1917), and other works, he tells of the 300000 miles he sailed in 40 years in the yacht which he gave as a hospital-ship during World War I. He founded (1886) and edited *The Naval Annual*, which continues to this day as *Brassey's Year Book*.

BRATBY, John (1928–) English artist and writer. Born in Wimbledon, London, he went to school at Tiffin Boys' School and studied at Kingston Art School and the Royal College of Art. He is a leading protagonist of English 'New Realism', with a reputation for being the *enfant terrible* of the artistic establishment; in the 1950s he was associated with the 'kitchen sink' school because of his preoccupation with working-class domestic interiors. He represented Great Britain at the Venice Biennale in 1956, and has a host of works in public collections. He has written several novels, including *Breakdown* (1960), with his own illustrations. He did the paintings for the 1958 film of **Joyce Carey**'s novel, *The Horse's Mouth*.

BRATIANU, Ion (1821–91), Romanian politician, father of **Ion Bratianu**. With his brother, Demeter (1818–92), he founded the Romanian Liberal party. He was premier from 1876 to 1888, Demeter holding the office for a short time in 1881.

BRATIANU, Ion (1864–1927) Romanian politician. As premier, he brought Romania into World War I against the Central Powers.· His brother, Vintila (1867–1930), was premier from 1927 to 1928.

BRATTAIN, Walter Houser (1902–87) American physicist, born in Amoy, China, co-inventor of the transistor. He grew up on a cattle ranch in the State of Washington, and was educated at the University of Oregon and at Minnesota. He then joined Bell Telephone Laboratories where he worked as a research physicist until his retirement in 1967, working on the surface properties of semiconductors. With **Bardeen** and **Shockley**, and using a mix of theory and experiment, he developed the point-contact transistor, using a thin germanium crystal. Soon afterwards, the junction transistor devised by Shockley, in the form of the silicon micro-chip, took the dominant place it has held in electronics ever since. He shared the Nobel prize for physics with Bardeen and Shockley in 1956.

BRAUDEL, Fernand (1902–85) French historian, born in Lorraine. He studied at the Sorbonne, and taught in Algerian schools (1923–32), in Paris (1932–35), and at the Saõ Paulo University, Brazil (1935–38). He wrote, from memory, his great work *La Mediterranée et le monde mediterranéen à l'époque de Philippe II* in a German prison camp in Lübeck throughout World War II, after which it won a doctorate and was published (1949) and later translated into English (1972–73). He became professor at the Collège de France (1949–72), was editor of the professional journal *Annales d'histoire économique et sociale*, wrote the first volume of *Civilisation matérielle et capitalisme* (1967) as well as its *Afterthoughts*, and a study of Italian achievements outside Italy, following the ideas of **Bloch** on the greater use of the social sciences and the pursuit of problems rather than catalogues of events. His final work, *The Identity of France*, continued his ideas on the study of environment and human behaviour and his utilization of geography and sociology. His great achievement was forcing historians to think of the human past in new terms by the stimulus of historical writing on a courageous and grand scale.

BRAUER, Adrian See **BROUWER**

BRAUN, Eva (1910–45) mistress of **Adolf Hitler**. She was secretary to Hitler's staff photographer, became Hitler's mistress in the 1930s and is said to have married him before they committed suicide together in the air-raid shelter of the Chancellery during the fall of Berlin.

BRAUN, Ferdinand (1850–1918) German physicist, born in Fulda. In 1909 he shared with **Guglielmo Marconi** the Nobel prize for physics for his work on wireless telegraphy and cathode rays.

BRAUN, Lili, née **von Kretschmann** (1865–1916) German socialist authoress and feminist, born in Halberstadt. She married the socialist writer and politician Heinrich Braun (1854–1927). Her best known book is *Im Schatten der Titanen* (1908).

BRAUN, Wernher von (1912–77) German-born American rocket pioneer, born in Wirsitz. He studied engineering at Berlin and Zürich and founded in 1930 a society for space travel which maintained a rocket-launching site near Berlin. Since rockets were outside the terms of the Versailles Treaty, the German army authorities became interested and by 1936, with Hitler's backing, von Braun was director of a rocket research station at Peenemünde, where he perfected and launched the famous V-2 rockets against Britain in September 1944. At the end of the war he surrendered, with his entire development team, to the Americans. He became a naturalized American in 1955 and a director of the US army's Ballistic Missile Agency at Huntsville, Alabama, and was chiefly responsible for the manufacture and successful launching of the first American artificial earth satellite, Explorer I, in 1958. He was director of the Marshal Space Flight Center (1960–70), where he developed the Saturn rocket for the Apollo 8 moon landing (1969). His books include *Conquest of the Moon* (1953) and *Space Frontier* (1967).

BRAWNE, Fanny See **KEATS, John**

BRAXFIELD, Robert Macqueen, Lord (1722–99) Scottish judge, born near Lanark. He attained eminence at the Scottish bar, particularly in feudal land law. He became a judge in 1776 and lord justice clerk of Scotland in 1788. As a judge, he was noted for his harshness towards political prisoners. Hard-headed, hard-hearted and hard-drinking, he was the original Lord Weir of **R L Stevenson**'s unfinished novel, *Weir of Hermiston* (1896).

BRAY, Thomas (1656–1730) English clergyman and philanthropist, born in Marton, Shropshire. Educated at All Souls' College, he became rector of Sheldon in 1690. He published *Catechetical Lectures* and other works. He established a system of parochial libraries in England, and also in Maryland, where he was sent as commissary from 1699 to 1706. Out of his library scheme grew the Society for Promoting Christian Knowledge (SPCK).

BRAYLEY, Edward Wedlake See **BRITTON, John**

BRAZIL, Angela (1868–1947) English writer of girls' school stories, born in Preston. She was a governess for some years before beginning to write tales notable for their healthy realism. Her best books include *The New Girl at St Chad's, A Fourth Form Friendship* and *Captain Peggie*.

BRAZZA, Pierre Savorgnan de (1852–1905) French explorer of Italian extraction, born in Rio de Janeiro. He entered the French navy in 1870, served in Gabon, and in 1876–78 explored the Ogowe. In 1878 the French government gave him 100000 francs for exploring the country north of the Congo, where he secured vast grants of land for France, and founded stations, including that of Brazzaville on the north shore of Stanley Pool.

BREADALBANE See **CAMPBELL**

BREAKSPEAR, Nicolas See **ADRIAN IV**

BRÉAL, Michel (1832–1915) French comparative philologist and mythologist, born in Rhenish Bavaria. In 1858 he settled in Paris, and in 1866 became professor of comparative grammar at the Collège de France. He founded the science of semantics with his *Essai de Sémantique* (1897), an exposition of principles for the study of the meaning of words.

BREAM, Julian Alexander (1933–) English guitarist and lutenist, born in London, where he made his début (1950). He was a protégé of **Andres Segovia**, has edited much music for guitar and lute, and many works have been specially written for him, by **Britten**, **Henze**, **Tippett**, **Walton** and others.

BREASLEY, Arthur Edward ('Scobie') (1914–) Australian jockey and trainer, born in Wagga Wagga. A successful rider for over 20 years before coming to Britain in 1950, he was retained to ride for the stable of Sir **Gordon Richards** in 1956. He was champion jockey in 1957, 1961, 1962 and 1963. In the Classics he won the Derby, on Santa Claus (1964) and Charlottown (1966), while Ki Ming gave him a 2000 Guineas win in 1951 and Festoon took the 1000 Guineas in 1954. He retired as a jockey in 1968 but made the move to trainer quickly and successfully, winning the Irish Derby with Ravi Tikkoo's Steel Pulse in 1972.

BREASTED, James Henry (1865–1935) American archaeologist and historian, born in Rockford, Illinois, the founder of American Egyptology and creator of Chicago University's Oriental Institute. He studied at Yale and Berlin before joining the faculty at Chicago in 1894. His five-volume *Ancient Records of Egypt* (1906) transcribed every hieroglyphic inscription then known, and he led expeditions to Egypt and Nubia (1905–07) to copy inscriptions that were perishing or had hitherto been inaccessible. In 1919, with funding from **John D Rockefeller**, he set up his own Oriental Institute to promote research on ancient Egypt and western Asia, establishing a field station, Chicago House, at Luxor five years later. Under his directorship, the Institute undertook notable excavations in the 1920s and 1930s in northern Palestine, at Khorsabad and Tell Asmar in Iraq, and (from 1931) at Persepolis, the Achaemenid capital of Iran. His other books include *The Development of Religion and Thought in Ancient Egypt* (1912), *Ancient Times* (1916), *The Conquest of Civilization* (1926) and *The Dawn of Conscience* (1933).

BRECHT, Bertolt Eugen Friedrich (1898–1956) German playwright and poet, born in Augsburg, perhaps Germany's greatest dramatist. He studied medicine and philosophy at Munich and Berlin Universities, and served briefly as a medical orderly in 1918. He won the Kleist drama prize in 1922 for his first two Expressionist plays, *Trommeln in der Nacht* (Drums in the Night), and *Baal*, followed by *Mann ist Mann* (Man is Man, 1926) with its clownish, inhuman soldiery. He was keenly interested in the effects produced by combining drama and music, and consequently collaborated with **Kurt Weill**, Eisler and Dessau in his major works. It was the *Dreigroschenoper* (Threepenny Opera, 1928), an adaptation of **Gay**'s *Beggar's Opera* in a sham Victorian London setting, with music by Kurt Weill, that established Brecht's reputation. A Marxist, he regarded his plays as social experiments, requiring detachment, not passion, from the observing audience. To achieve this, he introduced the 'epic' theatre, where the audience is required to see the stage as a stage, actors as actors, and not the traditional make-believe of the theatre. Thus, to prevent the audience from identifying themselves with a principal actor, the camp-following *Mutter Courage* (Mother Courage, 1941) is deliberately made to muff her lines, and *Puntilla* (1940) is given an increasingly ugly make-up. With **Hitler**'s rise to power in 1933, Brecht sought asylum in Denmark, Sweden, and Finland, journeyed across Russia and Persia, and in 1941 settled in Hollywood. His abiding hatred of Nazi Germany found expression in a series of short, episodic plays and poems collected under the title of *Furcht und Elend des dritten Reiches* (1945), and *Der aufhaltsame Aufstieg der Arturo Ui* (The Preventable Rise of Arturo Ui, 1958). He denied membership of the Communist party before a Senate sub-committee on un-American activities in 1946 and in 1948 accepted the East German government's offer of a theatre in East Berlin. The *Berliner Ensemble* was founded, producing under his direction his later plays, such as *Der kaukasische Kreidekreis* (The Caucasian Chalk Circle, 1949), and *Der gute Mensch von Sezuan* (The Good Woman of Setzuan, 1943), as well as touring in Western Europe, and visiting London shortly after his death with Helene Weigel, his widow, as the company's leading actress. Brecht, although apparently antipathetic towards the East German anti-Communist uprising in 1953 and a recipient of the Stalin peace prize (1954), proved as artist and thinker to be an embarrassment to the East German authorities. His opera *Lukullus* (1932–51), in which the Roman general has to account for his deeds before a tribunal-of-the-shadows, was withdrawn by order after the first night. *Galileo* (1938) underlined the moral that, however much the intellect may be oppressed, truth will out.

BRECKINRIDGE, John (1760–1806) American statesman, born near Staunton, Virginia. He became a member of congress in 1792 and, as attorney-general of Kentucky (1795–97), was largely responsible for the state's reformed penal code. He was a staunch supporter of **Jefferson**, who made him attorney-general of the USA in 1805.

BRECKINRIDGE, John Cabell (1821–75) vice-president of the USA, born near Lexington, Kentucky. He practised law there until 1847, when he was chosen major of a volunteer regiment for the Mexican war. He sat in congress 1851–55, and in 1856 was elected vice-president, with **Buchanan** as president. In 1860 he was the pro-slavery candidate for the presidency, but was defeated by **Lincoln**. A US senator from March to December 1861, he then was appointed a Confederate major-general in 1862, held important commands, was secretary of war in **Jefferson Davis**'s cabinet, and escaped to Europe, whence he returned in 1868.

BREHM, Alfred Edmund (1829–84) German naturalist, born in Renthendorf. He travelled in Africa, Spain, Norway, Lapland, Siberia, and Turkestan, and became keeper of the Hamburg Zoological Garden in 1863. He was the founder and director of the Berlin Aquarium in 1867. His *magnum opus* is the *Illustriertes Thierleben* on which many other natural histories are largely based.

BREITINGER, Johann Jakob (1701–76) Swiss critic and literary theorist, born in Zürich. Professor at the Collegium in Zürich, he was an adherent of the Anglo-German Romantic movement and a friend of **Bodmer**. He published *Critische Dichtkunst* (1740) and *Fabeln aus den Zeiten der Minnesinger* (1757).

BREITMANN, Hans See **LELAND, Charles Godfrey**

BREMER, Fredrika (1801–65) Swedish novelist, born near Åbo in Finland, and brought up near Stockholm. She is credited with the introduction of the realistic family novel into Swedish literature. Her novels include *Familjen H* (The Family H, 1831), *Grannarna* (The Neighbours, 1837), and *Hemmet* (The Home, 1839). Later she devoted herself to the education and emancipation of women, which informed her novels like *Hertha* (1856) and *Fader och dotter* (Father and Daughter, 1858). An inveterate traveller, journeys to Italy, Britain, Greece, Palestine and the USA supplied the material for two travel books, on the Old World and the New.

BREMOND, Henri (1865–1933) French critic and theologian, born in Aix-en-Provence. For 22 years a Jesuit (1882–1904), Bremond came under the influence of **Newman**, **Tyrrell** and the 'modernist' thinkers in the Catholic Church, gradually moving away from an orthodox religious position. His most extensive work is the *Literary History of Religious Feeling in France*, the final volumes of which were published after his death, and amongst his other books are *Sainte Chantal*, placed on the Index by the church, and numerous literary studies.

BRENAN, Gerald (1894–1987) English travel writer, Hispanophile and novelist, born in Malta, the son of an officer in an Irish regiment. After an itinerant boyhood he debunked with a donkey, drifting his way across Europe to the Balkans and back again. He went to Spain and settled in Yegen, an isolated village which became the focus of his classic *South from Granada* (1957). This was preceded by his best-known book, *The Spanish Labyrinth* (1943), still regarded as one of the most profound and perceptive studies of modern Spain. Other books include two volumes of memoirs, *A Life of One's Own* (1962) and *Personal Record* (1974), *The Literature of the Spanish People* (1951) and a novel, *Thoughts in a Dry Season* (1978).

BRENDAN, St (484–577) Irish abbot and traveller, traditionally the founder of the monastery of Clonfert in County Galway (561), and other monasteries in Ireland and Scotland. The Latin *Navigation of St Brendan* (c.1050) recounts his legendary voyage to a land of saints far to the west and north, possibly the Hebrides and the Northern Isles, or even Iceland. In old maps 'St Brendan's country' is placed west of the Cape Verde Islands.

BRENDEL, Alfred (1931–) Austrian pianist, born in Wiesenberg, Moravia. He made his début in Graz (1948) and is a distinguished interpreter of **Mozart**, **Beethoven**, **Schubert**, **Liszt** and **Schoenberg**. He tours internationally, giving master-classes and making frequent television appearances, and has written many perceptive essays on music.

BRENNAN, Christopher John (1870–1932) Australian poet and critic, born in Sydney of a Catholic family. Intended for the priesthood, after entering Sydney University he turned to the classics and philosophy. Going to Berlin University in 1892 to read philosophy, he was distracted by the exciting social and cultural life, and by French Symbolist poetry, which influenced his future writing. Returning to Sydney University in 1894, he was appointed associate professor of German literature in 1920 but was sacked five years later because of his marital problems and unconventional habits. He published only a select number of volumes of verse, the best of which was written before 1900; his sequence of verse, *The Wanderer* (1902), suggests the torment of his life. Some of his verse was published posthumously, and his criticism appeared mainly in journals, but he is also known for his co-editing of the standard college anthology *From Blake to Arnold* (1900), which contains much of his critical work.

BRENNER, Sydney (1927–) South African-born British molecular biologist, born in Germiston and educated at Witwatersrand University and Oxford. He joined the famed MRC Molecular Biology Laboratory in Cambridge in 1957, becoming its director in 1980. In the 1950s and 1960s he did notable work on the informational code of DNA, the 'blueprints' for all biological synthesis; and then in the 1970s moved to basic studies designed to relate, in detail, an animal's nervous system to its genetic make-up.

BRENT, Charles Henry (1862–1929) Canadian prelate and ecumenist, born in Newcastle, Ontario. He graduated from Trinity College, Toronto, and ministered in New York and Boston. After consecration in 1901 he was Anglican bishop of the missionary district of the Philippines, of Washington (1908), and of Western New York (1919). Largely responsible for organizing the ecumenical conferences at Stockholm (1925) and Lausanne (1927), he visualized a great church that would become the heir of the spiritual, moral and intellectual wealth of the Christian centuries. His books include *With God in the World* (1899), *The Conquest of Trouble* (1916), and *The Commonwealth: Its Foundations and Pillars* (1930).

BRENT-DYER, Elinor Mary (1894–1969) English author of the 'Chalet School' girls' stories, born in South Shields. Educated at Leeds University, she became a schoolmistress, and later headmistress of the Margaret Roper Girls' School in Hereford. Her first schoolgirl novel, *Gerry Goes to School*, appeared in 1922, inaugurating her 98 titles. Her fourth book, *The School at the Chalet* (1925), established her famous series by showing the 24-year-old Madge Bettany's successful attempt to found an English school in the Austrian Tyrol, to which Austrian as well as English parents were attracted. Centred on Jo Bettany, Madge's younger sister, the series sought to evangelize against English parochialism and xenophobia. Perhaps the best single title was *The Chalet School in Exile* (1940), a horrific if judicious account of the school's flight from Nazi rule with a grimly realistic depiction of homicidal persecution of Jews. Later stories were set in the Channel Islands, in Wales, and in the Bernese Oberland: the inevitable decline was offset for many years by the creation of another memorable character, the impetuous and gloriously frank Mary-Lou Trelawney. The final book in the series, *Prefects of the Chalet School*, was published posthumously in 1970.

BRENTANO, Bettina von See **ARNIM**

BRENTANO, Clemens von (1778–1842) German poet, uncle of **Franz** and **Lujo Brentano** and brother of **Bettina Arnim**, born in Ehrenbreitstein. He became a Roman Catholic in 1818 and withdrew to the monastery of Dülmen, near Münster (1818–24), where he recorded the revelations of the nun, **Anna Katharina Emmerich**. Thereafter he led a restless life, and showed plain signs of derangement some years before his death. In his earliest poems the peculiarities of the Romantic school are carried to excess. His dramatic productions, the best of which is *Die Gründung Prags*, are characterized by great dramatic power, and a wonderful humour. He was mostly successful in his novellas, particularly in the *Geschichte vom braven Kaspar*, and with his brother-in-law **Ludvig Achim von Arnim** he edited *Des Knaben Wunderhorn*, a collection of folk songs.

BRENTANO, Franz (1838–1917) German psychologist and philosopher, nephew of **Clemens von Brentano** and brother of **Lujo Brentano**, born in Marienberg. He became a Catholic priest in 1864 and taught philosophy at Würzburg until 1873 when he abandoned the priesthood, rejecting papal infallibility, and moved to teach at Vienna until retirement in 1895. He spent his later years in Florence and Zurich. He stressed the connection between psychology and philosophy and in his most important work, *Psychologie vom empirischen Standpunkt* (1874), developed the important doctrine of 'intentionality', characterizing mental events as involving the 'direction of the mind to an object'. Among his students were **Husserl**, **Meinong**, and **Masaryk**.

BRENTANO, Heinrich von (1904–64) West German statesman, born in Offenbach. A successful lawyer, he was one of the founders of the Christian Democratic party. He went into politics in Hesse in 1945 and was elected in 1949 to the Federal Diet at Bonn, where he played a prominent part in drafting the Constitution. He became foreign minister in 1955, aligning West Germany closely with the policies of the Atlantic Alliance, but resigned in 1961 to facilitate the formation of a coalition government of Dr **Adenauer**'s parties with the Free Democrats.

BRENTANO, Lujo (1844–1931) German political economist, born in Aschaffenburg in Bavaria, nephew of **Clemens von Brentano** and brother of **Franz Brentano**. In 1868 he went to England to study the condition of the working-classes, and especially trades associations and unions. The outcome of this was his *English Guilds* (1870) and *Die Arbeitergilden der Gegenwart* (2 vols, 1871–72). He became professor of his subject in five universities and wrote on wages, labour in relation to land, compulsory insurance for workmen, and an *Economic History of England* (1929). A prominent pacifist, he was awarded the Nobel peace prize in 1927.

BRENTFORD See **JOYNSON-HICKS**

BRENTON, Howard (1942–) English dramatist, born in Portsmouth. He wrote for fringe theatre companies during the late 1960s, and was resident dramatist at the Royal Court Theatre, London, from 1972 to 1973, where his play *Magnificence*, dealing with urban terrorism, was staged. *The Churchill Play* (1974), a bleak look at a future Britain governed by hard-liners using troops to brutalize trade unionists, was produced at the Nottingham Playhouse. *Weapons of Happiness* (1976) became the first new play to be produced at the National Theatre's recently-opened South Bank building. *The Romans in Britain* was premiered at the NT in 1980, and *The Genius*, on the nuclear arms race, at the Royal Court in 1983. He has also collaborated with **David Hare** on a number of projects, the most outstanding being *Pravda* (1985), a furiously ebullient satire on the cravenness of the national press. He has also written a political thriller, *Diving for Pearls* (1989).

BRENZ, Johann (1499–1570) German Lutheran reformer, born in Swabia. He was co-author of the Württemberg Confession of Faith, and his Catechism (1551) stands next to **Luther**'s in Protestant Germany.

BRETON, André (1896–1966) French poet, essayist and critic, born in Tinchebray, Normandy. In 1916 he joined the Dadaist group and was co-founder of the Dada magazine *Littérature* (1919), and collaborated with Philippe Soupault to write *Les Champs magnétiques*, which was described as 'an experiment in automatic writing'. In 1922 he turned to Surrealism, and in 1924 he published his first Surrealist manifesto and *Le Poisson soluble*, and became editor of *La Révolution surréaliste*. His major novel, *Nadja*, was published in 1928. In 1930 he joined the Communist party for a while. He spent the war years in the USA. His writings also include *Qu'est-ce que le surréalisme?* (1936).

BRETON, Nicholas (c.1545–c.1626) English poet, born in London, the son of a merchant, and stepson of **George Gascoigne**. Educated at Oxford, he became a prolific writer of all kinds of verse, prose and pamphlets. His best-known poem is *The Passionate Shepheard* (1604). His prose *Wits Trenchmour* (1597) is a fishing idyll on which **Izaak Walton** drew for *The Compleat Angler*. He also wrote a prose romance, *The Strange Fortune of Two Excellent Princes* (1600), and a collection of character observations, *Fantasticks* (1626).

BRETÓN DE LOS HERREROS, Don Manuel (1796–1873) Spanish dramatist, author of some 360 plays, mostly social comedies in which caricature rather than character is portrayed.

BRETONNEAU, Pierre (1778–1862) French physician, born in Tours. He was the first to name diphtheria and describe typhoid fever.

BRETSCHNEIDER, Karl Gottlieb (1776–1848) German theologian, born in Gersdorf in Saxony. He lectured in theology at Wittenberg (1804–06) and eventually became superintendent at Gotha, where he died. In his treatise on the gospel of St John (1820) he examines the arguments against St John's authorship. His *Manual of the Religion and History of the Christian Church* (trans 1857) reveals his dogmatic position. He allows full and reasoned criticism of the Christian dogmas while still recognizing the inspired nature of the Bible.

BREUER, Josef See **FREUD, Sigmund**

BREUER, Marcel Lajos (1902–81) Hungarian-born American architect and designer, born in Pécs. A student at the Bauhaus in Germany from 1920, he took charge of the furniture workshop by 1924. He designed probably the first modern tubular steel chair, the 'Wassily' (1925), and the well-known 'Cesca' cantilevered chair (1928). In England from 1935 to 1937, he was in partnership with the architect F R S Yorke, during which time he designed the laminated wood 'Isokon' long chair for Jack Pritchard (1936). In 1937 he joined **Walter Gropius** in the USA as associate professor of architecture at Harvard University (1937–46) and in architectural practice. Working independently after 1947, he designed the majority of his architectural projects, including the UNESCO building in Paris (with Bernard Zehrfuss and **Pier Luigi Nervi**). A significant figure in the 'Modern Movement', his classic furniture designs, in particular, represented major developments in materials and techniques.

BREUIL, Henri Édouard Prosper (1877–1961) French archaeologist. He trained as a priest, became interested in cave art in 1900, and was responsible the following year for the discovery of the famous decorated caves at Combarelles and Font-de-Gaume in the Dordogne. Noted for his studies of artistic technique and the detailed copying of hundreds of paintings in Europe, Africa, and elsewhere, he later became professor at the Collège de France (1929–47). His work marked the beginning of the study of palaeolithic art, as shown by his *Quatre cents siècles de l'art pariétal* (Four hundred Centuries of Cave Art, 1952).

BREWER, Ebenezer Cobham (1810–97) English clergyman, born in London. He took a first-class degree in law at Trinity Hall, Cambridge in 1835, one year after receiving orders. He then became a London schoolmaster. His most enduring work is his *Dictionary of Phrase and Fable* (1870), still a standard work of reference.

BREWER, John Sherren (1809–79) English scholar, born in Norwich. As professor of English at King's College, London, he spent nearly 20 years in the record office, editing the *Monumenta Franciscana* (1858), the works of **Roger Bacon** (1859) and **Giraldus Cambrensis** (1861), and volumes i–iv of the *Calendar of Papers of the Reign of Henry VIII* (1862–72).

BREWSTER, Sir David (1781–1868) Scottish physicist, born in Jedburgh. Educated for the Church, he became editor of the *Edinburgh Magazine* (1802), and in 1808 of the *Edinburgh Encyclopaedia*. He had previously been interested in the study of optics, and in 1816 he invented the kaleidoscope, and later improved Sir **Charles Wheatstone**'s stereoscope by introducing refracting lenses. In 1819 the *Edinburgh Philosophical Journal* took the place of the *Magazine*; and in 1831 Brewster was one of the chief originators of the British Association. In 1818 he was awarded the **Rumford** gold and silver medals for his discoveries on the polarization of light. In 1838 he was appointed principal of St Salvator and St Leonard's, St Andrews. He was principal of Edinburgh University from 1859.

BREZHNEV, Leonid Ilyich (1906–82) Russian politician, born in Dneprodzerzhinsk in the Ukraine, the son of a steelworker. He joined the Komsomol (Communist Youth League) in 1923 and, having trained as an agricultural surveyor, worked on the collectivization programmes in Belorussia and the Urals region during the 1920s. On his acceptance into the Communist party (CPSU) in 1931, he was sent back to Dneprodzerzhinsk in 1931, where he retrained as an industrial engineer and became head of the local metallurgical polytechnic. In 1938 he was appointed party propaganda chief at Dnepropetrovsk and impressed the new Ukrainian party chief, **Nikita Khrushchev**, with his organizational skills. Between 1941 and 1945 he served as a political commissar to the Southern Army and after the war was sent to Moldavia as party chief (1950–52) to 'sovietize' the newly-ceded republic. His work here drew the attention of the CPSU leader, **Joseph Stalin**, who inducted Brezhnev into the Secretariat and the Politburo, as a 'candidate' member, in 1952. Brezhnev was removed from these posts following Stalin's death in 1953, but, with Khrushchev's patronage, returned to favour in 1954, being sent to Kazakhstan to oversee implementation of the new 'virgin lands' agricultural programme. In 1956–57 Brezhnev returned to the Politburo and Secretariat, but was removed again in 1960, as criticism of Khrushchev mounted. He assumed the ceremonial post of state president and began to distance himself from the radical new domestic and foreign policies of Khrushchev. In July 1963, Brezhnev returned to the Politburo and Secretariat and was elected the new CPSU general secretary in October 1964, when Khrushchev was ousted, forming part of a new conservative and consensual coalition. During the 1960s, Brezhnev, packing the Politburo with Dnepropetrovsk colleagues, established himself as the dominant figure in the Soviet polity. He emerged as an international statesman during the early 1970s and in May 1977 gained the additional title of state president. During the later 1970s, however, as his health deteriorated, policy-making became paralysed and economic difficulties mounted. The Brezhnev era saw the Soviet Union establish itself as a military and political superpower, extending its influence in Africa and Asia. At home, however, it was a period of caution and, during the 1970s, of economic stagnation which has been much criticized by the new **Gorbachev** administration.

BŘEZINA, Otakar, properly **Václav Jebavy** (1868–1929) Czech poet, born in Pocatky. He was a leading exponent of Symbolism in Czech poetry in his collections *Polar Winds* (1897), *Temple Builders* (1899), *The Hands* (1901), and others.

BRIALMONT, Henri Alexis (1821–1903) Belgian military engineer, born in Venloo. An authority on fortification, he designed the fortifications of Antwerp, Liège, Namur, Bucharest and other towns.

BRIAN, (William) Havergal (1876–1972) English composer and writer on music, born in Dresden, Staffordshire. Championed by such figures as **Beecham**, **Wood**, **Tovey** and **Bantock**, his success seemed secure, but he suffered a long period of neglect after World War I. The vast scale of certain works, his 'unfashionable' style of expansive post-Romanticism, the sheer number of his works, and the vagaries of his private life all contributed to this. A revival of interest in his music occurred in the last decade or so of his life. He wrote 32 symphonies (No. 1, *The Gothic*, 1919–27; No. 32, 1968), a huge setting of **Shelley**'s *Prometheus Unbound*, a Violin Concerto and five operas (including *The Tigers*, 1916–19 and *Faust*, 1955–56). From 1904 to 1949 he wrote musical criticism distinguished by his eclectic outlook and perception.

BRIAND, Aristide (1862–1932) French socialist, born in Nantes. He was founder (with **Jean Jaures**) of *L'humanité* and framer of the law for the separation of church and state (1905). He was eleven times French premier and was foreign minister from 1925 to 1932. He shared the Nobel prize for peace with **Gustav Stresemann** and advocated a United States of Europe.

BRICKHILL, Paul Chester Jerome (1916–) Australian author, born in Sydney. Educated at Sydney University, he worked in journalism before serving with the Royal Australian Air Force during World War II. Shot down in North Africa, he was for two years a prisoner-of-war in Germany, in Stalag Luft III from which the intrepid escape was made, later described by him in *The Great Escape* (1951). His first published book, *Escape to Danger* (1946), collected many stories of prison-camp life. He went on to become the most successful non-fiction writer of the post-war period, with *The Dam Busters* (1951, later filmed), *Escape or Die* (1952), and the story of the legless air ace **Douglas Bader**, *Reach for the Sky* (1954, also filmed).

BRIDE, St See **BRIDGET**

BRIDGE, Frank (1879–1941) English composer and conductor, born in Brighton. He studied under **Stanford**, as **Britten** was later to study under him. He played the viola in leading quartets and conducted the New Symphony Orchestra from its inception at Covent Garden and often at the 'Proms'. He is best known for his string quartets, but his full orchestral works were less successful, except perhaps his 'Sea' suite.

BRIDGES, Robert Seymour (1844–1930) English poet and critic, born in Walmer, Kent. Educated at Eton and Corpus Christi College, Oxford, he then studied medicine at St Bartholomew's Hospital and practised until 1881. At university he met **Gerard Manley Hopkins**, with whom he became friendly, arranging for the posthumous publication of his poems in 1918. His first collection, *Poems*, appeared in 1873, and was followed by *The Growth of Love* (1876), a sequence of sonnets which was a popular success. He followed this with two long poems, *Prometheus the Firegiver* (1883) and *Eros and Psyche* (1885), but for the next decade he concentrated on plays and wrote eight, only one of which was performed in his lifetime. He made important contributions to criticism, with studies of **Milton** (1893) and **Keats** (1895), and wrote poems set to music by **Charles Parry**, as well as *A Practical Discourse on Hymn Singing* (1901). In 1912 he published his *Collected Poems* to wide public acclaim and in 1913 he was surprisingly appointed Poet Laureate, and produced *The Spirit of Man* (1916), an idiosyncratic anthology of prose and verse designed to lift the nation's spirits during World War I. After the war, he published *October and Other Poems* (1920) and, in his 85th year, *The Testament of Beauty*, a long poem in four parts whose philosophy is expressed in its title.

BRIDGET, or **Brigid,** or **Bride, St** (453–523) Irish abbess, said to be the daughter of an Ulster prince. She entered a convent at Meath in her fourteenth year, and founded four monasteries for women, the chief at Kildare, where she was buried. She was regarded as one of the three great saints of Ireland, the others being St **Patrick** and St **Columba**, and was held in great reverence in Scotland (as St Bride). Her feast day is 1 February.

BRIDGET, St, of Sweden See **BIRGITTA**

BRIDGEWATER See **EGERTON**

BRIDGMAN, Laura Dewey (1829–89) blind American deaf-mute, born in Hanover, New Hampshire. At the age of two a violent fever utterly destroyed her sight, hearing, smell, and in some degree taste. Dr **Samuel Howe** educated her at the Perkins institution, and she became a skilful teacher of blind deaf-mutes. She is referred to in **Charles Dickens**' *American Notes* (1842).

BRIDGMAN, Sir Orlando (1608–74) English conveyancer and judge. Educated at Queen's College, Cambridge, he practised as a conveyancer during the Civil War but at the Restoration became successively chief baron of Exchequer (1660), chief justice of the Common Pleas (1660) and lord keeper of the Great Seal (1667–72). Various developments in conveyancing are attributed to him; his book of precedents was popular and is still a source of information on the property law of that time. His opinions display learning and precision of thought and expression.

BRIDGMAN, Percy Williams (1882–1961) American physicist, born in Cambridge, Massachusetts. Educated at Harvard, he became professor of physics and mathematics there in 1919. He obtained under high pressure a new form of phosphorus, proved experimentally that viscosity increases with high pressure, and was awarded the Nobel prize for physics in 1946 for his work on high-pressure physics and thermodynamics.

BRIDIE, James, pseud of **Osborne Henry Mavor** (1888–1951) Scottish dramatist, born in Glasgow. He qualified as a doctor at Glasgow University and became a successful general practitioner and consultant. Always interested in the theatre, he seized his chance when the Scottish National Players produced his *Sunlight Sonata* in 1928 under the pseudonym of **Mary Henderson**. After that, he wrote a stream of plays, among them *The Anatomist* (1931), *A Sleeping Clergyman* (1933), *Mr Bolfry* (1943) and *Dr Angelus* (1947). He served in both world wars in the RAMC and after the second he became head of the Scottish Committee of CEMA and played a leading part in the foundation of the Glasgow Citizen's Theatre.

BRIDPORT, Lord See **HOOD, Alexander**

BRIEUX, Eugène (1858–1932) French dramatist and Academician, born in Paris of poor parents. He experienced many of the social evils which his powerful, didactic plays, leavened by wit, expose. His works include *The Evasion* (1896) and *Maternity* (1903).

BRIGGS, Henry (1561–1631) English mathematician, born in Warley Wood, Halifax. In 1581 he graduated at St John's College, Cambridge, and became a fellow in 1588. In 1596 he became the first professor of geometry at Gresham College, London, and in 1619 first Savilian professor of geometry in Oxford. He visited **John Napier** in 1616 and 1617 and, with Napier's agreement, proposed the use of the base 10 for logarithms instead of that used by Napier. This was an important simplification for the practical use of logarithms in calculation. He calculated and published logarithmic and trigonometric tables to 14 decimal places.

BRIGGS, Raymond (Redvers) (1934–) English children's illustrator and author, born in London, the son of a milkman. His early publications were conventional, such as *Midnight Adventure* (1961), but in 1966 his *Mother Goose Treasury* appeared with over 900 pictures, and his talent for eccentric comedy was established, winning him the Kate Greenaway Medal. *Father Christmas* (1973), another distinctive work, uses the comic-strip format, featuring a grumpy, expletory Santa, reluctantly braving the wintry elements. For this he was awarded his second Greenaway Medal. *Fungus the Bogeyman* (1977) brought him love and loathing, and *The Snowman* (1979) enchanted adults and children alike. A provocative as well as an entertaining artist, his anxiety for the future well-being of the planet is expressed in *When the Wind Blows* (1982).

BRIGHAM YOUNG See **YOUNG**

BRIGHT, John (1811–89) British Radical statesman and orator, born in Rochdale, son of a Quaker cotton-spinner. When the Anti Corn-Law League was formed in 1839 he was a leading member, and, with **Cobden**, engaged in free trade agitation throughout the country. In 1843 he became MP for Durham and strongly opposed the corn-laws until they were repealed. Like Cobden, he was a member of the Peace Society and energetically denounced the Crimean War (1854). Elected in 1857 for Birmingham, he seconded the motion against the Conspiracy Bill which led to the overthrow of **Palmerston**'s government. His name was closely associated with the Reform Act of 1867. In 1868 he accepted office as president of the board of trade but retired through illness in 1870, returning in 1881, as chancellor of the duchy of Lancaster. He retired from the **Gladstone** ministry in 1882, opposing his Home Rule policy (1886–88). Bright exerted a considerable influence on the Unionist party and was regarded as one of the most eloquent speakers of his time.

BRIGHT, Richard (1789–1858) English physician, born in Bristol. He studied at Edinburgh, London, Berlin, and Vienna, and from 1820 was connected with Guy's Hospital. He made many important medical observations ('Bright's disease' of the kidneys is named after him) and wrote numerous dissertations. His *Travels from Vienna through Lower Hungary* (1818) contains a valuable account of the Gypsies.

BRIGHT, Timothy (c.1551–1615) English inventor, doctor and clergyman, born in Yorkshire. He abandoned medicine for the church, and in 1588 was granted a teaching patent for a system of shorthand he had invented.

BRIL, Mattys (1550–84) Flemish landscape painter, born in Antwerp, brother of **Paul Bril**. He painted frescoes in the Vatican.

BRIL, Paul (1556–1626) Flemish painter, born in Antwerp, brother of **Mattys Bril**. He worked in Rome, and raised the prestige of landscape painting by his frescoes.

BRILLAT-SAVARIN, Anthelme (1755–1826) French politician, gastronome and writer, born in Belley. He was a deputy in 1789, and mayor of Belley in 1793. During the French Revolution he took refuge in Switzerland, and afterwards in America, where he played in the orchestra of a New York theatre; and from 1796 until his death was a member of the Court of Cassation. His *Physiologie du goût* (1825), an elegant and witty compendium of the art of dining, has been repeatedly republished and translated; an English form is *A Handbook of Gastronomy*, with 52 etchings by Lalauze (1884).

BRINDLEY, James (1716–72) English engineer and canal builder, born in Thornsett near Chapel-en-le-Frith of humble parentage. Apprenticed to a millwright, he became an engineer, and in 1752 contrived a water engine for draining a coalmine. A silk mill on a new plan, and several others of his works, recommended him to **Francis Egerton**, 3rd Duke of Bridgewater, who employed him (1759) to execute the canal between Worsley and Manchester—a difficult enterprise crowned with complete success (1772). He also commenced the Grand Trunk Canal, and completed the Birmingham, Chesterfield, and others; in all, constructing 365 miles of canals. He was illiterate all his life; most of his problems were solved without writings or drawings; and when anything specially difficult had to be considered, he would go to bed and think it out there.

BRINELL, Johann August (1849–1925) Swedish engineer and metallurgist. He invented the Brinell machine for measuring the hardness of alloys and metals.

BRINK, André (1935–) South African novelist, short-story writer, playwright, critic and translator, born in Vrede, Orange Free State. An Afrikaaner dissident, he has produced a prodigious body of work of uneven quality and has, almost single-handedly, contemporized Afrikaans novel writing. He emerged as a writer in the 1950s but it was not until his seventh novel—which he later translated into English as *Looking on Darkness* (1974)—was banned by the South African authorities that he began to attract international attention. Relating the story of a coloured actor who makes good in London and returns to South Africa to confront the apartheid régime, it won the author admiration, though more for his courage than his style. Subsequent books have been criticized for their sentimentality and sensationalism but the best—*Rumours of Rain* (1978), *Chain of Voices* (1982) and *States of Emergency* (1988)—are powerful narratives which highlight conditions in South Africa without resorting to propaganda. He received the **Martin Luther King** Memorial prize and the French Prix Medicis Étranger in 1980, has thrice won the CNA award, South Africa's most prestigious commendation, and has twice been runner-up for the Booker prize.

BRINK, Bernard ten (1841–92) Dutch philologist, born in Amsterdam. In 1870 he became professor of modern languages and literature at Marburg, in 1873 of English at Strasbourg. He was the author of *Chaucer-Studien* (1870), *Geschichte der englischen Literatur* (1874), *Chaucers Sprache und Verskunst* (1884), and *Beowulf-Untersuchungen* (1888).

BRINTON, Daniel Garrison (1839–99) medical doctor turned linguist, folklorist and writer on North American ethnology. He was an influential advocate of the doctrine that cultural similarities were due to independent invention rather than borrowing or diffusion.

BRINVILLIERS, Marie Madeleine, Marquise de (c.1630–1676) French murderess, daughter of Dreux d'Aubray, lieutenant of Paris. In 1651 she married the Marquis of Brinvilliers, who introduced her to a handsome young officer, Sainte Croix. He became her lover and was sent to the Bastille by her father. On his release the couple set about poisoning the marquise's family. Her father, brothers, and sisters died, as eventually did Sainte Croix himself, an accidental victim of his own poison. He left incriminating documents, and the marquise fled, but was arrested in Liège, taken to Paris, and executed.

BRION, Frederike Elisabeth (1752–1813) German pastor's daughter, born in Sesenheim, near Strasbourg. In 1770–71 she had a passionate love-affair with **Goethe**. She never married.

BRISBANE, Sir Thomas Makdougall (1773–1860) Scottish soldier and astronomer, born in Largs. At 16 he entered the army, and served with distinction in Flanders, the West Indies, Spain, and North America, and was promoted major-general in 1813. From 1821 to 1825 he was governor of New South Wales. He catalogued in Australia 7385 stars, and received the **Copley** medal from the Royal Society. Brisbane, the capital of Queensland, was named after him.

BRISCOE, Arthur John Trevor (1873–1943) English etcher, born in Birkenhead. He studied at the Slade School of Art and later in Paris. He served during World War I in the RNVR. On his return from Paris he purchased a boat and explored the French and British coasts and Dutch canals, from all of which he drew his inspiration. Almost his entire output of some 189 etchings are of seafaring subjects which were executed over a period of ten years.

BRISSOT DE WARVILLE, Jacques Pierre (1754–93) French revolutionary politician, born near Chartres. After completing his studies in Paris he abandoned the legal profession for that of journalism. His *Théorie des lois criminelles* (1780) was followed by his *Bibliothèque des lois criminelles* (1782–86), which established his reputation as a jurist. He was imprisoned for four months in the Bastille on the false charge of having written a brochure against the queen; to escape from a new term there he retired in 1787 to London, and next year visited North America as representative of the *Société des Amis des Noirs*. In 1789 he was present at the storming of the Bastille, and was elected representative for Paris in the National Assembly, where he exercised a predominant influence over all the early movements of the revolution. He also established *Le Patriote français*, which became the organ of the earliest Republicans. As the revolution proceeded, Brissot was recognized as the head of the Girondists or Brissotins. He contributed powerfully to the fall of the monarchy, and strongly urged war against Austria and England in 1792, and the diffusion of republican principles. In the Convention his moderation made him suspected, and, with 20 other Girondists, he was guillotined.

BRITANNICUS, in full **Claudius Tiberius Britannicus Caesar** (41–55) the son of the emperor **Claudius** and **Messalina**, born 41 or 42 and surnamed in honour of his father's triumph in Britain (43). Claudius' fourth wife, **Agrippina the Younger**, caused her husband to adopt her son **Nero**, and treat Britannicus as an imbecile; and Nero, after his accession, had his half-brother poisoned. He is the subject of a tragedy by **Racine**.

BRITTAIN, Vera Mary (1893–1970) English writer, born in Newcastle-under-Lyme. After studying at Oxford she served as a nurse in World War I, recording her experiences with war-found idealism in *Testament of Youth* (1933). As well as writing a number of novels, she made several lecture tours in the USA, promoting feminism and pacifism. In 1925 she married George Catlin, professor of politics at Cornell, and wrote the sequels, *Testament of Friendship* (1940) and *Testament of Experience* (1957). Her daughter is the English politician **Shirley Williams.**

BRITTAN, Sir Leon (1939–) English Conservative politician. Educated at Trinity College, Cambridge and Harvard, he qualified as a barrister. Politically active while still an undergraduate, he entered the House of Commons in 1974 and from 1979 held ministerial posts under **Margaret Thatcher**, including Treasury chief secretary (1981–83), home secretary (1983–85) and trade and industry secretary (1985–86). He resigned from the cabinet in 1986 because of his involvement in the political dispute over the sale of the Westland Helicopter company and returned to the back benches. In 1989 he was nominated as a vice-president of the European Commission with special responsibility for competition policy.

BRITTEN, Baron (Edward) Benjamin, of Aldeburgh (1913–76) English composer, born in Lowestoft. He studied the piano under Harold Samuel and composition under **Frank Bridge** before winning a scholarship to the Royal College of Music, where he worked under **John Ireland**; he was already a prolific composer, and some of his student works have survived to stand beside more mature compositions: notable among these is the set of choral variations, *A Boy was Born*. During the 1930s Britten supplied a great deal of incidental music for plays and documentary films, collaborating at times with **W H Auden**, whose poetry provided texts for the song cycles *Our Hunting Fathers* and *On This Island*. From 1939 to 1942 Britten worked in America, producing his large-scale instrumental works, the Violin Concerto and the *Sinfonia da Requiem*. After his return to Britain, his works were almost exclusively vocal and choral, apart from the Variations and Fugue on a Theme of Purcell (*The Young Person's Guide to the Orchestra*), the String Quartets Nos. 1 and 3, the Cello Symphony (1963), the Cello Sonata and three suites for solo cello (the last group of works all for the cellist **Rostropovich**). As well as the choral 'Spring' Symphony and many vocal and choral works, after 1945, when his first opera *Peter Grimes* won an immediate success, Britten wrote two further operas on a large scale, *Billy Budd* and *Gloriana*, the latter for the coronation of Queen **Elizabeth**, and five, including *The Turn of the Screw*, on a smaller scale he called 'chamber operas', with a basic orchestra of twelve players. Amongst his gifts was the skill to write with a simplicity that attracts amateur performers while losing nothing of its artistic and dramatic effectiveness; this quality is especially marked in the 'children's operas', *The Little Sweep*, incorporated in *Let's Make an Opera!* (1949), and *Noye's Fludde* (1958), a musical rendering of a 14th-century miracle play. His later operas include *A Midsummer Night's Dream* (1960), *Owen Wingrave* (1970) and *Death in Venice* (1973). In addition to his enormous activity as a composer, Britten was an accomplished pianist, usually heard as an accompanist, particularly of **Peter Pears**, with whom he and Eric Crozier founded in 1948 the annual Aldeburgh Festival, where several of his own works had their first performances. He was awarded a life peerage in 1976.

BRITTON, John (1771–1857) English topographer and antiquary, born in Kingston St Michael, near Chippenham. At 16 he went to London, and was in turn cellarman, clerk, and compiler of a song book and a dramatic miscellany. He was employed with Edward Wedlake Brayley (1773–1854) to compile *The Beauties of Wiltshire*; its success led to *The Beauties of England and Wales* (15 vols, 1803–14). He also compiled *Architectural Beauties of Great Britain* (1805–14), and *Cathedral Antiquities of England* (14 vols, 1814–35)

BRITTON, Nathaniel Lord (1859–1934) American botanist, born in Staten Island, New York. Originally a geologist, he became professor of botany at Columbia in 1891, and was the initiator and first director of the New York Botanical Garden (1896–1929). He wrote *Illustrated Flora of the Northern United States, Canada and the British Possessions* (1896–98), and *Flora of Bermuda* (1918).

BRITTON, Thomas (1654–1714) English coal-merchant, known as 'the musical small-coal man'. He founded a fashionable musical club over his shop in London, patronized by **Handel**, **Pepusch** and others. A student of the occult and a bibliophile, he helped to form the Harleian library in the British Museum and collected the Somers tracts of John, 1st Baron **Somers**.

BRIZIEUX, Julien Auguste Pélage (1803–58) French poet, born in Lorient. Much of his work, including a translation of **Dante**'s *Divina Commedia*, was influenced by Italian styles, but his verse also incorporated the folklore and dialect of Britanny.

BROAD, Charlie Dunbar (1887–1971) English philosopher, born in London, who was professor of moral philosophy in Cambridge from 1933 to 1953. His work is characterized by thorough, fair-minded analysis and appraisal, as in *Scientific Thought* (1930) and the two-volume *Examination of McTaggart's Philosophy* (1933, 1938), which contains most of his own original thought. He also had a strong interest in parapsychology and was president of the Society for Psychical Research.

BROADBENT, Donald Eric (1926–) English psychologist. He joined the scientific staff of the Medical Research Council's Applied Psychology Research Unit in Cambridge after World War II (director, 1949–58). A major figure in postwar experimental psychology, he was the most influential British psychologist in the movement to import ideas from communication theory and cybernetics into cognitive psychology. His first book, *Perception and Communication* (1958), was a milestone in the development of this field, and his work at the Applied Psychology Unit did much to advance the reputation of experimental psychology as an applied science. Since 1974 he has been a member of the external staff of the Medical Research Council, based in Oxford. He was awarded the American Psychological Association's Distinguished Scientist Award (1975).

BROADWOOD, John (1732–1812) Scottish piano manufacturer, born in Cockburnspath, Berwickshire. He walked to London to become a cabinet maker, married the daughter of the Swiss-born harpsichord-maker, Burkhardt Tschudi, and in 1770 founded with him the great London pianoforte house. His grandson, **Henry Fowler Broadwood** (1811–93), was also a great improver of the piano.

BROCA, Paul Pierre (1824–80) French surgeon and anthropologist, born in Sainte-Foy-le-Grande, Gironde. He first located the motor speech centre in the brain and did research on prehistoric surgical operations.

BROCH, Hermann (1886–1951) Austrian novelist and essayist, born in Vienna. He spent his early adult life working in his father's textile business and was over 40 when he went to Vienna University to study philosophy and mathematics. When the Nazis invaded Austria in 1938 he was imprisoned, but influential friends, including **James Joyce**, obtained his release and facilitated his emigration to America in 1940, where he remained until he died in abject surroundings. He is regarded as one of the greatest German writers of the 20th century, though he was a reluctant writer and his books reward only readers with perseverance. His masterpiece is *The Death of Virgil* (1946). Other notable books include *The Sleepwalkers* (3 vols, 1931–32), *The Unknown Quantity* (1935) and *The Spell*, published posthumously and first translated into English in 1987.

BROCKHAUS, Friedrich Arnold (1772–1823) German publisher, founder of the firm of Brockhaus in

Leipzig and publisher of the famous *Konversations-Lexikon*, begun by R G Löbel in 1796 and completed in 1811. An improved edition was begun in 1812, edited by Brockhaus. The business was carried on by his descendants. The first illustrated edition of the *Lexikon* was published in 1892–97; *Der Grosse Brockhaus* was begun in 1928.

BROCKHURST, Gerald Leslie (1891–1979) English artist and etcher, born in Birmingham. He studied at the Birmingham School of Art, and at the age of 22 won the Royal Academy's Gold Medal and Scholarship which took him to France and Italy. His etchings and lithographs are unsurpassed in meticulous detail and are almost entirely concerned with the themes of young womanhood and portraiture. He was influenced by the early Italian Renaissance painters and his acknowledged masterpiece, 'Adolescence', which was exhibited at the Royal Academy in 1933, is a fine example of his craftsmanship.

BROCKWAY, (Archibald) Fenner, Baron Brockway (1888–1988) English left-wing politician and pacifist, a founder of the Campaign for Nuclear Disarmament. He was born in Calcutta into a missionary family, and educated at the School for the Sons of Missionaries at Blackheath (now Eltham College) in England. As a young journalist he was converted to socialism by an interview with **Keir Hardie**. He joined the Independent Labour party and became a militant pacifist, and was imprisoned during World War I. In the 1930s he claimed to have been the last socialist to speak publicly in Germany before **Hitler** came to power (1933). He was elected to parliament for the first time in 1929–31, and again in 1950–64. He was made a life peer in 1964, and wrote more than a score of books, including his autobiographical volumes *Inside the Left*, *Outside the Right*, *Towards Tomorrow* and (in 1986), *98 not out*. He died six months short of his 100th birthday.

BROD, Max (1884–1968) Austrian novelist, biographer, essayist, poet and dramatist, born in Prague. He became a Zionist and emigrated to Palestine in 1939. Although he is known in the English-speaking world as the long-time friend, editor and biographer of **Franz Kafka**, he was a versatile and prolific writer in his own right.

BRODIE, Sir Benjamin Collins, (1783–1862) English surgeon, born at Winterslow Rectory, Wiltshire. He studied at St George's Hospital where he became surgeon. He advocated conservative treatment of diseases of joints, thereby reducing the number of amputations.

BROEDERLAM, Melchior (fl.1381–1409) Netherlandish painter, born in Ypres. He became court painter to **Philip the Bold**, Duke of Burgundy, in 1387, and was in Paris in 1390. For the Chartreuse de Champmol, Philip's main religious foundation, he was commissioned in 1392 to paint a pair of shutters for an altarpiece. Now held in Dijon, these are his only known surviving works. They are among the earliest examples of the elegant, refined richly-decorative style known as International Gothic. He was also a goldsmith and stained-glass designer, and worked on many secular decorative projects for the duke.

BROGAN, Sir Denis William (1900–74) Scottish historian, born in Rutherglen, near Glasgow, of Irish descent. Educated at Glasgow, Oxford, and Harvard, he became a fellow of Corpus Christi College, Oxford, in 1934, and professor of political science at Cambridge in 1939. He is known for his books on historical and modern America, such as *The American Political System* (1933) and *Introduction to American Politics* (1954), as well as more general works, such as *The English People* (1943) and *The French Nation* (1957).

BROGLIE, Achille Charles Léonce Victor (1785–1870) French politician, grandson of **Victor Broglie**, and son of Prince Claude Victor (1757–94). He distinguished himself as a Liberal politician and advocate of the abolition of slavery, and became foreign secretary and prime minister (1835–36) under **Louis-Philippe** (1757–94). An Academician, he published *Écrits et discours* (1863) and his *Souvenirs* (1866).

BROGLIE, Jacques Victor Albert (1821–1901) French historian and statesman, son of **Achille Charles Léonce Victor Broglie**. He was ambassador to Britain and twice premier (1873, 1877). His historical works include *L'Église et L'Empire romain au IVe siècle* (1856), a study of the empress Marie Thérèse (wife of **Louis XIV**), and two hostile works on **Frederick II, 'the Great'**.

BROGLIE, Louis César Victor Maurice, 6th Duc de (1875–1960) French physicist, grandson of Jacques Victor Albert (4th Duc). He was famed for his researches in X-ray spectra.

BROGLIE, Louis Victor, 7th Duc de (1892–1987) French physicist, younger brother of **Louis César Victor Maurice** (6th Duc). He did research on the quantum theory, and won the Nobel prize for physics in 1929 for his pioneer work on the undulatory theory of matter.

BROGLIE, Victor François (1718–1804) French soldier, son of **Jacques Broglie**. He was the most capable French commander in the Seven Years' War (1756–63). After the revolution he went into exile and entered Russian service.

BROKE, Sir Philip Bowes Vere (1776–1841) English naval commander, born in Broke Hall, Ipswich. He entered the navy in 1792, was promoted captain in 1801, and appointed to the frigate *Shannon* in 1806. In her he fought a memorable duel with the American frigate *Chesapeake*, off Boston, on 1 June 1813, which made 'brave Broke' a hero in popular song. He succeeded in capturing the *Chesapeake*, but was wounded so severely that he retired from active service.

BROME, Richard (d.c.1652) English dramatist, of whom little is known except that he had been in his earlier days servant to **Ben Jonson**, and that he wrote as many as 24 popular plays, the best being *The Northern Lass* and *The Jovial Crew*.

BROMFIELD, Louis (1896–1956) American novelist, born in Mansfield, Ohio, the son of a farmer. Educated at Cornell Agricultural College and Columbia University, he joined the French army in 1914, was awarded the *croix de guerre*, and returned to journalism in America. His novels include *The Green Bay Tree* (1924), *Early Autumn* (1926, Pulitzer prize), *The Strange Case of Miss Annie Spragge* (1928), *The Rains Came* (1937), *Until the Day Break* (1942), *Colorado* (1947), and *Mr Smith* (1951). His short stories include *Awake and Rehearse* (1929), and his plays *The House of Women* (1927).

BRONGNIART, Alexandre (1770–1847) French naturalist and geologist, born in Paris. From 1808 professor at the Sorbonne and Museum of Natural History, he was also director of the porcelain manufactory at Sèvres from 1800. He introduced the term *Jurassic* for the limestones and clays of the Cotswolds. His son Adolphe Théodore (1801–76) was a noted botanist.

BRONHILL, June, originally **June Gough** (1929–) Australian soprano, born in the mining town of Broken Hill, New South Wales, from which she adapted her stage name. After coming third to **Joan Sutherland** in the Sydney *Sun* Aria competition (1949), and winning it the following year, her home town raised funds to send her to London for further study. In 1954 she made an immediate success at Sadler's Wells in musicals such as *Robert and Elizabeth* and *The Sound of Music*, and in operetta, particularly as *The Merry Widow*. Later, she took the lead in *Lucia di Lammermoor* at Covent Garden, London (1959).

BRØNSTED, Johannes Nicolaus (1879–1947) Danish physical chemist, born in Varde. He studied engineering and chemistry at the Polytechnic Institute, Copenhagen, and became professor of chemistry there in 1908. He is known for a novel and valuable definition of acids and bases, the Brønsted-Lowry definition, which defines an acid as a substance with a tendency to lose a proton, and a base as a substance that tends to gain a proton.

BRONTË, originally **Brunty** or **Prunty,** the name of three sisters, **Anne, Charlotte** and **Emily**, remarkable in English literary history, born in Thornton, Yorkshire. They were the daughters of Patrick Brontë (1777–1861), a clergyman of Irish descent and his Cornish wife, Maria (1783–1821), and sisters of Maria and Elizabeth, who both died in childhood, and Branwell (1817–48), a brother who squandered his many talents. The family moved to Haworth, now part of Keighley, in 1820 when their father became rector there. After the mother's death from cancer, her sister came to look after the children. Their childhood, spent in the sole companionship of one another on the wild Yorkshire moors, was happy enough. Branwell's twelve toy soldiers inspired them to construct two fantasy worlds of their own, *Gondal* and *Angria*, which contained all the exotic places and was peopled by all the great figures they had read about. Incidents in these were described by the children in verse and prose in rival collections of notebooks. Such escapism did not prepare them for their harsh schooling at Cowan Bridge, but Roe Head, their second school, proved more amenable. Branwell's debts caused them to leave home and find employment, but they always returned to their beloved Haworth.

BRONTË, Anne, pseud **Acton Bell** (1820–49) She went as governess to the Inghams at Blake Hall in 1839 and to the Robinsons at Thorpe Green (1841–45), a post she had to leave because of Branwell's unfortunate love for Mrs Robinson. She shared in the joint publication, under pseudonyms, of the three sisters' *Poems* (1846), only two volumes of which were sold. Her two novels, *Agnes Grey* (1845) and *The Tenant of Wildfell Hall* (1848), although unsuccessful at the time, show a decided talent, if less vivid than that of her sisters.

BRONTË, Charlotte, pseud **Currer Bell** (1816–55) She returned in 1835 to her old school, Roe Head, as teacher, but gave up this post and two others, both as governess. Back at Haworth, the three sisters planned to start a school of their own and, to augment their qualifications, Charlotte and Emily attended the Héger Pensionat in Brussels (1842). Their plans foundered, however, and Charlotte returned to Brussels as an English teacher (1843–44) and formed an unreciprocated attachment to the married M Héger, whom she later scornfully satirized in *Villette* (1852). Her chance discovery of Emily's remarkable poems in 1845 led to the abortive joint publication, under pseudonyms, of the three sisters' *Poems* (1846). This provoked them all to novel-writing. *The Professor*, which did not achieve publication until Charlotte's death, dwells on the theme of moral madness, possibly inspired by Branwell's degeneration. It was rejected by her publisher, but with sufficient encouragement for her to complete her masterpiece, *Jane Eyre* (1847). This in essence, through the master-pupil love relationship between Rochester and Jane, constituted a magnificent plea for feminine equality with men in the avowal of their passions. It was followed in 1849 by *Shirley*, a novel set in the background of the Luddite riots. By now her brother and two sisters were dead, and she was left alone at Haworth with her father. *Villette*, founded on her memories of Brussels, was published in 1853. She married her father's curate, Arthur Bell Nicholls, in 1854 and died during pregnancy in the following year, leaving the fragment of another novel, *Emma*. Two stories, *The Secret* and *Lily Hart*, were published for the first time in 1978.

BRONTË, Emily Jane, pseud **Ellis Bell** (1818–48) In 1837 she became a governess in Halifax. She attended the Héger Pensionat in Brussels with Charlotte and in 1845 embarked upon a joint publication of poems after the discovery by the latter of her *Gondal* verse, including such fine items at *To Imagination*, *Plead for Me*, and *Last Lines*. Her single novel, *Wuthering Heights* (1847), an intense and powerful tale of love and revenge set in the remote wilds of 18th-century Yorkshire, has much in common with Greek tragedy.

BRONZINO, IL, properly **Agnolo di Cosimo di Mariano** (1502–72) Italian Mannerist painter, born in Monticelli. He was a pupil of Rafaello del Garbo and of **Pontormo**, who adopted him. He decorated the chapel of the Palazzo Vecchio in Florence, and painted the *Christ in Limbo* in the Uffizi (1552). His *Venus, Folly, Cupid and Time* is in the National Gallery, and his portraits include most of the **Medici** family, also **Dante**, **Boccaccio**, and **Petrarch**. His nephew, **Alessandro Allori,** and nephew's son, both Florentine painters, adopted his name.

BROOK, Peter Stephen Paul (1925–) British theatre and film director, educated at Westminster, Greshams and Magdalen College, Oxford. His involvement in the theatre began while at university—his first work as director was a production of **Marlowe**'s *Dr Faustus* presented in London in 1943. In 1944 he joined a film company which he left the following year to direct **Cocteau**'s *The Infernal Machine*, after which he directed many classical plays at the Birmingham Repertory Theatre, including a notable production of **Shakespeare**'s *King John*. In his first season at Stratford, in 1947, he showed his formidable originality in a *Romeo and Juliet* that did not meet with wide critical acclaim. From 1947 to 1950 he was also director of productions at the Royal Opera House, Covent Garden, directing a memorable **Dali**-designed *Salome*. During the 1950s he worked on many productions in Britain, Europe and America, including a French version of **Arthur Miller**'s *Death of a Salesman* at the Belgian National Theatre in 1951, and the 1953 revival of **Otway**'s *Venice Preserved*. In 1962 he returned to Stratford to join the newly-established Royal Shakespeare Company for which he directed, among other productions, the legendary **Paul Schofield** *King Lear* (1963), **Peter Weiss**'s *Marat/Sade* (1964), *U.S.* (1966), and in 1970 his greatly acclaimed *Midsummer Night's Dream*. Most of his work in the 1970s was done with the Paris-based Centre for Theatre Research, which he helped to set up in 1970 and with which he has travelled widely in Africa and Asia; in 1978 he again returned to Stratford to direct *Antony and Cleopatra*. Among his films are *The Beggar's Opera* (1952), *Lord of the Flies* (1962), *The Marat/Sade* (1967), *King Lear* (1969) and *Meetings With Remarkable Men* (1979). In 1988 he directed a production of *The Mahabharata* in Glasgow. Later Paris productions include a nine-hour adaptation of *The Mahabharata*, which subsequently toured the world. Brook's work in difficult to categorize and difficult to assess, although he is acknowledged to be 'the director's director'.

BROOKE, Sir Basil Stanlake See **BROOKE-BOROUGH**

BROOKE, Henry (c.1703–1783) Irish dramatist and novelist, born in Rantavan County Cavan. He became the friend of **Pope** and married his cousin and ward. His poem *Universal Beauty* (1735) is supposed to have suggested **Erasmus Darwin**'s *Botanic Garden*. His novel, *The Fool of Quality* (1766), is the sole survivor of his numerous works.

BROOKE, Sir James (1803–68) English soldier, and rajah of Sarawak. Born in Benares in India, and educated in Norwich, he sailed in 1838 in a schooner-yacht from London for Sarawak, a province on the northwest coast of Borneo, with the object of putting down piracy, and was made rajah of Sarawak (1841) for assistance rendered to the sultan of Borneo against Dayak rebel tribes. Brooke instituted free trade, framed a new code of laws, declared the Dayak custom of head-hunting a capital crime, and vigorously set about the extirpation of piracy. In 1857 Brooke, superseded in the governorship of Labuan but still acting as rajah of Sarawak, sustained successfully, with his native forces, a series of attacks by a large body of Chinese, who were irritated at his efforts to prevent opium-smuggling. He was succeeded as rajah in 1868 by his nephew Sir Charles Johnson (1829–1917), who changed his name to Brooke. He was succeeded in turn in 1917 by his son Sir Charles Vyner (1874–1963), who in 1946 ceded Sarawak to the British crown.

BROOKE, (Bernard) Joycelyn (1908–66) English novelist, poet and amateur botanist, born in Kent. After running away from boarding school twice he settled at Bedales before going to Worcester College, Oxford, emerging without distinction. He tried various occupations before joining the family wine firm. During World War II he enlisted in the Royal Army Medical Corps, and re-enlisted after the war; but the army in peacetime was not to his liking and following the critical success of *The Military Orchid* (1948) he bought himself out and thereafter devoted himself to writing. He followed this with the second and third parts of the overtly autobiographical trilogy (known subsequently as *The Orchid Trilogy*), *A Mine of Serpents* (1949) and *The Goose Cathedral* (1950), the former drawing heavily on his obsession with pyrotechnics. His works also include two volumes of poetry, *December Spring* (1946) and *The Elements of Death* (1952); a Kafkaesque novel, *The Image of a Drawn Sword* (1950), and botanical books.

BROOKE, Lord See **GREVILLE, Sir Fulke**

BROOKE, Rupert Chawner (1887–1915) English poet, born in Rugby. Educated at King's College, Cambridge, he travelled in Germany and visited the USA and Tahiti. He died a commissioned officer on Skyros on his way to the Dardanelles and was buried there. His *Poems* appeared in 1911, *1914 and Other Poems* in 1915, after his death. If lacking the insight of a maturer poet, his poetry was characterized by a youthful, self-probing honesty, a fresh perception, a gentle lyricism and comedy. These, together with his handsome appearance and untimely death, made him a favourite poet among young people in the interwar period.

BROOKE, Stopford Augustus (1832–1916) Irish clergyman and man of letters, born in Letterkenny, Donegal. An outstanding preacher, he was appointed a royal chaplain in 1872 but through inability to continue to believe in miracles, he seceded from the Church of England, but continued to preach in his proprietary chapel as Unitarian minister. He published numerous popular works, including *Theology in the English Poets* (1874), *Primer of English Literature* (1876), and *English Literature to the Conquest* (1898).

BROOKEBOROUGH, Basil Stanlake Brooke, 1st Viscount (1888–1973) Irish statesman, born in Fermanagh. Elected to the Northern Ireland parliament in 1929, he became minister of agriculture in 1933, of commerce in 1941, and prime minister from 1943 till his resignation in 1963. A staunch supporter of Unionist policy, he exhibited an unswerving determination to preserve the ties between Northern Ireland and the UK. He retired from politics in 1968.

BROOKES, Sir Norman Everard (1877–1968) Australian tennis player, born in Melbourne. He went to Wimbledon in 1905, winning the allcomers' singles title, and returned the following year to win the singles, doubles, and mixed doubles titles. In the same year, he and Anthony Wilding achieved Australasia's first victory in the Davis Cup. He won again at Wimbledon in 1914 and, after service in World War I, played Davis-Cup tennis until 1921, captaining six winning teams. He was also a national golf champion. He was appointed Chevalier du Légion d'Honneur by France, and was knighted in 1939.

BROOKNER, Anita (1928–) English novelist and art historian, born in London. An authority on 18th-century painting, she was the first woman Slade professor at Cambridge University (1967–68), and has been a reader at the Courtauld Institute of Art since 1977. She is the author of *Watteau* (1968), *The Genius of the Future* (1971) and *Jacques-Louis David* (1981). As a novelist she was a late starter, but in eight years (1981–88) she published as many novels, elegant, witty and imbued with cosmopolitan melancholy. Invariably, her main characters are women, self-sufficient in all but love. By winning the Booker prize, *Hôtel du Lac* (1984) has become her best-known novel and is regarded by many as her most accomplished. Other titles include *Family and Friends* (1985), and *Friends from England* (1987).

BROOKS, Charles William Shirley (1816–74) English journalist and novelist, born in London. He wrote dramas and newspaper articles. In 1870 he succeeded **Mark Lemon** as editor of *Punch*. His novels include *Aspen Court* (1855) and *The Gordian Knot* (1860).

BROOKS, Phillips (1835–93) American Protestant Episcopal bishop, born in Boston. He studied at Harvard, and after serving cures in Philadelphia and Boston, was consecrated bishop of Massachusetts in 1891. A keen thinker and powerful preacher, he opposed the theory of apostolic succession, but is best known for his Yale *Lectures on Preaching* (1877).

BROOKS, Van Wyck (1886–1963) American author and critic, born in Plainfield, New Jersey. He wrote biographical studies of **Mark Twain** (1920), **Henry James** (1925), and **Emerson** (1932), attacked American materialism, and won the Pulitzer prize with his *Flowering of New England* (1936), a study in literary history.

BROOM, Robert (1866–1951) Scots-born South African palaeontologist, born in Paisley. He graduated in medicine from Glasgow and practised in Australia before moving to South Africa in 1897 as a general physician. He was appointed professor of zoology and geology at Victoria College (1903–10), where in 1934 he became palaeontologist at the Transvaal Museum, Pretoria. In 1936 he began to study fossil hominids and concluded that **Raymond Dart** was correct in his view that *Australopithecus africanus* is an ancestor of man. In 1947 he found a partial skeleton of this hominid (*Australopithecus*) including the pelvis, which proved that he had walked upright, about 1–2 million years ago. His studies on human ancestry are given in his book *Finding the Missing Link* (1950). He also wrote *The Coming of Man* (1933).

BROONZY, Big Bill (William Lee Conley) (1898–1958) American blues singer, composer and musician, born in Scott, Mississippi. He began musical life as a fiddler, but switched to guitar when he moved to Chicago in 1920. He was one of the most eclectic stylists among the great blues performers, encompassing American folk-song and jazz as well as rural and urban blues. For much of his career his appearances were confined to small clubs and bars throughout the USA, but in the 1950s the folk-music revival and international interests in traditional jazz and blues brought him a wider audience, and he toured extensively, performing in Europe, Africa and South America.

BROSCHI, Carlo (1705–82) Italian singer, born in Naples. Under the name 'Farinelli' he became the most famous of castrato singers. He visited London in 1734; and in Spain was made a grandee, with a pension of £2000 a year.

BROSSE, Salomon de (1565–1626) French architect to **Marie de' Medici**. He designed the Luxembourg Palace in Paris (1615–20), and **Louis XIII**'s hunting lodge (1624–26), the nucleus of Versailles.

BROSSES, Charles de (1709–77) French historian, born in Dijon. Among his works were *Lettres sur Herculaneum* (1750), *Histoire des navigations aux terres australes* (1756), and *Du culte des dieux fétiches* (1760, the word *fétich* being first used by him in the sense now usual). He was president of the parliament of Burgundy when he died.

BROTHERS, Richard (1757–1824) English religious fanatic and ex-naval officer, born in Newfoundland. He announced himself in 1793 as the 'nephew of the Almighty', apostle of a new religion, the Anglo-Israelites. In 1795, for prophesying the destruction of the monarchy, he was sent to Newgate and subsequently to an asylum, but not before he had acquired a number of disciples, some of them men of influence and standing.

BROUGHAM, Henry Peter, 1st Baron Brougham and Vaux (1778–1868) Scottish jurist and politician, born in Edinburgh; his father was of an old Westmorland family, and his mother a niece of the historian **William Robertson**. Educated at the High School and Edinburgh University, he helped in 1802 to found the *Edinburgh Review*. His liberal views excluded him from hope of promotion in Scotland and in 1805 he settled in London; in 1806 he was secretary to a mission to Lisbon; and in 1808 was called to the English bar. Entering parliament in 1810, he carried an act making participation in the slave trade a felony. In 1812 he carried the repeal of the Orders in Council; but, contesting Liverpool against **George Canning**, was defeated, and remained without a seat till 1816, when he was returned for Winchelsea. He never acquired a very large practice at the bar, but he repeatedly distinguished himself by speeches of great vigour and ability—his most famous appearance being in defence of Queen **Caroline of Brunswick** (1820). His eloquence and boldness made him a popular hero for some time (1820–30). In 1822 he tried to use his power in support of a scheme of national education; and he did much for the establishment of London University, of the first Mechanics' Institute, and of the Society for the Diffusion of Useful Knowledge. In 1828 he delivered a masterly speech on the need for law reform. In 1830 he was returned for the county of York. The aristocratic Whigs found him indispensible for the Reform ministry; he was persuaded to accept a peerage and the chancellorship (1830), and assisted materially in carrying the Reform Bill, but his arrogance, self-confidence, and eccentricities made him as unpopular with his colleagues as he was on the bench. He went out with the Whig government in 1834, and on its reconstruction was shelved, never to hold office again. He was founder of the Social Science Association (1857); but it is as a law reformer that Brougham will be best remembered. In 1816 he introduced a bill amending the law of libel, and in 1827 made proposals for dealing with law reform on a large scale. He was responsible for the creation of the Judicial Committee of the privy council and the central criminal court. After he left office, he secured great changes in the law of evidence. As an orator and as a debater in parliament he was inferior only to Canning, though he often carried fiery declamation and fierce invective too far. His miscellaneous writings cover an almost incredible variety of subjects, but have little permanent value. His own *Life and Times* (3 vols, 1871), written in extreme old age, is very untrustworthy. The brougham (carriage) is named after him.

BROUGHTON, Lord See **HOBHOUSE, John Cam**

BROUGHTON, William Grant (1788–1853) English prelate, and first Anglican bishop of Sydney, born in Westminster, London. He worked as a clerk in East India House for five years before going to Cambridge. Ordained in 1818, he ministered in Hampshire before accepting an invitation from the Duke of **Wellington** to become the second archdeacon of New South Wales. He arrived in Sydney in 1829 to supervise a huge territory which extended over all of Australia and some regions beyond. When the post was elevated to a see in 1836 he became bishop of Australia. With the division in 1847 into more manageable dioceses he was restyled bishop of Sydney and metropolitan of Australia. A high churchman with Tractarian sympathies, he had to counter Anglicans of liberal and (to a lesser extent) of evangelical traditions, but he worked hard to lay this far-flung province of the Church of England on a sound foundation.

BROUNCKER, William, 2nd Viscount Brouncker of Castle Lyons (1620–84) Irish mathematician. Educated at Oxford, he was a founder member and first president of the Royal Society. He expressed π as a continued fraction, and found expressions for the logarithm as an infinite series. He was a friend of **Samuel Pepys**, often mentioned in his *Diary*.

BROUSSAIS, François Joseph Victor (1772–1838) French physician, born in St-Malo, founder of a theory of medicine which strongly resembles the Brunonian system of **John Brown** (1735–88). He served as a surgeon in the navy and army, and subsequently was appointed a professor at Val-de-Grâce. He viewed disease as the ultimate result of inflammation of the gastro-intestinal tract.

BROUWER, or **Bauer, Adriaen** (c.1605–1638) Flemish painter, born in Oudenarde. He studied at Haarlem under **Frans Hals**, and about 1630 settled at Antwerp, where he died of the plague. His favourite subjects were scenes from tavern life, country merry-makings, card players, smoking and drinking groups, and roisterers generally.

BROUWER, Luitzen Egbertus Jan (1881–1966) Dutch mathematician, born in Overschie. He showed precocious intellectual powers and entered Amsterdam University at the age of 16, where he was professor from 1912 to 1951. His doctoral thesis was on the foundations of mathematics, an area in which he continued to work throughout his life. He founded the intuitionist or constructivist school of mathematical logic, which does not accept the law of the excluded middle, and in which the existence of a mathematical object can only be proved by giving an explicit method for its construction. This places severe restrictions on much modern mathematics, and has not been accepted by mathematicians in general, though it continues to interest logicians and philosophers. He also made fundamental advances in topology, introducing the concept of simplicial approximation, the degree of a mapping, and proving the invariance of dimension, and the fixed point theorem named after him.

BROWN, Sir Arthur Whitten (1886–1948), British aviator, born in Glasgow of American parents. As navigator with Sir **John William Alcock** he made the first non-stop crossing of the Atlantic in a Vickers-Vimy biplane on 14 June 1919, and shared a £10000 prize given by the London *Daily Mail*. Both men were knighted after the flight.

BROWN, 'Capability' See **BROWN, Lancelot**

BROWN, Charles Brockden (1771–1810) American novelist, born of Quaker ancestry in Philadelphia. He was the first professional American writer. *Wieland* (1798), *Ormund* (1799), and *Jane Talbot* (1804), among many others, are Gothic romances, full of incident and subtle analysis, but extravagant in style.

BROWN, Ford Madox (1821–93) British historical painter, grandson of the physician **John Brown** (c.1735–1788), born in Calais. He studied art at Bruges, Ghent, and Antwerp; in Paris he produced his *Manfred on the Jungfrau* (1841), a work intensely dramatic in feeling, but sombre in colouring. He contributed to the Westminster cartoon competitions. A visit to Italy (1845) led him to seek a greater variety and richness of colouring, as in *Chaucer reciting his Poetry* (1851). He contributed verse, prose, and design to the Pre-Raphaelite *Germ*, and in his youth **Dante Gabriel Rossetti** worked in his studio. He was a close associate of **William Morris**, and in 1861 was a founder member of Morris, Marshall, Faulkner & Company (later Morris & Company) for which he produced some designs for furniture and stained glass. Among his maturer works are *Christ washing Peter's Feet* and *The Entombment*. He completed twelve frescoes for Manchester Town Hall, just before his death.

BROWN, George Alfred See **GEORGE-BROWN**

BROWN, George Douglas (1869–1902) Scottish writer, born in Ochiltree, Ayrshire, the illegitimate son of a farmer. Educated at the village school and Ayr Academy, he went to Glasgow University and Balliol College, Oxford, on a scholarship. He settled in London as a journalist, published a boys' adventure book, *Love and Sword* (1899), but made his name, under the pseudonym 'George Douglas', with *The House with the Green Shutters* (1901), a powerfully realistic novel, an antidote to the 'Kailyard School'. He died of pneumonia before completing two other novels.

BROWN, (James) Gordon (1951–) Scottish politician. The son of a Church of Scotland minister, he won a first in history at Edinburgh University before he was 20, and went on to complete his doctorate. While still a student there he was elected rector of Edinburgh University (1972–75). After experience as a lecturer and television journalist, he entered the House of Commons in 1983, as Labour member for Dunfermline East. Despite losing the sight of one eye in a sporting accident, he is an avid reader and meticulous researcher and this, combined with his formidable debating skills, made his rise within the Labour party unusually swift. At the age of 38 he topped the Labour party shadow cabinet poll.

BROWN, Henry Kirke (1814–86) American sculptor, born in Leyden, Massachusetts. He returned in 1846 from Italy to Brooklyn and executed statues of **Lincoln** and **Washington** in Union Square, New York, amongst many others.

BROWN, Herbert Charles (1912–) English-born American chemist, born in London. His family moved to Chicago when he was two. Despite acute financial difficulty he eventually studied at Chicago University and later became professor at Purdue University, Indiana. He shared, with **Georg Wittig**, the Nobel prize for chemistry in 1979 for their work in introducing boron compounds as important reagents in synthesis.

BROWN, James (1928–) American black pop singer, songwriter and producer, born in Barnwell, South Carolina. He began his professional career backed by a former gospel group, The Famous Flames, with whom he recorded his first 'cry' ballads, 'Please, Please, Please' and 'Try Me' (1958). Mixing gospel and blues roots with his own aggressive energy, he put together a band and roadshow which by 1962 had made him America's leading rhythm and blues star and earned him the nickname 'Soul Brother Number One'. 'Out Of Sight' (1964) brought him his first international success. During the late 1960s he courted controversy with what was perceived as an ambiguous stance on racial politics, recording both 'America Is My Home' and 'Say It Loud, I'm Black and I'm Proud'. An enduring influence on black pop music, he was one of the first entertainers to assume complete control of his own career. In 1988 he was jailed for six years on charges that included aggravated assault. His songs have included 'Papa's Got A Brand New Bag' (1965), 'It's A Man's Man's Man's World' (1966), 'Ain't It Funky Now' (1969), 'Sex Machine' (1970) and 'Get Up Offa That Thing' (1976).

BROWN, Jim (James) (1936–) American college and professional footballer, born in St Simon Island, Georgia. An All-American halfback at Syracuse University (1956), he had nine outstanding years with the Cleveland Browns in the National League (1957–66), during which he led the league eight times in rushing. Later he had a successful film career in Hollywood. He also made several forays into politics.

BROWN, John (1722–87) Scottish clergyman and theologian, born in Carpow, near Abernethy, Perthshire. A boy herdsman, he had little schooling, but taught himself Greek, Latin and Hebrew. For a time he was a pedlar; during 1745 he served in the Fife militia; he taught in several schools, and having studied theology in connection with the Associate Burgher Synod, in 1750 he was called to the congregation of Haddington. In 1768 he accepted the Burgher chair of divinity at Glasgow. In 1778 he published his immensely popular biblical commentary, *Self-Interpreting Bible*.

BROWN, John (c.1735–1788) Scottish physician, founder of the Brunonian system of medicine, born of poor parents in Bunkle parish, Berwickshire. He taught at Duns and Edinburgh, and after studying medicine became assistant to Professor **William Cullen**. Thinking himself slighted by the professor, he began to give lectures himself on a new system of medicine, according to which all diseases are divided into the sthenic, depending on an excess of excitement, and the asthenic; the former to be removed by debilitating medicines, and the latter by stimulants. He also condemned the practice of bloodletting.

BROWN, John (1800–59) American abolitionist, born in Torrington, Connecticut, of Pilgrim descent. He was sucessively tanner and land surveyor, shepherd and farmer; and, a strong abolitionist, wandered through the country on anti-slavery enterprises. He was twice married and had 20 children. In 1854 five of his sons moved to Kansas, and, joining them after the border conflict had begun, Brown became a leader in the strife. In reprisal, he once ordered five pro-slavery men at Pottawatomie to be shot. Osawatomie, Brown's home, was burned in 1856, and one of his sons killed. When the war in Kansas ceased, Brown began to drill men in Iowa. His next scheme was to establish a stronghold in the mountains of Virginia as a refuge for runaway slaves, and in 1859 he made a harebrained attack on the Federal arsenal at Harper's Ferry in Virginia. On the night of 16 October, with 18 men, he seized the armoury and took several citizens prisoner. On 18 October the arsenal was stormed by Colonel **Robert E Lee** with a company of marines. Brown and six men, barricading themselves in an engine-house, continued to fight until two of Brown's sons were killed and he was severely wounded. Tried by a Virginia court for insurrection, treason, and murder, he was convicted and hanged at Charlestown, Virginia. Four of his men were executed with him, and two others later. The song 'John Brown's body lies a-mouldering in the grave', commemorating the Harper's Ferry raid, was highly popular with Republican soldiers as a marching song in the Civil War.

BROWN, John (1810–82) Scottish physician and essayist, born in Biggar. He attended the High School of Edinburgh and studied medicine at the university there. He wrote *Horae subsecivae* (Leisure Hours, 1858–61) and *John Leech and other Papers* (1882). Humour and pathos are the chief features of his style, as exemplified in his essay on the human nature of dogs in 'Rab and his Friends' and 'Pet Marjorie', an essay on the child writer **Margaret Fleming**.

BROWN, Sir John (1816–96) English industrialist, founder of the Atlas Steel Works at Sheffield, employing 4500 workers. He invented the process of rolling armour-plate, and was one of the first to make rolled steel rails.

BROWN, John (1826–83) Scottish retainer, born in Craithenaird, Balmoral. For 34 years he was Queen **Victoria**'s personal attendant at Balmoral. He died at Windsor.

BROWN, Lancelot, known as **'Capability Brown'** (1716–83) English landscape-gardener, born in Kirkharle, Northumberland. He established a purely English style of garden lay-out, using simple artifices to produce natural effects, as at the laid-out gardens at Blenheim, Kew, Stowe, Warwick Castle, and others. He got his nickname from telling clients that their gardens had excellent 'capabilities'.

BROWN, Michael Stuart (1941–) American molecular geneticist, joint winner of the 1985 Nobel prize for physiology or medicine. He studied medicine at Pennsylvania and worked on the research staff at the National Institutes of Health (1968–71) before becoming professor at the Southwestern Medical School at Texas University in 1971. He conducted research into cholesterol metabolism with **Joseph Goldstein** at Texas, leading to the discovery of low-density or LDL receptors, for which they were awarded the Nobel prize.

BROWN, Oliver Madox (1855–74) English author and artist, born in Finchley, son of **Ford Madox Brown**. At twelve he painted a watercolour of considerable merit. In 1871 he wrote his first novel, *Gabriel Denver*, reprinted in his *Literary Remains* (1876) under its first title *The Black Swan*. He died of food poisoning.

BROWN, Peter Hume (1850–1918) Scottish historian, born near Haddington. He studied at Edinburgh and was author of Lives of **George Buchanan** (1890), **John Knox** (1895), and **Goethe** (1920), and wrote a *History of Scotland* (1898–1909). In 1898 he became editor of the Privy Council Register of Scotland, in 1901 professor of ancient Scottish history at Edinburgh and in 1908 historiographer royal for Scotland.

BROWN, Robert (1773–1858) Scottish botanist, born in Montrose, the son of an Episcopal clergyman. Educated at Aberdeen and Edinburgh, he served with a Scottish regiment in Ireland (1795). In 1798 he visited London, where his ability so impressed Sir **Joseph Banks** that he was appointed naturalist to **Matthew Flinders**'s coastal survey of Australia in 1801–05. He brought back nearly 4000 species of plants for classification. Appointed librarian to the Linnaean Society, he published *Prodromus Florae Novae Hollandiae et insulae Van-diemen* (1810). He adopted, with modifications, the **Jussieu** natural system of plant classification, thus encouraging its general acceptance in place of **Linnaeus**'s artifical 'sexual system'. In 1810 he received charge of Banks' library and splendid collections; and when they were transferred to the British Museum in 1827 he became botanical keeper there. He is renowned for his investigation into the impregnation of plants. He was the first to note that, in general, living cells contain a nucleus, and to name it. In 1827 he first observed the 'Brownian movement' of fine particles in a liquid, significant in shaping physicists' later ideas on liquids and gases.

BROWN, Thomas (1778–1820) Scottish philosopher, born in Kirkmabreck Manse, Kirkcudbrightshire. He studied first law then medicine at Edinburgh, and in 1810 became a colleague (and then successor) to **Dugald Stewart**. He had original contributions to make both to philosophy and psychology, but never developed these fully as a result of his early death and his own unfortunate preference for his indifferent poetical works.

BROWN, Thomas (1663–1704) English satirist, born possibly in Shifnal or, more probably, Newport, Shropshire. As a student at Christ Church College, Oxford, he produced his famous extempore adaptation of **Martial**'s 33rd epigram, 'Non amo te, Sabidi', at the demand of Dr **John Fell**, the dean: 'I do not love thee, Dr Fell'. After teaching at Kingston-on-Thames, he settled in London, where he made an uncertain living by writing scurrilous satirical poems and pamphlets, and published *Amusements Serious and Comical* (1700). He was buried in the Westminster cloisters near his friend, Mrs **Aphra Behn**.

BROWN, Trisha (1936–) American choreographer, born in Aberdeen, Washington. A meeting with the dancer **Yvonne Rainer** at a West Coast summer school under the direction of the experimental choreographer and dancer Anna Halprin, led her to New York in 1961. There, along with Rainer and others, she founded the experimental Judson Dance Company in 1962. Throughout the 1960s and 1970s she created a series of daringly original 'equipment pieces' where dancers were rigged in block and tackle harness to allow them to walk on walls or down the trunks of trees. *Walking of the Walls*, *Man Walking Down the Side of a Building* and *Spiral* are from this period, along with *Roof Piece* (1973), which dotted dancers across Manhattan roofs, signalling to one another. Between 1970 and 1976 she ran an improvisational group, Grand Union. In the late 1970s she began to work in traditional theatres, adding design and music to her pieces for the first time. **Robert Rauschenberg**, the American painter, designed for several of her works, including *Glacial Decoy* (1979) and *Set and Reset* (1983).

BROWN-SÉQUARD, Édouard (1817–94) French physiologist, born in Port Louis, Mauritius, the son of a Philadelphia sea captain and a lady called Séquard. He studied at Paris, devoted himself to physiological research, and received many prizes for his experiments on blood, muscular irritability, animal heat, the spinal cord, and the nervous system. He was professor of physiology at Harvard (1864), at the School of Medicine in Paris (1869–73), and the Collège de France (from 1878).

BROWNE, Edward Granville (1862–1926) English oriental scholar. Professor at Cambridge (1902–26), he devoted himself chiefly to Persian, and wrote a monumental *Literary History of Persia* (1902–24).

BROWNE, Edward Harold (1811–91) English prelate and theologian. He was Norrisian professor of divinity at Cambridge (from 1854), bishop of Ely (1864) and bishop of Winchester in 1873. His *Exposition of the Thirty-Nine Articles* (1850) is a standard work.

BROWNE, Felicia Dorothea See **HEMANS**

BROWNE, Hablot Knight, pseud **Phiz** (1815–82) English illustrator, born in Kennington, London. He was apprenticed to a line engraver, but soon took to etching and watercolour painting, and in 1833 gained a medal from the Society of Arts for an etching of 'John Gilpin'. In 1836 he became illustrator of *The Pickwick Papers*, and maintained his reputation by his designs for other works by **Dickens**. His son, Gordon F Browne (1858–1932), was a well-known book illustrator.

BROWNE, Charles Farrar, pseud **Artemus Ward** (1834–67), American humorist, born in Waterford, Maine. In 1858 he wrote for the *Cleveland Plaindealer* a description of an imaginary travelling menagerie, followed by letters in which grotesque spelling and a mixture of business platitudes and sermonizing served to convey sound sense and shrewd satire. In 1861, as Artemus Ward, he entered the lecture field, and started a panorama, whose artistic wretchedness gave rise to countless jokes. In 1864 he contracted tuberculosis; but in 1866 he went to London, where he contributed to *Punch*, and was very popular as 'the genial showman', exhibiting his panorama at the Egyptian Hall. His publications included *Artemus Ward, His Book* (1862), and *Artemus Ward, His Panorama* (1865).

BROWNE, Robert (c.1550–c.1633) English clergyman, founder of the Brownists, born in Tolethorpe, Rutland. After graduating from Cambridge in 1572, he became a schoolmaster in London, and an open-air preacher. In 1580 he began to attack the established church, and soon after formed a distinct church on congregational principles at Norwich. Committed to the custody of the sheriff, he was released through the influence of his kinsman, **William Cecil**, Lord Burghley; but in 1581, he was obliged to take refuge with his followers at Middelburg, in Holland. In 1584 he returned, via Scotland, to England, and reconciling himself to the church, in 1586 became master of Stamford grammar school, and in 1591 rector of Achurch, Northamptonshire. Of a very violent temper, he was sent to Northampton jail at the age of 80 for an assault on a constable, and he died in jail. The Brownists may be said to have given birth to the Independents or Congregationalists.

BROWNE, Sir Samuel James (1824–1901) British soldier, born in India, the son of a doctor. He joined the Indian army in 1849 and fought in the battles of Chilianwalla and Goojerat in the 2nd Sikh War (1848–49). During the Indian Mutiny (1857–58) he saw much service, including action at Lucknow and at Seerporah, where he lost his left arm and won a VC. He was promoted to general in 1888; the 'Sam Browne' sword-belt is attributed to him.

BROWNE, Sir Thomas (1605–82) English author and physician, born in London. Educated at Winchester College and at Pembroke College, Oxford, he studied medicine, travelled in Ireland, France, and Italy, continued his medical studies at Montpellier and Padua, graduated as Doctor of Medicine at Leiden and at Oxford, and settled in 1637 at Norwich, where he lived and practised the rest of his life. He was knighted by **Charles II** on his visit to Norwich in 1671. He was buried in the church of St Peter Mancroft. His greatest work is his earliest, the *Religio Medici*, written about 1635—a sort of confession of faith, revealing a deep insight into the dim mysteries of the spiritual life. The surreptitious publication of two editions in 1642 obliged him to issue an authorized edition in 1643. *Pseudodoxia Epidemica, or Enquiries into ... Vulgar and Common Errors* (1646), a strange and discursive amalgam of humour, acuteness, learning, and credulity, is by far the most elaborate of his works. *Hydriotaphia; Urn Burial* (1658), mainly a discussion of burial customs, shows all his vast and curious learning set in language of rich and gorgeous eloquence. The *Garden of Cyrus* (1658), the most fantastic of Browne's writings, aims to show that the number five pervaded not only all the horticulture of antiquity, but that it recurs throughout all plant life, as well as in the 'figurations' of animals. After his death appeared *Miscellany Tracts* (1683), *Letter to a Friend* (1690), and *Christian Morals* (1716), an incomplete work, evidently intended to be a continuation of the *Religio Medici*. Browne's favourite theme is the mystery of death.

BROWNE, Thomas A See **BOLDREWOOD, Rolf**

BROWNE, Tom (1870–1910) English strip cartoonist, illustrator and painter, born in Nottingham. The 'father of British comic style' with his creation of *Weary Willie and Tired Tim*, he was first apprenticed to a lithographer and freelanced his first strip to *Scraps* (1880). Moving to London, he quickly became a popular cartoonist for magazines, posters and picture postcards. When *Comic Cuts* was launched (1890), his bold linear style proved perfect for cheap reproduction, and he was soon drawing front pages for several comics a week. His two tramps, inspired by Don Quixote and Sancho Panza, were instantly popular, and continued to appear in *Chips* 40 years after his death.

BROWNE, Ulysses Maximilian, Count von, Baron de Camus (1705–57) Austrian soldier, born in Basel of an Irish Jacobite family. He became one of the foremost generals in the Austrian army, commanding forces in Italy in the War of the Austrian Succession (1740–48) and in the Seven Years' War (1756–63). He was killed at the battle of Prague.

BROWNE, William (1591–1643) English pastoral poet, born in Tavistock, Devon. Educated at Exeter College, Oxford, he entered the Inner Temple, and was then tutor to Robert Dormer, the future Earl of Carnarvon. His finest poetry is to be found in the three-volumed *Britannia's Pastorals* (1613–52) and in the *Inner Temple Masque* (1615).

BROWNING, Elizabeth, née **Barrett** (1806–61) English poet, born in Coxhoe Hall, Durham, wife of **Robert Browning**. She spent her girlhood mostly on her father's estate, at Hope Hill in Herefordshire. At 10 she read **Homer** in the original, and at 14 wrote an epic on *The Battle of Marathon*. In her teens she developed a tubercular complaint that damaged her spine, and was an invalid for a long time. The family ultimately settled in 50 Wimpole Street, London, in 1837. Her *Essay on Mind, and Other Poems*, was published in 1826 when she was 19. In 1833 she issued a translation of **Aeschylus**' *Prometheus Bound*. This was succeeded by *The Seraphim, and Other Poems* (1838), in which volume was republished the fine poem on **Cowper**'s grave. When she was staying at Torquay, her brother and a party of friends were drowned there in a boating expedition, and the shock confined her for many years to the sickroom. In 1844 appeared *Poems*, which contained 'The Cry of the Children', an outburst against the employment of young children in factories. In 1845 she first met Robert Browning, six years her junior, who freed her from her sickroom and a possessive father by marrying her the following year. They settled in Pisa (1846), and then Florence (1847), where their son Robert was born in 1849. They became the centre of a brilliant literary circle there. The *Poems* of 1850 contained an entirely new translation of the *Prometheus Bound*. In *Casa Guidi Windows* (1851) she expressed her sympathy with the regeneration of Italy. *Aurora Leigh* (1856) is a long narrative poem into which all the treasures of its writer's mind and heart have been poured. In *Poems before Congress* (1860) she again manifested her interest in Italian freedom. Her so-called *Sonnets from the Portuguese* (published in the *Poems* of 1850) are not translations at all, but express her own love for the country ('my little Portuguese' was Browning's pet name for her). Her *Last Poems* were published the following year.

BROWNING, John Moses (1855–1926) American gunsmith and inventor, born in Ogden, Utah, the son of a Mormon gunsmith. He produced his first gun from scrap metal at the age of 13. He patented a breech-loading single-shot rifle in 1879, and the Browning automatic pistol in 1911. The Browning machine gun (1917) and the Browning automatic rifle (1918) became standard army weapons for many years.

BROWNING, Oscar (1837–1923) English schoolmaster, historian and educational reformer, born in London. Educated at Eton and King's College, Cambridge, he was a fellow from 1859 until his death, since by never marrying he was therefore not obliged to vacate his fellowship. Assistant master and housemaster at Eton from 1860, he was dismissed in 1857 on unsubstantiated charges of intimacy with boys. He returned to King's unbroken in spirit, and became lecturer in history at King's, 1880, and university lecturer, 1883. An exceptionally popular tutor, he helped to found the Cambridge University day training college and was principal, 1891–1909. He retired to Rome and wrote most of his historical works in his last years, including *A History of the Modern World, 1815–1910* (2 vols, 1912). He was an indomitable optimist who never allowed misfortune to cloud his pleasure in life.

BROWNING, Robert (1812–89) English poet, and husband of **Elizabeth Browning**, born in Camberwell, the only son of a Bank of England clerk. He attended lectures briefly at University College, London and then travelled abroad. *Pauline*, a dramatic poem, written at the age of 20, was published anonymously in 1833. He made a visit to St Petersburg (Leningrad), and on his return *Paracelsus* (1835) won him some recognition in literary circles; but *Sordello* (1840) was a failure. He wrote several dramas and dramatic poems, which were published as 'Bells and Pomegranates' in *Dramatic Romances and Lyrics*, which also contained 'My Last Duchess' 'Soliloquy of the Spanish Cloister', 'The Pied Piper of Hamelin', 'Home Thoughts from Abroad', and many other familiar and much loved poems. In 1846 he married Elizabeth Barrett, and with her settled first in Pisa (1846) and then in Florence (1847); their son, Robert Barrett (1849–1912), who became a sculptor, was born there. In 1855 he published *Men and Women*, which contained such poems as 'Fra Lippo Lippi', 'Childe Roland to the Dark Tower Came', and 'Andrea del Sarte'. After the death of his wife (1861) he settled permanently in London with his son. His masterpiece, *The Ring and the Book*, published in four volumes (1868–69), is an epic dealing searchingly with passions of humanity, and has for its basis the narrative of a murder by an Italian count, as related by the various persons concerned. Browning's poetry is distinguished by its depth of spiritual insight and power of psychological analysis; and he invented new kinds of narrative structure which have taken the place of the epic and the pastoral. In his play, *Pippa Passes* (1841), for example, a girl's song binds together a variety of scenes. His other chief works are *Dramatis Personae* (1864), *Fifine at the Fair* (1872), *The Inn Album* (1875), *Pacchiarotto* (1876), and *Asolando* (1889).

BROWNLEE, John (1900–69) Australian operatic baritone, born in Geelong, Victoria. He studied at Melbourne and Paris, where he made his début in 1926. **Nellie Melba** then engaged him to sing opposite her in *La Bohème* at Covent Garden, London, thus beginning his distinguished international career. He was a regular soloist with the Paris Opéra until 1936, a founding soloist with the Glyndebourne Festival Opera, and made many records. He made his first appearance with the Metropolitan Opera, New York, in 1937 as Rigoletto and appeared there regularly until 1958. As director of the Manhattan School of Music he spent the remaining years of his life in Manhattan.

BROWNRIGG, Sir Robert (1759–1833) English soldier. Governor of Ceylon from 1811 to 1820, he conquered the Kandyan kingdom in 1814–15 and was promoted to general in 1819.

BROWNSON, Orestes Augustus (1803–76) American clergyman and writer, born in Stockbridge, Vermont. He was successively a Presbyterian, a Universalist, a Unitarian pastor and, from 1844, a Roman Catholic. He founded and edited *Brownson's Quarterly Review* (1844–65, and 1872 onwards), and wrote many books, including *The Convert* (1857) and *The American Republic* (1865).

BRUBECK, Dave (David Warren) (1920–) American pianist, composer and bandleader, born in Concord, California. Tutored from childhood by his mother, a classical pianist, he went on to study music at the College of the Pacific, Stockton, California, leading a twelve-piece jazz band and at the same time studying composition under **Darius Milhaud**. Towards the end of World War II he was stationed in Europe, leading a service band, but in 1946 he resumed his studies and began to make his reputation as an experimental musician with his Jazz Workshop Ensemble. He reached a wider public with the Dave Brubeck Quartet formed in 1951, including alto saxophonist Paul Desmond. Desmond's composition 'Take Five' in 5/4 time, became one of the most popular recordings in jazz. Brubeck has also composed larger works such as ballets, a mass, and pieces for jazz group and orchestra, and he continued to tour and record with small groups through the 1980s.

BRUCE, Christopher (1945–) English dancer-choreographer, born in Leicester. He studied tap, acrobatics and ballet, and on graduating from the Ballet Rambert School (1963) immediately joined the company. In 1967 he established his reputation in **Glen Tetley**'s *Pierrot lunaire*. Within two years of this he had choreographed his first piece for Rambert, *George Frideric*, an abstract dance laced with drama. Later works include *Ancient Voices of Children* (1975), *Cruel Garden* (1977, with **Lindsay Kemp**), *Ghost Dances* (1981) and *Swansong* (1987). His work is a fusion of classical and modern dance idioms, with a strong undercurrent of social consciousness. Since 1985 he has been associate choreographer of English National

Ballet (formerly London Festival Ballet). He is now a resident choreographer of Houston Ballet.

BRUCE, Sir David (1855–1931) Scottish microbiologist and physician, born in Australia, after whom the cattle disease brucellosis is named. As an officer in the Royal Army Medical Corps (1883–1919), he identified in Malta the bacterium that causes undulant fever in humans, named *Brucella* (1887). In 1895 in South Africa he also discovered that the tsetse fly was the carrier of the protozoal parasite (*Trypanosoma brucei*) responsible for the cattle disease nagana, and sleeping sickness in humans. He was commandant of the Royal Army Medical College in World War I.

BRUCE, Frederick Fyvie (1910–) Scottish classicist and biblical scholar, born in Elgin, Morayshire, son of a Plymouth Brethren preacher. He was educated at Aberdeen, Cambridge and Vienna, and taught at Edinburgh, Leeds and Sheffield before moving to the historic Rylands chair of biblical criticism and exegesis at Manchester (1959–78). A welcome speaker and lecturer in evangelical circles, he edited the *Evangelical Quarterly* (1949–80) and *Palestine Exploration Quarterly* (1957–71). An indefatigable writer, he produced commentaries on nearly every New Testament book. Among his many other works are *The Books and the Parchments* (1950), *Second Thoughts on the Dead Sea Scrolls* (1956), *Israel and the Nations* (1963), *New Testament History* (1969), *Paul and Jesus* (1974), *History of the Bible in English* (1979), the autobiographical *In Retrospect* (1980), and *The Real Jesus* (1985).

BRUCE, James (1730–94) Scottish explorer, known as 'the Abyssinian', born in Stirlingshire. He became consul-general in Algiers (1763–65), and in 1768 journeyed to Abyssinia by the Nile, Assouan, the Red Sea, and Massowah. In 1770 he reached the source of the Abbai, or headstream of the Blue Nile, then considered the main stream of the Nile. His *Travels to Discover the Sources of the Nile* was published in 1790, but contained such curious accounts of the manners of the Abyssinians that many considered them fictitious at the time.

BRUCE, James See **ELGIN, 8th Earl of**

BRUCE, Lenny, originally **Leonard Alfred Schneider** (1925–66) American satirical comedian, born in New York. He had a variety of jobs after leaving the US navy in 1946, and first appeared as a night-club performer in Baltimore. The satire and 'black' humour of his largely improvised act often overstepped the bounds of what was considered respectable; in 1961 he was imprisoned for obscenity, and in 1963, a year after his first appearance at the Establishment Club in London, he was refused permission to enter Britain to fulfil a further engagement. In May 1963 he was found guilty of illegal possession of drugs, and it was his use of these which contributed to his death three years later. He was one of the first comedians who sought to disturb rather than amuse with his observation of the violence and brutalities of the mid twentieth century.

BRUCE, Robert (c.1078–1141) Scottish nobleman, son of **Robert de Bruis (Bruce)**, a companion in arms of Prince David of Scotland, afterwards **David I**, from whom he got the lordship of Annandale. Robert renounced his allegiance to David in the war in England between **Stephen** and **Matilda**, niece of the king of Scots.

BRUCE, Robert (d.1245) Scotish nobleman, 4th Lord of Annandale. He married Isabel, second daughter of David, Earl of Huntingdon and Chester, brother of King **William the Lion**, and thus founded the royal house of Bruce.

BRUCE, Robert (1274–1329) king of Scotland from 1306, as **Robert I** hero of the Scottish War of Independence, born either at Turnberry or in Essex. In 1296, as Earl of Carrick, he swore fealty to **Edward I** at Berwick, and in 1297 renewed his oath of homage at Carlisle. Shortly after, with his Carrick vassals, he joined the Scottish revolt under **William Wallace**. He was appointed one of the four guardians of Scotland in 1298, but did not again fight against Edward until the final rising in 1306. His stabbing of John Comyn, the nephew of **Balliol** and a rival with a better claim to the throne, in the church of the Minorite Friars at Dumfries (10 February 1306), allowed him to assert his own rights and two months later he was crowned king at Scone. His career between 1306 and 1314 saw the emergence of a master of guerrilla warfare into a national leader, despite scepticism by some as to his legal status. Two defeats in 1306, one by an English army at Perth, the other by the lord of Argyll, a kinsman of the **Comyns**, at Dalry, forced him to flee, probably to Rathlin Island off the north coast of Ireland. The turnabout in his fortunes between 1307 and 1309 began, predictably, in his own territory of the south-west, with the defeat of an English force at Loudoun in May 1307. The death of Edward I the following July brought to the English throne a king, **Edward II**, who lacked his father's iron will and drive. By 1309 Robert was able to hold his first parliament, which was, however, attended only by Bruce supporters. Spectacular military success between 1310 and 1314, when he won control of northern Scotland, resolved the doubts of many. A series of strongholds were recaptured, leaving only Lothian outside his control. In early 1314 the castles of Edinburgh and Roxburgh also fell to him, leaving Stirling as the only English stronghold north of the Forth. The victory at Bannockburn, near Stirling, over a larger English army of nearly 20000 men on 24 June 1314 did not end the Anglo-Scottish war, which went on until 1328 or later, but it did virtually settle the Scottish civil war, leaving Robert I unchallenged. For ten years the north of England was raided and a second front was opened up by his brother, Edward, in Ireland in 1315. The Declaration of Arbroath, composed in 1320 by his chancellor, Bernard de Linton, and a mission to Avignon, finally persuaded Pope **John XXII** to recognize Robert as king in 1323. A truce with England brought hostilities to an end in 1323, but Robert took advantage of the accession of the young **Edward III** in 1327 to force the Treaty of Northampton (1328), which secured English acknowledgement of Scottish independence and his own right to the throne.

BRUCE, Robert (1554–1631) Scottish churchman, born in Airth, the son of the laird. He became laird of Kinnaird, and from 1587 to 1600 he was a presbyterian minister in Edinburgh. He annointed Queen **Anne of Denmark** at her coronation in 1590 as wife of **James VI** of Scotland, but he opposed James's attempts to introduce episcopacy, and was banished to Inverness in 1605. He wrote *Sermons on the Sacraments*.

BRUCE, Robert de, 5th Lord of Annandale (1210–95) Scottish nobleman. He did homage to **Henry III** in 1251, on the death of his mother, for her lands in England, and was made sheriff of Cumberland and constable of Carlisle. On the Scottish throne becoming vacant at the death in 1290 of **Margaret, 'Maid of Norway'**, granddaughter of **Alexander III, John de Baliol** and Bruce claimed the succession. **Edward I** of England as umpire decided in favour of Baliol in 1292. To avoid swearing fealty to his successful rival, Bruce resigned Annandale to his eldest son, **Robert de Bruce** (1253–1304).

BRUCE, Robert de (1253–1304) Scottish nobleman, eldest son of **Robert de Bruce** (1210–95). He is said to have accompanied **Edward I** of England to Palestine in 1269. In 1271 he married Marjory, Countess of Carrick, and in her right became Earl of Carrick. In 1292 he resigned the earldom to his eldest son, **Robert the Bruce** (1274–1329), the future King Robert I. On the death of his father in 1295 he did homage to Edward for his English lands, was made constable of Carlisle, and fought for the English against **John de Baliol**. On Baliol's defeat he applied to Edward for the crown, but was refused it.

BRUCE, Robert de Bruis (d.c.1094) Norman knight, who accompanied **William I, 'the Conqueror'** to England in 1066. The name is traced to the domain of Bruis near Cherbourg. He received extensive lands in Yorkshire.

BRUCE, Stanley Melbourne, 1st Viscount Bruce of Melbourne (1883–1967) Australian politician. He entered parliament in 1918, and represented Australia in the League of Nations Assembly. He was premier of Australia 1923–29, and from 1933 to 1945 was high commissioner in London and represented Australia at meetings of **Churchill**'s war cabinet. He settled in England for the last 20 years of his life.

BRUCE, Sir William, of Kinross (1630–1710) Scottish architect, born at Blairhall. He was appointed king's surveyor and master of works in 1671, and rebuilt the palace of Holyrood in Edinburgh from 1671 to 1679. He also designed part of Hopetoun House in West Lothian.

BRUCH, Max (1838–1920) German composer, born in Cologne. He became musical director at Coblenz in 1865, and conducted the Liverpool Philharmonic Society (1880–83), introducing many of his choral works. He is best known, however, for his violin concerto in G minor, the *Kol Nidrei* variations in which he employs the idioms of Hebrew and Celtic traditional melodies, and the *Konzertstück*.

BRUCKNER, Anton (1824–96) Austrian composer, born in Ansfelden. At ten he was deputizing for his schoolmaster father at the church organ, and in 1837 was a choral scholar at the Church of St Florian, where he himself became a teacher in 1845. His early sacred choruses reflect this background, and his sense of religion was always immensely strong. Later he became organist at Linz Cathedral. In 1856, feeling that he still needed a thorough grounding in compositional technique, he began a five-year correspondence course in advanced harmony and counterpoint with a Viennese teacher, Simon Sechter. Following this rigorous, self-imposed training and slow growth to maturity, Bruckner wrote his first orchestral works. After two 'apprentice' symphonies he wrote the Symphony No. 1 in 1865–66. At this time he came to admire **Wagner** and his music. 1868 saw the last of three great choral-orchestral Masses, and his appointment as professor at the Vienna Conservatory. Vienna remained his home thereafter; he became a university professor there in 1875, but never lost his simplicity of character and rural accent. He rarely travelled, but gave organ recitals in France (1869) and London (1871). The story of Bruckner's last 25 years is really that of his symphonies: his creation of new concepts of form and unity, and his struggle to achieve success in the face of critical opposition. His friends in Vienna included **Mahler**, **Wolf** and the conductors **Richter**, Levi, Mottle and **Nikisch**. He wrote a String Quintet for the violinist Hellmesberger. A *Te Deum* followed in 1884, the year his Seventh Symphony had an enormously successful première; but criticism of his Symphony No. 8 weakened his confidence and led to years of feverish revision of earlier scores. He thus lost time for new compositions and was beset by ill-health in his last six years, and so left the finale of the Ninth Symphony incomplete when he died.

BRUDENELL, James Thomas See **CARDIGAN**

BRUEGHEL, or **Breughel, Jan the Elder** (1568–1625) Flemish artist, younger son of **Pieter Brueghel**, called 'Velvet' Breughel. He painted still life, flowers, landscapes and religious subjects, generally on a small scale. His son, Jan the Younger (1601–78), imitated him closely.

BRUEGHEL, or **Breughel, Pieter the Elder** (c.1520–1569) Flemish artist, born in the village of Bruegel, near Breda. His name is variously spelt and he is called the Elder to distinguish him from his son, **Pieter Brueghel the Younger**. An early influence on his work was **Bosch**. He was made a master of the Antwerp guild in 1551 and then embarked upon a journey to Italy, although curiously he seems to have been unaffected by the Italian Mannerism he must have encountered. His work was highly regarded, particularly by **Rubens**, and much of it was bought for royal collections. His reputation went into decline, however, until the beginning of this century. The most typical pictures depict earthy peasants engaging in all sorts of activities against a backdrop of well-observed landscape, and the truthfulness of his rendering of peasant life and weather conditions marks his work out from the Italianate style of his Netherlandish contemporaries. More than mere mirrors of life around him, his pictures are often highly sophisticated moral commentaries derived from everyday sayings and proverbs. This genre reached its highest expression in his later works, *The Blind Leading the Blind* (1568), *The Peasant Wedding* (1568) and *The Peasant Dance* (1568). His principal works are in Vienna but there are two superb examples, *The Adoration of the Kings* and *The Death of the Virgin*, in the London National Gallery.

BRUEGHEL, or **Breughel, Pieter the Younger** (c.1564–1638) Flemish painter, son of **Pieter Brueghel the Elder**. He was called 'Hell' Breughel because he painted *diableries*, scenes with devils, hags or robbers.

BRUGMANN, Karl (1849–1919) German philologist, born in Wiesbaden. Professor of Sanskrit at Freiburg (1884) and Leipzig (1887), he wrote a *Comparative Grammar of the Indo-Germanic Languages* (1886–83), supplemented by three volumes on syntax by **Delbruck**. He was a leading exponent of the Neo-Grammarian school, stressing the fixity of sound laws.

BRUGSCH, Heinrich Karl (1827–94) German Egyptologist, born in Berlin. In 1853 he first visited Egypt, and subsequently alternated between Egypt and Germany as professor, or as consul for Germany. He was director of the School of Egyptology in Cairo, 1870–90. He helped to decipher demotic script, and published a hieroglyphic-demotic dictionary (1867–82). He wrote many books, including *Egypt under the Pharaohs* (1879).

BRÜHL, Heinrich, Count von (1700–63) Saxon politician. The unworthy prime minister of **Augustus III**, king of Poland and Elector of Saxony, with the basest sycophancy he humoured the whims of his luxurious master, draining the coffers of the state, and burdening the country with debt. He himself meanwhile maintained a splendid and costly establishment.

BRUHN, Erik Belton Evers (1928–86) Danish dancer and ballet director, born in Copenhagen. After a decade training at the Royal Danish Ballet School, he joined the company in 1947 to become the epitome of the elegant classical male dancer. An unrivalled exponent of the buoyant **Bournonville** style, he toured the world as guest performer with many companies, appearing to great acclaim in such ballets as *Sleeping Beauty* and *La Sylphide*. He was equally forceful in dramatic roles from the modern repertory (eg **Roland Petit**'s *Carmen*, **Birgit Cullberg**'s *Miss Julie*). He later took on character roles, including Dr Coppelius in his own production of *Coppelia* (1975). He was the director of the Royal Swedish Ballet (1967–72) and artistic director of the National Ballet of Canada (1983–86).

BRUMBY, Colin James (1933–) Australian composer and teacher, born in Melbourne, where he studied at the Conservatorium of Music. He subsequently studied in Europe with Philipp Jarnach and **Alexander Goehr**, returning to become senior lecturer at the University of Queensland, Brisbane, where he was head of the music department from 1975 to 1980, and is now associate professor. His considerable output includes two operas, nine operettas for younger audiences, nine concertos, *Alice: Memories of Childhood* for the Queensland Ballet, choral works, film scores and chamber music, much of which has been recorded. Major works include a flute concerto and his *Festival Overture on Australian Themes* (1982), a symphony (1982), *Ballade for St Cecilia* (1971), and *The Phoenix and the Turtle* (1974).

BRUMEL, Valeri Nikolayevich (1942–) Soviet athlete, born in Siberia. He won the Olympic gold medal in the high jump at Tokyo in 1964, and between 1960 and 1963 raised the world record to 2.28 metres.

BRUMMELL, George Bryan, called **Beau Brummell** (1778–1840) English dandy, born in London, the son of Frederick, Lord **North**'s private secretary, and grandson of a gentleman's gentleman. At Eton, and during a brief sojourn at Oxford, he was less distinguished for studiousness than for the exquisiteness of his dress and manners; and after four years in the army, having come into a fortune, he entered on his true vocation of arbiter of elegancies. A close friend and protégé of the Prince Regent (the future **George IV**), he quarrelled with him in 1813, and in 1816 gambling debts forced Brummell to flee to Calais. From 1830 to 1832 he held a sinecure consulate at Caen. He died there in the pauper lunatic asylum.

BRUNA, Dick (1927–) Dutch artist and writer. The creator of a highly successful series of dinky picture books for young children, he started in the book-trade but gave this up to concentrate on graphic art. His first book was *The Apple*, published in England in 1966, 13 years after it appeared in Holland. His great success came from 1959 onwards when his books began to appear in their now-familiar format. Many of these featured Miffy, others the small dog Snuffy. Among his most popular books is *B is for Bear*, first published in Dutch in 1967.

BRUNDAGE, Avery (1887–1975) American international athletics administrator, born in Detroit. He was a member of the US decathlon team in the 1912 Olympic games at Stockholm, but was far more influential in his long spell as president of the US Olympic Association from 1929 to 1953, and in his 20 years as president of the International Olympic Committee (1952–72). From a patrician background, he was criticized for his rigid adherence to the letter of the Olympian law and his insistence on the strictest tenets of amateurism, but he fought hard to preserve the games from some of the commercial excesses which have since afflicted them.

BRUNDTLAND, Gro Harlem (1939–) Norwegian Labour politician, and first woman prime minister of Norway, born in Oslo, the daughter of a doctor who became a cabinet minister. She studied medicine at Oslo and Harvard, qualifying as a physician. In 1960 she married a leader of the opposition Conservative party, Arne Olav, and they have four children. In 1969 she joined the Labour party and entered politics, after working in public medicine services in Oslo. She was appointed environment minister (1974–79) and then, as leader of the Labour party group, became prime minister in 1981. She was prime minister again in 1986, and in 1987 chaired the world commission on environment and development which produced the report *Our Common Future*. In 1988 she was awarded the Third World Foundation prize for leadership in environmental issues.

BRUNE, Guillaume Marie Anne (1762–1815) French soldier, and marshal of the First Empire, born in Brives-la-Gaillarde. He commanded the revolutionary army in the Netherlands (1799) and defeated the Russo-British forces (the latter commanded by **Frederick-Augustus**, Duke of York) at two battles of Bergen. He commanded under **Napoleon** in Italy (1800). On the emperor's return from Elba in 1815, Brune joined him, and was murdered by a royalist mob at Avignon.

BRUNEAU, Alfred (1857–1934) French composer and music critic, born in Paris. He studied at the Paris Conservatoire with **Massenet**. Although he wrote a choral symphony, lieder, and other works of a high order, he is best known for his operas based on **Zola**'s works, such as *Le Rêve* (1891) and *Messidor* (1897). On its first production, the latter suffered because of the composer's and Zola's unpopularity for championing **Dreyfus**. Three volumes of his criticisms were published in 1900–03.

BRUNEL, Isambard Kingdom (1806–59) English engineer and inventor, born in Portsmouth, son of Sir **Marc Isambard Brunel**. In 1823, after two years spent at the Collège Henri Quatre in Paris, he entered his father's office. He helped to plan the Thames Tunnel, and himself, in 1829–31, planned the Clifton Suspension Bridge, which was completed only in 1864 with the chains from his own Hungerford Suspension Bridge (1841–45) over the Thames at Charing Cross. He designed the *Great Western* (1838), the first steamship built to cross the Atlantic, and the *Great Britain* (1845), the first ocean screw-steamer (now preserved in Bristol). The *Great Eastern*, until 1899 the largest vessel ever built, was constructed to his design in collaboration (strained at times) with **John Scott Russell** from whose yard in Millwall the 'Great Ship' was launched at the second attempt in January 1858, three months late, and 40 years ahead of the technology of the time. In 1833 he was appointed engineer to the Great Western Railway, and constructed all the tunnels, bridges, and viaducts on that line. Among docks constructed or improved by him were those of Bristol, Monkwearmouth, Cardiff, and Milford Haven.

BRUNEL, Sir Marc Isambard (1769–1849) English engineer and inventor, born in Hacqueville near Rouen. During the French Revolution he escaped from Paris to the USA in 1793; in 1794 he was appointed to survey for the canal from Lake Champlain to the Hudson at Albany. He was afterwards an architect in New York, and chief engineer for the city. Returning to Europe in 1799, he married and settled in England. A plan submitted by him to the government for making block-pulleys by machinery was adopted in 1803, and on its completion in 1806 the saving on the first year was about £24000. He received £17000 as a reward. He constructed public works in Woolwich arsenal and Chatham dockyard, and made experiments in steam navigation on the Thames in 1812, but his scheme for steam-tugs was declined by the navy board. The destruction of his sawmills at Battersea by fire (1814) led to his bankruptcy (1821), when he was thrown into prison for debt. He was released on a grant of £5000 being made by the government. His most remarkable undertaking was the Thames Tunnel from Rotherhithe to Wapping (1825–43), for which he used the tunnelling shield he had patented in 1818.

BRUNELLESCHI, Filippo (1377–1446) Italian architect, goldsmith and sculptor. One of the figures responsible for the development of the Renaissance style in Florence, his chief claim to fame is the dome of the cathedral there. Erected between 1420 and 1461, it is (measured diametrically) the largest in the world and served as the model for **Michelangelo**'s design for Saint Peter's in Rome. Other well-known buildings by him in Florence are S Spirito, San Lorenzo, and the Ospedale degli Innocenti. He is said to have turned his talents to architecture after defeat by **Ghiberti** in the competition for the Florence Cathedral baptistery doors (the competition panels entered by both men are in the Bargello Museum). The wooden crucifix in the church of S Maria Novella was designed by him in private competition with **Donatello**. He is also to be noted for his innovations in the use of perspective.

BRUNER, Jerome Seymour (1915–) American psychologist, born in New York City, noted for his contributions to cognitive development and curriculum design. Educated at Duke University and Harvard, he was professor of psychology at Harvard (1952–72), Oxford (1972–80), and the New School for Social Research, New York. He has been exceptionally influential on both sides of the Atlantic. His book *The Process of Education* (1960) established his reputation as a curriculum innovator. In a number of works published in the 1960s he stressed the centrality of teaching for underlying cognitive structure and the usefulness of the 'spiral curriculum'. His humanities programme 'Man: A Course of Study', described in *Toward a Theory of Instruction* (1966), has been held to be a landmark in curriculum development. He has also pioneered techniques for investigating infant perception. The leading advocate of the value of the phenomenological tradition in psychology, he has attacked the radical behaviourism of **Burrhus Frederic Skinner** as having distracted the subject from a proper regard for the main problems of humanity.

BRUNET, Jacques Charles (1780–1867) French bibliographer, born in Paris. He compiled a great bibliographical dictionary, *Manuel du libraire et de l'amateur des livres* (1810).

BRUNHILDE (567–613) Frankish queen, the daughter of the Visigothic king Athanagild. She married King Sigbert of Austrasia, and afterwards, as regent for her two grandsons, Theodebert II, king of Austrasia, and Theodoric II, king of Burgundy, divided the government of the whole Frankish world with her rival **Fredegond**, who governed Neustria for the youthful Clotaire II. On Fredegond's death in 598 she seized Neustria, and for a time united under her rule the whole Merovingian dominions, but was overthrown by the Austrasian nobels under Clotaire II, and put to death by being dragged at the heels of a wild horse.

BRUNI, Leonardo (1369–1444) Italian humanist, born in Arezzo, and hence styled **Aretino**. Papal secretary in 1405–15, he then wrote *Historia Florentina*, and was made chancellor of Florence in 1427. Bruni aided the advance of the study of Greek literature mainly by his literal translations into Latin of **Aristotle**, **Demosthenes**, **Plato**, and others; he also wrote Lives of **Petrarch** and **Dante** in Italian.

BRÜNING, Heinrich (1885–1970) German statesman, born in Münster. He studied at Bonn and the London School of Economics, and was leader of the Catholic Centre party from 1929, and chancellor from 1930 to 1932, when he was forced to resign by the Nazis. In 1934 he left Germany. He was professor of government at Harvard (1939–52), and professor of political science at Cologne (1951–55).

BRUNNE See **ROBERT MANNYNG**

BRUNNER, (Heinrich) Emil (1889–1966) Swiss Reformed theologian, born in Winterthur, near Zürich. Following service as a pastor (1916–24), he became professor of systematic and practical theology at Zürich (1924–55), and visiting professor at the International Christian University, Toyko (1953–55). The author of nearly 400 books and articles, his reputation outside the continent was established by translations of *The Mediator* (1927) and *The Divine Imperative* (1937). *The Divine-Human Encounter* (1944) reveals his debt to **Martin Buber**'s 'I-Thou' understanding of the relationship between God and Man, but he parted company in 1934 with the dialectical theology of the early **Karl Barth** by holding that there *was* a limited universal revelation of God in creation.

BRUNNER, Heinrich (1840–1915) German legal historian, whose work has been fundamental for the study and understanding of early German law and institutions. His main works were *Deutsche Rechtsgeschichte* (1887) and *Grundzuge der deutschen Rechtsgeschichte* (1901).

BRUNNER, Thomas (1821–74) New Zealand explorer. At the age of 20 he joined the New Zealand Company as a surveyor and was sent as a first settler to the Nelson Haven site on South Island. In 1846 he set out to search for accessible grazing lands in the province, and explored extensively until 1848 when he arrived at the Buller outlet from Rotoiti after a journey of 550 days, during which he lived almost entirely off the land with the help of his loyal Maori guide, Kehu. In this time he had traced the two main rivers, the Buller and the Grey, from their source to the coast, and discovered coal, but without recognizing its significance. He later became chief surveyor and commissioner of public works.

BRÜNNICH, Morten Thrane (1737–1827) Danish naturalist and zoologist, born in Copenhagen, the son of a portrait painter. He studied theology and oriental languages, but turned to the natural sciences under the influence of **Linnaeus**. He wrote *A History of the Eider Duck* (1763), and in 1764 published a book on northern birds, *Ornithologia Borealis*, followed by *Entomologia* in the same year. As lecturer in natural history and economy at Copenhagen, he established a natural history museum, and wrote *Zoologiae fundamenta* (1771). Regarded as the founder of Danish zoology, Brünnich's Guillemot is named after him.

BRUNNOW, Philipp Ivanovich, Count von (1797–1875) Russian diplomat, born in Dresden. He entered the Russian service in 1818, and was Russian ambassador in London both before and after the Crimean War.

BRUNO, St (925–65) German prelate, known as Bruno the Great. The third son of **Henry the Fowler**, and brother of **Otto I, 'the Great'**, he was imperial chancellor in 940. In 953 he crushed a rebellion against Otto. He became archbishop of Cologne in 953, and Duke of Lorraine in 954. He was distinguished both for piety and learning. His feast day is 11 October.

BRUNO, St also known as **Boniface** (970–1009) German missionary, born in Querfurt. Educated at Magdeburg Cathedral School, he entered the monastery in Ravenna in 997. He worked as a missionary bishop in Poland, Hungary and the Ukraine. He reached Prussia but met fierce opposition, and was put to death with his companions. His feast day is 19 June.

BRUNO, Giordano (1548–1600) Italian philosopher and scientist, born in Nola near Naples. He became a Dominican friar but was too unorthodox to stay in the order, travelled widely, lecturing and teaching, in France, Germany, England and Italy. He propounded an extreme pantheistic philosophy whereby God animated the whole of creation as 'world-soul', and his enthusiastic championship of **Copernicus** and his astronomy brought him into conflict with the Inquisition. He was arrested in 1592 in Venice and after a seven-year trial was burned at the stake in Rome.

BRUNO OF COLOGNE, St (c.1030–1101) German churchman, born in Cologne, and founder of the Carthusian order. He became rector of the cathedral school at Reims, but, oppressed by the wickedness of his time, withdrew in 1084 to the wild mountains of Chartreuse, near Grenoble. Here with six friends he founded the austere Carthusian order on the site of the present Grande Chartreuse. In 1091, at the invitation of Pope **Urban II**, he established a second Carthusian monastery at Della Torre in Calabria, where he died. His feast day is 6 October.

BRUNOFF, Jean de and **Laurent de** (1899–1937, 1925–) French illustrators, father and son, creators of Babar the Elephant, hero of a series of picture books. Drawn originally by Jean, he first appeared in 1931 in *L'Histoire de Babar, le pétit éléphant* (trans 1933).

BRUNOT, Ferdinand (1860–1938) French philologist. Dean of the faculty of letters at the University of Paris, he wrote a history of the French language (1905–34) in relation to successive states of society.

BRUSILOV, Alexei (1856–1926) Russian soldier, born in Tiflis. He served in the war against Turkey (1877). In World War I he led the invasion of Galicia (1914) and in the Carpathians. From 1916 he distinguished himself on the eastern front, notably in command of South Western Army Group in the highly successful 'Brusilov Offensive' against the Austrians in 1916. He became chief of staff in 1917, but the second 'Ponsilov Offensive' was frustrated and his troops mutinied. After the revolution he commanded forces in the war against Poland (1920).

BRUSTEIN, Robert (1927–) American drama critic, teacher and director, born in New York. In 1966, as dean of the School of Drama at Yale University, he founded the Yale Repertory Theater. He is also director of the American Repertory Theater, which took up residence at Harvard University in 1980. He is the author of several books, including an erudite and entertaining book of collected essays under the title *Who Needs Theater* (1987).

BRUTUS, Lucius Junius (fl.500 BC) legendary Roman hero who established Republican government at Rome. The son of a rich Roman, on whose death **Lucius Tarquinius** seized the property and killed an elder brother, he himself escaped by feigning idiocy, from which he got his name (*Brutus* means 'stupid'). When popular indignation was roused at the outrage on **Lucretia**, he drove the royal family from Rome. He was elected one of the first two consuls (509 BC). He sentenced to death his own two sons for conspiring to restore the monarchy, and fell repelling an attack led by one of Tarquin's sons.

BRUTUS, Marcus Junius (85–42 BC) Roman politician. He sided with **Pompey** when the civil war broke out, but, after Pharsalial, submitted to **Caesar**, and was appointed governor of Cisalpine Gaul. He divorced his wife to marry Portia, the daughter of his master **Cato**. Cassius persuaded him to join the conspiracy against Caesar (44 BC); and, defeated by **Antonius Marcus** and **Augustus** at Philippi, he killed himself.

BRUYÈRE See **LA BRUYÉRE, Jean de**

BRY, Théodor de (1528–98) Flemish engraver and goldsmith, born in Liège. He settled in Frankfurt-am-Main about 1570 and established a printing house there. A well-known print of his is *The Procession of the Knights of the Garter under Queen Elizabeth*, the result of a visit to England.

BRYAN, William See **O'BRYAN**

BRYAN, William Jennings (1860–1925) American populist, lawyer and politician, born in Salem, Illinois, father of the feminist **Ruth Rohde**. He graduated from Illinois College in 1881, studied law at Chicago, and practised at Jacksonville and in Nebraska. Elected to congress in 1890, as Democratic candidate for the presidency he was crushingly defeated by **McKinley** in 1896 and 1900, and by **Taft** in 1908. A great populist stump-orator, founder and editor of *The Commoner*, he was appointed secretary of state by **Thomas Woodrow Wilson** (1913), but as an ardent pacifist resigned in June 1915 over America's second *Lusitania* note to Germany. He was leading an anti-Darwinian campaign when he died.

BRYANT, Bear (Paul Williams) (1913–83) American football coach, born in Kingsland, Arkansas. As a player (right end) with Alabama University football team, he won the 1935 Rose Bowl game. He started coaching in 1945 at Maryland, and from 1958 was coach at Alabama. He broke the all-time career victories record in 1981 with 315 victories (not broken until 1985), and is reported to have earned $450000 in a single season. He retired in 1982. At the university a hall and stadium are both named after him. He was previously head coach at Texas A and M college. In 1960 he wrote a book, *Building a Championship Football Team.*

BRYANT, William Cullen (1794–1878) American poet and journalist, born in Cummington, Massachusetts. He graduated in law and practised in Great Barrington, Massachusetts, from 1816, but in 1817 the majestic blank verse of *Thanatopsis* appeared. He continued to practise at the bar until 1825, but more and more turned to newspaper contributions in prose and verse, becoming co-owner and editor of the New York *Evening Post* in 1829. The paper was Democratic, but, having antislavery views, assisted in 1856 in forming the Republican party. Bryant's public addresses and letters to his paper on his visits to Europe and the West Indies were published in book form, and he also published volumes of his poetry.

BRYCE, David (1803–76) Scottish architect. In partnership with **William Burn** in Edinburgh, his speciality was the 'Scottish Baronial' style, exemplified in Fettes College and the Royal Infirmary, Edinburgh. He designed over 100 country houses.

BRYCE, James, 1st Viscount (1838–1922) British jurist and statesman, born in Belfast. He was educated at Glasgow High School and University, and Trinity College, Oxford, where he graduated in 1862 with a double first. Elected a fellow of Oriel, and called to the bar in 1867, he was Regius professor of civil law at Oxford, 1870–93, and entered parliament in 1880. Some of his teaching appeared as *Studies in History and Jurisprudence* (1901). In 1905 he was made Irish secretary, and from 1907 to 1913 was ambassador to the USA, signing the Anglo-American Arbitration Treaty in 1911. A strong home-ruler, he took an active interest in such issues as university reform and the eastern question. His works include *The Holy Roman Empire* (1864), *Transcaucasia and Ararat* (1877), and *The American Commonwealth* (1888).

BRYDEN, Bill (William) (1942–) Scottish stage director and dramatist, born in Greenock. He started as a documentary scriptwriter for Scottish Television (1963–64), before becoming assistant director at the Belgrade Theatre, Coventry (1965–67) and associate director of the Royal Lyceum Theatre, Edinburgh (1971–74). His productions at Edinburgh included two of his own plays, *Willie Rough* (1972), and *Benny Lynch* (1974), gritty dramas set in Scotland. From 1975 to 1985 he was an associate of the National Theatre, where he was director of the Cottesloe Theatre from 1978 to 1980. At the NT, he became particularly associated with directing plays by American authors. In 1985 he became head of drama for BBC Television Scotland. He has directed two films from his own screenplays: *Ill Fares the Land* (1982), and *The Holy City* (1985).

BRYDGES, Sir Samuel Egerton (1762–1837) English bibliographer and genealogist, born at Wootton House, Kent. He failed to establish his claim to the barony of Chandos, but was gratified with a Swedish knighthood in 1808 and an English baronetcy in 1814. He was MP for Maidstone 1812–18, and printed privately at the Lee Priory Press small editions of many rare Elizabethan books.

BRYUSSOV, Valery Yakovlevich (1873–1924) Russian poet, critic and translator, born in Moscow. He was one of the leaders of the Russian Symbolist movement which looked to France for its inspiration. Like **Balmont**, his best work was done before 1910, but unlike him his technique remained unimpaired to the last. He translated many of the major modernist writers in Europe, including **Verlaine**, **Mallarmé**, **Maeterlinck** and **D'Annunzio**. He became an enthusiastic Bolshevist in 1917 and worked tirelessly for that cause until his death.

BRZEZINSKI, Zbigniew (1928–) Polish-born American academic and politician, born in Warsaw, he settled in the USA and became a naturalized citizen in 1958. He taught at Harvard's Russian Research Center during the 1950s and then, as professor of public law and government, at Columbia University. A member of the state department's policy planning council during the **Johnson** administration, he became national security adviser to President **Carter** (1977–80) and was the chief architect of a tough human rights policy, directed against the Soviet Union. From 1981 he resumed his position at Columbia and taught at Georgetown University, producing influential works on strategic relations with the USSR and Japan.

BUBER, Martin (1878–1965) Austrian Jewish theologian and philosopher, born in Vienna. He studied philosophy at Vienna, Berlin and Zürich. He then became attracted to Hasidism, founded and edited a monthly journal *Der Jude* (1916–24), taught comparative religion at Frankfurt (1923–33), and directed a Jewish adult education programme until 1938 when he fled to Palestine to escape the Nazis and became professor of social philosophy at Jerusalem. He published profusely on social and ethical problems, but is best-known for his religious philosophy expounded most famously in *Ich und Du* (1923), contrasting personal relationships of mutuality and reciprocity with utilitarian or objective relationships.

BUCCLEUCH, Duke of See **SCOTT** family

BUCER, or **Butzer, Martin** (1491–1551) German Protestant reformer, born in Schlettstadt, in Alsace. He entered the Dominican order, and studied theology at Heidelberg. In 1521 he left the order, married a former nun, and in 1523 settled in Strasbourg. In the disputes between **Luther** and **Zwingli** he adopted a middle course. At the Diet of Augsburg he declined to subscribe to the proposed Confession of Faith, and afterwards drew up the *Confessio Tetrapolitana* (1530). He advised **Henry VIII** on his divorce from **Catherine of Aragon** (1533). At Wittenberg in 1536 he made an agreement with the Lutherans, but when attacked for his refusal to sign the *Interim* in 1548, he came to England on **Cranmer**'s invitation (1549) as Regius professor of theology at Cambridge, where he made many friends. In **Mary I**'s reign his remains were exhumed and burned. His chief work was a translation and exposition of the Psalms (1529).

BUCH, Leopold von (1774–1853) German geologist and traveller. He investigated volcanic processes and upheld the theory of 'elevation craters', since discarded.

BUCHAN, Earls of See under **COMYN, ERSKINE, David**, and **STEWART, Alexander**

BUCHAN, Hon Alastair Francis (1918–76) Scottish authority on geopolitics, the third son of **John Buchan** (Lord Tweedsmuir). Educated at Eton and Oxford, in 1939, when his father was governor-general of Canada, he was made junior fellow at Virginia University, but was commissioned in the Canadian army on the outbreak of World War II, taking part in the Dieppe Raid and becoming a major in the 14th Canadian Hussars. He graduated from *The Economist* (1948–51) to *The Observer* (1951–58), serving first as Washington and then as defence and diplomatic correspondent. He was director of the Institute for Strategic Studies from 1958 to 1969. In 1973 he delivered the Reith Lectures, published as *Change without War*, and was the author of a number of works on international relations as well as a life of **Walter Bagehot**, titled *The Spare Chancellor* (1959).

BUCHAN, Alexander (1829–1907) Scottish meteorologist, born in Kinnesswood, near Kinross. He became secretary of the Scottish Meteorological Society in 1860. He postulated the 'Buchan spells' theory, based on earlier statistics, that the British climate is subject to successive warm and cold spells falling approximately between certain dates each year.

BUCHAN, Elspeth, née **Simpson** (1738–91) Scottish religious, the wife of a potter. In 1784 she founded at Irvine a fanatical sect, the Buchanites, announcing herself to her 46 followers as the Woman of Revelations xii.

BUCHAN, John, 1st Baron Tweedsmuir (1875–1940) Scottish author and statesman, born in Perth, the son of a Free Church minister. He was educated at Hutcheson's Grammar School and Glasgow University and at Brasenose College, Oxford, where he won the Newdigate prize for poetry in 1898. In 1901 he was called to the bar and became private secretary to Lord **Milner**, high commissioner for South Africa. He returned in 1903 to become a director of Nelson's the publishers. During World War I he served on HQ staff until 1917, when he became director of information. He wrote *Nelson's History of the War* (1915–19), and became president of the Scottish History Society (1929–32). He was MP for the Scottish Universities (1927–35), and was raised to the peerage in 1935, when he became governor-general of Canada. In 1937 he was made a privy councillor, and chancellor of Edinburgh University. Despite his busy public life, Buchan wrote over 50 books, beginning with a series of essays, *Scholar Gipsies* (1896). His forte as a writer was for fast-moving adventure stories, which included *Prester John* (1910), *Huntingtower* (1922), *John MacNab*, and *Witch Wood* (1927). He became best known for his exciting counter-espionage thrillers featuring Richard Hanney, *The Thirty-Nine Steps* (1915), *Greenmantle* (1916), *The Three Hostages* (1924), and several others. Of his biographical works, *Montrose* (1928) and *Sir Walter Scott* (1932) are considered the best.

BUCHAN, William (1729–1805) Scottish physician, born in Ancrum, Roxburghshire. He was the author of the popular *Domestic Medicine: or The Family Physician* (1769).

BUCHANAN, Claudius (1766–1815) Scottish missionary, born in Cambuslang near Glasgow. In 1797 he became chaplain to the East India Company at Barrackpur, translated the Gospels into Persian and Hindustani, and made two tours through southern and western India. Returning in 1808 to England, he excited so much interest in Indian missions that before his death the first English bishop had been appointed to Calcutta.

BUCHANAN, George (c.1506–1582) Scottish scholar and humanist, born near Killearn in Stirlingshire. Because of straitened family circumstances he attended the local grammar school, but at the age of 14 was sent by an uncle to study Latin at the University of Paris. He returned to Scotland in 1523, and did service in the army of the Duke of Albany (the future King **James V**). Thereafter he was enrolled at St Andrews as a poor student, before returning to Paris, where he taught at the College of Sainte Barbe (1528–37). In 1537, King James appointed him tutor to one of his illegitimate sons, the future Earl of **Moray**, but he was soon charged with heresy at St Andrews after writing a satirical poem about friars, *Franciscanus*, which offended Cardinal **Beaton**. He fled to France, where he taught at Bordeaux (1539–42) with **Montaigne** as one of his pupils, and wrote two tragedies in Latin, *Jeptha* and *Baptistes*. In 1547 he went to teach at Coimbra in Portugal, where he was arrested by the Inquisition as a suspected heretic. During his confinement (1547–53) he made a Latin paraphrase of the Psalms, which was published in 1566 with a dedication to **Mary, Queen of Scots**. He returned to Scotland in 1561 and was appointed classical tutor to the 19-year-old queen, despite his acknowledged leanings towards Protestantism. The queen awarded him a handsome pension, and in 1566 he was appointed principal of St Leonard's College at St Andrews. He abandoned the queen's cause after the murder of Lord Darnley in 1567, and charged her with complicity in a scurrilous pamphlet, *Ane Detectioun of the Duings of Mary Quene* (1571). In 1567 he was elected moderator of the newly-formed General Assembly of the Church of Scotland, and later was appointed keeper of the privy seal of Scotland, and tutor to the four-year-old King **James VI** of Scotland (1570–78). He proved a hard task-master, but the king learned his classics thoroughly. Buchanan's main works were *De juri regni apud Scotos* (1579, an attack on the divine right of monarchs and a justification for the deposition of Mary), and a monumental but unreliable history of Scotland, *Rerum scoticarum historia* (20 vols), which he completed shortly before his death.

BUCHANAN, James (1791–1868) 15th president of the USA, born in Stony Batter, near Mercersburg, Pennsylvania, the son of an immigrant Irish farmer. He was educated at Dickinson College, and in 1812 was admitted to the bar, where he established a large practice. He was sent in 1832 to negotiate the first commercial treaty with Russia; became secretary of state in 1845 and till the close of **Polk**'s presidency in 1849 succeeded in settling the Oregon boundary question. On the nomination of the Democratic party, he was elected president in 1856. During his administration the slavery question came to a head. Buchanan was strongly in favour of the maintenance of slavery, and he freely supported the attempt to establish Kansas as a slave state. As the end of his term approached, it became evident that a conflict was impending, and the election of **Lincoln** precipitated the outbreak. After his retirement in March 1861, Buchanan took no part in public affairs; but in 1866 he published a defence of his administration.

BUCHANAN, James McGill (1919–) American economist, born in Tennessee and educated there and in Chicago. He was awarded the Nobel prize for economics in 1986 for his work on the theories of public choice. He has held numerous professorships since 1950, is currently at George Mason University (1983–) and, since 1969, has been director of the Center for Public Choice.

BUCHANAN, Ken (Kenneth) (1945–) Scottish boxer, born in Edinburgh. For almost ten years he was one of the world's leading lightweight boxers, being British champion from 1968 to 1971 and again from 1973 to 1974. He was European champion from 1974 to 1975 and World Boxing Association lightweight champion from 1970 to 1972. On retiring from the ring he entered the hotel business in Edinburgh, and later was associated with a boxing school for young fighters.

BUCHANAN, Robert Williams (1841–1901) English poet, novelist and playwright, born in Caverswall, Staffordshire. He was educated at Glasgow High School and University, where his closest friend was **David Gray**, with whom he set out for London in 1860. They found life hard in London and success came too late for Buchanan. He is noted for his attack in the *Spectator* on **Swinburne**, whom he called unclean, morbid and sensual, and on the pre-Raphaelites under the pseudonym of 'Thomas Maitland' in another article entitled 'The Fleshly School of Poetry' (1871). *London Poems* (1866) was his first distinct success. He also wrote many now-forgotten novels and plays.

BUCHEZ, Philippe Benjamin Joseph (1796–1865) French physician and socialist, born in Matagne-la-Petite. He published works on social science, history, and philosophy, striving to weld communism and Catholicism, and began the *Histoire parlementaire de la Révolution française* (1833–38). In 1848 he was president of the National Assembly.

BUCHMAN, Frank Nathan Daniel (1878–1961) American evangelist, born in Pennsburg, Pennsylvania, of devout Lutheran parents, founder of the 'Group' and 'Moral Rearmament' movements. Ordained in 1902, he was minister in charge of a hospice for under-privileged boys in Philadelphia (1902–07), travelled extensively in the east, and in 1921, believing that there was an imminent danger of the collapse of civilization, founded at Oxford the 'First Century Christian Fellowship'. For its propagation it led parties of young men, including some Oxford undergraduates, to many parts of the world. The movement was misleadingly labelled the 'Oxford Group', until 1938, when it began to rally under the slogan 'Moral Rearmament' (MRA). The Buchmanites did not regard themselves as a new sect, but as a catalyst for existing religious institutions. They emphasized divine guidance, constant adherence to the four cardinal principles of honesty, purity, unselfishness, and love, fostered by compulsory, public 'sharing' of their shortcomings. After World War II the movement emerged in a more political guise as an alternative to capitalism and communism. He wrote *The Oxford Group and its Work of Moral Rearmament* (1954) and *America Needs an Ideology* (1957).

BÜCHNER, Eduard (1860–1917) German chemist, born in Munich. He won the Nobel prize for chemistry in 1907 for demonstrating that alcoholic fermentation is due not to physiological but to chemical processes in the yeast.

BÜCHNER, Georg (1813–37) German dramatist and pioneer of Expressionist theatre, brother of **Ludwig**

Büchner, born in Goddelau near Darmstadt. He studied medicine and science, became involved in revolutionary politics and fled to Zürich where he died of typhoid at the age of 24. His best-known works are the poetical dramas *Dantons Tod* (1835) and *Woyzeck* (1837) (of which he left many unfinished manuscript versions) the true-life story of an uneducated and mentally-backward army private who killed his girlfriend in a fit of jealousy. It was used by **Alban Berg** as the basis for his opera *Wozzeck*. His sister Louise (1821–77) was also a poet and novelist.

BÜCHNER, Hans (1850–1902) German bacteriologist, brother of **Eduard Büchner**. Professor at Munich (1880–1902) and director of the Hygienisches Institut from 1894, he discovered that blood serum contains protective substances against infection.

BÜCHNER, Ludwig (1824–99) German physician and materialist philosopher, born in Darmstadt, brother of **Georg Büchner**. He lectured at Tübingen (1852), but his controversial *Kraft und Stoff* (1855) brought about his forced resignation and made him take up private practice at Darmstadt.

BUCK, Frank (1884–1950) American big-game hunter and collector, born in Gainesville, Texas. From 1911 he led several expeditions all over the world to capture wild animals for zoos and circuses. Perhaps the most celebrated hunter in the world, he was enormously popular as a lecturer, and wrote many books, including *Bring 'Em Back Alive* (1930), *Wild Cargo* (1931) and *Fang and Claw* (1935), which were turned into movies starring Buck himself.

BUCK, Pearl, née **Sydenstricker** (1892–1973) American novelist, born in Hillsboro, West Virginia. The daughter of Presbyterian Missionaries, she lived in China from childhood, went to the USA for her education, but returned to China as a missionary and teacher in 1921. She married another missionary, John Lossing Buck, in 1917, and divorced in 1934. Her earliest novels are coloured by her experiences while living in China. *The Good Earth* (1931), a runaway best-seller, earned her the 1938 Nobel prize for literature. In 1935 she returned to America, and most of her output after that date was concerned with the contemporary American scene. Her other novels on China include *Sons* (1932), *A House Divided* (1935), *Dragon Seed* (1942), and *Imperial Woman* (1956), and amongst other works are *What America Means to Me* (1944) and *My Several Worlds* (1955).

BUCK, Sir Percy Carter (1871–1947) English musical educationist, born in West Ham, London. He held successive posts at Wells and Bristol Cathedrals, was director of music at Harrow, and then at Dublin University (1910) and London University (1923). The author of several sound textbooks, he was responsible for the inauguration of the teachers' course at the Royal College of Music.

BUCKHURST, Lord See **SACKVILLE, Thomas**

BUCKINGHAM, George Villiers, 1st Duke of (1592–1628) English statesman, second son of Sir George Villiers, born at his father's seat of Brooksby, Leicestershire. In 1614 he was brought to the notice of **James I**, and was soon received into high favour, as successor to **Robert Carr**, Earl of Somerset. He was knighted, raised to the peerage as Viscount Villiers in 1616, and became Earl of Buckingham in 1617, Marquis in 1618. Offices and lands were heaped on him so profusely that, from a threadbare hanger-on at court, 'Steenie' became, with a single exception, the wealthiest noble in England. In 1623, while the proposed Spanish match for Prince Charles (the future **Charles I**) was in progress, Buckingham persuaded Charles to go to Madrid and prosecute his suit in person; the ultimate failure of the negotiations was largely owing to his arrogance. On his return Buckingham, now a duke, was made lord-warden of the Cinque Ports. He negotiated the marriage of Charles I with **Henrietta Maria** of France, and maintained his ascendancy after Charles's accession in 1625. But the abortive expedition against Cadiz exposed him to impeachment by the Commons, and only a dissolution rescued him. His insolence in making love to the queen of France next made mischief. In 1627 he appeared with an armament before Rochelle; but the Huguenots refused him admission within the harbour; and when his troops made an ill-supported descent on the neighbouring Île de Rhé, they were defeated, in spite of his brave conduct. For a second expedition to Rochelle he had gone down to Portsmouth, but was assassinated by a discontented subaltern, John Felton.

BUCKINGHAM, George Villiers, 2nd Duke of (1627–87) son of the 1st Duke, born in Wallingford House, London. After his father's assassination in 1628 he was brought up with **Charles I**'s children. At the outbreak of the Civil War he joined the royalists and served under Prince Rupert. In 1648 he joined the rising by Lord **Holland** in Surrey and barely escaped with his life, although his younger brother was killed. He went with **Charles II** to Scotland, and after the battle of Worcester went into exile. Returning secretly to England, in 1657 he married the daughter of Lord **Fairfax**, the parliamentary general to whom his forfeited estates had been assigned. At the Restoration he got them back and became a privy councillor and for the next 25 years he excelled the other courtiers in debauchery and wit. In 1667 he killed in a duel the Earl of Shrewsbury, whose countess, his paramour, looked on, disguised as a page. He was instrumental in **Clarendon**'s downfall and was a member of the infamous 'Cabal'. He lost influence to **Aldington**, and in 1674 was dismissed from government. He was author and part-author of several comedies, the wittiest *The Rehearsal* (1671), a parody of **Dryden**'s tragedies, but he is better remembered as the 'Zimri' of Dryden's *Absalom and Achitophel*.

BUCKLAND, Henry Seymour Berry, Baron (1877–1928) Welsh industrialist, born in Merthyr Tydfil, brother of Lords **Camrose** and **Kemsley**. A protégé of Lord **Rhondda**, he directed his enterprises when Rhondda served in the Cabinet. He promoted mergers within the coal industry in South Wales with the aim of greater efficiency. He also held interests in newspapers with his brothers. He died after a riding accident.

BUCKLAND, William (1784–1856) English geologist and clergyman, born in Tiverton. Educated at Oxford, he became reader in mineralogy there. He is known for his description of Kirkdale Cave, and his attempts to relate geology to the biblical description of the Creation. In 1845 he became dean of Westminster.

BUCKLE, George Earle (1854–1935) English journalist, born in Twerton vicarage, Bath. He was editor of *The Times* from 1884 to 1912. He completed Monypenny's *Life of Disraeli* (1914–20), and edited six volumes of Queen **Victoria**'s Letters (1926–32).

BUCKLE, Henry Thomas (1821–62) English historian, born in Lee, in Kent. Mostly self-educated, he mastered 18 foreign languages and amassed an enormous library to assist him in compiling a monumental *History of Civilization in England* (1857–61), only two volumes of which saw the light of day and in which he practised a scientific method of writing history, taking into account a country's climate, etc. He excelled as a chess player.

BUCKLEY, William (1780–1856) the 'Wild White Man' of Australia, a huge English convict who lived for 32 years with a tribe of aborigines. Born near Macclesfield, he was a bricklayer, then joined the army, but was transported to Australia in 1802 for stealing. He escaped the following year from a new convict settlement at Port Phillip, near Melbourne, was adopted by a native tribe, and lived with them for 32 years before being found by an expedition. He became a bodyguard to the colonel in command of the new colony, then moved to Van Diemen's Land (Tasmania), where he died.

BUCKMINSTER FULLER See **Fuller, Richard Buckminster**

BUCKNER, Simon Bolivar, Jr (1886–1945) American soldier, born in Munfordville, Kentucky, the son of a Civil War general. Educated at the US Military Academy, West Point, he commanded the Alaska Defense Force (1940) and took part in operations for the recapture of the Aleutian islands (1942–43). He commanded the 10th army in the Central Pacific command, and led the invasion of the island of Okinawa in April 1945. He was killed in action during the final stages of the capture of this key strategic objective of US Pacific strategy.

BUCKSTONE, John Baldwin (1802–79) English comedian, actor-manager and playwright, born in Hoxton. He played at the Surrey, Adelphi, Drury Lane, and Lyceum theatres, mostly as a comedian, and visited the USA in 1840 and then played at the Haymarket, where he was actor-manager (1853–78). He wrote 150 pieces for the stage.

BUDAEUS, Latinized form of **Guillaume Budé** (1467–1540) French scholar, born in Paris. Of his works on philology, philosophy, and jurisprudence, the best known are his *Annotationes in XXIV libros Pandectarum*, a work on ancient coins (1514), and the *Commentarii Linguae Graecae* (1519). **Louis XII** and **Francis I** also employed him in diplomacy. At his suggestion Francis founded the Collège de France. Though suspected of a leaning towards Lutheranism, he was royal librarian and founded the royal collection at Fontainebleau, which, moved to Paris, became the Bibliothèque Nationale. His collected works were published in 1557.

BUDD, William (1811–80) English physician, born in North Tawton, Devonshire. Working in Bristol, he advocated disinfection to prevent the spread of contagious diseases, such as typhoid fever, cholera, and rinderpest. His brother George (1808–82) was a celebrated London physician.

BUDD, Zola (1966–) South African athlete, born in Bloemfontein. Dogged by controversy, she set a world record time of 15.01.83 for the 5000 metres while still a South African citizen. In April 1984 she was accorded British citizenship on the strength of her parental background, and became eligible to participate in the 1984 Olympic Games. But her presence was not universally welcomed, and her disappointing performance was best remembered for her accidental clash with the American Mary Decker. She set further world records for the 5000 metres in 1984 and 1985, reducing the time to 14.48.07, but her refusal to condemn apartheid outright and her apparent lack of commitment to her British residency brought her career to a premature end.

BUDDHA, ('the enlightened') (c.563–c.483 BC) the title of Prince Gautama Siddhartha, the founder of Buddhism, born the son of the rajah of the Sakya tribe ruling in Kapilavastu, 100 miles north of Benares, in Nepal. When about 30 years old he left the luxuries of the court, his beautiful wife, and all earthly ambitions for the life of an ascetic; after six years of self-torturing austerity and extreme mortification he saw in the contemplative life the perfect way to self-enlightenment. According to tradition, he achieved enlightenment when sitting beneath a banyan tree near Buddh Gaya in Bihar. For the next 40 years he taught, gaining many disciples and followers, and died at the age of about 80 in Kusinagara in Oudh. His system was perhaps a revolutionary reformation of Brahmanism rather than a new faith, the keynote of it being that existence is necessarily miserable, and that 'Nirvana', or nonexistence, the chief good, is to be attained by diligent devotion to Buddhistic rules. The death of the body does not bring Nirvana: the unholy are condemned to transmigration through many existences. Buddhism spread steadily over India, and in the 3rd century BC was dominant from the Himalayas to Cape Comorin. In the earlier centuries of our epoch it began to decline, was relentlessly persecuted by triumphant Brahmanism in the 7th and 8th centuries, and stamped out of continental India (except Nepal) by invading Islam. But it had spread to Tibet, Ceylon, Burma, Siam, China, and Japan, where it is still powerful.

BUDDHAGHOSA (5th century) Indian Buddhist scholar, born near Buddh Gaya, or Ghosa, East India, the place of the **Buddha**'s enlightenment. He studied the Buddhist texts in Ceylon and is best known for the *Visuddhimagga*, 'The Path of Purity', a compendium of the Buddhist doctrines.

BUDÉ See **BUDAEUS, Guillaume**

BUDENNY, Simeon Mikhailovich (1883–1973) Russian soldier, the son of a Cossack farmer. He fought as a Cossack private in the Russo-Japanese war (1904–05) and as an NCO in World War I. After the revolution he became a Bolshevik and raised a Cossack unit to fight the White forces on the Don, and defeated the Whites in the battles of Tsaritsyn (1918–19). He served in the war against Poland (1920), and was made a marshal in 1935. In 1941 he commanded the South West sector against the German invasion, but was relieved by **Timoshenko** after a disaster at Kiev.

BUDGE, Don (John Donald) (1915–) American tennis player, born in Oakland, California. The son of a Scots immigrant, he retains his reputation as one of the greatest tennis players ever. In 1938 he became the first player to win all four Grand Slam events in the same year. 1937–38 saw him at his peak: in both years he won the Wimbledon singles, men's doubles (with his compatriot Gene Mako) and, with fellow-American Alice Marble, the mixed doubles. He turned professional in 1939.

BUDGELL, Eustace (1686–1737) English writer, born in Exeter. He was a cousin of **Joseph Addison**, and contributed miscellaneous essays to the *Spectator*. He lost a fortune in the South Sea Company collapse (1720), and degenerated to a Grub Street writer. He drowned himself in the Thames.

BUENO, Maria Esther (1939–) Brazilian lawn tennis player, born in São Paulo. She was almost the last of the essentially feminine women champions, relying on subtlety and placement. She won Wimbledon in 1959 and 1960 and again in 1964, and was US champion on four occasions. With the American, Darlene Hard, she won the Wimbledon doubles title five times and the US doubles four times. Ill-health brought her retirement from top-class tennis at the relatively early age of 29.

BUFF, Charlotte See **GOETHE**

BUFFALO BILL See **CODY, William Frederick**

BUFFON, George-Louis Leclerc, Comte de (1707–88) French naturalist, born in Montbard, in Burgundy, the son of a wealthy lawyer. After studying law at the Jesuit college in Dijon, he devoted himself to science, and while on a visit to England (1733) translated into French **Newton**'s *Fluxions*. In 1739 he was appointed director of the Jardin du Roi and the Royal Museum, and formed the design of his monumental *Histoire Naturelle* (44 vols, 1749–67), in which all the known facts of natural science were discussed. After receiving various high honours, he was made Comte de Buffon by **Louis XV**. His work was inclined to generalization, but he proposed several new theories (including a greater age to the earth than proposed in Genesis). His writings were influential in arousing interest in natural history, and foreshadowed the theory of evolution.

BUGATTI, Ettore (1882–1947) Italian car manufacturer, born in Milan. He began designing cars in 1899 and set up his works in Strasbourg (1907). In World War I he moved to Italy and later to France, where his racing cars won international fame in the 1930s.

BUGEAUD, Thomas (1784–1849) French soldier, born in Limoges. He served in the Napoleonic campaigns, and with great distinction in Algeria and Morocco (1836–44), his victory at Isly in 1844 over the emperor of Morocco's forces gaining him the title Duc d'Isly. In the February revolution of 1848 he commanded the army in Paris, where he later died of cholera.

BUGENHAGEN, Johann (1485–1558) German Lutheran reformer, also called Dr Pommer, born near Stettin. Converted to **Luther**'s views in 1620, he helped in the Reformation by organizing the church in many German cities. He also helped with the translation of the bible.

BUGGE, Sophus Elseus (1833–1907) Norwegian philologist, born in Larvik. He studied at Christiania (Oslo), Copenhagen, and Berlin, and in 1866 was appointed professor of comparative philology and Old Norse at the University of Copenhagen. In addition to writing on runic inscriptions, he contributed to the study of Etruscan, Italic, Celtic and the Romance languages. His major work was a critical edition of the Old Icelandic *Elder Edda* (1867).

BUHL, properly **Boulle, Charles André** (1642–1732) French cabinetmaker, born in Paris. In the service of **Louis XIV** he introduced *buhlwork*, a style of decorating furniture by inlaying metals, shells, and pearls, on ebony, which was carried on by his sons, Jean, Pierre, André, and Charles.

BUJONES, Fernando (1955–) American dancer, born in Miami, Florida, of Cuban extraction. He studied with **Alicia Alonso** in Havana and at the School of American Ballet in New York, and danced briefly with the Eglevsky Ballet. In 1972 he joined American Ballet Theatre, rising to the status of principal in 1974, the same year that he won the gold medal at Varna, Yugoslavia. Blessed with a technique that can be either elegant or electrifying, he has danced all the major classical roles for companies the world over. He is equally at home in the modern repertoire.

BUKOWSKI, Charles (1920–) German-born American poet, short-story writer and novelist, born in Andernach. As befits an underground writer, his world is one frequented by low lifers which he evokes, as one critic has said, in 'words nailed to the page'. His pared style, revealing an affinity with **Hemingway**, has been employed to effect in four novels, half a dozen collections of short stories and many volumes of verse. A cult figure who has not achieved popular success, he has a sardonic sense of humour and a liking for long titles, eg *Play the Piano Drunk Like a Percussion Instrument until the Fingers Begin to Bleed a Bit* (1979).

BULGAKOV, Mikhail Afanasievich (1891–1940) Russian writer, born in Kiev. He studied medicine, graduating in 1916. In 1920 he gave up his medical practice and went to Moscow, where he worked for some years as a reporter. His first published work was a collection of short stories, *Diavoliada* (1925). He had considerable success as a playwright in Russia and in the west, the most famous of his plays being *The White Guard* (1926), but with increasingly strict censorship they were taken out of production. Until 1936 he was literary adviser and assistant producer at the Moscow Arts Theatre under **Stanislavsky**. His experiences there are described in his unfinished novel *Black Snow* (1965, trans 1968). From 1936, until he went blind in 1939, he worked at the Bolshoi Theatre. Like his plays, his novels are satirical studies of contemporary life in Russia. In addition to *Black Snow* he wrote *The Heart of a Dog* (trans 1968) and *The Master and Margarita* (trans 1967).

BULGAKOV, Sergei Nikolayevich (1871–1944) Russian philosopher, economist, and Orthodox theologian, born in Livny, Central Russia. A professor of political economy at Kiev (1901–06) and then Moscow (1906–18), he became disillusioned with socialism after 1906 and became a priest in 1918. Expelled from Russia in 1923 like many other clergy, he was appointed dean and professor of the Orthodox Theological Academy in Paris (1925–44), where he expounded Sophiology, following **Vladimir Soloviev** and Florensky's interpretation of the eastern fathers. Bulgakov's belief that Sophia (the Divine Wisdom) mediates between God and the world implied a fourth person of the Trinity and attracted accusations of heresy. There are English editions of *The Orthodox Church* (1935) and *The Wisdom of God* (1937). Autobiographical notes and extracts from other French and Russian works appear in *A Bulgakov Anthology* (1976).

BULGANIN, Nikolai (1895–1975) Soviet politician, born in Nizhni-Novgorod (now Gorki). An early member of the Communist party, he was mayor of Moscow (1933–37) and a member of the Military Council during World War II. Created a marshal at the end of the war, he succeeded **Stalin** as minister for defence in 1946. After Stalin's death he became vice-premier in **Malenkov**'s government and was made premier after the latter's resignation in February 1955, a constitutional façade with **Khrushchev** wielding real power as first secretary of the party. 'B and K', unlike their predecessors, travelled extensively abroad in Yugoslavia, India, and Britain, and conducted propaganda by means of lengthy letters addressed to western statesmen, particularly over the disarmament question. Khrushchev ousted Bulganin from his nominal position in March 1958 and he suffered total political eclipse in August 1958, retaining only the minor post of chairman of the Soviet State Bank.

BULGARIN, Thaddeus (1789–1859) Russian author and journalist. He was a zealous supporter of reaction and of absolutism. His best novel is *Ivan Vyzhigin* (1829).

BULL, George (1634–1710) English prelate, born in Wells. He studied at Exeter College, Oxford, where he retired in 1649, having refused to take the Commonwealth Oath. Ordained in 1655, he took the small parish of St George's, Bristol, and eventually obtained the bishopric of St Davids (1705). His greatest work, the *Defensio Fidei Nicenae* (1685), was directed against Arians and Socinians; for his *Judicium Ecclesiae Catholicae* (1694) the thanks of the French clergy were sent to him through **Bossuet**.

BULL, John (c.1562–1628) English musician, born in Somerset. He was appointed organist in the Queen's Chapel in 1586, first music lecturer at Gresham College in 1597, and organist to **James I** in 1607. A Catholic, he fled abroad in 1613, and entered the archduke's service in Brussels; in 1615 he became organist of Antwerp Cathedral, and there he died. He was one of England's finest virtuoso composers and may be considered as one of the founders of contrapuntal keyboard music.

BULL, Olav Jacob Martin Luther (1883–1933) Norwegian lyric poet, born in Christiania (now Oslo). Because of his ardent love of nature evident in all his work, he has sometimes been compared with **John Keats**. Of his many volumes of verse, *Metope* (1927) is considered outstanding.

BULL, Ole Bornemann (1810–80) Norwegian violinist, born in Bergen. Rising to fame in Paris, he made triumphant tours of Italy, England, Scotland, Ireland, Russia, Germany, and Norway. From 1843 he was repeatedly in America, making enormous sums by his concerts, but losing heavily by land speculations, especially an attempt to found a Scandinavian colony in Pennsylvania. He was a noted eccentric.

BULLARD, Sir Edward Crisp (1907–80) English geophysicist, born in Norwich and educated in Cambridge. After working in naval research in World War II, he was professor at Toronto (1946–49), director of the National Physical Laboratory (1950–55) and director of the department of geodesy and geophysics at Cambridge (1964–74). He made the first satisfactory measurements of geothermal heat-flow through the oceanic crust, and helped to develop the theory of continental drift. His reintroduction of the idea of thermal convection currents in the Earth's core led him, independently of Elsasser, to the theory that they are responsible for the origin of the Earth's magnetism.

BULLEN, Arthur Henry (1857–1920) English editor, born in London. He edited **John Day**, **Thomas Campion**, and other Elizabethans, and founded at Stratford-on-Avon the Shakespeare Head Press (1904).

BULLEN, Frank Thomas (1857–1915) English writer. He was a sailor till 1883, and made notable additions to the literature of the sea, including *Cruise of the Cachalot* (1898). He also wrote *Recollections* (1915).

BULLER, Sir Redvers Henry (1839–1908) English soldier, born in Crediton, Devon. Educated at Eton College, he was commissioned into the 60th Rifles in 1858 and saw active service in the war with China (1860) the Red River expedition (1870), the Ashanti War (1874), the Kaffir War (1878) and the Zulu War (1879), where his rescue of fellow-soldiers in action at Inhlobane won him the VC. He was chief of staff in the 1st Boer War (1881), and served in Egypt and the Sudan. He was promoted lieutenant-general in 1894. He was commander-in-chief in the 2nd Boer War (1899–1900) and raised the siege of Ladysmith (1900), and was succeeded by **Roberts**. He commanded the 1st Army Corps (1901–06).

BULLETT, Gerald (1893–1958) English author, born in London. Educated at Jesus College, Cambridge, from 1914 his published work included fiction, poems, essays, biographies, anthologies, children's books, literary criticism, and plays. His novels include *The Pandervils*, *The Jury*, and *The Snare of the Fowler*.

BULLINGER, Heinrich (1504–75) Swiss reformer, the son of a priest. In 1529 he married a former nun, and became a disciple of **Zwingli**, whom he succeeded in 1531 as leader of the reformed party in Switzerland in its struggle with the Catholics, as well as with the Zealots and the Lutherans. He drew up the Helvetic Confessions of 1536 and 1566.

BULLOCK, Alan Louis Charles, Baron Bullock (1914–) English historian. Educated at Bradford Grammar School and Wadham College, Oxford, he was appointed censor of St Catherine's Society, Oxford (1952–62), vice-chancellor of Oxford University (1969–73), and Master of St Catherine's College, Oxford (1960–80). He was chairman of the National Advisory council on the Training and Supply of Teachers (1963–65), and of the Schools Council (1966–69). As chairman of the Committee on Reading and Other Uses of English Language from 1972 to 1974, the Bullock report (Report, *A Language for Life*, 1975), was a response to suggestions that reading standards were declining and offered practical guidance for the teacher of reading, writing, speech and language skills. It was much discussed and undoubtedly beneficial. He is also the author of numerous works on 20th-century Europe, including *Hitler: A Study in Tyranny* (1952).

BÜLOW, Carl Wilhelm Paul von (1846–1921) German soldier, brother of Prince **Bernhard Bülow**. He entered the army in 1864, and in 1914 commanded the German 2nd Army for the invasion of France and Belgium.

BÜLOW, Prince Bernhard Heinrich von (1849–1929) German statesman, born in Flottbeck, Holstein. He was chancellor (1900–09), foreign secretary (1897), count (1899) and prince (1905). He wrote *Imperial Germany* (trans, new ed 1916), and *Memoirs* (trans 1931–32).

BÜLOW, Hans Guido von (1830–94) German pianist and conductor, born in Dresden. He studied law, but under the influence of **Wagner** made himself the musico-political spokesman of the new German school. In 1851 he took pianoforte lessons from **Liszt**, married his daughter, Cosima (1857), and became an outstanding conductor. In 1864 he became court pianist and director of the music school at Munich, but resigned when his wife deserted him for Wagner in 1869. He undertook extensive conducting tours in England and America.

BÜLOW VON DENNEWITZ, Friedrich Wilhelm, Count (1755–1816) Prussian soldier. He entered the army in 1768 and served in the Rhine campaigns (1792–95) and the Napoleonic campaign of 1805–06. In 1813 he commanded in the first successful encounter with the French at Möckern. His victories at Grossbeeren and Dennewitz saved Berlin; he was prominent in the battle of Leipzig (1813), and by taking Montmartre finished the campaign of 1814. In 1815 he joined **Blücher** by forced marches, and came to **Wellington**'s aid at Waterloo. His brother, Dietrich Adam Heinrich (1757–1807), satirized the Prussian army system in *Der Feldzug von 1805* (1806).

BULTMANN, Rudolf Karl (1884–1976) German Protestant theologian, born in Wiefelstede, Oldenberg. Professor of New Testament at Marburg (1921–51), he maintained that while form criticism of the Gospels showed it was next to impossible to know anything about the historical **Jesus Christ**, faith *in* Christ, rather than belief *about* him, was what mattered. The Gospels' existential challenge was, however, blunted for modern man by difficulties with miracles and other aspects of the New Testament world-view, which therefore needed to be 'demythologized'. Such controversial views provoked sharp reaction: ultimately towards more confidence in the historicity of the Gospels or to a humanistic existentialism unconcerned with their subject. His books include *The History of the Synoptic Tradition* (1921), *Jesus and the Word* (1934), *Kerygma and Myth* (1953), Gifford Lectures on *History and*

Eschatology (1957), *Jesus Christ and Mythology* (1960), *Theology of the New Testament* (2 vols, 1952–55), *Existence and Faith* (1964), and *The Gospel of John* (1941).

BULWER, Henry Lytton (1801–72). English diplomatist and author, born in London, the elder brother of Lord **Edward Bulwer Lytton**. Educated at Harrow and Cambridge, he entered the diplomatic service in 1827, and was attaché at Berlin, Brussels, and The Hague. An advanced Liberal MP, he became secretary of embassy at Constantinople in 1837, where he negotiated a very important commercial treaty. As minister plenipotentiary in Madrid, he negotiated the peace between Spain and Morocco (1849). His outspokenness resulted in his expulsion, and in 1849 he proceeded to Washington, where he concluded the **Clayton**-Bulwer Treaty. He was ambassador to the Ottoman Porte (1858–65), and ably carried out **Palmerston**'s policy on the eastern question. Created Lord Dalling and Bulwer in 1871, he died in Naples. Among his works were *An Autumn in Greece* (1826), *Historical Characters* (1868–70), and an unfinished *Life of Palmerston* (1870–74).

BULWER-LYTTON See **LYTTON, 1st Baron**

BUNAU-VARILLA, Philippe Jean (1859–1940) French engineer. The chief organizer of the Panama Canal project, he was instrumental in getting the waterway routed through Panama instead of Nicaragua, worked to bring about the sale of the canal to the USA, incited the Panama revolution (1903) to further this end, was made Panamanian minister to the USA and negotiated the Hay-Bunau-Varilla Treaty (1903) giving the USA control of the Canal Zone. He wrote *From Panama to Verdun* (1940).

BUNBURY, Henry William (1750–1811) English caricaturist and sporting writer, born in Mildenhall, Suffolk. He became a squire in Norfolk, and found fame as an outstanding caricaturist with *Master of the Horse to the Doge of Venice*, which he illustrated with his own humorous designs. As a pioneer of the genre in Britain, he was the friend and equal of **Thomas Rowlandson** and **James Gillray**.

BUNCHE, Ralphe Johnson (1904–71) American administrator, born in Detroit, the grandson of a slave. He studied at Harvard, Capetown, the London School of Economics, and became assistant-professor of political science at Howard University, Washington (1928). During World War II he advised the government on African strategic questions, and as an expert on trusteeship territories drafted the appropriate sections of the UN Charter. As director (1947–54) of the UN Trusteeship department, he followed Count **Folke Bernadotte**, after the latter's assassination (1948), as UN mediator in Palestine and arranged for a cease-fire. Awarded the Nobel peace prize (1950), he became a UN under-secretary (1954–67) and played an important role in Suez, the Congo, and the Indo-Pakistan war of 1965. He was under-secretary-general from 1968.

BUNCHO, Tani (1773–1840) Japanese painter, born in Edo (Tokyo). The son of a poet, he was familiar with the styles of various schools (Kano, Tosa, Nagasagik, Masumyama, Shijo) and Chinese works, and attempted a synthesis of these with European techniques. An illustrator of books and a prolific painter of a variety of subjects, he excelled in landscapes. He also introduced the Nanga style of painting to Edo, which encouraged individualism and the expression of the artist's own feelings, a revolutionary concept for the period. Buncho was regarded as the greatest master of Edo in his time.

BUNIN, Ivan Alexeievich (1870–1953) Russian author, born in Voronezh. He wrote lyrics and novels of the decay of the Russian nobility and of peasant life, among them *The Village* (1910, trans 1923), *The Gentleman from San Francisco* (1914, trans 1922), his best-known work with its theme the vanity of all things earthly, and the autobiographical *The Well of Days* (1933, trans 1946). He lived in Paris after the Russian Revolution, and received the 1933 Nobel prize for literature.

BUNNY, Rupert Charles Wulsten (1864–1947) Australian artist, born in St Kilda, Victoria. He studied in Melbourne and then in London at Calderons preparatory school for the Royal Academy. He later moved to Paris where he exhibited first at the Old Salon, in 1890 receiving a 'Mention Honorable' and in 1900 a Bronze Medal at the Paris Exhibition. In 1901 he moved to the 'New' Salon and from then on spent most of his working life in Paris. In 1946 he held the first Loan Exhibition of an Australian artist at the National Gallery of Victoria. His work was not influenced by the prevailing Impressionist school but more by classical mythology; he later turned to large decorative and exotic scenes.

BUNSEN, Christian Karl Josias, Baron (1791–1860) Prussian diplomat, theologian, and scholar, born in Korbach, in Waldeck. He studied at Marburg, Göttingen, Copenhagen, Berlin, Paris, and Rome, where he was appointed (1818) secretary to the Prussian embassy at the papal court (where **Barthold Niebuhr** was ambassador), and in 1827 resident minister. He gave much time to the study of **Plato** and Egyptology, published much on church history, liturgical history, and biblical criticism, and was a great supporter of the Archaeological Institute. In 1841 he was sent to London on a special mission about an Anglo-Prussian bishopric in Jerusalem, and next year was appointed ambassador at the English court. In 1844 he drew up a constitution for Prussia on English lines. In the Schleswig-Holstein question he strongly advocated the German view. Differing from the court on the eastern question, he resigned in 1854, and lived at Heidelberg and Cannes.

BUNSEN, Robert Wilhelm (1811–99) German chemist and physicist, born in Göttingen. After studying at Göttingen, Paris, Berlin, and Vienna, he became professor of chemistry at Heidelberg in 1852. He shared with **Gustav Robert Kirchhoff** the discovery, in 1859, of spectrum analysis, which facilitated the discovery of new elements, including cesium and rubidium. He partially lost the sight of one eye, which caused him to forbid the study of organic chemistry in his laboratories. He invented the Bunsen burner, the grease-spot photometer, a galvanic battery, an ice calorimeter, and, with Sir **Henry Roscoe**, the actinometer.

BUNTING, Basil (1900–85) English poet, born in Northumberland. His career was one of neglect, and until the publication of *Loquitur* (1965) **Ezra Pound** seemed to be his sole aficionado. That, however, encouraged the growth of a cult following and Bunting attracted more admirers with his long poem, *Briggflatts* (1966). He assisted **Ford Maddox Ford** with *The Transatlantic Review* in Paris but he largely shunned literary society. His admirers have included **Read**, **Tomlinson**, **MacDiarmid** and **Creely**, but he has a greater following in the USA than in Britain despite attempts to revive interest. His *Collected Poems* appeared in 1968.

BUÑUEL, Luis (1900–83) Spanish film director, born in Calanda. He was educated at Madrid University. With **Salvador Dali** he achieved a *succès de scandale* with their surrealistic, macabre, poetic *Un*

Chien Andalou (1928) and *L'Age d'or* (1930). His first solo venture, *Las Hurdes* (1932), a documentary on Spanish poverty, was banned in Spain, and he eventually settled in Mexico (1947), his career in eclipse. *Los Olvidados* (1950), a realistic study of juvenile delinquency, re-established him, and later films, such as *Nazarin* (1958), *Viridiana* (1961), *Belle de Jour* (1966), *La Voie Lactée* (1969), *The Discreet Charm of the Bourgeoisie* (1972) and *That Obscure Object of Desire* (1977), illustrate his poetic, often erotic, use of imagery, his black humour, and his hatred of Catholicism, often expressed in blasphemy.

BUNYAN, John (1628–88) English writer and preacher, born in Elstow near Bedford, son of a 'brasever' or tinker. In 1644 he was drafted into the army, in June 1645 he returned to Elstow, and there about 1649 married a poor girl who brought with her two books which had belonged to her father, the *Plain Man's Pathway to Heaven* and the *Practice of Piety*. About this time Bunyan began to experience those deep religious experiences which he has described so vividly in his *Grace Abounding* (1666). In 1653 he joined a Christian fellowship which had been organized by a converted royalist major, and about 1655 he was asked by the brethren to address them. This led to his preaching in the villages round Bedford; and in 1656 he was brought into discussions with the followers of **George Fox**, which led to his first book, *Some Gospel Truths Opened* (1656), a vigorous attack on Quakerism. To this Edward Burrough, the Quaker, replied, and Bunyan replied in *A Vindication of Gospel Truths Opened* (1657). In November 1660 he was arrested while preaching in a farmhouse near Ampthill. During the twelve years' imprisonment in Bedford county gaol which followed, Bunyan wrote *Profitable Meditations* (1661), *I Will Pray with the Spirit* (1663), *Christian Behaviour* (1663), *The Holy City* (1665), *The Resurrection of the Dead* (1665), *Grace Abounding* (1666) and some other works. He was released after the Declaration of Indulgence of 1672, under which he became a licensed preacher, and pastor of the church to which he belonged. In February 1673, however, the Declaration of Indulgence was cancelled, and on 4 March, a warrant, signed by 13 magistrates, was issued for his arrest. Brought to trial under the Conventicle Act, Bunyan was sent to prison for six months in the town gaol. It was during this later and briefer imprisonment that he wrote the first part of *The Pilgrim's Progress*. When first issued in 1678 it contained no Mr Worldly Wiseman, and many passages were added in the second and third editions (1679). It is essentially a vision of life recounted allegorically as the narrative of a journey. There followed the *Life and Death of Mr Badman* (1680), the *Holy War* (1682), and *The Pilgrim's Progress, Second Part* (1684), containing the story of Christiana and her children. Bunyan became pastor at Bedford for 16 years until his death after a ride through the rain from Reading to London. He was buried in Bunhill Fields, the *Campo Santo* of the Nonconformists.

BUONAPARTE See **BONAPARTE**

BUONARROTI See **MICHELANGELO**

BUONONCINI See **BONONCINI**

BURBAGE, Richard (c.1567–1619) English actor, the son of James Burbage, himself an actor, and the builder of the Shoreditch and Blackfriars theatres. Richard made his début early, and had earned the title of 'Roscius', when the death of his father in 1597 brought him a share in the Blackfriars Theatre. In 1599, together with his brother Cuthbert, he pulled down the Shoreditch house, and built the famous Globe Theatre as a summer playhouse, while the Blackfriars was to be a winter one. He took as partners **Shakespeare, Heminge, Condell**, and others.

BURBANK, Luther (1849–1926) American horticulturalist, born in Lancaster, Massachusetts. He developed the Burbank potato, and in 1875 moved to Santa Rosa, California, where, by indefatigable experiment, he bred new fruits and flowers. The city of Burbank, California, is named after him.

BURCHARD (?965–1025) bishop of Worms. He compiled a collection of decretals of the popes, *Decretorum libri XX* or *Brocardus* (c.1020), based on the collection of Regino of Prum, the *Dionysio-Hadriana*, the False Decretals and some other works. This does not draw much from Roman law but takes a good deal from Carolingian capitularies, and the material is edited and modified to present Burchard's own views. A standard work until the time of **Gratian**'s *Decretum*, it is to a substantial extent a source of that work.

BURCHELL, William John (c.1782–1863) English botanist and naturalist, born in Fulham. He travelled in South Africa (1810–15), as described in his *Travels in the Interior of South Africa* (2 vols, 1822–24), and South America (1826–29), and collected many species new to science.

BURCHFIELD, Robert William (1923–) New Zealand-born English scholar and lexicographer, born in Wanganui. He was lecturer in English language, Oxford University (1952–63), tutorial fellow (1963–79), and senior research fellow from 1979. In 1957 he was appointed editor of a new *Supplement to the Oxford English Dictionary* which appeared in four volumes between 1972 and 1986. Among his other works are *The Oxford Dictionary of English Etymology* (1966; with **C T Onions** and G W S Friedrichsen) and *The English Language* (1985).

BURCKHARDT, Jacob Christopher (1818–97) Swiss historian, born in Basel. He studied theology and later art history in Berlin and Bonn, became editor of the *Basler Zeitung* (1844–45), and from 1858 to 1893 was professor of history at Basel University. He is known for his works on the Italian Renaissance and on Greek civilization.

BURCKHARDT, Johann Ludwig (1784–1817) Swiss traveller, born in Lausanne. In 1806 he was sent by the African Association to explore the interior of Africa. He went, disguised as an oriental, to Aleppo, where he studied for more than two years; then he visited and described Petra, before travelling up the Nile discovering the Temple of **Rameses II** at Abu Simbel. In 1814 he visited Mecca, where he was accepted not only as a true believer, but as a great Muslim scholar. While waiting for the Fezzan caravan, he died of dysentery at Cairo. His collection of oriental manuscripts was left to Cambridge University.

BURDETT, Sir Francis (1770–1844) English politician. Educated at Westminster and Oxford, he spent three years (1790–93) on the continent, and witnessed the French Revolution. In 1793 he married Sophia Coutts, daughter of **Thomas Coutts**, of the great banking family. Entering the House of Commons in 1796, he made himself conspicuous by opposing the war with France, and advocating parliamentary reform, Catholic emancipation, freedom of speech, prison reform, and other liberal measures. His candidature for Middlesex in 1802 involved him in four years' costly and fruitless litigation; in May 1807 he fought a duel with a Mr Paull. Burdett having in 1810 published, in **Cobbett**'s *Political Register*, a Letter to his Constituents, declaring the conduct of the House of Commons illegal in imprisoning a radical orator, the Speaker's warrant was issued for his arrest. For two days he barricaded his house; the people supported him, and in a street contest between them and the military one life was lost; but after two days an entry was forced, and Burdett conveyed to the Tower. The prorogation restored him to liberty. In 1820 a letter on the 'Peterloo massacre' brought three months' imprisonment and a fine. In 1835 he joined the Conservatives.

BURDETT-COUTTS, Angela Georgina, Baroness (1814–1906) English philanthropist, daughter of Sir **Francis Burdett**, and grand-daughter of **Thomas Coutts**. She inherited her grandfather's fortune in 1837 and used it to mitigate suffering. She established a shelter for fallen women, built model homes, and endowed churches and colonial bishoprics. In 1871 she received a peerage, and in 1872 she became the first woman to be given the freedom of the City of London. In 1881 she married William Ashmead-Bartlett (1851–1921), who assumed her name.

BÜRGER, Gottfried August (1747–94) German lyric poet and writer of ballads, born in Molmerswende, near Halberstadt, the son of the Lutheran pastor. In boyhood he displayed no inclination to study, but shaved a relish for verse. In 1764 he began to study theology, but in 1768 he migrated to Göttingen, and entered on a course of jurisprudence. His life here was wild and extravagant, and he might have sunk into obscurity but for the friendship which he happily formed with **Johann Heinrich Voss**, the two **Stolbergs**, and others. He studied closely the ancient and modern classics and translated **Percy**'s *Reliques*. He wrote many ballads, including *Lenore* (1773), which was translated by Sir **Walter Scott**. He married unhappily three times, speculated unwisely, and although a favourite poet of the German nation, he was left to earn his livelihood by translations and similar hack-work.

BURGER, Warren Earl (1907–) American judge, born in St Paul, Minnesota. Educated at the University of Minnesota, he taught and practised law in St Paul from 1931 before becoming assistant attorney-general of the USA (1953), and in 1955 judge of the US Court of Appeals for the District of Columbia. He was appointed chief justice of the US Supreme Court in 1969 and showed himself inclined to judicial restraint, restricting the liberal tendencies followed in previous years.

BURGES, William (1827–81) English architect and designer, born in London. He trained with the architect **Edward Blore**, and worked with **Matthew Digby Wyatt**. Much influenced by **Pugin** and **Viollet-le-Duc**, and fortified by his own scholarship, he employed a strong medieval element in both his architecture and his rather heavy-handed furniture. Castell Coch (1876–81), near Cardiff, a reconstruction on 13th-century foundations, was designed as a hunting lodge for the 3rd Marquess of **Bute**. It combines archaeological seriousness with imaginative exuberance. His other project for the marquess, Cardiff Castle (1868–81), is a more eclectic mixture of medieval and exotic styles again applied to the remains of a fortress. His other major works include Cork Cathedral (1862–76, for which he also designed stained glass), a house in Park Place, Cardiff (1870s) and his own house in Melbury Road, London (1875–78). He also designed wallpapers, metalwork and jewellery.

BURGESS, Anthony, pen name of **John Anthony Burgess Wilson** (1917–) English novelist, critic and composer, born in Manchester into a Catholic family of predominantly Irish background. His grandfather was a publican and his father ran a tobacconist's shop. His mother was of Scottish extraction, a singer and dancer, who died in the influenza epidemic of 1919. Educated at the Xaverian College, Manchester, he did odd jobs before going to the University of Manchester where he studied language and literature. He also taught himself music, and has composed a large number of works. In World War II he served in the Royal Army Medical Corps and entertained the troops with his compositions and piano-playing. He married in 1942, and after the war he taught in England before going to Malaya in 1954 where he trained teachers. He wrote his first novel, *A Vision of Battlements*, in 1953 but it was not published until 1965. In the far east he wrote the three novels which became *The Long Day Wanes*: *Time for a Tiger* (1956), *The Enemy in the Blanket* (1958), and *Beds in the East* (1959). Invalided out of the Colonial Service with a suspected brain tumour, he was given a year to live and wrote five novels in a year to provide for his prospective widow. But it was she who died first. In 1968 he married the Contessa Pasi and, beleaguered by death duties, went to live abroad where he has remained ever since, first in Italy, latterly in Monte Carlo and Switzerland. Among his many novels are his dark and violent vision of the future, *A Clockwork Orange* (1962), *Inside Mr Enderby* (1963), *Napoleon Symphony* (1974), *Earthly Powers* (1980), *Kingdom of the Wicked* (1985) and *Any Old Iron* (1989). He is fascinated by language, as his various works of exegesis demonstrate. He has also written biographies, books for children and libretti. An autobiography, *Little Wilson and Big God*, 'Being the First Part of the Confessions of Anthony Burgess', was published in 1987.

BURGESS, Guy Francis de Moncy (1910–63) English spy and traitor (see also **Donald MacLean**, **Kim Philby** and **Anthony Blunt**), son of a naval officer. He was educated at Eton, Royal Naval College, Dartmouth, and at Trinity College, Cambridge, where he became a communist. Recruited as a Soviet agent in the 1930s, he worked with the BBC (1936–39), wrote war propaganda (1939–41), and, ostensibly working for the BBC, served with MI5. After the war he was a member of the foreign office, and finally second secretary under Philby in Washington in 1950. Recalled in 1951 for 'serious misconduct', he, together with MacLean, disappeared to the Soviet Union in 1951 (although the Russians denied the fact until 1956), and died there.

BURGH, Hubert de (d.1243) English statesman. From 1215 to 1232 he was the patriotic justiciar of England, virtual ruler for the last four years, but now is chiefly remembered as the jailer of Prince **Arthur**. He was created Earl of Kent in 1227, and died at Banstead, Surrey. Walter de Burgh, Earl of Ulster, who died at Galway in 1291, was his grand-nephew.

BURGHLEY, or BURGHLEIGH See **CECIL**

BÜRGI See **BYRGIUS**

BURGKMAIR, Hans (1473–1531) German painter and wood-engraver, born in Augsburg. The father-in-law of the elder **Holbein** and the friend of **Dürer**, he is best known by his woodcuts, amounting to nearly 700.

BURGOYNE, John (1722–92) English soldier and dramatist. Educated at Westminster School, he entered the army in 1740. In 1743 he eloped with a daughter of the Earl of Derby, and lived for nine years in France (1747–56). In the Seven Years' War (1756–63) he distinguished himself in the Iberian peninsula by the capture of Valencia de Alcántara (1762), and sat in parliament as a Tory. He was sent out to America in 1774. He fought at Bunker Hill (1775). In 1777 he led an expedition from Canada, and took Ticonderoga; but was later forced to surrender to General **Gates** at Saratoga. Having gone over to the Whigs, he was commander-in-chief in Ireland in 1782–83. He was the author of plays including *The Maid of the Oaks* (1775) and *The Heiress* (1786).

BURGOYNE, Sir John Fox (1782–1871) English military engineer, the illegitimate son of **John Burgoyne**. Educated at Eton College and the Royal Military College, Woolwich, he served with Sir **John Moore** at La Coruña (1809), and served under **Wellington** through the Penisular War. In the Crimean War he was chief of the British engineering department, but was unjustly recalled. He was constable of the Tower (1865), and a field marshal (1868).

BURIDAN, Jean (c.1300–c.1358) French scholastic philosopher, probably born in Béthune, Artois. He studied under **William of Ockham** and taught in Paris. He published works on mechanics, optics, and in particular logic. He gave his name to the famous problem of decision-making called 'Buridan's Ass', where an ass faced with two equidistant and equally desirable bales of hay starves to death because there are no grounds for preferring to go to one bale rather than the other.

BURKE, Edmund (1729–97) Irish statesman and philosopher, born in Dublin. He was educated at a Quaker boarding-school and at Trinity College, Dublin. In 1750 he entered the Middle Temple, London, but soon abandoned law for literary work. His *Vindication of Natural Society*, in which, with well-concealed irony, he confutes **Bolingbroke**'s views of society by a *reductio ad absurdum*, was published anonymously in 1756, as also was his *Philosophical Inquiry into the Origin of our Ideas of the Sublime and Beautiful*. From 1761 to 1763 he was back in Dublin as private secretary to 'Single-speech Hamilton', then secretary for Ireland. In 1765 he became private secretary to the Marquis of **Rockingham**, at that time premier, and entered parliament for the pocket borough of Wendover. His eloquence at once gained him a high position in the Whig party. Rockingham's administration lasted only about a year; but though he held no office till the downfall of the **North** ministry in 1782, Burke's public activity never ceased till his death. Lord North's long administration (1770–82) was marked by the unsuccessful coercion of the American colonies, by corruption, extravagance, and reaction. Against this policy Burke and his Whig friends could only raise a strong protest. The best of Burke's writings and speeches belong to this period, and may be described as a defence of sound constitutional statesmanship against prevailing abuse and misgovernment. *Observations on the Present State of the Nation* (1769) was a reply to **George Grenville**; *On the Causes of the Present Discontents* (1770) treats of the **Wilkes** controversy. Perhaps the finest of his many efforts are the speech on *American Taxation* (1774), the speech on *Conciliation with America* (1775), and the *Letter to the Sheriffs of Bristol* (1777)—all advocating wise and liberal measures, which would have averted the troubles that ensued. Burke never systematized his political philosophy. It emerges with inconsistencies out of the writings and speeches mentioned above. Opposed to the doctrine of 'natural rights', he yet takes over the concept of 'social contract' and attaches to it divine sanction. But his support of the proposals for relaxing the restrictions on the trade of Ireland with Great Britain, and for alleviating the laws against Catholics, cost him the seat at Bristol (1780), and from that time till 1794 he represented Malton. When the disasters of the American war brought Lord North's government to a close, Burke was paymaster of the forces under Rockingham (1782), as also under Portland (1783). After the fall of the Whig ministry in 1783 Burke was never again in office, and, misled by party feeling, he opposed **Pitt**'s measure for free trade with Ireland and the Commercial Treaty with France. In 1788 he opened the trial of **Warren Hastings** by the speech which will always rank among the masterpieces of English eloquence. His *Reflections on the French Revolution* (1790) was read all over Europe and strongly encouraged its rulers to resist, but his opposition to it cost him the support of his fellow Whigs, notably that of **Fox**. In his *Appeal from the New to the Old Whigs*, *Thoughts on French Affairs*, and *Letters on a Regicide Peace*, he goes further, urging the government to suppress free opinions at home. He was buried in the little church at Beaconsfield, where in 1768 he had purchased the estate of Gregories. During his whole political life Burke was financially embarrassed, despite two pensions granted him in 1794. He ranks as one of the foremost political thinkers of England. He had vast knowledge of affairs, a glowing imagination, passionate sympathies, and an inexhaustible wealth of powerful and cultured expression; but his delivery was awkward and ungainly, and speeches which captivate the reader only served to empty the benches of the House of Commons. Although himself a Whig, Burke's political thought has become, with **Disraeli**'s, the philosophy of modern Conservatism.

BURKE, John (1787–1848) Irish genealogist, born in Tipperary. He was the compiler of *Burke's Peerage*—the first dictionary of baronets and peers in alphabetical order, published in 1826.

BURKE, Sir John Bernard (1814–92) Irish genealogist son of **John Burke**. He took over *Burke's Peerage* from his father and published it annually from 1847, as well as anecdotes of the aristocracy. An expert in heraldry, he was Ulster King of Arms (1853), and keeper of the state papers of Ireland (1855).

BURKE, Robert O'Hara (1820–61) Irish traveller and explorer of Australia, born in St Clerans, County Galway. As leader of the Burke and Wills expedition, he was one of the first white men to cross the Australian continent from south to north. Educated in Belgium, he served in the Austrian army (1840), joined the Irish constabulary (1848), and emigrated to Australia in 1853. While an inspector of police in Victoria he accepted the leadership, with **William Wills**, of an expedition to cross the continent. It set off from Melbourne, and, after many hardships, Burke and Wills and two other men reached the tidal marshes of the Flinders River at the edge of the Gulf of Carpentaria. Both Burke and Wills, and a third man, died of starvation on the return journey; the only survivor was **John King**.

BURKE, Thomas (1886–1945) English writer, born in London. He is best known for his *Limehouse Nights* (1916), but he was the author of about 30 books, mostly on aspects of London or about inns. These include *Nights in Town* (1915), *The Streets of London* (1941), and *The English Inn* (1930). He also made a fine reconstruction of the Thurtell and Hunt case in *Murder at Elstree* (1936). He published an autobiography, *The Wind and the Rain*, in (1924).

BURKE, Thomas Henry (1829–82) English politician. Permanent Irish under-secretary from 1868, he was brutally murdered with Lord Frederick Cavendish in Phoenix Park, Dublin.

BURKE, William (1792–1829) Irish murderer. With his partner William Hare (1790–1860) he committed a series of murders in Edinburgh, to supply dissection subjects to Dr **Robert Knox**, the anatomist. Hare, the more villainous of the two, was admitted king's evidence, and, according to Serjeant Ballantine, died some time in the 1860s, a blind beggar in London, while

Burke was hanged, to the general satisfaction of the crowd. **Bridie**'s play *The Anatomist* was based on the case.

BURLAMAQUI, Jean Jacques (1694–1748) Swiss jurist, professor of civil and natural law and also councillor and minister of state at Geneva. He wrote the influential *Principes du Droit Naturel* (1747) and *Principes du Droit Politique* (1751) which were important in their time. Seeking to derive natural law from God, human reason and moral instinct, he taught that domestic law and international law were based on natural law.

BURLEIGH See **CECIL**, and **BALFOUR, John, of Kinloch**

BURLINGAME, Anson (1820–70) American diplomat, born in New Berlin, New York. He was sent as US minister to China by **Lincoln**; and when returning was made Chinese envoy to the US and Europe. He negotiated the Burlingame treaty between China and the US (1868), establishing reciprocal rights of citizenship.

BURLINGTON, Richard Boyle, 3rd Earl of (1695–1753) Anglo-Irish politician and patron of the arts. A great admirer of **Palladio**, he was himself an enthusiastic architect. He refashioned the Burlington House of his great-grandfather, the first earl, in Piccadilly and by his influence over a group of young architects was responsible for fostering the Palladian precept which was to govern English building for half a century. He was lord high treasurer of Ireland in 1715.

BURMANN, Peter 'the elder' (1668–1741) Dutch historian. He studied law at Utrecht and Leiden, and became professor of history and rhetoric at Utrecht, afterwards of Greek at Leiden. His chief works are editions of the Latin classics.

BURMANN, Peter 'the younger' (1714–78) Dutch classical scholar, nephew of **Peter 'the elder'**. He studied at Utrecht, and became professor at Franeker, then at Amsterdam, and keeper of the public library there. He edited **Virgil**, **Aristophanes**, **Claudian**, **Propertius**, and a Latin anthology.

BURN, Richard (1709–85) English legal writer and historian, born in Winton, Westmorland. Educated at Oxford, he was vicar of Orton from 1736 and compiled *Justice of the Peace* and *Ecclesiastical Law*.

BURN, William (1789–1870) Scottish architect, born in Edinburgh. He trained under **Smirke** in London, and founded a successful business first in Edinburgh (with **David Bryce**), and then, after 1844, in London. He designed The Edinburgh Academy (1824), John Watson's Hospital and the Music Hall in Edinburgh, and the Custom House in Greenock.

BURNABY, Frederick Gustavus (1842–85) English soldier and traveller, born in Bedford. He joined the Royal Horse Guards Blue in 1859 (colonel, 1881). He travelled with General **Gordon** in the Sudan in 1875, and that winter journeyed across the Russian steppes on horseback (*Ride to Khiva*, 1876). In 1876–78 he travelled in Asia Minor and Armenia, writing thereafter *On Horseback through Asia Minor*. In 1882 he crossed the Channel to Normandy in a balloon.

BURNAND, Sir Francis Cowley (1836–1917) English dramatist and journalist. He was called to the bar in 1862, but the success of some early dramatic ventures altered his plans. He helped to start *Fun*, but in 1863 left that paper for *Punch*, of which he was editor (1880–1906). He wrote many burlesques, including *Black-Eyed Susan* (1866) and *Cox and Box*, with music by **Arthur Sullivan** (1867).

BURNE-JONES, Sir Edward Coley (1833–98) English painter, born in Birmingham of Welsh ancestry. He studied at Exeter College, Oxford, where he became the intimate friend of **William Morris** and **Dante Gabriel Rossetti**. In 1861 he became a founder member of Morris, Marshall, Faulkner & Company (later Morris & Company), for which he designed tapestries and stained glass. His early works, mostly in water-colour, such as *The Merciful Knight* (1864) and *The Wine of Circe* (1867), attain a greater brilliancy and purity of hue even than his later oils which, inspired by the early art of the Italian Renaissance, are characterized by a romantic and contrived mannerism. His subjects, drawn from the Arthurian romances and Greek myths, include *The Days of Creation*, *The Beguiling of Merlin*, *The Mirror of Venus* (1877), and *Pan and Psyche* (1878). His *Love and the Pilgrim* is in the Tate Gallery, London. His son, Sir Philip (1861–1926), was also a painter.

BURNES, Sir Alexander (1805–41) Scottish traveller and diplomat, born in Montrose, distantly related to **Robert Burns**. In 1821 he entered the Indian army, and his knowledge of oriental languages gained him rapid promotion. In 1832, wearing Afghan dress, he travelled through Peshawar and Kabul, and crossed the Hindu Kush to Balkh. From there he passed on to Bukhara, Astrabad, and Teheran, and, journeying through Isfahan and Shiraz, embarked at Bushire for India. In 1839 he was appointed political resident at Kabul, where he was murdered by the Afghan mob.

BURNET, Sir Frank Macfarlane (1899–1985) Australian physician and virologist, born in Traralgon, Victoria. Director of the Institute for Medical Research, Melbourne, he became a world authority on viral diseases, perfecting the technique of cultivating viruses in living chick embryos. He shared the 1960 Nobel prize for physiology or medicine with Sir **Peter Brian Medawar** for researches on immunological intolerance in relation to skin and organ grafting.

BURNET, Gilbert (1643–1715) Scottish churchman and Anglican historian, born in Edinburgh. At ten he entered Marischal College, Aberdeen, and applied himself first to law and then to divinity with such diligence that in 1661 he was admitted a probationer of the Church of Scotland. In 1663 he visited Cambridge, Oxford, and London, and the next year perfected his Hebrew under a rabbi from Amsterdam. In 1669, he was appointed professor of divinity at Glasgow; but in 1674, having brought on himself the enmity of his old patron the Duke of **Lauderdale**, he resigned his chair, and settled in London, where he associated with the Whig broad-church opposition and was made chaplain to the Rolls Chapel, and afterwards lecturer at St Clements, publishing several works, including in 1679–81 the first two volumes of his *History of the Reformation*. In 1680 he declined the bishopric of Chichester; in 1683 he attended the execution of his friend William, Lord **Russell** for complicity in the Ryehouse Plot. **Charles II** exhibited his unkingly spite by depriving him of his lectureship; and on **James II**'s accession Burnet went to the continent, and travelled through Europe, eventually taking Dutch nationality. In 1684 he met the Prince of Orange, with whom he became a great favourite. When **William III** came over in the 'Glorious Revolution' of 1688, Burnet accompanied him as royal chaplain, and in 1689 was appointed bishop of Salisbury. His first pastoral letter, founding William's right to the throne on conquest, gave so much offence to parliament that it was burned by the hangman. In 1699 he published his *Exposition of the thirty-nine Articles*, which was condemned as heterodox by the Lower House of Convocation. In 1714 he published the third volume of his *History of the*

Reformation. He also wrote a *History of My Own Time* (1724–34).

BURNET, Thomas (c.1635–1715) English clergyman, born in Croft, Yorkshire. He became clerk of the closet to **William III**, but had to resign the post in 1692 on account of his *Archaeologia Philosophica*, which treated the Mosaic account of the Fall as an allegory. His *Telluris Theoria Sacra* (1680–89), recomposed in English by the author, is a mere fanciful cosmogony. He was master of Charterhouse from 1685.

BURNETT, Frances Eliza, née **Hodgson** (1849–1924) English-born American novelist, born in Manchester, the daughter of a manufacturer. In 1865 she emigrated with her parents to Knoxville, Tennessee, where she married Dr Swan Moses Burnett in 1873 (divorced in 1898). Her first literary success was *That Lass o' Lowrie's* (1877). Later works included plays and her most popular story *Little Lord Fauntleroy* (1886), *The One I Knew Best of All* (1893, autobiographical), *The Little Princess* (1905) and *The Secret Garden* (1909).

BURNETT, James See **MONBODDO**

BURNETT, Sir William (1799–1861) Scottish physician and physician-general of the navy, born in Montrose. 'Burnett's fluid', a strong solution of zinc chloride used as a wood preservative, is named after him.

BURNEY, Charles (1726–1814) English musicologist, father of **Fanny Burney**, born in Shrewsbury. He studied music there, at Chester, and under Dr **Arne** in London, later giving lessons himself. After composing three pieces, *Alfred*, *Robin Hood*, and *Queen Mab*, for Drury Lane (1745–50), he went as organist to King's Lynn, Norfolk (1751–60). He travelled (1770–72) in France, Italy, Germany, and Austria to collect material for his *General History of Music* (1776–89), and his *Present State of Music in France and Italy* (1771). His *General History* was for long considered a standard work, superseding that of Sir **John Hawkins**, but its value has been stultified by its bias towards the then popular Italian style, to the neglect of **Bach** and his contemporaries. Burney also wrote a *Life of Metastasio*, and nearly all the musical articles in *Rees's Cyclopaedia*. In 1783 he became organist to Chelsea Hospital. He knew intimately many of the eminent men of his day, including **Burke**, Dr **Johnson** and **Garrick**.

BURNEY, Fanny, originally **Frances,** later **Madame D'Arblay** (1752–1840) English novelist and diarist, daughter of **Charles Burney**, born in King's Lynn. She educated herself by reading English and French literature and observing the distinguished people who visited her father. By ten she had begun her incessant scribbling of stories, plays, and poems; on her 15th birthday, in a fit of repentance for such waste of time, she burned all her papers, but she could not forget the plot of *Evelina*, her first and best novel, published anonymously in 1778, which describes the entry of a country girl into the gaieties of London life. Her father at once recognized his daughter's talent, and confided the secret to Mrs **Thrale**, who, as well as Dr **Johnson**, championed the gifted young authoress. *Cecilia* (1782), though more complex, is less natural, and her style gradually declined in *Camilla* (1796) and *The Wanderer* (1814). She was appointed a second keeper of the robes to Queen **Charlotte** in 1786, but her health declined; she retired on a pension and married a French émigré, General d'Arblay, in 1793. Her *Letters and Diaries* (1846) show her skill in reporting dramatically. As a portrayer of the domestic scene she was a forerunner of **Jane Austen**, whom she influenced.

BURNHAM, David Hudson (1846–1912) American architect and leader of the Chicago School, born in Henderson, New York. He worked in partnership with John Wellborn Root (1850–91), and later with Charles B Atwood. His pioneering designs into urban planning in Chicago were widely influential. He continued the Romanesque revival and developed the Richardsonian style. With Root, in Chicago, he designed the Women's Temple and Masonic Building (1890–92), now demolished, the Reliance Building (1890–95), and the conservative skyscraper design, Monadnock Building (1890–91). As chief of construction for the Chicago World's Fair (1893), he co-ordinated the creation of the White City, comprising formal monumental designs. The Rookery Building, New York (1901), the Selfridge Building, London (1908) and the Union Railroad Station, Washington, DC (1909) are examples of his later commissions.

BURNHAM, Forbes (1923–85) Guyanese politician. He studied law in London, and was co-founder of the Marxist-Leninist People's Progressive party (PPP) in 1949. In 1955 he broke away and was co-founder in 1957 of the more moderate, socialist People's National Congress (PNC). He became prime minister of Guyana in 1964 and led his country to independence two years later. In 1970 he declared the country a 'Co-operative Socialist Republic'. He won two elections, in 1968 and 1973, amid widespread claims of election-rigging. In 1980 a new constitution was adopted and he became executive president until his death in office.

BURNHAM, Harry Lawson Webster Lawson, 1st Viscount (1862–1933) English statesman, born in London. He was educated at Eton and Oxford, was Liberal and later Unionist MP, succeeded his father as director of *The Daily Telegraph* in 1903 and helped to frame the Representation of the People Act of 1918. He was president of the International Labour Conference and the Empire Press Union for several years. He is chiefly known, however, as chairman of the committees which inquired into the salaries of teachers and which recommended the Burnham Scales.

BURNOUF, Émile Louis (1821–1907) French philologist, and cousin of **Eugène Burnouf**. He directed the French school at Athens, and wrote on Sanskrit, Greek, the science of religion, Japanese mythology, and Latin hymnology.

BURNOUF, Eugène (1801–52) French philologist and orientalist, son of **Jean Louis Burnouf**, born in Paris. He became a member of the Académie des Inscriptions in 1832, and from then till his death was professor of Sanskrit at the Collège de France. His first works were on Pali (1826–27) and Zend MSS. His lithographed edition (1829–43) of the Vendidad-Sadé, part of the *Zend-Avesta*, and his *Commentaire sur le Yaçna* (1833), revealed the language and doctrine of **Zoroaster** to the western world. He attempted to decipher the cuneiform inscriptions of Persepolis (1836). In 1840 he published text and translation of the *Bhâgavata Purâna*, a system of Indian mythology, and in 1844 his *Histoire du Bouddhisme*.

BURNOUF, Jean Louis (1755–1844) French philologist, father of **Eugène Burnouf**. He was professor of rhetoric at the Collège de France (1817), inspector and librarian of the university, and member of the Académie des Inscriptions (1836). He translated **Tacitus** (1827–33).

BURNS, Sir George (1795–1890) Scottish shipowner, born in Glasgow. With his brother James (1789–1871) he pioneered steam navigation from Glasgow. In 1839, with **Samuel Cunard** and **Robert Napier**, he founded the future Cunard Line. He retired in 1858 and was succeeded by his son John (1829–1911), later Lord Inverclyde.

BURNS, John (1858–1943) British Labour politician, born of Scottish parentage in London. He worked as an engineer, took to socialism, and, elected MP for Battersea in 1892, became president of the local government board in 1905, and of the board of trade in 1914, but resigned when war began. He was the first working-man cabinet minister in Britain.

BURNS, Robert (1759–96) Scottish poet, born in Alloway near Ayr, the son of a small farmer. The boy's education, begun at a school at Alloway Mill, and continued by one John Murdoch, was thoroughly literary. Among early influences were the popular tales, ballads and songs of Betty Davidson, an old woman who lived with the poet's family. He read **Allan Ramsay**, and began to write a little. Acquaintance with sailors and smugglers broadened his outlook, and his interest in women made him a kind of rural Don Juan. The death of Burns's father in 1784 left him to try to farm for himself. Burns's husbandry at Mossgiel near Mauchline went badly; the entanglement with Jean Armour (1767–1834) began; and out of his poverty, his passion, his despair, and his desperate mirth, came the extraordinary poetic harvest of 1785. To this year belong the 'Epistle to Davie', 'Death and Dr Hornbook', 'The Twa Herds', 'The Jolly Beggars', 'Halloween', 'The Cotter's Saturday Night', 'Holy Willie's Prayer', 'The Holy Fair', and 'The Address to a Mouse'. The next year produced more excellent work, though much of the verse is satirical. 'The Twa Dogs' is a masterpiece of humour; 'The Lament' and 'Despondency' are fine works. In this year there was abundant trouble with Jean Armour, and there was a love episode involving 'Highland Mary' (Mary Campbell) and her subsequent death. Looking about for money to emigrate to Jamaica, Burns published the famous Kilmarnock edition of his poems (1786). Their fame spread, and with the money he received, he decided to leave Scotland for good. He was just about to sail when the praises and promises of admirers induced him to stay in Scotland. In winter he went to Edinburgh and was greeted with acclaim. On returning to the country, he 'fell to his old love again', Jean Armour; then, after a Highland tour, went back to Edinburgh, and began the epistolary flirtations with 'Clarinda' (**Agnes Maclehose**). By this date **James Johnson** had set about publishing his *Scots Musical Museum*, which contains all that is briefest and brightest of Burns. He contributed an astonishing number of the most beautiful, tender, passionate, and vivacious songs in any language, chiefly adapted to old Scottish airs, and moulded now and then on old Scots words. In 1788 he married Jean Armour. He took a lease of Ellisland farm, on the Nith, above Dumfries, and next year became an excise officer. 'Tam o' Shanter' (1790) was written in one day; by this time Ellisland had proved a failure. He left his farm, withdrew to Dumfries, flirted with the French Revolution, drank, wrote songs, expressed opinions then thought radical, and made himself unpopular with the local lairds. But in 1795 he turned patriot again. He died of endocarditis induced by rheumatism, and is buried in Dumfries. His humble origin and his identification with the Scottish folk tradition, which he rescued, refurbished, and in part embellished, are factors that help to explain his unwaning popularity as the national poet of Scotland.

BURNSIDE, Ambrose Everett (1824–81) American soldier, born in Liberty, Indiana. He served an apprenticeship to a tailor, but graduated at West Point in 1847. As colonel of volunteers in 1861, he commanded a brigade at Bull Run, and in February 1862 captured Roanoke Island. His corps was repulsed with heavy losses in the battle of Antietam (September 1862). He accepted command of the army of the Potomac reluctantly on the supersession of McClellan, and crossed the Rappahannock to attack **Lee** near Fredericksburg, but was repulsed with a loss of over 10000 men (December 1862). He was removed from command after another attempted crossing (January 1863). In 1863 he successfully held Knoxville, and in 1864 led a corps under **Grant** through the battles of the Wilderness and Cold Harbor. He was elected US senator in 1875. He lent his name to a style of side-whiskers he wore ('burnsides', now 'sideburns').

BURNSIDE, William (1852–1927) English mathematician, born in London. He entered St John's College, Cambridge in 1871, graduated second wrangler from Pembroke College in 1875, was a fellow of Pembroke until 1886, and was professor of mathematics at the Royal Naval College, Greenwich (1885–1919). He worked in mathematical physics, complex function theory, differential geometry, and probability theory, but his lasting work was in group theory. His *Theory of groups* (1897, 2nd ed 1911) was the first English textbook on the subject and is still of value, containing much new research of his own and posing the famous Burnside problem. This was not solved until 1962 by Walter Feit and John Griggs Thompson in probably the longest and most complicated proof ever published in the history of mathematics.

BURR, Aaron (1756–1836) American statesman, born in Newark, New Jersey. A graduate of Princeton, he was called to the bar in 1782, and was attorney-general 1789–91, US senator 1791–97, and vice-president of the USA 1800–04, having tied with **Thomas Jefferson** in the electoral college of 1800, but was defeated by a vote of the House of Representatives. His defeat in a contest for the governorship of New York led him to force a duel (11 July 1804) on Alexander Hamilton, his personal rival, whom he mortally wounded. Burr fled to South Carolina, and though indicted for murder, returned and completed his term as vice-president. He now prepared to raise a force to conquer Texas, and establish there a republic, and ultimately (said his enemies, unjustly) dismember the Union. This enterprise was proclaimed by the president, and Burr was tried for treason (1807). Acquitted, but with his reputation in shreds, he spent some wretched years in Europe, and in 1812 resumed his law practice in New York. There, shunned by society, he died.

BURRA, Edward (1905–76) English artist, born in London. He studied at the Chelsea School of Art and the Royal College of Art, and travelled widely in Europe and the USA. He is well known as a colourist, and his surrealist paintings of figures against exotic (often Spanish) backgrounds are invariably in watercolour. His picture *Soldiers* in this vein (1942) is in the Tate Gallery, London. He also designed for the ballet.

BURRELL, Sir William (1861–1958) Scottish shipowner and art collector, born in Glasgow, the son of a shipping agent. He entered his father's business at the age of 15, and during his lifetime he accumulated a magnificent collection of 8000 works of art from all over the world, including modern French paintings, which he gave in 1944 to the city of Glasgow, with provision for a gallery. In 1949 he gifted an art gallery and a number of pictures to Berwick-on-Tweed. The Burrell Collection was finally opened to the public in 1983 in a new gallery built for it on the south side of Glasgow.

BURRITT, Elihu (1810–79) American pacifist, known as 'the learned blacksmith', born in New Britain,

Connecticut. He worked as a blacksmith in his native town and at Worcester, Massachusetts, but devoted all his leisure to mathematics and languages. Through his published works and through his travels in the USA and Europe he was known as an apostle of peace. He founded the *Christian Citizen* in 1844. From 1865 to 1870 he was American consul in Birmingham, England.

BURROUGHS, Edgar Rice (1875–1950) American popular author, creator of Tarzan, born in Chicago. He served in the US cavalry and fought against the Apache Indians but was discharged when it was discovered he was under age. Thereafter he had several colourful occupations before he took to writing, his aim being to improve on the average dime novel. *Tarzan of the Apes* (1914) was his first book to feature the eponymous superhero, the son of a British aristocrat, abandoned in the jungle and brought up by apes. It spawned many sequels, films (Tarzan played, most memorably, by **Johnny Weismuller**), radio programmes and comic strips, making Burroughs a millionaire.

BURROUGHS, John (1837–1921) American naturalist and writer, born in Roxbury, New York. A teacher and later tax inspector, he settled down in 1874 on a farm near Aesopus, New York, where he built himself a secluded cabin for his studies. His books mostly deal with country life, and include *Wake-Robin* (1871), *Winter Sunshine* (1875), *Birds and Poets* (1877), and *Locusts and Wild Honey* (1879).

BURROUGHS, William Seward (1855–98) American inventor, born in Auburn, New York. He developed a mechanical calculating machine in 1885, and an adding machine in 1892.

BURROUGHS, William Seward (1914–) American author, born in St Louis, Mississippi. He graduated from Harvard in 1936 and wandered in the USA and Europe. In 1944 he became a heroin addict while doing odd jobs in New York. In 1953 he published *Junkie*, an account of his experiences as an addict, and his novels *The Naked Lunch* (1959) and *The Soft Machine* (1961) established him as a spokesman of the 'beat' movement of the late 1950s. Intensely interested in the juxtaposition of apparently random ideas and observations, his later work is concerned with innovations in the novel form, such as the techniques of 'cut-up' and 'fold-in', in which words and phrases are either cut out and pasted together or formed by cross-column reading. Other works include *The Experimentor* (1960, with Bryon Gysin), *The Ticket that Exploded* (1962), *The Yage Letters* 1963, (with **Allen Ginsberg**), *Dead Fingers Talk* (1963), *Nova Express* (1964), *The Wild Boys* (1971), *Exterminator!* (1973), *The Last Words of Dutch Schultz* (1975), *Ah, Pook is Here* (1971) and *Cities of the Red Night* (1981). His autobiography appeared in 1973.

BURROWS, Montagu (1819–1905) English historian, born in Hadley, near Barnet. He rose in the navy to commander (1852), and then, going up to Oxford, took a double first, and in 1862 became Chichele professor of modern history. Among his works are *Wyclif's Place in History* (1882) and an Autobiography (1908).

BURT, Sir Cyril Lodowic (1883–1971) English psychologist, born in London. Educated at Christ's Hospital and Jesus College, Oxford, and at Würzburg, he became professor of education at London (1924–31) and professor of psychology (1931–50). He was also psychologist to the London County Council, was consulted by the war office and the civil service commission on 'personnel selection' and was highly influential in the theory and practice of intelligence and aptitude tests, ranging from the psychology of education to the problems of juvenile delinquency. Since his death the authenticity of some of his research data has been questioned.

BURTON, Decimus (1800–81) English architect, son of a London builder. At the age of 23 he planned the Regent's Park colosseum, an exhibition hall with a dome larger than that of St Paul's, and in 1825 designed the new layout of Hyde Park and the triumphal arch at Hyde Park Corner. He designed the Palm House at Kew Gardens (1844–48) with engineer Richard Turner.

BURTON, John Hill (1809–81) Scottish historian and lawyer, born in Aberdeen. He studied law at Aberdeen and was called to the bar in Edinburgh, but turned to writing to supplement his income. He wrote biographies of **David Hume** (1846), and Lord **Lovat** and **Duncan Forbes** (1847). His major work was his *History of Scotland* (9 vols, 1853–70). In 1854 he was appointed secretary to the prison board of Scotland, and later a commissioner (1877). In 1867 he was appointed historiographer royal for Scotland.

BURTON, Michael Lord See **BASS, Michael Thomas**

BURTON, Richard, originally **Jenkins** (1925–84) Welsh stage and film actor, born in Pontrhydfen. A coal miner's son, he gained a scholarship to Exeter College, Oxford. He first appeared on stage in *Druid's Rest* at the Royal Court Theatre, Liverpool and, after national service in the RAF, returned to the stage in 1948, the same year as his film début in *The Last Days of Dolwyn*. He made his stage reputation in **Christopher Fry**'s *The Lady's Not for Burning* (1949), which was enthusiastically received on Broadway. A triumphant season at Stratford in 1951 preceded his first Hollywood film, *My Cousin Rachel* (1952), for which he received one of his seven Academy Award nominations. In 1954 he was the narrator in the famous radio production of **Dylan Thomas**'s *Under Milk Wood*. Hailed as one of the most promising Shakespearean actors of his generation, a well-publicized romance with **Elizabeth Taylor** during the making of *Cleopatra* in 1962 and their eventual marriage projected them both into the 'superstar' category, and he was able to command vast salaries for such highly successful films as *The Spy Who Came in from the Cold* (1965) and *Where Eagles Dare* (1969). Interest in his lifestyle was greater than in his performances, although his work in *Who's Afraid of Virginia Woolf* (1968) and *Equus* (1977) and *1984* was well-received.

BURTON, Sir Richard Francis (1821–90) English orientalist and explorer, born in Torquay, son of a colonel. His education, on the continent and in England was irregular, and included expulsion from Oxford. In 1842 he served in Sind under Sir **Charles Napier**, and having mastered Hindustani, Persian, and Arabic, made a pilgrimage to Mecca disguised as a Pathan (1853). In 1856 he set out with **John Hanning Speke** on the journey which led to the discovery (1858) of Lake Tanganyika. In 1861 he was consul at Fernando Pó, and went on a mission to Dahomey. He was subsequently consul at Santos in Brazil, at Damascus, and (1872) at Trieste. He was knighted in 1886. He amassed a vast store of notes, sociological, anthropological, often simply erotological; and for some of his translations (*The Perfumed Garden*, *Kama Sutra*, and his monumental annotated editon of the *Arabian Nights*, 16 vols, 1885–88) he resorted to private publication, so avoiding prosecution and making a considerable fortune in his last years. Lady Burton (née Isabel Arundell, 1831–96), shared in much of his travelling and writing; a devoted wife, she denied posterity her husband's last (incomplete) work, *The*

Scented Garden Men's Hearts to Gladden, and his journals, by burning the manuscript, after his death.

BURTON, Robert (1577–1640) English writer and clergyman, author of the *Anatomy of Melancholy*, born in Lindley, Leicestershire. Educated at Nuneaton, Sutton Coldfield, and Brasenose College, Oxford, in 1599 he was elected a student of Christ Church College. In 1616 he was presented to the Oxford vicarage of St Thomas, and about 1630 to the rectory of Segrave. Both livings he kept, but spent his life at Christ Church, where he died. The first edition of *Anatomy of Melancholy*, written under the pseudonym 'Democritus Junior', appeared in quarto in 1621. Four more editions in folio were published within the author's lifetime, each with successive alterations and additions; the final form of the book was the sixth edition (1651–52). One of the most interesting parts is the long preface, 'Democritus to the Reader', in which Burton gives indirectly an account of himself and his studies. This strange book is a vast and witty compendium of Jacobean knowledge about the 'disease' of melancholy, gathered from even the most out-of-the-way classical and medieval writers, as well as folklore and superstition.

BURY, Lady Charlotte Susan Maria (1775–1861) Scottish novelist, youngest child of the fifth Duke of Argyll. She married in 1796 Colonel John Campbell (d.1809), and in 1818 the Rev Edward John Bury (1790–1832). Beautiful and accomplished, she published 16 novels, including *Flirtation*, and *Separation*, and was reputedly the anonymous author of the spicy *Diary illustrative of the Times of George IV* (1838).

BURY, John Bagnell (1861–1927) Irish historian and classical scholar, born in County Monaghan. Educated at Trinity College, Dublin, he became professor of modern history (1893–1902) and Greek (1899–1902) at Dublin and thereafter Regius professor of modern history at Cambridge. He wrote a monumental *History of the Later Roman Empire* (1889) at the age of 28, and other major histories of Greece and Rome, and edited **Pindar** and **Gibbon**.

BUSBY, Sir Matt (1909–) Scottish footballer and football manager, born in Bellshill, Lanarkshire. After a comparatively undistinguished playing career with Manchester City and Liverpool, he became manager of Manchester United in 1945. Almost immediately the club won the FA Cup in 1948 and the League shortly afterwards. Rebuilding the team, he seemed likely to bring the European Cup to Britain for the first time in 1958 but his young side was largely wiped out in an air crash at Munich airport. He himself was severely injured, but patiently reconstructed the side until European Cup success eventually came in 1968.

BUSBY, Richard (1606–95) English schoolmaster, born in Lutton-Bowine, Lincolnshire. Educated at Westminster School and Christ Church College, Oxford, he was headmaster of Westminster from 1640 until his death. He was the prototype 17th-century headmaster, notable alike for learning, assiduity, and unsparing application of the birch. Among his pupils were **John Dryden**, **John Locke**, **Robert South**, and **Francis Atterbury**.

BUSCH, Adolf (1891–1952) German-born American violinist, born in Siegan, Westphalia. In 1919 he formed the Busch Quartet and Busch Trio with his brother Hermann (1897–1975) as cellist and his son-in-law **Rudolf Serkin** as pianist. He emigrated to America in 1939. Another brother, Fritz (1890–1951), was an eminent conductor and noted Mozartian, especially as music director of the Dresden Opera 1922–33, where he premiered operas by **Strauss** at Glyndebourne (1934–39), in South America (1940–45) and at the New York Metropolitan (1945–49).

BUSCH, Wilhelm (1832–1908) German cartoonist and writer, born near Hanover. He worked as an illustrator for the *Fliegende Blätter* (1859–71), and wrote satirical verse-stories with his own illustrations, such as *Max und Moritz* (1865, the prototypes for **Rudolph Dirks**' *Katzenjammer Kids*), and *Herr und Frau Knopp* (1876).

BÜSCHING, Anton Friedrich (1724–93) German geographer, the founder of statistical geography, born in Schaumburg-Lippe. The director of a gymnasium in Berlin, he wrote *Neue Erdbeschreibung* (1754–92). His son, Johann Gustav (1783–1829), published many works on German antiquities, literature, and art.

BUSENBAUM, Hermann (1600–68) German Jesuit theologian, born in Westphalia. He entered the Jesuit order in 1619 and became rector of the Jesuit College at Münster. His *Medulla Theologiae Moralis* (1645) became a standard authority in Jesuit seminaries, though several of its propositions were later condemned by the popes for their apparent support of regicide and the book was publicly burned in 1757.

BUSH, Alan Dudley (1900–) English composer and pianist, born in London. He studied at the Royal Academy of Music (1918–22): composition with **John Ireland** (1922–27) and piano with **Moiseiwitsch** and **Schnabel**. He was a notable composition teacher at the Royal Academy from 1925 to 1978, except when studying philosophy and musicology at Berlin University (1929–31) and serving in the Royal Army Medical Corps (1941–45). In 1924 he became active in the British working-class movement and founded the Workers' Music Association (1936), of which he has been president since 1941. His political and philosophical beliefs underlie much of his output which includes four operas (*Wat Tyler*, Leipzig 1953, *Men of Blackmoor*, Weimar 1956, *The Sugar Reapers*, Leipzig 1966, and *Joe Hill—The Man Who Never Died*, Berlin 1970); four symphonies and much other orchestral music; concertos for violin and piano; choral works including *The Winter Journey* (1946); folksong arrangements; songs including the cycle *Voices of the Prophets* (1952); many chamber works including *Dialectic* (1929) for string quartet; and a considerable quantity of piano music, organ works, etc. In 1980 he published his collected essays, *In My Eighth Decade*.

BUSH, George Herbert Walker (1924–) American Republican politician, and 41st president of the USA, born in Milton, Massachusetts, the son of a Connecticut senator. He served in the navy between 1942 and 1945, becoming its youngest pilot, before taking a degree in economics at Yale. He married Barbara Pierce (1925–), the daughter of a wealthy New York publisher, in 1945, and moved to Texas in 1948 where he made a fortune through establishing an oil-drilling business, before selling out his interests in 1966 and devoting himself to politics. Having run unsuccessfully for the senate in 1964, he was elected to the House of Representatives in 1966 and, after being defeated again in a race for the senate in Texas, was first appointed American ambassador to the United Nations (1971–73) and then Republican National Chairman (1973–74) by President **Nixon**. During the **Ford** administration, Bush was appointed special envoy to China (1974–75) and director of the CIA (1976). In 1980 he contested the Republican party presidential primaries and gained a surprise early victory at the Iowa caucuses, before losing ground to **Ronald Reagan**. Bush joined Reagan on the successful Republican 'ticket' in November 1980 and served as a loyal vice-president to Reagan for eight years, playing a significant role in the formulation and execution of foreign policy as head of a special emergency operations unit and as a peripatetic ambassador for the administration. His standing was damaged during 1987 by his indirect connection with the 'Iran-Contragate Scandal', but in 1988 Bush recovered to be elected president, defeating his Democrat challenger, **Michael Dukakis**.

BUSH, Vannevar (1890–1974) American electrical engineer and inventor, born in Everett, Massachusetts. He graduated from Tufts College and from the Massachusetts Institute of Technology. He devoted most of his considerable research effort from 1925 to the development of mechanical, electro-mechanical and latterly electronic calculating machines or analogue computers, which led directly to the digital computers universally used today. He also devised a cipher-breaking machine which was successful in breaking Japanese codes during World War II, and he was instrumental in setting up the 'Manhattan Project' in 1942 which led to the American atomic bomb.

BUSONI, Ferruccio Benvenuto (1866–1924) Italian pianist and composer, born in Empoli, Tuscany. An infant prodigy, he played in public at the age of nine, and at fifteen made a successful concert tour. In 1889 he became professor of the pianoforte at Helsinki, met **Sibelius**, and married (1890) Gerda Sjöstrand. He subsequently taught and played the pianoforte in Moscow, Boston, Berlin, Weimar, and Zürich, returning to Berlin in 1920. The influence of **Liszt** is apparent in his great pianoforte concerto. Of his four operas *Doktor Faust*, completed posthumously by a pupil in 1925, is his greatest work. Its superbly scored ballet music shows his debt to **Bizet**. He was a noted editor of the keyboard music of **Bach** and Liszt. His pupils included **Percy Grainger**, **Hindemith** and **Kurt Weill**. He wrote *Outline of a new Aesthetic of Music* (1906).

BUSS, Frances Mary (1827–94) English pioneer in women's education. At the age of 23 she founded the North London Collegiate School for Ladies and was headmistress 1850–94—the first woman to call herself a headmistress. She was immortalized in verse with **Dorothea Beale** of Cheltenham Ladies' College ('Miss Buss and Miss Beale, Cupid's darts do not feel').

BUSSY-RABUTIN, Roger, Comte de, properly **Roger de Rabutin, Comte de Bussy** (1618–93) French soldier, adventurer and writer. A raffish and dashing cavalry officer, he ruined his brilliant military prospects by getting himself imprisoned and exiled for his *Histoire amoureuse des Gaules*, a book of partly fictitious court scandals (1666). He conducted a long correspondence from exile with his cousin, **Mme de Sévigné**.

BUSTAMENTE, Sir (William) Alexander, originally **William Alexander Clarke** (1884–1977) Jamaican politician. Born near Kingston, the son of an Irish planter, he was adopted at the age of 15 by a Spanish seaman called Bustamente and spent an adventurous youth abroad before returning in 1932 to become a trade union leader. In 1943 he founded the Jamaica Labour party (JLP) as the political wing of his union, and in 1962, when Jamaica achieved independence, became its first prime minister. He was knighted in 1955.

BUTCHER, Rosemary (1947–) British choreographer, born in Bristol. The first dance graduate of Dartington College in Devon, she went to New York where she saw the experimental work of **Trisha Brown**, **Steve Paxton** and **Lucinda Childs**. She began choreographing her own work in 1976 and has made over 30 pieces, often performing them in unusual places—in art galleries and once even on a Scottish mountainside. Her work is minimal and is often made in conjunction with other artists. The fast-moving *Flying Lines* (1985) incorporates music by Michael Nyman and an installation by Peter Noble. The meditative *Touch the Earth* (1986) also has a Nyman score, and sculpture by the artist Dieter Pietsch.

BUTCHER, Samuel Henry (1850–1910) Irish classical scholar, born in Dublin. Educated at Marlborough and Trinity College, Cambridge, he was elected to an extraordinary fellowship at University College, Oxford, and in 1882 became professor of Greek at Edinburgh. He collaborated with **Andrew Lang** in one of the best prose translations of the *Odyssey* (1879) and is also well known for his work on **Aristotle**'s *Poetics* (1895). He was MP for Cambridge University from 1906.

BUTE, John Stuart, 3rd Earl of (1713–92) Scottish statesman. He succeeded his father in 1723, and about 1737 was made one of his lords of the bedchamber by **Frederick**, Prince of Wales. On the prince's death (1751), Bute became groom of the stole to his son, afterwards **George III**, whom he strongly influenced. He became the main instrument for breaking the power of the Whigs and establishing the personal rule of the monarch through parliament. He was made prime minister in 1762, replacing the popular **Pitt**, thus making him the most disliked politician in the country. He resigned in 1763, after the Seven Years' War.

BUTENANDT, Adolf Friedrich Johann (1903–) German biochemist, born in Bremerhaven-Lehe, who developed the chemistry of sex hormones. Educated at Marburg and Gottingen, he went on to work on sex hormones. In 1929 he isolated oestrone from pregnancy urine, in 1931 isolated the male hormone androsterone, and the same year married his laboratory assistant. He also investigated the chemical structure of progestin, and in all his work was heavily dependent on the microanalytical techniques pioneered by **Fritz Pregl**. He was awarded the 1939 Nobel prize for chemistry with **Leopold Ruzička**, but was forbidden to accept it by the Nazi régime.

BUTHELEZI, Chief Gatsha (1928–) South African Zulu leader and politician, born in Mahlabatini. Installed as chief of the Buthelezi tribe in 1953, he was assistant to the Zulu king Cyprian (1953–68) before being elected leader of Zululand in 1970. A political moderate, he became chief minister of KwaZulu, the black South African homeland, in 1976. He is founder-president of Inkatha, a para-military organization for achieving a non-racist democratic political system.

BUTLER, Alban (1710–73) English hagiographer, born in Appletree, Northampton. He was educated at Douai in France, became professor there and was for some time chaplain to the Duke of Norfolk. He later became head of the English College at St Omer. His great work, the *Lives of the Saints* (1756–59), primarily intended for edification, makes no distinction between fact and fiction. His nephew Charles (1750–1832), a lawyer, wrote on legal and theological subjects.

BUTLER, Benjamin Franklin (1818–93) American lawyer, general, and congressman, born in Deerfield, New Hampshire. Graduating at Waterville College, Maine, in 1838, and admitted to the bar in 1840, he became noted as a criminal lawyer, a champion of the working classes, and an ardent Democrat, both in the legislature and in the state senate. In 1861 he was appointed major-general of volunteers, and in 1862 took possession of New Orleans (1 May), where prompt and severe measures crushed all opposition. In December 'Beast Butler', as the Confederates called him, was superseded, but in November 1863 he received a command in Virginia, and next year made an expedition against Fort Fisher, near Wilmington. Elected to congress in 1866, he was prominent in the Republican efforts for the reconstruction of the southern states and the impeachment of President **Andrew Johnson**. In 1878 and 1879 he was nominated for governor of Massachusetts by the National party, and endorsed by Democrats, in 1882 elected, but in 1883 again defeated. His nomination for president in 1884 was not taken seriously.

BUTLER, Lady Eleanor (1745–1829) Irish recluse, born in Dublin. In 1779 she and her friend **Sarah Ponsonby** (1755–1831) resolved to live in seclusion, and settled in a cottage at Plasnewydd in the vale of Llangollen in Wales, accompanied by a maidservant. They became famous thoughout Europe as the 'Maids of Llangollen' or 'Ladies of the Vale', and attracted visitors from far and wide.

BUTLER, Elizabeth See **BUTLER, Sir William Francis**

BUTLER, Frances Pierce See **KEMBLE, Frances Anne**

BUTLER, George See **BUTLER, Josephine**

BUTLER, James See **ORMONDE**

BUTLER, Joseph (1692–1752) English moral philosopher and theologian, born in Wantage, Berkshire. From early on he seemed destined for the Presbyterian ministry, but in 1718 he graduated from Oriel College, Oxford, took Anglican orders, and was appointed preacher at the Rolls Chapel where he preached the *Fifteen Sermons* (published in 1726). That work sets out his ethical system, which he tries to base firmly on the empirical complexity of human nature and the distinctive human faculty of conscience, and which argues the ultimate compatibility of self-love and benevolence. He became, successively, bishop of Bristol (1738), dean of St Paul's (1740) and bishop of Durham (1750). His other great work was *The Analogy of Religion* (1736), a defence of revealed religion against the deists. He was buried in Bristol Cathedral.

BUTLER, Josephine Elizabeth, née **Gray** (1828–1906) English social reformer, born in Milfield. She promoted women's education and successfully crusaded against licensed brothels and the white-slave traffic, and against the Contagious Diseases Acts which made women in seaports and military towns liable for compulsory examination for venereal disease. She was married to George Butler (1819–90), canon of Winchester and author of educational works. She wrote *Personal Reminiscences of a Great Crusade* (1896).

BUTLER, Nicholas Murray (1862–1947) American educationist, co-winner (with **Jane Addams**) of the Nobel peace prize in 1931. Born in Elizabeth, New Jersey, he became professor of philosophy and education at Columbia University in 1890, and president 1901–45. He helped to found and organize what is now the Teachers' College, Columbia. He was the author of many books on public questions, mainly on the philosophy of education, and was president of the Carnegie Endowment for International Peace (1925–45).

BUTLER, Reginald Cotterell (1913–81) English sculptor, born in Buntingford, Hertfordshire. He trained as an architect and engineer, and was a lecturer at the Architectural Association School of Architecture from 1937 to 1939, and technical editor of the Architectural Press from 1946 to 1951, when he was appointed Gregory fellow of sculpture of Leeds University. In 1953 he won first prize in the international *Unknown Political Prisoner* sculpture competition. He was recognized as one of the leading exponents of 'linear' sculpture, and produced many constructions in wrought iron, although he later turned to a more realistic style.

BUTLER, Richard Austen, Baron (1902–82) English Conservative politician, born in Attock Serai, India, the son of a distinguished administrator. He was educated at Marlborough and Cambridge, was president of the University Union in 1924 and fellow of Corpus Christi College from 1925 to 1929, when he became MP for Saffron Walden, Essex. After a series of junior ministerial appointments from 1932, he was minister of education (1941–45). His name will always be closely associated with the forward-looking Education Act of 1944 which reorganized the secondary school system and introduced the '11-plus' examination for the selection of grammar school pupils. In **Churchill**'s 1951 government he was Chancellor of the Exchequer, and in 1955 introduced the emergency 'credit squeeze' budget, which was to be his last. In December he became lord privy seal (until 1959) and leader of the House of Commons (until 1961). Though tipped for the premiership after **Eden**'s resignation in 1957, **Macmillan** was chosen and Butler became home secretary (until 1962). First secretary of state and deputy prime minister (1962–63), he again narrowly lost the premiership to **Douglas-Home** in 1963, and became foreign secretary (1963–64). Once described as 'both irreproachable and unapproachable', he will go down as one of the most progressive, thoughtful, and dedicated of Tory leaders. In 1965 he was appointed master of Trinity College, Cambridge, and was made a life peer.

BUTLER, Samuel (1612–80) English satirist, born in Strensham, Worcestershire, the son of a small farmer. He was educated at Worcester grammar school, and perhaps Oxford or Cambridge. He was in the service of Elizabeth, Countess of Kent, and became a friend of the antiquarian, **John Selden**. After the Restoration, he became secretary to the Earl of Carbery, lord president of Wales, by whom he was appointed steward of Ludlow Castle. From 1670 to 1674 he was secretary to George Villiers, 2nd Duke of **Buckingham**. He is best known as the author of *Hudibras*. The first part appeared in 1663, the second in 1664, and the third in 1678. The poem, a burlesque satire on Puritanism, secured immediate popularity, and was a special favourite of **Charles II**. Despite the king's generosity he died in penury, and was buried in Westminster Abbey.

BUTLER, Samuel (1835–1902) English author, painter and musician, born in Langar Rectory, near Bingham, Nottinghamshire. He was educated at Shrewsbury and St John's College, Cambridge. Always quarrelling with his clergyman father, he gave up the idea of taking orders and became instead a sheep farmer in New Zealand. Passages from his *A First Year in Canterbury Settlement* (1863) reappeared in *Erewhon* (1872), a Utopian satire in which many of the conventional practices and customs are reversed. For example, crime is treated as an illness and illness as a crime, and machines have been abolished for fear of their mastery over men's minds. The dominant theme of its supplement, *Erewhon Revisited* (1901), is the origin of religious belief. Butler was greatly influenced by **Darwin**'s *Origin of Species*, and accepted the latter's theory of evolution, but not of natural selection. He returned to Britain in 1864, and from then on lived in London. For a time he studied painting, and his picture *Mr Heatherley's Holiday* is in the Tate Gallery. In a series of writings he tried to revive the 'vitalist' or 'creative' view of evolution, as in *Luck or Cunning* (1886), in opposition to Darwin's doctrine of natural selection. He loved music, especially **Handel**'s, and composed two oratorios, gavottes, minuets, fugues, and a cantata. In his later years he turned to scholarship and published translations of the *Iliad* (1898) and the *Odyssey* (1900). His essay *The Humour of Homer* (1892) is a remarkable piece of literary criticism. He is best known, however, for his autobiographical novel *The Way of All Flesh*, published posthumously in 1903, a work of moral realism on the causes of strife between different generations which left its mark on **George Bernard Shaw** and much 20th-century literature.

BUTLER, Sir William Francis (1838–1910) Irish soldier and author, born in Suirville, Tipperary. He joined the British army in 1858, and served in Canada from 1867 to 1873, where his experiences provided the material for his popular book, *The Great Lone Land* (1872). He served on the Red River expedition (1870–71), on the Ashanti expedition (1873), in the Sudan (1884–85), and in South Africa (1888–99). He published biographies of **Gordon** and Sir **Charles Napier**, and several travel books. In 1877 he married Elizabeth Southerden Thompson (1850–1933), battle-painter, born in Lausanne, who made her reputation with the *Roll Call* (1874) and *Inkermann* (1877).

BUTLEROV, Aleksandr Mikhailovich (1828–86) Russian organic chemist, born into a landed family in Chistopol, Prussia (now in the Soviet Union). Educated at the University of Kazan, he became professor of chemistry there in 1987. He spent the next few years travelling in Europe and studying in **Charles Wurtz**'s laboratory, where he met **F Kekulé**, **von Liebig**, **F Wöhler**, and **A S Couper**. On his return to Kazan he did much to expound their ideas in Russia, and he invented the term 'chemical structure'. In 1864 he correctly predicted the existence of tertiary alcohols, based on his grasp of structure theory; and he first introduced the idea of isomeric molecules existing in chemical equilibrium (tautomerism).

BUTLIN, Sir William Edmund, known as **'Billy'** (1899–1980) British holiday camp promoter, born in South Africa. He moved with his parents to Canada, and after serving in World War I, he worked his passage to England with only £5 capital. After a short period in a fun fair he went into business on his own. In 1936 he opened his first camp at Skegness, followed by others at Clacton and Filey. During World War II he served as director-general of hostels to the ministry of supply. After the war more camps and hotels were opened both at home and abroad.

BUTOR, Michel Marie François (1926–) French writer, born in Mons-en-Baroeul. He taught in Egypt, England, Greece, Switzerland and the USA and in French universities. He is 'professor extraordinaire' at the University of Geneva. He came to the fore in the 1950s, together with **Robbe-Grillet**, **Sarraute**, **Simon** and others who were known collectively as the New Novelists. His novels include *Passage de Milan* (1954), *L'emploi du temps* (1956), *Degrés* (1960), *Le génie du Piev* (1960) and *Repertoire* (1960). As well as fiction, he is noted as a writer of poetry, criticism and drama, and has collaborated with the Belgian composer Henri Pausseur in an opera, *Notre Faust* (1962).

BUTT, Dame Clara (1815–82) English contralto singer, born in Southwick. She made her début in 1892. **Elgar**'s *Sea Pictures* were especially composed for her.

BUTT, Isaac (1813–79) Irish politician, the first 'Home Ruler', the son of the Protestant rector of Stranorlar, and was born in Glenfin, County Donegal. Educated at Raphoe and Trinity College, Dublin, he was called to the Irish bar in 1838 and soon became active in politics. He represented Youghal as a 'Liberal Conservative' and in 1871 was returned for Limerick to lead the Home Rule party in the House of Commons, but met with little success.

BUTTERFIELD, Sir Herbert (1900–79) English historian, born in Yorkshire. A star pupil at the Trade and Grammar School, Keighley, he won a scholarship to Peterhouse College, Cambridge, of which he would later be fellow (1923–55) and master (1955–68), as well as lecturer (1930–44), professor of modern history (1944–63) and Regius professor (1963–68). He won initial recognition as a diplomatic historian with *The Peace-Tactics of Napoleon 1806–08* (1929), but followed it with a widely influential attack on historians who assumed inevitable (Protestant, English constitutional) progress in *The Whig Interpretation of History* (1931), while showing some wartime reassertion of nationalist sentiment in historical writing, in *The Englishman and his History* (1944). A profound if ill-written work, *George III, Lord North and the People 1779–1780* (1949), inspired later scholarship on whether Britain and Ireland almost had a revolution in 1780, while his *The Origins of Modern Science* (1949) inaugurated the subsequent world-wide development of the history of science. He returned to problems of historiography, confronting the search for objectivity with the Christian loyalties stemming from his deeply-held Methodism (*Christianity and History*, 1949), while attacking modern readiness to 'take the mind out of history' as shown by the school of Sir **Lewis Namier** (*George III and the Politicians*, 1957) and advocating deeper study of historical writing in the past. His other works include *The Statecraft of Machiavelli* (1940), *History of Human Relations* (1951), *Man and His Past* (1955) and *International Conflict in the Twentieth Century* (1960).

BUTTERFIELD, William (1814–1900) English architect, born in London. Associated with the Oxford Movement, he was a leading exponent of the Gothic revival, and was the architect of Keble College, Oxford; St Augustine's College, Canterbury; the chapel and quadrangle of Rugby; All Saints', Margaret Street, London; and St Albans, Holborn. He was also responsible for many controversial 'restorations'.

BUTTERICK, Ebenezer (1826–1903) American tailor and inventor, born in Sterling, Massachusetts. In 1859 he invented standardized paper patterns for garments.

BUTTERLEY, Nigel Henry (1935–) Australian composer and pianist, born in Sydney. He studied at the New South Wales Conservatorium, and later in London. He worked as a producer and planner for the music department of the Australian Broadcasting Commission from 1955, and in 1966 he won the prestigious Italia Prize with *In the Head the Fire*, a musical work for radio commissioned by the ABC. Other major works include *Fire in the Heavens*, which was performed at the opening of the Sydney Opera House in 1973, a violin concerto, *Meditations of Thomas Traherne*, *Letter from Hardy's Bay* and *Explorations for Piano and Orchestra*.

BUTTERWORTH, George (1885–1916) English composer, critic and folksong collector. His enormous promise is seen in his songs from *A Shropshire Lad* and the orchestral *The Banks of Green Willows*. He was killed in action at Pozières.

BUTZER See **BUCER, Martin**

BUXTEHUDE, Diderik, German **Dietrich** (c.1637–1707) Danish organist and composer, born in Oldesloe, Holstein. In 1668 he was appointed to the coveted post of organist at the Marienkirche, Lübeck. Here he began the famous *Abendmusiken*—evening concerts during Advent of his own sacred choral and orchestral music and organ works. In 1705 **Johann**

Sebastian Bach walked 200 miles across Germany from Arnstadt and **Handel** travelled from Hamburg to attend the concerts and to meet Buxtehude, outstanding in his time as an organist and as a composer. His principles of 'free' organ and pure instrumental works were later to be developed by Bach.

BUXTON, Sir Thomas Fowell, 1st Bart (1786–1845) English brewer and social reformer, born in Earls Colne, Essex. He was educated at Trinity College, Dublin, and married into the **Gurney** family of Norwich. As MP for Weymouth (1818–37) he worked for modification of the criminal law, abolition of the slave trade, and prison reform, succeeding **William Wilberforce** as head of the antislavery party in 1824.

BUXTORF, Johann (1564–1629) German Hebraist, born in Kamen, in Westphalia. In 1591 he became professor of Hebrew at Basel, where he died of the plague. His *Lexicon Chaldaicum, Talmudicum et Rabbinicum* was completed in 1639 by his son, Johann (1599–1664), who succeeded to the Hebrew chair, as also did his son Jakob (1645–1704), and *his* nephew Johann (1663–1732).

BUYS-BALLOT, Christoph Hendrik Diederik (1817–90) Dutch meteorologist, born at Kloetingen in Zeeland. He was the inventor of the aeroklinoscope and of a system of weather signals.

BYARS, Betsy Cromer (1928–) American children's novelist, born in Charlotte, North Carolina. She began to write in the 1960s but had no great impact until *The Summer of the Swans* (1970), the story of a girl and her retarded brother, which was awarded the Newbery Medal. Specializing in kitchen sink drama—contemporary realism—she produced a number of popular novels, at times perceptive and inventive, at others predictable and reminiscent of soap opera. Her titles include *The Eighteenth Emergency* (1973), *Goodbye, Chicken Little* (1979) and *The Animal, The Vegetable, and John D Jones* (1982).

BYNG, George, 1st Viscount Torrington (1663–1733) English naval commander, born in Wrotham, Kent. He entered the navy at 15, and in 1688 recommended himself to William of Orange (the future **William III**) by his zeal in the cause of the 'Glorious Revolution'. Promoted to rear admiral in 1703, he captured Gibraltar in 1704, and for his gallant conduct at the sea fight of Málaga was knighted by Queen **Anne**. In 1708 he commanded a squadron that frustrated a threatened landing in Scotland by the Old Pretender, **James Francis Edward Stewart**, and again in 1715. In 1718 as admiral of the fleet, he destroyed the Spanish fleet off Messina. In 1721 he was created viscount Torrington (not to be confused with **Arthur Herbert**, 8th Earl of Torrington).

BYNG, John (1704–57) English naval commander, fourth son of Admiral **George Byng**. He joined the navy at 14, and in 1745 had risen to the rank of rear admiral in the Mediterranean fleet as a result of his father's influence. In 1756, the year he was promoted admiral, he was sent with a poorly equipped squadron to relieve Minorca, at that time blockaded by a French fleet. He failed ignominiously, and was brought home under arrest. Acquitted of cowardice or disaffection, he was found guilty of neglect of duty, and condemned to death. He was shot on board the *Monarque* at Portsmouth.

BYNG, Julian Hedworth George, 1st Viscount Byng of Vimy (1862–1935) English soldier. Commissioned in the 10th Hussars in 1883, he served in the Sudan (1884) and South Africa (1899–1902). In World War I he commanded the 9th Army Corps in Gallipoli (1915), the Canadian Army Corps in France at the capture of Vimy Ridge (1916–17), and thereafter the 3rd Army (1917–18), executing the first large-scale tank attack at Cambrai (November 1917). Governor-general of Canada (1921–26), he was commissioner of the metropolitan police (1928–31).

BYNKERSHOEK, Cornelis van (1673–1743) Dutch judge and jurist, a judge of the Supreme Court of Holland and Zealand. He wrote on Roman law, notably *Observationum juris Romani* (1710–33), on Roman Dutch law, particularly *Quaestionum juris privati* (1744–47) and *Observationes tumultuariae* (decisions of the Supreme Court, 1704–43); he also wrote on international law, especially *De Dominio Maris* (1702), a classic of maritime law, *De Foro Legatorum* (1720), on diplomatic rights, and on war and neutrality in *Quaestiones juris publici* (1737), works which emphasized the importance of treaties and custom and usage of states as sources of international law. He is credited with proposing the three-mile rule, whereby a state can claim sovereignty over its territorial waters up to three miles from the coast.

BYRD, Harry Flood (1887–1966) American politician, born in West Virginia, the brother of **Richard Evelyn Byrd**. Educated at Shenandoah Valley Academy, he started work at the age of 15 on the Winchester *Star*. He took up apple and peach farming from 1906, was president of the Valley Turnpike Company (1908–18), and played an important part in the development of Virginia state highways. Elected to the state senate, he served from 1915 to 1925, becoming Democratic State Committee chairman in 1922, and was successfully nominated for governor (1926–30). He was unsuccessful in his attempt at presidential nomination in 1932. Appointed US senator for Virginia from 1933 to 1965, he became chairman of the Senate Finance Committee, and was distinguished for his extreme conservatism and support for segregation.

BYRD, Richard Evelyn (1888–1957) American explorer and aviator, born in Winchester, Virginia. Graduating from the US Naval Academy in 1912, he joined the navy's aviation service. With **Floyd Bennett** he made the first aeroplane flight over the North Pole (1926) for which they received the Congressional Medal of Honour. In 1929 he established a base, 'Little America', in the Antarctic and was the first to fly over the South Pole. He made four more expeditions to the Antarctic (1933–35, 1939–41, 1946–47 and 1955–56).

BYRD, William (1543–1623) English composer, born probably in Lincoln. His early life is obscure, but it is likely that he was one of the Children of the Chapel Royal, under **Tallis**. At the age of 20 he became organist of Lincoln Cathedral, where he remained until 1572, when he was made joint-organist with Tallis of the Chapel Royal. Three years later, Queen **Elizabeth** granted Byrd and Tallis an exclusive licence for the printing and sale of music, and their joint work of that year, *Piae Cantiones*, was dedicated to her. Byrd was associated with **John Bull** and **Orlando Gibbons** in *Parthenia* (1611), the first printed music for virginals. A firm Catholic, Byrd, who is often regarded as the greatest of the Tudor composers, was several times prosecuted as a recusant, but he wrote music of great power and beauty for both the Catholic and the Anglican services, as well as madrigals, songs, and music for strings.

BYRD, William (1674–1744) American tobacco planter, colonial official and diarist, born in Virginia, the son of William Byrd (1652–1704), pioneer planter and early Virginian aristocrat. During two periods in London (1697–1705 and 1715–26) as a student of law and a colonial agent, he showed himself an elegant socialite, a man of learning and many amours. In 1728 he took part in surveying the boundary line between

Virginia and Carolina, in 1737 he founded the town of Richmond, and in 1743 he became president of the council of state, of which he had been a member since 1709. At his mansion, 'Westover', he kept a magnificent library, and wrote a diary, published in 1958 as *The London Diary (1717–1721) and Other Writings*.

BYRGIUS, Justus, or **Jost Bürgi** (1552–1633) Swiss mathematician and inventor, born in the canton of St Gall. A court watchmaker, he assisted **Kepler** in his astronomical work, and invented celestial globes. He compiled logarithms, but did not publish them before **John Napier**.

BYRNE, Donn, pseud of **Brian Oswald Donn-Byrne** (1889–1928) Irish-American novelist and short-story writer, born in Brooklyn. He was educated at Dublin, the Sorbonne, and at Leipzig. A cowpuncher in South America and garage hand in New York, his works include *Messer Marco Polo* (1921) and *Hangman's House* (1926).

BYRNE, John (1940–) Scottish dramatist and stage designer, born in Paisley. He had designed plays for the 7:84 Theatre Company before writing his first play, *Writer's Cramp*, produced at the Edinburgh Festival Fringe (1977). *The Slab Boys* (1978), concerning the lives of employees at a carpet factory, grew into a trilogy with *Cuttin' A Rug* (1980), and *Still Life* (1983). Other plays include *Normal Service* (1979), and *Cara Coco* (1982). He wrote the highly acclaimed *Tutti Frutti* (1987), a BBC Scotland television series about an ageing pop group. He has designed stage sets for most of his own work, and many other productions.

BYROM, John (1692–1763) English poet and stenographer, born in Broughton, near Manchester. He studied medicine at Montpellier, but returned to England in 1716 to teach a new system of shorthand he had invented. In 1740 he succeeded to family estates. He patented his system in 1742; it was published in 1767 as the *Universal English Shorthand*. He was the author of the hymn 'Christian's awake! Salute the happy morn!'. His poetry was published in *Miscellaneous Poems* (1773).

BYRON, George Gordon, 6th Baron Byron of Rochdale (1788–1824) English poet of Scottish antecedents, born in London, son of the irresponsible and eccentric Captain 'Mad Jack' Byron (1756–91) and Catherine Gordon of Gight, Aberdeen, a Scottish heiress. His grandfather was admiral **John Byron**. His first ten years were spent in his mother's lodgings in Aberdeen, her husband having squandered her fortune in France. Byron was lame from birth, and the shabby surroundings and the violent temper of his foolish, vulgar and deserted mother produced a repression in him which explains many of his later actions. In 1798 he succeeded to the title on the death of 'the wicked lord', his great-uncle. He was educated at Aberdeen grammar school, then privately at Dulwich and at Harrow School, proceeding to Trinity College, Cambridge, in 1805, where he read much, swam and boxed, and led a dissipated life. An early collection of poems under the title of *Hours of Idleness* was reprinted with alterations in 1807 and was 'savagely cut up' by the *Edinburgh Review* in 1808. Byron replied with his powerful Popian satire *English Bards and Scotch Reviewers* (1809), and set out on his grand tour, visiting Spain, Malta, Albania, Greece, and the Aegean, returning after two years with 'a great many stanzas in Spenser's measure relative to the countries he had visited', which appeared under the title of *Childe Harold's Pilgrimage* in 1812 and were widely popular. This was followed by a series of oriental pieces such as the *Giaour* (1813), *Lara* (1814), and the *Siege of Corinth* (1816). During this time he dramatized himself as a man of mystery, a gloomy romantic figure, derived from the popular fiction of the day and not least from *Childe Harold*. He became the darling of London society, and lover of Lady **Caroline Lamb**, and gave to Europe the concept of the 'Byronic hero'. In 1815 he married an heiress, Anne Isabella Milbanke, who left him in 1816 after the birth of a daughter, Ada (later Countess of **Lovelace**). He was also suspected of a more than brotherly love for his half-sister, Augusta Leigh, and was ostracized. He left for the continent, travelled through Belgium and the Rhine country to Switzerland, where he met **Shelley**, and on to Venice and Rome, where he wrote the last canto of *Childe Harold* (1817). He spent two years in Venice and met the Countess Teresa Guiccioli, who became his mistress. Some of his best works belong to this period, including *Beppo* (1818), *A Vision of Judgment* (1822), and *Don Juan* (1819–24), written in a new metre (ottava rima) and in an informal conversational manner which enabled him to express the whole of his complex personality. He gave active help to the Italian revolutionaries and founded with **Leigh Hunt** a short-lived journal, *The Liberal*. In 1823 he joined the Greek insurgents who had risen against the Turks, and died of marsh fever at Missolonghi. His body was brought back to England and buried at Hucknall Torkard in Nottingham. His reputation declined after his death despite the championship of **Matthew Arnold**. On the continent he had a far-reaching influence both as the creator of the 'Byronic hero' and as the champion of political liberty, leaving his mark on such writers as **Hugo**, **De Musset**, **Leopardi**, **Heine**, **Espronceda**, **Pushkin**, and **Lermontov**.

BYRON, John ('Foulweather Jack') (1723–86) English naval officer, and grandfather of the poet Lord **Byron**. His account of his shipwreck on the coast of Chile in 1761 was used by Byron in *Don Juan*. He commanded a voyage round the world (1764–66), and was governor of Newfoundland (1769–72).

BYRON, Robert (1905–41) English writer on travel and architecture, Byzantinist and aesthete. Born in Wiltshire, he was educated at Eton and Merton College, Oxford, where he collected Victoriana. A visit to Mount Athos led to *The Station* (1928) which was followed by *The Byzantine Achievement* (1929) and *The Appreciation of Architecture* (1932). He is best-remembered, however, for his vivacious and erudite travelogues, which include *First Russia, Then Tibet* (1933) and *The Road to Oxiana* (1937), a minor masterpiece conceived as a collection of diary jottings. Typically aggressive in its assertions, it is suffused with humour and sensibility, and won the *Sunday Times* Literary award. A combative personality, his life was infused with passionate antagonisms and furious enthusiasms. He died during World War II when his ship was torpedoed.

C

CABALLÉ, Montserrat (1933–) Spanish soprano, born in Barcelona. In addition to her concert repertoire she enjoys enormous acclaim in a remarkable variety of stage roles from **Rossini** to **Puccini**, in contemporary opera, in Zarzuela, and in the German tradition (notably **Wagner** and **Strauss**). She has sung at Covent Garden, Glyndebourne, the Metropolitan Opera, La Scala, Mexico City and other main houses, and has made many recordings.

CABALLERO, Fernán, pseud of **Cecilia Francesca de Arrom** (1797–1877) Spanish novelist, born in Morges in Switzerland. She was the daughter of Nikolaus Böhl von Faber (1770–1836), a German merchant in Spain. She spent most of her childhood in Germany, but returned to Spain in 1813. She wrote on the history of Spanish literature and introduced in Spain the picturesque local-colour novel. The first of her 50 romances was *La Gaviota* (1849); others include *Elia*, *Clemencia*, and *La Familia de Alvareda*. She also collected Spanish folk tales.

CABANEL, Alexandre (1823–89) French painter, born in Montpellier. A strict classicist, he won great popularity as a portrait painter and as a teacher, and was, with **Bouguereau**, the most influential Academician of his day.

CABANIS, Pierre Jean Georges (1757–1808) French physician and philosophical writer, born in Cosnac, Charente-Inférieure. He attached himself to the popular side in the revolution. He furnished **Mirabeau** with material for his speeches on public education; and Mirabeau died in his arms. During the Terror he lived in retirement, and was afterwards a teacher in the medical school at Paris, a member of the Council of Five Hundred, then of the senate. His chief work is his *Rapports du physique et du moral de l'homme* (1802).

CABELL, James Branch (1879–1958) American novelist and critic, born in Richmond, Virginia. He made his name with his novel *Jurgen* (1919), the best known of a sequence of 18 novels, collectively known as *Biography of Michael*, set in the imaginary medieval kingdom of Poictesme and written in an elaborate, sophisticated style showing the author's fondness for archaisms. He also published a book of criticism, *Preface to the Past* (1936).

CABET, Étienne (1788–1856) French reformer and communist, born in Dijon. After the revolution of 1830 he was elected a deputy in 1831, but was exiled in 1834 for his radical pampleteering. He set out his social doctrine in a book, *Voyage en Icarie* (1840), a 'philosophical and social romance', describing a communistic utopia. In 1849 he led a group to Texas to found a utopian settlement called Icaria on the Red River, and later moved to Nauvoo in Illinois. He was president of the community from 1849, but withdrew in 1845 after internal disputes.

CABEZÓN, Antonio de (1500–66) Spanish composer. Blind from birth, he was the first major Spanish keyboard composer, noted for his keyboard pieces and vocal works.

CABLE, George Washington (1844–1925) American author, born in New Orleans. At the age of 19 he volunteered as a Confederate soldier. After the war he earned a precarious living in New Orleans, before taking up a literary career in 1879. In 1884 he went to New England. His Creole sketches in *Scribner's* made his reputation. Among his books are *Old Creole Days* (1879), *The Grandissimes* (1880), *The Silent South* (1885), *Bylow Hill* (1902), *Kincaid's Battery* (1908), and *Lovers of Louisiana* (1918).

CABOT, John (Giovanni Caboto) (1425–c.1500) Genoese-born Venetian navigator and explorer, hailed as the modern discoverer of North America. He moved to England and settled in Bristol c.1490. In 1497 under letters patent from King **Henry VII**, he sailed from Bristol with two ships in search of a route to Asia, accompanied by his three sons. On 24 June, after 52 days at sea, he sighted land (probably Cape Breton Island, Nova Scotia), and claimed North America for England. He is thought to have made further voyages in search of a Northwest Passage.

CABOT, Sebastian (c.1475–1557) Venetian navigator and cartographer, second son of **John Cabot**, born in Venice. He sailed with his father on expeditions in search of the Northwest Passage. In 1512 he made a map of Gascony and Guienne for King **Henry VIII**, then entered the service of King **Ferdinand the Catholic** of Aragon as a cartographer. In 1517 he was back in England to command an expedition which was apparently cancelled. In 1519 he returned to Spain, and as pilot-major for the emperor **Charles V** explored the coast of Brazil and the River Plate in 1526. After a failed attempt at colonization he was imprisoned and banished for two years to Africa. In 1533 he was once again appointed pilot-major in Spain, and in 1544 published an engraved map of the world (the only surviving copy is in the Bibliothèque Nationale in Paris). In 1548 he returned to England where he was made inspector of the navy by King **Edward VI**; in 1551 he founded the company of Merchant Adventurers of London.

CABRAL, or **Cabrera, Pedro Alvarez** (c.1467–c.1520) Portuguese navigator, and discoverer, in the same year as **Pinzon**, of Brazil. In 1500 he sailed from Lisbon in command of a fleet of thirteen vessels bound for the East Indies. Falling into the South American current of the Atlantic, he was carried to the unknown coast of Brazil, which he claimed on behalf of the king of Portugal. He then made for India; but, after losing seven of his ships, he landed at Mozambique, of which he was the first to give clear information, and, sailing thence to Calicut, established the first commercial treaty between Portugal and India. He returned to Lisbon in 1501.

CABRERA, Don Ramón (1810–77) Spanish Carlist leader in 1833–40 and 1848–49, born in Tortosa. He died at Wentworth near Staines, having married a wealthy English lady. In 1839 Don **Carlos** created him Count of Morella.

CABRERA INFANTE, Guillermo (1929–) Cuban-born British novelist, born in Gibara, Cuba. Educated at Havana University, he emigrated to England in 1966. Film critic, journalist and translator of **Joyce**'s *Dubliners* (1972), he is known chiefly for his fiction, particularly *Infante's Inferno* (1984), set in Havana during the 1940s and 1950s, which skilfully blurs the distinction between autobiography and fiction, in the process demythologizing the Don Juan legend in Hispanic culture.

CABRINI, St Francesca Xavier (1850–1917) Italian-born American nun, born Maria Francesca in Sant 'Angelo, Lodigliano. She founded the Missionary Sisters of the Sacred Heart (1880), emigrated to the USA in 1889 and became renowned as 'Mother Cabrini' for her social and charitable work. She founded 67 houses in the USA, Buenos Aires, Paris and Madrid. Canonized in 1946, she was the first American saint. Her feast day is 13 November.

CACCINI, Giulio (c.1550–1618) Italian composer and singer, born in Rome. With **Jacopo Peri** he paved the way for opera by setting to music the drama *Euridice* (1602). Particularly significant was his *Nuove Musiche* (1602), a collection of canzonets and madrigals.

CADALSO VASQUEZ, José de (1741–82) Spanish writer, born in Cadiz. By profession an army officer, he wrote as a hobby. He is best known for a prose satire—*Los eruditos a la violeta* (1772)—which ridicules pedantry. He was killed at the siege of Gibraltar.

CADBURY, George (1839–1922) English Quaker businessman, son of **John Cadbury**, the founder of the cocoa firm. In partnership with his elder brother Richard (1835–99) he took over his father's business in 1861, moved the factory and in 1894 established for the workers the model village of Bournville, near Birmingham, a prototype for modern methods of housing and town planning. In 1902 he became proprietor of the *Daily News*.

CADBURY, Henry Joel (1883–1974) American Quaker scholar, born in Philadelphia. Educated at Haverford College and at Harvard, he taught Bible at Haverford, Bryn Mawr, and Harvard, where he subsequently held a chair in divinity (1934–54). Active in the work of the American Friends Service Committee (he had two stints as chairman) and member of many learned societies, he wrote prolifically. Among his works were *Style and Literary Method of Luke* (1920), *The Peril of Modernizing Jesus* (1937), *George Fox's Book of Miracles* (1948), *The Book of Acts in History* (1955), and *Friendly Heritage* (1972).

CADBURY, John (1801–89) English Quaker businessman, son of Richard Tapper Cadbury, who had settled in Birmingham in 1794. He founded the cocoa and chocolate business of Cadburys.

CADE, Jack (d.1450) Irish rebel, leader of the insurrection of 1450. After an unsettled early career, he established himself in Kent as a physician. Outraged by the misgovernment of **Henry VI**, he marched on London with upwards of 40000 followers and defeated the royalist forces. After two days of strict control, his forces began to run amok and were eventually dispersed. Cade attempted to reach the coast but was killed in a garden near Heathfield in Sussex.

CADELL, Francis Campbell Boileau (1883–1937) Scottish painter, born in Edinburgh. He studied in Paris from 1899 to 1903, visited Munich in 1907, and returned to Edinburgh in 1909. In 1912 he founded the Society of Eight. One of the 'Scottish Colourists', he painted landscapes, interiors and still-life in broad patches of brilliant, high-keyed colour.

CADELL, Robert (1788–1849) Scottish publisher, partner from 1811 in the Edinburgh publishing house of Constable & Co. After its failure in 1825 he began business again, and realized a handsome fortune by his editions of Sir **Walter Scott**'s works.

CADILLAC, Antoine de la Mothe, Sieur (1656–1730) French soldier and colonialist, the founder of Detroit, born in Gascony. He went to America with the French army in 1683, and founded in 1701 the settlement of Fort-Pontehartrain du Détroit which became the city of Detroit. In 1711 he was appointed governor of Louisiana but returned to France in 1716 and died in his native Gascony.

CADOGAN, Sir Alexander George Montagu (1884–1968) English diplomat, son of **George Henry Cadogan**. Educated at Eton and Oxford, he was minister plenipotentiary at Peking (1933–35) and UK representative on the security council of the United Nations (1946–50). From 1952 to 1957 he was chairman of the British Broadcasting Corporation.

CADOGAN, George Henry, 5th Earl (1840–1915) English statesman, son of the 4th Earl, father of Sir **Alexander Cadogan**, born in Durham. He became under-secretary for war (1875) and for the colonies (1878) under **Disraeli**, but is best remembered as lord-lieutenant of Ireland (1895–1902), when, though criticized for weakness, he showed himself an able and unbiased administrator.

CADOGAN, William, 1st Earl Cadogan (1675–1726) English soldier, born in Dublin. He fought as a 'volunteer' at the Battle of the Boyne (1690), and was commissioned in the Inniskilling Dragoons. In 1703, with the rank of colonel, he was appointed quartermaster-general to **Marlborough** and led the march into Bavaria which ended in the victory of Blenheim (1704). At the head of his own regiment of horse he distinguished himself at the Helexem-Neerwinden river crossing at Oudenarde, and at Ramillies (1706). With Marlborough's fall from political favour he resigned all his appointments; but on the accession of **George I** was restored. In 1715 he succeeded the 2nd Duke of **Argyll** in Scotland in quelling the Jacobite rebellion. On Marlborough's death (1722) he was appointed commander-in-chief.

CADOUDAL, Georges (1771–1804) French insurgent, a miller's son from Auray in Lower Brittany. From 1793 to 1800 he led the royalist Chouans against the Republicans, and was guillotined for conspiring, with **Pichegru**, against **Napoleon**.

CADWALADR (d.1172) Welsh prince of Gwynedd. He conquered large parts of Wales with his older brother Owain until he was expelled by him (1143). He went to Ireland to seek help, where he was blinded by pirates, was reconciled to Owain, but eventually fled to England where **Henry II** restored him to his lands after the conquest of Wales (1158).

CADWALLON (d.634) pagan Welsh king of Gwynedd from c.625. With **Penda**, king of Mercia, he invaded the Christian kingdom of Northumbria in 633 and slew King **Edwin** at the battle of Heathfield (Hatfield Chase) near Doncaster. He ravaged the kingdom, according to the Venerable **Bede**, but was himself defeated and killed by King **Oswald** (St Oswald) of Bernicia at the battle of Heavenfield near Hexham in 634.

CAEDMON (7th century) Anglo-Saxon poet, the earliest Christian English poet known by name. According to the **Venerable Bede**, he was an unlettered herdsman who in his old age received a divine call in a dream to sing of the Creation. He then became a monk at Whitby under the rule of St **Hilda**, where he turned other biblical themes into vernacular poetry. But the original hymn of the Creation, a mere nine lines long, is the only extant poem that can be atributed to him with any certainty.

CAESALPINUS See **CESALPINO**

CAESAR, Gaius Julius (100 or 102–44 BC) Roman general and statesman, from an ancient patrician family. His aunt was the wife of **Marius**; in 83 BC Caesar married Cornelia, daughter of **Cinna**, and thus incurred the hostility of **Sulla**. He went to Asia (81), served against the pirates (75–74), was elected pontifex (73), supported the attack on Sulla's legislation (71–70), was quaestor in Spain (69), and supported one or both of **Pompey**'s commands (67–66). In 65 as curule aedile he spent lavishly on games and public buildings, was elected pontifex maximus in 63 and praetor for 62. Whether he was implicated in the conspiracy of **Catilina** in 63 is not clear. In 61 he governed the province of Hispania Ulterior, and on his return in 60 was elected consul for 59. He reconciled Pompey and **Crassus**, and with them established the informal alliance known as the 'First Triumvirate'. Caesar gave Pompey his daughter Julia in marriage, while he married Calpurnia. Next he obtained the provinces of Gallia Cisalpina, Gallia Transalpina, and Illyricum; for nine years (58–50) he conducted campaigns which extended Roman power in the west. In the first campaign he defeated the Helvetii and Ariovistus; in 57 the Belgic confederacy and the Nervii; and in 56 the Veneti and other peoples of Brittany and Normandy. He next invaded Britain (55). In 54, on a second invasion of Britain, he crossed the Thames, and enforced at least the nominal submission of the southeast of the island. On his return to Gaul, defeated by the rebellious Eburones, he exacted a terrible vengeance from their leaders. Visiting northern Italy, he had hastily to return in midwinter to quell a general rebellion headed by Vercingetorix. The struggle was severe; at Gergovia, the capital of the Arverni, Caesar was defeated. But by the capture of Alesia (52) he crushed the united armies of the Gauls. In the meantime Crassus had been defeated and killed in Asia (53) and Pompey was moving away from Caesar. The Senate called upon Caesar, now in Cisalpine Gaul, to resign his command and disband his army (50), and entrusted Pompey with large powers. His forces outnumbered Caesar's legions, but were scattered over the empire. Supported by his victorious troops, Caesar moved southwards (49). Pompey withdrew to Brundisium, pursued by Caesar, and from there to Greece (49); in three months Caesar was master of all Italy. After subduing Pompey's legates in Spain, he was appointed dictator. Pompey had gathered in Egypt, Greece, and the east a powerful army, while his fleet controlled the sea. Caesar, crossing the Adriatic, was driven back with heavy losses from Dyrrhachium. But in a second battle at Pharsalia (48), the senatorial army was routed, and Pompey himself fled to Egypt, where he was murdered. Caesar, again appointed dictator for a year, and consul for five years, instead of returning to Rome, went to Egypt where he engaged in the 'Alexandrine War' on behalf of **Cleopatra** (47). He overthrew a son of **Mithradates** in Pontus, and after a short stay in Rome, routed the Pompeian generals, Scipio and **Marcus Porcius Cato**, at Thapsus in Africa (46). After his victories in Gaul, Egypt, Pontus and Africa he had still to put down an insurrection in Spain by Pompey's sons (45). He now received the title of 'Father of his Country', was made dictator for life, and consul for ten years; his person was declared sacred, his statue placed in temples, his portrait struck on coins, and the month Quintilis renamed Julius in his honour. Ambitious plans were ascribed to him. He proposed to make a digest of the whole of Roman law, to found libraries, to drain the Pontine Marshes, to enlarge the harbour at Ostia, to dig a canal through the Isthmus, and to launch a war against the Dacians in central Europe and the Parthians in the east. In the midst of these vast designs he was assassinated on the Ides (15th) of March. The conspirators, mostly aristocrats led by **Brutus** and **Cassius**, believed that they were striking a blow for the restoration of republican freedom, which Caesar's autocracy was negating. But they merely succeeded in plunging the Roman world into a fresh round of civil wars, in which the Republic was finally destroyed. Caesar was of a noble presence, tall, thin-featured, bald, and close shaven. As general, if not as statesman, he ranks among the greatest in history. Highly talented, and with a wide range of interests, he was second only to **Cicero** as orator, and his historical writings (the Gallic and Civil Wars) are simple and direct; yet for all his genius, he failed to find a solution to the political problems of the late Republic, and it was left to his adopted son Octavianus (the future emperor **Augustus**) to achieve this.

CAESAR, Sir Julius (1558–1636) English judge, born in Tottenham, the son of Cesare Adelmare, physician to Queen **Mary I**. Judge of the Admiralty Court in 1584, Chancellor of the Exchequer in 1606, master of the rolls in 1614, he wrote *The Ancient State Authorities and Proceedings of the Court of Requests* (1597) and *Concerning the Private Council of the King* (1625).

CAGE, John (1912–) American composer, born in Los Angeles. He was a pupil of **Schoenberg** and of Henry Cecil. Associated with ultra-modernism, he has variously exploited the 'prepared piano' (distorting the sound of the instrument with objects placed inside); unorthodox musical notation in the form of pictures or graphics; indeterminacy in music or 'aleatory' music in which, following one method, a dice would be thrown to determine the elements of a composition; silence as an art form; and has also indulged in gleefully bizarre use of percussion. He has written copiously, illogically and often cleverly about music, and is an authority on mushrooms. His books include *Silence* (1961), *A Year from Monday* (1967), *M* (1973) and *Empty Words* (1979).

CAGLIARI, Paolo See **VERONESE**

CAGLIOSTRO, Count Alessandro di, properly **Giuseppe Balsamo** (1743–95) Italian adventurer, born in poverty in Palermo. At the monastery of Caltagirone he picked up a smattering of chemistry and medicine, and travelled Europe selling an 'elixir of immortal youth' with the help of a beautiful wife, Lorenza Feliciani. A gifted conman, he styled himself 'Count', and in London persuaded clients to invest in 'Egyptian freemasonry'. In 1785 he was involved with the Comtesse de **La Motte** and Cardinal **Rohan-Guéménée** in the Affair of the Diamond Necklace, which landed him in the Bastille. He was arrested in Rome in 1789 for peddling freemasonry, and died in prison.

CAGNEY, James (1899–1986) American film actor, born on New York's lower East Side. Graduating from vaudeville to musicals and the legitimate Broadway theatre, he was seen there in *Penny Arcade* (1929) and signed to a contract with Warner Brothers, making his film début in *Sinner's Holiday* (1930). A leading role in *Public Enemy* (1931) established him as the quintessential screen gangster, and he remained in that mould throughout the 1930s in such popular fare as *Lady Killer* (1933) and *The Roaring Twenties* (1939). Occasionally extending his range, as in *A Midsummer Night's Dream* (1935, as Bottom), his performance in *Yankee Doodle Dandy* (1942) earned him an Academy Award. Later, he offered incisive psychological portraits of the hoodlum in *White Heat* (1949) and *Love Me or Leave Me* (1955), whilst displaying his virtuoso comic skills in *Mister Roberts* (1955) and the frenetic *One, Two, Three* (1961). He retired in 1961, returning only for typically pugnacious roles, as in *Ragtime* (1981). A farmer, a painter and poet, he wrote an autobiography, *Cagney on Cagney*, in 1976.

CAGNIARD DE LA TOUR, Charles (1777–1859) French physicist, born in Paris. He invented a disc siren for measuring the frequency of sounds, and discovered the 'critical state' in liquids and their vapours.

CAGNOLA, Luigi, Marchese (1762–1833) Italian architect, a follower of **Palladio**. His masterwork was the triumphal *Arco della Pace*, of white marble, in Milan.

CAIGER-SMITH, Alan (1930–) English potter. He studied at Camberwell School of Arts and Crafts and King's College, Cambridge, prior to training in pottery at the Central School of Art and Design in 1954. He established the Aldermaston Pottery in 1955, producing fine examples of tin-glazed earthenware with free hand brushwork and, occasionally, rich lustres. His book, *Tin Glaze in Europe and the Islamic World*, was published in 1973.

CAILLAUX, Joseph (1863–1944) French politician, born in Le Mans. He became French finance minister in 1899, 1906, 1911, 1913, and 1925, premier in 1911. Arrested in 1918, he was convicted (1920) of corresponding with Germany during the war. Reprieved in 1924, he took part in war debt negotiations with the USA. In 1914 his second wife shot M Calmette, editor of *Le Figaro*, but was acquitted.

CAILLETET, Louis Paul (1832–1913) French ironmaster of Châtillon-sur-Seine. While engaged in research on the liquefaction of gases in 1877 he liquefied for the first time hydrogen, nitrogen, oxygen, and air by compression, cooling, and sudden expansion. This was also done by **Raoul Pictet** at about the same time.

CAILLIÉ, René (1799–1838) French explorer of north-west Africa, born in Mauze in Poitou. In 1827–28 he travelled from Sierra Leone to Timbuktu disguised as a Moorish trader, and won a prize of 10000 francs offered by the geographical society of Paris.

CAIN, James Mallahan (1892–1977) American thriller writer, born in Annapolis, Maryland. Often associated with **Dashiell Hammett** and **Raymond Chandler**, his earliest ambition was to emulate his mother and become a professional singer, and he studied assiduously towards this. Music remained his favourite recreation and it forms the background of some of his stories. He tried various jobs, was a reporter for many years and also taught journalism, but he always hankered after 'the great American novel'. He never quite managed to accomplish this but after moving to California he found the style which is his hallmark. It first emerged in *The Postman Always Rings Twice* (1934), in which an adulterous couple murder the woman's husband but betray each other, then in *Serenade* (1937), *Mildred Pierce* (1941), *Double Indemnity* (1943) and *The Butterfly* (1947). Several of his stories were filmed with what Cain described as 'legendary success', but the script credits went to others.

CAINE, Sir (Thomas Henry) Hall (1853–1931) English novelist, born in Runcorn. He trained as an architect, and became secretary to **Dante Gabriel Rossetti** from 1881 to 1882, and later published *Recollections of Rossetti* (1882). He wrote a number of popular novels, many of them set in the Isle of Man, including *The Shadow of a Crime* (1885), *The Deemster* (1887), *The Bondman* (1890), *The Scapegoat* (1891), *The Manxman* (1894), *The Eternal City* (1901) and *The Prodigal Son* (1904). He also wrote a *Life of Christ* (1938), and published an early autobiography, *My Story* (1908).

CAINE, Michael, originally **Maurice Micklewhite** (1933–) English film actor, born in the east end of London. He spent many years as a struggling small-part actor in a variety of media, before winning attention for his performance as an aristocratic officer in *Zulu* (1963). His belated stardom was consolidated with roles as down-at-heel spy Harry Palmer in *The Ipcress File* (1965) and its two sequels, and as the Cockney romeo *Alfie* (1966). A prolific performer, his reputation for consummate professionalism has withstood many inferior films and enhanced superior material like *Sleuth* (1972), *California Suite* (1978) and *Educating Rita* (1983). Nominated four times for the Academy Award, he won an Oscar for *Hannah and Her Sisters* (1986).

CAIRD, Edward (1835–1908) Scottish philosopher, born in Greenock, Renfrewshire, brother of **John Caird**. He became professor of moral philosophy at Glasgow (1886) and succeeded **Benjamin Jowett** as master of Balliol College, Oxford (1893–1907). One of the school of British idealists (with **T H Green** and **F H Bradley**), he published important studies of **Hegel** and **Kant**, and works on the evolution of religion.

CAIRD, John (1820–98) Scottish clergyman and philosopher, brother of **Edward Caird**. His *Religion in Common Life*, preached before Queen **Victoria** at Crathie in 1855, was said by Dean **Stanley** to be the greatest single sermon of the century. He was appointed professor of divinity at Glasgow in 1862, and was principal from 1873. He published *Sermons* (1858), *An Introduction to the Philosophy of Religion* (1880), and *Spinoza* (1888).

CAIRNES, John Elliot (1823–75) Irish economist, born in Castle Bellingham, County Louth. He was placed in his father's brewery; but, much against his father's will, went to Trinity College, Dublin. In 1856 he was appointed professor of political economy at Dublin, in 1859 at Queen's College, Galway, and in 1866 at University College London. He resigned his chair in 1872. His ten works include *Character and Logical Method of Political Economy* (1857), and *The Slave Power* (1862). Cairnes may be regarded as a disciple of **John Stuart Mill**, though differing from him on many points.

CAIRNS, Hugh MacCalmont Cairns, Earl (1819–95) British jurist and politician, born in County Down, Northern Ireland. Educated at Belfast and Trinity College, Dublin, he was called to the bar at the Middle Temple in 1844, entered parliament for Belfast in 1852, and quickly made his mark in the House as a debater. He became QC in 1856, in 1858 solicitor-general, in 1866 attorney-general under Lord **Derby** and then a lord justice of appeal, and in 1867 Baron Cairns. Under **Disraeli** he was made lord chancellor in 1868, and again in 1874, and was created Viscount Garmoyle and Earl Cairns in 1878. For some years he led the Conservatives in the upper House. He prepared measures for simplifying the transfer of land, and projected that fusion of law and equity which was carried out by the 1st Earl of **Selborne**, and secured the publication of *The Statutes Revised* (1870–85).

CAIRNS, Sir Hugh William Bell (1896–1952) Australian surgeon, born in Port Pirie. His medical studies at Adelaide University were interrupted by military service, but after World War I, a Rhodes Scholarship allowed him to continue his medical work, first at Oxford, and then at the London Hospital. His interest gradually shifted to neurosurgery, especially after a year's work with **Harvey Cushing**, and he made the London Hospital an international centre. In 1937 he became Nuffield professor of surgery at Oxford. During World War II he became adviser on head injuries to the ministry of health, and neurosurgeon to the army. He played a crucial role in organizing the evacuation and treatment of soldiers with neurological injuries and persuaded the army to make crash helmets compulsory for dispatch riders. Among his patients was **T E Lawrence**, following his fatal motorcycle accident in 1935.

CAIROLI, Benedetto (1825–89) Italian statesman, born in Pavia. In youth a revolutionary and a Garibaldian, he was in 1878 and 1879 Radical prime minister of Italy.

CAIROLI, Charlie (1910–80) French-born circus clown. The son of a juggler, he made his début as a circus performer at the age of five. He came to Britain in 1938 and was for 39 years a star attraction of the Blackpool Tower Circus, until ill-health forced his retirement a year before his death.

CAITANYA (c.1486–1533) Indian Hindu mystic, born in Nadia, Bengal. A Sanskrit teacher before becoming an itinerant holy man, following conversion in 1510 to a life of devotion to Krishna, he spent the latter part of his life in Puri, inspiring disciples in both Bengal and Orissa with his emphasis on joy and love of Krishna, and the place of singing and dancing in worship. Though he wrote little, he is also remembered for influencing the development of Bengali literature, previously held as much inferior to Sanskrit.

CAIUS, John (1510–73) English physician and scholar, co-founder of Gonville and Caius College, Cambridge. Born in Norwich, he became a student at Gonville Hall, Cambridge in 1529, and a fellow in 1533. He studied medicine at Padua under **Andreas Vesalius**, then lectured on anatomy in London (1544–64). President of the College of Physicians nine times, he was physician to **Edward VI**, **Mary I**, and Queen **Elizabeth**. In 1557 he obtained a charter to refound and enlarge his old Cambridge college, Gonville Hall (founded by Edmund Gonville in 1348), and in 1559 became the first master of Gonville and Caius College. A loyal Catholic, he had trouble with his Protestant colleagues, who burned his Mass vestments while he sentenced them to the stocks. He was the author of various critical, antiquarian and scientific books, notably *A Boke of Counseill against the Disease commonly called the Sweate, or Sweatying Sicknesse* (1552).

CAJANDER, Aimo Kaarlo (1879–1943) Finnish politician and forestry expert. He became professor of forestry at Helsinki, and was three times prime minister of Finland (1922, 1924, 1937–40).

CAJETAN, Italian **Gaetano,** properly **Thomas de Vio** (1469–1534) Italian prelate and theologian, born in Gaeta. In 1508 he became general of the Dominicans, in 1517 cardinal, in 1519 bishop of Gaeta, and in 1523 legate to Hungary. In 1518 he sought to induce **Luther** to recant at Augsburg.

CALAMITY JANE, nickname of **Martha Jane Burke,** née **Cannary** (c.1852–1903) American frontierswoman, born in Princeton, Missouri. She became a living legend for her skill at riding and shooting, particularly in the Gold Rush days in the Black Hills of Dakota. She teamed up with the renowned US marshal, Wild Bill Hickok (1847–76), at Deadwood, Dakota, before he was murdered. She is said to have threatened 'calamity' for any man who tried to court her, but in 1885 she got married.

CALAMY, Edmund (1600–66) English clergyman. He studied at Pembroke Hall, Cambridge (1616–19); and afterwards became domestic chaplain to the bishop of Ely. In 1626 he was appointed lecturer at Bury St Edmunds, but resigned when the order to read the *Book of Sports* was enforced (1636); in 1639 he was chosen minister of St Mary Aldermanbury, London. He was one of the chief authors of *Smectymnuus* (1641), a reply to Bishop **Joseph Hall**'s *Divine Right of Episcopacy*. He disapproved of the execution of **Charles I**, and of **Cromwell**'s protectorate, and was one of the deputation to **Charles II** in Holland. His services were recognized by a royal chaplaincy and the offer of the bishopric of Coventry and Lichfield, which he declined through conscientious scruples. Ejected for nonconformity in 1662, he continued to attend service in his old church, till, heartbroken by the Great Fire, he died. His son Edmund Calamy (1642–86), a prebendary of St Paul's, wrote *A Discourse about a Scrupulous Conscience*, dedicated to Judge **Jeffreys**.

CALAMY, Edmund (1671–1732) English puritan clergyman, grandson of **Edmund Calamy** (1600–66). He studied three years at Utrecht, and, declining **Carstares'** offer of a Scottish professorship, from 1694 was a Nonconformist minister in London. He visited Scotland in 1709, when Edinburgh, Glasgow, and Aberdeen all conferred degrees on him. His forty-one works include *Account of the Ejected Ministers* (1702) and an interesting autobiography, first published in 1829.

CALAS, Jean (1698–1762) French Huguenot, a tradesman of Toulouse. In 1761 he was accused, on the flimsiest evidence, of murdering his eldest son (a suicide) in order to prevent him becoming a Roman Catholic. He was found guilty, and executed by being broken on the wheel. A revision of the trial followed as a result of a campaign led by **Voltaire**, and the parliament at Paris in 1765 declared Calas and all his family innocent. **Louis XV** gave them 30000 livres, but neither the parliament of Toulouse nor the fanatical monks were ever brought to account.

CALDARA, Antonio (1670–1736) Italian composer, born in Venice. He became vice-kapellmeister in Vienna, and amongst his choral works are some outstanding examples of the polyphonic style. He also wrote many operas and oratorios, and some trio-sonatas in the style of **Corelli**.

CALDARA, Polidoro See **CARAVAGGIO**

CALDECOTT, Randolph (1846–86) English artist and illustrator. Starting as a bank-clerk in Whitstable and Manchester, he moved to London to follow an artistic career. He illustrated **Washington Irving**'s *Old Christmas* (1876), and numerous children's books like *The House that Jack Built* (1878) and **Aesop**'s Fables (1883). He also contributed to *Punch* and the *Graphic*. The Caldecott Medal has been awarded annually since 1938 to the best American artist-illustrator of children's books.

CALDER, Alexander (1898–1976) American artist and pioneer of kinetic art, born in Lawnton, Philadelphia, the son of the Scots-born American sculptor Alexander Milne Calder (1846–1923). He trained as an engineer (1915–19) before studying art at the School of the Art Students' League in New York (1923). In 1925 he began making wire-sculptures; in 1926 he exhibited paintings in the Artists' Gallery, New York, and in 1929 he had a one-man show in Paris. He specialized in abstract hanging wire constructions some of which were connected to motors (**Marcel Duchamp** christened them 'mobiles' in 1932). His best known works, however, were unpowered, relying upon air currents to set them rotating and casting intricate, ever-changing shadows.

CALDER, (Peter) Ritchie, Lord (1906–82) Scottish journalist and educationist, born in Forfar. Specializing in the spread of scientific knowledge to lay readers, he wrote numerous books including *Men Against the Desert* (1951), *Men Against the Jungle* (1954), *Living with the Atom* (1962) and *The Evolution of the Machine* (1968). He was made a life peer in 1966 and took the title Baron Ritchie-Calder of Balmashannar.

CALDERÓN DE LA BARCA, Pedro (1600–81) Spanish dramatist, born of good family in Madrid. After schooling under the Jesuits, he studied law and philosophy at Salamanca (1613–19), and during ten years' service in the Milanese and in Flanders saw much of men and manners that he afterwards utilized. On **Vega Carpio**'s death in 1635, he was summoned by **Philip IV** to Madrid, and appointed a sort of master of the revels. In 1640 the rebellion in Catalonia made him return to the army; but in 1651 he entered the priesthood, and in 1653 withdrew to Toledo. Ten years went by, and he was recalled to court and to the resumption of his dramatic activity, receiving, with other preferments, the post of chaplain of honour to Philip; and he continued to write for the court, the church, and the public theatres till his death. Castilian and Catholic to the backbone, Calderón wrote with perfect fidelity to the Spanish thought and manners of his age. His *autos sacramentales*, outdoor plays for the festival of Corpus Christi, number 72, and have been divided into seven classes—biblical, classical, ethical, 'cloak and sword plays', dramas of passion, and so forth; the finest of them is *El divino Orfeo*. Of his regular dramas 118 are extant.

CALDERWOOD, David (1575–1650) Scottish clergyman and ecclesiastical historian, minister of Crailing in Roxburghshire from 1604. In 1617 he joined in a protest against granting the power of framing new church laws to an ecclesiastical council appointed by King **James VI and I**, and was imprisoned and banished to Holland in 1619. There he published *Altare Damascenum* (1625), a massive defence of presbyterianism against episcopacy. After the king's death (1625), he returned to Scotland to become minister of Pencaitland, and spent years in collecting materials for his *History of the Church of Scotland*, published in 1678.

CALDWELL, Anne See **MARSH, George Perkins**

CALDWELL, Erskine (1903–87) American author, born in White Oak, Georgia. He worked amongst the 'poor whites' in the southern states, where he absorbed the background for his best-known work *Tobacco Road* (1932), of which the dramatized version by Jack Kirkland (1933) had a record run in New York. Other books include *God's Little Acre* (1933), *Sure Hand of God* (1947), *A Lamp for Nightfall* (1952), *Love and Money* (1954) and *Close to Home* (1962).

CALEPINO, Ambrogio (c.1435–1511) Italian lexicographer, born in Bergamo. An Augustinian monk, he compiled a Latin-Italian dictionary in 1502 which developed into a polygot dictionary of 11 languages.

CALETTI-BRUNI See **CAVALLI, Francesco**

CALGACUS (1st century) Caledonian chieftain in northern Britian, leader of the tribes defeated by **Agricola** at the battle of Mons Graupius. Agricola's biographer, **Tacitus**, attibutes to him a heroic speech on the eve of a battle, with a ringing denunciation of Roman imperialism ('They make a desolation, and call it peace').

CALHOUN, John Caldwell (1782–1850) American statesman, of Irish Presbyterian descent, born in Abbeville County, South Carolina. He studied at Yale, and became a successful lawyer. In Congress he supported the measures which led to the war of 1812–15 with Great Britain, and promoted the protective tariff. In 1817 he joined **Monroe**'s cabinet as secretary of war, and did good work in reorganizing the war department. He was vice-president under **John Q Adams** (1825–29), and then under **Jackson**. In 1829 he declared that a state can nullify unconstitutional laws; and his *Address to the People of South Carolina* (1831) set forth his theory of state rights. On the passing by South Carolina in 1832 of the nullification ordinance he resigned the vice-presidency, and entered the senate, becoming a leader of the states-rights movement, and a champion of the interests of the slave-holding states. In 1844, as secretary of state, he signed a treaty annexing Texas; but once more in the senate, he strenuously opposed the war of 1846–47 with Mexico. He, **Henry Clay**, and **Daniel Webster** were 'the great triumvirate' of American political orators.

CALIGULA, Gaius Caesar Augustus Germanicus (12–41) Roman emperor, the youngest son of **Germanicus Caesar** and **Agrippina**, born in Antium. Educated in the camp, he was nicknamed Caligula from his soldier's boots (*caligae*). He ingratiated himself with **Tiberius**, and, on his death (37), was found to have been appointed co-heir along with the Emperor's grandson Gemellus; the senate, however, conferred imperial power on Caligula alone. Ill-prepared for power and poor in health, his rule quickly evolved from promising beginnings to open and erratic despotism, though it is not easy to separate fact from fiction in a highly coloured and hostile tradition. He squandered the wealth left by Tiberius, banished or murdered his relatives, excepting his uncle **Claudius** and sister Drusilla (with whom he was suspected of committing incest), filled Rome with executions and confiscations, and received extravagant personal honours. Assassination terminated his brief but traumatic reign.

CALISHER, Hortense (1911–) American novelist and short-story writer, born in New York City. Her milieu is New York and her characters are usually drawn from the upper middle class. A powerful and precise writer, her novels—*The New Yorkers* (1969), *Queenie* (1971), *The Bobby-Soxer* (1986)—though frequently of novella length are less successful than stories like 'In Greenwich There Are Many Gravelled Walks', which aspire to classic status.

CALIXTUS, or **Callistus I** (d.222) pope (from 218 to 222). According to **Hippolytus**, his bitter opponent who became antipope in 217, Calixtus was originally a slave, and had twice undergone severe punishment for his crimes before he became a priest under Zephyrinus, whom he succeeded as pope. He was martyred.

CALIXTUS II (d.1124) pope from 1119 to 1124, formerly Guido, Count of Burgundy and archbishop of Vienne. In 1121 he overcame the antipope Burdinus (Gregory VIII), who was supported by the emperor Henry V, and in 1122 concluded with the emperor the concordat of Worms, which settled the Investiture Controversy.

CALIXTUS III (1378–1458) pope from 1455 to 1458, formerly Alfonso de Borja (Italian *Borgia*), born in Jativa in Spain. He was successively counsellor to **Alfonso V of Aragon**, bishop of Valencia, and cardinal. He laboured in vain to organize a crusade against the Turks, and raised to the cardinalate his nephew, Rodrigo Borgia, the future pope **Alexander VI**.

CALIXTUS, properly **Callisen Georg** (1586–1656) German Lutheran theologian, born in Medelbye in Schleswig. From 1603 he studied at Helmstedt, where, after travelling for four years, he was professor of theology. Although acknowledged by learned Romanists to be one of their ablest opponents, he was declared guilty of abominable heresy for some statements in his works which seemed favourable to Catholic dogmas, and others which approached too near to the Calvinistic standpoint. He was accused of apostasy at the conference of Thom in 1645, having been on more intimate terms with the Calvinistic than the Lutheran theologians. His friends in Brunswick, however, stood firmly by him, and he retained his chair till his death.

CALLAGHAN, (Leonard) James, Baron (1912–) English Labour statesman, educated at Portsmouth Northern Secondary School. He joined the staff of the inland revenue department in 1929. In 1945 he was elected Labour MP for South Cardiff and from 1950 represented South-east Cardiff. One of the chief contenders for the party leadership after the death of **Gaitskell**, in 1964 he was appointed Chancellor of the Exchequer in **Harold Wilson**'s government. In this capacity he introduced some of the most controversial taxation measures in British fiscal history, including the corporation and selective employment taxes. He was home secretary (1967–70) and foreign secretary (1974–76). In April 1976 he was elected prime minister on Harold Wilson's resignation, remaining in office until the general election of 1979. He resigned as leader of the opposition in 1980 and was made a life peer in 1987. His autobiography *Time and Chance* was published in 1987.

CALLAGHAN, Morley Edward (1903–) Canadian novelist, short-story writer and memoirist, born in Toronto of Irish descent. Now one of Canada's premier novelists, he was educated at Toronto University, and was befriended by **Hemingway** when a cub reporter on the Toronto *Daily Star*. They met up again in Paris, where his boxing prowess earned him Hemingway's respect, and he wrote about his time there in one of his most appealing books, *That Summer in Paris* (1963). He had been called to the bar in 1928, but Hemingway encouraged him to renounce law for literature and helped him get some of his stories published in expatriate literary magazines. In terms of publication, Callaghan's career has been strikingly uneven, periods of productivity mirrored by prolonged silence. His first novel was *Strange Fugitive* (1928) and his first collection of stories *A Native Argosy* (1930). From the late 1920s to the late 1930s he wrote six novels, finishing with *More Joy in Heaven* (1937). He returned to Toronto in 1929. His later novels include *The Loved and the Lost* (1951), *The Many Colored Coat* (1960), *A Fine and Private Place* (1975) and *A Time for Judas* (1983).

CALLAS, Maria Meneghini (1923–77) American operatic soprano, born in New York of Greek parents, She studied at Athens Conservatory, and in 1947 appeared at Verona in *La Gioconda*, winning immediate recognition. She sang with great authority in all the most exacting soprano roles, excelling in the intricate *bel canto* style of pre-Verdian Italian opera.

CALLCOTT, Sir Augustus Wall (1779–1844) English landscape painter, born in Kensington, London. He was appointed surveyor of royal pictures in 1834. His wife, Lady Maria Callcott (1785–42), wrote *Little Arthur's History of England*.

CALLENDAR, Hugh Longbourne (1863–1930) English physicist, born in Hatherop, Gloucestershire. Educated at Cambridge, he was professor of physics at McGill University, Montreal (1893), University College London (1898), and Imperial College of Science (1902). He devised a constant-pressure air thermometer which could measure up to 450°C, and also an accurate platinum resistance thermometer.

CALLES, Plutarco Elias (1877–1945) Mexican political leader. A former schoolmaster and tradesman, he took part in the revolt against **Porfirio Diaz** (1910), became governor of Sonora (1917–19) and secretary of the interior (1920–24). From 1924 to 1928 he was president of Mexico. In 1928 he retired to become a landowner and financier, but founded the National Revolutionary party in 1929 through which he controlled succeeding presidents. Known for his fanatical anticlericalism and for his efforts to restrict foreign influence in the oil industry, he was defeated by **Lázaro Cárdenas** and from 1936 to 1941 was exiled to the USA.

CALLIMACHUS (3rd century BC) Greek Hellenistic poet, grammarian, and critic, of Alexandria, born in Cyrene in Libya. He became head of the Alexandrian Library, and prepared a catalogue of it, in 120 volumes. He wrote numerous prose works which have not survived, a number of *Hymns* and *Epigrams*, and a long elegiac poem, *Aitia*, among others.

CALLISTRATUS (4th century BC) Athenian orator and statesman, whose eloquence is said to have fired the imagination of the youthful **Demosthenes**. In 366 he allowed the Thebans to occupy Oropus, and was prosecuted, but defended himself successfully in a brilliant speech. He was prosecuted again in 361 for his Spartan sympathies and was condemned to death, but went into exile before sentence was pronounced. He returned from exile in Macedonia, hoping to win public support, but was executed.

CALLISTUS See **CALIXTUS I**

CALLOT, Jacques (c.1592–1635) French etcher and engraver, born in Nancy. At the age of twelve he joined a band of gypsies, and travelled with them to Florence, but was sent home. In 1612 he went to Rome to study and then moved to Florence where he earned a reputation for his spirited etchings. In 1621 he returned to Nancy, where he was favourably received by the Duke of Lorraine. For **Louis XIII**, who invited him to Paris, he executed etchings of the siege of Rochelle, but refused to commemorate the capture of his native town. His 1600 realistic engravings cast vivid light on the manners of the 17th century, and his *Miseries of War* and his *Gypsies* are especially celebrated.

CALLOW, Simon (1949–) English actor, director and writer, born in London. He made his London début in *The Plumber's Progress* (1975), and joined Joint Stock in 1977, touring in several plays including **David Hare**'s *Fanshen* and **Howard Brenton**'s *Epsom Downs*. In 1978 he played the title roles in *Titus Andronicus* at the Bristol Old Vic, and **Brecht**'s *The Resistable Rise of Arturo Ui* at the Half Moon Theatre. At the National Theatre he played Orlando in *As You Like it* and **Mozart** in **Peter Shaffer**'s *Amadeus* (1979), and appeared in **Ayckbourn**'s *Sisterly Feelings* (1980). He returned to the NT in 1988 to play a shabby and ebullient Guy Burgess in *An Englishman Abroad*, part of **Alan Bennett**'s double bill, *Single Spies*. He has directed several new plays in fringe theatres and published an autobiography, *Being An Actor* (1984), and a biography of **Charles Laughton** (1987).

CALMETTE, (Léon Charles) Albert (1863–1933) French bacteriologist, born in Nice. A pupil of **Pasteur** and founder of the Pasteur Institute at Saigon, he was the discoverer of an anti-snakebite serum there. In 1895 he founded the Pasteur Institute at Lille (director, 1895–1919). He is best known for the vaccine BCG (Bacillus Calmette-Guérin), for inoculation against tuberculosis, which he jointly discovered with Dr Camille Guérin.

CALONNE, Charles Alexandre de (1734–1802) French statesman, born in Douai, studied law, and in 1783 was made controller-general of finance. As such he gained favour among the courtiers, who had complained of **Turgot** and **Necker**, by showering on them sums obtained by borrowing and increased taxation. In 1786, when the people could bear this no longer, Calonne advised the king to convoke the

Assembly of the Notables, and distribute the burden of taxation more equally. In opening the Assembly (1787), he described the general prosperity of France, but confessed that the annual deficit of the treasury had risen to 115 million francs, and that during 1776–86 the government had borrowed 1250 millions. The Notables demanded a statement of accounts; failing to satisfy them, he was banished to Lorraine. After this, he resided chiefly in England, until in 1802 **Napoleon** permitted him to return. He died very poor.

CALPRENÈDE, Gautier des Costes de la (1610–63) French author, officer of the guards and royal chamberlain of France. He wrote tragedies, tragicomedies, and the clever but tedious 'heroic romances', *Cléopâtre*, *Cassandre*, and others.

CALPURNIUS SICULUS, Titus (fl.mid 1st century) Latin bucolic poet. He is best known for his seven surviving Eclogues.

CALVAERT, Denis, or **Dionisio Fiammingo** (c.1540–1619) Flemish painter, born in Antwerp. He settled in Bologna, where he opened a school, among whose students were **Guido Reni**, **Domenichino**, and **Albani**, who afterwards, however, were pupils of the **Carracci**.

CALVERLEY, Charles Stuart (1831–84) English poet and parodist, born in Martley, Worcestershire, the son of a clergyman. He was educated at Marlborough, Harrow, Oxford and Cambridge. In 1858 he was elected a fellow of Christ's College, Cambridge, and in 1865 called to the bar, and settled in London. A fall on the ice in the winter of 1866–67 put an end to a brilliant career and his last years were spent as an invalid. One of the most gifted men of his time, he is remembered as a skilful parodist in his two little volumes, *Verses and Translations* (1862) and *Fly Leaves* (1872). His translation of **Theocritus** (1869) shows at once his scholarship and his mastery of English verse.

CALVERT, Frederick Crace (1819–73) English chemist, born in London. A consulting chemist in Manchester, he was largely instrumental in introducing carbolic acid as a disinfectant.

CALVERT, George See **BALTIMORE**

CALVI, Robert, originally **Gian Roberto Calvini** (1920–82) Italian banker and financier, convicted of illegal dealings, born in Milan. Working his way up through Banco Ambrosiano, he became its chairman in 1975, and continued to build a vast financial empire. In 1978, a report by the Bank of Italy on Ambrosiano concluded that several billion lire had been illegally exported. In May 1981, Calvi was indicted and arrested along with ten others. The trial began on 2 June. Calvi tried to commit suicide, but it is thought that the attempt was feigned. On 20 July he was found guilty and was sentenced to four years' imprisonment and was fined 16 billion lire. Calvi was released pending his appeal. Throughout the 1970s, he had become increasingly involved in Propaganda 2 (P2), a secret masonic lodge. In 1981, he also became entangled in the P2 scandal when the extent of its influence became publicly known. Members of parliament, leading financiers, intelligence officers and media magnates were implicated. By 1982, the bank hovered on the verge of financial collapse. It was temporarily saved by patronage letters from the Vatican's bank which, under the leadership of Paul Marcinckus, had jointly perpetrated with Ambrosiano several dubious business deals. On 10 June, Calvi flew to Rome. He was reported missing the next day. On 18 June, his body was found hanging from scaffolding under Blackfriars Bridge in London. His pockets were weighed down with bricks and concrete, and with a large amount of cash. A verdict of suicide was recorded, which was overturned in 1983, when an inquest delivered an open verdict on the death. The ramifications of the collapse of Banco Ambrosiano, of the Vatican's involvement and of the Mafia's possible involvement via P2 continued well after Calvi's death. Calvi's family still maintain that he was murdered.

CALVIN, John (1509–64) French theologian and reformer, born in Noyon, in Picardy, where his father, Gérard Caulvin or Cauvin, was procureur-fiscal and secretary of the diocese. He studied Latin in Paris from 1523 and later as a law student in Orléans received from the Scriptures his first impulse to theological studies. From Orléans he went to Bourges, where he learned Greek, published an edition of **Seneca**'s *De clementia* and began to preach the reformed doctrines. After a short stay (1533) in Paris, now a centre of the 'new learning' and of religious excitement, he visited Noyon. He went to Nerac, Saintonge, the residence of the queen of Navarre, Angoulême, and then to Paris again. Persecution raged so hotly that Calvin was no longer safe in France; at Basel he issued in 1536 his *Christianae Religionis Institutio*, with the famous preface addressed to **Francis I**. After a short visit to Italy, to Renée, Duchess of Ferrara, he revisited his native town, sold his paternal estate, and set out for Strasbourg, by way of Geneva, where **Guillaume Farel** persuaded him to remain and assist in the work of reformation. The citizens had asserted their independence against the Duke of Savoy; and magistrates and people eagerly joined with the reformers. A Protestant Confession of Faith was proclaimed, and moral severity took the place of licence. The strain, however, was too sudden and extreme. A spirit of rebellion broke forth under the 'Libertines', and Calvin and Farel were expelled from the city (1538). Calvin, withdrawing to Strasbourg, devoted himself to critical labours on the New Testament; and here in 1539 he married the widow of a converted Anabaptist. But in 1541 the Genevans, wearying of the Libertine licence, invited Calvin to return and after some delay, he acceded to their request. By his College of Pastors and Doctors, and his Consistorial Court of Discipline, he founded a theocracy, which was virtually to direct all the affairs of the city, and to control the social and individual life of the citizens. His struggle with the Libertines lasted 14 years, when the reformer's authority was confirmed into an absolute supremacy (1555). During that long struggle controversies also occurred between Calvin and **Castellio**, **Bolsec**, and **Servetus**. The last, whose speculations on the Trinity were abhorrent to Calvin, was apprehended at Vienna by the Catholic authorities (to whom Calvin forwarded incriminating documents), and was sentenced to be burned, but effected his escape, and in Geneva, on his way to Italy, was subjected to a new trial, condemned, and burnt to death (1553). Calvin's intolerance was approved by the most conspicuous Reformers, including the gentle **Melanchthon**. Through **Beza** he made his influence felt in the great struggle in France between the **Guises** and the Protestants. None can dispute Calvin's intellectual greatness, or the powerful services which he rendered to the cause of Protestantism. Stern in spirit and unyielding in will, he was never selfish or petty in his motives. He rendered a double service to Protestantism: he systematized its doctrine, and organized its ecclesiastical discipline. His commentaries embrace the greater part of the Old Testament and the whole of the New except the Revelation. In 1559 he founded a theological academy at Geneva that became the university.

CALVIN, Melvin (1911–) American chemist, born in Minnesota, of Russian immigrant parents. He became professor of chemistry at the University of California (1947–71) and head of the Lawrence Radiation Laboratory there (1963–80). He is best known for his researches into the role of chlorophyll in photosynthesis, for which he won the Nobel prize for chemistry in 1961.

CALVINO, Italo (1923–87) Italian novelist, essayist and journalist, born in Santiago de las Vegas, Cuba, of Italian parents. He grew up in San Remo on the Italian Riviera and was educated at the University of Turin. In 1940 he was forced to join the Young Fascists. He was a reluctant participant in the Italian occupation of the French Riviera, but in 1943 he was able to join the Resistance, and until 1945 he was with the Partisan forces fighting the Nazis in Liguria. Throughout the 1940s he wrote for the Communist paper *L'unità* and later he succeeded **Cesare Pavese** at Einaudi, the Turin-based publishers. His first novel, *The Path to the Nest of Spiders* (1947; trans 1956), was dubbed neo-realist but he became increasingly interested in fantasy, folktales and the nature of narrative. During the Cold War years of the 1950s he wrote three fantastic 'historical' novels, collectively titled *Our Ancestors* (1960; trans 1980). A complete translation of his *Fiabe Italiane* (1956) was published as *Italian folktales* in English in 1980. Regarded as one of the most inventive of the European modernists, he combined fantasy and surrealism with a hard, satirical wit and his later books are complex and profound. Seminal titles are *Invisible Cities* (1975), *The Castle of Crossed Destinies* (1977), *If on a Winter's Night a Traveller* (1981) and *Palomar* (1983). In 1973 he won the prestigious Italian literary award, the Premio Feltrinelli.

CALWELL, Arthur Augustus (1896–1973) Australian politician. A lifelong member of the Australian Labor party (ALP), as the responsible minister (1945–49), he oversaw the programme for a massive influx of one million Europeans into Australia in the decade immediately following Word War II. In 1960 he succeeded **H V Evatt** as leader of the ALP opposition.

CAM, or **Cão** (15th century) Portuguese explorer. In 1482 he discovered the mouth of the Congo, near whose bank an inscribed stone erected by him as a memorial was found in 1887. His voyages southwards along the west African coast later enabled **Bartholomew Diaz** to find the sea route to the Indian Ocean around the Cape.

CAMARA, Helder Pessoa (1909–) Brazilian Roman Catholic theologian and prelate, born in Fortaleza, Ceará State. Archbishop of Olinda and Recife, north east Brazil, from 1964 to 1984, he has been a champion of the poor and of non-violent social change in his native Brazil and in the Catholic Church at large through his influence at Vatican Council II, and received international recognition with the award of the Martin Luther King Jr Peace prize (1970) and the People's prize (1973). His theological and devotional writings have been translated into many languages, especially *Race Against Time* (1971), *Revolution Through Peace* (1971) and *Hoping Against All Hope* (1984).

CAMARGO, Maria Anna de (1710–70) French dancer, born in Brussels. She won European fame for her performances at the Paris Opera, where she made her début in 1726 in Jean Balon's *Les Caractères de la Danse*; and is said to have been responsible for the shortening of the traditional ballet skirt which allowed more complicated steps to be seen. She was also one of the first celebrities to lend her name to merchandizing shoes and wigs.

CAMBACÉRÈS, Jean Jacques Régis de (1753–1824) Duke of Parma and arch-chancellor of the Empire from 1804, born in Montpellier. The *Projet de Code Civil*, published in his name, formed the basis of the *Code Napoléon*.

CAMBIO See **ARNOLFO DI CAMBIO**

CAMBON, Joseph (1756–1820) French financier and revolutionary, born in Montpellier. During the Revolution he was a member of the Legislative Assembly and the Convention (1792), and although a moderate, he voted for the king's death. As head of the committee on finance (1793–95), he produced the 'Great Book of the Public Debt' in an attempt to stabilize the finances. He was banished as a regicide in 1815, and died near Brussels.

CAMBRENSIS See **GIRALDUS CAMBRENSIS**

CAMBRIDGE, Ada (1844–1926) English-born Australian novelist and poet, born in Norfolk. The second of ten children, her father was a gentleman farmer and she was educated privately. By the time she met and married George Cross at the age of 26, she had published short stories, poems and a book of hymns. They left almost immediately for Australia where her husband was to be a missionary priest, and settled eventually in Melbourne. In 1873 she began contributing to the *Australian* and published her first novella, *Up the Murray*, in 1875. A woman with a strong sense of class, her writing called attention to women's social position and encouraged them to think for themselves. She wrote 18 novels and attracted a wide English readership but was modest about her success, regarding herself fortunate to have been the first in the field. **Jane Austen** is the most obvious influence, and her best work is to be found in *A Marked Man* (1890), *The Three Miss Kings* (1891), *Not All In Vain* (1892), *Fidelis* (1895) and *Materfamilias* (1898).

CAMBRIDGE, George William Frederick Charles, 2nd Duke of (1819–1904) British soldier, born in Hanover, the only son of **George III**'s seventh son, Adolphus Frederick (1774–1850), 1st duke of Cambridge. He served briefly in the Hanoverian army before transferring to the British army. Promoted major-general in 1854, he fought at Alma and Inkermann in the Crimean War. From 1856 to 1895 he was commander-in-chief of the British army (field marshal from 1862).

CAMBYSES II, Persian **Kambujiya** (d.522) second King of the Medes and Persians. He succeeded his father, **Cyrus**, in 529 BC. He put his brother Smerdis to death and in 527 or 525 invaded and conquered Egypt. He meditated further conquests, but the Tyrian fleet refused to serve against Carthage; an army sent to seize the temple of Ammon is said to have perished in the desert; and one which he led in person to Nubia was likewise unsuccessful. When news came, in 522, that Gaumáta, a Magian, had assumed Smerdis' character, and usurped the Persian throne, Cambyses marched against him from Egypt, but died in Syria, either by accident or suicide.

CAMDEN, Charles Pratt, 1st Earl (1713–94) English jurist and statesman. Educated at Eton College and Cambridge, he was called to the bar in 1738. Chief justice of the common pleas, 1762–66, and lord chancellor from 1766 to 1770, he was president of the Council (1782–94), and was created Earl Camden in 1786.

CAMDEN, William (1551–1623) English antiquarian and historian, born in London, the son of a painter. Educated at Christ's Hospital, St Paul's School, and Oxford, he became second master of Westminster School in 1575 and headmaster in 1593. A dedicated scholar, he compiled a pioneering topographical survey of the British Isles in Latin, *Britannia* (1586, translated into English in 1610). In 1597 he was appointed Clarenceux king-at-arms. He also published a list of the epitaphs in Westminster Abbey (1600) a collection of old English historians (1603), a narrative of the trial of **Guy Fawkes** and the Gunpowder Plotters (1607), and *Annals of the Reign of Elizabeth to 1588* (1615). He was buried in Westminster Abbey.

CAMERARIUS, Joachim (1500–74) German classical scholar, who changed his original name of Liebhard into Camerarius because his forefathers had been *Kammerer* (chamberlains) to the bishops of Bamberg. A friend of **Melanchthon**, he embraced the Reformation at Wittenberg in 1521, and helped to formulate the Augsburg Confession of 1530. Professor of Greek and Latin at Tübingen (1535) and Leipzig (from 1541), he produced several editions of the classical authors, wrote a biography of Melanchthon (1566) and edited his letters (1569), and wrote *Epistolae Familiares* (3 vols, 1583–95) on contemporary affairs.

CAMERARIUS, Joachim (1534–98) German botanist, son of **Joachim Camerarius** (1500-74). Physician in Nürnberg, author of *Hortus medicus et philosophicus* (1588) and *Symbola et Emblem* (1590), he was one of the most learned physicians and botanists of his age.

CAMERARIUS, Rudolph Jacob (1665–1721) German physician and botanist, born in Tübingen. Director of the botanic garden at Tübingen and professor of botany, he was renowned for his experimental proof of sexuality in plants (*De Sexu Plantarum*, 1694)

CAMERON, Sir David Young (1865–1945) Scottish artist, born the son of a Glasgow minister. He studied at the Glasgow School of Art (1881–85) and was introduced to the collector George Stevenson who discovered his pen and ink drawings in 1887. As a result of this he gave up a career in business and concentrated on art. One of the finest and most romantic of British etchers, he followed the lead of **Whistler** and **Haden**. Turning to his native landscape for inspiration, he introduced drypoint to produce some of the most memorable images seen in British printmaking this century. He was appointed king's limner in 1933.

CAMERON, James Mark (1911–85) Scottish journalist, born of Scottish parents in Battersea, London. His career began as an office boy for the *Weekly News* (1935) and progressed, via Dundee and Glasgow, to Fleet Street in 1940. Rejected for military service, he worked as a sub-editor on *The Daily Express* (1940–45) and subsequently returned to reporting. Covering the atom bomb experiments at Bikini (1946) formed his anti-authoritarian views and convinced him to become a member of CND. He resigned from the *Daily Express* in 1950 and *Picture Post* in 1951 over points of principle before settling with the *New Chronicle* (1952–60) as a roving reporter on war, poverty and injustice. Renowned for his integrity, dry wit and concise summation of a situation, he painted literary pictures of some of the great events in world affairs, from the Vietnam War to ill-treatment of the underprivileged in India. A writer and presenter of many television programmes, including *Men of Our Time* (1963), the intermittent *Cameron Country* and the autobiographical *Once Upon a Time* (1984), his radio play *The Pump* (1973) won the Prix Italia and was dramatized for television in 1980. His books include *Witness in Vietnam* (1966) and the autobiography *Point of Departure* (1967).

CAMERON, John (c.1579–1625) Scottish theologian, known as the 'walking library', born in Glasgow. He was educated at Glasgow University, and in 1600 went to the Continent, where his erudition secured him appointments at Bergerac, Sedan, and Saumur. In 1622 he was appointed principal of Glasgow University. In less than a year, however, he returned to Saumur, and from there went to Montauban, where he received a divinity professorship. Here, as at Glasgow, his moderate Calvinist doctrine of passive obedience made him many enemies, one of whom stabbed him mortally in the street. His eight theological works, in Latin and French (1616–42), are said to be the foundation of **Amyraut**'s doctrine of universal grace (1634).

CAMERON, Julia Margaret, née **Pattle** (1815–79) British photographer. Born in Calcutta, she married an Indian jurist Charles Hay Cameron (1795–1880) in 1838, and died in Ceylon. At the age of 48 she was given a camera, and went on to become an outstanding amateur photographer in the 1860s. Her style influenced by her good friend **George Frederick Watts**, her close-up portraits of such Victorian celebrities as **Tennyson**, **Darwin**, **Carlyle**, and **Newman**, received permanent acclaim.

CAMERON, Richard (1648–80) Scottish Covenanter, born in Falkland in Fife. Having studied at St Andrews (1662–65), he became precentor and schoolmaster at Falkland under an Episopal incumbent, but was subsequently 'converted by the field preachers'. In 1678 he went to Holland, and returned in 1680 in time to publish the Sanquhar Declaration, in which he and his followers ('Cameronians') renounced their allegiance to the king and declared war on him and his agents. Retiring then, with some sixty armed comrades, to the hills between Nithsdale and Ayrshire, he succeeded in evading capture for a month. In 1680, however, the band was surprised by a body of dragoons on Airds Moss, near Auchinleck, and, after a brave fight, Cameron fell. His hands and head were fixed on the Netherbow Port, Edinburgh.

CAMERON, Simon (1799–1889) American statesman, born in Pennsylvania. He was a journeyman printer and newspaper editor. In 1845 he became a senator, was **Lincoln**'s secretary of war (1861–62), and minister plenipotentiary to Russia (1862–63), and died in New York.

CAMERON, Verney Lovett (1844–94) English explorer, born at Radipole near Weymouth. He entered the navy in 1857, taking part in the suppression of the slave trade. In 1872 he was appointed to command an African east coast expedition to relieve **David Livingstone**. Starting from Bagamoyo in March 1873, he met Livingstone's followers bearing his remains to the coast in August at Unyanyembe. He made a survey of Lake Tanganyika, and in the belief that the Lualaba was the upper Congo, he resolved to follow its course to the west coast; but native hostility prevented him from verifying this, and striking southwest he reached Benguela on 7 November 1875, the first European to cross Africa from coast to coast. In 1878 he travelled overland to India, to satisfy himself of the feasibility of a Constantinople–Baghdad railway; and in 1882, with Sir **Richard Burton**, he visited the Gold Coast. He died in a hunting accident.

CAMERON OF LOCHIEL, Donald, 'Gentle Lochiel' (c.1695–1748) Scottish Highland chieftain, grandson of Sir **Ewan Cameron of Lochiel**. His reluctant support of the young Pretender (**Charles Edward Stewart**) in 1745 encouraged other chieftains. Badly wounded at Culloden, he died in exile in France.

CAMERON OF LOCHIEL, Sir Ewen (1629–1719) Scottish Jacobite and chief of clan Cameron. Famous for his prodigious feats of strength, he led his clan against the parliamentary forces of the English Commonwealth, fought at Killiecrankie (1689), and supported the Earl of **Mar** in the 1715 Rising. He is said to have killed the last wolf in Scotland.

CAMILLUS, Marcus Furius (447–365 BC) Roman patrician who first appears as censor in 403 BC. He took Veii in 396, after a ten years' siege; and in 394 his magnanimity induced Falerii to surrender unconditionally. Condemned on a charge of misappropriating the booty, but really because of his patrician haughtiness, he went into banishment at Ardea (391); but, Brennus having captured and destroyed all Rome except the Capitol, he was recalled and appointed dictator, appearing according to the legend just as the garrison were about to purchase the Gauls' departure, and drove the invader from the town. He routed the Aequi, Volsci, and Etrusci; and in 367, though 80, he became for the fifth time dictator, and defeated the Gauls near Alba. He died of the plague.

CAMM, Sir Sydney (1893–1966) English aircraft designer, born in Windsor, Berkshire. Secretary of the Windsor Model Aeroplane Club (1912) and designer to Martinsyde Company (1914), he joined Hawker Engineering Company (later Hawker Siddeley Aviation) in 1923. By 1925 he was chief designer, a post he retained until his death. He had a unique design record of highly successful single-engined military aircraft, notably the Fury, Hart and Demon biplanes, and his first monoplane, the Hurricane; he also designed the Tornado, Typhoon, Tempest, and the jet-engined Sea Hawk, Hunter and the jet-jump Harrier, the only jet-lift type to enter long-term service with four air forces.

CAMOENS, Camões, Luis de (1524–80) Portuguese poet, born in Lisbon. He studied for the church as an 'honourable poor student' at Coimbra, but declined to take orders. His *Amphitriões* was acted before the university. Returning to Lisbon, probably in 1542, he fell in love with Donna Caterina Ataide, who returned his affection; but her father was against the marriage, and the poet had to content himself with passionate protestations in his *Rimas*—short poems after the model of the Italians. He was banished from Lisbon for a year, and joining a Portuguese force at Ceuta, served there for two years, losing his right eye because of a splinter. In 1550 he returned to Lisbon, where for the next three years he seems to have led a somewhat discreditable life; and having been thrown into prison for his share in a street affray, was released only on his volunteering to go to India. At Goa (1553–56) he engaged in two military expeditions, but his bold denunciations of the Portuguese officials at length led to an honourable exile in a lucrative post at Macao (1556). Returning to Goa (1558) he was shipwrecked and lost everything except his poem, *The Lusiads*. At Goa he was thrown into prison through the machinations of his former enemies; but at length, after an exile of 16 years, he returned to Portugal to spend the remainder of his life at Lisbon in poverty and obscurity. In 1572 he published *The Lusiads*, which had an immediate and brilliant success, but did little for the fortunes of its author, who died in a public hospital. In *The Lusiads* he did for the Portuguese language what **Chaucer** did for English and **Dante** for Italian—as well as making himself the interpreter of the deepest aspirations of the Portuguese nation. The Portuguese regard it as their national epic.

CAMP, Walter Chauncy (1859–1925) American footballer, born in New Britain, Connecticut, the 'father of American football'. At Yale University (1888–92) he helped to shape American football rules, introducing the eleven-man side (as against fifteen), the concept of 'downs' and 'yards gained', and the creation of a new points-scoring system. He also pioneered the notion of the All-American side, a somewhat bizarre concept since such a selection had no opposition abroad against which it could be measured.

CAMPAGNOLA, Domenico (c.1490–c.1564) Italian painter. A pupil of **Giulio Campagnola** and assistant of **Titian**, he is known for his religious frescoes in Padua, also for masterly engravings and line drawings in the manner of Titian.

CAMPAGNOLA, Giulio (1482–c.1515) Italian engraver, born in Padua. He designed type for **Aldus Manutius**, and produced fine engravings after **Mantegna**, **Bellini**, and **Giorgione**.

CAMPAN, Jeanne Louise Henriette (1752–1822) French educationist and writer, born in Paris. She was a friend of **Marie Antoinette** (1770–92), and after **Robespierre**'s fall opened a boarding-school at St Germain-en-Laye at which **Hortense de Beauharnais** was a pupil. In 1806 **Napoleon** appointed her head of the school at Ecouen for the daughters of officers of the Legion of Honour. She wrote *Vie privée de Marie Antoinette* (1823), *Journal anecdotique* (1824), and *Correspondance avec la Reine Hortense* (2 vols, 1835).

CAMPANELLA, Tommaso (1568–1639) Italian philosopher, born in Stilo in Calabria. Entering the Dominican order in 1583, he taught at Rome and Naples. He evolved an empirical, anti-Scholastic philosophy, as expounded in *Philosophia sensibus demonstrata* (1591), for which he was imprisoned and tortured by the Inquisition. He was arrested again in 1599 for heresy and conspiracy against Spanish rule, and was not finally released until 1626. From prison he wrote his famous utopian work, *City of the Sun* (c.1602), as well as other religious works and some poetry. He eventually fled to Paris in 1634, as a protégé of **Richelieu**.

CAMPBELL-BANNERMAN, Sir Henry (1836–1908) Scottish statesman, the second son of Sir James Campbell, lord provost of Glasgow from 1840 to 1843. He assumed the name Bannerman in 1872. Educated at Glasgow and Trinity College, Cambridge, he became Liberal MP for the Stirling burghs in 1868, was chief secretary for Ireland in 1884, and, having been converted to Home Rule for Ireland, war secretary in 1886, GCB in 1895, Liberal leader in 1899, and prime minister in 1905. He resigned on 4 April 1908, and died 11 April. A 'pro-Boer', he granted the ex-republics responsible government; and he launched the campaign against the House of Lords.

CAMPBELL ancient Scottish family, whose members have held the titles of **Argyll**, Breadalbane, and Cawdor. Sir Duncan Campbell of Lochow was created Lord Campbell in 1445, and his successor was created Earl of Argyll in 1457. From his younger son, Sir Colin Campbell of Glenorchy (c.1400–78), are descended the earls and marquises of Breadalbane and from the younger son of the second Earl of Argyll, who fell at Flodden in 1513, the earls of Cawdor.

CAMPBELL, Alexander (1788–1866) Irish-born American pastor, leader of the 'Disciples of Christ', otherwise known as 'Campbellites', born near Ballymena, Antrim. He emigrated to the USA with his father, Thomas (1763–1854), in 1809. In 1813 he succeeded his father as pastor of an independent church at Brush Run, Pennsylvania. He advocated a return to the simple church of New Testament times, and in 1826 published a translation of the New Testament, in which the word 'baptism' gave place to 'immersion'. In 1841 he founded Bethany College in West Virginia.

CAMPBELL, Charles Arthur (1897–1974) Scottish philosopher, born in Glasgow. A teacher of moral philosophy in Glasgow before becoming professor of philosophy at the University College of North Wales,

Bangor in 1932, he returned to Glasgow as professor of logic and rhetoric (1938–61). His unfashionable yet indefatigable pursuit of the traditional concerns of philosophy against the trend to reduce the subject to questions of linguistic analysis is demonstrated in *Scepticism and Construction* (1931), his 1953–55 Gifford lectures expanded as *On Selfhood and Godhood* (1957), and selected essays 1935–62 published as *In Defence of Free Will* (1967).

CAMPBELL, Colen (1679–1726) Scottish architect, born either in Nairn or in Argyll. He began as a lawyer, moving to London c.1710. His earliest recorded design was Shawfield Mansion, Glasgow (1712, demolished 1795). He was apparently associated with James Smith, a leading Scottish classicist architect, possibly as his pupil. A prime instigator of British neo-Palladianism, he produced an influential *Vitruvius Britannicus* (1712, 1718 and 1725) named after the Roman architect Vitruvius, and which was widely admired. His designs set precedents from which British Palladianism evolved. In 1728 he published a revision of **Palladio**'s *First Book of Architecture*. His best-known works include Rolls House (1717), Burlington House (1718–19) and Wanstead House (1714–20, demolished 1824), London; Mereworth Castle, Kent (1722–25), echoing a Palladian villa, Houghton Hall, Norfolk (1722–26), and Compton Place, Eastbourne (1726–27).

CAMPBELL, Sir Colin, Baron Clyde (1792–1863) Scottish soldier, born in Glasgow. His father was a carpenter, named Macliver, but Colin assumed the name of Campbell from his mother's brother, Colonel John Campbell, who in 1802 put him to school at Gosport. He was gazetted an ensign in 1808, and by 1813 had fought his way up to a captaincy, serving on the Walcheren expedition (1809), and through all the Peninsular war, where he was twice badly wounded. He took part in the expedition to the United States (1814), and then passed nearly 30 years in garrison duty at Gibraltar, Barbados, Demerara, and various places in England, in 1837 becoming lieutenant-colonel of the 98th foot. For the brief Chinese campaign of 1842 he was made a CB and for his brilliant sevices in the second Sikh war (1848–49) a KCB, thereafter commanding for three years at Peshawar against the frontier tribes. On the outbreak of the Crimean War in 1854 he was appointed to the command of the Highland Brigade; the victory of Alma was mainly his; and his, too, the spendid repulse of the Russians by the 'thin red line' in the battle of Balaclava. He was rewarded with a KGCB, with a sword of honour from his native city, and several foreign orders, and in 1856 was appointed inspector-general of Infantry. On the outbreak of the Mutiny (July 1857), Lord **Palmerston** offered him the command of the forces in India: he effected the final relief of Lucknow in November, was created Baron Clyde in July 1858, and brought the rebellion to an end by December. Returning next year to England, he was made a fieldmarshal. He died at Chatham, and was buried in Westminster Abbey.

CAMPBELL, Donald Malcolm (1921–67) English car and speedboat racer, son of Sir **Malcolm Campbell**. An engineer by training, with a reputation as a playboy, he sought to emulate his father's achievements. He set new world speed records several times on both land and water, culminating in 1964 with a water-speed record of 276.33 mph on Lake Dumbleyung in Australia, and a land-speed record of 403.1 mph at Lake Eyre salt flats in Australia. In an attempt to become the first man to break 300 mph on water, he was killed when his *Bluebird* turbo-jet hydroplane crashed on Lake Coniston in England.

CAMPBELL, George (1719–96) Scottish theologian, born in Aberdeen, and educated there at the grammar school and Marischal College. Abandoning law for divinity, he was in 1748 ordained minister, and in 1759 was appointed principal of Marischal College, and in 1771 professor of divinity. His works include *Dissertation on Miracles* (1762) in answer to **Hume**, *Philosophy of Rhetoric* (1776), and *Lectures on Ecclesiastical History* (1800).

CAMPBELL, John, 1st Baron Campbell (1779–1861) Scottish judge, born in Cupar, Fife, and lord chancellor of England. He studied for the church at St Andrews, turned to law and journalism, and was called to the English bar in 1806. A Whig MP (1830–49), he was knighted and made solicitor-general in 1832, and became attorney-general in 1834. As such he sponsored some important reforming Acts. Created a baron in 1841, he was appointed successively lord chancellor of Ireland (1841), chancellor of the duchy of Lancaster (1846), chief justice of the Queen's Bench (1850), and lord chancellor (1859). His *Lives of the Chief Justices* (1849–57) and *Lives of the Lord Chancellors* (1845–47) are disfigured by prejudiced comments and in later volumes by inaccuracy.

CAMPBELL, John Archibald (1859–1909) Scottish architect, regarded as an early pioneer of the vertical articulation of tall buildings. He studied at the École des Beaux Arts, Paris (1880–83). From 1886 to 1897 he was in partnership with John J Burnet in Glasgow with whom he produced the Athanaeum Theatre (1891) in a wilfully asymmetrical free style. One of his major independent works was The Northern Insurance Building in Glasgow (1908–09) where he contrasted a vertically proportioned Scots Renaissance façade with a functional rear elevation, and pioneered a steel frame which gave maximum daylighting from the cramped rear court. He also designed numerous houses, especially around his own at Bridge of Weir.

CAMPBELL, John Francis, of Islay (1822–85) Scottish folk-lorist, born on the Hebridean island of Islay and educated at Eton and Edinburgh University. He held offices at court, and was afterwards secretary to the lighthouse and coal commissions. An enthusiastic Highlander and profound Gaelic scholar, he collected folk-traditions which he translated in his *Popular Tales of the West Highlands* (4 vols, 1860–62).

CAMPBELL, John McLeod (1800–72) Scottish theologian and preacher, born in Kilninver, Argyll. He entered Glasgow University at the age of eleven, and was ordained minister of Rhu, near Helensburgh, in 1825. His views on the personal assurance of salvation and on the universality of the atonement led to his deposition for heresy in 1831. For two years he laboured in the Highlands as an evangelist, and then preached quietly without remuneration to a congregation that gathered round him in Glasgow (1833–59). From 1870 he lived in Rosneath, and died there. He wrote *Christ the Bread of Life* (1851), *The Nature of the Atonement* (1856), and *Thoughts on Revelation* (1862).

CAMPBELL, Lewis (1830–1908) Scottish classical scholar, born in Edinburgh. Educated at Edinburgh, Glasgow and Oxford, he took Anglican orders, and was professor of Greek at St Andrews, 1863–92. He is known especially for his editions and translations of **Sophocles** and **Plato**.

CAMPBELL, Sir Malcolm (1885–1949) English sportsman and racer, born in Chislehurst, Kent, holder of both the land and water speed records from 1927 onwards. In 1935 he became the first man to break 300 mph on land with 301.1291 mph at Bonneville Salt Flats, Utah. In 1939 he achieved his fastest speed on water with 141.74 mph. He called all his racing cars and speedboats *Bluebird* after the symbol of unattainability in the play of that name by **Maurice Maeterlinck**.

CAMPBELL, Mrs Patrick, née **Beatrice Stella Tanner** (1865–1940) English actress, born in Kensington of mixed English and Italian parentage. She married in 1884, and went on the stage in 1888. Though her mercurial temperament made her the terror of managers, she possessed outstanding charm and talent, and leapt to fame in *The Second Mrs Tanqueray* (1893). Her first husband died in South Africa in 1900; in 1914 she married George Cornwallis-West. She played Eliza in Shaw's *Pygmalion* (1914) and formed a long friendship with the author.

CAMPBELL, Reginald John (1867–1956) English clergyman, born in London. He entered the Congregational ministry in 1895 and was pastor of the City Temple, London (1903–15). In 1907 he startled the evangelical world by his exposition of an 'advanced' *New Theology*. He became an Anglican in 1916. He wrote a biography of **David Livingstone** in 1929. Other works included *The Call of Christ* (1933) and *The Peace of God* (1936).

CAMPBELL, (Ignatius) Roy Dunnachie (1901–57) South African poet and journalist, born in Durban. The violence of his personality and his enthusiasms give his work a brilliance quite distinct from its merit. He became an ardent admirer of all things Spanish and fought with **Franco**'s armies during the Civil War. His books of poetry include *The Flamingo Terrapin* (1924), *The Wayzgoose* (1928), *Adamastor* (1930), *The Georgiad* (1931), *Mithraic Emblems* (1936), and *Flowering Rifle* (1939). A collected edition of his poems appeared in 1949, and he published two autobiographical volumes: *Broken Record* (1934) and *Light on a Dark Horse* (1951).

CAMPBELL, Thomas (1777–1844) Scottish poet and journalist, born and educated in Glasgow. In 1797 he went to Edinburgh to study law; but he was more and more drawn to the reading and writing of poetry. *The Pleasures of Hope*, published in 1799, ran through four editions in a year. During a tour on the Continent (1800–01) he visited Hohenlinden, at Hamburg fell in with the prototype of his 'Exile of Erin', and sailed past the batteries of Copenhagen. In 1803 he married and settled in London, having refused the offer of a chair at Wilna, and resolved to adopt a literary career. He contributed articles to *The Edinburgh Encyclopaedia*, and compiled *The Annals of Great Britain from George II to the Peace of Amiens*. In 1809 appeared *Gertrude of Wyoming*; in 1818 he was again in Germany, and on his return he published his *Specimens of the British Poets*. In 1820 he delivered a course of lectures on poetry at the Surrey Institution; and from 1820 to 1830 he edited *The New Monthly Magazine*, contributing 'The Last Man' and other poems. He was buried in Westminster Abbey. 'Hohenlinden', 'Ye Mariners of England', and 'The Battle of the Baltic' are among his best-known poems.

CAMPBELL, William Wallace (1862–1938) American astronomer, born in Hancock County, Ohio. He joined the Lick Observatory in California in 1891, became its director (1901–30), and was also president of the University of California (1923–30). He is best known for his work on the radial velocity of stars. He led seven expeditions to study solar eclipses, and elucidated the sun's motion in the galaxy.

CAMPBELL, William Wilfred (1860–1919) Canadian poet, born in Kitchener, Ontario. An Anglican clergyman, he joined the Canadian civil service in 1891. He was author of *Lake Lyrics* (1889) and other volumes of poetry, and was editor of the *Oxford Book of Canadian Verse* (1906).

CAMPE, Joachim Heinrich (1746–1818) German educationist, born near Holzminden. After serving with **Johann Basedow** he founded an institution of his own, and in 1787 reorganized the school system in Brunswick, where he also established a large publishing house. He wrote some works on education, and a German Dictionary (5 vols, 1807–11); but his books for the young, such as *Robinson der Jüngere* were specially popular.

CAMPEGGIO, Lorenzo (1472–1539) Italian prelate, born in Bologna. He studied law, married early, and after his wife's death took orders. He was made bishop of Feltri (1512), a cardinal (1517), papal legate to England to incite **Henry VIII** against the Turks (1518), and bishop of Salisbury and archbishop of Bologna (1524). Joint judge with **Wolsey** in the divorce suit against **Catherine of Aragon**, he ended by displeasing all parties (1529).

CAMPEN, Jacob van (1595–1657) Dutch architect and painter, born in Haarlem. Greatly influenced by Italian style, he built the first completely classical building in Holland. His masterpiece was the Mauritshuis, The Hague (1633) for Prince Johan Maurits von Nassau; the interior was destroyed in 1704. Other works include Amsterdam Theatre (1637), based on **Palladio**'s Theatro Olympico, and Amsterdam Town Hall (1647–55, now the royal palace), a large classical building around two courts with a huge sculptured pediment depicting the oceans paying homage to Amsterdam, which was both a monument to the Peace of Munster and to the city itself.

CAMPENDONCK, Heinrich (1889–1957) German Expressionist painter, born in Krefeld. He was a member of the 'Blue Rider' group founded by **Marc** and **Kandinsky**.

CAMPENHOUT, François von (1779–1849) Belgian composer and violinist. He wrote several works, but is best remembered for *La Brabançonne*, the Belgian national anthem.

CAMPER, Pieter (1722–89) Dutch anatomist, born in Leiden. Professor at Franeker (1749–61), Amsterdam (1761–63), and Groningen (1763–73), he wrote a series of works on human and comparative anatomy, and discovered the large air content of the bones of birds.

CAMPESE, David Ian (1962–) Australian rugby player, born near Queanbeyan, one of the fastest wingers in international rugby. His powerful sprinting meant that by the time he played his 42nd international he had scored more than 30 tries, a record for international rugby. He followed the pattern of many modern rugby union top-grade players by playing for most of the year, appearing frequently in Italy and taking full advantage of the difference in playing seasons between the two hemispheres.

CAMPI, Antonio (c.1536–c.1591) Italian painter and architect, brother of **Giulio** and **Vincenzo Campi**. He was a successful imitator of **Correggio**.

CAMPI, Bernardino (1522–c.1592) Italian artist, the son of a goldsmith, and possibly a kinsman of **Antonio Campi**. He imitated **Titian** with such success that it has been difficult to distinguish the copies from the originals. His works may be seen in Mantua and Cremona.

CAMPI, Giulio (1502–72) Italian architect and painter, elder brother of **Antonio** and **Vincenzo Campi**. He studied under Giulio Romano and has left a fine altarpiece in San Abbondio in Cremona.

CAMPI, Vincenzo (1536–91) Italian painter, brother of **Antonio** and **Giulio Campi**. He excelled in small figures; also painted portraits.

CAMPIN, Robert (c.1375–1444) Dutch artist, known as the Master of Flémalle from his paintings in the Abbey of that name near Liège. About 1400 he settled in Tournai, where **Roger van der Weyden** and Jaques Daret were his pupils, and he is thought to have learnt technical secrets from Hubert, brother of **Jan van Eyck**. His *Madonna* and the pair of portraits of a man and his wife in the National Gallery, London, show him to have been a painter of rude vigour.

CAMPION, Edmund (1540–81) English Jesuit martyr, the son of a London tradesman. He was educated at Christ's Hospital and St John's College, Oxford, and was ordained an Anglican deacon in 1569; but he hankered after the old religion, and went to Dublin to help re-establish the university there. Suspected of leanings towards Rome, and fearing arrest, he escaped to Douai, and in 1573 joined the Society of Jesus in Bohemia. In 1580 he was recalled from Prague, where he was professor of rhetoric, to accompany **Robert Parsons** on the Jesuit mission into England. The audacity of his controversial manifesto known as Campion's 'Brag and challenge', which was followed by his *Decem Rationes*, or 'Ten Reasons', greatly irritated his opponents. In July 1581 he was caught near Wantage, and sent up to London, tied on horseback, with a paper stuck on his hat inscribed 'Campion, the seditious Jesuit'. Thrice racked, he was tried on a charge of conspiracy of which he was innocent, and hanged. With other sufferers in the same cause, he was beatified by **Leo XIII** in 1886, and canonized in 1970. His feast day is 1 December.

CAMPION, Thomas (1567–1620) English physician, poet, and composer, born in Witham in Essex. He studied at Cambridge and abroad, and set his own lyrics to music. As well as poetry in Latin and English he left several books of 'ayres' for voice and lute.

CAMPOAMOR, Ramón de (1817–1901) Spanish poet, born in Navia. He gave up a medical career for literature; but after some success during his lifetime, his work is now neglected. His short, epigrammatic poems, *Doloras*, *Pequeños poemas* and *Humoradas*, are the best known of his works.

CAMPOLI, Alfredo (1906–) Italian violinist, born in Rome. He went to London in 1911, and quickly won a reputation as a soloist. During the lean years of the 1930s he became better known for his salon orchestra. This was disbanded at the outbreak of World War II, after which he emerged as one of the outstanding violinists of his time.

CAMROSE, William Ewert Berry, 1st Viscount (1879–1954) Welsh newspaper proprietor, born in Merthyr Tydfil. After working on local newspapers, he founded (in 1901), with his brother Gomer Berry, 1st Viscount Kemsley, *The Advertising World.* In 1915 the brothers acquired the *Sunday Times* and during the 1920s gained control of more than a hundred national and provincial publications. In 1928 he became managing editor of the *Daily Telegraph*. He was raised to the peerage in 1941, and in 1947, at the time of the Royal Commission on the Press, published *British Newspapers and their Controllers*.

CAMUS, Albert (1913–60) French writer, born in Mondovi, Algeria, the son of a farm labourer. He studied philosophy at Algiers and, interrupted by long spells of ill-health, became actor, schoolmaster, playwright and journalist there and in Paris. Active in the French resistance during World War II, he became co-editor with **Sartre** of the left-wing newspaper *Combat* after the liberation until 1948, when he broke with Sartre and 'committed' political writing. Having earned an international reputation with his Existentialist novel, *L'Étranger* (The Stranger, 1942), 'the study of an absurd man in an absurd world', he set himself in his subsequent work the aim of elucidating some values for man confronted with cosmic meaninglessness. The essays *Le Mythe de Sisyphe* (1942; trans 1955), concerning suicide, and *L'Homme révolté* (1951; trans 1953), on the harm done by surrendering to ideologies, the magnanimous letters to a German friend (1945), a second masterpiece *La Peste* (The Plague, 1947), in which the plague-stricken city Oran symbolizes man's isolation, were followed by a return to extreme ironical pessimism in *La Chute* (The Fall 1956). *Le Malentendu* and *Caligula* (both 1945; trans 1947) are his best plays. His political writings are collected in *Actuelles I* (1950) and *II* (1953). He was awarded the 1957 Nobel prize for literature. He died in a car accident.

CAMUS, Armand Gaston (1740–1804) French revolutionary, born in Paris. In 1793 he was sent to take **Dumouriez** prisoner, but was himself with four colleagues seized and delivered over to the Austrians. After an imprisonment of 30 months, he was exchanged for the daughter of **Louis XVI**, and on his return to Paris was made member, and afterwards president, of the Council of Five Hundred, but resigned in 1797, and devoted his time to literature.

CANALETTO, real name **Giovanni Antonio Canal** (1697–1768) Italian painter, born and worked mostly in Venice. The son of a theatrical scene-painter, he studied in Rome under Panini but returned to Venice in 1730. Between 1746 and 1756 he worked in England, and on his return to Venice his views of the city became immensely popular with tourists, especially the English, thanks to the efforts of an English entrepreneur, Joseph Smith, who lived there. Smith's own collection was sold to King **George III** in 1758 and the British Royal Collection still has the best selection of Canalettos. He is essentially a topographical painter—even today his views of Venice are remarkably unchanged—but he often shows a sincere poetic response to his subjects. Unlike his rival **Guardi**, he enjoyed extraordinary commercial success. His nephew, Bernardo Bellotto, was also a painter.

CANARIS, Wilhelm (1887–1945) German naval commander, born in Aplerbeck, the son of a Westphalian industrialist of Greek descent. He entered the Imperial German Navy in 1905, and served in the *Dresden* at the battles of Coronel and the Falklands in World War I. He escaped from internment in Chile and made his way back to Germany, and served in U-boats in the Mediterranean. He retired with the rank of rear admiral in 1934. Though disapproving of aspects of the Nazi regime, he rose under **Hitler** to become admiral of the German navy and chief of the *Abwehr*, the military intelligence service of the high command of the armed forces. Associated with the 1944 bomb plot against Hitler, he was arrested, imprisoned and hanged in April 1945, just before the entry of the Russian army into Berlin.

CANDACE the name (or rather title) of the queens of Ethiopia in the first Christian century.

CANDELA, Felix (1910–) Spanish-born Mexican architect and engineer. He fled to Mexico in 1939 as a republican refugee from the Spanish civil war. He worked as construction foreman, builder, architect and structural engineer to become one of the world's foremost designers of slender reinforced concrete hyperbolic paraboloid shell roofs. His creations have included the Sports Palace for the Olympic Games in Mexico City (1968). He emigrated to the USA in 1971.

CANDLISH, Robert Smith (1806–73) Scottish ecclesiastic, born in Edinburgh. He was minister from 1834 of St George's, Edinburgh. After the Disruption (1843) he co-operated with Dr **Thomas Chalmers** in organizing the Free Church, and from Chalmers' death was its virtual leader. He was made moderator of the Free Assembly in 1861, and principal of the New College in 1862.

CANDOLLE, Alphonse Louis Pierre Pyrame de (1806–93) Swiss botanist, son of **Augustin Pyrame de Candolle**. He succeeded his father as professor at Geneva in 1842. He published the great *Géographie botanique raisonnée* (2 vols, 1855) and *Origine des plantes cultivées* (1883).

CANDOLLE, Augustin Pyrame de (1778–1841) Swiss botanist, born in Geneva. He studied chemistry, physics and botany at Geneva and Paris, and became professor of botany at Montpellier (1808) and Geneva (1817). His earliest work, on lichens (1797), was followed by *Astragalogia* (1802) and *Propriétés médicales des plantes* (1804). His new edition of *Flore française* appeared in 1805. The French government commissioned him to make a six-year botanical and agricultural survey of France (1806–12). He was the first to use the word 'taxonomy' for his classification of plants by their morphology, rather than physiology, as set out in his *Elementary Theory of Botany* (1813). He continued his work in *Regni Vegetabilis Systema Naturale* (1818–21) and the multi-volume *Prodromus Systematis Naturalis Regni Vegetabilis* which he began publishing in 1824.

CANETTI, Elias (1905–) Bulgarian man-of-letters, born in Russe into a community of Spanish-speaking Jews. In his formative years he moved between England, Switzerland, Austria and Germany. Since 1938 he has lived in Britain. The works for which he is best known are his novel on the growth of totalitarianism, *Auto-da-Fé* (1935, trans 1946), and a study of the behaviour of the mass, *Crowds and Power* (1960, trans 1962). In recent years his autobiographies, *The Tongue Set Free* (1977, trans 1979) and *The Torch in my Ear* (1980, trans 1982), have emphasized the origins of and inspiration for his life's work. He was awarded the Nobel prize for literature in 1981.

CANIFF, Milton (1907–88) American strip cartoonist, born in Hillsboro, Ohio. In 1922 he joined Associated Press to draw the daily jokes, *Mr Gilfeather* and *Gay Thirties*. He created his first daily strip, *Dickie Dare*, in 1933, the globe-trotting adventures of a young boy, then joined the *New York Daily News* to create a similar serial, *Terry and the Pirates* (1934), where the adventures grew increasingly adult as Terry grew older. In World War II, Caniff drew a sexy strip, *Male Call*, for servicemen. Suddenly abandoning *Terry*, he created a new series about an ex-pilot, *Steve Canyon* (1947), which continued until the artist's death.

CANNABICH, Christian (1731–98) German composer, born in Mannheim. He studied under **Stamitz**, becoming his successor as konzertmeister at the ducal court of Karl Theodor at Mannheim, and later at Munich. He composed over 100 symphonies as well as ballets, chamber works etc.

CANNING, Charles John, 1st Earl (1812–62) English statesman, third son of **George Canning** born in London. He was educated at Eton and Christ Church, Oxford, where he obtained high honours. He entered parliament in 1836 as Conservative member for Warwick, but next year was raised to the upper House as Viscount Canning by his mother's death, both his elder brothers having predeceased her. In 1841 he became under-secretary in the foreign office. Under Lord **Aberdeen** he was postmaster-general; and in 1856 he succeeded Lord **Dalhousie** as governor-general of India. The war with Persia was brought to a successful close in 1857. In the same year (10 May), the Indian Mutiny began with the outbreak at Meerut. Canning's conduct was described at the time as weak—he was nicknamed 'Clemency Canning'—but the general opinion later was that he acted with courage, moderation and judiciousness. In 1858 he became the first viceroy, and in 1859 was raised to an earldom.

CANNING, George (1770–1827) English statesman, born in London. His father died when he was one year old, leaving the family in poverty and his education was provided by his uncle, a banker. He attended Eton, Christ Church, Oxford and Lincoln's Inn. In 1794 he entered parliament as a **Pitt** supporter, and two years later was appointed an under-secretary of state. A strong advocate against slavery, he became treasurer of the navy under Pitt in 1801 and minister for foreign affairs in the Portland ministry (1807). In this post he helped foil **Napoleon** by planning the seizure of the Danish fleet. His disapproval of the Walcheren expedition led to a duel with secretary at war **Castlereagh**. After the collapse of the Portland ministry, he held no high office for many years. As MP for Liverpool (1812) he was eloquent in the cause of Catholic emancipation. He supported the **Liverpool** ministry until 1820 when he resigned over the government's action against Queen **Caroline**. On Castlereagh's suicide he became head of foreign affairs and as such infused a greater liberalism into the cabinet. He asserted British independence against the Holy Alliance, gave new impetus to commerce, and paved the way for a repeal of the corn-laws. On Lord Liverpool's resignation in 1827 he formed an administration with the help of the Whigs, but he died the same year. A remarkably acute and eloquent orator, he was buried in Westminster Abbey near Pitt.

CANNING, Sir Samuel (1823–1908) English engineer, born in Ogbourne St Andrew, near Marlborough. He was engineer-in-chief of the Atlantic cables of 1865–69 in **Brunel**'s steamship, the *Great Eastern*.

CANNING, Sir Stratford See **STRATFORD DE REDCLIFFE**

CANNIZZARO, Stanislao (1826–1910) Italian chemist, born in Palermo. He was professor of chemistry at Genoa, Palermo, and Rome. In 1860, while at Genoa, he marched with **Garibaldi**'s Thousand. He was the first to appreciate the importance of **Amedeo Avogadro**'s work in connection with atomic weights. He co-ordinated organic and inorganic chemistry, and discovered the reaction named after him.

CANNON, Annie Jump (1863–1941) American astronomer, born in Dover, Delaware. The daughter of a Delaware state senator, she was one of the first girls from Delaware to attend university (Wellesley College). She became deaf through contracting scarlet fever, entered Radcliffe College to study astronomy, and was appointed to the staff of the Harvard College Observatory in 1896. She worked there throughout her career; in 1938 she was appointed William Cranch Bond Astronomer. She reorganized the classification of stars in terms of surface temperature, and developed great skill in cataloguing stars; her classification of over 225000 stars brighter than 9th or 10th magnitude was a major contribution.

CANNON, Walter Bradford (1871–1945) American physiologist, born in Prairie du Chien, Wisconsin. He was associated with Harvard University as undergraduate, medical student and teacher for most of his life. He investigated many physiological problems, including digestion (he pioneered the use of X-rays for studying the movement of barium in the alimentary tract) and the functions of the autonomic (sympathetic and parasympathetic) nervous system. The sympathetic nerves, he argued, prepared an animal for 'fight or flight', through increasing heart rate, blood pressure, etc, and the two branches of the autonomic system acted together to maintain a large number of physiological functions, including the relatively constant composition of the body's fluids, temperature, etc. He coined the word homeostasis to describe this and developed the concept in his *Wisdom of the Body* (1932). During World War I, he studied the mechanism of traumatic shock on the battlefield. In 1939 he discovered sympathin, a stimulant for certain organs.

CANO, Alonso (1601–67) Spanish painter, sculptor and architect, born in Granada. He studied in Seville, with **Velasquez**, under **Pacheco**. In 1639 he was appointed court painter and architect. He designed the façade of Coranada Cathedral c.1664.

CANO, Juan Sebastian del (d.1526) Basque navigator, the first man to circumnavigate the globe, born in Guetaria on the Bay of Biscay. In 1519 he sailed with **Magellan** in command of the *Concepción*, and, after Magellan's death in the Philippines, safely navigated the *Victoria* home to Spain, arriving on 6 September 1522.

CANO, Melchior (1509–60) Spanish theologian, born in Tarancón. A Dominican, he became professor of theology at Valladolid, Alcalá de Henares, and Salamanca. His *Loci Theologici* (1563) laid the foundations of theological methodology.

CANOVA, Antonio (1757–1822) Venetian sculptor, born in the village of Possagno, and studied at Venice and Rome. After his *Theseus* (1782), he was regarded as the founder of a new school. He did not rigorously adhere to the severe simplicity of the antique, but infused into his works a peculiar grace such as characterized his *Cupid and Psyche*, which was produced soon after he had completed in 1787 the monument of Pope **Clement XIV**. Other works were a *Winged Cupid*, *Venus and Adonis*, a *Psyche holding a Butterfly*, *Penitent Magdalen*, and *Perseus with the head of the Medusa*, a second famous papal monument, and one at Vienna to an archduchess. In 1802 he was appointed by **Pius VII** curator of works of art, and was called to Paris to model a colossal statue of **Napoleon**. In 1815 the pope sent him again to Paris to recover the works of art taken from Rome, and he also visited England.

CÁNOVAS DEL CASTILLO, Antonio (1828–97) Spanish Conservative statesman and historian, born in Malaga. He became a member of the Cortes in 1854, and was premier 1875–81, 1884–85, 1890–92, and from 1895 till 8 August 1897, when, at the bath of Santa Agueda, Vitoria, he was shot by an anarchist in the presence of his wife.

CANROBERT, François Certain (1809–95) French soldier and marshal of France, born in St Céré in Lot. Educated at St Cyr, he distinguished himself in Algeria (1835–51) and supported the *coup d'état* of 1851. He commanded in the Crimea in 1854, and was wounded at the Alma. On St **Arnaud**'s death (1854) he assumed the chief command. He commanded at Magenta and Solferino (1859). In the Franco-German war of 1870–71 he was taken prisoner at the fall of Metz (1870). He was elected to the Senate in 1876.

CANT, Andrew (c.1590–1663) Scottish Covenanting minister. In 1638 he was sent to Aberdeen to persuade the inhabitants to subscribe the Covenant; and in November of that same year he was a member of the Glasgow Assembly which abolished Episcopacy. He was nevertheless a zealous royalist, and in 1641 preached before **Charles I** in Edinburgh. His son Andrew was principal of Edinburgh University, 1675–85.

CANTACUZENUS, John VI (1292–1383) Byzantine soldier and ruler, a powerful courtier in the reigns of **Andronicus II** and **III**. At the death of Andronicus III in 1341 he became guardian of his son, John V (1332–91), then nine years old. Cantacuzenus, however, proclaimed himself the child's 'colleague', and after a six-year civil war made himself emperor (1347) with John V as colleague. In a second war, during which the Turks occupied Gallipoli, he was forced to abdicate (1355). He retired to a monastery, where he died.

CANTELUPE, St Thomas de, or **St Thomas of Hereford** (c.1218–1282) English prelate, born in Hambleden near Henley-on-Thames. He studied at Oxford, Paris, and Orléans, and was made chancellor of Oxford University (1262). He supported the barons against **Henry III**, and was appointed chancellor of England by **Simon de Montfort** (1264–65). In 1275 he was appointed bishop of Hereford, where his justice and kindness became proverbial. Excommunicated by his archbishop in 1282, he took his case to Rome, but died on the way in Orvieto, and was canonized by Pope **John XXII** in 1320. His relics were brought to Hereford, where his shrine became almost as revered as that of **Becket** at Canterbury.

CANTH, Minna, née **Ulrika Vilhelmina Johnsson** (1844–97) Finnish playwright and feminist, born in Tampere. A powerful exponent of the Realist school, her best-known plays are *Työmiehen vaimo* (A Working-class Wife, 1885) and *Kovan onnen lapsia* (Children of Misfortune, 1988). Later she turned to Tolstoyan psychological dramas about women, as in *Anna Liisa* (1895).

CANTILLON, Richard (1697–1734) Irish-born French economist, born in Ballyheige, County Kerry. He became a prosperous financier in Paris and London, and wrote the authoritative *Essai sur la nature du commerce en général* (1755), which in many respects anticipated **Adam Smith** and **Malthus**. He was murdered by his cook during a robbery.

CANTON, John (1718–72) English physicist, born in Stroud. A schoolmaster in London, he was elected a fellow of the Royal Society in 1749. He invented an electroscope and an electrometer; originated experiments in induction; was the first to make powerful artificial magnets; and in 1762 demonstrated the compressibility of water.

CANTOR, Georg (1845–1918) Russian-born German mathematician, born in St Petersburg. He studied in Berlin and in 1877 became professor of mathematics at Halle. He worked out a highly original arithmetic of the infinite, extending the concept of cardinal and ordinal numbers to infinite sets. Other aspects of his ideas on the theory of sets of points have become fundamental in topology and modern analysis. He also did important work on classical analysis, particularly in trigonometric series. His work did not receive immediate acceptance, and this may have contributed to the mental illness which he suffered in later life.

CANTÚ, Cesare (1804–95) Italian historian and novelist, born in Brivio in the Milanese territory. Imprisoned as a liberal in 1833, he described the sorrows of a prisoner in a historical romance, *Margherita Pusterla* (1838). As well as his monumental history of the world, *Storia universale* (35 vols, 1836–42), he wrote a multitude of works on Italian history and literature, as well as lighter works, and *Manzoni*: *Reminiscinze* (2 vols, 1883).

CANUTE, or **CNUT** See **KNUT SVEINSSON**

CANYNGES, William (c.1399–1474) English merchant. Mayor of Bristol, and MP, he rebuilt St Mary

Redcliffe, and, having taken orders, in 1469 became dean of the college of Westbury.

CAO YU, pseud of **Wan Jiabao** (1910–) Chinese playwright, born in Tianjin. The most significant 20th-century dramatist in China, he studied western literature at Qinghua University (1930–34), where he was profoundly influenced by **Ibsen** and **Shaw** to attack the corruption of traditional society. His best-known work, *Thunderstorm*, was staged in 1935; his other major plays are *Sunrise* (1935), *Wilderness* (1936), *Metamorphosis* (1940), *Peking Man* (1940), and *Family* (1941), adapted from the novel by **Ba Jin**. He toured the USA in 1946, and after the foundation of the People's Republic in 1949 he was appointed to numerous official posts. In 1979 he wrote the play *The Consort of Peace*.

CAPA, Robert, originally **André Friedmann** (1913–54) Hungarian-born American photo-journalist, born in Budapest. After working in Berlin he moved to Paris in 1933 and recorded the Spanish Civil War (1935–37) and China under the Japanese attacks of 1938. In 1939 he emigrated to the USA and covered World War II in Europe from the invasion of Normandy; subsequently he reported on the early days of the state of Israel and was killed by a land mine in the Indo-China fighting, perhaps the first American casualty in Vietnam. His images of war were moving in their compassionate portrayal of the suffering of both soldiers and civilians. His brother, Cornell Capa (1918–), was also a photographer.

CAPABLANCA, José Raúl (1888–1942) Cuban chess player, born in Havana. At the age of four he learned chess by watching his father's games. Within nine years he had defeated the Cuban champion, Corzo, in a match. A local industrialist sponsored his education in the USA, where he took an engineering degree at Columbia University. His spare time was devoted to chess at the Manhattan Club, New York, where he achieved a sensational win in a 1909 match against American champion Marshall. On his first appearance in Europe he defeated most of the world's leading masters at the San Sebastian tournament, 1909. He had to wait until 1921 for an opportunity to play for the world championship, defeating **Lasker** without losing a game. Vain, conceited and lazy, he relied on a phenomenal natural talent, rather than on application, to maintain a record of near invincibility from 1921 to 1927. His defeat by **Alekhine** in 1927 was a major surprise, and despite further tournament successes he never received the opportunity to regain his title.

ČAPEK, Josef (1887–1945) Czech writer and painter, born in Schwadonitz, elder brother of **Karel Čapek**. His early literary works, written in collaboration with his brother, include the allegorical *Insect Play* (1921). From such anxious visions of the future he progressed to a philosophy of sceptical humanism which found expression in his one novel, *Stin Kapradiny* (1930), and in his essays. He died in Belsen.

ČAPEK, Karel (1890–1938) Czech author, born in Schwadonitz, brother of **Josef Čapek**. He is remembered above all for his play *R. U. R.* (Rossum's Universal Robots), produced in 1921, showing mechanization rampant. With his brother he wrote the *Insect Play* (1921), one of several pieces foreshadowing totalitarianism, as well as short stories on crime and mystery, prophetic science-fiction, and travel-books, such as *Letters from England* (trans 1925). His brilliant writings are full of social and political satire, and have been translated into English almost in their entirety.

CAPEL, Arthur, Lord (1610–49) English royalist. He was raised to the peerage in 1641, and fought for **Charles I** through the Civil War. Captured at Colchester in 1648, he escaped from the Tower, but was retaken and beheaded.

CAPEL, Arthur (1631–83) English politician, eldest son of **Arthur, Lord Capel**. Created earl in 1661, he was viceroy of Ireland (1672-77), and first lord-commissioner of the Treasury (1679). On the discovery of the Rye House Plot against **Charles II** he was sent to the Tower, where he was found with his throat cut —probably by his own hand.

CAPELL, Edward (1713–81) English scholar, born near Bury St Edmunds. He published an edition of **Shakespeare** (10 vols, 1768) based on the Folio and Quarto texts, and a full commentary, *Notes and Various Readings to Shakespeare* (3 vols, 1783).

CAPELLA, Martianus Mineus Felix (fl.480) North African scholar and writer. His *Satiricon*, a kind of encyclopaedia, highly esteemed during the middle ages, is a medley of prose and verse, full of curious learning.

CAPET, Hugo or **Hugh** (c.938–996) king of France from 987. Duke of Francia, he was elected king of France on the death of the last Carolingian **Louis V** (987). The Capetian dynasty he founded ruled France until 1328.

CAPGRAVE, John (1393–1464) English chronicler, theologian, and provincial of the Augustine Friars in England. Born in Lynn, Norfolk, he studied, probably at Cambridge, and was ordained priest about 1418, having already entered his order in Lynn. His works include Bible commentaries, sermons, *Nova legenda Angliae*, *De illustribus Henricis*, the lives of 24 emperors of Germany, kings of England, etc, and *Vita Humfredi Ducis Glocestriae*. Among his English works are a life of St Catherine in verse and *A Chronicle of England from the Creation to 1417*. *Ye Solace of Pilgrimes*, a description of Rome, has been assigned to him.

CAPITO, or **Köpfel, Wolfgang Fabricius** (1478–1541) reformer, born in Hagenau in Alsace. He entered the Benedictine order, and in 1515 became professor of theology at Basel. He approved of **Luther**'s action, but in 1519 entered the service of Archishop Albert of Mainz; he did not declare for the Reformation until later, when he became a Protestant leader in Strasbourg.

CAPO D'ISTRIAS, or **D'Istria, Ionnes Antonios, Count** (1776–1831) Greek statesman, president of the Greek republic, born in Corfu. In 1809, after holding a high position in the Ionian Islands, he passed to the diplomatic service of Russia. In 1828 he entered on a seven years' presidency of Greece; but imbued as he was with Russian ideas, his autocratic measures aroused discontent; and in October 1831, he was assassinated in a church at Nauplia. His feeble brother, Iony Augostinos (1778–1857), succeeded him, but resigned the following April.

CAPONE, Al (Alphonse) (1899–1947) American gangster, born in Brooklyn. He achieved worldwide notoriety as a racketeer during the prohibition era in Chicago, but until 1931 there was insufficient evidence to charge him with. Once caught, however, he was sentenced to ten years' imprisonment for tax evasion.

CAPOTE, Truman (1924–84) American author, born in New Orleans of Spanish descent. He spent much of his childhood in Alabama. He won several literary prizes while at school in New York but showed little ability in other subjects. His short story 'Miriam', published in the magazine *Mademoiselle*, was selected for the O Henry Memorial Award volume in 1946. *Other Voices, Other Rooms* (1948), his first novel, revealed his talent for sympathetic description of small-town life in the deep South, while *The Grass Harp* (1951) is a fantasy performed against a background of the Alabama of his childhood. Other works are

Breakfast at Tiffany's (1958), which was highly successful as a film, *In Cold Blood* (1966), a 'non-fiction novel' about a murder in Kansas, and latterly a collection of short pieces, *Music for Chameleons* and an unfinished novel *Answered Prayers*.

CAPP, Al, originally **Alfred Gerald Caplin** (1909–79) American strip cartoonist, born in New Haven, Connecticut. He studied at Designers Art School, Boston (1929) and entered strips as assistant to **Bud Fisher** on *Mutt and Jeff* (1930). Joining Associated Press he took on a daily joke, *Mr Gilfeather* (1932), then became assistant to Ham Fisher on *Joe Palooka* (1933), introducing hill-billy characters, and developed *L'il Abner* (1934). Capp's chunky artwork coupled with hilarious hill-billy dialogue soon made the strip a success, and fair Daisy Mae's never-ending pursuit of her bashful hero was a daily delight. *L'il Abner* inspired two films, a stage musical, and an animated series.

CAPPELLO, Bianco (1548–87) Italian noblewoman and courtesan. She was the mistress and (from 1579) wife, of Francesco de' Medici, Duke of Florence (1541–87), with whom she was supposed, but falsely in all likelihood, to have been poisoned by his brother, the Cardinal Ferdinando.

CAPRA, Frank (1897–) Italian-born American film director, born in Palermo but resident in the USA from the age of six. He took a degree in chemical engineering at the California Institute of Technology before moving into the film industry, initially as a gag writer for silent slapstick comedies. His most renowned work as a director celebrates the decency and integrity of the common man as he combats corruption and malfeasance in high places. He earned Academy Awards for *It Happened One Night* (1934), *Mr Deeds goes to Town* (1936) and *You Can't Take it with You* (1938). During World War II he made a series of patriotic documentaries but, after the commercial failure in 1946 of the whimsical *It's A Wonderful Life* (now a television perennial), his sure touch faltered and later films were pale imitations of past successes. He retired in 1964.

CAPRIVI, Georg Leo, Graf von (1831–99) German soldier and political leader, born in Berlin. Entering the Prussian army in 1849, he fought in the campaigns of 1864 and 1866, and in the Franco-Prussian war of 1870–71 was chief of staff to the 10th Army Corps. From 1883 to 1888, as head of the Admiralty, he reorganized the navy and then was made commander of his old army corps in Hanover. On **Bismarck**'s fall in 1890, he became imperial chancellor and Prussian prime minister. His principal measures were the army bills of 1892–93 and the commercial treaty with Russia in 1894. He was dismissed in 1894.

CAPUS, (Vincent Marie) Alfred (1858–1922) French writer, born in Aix-en-Provence. He left engineering for journalism, and became political editor of *Figaro*. He wrote *Qui perd gagne* (1890) and other novels, but is best remembered for his comedies of the Parisian bourgeoisie such as *La Veine* (1901).

CARACALLA (176–217) Roman emperor, the son of the emperor Septimius **Severus**, born in Lyons. He was originally named Bassianus, from his maternal grandfather, but his legal name was Marcus Aurelius Antoninus. Caracalla was a nickname given him from his long hooded Gaulish tunic. After his father's death at Eboracum (York), he ascended the throne in 211 as joint emperor with his brother Publius Septimius Antoninius Geta, whom he soon murdered. He next turned against all Geta's adherents, killing many including the great jurist **Papinianus**. His open reliance on the army alienated the senatorial class and earned him a hostile reputation in the historical tradition. He campaigned extensively abroad, in Germany, on the Danube, and in the east, and was assassinated while on his way from Edessa to Carrhae as he was preparing for war against the Parthians. His chief title to fame was the edict of 212 (the *Constitutio Antoniniana*) which granted Roman citizenship to all free members of the empire.

CARACCIOLO, Prince Francesco (1752–99) Neapolitan naval commander. He served with the British in the American War of Independence, then entered the service of Ferdinand of Naples and became supreme commander of the Neapolitan navy. In December 1798 he fled with the king before the French from Naples to Palermo, but returned to Naples in 1798 and entered the service of the 'Parthenopean Republic'. For two months he ably directed the operations of the revolutionists, but was captured trying to escape in peasant disguise, and was hanged.

CARACTACUS See **CARATACUS**

CARAN D'ACHE, pseud of **Emmanuel Poiré** (1858–1909) French caricaturist, born in Moscow. A contributor to many periodicals, he was a pioneer in the development of the *bande dessinée* (French comic strip), and a major influence on **H M Bateman**. Several collections of his works were published. His pseudonym came from the Russian word for *pencil*.

CARATACUS, or **Caradoc** (d.54) British chieftain, and son of Cunobelinus (**Cymbeline**). He fought against the Romans (43–50), but at length was completely overthrown by Ostorius near Ludlow. His wife and daughters fell into the hands of the victors; his brothers surrendered; and he himself was delivered up by Cartimandua, Queen of the Brigantes. He was carried to Rome in 51, and exhibited in triumph by the Emperor **Claudius**. According to tradition he died at Rome about 54.

CARAUSIUS, Marcus Aurelius (c.245–293) rogue Roman 'emperor' in Britain from 287 till his murder by one of his officers, Allectus, who set himself up as emperor in Britain in his stead. Originally a Batavian pilot, Carausius had been put in command of the Roman fleet in the Channel to ward off pirates.

CARAVAGGIO, Michelangelo Merisi da (1573–1610) Italian painter, born in Caravaggio. Trained in Milan, he moved to Rome in the 1590s. There, one of his works was noted by Cardinal del Monte. He soon became a master of realism and is widely regarded as the greatest Italian painter of the 17th century. His early work is strikingly homo-erotic: pubescent youths voluptuously portrayed in various guises. With his first two commissions, however, his style changed. The *Life of Saint Matthew* cycle in the Contarelli Chapel of the church of San Luigi dei Francese and the *Conversion of Saint Paul* and the *Crucifixion of Saint Peter* in the Cerasi Chapel of S Maria del Popolo, both in Rome, are highly original, strongly lit, intensely realistic figures emerging dramatically from dark shadow. His work was often controversial since he often used models off the street for biblical characters. In 1606 he fled Rome after killing a man, and spent the rest of his life as a refugee, moving between Naples, Sicily and Malta. In the latter he obtained the favour of the grand master but on making his way back to Rome he was wounded, lost all his baggage, caught a fever and, upon reaching the beach at Porto Ercole, lay down on a bank and died. Unlike the **Carracci** family he had no pupils, but his influence throughout the rest of the century was immense and a group of painters known as the Caravaggisti imitated his work.

CARAVAGGIO, Polidoro Caldara da (c.1492–1543) Italian painter, born in Caravaggio. He aided **Raphael**

in his Vatican frescoes. His *Christ bearing the Cross* is in Naples. He was murdered by his servant at Messina.

CARCO, Francis, pseud of **François Carcopino-Tusoli** (1886–1958) French author, born in Nouméa in New Caledonia. He first gained recognition with his volume of poems *La Bohème et mon coeur* (1912), and added to his reputation with a series of novels chiefly set in Paris's Latin Quarter.

CARDANO, Girolamo (1501–76) Italian mathematician, naturalist, physician, philosopher, gambler and astrologer, born in Pavia. He became famous as a physician and teacher of mathematics in Milan, became professor of medicine at Pavia (1543) and Bologna (1562). In 1551 he visited Scotland to treat the archbishop of St Andrews, and in London cast the horoscope of **Edward VI**. In 1570 he was imprisoned by the Inquisition for heresy, recanted and went to Rome in 1571 where he was given a pension by Pope **Pius V**. He died a few weeks after finishing his candid autobiography *De propria vita*. A strange mixture of polymath and charlatan, he wrote over 200 treatises on, among other things, physics, mathematics, astronomy, astrology, philosophy, music, and medicine. His most famous work is his treatise on algebra, the *Ars Magna*, in which the formulae for solving cubic and quartic equations were published for the first time. He was accused of plagiarism by Niccolo Tartaglia who claimed the solution of the cubic as his own, but the real credit should apparently go to Scipione da Ferro. Despite this the solution is still known as Cardan's formula.

CARDEN, Joan Maralyn (1937–) Australian operatic and concert soprano, renowned for her performances of **Mozart**, born in Melbourne, Victoria. A principal artist with the Australian Opera since 1971, she made her début at Covent Garden, London, in 1974 as Gilda in *Rigoletto*, a role she has since made her own. She has appeared at the Glyndebourne Festival, as Donna Anna in **Peter Hall**'s production of *Don Giovanni*, and with the English National Opera, the Scottish Opera and the Metropolitan, New York. Her repertoire extends from **Handel** to **Richard Strauss** and **Benjamin Britten**, and one of her most celebrated performances is of the four heroines in *The Tales of Hoffmann*.

CÁRDENAS, Garcia Lopez de (mid 16th century) Spanish explorer. On **Francisco Coronado**'s expedition to New Mexico he discovered the Grand Canyon of the Colorado in 1540.

CÁRDENAS, Lázaro (1895–1970) Mexican soldier and political leader, president of the Mexican Republic (1934–40), born in the Michoacán, the son of a peasant. He joined the revolutionary army in 1913, was a general by 1923 and governor of Michoacán from 1928 to 1932. He rose from relative obscurity through the patronage of former president **Plutarco Calles**. Cárdenas wrested control of the government from Calles and instituted a broad programme of social and economic reforms. The 'ejido' program granted thousands of acres to collectives and individuals, foreign oil holdings were expropriated and the petroleum industry nationalized, labour unions reformed and a system of state-capitalism established; an understanding was reached between Church and state; government institutions were strengthened and the old revolutionary chieftains weakened. Often wrongly accused of being a communist, Cárdenas carried out the long overdue promises of the 1910 revolution, ensuring Mexico's stability.

CARDEW, Michael (1901–82) English potter. After studying under **Bernard Leach** at St Ives (1923–26), he set up his own studio at Winchcombe in the Cotswolds. Influenced by early English pottery, he specialized in lead-glazed slipware for everyday use. In 1939 he moved to Wenford Bridge in Cornwall and experimented with stoneware and tin-glazes. In 1942 he took over the Achimota College on the Gold Coast, and started his own pottery at Vumé on the Volta, where he produced stoneware and strove to bring to West Africa a new industry capable of developing a modern West African art form, alongside the existing traditional craft.

CARDI See **CIGOLI**

CARDIGAN, James Thomas Brudenell, 7th Earl of (1797–1868) English cavalry officer, son of the 6th Earl of Cardigan, whom he succeeded to the title in 1837. He was MP for Marlborough (1818–29) and North Northamptonshire (1832). In 1824 he joined the army as a cornet, and in 1830 bought himself a command in the 15th Hussars as a lieutenant-colonel. His fiery temper brought him into conflict with fellow officers, and he was forced to resign in 1833. From 1836 to 1847 he commanded the 11th Hussars, on which he lavished his own money to make it a crack squadron; after a duel with one of his officers in 1841 he was acquitted on a legal technicality by the House of Lords. Appointed major-general in 1847, he commanded the light cavalry brigade ('the Six Hundred') in the Crimea, and led it to destruction with the fatal charge against enemy guns at Balaclava (1854). Received home as a hero, he was appointed inspector-general of the cavalry (1855-60). The knitted woollen jacket he wore against the cold of a Crimean winter is named after him.

CARDIN, Pierre (1922–) French fashion designer, born in Venice. After working during World War II for a tailor in Vichy, he went to Paris in 1944. He worked in fashion houses and on costume design, for example for **Cocteau**'s film *Beauty and the Beast* (1947). He opened his own house in 1953 and has since been prominent in fashion for both women and men. He extended his activities to other fields of design and business, which was regarded unfavourably by the world of couture. However, his standing as an original and influential designer is clearly established.

CARDOZO, Benjamin Nathan (1870–1938) American judge, born in New York. He sat on the bench of the New York Court of Appeals from 1913 to 1932, where he delivered many outstanding judgments, and in the US Supreme Court for six years, 1932–38, in which he handed down important opinions on congressional power, control of inter-state commerce and the relationship of the Bill of Rights to states' rights. He was generally liberal and favoured greater involvement of courts in public policy. He also wrote some very thoughtful books, now classics: *The Nature of the Judicial Process* (1921), *The Growth of the Law* (1924), and *The Paradoxes of Legal Science* (1928).

CARDUCCI, Giosuè (1835–1907) Italian poet, born in Valdicastello Pisa province, the son of a physician. In 1860 he became professor of Italian literature at Bologna, in 1876 was returned to the Italian parliament as a Republican, and in 1890 was nominated a senator. He published several volumes of verse, and was considered Italy's national poet. He was awarded the Nobel prize for literature in 1906.

CARELESS See CARLOS, William

CARÊME, Marie Antoine (1784–1833) French *chef de cuisine* and author. He wrote *La Cuisine Française*, etc. As **Talleyrand**'s cook, he played an important part at the Congress of Vienna.

CAREW, George, 1st Baron Carew of Clopton and **1st Earl of Totnes** (1555–1629) English soldier and administrator. Educated at Broadgates Hall, Oxford, he fought in the Irish wars (1575–83), interrupted in

1578 by a voyage to the New World with Sir **Humphrey Gilbert**. As lieutenant-general of ordnance in England he accompained **Essex** to Cadiz (1596) and the Azores (1597), and as president of Munster (1600–03) repressed the Earl of **Tyrone**'s rebellion. As master-general of ordnance (1608–17), he received, jointly with **Buckingham** and Cranfield, the monopoly for gunpowder manufacture (1621). He was governor of Guernsey (1610-21). A friend of **Raleigh**, he left important historical and antiquarian documents relating to Ireland.

CAREW, Thomas (1595–1639) English Cavalier poet, born in West Wickham, the son of a successful lawyer. He studied at Merton College, and entered the Inner Temple to study law in 1612. Between 1613 and 1616 he visited Holland as secretary to the ambassador, but was dismissed for slandering his employers. After three years in London he went to France in 1619–24, again as secretary to the ambassador. Afterwards he rose into high favour with **Charles I**. A friend of **Ben Jonson** and **Donne**, he wrote polished lyrics in the Cavalier tradition, particularly 'Rapture'.

CAREY, Henry (c.1690–1743) English poet and musician, born in Yorkshire, believed to have been an illegitimate son of a member of the Savile family. He published his first volume of poems in 1713. He wrote innumerable songs, witty poems, burlesques, farces, and dramatic pieces, sometimes composing the accompanying music. His best-known poem is 'Sally in our Alley'.

CAREY, Henry Charles (1793–1879) American political economist, born in Philadelphia. Thither his father, Mathew Carey (1760–1839), a journalist who had been imprisoned for nationalist opinions, had emigrated from Ireland in 1784, to become a successful publisher and author, known especially for his *Vindiciae Hibernicae*, written to confute **Godwin** and other English misrepresenters of Ireland. Henry Charles early became a partner in his father's book-selling business. When in 1835 he retired from business to devote himself to his favourite study, he was at the head of the largest publishing concern in the United States. Among his works were *Principles of Political Economy* (3 vols, 1837–40) and *Principles of Social Science* (3 vols, 1858–59). Originally a zealous free-trader, he came to regard free trade as an ideal, but impossible in the existing state of American industry: a period of protection was indispensable.

CAREY, James (1845–83) Irish builder and town councillor in Dublin, who joined the Fenians about 1861 and helped to found the 'Invincibles' in 1881. He betrayed his associates in the murder of Lord Frederick Cavendish and **Thomas Henry Burke** (the Phoenix Park murders), and on the voyage between Capetown and Natal was shot dead by a bricklayer, Patrick O'Donnell, who was hanged in London.

CAREY, Peter (1943–) Australian novelist, born in Bacchus Marsh, Victoria. He attended Geelong Grammar School before beginning a career as an advertising copywriter, after which he lived for a spell in London. His first book, *The Fat Man in History* (1974), was a collection of short stories, and he was quickly regarded as an innovative force in Australian writing, breaking free from the mould of realism to experiment with modes as diverse as absurdism, surrealism, science ficton and fable. His next book, *Bliss* (1981), explored the advertising world. In 1985 he published *Illywhacker* (Australian slang for a trickster or conman), an imaginative tour de force which was shortlisted for the Booker prize. In 1988 he won the Booker prize with *Oscar and Lucinda* (1988), an exuberant novel constructed on a Victorian scale, in which a compulsive gambler and a Sydney heiress fascinated with the manufacture of glass are bizarrely united.

CAREY, Sir Robert (c.1560–1639) English courtier, youngest son of Lord Hunsdon. For the last ten years of **Elizabeth**'s reign he was English warden on the Border marches. He was present at her deathbed (1603), and in 60 hours galloped with the news to Edinburgh. **Charles I** created him Earl of Monmouth.

CAREY, William (1761–1834) English missionary and orientalist, born in Paulerspury, near Towcester. Apprenticed to a shoemaker, he joined the Baptists in 1783, and three years later became a minister. In 1793 he and John Thomas were chosen as first Baptist missionaries to India, where he founded the Serampur mission in 1799, and from 1801 to 1830 was Oriental professor at Fort William College, Calcutta.

CARGILL, Donald (c.1619–1681) Scottish Covenanter, born in Rattray, near Blairgowrie. He studied at Aberdeen and St Andrews, and in 1655 was ordained minister of the Barony parish in Glasgow. Ejected for denouncing the Restoration, he became an indefatigable field preacher, fought and was wounded at Bothwell Brig (1679), and took part with **Richard Cameron** in the famous Sanquhar declaration (1680). Having excommunicated the king, the Duke of York, and others at Torwood, Stirlingshire, he was seized, and executed at the Mercat Cross in Edinburgh.

CARISSIMI, Giacomo (1605–74) Italian composer. Organist in Tivoli, Assisi, and from 1628 in Rome, he did much to develop the sacred cantata, and his works include the oratorio *Jephthah*.

CARL XVI GUSTAF (1946–) king of Sweden since 1973, the seventh sovereign of the House of **Bernadotte**, and grandson of King **Gustaf VI**. His father, Prince Gustav Adolf (1906–47), the heir apparent, was killed in an air crash, so Carl Gustaf became crown prince on his grandfather's accession in 1950. Educated at boarding school, he did military service, mainly with the navy (1966–68), and took a specially-designed one-year course at Uppsala University. Then followed a special programme of study into the operation of Sweden's social and political structure, and studies in economics at Stockholm University. On his accession in 1973, in accordance with the new constitution being discussed by the Riksdag (parliament), he became a 'democratic monarch' like his grandfather, although the constitution was not formally approved until 1975; he is head of state, but does not preside at cabinet meetings and is not supreme commander of the armed forces. In 1976 he married a commoner, Silvia Renate Sommerlath, (1943–), daughter of a West German businessman, whom he met when she was chief hostess at the Olympic Games in Munich in 1972. They have three children, Princess Victoria (1977–), hereditary Prince Carl Philip (1979–) and Princess Madeleine (1982–). Under a new Act of Succession (1980), Crown Princess Victoria is now heir to the Swedish throne. King Carl Gustaf is a keen sportsman, especially interested in yachting, skiing and hunting; he is also prominent in nature conservation and environmental issues.

CARLE, Eric (1929–) American picture book artist, born in Germany. Using a distinctive collage technique he has written and illustrated several children's books, but is best-known for *The Very Hungry Caterpillar* (1970), in which the voracious creature burrows through the pages of the book in search of delicacies.

CARLETON, Guy, 1st Baron Dorchester (1724–1808) British soldier, born in Strabane, County Tyrone. He served under **Cumberland** on the Continent, and under **Wolfe** in Canada. Governor of Quebec from 1775 to 1777, he successfully defended the city against the Americans under **Benedict Arnold**, whom he subsequently defeated again on Lake Champlain in 1776. In 1782–83 he was British commander-in-chief in America. He was governor of Quebec again from 1786 to 1789 and 1793 to 1796, and governor of Lower Canada from 1791 to 1796. As soldier and statesman he did much to save Canada for Britain.

CARLETON, Will (William McKendree) (1845–1912) American poet, born in Hudson, Michigan. He graduated at Hillsdale College, Michigan, and wrote *Farm Ballads* (1875), *City Ballads* (1885) and other works.

CARLETON, William (1794–1869) Irish novelist, born in Prillisk, County Tyrone, of peasant birth, the youngest of 14 children. He became a tutor and writer in Dublin, contributing sketches to the *Christian Examiner*, republished as *Traits and Stories of the Irish Peasantry* (1830). A second series (1833) was no less well received. In 1839 he published a long novel, *Fardorougha the Miser*, which was followed by *The Black Prophet* (1847), about the Famine, *The Tithe Proctor* (1849), *The Squanders of Castle Squander* (1852) and others.

CARLI, Giovanni Rinaldo (1720–95) Italian economist and antiquary. Professor of astronomy and navigation at Padua (1744), and president of the school of finance in Milan (1771), he wrote *Della Moneta* (1754–60) and *Antichità italiche* (1788–90).

CARLILE, Richard (1790–1843) English journalist and radical reformer, born in Ashburton, Devon. He became a chemist's boy and a tinman's apprentice. A disciple of **Thomas Paine**, he sold the prohibited radical weekly *Black Dwarf* throughout London in 1817. He then printed thousands of **Southey**'s *Wat Tyler*, reprinted **William Hone**'s *Parodies*, and wrote a series of imitations of them, for which he got 18 weeks in the King's Bench. This was the first of a series of imprisonments whose total amounted to nine years and four months, and which included sentences for publishing his own *Political Litany* and Paine's works, and a journal, *The Republican* (1819–26).

CARLILE, Wilson (1847–1942) Anglican clergyman, born in Buxton. In 1852 he founded the Church Army, and was made a prebendary of St Paul's in 1905.

CARLISLE, Lucy, Countess of (1599–1660) English courtier, second daughter of Henry **Percy**, 9th Earl of Northumberland. In 1617 she married James Hay, afterwards Earl of Carlisle (d.1636). Witty and beautiful, she was the friend of **Strafford**, and, after his fall, played an intricate game of intrigue, which in 1649 brought her for some months to the Tower.

CARLO DOLCI See **DOLCI**

CARLOMAN (751–71) Frankish prince, younger son of **Pepin the Short** and brother of **Charlemagne**, ruled the eastern Franks from 768. At his death Charlemagne took over his lands.

CARLOS, Don (1545–68) son of **Philip II** by his first wife, Maria of Portugal, born in Valladolid. He was sent to study at Alcalá de Henares, where he profited so little that the king invited a nephew, the Archduke Rudolf, to Spain, intending to make him his heir. Weak, vicious, and cruel, he early conceived a strong aversion towards the king's confidants, and in confession to a priest, on Christmas Eve 1567, betrayed his purpose to assassinate a certain person. As the king was believed to be the intended victim, this confession was divulged; and Don Carlos was tried and found guilty of conspiring against the life of his father. The sentence was left for the king to pronounce. Philip declared that he could make no exception in favour of such an unworthy son; but sentence of death was not formally recorded. Shortly afterwards Don Carlos died. The suspicion that he was poisoned or strangled has no valid evidence to support it.

CARLOS, Don (1788–1855) Spanish pretender, second son of **Charles IV** of Spain. On the accession of his niece **Isabella II** in 1833, he asserted his claim to the throne—a claim reasserted by his son, Don Carlos, Count de Montemolin (1818–61), and by *his* nephew, Don Carlos (1848-1909). Carlist risings, whose strength lay in the Basque provinces, occurred in 1834-39 and 1872-76.

CARLOS, or **Careless, William** (d.1689) English royalist soldier. After the battle of Worcester (1651), he hid with **Charles II** in the oak at Boscobel, and escaped with him to France.

CARLOVNA, Anna, née **Elisabeth Katharine Christinem**, (1718–46) regent of Russia. The daughter of Charles Leopold, Duke of Mecklenburg Schwerin, she was the niece of the empress **Anna Ivanovna**. In 1739 she married Prince Anton Ulrich, Duke of Brunswick. Their son, Ivan, was declared emperor of Russia at the age of eight weeks on the death of Anna Ivanovna, and Anna Carlovna was appointed regent. A year later, however, Ivan was deposed by the empress **Elizabeth Petrovna**, and Anna Carlovna was thrown into prison, where she died.

CARLSON, Carolyn (1943–) American dancer-choreographer, born in California. She studied at San Francisco Ballet School and with **Alwin Nikolais**, in whose company she danced from 1966 to 1971. After freelancing in Europe, she was invited to create a piece for the Paris Opera Ballet in 1973. Her solo was so well-received that a special post, *Danseuse étoile choreographique*, was invented for her. Her dream-like, ritualistic dance-spectacles and independent working methods had a great impact on French and European modern/experimental dance. From 1980 she directed her own troupe at Venice's Teatro Fenice, but later returned to Paris.

CARLSON, Chester Floyd (1906–68) American inventor, born in Seattle, Washington. He graduated in physics from the California Institute of Technology in 1930, then took a law degree and worked as a patent lawyer in an electronics firm. On his own he began to experiment with copying processes using photoconductivity and by 1938 had discovered the basic principles of the electrostatic 'xerography' process. Patented in 1940, it was subsequently developed and from 1959 marketed worldwide by the Xerox Corporation, and made him a multi-millionaire.

CARLSSON, Ingvar Costa (1934–) Swedish politician. Educated at Lund (Sweden) and North Western (USA) universities, he was secretary in the prime minister's office (1958–60) before entering active party politics. He became president of the youth league of the Social Democratic Labour party (SAP) in 1961, and in 1964 was elected to the Riksdag (parliament). After holding a number of junior posts (1967–76), he became deputy to **Olof Palme** in 1982 and succeeded him as prime minister and SAP leader after Palme's assassination in 1986.

CARLSTADT, properly **Andreas Rudolf Bodenstein** (d.1541) German reformer, born prior to 1483 at Carlstadt in Bavaria. In 1517 he joined **Luther**, who in 1521 rebuked his iconoclastic zeal, and whom he afterwards opposed on the question of the Eucharist. Accused of participation in the Peasants' War, he fled to Switzerland, and became professor of theology at Basel.

CARLTON, Richard (c.1560–c.1638) English composer. He was educated at Cambridge and spent most of his life as vicar of St Stephen's, Norwich, and as a minor canon of Norwich Cathedral. In 1601 he published a volume of madrigals and was a contributor to *The Triumphs of Oriana*, the volume of madrigals presented to Queen **Elizabeth** in 1603.

CARLUCCI, Frank Charles (1930–) American statesman, born in Scranton, Pennsylvania. Educated at Princeton and Harvard, he fought in the Korean War, and served as a career diplomat in Africa and South America. He returned to the USA in 1969 to work in the **Nixon** administration (1969–74) and then served, under presidents **Ford** (1974–76) and **Carter** (1977–81), as US ambassador to Portugal and, later, as deputy director of the CIA. A pragmatic and apolitical Atlanticist, he found himself out of step with the 'hawks' in the **Reagan** administration (1981–89) and left to work at Sears World Trade after barely a year as deputy secretary of defence. In 1986 he replaced Rear Admiral **John Poindexter** as National Security Adviser, and served as defence secretary from 1987, supporting Soviet-US arms reduction initiatives.

CARLYLE, Alexander, of Inveresk (1722–1805) Scottish churchman, known as 'Jupiter', born in Prestonpans. Minister of Inveresk from 1748, he was the friend of **Hume**, **Adam Smith**, **Smollett**, **John Home**, and others. With **William Robertson** the historian he led the moderate party in the Church of Scotland; he was Moderator of the General Assembly in 1770, and was made dean of the Chapel Royal in 1789. His autobiography was published in 1860.

CARLYLE, Jane Baillie, née **Welsh** (1801–66) wife of **Thomas Carlyle**. Born in Haddington, East Lothian, she was the only daughter of Dr John Welsh, from whom she inherited a small family estate at Craigenputtock in the moors of Dumfriesshire. She was tutored by the revivalist minister **Edward Irving**, who introduced her in 1821 to his friend Carlyle, whom she married in 1826. They lived at Craigenputtock from 1828 to 1834, and therafter at 5 Cheyne Walk, Chelsea. Forthright and quick-witted, she declined to become a writer despite Carlyle's promptings. The marriage was a difficult one, and they seem to have had considerable sexual problems; Carlyle was an unhappy, withdrawn, even tormented man, but she supported him loyally through his depressions and chronic ill-health. After her sudden death in 1866, Carlyle was grief-stricken and retired from public life. He wrote an anguished memoir of her in his *Reminiscences* (1881); he also edited her letters and diaries, which are full of vivid insights and quality writing, and were eventually published after his death in 1883.

CARLYLE, Thomas (1795–1881) Scottish historian, essayist and sage, born in Ecclefechan in Dumfriesshire, the son of a stonemason (and later farmer). Brought up in a strictly Calvinist and Secessionist home, he was educated at Ecclefechan village school, Annan Academy and Edinburgh University, where he studied arts and mathematics under Sir **John Leslie**. He graduated in 1813 and spent a year studying for the Secessionist Church in Edinburgh, but turned to teaching instead, at Annan Academy and then in Kirkcaldy (1816–18), where he met the revivalist minister **Edward Irving** who became a lifelong friend. He moved back to Edinburgh in 1818 to study law, but turned to private tutoring. He wrote several articles for Sir **David Brewster**, editor of the *Edinburgh Encyclopaedia*, and immersed himself in the study of German literature, publishing his first major essay, on **Goethe**'s *Faust*, in *The New Edinburgh Review* (1922). He translated **Legendre**'s *Elements of Geometry* from the French, and wrote an ambitious *Life of Schiller*, which was published in instalments in *The London Magazine* from October 1823 and in book form in 1825. His major work in this period was his translation of Goethe's *Wilhelm Meister*, which was published in 1824 and earned him the acquaintance of **Coleridge**, **Hazlitt**, **Thomas Campbell** and other literary figures in London. In 1825 he moved to the farm of Hoddam Hill, near his parents' farm of Mainhill in Dumfriesshire, where he prepared a four-volume collection of translations from various writers, *German Romance* (1827). In 1826, however, he married Jane Baillie Welsh (**Jane Carlyle**), and settled in Edinburgh, where he wrote articles for **Francis Jeffrey** in the *Edinburgh Review*. However in 1828 he moved to the estate of Craigenputtoch, near Dumfries, which Jane had inherited, where they lived for the next six years. There he began an unfinished novel, *Wotton Reinfred*, and wrote articles for the *Edinburgh Review*, and a *History of German Literature* (subsequently published in a series of essays). He also wrote his first major work on social philosophy, *Sartor Resartus*, which was published in instalments in *Fraser's Magazine* in 1833–34; it came out in book form in the USA in 1836 with an introduction by **Ralph Waldo Emerson**, who had visited him at Craigenputtoch. It was partly a satirical discourse on the value of clothes by 'Professor Teufelsdröckh', and partly a semi-autiobiographical discussion of creeds and human values. In 1834 they moved down to London, to 5 Cheyne Walk in Chelsea, where he spent the rest of his life. Here he completed his romantic history of *The French Revolution* (1837), despite the accidental burning of the manuscript of most of the first volume by **John Stuart Mill**'s maidservant. He was now established as a man of letters, and engaged in a series of lectures, collected as *On Heroes, Hero Worship and the Heroic in History* (1841), which adumbrated his advocacy of the need for a strong hero-figure as a nation's leader as the best remedy for society's ills. On this theme of strong, benevolent autocracy as the best protection of freedom he also wrote an important essay on *Chartism* (1839) and a major political essay *Past and Present* (1843). In 1845 he published *Oliver Cromwell's Letters and Speeches*, which revolutionized contemporary attitudes to the Protector and his dictatorship. Another collection of essays, *Latter Day Pamphlets* (1850), underlined his increasingly right-wing political attitudes, with their emphasis on duty, obedience and punishment. His most ambitious work was now published: a six-volume *History of ... Frederick the Great* (1858–65), a compelling portrait of the practical autocrat as a heroic idealist. In 1866 he was installed as lord rector of Edinburgh University with a rectorial address entitled *On the Choice of Books*. His wife died suddenly at this time and he wrote little more except for a minor work on *The Early Kings of Norway* (1875). He refused an honour from **Disraeli**, and was buried at his own wish in Ecclefechan, not Westminster Abbey. His cottage birthplace there is now in the care of the National Trust for Scotland.

CARMEN SYLVA (1843–1916) the pen-name of Elizabeth, queen of Rumania, who was born the daughter of Prince Hermann of Wied Neuwied, and married King (then Prince) **Carol I** of Rumania in 1869. Her only child, a daughter, died in 1874, and out of her sorrow arose her literary activity. Two poems, printed privately at Leipzig in 1880 under the name 'Carmen Sylva', were followed by *Stürme* (1881), *Leidens Erdengang* (1882; trans as *Pilgrim Sorrow* by H Zimmern, 1884), *Pensées d'une reine* (1882), *The Bard of Dimbovitza* (1891), *Meister Manole* (1892), and other works. In the war of 1877–78 she endeared herself to her people by her devotion to the wounded.

CARMONA, Antonio (1869–1951) president of Portugal from 1928. He entered the army in 1888 and became a general in 1922. After a military coup in 1926 he was made prime minister and minister of war, with dictatorial powers. In 1928 he was elected president for life by plebiscite. In 1932 he appointed **Antonio Salazar** as prime minister and virtual dictator.

CARNAP, Rudolf (1891–1970) German-born American philosopher and logician, born in Wuppertal. A lecturer in Vienna (1926–31) and Prague (1931–35), he moved to Chicago (1935–52) and then California. He was a leading member of the 'Vienna Circle' of logical positivists, who dismissed most traditional metaphysics as a source of meaningless answers to pseudo-problems. His important work on the foundations of knowledge, scientific method, logic and semantics is represented in *Der logische Aufbau der Welt* (1928), *Logische Syntax der Sprache* (1934), *Meaning and Necessity* (1947) and especially in *The Logical Foundations of Probability* (1950).

CARNARVON, George Edward Stanhope Molyneux Herbert, 5th Earl of (1866–1923) wealthy amateur Egyptologist, son of Henry Carnarvon. From 1907 he sponsored **Howard Carter**'s excavations of royal tombs at Thebes. He died shortly after the spectacular discovery of **Tut'ankhamun**'s tomb in the Valley of the Kings in 1922.

CARNÉ, Marcel (1909–) French film director, born in Paris. Initially an insurance clerk, he served his filmmaking apprenticeship as an assistant to such noted directors as Jacques Feyder and **René Clair**. He made a short documentary, *Nogent, Eldorado du Dimanche*, in 1929 and his fictional directorial début with *Jenny* in 1936. Over the next decade, in collaboration with poet and screenwriter **Jacques Prévert**, designer Alexandre Trauner and others, he created classic romantic melodramas, expressing the fatalistic mood of the period in films like *Quai des Brumes* (1938) and *Le Jour se Lève* (1939). *Les Enfants du Paradis* (1944), made during the German occupation, is a celebrated epic, evoking a romantic theatrical past with wit and sensitivity, and is considered his masterpiece. After the war, the stature and quality of his work sharply declined, although he remained an active director into the 1980s.

CARNEADES (c.214–129 BC) Greek philosopher, born in Cyrene. He became head of the Academy, which under his very different, sceptical direction became known as the 'New Academy'. He had the reputation of a virtuoso dialectician, who could argue equally persuasively for quite opposing points of view.

CARNEGIE, Andrew (1835–1918) Scottish-born American industrialist and philanthropist, born in Dunfermline, the son of a weaver. His father emigrated to Pittsburgh in 1848. After several jobs, including factory hand, telegraphist, and railway clerk, young Andrew invested his savings in oil lands, and after the Civil War (1861–65) in the business which grew into the largest iron and steel works in America. He retired in 1901, a multimillionaire, to Skibo Castle in Sutherland, Scotland and died in Lenox, Massachusetts. His benefactions exceeded £70 000 000, including public libraries throughout the USA and Britain, Pittsburgh Carnegie Institute, Washington Carnegie Institution, Hero Funds, Hague Peace Temple, Pan-American Union Building, and great gifts to Scottish and American universities, Dunfermline, and so on. Besides an autobiography (1920), he wrote *Triumphant Democracy*, *The Gospel of Wealth*, and *Problems of Today*.

CARNOT, Lazare Nicolas Marguerite (1753–1823) French revolutionary and statesman, born in Nolay, Côte d'Or, known as the 'organizer of victory' in the French revolutionary wars. He entered the army as an engineer, in 1791 became a member of the Legislative Assembly, and in the Convention voted for the death of **Louis XVI**. During a mission to the army of the north, he took temporary command and gained the victory of Wattignies. Elected into the committee of public safety and entrusted with the organization of the armies of the revolution, he raised 14 armies, and drew up a plan of operations by which the forces of the European reaction were repelled from the frontier. Though he endeavoured to restrict the power of **Robespierre**, he was accused after the Reign of Terror; but the charge was dismissed. Having as a member of the Directory opposed, in 1797, the extreme measures of **Barras**, his colleague, he was sentenced to deportation as a suspected royalist. Escaping to Germany, he wrote a defence which conduced to the overthrow of his colleagues in 1799. The coup d'état of 18th Brumaire (1799) brought him back to Paris, where in 1800, as minister of war, he helped to achieve the brilliant results of the Italian and Rhenish campaigns. He retired when he understood the ambitious plans of the emperor, but on his reverses hastened to offer his services, and received the command of Antwerp in 1814, which he heroically defended. During the Hundred Days he was minister of the interior; and after the second restoration (1830) was banished, and retired first to Warsaw, and then to Magdeburg, where he died. He was the author of *De la défense des places fortes* (1810).

CARNOT, Marie François Sadi (1837–94) president of the French Republic, born in Limoges. He studied at the École Polytechnique, and became a civil engineer. In 1871 he was chosen for the National Assembly, and was finance minister in 1879 and 1887. In 1887 he was elected president of the Republic and proceeded to stand firm against the Boulangist movement. He was stabbed to death at Lyon by an Italian anarchist.

CARNOT, Nicholas Léonard Sadi (1796–1832) French physicist, born in Paris, son of **Lazare Carnot**. The founder of the science of thermodynamics, he became a captain of engineers, but from 1819 concentrated on scientific research. In his sole published work, *Réflexions sur la puissance du feu* (1824), he applied for the first time scientific principles to an analysis of the working cycle and efficiency of the steam engine, arriving at an early form of the second law of thermodynamics and the concept of reversibility in the form of the ideal Carnot cycle.

CARO, Sir Anthony (1924–) English sculptor, born in London. He studied engineering at Cambridge but turned to sculpture after World War II, attending the Regent Street Polytechnic (1946) and the Royal Academy Schools (1947–52). From 1951 to 1953 he worked with Sir **Henry Moore**. He visited the USA in 1959, where he met avant-garde artists like **David Smith** and the critic Clement Greenberg. His work is abstract, typically large pieces of metal welded together and painted in primary colours. He has had major one-man exhibitions in London, Washington, New York, and Ottowa.

CAROL I (1839–1914) king of Romania from 1881. Born Prince Karl of Hohenzollern-Sigmaringen, he was elected Prince of Romania in 1866 and became Romania's first king in 1881. He promoted economic development and military expansion, and brutally crushed a peasant rebellion in 1907. He married (1869) Princess Elizabeth of Wied, a prolific writer under the pseudonym **Carmen Sylva**. At the outset of World War I, King Carol declared Romanian neutrality, but his successor (his nephew King Ferdinand I) declared for the Allies in 1916.

CAROL II (1893–1953) king of Rumania, 1930–40, the eldest son of King Ferdinand I (reigned 1914–27) and great-nephew of **Carol I**. His flamboyant private life created constant problems. In 1917 he made a morganatic marriage to Zizi Lambrini, whom he divorced to marry Princess Helen of Greece in 1921 and by whom he had a son, King **Michael**. In 1925 he renounced his right of succession to the throne, deserted his wife, and went into exile with his mistress Magda Lupescu. In 1930 he returned to Rumania and became king in a coup that overthrew his son. His reign was made chaotic by pressures from both Russia and Germany. In 1938, in an attempt to counter the pro-Nazi Iron Guard movement, he banned all political parties and created a Front of National Rebirth; but in 1940, after being compelled to cede northern Transylvania to Hungary, he was deposed through German influence in favour of his son, and fled into exile in Spain.

CAROLINE OF ANSPACH (1683–1737) queen of Great Britain and Ireland, wife of **George II**. The daughter of the Margrave of Brandenburg-Anspach, she married George, Electoral Prince of Hanover, in 1705, and went to England with him when his father became King **George I** in 1714. As Princess of Wales she established a glittering court of writers and politicians at Leicester House. She was a strong supporter of Sir **Robert Walpole**, and acted as regent during her husband's absences abroad. They had five children, including Frederick Louis (1707–51), the Prince of Wales and father of **George II**, and William Augustus, Duke of **Cumberland** (1721-65).

CAROLINE OF BRUNSWICK, Amelia Elizabeth (1768–1821) queen of Great Britain and Ireland, wife of **George IV**. The second daughter of Charles William, Duke of Brunswick-Wolfenbüttel, and of **George III**'s sister, Augusta, in 1795 she was married to the Prince of Wales, her first cousin. The marriage was disagreeable to him, and although she bore him a daughter, the Princess **Charlotte**, he made her live by herself at Shooters Hill and Blackheath, the object of much sympathy. Reports to her discredit led the king in 1806 to cause investigation to be made into her conduct, which was found to be imprudent, but not criminal. When George came to the throne in 1820, she was offered an annuity of £50000 to renounce the title of queen and live abroad; when she refused, and made a triumphal entry into London, the government instituted proceedings against her for adultery. Much that was very reprehensible was proved; but her husband's usage, and the splendid defence of Lord **Brougham**, caused such a general feeling in her favour that the ministry gave up the Divorce Bill. She assumed the rank of royalty, but was turned away from Westminster Abbey door at George IV's coronation a few days before she died.

CAROLUS-DURAN, properly **Charles Auguste Emile Durand** (1838–1917) French painter, born in Lille. He was strongly influenced by **Velasquez** and the Spanish school. He was the teacher of **Sargent**.

CAROSSA, Hans (1878–1956) German writer and physician, born in Tölz. A doctor in Bavaria, he became prominent with his autobiographical *Eine Kindheit* (1922). Other writings include *Rumänisches Tagebuch* (1924), a war diary, and numerous novels such as *Das Jahr der schönen Täuschungen* (1941).

CAROTHERS, Wallace Hume (1896–1937) American industrial chemist, who discovered nylon. Born in Burlington, Iowa, a teacher's son, he taught at various universities before concentrating on research. Working for the Du Pont Company at Wilmington, he produced the first successful synthetic rubber, Neoprene, and followed this with nylon. Despite his achievements, however, he committed suicide, and the patent for nylon, awarded posthumously, was given to the Du Pont Company.

CARPACCIO, Vittore (c.1455–1522) Italian painter, born in Venice. His most characteristic work is seen in the nine subjects from the life of St **Ursula**, which he painted (1490–95), for the school of St Ursula, Venice (now in the Accademia). The nine subjects from the lives of the Saviour, and Saints **Jerome**, **George**, and Tryphonius (1502–08) painted for the school of San Giorgio de Schiavoni are still preserved there. In 1510 he executed for San Giobbe his masterpiece, the *Presentation in the Temple*, now in the Accademia.

CARPEAUX, Jean Baptiste (1827–75) French sculptor, born in Valenciennes, in 1854 obtained the *Prix de Rome*. His *chef d'œuvre* was the marble group, *The Dance*, in the façade of the Paris Opera House of 1866.

CARPENTER, Edward (1844–1929) English social reformer and writer, born in Brighton. An Anglican priest, he left the church and visited the USA, where he made friends with **Walt Whitman** and others. In England he turned to socialism and the crafts movement inspired by **William Morris**, and became a sandal-maker and market-gardener. He wrote copiously, including *England's Ideal* (1885), *Civilization, its Cause and Cure* (1889), and an autobiography, *My Days and Dreams* (1916).

CARPENTER, Mary (1807–77) English educationist and reformer, born in Exeter, daughter of a Unitarian minister, and sister of **William Carpenter**. Trained as a teacher, she opened a girls' school in Bristol in 1829 and took an active part in the movement for the reformation of neglected children. In 1846 she founded a ragged school in Bristol, and several reformatories for girls. She visited India on four occasions, and published *Our Convicts* (1864), *The Last Days of Rammohun Roy* (1866), and *Six Months in India* (1868).

CARPENTER, William Benjamin (1813–85) English biologist, born in Exeter, brother of **Mary Carpenter**. He studied medicine at Bristol, London, and Edinburgh. His graduation thesis (1839) on the nervous system of the invertebrates led on to his *Principles of General and Comparative Physiology* (1839). In 1844 he was appointed professor of physiology at the Royal Institution, London, and professor of forensic medicine at University College (1849). He took part in a deep sea exploration expedition (1868–71), and he did valuable research on the Foraminifera. His other works are *Principles of Human Physiology* (1846), *The Microscope and its Revelations* (1856), *Principles of Mental Physiology* (1874), and *Nature and Man* (1888).

CARPENTER, William Boyd (1841–1918) English prelate, born in Liverpool. A favourite of Queen **Victoria**, he was made a royal chaplain (1879), canon of Windsor (1882) and bishop of Ripon (1884–1911), then canon of Westminster. He wrote *Some Pages of my Life* (1911) and *Further Pages* (1916), and was a great pulpit orator.

CARPENTIER, Alejo (1904–80) Cuban novelist, born in Havana. For many years he lived in France and Venezuela but he returned to Cuba after the revolution and served in several official government posts, though some critics find the political messages in his novels at best ambiguous. One of the major Latin American writers of this century, his numerous books include *El siglo de las luces* (1962, trans *Explosion in the Cathedral*, 1963), *El reino de este mundo* (1949, trans *The Kingdom of the World*, 1957) and *Los pasos perdidos* (1953, trans *The Lost Steps*, 1956).

CARPINI, (John of Plano) (c.1182–c.1253) Franciscan monk and traveller, born in Umbria. A disciple of **Francis of Assisi**, he was head of the mission sent by

Pope Innocent IV to the emperor of the Mongols, whose warlike advances had thrown Christendom into consternation. A big, fat man, more than 60 years old, he started from Lyon in April 1245, and, crossing the Dnieper, Don, Volga, Ural, and Jaxartes, in the summer of 1246 reached the Karakoram mountains, beyond Lake Baikal, where he met the supreme emperor. He returned to Kiev in June 1247, and so back to Lyon to report to the Pope. He was later appointed archbishop of Autivari.

CARPOCRATES OF ALEXANDRIA (2nd century) Greek religious leader. He founded the gnostic sect of Carpocratians, who sought through contemplation the union, or return, of the individual soul to God and claimed among their spiritual predecessors **Pythagoras**, **Plato**, **Aristotle** and **Jesus**.

CARPZOV, Benedict (1595–1666) German jurist and writer on law. Regarded as the founder of legal science in Germany, he did much to systematize German law, and held high offices in Dresden and Leipzig.

CARR, Robert, Earl of Somerset (c.1590–1645) Scottish courtier. Handsome and high-spirited, he became the favourite of **James VI and I**, who made him constitutional adviser, Viscount of Rochester (1611), Earl of Somerset (1611) and treasurer of Scotland (1613). He fell in love with Frances Howard (1592–1632), the wife of Robert Devereux, 3rd Earl of **Essex**; his plan to marry her was opposed by his friend, **Thomas Overbury**, who then died of poisoning in the Tower in 1613. By royal influence the divorce went through and Carr married the countess. But in 1614 he was displaced as royal favourite by George Villiers, 1st Duke of **Buckingham**, and in 1615 the couple were both arraigned for conspiring to murder Overbury. The countess pleaded guilty and was pardoned; but Carr, prosecuted by **Roger Bacon**, was imprisoned in the Tower until 1621, when he was pardoned.

CARR-BOYD, Ann Kirsten (1938–) Australian composer, teacher and music historian, born in Sydney, and educated at Sydney University. A leading authority on aboriginal and early Australian music, her many orchestral, chamber and instrumental compositions include *Symphony in Three Movements* (1964), *Three Songs of Love* (1975), *Festival* (1980), *Australian Baroque* (1984), and *Suite Veronese* (1985). Commissions include *Fanfare for Aunty* (1974), for the opening of the ABC's FM transmissions, and *The Bells of Sydney Harbour* (1979) for the Sydney Organ Society.

CARRA, Carlo (1881–1966) Italian painter, born in Quergneto, Alexandria. He studied at the Brera Academy, Milan, and aligned himself at first (1909–14) with the Futurists, with paintings like *Funeral of the Anarchist Galli* (1911). He was one of the signatories of the Futurist Manifesto at the Exhibition in Paris in 1911. In 1915 he met **Giorgio di Chirico** and was influenced by his 'metaphysical painting' movement. Carra's aim thereafter was, broadly, to synthesize the past and present: he sought, so to speak, a bridge between **Giotto** and **Cézanne**.

CARRACCI, Agostino (1557–1602) Italian engraver born in Bologna, brother of **Annibale** and cousin of **Ludovico Carracci**. He dabbled in poetry and literature, but made his reputation as a painter and a brilliant engraver on copper. His brother's jealousy is said to have driven him from Rome (where they did the frescoes in the Farnese palace) to Parma, where he died. He had an illegimate son, Antonio Marziale (1583–1618), also a painter.

CARRACCI, Annibale (1540–1609) Italian artist and leading member of a Bolognese dynasty, born in Bologna, brother of **Agostino Carracci** and cousin of **Ludovico Carraci**. He was responsible for the revival of Italian painting after the vapid excesses of the later Mannerist period. The chief influences on his style were **Raphael** and **Corregio**. A brilliant draughtsman—many of the family's drawings are in the Royal Collection at Windsor—only **Caravaggio** of the same generation is his equal. Apart from being the inventor of caricature in the modern sense, he was also a lively genre painter. In his greatest work, the ceiling of the Palazzo Farnese in Rome (1597–1600), he combines the influence of the antique with those of the High Renaissance masters, **Michelangelo** and Raphael, but adds to them an exuberance which was to become one of the foundations of Baroque painting. He was also the father of the idealized landscape which reached perfection in the hands of **Claude** and **Poussin**. **Domenichino** and **Reni** were both students at the Carracci Academy.

CARRACCI, Ludovico (1555–1619) Italian painter, born in Bologna, the son of a butcher. He studied art there and in Parma, Mantua and Venice, and became a distinguished teacher. With his cousins **Agostino Carracci** and **Annibale Carracci** he established in Bologna an 'eclectic' school of painting, the Accademia degli Incamminati. His own works include the *Madonna and Child Enthroned* and the *Transfiguration* (both still in Bologna).

CARRANZA, Bartholomaeus de (1503–76) Spanish theologian, born in Miranda in Navarre. A Dominican, he became professor of theology at Valladolid, and in 1554 accompanied **Philip II** to England, where he was confessor to Queen **Mary I**, and where his zealous efforts to re-establish Catholicism gained him the confidence of Philip and the archbishopric of Toledo. Here, however, he was accused of heresy, and imprisoned by the Inquisition in 1559. In 1567 he was removed to Rome, and confined in the castle of St Angelo. He died a few days after his release.

CARREL, Alexis (1873–1944) French-born American biologist, born in Ste Foy-lès-Lyon. A graduate of Lyon University, he moved to the Rockefeller Institute for medical research in New York in 1906. He discovered a method of suturing blood-vessels which made it possible to replace arteries, and was awarded the 1912 Nobel prize for physiology or medicine. He did much research on the prolongation of the life of tissues, and helped **Henry Dakin** develop 'Dakin's solution' for sterilizing deep wounds.

CARREÑO DE MIRANDA, Juan (1614–85) Spanish painter, born in Avilés. Assistant and successor of **Velasquez** at the Spanish court, he painted religious pictures and frescoes, as well as portraits.

CARRERAS, José Maria (1946–) Spanish lyric tenor, born in Barcelona and first sang at the Liceo there. He made his début at Covent Garden and at the Metropolitan Opera (1974), at La Scala (1975) and Salzburg (1976). After severe illness in the mid 1980s, he returned to the stage.

CARRIER, Jean Baptiste (1756–94) French revolutionary, born in Yolai, near Aurillac. In the National Convention he helped to form the Revolutionary Tribunal, voted for the death of the king, demanded the arrest of the Duke of **Orléans**, and assisted in the overthrow of the Girondists. At Nantes in 1793 he massacred in four months 16000 Vendéan and other prisoners, chiefly by drowning them in the Loire (the *noyades*), but also by shooting them, as in a battue. After the fall of **Robespierre** he was tried, and perished by the guillotine.

CARRIER, Willis Haviland (1876–1950) American engineer and inventor, born in Angola, New York, the pioneer of modern air-conditioning. He designed his first machine to control humidity for a New York printing plant in 1902. He formed the Carrier Engineering Corporation in 1915, and in 1939 invented a practical air-conditioning system for skyscrapers.

CARRIERA, Rosalba (1675–1757) Italian painter, born in Venice. She was famed for her flattering portraits and miniatures, some of them in pastel, especially on ivory.

CARRIÈRE, Eugène (1849–1906) French artist, born in Gournay-sur-Marne. He lived and worked in Paris, specializing in domestic groups and portraits. His soft tonalities inspired **Edmond de Goncourt** to call him 'the modern Madonna painter'.

CARRINGTON, Peter Alexander Rupert, 6th Baron Carrington (Ireland) (1919–) English Conservative politician. Educated at Eton and Sandhurst, he was virtually destined for high public office and, after service in World War II, held ministerial posts in the Conservative administrations of **Churchill** (1951–54), **Eden** (1954–56), **Macmillan** (1957–63), **Douglas-Home** (1963–64), **Heath** (1970–74) and **Thatcher** (1979–82). He also served as high commissioner to Australia (1956–59). As foreign secretary (1979–82) he was instrumental in establishing independence for Zimbabwe (1980). He resigned in 1982, accepting responsibility for the Argentinian invasion of the Falkland Islands. His last important position was secretary-general of NATO (1984–88).

CARRINGTON, Richard Christopher (1826–75) English astronomer, born in Chelsea. Educated at Cambridge, he made an important catalogue of stars at his private observatory in Redhill.

CARROLL, Charles, of Carollton (1737–1832) American statesman, born in Annapolis, Maryland, into a powerful Catholic family of Irish origin, the cousin of **John Carroll**, the first American Catholic bishop. Educated by the Jesuits in St Omer and at the Collège de Louis le grand in Paris, he became involved in the pamphlet wars of the mid 1770s on behalf of the colonies, served on the Annapolis Committee of Correspondence, the Maryland Revolutionary Convention and the Maryland Committee of Correspondence and Committee of Safety, and was the last survivor of the signatories of the Declaration of Independence. He later served in the Maryland Senate (1777–88, 1791–1801) and was the first senator from Maryland to the US senate (1789–92). His politics were markedly conservative, as his Catholicism and his wealth might suggest, thus his adhesion to the Revolutionary cause symbolized how drastic things were, and his stand was inspirational to other American Catholics as well as highly advantageous for Catholicism in the new USA. He later became director of the Baltimore and Ohio Railroad.

CARROLL, James (1854–1907) English-born American physician, born in Woolwich. He emigrated in childhood to Canada and the USA. Serving as a surgeon in the American army, and in association with **Walter Reed** did valuable research on yellow fever, deliberately infecting himself with the disease in the process (1900). In 1902 he became professor of bacteriology and pathology at Columbia and the Army Medical School.

CARROLL, John (1735–1815) American prelate, born in Upper Marlbro, Maryland, the first US Roman Catholic bishop. He entered the Jesuit Order in 1753 and was ordained priest in 1769. The Maryland priests petitioned **Pius VI** for a bishop in the US, and Carroll was appointed to the see of Baltimore in 1789. In 1808 he was made archbishop and the diocese was divided into four sees.

CARROLL, Lewis See **DODGSON, Charles**

CARRUTHERS, Jimmy (1929–) Australian boxer, born in Paddington, New South Wales. In the course of a very short professional boxing career—only 19 bouts, all of which were won—he established himself as the greatest of Australian boxers. He represented Australia as an amateur at the London Olympics of 1948 and had his first professional bout in 1950. He became world bantamweight champion by knocking out Vic Toweel, the South African title holder, in the first round in Johannesburg in November 1952, and then allowed his defeated opponent another bid for the title in South Africa. Again Carruthers won, this time in the tenth round. Two more successful title defences followed, against Henry (Pappy) Gault in Sydney and Chamren Songkitrat of Thailand in Bangkok. He retired while not yet 25 to become a boxing referee and pub owner. Seven years later he made a short and ill-advised return to the ring but he had lost his old speed and power.

CARSON, Christopher or **'Kit'** (1809–68) American trapper, born in Missouri. In 1831 he became a trapper and hunter. His knowledge of Indian habits and languages led to his becoming guide in **Frémont**'s explorations (1842–45), and Indian agent in New Mexico (1853).

CARSON, Edward Henry, Baron (1854–1935) British politician and judge. Born in Dublin, he was called to the Irish bar, became QC of the Irish (1880) and English bar (1894), Conservative MP for Dublin University (1892–1918) and the Duncairn division of Belfast (1918–21), solicitor-general for Ireland (1892) and for England (1900–06), attorney-general (1915), First Lord of the Admiralty (1917), and a member of the war cabinet, 1917–18. As leader of the Irish Unionists, he organized the Ulster Volunteers, and violently opposed Home Rule. He was a lord of appeal, 1921–29.

CARSON, John William (1925–) American television personality and businessman, born in Corning, Iowa. Active with magic tricks and mimicry in school theatricals, he served in the US navy from 1943 to 1946 and majored in journalism at Nebraska University after his discharge. Working in local radio and television from 1950, he hosted *Carson's Cellar* (1951) and wrote and performed on the *Red Skelton Show* (1954). Following *The Johnny Carson Show* (1955–56) and a stage appearance in *Tunnel of Love* (1958), he was engaged as an occasional host of *The Tonight Show*, a position that was rendered permanent in 1962. Consistently top of the ratings, his breezy, relaxed manner, comic monologue and selection of guests have made him an American institution and one of the country's highest-paid television performers. Carson Productions Group, formed in 1980, has been responsible for a variety of film and television productions. A night club performer and stand-up comedian, he also wrote *Happiness is a Dry Martini* (1965).

CARSON, Rachel Louise (1907–64) American naturalist and science writer, born in Springdale, Pennsylvania. She studied biology at Johns Hopkins University, taught at Maryland (1931–36) and worked as a marine biologist for the US Fish and Wildlife Service from 1936 to 1949. Her work in marine ecology established her position in the subject, but her wider reputation came with *The Sea Around Us* (1951), which warned of the increasing danger of large-scale marine pollution, and the hard-hitting *Silent Spring* (1962), which forcefully directed public concern to the problems caused by modern synthetic pesticides and their effect on food chains. The resulting controls in the USA on their use owe much to her work, which also contributed to the increasing ecological and conservationist attitudes which emerged in the 1970s and 1980s.

CARSON, Willie (William Fisher Hunter) (1942–) Scottish jockey, born in Stirling. A late developer, he was 19 years old before riding his first winner, and was further held back by a car accident in 1967. In 1972, however, he became the first Scotsman to be champion jockey and recorded his first Classic success, on High Top in the 2000 Guineas. Fiery and combative on the track, good-humoured and outgoing off it, he recorded a notable royal double for the Queen in 1977 when winning the Oaks and the St Leger on Dunfermline. He had to wait until 1979 for his first Derby winner, Troy, but immediately won again on Henbit in 1980.

CARSTAIRS, John Paddy, real name **John Keys** (1914–70) British novelist, film director, filmscript writer, and artist. He studied art at the Slade School, and painted a number of light-hearted landscapes in 3202 various media. His best-known novel is *Love and Ella Rafferty* (1947), and he also wrote the autobiographical *Honest Injun* (1943).

CARSTARES, William (1649–1715) Scottish clergyman, born in Cathcart, Glasgow, the son of a Presbyterian minister. He studied at Edinburgh and Utrecht, and became friend and adviser to the Prince of Orange (**William III**). Coming to London in 1672, he was arrested as a spy in 1675, and imprisoned in Edinburgh until 1679. In 1683 he was again arrested, and put to the torture of the boot and thumbscrew. After an imprisonment of a year and a half, he returned to Holland to be chaplain to the Prince of Orange, and afterwards secured good relations between the new king and the Church of Scotland. From 1693 to the death of the king in 1702 he could not have had more influence in Scottish affairs if he had been prime minister; he was popularly called 'Cardinal Carstares' by the Jacobites. He was elected principal of Edinburgh University in 1703, and in 1705-14 was four times moderator of the General Assembly. His influence helped to pass the Treaty of Union.

CARSTENS, Asmus Jakob (1754–98) German painter, born near Schleswig. He studied art at Copenhagen and in 1783–88 barely supported himself by portrait painting in Lübeck and Berlin before his *Fall of the Angels* gained him a professorship in the Academy of Art in Berlin in 1790. He lived in Rome from 1792, working on classical themes. He was a precursor of **Overbeck** and **Cornelius**.

CARSWELL, Sir Robert (1793–1857) Scottish pathologist and physician, born in Paisley. He studied medicine at Glasgow University, although his MD was from Marischal College, Aberdeen. He spent two extensive periods of study in Paris, where he put his considerable artistic talents to work in producing a fine series of pathological drawings ultimately published as *Illustrations of the Elementary Forms of Disease* (1837). He was professor of pathology at University College London until 1840, when ill health led him to accept an appointment as physician to **Leopold I**, the king of the Belgians.

CARTAN, Élie (Joseph) (1869–1951) French mathematician, born in Dolomieu, the son of a blacksmith. As a child his mathematical talent attracted attention and he received a scholarship first to the Lycée and then to the École Normale Supérieure. He was professor in Paris from 1912 to 1940. One of the most original mathematicians of his time, he worked on **Lie** groups and differential geometry, and founded the subject of analysis on differentiable manifolds, which is essential to modern fundamental physical theories. Among his discoveries are the theory of spinors, the method of moving frames and the exterior differential calculus. The novelty of his ideas and their somewhat obscure presentation delayed their understanding, and his importance was only fully appreciated during the later part of his life. He is now seen to be a seminal figure for much of the mathematics of this century.

CARTE, Richard D'Oyly (1844–1901) English impresario, born in London. After working in his father's musical instrument-making business he became a concert agent, and from 1875 produced the first operettas by **Gilbert** and **Sullivan**, with whom he formed a partnership. In 1881 he built the Savoy Theatre in London, the first to be lit by electricity. Another theatre building, a Royal English Opera House (1891), failed. After his death the D'Oyly Carte company continued to perform Gilbert and Sullivan in traditional style for many years.

CARTE, Thomas (1686–1754) English historian, born near Rugby. He was educated at both Oxford and Cambridge, and took holy orders. A Jacobite, in 1714 he resigned rather than take the oaths of allegiance to King **George I**. In 1722, as secretary of Bishop Allerbury, he was suspected of complicity in the conspiracy to restore the **Stewarts**, but escaped to France, where he remained till 1728. After his return, he published a *Life of James, Duke of Ormonde* (2 vols, 1736), and a *General History of England to 1654* (4 vols, 1747–55), whose prospects were blighted by an unlucky note, ascribing to the Young Pretender, **Charles Edward Stewart** the gift of touching for the king's evil.

CARTER, Benny (Bennet Lester) (1907–) American alto saxophonist, born in New York. Although also a trumpeter and clarinettist, it was his warm tone and elegant flowing lines on his main instrument, the alto saxophone, that set the swing era style. He was among the outstanding early writers of big band arrangements, composing for the Fletcher Henderson and Benny Goodman Orchestras among others. Carter has led big bands of his own, although none gained particular recognition. A spell in London in 1936 as musical director of the Henry Hall Orchestra had significant influence on the development of British jazz. Carter was composer-in-residence to the first Glasgow Jazz Festival in 1987.

CARTER, Elizabeth (1717–1806) English scholar and poet, born in Deal. She contributed verse to many publications, and was an accomplished linguist. Her best-known work is her translation of **Epictetus**. Among her friends were Dr **Johnson**, Sir **Joshua Reynolds**, **Burke**, and **Horace Walpole**.

CARTER, Elliot Cook Jr (1908–) American composer, born in New York City. At the age of 15 he was befriended by **Charles Ives** who introduced him to contemporary music. He studied at Harvard with **Walter Piston** and in Paris with **Nadia Boulanger**; taught Greek and mathematics at St John's College, Annapolis (1940–42); and subsequently taught music at Columbia and Yale universities and elsewhere. His first work to gain international recognition was a String Quartet (1953, the first of four quartets); this and subsequent works display an uncompromisingly intellectual and yet emotionally charged style, with the serial element extended to great rhythmic and metrical complexity. His output includes symphonies, other orchestral music, several concertos, songs and much chamber music. His collected writings were published in 1977.

CARTER, Henry See **LESLIE, Frank**

CARTER, Howard (1874–1939) English Egyptologist, born in Swaffham, Norfolk. He joined **Flinders Petrie**'s archaeological survey of Egypt as a draughtsman in 1891, drawing inscriptions and sculptures at Thebes and at the Dynasty XVIII temple of Hatshepsut at Deir el-Bahari. He subsequently served as inspector-general of the Egyptian Antiquities Department, from 1907 conducting his own research under the patronage of George Herbert, 5th Earl of **Carnarvon** (1866–1923). His discoveries included the tombs of Hatshepsut (1907), Tuthmoses IV and, most notably, in 1922 the virtually intact burial of the Dynasty XVIII king **Tut'ankhamun** (d.1352 BC). The work of emptying the chambers, photographing, conserving and despatching the treasures to Cairo occupied him for the rest of his life, and he failed through ill health to produce a final, detailed report.

CARTER, James Earl (Jimmy) (1924–) 39th president of the USA, born in Plains, Georgia. He graduated from the US Naval Academy in 1946 and served in the US navy until 1953, when he took over the family peanut business and other business enterprises. As governor of Georgia (1970–74) he expressed an enlightened policy towards the rights of blacks and women. In 1976 he won the Democratic presidential nomination over several much more prominent figures and went on to win a narrow victory over **Gerald Ford** for the presidency. Throughout his campaign he presented an air of informality, honesty, morality and religious fervour which appealed to an American electorate tired of the scandal and intrigue of the **Nixon** administration. On his election he promised to institute a populist form of government giving the people a greater say in the administration. He also promised to set up effective energy and health programmes, to concern himself with civil and human rights issues and to try to restrict the making of nuclear weapons. His presidency was notable for the Panama Treaty and Camp David (Middle East) agreements of 1978. Carter's popularity waned, however, during 1979–80 as a result of mounting economic difficulties and the seizure of USA embassy hostages by Islamic fundamentalists in Iran. He was defeated by the Republican **Ronald Reagan** in 1980. His memoirs were entitled *Keeping Faith* (1982).

CARTERET, John, 1st Earl Granville (1690–1763) English orator, diplomat, and statesman, son of Baron Carteret. Educated at Westminster School and Christ Church, Oxford, in 1719 he was ambassador extraordinary to Sweden and in 1721 was appointed one of the two foreign secretaries under **Walpole** and, as such, attended in 1723 the congress of Cambrai. From 1730 to 1742 he led in the House of Lords the party opposed to Walpole and became the real head of the next administration, although nominally only secretary of state. He was with **George II** at the battle of Dettingen (1743).

CARTERET, Philip (d.1796) English navigator. He sailed as lieutenant in **John Byron**'s voyage round the world (1764–66), and commanded the *Swallow* in **Samuel Wallis**'s expedition round the world (1766). Separated from Wallis while clearing the Strait of Magellan, he discovered Pitcairn and other small islands (one of the Solomons bears his name) and returned round the Cape of Good Hope to England in 1769.

CARTESIUS See **DESCARTES**

CARTIER, Sir Georges Étienne (1814–73) Canadian statesman, born in Antoine, Quebec. A lawyer by profession, he became attorney-general for Lower Canada in 1856, and was joint prime minister with Sir **John Macdonald** from 1858 to 1862. He worked for Canadian confederation and expansion in the west.

CARTIER, Jacques (1491–1557) French navigator, born in St Malo, discoverer of the St Lawrence River. Between 1534 and 1541 he made three voyages of discovery to North America searching for a westerly route to Asia.

CARTIER-BRESSON, Henri (1908–) French photographer, born in Paris. He studied painting with André Lhote in 1927–28 and after a trip to West Africa adopted photography as his chosen form of artistic expression, presenting his first exhibition in 1933; in the later 1930s he visited Mexico and the United States and worked as an assistant to the film director **Jean Renoir**. After the War, during which he escaped from imprisonment to join the Resistance, he developed his human interest style of black-and-white photography in worldwide travels, capturing the character and attitudes of contemporary life by recording at the 'moment of decision' without artificial preparation or composition. Publications include *Images á la sauvette* (The Decisive Moment, 1952), *The Europeans* (1955) and collections from many other parts of the world.

CARTLAND, (Mary) Barbara Hamilton (1901–) English popular romantic novelist, born in Edgbaston, Birmingham, and step-grandmother of Diana, Princess of Wales. She published her first novel, *Jigsaw*, in 1923, and has since produced well over 400 best-selling books, mostly novels of chaste romantic love designed for women readers, but also including biographies and books on food, health and beauty, and several volumes of autobiography. She earned a place in the *Guinness Book of Records* for writing 26 books in 1983. She married first (1927) Alexander George McCorquodale (d.1964), whom she divorced in 1933; and, second (1936), his cousin, Hugh McCorquodale (d.1963). By her first marriage she is the mother of Raine, Countess Spencer, step-mother of the Princess of Wales. An ardent advocate of health foods and fitness for the elderly, she has championed causes like the St John's Ambulance Brigade and providing camp-sites for Romany gipsies.

CARTWRIGHT, Edmund (1743–1823) English inventor and clergyman, brother of **John Cartwright**, born in Marnham, Nottinghamshire. Educated at Wakefield and University College, Oxford, he became rector of Goadby-Marwood, Leicestershire (1779), where on his glebe he made improvements in agriculture. A visit in 1784 to **Arkwright**'s cotton-spinning mills resulted in his invention of the power loom (1785). He built a weaving mill at Doncaster (1787), but attempts to put it to use met with fierce opposition; it was not till the 19th century that it came into practical use. Cartwright also took out patents for wool-combing machines (1790) and various other inventions; he even joined **Robert Fulton** in his efforts after steam navigation. His business went bankrupt in 1793, but in 1797 he patented an alcohol engine, and in 1809 the government made him an award of £10000.

CARTWRIGHT, John (1740–1824) English reformer, known as the 'Father of Reform', and elder brother of **Edmund Cartwright**. He served in the navy (1758–70), and in 1775 became major to the Nottinghamshire militia. He then began to write on politics, advocating annual parliaments, the ballot, and manhood suffrage, and afterwards taking up reform in farming, abolition of slavery, the national defences, and the liberties of Spain and Greece. In 1820 he was fined £100 for sedition.

CARTWRIGHT, Peter (1785–1872) American Methodist preacher, born in Amherst County, Virginia. He was ordained in Kentucky in 1806, and in 1823 removed to Illinois. In 1846 he was defeated by **Abraham Lincoln** in an election for congressman. He wrote his autobiography (1856), and *The Backwoods Preacher* (1869).

CARTWRIGHT, Thomas (1535–1603) English Puritan clergyman, born in Hertfordshire. He became in 1569 Lady Margaret professor of divinity at Cambridge, but was deprived for his nonconforming lectures and later several times imprisoned.

CARTWRIGHT, William (1611–43) English playwright, poet, and preacher, born in Northway, near Tewkesbury. He preached at Oxford, and wrote plays such as *The Royal Slave*, which was performed at Oxford before **Charles I** in 1636, and a play ridiculing Puritans, *The Ordinary*. He was one of the group of young playwrights known as the 'sons' of **Ben Jonson**.

CARUS, Karl Gustav (1789–1869) German scholar and physician, born in Leipzig. Professor at Dresden from 1814, he was a man of immense versatility: royal physician from 1827, a philosopher adherent of **Friedrich Schelling**, and a notable painter. He wrote several works of psychology, philosophy and literary criticism.

CARUSO, Enrico (1873–1921) Italian operatic tenor, born in Naples. He made his first appearance in *Faust* (1895), first appeared in London in 1902 and in New York the following year. The extraordinary power and musical purity of his voice, combined with his acting ability, won him recognition as one of the greatest tenors of all time.

CARVER, George Washington (c.1860–1943) American botanist and scientist, born of Negro slave parents in Missouri. He was renowned for his researches on agricultural problems and on commercial products such as peanut butter, and many others derived from peanuts and potatoes.

CARVER, John (c.1575–1621) English colonist in America. After emigrating to Holland in 1609 he joined the Pilgrim Fathers and became their agent for the expedition to the New World. He chartered the *Mayflower*, sailing in June 1620, and was elected first governor of the colony at New Plymouth, Massachusetts. He died within five months of their landing.

CARVER, Raymond (1939–88) American poet and short-story writer, born in Clatskanie, Oregon. He married at 18 and struggled for many years to provide for a young family and further his career as a writer. His first published story, 'Pastoral', was accepted by the *Western Humanities Review*. His collections include *Will You Please Be Quiet, Please?* (1976), *What We Talk About When We Talk About Love* (1981) and *Cathedral* (1983). Both his fiction and his poetry are remarkable for their spare narratives, focusing on a society of the lower and middle classes and dealing with people in a state of transition: couples breaking up, people between jobs, between sleeping and wakefulness. He wrote no novels. He was a Guggenheim Fellow in 1979 and was twice awarded grants by the National Endowment for Arts. He taught at the University of Iowa, the University of Texas and the University of California. Other books include *Fire: Essays, Poems, Stories* (1984), and books of poems: *Where Water Comes Together with Other Water* (1985) and *Ultramarine* (1985). *In A Marine Light: Selected Poems* appeared in the year he died.

CARVER, Richard Michael Power, 1st Baron (1915–) English soldier, born in Surrey. Educated at Winchester College, he was commissioned into the Royal Tank Corps in 1935. In World War II he served with distinction in North Africa (1941–43), in Italy (1943) and Normandy (1944). He commanded the 4th Independent Armoured Brigade in North West Europe (1944–45). He was chief of the General Staff (1971–73), and chief of the Defence Staff (1973–76). He has written several historical, biographical and strategic studies.

CARVER, Robert (c.1490–c.1567) Scottish composer, canon of Scone, and attached to the Chapel Royal of Scotland. Five of his Masses have survived, each displaying a florid style with free use of counterpoint; one is the only early 16th-century British example based on the *cantus firmus* 'L'Homme armé'. Of two surviving motets, *O bone Jesu* is for a remarkable 19 voice parts.

CARY, Henry Francis (1772–1844) English clergyman and translator, born in Gibraltar. Educated at Rugby, Sutton Coldfield, and Birmingham, he went to Christ Church, Oxford, and took holy orders in 1796. In 1805 he published a translation in blank verse of **Dante**'s *Inferno*, and in 1814 of the whole *Divina Commedia*. He afterwards translated **Pindar**'s *Odes* and **Aristophanes**' *Birds*, and wrote memoirs in continuation of **Johnson**'s *Lives of the Poets*. He was buried in Westminster Abbey.

CARY, John (c.1754–1835) English cartographer. His *New and Correct English Atlas* appeared in 1787. He prospered, and county atlases followed, with a large *New Universal Atlas* in 1808. In 1794 he undertook a road survey of England and Wales, the results of which were embodied in *Cary's New Itinerary* (1798). He was responsible for the *Improved Map of England and Wales etc* (1832) on the scale of half an inch to the mile.

CARY, (Arthur) Joyce Lunel (1888–1957) English novelist, born in Londonderry of English parents. He was educated at Tunbridge Wells and Clifton College and later studied art in Edinburgh and Paris, graduating (1912) at Oxford. He then served with the Red Cross in the Balkan war of 1912–13 and was decorated by the king of Montenegro. In 1913 he joined the Nigerian Political Service and fought in a Nigerian regiment in World War I. War injuries and ill-health dictated his early retirement after the war to Oxford, where he took up writing. Out of his African experiences emerge such novels as *Aissa Saved* (1932), *African Witch* (1936), and *Mister Johnson* (1939), a high-spirited, richly humorous study of a native clerk. In 1941 he was awarded the James Tait Black Memorial prize for *The House of Children*, and with the trilogy, *Herself Surprised* (1940), *To be a Pilgrim* (1942), and *The Horses's Mouth* (1944), Cary established himself. These were followed by *Moonlight* (1946) and *A Fearful Joy* (1949), and a later trilogy on the life of Chester Nimmo, a politician, *Prisoner of Grace* (1952), *Except the Lord* (1953), and *Not Honour More* (1955), and finally an unfinished novel with a religious theme *The Captive and the Free* (1959).

CARY, Lucius See **FALKLAND**

CARY, Sir Robert See **CAREY**

CARY, Tristram (1925–) English-born Australian composer and teacher, born in Oxford, the son of **Joyce Cary**. After service in the Royal Naval Volunteer Reserve, he went to Trinity College of Music, and pioneered the development of electronic music, establishing his own studio in 1952. He became a director of the celebrated Electronic Music Studios in London and from 1967 to 1974 was professor of electronic music at the Royal College of Music, London. In 1979 he joined Adelaide University, South Australia, where he became dean of music and is now honorary visiting research fellow. He has written much music for films, theatre, radio and television.

CASA, Giovanni della (1503–56) Italian author and prelate, born near Florence. He was appointed archbishop of Benevento in 1544. He is remembered for stylish lyric verse, and *Il Galateo ovvero De' Costumi* (1558), a manual of etiquette.

CASALS, Pablo (Pau) (1876–1973) Spanish cellist, conductor and composer, born in Vendrell, Tarragona.

He studied at the Royal Conservatory, Madrid, returning to Barcelona as professor of the cello at the Conservatory. After playing as leading cello in the Paris Opera from 1895 to 1898, he began to appear as a soloist. With **Jacques Thibaud** and **Alfred Cortot** he formed, in 1905, a trio famed for its performance of classical works. In 1919 he founded the Barcelona Orchestra, which he conducted until he left Spain at the outbreak of the Spanish Civil War in 1936, after which he did not return. In 1950 he founded at Prades, France, an annual festival of classical chamber music. His own compositions consist of choral and chamber works.

CASANOVA DE SEINGALT, Giacomo Girolamo (1725–98) Italian adventurer, whose name has become synonymous with amorous intrigues, born in Venice. In 1741 he was expelled from a seminary for scandalous conduct, and by 1750 had been secretary to a cardinal, an ensign in the Venetian army, an abbé, a gambler, an alchemist, and a violinist, working all over Europe. He was imprisoned in Italy in 1755 but made a daring escape in 1756, and for the next 20 years wandered through Europe, mocking the importance of the high and mighty and indulging in romantic escapades; everywhere he was introduced to the best society, and everywhere he found it expedient to move on in a hurry. He was the director of state lotteries in Paris, was knighted in the Netherlands, visited Russia but fled after a duel, worked as a spy for **Louis XV** and as a police informer for the Venetian Inquisition. In 1785 he found a haven as librarian for Count von Waldstein in his castle of Dux in Bohemia. His intimate and scandalous *Mémoires écrits par lui-même* were first published in edited form in Leipzig (12 vols, 1828–38); the complete edition was first published in 1960.

CASAS, Las See **LAS CASAS**

CASAUBON, Isaac (1559–1614) French scholar and humanist, born in Geneva, the son of refugee Huguenot parents. In 1583 he became professor of Greek at Geneva; in 1586 he married the daughter of the Geneva printer **Henri Stephens**. He was made Greek professor at Montpellier in 1596, and royal librarian at Paris in 1598. After the death of **Henry IV** his Protestantism exposed him to risk; and removing in 1610 to London, he was made a prebendary of Canterbury. His works include *De Satyrica Graecorum Poësi et Romanorum Satira* (1605), *De Libertate Ecclesiastica* (1607), the *Exercitationes contra Baronium* (1614), and editions of **Aristotle**, **Theophrastus**, **Persius**, **Suetonius**, and other classical authors.

CASELLA, Alfredo (1883–1947) Italian composer and musician, born in Turin. He studied piano at the Paris Conservatoire and first came to notice as a composer in 1908. His work was varied but mainly neo-classical in character, and includes three operas, two symphonies, concertos for cello, violin, and organ, as well as chamber music, many piano pieces and songs. He produced some noteworthy editions of classical composers and wrote books on **Stravinsky**, **Bach** and **Beethoven**, and an autobiography (1941).

CASEMENT, Sir Roger David (1864–1916) Irish patriot and British consular official, born in Sandycove, County Dublin. He went to Africa for the British colonial service, and condemned the treatment of native workers (1904). As consul-general at Rio de Janeiro he denounced Putumayo rubber atrocities. Knighted in 1911, he joined the Irish Volunteers in 1913, and at the outbreak of World War I went to Berlin to try to obtain German help for Irish independence. In April 1916 he was arrested on landing in Ireland from a German submarine to head the Sinn Fein rebellion. He was tried in England for high treason, and hanged. His controversial 'Black Diaries', revealing, among other things, homosexual practices, were long suppressed by the government, but ultimately published in 1959.

CASEY, Richard Gardiner, Baron Casey (1890–1976) Australian statesman, born in Melbourne. He was elected to the House of Representatives in 1931. He became first Australian minister to the USA in 1940, minister of state in the Middle East (a war cabinet rank) in 1942, and minister for external affairs in 1951. A life peerage was conferred on him in 1960.

CASH, Johnny (1932–) American country music singer, songwriter and guitarist, born in Kingsland, Arkansas into a cotton farming family, one of the greatest stars of country music. He worked in a car factory and spent four years in the USAF before moving to Memphis and signing to Sun records in 1955. Early songs included 'Cry, Cry, Cry' and 'I Walk The Line'. An interest in expressing counter-culture ideas in the language of country music was reflected in his association with **Bob Dylan** in the late 1960s. Nicknamed 'The Man In Black' after a 1971 hit of that name, other of his hits have included 'Don't Take Your Guns To Town' (1959), 'Ring of Fire' (1963), 'A Boy Named Sue' (1969) and 'A Thing Called Love' (1972).

CASH, Martin (1810–77) Irish-born Australian bushranger, born in Enniscorthy. In 1827 he was transported to Australia for seven years for theft and attempted murder. In 1831 he received his ticket-of-leave, but was soon on the run again, accused of cattle-stealing. He arrived in Hobart, Tasmania, in 1837 but three years later was sentenced to seven years for possession of stolen goods. With two others he escaped from the prison at Port Arthur, and took up a career of bushranging throughout Tasmania. After shooting a constable in 1843 he was sentenced to death, later commuted to life imprisonment on the penal settlement of Norfolk Island, where he became a model prisoner. He married a fellow-prisoner, received a pardon in 1853, returned to Hobart where he was appointed a constable and was for some years caretaker of the Botanic Gardens there.

CASIMIR the name of many Polish sovereigns. Under **Casimir I** in 1041, Christianity was established. **Casimir III**, the **Great** (1310-70), king from 1333, founded Cracow University (1364).

CASMIR-PÉRIER, Jean Pierre Paul (1847–1907) French statesman, born in Paris. He was a moderate Republican deputy from 1874, became under-secretary for instruction and for war, vice-president and president of the Chamber (1885–93), premier, December 1893 to May 1894, then again president of the Republic, but resigned in January 1895.

CASLON, William (1692–1766) English type-founder, born in Cradley, Worcestershire. He set up in business as a gun engraver and toolmaker in London in 1716, but soon began cutting type for printers, especially **William Bowyer**. His graceful 'old face' Caslon types were extensively used in Europe and the USA until the end of the 18th century, when they went out of fashion. Revived 50 years later, they have retained their popularity to the present day. His son William (1720–78) carried on the business.

CASORATI, Felice (1886–1963) Italian painter, born in Novara, Piedmont. A pupil of Vianello, he was one of the exponents of Italian Neoclassicism and is noted for his series of portraits of women, from which may be singled out the character studies of *The Heiress* and *The Cousin*.

CASS, Lewis (1782–1866) American statesman, born in Exeter, New Hampshire. He was called to the Ohio bar in 1803, but rose to be general in the war of 1812.

He was then for 18 years civil governor of Michigan, which under his skilful administration became a settled state. From 1831 to 1836 he was secretary of war, and in 1836–42 minister at Paris. He twice failed in a try for the presidency, sat in the senate 1845–57, and was secretary of state in 1857–60. His position was generally one of compromise, but he was bitterly hostile to Britain. He published works on the Indians (1823) and France (1840).

CASSAGNAC, Adolphe Granier de (1806–80) French journalist and politician. He came to Paris in 1832, where his vehement writing in the journals brought him many duels and law-suits. In 1840 he went to the West Indies and married a Creole. Until 1848 a zealous Orléanist, he became a strenuous imperialist, and as such represented his native department from 1852 to 1870. He became editor of the semi-official *Le Pays*.

CASSAGNAC, Paul Adolphe Marie de (1843–1904) French journalist and politician, son of **Adolphe Granier de Cassagnac**. He joined him on *Le Pays* (1866), and fought at Sedan in 1870. Violently imperialist, and as deputy (from 1876) troublesome to friends and foes, he edited the 'Victorist' organ *Autorité*.

CASSANDER (c.354–c.297 BC) son of **Antipater**, from 318 ruler, from 305 king of Macedonia. He put to death **Olympias**, the mother of **Alexander**; also Roxana (Alexander's wife) and her children; and married Thessalonica (Alexander's half-sister), for whom he built and named a city in Macedonia.

CASSATT, Mary (1845–1926) American impressionist painter, born in Allegheny, Pittsburgh. She studied in Spain, Italy and Holland, but worked mainly in France, where she was a pupil and close follower of Degas. Her *Woman and Child Driving* in the Philadelphia Museum is a typical work. She was also renowned for her etching and drypoint studies of domestic scenes.

CASSEL, (Karl) Gustav (1866–1945) Swedish economist, born in Stockholm. Professor there from 1904, he became known as a world authority on monetary problems.

CASSELL, John (1817–65) English publisher, the son of a Manchester innkeeper. After apprenticeship as a carpenter, he came to London in 1836 as a temperance advocate. In 1847 he started as a tea and coffee merchant, and in 1850 turned to writing and publishing educational books and magazines for the working classes (*Cassell's Magazine*, 1852).

CASSIAN, John, St (?360–c.435) Romanian-born monk and theologian. He spent some years as an ascetic in the Egyptian deserts, before being ordained by St **John Chrysostom** at Constantinople in 403. He instituted several monasteries in the south of France, including the Abbey of St Victor at Massilia (Marseilles), which served as a model for many in Gaul and Spain. Cassian was one of the first of the 'semi-Pelagians'. He was the author of *Collationes* (on the Desert Fathers), and a book on monasticism. His feast day is 23 July.

CASSIN, René (1887–1976) French jurist and statesman, born in Bayonne and educated at Aix and Paris universities. He was professor of international law at Lille (1920–29) and at Paris (1929–60), combining this with membership of the French delegation to the League of Nations (1924–38). During World War II he joined General **Charles de Gaulle** in London. He was principal legal adviser in negotiations with the British government and, in the later years of the war, held important posts in the French government in exile in London and Algiers, and subsequently in the Council of State (of which he was president, 1944–60) in liberated France. After the war he was increasingly concerned with the safeguarding of human rights. He was the principal author of the Universal Declaration of the Rights of Man (1948) and played a leading part in the establishment of UNESCO. He was a member of the European Court of Human Rights from 1959, and its president (1965-68). In 1968 he was awarded the Nobel prize for peace.

CASSINI, César François (1714–84) French astronomer, son of **Jacques Cassini**. In 1765 he succeeded his father as director of the Paris Observatory, and in 1744 began a topographical map of France.

CASSINI, Giovanni Domenico (Jean Dominique) (1625–1712) Italian-born French astronomer, born near Nice. In 1650 he became professor of astronomy at Bologna, and in 1669 became first director of the observatory at Paris. He greatly extended knowledge of the sun's parallax, the periods of Jupiter, Mars, and Venus, the zodiacal light etc.

CASSINI, Jacques (1677–1756) French astronomer, son and successor of **Giovanni Cassini**. He wrote on astronomy and electricity.

CASSINI, Jacques Dominique de, Comte (1748–1845) French astronomer and successor of **César François Cassini** as director of the Paris Observatory. He completed his father's topographical map. Ennobled, he was imprisoned for a time during the revolution.

CASSIODORUS, Flavius Magnus Aurelius (c.490–c.580) Roman historian and statesman, born in Scylaceum (Squillace) in Calabria. He was minister and counsellor to **Theodoric the Great**, king of the Ostrogoths in Italy, and after his death, chief minister to Queen Amalasontha. He retired c.540 to devote himself to study and writing. He founded monasteries, and promoted the transcription of classical MSS. He compiled an encyclopaedia on learning and the liberal arts for his monks, *Institutiones divinarum et saecularium litterarum*, and a history of the Goths which is no longer extant but which was summarized by **Jordanes**.

CASSIRER, Ernst (1874–1945) German-Jewish philosopher and historian of ideas, born in Wroclaw. Educated at various German universities, he was appointed professor of philosophy (1919), then rector (1930), at Hamburg, but resigned when **Hitler** came to power. He then taught successively at Oxford (1933–35), Göteborg (1935–41), Yale (1941–44) and Columbia (1944–45). He was attracted by neo-Kantianism and had a special interest in the formation of scientific and cultural concepts. His works include *Substanzbegriff und Funktionsbegriff* (1910), *Philosophie der Symbolischen Formen* (1923) and *Sprache und Mythos* (1925).

CASSIUS See **DIO CASSIUS**

CASSIUS, in full **Gaius Cassius Longinus** (d.42 BC) Roman conspirator. He was quaestor to **Crassus** in the Parthian war (54 BC), saving the credit of Roman arms after the commander's disastrous defeat and death, and as tribune of the people (49) attached himself to **Pompey**. After Pharsalia he was taken prisoner and pardoned by **Caesar**. In 44 BC as praetor he allied himself with the aristocrats who resented Caesar's supremacy, and won over **Marcus Brutus**; and the same year Caesar was murdered. But popular feeling blazed out, and **Antonius Marcus (Mark Antony)** seized his opportunity. Cassius fled to the east, united his forces with those of Brutus, and at Philippi, being routed, compelled his freedman to kill him.

CASSIVELLAUNUS British chief of the Catavellauni who fought against **Julius Caesar** on his second invasion, 54 BC.

CASSON, Sir Hugh (1910–) English architect. Educated at Cambridge, he was professor of interior design, Royal College of Art, from 1953 to 1975, and was planning adviser to several authorities after World War II. Among his works are *Homes by the Million* (1947), *Permanence and Prefabrication* (1947), and *Victorian Architecture* (1948). He was President of the Royal Academy from 1976 to 1984.

CASSON, Sir Lewis (1875–1969) English actor-manager and producer, born in Birkenhead. He is known especially for his productions of **Shakespeare** and **Shaw**. He married **Sybil Thorndike** in 1908, and was director of drama to CEMA from 1942 to 1945.

CASTAGNO, Andrea del, properly **Andrea di Bartolo de Simone** (1409–80) Florentine painter, born in Castagno, Tuscany. After early privations he attracted the attention of Bernardetto de' Medici, who sent him to study in Florence. His style shows the influence of **Masaccio** and **Donatello**. In about 1440 he painted some effigies of men hanged by their heels, which established his reputation as a painter of violent scenes. After doing some work in Venice he returned to Florence where he designed a stained-glass window for the cathedral. Soon after, he painted his celebrated *Last Supper* for S Apollonia, now in the Castagno Museum. His series of *Famous Men and Women*, painted for a villa at Legnaia, are now also in the Castagno Museum. His last dated work is the famous equestrian portrait of *Niccolò da Tolentino*—a companion piece to the fresco of *Sir Nicholas Hawkswood* by **Uccello**—in Florence Cathedral. In his own time he was praised as a draughtsman.

CASTAÑOS, Francisco Xavier de, Duke of Bailen (1756–1852) Spanish soldier. During the Peninsular War (1808–14) he compelled 18000 French to surrender at the battle of Bailén (1808), but was defeated by **Lannes** at Tudela. Under **Wellington** he took part in the battles of Albuera, Salamanca, and Vitoria (1813). In 1843 he was appointed guardian of Queen **Isabella II** of Spain.

CASTELAR Y RIPOLL, Emilio (1832–99) Spanish statesman and writer, born in Cadiz. He studied at Madrid, and was professor there of history and philosophy (1856–65). A leader of the republicans, he fled to Paris in 1866 but returned at the 1868 revolution, and in 1873 helped to bring about the downfall of King Amadeus I. He was made head of government in September 1873, but resigned in January 1874, and fled on **Alfonso XII**'s accession. He returned to Spain in 1876, and till his withdrawal from public life in 1893, he often spoke in the Cortes with all his old fire and eloquence. His writings include *La civilisazión en los cinco primeros siglos* (1859), *Vida de Byron* (1873), and political works.

CASTELLI, Ignaz Franz (1781–1862) Austrian poet, born in Vienna. He wrote *Kriegesliedes für die österreichische Armee* (1809), which was banned by **Napoleon**.

CASTELLIO, or **Chateillon, Sebastianus** (1515–63) French theologian, born in Savoy. He studied at Lyon, and about 1540, on **Calvin**'s recommendation, was appointed rector of a school at Geneva. His humanistic views embroiled him with the reformer; and in 1544 he was forced to migrate to Basel, where in 1553 he became Greek professor. He translated the Bible into Latin and French.

CASTELLO BRANCO, Camillo, Visconde de Correia Botelho (1825–90) Portuguese novelist. An illegitimate child whose love of literature and longing for adventure grew from his reading, he became one of the most important of modern Portuguese novelists, with a deep understanding of the life of his people. His work ranges from romances like *The Mysteries of Lisbon*, to closely observed, imaginative interpretations of the everyday Portuguese scene, such as *The Crime of Father Amara*. He was created viscount for his services to literature in 1885. He died by his own hand.

CASTELNAU, Michel de (1520–92) French soldier and diplomat in the service of **Henri II**. He was ambassador to England (1575–85). His *Mémoires* are of great historical value.

CASTELNAU, Noel Marie Joseph Edouard, Vicomte de Curiéres de (1851–1944) French soldier, born in Aveyron of a military, royalist, Catholic family. Educated at St Cyr, he served on the Loire in the Franco-Prussian War (1870–71). He was a member of the Conseil de Guerre in 1913 and took command of the Army of Lorraine in 1914. As commander of all French armies in France, he directed the Champagne offensive (1915), and became **Joffre**'s chief of staff.

CASTELNUOVO-TEDESCO, Mario (1895–1968) Italian composer, born in Florence. He studied under **Pizzetti**, began composing as a boy, and in 1926 brought out his opera *La Mandragola*, based on **Machiavelli**'s book. In addition to two other operas he produced orchestral and instrumental works, but is probably best known for his songs, especially his complete series of the lyrics from **Shakespeare**'s plays.

CASTI, Giambattista (c.1721–1803) Italian poet, born in Prato, Tuscany. He took holy orders, but in 1764 went to Vienna, where he became poet laureate. On **Joseph II**'s death he returned to Florence, and in 1798 went to Paris. He wrote the 48 *Novelle galanti* (1793), and *Gli animali parlanti* (1802), a political satire.

CASTIGLIANO, (Carlo) Alberto (1847–84) Italian civil engineer, born in Asti. He studied at the Polytechnic in Turin and worked as a railway engineer in northern Italy. He is noted for the introduction of strain energy methods of structural analysis in his two theorems of 1873 and 1875, the second of which also states the principle of least work. These theorems represented a great advance on the methods of classical theory of structures, especially in their application to statically indeterminate systems.

CASTIGLIONE, Baldassare, Count (1478–1529) Italian courtier and writer, born near Mantua. In 1505 he was sent by the Duke of Urbino as envoy to **Henry VII** of England, who made him a knight, and was later Mantuan ambassador at the papal court in Rome (1513–24). Thereafter he was papal nuncio for Pope **Clement VII** in Spain, from 1524. His chief work, *Il Cortegiano* (1528), is a manual for courtiers, in dialogue form, and was translated into English by Sir **Thomas Hoby** in 1561. His Italian and Latin poems are models of elegance. His Letters (1769–71) illustrate political and literary history.

CASTLE, Barbara Anne, née **Betts** (1911–) English Labour politician. Educated at Bradford Girls' Grammar School and St Hugh's College, Oxford, she married in 1944 Edward Cyril Castle (1907–), a journalist, worked in local government before World War II, and entered parliament in 1945 as MP for Blackburn. During the 1950s she was a convinced 'Bevanite', outspoken in her defence of radical causes. Chairman of the Labour party (1958–59), after Labour came into power in 1964 she attained cabinet rank as minister of overseas development (1964–65). She was a controversial minister of transport (1965–68), introducing a 70 mph speed limit and the 'breathalyzer' test for drunken drivers, in an effort to cut down road accidents. She took over the newly-created post of secretary of state for employment and productivity (1968–70) to deal with the government's difficult prices and incomes policy. In 1974 she became minister of health and social security. In 1976 when **James Callaghan** became prime minister she returned to the back benches, and became vice-chairman of the Socialist Group in the European parliament (1979–84). Two volumes of her diaries were published in 1980 and 1984.

CASTLE, Vernon and **Irene** (1887–1918 and 1893–1969) English champion ballroom dancers. He was originally Vernon Blythe, born in Norwich, England. She was Irene Foote, from New Rochelle, New York. They married in 1911 and were to rank among the most popular exhibition ballroom dancers and teachers in history, performing with great style and flair throughout America and Europe. He devised such famous dances as the One-step, the Maxixe, the Turkey-trot, the Castle Walk and the Hesitation Waltz. She retired from dancing after his death as an airman in the Royal Flying Corps.

CASTLE, William Ernest (1867–1962) American biologist, born in Ohio. Educated at Harvard, he became professor of geology there (1897) and later of genetics (1908–36), and carried out important research in the field of heredity and natural selection.

CASTLEREAGH, Robert Stewart, Viscount (1769–1822) British statesman, the son of an Ulster proprietor who in 1816 became marquis of Londonderry. Educated at Armagh and Cambridge (for one year), he entered the Irish parliament in 1790 as a Whig member for County Down. In 1795 he turned Tory, although he remained in favour of Catholic emancipation. As Irish chief-secretary from 1797 he devoted himself to promoting **Pitt**'s measure of union, but, with Pitt, retired from office when Pitt's Catholic pledges were defeated. War minister in 1806–07 and 1807–09, he was made scapegoat for the failed Walcheren expedition, the dispute ending in a duel with **Canning** in which Castlereagh was slightly wounded. In 1812 he achieved recognition as foreign secretary under Lord **Liverpool**, but despite his diplomatic success committed suicide. Britain and Europe were indebted to him for the 40 years of peace that succeeded **Napoleon**'s downfall, yet very few statesmen have been so disliked, and a shout of exultation was given as his coffin was carried into Westminster Abbey.

CASTNER, Hamilton Young (1859–99) American analytical chemist, born in New York. Educated at Columbia, he came to Britain in 1886 and invented a new process for the isolation of sodium from brine by electrolysis.

CASTREN, Matthias Alexander (1813–52) Finnish philologist, born in Trevola. A pioneer in the study of Finno-Ugrian, and Ural-Altaic, he carried out ethnographic researches in Lapland, Siberia, and China. One of his sons, Robert (1851–83), wrote on Finnish history.

CASTRIOTA, George See **SKANDERBEG**

CASTRO, Cipriano (c.1858–1924) Venezuelan dictator, born near San Antonio. He became supreme military leader (1899) and president (1902–08). His dictatorship involved Venezuela in financial troubles and a blockade of its ports (1902). Deposed in 1908, he died in exile.

CASTRO, Eugenio de (1869–1944) Portuguese poet, born in Coimbra. He became professor of Portuguese literature in his native town and travelled widely in Europe. In Paris he became interested in Symbolism, which, through his influence, especially with his *Oaristos* (1890), had an effect on Portuguese literature.

CASTRO, Fidel (1927–) Cuban revolutionary, son of a successful sugar planter. He studied law and practised in Havana, fighting cases on behalf of the poor and against the official corruption and oppression which were rife under President **Batista**. In July 1953, with his brother Raúl, also an ardent revolutionary, he led an unsuccessful rising and was sentenced to 15 years' imprisonment, but, released under an amnesty within a year, he fled to the USA and thence to Mexico, all the time organizing anti-Batista activities. In 1956 he landed in Cuba with a small band of insurgents, but was betrayed and ambushed, barely escaping into the Sierra Maestra mountains, from where he waged a relentless guerrilla campaign. The degeneration of Cuba into a police state brought many recruits to his cause, and in December 1958 he mounted a full-scale attack and Batista was forced to flee. Castro, prime minister from February 1959, proclaimed a 'Marxist-Leninist programme' adapted to local requirements. He set about far-reaching reforms in agriculture, industry, and education, not all immediately successful, but sufficiently so to enable his régime to gather strength. His overthrow of US dominance in the economic sphere and routing of the US-connived emigré invasion at the Bay of Pigs (April 1961) was balanced by consequent dependence on communist (mainly Russian) aid and the near-disaster of the 'missiles crisis' of 1962. Despite problems in sugar and tobacco production and two mass exoduses, Castro's popularity remained high. In 1979 he became president of the non-aligned countries movement despite Cuba's continuing substantial economic and political involvement with the USSR.

CASTRO, Guillén de (1569–1631) Spanish dramatist, born in Valencia. He commanded a Neapolitan fortress, but later lived in Madrid, and died in poverty. **Corneille** was deeply indebted to his *Las Mocedades del Cid* (c.1600).

CASTRO, Inez de (d.1355) daughter of a Spanish nobleman. In 1340 she came to Portugal in the train of her cousin Costança, the bride of the Infante, Dom Pedro (the future King Peter I). Her beauty captivated him, and, after Costança's death in 1345, he made her his mistress, in 1354 his wife. But on the orders of his father, Alfonso IV, she was stabbed to death.

CASTRO, João de (1500–48) Portuguese naval commander, born in Lisbon. He volunteered against the Moors at Tangiers, accompanied **Charles V** to Tunis, and had already fought and travelled in the East when in 1545 he sailed to India at the head of a small expedition, where he relieved the city of Diu. He was appointed Portuguese viceroy, but died in the arms of St **Francis Xavier**.

CATALANI, Alfredo (1854–93) Italian composer, born in Lucca. In 1886 he succeeded **Ponchielli** as professor at Milan Conservatory. He aimed to reform the Italian opera as **Wagner** had the German. His finest opera was his last, *La Wally* (1892).

CATCHPOLE, Margaret (1762–1819) English-born Australian pioneer, the subject of **Richard Cobbold**'s *Margaret Catchpole* (1845). Born near Ipswich, Suffolk, she was servant to the Cobbold family of brewers of that town. Twice sentenced to death, for stealing a horse and for subsequently escaping from Ipswich jail, she was transported to New South Wales in 1801, where she was assigned as a servant and nurse. She managed a farm, ran a store, acted as midwife and led a useful life in the community, dying of an illness brought about by helping a neighbour during the bad winter weather. Her letters home to her relations and to the Cobbold family, who retained an interest in her welfare, formed the basis of Cobbold's book and give a valuable account of early 19th-century life in the new colony.

CATENA, Vincenzo (c.1480–1531) Venetian painter. His early work derived strongly from **Giovanni Bellini** and **Cima da Conegliano**. In 1506 he was mentioned as a 'colleague' of **Giorgione**'s and by c.1510 the influence of this painter was apparent. His mature style blends elements of **Titian**, **Palma Vecchio** and other masters of the time. Though never a great originator, he was an educated man and a very competent artist whose best work is seen in his sensitive portraiture.

CATESBY, Mark (c.1679–1749) English naturalist, born in London. He travelled widely in North America in 1710–19 and 1722–26, and published *The Natural History of Carolina, Florida and the Bahama Islands* (1731–48).

CATESBY, Robert (1573–1605) English conspirator, involved in the Gunpowder Plot. A Northamptonshire Catholic of wealth and lineage, he had suffered much as a recusant both by fines and imprisonment. He was named as an accomplice in the Rye Plot (1603) against **James VI and I**, and in 1604 he was the chief instigator of the Gunpowder Plot. He was shot dead while resisting arrest.

CATHCART, Charles Murray, 2nd Earl (1783–1859) Scottish soldier, eldest son of Sir William, 1st **Earl Cathcart**. Styled as Lord Greenock from one of his titles, he joined the army in 1800. He served with high distinction in Italy (1805–06), Walcheren (1809), in the Peninsular War from 1810 to 1812 and at Waterloo (1815). From 1846 to 1849 he was commander-in-chief in British North America.

CATHCART, Sir George (1794–1854) Scottish soldier, son of Sir William 1st Earl **Cathcart**. He joined the army in 1810. He served as aide-de-camp to his father when military commissioner with the Russian army (1813–15), served with the Russians in the campaigns of 1812 and 1813, and with **Wellington** at Quatre Bras and Waterloo. After helping to suppress the Canadian rebellion of 1835, and being deputy-lieutenant of the Tower, in 1852 as governor of Cape Colony he brought to a successful end the 8th Kaffir war (1850–53). He was killed in command of the 4th division at Inkermann in the Crimea. He wrote valuable *Commentaries on the War in Russia and Germany in 1812–13* (1850).

CATHCART, Sir William Schaw, 1st Earl Cathcart (1755–1843) Scottish soldier and diplomat, son of the 9th Baron Cathcart. Educated at Eton and Glasgow, he abandoned law and entered the army, served in the wars in America, Flanders, and Germany. From 1803 to 1805 he was commander-in-chief in Ireland; in 1807 commanded the land forces at the bombardment of Copenhagen. Sent in 1813 as ambassador to St Petersburg, he accompanied Tsar **Alexander I** in his campaigns.

CATHELINEAU, Jacques (1759–93) French royalist leader, born in Pin-en-Mauge, Lower Anjou. In 1793 he led the Vendéans in rebellion, and achieved fame at the storming of Cholet. Supreme command was forced upon him after the victory of Saumur. He was mortally wounded while attacking Nantes.

CATHER, Willa Sibert (1876–1947) American fiction writer, poet and journalist, born on a farm near Winchester, Virginia. Her formative years were spent in Nebraska, and after university there (1891–95), her career began with a well-written but not significant volume of poetry, *April Twilights* (1903). She moved to New York as editor of *McClure's* magazine (1906–12). After her first novel, *Alexander's Bridge* (1912), she wrote a trilogy dealing with immigrants to the USA, the third of which, *My Antonia* (1918), is generally regarded as her best book. A homosexual who wrote primarily about independent women, she was a prolific writer, and other novels include *Death Comes for the Archbishop* (1927) and *One of Ours* (1922), which won the Pulitzer prize.

CATHERINE, St (d.307) traditionally a virgin of royal descent in Alexandria, who publicly confessed the gospel at a sacrificial feast appointed by the emperor Maximinus, and was beheaded, after being tortured on a spiked wheel (later known as a 'catherine' wheel). Her remains were miraculously spirited to Mount Sinai, where her shrine is on display in St Catherine's monastery there. Her feast day is 25 November.

CATHERINE I (1684–1727) empress of Russia, succeeded her husband **Peter I, the Great** in 1725. She was of lowly birth, probably of Lithuanian peasant stock, and was baptized a Roman Catholic with the name of Martha. Married as a young girl to a Swedish army officer who deserted her, she subsequently became mistress to a Russian general, Boris Sheremetev, and to the tsar's principal minister, Prince **Alexander Menshikov**. In 1705 she became mistress to Tsar Peter, changing her name to Catherine and converting to Orthodoxy in 1708. The tsar married her (his second wife) in 1712, following her distinguished conduct while on campaign with her husband during the wars against Sweden. In 1722 Peter passed a law allowing the tsar to nominate a successor and in 1724 chose Catherine, having her crowned empress in that year. After his death in 1725, Prince **Menshikov** ensured her succession to the throne. Although she continued her husband's reforms, she had neither Peter's strong will nor his sense of purpose. She was, however, concerned to alleviate conditions for the peasantry, lowering taxation and reducing the power of local bureaucracies. She was succeeded by Peter's grandson, **Peter II**.

CATHERINE II 'the Great' (1729–96) empress of Russia from 1762. Born in Stettin, the daughter of the Prince of Anhalt-Zerbst, she married Grand Duke **Peter**, heir to the Russian throne as **Peter III**, in 1745. She soon quarrelled with her husband, and became notorious for her love affairs with **Gregory Orlov** and then with **Stanislaw Augustus Poniatowski**. After Peter III's accession in 1762, Catherine was banished to a separate abode, till Peter was dethroned by a conspiracy, and Catherine was made empress. A few days afterwards Peter was murdered by Orlov and others. Catherine now made a show of regard for the Greek Church, although her principles were those of the French philosophers. The government was carried on with great energy, and the dominions and power of Russia rapidly increased. When discontent was voiced, the young Prince Ivan, the hope of the disaffected, was murdered in the castle of Schlüsselburg. From that time internal politics consisted of court intrigues for and against one favourite or another, **Grigori Potemkin** being the best known. The first partition of Poland in 1772 and the Turkish war (1774) vastly increased the empire; so did a war with Sweden (1790) and another Turkish war (1792). The second and third partitions of Poland, and the incorporation of Courland into Russia, completed the triumphs of Catherine's reign.

CATHERINE DE' MEDICI (1519–89) queen of France, and mother of three kings of France, born in Florence, the daughter of **Lorenzo de' Medici**, Duke of Urbino. In 1533, at the age of 14, she married Henri, Duke of Orléans, the future **Henri II** of France, second son of **Francis I**. She became queen on her husband's accession in 1547, but was constantly humiliated by Henry's mistress, Diane of Poitiers, who ruled him completely. When Henri died in 1559, she acted as queen regent during the brief reign of her eldest son, **Francis II** (1544–60), the first husband of **Mary Queen**

of Scots. She was also queen regent during the minority of her second son, **Charles IX** (1550–74), who succeeded to the throne in 1560, and whom she dominated throughout his reign. In the religious wars of 1562–69 (the struggle for power between Protestants and Roman Catholics), she at first supported the Protestant Huguenots against the **Guise** faction, but later supported the Guises and has traditionally been implicated in the fearful St Bartholomew's Day Massacre of 1572. Her third son, Henri of Anjou, having been elected king of Poland in 1573, succeeded to the French throne in 1574 as **Henri III**; but her political influence waned throughout his troubled reign.

CATHERINE OF ARAGON (1485–1536) queen of England, the first wife of **Henry VIII**, and youngest daughter of **Ferdinand** and **Isabella** of Spain. In 1501 she married the 15-year-old Prince Arthur, Prince of Wales, son and heir of **Henry VII**; Arthur died six months later, and in June 1503 she was betrothed to her brother-in-law, the 11-year-old Prince Henry. They were married in 1509, seven weeks after Henry's accession to the throne. Between 1510 and 1514 she bore him four children, who all died in infancy. In 1516 she gave birth to her only surviving child, Princess Mary, later Queen **Mary I** (Mary Tudor). In the years that followed, Henry's infidelities, and his anxiety for a son and heir, soured the marriage, and in 1527 he began to seek an annulment which would allow him to marry his latest favourite, **Anne Boleyn**. Despite strong opposition from the pope, Henry and Anne were secretly married in 1533, and the annulment of the marriage to Catherine was pronounced by Archbishop **Thomas Cranmer** a few months later. Catherine, who had offered a dignified, passive resistance throughout, was sent into retirement at Ampthill in Bedfordshire. In 1534 the pope pronounced her marriage valid, which provoked Henry's final break with Rome and the onset of the Reformation in England. Catherine steadfastly refused to accept the title of 'princess dowager', or to accept the Act of Succession (1534) which declared Princess Mary illegitimate. She died at Kimbolton House, Huntingdonshire, and was buried in Peterborough Abbey.

CATHERINE OF BRAGANZA (1638–1705) queen of England, the wife of **Charles II**, and the daughter of the Duke of Braganza (later King John IV of Portugal). A devout Roman Catholic, she married Charles in 1662, and suffered the humiliation of being forced to receive his mistress, **Barbara Villiers**, and their children, at court. Her own failure to bear children, and her extreme parsimony, alienated her from the people. Charles resisted all pressure for a divorce, but did force her to live apart from him in retirement. In 1692, seven years after Charles' death, she went home to Spain.

CATHERINE OF SIENA, St properly **Caterina Benincasa** (1347–80) Italian mystic, the daughter of a dyer in Siena. She became a Dominican at the age of 16, and so is their patron saint. Her enthusiasm converted hardened sinners, and she prevailed on Pope **Gregory XI** to return from Avignon to Rome. Christ's stigmata were said to have been imprinted on her body in 1375. She wrote devotional pieces, letters, and poems; her *Dialogue*, a work on mysticism, was translated in 1896. She was canonized in 1461. Her feast day is 30 April.

CATHERINE OF VALOIS (1401–37) queen of England, wife of King **Henry V**, and youngest daughter of King Charles VI ('the Foolish') of France. After a stormy courtship, when England and France went to war over Henry's dowry demands, she married Henry at Troyes in 1420. In 1421 she gave birth to a son, the future **Henry VI**. After Henry's death in France in 1422, she secretly married Owen Tudor, a Welsh squire, despite parliamentary opposition; their eldest son, Edmund, Earl of Richmond, was the father of **Henry VII**, the first of the Tudor kings of England. Catherine died at Bermondsey Abbey and was buried in Westminster Abbey.

CATILINA, Lucius Sergius, (anglicized as **Catiline)** (c.108–62 BC) Roman conspirator, born of an impoverished family. An adherent of **Sulla**, he was elected praetor in 68, and next year governor of Africa, but was disqualified from the consulship in 66 on charges of maladministration. Disappointed and crippled by debt, he entered into a conspiracy with other Roman nobles. In 63 he devised a plan for assassinating **Cicero** and the hostile senators, and other details of a complete revolution—details soon made known to Cicero. When the assassins came to the consul's house, they were repulsed; and when two days later Catilina appeared in the senate, Cicero made his famous speech against him. Catilina's reply was drowned in cries of execration. He escaped from Rome, but others of the conspirators were arrested and executed. Insurrections in several parts of Italy were suppressed; and in January 62 Catilina encountered the forces of the republic at Pistoria (now Pistoia). After a desperate battle he was defeated and slain.

CATINAT, Nicolas (1637–1712) French soldier and marshal of France, born in Paris. He defeated Amadeus II of Savoy at Staffarda (1690) and Marsaglia (1693). In the War of the Spanish Succession (1701–12) he commanded the French forces but was soon superseded.

CATLIN, George (1796–1872) American artist and author, born in Wilkes-Barre, Pennsylvania. He studied law, but soon turned to drawing and painting. During 1832–40 he was studying the Indians of the Far West, everywhere painting portraits (470 full length) and pictures illustrative of life and manners, now in the National Museum at Washington. He spent eight years in Europe with a Far West show; travelled (1852–57) in South and Central America; and again lived in Europe until 1871. His works include *Manners of the North American Indians* (2 vols, 1841), *The North American Portfolio* (1844), and *Last Rambles in the Rocky Mountains* (1868).

CATO, Dionysius (4th century) Roman writer, the supposed author of a 4th-century volume of 164 moral precepts in Latin dactylic hexameters, known as *Dionysii Catonis disticha de moribus ad filium*, which was a great favourite during the Middle Ages. An English version by Benedict Burgh was printed by **Caxton** before 1479.

CATO, Marcus Porcius, 'the Elder' (234–149 BC) also known as 'the Censor', Roman statesman and orator, born in Tusculum, of peasant stock. He distinguished himself in the 2nd Punic War (218–202) at the capture of Tarentum (209), and became successively quaestor, aedile, praetor, and consul (195). In Spain he crushed a formidable insurrection; and in 191 he gained glory in the campaign against Antiochus. Meanwhile, he strove to stem the tide of Greek refinement and luxury, and advocated a return to a simpler and stricter social life after the ancient Roman pattern. In 184 elected censor, he discharged so rigorously the duties of his office that 'Censor' became his permanent surname. He repaired watercourses, paved reservoirs, cleansed drains, raised the rents paid by the tax-farmers and reduced the contract prices paid by the state. More questionable reforms were those in regard to the price of slaves, dress, furniture, equipages, and the like. Good and bad innovations he opposed with equal intolerance. Sent on a mission to Carthage in 175, he was so impressed by the dangerous power of the Carthaginians that afterwards he ended every speech in the senate with the words 'Carthage must be destroyed' (*Carthago delenda est*). He lived to see the start of the 3rd Punic War (149–146). He wrote several works, of which only the *De Re Rustica* and a few fragments of his *Origines*, a summary of the Roman annals, have been preserved.

CATO, Marcus Porcius, 'the Younger' (95–46 BC), great-grandson of **Cato the Elder**, called 'Uticensis' from Utica the place of his death. Raised in the household of **Marcus Livius Drusus**, he served in the campaign against Spartacus (72 BC). Military tribune in 67, he brought back with him from Greece the Stoic philosopher Athenodorus. As quaestor (65–64) he carried through a rigorous reform into the treasury offices. As tribune (63) he delivered a famous speech denouncing **Caesar** as an accomplice of **Catilina**, and began a course of strenuous opposition to **Crassus**, **Pompey**, and Caesar, which hastened the formation of the first triumvirate. He was afterwards forced to side with Pompey, and after the battle of Pharsalia (48) escaped into Africa, and undertook the defence of Utica. When he had tidings of Caesar's decisive victory at Thapsus (46), he resolved to die rather than surrender; and, after spending the night reading **Plato**'s *Phaedo*, committed suicide.

CATROUX, Georges (1879–1969) French soldier, born in Algiers. He served in World War I, was governor-general of Indo-China (1939–40), commanded the Free French forces in Syria and the Near East in 1940–41, and became governor-general of Algeria in 1943. In 1945–46 he was ambassador in Russia.

CATS, Jacob (1577–1660) Dutch statesman and poet, born in Brouwershaven in Zeeland. After studying law at Leiden and Orléans, he settled at Middelburg. He rose to a position of authority in the state, and was twice ambassador in England (1627 and 1652). From then till his death, 'Father Cats' lived at his villa near the Hague, writing the autobiography printed in the 1700 edition of his Poems.

CATT, Carrie Clinton Chapman, née **Lane** (1859–1947) American reformer and pacifist, born in Ripon, Wisconsin. Educated at Iowa State College, she joined the staff of the National American Woman Suffrage Association in 1890, and later became its president (1900-04 and 1915–47), effecting dramatic changes in the organization and helping to bring about the 19th Amendment (1920), thus securing the vote for women. She helped establish the League of Women Voters (1919), and spent the later years of her life campaigning for world peace.

CATTELL, Raymond B (1905–) English psychologist, born in Devon. Educated at London University, where he took a PhD in psychology following a first degree in chemistry, he taught at Harvard, Clarke and Duke Universities before World War II, and after the war became research professor and director of the Laboratory of Personality Assessment at Illinois University. He later moved to the University of Hawaii. He applied the statistical techniques of factor analysis to the study of personality differences, with the aim of being able to establish psychological dimensions along which people could be measured and compared. He devised a lengthy questionnaire (the 16 PF scale) from which is derived a personality profile of 16 scores for the person tested. His contributions to psychology have been mainly methodological and theoretical, and he has written widely on various statistical techniques of multivariate analysis (ie, the analysis of empirical data in terms of many concurrent souces of variation), and is a recipient of the Wenner-Gren prize of the New York Academy of Science.

CATTERMOLE, George (1800–68) English water-colour painter and book illustrator, born in Dickleborough, Norfolk. He was known for his antiquarian and architectural paintings, and for his illustrations of Sir **Walter Scott**'s *Waverley Novels*.

CATULLUS, Gaius Valerius (c.84–c.54 BC) Roman lyric poet, born in Verona, the son of a wealthy and well connected family. He lived mainly in Rome, where he settled about 62 BC, and in his villas at Tibur and Sirmio. He began to write verses when a boy of 16. In Rome he became friendly with **Cicero**, the **Metelli**, Hortensius, and probably **Lucretius**; and in Rome he met 'Lesbia', a married woman to whom he sang in verses unequalled in the lyric poetry of passion. A final rupture seems to have happened in 57 BC, and in that year he accompanied the governor, Memmius, to his province of Bithynia. He returned to Rome disappointed in his hopes of enriching himself, and entered impetuously as an aristocrat into the contest of parties. A fiery, unscrupulous partisan, he assailed his enemies, including **Julius Caesar**, with equal scurrility and wit. His extant works comprise 116 pieces, many of them extremely brief, while the longest contains only some 400 lines. But in this slender body of poetry, there are, besides the magnificent love poems, graceful, playful verses of society, fierce, satiric poems, elaborate descriptive and mythological pieces (some of them adapted from the Greek), and the strange, wild, imaginative *Attis*. The text of the works, lost for more than three hundred years, was discovered in the 14th century at Verona.

CAUCHY, Augustin Louis, Baron (1789–1857) French mathematician, born in Paris. He studied to become an engineer, but ill health forced him to retire and teach mathematics at the École Polytechnique. After the 1830 revolution he exiled himself to Turin and Prague, and returned to Paris in 1838. He did important work on partial differential equations, the wave theory of light and the mathematical theory of elasticity, but is primarily remembered as the founder of the theory of functions of a complex variable which was to play a leading role in the development of mathematics for the rest of the 19th century. He wrote an influential *Cours d'analyse* (1821). In algebra he gave a definitive account of the theory of determinants, and developed the ideas of group theory which had appeared in the work of **Joseph Louis de Lagrange** and **Évariste Galois**.

CAULAINCOURT, Armand de (1772–1827) French soldier and statesman. A devoted supporter of **Napoleon**, he was made a general of division in 1805, and shortly after created Duke of Vicenza. He served as ambassador to Russia (1807–11) and minister for foreign affairs (1813–14). During the Hundred Days he resumed the office, receiving a peerage of France, of which he was deprived after the restoration.

CAUS, or Caulx, Salomon de (1576–1626) English Huguenot engineer, architect and inventor, born in Dieppe. He spent much of his time in England and Germany. His *Les Raisons des forces mouvantes avec diverses machines* (1615) anticipated the invention of the steam engine.

CAVACO SILVA, Anibal (1939–) Portuguese politician, born in Loule. After studying economics in Britain and the USA he became a university teacher and then a research director in the Bank of Portugal. With the gradual re-establishment of constitutional government after 1976, he was persuaded by colleagues to enter politics and was minister of finance (1980–81). In 1985 he became leader of the Social Democratic party (PSD) and prime minister. Under his cautious, conservative leadership, Portugal joined the European Community (EC) in 1985 and the Western European Union (WEU) in 1988.

CAVAFY, Constantine P, pen-name **of C P Kavafis** (1863–1933) Greek poet, born in Alexandria, Egypt, of a Greek merchant family. After his father's death in 1872 he was taken by his mother to England for five years, and apart from three years in Istanbul (1882–85) he spent the rest of his life in Alexandria, where he worked as a civil servant, making it the setting, either physical or symbolic, of much of his poetry. His work tends to diverge into the erotic—in which he was one of the first modern writers to deal explicitly with homosexuality—and the historical, in which he recreates the world of Greece and Alexandria in the Hellenistic period. His view of life is essentially tragic. His first book, containing 14 poems, was privately published when he was 41, and reissued five years later with an additional seven poems. He published no further work during his lifetime, preferring to distribute his work among his friends, but in recent years he has come to be regarded as one of the finest and most influential modern Greek poets. Some of his early verse was written in English, but it was not until the 1950s that his work became available in English translation. His best-known poems are, perhaps, his earlier ones, such as *I Polis* (The City) and *Perimenondas tous Varvarous* (Waiting for the Barbarians).

CAVAIGNAC, Louis Eugène (1802–57) French soldier, born in Paris, a son of General Jean Baptiste Cavaignac (1762–1829), a member of the National Convention. Exiled to Algeria as a republican (1832), he became governor-general there in 1848, but was soon recalled to Paris and became minister of war. As military dictator he quelled the formidable insurrection of June 1840. In the *coup d'état* of December 1851 he was arrested but soon released; and though he refused to adhere to the Empire, he was permitted to reside in France.

CAVALCANTI, Bartolommeo (1503–62) Florentine noble. He led a revolt against the **Medici**, and was afterwards employed by Pope **Paul III**.

CAVALCANTI, Guido (1230–1300) Italian poet and friend of **Dante**. He married a Ghibelline, and was banished by the **Guelfs.** He returned to Florence only to die. His works, which included ballads and love poetry, were translated by **Rossetti** and **Ezra Pound**.

CAVALCASELLE, Giovanni Battista (1820–97) Italian art historian, born in Legnano. One of **Garibaldi**'s revolutionaries, he became inspector of the Museo Nazionale in Florence and director of fine arts in Rome. He is noted for his joint authorship, with Sir **Joseph Archer Crowe**, of *Early Flemish Painters* (1856), *History of Painting in Italy* (1864–71), and other authoritative works.

CAVALIER, Jean (1681–1740) French insurgent, a baker of Anduze. In 1702 he became a leader of the Huguenot Camisards, being a prophet and preacher. He surrendered to **Villars** in 1704, and entered the service of Savoy. He settled with a British pension in England, and died in Chelsea, governor of Jersey.

CAVALIERI, Emilio de' (c.1550–1602) Italian composer, born in Rome. He lived mainly at the Florentine court of the Medici, where he was inspector general of arts. His dramatic works were forerunners of opera and oratorio.

CAVALIERI, Francesco Bonaventura (1598–1647) Italian mathematician, born in Milan. Professor at Bologna University, his 'method of indivisibles' began a new era in geometry and paved the way for the introduction of integral calculus.

CAVALLI, Francesco, originally **Caletti-Bruni** (1602–76) Italian composer, who assumed the name of his patron, born in Crema. A pupil of **Monteverdi**, he was organist and *maestro di capella* of St Mark's in Venice. As an opera and church composer he prepared the way for **Alessandro Scarlatti**.

CAVALLINI, Pietro (1259–1344) Italian painter and artist in mosaic, born in Rome, a contemporary of **Giotto**. His mosaics in S Maria in Trastevere are notable, as is the fragmentary *Last Judgement* fresco in S Cecilia in Trastavere. Both date from the early 1290s.

CAVE, Edward known as **'Sylvanus Urban'**, (1691–1754) English printer, born in Newton near Rugby, a cobbler's son. A journalist to trade, he set up a small printing office in London, and in 1731 founded the *Gentleman's Magazine*, which he edited under the pseudonym 'Sylvanus Urban, Gent'. **Samuel Johnson** became its parliamentary reporter in 1740.

CAVELL, Edith Louisa (1865–1915) English nurse, second daughter of the rector of Swardeston, Norfolk. In 1907 she became the first matron of the Berkendael Medical Institute in Brussels, which became a Red Cross hospital during World War I. In August 1915 she was arrested by the Germans and charged with having helped about 200 Allied soldiers to escape to neutral Holland. Tried by court-martial, she did not deny the charges and was executed.

CAVENDISH the surname of the ducal house of Devonshire, a family directly descended from the chief-justice, Sir John Cavendish, who in 1381 was beheaded at Bury St Edmunds by Jack Straw's followers; and from Sir William Cavendish of Cavendish, Suffolk (c.1505–1557), a brother of **Wolsey**'s biographer. His third wife, the celebrated 'Bess of Hardwick', afterwards Countess of **Shrewsbury**, brought Chatsworth into the family; and William, their second son, was in 1618 made Earl of **Devonshire**.

CAVENDISH, Spencer Compton, 8th Duke (1833–1908) eldest son of William, 7th Duke of Cavendish, but for 33 years known as Marquis of Hartington. He was educated at Trinity College, Cambridge, and entered parliament in 1857. Between 1863 and 1874 he held office as Lord of the Admiralty, under-secretary for war, war secretary, postmaster-general and, from 1871, chief secretary for Ireland. In February 1875, on **Gladstone**'s temporary abdication, he was chosen leader of the Liberal opposition, a post which he filled admirably and in 1880, on the fall of the **Disraeli** administration, was invited by the queen to form a ministry. He declined the offer, choosing to serve under Gladstone.

CAVENDISH, William, 1st Duke of Devonshire (1640–1707) English soldier and statesman, and builder of Chatsworth House. A steadfast Whig under **Charles II** and **James II**, he was leader of the anti-court and anti-Romanist party in the House of Commons, and was a strong supporter of the 'Glorious Revolution' of 1688 that brought **William III** to the throne. He was created Duke of Devonshire and Marquis of Huntingdon in 1694 in recognition of his services.

CAVENDISH, William, 4th Duke of Devonshire (1720–64) English statesman. The great-grandson of William, the 1st Duke of **Cavendish**, he was prime minister from 1756 to 1757.

CAVENDISH, William, 5th Duke of Devonshire (1748–1811) English nobleman. In 1774 he married the beautiful Lady Georgiana Spencer (1757–1806), a leader of society who gathered a glittering circle of literary and political friends, and was painted by **Gainsborough** and **Reynolds**.

'CAVENDISH' See **JONES, Henry**

CAVENDISH, George (c.1500–c.1562) English courtier and author. He became gentleman-usher to Cardinal **Wolsey** at least as early as 1527, and was in attendance to him until 1530. He afterwards retired to his house at Glemsford, in Suffolk, where he lived quietly with his wife. He wrote a *Life of Cardinal Wolsey* (1557, first published in 1641).

CAVENDISH, Henry (1731–1810) English natural philosopher and chemist, eldest son of Lord Charles Cavendish, and a grandson of the Duke of Devonshire, born in Nice. He attended Peterhouse College, Cambridge, but left without a degree. Having inherited a fortune from his uncle he lived as a recluse in London, and devoted his life to scientific investigations. In 1760 he discovered the extreme levity of inflammable air, now known as hydrogen gas—a discovery which led to balloon experiments; and later, he ascertained that water resulted from the union of two gases—a discovery which was made simultaneously by **James Watt**. The 'Cavendish Experiment' was an ingenious device for estimating the density of the earth. He also wrote on astronomical instruments. The Cavendish Physical Laboratory at Cambridge was named after him and contains most of his apparatus.

CAVENDISH, Thomas (c.1555–c.1592) English navigator, and circumnavigator of the globe, born in Trimley St Martin, near Ipswich. After squandering his patrimony at court, he shared in Sir **Richard Grenville**'s expedition to Virginia (1585). In 1586, he sailed with three ships for the Pacific, where he burned three Spanish towns and 13 ships; then, with a rich booty, but only his largest vessel, the *Desire*, he returned by the Cape of Good Hope to England, in 1588. Queen **Elizabeth** knighted him. A second expedition (1591) ended in utter disaster, and he died off Ascension.

CAVENDISH, William, Duke of Newcastle (1592–1676) English soldier and royalist, nephew of the first Earl of Devonshire. Educated at St John's College, Cambridge, he was created Knight of the Bath by **James II** in 1610 and Earl of Newcastle in 1628 by **Charles I** after munificent entertainment at the family seat at Welbeck. In 1638 he was appointed governor to his son, the future **Charles II**. His support of the king in the Civil War was generous. As general of all the forces north of the Trent, he had power to issue declarations, confer knighthood, coin money, and raise men; the last function he executed with great zeal. After Marston Moor (1644) he lived on the Continent, at times in great poverty, till the Restoration. In 1655 he was created Duke of Newcastle. He was author of two works on horsemanship, and of several plays. His second wife, Margaret Lucas (1624–74), also wrote poems and plays.

CAVENTOU, Joseph Bienaimé (1795–1877) French chemist, born at St Omer, he became professor at the École de Pharmacie, Paris. In 1817, in collaboration with **Pierre Joseph Pelletier**, he introduced the term *chlorophyll*. They also discovered quinine (1820), strychnine, brucine, and cinchonine.

CAVOUR, Count Camillo Benso di (1810–61) Italian statesman and restorer of Italian nationality, born in Turin of an ancient Piedmontese house. Unable to reconcile his liberal opinions with his position in the army, he retired in 1831. With Count Cesare **Balbo** in 1847 he established a newspaper, *Il Risorgimento*, in which he advocated a representative system; on his suggestion the king was petitioned for a constitution, and this was granted in 1848. He held an important place in **D'Azeglio**'s ministry, and succeeded him as premier from 1852 to 1859, when he started the Sardinian policy, making Sardinia a power in Europe. His measures greatly improved the country's financial status, and following Sardinia's participation in the Crimean War, he managed to bring the Italian question before the Congress of Paris in 1856. In 1858 he negotiated with **Napoleon III** to drive the Austrians out of Italy, but was bitterly disappointed when the peace of Villafranca left Venetia Austrian. He resigned briefly, but returned in 1860 and achieved his aim, seeing **Victor Emanuel II** declared king of Italy with only Rome and Venetia separate still.

CAXTON, William (c.1422–c.1491) the first English printer, born in the Weald of Kent, possibly at Tenterden. In 1438 he was apprenticed to a London mercer, and then went to Bruges in 1446, where he prospered and was in 1462–70 acting 'governor of the English nation', ie of the Merchant Adventurers. He had diplomatic dealings with Burgundy and the Hanseatic League. In 1471 he attached himself to the household of Margaret, Duchess of Burgundy, **Edward IV**'s sister. He probably learned the art of printing when he was in Cologne 1471–72. In Bruges he joined with the Flemish calligrapher Colard Mansion to set up a press; and in 1474 and 1475 he put through the press the first book printed in the English tongue, the *Recuyell of the Historyes of Troye*, which he himself had translated. *The Game and Playe of the Chesse* was another of his earliest publications. Late in 1476 he set up his wooden press in Westminster, where Tothill Street now is. The *Dictes or Sayengis of the Philosophres* (1477), translated from the French by the 2nd **Earl Rivers**, is the first book proved to have been printed in England. Of about 100 books printed by him over a third survive in unique copies or fragments only. Among the important books to come from his press were two editions of **Chaucer**'s *Canterbury Tales*, **Gower**'s *Confessio Amantics*, and **Malory**'s *Le Morte d'Arthur*.

CAYLEY, Arthur (1821–95) English mathematician, born in Richmond, Surrey. His father was an English merchant in St Petersburg and he lived in Russia till the age of eight. He graduated from Trinity College, Cambridge, as senior wrangler in 1842. Called to the bar in 1849, he wrote nearly 300 mathematical papers during 14 years' practice in conveyancing. In 1863 he was elected first Sadlerian professor of pure mathematics at Cambridge. His principal contributions to mathematics are his theory of invariants and covariants, and his work on matrices and analytical geometry; his collected mathematical papers fill 13 volumes.

CAYLEY, Sir George (1771–1857) English engineer and pioneer of aviation, born in Scarborough. He constructed and flew a glider with a wing area of 300 square feet, probably the first heavier-than-air machine. In 1853 he constructed the first successful man-carrying glider. He also interested himself in railway engineering, allotment agriculture, and land reclamation methods, invented a new type of telescope, artificial limbs, the caterpillar tractor, and the tension wheel. He helped to found the Regent Street Polytechnic, London.

CAYLUS, Anne Claude Philippe de Tubières, Comte de (1692–1765) French antiquarian, born in Paris. After serving in the Spanish War of Succession, he travelled in Italy and the Levant, returning to Paris in 1717 to devote himself to the study of antiquities. His multi-volume catalogue of antiquities, including material from Egypt and Europe as well as the classical world (1752–64), is one of the greatest antiquarian works of the Enlightenment.

CEADDA, St See **CHAD**

CEAUSESCU, Nicolae (1918–89) Romanian ruler, head of state from 1974. Born of peasant stock and educated at the Academy of Economic Studies, Bucharest, Ceausescu joined the Communist party in Romania at the age of 15. He was imprisoned twice during his youth for anti-Fascist activities, and in 1945 became secretary of the Bucharest branch of the Communist party. After holding numerous political posts, he became secretary-general of the Romanian Communist party in 1965 and president of the State Council in 1967, thereby attaining the leading position in both party and state. He was elected president of Romania in 1974. Re-elected in 1980 and 1985 he ruled in a personalized manner, promoting family members, including his wife Elena, to senior state and party positions. Despite his attempts to promote industrialization, Romania's economy, under his direction, badly stagnated from the later 1970s and there were serious human rights abuses, particularly against the country's ethnic Hungarian community. Internal opposition to Ceausescu's repressive and increasingly bizarre policies led to his dramatic overthrow in a bloody, revolutionary coup in 1989 in which the resource-starved army turned against him. He was caught attempting to flee the country and, along with his wife, was summarily tried and executed.

CECCHETTI, Enrico (1850–1928) Italian dancer, teacher and choreographer, born in Milan. He is most closely associated with Russia, where he worked from 1887 to 1902. After performing in Italy, London and the USA he settled in Russia, first as dancer with the Imperial Ballet in St Petersburg (Leningrad) and then as teacher, developing the talents of stars like **Anna Pavlova**. He was ballet master of **Diaghilev**'s Ballet Russes for 15 years. Though he choreographed several works, he is remembered for the influential ballet technique he developed, which is still highly regarded today.

CECIL (c.1500-c.1560) name of an English family of statesmen, descended from David Cecill, a sheriff of Northamptonshire (1532–33) and MP. The earldoms of Exeter and Salisbury characterize two branches of the family founded by two sons of **William Cecil, 1st Baron Burghley**. They became marquisates in 1789 (Salisbury) and 1801 (Exeter).

CECIL, Lord (Edward Christian) David Gascoyne (1902–86) English literary critic, younger son of **James Edward Hubert Gascoyne Cecil**. He was professor of English literature at Oxford from 1948 to 1970. Known chiefly as a literary biographer—**Cowper** (in *The Stricken Deer*, 1929), *Sir Walter Scott* (1933), *Jane Austen* (1935), *Thomas Hardy* (1943) and **Max Beerbohm** (*Max*, 1964)—he also wrote an effective political biography of **Melbourne** in two volumes—*The Young Melbourne* (1939) and *Lord M* (1954). He also published a collection of essays, *The Fine Art of Reading* (1957).

CECIL, David George Brownlow, 6th Marquis of Exeter, known as **Lord Burghley** (1905–) English athlete. He won the Olympic gold medal for the 400 metre hurdles (1928) and eight Empire championships. From 1936 he presided over the Amateur Athletic Association and the British Olympic Association, which was responsible for organizing the 1948 Olympic Games in London.

CECIL, Sir Edward, 1st Baron Wimbledon (1572–1638) English courtier, third son of Thomas, 1st earl of Exeter. He commanded in the Low Countries (1596–1610) and the unsuccessful expedition against Cadiz (1625), but avoided censure through **Buckingham**'s favouritism.

CECIL, James Edward Hubert Gascoyne, 4th Marquis of Salisbury (1861–1947) English Conservative politician, son of **Robert Cecil** (3rd Marquis of Salisbury) and father of **Robert Cecil** (5th Marquis of Salisbury) and Lord **David Cecil**. He served in the Boer war, was lord privy seal (1903–05), lord president of the Council (1922–23) and leader of the House of Lords (1925–29).

CECIL, Robert, 1st Earl of Salisbury (c.1563–c.1612) English statesman, son of **William Cecil**. He was made 1st Viscount Cranbourne by **James I** (1604) and earl (1605) in return for his services as **Elizabeth**'s secretary of state, in securing James's succession to the English crown. Lord treasurer from 1608, he remained James's chief minister till his death.

CECIL, Robert, 1st Viscount Cecil of Chelwood (1864–1958) English Conservative statesman, son of **Robert Cecil** (3rd Marquis of Salisbury). Educated at Eton and University College, Oxford, he was called to the bar in 1887, and entered parliament (1903). He was minister of blockade (1916–18), and as under-secretary for foreign affairs (1918) helped to draft the League of Nations Covenant and was British representative at various disarmament conferences. He was president of the League of Nations Union (1923–45) and thereafter an honorary life president of UNA. He resigned from the Cabinet because of the cruiser question with the United States (1927) and was awarded the Nobel peace prize (1937). He wrote books on commercial law, the church, and peace (1928 ff.), and his autobiography, *All the Way* (1949).

CECIL, Robert Arthur James Gascoyne-, 5th Marquis of Salisbury (1893–1972) English Conservative statesman, son of **James Edward Cecil**, born at Hatfield House and educated at Eton and Oxford. He became MP for South Dorset in 1929, and in 1935 as Viscount Cranborne became foreign under-secretary. He resigned with his chief, **Anthony Eden**, in February 1938 over the 'appeasement' of **Mussolini**. In the **Churchill** government of 1940 he became paymaster general and was dominions secretary till 1941 when he was called to the Lords. He was colonial secretary, and lord privy seal, and represented Britain at the founding conference of UNO at San Francisco. As leader of the Opposition in the House of Lords (1945–51) he counselled acceptance by the Tory majority of most of the legislation of the political and economic revolution. In the Churchill government of 1951 he became secretary of state for commonwealth relations and in 1952 lord president of the Council. From 1951 to 1957 he was leader of the House of Lords. In January 1957 he (and Churchill) advised the queen on the choice of **Harold Macmillan** (rather than **R A Butler**) as prime minister to succeed Anthony Eden. In March 1957 he resigned the lord presidency in protest against the government's action in releasing unconditionally Archbishop **Makarios** of Cyprus from his Seychelles exile. He conducted the affairs of the House of Lords—which he wished to see reformed (within limits)—with notable distinction and unmatched authority as one of the heads of 'the Establishment'.

CECIL, Robert Arthur Talbot Gascoyne, 3rd Marquis of Salisbury (1830–1903) English Conservative statesman, born at Hatfield House. Educated at Eton and Christ Church, Oxford, he was elected fellow of All Souls' (1853) and Conservative member for Stamford. In 1865 he became Viscount Cranborne and heir to the marquisate on the death of his elder brother, and he proved one of the most effective opponents of **Gladstone**'s Reform Bill of that year. In the **Derby** ministry (1866), Lord Cranborne became Indian secretary; but Lord Derby and **Disraeli** proceeding to concoct a reform bill, Lord Cranborne (like others) resigned, and fought against the measure with extreme pertinacity. In 1868 he succeeded his father as third marquis, and was the strongest opponent of the disestablishment of the Irish Church. In 1869 he was elected chancellor of the University of Oxford. In 1870 he supported the Peace Preservation Bill, but disapproved the Irish Land Act. The bill for abolishing religious tests in the universities gave him much trouble. In January 1874 parliament was dissolved, and the Conservatives came in with a great majority. Lord Salisbury again became secretary for India; but before the end of the year he had again come into collision with his chief on the Public Worship Regulation Act, being described by Disraeli as 'a great master of gibes and flouts and jeers'. In 1878 he succeeded Lord Derby as foreign secretary and accompanied Disraeli (Lord Beaconsfield) to the Berlin Congress. On the death of Disraeli, he succeeded to the leadership of the Conservative Opposition; in June 1885 he became prime minister and secretary of state for foreign affairs, and settled the 'Penjdeh incident'. The contentious Irish Home Rule Bill defeated the Liberals, and Lord Salisbury, backed by Liberal Unionists, was premier again in 1886 and in 1895, when a succession of foreign complications brought the country several times to the verge of war, only averted by the firm, and at the same time conciliatory, attitude of the British government. Turkish massacres in Armenia led to the reopening of the Eastern Question in an acute form, nearly resulting in a European conflagration. Hostilities with the United States seemed imminent owing to the interference of the latter country in a boundary dispute between British Guiana and Venezuela. Dr Jameson's filibustering expedition into the Transvaal at New Year 1896 led to critical relations with the republic, and revealed antagonism on the part of Germany. The jealousy of France at the British occupation of Egypt was actively aroused in April 1896 by Lord Salisbury entering upon the reconquest of the Sudan. And the Cretan insurrection, with the consequent crushing defeat of Greece by Turkey (1897), severely tested the Concert of the Powers. He resigned the foreign secretaryship in 1900; and having remained at the head of the government during the Boer War (1889–1902), retired from public life in July 1902.

CECIL, Thomas, 1st Earl of Exeter, 2nd Baron Burghley (1542–1623) English soldier, son of **William Cecil, Ist Baron Burghley** by his first wife. He served in the Scottish war (1573) and against the Armada (1588), and crushed **Essex**'s rebellion (1601). He was created Earl of Exeter in 1605.

CECIL, William, 1st Baron Burghley or **Burchleigh** (1520–98) one of England's greatest statesmen, father of **Thomas Cecil** and **Robert Cecil**, 1st Earl of **Salisbury** born in Bourn, Lincolnshire. He was the son of Richard Cecil of Burghley, Northamptonshire, who rose high in favour with **Henry VIII**, and left large estates at his death in 1552. Educated at Stamford and Grantham, young Cecil passed in 1535 to St John's College, Cambridge. In 1547 Henry VIII appointed him 'Custos Brevium' and in 1547, under the patronage of the Protector Somerset, he was made master of requests and his secretary in the following year. When Somerset fell from grace Cecil fell too, but in 1550 he returned to office as secretary of state and in 1551 was knighted. During **Mary I**'s reign he adopted Catholicism but had already entered into correspondence with **Elizabeth** who, in 1558, appointed him chief secretary of state. For the next 40 years he was the main architect of the successful policies of the Elizabethan era. He was created Baron Burghley in 1571 and lord high treasurer in 1572, an office he held until his death. He left lavish mansions which he had built or restored, including Burghley, Theobalds in Hertfordshire and Cecil House in the Strand.

CECILIA, St (d.230) Christian martyr, and patron saint of music. According to a highly dubious tradition, she was a Roman maiden of patrician birth compelled to marry a young pagan, Valerian, despite a vow of celibacy. She succeeded in persuading him to respect her vow, and converted him to Christianity. They were both put to death for their faith. Later tradition made her a singer, hence her association with music-making.

CECROPS traditionally the first king of Attica and the founder of Athens.

CELA, Camilo José (1916–) Spanish novelist, born in Iria Flavia, La Coruña. He attended Madrid University and served in **Franco**'s forces; his work is frequently interpreted as an eloquent, aggressive, idiosyncratic reaction to that error of judgment. He has been the dominant novelist in Spain for over 40 years. His first novel, *The Family of Pascual Duarte*, appeared in 1942 and was banned, having stunned readers with its seemingly gratuitous violence. The range of his work is vast and varied but he is best known for *La Colmena* (1951, trans 1953, *The Hive*) which recreates daily life in Madrid in the aftermath of the Spanish Civil War with great sensitivity and feeling for the plight of ordinary people. Others worthy of note are *Viaje a la Alcarría* (1948, trans 1948, *Journey to the Alcarria*) and *San Camilo* (1936, trans 1970). Eccentric, even scatological, he is a candid, combative protagonist who says what he thinks regardless of popularity. A member of the Spanish Royal Academy, he holds a plethora of honorary doctorates. In 1989 he was awarded the Nobel prize for literature.

ČELAKOVSKÝ, Ladišlav Josef (1834–1902) Bohemian botanist, son of the poet František Čelakovsky.. From 1880, he was professor of botany at Prague, notable for his plant morphological works and his *Flora von Böhers* (4 vols, 1867–80).

CELANO, Thomas of (d. c.1255) Italian monk, born in Celano in the Abruzzi. An early disciple of St **Francis of Assisi**, he wrote of his life. He spent the years 1221–28 in the Rhineland. He is reputed to be the author of the hymn *Dies Irae*.

CELESTINE name of five popes; Celestine I (422–32); II (1143–44); III (1191–98); IV (1241); and V, the Neapolitan Pietro di Morrone (1215–96), who, after a long life of ascetic severities, was reluctantly elected pope in 1294. He resigned his office after five months—'the great refusal'—for which **Dante** places him at the entrance of hell. He was imprisoned by his successor, **Boniface VIII**. He founded the Celestines, and was canonized in 1313.

CELINE, Louis-Ferdinand pseud of **L F Destouches** (1894–1961) French novelist, born in Paris, the son of a poor clerk and a lace seamstress. His education was rudimentary and he had various jobs until 1912 when he joined the cavalry. In the first year of World War I he was wounded in the head and shell-shocked in an action for which he was decorated. The suffering, both mental and physical, caused by his wounds dogged him to the end of his days. He was invalided out of the military, took a medical degree, worked as a staff surgeon at the Ford plant in Detroit and later ministered to the poor of Paris, the experience of which, he acknowledged, was invaluable to his literary endeavours. His first novel, *Voyage au Bout de la Nuit* (Journey to the End of Night, 1932), brought international acclaim, and his reputation was enhanced on the publication of his second novel, *Mort à Crédit* (Death on the Installment Plan, 1936). His use of the demotic and his insights into life among the lower classes have influenced many writers, among them **Sartre**, **Burroughs** and **Henry Miller**. In the late 1930s he was a declared anti-semite, and after the liberation of France (1944) he fled to Denmark. He was tried and sentenced to death *in absentia* but this was later reversed and he spent his last years in France, with partial paralysis, tinnitus and close to insanity. His final novels, *D'un Château à L'Autre* (1957) and *Nord* (1960), are ranked with his best.

CELLINI, Benvenuto (1500–71) Italian goldsmith, sculptor, and engraver, born in Florence, and author of one of the most interesting autobiographies ever written. Banished from Florence after a duel, he travelled to Rome, where his skill as an artist in metalwork gained him the favour of the highest nobles and prelates. By his own account he was an expert with sword and dagger as with his goldsmith's tools, and he apparently had no scruple in murdering or maiming any who endeavoured to thwart him. He states that at the siege of Rome in 1527 it was he who killed the **Constable Bourbon**, and that he afterwards shot down **William the Silent** (Prince of Orange) before the castle of St Angelo. He stood in high favour with Pope **Clement VII**, but was eventually flung into prison for the murder of a rival goldsmith. In 1534 he was pardoned and set free by **Paul III**, who wished him to engrave dies in the mint; soon afterwards, having spoken contemptuously of the pope's artistic tastes, he was cast into an *oubliette* of St Angelo. He escaped through his knowledge of the castle's vaults, but was immediately recaptured, and was only saved from the pope's vengeance by the intercession of Cardinal d'Este. For some years he lived alternately in Rome and Florence, Mantua and Naples. In 1537 he was honourably received at the court of **Francis I** of France, but soon returned to Florence, where he worked under the patronage of **Cosimo I de' Medici**, and where he executed his famous bronze *Perseus with the head of Medusa*. He began to write his autobiography in 1558, and died in Florence. His autobiography was first translated in 1822.

CELSIUS, Anders (1701–44) Swedish astronomer, born in Uppsala. In 1730 he became professor at Uppsala University, and in 1742 he devised the centigrade, or 'Celsius', scale of temperature. He advocated the introduction of the Gregorian calendar, and made observations of the aurora borealis. In 1740 he became director of the observatory at Uppsala that had been built in his honour.

CELSUS (2nd century) Roman philosopher. He was a Platonist who published one of the first anti-Jewish and anti-Christian polemics in his *True discourse* (c.178), which was sufficiently notable to merit a response from **Origen** in his *Contra Celsum* (c.248).

CELSUS, Aulus Cornelius (1st century) Roman writer. He compiled an encyclopedia on medicine, rhetoric, history, philosophy, war, and agriculture. The only extant portion of the work is the *De Medicina*, one of the first medical works to be printed (1478).

CENCI, Beatrice (1577–99) Italian beauty, and central figure of a tragedy by **Shelley** (1819). She was the youngest daughter of a wealthy Roman nobleman, Count Francesco Cenci, who conceived an incestuous passion for her. With her stepmother and her brother, Giacomo, she plotted his murder in 1598 by means of two hired assassins. The Cenci family were arrested and tortured, and all three were beheaded, by order of Pope Clement VIII.

CENDRARS, Blaise, originally **Frédéric Louis Sauser** (1887–1961) Swiss novelist, poet and traveller, born in Chaux-de-Fonds, Switzerland. His mother was a Scot and he regarded himself as a cosmopolitan. When he was 15 he ran away from home to work for a jewel merchant with whom he travelled through Russia, Persia and China. He later described this journey in a long poem, *Transsibérien* (1913). In 1910 he met **Apollinaire**, by whom he was much influenced. He wrote his first long poem in America, *Les Paques à New York* (1912) which, with *Transsibérien* and his third and last long poem, *Le Panama ou Les Aventures de Mes Sept Oncles* (written in 1918, published in 1931 in a translation by **John Dos Passos**), was important in shaping the spirit of modern poetry. He was careless with the truth and was fond of apocryphal stories but he did lose an arm fighting for the French Foreign Legion in World War I. A reluctant writer, his poetry is not particularly memorable but his best novels—*La Confession de Dan Yack* (1927–29; 1946; trans *Antarctic Fugue*, 1948), *Moravagine* (1926 trans 1969) and *L'Or* (1925; trans *Sutter's Gold*, 1926)—are less well-known than they ought to be.

CENTLIVRE, Susannah, née **Freeman** (c.1667–c.1723) English dramatist, born probably in Holbeach, Lincolnshire. She was first married at 16 and twice widowed. In 1700 she produced a tragedy, *The Perjured Husband*, and subsequently appeared on the stage in Bath in her own comedy, *Love at a Venture* (1706). In 1706 she married her third husband, Joseph Centlivre, head cook to Queen **Anne** at Windsor. Her 18 plays also included *The Gamester* (1705), *The Busybody* (1709) and *A Bold Stroke for a Wife* (1717).

CENTLIVRES, Albert van de Sandt (1887–1966) South African judge, born in Cape Town and educated at the South African College there. A Rhodes Scholar at Oxford, he became a judge of the Cape provincial division of the Supreme Court of South Africa in 1935, a judge of appeal in 1939 and chief justice from 1950 to 1957. Highly regarded as a judge, he played a substantial part in restoring Roman-Dutch law in South Africa and in extirpating various unfortunate importations from English law. As a result, the Appellate Division restricted the English concept of the duty of care in actions for negligent harm, and reasserted the Roman-Dutch approach, requiring for civil liability a wrongful act, *dolus* or *culpa*, and resulting patrimonial loss.

CERDIC (d.534) Saxon leader who invaded Britain, landing in Hampshire with his son Cynric in 495; by 500 he had created the kingdom of Wessex for himself and founded the West Saxon royal dynasty.

CEREZO AREVALO, Mario Vinicio (1942–) Guatemalan politician. Educated at San Carlos University, he joined the Christian Democratic party (PDCG), founded in 1968. From 1974 there was widespread political violence and democratic government was virtually suspended. With the adoption of a new constitution in 1985 the PDCG won the congressional elections and Cerezo became the first civilian president for 20 years.

CERINTHUS (c.100) Jewish Gnostic heretic, born in Alexandria. He is said to have lived in Ephesus contemporaneously with the aged apostle **John**.

CERUTTY, Percy Wells (1895–1975) Australian athletics coach and trainer, born in Prahan, Victoria. A childhood respiratory disease severely restricted his own athletic career, although in his middle fifties he became a noted distance runner, recording 162 kilometres within a 24-hour span. It is, however, as a coach that he is best remembered, being responsible for the development of the two great Australian middle distance runners, John Landy and **Herb Elliott**. Cerutty was in charge of the Australian team at the 1952 Olympic Games in Helsinki, and in 1954 Landy recorded only the second ever sub four-minute mile.

His success with **Herb Elliott**, who broke that barrier no fewer than 17 times and was never bested at that distance or at 1500 metres, was even more remarkable in the years 1956–62. Cerutty was a man of great asceticism and pioneered such concepts as training over sand dunes and the idea of the 'pain barrier'. He incorporated most of these ideas in his book, *Be Fit or Be Damned!* (1969).

CERVANTES SAAVEDRA, Miguel de (1547–1616) Spanish novelist, and author of *Don Quixote*, born in Alcalá de Henares, the son of a poor medical practitioner. In 1569 he published his first known work, a collection of pieces on the death of the queen. He then travelled to Italy in the service of Cardinal Giulio Acquaviva, and enlisted as a soldier. At the battle of Lepanto a gunshot wound maimed his left hand. After further service against the Turks in Tunis, he was returning to Spain in 1575 when the galley he sailed in was captured by Algerian corsairs, and with his brother Rodrigo and others he was carried into Algiers, where he remained in captivity for five years, during which he made four daring attempts to escape. In 1580 he was ransomed by the efforts of Trinitarian monks, Algiers traders, and his devoted family. Finding no permanent occupation at home, he drifted to Madrid, and tried a literary career. In 1584 he married Catalina de Salazar y Palacios (1565–1626). The marriage was childless, but Cervantes had an illegitimate daughter, Isabel de Saavedra (c.1585–1652). His first important work was *La Galatea*, a pastoral romance, printed at Alcalá in 1585. For some years he strove to gain a livelihood by writing plays, of which two only, *La Numancia* and *Los tratos de Argel*, have survived. In 1587 he became commissary to the fleet at Seville. In 1594 he was appointed as collector of revenues for the kingdom of Granada; but in 1597, failing to make up the sum due to the treasury, he was sent to prison in Seville, released on giving security, but not reinstated. Local tradition maintains that he wrote *Don Quixote* in prison at Argamasilla in La Mancha. In September 1604 leave was granted to print the first part of *Don Quixote*, and early in January 1605 the book came out at Madrid. It was immediately popular, though **Lope de Vega** wrote sneeringly of it; but instead of giving his readers the sequel they asked for, Cervantes busied himself with writing for the stage and composing short tales, or 'exemplary novels' as he called them, which came out as *Novelas Ejemplares* in 1613. His *Viage del Parnaso*, a poem of over 3000 lines in *terza rima*, reviews the poetry and poets of the day. In 1614 a pseudonymous writer brought out a spurious second part of *Don Quixote*, with an insulting preface, which served to spur Cervantes to the completion of the genuine second part (1615). While it was in the press he revised his various plays and interludes, and a little before his death, he finished the romance of *Persiles y Sigismunda*. For *Don Quixote* Cervantes ranks as one of the great writers of the world, though it is the most carelessly written of all great books. Cervantes wrote it in fits and starts and neglected it for his other work.

CESAIRE, Aimé Fernand (1913–) West Indian poet and playwright, born in Basse-Point, Martinique. One of the best-known poets and playwrights in the Third World, his reputation is based largely on two plays, *The Tragedy of King Christophe* (1963) and an original adaptation of Shakespeare's *The Tempest*. He is also noted for a long poem, the *Notebook of a Return to my Native Land* (1939) and for a biography of the revolutionary, *L'Ouverture* (1961). A militant Marxist and anti-colonialist, he played a large role in rallying decolonized Africans in the 1950s.

CESALPINO, Andrea, Latin **Caesalpinus** (1519–1603) Italian botanist, anatomist, physician and physiologist, born in Arezzo. The most original and philosophical botanist since **Theophrastus**, whose work he revived, he was the author of *De Plantis* (1583). He propounded a theory of the circulation of the blood and initiated scientific plant classification. He was professor of medicine and director of the botanic garden in Pisa, 1553–92, when he became physician to Pope Clement VIII.

CESARI, Giuseppe, or **Il Cavaliere d'Arpino** (c.1568–c.1640) Italian painter, born in Arpino. Honoured by five popes, he is best known for the frescoes in the Capitol at Rome, where he died.

CESAROTTI, Melchiore (1730–1808) Italian scholar and poet, born in Padua. Professor of Greek and Hebrew at Padua from 1768, his translations of **Macpherson**'s *Ossian* (1763) and the *Iliad* threw fresh life into Italian literature. His *Filosofia delle lingue* and *Filosofia del gusto* are the best of his works.

CESNOLA, Count Luigi Palma di (1832–1904) Italian-born American army officer and archaeologist, born near Turin. He fought in the Austrian, Crimean, and American Civil wars, and, having taken American citizenship (1865), became US consul in Cyprus. He was director of the New York Metropolitan Museum from 1879 until his death, and to it he presented his collection of antiquities.

CÉSPEDES, Pablo de (1536–1608) Spanish painter, born in Córdoba. He studied at Rome under **Michelangelo** and **Raphael**. In 1577 he became a canon at Córdoba, where he established a school of art, and was also active as an architect and writer. He painted the *Last Supper* in Córdoba cathedral.

CETEWAYO (d.1884) king of Zululand, 1873–83, and nephew of **Shaka**. When the British invaded Zululand in 1879 he destroyed the garrison at Isandhlwana, but was himself defeated at Ulundi and taken prisoner. After captivity in the Cape of Good Hope and England, he was restored by the British to part of his kingdom in 1883, but was soon driven out by his subjects and died at Ekowa.

CETTI, Francesco (1726–78) Italian Jesuit and naturalist, in whose honour the bird Cetti's Warbler (*Cettia cetti*) was named. Born in Mannheim, Germany, he was educated in Lombardy and at the Jesuit College in Monza. In 1766, at the request of Charles Emmanuel III, king of Sardinia, he was appointed professor of mathematics at the university of Sassari. A distinguished naturalist as well as theologian and philosopher, his great work was a monumental *Storia naturale della Sardegna* (1774–77).

CEULEN, Ludolph van (1540–1610) Dutch mathematician, born in Hildesheim. He devoted himself to finding the value of π and finally worked it out to 35 decimal places ('Ludolph's number'); it was inscribed on his tombstone at Leiden.

CEVA, Giovanni (?1647–1734) Italian geometer, born in Milan. He gave his name to a theorem on concurrent lines through the vertices of a triangle.

CÉZANNE, Paul (1839–1906) French artist, born in Aix-en-Provence. A contemporary and friend of **Zola**, with whom he shared an interest in literature, from 1859 to 1861 he studied law at Aix, entered his father's bank, and in 1862, persuaded by Zola, went to Paris and studied at the Académie Suisse. In Paris he met the circle of painters centred on **Manet**, but found himself not truly in accord with them, and thereafter worked mainly at Aix and l'Estaque, with occasional visits to Paris, where he exhibited at the first and third Impressionist exhibitions in 1874 and 1877. He was influenced by **Pissarro**, with whom he worked at

Auvers and Pontoise (1872–73). He abandoned his former sombre expressionism for the study of nature, as in the famous *Maison du Pendu* of this period in the Louvre, and began to use his characteristic glowing colours. In his later period (after 1886, when he became financially independent of his father) he emphasized the underlying forms of nature—'the cylinder, the sphere, the cone'—by constructing his pictures from a rhythmic series of coloured planes, painting not light but plastic form, and thus becoming the forerunner of Cubism. In 1886 he married Hortense Fiquet, with whom he had had a secret liaison since 1870: she is reputed to have had the occasional task of retrieving completed canvases, abandoned by her husband wherever he happened to have been working on them—for his passion was the actual painting of them, not the possession. Also in 1886, his friendship with Zola was ended by the publication of the latter's novel, *L'Œuvre*, in which the central figure, an unsuccessful and unbalanced Impressionist painter, is in many respects identifiable as Cézanne. Cézanne, who himself described his aim as being 'to make Impressionism something solid and durable like the art of the old masters', obtained recognition only in the last years of his life, and two exhibitions of his work were held by Vollard, in 1895 and 1899. His *L'Homme au chapeau de paille* (c.1871) is in the Metropolitan Museum, New York; his *Aix*: *Paysage rocheux* (c.1887) and *Le Jardinier* (c.1906) are in the Tate Gallery, London; and *La Vielle au chapelet* (c.1897–98) is in the National Gallery, London.

CH'I, Pai-shih (1863–1957) Chinese artist, born in Hsiang T'an, Hunan, into a poor farmer's home. In his boyhood and youth he was a carpenter and woodcarver and took up the study of painting only at 27. He also mastered calligraphy, poetry and seal-carving. Sometimes called China's **Picasso**, his art is deeply rooted in the folk tradition, with a direct and vivid style. His extensive travels and encounters with other artists and scholars enriched his art. Following the advice of fellow artist Ch'en Heng-K'o, he attempted to assimilate influences from the early Ch'ing individualists and to incorporate these into his earlier background of folk art. The innovative style which evolved reflected these influences together with a keen observation of nature. He painted birds, flowers, fruit and landscapes, and many other subjects with a theme from daily life previously considered to be inappropriate subjects for art. His spontaneous, calligraphic and even humorous style was unique. He was a prolific and versatile artist of genius whose school was established as the mainstream of contemporary Chinese painting.

CHABANEUA, François (1754–1842) French chemist, born in Nontron. He began as a student of theology but was expelled on account of his views on metaphysics. Professor of mathematics at Passy when only 17 and with no knowledge of the subject, he turned to the study of physics and chemistry. Later he became professor of mineralogy, physics and chemistry at Madrid, where he carried out the researches on platinum which resulted in 1783 in an ingot of malleable platinum.

CHABRIER, (Alexis) Emmanuel (1841–94) French composer, born in Ambert. His operas are *Gwendoline* (1886), *Le Roi malgré lui* (1887), and *Briséis* (unfinished), but the piece most performed today is his orchestral rhapsody *España*.

CHAD, Old English **Ceadda, St** (d.672) Anglo-Saxon churchman, born in Northumbria. A pupil of St **Aidan** in Lindisfarne, he spent part of his youth in Ireland, and in 664 became abbot of Lastingham, and in 666 bishop of York. Doubt having been cast on the validity of his consecration, he withdrew in 669, but was immediately made bishop of Mercia, fixing the see at Lichfield.

CHADLI, Benjadid (1929–) Algerian politician and soldier, born in Sebaa. In 1955 he joined the guerrillas (*maquisards*) who were fighting for independence as part of the National Liberation Front (FLN). Under **Houari Boumédienne**, defence minister in **Ben Bella**'s government, he was military commander of Algiers, and when Boumédienne overthrew Ben Bella in 1965 he joined the Revolutionary Council. He succeeded Boumédienne as secretary-general of the FLN and president in 1979.

CHADWICK, Sir Edwin (1801–90) English social reformer, born near Manchester. Called to the bar in 1830, he was appointed an assistant poor-law commissioner in 1832, and in his report (1833) he laid the foundation of the later systems of government inspection. He became secretary of the new Poor Law Board (1834–36).

CHADWICK, Sir James (1891–1974) English physicist, born near Macclesfield. He studied at Manchester, Berlin and Cambridge. He worked on radioactivity with **Ernest Rutherford** and in 1934, as a result of the **Curies**' work, was able to confirm the existence of the neutron which Rutherford had postulated in 1920. For this he was awarded the Nobel prize for physics in 1935. He built Britain's first cyclotron in 1935 at Liverpool and during World War II worked on the Manhattan Project (the atomic bomb) in America.

CHADWICK, Lynn (1914–) English sculptor, born in London. Trained as an architect, he turned to abstract constructions and mobiles in 1945. Like **Henry Moore**, he is an abstract artist whose work nevertheless carries suggestions of the human figure. His first one-man show was at Gimpel Fils, London in 1950. This was followed by others in New York, Venice and Zürich, and in 1956 he won the International Prize at the Venice Biennale.

CHADWICK, Roy (1893–1947) English aeronautical engineer, born in Farnworth, son of a mechanical engineer. Educated at the Manchester College of Technology, in 1911 he joined Alliott Verdon-Roe and Roy Dobson in the AVRO company, designing and manufacturing aeroplanes. During World War I he designed many famous types including the Avro 504 trainer. Other designs included the Baby (a truly light aircraft), Avian, Anson (used for RAF coastal reconnaissance) and in World War II the Manchester and the famous Lancaster heavy bombers. Following the war he designed the Tudor and Ashton, both jet-propelled. He was killed in a test flight of the Tudor II prototype.

CHAGALL, Marc (1889–1985) Russian-born French artist, born in Vitebsk. He studied at St Petersburg and in Paris. In 1914 he held a one-man show in Berlin, and for a short time was commissar of fine arts at Vitebsk, but in 1922 he left Russia and settled near Paris. He spent the years 1941–1947 in the USA. Books illustrated by him include **Gogol**'s *Dead Souls* and **La Fontaine**'s *Fables*, but he is most famous for his fanciful painting, in which a visual potpourri of animals, objects, and people from the artist's past life, from his dreams and from Russian folklore, is presented in an arbitrary colour scheme of blues, greens, yellows, and pinks, eg *Bouquet of Flying Lovers* (1947) in the Tate Gallery, London. The word 'Surrealist' is said to have been coined by **Apollinaire** to describe the work of Chagall. He wrote his autobiography, *Ma Vie*, in 1931.

CHAGAS, Carlos Ribeiro Justiniano (1879–1934) Brazilian physician and microbiologist, born in Oliveira, Minás Gerais. He studied at the Medical School of Rio de Janeiro, where he was introduced to the concepts and techniques of bacteriology and scientific medicine. After a few years in private practice, he joined the staff of the Instituto Oswaldo Cruz, where its founder and leading light, Oswald Cruz, befriended him. Much of Chagas's early work was concerned with malaria prevention and control. During one of his field missions, in Lassance, a village in the interior of Brazil, he first described a disease (Chagas' disease) caused by a trypanosome (he named the organism *T. Cruzi* after Cruz). Chagas elucidated its mode of spread through an insect vector, established the trypanosome's virulence in laboratory animals and described its acute and chronic course in human beings. On circumstantial evidence, some historians have suggested that **Charles Darwin** suffered from Chagas' disease.

CHAILLU, Paul du See **DU CHAILLU**

CHAIN, Sir Ernst Boris (1906–79) German-born British biochemist, born in Berlin of Russian Jewish extraction. After studying physiology and chemistry in Berlin, he fled from Nazi Germany to Britain, where he taught at Cambridge (1933–35) and Oxford (1935–48). With Sir **Howard Florey** at Oxford he was a key figure in the successful isolation of penicillin (discovered earlier by Sir **Alexander Fleming**), and all three shared the 1945 Nobel prize for physiology or medicine. He was director of the International Research Centre for Chemical Microbiology in Rome (1948–61), and professor of biochemistry at Imperial College, London (1961–73).

CHALIAPIN, Fedor Ivonivich (1873–1938) Russian bass singer of great power, born in Kazan. Also talented as an actor, he sang in opera at Tiflis (1892), Moscow (1896), and London (1913). He left Russia after the Revolution.

CHALKONDYLAS, Demetrios (1424–1511) Athenian scholar. He came after the Turkish conquest from Athens to Italy, and at Florence and Milan taught Greek, published grammars, and edited **Homer**, **Isocrates** and **Suidas**.

CHALKONDYLAS, Nikolaos (15th century) Greek historian, brother of **Demetrios Chalkondylas**. He wrote, about 1450, a history of the Turks and the fall of the Greek Empire.

CHALLEMEL-LACOUR, Paul Armand (1827–96) French politician, born in Avranches, one of the most gifted representatives of republicanism and anticlericalism. Foreign minister, senator, ambassador at Bern and in London, vice-president (1890), and president (1893) of the Senate, he wrote on philosophy, edited Madame **d'Épinay**'s works, and was an Academician.

CHALLIS, James (1803–82) English astronomer, born in Braintree, professor of astronomy at Cambridge (1836–82). In August 1846 he twice observed the planet Neptune without noting it before its discovery by the Berlin Observatory on 23 September.

CHALLONER, Richard (1691–1781) English prelate and writer, born in Lewes. He turned Catholic as a boy, went to the English College at Douai in 1704 and was ordained in 1716, remaining there as a professor until 1730. He then served as a missionary priest in London, until in 1741 he was consecrated titular bishop of Debra and coadjutor of Bishop Petre, whom he succeeded as vicar apostolic of the London district in 1758. During the 'No Popery' riots of 1780 he was secreted near Highgate. Among his 34 works are the *Catholic Christian Instructed* (1737), an answer to **Conyers Middleton**'s *Letters from Rome*; the *Garden of the Soul* (1740), still a most popular prayer book with English Catholics; his revision of the Douai version of the Bible (5 vols, 1750), *Memoirs of Missionary Priests 1577–1684* (2 vols, 1741), and *Britannia Sancta* (2 vols, 1745).

CHALMERS, Alexander (1759–1834) Scottish journalist and biographer, born in Aberdeen. He studied medicine there, but about 1777 became an active writer in London. He published editions of several major authors, and a glossary to **Shakespeare** (1797), but his reputation rests mainly on his monumental *General Biographical Dictionary* (32 vols, 1812–17).

CHALMERS, George (1742–1825) Scottish antiquarian, born in Fochabers in Moray. Educated at Aberdeen, he studied law at Edinburgh and from 1763 practised as a lawyer in Baltimore, Maryland until the outbreak of the American War of Independence whereupon he settled in London. He published biographies of **Defoe**, **Paine**, **Ruddiman** and **Mary, Queen of Scots**, and editions of the poetry of **Allan Ramsay** and Sir **David Lyndsay**. But his most ambitious project, unfinished at his death, was a monumental history of Scotland and its antiquities, *Caledonia: an Account, Historical and Topographical, of North Britain* (3 vols, 1807–24).

CHALMERS, George Paul (1833–78) Scottish artist, born in Montrose. He worked as errand boy to a surgeon, and apprentice to a shipchandler; but in 1853 came to Edinburgh, and studied art under **Robert Scott Lauder**. He is represented in the National Gallery of Scotland by *The Legend*.

CHALMERS, James (1782–1853) Scottish bookseller and inventor, born in Arbroath. A bookseller and newspaper publisher in Dundee, he advocated faster mail services in 1825, and invented adhesive postage stamps.

CHALMERS, Thomas (1780–1847) Scottish theologian and preacher, born in Anstruther. Educated at St Andrews, he was ordained minister of Kilmany in 1803. He carried on mathematical and chemistry classes at St Andrews in 1803–04, and in 1808 published an *Inquiry into National Resources*. In 1815 he became minister to the Tron parish in Glasgow, where his magnificent oratory, partly published as *Astronomical Discourses* (1817) and *Commercial Discourses* (1820), took the city by storm. In 1823 he accepted the moral philosophy chair in St Andrews, where he wrote his *Use and Abuse of Literary and Ecclesiastical Endowments* (1827). In 1827 he was transferred to the chair of theology in Edinburgh, and in 1832 published a work on political economy. In 1833 appeared his Bridgewater treatise, *On the Adaptation of External Nature to the Moral and Intellectual Constitution of Man*. Meanwhile, the struggles in regard to patronage became keener, until in 1843 Chalmers led the Disruption when he, followed by 470 ministers, seceded from the Church of Scotland, and founded the Free Church of Scotland, whose swift and successful organization was mainly due to his indefatigable exertions. He was the first moderator of its assembly, and principal of the Free Church College from 1843 to 1847, when he completed his *Institutes of Theology*. His works, in 34 volumes, deal especially with natural theology, apologetics and social economy. As a religious orator Chalmers was unrivalled.

CHALMERS, William (1748–1811) Swedish merchant, born in Gothenburg of British parents. He was representative in China of the Swedish East India Company (1782–93) and returned to Gothenburg a rich man. He left his fortune half to the Sahlgrenska Hospital and half to the foundation of the Chalmers'

Craft School (1829), which became the Chalmers' Technical University in 1937.

CHAM, pseud of **Amédée de Noé** (1819–79) French caricaturist, born in Paris, son of the Comte de Noé by an English mother. In 1843 he began a long connection with the French satirical magazine *Charivari*. *Cham* is French for *Ham*, the son of Noah.

CHAMBERLAIN, Sir (Joseph) Austen (1863–1937) English statesman, eldest son of **Joseph Chamberlain**. He was Chancellor of the Exchequer, 1903–06 and 1919–21, secretary for India, 1915–17, a member of **Lloyd George**'s War Cabinet, lord privy seal, leader of the House and Unionist leader, 1921–22. As foreign secretary, 1924–29, he was made KG in 1925, and shared with Charles Gates Dawes the 1925 Nobel peace prize for negotiating the Locarno Pact.

CHAMBERLAIN, Houston Stewart (1855–1927) English-born German author and propagandist, son of an admiral. He settled in Dresden in 1885, and in 1908 he moved to Bayreuth and married, as his second wife, Eva, daughter of **Richard Wagner**, and wrote in German on music, Wagner, **Kant** and philosophy. A committed supporter of the dogmas of Aryan supremacy, he was naturalized as a German in 1916.

CHAMBERLAIN, Joseph (1836–1914) English statesman, born in London. He was educated at University College School, entered Nettlefold's screw factory at Birmingham, and retired in 1874 with a fortune. A Radical politician, in 1868 he became a Birmingham town councillor, and in 1873–76 was mayor. Returned unopposed for Birmingham in 1876, he soon made his mark in Parliament, and in 1880 was appointed president of the board of trade, with a seat in the Cabinet. To his exertions was due the passing of the Bankruptcy Bill. Regarded as the leader of the extreme Radical party, he enunciated schemes for the regeneration of the masses, and during the general election of 1886 produced an 'unauthorized' programme, which included the readjustment of taxation, free schools, and the creation of allotments by compulsory purchase. In February 1886 he became president of the local government board, but resigned in March because of his strong objections to **Gladstone**'s Home Rule Bill, of which he became the most strenuous opponent. From 1891 he was leader of the Liberal Unionists, and in the coalition government of 1895 took office as secretary for the colonies, acquiring a great reputation as a colonial administrator, enhanced even during and after the South African War (1899–1902). In September 1903 he resigned office to be free to advocate his scheme of tariff reform, giving preferential treatment to colonial imports and protection for native manufactures. Subsequently, in 1919 and especially 1932, the scheme was carried out by his sons. In 1906 he practically withdrew from public life in consequence of ill-health. He was the first chancellor of Birmingham University, whose welfare he did much to promote.

CHAMBERLAIN, (Arthur) Neville (1869–1940) English statesman, son of **Joseph Chamberlain** by his second marriage. He was lord mayor of Birmingham, 1915–16, Chancellor of the Exchequer, 1923–24 and 1931–37, minister for health, 1924–29, and became prime minister in 1937. For the sake of peace, and with the country unprepared for war, he essayed 'appeasement' of Italy and Germany, but in the end, having meantime pressed on with rearmament, was constrained to go to war (1939). Criticism of his war leadership accompanied initial military reverses, and in 1940 he yielded the premiership to **Churchill**; and in ill-health, relinquished all office shortly before his death. Subsequent re-evaluations of his career have shown his policy of appeasement in a more favourable light, Britain, at the time, being ill-prepared for war.

CHAMBERLAIN, Owen (1920–) American physicist, born in San Francisco. He became a professor at the University of California after working on the Manhattan atomic bomb project (1942–46) and at the Argonne National Laboratory. In 1959 he was awarded the Nobel prize for physics jointly with his colleague **Emilio Segré** for research on the antiproton.

CHAMBERLAIN, Wilt (Wilton Norman) (1936–) American basketball player, born in Philadelphia. More than 7ft tall, and known as 'Wilt the Stilt', he began his professional career with the Harlem Globetrotters. In 1959 he signed for the Philadelphia (later San Francisco) Warriors of the National Basketball Association and at various times played with the New York Knickerbockers as well as with the Philadelphia Seventy-Sixers and the Los Angeles Lakers, with whom he played in championship-winning teams. He was on four occasions the NBA's Most Valuable Player.

CHAMBERLAND, Charles Édouard (1851–1908) French bacteriologist. A collaborator with **Pasteur**, he invented the unglazed porcelain filter.

CHAMBERLAYNE, William (1619–89) English poet. He practised as a physician at Shaftesbury, Dorset, and fought as a royalist at Newbury. His works are *Love's Victory, a Tragi-Comedy* (1658), and *Pharonnida, An Heroick Poem* (1659).

CHAMBERLIN, Thomas Chrowder (1843–1928) American geologist, born in Mattoon, Illinois. Educated at Beloit College, where he became professor of geology (1872–82), he was chief geologist of the Wisconsin Geological Survey and later professor of geology at Chicago (1892–1918). His best-known work was in connection with the fundamental geology of the solar system. His books include *The Origin of the Earth* (1916) and *The Two Solar Families, The Sun's Children* (1928).

CHAMBERS, Sir Edmund Kerchever (1866–1954) English scholar and critic, born in Berkshire. He was educated at Marlborough and Corpus Christi, Oxford, and was a civil servant with the Board of Education (1892–1926). He wrote important books on *The Medieval Stage* (1903), *The Elizabethan Stage* (1923), *Arthur of Britain* (1927) and *William Shakespeare* (1930).

CHAMBERS, Ephraim (c.1680–1740) English encyclopedist, born in Kendal. While apprenticed to a globemaker in London he conceived the idea of a *Cyclopaedia, or Universal Dictionary of Arts and Sciences* (2 folio vols, 1728). A French translation inspired **Diderot**'s great French *Encyclopédie*.

CHAMBERS, John Graham (1843–83) English sportsman, associated with the formulation of the 'Queensberry rules' for boxing. A champion walker and oarsman, he founded the Amateur Athletic Club in 1866 and drew up the rules for amateur athletic competitions. In 1867 he drew up the rules for boxing promulgated under the aegis of the 8th Marquis of **Queensberry**.

CHAMBERS, Raymond Wilson (1874–1942) English scholar, educated at University College, London, where he became professor of English language and literature (1922–41). His numerous learned works include studies of *Widsith* and *Beowulf*, an essay on *The Continuity of English Prose* (1932), editions of **Berner**'s translation of **Froissart** (6 vols, 1901–03, with **W P Ker**), and other texts.

CHAMBERS, Robert (1802–71) Scottish writer and publisher, younger brother of **William Chambers**, born in Peebles. He began business as a bookseller with his brother in Edinburgh in 1819, and wrote in his spare time. In 1824 he produced *Traditions of Edinburgh*. The success of *Chambers' Edinburgh Journal*, started by his brother in 1832, was considerably due to his essays and his literary insight. Later that year he and his brother combined to form the publishing house of W & R Chambers. In 1844 he published anonymously the pre-Darwinian *Vestiges of Creation*. A prolific writer of reference books, he edited the *Chambers Encyclopaedia* (1859–68) and *The Cyclopaedia of English Literature* (1842), and himself wrote *A Biographical Dictionary of Eminent Scotsmen* (1832–34), *Domestic Annuals of Scotland* (3 vols, 1858–61)), extracts from Scottish historical sources, and *The Book of Days* (2 vols, 1863, an almanac of historical data), which broke his health. His other works include *Popular Rhymes of Scotland* (1826), a *History of the Rebellions in Scotland*, *Life of James I*, *Scottish Ballads and Songs* (1829), *Ancient Sea Margins* (1848), *The Life and Works of Robert Burns* (4 vols, 1851), and *Songs of Scotland prior to Burns* (1862). His son Robert (1832–88) became head of the firm in 1883, and conducted the *Journal* until his death.

CHAMBERS, Sir William (1726–96) Scottish architect, born of Scottish ancestry in Stockholm. He studied in Italy and France and practised in England. He designed Somerset House (1776) and the pagoda in Kew Gardens, and wrote a *Treatise of Civil Architecture* (1759).

CHAMBERS, William (1800–83) Scottish publisher, brother of **Robert Chambers**, born in Peebles, the son of a cotton manufacturer. In 1814 he was apprenticed to a bookseller in Edinburgh, and in 1819 started in business for himself, first bookselling and later adding printing. Between 1825 and 1830 he wrote the *Book of Scotland* and, in conjunction with his brother Robert, a *Gazetteer of Scotland*. In 1832 he started *Chambers' Edinburgh Journal*, six weeks in advance of the *Penny Magazine*; and later joined Robert in founding the business of W & R Chambers. In 1859 he founded and endowed a museum, library and art gallery in his native town of Peebles. Lord Provost of Edinburgh from 1865 to 1869, he promoted a successful scheme for improving the older part of the city. He carried out at his own cost a restoration of St Giles' Cathedral. Besides many contributions to the *Journal*, he wrote a *Youth's Companion*, a *History of Peeblesshire* (1864), *Ailie Gilroy*, *Stories of Remarkable Persons*, *Stories of Old Families*, and a *Historical Sketch of St Giles' Cathedral* (1879).

CHAMBORD, Henri Charles Dieudonné, Comte de (1820–83) French **Bourbon** pretender as 'Henri V', grandson of King **Charles X** of France. Born in Paris after the assassination of his father, the Duc de **Berry**, he was taken into exile with the remaining Bourbons after the abdication of Charles in 1830. On Charles' death in 1836, he was proclaimed king of France by the Legitimist party. Another attempt was made after the fall of **Napoleon III** in 1870, but a motion for restoration of the monarchy was finally defeated in the National Assembly in 1874.

CHAMFORT, Nicolas Sébastian Roch (1741–94) French writer. He made an entrance into the literary circles of Paris, and lived for years 'by his wit, if not by his wits'. He joined the Jacobins at the outbreak of the French Revolution (1789), but his remarks on the Terror brought him into disfavour. Threatened with arrest, he tried to commit suicide and died after several days' suffering. His works include tales, dramas, *éloges*, brilliant maxims and even more admirably observed anecdotes (published posthumously in 1795).

CHAMISSO, Adelbert von (Louis Charles Adelaide de) (1781–1838) French-born German poet and biologist, born in Champagne. The French Revolution drove his parents to Prussia, and he served in the Prussian army (1798–1807). In Geneva he joined the literary circle of Madame **de Staël** and later studied at Berlin. In 1815–18 he accompanied a Russian exploring expedition round the world as naturalist, and on his return was appointed keeper of the Botanical Garden of Berlin. In 1819 he was the first to discover in certain animals what he called 'alternation of generations' (the recurrence in the life cycle of two or more forms). He wrote several works on natural history, but his fame rests partly on his poems, still more on his quaint and humorous *Peter Schlemihl* (1813), the story of the man who lost his shadow.

CHAMPAIGNE, Philippe de (1602–74) French painter of portraits and religious subjects, born in Brussels and trained as a landscapist there. After moving to Paris in 1621 he assisted with decorations for the Luxembourg palace with **Nicholas Poussin** and in 1628 was appointed painter to **Marie de' Medici** and was patronized by **Louis XIII** and Cardinal **Richelieu**. His portraiture is most similar to that of **Van Dyck**, particularly his triple portrait of the Cardinal which was painted for **Bernini** to use as a model for a bust of the great man. After 1647 he began to associate with a strict religious sect in Paris, called the Jansenists. Thereafter, his work becomes more austere and all traces of the Baroque influence of **Rubens** disappear.

CHAMPFLEURY, assumed name of **Jules Fleury-Husson** (1821–89) French author, born in Laon. He wrote several early pieces for the theatre, and a number of novels in Realist style. He became head of the Porcelain Museum in Sèvres, and published important studies on the history of caricature, literature, art and pottery.

CHAMPLAIN, Samuel de (1567–1635) French explorer and 'founder of Canada', born at Brouage in Saintonge. In 1603 he made his first voyage to Canada. From 1604 to 1607 he explored the coasts, and on his third voyage in 1608 he founded Quebec. He was appointed lieutenant of Canada in 1612. His explorations into the interior mapped many new areas. During the Anglo-French war, Quebec was seized by the English, and he successfully negotiated its return to French sovereignty.

CHAMPOLLION, Jean François (1790–1832) French founder of Egyptology, born in Figeac. Educated at Grenoble, he was devoted from his boyhood to the study of oriental languages, especially Coptic. In 1807 he went to Paris, subsequently becoming professor of history at Grenoble (1809–16). Best known for his use of the Rosetta Stone to decipher Egyptian hieroglyphics (1822–24), he was the first to place the study of early Egyptian history and culture on a firm footing. He was sent by the king on a scientific mission to Italy in 1824–26, and in 1826 was appointed conservator of the Egyptian collections. In 1828, he mounted a joint expedition with the Italian Ippolito Rosellini (1800–43) to record the monuments of the Nile as far south as Aswan; on his return he was made a member of the Académie des Inscriptions (1830), and a chair of Egyptology was founded for him at the Collège de France. He died a few months later. His *Precis du système hiéroglyphique* was published in 1824, the two volumes of *Monuments de l'Égypte et de la Nubie* posthumously in 1844 and 1889.

CHANCE, Britton (1913–) American biophysicist, born in Wilkes-Barre, Pennsylvania. He was educated at Pennsylvania University and became professor of biophysics there in 1949. His best-known work is his demonstration, in 1943, of the existence of a complex between an enzyme and its substrate; such complexes had long been presumed as an essential stage in enzyme action but had not been detected. He also did valuable work on problems of energy generation in biological cells.

CHANCELLOR, Richard (d.1556) English seaman. Brought up in the household of the father of Sir **Philip Sidney**, he was chosen in 1553 as 'pilot-general' of Sir **Hugh Willoughby**'s expedition in search of a northeast passage to India. The ships were parted in a storm off the Lofoten Islands, and Chancellor, after waiting seven days at Vardöhus, proceeded alone into the White Sea and travelled thence overland to the court at Moscow, where he concluded a treaty giving freedom of trade to English ships. Next spring he returned to England, where his optimistic reports led to the establishment of the Muscovy Company. In 1555 he made a second voyage to the White Sea and to Moscow. He was lost at sea on the way home in Aberdour Bay, Fife.

CHANCOURTOIS, Alexandre Emile Béguyer de (1819–86) French geologist. As professor of geology at the School of Mines in Paris, he was one of the first to suspect periodicity in the elements. His work went unnoticed at the time.

CHANDLER, Raymond (1888–1959) American novelist, born in Chicago. He was brought up in England from the age of seven, educated at Dulwich College and in France and Germany, and worked as a freelance writer in London. In 1912 he went to California, and served in the Canadian army in France, and in the RAF during World War I. After a variety of jobs, during the Depression he began to write short stories and novelettes for the detective-story pulp magazines of the day. On such stories he based his subsequent full-length 'private eye' novels, *The Big Sleep* (1939), *Farewell, My Lovely* (1940), *The High Window* (1942) and *The Lady in the Lake* (1943), all of which were successfully filmed. Chandler himself went to Hollywood in 1943 and worked on film scripts. He did much to establish the conventions of his genre, particularly with his cynical but honest anti-hero, Philip Marlowe, who also appeared in such later works as *The Little Sister* (1949), *The Long Goodbye* (1953) and *Playback* (1958).

CHANDLER, Richard (1738–1810) English archaeologist, born in Elson, Hampshire. He was educated at Winchester and at Queen's and Magdalen Colleges, Oxford. His *Marmora Oxoniensia* (1763) is an elaborate description of the Oxford marbles. He afterwards travelled through Greece and Asia Minor for the Dilettanti Society. The materials collected were given to the world in *Ionian Antiquities* (1769), *Inscriptiones Antiquæ* (1774), *Travels in Asia Minor* (1775), and *Travels in Greece* (1776).

CHANDOS a great English family, descended from a follower of **William I the Conqueror**. Its greatest member was Sir John Chandos, the **Black Prince**'s follower, who fell in battle, 1 January 1370; and its last representative in the direct male line was another Sir John (d.1428), whose sister married one Giles Brydges. Their descendant, Sir John Brydges, was lieutenant of the Tower under Queen **Mary I**, and was created Baron Chandos in 1554. James Brydges (1673–1744), eighth Lord Chandos, sat in parliament for Hereford from 1698 to 1714, and was created Duke of Chandos in 1719. In 1796 the title passed by marriage to the family of Grenville, till 1889 Dukes of Buckingham and Chandos.

CHANDOS, Oliver Lyttelton, 1st Viscount (1893–1972) English industrialist and politician. He belonged to a family with many political connections. After Eton and Cambridge, where he gained a blue for golf, he served in the Grenadier Guards in World War I, winning the DSO. By 1928 he was managing director of the British Metal Corporation, and during the years of depression played a big part in organizing international cartels in the metal world to mitigate the effects of the slump. On the outbreak of war in 1939 he became controller of non-ferrous metals, and in 1940 was made president of the board of trade, a seat in the House of Commons being found for him at Aldershot. He was subsequently minister of state in Cairo, and minister of production. When the Conservatives were returned to office in 1951 Lyttelton went to the colonial office, until his resignation from politics to return to business in 1954, when he was raised to the peerage. His period of office was a difficult one, with outbreaks of violence in Kenya and Malaya to contend with, and a constitutional crisis in British Guiana. However, he played a leading part in drawing up plans of constitutional reform and advance for many of the African colonial territories.

CHANDRAGUPTA, or **Sandracottus** (c.350–c.250 BC) Hindu emperor of Pâtaliputra or Palibothra, to whom **Megasthenes** was sent by **Seleucus I Nicator** (c.300 BC).

CHANDRASEKHAR, Subrahmanyan (1910–) Indian-born American astrophysicist, born in Lahore (now in Pakistan), who developed a theory of white dwarf stars. He studied at the Presidency College, Madras before going to Cambridge University. In 1936 he went to America and worked at the University of Chicago and the Yerkes Observatory. He studied the final stages of stellar evolution, showing that the final fate of a star (ie, as a supernova or as a white dwarf), depends on its mass. Massive stars will be unable to evolve into white dwarves, and this limiting stellar mass (about 1.4 solar masses) is called the Chandrasekhar limit.

CHANEL, Gabrielle, known as **Coco** (1883–1971) French couturier. Orphaned at an early age, she worked with her sister as a milliner until 1912, when she opened a shop of her own. After serving as a nurse during World War I, she opened a couture house in Deauville (1913) and in the Rue du Cambon in Paris (1924). It was from here that she was to revolutionize women's fashions during the 1920s. For the first time for a century women were liberated from the restriction of corsets; in 1920 she designed her first 'chemise' dress, and in 1925 the collarless cardigan jacket. The combination of simple elegance and comfort in her designs gave them immediate, widespread and lasting appeal, and many of the features she introduced, such as the vogue for costume jewellery, the evening scarf, and the 'little black dress', have retained their popularity. At the height of her career she managed four businesses, including the manufacture of her world-famous perfume, Chanel No. 5, and her great wealth and dazzling social life attracted great public interest. She retired in 1938, but made a surprisingly successful comeback in 1954, when, following her original style, she regained her prominence in the fashion world and became a legendary figure of the 20th century.

CHANEY, Lon (1883–1930) American film and stage actor, born in Colorado Springs, Colorado. Known as 'The Man of a Thousand Faces' from his skill at make-up and miming, he made his film début in 1913 and gained a reputation for his painstaking portrayal of deformed villains and other spine-chilling parts, most notably in *The Miracle Man* (1919), *The Hunchback of Notre Dame* (1923) and *The Phantom of the Opera* (1925). His son, Lon Chaney Jr (1907–73), was also an actor in horror films, and starred in a film version of **Steinbeck**'s *Of Mice and Men* (1939).

CHANG HENG (78–139) Chinese scholar and inventor, born in Wan (now Nanyang). He was the astronomer royal at the court of the later **Han** Emperors, and although none of his actual works has survived there are detailed accounts extant of several of his inventions. He introduced a complete armillary sphere at about the same time as **Ptolemy** did in the West, but he then went on to construct one that was water-powered and, it is thought, regulated by some primitive form of escapement, similar perhaps to that of the improved water clock he had built previously. He is also credited with the construction of the world's first seismograph, the central component of which was a large pendulum which would be set in motion by an earthquake shock. Round the pendulum eight dragon heads were positioned so that any movement would dislodge a ball from a dragon's mouth into the open mouth of a toad below, allowing the direction of the earthquake's centre to be estimated.

CHANGAMIRE the dynastic title of the rulers of southern Zimbabwe from 1480 until the mid 17th century. In 1480 a vassal-ruler of the Changa people took advantage of the weakness of the empire of Monomotapa to declare himself an independent amir (Changa Amir). During the 17th century the Changamire also conquered most of northern Zimbabwe (Mutapa) and formed a powerful barrier to the incursions of Portuguese traders, eager to obtain access to the substantial gold-mining industry there.

CHANGARNIER, Nicolas Anne Théodule (1792–1877) French soldier, born in Autun. He served in Algeria (1830–48) and was appointed its governor-general (1848), but returned to Paris to take command of the Paris garrisons and of the National Guard. After the *coup d'état* in 1851 he went into exile; in the Franco-Prussian war of 1870–71 he was taken prisoner at Metz with **Bazaine**. He was elected senator in 1875, and died at Versailles.

CHANNING, William Ellery (1780–1842) American clergyman, born in Newport, Rhode Island. He graduated at Harvard in 1798, and in 1803 was ordained to the Congregational Federal Street Church in Boston, where his sermons were famous for their 'fervour, solemnity, and beauty'. He was ultimately the leader of the Unitarians. In 1822 he visited Europe, and made the acquaintance of **Wordsworth** and **Coleridge**. Among his Works (6 vols, 1841–46) were his *Essay on National Literature*, *Remarks on Milton*, *Character and Writings of Fénelon*, *Negro Slavery*, and *Self-culture*.

CHANTREY, Sir Francis Legatt (1781–1841) English sculptor, and in his youth a painter, born in Norton, in Derbyshire. He was famed for his portrait statues and busts, and church monuments such as the Robinson children (1817) in Lichfield cathedral. He left the bulk of his fortune to the Royal Academy with life rent to his widow (d.1875) to purchase native works of art. The collection is now in the Tate Gallery.

CHANZY, Antoine Eugène Alfred (1823–83) French soldier, born in Nouart. He served in Algeria and Lombardy. In the Franco-Prussian War of 1870–71 he commanded the Second Army of the Loire after the battle of Orléans, and resisted the German advance. After his offensive at the battle of Le Mans he was forced to withdraw westwards. From 1873 to 1879 he was governor-general of Algeria and was chosen a life senator in 1875. He was put forward for the presidency in 1879, but instead was ambassador at St Petersburg from 1879 to 1881.

CHAPELAIN, Jean (1595–1674) French poet and critic. An original member of the Académie Française (1634), he had a high reputation as a critic. He also wrote *La Pucelle*, in 24 books (1656), which was savaged by **Boileau**.

CHAPLIN, Charlie (Sir Charles Spencer) (1889–1977) English film actor and director, born in Kennington, London, of theatrical parents. His father died when he was a child, leaving the family in straitened circumstances, and his first regular education was in the school at Hanwell Poor Law Institution. These hard times are often mirrored in the poignant contrasts of humour and sadness which are a feature of his early films. By the age of eight he was a seasoned stage performer, but his skill in comedy developed under Fred Karno. As a member of his vaudeville company he went to Hollywood in 1914 and entered the motion picture business, then in its infancy, making 35 films in his first year. In these early comedies he adopted the bowler hat, out-turned feet, moustache and walking-cane which became the hallmark of his consummate buffoonery in *The Kid* (1920), *The Gold Rush* (1924), *The Champion* (1915), *Shoulder Arms* (1918) etc. His art was essentially suited to the silent film and, realizing this, he experimented with new forms when sound arrived, as in *City Lights* (1931), with music only, and *Modern Times* (1936), part speech and part mime. Eventually he entered the orthodox sound film field with the satirical caricature of **Adolf Hitler** in *The Great Dictator* (1940). In *Limelight* (1952) he acted, directed and composed the music and dances. His left-wing sympathies caused him to fall foul of the rabid anti-Communist factions of post-war America, and he emigrated to Switzerland. Later, the biting satire of *A King in New York* (1957) mocked the American way of life. He was knighted in 1975.

CHAPLIN, Matilda See **AYRTON, William Edward**

CHAPMAN, George (c.1559–1634) English dramatist, born near Hitchin, Hertfordshire. He is thought to have had a university education, possibly at Oxford. He began to make a reputation in Elizabethan literary circles with his poems *The Shadow of the Night* (1594), and in 1595 saw the production of his earliest extant play, the popular comedy *The Blind Beggar of Alexandria*. His next comedy, *All Fools*, printed in 1605, was probably produced in 1599. In 1598 he wrote a continuation of **Marlowe**'s *Hero and Leander*. After partial translations from the *Iliad* in 1598 and 1610, the complete translation of *The Iliads of Homer, Prince of Poets*, appeared in 1611. Having finished the *Iliad*, he set to work on the *Odyssey* (1616), followed (about 1624) by the minor works. He joined **Ben Jonson** and **John Marston** in the composition of *Eastward Hoe* (1605), in which slighting references to the Scots earned the authors a jail sentence, and in 1606 published a graceful comedy, *The Gentleman Usher*. In 1607 appeared the tragedy *Bussy d'Ambois*, and in 1613 *The Revenge of Bussy d'Ambois*. *The Conspiracie* and *Tragedie of Charles, Duke of Byron* (1608) are also undramatic, but are full of fine poetry. His other plays are *The May Day* (1611), *The Widow's Tears* (1612), and *Caesar and Pompey* (1631). Two posthumous tragedies (1654), *Alphonous* and *Revenge for Honour*, bear his name, but it is doubtful that he wrote them. *The Ball*, a comedy, and *The Tragedie of Chabot* (1639) were the joint work of Chapman and **Shirley**. Among Chapman's nondramatic works are the epic philosophical poem *Euthymiae & Raptus* (1609), *Petrarch's Seven Penitentiall Psalmes* (1612), *The Divine Poem of Musaeus* (1616), and *The Georgicks of Hesiod* (1618).

CHAPMAN, Mark David (c.1955–) convicted American murderer. A security guard from Hawaii, he shot and killed former **Beatles** member John Lennon, on 8 December 1980, outside Lennon's apartment in

Manhattan. Much attention was paid at Chapman's trial to his psychiatric state, as his lawyer initially entered a plea of insanity which Chapman later overturned with a plea of guilty. Chapman had been a fan of the Beatles, and had idolized Lennon to the extent that he often imagined that he was Lennon. He was also obsessed with and inspired by **J D Salinger**'s novel *The Catcher in the Rye*, identifying strongly with the central character who regarded the world as phoney. Chapman was found guilty of murder and was sentenced to life imprisonment. He was also ordered to receive psychiatric treatment.

CHAPMAN, Sydney (1888–1970) English applied mathematician and geophysicist, born in Eccles. He studied engineering at Manchester and mathematics at Cambridge, and was professor at Manchester (1919–24), Imperial College, London (1924–46), and Oxford (1946–53). From 1954 he worked at the High Altitude Observatory at Boulder, Colorado, and the Geophysical Institute in Alaska. He made a major contribution to the kinetic theory of gases, and developed the theory of thermal diffusion. He also developed theories on geomagnetism, atmospheric tides, and geomagnetic storms.

CHAPMAN, Walter See **CHEPMAN**

CHAPONE, Hester, née **Mulso** (1727–1801) English essayist, born in Twywell, Northamptonshire. One of the 'blue-stocking' circle associated with **Elizabeth Montagu**, she wrote for the *Rambler* (No. 10), *Gentleman's Magazine* and other magazines, but is chiefly remembered for her *Letters on the Improvement of the Mind* (1772).

CHAPPE, Claude (1763–1805) French engineer and inventor, born in Brulon, Sarthe. He was studying for a career in the church when the French Revolution upset his plans, and he decided instead to pursue his interest in telegraphy. Failing in his attempts to construct apparatus for electrical telegraphy, he turned in 1793 to a hand-operated semaphore system which with government backing was quite extensively used in France up to about 1850. Repeater stations at distances of 10 to 12 km were required, and messages could be sent by day and by night with the aid of lamps on the semaphore arms. Later financial difficulties drove him to suicide.

CHAPPELL, Greg (Gregory Stephen) (1948–) Australian cricketer, born in Unley, South Australia, younger brother of **Ian Chappell**. One of the most graceful of modern batsmen, he played 87 times for his country and scored 24 Test centuries, and succeeded his brother as captain. At the Oval in 1972, he and his brother both made centuries in the same innings. He played in England for Somerset for two years.

CHAPPELL, Ian Michael (1943–) Australian cricketer, born in Unley, South Australia, elder brother of **Greg Chappell**. A more combative character than his brother, he played 75 times for Australia, scoring over 5000 runs and 14 Test centuries. A grandson of Victor Richardson, himself an Australian Test cricketer, Chappell's pugnacious, driving style of captaincy made Australia a side universally respected in the 1970s, if not always greatly liked.

CHAPPELL, William (1809–88) English antiquary, a member of a great London music publishing house. His *Collection of National English Airs* (2 vols, 1838–40) grew into *Popular Music of the Olden Time* (2 vols, 1855–59). Chappell took a principal part in the foundation in 1840 of the Musical Antiquarian Society, the Percy Society, and in 1868 of the Ballad Society. In 1874 he published the first volume of a *History of Music*.

CHAPTAL, Jean Antoine (Comte de Chantaloupe) (1756–1832) French statesman and chemist, born in Nogaret. As a member of the Senate he took a leading part in the introduction of the metric system of weights and measures. He was equally successful as a chemical manufacturer and a writer on industrial chemistry. He was ennobled by **Napoleon** and served as a minister in his Hundred Days (1815).

CHARCOT, Jean Baptiste (1867–1936) French explorer, son of **Jean Martin Charcot**, born in Neuilly. A doctor, he commanded two Antarctic expeditions in the *Français* (1903–05) and *Pourquoi Pas?* (1908–1910), and after World War I carried out hydrographic surveys off Greenland. He later went down with the *Pourquoi Pas?* off Iceland.

CHARCOT, Jean Martin (1825–93) French pathologist and neurologist, born in Paris. He worked at the Salpêtrière, from 1862, where he established a neurological unit. **Sigmund Freud** was among his pupils. He contributed much to knowledge of chronic and nervous diseases, and made important studies of hypnotism.

CHARD, John Rouse Merriott (1847–97) English soldier, born near Plymouth. As a lieutenant he was one of the eight men awarded the VC in 1879 for the defence of Rorke's Drift against 3000 Zulus, with 80 men of the 24th Regiment.

CHARDIN, Jean Baptiste Siméon (1699–1779) French painter, born in Paris, son of the king's billiard-table maker. He showed such promise as a student that he was selected to assist in the restoration of the royal paintings at Fontainebleau, and he later attracted attention as a signpainter. In 1728 he exhibited at the 'Exposition de la jeunesse', a series of still-life paintings which were so successful that he was elected to the Academy in the same year. He now emerged as a genre painter and produced many superb pictures of peasant life and domestic scenes. *Grace before Meat* (1740; Louvre), perhaps his masterpiece in this vein, earned the extravagant praises of **Diderot**. In 1755 he was appointed treasurer of the Academy, with an apartment in the Louvre. As an exponent of still life and genre Chardin is without equal in French painting, his composition and colouring is comparable with that of the best Dutch and Flemish masters, and he is free from both satire and sentimentality. An unassuming, serious bourgeois, he never travelled further than Fontainebleau, but spent the whole of his long, placid life in Paris.

CHARDIN, Sir John or **Jean** (1643–1713) French traveller, born in Paris. He went to India in 1663 to buy diamonds and stayed there and in Persia until 1677. In 1681 he settled as a Protestant in England, where he became court jeweller, and was knighted by **Charles II**.

CHARDONNE, Jacques, pseud of **Jacques Boutelleau** (1884–1968) French writer, born in Barbezieux. He wrote domestic novels mainly set in his native Charente, among them *Claire* (1931), *Les Destinées sentimentales* (1934–36) and *Romanesques* (1937). He also wrote essays and a chronicle of the French collapse in 1940.

CHARDONNET, Hilaire, Comte de (1839–1924) French chemist, born in Besançon. He was a pioneer of the artificial-silk (rayon) industry.

CHARGAFF, Erwin (1905–) Czech-born American biochemist, born in Czernowitz (now in the USSR). He studied in Vienna, Yale, Berlin and Paris before settling at Columbia University, New York, from 1935. His best-known work is on nucleic acids, the 'informational molecules' of all living cells, which make up the genes. His pioneering analytical studies on them formed an important part of the groundwork used by **Francis Crick** and **James Dewey Watson** in 1953 in their work on the double helical structure of nucleic acids, which created modern molecular biology.

CHARLEMAGNE, (Carolus Magnus, Charles the Great) (747–814) king of the Franks and Christian emperor of the west, grandson of **Charles Martel** and the eldest son of **Pepin III the Short**. On Pepin's death in 768 the Frankish kingdom was divided between Charlemagne and his younger brother **Carloman**; three years later, on Carloman's death, he became sole ruler. The first years of his reign were spent in strenuous campaigns to subdue and Christianize neighbouring kingdoms, particularly the Saxons to the north-east (772–77) and the Lombards of northern Italy (773), where he was crowned king of Lombardy. In 778 he led an expedition against the Moors in Spain, but withdrew the same year when his presence was required elsewhere; the celebrated rearguard action at Roncesvalles in which **Roland**, his chief paladin, is said to have been overwhelmed, gave rise to the heroic literature of the *Chanson de Roland*. In 782 the Saxons rose again in rebellion and destroyed a Frankish army at Süntelberg, which Charlemagne avenged by beheading 4500 Saxons. Other risings followed, but in 785 the Saxon leader, Widukind, submitted and accepted baptism, and became a loyal vassal. In 788, Charlemagne deposed the ruler of Bohemia and absorbed it into his empire. Farther to the east he subdued the Avars (Turko-Finnish nomads) in the middle Danube basin (795–96) to create an eastern 'March' to buttress his frontiers; to the west he created the so-called 'Spanish March' on the southern side of the Pyrenees (795). In 800 he swept into Italy to support Pope **Leo III** against the rebellious Romans, and on Christmas Day, 800, in St Peter's Church, was crowned by the pope Emperor of the Romans as 'Carolus Augustus'. The remaining years of his reign were spent in consolidating his vast empire which reached from the Ebro in northern Spain to the Elbe. Bishoprics were founded in the Saxon country; many of the Slavs east of the Elbe were subjugated. The emperor established his capital and principal court at Aachen (Aix-la-Chapelle), where he built a magnificent palace and founded an academy to which many of the greatest scholars of the age, like **Alcuin** of York, were invited. He himself could speak Latin and read Greek, and letters and Latin poems ascribed to him are still extant. He zealously promoted education, architecture, bookmaking and the arts, created stable administrations and good laws, and encouraged agriculture, industry and commerce. He fostered good relations with the east, and in 798 **Harūn al-Raschīd**, the caliph of Baghdad, sent ambassadors and a gift of a white elephant. His reign was a noble attempt to consolidate order and Christian culture among the nations of the west, a Carolingian renaissance, but his empire did not long survive his death, for his sons lacked both his vision and authority. He was buried at Aachen.

CHARLES (1887–1922) emperor of Austria (1916–18) and king of Hungary (1916–19), the last of the Habsburg emperors. The son of Archduke Otto and grand-nephew of Emperor **Franz Joseph**, he became heir presumptive in 1914 on the assassination at Sarajevo of his uncle, Archduke **Franz Ferdinand**. On his great-uncle's death in 1916 he proclaimed himself emperor of Austria as 'Karl I' and king of Hungary as 'Károly IV'. He made secret attempts (which failed) to withdraw Austria/Hungary from the war. In November 1918 he was deposed, and exiled to Switzerland the following year. In 1921 he made two unsuccessful attempts to regain the crown of Hungary, and was deported to Madeira, where he died the following year. In 1911 he married Zita of Bourbon-Parma; their son, Archduke Otto, is the present Habsburg claimant to the throne.

CHARLES I, called **the Bald** (823–77) king of France, son of **Louis the Pious** and grandson of **Charlemagne**, was king from 843 and Holy Roman Emperor (as **Charles II**) of the west from 875.

CHARLES II, called **the Fat** (839–88) king of France from 884. He had become Holy Roman Emperor in Germany (as **Charles III**) in 881, but was deposed after making a humiliating treaty with the Vikings in Paris in 887.

CHARLES III, called **the Simple** (879–929) king of France from 893. He ceded Normandy to the Vikings under **Rollo**, and was deposed in 922.

CHARLES IV, called **the Fair** (1294–1328) king of France from 1322. He was the last of the Capetian dynasty.

CHARLES V, called **the Wise** (1338–80) king of France from 1364. As Dauphin he acted as regent during the long captivity of his father John II, after the battle of Poitiers in 1356, and succeeded his father in 1364. He regained most of the territory lost to the English.

CHARLES VII (1403–61) king of France, son of Charles VI ('the Foolish') whom he succeeded in 1422. He then held only the southern provinces; Paris and the north were in the hands of the English, who proclaimed **Henry VI** of England king of France, and appointed the Duke of **Bedford** regent. Charles was compelled to evacuate Champagne and Maine; but in 1426, at Montargis, **Dunois** gained the first victory over the English, who in 1427 laid siege to Orléans. **Joan of Arc** roused the fervour of both nobles and people; the siege of Orléans was raised in May 1429; the English gradually lost all they had gained in France; and their cause became hopeless after the treaty concluded at Arras (1435) between the French king and Philip the Good, Duke of Burgundy. Bayonne fell in 1451, and with the death of Sir **John Talbot 1st Earl of Shrewsbury** under the walls of Castillon in 1453, the whole south finally passed to France, and the Hundred Years' War came to an end. In 1436 Charles had entered Paris. He devoted himself to the reorganization of the government, and under his rule France recovered in some measure from her terrible calamities. His last years were embittered by the conduct of his son, the Dauphin, afterwards **Louis XI**. His mistress and confidante from 1444 was **Agnes Sorel**.

CHARLES VIII (1470–98) king of France, called 'the Affable'. He succeeded his father, **Louis XI**, in 1483; in 1495–96 he failed in an attempt to secure the kingdom of Naples.

CHARLES IX (1550–74) king of France, second son of **Henri II** and **Catherine de' Medici**. He succeeded his brother, **Francis II**, in 1559. His reign was dominated by the religious wars between Protestants and Catholics. For most of the reign, the government was effectively in the hands of his mother who, together with Charles' younger brother, Henri (later **Henri III**), was largely responsible for the slaughter of the Parisian Huguenots at the St Bartholomew Day Massacre in 1572.

CHARLES X (1757–1836) king of France 1824–30, successor to his brothers **Louis XVI** and **Louis XVII**. The third surviving son of the Dauphin Louis, and grandson of **Louis XV**, he was born at Versailles and known as the Comte D'Artois before his accession in 1824. In 1773 he married Marie Theresa of Savoy. He fled to St Petersburg and then to England at the beginning of the Revolution and became leader of the émigrés, playing an inglorious part in abortive expeditions to France in 1795. He lived in England

(Hartwell) and Scotland (Holyrood) from 1795 until the Restoration, after the fall of **Napoleon** in 1814, when he appeared in France as lieutenant-general of the kingdom. After the second Restoration (1815) he became leader of the Ultraroyalists in their struggle with the Constitutionalists. When he acceded to the throne in succession to **Louis XVII** he attempted to restore the absolutism of the old French monarchy and became increasingly unpopular. In May 1830 he dissolved the Chamber of Deputies and tried to end the freedom of the press, but was overthrown by the July Revolution of 27–29 July. On 2 August he abdicated with his elder son, the **Duc d'Angoulême**, in favour of his young grandson, the **Comte de Chambord**, but the people of France insisted on the election of their 'citizen king', **Louis-Philippe**. Charles and his family fled to Scotland, and later lived in Prague; he died in Görz of cholera.

CHARLES I (1600–49) king of Great Britain and Ireland, born in Dunfermline, second son of **James VI and I** and **Anne of Denmark**. He was a sickly child, unable to speak till his fifth year, and so weak in the ankles that till his seventh he had to crawl upon his hands and knees. Except for a stammer, he outgrew both defects, and became a skilled tilter and marksman, as well as an accomplished scholar and a diligent student of theology. He was created Duke of Albany at his baptism, Duke of York in 1605, and Prince of Wales in 1616, four years after the death of Prince Henry had left him heir to the crown. The Spanish match with the Infanta Maria had been mooted as early as 1614; but it was not till 17 February 1623 that, with **Buckingham**, Charles started on a romantic incognito journey to Madrid. Nothing short of his conversion would have satisfied the Spanish and papal courts; and in October, he landed again in England, eager for rupture with Spain. The nation's joy was speedily dashed by his betrothal to the French princess, **Henrietta Maria** (1609–1669); for the marriage articles pledged him to permit her the free exercise of the Catholic religion, and to give her the upbringing of their children till the age of 13. In March 1625 Charles succeeded to the throne; in June he welcomed his little bright-eyed queen at Dover, having married her by proxy six weeks earlier. Barely a year was over when he packed off her troublesome retinue to France—a bishop and 29 priests, with 410 more male and female attendants. Thenceforth their domestic life was a happy one; and during the twelve years following the murder of Buckingham, in whose hands he had been a mere tool, Charles gradually came to yield himself up to her unwise influence, not wholly indeed, but more than to that of **Strafford** even, or **Laud**. Three parliaments were summoned and dissolved in the first four years of the reign; then for eleven years Charles ruled without one, in its stead employing subservient judges and the courts of Star Chamber and High Commission. In 1627 he had blundered into an inglorious French war; but with France he concluded peace in 1629, with Spain in 1630. Peace, economy and arbitrary taxation were to solve the great problem of his policy—how to get money, yet not account for it. The extension of the ship tax to the inland counties was met by **Hampden**'s passive resistance (1637); Laud's attempt to anglicize the Scottish Church, by the active resistance of the whole northern nation (1639). Once more Charles had to call a parliament: two met in 1640—the Short Parliament, which lasted three weeks, and the Long, which outlasted Charles. It met to pronounce Strafford's doom; and, his plot with the army detected, Charles sacrificed his loyal servitor to fears for the queen's safety, at the same time assenting to a second bill by which the existing parliament might not be dissolved without its own consent. That pledge, as extorted by force, Charles intended to disregard; and during his visit to Edinburgh, in the autumn of 1641, he trusted by lavish concessions to bring over the Scots to his side. Instead, he got entangled in dark suspicions of plotting the murder of the Covenanting lords, of connivance even in the Ulster massacre. Still, his return to London was welcomed with some enthusiasm, and a party was forming in the Commons itself of men who revolted from the sweeping changes that menaced both church and state. **Pym**'s 'Grand Remonstrance' justified their fears, and Charles seemed to jusfify the 'Grand Remonstrance' by his attempt to arrest the five members (4 January 1642); but that ill-stricken blow was dictated by the knowledge of an impending impeachment of the queen herself. On 22 August he raised the royal standard at Nottingham; and the four years' Civil War commenced, in which, as at Naseby, he showed no lack of physical courage, and which resulted at Naseby in the utter annihilation of his cause (14 June 1645). Quitting his last refuge, Oxford, he surrendered himself on 5 May 1646 to the Scots at Newark, and by them in the following January was handed over to the parliament. His four months' captivity at Holmby House, near Northampton; his seizure, on 3 June, by Cornet Joyce; the three months at Hampton Court; the flight on 11 November; the fresh captivity at Carisbrooke Castle, in the Isle of Wight—these led up to the 'trial' at Westminster of the 'tyrant, traitor, and murderer, Charles Stuart'. He had drawn the sword, and by the sword he perished, for it was the army, not parliament, that stood at the back of his judges. Charles faced them bravely, and with dignity. Thrice he refused to plead, denying the competence of such a court; and his refusal being treated as a confession on 30 January 1649, he died on the scaffold in front of Whitehall, with a courage worthy of a martyr. On the snowy 7th of February they bore the 'white king' to his grave at Windsor in **Henry VIII**'s vault; in 1813 the Prince Regent had his leaden coffin opened. Six children survived him—Charles and James, his successors; Mary, Princess of Orange (1631–60); Elizabeth (1635–50); Henry, Duke of Gloucester (1639–60); and **Henrietta Anne**, Duchess of Orléans (1644–70), the last born ten weeks after Charles's final parting from his queen.

CHARLES II (1630–85) king of Scotland and England from 1660, eldest son of **Charles I** and **Henrietta Maria**. During the Civil War (1642–46) he was sent as Prince of Wales, with a council, to govern the west of England, and was present at the battle of Edgehill (1642), but was soon forced into exile, first to Scilly and Jersey (where he met one of his mistresses, **Lucy Walter**, who later bore him a son, James, Duke of **Monmouth**) and finally to France. On the execution of his father in 1649 he assumed the title of king, and was proclaimed king in Edinburgh; he landed in Scotland in June, agreed to subscribe to the presbyterian Covenant, and despite a Scottish defeat at the battle of Dunbar at **Oliver Cromwell**'s hands, was crowned king at Scone on 1 January 1651. He invaded England, but was routed by Cromwell at the battle of Worcester in September and only escaped to France with great difficulty and after many adventures. He spent the next nine years in impoverished exile, mostly in France and the Netherlands. After the fall of the Protectorate in 1659, General **George Monk** negotiated the restoration of the monarchy, and Charles entered London in triumph on his birthday, 29 May 1660, after issuing his Declaration of Breda promising a general amnesty and liberty of conscience. In 1662 he married **Catherine of**

Braganza, but the union was childless. The restored monarchy survived a number of minor conspiracies and risings which the government, with the support of a strongly royalist parliament, exploited in order to pass severely repressive laws against dissenters and non-conformists; the king himself, tolerant in religious matters and personally inclined to favour Roman Catholicism, attempted to alleviate their lot by a Declaration of Indulgence in 1663, which was bitterly resented. Under the Lord Chancellor, Edward Hyde, Earl of **Clarendon**, the country enjoyed relatively sound and stable government; but an unsuccessful war with Holland (1665–67) led to Clarendon's downfall, to be replaced by a group of ministers known as the 'Cabal'. The Great Fire of London (1666), widely believed to have been the result of a Roman Catholic conspiracy, and the alarming growth in the power of **Louis XIV** of France, led to an upsurge in anti-Catholic sentiment. Charles had sold Dunkirk to France for £400000 in 1662, and now he was engaged in devious political negotiations with France behind the back of parliament. In 1670, with the aid of a small group of favoured ministers and of his sister, **Henrietta Anne** (Minette), Duchess of Orléans, he concluded with Louis a secret treaty, the Treaty of Dover, whereby he agreed to join the Catholic church with his brother James, Duke of York (the future **James II**), and enter into an alliance with France against Holland, in exchange for £200000 a year from Louis. The ensuing war with Holland (1672–74) was only slightly more successful than the previous one. James openly professed his belief in Catholicism, and in 1673 married a Catholic, **Mary of Modena**. Meanwhile, Charles had issued another Declaration of Indulgence (1672) annulling the penal laws against Catholics and dissenters, but parliament forced him to withdraw it the following year and passed the Test Act, which excluded all Roman Catholics from sitting in parliament or holding government office; and it was followed by repeated attempts in parliament to pass a bill to prevent James from succeeding to the throne, or to limit his powers should he do so (the Exclusion Crisis). In 1677, in the light of the queen's childlessness, popular sentiment forced the king to consent to the marriage of his niece, the Protestant **Mary**, to William of Orange (the future **William III**). In 1678 anti-Catholic feeling was whipped up to fever-point by the trumped-up revelations of **Titus Oates** about a supposed Popish Plot to murder the king. For three feverish years the future of the Stuart dynasty seemed once again to be hanging in the balance, while the deepening crisis gave rise to the party distinctions of Whig (favouring the exclusion of James) and Tory (opposing any alteration in the succession). With Tory support, Charles and his brother weathered the storm, ruthlessly remodelling borough government to exclude Whigs from power. From 1681, Charles ruled without parliament. Persecution of religious dissenters increased, particularly after the unmasking of the Rye House Plot (1683) to assassinate the king and his brother. But the succession was now safe, and on his deathbed Charles acknowledged his Roman Catholicism. He died without legitimate issue, but he had had many mistresses and many illegitimate offspring, most of whom he had acknowledged and ennobled.

CHARLES, (Philip Arthur George), Prince of Wales (1948–) prince of the UK, eldest son of Queen **Elizabeth** and Prince Philip, Duke of **Edinburgh**, and heir-apparent to the throne. He was given the title of Prince of Wales in 1958, and invested at Caernarvon in 1969. Educated at Cheam School in Berkshire and Gordonstoun in Scotland, he spent a term at Geelong Grammar School, Australia, in 1966, and studied at Trinity College, Cambridge, (1967-70). He served in the RAF and Royal Navy, 1971–76, and in 1981 married Lady Diana Frances, younger daughter of the 8th Earl Spencer. Their first child, Prince William Arthur Philip Louis, was born in 1982, and their second, Prince Henry Charles Albert David, in 1984.

CHARLES IV (1316–78) Holy Roman Emperor. He assumed the government of Bohemia after the blindness of his father, King **John**. He was elected king of Germany in 1347 and crowned Holy Roman Emperor in Rome in 1355, but unlike his predecessors tried to avoid being drawn into Italian conflicts. Instead, through shrewd diplomacy, he built up a dynastic empire based round his hereditary domains of Bohemia and Moravia, with his capital at Prague, where he founded the first university within the Empire (1348). His *Golden Bull* of 1356 became the new constitutional framework for the empire; it laid down procedure for the election of the monarch, excluded papal pretensions, and defined the rights of the seven electors, whose domains were declared indivisible. He was the first emperor since **Frederick I** to be succeeded by his son, **Wenceslas IV**.

CHARLES V (1500–58) Holy Roman Emperor 1519–56 and king of Spain as Charles I (1516–56), founder of the Habsburg dynasty. He was the son of Philip the Handsome (count of Flanders, son of the Holy Roman Emperor **Maximilian I** and briefly king of Spain as **Philip I**) and Joanna, the Infanta of Spain (daughter of **Ferdinand the Catholic** of Aragon and **Isabella of Castile**). Charles' father died in 1506, and his mother, a chronic melancholic who was regarded as insane, was kept in confinement in Spain for the rest of her life by her father, who assumed control of Castile. Charles and his sisters were brought up in Flanders by their aunt, the archduchess **Margaret of Austria**, who acted as Charles' regent in the Netherlands until 1515, when Charles was declared of age at the age of 15. In 1516 his maternal grandfather Ferdinand of Aragon died, and Charles inherited from him Spain, Naples and Spanish America. In 1519 his paternal grandfather, Maximilian, died, and Charles inherited from him the crown of Germany. In 1520 he was crowned Holy Roman Emperor at Aachen, having defeated **Francis I** of France for the election, and thereby became the most powerful monarch in Europe at the age of 19. The ensuing years were dominated by virtually continuous wars with France for possession of Italy, and by a series of fruitless attempts to achieve religious unity in Germany. In 1525 Francis was soundly defeated at the battle of Pavia and taken prisoner, but repudiated the subsequent treaty as soon as he was released. Charles thereupon invaded Italy against an alliance in which France was joined by Pope **Clement VII** and **Henry VIII** of England, and in 1527 captured and sacked Rome. The Treaty of Cambrai (1529) brought a temporary peace, and Charles made a triumphal procession through Italy and in 1530 was crowned by the pope in Bologna as emperor and king of Italy. War broke out again in 1536, when Francis invaded Savoy, and again in 1542, until a final truce was arranged through the Treaty of Crépy (1544). Meanwhile, Charles had also beaten off an attack by the Ottoman empire with the siege of Vienna by the sultan **Süleyman the Magnificent** in 1532. On the religious front, Charles worked hard to try to cope with the tide of Protestantism which threatened to split his empire. In 1521 he presided over the Imperial Diet of Worms, where **Martin Luther** was given a hearing but declared an outlaw. He also called the Diets of Augsburg (1530) and Regensburg (1541) which, however, failed to reconcile the differences between Catholics and Lutherans. In 1546 he took arms against the Lutheran princes (the League of Schmalkalden) and defeated them at Mühlberg (1547), and imposed the Augsburg Interim (1548) which condemned Lutheranism; but the harshness with which Charles treated the Protestant prisoners only provoked a rebellious uprising in Saxony where Charles was worsted and was forced to grant Protestantism legal recognition through the Treaty of Passau (1552) and the Peace of Augsburg (1555). Elsewhere, Charles extended Spanish dominions in the New World by the conquest of Mexico by **Cortés** (1519–21) and of Peru by **Pizarro** (1531–35). Towards the end of his long reign, his health broken by gout, Charles devoted himself to consolidating his vast dominions for the benefit of his heirs. In 1527 he had married Isabella of Portugal, by whom he had a son, Philip (the future **Philip II** of Spain). In 1553 he renounced his imperial crown in favour of his brother, **Ferdinand I** (although his abdication was not formally accepted until 1558), and in 1555–56 he resigned his kingdoms of Spain, the Netherlands, and the Spanish Americas to his son Philip. Having abdicated all his powers he retired to live in seclusion in the monastery of San Geronimo de Yuste, in Estremadura.

CHARLES I, king of Spain See **CHARLES V**, Holy Roman Emperor

CHARLES II (1661–1700) king of Spain from 1665, the last of the Spanish Habsburg kings, younger son and successor of **Philip IV**. He was weak minded from birth. During his minority (1665–75) his mother, Queen Mariana de Austria, acted as regent. In 1690 he joined the League of Augsburg and went to war against **Louis XIV** in the Grand Alliance (1688–97). Childless despite two marriages, he was induced to bequeath the crown to Philip of Anjou (**Philip V**), grandson of Louis XIV. The prospect of a union of the crowns of Spain and France under the house of **Bourbon** so alarmed other European powers that it precipitated the War of the Spanish Succession (1701–13).

CHARLES III (1716–88) king of Spain, 1759–88, younger son of **Philip V**, successor to his half-brother **Ferdinand VI**. He became Duke of Parma in 1731, and in the War of the Polish Succession (1734) conquered Naples and Sicily and became king over them as Charles IV. When he succeeded to the throne of Spain in 1759 he handed over Naples and Sicily to his third son, **Ferdinand I**. During the Seven Years' War (1756–63) he sided with France against Britain and lost Florida, but regained it in 1783 by siding with the Americans during the War of Independence (1775–83). At home he reformed the nation's economy, strengthened the crown's authority over the church, and expelled the Jesuits. He was succeeded by his son, **Charles IV**.

CHARLES IV (1784–1819) king of Spain 1788–1808, son and successor of **Charles III**. He was an ineffectual ruler, dominated by his wife Maria Louisa of Parma and her lover, **Manuel Godoy**, whom he appointed prime minister in 1792. During the Napoleonic wars Spain was in constant trouble; her fleet was destroyed by **Nelson** off Cape Trafalgar in 1805, and in 1807 France invaded. In 1808 Charles was forced to abdicate in favour of **Napoleon**'s brother, **Joseph Bonaparte**; he was given a pension by Napoleon, and died in Rome.

CHARLES, kings of Sweden See **KARL**

CHARLES, (Karl Ludwig Johann) (1771–1847) archduke of Austria, third son of the Emperor **Leopold II** and brother of the emperor **Francis II**, born in Florence. He entered the Austrian army in 1792 and became governor-general of the Netherlands (1793). As commander of the Austrian army on the Rhine in 1796, he defeated **Moreau** and **Jourdan** in several battles, drove the French over the Rhine, and took Kehl. He was forced back from the Tagliamento by **Napoleon** as he invaded Austria in 1797, but defeated Jourdain again at Stockach in 1799, only to be worsted by **Masséna**. In 1799 he was again victorious over Jourdan. Next year ill-health compelled him to accept the governor-generalship of Bohemia. Recalled after the Austrian defeat at Hohenlinden (1800) to the chief command, he checked the progress of Moreau. In 1805 he commanded against Masséna in Italy; then, after news of the crushing defeat at Austerlitz, he made a masterly retreat to Croatia. In 1809 he won the great battle of Aspern, but had to give best at the ferocious battle of Wagram, leading to the Treaty of Schonbrunn. He retired thereafter and became governor of Mainz in 1815.

CHARLES, (Mary) Eugenia, (1919–) Dominican politician, born in Pointe Michel. After qualifying in London as a barrister she returned to the West Indies to practise in what were the Windward and Leeward Islands. She entered politics in 1968 and two years later became co-founder and first leader of the centrist Dominica Freedom party (DFP). She became an MP in 1975. Two years after independence, the DFP won the 1980 general election and she became the Caribbean's first female prime minister. She was re-elected prime minister in 1985.

CHARLES, Jacques Alexandre César (1746–1823) French physicist, born in Beaugency (Loiret). He was the discoverer of Charles's Law connecting the expansion of gas with its rise in temperature and was the first to make a hydrogen balloon ascent (December 1783). He was professor of physics in Paris, where he invented several ingenious scientific instruments.

CHARLES, John (1932–) Welsh footballer, born in Swansea. One of the finest Welsh players of the postwar era, he played ten years with Leeds United as both centre-half and centre-forward before moving to Juventus in 1957. After a brief return to England he resumed his Italian career with Roma. A prolific goal scorer (42 goals in the 1953–54 season with Leeds), he was an automatic selection for his country, winning 38 Welsh caps over a 15-year period.

CHARLES, Robert (1936–) New Zealand golfer, born in Cartenton. An outstanding putter, in 1963 he became the only left-handed golfer to win the British Open championship, and 25 years later he was still performing creditably in the same competition. In 1963 he also won five US Tour events.

CHARLES ALBERT (1798–1849) king of Sardinia-Piedmont from 1831. The son of Prince Charles Emmanuel of Savoy-Carignan, he succeeded his father as prince of Carignan in 1800. At the Piedmontese rising of 1821 he was briefly appointed regent, but was soon arrested and exiled by the new king, Charles Felix. Appointed viceroy of Sardinia in 1829, he succeeded to the throne when Charles Felix, the last of the Savoy line, died in 1831. He introduced many liberal reforms, but in 1848 declared war on Austria, and was soundly defeated at the battles of Custozza (1846) and Novara (1849). Soon afterwards he resigned the throne in favour of his son **Victor Emmanuel II**, and retired to a monastery in Portugal.

CHARLES D'ORLÉANS See **ORLEANS**

CHARLES EDWARD See **STEWART**

CHARLES MARTEL, 'the Hammer' (c.688–741) ruler of the Franks from 719, progenitor of the Carolingian dynasty, and grandfather of **Charlemagne**. He was the illegitimate son of **Pepin II** of Héristal and in 714 he was chosen duke by the Austrasian (eastern)

Franks, defeated the Neustrian (western) Franks in 716, and in 719 became 'mayor of the palace' of Austrasia and real ruler of all the Frankish kingdom. He earned his nickname by his defeat of the Moors in a desperate battle at Tours, near Poitiers, in 732, thus turning back the tide of Arab conquest in Europe, then drove the Saracens out of Burgundy and Languedoc (737). He died in 741, leaving the Frankish kingdom to be divided between his sons Carloman and **Pepin III the Short**.

CHARLES OF ANJOU (1227–85) Angevin king of Naples and Sicily. The posthumous son of Louis VIII of France, he was invested with the crown of Naples and Sicily by Pope **Urban IV** (1265). After defeating his Hohenstaufen rivals **Manfred, King of Sicily** (1266) and **Conradin of Swabia** (1268), he and his French supporters had established control of the kingdom. He conquered Corfu and much of mainland Greece, and planned to capture Constantinople and re-establish the Latin Empire, but his schemes were wrecked by the revolt known as the Sicilian Vespers in 1282, which allowed Manfred's son-in-law, Peter III of Aragon, to seize the entire island of Sicily.

CHARLES OF VALOIS (1270–1325) second son of **Philip III** of France and Isabelle of Aragon. He was put forward as French claimant to the kingdom of Aragon which he was unable to conquer (1283–89), eventually receiving Anjou and Maine as compensation. He continued to figure in the diplomatic schemes of his brother **Philip IV** as unsuccessful candidate for the thrones of Constantinople (1301–07) and the Holy Roman Empire (1308), and achieved great influence during the short reigns of Philip's three sons **Louis X**, **Philip V** and **Charles IV**. Spending most of his life as a potential king in search of a kingdom, Charles died only three years before the French throne passed to his only son **Philip VI**, the first of the Valois dynasty.

CHARLES ROBERT (1288–1342) first king of Hungary of the Angevin dynasty. He claimed the throne (through his mother) on the death of the last male member of the House of Arpàd, Andrew III (1301), and after the defeat of rival claimants was crowned in 1310. He restored the royal authority in a struggle against the rebellious great magnates, whose lands he redistributed to the minor nobility, thus creating a new aristocracy loyal to him. The reforms which followed included the reorganization of military service and the introduction of a royal monopoly on gold and silver production. He married Elizabeth, daughter of **Casimir III** of Poland, and in 1337 obtained recognition of his son Louis, the future **Louis the Great** (1326–82), as heir also to the Polish throne.

CHARLES THE BOLD (1433–77) Duke of Burgundy, born in Dijon, son of Duke **Philip the Good** whom he succeeded in 1467. He married, first Catherine, the daughter of **Charles VII** of France; second, Isabella, daughter of **Charles Bourbon** (Constable of Bourbon); and third, in 1468, Margaret of York, sister of **Edward IV** of England. From his youth he was a declared enemy of **Louis XI** of France, nominally feudal superior of Burgundy, and he early formed an alliance with the Duke of Brittany and some of the great nobles of France (League of Public Weal). Their united forces ravaged Picardy, threatened Paris, defeated the king at Montlhéry, and extorted from him favourable terms. Richer and more powerful than any prince of his time, he conceived the design of restoring the old kingdom of Burgundy, and conquering Lorraine, Provence, Dauphiné and Switzerland. Louis invited him to a conference, and while he hesitated, stirred up the citizens of Liège to revolt. At the news Charles seized the king, and but for **Comines** would have put him to death. He compelled Louis to accompany him to Liège, and sanction by his presence the cruelties which he inflicted on the citizens. War raged between them till 1475, when Charles turned anew to his favourite scheme of conquest, and soon made himself master of Lorraine. Invading Switzerland, he stormed Granson, and hanged and drowned the garrison; but was terribly defeated by the Swiss near Granson (1476). Presently he besieged Morat, but sustained a more terrible defeat. The news that Duke René of Lorraine was attempting to recover his territories roused him from despair. He laid siege to Nancy; but his army was small, and his Italian mercenaries went over to the enemy. Charles fought with all his wonted recklessness, and perished in the battle. His daughter Mary of Burgundy married the emperor **Maximilian I**.

CHARLES THE GREAT See **CHARLEMAGNE**

CHARLET, Nicolas Toussaint (1792–1845) French painter and engraver, born in Paris. A pupil of **Gros**, he is known for his humorously-treated genre pictures and his lithographs celebrating the exploits of the Napoleonic wars.

CHARLEVOIX, Pierre François Xavier de (1682–1761) French Jesuit explorer of North America, born in St Quentin, Picardy. In 1720 he was sent by the French Regent to find a route to western Canada. For two and a half years he travelled by canoe up the St Lawrence River across the Great Lakes and down the Mississippi River to New Orleans, and was finally shipwrecked in the Gulf of Mexico. He became the only traveller of that time to describe the interior of North America in his *Histoire et description de la Nouvelle France* (1774).

CHARLIEU See **LABE**

CHARLOTTE (AUGUSTA), Princess (1796–1817) princess of Great Britain and Ireland, only daughter of King **George IV** and **Caroline of Brunswick**, who separated immediately after her birth. The heir to the British throne, she was brought up in strict seclusion. In 1813 she was betrothed to Prince William of Orange, but broke off the engagement in 1814. In 1816 she married Prince Leopold of Saxe-Coburg (the future King **Leopold I** of the Belgians), but died in childbirth the following year.

CHARLOTTE SOPHIA (1744–1818) queen of Great Britain and Ireland, wife of King **George III** and niece of the Duke of Mecklenburg-Strelitz. She married George shortly after his accession to the throne, in 1761, and bore him 15 children. Their eldest son was the future **George IV**, born in 1762.

CHARLTON, Bobby (Robert) (1937–) English footballer, born in Ashington, Northumberland, the younger brother of **Jack Charlton**. A fast and deadly striker, he was with the one club, Manchester United, throughout his career (1954–73), playing 754 games, scoring 245 goals, and winning five League championship medals, an FA Cup-winner's medal (1963), and a European Cup winner's medal (1968). He won 106 caps for England between 1957 and 1973, and was a member of the World Cup-winning side of 1966. After a brief spell of management with Preston North End, he turned to running highly successful coaching schools and also became a director of Manchester United.

CHARLTON, Jack (John) (1935–) English footballer, born in Ashington, Northumberland, elder brother of **Bobby Charlton**. A dour and uncompromising defender, he was a vital part of the great Leeds United side of 1965–75 under **Don Revie**'s management. He was almost 30 before he was capped for England, but then retained his place for five years. His playing days over, he became manager of Middlesborough (1973), Sheffield Wednesday (1977) and Newcastle United (1984). In 1986 he was unexpectedly appointed manager of the Republic of Ireland, and inspired the team to the semi-finals of the European Nations Cup in 1988.

CHARNLEY, Sir John (1911–82) English orthopaedic surgeon, born in Bury, Lancashire. He received his medical education at Manchester University, where he was a brilliant student. During World War II, he was an orthopaedic surgeon in the Royal Army Medical Corps. He then became a consultant to the Manchester Royal Infirmary. There and afterwards at Wrightington Hospital, Charnley developed the techniques in the 1950s and 1960s for the surgical replacement of arthritic hip joints. He played the key role in both the technology and the surgical techniques of hip replacements and his Centre at Wrightington became world famous.

CHARNOCK, Job (d.1693) English merchant. He joined the East India company in 1656, and became chief agent at Húglí. In 1690, when Húglí was under seige, he moved its factories to the mouth of the Ganges, thus founding Calcutta.

CHARPENTIER, Gustave (1860–1956) French composer, born in Dieuze, Lorraine. He wrote dramatic and choral works and composed both music and libretti of the operas *Louise* (1900) and *Julien* (1913). He wrote dramatic and choral works and succeeded his teacher, **Jules Massenet**, in the Académie des Beaux Arts.

CHARRON, Pierre (1541–1603) French theologian and philosopher, born in Paris. A close friend of **Montaigne**, he studied law but entered the church instead. He assailed the League in *Discours chrétiens* (1589), vindicated Catholicism in *Les Trois Vérités* (1594), and in his chief work, *De la sagesse* (1601), took a sceptical attitude towards all forms of religion.

CHARTERIS, Leslie, pseud of **Leslie Charles Bowyer Yin** (1907–) British-born American crime story writer, born in Singapore, the son of an English mother and a Chinese father. Educated at Cambridge, he is author of a series of books featuring a criminal hero, Simon Templar, 'the Saint', starting with *Meet the Tiger* (1928) and *Enter the Saint* (1930). He moved to the USA in 1932 and worked in Hollywood as a screenwriter. He was naturalized in 1941.

CHARTIER, Alain (c.1385–c.1435) French writer and courtier, born in Bayeux. He was secretary to **Charles VI** and **VII** and went on diplomatic missions to Germany, Venice and Scotland (1425–28). His much imitated poem, *La belle dame sans merci* (1424), is a piece of escapism in the midst of his preoccupation with the plight of France in the Hundred Years' War. This forms the backcloth of his two best works, the *Livre des quatre dames* (1415–16) in which four ladies on the morrow of Agincourt weep for their lost lovers, and the prose *Quadrilogue invectif* (1422), a debate apportioning the blame for France's ills between the people and the nobility. He also showed skill in handling the *ballade* and other lyrical forms.

CHASE, James Hadley, pseud of **René Raymond** (1906–) English novelist. He started the vogue for tough realism in gangster stories with his *No Orchids for Miss Blandish* (1939), the first of a number in similar vein.

CHASE, Salmon Portland (1808–73) American jurist and statesman, born in Cornish, New Hampshire. In 1830 he settled as a lawyer in Cincinnati, where he acted as counsel for the defence of fugitive slaves. In 1841 he helped to found the Liberty party, which brought about **Henry Clay**'s defeat in 1844. Chase was returned to the senate in 1849 by the Ohio Democrats, but separated from the party in 1852 when it committed itself to slavery. He was twice governor of Ohio (1855–59), and from 1861 to 1864 was secretary of the treasury. In 1864 **Abraham Lincoln** appointed him chief justice of the USA; as such he presided at the trial of President **Andrew Johnson** (1868). He died in New York.

CHASE, Samuel (1741–1811) American jurist, born in Somerset County, Maryland, the son of an immigrant English Anglican clergyman. He commenced law practice in Maryland, where as an Annapolis advocate he was quickly identified with rising Revolutionary sentiment in opposition to the Stamp Act. He was a delegate to the Continental Congresses from 1774 and signed the Declaration of Independence, later leading opposition to British peace proposals in 1778. He opposed the new Constitution but unexpectedly turned supporter of the **Washington** administration in 1795, and won nomination to the US Supreme Court in 1796. He delivered many distinguished opinions, stressing supremacy of national treaties over state laws, and inherent limitations on legislative powers. He was impeached in 1804 at the instance of President **Jefferson** for his partisan hostility to political offenders, but was eventually acquitted in 1805.

CHASE, William Merrit (1849–1916) American painter of landscapes, portraits and still-life, born in Franklin, Indiana. From 1872 to 1878 he studied in Munich under **Piloty**. After returning to the USA in 1878 he gained a great reputation as a teacher.

CHASLES, Michel (1793–1880) French geometer, born in Épernon. He entered the École Polytechnique in 1812, and became a military engineer. He resigned to devote himself to mathematics, taught at the École Polytechnique (1841–51) and became professor of geometry at the Sorbonne in 1846. He greatly developed synthetic projective geometry by means of cross-ratio and homographies without the use of co-ordinates. In 1867 he reported to the Academy that he had come into possession of autographs of **Pascal** which proved that Pascal had anticipated **Newton**'s discovery of the law of gravitation. Ultimately, however, he had to admit that these and several thousand other autographs (of **Julius Caesar**, **Dante**, **Shakespeare**, etc) were forgeries. The forger, Vrain-Lucas, was convicted in 1869.

CHASLES, Philarète (1798–1873) French scholar and writer, born in Mainvilliers, near Chartres. Jailed as a Jacobin, he fled on his release to England, where he acquired the knowledge of English books which he used for his essays on comparative literature. In 1837 he became librarian of the Bibliothèque Mazarine, and in 1841 professor of northern languages at the Collège de France.

CHASSÉ, David Hendrik, Baron (1765–1849) Dutch soldier, born in Thiel, in Guelders, nicknamed 'General Baïonette' by **Napoleon**. He joined the French army in 1789 and fought with great distinction in Germany and Spain. As lieutenant-general of the Dutch forces in 1815 he fought at Waterloo against his old comrades, the French. In the struggle for Belgian independence he held the citadel at Antwerp (1830–32), but finally surrendered to superior French and Belgian forces, with some Pontish naval assistance.

CHASSEPOT, Antoine Alphonse (1833–1905) French inventor. He was an employee in the Paris arsenal, and in 1863 produced the model of a rifle named after him, adopted by the French army in 1866. He subsequently became a hotelkeeper in Nice.

CHASSÉRIAU, Théodor (1819–56) Creole-French painter, born in Samana, San Domingo. He studied under **Delaroche** and **Ingres**, and executed murals and historical subject paintings. His *Tepidarium at Pompeii* and *Susanna* are in the Louvre.

CHASTELARD, Pierre de Boscosel de (c.1540–1563) French courtier in the service of King **Francis II** and **Mary, Queen of Scots**. Hopelessly in love with the widowed young queen, he followed her to Scotland, where he was twice caught trying to hide under her bed, and was executed.

CHATAWAY, Chris (Christopher John) (1931–) English athlete and politician, born in Chelsea, London. Educated at Sherborne School and Magdalen College, Oxford, he was one of Britain's finest middle-distance runners in the 1950s. A member of the Olympic team in 1952 and 1956, he helped **Roger Bannister** break the four-minute mile in 1954; later in the year he defeated **Vladimir Kuts** in the 5000 metres in an epic race in London, achieving a new world record time. In 1959 he entered parliament as a Conservative MP, and was minister of posts and telecommunications (1970–72) and minister for industrial development (1972–74) before taking up a career in the City.

CHATEAUBRIAND, François René, Vicomte de (1768–1848) French writer and statesman, born of a noble Breton family in St Malo. He served for a short time as an ensign, and in 1791 sailed to North America, spending eight months in the travels recounted in his *Voyage en Amérique*. Returning to France, he married, but forthwith joined the army of the émigrés, and was left for dead near Namur. From 1793 to 1800 he lived in London, teaching and translating. In 1797 he published an *Essai sur les Révolutions*. *Atala*, an unfinished Romantic epic of American Indian life (1801), established his literary reputation; and *Génie du christianisme* (1802), a vindication of the Church of Rome, raised him to the foremost position among the French men of letters of the day. In 1803 he was appointed secretary to the embassy in Rome, where he wrote his *Lettres sur l'Italie*, and in 1804 was sent as envoy to the little republic of Valais. But on the murder of the Duc **d'Enghien**, Chateaubriand refused to hold office under **Napoleon**. He set out for the East in 1806, visited Greece, Palestine and Egypt, and returned to France in 1807. Two years later he issued *Les Martyrs*, a prose epic of **Diocletian**'s persecutions. From 1814 to 1824 he gave support to the Restoration monarchy. He was made a peer and minister, and in 1822–24 was ambassador extraordinary at the British court. Disappointed in his hope of becoming prime minister, from 1824 to 1830 he figured as a Liberal. On the downfall of **Charles X** he went back to the royalists. During the reign of **Louis-Philippe** he occupied himself in writing his celebrated *Mémoires d'outre-tombe*. Parts of this eloquent autobiography appeared before his death; the whole, in six volumes, not till 1902. His writings also include the *Itinéraire de Paris à Jerusalem*; *Les Natchez*, a prose epic dealing with American Indian life; and two works of fiction, *René* and *Les Aventures du dernier des Abencérages* (1826), a tale of 16th-century Spain.

CHÂTELET-LOMONT, Gabrielle Émilie, Marquise du (1706–49) French scholar and writer, daughter of the Baron de Breteuil and mistress of **Voltaire**. An outstanding beauty, she learned Latin and Italian with her father, and after her marriage in 1725 to the Comte du Châtelet-Lomont she studied mathematics and the physical sciences. In 1773 she met Voltaire, who came to live with her at her husband's estate at Cirey. She wrote *Institutions de physique* (1740) and *Dissertation sur la nature et la propagation du feu* (1744), but her chief work was her translation into French of **Newton**'s *Principia Mathematica*, posthumoulsy published in 1759.

CHATELIER, Henry le (1850–1936) French chemist, born in Paris. In 1888 he discovered the law of reaction governing the effect of pressure and temperature on equilibrium. He devised a railway water-brake, an optical pyrometer, and made contributions to metallurgy and ceramics.

CHATHAM, William Pitt, 1st Earl of (1708–78) known as 'the elder Pitt', English statesman and orator, the younger son of Robert Pitt of Boconnoc, in Cornwall. Born in Westminster, he was educated at Eton and Trinity College, Oxford. He obtained a cornetcy in the Blues (1731), and in 1735 entered parliament for the family borough, Old Sarum. He sided with **Frederick**, Prince of Wales, then at deadly feud with the king, and offered, as leader of the young 'Patriot' Whigs, a determined opposition to **Walpole**. The latter being driven from power, the king found it necessary, in 1746, to allow Pitt's admission to the Broad-bottom administration; subsequently he was paymaster-general, but resigned in 1755. The Duchess of Marlborough had left him £10000 in 1744; and Sir William Pynsent left him £3000 a year and the Somerset estate of Burton-Pynsent, the family seat thenceforward of the Pitts. In 1756 Pitt became nominally secretary of state, but virtually premier. He immediately put into execution his own plan of carrying on the war with France, raised the militia, and strengthened the naval power; but the king's old enmity and German predilections led him to resign in April 1757, to be recalled in June, in obedience to the loud demands of the people. His war policy was characterized by unusual vigour, sagacity and success. French armies were beaten everyhere by Britain and her allies—in India, in Africa, in Canada, on the Rhine—and British fleets drove the few French ships they did not capture or destroy from almost every sea. But the prime mover of all these brilliant victories found himself compelled to resign (1761) when, through Lord **Bute**, the majority of the cabinet refused to declare war with Spain. Pitt received a pension of £3000 a year; and his wife, sister of **George Grenville**, was created Baroness Chatham. In 1766 he formed a new ministry, choosing for himself the almost sinecure office of privy seal, with a seat in the House of Lords as Viscount Pitt and Earl of Chatham. Ill-health prevented Chatham from taking any active part in guiding his weak and embarrassed ministry, and he resigned in 1768, to hold office no more. He spoke strongly against the arbitrary and harsh policy towards the American colonies, and warmly urged an amicable settlement of the differences. But when it was proposed to make peace on any terms, ill though he was, Chatham came down to the House of Lords (2 April 1778), and by a few broken words secured a majority against the motion. But exhausted by speaking, on rising again to reply to a query, he fell back into the arms of his friends, and died. He was honoured with a public funeral and a statue in Westminster Abbey; government voted £20000 to pay his debts, and conferred a pension of £4000 a year on his descendants. His imposing appearance and his magnificent voice added greatly to the attractions of his oratory. His character was irreproachable, though his haughtiness irritated even his friends. His eldest son, John, 2nd Earl of Chatham (1756–1835), commanded the luckless Walcheren Expedition (1809). His second son was **William Pitt**, 'the Younger'.

CHATRIAN See **ERCKMANN-CHATRIAN**

CHATTERJEE, Bankim Chandra (1838–94) Indian writer, born in Katalpura, Bengal. One of the most influential figures in 19th-century Indian literature, his novels included *Durges Nandini* (1864) and *Anandamath* (1882), a novel of the Sannyasi rebellion of 1772 from which the Nationalist song *Bande Mataram* ('Hail to thee, Mother'), was taken.

CHATTERTON, Thomas (1752–70) English poet, born in Bristol. His father, a sub-chanter in the cathedral, and master of a charity school, died before the boy was born. The mother, a poor schoolmistress and needlewoman, brought up her son and his sister beneath the shadow of St Mary Redcliffe, where their forefathers had been sextons (more probably masons) since the days of Queen **Elizabeth**. He was a scholar of **Colston**'s bluecoat hospital (1760–65), and then was apprenticed an attorney. Fascinated from boyhood by antiques, he wrote and published pseudo-archaic poems purporting to be the work of a 15th-century Bristol Monk, Thomas Rowley, a friend of a historical figure, a merchant called William Canynge. In 1769 he sent a history of painting in England, allegedly by Rowley, to **Horace Walpole**, who was only temporarily deceived. He was released from his apprenticeship in 1770 and left for London, where he worked on innumerable satires, essays and epistles, and a burlesque opera, *The Revenge*. But later that year he poisoned himself with arsenic. His 'Rowley' poems, although soon exposed as forgeries, are considered to have genuine talent, and he became a romantic hero to later poets. His story was dramatized by Alfred de Vigny in 1835.

CHATWIN, Bruce (1940–89) English writer and traveller, born in Sheffield. He worked at Sotheby's as an expert on modern art for eight years until he temporarily went blind. To recuperate, he went to Africa and the Sudan. He was converted to a life of nomadic asceticism and began writing beguiling books which defy classification, combining fiction, anthropology, philosophy and travel. They include *In Patagonia* (1977) which won the Hawthornden prize and the E M Forster Award of the American Academy of Letters; *The Viceroy of Ouidah* (1980); *On The Black Hill* (1982), winner of the Whitbread Literary award for the best first novel; *The Songlines* (1987) and *Utz* (1988), a novella which was short-listed for the Booker prize.

CHAUCER, Geoffrey (c.1345–1400) English poet, the son of John Chaucer, a vintner and tavern keeper in London, perhaps the John Chaucer who was deputy to the king's butler. In 1357 and 1358 he was a page in the service of the wife of Lionel, Duke of Clarence; he would seem to have been presently transferred to King **Edward III**'s household. In 1359 he served in the campaign in France, and was taken prisoner at 'Retters' (Réthel), but was soon ransomed, the king contributing £16 towards the required amount. He returned home in 1360. In 1367 the king granted him a pension. He is described as 'our beloved yeoman', and as 'one of the yeomen of the king's chamber', and in 1368 he was one of the king's esquires. In 1369 he first appeared as a poet, with his *Book of the Duchess*, on the death of **John of Gaunt**'s wife. In 1370 he went abroad on the king's service; in 1372–73 on a royal mission to Genoa, Pisa, Florence; in 1376, abroad again; in 1377, to Flanders and to France; in 1378, to Italy again. Meanwhile in 1374 he was appointed comptroller of the Customs and Subsidy of Wools, Skins, and Tanned Hides in the port of London; in 1382, comptroller of the Petty Customs; and in 1385 he was allowed to nominate a permanent deputy. In 1374 the king granted him a pitcher of wine daily; and John of Gaunt conferred on him a pension of £10 for life. In 1375 he received from the crown the custody of lands that brought him in £104. In 1386 he was elected a knight of the shire for Kent. The following writings certainly belong to the period 1369–87: *The Parliament of Fowls*, *The House of Fame*, *Troilus and Cressida*, and *The Legend of Good Women*; also what ultimately appeared as the Clerk's, Man of Law's, Prioress's, Second Nun's and Knight's Tales in the *Canterbury Tales*. Chaucer's earlier writings, including his translation of part of the *Roman de la Rose*, followed the current French trends, but the most important influence acting upon him during this middle period of his literary life was that of Italy. Much of his subject matter he derived from his great Italian contemporaries, especially from **Boccaccio**, but it was the spirit, not the letter of these masters which he imitated. The crowning work of the middle period of his life is *Troilus and Cressida*—a work in which his immense power of human observation, his sense of humour, and his dramatic skill are lavishly displayed. *The Legend of Good Women* has an admirable prologue, but was never finished. His next great subject was the *Canterbury Tales*. But about the end of 1386 he lost his offices, possibly owing to the absence abroad of John of Gaunt, and fell upon hard times. In 1389 he was appointed clerk of the King's Works, but this did not last and he fell into debt. In 1394 King **Richard II** granted him a pension of £20 for life; but the advances of payment he applied for, and the issue of letters of protection from arrest for debt, indicate his condition. On the accession in 1399 of **Henry IV**, John of Gaunt, he was granted a pension of 40 marks (£26 13s 4d), and his few remaining months were spent in comfort. After his death he was laid in that part of Westminster Abbey which through his burial there came afterwards to be called the Poets' Corner. His greatest achievement is the Prologue (1387) to the *Tales*, which, as a piece of descriptive writing, is unique. Chaucer was the first great poet of the English race, and he established the southern English dialect as the literary language of England. Many works have been ascribed to Chaucer, and were long printed in popular editions, that are certainly not his—eg, *The Court of Love*, *Chaucer's Dream*, *The Complaint of the Black Knight*, *The Cuckoo and Nightingale*, *The Flower and the Leaf*, and much of the extant *Romaunt of the Rose*.

CHAULIAC, Guy de (c.1300–1368) French surgeon, born in Chauliac in Auvergne. The most famous surgeon of the Middle Ages, he wrote *Chirurgia Magna* (1363), which was translated into French over a century later and used as a manual by generations of doctors.

CHAUMETTE, Pierre Gaspard (1763–94) French revolutionary, born in Nevers, a shoemaker's son. At the revolution he joined with **Camille Desmoulins**, and soon gained such popularity by his extreme sansculottism that he was appointed procurator of the Paris commune. His extravagances disgusted **Robespierre**, and he perished on the scaffold.

CHAUSSON, Ernest (1855–99) French composer, born in Paris. He studied under **Jules Massenet** and **César Franck**. Several of his orchestral works, including the *Poème* for violin and orchestra, and the symphony in Bb (1891), as well as a number of attractive songs, have kept their popularity.

CHAUVIRÉ, Yvette (1917–) French dancer and teacher, born in Paris. The leading French ballerina of her generation, she studied at the Paris Opera Ballet School before creating her first role for the company in 1936. In 1941 her mentor, company director **Serge Lifar**, promoted her to the rank of étoile, a position she held almost continually until her retirement from the stage in 1972. With her lyricism and technical finesse, she excelled in the classical repertoire and was a guest star with companies around the world. In 1970 she became director of the Académie Internationale de Danse in Paris.

CHAVANNES See **PUVIS de CHAVANNES**

CHÁVEZ, Carlos (1899–1978) Mexican composer, born in Mexico City. He supplemented casual musical teaching by study in New York and Europe, and, returning to Mexico, formed the Mexican Symphony Orchestra in 1928, becoming director of the National Conservatory. As an official in the Ministry of Fine Arts, Chávez's influence on every aspect of Mexican music was enormous. His works are little known outside his own country, partly owing to their large scale and demands for grandiose orchestral forces, but are influenced by Mexican folk music and include ballets, symphonies and concertos and an unusual *Toccata for Percussion* (1942).

CHAYEFSKY, Paddy (Sidney) (1923–81) American stage and television playwright, born in New York City. He is best known for *Marty* (1953) and *The Bachelor Party* (1954), sensitive and affecting plays about ordinary people.

CHEBYSHEV, Pafnutii Lvovich (1821–94) Russian mathematician, born in Okatovo, the son of a retired army officer. A graduate of Moscow University, he became an assistant at St Petersburg in 1847 and later professor (1860–82). In number theory he made important contributions to the theory of the distribution of prime numbers, and in probability theory he proved fundamental limit theorems. Later he studied the theory of mechanisms and developed a theory of approximation to functions by polynomials, which has become important in modern computing. The mathematical school that he founded at St Petersburg remained the dominant influence on Russian mathematics for the rest of the century.

CHEEVER, John (1912–82) American short-story writer and novelist. Born in Quincy, Massachusetts, he began telling stories when he was eight or nine. He sold his first story, 'Expelled', to *The New Republic* after he was thrown out of Thayer Academy in South Braintree, Massachusetts, at the age of 17. By the time he was 22 the *New Yorker* was accepting his work and for years he contributed a dozen stories a year to it. His first collection of stories was published in 1943 when he was in the army. After the war he taught composition and wrote scripts for television, but in 1951 a Guggenheim Fellowship allowed him to devote his attention to writing, and a second collection, *The Enormous Radio and Other Stories*, came out in 1953. His first novel, *The Wapshot Chronicle* (1957) won the National Book award and its sequel, *The Wapshot Scandal* (1964), was awarded the Howell's Medal for fiction. A steady stream of novels and stories followed, many of them focusing on the isolation and discontent of contemporary American life. Invariably funny and ironic, sad and sophisticated, these include *Bullet Park* (1969), *The World of Apples* (1973), *Falconer* (1977) and *The Stories of John Cheever*, winner of the Pulitzer prize and the National Book Critics award in 1979.

CHEKE, Sir John (1514–57) English scholar, born in Cambridge. Fellow of St John's College, Cambridge from 1529, he adopted the doctrines of the Reformation, and in 1540 was appointed the first regius professor of Greek at Cambridge. With Sir **Thomas Smith** he introduced the Erasmian pronunciation of Greek despite opposition from Bishop **Stephen Gardiner**. In 1554 he was appointed tutor to the Prince of Wales (later **Edward VI**), whose accession secured him a seat in parliament (1547), the provostship of King's College, Cambridge (1548) and a knighthood (1552). After the accession of **Mary I** he was imprisoned (1553–54) for having served as Latin secretary to Lady **Jane Grey**, and thereafter went abroad to teach. In 1556 he was lured to Belgium and treacherously seized, and brought back to the Tower where he was forced to recant his Protestantism publicly.

CHEKHOV, Anton Pavlovich (1860–1904) Russian author, born in Taganrog, the son of an unsuccessful shopkeeper and the grandson of a serf. He studied medicine at Moscow University and qualified as a doctor in 1884. As a student, he had written articles for various comic papers, and his first book, *Motley Stories* (Pëstrye Rasskazy), appearing in 1886, was successful enough for him to think of writing as a profession. He continued to regard himself as a doctor rather than a writer, though he practised very little except during the cholera epidemic of 1892–93. His magazine articles led to an interest in the popular stage of vaudeville and French farce, and, after the failure of his first full-length play, *Ivanov* (1887), he wrote several one-acters, such as *The Bear* (1889) and *The Proposal* (1889). In 1892 he settled on a farm estate at Melikhovo. His next full length plays, *The Wood Demon* (1889) and *The Seagull* (1896), were also failures and Chekhov had decided to concentrate on his stories (which had introduced him to his admired **Tolstoy** and **Gorky**) when Nemirovich-Danchenko persuaded him to let the Moscow Art Theatre revive *The Seagull* in 1898. Produced by **Stanislavsky**, who revealed its quality and originality, its reception encouraged him to write for the same company his masterpieces: *Uncle Vanya* (1900), *The Three Sisters* (1901) and *The Cherry Orchard* (1904). Meanwhile he continued to write short stories. In 1891 he wrote *Saghalien Island*, after a visit to a penal settlement which had a considerable effect on subsequent criminal legislation. In 1897 tuberculosis forced him to live either abroad or at Yalta in the Crimea. In 1900 he was elected fellow of the Moscow Academy of Science, but resigned when his fellow-member, Gorky, was dismissed by order of the tsar. In 1901 he married the actress Olga Knipper, who for many years after her husband's death was the admired exponent of female parts in his plays. Chekhov is perhaps the most popular Russian author outside his own country. His stories have strongly influenced many writers, and his plays are firmly established in the classical repertoires of Europe. His technique is impressionistic—almost *pointilliste*. In all his work he equates worldly success with loss of soul. It is the sensitive, hopefully struggling people, at the mercy of forces almost always too strong for them, who are his heroes. For this reason his work, though presenting a convincing picture of Russian middle-class life at the end of the 19th century, has a timeless quality, since it reflects the universal predicament of the 'little man'. Among his many short stories, the following are outstanding: *The Steppe*, *The Chorus Girl*, *The Duel*, *Ward No* 6, *The Darling*, *The Lady with the Dog*, *In the Ravine* and *The Bishop*.

CHELCICKY, Petz (c.1390–1460) Czech reformer and theologian, born probably in Chelčice in Bohemia. A radical follower of the Hussites, he abjured towns and commerce, and founded the sect which became the Moravian Brothers. The Christian doctrine of his *The Net of True Faith* (1450) was later promulgated by **Tolstoy**.

CHELMSFORD, Frederic Thesiger, 1st Baron (1794–1878) English judge. A midshipman in the navy, he exchanged the sea for law, and was called to the bar in 1818. He was made solicitor-general in 1844, attorney-general in 1845–46 and 1852, and Lord Chancellor in 1858 and 1866.

CHELMSFORD, Frederick John Napier Thesiger, 1st Viscount (1868–1933) English colonial administrator. He was governor of Queensland (1905–09), of New South Wales (1909–13), viceroy of India (1916–21), and First Lord of the Admiralty in 1924.

CHEMNITZ, Martin (1522–86) German Lutheran theologian, born in Treuenbrietzen, in Brandenburg. His skill in astrology led to his appointment as ducal librarian at Königsberg in 1549, and thenceforth he devoted himself to theology. His opposition to **Osiander** led him to Wittenberg (1553); and he was appointed a preacher at Brunswick in 1554, and 'superintendent' in 1567. His works include *Examen Councilii Tridentini* (1565–73) and *De duabus Naturis in Christo* (1571).

CHEN, Yi (1901–72) Chinese communist leader. He studied in France, and joined the Communist party on his return. He supported **Mao Zedong** in the struggle with the Kuomintang, and the Japanese (1934). He formed the 4th Route Army in Kiangsi (1940), and commanded the East China Liberation army (1946), restyled the 3rd (East China) Army (1948). He prepared an amphibious operation against Taiwan, but failed to capture Quemoy island in 1949. Created marshal of the People's Republic in 1955, he became foreign minister in 1958. He was dropped from the politburo during the Cultural Revolution in 1969.

CHEN NING YANG See **YANG**

CHÉNIER, Marie André (1762–94) French poet, born in Constantinople, the third son of the French consul-general and a Greek woman. At three he was sent to France, and at twelve was placed at the Collège de Navarre, Paris, where Greek literature was his special subject. At 20 he entered the army, and served for six months in Strasbourg; but disgusted with military life, returned to Paris and to strenuous study. To this period belong his famous idylls *Le Mendiant* and *L'Aveugle*. His health giving way, he travelled in Switzerland, Italy and the Archipelago. In 1786 he returned to Paris and began several ambitious poems, most of which remained fragments. The most noteworthy are *Suzanne*, *L'Invention* and *Hermès*, the last being an imitation of **Lucretius**. In 1787 he went to England as secretary to the French ambassador, but in 1790 he returned to Paris to find himself in the ferment of the Revolution, which at first he supported; but alarmed by its excesses he mortally offended **Robespierre** by pamphlets. He was thrown into prison, and after six months was guillotined on 25 July, just three days before the end of the Reign of Terror.

CHEOPS (26th century BC) Grecized form of **Khufu**, king of Memphis in Egypt, 2nd of the fourth dynasty. He is famous as the builder of the Great Pyramid. A son and successor, Chephren (Khafre) built the next largest pyramid.

CHEPMAN, Walter (c.1473–1538) the first Scottish printer. A notary and merchant in Edinburgh, in 1507 he received a patent from **James IV** to set up the first Scottish printing press, with an Edinburgh bookseller, Andrew Myllar. Little remains of their output apart from the *Aberdeen Breviary* (1510) and fragments of *The Wallace* by **Blind Harry**.

CHERBULIEZ, Charles Victor (1829–99) Swiss-born French novelist and critic, born in Geneva. At Paris, Bonn and Berlin, he studied first mathematics, then philology and philosophy, after which he lived in Geneva as a teacher. In 1864 he went to Paris to join the staff of the *Revue des Deux Mondes*, writing under the pseudonym of G Valbert. He was elected to the French Academy in 1881. His novels include *Le Roman d'une honnête femme* (1866), *Meta Holdenis* (1873), *Samuel Brohl et Cie* (1877), *L'Idée de Jean Têterol* (1878), *Noirs et rouges* (1881), *La Vocation du Comte Ghislain* (1888), and *Le Secret du précepteur* (1893). He also wrote many literary and political articles in the *Revue des Deux Mondes*.

CHERBULIEZ, Joel (1806–70) Swiss novelist and critic, born in Geneva, the son of a prosperous bookseller. He succeeded to his father's business, and edited the *Revue critique* from 1833. His *Lendemain du dernier jour d'un condamné* (1829) was a clever burlesque on **Victor Hugo**'s well-known *tour-de-force*, while his *Genève* (1867) was a solid contribution to the history of the city.

CHERENKOV, Pavel Alekseevich (1904–) Soviet physicist. In 1934 he noted the emission of blue light from water and other transparent media when atomic particles are passed through them at a speed greater than that of light. Subsequent researches by **Igor Tamm** and **Ilya Frank** led to a definite explanation of the 'Cherenkov effect' for which all three Soviet physicists shared the Nobel prize for physics in 1958. The principle was adapted in constructing a cosmic-ray counter mounted in *Sputnik III*.

CHERKASSKY, Shura Alexander Isaakovich (1911–) Russian-born American pianist, born in Odessa. He settled in America in 1922 and studied under Josef Hofmann at the Curtis Institute, Philadelphia. He excels in the Romantic repertoire and has toured and recorded widely.

CHERMAYEFF, Serge (1900–) American architect and designer, born in the Caucasus, educated in England. After a period in journalism, he became a director of Waring and Gillow (1928) for which he established a 'Modern Art Studio'. His early design work was for interiors, including studios for Broadcasting House, London (1931). He also designed textiles, radio-cabinets (for Ekco) and furniture; outstanding was a modular range called 'Plan' (1936). His architectural designs included the De La Warr Pavilion, Bexhill-on-Sea (1933–35), with **Erich Mendelsohn**, and some notable houses. In 1940 he emigrated to the USA where, in addition to his architectural work, he taught design and architecture. He held professorships at Harvard (1952–62) and Yale (1962–69).

CHERNENKO, Konstantin (1911–85) Soviet politician, born of peasant stock in Bolshaya Tes in Central Siberia. He joined the Komsomol (Communist Youth League) in 1929 and the Communist party (CPSU) in 1931. During the 1940s, he worked as a specialist in party propaganda in, first, Krasnoyarsk (Siberia) and, then, Moldavia, where he impressed **Leonid Brezhnev**, who was the first secretary of the CPSU in Moldavia between 1950 and 1952. Brezhnev adopted Chernenko as his personal assistant and brought him to Moscow to work in the central apparatus in 1956. He was inducted into the CPSU Central Committee in 1971, the secretariat in 1976 and into the politburo, as a full member, in December 1978. During his final years in power, Brezhnev sought to promote Chernenko as his heir-apparent, but on Brezhnev's death in November 1982 Chernenko was passed over in favour of **Yuri Andropov**. During the Andropov administration, he held the post of ideology secretary. However, when Andropov died in February 1984 Chernenko was selected as the CPSU's stop-gap leader by cautious party colleagues. In April 1984 Chernenko was also elected state president. As Soviet leader he sought to promote a new era of detente, but from July 1984, suffering from emphysema, he progressively retired from public view.

CHERNYSHEVSKI, Nicolai Gavrilovich (1828–89) Russian critic and novelist. A follower of the French socialists, he wrote on political and social matters such as Nihilism as well as literature, and was imprisoned in Siberia from 1862 to 1883 for revolutionary activities.

His *Aesthetic Relationship between Art and Reality* deals with his theory of the place of art in life, and his propagandist novel, *A Vital Question*, was written during imprisonment.

CHERUBINI, Maria Luigi Carlo Zenobio Salvatore (1760–1842) Italian composer, born in Florence. Showing early promise in composing church pieces, he studied at Bologna and Milan, and wrote a succession of operas, at first in Neapolitan, later (having moved to Paris) in French style, of which little is now heard apart from some of the overtures, such as that of *The Water-Carrier* (1800), his best opera. His later work was mainly ecclesiastical. In 1822 he became director of the Paris Conservatoire, which he brought to prominence. His work on counterpoint and fugue (1835) was a standard text.

CHERWELL, Frederick Alexander Lindemann, 1st Viscount (1886–1957) English physicist, born in Baden-Baden. He was educated at the University of Berlin and at the Sorbonne, where his work on the problems of atomic heat attracted the attention of distinguished physicists. In 1914 he became director of the RFC Experimental Physics Station at Farnborough. He was the first to evolve the mathematical theory of aircraft spin and put it into practice in a daring flight. He was professor of experimental philosophy at Oxford (1919–56) and director of the Clarendon laboratory, which he made one of the best on low-temperature research in Britain. A close friend of Sir **Winston Churchill**, he became his personal assistant in 1940. He was paymaster-general from 1942 to 1945 and again in the 1951 government, advising on nuclear research and scientific matters generally. He resigned in 1953 to resume his professorship, and was created viscount in 1956.

CHESELDEN, William (1688–1752) English surgeon, born in Somerby near Melton Mowbray. He was the first to perform operations for lateral lithotomy and iridectomy (removal of part of the iris). He wrote *The Anatomy of the Human Body* (1713).

CHESHIRE, Geoffrey Chevalier (1886–) English law teacher and jurist, born in Hartford, Cheshire. Educated at Denstone College and Merton College, Oxford, he was Vinerian professor of law at Oxford (1944–49). An outstanding teacher of law and a great expositor, he wrote three classic, authoritative works, *The Modern Law of Real Property* (1925), *Private International Law* (1935) and, with CHS Fifoot, *The Law of Contract* (1945), all of which have been repeatedly re-edited and cited in court.

CHESHIRE, Geoffrey Leonard (1917–) English philanthropist, educated at Stowe School and Merton College, Oxford. An outstanding pilot in the RAF in World War II, he was promoted Group Captain and won the VC in 1944 on completing a hundred bombing missions, often at low altitude, on heavily defended German targets. With **Penney** he was the official British observer of the destruction caused by the atomic bomb over Nagasaki (1945). This experience, together with his new-found faith in Roman Catholicism, made him decide to devote the rest of his life to the relief of suffering. He founded the 'Cheshire Foundation Homes' for the incurably sick in many countries. In 1959 he married Sue, Baroness **Ryder**, who founded the Sue Ryder Foundation for the sick and disabled of all age groups.

CHESNEY, Charles Cornwallis (1826–76) English soldier, nephew of **Francis Rawson Chesney**. He was professor of military history at Sandhurst (1858–64) and the Imperial Staff College from 1864. He was author of the *Waterloo Lectures* (1861) delivered at Sandhurst, criticizing **Wellington** and giving the credit to **Blücher**.

CHESNEY, Francis Rawdon (1789–1872) Irish soldier and explorer of the Euphrates, born at Annalong, County Down. In 1829 he surveyed the route for a Suez Canal; after 1831 he four times explored a route to India by rail and sea via Syria and the Euphrates. He commanded the artillery at Hong Kong in 1843–47.

CHESSMAN, Caryl Whittier (1922–60) American convict-author, born in St Joseph, Michigan. He was sentenced to death in 1948 on 17 charges of kidnapping, robbery and rape, but was granted eight stays of execution by the governor of California amounting to a record period of twelve years under sentence of death, without a reprieve. During this period he conducted a brilliant legal battle from prison, learnt four languages and wrote the best-selling books against capital punishment *Cell* 2455 *Death Row* (1956), *Trial by Ordeal* (1956) and *The Face of Justice* (1958). His ultimate execution provoked worldwide criticism of American judicial methods.

CHESTERFIELD, Philip Dormer Stanhope, 4th Earl of (1694–1773) English statesman, orator, wit and man of letters, born in London. He studied at Cambridge, made the Grand Tour, was member for St Germains in Cornwall from 1715 to 1722, for Lostwithiel from 1722 to c.1723. In 1726 he succeeded his father as 4th Earl of Chesterfield. In 1730 he was made lord steward of the household. Until then, as a Whig, he had supported **Walpole**; but being ousted from office for voting against an excise bill, he went over to the Opposition, and was one of Walpole's bitterest antagonists. He joined the **Pelham** ministry in 1744, made an excellent Irish lord-lieutenant in 1745, and was in 1746 one of the principal secretaries of state. Intimate with **Swift**, **Pope** and **Bolingbroke**, he drew from **Johnson** a famous indignant letter. Besides the well-known *Letters to his* [natural] *son*, he also wrote *Letters to his Godson and Successor*. His *Letters to Lord Huntingdon* appeared in 1923, his verse in 1927.

CHESTERTON, G K (Gilbert Keith) (1874–1936) English critic, novelist and poet, born in London. He was educated at St Paul's School and studied art at the Slade School, which he never practised professionally, although he contributed illustrations to the novels of his friend **Hilaire Belloc**. His first writings were for periodicals, and all through his life much of his best work went into essays and articles in *The Bookman*, *The Speaker*, *The Illustrated London News*, and his own *G.K's Weekly*, which was born in 1925 of the *New Witness* inherited from his brother a few years earlier. Tremendous zest and energy, with a mastery of paradox, a robust humour and forthright devotion characterize his entire output. He became a Roman Catholic in 1922, but this decision is clearly foreshadowed in his works, the best of which were published before that date. His two earliest books were the collections of poetry *The Wild Knight* and *Greybeards at Play* (both 1900); the works which followed include *The Napoleon of Notting Hill* (1904), liberal and anti-Imperialist in outlook, brilliant studies of **Browning** (1903), **Dickens** (1906) and **R L Stevenson** (1907); and the provocative *Heretics* (1908) and *Orthodoxy* (1908). The amiable detective-priest Father Brown, who brought Chesterton popularity with a wider public, first appeared in *The Innocence of Father Brown* (1911). Soon after his conversion Chesterton published his well-known Life of St **Francis of Assisi**, also one of St **Thomas Aquinas** (1933). His *Collected Poems* appeared in 1933, and his *Autobiography* posthumously in 1936. An ebullient personality, with a figure of Johnsonian proportions, absent-minded but quick-witted, he will go down as one of the most colourful and provocative writers of his day. His brother, Cecil Edward (1879–1918), wrote anti-liberal books and started, with Hilaire Belloc, the anti-bureaucratic paper *New Witness* in 1912. He married Ada Elizbeth Jones, journalist and writer, who pioneered the Cecil Houses for London's homeless women.

CHETHAM, Humphrey (1580–1653) English merchant and philanthropist, born in Manchester. He became a cloth manufacturer in Manchester, and was the founder of Chetham Hospital and a public library at Manchester.

CHETTLE, Henry (d.c.1607) English dramatist and pamphleteer, born in London, the son of a dyer. A printer by trade, he turned to writing when his printing-house failed. He edited **Robert Greene**'s *Groat's-worth of Wit* (1592), and in 1593 published a pamphlet, *Kind Harts Dreame*, apologizing for Greene's attack on **Shakespeare**. He wrote a picaresque romance, *Piers Plainnes Seven Yeres Prentiship* (1595), and from 1598 turned to writing plays for **Philip Henslowe**'s Rose Theatre in Bankside, especially *The Tragedy of Hoffman* (1602). He collaborated on many others, including *Robin Hood, Patient Grisel, The Blind-Beggar of Bethnal-Green* (with **John Day**) and *Jane Shore*. He also wrote an elegy for Queen **Elizabeth**, *England's Mourning Garment* (1603).

CHEVALIER, Albert (1862–1923) English entertainer, the son of a French teacher at the Kensington Grammar School. He appeared as an actor at the old Prince of Wales's in 1877, and in 1891 became a music-hall singer. Writing, composing and singing costermonger ballads, he immortalized such songs as 'My Old Dutch', and 'Knocked 'em in the Old Kent Road'. In 1901 he published *Before I Forget*.

CHEVALIER, Maurice (1888–1972) French film and vaudeville actor, born in Paris. He began his career as a child, singing and dancing in small cafés, and became dancing partner to **Mistinguett** at the Folies Bergères from 1909 to 1913. A prisoner during World War I, he won the Croix de Guerre, and became a member of the Legion of Honour. He first appeared in London in 1919 and 40 years later his individual, straw-hatted, *bon-viveur* personality was capable of scoring a popular success in the musical film *Gigi* (1958). Among the best of his earlier films were *The Innocents of Paris* (1929) and *The Love Parade* (1932). He wrote his autobiography in *Ma route et mes chansons* (translated as *The Man in the Straw Hat* in 1949), and *I Remember it Well* (1971).

CHEVALIER, Michel (1806–79) French economist, born in Limoges. He trained as an engineer. An ardent follower of the economist **St Simon**, he attached himself to **Enfantin**, and helped to compile the propagandist *Livre nouveau*. After six months' imprisonment in 1832, he retracted all he had written in the *Globe* (1830–32) against Christianity and marriage. He was sent by **Thiers** to inquire into water and railway communication in the United States (1832–33). Abandoning socialism, he was made a councillor of state in 1838; and in 1840 professor of political economy at the Collège de France. In 1845 he was returned by Aveyron to the Chamber of Deputies. After the revolution of 1848 he made onslaughts that were never met upon **Louis Blanc**'s socialism in articles collected as *L'Organisation du travail* (1848) and *Questions politiques et sociales* (1852). As a free-trader he aided **Cobden** in carrying into effect in 1860 the commercial treaty between France and England.

CHEVALLIER, Gabriel (1895–1969) French novelist, born in Lyons. He won wide acclaim with his *Clochemerle* (1934, English translation 1936), an earthy satire on petty bureaucracy, after a series of less successful psychological novels. Other books include *La Peur* (1930), *Clarisse Vernon* (1933), *Sainte-Colline* (1937), *Les Héritiers Euffe* (1945), *Le Petit général* (1951) and *Clochemerle Babylone* (1954).

CHEVREUL, Michel Eugène (1786–1889) French chemist, born in Angers. He studied chemistry at the Collège de France in Paris. He lectured at the Collège Charlemagne, and was a director of the Gobelins tapestry works. In 1830 he became professor and then director (1864–79) of the Museum of Natural History. Early discoveries were those of margarine, olein and stearin; and these studies and his theory of saponification opened up vast industries. Between 1828 and 1864 he studied colours.

CHEVROLET, Louis (1879–1941) Swiss-born American automobile designer and racing driver, born in La Chaux de Fords. He emigrated to the USA in 1900, became a racing car driver, and in his first motor race defeated **Barney Oldfield**. Thereafter he set records on every important racing circuit in the USA. In 1911 with William Crapo Durant he founded the Chevrolet Motor Company, but had little confidence in it and sold his interest to Durant in 1915, who incorporated it with General Motors in 1916. Other cars designed by Chevrolet won important races, including the Indianapolis in 1920 and 1921. He was also involved in motor boat racing, and an unsuccessful aircraft factory in Indianapolis. In 1936 he returned to work for General Motors in the Chevrolet Division, but only as a minor employee.

CHEYNE, George (1671–1743) Scottish physician, born in Methlick, Aberdeenshire. After studying at Edinburgh, he started a London practice in 1702. There rich living made him enormously fat (32 stone in weight), as well as asthmatic, but from a milk and vegetable diet he derived so much benefit that he recommended it in all the later of his twelve medical treatises. His *Essay of Health and Long Life* was eulogized by Dr **Johnson**.

CHEYNE, Thomas Kelly (1841–1915) English biblical scholar, born in London. He was chief editor of the *Encyclopaedia Biblica* (4 vols, 1900–03) and author of *Critica Biblica* and a number of works on the Old Testament. Educated at Merchant Taylors' School and Worcester College, Oxford, he became fellow of Balliol in 1868. He was Oriel professor of the interpretation of scripture at Oxford (1885–1908), canon of Rochester, and a member of the Old Testament Revision Board.

CHI'NG the last dynasty of imperial China, was founded by the Manchus following their conquest of China in 1644. **K'ang-hsi** (reigned 1662–1722) made concerted attempts to suppress corruption and reduce taxation and was also a great patron of the arts and sciences. During his reign Jesuit missionaries from France were allowed to settle in China and, with the emperor's permission, they were responsible for the first geographical survey of the empire in 1718. Much of the reign was taken up with military matters, the revolt of the Three Feudatories (1673–81) and wars with the Mongols and with Russia. Ch'ien-lung (reigned 1736–96) was a painter, poet and patron of the arts. The early years of his long reign were peaceful and prosperous but the latter half was marred by corruption at court. Military conquests and the suppression of internal rebellions, especially the White Lotus rebellion (1796–1807), were a considerable drain on the treasury. The emperor formally abdicated in 1796 although he continued to 'instruct' his son on the conduct of national affairs until his death in 1799. The dynasty entered a period of decline in the 19th century as China fell more and more under the domination of the European powers but did not finally collapse until the revolution of 1911, when China became a republic.

CHIABRERA, Gabriello (1552–1637) Italian poet, born in Savona. Educated at Rome, he served Cardinal Cornaro, but was obliged to leave for revenging himself upon a Roman nobleman. An enthusiastic student of Greek, he skilfully imitated **Pindar** and **Anacreon**, while his *Lettere Famigliari* introduced the poetical epistle into Italian.

CHIANG CHING See **JIANG QING**

CHIANG CHING-KUO (1910–88) Taiwanese politician. The son of **Chiang Kai-shek**, he studied in the Soviet Union during the early 1930s, returning to China with a Russian wife in 1937 at the time of the Japanese invasion. After the defeat of Japan in 1945 he held a number of government posts before fleeing with his father and the defeated Kuomintang (KMT: Nationalist party) forces to Taiwan in 1949. He became defence minister (1965–72), and was prime minister from 1972 to 1978. He succeeded to the post of KMT leader on his father's death in 1975 and became state president in 1978. Under his stewardship, Taiwan's post-war 'economic miracle' continued, but in the political sphere there was repression. During the closing years of his life, with his health failing, he instituted a progressive programme of political liberalization and democratization, which was continued by his successor, **Lee Teng-hui**.

CHIANG KAI-SHEK (1887–1975) Chinese general and statesman, born in Fenghwa, Chekiang, he received his military training at Tokyo, where he fell under the influence of **Sun Yat-sen**, for whom he fought in the 1911 revolution, and by whom he was put in charge of the Whampoa Military Academy, an establishment for training Kuomintang officers on the Russian model. In 1926 he commanded the army which set out to accomplish by military means the unification of China, a task which he completed by 1928. During this time he had opposed the infiltration of communism and rid the Kuomintang of its influence. As president of the republic (1928–31), he consolidated the nationalist régime by force of arms, but dangerous left-wing splinter groups retained a foothold in several areas and it was their survival which led to Chiang's ultimate downfall. Head of the executive from 1935 to 1945, he was also commander-in-chief of China united against Japanese aggression. During and after the war he allowed corrupt right-wing elements to become dominant in the Kuomintang, and the split with the communists was intensified. In 1948 the Kuomintang collapsed before the communist advance and Chiang was forced to withdraw with the remnant of the nationalist army to Formosa (Taiwan) where he then retained the office of president. There the Chinese national government, 'White China', trained new forces, aided by the USA, and breathed threats against the mainland. He wrote *Summing up at Seventy* (1957). His second wife, Mayling Soong (1901–) was educated at American universities, and distinguished herself in social and educational work, and wrote a number of works on China.

CHIARELLI, Luigi (1884–1947) Italian playwright, born in Trani. A journalist who took to the stage, he had his first play, *Vita intima*, performed in 1909. His great success was *La Maschera e il volta* (1916), a farcical comedy translated into nearly every European language.

CHICHELE, Henry (c.1362–c.1443) English prelate and diplomat. Envoy to the Vatican in 1405 and 1407, in 1408 he became bishop of St Davids, and in 1414 archbishop of Canterbury. He was the founder of two colleges at Oxford in 1437: St John's and All Souls.

CHICHESTER, Sir Francis (Charles) (1901–72) English adventurer and yachtsman, born in Barnstaple, Devonshire. Educated at Marlborough, he emigrated to New Zealand in 1919, where he made a fortune as a land agent. He became interested in flying, returned to Britain in 1929 for a course of instruction, and made a solo flight to Australia in a Gipsy Moth plane. In 1931 he was badly injured by a crash in Japan. He spent the war years in Britain as an air navigation instructor, afterwards starting a map-publishing business. In 1953 he took up yacht racing. He was found in 1957 to have lung cancer, but recovered and in 1960 won the first solo transatlantic yacht race, with his boat 'Gipsy Moth III', sailing from Plymouth to New York in 40 days. He made a successful solo cicumnavigation of the world (1966–67) in 'Gipsy Moth IV', sailing from Plymouth to Sydney in 107 days and from there back to Plymouth, via Cape Horn, in 119 days. He later sailed on to Greenwich Palace where he was knighted by the queen in the Grand Square, using the sword with which **Elizabeth** of England had knighted Sir **Francis Drake** nearly four centuries earlier. He wrote *The Lonely Sea and the Sky* (1964), and *Gipsy Moth Circles the World* (1967).

CHIFLEY, Joseph Benedict (1885–1951) Australian politician. In early life an engine driver, he entered parliament in 1928, became defence minister the following year, and was Labour prime minister 1945–49.

CHIGI a princely Italian family, whose founder, Agostino Chigi (d.1512) of Siena, known as 'il Magnifico', became banker to the popes in Rome, and was noted for his pomp and encouragement of artists like **Raphael**. He built the Villa Farnese in Rome (1509–11). A descendant, Fabio Chigi, became pope as **Alexander VII** (1655–67). Flavio Chigi (1810–85) was a nuncio and cardinal.

CHILD, Francis James (1825–96) American scholar, born in Boston, Massachusetts. He graduated from Harvard in 1846, and, after a year or two spent in Europe, was appointed to the chair of rhetoric in 1851, which he exchanged in 1876 for that of Anglo-Saxon and Early English literature. An authority on the ballad, his first work was *Four Old Plays* (1848); but more important were his annotated *Spenser* (5 vols, 1855) and *English and Scottish Ballads* (8 vols, 1857–59).

CHILD, Sir Josiah (1630–99) English writer and economist, son of a London merchant. He himself made a fortune of £200000 as a navy victualler at Portsmouth and a director of the East India Company. In his *Brief Observations concerning Trade and Interest* (1668) he explained his plans for the relief and employment of the poor, substituting districts or unions for parishes, and transporting paupers to the colonies. His brother, Sir John Child, also a member of the East India Company, was governor of Bombay.

CHILD, William (c.1606–1697) English composer, born in Bristol. He was organist at St George's Chapel, Windsor, from 1632, with an interlude during the Cromwellian régime. He wrote anthems and church services.

CHILDE, Vere Gordon (1892–1957) Australian archaeologist, born in Sydney. Educated at Sydney University and Oxford, he established a reputation with his first book, *The Dawn of European Civilisation* (1925), a brilliant and erudite work that charted the prehistoric development of Europe in terms of its various peoples and their archaeological cultures. With *The Most Ancient Near East* (1928) and *The Danube in*

Prehistory (1929) it established him as the most influential archaeological theorist of his generation. A lifelong Marxist and prodigious traveller and linguist, he was professor of archaeology at Edinburgh University (1927–46) and director of the University of London Institute of Archaeology (1946–56). A companionable, eccentric but essentially lonely man, he returned to Australia on retirement, jumping to his death in the Blue Mountains near Sydney soon after in an unnerving act of premeditated suicide.

CHILDERS, (Robert) Erskine (1870–1922) Anglo-Irish writer and nationalist, born in London. Educated at Haileybury and Trinity College, Cambridge, he was a clerk in the House of Commons from 1895 to 1910. He served as a volunteer in the 2nd Boer War (1899–1902). A skilled yachtsman, in 1903 he wrote a popular spy novel about a German invasion of Britain, called *The Riddle of the Sands*. In 1910 he devoted himself to working for Irish Home Rule, and used his yacht, the 'Asgard', to bring German arms to the Irish volunteers in 1914. Nonetheless he served in the Royal Navy in World War II. In 1921 he became a Sinn Fein member of the Irish parliament for County Widelow and minister for propaganda. He opposed the treaty that established the Irish Free State, joined the IRA, but was captured by the Free State authorities and executed. One of his sons, Erskine Hamilton Childers (1905–74), became the 4th president (1973–74).

CHILDS, George William (1829–94) American publisher, born in Baltimore. From 1864 he was the proprietor of the *Public Ledger* newspaper. His philanthropic gestures included memorials in England to **Cowper**, **George Herbert**, **Leigh Hunt** and **Shakespeare**.

CHILDS, Lucinda (1940–) American dancer and choreographer, born in New York, where she trained with **Merce Cunningham**. A founder member of the experimental Judson Dance Theatre (1962–64), she was greatly influenced by **Yvonne Rainer**, and developed a minimalist style of choreography often incorporating dialogue. After a five-year gap she made the first of her 'reductionist pattern pieces'in 1973. In 1976 she performed her own solo material in the **Robert Wilson/Philip Glass** opera *Einstein on the Beach*. Since the late 1970s she has embraced the work of other artists in her choreography. *Dance 1–5* was set to a 90-minute score by Philip Glass and film by sculptor and painter Sol le Witt. Other works include *Relative Calm* (1981), *Available Light* (1983) and *Premier Orage* (1984), the year she put her choreography on pointe for the first time.

CHILLINGWORTH, William (1602–43) English theologian, born in Oxford, the son of a prosperous citizen. In 1618 he became a scholar, in 1628 a fellow, of Trinity College. He embraced Catholicism, and studied at the Jesuit college at Doubai (1630–31). Later he renounced the Catholic faith (1634), and thereafter became involved in controversies with several Catholic divines; his answers are contained in his *Additional Discourses*. In the quiet of Lord Falkland's house at Great Tew in Oxfordshire he wrote *The Religion of Protestants, a Safe Way to Salvation* (1637). He left also nine sermons, and a fragment on the apostolical institution of episcopacy. In 1638 he took orders, and was made chancellor of Salisbury. In the Civil War he accompanied the king's forces, and before Gloucester devised a siege engine like the old Roman *testudo*. At Arundel Castle he fell ill, and after the surrender was lodged in the bishop's palace at Chichester, where he died.

CHIN SHIH HUANG TI See **SHIH HUANG TI**

CHIPIEZ, Charles See **PERROT, George**

CHIPPENDALE, Thomas (1718–79) English furniture designer, born in Otley, Yorkshire, the son of a joiner. In 1753 he set up a workshop in St Martin's Lane, London, and earned a reputation for graceful neoclassical furniture, especially chairs, which he made mostly from mahogany, then newly introduced from South America. His book, *The Gentleman and Cabinet Maker's Director* (1754), the first comprehensive trade catalogue of its kind, had a widespread influence on later craftsmen like **George Hepplewhite** and **Thomas Sheraton**. His style became increasingly eclectic and elaborate, including Rococo, Chinese and neo-Gothic. His son Thomas (1749–1822) carried on his business until 1813.

CHIRAC, Jacques René (1932–) French Conservative politician, born in Paris the son of a banker. He graduated from the prestigious Ecole Nationale d'Administration and worked in the Court of Accounts, before joining the government secretariat of President **Pompidou**. In 1967 he was elected to the National Assembly for the Correze constituency in central France and proceeded to build up a powerful base there as a department and regional councillor. During the Pompidou presidency (1969–74), Chirac served as a junior secretary in the finance ministry and then as agriculture and later industry minister, gaining the nickname 'the bulldozer' for his drive and determination. Between 1974 and 1976 Chirac served as prime minister to President **Giscard d'Estaing**, but the relationship was uneasy. On resigning as prime minister in August 1976, Chirac went on to establish the new neo-Gaullist Rassemblement (Rally) pour la République (RPR). He was elected mayor of Paris in 1977 and, despite unsuccessfully contesting the first ballot of the May 1981 presidential election, emerged as the National Assembly leader for the 'right coalition' during the Socialist administration of 1981–86. Following the 'right coalition's' victory in the March 1986 National Assembly elections, Chirac was appointed prime minister by President **Mitterand** in a unique 'co-habitation' experiment. However, he was subsequently defeated by Mitterrand in the presidential election of 1988.

CHIRICO, Giorgio de (1888–1978) Italian artist, born in Volo, Greece. He studied at Athens and Munich, working later in Paris, and with **Carrà** in Italy, where he helped to found the *Valori Plastici* review in 1918. About 1910 he began to produce a series of dreamlike pictures of deserted squares, eg, *Nostalgia of the Infinite*, dated 1911, in the Museum of Modern Art, New York. These have had considerable influence on the Surrealists, with whom he exhibited in Paris in 1925. His whole style, with that of **Carlo Carrin**, is often called 'metaphysical painting', a term which he reserved for his work after 1915, including semi-abstract geometric figures and stylized horses. In 1929 he wrote *Hebdomeros*, a dream novel, but in the 1930s he renounced all his previous work and reverted to an academic style, and to his study of the techniques of the old masters. He published his autobiography *Memorie della mia vita* in 1945.

CHISHOLM, Caroline (1808–77) English-born Australian social worker and philanthropist, born near Northampton. She married an officer in the army of the East India Company, based in Madras. In 1838 they settled in Windsor, New South Wales, but two years later Captain Chisholm returned to duty. Concerned at the plight of abandoned and impoverished immigrant women in the colony, Caroline Chisholm, with the approval of Governor **Gipps**, established an office to provide shelter for the new arrivals, and then set about finding them work. In the

1840s she cared for over 11000 women and children, thereby helping to alleviate the overcrowding in Sydney. She persuaded the British government to grant free passage to families of convicts already transported, and established the Family Colonization Loan Society, to which in 1852 the New South Wales government voted £10000 for her work. In 1854 she visited the gold-rush settlements of Victoria and publicized the appalling conditions there, but ill-health caused her to return to Sydney, and in 1866 she left for England where she received a civil pension of £100 a year.

CHISHOLM, Erik (1904–65) Scottish composer, born in Glasgow. He studied under **Tovey** and from 1930, as conductor of the Glasgow Grand Opera Society, produced many rarely heard works, including *The Trojans*, by **Berlioz**. In 1945 he was appointed professor of music at Capetown. His works include two symphonies, concertos for piano and violin, other orchestral music and operas.

CHISSANO, Joaquim (1939–) Mozambique politician, born in Chibuto. During the campaign for independence in the early 1960s he joined the National Front for the Liberation of Mozambique (Frelimo) and became secretary to its leader, **Samora Machel**. When internal self-government was granted in 1974 he was appointed prime minister. He then served under Machel as foreign minister, and on Machel's death in 1986 succeeded him as president.

CHITTENDEN, Russell Henry (1856–1943) American physiologist, born in New Haven, Connecticut. Educated at Yale and Heidelberg, he was one of the founders of the study of physiological chemistry in America. He was professor at Yale and later director of the Sheffield Scientific School. He wrote *Physiological Economy in Nutrition* (1905) and *Nutrition of Man* (1907).

CHLADNI, Ernst Florens Friedrich (1756–1827) German physicist, born in Wittenberg. The founder of the science of acoustics, he invented the euphonium. His study of the vibration of solid bodies resulted in the patterns known as Chladni figures.

CHLODOVECH, CHLODWIG See **CLOVIS**

CHLOPICKI, Joseph (1771–1854) Polish soldier and patriot. He served under **Napoleon**, was made a general by the Emperor Alexander, but became dictator in the Polish insurrection of 1830–31, and died in exile at Cracow.

CHOISEUL, Étienne François, Duc de (1719–85) French politican and minister of **Louis XV**. He served in the War of the Austrian Succession (1740–48), and, through Madame de **Pompadour**, became lieutenant-general in 1748, and Duc de Choiseul in 1758. He arranged in 1756 the alliance between France and Austria against **Frederick the Great** of Prussia, and made himself popular by the terms he obtained at the close of the Seven Years' War (1763), as also by his opposition to the Jesuits. He improved the army and navy, developed trade and industry, and reopened intercourse with India. He had spies in every court, and **Catherine the Great** nicknamed him *Le Cocher de l'Europe*. His power survived the death of his patroness in 1764, but Madame **du Barry** alienated Louis from his able minister, who retired in 1770 to his estate of Chanteloup.

CHOMSKY, Avril Noam (1928–) American linguist and political activist, born in Philadelphia, the son of a distinguished Hebrew scholar. Educated at Central High School, Philadelphia, he studied under Zellig S Harris at Pennsylvania, followed by a four-year junior fellowship at Harvard. In 1955 he began teaching modern languages and linguistics at the Massachusetts Institute of Technology, becoming a full professor in 1961, Ferrari P Ward professor of foreign languages and linguistics in 1966, and Institute professor in 1976. He is one of the founders of transformational generative grammar, and his book *Syntactic Structures* (1957) began a revolution in the field of linguistics, although his grammatical theories developed first out of his interest in logic and mathematics and were only later applied to the description of natural languages. He views language and other facets of human cognitive behaviour as being the result of innate cognitive structures built into the mind, and is strongly critical of empiricism. Among his other major works on linguistic theory are *Aspects of the Theory of Syntax* (1965), *Cartesian Linguistics* (1966), *The Sound Pattern of English* (1968, with Morris Halle), *Language and Mind* (1968, enlarged edition 1972), *Reflections on Language* (1975), *The Logical Structure of Linguistic Theory* (1975), *Lectures on Government and Binding* (1981), and *Language and Problems of Knowledge* (1987). Politically radical, he was an outspoken opponent of American military involvement in Vietnam, and published *American Power and the New Mandarins* (1969) and *At War with Asia* (1970). He has continued his critiques of American policy with *Peace in the Middle East* (1974), *Human Rights and American Foreign Policy* (1978), *The Political Economy of Human Rights* (1979, with Edward Herman), *Towards a New Cold War* (1982), *Turning the Tide* (1985), and *The Political Economy of the Mass Media* (1988, with Edward Herman).

CHOPIN, Frédéric (1810–49) Polish composer and pianist, born in Zelazowa Wola, a village near Warsaw, where his father, a Frenchman, had settled. He played in public at the age of eight; in 1825 he published his first work, a Rondo in C minor; from 1826–29 he studied at Warsaw Conservatory under Elsner; he then visited Vienna where he made a brilliant impression. In 1831 he went to Paris, where he found fame, and lost his health. Here he became the idol of the *salons*, giving lessons to a select clientèle of pupils, composing in his spare time. In 1836 he was introduced to **George Sand** (Madame Dudevant) by **Liszt**, spent the winter of 1838–39 with her in Majorca and lived at her home at Nohant until 1847, when they became estranged. He visited England in 1837 and 1848, playing in London, Manchester, Edinburgh and Glasgow. He died from consumption. On a groundwork of Slavonic airs and rhythms, notably that of the mazurka, Chopin raised superstructures of the most fantastic and original beauty; his style is so strongly marked as to amount to a mannerism. He seldom composed for the orchestra, but for the piano he wrote a great deal of superlatively artistic music. His compositions include 50 mazurkas, 25 *préludes*, two piano concertos, and a funeral march.

CHOPIN, Katherine ('Kate'), née **O'Flaherty** (1851–1904) American novelist, short story writer and poet, born in St Louis, Missouri, The daughter of an Irish immigrant and a French-Creole mother, she was well educated at the Sacred Heart convent, 'came out' in society and married Oscar Chopin, a Creole cotton trader from Louisiana by whom she had six children. It was a happy marriage, scarred only by business failure. After her husband died of swamp fever (1882) she returned with her children to St Louis where she began to compose sketches of her life in 'Old Natachitoches', such as *Bayou Folk* (1894) and *A Night in Acidie* (1897). This work gives no indication of the furore she aroused with the publication of a realistic novel of sexual passion, *The Awakening* (1899), which was harshly condemned by the public. Thereafter she wrote only a few poems and short stories. Interest in her work was revived largely by **Edmund Wilson**, and she has since been embraced by feminists as a fin de siècle iconoclast bravely articulating the plight of the 'lost' woman.

CHORLEY, Richard John (1927–) English geomorphologist, born in Minehead, Somerset. Educated at Minehead Grammar School and Exeter College, Oxford, he was a Fulbright scholar at Columbia University (1951–52) studying geology. After various lecturing appointments in North America and Britain he became first a reader (1970–74) then a professor of geography at Cambridge University (1974–). He is a leader in the group which challenged traditional geography and led to the British phase of the so-called 'quantitative revolution'. He used general system theory in the study of landforms, advocated geography as human ecology and developed the use of models in explanation. His publications include *The History of the Study of Landforms* (vols I & II, 1964, 1973), *Physical Geography* (1971), *Environmental Systems* (1978) and *Geomorphology* (1984).

CHOSROES I, or **Khosru** (6th century) Persian ruler. He reigned over Persia, 531–79, waged war against the Roman emperor **Justinian I** for 20 years, and at home promoted agriculture, commerce and science. His grandson Chosroes II (591–628) inflicted great disaster on the Byzantine empire, conquering Syria and Egypt.

CHOSROES I PARVIZ (d.628) Sassanid king of Persia, 588–627, grandson of **Chosroes I**. He conquered Syria, Palestine, Egypt and parts of Asia Minor (613–19) which almost brought the Byzantine empire to its knees, but the emperor **Heraclius** led a recovery and penetrated Persia, defeating him at Ninevah (627), after which he was deposed and executed by his son, Kavādh.

CHOU EN-LAI See **ZHOU ENLAI**

CHRÉTIEN DE TROYES (d. c.1183) French poet and troubadour, born in Troyes, in Champagne, and author of the earliest romances dealing with the King **Arthur** legend. The greatest of the French medieval poets, he was a member of the court of the Countess Marie de Champagne, daughter of **Louis VII**, and to whom he dedicated his metrical romance of courtly love, *Yvain et Lancelot*. His other romances were *Érec et Énide* (c.1160), *Cligès* (c.1164), and the unfinished *Perceval, ou Le Conte du Graal* (c.1180). His works enjoyed huge popularity throughout medieval Europe.

CHRISTALLER, Walter (1893–1969) German geographer, born in Berneck. Educated at Erlangen and Freiburg, he was an advocate of the method of deductive reasoning and originator of the 'central place theory' (1933) which was inspired by economic theory and arose from a study of tertiary economic functions in southern Germany. Although his ideas were not available in English until the 1960s this approach has been used extensively in the analysis of the spacing and arrangement of central places and it found practical application as a planning tool in North America and, after World War II, in the north-east polders of the Netherlands.

CHRISTENSEN, Harold, Lew and **Willam** (1904–89, 1909–84 and 1902–) American dancers, born in Utah to a family of music and dance teachers of Danish-Mormon descent. As youngsters all three toured in vaudeville, hoofing and performing classical dance. In 1932 Willam opened a ballet school in Portland, Oregon, from which emerged the Portland Ballet. In 1938 he became ballet master and choreographer of the San Francisco Opera Ballet, which within a few years became an independent institution for which he choreographed the first full-length American productions of *Coppelia*, *Swan Lake* and *The Nutcracker*. In 1951 he established in Salt Lake City the first dance department at an American university and, in the following year, the Utah Ballet, which since 1968 has been called Ballet West. Harold, having studied at the School of American Ballet and danced for various companies on both American coasts, retired from the stage in 1946 and took charge of the San Francisco Ballet School until 1975. As a member of the American Ballet, Lew was cast as the first American Apollo in **George Balanchine**'s ballet of the same name. In 1938 he choreographed *The Filling Station*, a piece of contemporary Americana, for Ballet Caravan, and in the mid 1940s he was on the faculty of the School of American Ballet and New York City Ballet. In the 1950s he replaced Willam as director and choreographer of the San Francisco Ballet, a position he held virtually until his death.

CHRISTIAN ten Scandinavian kings. See **KRISTIAN**

CHRISTIAN, Charlie (Charles) (1916–42) American jazz guitarist, born in Dallas, Texas, who learned to play a home-made 'cigar box' guitar as a child. His skill developed to the point where he was hired by bandleader **Benny Goodman** in 1939, playing mainly with the Goodman sextet rather than the big band. Christian pioneered the use of the amplified guitar as a solo instrument, freeing the guitar from a purely rhythmic role. He was one of the musicians whose after-hours sessions at Minton's Playhouse in New York laid the basis of the bebop revolution. His melodic facility and harmonic boldness establish him as the father of the modern jazz guitar.

CHRISTIAN, Fletcher (c.1764–c.1794) English seaman and ringleader of the mutiny against Captain **William Bligh** on the *Bounty* in 1789, born in Cockermouth in Cumberland. Educated at St Bees School and Cockermouth Grammar School, he declined to go to university and joined the navy instead at the age of 18. He served with Bligh on various ships and was selected by Bligh as midshipman on the *Britannia* sailing to the West Indies in 1787. A close friendship developed, and Bligh appointed him as first mate on the *Bounty* on a voyage to Tahiti to collect bread-fruit plants for the West Indies. After the mutiny Christian and eight other mutineers, including **John Adams**, took refuge on Pitcairn Island with some Tahitian men and women, where they founded a settlement. In all probability, Christian was killed by the Tahitians, along with three other mutineers. His brother, Edward Christian, was professor of law at Cambridge (1788–1823).

CHRISTIE a family of London auctioneers. The founder of the firm, in 1766, was James (1730–1803), two of whose sons were James (1773–1831), antiquary and auctioneer, and Samuel Hunter (1784–1865), student of magnetism and professor of mathematics at Woolwich (1806–50). Samuel's son, Sir William Henry Mahoney (1845–1922), was astronomer royal (1881–1910).

CHRISTIE, Dame Agatha Mary Clarissa, née **Miller** (1890–1976) English author, born in Torquay. Under the surname of her first husband (Colonel Christie, divorced 1928), she wrote more than 70 classic detective novels, featuring the Belgian detective, Hercule Poirot, or the village spinster, Miss Jane Marple. In 1930 she married Sir **Max Mallowan** (1904–1978), noted archaeologist, a professor at London University (1947–62). Between December 1953 and January 1954, she achieved three concurrent West End productions, *The Spider's Web*, *Witness for the Prosecution* and *The Mousetrap* (record-breaking run). Her best-known novels are *The Mysterious Affair at Styles* (1920), first featuring the Belgian detective Poirot; *The Murder of*

Richard Ackroyd (1926); *Murder at the Vicarage* (1930), introducing Miss Marple; *Murder on the Orient Express* (1934); *Death on the Nile* (1937); *And Then There Were Nine* (1941) and *Curtain* (1975), in which Poirot met his end. She also wrote under the pen-name 'Mary Westmacott'.

CHRISTIE, John Reginald Halliday (1898–1953) English murderer, born in Yorkshire. He was hanged for the murder of his wife and confessed to the murder by strangulation of five other women. He also confessed to the murder of Mrs Evans, wife of Timothy John Evans, who lived in the same house. Evans had been convicted and hanged for the murder of his infant daughter in 1950. He had been charged at the same time with the murder of his wife, but this was never heard. After a special inquiry instigated by the Home Office, and several fierce debates in the House of Commons, no definite conclusion was reached; but there was an increasing body of opinion that Evans was technically innocent and that Christie killed both Mrs Evans and the child, and in 1966 Evans was granted a free pardon. The trial of Christie, therefore, played an important part in altering legislation affecting the death penalty.

CHRISTIE, Julie (1940–) English actress, born in Chukua, Assam. A student at the Central School of Music and Drama, she worked in repertory before a television serial, *A is for Andromeda* (1962), led to a small film role in *Crooks Anonymous* (1962). Her portrayal of a free spirit in *Billy Liar* (1963) brought further offers and in 1965 she won an Academy Award for *Darling*. Judged to be the epitome of Swinging Sixties London, she consolidated her career with *Dr. Zhivago* (1965), *Far From the Madding Crowd* (1967) and *The Go-Between* (1971). Subsequent films have highlighted her involvement with a variety of political issues, although she returned to more mainstream productions with *Heat and Dust* (1982) and *Power* (1985).

CHRISTINA OF SPAIN See **MARIA CHRISTINA**

CHRISTINE DE PISAN (c.1363–1431) French poetess, born in Venice. She was daughter of an Italian who was court astrologer to **Charles V**. Brought up in Paris, in 1378 she married Étienne Castel, who became the king's secretary, but died in 1389. Left with three children and no money, she was obliged to call upon her literary talents and between 1399 and 1415 produced a number of brilliant works in both prose and verse, including a Life of **Charles V** for Philippe, Duke of Burgundy; *Cité des dames*, a translation from **Boccaccio**; and *Livres des trois vertus*, an educational and social compendium for women. Her love poems have grace and charm, but lack depth. Christine is noteworthy for her defence of the female sex, hitherto a target for satirists. Saddened by the misfortunes of the Hundred Years' war she withdrew to a nunnery in about 1418 but lived to write in celebration of **Joan of Arc**'s early successes in 1429.

CHRISTISON, Sir Robert (1797–1882) Scottish toxicologist, born in Edinburgh, the son of the professor of humanity. He studied toxicology in Paris under **Mathieu Orfila**. In 1822 he was appointed professor of medical jurisprudence at Edinburgh, and from 1832 professor of materia medica. He became physician to Queen **Victoria** (1848) and wrote a *Treatise on Poisons* (1829).

CHRISTO, originally **Christo Jaracheff** (1935–) Bulgarian-born American avant-garde artist, born in Gabrova. He studied art first in Sophia (1951–56), then briefly in Vienna (1957), before moving to Paris in 1958. In 1964 he moved permanently to New York. His work consists of wrapping objects (trees, cars, buildings) in canvas or plastic sheeting, or of creating 'assemblages' of stacked oil drums.

CHRISTOFF, Boris (1914–) Bulgarian bass-baritone, born in Plovdiv. He studied law in Sofia, then studied singing in Rome and Salzburg. His début recital was in Rome (1946); in 1947 he sang at La Scala in Milan, in 1949 at Covent Garden, and from 1956 in the USA. He excelled in the role of Boris Godunov, which he sang in the USSR.

CHRISTOPHE, Henri (1767–1829) king of Haiti. Born a slave on the island of Grenada, he joined the black insurgents in Haiti against the French in 1790, and with his gigantic stature and courage, proved an able lieutenant to their leader **Toussaint l'Ouverture**. In 1802 he gallantly defended Cape Haiti against the French. In 1806 he cut down the Emperor **Dessalines**, and in 1807 was appointed president. After years of civil war, he was proclaimed king of Haiti as Henri I in 1811, and ruled with enthusiasm. But his avarice and cruelty led to an insurrection, and he shot himself.

CHRISTOPHER, St Syrian Christian martyr, perhaps of the 3rd century AD. According to tradition, he was a man of gigantic stature. His name in Greek (*Christophoros*) means 'Christ-bearing', which gave rise to the legend that he had carried the Christ-child across a river. He is said to have suffered martyrdom under the emperor Decius (reigned 249–251). He is the patron saint of wayfarers, and now motorists. His feast day is 25 July.

CHRISTOPHERSEN, Henning (1939–) Danish politician, born in Copenhagen. A member of the Danish parliament (*Folketinget*) from 1971 to 1984, he led the Danish Liberal party (*Venstre*) from 1978 to 1984. During 1978 and 1979 he was minister of foreign affairs and from 1982 to 1984 was minister of finance and deputy prime minister. He has been a member of the EC Commission since 1984 and is a vice-president, in charge of economic and monetary co-operation.

CHRISTUS, Petrus (c.1420–1473) Netherlandish painter, who became a master in Bruges in 1444. He is often said to have been the pupil or assistant of **Jan van Eyck**, and certainly in both his style and his compositions he continued that master's tradition, though in a simplified and less profound manner. He may have visited Italy—he has been identified as the 'Piero di Burges' referred to in a Milanese document of 1457—and it has been speculated that he was an important source for the transmission of the Eyckian technique to Italian painters, in particular **Antonello da Messina**.

CHRISTY, Edwin Pearce (1815–62) American entertainer, born in Philadelphia, the originator of the Christy Minstrels show. He was singing with two assistants at a public house in Buffalo in 1842, but steadily increased the reputation of his troupe and the success of his 'black-face' ministrelsy in New York and London. Many of his songs were commissioned from **Stephen Foster**. He retired in 1855, and eventually threw himself out of a window during the American Civil War (1861–65).

CHRISTY, Henry (1810–65) English banker and archaeologist. With the Frenchman Édouard Lartet (1801–71) he explored the palaeolithic caves of the Dordogne from 1862, excavating in the valley of the Vézèe at Gorge d'Enfer, La Madeleine, Le Moustier and Les Eyzies.

CHRYSANDER, Friedrich (1826–1901) German musical historian, biographer and editor of **Handel**. He founded the Handel Society in 1856.

CHRYSIPPUS (c.280–c.206 BC) Stoic philosopher, born in Soli in Cilicia. He went to Athens as a youth and studied under **Cleanthes** to become the third and greatest head of the Stoa. He wrote over 700 works (only fragments remain) elaborating the Stoic system in what became its definitive and orthodox form.

CHRYSLER, Walter Percy (1875–1940) American automobile manufacturer, born in Wamego, Kansas. He started his working life as an apprentice in a Union Pacific Railroad machine shop. He worked his way up to become plant manager with the American Locomotive Company, but left in 1912 to become works manager of Buick Motor Company at half the salary. By 1916 he had become president, but resigned in 1919 (although Buick was by then the strongest division of General Motors) to become a director of Willys-Overland and Maxwell Motor Company in 1921. This became the Chrysler Corporation in 1925. He introduced the 'Plymouth' motor car and designed the first high compression engine. His autobiography, *The Life of an American Workman*, was published in 1937.

CHRYSOLORAS, Manuel (c.1355–1415) Greek scholar, born in Constantinople, the first to transplant Greek literature into Italy. About 1391 he was sent by the Byzantine emperor, John Palaeologus, to England and Italy to seek assistance against the Turks, and in 1397 he settled at Florence and taught Greek literature. He was afterwards employed by Pope **Gregory XII** in an attempt to promote a union of the Greek with the Roman Church, and in 1413 went with Pope **John XXII** to the Council of Constance, where he died. His chief work was a Greek grammar, *Erotematasive quaestiones*. His nephew, John Chrysoloras also taught Greek in Italy.

CHRYSOSTOM, St John (c.347–407) Syrian churchman, and one of the Doctors of the Church, born in Antioch, and named *Chrysostomos* from the Greek meaning 'Golden-Mouthed'. Trained by his pious mother Anthusa, he studied oratory for the career of advocate; but, in his twenty-third year, was baptized and ordained an *anagnóstés* or 'Reader'. After six years spent as a monk in the mountains, illness forced him to return in 380 to Antioch, where he was ordained deacon in 381 and priest in 386. The eloquence and earnestness of his preaching secured for him the reputation of the greatest orator of the church; and in 398 the emperor **Arcadius** made him archbishop of Constantinople. Chrysostom bestowed much of his revenues on hospitals, sought to reform the lives of the clergy, and sent monks as missionaries into Scythia, Persia and other lands. His zealous reproof of vices moved the empress **Eudocia** to have him deposed and banished in 403—first to Nicaea, and then to the Taurus mountains, and finally to Pityus on the Black Sea. Compelled to travel thither on foot, with his bare head exposed to a burning sun, the old man died on the way to Comana, in Pontus. His body was brought to Constantinople and reburied with honour in 438. His works are numerous, and consist of *Homilies*, *Commentaries* on the whole Bible, part of which have perished, *Epistles*, *Treatises* on Providence, the Priesthood, etc, and *Liturgies*. His feast day is 27 January.

CHU-TA, also **Pa Ta Shan Jen** (1626–1705) Chinese painter in the Ch'an (Zen) School of painting, born in Nan-ch'ang, Kiangsi. A relation of the **Ming** Royal House, he retired to a monastery and may have pretended madness in order to survive the purges of the Manchu conquerors. The bravura and individualism of his ink paintings of flowers, birds, fish and landscapes appealed to the Japanese, and his style has become synonymous with Zen painting in Japan. Mocking every rule of classical tradition, his witty and expressive individualism has been influential up to the present day in both Japan and China.

CHUBB, Charles (1772–1846) English locksmith. He patented improvements in 'detector' locks, originally (1818) patented by his brother, Jeremiah, of Portsea. He was in the hardware business in Winchester and Portsea, before settling in London. Under his son, John Chubb (1816–72), further patents were taken out.

CHUBB, Thomas (1679–1747) English deist, born in East-Harnham near Salisbury. Brought up in poor circumstances, he had little formal education, but had already contrived to pick up considerable learning, when a reading of the 'historical preface' to **William Whiston**'s *Primitive Christianity Revived* impelled him to write his own tract, *The Supremacy of the Father Asserted* (1715). A quarto volume of his tracts, published in 1730, made his name widely known. He also wrote *True Gospel of Jesus Christ Vindicated* (1739) and *Discourse on Miracles* (1741). His opinions drifted near to deism, yet he went to church, and regarded the mission of Christ as divine.

CHUDLEIGH, Elizabeth (1720–88) English courtesan and bigamist, Countess of Bristol and 'Duchess of Kingston'. Beautiful but illiterate, she had several liaisons at court before secretly marrying naval lieutenant, Augustus John Hervey, brother of the 2nd Earl of Bristol, in 1744. Having concealed the birth and death of a son, she obtained a separation from her husband; later, when courted by the 2nd Duke of Kingston, she denied the first marriage on oath and married him in 1769. On being left heiress to the Duke's estates in 1773, she was accused of bigamy by his nephew and found guilty in 1776. In the following year her marriage to Hervey, who had now succeeded his brother as 3rd Duke of Bristol, was declared valid. She was the prototype of 'Beatrix Esmond' in **Thackeray**'s *Esmond* and *The Virginians*.

CHULALONGKORN, Phra Paramindr Maha (Rama V) (1853–1910) king of Siam from 1868, son of King Maha Mong Kut, who was the model for the best-selling *The King and I*. He was educated by English teachers, acquiring Western linguistic and cultural skills, after which he went, as traditionally prescribed, to a Buddhist monastery where he remained until 20, having ceremonially succeeded his father in 1868. He toured India and Indonesia, abolished slavery, freed his subjects from approaching him on hands and knees, proclaimed liberty of conscience, built schools, hospitals, roads, railways and followed his father in extending the armed forces. He standardized the coinage, introduced posts and telegraphs, and policed, sanitized and electrified Bangkok. He sent his crown prince to study in Britain, visited Queen **Victoria** and ultimately paid for his westernization by being forced to accept treaties with France (weakening his power in Cambodia) and with Britain (removing his rule over Malayan islands). He is much more entitled to be called an enlightened despot than are the European rulers of the 18th century.

CHUN DOO-HWAN, (1931–) South Korean soldier and politician. Born in Taegu in Kyongsang province, he trained at the Korean military academy and was commissioned as a second lieutenant in the South Korean army in 1955. After further training at the US Army Infantry School, in 1960 he worked with the Special Airborne Forces group and in military intelligence. After President **Park**'s assassination in October 1979, he took charge of the Korean Central Intelligence Agency (KCIA) and led the investigation into Park's murder. He assumed control of the army and the government after a coup in 1979. In 1981 he was appointed president and retired from the army to head the newly formed Democratic Justice party (DJP). Under his rule, the country's 'economic miracle' continued, but popular opposition to the authoritarian nature of the régime mounted, which eventually forced his retirement in 1988.

CHUNDER SEN, Keshub (1838–84) Indian Hindu reformer. He was the chief developer after 1858 of the Theistic society called the *Brahma Samaj of India*, which originated with **Rammohun Roy**. He visited Europe in 1870.

CHUNG, Kyung-Wha (1948–) Korean-born American violinist, born in Seoul. She moved to New York in 1960 and studied at the Juilliard School of Music until 1967, when she made her début with the New York Philharmonic; her London début came three years later. Her sister Myung-Wha (1944–) is a distinguished cellist, and her brother Myung-Whung (1953–) a pianist and conductor who was appointed music director of the new Bastille Opera, Paris 1989.

CHURCH, Frederick Edwin (1826–1900) American landscape painter, born in Hartford, Connecticut. He travelled widely, and painted scenes of grandeur in South America, the Arctic regions, and the East.

CHURCH, Sir Richard (1785–1873) Irish soldier, born in Cork, the son of a Quaker merchant. He ran away from school to join the British army, and was commissioned in the 13th Foot (later Somerset Light Infantry) in 1800. He served with distinction in the British and Neapolitan services in the Mediterranean (1808–09) and with Greek troops (1812–15). He took part in the Greek War of Independence (1821–32), and was appointed generalissimo of the Greek insurgent forces in 1827. He led the revolution in Greece in 1815, and was promoted general in 1854, having earned the nickname of 'Liberator of Greece'. He became a Greek citizen before he died.

CHURCH, Richard Thomas (1893–1972) English author, born in London. He made his name first as a poet, but he is known also for his novels, literary criticism, travel books and stories, for children, especially *A Squirrel called Rufus*. His novel *The Porch* (1937) won the Femina Vie-Heureuse prize. He also published three volumes of autobiography.

CHURCH, Richard William (1815–90) English clergyman and scholar, born in Lisbon, nephew of Sir **Richard Thomas**. Educated at Wadham College, Oxford, in 1838 he was elected a fellow of Oriel College, Oxford, and in 1871 dean of St Paul's. A close friend of **Newman**, he wrote a history of the 'Oxford Movement' (1891) as well as a number of sermons, essays, historical works. He also wrote studies of **Dante**, **Spenser** and **Bacon**. He was the author of lives of St **Wulfstan** and St **Anselm**, and a book on *The Beginnings of the Middle Ages* (1877).

CHURCH, William (?1778–1863) American inventor. He devised the first typesetting machine, patented in England in 1822.

CHURCHILL, Arabella (1648–1730) English aristocrat, elder sister of John Churchill, 1st Duke of **Marlborough**, and mistress of King **James II**. In 1665 she entered the service of the Duchess of York, wife of the future James II, and soon became James's mistress. She was the mother by James of two daughters and two sons: James Fitzjames (Duke of **Berwick**), and Henry Fitzjames (Duke of Albermarle).

CHURCHILL, Caryl (1938–) English dramatist. Her first play was *Light Shining* (1976), about the Levellers. Her greatest commercial success has been *Serious Money* (1987), satirizing the world of the young, get-rich-quick City financial brokers. Other plays include *Cloud Nine* (1979), *Top Girls* (1982), *Fen* (1983), and *Softcops* (1984), all of greater dramatic quality than *Serious Money*.

CHURCHILL, Charles (1731–64) English satirical poet, born in Westminster, the son of a curate. He was educated at Westminster School and went on to John's College, Cambridge, but ruined his academic career with a clandestine marriage at the age of 17. With his father's help he was ordained priest in 1756, and at his father's death in 1758 succeeded him as curate of St John's, Westminster. But after a bankruptcy, a formal separation from his wife and a course of unclerical dissipation, he gave up the church (1763). His *Rosciad* (1761) had already made him famous and a terror to actors. *The Apology* (also 1761) was a savage onslaught on his critics, particularly **Smollett**. In *Night* (1762) he lengthily replied to critcisms of his life. *The Ghost* (1762) ridiculed Dr **Johnson** and others in over 4000 lines. He next helped **John Wilkes** in the *North Briton*, and heaped ridicule upon the Scots in *The Prophecy of Famine* (1763), an admirable satire. For *The Epistle to Hogarth* (1763) the artist retaliated with a savage caricature. Other works include *The Candidate* (1764), *Independence* (1794), and, unfinished, *The Journey* and the masterly *Dedication*. He died suddenly on a visit to Wilkes in France. He lacked the chief essential of true satire, a real insight into the heart of man, but possessed volubility in rhyming, boisterous energy, and an instinctive hatred of wrong.

CHURCHILL, John See **MARLBOROUGH**

CHURCHILL, Randolph Frederick Edward Spencer (1911–68) English journalist, son of Sir **Winston Churchill**. Educated at Eton and Christ Church College, Oxford, he served in World War II in North Africa and Italy and in the Middle East as an intelligence officer on the general staff. He was Conservative MP for Preston (1940–45). A pugnacious and forthright commentator on current affairs, he also wrote *The Rise and Fall of Sir Anthony Eden* (1959), and published two volumes of a full-length biography of his father (1966, 1967).

CHURCHILL, Lord Randolph Henry Spencer (1849–95) father of Sir **Winston Churchill**, third son of the 7th Duke of Marlborough, born in Blenheim Palace, and educated at Eton and Merton College, Oxford. Returned for Woodstock in 1874, in which year he married Jeanette (Jennie) Jerome, the beautiful daughter of a New York businessman, he became conspicuous in 1880 as the leader of a guerilla band of Conservatives known as the 'Fourth Party'; and soon had a considerable following among the younger Conservatives, who regarded him as the future leader of the Tory Democracy. After an attempt to defeat **John Bright** at Birmingham in 1885, he was returned for South Paddington. He was secretary for India in Lord **Salisbury**'s first ministry (1885–86), and then, in his second, Chancellor of the Exchequer and leader of the House of Commons from July to December 1886, when he resigned.

CHURCHILL, Sarah, née **Jennings** (1660–1744) English aristocrat, wife of John Churchill, 1st Duke of **Marlborough**. In 1673 she entered the service of the Duke of York (the future **James II**), and became a close friend of his younger daughter by Anne Hyde, Princess Anne (the future Queen **Anne**): in their private correspondence, Anne was called 'Mrs Morley' and Sarah was called 'Mrs Freeman'. After the 'Glorious Revolution' of 1688, when **William III** supplanted James II on the throne, she and her husband tried to draw Anne into Jacobite intrigues for the restoration of her father; but after Anne became queen, Sarah dominated her household and the Whig ministry. Queen Anne finally broke with the Marlboroughs in 1711, when Sarah was supplanted by a new favourite, her cousin Mrs Abigail Marsham. She had two daughters: Henrietta, who married (1698) Sidney, 1st

Earl of **Godolphin**; and Anne, who married (1700) a son of the 2nd Earl of **Sunderland**.

CHURCHILL, Sir Winston Leonard Spencer (1874–1965) English statesman, born at Blenheim Palace, Woodstock, Oxfordshire, the eldest son of Lord **Randolph Churchill**. He was educated at Harrow and Sandhurst and was gazetted to the 4th Hussars in 1895. His early army career included service with the Malakand field force in 1897 and with the 1898 Nile expeditionary force, when he fought hand-to-hand against the Dervishes at Omdurman. Acting as a London newspaper correspondent in the Boer War, he was captured in an ambush but successfully escaped with a £25 price on his head. In 1900 he became Conservative MP for Oldham, but his differences with the party widened and he joined the Liberals in 1906, becoming colonial under-secretary and from 1908 to 1910 president of the board of trade, when he introduced the labour exchanges. He became home secretary in 1910 and was involved in the 'Siege of Sidney Street' controversy in 1911. In that year of the threatening German 'Agadir incident' he became First Lord of the Admiralty. He developed a war staff, became the 'father of naval aviation' and generally organized the navy for the war he foresaw. In 1915 he was made the scapegoat for the Dardanelles disaster and joined the army in France. In 1917 he became **Lloyd George**'s minister of munitions, concentrating on the production of thousands of tanks (largely his own 'brain-child'). From 1919 to 1921 he was secretary of state for war and air and from 1924 —when he was returned for Epping as a 'Constitutionalist' supporter of the Conservatives—till 1929 he was Chancellor of the Exchequer. His spare-time occupations ranged from bricklaying (for which he held a union card) to editing the *British Gazette* during the 1926 General Strike. In the 'thirties he brooded in the political wilderness, increasingly angry at the National government's supineness in face of the arming dictators. Munich he prophetically called 'a total and unmitigated defeat'. When war came again he was back at the Admiralty. Then, in May 1940, when power slipped from the hands of **Neville Chamberlain**, he formed a Coalition government, the beginning of his 'walk with destiny' for which he considered all his earlier life but a preparation. He offered the British people nothing but 'blood, toil, tears and sweat' and with steely resolution led Britain alone against Germany and Italy, incomparably expressing the national spirit of resistance. During the war he worked round the clock, travelled 150000 miles, always making vital decisions, from shaping the Atlantic Charter in 1941 to devising the strategy of Alamein in 1942, from giving the highest priority to the battle against the U-boats and repelling the Luftwaffe assault on Britain to inspiring tortured Europe with his voice. He was on close personal terms with President F D **Roosevelt** while sustaining the often difficult alliance with the Soviet Union. Defeated in the July 1945 election at the height of his wartime fame, he became a pugnacious leader of the opposition. In international speeches he warned about the tyranny behind the Iron Curtain (his own phrase) and fostered the conception of European and Atlantic unity, later to bear fruit in NATO and other supranational organizations. In 1951, he became prime minister again at the age of 77, and when he laid down his office in 1955 he was the last surviving member of the great Allied war-winning triumvirate. Sir Winston, who called himself 'a child of the House of Commons', remained in old age a back-bencher who was looked on almost with veneration. In the last phase of his crowded years of public service—recognized by countless honours and decorations—he was often described as 'the greatest living Englishman'. He achieved a world reputation not only as an all-seeing strategist and inspiring war leader, but as the last of the classic orators with a supreme command of English; as a writer with an Augustan style, great breadth of mind and a profound sense of history; as a painter of no little talent; as the shrewdest—and sometimes the most impish—of political tacticians; as the seer who said (when the Commons was considering the perils and opportunities of the H-bomb age), 'the nations stand at this hour of human history before the portals of supreme catastrophe and measureless reward'; as a zestful social reformer who believed that there could be 'shining uplands' of welfare before mankind; as a figure who incarnated in himself the tumultuous sweep of modern history; and as an intensely human, rich and vivid personality whose abiding qualities were courage and imagination, passion and magnanimity, all in the service of a limitless patriotism. In 1908 he married Clementine Ogilvy Hozier, second daughter of Sir Henry and Lady Blanche Hozier, and grand-daughter of the Earl of Airlie. An indefatigable worker for charitable causes, she organized canteens for munitions workers during the First World War, and the Red Cross Aid to Russia fund during the Second. She served on many committees and held honorary degrees from Glasgow and Oxford universities. She was created a life peer in 1965, taking the title of Baroness Spencer-Churchill of Chartwell. Sir Winston's publications include *The World Crisis* (4 vols, 1923–29); *Marlborough* (4 vols, 1933–38); *The Second World War* (6 vols, 1948–54); *History of the English-Speaking Peoples* (4 vols, 1956–58).

CHURCHILL, Winston (1871–1947) American historian novelist, born in St Louis, Missouri. His works include *Richard Carvel* (1899) and *The Crisis* (1901).

CHURCHWARD, George Jackson (1857–1933) English locomotive engineer, born in Stoke Gabriel in Devon. He was chief mechanical engineer of the Great Western Railway from 1902 to 1921. Although not a great innovator he showed rare judgment in combining the best features of British and foreign locomotive practice in his designs, such as the 4-6-0 'Star' series introduced in 1906 which was the outstanding British express locomotive for the next 20 years. His use of longer stroke, longer valve travel, tapered boiler and higher steam pressure showed the way to other designers in the first half of the 20th century.

CHURCHYARD, Thomas (1520–1604) English soldier of fortune and writer, born in Shrewsbury. He served in Scotland, Ireland and the Low Countries under the Earl of **Surrey** and published many verse and prose pieces, the best-known being *The Legend of Shore's Wife* (1563, in *A Mirror for Magistrates*), and *Worthiness of Wales*.

CHURRIGUERA, Don José (1650–1725) Spanish architect, born in Salamanca. He was royal architect to **Charles II** and developed the extravagant style which has come down to us as Churri-gueresque. He designed Salamanca Cathedral. His brothers Joaquin (1674–1720) and Alberto (1676–1750) were also architects.

CHUTE, Anthony (d.?1595) Elizabethan poet, author of *Beawtie Dishonoured* (1593), largely plagiarized from **Churchyard**'s *Legend of Shore's Wife*. He was patronized by **Gabriel Harvey** and assailed by **Thomas Nashe** the satirist.

CHU TEH See **ZHU DE**

CHUTER-EDE, Baron of Epsom See **EDE**

CIALDINI, Enrico, Duke of Gaeta (1811–92) Italian soldier, born in Castelvetro. He studied medicine at Parma, but fled after the failed insurrection in Parma in

1830. In the Italian War of Independence against Austria (1848–49) he commanded a regiment of Piedmontese infantry, and again from 1859 to 1861, gaining two victories and capturing Gaeta and Messina. In 1862 he defeated **Garibaldi** at Aspromonte, and in 1864 he became a senator, and in the war of 1866 against Austria he occupied Venice.

CIANO, Count Galeazzo (1903–44) Italian politician, son-in-law of **Mussolini** and leading Fascist. As minister of propaganda (1935) and of foreign affairs (1936–43), he supported his father-in-law's expansionist and war policy, but, on early signs of its failure, opposed it; and in 1943 he contributed his vote to the fall of the régime. He was dragged from hiding by the now republican Fascists and, after trial, shot.

CIARAN the name of two Irish 6th-century saints, one the founder of Clonmacnoise, and the other bishop of Ossory.

CIBBER, Colley (1671–1757) English actor and dramatist, born in London, son of the Schleswig sculptor, Caius Gabriel Cibber (1630–1700), known for his *Melancholy* and *Raving Madness*. In 1690 he joined the Theatre Royal in Drury Lane, and there, except for short intervals, spent his whole career. In 1696 his first comedy, *Love's Last Shift*, established his fame both as dramatist and actor. As manager and playwright, he greatly improved the decency of the theatre. From 1730 he was poet laureate. He wrote *Apology for the Life of Mr Colley Cibber, Comedian* (1740).

CIBBER, Mrs, née **Susannah Maria Arne** (1714–66) English actress and singer, born in London, sister of the composer **Thomas Arne**. A fine contralto, she made her stage debut in her brother's *Rosamund* (1733), and the following year married Theophilus Cibber (1703–58, son of **Colley Cibber**); from then on she was known as 'Mrs Cibber'. **Handel** wrote parts for her in his *Messiah* and *Samson*. Thereafter she turned to drama and played opposite **David Garrick** at Drury Lane with enormous success.

CICERO, Marcus Tullius (106–43 BC) Roman orator, statesman, and man of letters, born in Arpinum in Latium, of a wealthy family. At Rome he studied law and oratory, Greek philosophy, and Greek literature. He saw military service in the war of 90–88 BC under Pompeius Strabo, the father of **Pompey The Great**. His first important speech, in his twenty-sixth year, was the successful defence of a client against a favourite of the dictator **Sulla**. After a visit to Athens, and a tour in Asia Minor, he was elected quaestor (76), and obtained an appointment in Sicily; at the request of the Sicilians he undertook his successful impeachment of the corrupt governor **Gaius Verres** in 70. In 66 he was praetor, and supported in a great speech (*Pro Lege Manilia*) the appointment of Pompey to conduct the war with **Mithradates VI**. In 63 he was consul, and foiled the plot of **Catilina** by the execution of five of the conspirators. The 'father of his country' was now for a brief space the great man of the day. But the tide soon turned. Cicero might have saved the country, but had violated the constitution—a Roman citizen could not be capitally punished save by the sentence of the people in regular assembly. **Publius Clodius**, now tribune, pressed the charge, and after Cicero had taken refuge at Thessalonica in 58, he was condemned to exile, and his house at Rome and his country houses at Formiae and Tusculum were plundered. But in 57 the people almost unanimously voted his recall. Now, however, he was no longer a power in politics; and, nervously sensitive to the fluctuations of public opinion, he could not decide between Pompey and the aristocracy and **Caesar** and the new democracy. Thus, though he ultimately inclined to Caesar, he lost the esteem of both parties, being regarded as a trimmer and time-server. In 52 he composed his speech in defence of Milo, who had killed Clodius in a riot. Next year he was in Asia, as governor of Cilicia. In 49–48 he was with Pompey's army in Greece, but after the defeat at Pharsalia (48) threw himself on Caesar's mercy. In 46–44 he wrote most of his chief works on rhetoric and philosophy, living in retirement and brooding over his disappointments. In 43, after Caesar's death, his famous speeches against **Marcus Antonius**, the *Philippics* were delivered, and cost him his life. As soon as Antony, Octavian and **Lepidus** had leagued themselves in the triumvirate, they proscribed their enemies, and Cicero's name was on the fatal list. Old and feeble, he fled to his villa at Formiae, pursued by the soldiers of Antony, and was overtaken as he was being carried in a litter. With calm courage he put his head out of the litter and bade the murderers strike. He was in his sixty-third year. As orator and pleader Cicero stands in the first rank; of his speeches the most famous are those against Verras and Catiline. As a politician he failed. As an essayist and letter-writer he is most attractive. His essays on 'old age', 'friendship' and 'duty' (*De Oficiis*) are still good reading; and his Tusculan disputations, his treatises on the 'nature of the gods' and 'true ends of human life' (*De Finibus*), illustrate the various ancient philosophies.

CID, El, properly **Rodrigo diaz de Vivar** (c.1043–1099) Spanish warrior hero, born in Burgos, immortalized as 'El Cid' (The Lord) or 'El Campeador' (The Champion). A vassal of Alfonso VI of Castile, he was a compound of condottiere and patriot, constantly fighting from 1065. In 1081 he was banished for an unauthorized raid, and began a long career as a soldier of fortune, serving both Spaniards and Moors. He besieged and captured Valencia (1093–94) and became its ruler.

CIDENAS (4th century BC) Babylonian astronomer, head of an astronomical school at Sippra. He discovered the precession of the equinoxes.

CIERVA, Juan de la (1895–1936) Spanish aeronautical engineer. In 1823 he invented the autogiro.

CIGOLI, properly **Ludovico Cardi** (1559–1613) Italian painter and architect of the later Florentine school, born in Cigoli, near Florence. He was invited to Rome by **Clement VII**.

CILEA, Francesco (1866–1950) Italian operatic composer, born in Palmi, Calabria. He was director of the Naples Conservatory from 1916 to 1936. He wrote several operas, of which the best-known is *Adriana Lecouvreur* (1902).

CILENTO, Lady Phyllis Dorothy, née **McGlew** (1894–1987) Australian medical practitioner, author and broadcaster, born in Sydney and educated at Adelaide University. After postgraduate work in Asia, Europe and the USA, she became lecturer in mothercraft and obstetrical physiotherapy at the University of Queensland. Her life's work, for which she was awarded the AM, was devoted to family planning, childbirth education, and nutrition, on which subjects she broadcast and wrote many books and newspaper columns. She married **Raphael West Cilento** in 1920.

CILENTO, Sir Raphael West (1893–1985) Australian medical administrator, born in Jamestown, South Australia. Educated at Adelaide University, he later became a medallist of the London School of Tropical Medicine. He was director of the Australian Institute of Tropical Medicine at Townsville, Queensland, from 1922, director of public health and quarantine in New Guinea (1924–28), director-general of health and medical services for Queensland

(1934–45) and sometime honorary professor of tropical and social medicine at the University of Queensland. Knighted in 1935, after World War II he served in Germany and New York, and worked with the United Nations from 1946 to 1951.

CILIAN, St (d.697) the Irish apostle of Franconia, martyred at Würzburg.

CIMA DA CONEGLIANO, Giovanni Battista (c.1460–1508) Venetian religious painter, born in Conegliano. He was strongly influenced by **Giovanni Bellini**. His *David and Jonathan* is in the National Gallery.

CIMABUÉ, Giovanni (c.1240–c.1302) Italian painter, born in Florence. His chief fame rests upon his role as the teacher of **Giotto**. Cimabué was the first artist to move away from the stylized and rigid conventions of Byzantine art. In doing this he paved the way for his pupil's humanistic naturalism which in turn forms the basis of Italian art. He is mentioned by **Dante** as having his reputation eclipsed by Giotto. Early critics attribute the famous *Rucellai Madonna* to him but this is now generally believed to be by **Duccio**. Cimabué is known to have been in Rome in 1272 and is documented as having been working on the mosaic figure of Saint **John** in the apse of Pisa Cathedral in 1302. He also executed several important works in the Lower Church of San Francesco at Assisi.

CIMAROSA, Domenico (1749–1801) Italian composer of operas, was born in Aversa. He studied music at Naples, and produced his first opera there in 1772. In 1789 he was summoned to St Petersburg by **Catherine II**, in 1792 to Vienna; and in 1793 he returned to Naples, where his comic opera, *Il Matrimonio segreto*, was repeated 70 times.

CIMON (d. 449 BC) Athenian soldier and statesman, the son of **Miltiades**, the conqueror at Marathon. He fought at the battle of Salamis (450 BC), and by 476 BC he was in supreme command of the Athenian forces in the patriotic struggle against the Persians, and captured Eïon, a town on the river Strymon. His greatest exploit was his destruction of a Persian fleet and army at the river Eurymedon (466 or 467). He led an unsuccessful expedition to support the Spartans during the Helot uprising in 462 BC, and was dismissed and ostracized (461). He was recalled in 454, and may have been instrumental in obtaining a five years' armistice with Sparta. He died at the siege of a town in Cyprus.

CINCINNATUS, Lucius Quinctius (5th century BC) Roman statesman and soldier, a favourite hero of the old Roman republic. In 460 BC he was chosen consul, and two years later dictator. The story goes that when the messengers came to tell Cincinnatus of his new dignity they found him ploughing on his small farm. He rescued the consul Minucius, who had been defeated and surrounded by the Aequi, and 16 days later, he laid down his dictatorship and returned to his farm.

CINEAS (d.270 BC) Greek politician from Thessaly. The friend and minister of **Pyrrhus**, the king of Epyrus, he was said to be the most eloquent man of his time.

CINNA, Lucius Cornelius (d.84 BC) Roman patrician and politician. He supported **Gaius Marius**. **Sulla**, after driving Marius from Rome, and before setting out against **Mithradates**, allowed Cinna to be elected consul on his swearing not to disturb the existing constitution. No sooner, however, had he entered office (87 BC) than he impeached Sulla, and agitated for Marius' recall. Cinna and Marius next declared themselves consuls after a cruel massacre. Marius died a few days later; and Cinna in 84 BC prepared to meet Sulla, but was slain by his own disaffected troops at the coast. During his fourth consulate his daughter Cornelia had been married to **Julius Caesar**.

CIPRIANI, Giambattista (1727–85) Italian historical painter, born in Florence. In 1755 he accompanied Sir **William Chambers** to London, where his graceful drawings, engraved by **Bartolozzi**, gained great popularity. He was a member of the St Martin's Lane Academy, and in 1768 was elected a foundation member of the Royal Academy.

CITRINE, Walter McLennan, 1st Baron Citrine of Wembley (1887–1983) English trade union leader, born in Wallasey. An electrician by trade, he held office in the ETU, 1914–23 and was general secretary of the TUC, 1926–46. From 1928 to 1945 he was president of the International Federation of Trades Unions, and was a member of the National Coal Board and chairman of the Miners' Welfare Commission, 1946–47. Knighted in 1935 and created a peer in 1946, he became chairman of the Central Electricity Authority in 1947. Efficient and versatile, a skilled trade-union diplomat, he was one of the more significant figures of the postwar social-democratic 'managerial revolution'.

CITROËN, André Gustave (1878–1935) French engineer and motor manufacturer, born in Paris. He was responsible for the mass production of armaments during World War I. After the war he applied these techniques to the manufacture of low-priced small cars. In 1934 he became bankrupt and lost control of the company which still bears his name.

CIVILIS, Claudius or **Julius** (fl.69–70) Dutch folk-hero, from Roman times. He was one of the favoured Batavian tribe who in opposition to Roman conscription and gubernatorial exactions took advantage of the imperial crisis after **Nero**'s fall to lead his people into revolt in alliance with the Germans (especially the Frisians) and then also the Gauls. Civilis seems to have been sufficiently Romanized to win over troops and captains. But **Vespasian**, once master of Rome, despatched Petillius Cerialis to end the revolt. Civilis refused terms of surrender, but Gauls and Roman mutineers were overawed and Civilis was defeated by the Romans at Trier in 70, and after further fighting fell back on sea-protected Batavia. Nothing more is known of him.

CIVITALI, Matteo (1435–1501) an Italian architect and sculptor, born in Lucca. His best work is seen in the cathedral there.

CI-XI, old style **Tz'u-Hsi** (1834–1908) empress dowager of China. She was presented as a concubine to the Manchu emperor Xianfeng (Hsien-Feng) and on his death, in 1861 became regent, initially to her infant son, Tongzhi (T'ung-chih), and then, following his death in 1874, to her nephew Guangxu (Kuang-hsu), despite a dynastic custom which forbade women to reign. A conservative force within the Chinese court and inveterate intriguer, she acquired the nickname the 'Old Buddha', and worked to frustrate the country's late 19th-century modernization programme. She remained dominant even after Guangxu (1871–1908) formally assumed imperial power in 1889; and from 1898, after the emperor had attempted to promote far-reaching reform, she confined him to the palace. In 1900 she helped foment the anti-foreigner Boxer agitation, and a day before her own death, she organized the murder of Guangxu.

CIXOUS, Hélène (1937–) French academic and feminist, born in Algiers into a Jewish family. Educated at the Lycée Bugeaud in Algiers, she moved to France in 1955 where she began to teach, at the same time taking further degrees in English. In 1965 she became an assistant lecturer at the Sorbonne and took an active part in the student uprisings of 1968. Later, as professor at Vincennes, she established experimental literature courses. Her work is mostly concerned with the relationship between psychoanalysis and language, especially in its significance for women, and in exploring the links between the writer and reader. Her publications include *Dedans* (winner of the 1969 Prix Médicis), *Neutre* (1972) and *La* (1979).

CLAIR, René, pseud of **René Lucien Chomette** (1898–1981) French film director, born in Paris. He established his reputation with avant-garde films like *Paris qui dort* (1923) and *Entr'acte* (1924), and developed his light comedy touch and whimsical irony in a string of successful films made in France, and later in America, including *The Italian Straw Hat* (1927), *Paris* (1930), *Le Million* (1931), *Quatorze Juillet* (1932), *The Ghost Goes West* (1935) and *It Happened Tomorrow* (1944). He returned to France in 1946, and his final film was *Les Fêtes Galantes* (1965).

CLAIRAUT, Alexis Claude (1713–65) French mathematician, born in Paris and admitted to the Académie des Sciences at 18. He worked on celestial mechanics, including the figure of the earth and the motion of the moon, and computed the date of the return of **Halley**'s comet in 1759.

CLAPARÈDE, Edouard (1873–1940) Swiss psychologist and educationist. After studies at Geneva, Leipzig and Paris, he founded the journal *Archives de psychologie* (1901). As professor at Geneva, he was director of the experimental psychology laboratory and in 1912 founded the J J Rousseau Institute for the study of educational science. An exponent of Functionalism, he pioneered studies in problem-solving and sleep.

CLAPEYRON, Bénoit Paul Émile (1799–1864) French civil engineer, born in Paris. He was educated at the École Polytechnique and the École des Mines. After some time in Russia he returned to France and was principally engaged in the construction of railways and bridges, including the design of locomotives where he was the first to make use of the expansive action of steam in the cylinder. For the analysis of beams resting on more than two supports he developed the 'Theorem of Three Moments', and in 1834 he published an exposition of **Sadi Carnot**'s classic but previously neglected paper on the power and efficiency of various types of heat engine.

CLAPPERTON, Hugh (1788–1827) Scottish explorer, born in Annan. At sea from the age of 13, he was sent in 1821 with **Dixon Denham** to discover the source of the Niger. They travelled south across the Sahara to Lake Chad in 1823; from there he pushed on alone to Sokoto, returning to England in 1825. The journey had thrown light on Bornu and the Houssa country, but the great problem of the source of the Niger was untouched. In a new attempt to resolve it he started again from the Bight of Benin in December 1825, travelling north in company with **Richard Lander** and others. The others died early on the journey, but Clapperton and Lander reached Sokoto where Clapperton was detained by the sultan and died.

CLARE, St, of Assisi (1194–1253) Italian Christian saint, daughter of Count Favorino Scifi, and elder sister of St **Agnes**. At the age of 18 she became a follower of St **Francis**, and with him and her younger sister founded the order of Poor Ladies of San Damiano ('Poor Clares', formerly called 'Minoresses'), of which she became abbess. She was canonized in 1255, and in 1958 she was designated patron saint of television by Pope **Pius XI** on the grounds that at Christmas 1252, when she was in her cell at San Damiano, she 'saw and heard' a service being held in the church of St Francis in Assisi. Her feast day is 12 August.

CLARE, John (1793–1864) English peasant poet, born in Helpstone, near Peterborough, the son of a poor labourer. Though almost without schooling, he studied **James Thomsons**'s *Seasons*, and began to cultivate verse writing as well as gardening. After serving in the Northamptonshire militia (1812–14), in 1817 he published *Proposals for Publishing a Collection of Trifles in Verse* at his own expense, but got no subscribers. It led, however, to the publication of his *Poems Descriptive of Rural Life* (1820), which had a good reception; but though the Marquis of Exeter and other patrons secured him £45 a year, he continued to live in poverty, and went insane. His other published works were *Village Minstrel* (1821), *The Shepherd's Calendar* (1827), and *Rural Muse* (1835). He was committed to an asylum in 1837, where he died.

CLARENCE, Duke of English ducal title occasionally conferred on the younger sons or brothers of English monarchs. It was first conferred in 1362 on Lionel of Antwerp (1330–80), third son of **Edward III** and **Philippa of Hainault**. Other notable Dukes were Thomas (son of **Henry IV**), who fell at the battle of Beaugé in 1421; **George** (brother of **Edward IV** and **Richard III**); William (later **William IV**), son of **George III**; and Prince William Albert Victor (1864–92), son of **Edward VII**.

CLARENCE, George, Duke of Clarence (1449–78) third son of Richard, Duke of **York**, and brother of **Edward IV** and **Richard III**: according to tradition, he was put to death in the Tower of London 'in a butt of Malmsey'. Created Duke of Clarence on Edward's accession in 1461, in 1469 he married Isabella, elder daughter of Richard Neville, Earl of **Warwick**, against Edward's wishes. He supported Warwick against his brother in the brief restoration of **Henry VI** in 1470, but deserted to his brother's side in 1471. He quarrelled with his other brother, Richard, Duke of Gloucester, over Richard's marriage to his sister-in-law Anne Neville in 1472, but was later reconciled. In 1478 he was impeached by his brothers for treason, and secretly executed.

CLARENDON, Edward Hyde, 1st Earl of (1609–74) English statesman, born in Dinton, near Salisbury, the third son of a Wiltshire squire. He sat in the Short Parliament of 1640 and the Long Parliament, where he criticized **Charles I**'s unconstitutional actions and supported the impeachment of **Strafford**. In 1641 he broke with the revolutionaries and became a royal adviser and when the civil war broke out followed the monarch to Oxford. On the king's defeat in 1646 he joined Prince Charles in Jersey. In 1651 he became chief adviser to **Charles II** in exile and on the restoration was created earl of Clarendon. He further increased his influence by marrying Anne, the daughter of the Duke of York. He introduced the 'Clarendon Code' to ensure the supremacy of the Church of England but his moderate policies were opposed by the extremists. He lost the confidence of Charles II when he criticized his private life, and the disasters of 1667, when the Dutch sailed up the Medway, finally confirmed his downfall. He died in exile in Rouen but was buried in Westminster Abbey.

CLARENDON, George William Frederick Villiers, 4th Earl of (1800–70) English statesman, born in London. His grandfather, Thomas Villiers, second son of the Earl of Jersey, having married in 1752 the heiress of the last Lord Clarendon of the Hyde family, was made Baron Hyde (1756) and Earl of Clarendon (1776). Having studied at Cambridge, he early entered the diplomatic service, and in 1833 was appointed ambassador at Madrid, where he employed his great influence in helping Espartero to establish a constitutional government. In 1838 he succeeded his uncle as 4th Earl, and in 1840 was made lord privy seal under **Melbourne**. When the Whigs fell (1841) he became an active member of the opposition; but warmly supported **Peel** and his own brother, **Charles Pelham Villiers**, in the abolition of the Corn Laws. Under **Russell** he became president of the Board of Trade in 1846 and from 1847 to 1852 was Irish viceroy. His impartiality helped to reconcile party exasperations, though it did not avert the bitter hatred of the Orangemen. He was thanked in the speech from the throne in 1848, and in 1849 received the Garter. Secretary of state for foreign affairs (1853), he incurred the responsibility for the Crimean War, and **Roebuck**'s resolution in 1855 cost him his office, which he resumed at **Palmerston**'s desire. He resumed his old office in 1865 and 1868.

CLARETIE, Jules, properly **Arsène Arnaud** (1840–1913) French novelist, born in Limoges. While a schoolboy in Paris he published a novel, and soon became a leading critic and political writer. His short story *Pierrille* (1863) was praised by **George Sand**. His novels also were generally popular. During the Franco-German war he sent a series of remarkable letters to the *Rappel* and *Opinion nationale*, and acquired the materials for a later series of bright and vigorous anti-German books of an historical character. He first made a hit on the stage with his Revolution plays, *Les Muscadins* (1874), *Le Régiment de Champagne* (1877) and *Les Mirabeau* (1878); in 1885 he became director of the Comédie Français.

CLARIN See **ALAS, Leopoldo**

CLARK, Charles Manning Hope (1915–) Australian historian and writer, born in Burwood, New South Wales, the son of a vicar, and great-great-great-grandson of **Samuel Marsden**, the 'flogging parson of Parramatta'. Educated at Melbourne Grammar School, Melbourne University and Oxford University, in 1949 he became the first professor of Australian history at the Australian National University, Canberra, becoming Emeritus professor in 1977. His two-volume *Select Documents in Australian History* (1950–55) and *Sources of Australian History* (1957) established his scholarly reputation. Clark was never far from the centre of controversy on political issues, and strong republican views informed his six-volume *History of Australia* (1962–88). Although criticized by academics, the *History*, along with his *Short History of Australia* (1963), has done much to popularize the study of Australian history in schools and colleges. In 1976 he gave the ABC Boyer Lectures on *The Discovery of Australia*.

CLARK, (John) Grahame Douglas (1907–) English archaeologist, born in Shortlands, Kent. Educated at Marlborough and Peterhouse, Cambridge, he taught at Cambridge from 1935, serving as Disney professor of archaeology (1952–74), and was master of Peterhouse (1973–80). His *Archaeology and Society* (1939) and *World Prehistory* (1961, 1977) pioneered the use of the archaeological record to document the economic and social life of prehistoric communities. Books such as *Prehistoric Europe: The Economic Basis* (1952) also played a major role in moving prehistory away from its preoccupation with typology and encouraging the newly emergent discipline of environmental archaeology. Of his many excavations, the most famous is that of the Mesolithic hunting settlement of the mid-eighth millenium BC at Star Carr near Scarborough, revealed 1949–51. *Archaeology at Cambridge and Beyond*, which appeared in 1989, has a strong autobiographical flavour, as have some of the essays in the collection *Economic Prehistory* published the same year.

CLARK, Jim (James) (1936–68) Scottish racing driver and world champion, born in Berwickshire. Educated at Loretto School in Musselburgh, he won his first motor race in 1956, and became Scottish Speed Champion in 1958 and 1959. In 1960 he joined the Lotus team as a Formula One driver, and thereafter won the world championship in 1963 and 1965. Also in 1965 he became the first non-American since 1916 to win the Indianapolis 500. In all, he won 25 Grand Prix events, breaking the record of 24 held by **Juan Fangio**. He was killed during practice for a Formula Two race at Hockenheim, in West Germany.

CLARK, Joe Charles Joseph (1939–) Canadian politician, born in High River, Alberta, and educated at Alberta and Dalhousie universities, where he was politically active. After a short period as journalist and university lecturer, he was elected to the Canadian House of Commons in 1972 and four years later became leader of the Progressive Conservative party (PCP). He defeated **Pierre Trudeau** in 1979 to become Canada's youngest prime minister, but was himself defeated a year later. In 1983 he was replaced as party leader by **Brian Mulroney** who, as prime minister in 1984, made Clark his external affairs minister.

CLARK, Josiah Latimer (1822–98) English electrical engineer, born in Great Marlow. In 1854 he patented a pneumatic delivery tube, and made important inventions in connection with submarine cables. He also invented a single-lens stereo-camera.

CLARK, Sir Kenneth Mackenzie, Baron (1903–83) English art historian, educated at Winchester and Trinity College, Oxford. Privately wealthy, he worked in Florence with **Bernard Berenson** and became an authority on Italian Renaissance art. He was keeper of the department of fine art at the Ashmolean Museum (1931–33), director of the National Gallery in London (1934–45), Slade professor of fine art at Oxford (1946–50, 1961–62), and professor of art history at the Royal Academy (1977–83). A major cultural influence in British life, he was chairman of the Arts Council (1953–60), and chairman of the Independent Television Authority (1954–57) at the launch of commercial television in Britain. He wrote several books, including studies on *Leonardo da Vinci* (1935 and 1939) and *Piero della Francesca* (1951) and two surveys, *Landscape into Art* (1949) and *The Nude* (1955). He achieved huge fame with his pioneering television series, *Civilisation* (1969), which stimulated widespread popular interest in art.

CLARK, Mark Wayne (1896–1984) American soldier, born in Maddison Barracks, New York, of a military family. He graduated from West Point Military Academy in 1917 and was wounded while on active service in Europe. In 1942 he was given a senior staff appointment as a major general. He was designated as Commander II Corps under **Eisenhower** for the invasion of North Africa, but subsequently became his deputy. Prior to the Allied landings in North Africa he was secretly landed in Algeria to make contact with friendly French officials, narrowly escaping capture by the Vichy Security Police. He commanded the 5th Army at the Salerno landing (1943) and Anzio, and the capture of Rome (1944) and was much criticized for choosing the latter instead of encircling the German forces. Commanding general of the US Forces in Austria after the war, he ceded nothing to Soviet hectoring. He commanded the US 6th Army in the Far East (1947–49), and relieved **Ridgeway** in command of UN forces in Korea (1952–53).

CLARK, Michael (1962–) Scottish dancer and choreographer, born in Aberdeen, where he took lessons in Scottish country dancing from the age of 4. Accepted by the Royal Ballet School at 13, he went on to dance with the Royal Ballet. A move to Ballet Rambert led to roles in **Richard Alston**'s *Dutiful Ducks* and *Soda Lake*. After studying with **Merce Cunningham** in New York for a short time, he began to choreograph. While developing his own style he worked as a dancer with **Karole Armitage** in Paris, starting his own company in 1984. His brilliantly original style incorporates punk, 1960s fantasy, nudity, video, platform shoes and giant hamburgers, but it is his keen, sculptural choreography which makes him one of the most inventive artists today. Major full-length productions include *Our caca phony H. our caca phony H* (1985), *No Fire Escape in Hell* (1986), *Because We Must* (1987) and *I Am Curious, Orange* (1988). Commissions include *Swamp* for Ballet Rambert (1986).

CLARK, Sir Wilfred Edward Le Gros (1895–1971) English anatomist, born in Hemel Hempstead. He qualified in medicine in London in 1916 and served as medical officer in Borneo before returning to teach anatomy at London and from 1934 to 1962 in Oxford. Distinguished for his work on the anatomy of primates and especially the brain, he helped expose in the 1950s the 'Piltdown Man' hoax involving **Charlie Dawson**.

CLARK, William Mansfield (1884–1964) American chemist. He was educated at Johns Hopkins University, where he later became professor of physiological chemistry. He did important research on hydrogen-ion concentration and on oxidation reduction equilibria.

CLARKE, Adam (1762–1832) English Wesleyan divine, born near Portrush. He was the author of a *Bibliographical Dictionary* (8 vols, 1802–06) and a well-known edition of the Holy Scriptures (8 vols, 1810–26) with a commentary. He denied the eternal sonship of Christ, though maintaining His divinity, and held that Judas repented unto salvation, and that the tempter of Eve was a baboon.

CLARKE, Alexander Ross (1828–1914) Scottish geodesist. He began as an army engineer and was later attached to the Ordnance Survey. He is remembered for his work on the principal triangulation of the British Isles, and for his book *Geodesy* (1880).

CLARKE, Arthur Charles (1917–) English writer of science fiction, born in Minehead, Somerset. He worked in scientific research before turning to fiction: he was a radar instructor in World War II, and originated the idea of satellite communication in a scientific article in 1945. A prolific writer and an unashamed entertainer, his themes are exploration — in both the near and distant future—and man's position in the hierarchy of the universe. His first book was *Prelude to Space* (1951) and while he is credited with some of the genre's best examples—*Rendezvous with Rama* (1973), *The Fountains of Paradise* (1979)—his name will always be associated first with *2001: A Space Odyssey* (1968), which, under the direction of **Stanley Kubrick**, became a highly successful film. He emigrated to Sri Lanka in the 1950s.

CLARKE, Austin (1896–1974) Irish poet and dramatist, born in Dublin where he was educated at the Jesuit Belvedere College and University College. He spent 15 years in England as a book reviewer and journalist before returning to Dublin in 1937. *The Vengeance of Fionn*, the first of 18 books of verse, was published in 1917. Like other earlier verse, it is markedly influenced by **Yeats** and his obsession with Irish mythology, but he shook this off and developed into a technically accomplished poet, sharply satirical, and critical, of Irish attitudes. His *Collected Poems* were published in 1974. He was also a noted playwright and an adherent of verse drama which he promoted through the Dublin Verse-Speaking Society which he formed in 1941. His plays, drawing heavily on Irish legend, were collected in 1963. His first novel, *The Bright Temptation* (1932), was banned in Ireland until 1954. *Twice Round the Black Church* (1962) and *A Penny in the Clouds* (1968) are autobiographical.

CLARKE, Charles Cowden (1787–1877) English Shakespearean scholar, born in Enfield, Middlesex, where his father kept a school where **Keats** was a pupil. He formed the friendship of **Leigh Hunt**, **Shelley**, **Hazlitt**, **Charles** and **Mary Lamb**. In 1820, he became a bookseller in London and soon a partner as music publisher with Alfred Novello, whose sister Mary Victoria (1809–98), he married in 1828; she compiled a *Concordance to Shakespeare's Plays* (1845). He gave public lectures on Shakespeare and other literary figures, some of which were published as *Shakespeare Characters* (1863), and *Molière Characters* (1865). With his wife he published *Shakespeare Key* (1879), an annotated edition of **Shakespeare** (1869), and *Recollections of Writers* (1878).

CLARKE, David Leonard (1937–76) English archaeologist, born in Kent. He studied at Dulwich College and at Peterhouse, Cambridge, of which he was a fellow (1966–76). His spirited teaching and writing—particularly in *Analytical Archaeology* (1967)—transformed European archaeology in the 1970s. Matched in impact only by the work of **Lewis Binford** in the USA, it demonstrated the central importance of systems theory, quantification, and clearly stated scientific reasoning in archaeology, and drew ecology, geography, and comparative anthropology firmly within the ambit of the subject for the first time. *Analytical Archaeologist* (1979) is a collection of his writings interlarded with the reminiscences of colleagues.

CLARKE, Edward Daniel (1769–1822) English traveller and mineralogist, born in Willingdon, Sussex. Educated at Tonbridge School and Jesus College, Cambridge, he travelled in Europe as tutor in noblemen's families (1790–99). In 1799–1802 he also traversed Finland, Russia, Scandinavia, the Middle East and Greece. In 1808 he was appointed first professor of mineralogy at Cambridge.

CLARKE, Frank Wigglesworth (1847–1931) American geologist, born in Boston. He was professor of physics at Howard University and at Cincinnati (1874–83), chief chemist to the US Geological Survey (1883–1925), and did much work on the recalculation of atomic weights.

CLARKE, Sir Fred (1880–1952) radical English educationist, born in Witney. Educated at elementary school and technical college, he studied modern history at Oxford. He became master of method at the Diocesan Training College, York (1903), and successively professor of education at Hartley University College, Southampton (1906–11), South African College and University of Cape Town (1911–29) and McGill University, Montreal (1929). He was adviser (1935) and director (1936–45) of the Institute of Education, London. He wrote a number of books including *Foundations of History Teaching* (1929), but his really influential work was *Education and Social Change* (1940). Termed 'the Beveridge of education', he foresaw the significance of education in the post-war period. As early as 1922 he had regarded **R H Tawney**'s *Secondary Education for All* programme as inadequate. Influenced by the refugee sociologist Karl Mannheim, he argued that after World War II the old class-divided education offered in Britain would be intolerable, especially at secondary level. 'We can hardly continue to contemplate an England where the mass of the people coming on by one educational path are to be governed for the most part by a minority advancing by a quite separate and more favoured path', he wrote in what was to be one of the outstanding education books of the century and a forerunner of the thinking behind the Education Act of 1944.

CLARKE, Gillian (1937–) Welsh poet, born in Cardiff and educated at the city's University College. She has published three collections of poetry, the latest being *Letting in the Rumour* (1989). She was editor of *The Anglo-Welsh Review* from 1976 to 1984, and since 1987 has been chairman of The Welsh Academy.

CLARKE, James Freeman (1810–88) American theologian, born in Hanover, New Hampshire. He studied at Harvard, became a Unitarian pastor, and in 1841 founded the Unitarian Church of the Disciples at Boston. He held a chair of natural theology at Harvard from 1867 to 1871. He wrote many books, including *Ten Great Religions* (1871) and *Self-Culture* (1882).

CLARKE, Jeremiah (c.1674–1707) English composer, born probably in London. He studied under **John Blow** at the Chapel Royal and became organist of Winchester College in 1692 and of St Paul's Cathedral three years later, following his master at the Chapel Royal in 1704. He committed suicide as the result of an unhappy love affair. The real composer of the *Trumpet Voluntary* long attributed to **Purcell**, Clarke wrote operas, theatre music, religious and secular choral works, and music for harpsichord.

CLARKE, Kenneth Harry (1940–) English politician. From Cambridge he was called to the bar in 1963 and practised on the Midland Circuit (1963–79). An active member of the progressive Bow Group in the Conservative party, he entered parliament, representing Rushcliffe, Nottinghamshire, in 1970. After junior posts in the **Heath** administration (1971–74) he entered **Margaret Thatcher**'s government in 1979 and built up a reputation as an affable and effective politician, capable of handling a controversial brief. In 1988 he was appointed to the key post of secretary of state for health, with the task of overseeing a major reform of the National Health Service.

CLARKE, Marcus (1846–81) Australian writer, born in London, the son of a London barrister. He emigrated to Australia in 1863 and joined the Melbourne *Argus*. His chief work was *For the Term of his Natural Life* (1874), a novel of the convict settlements.

CLARKE, Martha (1944–) American dancer-choreographer, born in Maryland. She studied dance as a child and later trained with **José Limón**, **Alvin Ailey**, **Charles Weidman** and **Anna Sokolow** at the American Dance Festival in Connecticut and with **Martha Graham**'s associate Louis Horst at New York's Juilliard School of Music. She spent a few seasons in Anna Sokolow's company before moving to Europe. On her return to the USA she became (1972) one of the first female members of Pilobolus, a collectively-run dance-theatre ensemble. As the troupe achieved worldwide popularity, Clarke and dancers Robby Barnett and Felix Blaska formed the trio Crowsnest. Since the mid 1980s, she has concentrated on unclassifiable dance-theatre productions such as *Garden of Earthly Delights* (1984), *Vienna: Lusthaus* (1986), *The Hunger Artist* (1987) and *Miracolo d'Amore* (1988).

CLARKE, Mary Anne, née **Thompson** (1776–1852) English courtier. She was mistress during 1803–07 to Frederick, Duke of **York**, and trafficked in commissions. Imprisoned for libel in 1813, she later settled in Paris.

CLARKE, Ronald William (1937–) Australian athlete, born in Melbourne. One of the greatest distance runners of all time, the ultimate prize of an Olympic medal nevertheless eluded him. As a youth he was selected to carry the Olympic torch at the Melbourne Games of 1956, but he first concentrated on his career as an accountant. At one time he held the world records at such varied distances as three miles, five miles, ten miles, 3000, 5000 and 10000 metres, but despite holding six world records simultaneously he only came sixth in the 10000 metres in Mexico City in 1968, and was so badly affected by the altitude that he collapsed on completion of the race and was revived with some difficulty, his heart having momentarily stopped beating. Although he had the reputation of being a better runner against the clock than against rivals, he lost only 25 of 500 races. He retired after the 1970 Commonwealth Games.

CLARKE, Samuel (1675–1729) English philosopher and theologian, born in Norwich. He studied in Cambridge, where he became a friend and disciple of **Newton**. He was chaplain to the bishop of Norwich (from 1698), to Queen **Anne** (from 1706) and became rector of St James' Westminster in 1709. His Boyle Lectures of 1704–05 contained his 'Demonstration of the Being and Attributes of God' and expanded the famous 'mathematical' proof of God's existence. His extensive correspondence with **Leibniz** (published in 1717) defended a Newtonian view of space, time and the universe.

CLARKE, Thomas James (1858–1916) Irish nationalist and revolutionary, born in Hurst Castle, Isle of Wight, where his father was a British soldier. His family emigrated to South Africa when he was a child, and returned to Ireland when he was 10. At 21 he emigrated to the USA, where he became involved in Clan-na-Gael, the clandestine American wing of the Irish Republican Brotherhood, promoting anti-British action. Sent to England in 1883, he was arrested for participation in the dynamite campaign against London civilians and was sentenced to penal servitude for life. He served 15 years under the most severe conditions, retaining his sanity by translating the Bible into shorthand twice. His post-release *Glimpses of an Irish Felon's Prison Life* is a work of stoicism, dignity and intransigence. On his release in 1898 he returned to the USA and became agent for the remilitarized **John Devoy** and married Kathleen Daly, niece of a fellow-dynamiter and fellow-prisoner John Daly (1845–1916), mayor of Limerick (1899–1901) after his release. Clarke returned to Ireland in 1907 as a US citizen and at his urging the Irish Republican Brotherhood set up a military council. Under Clarke's influence this brought about the Easter Rising of 1916, in which Clarke was a symbolic presence: after the surrender he was court-martialled and shot.

CLARKE, William Branwhite (1798–1878) English clergyman and geologist, born in East Bergholt, Suffolk. Educated at Dedham and Cambridge, he took holy orders. In 1839 he went out to New South Wales, and in 1841 discovered gold in the alluvium of the Macquarie.

CLARKSON, Thomas (1760–1846) English anti-slavery campaigner, born in Wisbeach, and educated at St Paul's School, and St John's College, Cambridge. He gained a prize for a Latin essay in 1785, on the question 'Is it right to make slaves of others against their will?' which in an English translation (1786) was widely read. In 1787, in association with **Wilberforce** and **Granville Sharp**, he formed an anti-slavery society and after the passing of the British anti-slavery laws (1807), wrote a *History of the Abolition of the African*

Slave-trade (2 vols, 1808). He campaigned for the abolition of slavery in the colonies and saw it attained in 1833.

CLAUDE, Georges (1870–1960) French chemist and physicist, born in Paris. He is noted for his work on gases, and is credited with the invention of neon lighting for signs.

CLAUDE LORRAINE, real name **Claude Gêlée** (1600–82) French landscape painter, born near Nancy. By tradition he is believed to have trained as a pastry-cook but by about 1613 he was in Italy where he was apprenticed to Cavaliere d'Arpino and the landscapist Agostino Tassi. In 1625 he returned to Nancy but in 1627 he was back in Rome and within three years had achieved a distinguished reputation as a landscape painter. In about 1635 he began recording his compositions in a book of drawings, the *Liber Veritatis* (now in the British Museum), to guard against copyists. The sources of his landscape style are the romanticized landscapes of the later Mannerists, **Elsheimer** and the Brills. He is somewhat restricted in his subjects and natural effects—he had little sympathy with nature in her wilder and sterner moods—and tends to be rather repetitive, but his colour is always harmonious and mellow. He also produced about 30 etchings. **Hamerton** pronounced *Le Bouvier* 'the finest landscape etching in the world'. Although his work may not be to the modern taste he was a major influence on virtually every landscape painter from the 17th to the 19th centuries, including **Watteau**, **Wilson** and **Turner**. The latter painted his *Dido Building Carthage* in emulation of Claude (London, National Gallery).

CLAUDEL, Camille (1864–1943) French sculptor, born in La Fère-en-Tardenois, daughter of a wealthy civil servant, and sister of the poet **Paul Claudel**. She decided to become a sculptor at an early age and in 1884 was introduced to **Auguste Rodin**. She became his student, model and mistress, producing works which, while close to his, nonetheless show great individuality and mastery. After a fiery relationship, Claudel and Rodin parted company in 1898, but she continued to sculpt and achieved great renown around 1900. However, the break with Rodin affected her mental stability and from 1913 until her death she was confined to various institutions.

CLAUDEL, Paul (1868–1955) French poet, essayist and dramatist, born in Villeneuve-sur-Fère. Now regarded as one of the major figures in French Catholic literature, it was long before he was recognized, even by his countrymen. He joined the diplomatic service and held posts in many parts of the world. This experience, with the early influence of the Symbolists, adds quality and richness to his work. His eight dramas, of which the most celebrated are *L'Annonce fait à Marie* (1892), *Partage de Midi* (1905), *L'Otage* (1909) and *Le Soulier de satin* (The Satin Slipper, 1921), have a Wagnerian grandeur and, in many cases, an anti-Protestant violence that make them too strong for popular taste. He wrote memorable poetry—*Cinq Grandes Odes* (1922) and *Corona Benignitatis Anni Dei* (1913)—and the libretti for two operas: *Jeanne d'Arc au bûcher* by **Honegger** and *Christophe Colombe* by **Milhaud**.

CLAUDIAN, (Claudius Claudianus) (4th century) the last of the great Latin poets. He came from Alexandria to Rome in AD 395, and obtained patrician dignity by favour of **Stilicho**, whose fall (408) he seems not to have long survived. A pagan, he wrote first in Greek, though he was of Roman extraction. Several epic poems by him, including *The Rape of Proserpine*, panegyrics on **Honorius**, Stilicho and others, invectives against **Rufinus** and Eutropius, occasional poems, and a Greek fragment, *Gigantomachia*, are still extant.

CLAUDIUS I, full name **Tiberius Claudius Drusus Nero Germanicus** (10 BC–54 AD) fourth Roman emperor, born in Lyon, younger son of **Drusus** senior, brother of the emperor **Tiberius**. He was largely kept out of public life by Tiberius, and his supposed imbecility saved him from the cruelty of **Caligula**, but he had devoted much time to the study of history, and wrote in Latin and Greek several works now lost. After Caligula's assassination (41), Claudius was found by the soldiers hiding in the palace, and proclaimed emperor. In his reign he was faced with the problems of restoring order and sound government after the excesses of Caligula, securing the co-operation of a reluctant senate who resented the manner of his accession, and compensating for his lack of a public career and military achievements of his own. Hence his reign was marked by expansion of the Roman empire. He created new provinces: the two Mauretanias (c.43), Thrace (46), and he inaugurated the conquest of Britain, taking part in the opening campaign in person (43). More than his predecessors, he sought to integrate provincials in the empire through the extension of Roman citizenship, as illustrated by a speech of his preserved on a bronze tablet from Lyon (48). He tried, unsuccessfully, to secure the co-operation of the senate in government, and his reign was marked by numerous executions. A hostile tradition portrays him as a weak personality, too influenced by his freedmen (some of whom achieved greater power than senators) and by his wives. The excesses of his third wife, **Messalina**, were notorious, and she eventually went through a form of public marriage with a young lover, whereupon Claudius had her executed (48). He next married his niece, **Agrippina the Younger**, who persuaded him to adopt **Nero**, her son by an earlier husband (50), although Claudius had a son of his own, **Britannicus**. Agrippina is believed to have poisoned Claudius with a dish of mushrooms to secure the succession of Nero.

CLAUDIUS, Appius (5th century BC) Roman decemvir. Consul in 47 BC, he was one of a ten-man commission (the decemviri) appointed in 451 in response to popular demand to publish Rome's first code of laws, the so-called Twelve Tables. The commission tried to hold on to power, but was forced to resign by a popular uprising in 449. In later legend he was cast as a figure of extreme wickedness.

CLAUDIUS, Appius (Caecus) (4th–3rd century BC) Roman statesman and law-giver, regarded by the Romans as being the 'father' of Latin prose and oratory. He was censor c.312–307 BC, and held several important posts. He promoted many reforms giving privileges to the plebeians, and built the Aqua Appia aqueduct and the Via Appia highway.

CLAUSEL, Bertrand (1772–1842) French soldier and marshal of France, born in Mirepoix. He obtained distinction in the Italian and Austrian campaigns, but more especially as commander in Spain in 1812. Condemned to death as a traitor after the downfall of **Napoleon** and the restoration of the **Bourbons**, he fled to the USA (1816), but in 1819 he was permitted to come back to France, and from 1835–1837 was governor of Algeria.

CLAUSEWITZ, Karl Marie von (1780–1831) Prussian soldier, born in Burg. He entered the Prussian army in 1792 and saw active service in the Revolutionary War (1793–94). He served as a Russian staff officer (1812), but returned to the Prussian service and in 1815 became chief of staff, taking part in the Waterloo campaign. From 1818 to 1830 he was director of the General War School in Berlin. His great treatise *Vom Kriege* ('On War' 1833) has had a major impact on strategic studies. He died of cholera in Breslau.

CLAUSIUS, Rudolf (1822–88) German physicist, born in Köslin. He studied at Berlin, and in 1869 became professor of natural philosophy at Bonn. He studied optics and electricity, and shared the honour with Lord **Kelvin** of establishing the second law of thermodynamics, tentatively enunciated in 1824 by **Sadi Carnot**, on a rigorously scientific basis.

CLAUSSEN, Sophus Niels Christen (1865–1931) Danish poet, born in Heletoft. He is generally regarded as the greatest symbolist poet of his country. He lived for many years in France, where he was influenced by the French symbolists, but brought a personal eroticism to nearly everything he wrote. He published several volumes of verse, and some plays. He also translated **Heine**, **Baudelaire** and **Shelley**. His *Samlede Vaerker* were published in seven volumes in 1910.

CLAVELL, James du Maresq (1924–) Australian-born American novelist, cinema scenarist, director and producer, born in Sydney. Though his screen credits include *The Fly* (1958), *The Great Escape* (1963) and *To Sir With Love* (1967), he is known primarily as the author of a series of chunky novels with an Oriental setting. *King Rat* was published in 1962 and was followed by *Tai-Pan* (1966), *Shogun* (1975) and *Noble House* (1981), ripping yarns and bestsellers.

CLAVERHOUSE See **DUNDEE**

CLAVIJERO, Francisco Xavier (1721–87) Brazilian Jesuit priest and historian, born in Vera Cruz. He wrote a valuable Italian *History of Mexico* (trans 1787).

CLAY, Henry (1777–1852) American politician, born in 'the Slashes', Hanover county, Virginia, the son of a Baptist preacher. From his employment in a grist-mill he was nicknamed 'the mill-boy of the Slashes'. At 15 he became an assistant clerk in the chancery court of Virginia; and in 1797 he was licensed to practise law, and went to Lexington, Kentucky, where he soon acquired a high reputation. He entered the lower house of congress in 1811, and was chosen its speaker, a post he filled for many years. As leader of the 'War Hawk' group he was active in bringing on the war of 1812 with Great Britain, and was one of the commissioners who arranged the treaty of Ghent which ended it (1814). By his course in regard to the 'Missouri Compromise' of 1820, he was given the nickname of 'the great pacificator'. He was US secretary of state (1825–29) and US senator (1831–42). In 1832 and 1844 he was an unsuccessful candidate for the presidency. The compromise of 1850 between the opposing free-soil and pro-slavery interests, by which he attempted to avoid civil war, was largely Clay's work.

CLAYTON, John (fl.c.1650) English scientist. Educated as a theologian, he first discovered that gas could be distilled from crude coal and stored, but did not realize the commercial importance of his discovery. He also did work on stained glass.

CLAYTON, John Middleton (1796–1856) American statesman, born in Sussex county, Delaware, studied at Yale, and practised as a lawyer. In 1829 he became a United States senator, and while secretary of state in 1849–50 he negotiated the Clayton-**Bulwer** Treaty with Britain.

CLEÄNTHES (c.331–232 BC) Greek Stoic philosopher, born in Assos in Troas. He studied under **Zeno of Citium** in Athens for 19 years and succeeded him as head of the Stoa in 262. His own contributions to Stoicism were especially in the areas of theology and cosmology, and his principal extant writing is the *Hymn to Zeus*.

CLEESE, John Marwood (1939–) English comic actor and writer, born in Weston-super-Mare. As a student at Cambridge he joined the Footlights Revue (1963) and subsequently appeared with them in London, New Zealand and New York. He appeared in the Broadway production of *Half a Sixpence* (1965) and returned to Britain to write and perform in such television series as *The Frost Report* (1966) and *At Last the 1948 Show* (1967). With Graham Chapman he wrote scripts for television (*Doctor in the House*, 1968) and film (*The Rise and Rise of Michael Rimmer*, 1969). He then joined *Monty Python's Flying Circus* (1969–74), an anarchic series that changed the face of British television humour with its inspired lunacy, surreal comedy and animated graphics. The troupe subsequently collaborated on such films as *The Life of Brian* (1979) and *The Meaning of Life* (1983). Tall and angular, he has specialized in explosive, manic eccentricity and physical humour, often involving silly walks. He enjoyed spectacular success as the writer and star of the series *Fawlty Towers* (1975 and 1979) and the film *A Fish Called Wanda* (1988). He also founded Video Arts Ltd, producing industrial training films, and, with Robin Skynner, wrote the bestseller *Families and How to Survive Them* (1983).

CLEGG, Samuel (1781–1861) English inventor, born in Manchester. He was taught some science by **John Dalton**, and then became an apprentice at **Boulton** and **Watt**'s engineering works, where he saw the early experiments of **William Murdock** with coal gas lighting. He left the firm in 1805 and continued to work on improved methods of producing coal gas, leading to his appointment in 1813 as chief engineer of the Chartered Gas Company, for whom in 1814 he successfully illuminated by gas an entire district of London. In the course of this work he patented several important innovations in gas production, including purification by lime, a gas meter, a self-acting gas pressure governor, and an advanced type of rotating retort that later came into general use in the gas industry.

CLELAND, John (1709–89) English novelist, born in London. He was educated at Westminster School, and after a spell in the consular service and in the East India Company, followed by vagrant travel in Europe, he published in 1750 a pornographic novel, *Fanny Hill, or the Memoirs of a Woman of Pleasure*, a best-seller in its time which achieved a second *succès de scandale* on its revival and prosecution under the Obscene Publications Act in 1963. He also wrote *Memoirs of a Coxcomb* (1751), and *The Surprises of Love* (1764).

CLELAND, William (c.1661–1689) Scottish Covenanter and poet. He studied at St Andrews, joined the Covenanters, and fought at Drumclog and Bothwell Brig (1679), and fled to Holland, where he studied at Leiden. He took part in the abortive rebellion by Archibald 9th Earl of **Argyll**, in 1685, and fled back to Holland. After the 'Glorious Revolution' of 1688 he returned to Scotland as colonel of the Cameronians, and fell in the defence of Dunkeld against the Jacobite rebels. His poetry was published posthumously (1697).

CLEMENCEAU, Georges (1841–1929) French statesman, born in La Vendée. He became a Paris physician, lived in the USA 1865–69, in 1871 was in the French National Assembly, and, sent in 1876 to the Chamber, became a leader of the extreme left. The destroyer of many ministries, he was himself premier 1906–09, 1917–20. 'The Tiger', as he was called, presided at the Peace Conference in 1919 and his intransigent hatred of Germany at that time may have contributed towards World War II. A brilliant journalist, he founded *L'Aurore*, and from 1918 was an Academician.

CLEMENS, Samuel Langhorne See **TWAIN, Mark**

CLEMENT, Clemens Romanus (d.?101) pope from 88 to 89 or 92 to 101, and the first of the Apostolic Fathers. He is reckoned variously as the second or third successor of St **Peter** in the see of Rome. He may have been a freedman of Jewish parentage belonging to the imperial household. He was the author of an *Epistle to the Corinthian Church* (c.95), which discusses social dissensions and the Resurrection. A tradition suggests that he was martyred.

CLEMENT IV, named **Guy Foulques** (d.1268) pope 1265–68. A Frenchman, he was the papal legate to England when he was elected pope. He supported **Charles of Anjou** and encouraged **Roger Bacon**.

CLEMENT V (c.1260–1314) pope from 1305 to 1314, formerly archbishop of Bordeaux. He suppressed the Knights Templars, and removed the seat of the papacy to Avignon (1308), a move disastrous to Italy.

CLEMENT VII (1478–1534) pope from 1523 to 1534, born **Guilio de' Medici**, cousin of Pope **Leo X**. A cunning diplomat but a most unlucky pope, he allied himself with **Francis I** against **Charles V**, was besieged by the Constable **Bourbon** and became his prisoner, and refused to sanction **Henry VIII**'s divorce.

CLEMENT XI (1649–1721) pope from 1700 to 1721. He issued the bull *Unigenitus* against the 'Gallican liberties' of the French church.

CLEMENT XIV, named **Ganganelli** (1705–74) pope from 1769 to 1774, an excellent and accomplished but much calumniated pontiff. In 1773 he suppressed the Jesuit order.

CLEMENT OF ALEXANDRIA, St (Titus Flavius Clemens) (c.150–c.215) a Church Father, probably born in Athens, but lived chiefly in Alexandria. He became head of the catechetical school (c.180–201) and together with his pupil **Origen** made it a celebrated centre of learning, until forced to flee to Palestine during the persecutions of Emperor **Severus**. His chief surviving works are *Who is the Rich Man that is Saved* and the trilogy of *The Missionary*, *The Tutor* and *The Miscellanies*.

CLEMENTE, Roberto Walker (1934–72) Puerto-Rican-born American baseball player, born in Carolina. An outstanding outfielder, he played for the Pittsburgh Pirates for 17 years (1955–72), making more than 3000 hits and 240 home runs. He led the National League in batting five times, and was in the World Series in 1971. In 1966 he was voted the Most Valuable Player (MVP). He was killed in an air-crash while flying on a relief mission to the victims of the earthquake at Managua in Nicaragua. In 1973 he was immediately elected to the National Baseball Hall of Fame without the usual five-year wait, and a racehorse named after him won the Epsom Derby that same year.

CLEMENTI, Muzio (1752–1832) Italian pianist and composer for the pianoforte, born in Rome. He was brought to England in 1766 by Peter Beckford, MP. He conducted the Italian Opera in London (1777–80), toured as a virtuoso in 1781, and later went into the piano-manufacturing business. In 1817 he wrote the *Gradus ad Parnassum*, on which subsequent piano methods have been based, and he left many charming and tuneful pieces.

CLEMENTIS, Vladimir (1902–52) Czech politician, born in Tesovec, Slovakia, and studied at Prague University. He became a Czech communist MP in 1935 and in 1945 vice-minister of foreign affairs in the first Czech postwar government. A chief organizer of the 1948 coup, he succeeded **Jan Masaryk** as foreign minister, but was forced to resign in 1950 as a 'deviationist'. Following a political purge, he was hanged.

CLEMENTS, Sir John Selby (1911–88) English actor and director. Educated at St Paul's School and St John's College, Cambridge, he first appeared on stage at the Lyric Hammersmith in 1930. His first marriage, to Inga Maria Ahlgren, was dissolved in 1946. In that year he married the actress Kay Hammond (d.1980), and they became one of Britain's most famous theatrical partnerships, especially in *Marriage à la Mode* and *The Beaux' Strategem* (500 performances at the Phoenix in 1949–50). In 1966 he was appointed director of Chichester Festival Theatre, for seven enormously successful seasons.

CLEOMENES I (d.490 BC) king of Sparta in the Agiad royal family, who reigned c.520–490 BC. He appears to have sought an extension of Sparta's power in the Peloponnese and in central Greece, while avoiding more distant overseas commitments. He expelled the Pisistratid tyranny from Athens in 510 BC (see **Pisistratus**) and sought repeatedly to bring Athens under Spartan influence, but failed on the opposition of the Corinthians and of his fellow king Demaratus. He inflicted a decisive defeat on Sparta's old rival Argos in c.494. On the other hand, he refused an invitation to intervene in Samos in c.517, and gave no support to the revolt of the Ionian Greeks from Persia in 499. He secured the depositon of his fellow king Demaratus in 491 by bribing the Delphic oracle, but when detected fled from Sparta, intrigued with the Arcadians, and was eventually recalled. According to **Herodotus**, he committed suicide, though foul play by the Spartans can easily be suspected.

CLEOMENES III (c.260–219 BC) king of Sparta in the Agiad royal family from 235 to 222 BC. Inspired by the example of **Agis IV**, whose widow he married, he conceived and eventually carried out (in 227) a revolutionary programme of reforms to augment Sparta's depleted citizen body and assert once more her ancient leadership in the Peloponnese. But his success alarmed **Aratus** of Sicyon, the leader of the Achaean League, who invited the Macedonian king Antigonus Doson to intervene. Defeated at Sellasia in 222, Cleomenes fled to Alexandria where he committed suicide after an unsuccessful uprising. **Plutarch**'s *Life of Cleomenes* is the principal source for his career.

CLEON (d.422 BC) Athenian soldier and politician, of humble origins. He worked as a tanner, and became leader of the War party during the Peloponnesian War (431–404). As a member of the Assembly he advocated (427 BC) the slaughter of the Mytilenean prisoners, who were saved by a last minute reprieve. His first great success was the reduction of Sphacteria, in which a Lacedaemonian force had long held out (424 BC). Success was largely due to his colleague **Demosthenes**, but many of his countrymen must have credited Cleon with military genius, for in 422 he was sent to oppose the Spartan **Brasidas** in Macedonia, but was killed at Amphipolis.

CLEOPATRA (69–30 BC) queen of Egypt, the last and most famous of the Macedonian dynasty of the Ptolemies. By the will of her father, Ptolemy Auletes (d.51 BC), she should have shared the throne with her younger brother, Ptolemy. She was ousted by Ptolemy's guardians, and was about to assert her rights, when **Julius Caesar** arrived in Egypt in pursuit of **Pompey** (48). Caesar took her side, and after the Alexandrine war placed her back on the throne (47). A son born to her the following year was claimed by her to be Caesar's (the boy, Caesarion, was later put to death by **Augustus**). She followed Caesar to Rome in

46, but left after his assassination. After the battle of Philippi (42), **Marcus Antonius** (Mark Antony) summoned her to Tarsus in Cilicia, and their meeting has been made famous in **Plutarch**'s account. They spent the following winter in Alexandria, but Antony then married Octavia (40), sister of Augustus, and did not see Cleopatra again till 37, by which time he had become estranged from his wife. He acknowledged the paternity of the twins Cleopatra had borne him in 40, and a third child was born in 36. From this time on, their personal and political careers were linked, though how far their aims coincided is not easy to determine. Cleopatra's ambition was most probably to achieve the restoration of Ptolemaic power to the heights it had once reached under **Ptolemy II Philadelphus**. But Antony's position in the East and his relations with Cleopatra were ambiguous and susceptible to distortion for propaganda purposes, and at length Augustus was successful in swaying Roman public opinion against his absent rival. War was declared against Cleopatra, who was presented as a threat to the power of Rome, and at the battle of Actium (31) Antony and Cleopatra were defeated and fled to Egypt. When Augustus appeared before Alexandria, Cleopatra opened negotiations with him to try to save her dynasty. Antony, misled by a false report of Cleopatra's death, committed suicide by falling on his sword. Finding that she could not move Augustus, and disdaining to grace his triumph, she killed herself, it is said, by causing an asp to bite her breast.

CLERICUS See **LE CLERC**

CLERK, Sir Dugald (1854–1932) Scottish engineer, born in Glasgow. He studied at Anderson's College, Glasgow, and in Leeds, intending to become a chemical engineer. Having studied the properties of petroleum oils, from 1877 he devoted himself to research on the theory and design of gas engines. In 1881 he patented a gas engine working on the two-stroke principle which became known as the Clerk cycle, extensively used for large gas engines and later for small petrol engines.

CLERK-MAXWELL, James see **MAXWELL, James Clerk**

CLEVE, Cornelis (1520–67) Flemish painter born in Antwerp, the son of **Joos van Cleve**. He specialized in portraits of the rich Flemish bourgeoisie. In 1554 he went to England, hoping for the patronage of **Philip II** of Spain, who was there for his marriage to **Mary I** (Mary Tudor), but his arrival coincided with that of a collection of pictures by **Titian** and others from Italy, which ousted the Flemish school from royal favour. The disappointment mentally deranged Cornelis, who never entirely recovered, being known thereafter as 'Sotte (ie mad) Cleve'. Some of his work is at Windsor Castle.

CLEVE, Joos van der Beke (c.1480–1540) Flemish painter, born in Antwerp. Most of his work was done there, though he also worked in Cologne and was invited to Paris to paint portraits of **Francis I** and his family. He is best known for his religious pictures and is sometimes called 'the Master of the Death of the Virgin' from two triptychs of that subject at Munich and Cologne.

CLEVELAND, Barbara Villiers See **VILLIERS**

CLEVELAND, John (1613–58) English Cavalier poet, born in Loughborough, Leicestershire, son of a poor clergyman who was ousted by parliament from the living of Hinckley in 1645. In 1627 he entered Christ's College, Cambridge, graduated BA four years later, and then moved to St John's College, where he was elected to a fellowship in 1634 and lived nine years as 'the delight and ornament of the society'. He vigorously opposed **Cromwell**'s election to the Long Parliament for Cambridge, and was for his loyalty himself ejected from his fellowship in 1645. He joined the Royalist army, and was appointed judge advocate at Newark, but was obliged to surrender with the garrison. In 1655 he was arrested at Norwich, but was released by Cromwell, who could admire the courageous manliness of the poor poet's letter addressed to him. In 1656 he published a volume containing 36 poems—elegies on **Charles I**, **Strafford**, **Laud** and Edward King, and also some stinging satires. Cleveland now went to live at Gray's Inn, where he died. In 1677 was published, with a short Life, *Clievelandi Vindiciae*. Extremely popular as a poet in his day, he is little read now.

CLEVELAND, Stephen Grover (1837–1908) the 22nd and 24th president of the United States, born in Caldwell, New Jersey, the son of a Presbyterian minister. In 1859 he was admitted to the bar, and began to practise at Buffalo. From 1863 to 1866 he was assistant district attorney for Erie County, and in 1870 was chosen sheriff. After filling the office of mayor of Buffalo, he was in 1882 elected governor in New York by a majority of 190000 votes. In 1884 he was nominated by the Democrats for the presidency, and took his seat as president in 1885. In a message to congress in 1887 he strongly advised a readjustment of the tariff on certain manufactured articles of import, and the duty-free admission of some raw materials. Protectionists classed the president's message as a free-trade document, but this was denied by the Democrats, and its doctrines were adopted at the convention of that party in 1888. In the following August, on the rejection of the proposed Fisheries Treaty with Canada by the Republican majority in the senate, the president sent a message to congress, declaring a policy of 'retaliation' against Canada to be necessary. At the election in November he was defeated by the Republican candidate, **Benjamin Harrison**, over whom, however, he secured a large majority in November 1892. In 1895 he evoked intense excitement throughout the whole civilized world by his application of the 'Monroe Doctrine' to Britain's dispute with Venezuela over the frontier question.

CLEVELEY, John (1747–86) and **Robert** (1747–1809), twin brothers, born in Deptford. From 1764 they were both marine painters.

CLIFF, Clarice (1899–1972) English ceramic designer. She attended local art schools at Tunstall and Burslem, and set up a design studio at Wilkinson's Newport Showroom where she developed a unique style using bold designs painted with stylized trees and abstract patterns in vivid colours with bold brushwork. By 1929 the Newport Pottery was given over entirely to the decoration of her work which was marketed under the name 'Bizarre', which also included work by contemporary artists such as **Vanessa Bell** and **Laura Knight**.

CLIFFORD a family descended from Walter (fl. 12th century) Richard FitzPonce's son, who by marriage, prior to 1138, acquired Clifford Castle on the Wye, 17 miles west of Hereford, and who then assumed the surname Clifford. He was the father of Fair Rosamond, **Henry II**'s mistress, who seems to have died about 1176, and to have been buried at Godstow Nunnery, near Oxford. The legend of her murder by Queen **Eleanor of Aquitaine** appears first in the 14th century; the Woodstock maze, the clue, the dagger and the poisoned bowl belong to a yet later age. Among Walter's descendants were the soldier-judge Roger de Clifford (d.c.1285), who by marriage with Isabella de Vipont got Brougham Castle in Westmorland (c.1270); John (1435–61), the savage Lancastrian; Henry

(1455–1523), the 'shepherd lord'; Henry (1493–1542), 15th Lord Clifford and 1st Earl of Cumberland; George, 3rd earl (1558–1605), naval commander, whose daughter, Anne (1590–1676), married first the Earl of Dorset, and then the Earl of Pembroke; and Henry, 5th and last earl (1591–1643). To a cadet branch belonged Thomas (1630–73), a Catholic member of the Cabal, who in 1672 was created Lord Clifford of Chudleigh.

CLIFFORD, John (1836–1923) English clergyman, born in Sawley near Derby. He studied at the Baptist College in Nottingham and at University College London, and from 1858 to 1915 was pastor of Praed Street Baptist Church in Paddington. A leading passive resister to the Education Act of 1902 and a strong Nonconformist Liberal, he was created first president of the Baptist World Alliance (1905–11).

CLIFFORD, William Kingdon (1845–79) English mathematician, born in Exeter. A precocious child, he entered King's College, London, at the age of 15, and then Trinity College, Cambridge, in 1863, where he graduated as second wrangler in 1867. As an undergraduate he was renowned for his gymnastic feats and is said to have hung by his toes from the cross-bar of a church weathercock. In 1871 he became professor of applied mathematics at University College, London. He remained there until his early death of tuberculosis. He wrote on projective and non-Euclidean geometry, and on the philosophy of science, including *The Common Sense of the Exact Sciences*, completed by **Karl Pearson** in 1885. He had a reputation as an excellent lecturer on science to popular audiences.

CLIFT, Edward Montgomery (1920–66) American film and stage actor, born in Omaha, Nebraska. After working in summer stock as a teenager he moved to New York and for ten years remained exclusively a stage performer. Finally succumbing to one of many film offers, he appeared in *Red River* (1946) and was briefly considered the most promising of post-war actors. Broodingly handsome, he was a slight, intense figure particularly adept at conveying the introspective turmoil of society's drifters and outsiders. His performances in *The Search* (1948), *A Place in The Sun* (1951) and *From Here to Eternity* (1953) earned him Academy Award nominations. A non-conformist, he turned down many prestigious films. A car accident in 1957 left him permanently scarred. Troubled by his homosexuality and beset by poor health, his subsequent career never fulfilled its early promise, although his sincerity and conviction remained evident, particularly in his last major role *Freud* (1962).

CLINTON, De Witt (1769–1828) American politician, admitted to the New York bar in 1788. He sat in the state legislature (1797) and in the state senate (1798–1802); and in 1802 he was elected to the US senate, but resigned in the same year on being appointed mayor of New York by his uncle. In this office he continued, save for two short intervals, until 1815; he was defeated by **Madison** in the presidential contest of 1812. He pressed the Erie Canal scheme, was elected governor of the state in 1817, and in 1825 opened the canal. He died in office at Albany.

CLINTON, George (1739–1812) American soldier and politician, born in Little Britain, New York. He fought with his father, Charles Clinton (1690–1773), and brother **James Clinton**, in the French and Indian War (1755–63), including the expedition against Fort Frontenac (1758). He was a member of the New York Provincial assembly (1768–75), and in 1775 attended the second Continental Congress. In the American War of Independence (1775–83) he was a brigadier of militia and in 1777 was chosen first governor of New York, a post he held for six successive terms (1777–95). To him was due the conception of the Erie Canal. In 1804 and again in 1808 he was elected vice-president of the United States.

CLINTON, Sir Henry (c.1738–1795) British soldier, born in Newfoundland, son of the Hon. George Clinton, governor of Newfoundland, and afterwards of New York. He first entered the New York militia and thereafter transferred to the Coldstream Guards. He served with distinction in the Seven Years' War (1756–63), and was promoted major-general in 1772. Sent to America in 1775, he fought at Bunker Hill, and in 1776 was repulsed in an attack on Charleston. After **Burgoyne**'s surrender in 1778, Clinton succeeded **Howe** as commander-in-chief. In 1780 he captured Charleston and the entire southern army; but after **Cornwallis**' capitulation at Yorktown in 1781, he resigned his command and returned to England, where in 1783 he published a *Narrative* of the campaign. In 1794 he was appointed governor of Gibraltar. Both sons, Sir William Henry (1769–1846) and Sir Henry (1771–1829), became soldiers and rose to the rank of general.

CLINTON, James (1736–1812) American soldier born in Little Britain, New York, brother of **George Clinton** and son of Charles Clinton (1690–1773), who had emigrated from Ireland to New York State in 1729. He fought with distinction in the French and Indian War (1755–63) and as a brigadier-general during the War of Independence (1775–83).

CLISSON, Olivier de (1336–1407) French knight, and lieutenant of Guienne. He was a comrade of Bertrand **du Guesclin**, whom he succeeded as constable of France in 1380.

CLITHEROW, St Margaret, née **Middleton** (c.1556–1586) English religious, called the 'Pearl of York'. The wife of a York butcher, she was converted to Catholicism in 1574. She harboured priests in her home, for which she was tried, condemned and pressed to death. She was canonized in 1970.

CLIVE, Kitty (1711–85) English comic actress, born in London. She was the daughter of William Raftor, a Jacobite lawyer from Kilkenny. She made her début at Drury Lane about 1728, where she continued to play till 1769, when she left the stage. About 1731 she had married George Clive, a barrister, but they soon parted. She was admired by **Garrick, Handel, Walpole** and Dr **Johnson**, the last remarking to **Boswell** that 'in the sprightliness of humour he never had seen her equalled'.

CLIVE OF PLASSEY, Robert, Baron (1725–74) English soldier and colonial administrator, born near Market Drayton of an old Shropshire family. The boy was brought up by an uncle near Eccles. In 1743 he joined the East India Company in Madras, where he tried, and failed, to commit suicide. In 1746 he was captured when the French took Madras, but escaped, and in 1751 made a daring dash upon Arcot, which he held with a small force against a French-Indian army for 53 days before being relieved. In 1753 he married Margaret Maskelyne, sister of the astronomer **Nevil Maskelyne**, and returned to England in triumph. In 1755 he returned to India as governor of Fort St David, and in 1757 was summoned from Madras to avenge the atrocity of the Black Hole of Calcutta. Calcutta was soon retaken; Chandernagore, the French settlement, captured; and at Plassey he defeated the Nawab of Bengal, **Suraja Dowlah**. For three years he was sole ruler in all but name of Bengal on behalf of the East India Company. In 1760 he returned to England, to be hailed by **Pitt** as 'a heaven-born general'. In 1761 he entered parliament as member for Shrewsbury, and in 1762 was raised to the Irish peerage as Baron Clive of Plassey. Meanwhile in India the Company's affairs had fallen into disorder, and Clive was sent out again in 1764 as governor and commander-in-chief of Bengal. He rooted out corruption and restored military discipline, and established British supremancy throughout India. On his return to England in 1767, however, he was faced with a parliamentary storm about his handling of the East India Company's affairs, and although ultimately vindicated in 1773, committed suicide soon afterwards.

CLODIUS, Publius C Pulcher (d.52 BC) a Roman tribune (58 BC). He brought about **Cicero**'s banishment, and tyrannized with his gladiators till he was slain by Milo.

CLOOTZ, Jean Baptiste du Val de Grâce, Baron, called **Anacharsis Clootz** (1755–94) born at Schloss Gnadenthal, near Cleves, and educated in Paris. While still young he traversed Europe under the name of Anacharsis, lavishing his money to promote the union of all nations in one family. In the French Revolution he saw the fulfilment of his dreams. He constituted himself the 'orator of the human race', and wearied the National Assembly with his ravings against Christianity. With all its folly his enthusiasm was honest, and he was both hated and feared by **Robespierre**, who involved him in Hébert's downfall, and he was guillotined. He wrote *Certitude des preuves du Mohammédisme* (London 1780) and *La République du genre humain* (1793).

CLOPINEL See **MEUNG**

CLOPTON, Sir Hugh (d.1497) English silk merchant and philanthropist, born in Stratford-on-Avon. A mercer in London, he became sheriff (1486) and mayor (1492). At Stratford he built New Place (c.1483), which was **Shakespeare**'s home from 1597 to 1616, and a stone bridge over the river.

CLOSE, Chuck (1940–) American artist, born in Menroe, Washington. He studied painting at Yale from 1962 to 1964 and since 1967 has lived in New York. In 1967–68 he began copying portrait photographs, painstakingly reproducing every detail, and has since continued with this 'Super-Realist' method. His works are often large scale and many are monochromatic. In the 1980s, he adopted the techniques of finger-painting and collage to achieve the same hyper-detailed results.

CLOSE, Dennis Brian (1931–) English cricketer, born in Rawdon in Yorkshire. An outstanding cricketing tactician, he played in only 22 Test matches, spread over 27 years. A fearless batsman, he performed the double of 1000 runs and 100 wickets in his first season in county cricket at the age of 19. Late in his career he moved to Somerset, which was transformed by his aggressive, professional approach.

CLOSE, Glenn (1947–) American actress, born in Greenwich, Connecticut. A student of anthropology and acting, she began her career in regional theatre before her Broadway début in *Love for Love* (1974). A versatile leading lady, her subsequent theatre work includes *The Crucifier of Blood* (1978), *Barnum* (1980–81), *The Singular Life of Albert Nobbs* (1982, for which she received an Obie Award) and *The Real Thing* (1984–85), for which she received a Tony. She made her television début in *Too Far to Go* (1979) and received an Emmy nomination for *Something About Amelia* (1984). Her cinema début in *The World According to Garp* (1982) was followed by several intelligent interpretations of goodness and virtue in such films as *The Big Chill* (1983) and *The Natural* (1984), before a radical change of image as the psychotic mistress in *Fatal Attraction* (1987) brought her international fame that was consolidated with the success of *Dangerous Liaisons* (1988). She was also the executive producer of the documentary *Do You Mean There Are Still Real Cowboys?* (1987).

CLOSTERMAN, John (1656–1713) German painter, born in Osnabrück. In 1681 he settled in England as a portraitist, notably of Queen **Anne**.

CLOTAIRE I, or **Chlotar** (6th century) king of all the Franks from 558. The son of the Frankish king **Clovis**, he inherited the kingdom jointly with his three brothers in 511, but gradually added to his holdings until with the death of his brother Childebert I in 558 he became ruler of all the Franks.

CLOTAIRE II (d.628) king of the Franks, grandson of **Clotaire I**. He assumed rule in 613 after a period of regency, recovered lost territories and extended rule over all the Franks.

CLOTILDA, St (474–545) queen of the Franks. The daughter of a Burgundian king, Childeric, she married the Frankish king **Clovis** in 493 and converted him to Christianity. After his death in 511 she lived a life of austerity and good works at the abbey of St Martin at Tours, where she died.

CLOUET, François (c.1516–1572) French portrait painter, born probably in Tours, son of **Jean Clouet**. He succeeded his father as court painter to **Francis I** and continued in that office under **Henri II**, **Francis II** and **Charles IX**. His masterpiece, the Louvre portrait of **Elizabeth of Austria**, is one of the finest examples of the period; that of **Mary Queen of Scots** in the Wallace Collection is attributed to him.

CLOUET, Jean, Jehan, or **Janet** (d. 1540/41) French portrait painter, probably the son of Jehan Clouet (c.1420–c.1480), a Flemish painter who came to France as court painter to the Duke of Burgundy. He became court painter to **Francis I**, whose portrait in the Louvre is supposed to be by him.

CLOUGH, Ann Jemima (1820–92) English educationist, sister of **Arthur Hugh Clough**. A vigorous proponent of higher education for women, she secured the admission of women to Manchester and Newcastle colleges. In 1871 she became the first principal of the first hall for women students at Cambridge, Newnham Hall, later called Newnham College.

CLOUGH, Arthur Hugh (1819–61) English poet, born in Liverpool, the son of a cotton merchant who emigrated to Charleston, USA, in 1823. The boy was sent back to England in 1828 and entered Rugby, where he became Dr **Thomas Arnold**'s most promising pupil and where he commenced his friendship with **Matthew Arnold**. Though he only got a 'second' at Balliol College, Oxford, in 1841, he was elected a fellow of Oriel College and there lived through the crisis which resulted in **Newman**'s conversion to Rome. His own difficulties with the Thirty-nine Articles led to his resignation in 1848. He became for a time principal of the new University Hall, attached to University College, Gower Street, which had a Unitarian bias little to Clough's liking ('the Sadducees', he called them). On his dismissal from University Hall he obtained an examinership in the education department. Before taking up that appointment he spent some months in Boston, Massachusetts, where he met the Boston Brahmins. Financial worries added to his religious troubles; in the year he got his fellowship at Oriel his father became a bankrupt. He seems not to have enjoyed much of a family life before his marriage to Blanche Smith in 1854. The last years of his short life were relatively happy. He enjoyed not only the friendship of the great Victorians, **Ruskin**, Arnold and **Carlyle**, but also of distinguished Americans of the Boston connection. At Oriel he was the self-confident leader of a group, Members of the Decade, and conducted reading parties in vacations to the Lakes and to Scotland. The latter resulted in a 'Long-vacation pastoral' called *The Bothie* (1848), which delighted those of his friends whom it did not outrage. His only other long poems were *Amours de voyage*, written in Rome in 1849; and *Dipsychus*, 1850, both published posthumously. Arnold hesitated for ten years to write his commemorative poem *Thyrsis*. The two-volume *Correspondence* published in 1957 shows that Clough's dilemma was not confined to the Thirty-nine Articles (to which after all he subscribed) but to the whole of what is now called the Establishment. He followed the revolutionary doctrines of **George Sand**, called himself a republican, disliked class distinction ('your aversion, the Gentleman') and the capitalist system.

CLOUGH, Brian (1935–) English footballer and manager, born in Middlesbrough. When injury terminated his playing career, he became a manager at an early age. He took Derby County and Nottingham Forest to League championship wins and, in the case of Nottingham Forest, two European Cup successes.

CLOVIO, Giulio, or **Jurni Glovichisch** (1498–1578) Italian miniaturist, born in Croatia. A monk for 50 years, he is best known for a series of twelve miniatures on the victories of the Emperor **Charles V**.

CLOVIS, (Old German **Chlodwig**) (465–511) Merovingian ruler of the Franks, grandson of **Merovech**. In 481 he succeeded his father, Childeric I, as king of the Salian Franks whose capital was at Tournai. In 486 he overthrew the last Roman governor in Gaul, Syagrius, near Soissons, and took control of the whole country between the Somme and the Loire, making his capital at Soissons. In 493 he married **St Clotilda** of Burgundy, through whom he was converted to Christianity in thanksgiving for a great victory over the Alemmani near Cologne in 496: with 2000 of his soldiers he accepted mass baptism by Remigius, bishop of Reims, on Christmas Day. He became a champion of orthodox Christianity against the heretic Arians; in 507 he defeated the Arian Visigoths under **Alaric II** at the crucial battle of Vouillé, near Poitiers, and took possession of the whole country as far as Bordeaux and Toulouse, but was checked at Arles by the Ostrogoth **Theodoric the Great**. He made his capital in Paris. When he died, his Frankish kingdom was divided between his four sons, who further enlarged the empire by conquest.

CLOWES, William (1779–1847) English printer, born in Chichester. In 1803 he started a London printing business carried on by his son, William (1807–83), and was the first printer to use steam-driven machines.

CLOWES, William (1780–1851) English non-conformist, born in Burslem. He became a potter, and in the course of a dissolute youth achieved an ephemeral reputation as a champion dancer. In 1805 he was converted to Methodism, becoming in 1810 a co-founder with **Hugh Bourne** of the Primitive Methodists.

CLUNE, Francis Patrick (Frank) (1893–1971) Australian writer of biography, history and travel, born in the dockside district of Woolloomooloo, Sydney, of Irish extraction. His early life was one of travel and adventure at sea, in Europe and America. He served with the Australian Imperial Forces in World War I and was wounded at Gallipoli. A vagabond life followed, and marriage, then a career in accountancy. At the age of 40, while recuperating from an ulcer, he decided to write the story of his early years; this was published as *Try Anything Once* (1933) and Clune was launched into a writing career. He wrote over 60 books, often in collaboration with P R ('Inky') Stephensen, and was one of Australia's best-selling writers. Of popular appeal, Clune's work such as *Rolling down the Lachlan* (1935), *Wild Colonial Boys* (1948) and *Ben Hall the Bushranger* (1947) aroused interest in stories of Australian history.

CLUNIES ROSS, Sir Ian (1899–1959) Australian veterinary scientist, born in Bathurst, New South Wales. His grandfather was Robert, a sea captain from the Shetlands whose brother John founded the Clunies Ross dynasty on the Cocos Islands. He joined the newly-formed [Australian] Council for Scientific and Industrial Research in 1926 but resigned in 1937 upon being appointed Australian representative on the International Wool Secretariat, where he served as chairman until 1940. That year he became professor of veterinary science at Sydney University, returning to the CSIR in 1946 as a member of its executive committee. When the CSIR became the [Australian] Commonwealth Scientific and Industrial Research Organization in 1949, Clunies Ross became its first chairman, a position he held until his death. He played a leading role in research for the sheep and wool industries, established a sheep biology laboratory in Sydney, and wrote over 60 scientific papers. He was a member of the Australian delegation to the League of Nations in 1938, and president of the Australian Institute of International Affairs from 1941 to 1945.

CLURMAN, Harold Edgar (1901–80) American theatre director and critic, born in New York City. In 1931 he was co-founder with **Lee Strasberg** of the Group Theater, best remembered for the fervent dedication of its members and its staging of a sequence of plays by **Clifford Odets**. The Group disbanded in 1940, and Clurman went on to work extensively on Broadway. He directed, among others, **Carson McCuller**'s *The Member of the Wedding* (1950) and **Arthur Miller**'s *Incident at Vichy* (1964). He also directed productions in London (**Giraudoux**'s *Tiger at the Gates* in 1955), Los Angeles, Israel and Japan. As a drama critic he wrote for the American magazine *The New Republic* (1949–53), and for the London *Observer* (1959–63). He published several books, including a history of the Group Theater, *The Fervent Years* (1945).

CLUSIUS See **LÉCLUSE**

CLUVERIUS, or **Clüver, Phillip** (1580–1622) German geographer and antiquarian, born in Danzig. Regarded as the founder of historical geography, he studied law at Leiden, and visited Norway, England, Scotland, France, Italy, etc. He wrote *Introductio in universam geographium* in 1624.

CLYDE, Lord See **CAMPBELL, Sir Colin**

CLYNES, Joseph Robert (1869–1949) English Labour politician, born in Oldham. He worked in a cotton mill from the age of ten and educated himself. Organizer of the Lancashire Gasworkers' Union (1891), he was president (1892) and secretary (1894–1912) of Oldham's Trade Council and, entering parliament (1910), was food controller (1918), vice-chairman (1922) and lord privy seal in Britain's first Labour cabinet (1924). As home secretary (1929–31), he refused to allow **Trotsky** to settle in Britain. He became a privy councillor (1918).

COANDA, Henri (1885–1972) Rumanian aeronautical engineer. He built the first jet-propelled aeroplane. This used a ducted fan, not a turbojet, and, because of a phenomenon not then understood, the hot exhaust gases set fire to the structure. Coanda later investigated this effect; the entrainment of a free jet alongside a curved surface: this now bears his name. He subsequently became an aircraft designer with the British & Colonial Aeroplane Company (later the Bristol Aircraft Company).

COATES, Eric (1886–1957) English composer, born in Hucknall, Nottinghamshire. He studied in Nottingham and at the Royal Academy of Music, working as violinist in chamber music groups until, in 1912, he became leading violist in the Queen's Hall Orchestra under Sir **Henry Wood**, who produced several of his early works at Promenade Concerts. Success as a composer of attractive light music enabled him to devote himself to composition after 1918. Among his best-known compositions are the *London Suite* (1933), *The Three Bears* (1926), the suites *Four Centuries* (1941) and *The Three Elizabeths* (1944), and a number of popular waltzes and marches.

COATES, Wells Wintemute (1895–1958) English architect, born in Tokyo. He was one of the principal figures of the modern movement in architecture, and practised as an architect from 1929. He studied in Canada and London, and in 1933 formed the MARS group of architects. He was responsible for the design of BBC studios, the EKCO laboratories, and many other buildings in Great Britain and in Canada, and he also played an important part in the development of industrial design. His work in this field included furniture and an innovative bakelite circular radio for EKCO.

COATS, Sir Peter (1808–90) and **Thomas** (1809–83), Scottish industrialists, born in Paisley. Their father founded the thread factory at Ferguslie, Paisley. They made many munificent gifts to Paisley, including a park, playgrounds, and an observatory.

COBB, Ty (Tyrus Raymond) (1886–1961) American baseball player, born in Narrows, Georgia, considered the outstanding offensive player of all time. Known as the 'Georgia Peach', he played for the Detroit Tigers (1905–26) and the Philadelphia Athletics (1926–28), and is the only player to have scored more than 4000 hits in major-league baseball. His career batting average was an astonishing .367, meaning that he had a hit more than once every three times at bat. He came first in the first ballot for the National Baseball Hall of Fame in 1936.

COBBE, Frances Power (1822–1904) Irish social worker and feminist, born in Newbridge near Dublin. She travelled in Italy and the East, and wrote *Cities of the Past* (1864) and *Italics* (1864). A strong theist, a supporter of women's rights, and a prominent anti-vivisectionist, she was associated with **Mary Carpenter** in the founding of ragged schools and published more than 30 works, mostly on social questions.

COBBETT, William (1763–1835) English writer and champion of the poor, born in Farnham, Surrey, the son of a small farmer. In 1784 he enlisted in the 54th Foot, taught himself to read and write, and served as sergeant-major in New Brunswick (1785–91), meanwhile studying rhetoric, geometry, logic, French and fortification. He bought his discharge in 1791, and brought charges of corruption against several of his officers, but went to France when he was not even called to give evidence at the court-martial. After mastering the language he sailed for America (1792). In Philadelphia he taught English to French refugees, opened a bookshop and published a paper called *Porcupine's Gazette* (1797–99). Under the pseudonym 'Peter Porcupine' he wrote fierce onslaughts on **Joseph Priestley**, **Tom Paine** and the native Democrats. Twice he was prosecuted for libel, and in 1800 he returned to England. The Tories welcomed him with open arms and in 1802 he started his weekly *Cobbett's Political Register*, which, with a three-months' break in 1817, continued till his death. Tory at first, he altered its politics in 1804, till at last it became the most uncompromising champion of Radicalism. He initiated the publication of *Parliamentary Debate* (1806, later taken over by **Luke Hansard**) and *State Trials* (1809). A great lover of the country, he purchased a model farm at Botley in Hampshire. He got two years in Newgate (1810–12) for his strictures on flogging in the army. In 1817 money muddles and dread of a second imprisonment drove him once more across the Atlantic and he farmed in Long Island, published a *Grammar of the English Lanuage* (1819) and, in 1819, ventured back to England. Botley had to be sold, but he started a seed-farm at Kensington and stood unsuccessfully for Parliament in 1821 and 1826. In 1831 he defended himself against a charge of sedition, and in 1832, after the First Reform Bill, he entered Parliament as member for Oldham. His celebrated *Rural Rides* (1830), a delightful picture of a vanishing world, were reprinted from the *Register*. He also published a savage *History of the Reformation* (1824–27), *The Woodlands* (1825), *Advice to Young Men* (1830), and 40 or 50 more works.

COBBOLD, Richard (1797–1877) English author, born in Ipswich. He wrote *Margaret Catchpole* (1845) and other works, and for 50 years was rector of Wortham, near Diss. His mother, Elizabeth (1767–1824), wrote poetry; and his third son, Thomas Spencer (1828–86), lectured in London on botany, zoology, comparative anatomy, geology and helminthology. He wrote *Entozoa* (1864), *Tapeworms* (1866) and *Human Parasites* (1882).

COBDEN, Richard (1804–65) English economist and politician, 'the Apostle of Free Trade', born in Heyshott, near Midhurst, Sussex. His father had to sell his farm in 1814; and Richard, the fourth of his eleven children, was sent for five years to a 'Dotheboys' school in Yorkshire. In 1819 he was received into an uncle's warehouse in London, where he showed great aptitude both as clerk and commercial traveller. In 1828 he and two friends entered into a partnership for selling calicoes by commission in London. They set up an establishment for calico-printing in Lancashire in 1831, and in 1832 Cobden settled in Manchester. In 1835 he visited the USA, and in 1836–37 the Levant. The result was two pamphlets, *England, Ireland, and America* (1835), and *Russia* (1836), the former preaching free trade and non-intervention, the latter directed against 'Russophobia'. He contested Stockport unsuccessfully on free-trade principles in 1837. In 1838 seven merchants of Manchester founded the Anti-Corn-Law League; its most prominent member was Cobden. His lectures all over the country and his speeches in parliament (to which Stockport returned him in 1841) were characterized by clear, quiet persuasiveness; and to them was in great part due, as **Peel** acknowledged, the abolition of the Corn Laws in 1846. Cobden's zeal for free trade in corn had, however, to such a degree withdrawn his attention from private business that he was now a ruined man, and a subscription of £80000 was raised in recognition of his services; with this in 1847 he re-purchased Dunford, the farmhouse in which he was born. As his health, too, had suffered he travelled for 14 months in Spain, Italy, Russia, etc, and during his absence was elected for both Stockport and the West Riding; he chose the latter constituency. He shared **Bright**'s unpopularity for opposing the Crimean war (1853–56); and on **Palmerston**'s appeal to the country to support him in his Chinese policy, of which Cobden was a strenuous opponent, he retired from the West Riding and contested Huddersfield, where, however, he was defeated (1857). In 1859 he revisited America, and meanwhile was elected for Rochdale. Palmerston offered him the presidency of the board of trade; but Cobden felt bound to decline. Ill-health forbade his taking further part in parliamentary proceedings, but in 1859–60 he arranged the treaty of commerce with France. Cobden spoke out strongly in favour of the North during the American Civil War (1861–65), and in 1864 strenuously opposed intervention in favour of Denmark. He was buried at Lavington, Sussex. His *Speeches on Questions of Public Policy* were edited by John Bright and Thorald Rogers (1870).

COBDEN-SANDERSON, Thomas James (1840–1922) English printer and bookbinder, born in Alnwick, Northumberland. A lawyer by training, he became a leader of the 19th century revival of artistic typography, working with **William Morris**, and in 1900 founded the Doves Press at Hammersmith from which was issued the beautiful *Doves Bible* (1903). In 1916 the press closed and Cobden-Sanderson threw the type into the Thames.

COBHAM, Lord See **OLDCASTLE**

COBORN, Charles, stage-name of **Colin Whitton McCallum** (1852–1945) Cockney comedian of Scottish descent. He spent his childhood in London's East End, went on the stage in 1875 and immortalized the songs 'Two Lovely Black Eyes' (1886) and 'The Man who Broke the Bank at Monte Carlo' (1890). In 1928 he published the autobiographical *The Man who Broke the Bank* (1928).

COBURN, John (1925–) Australian artist and tapestry designer, born in Ingham, Queensland. During war service in the Far East he studied the arts of India, Burma and China, which influenced his subsequent work using formalized leaf designs to make two-dimensional patterns of shape and colour. This style lent itself to large-scale tapestry design, and most of his work in this medium has been woven on the famous looms at Aubusson, France. It was there that Coburn worked from 1969 to 1972 on his best-known commissions, the *Curtain of the Sun* and *Curtain of the Moon* for the prosceniums of the new Sydney Opera House. His tapestries also hang in the Australian Embassy in Paris and in the John F Kennedy Center for the Performing Arts, Washington DC.

COCCEIUS, or **Koch, Johannes** (1603–69) German theologian, born in Bremen. In 1636 he became professor of Hebrew at Franeker, and in 1650 of theology at Leiden. His *Hebrew Lexicon* (1669) was the first tolerably complete one.

COCCEJI, Heinrich Freiherr von (1644–1719) German jurist, born in Bremen. He became professor of law at Heidelberg (1672), Utrecht (1689) and Frankfurt an der Oder (1690). His work on civil law (*Juris Publici Prudentia*, 1695) was a standard textbook for a long time. His youngest son, Samuel (1679–1755), also became professor at Frankfurt an der Oder in 1703, and was ultimately **Frederick II the Great**'s chancellor. He reformed the Prussian administration of justice, and wrote on law.

COCHISE (d.1874) American Apache chief, born in Arizona. He put up a fierce resistance to white settlement on his ancestral lands, terrorizing the settlers in the 1860s. With his base in the Dragoon Mountains, he eventually surrendered to General **George Crook** in 1871 and settled on a reservation.

COCHLAEUS, or **Dobneck, Johann** (1479–1552) German theologian and humanist, born near Nürnberg. He had a busy career as a teacher and chaplain, and was **Luther**'s most active critic at numerous confrontations, including the Diet of Worms (1521). He was the author of *Commentaria de actis et scriptis Lutheri* (1549).

COCHRAN, Sir Charles Blake (1872–1951) English theatrical producer, born in Lindfield in Sussex. He began his career as an actor, then turned impresario, becoming agent for **Mistinguett**, **Houdini** and other famous figures. His spectacular presentation of *The Miracle* (1911) won him renown as a producer, but after a number of successes, the failure of the Wembley rodeo venture in 1924 made him bankrupt. However, he made a rapid comeback with the brilliant **Noel Coward** musicals *This Year of Grace* (1928), *Bitter Sweet* (1929) and *Cavalcade* (1931). His most successful production was *Bless the Bride* by Herbert and Ellis (1947), which ran for 886 performances.

COCHRAN, Jacqueline (1910–80) American aviator, born in Pensacola, Florida. She received her pilot's licence in 1932, and became the first woman to fly in the Bendix transcontinental air race in 1935. In 1938 she secured the transcontinental record at 10 hours and 28 minutes. The International League of Aviators named her the world's outstanding woman pilot from 1937 to 1950 and in 1953. The first woman to pilot a bomber across the Atlantic in World War II, she became director of Women Auxiliary Service Pilots in the USAF in 1943. In 1953 she became the first woman to fly faster than sound (in an F-86 Sabre fighter). She made the first landing and take-off by a woman pilot from an aircraft carrier, and in 1964 flew faster than twice the speed of sound.

COCHRANE, Thomas, 10th Earl of Dundonald (1775–1860) Scottish naval commander, born in Annsfield, Hamilton. He entered the navy in 1793, and in 1800 received the command of a sloop, the *Speedy*, with which he took over 50 prizes in 15 months, including a 32-gun frigate. He was captured shortly afterwards by the French, but was speedily exchanged, and promoted to post-captain. After protecting the Orkney fisheries, he returned to prize-taking off the Azores in 1805, and by April had made £75000 of prize money for his own share. In 1805 he stood unsuccessfully for election to parliament for Moniton, but by judicious bribery was elected the following year. In 1807 he was returned for Westminster, and campaigned against naval abuses, but was ordered to the Mediterranean. In 1809 he was selected to burn the French fleet then blockaded in Aix Roads by Lord **Gambier**; the operation was only partly successful. Discredited and on half-pay, Cochrane pursued his crusade against naval corruption, until in 1814 he was arrested on a charge of fraud: he was accused, with two others, of spreading a rumour of **Napoleon**'s overthrow that sent up the funds, and then selling out upwards of a million sterling with a gross profit of £10000. The others were guilty; Cochrane, by some held innocent, was sentenced to pay a fine of £1000, to suffer a year's imprisonment, and to stand for an hour in the pillory. Westminster re-elected him, and in March 1815 he broke out of jail and reappeared in the House, to be forcibly removed and reimprisoned for the remaining three months of his sentence, and further fined £100. In 1818 he was in command of Chile's navy (1818–22) in the War for Freedom by Chile and Peru; he stormed the 15 strong forts of Valdivia (1819), and in two-and-a-half years made Chile mistress of her own waters. He took command of the Brazilian navy (1823–25), and later the Greek navy (1827–28). In 1831 he succeeded to the earldom of Dundonald, and in 1832 was granted a free pardon for past misdeeds. He was restored to the navy as a rear-admiral, and was later commander-in-chief on the North American station (1848–51), and rear admiral of the United Kingdom (1854). He was buried in Westminster Abbey.

COCKBURN, Sir Alexander James Edmund (1802–80) English judge and politician. In 1822 he entered Trinity Hall, Cambridge, and in 1829 was called to the bar, soon becoming distinguished as a pleader before parliamentary committees. In 1847 he became Liberal MP for Southampton, in 1850 solicitor-general, in 1851 attorney-general, in 1856 chief justice of the common pleas, and in 1859 lord chief justice. He prosecuted in the Palmer case, and presided over the **Tichborne** case. He represented Britain in the Alabama arbitration at Geneva.

COCKBURN, Alison, née **Rutherford** (1713–94) Scottish poet, born in Selkirkshire. For over 60 years she was a queen of Edinburgh society. Of her lyrics the best known is the exquisite version of 'The Flowers of the Forest' ('I've seen the smiling of Fortune beguiling'), commemorating a wave of calamity that swept over Ettrick Forest, and first printed in 1765. In 1777 she discerned in **Walter Scott** 'the most extraordinary genius of a boy'; in 1786 she made Burn's acquaintance.

COCKBURN, Henry Thomas (1779–1854) Scottish judge, born perhaps in Cockpen, but more probably in the Parliament Close of old Edinburgh. He entered the High School in 1787, and the university in 1793. Through a debating club he became the companion of **Francis Jeffrey**, **Francis Horner** and **Henry Brougham**. He was called to the Scottish bar in 1800; and in 1807 his uncle, the all-powerful Lord **Melville**, gave him an advocate-deputeship—a non-political post, from which, on political grounds, he 'had the honour of being dismissed' in 1810. He rose, however, to share, with Jeffrey the leadership of the bar. A zealous supporter of parliamentary reform, he became solicitor-general for Scotland in 1830, had the chief hand in drafting the Scottish Reform Bill and was elected lord rector of Glasgow University (1831); in 1834 he was made, as Lord Cockburn, a judge of the Court of Session; and three years later a lord of justiciary. He contributed to the *Edinburgh Review*, and was author of a *Life of Jeffrey* (1852), the delightful *Memorials of his Time* (1856), *Journal, 1831–44* (2 vols, 1874) and *Circuit Journeys* (1888).

COCKCROFT, Sir John Douglas (1897–1967) English nuclear physicist, born in Yorkshire. Educated at Manchester and Cambridge, he became Jacksonian professor of physics at Cambridge (1939–46). He and **Ernest Walton** succeeded in disintegrating lithium by proton bombardment (1932) and shared the Nobel prize for physics (1951). He assisted in the design of much special experimental equipment for the Cavendish Laboratory, including the cyclotron. During World War II, he was director of air defence research (1941–44) and of the Atomic Energy division of the Canadian National Research Council (1944–46). He became the first director of Britain's atomic energy establishment at Harwell in 1946. He was appointed master of Churchill College, Cambridge, in 1959.

COCKER, Edward (1631–75) London engraver who also taught penmanship and arithmetic. He was reputedly the author of *Cocker's Arithmetic* (1678), which went through 112 editions. Its reputation for accuracy gave rise to the expression 'according to Cocker', but it has been exposed as a poor and inaccurate forgery by his editor and publisher.

COCKERELL, Charles Robert (1788–1863) English architect, son of **Samuel Pepys Cockerell**. He travelled in the Levant and Italy (1810–17), was professor of architecture in the Royal Academy (1840–57), and designed the Taylorian Institute at Oxford and the Fitzwilliam Museum at Cambridge.

COCKERELL, Sir Christopher Sydney (1910–) English radio-engineer and inventor of the hovercraft, born in Cambridge. He worked on radar in World War II, and later worked on hydrodynamics. In 1953 he pioneered the amphibious hovercraft which rides on a cushion of jet-generated air. A prototype, the SRNI, made the Calais–Dover crossing in 1959.

COCKERELL, Samuel Pepys (1754–1827) English architect. He laid out Brunswick and Mecklenburg Squares in London; and designed the tower of St Anne's, Soho.

COCKERILL, John (1790–1840) English industrialist, born in Haslingden, Lancashire, the son of William Cockerill (1759–1832), an inventor who in 1807 established a factory at Liège for manufacturing spinning machines. John and an elder brother, having in 1812 taken over their father's business, in 1815 started a woollen factory at Berlin, and in 1817 the famous iron works at Seraing in Belgium.

COCKS, Michael Francis Lovell, Lord Cocks (1929–) English Labour politician. A graduate of Bristol University, he lectured there until entering the House of Commons in 1970 as Labour member for Bristol South. To the right of the party, he was often involved in battles with its left wing. He was a junior whip under **Harold Wilson** (1974–76) and opposition chief whip (1979–84). He lost his Commons seat in the 1987 general election and was made a life peer.

COCTEAU, Jean (1889–1963) French poet, playwright and film director, born in Maisons-Lafitte, near Paris. Success came early with *La Lampe d'Aladin* (1909), and he exploited it. He postured and preened and ran the gamut of experience, first a spectacular conversion to Roman Catholicism through **Jacques Maritain**; a derisive repudiation of his mentor; recourse to opium; and search for salvation through solitude; nevertheless he had astonishing success with whatever he touched. He figured as the sponsor of **Picasso**, **Stravinsky**, **Giorgio de Chirico** and the musical group known as *Les Six*, in complete accord with the Surrealist and Dadaist movements. He was actor, director, scenario writer, novelist, critic, artist, and all of his work was marked by vivacity and a pyrotechnic brilliance. He was elected to the French Academy in 1955. Significant works are his novels *Le Grand Écart* (1923), *Thomas l'Imposteur* (1923), *Les Enfants terribles* (1929), and plays: *Les Mariés de la Tour Eiffel* (1921), *Orphée* (1926), and *L'Aigle à deux têtes* (1946). His films include *Le Sang du poète* (1932), *La Belle et la bête* (1945), *Orphée* (adapted from his play, 1949) and *Le Testament d'Orphée* (1960).

CODRINGTON, Sir Edward (1770–1851) English naval commander, born in Dodington, Gloucestershire. He entered the navy in 1783 and in 1794 he was lieutenant of Lord **Howe**'s flagship in the action off Ushant. At Trafalgar, in 1805, he commanded the *Orion*. In 1826, as commander-in-chief of the Mediterranean squadron, he sought to advance Greek independence peacefully, in company with the French and Russian naval commanders. In this event the Turkish fleet was annihilated at the battle of Navarino (1827). He was admiral of the red in 1837, and in 1839 commander-in-chief at Portsmouth.

CODRINGTON, Sir Henry John (1808–77) English naval commander, son of Sir **Edward Codrington**. He entered the navy in 1823, was wounded at the battle of Navarino under his father's command (1827), and promoted lieutenant. He was present at the bombardment of Acre in 1840, and served in the Baltic during the Crimean War (1854–55). He was promoted admiral of the fleet in 1877.

CODRINGTON, Sir William John (1804–84) English army commander, son of Sir **Edward Codrington**. He entered the army in 1821, was promoted major-general in 1854, and distinguished himself during the Crimean War at the battles of Alma and Inkerman. He was governor of Gibraltar (1859–65).

CODY, Samuel Franklin (1862–1913) American-born British aviator, born in Texas. He came to England in 1896 and acquired British nationality. He experimented with man-lifting kites, participated in the planning and construction of the first British dirigible, and built an early aeroplane in 1908. He was killed in a flying accident.

CODY, William Frederick (1846–1917) American showman, known as Buffalo Bill, born in Scott Country, Iowa. An army scout and pony express rider, he earned his nickname after killing nearly 5000 buffalo in 18 months in pursuance of a contract to supply the workers on the Kansas Pacific Railway with meat. He served as a scout in the Sioux wars, but from 1883 toured with his Wild West Show. The town of Cody in Wyoming stands on part of his former ranch.

COE, Sebastian (1956–) English athlete, born in Chiswick. He won the 1500 metres gold medal and the silver medal in the 800 metres at both the 1980 Moscow Olympics and at Los Angeles four years later. In 1981 he broke the world record for the 800 metres, 1000 metres and the mile. Between September 1976 and June 1983 he did not lose the final of any race over 1500 metres or a mile. Following the 1990 Commonwealth Games, he retired from athletics to pursue a career in politics.

COELLO, Alonso Sánchez (c.1515–1590) Spanish portrait painter. He was court painter to **Philip II**, whose portrait by him is in the National Gallery.

COELLO, Claudio (1621–93) Spanish religious painter. He is known for the sacristy altarpiece in the Escorial and many other church-paintings in Toledo, Saragossa and Madrid.

COETZEE, John Michael (1940–) South African novelist, born in Cape Town. The political situation in his native country provides him with the base from which to launch his allegories and fables, attacking colonialism and demythologizing historical and contemporary myths of imperialism. His first work of fiction was *Dusklands* (1974), followed by *In the Heart of the Country* (1977), *Waiting for the Barbarians* (1980), *Life and Times of Michael K* (1983), for which he was awarded the Booker prize, and *Foe* (1986).

COGGAN, (Frederick) Donald, Baron (1909–) English prelate, born in London. He was educated at Merchant Taylors' School and St John's College, Cambridge. A lecturer in Semitic languages at Manchester (1931–34), professor of New Testament at Wycliffe College, Toronto (1937–44), principal of London College of Divinity (1944–56), bishop of Bradford (1956–61), he was archbishop of Canterbury from 1974 to 1980, when he was made a life peer. He is the author of several theological works, including *On Preaching* (1978) and *Mission to the World* (1982).

COGGESHALL, Ralph de (d.c.1227) English chronicler, a native of Cambridgeshire. He was abbot from 1207 to 1218 of the Cistercian abbey of Coggeshall, Essex, and continued the Latin Chronicle (*Chronicon Anglicanum*) kept at the Abbey, covering the period 1187–1224.

COGSWELL, Joseph Green (1786–1871) American bibliographer, born in Ipswich, Massachusetts. Professor of geology at Harvard (1820–23), he established the Round Hill School at Northampton, Massachusetts, with **George Bancroft** in 1823, edited the *New York Review* (1836–42), and from 1848 was superintendent of the **Astor** Library.

COHAN, Robert (1925–) American dancer, choreographer and director, born in Brooklyn, New York. After serving in World War II he dropped his career as a research naturalist to take up a training with the **Martha Graham** Company in New York. From 1946 to 1957 he was Martha Graham's partner, and created his first role in her *Diversion of Angels* (1948). Keen to develop his own choreography, he founded a company in 1957, but after five years returned to Graham's group, where he became co-director in 1966. From 1967 to 1983 he was the founding artistic director of London Contemporary Dance Theatre, which was to play a key role in the development of modern dance performance and education in Britain. His many works include *Cell* (1969), *Stages* (1971), *Class* (1975) and *Video-Life* (1987).

COHEN, Hermann (1842–1912) German-Jewish philosopher, born in Coswig, Anhalt. Professor of philosophy at Marburg (1876–1912), he founded the Marburg School of neo-Kantianism which applied Kantian methods to the presuppositions of science and whose other exponents included **Paul Gerhard Natorp** and **Ernst Cassirer**. He later taught at the Rabbinic seminary in Berlin and propounded a synthesis of Judaism and idealism which had a deep influence on such early 20th-century Jewish thinkers as **Martin Buber** and **Franz Rosenzweig**.

COHEN, Seymour Stanley (1917–) American biochemist, born and educated in New York. He did valuable early work in the 1940s using radioactive labelling of bacteriophage which suggested, but did not prove, that DNA plays a key part in heredity.

COHL, Emile, originally **Emile Courtet** (1857–1938) French cartoonist, born in Paris, the inventor of the animated cartoon film. He began as a jeweller's apprentice, but later became a pupil of the caricaturist, **André Gill**. His first cartoons were published in *Le Rire* (1880), and he was given a position as comedy film writer/director at the Gaumont Studio after accusing the company of basing scenarios on his comic strips. Using simple stick figures he produced the first frame-by-frame animated cartoon film, *Fantasmagorie* (1908), projecting it in negative so that it looked like chalk drawings on a blackboard. Sent to New York by Eclair Films he adapted the George McManus strip, *The Newlyweds and Their Baby*, into the first animated series (1912).

COHN, Ferdinand Julius (1828–98) German botanist and bacteriologist. Professor of botany at Breslau (1859) and founder of the Institute of Plant Physiology, he is regarded as the father of bacteriology in that he was the first to account it a separate science. He did important research in plant pathology, and worked with **Robert Koch** on anthrax.

COHNHEIM, Julius Friedrich (1839–84) German pathologist, born in Demmin, Pomerania (now part of Poland). His love for pathology was awakened by **Rudolf Virchow** in Berlin. He spent a year as Virchow's assistant and then occupied chairs in Kiel, Breslau and Leipzig. A superb microscopist and experimentalist, he worked on many problems, including infectious diseases and cancer. He also first elucidated completely the microscopical events of inflammation, and provided the first proof that tuberculosis was an infectious disease. His *Lectures on General Pathology* (1877) summarized the field.

COKE, Sir Edward (1552–1634) English jurist, born in Mileham of an old Norfolk family. From Norwich school he passed in 1567 to Trinity College, Cambridge, in 1571 to Clifford's Inn, in 1572 to the Inner Temple, and was called to the bar in 1578. His rise was rapid—from recorder of Coventry (1585), to member for Aldeburgh (1589), solicitor-general (1592), speaker of the House of Commons (1593), attorney-general (1594), chief justice of the common pleas (1606), chief justice of the King's Bench and privy councillor (1613). The rancour which he demonstrated in his prosecutions of **Essex** (1600), **Raleigh** (1603) and the Gunpowder conspirators (1605) has gained him little credit with posterity; but from 1606 he stands forth as a vindicator of the national liberties, opposing every illegal encroachment on the part of both church and crown. Alone of twelve judges, he resisted the royal prerogative; and in the Sir **Thomas Overbury** case (1616) he showed an indiscreet zeal to come at the real truth. He was removed from the bench on trivial grounds (1617), and though he was soon recalled to the council, his conduct in parliament from 1620 as a leader of the popular party, an opponent of Spain and of monopolies, estranged him for ever from the court. In 1621–22 he suffered nine months' imprisonment in the Tower; though still old, he carried his opposition into the next reign, the Petition of Right (1628) being largely his doing. Coke's four *Institutes* (1628–44) deal with tenures, of land, statutes, criminal law and the jurisdiction of the several law courts. The first of these is the so-called *Coke upon Littleton*—an elaborate commentary on Sir **Thomas Littleton**'s *Tenures* that, in spite of its defective etymologies, has still a real, if mainly historical, value. They are the earliest textbooks on the early modern common law, and were very influential. Eleven of the thirteen parts of his epoch-making Law Reports were published during his lifetime (1600–15).

COKE, Thomas (1747–1814) Welsh Methodist churchman, born in Brecon. He graduated in 1768 from Oxford, and became an Anglican curate in Somerset, but in 1777 joined the Methodists, and was attached to the London circuit. In 1784 he was appointed by **John Wesley** as the superintendent of the Methodist Church in America. He visited the USA nine times, and assumed the title of bishop in 1787. He died in the Indian Ocean on a missionary voyage to Ceylon. He published, besides religious works, extracts from his American *Journals* (1790), a *History of the West Indies* (3 vols, 1808–11), and, with Henry Moore, a *Life of Wesley* (1792).

COKE, Thomas William See **LEICESTER OF HOLKHAM**

COLBERT, Claudette, originally **Claudette Lily Chauchoin** (1903/05–) American actress, born in Paris. Educated in New York, she harboured an ambition to be a fashion designer but a bit part on stage in *The Wild Westcotts* (1923) converted her to acting. Her subsequent theatre work includes *The Marionette Man* (1924), *A Kiss in a Taxi* (1925) and the popular *The Barker* (1927). Her film début in *For the Love of Mike* (1927) led to a long-term contract with Paramount. Petite, saucer-eyed, apple-cheeked, with a deep-throated laugh, she gained attention as historical seductresses in *The Sign of the Cross* (1932) and *Cleopatra* (1934) but sparkled in screwball comedy where her intelligence, wit and glamour enhanced such films as *It Happened One Night* (1934, Academy Award), *Midnight* (1939) and *The Palm Beach Story* (1942). She retired from the cinema in 1961 but has occasionally been seen on stage, as in *The Kingfisher* (1978) and *Aren't We All?* (1984). She also returned to the cameras for the television mini-series *The Two Mrs Grenvilles* (1987).

COLBERT, Jean Baptiste (1619–83) French statesman, born in Reims. He obtained a post in the war office, and in 1651 entered the service of **Mazarin**. When, in 1661, he became the chief minister of **Louis XIV**, he found the finances in a ruinous condition, and immediately began his reforms. Dishonest administrators were imprisoned; farmers of the state revenues were forced to yield up the resources of the crown; the debts of the state were reduced by arbitrary composition; and in all the departments of finance order and economy were introduced, so that in ten years the revenue was more than doubled. He reorganized the colonies in Canada, Martinique and St Domingo, and founded others at Cayenne and Madagascar. In a few years he provided France with one of the strongest fleets in the world, with well-equipped arsenals and a splendid body of seamen. He improved the civil code, and introduced a marine code. The Academies of Inscriptions, Science and Architecture were founded by him. In short, Colbert was the patron of industry, commerce, art, science and literature—the founder of a new epoch in France. His aim was to raise the strength of France by developing every side of the national life. In this—often by arbitrary measures—he entirely succeeded during the early part of Louis's reign, but the wars and the extravagance of the court undid all that had been accomplished. Colbert died bitterly disappointed, and hated by the people as the cause of their oppressive taxes.

COLBURN, Zerah (1804–40) American child prodigy, born in Vermont. He displayed such powers of calculation that in 1810 his father left Vermont to exhibit him. He answered in 20 seconds such questions as 'How many hours in 1811 years?' and a few years later solved much more complicated problems with equal rapidity. He was shown in Great Britain and Paris; from 1816 to 1819 he studied at Westminster School at the expense of the Earl of Bristol. His father died in 1824, and he returned to America; here he was a Methodist preacher for nine years, and from 1835 professor of languages at Norwich, Vermont. His remarkable faculty disappeared as he grew to manhood.

COLCHESTER, Charles Abbot, 1st Baron (1757–1829) English jurist and speaker of the House of Commons, born in Abingdon. He was educated at Westminster and Christ Church, Oxford, and in 1779 entered the Middle Temple. Returned to parliament as a strong Tory in 1795, in his first session he improved the legislation regarding temporary and expiring laws; and it is due to his exertions that municipal bodies receive a copy of all new acts as soon as they are printed. To him too is mainly owed the Private Bill Office and the royal Record Commission, whose proceedings he superintended for many years. But his greatest service was in the Act (1800) for taking the first census. He was speaker from 1802 until 1817, when he retired with a peerage.

COLDSTREAM, Sir William (1908–87) English painter and teacher of art, born in Belford, Northumberland. He studied at the Slade School (1926–29) and joined the London Group in 1933. In 1937 he helped to found the Euston Road School, which promoted a quiet, sober realism, eschewing the fads and fashions of modern art. During World War II he was an official war artist in Italy and the Middle East. From 1949 he was Slade professor of fine art at University College, London. A highly skilled administrator, he helped reshape British art education, especially through his work on the national advisory committee (1958–71) which produced the two 'Coldstream Reports'.

COLE, George Douglas Howard (1889–1958) English economist, historian and detective-story writer, born in London. Educated at St Paul's School and Balliol College, Oxford, in 1925 he became reader there in economics and in 1944 Chichele professor of social and political theory. Historian, chairman (1939–46, 1948–50) and president from 1952 of the Fabian Society, he wrote numerous books on socialism, including Lives of **William Cobbett** (1925) and **Robert**

Owen (1925) and a history of the British working-class movements, 1789–1947 (1948), often in collaboration with his wife, Margaret Isobel Cole and her brother, Raymond Postgate. The Coles also collaborated in writing detective fiction.

COLE, Sir Henry (1808–82) English designer, writer and civil servant, born in Bath. As assistant keeper at the Public Records Office from 1838, he was responsible for saving many ill-preserved documents. He introduced the penny postage system and invented the adhesive stamp. Under the pseudonym 'Felix Summerley' he set up a firm for 'art manufacture', published illustrated children's books, and published the first Christmas card. He planned and largely organized the Great Exhibition of 1851 under the patronage of **Prince Albert**. He set up a national system of art education, and was director of the South Kensington Museum (1853–73) which became the Victoria and Albert Museum. His autobiography was published posthumously in 1884.

COLE, Thomas (1801–48) English-born American painter, born in Bolton. He went to America in 1819 and settled in Catshill, New York, and became founder of the Hudson River school of landscape painters. In 1830 two of his pictures appeared in the Royal Academy, and he afterwards made sketching tours through England, France, and Italy; but all his best landscapes were American, especially the *Voyage of Life* series.

COLEBROOKE, Henry Thomas (1765–1837) English orientalist, born in London. He became an official in India, made a study of Sanskrit and aroused interest in Asiatic language and culture by his essays and his *Sanskrit Grammar* (1805).

COLEMAN, Ornette (1930–) American alto saxophonist, multi-instrumentalist and composer, born in Fort Worth, Texas, whose experiments in free-form jazz and atonality from the mid 1950s attracted equal measures of praise and scepticism. Following early recordings with Don Cherry (pocket-trumpet) he persevered through a discouraging climate for avant garde jazz, becoming more generally accepted in the 1960s as a major innovator. A writer of jazz works in unconventional forms, he has also composed several classical pieces.

COLENSO, John William (1814–83) English clergyman, born in St Austell. A graduate of St John's College, Cambridge, he published *Miscellaneous Examples in Algebra* in 1848, *Plane Trigonometry* in 1851, and *Village Sermons* (1853). In 1853 he was appointed first Bishop of Natal. He soon mastered the Zulu language, prepared a grammar and dictionary, and translated the Prayer Book and part of the Bible. His *The Pentateuch and the Book of Joshua Critically Examined* (1862–79), which cast doubts upon biblical accuracy, was regarded as heretical and his Metropolitan, Bishop Gray of Capetown, went to great lengths in attempting to have him deposed, even publicly excommunicating him (1864). He also earned disfavour by championing dispossessed Negroes. He was eventually deposed in 1869.

COLEPEPER, or **CULPEPER John** (1600–60) English royalist, a native of Sussex. He served abroad, and was returned for Kent in 1640 to the Long Parliament. There he opposed the Grand Remonstrance, but supported episcopacy. In 1642 he was created Chancellor of the Exchequer, in 1643 Master of the Rolls, and in 1644 Lord Colepeper.

COLERIDGE, Hartley (1796–1849) English man of letters, eldest son of **Samuel Taylor Coleridge**, born in Clevedon, Somerset. He was brought up by **Southey** at Greta Hall, and educated at Ambleside school and Merton College, Oxford. His scholarship was great but unequal; his failures to win the Newdigate filled him with 'a passionate despondency'; and he forfeited an Oriel College fellowship by intemperance. He spent two years in London, tried taking pupils at Ambleside, occasionally writing for *Blackwood's Magazine*, lived for some time at Grasmere, and then went to live at Leeds with a publisher, for whom he wrote biographies, published under the titles of *Biographia Borealis* (1833) and *Worthies of Yorkshire and Lancashire* (1836). He subsequently lived at Grasmere, with two short intervals of teaching at Sedbergh. Provided for by an annuity, he continued to write poetry, and edited **John Ford** and **Massinger**. His days were spent in fitful study, lonely reverie, and wanderings over the Lake Country, with occasional bouts of intemperance. His poetry is graceful, tender and sincere.

COLERIDGE, John Duke, 1st Baron Coleridge (1821–94) English jurist, eldest son of the judge Sir John Taylor Coleridge (1790–1876), the nephew of the poet **Samuel Taylor Coleridge** and the biographer of **John Keble**. Educated at Eton and Oxford, he became successively solicitor-general (1868), attorney-general (1871), chief justice of the common pleas (1873), and lord chief justice of England (1880).

COLERIDGE, Samuel Taylor (1772–1834) English poet, son of a vicar of Ottery St Mary, Devon. The youngest of a very large family, he had an unhappy childhood, and was educated at Christ's Hospital and went to Jesus College, Cambridge, to study for the church. His university career was interrupted in 1793 by a runaway enlistment in the 15th Dragoons from which he was rescued by his family. On a walking tour in 1794 he met **Robert Southey** at Balliol College, Oxford, with whom he shared Romantic and revolutionary views. Together they planned a 'pantisocracy' or communist society on the banks of the Susquehanna, in Pennsylvania, but the idea came to nothing. In 1795 he married Sarah Fricker, a friend of Southey's, while her sister Edith married Southey. He had contributed some verses to the *Morning Chronicle* in 1793, and now he wrote, with Southey, a historical play, *The Fall of Robespierre*. He now became immersed in lecturing and journalism in Bristol, interspersed with itinerant preaching at Unitarian chapels. The Bristol circle provided Coleridge with generous friends—**Joseph Cottle** the bookseller, who published his first book of poems, *Poems on Various Subjects* (1796), which contained the 'Ode to France'. In 1797 the Coleridges moved to a cottage at Nether Stowey, Somerset, and later that year met **William** and **Dorothy Wordsworth**. The result was momentous for English poetry—from their discussions emerged a new poetry which represented a revulsion from neo-classic artificiality and, as a consequence, the renovation of the language of poetry. *Lyrical Ballads* (1798), which opened with Coleridge's 'Ancient Mariner' and closed with Wordsworth's 'Tintern Abbey', was thus in the nature of a manifesto. A visit to Germany with the Wordsworths (1798–99) followed. German philosophy and criticism influenced him greatly and he published translations of **Schiller**'s *Piccolomini* and *Wallenstein*. In 1800 he settled at Keswick and for a time, with the Wordsworths at Grasmere and Southey already resident at Keswick, it looked as if a fruitful career was opening out for him, but his moral collapse, due partly to opium, made the next few years a misery to him and his friends. His 'Ode to Dejection' (1802) is both a recantation of Wordsworth's animistic view of Nature and a confession of failure. From then on his association with Wordsworth was strained; his relations with Dorothy continued only through her devotion to him. He had a sojourn in Malta as secretary to the Governor from 1804 to 1806. In 1809 he began a weekly paper, *The Friend*, which ran for 28 issues and was published as a book in 1818. In 1810 he finally broke with Wordsworth and settled in London, where he engaged in various activities—miscellaneous writing and lecturing at the Royal Institution (his lectures on **Shakespeare** alone are extant). He also wrote a play, *Remorse* (1813), which had a mild success at Drury Lane. In 1816 he published 'Christabel' and the fragment, 'Kubla Khan', both written in his earlier period of inspiration. He had long relinquished the idea of renewing that inspiration and resigned himself, as he indicates in the close of 'Dejection', to philosophical speculation. His critical writing in these middle years is important also as the finest 'creative' criticism in the language, collected in *Biographia Literaria* (1817), *Aids to Reflection* (1825), and *Anima Poetae* (edited from his notebooks, 1895). He was a gifted poet and a writer of theological and politico-sociological works which have a relevance even today.

COLERIDGE, Sara (1802–52) English scholar, born at Greta Hall, Keswick, daughter of **Samuel Taylor Coleridge**. She was brought up in **Southey**'s household. In 1822 she translated Dobrizhoffer's *Historia de Abiponibus*, and in 1825 the 'Loyal Servitor's' memoirs of the Chevalier **Bayard**. In 1829 she married her cousin, Henry Nelson Coleridge, and helped to edit her father's writings. Her own works were *Pretty Lessons for Good Children* (1834) and *Phantasmion* (1837), a fairy tale. Her son, Herbert Coleridge (1830–61), educated at Eton and Balliol, was called to the bar, but, devoting himself to comparative philology, worked for the Philological Society's dictionary, and wrote a *Thirteenth Century Glossarial Index* (1859) and an essay on King **Arthur**.

COLERIDGE-TAYLOR, Samuel (1875–1912) English composer, born in London, the son of a West African doctor and an Englishwoman. He composed *Hiawatha* (1898–1900) and other popular cantatas and orchestral works.

COLET, John (c.1467–1519) English scholar and theologian, born in London, the son of Sir Henry Colet, twice Lord Mayor. He studied at Oxford, and about 1493 travelled to Italy, where he became acquainted with the views of **Savonarola**. Having returned to England in 1496, and been ordained priest, he lectured at Oxford on the Epistles of St Paul (1496–1504), opposing the interpretations of the scholastic theologians. In 1498 he met **Erasmus** in Oxford. In 1505 he was made Dean of St Paul's, and continued to deliver lectures on different books of Scripture, and preach against ecclesiastical abuses; charges of heresy were brought against him, but Archbishop **William Warham** refused to support them. With the large fortune he inherited from his father he endowed St Paul's School in 1509–12.

COLETTE, Sidonie Gabrielle (1873–1954) French novelist, born in Saint-Sauveur-en-Puisaye. Her early novels, the *Claudine* series, were published by her first husband, Henri Gauthier-Villars under his pen-name of 'Willy'. After their divorce in 1906 she appeared in music-halls in dance and mime, and out of this period came *L'Envers du music-hall* (1913). Her work is characterized by an intense, almost entirely physical preoccupation with immediate sense experiences. Her novels include *Chéri* (1920), *La Fin de Chéri* (1926), *La Chatte* (1933) *Gigi* (1945) and *The Stories of Colette* (trans 1958). In 1912 she married **Henry de Jouvenel**, and in 1935, Maurice Goudeket.

COLFAX, Schuyler (1823–85) American statesman, born in New York. Originally a newspaper editor, in 1868 he was elected vice-president of the United States, in **Grant**'s first term. Implicated, apparently unjustly, in the Crédit Mobilier charges of 1873, he spent the rest of his life in political retirement.

COLIGNY, Gaspard II de, seigneur de Châtillon (1519–72) French Huguenot leader, born in Châtillon-sur-Loing. He early distinguished himself in the wars of **Francis I** and **Henri II**. In 1552 he was made admiral of France, though he never commanded at sea; in 1557 he held St Quentin with a handful of men for 17 days against the army of Spain, but was taken prisoner. During his captivity in Spain (1557–59) he was converted to Protestantism. He became a leader of the Huguenots with Louis I de Bourbon, **Prince de Condé**; after the defeat of Dreux (1562), where Condé was taken prisoner, Coligny drew off the Huguenot remnant into Normandy. In the second Huguenot war, on Condé's death (1569), he was appointed generalissimo and brought about the favourable peace of St Germain (1570). **Catherine de' Medici**, however, alarmed at the growing power of the Huguenots and at Coligny's ascendancy over her son, **Charles IX**, determined to regain her power; and Coligny was one of the first victims in the Massacre of the Huguenots on St Bartholomew's Day, 1572.

COLLEONI, Bartolommeo (1400–75) Italian soldier and condottiere, born near Bergamo. He fought on both sides in the strife between Milan and Venice, where he finally settled in 1454, becoming generalissimo for life. He is the subject of a famous Venetian equestrian statue by **Verrochio**.

COLLETT, (Jacobine) Camilla, née **Wergeland** (1813–95) Norwegian novelist, born in Kristiansand, sister of **Hendrik Arnold Wergeland**. A champion of women's rights and social justice, she brought realism to Norwegian fiction in books like *Amtmandens døttre* (The Magistrate's Daughter, 1855), *I den lange neeter* (In the Long Nights, 1862), and *Sidtse blade* (*Last Page*, 1868–73).

COLLIER, Arthur (1680–1732) English philosopher, born in Steeple Langford rectory, where he himself became rector in 1704. His *Clavis Universalis* (1713) independently argues for the idealist conclusions Bishop **Berkeley** reached on the impossibility of the existence of an external world.

COLLIER, Jeremy (1650–1726) English clergyman and nonjuror, who refused the oath of allegiance to **William III** and Mary, born at Stow cum Quy, Cambridgeshire. His father was a clerical schoolmaster at Ipswich, and here and at Caius College, Cambridge, he was educated, afterwards becoming rector of Ampton near Bury St Edmunds, and lecturer at Gray's Inn. His reply to **Burnet**'s *Inquiry into the State of Affairs* (1688) cost him some months in Newgate. He next waged warfare on the crown with incisive pamphlets, and was arrested in 1692 on suspicion of being involved in a Jacobite plot. In 1696 he gave absolution to the would-be assassins Friend and Parkyns on the scaffold, for which offence he was outlawed. In 1697 he published his *Short View of the Immorality and Profaneness of the English Stage*, which fell like a thunderbolt among the wits. **Congreve** and **Vanbrugh** answered angrily, and were crushed anew by Collier. **Dryden** in the preface to his *Fables* (1700) acknowledged that he had been justly reproved. Collier continued to preach to a congregation of nonjurors, and was consecrated a nonjuring bishop in 1713. He upheld the 'usages', and laid himself open to a charge of holding Romish views. His largest works were the *Great Historical, Geographical, Genealogical, and Poetical Dictionary* (4 vols, folio, 1701–21). and *An*

Ecclesiastical History of Great Britain (2 vols, folio, 1708–14).

COLLIER, John Payne (1789–1883) English journalist and critic, born in London. He published editions of various authors, including **Shakespeare** and **Dodsley**, and a *History of English Dramatic Poetry*, and *Annals of the Stage to the Restoration* (1831). But he is chiefly remembered for his forgeries and falsification of old manuscripts, especially the so-called 'Perkins folio'. He was exposed in 1859.

COLLIER, John, known as **'Tim Bobbin'** (1708–86) English poet, born in Urmston, near Manchester, the son of the curate of Stretford. From 1729 he was usher or master of a school at Milnrow, near Rochdale. His rhyming satire, *The Blackbird*, appeared in 1739, and his *View of the Lancashire Dialect* (in humorous dialogue) in 1775.

COLLINGS, Jesse (1831–1920) English politician, born in Littleham-cum-Exmouth in Devonshire. Elected Radical MP for Ipswich in 1880, he sat for Bordesley as a Unionist (1886–1918), and was specially identified with the Agricultural Labourers' Union and measures for promoting allotments and smallholdings ('three acres and a cow'). He was under-secretary for the home office in 1895–1902.

COLLINGWOOD, Cuthbert, Lord (1750–1819) English naval commander, born in Newcastle-upon-Tyne. He entered the navy at the age of 11, and from 1778 his career was closely connected with that of **Nelson**, whom he followed up the ladder of promotion step by step. Among the great naval victories in which he played a prominent part, were those of Lord **Howe** off Brest in 1794; of Lord **Jervis** off Cape St Vincent in 1797; and of Nelson off Cape Trafalgar in 1805, where he held the second command. He died at sea, and was buried beside Nelson, in St Paul's Cathedral, London.

COLLINGWOOD, Robin George (1889–1943) English philosopher, historian and archaeologist, born in Coniston. Educated at Rugby and Oxford, he taught at Oxford and was professor of philosophy there (1934–41). He was an authority on the archaeology of Roman Britain, and much of his philosophical work was concerned with the relations of history and philosophy. He was at first much influenced by **Hegel** and **Croce**, but increasingly he saw philosophy as an irreducibly historical discipline, always exhibiting the presuppositions and concepts of its own time and culture. He was intellectually an unfashionable figure in his lifetime but was recognized as a writer of great style, originality and wide learning. His many books include: *Speculum Mentis* (1924), *Roman Britain and the English Settlements* (1936), *The Principles of Art* (1937), *Autobiography* (1939), *Essay on Metaphysics* (1940), *The New Leviathan* (1942), and two posthumous works *The Idea of Nature* (1945) and *The Idea of History* (1946).

COLLINGWOOD, William Gershom (1854–1932) English artist and archaeologist, born in Liverpool, the son of a landscape painter. He studied philosophy and aesthetics at Oxford, then trained as an artist for four years in London under **Alphonse Legros**. He moved to Coniston in the Lake District to be private secretary and collaborator to **John Ruskin**, and was for a time a professor at Reading University. He is best known for his archaeological studies on Viking remains in the north of England, and for his *Pilgrimage to the Saga-Steads of Iceland* (1899), copiously illustrated with his own water-colours.

COLLINS, Anthony (1676–1729) English theologian, born in Heston near Hounslow. Educated at Eton and Cambridge, he became a friend and disciple of **John Locke**. He was one of the English eighteenth-century deists, who held that God's nature and existence could be established by reason not revelation, and he published an *Essay concerning the Use of Reason* (1707), *Inquiry concerning Human Liberty* (1715) and *Discourse of the Grounds and Reasons of the Christian Religion* (1724); his best-known work was *A Discourse of Free-thinking* (1713), which provoked a brilliant reply from **Richard Bentley**.

COLLINS, Sir Benjamin See **BRODIE, Sir Benjamin**

COLLINS, Charles Allston (1828–73) English painter, second son of the artist William Collins (1788–1847) and brother of **William Wilkie Collins**. In early life he painted pictures in the Pre-Raphaelite style. In 1860 he married the younger daughter of **Charles Dickens**, and having already turned his attention to literature, produced *The Eye-witness* essays (1860), two novels, and other works.

COLLINS, Joan Henrietta (1933–) English actress, born in London. She made her film début in *Lady Godiva Rides Again* (1951) and used her sultry appeal and headline-catching private life to build a career as a durable international celebrity. By the 1970s she was appearing in low-budget horror films and softcore pornography, but her fortunes were revitalized with a leading role in the universally popular television soap opera *Dynasty* (1981–89). Married four times, she has written one volume of tell-all autobiography, *Past Imperfect* (1978), and a novel, *Prime Time* (1988). Her sister is the bestselling novelist Jackie Collins.

COLLINS, John Churton (1848–1908) English scholar and critic. Educated at King Edward's School, Birmingham, and Balliol College, Oxford, he edited the works of literary figures like **Cyril Tourneur** and Robert Greene, and wrote *Studies in Shakespeare* (1904), *Studies in Poetry and Criticism* (1905) and *Voltaire, Montesquieu and Rousseau in England* (1905). He became professor of English literature at Birmingham in 1904.

COLLINS, Michael (1890–1922) Irish politician and Sinn Fein leader, born near Clonakilty. He was largely responsible for the negotiation of the treaty with Great Britain in 1921. He was killed in an ambush between Bandon and Macroom.

COLLINS, Michael (1930–) American astronaut, born in Rome. He joined the USAF in 1952 after graduating from the US Academy at West Point, reaching the rank of lieutenant-colonel and becoming an experimental test pilot at the Air Force Flight Test Center, Edwards Air Force Base, California. He joined NASA as an astronaut in 1963 and was back-up pilot for Gemini 7 (a two-seater earth satellite capsule) before orbiting as co-pilot in Gemini 10, which was launched on 18 July 1966. On the historic Apollo II moon-landing mission in 1969 he was in the command module while **Neil Armstrong** and **Edwin Aldrin** set foot on the moon.

COLLINS, (William) Wilkie (1824–89) English novelist, elder son of the artist **William Collins** (1788–1847), born in London. He was educated partly at Highbury, but from 1836 to 1839 was with his parents in Italy. After his return he spent four years in business, and then was called to the bar, but gradually turned to literature, the Life of his father (1848) being his earliest production. His first work of fiction was a novel about the fall of Rome, *Antonina* (1850). With *Basil* (1852), he turned his attention to mystery, suspense and crime. His best work was written in the 1860s when he produced *The Woman in White* (1860), *No Name* (1862), *Armadale* (1866) and *The Moonstone* (1868). In all he produced more than a score of popular novels.

COLLINS, William (1721–59) English poet, born in Chichester, the son of a hatter. He was educated at Winchester and Magdalen College, Oxford, but having been pronounced 'too indolent even for the army', and dissuaded from entering the church, as the sole alternative he came to London to make a living by literature. During this period he spent an inheritance, in advance of receiving it, and was forced to live on credit, reduced at times to the greatest straits; Dr **Johnson** once rescued him from the bailiffs by obtaining an advance from a bookseller on the promise of Collins to translate the *Poetics* of **Aristotle**. It was during this period, however, that he wrote his *Odes*, upon which his fame rests. They attracted no notice at the time of publication (1747), and were little valued even by **Thomas Gray** and Dr Johnson. On the death of an uncle in 1749, Collins inherited £2000, which enabled him to retire to Chichester, and apparently to pursue a regular course of study. It was about this time that he met **John Home**, the author of *Douglas*, and gave him his 'Ode on the Superstitions of the Highlands', a poem in which, says **Lowell**, 'the whole Romantic School is foreshadowed'. His mental health broke down after a visit to France, and he died insane.

COLLINS, William (1788–1847) English landscape and figure painter, born in London, of a Wicklow family. He studied at the Royal Academy. He is remembered for his subject pictures of country scenes, such as *Blackberry Gatherers* and *The Bird-catchers* (1814).

COLLINS, William (1789–1853) Scottish publisher, born in Eastwood, Renfrewshire. A weaver by trade, he opened a private school for the poor in Glasgow in 1813. A friend of the evangelist **Thomas Chalmers**, in 1819 he set up business in Glasgow as a bookseller and publisher with Chalmer's brother. He specialized in church history and pioneered school textbooks.

COLLINSON, Peter (1694–1768) English botanist and naturalist, born in London. He became a woollen draper, trading with the American colonies, and through his business and Quaker associations introduced American plant species into Britain, and vice versa, thereby assisting horticultural progress in both countries. He had a garden first at Peckham, and then at Mill Hill.

COLLOT D'HERBOIS, Jean Marie (1751–96) French revolutionary, born in Paris. Originally a provincial actor, he was attracted by the revolution back to Paris and joined the Jacobin Club in 1791. His self-confidence, his loud voice and his *Almanach du Père Gérard* secured his election to the National Convention. In 1793 he became president of the Convention and a member of the murderous Committee of Public Safety. Sent by **Robespierre** to Lyon, he took bloody revenge by guillotine and grapeshot on the inhabitants for having once hissed him off the stage. He joined in the successful plot against Robespierre (1794), but himself was expelled from the Convention, and banished to Cayenne (1795), where he died.

COLM See **COLUMBA**

COLMAN, St (d.676) Irish monk of Iona. In 661 he became bishop of Lindisfarne, but in 664 withdrew to Iona on the defeat of the Celtic party at the Council of Whitby. He died in County Mayo.

COLMAN, George (1732–94) 'the Elder', playwright and manager, born in Florence, the son of the English envoy. He was educated at Westminster and Oxford, and called to the bar in 1755. In 1760 his first piece, *Polly Honeycombe*, was produced at Drury Lane with great success; next year came *The Jealous Wife*, and in 1766 *The Clandestine Marriage*, written in conjunction with **Garrick**. In 1767 he purchased, with three others, Covent Garden Theatre, and held the office of manager for seven years, until he sold his share. In 1776 he purchased the Haymarket Theatre from **Samuel Foote**, but was paralysed by a stroke from 1785.

COLMAN, George (1762–1836) 'the Younger', son of **George Colman** 'the Elder'. He was educated at Westminster, Oxford and Aberdeen. During his father's illness he acted as manager of the Haymarket and on his death the patent was transferred to him. As Examiner of Plays from 1824 he showed himself both arrogant and excessively precise. In industry he rivalled his father, and he made money by his *John Bull*, *Iron Chest*, *Heir at Law* and other comedies, and by songs like 'Mynheer Van Dunck'. He wrote *Random Records of My Life* (1830).

COLMAN, Ronald (1891–1958) English film and stage actor, born in Richmond, Surrey. His dashing good looks, mellifluous voice and gentlemanly manner made him a popular romantic leading man for three decades, and he was one of the few major Hollywood stars to survive the transition to the sound era. He made his screen début in 1919 in *The Live Wire* and starred in heroic parts in *The White Sister* (1923), *Raffles* (1930), *A Tale of Two Cities* (1935), *The Prisoner of Zenda* (1937) and *Random Harvest* (1942).

COLMAN, Samuel (1832–1920) American painter, born in Portland, Maine. He studied in Europe from 1860–62, was elected a member of the National Academy in 1862, and first president (1866–71) of the American Society of Painters in Watercolors. His pictures include scenes from Algeria, Germany, France, Italy and Holland.

COLOMB, Philip Howard (1831–99) Scottish naval officer and historian. He entered the navy in 1846 and served in the Burmese war (1852) and in China (1874–77). He devised the system of night signalling known as 'Colomb's Flashing Signals' (1858). He wrote *Naval Warfare* (1891) on the importance of naval supremacy, and was promoted vice-admiral in 1892.

COLOMBO, Joe Cesare (1930–71) Italian designer, born in Milan. Although interested in painting, sculpture and architecture, it was as an industrial designer that he found his métier. One of the most versatile Italian designers of the 1960s, his interests included lighting, glass, furniture and, in particular, multi-function storage furniture. A logical extension of this led him to design compact 'core' units containing all the requirements necessary for the living environment, furniture included. Such units, when placed in an empty space, required only connection to services to provided a fully functioning home. They included kitchen, bathroom and storage, and housed radio, music centre and television. The best example was his 'Total Furnishing Unit' (1971) for the exhibition 'Italy: The New Domestic Landscape' at the Museum of Modern Art, New York. This, and many of his designs, made much use of plastics, in which material he was very fluent.

COLONNA Roman family, which took its name from a village among the Alban Hills. From it have sprung a pope (**Martin V**), several cardinals, generals, statesman and noted scholars. One of its most prominent members was Vittoria Colonna (c.1492–1547). The daughter of the constable of Naples, at four years old she was betrothed to a boy of the same age; at seventeen they were married. After her husband's death in the battle of Pavia (1525), Vittoria found her chief consolation in solitude and the writing of poetry. During seven years of her widowhood she resided alternately at Naples and Ischia, and then in the convents of Orvieto and Viterbo. Later she lived in Rome, where she died. She was the close friend of **Michelangelo**, admired by **Ariosto**, and the intimate associate of the reforming party at the papal court. Her poems appeared at Parma in 1538.

COLQUHOUN, Patrick (1745–1820) Scottish merchant and reformer, born in Dumbarton. After visiting Virginia, he became a tobacco merchant in Glasgow and was Lord Provost in 1782. He founded the Glasgow Chamber of Commerce in 1783, the oldest of its kind in Britain. Moving to London in 1789 he became a police magistrate and wrote many reforming pamphlets, including *Police of the Metropolis* (1795).

COLQUHOUN, Robert (1914–62) Scottish artist, born in Kilmarnock. He studied at the Glasgow School of Art, and in Italy, France, Holland and Belgium. His enigmatic, dreamlike figures (eg, *Girl with a circus goat*) are usually presented in a characteristic colour scheme of reds and browns.

COLSTON, Edward (1636–1721) English merchant and philanthropist, born in Bristol. A Tory and high-churchman, he bestowed over £70000 in establishing or endowing almshouses, schools and other public benefactions. From 1689 he lived chiefly in Mortlake.

COLT, Samuel (1814–62) American inventor, born in Hartford, Connecticut. He ran away to sea in 1827, and about 1836 travelled over America, lecturing on chemistry. In 1836 he took out his first patent for a revolver, which after the Mexican War (1846–48) was adopted for the US army. He expended over $2500000 on an immense armoury in Hartford. He also worked on submarine mines, and a submarine telegraph.

COLTRANE, John William (1926–67) American saxophonist and composer, born in Hamlet, North Carolina. He emerged in the 1950s as one of the most influential jazz performers of the post-bebop era. Early saxophone lessons were followed by military service with a navy band, then professional work as a rhythm-and-blues player. After working with the **Dizzy Gillespie** Big Band and with such modernists as pianist **Bud Powell**, Coltrane began to shape his distinctive style when he joined the influential **Miles Davis** Quintet (1955). A formative period followed two years later, working with **Thelonious Monk**; when he rejoined Miles Davis in 1958 to take part in modal jazz experiments, the freedom from conventional harmonic structures profoundly affected his improvising style. The intensity of his attack and dense flow of notes influenced a generation of future saxophone players, as did Coltrane's adoption of the soprano saxophone as a second instrument to the tenor. He led his own small groups after 1960, showing the influence of Indian music and philosophy, and remaining a controversial avant garde figure. His most important compositions include 'Giant Steps' (1959) and 'A Love Supreme' (1964).

COLUM, Pádraic (1881–1972) Irish poet and playwright, born in County Longford, the son of the warden of a workhouse. He was educated at a school in Longford, and worked as a railway clerk in Dublin. He became a leader of the Irish literary revival, and wrote plays for the Abbey Theatre including *Broken Soil* (1903, later called *The Fiddler's House*), *The Land* (1905), and *Thomas Muskerry* (1910). He published his first collection of poems, *Wild Earth*, in 1907. In 1916 he was co-founder of the *Irish Review*. From 1914 he lived in the USA, where he and his wife (Molly Maguire) taught comparative literature at Columba University. He published two studies on Hawaiian folklore (1924 and 1926), the result of government-sponsored research. He wrote several further volumes of verse, including the lyric *She Moved Through the Fair*.

COLUMBA, St, also known as **Colmcille ('Colm of the Churches')** (521–97) Irish apostle of Christianity in Scotland, born into the royal warrior aristocracy of Ireland at Gartan in County Donegal. According to his 7th-century biographer, **Adomnán**, he studied under St **Finnian** at Clonard with St **Ciaran**. In 546 he founded the monastery of Derry. In 561, however, he was accused of having been involved in the bloody battle of Cuildreimhne, for which he was excommunicated and sentenced to exile; it was perhaps in this battle that he received the wound that left a livid scar on his side. In 563, at the advanced age of 42 and accompanied by 12 disciples, he set sail to do penance as a missionary, and found haven on the Hebridean island of Iona, where he founded a monastery that became the mother church of Celtic Christianity in Scotland. From Iona he travelled to other parts of Scotland, especially to the north to evangelize amongst the Picts, and won the respect of the pagan King Brude (Bridei) at his stronghold near Inverness (possibly the hill-fort at Craig Phadrig). He and his missionaries founded numerous churches in the islands of the Hebrides (hence his Gaelic name of Colmcille). A formidably energetic administrator, he organized his monastery on Iona as a school for missionaries, and played a vigorous role in the politics of the country. Although he spent the last 34 years of his life in Scotland, he visited Ireland on occasions, and towards the end of his life he founded the monastery of Durrow in Ireland. He was renowned as a man of letters; he wrote hymns, and is credited with having transcribed 300 books with his own hand; but he was also revered as a warrior saint, and his supernatural aid was frequently invoked for victory in battle. He died on Iona and was buried in the abbey.

COLUMBAN, or **Columbanus, St** (543–615) Irish missionary, 'the younger Columba', born in Leinster. He studied under **St Comgall** at Bangor in Down, and c.585 went to Gaul with twelve companions, and founded the monasteries of Anegray, Luxeuil and Fontaine in the Vosges country. His adherence to the Celtic Easter involved him in controversy; and the vigour with which he rebuked the vices of the Burgundian court led to his expulsion in 610. After a year or two at Bregenz, on Lake Constance, he went to Lombardy, and in 612 founded the monastery of Bobbio, in the Appenines, where he died. His writings, all in Latin, comprise a monastic rule, six poems on the vanity of life, seventeen sermons and a commentary on the Psalms (1878).

COLUMBUS, Christopher (1451–1506) Genoese explorer, and discoverer of the New World, born in Genoa, the son of a woolcomber. At 14 he went to sea, fought with Tunisian galleys, and about 1470, shipwrecked in a fight off Cape St Vincent, reached the shores of Portugal on a plank. In Lisbon he married Filippa Moniz. As early as 1474 he had conceived the design of reaching India by sailing westward—a design in which he was encouraged by a Florentine astronomer Paolo Toscanelli; in 1477 he 'sailed 100 leagues beyond Thule', probably to or beyond Iceland; and, having also visited the Cape Verde Islands and Sierra Leone, he began to seek a patron for his intended expedition. Finally, after seven years of alternate encouragement and repulse, his plans were accepted by **Ferdinand** and **Isabella** of Castile in April 1492. On Friday, 3 August, Columbus set sail in command of the small *Santa Maria*, with 50 men, and attended by two little caravels, the *Pinta* and the *Niña*, the whole squadron comprising only 120 adventurers.

He first made the Canary Islands; and though he found it hard to keep up the courage of his crews, new land was descried on Friday 12 October, probably Watling's Island in the Bahamas. He then visited Cuba and Hispaniola (Haiti), planted a small colony, and set sail with his two caravels (for the flagship had been wrecked). After an exceedingly tempestuous voyage, he re-entered the port of Palos on 15 March 1493, and was received with the highest honours by the court. He sailed on his second voyage on 25 September, with three carracks and 17 small caravels, and on 3 November sighted Dominica in the West Indies. After a succession of wretched quarrels with his associates, and a long illness in Hispaniola, he returned to Spain much dejected in 1496. His third voyage, begun in 1498, resulted in the discovery of the South American mainland. In 1500 Columbus and his brother were sent home in irons by a newly appointed royal governor; but the king and queen repudiated this action, and restored Columbus to favour. His last great voyage (1502–04), along the south side of the Gulf of Mexico, was accomplished in the midst of great hardships. He died at Valladolid, in Spain, and was buried in a monastery near Seville. In 1536 his remains were taken to Santa Domingo in Hispaniola; in 1899 they were brought back to Spain and deposited in Seville Cathedral in 1902.

COLUMELLA, Lucius Junius Moderatus (fl.1st century) Roman writer on agriculture, born in Gades in Spain. He wrote *De Re Rustica* (12 books), on arable and pasture lands, the culture of vines and olives, the care of domestic animals, gardening (in dactylic hexameters), and arboriculture.

COLVILLE, David (1813–97) Scottish industrialist born in Campbeltown, Glasgow. In 1871, employing 200 men, he began making malleable plates and angles for Scottish shipbuilders. In 1879 he built five of the largest Siemens furnaces for the production of steel, and in 1880 he obtained the contract to supply Siemans furnaces. In 1885 he took his three sons into partnership, but two of them died in 1916 and the third, John, became an MP. Thus the chairmanship passed to a former office boy, Sir John Craig (1874–1957), who made the firm the fourth largest steel concern in Great Britain.

COLVIN, Sir Sidney (1845–1927) English scholar, born in Norwood, Surrey. He studied at Trinity College, Cambridge, and became a fellow in 1869. He was elected Slade professor of fine art at Cambridge in 1873, director of the Fitzwilliam Museum in 1876, and keeper of the Department of Prints and Drawings in the British Museum (1884–1912). He edited the works of **Robert Louis Stevenson**, and wrote on **Dürer**, **Flaxman**, **Landor**, **Keats**, and others.

COMBE, Andrew (1797–1847) Scottish physician, born in Edinburgh, brother of **George Combe**. He began to practise there in 1823. In 1836 he was appointed physician to the king of the Belgians; but his health failed and he returned to Scotland, where in 1838 he became a physician to Queen **Victoria**. His *Principles of Physiology* (1834) was influential and went through 15 editions.

COMBE, George (1788–1858) Scottish phrenologist, moral philosopher and brother of **Andrew Combe**, born in Edinburgh, a brewer's son. He became a solicitor in 1812, and practised till 1837. Through **Johann Spurzheim** he became a convert to phrenology, and wrote *Essays on Phrenology* (1819) and *The Constitution of Man* (1828), which was violently opposed as inimical to revealed religion. He travelled and lectured in Britain, Germany and the USA, and published *Notes on the United States* (1841). In 1833 he married Cecilia (1794–1868), the daughter of **Sarah Siddons**. His ideas on popular education were carried out for some years in a school which he founded in Edinburgh in 1848.

COMBE, William (1741–1823) English writer and adventurer, born in Bristol, renowned as the creator of *Dr Syntax*. The illegitimate son of a wealthy London alderman, he inherited a fortune in 1762 and led the life of an adventurer and spent much time in debtors' jails. Educated at Eton and Oxford, he wrote metrical satires like *The Diaboliad* (1776), but made his name with his three verse satires on popular travel-books. Illustrated with cartoons by **Thomas Rowlandson**, they recounted the adventures of a clergyman schoolmaster on his holidays (based on **William Gilpin**), in *Dr Syntax in search of the Picturesque* (1809), *The Second Tour of Dr Syntax in search of Consolation* (1820), and *The Third Tour of Dr Syntax in search of a Wife* (1821). He also wrote the text for Rowlandson's *Dance of Death* (1815–16), *Dance of Life* (1816) and *Johnny Quae Genus* (1822), and for *The Microcosm of London* (1808).

COMBERMERE, Sir Stapleton Cotton, 1st Viscount (1772–1865) English soldier, born in Llewenny Hall, Denbighshire. Educated at Audlem and Westminster School, he entered the army in 1790, and served in Flanders (1743–44), South Africa (1795) and in India with the Light Dragoon Regiment (1796–1800). He was MP for Newark (1806–14). In the Peninsular War he commanded cavalry (1808–12), before being invalided out due to wounds. In 1815 he commanded the cavalry of the army of occupation in France. He was commander of the forces in the West Indies, 1817–20; commander-in chief in Ireland, 1822–25; and commander in India, 1825–30, where in 1827 he captured the Jat fortress of Bhartpur. He was made a viscount in 1827, constable of the Tower in 1852, and a field-marshal in 1855.

COMENIUS, or **Komenský, John Amos** (1592–1670) Czech educational reformer, born in Eastern Moravia. His parents belonged to the Moravian Brethren. He studied at Herborn (1612) and then at Heidelberg, became rector of the Moravian school of Prerau (1614–16) and minister at Fulnek, but lost all his property and library in 1621, when the town was taken by the Imperialists. Settling at Lissa in Poland (1628), he worked out his new theory of education, wrote his *Didactica Magna*, and was chosen bishop of the Moravian Brethren in 1632. He spoke four languages fluently and was a pioneer of new language teaching methods. In 1631 he published his *Janua Linguarum Reserata*, and in 1639 his *Pansophiæ Prodromus*. In 1641 he was in England by invitation of parliament, planning a Baconian College of all the sciences; but the civil war drove him to Sweden (1642). He returned to Lissa in 1648, and in 1650 went to Saros-Patak, Hungary. Here he composed his *Orbis Sensualium Pictus* (1658), the first foreign language text-book to use pictures as a 'visual aid' to learning. Finally, he settled in Amsterdam, and died at Naarden.

COMGALL, St (c.515–602) Irish abbot, born in Ulster. He founded about 558 the great abbey of Bangor, in County Down. He is said to have lived on the Hebridean island of Tiree for a time, and accompanied **St Columba** on his journey to the north of Scotland.

COMINES, Philippe de (1445–1509) French statesman and historian, born in the castle of Comines near Courtrai. In 1463 he entered the court of Burgundy, but in 1472 passed over to the service of **Louis XI** of France. He was rewarded with the rich fief of Talmont, married the heiress of Argenton and became one of

Louis's most trusted advisers. Louis's death brought him the loss of much property, and even eight months' imprisonment in an iron cage; but in 1493 he was restored to a measure of favour. He accompanied **Charles VIII** on his Italian expedition (1494), was present at the battle of Fornovo, and met **Machiavelli**. His *Mémoires* (1524) are the earliest French example of history as distinguished from the chronicle.

COMMODUS, Lucius Aurelius (161–92) Roman emperor from 180, the son of **Marcus Aurelius** and **Faustina**. Though carefully educated and groomed for the succession, he proved unable to live up to the example of his virtuous father, and his reign degenerated quickly into one of the worst chapters of Roman imperial despotism. At his father's death he was fighting the Marcomanni on the upper Danube, but at once concluded a treaty, and hastened to Rome. After the discovery of his sister Lucilla's plot against his life in 183, he gave uncontrolled vent to his savagery. At length his mistress, Marcia, had him strangled by Narcissus, a famous athlete. His death brought to an end the dynasty of the Antonine emperors.

COMNENUS (1057–1461) a family, originally Italian, of which many members occupied the Byzantine throne from 1057 to 1185 and that of Trebizond from 1204 to 1461. See **Alexius I**, **Isaac I**, and **Anna Comnena**. David Comnenus, the last in Trebizond, was executed at Adrianople in 1462, with all his family, by **Mohammed II**.

COMPTON, Arthur Holly (1892–1962) American physicist, born in Wooster, Ohio, the son of a Presbyterian minister, whose faith he inherited. He studied at Princeton and Cambridge, England, and held posts at Washington University in St Louis, and at Chicago. He won the 1927 Nobel prize for physics, jointly with **Charles Wilson**, for their work on the wavelength of scattered photons. A leading authority on nuclear energy, X-rays and nuclear chemistry, he was invited in 1941 to direct plutonium production for the atomic bomb. After quelling his religious doubts, he played a major part in the Manhattan Project at Chicago, in 1942 building the first reactor with **Fermi**. In 1958 he published *Atomic Quest*, describing the project.

COMPTON, Denis Charles Scott (1918–) English cricketer and journalist, born in London. An elegant and cavalier batsman, he first played for Middlesex in 1936, and was first capped for England the following year. He played in 78 Test matches, scoring 17 Test centuries. In his first-class career he scored over 38000 runs, including 123 centuries; his most brilliant year was in 1947, when he scored 3816 runs and 18 centuries. He was also a talented footballer, a member of the Cup-winning Arsenal team in 1950; he was capped for England in 1943. He retired from professional cricket in 1957 to take up journalism and broadcasting.

COMPTON, Fay (1894–1978) English actress, born in London, daughter of the actor Edward Compton (1854–1918) and sister of Sir **Compton Mackenzie**. She first appeared on the stage in 1911. After a successful US visit in 1914 she won acclaim in London as *Peter Pan* (1918), subsequently playing many famous parts, especially in plays by **Barrie** and in comedies such as **Dodie Smith**'s *Autumn Crocus* and *Call it a Day*.

COMPTON, Henry (1632–1713) English prelate, youngest son of the second Earl of Northampton. He entered the church in 1662, in 1674 he became bishop of Oxford, and in 1675 of London. He was tutor of the daughters of **James II** (**Mary** and **Anne**), but was suspended for two years for his Protestantism. He cordially welcomed William of Orange and crowned him **William III** with his wife Mary.

COMPTON, John George Melvin (1926–) St Lucian politician, born in Canouan in St Vincent and the Grenadines. He graduated at the London School of Economics and was called to the English bar. In 1951 he established a law practice in St Lucia and three years later joined the St Lucia Labour party (SLP), becoming deputy leader. He left in 1961 to form the United Workers' party (UWP). At independence in 1979 he was St Lucia's first prime minister. He was defeated in the same year by the Labour party but returned in 1982 and was narrowly re-elected in 1987.

COMPTON-BURNETT, Dame Ivy (1892–1969) English novelist, born in London. She graduated in classics from the Royal Holloway College, London University, and published her first novel, *Dolores*, in 1911. A prolific writer, her rather stylized novels have many features in common, such as they are set in upper-class Victorian or Edwardian society and the characters usually belong to a large family, spanning several generations. She was noted for her skilful use of dialogue, not because the language is appropriate to character but because it conveys the secret thoughts and understanding of the characters. Her works included *Pastors and Masters* (1925), *Brothers and Sisters* (1929), *Parents and Children* (1941), *Mother and Son* (1955, Tait Black Memorial Prize), *A Father and his Fate* (1957), *The Mighty and their Fall* (1961), and *A God and His Gifts* (1963).

COMRIE, Leslie John (1893–1950) New Zealand astronomer and pioneer in mechanical computation, born in Pukekohe. He was educated at Auckland University College and Cambridge. After teaching in the USA, he joined HM Nautical Alamanac Office in 1926, becoming superintendent (1930–36). Regarded as the foremost computer and table-maker of his day, in 1936 he founded the Scientific Computing Service Ltd,

COMTE, Auguste (1798–1857) French philosopher and social theorist, born in Montpelier. Usually regarded as the founding father of sociology, he was an unconventional and rebellious student at the École Polytechnique in Paris (1814–16), made a meagre living for a while teaching mathematics, and from 1818 came strongly under the influence of the social reformer **Saint-Simon**. His professional and personal life then became more precarious: in 1824 he broke violently with Saint-Simon; in 1825 he married, briefly and unhappily; in 1826 he began teaching philosophy, but suffered a breakdown, and although he continued teaching privately, he was largely supported in his later years by **J S Mill**, **George Grote** and other friends. He nonetheless completed at least two major works: the *Cours de Philosophie positive* (6 volumes, 1830–42) and the *Système de Politique positive* (1851–54). His 'Positivism' sought to expound the laws of social evolution, to describe the organization and hierarchy of all branches of human knowledge, and to establish a true science of society as a basis for social planning and regeneration; in this vision 'Humanity' itself becomes the object of religous reverence and love—'Catholicism minus Christianity', as **T H Huxley** dubbed it.

COMYN, Cumming, or **Cumyn** a family which took its name from the town of Comines near Lille, on the Franco-Belgian frontier. While one branch remained there, and gave birth to Philippe de **Comines**, another followed **William** of Normandy to England. In 1069 'the Conqueror' made Robert of Comines, or Comyn, Earl of Northumberland; his younger son, William, became chancellor of Scotland about 1133. By 1250 his descendants in Scotland included four Earls (Buchan,

Monteith, Angus and Athole) and 32 belted knights of the name of Comyn; but 70 years afterwards this great house was overthrown.

CONANT, Thomas Jefferson (1802–91) American biblical scholar. He filled chairs of languages in various colleges. He made new versions of both Old and New Testaments, translated **Heinrich Gesenius**' Hebrew grammar, and was one of the American committee for the revision of the Old Testament.

CONDAMINE, C M de La See **LACONDAMINE**

CONDÉ, Louis I de Bourbon, Prince de (1530–69) French nobleman and Huguenot leader in the Wars of Religion (1562–98), founder of the House of Condé. The youngest son of Charles de Bourbon, Duc de Vendôme, he distinguished himself on the field. At the accession of **Francis II** in 1559, under the regency of his mother, **Catherine de' Medici**, he joined the Huguenots and took part in the luckless Conspiracy of Amboise against the **Guise** faction, and escaped execution only by the death of the king in 1560. Appointed governor of Picardy by the regent, he fought the Guises again but was defeated at Dreux in 1562. He led the second Huguenot advance on Paris in 1567, but was defeated again, taken prisoner and shot.

CONDÉ, Louis II, 4th Prince de Bourban, Prince de Condé (1621–86) French nobleman, great-grandson of **Louis I**, and known as 'the Great Condé'. During the Thirty Years War he won brilliant victories against Spain at Rocroi (1643) and Lens (1648). He was recalled to suppress the first French uprising (Fronde) against Cardinal **Mazarin** and the regent, **Anne of Austria**, in 1649. In 1650 he rebelled and led the second Fronde, but fled to Spain, where he served for six years against his country, until he was defeated by **Turenne** and **Cromwell**'s Ironsides at the Battle of the Dunes in 1658. Pardoned in 1659, he became one of the outstanding generals of the young **Louis XIV**, who assumed power in 1661. He defeated the Spanish again in Franche-Comté in 1668, and commanded the French armies with Turenne in the Netherlands. His last battle, in 1674, was a marathon but indecisive engagement against William of Orange (the future **William III** of Britain). Thereafter he retired to Chantilly, where he enjoyed the company of literary friends like **Molière**, **Racine**, **Boileau** and **La Bruyère**.

CONDER, Charles Edward (1868–1909) English-born Australian painter and lithogapher, born in London. He arrived in Sydney in 1884, worked as a lithographer and contributed to the *Sydney Illustrated News*. In 1888 one of his oils was bought for the Art Gallery of New South Wales, and later that year he joined **Tom Roberts**, **Arthur Streeton** and **Frederick McCubbin** in their camp at Box Hill, Victoria. He also showed in the controversial '9 × 5 Impression' exhibition in the following year. In 1890 he went to Paris, where his portrait was painted by **Toulouse-Lautrec**, and later to London where he was influenced by **Whistler** and the 'Japonais' cult. From then until his death Conder worked in delicate water-colours on silk, and he is especially noted for his delicate fan designs.

CONDILLAC, Étienne Bonnot de (1715–80) French philosopher and psychologist, born in Grenoble. Though an ordained priest he was an associate of **Diderot**, **Rousseau** and others in the rationalizing and secularizing movements of the Enlightenment. He was also a great admirer of **John Locke** and in his *Essai sur l'origine des connaissances humaines* (1746) and *Traité des sensations* (1754) he argued that all knowledge depends ultimately on the senses and on the association of ideas. He also wrote on logic, language and economics.

CONDON, Edward Uhler (1902–74) American theoretical physicist, born in Alamogordo, New Mexico, distinguished for his research in atomic spectroscopy. Educated at the University of California, and Göttingen, and for a time a news reporter 'in tough Oakland', his many posts included chairs in physics at Washington, Minnesota and Colorado. In World War II he did notable work on the Manhattan (atomic bomb) project, as associate director with **Oppenheimer**, although he found the necessary secrecy and security difficult to bear; and he was afterwards director of a USAAF study of UFOs (Unidentified Flying Objects) from 1945 to 1951.

CONDORET, Marie Jean Antoine Nicolas Caritat, Marquis de (1743–94) French mathematician, born, the son of a cavalry officer, at Ribemont, near St Quentin. At 13, after distinguishing himself in the Jesuit school at Reims, he began his mathematical studies at the College of Navarre in Paris. His success was rapid and brilliant; and the high approval of **Clairaut** and **D'Alembert** determined his future. His *Essai sur le calcul intégral* (1765) won him a seat in the Academy of Sciences; in 1781 he entered the French Academy. He took an active part in the *Encyclopédie*. On the outbreak of the Revolution he made eloquent speeches and wrote famous pamphlets on the popular side, was sent by Paris to the Legislative Assembly in 1791, and in 1792 became president of the Assembly. He voted that the king should receive the most severe punishment except death, and, as deputy for Aisne in the National Convention, he sided usually with the Girondists. Accused and condemned by the extreme party, he found refuge in the house of a generous lady, Madame Vernet, for eight months; but, driven to change his place of concealment, was recognized and lodged in the jail of Bourg-la-Reine, where he was found dead the next morning. In his *Progrès de l'esprit humain* (1794), written in hiding, he insisted on the justice and necessity of establishing a perfect equality of civil and political rights between the individuals of both sexes, and proclaimed the indefinite perfectibility of the human race.

CONE, James Hal (1938–) American theologian, chief advocate of Black theology in the USA, born in Arkansas. A professor of systematic theology at Union theological seminary, New York, he has written extensively. His angry criticisms of the presuppositions of white theology in *A Black Theology of Liberation* (1970) were followed by the more measured *God of the Oppressed* (1975), *For My People* (1984), *Speaking the Truth* (1986), and the autobiographical *My Soul Looks Back* (1987); he also edited *Black Theology: A Documentary History* (1979) with Gayraud S Wilmore.

CONEGLIANO See **CIMA DA CONEGLIANO**

CONFUCIUS, Latin for **K'ung Fu-tzu, the Master K'ung** (551–479 BC) Chinese philosopher, born of an aristocratic but impoverished family in the state of Lu, part of the present province of Shantung. His father died in his third year and he married at 19, becoming a government official in Lu with a retinue of disciples, mostly young gentlemen whom he was preparing for government service. He was promoted to ministerial rank and enjoyed a successful and highly popular career, which eventually attracted jealousy and hostility and led to a breach with the ruler. In 497 he left Lu and for a dozen years became an itinerant sage, wandering from court to court seeking a sympathetic patron and attended by a company of his disciples. In about 485 he returned to Lu and spent his final years teaching and possibly writing. After his death his pupils compiled a volume of memorabilia, the *Analects*, which record the master's sayings and doings, but most of the other works attributed to him are later compilations which, like the philosophy of 'Confucianism' itself, are probably only loosely related to his own teachings. He emerges as a great moral teacher who tried to replace the old religious observances with moral values as the basis of social and political order. In his Way (*tao*) he emphasized the practical virtues of benevolence (*jen*), reciprocity (*shu*), respect and personal effort which were to be interpreted pragmatically with regard to individual circumstances and cases rather than any abstract system of imperatives. Succeeding generations revered him and Confucianism became, and remained until recently, the state religion of China.

CONGREVE, William (1670–1729) English dramatist and poet, born in Bardsey near Leeds. He was educated in Ireland at Kilkenny School and Trinity College, Dublin, where he was a fellow student of **Swift**. In London he entered the Middle Temple to study law, but never practised. His first publication was *Incognita, or Love and Duty Reconciled* (1692), a novel of cross-purposes and disguises which was written in a fortnight. His translation of the eleventh satire of **Juvenal** came out soon after in **Dryden**'s *Juvenal and Persius*. In January 1693 his comedy *The Old Bachelor*, produced under Dryden's auspices, with the celebrated **Anne Bracegirdle** as heroine, achieved brilliant success at a time when the theatre had been suffering a slump. His second comedy, *The Double Dealer* (November 1693), was in every way stronger than *The Old Bachelor*, but the satire on the heartless sexual morals of the time was aimed too directly at the theatre's best customers, and it failed to please. *The Mourning Muse of Alexis* (1695), a poetic dialogue on the death of Queen **Mary II** wife of **William III** was full of artificial conceits. *Love for Love*, generally regarded as Congreve's stage masterpiece, was first produced in 1695. It is more satirical, more vital and stronger in feeling than its predecessors; it also has a more coherent plot and truer characterization. In 1697 his only tragedy, *The Mourning Bride*, appeared, best remembered for the two overworked quotations 'music hath charms to soothe the savage breast' and 'hell hath no fury like a woman scorned'. He was next occupied busily in the famous **Jeremy Collier** controversy, defending the morality of the new stage (1698). His last play, *The Way of the World*, was produced in 1700, but was not a success. He wrote no more for the stage, apart from the words of a masque of *The Judgment of Paris*, set to music by **John Eccles** for a musical competition in 1701, and the undistinguished libretto of *Semele*, also to the music of Eccles, but later used by **Handel**. He was now almost blind owing to cataracts, but his support of the Whig party brought him a few sinecures which enabled him to live comfortably, writing occasional poems, until his death after a coach mishap. He was buried in Westminster Abbey.

CONGREVE, Sir William (1772–1828) English scientist, comptroller of the Woolwich Laboratory. Educated at Woolwich Academy, in 1808 he invented the Congreve rocket, first used in the Napoleonic wars. The first friction matches, called 'Congreves' (alluding to the rockets) were not invented by him but by **John Walker**. He became MP for Gatton (1818–28).

CONINGTON, John (1825–69) English classical scholar, born in Boston. Educated at Rugby and Magdalen College, Oxford, he became Latin professor at Oxford in 1854. His greatest work is his edition of *Virgil* (3 vols, 1861–68).

CONKLING, Roscoe (1829–88) American politician, born in Albany, New York. He sat in congress as a Republican, 1858–62, 1864–66; in the senate, 1867, 1873, 1879. In 1876 he received 93 votes for the presidential nomination; in 1880, supporting **Grant** and opposing **Blaine**, he split the Republican party.

CONNAUGHT, Prince Arthur, Duke of (1850–1942) British prince and soldier, third son of Queen **Victoria**. After training at the Royal Military Academy, Woolwich, he served in Canada, Gibraltar, Egypt and India (1869–90). Thereafter he was commander-in-chief in Ireland (1900–04), commander-in-chief of the Mediterranean (1907–09) and governor-general of Canada (1911–16). He was created Duke of Connaught and Strathearn in 1874. In 1879 he married Princess Louise Margaret of Prussia (1860–1917). Of their children, Margaret (1882–1920) married the future King **Gustav VI Adolf** of Sweden in 1905; and his son, Prince Arthur (1883–1938), was governor-general of South Africa from 1920 to 1923.

CONNELLY, Marc (Marcus Cook) (1890–1980) American dramatist, born in McKeesport, Pennsylvania. As a journalist who took to the theatre, he achieved several outstanding successes in collaboration with **George S Kaufman**, including *Dulcy* (1921), *To the Ladies* (1922), the amusing 'expressionist' *Beggar on Horseback* (1924), and *Hunter's Moon* (1958). His greatest individual success was *Green Pastures* (1930) adapted from Negro stories of the Deity and a Negro heaven, which won the Pulitzer prize.

CONNERY, Sean Thomas (1930–) Scottish film actor, born in Edinburgh. After a succession of jobs, including lifeguard and coffin-polisher, his powerful physique won him a role in the chorus line of the London stage production of *South Pacific* (1951). Sporadic film work followed, although there were more significant opportunities in television drama, particularly *Requiem for a Heavyweight* (1956). In 1962 he was cast in *Dr. No* as **Ian Fleming**'s secret agent James Bond, a part he subsequently played on seven occasions. The film's unexpected success established him as an international box-office attraction. Later films have allowed him to display his versatility, for example as an army rebel in *The Hill* (1965), a 19th-century union leader in *The Molly Maguires* (1969), a disturbed police officer in *The Offence* (1972) and a roistering adventurer in *The Man Who Would Be King* (1975). He won an Academy Award as an aging Irish cop with true grit in *The Untouchables* (1987).

CONNOLLY, Cyril Vernon (1903–74) English author and journalist. Educated at Eton and Oxford, he contributed to the *New Statesman* and other periodicals and wrote regularly for the *Sunday Times*. He was founder/editor of *Horizon* (1939–50) and briefly literary editor of the *Observer*. His only novel was *The Rock Pool* (1936). Among his works are *Enemies of Promise* (1938), which included a look at the prevailing literary scene and an autobiograpical fragment, *The Unquiet Grave* (1944), miscellaneous aphorisms and reflections, and various collections of essays. Inclined to sloth and prey to fitful depressions, his potential was greater than his achievement.

CONNOLLY, James (1868–1916) Irish Labour leader and insurgent, born in Edinburgh of Irish immigrant parents. He joined the British army at the age of 14 and was stationed in the Curragh and Dublin, but deserted to get married to an Irish girl in Scotland. Returning to Ireland in 1896 he organized the Irish Socialist Republican party and founded *The Workers' Republic*, the first Irish socialist paper. He toured the USA as a lecturer from 1902 to 1910; and helped found the Industrial Workers of the World ('Wobblies'). Back in Ireland, in 1913 with **James Larkin** he organized the great transport strike in Dublin. He organized socialist 'citizen armies', and took part in the Easter rebellion (1916) in command of the GPO.

Severely wounded, he was arrested and executed on 12 May, tied to a chair because he was unable to stand. He wrote *Labour in Irish History* (1912).

CONNOLLY, Maureen Catherine (1934–69) American tennis player, born in San Diego, California. Known as 'Little Mo', she made tennis history by becoming the first woman to win the so-called Grand Slam of the four major titles (British, American, French and Australian) in the same year (1953). She won the US title in three consecutive years (1951–53) and the Wimbledon singles in three consecutive years (1952–54). Soon after her last Wimbledon triumph she broke her leg in a riding accident and retired from tournament play.

CONNORS, Jimmy (James Scott) (1952–) American tennis player, born in East St Louis, Illinois. An extremely fit all-action player, he won four US singles titles and had two widely-spaced successes at Wimbledon (1974, 1982). His zest for the sport kept him at the top for many years.

CONRAD I (d.918) king of Germany, son of the Count of Franconia, and nephew of the Emperor Arnulf. Elected king on the extinction of the direct Carolingian line in 911, he gradually re-established the imperial authority over most of the German princes, carried on an unsuccessful war with France, and at last fell mortally wounded at Quedlinburg in a battle with the Hungarians.

CONRAD II (c.990–1039) king of Germany from 1024 and Holy Roman Emperor from 1027, son of the Duke of Franconia and founder of the Salian dynasty. In 1026 he crossed the Alps, crushed a rebellion in Italy, was crowned at Milan and was anointed Holy Roman Emperor by the pope in 1027. He was soon recalled to Germany to put down four revolts, which he achieved by 1033. In the same year he was crowned king of Burgundy; in 1036 a fresh rebellion recalled him to Italy; but this time he was forced to grant various privileges to his Italian subjects. Shortly after his return he died at Utrecht. He was succeeded by his son **Henry III**.

CONRAD III (1093–1152) king of Germany, and the first **Hohenstaufen** king of the Germans, son of Frederick of Swabia. While under 20, he had bravely supported Henry V, who in return granted him the duchy of Franconia in 1115. In 1125 he unsuccessfully contested the crown of Italy with the emperor Lothar III, on whose death the princes of Germany, fearing the growing preponderance of the **Guelf** party, offered Conrad the throne, and he was crowned at Anchen in 1138. He was immediately involved in a quarrel with Henry the Proud, Duke of Bavaria and Saxony, and head of the Guelfs in Germany, the struggle being continued under Henry's son, **Henry the Lion**. When St **Bernard of Clairvaux** preached a new crusade, Conrad set out for Palestine with a large army (1147). A new Bavarian rebellion was defeated before his death. He designated his nephew, **Frederick I Barbarossa**, as his successor.

CONRAD, Joseph, originally **Jozef Teodor Konrad Nalecz Korzeniowski** (1857–1924) Polish-born British novelist, born in Berdichev, in the Polish Ukraine, now in the USSR. His father was a revolutionary of literary gifts—he translated **Victor Hugo**'s *Les Travailleurs de la mer*—who was exiled to Vologda in 1862. In 1878 Joseph joined an English merchant ship and was naturalized in 1884 when he gained his certificate as a master. In the ten years that followed, he sailed between Singapore and Borneo, and this gave him an unrivalled background of mysterious creeks and jungle for the tales to follow. There was also an interlude in the Belgian Congo which provided exotic colour for his *Heart of Darkness*, one of his three finest short stories, the others being *Youth* and *Typhoon*. In 1896 he married and settled at Ashford in Kent, where he lived in seclusion for the rest of his days. Conrad's first novel was *Almayer's Folly* (1894), and then followed *An Outcast of the Islands* (1896), *The Nigger of the Narcissus* (1897), *Lord Jim* (1900), *Nostromo* (1904), *The Secret Agent* (1907) and *Under Western Eyes* (1911) before *Chance* (1914) made him famous. It was only then that *Lord Jim* was recognized as a masterpiece. Perhaps the short story was his true medium—*Tales of Unrest* (1898), *Youth* (1902) and *Twixt Land and Sea* (1912). His semi-autobiographical *The Mirror and the Sea* and his *Personal Record* testify to his high artistic aims. He also wrote *Victory* (1919), but his later works, *The Arrow of Gold* (1919) and *The Rescue* (1920), owed their popularity largely to his earlier work.

CONRAD, of Montferrat (d.1192) Italian crusader, distinguished himself during the defence of Tyre against Saladin (1187). In 1192 he was elected king of Jerusalem as consort of the heiress Isabella, daughter of Amalric I, but was murdered by the Assassins before he could be crowned.

CONRADIN, of Swabia (1252–68) the last **Hohenstaufen** emperor, the son of Conrad IV. His uncle, **Manfred**, had assumed the crown of Sicily on a rumour of Conradin's death, and Pope **Urban IV**'s hatred of the Hohenstaufens led him to offer the crown of the Two Sicilies to **Charles of Anjou**, who invaded Italy and slew Manfred at Benevento (1266). Conradin, invited by the Neapolitans to assert his rights, appeared in Italy with 10000 men, but was defeated near Tagliacozzo, taken prisoner, and executed.

CONRAN, Jasper (1959–) English fashion designer, born in London, the son of Sir **Terence Conran**. He trained at the Parsons School of Art and Design in New York, leaving in 1977, when he joined Fiorucci briefly as a designer. He produced his first collection of easy-to-wear, quality clothes in London in 1978.

CONRAN, Sir Terence Orby (1931–) English designer and businessman, born in Esher, Surrey. He founded and ran the Habitat Company (1971), based on his own success as a furniture designer and the virtues of good design and marketing. He has since been involved in the management of several related businesses such as Richard Shops, Conran Stores and Habitat Mothercare. His first wife, Shirley (née Pearce) Conran (b.1932), a designer and fashion editor, is the author of best-selling books like *Superwoman* (1975) and *Lace* (1982).

CONSALVI, Ercole (1757–1824) Italian statesman and prelate, born in Rome. He was made cardinal and secretary of state by Pope **Pius VII** (1800), and concluded the concordat with **Napoleon** (1801). At the Congress of Vienna he secured the restoration of the Papal States; as papal secretary he suppressed all monopolies, feudal taxes and exclusive rights. He was a liberal patron of science and art.

CONSCIENCE, Hendrik (1812–83) Flemish novelist, born in Antwerp. From 1866 he was director of the Wiertz Museum. His *Phantazy* (1837), a fine collection of tales, and his most popular romance, *De Leeuw van Vlaenderen* (1838), earned him a place as the father of the Flemish novel. His series of pictures of Flemish life, beginning with *Hoe man schilder wordt* (1843), carried his name over Europe.

CONSIDÉRANT, Victor Prosper (1808–93) French socialist, born in Salina. He became a disciple of **François Fourier** and on his death in 1837 took charge of his school and edited the *Phalange*. In 1849 he was accused of high treason, fled from France and in 1855 founded a socialist commune, *La Réunion*, in Texas, which flourished briefly then failed. He returned to France in 1869. The most important of his many writings are *Destinée sociale* (1834–38), *Débâcle de la politique* (1836) and *Le Socialisme devant le vieux monde* (1848).

CONSTABLE, Archibald (1774–1827) Scottish publisher, born in Carnbee, Fife. He became a bookseller's apprentice in Edinburgh in 1788, and in 1795 started as a bookseller on his own account, and quickly gathered round him the chief book-collectors of the time. He drifted into publishing, bought the *Scots Magazine* in 1801, and was chosen as publisher of the *Edinburgh Review* (1802). For his flair and respect for editorial independence he is regarded as the first modern publisher. He published for all the leading men of the time, and his quick appreciation of **Scott** became the envy of the book trade. In 1812 he purchased the copyright of the *Encyclopaedia Britannica*. But in 1826 came the financial crash which ruined Constable and plunged Scott heavily into debt. Nevertheless he was incorrigibly innovative and launched (1827) Constable's *Miscellany*, a series of volumes on literature, art and science, moderately priced to encourage sales among the common man; but he died before he could capitalize on its success.

CONSTABLE, Henry (1562–1613) English poet, the son of Sir Robert Constable of Newark. At 16 he entered St John's College, Cambridge, turned Catholic, and went to Paris. He was pensioned by King **Henri IV**, and seems to have been employed in confidential missions to England and Scotland. In 1592 he published his *Diana*, a collection of 23 sonnets; two years later, the second edition, containing 76, some by his friend, Sir **Philip Sidney**, and other poets.

CONSTABLE, John (1776–1837) English landscape painter, born in East Bergholt, Suffolk, where his father was a landowner and miller. Educated at Lavenham and Dedham, he assisted his father for a year in the mill (1794); but his love of art was irrepressible, and Sir **George Beaumont** prevailed on his family to send him to London, where he studied under **Ruisdael** and **Claude Lorraine** at the Royal Academy schools. He exhibited his first picture at the RA in 1802. In 1816 he married Mary Bicknell; and in 1828, on the death of her father, solicitor to the Admiralty, an inheritance of £20000 enabled Constable to devote himself exclusively to his landscape work. In 1821 he had a triumph with his *Haywain* in the Paris Salon, and in 1825 at Lille with his *White Horse*. Both gained gold medals and exercised a powerful influence upon **Delacroix** and other French artists. His later years were saddened by the deaths of his wife and his friend Archdeacon Fisher, by ill-health, and by great depression of spirits; but he worked steadily at his art, though his landscapes still were frequently unsold. Some of his finest landscapes, including the *Valley Farm*, *Cornfield* and *Haywain*, and over a score of other works, are in the National Gallery, and nearly as many in the Tate Gallery.

CONSTANS I, Flavius Julius (c.320–350) Roman emperor, youngest of three sons of **Constantine the Great**, in 337 he received Illyricum, Italy and Africa as his share of the empire. After defeating his brother Constantine at Aquileia (340), Constans became sole ruler of the West till his death at the hands of Magnentius.

CONSTANS II, Flavius Heraclius (630–68) Byzantine emperor. He succeeded his father Constantine III in 641. His reign was marked by the loss of Egypt and much of the Middle East to the Arabs. His despotism and church policies aroused antagonism, and he was murdered in his bath by a chamberlain five years after transferring his capital to Syracuse.

CONSTANT DE REBECQUE, Henri Benjamin (1767–1830) author and politician, born of French Huguenot ancestry in Lausanne. Educated at Oxford, Erlangen and Edinburgh, he settled in Paris in 1795 as a publicist. He entered the Tribunate in 1799, but was banished from France in 1802 for denouncing the despotic acts of **Napoleon**. After travelling in Germany and Italy with Madame de **Staël**, he settled at Göttingen. On Napoleon's fall in 1814 he returned to Paris; during the Hundred Days became one of Napoleon's councillors, though previously he had styled Napoleon a Genghis Khan; and after the second restoration of the **Bourbon**s wrote and spoke in favour of constitutional freedom. He was returned to the Chamber of Deputies in 1819, and became the leader of the liberal Opposition. He wrote *De la religion* (5 vols, 1824–31); but more important is a remarkable psychological novel, *Adolphe* (1816). His correspondence appeared in 1844, his *Oevres politiques* in 1875, his Letters to Madame Récamier and his family in 1882–88, and his *Journal intime* in 1895.

CONSTANTINE I, called **the Great,** properly **Flavius Valerius Aurelius Constantinus** (c.274–337) Roman Emperor, born in Naissus, in Upper Moesia. He was the eldest son of **Constantius Chlorus** and **Helena**, and first distinguished himself as a soldier in **Diocletian**'s Egyptian expedition (296), next under **Galerius** in the Persian war. In 305 the two emperors Diocletian and Maximian abdicated, and were succeeded by Constantius Chlorus and Galerius. Constantine joined his father, who ruled in the west, at Boulogne on the expedition against the Picts, and before Constantius died (306) he proclaimed his son his successor. Galerius did not dare to quarrel with Constantine, yet he granted him the title of Caesar only, refusing that of Augustus. Political complications now increased, until in 308 there were actually no fewer than six emperors at once—Galerius, Licinius and Maximian in the east; and Maximian, Maxentius his son, and Constantine in the west. Maxentius drove his father from Rome, and after some intrigues, Maximian died by suicide (309). Maxentius threatened Gaul with a large army. Constantine, crossing the Alps by Mont Cénis, thrice defeated Maxentius, who was drowned after the last great victory at the Milvian Bridge near Rome (312). Before the battle a flaming cross inscribed 'In this conquer' was said to have caused Constantine's conversion to Christianity; and the edict of Milan (313), issued conjointly with Licinius, gave civil rights and toleration to Christians throughout the empire. Constantine was now sole emperor of the West; and by the death of Galerius in 311 and of Maximian in 313, Licinius became sole emperor of the east. After a war (314) between the two rulers, Licinius had to cede Illyricum, Pannonia and Greece; and Constantine for the next nine years devoted himself vigorously to the correction of abuses, the strengthening of his frontiers and the chastizing of the barbarians. Having in 323 again defeated Licinius, and put him to death, Constantine was now sole governor of the Roman world. He chose Byzantium for his capital, and in 330 inaugurated it under the name of Constantinople ('City of Constantine'). Christianity became a state religion in 324, though paganism was not persecuted. In 325 the great Church Council of Nicaea was held, in which the court sided against the Arians and the Nicene Creed was adopted. Yet it was only shortly before his death that Constantine received baptism. The story of his baptism at Rome by Pope **Sylvester I** in 326, and of the so-called *Donation of Constantine*, long treated as an argument for the temporal power of the papacy, is utterly unhistorical. His later years were vicious, seeing the execution of his eldest son Crispus (326) for treason and of his own second wife Fausta (327) on some similar charge. He proposed to divide the empire between his three sons by Fausta: **Constantius**, Constantine II and **Constans I**; but in 340 Constantine II lost his life in war with Constans.

CONSTANTINE IV (d.685) Roman emperor from 668 to 685, who gave up much territory to the Bulgarians, Serbs and Croats.

CONSTANTINE V COPRONYMUS (718–75) Byzantine emperor, son of **Leo III**, crowned co-emperor at the age of two. On the death of his father (741) he defeated a revolt by his brother-in-law, Artabasdus, and thereafter intensified Leo's iconoclastic policies. A well-managed Council of the church (754) promulgated the destruction of icons, inaugurating an era of persecution of the orthodox party. A talented leader of soldiers, Constantine directed numerous expeditions against the Bulgarians, whom he defeated in battle in 763 and 773, and died on campaign.

CONSTANTINE VII PORPHYROGENITUS (905–59) Byzantine emperor, son of Leo VI. Although crowned emperor in 911, for over 30 years he was overshadowed by his father-in-law, the regent Romanus Lacapenus, who created his own sons co-emperors, but in 945 a struggle within this family allowed Constantine to seize sole power. A scholar rather than a ruler by nature, he wrote or compiled numerous works of history and geography, including the life of his grandfather **Basil I**.

CONSTANTINE XI PALAEOLOGUS DRAGASES (1404–53) the last Byzantine emperor, fourth son of Manuel II and the Serbian princess, Helen Dragaš. During the reign of his elder brother, John VIII, he and his other brothers jointly ruled the despotate of Morea, a Byzantine apanage in the Peloponnese, and on John's death (1448) Constantine succeeded to an empire consisting of little more than Constantinople and its environs, threatened by the vast Ottoman empire which surrounded it. His proclamation of the union of the Greek Church with Rome (1452) secured only limited military assistance from the West and was repudiated by his indignant subjects. Powerless to prevent the inevitable Ottoman siege, Constantine died fighting in the final Turkish assault.

CONSTANTINE I (1868–1923) king of Greece, 1913–17 and 1920–22, son and successor of **George I**. As a military commander he was unsuccessful in the Turkish War of 1897, but led the Greeks to victory in the Balkan War (1912–13). Brother-in-law to Kaiser **William II** of Germany, he insisted on Greek neutrality in World War I, but was forced to retire in favour of his son Alexander by the rival government of **Eleutherios Venzelos** and the Allies in 1917. In 1920 he was restored to the throne by plebiscite, but after a military revolt in 1922, abdicated again in favour of his son **George II**.

CONSTANTINE II, or **XII** (1940–) king of Greece, 1964–73, son and successor of **Paul I**. Soon after his accession in 1964 he married Princess Anne-Marie, younger daughter of **Frederik IX** of Denmark and sister of Queen **Margarethe** of Denmark. In April 1967 the 'Colonels' Junta' seized power in a military coup; the king made an abortive attempt to regain power, and fled into exile in Rome in December. He was formally deposed in June 1973, and the monarchy was abolished by national referendum in 1974. His heir is Crown Prince Paul (b.1967).

CONSTANTINE, Learie Nicholas, Baron Constantine (1902–71) West Indian cricketer and statesman, born in Trinidad. The grandson of a slave, he became one of the great all-round cricketers. The need to earn a living in Lancashire league cricket restricted him to only 18 Tests, but his dynamic fast bowling, furiously aggressive batting and peerless fielding remain in the minds of all who saw them. Against Northamptonshire in 1928 he accomplished the rare feat of scoring a century and taking a 'hat-trick' of three wickets with consecutive balls in the same match. During World War II he was appointed to look after the interests of the West Indians who had been sent to Britain to help in the war effort. He took a law degree and became a fearless opponent of racial discrimination, bringing an action in 1944 against a London hotel which had refused him accommodation. For his services to cricket and the West Indian community he was awarded a life peerage.

CONSTANTINE NIKOLAEVICH (1827–92) Russian grandduke, the second son of Tsar **Nicholas I**. In the Crimean War he commanded the Russian fleet, and held the British and French in check before Kronstadt. In 1865 and 1878 he became president of the council; in 1882 he was dismissed for revolutionary views.

CONSTANTIUS CHLORUS (c.250–306) Roman emperor, nephew of Claudius II Gothicus and father of **Constantine the Great**. He became Caesar in 292, had Britain, Gaul and Spain as his government, and, after re-establishing Roman power in Britain and defeating the Alemanni, became Augustus in 305. He died at York in 306.

CONSTANTIUS (317–61) third son of **Constantine the Great**. He was Eastern Roman emperor 337–361. He fought against the Persians, and after the death in 350 of his brother **Constans I** became sole emperor.

CONTE, Lamsana (c.1945–) Guinean politician and soldier. Formerly military commander of the Boke Region of West Guinea, on the death of President Seke Toure in 1984 he led a bloodless coup and set up a Military Committee for National Recovery (CMRN), with himself as president. He has done much to restore Guinea's international standing, and thousands of exiles have returned. In 1985 an attempt to overthrow him was thwarted by loyal troops.

CONTI, Armand de Bourbon (1629–66) French nobleman, founder of the House of Conti, a junior branch of the House of Condé. The brother of Louis II, Prince de **Condé** (the Great Condé), he took his title from the little town of Conti, near Amiens. He married the niece of Cardinal **Mazarin**. Although feeble and deformed, he was an enthusiastic warrior, campaigning in Spain and Italy.

CONTI, François Louis (1664–1709) French nobleman, Prince de la Roche-sur-Lyon et de Conti, younger son of **Armand de Bourbon Conti**. He married a granddaughter of **Louis II, Prince de Condé** (the Great Condé), and fought with great distinction in Hungary, and later at the battles of Steinkerke and Neerwinden. In 1697 he was elected king of Poland, but found the throne occupied by the time he arrived to receive the crown. In 1709 he was appointed commander of a French army during the War of the Spanish Succession, but died before he could take the field.

CONWAY, Henry Seymour (1721–95) English soldier and politician, and nephew of Sir **Robert Walpole**. An MP for various pocket-boroughs (1741–84), he saw active service at Dettingen (1743) and Fontenoy (1875) in the War of the Austrian Succession (1740–48). In the 1745 Jacobite Rising he was aide-de-camp to the Duke of **Cumberland** at the battle of Culloden (1745). Appointed lieutenant-general in 1759, he was secretary of state from 1765 to 1768 and governor of Jersey from 1772 to 1795.

CONWAY, Hugh pseud of **Frederick John Fergus** (1847–85) auctioneer in Bristol. He wrote clever newspaper verse and tales, but his greatest success was the melodramatic, *Called Back* (1884), also popular as a play.

CONWAY, Moncure Daniel (1832–1907) American abolitionist, born in Stafford County, Virginia. A Methodist turned Unitarian preacher, he lectured in England on the Civil War and became a pastor in London (1864–97). He published *Demonology and Devil-lore* (1879), *Thomas Carlyle* (1881), *The Wandering Jew* (1881) and *Life of Paine* (1892).

CONYNGHAM, Barry Ernest (1944–) Australian composer, lecturer and performer, born in Sydney. He studied under **Peter Sculthorpe** at Sydney University and **Raymond Hanson** at the State Conservatorium. Influenced by jazz in his early years, Conyngham has also used computer-generated sound, which he actively promotes, in his works. Japanese influences are also strong in his work. Much of his varied output is for film or theatre, including an opera *Edward John Eyre* based on the life of the explorer, *The Ballad of Bony Anderson*, and another opera *Ned* about **Ned Kelly**. Conyngham's other works include a cello concerto, and *Southern Cross*, a double concerto for piano and violin written for **Roger Woodward** and Wanda Wilkomirska. His concerto for contrabass and orchestra, *Shadows of Noh* was premièred in San Diego, USA, by Bertram Turetzky in 1989.

COOK, Arthur James (1883–1931) Welsh miners' leader, born in Wookey, Somerset. A coal miner in the Rhondda and a leading figure in the South Wales branch of the union, he became general secretary of the national union in 1924 and was one of the miners' leaders during the General Strike of 1926. A powerful orator, he fought successfully to hold the union together after the strike.

COOK, Eliza (1818–89) English poet, daughter of a London tradesman. She contributed to magazines from an early age, and issued volumes of poetry in 1838, 1864 and 1865. She wrote *Eliza Cook's Journal* (1849–54), much of it republished as *Jottings from my Journal* (1860).

COOK, Frederick Albert (1865–1940) American explorer and physician, born in Calicoon Depot, New York State. He studied medicine at the universities of Columbia and New York, before being invited to join an Arctic expedition as surgeon to Greenland in 1891 led by **Robert E Peary**. Two further expeditions to Greenland followed in 1893 and 1894, and a Belgian expedition to the Antarctic in 1897 led by Adrien de Gerlache was recounted by Cook in *Through the Antarctic Night* (1900). In 1906 he claimed to have made the first ascent of the highest mountain in North America, Mount McKinley, Alaska, reported in *To the Top of the Continent* (1908). In 1908 he claimed to be the first man to reach the North Pole. On 3 July 1907 he sailed from Gloucester, Massachusetts, crossed Ellesmere Island, and reached Axel Heilberg Island on 17 March 1908. From here he set off with four Inuit (Eskimos), of whom only two were said to have reached the North Pole with him on 21 April 1908. Although he was treated as a hero on his return, his claim to the Pole was questioned by Peary, who said his own visit on 6 April 1909 was the first. An investigative committee set up by Copenhagen University discredited both Cook's claim to be the first man to the North Pole and his ascent of Mount McKinley. He denied this vehemently both in public and in *My Attainment of the Pole* (1911). His subsequent imprisonment for fraud in 1923 brought his character into further question, and although he was pardoned shortly before his death the controversy continues to the present day.

COOK, James (1728–79) English navigator, born at Marton, Cleveland, Yorkshire, the son of an agricultural labourer. After a short time in a haberdasher's shop at Staithes, he was bound apprentice to Whitby ship-owners, and spent several years in the coasting and Baltic trade. In 1755 he entered the navy, and in 1759 became master. He was for eight years engaged in surveying about the St Lawrence and the shores of Newfoundland. In 1768–71, in command of the *Endeavour*, he conveyed to the Pacific the expedition for observing the transit of Venus. On the return, New Zealand was circumnavigated and charted; the east coast of Australia was surveyed and claimed for Britain; the strait between Australia and New Guinea was sailed through, and the voyage completed by way of Java and the Cape of Good Hope. Cook, now a commander, was given control of a second voyage of discovery in the *Resolution* and *Adventure*, in 1772–75, to discover how far the lands of the Antarctic stretched northwards, and sailed round the edge of the ice, reaching 71° 10' S., in long. 110° 54' W. During the intervals between the Antarctic voyages, Cook visited Tahiti and the New Hebrides, and discovered New Caledonia and other groups. Owing to Cook's precautions, there was only one death among his crews during all the three years. His next and last voyage (1776–79) was to discover a passage round the north coast of America from the Pacific, and was by way of the Cape, Tasmania, New Zealand, the Pacific Islands, the Sandwich Islands (now discovered), and the west coast of North America, which he surveyed from 45° N. as far as Icy Cape in Bering Strait, where he was compelled to turn back, reaching Karakakoa Bay in Hawaii, in January 1779. The natives, at first friendly, suddenly changed their attitude; and on 14 February, when Cook landed with a party to recover a stolen boat, he was set upon with sudden fury, and killed. Cook did more than any other navigator to add to our knowledge of the Pacific and the Southern Ocean.

COOK, Peter (1937–) English comedian and actor. He first achieved prominence as one of the writers and performers of *Beyond the Fringe* (1960), and a sequel *Behind the Fringe* (1971–72). He invented the stage character E L Wisty, a forlorn figure perplexed by the complexities of life. From 1965 to 1971 he collaborated with Dudley Moore in the irreverent television programme, *Not Only... But Also*. He has made regular film appearances, notably in *The Bed Sitting Room* (1970), and has long been associated with the satirical magazine, *Private Eye*.

COOK, Stanley Arthur (1873–1949) English bible scholar, born in King's Lynn. From 1932 to 1938 he was professor of Hebrew at Cambridge and wrote on Old Testament history. His works include *The Place of the Old Testament in Modern Research* (1932) and *An Introduction to the Bible* (1945). He was joint editor of the *Cambridge Ancient History*.

COOK, Thomas (1808–92) British railway excursion and tourist pioneer, born in Melbourne, Derbyshire. His first railway trip (a temperance one) was made from Leicester to Loughborough in 1841.

COOKE, (Alfred) Alastair (1908–) English-born American journalist and broadcaster, born in Manchester. A sympathetic and urbane commentator on current affairs and popular culture in the USA, he has reported for several British newspapers, written numerous books, including *A Generation on Trial* (1950) and *One Man's America* (1952), and edited *The Vintage Mencken* (1954). His 'Letter from America', first broadcast by the BBC in 1946, is the longest-running solo radio feature programme.

COOKE, Benjamin (1734–93) English composer of glees and anthems. He was organist of Westminster Abbey from 1762, as from 1802 was his son, Robert, who drowned himself in 1814.

COOKE, Deryck Victor (1919–76) English writer and broadcaster on music, born in Leicester. A distinguished **Mahler** scholar, he published a book on the composer (1960) and completed a realization of Mahler's Tenth Symphony (premiered 1964). He also wrote perceptively on **Bruckner** and **Wagner** (notably a posthumously published study of *The Ring*, 'I Saw the World End', 1979).

COOKE, George Frederick (1756–1812) English actor, born in Westminster. He made his début at Brentford in 1776, and between 1784 and 1800 was one of the leading actors of his day despite his heavy drinking. From 1801 to 1810 he played at Covent Garden both in comedy and in tragedy, and rivalled **Kemble** in the public favour. In 1810 he visited America. A monument in New York marks his grave, erected in 1821 by **Edmund Kean**, who regarded Cooke as the greatest of actors.

COOKE, Thomas (1703–56) English author, born in Braintree, Essex, best known as the translator of **Hesiod**. His criticisms of **Pope** in his *Battle of the Poets* (1725) earned him a place in the *Dunciad*.

COOKE, Sir William Fothergill (1806–79) English inventor, born in Ealing. He studied medicine, took up telegraphy, and in 1837 became Sir **Charles Wheatstone**'s partner. In 1845 they patented the single needle apparatus; in 1846 Cooke formed a company, which paid £120000 for the partners' earlier patents. In 1867 he got the Albert gold medal.

COOKSON, Catherine Ann (1906–) English popular novelist, born in Tyne Dock, County Durham. Her fiction is set in the north-east of England and is replete with tragedy, exploitation and romance. The author of more than 40 books, including the Mallen trilogy and the Tilly Trotter series, she is a favourite among habituées of the public library. *Our Kate* (1969) is autobiographical.

COOKWORTHY, William (1705–80) English porcelain manufacturer, born in Kingsbridge, Devon. A Plymouth pharmacist and a Quaker, he was the discoverer of kaolin near St Austell, in 1756, and established a china factory near Plymouth.

COOLEY, Denton Arthur (1920–) American cardiac surgeon, born in Houston, Texas. He received his MD from the Johns Hopkins University Medical School and in 1954 joined the staff of the Baylor University College of Medicine, where he was professor of surgery from 1962 to 1969 as well as the founder (1962) and chief of the surgical division of the Texas Heart Institute in Houston. With **Michael De Bakey** and others, he pioneered open-heart surgery as well as the surgical treatment of diseases of the arteries, especially the treatment of aortic aneurysms by graft replacement.

COOLIDGE, Calvin (1872–1933) 30th president of the USA (1923–29), born in Plymouth, Vermont, the son of a farmer and storekeeper. He became a lawyer and then governor of Massachusetts (1919–20), where he achieved renown in decisively using the state militia to break the Boston police strike in 1919. Vice-president from 1921 to 1923, he succeeded as president on **Warren Harding**'s death and was triumphantly re-elected by the Republicans in 1924. His term as president was marked by economic prosperity.

COOLIDGE, Susan, pseud of **Sarah Chauncy Woolsey** (1835–1905) American children's writer and literary critic, born in Cleveland, Ohio. She wrote the *Katy* books and other stories for girls, in an easy natural style, free from contemporary sentimentality.

COOLIDGE, William Augustus Brevoort (1850–1926) American mountaineer and historian, born in New York. After ordination as an Anglican priest (1883) he moved to Switzerland to study its geography and history. As an Alpinist he made about 1750 ascents between 1865 and 1900, including the first winter ascent of the Jungfrau in 1874.

COOLIDGE, William David (1873–1975) American physical chemist, born in Hudson, Massachussetts, best known as the developer of the type of modern vacuum X-ray tube widely used in research, industry and medicine. Educated at Massachusetts Institute of Technology and Leipzig, he spent much of his career with the General Electric Company at Schenectady, New York, and worked on the Manhattan atomic bomb project in World War II.

COOMARASWAMY, Ananda (1877–1947) Ceylon-born Indian author and scholar. He was a leader of the 20th-century cultural revival in India, especially in the field of art.

COOMBS, Herbert Cole ('Nugget') (1906–) Australian economist and banker, born in Perth, Western Australia. After studying at the London School of Economics, he joined the [Australian] Commonwealth Bank as an assistant economist, moving to the Treasury in 1939. He became a member of the board of the Commonwealth Bank in 1942, governor of the bank in 1949 and chairman of the board in 1951. When the bank's regulatory and trading functions were separated in 1959, Coombs became the inaugural governor of the newly-created Reserve Bank of Australia, a position he held until he retired in 1968. He was personal adviser to seven Australian prime ministers, and his opinion was accepted by both sides of the political spectrum. He also held other important positions, especially in the arts. Actively concerned in the affairs of the Australian National University, Canberra, he became pro-chancellor in 1959 and chancellor of the university in 1968. A keen supporter of environmental issues, he delivered the ABC's Boyer Lectures, 'The Fragile Pattern, Institutions and Man' in 1970.

COON, Carleton Stevens (1904–81) American anthropologist, born in Wakefield, Massachusetts. Educated at Harvard, he was professor there from 1934 to 1948, and at Pennsylvania (1948–63). His many archaeological expeditions led him to discover the remains of Aterian fossil man (N Africa, 1939), Hotu man (Iran, 1951) and Jebel Ighoud man No. 2 (Sierra Leone, 1965). His books included *A Reader in General Anthropology* (1948), *The Story of Man* (1954), *The Seven Caves* (1957) and the now discredited *Origin of Races* (1962).

COONEY, Ray (Raymond) (1932–) English dramatist, director and producer, born in London. He made his début as an actor in *Song of Norway* (1946), and appeared in several stage comedies and farces in the 1950s and 1960s. Best known as an author and director, his own first play, a farce, *One for the Pot*, appeared in 1961, and was followed by many others, including *Chase Me Comrade* (1964), *Move Over, Mrs Markham* (1969), *Two Into One* (1981), *Run for your Wife* (1983), and *Wife Begins at Forty* (1986). In 1983 he created the Theatre of Comedy, based at the Shaftesbury Theatre, London.

COOPER, Sir Alfred Duff, 1st Viscount Norwich (1890–1954) English politician, educated at Eton and Oxford. He served with the Grenadier Guards in World War I and was elected to parliament as a Conservative in 1924, becoming secretary for war 1935–37. He resigned from the office of First Lord of the Admiralty in 1938 in protest against **Chamberlain**'s 'appeasement' policy, but became minister of information under **Churchill** (1940–42), and ambassador to France (1944–47). He wrote lives of **Talleyrand** (1932), **Haig** (1935) and King **David** (1943), and other books. In 1919 he married Lady Diana Manners (1892–), daughter of the Duke of Rutland, who acted a leading role in **Max Reinhardt**'s famous *The Miracle* (1911–12). See her *Rainbow Comes and Goes* (1958), *The Light of Common Day* (1959), and *Trumpets from the Steep* (1960).

COOPER, Ashley See **SHAFTESBURY, Anthony Ashley Cooper**

COOPER, Sir Astley (1768–1841) English surgeon, born, a clergyman's son, at Brooke Hall, Norfolk. After studying in London and Edinburgh, he lectured on anatomy at St Thomas's Hospital (1789) and at the College of Surgeons (1793). In 1800 he became surgeon to Guy's Hospital, and in 1813 professor of comparative anatomy in the College of Surgeons. In his work he raised surgery from its primitive state to a science. He was the first man to tie the abdominal aorta in treating an aneurysm. In 1820 he removed a tumour from the head of King **George IV**, and was made a baronet, and in 1828 was appointed sergeant-surgeon to the king. His major work on *Anatomy and Surgical Treatment of Hernia* appeared in 1804–7, followed by *Dislocations and Fractures* (1822), *Anatomy and Diseases of the Breast* (1829–40), and *Anatomy of the Thymus Gland* (1832).

COOPER, Charles Alfred (1829–1916) English journalist, and editor of *The Scotsman* from 1876 to 1906, a Yorkshire Roman Catholic by birth. Educated at Hull Grammar School, he started his career as sub-editor on the *Hull Advertiser*. He went to London in 1861 to become a House of Commons reporter for the *Morning Star*, and was sub-editor (1862–68) before going to Edinburgh as assistant to Alexander Russel, editor of *The Scotsman*, whom he succeeded. He shared something of Russel's reform convictions, and was deeply impressed by **Rosebery**, rapidly becoming the rising star of Scottish Liberalism. He welcomed Rosebery's campaigns which ultimately resulted in the creation of the Scottish Office, but he broke from **Gladstone** on the first Irish Home Rule Bill and *The Scotsman* remained Unionist thereafter. He increased advertising, shrewdly bargaining goodwill in newspaper coverage. He travelled in Egypt and South Africa, publishing his reports (1891, 1895). His *An Editor's Retrospect* (1896) is valuable, perhaps being franker than he realized.

COOPER, Edith Emma See **FIELD, Michael**

COOPER, Gary (1901–61) American film actor, born in Helena, Montana. Originally a cartoonist, he moved to Los Angeles and began working as an extra and stunt rider in western films. A bit part in 1926 brought him a contract with Paramount Pictures and several years of minor roles before his work as the laconic cowboy in *The Virginian* (1929) made him a star. He spent the next three decades projecting a similar image: peace-loving and courageously determined. In light comedy and high adventure his many noteworthy credits include *The Lives of a Bengal Lancer* (1935), *For Whom the Bell Tolls* (1943) and *Friendly Persuasion* (1956). He won Academy Awards for his performances as the World War I Quaker hero *Sergeant York* (1941) and as the sheriff who stood alone in *High Noon* (1952).

COOPER, Dame Gladys (1888–1971) English actress, born in London. She made her début in 1905 and leapt to fame as Paula in *The Second Mrs Tanqueray* (1922). She achieved success in films as well as on the stage.

COOPER, James Fenimore (1789–1851) American novelist, born in Burlington, New Jersey. His father, a wealthy Quaker and Federalist member of Congress, moved to Cooperstown, New York, then in a wild frontier region of great natural beauty. Cooper entered Yale College in 1803, but was expelled during his third year for a prank. In 1806 he shipped as a common sailor, and in 1808 entered the navy as midshipman. He rose to the rank of lieutenant, but in 1811 resigned his commission and married Susan, a sister of Bishop De Lancey of New York, and settled down as a country gentleman. His first novel, *Precaution* (1819), was a failure; and the 32 which followed it were of uneven quality. The best were the stories of the sea and of Red Indians—*The Spy* (1821), *The Pilot* (1823), *The Last of the Mohicans* (1826), *The Prairie* (1826), *The Red Rover* (1827), *The Bravo* (1831), *The Pathfinder* (1840), *The Deerslayer* (1841), *The Two Admirals* (1842), *Wing-and-Wing* (1842) and *Satanstoe* (1845). His other writings include a scholarly *Naval History of the United States* (1839), and *Lives of Distinguished American Naval Officers* (1846). After visiting England and France, he was American consul at Lyons (1826–29), and then travelled in Switzerland and Italy till 1831. His later years were much disturbed by literary and newspaper controversies and litigation.

COOPER, John, also called **Giovanni Coprario** (c.1570–1626) English composer who studied in Italy and retained his Italianized name after his return to England in 1604. Winning a high reputation for his compositions, which include masques, songs and instrumental works as well as church music, he became music master to the children of **James VI and I** and to the composers William and **Henry Lawes**.

COOPER, Leon Neil (1930–) American physicist, and Nobel prize-winner, born in New York. Educated at Columbia University he contributed to the BCS (Bardeen-Cooper-Schrieffer) theory of superconductivity. After brief spells at the Institute for Advanced Study, Princeton, and the University of Illinois, where he collaborated with **John Bardeen** and **John Schrieffer**, followed by Ohio State University, he moved to Brown University, Providence, and was appointed professor of physics in 1962. He made a theoretical prediction that at low temperatures electrons in a conductor could act in bound pairs (Cooper pairs). The BCS theory accounts for superconductivity as being due to the fact that these pairs can move through a lattice with zero scattering by impurities because the pair is much larger than any impurity atom. All three shared the 1972 Nobel prize for physics.

COOPER, Paul (1869–1933) English architect and jeweller, born in London. He entered the office of J D Seddings in 1889, where he undertook architectural work for the Duke of Portland. He took lessons in jewellery in 1890 and was appointed head of the metalwork department at Birmingham School of Art in 1901. He abandoned his architectural career in 1898, enabling him to devote his time entirely to craft-work which dominated the rest of his working life. He produced an enormous amount of jewellery work throughout his career, all of which was meticulously detailed in his stock books.

COOPER, Peter (1791–1883) American manufacturer, inventor and philanthropist, born in New York. After starting a cloth-shearing business, a grocery store, and a glue factory, he erected the Canton Iron Works in Baltimore in 1828, and in 1830 built there *Tom Thumb*, the first locomotive engine ever made in America. He afterwards built an iron-wire factory in

New York and blast-furnaces in Pennsylvania; and helped Cyrus West in promoting the laying of the Atlantic cable. He invented a washing machine and many other devices. To provide the working classes with educational advantages, he erected and endowed the Cooper Union (1854–59) in New York.

COOPER, Samuel (1609–72) English miniaturist. His sitters included **Cromwell**, Mrs Samuel Pepys, **Milton**, **George Monck** and **Cosimo III de' Medici**, and he also produced several portraits of monarchs and nobility in the royal collection. His work is in the true oil portrait style, as distinct from the tinted drawing of earlier schools.

COOPER, Susie (Susan Vera) (1902–) English ceramic designer. She studied at Burslem School of Art under **Gordon Forsyth**, and set up her own firm in 1929 where she purchased earthenware from local firms which were decorated with her individual designs of simple patterns: coloured bands and polka dots and animals and flowers. She also used lithographic transfers and received her first major orders in 1935. She became the first royal designer for industry and has since received many important commissions which show the diversity and originality of her work. In 1961 her firm merged with R H & S L Plant which became part of the Wedgwood Group in 1966.

COOPER, or **COUPER, Thomas** (c.1517–1594) English prelate and lexicographer, born in Oxford, a tailor's son. Master of Magdalen College School, Oxford (1549–68), bishop of Lincoln (1570) and bishop of Winchester (1584), he published a *Thesaurus Linguae Romanae et Britannicae* (1565), which became known as 'Cooper's Dictionary'.

COOPER, Thomas (1805–92) English Chartist and poet, born in Leicester. Apprenticed to a shoemaker at Gainsborough, he taught himself Latin, Greek, Hebrew and French, and at 23 turned schoolmaster and Methodist preacher. He became leader of the Leicester Chartists in 1841, and got two years for sedition in Stafford jail. Here he wrote *The Purgatory of Suicides*, a poem in the Spenserian stanza, and *Wise Saws and Modern Instances* (1845). He published two novels, *Aldermand Ralph* (1853) and *The Family Feud* (1854), and in 1855 became a Christian lecturer.

COOPER, Thomas Mackay, Lord, of Culross of Dunnet (1892–1955) Scottish judge and legal scholar, born in Edinburgh. Educated at George Watson's College and Edinburgh University, he was successively lord advocate (1938), lord justice-clerk (1941) and lord justice-general of Scotland and lord president of the Court of Session (1947). An outstanding judge and leader of the court, in his judgments he stressed reliance on Scottish principles rather than incautious following of English precedents. Many of his judgments are of great and permanent value. He was also keenly interested in legal history and published *Select Scottish Cases of the Thirteenth Century* (1944) and edited *The Register of Brieves* (1946) and **Skene**'s *Regiam Majestatem* (1947).

COOPER, Tommy (1922–84) Welsh comic and magician, born in Caerphilly, Glamorgan. He first became interested in magic when given a present of tricks as a child. A member of the Horse Guards (1939–46), he began performing with the Combined Services Entertainment in the Middle East where he acquired his trademark headgear of a red fez. In 1947 he appeared at the Windmill Theatre and refined his act in clubs and music halls before achieving television renown in numerous variety shows and his own 1950s series *It's Magic*. His act thrived on his apparently inexpert ability to misperform elaborate tricks. He also made occasional appearances in films like *The Plank* (1967). He died during the transmission of the television show *Live From Her Majesty's*.

COOTE, Sir Eyre (1726–83) Anglo-Irish soldier born in Ash Hill, County Limerick. He entered the army early and saw service in Scotland, and from 1756 to 1762 served in India. It was he who induced **Clive** to risk the battle of Plassey (1757). In 1760 he defeated **Lally** at Wandiwash and his capture of Pondicherry in 1761 completed the downfall of the French in India. In 1777 he became commander-in-chief in India, and in 1781, his rout of **Haidar Ali** at Porto Novo saved the presidency for a second time.

COPE, Edward Drinker (1840–97) American naturalist and palaeontologist, born in Philadelphia. Professor at the university of Pennsylvania from 1889, he was a noted hunter of vertebrate fossils, and contributed materially to the discussion of evolution. His great rival in the fossil field was **Othniel Charles Marsh**.

COPE, Sir John (d.1760) English soldier. He was commissioned in the cavalry in 1707 and in the War of the Austrian Succession (1740–48) and in 1742 commanded the troops sent to assist the Empress **Maria Theresa** in 1742. On the landing of Prince **Charles Edward Stuart** in 1745, he was appointed commander-in-chief of the forces in Scotland. After a fruitless march to the Highlands, he returned by sea to Dunbar, and was routed at Prestonpans. He was held to ridicule in the song 'Hey, Johhny Cope'.

COPEAU, Jacques (1879–1949) French theatrical manager. As co-founder of the *Nouvelle Revue française* in 1908 and manager of the Théâtre du Vieux-Colombier, he had a profound influence on French dramatic art.

COPELAND, William Taylor (1797–1868) English china manufacturer, born probably at Stoke, son of William Copeland, the partner of **Spode**. He managed the Spode concerns in Stoke and London, from 1827 to 1833, later gaining control, and from 1846 onwards produced Parian (imitation marble) groups and statuettes, and bone china. He also invented a filter press for working clay, and was one of the founders of the North Staffordshire Railway. In 1835 he was Lord Mayor of London, and from 1837 to 1852 and 1857 to 1865 MP for Stoke-on-Trent.

COPER, Hans (1920–81) German-born British studio potter. He trained as an engineer before arriving in England in 1939, and worked with the Pioneer Corps before joining the Studio of **Lucie Rie** as an assistant in 1947. He contributed works to her Berkeley Galleries Exhibitions in 1950 and 1951, and in 1958 established his own workshop in Hertfordshire. His work mainly consisted of thrown vases which are more sculptural and decorative than domestic. He worked as a consultant to a development group concerned with the use of clay products in building. Originally a painter and sculptor, he is widely remembered as one of the most influential of British studio potters. He moved to London in 1969 and later to Somerset.

COPERARIO See **COOPER, JOHN**

COPERNICUS, Nicolas (1473–1543) Polish astronomer, and the founder of modern astronomy, born in Toruń, Poland. His father was a Germanized Slav, his mother a German; Poland and Germany both claim the honour of producing him. Brought up under his uncle, the bishop of Ermeland, from 1491 on he studied mathematics, optics and perspective at Cracow University, and in 1496 canon law at Bologna. In 1497 he was appointed canon of Frauenburg, the cathedral city of Ermeland, on the Frisches Haff. The year 1500 he spent at Rome, where he lectured on astronomy, and (6 November) 'observed an eclipse of the moon'. In 1501 he began the study of medicine at Padua; in 1503 he was made doctor of canon law at Ferrara; in 1505 he left Italy for Prussia. 'Scholasticus' of Breslau till 1538, and canon of Frauenburg, he never became a priest. As medical attendant and secretary to his uncle, he lived with him (1507–12) in the princely castle of Heilsberg, 46 miles from Frauenburg. After his uncle's death in 1512, he lived at Frauenburg, not merely studying the stars, but executing with vigour the offices of bailiff, military governor, judge, tax collector, vicar-general, physician and reformer of the coinage. His difficulties were increased by the intrigues and wars by which West Prussia was restored to the Teutonic Knights and incorporated with Brandenburg. His *De Revolutionibus*, proving the sun to be the centre of the universe, was completed in 1530 and published just before his death in 1543. He also published a Latin translation of the Epistles of Theophylactus Simocatta and a treatise on trigonometry.

COPLAND, Aaron (1900–) American composer, born in Brooklyn, New York. He studied under Rubin Goldmark, the teacher of **George Gershwin** in New York, and followed this with three years of study in France, under **Nadia Boulanger**. His music quickly gained appreciation after his return to America in 1924, and a Guggenheim Fellowship—the first to be awarded to a composer—in 1925 marked the progress of his reputation. A series of early works influenced by **Stravinsky**, neoclassical in outlook and employing jazz idioms, was followed by compositions in which he tapped a deeper vein of American tradition and folk music, of which the ballets *Billy the Kid* (1938) and *Appalachian Spring* (1944), and *A Lincoln Portrait* (1942), for orator and orchestra, are typical. As well as ballets and impressive film scores, he has composed two operas and three symphonies. He published his autobiography, *Composer from Brooklyn* in 1984.

COPLESTON, Frederick Charles (1907–) English Catholic philosopher, born near Taunton and educated at Marlborough. He entered the Society of Jesus in 1930 and was ordained in 1937; he became professor at Heythrop College in 1939 and at the Gregorian University in Rome in 1952. He has published many critical studies of philosophers and is the author of the monumental eight-volume *A History of Philosophy* (1946–66). He took part in a famous broadcast debate with **Bertrand Russell** in 1948 on 'the existence of God'.

COPLEY, Sir Godfrey (d.1709) English philanthropist, born in Yorkshire. He left a fund in trust to the Royal Society which has been applied since 1736 to the provision of the annual 'Copley Medal' for philosophical research.

COPLEY, John Michael Harold (1933–) English theatrical producer, born in Birmingham. After a brief career on the stage, Copley became stage manager at Sadler's Wells in 1953, both for the ballet and the opera companies. In 1960 he joined the Covent Garden Opera Company as deputy stage manager, becoming resident producer in 1972. He has since produced most of the standard operatic repertoire, both at Covent Garden and at the London Coliseum, and also the Royal Silver Jubilee Gala at Covent Garden in 1977. He has produced for many opera houses and festivals in Europe, the USA and Canada, and has had a long and successful connection with the Australian Opera since his *Fidelio* in 1970, with productions including *Zauberflote* in 1973, and the Australian première of **Janáček**'s *Jenufa*. He has also directed for the Victorian State Opera.

COPLEY, John Singleton (1737–1815) American portrait and historical painter, born in Boston, Massachusetts, of Anglo-Irish parents, lately of Limerick. At 16 he was executing portraits; in 1755 **Washington** sat for him. In 1774 he left for England, where he was well received by **Reynolds**, **West** and **Strange**, and was commissioned to paint the king and queen for Governor Wentworth. He studied in Italy, and returned to London at the end of 1776. *The Death of Chatham* (1779–80) and the still finer *Death of Major Peirson* (1783) are both in the Tate Gallery. Other works include an enormous canvas of the Siege of Gibraltar painted for the City of London (1786–91) and a group of the royal princesses in Buckingham Palace. His son was the future Lord **Lyndhurst**.

COPPARD, Alfred Edgar (1878–1957) English short-story writer and poet, born in Folkestone. His schooling ceased when he was nine, and after being an office boy, then an accountant, he became a professional writer in 1919. In 1921 he published *Adam and Eve and Pinch Me*, and soon became celebrated for his tales of country life and character. His prose is remarkable for its detailed observation and poetic quality. Other volumes of stories include *The Black Dog* (1923), *The Field of Mustard* (1926) and *Lucy in Her Pink Jacket* (1954). His *Collected Poems* appeared in 1928. His autobiography *It's Me, O Lord!* was published in 1957.

COPPÉE, François (1842–1908) French poet, born in Paris. For three years a war-office clerk, he soon turned to poetry, and with *Le Relinquaire* (1866) and *Les Intimités* (1867) gained the front rank of the 'Parnassiens'. Later volumes of poetry were *Les Humbles* (1872), *Le Cahier rouge* (1874), *Olivier* (his one long poem), *Les Récits et les élégies* and *Contes en vers*. His earliest dramatic poem, *Le Passant* (1869), owed much to **Sarah Bernhardt**, and was followed by *Deux Douleurs*, *L'Abandonnée*, *Le Luthier de Crémone*, *La Guerre de Cent Ans*, *Madame de Maintenon* (1881), *Severo Torelli* (1883), *Les Jacobites* (1885), *Le Pater* (1890), *Pour la couronne* (1895). He won fame in yet another field with his *Contes en prose*, *Vingt Contes nouveaux*, and *Contes rapides*.

COPPI, Fausto (1919–60) Italian racing cyclist. Although his career was interrupted by World War II he won the Tour of Italy five times and the Tour de France twice, the first man to win both in the same year (1949 and 1952). His riding skill depended on strength, tenacity and a fast start rather than sheer pace, and his finishing sprint was always unremarkable, although his winning margins were often huge.

COPPOLA, Francis Ford (1939–) American filmmaker, born in Detroit, Michigan. A graduate of the University of California, Los Angeles, he worked on low-budget productions before being allowed to direct the horror film *Dementia 13* (1963). An accomplished screenwriter, he won an Academy Award for *Patton* (1970); and throughout his career his prodigious directorial output has interspersed epic statements on power and patriarchy with more intimate portraits of personal failure and alienation. The commercial success of *The Godfather* (1972) and, to a lesser extent, *Apocalypse Now* (1979) allowed him to form his own company, American Zoetrope, which has supported directors like George Lucas and **Wim Wenders**. Beset by monetary difficulties throughout the 1980s, he has still created works as diverse as the romance *One from the Heart* (1982), the existentialist *Rumble Fish* (1983) and *Tucker* (1988), a biography of the maverick automobile designer Preston Tucker, that suggested a strong affinity with the director's own quest for independence and innovation.

COQUELIN, Benoît Constant (1841–1909) French actor, known as Coquelin aîné, born a baker's son in Boulogne. He was admitted to the conservatoire in 1859, and made his début at the Théâtre Français in

1860. Here, and after 1897 at the Porte St Martin, he played with continued success, both in classical pieces and in roles created by himself, standing unrivalled in the broader aspects of comedy.

CORAM, Thomas (c.1668–1751) English philanthropist, born in Lyme Regis, Dorset. A shipwright by trade, he went to America in 1693 and settled at Taunton, Massachusetts (1694–1704). There he strengthened the Anglican church, and promoted settlement schemes in Georgia and Nova Scotia. Back in London (c.1720) he projected and founded the Foundling Hospital (1741), of which **Hogarth** was a patron.

CORBET, Richard (1582–1635) English poet and prelate, the son of a gardener in Ewell, Surrey. He was educated at Westminster School then passed to Oxford, and in 1620 was made dean of Christ Church. In 1624 he was consecrated bishop of Oxford, and in 1632 translated to Norwich. His *Certaine Elegant Poems* (1647) reflect the jovial temper of the man. His longest piece is *Iter Boreale*, a holiday tour of four students; the best and best known is the *Fairies' Farewell*.

CORBETT, 'Gentleman Jim' (James John) (1866–1933) American pugilist and World Champion. Born in San Francisco, he won the world heavyweight championship in 1892 by knocking out **John L Sullivan** in the 21st round, and lost it in 1897 to **Robert Fitzsimmons** in the 4th round. He failed to regain his title in two fights with his former sparring partner, **James J Jeffries**, in 1900 and 1903. Corbett, who is said to have introduced 'science' into the art of pugilism, also made several appearances on stage and in films.

CORBETT, Ronnie (Ronald Balfour) (1930–) Scottish comedian, born in Edinburgh. After national service in the RAF and 18 months as a civil servant in the department of agriculture, he branched out into showbusiness via amateur dramatics, seaside shows and stand-up comedy, making an early film appearance in *You're Only Young Once* (1952). Spotted in Danny La Rue's nightclub by **David Frost**, he appeared on television in *The Frost Report* (1966–67) and *Frost on Sunday* (1968–69). His diminutive stature, impish sense of fun and inimitably discursive delivery of comic monologues soon gained him national popularity and his own series have included *No, That's Me Over Here* (1970) and *Sorry!* (1981–88). A fruitful partnership with **Ronnie Barker** led to the long-running *The Two Ronnies* (1971–87) and numerous cabaret appearances. His stage work includes *Twang!* (1965) and many pantomimes, notably *Cinderella* (1971–72) at the London Palladium. Later film appearances comprise *Casino Royale* (1967) and *No Sex Please, We're British* (1972). A keen amateur golfer, he has written *Armchair Golf* (1986).

CORBIN, Arthur Linton (1874–1967) American legal scholar, born in Linn County, Kansas. Educated at the University of Kansas and Yale, he taught for many years at Yale where he transformed the educational system. His major interest was contract law, a field in which he was the national leader, and his major work was *A Comprehensive Treatise on the Working Rules of Contract Law* (1950). He also produced many smaller works on contract law and numerous scholarly articles.

CORDAY, Charlotte, in full **Marie Charlotte Corday d'Armont** (1768–93) French murderess, born in St Saturnin near Sées (Orne). Despite her aristocratic background she initially welcomed the French Revolution. The behaviour of the Jacobins, however, so horrified her that she resolved to kill one of the chief revolutionaries, either **Robespierre** or **Marat**. Going to Paris, and hearing of Marat's demand for 200 000 more victims, she gained admittance to his house by pretending to be a messenger. When she arrived Marat was having a bath, and his heartless comment about the fugitive Girondists ('I will have them all guillotined at Paris') incited her to stab him to death. Unrepentant, she was brought before the Revolutionary Tribunal and guillotined.

CORDOBES, El, real name **Manuel Benitez Pérez** (1937–) Spanish matador, born in Palma del Rio. The idol of the crowds in the 1960s, his athleticism and vulgarity in the ring shocked purists who saw him as more of an acrobat than a torero, but his theatrical style and disregard of danger made him the highest paid matador in history. He retired in 1972.

CORDOVO See **GONSALVO DE CORDOBA**

CORELLI, Arcangelo (1653–1713) Italian composer, surnamed 'Il divino', born in Fusignano near Bologna. His Concerti grossi and his solo and trio sonatas for violin mark an epoch in chamber music, and had great influence on **J S Bach** and on contemporary string technique.

CORELLI, Marie, pseud of **Mary Mackay** (1855–1924) English popular romantic novelist, born in London, the illegitimate child of Charles Mackay, a journalist, and Ellen Mills, a widow whom he later married as his second wife. She was educated by governesses and trained as a pianist, but though accomplished her métier was writing, to which she devoted herself from 1885. *A Romance of Two Worlds* (1886) marked the beginning of an unprecedented career as a bestseller. A self-righteous, sentimental moralist, lacking self-criticism or a sense of the absurd, she was the writer that critics loved to hate. Later in a prolific career she refused reviewers access to her latest books, but her aficionados included **Gladstone** and **Oscar Wilde** and her readership was immense. Her novels include *Thelma* (1887), *Barabbas* (1893), *God's Good Man* (1904), *The Devil's Motor* (1910), *Eyes of the Sea* (1917) and *The Secret Power* (1921).

CORI, Carl Ferdinand (1896–1984) Czech-born American biochemist, born in Prague; he and his wife, Gerty Theresa Cori (1896–1957), also a biochemist, shared the 1947 Nobel prize for physiology or medicine, only the third husband-and-wife team to do so after the **Curies** in 1903 and the **Joliot-Curies** in 1935. They both studied medicine at Prague, marrying when they graduated, and at Trieste. In 1922 they emigrated to the USA, and both became professors at the Medical School at the Washington University in St Louis from 1931. They conducted research into carbohydrate metabolism and the enzymes of animal tissue. They shared the Nobel prize with **Bernardo Houssay**. After Gerty's death, Cori worked at the Massachusetts General Hospital, from 1967.

CORINTH, Louis (1858–1925) German painter, born in Tapiau, East Prussia. He studied at Königsberg and Munich and under **Bouguereau** in Paris. From conventional nude, landscape painting and especially portraiture, his style became markedly Impressionistic, as in *Under the Chandelier* (1905), *After a Bathe* (1906) and his many *Waldensee* views, while later work, eg, *Georg Brandes* (1924), verged on Expressionism. From 1900 he lived in Berlin and with **Marx Liebermann** and **Slevogt** led the secession movement, of which he became president (1915) against the Berlin academic school.

CORIOLANUS, Gaius, or **Gnaeus Marcius** (5th century BC) legendary Roman hero, so named from the courage he showed at the capture of the Volscian town of Corioli (439 BC). Later banished from Rome, he took refuge with the Volscians, and aided them against Rome. His victories alarmed the Romans, who on his approach (488 BC) sent deputations to plead with him.

He was deaf to every entreaty. At last, the noblest matrons, headed by his mother Veturia, and his wife Volumnia, leading her two children, came to his tent. Their tears moved him, and he led back the Volsci.

CORK, Earl of See **BOYLE**

CORKERY, Daniel (1878–1964) Irish cultural leader, born in Cork. Educated at University College, Cork, he was professor of English there from 1931 to 1947. He published a collection of short stories, *A Munster Twilight* (1917), depicting ethnic and class division in Irish life, and a novel, *The Threshold of Quiet* (1917). He made a great attack on the literary historians who saw Ireland in terms of the 18th-century 'Big House', in his *The Hidden Ireland* (1925). He profoundly influenced new Irish writers such as **Frank O'Connor** and **Sean O'Faolain** and his love of the Irish language was the basis of his literary evangelism, as revealed in his *The Fortunes of the Irish Language* (1954). He also wrote *Synge and Anglo-Irish Literature* (1931) and several plays. He was elected to the Irish Senate in 1951.

CORLISS, George Henry (1817–88) American engineer and inventor, born in Easton, New York. Of his many improvements to the steam engine the most important were the Corliss valve with separate inlet and exhaust ports, and his use of springs to assist in opening and closing valves more quickly. In 1856 he founded the Corliss Engine Co which for the Philadelphia Centennial Exhibition of 1876 supplied a huge 1400 hp engine which worked continuously for six months, driving all the machines in the exhibition.

CORMACK, Allan (1924–) South African-born American physicist, joint winner of the 1979 Nobel prize for physiology or medicine. He studied physics and engineering at Cape Town University and did graduate work at Cambridge. He worked as a medical physicist at Groote Shuur Hospital in Johannesburg before moving to the USA as professor of physics at Tufts University in 1956. His work pioneered the development of computerized axial X-ray tomography scanning (CAT). He shared the Nobel prize with the English electrical engineer, Sir **Godfrey Hounsfield**, who had independently developed a similar device.

CORNARO, Caterina (1454–1510) Venetian noblewoman, cousin of Cardinal **Bembo**, and queen of Cyprus from 1473 to 1489. She succeeded her husband, James II, on the throne at his death eight months after their marriage. In 1489 she was forced to abdicate in favour of a Venetian republic, and set up a kind of court for poets and scholars at Asolo, near Bassano.

CORNARO, Luigi Alvise (1475–1566) Venetian architect, author of *Discorsi della vita sobria*. At the age of 40, finding his health much impaired by intemperance, he adopted strict rules both in meat and drink, and lived to a cheerful old age. He was 83 years old when he published his celebrated book, which was translated into English in 1779.

CORNEILLE, Guillaume, properly **Cornélis van Beverloo** (1922–) Belgian painter, born in Liége. A leading European exponent of 'action' painting, his works include *Drawing in Colour*, belonging to the 'and the country loses itself in Infinity' series (1955), and *Summer Flowers* (1958).

CORNEILLE, Pierre (1606–84) French dramatist, born in Rouen, where he tried to obtain a barrister's practice. In 1629 he removed to Paris, where his comedy *Mélite*, already performed at Rouen, proved highly successful. It was followed by *Clitandre*, *La Veuve*, *La Galerie du Palais*, *La Suivante* and *La Place Royale*. In these early pieces intricate and extravagant plots are handled with ingenuity, but the writer's poetic genius flashes out only in occasional verses. For a time Corneille was one of **Richelieu**'s 'five poets', engaged to compose plays on lines laid down by the cardinal; among the pieces thus produced were *Les Tuileries*, *L'Aveugle de Smyrne* and *La Grande Pastorale*. Corneille, however was too independent to retain Richelieu's favour. *Médée* (1635) showed a marked advance on his earlier works; and in 1636 *Le Cid* took Paris by storm. Richelieu ordered his literary retainers to write it down; but adverse criticism was powerless against the general enthusiasm. *Horace*, founded on the story of the Horatii, and *Cinna*, appeared in 1639; *Polyeucte*, a noble tragedy, in 1640; and *La Mort de Pompée* in 1641. *Le Menteur* (1642) entitles Corneille to be called the father of French comedy as well as of French tragedy. *Théodore* was brought out in 1645, and *Rodogune* in 1646. Between 1647—when he was made an academician—and 1653 Corneille produced *Héraclius*, *Don Sanche d'Aragon*, *Andromède*, *Nicomède*, and *Pertharite*. These pieces, of which the last was damned, show a decline in dramatic and poetic power; and Corneille occupied himself with a verse translation of the *Imitatio Christi*. He returned to the stage in 1659 with *Œdipe*, which was followed by *La Toison d'or*, *Sertorius*, *Sophonisbe*, *Othon*, *Agésilas*, *Attila*, and *Tite et Bérénice* (1670). In 1671 he joined **Molière** and Quinault in writing the opera *Psyché*. His last works were *Pulchérie* (1672) and *Suréna* (1674). After his marriage in 1640 he lived habitually in Rouen until 1662, when he settled in Paris. During his later years his popularity waned before that of **Racine**, whose cause was espoused by **Boileau** and the king. A master of the Alexandrine verse form, he concerned himself with moral and mental conflict rather than physical action.

CORNEILLE, Thomas (1625–1709) French playwright, brother of **Pierre Corneille**, born in Rouen. He was a dramatist of merit, his tragedies—*Camma*, *Laodice*, *Pyrrhus*, *Bérénice*, *Timocrate*, *Ariane*, *Bradamante*, and others—being in general superior to his comedies. He also wrote a verse translation of **Ovid**'s *Metamorphoses*.

CORNELIA See **GRACCHUS**

CORNELIUS, Peter (1824–74) German composer, born in Mainz, the nephew of **Peter von Cornelius**. Going to Weimar in 1852, he became devoted to **Liszt**, **Wagner** and the New German school, and produced his famous comic opera, *The Barber of Baghdad* (a failure in 1858), and his grand opera, *Der Cid* (1865).

CORNELIUS, Peter von (1783–1867) German painter, born in Düsseldorf. In 1811 he joined the group of **Veit, Friedrich**, **Schadow** and **Overbeck** in Rome, and aided in the decoration of the Casa Bartoldi. From Rome he went to Düsseldorf, where he became director of the academy; in 1819 he was called to Munich. Here he remained till 1841, and executed the large frescoes of Greek mythology in the Glyptothek and the New Testament frescoes in the Ludwigskirche, which was built to give scope for his genius. In 1841 he was appointed director of the Berlin Academy. Among his productions at Berlin are the frescoes for the Campo Santo, or royal burial place, the finest being his *Four Riders of the Apocalypse*.

CORNELIUS NEPOS See **NEPOS**

CORNELL, Ezra (1807–74) American industrialist and philanthropist, and one of the co-founders of Cornell University, born in Westchester Landing, New York. He began as a carpenter and millwright, and in association with **Samuel Morse** devised insulation for telegraph wires on poles. He founded and organized telegraph companies, including the Western Union Telegraph in 1855. In 1865, in association with Andrew Dickson White, he founded and heavily endowed

Cornell University, which opened in Ithaca, New York, in 1868.

CORNELL, Joseph (1903–72) American artist, born in Nyach, New York. A self-taught artist, he was one of the first exponents of a form of sculpture called 'assemblage', in which unrelated objects are brought together to create new forms and sometimes suprising juxtapositions. His 'boxes' contain evocative and poetic collections of bric-à-brac which, due to their irrational nature, can be described as Surrealist. His first one-man exhibition was in New York in 1932 and his work has been included in many subsequent exhibitions of Surrealist art.

CORNELL, Katharine (1898–1974) American actress, producer and manager, born in Berlin of American parents. She was educated in New York, and made her first stage appearance in 1916. She appeared in many stage productions such as *The Green Hat*, *The Letter* and *The Age of Innocence* before embarking on a career as producer. Her own productions include a number of Shakespearean and Shavian classics, *The Constant Wife*, *The First-Born* and *Dear Liar*.

CORNFORTH, Sir John Warcup (1917–) Australian organic chemist, born in Sydney. Educated at the universities of Sydney and Oxford, he joined the staff of the Medical Research Council in 1946. He served as the director of the Milstead Laboratory of Chemical Enzymology from 1962, and in 1975 became the Royal Society research professor at Sussex University. He showed how cholesterol is synthesized in the living cell, and followed this by notable work on the stereochemistry of enzyme-catalyzed reactions; for this work he was awarded the 1975 Nobel prize for chemistry, shared with **Vladimir Prelog**.

CORNWALL, Barry See **PROCTER, Bryan Waller**

CORNWALLIS, Charles, 1st Marquis Cornwallis (1738–1805) English soldier, born in London, son of the 1st Earl Cornwallis. Educated at Eton and the Military Academy of Turin, he served as aide-de-camp to the Marquis of **Granby** during part of the Seven Years' War. In the American War of Independence (1775–83), although he opposed the taxation of the American colonists, he accepted a command in the war, and with an inferior force defeated **Gates** at Camden in 1780 and more than held his own at Guildford (1781). Later that year he was beseiged at Yorktown, Virginia, and forced to surrender—a disaster that proved the ruin of the British cause in America. From 1786 to 1793 he was governor-general of India and commander-in-chief, and distinguished himself by his victories over **Tippoo Sahib**. As lord-lieutenant of Ireland (1798–1801), with **Castlereagh** for secretary, he crushed the 1798 rebellion, and showed a rare union of vigour and humanity. As plenipotentiary to France he negotiated the peace of Amiens in 1802. Reappointed governor-general of India in 1804, he died at Ghazipur.

CORNYSHE, William (c.1465–1523) English composer at the courts of **Henry VII** and **Henry VIII**, where he was employed as musician, actor and producer of entertainments. In 1509 he became master of the Children of the Chapel Royal, and was in charge of the music at the Field of Cloth of Gold, 1520. He composed religious and secular choral works.

CORONADO, Francisco Vázquez de (1510–54) Spanish conquistador and explorer of Mexico, born in Salamanca. In 1540 he commanded an expedition which penetrated into what is now the southwest of the USA and discovered the Grand Canyon of Colorado.

COROT, Jean Baptiste Camille (1796–1875) French landscape painter, born in Paris, and educated at Rouen. He became an assistant in a Paris drapery establishment, but in 1822 took up the systematic study of art. In 1825 he settled in Rome; in 1827 he returned to Paris, and contributed his *Vue prise à Narni* and his *Campagne de Rome* to the Salon. His main sketching ground was at Barbizon, in the Forest of Fontainebleau; but he made two other visits to Italy in 1835 and 1843. It was not until about 1840 that he developed fully his style, characterized by great breadth and delicacy, and sacrificing accuracy of detail to unity of impression and harmony of general effect. Among his masterpieces are *Danse de nymphes*, *Homère et les bergers*, *Orphée*, *Joueur de flûte* and *Le Bûcheron*.

CORREGGIO, Antonio Allegri da (c.1494–1534) Italian painter, born in Correggio, near Parma. He studied art under his uncle and three other masters. In 1514 he painted for the Franciscan convent a *Virgin Enthroned*, now in the Dresden Gallery; in 1518 he began his great series of mythological frescoes for the convent of San Paolo at Padua. From 1521 to 1524 he was engaged upon *The Ascension* in the cupola of the Benedictine church of San Giovanni. The decoration of the cathedral of Parma was commissioned in 1522. Meanwhile he was also much occupied with easel pictures. Among these are the *Ecce Homo* (National Gallery, London) and his celebrated version of the shepherds at Bethlehem, commissioned in 1522, now in the Dresden Gallery, a work of marvellous softness and delicacy. Five years later he painted *Il Giorno*, an exquisite picture of **St Jerome** (Parma Gallery). In 1530 he removed from Parma to his native town, and purchased an estate. The *Jupiter and Antiope* of the Louvre, the *Education of Cupid* of the National Gallery, the *Danae* of the Borghese Gallery, and the *Leda* of the Berlin Museum, have been assigned to the painter's later years; the *Reading Magdalene*, of which the picture in the Dresden Gallery is now regarded as merely a 17th century copy, was completed in 1528. His only son Pomponio was born in 1521, and was alive in 1593. He also was a painter, and an altarpiece by him is in the Academy at Parma.

CORRENS, Carl Franz Joseph Erich (1864–1933) German botanist and geneticist, born in Munich. From 1914 he was the first director of the Kaiser-Wilhelm Institut für Biologie at Berlin, and with **Hugo de Vries** and Tschermak was a rediscoverer of **Mendel**'s law of heredity.

CORRIGAN, Mairead (1944–) Irish peace activist, born in Belfast, founder with Betty Williams of the Northern Ireland Peace Movement in 1976. A Roman Catholic secretary in Belfast, she started organizing peace petitions in the face of the sectarian violence in Northern Ireland. The initiative became a mass movement of Roman Catholic and Protestant women known as the 'Community of the Peace People'. She shared with Betty Williams the 1977 Nobel peace prize.

CORSSEN, Wilhelm Paul (1820–75) German philologist, born in Bremen. He studied under **Boeckh** and **Lachmann** and was professor at Schulpforta (1846–66), and then settled in Berlin. His earliest great work is his treatise on the pronunciation of Latin (2 vols, 1858–59); the second (2 vols, 1874–75) tried to prove that Etruscan was cognate with Latin.

CORT, Henry (1740–1800) English ironmaster, and navy agent in London. He was the inventor of the 'puddling' process for purifying iron. Ruined by a prosecution for debt, he was ultimately pensioned.

CORTAZAR, Julio (1914–84) Argentinian/French writer, born in Brussels. He grew up in Argentina where he was educated. From 1935 to 1945 he taught in secondary schools in several small towns and in Mendoza, Argentina. From 1945 to 1951 he was a translator for publishers, then moved to Paris where he lived until his death, writing and freelancing for Unesco. He is one of the most widely recognized Spanish-American writers outside the Spanish-speaking world, owing this particularly to the filming of *Hopscotch* (*Rayuila*, 1963; trans 1963), and of a short story, 'Blow-Up' (from *Blow-Up and Other Stories*, 1968), by the Italian director **Michelangelo Antonioni**. Others of his novels which have been translated include *Los premios* (1960; trans *The Winners*, 1965) and *62: modelo para armar* (1962, trans 1962: *A Model Kit*, 1972).

CORTÉS, Hernando (1485–1547) Spanish conquistador and conqueror of Mexico, born of noble family in Medellin, in Estremadura. In 1504 he sailed for San Domingo, and accompanied **Diego Velázquez de Cuellar** in his expedition to Cuba. Fired by the discoveries of **Alvarado** and others, Velázques fitted out a small expedition of 550 men with 17 horses and 10 cannon against Mexico, the command of which he gave (1518) to Cortés. He landed first in the Yucatán, and subjugated Tabasco. At San Juan de Ulua, messengers from **Montezuma II**, the Aztec king, reached him, bringing presents. Having founded Vera Cruz, and burnt his ships, he marched to Tlacala, whose warlike inhabitants, subdued after hard fighting, became henceforward his faithful allies. After some delay he started on his march to Mexico, with his Tlacalan allies. He escaped a dangerous ambush at Cholula, and on 8 November 1519, he reached the capital, Tenochtitlán, where he was well received by Montezuma. Montezuma was abducted to the Spanish quarters, and forced to submit to a public act of vassalage to Spain. In 1520 Cortés marched to the coast, leaving Alvarado in command to deal with a force sent by Velázquez to arrest him, under **Narvaez**, and succeeded in winning them to his side. Meanwhile Alvarado's harshness had provoked the Mexicans to revolt, and Cortés was forced to evacuate Tenochtitlán with terrible losses (the 'Night of Sorrows'). In retreat, Cortés overcame a hugh Aztec army at Otumba, and eventually reached Tlaxcala. After rebuilding his forces he laid siege to Tenochtitlán in 1521, which he captured and razed to the ground, building Mexico City in its place. In 1522 he was appointed governor and captain-general of New Spain. He sent Alvarado to subdue Guatemala (1524–25), and he himself made an expedition to Honduras (1524–26). In May 1528 he went back to Spain, was received with honour by **Charles V**, and created a marquis. He returned in 1530 as captain-general, but not as civil governor, of New Spain. Poor and broken in health, he returned to Spain in 1540, where he accompanied Charles in his unhappy expedition against Algiers, and died neglected near Seville. His body was translated to Tezcuco in 1562, to Mexico City in 1629.

CORTONA, Pietro Berrettini da (1596–1669) Italian painter and architect, born in Cortona. With **Bernini** he ranks as one of the great figures of the Baroque in Rome. With Lanfranco and **Guercino** he was the founder of the Roman High Baroque style in painting. He specialized in highly illusionistic ceiling painting in which paint is combined with stucco and gilt to create magnificent, awe-inspiring effects. The greatest of these is his *Allegory of Divine Providence* and *Barberini Power* (1633–39) in the Palazzo Barberini in Rome. There is similar work in the apse of the church of Santa Maria in Vallicella and the Palazzo Pitti in Florence. Although he once said that he regarded architecture as a pastime, his church of SS Martina e Luca in Rome is of high quality. His easel painting is usually less impressive.

CORTOT, Alfred (1877–1962) French pianist and conductor, born in Nyon, Switzerland, of French parents. After winning the first prize for piano-playing at the Paris Conservatoire in 1896, he became known in France as an outstanding player of **Beethoven**'s concertos. In 1902 he formed the Société de Festival Lyrique, which gave the first Paris performance of *Götterdammerung* under his baton. In 1905, with **Jacques Thibaud** and **Pablo Casals**, he founded a trio whose chamber music performances won great renown. Principally known in later years as an exponent of **Chopin**'s music, he was professor of the pianoforte at the Paris Conservatoire from 1917 to 1920 and author of several books on musical appreciation, interpretation and piano technique.

CORVINUS, Matthias See **MATTHIAS**

CORVISART-DESMARETS, Jean Nicolas, Baron de (1755–1821) French physician, born in Voliziers in Champagne. As professor at the Collège de France, he popularized the method of percussion in diagnosing heart diseases.

CORY, Charles Barney (1857–1921) American naturalist and traveller, born in Boston, the son of a millionaire. A fine sportsman (shooting, golf, billiards), he developed an early interest in ornithology and travelled widely in the eastern USA and the Caribbean. A founder-member of the American Ornithologists' Union, he published *The Birds of the Bahamas* (1878) and various other bird books. In 1906 he lost all his inherited fortune, and moved to Chicago, where he became curator of zoology at the Chicago Field Museum, and published his monumental *Birds of the Americas* (4 vols, 1918–19). Cory's Shearwater was named in his honour.

CORY, William Johnson (1823–92) English poet, born in Torrington, Devon. Educated at Eton and King's College, Cambridge, he was assistant-master at Eton from 1845 to 1872. He was author of a book of poems, *Ionica, Poems* (1858, enlarged 1891).

CORYATE, Thomas (c.1577–1617) English traveller, born in Odcombe Rectory, Somerset. He entered Gloucester Hall, Oxford, in 1596, but left without a degree, and after the accession of King **James I** in 1603 became a court jester. In 1608 he set out on a journey on foot of 1975 miles through Paris, Lyons, Turin, Venice, Zürich and Strasbourg, and in 1611 published *Coryat's Crudities: Hastily gobled up in Five Moneth's Travels*. Dedicating his travel-worn shoes in Odcombe Church, he started for Constantinople, Greece, Smyrna, Alexandria, Palestine, Mesopotamia, Persia, Afghanistan and Agra. He died in Surat.

COSBY, Bill (William Henry) (1937–) American comedian, born in North Philadelphia. After service in the US navy (1956–60), he enrolled at Temple University, Philadelphia, on a track and field scholarship. He began performing as a nightclub comic and abandoned his studies to pursue this career full time. An appearance on *The Tonight Show* in 1965 led to him being cast in the television series *I Spy* (1965–68) where his role won him three consecutive Emmy Awards and broke new ground in the portrayal of blacks on screen. Subsequent television series included *The Bill Cosby Show* (1969–71) and *Fat Albert and the Cosby* (1972–84). A congenial figure, his wholesome humour is based on quirky observations of the world around him and offbeat anecdotes based on personal experience. He made his film début in *Hickey and Boggs* (1971) and has appeared in *Uptown Saturday Night* (1974), *California Suite* (1978) and *Leonard: Part VI* (1987). Involved with children's educational television for many years, and a frequent personality in commercials, his series *The Cosby Show* (1984–), an inoffensive domestic comedy, has consistently topped the ratings and made him one of the wealthiest men in showbusiness. He has recorded more than 20 albums and won 8 Grammy Awards, whilst his book *Fatherhood* (1986) was a bestseller.

COSGRAVE, Liam (1920–) Irish politician, son of **William Thomas Cosgrave**. Educated at St Vincent's College, Castleknock, Dublin, he was called to the bar in 1943 and was a member of the Dail (1943–81). He was minister for external affairs (1954–57), leader of the Fine Gael party (1965–77) and president (1973–77).

COSGRAVE, William Thomas (1880–1965) Irish politician. He was first president of the executive council of the Irish Free State (1922–32), and then leader of the Opposition (1932–44).

COSIMO, Agnolo di See **BRONZINO**

COSIMO, Piero di See **PIERO DI COSIMO**

COSIN, John (1594–1672) English prelate, born in Norwich. Educated there and at Caius College, Cambridge, he became a fellow, and after various preferments, master of Peterhouse College, Cambridge (1635), and dean of Peterborough (1640). An intimate friend of **Laud**, he had already come into collision with the Puritans about his ritualistic reforms, and, deprived in 1641 of his benefices and ejected by order of the House of Commons from Peterhouse (1644), he retired to Paris. At the Restoration he recovered his preferments, and in 1660 he was consecrated bishop of Durham. During his first seven years he spent £34 500 upon his two castles, his cathedral, the library at Durham, and deeds of general benevolence. He sternly repressed Puritan and Roman Catholic recusancy alike; for, however devoted to ancient ritual and order, he hated popery, and never ceased to regret the perversion of his own 'lost son' who had turned Roman Catholic. All Cosin's writings are inconsiderable save his *Collection of Private Devotions* (1627), which was denounced by **Prynne** in his *Brief Survey of Mr Cozen's Cozening Devotions*. A lasting service to the church was his contribution, invaluable from his profound liturgical learning, to the final revision (1661) of the Prayer Book.

COSMAS, and **DAMIAN, SS** (d.303) Arabian brothers, said to have been physicians at Ægæa in Cilicia, who were cast into the sea as Christians, but rescued by an angel. Thereafter, burning and stoning having proved ineffectual, they were beheaded.

COSMAS, called **Indicopleustes,** meaning **'Indian Traveller'** (fl.6th century) a merchant of Alexandria. After much travel in Ethiopia and part of Asia, he returned to Egypt about 550, and in monastic retirement wrote a Greek work on Christian Topography to prove the authenticity of the Biblical account of the world.

COSQUIN, Emmanuel (1841–1922) French folklorist, born in Vitry-le-François in Marne, where his father was a notary. In his *Contes populaires de Lorraine* (2 vols, 1886) he argued for the transmission of European folk tales from India within the historical period.

COSSA, Francesco del (?1435–1477) Italian artist, born in Ferrara. His work was similar to that of **Tura**, and often equally austere, but in his most famous work, the frescoes in the Palazzo Schifanoia at Ferrara, which were commissioned by Borso **d'Este**, he produced a number of gay mythological and court scenes. He also worked in Bologna.

COSTA, Isaac Da See **DA COSTA**

COSTA, Joaquin (1846–1911) Spanish historian and writer, born in Monzon, Huesca. He was a crusader for the political and economic regeneration of Spain and an investigator of Spain's oldest traditions. His work includes *Juridical and Political Studies* (1884) and *Agrarian Collectivism in Spain* (1898).

COSTA, Lorenzo (c.1460–1535) Italian painter, born in Ferrara. His *Madonna and Child Enthroned* is in the National Gallery in London. In 1506 he went to Mantua, where he succeeded **Mantegna** as court painter.

COSTA, Lucio (1902–) Brazilian architect, born in Toulouse of Franco-Brazilian parents and considered the father of modern Brazilian architecture. He studied in Rio de Janeiro. Influenced by **Gropius**, **Mies van der Rohe** and **Le Corbusier**, from 1948 to 1954 he designed the award-winning Eduardo Gunile Apartments. In 1956 his plan for the city of Brasilia was chosen by an international jury for its clarity and ability to integrate monumentality and daily life. He now devotes his time to the Brazilian Society for Historical Preservation, and is an authority on the colonial architecture of Brazil.

COSTA, Manuel Pinto da (1937–) Sao Tome politician, born in Agua Grande. In 1972 he founded the Movement for the Liberation of Sao Tome and Principe (MLSTP) in Gabon and in 1974, taking advantage of a military coup in Portugal, returned and persuaded the new government in Lisbon to recognize the MLSTP as the sole representative of the people and to grant independence a year later. He became president in 1975 and set his country on a politically non-aligned course.

COSTA, Sir Michael (1810–84) Italian conductor and composer, born in Naples. Trained at the conservatory there, he settled in England (1828), and in 1831 his ballet of *Kenilworth* was pruduced with success. He was conductor at the King's Theatre (1832), at Covent Garden (1846), to the Philharmonic Concerts (1846) and to the Sacred Harmonic Society (1848). His oratorio *Eli*, produced at the Birmingham Festival of 1855 (where he conducted till 1879), raised him to eminence; *Naaman*, less successful, was first sung at Birmingham in 1864. From 1857 till 1877 he conducted at the Handel Festival, and in 1871 he became director of Her Majesty's Opera. He composed ballets and operas, including *Malek Adhel* (1838) and *Don Carlos* (1844).

COSTELLO, Elvis, real name **Declan Patrick McManus** (1955–) English singer-songwriter, born in Paddington, London, the most important songwriter to emerge from the English new wave of the late 1970s and one of the finest pop chroniclers of Britain in the 1980s. The son of big band singer Ros McManus, he started his own career with the unrecorded band Flip City and as a solo folk club singer. Signed to Stiff Records in 1977, his début album *My Aim Is True* immediately established his reputation as an intense and vitriolic musician. For his second album, *This Year's Model* (1978), he was joined by the Attractions —a three-piece group consisting of Steve Nieve, Pete Thomas and Bruce Thomas who worked with Costello on most of his albums over the next eight years, although Costello also collaborated with many other musicians. His albums have included *Get Happy* (1980), *Almost Blue* (1981, a collection of country and western songs), *Imperial Bedroom* (1982), *Goodbye Cruel World* (1984) and *King of America* (1986).

COSTELLO, John Aloysius (1891–1976) Irish politician, born in Dublin and educated at University College, Dublin. Called to the bar in 1914, he was attorney-general from 1926 to 1932. In 1948 he became prime minister of a government of several parties of which his own Fine Gael party was the chief. As a foremost constitutional lawyer, one of his first acts was to repeal the External Relations Act, which paved the way that year for the formal change from the State of Eire to the Republic of Ireland. On the defeat of his government by **De Valera**'s Fianna Fail party in 1951, he became leader of the Opposition in the Dail, from 1954 to 1957 was premier, and again Opposition leader until 1959.

COSTER See **JANSZOON, Laurens**

COSTER, Charles de (1827–79) Belgian storyteller, born in Munich. He studied at Brussels. His most famous work, the prose epic *The Legend of Tyl Ulenspiegel* (1866, trans 1918), took ten years to write.

COSTER, Dirk (1889–1950) Dutch physicist, professor of physics and meteorology at Groningen. In 1923, while working in Copenhagen, he discovered the element hafnium.

COSWAY, Richard (c.1742–1821) English miniaturist, born in Tiverton. He painted in oils *à la* Correggio, but it was in portraiture that he made his mark, and soon his miniatures were 'not only fashionable, but the fashion itself'. The Prince of Wales appointed him painter-in-ordinary. In 1781 he married the Irish-Italian Maria Hadfield (1759–1838), herself a skilful artist, who established a conventual school at Lodi, and was made a baroness by **Francis I**.

COTES, Roger (1682–1716) English mathematician, born in Burbage, near Leicester. He was educated at St Paul's School, London, and Trinity College, Cambridge, where he became a fellow in 1705, and Plumian professor of astronomy and natural philosophy in 1706. In 1713 he took holy orders. He collaborated with **Isaac Newton** in revising the second edition of Newton's *Principia* and contributed a preface defending Newton's methodology. 'Had Cotes lived', said Newton, 'we might have known something.' His posthumously published *Harmonia mensurarum* (1722) contains work on logarithms and integration.

COTGRAVE, Randle (d.?1634) English lexicographer, born in Cheshire. Educated at St John's College, Cambridge, he became secretary to **William Cecil**, 1st baron Burghley. In 1611 he published a French-English dictionary, the earliest in Britain.

COTMAN, John Sell (1782–1842) English landscape water colourist, born and educated at Norwich. His well-to-do parents sent him to study art in London, whence he made journeys all over Britain sketching architecture and the countryside. In 1806 he went back to his birthplace and became a leading member of the 'Norwich School', but from 1811 to 1823 lived in Yarmouth, where he executed some fine oil paintings and etchings. He left Norwich in 1834 and became, thanks to the good offices of **Joseph Turner**, drawing master of King's College, London. His work exhibits a variety of styles, the best being characterized by masterly arrangement of masses of light and shade, with a minimum of modelling, giving an effect reminiscent of a Japanese print or a modern poster, as in his famous *Chirk Aqueduct* and *Greta Bridge*.

COTTA a publishing-house established in Tübingen in 1640. The family came originally from Italy. Its most prominent members have been Johann Friedrich (1701–79), theological professor at Tübingen, Göttingen and Jena; and his grandson, Johann Friedrich, Freiherr Cotta von Cottendorf (1764 –1832). Educated at Tübingen, and for some time an advocate, in 1787 he undertook the family business. In 1795 he established the famous *Horen*, a literary journal, under **Schiller**'s editorship. Already in 1793 he had sketched out the plan for the *Allgemeine Zeitung* (1798). The *Almanach für Damen* (1797) and other periodicals were no less successful. Cotta now likewise published the works of Schiller, **Goethe**, **Herder**, **Fichte**, **Schelling**, **Johann Paul Richter**, **Tieck**, **Voss**, the **Humboldts**, and others. In 1810 he moved to Stuttgart, and in 1824 introduced the first steam printing press into Bavaria. In the diet of Württemberg, and as president of the Second Chamber, he was always the fearless defender of constitutional rights. He was the first Württemberg proprietor to abolish serfdom on his estates.

COTTIN, Sophie, née **Risteau** (1770–1807) French writer. At 17 she married a Parisian banker, who left her a childless widow at 20. For comfort she turned to letters, wrote verses and a lengthy history, and romantic fiction. She had already written *Claire d'Albe* (1799), *Mathilde* (1805) when in 1806 she wrote her most successful work, *Élisabeth, ou les exilés de Sibérie*.

COTTON, Charles (1630–87) English writer, born at his father's estate of Beresford in Staffordshire. His father was a warm friend of **Ben Jonson**, **Selden**, **Donne** and other illustrious men. The boy travelled on the Continent, and early wrote verses which were circulated privately. In 1656 he married his cousin Isabella, half-sister of the regicide **John Hutchinson** (1615–64). Though a sincere loyalist, he seems to have lived securely enough under the Commonwealth, and the decay of his father's estate was due mainly to unprosperous lawsuits. In 1664 he issued anonymously his burlesque poem, *Scarronides, or the First Book of Virgil Travestie*, added to in later editions in grossness as well as in bulk. Later works are his *Voyage to Ireland in Burlesque* (1670), *Burlesque upon Burlesque* (1675), *Planter's Manual* (1675), and a treatise on fly-fishing contributed in 1676 to the fifth edition of Walton's *Compleat Angler*. He also published a masterly translation of Montaigne's *Essays* (1685).

COTTON, George Edward Lynch (1813–66) English teacher and bishop. Educated at Westminster School and Trinity College, Cambridge, from 1836 he was a master at Rugby School under **Thomas Arnold** and **Archibald Campbell Tait**; in *Tom Brown's School Days* he appears as 'the young master'. In 1852 he became head of Marlborough College, which he raised to a position among the first schools of England, and in 1858 Bishop of Calcutta, where he founded schools for the children of the poorer Anglo-Indians and Eurasians. He was drowned in the Ganges.

COTTON, Sir (Thomas) Henry (1907–87) English golfer, born at Holmes Chapel, Cheshire. Educated at Alleyn's School, he soon became a professional golfer. In the 1930s and 1940s he almost single-handedly fought off the American challenge in the British Open Championship, winning in 1934, 1937 and 1948. He won many other titles, and played in the Ryder Cup against America four times between 1929 and 1953. In his latter years he ran a golf complex in Portugal and was much in demand as a teacher and consultant.

COTTON, John (1585–1652) English Puritan clergyman, born in Derby, and known as 'The Patriarch of New England'. He was a tutor at Cambridge, and from about 1612 held a charge at Boston, Lincolnshire. Cited for his Puritan views before **Laud**, in 1633 he emigrated to Boston, Massachusetts, where he preached till his death. He became the head of Congregationalism in the USA. His many works include a catechism, forms of prayer, and his defence against **Roger Williams** of the civil authority in religious matters. He also wrote *The Keys of the Kingdom of Heaven* (1644) and *Spiritual Milk for Babes* (1646).

COTTON, Sir Robert Bruce (1571–1631) English antiquary, born in Denton, Huntingdonshire. He was educated at Westminster School (where his master was the antiquarian, **William Camden**), and went on to Jesus College, Cambridge. At Cotton House in Westminster, on the site of the present House of Lords, he accumulated books, manuscripts, coins, etc, dispersed by the dissolution of the monasteries. His papers at the Antiquarian Society spread wide the reputation of his learning; King **James VI and I** created him a baronet in 1611, and frequently consulted him. But he kept the scholar in prison for eight months in connection with the **Overbury** case (1615–16). Cotton, returned to parliament in 1604, from about 1620 identified himself with the constitutional opposition to the crown. His protest against the proposed debasement of the coinage by King **Charles I** (1626), his frank criticism of kingcraft in his *Raigne of Henry III* (1627), his *Dangers wherein the Kingdon now Standeth* (1628), and the frequent meeting in his house of Sir **John Pym**, **Selden** and Sir **Edward Coke**, marked him out to the court as an enemy. A seemingly ironical tract, *A Proposition to Bridle the Impertinency of Parliaments*, having fallen into **Stafford**'s hands, it was found on inquiry that the original was in Cotton's library, from which a copy had been made, though without his knowledge. Cotton was flung into prison, but released on the occasion of the birth of an heir to the throne (May 29, 1630). His library, however, was not restored to him. Fourteen of his tracts were collected as *Cotton's Posthuma* in 1651. His son, Sir Thomas (1594–1662), had the books restored to him and greatly increased the library; and his great-grandson, Sir John (1679–1731), in 1700 bestowed them on the nation.

COTTON, Sir Stapleton See **COMBERMERE**

COTY, François (1874–1934) French industrialist and newspaper proprietor, born in Ajaccio in Corsica. He built up the famous perfumery firm which bears his name, obtained control of *Figaro* in 1924 and founded the *Ami du Peuple* in 1928. He was a member of the Corsican Senate.

COTY, René (1882–1962) French statesman, the last president of the French Fourth Republic (1953–59), born at Le Havre. A barrister, he was elected a Left Republican deputy in 1923, entered the Senate in 1935 and was minister of reconstruction in 1947, and in 1953 president of France. After the constitutional crisis precipitated by the generals in Algeria in May 1958, he powerfully assisted the return to power of General **de Gaulle** and the consequent birth of the new constitution and 5th Republic in January 1959, with de Gaulle as his successor.

COUCH, Sir Arthur Quiller (1863–1944) English man of letters, born in Bodmin, in Cornwall. He was educated at Clifton College and Trinity College, Oxford, where he was a lecturer in classics (1886–87). After some years of literary work in London and in Cornwall, where he lived from 1891, he became professor of English literature at Cambridge in 1912. He edited the *Oxford Book of English Verse* (1900) and other anthologies, and published volumes of essays, criticism, poems, and parodies, among them *From a Cornish Window* (1906), *On the Art of Writing* (1916), *Studies in Literature* and *On the Art of Reading* (1920). He is also remembered for a series of humorous novels set in a Cornish background, written under the pseudonym 'Q'.

COUÉ, Émile (1857–1926) French pharmacist and hypnotist, and pioneer of 'auto-suggestion'. As a pharmacist in Troyes from 1882 he took up the study of and became a psychotherapist, and in 1910 opened a free clinic in Nancy. His system became world-famous as 'Couéism', expressed in the famous formula 'Every day, in every way, I am becoming better and better'.

COUES, Elliot (1842–99) American ornithologist, born in Portsmouth, New Hampshire. An army surgeon by profession, he became secretary of the US Northern Boundary Commission, and wrote *Key to North American Birds* (1872).

COULANGES See **FUSTEL DE COULANGES**

COULOMB, Charles Augustin de (1736–1806) French physicist, born in Angoulême. He experimented on friction, and invented the torsion balance for measuring the force of magnetic and electrical attraction. The coulomb, the unit of quantity in measuring current electricity, is named after him.

COULTON, George Gordon (1858–1947) English historian, born in King's Lynn. He became a lecturer at Cambridge, Oxford, Toronto and Edinburgh. His many works include *Five Centuries of Religion* (1923 *et seq.*), *The Medieval Village* (1925), *Art and the Reformation* (1928), *Life in the Middle Ages* (1928–29), and *Medieval Thought* (1939). He wrote an autobiography, *Fourscore Years* (1943).

COUPER, Archibald Scott (1831–92) Scottish organic chemist, born in Kirkintilloch, the pioneer of structural organic chemistry. The son of a cotton-weaving mill owner, he studied classics at Glasgow and philosophy at Edinburgh, then turned to chemistry and travelled in Germany, and studied in Paris under **Charles Adolphe Wurtz**. In 1858 he asked Wurtz to present to the French Academy a paper he had written *On a New Chemical Theory* in which he argued that carbon had a valence of two or four; and that its atoms could self-link to form chains. This is fundamentally important in assigning structural formulae to organic compounds. Unfortunately Wurtz procrastinated in his presentation and **Friedrich Kekulé von Stradonitz** published first. In many ways Couper's ideas were ahead of Kekulé's, but Kekulé forcefully pressed his superiority, Couper quarrelled with Wurtz, returned to Edinburgh ignored as a chemist, and suffered a permanent depressive illness. Kekulé's successor at Bonn discovered Couper's early work in which he had used the graphic formulae, and his paper on chemical theory, and Couper's work was given belated recognition.

COUPERIN, Charles (1638–79) French organist and composer, born in Chaumes-en-Brie, one of the first generation of a celebrated family of musicians. He succeeded his brother **Louis Couperin** as organist of the church of Saint-Gervais, Paris.

COUPERIN, François, known as **'le Grand'** (1668–1733) French organist and composer, son of **Charles Couperin**, born in Paris. He was taught by his father, whom he eventually followed as organist of Saint-Gervais in 1685, holding the post until his death. In 1693 he became organist to **Louis XIV**, and in 1717 composer-in-ordinary of chamber music to the king, having previously been harpsichord teacher of the royal children. Internationally famous as a harpsichord composer whose principles are enunciated in his textbook *L'Art de toucher le clavecin*, he had a profound influence on **J S Bach**. His other compositions include many chamber concertos as well as motets and other church music.

COUPERIN, Louis (1626–61) French violinist, organist and composer, brother of **Charles Couperin**. He was introduced to Paris and the court by Chambonnières, and was appointed organist of Saint-Gervais.

COUPERUS, Louis (1863–1923) Dutch poet and novelist, born in The Hague. He wrote a powerful tetralogy, *The Books of the Small Souls*.

COURANT, Richard (1888–1972) German-born American mathematician, born in Lublinitz. He studied in Breslau, Zürich and, as a pupil of **David Hilbert**, at Göttingen, where he became professor in 1920, founding the Mathematics Institute in 1929. In 1933 he was forced by the Nazis to retire and after a year at Cambridge, he went to the USA where he became professor at New York University (1934), and director of the Institute of Mathematical Sciences (later the Courant Research Institute) from 1953 to 1958. His work in applied analysis, particularly in partial differential equations and the **Dirichlet** problem, was always motivated by its physical applications. His textbook *Methoden der mathematischen Physik* (1924–27), written jointly with Hilbert, immediately became a classic. *What is mathematics*? (1941, written with H Robbins), attempts to explain mathematics to the layman.

COURBET, Gustave (1819–77) French painter, born in Ornans, the son of a farmer. He studied law in Paris, but turned to painting. He had little formal art training and scorned the rigid classical outlook, preferring Flemish and Spanish models, especially **Velazquez**. The founder of Realism, in 1844 he began exhibiting pictures in which everyday scenes were portrayed with complete sincerity and absence of idealism, as *Peasants of Flazey* and *Funeral at Ornans*, both of which were condemned as 'socialistic' though not painted with any political intent. Perhaps his most famous canvas is the large *Studio of the Painter: an Allegory of Realism*, in the Louvre, a kind of synthesis of his outlook, containing the various types of model which he favoured, some of his friends, and the painter himself. Republican in sympathies, he joined the Commune in 1871, and on its suppression was imprisoned and fined for his part in the destruction of the Vendôme Column. On his release in 1873 he fled to Switzerland and died there at Vevey.

COURIER, Paul Louis (1772–1825) French writer, born in Paris. He was a polished translator from Greek, and a master of irony. In 1816 he issued the *Pétition aux deux chambres*, a scathing exposure of the wrongs of the peasantry. His masterpiece, *Simple Discours de Paul Louis, Vigneron* (1821), derided the scheme to purchase Chambord for the Duc de Bordeaux by a 'national offering', and he was imprisoned. He was assassinated on his estate in Touraine.

COURNAND, André Frédéric (1895–) French-born American physician, born in Paris. He was educated at the Sorbonne, emigrating to the USA in 1930 and becoming an American citizen in 1941. A specialist in heart surgery, he was awarded the Nobel prize for physiology or medicine jointly with **Werner Forssman** and **Dickenson Richards** for developing cardiac catheterization. In 1960 he became professor of clinical physiology at Columbia University, and in 1964 Professor Emeritus of medicine.

COURRÈGES, André (1923–) French fashion designer, born in Pau. He studied civil engineering but later turned to fashion, in Paris. Trained by **Balenciaga** from 1952 to 1960, he opened his own house in 1961. Famous for his stark, futuristic, 'Space Age' designs, he introduced the miniskirt (1964), and has featured trouser suits for women, and white boots. Since 1966 he has produced ready-to-wear as well as couture clothes.

COURT, Margaret née **Smith** (1924–) Australian tennis player, born in Albury, New South Wales. Tall and powerful, she was the first Australian to win the Wimbledon women's singles title in 1963 (and again in 1965 and 1970). In 1970 she became the second woman, after **Maureen Connolly**, to win the Grand Slam of the four major titles (British, American, French and Australian) in a single year; she also won the Grand Slam in mixed doubles (with Ken Fletcher) in 1963. In addition she won the Australian singles title 11 times and the US title seven times.

COURTAULD, Samuel (1876–1947) English industrialist, descendant of Samuel Courtauld (1793–1881), founder of the silk manufacturing company in 1816. As chairman of Courtaulds Limited he promoted the British rayon and nylon industry, and was a patron of art and music. He built the Courtauld Institute of Art in Portman Square, London, and donated it with his art collection, to London University.

COURTELINE, Georges, pseud of **Georges Moinaux** (1860–1929) French dramatist, born in Tours. He wrote satirical comedies, many of them one-acters, including *Boubouroche* (1893), *Un Client sérieux* (1897) and *Le Commissaire est bon enfant* (1900). He also published novels, as *Le Train de* 8^h47 (1888, later dramatized) and *Messieurs les Ronds-de-cuir* (1893).

COURTENAY, Sir William (c.1796–1838) the name assumed in 1832 by a crazy Cornishman, John Nichols Thom, who claimed to be a Knight of Malta and heir to the earldom of Devon. A political and religious maniac, and sometime inmate of Kent County lunatic asylum, he gathered about a hundred scythe-armed followers, asserted that he was the Messiah and possessed the stigmata and the power to work miracles. He was killed with eight of his disciples in Blean Wood, near Canterbury, in a skirmish with troops sent from the city to apprehend him.

COURTENEY, Tom (Thomas) (1937–) English actor, born in Hull. He made his professional début in 1960, as Konstantin in **Chekhov**'s *The Seagull*, with the Old Vic company in Edinburgh. He has since appeared in a diverse repertoire. He played Hamlet at the 1968 Edinburgh Festival, and won great acclaim for his performance as Norman in the **Ayckbourn** comedy trilogy, *The Norman Conquests* (1974). Other stage appearances include leading roles in *The Dresser* (1980), and the title role in the musical, *Andy Capp* (1982). A distinguished film actor, his first appearance was in *The Loneliness of the Long-Distance Runner* (1962). Subsequent films include *Billy Liar*, *King Rat*, *Doctor Zhivago* and *One Day in the Life of Ivan Denisovitch*.

COURTHOPE, William John (1842–1917) English poet and critic, born in South Malling vicarage, near Lewes. He was educated at Harrow School and Corpus Christi College and New College, Oxford, where he was professor of poetry (1895–1901). In 1892–1907 he was first civil service commissioner. Among his critical works are *Addison* (1883), *Pope* (1889) and *History of English Poetry* (6 vols, 1895–1909). He also published some charming verse.

COURTNEIDGE, Dame Cicely (Esmerelda) (1883–1980) English actress of light musical comedies, born in Sydney, New South Wales. A child actress from the age of eight, she made her London début at 14 in a musical version of *Tom Jones*. She later became widely known as an actress in musicals, pantomime and revue, having a great success in *By-the-Way* in 1935, which also starred her husband, Jack Hulbert (1892–1978). They appeared together in many shows such as *Clowns in Clover* in 1927, *Under Your Hat* in 1938, and *Something in the Air* in 1943. She also appeared in several straight comedies, including her final West End stage appearance in *Move Over, Mrs Markham*, by **Ray Cooney** (1971). She published an autobiography, *Cicely*, in 1953.

COURTNEY, Leonard Henry, 1st Baron Courtney of Penwith (1832–1918) English politician, born, a banker's son, in Penzance. Educated at St John's College, Cambridge, made a fellow (1856), he was called to the bar, and from 1872 to his visit to India (1875–76) was professor of political economy at

University College London. He wrote for *The Times*, and his pamphlets and magazine articles placed him among the ablest and most advanced *doctrinaire* Liberals, an early advocate for proportional representation and a wide extension of local government. He represented Cornish constituencies 1876–1900, and held minor offices.

COURTOIS, Bernard (1777–1838) French chemist. In 1811 he discovered iodine while studying the liquor obtained in leaching the ashes of burnt kelp.

COUSIN, Jean (1501–c.1590) French sculptor, glass-stainer and painter, born in Soucy, near Sens. He was responsible for the stained glass in the church of Saint-Gervais in Paris, in Sens Cathedral, and the Sainte Chapelle in Vincennes.

COUSIN, Victor (1792–1867) French philosopher, born in Paris. A charismatic lecturer and teacher who also had a lively, if uneven, public career, he studied under **Royer-Collard** and became lecturer at the École Normale at Paris in 1815. In 1817 he visited Germany to study German philosophy and met **Hegel**, **Carl Jacobi** and **Schelling**. His liberalism occasioned various professional setbacks, but he prospered after the revolution of 1830 when his friend **Guizot** became prime minister. He became a member of the Council of Public Instruction (1830), a peer of France and Director of the École Normale (1832), and Minister of Public Instruction under **Thiers** (1840). He was sympathetic to the revolution of 1848 and assisted **Cavaignac**, but retired from public life in 1849 and lived for many years in the Sorbonne. He was an eclectic in philosophy and published many historical studies and commentaries, including a translation of **Plato** and editions of **Proclus**, **Descartes**, **Abelard** and **Pascal**. His most original work was *Du vrai, du beau, et du bien* (1854).

COUSINS, Frank (1904–86) British trade-union leader, born at Bulwell, Nottingham, a miner's son. He worked in the pits at 14, turned lorry driver and by 1938 was a full-time union organizer. In 1955 he was appointed general secretary of the Transport and General Worker's Union. He played a controversial part in the London transport strike (1958) and, defying the TUC and the leaders of the Labour Party, aligned his union behind a near unilateral nuclear disarmament policy in 1958. In 1965 he was elected MP for Nuneaton, having been appointed minister of technology (1964), a post he resigned in 1966 because of the government's economic policy, resuming his former union post. He also gave up his parliamentary seat the same year. He was chairman of the Community Relations Commission 1968–70.

COUSINS, Samuel (1801–87) English engraver, born in Exeter. In 1814 he was apprenticed to **Samuel William Reynolds**, the mezzotinter, and in 1826 started on his own account, and produced the 'Master Lambton' after Sir **Thomas Lawrence**, which at once established his reputation. It was followed by a long series of plates after Sir **Joshua Reynolds**, Lawrence, **Landseer**, **Millais**, etc.

COUSTEAU, Jacques Yves (1910–) French naval officer and underwater explorer, born in Saint-André, Gironde. He invented the Aqualung diving apparatus (1943), and a process of underwater television. In 1945 he founded the French Navy's Undersea Research Group, and became commander of the oceanographic research ship *Calypso* in 1950. He won Academy Awards for his films *The Silent World* (1956), *The Golden Fish* (1960) and *World Without Sun* (1964). In 1957 he was appointed director of the Institute of Oceanography in Monaco.

COUSTOU, Guillaume (1678–1746) French sculptor, brother of **Nicolas Coustou**. He was the sculptor of the *Chevaux de Marly* at the entrance of the Champs Elysées, Paris, and many other spectacular works.

COUSTOU, Guillaume (1716–77) French sculptor, son of **Guillaume Coustou** (1678–1746). He left works including the bronze bas-relief *Visitation* at Versailles, and the mausoleum of the dauphin (father of **Louis XVI**) in the cathedral at Sens.

COUSTOU, Nicolas (1658–1733) French sculptor brother of **Guillaume Coustou** (1678–1746). He was the sculptor of the *Descente de Croix* at Notre Dame.

COUSY, Bob (Robert Joseph) (1928–) American basketball player, born in New York City, considered to be one of the greatest players ever. He played professionally with the Boston Celtics from 1950 to 1963, then went on to coach with the Cincinatti Royals and the Kansas City-Omaha Kings. He became a sports commentator and was elected to basketball's Hall of Fame in 1971. He has been the author of several books on the sport, including *Basketball in my Life* (1956) and *The Killer Instinct* (1976).

COUTHON, Georges (1756–94) French revolutionary, born in Orcet, near Clermont, in Auvergne. An advocate at the outbreak of the Revolution, he was sent by Puy de Dôme to the National Convention, where he demonstrated his hatred of the priesthood and the monarchy. In July 1793 he became a member of the committee of public safety. At Lyons he crushed the insurrection with merciless severity (1793), and helped to usher in the Terror. **Robespierre**'s fall brought down Couthon also; he was thrown into prison, freed by the mob with whom he was popular, recaptured by the soldiers of the Convention, and executed, with **Saint-Just** and Robespierre.

COUTTS, Thomas (1735–1822) Scottish banker, son of the Edinburgh merchant and banker John Coutts (1699–1751) who was lord provost in 1742–44. He founded the London banking-house of Coutts & Co. with his brother James, on whose death in 1778 he became sole manager. Keen and exact in matters of business, he left £900000. By his first wife, a servant of his brother's, he had three daughters, who married the Earl of Guilford, the Marquis of Bute and Sir Francis Burdett; in 1815 he married the actress **Harriot Mellon**. His grand-daughter was **Angela Burdett-Coutts**.

COVENTRY, Sir John (d.1682) English royalist. He sat in the Long Parliament (1640), and at the Restoration was made a Knight of the Bath. Elected for Weymouth in 1667, he asked, during a debate on playhouses (October 1670) a question reflecting on the king's amours. **Charles II** and his minions were furious, and one night Coventry was pulled from his coach and his nose slit to the bone. The 'Coventry Act' made maiming a capital offence.

COVERDALE, Miles (1488–1568) English Protestant reformer and biblical scholar, born in Yorkshire. He studied at Cambridge, was ordained priest at Norwich in 1514, and joined the Augustinian Friars at Cambridge, where he was converted to Protestantism. He lived abroad from 1528 to 1534 to escape persecution; and in 1535 published in Zürich the first translation of the whole Bible into English, with a dedication to **Henry VIII**. The Prayer Book retains the Psalms of this translation, and many of the finest phrases in the Authorized Version of 1611 are directly due to Coverdale. In 1538 he was sent by **Thomas Cromwell** to Paris to superintend another English edition of the Scriptures. **Francis I** had granted a licence, but during the printing an edict was issued prohibiting the work. Many of the sheets were burned, but the presses and types were hastily carried over to London. Grafton and Whitchurch, the noted printers of that day, were thus enabled to bring out in 1539, under Coverdale's superintendence, the 'Great Bible', which was presented to Henry VIII by Cromwell. The second 'Great Bible', known also as 'Cranmer's Bible' (1540), was also edited by Coverdale, who on Cromwell's fall found it expedient to leave England. While abroad he married and acted as Lutheran pastor in Rhenish Bavaria. In March 1548 he returned to England, was well received through **Cranmer**'s influence, and in 1551 was made bishop of Exeter. On **Mary I**'s accession he was deprived of his see, but was allowed to leave the country, at the earnest intercession of the king of Denmark, whose chaplain, Dr Macchabaeus (MacAlpine), was Coverdale's brother-in-law. Returning to England in 1559, he did not resume his bishopric, but in 1564 he was collated by **Grindal** to the living of St Magnus, near London Bridge, which he resigned from growing Puritan scruples about the liturgy in 1566.

COWARD, Sir Noel Pierce, (1899–1973) English actor, dramatist, and composer of light music, born in Teddington. At the age of 14 he appeared in *Peter Pan*, and thereafter in other plays, including many of his own. His first play *I'll Leave It to You* (1920), was followed by many successes, including *The Vortex* (1924), *Hay Fever* (1925), *Private Lives* (1930), *Blithe Spirit* (1941), *This Happy Breed* (1943) and *Nude With Violin* (1956), all showing his strong satiric humour and his unique gift for witty dialogue. He wrote the music for, among others, his operetta *Bitter Sweet* (1929) and his play *Cavalcade* (1931), and for a series of revues, including *Words and Music* (1932), with its 'Mad Dogs and Englishmen', *This Year of Grace* (1928) and *Sigh No More* (1945). He produced several films based on his own scripts, including *In Which We Serve*, *Blithe Spirit* and *Brief Encounter*. He published two autobiographies, *Present Indicative* (1937) and *Future Indefinite* (1954).

COWDREY, Michael Colin (1932–) English cricketer, born in India. Educated at Tonbridge School (where he played in his school XI at the age of 13) and Brasenose College, Oxford, he was captain of the Oxford XI in 1954 when he was already a Kent player. A magnificent batsman and outstanding slip-fielder, he played in a record 114 Tests for England (23 as captain), despite being dogged by injuries and illness; and he made six tours of Australia, also a record. In his long first-class career (1951–75) he was captain of Kent from 1957 to 1971, and scored 107 centuries, of which 22 were in Test matches. His son, Chris Cowdrey, has also captained Kent and England.

COWELL, Edward Byles (1826–1903) English Sanskrit scholar, born in Ipswich. From 1856 he was professor of history in the new Presidency College at Calcutta, and principal of the Sanskrit College (from 1858). In 1867 he was appointed professor of Sanskrit at Cambridge. He edited and translated several important texts.

COWELL, Henry Dixon (1897–1965) American composer, born in Menlo Park, California. Noted as a leader of the avant-garde in American music, he developed many of the idiosyncrasies of his style while young, before undertaking orthodox studies in the Universities of California and New York. His book, *New Musical Resources* (1919), and *The New Musical Quarterly*, of which he was founder (1927), reflect his interest in experimental composition perhaps more than his own works, where 'progressive' styles appear with more traditional types of material. He composed 20 symphonies and a large number of other orchestral works.

COWELL, John (1554–1611) English jurist, born in Ernsborough, Devon. He was educated at Eton and King's College, Cambridge, where he became regius professor of civil law in 1594. His *Interpreter* (1607), a glossary of the legal meanings of words, was assailed by Sir **Edward Coke** for its controversial interpretation of the monarchy, and parliament ordered it to be burnt by the common hangman.

COWEN, Sir Frederic Hymen (1852–1935) English composer, born in Kingston, Jamaica. He was brought as a child to England. He composed operas, cantatas, oratorios, half-a-dozen symphonies, a number of overtures, pianoforte pieces, and minor works, and some 300 songs. In 1888–92 and 1900–07 he was conductor of the Philharmonic, in 1900–10 of the Scottish Orchestra. He published *My Art and My Friends* in 1913.

COWEN, Sir Zelman (1919–) Australian jurist, administrator and writer, born in St Kilda, Victoria. After serving in World War II with the Royal Australian Navy, he studied law at Oxford University. He became a fellow of Oriel College in 1947, and returned there as provost in 1982. From 1951 Sir Zelman was professor of public law, and dean of the faculty of law, at Melbourne University, and in 1967 was appointed emeritus professor. He was vice-chancellor of the University of New England, New South Wales (1966–70) and of the University of Queensland (1970–77). In 1977 he succeeded Sir **John Kerr** as governor-general of the Commonwealth of Australia, beginning 'a period of healing' after the controversy of the previous years. A regular broadcaster and commentator, he delivered the ABC's Boyer Lectures on 'The Private Man' in 1969. He was appointed chairman of the UK Press Council in 1983.

COWLEY, Abraham (1618–67) English poet, born in London, the seventh and posthumous child of a stationer. Attracted to poetry by the *Faërie Queen*, he wrote excellent verses at ten, and at fifteen published five poems. From Westminister School he proceeded in 1637 to Trinity College, Cambridge, and while there wrote, among many other pieces, a large portion of his epic the *Davideis*, its hero **David**. During the Civil War he was ejected from Cambridge (1644) but studied at Oxford for another two years. In 1646 he accompanied or followed the queen to Paris, was sent on Royalist missions, and carried on her correspondence in cipher with the king. He returned to England in 1654 and in 1655 was arrested, released on £1000 bail, and took the Oxford MD (1657). On **Oliver Cromwell**'s death he returned to Paris, but came home to England at the Restoration, and received a comfortable provision.

COWLEY, Malcolm (1898–1989) American critic and editor, born in Belsano, Pennsylvania. His father was a doctor, which enabled him to attend Harvard, though he had to struggle to make a living as a neophyte writer in New York and Paris. The experience of hardship, however, proved useful when he came to write *Exile's Return* (1934), about the illustrious group of American writers who convened in Paris after World War I. He returned to the theme with *A Second Flowering: Works and Days of the Lost Generation* (1973), and *The Dream of the Golden Mountains: Remembering the 1930s* (1980). He also published a volume of poetry, *Blue Juniata* (1929), and several volumes of essays. Long associated with *The New Republic* as literary editor (1929–44), and responsible for recognizing the talent of **John Cheever**, he is credited with resuscitating the career of **William Faulkner** by editing a Viking Portable selection of his work (1949).

COWPER, William (1666–1709) English surgeon and anatomist, born in Petersfield, in Sussex. He settled as a surgeon in London, and wrote *The Anatomy* *of Human Bodies* (1698), and discovered Cowper's glands.

COWPER, William (1731–1800) English poet, son of the rector of Great Berkhamstead, Hertfordshire. He was educated at Westminster School, where **Warren Hastings** and the poet **Charles Churchill** were contemporaries. In 1752 he took chambers in the Middle Temple and was called to the bar in 1754. He made no attempt to practise, but showed signs of mental instability. In 1763 he tried to commit suicide when he was offered the sinecure job of a clerkship in the House of Lords, involving a formal examination. Cured temporarily from his breakdown, he was received into the household of a retired evangelical clergyman, Morley Unwin, who with his wife Mary contrived to make the poet's stay at Huntingdon happy. On the death of Mr Unwin his widow removed with her children to Olney, in Buckinghamshire, which was henceforth to be associated with the name of Cowper. Unfortunately the curate of Olney, John Newton, was precisely the person to undo the work of tranquillizing the sick man. His gloomy piety, imposed on the poet, eventually caused a recurrence of his malady (1773), but the fruit of their association was the *Olney Hymns* (1779), to which Cowper contributed some hymns which are still favourites. In 1779 Newton accepted a charge in London and his absence was at once reflected in a restoration of the poet's spirits. Mrs Unwin suggested to him the writing of a series of moral satires which were published in 1782 (*Poems*) along with some occasional pieces which show the lighter side of his talent. Further to engage him in literary activity, Lady Austen now appeared on the scene (1781) as the occupant of Newton's vicarage. It is not known why her friendship with the poet was interrupted two years later, but *The Task*, published in 1785, came from her suggestion. Cowper's cousin, Lady Hesketh, took her place as literary director (1786), but Cowper seems to have exhausted himself as a creative poet and now turned only to translations—the **Homer**, which was not successful (1791), **Milton**'s Latin poems and some French and Italian translations. His genius, however, was still apparent in the short or occasional piece: 'On Receiving My Mother's Picture', 'To Mary' and 'Yardley Oak' (1791). Out of the darkest period, after Mrs Unwin's death in 1796, comes the wonderful, if tragic, 'Castaway'. The lighter side of Cowper's genius—the comic ballad 'John Gilpin', 'Table Talk', and the burlesque opening of *The Task*, a long poem on rural themes—should not be overlooked, but he is generally regarded as the poet of the evangelical revival and as the precursor of **Wordsworth** as a poet of Nature.

COWPER, William Cowper, Earl (c.1664–1723) English jurist. He became a barrister in 1688, MP for Hertford in 1695, lord keeper of the Great Seal in 1705, Baron Cowper in 1706, Lord Chancellor in 1707 and 1714, and Earl Cowper in 1718, in which year he resigned, and from a Whig became a leader of the opposition. He played a large part in negotiating the Union with Scotland (1707), made a substantial contribution to the development of modern equity and was well regarded as a judge.

COX, Brian (1946–) Scottish actor, teacher and director, born in Dundee. He made his London début as Orlando in *As You Like It* in 1967; his subsequent West End appearances include **Alan Bennett**'s *Getting On* (1971) and **Eugene O'Neill**'s *Strange Interlude* (1984). At the Royal Court he won huge acclaim for his performance as a police inspector in *Rat in the Skull* (1984). At the National Theatre, he appeared in *Tamburlaine* (1976), *Julius Caesar* (1977) and *Danton's Death* (1982). At the Royal Shakespeare Company his performances include Danton in **Pam Gems**'s *The Danton Affair* (1986), Petruchio in *The Taming of the Shrew* (1987), and the title role in *Titus Andronicus* (1987). He has made several television and film appearances, has taught drama extensively in London and became the first British actor to teach at the Moscow Art Theatre School.

COX, David (1783–1859) English landscape painter, born near Birmingham; a pupil of John Varley, he taught as a drawing-master from 1814 to 1826 in Hereford, publishing *A Treatise on Landscape Painting*. In 1813 he joined the Society of Painters in Watercolours, to whose exhibitions he was a regular contributor. In 1839 he turned his attention seriously to oil-painting, and executed about a hundred works in oil. In 1841 he settled at Harborne, near Birmingham, where he died. It was during this period that he produced his greatest works. They mainly owe their inspiration to the scenery of North Wales, and especially of Bettws-y-Coed, which he visited every autumn. The Birmingham Art Gallery has many examples of his work both in oil and watercolour, as also has the Tate Gallery. His son, David Cox (1809–85), was also a noted watercolourist.

COX, George William (1827–1902) English historian and mythologist, born in India. Educated at Rugby School and Trinity College, Oxford, he took holy orders in 1850. Among his works were *Tales of Ancient Greece* (1886), *Aryan Mythology* (1870), *History of Greece* (1874), *Comparative Mythology and Folklore* (1881), *Lives of Greek Statesmen* (1886), and *Life of Colenso* (1888).

COX, Richard (1500–81) English prelate and Protestant reformer, born in Whaddon, Buckinghamshire. Educated at Eton and King's College, Cambridge, he became headmaster of Eton and a favourite of Archbishop **Cranmer**. As vice-chancellor of Oxford (1547–52) he proscribed books, pictures and statues smacking of 'popery'. On the accession of Queen **Mary I** he was imprisoned, and then went into exile in Frankfurt, where he was a bitter opponent of **John Knox** and his Calvinist doctrines. Back in England, he was appointed Bishop of Ely (1559–80).

COX, William (1764–1837) English-born pioneer Australian road builder, born in Wimbourne Minster, Dorset. He arrived in Australia in 1800 as a lieutenant in the New South Wales Corps, and purchased land which he farmed. In 1814 Governor **Lachlan Macquarie** made him superintendent of works for a new road over the Blue Mountains, which was to reach the rich farming land of the central plains and the town of Bathurst, the first European settlement west of the Great Dividing Range. With 30 strong convict labourers Cox constructed, in just six months, 101 miles of road through rugged hills with precipitous gradients, building more than a dozen bridges to cross the mountain streams. The party started from Penrith, New South Wales, in July 1814 and reached Bathurst in January the following year, a road-building feat unequalled for many years. He received the first grant of land in the new district, returned to farming, and established a flock of sheep famous for the quality of its wool. He was appointed magistrate and later provisioned John Oxley's expeditions into western New South Wales, the new territory which had been opened up by Cox's road.

COXCIE, Michael See **COXIE**

COXE, Henry Octavius (1811–81) English librarian, born in Bucklebury, Berkshire. Educated at Westminster and Oxford, he entered the British Museum in 1833, and in 1838 the Bodleian Library, of which he became head in 1860. In 1857 he had toured the Levant, discovering many codices. He was rector of Wytham near Oxford, from 1868. Among his works were editions of **Roger of Wendover**'s *Chronicle* (1841–44) and **John Gower**'s *Vox Clamantis*; also catalogues of MSS in the Oxford Colleges and the Bodleian.

COXE, William (1747–1828) English historian, born in London. He was educated at Eton and King's College, Cambridge, of which he became a fellow in 1768. He was the author of *History of the House of Austria* and 13 other works of history and travel. He spent much of 20 years on the Continent, and died a prebendary of Salisbury and archdeacon of Wiltshire.

COXIE, Coxcie or **Coxius, Michiel** (1499–1592) Flemish painter, born in Mechelen. He introduced the Italian classical style into Flanders. Frescoes in S Maria dell' Anima at Rome are his work. He was court painter to **Philip II** of Spain.

COXWELL, Henry Tracey (1819–1900) English aviator, born in Wouldham rectory, near Rochester. Educated for the army, he became a surgeon-dentist in London. From boyhood he had taken a keen interest in ballooning, and in 1845 established the *Aerostatic Magazine*, thereafter making some 700 ascents—the most remarkable in 1862, when he reached, with **Glaisher**, a height of over seven miles.

COYSEVOX, Antoine (1640–1720) French sculptor, born in Lyon. He became court sculptor to **Louis XIV** in 1666 and was responsible for much of the decoration at the palace of Versailles, most notably the Galérie des Glaces and the Salon de la Guerre (containing an important relief equestrian sculpture of the king). His vigorous and decorative Baroque style—ultimately derived from **Bernini**—was appropriate for the flamboyance of the French court, though he also sculpted very fine portrait busts of, and memorials to, many important figures of the time, including **Charles Le Brun**, Cardinal **Mazarin** and **Jean Baptiste Colbert**.

COZENS, Alexander (d.1786) English watercolour painter, believed to be one of the two illegitimate sons of **Peter the Great** by a woman from Deptford who accompanied the Tsar to Russia. After studying in Italy, he came to England in 1746. In 1785 he published a treatise describing his method of using accidental ink-blots as the basis for landscape compositions.

COZENS, John Robert (1752–c.1799) English watercolour landscape painter, son of **Alexander Cozens**, born in London. In 1776 he visited Switzerland, and in 1783 returned from Italy. In 1794 his mind gave way, and in his later days he was befriended by Sir **George Beaumont** and Dr Munro. **Turner** and **Girtin** copied his drawings, and **John Constable** pronounced that 'his works were all poetry', that he was 'the greatest genius that ever touched landscape'.

COZZENS, James Gould (1903–78) American writer, born in Chicago. He published his first novel, *Confusion* (1924) while a student at Harvard at the age of 19. He fought with the American air force in World War II, and on his release from service wrote the Pulitzer prizewinning *Guard of Honour* (1948). Among his other works are *S.S. San Pedro* (1931), *Ask Me Tomorrow* (1940), *The Just and the Unjust* (1942), *By Love Possessed* (1958) and *Children and Others* (1965).

CRAB, Roger (c.1621–1680) English hermit. He served (1642–49) in the parliamentary army and then set up in business as a 'haberdasher of hats' at Chesham, Buckinghamshire; but in 1651 sold off his stock-in-trade, distributing the proceeds among the poor, and took up his residence in a hut, his sole drink water, and his food bran, turnip-tops, dock-leaves and grass. He published *The English Hermite*, *Dagon's Downfall* and a tract against Quakerism; and died in Bethnal Green.

CRABBE, George (1754–1832) English poet, born in Aldeburgh on the Suffolk Coast, son of a 'salt-master' and warehousekeeper. His father's violence was offset by his mother's piety. Two of his three brothers perished at sea. His schooling was irregular, but he managed to pick up enough surgery in a nine month's course in London to enable him to set up poorly as a surgeon in Aldeburgh. This was not his chosen career, for he had already published *Inebriety, a Poem* in 1775 and *The Candidate*. He ventured into the literary world in London in 1780, but lived in poverty, unrelieved by appeals to various patrons of letters, until a favourable answer from **Edmund Burke** changed the course of his life. As the guest of Burke at Beaconsfield, he met the noted men of the day, published *The Library* (1781), and patronage flowed in. He was ordained in 1782 and the next year was established in the Duke of Rutland's seat at Belvoir with the prospect of various livings to follow his chaplaincy there. After his marriage to Sarah Elmy (1783) he spent happy years in charges in Suffolk (1792–1805); returned to Muston in Leicestershire; and finally settled in Trowbridge, Wiltshire. In 1783 *The Village*, a harshly realistic poem about village life sponsored by Burke and Dr **Johnson**, brought him fame. Twenty-four years passed before *The Parish Register* (1807) revealed his gifts as a narrative poet. He followed this with *The Borough* (1810), a collection of 24 tales in letter-form (which were later to form the basis of **Benjamin Britten**'s opera, *Peter Grimes*). *Tales* followed in 1812, showing no diminution of his powers of narrative and character-drawing. *Tales of the Hall* (1819) concluded this remarkable output of narrative genius. Crabbe's manner suited all tastes—he is still read because of his veracity and his masterly genre painting of humble and middle-class life. His strict moralism—the miseries of the poor are due to sin and insobriety—seems strange to the modern reader, but the grim stories of madness as in 'Sir Eustace Grey' (*Parish Register*) and the comic wooing in 'The Frank Courtship' (*Tales*), show his craft at its best.

CRADDOCK, Charles Egbert, pseud of **Mary Noailles Murfree** (1850–1922) American writer, born in Murfreesboro, Tennessee. She published short stories in the *Atlantic Monthly* from 1878, published as *In the Tennessee Mountains* (1884), and thereafter became a prolific novelist of mountain backwoods life.

CRAIG, Christopher (c.1936–) convicted British murderer. On Sunday 2 November 1952, he and his friend **Derek Bentley** broke into a confectionery warehouse in Croydon. They were seen climbing over the fence, and the police were alerted. Bentley, who was later found to be carrying a knife and a knuckleduster, and Craig, who was armed with a gun, were approached by the police. Bentley was quickly apprehended, but Craig fired several shots, initially wounding one policeman and then killing another. In a suicide attempt, he threw himself off the roof of the building, but he only succeeded in fracturing his spine. Both boys were eventually arrested and charged. A secret cache of arms was found in Craig's house which further stirred the imagination of the press and the public. The case was heard on 4 December 1952. Craig's defence claimed that his actions were invoked by the violent comics and films for which he had an insatiable appetite. He and Bentley were both found guilty. Craig was sentenced to an indefinite period of detention, as he was too young to receive the death penalty. Bentley was sentenced to be hanged. Despite vigorous attempts by Bentley's family and by members of parliament to gain a reprieve, Bentley was hanged. Craig was released from prison in 1963.

CRAIG, Edward Gordon (1872–1966) English actor and stage designer, the son of **Ellen Terry** and **William Godwin**. He was for eight years an actor under Irving, retiring from the stage in 1897; but it was his understanding of the actor's point of view that gave him his special approach to theatrical design. His aim of simplifying the scene and emphasizing the actors was too advanced for England, where his three productions for his mother were failures; but he was acclaimed in Germany, Italy and Russia, where he produced *Hamlet* (1912) at the Moscow Arts Theatre. In 1905 he met **Isadora Duncan**, with whom he travelled through Europe. He settled in Italy in 1906, published a quarterly, *The Mask*, from 1908 to 1929, and founded a theatrical art school in Florence in 1913. He greatly influenced scenic design in America and Europe, and his published works include *On the Art of the Theatre* (1911), *Towards a New Theatre* (1913), *Ellen Terry and Her Secret Self* (1931), and the autobiographical *Index to the Story of My Days* (1957).

CRAIG, James, 1st Viscount Craigavon (1871–1940) Ulster politician, born in Belfast. A Unionist MP on the British Parliament (1906–21), he was resolutely opposed to Home Rule for Ireland as it might affect Ulster. When the Stormont Parliament was established in 1921, he became the first prime minister of Northern Ireland (1921–40).

CRAIG, Sir James Henry (1748–1812) British soldier, born in Gibraltar. He joined the army at 15 and served with distinction in America where he was wounded at Bunker Hill and helped capture Ticonderoga (1777). In 1795, as major general, he took Cape Colony and served as its governor from 1795 to 1797. He was governor general of Canada from 1807 to 1811.

CRAIG, John (1512–1600) Scottish reformer. He lost his father at Flodden (1514), and was educated at St Andrews. He joined the Dominicans there, but fell under suspicion of heresy, and after a brief imprisonment (1536) went to Rome. Through Cardinal **Reginald Pole** he gained admission to the Dominican convent of Bologna; but Calvin's *Institutes* converted him to Protestantism. On 18 August 1559, he was lying in the dungeon of the Inquisition, condemned to suffer next morning at the stake, when Pope **Paul IV** died, and the mob set the prisoners at liberty. A bandit befriended him; a dog brought him a purse of gold; he escaped to Vienna, and there preached in his friar's habit, one of his listeners being the Archduke Maximilian. Presently the new pope, learning his whereabouts, demanded his surrender; but Maximilian gave him a safe conduct, and in 1560 he returned to Scotland. In 1563 he was appointed coadjutor to **John Knox**; in 1567 incurred some censure for proclaiming, under strong protest, the banns between **Mary, Queen of Scots** and **Bothwell**: and in 1572 was sent to 'illuminate the dark places' in Angus and Aberdeenshire. He came back to Edinburgh in 1579 as a royal chaplain, had a share with **Andrew Melville** in the Second Book of Discipline, and drew up the 'Confession of Faith'.

CRAIG, Sir Thomas of Riccarton (1538–1608) Scottish writer on feudal law, born either in Craigfintray (Aberdeenshire) or in Edinburgh. From St Andrews University he passed in 1555 to Paris, and in 1563 was admitted a Scottish advocate, being next year appointed justice-depute of Scotland, and in 1573 sheriff-depute of Edinburgh. Besides an epithalamium on the marriage of **Mary, Queen of Scots** to Lord Darnley, several more Latin poems, and the masterly *Jus Feudale* (1608), which is a Scottish legal classic relating the development of Scots law to that of European systems, he wrote *De Unione Regnorum* (Scottish Hist Soc 1910), and Latin treatises on **James VI**'s right to the English throne and on the homage controversy between Scotland and England.

CRAIGIE, Sir William Alexander (1867–1957) Scottish philologist and lexicographer, born in Dundee. Educated in Dundee and at St Andrews, he went to Balliol College, Oxford, for a year before going to Copenhagen to study Old Icelandic. While he was assistant to the professsor of Latin at St Andrews (1893–97), he produced *Scandinavian Folk-Lore* (1897). In 1897 he joined Sir **James Murray** in the compilation of the *Oxford English Dictionary* (joint editor, 1901–33). In 1916 he was appointed professor of Anglo-Saxon at Oxford, and in 1925–36 was professor of English at the university of Chicago, where he compiled the *Historical Dictionary of American English* (4 vols, 1936–44). From 1936 to 1955 he was editor of the *Dictionary of the Older Scottish Tongue*. A scholar of encyclopedic knowledge, he also wrote *The Icelandic Sagas* (1913), *The Pronunciation of English* (1917, *Easy Readings in Anglo-Saxon* (1923), *The Poetry of Iceland* (1925), and a monumental study of Iceland *rímur* ('rhymes'), *Sýnisbók íslenkra rímna* (3 vols, 1952).

CRAIK, Dinah Maria, née **Mulock** (1826–87) English novelist, born in Stoke-upon-Trent. Settling in London at 20, she published *The Ogilvies* (1849), *Olive* (1850), *The Head of the Family* (1851), and *Agatha's Husband* (1853). Her best-known novel was *John Halifax, Gentleman* (1857). In 1865 she married George Lillie Craik, nephew of **George Lillie Craik**, a partner in the publishing house of Macmillan.

CRAIK, George Lillie (1798–1866) Scottish scholar, born in Kennoway, Fife. He studied for the Church at St Andrews, but went to London in 1826, and in 1849 became professor of history and English literature at Queen's College, Belfast. He wrote *The History of English Literature and the English Language* (1861). His youngest daughter, Georgiana Marion (1831–95; Mrs May), was a popular novelist.

CRAIK, Kenneth J W (1914–45) Scottish experimental psychologist. Educated at Edinburgh and Cambridge, he spent much of World War II on applied military research on topics which included servomechanisms and 'human factors' in design. In 1944 he was appointed director of the new Unit for Research in Applied Psychology at Cambridge set up by the Medical Research Council. He pioneered that major modern psychological school of thought in which the mind is considered as a complex example of an information-processing system. The development of this metaphor, with the help of digital computers, is known nowadays as Cognitive Science. He died tragically early following a cycling accident in Cambridge on the eve of VE Day. His writings establish him as an original thinker, whose ideas have been of lasting influence in postwar experimental and physiological psychology.

CRAM, Steve (Steven) (1960–) English middle distance runner, born in Jarrow. As a young athlete, he was inspired by the feats of another runner from the north-east of England, **Brendan Foster**, and emerged from the shadows of **Sebastian Coe** and **Steve Ovett**, who had dominated 800 metre and 1500 metre running. He won the 1500 metre titles in the World Championships (1983), European Championships (1982) and Commonwealth Games (1982), as well as the silver medal in the 1984 Olympics. His elegant style, effortless acceleration and striking golden hair made him a favourite at track meetings. He broke three world records in just 19 days in 1985, at 1500 metres, one mile and 2000 metres.

CRAMER, Johann Baptist (1771–1858) German-born pianist, born in Mannheim, the son of Wilhelm Cramer (1745–99), a British musician who settled in London in 1772. From 1788 he undertook concert tours on the Continent, and gained a high reputation. He founded in 1828 the London musical publishing firm of Cramer and Co, and, after some years' residence in Paris, died in London. Most of his compositions are forgotten, except for his *Études*, which is an important work.

CRAMPTON, Thomas Russell (1816–88) English engineer, born in Broadstairs. He was a pioneer of locomotive construction and was responsible for the first successful cross-channel submarine cable, between Dover and Calais, in 1851. He built the Berlin waterworks (1855), and many railway systems.

CRANACH, Lucas, called **'the Elder'** (1472–1553) German painter, born in Kronach, near Bamberg. He seems to have been instructed by his father, and was court painter at Wittenberg to the Elector Frederick the Wise of Saxony. In 1509 he accompanied an embassy to the emperor **Maximilian I**, and while in the Netherlands portrayed the future **Charles V**. In 1537, and again in 1540, he was elected burgomaster of Wittenberg. He repaired to Augsburg in 1550 to share the captivity of John Frederick, and on the Elector's release (1552) went with him to Weimar, where he died. His paintings include sacred and a few classical subjects, hunting scenes and portraits. He was closely associated with the German Reformers, many of whom (including **Luther** and **Melanchthon**) were portrayed by himself and his pupils. A *Crucifixion* in the Stadkirche, Weimar, is his masterpiece. His wood engravings are numerous. Of three sons, all painters, the second, Lucas the Younger (1515–86), painted so like his father that their works are difficult to distinguish.

CRANBORNE, Viscount See **CECIL**

CRANBROOK, Gathorne Gathorne-Hardy, 1st Earl (1814–1906) English politician, born in Bradford. Educated at Shrewsbury and at Oriel College, Oxford, he was called to the bar in 1840, and in 1856 was returned as Conservative MP for Leominster. In 1865 he defeated **Gladstone** in the famous Oxford University election; in 1878 he was made Viscount and in 1892 Earl Cranbrook. He was under-secretary for the home department (1858–59), president of the poor law board (1866–67), home secretary (1867–68), war secretary (1874–78), secretary for India (1878–80) and lord president of the council (1885–92).

CRANE, Harold Hart (1899–1932) American poet, born in Garrettsville, Ohio. He had little formal education and resisted attempts to place him in the business world, but worked as an advertising copywriter in New York before he found a patron who gave him the wherewithal to travel and devote himself to poetry. A pederastic alcoholic, given to troughs of shame and remorse, he placed a heavy burden on his friends' tolerance and wallets. Nevertheless he managed to write two long, symbolic poems—*White Buildings* (1926) and *The Bridge* (1930)—variously hailed as masterpieces and unintelligible, and he has emerged as one of America's major poets. Returning to America from Mexico, where he had attempted unsuccessfully to write an epic poem on *Montezuma*, and convinced he had betrayed the woman with whom he was in love, he drowned himself by leaping from a steamboat into the Caribbean.

CRANE, Stephen (1871–1900) American writer and war correspondent, born in New Jersey. He worked as a journalist in New York before publishing his first novel, *Maggie: A Girl of the Streets* (1893). His reputation, however, rests on *The Red Badge of Courage* (1895), which relates vividly the experiences of a soldier in the American Civil War. He had no personal experience of the war but the book was received with acclaim, in particular for its psychological realism. He never repeated its success but was lionized by literary London (befriended by **Joseph Conrad** and meeting **H G Wells**) before succumbing to tuberculosis in Baden Baden.

CRANE, Walter (1845–1915) English painter and illustrator, born in Liverpool, the son of the portrait painter Thomas Crane (1808–59). As an apprentice to the wood engraver, **William James Linton**, he came under the influence of the pre-Raphaelites, and became a leader with **William Morris** in the Arts and Crafts movement, and in early socialism. He was particularly celebrated as an illustrator of children's books. His finest achievement was his illustrated edition of **Spenser**'s *Faerie Queen* (1894–96). In his paintings he was much influenced by **Botticelli**. He was director of Manchester School of Art (1893–96), Reading College (1896–98), and principal of the Royal College of Art (1898–99).

CRANKO, John (1927–73) South African choreographer, born in Rustenburg. From the age of 16, when he made a piece for the Cape Town Ballet Club, choreography was his overriding interest. In 1946 he moved to Britain to study, and joined Sadler's Wells Theatre Ballet (1946–61, resident choreographer in 1950). He made over 30 dances, including *Pineapple Poll* (1951), and his first full length ballet *Prince of the Pagodas* with music by **Benjamin Britten** (1957). He also wrote the musical revue *Cranks* (1955). In 1961 he moved to Germany to become artistic director of the Stuttgart Ballet, which he shaped into a company of international renown. With a love of drama and physical intensity, he choreographed ballets like *Romeo and Juliet* (1958), *Onegin* (1969) and *Carmen* (1971). One-act ballets include *Jeu de Cartes* (1965) and *Initials R.B.M.E.* (1972).

CRANMER, Thomas (1489–1556) English prelate and archbishop of Canterbury, born in Aslacton or Aslockton, Nottinghamshire. He was sent in 1503 by his widowed mother to Jesus College, Cambridge, where in 1510 he obtained a fellowship. He forfeited it by his marriage with 'black Joan' of the Dolphin tavern, but regained it on her death before the year's grace was up, and took holy orders in 1523. During an epidemic of the plague, he left Cambridge for Waltham in 1529 with two pupils. Here he met **John Foxe** and **Stephen Gardiner** and with them discussed **Henry VIII**'s proposed divorce from **Catherine of Aragon**. Cranmer suggested an appeal to the universities of Christendom, which pleased Henry, and he subsequently became a counsel in the suit. He was appointed a royal chaplain and archdeacon of Taunton; was attached to the household of **Ann Boleyn**'s father (Anne at the time being Henry's paramour); and was sent on two embassies, to Italy in 1530 and to **Charles V** in Germany in 1532. At Rome, Pope **Clement VII** made him grand penitentiary of England. At Nuremberg he met and married a niece of the reformer **Osiander**; soon afterwards a royal summons reached him to return as **Warham**'s successor, as archbishop of Canterbury. He sent his wife secretly over, and himself following, was consecrated in March. He took the oath of allegiance to the pope, with a protest that he took it 'for form's sake'. In May, Cranmer pronounced Catherine's marriage null and void *ab initio* and the private marriage to Anne Boleyn, four months earlier, valid; in September he stood godfather to Anne's daughter **Elizabeth**. In 1536 he annulled Henry's marriage with Anne Boleyn, divorced him from **Anne of Cleves** (1540), informed him of **Catherine Howard**'s premarital affairs, then strove to coax her into confessing them (1541). He did what he dared to oppose the Six Articles of 1539, which sought to impose uniformity of dogma; one of these made the marriage of priests punishable with death, whereupon he sent his wife away to Germany and did not recall her until 1548. He was a kindly and humane man by nature, but nevertheless his episcopacy saw the burning of **Frith** and Lambert for denying transubstantiation (1533–38), of Friar Forest for upholding the papal supremacy (1538), of two Anabaptists (1538), of Joan Bocher for denying **Christ**'s humanity (1550), and of a Dutch Arian (1551). He promoted the translation of the Bible and a service-book, and curtailed the number of holy days. In 1547 Henry died, and Cranmer sang mass of requiem for his soul. He had been slowly drifting into Protestantism, but now was quickly swept into great religious changes. In 1548 he compiled **Edward VI**'s First Prayer Book (which converted the mass into communion), composed the 42 articles of religion (1553), later called the 39 Articles, and in 1552 rephrased the Prayer Book. During this, as during the preceding reign, he meddled little with affairs of state though he was one of the council of regency. What he did do was not too creditable. In gross violation of the canon law he signed **Thomas Seymour**'s death warrant (1549); he had a chief hand in the depostion and imprisonment of Bishops Bonner, Gardiner and Day; and, won over by the dying boy-king's pleading, he reluctantly subscribed the instrument diverting the succession from **Mary** to Lady **Jane Grey** (1553). By this he was guilty of conscious perjury, yet when the twelve-days' reign was over he made no attempt to flee. On 14 September he was sent to the Tower, on 13 November was arraigned for treason, and, pleading guilty, was condemned to die. In March 1554 he went to Oxford where he bravely faced his trial before the papal commissioner, whose jurisdiction he refused to recognize. In October, from jail, he witnessed **Latimer**'s and **Ridley**'s martyrdom; and on 14 February 1556, he was formally degraded. In rapid succession he signed seven increasingly submissive recantations. The last he transcribed on 21 March, and was immediately taken to St Mary's Church, where he heard that he was to be burnt. When the time came for him to read his recantation, he retracted all that he had written. Taken to the stake, he thrust his right hand into the flame and kept it there, crying: 'This hath offended! Oh this unworthy hand!'. Among Cranmer's 42 writings are his prefaces to the Bible (1540) and the First Prayer Book (1549); the *Reformatio Legum Ecclesiasticarum* (1571), and *A Defence of the Doctrine of the Sacrament* (1550).

CRANWORTH, Robert Monsey Rolfe, Lord (1790–1868) English judge, born in Cranworth, Yorkshire. Educated at Winchester and Trinity College, Cambridge, he became solicitor-general in 1834 and 1835–39, a baron of Exchequer in 1839, a vice-chancellor in 1850, a lord justice of appeal in 1851 and Lord Chancellor in 1852–58 and 1865–66. He initiated work on the consolidation and simplification of the statute law, contemplated codification (a Code Victoria), and started the series of statute law revision acts. He secured the passing of a common law procedure act and reforms in conveyancing. A sound and acute judge, he set in motion many beneficial reforms.

CRASHAW, Richard (c.1613–1649) English religious poet, born in London, the only son of the Puritan poet and clergyman William Crashaw (1572–1626). From the Charterhouse he proceeded in 1631 to Pembroke Hall, Cambridge, and c.1636 became a fellow of Peterhouse College. In 1634 he published a volume of Latin poems, *Epigrammatum Sacrocorum Liber* (2nd ed 1670), in which occurs the famous line on the miracle at Cana: '*Nymphas pudica Deum vidit et erubuit*' (the modest water saw its God and blushed). His Catholic leanings prevented him from receiving Anglican orders, and in 1643 he lost his fellowship for refusing to take the Covenant. He went to Paris and embraced Catholicism, and in 1646 published his *Steps to the Temple*, republished at Paris in 1652, under the title *Carmen Deo Nostro*, with twelve vignette engravings designed by Crashaw. Soon afterwards he was introduced by John Cowley to Queen **Henrietta Maria**, who recommended him at Rome; and in April 1649 he became a subcanon at Loretto, but died four months afterwards.

CRASSUS, Lucius Licinius (140–91 BC) Roman orator. In 95 he was elected consul, along with Quintus Scaevola; and during their consulship a rigorous law was enacted banishing from Rome all who had not the full rights of citizens, which was one of the chief causes of the Social War (90–88). Crassus is the chief speaker in **Cicero**'s *De Oratore*, and represents the writer's own opinions.

CRASSUS, Marcus Licinius (c.115–153 BC) Roman financier and politician, known as 'Dives', 'The Rich'. He was a protégé and supporter of **Sulla** in the civil war against **Gaius Marius** (88–82 BC) and distinguished himself in the battle against the Samnites at the gates of Rome. As praetor he crushed the revolt of **Spartacus** at the battle of Lucania (71), and in 72 was made consul with **Pompey**, a colleague whom he hated. **Caesar** valued the friendship of Crassus, the richest of Roman citizens. About 60, Caesar, Pompey and Crassus entered into the first triumvirate. In 55, as consul with Pompey, Crassus had Syria assigned him for his province, and in war against the Parthians, misled by a treacherous guide, he was utterly defeated in the plains of Mesopotamia. Retreating towards Armenia, he was beguiled into a conference with the Parthian general Surenas, and slain.

CRATES OF ATHENS (early 3rd century BC) Greek philosopher who succeeded Potemo and preceded **Arcesilas** as head of the Academy. Not to be confused with Crates of Tarsus, who was head of the Academy about 130 BC, or Crates of Thebes, a disciple of **Diogenes of Sinope** in the fourth century BC. His main claims to fame were that he was teacher of **Zeno of Citium** and that he had sex in public to make a philosophical point about social conventions.

CRATES, of Chalkis (fl.335–325 BC) Greek engineer, one of several who carried out notable works for **Alexander the Great,** including the building of the new city and port of Alexandria in the Nile delta. Other projects with which he is thought to have been concerned include works of drainage, irrigation and water supply, as well as an attempt to drive two tunnels each more than a mile long which, however, was abandoned before completion.

CRATINUS (c.519–423 BC) Greek comic poet. Next to Eupolis and **Aristophanes**, he best represents the Old Attic comedy. He limited the number of actors to three, and was the first to add to comedy the interest of biting personal attack; even **Pericles** did not escape his pen. Of his 21 comedies, nine of which obtained the first public prize, on one occasion beating Aristophanes' *Clouds*, only some fragments are extant, collected in Meineke's *Fragmenta Comicorum Graecorum* (Berlin 1840). A younger Cratinus, a contemporary of **Plato**, belonged to the Middle Comedy.

CRATIPPUS (1st century BC) Peripatetic philosopher, a native of Mitylene, and a contemporary of

Cicero, whose son Marcus he instructed at Athens in 44 BC. Pompey visited him after Pharsalia, and **Marcus Brutus** turned aside to Athens to hear him, even while making preparations to meet **Octavianus Augustus** and **Marcus Antonius**. Nothing that he wrote has survived.

CRAVEN, Daniel Hartman (1911–) South African rugby player and administrator, born in Lindley, Orange Free State. A versatile player who represented his country in four different positions, he was captain of South Africa against the visiting Lions side in 1938. He was also for many years coach to Stellenbosch University, but it is as an adminstrator that his greatest contribution was made to the Rubgy Union game. He became chairman of the South African Rugby Board in 1956 and over the next 30 years worked untiringly to keep South Africa within the Rugby Union fold and, later, to have it reinstated.

CRAVEN, William, Earl of Craven (1606–97) English soldier, son of a lord mayor of London. He served in the Low Countries on behalf of **Elizabeth of Bohemia**, daughter of **James VI and I** and was taken prisoner with her son, Prince **Rupert**, purchasing his liberty in 1639 and subsequently attaching himself to the exiled queen's court at The Hague. A man of great wealth, he assisted **Charles I** financially, and his estates were sequestered in 1652 but returned at the Restoration. He was made an earl by **Charles II** in 1664 and a number of offices were bestowed upon him, including that of lord-lieutenant of Middlesex, but he retained his attachment to Elizabeth of Bohemia.

CRAWFORD AND BALCARRES, Alexander William Crawford Lindsay, 25th/8th Earl of (1812–80) Scottish nobleman, born in Muncaster Castle, Cumberland, and educated at Eton and Trinity College, Cambridge. His researches enabled him in 1848 to establish his father's claim to the Crawford title (the premier earldom of Scotland; cr 1398). A great book-collector, he wrote *Letters on the Holy Land* (1838), *Progression by Antagonism* (1846), *Sketches of the History of Christian Art* (1847), *Lives of the Lindsays* (1849) and *The Earldom of Mar* (1882). He died in Florence; his body, stolen from the mausoleum at Dunecht, near Aberdeen, was found in a nearby wood some months afterwards.

CRAWFORD, Joan, originally **Lucille Le Sueur** (1906–77) American film actress, born in San Antonio, Texas. A chorus girl, she arrived in Hollywood in 1924 to work as an extra at M-G-M, and gained some recognition in films like *Our Dancing Daughters* (1928), and *Our Blushing Brides* (1930). She created a niche for herself as the star of many formula melodramas, usually as a working-class girl with her sights set on wealth and sophistication, and became the archetypal glamorous Hollywood Movie Queen. She was declared 'box-office poison' in 1938, but returned as the wickedly witty husband-stealer in *The Women* (1939). Later, she continued to suffer in jewels and ermine as the older woman beset by emotional problems, in *Mildred Pierce* (1945, Academy Award) and *Whatever Happened to Baby Jane*? (1962), a stylish exercise in gothic horror, but she retired after *Trog* (1970). An autobiography, *Portrait of Joan*, appeared in 1962 and her adopted daughter Christina wrote a scathing attack on her domestic tyranny in *Mommie Dearest* (1978).

CRAWFORD, Sir John Grenfell (1910–85) Australian economist and administrator, born in Hurstville, Sydney, and educated at Sydney University. He held various senior positions in agricultural and rural economics including director of the [Australian] Commonwealth Bureau of Agricultural Economics (1945–50). He was senior agricultural advisor to the World Bank, and a member of its economic mission to India (1964–65). He held the chair of economics at the Australian National University, Canberra (1960–67) and was vice-chancellor there (1968–73). He had a strong interest in developing countries, and was sometime chairman of the Papua New Guinea Development Bank, and chancellor of the University of Papua New Guinea from 1972 to 1975. He received many honours for his work, including the Japanese Order of the Sacred Treasure in 1972, and was president of the Australian and New Zealand Association for the Advancement of Science (1967–68).

CRAWFORD, Michael (1942–) English actor, and one of Britain's leading performers in musicals. As a boy he was in the original cast of **Benjamin Britten**'s *Let's Make an Opera* (1949), and *Noah's Flood* (1958). His performance in *No Sex Please, We're British* (1971) established him as a highly-gifted comedy actor. He went on to star in such musicals as *Billy* (1974), *Flowers for Algernon* (1979), and *Barnum* (1981). In the 1970s the television series *Some Mothers Do 'Ave 'Em*, in which he played the accident-prone misfit Frank Spencer, made him a household name in Britain. His performance in **Andrew Lloyd Webber**'s *The Phantom of the Opera* (1986) was universally praised. His films include *The Knack* (1964), *How I Won the War* (1966), *Hello Dolly* (1968) and *Condorman* (1980).

CRAWFORD, Osbert Guy Stanhope (1886–1957) English archaeologist and pioneer aerial photographer, born in Bombay. Educated at Marlborough, he studied classics and then geography at Keble College, Oxford, and developed an interest in field archaeology. Serving with the Royal Flying Corps on the Western Front in World War I, he identified the potential of aerial photography in archaeology, his enthusiasm culminating in the classic album *Wessex from the Air* (1928). He served as the first archaeology officer of the Ordnance Survey (1920–40) and did much to develop the cartographic recording of archaeology, especially in period maps such as the *Ordnance Survey Map of Roman Britain* (1924). In 1927 he founded the journal *Antiquity*, which he edited until his death. His idiosyncratic *Archaeology in the Field* appeared in 1953 and an autobiography, *Said and Done*, in 1955.

CRAWFORD, Thomas (1814–57) American sculptor, born in New York City. He studied in Rome with **Thorvaldsen**. His works include the fine Washington monument at Richmond and the bronze figure of Liberty surmounting the dome of the capitol at Washington.

CRAWFORD, William Harris (1772–1834) American politician, born in Virginia. He practised law at Lexington, Georgia, and was elected to the state senate in 1802 and to the US senate in 1807 and 1811. Appointed minister to France in 1813 and secretary of the treasury in 1816, he was a Democratic candidate for the presidency in 1824.

CRAWFURD, John (1783–1868) Scottish orientalist, born on Islay. He served (1803–27) as an East Indian army doctor, he was envoy to Siam, and in 1823 succeeded Sir **Thomas Stamford Raffles** as administrator of Singapore.

CRAXI, Bettino (1934–) Italian politician, born in Milan. After being active in the Socialist Youth Movement he became a member of the Central Committee of the Italian Socialist party (PSI) in 1957, a member of the National Executive in 1965, was deputy secretary, 1970–76, and became general secretary in 1976. After the general election of July 1983 he became Italy's first socialist prime minister, successfully leading a broad-based coalition until 1987.

CRAY, Seymour R (1925–) American computer designer, born in Chippewa Falls, Wisconsin. Educated at Wisconsin University, he has made his name synonymous with the word 'supercomputer'. He established himself at the forefront of large-scale computer design through his work at Engineering Research Associates, Remington Rand, UNIVAC and Control Data Corporation. In 1972 he organized Cray Research Inc in Chippewa Falls to develop and market the most powerful computer systems available. He is now a consultant director of the firm.

CREASY, Sir Edward Shepherd (1812–78) English jurist and historian, born in Bexley, Kent. From Eton College he passed to King's College, Cambridge, and in 1834 was elected a fellow. Called to the bar in 1837, he went on the home circuit for over 20 years, and in 1840 was appointed professor of history at London University, and in 1860 chief-justice of Ceylon. In 1870 he came home invalided on a year's leave of absence, in 1871 went out again, but had to return finally in 1873. He was author of *The Fifteen Decisive Battles of the World* (1851), *Invasions of England* (1852), and *History of the Ottoman Turks* (1854–56).

CRÉBILLON, Claude Prosper Jolyot de (1707–77) French novelist, younger son of **Prosper Jolyot de Crébillon**, born in Paris. After writing a number of slight pieces for the stage, he acquired great popularity as an author of licentious stories. In 1740 he married an Englishwoman, Lady Stafford. The indecency of his *Le Sopha, conte moral*, having offended Madame **de Pompadour**, he was banished from Paris for five years, but on his return in 1755 was appointed to the censorship.

CRÉBILLON, Prosper Jolyot de (1674–1762) French dramatist, born in Dijon. He studied in Paris for the law. His tragedy of *Idoménée* was successfully produced in 1703. It was followed by *Atrée et Thyeste* (1707), *Électre* (1709), and *Rhadamiste et Zénobie* (1711), his masterpiece. After writing several other pieces, Crébillon fell into neglect and produced nothing for over 20 years. He was then pushed forward as a dramatic rival to **Voltaire** by Madame **de Pompadour**, elected to the Academy, awarded a pension of 1000 francs, and appointed royal censor and a royal librarian. His *Catilina* was brought out with great success in 1748. Among his other works were *Xerxès*, *Sémiramis*, *Pyrrhus*, and *Le Triumvirat*.

CREDI, Lorenzo di (1459–1537) Italian painter, born in Florence. He was the fellow-pupil, lifelong friend, and executor of **Leonardo da Vinci**. He painted mainly Holy Families, and executed his works with great craftsmanship. Examples may be seen in the National Gallery and the Louvre.

CREECH, Thomas (1659–1700) English classical scholar, born in Blandford. Headmaster of Sherborne and rector of Welwyn, Hertfordshire, he translated **Lucretius** into heroic rhyming couplets, and also translated other authors. He committed suicide by hanging.

CREECH, William (1745–1815) Scottish publisher, born in Newbattle, Midlothian. He studied medicine at Edinburgh, but became a partner in a printing firm in 1771 and sole proprietor in 1773. His premises became a centre of literary and social activity in Edinburgh. He published the first Edinburgh edition of **Robert Burns**, the works of **Robert Blair**, **Beattie** and **Dugald Stewart**, and **Henry Mackenzie**'s periodicals, *The Mirror* and *The Lounger*.

CREED, Frederick George (1871–1957) Canadian inventor, born in Nova Scotia. He came to Glasgow in 1897 and there perfected the Creed teleprinter, used in news offices all over the world.

CREELEY, Robert (1926–) American poet, born in Arlington, Massachusetts. Appointed to the faculty at Black Mountain College in North Carolina he was linked with the Black Mountain school of poets. In the mid-1950s he moved to California where he mixed with prominent 'beat' writers like **Kerouac** and **Ginsberg**. His poems, characterized by dense syntax and abrupt endings, have appeared in numerous collections including *If You* (1956), *The Whip* (1957), *For You: Poems 1950–60* (1962), *St Martin's* (1971) and *The Collected Poems of Robert Creeley, 1945–75* (1982). He has written one novel, *The Island* (1963); other prose appears in *The Collected Prose of Robert Creeley: A Story* (1984).

CREEVEY, Thomas (1768–1838) English politician and diarist. He was a Whig MP for Thetford in 1802, and later Appleby, and became treasurer of ordnance (1830) and treasurer of Greenwich hospital. He is remembered for the *Creevey Papers*, a journal important as a source of Georgian social history.

CREIGHTON, Mandell (1843–1901) English historian, born in Carlisle. A fellow of Merton College, Oxford, from 1866, he became first professor of ecclesiastical history at Cambridge in 1884, bishop of Peterborough in 1891, and of London (1896). His chief works are *Simon de Montfort* (1876), *History of the Papacy during the Reformation Period* (5 vols, 1882–94) and *Queen Elizabeth* (1897).

CREMER, Sir William Randal (1838–1908) English pacifist, born in Fareham. An active trade unionist, he was a strong advocate of British neutrality in the Franco-Prussian war, and founded the Workmen's Peace Association, the germ of the International Arbitration League. A radical MP from 1885, he edited the peace journal *Arbitor* from 1889. In 1903 he won the Nobel peace prize.

CRÉMIEUX, Benjamin (1888–1944) French writer and critic, born in Narbonne. He is known for his works on modern European literature, including the *XXe siècle* (1924) and for his translation of the plays of **Pirandello**. He died in Buchenwald concentration camp.

CREON according to Greek legend, the brother of Jocasta, wife of Laius, king of Thebes. When Laius was killed, Creon offered the hand of Jocasta and the kingdom to anyone who would free Thebes from the scourge of the Sphinx. **Oedipus**, son of Laius and Jocasta, who had already unwittingly killed his father, succeeded in this and married his mother Jocasta. After the fall of Oedipus, Creon became king of Thebes and took under his care the children of Oedipus and Jocasta. **Sophocles**' tragedy *Antigone* tells how one of these, Polynices, was denied burial by Creon after attacking Thebes together with other chieftains (the Seven against Thebes), and being killed in combat by his brother Eteocles. Antigone, sister of Polynices, defied the order, and was punished by Creon by being buried alive. Creon's son Haemon, who was betrothed to Antigone, then committed suicide on her body.

CRERAR, Henry Duncan Graham (1888–1965) Canadian soldier, born in Hamilton, Ontario, of Scottish parentage. Educated at Upper Canada College and Royal Military College, Kingston, he worked as a civil engineer while holding a commission in the militia. In World War I he served with the Canadian Artillery in France. In World War II he was chief of Canadian Army Staff (1940–41), commanded the 2nd Canadian Division (1942) and the Canadian Corps in Italy (1942–44) and succeeded **Andrew McNaughton** in command of the Canadian Land Forces in Europe (1944).

CRESCAS, Hasdai ben Abraham (1340–c.1410) Spanish philosopher and Hebrew poet, born in Barcelona. He became a member of the Aragonese court of

John I and Crown Rabbi of Aragon. His *Or Adonai* (Light of the Lord) criticizes **Maimonides** and stresses the limitations of human reason and the need for love and for mystical communion with God. He was an important influence on **Giordano Bruno**, **Spinoza** and others.

CRESPI, Giovanni Battista (c.1557–1633) Italian painter, architect and sculptor born in Cerano. His best works are in Milan, where he was chiefly active.

CRESPI, Giuseppe Maria, called **Lo Spagnuolo** (1665–1747) Italian painter of the Bolognese school, born in Bologna. He painted religious and mythological subjects showing the influence of the Eclectic school of the **Carracci**.

CRETZSCHMAR, Philipp Jakob (1786–1845) German naturalist and physician, born in Sulzbach, the son of a Lutheran minister. He studied medicine at Würzburg and Halle, and after army service settled in Frankfurt where he practised as a doctor and taught zoology. In 1817 he founded the Senckenberg Natural History Society in Frankfurt, and made the ornithological contributions to the works of **Eduard Rüppell**. Cretzschmar's Bunting was named in his honour.

CREUZER, Georg Friedrich (1771–1858) German historian and philologist, born in Marburg. Professor of philology and ancient history at Heidelberg (1804–45), his first and greatest work was his *Symbolik und Mythologie der alten Völker, besonders der Griechen* (4 vols, 1810–12).

CRIBB, Tom (1781–1848) English prizefighter, and bare-knuckles champion of the world. Born in Bitton, Gloucestershire, he won his first public contest in 1805 against the black American Bill Richmond after 76 rounds. After being taken over by **Robert Barclay-Allardice**, he twice defeated Jem Belcher for the bare-knuckles championship (1807 and 1809), and also defeated the American black pugilist Tom Molineaux (1810 and 1811). He retired with an unbeaten record and became a publican in London.

CRICHTON, James (1560–c.1585) Scottish prodigy and epitome of the Scottish Enlightenment, known as 'the Admirable'. The son of the Scottish Lord Advocate, he was born in Cluny, Perthshire, and educated at St Andrews, where his tutor was **George Buchanan**. After graduating in 1575, he earned a tremendous reputation as a scholar, poet, linguist and swordsman on the Continent. He spent two years in France as a teenager, apparently in the French army, delivered a Latin oration before the senate in Genoa in 1579, took part in a great scholastic disputation in Venice in 1580, and again in Padua in 1581. Later he went to Mantua in the service of the duke, and was killed in a nocturnal brawl by the duke's son. His popular reputation rests on the fantastic account of his exploits written by Sir **Thomas Urquhart** in his panegyric on the Scots nation, *The Discoveryie of a Most Exquisite Jewel* (1652). 'Admirable Crichton' became synonymous with all-round talents, the ideal man; the phrase was used by **J M Barrie** for his play about a perfect butler, *The Admirable Crichton* (1902).

CRICK, Francis Harry Compton (1916–) English molecular biologist, educated at Mill Hill School and the universities of London and Cambridge. From 1949 he carried on research in molecular biology at the Cavendish Laboratory. With **James D Watson** in 1953 he constructed a molecular model of the complex genetic material deoxyribonucleic acid (DNA); later researches on the nucleic acids led to far-reaching discoveries concerning the genetic code. With Watson and **Maurice H Wilkins** he was awarded the Nobel prize for medicine and physiology in 1962.

CRILE, George Washington (1864–1943) American surgeon and physiologist, born in Chilo, Ohio. He spent much of his working life as student, teacher and practitioner, in Cleveland; he was founder and first director of the Cleveland Clinic Foundation (1921–40). He did important experimental work on the causes and prevention of surgical shock (abnormally low blood pressure), and devised a method (which he called 'anoci-association') of combining drugs and anaesthetics which relaxed the patient and made surgical complications easier to control. He was also an early advocate of blood-pressure monitoring during operations, and used adrenaline and saline and blood transfusions to help combat surgical shock. He developed several operations for the endocrine glands, though some of his later physiological speculations were rather eccentric.

CRILLON, Louis des Balbes de Berton de (1541–1615) French soldier called 'Le Brave', born in Murs in Provence. As a young man he covered himself with glory at the siege of Calais (1558) and the capture of Guines. In the religious wars he fought against the Huguenots at Dreux (1562), Jarnac and Moncontour (1569). Wounded at Lepanto (1571) while serving with the Knights of Malta, he was yet sent to carry the news of the victory to the Pope and the French king. He abhorred the massacre of St Bartholomew, but took part in the siege of La Rochelle in 1573, and eventually died at Avignon.

CRIPPEN, Hawley Harvey (1862–1910) American murderer, born in Michigan. He studied medicine and dentistry in Michigan and in London (1883), and in 1896 returned to London, settling there with his second wife, Cora Turner, an unsuccessful opera singer and music hall star, who made his life miserable. Falling in love with his secretary, Ethel le Neve, Crippen poisoned his wife after a party at their home at Hilldrop Crescent, Holloway, dissected the body, and, having destroyed the bones by fire, interred the remains in the cellar. He told his wife's friends that she had left for America and had suddenly died there. After the police had unsuccessfully investigated the disappearance, Ethel, now living with Crippen, took fright, and the pair fled to Antwerp, where they boarded an Atlantic liner as Mr and Master Robinson. The suspicious captain, who had read reports of the second and successful search at Hilldrop Crescent, contacted Scotland Yard by radio-telegraphy (the first use of radio for police purposes), a detective disguised as a pilot was dispatched by a faster vessel, and the couple were arrested. They were both tried at the Old Bailey, and Crippen was executed at Pentonville.

CRIPPS, Charles Alfred, 1st Baron Parmoor (1852–1941) English lawyer and statesman. He wrote a standard work on the law of compensation (1881); sat as a Conservative MP (1895–1900, 1901–06, 1910–14); after 1914 he sat in the Judicial Committee of the privy council. In World War I he upheld the right of conscientious objection; afterwards he championed the League of Nations; and, as lord president of the Council, was in the Labour governments of 1924 and 1929–31.

CRIPPS, Sir Richard Stafford (1889–1952) English Labour statesman, economist, chemist and patent-lawyer, born in London son of **Charles Alfred Cripps**, and of Theresa, sister of **Beatrice Webb**. At Winchester, he won a scholarship to New College, Oxford, his chemistry papers attracting the attention of Sir **William Ramsay**, who persuaded him to work in his laboratory at University College London instead. At 22 he was part-author of a paper read before the Royal Society. He also pursued legal studies and was called to the bar in 1913, became the youngest barrister in the country in 1926 and made a fortune in patent and compensation cases. In 1930 he was appointed solicitor-general in the second Labour government, but refused to serve in **MacDonald**'s Coalition. From then until the outbreak of World War II, Cripps was associated with a succession of extreme left-wing movements, at first pacific in character, but later, as the Nazi threat increased, concerned with rallying everyone, and not only socialists, to active opposition to **Chamberlain**'s policy of appeasement, in a 'Popular Front' which brought about his expulsion from the Labour party in 1939 and forced him to sit as independent MP throughout the war. In 1940 he became ambassador to Moscow. The year 1942, however, under Churchill's leadership, saw his extraordinary rise to political power. In February he became lord privy seal and leader of the Commons, during the summer he was sent to India with the famous 'Cripps offer' of dominion status for a united India, rejected by both **Gandhi** and **Jinnah**, and finally in November he succeeded **Beaverbrook** in the vital post of minister of aircraft production which he held for the remainder of the war. When Labour came to power in July 1945, Cripps was readmitted to the party and appointed president of the board of trade. In 1947 he became the first minister of economic affairs and within a few weeks succeeded **Dalton** as Chancellor of the Exchequer. In this last office Cripps established a moral and intellectual ascendancy over parliament and the country, scarcely known since **Gladstone**. His at first unpopular policy of 'austerity' caught the public conscience. The trade unions took the unprecedented step of imposing a voluntary wage freeze. He only began to be challenged when he devalued the pound in September 1949. Illness from overwork forced his resignation in October 1950, leaving behind a number of brilliant disciples. Cripps firmly believed that politics was a proper sphere for the practice of Christianity. He was elected rector of Aberdeen University (1942–45). He wrote *Towards a Christian Democracy* (1945).

CRISPI, Francesco (1819–1901) Italian statesman, born at Ribera, Sicily. He was called to the bar, but, joining the revolutionary movement of 1848, had to flee to France. He organized the successful movement of 1859–60, and re-entered Sicily with **Garibaldi**. In the restored kingdom of Italy he became deputy, president of the chamber, minister, and from 1887 to 1890, and again in 1894, premier—a member of the Left, strongly anticlerical, and maintaining the alliance with Germany at the cost even of alienating France. A bank scandal vilification failed, but in 1896 the Abyssinian disaster of Adowa compelled his resignation.

CRISPIN, St (martyred 287) Christian martyr. According to legend, under the reign of **Diocletian** he fled from Rome, with his brother St Crispinian, and worked as a shoemaker in Soissons, while striving to spread Christianity. He and his brother suffered martyrdom in 287 by being thrown into molten lead. Their feast day is 25 October.

CRISTOFORI, or **Cristofali, Bartolommeo** (1655–1731) Italian harpsichord-maker, born in Padua, the inventor about 1710 of the pianoforte.

CRITIAS (c.460–403 BC) Athenian orator and politician, a pupil of **Socrates**. Implicated with **Alcibiades** in the mutilation of the Hermae on the eve of the Sicilian expedition (415), he nonetheless escaped punishment. In 411 he took part in the oligarchical revolution that set up the government of Four Hundred. Exiled in 406, he returned in 404, and as a strong supporter of Sparta became one of the Thirty Tyrants set up by the Spartans after their defeat of Athens at the end of the Peloponnesian War (431–404). In the same year he fell at Munychia, resisting **Thrasybulus** and the exiles. He had a high reputation as an orator, and wrote poetry and tragedies.

CRIVELLI, Carlo (c.1430–1495) Italian painter of the Venetian school. Trained probably by the **Vivarini** family in Venice, he spent most of his time working elsewhere in the Marches. His style is a highly individual and rather precious combination of old-fashioned International Gothic opulence with the new Renaissance passion for setting figures in architectural frameworks and against landscapes. His style of draughtmanship is not dissimilar to that of **Botticelli** but the impression given by his works is more overpowering. His *Annunciation* is in the London National Gallery.

CROCE, Benedetto (1866–1952) Italian idealist, philosopher, historian, critic and senator, born in Pescasseroli, Aquila. He was buried and lost his parents and sister in an earthquake on the island of Ischia (1883), studied at Rome, and in Naples devoted himself at first to literature and antiquarian studies, founding the bimonthly review, *La Critica*, in 1903. He developed a phenomenology of the mind (*Lo Spirito*) in which the four principal activities of the mind, art and philosophy (theoretical), political economy and ethics (practical), do not oppose, as they do for **Hegel**, but complement each other. His theory of aesthetics, with its denial of the physical reality of the work of art, is set out in the first volume of *Lo Spirito* and considerably influenced **Robin Collingwood**. In 1910, Croce became senator and was minister of education (1920–21) when with the rise of **Mussolini** he had to resign his professorship at Naples. His opposition to totalitarianism continued to find expression in many anti-Hegelian, anti-Marxian and anti-Fascist articles and studies, not least in *History as the Story of Liberty* (trans 1941), for which he was severely censured by his pro-Fascist colleague, **Giovanni Gentile**. With the fall of Mussolini in 1943, he played a leading role in resurrecting Liberal institutions in Italy. He also wrote literary studies of **Goethe**, **Dante**, **Ariosto** and **Corneille**.

CROCKER, Chester Arthur (1941–) American statesman. Educated at Ohio State and Johns Hopkins universities, he worked as a journalist on *African Report* during the mid 1960s and as a lecturer at the American University (1969–70). During the **Nixon** administration, he served briefly on the National Security Council as a staff officer (1970–72), before returning to academic life at Georgetown University, becoming its director of African studies in 1976. An expert on southern African politics, he joined the **Reagan** administration (1981–89) as assistant secretary of state for African affairs, being placed in effective charge of its new policy of 'constructive engagement' with Pretoria. This bore partial fruit with a peace settlement for Namibia.

CROCKETT, David, known as **Davy** (1786–1836) American frontiersman, born in Greene County, Tennessee. He distinguished himself against the Creek Indians in **Andrew Jackson**'s campaign of 1814, in 1821 was elected to the Tennessee state legislature, and in 1826 to the congress. He died fighting for Texas at the battle of the Alamo.

CROCKETT, Samuel Rutherford (1859–1914) Scottish popular novelist, born in Little Duchrae, Kirkcudbright, of tenant-farming stock. Paying his way by journalism and travelling tutorships, he attended Edinburgh University and New College, Edinburgh. Becoming a Free Church minister in Penicuik, he wrote sardonic congregational sketches, of which 24, collected as *The Stickit Minister* (1893), brought immediate fame; this was consolidated in 1894 by *The*

Raiders, *The Lilac Sunbonnet* (a seemingly innocent love story which ridiculed narrow religious sects) and two novellas. Resigning the ministry for full-time writing in 1895, he wrote a variety of books, from tales of Covenanting and medieval Scotland, to European historical romances and (often sensational) stories of mining, industrialism and Edinburgh slums. His posthumous works include one detective and one theological science-fiction novel.

CROESUS (6th century BC) the last king of Lydia. He succeeded his father, Alyattes, in c.560 BC. He made the Greeks of Asia Minor his tributaries, and extended his kingdom eastward from the Aegean to the Halys. His conquests, his mines, and the golden sand of the Pactolus made his wealth proverbial. **Cyrus the Great** defeated and imprisoned him (546); the manner of his death is lost in legend.

CROFT, Sir Herbert (1751–1816) English scholar. He was the vicar of Prittlewell, Essex, from 1786 but from 1802 lived as a bankrupt debtor on the Continent. He wrote a memoir of **Edward Young** for **Samuel Johnson**'s *Lives of the Poets*. He also wrote *Love and Madness* (1780).

CROFT, William (1677–1727) English organist and composer, born in Nether Eatington, Warwickshire. In 1700 he became a chorister in the Chapel Royal, in 1704 joint organist, and in 1707 sole organist. In 1708 he succeeded his teacher, **John Blow**, as organist of Westminster Abbey and choirmaster of the Chapel Royal; and in 1713 he took his Mus.Doc. at Oxford. Thirty of his anthems for state ceremonies were printed in 1724.

CROKE, Thomas William (1824–1902) Irish prelate, born in Ballyclough, County Cork. Educated in Paris and Rome, he is said to have fought at the barricades during the 1848 Revolution. A close friend of Cardinal **Manning**, in 1870 he became Roman Catholic bishop of Auckland, New Zealand. In 1875 he was promoted archbishop of Cashel and Emly. A strong nationalist, he backed the Gaelic League and the Land League, and supported the leadership of **Charles Parnell**. Croke Park in Dublin is named after him.

CROKER, John Wilson (1780–1857) Irish politician and essayist, born in Galway, the son of the surveyor-general of Irish customs. Educated at Trinity College, Dublin, in 1800 he entered Lincoln's Inn, and in 1802 was called to the Irish bar. Two satires on the Irish stage (*On the Present State of the Irish Stage*, 1804) and on Dublin society (*Intercepted Letters from Canton*, 1804) proved brilliant hits; so did his *Sketch of Ireland Past and Present* (1807), a pamphlet advocating Catholic emancipation. Elected MP for Downpatrick in 1807, in 1809 he helped to found the *Quarterly Review*, to which he contributed 260 articles. He was rewarded with the lucrative secretaryship of the Admiralty (1809–30) for his warm defence of Frederick, Duke of **York** in the case of **Mary Anne Clarke**. After 1832, he refused to re-enter parliament and would not even take office under **Peel**, his old friend (1834). He fell out with Peel over the repeal of the Corn Laws (1846). Among the 17 works that he wrote or edited were his *Stories for Children from English History* (1817), which suggested the *Tales of a Grandfather*; the *Suffolk Papers* (1823); his edition of **Boswell**'s *Life of Johnson* (1831); and *Essays on the Early French Revolution* (1857). He is better remembered for his attack on **Keats**, and **Macaulay**'s attack on him (Macaulay 'detested him more than cold boiled veal'); and as the originator of the term Conservative, a founder of the Athenaeum Club, and the 'Rigby' of **Disraeli**'s *Coningsby*.

CROKER, Richard, known as **'Boss Croker'** (1841–1922) Irish-born American politician, born in County Cork. His family emigrated to New York when he was a child. He entered New York City politics in 1862, joining the 'Young Democracy' faction opposed to Mayor Tweed in 1868. He secured control of the Tammany Hall machine in 1886 and, as 'Boss Croker', dominated Democratic party politics for the next 16 years, surviving a major corruption scandal involving the police department in 1894. After the election as mayor in 1901 of the reforming idealist Seith Low (1850–1916), he left the USA (1903) and spent the rest of his life on a large estate in Ireland.

CROKER, Thomas Crofton (1798–1854) Irish antiquary and folklorist, born in Cork. From 1818 to 1859 he was a clerk at the Admiralty. As a boy of 14 he had begun to collect songs and legends of the Irish peasantry and in 1818 he sent **Thomas Moore** nearly 40 old Irish melodies. In 1825 he published anonymously his *Fairy Legends and Traditions of the South of Ireland*, a work which charmed Sir **Walter Scott** and was translated into German by the brothers **Grimm** (1826). A second series followed in 1827. Of nearly 20 more works the best were *Researches in the South of Ireland* (1824), *Legends of the Lakes* (1829), *The Adventures of Barney Mahoney* (1832) and *Popular Songs of Ireland* (1839).

CROLL, James (1821–90) Scottish physicist, born in Little Whitefield, near Coupar-Angus. He received an elementary school education, but in science was wholly self-trained. Successively millwright, insurance-agent and keeper of the museum of Anderson's College, Glasgow, he was on the Scottish Geological Survey, 1867–81. Among his works were *Climate and Time* (1875) and *The Philosophic Basis of Evolution* (1890).

CROLY, George (1780–1860) Irish poet, romance-writer, biographer and Anglican preacher, born in Dublin. Educated at Trinity College, he took orders in 1804, and went to London in 1810, in 1835 becoming rector of St Stephen's, Walbrook. From 1817 he published some 40 works—the best-known the weird romance of *Salathiel*, based on the legend of the Wandering Jew.

CROME, John ('Old Crome') (1768–1821) English landscape painter, born in Norwich. He was mainly influential in founding, in 1803, the Norwich Society of Artists, of which he was president in 1808. He occasionally visited London, where he exhibited in the Academy and the British Institution; and a tour through Belgium and France in 1814 resulted in *The Fishmarket on the Beach*, *Boulogne* and *The Boulevard des Italiens*, *Paris*. But his subjects were nearly always derived from the scenery of his native county, which, though founding on the Dutch landscapists, he treated in a singularly direct and individual fashion. He practised, though rarely, as a watercolour painter; and his etchings of *Norfolk Picturesque Scenery* were published in 1834. His son, John Berny Crome (1794–1842), known as 'Young Crome', was also a landscape painter.

CROMEK, Robert Hartley (1770–1812) English engraver, born in Hull. He published **Robert Blair**'s *The Grave*, with engravings after **William Blake**. He visited Scotland to collect and publish the *Reliques of Burns* (1808) and *Select Scottish Songs* (1810), and meeting **Allan Cunningham**, published his literary fabrications in *Remains of Nithsdale and Galloway Song* (1810).

CROMER, Evelyn Baring, Earl (1841–1917) English colonial administrator, born in Cromer. He was private secretary to his cousin, Lord **Northbrook**, when viceroy of India (1872–76), British controller-general of Egyptian finance (1879–80), finance minister of India

(1880-83), and agent and consul-general in Egypt (1883–1907). He reformed Egyptian administration and agricultural policies, and put its finances on a good footing. Among his published works were *Modern Egypt* (1908), *Abbas II* (1915), and *Political and Literary Essays* (1908–16).

CROMPTON, Richmal, original surname **Lamburn** (1890–1969) English writer, and author of the *Just William* books, born in Bury, Lancashire. She was educated in Lancashire and Derby and at Royal Holloway College, London. An honours graduate in classics (1914), she taught for some years, but was struck down with poliomyelitis in 1923. She published 50 adult titles thereafter but she is best known for her 38 short-story collections (and one novel, *Just William's Luck*) about the perpetual schoolboy, the eleven-year-old William Brown. Children loved the judicious deliberation with which William's incursions and imitations are described in their reduction of ordered adult life to chaos.

CROMPTON, Rookes Evelyn Bell (1845–1940) English engineer, born near Thirsk, a pioneer of electric lighting and road transport. While still a schoolboy he designed and built first a model and then a full-size steam road locomotive, continuing with this work after army service in India. His road steamers were technically successful but could not compete with the rapid development of the railways in the second half of the 19th century. On his return to Britain he became involved in the generation and distribution of electricity for lighting, on which he became an international authority. He strongly supported standardization in industry and was concerned in the establishment of the National Physical Laboratory and what is now the British Standards Institution.

CROMPTON, Samuel (1753–1827) English inventor of the spinning-mule, born in Firwood, near Bolton, Lancashire, the son of a small farmer. After working at various jobs, he set out to invent a spinning machine that would improve on that of **James Hargreaves**. In 1779, after five years' work, he produced his spinning mule, so called because it was a cross between Hargeaves' water-frame and **Arkwright**'s spinning jenny. Too poor to apply for a patent, he sold the rights to a Bolton manufacturer for £67. In 1812 he was granted a reward of £5000 by the House of Commons. He tried bleaching at Over Darwen, then failed as a partner in a cotton firm. Some friends purchased him an annuity of £63. He died at Bolton.

CROMWELL, Oliver (1599–1658) English soldier and statesman, lord protector of England, 1653–58, born in Huntingdon. He was the younger son of Sir Henry Cromwell of Hinchinbrook, whose father (Richard Williams, a Welshman) had taken the surname of his uncle and patron, **Thomas Cromwell**, Earl of Essex. His mother was a daughter of Sir Thomas Steward of Ely, and he was first cousin to the great parliamentarian, **John Hampden**. He was educated at Huntingdon Grammar School and Sydney Sussex College, Cambridge. In 1617 he inherited a modest estate at Huntingdon, went to London to study law, and in 1620 married Elizabeth Bourchier, the daughter of a prosperous London merchant. He sat as MP for Huntingdon in the stormy parliament of 1628–29, during which he became a convinced critic of King **Charles I**. After the dissolution of parliament by the king he returned to farming, first at Huntingdon and then St Ives and later at Ely, where he had been left property by an uncle. He sat for Cambridge in the Short Parliament of 1640 that refused the king a grant of money for the Bishops' War. In the Long Parliament that followed it (1640) he moved the second reading of the bill for annual parliaments, and was a vehement supporter of Puritanism. At the outbreak of the first stage of the Civil War (1642) he organized his district for parliament and raised a troop of cavalry which he captained at the Battle of Edgehill (23 October 1642). In 1643 he formed his formidable regiment of Ironsides, and won the battle of Gainsborough (28 July). At Marston Moor (2 July 1644) his cavalry charge won the day. He now emerged as the leader of the Independents who demanded religious tolerance and vigorous prosecution of the war, as against the Presbyterian aristocrats and parliamentarians who wanted to make terms with King Charles. As commander of the New Model Army under the supreme command of **Thomas Fairfax** he decisively defeated the king at Naseby (14 June 1645). He marched on London to coerce the Presbyterians in parliament, and was probably responsible for abducting the king from Holmby in 1647. Although prepared to mediate between the king, the army and parliament, he failed to persuade the king to accept constitutional limitations, and his attitude hardened after the king's intriguing with his partisans while a prisoner on the Isle of Wight, which led to the outbreak of the second phase of the Civil War (1648). Cromwell swiftly put down a Royalist insurrection in Wales, and defeated the Scots under James, 3rd Marquis of **Hamilton**, at the Battle of Preston (1648). Cromwell now actively pressed for the prosecution of the king, and was one of the signatories of the death warrant in January 1649. After the execution (30 January), the monarchy was abolished and a commonwealth established, with Cromwell as chairman of the Council of State. As army commander and lord lieutenant of Ireland he ruthlessly concluded the Civil War there by storming Drogheda and Wexford and massacring their garrisons (1649). In 1650 he turned his attention to Scotland, where Charles's son, **Charles II**, had been acclaimed king; Cromwell defeated a Scottish army under **David Leslie** at Dunbar (1650), and finally subdued the Scottish thrust under Charles II at Worcester (3 September 1651), the battle which effectively ended the Civil War. He thereupon united the three kingdoms of England, Scotland and Ireland. In 1653 he contemptuously dissolved the Rump of the Long Parliament, and called a Puritan Convention, nicknamed the Little, or **Barebone**'s, Parliament, which was also quickly dismissed. Cromwell was now (16 December 1653) declared lord protector on the adoption of a new constitution, the Instrument of Government, designed to create a balance between the army and parliament. As lord protector he ruled by decree and ordinance until such time as parliament should meet. He reorganized the Church of England and established Puritanism, but upheld religious toleration; he provided judicial administration in Scotland (which prospered under his rule), and gave Ireland representation in parliament. In 1655 he dissolved parliament, and made a short-lived attempt to decentralize administration by putting ten major-generals in charge of ten districts in England. In 1656 he called a new parliament, which offered him the crown in 1657 in its 'Humble Petition and Advice', but Cromwell, after some hesitation, refused it, but accepted the right to name his successor, his son **Richard Cromwell**, as lord protector. But his relations with parliament remained strained, and he dissolved it again in 1658. In his foreign policy he ended the war with Portugal (1653) and Holland (1654), made treaties with France against Spain in 1655 and 1657, and defeated the Spanish at the Battle of the Dunes (1658) and took Dunkirk. He died in September 1693 and was buried in the tomb of the kings at

Westminster Abbey, but after the Restoration in 1660 he was attainted; his body was disinterred and hung from the gallows at Tyburn, and afterwards buried there. He was briefly succeeded as lord protector by Richard. His daughter, Bridget, married **Henry Ireton**.

CROMWELL, Richard (1626–1712) English statesman, third son of **Oliver Cromwell** and briefly his successor as lord protector of England (1658–59). He served in the parliamentary army, and sat in parliament in 1654 and 1656, and was a member of the Council of State in 1657. In September 1658 he succeeded his father as lord protector (his two elder brothers having died); but he soon fell out with parliament, which he dissolved in 1659. He recalled the Rump Parliament of 1653, but found the task of ruling beyond him, and was forced to abdicate in May 1659. After the Restoration (1660) he lived abroad, in France and Geneva, under the alias 'John Clarke', but returned to England in 1680, and spent the rest of his life at Cheshunt.

CROMWELL, Thomas, Earl of Essex (c.1485–1540) English statesman, born in Putney, London, the son of a blacksmith and brewer. He spent some years on the Continent (1504–12), where he may have served in the French army in Italy, and gained experience as a clerk and trader. In England from 1513 he became a wool-stapler and scrivener, as well as practising some law. In 1514 he entered the service of Cardinal **Wolsey**, and entered parliament in 1523. In 1525 he acted as Wolsey's chief agent in the dissolution of the smaller monasteries, and as his general factotum for the endowment of his colleges at Ipswich and Oxford. In 1529 he pleaded successfully in the House of Commons in favour of quashing the Bill of Attainder against Wolsey. In 1530 he entered the service of King **Henry VIII** and quickly became his principal adviser, as privy councillor (1531), Chancellor of the Exchequer (1533) and secretary of state and master of the rolls (1534). He was the guiding hand behind the Reformation acts of 1532–39 that produced the Act of Supremacy (1534) that made the king head of the English Church. As vicar-general from 1535, and as lord privy seal and the king's deputy as the head of the church (from 1536), he organized the dissolution of the monasteries (1536–39), thereby earning the nickname of *malleus monarchorum*—'hammer of the monks'. He exerted himself single-mindedly to the establishment of the absolute authority of the crown and the Protestantization of the church. He was appointed lord great chamberlain in 1539 and ennobled as the Earl of Essex in 1540; but he lost favour with the king after negotiating the disastrous marriage with **Anne of Cleves**; he was sent to the Tower, condemned by parliament under a Bill of Attainder, and executed.

CRONIN, Archibald Joseph (1896–1981) Scottish novelist, born in Cardross, Dumbartonshire. He graduated in medicine at Glasgow in 1919, but in 1930 abandoned his practice as a result of a breakdown in his health, and turned to literature. He had an immediate success with his autobiographical novel *Hatter's Castle* (1931). Subsequent works include *The Citadel* (1937), *The Keys of the Kingdom* (1941), *Beyond this Place* (1953), *Crusader's Tomb* (1956) and *A Song of Sixpence* (1964). The medical stories in his Scottish novels formed the basis of the popular radio and television series *Dr Finlay's Casebook* in the 1960s.

CRONIN, James Watson (1931–) American physicist, born in Chicago. Together with **Val Fitch**, he demonstrated the non-conservation of parity and charge conjugation in particle reactions. He was educated at Chicago and after working at the Brookhaven National Laboratory he moved to Princeton, becoming professor of physics in 1965, and at Chicago from 1971. In 1956 **T D Lee** and **C N Yang** had shown to the surprise of physicists that parity was not conserved in weak interactions between subatomic particles. In 1964, together with Fitch, J Christensen and R Turlay, Cronin made a study of neutral kaons and discovered that a combination of parity and charge conjugation was not conserved either, thus violating CP-conservation. This was an important result since it was known that a combination of parity, charge conjugation and time is conserved, implying that the decay of kaons is not symmetrical with respect to time reversal. Cronin and Fitch shared the 1980 Nobel prize for physics for their work in particle physics.

CRONJE, Piet (1835–1911) South African soldier. In the 1st Boer War (1880–81) he captured Potchefstroom (1881). He overpowered the **Jameson** Raiders in 1886. In the 2nd Boer War (1899–1900) he defeated the British (1881 and 1899–1900) at Magersfontein (1899) but surrendered to **F S R Roberts** at Paardeberg (1900).

CRONKITE, Walter Leland, Jnr (1916–) American journalist and broadcaster, born in St Joseph, Missouri. A student of political science, economics and journalism at Texas University (1933–35), he dropped out in his junior year to work for the Houston *Post* and later at KCMO radio in Kansas City as a news and sports reporter. Employed by the United Press (1939–48), he provided vivid eyewitness accounts of the war in Europe and remained to cover the Nuremberg trials and work as the bureau chief in Moscow (1946–48). At CBS from 1950, he hosted a number of shows and narrated *You Are There* (1953–56) but became a national institution as the avuncular anchorman of the *CBS Evening News* (1962–81) where his studious impartiality and informative, straightforward reporting earned him a reputation for honesty and trust. He also hosted such specials as *Sabotage in South Africa* (1962), *D-Day Plus 20 Years* (1964) and *Vietnam: A War That Is Finished* (1975).

CRONSTEDT, Axel Fredrik, Baron (1722–65) Swedish metallurgist. He first isolated nickel (1751) and noted its magnetic properties. He made a useful chemical classification of minerals and also discovered a zeolite (a water-softening silicate).

CROOK, George (1829–90) American soldier, born in Ohio. He fought on the Federal side in the Civil War (1861–65), commanding the army of West Virginia in 1864. He fought in the Indian wars (1866–77) in Idaho and Arizona (1873). He captured **Cochise** and pacified the Apaches (1871), fought in the Sioux War (1876), and fought the Apaches again under **Geronimo** (1882–86).

CROOKES, Sir William (1832–1919) English chemist and physicist, born in London. A pupil and assistant of **August Hoffmann** at the Royal College of Chemistry, he superintended the meteorological department of the Radcliffe Observatory, Oxford, and from 1855 lectured on chemistry at the Science College, Chester. He was a high authority on sanitation; discovered the metal thallium in 1861, the sodium amalgamation process in 1865 etc; improved vacuum tubes and promoted electric lighting; invented the radiometer (1873–76) and the spinthariscope; and was the author of *Select Methods of Chemical Analysis* (1871), and of works on diamonds, beetroot sugar, wheat, dyeing, calico-printing and psychical research.

CROSBY, Fanny (Frances Jane), later **Mrs Van Alstyne** (1820–1915) American hymnwriter, born in Southeast, New York. Blind from infancy, she was pupil and teacher in New York City's Institute for the Blind. She composed about 6000 popular hymns, including 'Safe in the arms of Jesus' (played at President **Grant**'s funeral), 'Pass me not, O gentle Saviour' (reportedly a favourite of Queen **Victoria**), and 'Rescue the perishing' (prompted by her mission work on New York's Lower East Side). She would not allow blindness to interfere with her almost constant round of activities. **Moody** and Sankey acknowledged a great debt to her.

CROSBY, Bing (Harry Lillis) (1904–77) American singer and film star, born in Tacoma, Washington. He began his career playing the drums in the evening while he was still at school and later became one of the trio known as **Paul Whiteman**'s Rhythm Boys. He made his feature film début in *King of Jazz* (1930). From the 1930s onwards his distinctive crooning style made him a top attraction on radio, a feat he repeated later on television, and one of the greatest sellers of records this century—his version of *White Christmas* sold over 30 million copies. Consistently among the most popular pre-war film stars, his partnership with **Bob Hope** resulted in a series of '*Road to . . .*' comedies and he won an Academy Award for *Going My Way* (1944). Later notable films include *The Bells of St Mary's* (1945), *Blue Skies* (1946), *White Christmas* (1954), *The Country Girl* (1954) and *High Society* (1956). A keen golfer, he continued to record and perform sell-out concerts until his death on a golf course in Spain.

CROSS, Charles Frederick (1855–1935) English chemist. With Edward John Bevan (1856–1921) he invented the modern method of producing artificial silk.

CROSS, Henri Edmond See **SIGNAC, Paul**

CROSS, Marian See **ELIOT, George**

CROSSLEY, Ada Jemima (1871–1929) Australian contralto, born in Tarraville, Victoria. After promising her parents 'never to sing in opera', she left for London in 1894 to study under Sir **Charles Santley**, and later under Madame Blanche Marchesi, making her début at the Queen's Hall, London, in 1895. After standing in at short notice for the indisposed **Clara Butt**, she was in demand for oratorios and festivals all over Great Britain, and within two years had given five 'command performances' for Queen **Victoria**. Her considerable repertoire included sacred songs and ballads; she sang in seven languages and was greatly admired both for her voice and for her interpretative skills. She toured the USA in 1902 and 1903, and recorded for the new Victor Company, later becoming an established international recording artist. She returned to Australia for two tours in 1903–1904 and 1907–1908, with supporting artists including the young **Percy Grainger**. She later reduced her commitments but performed at many charity concerts during World War I.

CROSSLEY, Sir Francis (1817–72) English carpet manufacturer and philanthropist, born in Halifax. He was Liberal MP for Halifax from 1852 to 1859 (then for the West Riding), and presented a public park (1857) to Halifax besides almshouses and an orphanage.

CROSSMAN, Richard Howard Stafford (1907–74) English Labour politician. The son of a judge who was a strong Conservative and a personal friend of **Clement Attlee**, he was educated at Winchester and New College, Oxford, where, after gaining a first-class degree, he stayed on as a fellow, philosophy tutor and lay dean. Having become leader of the Labour group on the Oxford City Council, he left the university in 1937 to lecture for the Workers' Educational Association and join the staff of the *New Statesman*. During World War II he worked in political and psychological warfare, and in 1945 became the Labour MP for Coventry East. A Bevanite activist, his brilliant intellect, and also perhaps his prosperous middle-class background, contributed towards causing the distrust sometimes shown towards him by his colleagues, and neither Attlee nor **Gaitskell** appointed him to high government office, though he was front bench spokesman on pensions under Gaitskell until he resigned in 1960. **Harold Wilson**, however, whom he had supported for leadership of the Labour party on Gaitskell's death in 1963, brought him into the Cabinet as minister of housing and local government, 1964–66, and leader of the House of Commons, 1966–69. His last office was secretary of state for social services and head of the department of health, and in 1970, on the defeat of the government, he returned to the *New Statesman* as editor until in 1972 the reorganizing of the paper forced his retirement. He will perhaps be best remembered for his political diary which he began in 1952 during the internal struggles of the party, wishing to make a detailed record of the day-to-day workings of government as they occurred, rather than a reasoned and sifted account viewed with hindsight. Published in three volumes, in 1975, 1976 and 1977 the diaries provide an invaluable insight into the Wilson administration. He also wrote an influential foreword to a new edition of **Walter Bagehot**'s 'English Constitution'.

CROTCH, William (1775–1847) English composer, born in Norwich. A carpenter's son, at two he could play *God Save the King*, and in 1779 was performing in London as a musical prodigy. In 1797 he became professor of music at Oxford, and in 1822 first principal of the Royal Academy of Music. He composed many pieces for the organ and piano, two oratorios, ten anthems, and wrote *Elements of Musical Composition* (1812) and *Styles of Music of all Ages* (1807–18).

CROWE, Sir Joseph Archer (1825–96) English art-writer and journalist, born in London. He studied art for seven years in Paris and travelled on the Continent, where in 1847 he met **Cavalcaselle**. He was a special correspondent in the Crimea, Indian Mutiny and the Franco-Austrian war; and from 1857 to 1859 was director of the School of Art at Bombay. In 1860 he was appointed consul-general at Leipzig and afterwards at Düsseldorf; in 1882 commercial attaché at Paris.

CROWE, Mrs See **BATEMAN, Kate Josephine**

CROWLEY, (Edward) Aleister, originally **Alexander** (1875–1947) English writer and 'magician'. He became interested in the occult while an undergraduate at Cambridge at the time of the 'magic revival' of the late 19th century, and was for a time a member of the Order of the Golden Dawn which **W B Yeats** also joined. Expelled for extreme practices, he founded his own order, the Silver Star, and travelled widely, settling for several years in Sicily with a group of disciples at the Abbey of Thelema near Cefalù. Rumours of drugs, orgies and magical ceremonies involving the sacrifice of babies culminated in his expulsion from Italy. In 1921 a series of newspaper articles brought him the notoriety he craved—he liked to be known as 'the great beast' and 'the wickedest man alive'—and certainly many who associated with him died tragically, including his wife and child.

CROWLEY, Bob (Robert) (1954–) English stage designer. One of the finest of contemporary stage designers, he has worked at the Bristol Old Vic, the Royal Exchange, Manchester, Greenwich Theatre and the National Theatre, where he designed **Bill Bryden**'s revival of *A Midsummer Night's Dream* (1982) and **Howard Davies**'s production of **Ibsen**'s *Hedda Gabler* (1989). He has also worked extensively at the Royal Shakespeare Company.

CROWQUILL, Alfred See **FORRESTER**

CROWTHER, Geoffrey, Baron Crowther (1907–72) English economist, born in Claymont, Delaware, USA. He was educated at Leeds Grammar School, Oundle, Clare College, Cambridge, Yale and Columbia universities. On the staff of *The Economist* from 1932, he was editor from 1938 to 1956. The *Crowther Report* (1959), produced during his period as chairman of the Central Advisory Council for Education (1956–60), held that 'the richest vein of untapped human resources' was those of middling ability, and recommended the raising of the school-leaving age to 16, the establishment of county colleges for those up to 17 not in full-time education, and more coherent, vocational education. It was the first British education report to seek systematic sociological answers and to consider the implications of economic and social change for the education of young people.

CROWTHER, Samuel Adjai (1809–91) African missionary, born in Ochugu, in West Africa. He was carried off as a slave in 1819, and sold more than once, but rescued by a British man-of-war and landed at Sierra Leone in 1822. He was baptized in 1825, taking the name of a London vicar, conducted a mission school at Regent's Town, and accompanied the Niger expeditions of 1841 and 1854. He was ordained in London in 1842, and was consecrated bishop of the Niger territory in 1864. He translated the Bible into Yoruba.

CROZIER, Eric See **BRITTEN, Benjamin**

CRUDEN, Alexander (1701–70) Scottish bookseller, born in Aberdeen. Educated at Marischal College, Aberdeen, in 1732 he started as a bookseller in London. In 1737 he published his biblical *Concordance of the Holy Scriptures*. From then on he suffered frequent bouts of insanity. Working as a printer's proof-reader he assumed the title of 'Alexander the Corrector', and in 1755 began to travel the country reproving Sabbath-breaking and profanity.

CRUFT, Charles (1852–1939) English showman. He was for many years general manager of James Spratt, dog-biscuit manufacturers. He organized the first dog show in 1886, and the annual shows since then have become world-famous. Through his influence the popularity of dogs has increased and the standards of dog-breeding have been greatly improved.

CRUICKSHANK, Andrew (1907–88) Scottish actor, born in Aberdeen, who became known worldwide for his portrayal of Dr Cameron in the BBC television series *Dr Finlay's Casebook*. Educated at Aberdeen Grammar School, he was intended for a career in civil engineering, but found his way into provincial repertory theatres instead. He reached the London stage in 1935, where he became an actor of distinction and took part in several long-running plays like *Dial 'M' for Murder*, *The House by the Lake* and *Alibi for a Judge* (1955).

CRUIKSHANK, George (1792–1878) English caricaturist and illustrator, born in London, younger son of Isaac Cruickshank (c.1756–1811) and brother of Isaac Robert Cruickshank (1789–1856), both caricaturists. After illustrating some children's books and songs, he made his name as a political caricaturist with *The Scourge* (1811–16) and *The Meteor* (1813–14). He contributed fine coloured etchings to the *Humorist* (1819–21) and *Points of Humour* (1823–24). His book illustrations included the etchings for *Peter Schlemihl* (1823) and **Grimm**'s *German Popular Stories* (1824–26). He also illustrated **Charles Dickens**' *Sketches by Boz* (1836) and *Oliver Twist* (1838), **Thackeray**'s *Legend of the Rhine*, and a series of books by **William Harrison Ainsworth**: *Jack Sheppard*, *Guy Fawkes*, *The Tower of London*, *Windsor Castle*, and *The Miser's Daughter*. From 1835 onwards he issued the *Comic Almanack*, one of the precursors of *Punch*. In his latter years he devoted much of his work to the cause of temperance, with a series of plates entitled *The Bottle* (1847), *The Drunkard's Children* (1848), and his magnificent cartoon *Worship of Bacchus* (1862). He is buried in St Paul's.

CRUVEILHIER, Jean (1791–1874) French anatomist, born in Limoges. A pioneer of the descriptive method, he was the first to describe multiple sclerosis, and progressive muscular atrophy (Cruveilhier's paralyses). He became professor of pathology at Montpellier in 1824 and of pathological anatomy in Paris in 1836.

CRUYFF, Johann (1947–) Dutch footballer, born in Amsterdam. He was one of several Dutch players who came to the fore in the late 1960s and his tall, raking stride and powerful raiding made him one of the great European forwards of his time. With Ajax Amsterdam he won three European Cup medals in succession and was European Footballer of the Year in 1973 and 1974. In 1974 he was captain of the Dutch side which lost to West Germany in the final of the World Cup. He afterwards moved to Barcelona where he never quite recaptured the form of his earlier years in Holland.

CSIKY, Gregor (1842–91) Hungarian dramatist, born in Pankota, Vilagos. A professor of theology at Temesvar seminary, he published some tales from religious history (Photographs from Life), and in 1875 a comedy, *Jaslot* (The Oracle), which was a success. Other plays followed, comedies like *Mirkány Kariar* and *Anna*, and tragedies, *Janus*, *The Magician*, *Theodora*. He also translated **Sophocles**, **Plautus**, and **Molière** into Hungarian, as well as several English plays. *Az Ellenallhatatlan* (The Irresistible), which won a prize from the Hungarian Academy, typifies his talent for a direct, fresh approach to his subject.

CSOKONAI VITEZ, Mihaly (1773–1805) Hungarian poet, born in Debrecen, Hungary. He was professor of poetry at the university there until his way of life lost him the post. His fame persists, however, chiefly through his lyrics, which are based on old Hungarian folksongs. Among his works are *Magyar-Musa* (1797), *Anacreontic Poems* (1903), and *Dorottya* (1804), a mock-heroic poem.

CSOMA DE KÖRÖS, Alexander (1784–1836) a Hungarian traveller and orientalist, born in the Transylvanian village of Körös. In 1820 he started for Central Asia, finding his way in Asiatic dress by Baghdad and Tehran to Bokhara, thence by Kabul and Lahore to Kashmir and Tibet, which he visited for the third time (1827–31). At Calcutta he completed his Tibetan grammar and dictionary and was appointed librarian to the Asiatic Society. He died on another journey to Tibet.

CTESIAS (5th century BC) Greek historian and physician. He was physician to **Artaxerxes II Mnemon** of Persia, and accompanied him in the expedition against his rebellious brother **Cyrus** (401 BC). He wrote a history of Persia in 23 books, *Persika*, of which only fragments remain.

CTESIBIUS (2nd century BC) Alexandrian Greek, the inventor of the force-pump and water organ, and improver of the clepsydra or water-clock. He was the teacher of **Hero of Alexandria**.

CUBITT, Thomas (1788–1855) English builder, born in Buxton. He revolutionized trade practices in the building industry, and was responsible for many large London projects, including Belgravia, and the east front of Buckingham Palace.

CUBITT, Sir William (1785–1861) English civil engineer, born in Dilham, Norfolk. He was a miller, a cabinetmaker and a millwright until 1812, and then chief engineer in **Robert Ransome**'s Orwell Works at Ipswich, in which he was a partner (1821–26). He removed to London in 1823. The Bute Docks at Cardiff, the Southeastern Railway and the Berlin waterworks were constructed by him. He also invented the treadmill and was associated with the construction of the Great Exhibition buildings (1851). He was Lord Mayor of London in 1860–61. Cubitt Town on the Isle of Dogs is named after him.

CUDWORTH, Ralph (1617–88) English philosopher and scholar, born in Aller in Somerset, and the leading member of the Cambridge Platonists. He became student, then fellow, at Emmanuel College, Cambridge. In 1645 he was appointed Master of Clare Hall and Regius professor of Hebrew. He held the College living of North Cadbury in succession to **Benjamin Whichcote**. In 1654 he was translated to the mastership of Christ's College, Cambridge where he lived until his death. His monumental work, *The True Intellectual System of the Universe* (1678), was a systematic but unwieldy and uncompleted treatise which aimed to refute determinism and materialism and to establish the reality of a supreme divine intelligence. An important work on ethics, directed against **Hobbes**, was published posthumously in 1731 as *Treatise concerning Eternal and Immutable Morality*.

CUEVA, Juan de la (c.1550–1607) Spanish poet and dramatist, born in Seville. He is known especially for his use of new metrical forms and his introduction of historical material into the drama.

CUGNOT, Nicolas Joseph (1725–1804) French military engineer. About 1770 he invented a three-wheeled steamdriven artillery carriage with a speed of 2–3 mph. Lack of support prevented further development.

CUI, César Antonovich (1835–1918) Russian composer, born in Vilna, the son of a French teacher. An expert on fortification, he became lieutenant-general of engineers. Practically a self-taught musician, he composed *William Ratcliff* (1861) and other operas.

CUJACIUS, properly **Jacques de Cujas** or **Cujaus** (1522–90) French jurist, born in Toulouse. He was professor at Valence and Bourges. The leading jurist of his time, he wrote extensively on Roman law. His complete works were edited by Fabrot (10 vols, 1658).

CUKOR, George (1899–1983) American film director, born in New York City. Involved with the theatre from an early age, he made his Broadway début with *Antonia* (1925). In Hollywood he worked as a dialogue director on *River of Romance* (1929) before making his directorial début with *Grumpy* (1930). *A Bill of Divorcement* (1932) and *Little Women* (1983) began a 50-year association with **Katharine Hepburn** that resulted in a succession of polished entertainments including *The Philadelphia Story* (1940), *Adam's Rib* (1949) and *Love Among the Ruins* (1975). Drawn to sophisticated comedies and literary subjects, he enjoyed a reputation for his sensitive handling of many major stars in films like *Camille* (1936, with **Greta Garbo**), *The Women* (1939), *Gaslight* (1944, with **Ingrid Bergman**), *Born Yesterday* (1950, with Judy Holliday) and *A Star is Born* (1954, with **Judy Garland**). He won an Academy Award for *My Fair Lady* (1964).

CULLBERG, Birgit Ragnhild (1908–) Swedish dancer, choreographer and ballet director, born in Nyköping. Her ballets are influenced by modern dance and characterized by their strong dramatic content, often of a psychological nature. She studied in England with **Kurt Jooss** (1935–39), and later in New York with **Martha Graham**. In the mid 1940s she toured the Continent with Svenska Dansteatern, a group she co-founded with Ivo Cramér. Her best-known work *Miss Julie*, dates from 1950. She was resident choreographer of the Royal Swedish Ballet (1952–57), after which she freelanced for companies including American Ballet Theatre and Royal Danish Ballet. She formed the Cullberg Ballet at the Swedish National Theatre in 1967, for which her sons Niklas and Mats Ek have danced and choreographed.

CULLEN, Countée (1903–46) American Black poet, born in New York. A leader of the so-called Harlem Renaissance, he began his literary career with *Color* (1925), a book of poems in which classical models such as the sonnet are used with considerable effect. He published several subsequent volumes of verse, and a novel *One Way to Heaven* (1932), and collaborated with Arna Bontemps in the play *St Louis Woman* (1946).

CULLEN, Paul (1803–78) Irish prelate, born in Prospect, County Kildare. After a brilliant course in the College of Propaganda at Rome he was ordained priest in 1829, and was successively vice-rector and rector of the Irish College in Rome and rector of the College of Propaganda. In 1850 consecrated archbishop of Armagh and primate of Ireland, and transferrred to Dublin in 1852, he helped to found the Catholic university in 1854 and Clonliffe College (the Dublin diocesan seminary) in 1859. His denunciations of Fenianism made him many enemies among the more hot-headed Irishmen but greatly increased the respect of English Protestants. He was created a cardinal priest in 1866, the first Irishman to attain that dignity.

CULLEN, William (1710–90) Scottish physician, born in Hamilton. After studying at Edinburgh he started a practice in Hamilton, where **William Hunter** became one of his pupils. In 1740 he set up as a physician in Glasgow, and lectured on medicine. In 1751 he was appointed to the chair of medicine; in 1755 he moved to Edinburgh, where for 35 years he occupied successively the chairs of chemistry, institutes of medicine, and medicine. He is largely responsible for the recognition of the important part played by the nervous system in health and disease. He bitterly opposed the Brunonian system (see **John Brown**). His chief works were *Synopsis Nosologiae Methodicae* (1769), *Institutions of Medicine* (1772), *Practice of Physic* (1776–84), and *Treatise of Materia Medica* (1789).

CULLMANN, Oscar (1902–) German biblical scholar and theologian, born in Strasbourg. As professor at Basle (from 1938) and Paris (from 1948), he was the chief representative in New Testament studies of the 1950s and 1960s 'biblical theology' movement and an exponent of the concept of Salvation-history (*Heilsgeschichte*). In *Christ and Time* (1951), *Salvation in History* (1967), and *Immortality of the Soul or Resurrection of the Dead?* (1958), he maintains that biblical thinking is essentially historical. God reveals Himself in historical events, not the isolated personal challenges of **Bultmann**'s existential demythologizing approach. He has also written *The Christology of the New Testament* (1959), *Peter: Disciple, Apostle, Martyr* (1953), and several studies of early Church worship and practice.

CULMANN, Karl (1821–81) German engineer, born in Bergzabern. He graduated from the Polytechnikum in Karlsruhe, and from 1855 taught at the polytechnic institute in Zürich. His principal work was in graphical statics which he systematized and elevated into a major method of structural analysis, introducing the use of force and funicular polygons and the method of sections.

CULPEPER, John See **COLEPEPER**

CULPEPER, Nicholas (1616–54) English physician, born in London. He studied at Cambridge, and in 1640 started to practise astrology and physic in Spitalfields, London. In 1649 he published an English translation of the College of Physicians' Pharmacopoeia, *A Physical Directory*, renamed in 1654 *Pharmacopoeia Londinensis, or the London Dispensatory*. This infringement of a close monopoly, together with his Puritanism, brought him many enemies. In 1653 appeared *The English Physician Enlarged, or the Herbal*. Both books had an enormous sale, the latter forming the basis of subsequent herbalism in the English-speaking world.

CULVERWEL, Nathanael (c.1618–c.1651) English philosopher and clergyman, born in Middlesex. One of the school of Cambridge Platonists who tried to establish a rational philosophical basis for Christianity, he became a fellow at Emmanuel College, Cambridge in 1642, but very little else is known of his life. He died young, and his *Discourse of the Light of Nature* was published posthumously in 1652.

CUMBERLAND, Dukes of See **ERNEST AUGUSTUS**

CUMBERLAND, Earls of See **CLIFFORD**

CUMBERLAND, Richard See **ERNEST AUGUSTUS, king of Hanover**

CUMBERLAND, Richard See **GEORGE V, king of Hanover**

CUMBERLAND, Richard (1631–1718) English philosopher and theologian, born in London. Educated at St Paul's School and Magdalene College, Cambridge, he was successively rector of Brampton, Northamptonshire (1658), vicar of All Saints, Stamford (1667), and bishop of Peterborough (1691). He is associated with the Cambridge Platonists. His *De legibus naturae* (1672) was written as a direct response to **Hobbes** and in some respects anticipated utilitarianism in espousing a principle of universal benevolence.

CUMBERLAND, Richard (1732–1811) English playwright, born in the lodge of Trinity College, Cambridge, maternal grandson of Dr **Richard Bentley**. From Bury St Edmunds and Westminster School he went to Trinity College, Cambridge, and was a fellow at 20. Becoming private secretary to Lord Halifax in 1761, he gave up his intention of taking orders. He was secretary to the board of trade from 1776 to 1782. Thereafter he retired to Tunbridge Wells, where he wrote farces, tragedies, comedies, pamphlets, essays and two novels, *Arundel* and *Henry*. Of his sentimental comedies the best are *The Brothers* (1769), *The West Indian* (1771), *The Fashionable Lover* (1772), *The Jew* (1794) and *The Wheel of Fortune* (1795). He was caricatured by **Sheridan** in *The Critic* as Sir Fretful Plagiary.

CUMBERLAND, William Augustus (1721–65) English military commander, the second son of **George II**. Adopting a military career, he was wounded at Dettingen in 1743, and defeated, not ingloriously, at Fontenoy by Marshal **Saxe** in 1745. Sent next to crush the 1745 Jacobite Rising in Scotland, he did so effectually at Culloden (1746), and by his cruelties earned the lasting title of 'Butcher'. In the latter stages of the War of the Austrian Succession he was defeated by Saxe at Langfeld (1747). In the Seven Years' War he had to surrender at Kloster-Zeven (1757), after which he retired.

CUMMING See **COMYN**

CUMMINGS, E E (Edward Estlin) (1894–1962) American writer and painter, born in Cambridge, Massachusetts. Educated at Harvard, he is celebrated for his verse characterized by typographical tricks and eccentric punctuations, signed 'e e cummings', starting with his first volume *Tulips and Chimneys* (1924). His best-known prose work, *The Enormous Room* (1922), describes his wartime internment—through an error by the authorities—in France. He also wrote a travel diary, a morality play, *Santa Claus* (1946), and a collection of six 'non-lectures' delivered at Harvard entitled *i* (1953). He studied art in Paris, and a collection of his drawings and paintings was published in 1931.

CUMMINS, Maria Susanna (1827–66) American writer, born in Salem, Massachusetts. Her first novel, *The Lamplighter* (1854), was a popular success.

CUMYN See **COMYN**

CUNARD, Sir Samuel (1787–1865) Canadian shipowner, born in Halifax, Nova Scotia. He succeeded early as a merchant and shipowner, emigrated to Britain in 1838, and, for the new steam rail service between Britain and America, joined with George Burns, Glasgow, and David McIver, Liverpool, in founding (1839) the British and North American Royal Mail Steam Packet Company, later known as the Cunard Line. The first passage (1840) was that of the *Britannia*, in 14 days 8 hours.

CUNLIFFE, Barrington Windsor (Barry) (1939–) English archaeologist, born in Portsmouth. Educated at St John's College, Cambridge, he taught at Bristol and Southampton and in 1972 became professor of European archaeology at Oxford. Much influenced by **Mortimer Wheeler**, he has the same hunger for archaeological discovery, commitment to disciplined excavation and writing, and flair for communication. An active fieldworker even as a schoolboy, he established a reputation in his 20s with spectacular excavations at the Roman palace of Fishbourne near Chichester (1961–67). He has since worked to notable effect in Roman Bath, and three sites in Wessex: the Roman fort of Portchester near Portsmouth, the Iron Age hillfort at Danebury near Stockbridge, and the late prehistoric trading settlement at Hengistbury Head near Christchurch. Among his general books are *Iron Age Communities in Britain* (1974), *The Celtic World* (1979), and *Greeks, Romans and Barbarians* (1988).

CUNNINGHAM, Sir Alan Gordon (1887–1983) English soldier, brother of Admiral Lord **Cunningham**. Educated at Cheltenham College and the Royal Military Academy, he served with distinction in World War II. From Kenya in 1941 he struck through Italian Somaliland and freed Abyssinia and British Somaliland from the Italians. He was high commissioner for Palestine (1945–48).

CUNNINGHAM, Allan (1784–1842) Scottish poet and man of letters, born in the parish of Dalswinton, Dumfriesshire. His father was neighbour of **Robert Burns** at Ellisland; and Allan, a boy of twelve, was present at the poet's funeral. At ten he was apprenticed to a stonemason, but continued to pore over songs and stories. His first publications were his sham-antique verse and prose contributions to **Cromek**'s *Remains of Nithsdale and Galloway Song* (1810). He already knew **James Hogg**, and through him he gained the acquaintance of Sir **Walter Scott**, with whom 'Honest Allan' was always a great favourite. He moved to London, and became one of the best-known writers for the *London Magazine*, as well as manager in **Chantrey**'s sculpture studio (1815–41). Among his works were *Traditional Tales of the English and Scottish Peasantry* (1822); *Songs of Scotland, Ancient and Modern* (1825); *Lives of the most Eminent British Painters, Sculptors,* *and Architects* (6 vols, 1829–33); and *Life of Wilkie* (3 vols, 1843).

CUNNINGHAM, Allan (1791–1839) English botanist and explorer, born in Wimbledon, Surrey. He became clerk to the curator of Kew Gardens, and then plant collector for Sir **Joseph Banks**, first in Brazil and then, in 1816, in New South Wales. While searching for new specimens Cunningham made many valuable explorations of the hinterland of New South Wales and Moreton Bay, Queensland. He also visited New Zealand and Norfolk Island, returning to Kew in 1831 to classify his specimens. He was offered the post of colonial botanist for New South Wales, but turned it down in favour of his younger brother Richard Cunningham (1793–1835). When his brother was killed by aborigines, he accepted the renewed invitation and returned to Sydney in 1837. He found that his duties included managing what he termed the 'Government Cabbage Garden' and growing vegetables for Governor **Gipps**'s table, so he resigned and left for New Zealand, but returned to Sydney six months later in bad health and died there. His writings and most of his collections are preserved at Kew, and many indigenous Australian trees now bear his name.

CUNNINGHAM, Andrew Browne, 1st Viscount Cunningham of Hyndhope (1883–1963) English naval commander, brother of Sir **Alan Cunningham**. Educated at Stubbington and HMS *Britannia* at Dartmouth, he entered the navy in 1898. He commanded a destroyer in World War I, and in World War II he was admiral commander-in-chief of British naval forces in the Mediterranean (1939–43). He defeated the Italian navy at Taranto (1940) and Cape Matapan (1941), and was in command of Allied naval forces for the invasion of North Africa (1942), and Sicily and Italy (1942). He was promoted Admiral of the Fleet in 1943, and was First Sea Lord from 1943 to 1946.

CUNNINGHAM, Glenn (1909–) American middle distance runner, born in Atlanta, Kansas. He overcame severe burns on his legs in childhood to become one of the greatest milers of his time. After finishing fourth in the 1500 metres at the 1932 Olympics, he broke the world mile record in 1934 (4: 6.7) and was expected to go on and win gold in 1936, but finished second behind **Jack Lovelock**, who broke the world record in the process.

CUNNINGHAM, Imogen (1883–1976) American photographer, born in Portland, Oregon. After working with **Edward Curtis**, she opened her own portrait studio in Seattle in 1910, but her personal style was pictorial romanticism, particularly in still-life flower studies. In 1915 she married a photographer, Roi Partridge, and moved to San Francisco, continuing with a soft-focus sentimental style until 1932, when she met **Edward Weston** and was converted to his 'straight photography' purists, Group f/64, which insisted on sharply-defined images and precise tonal gradation. After the break-up of the Group she continued with her portrait gallery for almost another 40 years, and in her nineties was still teaching at the Art Institute in San Francisco.

CUNNINGHAM, John (1917–) English military and civil aircraft pilot, born in Croydon, Surrey. He attended the Whitgift School and was apprenticed to the De Havilland Aircraft Company at Hatfield (1935–38), joining the Auxiliary Air Force in August 1935. He became a group captain in 1944, specializing in night defence against German bombers, earning the title 'Cat's Eyes Cunningham' during this period. After World War II he became chief test pilot of the De Havilland Aircraft Company (1946–78), and an executive director of De Havilland Aircraft in 1958 and of Hawker Siddeley Aviation (1963–77). Group Captain Cunningham retired from British Aerospace in 1980. He is the chairman of the De Havilland Flying Foundation, founded in memory of Sir **Geoffrey De Havilland**, which gives grants to encourage young people to take part in flying.

CUNNINGHAM, Merce (1919–) American choreographer and dancer, born in Washington. He appeared with the Martha Graham Dance Company from 1939 to 1945, began to choreograph himself in 1942, and gave his first solo concerts, with the composer **John Cage**, in 1944. His choreographic works include *Suite for Five* (1956), *Antic Meet* (1958), *Aeon* (1961), *Scramble* (1967), *Landrover* (1972) and *Travelogue* (1977). In 1953 he founded the Merce Cunningham Dance Company. He is credited with redefining modern dance and evolving a new vocabulary for it.

CUNNINGHAM, William (1805–61) Scottish churchman and theologian, born in Hamilton, a chief leader of the Disruption. Educated at Edinburgh, he became minister at Greenock (1830) and Edinburgh (1834), then professor (1843) and principal (1847) at the Free Church College, writing on theology and church history.

CUNNINGHAM, William (1849–1919) Scottish economist, born in Edinburgh. Educated at Edinburgh and Cambridge, he taught history at Cambridge, was professor of economics at King's College, London (1891–97), and in 1907 was made archdeacon of Ely. He was author of the pioneering *Growth of English Industry and Commerce* (1882), which in revised form remained a standard work for many years, reaching a 6th edition in 1929.

CUNNINGHAME GRAHAM, Robert Bontine (1852–1936) Scottish author and politician, grandson of **Robert Cunninghame Graham**, born in London. He was educated at Harrow and from 1869 was chiefly engaged in ranching in the Argentine, until he succeeded to the family estates in 1883. In 1879 he had married a Chilean poetess, Gabriela de la Belmondiere. He was Liberal MP for North-West Lanarkshire (1886–92) and was imprisoned with **John Burns**, the socialist leader, for 'illegal assembly' in Trafalgar Square during a mass unemployment demonstration in 1887. He was the first president of the Scottish Labour party in 1888. He travelled extensively in Spain and Morocco (1893–98), where an incident described in his *Mogreb-El-Acksa* (1898) inspired **Shaw**'s *Captain Brassbound's Conversion*. He wrote a great number of travel books, but is best known for his highly individual, flamboyant essays and short stories, collections of which are entitled *Success* (1902), *Faith* (1909), *Hope* (1910), *Charity* (1912) and *Scottish Stories* (1914). He was elected the first president of the National party of Scotland in 1928, and of the Scottish National party in 1934. **Conrad** and **Hudson** were among his close literary friends. He died in Argentina, where he was known as 'Don Roberto'.

CUNNINGHAME GRAHAM, Robert, originally **Robert Graham** (d.1797) Scottish laird and songwriter, born on the family estates at Gartmore, Stirlingshire. His mother was a daughter of the 12th Earl of Glencairn. He was educated at Glasgow University. He became a planter and receiver-general in Jamaica, was chosen rector of Glasgow University on his return in 1785 and became an MP (1794–96). He warmly supported the French Revolution, moved an abortive bill of rights and composed 'If doughty deeds my lady please' and other lyrical poems. On the death of the last Earl of Glencairn in 1796, he succeeded to the latter's estates and changed his name to Cunninghame Graham.

CUNOBELINUS See **CYMBELINE**

CURETON, William (1808–64) English Syriac scholar, born in Westbury, Shropshire. In 1837 he entered the British Museum as assistant-keeper of MSS, and brought to light a Syriac version of the Epistles of **Ignatius** and the 'Cureton Gospels'. He was a canon of Westminster.

CURIE, Marie (originally **Manya)** née **Sklodowska** (1867–1934) Polish-born French physicist and wife of **Pierre Curie**, born in Warsaw. After graduating from the Sorbonne in Paris, she married (1895) and worked with her husband on magnetism and radioactivity (a term she invented in 1898), and isolated radium, and polonium (which she named after her native Poland). She and her husband were jointly awarded the Nobel prize for physics in 1903, with **Antoine Henri Becquerel**. After her husband's death in 1906 she succeeded him as professor of physics at the Sorbonne. In 1910 she isolated pure radium and was awarded the Nobel prize for chemistry in 1911. She was director of the research department at the Radium Institute in Paris (1918–34), and honorary professor of radiology at Warsaw (1919–34). Her elder daughter was the nuclear physicist, **Irène Joliot Curie**; her second daughter Eve (1904–), became well-known as a musician and writer, and in World War II worked in the USA on behalf of the French Resistance movement. She wrote a Life of her Mother (English trans 1938).

CURIE, Pierre (1859–1906) French chemist, son of a Paris physician and husband of **Marie Curie**. He did research on magnetism and radioactivity with his wife, for which they were jointly awarded the Nobel prize for physics in 1903, with **Antoine Henri Becquerel**. Professor of physics at the Sorbonne, he was killed in a traffic accident in Paris when he was knocked down by a cart.

CURLEWIS, Sir Adrian Herbert (1901–85) Australian judge, surfer and administrator, born in Sydney. Son of Judge Herbert Curlewis (1869–1942) and novelist **Ethel Turner**, he studied law at Sydney University, and was a judge of the New South Wales district court from 1948 to 1971. He was president of the Surf Life-Saving Association of Australia (1933–74, then life governor), and president of the International Council of Surf Life-Saving (1956–73). As chairman of the International Convention of Life-Saving Techniques in 1960, he was an outstanding advocate for the adoption of mouth-to-mouth resuscitation (the 'kiss of life' method) which has saved countless lives.

CURLL, Edmund (1675–1747) English bookseller and pamphleteer. He was satirized by **Pope** in the *Dunciad*. He was twice (1716 and 1721) at the bar of the House of Lords for publishing matter regarding its members and was tried and convicted for publishing obscene books (1725). He was fined (1728) for the issue of *A Nun in Her Smock* and *De Usu Flagrorum*, and pilloried for his *Memoirs of John Ker of Kersland*. His announcement of *Mr Pope's Literary Correspondence* (1735) led to the seizure of the stock, and furnished Pope (who instigated its publication) with a sufficient excuse for the issue of an authentic edition (1737–41). Curll did not deal solely in works of a doubtful nature, as a list of his contains 167 standard works. His *Curliad* (1729) is styled a 'hypercritic upon the Dunciad Variorum'. It was of Curll's biographies that **John Arbuthnot** wittily said they had added a new terror to death.

CURRAN, John Philpot (1750–1817) Irish orator, born in Newmarket in County Cork. After Trinity College, Dublin, he spent two years at the Middle Temple, London, and was called to the Irish bar in 1775. Here he earned a considerable reputation for his wit and powers of advocacy but when he entered the Irish parliament in 1783 he met with less success. In the course of his turbulent career he fought five duels, all without serious injury. Although a staunch Protestant he had great sympathy for his Catholic fellow countrymen. He strongly opposed the Union which he described as 'the annihilation of Ireland'. He was master of the rolls in Ireland from 1806 to 1814 but towards the end of his life had serious domestic problems and failing health.

CURRIE, James (1756–1805) Scottish physician and editor, born in Kirkpatrick-Flemish manse, Dumfriesshire. He studied medicine at Edinburgh and Glasgow, and from 1780 practised in Liverpool. His chief medical work was *Reports on the Effects of Water in Febrile Diseases* (1797); but he is best remembered as the first editor of **Robert Burns** (1800) with a life and criticism of the writings, undertaken solely for the benefit of Burns' family.

CURTIN, John (1885–1945) Australian trade-union leader, journalist and Labour politician, born in Creswick, Victoria. In 1941 he became premier and in the Japanese war proved a far-seeing and intrepid national leader.

CURTIS, Charles Gordon (1860–1953) American inventor, born in Boston. He graduated at Columbia University as a civil engineer in 1881, then took his LL B at the New York Law School in 1883 and practised as a patent lawyer for the next eight years. He is best known for his invention of the Curtis impulse steam turbine in 1896, twelve years after the reaction turbine had been patented by Sir **Charles Parsons**. Present-day machines usually combine impulse and reaction stages for maximum efficiency.

CURTIS, Edward Sheriff (1868–1952) American photographer and writer, born in Madison, Wisconsin. Brought up in Seattle, Washington, he devoted almost the whole of his career from 1896 to the major enterprise of recording the North American Indian tribes and their way of life, which was to vanish almost completely during the 35 years of his study. With financial assistance from **J Pierpoint Morgan**, he published the first of 20 volumes in 1907, combining evocative and detailed photographs with an equally informative text. In all, he took some 40 000 negatives, many hundreds of which were reproduced as large photogravure plates illustrating his volumes, the last appearing in 1930. In contrast to earlier American photographers who portrayed the Indians as warriors, Curtis stressed their peaceful arts and culture, perhaps in idealized terms.

CURTIS, George William (1824–92) American man of letters, born in Providence, Rhode Island. After four years in Europe (1846–50) he joined the staff of the New York *Tribune*, and was one of the editors of *Putnam's Monthly* from 1852 to 1869. He began the 'Editor's Easy Chair' papers in *Harper's Monthly* in 1853, and became principal leader-writer for *Harper's Weekly* on its establishment in 1857. A novel, *Trumps* (1862), and most of his books appeared first in these journals.

CURTIS, Heber Doust (1872–1942) American astronomer, born in Muskegon, Michigan. He did notable work on the nature of spiral nebulae. He studied classics at Michigan University, then moved to California where his interest in astronomy seems to have begun. He became director of Michigan University observatory in 1930. He was convinced that spiral nebulae were isolated independent star systems, and that they lay beyond our galaxy. This view was strongly contested, but in 1924 **Edwin Hubble** demonstrated that the spiral Andromeda nebula lay well beyond our galaxy, confirming Curtis's ideas.

CURTIS, Tony (1946–) Welsh poet, born in Carmarthen and educated at University College, Swansea, and Goddard College, Vermont. He has published four collections of verse, a collection of prose-poems and short stories, two volumes of critical essays, and has edited several anthologies. A senior lecturer in English at the Polytechnic of Wales, he was chairman of The Welsh Academy from 1984 to 1987. In 1984 he won first prize in the National Poetry Competition.

CURTISS, Glen Hammond (1878–1930) American air pioneer and inventor, born in Hammondsport, New York. Originally a bicycle mechanic, he established a motorcycle factory in Hammondsport in 1902, and in 1905 set a world speed record of 137 mph on a motorcycle of his own design. He also designed motors for airships, and with **Alexander Graham Bell** formed the Aerial Experiment Association (1907). He gained the Scientific American Award in 1908 for the first public one-kilometre flight in the USA with his third aeroplane, the *June Bug*, flying at 40 mph. He won the James Gordon Bennett Cup in France in 1909 in his *Golden Arrow* at 46.65 mph. In 1911 he invented the aileron, and also flew the first practical seaplane (Hydroplane) which he patented, as well as the flying boat. During World War I he produced military aircraft like the JN-4 (Jenny), the Navy-Curtiss flying boat, speedboats and Liberty engines. He was design adviser to his Curtiss Aeroplane and Motor Company at the time of his death.

CURTIUS, Ernst (1814–96) German classical archaeologist, brother of **Georg Curtius**, born in Lübeck. He studied at Bonn, Göttingen and Berlin, visited Athens with Brandis in 1837, and accompanied Otfried Müller in his travels through Greece. Tutor (1844–49) to the crown prince Frederick of Prussia (the future **Frederick III**), he became successively professor at Göttingen (from 1856) and then Berlin (from 1868). An energetic excavator of high standards, he worked most notably at Olympia under the auspices of the German Archaeological Institute (1875–80), assisted first by the architect Friedrich Adler, later by the young **Wilhelm Dörpfeld**. Over £30000 was spent on the work, the expenses of the last season being borne personally by the emperor **William I**.

CURTIUS RUFUS, Quintus (1st century) Roman historian. About AD 41–54 he wrote a history of **Alexander the Great**, *De Rebus Gestis Alexandri Magni*, in ten books, of which the first two have been lost and the text of the remainder is imperfect. It has little value as history; but its style, if mannered, is elegant.

CURTIUS, Georg (1820–85) German philologist, born in Lübeck, and brother of **Ernst Curtius**. One of the greatest of Greek scholars, he was professor of classical philology at Prague (1849), Kiel (1854), and Leipzig (1862–65). The chief of his many works were *Griechische Schulgrammatik* (1852), *Erläuterungen* to the foregoing (1863), *Grundzüge der griechischen Etymologie* (1858), and *Das griechisches Verbum* (1873–76).

CURTIUS, Mettus or **Mettius** (4th century BC) a noble Roman youth who in 362 BC is said to have leapt on horseback into a chasm which had opened in the forum, and which the soothsayers declared could only be filled by throwing into it the most precious treasure of Rome.

CURTIUS, Theodor (1857–1928) German organic chemist, professor at Heidelberg from 1897, known especially for his discovery of hydrazine (1887) and other organic compounds.

CURWEN, John (1816–80) English musician, the apostle of the Tonic Sol-fa system, born in Heckmondwike, Yorkshire, the son of an Independent minister. In 1844 he was settled as Independent minister at Plaistow. In 1841 he began to advocate the sol-fa system; in 1843 his *Grammar of Vocal Music* appeared; in 1864 he resigned his ministry and gave himself wholly to the cause.

CURWOOD, James Oliver (1878–1927) American writer, born in Owosso, Michigan. He was the author of popular novels of outdoor life, such as *The Courage of Captain Plum* (1908), *The Grizzly King* (1917) and *The Alaskan* (1923).

CURZON, George Nathaniel, Marquis Curzon of Kedleston (1859–1925) English statesman, born at Kedleston Hall in Derbyshire, eldest son of Baron Scarsdale. After a promising career at Eton, he failed to take a first in classics at Oxford, but his subsequent brilliance gained him a fellowship of All Souls College in 1883. In 1886 he was elected MP for Southport, and the following year began extensive travels all over the East which gave him the extraordinary insight into oriental affairs and the personal contact with eastern rulers which fitted him for his later work at the Foreign Office and in India. Three authoritative books, on Asiatic Russia (1889), on Persia (1892) and on problems of the Far East (1894), were the outcome of his journeys. He became under-secretary for India in 1891, and for foreign affairs in 1895. In 1898, aged only 39, he was chosen viceroy of India and was given an Irish barony, having been unwilling to accept an English peerage with its accompanying bar from the House of Commons. A controversial and often turbulent viceroy, constantly at war with his officials, he introduced many reforms, both social and political, including the establishment of the NW Frontier Province and the partition of Bengal. After the arrival of Lord **Kitchener** as commander-in-chief in 1902, a difference of opinion arose over the dual control system then in force in the Indian Army. The government, finding Curzon's régime too dynamic for its liking, manipulated this crisis in such a way as to procure his resignation, and he left India, a disappointed man, in 1905. Relegated to the political wilderness, he devoted himself to art and archaeology and to the question of university reform. He returned to politics as lord privy seal in the Coalition of 1915, and became a member of **Lloyd George**'s War Cabinet in 1916, in which year he received the Garter. In 1919 his long-standing ambition to become foreign secretary was fulfilled, but in the unhealthy atmosphere of postwar foreign politics his optimistic planning was doomed to frustration, as in the failure of the Persian treaty (1919) and in the constant thwarting of his efforts by Lloyd George. In 1921 he was created a marquis, and as delegate to the Lausanne conference in 1922–23 he won a resounding success by his firm attitude at a time when British prestige had fallen dangerously low. On the resignation of **Andrew Bonar Law** in May 1923 he clearly hoped for and expected the premiership, and the choice of **Stanley Baldwin** was a great blow, but he offered his support and continued as foreign secretary until 1924. Curzon's handling of affairs was characterized by great self-confidence and decision and an unshakable faith in his own infallibility which brought him an unfortunate reputation for unapproachability and pomposity—his parliamentary manner was likened to that of 'a divinity addressing blackbeetles'—but his energy and ability and his courage in the face of bitter disappointments and physical handicap (he suffered from spinal curvature from an early age) stamp him as one of the outstanding figures of the century.

CURZON, Robert, Lord Zouche (1810–73) English diplomat and scholar, born in London. Educated at Charterhouse and Christ Church, Oxford, he travelled in the Levant in search of manuscripts (1833–37), was an *attaché* at Constantinople, and wrote *A Visit to the Monasteries in the Levant* (1849).

CUSACK, Cyril (1910–) Irish actor, director and playwright, born in Durban, South Africa. Having been a child actor, he joined the Abbey Theatre, Dublin in 1932, remaining there for 13 years and appearing in over 65 plays, including the major works of **O'Casey**, **Synge** and **Shaw**. He made his first appearance in London in **Eugene O'Neill**'s *Ah, Wilderness* in 1936. In 1945, he left the Abbey to form his own company, touring Ireland with a repertory of Irish and European plays, and making several visits abroad. He has also made a name with telling cameo parts in films.

CUSACK, (Ellen) Dymphna (1902–81) Australian author, born in Wyalong, New South Wales. Educated at Sydney University, she trained as a teacher. The first of her twelve novels, *Jungfrau*, was published in 1936, followed in 1939 by *Pioneers on Parade* which was written jointly with **Miles Franklin**. Illness forced her to retire from teaching in 1944, but in 1948 she won the [Sydney] *Daily Telegraph* novel competition with *Come In Spinner*, written in collaboration with Florence James and published in 1951. This story of the intertwined lives of a group of women in wartime Sydney, the effects of the absence of their menfolk and the presence of American servicemen, was an immediate success. She wrote nine other novels and eight plays, which illustrate her preoccupation with social and political disadvantage. They have been translated into over 30 languages, and her plays have been broadcast by the BBC and the ABC. She edited and introduced *Caddie, the Story of a Barmaid* (published 1953, filmed 1976).

CUSHING, Caleb (1800–79) American statesman, born in Salisbury, Massachusetts. He was admitted to the bar in 1821, sat in the state legislature and senate, and was elected to congress in 1835–43. He arranged the first treaty between China and the United States in 1844; raised and commanded a regiment in the war with Mexico; and was US attorney-general from 1853 to 1857, counsel for the US at the Geneva Conference in 1872, and minister to Spain from 1874 to 1877.

CUSHING, Harvey Williams (1869–1939) American neurosurgeon, born in Cleveland, Ohio. Educated at Yale and Harvard, he became professor of surgery at Harvard (1912–32) and of neurology at Yale (1932–37) he made a special study of the brain and the pituitary gland. Apart from his medical works, he won a Pulitzer prize in 1926 for his biography of the Canadian physician, Sir **William Osler**.

CUSHING, Peter (1913–) English actor, born in Kenley, Surrey. A student of voice production at the Guildhall School of Music and Drama, he worked as an assistant stage manager at Worthing Repertory Company before making his stage début in *The Middle Watch* (1935). A trip to the USA resulted in his Hollywood film début in *The Man in the Iron Mask* (1939) and a New York stage appearance in *The Seventh Trumpet* (1941). After the war he established himself as a classical actor with the Old Vic Company (1948–49) and was named Best Television Actor for his part in **Orwell**'s *1984* (1955). However, lasting fame has stemmed from a long association with the gothic horror films produced by Hammer in which his cadaverous figure and gentlemanly manner brought conviction to a succession of misguided scientists and vampire hunters in films like *The Curse of Frankenstein* (1956), *Dracula* (1958) and *The Mummy* (1959). His numerous other films include *Hamlet* (1948), *Dr. Who and the Daleks* (1965), *Tales from the Crypt* (1972) and *Star Wars* (1977). He has also enjoyed a long screen association with the character of Sherlock Holmes that includes a 1968 television series and the film *The Hound of the Baskervilles* (1959). He has published two volumes of autobiographical reminiscences: *An Autobiography* (1986), and *Past Forgetting* (1988).

CUSHMAN, Charlotte Saunders (1816–76) American actress, born in Boston, US. She appeared first in opera in 1834, and as Lady Macbeth in 1835. In 1844 she accompanied **William Charles Macready** on a tour through the northern states, and afterwards appeared in London, where she was well received in a range of characters that included Lady Macbeth, Rosalind, Meg Merrilees, and Romeo—her sister Susan (1822–59) playing Juliet.

CUST, Sir Lionel Henry (1859–1929) English art historian. He was director of the National Portrait Gallery (1895–1909), surveyor of the king's pictures (1901–27), and the author of many works, especially on **Van Dyck** and on the royal collections.

CUSTER, George Armstrong (1839–76) American soldier, born in New Rumley, Ohio. He graduated at West Point in 1861, and served with distinction through the Civil War. As a cavalry commander in the west, he several times defeated the hostile Indians; but on 25 June 1876, he attacked the Sioux under Chief **Sitting Bull** on the Little Bighorn, in Montana, and he and his 264 men were all destroyed ('Custer's Last Stand').

CUTHBERT, St (c.635–687) Anglo Saxon churchman and missionary, born probably in Lauderdale, in the Scottish Borders (then part of Northumbria). In 651 he was a shepherd boy there, and while watching his flock by night had a vision which made him resolve to become a monk. The same year he entered the monastery of Old Melrose, and in 660 accompanied its abbot, St Eata, to a new foundation at Ripon. In consequence of the dispute about Easter, Eata returned to Melrose (661), and Cuthbert, having accompanied him, was elected prior. He travelled widely in the north of England as a missionary, and many miracles were reported. In 664 he left Melrose for the island monastery of Lindisfarne, of which he became prior, his old master, Eata, being abbot. But in 676 he left Lindisfarne for a hermit's cell built with his own hands on Farne Island (Inner Farne). Here in 684, he was visited by Ecgfrith, king of Northumbria, who came entreating him to accept the bishopric of Hexham. He reluctantly complied, but shortly after exchanged the see of Hexham for that of Lindisfarne. Still thirsting after solitude, at the end of two years he returned to his cell, where he died. His body was elevated with a coffin-reliquary in 689, and the magnificent Lindisfarne Gospels book was made for the occasion. The fame of St Cuthbert had been great during his life; it became far greater after his death. Churches were dedicated to him from the Trent and Mersey to the Forth and Clyde. His body remained (incorrupt, as was believed) at Lindisfarne till 875, when the monks moved it inland at the time of the Viking incursions. After many wanderings it found a resting-place at Chester-le-Street in 883; in 995 it was translated first to Ripon and then, in 999, to Durham. Here, enclosed in a costly shrine, and believed to work miracles daily, it remained till the Reformation. The grave was opened in 1826, when inside a triple coffin his skeleton was found, still apparently entire, wrapped in fives robes of embroidered silk. His feast day is 20 March.

CUTTS, John Cutts, Baron (1661–1707) English soldier. He fought for **William III** at the battle of the Boyne (Ireland) in 1690, and was a hero of the siege of Namur (Netherlands) in 1695. He served under **Marlborough** in the Low Countries, and was third in command at the battle of Blenheim (1704).

CUVIER, Georges (Léopold Chrétien Frédéric Dagobert) (1769–1832) French anatomist, known as the father of comparative anatomy and palaeontology. Born in Montbéliard, he studied for the ministry at Stuttgart; and his love for zoology was confirmed by residence as a tutor on the Normandy coast (1788–94). In 1795, through **Geoffroy Saint-Hilaire**, he was appointed assistant professor of comparative anatomy in the Jardin des Plantes at the Museum of Natural History in Paris and in 1789 professor of natural history at the Collége de France. After the Restoration he was made chancellor of the University of Paris, and admitted into the cabinet by **Louis XVIII**. His opposition to the royal measures restricting the freedom of the press lost him the favour of **Charles X**; but under **Louis-Philippe** he was made a peer of France in 1831, and in the following year minister of the interior. He died of paralysis. In his plans for national education, in his labours for the French Protestant Church, and in scientific work, he was indefatigable. He was conspicuous for an unsurpassed grasp of facts rather than for originality or power of generalization, and proved a formidable opponent of the Theory of Descent. He originated the natural system of animal classification (although his four types are now known to give a false simplicity to nature). His studies of animal and fish fossils linked palaeontology to comparative anatomy, through his reconstructions of the extinct giant vertebrates of the Paris basin. Among Cuvier's more important works are: *Leçons d'anatomie comparée* (1801–05), *L'Anatomie des mollusques* (1816), *Les Ossements fossiles des quadrupèdes* (1812), *Histoire naturelle des poissons* (1828–49), written in concert with the French zoologist Achille Valenciennes, and *Le Règne animal distribué d'après son organisation* (1817).

CUVILLIÉS, François de (1695–1768) Bavarian architect, born in Belgium. Taken as court dwarf and architect by Maximilian Emmanuel, Elector of Bavaria, he was trained in Paris under Jacques-François Blondel. Becoming a leading exponent of the French Règence and rococo in Bavaria, he used natural motifs especially in the Amelienburg Pavilion (1734–39) at Schloss Nymphenburg, an exquisitely refined fantasy. He later adopted a heavier style, as seen in Residenztheater (1750–53), where a mass of rococo elements combine to produce a baroque heaviness. From 1738 he published a series of books of ornamental design which were influential throughout the Empire. His achievement was the creation of a more excessive rococo derived from France but seen through Bavarian eyes.

CUYP, or **Cuijp, Albert** (1620–91) Dutch painter, born in Dordrecht, son of Jacob Gerrits Cuyp (c.1575–1649), also a portrait painter. He travelled along his local rivers making sketches and studies from nature but unlike many of his peers never went to Italy. Although he had little influence on the history of Dutch painting, he is widely regarded as being one of the greatest Dutch landscapists. Excelling at capturing golden sunlight in scenes of munching cattle, his works are difficult to date and there are a great number of them even though he painted very little in the last decade of his life after marrying into a rich family. During the 18th and 19th centuries he was particularly appreciated in England with the result that a great number of his works are still in English collections.

CYMBELINE, or **Cunobelinus** (1st century) British chief of the Catevellauni tribe, described by **Suetonius** as 'rex Britannorum'. Several of his coins are extant. **Shakespeare**'s Cymbeline is loosely based on him, through **Holinshed**.

CYNEWULF (c.700–c.800) Anglo-Saxon poet and scholar, from Mercia or Northumberland. His identity is known only from his own runic inscription on texts. The works attributed to him are now restricted to four poems in the *Exeter Book* and the *Vercelli Book*: *The Ascension of Christ* and *Elene* (in the Exeter Book), and *St Juliana* and *The Fates of the Apostles*.

CYPRIAN, St, Thascius Caecilius Cyprianus (c.200–258) Christian martyr, born probably in Carthage, and one of the great fathers of the church. After teaching rhetoric in Carthage, he became a Christian about 245. He was made a bishop in 248, when his zealous efforts to restore strict discipline soon brought him a host of enemies. In the persecution under **Decius** he had to seek safety in flight; and after his return to Carthage in 251 the rest of his life was a constant struggle to hold the balance between severity and leniency towards the 'Lapsed' (ie, those who had conformed for a time to heathenism). Excommunicated by Pope **Stephen I** for denying the validity of heretic baptism, at a synod in Carthage in 256 Cyprian maintained that the Roman bishop, in spite of St **Peter**'s primacy, could not claim judicial authority over other bishops. He wrote a treatise on church unity, *De unitate ecclesiae*. During the persecution of the reign of **Valerianus** he was beheaded in Carthage. His feast day is 6 September.

CYPSELUS (c.655–625 BC) tyrant of Corinth and one of the earliest in a series of self-made rulers who arose in many Greek cities in the 7th and 6th centuries. He seized power against the narrow and exclusive oligarchy of the Bacchiads who had ruled Corinth since the 8th century, and founded the Cypselid dynasty. The earliest account of his rule in **Herodotus** is unfavourable, yet the tradition preserves indications that Cypselus' rule enjoyed some popular support. He founded colonies in north-west Greece and cultivated good relations with the Oracle of Apollo at Delphi. He was succeeded by his son **Periander**.

CYRANKIEWICZ, Jozef (1911–89) Polish politician. He became secretary of the Socialist party in Cracow in 1935. He was taken prisoner by the Germans in 1939, escaped and organized resistance in the Cracow Province and was sent to Auschwitz in 1941. In 1945 he became secretary-general of the Socialist party and was prime minister from 1947 to 1952. He resumed the premiership in 1954, held it until 1970, was chairman of the Council of State, 1970–72, and, from 1973, of the All-Poland Peace Committee.

CYRANO DE BERGERAC, Savinien (1619–55) French writer and dramatist, born in Paris. As a soldier, in his youth he fought more than a thousand duels, mostly on account of his monstrously large nose. His works, often crude, but full of invention, vigour, and wit, include a comedy, *Le Pédant joué* (1654), and the satirical science fantasy *Histoire comique des états de la lune et du soleil* (trans Aldington 1923). He was the subject of **Rostand**'s play, *Cyrano de Bererac* (1897).

CYRENIUS (d.21) a Greek form of Publius Sulpicius Quirinus, named in Luke ii as governor of Syria. He was appointed governor in AD 6, but may have also held the post some years earlier.

CYRIL, St (827–69) Christian missionary, born in Thessalonica. He and his brother, St Methodius

(826–85) were known as the Apostles of the Slavs. Cyril, who is traditionally regarded as the inventor of the Cyrillic alphabet, had been a disciple of **Photius**, and was surnamed 'the philosopher'. He preached the gospel to the Tartar Khazars to the northeast of the Black Sea (c.860), while Methodius evangelized the Bulgarians of Thrace and Moesia (c.863). At the request of the Duke of Moravia, the brothers prepared a Slav translation of the Scriptures and chief liturgical books. Their use of the vernacular in the liturgy aroused the opposition of the German Roman missionaries, and the brothers were summoned to Rome to explain their conduct, and Cyril died there in 869. Methodius, who in the same year was consecrated at Rome bishop of the Moravians, completed the evangelization of the Slavs. Called to Rome a second time in 879 to justify his celebration of the mass in the native tongue, he gained the approval of Pope John VIII, returned to his diocese in 880, and probably died at Hradiště on the Morava. Both brothers were recognized as saints by the Roman Catholic Church, after having been condemned as Arians by several popes. Their feast day is 7 July.

CYRIL OF ALEXANDRIA, St (376–444) Christian ecclesiastic, born in Alexandria, one of the doctors of the church. He was brought up under the care of his uncle Theophilus, whom, after some years spent as a monk in the Nitrian desert, he succeeded as archbishop of Alexandria in 412. A champion of orthodoxy, he closed the churches of the followers of **Novatian** immediately, and in 415 expelled the Jews from Alexandria. He was at least indirectly connected with the shameful murder of **Hypatia**, the philosopher, in 415. The latter part of his life was spent in the relentless persecution of **Nestorius**. The council of Ephesus condemned Nestorius, with his doctrine of the two natures in Christ. After this, John of Antioch and his adherents (numbering from 30 to 40 bishops), who had arrived at Ephesus too late, constituted a synod of their own which condemned Cyril. The emperor confirmed both of these depositions; but Cyril kept his patriarchate till his death. Among his extant works are a defence of Christianity, written against the emperor **Julian** in 433; and a series of homilies and treatises on the Trinity, the Incarnation, and the worship of God in spirit and in truth. His feast day is 9 February.

CYRIL OF JERUSALEM, St (c.315–386) Christian ecclesiastic, born in Jerusalem, and a Doctor of the Church. He was ordained presbyter about 345, tried to be neutral during the Arian controversies, and in 351 was ordained bishop of Jerusalem. He was twice expelled from his see, in 358 and by a synod at Constantinople in 360; but on the accession of **Julian** in 361 he returned to his flock till 367, when, by order of Valens, he was again expelled. He returned again on the death of Valens in 378, and took part, on the orthodox side, in the second Council of Constantinople. He was the author of 23 *Katéchéseis* (instructions to catechumens). His feast day is 18 March.

CYRILLUS LUCARIS See **LUCARIS**

CYRUS THE GREAT (d.529 BC) founder of the Persian empire, was the fourth in a line of kings of Anzan, in Susiana (called by the Hebrews *Elam*), who formed a branch of the Persian royal dynasty of the **Achaemenids**. Cyrus was the son of Cambyses I, grandson of Cyrus I, and great-grandson of Teispes, who was also the great-grandfather of Hystaspes, the father of **Darius**. In the third or sixth year of Nabonidus, king of Babylon (553 or 550 BC), Cyrus, 'king of Elam', made **Astyages**, king of Media, a prisoner, and took his capital, Ecbatana, the Median army having mutinied. By 548 he was 'King of Persia'. Favoured by a revolt of the tribes on 'the Lower Sea', or Persian Gulf, he advanced on Babylon and, after giving battle at Opis, took Sippara (Sepharvaim) and Babylon itself in 539. Cyrus, a polytheist, at once began a policy of religious conciliation. The nations who had been carried into captivity in Babylon along with the Jews were restored to their native countries, and allowed to take their gods with them. The empire of Lydia had fallen before the army of Cyrus some years before (in or about 546), and after the conquest of Babylonia he was master of all Asia from the Mediterranean to the Hindu Kush. The conqueror's hold over Asia Minor and Syria was much strengthened by his friendly relations with the Phoenicians and the Jews; in the Old Testament he is called the Shepherd and the Anointed of Jehovah. After he had extended his empire from the Arabian desert and the Persian Gulf in the south, to the Black Sea, the Caucasus and the Caspian in the north, he died in 529 though there are conflicting legends as to the manner of his death. Before his death he had made his son and successor Cambyses II 'king of Babylon'. The *Cyropaedia* of **Xenophon** is an historical romance.

CYRUS THE YOUNGER (424–401 BC) second son of **Darius II** and Parysatis. He conspired against his brother **Artaxerxes II Mnemon** (404), and was sentenced to death, but afterwards pardoned and restored to his position in Asia Minor. In 401 he left Sardis at the head of a large army of Asiatics and Greek mercenaries, encountered his brother at Cunaxa, 500 stadia from Babylon, and was there defeated and slain.

CZARTORYSKI, Adam Jerzy (1770–1861) Polish statesman, son of Prince Adam Czartoryski (1734–1823), born in Warsaw, and educated at Edinburgh and London. He fought against Russia in the Polish insurrection of 1794, and, sent to St Petersburg as a hostage, gained the friendship of the imperial grand duke **Alexander** and the confidence of the emperor **Paul**, who made him ambassador to Sardinia. When Alexander ascended the throne he appointed him assistant to the minister of foreign affairs. As curator of the university of Wilna (1803) he exerted all his influence to keep alive a spirit of nationality; and when some of the students were sent to Siberia, Czartoryski resigned his office. He threw himself into the Revolution of 1830 with all his heart. He was elected president of a provisional government, and summoned a national diet which in January 1831 declared the Polish throne vacant and elected Czartoryski head of the national government. He immediately devoted half of his large estates to the public service; and, though in August he resigned his post, continued to fight as a common soldier. After the suppression of the rising, Czartoryski—excluded from the amnesty and his Polish estates confiscated—escaped to Paris, where he afterwards resided, the liberal friend of his poor expatriate countrymen. In 1848 he freed all his serfs in Galicia, and during the Crimean war he endeavoured to induce the allies to identify the cause of Poland with that of Turkey. He refused the amnesty offered to him by **Alexander II**, and died near Paris.

CZERNY, Karl (1791–1857) Austrian pianist and composer, born in Vienna. He studied under **Beethoven** and **Clementi**, and himself taught **Liszt**, Thelberg and Döhler. His piano exercises and studies were widely used.

D

DABROWSKI See **DOMBROVSKI**

DACKO, David (1930–) Central African Republic politician, born in M'Baiki. In 1960 he became the first president of the republic following the accidental death of his uncle Barthelemy Boganda, a leading campaigner for independence and the president-designate. He was overthrown by **Jean Bedel Bokassa** in 1965. In 1976, he agreed to return as Bokassa's adviser, and ousted him in turn with French help in 1979. He was re-elected president for a six-year term in 1981, but within seven months was removed by the army chief-of-staff, André Kolingba.

DADD, Richard (1819–87) English painter, born in Chatham, Kent. He studied at the Royal Academy Schools, travelled extensively in Europe and the Middle East, and was considered a promising young artist. However, in 1843 he suffered a mental breakdown and murdered his father. He was sent first to the asylum of Bethlem, where he spent 20 years, and subsequently to Broadmoor, where he died. He is best known for the fantastically detailed fairy paintings which made up the bulk of his output after his incarceration; *The Fairy-Feller's Master Stroke* (1855–64) is a typical example.

DAENDELS, Herman Willem (1762–1818) Dutch soldier and colonialist, born in Hattem, in Guelderland. He joined the French Revolutionary army in 1793, but in 1806 entered Dutch service and was appointed governor-general of the Dutch East Indies (1808–11). In 1815 he was entrusted with the organization of the Dutch colonies on the coast of Africa, where he died.

DAFYDD, AP GRUFFYDD (d.1283) prince of Gwynnedd in north Wales, brother of **Llywelyn ap Gruffudd**. He opposed his brother's accession, but eventually supported him in his battles with the English. He succeeded his brother in 1282 but was betrayed and executed in 1283, the last native prince of Wales.

DA GAMA See **GAMA**

DAGOBERT I (605–39) Merovingian king and son of **Clotaire II**. King of Austrasia from 623, he ruled over a combined Frankish kingdom from 629. Subsequently he set his sons over Neustria and Austrasia.

DAGOBERT II king of Austrasia, (ruled 676–79) son of Sigibert III, after whose death in 656 he was banished to an Irish monastery. He was recalled and made king in 676, but was assassinated after a short reign.

DAGUERRE, Louis Jacques Mandé (1789–1851) French photographic pioneer and painter, inventor of the 'daguerrotype'. Born in Cormeilles, he was a scene painter for the opera in Paris. From 1826 onwards, and partly in conjunction with **Joseph Nicéphore Niepce**, he perfected his 'daguerrotype' process in which a photographic image is obtained on a copper plate coated with a layer of metallic silver sensitized to light by iodine vapour.

DAHL, Anders (18th century) Swedish botanist. A pupil of **Linnaeus**, the genus *Dahlia* is named after him.

DAHL, Johann Christian Clausen (1788–1857) Norwegian landscape painter. From 1821 he was professor of painting at Dresden.

DAHL, Michael (1656–1743) Swedish portrait painter, born in Stockholm. In 1688 he settled in London, and painted royalty and other notables. His works can be seen in the National Portrait Gallery.

DAHL, Roald (1916–) British children's author, short-story writer, playwright and versifier, born in Llandaff, Glamorgan, of Norwegian parentage. His first stories were based on his wartime experiences in the RAF and were collected in *Over to You* (1946). Subsequent collections achieved enormous popularity and include *Someone Like You* (1954), *Kiss, Kiss* (1960) and *Switch Bitch* (1974). Plot is paramount to Dahl and when he began to run short of good ones he turned to writing books for children. He is among the most popular children's authors of all time but many parents, teachers and librarians disapprove of his anarchic rudeness and violence. *Charlie and the Chocolate Factory* (1964) is his best-known book and was successfully filmed. Others include *James and the Giant Peach* (1961), *The Enormous Crocodile* (1978), *The BFG* (1982) and *Matilda* (1988). *Boy* (1984) is autobiographical.

DAHLGREN, John Adolphus Bernard (1809–70) American naval commander, born in Philadelphia. He joined the navy in 1826 and did much to advance the science of naval gunnery by founding an ordnance workshop at Washington, where he designed a new type of naval gun (1850). He commanded the South Atlantic blockade squadron in the Civil War.

DAHLGREN, Karl Fredrik (1791–1844) Swedish poet and humorist, born at Stensbruk in Ostergötland. He studied at Uppsala, and from 1815 was a preacher at Stockholm. His works—novels, tales, poems, dramas—fill five volumes (1847–52).

DAHLMANN, Friedrich Christoph (1785–1860) German historian, born in Wismar. He studied at Copenhagen and Halle, became professor of history at Kiel in 1813, and of political science at Göttingen in 1829, where he published (1830) his *Quellenkunde der deutschen Geschichte*. Banished in 1837 by the king of Hanover, he went to Leipzig, next to Jena, where he wrote his masterpiece, *Geschichte von Dänemark* (3 vols, 1840–43). In 1842 he became professor of history at Bonn, and in the movement of 1848 headed the constitutional liberals.

DAHN, Julius Sophus Felix (1834–1912) German historian and poet, born in Hamburg, the son of the actor, Friedrich Dahn (1811–89). He studied at Munich and Berlin, and became professor of German jurisprudence at Königsberg and Breslau. He wrote a number of novels, plays and books of poetry, and a notable history, *Die Könige der Germanen* (1861–1911).

DAHRENDORF, Ralf Gustav (1929–) German sociologist, born in Hamburg. Educated at Hamburg University and the London School of Economics, he held a succession of academic posts at universities in Germany and the USA in the 1950s and 1960s. He wrote *Class and Class Conflict in Industrial Society* (1957) and *Society and Democracy in Germany* (1965). In 1967 he joined the liberal Free Democrats (FDP) and briefly represented the party in the federal Bundestag and Baden-Wurttemberg Landtag. From 1970 to 1974 he was a member of the European Community Commission and then moved to Britain to become director of the LSE (1974–84), and wrote *Life Chances* (1980), a work which stresses the need to broaden the range of opportunities available to each individual. In 1987 he was appointed warden of St Anthony's College, Oxford.

DAIMLER, Gottlieb, Wilhelm (1834–1900) German engineer and inventor, born in Schorndorf. After 1872 he worked with Otto and Eugen Langen (1833–95) on improving the gas engine. In 1885 he built one of the earliest roadworthy motor cars, using a high-speed internal combustion engine, and founded the Daimler-Motoren-Gesellschaft in Cannstatt in 1890.

DAKIN, Henry Drysdale (1880–1952) English chemist, born in London. Noted for his researches on enzymes and his work on antiseptics, he developed 'Dakin's' or the 'Carrel-Dakin' solution (a 0.5% solution of sodium hypochlorite), widely used for treating wounds in World War I.

DALADIER, Édouard (1884–1970) French politician, born in Carpentras, became in 1927 leader of the radical socialists, and in 1933 minister of war and prime minister of a short-lived government. Again minister of war, in January 1934 he was asked to form a cabinet, but his government immediately met the full force of the repercussions of the **Stavisky** crisis, and lasted only a few weeks. In 1936 he became war minister in the Popular Front cabinet, and in 1938 again took office as premier. Pacifist in outlook, he supported 'appeasement' and was a signatory of the Munich Pact. In 1940 he resigned, became successively war and foreign minister, and on the fall of France was arrested and interned until 1945.

DALAI LAMA (Tenzin Gyatso) (1935–) Spiritual and temporal head of Tibet. Born in Taktser, in Amdo province, into a peasant family, he was designated the 14th Dalai Lama in 1937 by the monks of Lhasa who were convinced, from his actions, that he was the reincarnation of the Compassionate Buddha. He was enthroned at Lhasa in 1940, but his rights were exercised by a regency until 1950. He fled to Chumbi in southern Tibet after an abortive anti-Chinese uprising in 1950, but negotiated an autonomy agreement with the People's Republic the following year and for the next eight years served as nominal ruler of Tibet. After China's brutal suppression of the Tibetan national uprising of 1959 he was forced into permanent exile, settling, with other Tibetan refugees, at Dharamsala in Punjab, India, where he established a democratically-based alternative government. A revered figure in his homeland, the Dalai Lama has for long rejected Chinese overtures to return home as a figurehead, seeking instead full independence. In 1988, however, he modified this position, proposing the creation of a self-governing Tibet in association with China. He was awarded the 1989 Nobel prize for peace in recognition of his commitment to the non-violent liberation of his homeland.

D'ALBRET, Jeanne See **JEANNE D'ALBRET**

DALCROZE See **JACQUES-DALCROZE**

DALE, David (1739–1806) Scottish industrialist and philanthropist, born in Stewarton, Ayrshire, the son of a grocer. He was apprenticed to a Paisley weaver, then travelled the country as an agent buying up homespun linen, and became a clerk to a Glasgow silk mercer. In 1763 he set up his own business in Glasgow, importing linen yarn from Holland and Flanders. He was a founder member in 1768 of an independent dissenting sect, the 'Old Scotch Independents', who were firm believers in practical Christianity, and became their best-known lay preacher. In 1777 he married the daughter of an Edinburgh director of the Royal Bank of Scotland, and was appointed the first Glasgow agent of the bank in 1783. In 1784 he met **Richard Arkwright**, who was being given the freedom of Glasgow, and set up a business partnership to build cotton mills at New Lanark, near the Falls of Clyde; but the partnership was dissolved in 1785 when Arkwright lost his legal battle over patents for his 'water-frame' machines. Spinning began at New Lanark in 1786, followed by a mill at Blantyre in 1787. From 1791 he was concerned with alleviating the plight of impoverished Highlanders tempted to emigrate; he gave work and housing at New Lanark to destitute would-be emigrants from the Western Isles shipwrecked off the west coast, and started industrial ventures to provide more work, with spinning mills at Spinningdale in Sutherland and at Oban. He also employed hundreds of pauper children from Edinburgh and Glasgow at New Lanark, providing a school as well as accommodation for them. He became one of the first directors of the Glasgow Royal Infirmary in 1795, which was opened that year to help the sick and diseased poor. In 1799 he sold the New Lanark mills, with their tradition of benevolent management, to his son-in-law, **Robert Owen**. He retired to Cambuslang, where he died.

DALE, Sir Henry Hallett (1875–1968) British physiologist, born in London. Educated at Cambridge and London, he became director of the National Institute for Medical Research, London in 1928. He discovered acetylcholine, and in 1936 he shared with **Otto Loewi** the Nobel prize for physiology or medicine for work on the chemical transmission of nerve impulses.

DALÉN, Nils Gustav (1869–1937) Swedish engineer and inventor. Educated at Göteborg and Zürich, he invented automatic acetylene lighting for unmanned lighthouses and railway signals, for which he was awarded the Nobel prize for physics in 1912. He was blinded a year later by an explosion in a chemical experiment, but continued to work till his death.

DALGARNO, George (c.1626–1687) Scottish educationist, born in Old Aberdeen. He studied at Marischal College, and kept a school for 30 years in Oxford. He published a book on philosophy using letters of the alphabet for ideas, *Ars Signorum, vulgo Character Universalis* (1661) and a deaf-and-dumb sign-language, *Didascalocophus, or the Deaf and Dumb Man's Tutor* (1680).

DALGLISH, Kenneth Mathieson (1951–) Scottish footballer and manager, born in Glasgow. One of Scotland's greatest internationals, he won 102 caps for his country. He joined Glasgow Celtic in 1967 and in ten years there won every honour in the Scottish game. Transferred to Liverpool in August 1977 for a then record fee between two British clubs of £440000, he won every major English honour in addition to three European Cups. Unusually, Dalglish combined great skill with extreme durability and rarely missed a match. Unexpectedly invited to manage Liverpool while he was still a player, he confounded the pundits by being an instant success. In his first season, Liverpool won both Cup and League. He is the only player to have scored 100 goals in both English and Scottish football.

DALHAM See **DALLAM**

DALHOUSIE, James Andrew Broun-Ramsay, Marquis of (1812–60) 'greatest of Indian proconsuls', third son of the 9th Earl of Dalhousie born at Dalhousie Castle, Midlothian. Educated at Harrow and Christ Church College, Oxford, he succeeded in 1832, by the death of his only remaining brother, to the courtesy title of Lord Ramsay. In 1835 he stood unsuccessfully for Edinburgh as a Conservative; in 1837 was elected for Haddingtonshire; in 1838, on the death of his father, entered the House of Lords as Earl of Dalhousie. In 1843 **Peel** appointed him vice-president of the board of trade, and in 1845 he succeeded **Gladstone** as president. When Peel resigned office in 1846, Lord **John Russell** asked Dalhousie to remain at the board of trade in order to carry out the regulations he had framed for the railway system. In 1847 he was appointed governor-general of India—the youngest viceroy ever sent there. His Indian administration was not less successful in the acquisition of territory than in developing Indian resources and improving the administration. Pegu and the Punjab were conquered; Nagpur, Oudh, Sattara, Jhansi and Berar annexed. Railways on a colossal scale were planned and commenced; 4000 miles of telegraph were spread over India; 2000 miles of road were bridged and metalled; the Ganges Canal was opened; and important irrigation works all over India were executed. Noteworthy also are Dalhousie's energetic action against suttee, thuggee, female infanticide and the slave-trade; the organization of the Legislative Council; the improved training of the civil service, which was opened to all natural-born British subjects, black or white; the development of trade, agriculture, forestry, mining and the postal service. In 1848 he was made a KT; in 1849 received the marquisate and the thanks of parliament. Broken in health, he left India in 1856.

DALI, Salvador (1904–89) Spanish artist, born in Figueras. After studying at the Academy of Fine Arts, Madrid, he moved to Paris and joined the Surrealists in 1928, and became one of the principal figures of the movement. He made a deep study of abnormal psychology and dream symbolism, and represented 'paranoiac' objects in landscapes remembered from his Spanish boyhood with almost academic realism and highly finished craftsmanship. In 1940 he settled in the USA, and later became a Catholic and devoted his art to symbolic religious paintings. His publications include *The Secret Life of Salvador Dali* (1942) and the Surrealist novel *Hidden Faces* (1944). He collaborated with **Luis Buñuel** in producing the Surrealist films *Le Chien Andalou* (1928) and *L'Age d'Or* (1930). His painting *The Persistence of Memory* (1931) (known as the *Limp Watches*) is in the Museum of Modern Art, New York, and his *Christ of St John of the Cross* (1951) is in Glasgow Art Gallery.

DALIN, Olof von (1708–63) Swedish author and historian, the most influential literary figure of the Swedish Enlightenment. He published anonymously Sweden's first moralizing periodical, *Then svänska Argus* (The Swedish Argus, 1732–34), in the tradition of **Addison** and **Steele**'s *The Tatler* and *The Spectator*; influenced by **Swift**, it achieved enormous influence and popularity and is regarded as the foundation stone of modern Swedish prose. As tutor to the future King **Gustav III** (1751–56), he laid the foundations for a period of royal cultural patronage. He compiled a monumental history of Sweden (1747–62); among his many varied works were a verse tragedy, *Brynilda* (1738), and his prose allegorical masterpiece, *Sagan om hästen* (The Story of the Horse, 1740).

DALLAM, Ralph (d.1672) English organ-builder, who built organs for St George's Chapel, Windsor, and for Greenwich church.

DALLAM, Robert (1602–65) English organ-builder, son of **Thomas Dallam**. He was responsible for organs at New College, Oxford, York Minster, St Paul's Cathedral, Jesus College, Cambridge (1634), Canterbury Cathedral (1635), and St Mary Woolnoth (destroyed in the Fire of London).

DALLAM, Thomas (c.1599–c.1630) English organ-builder. He built organs for King's College, Cambridge, and for Worcester Cathedral.

DALLAPICCOLA, Luigi (1904–75) Italian composer and teacher. His compositions, making wide use of twelve-note technique, include songs, a piano concerto, two operas (*The Prisoner* and *Ulisse*), a ballet, *Marsyas*, and orchestral and choral works such as *Canti di Prigionia*, and were influential on American composition.

DALLAS, Alexander James (1759–1817) American lawyer, born in the West Indies of Scottish parents. He went to the USA in 1783, settled in Philadelphia, and was later secretary of the Treasury and war-secretary under President **Madison**.

DALLAS, George Mifflin (1792–1864) American lawyer and statesman, born in Philadelphia, the son of **Alexander James Dallas**. After graduating at Princeton College in 1810 he was admitted to the bar and entered the diplomatic service. In 1831 he was sent to the US senate by Pennsylvania. He was US minister to Russia, 1837–39, and in 1844 was elected vice-president of the USA. In 1846 his casting vote as president of the senate repealed the protective tariff of 1842, though he had been a Protectionist. Dallas in Texas is named after him. He was minister to Britain (1856–61). His writings include *Letters from London* (1869), a life of his father (1871), and his *Diary*.

DALLING, Lord See **BULWER, Henry Lytton**

DALOU, (Aimé) Jules (1838–1902) French sculptor, born in Paris. He was the pupil of **Carpeaux**, and after being the curator of the Louvre during the Commune, he fled to England in 1871, and taught at the Royal College of Art. His realistic modelling influenced many English sculptors of the time. His well-known monument, *Triumph of the Republic*, is in Paris.

DALRYMPLE, Sir David See **HAILES, Sir David Dalrymple**

DALRYMPLE, Sir John, later **Dalrymple Hamilton Macgil, 4th baronet of Cranstoun** (1726–1810) Scottish historian, descended from a distinguished Scottish legal and political family. Educated at Edinburgh and Cambridge, he was admitted to the Scottish bar in 1748, and was for a time solicitor to the board of excise. He published *An Essay towards a General History of Feudal Property in Great Britain under various Heads* (1757). He travelled on the Continent and obtained vital copies from Jacobite archives which revealed for the first time that leading Whig politicians were drawing financial support from **Louis XIV** and, after his exile, **James II** of England, thus implicating among others **Algernon Sidney** and John Churchill, later Duke of **Marlborough**. These he published as appendices to his *Memoirs of Great Britain and Ireland from the Dissolution of the Last Parliament until the Sea Battle of La Hogue* (3 vols, 1771, and 1790). He also discovered how to make soap from herrings, and defended the playwright **John Home** as a lay member of the General Assembly of the Church of Scotland for having staged his play *Douglas* in 1756.

DALTON, Hugh, Baron Dalton of Forest and Frith (1887–1962) British Labour politician, born at Neath, Glamorgan. He was educated at Eton, King's College, Cambridge, and the London School of Economics, served in World War I and was a Labour MP (1924–31 and from 1935). He became minister for economic warfare (1940) and president of the board of trade (1942) in **Churchill**'s war-time coalition. In 1945 he became Labour Chancellor of the Exchequer, nationalized the Bank of England (1946) but resigned in consequence of 'budget leakages' to a journalist in November 1947. He was made a life peer in 1960. He published *Call back Yesterday* (1953) and his memoirs, *High Tide and After* (1962).

DALTON, John (1766–1844) English chemist, born at Eaglesfield, near Cockermouth, the son of a Quaker weaver. After 1781 he became assistant in a boarding-school kept by a cousin in Kendal, of which in 1785 he and a brother became the proprietors. Here his love of mathematical and physical studies was developed, and here in 1787 he commenced a meteorological journal continued all his life, recording 200000 observations. He collected butterflies and gathered a great *hortus siccus* and herbarium. In 1793 he was appointed teacher of mathematics and science in New College, Manchester, and later supported himself in Manchester by private tuition. In 1794 he first described colour blindness ('Daltonism'), exemplified in his own case and that of his brother. His chief physical researches were on mixed gases, the force of steam, the elasticity of vapours and the expansion of gases by heat, his law of partial pressures being also known as *Dalton's law*; and in chemistry on the absorption of gases by water, on carbonic acid, carburetted hydrogen, etc, while his atomic theory elevated chemistry to a science. Dalton was unquestionably one of the greatest of chemists. In his habits he was simple, in manners grave and reserved but kindly. He 'never found time' to marry.

DALTON, Sir John Neale (1839–1931) English clergyman and philanthropist, born in Kent, the son of a clergyman. Educated at Blackheath and Cambridge, he occupied various curacies and was chosen by Queen **Victoria** as tutor to her grandsons Albert Victor and George (the future **George V**), whom he taught from 1871 to 1884. He was canon and steward of St George's Chapel at Windsor from 1884, and proved himself a distinguished antiquarian, inspired singing master and ruthless autocrat. His insistence on disinterring the corpse of **Henry VI** before a scholarly audience including **Montague James** seems to have inspired the sardonic portrait in James's ghost story *An Episode of Cathedral History*. He published valuable works, including *Ordinale Exon*: (3 vols, 1908, 1926), *The Collegiate Church of Ottery St Mary* (1917), and *The Book of Common Prayer, Proposals, and Suggestions* (1920). His *protégés* included the navvy poet **Patrick MacGill** whom he brought to the Windsor Cloisters as his secretary. His son was the politician **Hugh Dalton**, and he himself had strong socialist ideas.

DALY, (John) Augustin (1838–99) American dramatist and manager, born in Plymouth, North Carolina. After a career as a drama critic, he went into management, opening the Fifth Avenue Theatre, New York, in 1869, and his own theatre, Daly's, in 1879, with the company of which he visited London in 1884. In 1893 he opened the London Daly's with Ada Rehan in *The Taming of the Shrew*. He wrote and adapted nearly one hundred plays, of which the best was *Horizon* (1871), though the most popular were melodramas such as *Under the Gaslight* and *Leah the Forsaken*. He was chosen by **Tennyson** to adapt *The Foresters* for the stage in 1891.

DALY, Mary (1928–) American feminist and theological writer, born in Schenectady, New York. She studied theology at St Mary's College, Indiana, and Fribourg University, Switzerland, and has taught at Fribourg (1959–66) and Boston College (from 1969). Having analyzed the effects of male bias in *The Church and the Second Sex* (1968), she abandoned her attempts to reform official Roman Catholic attitudes and became a post-Christian radical feminist in *Beyond God the Father* (1973). Her emphasis on pre-Jewish/Christian religion and women's personal experience is developed in *Gyn/Ecology:* The Metaethics of Radical Feminism (1978) and *Pure Lust: Elemental Feminist Philosophy* (1984).

DALYELL, or **Dalzell, Thomas** (c.1615–1685) Scottish royalist soldier, known as the 'Muscovy general', born at The Binns, West Lothian. The son of a laird, he served in the unsuccessful expedition against Rochelle led by the 1st Duke of **Buckingham** (1628), and fought for the royalists in Ireland in the 1640s. In the attempted revolution he was taken prisoner at Worcester (1651), but escaped from the Tower of London in 1652 and joined **Charles II** in exile. In 1655 he entered the service of Russia and fought against the Tartars and Turks. In 1666, appointed commander-in-chief in Scotland, he defeated the Covenanters at Rullion Green in the Pentlands. He was commander-in-chief again from 1679 to 1685 charged with the bloody suppression of the Convenanters. He raised the Royal Scots Greys in 1681.

DALZELL, Thomas See **DALYELL**

DALZIEL, Edward (1817–1905) English engraver, born in Wooler. The fifth of the twelve sons of a Northumbrian artist, in 1839 he joined his brother George in London, and gradually built up (with a third brother, Thomas) the great business of the *Brothers Dalziel*, wood-engravers.

DAM, Carl Peter Henrik (1895–1976) Danish biochemist. He was professor at Copenhagen (1923–40) and in 1940 went to the USA where he taught at the University of Rochester (1942–45) and became a member of the Rockefeller Institute for Medical Research (1945). He was also on the staff of the Polytechnic Institute, Copenhagen (1941–65). For his discovery of the coagulant agent vitamin K (1934) he shared the Nobel prize for physiology or medicine in 1943 with the American biochemist **Edward Doisy**.

DAMALA See **BERNHARDT, Sarah**

DAMASUS I, St (c.304–384) pope from 366 to 384. A Roman deacon, possibly of Spanish descent, his election was violently contested, but confirmed by **Valentinian I**. He opposed Arianism, and condemned **Apollinaris the Younger** at the Council of Constantinople in 381. In 382 he proclaimed the primacy of the see of Rome. He restored the catacombs and wrote epitaphs for the tombs of the martyrs. He commissioned St **Jerome**, his secretary, to undertake the Vulgate Version of the Bible. His feast day is 11 December.

DAMASUS II, originally **Poppo** (d.1048) bishop of Brixen, he was elected pope in 1048 in opposition to **Benedict IX**, but died 23 days later.

DAMIANI, Pietro, or **St Peter Damian** (1007–72) Italian ecclesiastic, born in Ravenna, and one of the Doctors of the Church. He herded swine in boyhood, but joined the hermitage at Fonte Avellana in 1035 and rose to be cardinal and bishop of Ostia (1057). He supported the policy of Hildebrand (**Gregory VII**) without sharing his arrogance, and laboured strenuously to reform the clergy, then at a low ebb of immorality and indolence. He died in Faenza. His feast day is 23 February.

DAMIANUS, St See **COSMAS**

DAMIEN, Father Joseph, properly **De Veuster** (1840–89) Belgian missionary, renowned for his great work among the lepers of the Hawaiian island of Molokai, where he lived from 1873 until his death from the disease.

DAMIENS, Robert François (1714–57) French servant who attempted to assassinate **Louis XV**. On 4 January 1757, he went to Versailles, next day followed the king about everywhere, and about 6pm, as the king was entering his carriage, stabbed him. He was seized, and nearly three months later slowly tortured to death, being finally torn to pieces by four horses.

DAMOCLES (4th century BC) a courtier of **Dionysius the Elder**, tyrant of Syracuse. Having extolled the happiness of royalty he was invited to a sumptuous royal feast; but on looking upwards he saw a keen-edged sword suspended over his head by a single horse-hair—the 'Sword of Damocles'.

DAMON and **PHINTIAS (PYTHIAS)** (4th century BC) Pythagorean philosophers and proverbial friends. The story goes that Phintias was condemned to death for plotting against the tyrant **Dionysius the Elder** of Syracuse. He begged to be allowed to go home to settle his affairs and Damon pledged his own life as hostage. Phintias duly returned at the last moment to save Damon's life and Dionysius was so moved by their mutual devotion that he pardoned him.

DAMPIER, William (1652–1715) English navigator and hydrographer, born near Yeovil. He gained a great knowledge of hydrography in voyages to Newfoundland, Bantam, Jamaica and Campeachy Bay. After two years among the lawless logwood cutters of Yucatán, he joined in 1679 a band of buccaneers who crossed the Isthmus of Darien and ravaged the coast as far south as Juan Fernández. In another expedition (1683), after seizing a Danish ship at Sierra Leone, he coasted along the shores of Chile, Peru and Mexico, sailing thence across the Pacific, and touching at the Philippines, China and Australia. Marooned on Nicobar Islands (1688) he made his way in a native canoe to Atchin, and got back to England (1691), where he published his interesting *Voyage round the World* (1697). He conducted (1699–1700) a voyage of discovery to the South Seas, in which he explored the north-west coast of Australia, also the coasts of New Guinea and New Britain, giving his name to the Dampier Archipelago and Strait. On the return voyage he was wrecked off Ascension, and lived with his crew on turtles and goats for five weeks, until relieved. The old buccaneer was a better pilot than commander, and his cruelty to his lieutenant led to his being court-martialled. Yet in 1703 he was re-appointed to the command of two privateers (the master of one of them **Alexander Selkirk**) to the South Seas, when he was said to have been guilty of drunkenness, brutality and even cowardice. Dampier returned home at the close of 1707, poor and broken, nor did his angry *Vindication* re-establish his reputation. Next year he sailed again as pilot to a privateer, which rescued Selkirk, and returned in 1711.

DAMROSCH, Leopold (1832–85) German-born American conductor and composer, born in Posen. He was leader of the Weimar court orchestra under **Liszt** (1857–59) and conductor at Breslau (1859–60 and 1862–71) before emigrating to New York, where he ultimately became conductor at the Metropolitan Opera House and did much to popularize **Wagner** in the United States. His son, Walter Johannes (1862–1950), born in Breslau, also became well known as a conductor and composed several operas.

DANA, Charles Anderson (1819–97) American newspaper editor, born in Hinsdale, New Hampshire. He spent two years at Harvard, and was a member of the Brook Farm community (1841–46) with **George Ripley**. From 1848 to 1862 he edited the New York *Tribune*, which opposed the extension of slavery to new territories. From 1863 to the close of the Civil War he was assistant-secretary of war. In 1867 he purchased the New York *Sun*, and successfully managed it on democratic lines. He published translations and anthologies, collaborated in a Life of **Ulysses Grant** (1868), and with George Ripley edited the *New American Cyclopaedia* (1857–63) and the *American Cyclopaedia* (1873–76).

DANA, James Dwight (1813–95) American mineralogist and geologist, born in Utica, New York. A graduate of Yale, he was a scientific observer on the US exploring expedition under Charles Wilkes (1838–42), visiting the Antarctic and Pacific, during which Dana's ship was wrecked. With his father-in-law, **Benjamin Silliman**, he edited the *American Journal of Science* from 1840. He was professor of natural history (1849–64) and geology (1864–90) at Yale. Among his works are *Manual of Mineralogy* (1848), two treatises on corals, *Textbook of Geology* (1864) and *Hawaiian Volcanoes* (1890).

DANA, Richard Henry (1787–1879) American poet and prose writer, born in Cambridge, Massachusetts. He was educated at Harvard, and admitted to the bar at Boston in 1811. In 1818 he became associate editor of the *North American Review*, to which he contributed. His *Dying Raven* (1821), *The Buccaneer* (1827) and some others of his poems were warmly praised by critics, but his best work was in criticism.

DANA, Richard Henry (1815–82) American author and lawyer son of **Richard Henry Dana**. While a student at Harvard, he shipped as a common sailor, and made a voyage round Cape Horn to California and back, which he described in *Two Years before the Mast* (1840). After graduating in 1837 he was admitted to the Massachusetts bar in 1840, and was especially distinguished in maritime law. Among his works are *The Seaman's Friend* (1841) and *To Cuba and Back* (1859). He also edited Wheaton's *International Law*, and was a prominent free-soiler and Republican.

DANBY, Francis (1793–1861) Irish painter, born near Wexford, Killinick County. He studied art at Dublin, moved to Bristol in 1813 but left England for Switzerland in 1829 when his marriage broke up. He painted landscapes and large biblical and historical subject pictures.

DANBY, Lord See **LEEDS, Duke of**

DANCE, George (1700–68) English architect. He designed the Mansion House (1739) and many other London buildings.

DANCE, George (1741–1825) English architect and painter, son of **George Dance** (1700–68). He rebuilt Newgate Prison (1770–83), and was one of the original Royal Academicians.

DANCER, Ann See **BARRY, Spranger**

DANCOURT, Florent Carton (1661–1725) French dramatist, actor and court favourite. He became devout in his old age, which he spent in retirement in the country. He excelled in depicting the stupidity of the peasantry and the follies of the *bourgeoisie*.

DANDOLO, Enrico (c.1108–c.1205) Venetian statesman and soldier, eminent in learning, eloquence and knowledge of affairs. In 1173 he was sent as ambassador to Constantinople, and in 1192 was elected doge. As such, he defeated the Pisans, and in 1201 marched at the head of the Fourth Crusade, and subdued Trieste and Zara, the coasts of Albania, the Ionian Islands and Constantinople (1203). When the emperor Alexius was murdered by his own subjects, Dandolo laid siege to Constantinople and took it by storm again in 1204. He established there the empire of the Latins, and caused Count **Baldwin I** of Flanders to be chosen emperor. Other important members of the family include Giovanni, doge 1280–89; Francesco, doge 1328–39; Andrea, doge 1342–54.

DANDY, Walter Edward (1886–1946) American neurosurgeon, born in Sedalia, Missouri. He went to Johns Hopkins University for his medical training, where **Harvey Cushing** encouraged his interests in neurosurgery, and Dandy remained on the staff there until his death. He did important work on the pathophysiology and surgical treatment of hydrocephalus and developed a number of fundamental diagnostic and neurosurgical techniques. He also demonstrated the significance of ruptured vertebra disks in cases of low back pain and pioneered spinal surgery. Dandy and Cushing unfortunately later quarrelled and remained bitter rivals for the leadership of the American neurosurgical community.

DANE, Clemence, pseud of **Winifred Ashton** (?1891–1965) English novelist and playwright, born in Blackheath, London. Her novels included *Regiment of Women* (1917), *Legend* (1919), *Broome Stages* (1931) and *The Flower Girls* (1954), the last two dealing with theatrical families. Many of her plays achieved long runs, including *A Bill of Divorcement* (1921); the ingenious reconstruction of the poet's life in *Will Shakespeare* (1921); the stark tragedy of *Granite* (1926) and *Call Home the Heart* (1927).

DANE, Nathan (1752–1835) American lawyer and statesman, born in Ipswich, Massachusetts. A delegate to the Continental Congress in 1785 and later a commissioner to revise the statutes of Massachusetts, he published a nine-volume *General Abridgement and Digest of American Law*, the first comprehensive work on US law, in 1823–29. He arranged that the income from this work be used to establish a chair in the Harvard Law School provided that **Joseph Story** was the first holder; as Dane professor, Story published his outstanding series of *Commentaries* and revitalized the School.

DANGERFIELD, Thomas (1650–85) English criminal and inventor of the Meal-tub Plot, he was the son of a farmer in Essex. He had been a thief, vagabond and soldier on the Continent, pseudo-convert to Catholicism and among other things a coiner, when in 1679 he accused the presbyterians of plotting to destroy the government. Imprisoned when this was shown to be a lie, he excused himself as having been deceived by a tale invented by the Roman Catholics to screen a plot of their own against the king's life. Papers proving this would, he alleged, be found in a meal-tub in the house of a lady (who was tried and acquitted). For this he was whipped and pilloried, and on returning from Tyburn was killed by a blow in the eye from a bystander who struck him with a cane.

DANIEL, Arnaut (fl. late 12th century) Provençal poet, born at the Castle of Rebeyrac, in Périgord, of poor but noble parents. He became a member of the court of **Richard Cœur de Lion** and was esteemed one of the best of the troubadours, particularly for his treatment of the theme of love. He introduced the sestina, the pattern of which was later adapted by **Dante** and **Petrarch**.

DANIEL, Glyn Edmund (1914–86) Welsh archaeologist, born in Barry. Educated at University College, Cardiff, and St John's College, Cambridge, he lectured at Cambridge (1945–74) and was professor of archaeology (1974–81). A companionable bon viveur with a Celtic relish for anecdote, his career was devoted less to excavation and research than to stimulating popular interest in archaeology through writing, editing, and broadcasting. He was a pioneer historian of archaeology and an energetic editor, both of the journal *Antiquity* (1958–86) and of the book series *Ancient Peoples and Places* published by Thames and Hudson from 1955. On television he achieved particular popularity in the 1950s as chairman of the archaeological panel game *Animal, Vegetable, Mineral?* An autobiography, *Some Small Harvest*, appeared in 1986.

DANIEL, Samuel (1562–1619) English poet, the son of a music-master, born near Taunton. He entered Magdalen Hall, Oxford, in 1597, but left it without a degree. He was sometime tutor at Wilton to William Herbert, son of the Earl of Pembroke, afterwards at Skipton to Anne Clifford, daughter of the Earl of Cumberland. In 1604 he was appointed to read new plays; in 1607 became one of the queen's grooms of the privy chamber, and from 1615 to 1618 had charge of a company of young players at Bristol. He then retired to a farm which he possessed at Beckington, in Somerset. Daniel was highly commended by his contemporaries, although **Ben Johnson** described him as 'a good honest man...but no poet'. **Coleridge**, **Lamb** and **Hazlitt** all praised him. His works include sonnets, epistles, masques and dramas; but his chief production was a poem in eight books, *A History of the Civil Wars between York and Lancaster*. His *Defence of Ryme* (1602) is in admirable prose.

DANIELL, John Frederic (1790–1845) English chemist, born in London. Professor of chemistry at King's College, London, from 1831, he wrote an *Introduction to Chemical Philosophy* (1839). He invented a hygrometer (1820), a pyrometer (1830) and the Daniell electric cell (1836).

DANILOVA, Alexandra (1904–) Soviet dancer and teacher, born in Peterhof (Petrodvorets). One of the most popular and versatile ballerinas of her day, she trained at the Imperial Ballet School before joining the Maryinsky Theatre (now Kirov Ballet) in 1922. She left the USSR on a 1924 tour, never to return. That same year she was engaged by **Sergei Diaghilev** for his Ballets Russes until 1929. She was a member of Colonel **de Basil**'s Ballet Russe (1933–38) and its splinter group the Ballet Russe de Monte Carlo (until 1952), as well as making guest appearances with many companies. She formed her own group, Great Moments of Ballet (1954–56) before retiring in 1957. Afterwards she staged ballets for opera companies and in collaboration with **George Balanchine**, at whose School of American Ballet she has earned a reputation as a superb teacher.

D'ANNUNZIO, Gabriele (1863–1938) Italian writer, adventurer and political leader, born in Pescara. Starting as a journalist on the *Tribuna* in Rome, he made his name as a poet with several volumes of poetry starting in 1879 with *Primo vere*. During the 1890s he wrote 'Romances of the Rose' a trilogy of novels with Nietzschean heroes, *Il Piacere* (1889), *L'Innocente* (1892), and *Il Trionfo della morte*. *Le Vergini delle rocce* (1896) is one of a 'Lily' trilogy; *Il Fuoco* (1900), first of a 'Pomegranate' series. Elected a parliamentary deputy (1897–1900), he became notorious for his passionate affair with the actress Leonaro Druse, for whom he wrote several plays, including *La Città morta* (1898), *La Gioconda* (1899), *Francesca da Rimini* (1901) and *La figlia di Jorio* (1904). *Le Martyre de St Sébastien* (1911) is a mystery play. Grace, voluptuousness and affection characterize this apostle of a new Renaissance. An enthusiastic patriot, he urged Italian entry into World War I, and served as a soldier, sailor and finally airman. In 1916 he lost an eye in combat in the air, and in 1918 carried out a sensational aerial reconnaissance over Vienna. In 1919 he seized and held Fiume, despite the Allies, and ruled as dictator until he was removed by the Italian government (1920). He became a strong supporter of the Fascist party under **Mussolini**.

DANTAS, Julio (1876–1962) Portuguese dramatist, poet and short-story writer, born in Lagos. In his light lyrical poems and stories he displayed considerable talent, but his heavier work, such as historical dramas, attempted under the influence of the Norwegian and French schools, was less successful. His *A ceia dos cardeais* (1902) was translated by H A Saintsbury as *The Cardinal's Collation* (1927).

DANTE ALIGHIERI (1265–1321) Italian poet, born in Florence, a lawyer's son of the noble **Guelf** family. He was baptized Durante, afterwards abbreviated to Dante. According to his *La Vita Nuova* (c.1292), he first set eyes on his lifelong love, Beatrice Portinari (c.1265–1290), at the age of nine in 1274. There is no evidence that she returned his passion; she was married at an early age to one Simone de' Bardi, but neither this nor the poet's own subsequent marriage interfered with his pure and Platonic devotion to her, which intensified after her death. The story of his boyish but unquenchable passion is told with exquisite pathos in *Vita Nuova*. Shortly after, Dante married Gemma Donati, daughter of a powerful Guelf family. In 1289 he fought at Campaldino, where Florence defeated the Ghibellines, and was at the capitulation of Caprona. He was registered in one of the city guilds—that of the Apothecaries—being entered as 'Dante d'Aldighieri, *Poeta*'. In 1300, after filling minor public offices, and possibly going on some embassies abroad, he became one of the six priors of Florence but for only two months. It was towards the 'White Guelfs', or more moderate section, that his sympathies tended. As prior, he procured the banishment of the heads and leaders of the rival factions, showing characteristic sternness and impartiality to **Guelf** and Ghibelline, White and Black, alike. In 1301, in alarm at the threatened interference of Charles of Valois, he was sent on an embassy to Rome to Pope **Boniface VIII**. He never returned from that embassy, nor did he ever again set foot in his native city. Charles espoused the side of the *Neri* or Blacks, and their victory was complete. He was banished from Florence in 1309 and sentenced to death in absentia. From then on he led a wandering life, first in Verona, in Tuscany, in the Lunigiano, near Urbino, and then Verona again. He eventually settled in Ravenna (1318), where for the most part he remained until his death. He was buried with much pomp at Ravenna, where he still lies, restored in 1865 to the original sarcophagus. Dante had seven children, six sons and one daughter, Beatrice, a nun at Ravenna; but his family became extinct in the 16th century. His most celebrated work is the *Divina Commedia*, begun around 1307, his spiritual testament, narrating a journey through Hell and Purgatory, guided by **Virgil**, and finally to Paradise, guided by Beatrice. It gives an encyclopaedic view of the highest culture and knowledge of the age all expressed in the most exquisite poetry. The *Divina Commedia* may be said to have made the Italian language, which was before so rude and unformed that Dante himself hesitated to employ it on such a theme, and is said to have begun his poem in Latin. The next most important work is the fragment called the *Convito*, or *Banquet*, which takes the form of a commentary on some of the author's *canzoni*, or short poems, of which there are only three, though the work, if completed, would have contained fourteen. The *De Monarchia* (in Latin) expounds Dante's theory of the divinely intended government of the world by a universal pope. Another unfinished work, *De Vulgari Eloquentia*, discusses the origin of language, the divisions of languages, and the dialects of Italian in particular. *Canzoniere* is a collection of short poems, *canzoni*, sonnets, etc; and, finally, there are a dozen epistles addressed mainly to leading statesmen or rulers. There are also some *Eclogues* and other minor works, as well as several of doubtful authenticity.

DANTON, Georges Jacques (1759–94) French revolutionary leader, born of peasant stock in Arcis-sur-Aube. At the outbreak of the French Revolution he was practising as an advocate in Paris, where he had instituted the Cordeliers' Club with **Marat** and **Camille Desmoulins**. Soon it became the rallying point of all the hotter revolutionists. There the tall brawny man, with harsh and daring countenance, beetling black brows, and a voice of enormous power, thundered against the aristocrats. He fled to England in 1791, but in 1792 he became minister of justice in the new republic following the fall of the monarchy. The advance of the Prussians in 1792 for a moment struck panic to the heart of France; but on 2 September he uttered the famous words: 'Pour les vaincre, pour les atterrer, que faut-il? De l'audace, encore de l'audace, et toujours de l'audace.' He was elected to the National Convention, and voted for the death of the king in January 1793. He was one of the nine original members of the Committee of Public Safety, and frequently went on missions to **Dumouriez** and other republican generals. In the Convention he was regarded as the head of government, and directed his energies against the Girondists, or moderate party, on whose fall (October 1793) the extremists found themselves supreme. As president of the Jacobin Club he now tried to conciliate domestic hatreds and achieve stable government. He strove to abate the pitiless severity of the Revolutionary Tribunal, which he had himself set up, but began to lose power to **Robespierre** as the Reign of Terror developed. For a while Danton went to his native Arcis, and forgot all the machinations of his enemies in the quiet of domestic happiness with his second wife. But in March 1794 he and his followers were arrested and brought before the Revolutionary Tribunal, charged with conspiracy to overthrow the goverment. His defence was sublime in its audacity, its incoherence, its heroism and magnificent buffoonery. In the first two days of his trial his mighty voice and passionate eloquence moved the people so greatly that the committee concocted a decree to shut the mouths of men who had 'insulted Justice'; and on 5 April he was guillotined.

DANTZIG, Rudi von (1933–) Dutch dancer, choreographer and ballet director, born in Amsterdam. He studied with Sonia Gaskell, making his début in 1952 in her Ballet Recital Group, later known as the Netherlands Ballet and, eventually, Dutch National Ballet. He became her choreographer, assistant, co-director and, eventually, the company's sole director. He was one of the founding members of Netherlands Dance Theatre, a group that broke away from the Netherlands Ballet in 1959. His ballets are marked by their strong social themes, mix of academic and modern dance vocabularies, often abstract music scores and some technical experimentation.

DA PONTE, Giacomo See **BASSANO, Jacopo da**

DA PONTE, Lorenzo, originally **Emanuele Conegliano** (1749–1838) Italian poet, born in Ceneda near Venice of Jewish parents. He was converted to Roman Catholicism and became professor of rhetoric at Treviso until political and domestic troubles drove him to Vienna, where as a poet to the Court Opera he wrote the libretti for **Mozart**'s operas *The Marriage of Figaro* (1786), *Don Giovanni* (1787) and *Così fan Tutte* (1790). In London he taught Italian and sold boots; in 1805 he moved to New York, where he sold liquor, tobacco and groceries and ended up as professor of Italian literature at Columbia College from 1825.

DAQUIN, or **d'Aquin, Louis Claude** (1694–1772) French composer, organist and harpsichordist, born in Paris. A noted child prodigy, he played before **Louis XIV** when six years old and displaced his master, Marin de la Guerre, as organist of the Sainte Chapelle in 1706. He held many official posts, defeating **Rameau** in the contest for one in 1727, and became organist of the Chapel Royal in 1739. His works include religious music, and pieces for the organ and harpsichord, the most famous of which is *Le Coucou*.

D'ARBLAY, Madame See **BURNEY, Fanny**

DARBOY, Georges (1813–71) French prelate, born in Fayl-Billot, in Haute-Marne. In 1859 he was made bishop of Nancy, in 1863 archbishop of Paris. He upheld the Gallican theory, waged a long struggle with the Jesuits and at the Vatican Council opposed the dogma of papal infallibility, but when it was adopted was one of the first to submit. During the German siege of Paris (1870–71) he was unceasing in labours of benevolence, and under the Commune he refused to leave his flock. Arrested as a hostage by the Communards in 1871, he was shot in the court of the prison of La Roquette.

DARBY, Abraham (c.1678–1717) English iron-master, born near Dudley in Worcestershire. He founded the Bristol Iron Company (1708), and is generally acknowledged to be the first man, in 1709, to use coke successfully in the smelting of iron. Charcoal had become increasingly scarce and was too soft to allow larger furnaces to be used; coal itself was almost always contaminated with sulphur and other undesirable impurities; coke had neither of these disadvantages, though at first it was not possible to produce high quality wrought iron with the new fuel. His works at Coalbrookdale produced the finest iron yet made.

DARBY, Abraham (1711–63) English iron-master, son of **Abraham Darby** (c.1678–1717). He is reputed to have discovered how to produce wrought iron from coke-smelted ore, but if he did he kept the process such a close secret that no details of it are known. In fact, it is likely that the first man to achieve this on a commercial scale was **Henry Cort** in the 1780s with his puddling process. The Darby foundry at Coalbrookdale did, however, manufacture large numbers of cast-iron cylinders for **Newcomen**'s atmospheric steam engines, and later the first high-pressure steam boiler for **Trevithick**.

DARBY, Abraham (1750–91) English iron-master and engineer, son of **Abraham Darby** (1711–63). He raised the art of iron-founding to new heights in both decorative embellishment and structural prefabrication. His greatest achievement, the world's first cast iron bridge of 100 ft span, was designed and built in the Darby foundry and erected over the River Severn in 1779. It is still in use as a footbridge.

DARBY, Sir Henry Clifford (1909–) Welsh geographer, born in Glamorgan. He was educated at Neath County School and St Catharine's College, Cambridge. Following appointments at Cambridge and important wartime posts, he became the first professor of geography at Liverpool (1945–49). He was later professor at University College, London (1949–66) and at Cambridge (1966–76). His particular interest has been in medieval geography. He was a leader in promoting the relationships between geography and other subjects, especially history, and was an organizer of the study of *Domesday Book* (general editor, *The Domesday Geography of England*, 7 vols, 1952–77) and the historical geography of the Fenlands.

DARBY, John Nelson (1800–82) English churchman, born in London, the principal founder in 1830 of the Plymouth Brethren, and in 1840 an exclusive sect of it known as 'Darbyites'. Educated at Westminster School and Trinity College, Dublin, he was for a year or two an Anglican clergyman, and died in Bournemouth. He wrote 30 works.

D'ARC See **Joan of Arc**

D'ARCY, Margaretta See **ARDEN, John**

DARCY, Patrick (1598–1668) Irish constitutional nationalist theoretician, born in Galway, the seventh son of a Roman Catholic baronet of English descent. He sat for Navan, County Meath, in the Irish parliament of 1634, rose to prominence by 1640 and made common cause with his Irish-Gaelic fellow-Catholics in the Confederation of Kilkenny (1641). He replied before an Irish House of Lords committee on behalf of the Irish Commons to the answers of the Irish judges to 21 constitutional questions previously proposed to them by the Commons, arguing against the judges that no law of the English parliament can have force in Ireland unless enacted by the Irish parliament. Darcy was a negotiator for the Catholic Confederates with **Charles I**'s deputy **Ormonde** in 1649 and was then appointed a commissioner of the peace throughout Ireland, an appointment abrogated by the arrival of **Cromwell**.

DARCY, Thomas, Baron of Templehurst (1467–1537) English soldier and statesman, born in Yorkshire. He held a number of offices, was ennobled in 1505 and made warden of the east marches. He commanded forces in the field in Spain and France (1511–13). He was one of **Wolsey**'s chief accusers in 1529, and lost favour with **Henry VIII** by speaking against the divorce of **Catherine of Aragon**. An opponent of the dissolution of the monasteries, he was condemned for taking part in the Pilgrimage of Grace (1536), but was pardoned, only to be condemned again and beheaded for treason.

DARGOMIZHSKY, Alexander Sergeievitch (1813–69) Russian composer, born in Tula. At the age of 22 he retired from government service to devote himself to music and composed his first opera, *Esmeralda*, which was regarded as a work of extreme realism. Later, under the influence of the Russian nationalist composers, his setting of Pushkin's *The Stone Guest* (completed by **Rimsky-Korsakov**) anticipated the work of **Moussorgsky** in dramatic power and naturalistic treatment of words. He had little success in his lifetime except in Belgium, where he introduced his orchestral works in 1864.

DARÍO, Rubén, pen-name of **Felix Rubén García Sarmiento** (1867–1916) Nicaraguan poet. He lived a wandering life of a journalist, full of amours and diplomatic appointments, and died of pneumonia. He inaugurated the Spanish American modernist movement with his major works, *Azul* (1888), and *Prosas Profanas* (1896), showing Greek and French (Parnassian and Symbolist) influence, which gave new vitality to Spanish poetry.

DARIUS I (548–486 BC) king of Persia, the son of Hystaspes, of the family of the **Achaemenids**, he ascended the Persian throne in 521, after putting to death the Magian Gaumata, who pretended to be Cambyses' brother. He had for several years to contend with revolts in many parts of his dominions, especially Babylon. He reorganized the administration and finances of the Persian empire, making Susa the capital, while he pushed his conquests as far as the Caucasus and the Indus. In his expedition against the Scythians in c.515, after carrying a large army across the Bosporus on a bridge of boats, and subduing Thrace and Macedonia, he was led on by the retreating Scythians as far as the Volga, and returned to the Danube. His expedition against the Athenians to punish them for supporting the 'Ionian revolt' (499–94) was decisively defeated at Marathon (490). He died in 486, before the Egyptian revolt (487) had been subdued and in the midst of preparations for a second expedition against the Athenians, and was succeeded by **Xerxes I**. Darius was a Persian by birth, and bred in the Zoroastrian faith, which under him became the state religion.

DARIUS II, surnamed **Ochus**, called by the Greeks **Nothos**, 'bastard' (5th century BC) king of Persia, an illegitimate son of **Artaxerxes I**. He seized power in the dynastic struggle which followed his father's death, but was the tool of his cruel half-sister and spouse Parysatis, and his reign was a long series of struggles and revolts ruthlessly suppressed. After the failure of the Sicilian expedition of the Athenians in 413, Darius resumed active Persian intervention in Greek affairs. He died at Babylon, and was succeeded by his eldest son, **Artaxerxes II**.

DARIUS III, surnamed **Codomannus** (4th century BC) king of Persia, son of a daughter of **Artaxerxes II**, and king from 336. He was defeated by **Alexander the Great** at the Granicus (334), at Issus (333) and at Gaugamela or Arbela (331), and, during flight, treacherously slain by a satrap, **Artaterxes** (Ardashir).

DARK, Eleanor, née **O'Reilly** (1901–) Australian novelist, daughter of the writer Dowell O'Reilly, born and educated in Sydney. Employed briefly as a stenographer, she married a general practitioner in 1922 and a year later moved to Katoomba in the Blue Mountains. Her earliest writings, short stories and verse, were contributed from 1921 to various magazines, mostly under the pseudonym 'Patricia O'Rane' or 'P. O'R'. *Slow Dawning*, her first novel, was completed in 1923 but she had to wait until 1932 to see it published. Her other novels include *Prelude to Christopher* (1934), *The Little Company* (1945), *Lantana Lane* (1959) and the historical trilogy, *The Timeless Land* (1941), *Storm of Time* (1948) and *No Barrier* (1953). A writer of ideas, and a committed socialist and feminist, she was awarded the Australian Literature Society's Gold medal in 1934 and 1936, and in 1978 received the Australian Society of Women Writers' Alice award.

DARLAN, Jean Louis Xavier François (1881–1942) French naval officer and politician. He passed through the École Navale in 1899, becoming *Capitaine de corvette* in 1918 and attaining Flag rank in 1929. A pronounced 'political' and frequently termed 'l'Admiral des boulevardes', he became in turn minister of the navy and mercantile marine, vice-president of the Council of Ministers, and secretary of state for foreign affairs and the navy. During the Vichy régime he was admiral of the Fleet, vice premier, foreign minister and so called minister for national defence. In North Africa, as representative of the Vichy administration, he ordered resistance to cease. He was assassinated.

DARLEY, Felix Octavius Carr (1822–88) American artist, born in Philadelphia. He was illustrator of **Washington Irving**, **Fenimore Cooper**, **Dickens**, etc.

DARLEY, George (1795–1846) Irish poet and mathematician, born in Dublin. Educated at Trinity College, Dublin, from c.1822 he lived in London, and worked on the staff of the *London Magazine*. He published a volume of verse, *The Errors of Ecstasie* (1822) and a collection of prose stories, *Labours of Idleness* (1826). He also wrote a pastoral drama, *Sylvia* (1827) and the unfinished poem *Nepenthe* (1835). He wrote essays on dramatic criticism, and also published mathematical textbooks.

DARLING, Charles John, 1st Baron Darling (1849–1936) English judge, born in Colchester. Educated privately and articled to a Birmingham solicitor, he was called to the bar (1874) and joined the Oxford circuit. A freelance journalist, he was Conservative MP (1888-97) when his appointment as a judge of the King's Bench aroused widespread controversy. He presided over the Steinie Morrison (1911) and Armstrong (1922) murder trials, the Romney picture (1917) and Pemberton Billing (1918) cases, heard the **Crippen** (1910) and **Casement** (1916) appeals, deputized for the lord chief justice, Lord **Reading**, when the latter was ambassador in Washington (1914–18) and was a member of several royal commissions. In his august office, his wit and humour tended to get the better of him, just as they enlivened his volumes of light verse, *Scintillae Juris* (1877), *On the Oxford Circuit* (1909), etc. On his retirement, he was raised to the peerage (1924).

DARLING, Grace (1815–42) English heroine, born in Bamburgh, Northumberland, with her father, William Darling (1795–1860), lighthouse keeper on one of the Farne Islands. On 7 September 1838, she rescued the survivors of the *Forfarshire*.

DARLING, Jay Norwood, known as **Ding** (1876–1962) American cartoonist, born in Norwood, Michigan. As a staff cartoonist on the Des Moines *Register* (1906–49) and the New York *Tribune* (later *Herald Tribune*) from 1917 to 1949, he won the Pulitzer prize in 1923 and 1943. An active wildlife conservationist, he was chief of the US Biological Survey (1934–35) and president of the National Wildlife Federation (1936).

DARLINGTON, William (1782–1863) American botanist. He was born in Birmingham, Pennsylvania. The California pitcher plant (*Darlingtonia*) is named after him.

DARMESTETER, Arsène (1846–88) French philologist and lexicographer. Professor of Old French at the Sorbonne (1881–88), he helped to compile the *Dictionnaire général de la langue française* (1890–1900).

DARNLEY, Henry Stewart, Lord See **MARY, QUEEN OF SCOTS**

DARROW, Clarence Seward (1857–1938) American attorney, born in Kinsman, Ohio. Admitted to the bar in 1878, he began as a small-town Ohio lawyer, but moved to Chicago in 1887. From 1894 he acted for labor union officials, but later became a defense counsel in several sensational trials, including the defence of the 'thrill' murderers, Nathan Leopold and Richard Loeb (1924), whom he saved from the electric chair. His books include *Crime: Its Cause and Treatment* (1922).

DART, Raymond Arthur (1893–1988) Australian-born South African anatomist, born in Toowong. He graduated in medicine at Sydney in 1917, and became professor of anatomy at Witwatersrand University in Johannesburg in 1923. In 1925 he described an ape-like infant part-skull found in Botswana which he considered to be a human ancestor, and named *Australopithecus africanus*. Later work by Dart and others supports this view, and indicates that bipedalism preceded brain expansion; whether the australopithecines were tool-users, and in the direct ancestral line to *homo sapiens*, remains uncertain.

DARU, Pierre Antoine, Comte (1767–1829) French military administrator and historian, born in Montpellier. He entered the army at 16, was imprisoned during the Terror, but was appointed secretary of the war industry in 1800 and intendant-general in Austria and Prussia. He was minister of war from 1811, and later was ennobled by **Louis XVIII**. He wrote a history of Venice, and of Britain.

DARUSMONT, Frances, See **WRIGHT, Frances**

DARWIN, Charles Robert (1809–82) English naturalist, born in Shrewsbury, the originator (with **Alfred Russel Wallace**) of the theory of evolution by natural selection. The grandson of **Erasmus Darwin** and of **Josiah Wedgwood**, he was educated at Shrewsbury grammar school, studied medicine at Edinburgh (1825–27), and then, with a view to the church, entered Christ's College, Cambridge, in 1828. Already at Edinburgh he was a member of the local Plinian Society; he took part in its natural history excursions, and read before it his first scientific paper—on Flustra or sea-mats. His biological studies seriously began at Cambridge, where the botanist John Stevens Henslow encouraged his interest in zoology and geology. He was recommended by Henslow as naturalist to HMS *Beagle*, then about to start for a scientific survey of South American waters (1831–36) under its captain, **Robert Fitzroy**. He visited Tenerife, the Cape Verde Islands, Brazil, Montevideo, Tierra del Fuego, Buenos Aires, Valparaiso, Chile, the Galapagos, Tahiti, New Zealand, Tasmania and the Keeling Islands, in which last he started his famous theory of coral reefs. During this long expedition he obtained the intimate knowledge of the fauna, flora and geology of many lands which equipped him for his later many-sided investigations. By 1846 he had published several works on the geological and zoological discoveries of his voyage, on coral reefs, volcanic islands, etc—works that placed him at once in the front rank of scientists. He formed the friendship of Sir **Charles Lyell**, was secretary of the Geological Society from 1838–1841, and in 1839 married his cousin, Emma Wedgwood (1808–1896). From 1842 he lived at Downe, Kent, as a country gentleman among his garden, conservatories, pigeons and fowls. The practical knowledge thus gained (especially as regards variation and interbreeding) proved invaluable; private means enabled him to devote himself unremittingly, in spite of continuous ill-health, to science. At Downe he addressed himself to the great work of his life—the problem of the origin of species. After five years collecting the evidence, he 'allowed himself to speculate' on the subject, and drew up in 1842 some short notes, enlarged in 1844 into a sketch of conclusions for his own use. These embodied in embryo the principle of natural selection, the germ of the Darwinian Theory: but with constitutional caution Darwin delayed publication of his hypothesis which was only precipitated by accident. In 1858 **Alfred Russel Wallace** sent him a memoir on the Malay Archipelago, which, to Darwin's surprise, contained in essence the main idea of his own theory of natural selection. Lyell and **Joseph Hooker** persuaded him to submit a paper of his own, based on his 1844 sketch, which was read simultaneously with Wallace's before the Linnean Society on 1 July 1858, neither Darwin nor Wallace being present at that historic occasion. Darwin now set to work to condense his vast mass of notes, and put into shape his great work on *The Origin of Species by Means of Natural Selection*, published in November 1859. That epoch-making work, received throughout Europe with the deepest interest, was violently attacked and energetically defended, but in the end succeeded in obtaining recognition (with or without certain reservations) from almost all competent biologists. From the day of its publication Darwin continued to work at a great series of supplemental treatises: *The Fertilisation of Orchids* (1862), *The Variation of Plants and Animals under Domestication* (1867), and *The Descent of Man and Selection in Relation to Sex* (1871), which derived the human race from a hairy quadrumanous animal belonging to the great anthropoid group, and related to the progenitors of the orang-utan, chimpanzee and gorilla. In it Darwin also developed his important supplementary theory of sexual selection. Later works were *The Expression of the Emotions in Man and Animals* (1873), *Insectivorous Plants* (1875), *Climbing Plants* (1875), *The Effects of Cross and Self Fertilisation in the Vegetable Kingdom* (1876), *Different Forms of Flowers in Plants of the same Species* (1877), *The Power of Movement in Plants* (1880) and *The Formation of Vegetable Mould through the action of Worms* (1881). Though not the sole originator of the evolution hypothesis, nor even the first to apply the conception of descent to plants and animals, Darwin was the first thinker to gain for that concept a wide acceptance among biological experts. By adding to the crude evolutionism of **Erasmus Darwin, Lamarck** and others his own specific idea of natural selection, he supplied to the idea a sufficient cause, which raised it at once from a hypothesis to a verifiable theory. He also wrote a biography of Erasmus Darwin (1879), and was buried in Westminster Abbey. His son, Sir Francis, (1848–1925), also a botanist, became reader in botany at Oxford (1888) and produced Darwin's *Life and Letters* (1887-1903). Another son, Sir George Howard (1845–1913) was professor of astronomy at Cambridge (1883–1912), and was distinguished for his work on tides, tidal friction, and the equilibrium of rotating masses.

DARWIN, Erasmus (1731–1802) English physician and poet, born near Newark. He studied at Cambridge and Edinburgh, and at Lichfield became a popular physician and prominent figure from his ability, his radical and freethinking opinions, his poetry, his eight-acre botanical garden, and his imperious advocacy of temperance in drinking. After his second marriage in 1781, he settled in Derby, where he founded a Philosophical Society. By his first wife he was grandfather of **Charles Darwin**; by his second, of **Francis Galton**. He anticipated **Lamarck**'s views on evolution, and also those of his own grandson. He wrote a long verse work, *The Botanic Garden* (1789). His chief prose works are *Zoonomia, or the Laws of Organic Life* (1794–96), and *Phytologia* (1799).

DASENT, Sir George Webbe (1817–96) English scholar of Scandinavian studies and folklorist, born in St Vincent, where his father was attorney-general. He was educated at Westminster School, King's College, London, and Magdalen Hall, Oxford, and was called to the bar in 1852. He was an assistant editor on the London *Times* (1845–70), and married a sister of its editor, **John Thaddeus Delane**. He often acted as civil service examiner in English and modern languages, was a professor at King's College, London, from 1853 and from 1872 to 1892 was a civil service commissioner. He is best known as a popular translator of classical Icelandic literature, including *The Prose or Younger Edda* (1842), *The Saga of Burnt Njal* (1861) and the *Story of Gisli the Outlaw* (1866). He also published *Popular Tales from the Norse* (1859) and *Tales from the Fjeld* (1874), both from the Norwegian of **Asbjörnsen**.

DASHKOVA, Ekaterina Romanovna (1743–1810) Russian princess and author, born in St Petersburg. In 1759 she married Prince Dashkov (d.1762). She was an intimate friend and leading supporter of the Empress **Catherine II, the Great** in the conspiracy that deposed her husband, **Peter III**, in 1762. She travelled widely in Europe, and was director of the Academy of Arts and Sciences in St Petersburg (1783-96). She wrote several plays, and was the first president of the Russian Academy (1783). On Catherine's death in 1796 she was ordered by the new emperor, her son **Paul**, to retire to her estates at Novgorod.

DASHWOOD, Edmée Elizabeth See **DELAFIELD, E M**

DASHWOOD, Sir Francis (1708–81) English courtier and profligate, who succeeded his uncle as 15th Baron Le Dispencer (1762). He was an MP from 1741 to 1763, Chancellor of the Exchequer (1761–62) and postmaster-general (1766–81). In the 1740s he earned notoriety as the founder of a secret society, the Knights of St Francis of Wycombe, which became known as the 'Mad Monks of Medmenham' because of their obscene cavortings in the ruins of Medmenham Abbey.

DASSAULT, Marcel, originally **Marcel Bloch** (1892–1986) French aviation pioneer, industrialist and politician, born in Paris. While a schoolboy he saw one of the **Wright** brothers in flight, and was inspired to study aeronautical design and electrical engineering. After graduating from the École Nationale Supérieure de L'Aéronautique (1913), he joined Henri Potez in building aircraft during World War I. He spent several years in property speculation, then rejoined Potez to build twin-engined and tri-motor war planes. During World War II he was imprisoned in Buchenwald concentration camp, and was later converted from Judaism to Roman Catholicism. Following the war he adopted the name Dassault (which had been his brother's code name in the French Resistance), and founded his own company, Général Aéronautique Marcel Dassault. Building a series of highly successful craft in the 1950s, such as the Mystère and Mirage, guided weapons and specialized equipment, he became one of the wealthiest men in France. He was deputy in the National Assembly from 1951 to 1955, was deputy for the Oise (1957–58), and was elected to the National Assembly in 1986.

DASWANTH, also **Daswarth** or **Dasvanth** (16th century) Indian Mogul painter at the court of the emperor **Akbar the Great**. Akbar was interested in the development of an Indian school of painting and established an academy in which about 100 Hindu artists worked under the guidance of Persian painters. Daswanth was one of its leading three artists. Most of the surviving paintings of the 'Hamzanama', the adventures of Amir Hamza, the uncle of the prophet leader, were painted here during Akbar's reign. The composition and architectural ornaments were Persian in origin: the costumes, landscapes and figures began to show an Indian quality, which was also evident in the toning down of the original, brilliant colour scheme.

D'AUBIGNÉ, Jean Henri Merle (1794–1872) Swiss historian of the Reformation, born in Eaux-Vives, near Geneva. He studied at Berlin under **Neander**, and in 1818 became pastor of the French Protestant church in Hamburg. In 1823 he was appointed court preacher at Brussels. Returning to Geneva, he took part in the institution of the new Evangelical Church, and filled its chair of church history until his sudden death. His *Histoire de la Réformation du XVIe siècle* (1835–53) enjoyed immense popularity; other works were *Germany, England, and Scotland* (1848); a vindication of **Cromwell** (1848); *Trois siècles de lutte en Écosse* (1849); and *Histoire de la Réformation en Europe au temps de Calvin* (1863–78).

D'AUBIGNÉ, Théodore Agrippa (1552–1630) French soldier and scholar, born near Pons in Saintonge. Of noble family, but poor, he distinguished himself as a soldier in 1567 in the Huguenot cause, and was appointed vice-admiral of Guienne and Brittany by King **Henri IV**. His severe and inflexible character frequently embroiled him with the court; and after Henri's assassination (1610) he withdrew to a life of literary activity in Geneva, leaving a worthless son, Constant. His *Histoire universelle, 1550–1601* (1616–20) was burned in France by the common hangman. His biting satire is shown in his *Aventures du baron de Foeneste* (1617) and in his *Confession catholique du Sieur de Sancy* (1660). His granddaughter was Madame de **Maintenon**.

DAUBIGNY, Charles François (1817–78) French artist, born in Paris, a pupil of **Delaroche**. A member of the Barbizon school, he painted landscapes, especially moonlight and river scenes, a number of which are to be seen in the National Gallery in London.

DAUBRÉE, Gabriel Auguste (1814–96) French geologist and mineralogist, born in Metz. Professor of mineralogy and director of the École des Mines at Paris, he was a pioneer of experimental geology and wrote on that subject, and on crystalline rocks. The mineral daubreelite is named after him.

DAUDET, Alphonse (1840–97) French writer, born in Nîmes. After being educated at the Lyons Lycée he became an usher at Alais; but, when only 17, set out for Paris with his older brother, Ernest (1837–1921), who became a journalist and novelist of some mark, and both obtained appointments as clerk or private secretary in the office of the Duke of Morny. Alphonse's poem *Les Amoureuses* (1858) was followed by theatrical pieces (written partly in collaboration), *La Dernière Idole* (1862), *L'Oeillet blanc* (1865), *Le Frère aîné* (1868), *Le Sacrifice* (1869), *Lise Tavernier* and particularly *L'Arlésienne* (1872, with music by **Bizet**). His best-known work is his series of sketches and short stories of Provençal life, originally written for *Le Figaro*, especially *Lettres de mon moulin* (collected 1869), *Robert Helmont* (1874), *Contes du lundi* (1873) and the charming extravaganza of *Tartarin de Tarascon* (1872), continued in *Tartarin sur les Alpes* (1885) and *Port Tarascon* (1890). *Le Petit Chose* (1868) is full of pathos and of reminiscences of his own early struggles. He also published long naturalistic novels, on the social conditions of the day, such as *Fromont jeune et Risler aîné* (1874), *Jacks* (1876), *Le Nabab* (1877) and *Numa Roumestan* (1881). In *L'Évangéliste* (1883) the Salvation Army was introduced; *Sapho* (1884) is a tale of the infatuation of a young man for a courtesan; and in *L'Immortel* (1888) all the author's powers of ridicule are turned against the French Academy. His wife, Julia Allard Daudet (1845–1940), also published poetry.

DAUDET, Léon (1867–1942) French writer and political activist, son of **Alphonse Daudet**. He studied medicine but turned to journalism, and in 1899 helped to found the right-wing royalist newspaper *Action française*, of which he became editor in 1908. He sat in the Chamber of Deputies from 1919 to 1924. In 1925 his son was assassinated and subsequently he spent some time in Belgium as a political exile. He wrote several novels, but is best remembered for his numerous memoirs and critical works, especially *Le Stupide XIXe siècle* (1922).

D'AUMALE See **AUMALE, Duke of**

DAUMER, Georg Friedrich (1800–75) German philosopher and writer, born in Nuremburg, where he became a teacher and guardian of the 'wild boy' **Kaspar Hauser**. He veered from a bitter antagonism to Christianity (as in *Geheimnisse des christlichen Altertums*, 1847) to a dogmatic Catholicism and support for Ultramontanism (explained in his *Meine Konversion*, 1859).

DAUMIER, Honoré (1808–78) French caricaturist and painter, born in Marseilles. As a child he was taken to Paris and entered a lithographer's studio. He made his name as a satirical caricaturist, working for *La Caricature*, *Charivari* and other periodicals, and was imprisoned for six months for a caricature of **Louis-Philippe** in 1832. He made more than 4000 lithographs and 4000 caricatures in all. Later he worked as a serious painter of strongly realistic subject pictures, such as *Don Quixote* and *The Third Class Carriage*, and also as a sculptor. In his old age he became blind and was befriended by **Corot**.

DAUN, Leopold Joseph, Graf von (1705–66) Austrian soldier, born in Vienna. He served against the Turks and through the War of the Austrian Succession (1740–48), and was promoted field marshal in 1754. As Austrian commander-in-chief in the Seven Years' War (1756–63), he neutralized the Austrian defeat under

Ulysses Browne near Prague by driving **Frederick II, the Great**, who had beleaguered that city, to Kolin, and forcing him to evacuate Bohemia (1757). Defeated at Lentlen (December 1757) he gained a substantial victory at Hochkirch (October 1758), and came near to annihilating the Prussian army. In 1759 at Maxen he forced General Finck to surrender with 11000 men. After this, however, he gained no important successes, Frederick having grasped the tactics of 'the Austrian **Fabius Cunctator**'.

DAURAT or **Dorat, Jean** (c.1510–1588) French scholar and poet. As president of the Collège de Coqueret he superintended the studies of **Ronsard**, **Joachim du Bellay**, **Baif** and **Belleau**. These poets, with whom he was united in the famous Pléiade, he carefully trained for the task of reforming the vernacular and ennobling French literature by imitation of Greek and Latin models. He himself wrote copious verse in Greek and Latin, and was appointed court poet by **Charles IX**.

DAUSSET, Jean (1916–) French immunologist, born in Toulouse. He studied medicine in Paris, and was professor of medicine there from 1958 to 1977, and professor of experimental medicine at the College of France from 1977. Service in a blood transfusion unit in World War II led to his special interest in transfusion responses and the way they can lead to antibody production. His results led to 'tissue typing' which greatly reduced rejection risks in organ transplant surgery. He shared the 1980 Nobel prize for physiology or medicine with **George Snell** and **Baruj Benacerraf**.

DAVAINE, Casimir Joseph (1812–82) French physician and microbiologist, born in St-Amand-les-Eaux. After studying at Tournai and Lille, he went to Paris in 1830 for his medical course. He practised medicine in Paris, and while he never held an official university position he contributed a steady stream of important experimental papers, mostly to do with the role of micro-organisms in the causation of human and animal diseases. He developed procedures to identify parasitical worms, and first identified the anthrax bacillus in the blood of animals dying from anthrax. He was an advocate of the germ theory of disease at the Academy of Medicine before it was taken up by **Pasteur**, who always appreciated Davaine's work.

D'AVENANT, Sir William (1606–68) English poet and playwright, born in Oxford, the son of an innkeeper. His father kept the Crown, a tavern at which **Shakespeare** used to stop on the way between London and Stratford, thereby giving rise to the rumour that D'Avenant was Shakespeare's illegitimate son. At the age of twelve he wrote an 'Ode in Remembrance of Master Shakespeare', not printed, however, until 1638. After a short period of study at Lincoln College, Oxford, he became page to Frances, Duchess of Richmond; next he joined the household of the aged poet, **Fulke Greville**, Lord Brooke. In 1628 he turned to writing for the stage. During the next ten years he produced many plays, including *The Cruel Brother* (1630) and *The Wits* (1636). In 1638, at the request of the queen, **Henrietta Maria**, he was appointed poet laureate in succession to **Ben Jonson**. About the same time he lost his nose through an illness—a calamity which exposed him to public ridicule. Later he became manager of Drury Lane Theatre. During the Civil War he was knighted by King **Charles I** for his gallantry at the siege of Gloucester (1643). In 1650 he was imprisoned in the Tower for two years, where he completed his epic, *Gondibert* (1651). He is considered to have been the founder of English opera with his *Siege of Rhodes* (1656), and opened a theatre, the Cockpit, in Drury Lane in 1658.

DAVID-NEEL, Alexandra (1868–1969) French oriental scholar and traveller in Tibet, born in Paris. She studied Sanskrit in Sri Lanka and India, and toured internationally as an opera singer. She married an engineer, Phillippe François Neel, who was to be her main sponsor in Tunis in 1904, but she continued to study and travel in Europe until 1911 when she returned to India, visiting the Dalai Lama in exile at Darjeeling and studying Tibetan Buddism. Invited to Sikkim, she over-wintered in a high mountain cave with a holyman and her life-long servant, Yongden. Having travelled illegally to Tashilhumpo in Tibet, she was expelled from India in 1916 and went to Burma, Japan and Korea with Yongden, arriving in Beijing on 8 October 1917. Together they travelled 2000 miles to the Kumbum monastery near the Koko Nor and on to Chengdu through northern Tibet, Mongolia and across the Gobi Desert before she donned the disguise of a Tibetan pilgrim, as described in *My journey to Lhasa* (1927). They returned to Tibet in 1934 to work at Kanting until forced to leave by the Japanese advance of 1944, and retired to Digne in France, where she died aged 100 years.

DAVID, or **Dewi, St** (5th century) the patron saint of Wales. According to the *Annales Cambriae* (10th century) he died in 601, bishop of Moni Judeorum, or Menevia, afterwards St David's. He presided over two Welsh Synods, at Brefi and 'Lucus Victoriae'.

DAVID (Hebrew, 'beloved') the first king of the Judean dynasty of Israel. He was the youngest son of Jesse of Bethlehem, and distinguished himself by slaying the Philistine champion, Goliath. **Saul** appointed him to a military command, and gave him his daughter Michal as a wife; but he had soon to flee from the king's jealousy. In the cave of Adullam, near Gath, he gathered a troop of 400 freebooters, with whom he ranged through the country between Philistia and the Dead Sea. Saul's expeditions against him put him to great straits, and for over a year David became a vassal of the Philistine king of Gath. After the death of Saul and Jonathan at Gilboa, he reigned for seven-and-a-half years in Hebron over the tribe of Judah, while Ishbosheth, Saul's son, ruled the rest of Israel. On the death of Ishbosheth, all Israel chose David as king. He conquered the independent city of Jebus (Jerusalem) and made it the political and religious centre of his kingdom, building a palace for himself on its highest hill, Zion (the 'city of David'), and placing the Ark of the Covenant there under a tent. In the course of a few years the conquest of the Philistines, Moabites, Aramaeans, Edomites and Ammonites reduced the whole territory from Egypt to the Euphrates. The last years of his long reign of 32 years in Jerusalem were troubled by attempted revolutions by his sons Absalom and Adonijah. The death of the greatest of the kings of Israel took place at earliest 1018, at latest 993 BC. He was succeeded by **Solomon**, his son by Bathsheba.

DAVID I (c.1080–1153) king of Scotland from 1124, the youngest of the six sons of **Malcolm Canmore** and St **Margaret**. He was sent in 1093 to England along with his sister Matilda (who in 1100 married **Henry I** of England), and remained for several years at the English court. In 1107, when his elder brother **Alexander I** succeeded to the throne, David became Prince of Cumbria, with a territory which besides part of Cumberland, included all southern Scotland except Lothian. By his marriage in 1113 to Matilda, widow of the Norman Earl of Northampton and daughter of the Saxon Earl of Northumbria, he became Earl of Huntingdon. In 1124 he succeeded his brother on the Scottish throne. Although complicated by David's possession of large estates in England, which had entailed his swearing fealty to Henry I's daughter,

Matilda, Empress Maud, in 1127, Anglo-Scots relations remained generally good until the death of Henry and accession of **Stephen** in 1135. His invasion of northern England in support of **Mathilda**'s claims resulted in the Treaty of Durham (1136), by which he retained Cumbria and refused homage to Stephen, but allowed his son to do homage in respect of his estates at Huntingdon. An uneasy peace was followed by open warfare in 1138 and a further treaty made at Durham in 1139, which brought the earldom of Northumberland to his son, Henry (d.1152). His reign was remarkable for enhancing the monarch's prestige, consolidating a feudal settlement of Scotland, and revitalizing and transforming the Scottish church. The kingdom of the Scots, which was always how he termed his realm, began to be seen as a clearly defined entity; massive grants were made to Norman and English knights in southern Scotland by feudal tenure, but elsewhere there was considerable continuity, old custom and law being redefined and harmonized with feudal practice to produce a common law of Scotland. Sheriffdoms and justiciars were erected; a chain of castles was built in the south to act as centres of royal and baronial authority; burghs were founded, especially on the east coast, by royal charter and given specific privileges to encourage trade. David, like **Alexander I**, resisted English claims of jurisdiction over the Scottish church. The claim that he founded a diocesan episcopate is exaggerated, for the organization of the Scottish church, like that of the kingdom as a whole, became in his reign an amalgam of the new and the old. By 1154 there were ten dioceses, but only three—Caithness, Moray and Ross—were wholly new creations. Royal patronage of the religious orders was more dramatic: during his reign more than 20 religious houses were founded, such as the Cistercians at Melrose and the Premonstratensians at Dryburgh. By 1154 the transformation of the Scottish church that had begun with Malcolm Canmore and St Margaret was near-complete.

DAVID II (1324–71) king of Scotland from 1329, only surviving son of King **Robert I**, born in Dunfermline, and married in 1328 to **Edward II**'s daughter, Joanna. In 1329 he succeeded his father, and in 1331 was crowned, with his child queen, at Scone. In 1334 the success of **Edward Balliol** and **Edward III**'s victory at Halidon Hill forced David's guardians to send him and his consort to France, from where he returned in 1341. Five years later he invaded England, but at Neville's Cross, near Durham, was routed and captured (17 October, 1346). He remained a prisoner for 11 years until 1357 when he was released on promise of a ransom of 100 000 marks. The treaty of 1357 brought 27 years of truce, but strains over payment of the ransom forced pursuit of more revenue, particularly through customs duties and direct taxation, and caused resentment when the hostages of 1357 were abandoned in 1363 as a result of defaulting on payments. Yet he maintained a firm grip of his kingdom, with little sign of the tensions between king and magnates which afflicted later reigns, until his sudden death. He was succeeded by his sister's son, **Robert II**, for despite a second marriage to Margaret Drummond of Logie in 1363, a year after Queen Joanna died, he left no issue.

DAVID, (Père) Armand (1826–1900) French Lazarist missionary and naturalist, best known for his work in China. After teaching in Italy (1851–61), he was ordained and sent to do missionary work at Tche-li and Peking. He explored Mongolia (1866), Tibet (1860–70) and central China (1872–74), sending specimens to the Natural History Museum in Paris. *Plantae Davidianae* (1884–86) catalogued his plant collections.

DAVID, Félicien (1810–76) French composer, born in Cadenet. He was first a chorister in Aix cathedral, then entered the Paris Conservatoire. He became an ardent disciple of St Simon and of Enfantin; finally, on the break-up of the brotherhood in 1833, he travelled to the East. In 1835 he returned to Paris, but remained in obscurity till his *Désert* (1844), a grand 'Ode-symphonie', had a sudden and complete success. He failed to retain his popularity, but the oriental devices and motifs which he used influenced many other composers.

DAVID, Gerhard (c.1460–c.1523) Flemish painter, born in Oudewater in Holland. In 1484 he entered the Painters' Guild of Bruges, of which he became dean in 1501. Among his best works are the two *Justice Scenes* of 1498 in Bruges.

DAVID, Jacques Louis (1748–1825) French painter, born in Paris. He gained the 'prix de Rome' in 1774, and in Rome devoted himself to drawing from the antique. On his return to France his *Belisarius* (1780) procured his admission to the Academy. Soon afterwards he married, and visited Italy again and also Flanders. It is in the works of this period, such as the *Oath of the Horatii* (1784), *Death of Socrates* (1788), and *Brutus Condemning his Son* (1789), that the Neoclassical feeling is first clearly visible. David entered with enthusiasm into the Revolution, and in 1792 became a representative for Paris in the Convention. He voted for the death of **Louis XVI**, was a member of the Committee of Public Safety, and was the artistic director of the great national fêtes founded on classical customs. After **Robespierre**'s death he was twice imprisoned, and narrowly escaped with his life. Released in 1795, he produced his masterpiece, *The Rape of the Sabines* (1799), and in 1804 was appointed court painter by **Napoleon**. After the **Bourbon** restoration he was banished in 1816 as a regicide, and died in Brussels.

DAVID, Pierre Jean, called **David d'Angers** (1789–1856) French sculptor, born in Angers, the son of a wood carver. He studied under **Jacques Louis David** in Paris, and in 1811 his *rilievo* of the *Death of Epaminondas* gained the 'grand prix', and David proceeded to Rome, where he was influenced by **Ingres** and **Canova**. From 1835 to 1837 he executed the pediment of the Pantheon, in Paris, his most prestigious commission; he was also a prolific sculptor of portrait busts and medallions. In the Angers museum 200 of his works are preserved, as well as 400 of his medallions and many drawings.

DAVIDS, Thomas William Rhys (1843–1922) English orientalist, born in Colchester. Educated at Brighton and Breslau, in 1866 he entered the Ceylon civil service. In 1877 he was called to the bar in London. and was professor of Pali and Buddhist Literature in University College, London (1882–1912), and of comparative religion in Manchester (1904–15). He wrote many books on Buddhism, including *Buddhist India* (1903) and *Early Buddhism* (1908).

DAVIDSON, Donald (1917–) American philosopher, born in Springfield, Massachusetts, currently professor at the University of California, Berkeley. He has been one of the most influential analytical philosophers over the last two decades, with original, and interrelated, contributions to the philosophy of language, mind and action. He is the author of *Essays on Action and Events* (1980) and *Inquiries into Truth and Interpretation* (1983).

DAVIDSON, John (1857–1909) Scottish poet, novelist and dramatist, born in Barrhead, Renfrewshire, the son of an Evangelical minister. Educated at the

Highlander's Academy, Greenock, where he became a pupil-teacher (1872–76), and Edinburgh University, he became an itinerant teacher in Scotland. He had started to write in 1885 (four verse dramas, and a couple of novels), and in 1888 *Fleet Street Eclogues* (1893) and *Ballads and Songs* (1894). **T S Eliot** later acknowledged a debt to the urban imagery and colloquialism of 'Thirty Bob a Week'. He produced some further verse dramas, and eventually committed suicide.

DAVIDSON, Randall Thomas, Baron Davidson of Lambeth (1848–1930) Scottish Anglican prelate and archbishop of Canterbury, born in Edinburgh. He studied at Harrow and Trinity College, Oxford, and was chaplain to Archbishop **Tait** (his father-in-law) and to Queen **Victoria**, dean of Windsor, bishop of Rochester (1891) and of Winchester (1895), and archbishop of Canterbury (1903–28). He wrote the Life of Archbishop Tait in 1891.

DAVIDSON, Thomas (1840–1900) Scottish writer, born in Deer, Aberdeenshire. He studied at Aberdeen, and from 1867 lived in the USA. An indefatigable and original thinker and teacher, he wrote works on medieval philosophy, **Rosmini-Serbati**, education and art.

DAVIE, Alan (1920–) Scottish painter, born in Grangemouth, the son of a painter and etcher. He studied at Edinburgh College of Art (1937–40). During wartime service with the Royal Artillery he concentrated on his other major pursuit, as a jazz saxophonist. His early work showed the influence of **Klee** and **Picasso**. In 1948, on a travelling scholarship tour of Europe, he was introduced, in Venice, to the work of **Pollock** and **Rothko**, and his paintings in the subsequent decade had much in common with contemporary American Abstract Expressionism. His imaginative use of pictographic images suggestive of myth and magic, increasingly bold and colourful since the early 1970s, reflects his preoccupation with Zen and oriental mysticism.

DAVIES, Christian, known as **'Mother Ross'** (1667–1739) Irish woman soldier, born in Dublin, who served for many years in the army as a man. She inherited an inn in Dublin, but went to Flanders in search of her husband, Richard Welsh, who had been pressed into **Marlborough**'s army. There she enlisted as a private under the name of Christopher Welsh, and fought in the battle of Blenheim (1704) and other battles, and eventually was reunited with her husband in 1706. When he was killed at the battle of Malplaquet (1709) she married a grenadier, Hugh Jones, who was killed the following year. In England she was presented to Queen **Anne**, and returned to Dublin where she married another soldier, called Davies. She died in Chelsea Pensioners' Hospital for old soldiers.

DAVIES, Clement (1884–1962) Welsh politician, born in Llanfyllin, Montgomeryshire. He was educated at Llanfyllin and Trinity Hall, Cambridge, and was called to the bar in 1909. He became Liberal MP for Montgomeryshire in 1929, and in 1945 he was elected Leader of the decimated Liberal party in the House of Commons, holding this office until September 1956, when he resigned. He stubbornly refused all ministerial offices offered by the Conservative Governments, did not enter into any political agreements with either of the two great parties and thus kept the Liberal party a separate political entity. He conducted a brilliant parliamentary defence of **Seretse Khama** against the actions of successive Labour and Conservative colonial secretaries.

DAVIES, David (1818–90) Welsh industrialist and politician, born in Llandinam, Montgomeryshire. He worked his way up from being 'top sawyer' in a local saw mill, through building and contracting work to railway construction in mid-Wales, and later became owner of the Ocean Colliery in the Rhondda. A dispute with the Bute family interests in Cardiff docks led to his defiantly building his own docks at nearby Barry from which to ship his coal exports. He was a director of a number of railway companies but spoke out freely when he considered things were going wrong and resigned if matters were not rectified. He was elected Liberal MP for Cardigan in 1874, but in 1886 he resigned the Liberal whip.

DAVIES, David, 1st Baron (1880–1944) Welsh philanthropist, born in Llandinam, Montgomeryshire, grandson of the industrialist **David Davies**, whose great wealth he inherited. With his two sisters, Gwendoline and Margaret, he was a major benefactor of the University College of Wales, Aberystwyth, the National Library of Wales, and of a chain of TB sanatoria established in memory of King **Edward VII**. A Liberal MP for Montgomeryshire (1906–29) and close associate of **Lloyd George**, after World War I he turned his attention to support for the League of Nations and to attempts to set up an International Police Force, which never materialized. In 1933 he founded the New Commonwealth Society. He erected the Temple of Peace and Health in the centre of Cathays Park in Cardiff.

DAVIES, Sir Henry Walford (1869–1941) Welsh composer, organist and broadcaster, born in Oswestry. He became professor of music at Aberystwyth (1919–26), organist of St George's Chapel, Windsor (1927–32) and master of the King's Music (1934–41). He was a prolific composer of religious music, and an influential educationist through his radio talks on music.

DAVIES, Howard (1945–) English stage director, born in Reading. After taking a director's course at Bristol University, he became associate director of Bristol Old Vic, and joined the Royal Shakespeare Company in 1975. He became an associate director to establish and run the Warehouse, the RSC's London studio theatre (1977–82). His other RSC work includes a cool, Brechtian *Macbeth* in 1982, *Henry VIII* (1983), and *Troilus and Cressida* (1985), which he set during the Crimean War. He also directed **Saroyan**'s *The Time of Your Life*, and **Christopher Hampton**'s *Les Liaisons Dangereuses* at The Other Place. He became a National Theatre associate director in 1988.

DAVIES, Hubert Henry (1876–1917) English playwright, born in Woodley, Cheshire. He was a journalist in San Francisco, returned to England in 1901, and disappeared in 1917. His plays included *Cousin Kate* (1903) and *The Mollusc* (1907).

DAVIES, Idris (1905–53) Welsh poet, born in Rhymney, Gwent. He left school at 14 to become a miner in the pit where his father worked. He later took a correspondence course and went on to study at Loughborough College and Nottingham University, qualifying as a teacher. He published three volumes of verse, his work fired with anger and indignation at the social injustices that he had witnessed. From 1932 to 1951 he worked as a school-teacher, in the East of London and (after World War II) in Rhymney Valley.

DAVIES, Sir John (1569–1626) English poet and statesman, born in Tisbury, Wiltshire. Educated at Winchester School, Queen's College, Oxford, and the Middle Temple, he was called to the bar in 1595. Entering politics, he was returned to parliament for Corfe Castle and after the death of **Elizabeth** found favour with **James I** who sent him to Ireland as solicitor-general. Three years later he was made Irish attorney-general and knighted. In Ireland he supported severe repressive measures and took part in the plantation of Ulster. He returned to the English parliament in 1614, representing Newcastle-under-Lyme, and practised as king's serjeant in England. He had been nominated chief justice a month before his death of apoplexy. In 1622 he collected in one volume his three chief poems—*Orchestra, or a Poeme of Dancing* (1596); *Nosce Te Ipsum* (1599), a long didactic piece on the soul's immortality; and *Hymns to Astraea* (1599), a collection of clever acrostics on the name Elizabeth Regina.

DAVIES, Lynn (1942–) Welsh athlete, born in Nantymoel, Glamorgan. An outstanding long-jumper, he was the first Welshman ever to win an Olympic gold medal, at Tokyo in 1964. In the four years between Tokyo and Mexico in 1968 he added more than six inches to his personal best length but, like all other competitors, he was destroyed by **Bob Beamon**'s record leap.

DAVIES, (William) Robertson (1913–) Canadian novelist, playwright, essayist and critic, born in Thamesville, Ontario. Educated in Canada and Balliol College, Oxford, he has taught, acted (he was Sir **William Tyrone Guthrie**'s literary assistant) and been a journalist, and was editor of the *Examiner* (Peterborough, Ontario) from 1942 to 1963, and was a professor of English at the University of Toronto (1960–81). His first novel was *Tempest-Tost* (1951), the first of 'The Salterton Trilogy', but he is best known for 'The Deptford Trilogy'—*Fifth Business* (1970), *The Manticore* (1972), and *World of Wonders* (1975). This work evolved from his earlier books set in Salterton, an imagined Ontario city, patently Kingston, which is dominated by its old families, Anglican church, military school, university, and belief in the virtues of England and the English. Now a writer of international repute, *What's Bred in the Bone* (1985) was shortlisted for the Booker prize.

DAVIES, Sarah Emily (1830–1921) English feminist and educational reformer, born in Southampton. A vigorous campaigner for higher education for women, in 1869 she founded a small college for women students at Hitchin, which was transferred to Cambridge as Girton College in 1873. She was mistress of Girton from 1873 to 1875, and honorary secretary 1882–1904. As a member of the London School Board (1870–73), she agitated for London degrees for women, which were granted in 1874.

DAVIES, Siobhan (1950–) English choreographer and dancer, born in London. One of the first to study with London Contemporary Dance Theatre in the late 1960s, she began to choreograph early on in her career, becoming resident choreographer with the company in 1971, when she retired as a dancer. She created 17 pieces for LCDT including *New Galileo* (1984) and *Bridge the Distance* (1985). While still at LCDT, she also worked under commission for Ballet Rambert (*Celebration*, 1979), ran Siobhan Davies and Dancers for a short period during 1981, and became a founding member of Second Stride (a development of **Richard Alston**'s Strider) in 1982, for which she made six pieces. Working in a style which ranges from personal to abstract, she is also eclectic in her choice of music which includes scores by **Benjamin Britten**, Michael Nyman and Brian Eno. In 1987 she left LCDT and travelled to the USA on a Fullbright Arts Fellowship with her husband, photographer David Buckland, with whom she also has a working relationship. In 1988 she formed the Siobhan Davies Company. Her new work includes *Wyoming* (1988) and *White Man Sleeps* (1988).

DAVIES, Stephen Owen, known as 'SO' (1886–1972) Welsh politician and trade unionist, born in Abercwmboi, Glamorganshire. He was intended for the non-conformist ministry, but became active in socialist politics and went into the coal mines, and was soon appointed a union official with a reputation for militancy. He was deeply influenced by the Russian Revolution and proved to be a rebellious member of the Labour parliamentary party after he was elected MP for Merthyr Tydfil in 1934. A firm advocate of Welsh self-government, he supported Welsh cultural and educational institutions. Davies was critical of the National Coal Board and the government after the Aberfan Disaster and this, combined with his great age, led the constituency party to replace him as the official candidate in 1970. He stood as an independent socialist and won in June 1970.

DAVIES, William Henry (1871–1940) Engish poet, born in Newport, Monmouthshire, the son of a publican. Emigrating to the USA at the age of 22, he lived partly as a tramp and partly as a casual workman until the loss of a leg whilst 'jumping' a train caused him to return to England, where he began to write and lived the life of a tramp and pedlar in order to raise sufficient money to have his poems printed by a jobbing printer. A copy of this first work, *A Soul's Destroyer*, came into the hands of **George Bernard Shaw**, who arranged for its regular publication in 1907. The success of this book was consolidated by *The Autobiography of a Super-tramp* (1908). He continued to publish volumes of poems and lyrics, gathered in the *Collected Poems* (1943), two novels, and the prose *Adventures of Johnny Walker, Tramp* (1926). He continued his autobiography with *Beggars* (1909), *The True Traveller* (1912), *A Poet's Pilgrimage* (1918) and *Later Days* (1925).

DAVILA, Enrico Caterino (1576–1631) Italian historian and soldier, born near Padua. He entered the service of France under **Henri IV**, and then that of Venice. He was shot near Verona by an assassin. His great work is the *Storia delle guerre civili di Francia, 1558–98* (1630; trans 1647).

DA VINCI See **LEONARDO DA VINCI**

DAVIOT, Gordon See **MACKINTOSH, Elizabeth**

DAVIS, Bette (1908–89) American actress, born in Lowell, Massachusetts. After studying at the John Murray Anderson school, she worked with repertory and summer stock companies before a screen test led to a film contract and her début in *Bad Sister* (1931). Highly dedicated, her style was electrifying, and she illuminated a vast gallery of characters, bringing an emotional honesty to the most unprepossessing of melodramas. A prime box-office attraction between 1937 and 1946, she was nominated on ten occasions for the Academy Award, winning for *Dangerous* (1935) and *Jezebel* (1938). Latterly more often on television, she won the Emmy for *Strangers* (1979). Married four times, she wrote several volumes of autobiography: *The Lonely Life* (1962), *Mother Goddam* (1975, with Whitney Stine) and *This 'n' That* (1987, with Michael Herskowitz).

DAVIS, Sir Colin Rex (1927–) English conductor, born in Weybridge, Surrey. Educated at Christ's Hospital and the Royal College of Music, he was assistant conductor of the BBC Scottish Orchestra (1957–59) from where he went to Sadler's Wells to be conductor (1959), principal conductor (1960) and musical director (1961–65). He was chief conductor of the BBC Symphony Orchestra (1961–71) and musical director at Covent Garden (1971–86). He became principal guest conductor for the Boston Symphony Orchestra in 1972 and for the London Symphony Orchestra in 1974, and chief conductor of the Bavarian

Radio Symphony Orchestra in 1981. At Covent Garden he gained his reputation as a **Wagner** conductor of international standing with *The Ring*, and conducted at the Bayreuth Festival in 1977; he is a noted interpreter of **Berlioz**.

DAVIS, Dwight Filley (1879–1945) American public official, born in St Louis, Missouri. In 1900 he donated an international challenge cup for lawn tennis, competed for annually. The Davis Cup signifies the world team championship.

DAVIS, Fred (1913–) British billiards and snooker champion, younger brother of **Joe Davis**. Like his brother, he was world billiards champion on several occasions, and in 1948 succeeded his brother as world snooker champion—the first of ten championships.

DAVIS, Jefferson (1808–89) president of the Confederate States, born in Christian County, Kentucky. He studied at West Point, and served in several frontier campaigns, but resigned his commission in 1835. He entered congress in 1845 for Mississippi, and served with distinction in the Mexican war (1846–47) as colonel of volunteers. He was sent to the senate in 1847, 1848 and 1850; and from 1853 to 1857 was secretary of war. Returning to the senate, he succeeded **Calhoun** as leader of the extreme States Rights party, and as such carried in the senate (May 1860) his seven resolutions asserting the inability of congress or the legislatures of the territories to prohibit slavery. The lower house of congress refused to concur; the failure of the Democractic National Convention at Charleston to adopt like resolutions caused the disruption of the Democratic party; and the election of **Abraham Lincoln** to the presidency was an immediate result. In January 1861 Mississippi seceded from the Union; a few weeks later Davis was chosen provisional president of the Confederate States, an appointment confirmed for six years in November. The history of his presidency is that of the war of 1861–65. In May 1865, after the collapse of his government, Davis was captured by Union cavalry, imprisoned for two years in Fortress Monroe on Hampton Roads, then released on bail. Though indicted for treason, he was never brought to trial; and he was included in the amnesty of 1868. After 1879 he resided on an estate bequeathed to him in Mississippi. In 1881 he published *The Rise and Fall of the Confederate Government*. In 1893 his remains were translated to Richmond.

DAVIS, Joe (1901–78) British billiards and snooker champion. Born in the village of Whitwell, near Chesterfield, as a small child he watched the clients at his father's hotel playing billiards, and took up the game himself at the age of ten; two years later he made his first break of 100. In 1928 he won the billiards championship, which he held till 1933; the following year a new event was introduced, and while Walter Lindrum became the world champion, Davis continued to hold the United Kingdom championship. In 1927 he won the first world professional snooker championship and was never beaten until he retired from competitive snooker and billiards in 1946. He continued to play both games, and in 1955 made the maximum snooker break of 147 which 2 years later was officially recognized by the Billiards Association and Control Council as the world record. He was awarded the OBE in 1963. His younger brother, **Fred Davis,** followed the same career, winning the first of his ten world championships in 1948. The Davis brothers are the only players to have won both the World Billiards and the World Snooker Championships.

DAVIS, John (c.1550–1605) English navigator, born in Sandridge, near Dartmouth. Between 1585 and 1587 he undertook three Arctic voyages in search of a Northwest passage. In the last voyage he sailed as far as 73° N lat, and discovered Davis Strait. He fought against the Spanish Armada in 1588, and took part in an unsuccessful venture with **Thomas Cavendish**, sighting the Falkland Islands on the return journey. He invented navigational instruments like Davis's quadrant. He also made two ill-fated voyages towards the South Seas and as pilot of a Dutch vessel to the East Indies. On his last voyage he was killed by Japanese pirates off Singapore. He wrote *World's Hydrographical Description* (1595) and *The Seaman's Secrets* (1594).

DAVIS, Judy (1955–) Australian actress, born in Perth. Originally a singer in jazz and pop groups, she studied at the National Institute of Dramatic Arts in Sydney (1974–77) and made her film début in *High Rolling* (1976). After graduating, she worked with the Adelaide State Theatre Company, appearing in such plays as *Visions* (1978). Her performance as the strong-willed, 19th-century heroine of the film *My Brilliant Career* (1979) earned her international attention. An uncompromising actress, she has portrayed a range of forceful individuals in such films as *Winter of Our Dreams* (1981) and *Heatwave* (1981) whilst continuing a parallel stage career with *Piaf* (1980), *Lulu* (1981) and in London, *Insignificance* (1982). Her work in *A Passage to India* (1984) brought her an Academy Award nomination but she has spurned international offers in order to appear in Australian films like *Kangaroo* (1986) and *High Tide* (1987).

DAVIS, Miles Dewey (1926–) American jazz trumpeter and bandleader, born into a wealthy middle-class black family in Alton, Illinois, and brought up in St Louis. He took up the trumpet at 13 and, while receiving private tuition and playing in his high school band, he was performing with a local rhythm-and-blues group. In 1944 he began studies at the Juilliard School of Music, New York, but left to perform in the 52nd Street clubs where the new bebop style was emerging. At 19, he became a member of the foremost of these groups, the **Charlie Parker** Quintet. Although not then the most technically accomplished of jazz trumpeters, Davis played in an understated style that became highly influential, and he continued to be at the forefront of new stylistic departures. In 1948, working with pianist-arranger **Gil Evans**, he led a nonet that inspired the 'cool jazz' school. In the late 1950s, his quartet featuring saxophonist **John Coltrane** introduced a 'modal' approach which broke away from the harmonic principles previously accepted in jazz. Ten years later, his bands were featuring electronic instruments and synthesizers as well as rock-style rhythms. From 1975 to 1980, Davis retired from performing but he returned thereafter, further developing the use of electronics but using a commercial approach that did not find favour with all of his previous followers.

DAVIS, Richard Harding (1864–1916) American writer, born in Philadelphia. He wrote novels, short stories and plays, and was a famous war correspondent.

DAVIS, Steve (1958–) English snooker player, born in London. Between 1980 and 1985 he won three world titles, and of 96 major matches played he won all but eleven. Calm and imperturbable, he was distinguished by the maturity of his play even while very young. In 1985 he lost on the final black of the world championship to Dennis Taylor in a 35-frame match in what is universally regarded as the finest-ever televised snooker match. For almost all of the 1980s he was ranked as the world's leading player.

DAVIS, Stringer See **RUTHERFORD, Dame Margaret**

DAVIS, Stuart (1894–1964) Amercan painter and graphic artist, born in Philadelphia. He studied art with **Robert Henri** in New York (1910–13), and worked with John French Sloan (1871–1951) as as illustrator for the left-wing journal, *The Masses* (1913–16). The Armory Show in 1913 converted him to avant-garde French art, especially Cubism. He tried to develop a specifically American modernism; his imitation collages like *Lucky Strike* (1921) anticipated Pop Art by 35 years.

DAVIS, William Morris (1850–1934) American geomorphologist, born in Philadelphia. Professor of geology at Harvard, where he was educated, he introduced the term *peneplain* into physical geography to describe a rolling lowland, and was the first to formulate the doctrine of the 'cycle of erosion'.

DAVISON, Emily (1872–1913) English suffragette, born in Blackheath. Educated first at London University and then Oxford, where she took a first in English, in 1906 she became a militant member of the Women's Social and Political Union. Her activities included stone-throwing, setting alight letterboxes and attacking a Baptist minister whom she mistook for **Lloyd George**. Frequently imprisoned, she often resorted to hunger-striking, and was repeatedly force-fed. Once, while in Holloway prison, she attempted suicide in protest against force-feeding. In the 1913 Derby, wearing a WSPU banner, she tried to catch the reins of the king's horse and was trampled underfoot, dying several days later.

DAVISON, William (c.1541–1608) Queen **Elizabeth**'s secretary in 1586–87, and her stalking-horse in the execution of **Mary, Queen of Scots**, after which he was imprisoned for two years in the Tower.

DAVISSON, Clinton Joseph (1881–1958) American physicist, born in Bloomington, Illinois. He was educated at Chicago and Princeton, where he was instructor in physics before taking up industrial research at the Bell Telephone Laboratories. In 1927, with **Lester Halbert Germer**, he discovered the diffraction of electrons by crystals, thus confirming **Louis Victor de Broglie**'s theory of the wave properties of electrons. In 1937 he shared the Nobel prize for physics with **George Paget Thomson**.

DAVITT, Michael (1846–1906) Irish nationalist, founder of the Irish Land League, born a peasant's son, at Straid, County Mayo. Evicted from their smallholding, the family emigrated to Haslingden in Lancashire (1851); and here in 1857 the boy lost his right arm through a machinery accident in a cotton factory. In 1866 he joined the Fenian movement, and was sentenced in 1870 to 15 years' penal servitude. He was released in 1877 and, supplied with funds from the States, began an anti-landlord crusade which culminated in the Land League (21 October 1879). Davitt was thenceforward in frequent collision with the government, and from February 1881 to May 1882 was imprisoned in Portland for breaking his ticket-of-leave. His *Leaves from a Prison Diary* were published in 1885. A strong Home Ruler, but socialistic on the question of land nationalization, after the split in the party he opposed **Parnell**, and was returned to parliament in 1892 as an anti-Parnellite, but unseated on the ground of clerical intimidation. In 1895 he was returned unopposed by South Mayo, but resigned in 1899.

DAVOUT, Louis Nicolas (1770–1823) French soldier born in Annoux in Burgundy. He was educated with **Napoleon** at the military school of Brienne. As general he accompanied Napoleon to the East, and mainly secured the victory at Aboukir (1799). A marshal of the empire (1804), he acted a brilliant part at Austerlitz (1805) and Auerstädt (1806), and was made Duke of Auerstädt (1808). At Eckmühl and Wagram (1809) he checked the Austrians' attack, and in 1811 was created Prince of Eckmühl. As governor of Poland he ruled that country with the harshest despotism; in the Russian campaign of 1812–13 he gathered fresh laurels on the fields of Mohilev and Vitebsk. After the retreat from Moscow he became governor-general of the Hanse towns, and at Hamburg maintained a régime of repression till the first restoration of the Bourbons. On Napoleon's return from Elba in 1815, Davout was appointed war minister; and after Waterloo he received the command of the remnant of the French army under the walls of Paris. In 1819 he was made a peer of France.

DAVY, Edward (1806–85) English physician and scientist, born in Ottery St Mary, Devon. He invented the electric relay and deserves to stand alongside **Wheatstone** and **Cooke** as one of the inventors of wireless telegraphy. Trained in medicine, Davy commenced business in London as a chemist, but at about 30 he began experimenting with telegraphy. He lectured and wrote many papers on the subject, and demonstrated his system over a mile-long wire in Regents Park, London. He emigrated to Adelaide, South Australia, in 1838, where he involved himself in civic affairs and continued his experiments, on subjects including starch production and the smelting of copper. In 1853 he moved to Victoria where he made an unsuccessful attempt at farming, after which he returned to medicine which he practised for the rest of his life, and became involved in local affairs. In recognition of his earlier achievements he was made an honorary member of the Society of Telegraph Engineers in 1885.

DAVY, Sir Humphry (1778–1829) English chemist and science propagandist, born in Penzance, a woodcarver's son. Educated there and in Truro, in 1795 he was apprenticed to a Penzance surgeon. In 1797 he took up chemistry and was taken on by **Thomas Beddoes** as an assistant at his Medical Pneumatic Institution in Bristol. Here he experimented with various newly-discovered gases, and discovered the anaesthetic effect of laughing gas. In 1799 he published *Researches, Chemical and Philosophical*, which led to his appointment as lecturer at the Royal Institution (1801). From his first lecture he was hugely popular, his eloquence and the novelty of his experiments attracting large audiences. As a result he gained sufficient funding to research into electrochemistry. In 1813 he published his *Elements of Agricultural Chemistry*, consolidating the reputation already established by his Bakerian lecture *On Some Chemical Agencies of Electricity* (1806). This was followed in 1807 by his discovery that the alkalis and alkaline earths are compound substances formed by oxygen united with metallic bases. Through his experiments he discovered the new metals potassium, sodium, barium, strontium, calcium and magnesium. In 1812 he was knighted, and shortly after married Jane Apreece (1780–1855), a wealthy Scottish widow. Accepted as the leading British scientist of the day, he resigned the chemical chair of the Royal Institution and travelled abroad investigating his theory of volcanic action with his assistant **Faraday**. In 1815 he invented a safe lamp for use in gassy coalmines, allowing deep coal seams to be mined despite the presence of firedamp (CH_4FCR_1). Although his reputation exceeds his achievements (which were nevertheless considerable), he was a talented, energetic scientist. One of his greatest contributions was to sell the idea of science to industrialists. He also excited considerable interest in electrochemistry; he was described by **Berzelius** as leaving 'brilliant fragments' rather than major contributions to scientific theory.

DAVYS, John See **DAVIS, John**

DAWES, Charles Gates (1865–1951) Republican vice-president of the USA under **Coolidge,** 1925–29, financier and general, born at Marietta, Ohio. He was head of the commission which drew up the 'Dawes plan' (1924) for German reparation payments. He was awarded the Nobel peace prize for 1925.

DAWES, Sophia (1790–1840) English adventuress, born in St Helens in the Isle of Wight. She was a fisherman's daughter, an inmate in a workhouse, an officer's mistress, a servant in a brothel, mistress to the Duc de Bourbon, wife (1818) to his aide-de-camp, the Baron de Feuchères, and perhaps the Duc's murderess (1830).

DAWKINS, Richard (1941–) British ethologist. Educated in Oxford, he taught at the University of California before returning to Oxford in 1970. His work on animal behaviour emphasizes that apparently altruistic behaviour is designed to ensure survival of the species (*The Selfish Gene*, 1976) and this and wider views on behaviour and evolution have been developed in *The Blind Watchmaker* (1988).

DAWKINS, Sir William Boyd (1837–1929) Welsh geologist, born at Buttington vicarage, near Welshpool. Educated at Rossall School and Jesus College, Oxford, he joined the Geological Survey in 1861, became curator of Manchester Museum in 1870, and first professor of geology in Manchester in 1872. He wrote *Cave-hunting; or, Caves and the Early Inhabitants of Europe* (1874); and *Early Man in Britain* (1880).

DAWSON OF PENN, Bertrand Edward, 1st Viscount (1864–1945) English physician, born in Purley. He was physician-in-ordinary successively to **Edward VII**, **George V**, **Edward VIII**, **George VI** and Queen **Mary**. He was a major influence in the organization of medical services in inter-war Britain.

DAWSON, Charles (1864–1916) English solicitor and antiquarian, born in Sussex. An amateur geologist, he was the victim (or perpetrator?) of the celebrated 'Piltdown skull' hoax, when cranial fragments, found by him at Piltdown from 1908 to 1912, together with parts of a jawbone unearthed later, were accepted by anthropologists as the 'Missing Link' in **Darwin**'s theory of evolution, and as such one of the greatest discoveries of the age, being named after him *Eoanthropus Dawsoni* ('Dawson's Dawn Man'). Many experts had doubts, but it was not until 1953 that the skull was formally denounced as a fake, after scientific tests had established that the jawbone was that of a modern ape, coloured to simulate age, that the cranium had also been stained to match the gravel deposits in which it was found, and that the fragments had clearly been 'planted' on the site.

DAWSON, George Mercer (1849–1901) Canadian geologist, son of Sir **John William Dawson**, born in Pictou, Nova Scotia. Educated at McGill University, he did much pioneer geological work in British Columbia and the Yukon, where Dawson City was named after him.

DAWSON, Henry (1811–78) English landscape painter, born in Hull. Until 1835 he was a Nottingham lace-maker, then took to art, and died at Chiswick, the price of his pictures having risen from £5 or less to £800 or more. He specialized in marine and river scenes, such as *The Wooden Walls of Old England*, perhaps his best-known work.

DAWSON, James (1717–46) English Jacobite, the son of a Manchester apothecary. He studied for the church at St John's College, Cambridge, but having held a captaincy in Prince **Charles Edward Stewart**'s army, was hanged, drawn and quartered on Kensington Green. His sweetheart, Jenny Dawson, died in her coach there simultaneously. The incident gave rise to the **Shenstone** ballad 'Jenny Dawson'.

DAWSON, Sir John William (1820–99) Canadian geologist, born in Pictou, Nova Scotia. He studied at Edinburgh, and afterwards devoted himself to the natural history and geology of Nova Scotia and New Brunswick. From 1855 to 1893 he was principal of McGill University, Montreal. He was an authority on fossil plants and was a systematic anti-Darwinian. Among his works are *Acadian Geology* (1855), *Origin of the World* (1877), *Fossil Men* (1878), and *Relics of Primeval Life* (1897).

DAWSON, Peter (1882–1961) Australian bass-baritone, born in Adelaide, South Australia. He won a solo competition at Ballarat, Victoria, in 1901 and the following year left for London, where he studied for three years with Sir **Charles Santley** and toured with Madame **Albani**. He later returned to tour Australia with Amy Castle's company. He made his début in grand opera at Covent Garden in 1909, and appeared regularly in oratorios, but he was best known for his ballad singing. From 1904, when he cut a cylinder record for the Edison-Bell company, until 1957 when he made a microgroove stereo recording for EMI, Dawson was a prolific recording artist, using a variety of pseudonyms, including Will Danby, Hector Grant and Will Strong. Many of the ballads he sang were written by Dawson himself, under the name J P McColl.

DAY, Doris, originally **Doris Kappelhoff** (1924–) American singer and film actress, born in Cincinnati. A vocalist with several big bands and a radio favourite in the 1940s, she made her film début in *Romance on the High Seas* (1948). Her sunny personality, singing talent and girl-next-door image made her an asset to many standard Warner Brothers musicals of the 1950s. More satisfying material followed with *Calamity Jane* (1953), *Young at Heart* (1954) and *The Pajama Game* (1957). A top selling recording artist, she was also able to prove her dramatic worth in *Storm Warning* (1950) and *Love Me or Leave Me* (1955). The popularity of the lightweight sex comedy *Pillow Talk* (1959) earned her an Academy Award nomination and a further career as the perennial virgin in a series of frothy farces where she was often partnered by Rock Hudson. She retired from the screen after *With Six You Get Egg Roll* (1968), but appeared occasionally on television and also in *The Doris Day Show* (1968–73). Her autobiography, *Doris Day, Her Own Story* (1976), revealed much of the personal heartache and turmoil beneath her apparently carefree vivacity.

DAY, Dorothy (1897–1980) American writer and radical social reformer, born in Brooklyn, New York. A life-long socialist, she worked in the New York slums as a probationary nurse. Converted to Catholicism in 1927, she co-founded the monthly *Catholic Worker* in 1933, drawing on her earlier experience as a reporter on Marxist publications like *Call* and *The Masses* in lower east side Manhatten. Under the influence of the French itinerant priest Peter Maurin (1877–1949), she founded the Catholic Worker Movement, which established 'houses of hospitality' and farm communities for people hit by the Depression as described in her *House of Hospitality* (1939). A pacifist and a fervent supporter of farm-worker unionization in the 1960s, she helped turn her church's attention to peace and justice issues. Her autobiography, *The Long Loneliness*, was published in 1952. Other works include the autiobiographical novel *The Eleventh Virgin* (1924), and *On Pilgrimage: the Sixties* (1972).

DAY, John (1522–84) English printer, born in Dunwich. One of the first English music printers, he produced the earliest church service book with musical notation (1560), and in the same year Archbishop **Matthew Parker**'s English version of the psalms, with music by **Tallis** and others. His most celebrated publication was **John Foxe**'s *Actes and Monuments* (1563), better kown as the *Book of Martyrs*.

DAY, John (1574–?1640) English Jacobean dramatist. He studied at Caius College, Cambridge, and is mentioned in **Henslowe**'s *Diary* in 1598 as an active playwright and collaborated freely with **Chettle**, **Dekker**, and others. His works, privately printed by **Arthur Henry Bullen** in 1881, include a graceful comedy, *Humour out of Breath*, and *The Parliament of Bees*, an allegorical masque.

DAY, Sir Judson Graham (1933–) Canadian-born British business executive, born in Halifax, Nova Scotia. Educated in Canada, he spent eight years in private practice as a lawyer before joining Canadian Pacific in 1964. In 1975 he went to British Shipbuilders as deputy chairman and chief executive designate, but left in 1977 to take a chair at Dalhousie University. Four years later he became a vice-president of Dome Petroleum for a short period. In 1983 he returned to British Shipbuilders as chairman and chief executive, moving to the Rover Group plc as chairman and chief executive in 1986.

DAY, Sir Robin (1923–) English journalist and broadcaster, born in London. After service in the Royal Artillery (1943–47), he studied law at St Edmund Hall, Oxford (1947–51) and was called to the bar in 1952. After employment for the British Council in Washington, he became a freelance broadcaster in 1954, working at ITN from 1955 to 1959. He left to join the BBC's *Panorama*, which he presented from 1967 to 1972. He brought an acerbic freshness to interviewing techniques and has proved a formidable inquisitor of political figures. His radio work includes *It's Your Line* (1970–76) and *The World at One* (1979–88), while his television credits include *Question Time* (1979–89). The recipient of the Richard Dimbleby Award for Factual Television (1974), he stood unsuccessfully for parliament as a Liberal in 1959. Among his books are *The Case for Televising Parliament* (1963) and *Day by Day* (1975).

DAY, Thomas (1748–89) English writer and barrister, born in London. Educated at Charterhouse and Corpus Christi College, Oxford, he formed a close friendship with **Richard Lovell Edgeworth**. In 1765 he entered the Middle Temple, in 1775 was called to the bar, but never practised. A disciple of **Rousseau**, he brought up an orphan blonde and a foundling brunette, one of whom, he presumed, would become his wife. That scheme miscarried; and he proposed first to Honora and next to Elizabeth Sneyd. She sent him to France to acquire French graces but on his return she laughed at him. Finally in 1778 he married an appreciative heiress, Esther Milnes, and spent eleven happy years with her, farming on philanthropic and costly principles in Essex and Surrey, till he was killed by a fall from a colt he was breaking in. He was the author of a long children's tale *The History of Sandford and Merton* (3 vols, 1783–89), and a long poem, *The Dying Negro* (1773).

DAYAN, Moshe (1915–81) Israeli soldier and statesman, born in Palestine. A founder of the Haganah underground militia, in 1939 he was imprisoned by the British, but two years later he was freed to serve in the British Army in World War II, losing an eye in battle in 1941. In 1948 he was commissioned as an officer in the Israeli Army and was chief of staff when Israel conquered Gaza and Sinai in the Suez War of 1956. In 1958 he left military service to study at the Hebrew University in Jerusalem. Dayan was elected to the Knesset as a Labour member in 1959 and made minister of agriculture by **Ben-Gurion** (1959–64). He left the Labour party in 1966 to set up the Rafi party with Ben Gurion. In 1967 as a member of the opposition, he was appointed defence minister, and masterminded the Israeli victory in the Six-Day War. Dayan immediately became a symbol of Israeli dash and courage and he went on to achieve another notable feat, that of clearing Jerusalem of Arab/Jewish barriers and mines and declaring it a free city. Defence minister again from 1969 to 1974, his reputation was tarnished by Israel's disastrous start to the 1973 (Yom Kippur) War, and he was dropped from the cabinet the following year. In 1977, as foreign minister, he played a vital role in securing the historic peace treaty with Egypt. He resigned (1979) from the **Begin** government in protest at what he regarded as its inflexible approach to negotiations on eventual Palestinian autonomy in the Israeli-occupied West Bank and Gaza Strip. In 1981 he launched a new centre party, but died the same year. He wrote *Diary of the Sinai Campaign* (1966) and *Living with the Bible* (1978).

DAYE, Stephen (c.1610–1668) American printer, born in London. In 1639 he set up at Harvard the first New England printing press.

DEÁK, Francis (1803–76) Hungarian statesman, born in Söjtör, Zala. He practised as an advocate, entered the national diet in 1832, and played the part of a moderate, becoming in 1848 minister of justice. Hailed in 1861 as leader in the diet, by his efforts Hungary's constitution was restored in 1867 and the dual monarchy of Austria-Hungary established.

DEAKIN, Alfred (1857–1919) Australian statesman, born in Melbourne. He became minister of public works and water supply, and solicitor-general of Victoria, and, under the Commonwealth, attorney-general (1901) and prime minister (1903–04, 1905–08, 1909–1910).

DEAKIN, Arthur (1890–1955) British trade union leader, born in Sutton Coldfield. He began work on 4 shillings a week at 13 in a Dowlais, South Wales, steel works. A full-time trades union official from 1919, he became in 1935 assistant to **Ernest Bevin**, general secretary of the Transport and General Workers Union, following the Bevin tradition that a trade union leader should be a first-class organizer rather than an 'agitator'. In 1945 he became general secretary of the 1 300 000-strong union and was president of the World Federation of Trade Unions from 1945 to 1949, when he led the British withdrawal from the organization because of its Communist domination. Subsequently he was one of the founders of the International Confederation of Free Trade Unions. He was chairman of the TUC in 1951 and continued to be one of the most influential members of its General Council till his death.

DEAN, Christopher (1958–) English ice-skater, born in Nottingham. With his partner **Jayne Torvill**, he set a new standard in their sport. They started skating together in 1975. They were six times British champions (1978–83) and won the 'Grand Slam' of World, Olympic and European ice-dance titles in 1984. A policeman before he took up skating full-time, his artistry on the ice was close to perfection. His amateur career reached a pinnacle with the haunting interpretation of **Ravel**'s 'Bolero'. After turning professional in 1985 he continued to tour the world with Torvill in their own ice show.

DEAN, 'Dixie' (William Ralph) (1907–80) English footballer and record goal-scorer, born in Birkenhead.

The son of an engine-driver, he voluntarily attended Borstal for part of his schooling because it had better football facilities. He turned professional with Tranmere Rovers at the age of 16, and scored 27 goals in 27 matches in the following season. He joined Everton in 1925, for whom he scored 349 goals in 399 games. In 1938 he played for Notts County for one season before injury ended his career. Despite a severe motor-cycle accident in 1926 which fractured his skull, he is considered by many the greatest centre-forward of all time, particularly as a header of the ball; he still holds the remarkable scoring record of 60 League goals in one season.

DEAN, James Byron (1931–55) American film actor, born in Indiana. After leaving school he started acting at California University and in 1952 he moved to New York, where he eventually got a part in *See the Jaguar* on Broadway. He gained overnight success in the film *East of Eden* (1955). He made only two more films, *Rebel Without a Cause*, also in 1955, and *Giant*, released the following year, before his death in a car crash. In just over a year he had become the personification of contemporary American youth, restless, purposeless and deprived of security and direction. He became a cult figure, and for many years after his death remained a symbol of youthful rebellion and self-assertion.

DEAN, Laura (1945–) American dancer, choreographer and teacher, born in Staten Island, New York. She studied at Manhattan's High School of Performing Arts and School of American Ballet, danced in **Paul Taylor**'s company (1965–66), and worked with **Meredith Monk**, Kenneth King and **Robert Wilson**. She began choreographing in 1967, developing a style all her own based on an interest in simple, repetitive movement—spinning, stamping, jumping—aligned to rhythmic music. Formed in 1976, Laura Dean Dancers and Musicians mainly features her own scores and those of composer Steve Reich. She has made dances for other companies, including Joffrey Ballet and New York City Ballet.

DEANE, Richard (1610–53) English parliamentary commander and regicide, born in Temple Guiting, Gloucestershire. During the Civil War he commanded the parliamentary artillery in Cornwall and at Naseby (1645), and led the right wing at Preston (1648). He was a commissioner at the trial of **Charles I**, and one of the signatories of the king's death warrant. Later he held commands on both land and sea. He was major general at the battle of Worcester (1651), and commander-in-chief in Scotland (1652). He was general at sea with **Robert Blake** at the battle of Portland (1653) and was killed in the battle of Solebay later that year.

DEAT, Marcel (1894–1955) French politician, born in Guerigny, founder in 1933 of the Socialist party of France, which was Fascist in outlook. His pro-Nazi sympathies procured him the post of minister of labour in the Vichy government, and having achieved notoriety by his ruthless deportations of French workers to Germany, he fled thither himself in 1945, was sentenced to death *in absentia*, but evaded arrest until his death in Turin.

DE BAKEY, Michael Ellis (1908–) American cardiovascular surgeon, born in Lake Charles, Louisiana. He received his medical training at Tulane University, where he subsequently taught surgery until 1948, when he moved to Baylor University College of Medicine in Houston, Texas. There, with **Denton Cooley** and others, he developed a centre of international reputation in the field of cardiovascular surgery. De Bakey himself was particularly involved in the surgical treatment of aortic aneurysms and arterial occlusion through replacement with grafts, but also contributed to other aspects of surgery, including gastric.

DE BARY, Heinrich Anton (1831–88) German botanist, born in Frankfurt-am-Main, the founder of modern mycology. Successively professor of botany at Freiburg, Halle and Strasbourg, he was the first rector of its reorganized university. He studied the morphology and physiology of the fungi and the Myxomycetae.

DE BASIL, Colonel Wassili, originally **Vasily Grigorievich Voskresensky** (1881–1951) Russian ballet impresario, personality and publicist, born in Kaunas. Originally an army officer, he began his theatrical career in Paris as assistant to Prince Zeretelli, director of an itinerant Russian opera company. In 1932 he and **René Blum** co-founded the Ballet Russe de Monte Carlo, heir to **Sergei Diaghilev**'s Ballets Russes. The company gained considerable international acclaim with its high calibre dancers.

DE BAY See **BAJUS, Michael**

DE BEAUVOIR, Simone (1908–86) French novelist and feminist, celebrated also for her lifelong association with **Jean-Paul Sartre**. Born in Paris, she first met Sartre as a student at the Sorbonne, where she was a professor (1941–43), and she contributed substantially and distinctively to the Existentialist movement which flowered mid-century. Her study of women's social situation and historical predicament, *Le deuxième sexe* (1949), translated as *The Second Sex* (1953), was hailed as a pioneering feminist text. Her more autobiographical writings and novels include *Les Mandarins* (1954), winner of the Prix Goncourt; *Mémoires d'une jeune fille rangée* (1958), translated as *Memoirs of a Dutiful Daughter* (1959); *La Force de l'âge* (1960), translated as *The Prime of Life* (1963); *La Force des Choses* (1963), translated as *The Force of Circumstance* (1965); *Une Mort très douce* (1964), translated as *A Very Easy Death* (1972); *Toute compte fait* (1972), translated as *All Said and Done* (1974); and *La Cérémonie des adieux* (1981).

DE BEER, Sir Gavin Rylands (1899–1972) British zoologist, born in London. He served in both world wars and between them graduated from Oxford and then taught there (1923–38). After World War II he was professor of embryology in London, and from 1950 to 1960 he was director of the British Museum (Natural History). His work refuted some early theories in embryology; and he went on to contribute to theories of animal evolution, and to historical problems such as the origin of the Etruscans.

DE BONO, Edward Francis Charles Publius (1933–) Maltese-born British psychologist and author. He took a degree in medicine at the Royal University of Malta, then went as a Rhodes Scholar to Christ Church College, Oxford, where he read psychology, physiology and medicine. From 1976 to 1983 he was a lecturer in medicine at Cambridge, and is involved with a number of organizations to promote the skills of thinking, which break out of the trammels of the traditional, including the Cognitive Research Trust, Cambridge (director since 1971).

DE BONO, Emilio (1866–1944) Italian Fascist politician and general, born in Cassano d'Adda. He was a quadrumvir in **Mussolini**'s march on Rome (1922), governor of Tripolitania (1925), colonial secretary (1939) and commanded the Italian forces invading Abyssinia (1935). He voted against Mussolini in the Fascist Supreme Council (1943) and was summarily tried and executed as a traitor by neofascists in Verona.

DEBRAY, Regis (1941–) French Marxist theorist. Educated at the École Normale Supérieure, he gained international fame through his association with the Marxist revolutionary **Ernesto Che Guevara** in Latin America during the 1960s and, in 1967, was sentenced to 30 years' imprisonment in Bolivia. He was released from jail in 1970 and in 1981 was appointed a specialist adviser to President **Mitterrand** on Third World affairs. His most influential writings have been *Strategy for Revolution* (1970) and *The Power of the Intellectual in France* (1979), the latter a broadside against the growing influence of 'mediacrats'.

DEBRETT, John (c.1750–1822) English publisher. He took over a publishing house in London in 1781, and compiled his *Peerage of England, Scotland and Ireland*, which first appeared in 1802.

DEBREU, Gerard (1921–) French-born American economist, born in Calais. Educated at the University of Paris (PhD in economics, 1946), he went to the USA in 1950 as a researcher with the Cowles Foundation at Chicago University, and became a professor at Yale (1955–61) and then professor of mathematics and economics at the University of California at Berkeley from 1962. His work on the equilibrium between prices, production and consumer demand in a free-market economy was recognized by the award of the Nobel prize for economics in 1983. He wrote *Theory of Value: An Axiomatic Analysis of Economic Equilibrium* (1959), and a collection of essays, *Mathematical Economics* (1983).

DE BROGLIE, Louis-Victor Pierre Raymond, 7th Duke (1892–1987) French physicist, born in Dieppe, France, into an old Piedmontese family. He is known as the discoverer of the wave nature of particles. He studied history, but service at the Eiffel Tower radio station during World War I initiated his interest in science, and he took a doctorate at the Sorbonne (1924). Influenced by **Einstein**'s work on the photo-electric effect which he interpreted as showing that waves can behave as particles, De Broglie put forward the converse idea—that particles can behave as waves. The waves were detected experimentally by **Clinton Davisson** and L H Germer in 1927, and separately by **G P Thomson**, and the idea of wave-particle duality was used by **E Schrödinger** in his development of quantum mechanics. De Broglie was awarded the Nobel prize for physics in 1929.

DEBS, Eugene Victor (1855–1926) American politician and union leader, born in Terre Haute, Indiana. He organized the American railway union in 1893 and founded the Socialist party, standing unsuccessfully as its candidate in all the presidential elections between 1900 and 1920, except that of 1916. His pacifism during World War I brought him imprisonment from 1918 to 1921.

DEBURAU, Jean Gaspard (1796–1846) French actor, born in Bohemia. He developed mime into a fine art and romanticized the traditional harlequinade by the introduction of the Pierrot motif.

DEBUSSY, Claude Achille (1862–1918) French composer, born in St Germain-en-Laye. He received his musical education at the Paris Conservatoire (1873–84), studying piano under Marmontel. In 1879 he travelled Europe as the 'musical companion' of **Tchaikovsky**'s friend Mme von Meck, and in 1884 he won the Prix de Rome with his cantata *L'Enfant prodigue*. His early work was influenced by **Wagner**, for whom he had a great admiration, but he branched off into a more experimental and individual vein in his first mature work, the *Prélude à l'après-midi d'un faune*, evoked by **Mallarmé**'s poem, which first won him fame. He added further to his reputation with his operatic setting of **Maeterlinck**'s *Pelléas et Mélisande*, begun in 1892 but not performed until 1902, and some outstanding piano pieces, *Images* and *Préludes*, in which he moved further from traditional formulae and experimented with novel techniques and effects, producing the pictures in sound which led his work to be described as 'musical Impressionism'. He extended this new idiom to orchestral music in *La Mer* (1905), the orchestrated *Images*, and other pieces, and later elaborated his piano style still further, as in the scintillating *Feux d'artifice* and the atmospheric *La Cathédrale engloutie*. In his later period he composed much chamber music, including pieces for the flute and the harp, two instruments peculiarly suited to his type of music. Debussy in his private life was shy and reserved, particularly in his last years, which were clouded by his suffering from cancer, but although he did not socialize much, he frequented literary circles. In 1899 he married Rosalie Texier, a dressmaker, whom he left in 1904 for Emma Bardac, who became his wife in 1905. His compositions, intensely individual, explored new and original avenues of musical expression, and had a profound effect on French music in general and piano music in particular at the turn of the century.

DEBYE, Peter Joseph Wilhelm (1884–1966) Dutch-born American physicist, born in Maastricht. Educated at Munich (where he later lectured), he was professor successively at Zürich, Utrecht, Göttingen and Leipzig, and director of the Kaiser Wilhelm Institute for Physics, Berlin, 1935–40. In 1936 he was awarded the Nobel prize for chemistry. In 1940 he went to the USA as professor of chemistry at Cornell. He was specially noted for his work on molecular structure. He was also a pioneer in X-ray powder photography

DECAMPS, Alexandre Gabriel (1803–60) French painter, born in Paris. A pioneer of the Romantic school, he was a great colourist, specializing in Oriental scenes and biblical subjects. One of his best pictures, *The Watering Place*, is in the Wallace collection in London.

DECATUR, Stephen (1779–1820) American naval commander, born in Sinepuxent, Maryland, of French descent. He became a midshipman in 1798, served against the French, and in the war with Tripoli (1801–05) gained great distinction burning the captured *Philadelphia* off Tripoli, and then escaping under the fire of 141 guns. Promoted captain in 1804 and commodore in 1810, in the war with England in 1812 he commanded the *United States* in an action that captured the British frigate *Macedonian*. In 1815 he chastised the Algerians for piracy, and compelled the Dey to declare the American flag inviolable. He was killed in a duel by Commodore James Barron.

DECAZES, Elie, Duc (1780–1860) French statesman. He was called as a French advocate and judge to the Hague by the king (1806), supported the **Bourbon** restoration, and after 1815 was the moderate liberal minister of **Louis XVIII**, who made him a duke. He was ambassador in London (1820–21), and held dignities under **Louis-Philippe**. Later he developed the coalfields on his estates in Aveyron. His eldest son, Louis Charles (1819–86), was foreign minister from 1873 to 1877.

DECIUS, Caius Messius Quintus Trajanus (c.200–251) Roman emperor. He was born in Lower Pannonia, and was sent in 249 by the emperor Philip the Arab to reduce the rebellious army of Moesia. The soldiers proclaimed him emperor against his will, and Philip encountered him near Verona, but was defeated and slain. Decius' brief reign was one of warring with the Goths, and he was killed near Abricium in 251. Under him the Christians were persecuted with great severity.

DECKEN, Karl Klaus von der (1833–65) German traveller, born in Kotzen, Brandenburg. After serving in the Hanoverian army (1851–60), he began a journey from Zanzibar to Lake Nyasa, which failed through treachery. In 1862 he climbed Kilimanjaro to the height of 13 780 feet. He was murdered by a Somali on an East African expedition.

DECKER, Sir Matthew (1679–1749) Dutch-born English merchant and political economist, born in Amsterdam. He came to London in 1702, and having made a fortune in commerce, received a baronetcy in 1716, and became an MP (1719–22). He published anonymously two pamphlets: one (1743) proposed to raise all the public supplies from a tax upon houses; the other (1744) contained many good arguments for free trade.

DECKER, Thomas See **DEKKER**

DE COSTER, Charles See **COSTER**

DEDEKIND, Julius Wilhelm Richard (1831–1916) German mathematician, born in Brunswick. He attended the University of Göttingen, where he wrote his doctoral thesis under **Carl Friedrich Gauss** in 1852. From 1854 to 1858 he taught at Göttingen, then in Zürich, and returned to Brunswick in 1862 as professor at the Polytechnic. He gave one of the first precise definitions of the real number system, did important work in number theory, and introduced many concepts which have become fundamental in all modern algebra, in particular that of an 'ideal', building on the work of **Ernst Kummer**.

DE DUVE, Christian René (1917–) English-born Belgian biochemist, born in Thames Ditton, Surrey. He studied medicine at Louvain and returned there to teach in 1947. He was professor of biochemistry there from 1951, and from 1962 also held a chair of biochemistry at Rockefeller University, New York. He is best known as the discoverer of lysosomes, small organelles within cells which contain enzymes; their malfunction causes some metabolic diseases, such as cystinosis. For this and other discoveries on the structure and biochemistry of cells he shared the 1974 Nobel prize for physiology or medicine with Albert Claude and **George Palade**.

DEE, John (1527–1608) English alchemist, geographer and mathematician, born in London. Educated in London, Chelmsford, and at St John's College, Cambridge, he became one of the original fellows of Trinity College, Cambridge (1546). He earned the reputation of a sorcerer by his mechanical beetle in a representation of Aristophanes' *Peace*, and the following year he fetched from the Low Countries sundry astronomical instruments. As astrologer to Queen **Mary I**, he was imprisoned but acquitted on charges of compassing her death by magic (1555). Queen **Elizabeth** showed him considerable favour, making him warden of Manchester College in 1595. For most of his life he was concerned with the search for the Northwest Passage to the Far East, aiding the exploration by his navigational and geographical knowledge. A dabbler in necromancy and magic, he claimed to have found in the ruins of Glastonbury a quantity of the Elixir; and his assistant, Edward Kelley, professed to confer with angels by means of Dee's magic crystal, and talked him into consenting to a community of wives. He wrote numerous works on logic, mathematics, astrology, alchemy, navigation, geography and the calendar (1583), but died in poverty and is buried in Mortlake Church, London. His eldest son, Arthur (1579–1651), was likewise an alchemist, and a friend of Sir **Thomas Browne**.

DEEPING, (George) Warwick (1877–1950) English novelist, born in Southend. He trained as a doctor, but devoted himself to writing. It was not until after World War I, in which he served, that he gained recognition as an author with his bestseller, *Sorrell and Son* (1925), which was later filmed. Other novels include *Old Pybus* (1928) and *Roper's Row* (1929). In his stories, all sentimental, good breeding is represented as the cardinal virtue.

DEFFAND, Marie de Vichy-Chamrond, Marquise du (1697–1780) French salon hostess, educated in a Paris convent. As a girl she became famous for her wit, audacity and beauty. In 1718 she married the Marquis du Deffand, but they soon separated, and for a number of years she ran a brilliant salon frequented by leading figures in Paris literary society. She was a correspondent of **Voltaire**, **Montesquieu** and **D'Alembert**. In 1753 she became blind, and in 1754 invited Mademoiselle **de Lespinasse** to live with her and help her to preside over her salon. Ten years later Mademoiselle de Lespinasse departed after a quarrel, taking away with her D'Alembert and others of the elder lady's former admirers. From 1766 Madame du Deffand corresponded with **Horace Walpole**, who offered help when she fell into financial trouble.

DEFOE, Daniel (1660–1731) English author and adventurer, born in Stoke Newington, London, the son of a butcher. He appears to have travelled widely on the Continent before setting up in the hosiery trade in London in 1683. He took part in **Monmouth**'s rebellion and joined **William III**'s army in 1688. Up to 1704 he strenuously supported the king's party and earned William's favour with his satirical poem *The True-born Englishman* (1701), an attack on xenophobic prejudice. In Queen **Anne**'s reign he ran into trouble with his famous satire *The Shortest Way with the Dissenters* (1702), the irony of which at first deceived the High Church party, but which eventually cost him a ruinous fine, the pillory and imprisonment during the Queen's pleasure. In Newgate prison he managed to continue his pamphleteering on such questions as 'occasional conformity' and wrote a mock-pindaric *Hymn to the Pillory*. In 1704, after his release, he founded a newspaper, *The Review*, which is of importance in the history of journalism. Appearing thrice weekly up to 1713, it aimed at being an organ of commercial interests, but also expressed opinions on political and domestic topics, thus initiating the modern lead article. The 'Scandal Club', one of its features, anticipates the *Tatler* and *Spectator*. As well as writing *The Review* single-handed, he wrote, among much pamphleteering, the astonishingly vivid ghost story *The Apparition of One Mrs Veal*, allegedly, like so many of his fictions, a true account of an actual happening. After 1704 his political conduct becomes highly equivocal. He undertook various secret commissions for the Tory minister **Harley**, including dubious dealings with the Scottish commissioners for Union in 1706–07. On Harley's fall in 1708 he supported Nottingham's ministry and he again changed his coat on the return of Harley in 1710. On the accession of the House of Hanover in 1714 he tried to justify his career as a double-agent in his *Appeal to Honour and Justice* (1715). He now turned to the writing of fiction which was all passed off as actual history. In 1719–20, at the age of nearly 60, he published his best-known work, *Robinson Crusoe*. Among the other six fictions—the *Journal of the Plague Year* (1722) seems to have had a source in an actual diary—the most vivid is *Moll Flanders* (1722), which is still one of the best tales of low life. He did not repeat this triumph in *Roxana* (1724). *Memoirs of a Cavalier* and the brilliant (but unequal) *Captain Singleton* (both in 1720), along with *Captain Jack* (1722), make up an extraordinary outpouring of creative writing in these few years. He continued to write with unabated vigour, including a three-volume travel book (*Tour through the Whole Island of Great Britian*, 1724–27), *The Great Law of Subordination Considered* (1724), *The Complete English Tradesman* (1726), *Plan of the English Commerce* (1728), and *Augusta Triumphans, or the Way to make London the Most Flourishing City in the Universe* (1728). A writer of astonishing versatility, and the founder of British journalism, he published more than 250 works. He was buried in Bunfield Hills.

DE FOREST, Lee (1873–1961) American physicist and inventor, born in Council Bluffs, Iowa, and educated at Yale and Chicago. A pioneer of radio and wireless telegraphy, he patented more than 300 inventions and is known as the 'father of radio' in the USA. He introduced the grid into the thermionic valve, and invented the 'audion' and the four-electrode valve. He also did much early work on sound reproduction and on television.

DEFREGGER, Franz (1835–1921) Austrian painter, noted for his scenes of Tyrolean peasant life.

DEGAS, (Hilaire Germain) Edgar (1834–1917) French artist, born in Paris. After studying at the École des Beaux-Arts under Lamothe, a pupil of **Ingres**, he went to Italy, where he was influenced by the art of the Renaissance painters. On his return to Paris he associated with the Impressionists and took part in most of their exhibitions from 1874 to 1886. He was also influenced by Japanese woodcuts, and, in the seemingly casual composition of his paintings, by photography. He travelled in Spain and Italy and visited New Orleans, USA, in 1872–73, but most of his paintings and pastels of dancers and women at their toilet were produced in his Paris studio, often with the aid of wax and clay models. His interest lay in precision of line and the modelling of the human form in space. *Miss Lola at the Cirque Fernando* (1879) is in the Tate Gallery, *Rehearsal of the Ballet* (c.1874) is in the Louvre, *Dancer Lacing her Shoe* (c.1878) is in the Paris Museum of Impressionism, *Dancer at the Bar* is in the Metropolitan Museum, New York, and the well-known *Cotton-brokers Office* (1873) is in Pau Museum. Latterly, because of failing sight, he concentrated on sculpture.

DE GASPERI, Alcide (1881–1954) Italian politician, born in Pieve Tesino in the Austrian province of Trentino. Educated at Vienna University, he edited the journal *Il Nuovo Trentino* from 1906, and was elected to the Austrian parliament, 1911–16, and in 1919. After Trentino was united with Italy, he became a member of the Italian Chamber of Deputies until 1925, when the Fascist régime of **Mussolini** banned political activity. A founder of the Italian Popular party, he was arrested in 1926 but found refuge in the Vatican until Mussolini's overthrow in 1943. From 1945 he was a leading force in the creation of the Christian Democratic party (DC) and, as prime minister (1945–53), was Italy's most notable post-war politician.

DE GAULLE, Charles André Joseph Marie (1890–1970) French general and first president of the Fifth Republic, born in Lille. He fought in World War I, from which he emerged an enthusiatic advocate of the air-armour combination on which Germany was to found its *blitzkrieg* of 1940. His book, *The Army of the Future* (1940), aroused considerable comment; but his efforts to modernize and revivify the French army made little progress. With the fall of France, June 1940, de Gaulle fled to England to raise the standard of the 'Free French'. The failure of the Gaullist attempt to capture Dakar, together with the general's prickly, unaccommodating conduct of policy, combined to render his collaboration in the North African landings inadvisable; while his reconciliation with his military superior, the ex-prisoner of war General **Giraud**, was never much more than a gesture for the press cameras. Entering Paris at the head of one of the earliest liberation forces in August 1944, de Gaulle became head of the provisional government; but, being strongly suspected of aspirations towards an authoritarian rule, he withdrew to the political sidelines. He continued to exercise such widespread influence, however, that in May 1958, with the troubles in North Africa precipitating the collapse of all responsible government, he was called upon to head a temporary administration. A referendum confirmed to him powers as prime minister greater than any one Frenchman had enjoyed for decades, and he emerged triumphant as the one man able to inspire confidence after the melancholy post-war procession of vacillating leaders. In the elections which followed the adoption of his new constitution (November 1958) his supporters won an overwhelming victory, though he had handed over the party leadership to Soustelle and was himself elected first president of the Fifth Republic in December 1958 with greater powers than that office had previously bestowed. His extremely successful, if high-handed, foreign policy encompassed: the granting of independence to all French African colonies (1959–60); negotiation of the Evian agreements with strife-torn Algeria, which became independent in 1962 (de Gaulle surviving repeated political crises by a lavish use of the referendum); his insistence despite US pressure on developing an independent French nuclear deterrent; consolidation of a new friendship with Federal Germany; his refusal of any concessionary terms and thus effective blocking of Britain's entry into the Common Market in 1962–63 and 1967; belated recognition of the Peking government (1964); and a triumphant succession of state visits, including Russia in 1966. In 1965 he was re-elected only by a second vote. His position was confirmed by his party's overwhelming victory at the general election following the 'students' revolution' in May 1968, but in April 1969 he was forced to resign as president after the defeat of his referendum proposals for senate and regional reforms.

DE GUBERNATIS, Angela See **GUBERNATIS**

DE HAVILLAND, Sir Geoffrey (1882–1965) English aircraft designer, born near High Wycombe. He built his first plane in 1908 and became director of the firm bearing his name, which produced many famous aircraft, including the Tiger Moth (1930), the Mosquito (of revolutionary plywood construction, (1941) and the Comet jet airliner (1952). He established a height record for light aircraft in 1928, and won the King's Cup air race at the age of 51.

DEHMEL, Richard (1863–1920) German poet, a forester's son, born in Wendisch-Hermsdorf, Brandenburg. He wrote intellectual verse showing the influence of **Nietzsche**.

DE HONNECOURT See **VILLARD DE HONNECOURT**

DEIGHTON, Len (Leonard Cyril) (1929–) English thriller writer, born in London. He became, variously, an art student, a railway platemaker and a BOAC steward. His first novel, *The Ipcress File* (1962), was written when he was 33 and became a bestseller, as have almost all his books. Flip, entertaining and exciting, along with **John Le Carré**, **Graham Greene** and **Eric Ambler** he has been responsible for taking the spy novel out of the genre ghetto into mainstream literature. Notable titles are *Funeral in Berlin* (1965), *Only When I Larf* (1968) and the *Game, Set and Match* trilogy: *Berlin Game* (1984), *Mexico Set* (1985), and *London Match* (1986).

DÉJAZET, Pauline Virginie (1799–1875) French actress, born in Paris. From the age of five she played children's roles with marvellous precocity, and later became famous for her soubrette and 'boy' parts (*déjazets*). From 1859 to 1868 she managed, with her son, the Folies-Dramatiques, renamed the Théâtre Déjazet.

DE KEERSMAEKER, Anne Teresa (1960–) Belgian dancer and post-modern choreographer, born in Mechelen. She studied at the Mudra School in Brussels, and in New York, and created a style which blends the abstract qualities of new American dance with the expressionist energies of Europeans like **Pina Bausch**. Her own company, Rosas, premiered in 1983 with *Rosas Danst Rosas*. She has set her pieces to both minimalist and classical music and has used film and speech in her work. Her recent interests in dance theatre led to a staging of *Verkommenes Ufer Medea-material Landschaft mit Argonauten*, by East German writer Heiner Müller. Other work includes *Elena's Aria* (1984) and *Bartók/Aantekeningen* (1986), a piece about the modern woman which transforms high-heeled restriction into school-girl freedom with precision choreography.

DEKKER, Eduard Douwes, pseud **Multatuli** (1820–87) Dutch government official and writer, born in Amsterdam. He served for many years in the Dutch civil service in Java, and in his novel *Max Havelaar* (1860), and in many bitter satires, he protested against the abuses of the Dutch colonial system.

DEKKER, Thomas (c.1570–c.1641) English dramatist and pamphleteer, born in London. Around 1598 he was employed by **Philip Henslowe** to write plays, and in 1600 published two comedies, *The Shoemaker's Holiday, or the Gentle Craft*, and *The Pleasant Comedy of Old Fortunatus*. His next play (with **John Marston**) was *Satiromastix* (1602), which held up to ridicule **Ben Jonson**, who in 1619 had said that Dekker was a knave. In 1603 he published a pamphlet, *The Wonderful Year*, which gives a heartrending account of the plague. To the same date belongs the tract, *The Bachelor's Banquet*, in which he describes with gusto the ills of henpecked husbands. His most powerful writing is seen in *The Honest Whore* (Part I, written with **Thomas Middleton**, in 1604; Part II, which was his own work, in 1630). In 1607 he published three plays written in conjunction with **John Webster**, the *Famous History of Sir Thomas Wyat*, *Westward Ho!* and *Northward Ho!*. The pamphlet *Bellman of London* (1608) gives a lively account of London vagabonds; and he pursued the subject in *Lanthorn and Candlelight* (1608). In *The Gull's Hornbook* (1609) the life of a town gallant is racily depicted. He also published a devotional work, *Fowre Birds of Noahs Ark* (1609). The excellent comedy, *The Roaring Girl* (1611), was written partly in collaboration with Middleton. From 1613 to 1616 he was mostly in prison for debt. With **Philip Massinger** he composed the *Virgin Martyr* (1622). *The Sun's Darling*, licensed in 1624, but not printed until 1656, was written in conjunction with **John Ford**. A powerful tragedy, *The Witch of Edmonton* (1623) was written with Ford and **William Rowley**. In 1637, he republished his *Lanthorn and Candlelight* as *English Villainies*. He was also the author of masques and entertainments.

DE KLERK, F W (Frederik Willem) (1936–) South African politician. Born into a political family and a graduate of Potchestroom University, he established a legal practice in Vereeniging and became active in the National party, entering the South African parliament, representing Vereeniging, in 1972, and then served in the cabinets of **B J Vorster** and **P W Botha** (1978–89). De Klerk also became National party leader for the Transvaal in 1982 and in February and August 1989 successively replaced the ailing Botha as National party leader and acting state president. Projecting himself as a pragmatic and accessible conservative who sought gradual reform of the apartheid system and improved diplomatic relations, in September 1989 he secured electoral victory for his party, but with a reduced majority. In February 1990 he ended the 30-year-old ban on the African National Congress (ANC) black opposition movement and sanctioned the release from imprisonment of its effective leader **Nelson Mandela**.

DE KOONING, Willem, or **William** (1904–) Dutch-born American painter, born in Rotterdam. He emigrated to the USA in 1926, and is one of the leaders of the modern American nonfigurative artists, but his controversial series of *Woman* (1950–53) is Expressionist.

DE LA BECHE, Sir Henry Thomas (1796–1855) English geologist, born near London. In 1820 he published a paper on the temperature and depth of Lake Geneva; in 1824 he visited Jamaica, and published one on its geology. Other works include a *Manual of Geology* (1831) and a *Geological Observer* (1853). In 1832 he was appointed first director of the newly established Geological Survey of Great Britain. He founded the Geological Museum and the Royal School of Mines.

DELACROIX, Ferdinand Victor Eugène (1798–1863) French painter, born in Charenton, the son of Charles Delacroix (1741–1805), who had been foreign minister under the Directory, and prefect of Marseilles. As a boy he developed a love of art, and in 1861 he entered the studio of **Guérin**, where his fellow-pupil was **Géricault**, whose famous *Raft of the Medusa* gave him early inspiration. In 1822 he exhibited at the Institute *Dante and Vergil in Hell*, and in 1824 *The Massacre at Chios* (now in the Louvre). Both of these pictures, particularly the latter, with its loose drawing and vivid colouring, shocked the devotees of the austere and statuesque classical style, and aroused a storm of criticism. **Constable**'s *Haywain*, which was hung in the same exhibition, profoundly impressed Delacroix, who moved even further away from the traditional treatment in brilliant canvases of historical and dramatic scenes, often violent or macabre in subject, among them *The Execution of Faliero*, now in the Wallace collection, and the famous *Liberty Guiding the People* (1831, Louvre). A journey to Morocco and Spain with a diplomatic mission in 1832 led to several pictures with an oriental flavour, such as *Algerian Women* (1834), and he also turned to literary themes, notably from **Shakespeare** and **Torquato Tasso**. In 1838 he began work on a series of panels for the library of the Chamber of Deputies, choosing as his subject the history of ancient civilization, but despite this official recognition and despite the fact that the Government had bought his *Massacre at Chios*, he was regarded as a rebel in the art world and was not elected to the Institute until 1857. Perhaps the greatest figure in 19th century French art, Delacroix was one of the most accomplished colourists of all time, and was responsible for shifting the emphasis away from the meticulous but pallid techniques of **Ingres** and **David**. A man of immense energy, he interested himself in politics and literature (he was a friend of **George Sand**, whom he painted), and assiduously kept a daily journal from the age of 23 until the year of his death, recording fascinating details of his life and work.

DELAFIELD, E M, pseud of **Edmée Elizabeth Monica Dashwood,** née **de la Pasture** (1890–1943) English novelist, born in Llandogo, Monmouth. She married in 1921, and was the author of several novels, and a series beginning with *Diary of a Provincial Lady* (1931).

DE LA MARE, Walter (1873–1956) English poet and novelist, born in Charlton in Kent, of Huguenot descent. Educated at St Paul's Choir School, he went to work for the Standard Oil Company in 1890, and wrote in his spare time. He retired on a state pension in 1908 to take up full-time writing. The promise of his first book of verse, *Songs of Childhood* (1902, by 'Walter Ramal'), his prose romance *Henry Brocken* (1904), his children's story *The Three Mulla Mulgars* (1910) and his novel of the occult *The Return* (1910) was fulfilled in his volumes of poetry *The Listeners* (1912), *Peacock Pie* (1913) and *The Veil* (1921), in the fantastic novel *Memoirs of a Midget* (1921), and in books of short stories such as *On the Edge* (1930). Romanticist and musician in words, De la Mare has delighted children and grown-up readers alike by the delicate enchantments and humour of his *Märchen* world. In 1953, he published a new volume of lyrics, *O Lovely England*.

DELAMBRE, Jean Joseph (1749–1822) French astronomer, born in Amiens. He studied under **Joseph Lalande**, and attracted attention by his tables of the motion of Uranus. From 1792 to 1799, with Pierre Méchain (1744–1804), he measured the arc of the meridian between Dunkirk and Barcelona.

DELANE, John Thaddeus (1817–79) English journalist, born in London. He graduated in 1839 from Magdalen Hall, Oxford, where he was more famous for horsemanship than reading. **John Walter**, however, his father's neighbour in Berkshire and proprietor of *The Times*, had noticed him, and in 1841 he became joint editor of *The Times*. For 36 years he held this post, helped for 25 of them by **George Dasent**. Under him *The Times* attained a circulation and an influence unparalleled in journalism. He did not write articles, but contributed excellent reports and letters. His exposure of the railway mania, his attacks upon the management of the Crimean War, and his strong opposition to Britain's assisting Denmark in 1864 were noteworthy. He resigned in 1877.

DELANY, Mary, née **Granville** (1700–88) English lady of letters, born in Coulston, Wiltshire. The niece of Lord Lansdowne, she married first, in 1718, Alexander Pendarves (1659–1724); and secondly, in 1743, the Rev Patrick Delany (1685–1768), an Irish divine, **Swift**'s friend, and the author of a dozen volumes. After his death she lived chiefly in London. Her admired 'paper-mosaics', or flower work, have long since faded; but she is remembered through her patronage of **Fanny Burney** and by her *Autobiography and Correspondence* (6 vols, 1861–62).

DE LA RENTA, Oscar (1932–) American fashion designer, born in Santo Domingo, in the Dominican Republic. After studying art in Santo Domingo and Madrid, he worked at **Balenciaga**'s couture house in Madrid. He joined the house of Lanvin-Castillo in Paris in 1961, but after two years went to **Elizabeth Arden** in New York. In 1965 he started his own company. He has a reputation for opulent, ornately trimmed clothes, particularly evening dresses, but also designs daywear and accessories.

DELAROCHE, Hippolyte, known as **Paul** (1797–1856) French painter, born in Paris. He studied under Gros, and specialized in romantic historical subjects such as the *Death of Queen Elizabeth* (1827), and *Execution of Lady Jane Grey* (1834). From this period until 1841 he was engaged on his grandest work—the mural (*Apothesis of Art*) in the École des Beaux Arts, in the execution of which he was aided by **Armitage** and other of his pupils.

DE LA ROCHE, Mazo (1885–1961) Canadian novelist, born in Newmarket, Ontario. She wrote *Jalna* (1927), the first of a series of novels about the Whiteoak family. *Whiteoaks* (1929) was dramatized with considerable success. Her autobiography, *Ringing the Changes*, was published in 1957.

DE LA RUE, Warren (1815–89) British astronomer and physicist, born in Guernsey. He was educated at Paris, and early entered his father's business—the manufacture of paperwares—for which his inventive genius devised many new processes, including an envelope-making machine. He invented the silver chloride battery and did research on the discharge of electricity in gases. A pioneer of celestial photography, he invented the photoheliograph.

DELAUNAY, Robert (1885–1941) French painter, born in Paris. Originally apprenticed to a stage designer, he turned to painting in 1905 and his first works are painted in a colourful Divisionist technique. Under the influence of **Cézanne** he subdued his palette, but later returned to high-key colour in a series of pictures of Saint-Severin and the Eiffel Tower by which he is best known. Later he started isolating areas of pure colour in his pictures, a method he called Orphism. He saw this movement as a logical development of Impressionism and Neo-Impressionism. The breaking up of the surface of his pictures into planes of colour eventually led to almost pure abstraction. In 1912 he was visited by members of the Blaue Reiter group upon whom he was to exert considerable influence, and by 1914 he was thought the most significant painter in Paris.

DELAUNAY, Sonia Terk, née **Stern** (1885–1979) Russian-born French painter and textile designer, born in the Ukraine, the daughter of a factory owner. Brought up in St Petersburg (Leningrad), she studied art at Karlsruhe and in Paris where, in 1905, she attended the Académie de la Palette. In 1909 she made a marriage of convenience with the art critic Wilhelm Uhde, but that ended shortly, and in 1910 she married the French painter Robert Delaunay and together they founded the movement known as Orphism; in 1918 they designed sets and costumes for **Diaghilev**. She was a textile designer of international importance, and her work was included in the 'Exposition des Arts Décoratifs' in 1925.

DELAVIGNE, Jean François Casimir (1793–1843) French dramatist, satirist and lyricist, born in Le Havre. He became popular through his *Messéniennes* (1818), satires upon the Restoration. *Les Vêpres siciliennes* (1819), a tragic piece, was followed by *L'École des vieillards* and *Les Comédiens* (1821), *Louis XI*, (partly based on *Quentin Durward*, 1833), and *La Fille du Cid* (1839).

DE LA WARR, Thomas West, 3rd or **12th Baron** (1577–1618) English soldier and colonist. After serving under the Earl of **Essex** he was appointed the first governor of Virginia in 1610. Returning to England in 1611, he wrote the *Relation* on Virginia. He died on a return voyage to Virginia. The state of Delaware is named after him.

DELBRÜCK, Berthold (1842–1922) German linguist, born in Putbus, Prussia (now East Germany). He was professor of Sanskrit and comparative linguistics at Jena University from 1870 to 1912. He was the first Indo-Europeanist to study comparative syntax, his major work being the three volumes on syntax in the five-volume *Comparative Grammar of the Indo-Germanic Languages* (1886–93; 2nd enlarged edition

1897–1916), to which **Karl Brugmann** contributed the two volumes on phonology and morphology.

DELBRÜCK, Hans (1848–1929) German military historian, a native of Rügen. He was professor at Berlin (1885–1919), and from 1883 to 1919 was editor of the *Preussische Jahrbücher*. He wrote a number of military histories.

DELBRÜCK, Max (1906–81) German-born American biophysicist, born in Berlin. He studied physics in Göttingen, worked in chemistry in Berlin, and moved to biology from 1937 at the California Institute of Technology. There he did much to create bacterial and bacteriophage genetics, and in 1946 showed that viruses can recombine genetic material. His ideas in molecular biology inspired others, and he shared with Salvador Luvia and **Alfred Hershey** the 1969 Nobel prize for physiology or medicine for his work in viral genetics.

DELCASSÉ, Théophile (1852–1923) French statesman. He was foreign minister 1898–1905, 1914–15, promoted the *entente cordiale* with Britain and figured in Moroccan crises.

DELEDDA, Grazia (1875–1936) Italian writer. She made her name with peasant stories of her native Sardinia, and won the 1926 Nobel prize for literature.

DE LEON, Daniel (1852–1914) Dutch-born American radical, born in Curaçao, the son of a Jewish surgeon in Dutch colonial military service. He studied in Hildesheim, Germany, and then in Amsterdam, emigrating to the USA in 1874. He worked on a Spanish newspaper for Cuban liberation and taught in Westchester County, New York, while studying law at Columbia, afterwards practising in Texas, and then lecturing in Latin American diplomacy at Columbia from 1883 to 1889. He supported the Socialist Labor party from 1890, which made him its national lecturer and candidate for governor of New York (unsuccessfully) in 1891. He edited the party journal, *The People* (1890–1914). He founded the Socialist Trade and Labor Alliance in 1895, but a split developed in protest against his authoritarianism and the seceders of 1899 ultimately became the Socialist party of America. He assisted in the formation of the Industrial Workers of the World (1905), merging it with his Alliance, but broke away from them and founded a rival body, the Workers' International Industrial Union. He wrote several Marxist treatises such as *The Socialist Reconstruction of Society*, translated **Marx**'s *Eighteenth Brumaire of Louis Bonaparte* and profoundly influenced **Lenin**'s theoretical writings.

DELESCLUZE, Louis Charles (1809–71) French radical politician and journalist, born in Dreux. His republican agitation at the 1830 Restoration eventually drove him from France to journalism in Belgium (1835), but the February Revolution (1848) brought him back to Paris where his pen made him popular with the rabble but brought him imprisonment and he was ultimately transported until 1859. (See his *De Paris á Cayenne*; *Journal d'un transporté*, 1867.) In 1868 he started the *Réveil*, to promote the International; in the Paris Commune (1871) he played a prominent part, and died on the last barricade.

DELFONT, Bernard, Baron See **GRADE, Lew, Baron**

DELIBES, Léo (1836–91) French composer, born in St Germain du Val, Sarthe. In 1865 he became second director at the Grand Opera, and in 1880 a Conservatoire professor. He wrote light operas, of which *Lakmé* had the greatest success, but is chiefly remembered for the ballet *Coppélia* (1870), which has remained a prime favourite.

DELILLE, Jacques (1738–1813) French poet, born near Aigues-Perse in Auvergne. His verse translation of **Virgil**'s *Georgics* (1769) was very popular, and was praised by **Voltaire**. After holding a canonry at Moissac, he was presented by the Comte d'Artois with the abbacy of Saint-Severin. *Les Jardins* (1782), a didactic poem, was generally accepted as his masterpiece. The Revolution compelled Delille to leave France. He travelled in Switzerland and Germany, and then in London spent 18 months translating *Paradise Lost*. After his return to France in 1802 he produced a translation of Virgil's *Aeneid* (1804), and volumes of verse in *L'Imagination* (1806), *Les Trois Règnes de la nature* (1809) and *La Conversation* (1812). During his life he was regarded by his countrymen as the greatest French poet of the day, and was even declared the equal of Virgil and **Homer**; but his fame was short-lived.

DELISLE, Joseph Nicolas (1688–1768) French astronomer, born in Paris. A pioneer in solar study, he founded a famous school of astronomy in St Petersburg in 1726. He was also noted for his study of the transits of Venus and Mercury.

DELISLE, Leopold Victor (1826–1910) French librarian and palaeographer, born in Valognes. He entered the manuscript department of the Bibliothèque Nationale in 1852, and became curator in 1871 (administrator, 1874). He made important contributions to bibliography and literary history, especially in his work on *Recueil des historiens des gaules et de la France*.

DE LISLE, Rouget See **ROUGET DE LISLE**

DE L'ISLE, Sidney William Philip, 1st Viscount De L'Isle (1909–) English soldier, businessman and statesman, educated at Eton and Magdalene College, Cambridge. He served with the Grenadier Guards during World War II in France and Italy and was awarded the VC at Anzio. He was elected to parliament in 1944, but on the death of his father in the following year he entered the House of Lords as the 6th Baron De L'Isle and Dudley. He became a privy councillor in 1951 and until 1955 was secretary for air in **Churchill**'s first post-war ministry. He was created 1st Viscount De L'Isle in 1956, and was governor-general of Australia from 1961 to 1965. In his capacity as a chartered accountant he holds many business directorships, trusteeships and charitable appointments.

DELITZSCH, Franz Julius (1813–90) German Old Testament scholar, orientalist, and Hebraist, born in Leipzig. He became professor of theology at Rostock in 1846, at Erlangen in 1850, and at Leipzig in 1867. One of the foremost among conservative German theologians, he exercised great personal influence over a generation of Leipzig students, and a long series of profoundly learned books extended a sound knowledge of Old Testament exegesis in Germany, England and America. His son, Friedrich (1850–1922), in 1877 became professor of Assyriology at Leipzig, in 1893 at Breslau, in 1899 at Berlin.

DELIUS, Frederick (1862–1934) English composer, of German Scandinavian descent, born in Bradford. Despite his musical gifts, his parents planned a commercial career for him, but when he was 20 he went to Florida as an orange planter, in his leisure studying music from books and scores. He entered Leipzig Conservatory in 1886, but was influenced more by **Grieg**, who befriended him there, than by his teachers. After 1890 he lived almost entirely in France, composing prolifically in an individual style unconnected with any traditional school. He wrote six operas, including *Koanga* (1897) and *A Village Romeo and Juliet* (1901), concertos for violin, cello, piano and a violin and cello, small orchestral works, and larger choral and orchestral pieces, *Appalachia*, *Sea Drift* and

A Mass of Life, which are less familiar. In 1924, seized by paralysis, he became helpless and totally blind, but with the assistance of Eric Fenby, who became his amanuensis in 1928, he produced a group of final works, including the complex *A Song of Summer*, *Idyll* and *Songs of Farewell*.

DELIUS, Nikolaus (1813–88) German Shakespearian scholar, born in Bremen. He became extraordinary professor in 1855 at Bonn, and professor in 1863. His early lectures were on Sanskrit and the Romance tongues, but he afterwards devoted himself to English and Shakespeare. He was responsible for the first critical edition of Shakespeare's works in Germany (7 vols, 1854–61).

DELL, Ethel Mary (1881–1939) English novelist, born in Streatham. As a writer of light romantic novels she enjoyed a tremendous vogue in the years between the wars. Her books include *The Lamp in the Desert* (1919), *The Black Knight* (1926) and *Sown Among Thorns* (1939).

DELLA CASA, Lisa (1919–) Swiss soprano, born in Burgdorf near Berne. She studied in Zürich, and first appeared at Solothurn-Biel in 1943, subsequently joining the company at the Stadttheater, Zürich. Her appearance at the Salzburg Festival of 1947 led to her engagement with Vienna State Opera Company. A specialist in the operas of **Richard Strauss**, she shares with Lotte Lehmann (1888–1976) the distinction of having sung all three soprano roles in *Der Rosenkavalier*.

DELLA ROBBIA See **ROBBIA**

DELLER, Alfred George (1912–79) English countertenor, born in Margate, Kent. He joined his first church choir at the age of eleven, and in 1943, while a member of Canterbury Cathedral Choir, he was heard by **Michael Tippett** who was looking for a countertenor to sing music by **Purcell**, and arranged his first London concert. In 1946 he made his radio début in the inaugural broadcast of the BBC's Third Programme, and in 1947 began a full-time musical career. He made many recordings of early English songs, notably those of **Dowland** and Purcell, and in 1950 formed the Deller Consort, a small group of musicians devoted to the authentic performance of early music. In 1963 he founded the Stour Music Festival, at which he performed and conducted. Many composers wrote for his voice, including **Benjamin Britten**, who created the part of Oberon in *Midsummer Night's Dream* for him, and it was largely due to him that the counter-tenor voice regained its popularity in performance and teaching.

DELOLME, Jean Louis (1740–1806) Swiss jurist and writer, born in Geneva. An advocate in Geneva, he came to England in c.1769, where in spite of his literary activity, he lived in great poverty, always in debt and repeatedly in prison. Having inherited a small property, he returned to Geneva in 1775. He is remembered for his *Constitution of England* (Fr 1771, Engl 1775), *History of Flagellants* (1782) and *Strictures on the Union* (1796).

DELONEY, Thomas (c.1550–1600) English balladist and writer of fiction. A London silk-weaver, he wrote and distributed stories in pamphlet form like *Jack of Newbury*, *Thomas of Reading* and *Gentle Craft*, which with their lively dialogue and characterization, foreshadow the later novel.

DE LONG, George Washington (1844–81) American arctic explorer, born in New York. In 1879 he commanded the *Jeanette* in an attempt to reach the North Pole via the Bering Strait. Having abandoned his ship in the pack ice in 1881, he travelled 300 miles by sledge and boat to the Siberian coast, but only two of his crew reached safety.

DELORME, Marion (1613–50) French courtesan, born in Paris, where at an early period of her life her beauty and wit gathered a group of high-born lovers round her—among them the 1st Duke of **Buckingham**, **Saint-Évremond**, the Duc de Brissac and the Duc de Gramont. Even **Richelieu** was not insensible to her charms, and caused her to be separated from the Marquis de Cinq-Mars, whose mistress she was until he was executed in 1642. During the early days of the Fronde uprising (1648–53) her house was the rallying-point of its chiefs, and **Mazarin** was about to imprison her when she suddenly died.

DELORME, Philibert (c.1510–1570) French architect, born in Lyons. Royal architect to **Henri II**, he built the Tuileries for **Catherine de' Medici**, and the châteaux of Anet, Meudon, etc.

DELORS, Jacques (1925–) French socialist politician and European statesman. The son of a Paris bank employee, he served as social affairs adviser to prime minister Jacques Chaban-Delmas (1969–72). He joined the Socialist party in 1973 and represented it in the European parliament from 1979, chairing the economic and monetary commission. He served as minister of economy and finance in the administration of President **Mitterrand** (1981–84), overseeing a programme of austerity (*rigueur*). After being passed over for the post of prime minister in 1984, he left to become president of the European Commission in 1985. As Commission president, he oversaw significant budgetary reforms and the move towards a free Community market in 1992, with increased powers residing in Brussels. He was elected to a second four-year term as president in 1988.

DE LOS ANGELES, Victoria (1923–) Spanish lyric soprano, born in Barcelona, where she gave her first public concert (1944). Her operatic début was at the Liceo theatre, Barcelona, 1945; she then performed at the Paris Opera and La Scala, Milan (1949), Covent Garden (1950), the New York Metropolitan (1951) and subsequently at all the great houses and festivals throughout the world. She notably portrayed Carmen, Dido, **Puccini**'s heroines, **Mozart** roles, and Elisabeth in *Tannhäuser* (Bayreuth, 1961). After retiring from the stage in 1969 she continued to give recitals.

DEL RIO, Andrés Manuel (1764–1849) Spanish mineralogist, born in Madrid. He became professor of mineralogy at the Mexico School of Mines in 1793, and in 1801 discovered the metal vanadium.

DELSARTE, François Alexandre Nicolas Chéri (1811–71) French singing teacher and theoretician, born in Solesmes. Trained as a singer, he formulated theories on the movement and control of the body for singers which were developed by his students into the areas of acting and dance. It is not clear whether his theories were documented by his daughter Anna or his French patron Abbé Delsolemene, but it is these notes which have survived and been developed for use today.

DELUC, Jean André (1727–1817) Swiss geologist, meteorologist and physicist, born in Geneva. He tried to prove that creation as described in the Bible was consistent with science. He investigated atmosphere, the density of water, invented a hygrometer and was the first to record accurately the heights of mountains by the barometer. He settled in England in 1773, and was reader to Queen **Charlotte Sophie**, until his death at Windsor Castle.

DELVAUX, Paul (1897–) Belgian Surrealist painter, born in Antheit. He has lived mainly in Brussels, where he studied, and exhibited mainly Neo-Impressionist and Expressionist pictures until 1935. He was influenced by **Chirico** and **Magritte**, and produced a series of paintings depicting nude and semi-nude girls in dreamlike settings (eg, *The Call of the Night*), using a palette which gradually increased in brightness.

DELVIG, Anton Antonovitch, Baron von (1798–1831) Russian poet, born in Moscow. He studied with **Pushkin** at the Tsarskoé Sélo school and became keeper of the public library at St Petersburg. From 1825 to 1831 he published the almanac *Flowers from the North*.

DEMADES (c.380–319 BC) Athenian orator and politician. A bitter enemy to **Demosthenes**, he supported **Philip II** of Macedon, and after the battle of Chaeronea (338) secured an honourable peace. He also secured lenient treatment for Athens after the revolt of 335. In 332, after **Antipater** had crushed a revolt against Macedonian rule in the Lainian War, Demades procured the death of Demosthenes and his followers, but was himself executed by Cascander, the son of Antipater.

DEMARÇAY, Eugène Anatole (1852–1904) French chemist. In 1896 he discovered spectroscopically the element europium, and also gave spectroscopic proof of the discovery of radium.

DEMARCO, Richard (1930–) Scottish artist, broadcaster and teacher, born in Edinburgh where he studied at the College of Art (1949–53). A vivid, outspoken personality, he has been a leading promoter of modern art in Scotland, including the work of such international figures as **Joseph Beuys**, as well as contemporary Scottish artists, especially at the Edinburgh Festival since 1967, and has presented annual programmes of theatre, music, and dance. He was co-founder of the Traverse Theatre Club, and director (from 1966) of the Richard Demarco Gallery.

DEMBINSKI, Henryk (1791–1864) Polish soldier, born near Cracow. He entered the Polish army in 1809, and fought under **Napoleon** against Russia and at Leipzig (1813). In the Polish revolution of 1830 he was commander-in-chief; in 1833 he entered the service of **Mehemet 'Ali**. On the outbreak of the Hungarian insurrection in 1848, **Kossuth** appointed him commander-in-chief. He was hampered by the jealousy of **Görgei**, and after the defeat of Kapolna (1849) was forced to resign. On Kossuth's resignation he fled to Turkey, but in 1850 returned to Paris. He was author of *Mémoires* (1833) and four other works.

DEMETRIUS the name of several kings of Macedonia, of whom the one surnamed Poliorcetes (283 BC), 'besieger of cities', was the son of **Antigonus Monophthalmos**. He assumed the royal title together with his father in 306, and was king in Macedonia from 294 till his expulsion in 288. He died the prisoner of **Seleucus I** in 283. Several of the Seleucid kings of Syria were also called Demetrius.

DEMETRIUS See **DMITRI**

DEMETRIUS PHALEREUS (c.350–c.283 BC) Greek orator and statesman, so named from the Attic seaport of Phalerum, where he was born. Educated with **Menander** in the school of **Theophrastus**, he entered (c.325) on public life, in 317 was entrusted by **Cassander** with the government of Athens, and satisfactorily discharged its duties for ten years. Latterly he became dissipated; and when Demetrius Poliorcetes captured Athens in 307 he had to flee—first to Thebes and next to the court of **Ptolemy (I) Soter** at Alexandria, where he was involved with the establishment of the great Alexandrian library. On Ptolemy's death in 283 he retreated to Busiris in Upper Egypt, and died there of a snake-bite.

DEMIDOV Russian family descended from a blacksmith at Tula, who in the time of **Peter I, the Great** amassed an immense fortune as a manufacturer of arms. Prince Anatole (1813–70) wrote *Voyage dans la Russie méridionale* (4 vols, 1839–49).

DE MILLE, Agnes (1909–) American dancer, choreographer and writer, born in New York City, niece of the film director **Cecil B de Mille**. After graduating from the University of California, she went to London and danced with **Marie Rambert**'s company in the original production of **Antony Tudor**'s *Dark Elegies*. *Three Virgins and a Devil* (1941) marked her breakthrough into choreography and with Broadway in her sights she moved into show business. Irrepressible, she went on to choreograph for such hit musicals as *Oklahoma* (1943), *Carousel* (1945), *Brigadoon* (1947), *Gentlemen Prefer Blondes* (1949) and *Paint Your Wagon* (1951). She is also known for her wit and eloquent public speaking, and her contribution to television and film. Her books include *Dance to the Piper* (1952), *The Book of Dance* (1963), *American Dances* (1980).

DE MILLE, Cecil Blount (1881–1959) American film director, born in Ashfield, Massachusetts. He acted on the stage and wrote unsuccessful plays before discovering Hollywood with **Samuel Goldwyn** (with whom he founded Paramount Films) as a suitable place for shooting the first American feature film, *The Squaw Man* (1914). With the Gloria Swanson comedy, *Male and Female* (1919), he became the most 'advanced' of American film directors. Through *The Ten Commandments* (1923, re-made in cinemascope dimensions in 1956), *The Sign of the Cross* (1932), *The Plainsman* (1936) and *Reap the Wild Wind* (1942) he made a reputation for box-office mastery of the vast film spectacle, on the formula of a high moral theme, enlivened by physical violence and sex, a notable exception being the filmed Passion play, *King of Kings* (1927). He also organized the first commercial passenger airline service in the US in 1917. In 1938 he declined nomination to the US Senate.

DEMIREL, Suleyman (1924–) Turkish politician. He qualified as an engineer at Istanbul Technical University and worked on hydro-electric schemes in the USA and Turkey before making the transition from public service to politics. In 1964 he became president of the centrist Justice party (JP), now subsumed in the True Path party (TPP). He served three terms as prime minister from 1965, until a military coup in 1980 resulted in a three-year ban on political activity. He was placed in detention but released in 1983.

DE MITA, Luigi Ciriaco (1928–) Italian politician, born in Fusco, Avellino province. He joined the Christian Democratic party (DC) and in 1963 was elected to the Chamber of Deputies. He held a number of ministerial posts in the 1970s and in 1982 became DC secretary-general. In 1988, following a series of unsuccessful attempts to form a stable coalition, he accepted the challenge and became prime minister.

DEMOCRITUS (c.460–c.370 BC) Greek philosopher, born in Abdera in Thrace and supposedly known as 'the laughing philosopher' in the ancient world because of his wry amusement at human foibles. He was one of the most prolific of ancient authors, publishing works on ethics, physics, mathematics, cosmology and music, but only fragments of his writings (on ethics) survive. He is best known for his physical speculations, and in particular for the atomistic theory he developed from **Leucippus**, whereby the world consists of an infinite number of minute particles whose different combinations account for the different properties and qualities of all the world's contents. He was an important influence on **Epicurus**

and **Lucretius**, and he was the subject of **Karl Marx**'s PhD thesis.

DEMOGEOT, Jacques Claude (1808–94) French *littérateur*, born in Paris. He lectured at Beauvais, Rennes, Bordeaux and Lyons, and was professor of rhetoric at the Lycée St Louis at Paris, and later at the Sorbonne. Among his works were *Les Lettres et les hommes de lettres au XIX*[e] siècle (1856); *Histoire de la littérature française* (1857); *Tableau de la littérature française au XVII*[e] siècle (1859); and *Histoire des littératures étrangères* (2 vols, 1880).

DE MOIVRE, Abraham (1667–1754) French mathematician, born in Vitry, in Champagne. A Protestant, he came to England in about 1686, after the revocation of the Edict of Nantes, and supported himself by teaching. **Newton**'s *Principia* whetted his devotion to mathematics and he became known to the leading mathematicians of his time. In 1697 he was elected an FRS and helped to decide the famous contest between Newton and **Leibniz** on the origins of the calculus. His principal work is *The Doctrine of Chances* (1718) on probability theory, but he is best remembered for the fundamental formula on complex numbers known as De Moivre's theorem.

DE MORGAN, Augustus (1806–71) English mathematician, born in Madura, Madras Presidency, the son of an Indian army colonel. Educated at several English private schools, he 'read algebra like a novel', went up to Trinity College, Cambridge, where he graduated fourth wrangler (1827), and in 1828 became first professor of mathematics in University College, London. In 1831 he resigned this office, but resumed it from 1836 to 1866. He was one of the founders of the London Mathematical Society and its first president in 1865. He wrote a number of mathematical text books, but his most important work was in symbolic logic. He also had a deep knowledge of the history of mathematics and contributed 850 articles to the *Penny Cyclopaedia*.

DE MORGAN, William Frend (1839–1917) English Pre-Raphaelite ceramic artist and novelist, son of **Augustus De Morgan**, born in London. He studied art at the Academy Schools, and started as a designer of tiles and stained glass, but became interested in pottery, and in 1871 established a kiln in Chelsea, where he turned out glazed ware in beautiful blues and greens. These won much praise in artistic circles but made little money. In 1905 he abandoned pottery and, at the age of 65, he began writing novels in a whimsical Dickensian manner, like *Joseph Vance* (1906), *Alice-for-Short* (1907) and *Somehow Good* (1908). His wife, Evelyn Pickering (1855–1919), whom he married in 1887, was a Pre-Raphaelite painter.

DEMOSTHENES (d.413 BC) Athenian soldier. During the Peloponnesian Wars (431–404) he captured Anacterium (425) and helped assist **Cleon** to reduce Sphacteria, but failed to conquer Boeotia in 424. In 413, having been sent to Sicily to the relief of **Nicias**, he was captured by the Syracusans during a brave rearguard action and was put to death.

DEMOSTHENES (384–322 BC) Athenian orator and statesman, the greatest of the Greek orators, born in Athens. He lost his father (a cutler) at the age of seven, but the fortune bequeathed to him was reduced by the neglect or fraud of his guardians; when he came of age he prosecuted them, and gained his cause, but most of his inheritance was irretrievably lost. This litigation compelled Demosthenes to the study of the law, and to the pursuit of it as a livelihood. Up to the age of 30 he confined himself to 'speechwriting', and gained repute as a constitutional lawyer. His most famous constitutional law speech was delivered personally in support of Ctesippus against Leptines (354). He now made his first appearance as a politician, but continued to practise as a speechwriter until he was 40, by which time he had made a fortune that allowed him to devote himself exclusively to politics. At the beginning of his political career danger threatened Greece from **Philip II** of Macedon; Demosthenes from the outset advocated a policy which might have saved Athens and Greece. Intelligent as was the Athenian democracy, it was only when events justified Demosthenes that his policy was adopted. Philip's attack on the state of Olynthus gave occasion to the *Olynthiacs* (349), which, with the orations against Philip, the *Philippics* (351, 334 and 341), are Demosthenes' greatest speeches. Athens made war with Philip on behalf of Olynthus; but, having failed to save the city, found peace expedient. From 346 to 340 Demosthenes was engaged in forming an anti-Macedonian party and in indicting **Aeschines** for betraying Athens. War broke out again in 340, and ended in the fatal battle of Chaeronea (338). Athens did not withdraw her confidence from Demosthenes; but the Macedonian party siezed on a proposal to present him with a public crown as an occasion for his political destruction. The trial was held in 330, when in the famous speech *On the Crown* Demosthenes gloriously vindicated himself against Aeschines. In 324 Harpalus, the treasurer of **Alexander the Great**, absconded to Athens with an enormous sum of money. It was placed in the state treasury, under the care of Demosthenes and others, and when Alexander demanded it, half was missing. Demosthenes was accused and condemned, but escaped from prison into exile. In 323 Alexander died, and Demosthenes was recalled to head a fruitless attempt to throw off the Macedonian yoke. The battle of Crannon ended the revolt, Demosthenes fled the island of Calaureia under sentence of death from **Demades**, and there took poison to avoid being captured alive.

DEMPSEY, Jack (William Harrison) (1895–1983) American boxer and world heavyweight champion, born in Manassa, Colorado (hence his nickname of 'The Manassa Mauler'). He worked in copper mines before taking to the ring as 'Kid Blackie' in 1914. In 1919 he defeated Jess Willard to win the world heavyweight title, which he lost to **Gene Tunney** in 1926. In a re-match the following year, Tunney was saved by a 'long count' after a knock-down, and went on to win the fight on points. Dempsey retired from the ring in 1940 and became a successful restaurateur on Broadway in New York.

DEMPSTER, Thomas (c.1579–1625) Scottish scholar and poet, born in Aberdeenshire. Educated at Turriff, Aberdeen, Cambridge, Paris, Louvain, Rome and Douai, he held several provincial professorships, and was a professor at Paris for seven years. He was a skilled swordsman, but unruly of temper, and a brawl with his students drove him to England. He married a beautiful wife there, and then, finding his Catholicism a bar to preferment, returned to the continent, where he obtained a professorship at Pisa in 1616. His wife's infidelities marred his peace of mind, and he removed to Bologna where he became professor of humanities, and where he died. His not too veracious autobiography forms part of his *Historia Ecclesiastica Gentis Scotorum* (1627)—an erudite work in which, however, his desire to magnify his country often led him to forge the names of persons and books that never existed, and to claim as Scotsmen writers whose birthplace was doubtful.

DEMUTH, Charles (1883–1935) American painter and book illustrator, born in Lancaster, Pennsylvania. He studied at the Pennsylvania Academy of the Fine

Arts. From 1912 to 1914 he was in Paris where he met **Gertrude Stein** and saw the work of the early Cubists whose ideas he took back to America. From 1919 he was a major exponent of 'Precisionism', with its hard outlines and semi-abstract treatment of industrial or urban scenery, as seen in *My Egypt* (1927), a view of grain elevators.

DENCH, Dame Judi, originally **Judith Olivia Dench** (1934–) English actress, born in York. A student at the Central School of Speech Training and Dramatic Art, she made her stage début as Ophelia in *Hamlet* (1957) in Liverpool. A member of the Old Vic Company from 1957 to 1961, she matured into one of Britain's most distinguished classical actresses, appearing with all of the most prestigious theatre companies where her distinctive voice, feline features and versatility have brought warmth and emotional veracity to a kaleidoscope of characters from the sensual to the homely. A selection of her numerous stage appearances includes *Macbeth* (1963), *Cabaret* (1968), *The Good Companions* (1974), *Mother Courage* (1984), and *Antony and Cleopatra* (1987). Her television credits encompass many individual plays and the popular situation comedy *A Fine Romance* (1981–84) in which she co-starred with Michael Williams (1935–), her husband since 1971. She made her film début in *The Third Secret* (1964) and is only now a regular film performer with incisive character parts in *A Room With a View* (1985), *A Handful of Dust* (1987) and *Henry V* (1989). She was created DBE in 1988 and made her directorial début in the same year with a production of *Much Ado About Nothing*.

DENCK, Hans (c.1495–c.1527) German Anabaptist theologian, born in Habach, Bavaria. He became rector of the Sebaldusschule in Nuremberg in 1523. From 1524 he preached a doctrine resembling Evangelical Quakerism in various parts of Germany, and in 1525 was expelled from the school, whereupon he became a leader of the Anabaptists in Augsburg. He wrote a commentary on the book of Micah (1531) and other learned works.

DENEUVE, Cathérine, originally **Cathérine Dorléac** (1943–) French actress, born in Paris. Part of a theatrical family, she made her film début in *Les Collégiennes* (1956) and was occasionally cast as the sister of her real-life sister, actress Françoise Dorléac (1941–67). Her own career took off with the unexpected popularity of the musical *Les Parapluies de Cherbourg* (1964). Stunningly beautiful, her remoteness and image of exterior calm concealing passion or intrigue were seen to great effect as a psychopath in *Repulsion* (1965) and a bourgeois housewife turned prostitute in *Belle de Jour* (1967). Established as a major star, her other successes include *Tristana* (1970), *Le Sauvage* (1975) and *Le Dernier Métro* (1980). She has also made selective appearances in English language productions like *April Fools* (1969) and *Hustle* (1975). Married to the photographer **David Bailey** from 1965 to 1970, she has a child by director Roger Vadim (1963) and another by actor **Marcello Mastroianni** (1972).

DENG XIAOPING, (old style **Teng Hsiao-ping),** (1904–) Chinese Communist politician. Born in Sichuan province into a middle-class landlord family, he joined the Chinese Communist party (CCP) in 1925 as a student in Paris, where he met a fellow-student, **Zhou Enlai**, and adopted the name Xiaoping, 'Little Peace'. He later studied in Moscow (1926), took part in the 1934–36 Long March and served as a political commissar to the People's Liberation Army (PLA) during the civil war (1937–49). He entered the CCP politburo in 1955 and headed the secretariat during the early 1960s, working closely with President **Liu Shaoqi**. During the 1966–69 Cultural Revolution he was branded a 'capitalist roader' and sent for 're-education' in a tractor factory in Nanchang, but was rehabilitated by his patron Zhou Enlai in 1973, becoming vice-premier. When Zhou died in 1976 he was again forced into hiding, but following popular protests he was reinstated in 1977 and by December 1978, although nominally only a CCP vice-chairman, state vice-premier and chief-of-staff to the PLA, had become the controlling force in China. Working with his protégés **Hu Yaobang** and **Zhao Ziyang** he proceeded to introduce a pragmatic new economic modernization programme. Despite retiring from the politburo in 1987, he remained influential, serving as the nation's 'paramount leader'. He attempted to create a 'socialism with Chinese characteristics', but his reputation was tarnished by his sanctioning of the army's massacre of more than 2000 unarmed pro-democracy demonstrators in Tiananmen Square, Beijing, in June 1989.

DENHAM, Dixon (1786–1828) English traveller in Africa, born in London. The comrade of **Hugh Clapperton** he reached Lake Chad in 1823 and explored in Sudan. He was appointed lieutenant-governor of Sudan in 1827.

DENHAM, Sir John (1615–69) Irish poet, born in Dublin, the only son of an Irish judge of English birth. He was educated in London and at Trinity College, Oxford. He studied law at Lincoln's Inn, and was called to the bar in 1639. At the outbreak of the Civil War he was high-sheriff of Surrey, and immediately joined the king. He fell into Sir **William Waller**'s hands on the capture of Farnham Castle, and was sent as a prisoner to London, but he was soon freed and went to Oxford. In 1641 he produced *The Sophy*, a historical tragedy of the Turkish court which was performed to great applause at Blackfriars; and in 1642 he published a long poem, *Cooper's Hill*, a topographical description of the scenery around Egham, which **Pope** imitated in his *Windsor Forest*. In 1648, being discovered in the performance of secret services for **Charles I**, he fled to Holland and France. In 1650 he collected money for the young king **Charles II** from the Scots resident in Poland, and several times visited England on secret service. At the Restoration he was appointed surveyor-general of works, and in 1661 created a Knight of the Bath. He was a better poet than architect, but he had **Christopher Wren** as his deputy. He was buried in Poet's Corner in Westminster Abbey.

DENIFLE, Heinrich Seuse (1844–1905) Austrian Catholic historian, born in Tirol. A Dominican, he became assistant archivist at the Vatican. He compiled the *Chartularium Universitatis Parisiensis* (6 vols, 1889–97), and wrote *Geschichte der Universitäten im Mittelalter*, *Luther und Luthertum*, and other works.

DENIKIN, Anton Ivanovich (1872–1947) Russian soldier. He entered the army at the age of 15, and rose to lieutenant general in World War I. After the Revolution of 1917 he led the White Army in the south against the Bolsheviks (1918–20). He won the Ukraine, but was defeated by the Red Army at Orel (1919), and in 1920 resigned his command and escaped to Constantinople. Thereafter he lived in exile in France (1926–45) and the USA (1945–47), and wrote books on his military experiences.

DE NIRO, Robert (1943–) American actor, born in New York City. A student of acting with Stella Adler and **Lee Strasberg**, he worked off-Broadway before making his film début as an extra in *Trois Chambres à Manhattan* (1965). Supporting roles followed, including the critically acclaimed *Bang the Drum Slowly* (1973) and *The Godfather, Part II* (1974) for which he received an Academy Award. Graduating to leading man status, he has become noted for his chameleon-like versatility and an obsessive quest for authenticity in his characterizations. His many films include *Taxi Driver* (1976), *The Deerhunter* (1978), *King of Comedy* (1982) and *Midnight Run* (1988). He received a further Academy Award for his portrayal of boxer Jake La Motta in *Raging Bull* (1980).

DENIS, St, properly **Dionysius** (d.c.250) patron saint of France. An Italian by birth he was, according to tradition, sent from Rome about 250 to preach the gospel to the Gauls, and became the first bishop of Paris. Under the persecutions of the emperor **Valerian** he was beheaded on Montmartre ('Martyrs' Hill'). Later his legend was confused with that of **Dionysius the Areopagite**, and he was supposed to have carried his own head to his burial place, the site of the abbey church of Saint-Denys. His feast day is 9 October.

DENIS, Maurice (1870–1943) French artist and art theorist, born in Grandville. He was one of the original group of Symbolist painters, and then the Nabis ('prophets'), influenced by **Gauguin**. Some of his comments on the aesthetics of the modern movement have obtained a wide currency. He wrote *Théories* (1913), *Nouvelles théories* (1921), *Histoire de l'art religieux* (1939) and a study of *Sérusier* (1942). He executed some huge murals for the Théâtre des Champs Élysées and the Petit Palace. In 1919 he founded, with Desvalliéres, the Studios of Sacred Art, devoted to the revival of religious painting, but perhaps his most famous picture is the *Hommage à Cézanne* (1900), in the Musée d'Art Moderne, Paris.

DENISON, Edmund Beckett See **GRIMTHORPE**

DENMAN, Thomas, 1st Baron (1779–1854) English jurist, born in London. Educated at Eton and St John's College, Cambridge, he entered Lincoln's Inn in 1806. With **Henry Brougham** he defended Queen **Caroline** (1820), and shared his consequent popularity. He was Whig MP for Wareham and Nottingham, 1818–26, and was attorney-general in Earl **Grey**'s administration from 1830 to 1832. He became lord chief-justice in 1832, and was raised to the peerage in 1834. He retired from the bench in 1850.

DENMAN, Thomas 3rd Baron (1874–1954) succeeded in 1894, and was governor-general of Australia from 1911 to 1914.

DENNERY, Adolphe Philippe (1811–99) French playwright, born in Paris. He was clerk to a notary, but from 1831 produced 133 dramas, vaudevilles and plays, the most successful being *Marie Jeanne* (1845). He also wrote the libretti for **Gounod**'s *Le Tribut de Zamora* (1881) and **Massenet**'s *Le Cid* (1885). He was the creator of the Norman watering-place, Cabourg.

DENNESS, Michael (1940–) Scottish cricketer, born in Bellshill, Lanarkshire. Having learned his cricket in Scotland, he went on to captain Kent and England. In his first-class career he made over 25000 runs and hit four Test centuries. With K R Fletcher of Essex he holds the Test record for a fourth wicket partnership of 266 against New Zealand, at Auckland in 1974–75.

DENNING, Alfred Thompson, Baron of Whitchurch (1899–) English judge. Educated at Andover Grammar School and Magdalen College, Oxford, he was called to the bar in 1923, became a KC in 1938, and a judge of the High Court of Justice in 1944, a lord justice of appeal in 1948, lord of appeal in ordinary, 1957 and master of the rolls 1962–82. In 1963 he held the inquiry into the circumstances of **John Profumo**'s resignation as secretary of state for war. As master of the rolls he showed a profound regard for justice but was responsible for many controversial decisions. Among his many legal publications are *The Road to Justice* (1955), *The Discipline of Law* (1979), *What Next in the Law* (1982), and several autobiographical books.

DENNIS, John (1657–1734) English critic and playwright, born in London. He was educated at Harrow and Caius College, Cambridge. After a tour through France and Italy, he took his place among the wits and men of fashion, and produced biting criticism to support the Whigs. He wrote nine plays, but had little success with them, including a satire, *A Plot and No Plot* (1697), and *Rinaldo and Armida* (1699). **Pope**'s *Essay on Criticism* (1711) contained a contemptuous allusion to another play, *Appius and Virginia* (1709), answered by Dennis the next month in *Reflections Critical and Satirical*, which commenced a long feud. Among his critical works are *The Grounds of Criticism in Poetry* (1704) and *An Essay on the Genius and Writings of Shakespeare* (1712).

DENNY-BROWN, Derek Ernest (1901–81) New Zealand-born American neurologist, born in Christchurch. He received his early medical training at the University of New Zealand and then went on a Beit Fellowship to Oxford, where he worked with **Charles Sherrington**. After clinical work in London, and a brief spell as consultant neurologist at St Bartholomew's Hospital, he went to Harvard in 1941, where he remained. He was equally at home in the laboratory or at the bedside, and was particularly interested in the diseases of the basal ganglia and of the muscles.

DENT, Edward Joseph (1876–1957) English musician, born in Yorkshire. Professor of music at Cambridge, 1926–41, he made translations of many libretti, and wrote an opera, and lives of **Scarlatti**, **Busoni** and **Handel**. In 1923 he helped to found the International Society for Contemporary Music.

DENT, Joseph Mallaby (1849–1926) English publisher. He worked as a book binder in London before opening his own bookbinding business in 1892. In 1888 he founded the publishing house of J M Dent & Sons, which brought out the pocket-sized *Temple Classics* from 1893, and also *Everyman's Library* from 1904.

DENTATUS, Manius Curius (d.270 BC) Roman general, famed for his noble simplicity. Between 290 and 274 BC he defeated the Samnites and Sabines, **Pyrrhus**, and the Lucanians.

DEPARDIEU, Gérard (1948–) French actor, born in Châteauroux. An unruly child, he was encouraged to enter dramatics as a therapy and made his film début in *Le Beatnik et le minet* (1965). He continued in occasional film roles whilst appearing on stage and television, including the series *L'Inconnu* (1974). In the cinema his lumbering giant's physique and peasant's looks were seen in an increasing variety of roles as he gained a reputation as one of the busiest and most skilled actors of his generation. Able to combine strength and gentleness, his many notable films include *Le Dernier Métro* (1980), *Danton* (1982), *Le Retour de Martin Guerre* (1982), *Jean De Florette* (1986) and *Sous Le Soleil de Satan* (1987). He also directed *Le Tartuffe* (1984).

DE QUINCEY, Thomas (1785–1859) English critic and essayist, born in Manchester, the son of a merchant. He was educated at Manchester Grammar School, where he proved an apt pupil. In 1802 he ran away from school and wandered in Wales, and then to London, where he lived with a young prostitute called Ann. (He described this episode in his *Confessions of an English Opium-eater*, 1822.) Reclaimed from this wandering he spent a short time at Worcester College, Oxford. It was here that he became addicted to opium. A visit to his mother in Bath brought him into contact with **Coleridge**, then resident in Bristol, and through him with **Southey** and **Wordsworth**. When these poets settled at the Lakes. De Quincey visited them there and, after a brief sojourn in London (which enabled him to make the acquaintance of **Lamb**, **Hazlitt** and others of the 'Cockney' school), he went to stay in Grasmere in 1809. In 1816 he married Margaret Simpson, by whom he had three daughters and five sons, two of the latter distinguishing themselves as soldiers. De Quincey now set up as an author. Except for *The Logic of Political Economy* (1841) and an unsuccessful novel, his whole literary output, including the *Confessions*, consisted of magazine articles. The *Confessions* appeared as a serial in *The London Magazine*, 1821, and at once made him famous. Visits to London varied his existence at the Lakes, but in 1828 the lure of the Edinburgh literary scene drew him to the northern capital, where he lived and worked till his death in 1859. For 20 years he lent distinction to *Blackwood's Magazine*, *Tait's Magazine* and, occasionally, *The Quarterly*, with articles like *Murder Considered as one of the Fine Arts* (1827), *Lake Reminiscences* (1834–40), the fantasies *Suspiria De Profundis* (1845) and *Levana and Our Ladies of Sorrows* (1845), and the 'Dream Fugue' at the end of *The English Mail-Coach*, and *Vision of Sudden Death* (1849).

DERAIN, André (1880–1954) French artist, born in Chatou. He is most famous for his Fauve pictures, executed from 1904 to 1908, when he was associated with **Vlaminck** and **Matisse**. Later landscape pictures show a romantic realism influenced by **Cézanne**. He also designed for the theatre (notably the **Diaghilev** ballet) and illustrated several books.

DERBY, Earl of a title conferred in 1485 by **Henry VII** on Thomas, second Lord Stanley two months after Bosworth Field, where he had contributed to the victory of Richmond (later **Henry VII**) by withdrawing his promised support for **Richard III**. The Stanleys were descended from Adam de Aldithley, who attended Duke **William** to England in 1066, and whose grandson, having married the heiress of Thomas Stanley, of Stafford, exchanged the manor of Thalk in that county, his wife's marriage portion, for Stoneley, in Derbyshire, and assumed the surname of Stanley. In 1405 Sir John Stanley, who had married the heiress of Lathom, got a grant of the Isle of Man, which he and his descendants ruled till 1736.

DERBY, Edward Geoffrey Smith Stanley, 14th Earl (1799–1869) English statesman, born at Knowsley Hall, Lancashire. He was educated at Eton and Christ Church College, Oxford and entered parliament for Stockbridge in 1820. In 1830 he became chief-secretary for Ireland and in 1833 colonial secretary. In this capacity he carried the emancipation of West Indian slaves. In 1831 he seceded from the Whigs and, declining to join the **Peel** administration, he and his supporters, dubbed Stanleyites, maintained an independent position. In 1844 he resigned his Commons seat and went to the Lords as Baron Stanley of Bickerstaffe. When Peel attempted to repeal the Corn Laws, Stanley headed the Protectionists in the Upper House, and was seen as Conservative leader. In 1851 he succeeded his father as Earl Derby and became prime minister for a brief period. He returned as premier in 1858, but resigned the following year on a vote of confidence. Returning to power in 1866, he passed the Reform Act of 1867 in conjunction with **Disraeli**, to whom he passed the premiership in 1868. He was an accomplished scholar and an excellent parliamentary speaker.

DERBY, Edward Henry Smith Stanley, 15th Earl, (1826–93) eldest son of the 14th Earl of **Derby**, born at Knowsley Hall, and educated at Rugby and Trinity College, Cambridge. In 1848 he became MP for Lynn, and in 1852 was appointed foreign under-secretary in his father's first ministry. After declining to join **Palmerston**'s ministry in 1855, he became secretary for India in his father's second administration (1858–59), and carried the measure transferring the government of India to the Crown. He was foreign secretary in the third Derby and first **Disraeli** ministries (1866–68). In 1874 he again became foreign secretary under Disraeli; but resigned in March 1878 when the majority of the Cabinet determined to support Turkey by occupying Cyprus. In 1880 he definitely joined the Liberal party, and was colonial secretary (1882–85), but seceded on Home Rule.

DERBY, James, 7th Earl (1606–51) English soldier, known as the 'Great Earl of Derby'. He fought on the Royalist side throughout the Civil War. After the battle of Worcester in 1651, he helped **Charles II** to make his escape but was himself captured by the Parliamentary forces and beheaded at Bolton. His countess, Charlotte de la Trémouille (d.1663), is famous for her heroic defence of Lathom House (1644) and of the Isle of Man (1651).

DERÈME, Tristan, pseud of **Phillippe Huc** (1889–1941) French poet of the *fantaisiste* school. His works include *La Verdure dorée* (1922, incorporating eight previous collections of poems), and *L'Enlèvement sans clair de lune* (1924).

DERINGER, Henry (19th century) American manufacturer of small arms, born in Easton, Philadelphia. He supplied rifles to the US army, and in 1852 invented the pocket pistol known as a 'der(r)inger'.

DERNESCH, Helga (1939–) Austrian operatic soprano, born in Vienna, where she studied at the Conservatory. She made her début in Berne (1961) and at Covent Garden in 1970. She has sung throughout Europe and the USA, and is specially noted for her portrayals of **Wagner**, **Strauss** and the modern German repertory. Since 1979 she has sung mezzo-soprano roles.

DE ROBURT, Hammer (1923–) Nauruan politician. Educated at Nauru Secondary School and Geelong Technical College in Victoria, Australia, he worked as a teacher in Nauru from 1940 but was deported to Japan in 1942 after the country's occupation. After his release in 1946, he worked as an education liaison officer and teacher. He became head chief of Nauru in 1956 and was elected the country's first president in 1968. Apart from brief breaks (1976–78 and 1986), he remained president until August 1989, when he was ousted on a no-confidence motion and replaced by Kenas Aroi who is, allegedly, his 'unacknowledged natural son'.

DE ROS, Georgiana, Lady (1795–1891) daughter of the Duke of Richmond, in 1824 she married William, Lord de Ros (1797–1874). A friend of the Duke of **Wellington**, she knew 19 prime ministers.

DE ROSSI, Giovanni Battista See **ROSSI**

DÉROULÈDE, Paul (1846–1914) French politician and poet, born in Paris. A fervid nationalist, and the author of patriotic verses, his writings called for revenge on Germany, and he was active in the campaign against **Dreyfus**. In 1900 he was exiled for ten years for sedition, but returned in 1905.

DEROZIO, Henry Louis Vivian (1809–31) Eurasian poet and patriot, born in Calcutta. At 19 he had published two books of poems and was lecturing on English history and literature at the Hindu College, Calcutta. In the next four years he had translated **de Maupertuis**, lectured on philosophy, written a critique on **Kant** and edited four journals. He became involved in local politics, and instigated so much freethinking and social rebelliousness that he was dismissed from the College a few months before he died. Much of his verse is imitatively ornamental, but some of his sonnets put him among the lesser Romantics.

DERRIDA, Jacques (1930–) French philosopher, born in El Biar, Algiers. He studied in Paris and taught at the École Normale Supérieure from 1965. In 1967 he published three influential books on language and meaning: *La Voix et le phénomène*, *De la Grammatologie* and *L'Écriture et le différence*. His later publications include *Marges de la philosophie* (1972), *La Dissémination* (1972), *La Vérité en peinture* (1978) and *La Carte Postale* (1980). His work is highly original, often controversial and at times obscure, but has attracted great interest from a wide range of intellectuals and academics in the English-speaking world, spanning literary criticism, psychoanalysis and linguistics as well as philosophy. He stresses the primacy of the written over the spoken text ('there is nothing outside the text') and recommends a strategy of interpretation called 'deconstruction', which has consequently become a fashionable technique in many disciplines.

DE RUYTER, Michiel Adrianszoon See **RUYTER**

DERWENTWATER, James Radcliffe, 3rd Earl of (1689–1716) English Jacobite, born in London, and brought up in St Germain, where he was a companion of Prince **James Edward Stewart**, the 'Old Pretender'. He succeeded as 3rd earl in 1705, on the death of his father, who had married Lady Mary Tudor, **Charles II**'s daughter by Moll Davis. In 1715, at the time of the Jacobite Rising, warrants were issued against several gentlemen in the north, one of them against the young Catholic earl; but he fled from Dilston, his seat in Northumberland, and soon placed himself at the head of a few retainers. From this point the history of the earl becomes the history of the Rebellion which ended in the disastrous encounter at Preston. Derwentwater bore himself with heroism, but, with most of the rebel leaders, was taken prisoner, and conveyed to the Tower. At his trial for high treason at Westminster Hall he pleaded guilty, and threw himself on the king's mercy. Every effort for a pardon failed, and he was beheaded on Tower Hill.

DERZHAVIN, Gavril Romanovich (1743–1816) Russian poet, born in Kazan. In 1762 he entered the army as a private. His poetry is almost entirely lyrical, highly imaginative, and marks him as one of Russia's most original poets. His talents soon gained him promotion. In 1791 he became secretary of state, in 1800 imperial treasurer, and in 1802 minister of justice. He published much lyric poetry, and is considered one of Russia's greatest poets.

DES PÉRIERS, Bonaventure (c.1500–1544) French writer, born in Autun. He was a member of the court of men of letters assembled by **Margaret of Navarre**. In a dialogue, *Cymbalum mundi* (1537), under the pretence of attacking the superstitions of the ancients, he satirized the religious beliefs of his own day. The book raised a storm of indignation, against which Margaret was powerless to shield him; and rather than fall into the hands of his persecutors he is said to have killed himself. His *Nouvelles Récréations et joyeux devis* (1558) consists of 129 short stories, both comic and romantic. Des Périers has often been attributed with the chief authorship of Margaret's *Heptameron*.

DES PRES, Josquin (c.1440–1521) Franco-Flemish composer, born probably in Condé, where he died. Possibly a pupil of **Okeghem**, he was composer to the Sforza family in Milan and Rome, **Louis XII** of France and the Duke of Ferrara. A master of polyphony, he left a number of valuable masses, motets and secular vocal works. **Charles Burney** called him 'father of modern harmony'.

DESAGULIERS, John Theophilus (1683–1744) French-born British scientist and inventor, born in La Rochelle of Huguenot parents. Educated at Oxford, he became experimental assistant to Sir **Isaac Newton** and later lectured, wrote and performed experiments to popularize Newtonian theories and their practical applications. He proposed a scheme for heating vessels such as salt-boilers by steam instead of fire, and he improved the design of **Thomas Savery**'s steam engine by adding a safety valve and using an internal water jet to condense the steam in the displacement chambers.

DESAI, Anita, née **Mazumdar** (1937–) Indian novelist, born in Mussoorie, Uttar Pradesh, the daughter of a Bengali father and a German mother. Educated at Delhi University, her works include novels for adults and children and short stories. *Clear Light of Day* (1980) and *In Custody* (1980) were both short-listed for the Booker prize and *The Village by the Sea* won the Guardian award for children's fiction in 1982. Her most recent novel is *Baumgartner's Bombay* (1988), the grim story of a German expatriate washed up in India.

DESAI, Morarji Ranchhodji (1896–) Indian politician, born in Gujarat. Educated at Bombay University, Desai was a civil servant for twelve years before embarking on a long and varied political career. He joined congress in 1930, but was twice imprisoned as a supporter of **Mahatma Gandhi**'s Civil Disobedience campaign before becoming (1937–39) revenue minister in the Bombay government—his first official post. Desai was again imprisoned (1941–45), for his part in the 'Quit India' movement, before again serving as Bombay's revenue minister (1946) and later, home minister and chief minister (1952). Four years later, he entered central government, first as minister for commerce and industry (1956–58) then as finance minister, resigning in 1963 to devote himself to party work. He was a candidate for the premiership the following year, and again in 1966 when he was defeated by **Indira Gandhi**. Mrs Gandhi eventually invited him to become deputy premier and minister of finance, but Desai resigned two years later over differences with the premier. In 1974 he supported political agitation in Gujarat, and the following year he began a fast in an attempt to force Mrs Gandhi to order elections in the state. Desai was subsequently detained when a state of emergency was proclaimed. Soon after his release in 1977 he was appointed leader of the Janata party, a coalition opposed to Mrs Gandhi's rule, and Desai finally became prime minister after the elections that same year. The Janata government was, however, characterized by much internal strife, and Desai was forced to resign in 1979.

DESAIX DE VEYGOUX, Louis Charles Antoine (1768–1800) French soldier, born in St Hilaire-d'Ayat in Auvergne. He entered the army at 15, and in 1796 covered himself with glory in **Moreau**'s famous retreat through the Black Forest. Behind the ruinous fortress of Kehl he resisted the Austrians for two months, only capitulating, in 1797, when his ammunition was spent. His greatest achievement was the conquest of Upper Egypt, after an eight months' campaign (1799). He was killed in action in the battle of Marengo.

DESALVO, Albert (d.1973) convicted American sex offender. After his arrest in late 1964 for sex attacks on women in their homes, DeSalvo confessed to a psychiatrist that he was the Boston Strangler who had murdered and sexually assaulted 13 women between 1962 and 1964 in Boston. He was never tried for the murders, because under Massachusetts law a doctor who receives information from a suspect cannot use it as evidence. His defence lawyer, **Francis Lee Bailey**, claimed that he made another confession in July 1965 after an agreement that conversations with him would not be used in court. He was sentenced to life imprisonment for his other crimes. In November 1973 he was found stabbed to death in his cell in Walpole Prison, Massachusetts.

DESANI, Govindas Vishnoodas (1909–) African-born American novelist, born in Nairobi, Kenya. He went to Britain in 1926 and from 1928 was a correspondent for the *Times of India*, Reuters, and Associated Press. In the late 1930s he was a lecturer on antiquities for Bombay Baroda and Central India Railway and later lectured in England before becoming a broadcaster during World War II. From 1952 to 1966, pursuing a dual interest in yoga and meditation, he visited Buddhist and Hindu monasteries. Throughout the 1960s he filed a provocative column with the *Illustrated Weekly for India*. He has been an American citizen since 1979. His prose-poem *Hali* (1950) and some uncollected stories notwithstanding, his claim to posterity is dependent on *All About H. Hatterr* (1948). It reprinted the week after publication, then was neglected for several decades before being resurrected as a modern classic and placed on a pedestal alongside **Joyce** and **Flann O'Brien**.

DESARGUES, Girard (1591–1661) French mathematician, born in Lyons. By 1626 he was in Paris, and took part as an engineer in the siege of La Rochelle in 1628. He founded the use of projective methods in geometry, inspired by the theory of perspective in art, and introduced the notion that parallel lines 'meet at a point at infinity'. From 1645 he began a new career as an architect in Paris and Lyons.

DÉSAUGIERS, Marc (1772–1827) French composer and writer of songs and vaudeville plays, born in Fréjus, son of the composer Marc Antoine Desaugiers (1742–93). He lived in Paris from 1797 after adventurous years in San Domingo and elsewhere. He was director of the Théâtre du Vaudeville in Paris from 1815.

DESAULT, Pierre Joseph (1738–95) French surgeon and anatomist. He founded the first school of clinical surgery in France.

DESBARRES, Joseph Frederick Wallet (1722–1824) English military engineer of Huguenot parentage. At the siege of Quebec (1759) he was aide-de-camp to **Wolfe**. He surveyed the coast of Nova Scotia from 1763 to 1773; was lieutenant-governor of Cape Breton (1784–1805) and Prince Edward Island (1805–13). He died at Halifax, Nova Scotia, at the age of 102.

DESCARTES, René (1596–1650) French philosopher and mathematician, undoubtedly one of the great figures in the history of Western thought and usually regarded as the father of modern philosophy. He was born near Tours in a small town now called la-Haye-Descartes, and was educated from 1604 to 1614 at the Jesuit College at La Flèche. He did in fact remain a Catholic all his life, and he was careful to modify or even suppress some of his later scientific views, for example his sympathy with **Copernicus**, mindful no doubt of **Galilei**'s condemnation by the Inquisition in 1634. He studied law at Poitiers, graduating in 1616; then from 1618 he enlisted at his own expense for private military service, mainly in order to travel and to have the leisure to think. He was in Germany with the army of the Duke of Bavaria one winter's day in 1619 when he had his famous intellectual vision in the 'stove-heated room': he conceived a reconstruction of the whole of philosophy, and indeed of knowledge, into a unified system of certain truth modelled on mathematics and supported by a rigorous rationalism. From 1618 to 1628 he travelled widely in Holland, Germany, France and Italy; then in 1628 returned to Holland where he remained, living quietly and writing until 1649. Few details are known of his personal life, but he did have an illegitimate daughter called Francine, whose death in 1640 at the age of five was apparently a terrible blow for him. He published most of his major works in this period, the more popular ones in French, the more scholarly ones first in Latin. The *Discourse de la Méthode* (1637), the *Meditationes de prima Philosophia* (1641) and the *Principia Philosophiae* (1644) set out the fundamental Cartesian doctrines: the method of systematic doubt; the first indubitably true proposition, *cogito ergo sum*; the idea of god as the absolutely perfect Being; and the dualism of mind and matter. Other philosophical works include *Regulae ad directionem ingenii* (composed in the later 1620s, but unfinished and published posthumously in 1701) and *Les Passions de l'âme* (1649). He also made important contributions in astronomy, for example with his theory of vortices, and more especially in mathematics, where he reformed algebraic notation and helped found co-ordinate geometry. In 1649 he left Holland for Stockholm on the invitation of Queen **Kristina** who wanted him to give her tuition in philosophy. These lessons took place three times a week at 5 am and were especially taxing for Descartes whose habit of a lifetime was to stay in bed meditating and reading until about 11 am. He contracted pneumonia and died. His last words were supposedly *Ça mon âme, il faut partir* ('So my soul a time for parting'). He was buried in Stockholm but his body was later removed to Paris and eventually transferred to Saint-Germain-des-Prés.

DESCHAMPS, Eustache, called **Morel** (c.1345–c.1406) French poet, born in Vertus in Champagne. He was brought up by **Machaut**, who may have been his uncle and who probably taught him his craft. A soldier, a magistrate, a court favourite and a traveller in Italy and Hungary, he held important posts in Champagne, but after his patron, **Charles V**, died, his possessions were ravaged by the English. He composed 1175 lyrics, besides *Le Miroir de mariage*, a long poem satirizing women, and several poems in the current fashion, deploring the miseries of the Hundred Years' War.

DE SICA, Vittorio (1902–74) Italian filmmaker, born in Sora. A graduate of Rome University, he began in the film industry as an actor, making his début in *Il Processo Clémenceau* (1918). Appearing with a variety of theatre companies he also became a matinée film idol in the 1930s before turning to direction. In the immediate post-war years he was at the forefront of the neo-realist movement, depicting the social problems of battle-ravaged Italy with compassion and sensitivity in films like *Sciuscia* (Shoeshine, 1949), *Ladri di Biciclette* (Bicycle Thieves, 1948) and *Umberto D* (1952). Later films tended to be more lighthearted although *La Ciociara* (Two Women, 1960) and *Il Giardino dei Finzi Contini* (The Garden of the Finzi Continis, 1970) recalled the impact of earlier triumphs. An avuncular character actor, he also played minor roles in scores of international productions.

DESIDERIO DA SETTIGNANO (1428–64) Florentine sculptor in the early Renaissance style, born in Settignano near Florence and influenced by **Donatello** and **Della Robbia**.

DESMARETS, Jean, Sieur de Saint-Sorlen (1596–1676) French writer. A protégé of **Richelieu**, he was the author of many volumes of poetry and critical works, notably *Comparaison de la langue et la poésie* *française avec la grecque et la latine* (1670). He was the first chancellor and co-founder of the Académie française, and a protagonist in the ancients versus moderns controversy.

DESMOND, Earl of a title conferred in 1329 on Maurice Fitzgerald along with County Kerry, and last borne by Gerald Fitzgerald, 15th Earl, who in 1579–80 rebelled against Queen **Elizabeth**, sacked Youghal by night and was proclaimed a traitor. He escaped the fate of the garrison at Smerwick, but was driven at last from his strongholds, wandered about for over two years, and was killed (1583) in a cabin in the Kerry mountains.

DESMOULINS, Camille (1760–94) French revolutionary and journalist, born in Guise. He studied law along with **Robespierre** at the Collège Louis le Grand in Paris, but owing to a stutter never practised. His notions of classical republicanism found vent in his pamphlets, *La Philosophie du peuple français* (1788) and *La France libre* (1789), the latter published the day after the destruction of the Bastille, where he played a dramatic part. His *Discours de la Lanterne* procured him the sinister title of 'Procureur-général de la Lanterne'. In November 1789 he began the brilliantly witty, cruelly sarcastic *Révolutions de France et de Brabant* which appeared weekly until July 1792. His *Tribune des patriotes*, however, died in its fourth number. Desmoulins had been a member of the Cordeliers' Club from its foundation, and early clung to **Danton**. Elected by Paris to the National Convention, he voted for the death of the king. In the struggle between the Girondists and the Mountain he took an active part, and in May 1793, urged on by Robespierre, published his truculent *Histoire des Brissotins*. On 5 December he brought out the *Vieux Cordelier*, an eloquent expression of Desmoulins' and Danton's longing for clemency. Robespierre took fright at the reception of the third number, and soon became actively hostile. On 30 March 1794, Desmoulins was arrested with Danton; on 5 April he died by the guillotine. A fortnight later his beloved wife, Lucile Duplessis (1771–1794), whom he had married in 1790, followed him to the same doom.

DESPARD, Charlotte, née **French** (1844–1939) English social reformer, a sister of **John French** (1st Earl of Ypres). She was an advocate of women's rights, and Irish self determination. Her politics seriously embarrassed her brother during his viceroyalty of Ireland.

DESPARD, Edward Marcus (1751–1803) Irish conspirator, born in Queen's County, Ireland. At the age of 15 he obtained an ensigncy and from 1772 to 1790 did good service in the West Indies, but was then recalled on frivolous charges, proved (1792) to be baseless. His demands for compensation brought him two years' imprisonment (1798–1800). On his release he became involved in a crack-brained conspiracy to assassinate the king and to seize the Tower and Bank of England. For this, with six associates, he was drawn on a hurdle, hanged and beheaded.

DESPAUTERIUS, Johannes (c.1460–1520) Flemish scholar. He wrote a Latin grammar which was much used in Scotland before the Reformation.

DESPENCER, Lord le See **DASHWOOD, Sir Francis**

DESPENSER, Hugh (1262–1326) English baron. After the death of **Piers de Gaveston** (1312), he became chief adviser to **Edward I** but was banished with his son, Hugh (1321). Recalled the next year by **Edward II** he was created Earl of Winchester. After Queen **Isabella**'s landing in England in 1326 he was captured by the Queen's party and hanged at Bristol, as was his son at Hereford.

DESPIAU, Charles (1874–1946) French sculptor, born in Mont-de-Marsan. He was discovered by **Rodin**, who took him as a pupil. He is noted for his severely Neoclassical portrait busts.

DESPRÉAUX See **BOILEAU**

DESSALINES, Jean Jacques (c.1758–1806) emperor of Haiti, born in Guinea. Imported into Haiti as a slave, he was bought by a French planter, whose name he assumed, and in the slave revolt of 1791 was second only to **Toussaint L'Ouverture**. After the first compromise he became governor of the southern part of the island, but after the arrest of Toussaint in 1802 he renewed the war, and after infamous cruelties compelled the French to evacuate Haiti in October 1803. He was created governor in January 1804, and on 8 October was crowned emperor as Jean Jacques I. But his cruelty and debauchery soon alienated even his firmest adherents, and while trying to repress a revolt he was cut down by **Christophe**, who succeeded him.

DESSAU, Paul (1894–1979) German composer and conductor, born in Hamburg. After studies in Berlin, his career began as an opera coach. He conducted opera at Cologne from 1919, Mainz from 1923 and the Berlin State Opera from 1925. During the Nazi era he moved to Paris (1933) and the USA (1939). From 1942 he collaborated with **Brecht**, writing incidental music for *Mutter Courage* and other plays. Like Brecht, he settled in East Berlin in 1948, and produced the operas *Die Verurteilung des Lukullus* (text by Brecht), *Puntila* (text after Brecht), *Lanzelot* and *Einstein*. Dramatic qualities, constantly dazzling inventiveness and deep socialist commitment are also evident in his orchestral, choral and chamber works, and in his many songs.

DESTOUCHES, Philippe, originally **Néricault** (1680–1754) French playwright, born in Tours. He wrote 17 comedies, including *Le Philosophe marie* (1727) and *Le Glorieux*, his masterpiece (1732).

DETAILLE, Jean Baptiste Edouard (1848–1912) French battle painter of the school of Meissonier, born in Paris. He painted battle scenes while serving in the Franco-Russian war, also portraits, including *Edward VII and the Duke of Connaught*, in the Royal Collection.

DEUTSCHER, Isaac (1907–67) Polish-born British Marxist historian of Russia, born in Cracow. A journalist, he joined the Communist party in 1926 and edited Communist periodicals until his expulsion in 1932 for leading an anti-Stalinist opposition. He went to London in 1939, and worked on the editorial staff of *The Economist* (1942–49) and *The Observer* (1942–47), reporting extensively from Europe (1946–47). His *Stalin, a Political Biography* (1949) was a landmark in emancipating Marxists from Stalinophilia. His great biography of **Trotsky** appeared in three volumes: *The Prophet Armed* (1954), *The Prophet Unarmed* (1959), and *The Prophet Outcast* (1963). He was an inspirational essayist as shown in *Heretics and Renegades* (1955) and a fine independent critic of the Cold War as in *The Great Contest* (1960). A visiting professor at many US universities in the 1960s, he was prominent in the 'Teach-In' movement against the US's undeclared war in Vietnam. He also wrote *The Unfinished Revolution: Russia 1917–1967* (1967).

DE VALERA, Éamon (1882–1975) Irish statesman, born in Brooklyn, New York, of Spanish-Irish parentage. He was brought up in Bruree, County Limerick, by a labourer uncle, until he won scholarships to school and university-level education at Blackrock College, Dublin, after which he was a mathematics teacher. Taking up Irish, he joined the Gaelic League and married his teacher Sinéad Ni Flannagáin (subsequent author of delicate and enjoyable Gaelic fairy stories). Under the influence of **Thomas MacDonagh** he rose in the Irish Volunteers, leading his men into action in the Easter Rising of 1916, from which his sentence of execution after court-martial was commuted after intervention by the US consul. As senior survivor he was elected MP for East Clare after release from jail (1917), and became the symbolic focus of nationalist opposition to conscription (1918). Re-arrested he thus helped his Sinn Fein party to massive electoral victory (1918) and after a sensational escape he toured the USA as president of the Irish Republic (actually of Dáil Éireann, the secret assembly of Irish MPs refusing participation at Westminster), 1919–20. He drew in massive funds and moral support. Guerrilla warfare had exploded in Ireland without him and on his return he was believed a more moderate influence than **Michael Collins**, but ultimately Collins signed the Anglo-Irish Treaty of 1921 and met with de Valera's anger. Narrow victory for the Treaty in the Dáil caused de Valera's resignation as president. He played only a symbolic part in the anti-Treaty forces during the civil war (1922–23), but was ultimately imprisoned (1923–24) and in 1926 formed a Republican opposition party which entered the Irish Free State Dáil (1927), and which brought him to power there in 1932. He snapped most remaining links of constitutional dependence on Britain with consequent economic war, and produced and had ratified a new constitution (1937) under which his prime ministerial title was altered to taoiseach (to which he was re-elected until 1948, and then once more in 1951 and 1957). In international affairs he pursued neutrality, all the more because of anti-democratic threats from Right and Left. He served as head of state (president) from 1959 to 1973.

DE VERE, Aubrey Thomas (1814–1902) Irish poet, born in Curragh Chase, County Limerick, the son of Sir Aubrey De Vere (1788–1846). Educated at Trinity College, Dublin, he became a friend of **Newman**, **Wordsworth** and **Tennyson**. In addition to many volumes of poems he published poetical dramas on **Alexander the Great** (1874) and **Becket** (1876), *Essays on Poetry* (2 vols, 1887), and works on Irish ecclesiastical politics and literary criticism.

DEVEREUX See **ESSEX, Earl of**

DEVILLE See **SAINTE-CLAIRE DEVILLE**

DEVINE, George (1910–65) English stage director, administrator, teacher and actor. He began his career during the 1930s as an actor, and from 1936 to 1939 he taught at the London Theatre Studio. After World War II he was director of the Old Vic School. In 1956 he founded the English Stage Company, which took up residence at the Royal Court Theatre, London. With plays such as **John Osborne**'s *Look Back in Anger* and **John Arden**'s *Serjeant Musgrave's Dance*, he not only restored prestige to English theatre but set drama on a new course by encouraging the work of new writers. He made a return to acting in the year of his death: in Osborne's *A Patriot for Me* (1965). The George Devine Award, inaugurated in 1966, gives encouragement to young theatre practitioners.

DEVIS, Arthur (1711–87) English painter, born in Preston. By the 1740s he had settled in London and was painting small portraits and conversation pieces depicting, in fine detail, solidly middle-class patrons set within their own interiors or gardens. His brother Anthony (1729–1816) was a landscape painter, and his son, Arthur William (1762–1822), while in the service of the East India Company, produced paintings, which were engraved, of the arts and industry of Bengal.

DEVLIN, Bernadette See **McALISKEY**

DEVLIN, Joseph (1872–1934) Irish nationalist, born in Belfast, the son of poor parents. An Ulster Catholic constitutional nationalist politician and machine boss, he was educated by the Christian Brothers. He built up Belfast Catholic nationalism on ghetto lines of mutual favour-sharing with close clerical links, learning from the prevailing Protestant use of Masonic-style organizations so that his command over the local section of the international Ancient Order of Hibernians functioned on firm use of rewards and comrades. The disarray of Irish nationalist politics caused by the **Parnell** divorce split meant that Belfast, up till then an area where Home Rule politics were directed from Dublin as far as parliamentary hopes were concerned, was now made very much self-dependent. Devlin established good relations with the reunited Irish party under **John Redmond** and **John Dillon** to the extent of being made Nationalist MP for Kilkenny North (1902–06), but then captured and retained West Belfast. In the general election of 1918 Irish repudiation of his party was not shared by Ulster Catholics who by a majority rejected Sinn Féin candidates: Devlin himself defeated **Éamon de Valera** who in other contests was invincible. The Northern Ireland settlement of 1920, confirmed in 1922 and 1925, abandoned the Ulster Catholics to Protestant Unionist overlordship; Devlin as leader oscillated between ostracism of the new sub-state and ineffectual opposition tactics, but he consolidated his own politico-economic machine over Catholics, as was shown by his representation in the Stormont parliament at various times of Armagh, Tyrone, Fermanagh and Catholic Belfast.

DEVORGILLA See **BALIOL family**

DEVOY, John (1842–1928) Irish-born American journalist and nationalist, born in Kill, County Kildare, the son of a labourer. He served in the French Foreign Legion and the British army where he became an agent for the 'Fenian' secret society, oath-bound to seek an Irish Republic. He assisted in the rescue of the Fenian 'chief' **James Stephens** from prison before trial in 1865, and was himself seized in 1866 and sentenced to 15 years' imprisonment for organizing cells. Amnestied on condition of exile from the UK he settled in the USA as a journalist on the New York *Herald*, and helped organize Clan-na-Gael, displacing the increasingly moribund Fenian Brotherhood. It rescued Fenian prisoners from Australia (1876), offered terms of alliance ('the New Departure') in 1878 to **Parnell** (which he ignored), but supported him in any event with fund-raising, tour-planning, establishing Land League American branches, and so on. The Parnell split drove Devoy away from constitutionalism and his paper the *Gaelic American* returned to Anglophobian organization. Through **T J Clarke** he helped tie the Easter Rising of 1916 to alliance with Germany in World War I, and subsequently roused American support for the victims of its repression. His hatred of **Woodrow Wilson** may have weakened the Irish cause; in any event, **Éamon de Valera** as president of Dáil Éireann ultimately broke with him during his 1919–20 tour and kept the Irish cause free from identification with any one American political faction as Devoy now wished. He wrote *Recollections of an Irish Rebel* (1928).

DEVRIENT, Carl August (1797–1872) German actor, nephew of **Ludwig Devrient** and brother of **Philipp** and **Gustav Devrient**. He played lovers' parts, and married the *diva*, Madame Schröder-Devrient (1805–60).

DEVRIENT, Gustav Emil (1803–72) German actor, the most gifted brother of **Carl** and **Philipp Devrient.** He became identified with such characters as Hamlet, Tasso, and especially Posa.

DEVRIENT, Ludwig (1784–1832) German actor, distinguished both in comedy and tragedy, and especially in playing Shakespearean characters.

DEVRIENT, Max (1857–1929) German actor, son of **Carl Devrient**. He upheld the family tradition, and was much admired as Petruchio in *The Taming of the Shrew*.

DEVRIENT, Philipp Edouard (1801–77), German actor, brother of **Carl** and **Gustav Devrient**. He was a baritone singer and actor, and wrote many plays and the valuable *Geschichte der deutschen Schauspielkunst* (5 vols, 1848–74); he edited **Shakespeare** with his son Otto (1838–94), also an actor, manager and playwright.

DE VRIES, Hugo (Marie) de (1848–1935) Dutch botanist and geneticist, born in Haarlem, the son of a Dutch prime minister. The first instructor in plant physiology in the Netherlands, he studied at Leiden, Heidelberg and Würzburg and became professor of botany at Amsterdam (1878–1918). From 1890 he devoted himself to the study of heredity and variation in plants, significantly developing Mendelian genetics and evolutionary theory. His major work was *Die Mutationstheorie* (The Mutation Theory, 1901–03).

DE VRIES, Peter (1910–) American novelist, born in Chicago of Dutch immigrant parents. He was educated at Dutch Reformed Calvinist schools but rebelled against their puritanism. He was the editor of a community newspaper in Chicago before working as a vending-machine operator, toffee-apple salesman, radio actor, furniture mover, lecturer to women's clubs, and associate editor of *Poetry*. In 1943 he lured **James Thurber** to Chicago to give a benefit lecture for *Poetry* and Thurber subsequently encouraged him to write for *The New Yorker*. This he did, later joining the editorial staff, and latterly restricting his contribution to captions for cartoons. A satirist in his mentor's mould, he plays with words like **Perelman** and is an inveterate (and inventive) punster and epigrammatist. He has written more than 20 novels, though none has eclipsed the reception of his first, *The Tunnel of Love* (1954).

DEWAR, Sir James (1842–1923) Scottish chemist and physicist, born in Kincardine-on-Forth. Educated at Dollar Academy, Edinburgh University and Ghent, he became professor of natural experimental philosophy at Cambridge in 1875. He liquified and froze many gases, invented the vacuum flask and (with Sir **Frederick Abel**) discovered cordite.

D'EWES, Sir Simonds (1602–50) English antiquary, born in Coxden, near Chard. As MP for Sudbury, he sat in the Long Parliament, and was expelled by Col. **Thomas Pride** in 1648. He collected the *Journal of all the Parliaments During the Reign of Queen Elizabeth* (published in 1682), and transcribed many ancient documents (now lost) of great historical value. He also compiled an (unpublished) Anglo-Saxon Dictionary.

DE WET, Christian (1854–1922) Boer soldier and politician. A celebrated big game hunter, he became conspicuous in the 1st Boer War in the Transvaal of 1880–81; and in the 2nd Boer War (1899–1902). He wrote a book on the war, and in 1907 he became minister of agriculture of the Orange River Colony. In 1914 he joined the Afrikaner insurrection, but was captured in the field. Sentenced to six years' imprisonment, he was released in 1915.

DE WETTE, Wilhelm Martin Leberecht (1780–1849) German biblical critic, born in Ulla, near Weimar. He studied from 1799 at Jena, and became professor at Heidelberg in 1809, and in 1810 at Berlin. A letter sent in 1819 to his friend, the mother of Karl Ludwig Sand (the assassin of the playwright **Kotzebue**), cost him his chair. In 1822 he became professor of theology at Basel. He wrote introductions to the Old and New Testaments, and a manual of Hebrew archaeology.

DEWEY, George (1837–1917) American naval commander, born in Montpelier, Vermont. He graduated from the naval academy, and during the Civil War (1861–65) served with Admiral **Farragut**. As commander of the US Asiatic squadron (1897–99) he was in Hong Kong when war was declared with Spain in 1898. He set sail directly for the Philippines and destroyed the Spanish fleet in Manila Bay without the loss of a single man.

DEWEY, John (1859–1952) American philosopher and educational theorist, born in Burlington, Vermont. He began his professional career as a high-school teacher, but went on to a series of university positions at Johns Hopkins, Michigan, Chicago and eventually Columbia, where he was professor of philosophy from 1904 until retirement in 1930. He was a leading exponent of pragmatism, in succession to **Charles Peirce** and **William James**, and he stressed the instrumental function of ideas and judgments in problem-solving. He published widely on psychology and education as well as philosophy, and his many works include: *The School and Society* (1899), *Reconstruction in Philosophy* (1920), *Experience and Nature* (1925), *The Quest for Certainty* (1929), and *Experience and Education* (1938).

DEWEY, Melvil (1851–1931) American librarian, born in Adams Centre, New York, and founder of the 'Dewey System' of book classification by decimals. He designed the system for the Amherst College Library in 1876. He became chief librarian and professor of library economy at Columbia (1883–88), and director of the New York State Library (1889–1906).

DEWEY, Thomas Edmund (1902–71) American politician, born in Owosso, Michigan. After studying law at the universities of Michigan and Columbia, he became district attorney for New York County in 1937, and governor of New York State in 1942, being re-elected to this office in 1946 and 1950. He was Republican nominee for president in 1944 and 1948, when by virtue of the 'Dewey machine', his campaign organization, he appeared to be a much stronger candidate than President **Truman**.

DEWI, St See **DAVID**

DE WITT, Jan (1625–72) Dutch statesman, born in Dort, the son of Jacob de Witt, a vehement opponent of **William II**, Prince of Orange. Jan was one of the deputies sent by the States of Holland in 1652 to Zeeland, to dissuade that province from adopting an Orange policy. In 1653 he was made grand pensionary. The Orange party, during the war between England and Holland, was ever striving to increase the power of the young prince (afterwards **William III**); the republican (or oligarchic) party, composed of the nobles and the wealthier burgesses, with De Witt at their head, on the other hand sought to abolish the office of stadhouder. In 1654, on the conclusion of the war, a secret article in the treaty drawn up between De Witt and **Cromwell** deprived the House of Orange of all state offices. After the restoration of **Charles II**, De Witt leaned to the side of France, all the more during the two years' renewal of hostilities with England (1665–67).

DEXTER, John (1925–90) English stage director. He began as an actor in repertory and television before becoming a director in 1957. During the next 20 years, he directed 15 plays for the Royal Court Theatre, London, and became an associate of the National Theatre, 1963–66. He co-founded the New Theatre Company in 1986. In New York his direction of *Equus* won him a Tony award in 1974. He was director of the

Metropolitan Opera, New York, 1974–81. He also directed opera in London, Paris and Hamburg.

DEXTER, Ted (Edward Ralph) (1935–) English cricketer and sports commentator, born in Milan. Educated at Radley School, he became captain of England and scored 4502 runs, including eight Test centuries. Something of a throw-back to Corinthian times, his imperious batting earned him the nickname of 'Lord Ted' and he has some claim to be considered the last of the old-style amateur players. He excelled in most sports and was a particularly fine golfer. In 1964 he stood unsuccessfully for parliament as a Conservative against **James Callaghan**. In 1989 he was appointed chairman of the Test Selection board with far-reaching increases of authority.

D'HÉRELLE, Felix (1873–1949) French-Canadian bacteriologist, born in Montreal. He studied there and worked in central America, Europe and Egypt before holding a chair at Yale from 1926 to 1933. He was a discoverer in 1915 of bacteriophage, a type of virus which infects bacteria. Thereafter he tried to use 'phage' therapeutically, but without a success accepted by other workers; however, phage later proved of great value in research in molecular biology.

DHULEEP SINGH (1838–93) ruler of Lahore, son and successor of **Ranjit Singh**. He was deposed and pensioned in 1849, turned Christian (until 1886 when he sought in vain to re-establish himself), and lived for years as a Suffolk squire.

DI STEFANO, Alfredo (1926–) Argentinian footballer and coach, born in Buenos Aires of Italian descent. He first came to prominence in Colombia with the Bogota club, Millionarios. His lasting fame rests on his spell with Real Madrid, during which time he played in five European Cup successes. Tall, elegant and deadly, he did not like competition from clubmates and had **Didi** removed from the Real Madrid staff. With the Hungarian **Ferenc Puskas** he formed a partnership of equals, however; between them they scored all the goals in Real Madrid's 7–3 win over Eintracht Frankfurt at Hampden Park, Glasgow, in the European Cup Final of 1960, Di Stefano scoring three. Later he became a coach and took Valencia to the Spanish League Championship in 1971.

DIAGHILEV, Sergei Pavlovich (1872–1929) Russian impresario, born in Novgorod. He obtained a law degree, but his real preoccupation was with the arts. In 1898 he became editor of *Mir Iskousstva* (World of Art) and during the next few years arranged exhibitions and concerts of Russian Art and Music. In 1908 he presented *Boris Godunov* in Paris, and the next year brought a ballet company to the Châtelet. His permanent company, Ballet Russe de Diaghilev, was founded in 1911 (with headquarters in Monte Carlo, and **Enrico Cecchetti** as ballet master) and remained in existence for 20 years, triumphantly touring Europe, despite constant financial anxiety. Most of the great dancers, composers and painters of this period—among them the choreographers and dancers **Nijinsky**, **Massine** and **Balanchine**; artists **Bakst**, **Picasso** and **Goncharova**; and composers **Satie** and **Stravinsky**—contributed to the success of his Ballet Russe, and many owed their subsequent fame to their association with the company. A temperamental tyrant, who combined ruthlessness with charm, he was an aesthetic catalyst whose mere presence seemed to activate the creation of works of art.

DIANE DE FRANCE (1538–1619) Duchess of Angoulême, a natural daughter of **Henri II** of France and a Piedmontese (according to others, of **Diane de Poitiers**). Formally legitimized, she was married first to a son of the Duke of Parma, next to the eldest son of the 1st Duke of **Montmorency**. She enjoyed great influence at court under **Henri IV**, and superintended the education of the future **Louis XIII**.

DIANE DE POITIERS (1499–1566) mistress of **Henri II** of France, was married at 13, and left a widow at 32; presently she won the affections of the boy dauphin, already wedded to **Catherine de' Medici**. On his accession (1547) Diane enjoyed great influence, and was made Duchess of Valentinois. After his death (1559) she retired to her Château d'Anet.

DÍAZ DE LA PEÑA, Narciso Virgilio (1807–76) French landscape painter, born in Bordeaux of Spanish parentage. Left an orphan, he was educated by a Protestant pastor at Bellevue, near Paris. At 15 he was apprenticed to a porcelain painter; in 1831 he began to exhibit in the Salon. His favourite subjects were landscapes with nymphs, lovers, and satyrs; and his *forte* was colour.

DÍAZ DEL CASTILLO, Bernal (c.1492–1581) Spanish soldier and historian of the conquest of Mexico. He was one of the handful of conquistadors who accompanied **Cortés** in 1519. His *Historia de la conquista de la Nueva España* (1904; trans 1908–16), written at the age of 84, is invaluable.

DIAZ, or **Dias, Bartolomeu** (c.1450–1500) Portuguese navigator. At the royal court of Aragon he met many scientists, among others the German cosmographer **Martin Behaim**. In 1486 King John II gave him the command of two vessels to follow up the discoveries already made on the west coast of Africa. Diaz soon reached the limit which had been attained in South Atlantic navigation, and first touched land in 26° S lat. Driven by a violent storm, he sailed round the southern extremity of Africa, the Cape of Good Hope, without immediately realizing the fact, and discovered the southernmost point of Africa, so opening the route to India. He outfitted **Vasco da Gama**'s expedition of 1497 and travelled with them as far as the Cape Verde Islands. He established a number of trading posts before joining the expedition of Cabral, the discoverer of Brazil, but was lost in a storm after leaving Brazil.

DÍAZ, (José de la Cruz) Porfirio (1830–1915) Mexican soldier and president of Mexico from 1876 to 1880 and 1884 to 1911. Born in Oaxaca City to a modest meztizo family, he studied for the priesthood and then for the law. As a student of **Benito Juárez** he opposed the dictatorship of **Santa Anna**, joined the Oaxaca National Guard and rose to the rank of general. Hero of the War of Reform (1857–60) and the French Intervention (1861–67), Juárez's most loyal and effective officer was shunned by his old teacher in peacetime. Díaz retired from public life during Juárez's third term (1867–71). In 1871 he rebelled against the unconstitutional fourth re-election of Juárez, accepting government amnesty after Juárez's death. In 1876 he rebelled again in support of the principle of no re-election, and won the presidency. When his term ended (1880) he relinquished office peacefully to Manuel González, was elected again in 1884 and ruled without interruption thereafter until he was deposed in 1911. His rule was characterized by the conciliation of differences between interests and factions. He and his positivist advisers pursued a programme of 'peace and progress', attracting foreign investment to modernize Mexico, which produced a remarkable growth in railroads and other material improvements. But eventually the dictator's age and his neglect of political and social reforms led to the 1910 revolution of **Francisco Madero**. Negotiations between agents of Madero and the Mexican government sent Díaz into exile in Europe, where he died in poverty.

DIBDIN, Charles (1745–1814) English songwriter, born in Southampton. He early attracted notice by his singing, and, while still a boy, composed an operetta, *The Shepherd's Artifice*, which was produced at Covent Garden in 1762. He subsequently lived an unsettled life as an actor and composer of stage music, and in 1788 began a series of musical entertainments which enjoyed some popularity. He wrote nearly a hundred sea songs—among the best 'Poor Jack' and 'Tom Bowling'. He also wrote nearly 70 dramatic pieces. Two of his sons, Charles (1768–1833) and Thomas John (1771–1841), wrote songs and dramas. In 1803 he published his autobiography.

DIBDIN, Thomas Frognall (1776–1847) English bibliographer, born in Calcutta, a nephew of **Charles Dibdin**. Orphaned at four, he was brought up by an uncle and took orders in 1804, and held charges near Newmarket and in London. After publishing *Introduction to the knowledge of Rare and Valuable Editions of the Greek and Roman Classics* (1802), he became librarian to the 2nd Earl of **Spencer** at Althorp. He wrote *Bibliomania* (1809); *Bibliotheca Spenceriana* (1814–15); *The Bibliographical Decameron* (1817); *Reminiscences of a Literary Life* (1836); and *Bibliographical Tour in the Northern Counties of England and Scotland* (1838).

DIBELIUS, Karl Friedrich Otto (1880–1967) German Lutheran churchman and ecumenical leader, born in Berlin. Suspended from church duties as general superintendent of the Kurmark following a 1933 sermon to Nazi leaders stating that 'the dictatorship of a totalitarian state is irreconcilable with God's will', he continued to support the Confessing Church, despite being forbidden to speak or publish. As bishop of Berlin (1945–61), chairman of the Council of the Evangelical Church in Germany (1949–61), and a president of the World Council of Churches (1954–61), he defended religious freedom in East Berlin and encouraged ecumenism. He wrote an autobiography, *In the Service of the Lord* in 1965. His theologian cousin, Martin Dibelius (1883–1947), pioneered the use of Form Criticism (*Formgeschichtliche*) in New Testament studies, as in *From Tradition to Gospel* (1934).

DICEY, Albert Venn (1835–1922) English jurist. Vinerian professor of law at Oxford (1882–1909), he wrote *Law of the Constitution* (1885), *Conflict of Laws* (1896), and *Law and Public Opinion in England* (1905), all works of enduring importance. In his later years he campaigned vigorously against Irish Home Rule.

DICK, James (1743–1828) Scottish merchant and philanthropist, born in Forres. He made a fortune in American trading with the West Indies, and left the 'Dick Bequest' to promote higher learning in the parish schools of the counties of Moray, Banff and Aberdeen.

DICK, Philip Kindred (1928–) American writer of science fiction, born in Chicago, Illinois. Educated at Berkeley High School, he has worked as a record store manager and as a radio announcer. His career has two distinct phases; the first, from 1952 to 1955, remarkable for a profusion of short stories, the second, starting in 1962, notable for a torrent of novels. Despite a penchant for modish titles—*Do Androids Dream of Electric Sheep?* (1968) and *Galactic Pot-Healer* (1969), the story of a master-potter who has never thrown his own pots—he is not so much interested in technological gimickry and space-age jargon as in his characters. A spare and humorous writer, he was given the Hugo award in 1963.

DICK, Robert (1811–66) self-taught Scottish geologist and botanist, born in Tullibody. From 1830 he was a baker in Thurso.

DICK-READ, Grantly (1890–1959) English gynaecologist. He studied at St John's College, Cambridge, and the London Hospital. His unorthodox work, *Natural Childbirth* (1933), with its rejection of anaesthetics during childbirth and its advocacy of prenatal relaxation exercises, caused bitter controversy, but later found common acceptance. In 1948 he emigrated to South Africa where he conducted a tour of African tribes in 1954 investigating childbirth.

DICKE, Robert, Henry (1916–) American physicist, born in St Louis, Missouri. He studied physics at Princeton and Rochester, and spent his career at Princeton as professor of physics from 1957. Independently of **Alpher**, **Gamow** and Herman, he deduced in 1964 that a 'Big Bang' origin of the universe should have left an observable remnant of microwave radiation; and this was detected by **Penzias** and **R W Wilson**. In the 1960s he carried out important work on gravitation, including the proposal that the gravitational constant (G) slowly decreases with time (the Brans-Dicke theory, 1961).

DICKENS, Charles (1812–70) English author, born in Landport, then a little suburb of Portsmouth. His father was John Dickens, a clerk in the navy pay office, and at that time attached to Portsmouth dockyard. In 1814 he was transferred to London, and in 1816 to Chatham, where, already a great reader, he got some schooling. In 1821 the family fell into trouble; reforms in the Admiralty made his father redundant and they had to leave Chatham, and moved to London, where they took a small house in Camden Town. But the father was soon arrested for debt in 1824 and sent to the Marshalsea prison with his whole family, apart from Charles, who was sent to work in a blacking factory at Hungerford Market, where, with half a dozen rough boys, he labelled the blacking bottles. Not only were his days passed in this wretched work, but the child was left entirely to himself at night, when he had four miles to walk to his lonely bedroom in lodgings in Camden Town. On Sundays he visited his parents in the prison. On his father's release they all went back to Camden Town, and the boy was sent again to school, an academy in the Hampstead Road, for three or four years, after which he worked for a solicitor as an office boy (1827). Meantime, however, his father had obtained a post as reporter for the *Morning Herald*, and Charles decided also to attempt the profession of journalist. He taught himself shorthand; and he visited the British Museum daily to supplement some of the shortcomings of his reading. In 1828 he became a reporter of debates at the House of Commons for the *Morning Chronicle*, but at that time he was only interested in being an actor. It was not until 1835 that he succeeded in getting permanent employment on the staff of a London paper as a reporter and in this capacity he was sent around the country. Meanwhile in December 1833, the *Monthly Magazine* published a sketch 'Dinner at Poplar Walk', under the pen-name 'Boz' (the nickname of his younger brother, Augustus Moses). Other papers followed, but produced nothing for the contributor except the gratification of seeing them in print. He soon made an arrangement to contribute papers and sketches regularly to the *Evening Chronicle*, continuing to act as reporter for the *Morning Chronicle*, and getting his salary increased. The *Sketches by Boz* were collected and published early in 1836, the author receiving £150 for the copyright; he later bought it back for eleven times that amount. In the last week of March of that year appeared the first number of the *Pickwick Papers*; three days afterwards he married Catherine, the daughter of his friend George Hogarth, editor of the

Evening Chronicle. She bore him seven sons and three daughters between 1837 and 1852, three of whom predeceased him; in 1858 husband and wife separated. Success having definitely come his way, Dickens for the rest of his life allowed himself scant respite. In fulfilment of publishers' engagements he produced *Oliver Twist* (1837–39) which appeared in *Bentley's Miscellany*, which Dickens edited for a time, *Nicholas Nickleby* (1838–39), and *Master Humphrey's Clock*, a serial miscellany which resolved itself into the two stories, *The Old Curiosity Shop* (1840–41), and *Barnaby Rudge* (1841). From then on a great part of Dickens's life was spent abroad, especially notable being his visits to America in 1842 and 1867–68, his stay in Genoa in 1844–45 and in Lausanne in 1846, and his summers spent in Boulogne in 1853, 1854, and 1856. Meanwhile there came from his pen an incessant stream: *American Notes* (1842), *Martin Chuzzlewit* (1843), *The Christmas Tales—A Christmas Carol, The Chimes, The Cricket on the Hearth, The Battle of Life, The Haunted Man* and *The Ghost's Bargain* (1843, 1846 and 1848); *Pictures from Italy* (1845), *Dombey and Son* (1846–48), *David Copperfield* (1849–50), *Bleak House* (1852–53), *A Child's History of England* (1854), *Hard Times* (1854), *Little Dorrit* (1855–57), *A Tale of Two Cities* (1859), *The Uncommercial Traveller* (1861), the Christmas numbers in *Household Words* and *All the Year Round*, *Great Expectations* (1860–61), *Our Mutual Friend* (1864–65), and *The Mystery of Edwin Drood* (1870, unfinished). To this long roll must be added public readings (1858–70), both in this country and in America, private theatricals, speeches, innumerable letters, pamphlets, plays, the running of a popular magazine—first (1850) called *Household Words* and then (1859) *All the Year Round*. He died suddenly at Gadshill, near Rochester (the place he had coveted as a boy, and purchased in 1856), and was buried in Westminster Abbey.

DICKINSON, Emily Elizabeth (1830–86) American poet, born in Amherst, Massachusetts, the daughter of an autocratic lawyer who became a Congressman. She was educated at Amherst Academy and Mount Holyoke Female Seminary in South Hadley. She spent her whole life in the family home at Amherst. A mystic by inclination, she withdrew herself at 23 from all social contacts and lived an intensely secluded life, writing in secret over a thousand poems. All but one or two of these remained unpublished until after her death, when her sister Lavinia brought out three volumes between 1891 and 1896 which were acclaimed as the work of a poetic genius. Further collections appeared, as *The Single Hound* (1914), and *Bolts of Melody* (1945). Her lyrics, intensely personal and often spiritual, show great originality both in thought and in form, and have had considerable influence on modern poetry.

DICKINSON, Goldsworthy Lowes (1862–1932) English essayist and intellectual. A lecturer at Cambridge from 1896 to 1920, he was the author of such popular books as *The Greek View of Life* (1896), *The Meaning of Good* (1901), *Religion and Immortality* (1911) and a pacifist work, *War: its Nature, Cause and Cure* (1923).

DICKSEE, Sir Frank (Francis Bernard) (1853–1928) English painter. He is remembered for several much-reproduced historical subject paintings, such as *Romeo and Juliet*, and *The Passing of Arthur*. His sister, Margaret Isabel (1858–1903), painted several equally well-remembered canvases, such as *The Children of Charles I* and *Swift and Stella*.

DICKSON, Alec (Alexander Graeme) (1914–) Scottish educationist, born in London. A pioneer of community service involving young volunteers from the UK, he was educated at Rugby School and New College, Oxford. He trained as a journalist on the *Yorkshire Post*, but after war service in Africa he set up Community Service Volunteers (CSV) to enable young people to give voluntary service to the community in Britain. Since 1984 he has been consultant to International Baccalaureate schools worldwide. His publications include *A Community Service Handbook* (with his wife Mora Dickson, 1967); *School in the Round* (1969); *A Chance to Serve* (1976), and *Volunteers* (1983).

DICKSON, Leonard Eugene (1874–1954) American mathematician, born in Independence, Iowa. He studied at the University of Texas, and taught at Chicago for most of his life. He did important work in group theory, finite fields and linear associative algebras, and his encyclopaedic *History of the theory of numbers* (1919–23) is the definitive work on the subject.

DIDELOT, Charles-Louis (1767–1837) French dancer, choreographer and teacher, born in Stockholm, Sweden, where his father was principal dancer at the Royal Theatre. The king sent him to Paris for ballet training, and he made his début there. In London he choreographed the most famous of his more than 50 ballets, *Zephyr and Flora* (1796), in which his use of wired flying apparatus caused a sensation. From 1801 to 1811 he was master choreographer and teacher at the Imperial Ballet in St Petersburg, where he introduced a complete system of reforms influenced by his own French training. He returned there in 1816, having spent the interim in London and Paris. He was noted for his intense, innovative interests in stagecraft and costuming, his almost sculptural direction of group scenes, and the dramatic clarity he brought to the ballet storyline.

DIDEROT, Denis (1713–84) French man of letters, born in Langres in Champagne, the son of a master cutler. Trained by the Jesuits at home and in Paris, he refused to become either a lawyer or a physician, and was thrown upon his own resources, and worked as tutor and bookseller's hack (1734–44). In 1743 he married a young seamstress, who contrived to bring about a temporary reconciliation between father and son; but the marriage was not happy, and he had many love affairs. His *Pensées philosophiques* was burned by the parlement of Paris in 1746, and in 1749 he was imprisoned for his *Lettre sur les aveugles*. In 1746 he had published his first novel, *Les Bijoux indiscrets*. The bookseller Le Breton now invited him to edit an expanded translation of **Ephraim Chambers**'s *Cyclopaedia* (1727) with **D'Alembert**. In Diderot's hands the character of the work was transformed. He enlisted nearly all the important French writers of the time as contributors, and, in place of a compendium of useful information, produced a work of propaganda for the *philosophe* party. For some 20 years he retained his post in spite of dangers and drawbacks. The sale of the book was again and again prohibited, and its editor ran a constant risk of imprisonment or exile. D'Alembert abandoned him in despair in 1758. But his marvellous energy, his varied knowledge, and his faculty of rallying his fellow workers, enabled him to carry his vast undertaking to a successful conclusion. The first volume of the *Encyclopédie, ou Dictionnaire Raisonné des Sciences, des Arts et des Métiers* appeared in 1751; the 35th and last in 1776. In his later years he was rescued from financial difficulties by **Catherine II, the Great** of Russia, to whom in 1773 he paid a five-month visit. He died of apoplexy. One of the most prolific and versatile of writers, he was a novelist and a dramatist, a satirist, a philosopher, a critic of pictures and books, and a brilliant letter writer. His works also include *Pensées sur l'interprétation de la Nature* (1754), and two novels: *La Religieuse*, an exposure of convent life; and the **Sterne**-like *Jacques le Fataliste*, both published in 1796. In *Le Neveu de Rameau* (1721), an imaginary conversation between the author and a parasite, the follies of society are laid bare with sardonic humour and piercing insight. His plays were somewhat unsuccessful examples of melodrama, the best efforts being two short pieces which were never acted: *La Pièce et le prologue* and *Est -il bon? Est-il méchant?* His letters to Sophie Volland form the most interesting section of his voluminous correspondence. As a critic he stood far in advance of his contemporaries, and anticipated the Romanticists. His *Salons*, remarks on pictures exhibited, are the earliest example of modern aesthetic criticism.

DIDI, professional name of **Valdir Pereira** (1928–) Brazilian footballer, born in Campos and always known by the affectionate diminutive. Despite a slightly crippled right leg, he was the master strategist of the Brazil side which won the 1958 World Cup in Sweden. A spell with Real Madrid was unsuccessful because of a personality clash with **Alfredo Di Stefano**, but he later managed the Peruvian national side which reached the quarter-finals of the World Cup in Mexico in 1970.

DIDION, Joan (1934–) American writer, born in Sacramento, California. She was educated at the University of California at Berkeley (1952–56) and married the writer John Gregory Dunne in 1964. From 1956 to 1963 she was associate feature editor of *Vogue* in New York and has worked and written for the *Saturday Evening Post*, *Esquire*, and *National Review*. Her columns were published as *Slouching Towards Bethlehem* (1968) and *The White Album* (1979). Her novels portray contemporary social tensions in a laconic style that has aroused much admiration. *Run River* (1963) was her first novel, but she is best known for *A Book of Common Prayer* (1977), set in a banana republic devoid of history, and *Democracy* (1984), about the long and amorous affair between a politician's wife and Jack Lovett, a man who embodies everything her ambitious husband is not.

DIDIUS JULIANUS, Marcus (c.135–193) Roman soldier and emperor. A former governor of Gaul, he purchased power on 28 March 193 by bribing the praetorian guard in a famous 'auction of the empire' held after the death of **Pertinax**. He did not hold power for long, as the Senate soon declared for his rival **Lucius Septimius Severus** and deposed him; he was murdered in his palace on 1 June.

DIDOT, Firmin (1764–1836) French printer, grandson of **François Didot** and brother of **Pierre Didot**. As a printer, and especially as an engraver and founder, he raised the family name to the highest eminence. He revived and developed the stereotyping process, and produced fine editions of many classical, French and English works. He became a deputy, and obtained some reputation as an author by his tragedies, *La Reine de Portugal* and *La Mort d'Annibal*, and several volumes of metrical translations from the classics. His sons, Ambroise (1790–1876) and Hyacinthe (1794–1880), carried on and transmitted the business, as the firm of Firmin Didot Frères.

DIDOT, François (1689–1757) French printer and publisher, founder of a great printing dynasty. His two sons were François Ambroise (1730–1804) and Pierre François (1732–95).

DIDOT, Henri (1765–1852) French engraver and letter founder, grandson of **François Didot**. He produced very beautiful 'microscopic' types.

DIDOT, Pierre (1760–1853) French publisher, grandson of **François Didot**. He brought out the magnificent Louvre editions of **Virgil**, **Horace**, **Racine** and **La Fontaine**, besides **Boileau**'s works and **Voltaire**'s *Henriade*.

DIEBENKORN, Richard (1922–) American painter, born in Portland, Oregon. In 1946 he enrolled at the California School of Fine Arts, San Francisco, where he taught from 1947 to 1950. During the 1950s he developed a style close to Abstract Expressionism while retaining suggestions of the Californian landscape and of city motifs; his two major series of paintings, developed over many years, focus on Berkeley and Ocean Park. The loose, gestural brushwork of the 1950s gave way to more geometrical compositions during the 1960s and 1970s. Diebenkorn evokes the dazzling Californian light by using bright, semi-translucent colours, particularly blues and yellows.

DIEBITSCH, Hans Karl Friedrich, Count (1785–1831) German-born Russian soldier, born in Silesia. He joined the Russian army in 1801, and was a major-general in the campaigns of 1805 and 1812–14. In the Russo-Turkish war of 1828–29 he won the surname of Sabalkanski ('crosser of the Balkans'), and was promoted field-marshal. He died of cholera while suppressing the Polish insurrection of 1830–31.

DIEFENBACH, Lorenz (1806–83) German philologist, born in Ostheim in Hesse. He studied at Giessen, travelled much, and was twelve years pastor and librarian at Solms-Laubach. In 1848 he settled at Frankfurt, where he was second librarian (1865–76). His industry was enormous, embracing poetry and romances, besides many philological works, especially *Celtica* (1839–40), a significant work in Celtic studies.

DIEFENBAKER, John George (1895–1979) Canadian Conservative politician, born at Normanby Township, Ontario, educated at the University of Saskatchewan and called to the Saskatchewan bar in 1919. In 1940 he entered the Canadian Federal House of Commons and became leader of the Progressive Conservatives in December 1956. In June 1957 he became prime minister of Canada when the Liberal party was defeated after 22 years in office, but lost office again in April 1963. He retired from politics in 1968 after four years as leader of the opposition.

DIEFFENBACH, Johann Friedrich (1792–1847) German surgeon, born in Königsberg. Professor of surgery at Berlin from 1840, he was a pioneer of transplant surgery.

DIELS, Otto (1876–1954) German chemist, born in Hamburg. Professor of chemistry at Kiel University (1916–1948), with his pupil **Kurt Alder** he demonstrated in 1928 the 'diene synthesis' (Diels-Alder reaction), which is of far-reaching importance, especially in the plastics and petrochemicals industry. They shared the Nobel prize for chemistry in 1950.

DIEMEN, Antony Van See **TASMAN**

DIEREN, Bernard van (1884–1936) Dutch composer, critic and author, born in Rotterdam, resident in England from 1909. Trained as a scientist, he began to study music seriously in his twenties, and his earliest surviving works date from 1912. His complexity of style and concentration of utterance, as well as his refusal to compromise for popular taste, leave his work little known, despite the enthusiasm of a small band of disciples. He wrote a study of the sculptor **Epstein** (1920) and a volume of musical essays, *Down Among the Dead Men*. His compositions include an opera, *The Tailor*, and a *Chinese Symphony* for soloists, choir and orchestra, as well as numerous songs and chamber compositions.

DIESEL, Rudolph (Christian Karl) (1858–1913) German engineer, born in Paris. He studied at the Munich Polytechnic and trained as a refrigeration engineer, but in 1885 began work on internal combustion engines. Subsidized by Krupps he set about constructing a 'rational heat motor', demonstrating the first practical compression-ignition engine in 1897. The diesel engine achieved an efficiency about twice that of comparable steam engines. He spent most of his life at his factory at Augsburg but in 1913 he vanished from the Antwerp-Harwich mail steamer, and was presumed drowned.

DIESTERWEG, Friedrich Adolf Wilhelm (1790–1866) German educationist, born in Siegen. As head of the Berlin state school seminary he introduced **Pestalozzi**'s methods into Germany.

DIETRICH, Marlene, originally **Maria Magdalena von Losch** (1904–) German-born American film actress and cabaret performer, born in Berlin. She made her film début as a maid in *Der Kleine Napoleon* (1922), but it was her performance in Germany's first sound film *The Blue Angel* (1930) as the temptress Lola that brought her international attention and a contract to film in Hollywood. Under the direction of Josef von Sternberg she created an indelible image of enigmatic sexual allure in a succession of exotic and glamorous films like *Morocco* (1930), *Blond Venus* (1932), *The Scarlet Empress* (1934) and *The Devil Is a Woman* (1935). Labelled 'box-office poison' in 1937, she returned in triumph as brawling saloon singer Frenchie in *Destry Rides Again* (1939). Later film work tended to exploit her legendary mystique, although she was effective in *A Foreign Affair* (1948), *Rancho Notorious* (1952) and *Judgment at Nuremberg* (1961). After extensive tours to entertain troops during World War II she developed a further career as an international chanteuse and cabaret star. Increasingly reclusive she refused to be photographed for the 1984 documentary *Marlene*, but contributed a pugnacious vocal commentary.

DIETRICH OF BERN See **THEODORIC the Great**

DIETZENHOFER German family of architects, consisting of five brothers over the period 1643 to 1726. Their work was of great importance in the development of the late baroque in central Europe. The successors of **Borromini** and **Guarini** and the precursors of **Neumann**, a good example of their work is Christoph's St Nicholas in the Lesser Town Prague (1703–11), in which a system of ogival vaults supported on deep wall pillars are arranged to create a spatial syncopation. The work of the brothers is brought to a logical conclusion by Christoph's son Killian Ignaz in St Nicholas in the Old Town (1732–37) where a greater spatial awareness is gained through complexity and lighting.

DIEUDONNÉ, Jean Alexandre (1906–) French mathematician, born in Lille. He studied at the École Normale Supérieure, and has held chairs in Rennes, Nancy, Chicago, the Institut des Hautes Études Scientifiques, and finally Nice (1964–70). The leading French mathematician of his generation, he has worked in many areas of abstract analysis, **Lie** groups, algebraic geometry, and the history of mathematics. His *Éléments d'analyse* (1960–82) in nine volumes carries on the French tradition of the definitive treatise on analysis. As a founder of the **Bourbaki** group, his ideas on the presentation of mathematics, laying great stress on precise abstract formulation and elegance, have marked out a distinctively French school of mathematical writing whose influence has lasted for some 50 years.

DIEZ, Friedrich Christian (1794–1876) German Romance philologist, born in Giessen, and educated there and at Göttingen. In 1818 he saw **Goethe** at Jena, and by him was directed to the study of Provençal. From 1822 he lived in Bonn, and in 1830 became professor of romance languages there. His *Altspanische Romanzen* (1821) was followed by a series of works on Romance languages, including the *Grammatik der romanischen Sprachen* (1836–38).

DIGBY, Sir Kenelm (1603–65) English diplomat and writer, born in Gayhurst, near Newport Pagnell. His father was a convert to Catholicism and Kenelm was himself brought up in the faith. After leaving Gloucester Hall, Oxford without a degree, he spent nearly three years abroad where, in Madrid, he fell in with Prince **Charles**. He followed him back to England, was knighted and entered his service. After his wife's death he went into seclusion and became a Protestant, but soon announced his reconversion and during the Civil War was imprisoned and had his estates confiscated. Despite this, he was successful in establishing close relations with **Cromwell**. At the restoration he retained his office as chancellor to Queen **Henrietta Maria**. Digby was a founder member of the Royal Society (1663) but established a considerable reputation for duplicity, being described by **Stubbs** as 'the very Pliny of our age for lying'.

DIGBY, Kenelm Henry (1800–80) English writer, the youngest son of the dean of Clonfert. Educated at Trinity College, Cambridge, in 1822, he published a survey of medical customs, *The Broad Stone of Honour*. Converted to Roman Catholicism, he published *Mores Catholici* (1831–40) and other works, and some poetry.

DIGGES, Leonard (1520–?1559) English applied mathematician, known for his valuable work in surveying, navigation, and ballistics. He was probably self-educated, but his books on surveying and navigation went through many editions in the 16th century. His work in ballistics, based on his own experiments, appeared as *Stratioticos* (1579), published by his son, Thomas (d.1595). He took part in **Thomas Wyatt**'s rebellion in 1554, was condemned to death, but later pardoned and fined.

DILKE, Charles Wentworth (1789–1864) English critic and journalist. He graduated from Cambridge, served for twenty years in the navy pay office and edited *Old English Plays* (6 vols, 1814–16). In 1830 he became proprietor of the *Athenaeum*, and edited it until 1846, when he took over the *Daily News* and managed it for three years.

DILKE, Sir Charles Wentworth (1810–69) English gentleman, born in London. The son of **Charles Wentworth Dilke**, he was educated at Westminster, and Trinity Hall, Cambridge. He studied law, but never practised. One of the most active originators of the Great Exhibition of 1851, he refused a knighthood and a large reward, but in 1862 accepted a baronetcy. In 1865 he became Liberal MP for Wallingford, and in 1869 went as English commissioner to the horticultural exhibition at St Petersburg, where he died suddenly.

DILKE, Sir Charles Wentworth (1843–1911) English radical politician, son of Sir **Charles Dilke** (1789–1864), born in Chelsea. He graduated from Trinity Hall, Cambridge, as head of the law tripos in 1866, and was called to the bar. His travels in Canada and the United States, Australia and New Zealand he described in *Greater Britain* (1868). He was returned to parliament for Chelsea in 1868. A doctrinaire Radical, and once at least an avowed Republican, he yet held office as under-secretary for foreign affairs and president of the Local Government board under **Gladstone**. In 1885 he married the widow of **Mark Pattison** (née Emilia Frances Strong), herself the author of *Claude Lorrain*, *sa Vie et ses Oeuvres* (1884), *The Shrine of Death* (1886), etc. His connection with a Mrs Crawford, and a divorce case, led to defeat in 1886 and temporary retirement. But for this, he might have been Gladstone's successor. Author of *European Politics* (1887), *Problems of Greater Britain* (1890) and *The British Empire* (1899), he organized the Labour members into an influential party, was an authority on defence and foreign relations. He returned to public life in 1892 as MP for the Forest of Dean.

DILL, Sir John Greer (1881–1944) English soldier, educated at Cheltenham College and the Royal Military College Sandhurst. He served with the East Lancashire Regiment in the 2nd Boer War (1899–1902) and World War I, in which he was decorated and promoted brigadier general. In World War II he commanded I Corps in France, and became chief of the Imperial General Staff (1940–41). Endowed with profound strategical insight and outstanding organizational ability, he was head of the British Service Mission in Washingon from 1941. He was buried in Arlington Cemetery and posthumously decorated by the US president.

DILLENIUS, Johann Jacob (1687–1747) German botanist and botanical artist, born in Darmstadt. He came to England in 1721, and from 1734 was first Sherardian professor of botany at Oxford. He was the author and artist of *Hortus Elthamensis* (1732) and *Historia Muscorum* (1741), of fundamental importance in the study of mosses.

DILLINGER, John (1903–34) American gangster, born in Indianapolis. Specializing in armed bank robberies, he terrorized his native state of Indiana and neighbouring states. After escaping from Crown Point county jail, where he was being held on a murder charge, he was betrayed by his girfriend's landlady and shot dead by FBI agents in Chicago.

DILLMANN, (Christian Friedrich) August (1823–94) German orientalist, born in Württemberg. He studied at Tübingen under **Heinrich Ewald**, and in 1846–48 visited the libraries at Paris, London and Oxford, cataloguing Ethiopic MSS. He became professor of oriental languages at Kiel in 1860, but was transferred in 1864 to the chair of Old Testament Exegesis at Giessen, and in 1869 to Berlin. The first authority on the Ethiopic languages, his main work was *Lexicon linguae aethiopicae* (1862–63).

DILLON, John (1851–1927) Irish nationalist politician, born in Blackrock, County Dublin, the son of the nationalist John Blake Dillon (1816–66). Educated at the Catholic University medical school in Dublin, he qualified as a surgeon but turned to politics. He became a committed supporter of **Parnell** in the Land League and in 1880 was returned for County Tipperary. In parliament he distinguished himself by the violence of his language, while speeches delivered by him in Ireland led to his imprisonment in 1881, 1881–82 and in 1888. From 1885 to 1918 he sat for East Mayo. After the divorce case involving Parnell in 1890 he became leader of the Anti-Parnellite group (1896–99), but resigned in favour of **Redmond** (1900). In 1918 he became leader of the remnant of the Irish Nationalist party, but was defeated in the election of 1919 by **De Valera** and retired from politics.

DILTHEY, Wilhelm (1833–1911) German philosopher and historian of ideas, born in Biebrich, Hesse. He was a student of the great historian **Leopold von Ranke** and became professor at Basel, Kiel, Breslau and finally Berlin (1882–1911). He was much influenced by **Kant** and is himself a key figure in the idealist tradition in modern social thought. One of his central themes is the radical distinction he made between the natural sciences (*Naturwissenshaften*) and the human sciences (*Geisteswissenschaften*), the former offering explanations of physical events through causal laws, the latter offering understanding (*verstehen*) of events in terms of human intentions and meanings. He developed a theory of hermeneutics for the interpretation of historical texts, and favoured biography as the best historical method; his own biographies include studies of **Schleiermacher**, the young **Hegel**, **Lessing** and **Goethe**. He was an important influence on **Collingwood** and **Ortega y Gasset** in their espousal of historical relativism, and he developed a typology of world-views (*Weltanschauungen*) which would set out the different ways of conceiving our relation to the world.

DIMAGGIO, Joe (Joseph Paul) (1914–) American baseball player, born in Martinez, California, and known as 'Joltin' Joe' and 'the Yankee Clipper'. A powerful and elegant centre fielder and hitter, he played for 15 seasons with the New York Yankees. His greatest achievement was hitting safely (recording a hit) at least once in 56 consecutive games in the 1941 season. He won the batting championship twice (1939 and 1940), and was voted Most Valuable Player (MVP) three times. In 1954 he married (briefly) the film actress **Marilyn Monroe**.

DIMBLEBY, Richard (1913–65) English broadcaster. He was educated at Mill Hill School, and worked on the editorial staff of various newpapers before being appointed first news observer of the BBC in 1936. In 1939 he became the BBC's first war correspondent and was the first radio man in Berlin and at Belsen. In 1946 he decided to become a freelance broadcaster and gave commentaries on many major events, particularly royal occasions, and the funerals of **Kennedy** and **Churchill**. He took part in the first Eurovision relay in 1951 and in the first live TV broadcast from the Soviet Union in 1961.

DIMITROV, Georgi Mikhailovich (1882–1949) Bulgarian Communist politician, born in Pernik. A printer by trade, he began his political career as a union activist and served as a Socialist member of parliament from 1913 to 1918. After helping to form the Bulgarian Communist party in 1919, he directed the underground Communist movement which unsuccessfully attempted to overthrow kings **Ferdinand I** and Boris III, and was forced to flee to the Soviet Union in 1923. He became active in the Communist International (Comintern), heading its European section in Berlin (1929–33), and was accused of complicity in the burning of the Reichstag in February 1933. After a skilful defence he was acquitted, but deported to Moscow, where he became secretary-general of the Comintern (1935–43) and directed Bulgarian resistance to Nazi occupation (1944–45). He returned to Bulgaria in 1945 as head of the transitional government and became prime minister in 1946. Despite overseeing the 'Sovietization' of the republic, he fell out of favour with **Stalin** because of his close relations with **Tito**. He died in Moscow while undergoing medical treatment.

DIMITRY See **DMITRI**

DINE, Jim (1935–) American artist, born in Cincinatti, Ohio. He studied at Ohio University and the Boston Museum of Fine Arts School. In 1959 he exhibited his first series of objects as images, alongside **Claes Oldenburg**, with whom he has occasionally collaborated since on artistic projects. One of the foremost American Pop artists, he had his first one-man show at the Reuben Gallery, New York, in 1960. He has since turned to more traditional representational painting.

DINESEN, Isak See **BLIXEN, Karen**

DING LING, pseud of **Jiang Bingzhi** (1904–86) Chinese novelist and short-story writer, born in Linli County, Hunan Province. A radical feminist, her father died when she was three and her mother flouted tradition by enrolling in school and becoming a teacher. Jiang was educated at Beijing University, where she attended left-wing classes and started publishing stories of rebelliousness against traditional society, such as *The Diary of Miss Sophia* (1928), which dealt candidly with questions of female psychology and sexual desires, *Birth of an Individual* (1929), and *A Woman* (1930). She joined the League of Left-Wing Writers in 1930 and became editor of its official journal. She joined the Communist party in 1932, and after a spell of imprisonment, escaped to the Communist base at Yenan, where she became a star attraction for Western journalists. Her outspoken comments on male chauvinism and discrimination at Yenan led to her being disciplined by the party leaders, until her novel, *The Sun Shines over the Sanggan River* (1948), about land-reform, restored her to favour. In 1958, however, she was 'purged', and sent to raise chickens in the Heilongjiang reclamation area known as the Great Northern Wilderness (Beidahuang). She was imprisoned (1970–75) during the Cultural Revolution, but rehabilitated by the party in 1979, and published a novel based on her experiences in the Great Northern Wilderness, *Comrade Du Wanxiang*.

DINGAAN (d.1840) Zulu king, from 1828, and half brother of **Shaka**, whose murder he instigated. Having admitted the Boers in 1837 he treacherously massacred the colonists in Natal, but was defeated by **Andries Pretorius** at Blood River on 16 December 1838 ('Dingaan's Day'). He fled to Swaziland, where he was overthrown and killed by one of his brothers.

DINGELSTEDT, Franz von (1814–81) German poet and novelist, born in Halsdorf, near Marburg. He was royal librarian at Württemberg from 1843 to 1850, and director of the court theatres at Munich, Weimar and Vienna.

DINIZ, Denis (1261–1325) king of Portugal from 1279. He founded the University of Lisbon in 1290 and Coimbra in 1307, negotiated the first commercial treaty with England in 1294, formed the Portuguese navy in 1317, introduced improved methods of land cultivation, founded agricultural schools and was both a patron of literature and music and a prolific poet.

DINIZ DA CRUZ E SILVA, Antonio (1731–99) Portuguese poet, born in Lisbon. He took a law degree at the University of Coimbra in 1753, and became a founder member of the *Arcadia Lusitana*, a society dedicated to the revival of national poetry. He wrote the epic poem, *O Hyssope*, and *Odes Pindaricas*, lyrics which earned him the title of the 'Portuguese Pindar'. His later life was spent in Brazil.

DINWIDDIE, Robert (1693–1770) Scottish colonial administrator, born near Glasgow. He was appointed collector of customs for Bermuda in 1727 and surveyor-general for southern America in 1738. Appointed lieutenant-governor of Virginia in 1751, he tried to prevent French occupation of the Ohio district in 1753. He sent a young surveyor, **George Washington**, to demand a French withdrawal, followed by troops in 1754, but Washington was forced to surrender at Fort Necessity. In 1755 General **Edward Braddock** was defeated near Fort Duquesne in Ohio, thus precipitating the French and Indian War (1755–63). Dinwiddie was recalled in 1758.

DIO CASSIUS (c.150–c.235) Roman historian, born in Nicaea, in Bithynia. About 180 he went to Rome, held successively all the high offices of state, was twice consul, and enjoyed the intimate friendship of **Alexander Severus**, who sent him as legate to Dalmatia and Pannonia. About 229 he retired to his native city. Of the 80 books of his *History of Rome*, from the landing of Aeneas in Italy down to 229 AD, only 19 (xxxvi–liv) have survived complete. These embrace the period 68 BC–10 AD. The first 24 books exist in the merest fragments: of the last 20 we have Xiphilinus' 11th-century epitome. The *Annals* of Zonaras, too, followed Dio Cassius so closely as to be almost an epitome.

DIOCLETIAN, properly **Gaius Aurelius Valerius Diocletianus** (245–313) Roman emperor and one of the chief architects of the Roman recovery after the troubles of the 3rd century, he was humbly born near Salona, in Dalmatia. He served with distinction under **Probus** and **Aurelian**, accompanied Carus on his Persian campaign, and was proclaimed emperor in 284 by the army at Chalcedon. Diocletian's first years of government were so troubled by the incursions of barbarians that he took Maximian as colleague in the empire, assigning to him the western division (286). Still menaced on both eastern and western fronts, he subjected the Roman empire to a fourfold division, **Constantius Chlorus** and **Galerius** being proclaimed Caesars (292). Diocletian retained the East, with Nicomedia as his seat of government; Maximian kept Italy and Africa; Constantius took Britain, Gaul and Spain; while Galerius had Illyricum and the valley of the Danube. Britain, after maintaining independence under **Carausius** and Allectus, was in 296 restored to the empire; the Persians were defeated in 298; and the Marcomanni and other northern barbarians were driven beyond the Roman frontier. In 303 there was severe persecution of the Christians. Diocletian abdicated in 305, compelling Maximian to do likewise; and, building a palace (now the heart of modern Split) near Salona on the coast of Dalmatia, he devoted himself to philosophic reflection and gardening.

DIODATI, Charles (c.1608–1638) English physician and scholar, nephew of **Jean Diodati**. The son of a refugee Italian doctor who had married an English wife, he was a schoolfellow of **John Milton** at St Paul's School, and remained a close friend. Milton addressed to him two of his Latin elegies and an Italian sonnet, and lamented his death in the pastoral *Epitaphium Damonis*.

DIODATI, Jean (1576–1649) Swiss Calvinist theologian, born in Geneva. He became professor of Hebrew there in 1597, pastor of the reformed church in 1608, and in 1609, on **Beza**'s death, professor of theology. He was a preacher at Nîmes (1614–17), and Genevese representative at the Synod of Dort. He is remembered for his Italian translation of the Bible (1607) and his *Annotationes in Biblia* (1607).

DIODORUS SICULUS (1st century BC) Greek historian, born in Agyrium, Sicily. He travelled in Asia and Europe, and lived in Rome, collecting for 30 years the materials for his immense *Bibliothēkē Historikē*, a history of the world in 40 books, from the creation to the Gallic wars of **Caesar**. The first five books are extant entire; the next five lost; the next ten complete; and of the reminder fragments remain. The style is clear and simple, if monotonous.

DIOGENES LÄERTIUS (fl.2nd century) Greek writer, born in Läerte in Cilicia. His *Lives of the Greek Philosophers*, in ten books, gives a second-hand account of the principal Greek thinkers.

DIOGENES OF APOLLONIA (5th century BC) Greek philosopher who continued the pre-Socratic tradition of speculation about the primary constituent of the world, which he identified as air, operating as an active and intelligent life-force. He was caricatured along with **Socrates** in **Aristophanes**' comedy *The Clouds* in 423 BC.

DIOGENES OF SINOPE (c.410–c.320 BC) Greek philosopher and moralist, a native of Sinope in Pontus. He came to Athens as a young man and became a student of **Antisthenes**, with whom he founded the Cynic sect. The Cynics preached an austere asceticism and self-sufficiency, and Diogenes became legendary for his ostentatious disregard of domestic comforts and social niceties. He was said to have lived in a tub ('like a dog', the origin of the term 'Cynic'). When **Alexander the Great** visited him and asked what he could do for him he answered, 'you could move away out of the sun and not cast a shadow on me'. According to another story he would wander through Athens by daytime with a lamp 'looking for an honest man'. Later in life he was captured by pirates while on a sea-voyage and was sold as a slave to Xeniades of Corinth; he was soon freed, was appointed tutor to the children and remained in Corinth for the rest of his life.

DION (409–353 BC) Syracusan magnate, both brother-in-law and son-in-law of the elder **Dionysius**. This connection with the tyrant brought him great wealth, but he fell out with **Dionysius the Younger**, who banished him in 366. Thereupon he retired to Athens to study philosophy under **Plato**. A sudden attack upon Syracuse made him master of the city (357), but his severity alienated the Syracusans, and he was murdered.

DION or **DIO CHRYSOSTOMUS** (c.40–c.112) Greek orator and philosopher, nicknamed 'Golden-Mouthed', born in Prusa, in Bithynia. He came to Rome under **Vespasian**, but was banished by **Domitian**. He next visited—in the disguise of a beggar, and on advice of the Delphic oracle—Thrace, Mysia and Scythia. On **Nerva**'s accession (96) he returned to Rome, and lived in great honour under him and **Trajan**. Eighty (two perhaps spurious) orations or treatises on politics, morals, philosophy, etc are extant, besides fragments.

DIONYSIUS EXIGUUS (d.556) Scythian Christian scholar, abbot of a monastery in Rome. One of the most learned men of his time, he fixed the dating of the Christian era in his *Cyclus Paschalis* (525).

DIONYSIUS OF ALEXANDRIA, St (c.200–264) Greek theologian, known as 'the Great'. A pupil of **Origen**, he succeeded him as head of the catechical school in Alexandria in 231. He became bishop of Alexandria in 247. In the persecutions under **Decius** he escaped to a refuge in the Libyan desert, but was restored at the death of Decius in 251. He was banished again in 257, under **Valerian**, but returned in 261. Only fragments of his writings have survived. His feast day is 17 November.

DIONYSIUS OF HALICARNASSUS (1st century BC) Greek critic, historian and rhetorician. From 30 BC he lived and worked in Rome. He wrote, in Greek, *Rōmaïkē Archaeologia*, a history of Rome down to 264 BC, a mine of information about the constitution, religion, history, laws and private life of the Romans. Of its 20 books, only the first nine are complete. He also wrote a number of critical treatises on literature and rhetoric, particularly *On the Arrangement of Words*.

DIONYSIUS THE AREOPAGITE Greek or Syrian churchman, one of the few Athenians converted by the apostle **Paul** (Acts xvii. 34). Tradition makes him the first bishop of Athens and a martyr. The Greek writings bearing his name were written, not by him, but probably by an unknown Alexandrian of the early 6th century AD. They include the treatises *On the Heavenly and Ecclesiastical Hierarchies*, *On Divine Names*, *On Mystical Theology*, and a series of ten *Epistles*, and had a great influence on the development of theology.

DIONYSIUS THE ELDER (431–367 BC) tyrant of Syracuse, who made himself absolute ruler of his native city in 405. After ferociously suppressing several insurrections and conquering some of the Greek towns of Sicily, he began war with the Carthaginians in 398. At first successful, he soon suffered reverses, but took advantage of a pestilence in the Carthaginian fleet to gain a complete victory. In 392 the Carthaginians renewed hostilities, but were defeated and Dionysius concluded an advantageous peace. He now turned his forces against Lower Italy, and in 387 captured Rhegium. From this time he exercised influence over the Greek cities of Lower Italy, while his fleets swept the Tyrrhenian and Adriatic seas. In 383 and again about 368 he renewed the war with the Carthaginians, whom he wished to drive out of Sicily, but died suddenly next year. He was a poet and patron of poets and philosophers but a hostile tradition depicts him as the destroyer of Greek liberties.

DIONYSIUS THE YOUNGER tyrant of Syracuse, son of **Dionysius the Elder**, succeeded in 367 BC. Reportedly indolent and dissolute, he fell out with **Dion** who had invited **Plato** to Syracuse. Dion was banished, but ten years afterwards expelled Dionysius. He fled to Locri, and made himself master of the city, which he ruled despotically, till in 346 dissensions in Syracuse enabled him to return there. But in 343 **Timoleon** came to free Sicily, and Dionysius was exiled to Corinth.

DIONYSIUS THRAX (fl.c.100 BC) Greek grammarian, a native of Alexandria, who taught at Rhodes and at Rome. His *Technē Grammatikē* is the basis of all European works on grammar.

DIOPHANTUS (fl.3rd century) Greek mathematician, who lived at Alexandria. Little of his work has survived; the largest work is the *Arithmetica* which deals with the solution of algebraic equations and, in contrast to earlier Greek work, uses a rudimentary algebraic notation instead of a purely geometric one. In many problems the solution is not uniquely determined, and these have become known as Diophantine problems. The study of Diophantus's work inspired **Pierre de Fermat** to take up number theory in the 17th century with remarkable results.

DIOR, Christian (1905–57) French couturier, born in Granville, Normandy. He first began to design clothes in 1935, and founded his own Paris house in 1947. He achieved worldwide fame with his long-skirted 'New Look' in that year, followed by the 'A-line', the 'Holine trapeze look', and 'the Sack'.

DIORI, Hamani (1916–89) Niger politician. Educated in Benin and Senegal, he sat in the French National Assembly, representing Niger Territory (1946–51 and 1956–58). In 1958 he became prime minister of Niger and its first president two years later. With good relations with France, he seemed to have established one of the most stable régimes in Africa and was re-elected in 1965 and 1970, but opposition within his party, the Niger Progressive party (NPP), led to his overthrow in 1974 in a coup led by army chief of staff, **Seyni Kountche**.

DIOSCORIDES, Pedanius (fl.1st century) Greek physician from Anazarb in Cilicia. He wrote *De materia medica*, the standard work on the subject for many centuries.

DIOUF, Abdou (1935–) Senegalese politician, born in Louga in north-west Senegal. After studying at Paris University he returned to work as a civil servant before entering politics. After holding a number of posts he became prime minister in 1970 under President **Léopold Sédar Senghor**. When Senghor retired at the end of 1980 Diouf succeeded him. In 1982 he became president of the loose confederation of Senegambia and was re-elected president of Senegal in 1983 and 1988. He was chairman of the Organisation of African Unity (OAU) in 1985–86.

DIPPEL, Johann Konrad (1673–1734) German theologian and alchemist, born in Burg Frankenstein, near Darmstadt. As a chemist in Berlin, he invented a panacea known as 'Dippel's Animal Oil', a distillation of animal bone and offal. He also discovered Prussian blue.

DIRAC, Paul Adrien Maurice (1902–84) English mathematical physicist, born in Bristol. His work on quantum mechanics led to a complete mathematical formulation of the relativity theory of **Albert Einstein**, in *The Principles of Quantum Mechanics* (1930). Professor of mathematics at Cambridge (1932–69), he was awarded the Nobel prize for physics in 1933, with **Edwin Schrödinger**. He became professor of physics at Florida State University in 1971.

DIRCEU See **GONZAGA, Thomás**

DIRICHLET, Peter Gustav Lejeune (1805–59) German mathematician, born in Düren, the son of the local postmaster. He showed a precocious interest in mathematics and entered the Collège de France in Paris in 1822. After teaching privately, he became extraordinary professor at Berlin in 1828, and succeeded **Carl Friedrich Gauss** as professor at Göttingen in 1855. His main work was in number theory, **Fourier** series, and boundary value problems in mathematical physics.

DIRKS, Rudolph (1877–1968) German-born American strip cartoonist, born in Heinde, the son of a wood-carver who brought him to Chicago at the age of seven. He started selling joke cartoons to *Life* magazine in 1894, then joined the *New York Journal* where he created the long-running strip, *The Katzenjammer Kids* (1897) based on **Wilhelm Busch**'s *Max und Moritz*. Dirks later retitled his characters as *The Captain and the Kids* (1914), while the original *Katzenjammer Kids* continued in parallel for decades. Dirks retired in 1958 and his strip was continued by his son, John.

DISNEY, Walt (Walter Elias) (1901–66) American artist and film producer, born in Chicago. Universally known as the creator of Mickey Mouse (who first appeared as a sound cartoon in 1928), he had previously produced several series of animated cartoons. He broke new ground with his full-length coloured cartoon films, of which the first was *Snow White and the Seven Dwarfs* (1937), and which included *Pinocchio* (1940), *Dumbo* (1941), *Bambi* (1942), *Lady and The Tramp* (1955), *Sleeping Beauty* (1959), etc, and also, in 1940, *Fantasia*, the first successful attempt to realize music in images. In 1948 he began directing his series of coloured nature films, including *The Living Desert* (1953). He also directed several swashbuckling colour films for young people, such as *Treasure Island* (1959) and *Robin Hood* (1952). He built Disneyland amusement park in California in 1955 and Disney World in Florida in 1971.

DISRAELI, Benjamin, 1st Earl of Beaconsfield (1804–81) British statesman and novelist, born in London, the eldest son of **Isaac D'Israeli**, who, lax in the Jewish faith, had him baptized in 1817. He was educated at a private school at Walthamstow by a Unitarian minister, was articled to a solicitor and kept nine terms at Lincoln's Inn. In 1826 he became the talk of the town with his first novel, *Vivian Grey*. Returning from his grand tour in 1831, he fought four elections unsuccessfully before entering parliament for Maidstone in 1837. His maiden speech, too ornate, was drowned in shouts of laughter except the closing words 'ay and though I sit down now, the time will come when you will hear me'. A reckless back-bencher at first, his marriage to Mrs Wyndham Lewis, the widow of a fellow MP, steadied him somewhat and by 1842 he was head of the 'Young England' group of young Tories. **Peel** did not reward Disraeli's services with office and on the former's third 'betrayal' of his party on the repeal of the Corn Laws (1846) Disraeli made a savage onslaught on his leader in the name of the Tory Protectionists and brought about his political downfall. At the same time he wrote two political novels, *Coningsby* (1844) and *Sybil* (1846), in which his respect for tradition is blended with 'Young England' radicalism. As Chancellor of the Exchequer and leader of the Lower House in the brief **Derby** administration of 1852, he coolly discarded Protection, and came off on the whole with flying colours; still, his budget was rejected, mainly through **Gladstone**'s attack on it, and Gladstone succeeded him in the **Aberdeen** coalition ministry. In 1858 he returned, with Lord Derby, to power, and next year introduced a petty measure of parliamentary reform—his 'fancy franchise' bill—whose rejection was followed by his resignation. For seven years the Liberals remained in office; and Disraeli, in opposition, displayed talent as a debater, and a spirit and persistency under defeat that won for him the admiration of his adversaries. As Chancellor of the Exchequer in the third Derby administration (1866), he introduced and carried a Reform Bill (1867). In February 1868 he succeeded Lord Derby as premier; but, in the face of a hostile majority, he resigned in December. On this occasion Mrs Disraeli was raised to the peerage as Viscountess Beaconsfield. She died in 1872. Disraeli returned to power in 1874 and from this time his curious relationship with Queen **Victoria** began. In 1875 he made Britain half-owner of the Suez Canal; and in 1876 he conferred on the Queen the new title of Empress of India, himself the same year being called to the Upper House as Earl of Beaconsfield. The Bulgarian insurrection which was brutally put down by the Turks did not move Disraeli as it did Gladstone. The Russians threatened Constantinople and at length a British fleet was dispatched to the Dardanelles, but war was averted by Disraeli's diplomacy at the Congress of Berlin (1878). Russia agreed to respect British interests, the Turkish empire was drastically reduced and Britain's share was 'Peace with honour' and Cyprus. **Bismarck** was full of admiration for Disraeli: 'Der alte Jude, das ist ein Mann'. But the increase of taxation and loss of trade brought about a catastrophic defeat for the Tories at the polls in 1880. Disraeli retired to novel writing. He was buried at Hughenden, near High Wycombe.

D'ISRAELI, Isaac (1776–1848) English man of letters, born in Enfield, the son of a Jewish merchant of Italian descent and father of **Benjamin Disraeli**. In 1801 he became a British subject. His *forte* was in literary illustrations of persons and history, as in his *Curiosities of Literature* (1791–1834), *Calamities of Authors* (1812) and a commentary on **Charles I** (1831).

D'ISTRIA, Dora See **GHIKA, Helena**

DITTERSDORF, Karl Ditters von (1739–99) Viennese composer and violinist, a friend of **Haydn**. He wrote 13 Italian operas, and much orchestral and piano music.

DIX, Dorothea Lynde (1802–87) American humanitarian and reformer, born in Hampden, Maine. At the age of 19 she established her own school for girls in Boston (1821–35), and then devoted her life to prison reform and the care of the insane in proper state asylums. Throughout the Civil War she served as superintendent of women nurses in the army.

DIX, John Adams (1798–1879) American soldier and politician, born in Boscawen, New Hampshire. From 1833 he was successively secretary of state of New York, US senator, and US secretary of the Treasury. In the Civil War as major-general he rendered effective service to the cause of the Union. He was minister to France (1866–69) and governor of New York (1873–75).

DIX, Otto (1891–1969) German realist painter, born in Gera-Unternhaus. He is best known for his etchings and paintings of World War I casualties, portrayed with biting realism, and of Berlin prostitutes in the decadent post-war period. A brilliant and savage portraitist and social commentator, his work was regarded as unwholesome by the Nazis who included it in the famous exhibition of Degenerate Art. After World War II he painted mostly religious subjects in isolation at Hemmenhofen.

DIXON, Denham (1786–1828) English army officer and explorer, born in London. Educated at Merchant Taylor's School, he served with distinction in the Napoleonic wars, and in 1821 was sent as expedition leader to join **Hugh Clapperton** and Walter Oudney on their expedition to discover the source of the Niger (1821–25). In 1827 he was appointed governor of Sierra Leone, where he died of fever. Denham's Bustard was named in his honour.

DIXON, Jeremiah See **MASON, Charles**

DIXON, Sir Owen (1886–1972) Australian judge. Justice of the Supreme Court of Victoria (1926), of the High Court of Australia (1929–52) and then chief justice of that court (1952–64), he was a great master and judicial expositor of the law. In constitutional cases he turned interpretation of the Australian constitution in new directions, substantially helping to make it a guarantee of freedom of trade and commerce between the states. He served also as Australian minister to the USA (1942–44).

DIXON, Sir Pierson John (1904–65) English diplomat, born in Englefield Green, Surrey. He became, after a distinguished career in the foreign service, ambassador to Czechoslovakia from 1948 until 1953, when he was made permanent UK delegate to the UN. He was ambassador to France from 1960.

DIXON, Richard Watson (1833–1900) English poet, born in Islington. He studied at King Edward's School, Birmingham, Pembroke College, Oxford, and became a canon of Carlisle in 1874 and vicar of Warkworth in 1883. A member of the Pre-Raphaelite circle with **Burne-Jones** and **William Morris**, he wrote seven volumes of poetry and a *History of the Church of England* (6 vols, 1877–1902).

DIXON, William Hepworth (1821–79) English writer, born in Manchester. Two series of papers in the *Daily News* on 'The Literature of the Lower Orders' and 'London Prisons' attracted attention, and in 1850 he published *John Howard, and the Prison World of Europe*. *William Penn* (1851) is a defence against **Macaulay**'s attack. From 1853 to 1869 Dixon was editor of the *Athenaeum*. He wrote a number of works on political history. His second son Harold Baily (1852–1930), was a chemist, and was known for his work on gases. He was professor of chemistry at Manchester 1886–1922.

DJILAS, Milovan (1911–) Yugoslav politician, born in Montenegro. A lifelong friend of **Tito**, Djilas rose to a high position in the Yugoslav Government as a result of his wartime exploits as a partisan. He was discredited and imprisoned as a result of outspoken criticism of the Communist system as practised in Yugoslavia, but was released from prison under amnesty at the end of 1966. He wrote *The New Order* (1957), *The Unperfect Society: Beyond the New Class* (1966), etc, and two autobiographical volumes, *Land without Justice* (1958) and *Memoir of a Revolutionary* (1973). He was formally rehabilitated by the Yugoslav authorities in 1989.

DMITRI, or **Demetrius** (1583–91) Russian prince, youngest son of Tsar **Ivan the Terrible**. He was murdered by the regent **Boris Godunov**, but about 1603 was personated by a runaway Moscow monk, Grigoriy Otrepieff, the 'false Demetrius', who was crowned tsar by the army in 1605 but killed in 1606 in a rebellion. A second and a third 'false Demetrius' arose within the next few years, but their fate was no better.

DOBBIE, Sir William George Sheddon (1879–1964) English soldier, born in Madras. Educated at Charterhouse and the Royal Military Academy, Woolwich, he joined the Royal Engineers and served in South Africa in the 2nd Boer War (1899–1902). He was GOC in Malaya from 1935 to 1939, and governor of Malta from 1940 to 1942 during its resolute resistance to incessant German and Italian air attack.

DOBELL, Bertram (1841–1914) English bookseller and bibliophile. He discovered and edited the works of **Traherne** and **William Strode**, and edited the poems of **James Thomson**.

DOBELL, Sydney Thompson (1824–74) English poet, born in Cranbrook, Kent. He worked with his father as a wine merchant in London and Cheltenham, but lived for some time in the Scottish Highlands and abroad, and became a passionate advocate of oppressed nationalities. His dramatic poem, *The Roman* (1850), was written in sympathy with Italian aspirations for unity, and he also wrote sonnets on the Crimean War (1855) and *England in Time of War* (1856). His chief works were in the style of the so-called Spasmodic School, caricatured by **Aytoun**, appearing under the pseudonym Sydney Yendys.

DOBELL, Sir William (1899–1970) Australian portrait-painter, born in Newcastle, New South Wales. He was apprenticed to a local architect, but moved to Sydney and studied at the Julian Ashton Art School. In 1929 he won a scholarship, studied at the Slade School of Art, in London, and exhibited at the Royal Academy. Returning to Sydney he worked during World War II in a camouflage unit with other artists including Joshua Smith. Dobell's portrait of Smith won the Archibald prize in 1944 and became the centre of a bitter artistic storm. Dobell won the ensuing legal battle but it resulted in permanent damage to his health. He was further vindicated in 1948 by not only winning the Archibald again, but also the Wynne prize for landscape painting. In 1959 he won the Archibald for a third time and the following year was commissioned by *Time* magazine to paint a portrait of the then prime minister of Australia, Sir **Robert Menzies**. Three further cover portraits were published by the magazine, and in 1964 his career was crowned by a retrospective exhibition at the Art Gallery of New South Wales. On his death Dobell left all his estate to establish the art foundation which bears his name.

DÖBEREINER, Johann Wolfgang (1780–1849) German chemist, born at Bug bei Hof in Bavaria. Professor at Jena from 1810, he is remembered as the inventor of 'Döbereiner's Lamp', in which hydrogen, produced in the lamp by the action of sulphuric acid on zinc, burns on contact with a platinum sponge.

DOBRÉE, Bonamy (1891–1974) English literary scholar. He was professor of English literature at Leeds (1936–55), and wrote on Restoration Comedy (1924) and Tragedy (1929), **Chesterfield** (1932), **Wesley** (1933), **Pope** (1951), **Kipling** (1951), and **Dryden** (1956).

DOBROLYUBOV, Nikolai Alexandrovich (1836–61) Russian literary critic, born in Nijni Novgorod. He was influenced by **Belinsky** and **Chernyshevski** and became the most influential figure in 19th-century Russian criticism of the 'socio-utilitarian' school.

DOBROVSKY, Joseph (1753–1829) Czech scholar, born in Gyermet near Raab in Hungary, the founder of Slavonic philology. He studied at Prague, in 1772 became a Jesuit, and was teacher, tutor and editor of a critical journal. In 1792 he visited Denmark, Sweden and Russia to search for Bohemian books and MSS carried off in the Thirty Years' War. In 1822 he published the first grammar of Old Church Slavonic (*Institutiones linguae slavicae dialecti veteris*).

DOBRYNIN, Anataoly Fedorovich (1919–) Soviet diplomat and politician, born in Krasnoya Gorka, near Moscow. He was educated at a technical college and worked as an engineer at an aircraft plant during World War II. He joined the diplomatic service in 1941, serving as counsellor at the Soviet Embassy in Washington (1952–55), assistant to the minister for foreign affairs (1955–57), under-secretary at the UN (1957–59) and head of the USSR's American Department (1959–61), before being appointed Soviet ambassador to Washington, 1962–86. A member of the Communist party (CPSU) since 1945, he became a full member of its central committee in 1971. In 1986, the new Soviet leader, **Mikhail Gorbachev**, appointed him secretary for foreign affairs and head of the International Department. He retired in 1988.

DOBSON, Frank (1888–1963) English sculptor, born in London. He was associated with the London Group for many years, and was professor of sculpture at the Royal College of Art until 1953. His sculptures show an extraordinary feeling for plastic form, and his very individual style (with simplified contours and heavy limbs) is shown at its best in his female nudes. Among his best known works are *The Man Child*, *Morning*, and a bust of **Osbert Sitwell**.

DOBSON, Henry Austin (1840–1921) English poet, born in Plymouth. He was educated at Beaumaris, Coventry, and Strasbourg as a civil engineer like his father, but from 1856 to 1901 was a board of trade clerk. His earliest poems, published in 1868 in *St Paul's Magazine*, were followed by *Vignettes in Rhyme*, *Proverbs in Porcelain*, *Old World Idylls*, *At the Sign of the Lyre*, *The Story of Rosina* and *Collected Poems* (1923). Often in rondeau, ballade or villanelle form, these poems are marked by rare perfection. In prose he published monographs of **Fielding** (1883), **Steele**, **Thomas Bewick** (and his pupils), **Horace Walpole**, **Hogarth**, **Goldsmith**, **Fanny Burney** and **Richardson** (1902); and *Eighteenth Century Vignettes* (1892–96), *Four Frenchwomen*, and other collections of graceful and erudite essays.

DOBSON, William (1610–46) English portrait painter, born in London. He succeeded **Van Dyck** in 1641 as serjeant-painter to **Charles I**, and painted portraits of him, the Prince of Wales, and Prince **Rupert**. His affairs got into confusion, and he was imprisoned for debt, and died in poverty shortly after his release.

DOBZHANSKY, Theodosius (1900–75) Russian-born American geneticist, born in Nemirov in the Ukraine. He studied zoology at Kiev and taught genetics in Leningrad before going to the USA to join **Thomas Hunt Morgan** at Columbia in 1927 to work on the genetics of the fruit fly *Drosophila*. He taught thereafter at the California Institute of Technology (1929–40), Columbia (1940–62) and Rockefeller University, New York (1962–71). He showed that the genetic variability in a population is large, including many potentially lethal genes which nevertheless confer versatility when the population is exposed to environmental change. His influential work is described in *Genetics and the Origin of Species* (1937) and in *Genetics and the Evolutionary Process* (1970). His work gave the experimental evidence which linked Darwinian evolutionary theory with **Mendel**'s laws of heredity; and he applied his ideas to the concept of race in man, defining races as Mendelian populations differing in gene frequencies, as in his *Mankind Evolving* (1962).

DOCHERTY, Tommy (Thomas Henderson) (1928–) Scottish footballer and manager, born in Glasgow. In a tempestuous career he played 25 times for Scotland and managed ten clubs including Aston Villa, Manchester United, Derby County and Queen's Park Rangers. From September 1971 he managed the Scotland side for just over a year. A superb short-term motivator, he frequently fell out with his employers. On leaving football he built a successful career as an after-dinner speaker.

DOCKWRA, or **Dockwray, William** (d.1716) English merchant, based in London. In 1683 he devised a new penny postal system in London, and was alternately favoured and persecuted by the authorities.

DOCTOROW, Edgar Lawrence (1931–) American novelist, born in New York City. He was educated at Bronx High School of Science, Kenyon College and Columbia University. From 1960 to 1964 he was editor of the New American Library and has held teaching posts in several colleges and universities. His first novel was *Welcome to Hard Times* (1961), followed by *Big as Life* (1966) and *The Book of Daniel* (1971), based on the story of the **Rosenbergs**, executed for spying. *Ragtime* (1975) is generally regarded as his *tour de force*, in which he recreates the atmosphere of the Ragtime era with wit, accuracy and appealing nostalgia. It was filmed in 1981. Later books include *Loon Lake* (1980) and *The World's Fair* (1986).

DOD, Charles Roger Phipps (1793–1855) Irish journalist, born in Drumlease vicarage in Leitrim. He came to London in 1818, and for 23 years worked on *The Times*. He started the *Parliamentary Companion* (1832) and a *Peerage* (1841).

DODD, Charles Harold (1884–1973) Welsh biblical scholar and Congregational pastor, born in Wrexham. He graduated from Oxford and served a Congregational church in Warwick. He returned to lecture at Oxford, held a theological chair at Manchester, then was elected to the Norris-Hulse chair of divinity at Cambridge (1936–49)—the first Nonconformist incumbent for nearly three centuries. In 1949 he became general director for the New English Bible translation. His own publications included *The Apostolic Preaching and Its Developments* (1936), *According to the Scriptures* (1952), and *Historical Tradition in the Fourth Gospel* (1963).

DODD, Ken (Kenneth) (1929–) English stand-up comedian, singer and actor, born in Liverpool. He made his début at the Empire Theatre, Nottingham, in 1954, and played summer seasons all round Britain for the next ten years. He created a record at his London Palladium début in 1965 by starring in his own 42-week season of *Doddy's Here*. He has since appeared regularly on stage in variety and pantomime, on the radio and, occasionally, on television. He has also had hits with songs such as *Tears* and *Happiness*.

DODD, William (1729–77) English forger, born in Bourn, Lincolnshire. He graduated from Clare Hall, Cambridge (1750), married, took orders and became a popular preacher. He published a series of edifying books, and was made king's chaplain (1763) and tutor to Philip Stanhope, Lord Chesterfield's nephew. But, despite his large income, he fell hopelessly into debt. His attempt to buy the rich living of St George's, Hanover Square, led to his name being struck off the list of chaplains (1774). He left England, and was well received by his pupil, now Lord Chesterfield, at Geneva, and presented to the living of Wing in Buckinghamshire. However, but sinking deeper and deeper into debt, he sold his chapel, and in February 1777 offered a stockbroker a bond for £4200 signed by Chesterfield. It proved to be a forgery, and Dodd, though he refunded a great part of the money, was tried and sentenced to death. Extraordinary efforts were made by Dr **Johnson** and others to secure a pardon; but the king refused to reprieve him, and Dodd was hanged.

DODDRIDGE, Philip (1702–51) English Nonconformist clergyman, born in London. Determined to enter the Nonconformist ministry on the advice of the famous **Samuel Clarke**, he studied at Kibworth Academy, Leicestershire, from 1719 and in 1723 became pastor of a congregation there. In 1729 he settled in Northampton as minister and president of a theological academy. He died in Lisbon, where he had gone for his health. He was the author of *On the Rise and Progress of Religion in the Soul* (1745), and several hymns, including 'Hark, the glad sound, the Saviour comes', and 'O God of Bethel, by whose hand'.

DODDS, Alfred Amédée (1842–1922) French soldier, born in Saint Louis (Senegal). He served with distinction in the Franco-Prussian war (1870–71). In 1892 he led the French force in the 2nd Dahomey-French war and annexed the country.

DODDS, Johnny (John M) (1892–1940) American jazz clarinettist, born in New Orleans. Self-taught, his measured embroideries typified the role of his instrument in the early three-part ensemble style. Recordings in the 1920s with **King Oliver** and **Louis Armstrong** secured this reputation; but although he recorded little after 1929, his influence continues among clarinet players in the New Orleans style.

DODGE, Grenville Mellen (1831–1916) American soldier and engineer, born in Danvers, Massachusetts. He fought in the Civil War, and was promoted to major-general in 1864. After the war, as chief engineer of the Union Pacific Railway from 1866 he was responsible for the construction of some of the most famous American railroads.

DODGE, Henry (1782–1867) American politician and pioneer, born in Vincennes, Indiana. He served in the war of 1812 and the Black Hawk war of 1832, and became famous as a frontiersman. In 1836 he was appointed governor of the Territory of Wisconsin and became a member of the House of Representatives in 1841. He was US senator for Wisconsin, 1848–57.

DODGE, Mary Elizabeth, née **Mapes** (1838–1905) American writer, born in New York. She married William Dodge, a lawyer, in 1851, and after his death in 1858 turned to writing books for children, especially *Hans Brinker; or, The Silver Skates* (1865), which became a children's classic, and other works. From 1873 she was the editor of *St Nicholas Magazine*.

DODGE, Theodore Ayrault (1842–1909) American soldier and military historian, born in Pittsfield, Massachusetts. He fought in the Civil War, losing a leg at Gettysburg, and wrote *A Bird's-eye View of our Civil War* (1885), *Alexander* (1890), *Hannibal* (1891), *Caesar* (1892), etc.

DODGSON, Charles Lutwidge, pseud **Lewis Carroll** (1832–98) English writer, nonsense versifier and mathematician, born in Daresbury, near Warrington, the third of eleven children. His pseudonym derived from his first two names: Lutwidge is the same as Lutwig, of which Lewis is the anglicised version, and Carroll is a form of Charles. Throughout his childhood, with his siblings, he invented and played many board games, acrostics and other puzzles. He was educated at Rugby and Christ Church College, Oxford, where he lectured in mathematics after 1855 and took orders in 1861. *Alice's Adventures in Wonderland* (1865), his most famous book, had its origin in a boat trip which he made with Alice Liddell and her sisters, Lorina and Edith, the daughters of the Dean of his college, **Henry George Liddell**, 'all in the golden afternoon' of 4 July 1862. Originally he intended calling it *Alice's Adventures Underground.* A sequel, *Through the Looking-Glass and What Alice Found There*, appeared in 1871. Illustrated by Sir **John Tenniel**, both are superficially similar: in each Alice meets a succession of fantastic characters (Tweedledee and Tweedledum, the White Rabbit and the March Hare, Humpty-Dumpty) and each ends grandly, one with a trial, the other with a banquet. Each has been translated into many languages and there have been innumerable editions, many illustrated by distinguished artists. Their success among Victorian children was doubtless due to the fact that Dodgson eschewed moralising. His other works include *Phantasmagoria and other poems* (1869), *The Hunting of the Snark* (1876), *Rhyme? and Reason?* (1883) and *Sylvie and Bruno* (1889 and 1893). Of his mathematical works *Euclid and his Modern Rivals* (1879) is still of interest. He was also a pioneer photographer, and took many portraits of young girls with whom he seemed to empathize particularly. His diaries appeared in 1953, and an edition of his letters in 1979.

DODINGTON, George, originally named **Bubb,** later **1st Baron Melcombe** (1691–1762) British politician, the son of an Irish fortune-hunter or apothecary. He took the name Dodington in 1720 on inheriting an estate from his uncle. He has become the prototype of the time-serving politician: MP from 1715 to 1754, he switched loyalties with ease until he attained high office and an eventual peerage as Lord Melcombe (1761). However, he spoke out bravely against the execution of Admiral **John Byng** in 1757. His *Diary*, published posthumously in 1784, betrays the venality of politics in his day.

DODS, Marcus (1834–1909) Scottish clergyman and scholar. He was minister of Renfrew Free Church, Glasgow (1864–89), and professor of New Testament exegesis at the (United) Free Church College in Edinburgh (1889), and principal (1907). He published several theological works and commentaries on scripture.

DODSLEY, Robert (1704–64) English playwright, born in Mansfield, Nottinghamshire. He was apprenticed to a stocking weaver, but, probably ill-treated, ran away and became a footman. He spent his spare time reading, and in 1732 published *A Muse in Livery*. His *Toy Shop*, a dramatic piece, was through **Pope**'s influence acted at Covent Garden in 1735 with great success. With his profits, and £100 from Pope, he set up as bookseller, but still continued to write bright plays, including *The King and the Miller of Mansfield* (1737), *The Blind Beggar of Bethnal Green* (1741) and *Rex et Pontifex* (1745), which were collected as *Trifles* (1745). In 1738 he bought *London* from the yet unknown Dr **Johnson** for ten guineas. Other famous authors for whom he published included Pope, **Edward Young**, **Akenside** and **Goldsmith**, and he founded the *Annual Register* with **Edmund Burke** in 1759. With a tragedy, *Cleone* (1758), acted at Covent Garden with extraordinary success, he closed his career as a dramatist. He is chiefly remembered for his *Select*

Collection of Old Plays (12 vols, 1744–45) and his *Poems by Several Hands* (3 vols, 1748; 6 vols, 1758).

DOE, Samuel Kenyon (1950–) Liberian politician and soldier, born in Tuzon in Grand Gedeh county. He joined the army as a private in 1969, reaching the rank of master sergeant ten years later. In 1980 he led a coup, in which President William Tolbert was killed, and replaced him as head of state. The following year he made himself general and army commander-in-chief. In 1984 he established the National Democratic party of Liberia (NDPL), and in 1985 was narrowly elected president.

DOESBURG, Theo van, originally **Christian Emil Marie Kupper** (1883–1931) Dutch painter, architect and writer, born in Utrecht. He began as a poet, but took up painting and exhibited at The Hague in 1908. With **Piet Mondrian** he founded the avant-garde magazine *De Stijl* (1917–31), and devoted himself to propagating the new aesthetic ideas of this movement, based on a severe form of geometrical abstraction known as Neo-Plasticism. By 1921 he was in touch with **Le Corbusier**, and with the leading figures of the Bauhaus design school at Dessau. He later became increasingly involved in architectural projects.

DOESBURG van See **MONDRIAN, Piet**

DOGGETT, Thomas (c.1660–1721) Irish travelling actor, born in Dublin. He came to London in 1691 and prospered as a comic actor, wrote a play called *The Country Wake* (1696), and became past-proprietor of the Haymarket Theatre. In 1716, to honour the accession of King **George I**, he founded a sculling prize, 'Doggett's Coat and Badge', still competed for by Thames watermen on 1 August.

DOHNANYI, Ernst (Erno) von (1877–1960) Hungarian composer and pianist, born in Pressburg. He achieved some success with his opera *The Tower of Voivod* (1922), but is perhaps best known for his piano compositions, especially *Variation on a Nursery Theme*, for piano and orchestra.

DOISY, Edward Adelbert (1893–) American biochemist, born in Hume, Illinois. He studied at Harvard, and was director of the department of biochemistry at St Mary's Hospital, St Louis (1924–65). In collaboration with the American embryologist Edgar Allen (1892–1943) he conducted research on reproduction and hormones, and studied the female sex hormones estrone (1929), estriol (1930) and estradiol (1935). In 1939 he isolated two forms of the coagulant agent Vitamin K (discovered earlier by **C P H Dam**), and they shared the 1943 Nobel prize for physiology or medicine. He wrote *Sex Hormones* (1936) and *Sex and Internal Secretions* (1939).

DOLABELLA, Publius Cornelius (c.70–43 BC) Roman politician and **Cicero**'s profligate son-in-law, in 49 he sought refuge from his creditors with **Caesar**. Two years later, having obtained the tribuneship, he brought forward a bill cancelling all debts, which led to bloody struggles in Rome. On Caesar's murder (44) he usurped the consulate, and made a great display of republican sentiments until **Antonius** gave him the province of Syria. He murdered at Smyrna the proconsul, Trebonius, and proceeded to wring money from the towns of Asia with a recklessness that brought about his outlawry. Laodicea, in which he had shut himself up, was taken by **Cassius**, and Dolabella bade one of his own soldiers kill him.

DOLCI, Carlo (1616–86) Italian painter, born in Florence. His works, which are scattered over all Europe, include many Madonnas, *St Cecilia* (Dresden), *Herodias with the Head of John the Baptist* (Dresden) and the *Magdalen* in the Uffizi at Florence.

DOLCI, Danilo (1925–) Italian social worker, 'the **Gandhi** of Sicily', born in Trieste. He qualified as an architect, but, witnessing the death of an infant from starvation in Sicily, decided to fight poverty there. Fasting, and with a mouth-organ, he managed to extract municipal funds to launch his campaign in three of Sicily's poorest towns—Trappeto, Partinico and Montalepre—building schools and community centres to teach the people the methods by which they could raise themselves by their own efforts, helped by funds and social workers from many European countries. Opposed by the government, his own church and the Mafia, he was imprisoned in 1956 for four months for leading a gang of unemployed in repairing a road, unpaid and without permission, ie, an 'upside down strike', and again in 1957 for obscenity in publishing the pathetic life stories of little boys who sold themselves for vice in return for food. Although neither Communist nor fellow-traveller, he was awarded the Lenin peace prize in 1956. His books include *To Feed the Hungry* (trans, 1959), *Waste* (trans, 1963), *The Man Who Plays Alone* (trans, 1969) and *Sicilian Lives* (trans, 1982), and some published poetry.

DOLET, Étienne (1509–46) French printer and humanist, born in Orleans, and known as 'the martyr of the Renaissance'. At the university of Paris he was set upon a lifelong study of **Cicero**; in Venice (1526–32) he imbibed the spirit of humanism. At Lyons, his residence from 1534, he wrote *Dialogus de imitatione ciceroniana* (1535) against **Erasmus**, and came under strong suspicion of heresy. He killed a man in self-defence and fled to Paris, where friends intervened with the king (1537). In Lyon he set up a printing press, on which he printed translations of the classics, as well as Erasmus and **Rabelais**. He was arrested more than once for publishing heretical books. In 1544 he was found guilty of heresy (on a charge mainly based on an alleged mistranslation of **Plato**, in which he was accused of denying the immortality of the soul) and was burned at Paris. His chief contribution to classical scholarship was his *Commentaries on the Latin Language* (1536–38).

DOLGORUKOVA, Katharina, Princess Yourieffskaia (1847–1922) Russian noblewoman, mistress of the emperor **Alexander II**, who married her in 1880 after his first wife's death. Under the pseudonym of Victor Laferté, she published *Alexandre II, Détails inédits sur sa vie intime et sa mort* (1882). Her *Mémoires* (1890) were suppressed by the Russian government.

DOLIN, Anton, stage name of **Patrick Healey-Kay** (1904–83) British dancer and choreographer, born in Slinfold, Sussex. He studied under Grace and Lilly Cone, Serafoma Astafoeva and **Bronislava Nijinska**; and was a principal with **Diaghilev**'s Ballet Russe, from 1924, with whom he danced in **Fokine**'s *Spectre de la Rose* and **Balanchine**'s *Le Bal* and *The Prodigal Son*. He was a founder member of the Camargo Society and a principal with the Vic-Wells Ballet during the 1930s. His next move was to co-found the (Alicia) Markova-Dolin Ballet. The partnership became known particularly for their interpretations of *Giselle*. From 1950 to 1961 he served as London Festival Ballet's first artistic director, choreographing for the company. His list of works includes *Rhapsody in Blue* (1928), *Variations for Four* (1957) and *Pas de deux for Four* (1967). He wrote *The Life and Art of Alicia Markova* (1953) and published his autobiography in 1960.

D'OLIVEIRA, Basil Lewis (1931–) South African-born cricketer, born in Cape Town. As a Cape Coloured he had no prospects of first-class cricket within South Africa, but was brought to England to play league cricket in Lancashire and eventually joined Worcestershire. Selected for England, he played 44 times and scored five Test centuries. He was chosen for the 1968–69 England tour of South Africa, and the refusal of the South African government to admit him led to the cancellation of the tour and the subsequent exclusion of South Africa from international cricket.

DOLLFUSS, Engelbert (1892–1934) Austrian statesman, born at Texing. He studied at Vienna and Berlin, became leader of the Christian Socialist party, and in 1932 chancellor. In 1933 he suspended parliamentary government, drove the Socialists into revolt and crushed them. Purged of its Socialist majority, parliament then granted Dollfuss power to remodel the state. In 1934 conflict with the Nazis culminated in his murder on 25 July.

DÖLLINGER, Johann Joseph Ignaz von (1799–1890) German Catholic theologian, born in Bamberg. He was professor of ecclesiastical history and law at Munich almost continuously from 1826 to 1871, when he was elected rector. A staunch Ultramontane, he published *Die Reformation* (1846–48); but in 1857 a visit to Rome caused a change in his opinions. In 1870 the Vatican Council promulgated the decree of papal infallibility, and in March 1871 Döllinger issued a letter withholding his submission. Excommunicated, he took a leading part in the summoning of the congress in Munich out of which arose the Old Catholics. From this time Döllinger advocated the union of the various Christian churches in lectures, and, in two conferences, agreement was reached on various points with the Anglican and Orthodox churches. He published a history of moral controversies in the Catholic church since the 16th century (1888), *Akademische Vorträge* (1888–91) and other books. He represented his university in the Bavarian Chamber from 1845 to 1847, and onwards from 1849, and sat in the Frankfurt Parliament of 1848–49.

DOLLO, Louis Antoine Marie Joseph (1857–1931) Belgian palaeontologist, born in Lille. After studying there, in 1882 he became assistant (keeper, 1891) of mammals in the Royal Museum of Natural History in Brussels. In 1893 he enunciated Dollo's law of irreversibility in evolution.

DOLLOND, John (1706–61) English optician, born in London of Huguenot parentage. A silk weaver to trade, in 1752 he turned optician, and devoted himself with the help of his son Peter (1738–1820) to the invention of an achromatic telescope.

DOLMETSCH, Arnold (1858–1940) French-born British musical-instrument maker, born in Le Mans. In 1883 Dolmetsch came to England to study at the Royal College of Music. Deeply interested in early music and original instruments, he became involved in their restoration and manufacture around 1890. From 1892 he gave concerts at the Century Guild owned by **A H Mackmurdo**. He exhibited a harpsichord at the Arts and Crafts Exhibition in 1896 and his clavichord of 1897 was decorated by **Burne-Jones**. In 1919 he made the first modern recorder and in 1928 the Dolmetsch Foundation was established to support his work. He was the author of *The Interpretation of the Music of the Seventeenth and Eighteenth Centuries* (1893).

DOLOMIEU, Déodat Guy Gratet de (1750–1801) French geologist and mineralogist, born in Dolomieu in Dauphiné. Renowned for his researches on volcanic rocks, he gave his name to 'dolomite'.

DOMAGK, Gerhard (Johannes Paul) (1895–1964) German biochemist, born in Brandenburg. He studied at Kiel and taught at Greifswald and Münster before becoming director of the I G Farbenindustrie Laboratory for Experimental Pathology and Bacteriology in 1927. He discovered the chemotherapeutic properties of sulphanilamide, and thus ushered in a new age in chemotherapy. In 1939, on instruction from the German government, he refused the Nobel prize for physiology or medicine.

DOMAT, Jean (1625–96) French jurist and judge at Clermont-Ferrand. In an attempt to extract the general ideas and principles from Roman law and Christian teaching for use by lawyers, he compiled *Les Lois Civiles dans Leur Ordre Naturel* (3 vols, 1689–94), a work translated and copied elsewhere, and which influenced the French Civil Code of 1808.

DOMBROVSKI, or **Dabrowski, Jan Henryk** (1755–1818) Polish soldier, born near Cracow. He fought against Russia with **Kosciuszko** (1792–94), then formed a Polish legion in the French army and took a distinguished part throughout the Napoleonic campaigns. On **Napoleon**'s fall he returned to Poland, and was appointed by the emperor **Alexander I** a general of cavalry and Polish senator.

DOMENICHINO, or **Domenico, Zampieri** (1581–1641) Italian painter of the Bolognese school, born in Bologna. His masterpiece is the *Last Communion of St Jerome* (1614), in the Vatican.

DOMENICO VENEZIANO (c.1400–1461) Italian painter, known for his altarpiece in the Uffizi at Florence, and represented in the National Gallery by a *Madonna and Child.*

DOMETT, Alfred (1811–87) English poet and politician, born in Camberwell, like his lifelong friend, **Robert Browning** (who calls him 'Waring' in his poem of that name). He studied at St John's College, Cambridge; and was called to the bar in 1841. He went to New Zealand in 1841, and became prime minister (1862–63) and later registrar of land (1865–71), before returning to England. He published some verses on his New Zealand experiences.

DOMINGO, Placido (1941–) Spanish tenor, born in Madrid. He moved to Mexico with his family and attended the National Conservatory of Music, Mexico City, studying piano and conducting. In 1959 he made his début as a baritone, taking his first major tenor role, that of Alfredo in *La Traviata*, in 1960, and from 1962 to 1965 was a member of the Israeli National Opera. He first sang in New York in 1965, at La Scala in 1969 and Covent Garden in 1971. His controlled, intelligent vocal technique and superb acting have made him one of the world's leading lyric-dramatic tenors, and among his successes have been **Puccini**'s *Tosca*, **Meyerbeer**'s *L'Africaine*, **Verdi**'s *Othello*, **Bizet**'s *Carmen*, and **Offenbach**'s *Contes d'Hoffman*. He published his autobiography in 1983.

DOMINGUÍ, Luis Miguel (1926–) Spanish matador, born in Madrid. He became a first-rank matador at the age of 18, his style marked by an unflurried elegance and disdain. This sometimes angered the crowds but for purity of style and unruffled, detached courage no matador has ever bettered him. A friend of **Hemingway** and **Picasso**, he retired in 1961, but made a triumphant return to the bull-ring in 1971.

DOMINIC, St (c.1170–1221) Spanish religious. In 1216 he founded the Order of Friars Preachers. Born in Calaruega in Old Castile, he studied at Palencia, acquiring such a name for piety and learning that in 1193 the bishop of Osma made him a canon, and relied on his help to reform the whole chapter according to the Augustinian rule. He led a life of rigorous asceticism and devoted himself to missionary labours among Muslims and 'heretics'. In 1204 he accompanied his bishop on a political mission, and had to travel round the south of France three times. He undertook conversion of the Albigenses and travelled from place to place on foot, St **Paul**'s epistles in his hands, and preaching everywhere. He continued his labours for ten years, and gathered like-minded companions round him, for whom he founded the first house of his order at Toulouse. He also set up an asylum for women in danger from heretical influence, which developed into an order of nuns. Events occurred during the Inquisition which left a deep stain on his memory and that of his order, associating it closely with the Inquisition. **Innocent III**, incensed by the murder of his legate, Peter of Castelnau, called the barons of northern France, led by **Simon de Montfort**, to a crusade against the heretics; and Dominic became a consenting party to these cruelties. In 1215 he went to the fourth Lateran Council, and Innocent III promised approval of his new order on condition that it adopted an old rule. Dominic chose the rule of St **Augustine**, and next year the authorization was given by Honorius III. Dominic became 'Master of the Sacred Palace', an office which has continued hereditary in the order. In 1220 the Dominicans, in imitation of their Franciscan brethren, adopted a poverty so rigid that not even the order as a corporation could hold houses or lands, and thus they forced themselves to become mendicants or beggars. Dominic died at Bologna. He had lived to see his order occupying sixty houses and divided into eight provinces. It had spread to England, where from their dress they were called Black Friars; to northern France, Italy, Spain and Austria. He was canonized in 1234 by his friend **Gregory IX**.

DOMINICI, Gaston (1877–1965) French farmer, and central figure in a controversial murder case, born in Digne, Provence. He was sentenced to death in 1954 after prolonged inquiries and a much debated confession (afterwards retracted) for the murder near Lurs, Provence (1952), of Sir Jack Drummond (a British nutrition expert), his wife and their eleven-year-old daughter. The case was officially closed, 1956, with Dominici still in a Marseilles prison hospital. In 1957 his sentence was formally commuted to life imprisonment.

DOMINIS, Marco Antonio de (1566–1624) Italian prelate, born in the Dalmatian island of Arbe. As archbishop of Spalato from 1600 he became involved in a quarrel between the papacy and Venice, and resigned his see for reasons given in his *Consilium Profectionis* (1616). In 1616 he went to England, where he was converted to Anglicanism and in 1618 was appointed by **James VI and I** master of the Savoy, and in 1619 dean of Windsor. In his *Consilium Profectionis* and *De Republica Ecclesiastica* (1617) he disputed the supremacy of the pope; in 1619 he published without authority **Sarpi**'s *History of the Council of Trent*. His enemy **Paul V** died in 1620, and was succeeded by **Gregory XV**, a relative of de Dominis, who wanted to return to the Catholic Church. He left England in 1622, and while waiting in Brussels denounced the Church of England and recanted in his *Consilium Reditus ex Angliae consilium*. He went on to Rome, but was seized by the Inquisition, and died in prison. He published his *De Radiis Visus et Lucis in Vitris Perspectivis et Iride* in 1611.

DOMITIANUS, Titus Flavius (51–96) Roman emperor, a son of **Vespasian**; he succeeded his elder brother **Titus** as emperor in 81. He ruled well at first, but his autocratic manner and severity alienated the Roman upper classes, and his reign declined into violence and terror. He eventually fell victim to one of many conspiracies, and the Flavian dynasty came to an end with him.

DON CARLOS See **CARLOS**

DONALDSON, James (1751–1830) Scottish newspaper proprietor and philanthropist, born in Edinburgh. He inherited the *Edinburgh Advertiser*, and left about £240000 to found a 'hospital' (school) for 300 poor children. It was built in 1842–51 from designs by **William Playfair** at a cost of about £120000; it subsequently became Donaldson's School for the Deaf.

DONALDSON, Sir James (1831–1915) Scottish educational administrator and classical scholar, born in Aberdeen. Despite humble circumstances he was educated at Aberdeen Grammar School and University. He studied briefly at New College, London, with a view to joining the Congregationalist ministry but left to further his classical and theological studies in Berlin where he discovered the psychology of education and the work of **Herbart** and **Beneke**. From 1852 to 1854 he was assistant to the professor of Greek at Edinburgh; from 1854 to 1856 was rector of Stirling High School; and was classical master, 1856–66, and then rector, 1866–81 at Edinburgh High School. He was professor of humanity, Aberdeen University, 1881–86; principal of the United College at St Andrews, 1886–90, and principal and vice-chancellor of St Andrews University from 1890 to his death. His most significant work of scholarship, *A Critical History of Christian Literature and Doctrine from the Death of the Apostles to the Nicene Council*, was published in three volumes, 1864–66. He was active in educational politics and promoted the Education Act of 1872 which established primary education in Scotland on a compulsory basis.

DONALDSON, John Francis, Lord, of Lymington (1920–) English judge. Educated at Charterhouse and Trinity College, Cambridge, his practice was mainly in commercial cases; he became a judge in 1966, a lord justice of appeal in 1979 and master of the rolls in 1982. As such he acted vigorously to expedite the hearing of cases.

DONALDSON, John William (1811–61) English philologist, born in London, of Haddington ancestry. Educated at Trinity College, Cambridge, he became a fellow and tutor there. He was a spectacularly unsuccessful headmaster of Bury St Edmunds grammar school (1841–55); thereafter he tutored at Cambridge with great success. His *New Cratylus* (1839) was the first attempt on a large scale to familiarize Englishmen with German principles of comparative philology.

DONAT, Aelius See **DONATUS**

DONAT, Robert (1905–58) English film and stage actor of Polish descent, born in Manchester. Elocution lessons to cure a stammer led to his involvement with the theatre and his stage début with a small part in *Julius Caesar* (1921). He spent several years touring with the Benson Company before joining Liverpool Rep in 1928. His London début in *Knave and Queen* (1930) was followed by successes in *Saint Joan* (1931) and *Precious Bane* (1932) which brought him a contract with **Alexander Korda**. His handsome demeanour, natural manner and melodious voice made him one of the most popular stars of 1930s British cinema in films like *The Private Life of Henry VIII* (1932) and *Goodbye Mr. Chips* (1939), which earned him an Academy Award. A chronic asthmatic, his later career was blighted by ill-health. He nevertheless remained in demand and continued to give much-admired performances. He died shortly after completing a poignant performance as the Chinese mandarin in *Inn of the Sixth Happiness* (1958).

DONATELLO, real name **Donato di Niccolo** (c.1386–1466) Florentine sculptor. One of the most important artists of 15th-century Italy, he trained in the Florence Cathedral workshop under **Ghiberti** and received his first commission in 1408. In many ways he can be considered the founder of 'modern sculpture' since he was the first since classical times to produce works which are fully rounded and independent in themselves and not mere adjuncts of their architectural settings. The evolution of his highly-charged and emotional style can be traced in a series of figures of saints he executed for the exterior of Orsanmichele and another series of prophets for the Campanile, in which his interest in classical antiquity is evident. In the 1420s, in partnership with Michelozzo, he produced the monument to the antipope **John XXIII** in the Baptistery which was influential on all subsequent tomb design. In 1443 he migrated to Padua where he produced the bronze equestrian portrait of the military commander known as Gattemelata: the first lifesize equestrian statue since antiquity. The celebrated bronze statue of **David** is a key work of the Renaissance as is the multiple-viewpoint *Judith and Holofernes* in the Piazza della Signoria in Florence. The anguished, expressive statue of Mary Magdalene has no counterpart elsewhere in the 15th century and not until **Michelangelo** was his expressive power equalled.

DONATI, Giambattista (1826–73) Italian astronomer, born in Pisa. Director of the observatory at Florence, he discovered the brilliant comet ('Donati's comet') of 1858. Noted for his researches on stellar spectra, he was the first to observe the spectrum of a comet.

DONATUS, Aelius (fl.4th century) Roman grammarian. He taught grammar and rhetoric at Rome about 360 AD, amongst others to St **Jerome**. His treatises form a pretty complete course of Latin grammar (*Ars grammatica*), and in the middle ages were the only textbooks used in schools, so that the word 'Donat' came, in western Europe, to mean 'grammar book'. He also wrote a commentary on **Terence**.

DONATUS MAGNUS bishop (312) of Carthage. He was a leader of the Donatists, a 4th-century puritan Christian sect in North Africa.

DONDERS, Franciscus Cornelis (1818–89) Dutch oculist and professor of physiology at Utrecht. He improved the efficiency of spectacles by the introduction of prismatic and cylindrical lenses, and wrote on the physiology of the eye.

DONDI, Giovanni de' and **Jacopo de'** ((1318–89) and (1290–1359)) Italian horologists and physicians, son and father, born in Chioggia and Padua. Both studied medicine at the University of Padua, and both returned there as teachers. First Jacopo designed and built an astronomical clock for the prince of Padua which he completed in 1344, then Giovanni began in 1348 to construct an even more sophisticated one on which he was engaged for the next 18 years. In addition to the usual planetary motions it showed the feasts of the church calculated in accordance with a perpetual calendar, and Giovanni described every detail of its construction in his *Planetarium*. The clock was so far ahead of its time, however, that only one replica is known to have been made until the 20th century.

DÖNITZ, Karl (1891–1980) German naval commander, born in Grünau, near Berlin. He entered the navy as a sea-cadet in 1910 and served on the light cruiser *Breslau* (1912–16). In 1916 he joined the submarine service and became a staunch advocate and supporter of U-boat warfare. In 1936 he was appointed commander of **Hitler**'s U-boat fleet, which he himself had developed in secret and in 1943 succeeded **Raeder** as grand admiral and c-in-c for the German navy. Becoming Führer on the death of Hitler, he was responsible for the final surrender to the Allies, and in 1946 was sentenced to ten years' imprisonment for war crimes.

DONIZETTI, Gaetano (1797–1848) Italian composer, born in Bergamo. He studied music at Bergamo and Bologna. His first opera, *Enrico di Borgogna*, was successfully produced in 1818 at Venice, and was followed by others in rapid succession, but the work which carried his fame beyond Italy was *Anna Bolena*, produced at Milan in 1830. *L'Elisir d'amore* (1832) and *Lucrezia Borgia* (1833) also achieved lasting popularity. On his earliest visit to Paris, in 1835, his *Marino Faliero* met with little acclaim, but immediately afterwards *Lucia di Lammermoor* took the Neapolitan public by storm. In 1840 he revisited Paris, and brought out *La Fille du régiment*, *Lucrezia Borgia* and *La Favorita*, the last act of which is his masterpiece, and was written in three to four hours. In 1843 the comic opera *Don Pasquale* was well received; but the gloomy theme of *Dom Sébastien* almost precluded success. *Catarina Cornaro* (1844) was a failure. Stricken by paralysis, he fell into imbecility, and died in Bergamo.

DONKIN, Bryan (1768–1855) English engineer and inventor, born in Sandoe, Northumberland. He was first a land agent but then became apprenticed to a mechanic and within a few years (in 1804) had developed the first automatic paper-making machine. He continued to improve the machine and by 1850 had built almost 200 of them, effecting a radical change in the paper-making industry. With Richard Bacon in 1813 he patented one of the first rotary printing machines, but this was not successful. He also improved on the food-preserving invention of **Appert** by using sealed tins instead of glass jars, and built a factory to supply the Royal Navy with canned meat and vegetables.

DONLEAVY, James Patrick (1926–) American-born Irish author, born in Brooklyn, New York, of Irish parents. After serving in the American navy during World War II he studied microbiology at Trinity College, Dublin, and became a friend of **Brendan Behan**. While living on a farm in Wicklow he began painting, then wrote his first novel, *The Ginger Man*, published in 1955. Picaresque, bawdy, presenting an apparently totally irrational hero, it was hailed as a comic masterpiece. The novels, plays and stories that followed are on the same theme, that of his own 'dreams and inner desires', and have been described as paler versions of *The Ginger Man*. He became an Irish citizen in 1967 and among his other works are *A Singular Man* (1963), *Meet My Maker*, *The Mad Molecule* (short stories: 1964), *The Beastly Beatitudes of Balthazar B* (1968), written as a play in 1981, *The Onion Eaters* (1971), *A Fairy Tale of New York* (1973, a novel written from the play of 1960), *The Destinies of Darcy Dancer, Gentleman* (1971), *Schultz* (1980), and *Are you Listening, Rabbi Low?* (1987).

DONN-BYRNE See **BYRNE**

DONNAY, Maurice (1859–1945) French dramatist, born in Paris. His *Amants* (1895) achieved considerable popularity, as did *Lysistrata* (1920), an adaptation of **Aristophanes**, and several other works showing a novel approach to contemporary social problems.

DONNE, John (?1572–1631) English poet, born in London, the son of a prosperous ironmonger, but connected through his mother with Sir **Thomas More**. Though a Catholic, he was admitted to Hart Hall, Oxford, and later graduated at Cambridge, where his friendship with Sir **Henry Wotton** began. He decided to take up law and entered Lincoln's Inn in 1592. After taking part in the 2nd Earl of **Essex**'s two expeditions to Cadiz in 1597 and the Azores, 1598 (reflected in his poems 'The Storm' and 'The Calm'), he became (1598) secretary to Sir **Thomas Egerton**, keeper of the Great Seal, whose justice he celebrated in his fourth satire. His daring pieces and brilliant personality pointed to a career as notable as that of his great contemporary **Bacon**, but his secret marriage to Egerton's niece, Anne More, caused him to be dismissed and thrown into prison. Having turned Protestant, he lived at Mitcham in Surrey, but still sought favour at the Court with an eye to employment. The work he undertook under the direction of Thomas (later Bishop) Morton was a religious polemic against the Catholics. He had already written his passionate and erotic poems, *Songs and Sonets* and his six *Satires* and his *Elegies*, but published no verse until 1611 when his *Anniversarie* appeared, a commemorative poem for Elizabeth Drury, daughter of his benefactor, Sir Robert Drury, whose house in the Strand offered hospitality to the poet when in London. A second *Anniversarie* followed, really a 'meditatio mortis' displaying his metaphysical genius at its best. His religious temper is seen in more lyrical form in the *Divine Poems*, some of which certainly date from before 1607. These, like most of his verse, were published posthumously but his pieces circulated widely among learned and aristocratic friends. How difficult his journey to the Anglican faith was may be judged from the satirical 'Progresse of the Soule' (1601). This ugly unfinished poem is antiheretical, but also sceptical in a disturbing way. Donne's hesitation over some ten years to take orders is variously explained as due to a Hamlet-like indecision, or to a sense of unworthiness because of his profligate youth, or to his still having an eye on civil employment. He now courted the distinguished ladies of the time, in verse letters of laboured but ingenious compliment, among them Mrs Herbert and the Countess of Bedford. More injurious to his name was a splendid piece for the marriage of the king's favourite, Robert Carr, to the divorced Countess of Essex: a scandalous poem for a scandalous wedding. In Funeral poems, of which the first and second *Anniversaries* are the most brilliant, he also paid court to the great. His prose works of this period include *Pseudo-Martyr* (1610), which is an acute polemic against the Jesuits. More interesting is his *Biothanatos*, which discussed the question of suicide, towards which he says in his preface, 'I have often ... a sickly inclination'. He decides that suicide is permissible in certain cases, a conclusion at variance with that affirmed in his third *Satire*, but confirmed in a letter to his friend Sir **Henry Wotton**. King **James VI and I** encouraged him to go into the Church (1614), and promoted him, after several charges, to the deanship of St Paul's in 1621 when he relinquished his readership at Lincoln's Inn. Several of his sermons are still extant. In this middle period of his life he accompanied his patron, Sir Robert Drury, to France and Spain. In 1619 and 1620 he was in Germany, where he preached one of his noblest sermons before the exiled Queen **Elizabeth of Bohemia**, King James's daughter. Donne's creative years fall into three periods: from 1590 to 1601, a time of action, marked by passion and cynicism; from his marriage to his ordination in 1614, a period of anguished meditation and flattery of the great; and the period of his ministry, which includes two sonnet sequences, *La Corona* and *Holy Sonnets*, the latter containing (no xvii) an anguished tribute to his wife, who died in 1617. Also of this period are the fine 'Hymne to God, the Father', 'To God My God, in my Sicknesse', and 'The Author's Last Going into Germany'.

DONNELLY, Ignatius (1831–1901) American politician and writer, born in Philadelphia. After qualifying for the bar in 1852, he moved to Minnesota in 1856, becoming lieutenant-governor and governor (1859–63) and later Radical Republican Congressman (1863–69). He became identified with reform, editing the *Anti-Monopolist* and later the *Representative*, and was for several years president of the State Farmers' Alliance in Minnesota, a forerunner of the Populist party, which nominated him for vice-president. As a prophet of reform his most enduring legacy is a horrific novel, *Caesar's Column* (1891), predicting tyranny and oppression. His powerful imagination and realism on the pitfalls ahead of reform were tarnished by his anti-semitism for which US Populism as a whole has been somewhat unjustly blamed. His *Atlantis, The Antediluvian World* (1882) was a highly popular development of the idea of a former continent drowned under the Atlantic Ocean. His *The Great Cryptogram* (1888) sought to prove **Bacon** had written the plays usually attributed to **Shakespeare** and had hidden ciphered messages in the plays declaring his authorship.

DONOGHUE, Steve (Stephen) (1884–1945) English jockey, born in Warrington. He won the Derby six times between 1915 and 1925, beating **Fred Archer**'s record of five Derby wins, and including a hat-trick of three successive Derbies (Humorist in 1921, Captain Cuttle in 1922, and Papyrus in 1923). He also won the Queen Alexandra Stakes at Ascot for six consecutive years on Brown Jack (1929–34).

DONOSO, (Yanez) José (1928–) Chilean novelist, born in Santiago. He attended the University of Chile and spent two years at Princeton on a Doherty Foundation Fellowship (1949–51). In his time a longshoreman, teacher, editor and journalist, his first collection of short stories won Chile's Municipal prize in 1951, and in 1962 he received the William Faulkner Foundation prize for Chile, for his novel *Coronation* (1957, trans 1965). His work reflects urban life and its complications, madness, opulence and decay, and several novels have been translated into English: *The Obscene Bird of Night* (1970, trans 1973); *Sacred Families* (1977, trans 1978); and *A House in the Country* (1978, trans 1984).

DOOLEY, Mr See **DUNNE, Finley Peter**

DOOLITTLE, Hilda, known as **H D** (1886–1961) American imagist poet, born in Bethlehem, Pennsylvania, the daughter of a professor of astronomy. She was educated at Gordon School and the Friends' Central School in Philadelphia, and Bryn Mawr College (1904–06). She lived in London from 1911 and married **Richard Aldington** in 1913. After their divorce in 1937, she settled near Lake Geneva. Her many volumes of poetry include *Sea Garden* (1916), *The Walls do not Fall* (1944), *Flowering of the Rod* (1946) and *Helen in Egypt* (1961). She also wrote several novels, notably *Palimpsest* (1926), *Hedylus* (1928), *Bid Me to Live* (1960), and *Tribute to Freud* (1965).

DOOLITTLE, James Harold (1896–) American air force officer. An aviation enthusiast who was called up from reserve at the outbreak of war with Japan, he commanded 16 B-25 bombers which took off from Admiral **Halsey**'s aircraft carriers to raid Tokyo in April 1942, with decisive effects on Japanese naval strategy. He and other survivors landed in China. He later commanded the 12th Army Air Force (AAF) in North Africa, the 15th AAF in Italy (1943) and 8th AAF in Britain for operations in North West Europe (1944). After the war he was vice-president and director of Shell Oil (1945–59).

DOPPLER, Christian Johann (1803–53) Austrian physicist, born in Salzburg. In 1851 he was appointed professor of physics at Vienna. 'Doppler's principle', which he enunciated in a paper in 1842, explains the variation of frequency observed, higher or lower than that actually emitted, when a vibrating source of waves and the observer respectively approach or recede from one another.

DORA D'ISTRIA See **GHIKA, Helena**

DORAN, John (1807–78) English journalist and theatre historian, born in London. He brought out a melodrama, *Justice, or the Venetian Jew*, in 1824, followed by many other works, including *A Lady of the Last Century* (1873, an account of Mrs **Montagu**), *Mann and Manners* (1876, the letters of Sir **Horace Mann** to **Horace Walpole**), and books on kings and queens and on stage history. He was repeatedly acting-editor of the *Athenaeum*, edited the *Church and State Gazette* (1841–1852), and was editor of *Notes and Queries* (1870–78).

DORAT, Jean See **DAURAT**

DORÉ, Gustave (1832–83) French painter and book illustrator, born in Strasbourg. He first made his mark by his illustrations to **Rabelais** (1854) and to *The Wandering Jew* and **Balzac**'s *Contes drolatiques* (1865). These are followed by illustrated editions of **Dante**'s *Inferno* (1861), the *Contes* of **Perrault** and *Don Quixote* (1863), the *Purgatorio* and *Paradiso* of Dante (1868), the Bible (1865–66), *Paradise Lost* (1866), **Tennyson**'s *Idylls of the King* (1867–68), **La Fontaine**'s *Fables* (1867), and many other series of designs, which in the end deteriorated. He also executed much in colour.

DORIA, Andrea (c.1466–1560) Genoese commander and statesman, born in Oneglia of an ancient princely house. After serving under various Italian princes he returned to Genoa in 1501. In 1513 he received command of the Genoese fleet, and in 1519 defeated the Turkish corsairs off Pianosa. In 1522 the imperial faction were restored to power in Genoa, and Doria, an anti-imperialist, transferred his allegiance to **Francis I** of France. In command of the French fleet, he defeated the emperor **Charles V**, blockaded Genoa, and proclaimed the independence of the republic in 1527. In 1529, fearing the predominance of Francis, he transferred his allegiance to Charles V, entered Genoa amid popular acclamation, and established an aristocratic government which lasted to the end of the republic in 1797. The emperor gave him the order of the Golden Fleece and the princeship of Malfi. He continued his war against the Turks and **Barbarossa**, but had as many reverses as successes. His later years were disturbed by the conspiracy of the Fieschi in 1547 that forced him to flee the city and stained by his savage revenge for their murder of his nephew Gianettino.

DORISLAUS, Isaac (1595–1649) Anglo-Dutch diplomat, born in Alkmaar in Holland. He came to England about 1637. For some months he was history lecturer at Cambridge, and in 1640 he was appointed judge-advocate. He sided with the parliament, helped to bring **Charles I** to his doom, and in 1649 was sent to Holland to bring about an alliance with England. He was assassinated by twelve exiled royalists.

DORN, Friedrich Ernst (1848–1916) German chemist, born in Guttstadt. Educated at Königsberg, he is known for his discovery of radon (or radium emanation).

DORNBERGER, Walter Robert (1895–1980) German-born American rocket engineer, born in Giessen Hesse. An engineer and officer in the German army, he set up an experimental rocket station at Kummersdorf which successfully fired a 650lb-thrust motor in 1932. By 1934 he had designed a 3300lb-thrust rocket which reached a height of 1.5 miles. In World War II the work was transferred to Peenemünde where in 1942 a 46-foot 14-ton rocket was launched to the edge of the atmosphere. In 1944–45, 1500 of these V-2 rockets with explosive warheads were launched against England and 2000 into Antwerp, Belgium. After spending three years as a prisoner of war in England (1945–47), he went to the USA as a consultant to the air force. In 1950 he joined the Bell Aircraft Corporation, and worked on the Rascal air-to-surface missile and the Dyna-Soar manned Space Glider programme. He wrote *V2* (1952), an account of his work in jet propulsion.

DORNIER, Claudius (1884–1969) German aircraft designer, born in Kempten. After entering the service of Graf von Zeppelin, he designed the first all-metal aircraft in 1911, and in 1914 founded the Dornier works at Friedrichshafen on Lake Constance. He manufactured seaplanes and flying-boats, including the famous twelve-engined Do X (1929), and the Dornier twin-engined bomber which was a standard Luftwaffe type in World War II.

DOROTHEA OF ZELL See **KÖNIGSMARK, Count Philipp Christoph von**

DÖRPFELD, Wilhelm (1853–1940) German archaeologist, born in Barmen, son of Friedrich Wilhelm Dörpfeld (1824–93), the noted educationist. He was **Schliemann**'s collaborator and successor at Troy, and professor at Jena 1923. The chronology of Troy set out in his *Troja und Ilion* (1902) served to date European prehistory for the first 30 years of the 20th century.

DORS, Diana, originally **Diana Fluck** (1931–84) English actress, born in Swindon, Wiltshire. A student at RADA, she made her film début in *The Shop at Sly Corner* (1946) and was signed to a long-term contract with Rank who groomed her for stardom in their 'Charm School'. Promoted as a sex symbol, she was cast in various low-budget comedies, and despite an effective dramatic performance in *Yield to the Night* (1956) and various highly-publicized visits to Hollywood she was soon seen in blowsy supporting assignments. Her accomplished stage work in *Three Months Gone* (1970) brought her a selection of good character parts in films like *Deep End* (1970) and *The Amazing Mr. Blunden* (1972). Later roles were undistinguished but her personal popularity never dimmed as she performed in cabaret and as a television agony aunt. She returned to the screen in *Steaming* (1984) immediately prior to her death.

D'ORSAY, Alfred Guillaume Gabriel, Count (1801–52) French socialite, the 'last of the dandies', born in Paris. In 1822 he attached himself to Lady Blessington. In 1827 he married Lady Harriet Gardiner, Lord Blessington's fifteen-year-old daughter by a former wife. In 1829 Lord Blessington died, and d'Orsay, separated from his wife, took up his residence next door to Lady Blessington's in London where for 20 years they defied the conventions in a society of authors, artists and men of fashion. An intimate friend and supporter of **Louis Napoleon**, he naturally looked for a position when the exile became prince-president and d'Orsay a bankrupt; but the directorship of Fine Arts in Paris was conferred upon him only a few days before his death.

DORSET, Earls of See **SACKVILLE**

DORSEY, Tommy (Thomas) (1905–56) American trombonist and bandleader, born in Shenandoah, Pennsylvania, the son of a bandleader. Renowned for his sweet-toned instrumental style, his work hovered between jazz and dance music. His big bands, sometimes co-led by his brother Jimmy (1904–57, alto saxophone, clarinet), nevertheless included many accomplished jazz soloists. The Dorsey Brothers Orchestra existed from 1932 to 1935, reforming again in 1953 until Tommy's death. Both brothers were in great demand as session musicians in the late 1920s, with the expansion of radio in the USA, and their fame was revived through a regular television show in the 1950s.

DOS PASSOS, John Roderigo (1896–1970) American novelist, playwright, travel writer and poet, born in Chicago. The grandson of a Portuguese immigrant, he was educated at Choate and Harvard. In 1916 he went to Spain to study architecture but was caught up in World War I and served in the US Medical Corps. Thereafter he lived in the USA but travelled widely on journalistic assignments. In middle age he led a simple life on Cape Cod and later he and his wife moved to his father's farm at Spence's Point, Virginia, where he had spent summers as a boy. He had a precocious start as an author, publishing *One Man's Initiation* in 1917 when he was 21. *Three Soldiers* (1921) confirmed his talent and in *Manhattan Transfer* (1925) his confidence and ambition grew, foreshadowing the monumental *U.S.A.* triology: *42nd Parallel* (1930), *1919* (1932) and *The Big Money* (1936). A digressive, dynamic epic, it is a mishmash of newsreel footage, snatches of popular songs, brief but vivid sketches of public figures and prose-poetry. Something of a curate's egg, in bulk it is the 'great American novel'. He also wrote three plays. An anti-capitalist, Dos Passos wrote a second triology, *District of Columbia* (1939–49; 1952), less radical in its criticism of the free-enterprise system. His later work continued the trend towards conservatism. *The Best Times* (1966), his last book, was a reminiscence of his boyhood and early manhood.

DOS SANTOS, Jose Eduardo (1942–) Angolan politician. Born in Luanda, he joined the People's Movement for the Liberation of Angola (MPLA) in 1961 and was forced into exile in what is now Zaire while the struggle for independence developed into a civil war between the MPLA and the National Union for the Total Independence of Angola (UNITA). In Zaire he founded the MPLA Youth and in 1963 was sent to Moscow to study petroleum engineering and telecommunications. He returned to Angola in 1970 and rejoined the war (which continued after independence in 1975) between the government, assisted by Cuba, and UNITA, supported by South Africa. He held key positions under President Agostinho Neto and when Neto died in 1979, succeeded him. By 1989, with US help, he had negotiated the withdrawal of South African and Cuban forces, and a ceasefire between MPLA and UNITA.

DOSHI, Balkrishna Vithaldas (1927–) Indian architect, born in Poona. He was educated there and in Bombay. He worked as senior designer with **Le Corbusier** at Chandigarh and Ahmedabad (1951–57). In 1956 he joined Stein and Bhalla in partnership. His architectural aesthetic derived from the vernacular, traditional and functional styles of India, the user of local materials and craftsmanship: he was influenced by the late works of Le Corbusier and **Louis Kahn**. His architectural works include the City Hall, Toronto (1958), several mills (1958–77) and the Indian Institute of Management (1962–74, with Kahn), in Ahmedabad, and Vidyadhar Nagar New Town, Jaipur.

DOSSI DOSSO, properly **Giovanno di Nicolò Lutero** (1479–1542) Italian religious painter, born near Mantua, a friend of **Ariosto**. He painted some pictures jointly with his brother Battista.

DOSTOYEVSKY, Fyodor Mikhailovich (1821–81) Russian novelist, born in Moscow, the second son of a physician's seven children. His mother died in 1837 and his father was murdered by his serfs a little over two years later. After leaving a private boarding school in Moscow he studied from 1838 to 1843 at the Military Engineering College at St Petersburg, graduating with officer's rank. His first published short story was 'Poor Folk' which gained him immediate recognition. In 1849 he was arrested and sentenced to death for participating in the socialist 'Petrashevsky circle', but was reprieved and sent to Siberia, where he was confined in a convict prison at Omsk until 1854. From this experience grew *The House of the Dead* (1860). In 1861 he began the review *Vremya* (Truth) with his brother Mikhail and he spent the next two years travelling abroad, which confirmed his anti-European outlook. At this time he met Mlle Suslova, the model for many of his heroines, and succumbed to the gaming tables. He fell heavily into debt but was rescued by Anna Grigoryevna Smitkina, whom he married in 1867. They lived abroad for several years but he returned to Russia in 1871 to edit *Grazhdanin*, to which he contributed his 'Author's Diary'. Like **Dickens**, Dostoyevsky was both horrified and fascinated by the Industrial Revolution and his fiction is dark with suffering caused by poverty and appalling living conditions, crime and the exploitation of children. Second only to **Tolstoy**, his novels—*Crime and Punishment* (1866), *The Idiot* (1868), *The Devils* (1872) and *The Brothers Karamazov* (1880)—were and are profoundly influential, and their impact on **Robert Louis Stevenson**'s *Dr Jekyll and Mr Hyde* (1886), among many others, is conspicuous.

DOU, or **Douw, Gerard** (1612–75) Dutch painter, born in Leiden. He studied under **Rembrandt** (1628–31), and at first mainly occupied himself with portraiture, but soon turned to *genre*. His 200 works include his own portrait, his wife's and *The Poulterer's Shop*, in the National Gallery, London; and his celebrated *Dropsical Woman* (1663), with ten others, in the Louvre.

DOUDART DE LAGRÉE, Ernest-Marc-Louis de Gonzague (1823–68) French explorer who led the Mekong River Expedition (1866–68) which was charged with assessing the possibility of a navigable waterway to China. Educated at the École Polytechnique in Paris, he joined the Navy and served in the Crimean War. He became French representative at the court of King Norodom of Cambodia in 1863. The Mekong River Expedition left Saigon in June 1866 and made the first survey of the ruined temples of Angkor before continuing northwards, crossing the Sambor rapids and going on to the forbidding Khone Falls on the Laos border, showing that the river was unsuitable for commercial traffic. Their scientific work continued but Doudart de Lagrée died in Huitse after persistent illness, and leadership of the expedition was taken over by **Francis Garnier**.

DOUGHTY, Charles Montagu (1843–1926) English travel writer and poet, born at Theberton Hall in Suffolk, the son of a clergyman, and educated at Caius College, Cambridge. Out of two years' travel and hardship in Arabia (1875–77), slowly grew his masterpiece of philological virtuosity, *Travels in Arabia Deserta* (1888), written in austere, didactic prose. He also wrote epic poems and plays, including *The Dawn in Britain* (1906) and *Mansoul* (1923).

DOUGLAS a family which includes William the Hardy, crusader, who harried the monks of Melrose, and was the first man of mark who joined **Wallace** in the rising against the English in 1297. His son, the Good Sir James Douglas (c.1286–1330), called also 'the Black Douglas' from his swarthy complexion, was **Robert the Bruce**'s greatest captain in the War of Independence. The hero of 70 fights, he was slain in Andalusia, bearing the heart of Bruce. His son William fell at Halidon Hill; and the next Lord of Douglas, Hugh, brother of Sir James, and a canon of Glasgow, made over the now great domains of the family in 1342 to his nephew Sir William.

DOUGLAS, Earls of Angus, the first of whom, William, 1st Earl of Douglas (?1327–1384), while securing the earldom of Mar also secured the affections of the young widow of his wife's brother, Margaret, Countess of Angus and Mar. The issue of this amour was a son, George, 1st Earl of Angus, who in 1389 had a grant of his mother's earldom of Angus. George, 4th Earl (c.1412–1462), aided the king against the Douglases in 1454; his loyalty was rewarded by a grant of their old inheritance of Douglasdale and other lands; and so, in the phrase of the time, 'the Red Douglas put down the Black'. His son Archibald, 5th Earl (c.1449–1514), was nicknamed Bell-the-Cat from the lead he took against Lord Cochrane at Lauder; he filled the highest offices in the state and added largely to the family possessions. His grandson Archibald, 6th Earl (c.1489–1557), in 1514 married **Margaret Tudor**, widow of **James IV** of Scotland. By this marriage was a daughter, Margaret, who on marrying the 4th Earl of Lennox, became the mother of Darnley, **Mary, Queen of Scots'** husband and **James VI and I**'s father. The Earl of Angus had for a time supreme power in Scotland, but in 1528 **James V** escaped from his hands, and sentence of forfeiture was passed against him and his kinsmen. On James's death in 1542 Angus was restored to his estates and honours. He was succeeded by his nephew, David, whose son, Archibald, the 'Good Earl' (1558–88), died without male issue, and the earldom passed to a kinsman, William Douglas of Glenbervie.

DOUGLAS, Earls of Douglas the Douglases had since the time of William the Hardy (see **Douglas** family) held the title of Lords of Douglas; in 1358 Sir William (c.1327–1384) was made Earl of Douglas, and by marriage became Earl of Mar about 1374. His son, James, 2nd Earl of Douglas (c.1358–1388), fell at Otterburn, leaving no legitimate issue. His aunt had married for her second husband one of her brother's esquires, James of Sandilands, and through her Lord Torphichen, whose barony was a creation of **Mary, Queen of Scots**, in 1564, is now the heir general of the House of Douglas. The Earldom of Douglas meanwhile was bestowed on an illegitimate son of the Good Sir James—Archibald (c.1328–1400), Lord of Galloway, surnamed the Grim. By his marriage with the heiress of Bothwell he added that barony to the Douglas domains; and he married his only daughter to the heir-apparent of the Scottish crown (David, Duke of Rothesay, son of **Robert III**, murdered in 1402) and his eldest son to Margaret, eldest daughter of Robert III. His son, Archibald, 4th Earl (c.1369–1424), called 'Tyneman' ('loser'), was wounded and taken prisoner by Hotspur (see **Percy** family) at Homildon Hill in 1402, next year by Shrewsbury was again wounded and taken prisoner and, repairing to France, was made Duke of Touraine, and fell at Verneuil. His son Archibald, 5th Earl (c.1391–1439), fought in the French wars. His son, William, 6th Earl (c.1423–1440), was decoyed into Edinburgh Castle by **James II**, and beheaded, along with his brother David. His Scottish earldom was bestowed on his grand-uncle (the second son of Archibald the Grim), James the 'Gross' (c.1371–1443), who in 1437 had been made Earl of Avondale. His son William, 8th Earl, (c.1425–1452), was for a time all-powerful with James II, who made him lieutenant-general of the realm; he afterwards entered into a confederacy against the king, by whom he was stabbed in Stirling Castle. His brother James, 9th and last Earl (1426–88), in 1454 made open war against James II. The issue seemed doubtful until the **Hamiltons** sided with the king, and Douglas fled to England. His brothers, who still maintained the struggle, were defeated at Arkinholm (Langholm) in May 1455; and the earldom of Douglas came to an end by forfeiture. The last earl lived many years in England, leagued himself in 1484 with the exiled Duke of Albany, was defeated and taken prisoner at Lochmaben and died in the abbey of Lindores.

DOUGLAS, Earls of Morton Sir Andrew de Douglas, who appears in record in 1248, was apparently a younger son of Sir Archibald, the second chief of the house. His great-grandson, Sir William Douglas, the 'Knight of Liddesdale' (c.1300–1353), was assassinated by his kinsman, William, 1st Earl of Douglas. The grandson of his nephew, Sir James Douglas of Dalkeith, married a daughter of **James I**, and in 1458 was created 1st Earl of Morton. His grandson, the 3rd earl, dying without male issue in 1553, the earldom devolved on his youngest daughter's husband, the Regent **Morton**, and from him the present Earl of Morton is descended. James, 2nd earl of Douglas and Mar, had an illegitimate son, Sir William Douglas of Drumlanrig, whose descendants were created Viscounts of Drumlanrig in 1628, Earls of Queensberry in 1633, Marquises of Queensberry in 1681, Dukes of Queensberry in 1683, Earls of March in 1697, and Earls of Solway in 1706. On the death of the 4th Duke of **Queensberry** in 1810, that title went to the Duke of Buccleuch; the title of Marquis of Queensberry went to Sir Charles Douglas of Kelhead; and that of Earl of March to the Earl of Wemyss. In 1646 the third son of the 1st Marquis of Douglas was created Earl of Selkirk; in 1651 the eldest son was created Earl of Ormond, in 1661 Earl of Forfar; and in 1675 the fourth son was created Earl of Dumbarton. In 1641 the second son of the 10th Earl of Angus was created Lord Mordington. In 1633 Sir Robert Douglas (c.1574–1639) was created Viscount Belhaven.

DOUGLAS, Lord Alfred Bruce (1870–1945) English poet, son of the 8th Marquis of **Queensberry**. He wrote a number of brilliant sonnets, collected in *In Excelsis* (1924) and *Sonnets and Lyrics* (1935). He is remembered for his association with **Oscar Wilde**, to which his father objected, thereby provoking Wilde to bring the ill-advised libel action which led to his own arrest and imprisonment.

DOUGLAS, David (1798–1834) Scottish botanist, born in Scone, Perthshire. He travelled in North America as a collector for the Horticultural Society of London, and discovered many trees, shrubs and herbaceous plants which he introduced to Britain, including the Giant Fir (*Abies grandis*) in Western North America in 1825. The Oregon Pine (*Pseudotsuga menziesii*) was renamed the Douglas fir after him, as was the Douglas squirrel. He was gored to death by a wild bull in the Sandwich Islands.

DOUGLAS, Donald Wills (1892–1981) American aircraft designer and manufacturer, born in Brooklyn, New York. He attended the US Naval Academy in 1909, and Massachusetts Institute of Technology (MIT) in 1912, graduating in 1914. Chief engineer to the **Glenn L Martin** Aircraft Company in 1915, in 1920 he set up his own company (Davis-Douglas Co) in California. His Douglas World Cruisers made a historic round-the-world flight in 1924, and the all-metal low wing Douglas DC-2 transport of 1934 was second in the England-Australia Air Race, with 14 passengers. The DC-3 (C-47, Dakota) followed in 1936, and the DC-4, -6 and -7 and the jet-engined transports DC-8, -9 and -10. During World War II he produced the B-19 bomber and other craft. He was chairman of his company, Douglas Aircraft, until it merged with McDonnell Aircraft as the McDonnell Douglas Corporation in 1967.

DOUGLAS, Gavin (c.1474–1522) Scottish poet and prelate, born at Tantallon Castle, East Lothian, the third son of Archibald, 5th Earl of Angus. Educated at St Andrews and possibly Paris for the priesthood, from 1501 to 1514 he was dean or provost of the Collegiate Church of St Giles, Edinburgh. After the battle of Flodden (1513), in which King **James IV** fell, Douglas's nephew, the 6th Earl of Angus, married the widowed queen, **Margaret Tudor**. Through her influence, he obtained the bishopric of Dunkeld (January 1515), but was imprisoned under an old statute for receiving bulls from the pope, and not consecrated until more than a year after. On the fall of Angus in 1521, the bishop fled to England to obtain the aid of **Henry VIII**, but died suddenly of the plague in London. His works include *The Palice of Honour*, presumably written in 1501, an allegory of the life of the virtuous man, and a magnificent translation of **Virgil**'s *Aeneid*, with prologues, finished about 1513, the first version of a Latin poet published in English. He may also have written *King Hart*, an allegory about the control exercised by the heart in human personality and behaviour.

DOUGLAS, George See **BROWN, George Douglas**

DOUGLAS, Sir Howard (1776–1861) English soldier, born in Gosport, the son of an admiral. Commissioned in the Royal Artillery in 1794, he served in Canada, the Netherlands and the Peninsula, and was governor of New Brunswick (1823–29), where he founded Fredericton University. He was lord high commissioner of the Ionian Islands (1835–40), and MP for Liverpool (1842–46), and promoted general in 1851. He wrote on bridge construction and fortifications, and a *Treatise on Naval Gunnery* (1820).

DOUGLAS, John (1721–1807) Scottish prelate, the son of a Pittenweem shopkeeper. He was educated at Dunbar and Oxford and, as an army chaplain, was present at Fontenoy (1745). He became bishop of Carlisle (1787), dean of Windsor (1788) and bishop of Salisbury (1791). He wrote much—a defence of **Milton** from **Lauder**'s charge of plagiarism (1750), the famous *Letter on the Criterion of Miracles* (1754) against **David Hume**, ironical attacks on the Hutchinsonians, and political pamphlets.

DOUGLAS, Mary, née **Tew** (1921–) English social anthropologist, born in Italy. She studied at Oxford, and carried out fieldwork among the Lele of the Belgian Congo (Zaire) in 1949–50 and 1953. From 1970 until 1978 she was professor of social anthropology at University College, London. In 1977 she moved to the USA, becoming Avalon professor of the humanities at Northwestern University in 1980. She is especially known for her studies of systems of cultural classification and beliefs about purity and pollution, as in *Purity and Danger* (1966) and *Natural Symbols* (1973). In addition, she has contributed significantly to economic anthropology in *The World of Goods* (1980), and to the study of moral accountability, in *Cultural Bias* (1978) and *Risk and Culture* (1982).

DOUGLAS, (George) Norman (1868–1952) Scottish novelist and essayist, born in Tilquhillie on Deeside. His mother was part-German and he was educated at Uppingham School and at Karlsruhe, and joined the Foreign Office in 1894. He served in St Petersburg before settling in Capri in 1896, where his circle embraced **Compton Mackenzie**, **Ouida** and **D H Lawrence**. His first book, *Unprofessional Tales* (1901), was co-authored with his wife and published under the pseudonym 'Normyx'. *Siren Land* (1911) was, however, the book that first attracted critical attention. An account of his travels in southern Italy, it is an exotic collage of anecdote, philosophy and myth. *Old Calabria* (1915) garnished his reputation and is a minor classic. Other travel books are *Fountains in the Sun* (1912), *Alone* (1921) and *Together* (1923). Of his novels, *South Wind* (1917) is the most famous. Set in Nepenthe (Capri) among a floating population of expatriates, it is an unapologetic celebration of hedonism to which its author was a happy convert. *Looking Back* (1933) is an unusual autobiography, in which he recalls his life and his friends by taking up their calling cards and describing them one by one, at length or tersely depending on his mood.

DOUGLAS, Robert (1594–1674) Scottish Presbyterian minister, chaplain to a Scottish regiment in Swedish service, and minister in Edinburgh from 1641. He preached at the coronation of **Charles II** in Scotland in 1651, but after the Restoration would not acknowledge episcopacy, and resigned his charge. He was admitted to a charge in Pencaitland by the Declaration of Indulgence of 1669.

DOUGLAS, Stephen Arnold (1813–61) American political leader, born in Brandon, Vermont. He became attorney-general of Illinois in 1834, member of the legislature in 1835, secretary of state in 1840, and judge of the supreme court in 1841. He was returned to congress in 1843–44–46, and to the US senate in 1847–52–58. His policy was to 'make the United States an ocean-bound republic', and in the question of slavery he maintained that each territory should decide whether it should be a free or a slave state. In 1860 he was nominated for the presidency, but was defeated by **Lincoln**.

DOUGLAS, Sir William Fettes (1822–91) Scottish landscape and figure painter, born in Edinburgh. He painted *Hudibras and Ralph visiting the Astrologer*, and *David Laing in his Study*, and was appointed curator of the National Gallery of Scotland in 1771.

DOUGLAS, William Orville (1898–1980) American judge, born in Maine, Minnesota. Educated at Whitman College and Columbia University, he was a law professor at Yale, then a member (1934) and chairman (1937–39) of the Securities and Exchange Commission. A strong supporter of the New Deal, he was appointed to the Supreme Court in 1939. As a justice he strongly supported civil rights and liberties, and guarantees of freedom of speech and of the press. He wrote *We the Judges* (1956), *A Living Bill of Rights* (1961) and autobiographical works and many books on his travels.

DOUGLAS, Sir William Sholto, 1st Baron Douglas of Kirtleside (1893–1969) English air force officer, educated at Tonbridge school and Lincoln College, Oxford. He served in World War I as a fighter pilot. After a brief career as a commercial test pilot, he rejoined the Royal Air Force, and at the outbreak of World War II was assistant chief of air staff. He became AOC successively of Fighter Command (1940–42), Middle East Air Command (1943–44) and Coastal Command (1944–45), and directed the successful anti-submarine campaign which played a decisive part in the later stages of the war. After the war he commanded the British Air Force of Occupation in Germany (1945–46), and, having been made a marshal of the RAF in 1946, became military governor of the British zone of occupation (1946–48). He was chairman of British European Airways from 1949 to 1964.

DOUGLAS-HOME, Sir Alexander Frederick See **HOME OF THE HIRSEL**

DOUGLAS-HOME, William (1912–) Scottish playwright, born in Edinburgh and author of *Now Barabbas*, *The Chiltern Hundreds*, *The Manor of Northstead*, *The Reluctant Debutante*, *The Reluctant Peer* and other plays.

DOUGLASS, Andrew Ellicott (1867–1962) American astronomer, and 'father of dendrochronology', born in Windsor, Vermont. After research work at the Lowell Observatory at Flagstaff, Arizona, he became professor of physics and astronomy at Arizona University (1906) and later director of the Stewart Observatory (1918–38). He investigated the relationship between sunspots and climate by examining and measuring the annual growth-rings of long-lived Arizona pines and sequoias; he noted that variations in their width corresponded to specific climatic cycles, creating patterns which can be discerned in timbers from prehistoric archaeological sites and providing a time-sequence for dating purposes. He coined the term 'dendrochronology' ('tree-dating') in his *Climatic Cycles and Tree Growth* (3 vols, 1919–36).

DOUGLASS, Frederick, originally **Frederick Augustus Washington Bailey** (1817–95) American abolitionist, born a slave in Tuckahoe, near Easton, Maryland. In 1838 he escaped from a Baltimore shipyard, and changed his name. He settled in New Bedford, Massachusetts, and became an agent of the Massachusetts Anti-Slavery Society. He lectured on slavery (1845–47) in Great Britain, where £150 was collected to buy his freedom. In 1847 he started *Frederick Douglas's Paper* at Rochester, New York. He held various public offices and was US minister to Haiti (1889). He wrote *Narrative of the Life of Frederick Douglas* (1845) and *Life and Times* (1881).

DOUHET, Giulio (1869–1930) Italian general, born in Caserta, renowned as a military aviation strategist. In 1909 he foresaw the importance of air supremacy and from 1912 to 1915 was commander of Italy's first military aviation unit. He made himself unpopular by advocating a strong air force, and in 1916 was court-martialled and imprisoned for publicly deploring Italy's aerial weakness, but was released when the truth of his claims was shown by the defeat of Italian arms by the Austrian air force at Caporetto. He became head of the Italian Army Aviation Service in 1918 and was promoted to general in 1921. His writings on strategic bombing and the future devastation of major cities by mass bomber raids, such as *Il domino dell'aria* (The Command of the Air, 1921), influenced attitudes to civil defence prior to World War II.

DOULTON, Sir Henry (1820–97) English pottery manufacturer, born in Lambeth, London. He entered his father's pottery there, and in 1846 introduced stoneware drain pipes instead of flat-bottomed brick drains; in 1848 he started works, later the largest in the world, near Dudley. He furthered the revival in art pottery.

DOUMER, Paul (1857–1932) French statesman, born in Aurillac. He was a working jeweller, journalist, deputy (1888), and then governor-general of French Indo-China (1897–1902), president of the chamber (1905–06), of the senate (1927–31), of the republic (1931–32). He was shot by a mad Russian émigré, Gorgalov.

DOUMERGUE, Gaston (1863–1937) French statesman and first Protestant president of the French Republic (1924–31), born in Aigues-Vives. He was premier in 1913–14, 1934 (when he failed to carry constitutional changes); and president of the senate 1923–24.

DOUMIC, René (1860–1937) French critic, born in Paris. He was editor of the *Revue des Deux Mondes* from 1916. He wrote *Les Hommes et les idées du XIXe siècle* (1903), and *Études sur la littérature française* (6 vols, 1896–1909).

DOUW, Gerard See **DOU**

DOVE, Arthur Garfield (1880–1946) American painter, born in Canadaigua, New York. From 1903 he earned his living as a commercial illustrator. He travelled in Europe from 1907 to 1909, studying art. In 1910 he began a series of abstract paintings which bear comparison with contemporary works by **Kandinsky**, and in the 1920s he experimented with collage incorporating mirrors, sand and metal. His later abstract work is suggestive of natural organic forms.

DOVE, Heinrich Wilhelm (1803–79) German meteorologist, born in Liegnitz. He was professor of natural philosophy at Königsberg and Berlin. Besides other optical discoveries, he applied the stereoscope to the detection of forged banknotes. His *Distribution of Heat* was published in 1853 by the British Association, and his *Das Gesetz der Stürme* (1857) has also been translated.

DOVER, Thomas (1660–1742) London physician, born in Warwickshire, the inventor of 'Dover's Powder', to provoke sweating. In 1709, as second captain of the privateer *Duke*, he rescued **Alexander Selkirk** from one of the Juan Fernández islands.

DOW, Gerard See **DOU**

DOW, Neal (1804–97) American temperance reformer, born in Portland, Maine. As mayor of Portland, he was the author of the Maine Liquor Law (1851), a stringent prohibition measure. In 1880 he was the Prohibition candidate for the presidency.

DOWDEN, Edward (1843–1913) Irish critic, born in Cork. He was educated at Queen's College, Cork, Trinity College, Dublin, and in 1867 became professor of English literature there, only four years after graduating. He wrote several books on **Shakespeare** (1875–93), as well as *Studies in Literature* (1888–95), *Southey* (1879), *Life of Shelley* (1886), *History of French Literature* (1897), *A Woman's Reliquary* (poems, 1913), *Letters*, and *Poems* (1914).

DOWDEN, John (1840–1910) Irish prelate and theologian, born in Cork, brother of **Edward Dowden**. He became Episcopal bishop of Edinburgh in 1886 and wrote on the Scottish liturgy, the Celtic Church, the medieval Church in Scotland, and the *Bishops of Scotland* (1912).

DOWDING, Hugh Caswell Tremenheere, 1st Baron (1882–1970) Scottish air force chief, born in Moffat. Educated at Winchester and the Royal Military Academy, Woolwich, he joined the Royal Artillery in 1900. He transferred to the Royal Flying Corps in 1914 and was decorated for service in World War I. As commander-in-chief of Fighter Command (1936–40), he organized the air defence of Britain; despite the disasters to France in May–June 1940 he stood for the retention of his force at home, and in August–September the German air force was defeated in the momentous Battle of Britain. He was relieved of his post in November 1940 and made representative of the minister for aircraft production in the USA (1940–42) before he retired and was created a peer in 1943. He became interested in spiritualism, and his *Many Mansions* (1943) had communications attributed to men killed in the war.

DOWELL, Anthony (1943–) English dancer, born in London. He trained at Sadler's Wells and the Royal Ballet School. A skilful and elegant technician, he first performed with the Royal Ballet in 1961 and was chosen to partner **Antoinette Sibley** in **Ashton**'s *The Dream*, a partnership which was to be one of the most magnificent of its time. He was promoted to principal dancer in 1966 and since then has danced all the major roles in the classical repertoire as well as having many new roles created for him by major choreographers, some of the most notable being in *Monotones* (1965), *Enigma Variations* (1968) and *A Month in the Country*

(1976), all by Ashton, *Shadowplay* (1967) by **Tudor**, *Manon* (1974) by **MacMillan** and *Four Schumann Pieces* (1975) by **Hans van Manen**. Though he spent a season with American Ballet Theatre, Dowell has been closely connected with the Royal Ballet all his life and after two years as assistant to the director took over as director of the company in 1986.

DOWIE, John Alexander (1847–1907) Scots-born American religious leader, born in Edinburgh. He emigrated to Australia in 1860 and became a Congregational pastor in Sydney. In 1888 he emigrated to the USA, where he organized the Christian Catholic Church in Zion (1896). He became a faith healer, and proclaimed himself 'Elijah the Restorer', and in 1901 he founded near Chicago the prosperous industrial and banking community called 'Zion City'. He was deposed from his autocratic rule there in 1906.

DOWLAND, John (1563–1626) English lutenist songwriter, born possibly in Westminster. In 1588 he took a music degree at Oxford, later also graduating at Cambridge. Having failed, as a Catholic, to become a court musician to Queen **Elizabeth**, he entered the service of the Duke of Brunswick in 1594, and subsequently went to Italy, where he met with some English papist refugees. Fearing for his own reputation he wrote to Sir **Robert Cecil** denouncing them, an action which appears to have restored him to favour in England, where he returned in 1596. His *First Books of Songes or Ayres of Foure Partes with Tableture for the Lute* appeared in 1597 and ran to five editions by 1613. In 1598 he became lutenist to **Kristian IV** of Denmark, and his second (1600) and third (1603) books of 'ayres' appeared while he was abroad, though he was back in London by 1605, the year in which he brought out his *Lachrymae*, which contains some of the finest instrumental consort music of the period, dedicated to **Anne of Denmark**. Though as a lutenist he was the greatest virtuoso of the age, and his song accompaniments for that instrument are far in advance of his time, he is now remembered above all for the plaintive beauty of 'Weep you no more, sad fountains', 'Awake, sweet love', and many other exquisite songs, dismissed perfunctorily in the 19th century, but today numbered amongst the greatest of all time.

DOWLING, Stephen (1904–86) English strip cartoonist, born in Liverpool, the creator of the fantasy super-hero *Garth* (1942). After art studies and advertising agency work he teamed with his brother, copywriter Frank Dowling, to create newspaper strips, starting with *Tich* (1931) in the *Daily Mirror*, followed by *Ruggles* (1935–60), a family soap opera, and *Belinda Blue-Eyes* (1936–42), before the enormously successful *Garth*.

DOWNES, Terry (1936–) English boxer, born in Paddington, London. In the great line of Cockney boxers, he was British middleweight champion 1958–59 and again 1959 to 1962. He held the world championship from 1961 to 1962 and during his career won 35 out of 44 professional bouts.

DOWNING, Sir George, 1st Bart (c.1623–1684) English soldier and diplomat, born in Ireland. He emigrated to New England with his parents in 1638 and attended the newly founded Harvard College. Returning to England, he fought for parliament and later undertook several diplomatic missions for **Cromwell**, including that of ambassador to the Hague, where he associated with the royalist exiles and contrived to run with the hare and hunt with the hounds to such good effect that at the Restoration he continued as ambassador and received other offices, as well as a baronetcy (1663). As a diplomat he was an expert in commercial matters, but achieved a reputation for contentiousness and duplicity which led **Charles II** to use him as an instrument in provoking the Dutch to war. Downing Street in London was named after him.

DOWNING, Sir George, 3rd Bart (1684–1749) English landowner, born in Cambridgeshire, grandson of Sir **George Downing**, and founder of Downing College, Cambridge. Being childless, he stipulated that his estates should pass to each of four cousins in turn, and if they died without issue the money should be used to found a college named after him. Even when the last cousin died childless in 1764, the widow refused to give up the estates, and Downing College did not receive its charter until 1800.

DOWSING, William (c.1576–1679) English Puritan, born in Laxfield, Suffolk. In 1644 he purged over 150 churches in that county of stained glass, brasses, paintings and other relics of popery. He was also responsible for much iconoclasm in Cambridgeshire.

DOWSON, Ernest Christopher (1867–1900) English poet of the 'decadent' school, born in Kent. He studied at Oxford, and became part of the 'Rhymers' Club group, and was a friend of **Arthur Symons** and **W B Yeats**. He spent the rest of his life in France, where he died of alcoholism. He wrote delicate verse and translated French classics.

DOYLE, Sir Arthur Conan (1859–1930) Scottish writer of detective stories and historical romances, nephew of **Richard Doyle**, born of Irish parentage in Edinburgh. He was educated at Stonyhurst and in Germany, and studied medicine at Edinburgh. Initial poverty as a young practitioner in Southsea and as an oculist in London coaxed him into authorship. His debut was a story in *Chamber's Journal* (1879), and his first book introduced that prototype of the modern detective in fiction, the super-observant, deductive Sherlock Holmes, his good-natured doctor friend Dr John Watson, and the whole apparatus of detection mythology associated with Baker Street. *The Adventures of Sherlock Holmes* were serialized in the *Strand Magazine* (1891–93). They were so popular that when Conan Doyle, tired of his popular creation, tried to kill off his hero on a cliff, he was compelled in 1903 to revive him. The serials were published as books with the titles, *The Sign of Four* (1890), *The Hound of the Baskervilles* (1902), etc. Conan Doyle, however, set greater stock by his historical romances, *Micah Clarke* (1887), *The White Company* (1890), *Brigadier Gerard* (1896) and *Sir Nigel* (1906), which have greater literary merit but are underrated. A keen boxer himself, *Rodney Stone* (1896) is one of his best novels. *The Lost World* (1912) and *The Poison Belt* (1913) are essays into the pseudo-scientifically fantastic. He served as a physician in the 2nd Boer War (1899–1902), and his pamphlet, *The War in South Africa* (1902), correcting enemy propaganda and justifying Britain's action, earned him a knighthood (1902). He used his detective powers to some effect outside fiction in attempting to show that the criminal cases of the Parsee Birmingham lawyer, Edaljee (1903), and **Oscar Slater** (1909) were instances of mistaken identity. He wrote on spiritualism to which he became a convert in later life.

DOYLE, Sir Francis Hastings Charles, 2nd Bart (1810–88) English poet, born in Nunappleton near Tadcaster. Educated at Eton and Christ Church, Oxford, he was called to the bar, held offices in the customs, and from 1867 to 1877 was professor of poetry at Oxford. His two series of Oxford lectures he published in 1869 and 1877. His verse collections 1834 (enlarged 1840) and 1866, are unmemorable save for such ballads of British military fortitude as 'The Loss of the *Birkenhead*', and 'The Private of the Buffs'.

DOYLE, John (1797–1868) Irish political cartoonist, born in Dublin into an impoverished Roman Catholic family. He settled in England in 1921, where his loyalties were to liberal figures who brought about Catholic emancipation and reform. He revolutionized the art of caricature from the 18th-century grotesques. His subjects were striking likenesses, handled with dignity but not deference: royalty made slightly ludicrous; **Wellington** (to whom Doyle bore a striking physical resemblance) handled critically as a politician but affectionately as a person; 'John Bull' made an embodiment of radical public opinion, rough and honest. Doyle's 'Political Sketches' were issued as large single prints, collected in portfolios and signed 'H.B.' (from two IDs, his Latin initials, one on top of the other). Few knew H.B.'s identity. He could be hilariously apposite in placing politicians in Biblical or mythological settings. Doyle was widowed young and brought up an artistically talented family, including **Richard Doyle** and Charles, father of **Arthur Conan Doyle**.

DOYLE, Richard (1824–83) English caricaturist, book illustrator and watercolour painter, born in London. Trained by his father, himself the noted caricaturist 'H.B.' (**John Doyle**), he became a contributor to *Punch* in 1843, designed the famous cover that was used from 1849 to 1956, furnished the well-known 'Ye Manners and Customs of ye Englyshe' and the first of the famous 'Brown, Jones, and Robinson' travel and other adventures. In 1850 he left, resenting, as a Catholic, attacks on 'papal aggression'. He also illustrated **Ruskin** (*King of the Golden River*), **Thackeray** (*Newcomes*), **Dickens** (*Battle of Life*), and **Leigh Hunt**.

DRABBLE, Margaret (1939–) English novelist, born in Sheffield. Her elder sister is the novelist A S Byatt. The family was bookish; her father was a barrister, then a circuit judge, and, in retirement, a novelist. Her mother was an English teacher. She was educated at the Mount School, York (the Quaker boarding school where her mother taught), and at York University and Newnham College, Cambridge. She married the actor Clive Swift, acted briefly, then turned to writing. Divorced from her first husband in 1972 (after having three children), she married the biographer **Michael Holroyd** in 1982. Often mirroring her own life, her novels are concerned with middle-class women with middle-class concerns and have been derogatorily dubbed 'Hampstead' novels. *A Summer Bird-Cage* (1963), *The Garrick Year* (1964), *The Millstone* (1965), *Jersualem the Golden* (1967), *The Needle's Eye* (1972), *The Ice Age* (1977), *The Middle Ground* (1980) and *The Radiant Way* (1987) are among her titles. She was the editor of the 5th edition of the *Oxford Companion to English Literature*, and has written biographies of **Virginia Woolf** (1973) and **Arnold Bennett** (1974).

DRACHMANN, Holger Henrik Herholdt (1846–1908) Danish writer and artist, born in Copenhagen of a German family. The foremost modernist poet in Denmark, he travelled widely in Europe and published several volumes of verse, and also wrote novels and plays. He was also a marine painter, with a good knowledge of seafaring.

DRACO (7th century BC) Athenian law-giver, Archon at Athens in 621 BC, he revised the laws of Athens with admirable impartiality; but the severity of his penalty—death for almost every offence—made the strict execution of his code (since proverbial for its rigour) unpopular, and it was superseded by that of **Solon**.

DRAGHI, Giovanni Battista (17th century) Italian musician at the court of King **Charles II** in London. He wrote instrumental interludes for **Shadwell**'s *Psyche* (1674), and was organist to Queen **Catherine of Braganza** (1677). He took part in the celebrated organ-building competition between **Renatus Harris** and **Bernard Smith** (1674).

DRAKE, Edwin Laurentine (1819–90) American oil pioneer, born in Greenville, New York, the son of a farmer. He started as a railway conductor, later becoming a stockholder in the Pennsylvania Rock Oil Company, which sent him in 1857 to inspect its property at Oil Creek. Being favourably impressed with the location he secured a lease himself and after three months of drilling struck oil on 27 August 1859 at a depth of 69 feet, with an initial yield of 40 barrels a day. Having thus initiated the huge oil industry of today, he unfortunately failed to patent his invention of a tube down to bedrock to protect the drill-hole, and by 1863 he had lost his savings in oil speculation and spent the rest of his days in ill-health and poverty.

DRAKE, Sir Francis (c.1540–1596) English navigator and pirate, born in Crowndale, near Tavistock. He worked in the coasting trade from the age of 13, but by 1565 was voyaging to Guinea and the Spanish Main. In 1567 he commanded the *Judith* of 50 tons in his kinsman **John Hawkin**'s ill-fated expedition to the Gulf of Mexico; and in 1570 and 1571 sailed to the West Indies to make good the losses he had then sustained from the Spaniards. In 1572, with two small ships, the *Pasha* and *Swan*, and a privateer's licence from Queen **Elizabeth**, he plundered on the Isthmus of Panama and became the first Englishman to see the Pacific Ocean. On his return to Plymouth in 1573 he became a popular hero. In 1577 he fitted out the *Pelican* of 100 tons, the *Elizabeth* of 80 tons, and three smaller vessels, to explore the Strait of Magellan, where Drake changed his own ship's name to the *Golden Hind*. On entering the Pacific violent tempests were encountered for 52 days during which the *Marigold* foundered with all hands and the *Elizabeth* returned home. Drake sailed north alone, to Vancouver; but failing to find a North-West Passage back into the Atlantic he turned south and struck across the Pacific, and for 68 days did not sight land until he made the Pelew Islands. After refitting in Java, he headed for the Cape of Good Hope, and arrived in England in September 1580, the first Englishman to circumnavigate the world. The queen, in the face of Spanish protests, was at first uncertain how to receive him, but at length paid a visit to his ship at Deptford and knighted him. In the autumn of 1585 he sailed against the Spanish Indies, harrying Hispaniola, Cartagena and the coast of Florida, and brought home the 190 dispirited Virginian colonists, with tobacco and potatoes. Early in 1587 he sacked Cadiz; and in 1588, as vice admiral under Howard, took a leading part in harassing the Spanish Armada as it passed through the English Channel. Off Portland he captured the galleon *Rosario*. In 1589 he led a large expedition to aid the Portuguese against Spain, but the mission was unsuccessful. He died on an expedition, with Sir **John Hawkins**, to the West Indies.

DRAKE, Samuel Gardner (1798–1875) American antiquarian and historian, born in Pittsfield, New Hampshire. He published many reprints and valuable works on the early history of New England, including *Indian Biography* (1832) enlarged as *Book of the Indians* (1841).

DRAPER, Henry (1837–82) American astronomer and pioneer of astronomical photography, born in Prince Edward County, Virginia. His father was the chemical physicist **John William Draper** who, using **Daguerre**'s process, took what is probably the oldest surviving photographic portrait (of his sister Dorothy) in 1840, and in the same year photographed the Moon. Henry graduated in medicine at City University, New York, and taught natural science, and later physiology at the City of New York University (1860–82). He retired in 1882 in order to devote himself full time to astronomical research. With a 71-cm (28-inch) reflecting telescope he applied the new technique of photography to astronomy. In 1872 he obtained a photograph of a stellar spectrum (Vega); by 1882 he had photographed over 100 stellar spectra, and the Orion nebula. He showed photographic methods to be an important means of studying the heavens.

DRAPER, John William (1811–82) British-born American author and man of science, born in St Helens, near Liverpool. In 1831 he emigrated to Virginia, in 1839 became professor of chemistry in the University of New York, and from 1850 to 1873 was president of its medical department. Among his works are *On the Forces that Produce the Organisation of Plants* (1844), *Physiology* (1856), *History of the Amercian Civil War* (1867–70), and *Scientific Memoirs* (1878).

DRAPER, Ruth (1889–1956) American diseuse and monologist, born in New York. She made her stage début in 1915. Following successful solo appearances for the American troops in France in 1918, she toured extensively, appearing in 1926 before **George V** at Windsor. Her repertoire comprised 36 monologues, of her own devising, and embraced 57 characters. She was the recipient of many doctorates, including the LLD from Edinburgh University in 1951 when she was also made a CBE.

DRAYTON, Michael (1563–1631) English poet, born in Hartshill near Atherstone, Warwickshire. He became a page in a wealthy household and spent the rest of his life in the households of patrons. His earliest work was *The Harmony of the Church* (1591), a metrical rendering of scriptural passages, which gave offence to the authorities, and was condemned to be destroyed. In 1593 he published a volume of eclogues, *Idea, the Shepherd's Garland*, which afterwards underwent considerable revision, and the first of his 'historical legends' in verse, *Piers Gaveston*. His first important poem, *Mortimeriados* (1596), recast in 1603 as *The Barons' Wars*, has some fine passages. *England's Heroical Epistles* (1597) has more polish and is more even than many of Drayton's other works. *Poems, Lyric and Pastoral* (c.1606) contains some of his most familiar poems, including the *Ballad of Agincourt* and *Fair Stood the Wind for France*. The first eighteen 'songs' or books of Drayton's greatest work, *Polyolbion*, were published in 1613, with annotation by **John Selden**, and the complete poem, the product of vast learning and the labour of years, appeared in 1622. In it he aimed at giving 'a chorographical description of all the tracts, rivers, mountains, forests, and other parts of Great Britain'. In 1619 he collected in one volume all the poems (except *Polyolbion*) which he wished to preserve. In 1627 he published a new volume of miscellaneous poems, among them the whimsical and delightful *Nymphisdia, the Court of Fairy*, a triumph of ingenious fancy. His last work, *The Muses' Elysium* (1630), contains some pastoral poems of finished elegance. He was buried in Westminster Abbey.

DREBBEL, Cornelis Jacobszoon (c.1572–1633) Dutch-born British inventor, born in Alkmaar. Apprenticed to a painter and engraver in Haarlem who was also an alchemist, he acquired an interest in chemistry and later in various branches of technology. He prepared a map of Alkmaar and designed a water-supply system for the town, then in 1604 moved to England where he spent most of the rest of his life. Among his inventions were a clock driven by changes in atmospheric pressure, a new method for the manufacture of sulphuric acid, a thermostat which could regulate the supply of air to a furnace, and a rudimentary submarine (1620) which was successfully tested in the river Thames.

DREES, Willem (1886–1988) Dutch politician, born in Amsterdam. After a short period in a bank he moved to the Hague as a government stenographer and then entered politics, joining the Socialist Democratic Workers' party and becoming its chairman in 1911. He sat in the Second Chamber from 1933 until the German invasion of 1940, after which he played an important part in the resistance movement. In 1947, as minister of social affairs, he introduced the state pension and then became prime minister (1948–58). A modest, puritanical man, he became the most durable figure in Dutch politics, a special stamp being issued to commemorate his 100th birthday.

DREES, Willem (1922–) Dutch economist and politician, son of **Willem Drees** (1886–1988). After graduating at the Netherlands School of Economics, Rotterdam, he joined the International Monetary Fund (IMF) in Washington (1947–50), and then worked in the Dutch embassy in Jakarta (1950–55). He returned to the Netherlands as director of the budget in the ministry of finance as well as being professor of public finance at Rotterdam.

DREISER, Theodore Herman Albert (1871–1945) American novelist, born in Terre Haute, Indiana. The eleventh and penultimate child of a poor Catholic German immigrant father, he was brought up on the breadline and left home at 15 for Chicago. He did odd jobs before becoming a highly successful journalist and wrote *Sister Carrie* (1900), a powerful and frank treatment of a young working girl's climb towards worldly success. The publisher, fearful of accusations of obscenity, was diffident in its promotion and it flopped commercially. Dreiser next wrote *Jennie Gerhardt* (1911) on a similar theme, which established him as a novelist. There followed the first parts of a trilogy about Frank Cowperwood, a power-hungry business tycoon: *The Financier* (1912), *The Titan* (1914), and *The Stoic* (published posthumously in 1947). *The Genius* was published in 1915 and ten years later came *An American Tragedy* (1925), based on a real-life murder case, which, despite reservations about its author's leaden prose, has survived as a classic. A large, egocentric man with an excessive sexual appetite, his work in the last decades of life was unremarkable and his reputation was sullied by his jealousy of **Sinclair Lewis**'s receipt of the Nobel prize for literature in 1930 and by his alleged plagiarism of a book on Russia by Dorothy Thompson, Lewis's wife.

DRELINCOURT, Charles (1595–1669) French divine, born in Sedan. A Protestant pastor in Charenton, near Paris, from 1620, he wrote, among other works, *Consolations against the Fear of Death* (1651), to a fourth edition of the English translation of which was attached Defoe's *Apparition of one Mrs Veal* (1716).

DRESSER, Christopher (1834–1904) English designer and writer, born in Glasgow. His first area of study was botany, in which he excelled as a draughtsman, and from which he developed the stylized plant motifs which became the basis for his interest in decorative design. He contributed to **Owen Jones**'s *Grammar of Ornament* and later wrote *The Art of Decorative Design* (1862) and *The Principles of Decorative Design* (1873). As something of a pioneer consultant designer, he designed glass, ceramics and cast iron furniture for a number of manufacturers, but his outstanding works were well researched items of functional metalwork such as teapots and soup tureens. These, in their unadorned, geometric forms, are some of the most strikingly 'modern' designs of the 19th century.

DREYER, Carl Theodor (1889–1968) Danish film-maker, born in Copenhagen, and raised in a strict Lutheran family. His early career as a journalist brought him into contact with the developing film industry and he began writing scripts in 1912. He made his début as a director with *Praesidenten* (The President, 1919). Works like *Blade af Satans Bog* (Leaves from Satan's Book, 1920), *La Passion de Jeanne d'Arc* (1928) and *Vampyr* (1932) combine technical experimentation with a desire to explore spiritual themes and the influence of evil through torment and martyrdom. An exacting perfectionist whose work rarely found commercial favour, he returned to journalism in the 1930s and subsequently concentrated on documentaries. Infrequent fictional works like *Vredens Dag* (Day of Wrath, 1943) and *Ordet* (The Word, 1955) continued his fascination with spirituality and deliverance through death. His last film was *Gertrud* (1964), about a woman seeking perfect love, although until his death he continued to work on a long-cherished project to film the life of **Jesus Christ**.

DREYFUS, Alfred (c.1859–1935) French army officer, born in Mülhausen in Alsace, the son of a rich Jewish manufacturer. He was an artillery captain on the general staff when, in 1893–94, he was unjustly accused of delivering to a foreign government documents connected with the national defence. He was court-martialled, degraded, and transported for life to Devil's Island. The efforts of his wife and friends to prove him an innocent victim of malice, injustice and forgery plunged France into a chaos of militarism and anti-semitism which provoked **Émile Zola** to assail the government in his celebrated *J'accuse* (1898). Colonel Georges Picquart (1854–1914), who first threw doubts on the verdict, was dismissed from the army and imprisoned (but later rehabilitated) in an attempt by the authorities to prevent a retrial; but later in the year, Major Hubert Joseph Henry (1846–98), who as chief of military intelligence had forged the papers for the original trial with Major **Marie Charles Esterhazy**, confessed and committed suicide in prison. The case was tried again and Dreyfus was found guilty but pardoned. It was not until 1906, when anti-semitism in France had died down, that the verdict was reversed by a civilian court. Dreyfus was restored to his army rank and fought in World War I and was awarded the Legion of Honour.

DREYFUSS, Henry (1903–72) American designer and writer on design, born in New York. After an early career in stage design, in 1928 he opened his own design office which continued in practice after his death (he and his wife committed suicide). An important aspect of his work was his pioneering research into anthropometry, a study with clear implications for design. The results of this study are evident in his books *Designing for People* (1955) and *The Measure of Man* (1959). Not surprisingly, functionalism took precedence over style in his design work. He was also concerned with the ethical standards of his profession, and restricted the number of his clients partly to prevent a conflict of commitment. Among the products which he designed were Bell telephones, Hoover vacuum cleaners, RCA televisions, John Deare agricultural machinery and Lockheed airliner interiors.

DREYSE, Johann Nikolaus von (1787–1867) German gunsmith, born in Sömmerda near Erfurt. He founded iron works there, and invented a muzzle-loading, and in 1836 a breech-loading, needle-gun, both adopted by the Prussian army in 1841.

DRIESCH, Hans Adolf Eduard (1867–1941) German physiologist and philosopher, born in Kreuznach. Professor of philosophy at Heidelberg (1911), Cologne (1920), and Leipzig (1921), he pioneered experiments in embryology, and wrote works on the organism, vitalism and individuality.

DRINKWATER, later **Drinkwater Bethune, John** (1762–1844) English historian, born in Warrington. He served through the famous siege of Gibraltar (1779–83), of which he wrote a classic History (1785).

DRINKWATER, John (1882–1937) English poet, dramatist, and critic, born in Leytonstone. He was an insurance clerk who achieved an immediate success with his play *Abraham Lincoln* (1918), which he followed with *Mary Stuart*, *Oliver Cromwell* (both published in 1921), *Robert E. Lee* (1923) and a comedy *Bird in Hand* (1927). His first volume of poems appeared in 1923, and he also wrote critical studies of **Morris**, **Swinburne** and **Byron**, and of lyric poetry. He was one of the founders of the Pilgrim Players and became manager of the Birmingham Repertory Theatre.

DRIVER, Sir Godfrey Rolles (1892–1975) English biblical scholar, son of **Samuel Rolles Driver**. He was professor of Semitic philology at Oxford (1938–62); from 1965 to 1970 he was joint director of the project to develop the new translation of the *New English Bible*.

DRIVER, Samuel Rolles (1846–1914) English Old Testament scholar, born in Southampton. He succeeded **Edward Pusey** as regius professor of Hebrew at Oxford (1882–1914). He was a member of the Old Testament revision committee (1875–84), and wrote *Notes on Samuel* (1890) and *Introduction to the Literature of the Old Testament* (1891).

DROBNY, Jaroslav (1921–) Czechoslovakian tennis player and all-round sportsman. Born in Prague, he first came to prominence as a member of the Czech ice-hockey side which won an Olympic silver medal in 1948. In the same year he was rendered homeless by the Communist take-over of Czechoslovakia, and he competed in tennis first of all as a stateless player and then under the banner of Egypt. His left-handed service was peculiarly difficult to handle, but he lost two Wimbledon finals, to Ted Schroeder (1949) and **Frank Sedgman** (1951) before taking the title in 1954 in one of the tournament's most memorable finals, against **Ken Rosewall** of Australia.

DROESHOUT, Martin (17th century) Flemish engraver, resident in London, widely known by his portrait of **Shakespeare**, prefixed to the folio edition of 1623.

DROSTE-HÜLSHOFF, Annette Elisabeth, Baroness von (1797–1848) German poet, born in Westphalia. Commonly regarded as Germany's greatest woman writer, she led a retired life and from 1818 to 1820 wrote intense devotional verses, eventually published as *Geistliche Jahre* in 1851. She wrote in a more restrained and classical style than that of most of her contemporaries, especially her ballads and lyrics, though her long narrative poems, notably *Das Hospiz am Grossen Sant Bernard* (1825) and *Die Schlacht in Loener Bruch*, were influenced by **Byron**. She also wrote a novella, *Die Judenbuche* (1841).

DROUET, Jean Baptiste, Comte d'Erlon (1765–1844) French soldier, born in Reims. In the Napoleonic wars he served in the campaigns of the Moselle, Meuse, Sambre and Peninsula. At the first restoration, the **Bourbons** gave him a command, but on

Napoleon's return he was put under arrest in Lille citadel. He seized and held it for the emperor, who made him a peer of France; and at Waterloo (1815) he commanded the first *corps d'armé*. After the capitulation of Paris he fled to Bavaria, returned on the July Revolution (1830), was governor-general of Algeria 1834–35, and was made marshal of France in 1843.

DROUOT, Antoine, Comte (1774–1847) French soldier, born in Nancy. General of artillery, he was aide-de-campe to **Napoleon**, who called him 'le Sage de la Grande Armée'.

DROZ, Antoine Gustave (1832–95) French novelist, born in Paris. He was grandson of Jean Pierre Droz (1746–1823), an engraver of medals. He had devoted himself to art till he made his first and greatest success with *Monsieur, Madame, et Bébé* (1866). Later came *Entre nous* (1867), *Les Étangs* (1876), *L'Enfant* (1885), and others.

DRUCE, George Claridge (1850–1932) English botanist and pharmacist, born in Potter's Bar, Northamptonshire. In 1879 he opened a chemist's shop in Oxford, and in 1895 became Fielding curator in the department of botany at the Ashmolean Museum. He published Floras of Oxfordshire (1886), Berkshire (1890), Buckinghamshire (1930), and *Comital Flora of the British Isles* (1932).

DRUCKER, Peter Ferdinand (1909–) Austrian-born American management consultant, born in Vienna. Educated in Austria and England, he became an economist with a London international bank before going to live in the USA in 1937. He was professor of philosophy and politics at Bennington College (1942–50), professor of management at the Graduate School of Business, New York University (1950–72), and was appointed professor of social sciences at the Claremont Graduate School in California in 1972. He is well known as a management consultant and has written over 20 successful textbooks on management, including *The Effective Executive* (1967), *Management: Tasks, Practices, Responsibilities* (1974), and *The Age of Discontinuity* (1969). He has also written two novels.

DRUMMOND, Annabella (c.1350–1402) Scottish queen, born at Stobhill near Perth, the daughter of Sir John Drummond of Stobhill. In 1367 she married John Stewart, afterwards **Robert III** of Scotland.

DRUMMOND, Dugald (1840–1912) Scottish locomotive engineer, born in Ardrossan, Ayrshire. The chief mechanical engineer of the London & South Western Railway from 1905, he made his reputation in Scotland in 1876–78 with the 4-4-0 'Abbotsford' class, examples of which were still running in the 1960s. His younger brother, Peter (1850–1918), born in Polmont, Stirlingshire, was also a locomotive engineer with the Highland and Glasgow & South Western Railways.

DRUMMOND, George (1687–1766) Scottish entrepreneur and philanthropist, born in Perthshire, and known as the founder of the New Town in Edinburgh. An anti-Jacobite Whig, he fought at the battle of Sheriffmuir (1715) and commanded a company in the 1745 Rising. A skilled accountant, he worked on the accounts for the Union of Parliaments in 1707, and was appointed accountant-general of excise. In 1716 he became a member of Edinburgh town council, treasurer in 1717, and was six times lord provost of Edinburgh between 1725 and 1764. He was the driving force behind the building of the Royal Infirmary (1738), the building of the Royal Exchange (1760, now the City Chambers), the expansion of Edinburgh University, and the proposal to create a New Town to the north of Princes Street. He drained the Nor'Loch (1759), and in 1763 laid the foundation stone of the North Bridge.

DRUMMOND, Henry (1786–1860) English banker, politician and religious leader, born in Albury, Surrey. He was MP for Plumpton Earls from 1810 to 1813, and West Surrey (1847–60). He lived for a time near Geneva and continued **Robert Haldane**'s campaign against the creed of Socinianism founded by **Faustus Socinus**. He founded a chair of economics at Oxford (1825), and became the founder and chief prophet of the Catholic Apostolic, or Irvingite, church, based on the messianic creed of **Edward Irving**.

DRUMMOND, Henry (1851–97) Scottish evangelical theologian and biologist, born in Stirling. He studied at Edinburgh, and in 1877 became lecturer (professor, 1884) of natural science at the Free Church College, Glasgow. He travelled in the Rocky Mountains, Central Africa, Japan, and Australia. He attempted to reconcile Christianity and Darwinism in such works as *Natural Law of the Spiritual World* (1883), *The Ascent of Man* (1894), and *Tropical Africa* (1888).

DRUMMOND, Sir Jack Cecil See **DOMINICI, Gaston**

DRUMMOND, James Eric, 16th Earl of Perth (1876–1951) British statesman, born in Fulford, Yorkshire. He was first secretary-general of the League of Nations (1919–1932), and ambassador in Rome (1933–39).

DRUMMOND, Margaret (c.1472–1502) Scottish gentlewoman, youngest daughter of Lord Drummond. One of the many mistresses of King **James IV** of Scotland, she enjoyed royal favour in 1496 and bore him a daughter. She and two of her sisters died suddenly after a suspect breakfast.

DRUMMOND, Thomas (1797–1840) Scottish engineer and statesman, born in Edinburgh. Educated there and at Woolwich, he entered the Royal Engineers in 1815, and in 1820 joined the ordnance survey, whose work was immensely facilitated by his improved heliostat and lime-light (the 'Drummond Light'); the latter was also developed at about the same time by Sir **Goldsworthy Gurney**. He became head of the boundary commission under the Reform Bill; and under-secretary for Ireland (practically its governor) in 1835. Here he gained the affection of the people; his was the memorable saying, 'Property has its duties as well as its rights' (1838).

DRUMMOND, William of Hawthornden (1585–1649) Scottish poet, born in Hawthornden, near Roslin in Midlothian, the son of a courtier to King **James VI and I**. He was educated at the High School of Edinburgh, graduated MA at Edinburgh in 1605, studied law at Bourges and Paris, and on his father's death in 1610 became laird of Hawthornden. He devoted his life to poetry and mechanical experiments. He was on the point of marrying Euphemia Cunningham of Barns when the lady died on the eve of their wedding (1615). He took a mistress, by whom he had three children, and married Elizabeth Logan of Restalrig in 1630. He had to subscribe to the National Covenant of 1638 but witnessed its triumph with a sinking heart that the most sarcastic verses could not relieve. His death was hastened by grief for **Charles I**'s execution. Drummond enjoyed the friendship of **Ben Jonson**; the last paid him a memorable visit in 1618–19. Drummond's *Notes* of their talk is a charming chapter of literary history. His chief works are the pastoral lament *Tears on the Death of Moeliades* (ie, Prince Henry, 1613); *Poems, Amorous, Funereall, Divine, Pastorall in Sonnets, Songs, Sextains, Madrigals* (1614); *Forth Feasting* (1617); and *Flowers of Sion* (1623). In prose he wrote *A Cypress Grove* (1630) and a *History* *of the Five Jameses*. He also wrote a *History of Scotland 1423–1524* posthumously published in 1655.

DRURY, Alfred (1857–1944) Engish sculptor, born in London. Among his works are *St Agnes* (Chantrey Collection, 1896), **Edward VII** (1903), Sir **Joshua Reynolds** (Burlington House quadrangle, 1931) and the *London Troops* war memorial at the Royal Exchange.

DRURY, Dru (1725–1803) English naturalist and silversmith, born in London. He devoted himself to entomology, and published *Illustrations of Natural History* (3 vols, 1770–82), with over 240 figures by Moses Harris of exotic insects. His *Exotic Entomology* was published in 1837, with over 650 figures.

DRUSUS, Marcus Livius Roman politician, tribune of the people in 122 BC, opposed the democratic policy of his colleague, **Gracchus**.

DRUSUS, Marcus Livius (d.91BC) Roman politician, son and namesake of **M Livius Drusus**. Though identified by birth and sympathy with the senators, he renewed some of the most liberal measures of the **Gracchi**, and advocated the claims of the Italians to Roman citizenship. He was assassinated.

DRUSUS, Nero Claudius or **Drusus Senior** (39–9 BC) Roman soldier, son of Livia Drusilla, stepson of the emperor **Augustus**, and younger brother of the Emperor **Tiberius**. His campaign against the Rhaeti and other Alpine tribes (15 BC) was celebrated by **Horace** in his *Odes*. Until his death he was engaged chiefly in establishing Roman supremacy in Germany, and received the title Germanicus; the celebrated **Germanicus Caesar** was his son.

DRUTEN, John van (1901–57) English-born American playwright, born in London. He became famous with the production of his play *Young Woodley* in 1928. After several years and considerable success in the USA, he was granted American citizenship in 1944. *The Voice of the Turtle*, his most successful play with an American setting, was produced in 1943. He published his autobiography, *The Way to the Present* in 1938.

DRYDEN, John (1631–1700) English poet, born at the vicarage of Aldwinkle All Saints, Northamptonshire, where his maternal grandfather was rector. He was educated at Westminster School under **Richard Busby** and at Trinity College, Cambridge, where he stayed until 1657. Going up to London in that year he attached himself to his cousin Sir Gilbert Pickering, **Cromwell**'s chamberlain, in the hope of employment, which he might well have expected since on both sides his people were parliamentarians. His *Heroic Stanzas*, in quatrains, on the death of Cromwell (1658), was soon followed by his *Astrea Redux* (1660), celebrating the Restoration in heroic couplets, which was to be his staple measure even in the plays which soon poured from his pen for the amusement of 'a venal court'. The first of these 'heroic' verse plays to take the public taste was *The Indian Emperor* (1665), dealing with the conquest of Mexico by **Cortes** and his love for the Emperor's daughter, and the last was *Aurungzebe* (1676). In 1663 he married Lady Elizabeth Howard, eldest daughter of the earl of Berkshire. In 1667 he published *Annus Mirabilis, The Year of Wonders, 1666*, which established his reputation, and he was appointed poet laureate in 1668 following Sir **William D'Avenant**, and historiographer royal in 1670. Meanwhile he was turning out a series of comedies for the stage, including *The Rival Ladies* (1664, in rhymed verse), and culminating with *Marriage-á-la-Mode* (1673). He used blank verse for *All for Love* (1678), his best play and not unworthy to be placed beside **Shakespeare**'s *Antony and Cleopatra*. His adaptation of another of Shakespeare's plays, *Troilus and Cressida*, the following year, was by comparison a failure. Adaptation was a means of keeping up with the demands of the theatre on his service; he had already adapted *The Tempest* in 1670; **Milton**'s *Paradise Lost* (as *The State of Innocence*), 1677; and **Thomas Corneille**'s *The Mock Astrologer* (1668). He wrote a series of important critical essays as prefaces to his plays, including his charming *Essay of Dramatic Poesy* (1668), and the *Defence of the Epilogue* (to that popular play *The Conquest of Granada*, 1670). In 1680 he began a series of satirical and didactic poems, starting with the most famous, *Absalom and Achitophel* (1681), and followed by *The Medal* (1682) and *MacFlecknoe* (1684), written some years before, which did much to turn the tide against the Whigs. To this era also belong the didactic poem *Religico Laici* (1682), which argues the case for Anglicanism, and the much finer *The Hind and the Panther*, marking his conversion to Rome in 1685. A place in the Customs (1683) was his reward for his political labours. At the Revolution of 1688 he lost the poet laureateship and took to translation as a means of living. Of these his fine translation of **Virgil** was most profitable, that of **Juvenal** and **Persius** was prefaced by a *Discourse Concerning the Origin and Progress of Satire*, which had all his old ease and urbanity. His final work, published in 1699, was *Fables, Ancient and Modern* which, with its paraphrases of **Chaucer**, **Ovid** and **Boccaccio**, has delighted generations of readers. These works are only the most outstanding of a lifetime's industry. Dryden is transitional between the metaphysical poets of the school of **Donne** and the neoclassic reaction which he did so much to create.

DRYGALSKI, Erich Dagobert von (1865–1949) German geophysicist and explorer, born in Königsberg. He headed expeditions to Greenland (1891–93), and in the *Gauss* to the Antarctic (1902–03), where he discovered and named the Gaussberg volcano.

DRYSDALE, Sir (George) Russell (1912–81) English-born Australian painter, born in Sussex. His family settled in Melbourne in 1923 and, although he originally intended to work on the land, he attended art school. In 1939 he took part in the first exhibition of the Contemporary Art Society of Australia. Eventually he settled in Sydney and decided to paint fulltime and, in 1942, had his first one-man exhibition. **Kenneth Clark** encouraged him to exhibit in London in 1950. In 1954 he represented Australia at the Venice Biennale. His paintings of the Australian outback often stress drought and erosion, and show the influence of abstract and Surrealist art.

DUARENUS, properly **Francois Douaren** (1509–59) French humanist jurist, professor at Bourges and a rival of **Jacques de Cujacius**. He wrote a *Pro libertate ecclesiae Gallicae* (1551), *Commentarius in Consuetudines Feudorum* (1558) and a Commentary on **Justinian**'s *Digest*.

DUARTE, José Napoléon (1925–90) El Salvador politician. Trained as a civil engineer in the USA at the University of Notre Dame in South Bend, Indiana, he founded the Christian Democratic party (PDC) in 1960. After serving as mayor of El Salvador (1964–70), he was elected president in 1972 but was soon impeached and exiled for seven years in Venezuela. He returned and in 1980 regained the presidency, with US backing. He lost the 1982 election and for two years witnessed a fierce struggle between right- and left-wing elements. He returned as president in 1984 but in 1988, stricken by terminal cancer, was forced to resign.

DU BARRY, Marie Jean, née **Bécu, Comtesse** (1741–93) French courtesan, mistress of **Louis XV**. Born in Vaucouleurs, the daughter of a dressmaker, she became a shopgirl in Paris and was introduced to society as 'Mademoiselle Lange' by her lover, Jean du Barry. Presented at court, in 1768 she caught the fancy of the elderly king, who married her off to Jean's brother, a superannuated courtier, the comte Guillaume du Barry, in order to qualify her as an official court mistress. She helped to bring about the downfall of the finance minister, the Duke of **Choiseul**, and wielded considerable influence, but was unpopular with the public and squandered vast sums of money. She was banished from court after Louis' death in 1774. During the French Revolution she was brought before the Revolutionary Tribunal, charged with having wasted the treasure of the state, and guillotined.

DUBČEK, Alexander (1921–) Czechoslovakian statesman, born in Uhrovek, Slovakia. He lived from 1925 to 1938 in the Soviet Union, where his father was a member of a Czechoslovakian industrial co-operative. He joined the Communist party in 1939, fought as a Slovak patriot against the Nazis (1944–45), and gradually rose in the party hierarchy until in January 1968 he became first secretary. He introduced a series of far-reaching economic and political reforms, including abolition of censorship, increased freedom of speech, and suspension of ex-president Novotny and other former 'Stalinist' party leaders. Despite his avowed declaration of democracy within a Communist framework, his policy of liberalization led in August 1968 to the occupation of Czechoslovakia by Soviet forces. In 1969, however, after having been unable to break down the policy of passive disobedience and peaceful demonstration by the people, the Russians exerted strong pressure on the Czechoslovak government, and Dubček was replaced as first secretary by **Husak**. He was elected president of the Federal Assembly by the two houses of parliament, but expelled from the Presidium in September and deprived of party membership in 1970. He subsequently worked as a clerk in a lumber yard in Slovakia. Following the overthrow of the existing Communist régime in November 1989 in a bloodless 'Velvet Revolution', he dramatically re-emerged from retirement to be elected chairman of the country's federal assembly in December 1989.

DUBOIS, Guillaume (1656–1723) French prelate, born in Brives-la-Gaillarde, the son of a poor apothecary. He was first tutor and then secretary to the Duc de Chartres; and when the latter (now Duke of **Orléans**) became regent in 1715, Dubois was virtually all powerful. He was appointed foreign minister and archbishop of Cambrai (1720), a cardinal (1721), and prime minister of France (1722).

DUBOIS, Marie Eugène François Thomas (1858–1940) Dutch palaeontologist, born in Eijsden. He studied medicine in Amsterdam and taught there from 1899. His interest in the 'missing link' between the apes and man took him to Java in 1887, where in the 1890s he found the humanoid remains named as *Pithecanthropus erectus* (Java Man) and which he claimed to be the missing link. His view was contested and even ridiculed; and when in the 1920s it eventually became widely accepted, Dubois began to insist that the fossil bones were those of a giant gibbon, and maintained this view until his death.

DUBOIS, Paul (1829–1905) French sculptor, born in Nogent-sur-Seine. He studied law before turning to art. His works include a portrait bust of **Pasteur** and an equestrian statue of **Joan of Arc**. He was director of the École des Beaux-Arts from 1878.

DUBOIS, William Edward Burghardt (1868–1963) American Black writer and editor, born in Great Barrington, Massachusetts. He studied at Fisk University, Tennessee, and at Harvard, where his doctoral thesis was on the suppression of the African slave trade. He was professor of economics and history at Atlanta University (1897–1910). He was co-founder of the National Association for the Advancement of Coloured People (1909), and edited its magazine, *Crisis* (1910–34). He wrote a number of important works on slavery and the colour problem, including *The Souls of Black Folk* (1903), *John Brown* (1909), *The Negro* (1915), *The Gift of Black Folk* (1935), and *Colour and Democracy* (1945). He also wrote a novel, *The Dark Princess* (1928). A passionate advocate of radical Black action he joined the Communist party in 1961, and moved to Ghana at the age of 91, where he became a naturalized citizen just before he died.

DU BOS, Charles (1882–1939) French writer, born in Paris. He wrote critical works on **Byron**, **Mauriac**, **Gide**, and others and published a collection in seven volumes of critical essays under the title *Approximations* (1922–27). His *Qu'est-ce que la littérature* published posthumously in 1945, contains a 'Hommage' by a number of writers including **Charles Morgan**.

DUBOS, René Jules (1901–82) French-born American bacteriologist, born in Saint-Brice. He became an American citizen in 1938 and worked at Rockefeller University in New York City from 1927. In 1939 he discovered tyrothricin, the first commercially produced antibiotic.

DUBRICIUS, St (d.612) Welsh religious, and the traditional founder of the Welsh bishopric of Llandaff.

DUBUFFET, Jean (1901–85) French painter and printmaker, born in Le Havre. He enrolled at the Académie Julian in Paris in 1918, but never studied seriously, enjoying life as the son of a rich wine-merchant whose business he took over in 1925. He began painting again during World War II, when he invented the concept of Art Brut and pioneered the use of rubbish such as discarded newspapers, broken glass, rough plaster daubed and scratched like an old wall, to create 'pictures'. Regarded as a forerunner of the Pop Art and Dada-like fashions of the 1960s, his collected writings were published in 1967.

DU CAMP, Maxime (1822–94) French poet, novelist, journalist, born in Paris. He travelled in the East. He wrote books on Paris and was a founder of the *Revue de Paris* (1851).

DU CANGE, Charles Dufresne, Sieur (1610–88) French scholar, born in Amiens. He became a parliamentary advocate in Paris. A pioneer in the historical study of languages, his chief productions were *Glossarium ad Scriptores Mediae et Infimae Latinitatis* (Paris 1678) and *Glossarium ad Scriptores Mediae et Infimae Graecitatis* (1688).

DUCCIO DI BUONINSEGNA (c.1260–c.1320) Italian painter, founder of the Sienese school, in whose work the Byzantine tradition in Italian art is seen in its most highly-developed state. His masterpiece is the *Maestà* for the altar of Siena cathedral (1311), and the *Rucellai Madonna* in S Maria Novella at Florence, long attributed to **Cimabue**, is now generally considered to be his work. He is represented in the National Gallery by the *Annunciation*, *Christ Healing the Blind Man*, and the *Transfiguration*.

DU CHAILLU, Paul Belloni (1831–1903) French-born American traveller, born in Paris. From 1855 he spent four years exploring the interior of West Africa. His *Explorations in Equatorial Africa* (1861) made important contributions to geographical, ethnological, and zoological science, especially as to the source of the Ogowé River, the Fans and the gorilla, but was received at first with much distrust.

DUCHAMP, Marcel (1887–1968) French-born American painter, brother of **Jacques Villon** and half-brother of Raymond Duchamp-Villon (1876–1918), the sculptor. Associated with several modern movements including Cubism and Futurism, he shocked his generation with such works as *Coffee-Mill* (1911) and *Nude descending a staircase* (1912; Philadelphia), and was one of the pioneers of Dadaism, the anti-art protest, which exalted the presentation of energy and change above timeless, classical aesthetic values and fulminated against mechanization. In 1915 he left Paris for New York, where he introduced the mobile and the 'found object', and laboured eight years on a ten-foot-high composition in glass and metal, *The Bride Stripped Bare by Her Bachelors Even*, known as *The Large Glass* (1915–23; Philadelphia), in which many of the shapes were obtained by chance effects, dust blown on to the drawings, etc. This he described in his *Green Box* notes (1933). He edited the American art magazine, *VVV* (1942–44), and became an American citizen in 1955.

DUCHAMP-VILLON, Raymond (1876–1918) French sculptor, born in Damville, Normandy, brother of **Jacques Villon** and half-brother of **Marcel Duchamp**. He began as a medical student, turning to sculpture in 1898, and by 1914 was one of the leading Cubist sculptors in Paris. His most striking work was the bronze *Horse* (1914), in which realism is rejected in favour of an abstract swirl of forms that captures the energetic movement of the animal.

DU CHÂTELET See **CHÂTELET-LOMONT**

DUCHENNE, Guillaume Benjamin Amand (1806–75) French physician, educated at Douai and Paris. A pioneer in electrophysiology and the founder of electrotherapeutics, he was the first to describe locomotor ataxia, in 1858. His works include *L'Electrisation localisée* (1855) and *Physiologie des mouvements* (1867).

DUCHESNE, André, Latin **Chesnius** or **Quercetanus** (1584–1640) French historian. He was royal historiographer, and is known as the 'Father of French history'. He wrote histories of England, Scotland, and Ireland, of the popes down to **Paul V**, and of the House of Burgundy. He also made collections of the early Norman and French histories.

DUCHESNE, Père See **HÉBERT, Jacques René**

DUCIS, Jean François (1733–1816) French poet and playwright, born in Versailles. He is best known for his adaptations of **Shakespeare** for the French stage without knowing English.

DUCK, Stephen (1705–56) English ploughman-poet and scholar, born in Charlton in Wiltshire of humble parents. A self-educated farm-labourer, his verses came to the attention of Queen **Caroline**, who awarded him a pension and made him a Yeoman of the Guard in 1733. He published *Poems on Several Occasions* in 1736. He took holy orders in 1746 and was made rector of Byfleet in 1752, but committed suicide by drowning.

DUCKWORTH, Sir John Thomas (1748–1817) English naval commander, born in Leatherhead. He went to school at Eton, but left early to join the navy as a volunteer, and in 1759 saw action in the battles of Lagos Bay and Quiberon Bay, under **Hawke**. He served at sea in the War of American Independence (1775–83) and the French revolutionary wars (1792–1800), including the battle of Ushant (1794). In 1801 he captured Swedish and Danish possessions in the West Indies, and was commander-in-chief at Jamaica from 1803 to 1813.

DUCLOS DU HAURON, Louis (1837–1920) French scientist, born in Langon. Interested in photography from 1859, his publication *Les Couleurs en Photographie* in 1869 outlined for the first time all the principles of additive and subtractive colour reproduction, although at that period suitably sensitive photographic materials were not available. In 1878 he published *Photographie en Couleur*, describing practical methods which he patented, and in 1891 proposed the anaglyph method of viewing stereoscopic images. Although honoured towards the end of his life for his pioneering contributions, he died in penury.

DUDDELL, William du Bois (1872–1917) English engineer. He worked on radiotelegraphy and in 1897 invented an improved version of the oscillograph. He also designed a high-frequency generator. The Physical Society instituted the Duddell Medal in his honour.

DUDEVANT, Madame See **SAND, George**

DUDLEY, Dud (1599–1684) English ironmaster, illegitimate son of the 5th Baron Dudley. He was the first to attempt, with only limited success, the smelting of iron with coal in 1619. He wrote *Metallum Martis* (1665).

DUDLEY, Edmund (c.1462–1510) English lawyer and privy councillor. He was Sir **Richard Empson**'s partner in carrying out the detested policy of **Henry VII**, whose son and successor sent him to the block. He was also father of the Duke of Northumberland. See (Lady **Jane Grey**) and **Leicester**.

DUDLEY, Lord Guildford (d.1554) fourth son of the Lord Protector John Dudley, Earl of **Warwick** (Northumberland), and briefly husband of Lady **Jane Grey**. His father married him to the unwilling Jane Grey on 21 May 1553 as **Edward VI** lay dying, and then proclaimed her queen on 9 July. After the accession of **Mary I** (Edward's sister), Dudley and his wife were imprisoned and beheaded on Tower Hill on 12 February.

DUDLEY, Sir Robert (1573–1649) English nobleman, illegitimate son of the 1st Earl of Leicester by Lady Sheffield. After studying at Christ Church, Oxford, he made a voyage to the West Indies (1594–95), was knighted by **Essex** on the Cadiz expedition (1596), joined Essex's plot (1601), and, after a vain attempt to establish his legitimacy, quit England in 1605, deserting wife and daughters, and taking a mistress with him. He turned Roman Catholic, and lived chiefly at or near Florence, busy with naval inventions; in 1620 the Emperor **Ferdinand III** created him Duke of Northumberland and Earl of Warwick in the Holy Roman Empire.

DUDLEY, William (1947–) English stage designer, born in London, educated at St Martin's and the Slade Schools of Art, London. He designed his first stage set for *Hamlet* at the Nottingham Playhouse in 1970. He subsequently designed many productions for the Royal Court, including **Alan Bennett**'s *Kafka's Dick* in 1986. He has worked extensively at the National Theatre, and the Royal Shakespeare Company. He has also worked extensively in opera in Britain and abroad, and designed **Peter Hall**'s production of *The Ring* at Beyreuth in 1983.

DUDOK, Willem Marinus (1884–1974) Dutch architect. Trained as an army engineer, he became city architect of Hilversum in 1915. Mixing modern and traditional elements, his fully developed style is characterized by dramatic massing of asymmetrical plain brick blocks, deep-set windows and vertical elements. The Hilversum Town Hall (1928–30) was his master-work, a skilful juxtaposition of masses in a formal setting of pools and gardens. His most important building outside Hilversum was the Bijenkorf Department Store in Rotterdam (now demolished) where large areas of glazing contrasted with plain brickwork. Dudok had no successors, but was widely imitated abroad.

DUESBURY, William (1725–86) English china maker, born in Cannock, Staffordshire. In 1755 he moved to Derby, and founded a china manufacture there.

DUFAURE, Jules Armand Stanislas (1798–1881) French statesman, born in Saujon, Charente Inférieure. He was premier of France in 1876 and 1877–79.

DU FAY, Charles François de Cisternay (1698–1739) French chemist. As superintendent of gardens to the king of France, he discovered the two kinds of electricity, positive and negative, and carried out research on phosphorus and double refraction.

DUFAY, Guillaume (c.1400–1474) French composer, the most celebrated 15th-century composer. A choirboy at Cambrai, he returned there as canon in 1439 after extensive travel and residence in Italy. Almost 200 of his works are extant, including eight complete Masses, many motets and songs. His warmth of emotion, strong sense of melody and pioneering of the *cantus firmus* Mass greatly influenced Renaissance composers.

DUFF, Alexander (1806–78) Scottish missionary, born near Pitlochry. In 1829 he became the first Scottish missionary to India, and in 1830 opened a college in Calcutta combining religious teaching with Western science. In 1843, at the time of the Disruption in Scotland, he joined the Free Church, and had to give up his college; but he built another one, and soon his work was on a greater scale than before. In 1844 he helped to start the *Calcutta Review*. He was moderator of the Free Church Assembly in 1851, and again in 1873. He was one of the founders of the University of Calcutta, but because of persistent ill-health he had to leave India permanently in 1863. He endowed a missionary chair in New College, Edinburgh, of which he was the first occupant.

DUFF, Sir Lyman Poore (1865–1955) Canadian judge, judge of the Supreme Court of British Columbia (1904–06) and of the Supreme Court of Canada (1906–33) and chief justice of that court (1933–44). He had a very extensive knowledge of law, both common law and the modern civil law of France and Quebec, and wrote leading opinions on many important constitutional decisions. His influence was particularly significant on the question of distribution of powers between the Federal Government and the provinces, and on that of upholding the Federal Government's power to abolish, without the consent of the provinces, appeals to the privy council. He also sat on the judicial committee of the privy council (1919–46).

DUFFERIN AND AVA, Frederick Temple Hamilton Temple Blackwood, 1st Marquis of (1826–1902) English statesman, born in Florence. He succeeded his father as 5th baron Dufferin in 1841, and from Eton passed to Christ Church, Oxford. In 1860 he was sent by Lord Palmerston to inquire into the religious massacres in Syria, and on his return was created a KCB. He was under-secretary for India (1864–66) and for war (1866); chancellor of the duchy of Lancaster (1868–72); and governor-general of Canada (1872–78), having been created an earl in 1871. From 1879 to 1882 he was ambassador at St Petersburg, and then was transferred to Constantinople. In 1884 he succeeded Lord Ripon as viceroy of India.

DUFFY, Sir Charles Gavan (1816–1903) Irish nationalist, made KCMG in 1873, born in County Monaghan. He helped to start the *Nation* (1842), the Young Ireland organ, and for twelve years engaged in agitation, being tried for sedition and treason. On the break-up of the Independent Irish party, he emigrated in 1856 to Australia, where after the establishment of the Victorian constitution, he became in 1857 minister of public works, of lands in 1858 and 1862, and prime minister in 1871. In 1877 he was elected speaker of the Legislative Assembly. His *Ballad Poetry of Ireland* became a household book in his native country. In 1880, when he returned to Europe, appeared his *Young Ireland*, 1840–50 (final ed 1896), followed in 1883 by *Four Years of Irish History, 1845–49*, and in 1898 by *My Life in Two Hemispheres*.

DUFOUR, Guillaume Henri (1787–1875) Swiss soldier and writer on military matters. He served in the French army (1807–14), and founded the military academy at Thun in Switzerland in 1818. Chief of staff of the Swiss army from 1831, he commanded the new Swiss federal forces against the Sonderbund in 1847. He was also responsible for a topographical map of Switzerland (1864) and presided over the Geneva Convention in 1864 that led to the foundation of the Red Cross.

DUFRESNE, Charles See **DU CANGE**

DUFY, Raoul (1877–1953) French artist and designer, born in Le Havre. In 1900 he won a scholarship to the École des Beaux-Arts in Paris, and was much influenced by the brightness and colour of Fauvism, which he did much to popularize; later he abandoned it, but retained his singing blues and reds. From 1907 he worked in woodcut and engraved many book illustrations, including **Guillaume Apollinaire**'s *Bestiary* (1911), and produced woodcuts for making printed silk fabrics for dress designers. He also made pottery and tapestries, but in 1919 he returned to painting on the Riviera, where he produced a notable series of seascapes, bathers, sailing regattas and racecourse scenes.

DUGDALE, Sir William (1605–86) English antiquary, born in Shustoke, near Coleshill, Warwickshire. He studied law and history under his father, soon after whose death he purchased the neighbouring manor of Blythe (1625). In 1638 he was created a pursuivant-at-arms extraordinary and in 1640 Rouge Croix pursuivant. During the Great Rebellion he adhered to the royalist cause, and from 1642 to 1646 was at Oxford, the king's headquarters, being made an MA and Chester herald, while pursuing his antiquarian researches. He lived in obscurity during the Commonwealth, but on the Restoration received the office of Norroy, and in 1677 was promoted to be Garter Principal King of Arms, at the same time receiving a knighthood. His works include the *Monasticon Anglicanum* (1655–1661–73), a history of English religious foundations (Eng ed 6 vols, 1817–30); *Antiquaries of Warwickshire* (1656); *History of Imbanking and Drayning* (1662); *Origines Juridiciales*, a history of the English legal system (1666), and *Baronage of England* (3 vols, 1675–76).

DUGHET, Gaspard, also called **Gaspard Poussin** (1615–75) Italian painter, born in Rome of French descent. His sister married **Nicholas Poussin** and he called himself after his more famous brother-in-law. He specialized in landscapes which, while modelled on the Roman countryside, combine the classical manner of Poussin and the more lyrical style of **Claude Lorraine**. His works were avidly collected by 18th-century English travellers to Rome and were often taken as models for landscaped gardens and parks.

DUGUAY-TROUIN, René (1673–1736) French seaman, born in St Malo. A privateer from 1689, he was given the command of a frigate in 1697. In 1707 he engaged a British fleet at the entrance to the Channel, burning one ship, and capturing three others and 60 transports. In 1711 he captured and sacked Rio de Janeiro. In 1731 he was sent into the Levant.

DUGUIT, Leon (1859–1928) French jurist, professor of constitutional law at Bordeaux. He was author of *Transformations Générales du Droit privé depuis Le Code Napoléon* (1922), *Transformations du Droit Public* (1913), *Traité du Droit Constitutionel* (1921–25) and other works. His view of law was of something based on social solidarity through division of labour, a spontaneous product of circumstances; he believed that the inter-dependence of groups created a spontaneous self-regulation of human behaviour in society. For individual rights he proposed that the protection of social functions and law existed to ensure fulfilment of the need for social solidarity.

DUHAMEL, Georges (1884–1966) French novelist, poet and man of letters. He originally studied medicine and worked as an army surgeon in World War I. This provided the background for *La Vie des martyrs* (1917) and *Civilisation* (1918, awarded the Prix Goncourt). Many of his 50 volumes of vigorous, skilful writing have been translated. They include *Salavin* (1920–32), *News from Havre* (1934), *The Pasquier Chronicles* (1933–44), *Why France fights* (1940) and *Light on my Days* (1948, autobiographical). He edited *Mercure de France*.

DUHAMEL DU MONCEAU, Henri-Louis (1700–82) French technologist, born in Paris. Showing versatility in the range of problems he attacked as an academician, he proved the distinction between what we would now call potassium and sodium salts, showed that soda can be made from rock-salt, and improved the making of starch, soap, and brass. He reviewed agricultural practice and introduced **Tull**'s methods into France.

DUHEM, Pierre Maurice Marie (1861–1916) French philosopher of science and physicist, born in Paris. He held teaching positions at Lille, Rennes and Bordeaux. A devout Catholic all his life, his early scientific work was in thermodynamics and many of his ideas were well in advance of their time. He made important contributions to the history of science, in particular reviving an interest in medieval science in such works as *L'Évolution de la méchanique* (1903), *Origines de la statique* (1905–06), *Études sur Léonard de Vince* (3 vols, 1906–13) and *Système du monde* (10 vols, 1913 ff). His philosophical views are developed in *La Théorie physique, son objet et sa structure* (1906) and *Sauver les phénomènes* (1908), and present a formalistic account of science, whereby scientific theories and models should be regarded as useful predictive devices and psychological aids rather than direct descriptions or explanations of the world.

DÜHRING, Karl Eugen (1833–1921) German philosopher and political economist, born in Berlin. He became quite blind before he was 30. As a philosopher he was positivist and anti-Hegelian; as an economist he was influenced by **Henry Charles Carey**.

DUILIUS, Gaius (3rd century BC) Roman general. As consul in 260 BC he led 143 new Roman galleys to a decisive victory over the Carthaginians off Myle, by the first use of new devices nicknamed *corvi* (ravens), combined grappling-hooks and boarding-bridges.

DUJARDIN, Félix (1801–60) French zoologist, born in Tours. He taught at Tours, Toulouse and Rennes, and investigated foraminifera, protozoa, and invertebrates.

DUKAKIS, Michael (1933–) American politician, born in Boston, Massachusetts, the son of hardworking Greek immigrants. After studying law at Harvard and serving in Korea (1955–57), he concentrated on a political career in his home state. Elected as a Democrat to the Massachusetts legislature in 1962, he became state governor in 1974. His first term was unsuccessful, marred by an unwillingness to compromise, and he was defeated in 1978. However, he returned as a 'reformed man' in 1982, committed to work in a more consensual manner, and was elected governor again. Presiding over a high-tech driven boom, the 'Massachusetts miracle', he was re-elected by an increased margin in 1986 and captured the Democratic party's presidential nomination, presenting himself as a neo-liberal. He was defeated by the Republican **George Bush**.

DUKAS, Paul (1865–1935) French composer, born in Paris. Some of his work was classical in approach, but he tended mainly towards musical Impressionism. His best-known work is the symphonic poem *L'Apprenti sorcier* (1897); the opera *Ariane et Barbe-Bleue* is also noteworthy. He wrote some musicological books, and edited works by **Rameau** and **Scarlatti**.

DULAC, Edmund (1882–1953) French-born British artist and book illustrator, born in France. He is best known for his illustrations of classics and fairy tales. He designed the coronation stamp for 1937 and 1953.

DULBECCO, Renato (1914–) Italian-born American molecular biologist, born in Catanzaro. He studied medicine at Turin, moved to the USA in 1947, to Indiana University, and worked at the Salk Institute, California, from 1963. He showed how certain viruses can transform some cells into a cancerous state, giving a valuable simple model system for which he shared the 1975 Nobel prize for physiology or medicine with his former students, **David Baltimore** and **Howard Temin**.

DULLES, Allen Welsh (1893–1969) American Intelligence overlord, brother of **John Foster Dulles**, born in Washington, DC, into a clerical family with diplomatic links. He was educated at Princeton, and after 'educational work' in Allahabad, India, entered the US diplomatic service with the advantage of his uncle, **Robert Lansing**, being secretary of state. He had served at Vienna, Berne, Paris, Berlin and Istanbul by 1920. He was chief of Division of Near Eastern Affairs, Department of State (1922–26) and worked for a law firm with powerful international links from 1926 to 1942. In World War II he served in Europe with the US Office of Strategic Services (1942–45), and played an important part in arranging the surrender of Italian forces without Russian knowledge, as described in his *The Secret Surrender* (1966). When the **Truman** administration decided on the formation of the Central Intelligence Agency, Dulles was made deputy director (1951), becoming director in 1953 coincident with his brother John Foster Dulles becoming secretary of state. Under his direction the Agency had some success in clandestine operations, assisting in right-wing coups in Guatemala and Iran which were believed to be in the American interest, but the 1961 disaster at the Bay of Pigs in the attempt to overthrow **Fidel Castro** in Cuba brought American recrimination on the head of the **Kennedy** administration, which responded by making a scapegoat of the CIA. Dulles resigned under pressure. Two years later he served on the Warren Commission investigating Kennedy's death. He also wrote *The Craft of Intelligence* (1963).

DULLES, John Foster (1888–1959) US politician, brother of **Allen Welsh Dulles**, born in Washington, DC, and educated at Princeton University and the Sorbonne. As a young lawyer from a family with a diplomatic tradition he attended the Hague Conference of 1907. At the conference of Versailles he was adviser to President **Wilson** and was principal US spokesman on the Reparations Commission. In the interwar years he combined legal work in America with international conferences of churchmen and others concerned with advancing Christian ideals in world affairs. During World War II he was a strong advocate of a world governmental organization. In 1945 he was adviser to Senator **Vandenberg** at the Charter Conference of the United Nations. In 1946, in 1947 and in 1950 he was US delegate to the General Assembly. In January 1953 he became US secretary of state, opening a vigorous diplomacy of personal conferences with statesmen in other countries. By the end of 1954 he had travelled nearly 180000 miles and had visited more than 40 countries, signing treaties and agreements and drawing the attention of the Western nations more strongly to the threat of Communism. In 1954 he launched the concept of SEATO and backed the plan to bring Western Germany into NATO. In 1956, after the nationalization of the Suez Canal by President **Nasser** of Egypt, he proposed the Suez Canal Users' Association. Later he opposed the Anglo-French military intervention and was himself strongly opposed by much British Conservative opinion. Though President **Eisenhower** hailed him in 1957 as 'one of the greatest of our secretaries of state', the western world was apt to criticize his inflexible thinking and his occasional rashness, and to consider him a tactician rather than a creator of memorable policies; but no one questioned his dedicated belief that a moral purpose should inform international affairs. He was awarded the highest American civil decoration, the Medal of Freedom, shortly before his death from cancer. He published *War, Peace and Change* (1939), and *War or Peace* (1950).

DULONG, Pierre Louis (1785–1838) French chemist, born in Rouen. He trained first as a doctor and later became professor of chemistry and then of physics in Paris. In 1813 he discovered the explosive nitrogen trichloride. With **Alexis Thérèe Petit** he did research on heat and enunciated the law of the constancy of atomic heats (1819).

DUMAS, Alexandre, in full, **Alexandre Dumas Davy de la Pailleterie** (1802–70) French novelist and playwright, born in Villers-Cotterets, the son of General Alexandre Davy-Dumas and Marie Labouret, daughter of a tavern keeper and small landowner. After an idle youth, he went to Paris in 1823 and obtained a clerkship in the bureau of the Duc **d'Orléans** and spent some years writing. A volume of short stories and a couple of farces, however, were his only production when, at 27, he became famous for his *Henri III* (1829), performed at the Théâtre Français, which revolutionized historical drama. In 1831 he did the same for domestic tragedy with *Antony*, failed in verse with *Charles VII chez ses grands vassaux*, and scored a tremendous success with *Richard Darlington*. In 1832 he carried the romantic 'history' to its culmination in *La Tour de Nesle* (in collaboration with Gaillardet). In that same year he fell ill with cholera, went to Switzerland to recuperate, and wrote for the *Revue des Deux Mondes* the first of his famous and delightful *Impressions de voyage*. A prodigious worker, he would, after months of writing, refresh himself with a round of travel, and he always published his experiences, as in *En Suisse* (1832), *Le Midi de la France* (1840), and *Le Caucase* (1859). But it was as a storyteller that he gained enduring success. He worked with about 90 collaborators in all and disagreed violently with some of them. He borrowed indiscriminately, and brought to his borrowings his own immense and radiant personality. Still, it is undeniable that his thefts were many and flagrant. **Trelawny**'s *Adventures of a Younger Son*, for instance, appears in his collected works, and it is said that he was with difficulty restrained from signing a book of the *Iliad* which someone else had turned into prose. He decided to put the history of France into novels, and his earliest attempt was *Isabelle de Bavière* (1836). It was followed by *Pauline* (1838), *Acté* (1839), *Othon l'archer* (1840)—and others all on different lines. Then he turned again to the historical vein in *Le Chevalier d'Harmenthal* and *Ascanio* (1843). For the amazing decade that followed he wrote unparalleled literature. In 1844, with a number of digressions into new provinces such as *Cécile*, *Fernande*, *Amaury*, *The Count of Monte Cristo*, there appeared *Les Trois Mousquetaires*. In 1845, *Vingt ans après*, *La Fille du régent*, and *La Reine Margot*; in 1846, *La Guerre des femmes*, *Maison Rouge*, *Le Bâtard de Mauléon*, *La Dame de Monsoreau*, and *Les Mémoires d'un médecin*; in 1848, *Les Quarante-cinq* and the beginnings of *Bragelonne* which was finished in 1850; and in 1849, *Le Collier de la reine*. The next two years witnessed productions as varied as *La Tulipe noire* and *Le Trou de l'enfer* (1850), and *La Femme au collier de velours* (1851). In 1852 the historical masterpiece *Olympe de Clèves* was produced. Between that year and 1854 were produced the ten delightful volumes of *Mes Mémoires*, with *Ange Pitou* and *La Comtesse de Charny*. Other achievements in the romance of French history were *Ingénue* (1854), *Les Compagnons de Jéhu* (1857), *Les Louvres de Machecoul* (1859) and *Les Blancs et les bleus* (1867–68), with which the sequence ended. The list is incomplete, and reference can only be made in passing to the rest of his work during this period, such as drama (the great historical novels were dramatized—the *Mousquetaires* cycle supplied at least three plays—as also were *Monte Cristo* and others), history, *causerie*, journalism, etc. Dumas took a conspicuous part in the Days of July; in 1837 he received the red ribbon; in 1842 he married Mlle Ida Ferrier, from whom he promptly separated. In 1855 he went for two years into exile at Brussels; from 1860 to 1864 he was helping **Garibaldi** in Italy, and conducting and writing a journal, and in 1886 he produced the last but one of his plays. By this time the end was near; he sank under his work. He had gone through a series of fortunes, and he left Paris for the last time with only a couple of napoleons in his pocket. He went to his son's villa in Dieppe, and stayed there until his death.

DUMAS, Alexandre, known as **'Dumas fils'** (1824–95) French writer, illegitimate son of **Alexandre Dumas**, born in Paris when his father was only 22 years old. He was soon legitimized, and at 16, after a course of training at the Institution Goubaux and the Collège Bourbon, he left school for the world of letters and the society to which his father, then almost at his peak, belonged. He was basically respectable, however, and having sown some wild oats settled down to serious work. He started in fiction and succeeded and went on to drama. He took to theorizing about art, morals, politics, religion even and was successful. His novels—from *La Dame aux camélias* (1848) to *L'Affaire Clémenceau* (1864)—are all readable, and the former was a great success in dramatic form (1852). His essays, letters, speeches, and prefaces generally are brilliant. Of his 16 plays, *Le Demi-Monde* (1855), *Le Fils natural* (1856), *Les Idées de Mme Aubray* (1867), *Une Visite de noces* (1871), *Monsieur Alphonse* (1873), and *Denise* (1885) are masterpieces. Other famous dramas in which he had a share are *Le Supplice d'une femme* (1865), whose chaotic original is due to **Émile de Girardin**; *Héloïse Paranquet* (1866), in collaboration with Durantin; and *Les Danicheff* (1876). He may have assisted **George Sand** in preparing several of her works for the stage, and he completed and produced his father's *Joseph Balsamo* (1878).

DUMAS, Jean Baptiste André (1800–84) French organic chemist, born in Alais, Gard. He studied at Geneva, where he attracted notice, and went to Paris

(1821) where he became an assistant, then lecturer, at the École Polytechnique. He was leader of a group of chemists who rejected **Berzelius**' theories and, by propounding new ideas on the theories of relations between organic compounds, laid the foundations for **Kekulé**'s later work. From work which began by examining choking fumes from candles, Dumas developed a theory of substitution in organic compounds which conflicted with Berzelius' ideas, and went on to classify these into types. He became professor of chemistry at the Athenée, the École centrale (which he founded) and the Sorbonne. In 1848 he moved into politics, becoming master of the Mint in 1868. His major works were *Traité de chimie appliquée aux arts* (1828) and *Leçons sur la philosophie chimique* (1838).

DU MAURIER, Dame Daphne (1907–89) English novelist, daughter of Sir **Gerald Du Maurier**. She was the author of a number of successful period romances and adventure stories, including *Jamaica Inn* (1936), *Rebecca* (1938), *Frenchman's Creek* (1942), and *My Cousin Rachel* (1951), many of which have been filmed. Later books included *The Flight of the Falcon* (1965), *The House of the Strand* (1969), *The Winding Stair*, a study of **Francis Bacon** (1976), and *The Rendezvous and other Stories* (1980).

DU MAURIER, George Louis Palmella Busson (1834–96) French-born British artist, cartoonist and novelist, born in Paris. He was the grandson of émigrés who had originally fled to England at the Revolution; in 1851 he went to London himself and studied chemistry, but returned to Paris to study art there and in Antwerp and Düsseldorf. Back in England he made his name as an illustrator, with new editions of **Thackeray**'s *Esmond* and his ballads, **Foxe**'s *Book of Martyrs*, and stories in periodicals like *Once A Week* and the *Cornhill Magazine*. Finally he joined the staff of *Punch* (1864–96), where he became best known as a gentle satirist of middle and upper-class society (some of his illustrations were collected as *English Society at Home*, 1880). He also wrote and illustrated three novels, *Peter Ibbetson* (1891), *The Martian* (1897), and the phenomenally successful *Trilby* (1894), the story of a young singer under the mesmeric influence of another musician, Svengali.

DU MAURIER, Sir Gerald (1873–1934) British actor-manager, younger son of **George du Maurier**. He was educated at Harrow, and left a business career for the stage, making his reputation in criminal roles, beginning with *Raffles* (1906). He became joint manager of Wyndham's theatre (1910–25), and was knighted in 1922 for his services to the stage. He was manager of the St James's Theatre from 1926 until his death.

DUMONT, Louis Charles Jean (1911–) French social anthropologist, born in Greece. He carried out fieldwork on southern India and is well known for his studies of caste, as in *Homo hierarchicus* (1967), in which he distinguishes between the holistic, hierarchical ideology of traditional Indian society and the individualistic, egalitarian ideology of the modern West. The latter is explored in *Homo aequalis* (1977) and *Essais sur l'individualisme* (1983).

DUMONT, Pierre Étienne Louis (1759–1829) Swiss churchman, the apostle of Benthamism, born in Geneva. In 1783 he accepted the charge of the French Protestant church at St Petersburg. In 1785 he became tutor in London to the sons of Lord Shelbourne, afterwards Marquis of Lansdowne, his talents and liberalism recommending him to the Whigs. During the early years of the French Revolution he was at Paris, and became attached to **Mirabeau**, regarding whom he has given much information in his *Souvenirs sur Mirabeau* (1832). In 1791 he returned to England and met **Jeremy Bentham**. This was the event of his life. Convinced of the value of Bentham's views on legislation, he obtained permission to edit his unpublished writings. The results appeared in his *Traité de législation civile et penale* (1802), *Théorie des peines et des récompenses* (1811), etc. Dumont returned to Geneva in 1814, and became a member of the representative council. He died in Milan.

DUMONT D'URVILLE, Jules Sébastien César (1790–1842) French naval-explorer, born in Condé in Calvados. He entered the navy in 1807. During hydrographic surveys of the eastern Mediterranean (1819–20) he secured the statue of the *Venus de Milo* for France. He first visited the Pacific as a member of the Louis-Isidore Duprey biological expedition (1822–15) and on his return proposed a second voyage. Sailing in the *Astrolabe*, he searched for and successfully found the sunken remains of **La Pérouse**'s ship on the reefs of Vanikoro and also collected much important information on the ethnic groups, plants and geology of the Pacific islands, revising the majority of existing maps (1826–29). From 1837 to 1840 he sailed to the Antarctic via the Magellan Strait but was stopped by ice at 63° S and sailed along it for 250 miles before returning to Chile to resupply; the following year he again returned south from Tasmania and this time getting inside the ice barrier discovered Adelie and Joinsville Islands, so giving France its claim to Antarctica. He was promoted to rear admiral on his return. Forty-nine volumes of text and maps record his voyages. He was killed with his wife and son in a train crash near Versailles.

DUMOURIEZ, Charles François (1739–1823) French soldier, born in Cambrai. From 1757 he served with distinction during the Seven Years' War. He was imprisoned for trying to help dissidents in Poland, but in 1778 **Louis XVI** made him commandant of Cherbourg. In 1790 he became one of the Jacobins, and was appointed commandant at Nantes. He now attached himself to the Girondists, and was appointed minister of foreign affairs in 1792, but resigned to command the northern army against Austria and Prussia. By a series of bold and rapid manoeuvres he prevented the allies from sweeping over Champagne, defeated the Prussians at Valmy (September, 1792), and overthrew the Austrians at Jemappes. The campaign of 1793, aiming at the conquest of the Netherlands, opened with the siege of Maestricht; Breda and other places were taken by the French; but at Neerwinden (March 1793) he sustained a severe defeat from the Austrians. His leanings towards constitutional monarchy aroused the suspicion of the revolutionists, and soon he was denounced as a traitor and summoned to Paris. To save his head he went over to the Austrian camp. After wandering through many countries of Europe, he finally settled in England, and died at Turville Park near Henley-upon-Thames. Besides pamphlets, Dumouriez wrote *Mémoires* (1794).

DUNANT, Jean Henri (1828–1910) Swiss philanthropist, born in Geneva. He inspired the foundation of the International Red Cross after seeing the plight of the wounded on the battlefield of Solferino (1859). His efforts brought about the conference at Geneva (1863) from which came the Geneva Convention (1864). In 1901, with **Frédéric Passy**, he was awarded the first Nobel peace prize.

DUNBAR, Paul Lawrence (1872–1906) American poet, born in Dayton, Ohio, the son of escaped Negro slaves. He gained a reputation with *Lyrics of Lowly Life* (1896), many of which were in dialect. He published several other volumes of verse, and four novels. His *Complete Poems* appeared in 1913.

DUNBAR, William (c.1460–c.1520) Scottish poet, born probably in East Lothian. He seems to have studied at St Andrews University from 1475 to 1479. He became a Franciscan novice, and visited every flourishing town in England. He preached at Canterbury but he later left the order. He appears next to have been secretary to some of **James IV**'s numerous embassies to foreign courts. In 1500 he obtained a pension from the king. In 1501 he visited England, probably with the ambassadors sent to arrange the king's marriage to **Margaret Tudor**, daughter of **Henry VII**. Early in 1503, before the queen's arrival, he composed in honour of the event his most famous poem, *The Thrissil and the Rois*, perhaps the happiest political allegory in English literature. He seems now to have lived chiefly about court, writing poems and sustaining himself with the vain hope of church preferment. In 1508 **Walter Chepman** printed seven of his poems—the earliest specimen of Scottish typography. He visited the north of Scotland in May 1511, in the train of Queen **Margaret**, and his name disappears altogether after the battle of Flodden (1513). He was certainly dead by 1530. He reached his highest level in his satires, *The Twa Marriit Wemen and the Wedo*, and *The Dance of the Sevin Deadly Synnis*. His *Lament for the Makaris* is a masterpiece of pathos.

DUNCAN I See **MACBETH**

DUNCAN, Adam, Viscount (1731–1804) Scottish naval commander, born in Dundee. He entered the navy in 1746, and commanded the *Valiant* in the sack of Havana (1762). He commanded the *Monarch* at Cape St Vincent (1780), and as admiral took command in 1795 of the North Sea Squadron to watch the Dutch fleet (Holland and France being at war with Britain). His blockade of the Texel was effective, and Dutch trade was almost ruined. In the spring of 1797 the mutiny of the Nore spread to Duncan's seamen, and his position was for some weeks critical. In the autumn he gained a brilliant victory over Ian De Winter, the Dutch admiral, at Camperdown.

DUNCAN, Henry (1774–1846) Scottish clergyman, born in Lochrutton. From 1799 he was minister of Ruthwell, Dumfriesshire, where he restored the 7th-century runic cross now in Ruthwell Kirk. In 1810 he established at Ruthwell the first savings bank. He founded the newspaper *Dumfries and Galloway Courier* in 1809. At the time of the Disruption in 1843 he joined the Free Church.

DUNCAN, Isadora (1878–1927) American dancer, born in San Francisco. She travelled widely in Europe demonstrating her fluid new style of dancing, inspired by classical, particularly Greek, mythology, art and music. She remains one of the most influential and controversial figures in dance and as well as a prolific creator, founded schools in Berlin, Salzburg, Vienna and Moscow. In Moscow she married (1922) a young Russian poet, Sergei Yesenin (1895–1925), who later committed suicide. Her private life gave rise to considerable scandal, particularly after her children had been killed in a motor accident. She herself was accidentally strangled when her scarf caught in the wheel of her car. She published her autobiography, *My Life* in 1928.

DUNCAN, Robert Edward, originally **Edward Howard Duncan** (1919–) American poet, born in Oakland, California. He was adopted in 1920 and named Robert Edward Symmes. Educated at the University of California, he was editor of *Experimental Review* (1938–40), *Phoenix and Berkeley Miscellany* (1948–49). Aligned with the 'Black Mountain' poets, and influenced by **George Barker** and **Ezra Pound**, his collections include *Heavenly City, Earthly City* (1947), *The Opening of the Field* (1960), *Roots and Branches* (1964), and *The Years as Catches* (1966).

DUNCAN, Thomas (1807–45) Scottish painter, born in Kinclaven, Perthshire. He is best known for historical and genre works, many with a Jacobite flavour, as *Prince Charles's Entry into Edinburgh after Prestonpans*, and *Charles Edward Asleep after Culloden*.

DUNCAN-SANDYS, Duncan Edward, Baron, originally **Sandys** (1908–87) British Conservative politician, and founder of the Civic Trust (1956). He was educated at Eton and Magdalen College, Oxford, worked for the diplomatic service (1930–33), and in 1935 entered politics as MP for Norwood, London (1935–45, subsequently Streatham, 1950–74). In 1951 he was made minister of supply in the **Churchill** government; in 1954 became minister of housing and local government, and introduced the Clean Air Act and the concept of Green Belts round cities. As minister of defence (1957–59) he inaugurated a controversial programme of cutting costs and streamlining the forces. He was subsequently minister of aviation (1959–60), secretary of state for commonwealth relations (1960–64), and for the colonies (1962–64). In 1935 he married Diana, daughter of Sir Winston Churchill (divorced 1960). He published two books, *European Movement and the Council of Europe* (1949) and *The Modern Commonwealth* (1961), and was made a life peer in 1974.

DUNCKER, Maximilian Wolfgang (1811–86) German historian, born in Berlin, the son of a well-known bookseller, Karl Duncker (1781–1869). He became extraordinary professor of history at Halle in 1842; was in the National Assembly (1849), and as a Liberal in the Prussian chamber (1849–52) was called to a Tübingen chair in 1857, and recalled in 1859 to Berlin to fill a post in the ministry of state. From 1867 to 1874 he was director of the state archives of Prussia. His greatest work is his *History of Antiquity* (1852–86).

DUNCOMBE, Thomas Slingsby (1796–1861) English politician, born near Boroughbridge, and educated at Harrow. He was Radical MP for Hertford (1826–32), and for Finsbury from 1834. In 1842 he presented the Chartist petition to parliament.

DUNDAS, of Arniston, a Scottish family distinguished for legal and political talent. Sir James Dundas, the first of Arniston, was knighted by **James VI and I**, and was governor of Berwick. His son, Sir James, was a judge of the Court of Session under the title of Lord Arniston (1662), but was deprived of his office for refusing to abjure the Covenant. He died in 1679. His eldest son, Sir Robert, who also rose to the bench, died in 1726.

DUNDAS, Henry, 1st Viscount Melville and Baron Dunira (1742–1811) Scottish jurist and statesman, son of Robert Dundas, Lord Arniston (1685–1753). Admitted to the Scottish bar in 1763, his assiduity, ability and family influence soon procured him advancement, and he was successively advocate-depute and solicitor-general. In 1774 he became MP for Midlothian, in 1775 lord advocate, in 1777 keeper of the signet for Scotland. His career in parliament was highly successful, though not very creditable to his consistency. Elected in opposition to the ministry, he soon became a strenuous supporter of Lord **North**, and one of the most obstinate defenders of the war with America. When North resigned in 1781, Dundas continued as lord advocate under Lord **Rockingham**. On the formation of the coalition he passed over to **William Pitt**, and became his ablest coadjutor. When Pitt returned to power in

1784, Dundas was appointed president of the Board of Control, and he introduced a bill for restoring the Scottish estates forfeited after the 1745 Jacobite rebellion. Secretary of state for the Home Department (1791), he also held a number of other offices; and many of the most important public measures originated with or were promoted by him. He resigned with Pitt in 1801, and in 1802, under the Addington (see **Sidmouth**) administration, was made Viscount Melville and Baron Dunira. For 30 years he was the effective ruler of Scotland. In 1805 he was impeached for 'gross malversation and breach of duty' as treasurer of the navy. The fortnight's trial before his peers acquitted him on all charges involving his honour. Thereafter he lived mostly at Dunira, his seat near Comrie.

DUNDAS, Robert (1713–87) Scottish judge, son of **Robert Dundas**. He was admitted to the Scottish bar in 1738, and rose to be lord advocate (1754) and lord president of the Court of Session (1760).

DUNDAS, Robert, Lord Arniston (1685–1753) son of a Scottish judge, Sir Robert Dundas (Lord Arniston, 1689–1720). In 1717 he became solicitor-general, in 1720 lord advocate, and as MP for Midlothian from 1722 distinguished himself by his attention to Scottish affairs. Sir **Robert Walpole** coming into power in 1725, Dundas resigned his office, when he was elected dean of the faculty of advocates. In 1737 he was raised to the bench, as Lord Arniston. He became lord president of the Court of Session in 1748.

DUNDEE, John Graham of Claverhouse, 1st Viscount (c.1649–1689) Scottish soldier, known as 'Bonny Dundee' or 'Bloody Claverse'. He studied at St Andrews University, and then served in both the French and Dutch armies as a professional soldier. In 1674 at the battle of Seneff he is said to have saved the life of William of Orange (**William III**). In 1677 he returned to Scotland, and became lieutenant in a troop of horse commanded by his kinsman, the Marquis of **Montrose**, against the Covenanters. At Drumclog (1679) he was routed by an armed body of Covenanters, but three weeks later he commanded the cavalry at Bothwell Brig, where the Covenanters were defeated. From 1682 to 1685 he was active in hunting down Covenanters in the south-west of Scotland. When William III landed in England in 1688 at the start of the 'Glorious Revolution' he marched into England in support of **James II**, and was created Viscount Dundee. He was allowed to withdraw unscathed by William, and in Scotland, after leaving the Convention of 1689, raised an army in the Highlands. He defeated the loyalist forces in a fierce encounter at Killiecrankie (July 1689) but was mortally wounded in the hour of victory, and buried in the church at Old Blair.

DUNDONALD, Thomas Cochrane See **COCHRANE**

DUNEDIN, Andrew Graham Murray, Viscount, of Stenton (1849–1942) Scottish judge, born in Edinburgh. Educated at Harrow and Trinity College, Cambridge, he became an MP and successively solicitor-general for Scotland (1891–92 and 1895–96), lord advocate (1896–1903) and secretary for Scotland (1903–05) before becoming lord justice-general of Scotland and lord president of the Court of Session (1905–13) and then a lord of appeal in ordinary (1913–32). A highly skilled lawyer with a great grasp of principle, particularly in feudal land law, he was an excellent expositor and a very distinguished judge.

DUNÉR, Nils Christofer (1839–1914) Swedish astronomer. Educated at Lund, he became professor of astronomy at Uppsala and director of the observatory there (1888–1909). He made a study of variable and double stars, and was an expert on stellar spectroscopy.

DUNGLISON, Robley (1798–1869) English-born American physician, born in Keswick. He studied medicine in London, Edinburgh, and Erlangen. Invited to the USA in 1825 by President **Thomas Jefferson** to be professor of medicine at the University of Virginia, he was also professor at Maryland (1833) and Jefferson Medical College, Philadelphia (1836).

DUNHAM, Katherine (1910–) American dancer, choreographer and teacher, born in Chicago. She studied anthropology at Chicago and researched dance in the West Indies and Caribbean before her 1938 appointment as dance director of the Federal Theatre Project. Her first New York concert in 1940 launched her career as a leading choreographer of Afro-American dances. She subsequently worked on Broadway (most importantly for the 1940 musical *Cabin in the Sky*) and Hollywood (including *Stormy Weather*, 1943), while developing a successful formula for live black performance revues. Her Dunham School of Dance (1945–55) exerted considerable influence on the direction of American black dance with its combination of elements of classical ballet, modern and Afro-Caribbean techniques. She choreographed for opera, toured extensively with her own company and wrote several books about her field. She published her autobiography, *A Touch of Innocence*, in 1959.

DUNHILL, Thomas Frederick (1877–1946) English composer and teacher, born in London. He studied under **Charles Stanford** and taught at the Royal College of Music. In 1907 he organized concerts to publicize the works of younger British composers. He made his name with chamber works, songs, and the light opera *Tantivy Towers* (1931) to words by **A P Herbert**.

DUNLOP, Frank (1927–) English stage director and administrator, born in Leeds. After founding and directing Piccolo Theatre, Manchester, in 1954, he became an associate director of the Bristol Old Viv in 1956. From 1961 to 1964 he was director of Nottingham Playhouse, opening the first season in the new building. In 1965, he directed *Saturday Night and Sunday Morning* in the West End, and in 1966 directed Pop Theatre, a company he founded himself, in *The Winter's Tale* and **Euripides**'s *The Trojan Women* at the Edinburgh Festival. He became associate director at the National Theatre, 1967–71, and administrator 1968–71. He founded the Young Vic in 1970, and was the company's director until 1978 and from 1980 until 1983. He was appointed director of the Edinburgh Festival in 1984.

DUNLOP, John Boyd (1840–1921) Scottish inventor, born in Dreghorn, Ayrshire, and generally credited with inventing the pneumatic tyre. He became a veterinary surgeon in Edinburgh and then Belfast from 1867; in 1887 he fitted his child's tricycle-wheels with inflated rubber hoses instead of solid rubber tyres. The principle had already been patented, in 1845, by a Scottish engineer, Robert William Thomson (1822–73), but in 1889 Dunlop formed a business that became the Dunlop Rubber Company Ltd, produced commercially practical pneumatic tyres for bicycles and, later, motor cars.

DUNLOP, Ronald Ossary (1894–1973) Irish painter, born in Dublin. He studied at the Manchester and Wimbledon Schools of Art. A member of the London Group, he is best known for his palette-knife painting with rich impasto and glowing colour. His work is represented in the Tate Gallery, London, and many provincial galleries, and his writings on art include *Landscape Painting* (1954) and the autobiographical *Struggling with Paint* (1956).

DUNN, Douglas (1942–) American post-modern dancer and choreographer, born in Palo Alto, California. While at Princeton he studied dance, moving later to New York and the **Merce Cunningham** studio. While working for the Cunningham company (1969–73) he met **Yvonne Rainer**. As well as performing in her work (including *Continuous Project Altered Daily*, 1969–70), he joined her as one of the founders of the experimental dance group Grand Union with which he was associated for six years until 1976. During that time, he made a solo piece, *101*, which required him to lie motionless for four hours a day, six days a week for two months. With *Lazy Madge* (1975) he built a dance piece for 8–10 dancers which lasted over several seasons (1975–79). In 1977 he founded his own company. His choreography is fun, original and loose-limbed. He created *Pulcinella* for Paris Opera Ballet in 1980.

DUNNE, Finley Peter (1867–1936) American humorist, born in Chicago. He worked as a journalist there, and was editor of *Chicago Journal* (1897–1900). With his creation of the philosopher-bartender 'Mr Dooley' he became from 1900 the exponent of American-Irish humorous satire on current personages and events, in *Mr Dooley in Peace and War* (1898) and many other books.

DUNNE, John William (1875–1949) English inventor and philosopher. He designed the first British military aeroplane (1906–07) and wrote the best-selling speculative works *An Experiment with Time* (1927), *The Serial Universe* (1934), *The New Immortality* (1938) and *Nothing Dies* (1940).

DUNNING, John Ray (1907–75) American physicist. In 1940 he was one of the team of scientists which prepared the way for the atomic bomb by obtaining experimental verification of uranium-235 fission by slow neutrons.

DUNNING, William Archibald (1857–1922) American historian and educator, born in Plainfield, New Jersey. He studied and taught at Columbia University, New York, until his death. His major work was a three-volume *History of Political Theories* (1916), spanning two thousand years of European thought, but his chief significance lies in his direction of doctoral research on US history. In particular the 'Dunning School' (apart from his prize pupil, **Ulrich B Phillips**) produced detailed studies of individuai states under Reconstruction, which from 1900 to 1960 expounded the view to American historians and public that Reconstruction had been a corrupt, vindictive and disastrous experiment bound to fail because of the allegedly innate inferiority of blacks.

DUNOIS, Jean, Count of Dunois and Longueville (1402–68) known as the 'Bastard of Orléans', born in Paris, the illegitimate son of Louis I, Duke of Orléans, brother of **Charles VI**. His first great achievement was the defeat of the English at Montargis (1427); next he threw himself into Orléans with a small force, and defended it till its relief by **Joan of Arc** forced the English to raise the siege (1429). Dunois and the Maid of Orléans now won the battle of Patay, after which he marched through the provinces overrun by the English, and took the fortified towns. Shortly after Joan of Arc's death, he took Chartres, the key to Paris, forced **Bedford** to raise the siege of Lagny and chased the enemy from Paris (1436). He soon deprived them of all their conquests except Normandy and Guienne. From 1448 to 1450 he drove them from Normandy, and in 1455 from Guienne also, and secured the freedom of France. For joining the league of the nobles against **Louis XI** he was deprived of all his possessions, which were, however, restored to him under the treaty of Conflans (1465).

DUNOYER DE SEGONZAC See **SEGONZAC**

DUNRAVEN, Windham Thomas Wyndham-Quin, 4th Earl of (1841–1926) Irish politician, born at Adare Manor, Limerick. He studied at Christ Church, Oxford, acted as *Daily Telegraph* correspondent in Abyssinia and the Franco-German war, and succeeded as fourth earl in 1871. He was under-secretary for the colonies (1885–87), and Irish Free State senator from 1922. In addition to reminiscences, he wrote on Irish reform and devolution, *The Great Divide* (1874), *Self-Instruction in Navigation*; and in 1893 and 1895 contested the America Cup with his yachts *Valkyrie II* and *III*.

DUNS SCOTUS, John (c.1265–1308) Scottish scholastic philosopher who rivalled **Aquinas** as the greatest theologian of the middle ages but whose brief life is scantily documented. He was probably from Duns, Berwickshire; he became a Franciscan and was ordained priest in St Andrews Church, Northampton in 1291. He studied and taught at Oxford and Paris, probably also in Cambridge, and finally at Cologne where he died and was buried. His writings were mainly commentaries on the Bible, **Aristotle** and the *Sentences* of **Peter Lombard** and were left in various stages of completeness at his death. His associates collected and edited them (not always very responsibly), and the main works in the canon are now taken to be: The *Opus Pariense* (the Parisian Lectures, as recorded by a student), the *Opus Oxiense* (the Oxford lectures, also known as the *Ordinatio*, and probably revised by the author), the *Tractatus de Primo Principio* and the *Quaestiones Quodlibetales*. His philosophy represents a strong reaction against both Aristotle and Aquinas. He propounded the primacy of the individual (in the dispute about universals), and the freedom of the individual will. He saw faith as the necessary foundation of Christian theology, but faith was for him exercised through an act of will and was practical, not speculative or theoretical. The Franciscans followed Scotus as the Dominicans did Thomas Aquinas; he was known by contemporaries as *Doctor Subtilis* for the refinement and penetration of his criticisms of Thomism, but in the Renaissance the Scotists were dubbed 'Dunses' (hence 'dunce') for their obstinacy and conservatism. More recently he has, however, been admired by figures as diverse as **Charles Peirce**, **Martin Heidegger** and **Gerald Manley Hopkins**, who found him 'of realty the rarest veinèd unraveller'.

DUNSANY, Edward John Moreton Drax Plunkett, 18th Baron (1878–1957) Irish novelist, poet and playwright, born in London. Educated at Eton and Sandhurst, he succeeded to the title in 1899, served in the 2nd Boer War with the Coldstream Guards, and thereafter settled in Ireland at Dunsany Castle in County Meath. In World War I he was an officer of the Inniskilling Fusiliers. By World War II, he was Byron professor of English literature in Athens. His literary works are highly poetic and imaginative. They began in 1905 with the mythological novel *The Gods of Pegana*. At **Yeats**'s invitation he wrote many plays for the Abbey Theatre, including *The Glittering Gate* (1909) and *The Laughter of the Gods* (1919). His verse is contained in *Fifty Poems* (1930) and *Mirage Water* (1939). He also wrote an autobiographical series: *Patches of Sunlight* (1938), *While the Sirens Slept* (1944), *The Sirens Wake* (1945) and *To Awaken Pegasus* (1949).

DUNSTABLE, John (c.1390–1453) English composer, of whose life almost nothing is known. He was an important early exponent of counterpoint, and he wrote motets, masses and secular songs including the three-part *O Rosa bella*.

DUNSTAN, St (c.909–988) Anglo-Saxon prelate, the son of a West Saxon noble, and archbishop of Canterbury from 959. He was educated at the abbey, and spent some time at the court of King **Athelstan** but was banished for practising unlawful arts. He took monastic vows and retired to Glastonbury where he devoted himself to studying. Recalled on the accession of Athelstan's brother King **Edmund**, he was appointed abbot of Glastonbury (945). In this post he began to implement great reforms, turning Glastonbury into a centre of religious teaching. At the same time he became Edmund's treasurer and adviser, but on his death in 955 and the accession of Edwy, lost his influence. He fled to Flanders and Ghent where he first saw the strict Benedictine discipline which he was later to introduce into England. In 957 he was recalled by **Edgar**, who was now king of the country north of the Thames, and was created bishop of Worcester and of London (959). In that year, on Edwy's death Edgar became king of the entire country. One of his first acts was to appoint Dunstan archbishop of Canterbury, and Dunstan's wise counsel greatly contributed to the peace and prosperity of his reign. With Oswald, archbishop of York, Dunstan crowned Edgar at Bath in 973, a formal declaration of the unity of the kingdom. Dunstan strove to elevate the lives of the clergy and make them real teachers of the people in secular as well as religious matters. He made the payment of tithes by landowners obligatory, but did not entirely surrender the liberties of the church to Rome. On Edgar's death he declared for **Edward** 'the Martyr', Edgar's elder son, and crowned him. On Edward's murder (978) the two archbishops crowned **Æthelred**, whose hostility ended Dunstan's political career. His feast day is 19 May.

DUNSTERVILLE, Lionel Charles (1865–1946) English soldier. He was a schoolmate, at Westward Ho College, of **Rudyard Kipling**, who based his famous schoolboy character 'Stalky' on him. He commanded the Baku expedition of 1918, which he described in *The Adventures of Dunsterforce* (1920).

DUNTON, John (1659–1733) English bookseller, born in Graffham, Huntingdonshire, of a family of clergymen. He was apprenticed to a London bookseller, took a shop, married happily, made some lucky ventures, but was ultimately involved in financial troubles. He visited America, Holland, and Cologne, settled somehow with his creditors, and kept shop for ten years with fair prosperity; his *Athenian Gazette* was specially successful. He married a second time unhappily, and under the real and imaginary troubles of his later years his mind became deranged. His extraordinary *Life and Errors of John Dunton* (1705) throws interesting sidelights on the book trade of the time.

DUPANLOUP, Félix Antoine Philibert (1802–78) French prelate and educationist, born in St Félix in Savoy. Vicar-general of Paris in 1838 and bishop of Orléans in 1849, he tolerated the Jesuits, and defended the temporal authority of the pope, although protesting openly against the infallibility dogma. However, once it was published he signified his acceptance of it. He was responsible for the Falloux Law of 1850 which allowed the establishment of independent secondary schools. In 1871 he was elected deputy for Orléans to the National Assembly; and from this time until his death, he struggled courageously against the constant attacks upon the church both in the Assembly and outside. He entered the Senate in 1876 for life. He wrote various books on education and marriage.

DUPARC, Henri, in full **Marie Eugène Henri Fouques-Duparc** (1848–1933) French composer. He studied under **César Franck**, and, although he wrote a variety of works, he is remembered for his songs, based on poems by **Baudelaire** and others and which, though only 15 in number, rank among the world's greatest.

DUPLEIX, Joseph François (1697–1763) French colonial administrator, born in Landrecies. In 1720 he was appointed to a seat in the French East India Council at Pondicherry. In 1730 he became superintendent at Chandernagore, in 1741 governor-general of all the French Indies; and his skilful diplomacy among the native princes almost made the Carnatic a French province. His power alarmed the English company. When war broke out in Europe between France and England, **La Bourdonnais**, who had taken Madras, was bribed with £40000 to restore it to the English on payment of a ransom. This Dupleix refused to accede to, and violent disputes resulted in La Bourdonnais' recall. Several brilliant engagements took place between the French and the Nawab of the Carnatic, who endeavoured to seize Madras, but was forced to raise the siege. An attack on the English at Fort St David failed, but Dupleix's science and courage were displayed in the defence of Pondicherry, which Admiral **Boscawen** in vain attacked for five weeks. But Dupleix's ambitious project of founding a French empire in India on the ruins of the Mogul monarchy was frustrated by **Clive**; though the struggle continued until Dupleix's recall in 1754. The French Company refused to reimburse him for the vast sums he had spent out of his (alleged) private fortune, and he died in poverty and neglect in 1763.

DUPOND, Patrick (1959–) French dancer, born in Paris. He was the youngest dancer ever accepted into the Paris Opera Ballet (at the age of 15), and at 17 won top honours at the Varna international competition. In 1980 he reached the rank of *étoile*, and he has since been a guest performer with various companies around the world. A dazzling, rule-bending virtuoso, one of his most notable roles is that of **Nijinsky** in **John Neumeier**'s tribute to Vaslav (1979). In 1988 he became artistic director of Ballet de Nancy.

DUPONT, Pierre (1821–70) French popular poet and songwriter, born in Lyons. He was the author of *Le Chant des ouvriers*.

DU PONT, Pierre Samuel (1870–1954) American businessman and management innovator, born in Wilmington, Delaware. A graduate of Massachusetts Institute of Technology, he joined the family gunpowder company. In 1902 he bought the company with his cousins, Thomas Coleman Du Pont and Alfred Eugene Du Pont, and decentralized many of its activities, although family control was maintained. As president (1915–20) he also introduced and developed many new industrial management techniques, including a systematic approach to strategic planning, control systems, and the pioneering of modern industrial accounting methods. He became president of General Motors (GM) in 1920 after the Du Pont company had rescued it from near bankruptcy. He reorganized GM and appointed **Alfred Sloan** as its chief executive officer.

DUPONT, Samuel Francis (1803–65) American naval officer, born in Bergen Point, New Jersey. He entered the navy in 1815, and commanded a sloop during the Mexican War in the Gulf of California and off San Diego. In the Civil War he organized the blockade of the South Atlantic area by Federal naval forces, and captured the ports of South Carolina and Georgia. He was unjustly blamed for the failure of the

Federal attack on Charleston in 1863 and relieved of his command.

DU PONT NEMOURS, Eleuthère Irénée (1771–1834) French-born American industrialist, born in Paris, younger son of **Pierre-Samuel Du Pont de Nemours**. He worked in his father's printing plant until it was closed down in 1797. He emigrated to the USA (1800), and in 1802 established in Wilmington, Delaware, a gunpowder factory which developed into one of the world's largest chemical concerns.

DU PONT DE NEMOURS, Pierre-Samuel (1739–1817) French-born American economist. A disciple of **Quesney**, after a stormy political life he settled in the USA.

DU PONT DE NEMOURS, Victor-Marie (1767–1827) French-born American diplomat and industrialist, born in Paris, elder son of **Pierre-Samuel Du Pont de Nemours**. He went to the USA in 1787 as an attaché at the French legation, and was aide-de-camp to **Lafayette** (1789–91). He settled in the USA after 1800 and became a businessman but without his brother's success.

DU PRÉ, Jacqueline (1945–87) English cellist, born in Oxford. She studied at the Guildhall School of Music with William Pleeth, with **Tortelier** in Paris, **Casals** in Switzerland and **Rostropovich** in Moscow. She made her concert début at the Wigmore Hall aged 16, and subsequently toured internationally. In 1967 she married the pianist **Daniel Barenboim**. After developing multiple sclerosis in 1972 she pursued a teaching career, including televised master-classes.

DUPRÉ, Jules (1812–89) French landscape painter of the Barbizon school, born in Nantes. He studied in England with **Constable**, and was a leader of the Barbizon school.

DUPRÉ, Marcel (1886–1971) French organist, born in Rouen. An exceptional improvizer, he was chief organist at St Sulpice Church, Paris, and Notre Dame Cathedral. He became professor at the Paris conservatoire (1926), won the Prix de Rome for composition in 1914, and was acclaimed all over Europe for his organ recitals.

DUPUYTREN, Guillaume, Baron (1777–1835) French surgeon. From 1812 he was professor of clinical surgery in Paris, and surgeon to **Louis XVIII** and **Charles X**. He invented many surgical instruments, and devised surgical techniques for many conditions, including Dupuytren's contracture.

DUQUESNE, Abraham, Marquis (1610–88) French naval officer, born in Dieppe. He distinguished himself from 1637 to 1643 in the war with Spain. In the Swedish service (1644–47) he rose to vice admiral and won victories over a Danish-Dutch naval alliance. Returning to France, he reduced Bordeaux, which had declared for the Fronde (1650). He defeated **De Ruyter** and **Tromp** several times in 1672–73, and the united fleets of Spain and Holland off Sicily in 1676. On the revocation of the Edict of Nantes, Duquesne was the only Protestant excepted.

DURAN See **CAROLUS-DURAN**

DURAND, Asher Brown (1796–1886) American painter, engraver and illustrator, born in New Jersey. He served an engraving apprenticeship from 1812 and, as well as producing reproductions of the work of American artists, made his own engravings of famous contemporary Americans. Between 1835 and 1840 he also painted portraits of eminent Americans. After a visit to Europe in 1840 he was associated with the Hudson River School and painted Romantic and dramatic landscapes. His graphic work strongly influenced the design of US paper currency.

DURAND, Sir Henry Marion (1812–71) English soldier, the son of a cavalry officer. Trained at Addiscombe, he served in the Afghan war (bursting in the gates of Ghazni, 1839) and the Sikh war. As agent in Central India he rendered valuable service during the Mutiny, and was subsequently a member of the Indian Council, and governor-general of the Punjab.

DURAND, Madame See **GRÉVILLE, Henry**

DURANDUS, Gulielmus (1237–96) French jurist, born in Puimisson near Béziers. He studied canon law at Bologna and Modena, and had held various offices under several popes, when in 1286 he became bishop of Mende, still, however, remaining in Rome. His most famous work is his *Speculum Judiciale* (1271, first printed in 1474).

DURANTE, Francesco (1684–1755) Italian composer, born in Fratta Maggiore. Head of the Conservatorio di Santa Maria di Loreto, in Naples (1742–45), he wrote a wide variey of church and chamber music.

DURAS, Marguerite, pseud of **Marguerite Donnadien** (1914–) French novelist, born in Indo-China. She studied law and political science at the Sorbonne in Paris. During World War II she took part in the Resistance at great risk to herself as a Jewess. Considered one of the great European writers of the 20th century, her books include the semi-autobiographical *La Douleur* (1945) and *The Lover* (1984, Prix Goncourt), novels like *The Sea Wall* (1950), *Le Vice-Consul* (1966) and *Destroy, She Said* (1969), film scripts like *Hiroshima Mon Amour* (1960), and a play (*La Musica*).

DURBIN, Deanna, originally **Edna Mae** (1921–) Canadian entertainer, born in Winnipeg, Manitoba. When the family moved to California, her singing voice attracted the attention of talent scouts and she appeared in the short film *Every Sunday* (1936). Signed to a studio contract, and already popular on radio, she became an immediate star with the release of *Three Smart Girls* (1936). A high-spirited youngster with a lilting soprano and a charmingly fresh personality, she captivated audiences with a succession of lighthearted folderols that included *One Hundred Men and a Girl* (1937), *Mad About Music* (1938) and *Three Smart Girls Grow Up* (1939). Weathering the transition to adulthood, her flair for comedy was evident in *It Started With Eve* (1941) and she gave creditable dramatic performances in *Christmas Holiday* (1944) and *Lady on a Train* (1945). Lacking showbusiness ambitions, she made her last film in 1948 and has enjoyed a long and contented retirement near Paris.

DÜRER, Albrecht (1471–1528) German painter and engraver, born in Nuremberg, the son of a goldsmith from Hungary. In 1486 he was apprenticed to **Michael Wolgemut**, the chief illustrator of the Nürnberg Chronicle, and in 1490 started on his four years' travels. Then, having married and visited Italy, he worked again for a while under Wolgemut, and in 1497 started on his own account, and executed many paintings, among them the Dresden triptych, and the Baumgartner altarpiece at Munich. In 1498 he published his first great series of designs on wood, the illustrations of the Apocalypse. The copperplates of this period include *The Prodigal Son* (1500) and *Adam and Eve* (1504). From 1505 to 1506 he visited Venice, and there produced the *Feast of the Rosaries*, now the property of Strahow monastery, Prague. On (or before) his return he painted *Adam and Eve* (1507), now at Madrid; and *Assumption of the Virgin*—a triptych, whose centre was destroyed by fire at Munich in 1674. It was followed in 1511 by the *Adoration of the Trinity*, in the Vienna Gallery. Dürer was much employed by **Maximilian I**, of whom he executed several portraits, and for whose prayer book he made 43 pen and ink drawings, and in whose honour he drew the *Triumphal Car* and (with others) the *Triumphal Arch*, which were engraved on wood, the latter on 92 blocks, forming a surface of 100 square feet—the largest known woodcut. From 1520 to 1521 Dürer visited the Netherlands. At Antwerp he made the acquaintance of **Erasmus**; and he was present at the coronation of **Charles V**, who appointed him his court painter. During his later years he met **Luther** and showed great sympathy with the Reformation. As an engraver on metal and a designer of woodcuts he ranks even higher than as a painter. His work is distinguished by an unerring perception of the capabilities of the material, his metalplates being executed with extreme finish and refinement; while his woodcuts are boldly drawn with a broad expressive line. His copperplates, over 100 in number, include the *Little Passion* (16 plates, 1508–13); the *Knight, Death, and the Devil* (1513); *St Jerome in his Study*, and *Melancholia* (1514). He may also be regarded as the inventor of etching, as he produced several plates in which all the lines are bitten with acid. His woodcuts are about 200 in number, including the *Greater Passion*, 12 subjects; *The Little Passion*, 37 subjects; and *The Apocalypse*, 16 subjects. He also wrote several treatises on measurement and human proportion.

DUREY, Louis (1888–1979) French composer, born in Paris. His musical education did not begin until he was 22. In 1916, under the influence of **Erik Satie**, he became one of the group of young French composers known as 'The Six', but broke with them in 1921. He has written large orchestral and choral works, but is chiefly known for his songs and chamber music.

D'URFREY, Thomas (1653–1723) English dramatist and songwriter, born in Exeter of Huguenot ancestry. He was a nephew of **Honoré d'Urfé** (1568–1625), author of the famous romance of *Astrée*. He soon became a prolific playwright, his comedies especially being popular. Among these were *The Fond Husband* (1676), *Madame Fickle* (1677), and *Sir Burnaby Whig* (1681). In 1683 he published his *New Collection of Songs and Poems*, which was followed by a long series of songs, collected as *Wit and Mirth, or Pills to Purge Melancholy* (6 vols, 1719–20). Meanwhile he had written some plays, which were criticized as being immoral by **Jeremy Collier**. His fortunes declined as his comedies ceased to please.

DURHAM, John George Lambton, Earl of (1792–1840) English statesman, born in London. On his father's death in 1797 he inherited Lambton Hall, Durham, which had been in the family for over six centuries. Educated at Eton, he served for two years in the dragoons, and in 1813 was returned as a Whig of his native county. He was a strong liberal, and in 1821 brought forward a scheme for parliamentary reform much more advanced than that of 1832. In 1828 he was created Baron Durham. In the administration of his father-in-law, Lord **Grey** (1830), he was lord privy seal, and one of the four persons who drew up the Reform Bill. Resigning office in 1833, he was made an earl, and from 1835 to 1837 was ambassador-extraordinary to St Petersburg. In 1838 he was appointed governor-general of Canada where, owing to the revolt of the French in Lower Canada, the constitution had been suspended. His measures were statesmanlike but dictatorial, and the House of Lords voted disapproval of some of his acts.

DURKHEIM, Emile (1858–1917) pioneer French sociologist, generally regarded as one of the founders of the discipline. Educated at the Ecole Normale Supérieure, he taught at the University of Bordeaux from 1887 to 1902, and at the Sorbonne from 1902 to 1916. He was appointed to the first chair of sociology in France in 1913. Durkheim believed that sociology should be rigorously objective and scientific, and he developed a systematic sociological methodology based on the view that what he called 'social facts', that is, social phenomena, should be treated as 'things' to be explained solely by reference to other social facts, not in terms of any individual person's actions. This approach is presented in his methodological writings and is applied particularly in his study of suicide. Also central to his work is the idea that societies are held together by means of a 'conscience collective', powerful beliefs and sentiments that are shared in common by members of the society, and that exert a strong influence on individuals' behaviour. This is seen both in his study of the division of labour and in his analysis of the social basis of religion, which he regarded as having been created by society as a means of expressing its ideals and unifying itself. In addition to his contribution to sociology, Durkheim's writings have also been influential among anthropologists and historians.

DURONCERAY, Marie See **FAVART, Charles Simon**

DURRELL, Gerald Malcolm (1925–) English writer and naturalist, brother of **Lawrence Durrell**, born in Jamshedpur, India. His interest in zoology was sparked off when his family moved to Corfu in the 1930s where he kept a menagerie of local animals. As he wrote in his bestselling memoir, *My Family and Other Animals* (1956), it was like living 'in one of the more flamboyant and slapstick comic operas'. He has since combined writing with zoology and has published many popular books and made wildlife films. In 1958 he founded the Jersey Zoological Park, about which he wrote *The Stationary Ark* (1976).

DURRELL, Lawrence George (1912–) English novelist, poet, travel writer and playwright, born in Julundur, India, and brother of **Gerald Durrell**. He lived in India until he was ten when his family moved back to England. He took numerous odd jobs—in night clubs, as an estate agent and the Jamaica police—and once said he had been driven to writing 'by sheer ineptitude'. He convinced his family that life would be more congenial in a warmer climate and they moved to Corfu until the outbreak of World War II. He moved to France in 1957 but has travelled widely as a journalist and in the service of the Foreign Office. His first novel was *Pied Piper of Lovers* (1935) and his second, *Panic Spring*, appeared two years later under the pseudonym Charles Norden, so woeful were the sales of its predecessor. He made his name with the 'Alexandria Quartet'—*Justine* (1957), *Balthazar* (1958), *Mountolive* (1958) and *Clea* (1960)—a complex, interlocking series set in Egypt, remarkable for its sensuous language, intrigue and devious plotting, the nature of modern love being its central topic. He followed this with a two-novel sequence, *Tunc* (1968) and *Nunquam* (1970). The *Avignon Quincunx*—*Monsieur* (1974), *Livia* (1978), *Constance* (1982), *Sebastian* (1983) and *Quinx* (1985)—is also conceived on a grand and elaborate scale. His generous output includes travel books, *Prospero's Cell* (1945) and *Bitter Lemons* (1957), verse (*Collected Poems, 1931–1974*), comic sketches, criticism, plays and a children's novel, *White Eagles Over Serbia* (1957). His long friendship with **Henry Miller** is recorded in their correspondence published in 1988.

DÜRRENMATT, Friedrich (1921–) Swiss author, born in Konolfingen, Bern, the son of a pastor; he studied there and at Zürich and turned from painting to writing. The theme which recurs in all his work is that life is a calamity which has to be accepted for what it is but without surrender. His novels include the detective story *Der Richter und sein Henker* (1952), *Der Verdacht* (1953), *Die Panne* (1956), and his plays *Romulus der Grosse* (1949) and *Die Ehe des Herrn Mississippi* (1952), which established his international reputation. *Ein Engel kommt nach Babylon* (1953) is a parable in which an angel brings chaos instead of happiness, and *Der Besuch einer alten Dame* (1956) describes the return of an old lady to her native village to revenge herself on a seducer. Other plays include *The Physicists* (1962), *Play Strindberg* (1969), *Portrait of a Planet* (1970), and a novel, *Der Sturz*, published in 1971.

DURUY, Victor (1811–94) French historian and educationist, born in Paris. He became professor of history in the Collège Henri IV (1833), and minister of public instruction (1863–69). He introduced secondary education for girls and modern studies into school curricula, and wrote a history of the Romans (1789).

DUSE, Eleonora (1859–1924) Italian actress, born near Venice. She rose to fame in Italy, then triumphed (1892–93) in Vienna, Berlin, New York, London, etc. She returned to the stage in 1921 after years of retirement. **D'Annunzio** owed much to her histrionic genius. 'The Duse' ranks among the greatest actresses of all time.

DUSHAN See **STEPHEN DUSHAN**

DUSSEK, Jan Ladislav (1760–1812) Czech composer and pianist, born in Czaslau in Bohemia. In Amsterdam he produced his earliest works for the piano, and in London (1788–1800) he was very popular. From 1803 to 1806 he was instructor to Prince Louis Ferdinand of Prussia, and in 1808 he entered **Talleyrand**'s service. He composed over 30 sonatas.

DUTENS, Louis (1730–1812) French-born British historian, born in Tours of Huguenot parentage. He emigrated to England, went to Turin as chaplain to the English embassy (1758–62), and remained as *chargé d'affaires*. He held a pension of £300, in 1766 was presented to the rich sinecure living of Elsdon in Northumberland, travelled much, and was made historiographer royal. He undertook the first comprehensive edition of **Leibniz**'s works (1768).

DUTROCHET, René Joachim Henri (1776–1847) French physiologist, born in Néon. He qualified in medicine at Paris, and became physician to **Joseph Bonaparte** of Spain. He was the first to study and to name osmosis.

DUTT, Michael Madhu Sudan (1824–73) Indian poet, born in Sagandari, Bengal. He absorbed European culture, became a Christian and wrote poetry and drama in English and Bengali, such as the plays *Sarmishtha* (1858), *Padmavati* (1859), and the blank verse epics *Tillotama* (1860) and *Meghanad-Badha* (1861).

DUUN, Olav (1876–1939) Norwegian novelist, born in Namsdal. He worked as a teacher from 1904 to 1926. An important representative of new Norwegian writing in *Landsmål* ('national language', renamed *Nynorsk*, New Norwegian) between the wars, he made his reputation with a major series of saga-like novels about four generations of peasant landholders in Namsdal in *Juvikfolke* (The People of Juvik, 6 vols, 1918–23).

DUVAL, Claude (1643–70) French highwayman, born in Domfront, Normandy. He came to England at the Restoration in the train of the Duke of Richmond. Soon taking to the road, he pursued a successful career until, captured while drunk, he was hanged at Tyburn.

DUVALIER, François (1907–71) known as **Papa Doc**, president of Haiti from 1957. Born in Port-au-Prince, he trained in medicine, and became director of the public health service in 1946 and minister of health in 1949. After the military coup in 1950 he opposed the government, and in 1957 was overwhelmingly elected president in army-supervised elections. His rule became autocratic and murderous, through the civil militia of the so-called Tonton Macoutes. A professed believer in Voodoo, he fought off invasions and threatened uprisings with American economic help. He was succeeded by his son, **Jean-Claude** ('Baby Doc').

DUVALIER, Jean-Claude (1951–) Haitian politician, born in Port-au-Prince, son of **François 'Papa Doc' Duvalier** . After studying law at the University of Haiti he followed his father into politics, becoming known as 'Baby Doc'. At the age of 20 he became president-for-life, ruling, as had his father, through a private army. In 1986 he was deposed in a military coup led by General Henri Namphrey and went into exile in Grasse, in the south of France.

DUVEEN, Joseph, 1st Baron Duveen of Millbank (1869–1939) English art dealer who established significant collections in the USA and Europe. Starting in his father's antique shop, he developed a business in the USA specializing in Old Masters. He was a benefactor of the National Gallery, and gifted a gallery in the British Museum to house the Elgin marbles.

DVOŘÁK, Antonin (1841–1904) Czech composer, born near Prague. His father was a butcher, and he worked for a while in the business, but showed such musical talent that he was sent to the organ school in Prague in 1857. In 1859 he began to earn his living playing the viola in an orchestra and giving lessons, but all the while he was composing in secret. It was not until 1873 that he attracted attention with his *Hymnus*, a nationalistic cantata based on Halek's poem *The Heroes of the White Mountain*. In 1873 he married, and from 1874 to 1877 was organist at St Adalbert's church in Prague, during which time he made a name for himself with several compositions which were promising enough to bring him to the notice of the authorities and secure himelf a state grant. In 1877 **Brahms** became a member of the committee which examined the compositions of grant holders. He recognized Dvořák's talent and introduced his music to Vienna by sponsoring the publication of the *Klänge aus Mähren*, which were followed by the *Slavonic Dances*, a commissioned work. Brahms's friendship was a great influence and stimulus in the life of the young composer. His work, basically classical in structure, but leavened with colourful Slavonic motifs, won increasing recognition, culminating in European acclaim for his *Stabat Mater*, first performed in London in 1883. He had now written six symphonies and much chamber and piano music, and enjoyed a worldwide reputation which brought him in 1891 the offer of directorship of the New York Conservatory. It was in America that he wrote his ninth symphony, the ever-popular 'From the New World', containing themes redolent of American folk music yet retaining a distinct Slavonic flavour. The beautiful solo for cor anglais in the slow movement is firmly established as a world favourite among classical melodies. At this time he also wrote some of his best chamber music. He returned to Prague in 1895. The last period of his life was spent composing chiefly orchestral music, but he also wrote three more operas, including *Rusalka* (1901) and *Armida* (1904) which, like their predecessors, were not highly successful.

DWIGHT, John English potter, born in Oxfordshire. At his pottery in Fulham from 1671 to 1698, he patented a 'transparent earthenware' resembling porcelain, thus pioneering the English pottery industry.

DWIGHT, Theodore (1764–1846) American journalist and politician, brother of **Timothy Dwight**. He sat in the House of Representatives (1806–07), wrote in support of the Federalist party, edited the Albany *Daily Advertiser* (1815–17), and founded its New York namesake, which he edited (1817–36). His son Theodore (1796–1866) edited *Dwight's American Magazine* (1845–52), and wrote travel books.

DWIGHT, Timothy (1752–1817) American clergyman and educationist, born in Northampton, Massachusetts. Headmaster of Hopkins Grammar School in New Haven (1769–71) and a tutor at Yale from 1771, he was a chaplain with the Continental Army during the War of Independence (1775–83), and thereafter became minister of Greenfield Hill, Connecticut, where he also successfully conducted an academy. In 1795 he was elected president of Yale College and professor of divinity. His principal works are an epic poem, *The Conquest of Canaan* (1785), *Theology Explained and Defended* (1818) and *Travels in New England and New York* (1821). His grandson, Timothy Dwight (1828–1916), was president of Yale from 1886 to 1899, and a member of the American committee for revising the English Bible.

DYCE, Alexander (1798–1869) Scottish critic, born in Edinburgh. He edited **Peele** (1828–39), **Webster** (1830), **Greene** (1831), **Shirley** (1833), **Middleton** (1840), **Beaumont** and **Fletcher** (1843–46), **Marlowe** (1850), **Shakespeare** (1857) and others, as well as writing *Recollections of the Table-talk of Samuel Rogers* (1856).

DYCE, William (1806–64) Scottish historical and religious painter, born in Aberdeen. In 1825 he went to Rome, where he developed sympathies with the Nazarenes, which he transmitted to the Pre-Raphaelites. From 1844 professor of fine arts at King's College, London, he executed frescoes in the new House of Lords, Osborne House, Buckingham Palace, and All Saints', Margaret Street. He died at Streatham.

DYCK, Sir Anthony Van See **VAN DYCK**

DYER, Anson, originally **Ernest Anson-Dyer** (1876–1962) English animator, born in Brighton. Hailed as 'Britain's answer to **Walt Disney**', he studied at Brighton Art School, and designed stained glass windows before trying animation with a series of *Dicky Dee's Cartoons* (1915). For the Cartoon Film Company he produced the bi-monthly *John Bull's Animated Sketchbook* (1916), followed by ten *Kine Komedy Kartoons* (1917). After World War I he made a series of *Shakespeare Burlesques* (1920). In 1935 he began a delightful series of colour cartoons based on the **Stanley Holloway** character, *Old Sam*, his biggest popular success.

DYER, Sir Edward (c.1545–1607) English poet and diplomat, born in Sharpham Park, Somerset. He studied at Balliol College or Broadgates Hall, Oxford, and became a courtier. 'My Mind to Me a Kingdom is' is the best-known of his poems.

DYER, George (1755–1841) English man of letters, **Charles Lamb**'s friend, born in London. From Christ's Hospital he went to Emmanuel College, Cambridge, taking his BA in 1778. In 1792 he settled in Clifford's Inn, London, and, with 'poems' and a vast mass of hack work, produced the *History of the University of Cambridge* (1814) and *Privileges of the University of Cambridge* (1824). He contributed 'all that was original' to Valpy's classics (141 vols, 1809–31), and became totally blind soon after his life's work was done.

DYER, John (1699–1757) Welsh poet and painter, born in Llanfynydd parish, Dyfed. Educated at Westminster School, he abandoned law for art, and in 1725 published his most successful work, *Grongar Hill*, notable for its warmth of feeling, simplicity and exquisite descriptions of landscape. The poem, which advocates a 'quiet in the soul', was inspired by the scenery of the valley of the river Towey in Carmarthenshire, and was written while he was an itinerant painter. In 1750 he published *The Ruins of Rome*, and was ordained the following year. Thereafter he held various livings in Leicestershire and Lincolnshire. His longest work, *The Fleece* (1757), a didactic poem, is praised by **Wordsworth** in a sonnet.

DYLAN, Bob, originally **Robert Allen Zimmerman** (1941–) American singer and song-writer, born in Duluth, Minnesota. Under the early influence of pioneering folk-singer and song-writer **Woody Guthrie**, Dylan revived the folk tradition in American music, with its social and political concerns, in the early 1960s. With an unconventional vocal style, he was immediately influential and many of his songs, notably 'Blowing in the Wind' and 'The Times They are a-Changin'' were widely performed and imitated. Quickly tiring of his unsought role as spokesman for his generation, he turned in 1965 to rock and roll music. The use of amplified instruments alienated many of his early admirers but the songs—including 'Mr Tabourine Man', 'Desolation Row', 'Like a Rolling Stone'—had a profound effect. Self-consciously literary and often the product of Dylan's experiments with hallucinogenic drugs, they were treated by many critics as poetry rather than popular song and raised the latter form to new heights. After a motorcycle accident in 1966 Dylan briefly retired from public view, emerging to record more personal songs in a Country and Western style. The 1970s saw the singer, who had been born into the Jewish faith, embracing evangelical Christianity and, once again, rock and roll. In the 1980s he returned to Judaism and while there was a slackening in his productivity he remained one of the seminal influences on popular song-writing. His record albums include *The Freewheelin' Bob Dylan* (1963), *Another Side of Bob Dylan* (1964), *Blonde on Blonde* (1966), *John Wesley Harding* (1968), *Nashville Skyline* (1969), *Blood on the Tracks* (1973), *Slow Train Coming* (1979) and *Infidels* (1983).

DYMOKE, Sir John (d.1381) English knight. By his marriage (c.1350) with the heiress of the **Marmions** he got the Lincolnshire manor of Scrivelsby, and became king's champion at **Richard II**'s coronation. The function (to challenge all-comers to the king's title) was last exercised at **George IV**'s coronation by Henry Dymoke (1801–65), but Dymokes bore the standard of England at the coronations of **Edward VII**, **George V**, **George VI**, and Queen **Elizabeth**.

DYMPNA (9th century) Irish princess, said to have been slain by her father at Gheel in Belgium for resistance to his incestuous passion. She is the patron of the insane.

DYSON, Sir Frank Watson (1868–1939) English astronomer, born in Measham. Astronomer-royal for Scotland (1905–10) and England (1910–33), he is known for his work on the distribution of stars and on solar eclipses.

DYVEKE, 'little dove' (1491–1517) the nickname of a Dutch adventuress, born in Amsterdam, who became the mistress of King **Kristian II** of Denmark. She met him in 1507 in Bergen, where her mother, Sigbrit Willums, had an inn. They both went to Denmark with him in 1511, where her mother gained great influence, and the hatred of the nobles. Dyveke died suddenly, probably by poison.

DZERZHINSKY, Felix Edmundovich (1877–1926) Russian revolutionary, of Polish descent. In 1897 he was exiled to Siberia for political agitation, fought in the 1905 revolution, and in 1917, as one of the organizers of the *coup d'état*, became chairman of the secret police and a member of the Bolshevik central committee. After 1921 he reorganized the railway system, and was chairman of the supreme economic council, 1924–26.

DZIERZON, Jan (1811–1906) Polish-born apiculturalist, born at Lowkowitz in Upper Silesia. He discovered parthenogenesis in bees and introduced a new type of hive. He wrote *Rationelle Bienenzucht* (1861).

E

EADGAR See **EDGAR**

EADIE, John (1810–76) Scottish theologian and scholar, born in Alva. He published *Biblical Cyclopaedia* (1848), *Ecclesiastical Encyclopaedia* (1861), a number of commentaries, and a critical history of *The English Bible* (1876).

EADMER (d.c.1124) English monk of Canterbury and historian, the devoted friend of Archbishop **Anselm**, to whom he had been sent by Pope **Urban**. In 1120 at **Alexander I**'s request he became bishop of St Andrews. He was the author of *Historian Novorum in Anglia* (c.1115) and a *Vita Anselmi* (c.1125).

EADS, James Buchanan (1820–87) American engineer and inventor, born in Lawrenceburg, Indiana. He invented a diving bell and founded a salvage company that made a fortune from sunken river steamboats. In 1861 he built in 100 days eight ironclad Mississippi steamers for the government, followed by other ironclads and mortar-boats. He built the steel triple arched Eads Bridge (1867–74) across the Mississippi at St Louis, with a central span of 520 feet. His works for improving the Mississippi mouth were completed in 1875–79.

EAGLES, John See **ECCLES**

EAKINS, Thomas (1844–1916) American painter and photographer, born in Philadelphia. Trained in Paris, he was influenced by **Manet** and went on to become the leading American realist painter. Extremely fond of river scenes of boating and bathing, he used these themes to exhibit his mastery of light effects. Into America he introduced European educational techniques. In the 1870s he allowed both sexes to draw from the nude model at his class in the Pennsylvania Academy, but as a result was forced to resign. His interest in photography led him to extend the advances made by **Muybridge** in his studies of figures in motion, and his composite plates inspired **Duchamp**'s *Nude Descending the Staircase*. Lucky enough to have a private income, he was never obliged to bow to the restrictive attitudes of the American art establishment.

EALDHELM See **ALDHELM**

EALDRED See **ALDRED**

EALHWINE See **ALCUIN**

EAMES, Charles (1907–78) American designer, born in St Louis, Missouri. After an incomplete course in architecture, he set up an office in 1930 as an architect and industrial designer before teaching at Cranbrook Academy of Art from 1936. He collaborated with colleagues **Eero Saarinen** and Ray Kaiser on highly original furniture designs for a competition organized by **Eliot Noyes** at the Museum of Modern Art, New York, in 1940. The designs of this period used new materials such as moulded plywood, new foam upholstery and steel rod frames with great assurance and versatility. Having married Ray Kaiser (c.1916–1988) in 1941, he designed his one complete piece of architecture, their house in Santa Monica, California (1949). Constructed entirely from standard building components, it was a prototype of worldwide interest. He is known best for his furniture, including the celebrated 'Lounge Chair' produced in close collaboration with the manufacturer Herman Miller (1956), originally designed for his friend **Billy Wilder**. He was also very original and effective in his approach to graphics and exhibition design, and in the films he produced for IBM and the US government.

EANES, Antonio Ramalho dos Santos (1935–) Portuguese politician and soldier, born in Alcains, the son of a building contractor. After studying law he joined the army, serving in Goa, Macao and Mozambique. In 1974 he joined the Armed Forces Movement of dissident young officers which overthrew Marcello Caetano, and thereafter his military responsibilities included head of television programming. He became chief-of-staff in 1975 at the age of 40. In 1976 he was elected president, a post which he held for ten years.

EARDLEY, Joan (1921–63) English painter, born in Warnham, Sussex. She began her studies at Goldsmith's College of Art, London (1938) but moved to Glasgow where she enrolled at the School of Art in 1940. After the war she studied at Hospitalfield, Arbroath, and at Glasgow School of Art, winning various prizes and travelling to France and Italy on a Carnegie bursary. Greatly influenced by **Van Gogh**, both technically and in terms of her choice of subjects, in 1949 she took a studio in Cochrane Street, Glasgow, and began to paint poor children of the nearby tenements. In 1950 she first visited Catterline, the tiny fishing village on the north-east coast of Scotland which inspired her finest landscapes and seascapes. Here she lived and worked until her death.

EARHART, Amelia (1898–1937) American airwoman, born in Atchison, Kansas. She was the first woman to fly the Atlantic—Newfoundland to Burry Point, Wales, on 17 June 1928. Her plane was lost over the Pacific in July 1937. Her autobiography, *Last Flight* (1938), was edited by her husband, George Palmer Putnam.

EARLE, John (c.1601–1665) English prelate, born in York. In 1641 he became tutor to **Charles II**, then Prince of Wales, and also served him as chaplain during his exile in France. He became bishop of Worcester (1662), and of Salisbury (1663). He published anonymously (1628) *Microcosmographie*, a set of witty character sketches and epigrammatic essays.

EARLE, William (1833–85) English soldier, born in Liverpool. Educated at Winchester, he was commissioned in 1854 and served in the Crimean War (1851–55). He served in Canada and India, becoming major general in 1880. He commanded the garrison of Alexandria from 1882 to 1884, and was killed while leading a column of the **Gordon** rescue expedition.

EARLOM, Richard (1743–1822) English mezzotinter, born in London. He engraved more than 60 plates after **Claude Lorraine**'s *Liber Veritatis*, and was responsible for the well-known set of **Hogarth**'s *Marriage à la Mode*.

EARLY, Jubal Anderson (1816–94) American soldier, born in Franklin County, Virginia. He commanded a Confederate brigade at Bull Run, and a division at Fredericksburg and Gettysburg (1863). In 1864, after some successes, he was thrice defeated by **Sheridan** and **Custer** on a raiding expedition down the Shenandoah Valley towards Washington, and was relieved of his command after a rout at Waynesboro.

He fled to Canada (March 1865), but returned in 1869 to his former profession as a lawyer in Virginia.

EAST, Sir Alfred (1849–1913) English painter and etcher, born in Kettering, where there is a gallery devoted to his work. He studied at the Glasgow School of Art, and is best known for his landscapes of Japan, which he visited in 1889. From 1902 he produced a large number of etchings, and in 1906 he wrote *The Art of Landscape Painting in Oil Colour*.

EAST, Sir Edward Hyde (1764–1847) English judge, born in Jamaica. Starting as an MP, he served as chief justice of Bengal (1813–22) and later sat in the privy council on Indian Appeals. As a young man he reported cases in the King's Bench and also wrote an important *Pleas of the Crown: or a General Treatise on the Principles and Practice of the Criminal Law* (2 vols, 1803).

EAST, Michael (c.1580–1648) English composer and organist. He probably spent several years in the service of Sir **Christopher Hatton** and was subsequently organist of Lichfield Cathedral. His works include church music and madrigals, and he was a contributor to *The Triumphes of Oriana*, the madrigal collection dedicated to Queen **Elizabeth** in 1603.

EASTHAM, George (1936–) English footballer, born in Blackpool. A good but not outstanding player his importance lies in the court case he pursued, *Eastham* v *Newcastle United and others*, in which he established the right of professional footballers to freedom of contract. This case, heard in 1961, led to a decision that the retain and transfer lists then operating were in restraint of trade and should be abolished. This outcome revolutionized the pay structure in association football.

EASTLAKE, Sir Charles Lock (1793–1865) English historical painter, born in Plymouth. He studied under **Haydon**, and made his name with two full-length portraits of **Napoleon** sketched while a prisoner on HMS *Bellerophon* in Portsmouth harbour (1815). He produced many Italianate genre paintings, and became a director of the National Gallery from 1855. He is also remembered for his *Materials for the History of Oil Painting* (1847).

EASTLAKE, Charles Locke (1836–1906) English architect, furniture designer and writer, born in Plymouth, protégé of his uncle, the painter Sir **Charles Lock Eastlake**. He is best known for his writing. Probably his most important book, *Hints on Household Taste in Furniture, Upholstery and Other Details* (1868), developed an aesthetic reasoning in reaction to 19th-century excesses. It was especially influential in the USA where it, and the robust furniture it illustrated, gave rise to the 'Eastlake' style. Another major book, *A History of the Gothic Revival*, was published in 1872. He was assistant secretary of the RIBA from 1866, secretary from 1871 to 1877 and a keeper at the National Gallery in London (1878–98).

EASTMAN, George (1854–1932) American inventor and philanthropist, born in Waterville, New York. He turned from banking to photography, producing a successful roll-film (1884), the 'Kodak' box camera (1888), and joining with **Edison** in experiments which made possible the moving-picture industry. He formed the Eastman Kodak Co in 1892 and produced the Brownie camera in 1900. He was the founder of the Eastman School of Music in Rochester, New York.

EASTWICK, Edward Backhouse (1814–83) English orientalist, born in Warfield, Berkshire. After service with the East India Company he was appointed (1845) professor of Hindustani at Haileybury College, and assistant political secretary in the India Office (1859). He was secretary of legation in Persia in 1860–63. He was MP for Penryn and Falmouth (1868–74). He produced many translations from the Persian, notably the *Gulistan* of Sádi; a *Hindustani Grammar* (1847); *Journal of a Diplomate in Persia* (1864); and translated **Franz Bopp**.

EASTWOOD, Clint (1930–) American actor and director, born in San Francisco. An athletic youngster, he worked as a lumberjack and lifeguard before being signed to a standard Universal contract, making his film début in *Revenge of the Creature* (1955). He found television fame in *Rawhide* (1958–65) and then became a star in Italian 'spaghetti' westerns as the laconic gunslinger who was known as The Man with No Name. In America he proved a consistent box-office attraction in adventure films and as tough detective *Dirty Harry* (1971). He made his directorial début with the thriller *Play Misty for Me* (1971) and has placed his signature on works which reflect his personal interests like *Bronco Billy* (1980) and *Bird* (1988). From 1986 to 1988 he was mayor of Carmel, where he now lives.

EATON, Margaret, née **O'Neill,** known as **'Peggy'** (1799–1879) American socialite, born in Washington, DC, daughter of a Washington innkeeper. She married first (1816) John Timberlake, who died in 1828. In 1829 she married John Henry Eaton, secretary of state for war under President **Jackson**. The wives of the other cabinet ministers refused to mix with her because of her alleged premarital intimacy with Eaton and because of her birth, forcing Eaton to resign (1831) despite the strenuous efforts of Jackson, who even transferred his support to a presidential candidate, **Martin Van Buren**, favourably disposed towards her. A great social success in Europe when her husband became ambassador to Spain (1836), she married a young dancing instructor after the former's death.

EBAN, Abba, originally **Aubrey Solomon** (1915–) Israeli diplomat and politician, born in Cape Town, South Africa. Educated in England, he taught oriental languages at Cambridge before serving as a liaison officer at Allied HQ during World War II. In 1944 he worked in the Middle East Arab Centre in Jerusalem and in 1948 was Israeli UN representative in New York and then ambassador in Washington (1950–59). He returned to Israel where he won a seat in the Knesset and joined **David Ben-Gurion**'s government. Between 1959 and 1974 he held several posts, under various prime ministers, and was foreign minister for eight years (1966–74). In the 1989 general election he was unexpectedly defeated by the opposition leader **George Price**.

EBBA, St (d.c.670) Northumbrian princess, who founded the double monastery of Coldingham, and ruled it as abbess till her death.

EBBINGHAUS, Hermann (1850–1909) German experimental psychologist. He carried out pioneering experimental researches on memory to investigate higher mental processes, and discovered the so-called 'forgetting curve'. He published his findings in *Über das Gedächtnis* (1885).

EBERS, Georg Moritz (1837–98) German Egyptologist and novelist, born in Berlin. Lecturer (1865) and professor (1868) at Jena, he visited the East in 1869, and from 1870 to 1889 was professor of Egyptology at Leipzig. He discovered and published (1875) the celebrated hieratic medical *Papyrus Ebers*, and wrote on Biblical sites in Goshen, Sinai and Egypt. He is best known as the author of numerous historical novels based on ancient Egypt.

EBERT, Friedrich (1871–1925) German statesman, first president of the German Republic (elected February 1919), was born in Heidelberg, a tailor's son. A saddler at Heidelberg, he became a Social Democrat journalist and Reichstag member (1912). Chairman of his party (1913), he was a Majority Socialist leader in the revolution of 1918.

EBERT, Karl Egon (1801–82) Bohemian poet, born in Prague. His poems include the national epic *Vlasta* (1829).

ECCLES, or **EAGLES, John** (c.1650–1735) English composer, born in London of a branch of the family of **Solomon Eccles**. He became master of the King's Band of Musick in 1700, composed the music for the coronation of Queen **Anne** and published many volumes of theatre music, songs and masques. Two other brothers, Henry (c.1652–1742) and Thomas (after 1652–after 1735), were violinists. The former achieved success in Paris but little is known of the latter, except that he played in London taverns.

ECCLES, Sir John Carew (1903–) Australian neurophysiologist, educated at Melbourne and Oxford. He was director of the Kanematsu Institute of Pathology at Sydney (1937), then professor of physiology at Otago University (1944–51) and the Australian National University, Canberra. In 1968 he moved to the State University of New York at Buffalo. He was awarded the 1963 Nobel prize for physiology or medicine, with Sir **Alan Hodgkin** and Sir **Andrew Huxley**, for discoveries concerning the functioning of nervous impulses. In 1990 he was awarded the AC.

ECCLES, Solomon (c.1617–1682) English musician, born in London. He taught the virginals and viols until he became a Quaker in 1660, when he burned his instruments and books and became a shoemaker. During the Great Plague he ran naked through the streets with a brazier of burning sulphur on his head, prophesying disaster. In 1667 he published *A Musick Lector*, a discussion on whether or not music was from God. He accompanied **George Fox** to the West Indies in 1671 to spread Quakerism, and was prosecuted for sedition at Barbados in 1680.

ECEVIT, Bülent (1925–) Turkish writer and statesman, born in Istanbul. After working as a government official and a journalist, Ecevit became an MP for the centre-left Republican People's party in 1957. He was minister of labour for four years, and in 1966 became secretary-general of his party and subsequently (1972) chairman. He became prime minister of a coalition government in 1974, but resigned later that year over differences of opinion with the other coalition party. Ecevit again became prime minister in 1978, but his government only lasted for 22 months. Turkey experienced a military take-over in 1980, and Ecevit was imprisoned twice for criticizing the military regime. A distinguished poet and writer, Ecevit was committed to maintaining Turkey's independence within NATO and to improving the country's traditionally poor relations with neighbouring Greece. In 1987 he announced his retirement from active politics.

ECHEGARAY Y EIZAGUIRRE, José (1833–1916) Spanish dramatist, born of Basque descent in Madrid in 1833. He taught mathematics, held portfolios in various ministries (1868–74), then won literary fame by many plays in prose and verse, received the Nobel prize for literature (1904), returned to politics as minister of finance (1905), and to science as professor of physics, Madrid University (1905). His masterpiece was *The Great Galeoto* (1881).

ECK, Johann Mayer von (1486–1543) German Catholic theologian, born in Egg in Swabia. Professor of theology at Ingolstadt (1510), he was the ruling spirit of that university until his death. He disputed with **Luther** at Leipzig in 1519, and wrote his *De Primatu Petri* and went to Rome in 1520, to return with the bull which declared Luther a heretic. He also disputed with **Melanchthon** at Worms (1540) and with **Ratisbon** at Worms (1541).

ECKART, Johannes See **ECKHART**

ECKENER, Hugo (1868–1954) German aeronautical engineer, born in Flensburg. He became a friend of Count **Zeppelin** and in 1911 was made a director of his airship company. In 1924 he piloted the ZR3, later called the *Los Angeles*, from Friedrichshafen to Lakehurst, New Jersey, on the first flight by an airship directly from continental Europe across the Atlantic. He built the *Graf Zeppelin* (1929) in which he circumnavigated the world, and made many other notable flights.

ECKERMANN, Johann Peter (1792–1854) German author, born in Winsen in Hanover. He studied at Göttingen. The publication of his *Beiträge zur Poesie* (1823) led to his move to Weimar, where he assisted **Goethe** in preparing the final edition of his works. He achieved fame by his *Conversations with Goethe* (1837, trans 1839).

ECKERT, John Presper (1919–) American engineer and inventor, born in Philadelphia. He graduated in electronic engineering at the University of Pennsylvania where he remained for a further five years as a research associate. From 1942 to 1946, with **John W Mauchly**, he worked on the Electronic Numerical Integrator And Calculator (ENIAC), one of the first modern computers; it weighed several tons, used thousands of valves and resistors, and required 100 kW of electric power. He and Mauchly continued to develop improved versions of their computer, including UNIVAC I which in 1951 became one of the first computers to be sold commercially. Eckert himself has been granted more than 85 patents for his electronic inventions.

ECKFORD, Harry (1775–1832) Scottish-born American naval architect, born in Irvine. He went out to Quebec in 1790 and New York in 1796, and from 1800 built up a reputation for strong and speedy sailing ships. He built the famous early steamship *Robert Fulton* (1822).

ECKHART, Johannes, called **Meister Eckhart** (c.1260–1327) German mystic, born in Hochheim near Gotha. He entered the Dominican order, studied and taught in Paris, acted as prior of Erfurt and as vicar of his order for Thuringia, was Dominican provincial in Saxony. 1303–11, vicar-general of Bohemia, 1307, and from 1312 preached at Strasbourg, Frankfurt and Cologne. Eckhart's teaching is a mystic pantheism, which influenced later religious mysticism and speculative philosophy. In 1325 he was accused of heresy by the archbishop of Cologne, and two years after his death his writings were condemned by Pope **John XXII**. His extant works consist of Latin and German sermons and tractates.

ECO, Umberto (1932–) Italian novelist and semiotician, born in Alessandria in Piedmont. A student of philosophy at Turin University, he was awarded a doctorate for his thesis on St **Thomas Aquinas**. He taught at Turin (1956–67), and was appointed professor of semiotics (the study of signs in all realms of culture) at the University of Bologna in 1971. Imbued with a 'taste and passion' for the Middle Ages, he undertook a prolonged study of the commentary of Beatus of Liébana, an 8th-century saint, on the *Book of Revelation* and of 11th-century illuminations, all of which bore fruit in *The Name of the Rose* (1980). A suspense story set in a medieval monastery, centring on the criminal investigation of Brother William of Baskerville, an English Franciscan, it is indebted to **Conan Doyle**'s *Sherlock Holmes* despite having been described as 'a completely semiotic book'. It was an international bestseller and successfully translated to celluloid in a film of the same name directed by Jean-Jaques Arnaud and starring **Sean Connery**. *Foucault's Pendulum*, his second novel, was published in 1989.

EDDERY, Pat (Patrick James John) (1952–) Irish jockey, born in Newbridge. He was champion jockey from 1974 to 1977, and had several successes in the Classics, including Derby winners in 1975 and 1982, while he also won the Oaks twice, as well as the St Leger. He also had a particularly good record in France, winning the Prix de l'Arc de Triomphe in 1980, 1985, and 1986.

EDDINGTON, Sir Arthur Stanley (1882–1944) English astronomer, born in Kendal. Professor (1913) and observatory director (1914) at Cambridge, he was considered by many the greatest of modern English astronomers. His work in the inter-war years did much to establish **Albert Einstein**'s theories, which he also presented to a wider public in his *Mathematical Theory of Relativity* (1923). Other notable works are *Space, Time and Gravitation* (1920), *Stars and Atoms* (1927) and *The Expanding Universe* (1933).

EDDY, Mary (Morse), née **Baker** (1821–1910) American founder of the Christian Science Church, born in Bow, New Hampshire and brought up as a Congregationalist. She was frequently ill as a young woman. After a brief first marriage (to George Glover, 1843–44), she was married a second time, in 1853, to Daniel Patterson (divorced in 1873). In the 1860s she tried all kinds of medication, but turned to faith healing and in 1862 came under the influence of Phineas T Quimby (1802–66). While recovering from a severe fall in 1866 she turned to the Bible for a spiritual and metaphysical system she called Christian Science, explaining her beliefs in *Science and Health with Key to the Scriptures* (1875), which proclaimed the illusory nature of disease. She married Asa G Eddy in 1877, and in 1879 founded at Boston the Church of Christ, Scientist. Her church attracted great numbers of followers. She founded various publications, including the *Christian Science Journal* (1883), and the *Christian Science Monitor* (1908).

EDE, James Chuter, Baron Chuter-Ede (1882–1965) English politician, born in Epsom, He was educated at Epsom National School, and Dorking High School, Battersea Pupil Teachers' centre, and Christ's College, Cambridge. Assistant master at Surrey elementary schools, 1905–14, he was MP for Mitcham, 1923, and for South Shields, 1929–31, 1935–64. As minister of education, 1940–45, he helped to bring about the Education Act of 1944. He was home secretary, 1945–51, during which time he introduced the Criminal Justice Act of 1948 and was involved in controversy on capital punishment. He was leader of the House of Commons in 1951. A nonconformist with a passion for political liberty, he was greatly depended upon by **Richard Butler** for his knowledge of the local authorities.

EDELFELT, Albert Gustav (1854–1905) Finnish artist, born in Porvoeo. He worked in many different media in a naturalistic style. Among his best works are a portrait of **Pasteur**, *Christ and the Magdalene* and *Women in the Churchyard*.

EDELINCK, Gerard (1649–1707) Flemish copper engraver, born in Antwerp. In 1665 he went to Paris, where he produced more than 300 engravings and portraits. His portrait of **Dryden**, after **Kneller**, is his best known work.

EDELMAN, Gerald Maurice (1929–) American biochemist, born in New York City. He began to work on human immunoglobulins in 1960 at Rockefeller University, where he became professor of biochemistry in 1966. By 1969 his results, together with **Rodney Robert Porter**'s studies in England on a typical antibody (human immunoglobulin IgG), allowed a fairly detailed picture to be deduced of its Y-shaped molecule, which is likely to be typical of antibodies in general. For their discoveries concerning the chemical structure of antibodies, Edelman and Porter shared the 1972 Nobel prize for physiology or medicine.

EDEN, Sir (Robert) Anthony, 1st Earl of Avon (1897–1977) English statesman, born at Windlestone Hall, Bishop Auckland. He was educated at Eton and Christ Church, Oxford. He won the MC in 1917, and became Tory MP for Warwick and Leamington in 1923, holding the seat till his resignation in 1957. In 1931 he became foreign under-secretary, in 1934 lord privy seal and in 1935 foreign secretary. He resigned in 1938 following differences with the prime minister, **Neville Chamberlain**, principally on policy towards Fascist Italy. On the outbreak of World War II he became dominions secretary. In 1940 he was Sir **Winston Churchill**'s secretary of state for war, issuing the historic appeal that brought the Home Guard into being. In December 1940 he was foreign secretary again. Strenuous wartime work, which included negotiations of a 20-year treaty of alliance with the Soviet Union in 1942, culminated in his leadership of the British delegation to the 1945 San Francisco conference which established the United Nations. With Labour in power from 1945 to 1951, he was deputy leader of the opposition, returning to the foreign office once more in 1951 in Churchill's government. His peak year of patient negotiation was 1954, marked by settlements in Korea and Viet Nam (Indo-China), by the emergence of a new political pattern in Western Europe backed by a British military guarantee, and by a new agreement with Egypt for the withdrawal of British forces from the Suez Canal Zone. He succeeded Churchill as prime minister in April 1955, a year marked by the 'summit' conference at Geneva with the heads of America, France and the Soviet Union, In November 1956 he ordered British and French forces to occupy the Suez Canal Zone ahead of the invading Israeli army. His action was condemned by the United Nations and caused a bitter and prolonged controversy in Britain which did not subside when he ordered a withdrawal. In failing health, he abruptly resigned the premiership on 9 January 1957. He was created an earl in 1961. Eden's gracious, debonair manner concealed strong political convictions and fixity of purpose. Regarded as one of the Western world's most experienced statesmen, his supreme aim was world peace based on respect for law. He wrote *Place in the Sun, Foreign Affairs* (1939), *Freedom and Order* and *Days for Decision* (1949), his memoirs (3 vols, 1960–65) and an account of his pre-political life, *Another World* (1976).

EDEN, George, 1st Earl of Auckland (1784–1849) English statesman, son of Sir **William Eden**, born in Eden Farm, Beckenham. He succeeded as 2nd baron in 1814. A steadfast supporter of reform, he held two or three offices, and in 1835 was appointed governor-general of India. He plunged into the unhappy Afghan war in 1838, and was superseded in 1841. He was created an earl in 1839.

EDEN, William, 1st Baron (1744–1814) English statesman and diplomat, third son of Sir Robert Eden, Bart, of West Auckland, Durham. He was educated at Eton and Oxford, and called to the bar in 1768. In 1772 he was appointed under-secretary of state, and afterwards president of the board of trade, commissioner to treat with the American insurgents, chief secretary to the Irish viceroy, minister-plenipotentiary to France (negotiating **Pitt**'s commercial treaty with that country in 1786), ambassador to Spain, ambassador to Holland, and postmaster-general. In 1788 he was raised to the Irish, in 1793 to the British, peerage.

EDERLE, Gertrude Caroline (1906–) American swimmer, the first woman to swim the English channel. She won a gold medal at the 1924 Olympic Games as a member of the US 400-metre relay team, and two bronze medals. On 6 August 1926 she swam the Channel from Cap Gris Nez to Kingsdown in 14 hours 31 minutes, very nearly two hours faster than the existing men's record. Later she turned professional.

EDGAR THE ÆTHELING (c.1050–c.1125) English prince, son of **Edward the Ætheling** and grandson of **Edmond II 'Ironside'**, and legitimate heir to the English throne on the death of his great-uncle **Edward 'the Confessor'** in 1066. He was born during his father's exile in Hungary, and came to England with his father as a child in 1057. When Edward the Confessor died, he was passed over as king in favour of the military strong-man, **Harold Godwinsson**. After Harold's defeat and death at Hastings, some English nobles supported the Ætheling's claims against **William I, the Conqueror**, but he was compelled to make submission to William in 1067. In the following year he fled with his mother and sisters to Scotland, where king **Malcolm III, Canmore** received them well and married his sister, St **Margaret**. Malcolm Canmore embraced his cause and made incursions into the north of England, but in 1074 the Ætheling made peace with William and entered his service, leading the Norman expedition that conquered Apulia in 1086 and an expedition to Scotland in 1097 to depose a usurper and put Malcolm's son Edgar on the throne.

EDGAR, or **Eadgar** (944–75) king of the English. The younger son of King **Edmund** of Wessex, he was made king of Northumbria and Mercia in 957 in favour of his brother Eadwig, and succeeded to Wessex as well on his brother's death in 959, thus becoming ruler of a united England. He recalled St **Dunstan** from exile and made him his closest adviser and archbishop of Canterbury. In 973 he was formally crowned and received the submission of all the kings in Britain, who rowed him ceremonially on the river Dee. Guided by Dunstan, his reign was one of secure peace and prosperity, and the acceptance of the Danelaw as a separate but integral part of England, under his nominal authority. He is renowned for his part in reviving the English church. By his first wife he had a son, the future **Edward the Martyr**; by his second wife, Ælfryth, another son, the future **Æthelred II** ('the Unready').

EDGAR, David (1948–) English dramatist. He studied drama at Manchester University before becoming a journalist in Bradford, and wrote several plays for touring fringe theatre companies before deciding to write for the stage full time. *Destiny* (1976), a large-scale play looking at the roots of Fascism in British society, was produced by the Royal Shakespeare Company. His eight-hour adaptation of **Dickens**' *The Life and Adventures of Nicholas Nickleby* for the RSC (1980), brought his work to a massive audience. *Maydays* (1983), the first contemporary play to be presented by the RSC at the Barbican Theatre in London, was similarly ambitious. *Entertaining Strangers* (1985) set in 19th-century Dorchester of the 1830s and 1850s, counterpoints the commercial ambitions of the owner of a brewery with the fury of a fundamentalist preacher against the backdrop of industrialization and a cholera epidemic.

EDGERTON, Harold Eugene (1903–90) American electrical engineer, born in Fremont, Nebraska. In 1934 he became professor of electrical engineering at the Massachusetts Institute of Technology. A specialist in stroboscopes and high-speed photography, he produced a krypton-xenon gas arc which was employed in photographing the capillaries in the white of the eye without hurting the patient.

EDGERTON, Sidney (1818–1900) American politician, born in New York. He sat in Congress (1859–63), became first chief justice of Idaho Territory and as such was a founder of the new state (1864) of Montana, of which he was made the first governor.

EDGEWORTH, Francis Ysidro (1845–1926) Irish economist, born in Edgeworthstown, County Longford, nephew of **Richard Lovell Edgeworth**. Professor of political economy at Oxford (1891–1922), and first editor of the *Economic Journal* (1891–1926), he was perhaps the most outstanding mathematical economist of his time. Best known for his *Mathematical Psychics* (1881), he also carried out important work in the field of statistical theory.

EDGEWORTH, Maria (1767–1849) Irish novelist, eldest daughter of the inventor and educationist **Richard Lovell Edgeworth**, born in Blackbourton, Oxfordshire. After being educated in England, she returned to Edgeworthstown in County Longford, Ireland in 1872 to act as her father's assistant and governess to his many other children. With her father, and to illustrate his educational ideas, she published *Letters to Literary Ladies* (1795), *The Parent's Assistant* (1796) and *Practical Education* (1798). In 1800 she published her first novel, *Castle Rackrent*, which was an immediate success, followed by *Belinda* in 1801. She received praise from Sir **Walter Scott** and was lionized on a visit to London and the Continent, where she turned down a proposal of marriage from the Swedish Count Edelcrantz for the sake of her father. The next of her 'social novels' of Irish life was *The Absentee* (1809), followed by *Ormond* (1817). All her works were written under the influence of her father, which may have inhibited her natural story telling talent. After her father's death (1817) she did little more writing apart from a late novel, *Helen* (1834), but devoted herself to looking after the family property, and 'good works'. She is also remembered for children's stories.

EDGEWORTH, Richard Lovell (1744–1817) Anglo-Irish inventor and educationist, born in Bath. With his great friend **Thomas Day** he studied at Corpus Christi, Oxford, and while there made the first of his four marriages. He then studied law for a time, but following a stay in France, he returned in 1773 to live mainly on the family estate at Edgeworthstown, County Longford, an energetic and intelligent landlord. A prolific inventor, he produced many mechanical devices, including a semaphore, a velocipede and a pedometer. Through his inventions he came in touch with **Erasmus Darwin** and so with the Lichfield circle and with his second and third wives, Honora and Elizabeth Sneyd. The father of 22 children, the eldest educated on **Rousseau**'s system, he held noteworthy theories of education and published these in *Practical Education* (written with his daughter, **Maria Edgeworth**, in 1798) and *Professional Education* (1808). He wrote much also on mechanical subjects. In politics he advocated parliamentary reform and Catholic emancipation, and, as a member of the last Irish parliament (1798–99), spoke for union but voted against it.

EDGEWORTH DE FIRMONT, Henry Essex (1745–1807) Irish churchman, known as the 'Abbé Edgeworth', born in Edgworthstown, County Longford, son of the Protestant rector there who turned Catholic and settled in Toulouse. Educated at the Jesuit College and the Sorbonne, he was ordained a priest and took the surname De Firmont from Firmount, the family property. In 1791 he became confessor to Madame Elizabeth, sister of **Louis XVI**

and in 1793 to her brother just before his death. After attending them both to the scaffold he escaped to England (1796), and as chaplain attended **Louis XVIII** at Mitau, where he died.

EDINBURGH, Duke of, Prince Alfred Ernest Albert See **SAXE-COBURG-GOTHA**

EDINBURGH, Duke of, Prince Philip (1921–) consort of Queen Elizabeth. Son of Prince Andrew of Greece and Princess Alice of Battenburg, and grandson of **George I** of Greece and great grandson of Queen **Victoria**, he was born in Corfu and educated at Cheam, Gordonstoun and Dartmouth Naval College, he entered the Royal Navy in 1939 as Lieut Philip Mountbatten. In 1941 he joined HMS *Valiant*, on which he fought in the battle of Cape Matapan, subsequently serving in the Pacific on HMS *Whelp*. In 1947 he became a naturalized British subject as Philip Mountbatten, and on 20 November 1947, as the Duke of Edinburgh, he married his third cousin Princess Elizabeth the future Queen **Elizabeth**. As a prince of the UK since 1957, he has shown a keen and occasionally outspoken interest in science and the technology of industry, as well as in youth adventure training and world wildlife. He is also a keen sportsman, a yachtsman and a qualified airman. His speeches and essays were published in *Men, Machines and Sacred Cows* (1984).

EDISON, Thomas Alva (1847–1931) American inventor and physicist, born in Milan, Ohio, the most prolific inventor the world has ever seen. Expelled from school for being retarded, he became a railroad newsboy on the Grand Trunk Railway, and soon printed and published his own newspaper on the train, the *Grand Trunk Herald*. During the Civil War (1861–65) he worked as a telegraph operator in various cities, and invented an electric vote recording machine. In 1871 he invented the paper ticker-tape automatic repeater for stock exchange prices, which he then sold in order to establish an industrial research laboratory at Newark, New Jersey, which moved in 1876 to Menlo Park, New Jersey, and finally to West Orange, New Jersey, in 1887. He was now able to give full scope to his astonishing inventive genius. He took out more than 1000 patents in all, including the gramophone (1877), the incandescent light bulb (1879), and the carbon granule microphone as an improvement for **Bell**'s telephone. Amongst his other inventions were a megaphone, the electric valve (1883), the kinetoscope (1891), a storage battery, and benzol plants. In 1912 he produced the first talking motion pictures. He also discovered thermionic emission, formerly called the 'Edison Effect'.

EDITH See **EDWARD 'the Confessor'**

EDMONDS, Thomas Rowe (1803–89) English economist and statistician. He advocated the abolition of private ownership in industry and a two-hour day for workers, compiled life tables (1832) and wrote on political economy (1828) and the principle of population (1832).

EDMUND, St (c.841–70) king of East Anglia. According to tradition, he was the son of a Frankish king and succeeded **Offa** of Mercia as his adopted heir. When the great Danish invasion army of 865 descended on East Anglia in 870, Edmund met them at Hoxne, in Suffolk, and was defeated and killed. Tradition claims that he was taken captive, and when he refused to abjure his Christian faith he was tied to a tree and shot to death with arrows by the pagan Danes. A miracle cult quickly sprang up and in 903 his remains were translated from Hoxne to Bury St Edmunds.

EDMUND, St, originally **Edmund Rich** English ecclesiastic and scholar, born in Abingdon. He studied and taught at Oxford and Paris, and acquiring fame as a preacher, was commissioned by Pope **Gregory IX** to preach the Sixth Crusade throughout England (c.1227). In 1234 he was made archbishop of Canterbury. He attached himself to the national party, whose spokesman he became against **Henry III**, even threatening him with excommunication if he did not dismiss foreign favourites. But his gentleness, generosity, austerity and purity put him out of joint with the age. His authority was diminished by the arrival of the papal legate, Cardinal Otho, in 1237, and in 1240 he retired to the abbey of Pontigny in France, and died the same year. The last archbishop of Canterbury to be canonized, his feast day is 16 November. St Edmund Hall, Oxford, was named in his honour.

EDMUND I (921–46) king of the English, the son of **Edward the Elder**. In 939 he succeeded his half-brother, **Athelstan**, by whose side he had fought at the battle of Brunanburh in 937. He re-established English control of Mercia against the Norse Vikings of Northumbria, and re-conquered from them the 'Five Boroughs' of the Danelaw whose Danish settlers now regarded themselves as English citizens. He subdued the Norsemen in Cumbria and Strathclyde, which he entrusted to **Malcolm I** of Scotland as an ally. In 946 he was killed at Pucklechurch in Gloucestershire by an outlawed robber.

EDMUND II, 'Ironside' (c.981–1016) king of the English for a few months in 1016. The son of **Æthelred 'the Unready'** and half brother of **Edward 'the Confessor'**, he defied his father in 1015 by marrying the widow of a Danish earl in Mercia who had been murdered at the king's command, and was accepted as lord of most of Mercia. When **Knut Sveinsson** (Canute) invaded England that summer, Edmund raised an army in Mercia, and when his father died in April 1016, he was chosen king by the beleaguered defenders of London, while Knut was chosen king by the Witan (Council) in Southampton. After a series of brilliant but inconclusive engagements, for which he earned the nickname of 'Ironside', Edmund defeated the Danes at Oxford in Kent but was routed in a fierce battle at Ashingdon in Essex. By a compromise with Knut, it was agreed that Edmund should have Wessex and Knut have Mercia and Northumbria, and that whoever survived the other would succeed to the whole realm. A few weeks later, in November 1016, Edmund died and Knut became king of England. Edmund's two sons were taken for safe keeping to Hungary; the elder, **Edward the Ætheling**, became the legitimate heir-apparent to the throne of his uncle, Edward the Confessor.

EDMUNDS, George Franklin (1828–1919) American senator, born in Richmond, Connecticut. He sat in the state legislature and senate, and in the US senate (1866–91), after which he was president *pro tempore* after **Arthur** became president. He took an active part in the prosecution of President **Johnson**, and was author of the 'Edmunds Act' for the suppression of polygamy in Utah.

EDRICH, William John (1916–86) English cricketer, born in Norfolk. As a batsman he is always associated with his Middlesex partner, **Denis Compton**, but took longer to develop. One of a family which supplied five cricketers to the first-class game, he played 39 Tests and in 1938 became one of a handful of players to have scored 1000 runs before the end of May. With Compton he shared a record third wicket Test partnership of 370 against South Africa at Lord's in 1947. After World War II he reverted to amateur status to make himself available for the England captaincy, but was never selected for the post.

EDRISI, or **Idrisi** (c.1100–64) Arabic geographer, born in Ceuta. He studied at Córdoba, and travelled in Spain, Barbary and Asia Minor. He then settled at the court of Roger II of Sicily, who invited him to write a description of the earth. For this end travellers were sent on journeys of exploration, and were directed to send him an account of all they had seen or heard. This occupied many years, and Edrisi's Description of the World (*Nuzhat-el-Mushtâk*), or 'Book of Roger', as it was also called, was not completed till 1154. Unequal in execution, it yet stands in the very first rank of medieval geographies.

EDWARD THE ELDER (c.870–c.924) king of Wessex and son of **Alfred the Great**, succeeded his father in 899. During his vigorous reign he brought back under English rule the whole of the Danelaw south of the Humber, took control of Mercia in 918 after the death of his sister **Æthelflæd** (the 'Lady of the Mercians'), and subdued the Scots, the Norsemen in Northumbria, and the Welsh Britons of Strathclyde.

EDWARD THE MARTYR, St (c.963–78) Anglo-Saxon king of England. The elder son of King **Edgar**, he succeeded to the throne as a boy of twelve in 975. His accession provoked rival claims on behalf of his younger half-brother, **Æthelred II** the 'Unready'; and in 978 he was treacherously murdered by Æthelred's household at Corfe Castle in Dorset. He was canonized in 1001.

EDWARD 'THE CONFESSOR' (c.1003–66) king of England from 1042, and last Anglo-Saxon king of the old time. He was born at Islip in Oxfordshire, the elder son of **Æthelred, 'the Unready'** by his wife **Emma**, daughter of Richard, Duke of Normandy, and half-brother of **Edmund 'Ironside'**. After the death of Æthelred in 1016 the throne of England passed (via Edmund Ironside) to **Knut Sveinsson** (Canute), who promptly summoned Æthelred's widow Emma from Normandy and married her, and had a son by her, **Hardaknut**. Edward stayed on in Normandy during Knut's reign and became closely involved in religion, taking a vow of chastity. In 1041 he was recalled to the English court by his half-brother Hardaknut, and succeeded him on the throne the following year through the influence of the powerful Earl **Godwin** of Wessex, whose only daughter, Edith, he married in 1045. He was deeply influenced by Norman favourites, and the history of his reign is in part the story of the struggle of the Norman, or 'court', party with the 'national' party led by Godwin and his son, **Harold Godwinsson**, who were declared outlaws for a time (1051) but restored to favour in 1053. Edward founded Westminster Abbey, but was too ill to attend the consecration at Christmas, 1065; he died in January, 1066. Although his legitimate heir was his grandson, **Edgar the Ætheling** (the grandson of **Edmund 'Ironside'**), on his deathbed he allegedly nominated Harold Godwinsson as the successor to the throne. He was buried in Westminster Abbey and became the subject of a cult which saw him canonized in 1611.

EDWARD I (1239–1307) king of England, known as the 'Hammer of the Scots'. He was the elder son of King **Henry III** and **Eleanor of Provence**. In 1254 he married **Eleanor of Castile**, the half-sister of King **Alfonso X** of Leon and Castile, and received from his father responsibilities in Gascony, Ireland and Wales, where he learned his first lessons in warfare campaigning against Prince **Llewelyn ap Gruffud** of Gwynedd. In a struggle between King Henry and his barons, Edward sided for a time with **Simon de Montfort**; but when de Montfort raised a rebellion in 1264 he fought with his father at the battle of Lewes where the king was captured (mainly through Edward's rashness). He was held hostage for his father but escaped, and with Welsh support brought Simon de Montfort to battle at Evesham in 1265 and killed him. He won great renown as a knight on the Eighth (and last) Crusade of 1270, on which his wife Eleanor accompanied him. He succeeded to the throne on his father's death in 1272 but did not return to England for his coronation until 1274. He received the homage of **Alexander III** of Scotland for his lands in England, but had to force Prince Llewelyn into submission in 1276. After the defeat and death of Llewelyn in Radnorshire in 1282, the principality was formally annexed to the English crown by the Statute of Wales in 1284. In 1289 he betrothed his infant son Prince Edward (the future **Edward II**) to **Margaret**, infant queen of Scotland, the 'Maid of Norway'; but the Maid died at sea the following year, and Edward's hope of uniting the kingdoms of England and Scotland under a single crown through marriage were dashed. Chosen to be arbiter over the succession to the vacant Scottish throne, he decided against **Robert de Bruce**, Earl of Carrick, in favour of **John Baliol**, who on his accession in 1292 swore homage for the whole kingdom of Scotland. Troubles in France now engaged his attention; and to quell discontent at home, in 1295 he summoned an assembly of the three estates (later called the Model Parliament). The growing exasperation of the Scots flared into open rebellion in 1296: Edward marched north, captured Berwick, penetrated as far north as Aberdeen, stripped John Baliol of his crown at Montrose, and carried the Coronation Stone of Scone back to England. At Berwick on his way home he received the fealty of the Scottish clergy, barons and gentry whose names fill the *Ragman Roll*. The French problem (over Gascony) was mollified when he married Margaret, the sister of **Philip IV** of France (his first wife, Eleanor of Castile, had died in 1290). Meanwhile the Scots were up in arms again, led by the heroic **William Wallace**, who had won a great victory at Stirling Bridge (1297) and ravaged England from Newcastle to Carlisle; Edward marched north and defeated him soundly at Falkirk (1298). Wallace was betrayed to the English in 1305, and savagely executed; in that same year, Edward prepared a new constitution for Scotland, with representation in the English parliament. But Scotland was not subdued; **Robert the Bruce** (son of Robert de Bruce) had himself crowned king of the Scots as Robert I at Scone in 1306. Edward, old and infirm by then, marched north, but died near Carlisle in August 1307. He charged his son, Prince Edward, to carry his bones with the army until he had utterly subdued the Scots; but Edward buried him in Westminster with the inscription *Scotorum malleus*—'Hammer of the Scots'.

EDWARD II (1284–1327) king of England from 1307, the son of **Edward I** and **Eleanor of Castile**. Born in Caernarvon in Wales, in 1301 he was created Prince of Wales, the first English heir-apparent to bear that title. He accompanied his father on his Scottish campaigns, but was absent at his death, and, instead of carrying out his dying request, returned to London and the companionship of his favourite, the Gascon, Piers de Gaveston. He created him Earl of Cornwall, and on his departure for France in 1308 to marry **Isabella**, daughter of **Philip IV**, left him guardian of the kingdom. The indignant nobles demanded Gaveston's banishment, and twice he was forced to leave England; at length they rose, captured, and executed him in 1312. In 1314 Edward invaded Scotland with a large army. At Bannockburn, however, on 24 June, he was defeated with immense slaughter by **Robert the Bruce**

who, by going on to capture Berwick in 1318 undid virtually every trace of the conquest of Edward I. The disaster of Bannockburn was followed by risings in Wales and Ireland, and two seasons of unprecedented famine and pestilence. From this time the influence of Thomas, Earl of Lancaster, was supreme; but in 1321, with the aid of his new favourites, Hugh le Despenser and his son, Edward overthrew Lancaster, and put him to death. Edward then invaded Scotland for the last time with no particular success, and in 1323 concluded a truce for thirteen years. A dispute now arose with **Charles IV** of France, brother of his wife, Isabella, in regard to Edward's territories in that country. Charles seized these, whereupon Edward sent Isabella to effect an amicable arrangement. She despised her husband, hated the Despensers, and had fallen in love with Roger de Mortimer, one of the disaffected nobles. In 1326 she landed with a large body of malcontents on the coast of Suffolk; the Despensers were executed, and Edward, taken captive, was forced to abdicate. In the following year he was murdered in Berkeley Castle.

EDWARD III (1312–77) king of England from 1327, the son of **Edward II**. During his minority the country was really governed by his mother, **Isabella**, and her lover, Roger de Mortimer. In 1328 Edward married **Philippa of Hainault**, and two years later put Mortimer to death, and banished his mother to Castle Rising. Invading Scotland to assist **Edward Baliol** who, on the death of **Robert the Bruce**, had got himself crowned at Scone in opposition to the boy king **David II**, Edward defeated the Scots at Halidon Hill, near Berwick, in 1333, whereupon Baliol did homage to Edward for his possessions, but a few months later had to flee the kingdom. Despite successive English invasions the Scots rallied each time. **Charles IV** of France having died without a son in 1328, Edward claimed the crown in right of his mother, Isabella, sister of Charles. He declared war against **Philip VI** in 1337, raising money by tallages, forced loans, and by seizing wool. Despite the brilliant sea victory at Sluys in 1340, he was at first unsuccessful, and soon found himself compelled to purchase the grants of money necessary for the war with concessions of privileges, which he occasionally evaded. At length in 1346, accompanied by his eldest son, **Edward the Black Prince**, he again invaded France, conquered a great part of Normandy, marched to the gates of Paris, and in August 1346, inflicted a terrible defeat on the French at Crécy. After some further successes, and the fall of Calais after a year's siege, a truce for a few months was concluded. Meanwhile the Scots, in 1346, had been defeated at Neville's Cross near Durham, and their king, David II, taken prisoner, while in 1349 the Black Death had carried off a third of the population of England. The war began anew in 1355, and next year, on 19 September, the Black Prince obtained a brilliant victory at Poitiers, where King **John II** of France was taken prisoner. The Scottish king was released under promise of a ransom of 100000 marks in 1357, and King John in 1360, when a peace was concluded. John, finding it impossible to raise his proposed ransom, returned to captivity, and died in London in 1364. The Black Prince was obliged in 1374 to conclude a truce for three years; and, for all his brilliant victories, Edward was at the last unsuccessful. Neither in Scotland nor in France did he realize his desires. Affairs at home were no less unsatisfactory in his last years, and public finance drifted hopelessly into ruin. He quarrelled with his parliaments, and saw public discontent sap loyalty, while he gave himself up to the influence of the rapacious Alice Perrers (his wife's lady-in-waiting), who became his mistress from 1366, and let the government slip into the hands of his fourth son, **John of Gaunt**. The Black Prince, who had headed a party opposed to his father's policy, died in 1376, and the king himself died almost alone and friendless the following year.

EDWARD IV (1442–83) king of England from 1461, the son of Richard, Duke of York, and Cicely Neville, daughter of the first Earl of Westmorland. Born at Rouen, he bore the title of Earl of March. On his father's defeat and death at Wakefield (30 December, 1460), he found himself head of a strong party. He at once set out from Gloucester, defeated the Lancastrians of **Henry VI** at Mortimer's Cross (2 February, 1461), lost in the person of **Warwick** the second battle of St Albans (17 February); but on the 26th of the same month, taking advantage of the reaction of the south, entered London in triumph as king. On 29 March, he secured the crown by the battle of Towton, near York. Queen **Margaret** kept up the struggle in the north, but her defeats at Hedgeley Moor and Hexham (1464) and the capture of Henry VI (1465) in the meantime crushed her hopes. The young Edward was handsome and frank in manners, and quickly became popular. The commons granted him the wool tax and tonnage and poundage for life. But he imperilled his popularity by his licentiousness; and his ill-advised marriage (1464) with Elizabeth Woodville displeased Warwick and many of his nobility, whose disaffection was increased by the honours heaped upon the queen's relations. Warwick won over the king's brother, the Duke of **Clarence**, and married him to his daughter Isabel. Meantime popular discontent culminated in insurrections in the north. Warwick crossed to France, and made friends with his ancient enemy, Queen Margaret, and cemented the alliance by marrying his daughter Ann to her son, Prince Edward. In September 1470 Warwick landed in England, and Edward, deserted on every side, fled to Flanders; six months later he landed at Ravenspur to meet Warwick. Clarence now came over to his side, and in the battle at Barnet, 14 April 1471, the 'Kingmaker' fell on the field of his defeat. Edward put an end to the war by the victory over Queen Margaret at Tewkesbury (4 May). He showed his savagery by the murder of Prince Edward and his vengeance upon the other captives. The night of his arrival in London Henry VI died in the Tower—of a broken heart, as was given out; and Edward used his power to extort money by forced loans. In 1478 he stained his name by the private execution of Clarence in the Tower and Edward's partisanship of Burgundy against France brought no glory. He died suddenly on 9 April 1483, worn out by his debaucheries. He had, however, instituted a programme of governmental reform which, in many senses, foreshadowed the work of the Tudors.

EDWARD V (1470–83) king of England in 1483, son of **Edward IV**, and one of the 'Princes in the Tower'. On the death of his father, his maternal uncle, Earl Rovers, set out with him from Ludlow for London. But Richard, Duke of Gloucester (the future **Richard III**), got possession of him at Northampton, brought him to the capital on 4 May 1483, and the same month was appointed Protector. In June his brother, the young Duke of York, also fell into Richard's hands. The two boys were removed to the Tower, and never more heard of. In 1674 some bones were discovered and re-interred as theirs in Westminster Abbey. There is at least no doubt that they were murdered.

EDWARD VI (1537–53) king of England and Ireland from 1547, son of **Henry VIII** and his third wife, **Jane Seymour**. Since Edward was only ten years old at his succession, the government was at first entrusted to a lord protector, the king's uncle, **Edward Seymour**,

Duke of Somerset, who attempted to resolve the economic, social and religious problems of the realm without resorting to the autocratic methods of Henry VIII. The publication of the first *Book of Common Prayer* in 1549 was an important step towards the establishment of uniform observance in the newly-reformed English church, but it was the immediate cause of the Western Rebellion in the south-west and of **Robert Ket**'s rebellion in East Anglia. Somerset's moderate religious policy pleased neither adherents of the old faith nor the more zealous Protestants, while his cautious approach towards popular discontent worried those who advocated a harder line. He was executed in 1552 and replaced by John Dudley, Earl of **Warwick** and Duke of Northumberland, who had achieved a considerable ascendancy over the precocious boy-king. A ferocious Treason Act (1549) had reversed the policy of Somerset while, in religious affairs, the more vigorous reformers were now given their head. A revised prayer book was produced and the Forty-Two Articles (1551), intended to give the English church a definitive creed, were confirmed by a second Act of Uniformity (1552). The king's health, never robust, deteriorated suddenly in 1553 and Northumberland made efforts to induce the dying boy to alter the succession in favour of his own daughter-in-law, Lady **Jane Grey**, to the exclusion of his Catholic half-sister, Mary Tudor (**Mary I**).

EDWARD VII (1841–1910) king of Great Britain and Ireland from 1901, eldest son (Albert Edward) of Queen **Victoria** and Prince **Albert**. Born in Buckingham Palace, he served a 60-year apprenticeship as Prince of Wales during his mother's long reign. He was educated privately, and also at Edinburgh University, Christ Church College, Oxford, and Trinity College, Cambridge. In 1860 he made the first tour of Canada and the USA undertaken by a royal prince; and in 1861, after his father's death, took his seat in the House of Lords as Duke of Cornwall. In 1863 he married Princess **Alexandra**, eldest daughter of King **Kristian IX** of Denmark. Considered too frivolous for responsibility by his mother, he cut a prominent figure in European café society, conspicuously devoted to a lifestyle of horse-racing, theatre-going, and yachting. He had several mistresses, and caused a scandal by being cited as a witness in a divorce suit in 1870. He succeeded to the throne in 1901. As king he restored vitality and flair to the monarchy, and endeavoured to promote international amity by visits to Continental capitals, preparing the way for the Entente Cordiale of 1904 with France and the Anglo-Russian agreement of 1907. He and Queen Alexandra had six children: Albert Victor, Duke of **Clarence** (1864–92); George, later King **George V** (1865–1936); Louise, Princess Royal (1867–1931); Victoria (1868–1935); Maud (1869–1938), who married King **Haakon VII** of Norway; and Alexander (born and died in 1871).

EDWARD VIII (1894–1972) king of Great Britain and Ireland (1936), eldest son of **George V**, he was born at White Lodge, Richmond, Surrey, and educated at Osborne, Dartmouth, and Magdalen College, Oxford. As Prince of Wales he was in the navy and (in World War I) the army, travelled much, and achieved considerable popularity. He succeeded his father, 20 January 1936, but abdicated 11 December on account of general disapprobation of his proposed marriage to Mrs Ernest Simpson. He was thereupon given the title of Duke of Windsor, and the marriage took place on 3 June 1937. From 1940 to 1945 he was governor of the Bahamas. See his *A King's Story* (1951). His wife, the Duchess of **Windsor**, was born Bessie Wallis Warfield at Blue Ridge Summit, Pennsylvania. In 1916 she married Lieutenant E W Spencer of the US Navy, but in 1927 the marriage was dissolved. The following year she married in London Ernest Simpson, an American-born Englishman. Well known in London Society in 1930, she met Edward the Prince of Wales at a country house party. In 1936, the year of the Prince's accession, she obtained a divorce in England, and the king subsequently made clear to **Stanley Baldwin** and his government his determination to marry her even if it meant giving up the throne. See her *The Heart has its Reasons* (1956).

EDWARD, HRH The Prince Edward Antony Richard Louis (1964–) British prince, third son of Queen **Elizabeth**. Educated at Gordonstoun School, Scotland, he then spent several months as a house tutor in New Zealand at Wanganui School. After graduating from Cambridge with a degree in history, he joined the Royal Marines in 1986 but left the following year and began a career in the theatre as a production assistant with **Andrew Lloyd Webber**'s Really Useful Theatre Company.

EDWARD THE ÆTHELING, 'Prince' (d.1057) English nobleman, son of **Edmund 'Ironside'** and nephew of the childless **Edward 'the Confessor'**. After Edmund's death in 1016, he was taken for safe keeping to Hungary and married a lady of the royal house, by whom he had a son, **Edgar the Ætheling**. When it became apparent that the ascetic Edward the Confessor would never have an heir, Edward the Ætheling was recognized as the proper heir to his throne. An embassy was sent to the Continent in 1054 to bring him back to England; but he died shortly after landing in England in 1057.

EDWARD THE BLACK PRINCE (1330–76) English nobleman, eldest son of **Edward III**, created Earl of Chester (1333), Duke of Cornwall (1337) and Prince of Wales (1343). In 1346, as a youth of 16, he commanded the right wing at the battle of Crécy, and is said to have won from his black armour his popular title—a title first cited in the 16th century. In 1355–56 he undertook two marauding expeditions in France, the second signalized by the great victory of Poitiers. In 1361 he married his cousin, Joan the 'Fair Maid of Kent' (1328–85), who bore him two sons, Edward (1365–70) and the future **Richard II**; in 1362 his father created him Prince of Aquitaine, and next year he departed to take possession of his principality. In 1367 he espoused the cause of **Pedro 'the Cruel'** of Castile and restored him to the throne, at Navarrete winning his third great victory and taking **Bertrand Du Guesclin** prisoner; in 1370, worn out by sickness, he mercilessly sacked Limoges. He returned to England in 1371, mortally ill, and took no further part in public life.

EDWARDES, George (1852–1915) English theatrical manager, born in Clee, Lincolnshire, the son of a customs officer. In 1881 he became business manager at the Savoy Theatre, leaving in 1885 to enter into partnership with John Hollinshead at the Gaiety; in 1886 he took over the sole management. In 1893 he built Daly's Theatre for **Augustin Daly**. He is known as the father of musical comedy, the form of which he standardized by his gift of foreseeing public taste and recognizing and developing talent. His many successes include *The Geisha*, *The Merry Widow*, *The Gaiety Girl* and *The Quaker Girl*.

EDWARDES, Sir Herbert Benjamin (1819–68) English soldier and colonial official. He entered the East India Company's army in 1840, and served as ADC to General **Gough** in the 1st Sikh War (1845–46) and as assistant to Sir **Henry Lawrence** in 1847. Commissioner of Peshawar (1853–59), he was active in the Mutiny (1857–58). Edwardesabad in North-west Frontier Province was named after him.

EDWARDES, Sir Michael (Owen) (1930–) South African-born British business executive, born in South Africa of a Welsh father. Educated at Grahamstown University, he joined the Chloride Group of companies in Africa in 1951. In 1966 he first worked in Britain, as commercial director and then as general manager of Chloride's smallest subsidiary, Alkaline Batteries. He proved his skills in 'turning round' an ailing company, by defining sound business targets and building a team of competent and enthusiastic executives to achieve them. In 1974 he was appointed chairman of the Chloride Group and, in 1977, was challenged to rescue British Leyland from commercial collapse. Many knowledgeable people considered the task to be impossible, particularly in view of BL's bad industrial relations record. But in five years Edwardes's strong leadership and expectations of excellence had pulled Britain's major motor manufacturer 'Back from the Brink' (the title of the book he wrote about the experience in 1983). From 1982 to 1988 he was non-executive chairman of Chloride.

EDWARDS, Amelia Ann Blandford (1831–92) English novelist and Egypytologist, born in London. She was the author of *My Brother's Wife* (1855), *Debenham's Vow* (1869) and *Lord Brackenbury* (1880). She was founder of the Egyptian Exploration Fund, and contributed papers on Egyptology to the principal European and American journals, and wrote *A Thousand Miles up the Nile* (1877), and *Pharaohs, Fellahs, and Explorers* (1891).

EDWARDS, Gareth Owen (1947–) Welsh rugby player, born in Gwaun-cae-Gurwen near Swansea. With **Barry John** he formed a wonderful half-back partnership, but he also played full-back or centre. He was first capped for Wales while in his teens, and was appointed captain before he was 21. He won 63 caps, including 10 'B' internationals.

EDWARDS, Sir George Robert (1908–) English aircraft designer, born in Higham's Park, Essex. He graduated in engineering from London University in 1935, and joined the design staff of Vickers-Armstrong at Weybridge, where he was experimental manager in World War II, becoming chief designer in 1945. Responsible for Viking, Valiant, Viscount and Vanguard aircraft, he was managing director and later chairman of the British Aircraft Corporation. He received the US Guggenheim Award and the Royal Aeronautical Society Gold Medal.

EDWARDS, Jonathan (1703–58) American philosopher and theologian, born in East Windsor, Connecticut, grandson of **Solomon Stoddard**. He was educated at Yale and succeeded his grandfather as minister of the Congregationalist Church at Northampton, Massachusetts (1727–50). Renowned for his powerful preaching and hardline Calvinism, he helped inspire the revivalist movement known as the 'Great Awakening'. He was dismissed in 1750 for his overzealous orthodoxy and became a missionary to the Housatonnuck Indians at Stockbridge, Massachusetts, and eventually in 1757 became president of the College of New Jersey (now Princeton University). He is regarded as the greatest theologian of American puritanism, his main doctrinal work being the *Careful and Strict Enquiry into the Modern Prevailing Notions of that Freedom of the Will* (1754).

EDWARDS, Jonathan (1745–1801) American theologian, born in Northampton, Massachusetts, son of **Jonathan Edwards** (1703–58). He graduated from New Jersey, and in 1769 became pastor at White Haven, Connecticut, in 1796 at Colebrook, Connecticut, and in 1799 president of the new college at Schenectady, New York. His works include *A Dissertation concerning Liberty and Necessity* (1797) and *On the Necessity of the Atonement* (1785).

EDWARDS, Robert Walter Dudley (1910–88) Irish historian, one of the founders of modern Irish historiography. Born in Dublin of an English father and Irish mother, he was a brilliant student at University College, Dublin and then at the Institute of Historical Research, University of London. In 1938, with T W Moody, he founded the authoritative journal, *Irish Historical Studies*. In 1945 he was appointed professor of modern Irish history at University College, Dublin (he retired in 1979). An outstanding teacher, his most important published work was *Church and State in Tudor Ireland* (1936).

EDWIN, St (c.585–633) king of Northumbria from 616. He was the son of Ælla, king of Deira, who died in 588, at which point Deira was seized by the king of Bernicia. Edwin was taken to safety at the court of King Rædwald of East Anglia; and eventually, in 616, supported by Rædwald, Edwin invaded Deira and killed Æthelfrith of Bernicia in a great battle on the banks of the river Idle. Edwin had thereby created for the first time a united Northumbrian kingdom, which he extended as far north as the Lothians in Scotland and as far west as Anglesey and the Isle of Man. With the death of Rædwald (c.625) he assumed overlordship of East Anglia, and was soon master of all England except Kent. A pagan, he asked for the hand of Princess Æthelburh, daughter of **Æthelbert**, king of Kent, who had been converted to Christianity by St **Augustine**, but was refused until he agreed to countenance Christianity. They married in 625, and Æthelburh took north with her a Roman chaplain, **Paulinus**, who converted Edwin and all his court to Christianity in 627. In 633, Northumbria was invaded by **Cadwallon** of Wales and **Penda** of Mercia, and Edwin was killed in battle near Hatfield Chase.

EGAN, Sir John Leopold (1939–) English industrial executive, born in Coventry. Educated at Imperial College, London, as a petroleum engineer, he spent five years in the oil industry before taking a degree at London Business School. In 1968 he entered the motor industry, first with General Motors, then with British Leyland and Massey Ferguson. In 1980 he became chairman and chief executive of the then ailing Jaguar company, and restored the company's high reputation in Britain and abroad.

EGAN, Pierce (1772–1849) English sporting writer, born in London. A London journalist, he was the author of many works, including *Boxiana; or Sketches of Antient and Modern Pugilism* (1812–13). He achieved fame with his description of the life of a 'man about town', *Life in London*, published in serial form in 1820 and as a book in 1821, with coloured illustrations by the brothers **Cruikshank**. In 1824 he launched a weekly sporting journal *Pierce Egan's Life in London*, incorporated into *Sporting Life* in 1859. His son, 'Pierce the Younger' (1814–80), was also a journalist and writer, and published dozens of 'cheap' novels.

EGAS MONIZ, António Caetano de Abreu Freire (1874–1955) Portuguese neurosurgeon and diplomat. Professor of neurology at Coimbra (1902) and Lisbon (1911–44), he developed prefrontal lobotomy for the relief of schizophrenia, and in 1949 shared the Nobel prize for physiology or medicine with **Walter Hess**. He was a deputy in the Portuguese parliament (1903–17), foreign minister (1918), and led the Portuguese delegation to the Paris Peace Conference.

EGBERT (d.839) king of the West Saxons, and first ruler of all the English. The son of Ealhmund of Kent, he was driven into exile by the powerful **Offa** of Mercia, and spent some years at the court of **Charlemagne**. In

802 he returned to England and was recognized as king of Wessex in opposition to Mercian influence. In 825 he finally ended the hegemony of Mercia by an overwhelming victory at the battle of Ellendun, near Swindon, and four years later he conquered Mercia itself, and the Northumbrians accepted his overlordship (829). For this he was hailed as *Bretwalda*, 'sole ruler of Britain'. But by 830 he had lost Mercia again. In his last years, Egbert had to repel incursions by Viking pirates, and in 839 he defeated an alliance of Cornish insurgents and Danish invaders at the battle of Hingston Down, near the river Tamar.

EGEDE, Hans (1686–1758) Norwegian missionary, known as the 'Apostle of Greenland'. A pastor at Vagen (1707–17), he learned to speak the language of the Inuit (Eskimo), and in 1721 set out with his family as the first missionary to Danish Greenland. He founded a permanent mission there (1721–36), and returned to Copenhagen where he founded a seminary for training missionaries to Greenland and was appointed bishop (1740). He wrote *Det gamle Grönlands nye Perlustration* (1729), and published the first book written in Inuit (1742). His son, Paul (1708–89), succeeded him as bishop, and translated the New Testament (1766), as well as a catechism (1756) and prayer book (1783).

EGERTON an English family including Earls and Dukes of Bridgewater, Earls of Ellesmere and their descendants.

EGERTON, Francis, 1st Earl of Ellesmere (1800–57) English statesman, second son of the 1st Duke of Sutherland, born in London, and educated at Eton and Christ Church College, Oxford, He was Irish secretary (1828–30) and secretary for war (1830). In 1833, on succeeding to the Bridgewater estates, he assumed the name of Egerton, and in 1846 was created Earl of Ellesmere. He translated *Faust* etc.

EGERTON, Francis, 3rd Duke of Bridgewater (1736–1803) English aristocrat known as the 'father of British inland navigation'. From 1759 he constructed, after the plans of **James Brindley**, the earliest canal in England, 42 miles long, uniting Worsley with Manchester and Runcorn on the Mersey above Liverpool, known as the Bridgewater Canal.

EGERTON, Francis Henry, 8th Earl of Bridgewater (1756–1829) son of John Egerton, bishop of Durham, clergyman and antiquarian. He was a prebendary of Durham, but lived in Paris for many years and kept his house and garden full of animals dressed up like manikins, because he was fond of shooting. He left £8000 to be paid to the author of the best treatise on the subject of God manifested in Creation, which was eventually awarded to eight authors of the 'Bridgewater Treatises'.

EGERTON, John, 1st Earl of Bridgewater (1579–1649) son of Sir **Thomas Egerton**. His induction as lord-lieutenant of Wales at Ludlow Castle (1634) provided the occasion for **Milton**'s *Comus*.

EGERTON, Sir Thomas, Baron Ellesmere and **Viscount Brackley** (1540–1617) English lawyer and statesman. Educated at Brasenose College, Oxford, and Lincoln's Inn, he was called to the bar in 1572. Acquiring a large practice in Chancery, he became solicitor-general in 1581, a confidant of Queen **Elizabeth** and **James VI and I**, a friend of **Francis Bacon** and **Essex**. He took part in the trial of **Mary, Queen of Scots**, (1586) and of Essex (1600–01), and became lord chancellor in 1603. In the struggle with Sir **Edward Coke** and the courts of common law, he maintained the supremacy of his own court. He wrote a *Privileges of Prerogative of the High Court of Chancery* (1641).

EGGE, Peter Andreas (1869–1959) Norwegian novelist, born in Trondheim. Of humble peasant stock and too poor to pursue his education, he was discovered by **Knut Hamsun**, who arranged for the publication of his first novel, *Common People* (1891). His first real success was with *The Heart* (1917), which is a serious and penetrating study of marriage between two dissimilar personalities, and *Hansine Solstad* (1926), a delicate, sympathetic description of a woman wrongfully accused of theft in her youth, whose supposed crime dogs her through life. Egge also wrote plays in which he followed **Ibsen** in creating drama from defects of character.

EGGLESTON, Edward (1837–1902) American writer and pastor, born in Vevay, Indiana. He was a Methodist minister in Minnesota, and editor of journals like *Little Corporal*, *National Sunday School Teacher*, and *Hearth and Home*. He also wrote several classic novels, including *The Hoosier Schoolmaster* (1871) and *The Faith Doctor* (1891).

EGIDIUS See **GILES, St**

EGILSSON, Sveinbjörn (1791–1852) Icelandic philologist and lexicographer, born in Innri-Njarðvík, the son of a farmer. He studied theology at Copenhagen University (1814–19), then returned to Iceland to teach classics at the Latin School at Bessastaðir (1819–46), becoming headmaster when it was moved to Reykjavík. He translated **Homer**'s *Odyssey* (1829–40) and *Iliad* (1855) into magnificent Icelandic prose, edited the Icelandic *Sturlunga Saga* (1817–20), and translated into Latin most of the *Legendary Sagas* (1825–37) and the *Snorra Edda* (1848–49). But his major achievement was a dictionary of skaldic poetry, *Lexicon poeticum antiquae linguae septentrionalis*, published after his death (1854–60).

EGINHARD See **EINHARD**

EGLINTON AND WINTON, Archibald William Montgomerie, 13th Earl of (1812–61) twice lord-lieutenant of Ireland. A well-known patron of the turf and field-sports, he is chiefly remembered for his splendid reproduction of a tournament at Eglinton Castle in 1839. Among the knights was **Louis Napoleon**.

EGMONT, Lamoral, Count of, Prince of Gavre (1522–68) Flemish statesman and soldier, born in the castle of La Hamaide, in Hainault. He accompanied the emperor **Charles V** to Algiers in 1541 and in all his later campaigns, distinguished himself at St Quentin (1557) and Gravelines (1558), for which he was made governor of Flanders and Artois. He now sided with the party in the Netherlands that opposed **Philip II**'s Catholic policy, and left the state council in 1565. He went on a special mission to Spain in 1565 to tell him of conditions in the Netherlands, and when insurrections took place, he broke with the Prince of Orange and the 'Beggars' League'. He seemed to have restored order and to have gained the confidence of the Duke of **Alva**, now (1567) lieutenant-general to the Netherlands; but suddenly he was seized, condemned to death, and beheaded in Brussels.

EHRENBERG, Christian Gottfried (1795–1876) German naturalist, born in Delitzsch in Prussian Saxony. Professor at Berlin from 1839, he travelled in Egypt, Syria, Arabia and Central Asia. His works on microscopic organisms founded a new branch of science, and he discovered that phosphorescence in the sea is caused by living organisms.

EHRENBURG, Ilya Grigorievich (1891–1967) Russian writer, born in Moscow. In 1908 he was imprisoned for revolutionary activities, but escaped to Paris, where he worked as a journalist until 1917, when he returned to Russia but went back to Paris as a correspondent. Among his best works are *The Extraordinary Adventures of Julio Jurenito* (1921), a satire on the aftermath of World War I, *The Fall of Paris* (1941) and *The Storm* (1947), both novels about World War II, and *The Thaw* (1954), a novel about the de-Stalinization period. He published his memoirs *People, Years, Life* in six volumes from 1960 to 1966.

EHRLICH, Paul (1854–1915) German bacteriologist, born of Jewish family in Strehlen (now Strzelin), Silesia. A pioneer in haematology and chemotherapy, he synthesized Salvarsan as a treatment for syphilis, and propounded the side-chain theory in immunology. He was joint winner, with **Ilya Mechnikov**, of the 1908 Nobel prize for physiology or medicine.

EICHENDORFF, Joseph Freiherr von (1788–1857) German poet, novelist and critic, born near Ratibor. He is best remembered for his romantic lyrics. His novels include *Aus dem Leben eines Taugenichts* (1826) and *Das Marmorbild* (1826).

EICHHORN, Johann Gottfried (1752–1827) German theologian and biblical scholar, born in Dörrenzimmern in Franconia. In 1775 he became professor of oriental languages at Jena, in 1788 at Göttingen. His Introductions to the Old and New Testaments (1780–1814) were the first attempt to apply the ordinary methods of literary criticism to Scripture. He derived each of the four gospels from one original Greek gospel.

EICHMANN, Karl Adolf (1906–62) Austrian Nazi war criminal, born in Solingen. A fanatical anti-Semite, he became a member of the SS and organized anti-Jewish activities, particularly their deportation to concentration camps. Captured by US forces in 1945, he escaped from prison some months later, having kept his identity hidden, and in 1950 reached Argentina. He was traced by Israeli agents and in 1960, seized, taken to Israel, condemned for 'crimes against humanity' and executed.

EIFFEL, (Alexandre) Gustave (1832–1923) French engineer, born in Dijon, designer of many notable bridges and viaducts. The Eiffel Tower, 985 feet high, was erected in 1887–89 on the Champ-de-Mars in Paris at a cost of £260000 for the World Exhibition of 1889, and was the highest building in the world until 1930. In 1893 he was condemned to two years' imprisonment and fined for breach of trust in connection with the abortive French Panama Canal scheme.

EIGEN, Manfred (1917–) West German physical chemist, born in Bochum. Educated in Göttingen, he directed the Max Planck Institute for Physical Chemistry there from 1964. He developed methods for the study of very fast chemical reactions, and for this work shared the Nobel prize for chemistry in 1967, with **Ronald Norrish** and Sir **George Porter**.

EIJKMAN, Christiaan (1858–1930) Dutch physician and pathologist. He investigated beri-beri in the Dutch East Indies, and was the first to produce a dietary deficiency disease experimentally and to propose the concept of 'essential food factors', later called vitamins. He shared the 1929 Nobel prize for physiology or medicine with Sir **Frederick Hopkins**.

EINAUDI, Luigi (1874–1961) Italian statesman. He was professor of public finance at Turin (1902–49), senator (1915–45), president of Italy (1948–55).

EINEM, Gottfried von (1918–) Austrian composer, born in Bern, Switzerland. His most successful works have been for the stage, including several ballets and the operas *Dantons Tod* (1947) and *Der Besuch der alten Dame* (1971). He has also written orchestral, choral and chamber music, concertos and many songs.

EINHARD, or **Eginhard** (c.770–840) Frankish historian, born in East Franconia. He was sent to the court of **Charlemagne**, where he became a pupil of **Alcuin** and a favourite of the emperor, and of his successor **Louis I, 'the Pious'**. For years lay abbot of various monasteries, he ultimately retired to Mühlheim. His *Life of Charlemagne* (c.820) is the great biographical work of the middle ages. His *Annales Francorum* embraces the period 741–829; his *Epistolae* number 62.

EINSTEIN, Albert (1879–1955) German-Swiss-American mathematical physicist, who ranks with **Galilei** and **Newton** as one of the great conceptual revisors of man's understanding of the universe. Born in Ulm, Bavaria, of Jewish parents, he was educated at Munich, Aarau and Zürich. He took Swiss nationality in 1901, was appointed examiner at the Swiss Patent Office (1902–05), and began to publish original papers on the theoretical aspects of problems in physics. He achieved world fame by his special and general theories of relativity (1905 and 1916), and won the 1921 Nobel prize for physics for his work. The special theory provided a new system of mechanics which accommodated **James Clerk Maxwell**'s electromagnetic field theory, as well as the hitherto inexplicable results of the **Michelson-Morley** experiments on the speed of light. He showed that in the case of rapid relative motion involving velocities approaching the speed of light, puzzling phenomena such as decreased size and mass are to be expected. His general theory accounted for the slow rotation of the elliptical path of the planet Mercury, which Newtonian gravitational theory failed to do. In 1909 a special professorship was created for him at Zürich, in 1911 he became professor at Prague, in 1912 he returned to Zürich and from 1914 to 1933 was director of the Kaiser Wilhelm Physical Institute in Berlin. By 1930 his best work was complete. After **Hitler**'s rise to power he left Germany and from 1934 lectured at Princeton, USA, becoming an American citizen and professor at Princeton in 1940. In September 1939 he wrote to President **Roosevelt** warning him of the possibility that Germany would try to make an atomic bomb, thus helping to initiate the Allied attempt (the Manhattan Project). After the war he urged international control of atomic weapons and protested against the proceedings of the un-American Activites Senate Subcommittee which had arraigned many scientists. He spent the rest of his life trying, by means of his unified field theory (1950), to establish a merger between quantum theory and his general theory of relativity, thus bringing subatomic phenomena and large-scale physical phenomena under one set of determinate laws. His attempt was not successful. His works include *About Zionism* (1930) and *Why War* (1933, with **Sigmund Freud**).

EINSTEIN, Alfred (1880–1952) German musicologist, born in Munich. In 1933 he fled the Nazi régime and went to live in Florence and London. He collaborated in several well-known musical reference books, including *Eaglefield's Dictionary of Modern Music*, but is perhaps best remembered for his work on **Mozart**, especially the revision of Köchel's catalogue. He was a cousin of the physicist **Albert Einstein**. His posthumous *Essays on Music* were published in 1958.

EINTHOVEN, Willem (1860–1927) Dutch physiologist, born in Semarang, Dutch East Indies. He became professor of physiology at Leiden in 1886. In 1903 he invented the string galvanometer, causing great advances in electrocardiography, and was awarded the 1924 Nobel prize for physiology or medicine.

EISENHOWER, Dwight David (1890–1969) American general and 34th US president, born in Denison, Texas, of immigrant stock originating in the Rhineland. He graduated from West Point Military Academy in 1915. Taking the war college course in 1928 and gaining experience under the secretary for war, by 1939 he had become chief military assistant to General **MacArthur** in the Philippines. On the war's outbreak he obtained leave to return to troop duty in the US. Carefully groomed for the responsibility by General **George C Marshall**, in 1942 he assumed command of allied forces mustered for the amphibious descent on French North Africa. Without experience of high command, but perceptive and assimilative, he rapidly learned to translate strategic theory into terms of practical action. At the same time he exhibited a rare genius for smoothly co-ordinating the activities of an interallied staff, perhaps his most valuable contribution to the war effort. His successful conduct of the North African venture, plus the preponderant American element in the forces earmarked for 'Operation Overlord', led to his selection as supreme commander for the 1944 cross-Channel invasion of the Continental mainland; which he resolutely launched despite unnervingly capricious weather conditions. With an acute appreciation of the psychology of his US forces, his strategical preference for the drive to cross the Rhine was for a shoulder-to-shoulder advance in line; a choice of method that found some justification in the failure of the 'left-hook' stroke at Arnhem. But his reluctance to push on beyond the Elbe and occupy Berlin, and his quiescence in the hasty dismantling of the Anglo-American armies, resulted in Russia's emergence as the leading military power in Europe. Among many honours, he received an honorary OM in 1945, and in 1948 became for a while president of Columbia University. With the establishment of NATO in 1950 he was made supreme commander of the combined land forces, but in 1952 the popularity which he had gained in Europe swept him to nomination and ultimate victory in the presidential elections. Standing as a Republican, he won by a large majority despite the even balance of parties in the house, and was re-elected in 1956. During his presidency the US government was preoccupied with foreign policy and the campaign against Communism, and undercurrents of extremism and excess of zeal often placed the president in an invidious position, but his political inexperience was balanced by sincerity, integrity and a flair for conciliation. During recent years his presidency has been subject to a favourable reassessment, now seen as maintaining stablility during a difficult period.

EISENSTAEDT, Alfred (1898–) German-born American photojournalist, born in Dirschau (now Tczew, Poland). He moved with his family to Berlin in 1906, and served in the German army in World War I. He started freelancing as a photojournalist in the 1920s, and emigrated to the USA in 1935, where he became one of the original photographers working on *Life* (1936–72). Voted Photographer of the Year in 1951, his worldwide assignments and telling photo essays made him one of the outstanding practitioners of the century. His publications include *Witness to Our Time* (1966), *The Eye of Eisenstaedt* (1969) and *Photojournalism* (1971).

EISENSTEIN, Sergi Mikhailovich (1898–1948) Russian film director, born in Riga. He served in the Red Army during the Russian Revolution (1916–18), and after training in theatrical scene painting was appointed to make propaganda films on the history of the revolution with *The Battleship Potemkin* (1925) on the 1905 mutiny, and *Ten Days That Shook The World* (1928), on the October Revolution. His substitution of the group or crowd for the traditional hero, and his consummate skill in cutting and recutting to achieve mounting impressionistic effects as in the macabre Odessa steps sequence of *The Battleship Potemkin* greatly influenced film art. Later he made the patriotic epic *Alexander Nevski* (1938), *The Magic Seed* (1941) and the masterpiece *Ivan the Terrible* (1944) with its sequel *The Boyars Plot*, the last named being banned in the Soviet Union for many years.

EISLER, Hanns (1898–1962) German composer, born in Leipzig. He studied under **Schoenberg** at the Vienna Conservatory, 1919–23. A committed Marxist, he wrote political songs, choruses and theatre music, often in collaboration with **Brecht**. From 1933 he worked in Paris, London and Copenhagen, and moved to Hollywood in 1938, teaching and writing film music. Denounced in the **McCarthy** anti-Communist trials, he returned to Europe in 1948. He settled in East Germany in 1952, composing popular songs and organizing workers' choirs. He wrote about 600 songs and choruses, music for over 40 films and for nearly 40 plays. In his orchestral and chamber music he often adopted sophisticated techniques including the 12-note method.

EISNER, Kurt (1867–1919) German journalist and politician, born in Berlin, leader of the Bavarian revolution of 1918–19. First president of the Bavarian republic, he was assassinated in Munich.

EISNER, Will (William Erwin) (1917–) American comicbook artist and writer, born in New York. After studying at the Art Students League he became staff artist on the *New York American*. In 1936 he submitted a strip, *The Flame*, to a new comicbook, *Wow*, and in 1937 he set up the first 'shop' for mass-producing strips for *Wags*, in which he developed *The Flame* into the long-running weekly serial *Hawks of the Seas*. In 1940 he produced the first comicbook insert for Sunday newspapers, starring his own character, *The Spirit*.

EKEBERG, Anders Gustaf (1767–1813) Swedish chemist and mineralogist. Professor of chemistry at Uppsala, he discovered the element tantalum in 1802, choosing the name because of the tantalizing work involved in finding something to react with it.

EKELÖF, (Bengt) Gunnar (1907–68) Swedish poet. A leader of the post-war modernists, he is considered one of the most significant Swedish poets of this century. Much influenced by the French Symbolists, he published his first book of poetry, *Sent på jorden* (Late Arrival on Earth), in 1932, followed by *Dedikation* (Dedication, 1934), *Sorgen och stjärnan* (Sorrow and the Star, 1936) and *Färjesång* (Ferry Song), 1941. *En Mölna-elegi* (1960), which is concerned with the nature of time, was translated into English (A Mölna Elegy, 1979), as were his *Selected poems* (1966) and *Guide to the Underworld* (1967).

EKELUND, Vilhelm (1880–1949) Swedish poet and essayist. A symbolist and early modernist, his works include poetry such as *Stella Maris* (1906), and volumes of essays inspired by **Nietzsche**, including *Classical Ideal* (1909).

EKHOF, Konrad (1720–78) German actor and playwright, born in Hamburg. He founded an experimental dramatic academy in Schwerin in 1753, and later opened a theatrical school in Hamburg, where he lived for most of his career. A leading member successively of the famous Schönemann and Ackermann companies and of the national theatre at Hamburg, he did much to raise the standard of acting in Germany. From 1774 he was co-director of the Court Theatre at Gotha.

EKMAN, Vagn Walfrid (1874–1954) Swedish oceanographer, born in Stockholm, the son of an oceanographer. Educated at Uppsala University, he worked at the International Laboratory for Oceanographic Research in Oslo (1902–08) before returning to Sweden, where he was appointed professor of mathematical physics at Lund (1910–39). He explained the variation in direction of ocean currents with depth. His work originated from an observation made by the Norwegian explorer **Nansen** who noted that the path of drifting arctic sea ice did not follow the prevailing wind direction, but deviated 45 degrees to the right. Ekman explained this as an effect of the Earth's rotation (Coriolis force). He also showed that the general motion of near-surface water is the result of interaction between surface wind force, the Coriolis force, and frictional effects between different water layers. The resulting variation of water velocity with depth is known as the Ekman spiral.

EL MALAKH, Kamal (1918–) Egyptian archaeologist. In 1954 he recovered from a stone-slabbed pit in the shadow of the Great Pyramid a dismantled cedarwood rowing boat, probably one of the funeral vessels of King **Cheops** (d.2566 BC). Reconstructed, it measures 43.6m long with a beam of 5.9m.

ELAGABALUS See **HELIOGABALUS**

ELCANO See **CANO, Juan Sebastian de**

ELDER, Sir Thomas (1818–97) Scottish-born Australian pastoralist and entrepreneur, born in Kirkcaldy. He emigrated to Adelaide, South Australia, in 1854 where he joined his brother, Alexander, in the firm of Elder and Company. They financed copper mines in South Australia. With the proceeds and in partnership with **Robert Barr Smith**, who was to marry Thomas's sister Joanna, Thomas founded the firm of Elder, Smith & Co in 1863. This grew into one of the world's largest wool-broking firms, which built up extensive pastoral holdings to source the supply of wool, stretching into Western Australia and Queensland. He brought in camels to provide efficient transport in the outback, and Afghans to manage them. His stud of camels was invaluable, especially for some of the early expeditions into the 'centre' made by **Warburton, Ross, Giles** and Lewis, all of whose expeditions were financed by Elder. He was appointed GCMG in 1887. The company which he helped establish is perpetuated in the international brewing and resources group Elders IXL.

ELDH, Carl (1873–1954) Swedish sculptor. He studied in Paris (1896–1903) and his early work was much influenced by **Rodin**. His mature work after his return to Sweden is characterized by an idealized social realism. Among his public works are the **Strindberg** and **Branting** monuments in Stockholm, the young **Linnaeus** in Uppsala and **Engelbrekt** in Arboga. He produced many portrait busts of the figures of his day.

ELDON, John Scott, 1st Earl of (1751–1838) English lawyer and politician, born in Newcastle. He became MP (1782), solicitor-general (1788), attorney-general (1793), and lord chancellor (1801). Opposed to reform and religious liberty, he was noted in the education world for his judgment in the Leeds Grammar School case of 1805. Application had been made to use part of the endowment for teaching modern subjects, including French and German. Eldon held that governors would have to seek a change of the statutes to do so, as a grammar school was 'for reading grammatically the learned languages', in the words of Dr **Samuel Johnson**. He did not, however, as is commonly alleged, discourage the governors from seeking the proper power to extend the curriculum.

ELDRIDGE, Roy (David) known as **Little Jazz** (1911–89) American trumpet player, born in Pittsburgh, Pennsylvania. His originality and technical facility made him a jazz virtuoso to compare with **Louis Armstrong** and **Dizzy Gillespie** (on whom he was an early influence). He learned to play the drums as a child, before progressing to bugle and then trumpet. During the 1920s he worked with a succession of travelling shows, a carnival band and various lesser-known jazz groups until 1930, when he moved to New York. A passionate improviser, able to play with ease in the ultra-high register, he was in demand as a featured soloist with top bands of the 1930s, such as McKinney's Cotton Pickers and the Teddy Hill and **Fletcher Henderson** Orchestras. He continued to perform until suffering a stroke in 1980.

ELEANOR OF AQUITAINE (c.1122–1204) queen of France and of England, daughter of the Duke of Aquitaine, whom she succeeded as Duchess of Aquitaine. In 1137 she married Prince Louis, who became King **Louis VII** of France a month later. She led her own troops on the Second Crusade (1147–49), dressed as an Amazonian warrior. In 1152 the marriage was annulled on the ground of consanguineity, and in the same year Eleanor married Henry Plantaganet, Count of Anjou, who became **Henry II** of England in 1154. As a result of Henry's infidelities she supported their sons, Richard and John, in a rebellion against him, and was imprisoned (1174–89). She acted as regent for her son **Richard I** during his crusading campaigns abroad (1189–94), and raised the ransom for his release. In 1200 she led the army that crushed a rebellion in Anjou against her second son, King **John**.

ELEANOR OF CASTILE (c.1245–1290) daughter of **Ferdinand III** of Castile. In 1254 she married the future **Edward I** of England. She accompanied him to the Crusades (1270–73), and is said to have saved his life by sucking the poison from a wound. She died in Harby, Nottinghamshire, and the 'Eleanor Crosses' at Northampton, Geddington and Waltham Cross are survivors of the nine erected by Edward at the halting places of her cortège. The last stopping place was Charing Cross, where a replica now stands.

ELEANOR OF PROVENCE (1223–91) daughter of Raymond Berengar IV, count of Provence. In 1236 she married **Henry III** of England. In the Barons' War of 1264 she raised an army of mercenaries in France to support her husband, but her invasion fleet was wrecked. After the accession of her son, **Edward I**, in 1272 she retired to a convent.

ELEONORA OF ARBOREA (c.1350–1404) Sardinian ruler, regarded as the national heroine of Sardinia, daughter of a district chieftain (*giudice*). In 1383 she defeated an incursion from Aragon and became regent of Arborea for her infant son, Frederick. In 1395 she introduced a humanitarian code of laws, *Carta di Logu*, which was far ahead of its time. Her statue stands in the Piazza Eleonora in Oristano. She gave special protection to hawks and falcons, and Eleonora's Falcon is named after her.

ELGAR, Sir Edward (1857–1934) English composer, born in Broadheath near Worcester. The son of an organist and music dealer, he was, apart from violin lessons, self-taught. In his youth, as well as composing, he worked as an orchestral violinist and became conductor of the Worcester Glee Club and the County Asylum Band, and organist of St George's Roman Catholic Church, Worcester, in succession to his father. He married in 1889 and settled two years later in Malvern, where he devoted himself to composition and to winning gradual acceptance, particularly among provincial choral societies. The *Enigma Variations* (1899) and the oratorio *The Dream of Gerontius* (1900) won recognition in Germany and consolidated his position as the leading figure in English music. After the Elgar Festival, held in London in 1904, he was knighted. His further works included the oratorios *The Apostles* and *The Kingdom*, two symphonies and concertos for violin and cello as well as incidental music and, during World War I, topical occasional music. After his wife's death in 1920, he composed little, leaving an opera and a symphony incomplete at his death. From 1924 he was master of the King's Musick. He was the first figure of outstanding genius produced by the English musical renaissance, and his superb command of the orchestra and his mastery of late nineteenth-century musical styles within his own personal idiom were extremely influential in bringing English music back into the world's regard.

ELGIN, Earls of Scottish peers of the Bruce family.

ELGIN, James Bruce, 8th Earl of Elgin and 12th Earl of Kincardine (1811–63) son of the 7th Earl of **Elgin**, born in London. As governor of Jamaica (1842–46) and as governor-general of Canada (1847–54), he displayed great administrative abilities. While on his way to China in 1857, as plenipotentiary, he heard at Singapore of the Indian mutiny, and diverted the Chinese expedition thither—thus delaying his own mission which, after some military operations and diplomacy, issued in the treaty of Tientsin (1858). He also negotiated a treaty with Japan, and on his return home became postmaster-general. In 1860 he was again in China to enforce the treaty, and in 1861 became governor-general of India. He died at Dharmsala in the Punjab.

ELGIN, Thomas Bruce, 7th Earl of Elgin and 11th Earl of Kincardine (1766–1841) British diplomat and art connoisseur. While ambassador to the Ottoman sultan (1799–1803) he became interested in the decorated sculptures on the ruined Parthenon at Athens, and, because they were in danger of wilful damage and destruction, arranged for some of them to be transported to England. This action brought criticism and accusation of vandalism, but the earl was vindicated by a government committee and the Elgin Marbles were purchased for the nation in 1816 and ultimately placed in the British museum.

ELGIN, Victor Alexander Bruce, 9th Earl of Elgin and 13th Earl of Kincardine (1849–1917) son of the 8th Earl of **Elgin**, born in Montreal, he was educated at Eton and Balliol College, Oxford. A Liberal, he was viceroy of India from 1893 to 1898, and from 1905 to 1908 colonial secretary.

ELHUYAR, Don Fausto d' (1755–1833) Spanish chemist. In 1783, with his brother Don Juan José, he extracted metallic wolfram from wolframite. He later became director of mines, first in Mexico, then in Spain.

ELIA, Charles See **LAMB**

ELIADE, Mirca (1907–86) Romanian historian and philosopher of comparative religion, born in Bucharest. A student of Indian philosophy and Sanskrit at Calcutta University (1928–31) before becoming a lecturer in the history of religion and metaphysics at Bucharest from 1933 to 1939, he served in the diplomatic service during World War II, and later taught at the Sorbonne (1946–48) and Chicago University (1957–85). A pioneer in the systematic study of world religions, he published numerous books and papers, incuding *The Myth of the Eternal Return* (1949), *Patterns in Comparative Religion* (1958), *Yoga:* Immortality and Freedom (1958), *The Sacred and the Profane* (1959), *A History of Religious Ideas, I–III* (1978–85), and two volumes of autobiography (1982, 1988) covering the years 1907–60. He was editor-in-chief of *The Encyclopaedia of Religion* (1987), and wrote a number of novels, including *The Forbidden Forest* (1955).

ELIGIUS, St See **ELOI**

ELIJAH, Greek **Elias** (fl.c.900 BC.) Old Testament figure, the greatest of the prophets of Israel. He lived during the reigns of **Ahab** and Ahaziah, and fiercely attacked the cult of Baal among the Israelites.

ELIOT, Charles William (1834–1926) American educationist, mathematician and chemist, born in Boston. As president of Harvard College (1869–1909) he carried out radical reforms of its faculties and teaching methods and turned it into a full university. During his tenure it doubled in strength, and the old undergraduate curriculum was abandoned for an optional system of studies. He also organized a graduate school of arts and sciences, and helped to establish Radcliffe College. He published two manuals of chemistry and several books on education, and was editor of the *Harvard Classics*.

ELIOT, George, pen-name of **Mary Ann** or **Marian Evans** (1819–80) English novelist, born on Arbury Farm in Astley. In her father, Robert Evans, a Warwickshire land agent, a man of strong character, were seen many of the traits transferred by his daughter to Adam Bede and Caleb Garth. She lost her mother, whom she loved devotedly, in 1836, and soon afterwards took entire charge of the household. Masters came from Coventry to teach her German, Italian and music—of the last she was passionately fond throughout her life. She was also an immense reader. In 1841 her father moved to Coventry, and there she met Charles Bray, a writer on the philosophy of necessity from the phrenological standpoint, and his brother-in-law, Charles Hennell, who had published in 1838 a rationalistic *Inquiry concerning the Origin of Christianity*. Under their influence she rejected her earlier evangelical Christianity. In 1844 she took on the laborious task of translating **Strauss**'s *Leben Jesu* (published in 1846). After her father's death in 1849 she travelled on the Continent with Mr and Mrs Bray; returning to England in 1850 she began to write for the *Westminster Review*. She became assistant editor in 1851, and the centre of a literary circle, two of whose members were **Herbert Spencer** and **George Henry Lewes**. She translated **Feuerbach**'s *Essence of Christianity* (1854), the only book that bore her real name. Gradually her intimacy with Lewes grew, and in 1854 she formed a liaison with him which lasted until his death in 1878. In July 1854 she went abroad with him, staying three months in Weimar, where he was preparing for his *Life of Goethe*. After a longer stay in Berlin, they returned and lived first in Dover, then in East Sheen, then in Richmond. In 1856 she attempted her first story, 'The Sad Fortunes of the Rev. Amos Barton', the beginning of the *Scenes of Clerical Life*. It came out in *Blackwood's Magazine* in 1857, and at once showed that a new author of great power had risen. 'Mr Gilfil's Love Story' and 'Janet's Repentance' followed quickly. Her first novel, *Adam Bede* (1859) had an enormous success. *The Mill on the Floss* (1860), *Silas Marner* (1861), *Romola* (1863) and *Felix Holt* (1866) appeared next in succession. Her first poem, *The Spanish Gypsy* (1868), was followed next year by *Agatha*, *The Legend of Jubal* and *Armgart*; and in 1871–72 appeared *Middlemarch*, generally considered her greatest work. After that came *Daniel Deronda* (1876), her last great novel. After the death of Lewes, she was coaxed to write *Impressions of Theophrastus Such* (1879), a volume of somewhat miscellaneous essays. She fell in love again with a banker 20 years her junior, John Walter Cross (died 1924), a friend of long standing whom she married in May 1880. She died a few months later, and was buried in Highgate Cemetery, in the grave next to that of Lewes. As a novelist, George Eliot will probably always stand among the greatest of the English school; her pictures of farmers, tradesmen, and the lower middle class, generally of the Midlands, are hardly surpassed in English literature.

ELIOT, Sir John (1592–1632) English statesman, born in Port Eliot, near St Germans, Cornwall. He entered parliament in 1614, was knighted in 1618 and in 1619 was appointed vice-admiral of Devon. Formerly a follower of **Buckingham**, he broke with him in 1625 and was largely instrumental in securing his impeachment. In 1628 Eliot denounced arbitrary taxation and helped to force the Petition of Right from **Charles I**. After further protests against the king, he was sent, with eight others, to the Tower where he was kept in confinement until his death, from consumption.

ELIOT, John (1604–90) English missionary, known as the 'Apostle to the Indians', born in Widford, Hertfordshire. He graduated at Cambridge, took orders, left England on religious grounds and settled in Roxbury, Massachusetts, where he served as pastor. In 1646 he began to preach to the Indians at Nonantum nearby, establishing his native converts, who numbered 3600 in 1674, in 14 self-governing settlements nearby. But the numbers diminished after the war with a native King Philip (1675), and at the hands of the English. He was the author of *A Primer or Catechism, in the Massachusetts Indian Language* (1653). He also translated the Bible into the Indian language (1661–63), which was the first Bible printed in America. His book *The Christian Commonwealth* (1659) was suppressed for its republican sentiments.

ELIOT, Sir Thomas See **ELYOT**

ELIOT, T S (Thomas Stearns) (1888–1965) American-born British poet, critic and dramatist, born in St Louis, Missouri. After four years at Harvard, 1906–10 (where the chief influence upon his development was that of **Irving Babbitt** with his 'selective' humanism and his resistance to modern trends) he spent a year in Paris, attending lectures and improving his command of the French language. He returned to Harvard to study philosophy for three years. He had distinguished teachers, such as **Josiah Royce** and **George Santayana**, and, for a time, **Bertrand Russell**. A travelling scholarship from Harvard took him to Merton College, Oxford, for a year, where he worked on a doctoral dissertation on **F H Bradley**, and read **Plato** and **Aristotle** under H H Joachim. Persuaded by **Ezra Pound**, to whom he had shown his poems, he remained in England where he lived from then on (1911), taking up naturalization in 1927. After teaching for a term in High Wycombe, and for a year at Highgate Junior School, he worked for eight years in Lloyds Bank before becoming a director of the publishing firm of Faber. The enthusiastic support of Pound led to the publication of Eliot's first volume of verse, *Prufrock and Other Observations* (1917). He was introduced by Bertrand Russell into the Bloomsbury Circle, where the quality of his work was immediately recognized. His next two small volumes, *Ara vos prec* (1920) and the more important *The Waste Land* (1922), were published by **Leonard** and **Virginia Woolf** at the Hogarth Press. *The Hollow Men* which followed in 1925 gave more excuse for regarding Eliot at that point as a cynical defeatist. *The Waste Land* had appeared in the first number of *The Criterion*, a quarterly review which Eliot edited from 1923 to 1939. *The Criterion* aimed at impartiality in presenting opposed political philosophies and is indispensable for a study of ideas, political and religious, betweeen the wars, as well as for the literary developments, both here and abroad during that period. In 1927, the year in which he became a British subject, Eliot was baptized and confirmed, having been raised as a Unitarian. The publication of a volume of essays *For Lancelot Andrewes* (1928) gave his first public statement of his adherence to the Anglo-Catholic movement within the Church of England. *Ash Wednesday* (1930) is the first fruit of this new sacramental attitude. The religious plays *The Rock* (1934) and *Murder in the Cathedral* (1935) which followed sealed his reputation as the poet who had revived the verse play in the interests of Catholic devotion. His later dramas, *The Cocktail Party* (1950), *The Family Reunion* (1939), *The Confidential Clerk* (1954) and *The Elder Statesman* (1958), were to aim at being West End successes rather than sacred plays in church precincts, but Catholic doctrine inspired all these plays, sometimes to the embarrassment of critics and audience alike. Before this incursion into the theatre world he produced his greatest work, *Four Quartets* (1944), which, despite its obscurity, is one of the greatest philosophical poems in the language. The most rewarding is probably the last, *Little Gidding*. Eliot's critical work consists of literary criticism, such as *The Sacred Wood* (1920, on Jacobean dramatists), the admirable *Homage to Dryden* (1924), *The Use of Poetry and the Use of Criticism* (1933), *Elizabethan Essays* (1934) and *On Poetry and Poets* (1957). When writing or lecturing on literature generally he could be very provocative, as in his *Modern Education and the Classics* (1934), where he said that the Classics were to be studied not for their own sake but as a buttress for the Faith; and in *After Strange Gods* (1936), where he tries to stretch some great writers on the Procrustean bed of 'Christian Sensibility'. In social criticisms, as in *The Idea of a Christian Society* (1939) and *Notes Towards the Definition of Culture*, he is hierarchal and undemocratic. The new poetry, as announced by Ezra Pound, **T E Hulme** and Eliot, was to be related to modern life and expressed in modern idiom, preferably in free verse. Rhetoric and romantic clichés were to be avoided. In his late essay 'Milton II', in *On Poetry and Poets*, he confessed that he and his friends had insisted over much on these ideas and this was a sort of recantation for his abuse of Milton. But critics today have no doubt of the salutary effect of their crusade and of Eliot's poetry as having justified it. In 1948 he was awarded the Nobel prize for literature.

ELIOTT, George Augustus See **HEATHFIELD**

ELIZABETH, St (1207–31) Hungarian princess, daughter of Andreas II of Hungary, born in Sáros, Patak. At the age of four she was betrothed to Louis IV, landgrave of Thuringia, and educated at his father's court, the Wartburg, near Eisenach. At fourteen she was married, and a boy and two girls were the fruit of their union. Louis, who admired her for her long prayers and ceaseless alms-giving, died as a crusader at Otranto in 1227, whereupon Elizabeth was deprived of her regency by her husband's brother, and exiled on the plea that she wasted state treasures by her charities. After severe privations, she was received into the monastery of Kitzingen by the abbess, her aunt. Later she retired to a cottage near the castle of Marburg and lived in cloistered simplicity for the remainder of her days. She was canonized by Pope **Gregory IX** in 1235.

ELIZABETH (1596–1662) queen of Bohemia, eldest daughter of **James VI and I** of Scotland and England and **Anne of Denmark**, she married **Frederick V**, elector palatine, in 1613. Intelligent and cultured, she enlivened the court at Heidelberg by her presence and, with Frederick's championship of the Protestant cause and his brief, unhappy winter as king of Bohemia, Elizabeth was known variously as 'the Winter queen' or 'the Queen of Hearts' and became a potent symbol of the Protestant cause in Europe. Driven from Prague and deprived of the palatinate by Maximilian of Bavaria, the couple lived in exile in the Hague with their numerous children, continually beset by financial difficulties. Frederick died in 1632, but Elizabeth outlived him by 30 years. Her son, Charles Louis, was restored to the palatinate in 1648, but his mother remained in Holland. She died in London in 1662 while on a visit to her nephew, the newly-restored **Charles II** of England.

ELIZABETH I (1533–1603) queen of England and Ireland from 1558, daughter of **Henry VIII** and his second wife, **Anne Boleyn**. When her father married his third wife, **Jane Seymour** in 1536, Elizabeth and her elder half-sister Mary Tudor (the future **Mary I**) were declared illegitimate by parliament in favour of Jane Seymour's son, the future **Edward VI**. Her childhood was precarious but well educated, and unlike her sister she was brought up in the Protestant faith. In 1549, during the reign of Edward VI, she rejected the advances of **Thomas Seymour**, Lord High Admiral of England, who was subsequently executed for treason. On Edward's death she sided with her half-sister Mary against Lady **Jane Grey** and the Earl of **Warwick** (Northumberland), but her identification with Protestantism aroused the suspicions of her Catholic sister, and she was imprisoned in the Tower. Her accession to the throne in 1588 on Mary I's death was greeted with general approval as an earnest advocate of religious tolerance after the ferocious persecutions of the preceding reigns. Under the able guidance of Sir **William Cecil** (later Lord Burleigh) as secretary of state, Mary's Catholic legislation was repealed, and the church of England fully established (1559–63). Cecil also gave support to the Reformation in Scotland, where **Mary, Queen of Scots** had returned to Scotland in 1561 to face conflict with the Calvinist reformers led by **John Knox**. Imprisoned and forced to abdicate in 1567, in 1568 Mary escaped to England, where she was placed in confinement and soon became a focus for Catholic resistance to Elizabeth. The Northern rebellion of 1569 was followed by the **Ridolfo** plot the following year; and in 1570 the papal bull, *Regnans in Excelsis*, pronounced Elizabeth's excommunication and absolved her Catholic subjects from allegiance to her. Government retribution against English Catholics, at first restrained, became more repressive in the 1580s. Several plots against the queen were exposed, and the connivance of Mary in yet another plot in 1586 (the **Babington** conspiracy) led to her execution at Fotheringay Castle in 1587. The harsher policy against Roman Catholics, England's support for the Dutch rebellion against Spain, and the licensed piracy of men like Sir **John Hawkins** and Sir **Francis Drake** against Spanish possessions in the New World, all combined to provoke an attempted Spanish invasion in 1588. The Great Armada launched by **Philip II** of Spain reached the English Channel, only to be dispersed by storms and English harassment, and limped back to Spain after suffering considerable losses. For the remainder of her reign, Elizabeth continued her policy of strengthening Protestant allies and dividing her enemies. She allowed marriage negotiations with various foreign suitors but with no real intention of getting married, or of settling the line of succession; but with the death of Mary, Queen of Scots, she was content to know that the heir-apparent, **James VI** of Scotland, was a Protestant. She indulged in romances with court favourites like Robert Dudley, Earl of **Leicester**, and later with Robert Devereux, Earl of **Essex**, until his rebelliousness led to his execution in 1601. Her fiscal policies caused growing resentment, with escalating taxation to meet the costs of foreign military expeditions, and famine in the 1590s brought severe economic depression and social unrest, only partly alleviated by the Poor Law of 1597 which charged parishes with providing for the needy. England's vaunted sea-power stimulated voyages of discovery, with Drake circumnavigating the known world in 1577 and Sir **Walter Raleigh** mounting a number of expeditions to the North American coast in the 1580s, but England's only real Elizabethan colony was Ireland, where opportunities for English settlers to enrich themselves at the expense of the native Irish were now exploited more ruthlessly than ever before and provoked a serious rebellion under **Hugh O'Neill**, Earl of Tyrone, in 1597. At Elizabeth's death in March, 1603, the Tudor dynasty came to an end and the throne passed peacefully to the Stuart James VI of Scotland as James I of England. Her long reign had coincided with the emergence of England as a world power and the flowering of the English Renaissance; and the legend of the 'Virgin Queen', assiduously promoted by the queen herself and her court poets and playwrights, outlived her to play a crucial part in shaping the English national consciousness.

ELIZABETH II (1926–) queen of Great Britain and Ireland, formerly Princess Elizabeth Alexandra Mary, born in London. She was proclaimed Elizabeth II on the death of her father, **George VI**, on 6 February 1952, and crowned on 2 June 1953. In December 1952 were announced the styles of the royal title as applicable to the Commonwealth countries, in all of which the queen is accepted as head of the Commonwealth; she is queen of the United Kingdom, Canada, Australia, New Zealand, and of several other more recently independent countries. Her husband was created Duke of Edinburgh on the eve of their wedding (20 November 1947), and styled Prince Philip in 1957. They have three sons, Prince **Charles** Philip Arthur George, Prince **Andrew** Albert Christian Edward, and Prince **Edward** Anthony Richard Louis and a daughter, Princess **Anne** Elizabeth Alice Louise.

ELIZABETH, originally **Lady Elizabeth Bowes-Lyon** (1900–) Queen Mother, and queen-consort of Great Britain. She was born at St Paul's Walden Bury, Hertfordshire, on 4 August, her father becoming 14th Earl of Strathmore in 1904. Much of her childhood was spent at Glamis Castle in Scotland, where she helped the nursing staff in World War I. In 1920 she met the Duke of York, second son of **George V**; they were married in April 1923. Princess Elizabeth (later Queen **Elizabeth II**) was born in 1926 and Princess **Margaret** in 1930. The Duchess accompanied her husband on a long tour of Australasia in 1927 and, after he came to the throne as King **George VI** in 1936, she scored striking personal success in royal visits to Paris (1938) and to Canada and the USA (1939). She was with the king when Buckingham Palace was bombed in 1940, travelling with him to visit heavily damaged towns throughout the war. In 1947 she became the only queen-consort to tour South Africa. After George VI's death (1952), the Queen Mother continued to undertake public duties, flying thousands of miles each year and becoming a widely-loved figure. She never retired and, from 1953 onwards, found a new interest in restoring the Castle of Mey, on the Pentland Firth, as her favourite Scottish home. In 1978 she became lord warden of the Cinque Ports, the first woman to hold the office.

ELIZABETH, Madame (1764–94) French princess, sister of **Louis XVI**, whose fate she shared heroically, like him being guillotined.

ELIZABETH OF BAVARIA See **FRANZ JOSEPH**

ELIZABETH OF PARMA See **FARNESE, Elizabeth**

ELIZABETH OF RUMANIA See **CARMEN SYLVA**

ELIZABETH PETROVNA (1709–62) empress of Russia from 1741, younger daughter of **Peter I, the Great** and **Catherine I**. Passed over for the throne on earlier occasions, she came to power in 1741 in a military coup which ousted the infant Ivan VI (1740–64). An easy-going, genial character, she created a brilliant court and superintended a renaissance of Russian arts; she founded the University of Moscow (1755) and the Academy of Fine Arts in St Petersburg (1758), and built the Winter Palace in St Petersburg (now Leningrad). She was a patron of the Russian scientist and poet **Mikhail Lomonosov**. She made war with Sweden (1741–43) which came to a successful conclusion with the Treaty of Abö, and plunged Russia into the Seven Years' War (1756–63), motivated by a dislike of **Frederick II, the Great**. She was succeeded by her nephew **Peter III**, whom she had designated as her successor in 1742.

ELKIN, Stanley Lawrence (1930–) American author and academic, born in Brooklyn, New York. He was educated at the University of Illinois where he took a PhD. While his stories in *Criers and Kibitzers, Kibitzers and Criers* (1966) have their champions, and *The Living End* (1979)—three stories about heaven and hell—is his most widely read book, he is pre-eminently a novelist. *Boswell* (1964), about a professional wrestler obsessed with death and greatness, marked his début and was followed by *A Bad Man* (1967), *The Dick Gibson Show* (1971) and *The Franchiser* (1976), all fixated with modern America. *George Mills* (1982) and *The Magic Kingdom* (1985) are set, respectively, in Sultanic Turkey and contemporary St Louis.

ELKINGTON, George Richards (1801–65) English inventor and manufacturer. Based in Birmingham, from 1832 he introduced electroplating in conjunction with his cousin, Henry Elkington (1810–52).

ELLENBOROUGH, Edward Law, 1st Earl of (1790–1871) English politician, eldest son of Baron Ellenborough (1750–1818), lord chief-justice from 1802. He became a Tory MP (1813) and held office under several administrations, becoming governor-general of India (1841). Parliament approved his Afghan policy in 1843, but his treatment of the civil servants, and his policy of conciliating the natives by apparent sanction of idolatry, led to his recall in 1844. Created Viscount Southam and Earl of Ellenborough, he was First Lord of the Admiralty under **Peel** in 1846. In 1858 he was minister for India, but the publication of a dispatch in which he rebuked Viscount **Canning** forced him to resign. In 1863 he expressed strong sympathies with Poland, and in 1864 advocated British intervention in favour of Denmark.

ELLERY, William (1727–1820) American politician, born in Newport, Rhode Island, sat in the congress of 1776, and was a signatory of the Declaration of Independence.

ELLESMERE See **EGERTON**

ELLET, Charles (1810–62) American civil engineer, born in Bucks County, Pennsylvania. Called the 'Brunel of America', he was educated in France, built the first wire suspension bridges in America, including one over the Schuylkill River at Fairmount (1842) and another over the Ohio River at Wheeling (1849). He also constructed the James River and Kanawha Canal, and having advocated and demonstrated the use of ram-boats, built and commanded a fleet of them on the Mississippi, capturing Memphis (1862), but was killed in action.

ELLICOTT, Charles John (1819–1905) English prelate and scholar. He was professor of divinity at King's College, London, (1858), Hulsean lecturer (1859) and professor (1860) of divinity at Cambridge, dean of Exeter (1861) and bishop of Gloucester and Bristol (1863–97): he was bishop of Gloucester alone from 1897. Chairman for eleven years of the New Testament Revision Committee, he published commentaries on Galatians, Ephesians, etc, and works on the Sabbath, scriptures and scepticism.

ELLINGTON, Duke (Edward Kennedy) (1899–1974) American pianist, composer and bandleader, born in Washington, DC. He received his only formal musical education as a child through elementary piano lessons, but he was influenced while young by church music and burlesque theatre. After forming bands to play at parties and dances he led his first regular group, the Washingtonians, in New York in 1924. During the following three years, his band increased in size from six to ten or more players and a long residency at the Cotton Club, Harlem, with radio and recording contracts, placed him in the forefront of orchestral jazz, a position he maintained throughout his career. Until 1931 his music was largely written and performed as the accompaniment for dance shows; but he began to emerge as the most important of jazz composers, producing about 2000 works, often written specifically for performance by his outstanding instrumentalists. Many pieces, such as 'Mood Indigo' and 'Sophisticated Lady', became part of the standard jazz repertoire. Duke Ellington, often assisted by composer-arranger Billy Strayhorn, wrote several extended works and suites—notably 'Such Sweet Thunder'—which are unusual in jazz. He also wrote and performed film music, the most important of which was for *Anatomy of a Murder* (1959) and *Paris Blues* (1961). From the 1930s, his orchestras were usually composed of around 16 musicians.

ELLIOT, Jean or **Jane** (1727–1805) Scottish lyricist, the author of 'The Flowers of the Forest', the daughter of Sir Gilbert Elliot of Minto House, Teviotdale. She lived in Edinburgh (1756–1804), but died at the family seat, or at Monteviot. Her eldest brother, Sir Gilbert Elliot (1722–77), was himself a song-writer; whilst John (d.1808), the third brother, was a distinguished admiral.

ELLIOT, Walter (1888–1958) Scottish politician. Conservative MP for Lanark (1918–1923), Kelvingrove (1924–45) and Scottish Universities (1946–49), he was secretary of state for Scotland (1936–38) and minister of health (1938–40). Also known as a writer and broadcaster, he published *Toryism and the Twentieth Century* (1927). His wife, Baroness Katharine Elliot of Harwood (1903–) was created Scotland's first life peeress in October 1958.

ELLIOTSON, John (1791–1868) English physician, born in London. In 1831 he became professor at London University, and helped to establish University College Hospital. His conversion to mesmerism (1837) cost him his professorship in 1838, but hardly injured his large practice. One of the first to use the stethoscope, he experimented on the action of drugs, encouraged clinical study, and founded the Phrenological Society.

ELLIOTT, Denholm (1922–) English actor, born in London. He studied at RADA prior to service in the RAF during World War II when he spent three years in a prisoner of war camp. He made his stage début at Amersham in *The Drunkard* (1945) and his London début the following year in *The Guinea Pig*. *Venus Observed* (1950) won him the Clarence Derwent Award, whilst his New York début in *Ring Round the Moon* (1950) received the Donaldson Award. Following his film début in *Dear Mr. Prohack* (1949) he played breezy juveniles and heroic servicemen in films like *The Cruel Sea* (1953) and *They Who Dare* (1954). *Nothing But the Best* (1964) launched a second career as a distinguished character star illuminating a gallery of rogues, bounders and life's losers—sometimes seedy—in films like *Alfie* (1966), *Saint Jack* (1979) and *September* (1987). A prolific performer in all media, and an inveterate scene-stealer, he won British Film Awards for *Trading Places* (1983), *A Private Function* (1984) and *Defence of the Realm* (1985).

ELLIOTT, Ebenezer (1781–1849) English industrialist, radical and poet, known as the 'Corn Law Rhymer', born in Rotherham. He turned to poetry while working in his father's iron foundry, published several volumes, but made a prosperous living as a master-founder in Sheffield. He is chiefly remembered for his denunciations of social evils, especially the 'bread tax' (corn-laws); his *Corn-Law Rhymes* was first published in 1831. He also wrote *The Village Patriarch*, and *Love*, and a political exhortation, *Battle Song*.

ELLIOTT, Grace Dalrymple (c.1758–1823) Scottish courtesan, the daughter of an Edinburgh advocate, Hew Dalrymple. In 1771 she married Sir John Elliott, MD (1736–86), who divorced her in 1774. She was the mistress successively or simultaneously of Lord Valentia, Lord Cholmondley, the Prince of Wales (the future **George IV**), Charles Windham, **George Selwyn**, Philippe Égalité (Duke of **Orléans**), and many others. She died at Ville d'Avray near Sèvres, leaving an interesting but untrustworthy *Journal of My Life during the Revolution*, published in 1859 by her granddaughter.

ELLIOTT, Herbert James (1938–) Australian athlete, born in Perth. Winner of the gold medal in the 1500 metres at the 1960 Olympics in Rome, his time of 3.35.6 for that event was unbeaten for 7 years. He was never beaten on level terms over a mile or 1500 metres, and he ran the sub-4-minute mile 17 times. He was noted for the rigour and severity of his training schedule.

ELLIOTT, John Dorman (1941–) Australian businessman, born in Melbourne, Victoria, and educated at Melbourne University. He was a management consultant with the McKinsey organization for six years and in 1972, after extensive research, bought a stake in the jam manufacturing company of Henry Jones (IXL) Limited. A series of mergers and takeovers followed, first with Elder, Smith & Co and then with the Melbourne-based 'Fosters' company, Carlton and United Brewers. The resultant group, Elders IXL, is now organized into four divisions—brewing, resources, pastoral, and finance. Managing director from 1981, and chairman and chief executive from 1985, Elliott holds a substantial interest in the group. He was treasurer and is now president of the Liberal party of Australia.

ELLIS, originally **Sharpe, Alexander John** (1814–90) English philologist. Educated at Shrewsbury, Eton and Trinity College, Cambridge, he wrote much on mathematical, musical and philological questions, and did more than any other scholar to advance the scientific study of phonetics, of early English pronunciation, and of existing English dialects. His major work was *Early English Pronunciation* (1869–89).

ELLIS, George (1753–1815) British satirist and poet, born in Grenada, West Indies, the son of a planter. He won early popularity with his *Poetical Tales by Sir Gregory Gander* (1778), and contributed satires on **Pitt** and others to the *Rolliad*, though later he was co-founder with **George Canning** of the Tory *Anti-Jacobin*. A friend of Sir **Walter Scott** he edited *Specimens of Early English Poets* (1790) and *Specimens of Early English Romances in Metre* (1805).

ELLIS, Sir Henry (1777–1869) English librarian and antiquary. He was principal librarian at the British Museum from 1827 to 1856. His works include *Introduction to Domesday Book* (1833), *Original Letters Illustrative of English History* (1824–46), and an edition of Brand's *Antiquities* (1813).

ELLIS, Henry Havelock (1859–1939) English physician and writer on sex, born in Croydon, the son of a sea captain. He travelled widely in Australia and South America before studying medicine at St Thomas's Hospital, London. In 1891 he married Edith Lees and throughout his life had a number of female followers, notably **Olive Schreiner**. His interest in human biology and his own personal experiences led him to compile his seven-volume *Studies in the Psychology of Sex* (1897–1928, revised ed 1936), the first detached treatment of the subject unmarred by any guilt feelings, which caused tremendous controversy, and was banned in Britain. A brilliant literary expositor, he founded the 'Mermaid' series of Elizabethan and Jacobean dramatists and wrote *My Life* (1940).

ELLIS, Ruth, née **Neilson** (1926–55) convicted murderer, born in Rhyl, Wales. A night-club hostess, in a jealous rage she repeatedly shot her former lover, David Blakely, a racing-car driver, outside a Hampstead pub on 10 April 1955. The case achieved notoriety as a 'crime passionnel'—Blakely was trying to extricate himself from their tempestuous, often violent, relationship at the time of his murder. Ellis was the last woman to receive the death penalty in Britain, and was hanged on 13 July 1955.

ELLIS, Thomas Edward (1859–99) Welsh politician, born near Bala, Merionethshire. Educated at New College, Oxford, he was elected Liberal MP for Merionethshire in 1886 and became chief Liberal whip in 1894. He worked hard for Welsh education and culture and argued for Welsh self-government. His early death cut short a career which could have made him a major influence in national as well as Welsh Liberal politics.

ELLIS, Walter Scott (c.1932–) convicted Scottish thief. He first came to public attention when he was tried in October 1961 for the murder of John Walkenshaw, a Glasgow taxi driver, who had been shot in the head in Tormusk Road, Castlemilk on 23 July. The evidence against Ellis included glass splinters in his shoe, which were thought to have been planted there. Ellis had taken a taxi home that night, but took a route which did not include the location of the murder. Fingerprints were discovered in the taxi which were not Ellis's. He was found not guilty. Taxi-drivers jeered outside the courtroom. In the mid 1960s he was charged with and convicted of house-breaking. A subsequent charge in 1965 of writing threatening letters to the prosecutor and the procurator fiscal who were in attendance at the house-breaking trial led to a verdict of not guilty. In July 1966 Ellis was charged with armed bank robbery. After a long trial, he was found guilty and was sentenced to 21 years' imprisonment. In total, 19 convictions preceded this one.

ELLIS, William (1794–1872) English missionary to the South Sea Islands, born in London. His wife's illness obliged him to return home in 1825, after which he became secretary to the London Missionary Society. In 1838 he published a history of Madagascar, and after 1853 he made four visits to the island. His works included *Madagascar Revisited* (1867) and *The Martyr Church of Madagascar* (1870).

ELLIS, William Webb (1805–72) English sportsman and reputedly the inventor of rugby football. According to a rather doubtful tradition, he was a pupil at Rugby School in 1823 when he broke the rules by picking up and running with the ball during a game of association football, thus inspiring the new game of rugby.

ELLISON, Ralph Waldo (1914–) American novelist, born in Oklahoma City, Oklahoma. Bookish as well as musical, he studied music at Tuskagee Institute and served during World War II in the US Merchant Marine. He met **Richard Wright** in 1937, through whom he became aware of social and racial injustice, and who encouraged him to write. *Invisible Man* (1952), his only novel, is the quest of a nameless black man, travelling from South to North, in search of a personal and racial identity. Allusive but highly original and ingenious, it had a seminal influence on other black writers and won the National Book award. He was Albert Schweitzer professor in the humanities at New York University (1970–79). He has also published two books of essays, *Shadow and the Act* (1964) and *Going to the Territory* (1986).

ELLISTON, Robert William (1774–1831) English actor, born in London. In 1791 he ran away and made his début on the stage at Bath. In 1796 he appeared at the Haymarket and Covent Garden; in 1804–09 and 1812–15 he was a member of the Drury Lane company; and in 1819 he became lessee and manager of the theatre, from which in 1826 he retired a bankrupt. He afterwards played in the Surrey Theatre; but dissipation shattered his health.

ELLMANN, Richard (1918–87) American biographer and academic, born in Detroit, Michigan. He graduated from Yale University and after the war he lived in Dublin for a year, where he wrote his first book, *Yeats; the Man and the Mask* (1948). Some ten years later came his masterful biography of **James Joyce**, now accepted as one of the pinnacles of 20th-century biography, as much for its elegant composition as its astute judgment and erudition. A professor at Northwestern University, Illinois, until 1968, he moved to Oxford in 1970 as Goldsmiths' professor of English literature, where he remained till his death. His biography of **Oscar Wilde** (1987), a 20-year labour of love, was published posthumously to universal acclaim. Selected essays were published under the title, *a long the riverrun* in 1988.

ELLSWORTH, Lincoln (1880–1951) American explorer, born in Chicago, the son of a millionaire financier. He was the first person to fly over both the North Pole (in the airship *Norge* with **Umberto Nobile** and **Roald Amundsen** in 1926) and the South Pole (in 1935). In his Antarctic explorations (1935 and 1939), he claimed over a million square kilometres of territory for the USA (Ellsworth Land). He led an expedition to the Andes in 1924, helped survey the route for the Canadian transcontinental railway, and in 1931 financed Sir **George Hubert Wilkins'** transarctic submarine expedition in the *Nautilus*.

ELLWOOD, Thomas (1639–1713) English Quaker, born in Crowell in Oxfordshire. At the age of 20 he was converted to Quakerism. He befriended **Milton** in 1662, and in 1665 hired a cottage in Chalfont St Giles, so that Milton could escape the plague in London. Milton gave him the manuscript of *Paradise Lost* to read; Ellwood's criticisms inspired Milton to write *Paradise Regained*.

ELMAN, Mischa (1891–1967) Russian-born American violinist, born in Talnoye in the Ukraine. A child prodigy, his débuts were in Berlin (1904), London (1905) and New York (1908). He settled in the USA in 1911 and became an American citizen in 1923.

ELMS, Lauris Margaret (1931–) Australian operatic and lieder singer, born in Melbourne, Victoria. She studied in Paris and made her début in 1957 at Covent Garden in **Verdi**'s *Un Ballo in Maschera*, and became principal resident artist there. She toured Australia with **Joan Sutherland** in 1965, and appeared at the royal opening of the Sydney Opera House in 1973. She has appeared with all leading Australian companies, and is renowned for her Azucena in Verdi's *Il Trovatore*. She has broadcast frequently and gives regular lieder recitals with pianist Geoffrey Parsons. She has made a number of acclaimed recordings including *Peter Grimes* under the composer **Benjamin Britten**.

ELMSLEY, Peter (1773–1825) English classical scholar, known for his editions of **Euripides**, **Sophocles**, and other classical writers. From 1768 he was incumbent of Little Horkesley near Colchester. In 1823 he was appointed principal of St Alban's Hall, Oxford, and Camden professor of ancient history.

ELOI, or **Eligius, St** (588–658) bishop of Noyon and apostle of Flanders. He was originally a goldsmith, and so became patron of smiths.

ELPHINSTONE, George Keith, Viscount Keith (1746–1823) Scottish naval officer, born in Elphinstone Tower, Stirling. He entered the navy in 1761 and fought in the American War of Indpendence (1775–83). In the French revolutionary wars (1792–1800) he helped capture Toulon. Promoted rear admiral, he commanded the expedition that captured Cape Town (1795) and Ceylon (1796). He helped to quell the Nore mutiny in 1797, and took Malta and Genoa (1800). He landed **Abercromby**'s army at Aboukir Bay (1801). As commander of the Channel fleet (1812–15), he arranged **Napoleon**'s transfer to St Helena.

ELPHINSTONE, Mountstuart (1779–1859) Scottish colonial administrator and historian, 11th Lord Elphinstone. He entered the Bengal civil service in 1795, served with distinction on **Wellesley**'s staff (1803) at the battle of Assaye, and was appointed resident at Nagpur. In 1808 he was sent as the first British envoy to Kabul; and as resident from 1810 at Poona both ended the Mahratta war of 1817 and organized the newly-acquired territory. He was governor-general of Bombay (1819–27), where he founded the system of administration, and did much to advance state education in India. He returned to Britain in 1829, and, declining the governor-generalship of India, lived in comparative retirement until his death at Limpsfield, Surrey. He wrote a *History of India* (1841) and an incomplete *Rise of British Power in the East* (published in 1887).

ELPHINSTONE, William (1431–1514) Scottish churchman and statesman, born in Glasgow. He was ordained priest, spent five years in France, and lectured on law at Paris and Orleans. He returned to Scotland, was appointed bishop of Ross (1481) and Aberdeen (1488). For four months before the death of **James III** (1488) he was chancellor. Under **James IV** he was ambassador to France (1491), and keeper of the privy seal from 1492. It was chiefly through his influence that the first printing-press—that of **Walter Chepman** and Andrew Myllar—was established in Scotland. The University of Aberdeen (King's College) was founded by him in 1494. Additions to the cathedral and a stone bridge over the Dee were also due to him. The fatal battle of Flodden broke his spirit, and he died in Edinburgh not long after. His *Breviarium Aberdonense* was printed by Chepman and Myllar in 1509–10.

ELSHEIMER, Adam (1578–1610) German painter, born in Frankfurt. He worked in Venice after 1598 and in Rome after 1600. Basing his style on a close study of **Tintoretto** and other Italian masters, he excelled in the portrayal of atmosphere and effects of light, and exerted a profound influence on the development of German landscape painting.

ELSSLER, Therese (1808–78) and **Fanny** (1810–84), Austrian sisters and celebrated dancers, born in Vienna. Of the two, the younger, Fanny, was the more fêted, dancing her way through more than 25 years of successful world touring, first in Europe and from 1840 to 1842 in the USA, the only major Romantic ballerina to go there. As well as joining her sister on stage as a performer, Therese was one of the few female choreographers of the time. Fanny retired 1851; and Therese in 1850 married Prince Adalbert of Prussia, nephew of **Frederick William III**.

ELSTER, Julius (1854–1920) German physicist. He collaborated with **Hans Friedrich Geitel** in producing the first photoelectric cell and photometer and a Tesla transformer. Among other achievements, they determined in 1899 the charge on raindrops from thunderclouds, showed that lead in itself is not radioactive, and that radioactive substances producing ionization cause the conductivity of the atmosphere.

ELSTRACKE, Renold (c.1590–1630) Belgian engraver, born probably in Hasselt. One of the earliest engravers in England, he worked chiefly for booksellers, and his engravings, including portraits of the kings of England, **Mary, Queen of Scots**, etc now have great rarity value.

ELTON, Charles Sutherland (1900–) English ecologist born in Liverpool. He studied at Liverpool College and New College, Oxford, and spent most of his career there (1936–67). His four Arctic expeditions in the 1920s and his use of trappers' records for fur-bearing animals led to his classic books on animal ecology; and his talents were turned to reduction of food loss in World War II through his studies of rodent ecology. His work on animal communities led to recognition of the ability of many animals to counter environmental disadvantage by change of habitats, and to use of the concepts of 'food chain' and 'niche'. His books include *Animal Ecology* (1927), *Animal Ecology and Evolution* (1930) and *The Pattern of Animal Communities* (1966).

ELTON, Oliver (1861–1945) English literary historian, professor at Manchester (1890–1900) and Liverpool (1900–26). He is best known for his *Survey of English Literature* (6 vols, 1912–28), and a critical study of *The Augustan Ages* (1899).

ÉLUARD, Paul, pseud of **Eugène Grindal** (1895–1952) French poet, born in Saint-Denis, and founder with **André Breton** and **Louis Aragon** of the Surrealist movement. His early poetry showed this influence, as in *Le Devoir et l'inquiétude* (1917), *Capitale de la douleur* (1926) and *La Rose publique* (1934), but in 1938 he broke with the movement and adopted a more militant tone. During World War II he was active in the Resistance and joined the Communist party in 1942, circulating his poetry secretly (*Poésie et vérité*, 1942, and *Au rendez-vous allemande*, 1944). His post-war poetry was more lyrical and personal, especially his last volume, *Le Phénix*

ELVEHJEM, Conrad Arnold (1901–62) American biochemist, born in McFarland, Wisconsin. He studied and spent his entire career at Wisconsin University, ultimately as president from 1958 to 1962. In 1937 he showed that nicotinic acid cured two related deficiency diseases, canine blacktongue and human pellagra; it is now known as vitamin B6. He also showed that certain elements are essential in animal nutrition at trace levels, including copper, cobalt, and zinc.

ELWIN, Whitwell (1816–1900) rector of Booton, Norfolk. He was editor of the *Quarterly Review* (1853–60), and of the standard edition of **Pope**'s works (completed by **Courthope**).

ELYOT, Sir Thomas (c.1490–1546) English scholar and diplomat, born in Wiltshire, son of a jurist. Educated at Oxford and the Middle Temple, in 1523 he became clerk of the privy council. In 1531–32, as ambassador to the emperor **Charles V**, he visited the Low Countries and Germany, having orders to procure the arrest of **Tyndale**. His chief work, *The Boke Named the Gouernour* (1531), is the earliest English treatise on moral philosophy. He also wrote a medical handbook, based on classical sources, *The Castel of Helth* (1538), and compiled the first English *Dictionary* (1538).

ELYTIS, Odysseus, pseud of **Odysseus Alepoudelis** (1911–) Greek poet, born in Heraklion, Crete. Educated at Athens University and at the Sorbonne, Paris, he has worked in broadcasting and as a critic of art and literature. His pseudonym is said to combine the three most prevalent themes in his work: Greece, hope and freedom. Deeply influenced by the surrealists, both French and Greek, his career as a poet began in the 1930s. His early poems exude a love of Greece, sun and life but after war experience in Albania a natural *joie de vivre* is set against violence and the imminence of death. His greatest achievement is *To axion esti* (1959, trans *The Axion Esti*, 1974), a long optimistic poem which took 14 years to write. In 1979 he was awarded the Nobel prize for literature.

ELZEVIR a Dutch family of printers at Leiden, Amsterdam and elsewhere, who between 1592 and 1681 issued some 1600 beautiful editions of Latin, French and Italian classics—many of them bibliographical prizes. The founder of the family, Louis (1540–1617), was born in Louvain, and settled in Leiden. Five of his sons carried on the business—Matthias, Louis, Aegidius (Giles), Jodocus (Joost) and Bonaventura; and Abraham and Isaac, sons of Matthias, were also notable. A Daniel, another Louis, another Abraham, and Peter, all maintained the traditions of the house.

EMANUEL I, also **Manuel 'the Fortunate'** (1469–1521) king of Portugal, succeeded John II in 1495. His reign, marred only by persecution of the Jews, was the golden age of Portugal. He prepared the code of laws which bears his name, and made his court a centre of chivalry, art and science. **Vasco da Gama**'s voyage round the Cape, **Cabral**'s discovery of Brazil and the expeditions under **Albuquerque** and others, encouraged by Emanuel, did much to make Portugal the first naval power of Europe and the centre of commerce.

EMECHETA, (Florence Onye) Buchi (1944–) British novelist, born near Lagos, Nigeria. She was educated at the Methodist Girls' High School, Lagos, and the University of London, and has worked as a teacher, librarian and social worker. She came to England with her student husband in 1962 and has since lived in London with her five children. Writing of marriage as a battle of the sexes, her novels are powerful social documents, graphic in their depiction of man's inhumanity to woman (she separated from her husband). Relevant titles are *In the Ditch* (1972), *Second-Class Citizen* (1974), *The Bride Price* (1976), *The Slave Girl* (1977) and *The Joys of Motherhood* (1979).

EMERSON, Ralph Waldo (1803–82) American poet and essayist, born in Boston of a long line of ministers. He graduated at Harvard in 1821, and after teaching at different places, became in 1829 pastor of the Second Church (Unitarian) in Boston, and married his first wife, Ellen Louisa Tucker (d.1832). In that year he preached views on the Lord's Supper which were disapproved by the majority of his congregation; this led him finally to resign his pulpit. In 1833 he went to Europe, and visited **Carlyle** at Craigenputtock, next year beginning that 38 years' correspondence which shows the two men with all their characteristics, different as optimist and pessimist, yet with many profound sympathies. In 1834 he removed to Concord. In 1835 he married his second wife, Lydia (Lidian) Jackson (1802–92). In 1836 he published a prose rhapsody entitled *Nature*, which, like his earlier poems, was read by few, and understood by fewer still, but which contains the germs of many of his later essays and poems. It was followed by 'The American Scholar', an oration delivered at Harvard University. These two publications, the first in the series of his collected works, strike the keynote of his philosophical, poetical and moral teachings. The 'address before the Divinity Class, Cambridge, 1838', which follows them, defined his position in, or out of, the church in which he had been a minister. A plea for the individual consciousness (as against all historical creeds, bibles, churches) for the soul of each man as the supreme judge in spiritual matters, it produced a great sensation, especially among the Unitarians, and much controversy followed in which Emerson took no part. In 1849 he revisited England to lecture on *Representative Men* (published in 1850). His *English Traits* appeared in 1856, *The Conduct of Life* in 1860, *Society and Solitude* in 1870, *Letters and Social Aims* in 1876. The idealist or transcendentalist in philosophy, the rationalist in religion, the bold advocate of spiritual independence, of intuition as a divine guidance, of instinct as a heaven-born impulse, of individualism in its fullest extent, making each life a kind of theocratic ego-ism—this is the Emerson of his larger utterances. For him nature was a sphinx, covered with hieroglyphics, for which the spirit of man is to find the key.

EMETT, Rowland (1906–) English cartoonist and designer of eccentric mechanical displays, born in London. He studied art at Birmingham College and worked in a local commercial studio until 1939. A draughtsman during World War II, he helped develop the jet engine. After his earliest joke drawings for *Punch* (1939) he evolved a unique and fantastic style depicting a quaint, Victorian world of his own, culminating in Nellie the steam engine of the Far Tottering and Oyster Creek Railway. His cartoons came alive when he built a replica of his railway for the Festival of Britain (1951). Many working models followed, including the famous Guinness Clock.

EMIN PASHA, originally **Eduard Schnitzer** (1840–92) German doctor and explorer, born of Jewish parents at Neisse. He studied medicine at Breslau and Berlin, practised at Scutari (Albania), where he adopted the Moslem faith, and after 1876, as Emin Effendi, was in the Egyptian service, becoming bey and pasha. General **Gordon** appointed him chief medical officer of the Equatorial Province, and in 1878 made him governor of the province. A skilful linguist, he added enormously to the knowledge of African languages, made important surveys and wrote valuable geographical papers, and sent to Europe rich collections of plants and animals. Isolated by enemies, he was 'rescued' by **H M Stanley**'s expedition in 1889, accompanied Stanley to Zanzibar, but immediately returned to extend the German sphere of influence about Lake Victoria. He never regained his old influence, and was marching for the west coast when he was murdered by Arabs in the Manyema country.

EMINESCU, Mihail (1850–89) Rumanian poet, born in Ipotesti. He studied at Czernowitz, Vienna and Berlin, and wrote lyric verse which was widely read and translated. His works were collected in four volumes in 1939.

EMLYN, Thomas (1663–1741) English Presbyterian clergyman, born in Stamford. The first in England to describe himself as 'Unitarian', he was imprisoned and fined for blasphemy (1702–05). He died in London.

EMMA (d.1052) queen of England as consort first of **Æthelred II, 'the Unready'** and then of **Knut Sveinsson** (Canute). The daughter of Richard, Duke of Normandy, she married Æthelred in 1002, by whom she was the mother of **'Edward the Confessor'**. When **Svein Haraldsson, 'Fork-Beard'** invaded England in 1013 she fled home to Normandy for safety with Æthelred, and stayed there with her son Edward when Æthelred returned for a brief resumption of his reign (1014–16). In 1017 she was summoned to England to marry Æthelred's successor, Knut Sveinsson, by whom she had a son, **Hardaknut**. On Knut's death in 1035 she tried to put her son Hardaknut on the throne but was thwarted by her stepson, **Harold Harefoot** (Knut's son by his English mistress Ælgifu) and fled to the court of Baldwin the Pious, Count of Flanders and father-in-law of **William I, the Conqueror**. She returned to England with Hardaknut on his election as king in 1040; but after Hardaknut's death in 1042 she found no favour with his successor, her other son, Edward the Confessor. In 1043 she had all her lands and property confiscated by him, apparently for favouring a rival claimant to the English throne, **Magnus 'the Good'** of Norway.

EMMERICH, Anna Katharina, called **the Nun of Dülmen** (1774–1824) German visionary and nun, born near Coesfeld. She entered the Augustinian order in 1802, and from 1812 bore the stigmata of Christ's passion. Her revelations were recorded by the poet **Clemens von Brentano**.

EMMET, Robert (1778–1803) Irish nationalist, born in Dublin, son of the viceroy's physician. He left Trinity College, Dublin, in 1789 to join the United Irishmen, travelled on the Continent, interviewed **Napoleon** and **Talleyrand** in 1802 on behalf of the Irish cause, and returned the next year to spend his fortune of £3000 on muskets and pikes. With a few confederates he plotted to seize Dublin Castle and secure the viceroy, in conjunction with the expected French invasion of England, but was forced to begin his insurrection prematurely, and the rising resulted only in a few ruffianly murders (July, 1803). Emmet escaped to the Wicklow mountains, but returning for a last meeting with his sweetheart, Sarah Curran, daughter of the orator **John Curran**, was arrested, tried on 19 September 1803, and hanged the following day.

EMMET, Thomas Addis (1764–1827) Irish barrister and nationalist, brother of **Robert Emmet**. In 1798 he was arrested as a United Irishman. After three years' detention he went in 1802 to Holland and France, and thence in 1804 to New York.

EMPECINADO, ('the Stubborn'), nickname of **Don Juan Martin Diaz** (1775–1823) Spanish soldier and patriot. He acquired great distinction as a guerrilla leader against the French in the Peninsular War (1808–14). He became a general in 1814, but for petitioning **Ferdinand III** to re-establish the Cortes was banished to Valladolid (1818). On the outbreak of the insurrection in 1820 he joined the Constitutionalists; and on the Absolutists' triumph in 1823 he was exposed in an iron cage, and finally stabbed by a soldier.

EMPEDOCLES (fl.c.450 BC) Greek philosopher and poet, from Acragas (now Agrigento) in Sicily, who by tradition was also a doctor, statesman and sooth-sayer. He attracted various colourful but apocryphal anecdotes—such as the story that he jumped into Etna's crater to start a rumour about his likely divinity. His thought reflects both the Ionian and the Eleatic traditions, but we have only fragments of his writings from two long poems: *On Nature* describes a cosmic cycle in which the basic elements of earth, air, fire and water periodically combine and separate under the dynamic motive forces of Love and Hate; *Purifications* has a Pythagorean strain and describes the fall of man and the transmigration and redemption of souls.

EMPSON, Sir Richard (d.1510) English politician. In 1491 he became speaker of the House of Commons, and in 1504, now a knight, high steward of Cambridge University and chancellor of the duchy of Lancaster. Throughout **Henry VII**'s reign he was employed in exacting taxes and penalties due to the crown. His conduct, defended by himself as strictly legal, was by the people regarded as infamous and tyrannical, and in the second year of **Henry VIII**'s reign he was convicted of tyrannizing and of constructive treason, and beheaded on Tower Hill with his partner **Edmund Dudley**.

EMPSON, Sir William (1906–84) English poet and critic, born in Howden, Yorkshire. He was educated at Winchester and Magdalene College, Cambridge, where he studied mathematics and literature. His first work of criticism was his university dissertation, published as *Seven Types of Ambiguity* (1930). From 1931 to 1934 he was professor of English literature in Tokyo, and at Peking (1937–39 and 1947–53), having been in the meantime with the BBC's Far Eastern Service. In 1953 he became professor of English literature at Sheffield University. His other critical works included *The Structure of Complex Words* (1951) and *Milton's God* (1961). His *Collected Poems*, noted for their wit, concentration and complexity of thought, were published in 1955.

ENCINA, or **Enzina, Juan de la** (c.1469–c.1534) Spanish dramatist and poet, born near Salamanca. He was successively secretary to the first Duke of **Alva**, musical director in Pope **Leo X**'s chapel at Rome, and prior of León in Spain. Besides his *Cancionero* (1496), he wrote in 1521 a poetical account of his pilgrimage to Jerusalem. His fame rests on 14 dramatic poems, 7 of which were the first secular poems to be dramatized in Spain (1492).

ENCKE, Johann Franz (1791–1865) German astronomer, born in Hamburg. He was director of the Seeberg Observatory in Switzerland (1822–25), and subsequently became secretary of the Academy of Sciences at Berlin and director of the Observatory. Having determined the orbit of the comet of 1680, he next solved the problem of the sun. In 1819 he proved that the comet discovered by Jean Louis Pons in 1818 revolves in about 1200 days, and had been already observed in 1786, 1795 and 1805; it has since been called Encke's comet.

ENDECOTT, John (c.1588–1665) English colonist, born in Dorchester. In 1628 he landed in America as manager of a plantation near Salem, where he established an independent Puritan church. After **John Winthrop** arrived as governor with the main body of colonists in 1630, he served as an assistant. He headed a sanguinary expedition against the Indians in 1636, was deputy-governor 1641–44, 1650 and 1654, and governor six times from 1644 to 1665. He died in Boston.

ENDERBY, Samuel (fl.1830–39) English entrepreneur, General Gordon's grandfather, one of a firm of London merchants who (1830–39) fitted out three Antarctic expeditions. The name Enderby Land was given in 1831 to a tract of Antarctica by its discoverer, John Biscoe, a whaler employed by the company.

ENDERS, John Franklin (1897–1985) American bacteriologist, born in West Hartford, Connecticut. He studied literature at Harvard but switched to bacteriology and took his PhD there. He researched antibodies for the mumps virus, and in 1946 founded a laboratory for poliomyelitis research at Boston. He shared with **Frederick Robbins** and **Thomas Weller** the 1954 Nobel prize for physiology or medicine for the cultivation of polio viruses in human tissue cells, thus greatly advancing virology and making possible the development of a polio vaccine by **Jonas Edward Salk**. In 1962 he developed an effective vaccine against measles.

ENDLICHER, Stephen Ladislaus (1804–49) Austrian botanist, born in Pressburg (now Bratislava, Czechoslovakia). Professor of botany at Vienna from 1840, he formulated a system of plant classification. His great work was *Genera Plantarum* (1836–40).

ENDO, Shusako (1923–) Japanese novelist and short story writer, born in Toyko. After his parents divorced, he and his mother converted to Roman Catholicism. He graduated in French literature from Keio University, then studied for several years in Lyon. Widely regarded as the leading writer in Japan, he has won many literary awards. In 1981 he was elected to the Nihon Geijutsuin, the Japanese Arts Academy. His books include *Silence* (1966), *The Sea and Poison* (1972), *Wonderful Fool* (1974), *Volcano* (1978), *When I Whistle* (1979) and *Stained Glass Elegies* (1984). Inveterately a moralist, he is often labelled 'the Japanese **Graham Greene**'.

ENESCO, Georges, originally **Enescu, George** (1881–1955) Romanian composer, born in Dorohoiu. He studied in Vienna and under **Massenet** and **Fauré** at Paris. Successful as a virtuoso and teacher of the violin (his pupils included **Yehudi Menuhin**), he was also active as a composer. His works include music in Romanian national style, an opera, *Oedipus*, three symphonies and orchestral and chamber music.

ENFANTIN, Barthélemy Prosper (1796–1864) French economist and industrialist, son of a Paris banker. He was expelled from the École Polytechnique in 1814 for having with other pupils fought against the Allies on Montmartre. From 1825 an ardent follower of **Saint-Simon**, whom, however, he saw only once, after the July revolution of 1830 he associated himself with **Bazard** for the propagation of Saint-Simonism, but they soon quarrelled over the question of marriage and the relation of the sexes. Enfantin recognized two sorts of marriage, one permanent, the other temporary; the government prosecuted him, and in 1832 'Père Enfantin' was sentenced to two years' imprisonment and a fine of 100 francs. Released in a few months, he found employment in Egypt as an engineer; went out to Algiers as one of a scientific commission, and wrote *Colonisation de L'Algérie* (1843). After the revolution of 1848 he edited the short-lived *Crédit Public*; and subsequently held an important post in a railway office. He played a prominent part in the Suez Canal project. His principal works are *Doctrine de Saint-Simon*, in conjunction with others (1830); *Traité d'écomonie politique* (1831); and *La Religion Saint-Simonienne* (1831).

ENGEL, Johann Carl Ludwig (1778–1840) Finnish architect, born in Berlin. He planned the layout of Helsinki as capital of Finland, and designed many churches and public buildings.

ENGEL, Johann Jakob (1741–1802) German writer. He wrote the novel *Herr Lorenz Stark* (1795) and popular philosophical books.

ENGELBREKT, (Engelbrektsson) (c.1390–1436) Swedish rebel and military commander, born in Bergslagen of an iron mining family of German ancestry. When the wars of **Erik VIII of Pomerania** (the Kalmar Union king of Denmark, Norway and Sweden) disrupted the Swedish export of iron, he led a rebellion against the king. He forced the Council of the Realm to retract its oath of loyalty to Erik and, at a meeting in Arboga in 1435 ('the first Swedish Parliament'), he was appointed commander-in-chief of the Realm. Within months the Council reversed its decision, but a year later Erik was again excluded and Engelbrekt re-appointed commander. He was murdered in a personal quarrel shortly afterwards. His reputation as a hero of national liberation has ensured him a place in literature, not least in a play by **Strindberg**.

ENGELS, Friedrich (1820–95) German socialist, the fellow-labourer with **Marx** and founder of 'scientific socialism', born in Barmen. From 1842 he lived mostly in England. Having gained experience from working in his father's cotton-factory in Manchester and established contacts with the Chartist movement, he wrote *Condition of the Working Classes in England in 1844* (1845). He first met Marx at Brussels in 1844 and collaborated with him on the Communist Manifesto (1848) and returned to Germany with his mentor in 1848–49 to work on the *Neue Rheinische Zeitung* and fight on the barricades at Baden during the unsuccessful revolution of that year. After Marx's death in 1883, Engels devoted the remaining years of his life to editing and translating Marx's writings, including the second (1885) and third (1894) volumes of the influential *Das Kapital*, which established the materialist interpretation of history.

ENGHIEN, Louis Antoine Henri de Bourbon, Duke of (1772–1804) French soldier, born in Chantilly, the only son of Henry Louis Joseph, Prince de Condé. In 1792 he joined the corps of *émigrés* assembled on the Rhine, and commanded the vanguard from 1796 to 1799. At the peace of Lunéville (1801) he went to reside in Baden. When **Cadoudal**'s conspiracy against **Napoleon** in 1804 was discovered, Bonaparte chose to believe in D'Enghien's complicity, and, violating the neutral territory of Baden, captured the duke and took him to Vincennes. In March 1804, he was shot in the castle moat. **Fouché** said of this act that it was worse than a crime—it was a blunder.

ENGLER, (Gustav Heinrich) Adolf (1844–1930) German systematic botanist, born in Sagan, Silesia (now Zagan, Poland). He became curator of the Botanische Staatsanstalt in Munich, then in 1884 professor of botany at Breslau (now Wroclaw) and in 1889 professor at Berlin. Besides writing the *Syllabus der Pflanzenfamilien* (1892), and many other works, in 1888 he started (with Prantl) and edited *Die natürliche Pflanzenfamilien* surveying all the families and genera of plants according to his system of natural classification, for many years the most widely used.

ENGLISH, Thomas Dunn (1819–1902) American physician, lawyer and ballad-writer whose memory survives in his poem 'Ben Bolt'. This was a popular song during the Civil War, but gained worldwide prominence when **Du Maurier** introduced it in *Trilby*. He was also the author of more than 50 now-forgotten plays.

ENNIUS, Quintus (c.239–169 BC) Roman poet, born in Rudiae in Calabria, and probably of Greek extraction. He is said to have served in the wars, and returned from Sardinia to Rome with **Cato, 'the Elder'**. Here he taught Greek, gained the friendship of **Scipio Africanus the Elder**, and attained the rank of Roman citizen. He introduced the hexameter into Latin; his versification, if rough and unpolished, is vigorous. Of his tragedies, comedies, satires and *Annales*, an epic poem in 18 books chronicling Roman history, only fragments survive.

ENOCH, or **Thenew** See **KENTIGERN, St**

ENQUIST, Per Olov (1934–) Swedish playwright and novelist. His best-known work for the theatre is a collection of three plays published in 1981 under the collective title *Triptych*, comprising *Lesbian Night* (about **Strindberg** and his wife), *To Phaedra*, and *The Life of the Slow-Worms* (about **Hans Christian Andersen**). His major novel is *The Legionaries* (1968), a controversial documentary about the expulsion of Baltic refugees to Russia from Sweden after World War II.

ENRÍQUEZ GÓMEZ, Antonio, properly **Enríquez de Paz** (1602–c.1662) Spanish playwright and poet, born in Segovia, the son of a baptized Portuguese Jew. In 1636 he fled to France to escape the Inquisition, and became major duomo to **Louis XIII**. He wrote comedies, a mystic poem, and an epic, *El Sansón nazareno* (1656). Later he professed the Jewish faith, and in 1660 his effigy was burned at a Seville auto-da-fé.

ENSOR, James Sidney, Baron (1860–1949) Belgian painter and engraver, born in Ostend of Anglo-Belgian parentage. Although he trained at the Brussels Academy he rarely left Ostend and was neglected for much of his life. Now he is accorded major status as a pioneer/precursor of Expressionism. He is best known for his macabre carnival paintings of fighting skeletons and masked revellers which owe a great deal to **Bosch, Brueghel** and **Goya**, as in his *Entry of Christ into Brussels* (1888). His later work is less fierce.

ENSOR, Sir Robert Charles Kirkwood (1877–1958) English radical journalist and historian, born in Somerset. Educated at Winchester and Oxford, he joined the *Manchester Guardian* as leader-writer, and edited an anthology of speeches and writings of theoretical significance, *Modern Socialism* (1904). Active in the Labour movement, he served on the administrative council of the Independent Labour party and the executive committee of the Fabian Society (1907–19), winning membership of the London County Council (1910–13). He was called to the bar in 1903 but left it to become leader writer on the liberal *Daily News* (1909–11), and was chief leader-writer on the radical *Daily Chronicle* (1912–30). He refused *The Times*'s offer to become Berlin correspondent after the war, but left the *Daily Chronicle* when it merged with the *News*. He was a lecturer at the London School of Economics (1931–32), and held various other academic posts. Chosen to write the late Victorian volume of the *Oxford History of England*, his *England 1870–1914* (1936) was a masterpiece, brilliantly mingling personal knowledge with massive research. His *Courts and Judges* (1933) compared British, French and German systems.

ENVER PASHA (1881–1922) Turkish nationalist, and a Young Turk leader in the revolution of 1908. Turkish minister for war in 1914, he fled to Russia in 1918 after the Turkish surrender, and was killed in an insurrection in Turkestan.

ENZINA, Juan de la See **ENCINA**

ÉON DE BEAUMONT, Charles Geneviève Timothé d' (1728–1810) the 'Chevalier d'Éon', born at Tonnerre, Burgundy, was sent to London in 1762 as secretary of embassy, and in 1763 was made minister plenipotentiary. In 1774 the French ministry recalled him, fearing he might betray secrets to the British government. After much negotiation Éon surrendered certain compromising papers, and submitted to the condition imposed by **Louis XVI** of wearing feminine garb, which he had often before assumed as a disguise. In 1785 he returned to London, where he gave exhibitions in fencing, till in 1796 he was disabled by an accidental wound. After his death a post-mortem settled the moot question of his sex. He published *Loisirs du Chevalier d'Éon* (13 vols, Amsterdam 1774) etc, but the *Mémoires* (1837) which bear his name are not genuine.

EÖTVÖS, Joseph, Baron (1813–71) Hungarian author and statesman, born in Budapest. He became an advocate in 1833, but soon devoting himself to literature, published a work on prison reform, and the novels, *The Carthusian* (1838–41), *The Village Notary* (1846) and others. In the revolution of 1848 he was minister of public instruction, and again under **Andrássy** in 1867–71 after three years of exile.

EPAMINONDAS (c.418–362 BC) Theban general and statesman. He led a retired life till his 40th year, but after the stratagem by which his fellow-citizens expelled the Spartans (379 BC), he joined the patriots; and, when sent to Sparta in 371 to negotiate peace, displayed as much firmness as eloquence. When war was resumed, he defeated the Spartans and their allies at Leuctra (371) by innovative tactics involving combined cavalry and infantry manoeuvres. Two years later, with **Pelopidas**, he marched into the Peloponnesus, and incited some of the allies to desert Sparta. On his return to Thebes, he was accused of having retained the supreme power beyond the lawful time, but was acquitted in consequence of his able defence. In 368 war was renewed, and Epaminondas made a somewhat unsuccessful invasion into the Peloponnesus. To atone for this he advanced into Arcadia, and near Mantinea broke the Spartan phalanx, but was mortally wounded.

EPÉE, Charles Michel, Abbé de l' (1712–89) French educationist, born in Versailles. He became a preacher and canon at Troyes, but was deprived as a Jansenist. In 1765 he began to educate two deaf and dumb sisters, and invented a language of signs. He also pioneered the use of 'spatial aids' to assist the memorizing of, for example, vocabulary by associating words with particular locations in space. His attempts succeeding, at his own expense he founded a deaf and dumb institute, which was converted into a public institution two years after his death.

EPHIALTES an Athenian statesman, predecessor of **Pericles** in the leadership of the democratic party. He was assassinated in 457 BC.

EPHRAEM SYRUS, St (c.306–378) Syrian churchman, born in Nisibis. After its capture by the Persians in 363, he removed to a desert school near Edessa (Urfa in modern Iraq). Devoting himself to prayer, fasting, and the study of the Scriptures, Ephraem's orthodoxy, asceticism and learning were the admiration of his contemporaries; and his works, written in a fervid and popular style, maintain his reputation as an orator and poet. Part of them have come down to us in Syriac, part in Greek, Latin and Armenian translations. His feast day is 18 June.

EPICHARMUS (c.540–450 BC) Greek poet, born in Cos, who spent his last years at the court of Hiero of Syracuse. Fragments of his works survive, and the titles of 35, on topics mythological, social and political.

EPICTETUS (1st century) Greek Stoic philosopher and moralist, born in Hieropolis. At first a slave in Rome, he was freed and taught philosophy there until banished by the emperor **Domitianus** along with other philosophers in 90 AD when he settled at Nikopolis in Epirus. His pupil **Arrian** the historian collected his sayings into a manual entitled the *Enchiridion* and into eight volumes of *Discourses*, of which four survive. He taught a gospel of inner freedom through self-abnegation, submission to providence and the love of one's enemies.

EPICURUS (341–271 BC) Greek philosopher and founder of the Epicurean school, born in Samos. He visited Athens at the age of 18; taught for a while at Mitylene and at Lampsacus, and returned to Athens in about 306 to open his famous school in the Garden where he stayed to attract many devoted followers. The Garden became the model for other Epicurean communities, or communes, where members could escape ordinary society and live peacefully in friendship. He supposedly wrote some 300 volumes, but only three letters and a few fragments survive and most of our knowledge of his doctrines comes from **Cicero**, **Plutarch** and in particular, **Lucretius**. His whole philosophy was designed to promote detachment, serenity, and freedom from fear. Pleasure is the only good and the only goal of morality. But the term 'Epicurean' now has a misleading connotation. For Epicurus, true pleasure is not sensuality; it is the absence of pain and anxiety, and is cultivated through simplicity and temperance. These ethical views are supported by a materialistic psychology and an atomistic physics (largely derived from **Democritus**) which demonstrate that the world operates on mechanical principles and that neither death nor the gods are to be feared; the gods do not intervene in the world or punish the guilty; the human soul and body are a combination of atoms that dissolve and perish together. Epicureanism and Stoicism were the two great philosophies of the Hellenic period, and both found many adherents in Rome and endured for many centuries.

EPIMENIDES semi-legendary Greek poet and priest, born in Crete in the 7th or 6th century BC. He is said to have lived 299 years, during 57 of which he received in sleep the divine inspiration that determined his future career. (**Goethe** wrote a poem on the subject, *Des Epomenides Erwachen*.) Epimenides is supposed to have gone to Athens about 600 BC, where he stayed and with **Solon** reformed the Athenian constitution. He was the 'prophet' quoted by St **Paul** in Tit, i 12, but it is unlikely that he wrote the epic poems ascribed to him.

ÉPINAY, Louise Florence, née **Tardieu d'Esclavelles** (1726–83) French writer, born in Valenciennes. At the age of 19 she married a worthless cousin, and subsequently held a brilliant salon at La Chevrette and formed liaisons with **Rousseau**, **Friedrich Melchior, Grimm**, and others. Her *Conversations d'Émilie* (1774), a work on education, won her a gold medal from the French Academy.

EPIPHANES See **ANTIOCHUS IV**

EPIPHANIUS, St (c.315–403) Christian church father, born in Palestine. He founded a monastery near Eleutheropolis in 335. He was bishop of Constantia in Cyprus from 367 till his death. He showed intolerance to St **John Chrysostom** and proclaimed **Origen** a heretic in 394. He wrote several works against Arianism and various other heresies.

EPISCOPIUS, or Biscop, Simon (1583–1643) Dutch theologian, born in Amsterdam. He studied at Leiden under **Arminius** and **Gomarus**, and succeeded to the latter's chair in 1612. He and twelve other Arminians were banished by the Synod of Dort (1618); and in the Spanish Netherlands he wrote his famous Arminian *Confessio* (1622). On the renewal of the war between Spain and Holland, he found refuge in France, and published a series of able controversial treatises. Permitted to return in 1626, he was a professor at the Arminian College at Amsterdam from 1634, where he produced his *Institutiones theologicae* and *Responsio*. Episcopius lays the utmost stress on the personal responsibility of man in relation to divine grace, denies the doctrine of original sin, and treats Christian faith as the potentiality of moral conduct. The Son and the Holy Spirit are only subordinately partakers of divine power and glory—a rationalist development of Arminian doctrine far beyond the Five Articles, but finally adopted by the Arminian party.

EPSTEIN, Sir Jacob (1880–1959) American-born British sculptor, born, a Russian-Polish Jew, in New York. He studied at the École des Beaux-Arts in Paris. He became a British subject, and his early commissions included 18 nude figures for the façade of the British Medical Association building in the Strand (1907–8) and *Night and Day* (1929) for the London Transport Building. These and later symbolic sculptures, such as the marble *Genesis* (1930), the *Ecce Homo* (1934), and the alabaster *Adam* (1939), resulted in great controversy, and accusations of indecency and blasphemy. He was an outstanding modeller of portrait heads, cast in bronze, of celebrities, such as **Conrad**, **Einstein**, **Eliot** and **Shaw**, and of children, such as *Ester* (1944), his youngest daughter. He also executed two bronze *Madonna and Child* works, (1927, Riverside Church, New York; 1950, Holy Child Jesus Convent, London). In the 1950s, his last two large commissioned works, the aluminium *Christ in Majesty* (Llandaff Cathedral) and *St Michael and the Devil* (Coventry Cathedral), won more immediate critical acclaim.

ÉRARD, Sébastien (1752–1831) French pianoforte maker, born in Strasbourg. At his Paris workshop he was the inventor of the harp with double pedals, of the mechanical harpsichord, and of the piano with double escapement.

ERASISTRATUS OF CEOS (b.3 BC) Greek physician. He founded a school of anatomy at Alexandria, and is considered one of the pioneers of modern medicine. He is said to have been the first to trace arteries and veins to the heart.

ERASMUS, Desiderius (c.1466–1536) Dutch humanist and scholar, one of the most influential Renaissance figures, born in Rotterdam. Educated by the Brethren of the Common Life at Deventer, he joined an Augustine monastery at Steyn near Gouda in 1487, and was ordained a priest in 1492. But he was already reacting against scholasticism and was drawn to the Humanists. He studied and taught in Paris, and later in most of the cultural centres in Europe, including Oxford (1499) and Cambridge (1509–14), where he was professor of divinity and of Greek. He travelled widely, writing, teaching and meeting Europe's foremost intellectuals (including **John Colet** and **Thomas More**, while in England), the very model of a cultivated and dedicated scholar. He published many popular, sometimes didactic works like *Adagia* (*Adages*, 1500, 1508), *Enchiridion Militis Christiani* (*Handbook of a Christian Soldier*, 1503), and the famous *Encomium Moriae* (*In Praise of Folly*, 1509). He also published scholarly editions of classical authors and the Church Fathers, and edited the Greek New Testament (1516). He became strongly critical of the pedantries and abuses of the Catholic Church and his *Colloquia familiaria* of 1518 helped prepare the way for **Martin Luther** and the Reformation; but he also came to oppose the dogmatic theology of the Reformers and specifically attacked Luther in *De Libero Arbitrio* (1523). Despite these controversies he enjoyed great fame and respect in his last years, which he spent in Basel. The story of his father's life forms the theme of **Charles Reade**'s *The Cloister and the Hearth*.

ERASTUS, Thomas, properly **Liebler,** or **Lieber,** or **Lüber** (1524–83) Swiss theologian, and physician, born in Swiss Baden. He studied theology at Basel, philosophy and medicine in Italy, and was appointed physician to the counts of Henneberg. Professor of medicine at Heidelberg and physician to the elector palatine (1558), he became professor of ethics at Basel in 1580, and died there. Erastus was a skilful physician, and a vigorous writer against **Paracelsus** and witchcraft. In theology he was a follower of **Zwingli**, and represented his view of the Lord's Supper at Heidelberg in 1560 and Maulbronn in 1564. In England the name of Erastians was applied to the party that arose in the 17th century, denying the right of autonomy to the church which was not maintained nor denied by Erastus. **John Lightfoot** and **John Selden** were Erastians in this sense.

ERATOSTHENES (c.276–194 BC) Greek mathematician, astronomer and geographer, born in Cyrene. He became the head of the great library at Alexandria, and was the most versatile scholar of his time, known as 'pentathlos', or 'all-rounder'. He measured the obliquity of the ecliptic and the circumference of the earth with considerable accuracy. In mathematics he invented a method, the 'sieve of Eratosthenes', for listing the prime numbers, and a mechanical method of duplicating the cube. He also wrote on geography, chronology and literary criticism, but only fragments of all this work remain.

ERCILDOUNE See **THOMAS THE RHYMER**

ERCILLA Y ZÚÑIGA, Alonso de (1553–c.1595) Spanish poet, born in Bermeo on the Bay of Biscay. He entered the service of **Philip II**, and accompanied him in 1554 to England on the occasion of his marriage to Queen **Mary I**. Shortly after, he joined the expedition against the Araucanians in Chile whose heroism inspired his monumental epic poem, *La Araucana* (1569–89). An unfounded suspicion of his complicity in an insurrection nearly led to his execution. Fearing for his life, he returned to Spain, but Philip treated him with indifference so he made a tour through Europe, and for some time was chamberlain to the Emperor **Rudolf II**. In 1580 he returned to Madrid, where he lived in poverty till his death.

ERCKER, Lazarus (c.1530–c.1593) Bohemian metallurgist, born in Annaberg (now in West Germany). He wrote the first systematic account of analytical and metallurgical chemistry. He served under Emperor Rudolf II as chief superintendent of mines of the Holy Roman Empire and Bohemia, and was reputed to be both well-informed and a careful observer. However, his extensive influence was due to his book *Beschreibung allerfürnemisten mineralischen Ertzt und Berckwerksarten* (Prague,1574; Description of Leading Ore Processing and Mining Methods). The book was still being translated and published until the mid 18th century.

ERCKMANN-CHATRIAN (1822–99) the compound name of two French writers—Lorrainers both, **Émile Erckmann** (1822–99) born in Phalsbourg, and Alexandre Chatrian (1826–90) in Abreschwiller. Their literary partnership dates from 1848, but they had little success till the publication of *L'Illustre Docteur Mathéus* (1859). *Le Fou Yégof* (1862) is one of a series of novels, to which also belong *Histoire d'un conscrit* (1864), *Waterloo* (1865) and *Le Blocus* (1867). Well-known plays by them are *Le Juif polonais* (1869; in English *The Bells*), *L'Ami Fritz* (1876), *Les Rantzau* (1882), and *La Guerre* (1885). After the annexation of Alsace-Lorraine to Germany, a strong anti-German feeling was shown in several of their books—the best of these *L'Histoire d'un plébiscite* (1872). They had quarrelled over money just before Chatrian died.

ERHARD, Ludwig (1897–1977) German economist and politician, born in Furth, in North Bavaria. The son of a Catholic farmer turned haberdasher and Protestant mother, he was brought up as a Protestant and studied economics at Nuremberg's handelschochschule. His career was held back during the 1930s as a result of his refusal to join the Nazi party. However, immediately after World War II he became professor of economics at Munich. In 1949 he was elected to the federal parliament (Bundestag) at Bonn and was appointed finance minister in the Adenauer Christian Democrat administration. He was the pioneer of the West German 'economic miracle' of recovery from wartime devastation, devising a successful policy of social free enterprise (Marktwirtschaft).

ERICKSON, Arthur Charles (1924–) Canadian architect, born in Vancouver. Educated at British Columbia and McGill universities, he established Arthur Erickson architects after various partnerships. Powerful articulation and theatricality mark his designs, and a strong preoccupation with technology and materials. The influences of **Le Corbusier**, **Louis Kahn** and Brutalism are evident in his works. He received international recognition with the Simon Fraser University buildings, British Columbia (1963), confirmed by his avant-garde design of Lethbridge University, Alberta (1971). Further major works include the Canadian Pavilion at Expo '70, Osaka, the Museum of Anthropology, British Columbia (1971–77), and Roy Thomson Hall, Toronto, (1976–80).

ERICSON, Nils (1802–70) Swedish engineer, brother of the inventor **John Ericsson**. After supervising the building of the new Trollhättan canal and the Saima canal in Finland, he became director of state railway building (1854–62) and was responsible for the main lines in southern and central Sweden.

ERICSSON, John (1803–89) Swedish-born American inventor, born in Långbanshyttan, Värmland. He served as an officer of engineers in the Swedish army (1816–26), and in 1826 moved to England, where he set up as an engineering consultant. In 1829 he built a formidable rival to **Stephenson**'s *Rocket*; in 1836 he patented, six weeks after Sir **Francis Pettit Smith**, one of the first successful screw-propellers. In 1839 he went to the USA, where he designed the warship *Princeton*, the first steamer with engines and boilers entirely below the water-line, and brought out his improved caloric engine and numerous other inventions. He became a naturalized citizen in 1848. In 1861, during the Civil War, he designed the ironclad *Monitor* (the first warship with an armoured revolving turret), and in 1862 a number of similar vessels for the American navy. His inventions largely revolutionized navigation and the construction of warships, including *The Destroyer* (1878), which could launch submarine torpedoes.

ERIGENA, John Scotus (c.810–c.877) Irish philosopher and theologian, born in 'Scotia' (now Ireland), and also known as John the Scot, an enigmatic and singular figure who stands outside the mainstream of medieval thought. He taught at the Court of **Charles I, the Bald** in France, then supported **Hincmar** in the predestination controversy with his *De Praedestinatione* (851) which the Council of Valence condemned as *pultes Scotorum* (Irishman's porridge) and 'an invention of the devil'. He also translated into Latin and provided commentaries on the Greek writings of the theologians of the Eastern church. His major work *De Divisione Naturae* (c.865) tried to fuse Christian and neoplatonic doctrines and to reconcile faith and reason, but his work was later condemned for its pantheistic tendencies and eventually placed on the Index by **Gregory XIII** in 1685. Tradition has it that, having become Abbot of Malmesbury, he was stabbed to death by his scholars with their pens 'for trying to make them think'.

ERIK Fourteen kings of Sweden (and some of Denmark and Norway as well), of whom the first six are more or less legendary.

ERIK HARALDSSON, 'Blood-axe' (d.954) king of Norway from 942 to 947 and later of the Viking kingdom of York from 948. The eldest son of **Harald I Halfdanarson ('Fine Hair')**, he succeeded to the throne of Norway in 942 when his father abdicated in his favour at the age of 80. His wife was Gunnlaug, the imperious and ruthless sister of King **Harald Gormsson ('Blue-Tooth')** of Denmark. His reign in Norway was marked by much violence, and Erik killed several of his half-brothers who had rebelled against him. He was deposed by his youngest brother, **Haakon I Haraldsson** in 947 and sought refuge in England, where he was accepted as king in York of the Norse realm in Northumbria. He was eventually expelled in 954 and killed in battle at Stainmore in Yorkshire.

ERIK 'the Saint' (12th century) patron saint of Sweden. He became king of Sweden c.1155. He is said to have led a Christian crusade for the conversion of Finland; also to have been murdered at mass in Uppsala by a Danish pretender to his throne. He was married to Kristina, and became father of King Knut Eriksson (d. c.1195).

ERIK VIII, (Erik of Pomerania) (1382–1459) king of Denmark, Sweden and Norway from 1397. The son of Duke Wratislaw VII of Pomerania and Maria, niece of Queen **Margareta**, he was adopted as heir to the triple monarchy by his great-aunt, in 1389, and crowned at Kalmar in Sweden in 1397 when the treaty of union between the three countries was formally sealed. In 1405 he married Philippa, the daughter of King **Henry IV** of England. It was not until 1412, however, on Queen Margareta's death, that he gained actual power. Aggressive commercial and military policies against the Hanseatic League that ultimately failed led to economic disasters that fomented rebellion, and he was deposed by all three countries one by one: Sweden and Denmark in 1438, and Norway in 1442. He was succeeded by his nephew, Kristofer of Bavaria.

ERIK XIV (1533–77) king of Sweden from 1560 to 1569, eldest son and successor of **Gustav I Vasa**. Tutored by a German Lutheran nobleman, his outlook was that of a Renaissance prince, albeit highly unstable. Suspicious of others to the point of paranoia, in 1563 he imprisoned his half-brother Johan, who had been made Duke of Finland by Gustav Vasa, for treason and launched a seven-year war against the Denmark of **Frederik II** for control of the Baltic ports, which ended inconclusively with the Peace of Stettin (1570). Erik XIV's mental stability deteriorated progressively. He was an indefatigable suitor for the hand of Queen **Elizabeth** of England (and even **Mary, Queen of Scots**); he had several of his courtiers butchered on suspicion of treason; and he married privately a soldier's daughter, Karin Månsdotter, who alone seemed capable of controlling his paroxysms of fury. Her coronation as queen in 1568 provided a pretext for rebellion, and Stockholm was taken over by Erik's youngest brother, Duke Karl, the future **Karl IX** (Charles IX). Erik himself was dethroned early in 1569 in favour of his brother Johan as King **Johan III**; he spent the rest of his days in captivity, listening to music and writing psalms, until he died, probably of arsenic poisoning, in 1577.

ERIK THE RED (10th century) Norwegian sailor, who explored the Greenland coast and founded the Norse colonies there (985). His son, **Leif Eriksson**, landed in 'Vínland', often identified as America (c.1000). Both men are the subject of Icelandic sagas.

ERINNA (7th century BC) Greek poet, the intimate friend of **Sappho**, born either in Rhodes or on the island of Telos. Though she died at the age of only 19, she won fame for her epic, *The Distaff*, on the joys of childhood, only four lines of which are extant.

ERIUGENA, Johannes Scotus See **ERIGENA**

ERIXSON, Sven, known as **X-et** (1899–1970) Swedish artist, born in Tumba. He spent much time in the Mediterranean countries and took his motifs from there as well as from Sweden. His enormously colourful paintings, with their mixture of folk-art and naïvism, full of incident and story from everyday life, gave him great popularity and made him much in demand for large-scale public commissions, such as his tapestry *Melodies on the Square* (1937–39) in the Concert Hall in Gothenburg. He was also active as a scenic artist in the theatre.

ERLANGER, Joseph (1874–1965) American physiologist, born in San Francisco. Professor of physiology successively at the Johns Hopkins University, Wisconsin and Washington, he shared with his former student **Herbert Gasser** the 1944 Nobel prize for physiology or medicine for their work on nerve fibres and nerve impulse transmission. They wrote *Electrical Signs of Nervous Activity* (1937).

ERLE, Sir William (1793–1880) English judge, born in Fifehead-Magdalen, Dorset. Educated at Winchester and New College, Oxford, he became a judge in 1844 and chief justice of the Common Pleas (1859–66). He was more a practical that a philosophical judge and recognized that law must change with social conditions. He was chairman of the Royal Commission on Trade Unions of 1867–69, which recommended that trade unions should be legalized subject to certain legal controls, and for that commission he wrote a valuable memorandum on trade union law.

ERMANARIC, Icelandic **Jörmunrekkr** (fl.c.375) king of the Ostrogoths, the oldest historical personage depicted in the heroic lays of Scandinavia. He built up a huge empire centred on the Dnieper, but was overthrown by the Huns, and may have committed suicide when wounded. In Germanic legend he is depicted as a cruel tyrant who had his wife trampled to death by wild horses, and was mortally wounded by her brothers in a suicidal revenge attack.

ERNEST AUGUSTUS (1771–1851) king of Hanover, **George III**'s fifth son. In 1786 he was sent to the University of Göttingen; in 1790 entered the Hanoverian army; at Tournay lost his left eye (1794); in 1799 was created Duke of Cumberland; and in the House of Lords showed himself a strong Tory and staunch Protestant. In 1815 he married the Princess Frederica of Mecklenburg-Strelitz, and in 1837 under the Salic law succeeded William IV as King Ernest I of Hanover. His policy was in all respects reactionary; but in 1848 he did so far yield to the storm as just to save his throne by the unwilling concession of liberal reforms.

ERNESTI, Johann August (1707–81) German classical and biblical scholar, born in Tennstedt. Professor at Leipzig from 1742, he edited many classical texts, and was the chief founder of a correct exegesis of scripture by the laws of grammar and history.

ERNST, Max (1891–1976) German painter and sculptor, born in Brühl, near Cologne. After studying philosophy and psychiatry at Bonn, he turned to painting, and in 1918 founded at Cologne the German Dada group. Later, in Paris, with **Éluard** and **Breton**, he participated in the Surrealist movement. He invented the technique of frottage (pencil rubbings on canvas). He settled in the USA in 1941, but returned to France in 1953. He won the Venice Biennale prize (1954).

ERNULF, or **ARNULF** (1040–1124) French Benedictine monk. Appointed prior of Canterbury by **Anselm**, he was subsequently abbot of Peterborough (1197) and bishop of Rochester (1114). He was remarkable for his skill in canon law and personal saintliness and compiled a great collection of documents about his own church, laws and papal decrees, which from the old name of the see (*Hrofe-ceaster*) was known as the *Textus Roffensis*. As 'Ernulphus' he was comprehensively cursed in Book III of **Sterne**'s *Tristram Shandy*.

ERPENIUS, properly **Thomas van Erpen** (1584–1624) Dutch Orientalist, born in Gorkum. He studied at Leiden, and at Paris learned Arabic from an Egyptian. In 1613 he became professor of Oriental Languages at Leiden, where he erected an Arabic press in his own house. His *Grammatica Arabica* (1613) enjoyed undisputed supremacy for two hundred years, like his *Rudimenta* (1620). His other works were *Proverborum Arabicorum Centuriae Duae* (1614), and an edition of El-Mekin (1625).

ERSCH, Johann Samuel (1766–1828) German bibliographer, born in Grossglogau. He studied at Halle, and in 1800 became librarian to the University of Jena, professor of geography and statistics at Halle (1803), and in 1808 also principal librarian. In 1818, he commenced the publication at Leipzig of the famous *Allgemeine Encykolpädie*. By his *Handbuch der deutschen Litteratur seit der Mitte des 18 Jahrhundent* (1812–14) he established modern German bibliography.

ERSHAD, Lieutenant-General Hossain Mohammad (c.1929) Bangladeshi soldier-politician, born in Rangpur in northern Bangladesh. He was educated at Dhaka University, before joining the Pakistan army and undergoing training at the officers' colleges at Kohat and Quetta in West Pakistan. He subsequently served in East Pakistan, rising to the rank of colonel during the 1971 civil war. In 1975 he underwent further training at the National Defence College in New Delhi (India) and, following promotion to the rank of major-general, served as deputy chief-of-staff to the Bangladesh army between 1975 and 1978. He became chief-of-staff in 1979 and was appointed a lieutenant-general in 1979. Ershad assumed power in a military coup in 1982 and proceeded to govern, first as chief martial law administrator (March–October 1982) and then as prime minister, before becoming president in December 1983. As president, he proceeded to introduce a new rural-orientated economic programme. He was re-elected president in October 1986 and lifted martial law in November 1986, but faced continuing political opposition and demands for a full return to civilian rule.

ERSKINE, David Stewart, 11th Earl of Buchan (1742–1819) Scottish nobleman, brother of **Henry Erskine** and **Thomas Erskine**. A noble antiquarian, if considered somewhat eccentric and vain, he founded the Society of Antiquaries of Scotland and brought about a reform in the election of Scottish peers.

ERSKINE, Ebenezer (1680–1754) Scottish clergyman, born at Chirnside, the son of the minister there, and brother of **Ralph Erskine**. The founder of the Secession Church in Scotland in 1733, he was minister of Portmoak in Kinross-shire from 1703 to 1711, and then of Stirling. He took the Evangelical side in the rise of the Marrow Controversy in 1718 (over the place of Grace as opposed to Works). In the patronage dispute of 1733 he advocated the right of the people to choose their own pastors, and with three other ministers was suspended and then deposed. The sentence was revoked in the next year, but Erskine declined to return unless the evils he had contended against were removed. The invitation remained open until 1740, when he was finally deposed. Meanwhile, in 1733, he and the three other ministers formed an Associate Presbytery, setting up the Secession Church of Marrowkirk. In the divisions of 1747 (Seceders into Burghers and Anti-burgers), Erskine headed the Burghers.

ERSKINE, Henry (1746–1817) Scottish jurist and writer, born in Edinburgh, brother of **David Stewart Erskine** and **Thomas Erskine**. He joined the Scottish bar in 1768, became lord advocate (1783), and dean of the faculty of advocates (1785), but was deposed in 1796 for supporting at a public meeting a resolution against the government's Seditious Writings Bill. Returned by the Haddington burghs in March 1806, and in November by the Dumfries Burghs, he was again lord advocate (1806–07). He published metrical translations from the classics, *The Emigrant* (1773) etc. The recorded fragments of his speeches justify his high reputation as an orator and a wit.

ERSKINE, John (1509–91) of Dun, Scottish reformer. He took an active share in public affairs, steadfastly supporting the reformed preachers, especially **Wishart** and **Knox**, while his moderate and conciliatory temper gave him influence even with the Catholics and the Court. From 1560 to about 1589 he was a superintendent for the reformed district of Angus and Mearns. Although a layman, he was five times moderator of the General Assembly, and was one of the compilers of the *Second Book of Discipline* (1578).

ERSKINE, Ralph (1685–1752) Scottish clergyman, brother of **Ebenezer Erskine**. Minister of Dunfermline from 1711, he joined his brother in the Secession (Associate Presbytery) in 1737, and also took part with the Burghers in the splits of 1747. His sermons were greatly prized and many of them were translated into Dutch. His *Gospel Sonnets* and *Scripture Songs* are well known. His *Practical Works* were published in 1764.

ERSKINE, Thomas (1788–1870) Scottish religious writer, born in Linlathen. He was admitted advocate in 1810, but ceased to practise after his elder brother's death gave him the estate of Linlathen, near Dundee. He published several religious works, his cardinal belief being ultimate universal salvation. His Letters were published in 1878.

ERSKINE, Thomas, 1st Baron (1750–1823) Scottish jurist, born in Edinburgh, brother of **David Erskine** (11th Earl of Buchan) and **Henry Erskine**. In 1764 he was sent to sea, in 1768 bought a commission in the 1st Royals, and at Minorca (1770–72) studied English literature. Quitting the army, he entered Lincoln's Inn (1775) and Trinity College, Cambridge (1776), where he took an honorary MA in 1778, just before being called to the bar. His success was immediate and unprecedented. His brilliant defence (1778) of Captain Baillie, lieutenant-governor of Greenwich Hospital, who was threatened with a criminal prosecution for libel, overwhelmed him with briefs. The next year saw an equally successful defence of Admiral Lord **Keppel**, and in 1781 he secured the acquittal of Lord **George Gordon**. In 1783 he became a king's counsel, and MP for Portsmouth. His first appearance in the House of Commons was a failure and he never became a parliamentary orator. His sympathy with the French Revolution led him to join the 'Friends of the People', and to undertake the defence in many political prosecutions of 1793–94. His acceptance of a retainer from **Thomas Paine** cost him the attorney-generalship to the Prince of Wales (held since 1786); his speeches for Paine, the Scottish radical, **Thomas Hardy** (1794) and **John Horne Tooke** (1794) are among the finest specimens of forensic skill. That for Hadfield (1800), indicted for shooting at **George III**, was a destructive analysis of the current theory of criminal responsibility in mental disease. In 1802 he was appointed chancellor to the Prince of Wales, an ancient office revived in his favour. In 1806 he was appointed Lord Chancellor but resigned the following year and gradually retired into private life. He published a pamphlet on army abuses in 1772; a discussion of the war with France in 1797; a political romance, *Armata*; a pamphlet in favour of the Greeks; and some poems. His decisions as Lord Chancellor were styled the 'Apocrypha', and have added nothing to his fame. His reputation was solely forensic, and in this respect is unrivalled in the history of the English Bar.

ERSKINE of Carnock, John (1695–1768) Scottish jurist. Called to the bar in 1719, he became in 1737 professor of Scots law at Edinburgh. His two works are still held in deserved repute—*Principles of the Law of Scotland* (1754) and the more important *Institutes of the Law of Scotland* (1773), which is one of the classics of Scots law.

ERTZ, Susan, pen-name of **Mrs Ronald McCrindle** (c.1894–1985) American novelist, born in Walton-on-Thames. She was the author of many popular novels including *Madame Claire* (1922) and *The Prodigal Heart* (1950).

ERVINE, St John Greer (1883–1971) Irish playwright and author, born in Belfast. In 1900 he emigrated to London, where he wrote novels and plays. From 1915 to 1916 he was manager of the Abbey Theatre, Dublin, where his first plays (*Mixed Marriage*) (1911) and *Jane Clegg* (1914) were produced. After World War I, in which he served with the Dublin Fusiliers and lost a leg, he won a high reputation as a drama critic, working on *The Observer* and *The Morning Post*, and for the BBC (1932). His most successful plays are perhaps *Anthony and Anna* (1926), *The First Mrs Fraser* (1929) and *Robert's Wife* (1937); other publications include seven novels and several biographies.

ERZBERGER, Matthias (1875–1921) German politician, born in Buttenhausen, Württemberg. He became controversial when, as German propaganda minister, he began to advocate peace without annexations as early as 1917 and again (1918–19) when, as a member of the armistice delegation, he advocated acceptance, despite fierce German opposition, of the terms of the Versailles Treaty. Finance minister and vice-premier in 1919, he drastically reformed the tax system and nationalized the German railways. Unsuccessful in a libel action against an unscrupulous political opponent, he resigned in February 1921 and was assassinated by members of an extremist group on 26 August. He wrote *The League of Nations, the Way to World Peace* (1918; trans, 1919), etc.

ES-SA'ID, Nuri, officially **Nouri Said Pasha** (1888–1958) Iraqi politician, born in Kirkuk. Educated at the Istanbul Staff College for the Turkish Army, he fled to Egypt when his Pan-Arab activities became suspect. In World War I he fought against the Turks under King **Hussein** of the Hejaz. In 1921 he became Iraq's first chief of the General Staff and a year later defence minister. From 1930 he filled the office of prime minister many times until he was assassinated in July 1958 after the *coup d'état* of Brigadier **Kassem.**

ESAKI, Leo (1925–) Japanese physicist, born in Osaka, known for his discovery of the tunnel diode. He was educated at Tokyo University, working for his doctorate on semi-conductors. He investigated conduction by quantum mechanical 'tunnelling' of electrons through the potential energy barrier of a germanium p-n diode. He used the effect to construct a device with diode-like properties, the tunnel (or Esaki) diode. Their very fast speeds of operation, small size, low noise and power consumption, give these diodes widespread application in computers and microwave devices. He shared the Nobel prize for physics in 1973 for work on tunnelling effects with **Brian Josephson** and **Ivar Giaever**.

ESARHADDON (d.669 BC) king of Assyria, a younger son of **Sennacherib**, whom he succeeded in 680 BC. He achieved the conquest of Egypt (675–671). A great builder, he established the city of Nineveh. He was succeeded by his son, Ashurbanipal (**Sardanapalus**).

ESCHENBACH, Wolfram von See **WOLFRAM**

ESCOBAR MENDOZA, Antonio (1589–1669) Spanish Jesuit casuist, born in Valladolid. He wrote *Liber Theologiae Moralis* (1652–63, 7 vols), which was publicly burnt in Paris and violently attacked by **Pascal** in his *Lettres á un provincial*.

ESCOFFIER, Auguste (c.1847–1935) French chef. After service with a Russian grand-duke, he became *chef de cuisine* to the general staff of the Rhine army in the Franco-Prussian war (1871) and of the Grand Hotel, Monte Carlo, before César Ritz persuaded him to come to the Savoy, London, and finally to the Carlton. He invented the *bombe Nero* of flaming ice, *pêche melba* etc, and wrote the *Guide culinaire* (1903) and *Ma Cuisine* (1934).

ESOP See **AESOP**

ESPARTERO, Baldomero (1792–1879) Spanish soldier and politician, the son of a cartwright in a village of La Mancha. From 1815 to 1825 he was in South America, fighting against insurgents. After the accession of **Isabella II** in 1833, he helped defeat the Carlist supporters of her uncle **Don Carlos**, drove Don Carlos from Spain (1884) and was made Duke of Vitoria. In 1840 he was appointed regent for Isabella in place of her mother, Maria Christina, but in 1843 was driven out by **Narvaez**. He lived abroad in England and in retirement in Spain, but in 1854, with **Leopold O'Donnell**, led a successful revolution. In 1856 he resigned as head of the revolutionary government in favour of O'Donnell. In 1870 his name was put forward for the throne; but in 1875 he tendered his allegiance to **Alfonso XII** after his accession.

ESPERT, Nuria (1935–) Spanish actress and stage director. She began her professional career at 12, at 16 played Juliet and at 19, Medea. At 24 she co-founded the Nuria Espert Theatre Company, which she still leads. She has played the title role in *Hamlet*, and both Prospero and Ariel in the same production of *The Tempest*. Other productions include **Brecht**'s *The Good Person of Setzuan* and **Wilde**'s *Salomé*. She has appeared as an actress in productions all over the world. In 1986, she directed a revival of **Lorca**'s *The House of Bernarda Alba* in London, and also **Puccini**'s *Madame Butterfly* for Scottish Opera.

ESPINEL, Vicente de (1551–1624) Spanish writer, born in Ronda. He served as a soldier in France and Italy, meeting with some of the adventures related in his *Life of Marcos de Obregón* (1618), a book largely drawn upon by **Lesage** for his *Gil Blas*. After his return to Spain he took holy orders. He also published a volume of poems (1591) and a translation of the *Ars Poetica* of **Horace**. He was, if not the inventor, the improver of the ten-line stanza, and added the fifth string to the guitar.

ESPRONCEDA, José de (1808–42) Spanish poet and revolutionary, born in Almendralejo in Estremadura. He wrote romantic poems in the Byronic manner and is considered by some the greatest lyricist of his time.

ESPY, James Pollard (1785–1860) American meteorologist, born in Pennsylvania. His *Philosophy of Storms* (1841) earned him the nickname of 'The Storm King'. Appointed in 1843 to the Washington Observatory, he laid the basis of the Weather Bureau.

ESQUIROL, Jean Étienne Dominique (1772–1840) French physician, born in Toulouse. He served in the military lazaretto at Narbonne (1794), and was appointed physician to the Salpêtrière at Paris (1811). After 1817 he delivered clinical lectures on brain diseases; in 1818 he secured the appointment of a commission on abuses in madhouses; in 1825 he became first physician to the *Maison des Aliénés* while managing the asylum at Charenton. The July Revolution deprived him of his public offices. Esquirol's writings embrace the whole treatment of insanity, especially *Des Maladies Mentales* (1838).

ESQUIROS, Henri Alphonse (1814–76) French poet and politician, born in Paris. He published poems and romances. For his *Évangile du peuple* (1840), a democratic commentary on the life of Jesus, he was fined and imprisoned; this inspired his *Chants d'un prisonnier*. His *Vièrges folles*, *Vièrges martyres* and *Vièrges sages* (1841–42) showed more of his socialistic sympathies. After the revolution he became a member of the Legislative Assembly, but the *coup d'état* of 1851 drove him to England, where he gathered the materials for his *English at Home*, *Cornwall and its Coasts*, and *Religious Life in England*. In 1870 he was administrator of Bouches-du-Rhône, and was sent to the National Assembly (1871) and the Senate (1875).

ESSEX, Earl of a title borne successively by Mandevilles, Bohuns, Bourchiers (Devereux's ancestors), **Thomas Cromwell** and the Devereux.

ESSEX, Robert Devereux, 2nd Earl (1566–1601) Elizabethan soldier and courtier, eldest son of **Walter, 1st Earl**, born in Netherwood near Bromyard. At 15 he took his MA from Trinity College, Cambridge. Under **Leicester**, who had become his stepfather in 1580, he first saw service in the Netherlands (1585–86), and distinguished himself at Zutphen. Back at court, he quickly rose in the favour of Queen **Elizabeth**, only seriously interrupted by his clandestine marriage in 1590 with **Frances Walsingham**, widow of Sir **Philip Sidney**. In 1591 he commanded the forces despatched to help **Henri IV** of France against the League; in 1593 he became a privy councillor, and by 1594 was acting as a sort of foreign secretary. His was the principal glory of the capture of Cadiz (1596); but his, too, largely the failure next year of an expedition to the Azores to capture a Spanish treasure ship. In 1597 he became Earl Marshal, in 1598 chancellor of Cambridge; but his great quarrel with Elizabeth, when he turned his back on her, and she boxed his ears, meant that they were never properly reconciled. His six months' lord-lieutenancy of Ireland proved a failure; and, concluding a truce with **Hugh O'Neill**, Earl of Tyrone, he hurried back to England. Elizabeth received him not ungraciously at first; but imprisonment followed, and deprivation of all his dignities. Then he formed the mad plot for removing Elizabeth's counsellors, and on 8 February 1601 attempted to raise the city of London. On the 19th he was found guilty of high treason, and on the 25th beheaded in the Tower. A patron of letters, Essex was himself a sonneteer.

ESSEX, Robert Devereux, 3rd Earl (1591–1646) English parliamentary soldier, eldest son of **Robert, 2nd Earl**. In 1604 the earldom was restored to him after his father's execution for treason in 1601. In 1606 he married Frances Howard (1592–1632), who soon got embroiled in The **Overbury** affair. From 1626 Essex attached himself to the popular party; in July 1642 he received the command of the Parliamentary army. He was brave personally, but a very poor general; and to him the prolongation of the war was largely due. The drawn battle of Edgehill, the capture of Reading, and the relief of Gloucester were followed by his blundering march into Cornwall, whence he fled by sea. In April 1646 he resigned the command, and on 14 September he died. The title died with him; but in 1661 it was revived in favour of Arthur, Lord Capel (1631–83), ancestor of the present earl.

ESSEX, Walter Devereux, 1st Earl (cr 1572), **2nd Viscount Hereford** (1541–76) the scion of an old Herefordshire house, he earned notoriety as the merciless colonizer of Ulster from 1573. As earl marshall of Ireland he dealt severely with the rebellious Sorley Boy MacDonnell and his followers.

ESTAING, Charles Hector Théodat, Comte d' (1729–94) French naval officer. He served in the East Indies, and was captured twice by the British. He became a lieutenant-general in 1767. Later, as a vice-admiral, in 1778 he commanded French naval forces against the British in the American War of Independence, and captured St Vincent and Grenada in 1779, but his operations on the mainland were unsuccessful. During the French Revolution he was guillotined for writing in support of **Marie Antoinette**.

ESTE (1000–1875) Italian family who became rulers of Ferrara towards the end of the 12th century and maintained their hegemony over the city until 1598 when it was incorporated into the papal states. Azzo D'Este (1205–64), the first marquess, had established his authority over the area by the time of his death, and the office of *signore* of Ferrara was made hereditary in the family during the time of his son, Obizzo (d.1293), and the territories of Modena and Reggio were annexed to it. Niccolo III (1383–1441) brought peace and security to the state during his long reign while his sons and successors Leonello (1407–50), Borso (1413–71) and Ercole (1431–1505) were notable patrons of the arts and of humanist scholarship, a tradition continued by Isabella (1474–1539) and Beatrice (1475–97), daughters of Ercole, who married respectively Francesco Gonzaga of Mantua and Lodovico Sforza of Milan. Alfonso I (d.1534) quarrelled with popes **Julius II** and **Leo X** and lost the family's papal fiefs in 1527 while his son Ippolito (d.1572) erected the magnificent Villa d'Este at Tivoli. Although Ferrara was lost in 1598, the family retained the duchy of Modena until 1859 when Francis V (1819–75) resigned his territories to **Victor Emmanuel**.

ESTELLA See **PRIMO DE RIVERA**

ESTERHÁZY (1600–1866) a powerful family of Hungary, divided into several branches. Count Paul Esterházy of Fraknó (1635–1713), Austrian field marshal, for his successes against the Turks was made a prince of the empire in 1687. Prince Nicholas IV (1765–1833) formed a splendid collection of pictures at Vienna, and by extravagance brought his vast estates into sequestration. **Napoleon** in 1809 made overtures to Prince Esterházy respecting the crown of Hungary. His son, Prince Paul Anton (1786–1866), represented Austria at London until 1842, and in 1848 was minister of foreign affairs. He added by his magnificence to the burdens on the family property, which was again sequestrated in 1860.

ESTES, Richard (1932–) American painter, born in Keewane, Illinois. He studied at the Art Institute of Chicago from 1952 to 1956 and in 1959 moved to New York. For several years he worked in the illustration and advertizing industry before becoming a full-time painter in 1966. In the late 1960s he began painting precise copies of photographs, particularly of New York street-scenes. His meticulously detailed 'Super-Realist' works can easily be confused with photographs.

ESTHER (5th century BC) Biblical queen, a foster-daughter of the Jew Mordecai. According to the *Book of Esther* she was chosen by the Persian king Ahasuerus (**Xerxes**) as his wife in place of the disgraced queen Vashti, and brought about the deliverance of her people.

ÉSTIENNE See **STEPHENS** family

ESTRÉES, Gabrielle d' (c.1570–1599) French noblewoman. The mistress of **Henri IV** of France from about 1590, she was created Marquise de Monceaux and Duchesse de Beaufort. Henri was about to divorce his queen in order to marry her, when she died suddenly in Paris. From their illegitimate offspring the house of Vendôme was descended.

ETHELDREDA, St (Æthelthryth) (c.630–679) also known as St **Audrey**, founder of a monastery at Ely and revered as a virgin saint, although twice married. The daughter of King Anna of East Anglia, she was widowed after three years of her first marriage, which was said never to have been consummated. In 660 she married Ecgfrith, future king of Northumbria, but refused to consummate it. Instead she took the veil and withdrew to the double monastery at Coldingham founded by her aunt, Æbbe, and in 672 founded a double monastery herself on the isle of Ely, of which she was appointed abbess.

ETHELE See **ATTILA**

ETHEREGE, Sir George (?1635–92) a Restoration dramatist, he was born probably in Maidenhead. Secretary to the ambassador at Constantinople (1668 to 1670 or 1671), he married a wealthy widow, and in 1685 was sent to be resident at the Imperial court at Ratisbon. He varied the monotony of this banishment with coursing, drinking, play, flirtation with actresses and correspondence with **Middleton**, **Dryden** and **Betterton**. He seems to have died in Paris. In English literature he is founder of the comedy of intrigue. He sought his inspiration in **Molière**, and out of him grew the legitimate comedy of manners and the dramatic triumphs of **Sheridan** and **Goldsmith**. His three plays are *The Comical Revenge or, Love in a Tub* (1664); *She Would if She Could* (1668); and *The Man of Mode or, Sir Fopling Flutter* (1676)—all highly popular in their day.

ÉTIENNE See **STEPHENS family**

ETTMÜLLER, Ernst Moritz Ludwig (1802–77) German scholar, born in Gersdorf in Saxony. From 1863 professor of German literature at Zürich, he contributed enormously to the knowledge of middle high and low German. In 1840 he edited *Beowulf*, and in 1852 published his *Lexicon Anglo-Saxonicum*. He also worked in old Norse.

ETTY, William (1787–1849) English painter, born in York, the son of a baker. He was apprenticed to a printer in Hull, but in 1806 he went to London and studied in the Royal Academy schools; for a year he was a pupil of Sir **Thomas Lawrence**. In 1822–23 he spent 18 months in Italy, half of them at Venice, where he was deeply influenced by the Venetian masters. Renowned for his nudes, he depicted historical and classical subjects, like *The Combat* (1825), now in the National Gallery of Scotland, but he was perhaps at his best when working on a less ambitious scale.

ETZEL See **ATTILA**

EUCKEN, Rudolf Christoph (1846–1926) German philosopher, born in Aurich in East Friesland. He became professor at Basel (1871) and at Jena (1874), and won the Nobel prize for literature in 1908. He propounded a distinctive philosophy of ethical activism, broadly in the idealist tradition of **Kant**, and sought to identify and vindicate the spiritual significance of history and life. His works include *Philosophie der Geschichte* (1907), *Der Sinn und Wert des Lebens* (1908) and *Mensch und Welt* (1918).

EUCLEIDES OF MEGARA Greek philosopher, a disciple of **Socrates**, mentioned by **Plato** as one of those present during Socrates' last hours. He founded a school of 'Megarians', who were evidently influenced by **Parmenides** as well as by Socrates and are associated with various developments in logic like the 'liar paradox' (attributed to one of their number, Eubulides). Nothing of their writings survives.

EUCLID (fl.300 BC) Greek mathematician. He taught in Alexandria, where he appears to have founded a mathematical school. His *Elements* of geometry, in 13 books, is the earliest substantial Greek mathematical treatise to have survived, and is probably better known than any other mathematical book, having been printed in countless editions; with modifications and simplifications it was still being used as a school textbook in the earlier part of the 20th century. It was the first mathematical book to be printed and has stood as a model of rigorous mathematical exposition for centuries, though this aspect of it has been severely criticized by **Bertrand Russell** among others. He wrote other works on geometry, and on astronomy, optics and music, many of which are lost.

EUDOCIA (401–65) Byzantine princess, the beautiful and accomplished daughter of an Athenian professor of rhetoric. She was chosen by the all-powerful Pulcheria to be the wife of her brother, the weak-minded emperor, **Theodosius II**. She renounced paganism, changing her name from Athenais, and was married to Theodosius in 421. Soon violent rivalry arose between the sisters-in-law. Eudocia supported **Nestorius** and was worsted; later Pulcheria was banished, and Eudocia triumphantly backed **Eutyches**, head of an opposite heresy. But shortly before the emperor's death (450) Pulcheria regained her influence, while Eudocia retired to Jerusalem to end her life in works of piety. She wrote a panegyric on Theodosius' victories over the Persians, paraphrases of Scripture, hymns and poetry.

EUDOXUS OF CNIDUS (408–353 BC) Greek mathematician, astronomer and geographer. Thought to have been a member of **Plato**'s Academy, he spent over a year studying in Egypt with the priests at Heliopolis, and formed his own school in Cyzicus. He made many advances in geometry, and it is possible that most of **Euclid**'s book xii is largely his work. He drew up a map of the stars and compiled a map of the known areas of the world. He correctly recalculated the length of the solar year, and his philosophical theories are thought to have had a great influence on **Aristotle**.

EUGENE OF SAVOY, Prince, properly **François Eugène de Savoie Carignan** (1663–1736) Austrian soldier, born in Paris, the youngest son of the prince of Savoy Carignan and a niece of Cardinal **Mazarin**. After his father's death (1673), his mother's banishment from court by **Louis XIV** and Louis's refusal to give him a commission, he renounced his country and, at 20, entered the service of the emperor **Leopold I** against the Turks. He displayed extraordinary courage and talent at the siege of Vienna in 1683 and gained rapid promotion. In the war against Louis XIV in Italy, he distinguished himself; field-marshal in 1693, he defeated the Turks with immense slaughter in 1697 at Zenta, putting an end to their power in Hungary. The War of the Spanish Succession (1701) recalled him to the army of Italy, but though he inflicted several defeats upon the French, he was prevented from effecting much by the smallness of his forces and the skill of the Duke of Vendôme, who defeated him at Luzzara in 1702. In command of the imperial army he helped **Marlborough** at Blenheim (1704). Eugène was checked at Cassano (1705) by Vendôme, but afterwards crushed the French in a defeat which closed their career in Italy. He shared with Marlborough the glory of Oudenarde (1708) and Malplaquet (1709), but, crippled by the withdrawal of Holland and England, was unable to withstand the enemy of the Rhine, and his defeat by **Villars** at Denain (1712) was followed by other disasters, until the peace of Rastadt (1714) ended the war. In the renewal of the war (1716) against the Turks, Eugène defeated an army of 150000 men at Peterwardein, took Temesvar, and in 1717, after a desperate battle, carried Belgrade. In a new war with France over the crown of Poland, Eugéne was only able to keep the enemy out of Bavaria. After the peace he returned to Vienna.

EUGÉNIE, Empress See **NAPOLEON III**

EUGENIUS I, St pope (654–57). He succeeded St **Martin I**, who had been forced into exile. Like Martin, he fell foul of the emperor **Constans II** on the question of Monothelitism, but was saved from the consequences by the advance of the Islamic invaders.

EUGENIUS II pope (824–27). Though elected under doubtful circumstances to further Frankish interests, he is said to have fulfilled his office with dignity and wisdom.

EUGENIUS III, originally **Bernardo Paganelli**, pope from 1145 to 1153, he was a Cistercian monk, born near Pisa. His predecessor (Lucius II) having died during a rebellion against the papacy in Rome, he was obliged to flee to Viterbo immediately upon his election. Soon after his return he was again driven out by a revolt initiated by **Arnold of Brascia** and turned his attention to promoting a second Crusade in France.

EUGENIUS IV, originally **Gabriele Condulmer** (1383–1447) pope from 1431. A Venetian, he quarrelled with the reforming Council of Basel, convoked by his predecessor **Martin V**, which sought to limit papal power. Driven from Rome in 1434 by the Colonnas, he opened a new council, first at Ferrara, next at Florence, and excommunicated the bishops assembled at Basel. The council of Basel deposed him in 1439 and elected Amadeus, Duke of Savoy, as **Felix V**. At the Council of Ferrara, John Palaeologus II, emperor of Constantinople, appeared with 20 Greek bishops, and a union between the Greek and Latin Churches was effected for a short time in 1439. In 1444 Eugenius entered Rome again.

EUHEMERUS (fl.c.300 BC) Greek philosopher and mythographer, probably from Messene in Sicily. He wrote *Sacred History*, which 'euhemerized' Greek mythology by explaining the gods as distorted representations of warriors and heroes from remote history.

EULER, Leonhard (1707–83) Swiss mathematician, born in Basel, where, though destined by his father for theology, he studied mathematics under **Jean Bernoulli**. In 1727 he went to St Petersburg to join Bernoulli's sons at the Academy of Sciences newly founded by **Catherine II**, where he became professor of physics (1731) and then of mathematics (1733). In 1738 he lost the sight of one eye. In 1741 he moved to Berlin at the invitation of **Frederick II, the Great** to be director of mathematics and physics in the Berlin Academy, but returned to St Petersburg in 1766 after a disagreement with the king. He became totally blind but still continued to publish, and remained in Russia until his death. He was a giant figure in 18th-century mathematics, publishing over 800 different books and papers, almost all in Latin, on every aspect of pure and applied mathematics, physics and astronomy. In analysis he studied infinite series, differential equations, introduced many new functions, including the gamma function and elliptic integrals, and created the calculus of variations. His *Introductio in analysin infinitorum* (1748) and later treatises on differential and integral calculus and algebra remained standard textbooks for a century and his notations such as *e* and π have been used ever since. In mechanics he studied the motion of rigid bodies in three dimensions, the construction and control of ships, and celestial mechanics. For the princess of Anhalt-Dessau he wrote *Lettres à une princesse d'Allemagne* (1768–72) giving a non-technical outline of the main physical theories of the time. He had an amazing technical skill with complicated formulae and an almost unerring instinct for the right answer, though he was a little concerned with the questions of rigour which would occupy later generations. He had a prodigious memory, which enabled him to continue mathematical work though totally blind, and he is said to have been able to recite the whole of **Virgil**'s *Aeneid* by heart.

EULER-CHELPIN, Hans Karl August Simon Von (1873–1964) German-born Swedish biochemist. After studies at Berlin, Göttingen and Paris, he became lecturer in physical chemistry at Stockholm (1900), and afterwards professor of chemistry and director of the Stockholm Biochemical Institute (1929). With Sir **Arthur Harden** he was awarded the Nobel prize for chemistry in 1929 for researches on enzymes and fermentation.

EUMENES I king of Pergamon, reigned 263–241 BC, and successfully drove off **Antiochus I** c.262 BC. Though an independent ruler, he did not take on the royal title.

EUMENES II king of Pergamon, son of Attalus I, reigned 197–159 BC. During his reign Pergamon reached the zenith of its importance. Eumenes was an ally of Rome against **Antiochus III** and against Macedonia. He made Pergamon a centre of learning, founded a great library, and had the famous sculptured Altar of Pergamon built (now in Berlin museum).

EUMENES OF CARDIA (c.360–316 BC) Macedonian soldier, one of the ablest generals of **Alexander the Great**, after whose death he became governor of Cappadocia, Paphlagonia and part of Pontus. He was ultimately defeated in 317 BC by **Antigonus Cyclops** and executed.

EUNOMIUS (d.c.399) Cappadocian prelate. He was bishop of Cyzicus around 360 but was deposed for his Arian views. With **Aëtius** he became the leader of an extreme sect of Arians, known as the Anomoeans or Eunomians. Born in Cappadocia, he laboured under the Arian Aëtius in Alexandria, was bishop of Cyzicum about 360, but soon had to resign.

EUPHRANOR (4th century BC) Greek painter and sculptor from Corinth, famed for his decoration of the Stoa Basileios at Athens.

EUPHRONIOS (fl.late 6th century–5th century BC) Greek potter and vase painter. His name is inscribed—as either painter or potter—on 15 vessels which constitute some of the finest surviving examples of vessels painted in the so-called 'red figure' style.

EUPOLIS See **CRATINUS**

EURIPIDES (480 or 484–406 BC) Greek dramatist, latest of the three Greek tragedians, who abandoned painting for literature. Of about 80 of his dramas known to us, we possess 18 complete. He won the tragic prize only five times, and he died at the court of Archelaus, king of Macedonia. He did not take much part in public life; in politics he was moderate, approving of a democracy, but not of demagogues. The names and probable order of his plays are: *Alcestis*, *Medea*, *Hippolytus*, *Hecuba*, *Andromache*, *Supplices*, *Heraclidae*, *Troades*, *Helena*, *Phoenissae*, *Orestes*; the *Bacchae* and *Iphigenia in Aulis* were put on the Athenian stage only after the author's death; and it is uncertain to what period belonged the *Ion*, *Hercules Furens*, *Iphigenia in Tauris*, *Electra*, and *Cyclops*, whilst it is doubtful whether the *Rhesus* is genuine. The skill of Euripides as a playwright is of the highest order; he can construct plots which are exciting beyond anything attempted by his predecessors, and he has an unerring instinct for 'situation'. But in his desire to get on to the situation as rapidly as possible, he substitutes a bald prologue for a proper exposition and instead of working out the dénouement, makes a *deus ex machina* cut the knot of the situation. To the same end he sacrifices consistency in character drawing. His popularity increased after his death; his plays were 'revived' more frequently than those of **Aeschylus** or **Sophocles** and the number that have survived is greater than both of theirs put together. The oldest MSS known to us go back only to the 12th century, and are very corrupt. The *editio princeps* (Florence, 1496) contains only 4 plays; the Aldine (1503), 18.

EURYTUS OF CROTON (late 5th century BC) Greek philosopher, a follower of **Pythagoras**, known only for the reported story that he used pebbles to represent the essential definitions of physical objects.

EUSDEN, Laurence (1688–1730) English poet, born in Spofforth. He became poet laureate in 1718, but not on account of his poetic genius, merely because he had celebrated the marriage (1717) of the Duke of Newcastle (who was responsible for nominations for the position). He wrote little of value, was lampooned by **Pope**, and died rector of Coningsby, Lincolnshire.

EUSEBIO, Silva Ferreira da (1942–) Portuguese footballer, born in Mozambique. One of the first great players to emerge from the African continent, he had a long and successful career with Benfica of Lisbon, with whom he won European Cup medals. He was nominated as European Footballer of the Year in 1965 and in the Centenary Match to mark the foundation of the FA he played for the Rest of the World against England in 1963. In the World Cup of 1966 he was the top goal-scorer.

EUSEBIUS OF CAESAREA (c.264–340) Palestinian theologian and scholar, known as the Father of Church History, was born probably in Palestine. He became bishop of Caesarea about 313, and in the Council of Nicaea was the head of the semi-Arian or moderate party, which was averse to discussing the nature of the Trinity, and would have preferred the language of scripture to that of theology in speaking about the Godhead. His *Chronicon*, a history of the world to 325, is valuable as containing extracts from lost works. His *Praeparatio Evangelica* is a collection of such statements in heathen authors as support the evidences of Christianity; its complement is the *Demonstratio Evangelica* in 20 books, ten of which are extant, intended to convince the Jews of the truth of Christianity from their own scriptures. His great work, the *Ecclesiastical History*, is a record of the chief events in the Christian church down to 324. Other works, all likewise in Greek, are his *De Martyribus Palestinae*, treatises against Hierocles and Marcellus, the *Theophania* (discovered in 1839), and a life of **Constantine**.

EUSEBIUS OF EMESA (295–359) Greek prelate, born in Edessa, a favourite of the emperor **Constantine**. In 341 he declined the bishopric of Alexandria, vacant by the deposition of **Athanasius**, but was afterwards bishop of Emesa in Syria.

EUSEBIUS OF NICOMEDIA (d.342) Syrian prelate. He was bishop first of Beryta (Beyrout) in Syria, and then of Nicomedia. He defended **Arius** at the Council of Nicaea (325) and afterwards became the head of the Arian party. Exiled to Gaul for his views, he came back in 328 and influenced the emperor **Constantine** to move towards Arianism, and baptized him in 337, just before his death. He had also been responsible for the deposition of **Athenasius** in 335. In 339 he was appointed patriach of Constantinople, and enjoyed the favours of the emperor **Constantius**.

EUSTACHIO, Bartolommeo (1520–74) Italian anatomist and pioneer of modern anatomy. He discovered the Eustachian tube in the ear and the Eustachian valve of the heart. He was professor of anatomy at Rome when he died. He wrote *Opuscula Anatomica* (1564) and *Tabulae Anatomicae* (1714).

EUSTATHIUS Greek scholar and commentator, born in Constantinople. Archbishop of Thessalonica from 1160 and of Myra from 1174, he was the author of numerous chronicles and commentaries on classical writers. His commentary on **Homer** and other writings contain extracts from works no longer in evidence.

EUSTATHIUS OF ANTIOCH, St (fl. c.325) bishop of Antioch from 324. He steadfastly opposed the Arians in the Council of Nicaea (325), for which he was deposed in 330.

EUTHYMIDES (fl.late 6th century–early 5th century BC) Greek vase painter of the so-called 'red figure' style. He was a contemporary of **Euphronios** and, seemingly, a rival as, amongst the six surviving signed vessels, one is inscribed with the words: 'Euphronios never did anything like it'. His painted figures are amongst the earliest to show foreshortened limbs.

EUTROPIUS (fl. 4th century) Roman historian. He was secretary to the emperor **Constantine** and fought against the Persians under **Julian**. He wrote a survey of Roman history, *Breviarium Historiae Romanae*, from the foundation of the city to 364 AD. Written in simple, concise style, it may have been intended for the use of schools.

EUTYCHES (c.384–c.456) archimandrite at Constantinople. He was the founder of 'Eutychianism', holding that after the incarnation, the human nature became merged in the divine, and that **Jesus Christ** had therefore but one nature. He was condemned by a synod at Constantinople in 448; but the council of Ephesus (449) decided in his favour and restored him, deposing his opponents. The council of Chalcedon (451) annulled this decision, and Eutyches died in banishment. His sect was put down by penal laws.

EUWE, Max (Machgielis) (1901–81) Dutch chess player, born near Amsterdam, and world champion (1935–37). He was the only amateur to win the world championship in the history of chess, by defeating **Alexander Alekhine**; he lost the title in a return match two years later. His first career was as a professor of mathematics and mechanics, in which he gained a doctorate in 1926. After his academic retirement he served as president of FIDÉ (Fédération Internationale des Échecs), 1970–78, arbitrating over the turbulent **Fischer-Spassky** world championship match in Reykjavík, Iceland in 1972. A prolific annotator, he contributed more to the literature of chess than any other great master.

EVAGRIUS, known as **Scholasticus** (c.536–c.600) Byzantine church historian, born in Epiphanica in Syria. Patriarch of Antioch, his Greek *Ecclesiastical History*, 431–594, was a continuation of that of **Eusebius of Caesarea**.

EVALD, Johannes See **EWALD**

EVANS, Sir Arthur John (1851–1941) English archaeologist, son of Sir **John Evans**. He was a curator at the Ashmolean Museum, Oxford (1884–1908), where he developed an interest in the ancient coins and seals of Crete. Between 1899 and 1935 he excavated the Bronze Age city of Knossos (modern Kephala), discovering the remains of the civilization which in 1904 he named 'Minoan' after Minos, the Cretan king of Greek legend. He later rebuilt and repainted substantial parts of the Minoan palace in an effort to recreate its original appearance.

EVANS, Caradoc, pseud of **David Evans** (1878–1945) Welsh short-story writer and novelist, born in Llanfihangel-ar-Arth, Dyfed. He spent much of his childhood at Rhydlewis, but left home in 1893, working as a shop assistant in Carmarthen, Barry, Cardiff and finally London. While in London, he attended evening classes and eventually found employment as a journalist in 1906. His collections of short stories, *My People* (1915), *Capel Sion* (1916) and *My Neighbours* (1919), savagely exposed the hypocrisies, lust and greed of the Chapel-going people of his native West Wales. His play, *Taffy* (1923), was in similar vein and in his own time he was vilified by the Welsh as a traitor for his assaults on many cherished aspects of the Welsh way of life, from Nonconformity and the Eisteddfod to the integrity and intelligence of the common people.

EVANS, Dame Edith (1888–1976) English actress, born in London. She earned an enviable reputation for her versatility, appearing in many **Shakespeare** and **Shaw** plays, and in others, including *The Way of the World*, *The Late Christopher Bean*, *Daphne Laureola*, and *The Importance of Being Earnest* (as Lady Bracknell, also on film). During World War II she entertained the troops at home and abroad, and in 1946 was created DBE. In 1948, she made her first film appearance in *The Queen of Spades*.

EVANS, Frederick Henry (1853–1943) English photographer. Retiring from his profession as a bookseller in 1898, he devoted himself to architectural photography, especially of the cathedrals of England, emphasizing their structural rhythms and repetitions. He found similar order and pattern in his studies of trees and in photomicrographs as well as in his austerely-formed landscapes. His best work was done in the early years of the 20th century, but he remained unsympathetic to the modern activism then emerging.

EVANS, Sir George De Lacy (1787–1870) British soldier, born in Moig in Ireland. He served in India, the Iberian Peninsula, America and at Waterloo. An advanced Liberal, he sat for Rye (1831–32), and for Westminster (1833–65), with the exception of the years 1841–46. During 1835–37 he commanded the 'Spanish Legion' for Queen **Isabella II** against the Carlists, and performed creditable exploits. In the Crimea (1854) he commanded the second division, was hotly engaged at Alma, and during the siege of Sebastopol gallantly repelled a fierce sortie.

EVANS, Gil (Ian Ernest Gilmore Green) (1912–88) Canadian jazz pianist, composer and arranger, born in Toronto of Australian parents. A self-taught musician, he spent his childhood in Washington State and California. His first influential work was done between 1944 and 1948 when, apart from three years' military service, he was principal arranger for the Claude Thornhill Orchestra. Although basically a dance orchestra, its use of french horns and tuba to create dense textures attracted the interest of young jazz performers. The result was a series of collaborations, starting in the late 1940s, between Evans and **Miles Davis** which led to the emergence of the 'cool jazz' style. As an arranger and conductor, Evans continued to collaborate with Davis until 1960, covering a very influential period in the trumpeter's career. Evans went on to lead and write for a range of groups until his death, and was one of the first modern jazz arrangers to use electronics and rock influences successfully in combination with the swing and bebop idioms.

EVANS, (Thomas) Godfrey (1920–) English cricketer, born in Finchley. One of the greatest of England wicket-keepers, he was educated at Kent College, Canterbury and joined the Kent county staff at the age of 16. First capped for England in 1946, he played in 91 Test matches, and made many new records in his time, including 218 Test dismissals (75 against Australia). He was also a bustling quick-scoring bat, and was the first wicket-keeper to have dismissed more than 200 batsmen and scored 2000 runs in Test cricket. He scored two Test centuries and held records for both the fastest scoring and the slowest (his ten not out in 133 minutes against Australia at Adelaide in 1946–47 saved the match). After his retirement he went into public relations.

EVANS, Harold (1928–) English journalist, born in Manchester. Starting as a weekly reporter at the age of 16, he went on to take an MA at Durham University, and a Harkness Fellowship at the University of Chicago. Before finding his way to Fleet Street, he was an assistant editor on the *Manchester Evening News* and editor of the *Northern Echo*. He was the editor of the *Sunday Times* for 14 years from 1967 and was a pioneer of investigative journalism, successfully appealing to the European Court of Human Rights against the suppression by the House of Lords of articles exposing the Thalidomide scandal. He was editor of *The Times* (1981–82) but he resigned after its controversial takeover by **Rupert Murdoch**'s News International. Subsequently he has worked for Condé Nast. His books include five respected manuals on the craft of journalism, and *Good Times, Bad Times* (1983).

EVANS, Sir John (1823–1908) English industrialist and archaeologist, born at Britwell Court. A paper manufacturer, he was a keen antiquarian and collector of ancient implements and old coins. He published *The Coins of the Ancient Britons* (1864) and *Ancient Stone Implements, Weapons, and Ornaments of Great Britain* (1872).

EVANS, Marian or **Mary Ann** See **ELIOT, George**

EVANS, Merlyn (1910–73) Welsh painter, born in Cardiff. He studied at the Glasgow School of Art. His paintings are mainly surrealist in character, with semi-abstract figures. In 1966 he won the Gold Medal for Fine Art at the National Eisteddfod of Wales.

EVANS, Oliver (1755–1819) American inventor, born in Newport, Delaware. In 1777 he invented a high-speed machine for making textile cards. In 1785 he created the first continuous production line, with improved machinery in a flour mill. He also built some of the earliest successful high-pressure steam engines, improving considerably on **James Watt**'s invention. His amphibious steam dredging machine of 1804 is considered the first American steam carriage to run on the roads.

EVANS, Timothy John See **CHRISTIE, John Reginald Halliday**

EVANS, Walker (1903–75) American photographer, born in St Louis, Missouri. In 1933 he started as an architectural photographer but moved to social studies and from 1935 began to record the life of rural depression in the Southern states for the US government Farm Security Administration (FSA), although he left this organization a few years later. The two themes were combined in his *American Photographs* (1938), the first section of which shows members of society and the second its buildings, all the images being intended to be viewed in sequence. He worked with the writer **James Agee** for *Fortune* magazine to document the lives of the share-croppers of the Deep South, eventually published as *Let Us Now Praise Famous Men* (1941). During his years as associate editor of *Fortune* (1945–65) he continued with architectural studies, but particularly outstanding were his records of people in the New York City subways, published in 1966 as *Many Are Called*. He was professor of graphic design at Yale from 1965 to 1974.

EVANS-PRITCHARD, Sir Edward Evan (1902–73) English social anthropologist, born in Crowbridge, Sussex. He studied history at Oxford, and succeeded his teacher **Alfred Radcliffe-Brown** to the chair of social anthropology (1946–70). He carried out fieldwork in East Africa in the 1920s and 1930s among the Azande and the Nuer, resulting in a number of classic monographs including *Witchcraft, Oracles and Magic among the Azande* (1937), *The Nuer* (1940) and *Nuer Religion* (1956). Though strongly influenced by the sociological theory of **Emile Durkheim**, he came to reject Radcliffe-Brown's view that social anthropology could be regarded as a natural science of society, choosing instead to emphasize its affinity with history, requiring interpretation and translation rather than scientific explanation. His later work on religion was strongly coloured by his own experience of conversion to Catholicism.

EVARTS, William Maxwell (1818–1901) American lawyer and statesman, born in Boston. He was defence counsel for President **Andrew Johnson** in the impeachment proceedings of 1868, US attorney-general, US counsel before the *Alabama* Tribunal in Geneva in 1872, from 1877 to 1881 secretary of state, and sat in the senate from 1885 to 1891.

EVATT, Herbert Vere (1894–1965) Australian jurist and statesman, born in East Maitland, South Australia. He studied at Sydney University, where he became tutor in philosophy and legal interpretation. He served in the New South Wales State Assembly, took silk in 1929 and was justice of the High Court of Australia from 1930 to 1940. He entered the federal parliament as a Labour member in 1940. As minister of external affairs (1941–49), he was a frequent visitor to Britain and delegate at international conferences. He represented Australia in **Churchill**'s war cabinet, and was leader of the opposition in the federal parliament, 1951–60, when he became chief justice of New South Wales until his retirement in 1962. He wrote *The King and his Dominion Governors* (1936) and some other works on constitutional law.

EVELYN, John (1620–1706) English diarist and author, born of wealthy parentage in Wotton, near Dorking. He was brought up in Lewes (1625–37), then entered Balliol College, Oxford, and in 1640 the Middle Temple. He witnessed **Strafford**'s trial and execution, and in November 1642 joined the king's army for three days. The Covenant being pressed on him, he travelled for four years on the Continent. In Paris in 1647 he married the ambassador's daughter, Mary Browne (1635–1709), and in 1652 settled at Sayes Court, Deptford. He spent a lot of time at court after the Restoration and acted on public committees and from 1685 to 1687 was one of the commissioners of the privy seal. From 1695 to 1703 he was treasurer of Greenwich Hospital and was a prominent fellow of the Royal Society. In 1694 he removed to his brother's at Wotton, and let Sayes Court to Admiral **Benbow**, who sublet it to **Peter I, the Great**. Evelyn, as active and intelligent as he was honest and God-fearing, was yet neither sage nor hero. He was always active in Church affairs and was especially prominent in the rebuilding of St Paul's Cathedral. He dealt with a multitude of subjects. Of his three dozen works the chief are *Fumifiguim, or the Inconvenience of the Air and Smoke of London dissipated* (1661); *Sculptura, or the Art of Engraving on Copper* (1662); *Sylva, or a Discourse of Forest-trees* (1664); and the delightful *Diary* (discovered in an old clothes-basket at Wotton in 1817), covering the years 1641–1706 and containing vivid portraits of his contemporaries.

EVERDINGEN, Allart van (1621–75) Dutch landscape painter and etcher, born in Alkmaar. He worked in the style of **Ruisdael**; his brother, Caesar (1606–79), was an historical and portrait painter.

EVEREST, Sir George (1790–1866) English military engineer and later surveyor-general of India. He completed the trigonometrical survey of the Indian sub-continent in 1841. Mount Everest is named after him.

EVERETT, Alexander Hill (1790–1847) American diplomat, born in Boston. He was appointed minister at the Hague in 1818, at Madrid in 1825. Proprietor and editor of the *North American Review* (1829–35), and elected to the Massachusetts legislature, in 1840 he was appointed US agent in Cuba, and in 1845 commissioner to China. His principal works are two series of *Critical and Miscellaneous Essays* (1845–47).

EVERETT, Edward (1794–1865) American statesman and scholar, brother of **Alexander Everett**, born in Dorchester, Massachusetts. He graduated at Harvard in 1811, and in 1815 was elected professor of Greek there. In 1820 he became editor of the *North American Review*, and in 1824 a member of the US congress. From 1835 to 1838 he was four times governor of Massachusetts, and from 1841 to 1845 minister at the court of St James's. He was president of Harvard 1846–49, in 1852 succeeded **Daniel Webster** as secretary of state, and in 1853 was returned to the US senate. He wrote *Defence of Christianity* (1814); poems; *Orations and Speeches* (1836–59); and the memoir prefixed to Daniel Webster's works (1852).

EVERSLEY See **SHAW-LEFEVRE**

EVERT, Chris (Christine Marie) (1954–) American tennis player, born in Fort Lauderdale, Florida. Arctic-cool on the courts (hence her nickname, Ice Maiden) she won three times at Wimbledon and took her own native American title six times; in a long Wightman Cup career which stretched from 1971 to 1982 she never experienced defeat in a singles match. She was married for a time to the English tennis player, John Lloyd, and was co-author with him of *Lloyd on Lloyd* (1985).

ÉVREMOND See **SAINT-ÉVREMOND**

EWALD, Heinrich Georg August von (1803–75) German orientalist and theologian, born in Göttingen, where he studied and became professor both of philosophy and of oriental languages. He was deprived of office in 1837 for refusing to take the oath of allegiance to the king of Prussia. He is best known for his *Hebrew Grammar* (1827), his *History of Israel* (1843–52) and a number of biblical works.

EWALD, Johannes (1743–81) Danish Romantic poet and dramatist, born in Copenhagen, and writer of the Danish national anthem. At the age of 15 he ran away from home to fight in the Seven Years' War (1756–63), then turned his attention to writing. He was one of the first Danish poets to use national legends and myths as material, as in his Biblical drama *Adam og Eva* (1769), the historical drama *Rolf Krage* (1770) and the lyrical drama *Balders Död* (1773). He also wrote an operetta, *Fiskerne* (The Fishermen, 1779), which contains the song 'King Kristian stood by the lofty mast', which is now the Danish national anthem.

EWART, James Cossar (1851–1933) Scottish zoologist, born in Penicuik. Professor of natural history at Aberdeen (1879–82) and Edinburgh (1882–1927), he carried out notable experiments in animal breeding and hybridization and disproved the theory of telegony.

EWART, William (1798–1869) English politician and reformer, born in Liverpool. He was Liberal MP (1828–68) for Bletchingly, Liverpool, Wigan, and the Dumfries Burghs. He played a leading part in humanitarian reforms, including the abolition of capital punishment for minor offences and of hanging prisoners in chains. He carried a free libraries bill in 1850.

EWELL, Richard Stoddart (1817–72) American soldier, born in Georgetown, DC. He served in Mexico and against the Apaches; but in the Civil War he resigned from the army to join the Confederates in 1861, and served under **Jackson** and **Lee**. He fought at Gettysburg and the Wilderness, and commanded the defences of Richmond. He was eventually captured with his entire force at Sailor's Creek in April 1865.

EWING, Sir (James) Alfred (1855–1935) Scottish engineer and physicist, born in Dundee. He was professor of engineering at Tokyo (1878–83) and Dundee (1883–90), of mechanism at Cambridge (1890–1903), director of naval education (1903–1916), and principal of Edinburgh University (1916–1929). During World War I he worked on the deciphering of intercepted messages.

EWING, Julianna Horatia, née **Gatty** (1841–85) English writer for children, daughter of Margaret Gatty (1809–73), also a children's writer. Born in Ecclesfield, Yorkshire, she soon began to compose nursery plays, which are said to have suggested to her mother the starting of *Aunt Judy's Magazine* (1866), which she later edited, publishing in it many of her charming stories, such as *Jackanapes*. Her numerous books included *A Flat Iron for a Farthing* (1870), *Lab-lie-by-the-Fire* (1873) and *Daddy Darwin's Dovecot* (1881).

EWING, William Maurice (1906–) American marine geologist, born in Lockney, Texas, and raised on a farm. He made the first measurements of the thickness of the oceanic crust and discovered the global extent of mid-ocean ridges. After an education at the Rice Institute, Houston and a teaching post at Lehigh University, Pennsylvania, he joined the Lamont-Doherty Geological Observatory, New York, in 1944 and did much to make it into one of the world's leading geophysical research institutes. He pioneered marine seismic techniques, which he used to show that the oceanic crust is much thinner (5-8 km thick) than the continental crust (c.40 km thick). The Mid-Atlantic Ridge had been discovered when cables were laid across the Atlantic. Ewing demonstrated the global extent of mid-ocean ridges, and in 1957 discovered a deep central rift in them. His work showed that the ocean sediment thickness increases with distance from the mid-ocean ridge. This supported the sea-floor spreading hypothesis proposed by H H Hess, an important part of plate tectonics.

EWINS, Arthur James, (1882–1957) English chemist, born in London. Educated at Alleyn's School, Dulwich, and at London University (Chelsea Polytechnic), in 1936–37 he conducted the researches ending in the preparation of sulphapyridine (M & B 693), of great value in the treatment of pneumonia, etc.

EWORTH, Hans (c.1520–after 1573) Flemish painter. He was recorded in the Antwerp Guild in

1540, but was active chiefly in England, being based in London from c.1545 for about 20 years. His surviving paintings are mainly portraits (signed with the monogram HE), though he is known also to have undertaken work for masques and pageants. In their careful technique and delicate rendering of detail his portraits owe much to **Holbein**, but in style and imagery they are more closely related to the sophisticated Mannerism fashionable in contemporary European court circles. Among his most elaborate allegorical portraits is **Sir John Lutterell** (1550).

EXEKIAS, or **Execias** (fl.second half 6th century BC) Greek potter and vase painter who worked in the so-called 'black figure' style. The most famous of his vessels—on which is inscribed 'Exekias made and decorated me'—is in the Vatican Museum and depicts Achilles and Ajax playing dice.

EXETER, Earls of See **CECIL**

EXMOUTH, Edward Pellew, 1st Viscount (1757–1833) English naval commander, born in Dover. He entered the navy at 13 and attracted notice in the battle on Lake Champlain (1776). He was captured at Saratoga in 1777. In 1793, in command of a frigate, he captured a much larger French frigate, and was knighted: in 1796, for acts of personal bravery, he was created a baronet. In 1798 he was sent to the French coast, where many of his most brilliant actions took place. In 1804 he was appointed commander-in-chief in India, from whose seas he drove the French cruisers; he was afterwards made commander-in-chief in the North Sea and in the Mediterranean. In 1814 he was promoted admiral, and in 1816 was sent to Algiers to enforce the treaty abolishing Christian slavery. With a fleet of 25 English and Dutch vessels he bombarded the city for nine hours, and inflicted such immense damage that the Dey consented to every demand.

EYADEMA, (Etienne) Gnassingbe (1937–) Togolese politician and soldier, born in Pya, in Lama Kara district. He joined the French army in 1953 and, after extensive foreign service, became army commander-in-chief, in 1965, with the rank of lieutenant-general. Two years later he led a bloodless coup to oust President Nicolas Grunitzky. He banned all political activity until he had founded a new organization, the assembly of the Togolese People (RPT), as the only legal party. Although there have been several attempts to overthrow him, he has begun to introduce a degree of democracy into the political system.

EYCK, Jan van (c.1389–1441) Netherlandish painter, born near Maastricht, the greatest Flemish artist of the 15th century. He was successively in the service of John of Bavaria, Count of Holland, and **Philip 'the Good'** of Burgundy, for whom he undertook diplomatic missions in Spain and Portugal. From 1431 he lived in Bruges. All the works which can be definitely attributed to him date from these last ten years of his life. During this period there is evidence of his increasing wealth and importance as court painter, diplomat and city official. The Eyckian style is created from a meticulous attention to detail, accuracy in rendering textures and superbly realistic light effects. The resulting realism has never been bettered. In the hands of Jan van Eyck the oil-technique attained near-perfection. **Vasari** incorrectly attributes the invention of the technique to him; however, it does seem that the 'secret' was transmitted to the Italian school by his pupil Petrus Christus via **Antonello da Messina**. There are three works by him in the National Gallery, London, including the superb *Man in a Red Turban* which some have thought to be a self-portrait, and the mysterious Arnolfini marriage portrait. By far his most famous work is the altarpiece *The Adoration of the Holy Lamb* in the church of Saint Bavon at Ghent. Commissioned by Jodocus Vyd, it consists of 24 panels and is regarded as the greatest masterpiece of early Flemish art. There has been much controversy over an inscription on the frame which seems to suggest that the work was begun by his brother Hubert, but in 1951 a committee of experts decided there was no evidence of any other hand. During every major European conflict the altarpiece has been looted from Ghent, but has always miraculously found its way back.

EYDE, Samuel (1866–1940) Norwegian engineer, born in Arendal. He was educated in Germany where he worked as a structural engineer for some time. He became increasingly interested in the potential for electro-chemical industries in his native land, and with **Kristian Birkeland** developed an economic electric arc process for the fixation of nitrogen, using Norway's abundant hydro-electric power.

EYRE, Edward John (1815–1901) English explorer and colonist, the son of a Yorkshire clergyman. He emigrated to Australia at 17, settled on the Lower Murray as a sheep farmer, and was appointed a magistrate. In 1840–41 he explored the region between South and Western Australia, and discovered Lake Eyre. In 1847 he became governor of New Zealand, in 1854 of St Vincent, and in 1862 of Jamaica. In 1865 he suppressed a native rebellion at Morant Bay with the utmost severity; the alleged ring-leader (a wealthy Baptist mulatto who was also a member of the Jamaica House of Assembly) was court-martialled and hanged. Eyre was recalled to England and prosecuted amidst great public controversy, but was cleared.

EYRE, Richard (1943–) English stage director, born in Barnstaple. He began his career in 1965 at the Phoenix, Leicester. He became associate director of the Lyceum Theatre, Edinburgh, in 1967 and director of productions from 1970 to 1972. From 1973 to 1978 he was artistic director of the Nottingham Playhouse. From 1978 to 1981 he was producer of the BBC Television *Play for Today* series. Other television plays include *Tumbledown* (1988), a Falklands War saga. He has made three films, including *The Ploughman's Lunch* (1983). He was associate director of the National Theatre, London (1980–86), and in 1988 was appointed director.

EYSENCK, Hans Jurgen (1916–) German-born British psychologist, born in Berlin, probably the best-known name in postwar British psychology. Educated in France and at London University (BA 1938, PhD 1940, DSc 1964), he began his career in the field of clinical psychology, which led on to psychometric researches into the normal variations of human personality and intelligence. Throughout his career he has been an outspoken critic of loose thinking published in the name of psychology, particularly of claims made without adequate empirical evidence. A prolific and gifted writer, he has been a merciless critic of psychoanalysis in its various forms. He has frequently championed the view that genetic factors play a large part in determining the psychological differences between people, and has often held controversial views, particularly with his study of racial differences in intelligence in *Race, Intelligence and Education* (1971). This, combined with the polemical tone he has sometimes adopted, may have lessened the international impact of his writings. From 1955 to 1983 he was professor of psychology at the Insititute of Psychiatry of London University. He is a recipient of the American Psychological Association's Distinguished Scientific Award (1988).

EYVINDUR, known as **Skáldaspillir (The Plagiarist)** (d.c.990) Norwegian court poet of the Viking Age, properly **Eyvindur Jónsson**. Born of a noble family, he was a devoted follower of King **Haakon I, 'the Good'** of Norway, whom he eulogized in his *Hákonarmál*. He later wrote a eulogy in praise of Earl Haakon of Norway (*Haleygjatal*), and an *Íslendingadrápa* about Icelanders.

EZEKIEL Old Testament prophet, successor to **Isaiah** and **Jeremiah**. According to the *Book of Ezekiel*, he was carried captive to Mesopotamia by **Nebuchadrezzar** in 597 BC. The prophecies were composed during the Babylonian captivity, and looked forward to a new Jerusalem after the destruction of the old.

EZRA the Scribe, Old Testament reformer. He was living in Babylon either during the reign of **Artaxerxes Longimanus**, or, during that of **Artaxerxes II**, about 70 years later. He was commissioned to lead a band of his fellow countrymen from Babylon to Jerusalem (458 or 397 BC), to reorganize the returned Jews there. He is believed to have arranged the books of the Mosaic law (the Pentateuch) as they are now. The *Book of Ezra* records the return of the Jews after the Babylonian captivity in c.537 BC, and the rebuilding of the Temple.

F

FABER, Cecilia See **CABALLERO, Fernán**

FABER, Frederick William (1814–63) English hymn writer, born in Calverley, Yorkshire. He graduated from Oxford, where he won the Newdigate prize for poetry (1836). He took Anglican orders, but under the influence of **John Newman** he turned Catholic and founded in 1845 a lay community of converts (the 'Wilfridians'). He wrote many theological works, but is remembered for his *Hymns* (1861) which include 'My God, how wonderful Thou art' and 'Hark, hark my soul'.

FABER, John (1684–1756) English mezzotint engraver, son of John Faber 'the Elder' (c. 1660–1721, a draughtsman and engraver from the Hague). His chief works are the portraits of the *Kit-Cat Club* and *The Beauties of Hampton Court*.

FABERGÉ, Peter Carl (Karl Gustavovich Fabergé) (1846–1920) Russian goldsmith and jeweller of Huguenot descent, born in St Petersburg. Educated in Dresden, Italy, France and England, he inherited his father's establishment in 1870. Fabergé moved from the design and manufacture of conventional jewellery to the creation of more elaborate and fantastic objects, most famous of which are probably the celebrated imperial Easter eggs, first commisioned by **Alexander III** for his tsarina in 1884. Fabergé's skilled artists and craftsmen in his workshops produced exceptionally delicate and imaginative flowers, animals, groups of figures, etc, much prized by Russian, European and Asian royalty. He died in exile in Lausanne after his business had been destroyed by the events of the Russian revolution.

FABIUS the name of a patrician family of Rome. In 481 BC the Fabii were decoyed into an ambush by the Veientes, and all but one out of 306 men were killed.

FABIUS Quintus Fabius Rullianus (4th century BC), Roman general in the second Samnite war. He was dictator (315 BC), censor (304 BC) and six times consul.

FABIUS, Caius Fabius, surnamed **Pictor ('Painter')** (4th century BC) Roman general. He earned his surname by decorating the temple of Salus in Rome with the earliest known Roman paintings (304 BC).

FABIUS, Laurent (1946–) French socialist politician. The son of a wealthy Jewish art dealer in Paris, he had a brilliant academic career at the École Normale Supérieure and the École Nationale d'Administration. He joined the Council of State as an auditor in 1973 and became economic adviser to the Socialist party (PS) leader, **François Mitterrand**, in 1976. Elected to the National Assembly in 1978, representing the Seine-Maritime constituency, he was appointed budget minister when the PS gained power in 1981, and minister for research and industry in 1983. In 1984 he was appointed prime minister at the age of 37, in an effort to revive the PS's sagging fortunes. He introduced a liberal, 'freer market' economic programme, which had some success, but resigned following his party's electoral defeat in March 1986. A popular and moderate 'social democrat', he heads an influential faction within the PS.

FABIUS, Quintus Fabius Maximus Verrucosus, known as **'Cunctator'** (d.203 BC) Roman soldier, five times consul and twice censor. In the 2nd Punic War (218–202 BC) he was elected dictator (217 BC) after the Roman defeat at Lake Trasimene, and by his defensive tactics was known as Cunctator ('Delayer'). Avoiding direct encounters, he carried on guerrilla warfare and allowed Rome to muster her forces. The derisive nickname took on an honourable connotation after the disastrous Roman defeat at Cannae (216), and the 'Fabian' tactics were resumed. In 209 he recovered Tarentum and was made consul for the fifth time. He died just before the successful conclusion of the war.

FABIUS, Quintus Fabius Pictor Roman general, grandson of **'Cunctator' Fabius**. He wrote (in Greek) tne first Roman history in prose.

FABRE, Ferdinand (1830–98) French novelist, born in Bédarieux. He wrote *L'Abbé Tigrane* (1873) and other stories of rustic life in Cévennes.

FABRE, Jean Henri (1823–1915) French entomologist (the 'Insects' Homer'), born in St Léon, Aveyron. He taught in schools at Carpentras, Ajaccio and Avignon before retiring to Sérignan in Vaucluse, where he continued until his death. His *Souvenirs entomologiques* (10 vols, 1879–1907) are masterpieces of minute and patient observations.

FABRE D'ÉGLANTINE, Philippe François Nazaire (1750–94) French dramatist, poet, and revolutionist, born in Carcassone. He wrote *Le Philinte de Molière* (1790), a sequel to Molière's *Le Misanthrope*. A member of the National Convention, he devised some of the new names of months for the Revolutionary Calendar, but, having fallen out of favour with **Robespierre**, was eventually guillotined.

FABRIANO, Gentile da, properly **Niccolo di giovanni di Massio** (?1370–?1427) Italian painter, born in Fabriano in the Marches. Along with **Ghiberti** he is the major exponent in Italy of the International Gothic Style. He first achieved fame with his decorations for the Doge's Palace in Venice (all now lost) and then went on to work throughout Italy's main centres before reaching Rome where he executed frescoes in the church of San Giovanni in Laterano (also lost). His greatest surviving work is the *Adoration of the Magi*, now in the Uffizi Gallery, Florence, and in this work all the main facets of Gentile's opulent style can be studied: complex lighting effects, rich use of colour and gilding and careful attention to detail. The overall impression is intensely decorative. Gentile's style is often considered as 'old fashioned' for the period by art historians, but in comparison with that of his contemporary **Masaccio**, Gentile's work was thought the most advanced in his own day.

FABRICIUS, David (1564–1617) German astronomer and clergyman, born in Esens. In 1586 he discovered the first variable star (Mira, in the constellation Cetus). He was pastor at Resterhaave and Osteel in East Friesland, where he was murdered.

FABRICIUS, Hieronymus, or **Girolamo Fabrici** (1537–1619) Italian anatomist, born in Acquapendente. He studied at Padua under **Gabriele Falloppio** and succeeded him as professor of anatomy there (1562). One of his pupils was **William Harvey**.

FABRICIUS, Johannes (1587–1615) German astronomer and physician, son of **David Fabricius**. He discovered the sun's spots and its revolution.

FABRICUS, Johann Christian (1745–1808) Danish entomologist, born in Tondern in Schleswig, one of the founders of entomological taxonomy. In 1775 he became professor of natural history at Kiel. His classification of insects was based on the structure of the mouth.

FABRITIUS, Carel (1622–54) Dutch painter, born in Beemster. He worked under **Rembrandt** around 1641 and lived mainly at Delft, where he was killed in an explosion. He is important for the influence of his sensitive experiments in composition and the painting of light (as in the tiny *View of Delft*, 1652, in the National Gallery, London) upon his pupil **Vermeer**. Some of his paintings have been attributed to his brother Barent (1624–73), also a pupil of Rembrandt.

FABRY, Marie Paul Auguste Charles (1867–1945) French physicist. He became professor at Marseilles (1904) and the Sorbonne (1920). Inventor of the Fabry-Perot interferometer, he is also known for his researches into light in connection with astronomical phenomena.

FABYAN, Robert (d.1513) English chronicler. A clothier, he was sheriff of London in 1493. His history, *The New Chronicles of England and France* (1516), comes down in its second edition (1533) to the death of **Henry VII**. From the accession of **Richard I** it takes the form of a London chronicle, this being its chief value.

FACCIOLATI, Jacopo (1682–1769) Italian philologist and lexicographer. Professor at Padua, he brought out (1715–19) a new edition of **Calepino**'s polyglot dictionary, *Lexicon Undecim Linguarum*, in collaboration with Egidio Forcellini (1688–1768). They also worked on a new Latin dictionary, *Totius Latinitatis Lexicon* (1771).

FADEYEV, Aleksandr Aleksandrovich, pseud **Bulgya** (1901–56) Russian novelist of the socialist realism school. He was deeply influenced by **Tolstoy**, and wrote *The Rout* (1927) set in the Russian civil war, and *The Young Guard* (1945) portraying Russian resistance against the Germans in World War II. As general-secretary of the Soviet Writers' Union (1946–55) he mercilessly exposed any literary 'deviationism' from the party line but became himself a target and, compelled to revise the last-named work (1951), took to drink and finally shot himself.

FAED, John (1819–1902) Scottish painter, born in Burley Mill, Kirkcudbrightshire, brother of **Thomas Faed**. He studied at the Edinburgh School of Design from 1841, and became a noted painter of miniatures in London. He also painted figure subjects like *The Cottar's Saturday Night* (1854).

FAED, Thomas (1826–1900) Scottish painter, born in Burley Mill, Kirkcudbrightshire, brother of **John Faed**. He studied at the Edinburgh School of Design, and was elected an associate of the Royal Scottish Academy in 1849 when he produced *Scott and his Friends at Abbotsford*, engraved by his brother. He went to London in 1852 and made his name with paintings of humble incidents in Scottish life. Elected RA in 1864, he resigned in 1893.

FAGAN, Garth (1940–) Jamaican dancer, choreographer and artistic director, born in Kingston. As a teenager he toured Latin America with Ivy Baxter and Rex Nettleford's Jamaican National Dance Company. He later attended college in the USA and danced with, and choreographed for, several Detroit-based companies. Soon after joining the faculty of the State University of New York, Brockport (1970), he began teaching untrained urban youths at nearby Rochester. The fruit of these classes was The Bottom of the Bucket But... Dance Theatre, shortened to Bucket Dance Theatre a decade later. He fashioned his pupils into a disciplined professional ensemble who expertly convey the Fagan style, a fusion of modern and jazz dance with the influences of both Afro-Caribbean and classical ballet movement. He occasionally choreographs dances for other companies and directs stage shows.

FAGUET, Émile (1847–1916) French literary critic, born in La Roche sur Yon, Vendée. Professor of French literature at the Sorbonne from 1890, he wrote a number of great works of literary history, among them *Politiques et moralistes du XIXe siècle* (1891–1900), *Histoire de la littérature française* (1900–01), and *Le Féminisme* (1910).

FAHRENHEIT, Gabriel Daniel (1686–1736) German physicist, born in Danzig, who lived and worked in Holland. In 1709 he devised a thermometer that used alcohol, and about 1714 he invented the mercury thermometer. He also devised the temperature scale named after him, fixing the freezing point at 32° to avoid negative measurements. He was the first to show that the boiling point of liquids varies at different atmospheric pressures.

FÂ-HSIEN (fl.400) Chinese Buddhist monk and traveller. At the beginning of the 5th century AD, he made a pilgrimage to India across the Takla Makan desert and Pamirs, following the Upper Indus River south to Sri Lanka in search of holy texts. He returned by sea through south-east Asia.

FAIDHERBE, Louis Léon César (1818–89) French soldier and scholar, born in Lille. As governor of Senegal (1854) he greatly extended the frontiers of his province (1858–61). In the Franco-Prussian War, commanding the army of the North, he was defeated near St Quentin in 1871. After the peace he was dispatched by the French government to Egypt to study the monuments. He wrote on Numidian and Phoenician inscriptions (1870–74), the anthropology of Algiers and the French Sudan (1874–84), a work on Sénégal (1889), and treatises on the Fula (or Poul) and Berber languages (1875–77), besides *Campagne de l'armée du nord* (1871).

FAIRBAIRN, Andrew Martin (1838–1912) Scottish Congregational theologian, born in Inverkeithing. He is known for his brilliant essays in the *Contemporary Review*, and his *Studies in the Philosophy of Religion and History* (1876), and *Christ in Modern Theology* (1894). From 1888 to 1909 he was principal of Mansfield College (Congregational), Oxford.

FAIRBAIRN, Sir William (1789–1874) Scottish engineer, born in Kelso. In 1804 he was apprenticed to an engine-wright at North Shields, where he studied mathematics, and made the acquaintance of **George Stephenson**. Moving to Manchester in 1817 he began making machinery for cotton-mills etc, and in 1830 he took a lead in making iron boats; his works at Millwall, London (1835–49), turned out hundreds of vessels. For Stephenson's bridge over the Menai Strait he invented the rectangular tube ultimately adopted; and he erected a thousand bridges upon this principle. He aided **Joule** and Lord **Kelvin** in 1851 in investigations, and guided the experiments of the government committee (1861–65) on the use of iron for defensive purposes.

FAIRBANKS, Douglas Elton, Senior, originally **Ullman** (1833–1939) American film actor, born in Denver, Colorado. He first appeared in stage plays in 1901, but in 1915 went into films and made a speciality of swashbuckling hero parts, as in *The Three Musketeers* (1921), *Robin Hood* (1922) and *The Thief of Baghdad* (1924) in which he did all his own stunts. He was a founder of United Pictures. In 1920 he married **Mary Pickford** (divorced 1935). His son **Douglas Fairbanks, Junior** followed in his footsteps.

FAIRBANKS, Douglas, Junior (1909–) American film actor, son of **Douglas Fairbanks, Senior**. In his youth he made Hollywood movies in the style of his father, like *Catherine the Great* (1934), *The Prisoner of Zenda* (1937) and *Sinbad the Sailor* (1947), and also gained a reputation as a producer. He later became interested in international affairs, and made a name for himself as a diplomat. He distinguished himself in World War II, winning the British DSC and the American Silver Star. He was created an honorary KBE in 1949.

FAIREY, Sir (Charles) Richard (1887–1956) English aeronautical inventor and industrialist, born in Hendon, London. He studied electrical engineering at Finsbury Technical College and embarked first on an electrical career. He was also a skilled model aircraft builder, and became chief engineer to aircraft manufacturers Short Brothers in 1913. He formed Fairey Aviation Company in 1915, starting by building Short designs. Over 100 different types were produced during his 40 years as head of the firm and by 1925 half the aircraft in the RAF were of Fairey origin. Famous types from his factory include: Fox, Long-Range Monoplane, Hendon, Fantome, Swordfish, Albacore, Barracuda, Gannet, and Firefly. After World War II the company worked on guided weapons and helicopters and the Fairey 'Delta' was the first aircraft to fly at over 1000 mph (1132 mph) in 1956, just prior to his death. In 1927 he took up yachting, designing advanced hulls and winning many races.

FAIRFAX, Edward (c.1580–1635) English scholar, son of Sir Thomas Fairfax of Denton in Yorkshire. His life was spent in literary pursuits, at Fewston, near Otley, and his translation of **Tasso**'s *Gerusalemme Liberata* (1600) is noteworthy. His *Discourse of Witchcraft* (1621) was published in the *Miscellanies* of the Philobiblon Society (1858–59).

FAIRFAX, John (1804–77) English-born Australian newspaper proprietor, born in Warwick. In 1828 he founded a newspaper in the neighbouring town of Leamington, and in 1835 became part-owner of another. After twice successfully defending a libel action he was unable to meet his costs and was declared insolvent. He left England with his family and arrived in Sydney in 1838. Three years later he bought with a partner, on credit, the established daily newspaper *The Sydney Herald* which in 1842 became *The Sydney Morning Herald*. For the first few years the two partners performed every function, writing, editing and printing, and their success was such that in 1851 Fairfax returned to Leamington and repaid all his creditors in full. He also purchased a steam printing-press which on its arrival in Sydney in 1853 became the first of its kind to print a newspaper in Australia.

FAIRFAX, Thomas, 3rd Baron Fairfax of Cameron (1612–71) English parliamentary soldier, son of Ferdinando, Lord Fairfax, born in Denton, Yorkshire. From 1629 he served in Holland, under Sir Horace, 1st Baron **Vere**, whose daughter Anne he married (1637). In the Civil War (from 1642) he was general of Parliamentary horse and after distinguished action at Marston Moor (1644), was appointed to succeed the 3rd Earl of **Essex** in the supreme command in 1645 and defeated **Charles I** at the decisive battle of Naseby. In 1650, on Fairfax's refusal to march against the Scots, who had proclaimed **Charles II** king, **Cromwell** was appointed commander-in-chief, and Fairfax withdrew into private life. After Cromwell's death he assisted **Monk** against **John Lambert**; and was head of the commission dispatched to The Hague in 1660 to arrange for the return of Charles II.

FAIRFIELD, Cicily Isabel See **WEST, Dame Rebecca**

FAIRWEATHER, Ian (1891–1974) Scottish-born Australian painter, born in Bridge of Allan. After serving in the army in World War I he attended the Slade School of Art in London from 1920, where he developed an interest in Oriental art. He eventually became a student of Chinese and his painting was very much influenced by the art of non-European cultures. From 1924 he travelled extensively, living and working in, amongst other places, Germany, Canada, China, Japan, India, as well as Australia. In 1940 he served as a captain in the British army in India until, invalided out in 1943, he returned to Australia. In 1952 he attempted to sail from Darwin to Indonesia in a home-made raft. Although he eventually landed, he had been presumed lost at sea and an obituary had already appeared in the Australian press. After several more adventures, he returned to Australia in 1953 and, from that time until his death, he lived and worked in a hut he built on Bribie Island off the Queensland coast.

FAISAL I (1885–1933) king of the Helaz, born in Ta'if, son of **Hussein-ibn-Ali**. He played a prominent role in the Arab revolt against Turkey, 1916–18 and became king of Iraq in 1921.

FAISAL II, in full **Faisal ibn Ghazi ibn Faisal el Hashim** (1935–58) king of Iraq, was born in Baghdad, great-grandson with King **Hussein** of **Hussein-ibn-Ali**. He succeeded his father, King Ghazi, who was killed in an accident, in 1939. After an education at Harrow he was installed in 1953 as the third king of modern Iraq, thus ending the regency of his uncle, Emir Abdul Illah. He paid a state visit to Britain in 1956. Although in 1956, in the aftermath of the Suez intervention, he formally declared that Iraq would continue to stand by Egypt, rivalry later grew between the two incipient Arab blocs. In 1958 he therefore concluded with his cousin King Hussein of Jordan a federation of the two countries in opposition to the United Arab Republic of Egypt and Syria. In July that year, he and his entire household were assassinated during a military *coup d'état* and Iraq became a republic.

FAITHFULL, Emily (1835–95) English publisher and feminist, born at Headley Rectory, Surrey. In 1860 she founded in London a printing house with women compositors, and was appointed printer and publisher-in-ordinary to Queen **Victoria**. In 1863 she started the *Victoria Magazine*, advocating the claims of women to remunerative employment; and in 1868 she published *Change upon Change*, a novel.

FAITHORNE, William (1616–91) English engraver, born in London. He fought as a royalist, and having been banished for refusing allegiance to **Cromwell** spent several years in Paris, where he made engravings of prints from the vast collection of the Abbé de Villeloin. Allowed home in 1650, he achieved fame as a portraitist and also engraved Newcourt's maps of London and Westminster, and of Virginia and Maryland. He published *The Art of Graving and Etching* in 1662.

FAJANS, Kasimir (1887–1975) Polish-born American physical chemist, born in Warsaw. Educated at Leipzig, Heidelberg and Manchester, he was professor of chemistry at Munich (1917–35), then at Michigan (1936–57). He formulated the theory of isotopes, and contributed valuable research in connection with uranium X_1, the age of minerals in Norway, and the energies of hydration of ions. He wrote *Radio-activity and Latest Developments in the Study of Chemical Elements* (1919) and *Radio-elements and Isotopes* (1931).

FALCO, Louis (1942–) American modern dancer and choreographer, born in New York City. After studying with **José Limón**, **Martha Graham**, and Charles Weidman, he joined the Limón company in 1960. In his ten years with them he performed in Limón's *The Demon*, *Missa Brevis*, *The Winged*, and *The Exiles and Psalms*. In 1967 he formed his own company and began to choreograph. His works, popular with audiences, have since been included in the repertoires of many of the world's major contemporary dance companies including Boston Ballet, Rambert Dance Company and Netherlands Dance Theatre. His film work includes the dance element of the successful theatre school story, *Fame* (1980).

FALCONE, Aniello (1600–56) Italian artist. He founded a school of battle painters in Naples, and was the teacher of **Salvator Rosa**.

FALCONER, Hugh (1808–65) Scottish botanist and palaeontologist, born in Forres. He studied medicine at Edinburgh, joined the Bengal medical service, became keeper of the botanic garden at Sahāranpur (1832), and discovered many fossils in the Siwālik hills. He made the first experiments in growing tea in India. Back in England for his health (1842), he wrote on Indian botany and palaeontology, arranged Indian fossils in the British Museum and East India House, and prepared his great illustrated folio, *Fauna Antiqua Sivalensis* (1846–49). He returned to India in 1847 as superintendent of the botanic garden and professor of botany at Calcutta. His *Palaeontological Memoirs and Notes* were published in 1868.

FALCONER, Ion Keith (1856–87) Irish orientalist, missionary and athlete, third son of the Earl of Kintore. While at Cambridge he began evangelistic work, continued at Mile End in London. A keen cyclist, he defeated the then fastest rider in the world (1878), and rode from Land's End to John o' Groats. Professor of Arabic at Cambridge, he had settled at Shaikh Othman near Aden as a Free Church missionary, when he died of fever. In 1885 he translated the Fables of Bidpai.

FALCONER, William (1732–69) Scottish poet and seaman, born in Edinburgh. A barber's son, he went to sea, and soon was shipwrecked off Greece, this voyage forming the subject of his long poem, *The Shipwreck* (1762). He then entered the royal navy, being appointed in 1769 purser on the frigate *Aurora*, which foundered with all hands near Capetown. His *Demagogue* (1764), is a satire on **Wilkes** and **Marlborough**, and he was also author of the *Universal Marine Dictionary* (1769).

FALCONET, Étienne Maurice (1716–91) French sculptor, born in Paris. A pupil of **François Le Moyne**, he was director of sculpture at the Sèvres Porcelain Factory from 1757 to 1766. His figures of Venus, bathers and similar subjects epitomize the rococo style of the period of **Louis XV** and were very popular with patrons such as Mme **de Pompadour**. It was through the influence of **Denis Diderot** that **Catherine II** invited him to Russia in 1766 to execute what is his most impressive work, an equestrian monument to **Peter I, the Great** in St Petersburg (Leningrad). After suffering a stroke in 1783, he turned to writing art theory, nine volumes of which had been published by 1787.

FALDO, Nick (Nicholas Alexander) (1957–) English golfer, born in Welwyn Garden City. He had early successes in winning the Professional Golfing Association championships in 1978, 1980 and 1981, and in 1987 won the Open Championship at Muirfield in appalling conditions. A year later he lost the US Open tournament in a play-off with Curtis Strange. In 1989 he won the US Masters, and successfully defended his title in 1990.

FALGUIÈRE, Jean Alexandre Joseph (1831–1900) French sculptor and painter, born in Toulouse, celebrated for his portrait statues rather than his larger compositions. Several sculptures and paintings are in the Luxembourg in Paris; his statue of Lafayette stands in Washington, DC.

FALIERO, Marino (c.1274–1355) doge of Venice. He defeated the Hungarians at Zara in 1346, captured Capo d'Istria, was ambassador to Rome and Genoa, and became Doge in 1354. The following year, after conspiring unsuccessfully to overthrow the oligarchs, he was arrested and beheaded. His fate is the theme of tragedies by **Byron** and **Swinburne** and of a famous painting by **Delacroix**.

FALK, Adalbert (1827–1900) Prussian statesman, born at Metschkau, Silesia. As minister of public worship (1872–79) he was instrumental in carrying the May laws (1873–1875) against the hierarchical supremacy of the Church of Rome.

FALK, Johann Daniel (1768–1826) German writer and philanthropist, born in Danzig. He founded the 'company of friends in need' for helping destitute children, and established the Falk Institute at Weimar. Of his writings the best known are his satirical works like *Der Mensch* (1795) and a study on Goethe.

FALKEBERGET, Johann Petter, originally **Lillebakken** (1879–1967) Norwegian novelist, born in Nordre-Rugel. A miner from the age of eight, and the son of a miner, he wrote realistic novels of working class life in his area. His first novel was *Svarte Fjelde* (Black Mountains, 1907). He also wrote *Den fjerde nattevakt* (The Fourth Night-Watch, 1923), and two trilogies, *Christianus Sextus* (1927–35) and *Nattens brød* (Night's Bread, 1940–59).

FALKEHAYN, Erich von (1861–1922) German soldier, born near Graudenz in West Prussia. He served as an adviser with the Chinese army, and with the International force in the Boxer Rebellion (1900). He was Prussian war minister in 1913 and succeeded **Moltke** as chief of general staff in September 1914. He was relieved of command after the failure of his offensive strategy which caused enormous bloodshed at Verdun in August 1916. He directed the 'push' against Warsaw in 1915, and commanded in the invasion of Rumania, 1916–17. He was transferred to Palestine in July 1917. His last command was in Lithuania in 1918.

FALKENDER, Marcia Matilda, Baroness (1932–) British political worker. She took a history degree at Queen Mary College, London, then worked at Labour party headquarters before becoming private and political secretary to Prime Minister **Harold Wilson** (1956–73). Her background influence during the 1964–70 Labour government is chronicled in her book *Inside No. 10* (1972). She was given a life peerage in 1974.

FALKLAND, Lucius Cary, Viscount (1610–43) English statesman and writer, born probably in Burford, Oxfordshire, and educated at Trinity College, Dublin. On his father's death, in 1633 he inherited the title Viscount Falkland and his house at Tew, in Oxon, became the centre for the brightest intellects of Oxford and London, including **Sheldon**, **Morley**, **Hammond**, Earle, Chillingworth, John Hales and **Clarendon**. In 1639 he entered parliament as member for Newport (Isle of Wight) and, although mistrusting his character, took **Charles I**'s side against intolerant Presbyterianism. In 1642 he accepted the secretaryship of state and when war broke out loyally supported the king. He was killed at Newbury on 20 September, 1643.

FALKNER, William Harrison See **FAULKNER**

FALLA, Manuel de (1876–1946) Spanish composer, born in Cadiz. He studied the piano as a child, and the failure of a comic opera in 1902 moved him to spend two years in study under **Pedrell**, so that by 1905 he was awarded prizes both for his piano-playing and for his opera *La Vida Breve*. During his seven years in Paris, up to the outbreak of World War I, he composed in a less exclusively national style, but after his return to Spain his music gradually returned to his original colourful Spanish idiom. His international fame was crowned by the success of his ballet, *The Three-Cornered Hat*, in 1919. With the outbreak of the Spanish Civil War, he settled in South America. Commonly accepted as the greatest of the group of Spanish composers active in the early 20th century, his works include the opera *Master Peter's Puppet Show*, the ballet *Love the Magician* and the piano and orchestra suite *Nights in the Gardens of Spain*.

FALLADA, Hans, pseud of **Rudolf Ditzen** (1893–1947) German writer, born in Greifswald. He achieved international fame with his novel of German social problems, *Kleiner Mann, Was Nun?* (1932), translated into English as *Little Man, What Now?*

FALLERSLEBEN See **HOFFMANN, August**

FALLIÈRES, Armand (1841–1931) French president (1906–13), born in Agen, became an advocate, deputy, premier (1883), and president of the senate, 1899–1906.

FALLMERAYER, Jakob Philipp (1790–1861) German historian, born in Tschötsch. In 1826 he became professor of history and philology at Landshut. He wrote on the empire of Trebizond (1827) and on the Morea (1830–36). He insisted that the modern Greeks are mainly Slavonic in origin.

FALLOPPIO, Gabriele, Italian **Gabriele Falloppia** (1523–62) Italian anatomist, born in Modena. He became professor of anatomy at Pisa (1548) and Padua (1551), and specially studied the bones and the organs of generation; the Fallopian tube connecting the ovaries with the uterus is named after him.

FALLOUX, Fréderic Alfred Pierre, Comte de (1811–86) French politician and writer, born in Angers. A liberal Catholic, he drew attention by two legitimist works—*L'Histoire de Louis XVI* (1840) and *L'Histoire de Saint Pie V* (1884). Falloux was minister of public instruction for ten months under **Louis Napoleon**, but after the *coup d'état* he retired from public life. He was a member of the French Academy.

FALLS, Cyril Bentham (1888–1971) English military historian, educated at Bradfield College, Portora Royal School, Enniskillen, and London University. He served as a staff officer in World War I and won the *Croix de Guerre*. He was military correspondent of *The Times* (1939–53) and Chichele professor of the history of war at Oxford (1946–53). He wrote the official history of the British campaigns in Egypt, Palestine, Macedonia and France, studies of **Rudyard Kipling** and Marshal **Foch**, *A Short History of the Second World War* (1948), *The First World War* (1960), and other works.

FALSTAFF See **OLDCASTLE, Sir John** and **FASTOLF, Sir John**

FALWELL, Jerry (1933–) American Baptist evangelist, born in Lynchburg, Virginia. He studied engineering at Lynchburg, but after a religious conversion graduated from Baptist Bible College, Springfield, Missouri, and in 1956 became pastor of Thomas Road Baptist Church, Lynchburg, which he founded. There he inaugurated the television 'Old-Time Gospel Hour', and founded Liberty Baptist College. In 1979 he founded Moral Majority Inc., forming a rallying point for conservative opinion in the 1980 and 1984 Presidential election campaigns. In 1982 an influential publication listed him among the 20 most prominent people in America. He wrote *Listen, America!* (1980), *The Fundamentalist Phenomenon* (1981), and *Wisdom for Living* (1984).

FAN K'UAN (fl.c.990–1030) Chinese landscape painter, born in Hua-yuan, Shensi Province, a representative of the Monumental Style of Chinese painting which began between the fall of the T'ang dynasty and the foundation of the Sung dynasty in 960. The painted silk hanging scroll, *Travelling in Streams and Mountains* (Palace Museum, Taiwan), one of the few surviving paintings of the period, and possibly the greatest single example of the style, is attributed to Fan K'uan. Based on the practice of Taoism and the contemplation of nature—in his case the austere grandeur of the Shensi mountains to which he retired—his work led contemporary critics to attribute to him a power of creation which mirrors that of nature itself.

FANEUIL, Peter (1700–43) American merchant and philanthropist, born in New Rochelle, New York. He made a fortune in Boston and built the Faneuil Hall in Boston, known as 'the cradle of American liberty' (1742), and presented it to the town.

FANFANI, Amintore (1908–) Italian politician. A former professor of political economics, Fanfani was prime minister five times—briefly in 1954, 1958–59, twice from 1960 to 1963, and 1982–83. Nominated a life senator in 1972, he was president of the Italian senate 1968–73 and 1976–82. He is a member (and former secretary and chairman) of the Christian Democratic Party. He was prime minister 1980–81, briefly in 1983, and again briefly in 1987.

FANGIO, Juan Manuel (1911–) Argentine racing driver, born in Balcarce of Italian descent. He served his racing apprenticeship first as a mechanic and then driving a car he had built himself in South American events. He first took part in European Grand Prix racing in 1949, and in 1951 won the first of his five world championships; he was world champion again for four consecutive years from 1954 to 1957. His record of 24 Grand Prix wins was only bettered ten years later by **Jim Clark**.

FANSHAWE, Richard (1608–66) English scholar and diplomat, born at Ware Park, Hertfordshire. He studied at Jesus College, Cambridge, and went abroad to study languages. In the Civil War he fought for the Royalists, and while at Oxford married in 1644 Anne Harrison (1625–80). In 1648 he became treasurer to the navy under Prince **Rupert**, in 1651 was taken prisoner at Worcester, and on **Cromwell**'s death withdrew to the Continent. After the Restoration he was appointed ambassador at the courts of Portugal and Spain, and died suddenly at Madrid. He translated **Horace**, **Guarini**'s *Pastor Fido*, and **Camoens**' *Lusiad*. Lady Fanshawe's charming Memoirs were published in 1829.

FANTIN-LATOUR, (Ignace) Henri Joseph Théodore (1836–1904) French painter and printmaker, born in Grenoble. Having first been taught by his father, he went on to study at the École des Beaux Arts under **Courbet** and was a regular exhibitor at the French Salon from 1861 to 1899. Despite his academic background he also showed work at the controversial Salon des Refusés of 1863, and became friendly with some of the most advanced painters of his day, such as **Manet**, **Whistler** and Courbet. He made several visits to London and exhibited at the Royal Academy. His subject matter was varied: in France he was particularly admired for his portrait groups, in England for his still-lifes, especially of flowers. He was a great devotee of Romantic composers such as **Berlioz**, and especially of **Wagner**, and made a series of lithographs illustrating their music.

FARADAY, Michael (1791–1867) English chemist and physicist, creator of classical field theory. Born in

Newington Butts near London, the son of a blacksmith, he was apprenticed to a bookbinder whose books sparked his interest in science. In 1813, after applying to **Humphry Davy** for a job, he was taken on as his temporary assistant, accompanying him soon after on an 18-month European tour during which he met many top scientists and gained an irregular but invaluable scientific education. In 1827 he succeeded to Davy's chair of chemistry at the Royal Institution, in that year publishing his *Chemical Manipulation*. His early publications on physical science include papers on the condensation of gases, limits of vaporization and optical deceptions. He was the first to isolate benzene, and he synthesized the first chlorocarbons. His great life work, however, was the series of *Experimental Researches on Electricity* published over 40 years in *Philosophical Transactions*, in which he described his many discoveries, including electromagnetic induction (1831), the laws of electrolysis (1833) and the rotation of polarized light by magnetism (1845). He received a pension in 1835 and in 1858 was given a house in Hampton Court. As adviser to the Trinity House in 1862 he advocated the use of electric lights in lighthouses. Greatly influential on later physics, he nevertheless had no pupils and worked with only one long-suffering assistant. He is generally considered the greatest of all experimental physicists.

FAREL, Guillaume (1489–1565) French Reformer, born in Gap in Dauphiné. He studied in Paris, and became a convert to Protestantism in 1521. He fled to Basel, and in 1524 he supported 39 Protestant theses. He moved to Geneva in 1532 and after being twice compelled to leave, settled there in 1534; and in 1535 the town council proclaimed the Reformation. The severity of the ecclesiastical discipline imposed by **Calvin** produced a reaction, so that in 1538 the two reformers were expelled from the city. He became a pastor in Neuchâtel in 1538, and worked there for the rest of his life.

FARGUS, Frederick John See **CONWAY, Hugh**

FARIA Y SOUSA, Manuel de (1590–1649) Portuguese poet, born near Pombeiro. He went to Madrid c.1613, and from 1631 to 1634 was secretary to the Spanish embassy in Rome. He wrote on Portuguese history and on **Camoens**, and left approximately 200 Portuguese sonnets, twelve eclogues, and three treatises on poetry.

FARIGOULE, Louis See **ROMAINS, Jules**

FARINA, Battista (1893–1966) Italian automobile designer, born in Turin. Early in his career in the 1920s he worked at the Fiat factory and visited the USA, where he studied Ford's production methods, before setting up his own bodywork establishment in 1930 in Turin. Although always associated with classic designs for the prestigious Italian makers like Ferrari, Lancia and Alfa-Romeo, he also designed for mass-production. Among his firm's successful popular cars were Austin's innovative A40 'hatchback' of 1958, and the 1100 model (actually designed by his son Sergio) which appeared under a number of BMC names after 1963. His nickname, Pinin, was adopted in the company name—Pininfarina—in 1961.

FARINA, Johann Maria (1685–1766) Italian perfumier, born in Novara. He settled in Cologne in 1709, and invented eau-de-Cologne.

FARINACCI, Roberto (1892–1945) Italian politician, born at Isernia. He became Fascist party secretary (1924–26), a member of the Fascist grand council (1935) and minister of state (1938). An ardent racialist and anti-Semite, notorious for his extremism and pro-Nazi tendencies, he edited the *Regime Fascista*, the party organ. He was ultimately captured and shot, on the same day and by the same band of partisans as **Mussolini**, while attempting to flee to Switzerland.

FARINELLI, Carlo See **BROSCHI**

FARINI, Luigi Carlo (1812–66) Italian statesman, born near Ravenna. He practised medicine and later held various public offices, finally becoming minister of commerce in **Cavour**'s last cabinet, and premier for three months from December 1862. His *Il Stato Romano* was translated into English by **Gladstone** (1851–54); his *Storia d'Italia* is a continuation of Botta's work.

FARJEON, Eleanor (1881–1965) English writer. She wrote fantasies and children's stories, and collaborated with her brother Herbert in *Kings and Queens* (1932). There is a Farjeon award for outstanding work in children's books.

FARMAN, Henri (1874–1958) French pioneer aviator and aircraft manufacturer. With his brother Maurice (1878–1964) he made the first flight in a Voisin biplane (1908) which they had built. In 1912 they established a factory at Boulogne-sur-Seine to manufacture the Farman biplane, and built the first long-distance passenger plane, the *Goliath* in 1917.

FARMER, John (c.1565–c.1605) English composer. Organist of Christ Church Cathedral, Dublin, he is chiefly noted for his madrigals.

FARMER, Richard (1735–97) English churchman and writer, born in Leicester. A graduate of Emmanuel College, Cambridge, he helped **Johnson** with Cambridge notes for his *Lives of the Poets*. His *Essay on the Learning of Shakespeare* (1767) showed that the great dramatist derived his knowledge of the ancients from translations. He became master of Emmanuel (1775), chief librarian to the university (1778), and prebendary at Lichfield (1780), Canterbury (1782) and St Paul's (1788).

FARNABY, Giles (c.1563–1640) English composer, born probably in Truro. Few details of his career are known, but he spent most of his active life in London. His works include madrigals and settings of the psalms in verse paraphrases for East Psalter, but he is best remembered for his keyboard music.

FARNBOROUGH, Lord See **MAY, Sir Thomas Erskine**

FARNESE, Alessandro (1468–1549) Italian prelate, raised to the papal see in 1534 as **Paul III**. He founded the duchy of Parma and Piacenza.

FARNESE, Alessandro (1546–92) Spanish soldier, later 3rd Duke of Parma, born in Rome, the son of the 2nd Duke and Margaret (illegitimate daughter of the emperor **Charles V**), and nephew of **Philip II** of Spain. He distinguished himself under his uncle **John of Austria** at the sea battle of Lepanto (1571), but became one of the great land-force commanders of his era, as well as a gifted diplomat. He joined his uncle in the Spanish Netherlands in 1577, defeated the rebellious Dutch at Gembloux (1578) and captured Maastricht (1578). As governor-general himself he captured Antwerp in 1585. He prepared forces for the invasion of England in concert with the Great Armada in 1588. In 1590 he compelled **Henri IV** of France to raise the siege of Paris.

FARNESE, Elizabeth, or **Isabella** (1692–1766) Spanish queen, daughter of the Duke of Parma. She became the second wife of **Philip V** of Spain in 1714 and warmly supported **Alberoni**'s policy. She dominated her weak husband, and worked to secure the future of her sons, Philip and the future **Charles III** of Spain.

FARNOL, John Jeffrey (1878–1952) English author, born in Aston. He lived from 1902–1910 in the USA as a scene painter. His first successful novel was *The Broad*

Highway (1910), and he went on to establish a reputation for romantic adventure stories in a period setting, such as *The Amateur Gentleman* (1913), *The Geste of Duke Jocelyn* (1919) and *Peregrine's Progress* (1922).

FAROUK I (1920–65) king of Egypt from 1937 to 1952, born in Cairo. He was educated privately in England. Ascending the throne in 1937, he dismissed the premier, Nahas Pasha, and for a while devoted himself to schemes of economic development and land reform. In 1942, with Axis troops threatening Egypt, Britain insisted on the re-appointment of Nahas Pasha. After the war, his lifestyle became increasingly flamboyant. In 1948 he dissolved his first marriage with Princess Farida and married Narriman Sadek in 1951. General **Neguib**'s *coup d'état* in July 1952 forced Farouk to abdicate. He was exiled in Italy and in 1959 he became a citizen of Monaco.

FARQUHAR, George (c.1677–1707) Irish playwright, born in Londonderry, possibly in 1677 (but he is said to have fought at the Boyne). Educated at Trinity College, Dublin, he became an actor in a Dublin theatre, but proved an indifferent performer. The accidental wounding of a fellow actor so shocked him that he quitted the boards, and shortly after received a commission in a regiment stationed in Ireland. His first comedy, *Love and a Bottle* (1698), proved a success. His *Constant Couple* (1700) met with an enthusiastic reception, and to it he wrote a sequel, *Sir Harry Wildair*. In 1703 he produced *The Inconstant*, founded on **Fletcher**'s *Wild Goose Chase*. Having married in the same year, he fell into pecuniary difficulties, and died in poverty. During his last illness he wrote the best of his plays, *The Beaux' Stratagem*, and died while its wit and invention were making the town roar with delight. *The Recruiting Officer* had been produced with success in 1706. Farquhar is one of the best of our comic dramatists, and has on the whole more variety and character than any of his compeers.

FARR, William (1807–83) English statistician, born in Kenley, Shropshire. He studied medicine and worked at medical statistics, becoming a pioneer in the application of 'vital statistics'. In 1838 he became superintendent of the statistical department of the registrar-general.

FARRAGUT, David Glasgow (1801–70) American naval commander, born of Spanish origin near Knoxville, Tennessee. Entering the navy in 1810, he saw service against the British in 1812, and against pirates in 1820. In the civil war he served with the Federal forces and commanded the armament fitted out for the capture of New Orleans (1862). He took part in the siege and capture of Vicksburg (1863), and destroyed the enemy's gunboats in Mobile Bay, leading to the town's surrender. He was made vice admiral, the grade being created for him by special act of congress, as was also that of admiral (1866). He was the adopted son of **David Porter**.

FARRANT, Richard (1530–80) English musician, organist of St George's Chapel and of the Chapel Royal. He composed a morning and evening service, two anthems, and parts of other services.

FARRAR, Frederic William (1831–1903) English clergyman and writer, born in Bombay. He was ordained in 1854, taught at Harrow, became headmaster of Marlborough (1871–76), honorary chaplain to Queen **Victoria** (1869–73), and later became a chaplain-in-ordinary. He was made a canon of Westminster and rector of St Margaret's in 1876, archdeacon of Westminster in 1883, chaplain to the House of Commons in 1890, and dean of Canterbury in 1895. His theological writings were many, but he is chiefly remembered for the best seller *Eric, or Little by Little* (1858), one of several school stories that he wrote.

FARRELL, James Thomas (1904–79) American novelist, short-story writer, critic and essayist, born in Chicago. He paid for his own education at the University of Chicago (1925–29) and lived in Paris in the early 1930s. A lapsed Catholic and a naturalist in the mould of **Zola**, he owes most to the style of **Sherwood Anderson**. His first novel was *Young Lonigan* (1932) which began the *Studs Lonigan* trilogy of life on Chicago's South side, realistically and graphically expressed. The other volumes were *The Young Manhood of Studs Lonigan* (1934) and *Judgement Day* (1935). An accomplished study of defeat (the hero dies aged 29), it was a landmark in American fiction. This was followed by a five-novel sequence centred on Danny O'Neill (1936–53), and another trilogy, on Bernard Clare (1946–52). He published more than 50 novels in all.

FARRELL, Suzanne (1945–) American ballerina, born in Cincinnati, Ohio. At the age of 16 she graduated from the School of American Ballet to the New York City Ballet, where she quickly became a major muse of choreographer-artistic director **George Balanchine**. She and her husband, dancer Paul Majia, left the company to join **Maurice Béjart**'s Ballet of the 20th Century (1970–74). Upon her return to NYCB in 1975, she formed a fruitful onstage partnership with dancer **Peter Martins**. Long, strong and supple, with an exceptional sensitivity to music, she is the ideal Balanchine dancer and a ballerina against whom all others must be judged.

FARREN, Elizabeth (c.1759–1829) English actress, famous at Drury Lane and the Haymarket in aristocratic roles such as Lady Teazle and Lydia Languish.

FARREN, William (1786–1861) English actor and theatre manager, celebrated for his interpretation of elderly roles in 18th-century comedy. His son Henry (c.1826-60) was also an actor.

FARREN-PRICE, Ronald William (1930–) Australian pianist, born in Brisbane, Queensland. Educated at Melbourne University, he then studied in Germany and, under **Claudio Arrau**, in London. Since 1967 he has toured extensively in the USA, England and Europe, and was the first Australian pianist to tour the USSR. A regular broadcaster and recitalist, he has performed as a soloist with many major orchestras, and has recorded widely. In 1955 he joined the Melbourne Conservatorium of Music (now the faculty of music at Melbourne University) where he became reader in music.

FARRER, Reginald John (1880–1920) English botanist, plant-collector and writer, born in Clapham, Yorkshire. He travelled extensively in Europe and Japan, China (1914–16) and Upper Burma (1919–20). He wrote eight plays and a novel, six travel books, and five horticultural works: *My Rock-Garden* (1907), *Alpines and Bog-Plants* (1908), *In a Yorkshire Garden* (1909), *The Rock-Garden* (1912), and *The English Rock-Garden* (2 vols, 1919).

FARRER, William James (1845–1906) English herborist, born in Docker, Westmorland. He studied medicine at Cambridge, but tuberculosis forced him to give up and emigrate to Australia in 1870. He found work as a surveyor, but in 1886 he settled on his own property near Tharwa, New South Wales, where an early interest in grasses led him to systematic experiments with various varieties of wheat. He cross-bred over 200 strains each year in an endeavour to find one which would be resistant to diseases such as rust yet would give desirable baking qualities, while being suitable for Australian climatic conditions and farming methods. He pioneered scientific wheat-breeding and introduced many valuable varieties for stock and for commercial use, culminating in his 'Federation' strain of 1901. Farrer's work was almost solely responsible for the growth and success of the Australian wheat industry.

FARRÈRE, Claude, pseud of **Frédéric Charles Pierre Édouard Bargone** (1876–1957) French novelist, born in Lyon. He was a naval officer (1899–1919) who turned to writing. He made his name with novels of the exotic and tales of travel and adventure. Works include *Fumée d'opium* (1904) and *Les condamnés à mort* (1920).

FARSON, James Negley (1890–1960) American author, born in Plainfield, New Jersey. He trained as a civil engineer but came to England and went from there to Russia, where he had an export business and where he witnessed the 1917 revolution. From then on he led an adventurous life as airman, sailor and journalist, which is reflected in his varied works. These include *Sailing Across Europe* (1926), *Seeing Red* (1930), *Bomber's Moon* (1941) and *A Mirror for Narcissus* (1957).

FASCH, Johann Friedrich (1688–1758) German composer, born in Buttelstedt, Weimar. He was educated at the Thomasschule, Leipzig, and founded the *Collegium Musicum* there, the forerunner of the *Gewandhaus* concerts. After a roving life he was in 1722 appointed kapellmeister at Zerbst. He wrote overtures in the style of **Telemann**, orchestral suites, greatly admired by **J S Bach**, three operas, since lost, and also several masses, a *requiem*, trios and sonatas. His son, Carl Friedrich Christian (1736–1800), born in Zerbst, was a harpsichordist and composer, and was appointed accompanist to **Frederick II, the Great**, who played the flute, in 1756. He was twice visited by **Beethoven** (1796).

FASSBINDER, Rainer Werner (1946–82) West German film director, born in Bad Wörishofen. He began his career as an actor in fringe theatre in Munich, founding his own 'anti-theatre' company, for whom he wrote original works and adapted classical pieces. Moving into films, he was greatly influenced by the French director **Jean-Luc Godard**, believing that films should have a social purpose rather than exist simply as escapist entertainment. His first film to gain international recognition was *Why Does Herr R. Run Amok* (1979) and this was followed by a succession of films, often as many as four a year. These were usually politically committed criticisms of contemporary Germany, contrasting personal failure and frustration with the country's superficial economic success, and illustrating the misuse of power and social oppression. Among these were *The Bitter Tears of Petra von Kant* (1972, an adaptation of one of his own theatre pieces), *Effi Briest* (1974, based on a classic novel of the 1890s by **Theodor Fontane** on the theme of hypocritical bourgeois morality), and *The Marriage of Maria von Braun*, the story of a frustrated marriage and an allegory of post-war Germany, which won the first prize at the 1979 Berlin Film Festival. Before his death he had completed two films, *Lili Marleen* and *Lola*, of a planned series dealing with recent German history as seen through the eyes of women.

FASTOLF, Sir John (1378–1459) English soldier, born in Caister. He distinguished himself at Agincourt (1415), and still more at the 'Battle of the Herrings' (1429), so called because, while convoying supplies to the English besiegers of Orléans, he formed a *laager* of herring barrels, and beat off a whole French army. Later in the same year he was less successful against **Joan of Arc**, and at Patay, according to **Monstrelet**, displayed such cowardice that the Duke of Bedford stripped him of his Garter. This, however, is questionable; he rather seems to have retained all his honours till in 1440 he came home to Norfolk, and in 1441 was granted a pension of £20 'for notable and praiseworthy service and good counsel'. His Norfolk life is mirrored faithfully in the *Paston Letters*. His identification with 'Sir John Falstaff' is at least incomplete, for **Oldcastle** was certainly **Shakespeare**'s prototype.

FĀTIMA (7th century) Arab religious figure, youngest daughter of **Muhammad**. She was the wife of his cousin **Ali**; from them descended the **Fatimids**, who ruled over Egypt and North Africa (969–1171), and later over Syria and Palestine.

FATIMIDS an Arab dynasty tracing its descent from **Fātima**, daughter of **Muhammad**, and her husband **'Alī**. The dynasty came to prominence through its leadership of the Ismā'īlī movement, a branch of Shīa Islam which believed that the government of the Muslim community should reside in a series of divinely guided *imāms* drawn from the family of the prophet. The first Fatimid publicly to proclaim himself was 'Ubayd Allāh (871–934), who in 910 established himself as caliph in North Africa with the support of the Berber Kutāma people, taking the title al-Mahdī ('rightly guided one'). Al-Mu'izz (931–75), caliph from 952, conquered Egypt and built a new capital at Cairo; he and his successors extended their rule to Palestine, Syria and the holy places of Mecca and Medina. The principal aim of the Fatimids was the establishment of a universal caliphate, to be attained both by military means and by the maintenance of a vast missionary network intended to subvert the rule of their **'Abbasid** rivals and to propagate the Ismaīlī faith throughout the Middle East; however, the Sunni Muslims and Coptic Christians who constituted the majority of the Egyptian population were left in relative peace, except during the turbulent reign of **al-Hakim**. That of al-Mustansir (1029–94), caliph from 1036, marked a turning point in Fatimid fortunes, with the independence of the Zirid emirs in North Africa, and the loss of much of Syria to the Seljuks, while from 1099 Palestine was conquered by the Frankish crusaders. By this time the caliphs, who were frequently minors, had fallen under the domination of viziers and generals, and in the course of the 12th century, Egypt came under increasing pressure from the Franks of Jerusalem and **Nūr al-Dīn**, the ruler of Muslim Syria, who recognized the religious authority of the 'Abbasids. In 1168 Egypt was occupied by a Syrian army, and on the death of al-'Adid (1171) the caliphate was abolished by Nūr al-Dīn's general **Saladin**.

FAUCHER, Léon (1803–54) French journalist and politician, born in Limoges. He edited *Le Temps* and other papers (1830–42), wrote *Études sur l'Angleterre* (1845) and after the 1848 revolution became minister of public works and of the interior. The *coup d'état* ended his political career.

FAULKNER, William (1897–1962) American novelist, born near Oxford, Mississippi. His school career was undistinguished and he was rejected by the US army when America entered World War I but he became a pilot in the Canadian Flying Corps. Later he attended Mississippi University and did odd jobs. While working in New Orleans he met **Sherwood Anderson** who offered to recommend his first novel —*Soldier's Pay* (1926)—to a publisher on condition that he did not have to read it. Others followed but their sales were unremarkable. In 1929, the year of his marriage, he took a job as a coal-heaver and while on night-work at a local power station is said to have written *As I Lay Dying* (1930) between midnight and

4am during a space of six weeks. *Sanctuary* (1931) was intended as a pot-boiler and was more successful commercially but it is novels like *The Sound and the Fury* (1929), *Light in August* (1932), *Absalom, Absalom!* (1936), *The Hamlet* (1940) and *Intruder in the Dust* (1948) that account for his high reputation. In *Sartoris* (1929) he first describes the decline of the Compson and Sartoris families, indicative of the Old South, and the rise of the nouveau riche Snopes, which dominate the so-called 'Yoknapatawpha' novels, set in and around Jefferson in the imaginary Yoknapatawpha County. The tone of the novels is invariably sombre and elegiac but the prose sings like lyric poetry and Faulkner is revered as one of the modern masters of the novel. He was awarded the 1949 Nobel prize for literature.

FAUNTLEROY, Henry (1784–1824) English banker and forger, son of a Dorset bank clerk who had formed a private bank in London. He succeeded his father in 1807 as managing partner when the firm was in difficulties, and commenced a massive fraud which brought forgery to something near an exact science. He was arrested in September 1824, tried and found guilty of forging with intent to defraud the Bank of England and other parties of around £20000, and after unsuccessful appeals was hanged.

FAURE, Edgar (1908–88) French statesman, born in Béziers. Trained as a lawyer in Paris, he entered politics as a Radical-Socialist, and was minister of finance and economic affairs in 1950 and 1951, holding this office again in 1954 and in 1958. He served as président du Conseil des Ministres from February 1955 to January 1956, was professor of law at Dijon University (1962–66), and became minister of agriculture in 1966, minister of education in 1968, minister of state for social affairs in 1969, and president of the National Assembly 1973–78. He was a member of the European Parliament from 1979.

FAURE, François Félix (1841–99) president of the French Republic, born in Paris. A Roman Catholic, though of Protestant ancestry, and a Moderate Republican, he was first a journeyman currier in Touraine, ultimately a merchant and shipowner at Le Havre. He served as a volunteer in the Franco-German war, in 1881 became deputy for Le Havre, and, after holding posts in several administrations, in January 1895 succeeded **Casimir Périer** as president.

FAURÉ, Gabriel Urbain (1845–1924) French composer, born in Pamiers. He became *maître de chapelle* (1877) and organist (1896) at La Madeleine, Paris, and director of the Conservatoire (1905–20). Though chiefly remembered for his songs, including the evergreen *Après un rêve*, he also wrote operas and orchestral pieces, such as *Masques et bergamasques*, in which he experimented with subtle tonalities.

FAUST, Johann See **FUST**

FAUSTINA, Annia Galeria, known as **'the Elder'** (d.141), Roman empress, wife of **Antoninus Pius**.

FAUSTINA, Annia Galeria (d.175) Roman empress, known as **'the Younger'**, daughter of **Faustina the Elder**. She married her cousin **Marcus Aurelius**, and bore him at least 12 children. Like her mother, she was reputed to be promiscuous and faithless, but this was probably baseless.

FAVART, Charles Simon (1710–92) French dramatist, born in Paris, the son of a pastrycook. He began writing comic opera, and the success of his first production, *Deux Jumelles* (1734), obtained for him financial backing which enabled him to continue with this genre. He married in 1745 Marie Justine Benoîte Duronceray (1727–72), a talented actress of the Opéra-Comique with whom he pioneered a new realism in costume. At the end of 1745 the Opéra-Comique, which he was directing, was obliged to close, and the Favarts went to Flanders with a company of actors attached to Marshal **de Saxe**, who made an unscrupulous attempt to procure Mme Favart as his mistress. When she fled from him he took out *lettres de cachet* against her husband, who had to remain in hiding until 1750, when the marshal's death put an end to the persecution, and Favart was able to return to Paris and write more comic operas. Among the best out of more than 100 are *Bastien et Bastienne*, *Ninette à la cour* and *Les Trois Sultanes*.

FAVRE, Jules Claude Gabriel (1809–80) French lawyer and politician, born at Lyon. He took part in the July revolution of 1830, defended **Orsini**, became a Republican leader, and after the fall of **Napoleon III** became foreign minister, in which capacity he negotiated the treaty of Frankfurt in 1871.

FAWCETT, Henry (1833–84) English political economist and reformer, husband of **Millicent Garrett Fawcett** (m.1867), born in Salisbury. Blinded in a shooting accident in 1858, he became professor of political economy at Cambridge in 1863, and was elected Liberal MP in 1865. He advocated women's suffrage and helped pass the Reform Act of 1867. As postmaster-general from 1880 he introduced the parcel post, postal orders and sixpenny telegrams.

FAWCETT, Dame Millicent, née **Garrett** (1847–1929) English suffragette and educational reformer, wife of **Henry Fawcett** (m.1867) and younger sister of **Elizabeth Garrett Anderson**, born in Aldeburgh, Suffolk. She opposed the militancy of the **Pankhursts**, but campaigned for women's suffrage and higher education for women. She was a founder of Newnham College, Cambridge (1871), and was president of the National Union of Women's Suffrage Societies (1897–1919). She wrote *Political Economy for Beginners* (1870), and *The Women's Victory—and After* (1920).

FAWCETT, Percy Harrison (1867–1925) English explorer, born in Torquay. He entered the army at 19, rose to become lieutenant-colonel, and after service in Ceylon, Hong Kong and elsewhere was in 1906 given a border delimitation assignment on behalf of the Bolivian government. This led to several hazardous expeditions in the Mato Grosso area in search of traces of ancient civilizations. In 1925 he disappeared with his eldest son near the Xingú River.

FAWKES, Francis (1720–77) English poet and translator of the classics. He was the vicar of Orpington in Kent for 20 years. The comic song 'The Brown Jug' is his best-known piece.

FAWKES, Guy (1570–1606) English conspirator, born in York of Protestant parentage. Becoming a Catholic at an early age, he served in the Spanish army in the Netherlands (1593–1604), then crossed to England at **Robert Catesby**'s invitation. Inspired with fanatical zeal for his religion, he plotted with several Catholics to blow up King **James I**, his ministers and the members of both Houses of Parliament, on 5 November 1605. Caught red-handed with the gunpowder in the cellar of the Palace of Westminster, he was tortured, tried and hanged.

FAWKNER, John Pascoe (1792–1869) English-born Australian pioneer and founder of Melbourne, born in Cripplegate, London. His father was sentenced to transportation and, with his family, arrived in the colony of Port Phillip in 1803. When that colony was abandoned, the convicts and settlers were shipped across to Van Diemen's Land (now Tasmania) where the Fawkner family secured a land grant. He was involved in various enterprises, but in 1835 he engaged a ship to explore Western Port and Port Phillip Bay on the mainland of Australia, and made camp at the mouth of the Yarra River, the future site of the city of Melbourne. Fawkner's camp was found by another party of Tasmanian settlers, led by **John Batman**, who had previously 'purchased' land from the local aboriginal tribe. The new town prospered and Fawkner became a member of its council and later, when the new colony was separated from New South Wales, a member of the first legislative council for Victoria.

FAY, András (1786–1864) Hungarian poet, playwright and novelist. He lived in Budapest, and was a pioneer of the social novel. He also wrote a set of fables in the manner of **Aesop** which achieved great success.

FAYE, Hervé Auguste Étienne (1814–1902) French astronomer, born in Benoît-du-Sault. He became in 1873 professor of astronomy at the École Polytechnique, and in 1878 director of the Paris Observatory. In 1843 he discovered Faye's comet.

FAZY, Jean James (1794–1878) Swiss journalist, publicist and statesman, born in Geneva. He founded the *Revue de Genève*, and became the leading spirit in the Radical movement (1846), and until 1862 was the real ruler of Geneva, which he modernized. He wrote a *History of Geneva* (1838–40) and on constitutional law. He was deposed in 1862 and fled to Paris, where he edited *La France Nouvelle*. He later returned to Geneva and became professor of international law there (1871).

FEATHER, Victor Grayson, Baron Hardie (1908–76) British Trade Union leader. Educated at Hanson Grammar School, Bradford, he began work at 14, and joined the Shopworkers' Union. Shop steward at 15 and chairman of his branch committee at 21, he was a stirring speaker and in 1937 joined the staff of the TUC. Assistant secretary from 1947 to 1960, he travelled widely, reorganizing trade unions in Europe after the war, and in India and Pakistan in 1957. In 1969 he succeeded **George Woodcock** as general secretary, and achieved success in restoring industrial peace following the economic crisis despite opposition from the TUC's left wing. He fought the Conservative government's anti-union Industrial Relations bill and when this became law in 1972 he joined representatives of British industry to establish an independent advisory organization to settle labour disputes. He retired in 1973, becoming president of the European Trade Union until 1974, when he became a life peer.

FECHNER, Gustav Theodor (1801–87) German physicist, psychologist and philosopher, born in Gross-Särchen. He became professor of physics at Leipzig in 1834, working mainly on galvanism, electromagnetism and colour. He subsequently became interested in the connections between physiology and psychology, explored in his *Elemente der Psychophysik* (1860), and helped to formulate the **Weber**-Fechner Law relating stimuli to sensations. He also published *Das Büchlein vom Leben nach dem Tode* (1836) and *Vorschule der Aesthetik* (1876).

FECHTER, Charles Albert (1824–79) English actor, born in London. He was famed for his interpretations of Hamlet and Othello. He became lessee of the Lyceum Theatre and later went to the USA.

FEDDEN, Sir (Albert Hubert) Roy (1885–1973) English aero-engine designer, born in Bristol. After training as an engineer at Bristol Merchant Venturers Technical College, he joined Brazil Straker and Co in Bristol (1906) and produced Rolls-Royce aero-engines during World War I. He took his aero-engine design 'Jupiter' to form the engine department of the Bristol Aeroplane Company in 1920, where he was chief engineer until 1942. Initiating a famous range of piston engines—Mercury, Pegasus, Perseus, Taurus, Hercules and Centaurus—he was also notable for his unique development of the sleeve-valve engine. He held a variety of governmental and international posts until 1960, and was president of the Royal Aeronautical Society in 1938, 1939 and 1945.

FEHLING, Hermann von (1812–85) German chemist, born in Lübeck. Professor of chemistry at Stuttgart, he introduced the solution which bears his name.

FEININGER, Lyonel Charles Adrian (1871–1956) American artist and cartoonist, born in New York of German immigrant parents. He studied music in New York and then in Germany, where he turned to art and studied in Berlin and Hamburg, and then worked as a newspaper strip cartoonist. From 1907 he devoted himself to serious painting, working in a style reminiscent of Cubism. After World War II he taught at the Bauhaus at Weimar (1919–24) and Dessau (1925–33). When the Nazis came to power he returned to the USA where, with **Gropius** and **Mies van der Rohe**, he founded the Chicago Bauhaus.

FEISAL II See **FAISAL II**

FEITH, Rhijnvis (1753–1824) Dutch poet, born in Zwolle. He became mayor there in 1780. He wrote some sentimental love novels, and the lyrical *Oden en Gedichten* (1796–1810). Of his tragedies, the best known are *Thirza* (1784), *Johanna Gray* (1791), and *Ines de Castro* (1793). He published a collection of criticisms, *Brieven* (1784–94).

FELD, Eliot (1942–) American dancer, choreographer and artistic director, born in Brooklyn, New York. He trained in both the classical and modern idioms at the School of American Ballet and appeared in the 1957 Broadway and 1961 Hollywood versions of *West Side Story* before joining American Ballet Theatre (ABT) in 1963, where he quickly rose to the status of soloist, especially in character roles. Thanks to the support of **Jerome Robbins**, he made his choreographic début in 1967 with *Harbinger* and *At Midnight*, for which he was hailed as Robbins' natural successor. He left ABT to found the short-lived American Ballet Company (1969–71), rejoined ABT for a few seasons and formed Eliot Feld Ballet in 1974. He is a prolific choreographer with a gift for setting neo-classical, folk-influenced and even gymnastic movement to a wide range of music. In 1978 he started the New Ballet School, an organization that offers inner-city children the chance to become dance professionals.

FELIX II (d.365) the first antipope, being consecrated when **Liberius** was banished (355) for refusing to condemn **Athanasius**. When Liberius was restored (357) Felix retired; but he was ultimately regarded as a saint and martyr.

FELIX III (d.492) pope 483–492. Under him the first disruption between the churches of the east and west began.

FELIX IV (d.530) pope 526–530, was appointed by **Theodoric**.

FELIX V See **AMADEUS VIII**

FELIX, Marcus Antonius (1st century AD) a Roman procurator of Judaea in the time of the apostle **Paul** (Acts xxiv), was a freedman of **Claudius I** and brother of his favourite Pallus. **Josephus** says he cleared the country of robbers and suppressed the chaotic seditions of the Jews; but his cruelty, lust and greed were unbounded. Recalled in AD 62, he narrowly escaped execution.

FELL, John (1625–86) Anglican divine, with three others contrived to maintain the Church of England services during the Commonwealth; after the Restoration he was made dean of Christ Church, Oxford royal chaplain and DD. He governed the college strictly, restored its buildings, was liberal to poor scholars, and did much to promote learning. In 1676 he became bishop of Oxford. He rebuilt the episcopal palace at Cuddesdon. 'I do not like thee Doctor Fell' is ascribed to **Tom Brown**.

FELLER, William (1906–70) Yugoslav-born American mathematician, born in Zagreb. He studied at Zürich and Göttingen, and after teaching at Kiel, left Germany in 1933 for Stockholm. In 1939 he emigrated to the USA, holding chairs at Brown (1939–45), Cornell (1945–50) and Princeton (1950–70). His work in probability theory introduced new rigour without losing sight of practical applicability, and his textbook *Introduction to probability theory and its applications* (1950) is an enormously influential classic, unique as a textbook starting from first principles, yet containing original research often leading to surprising results, and packed with practical examples.

FELLINI, Federico (1920–) Italian film director, born in Rimini. Educated at Bologna University, he started as a cartoonist, journalist and scriptwriter, before becoming an assistant film director in 1942. His highly individual films include *I Vitelloni* (1953), *La Strada* (1954; foreign film Oscar winner, 1957), *Le Notte di Cabiria* (1957; Oscar winner, 1958), *Giulietta degli Spiriti* (1964), *Satyricon* (1969), *Fellini's Roma* (1972), *Amarcord* (1974), *Casanova* (1976), *Orchestra Rehearsal* (1979), *City of Women* (1981) and *The Ship Sails On* (1983). His most famous and controversial work, *La Dolce Vita* (1960; Cannes Festival prize winner), was a *succès de scandale* for its cynical evocation of modern Roman high life. *Otto e Mezzo* (1963) is his most obviously autobiographical work, juxtaposing the dreams and fantasies of its film director hero against the baroque settings of the film world. In 1943 he married the actress Giulietta Masina, star of several of his films, most notably *La Strada* and *Ginger and Fred* (1986).

FELLOWES, Edmund Horace (1870–1951) English musicologist. From 1900 he was a minor canon at St George's, Windsor. He edited *The English Madrigal School* (36 vols, 1912–24) and *The English School of Lutenist Songwriters* (31 vols, 1920–28).

FELLOWS, Sir Charles (1799–1860) English archaeologist. In 1838 he discovered the ruins of Xanthus, ancient capital of Lycia, and those of Tlos, and in 1839 the ruins of 13 cities; from these he later selected marbles, casts, and other artefacts for the British Museum.

FELLTHAM, Owen (c.1602–1668) English writer, born in Suffolk. He lived in Great Billing, Northants, and was the author of a series of moral essays, *Resolves, Divine, Morall, Politicall* (1620–28).

FÉNELON, François de Salignac de la Mothe (1651–1715) French prelate and writer, born in the château de Fénelon in Périgord. At 20 he entered the seminary of St Sulpice in Paris, and was ordained in 1675. After some time spent in parochial duties, he became director of an institution for women converts to the Catholic faith in 1678. Here he wrote *Traité de l'éducation des filles* (published in 1678), urging a more liberal education for women, and criticizing the coercion of Huguenot converts. At the revocation of the Edict of Nantes (1685) he was sent to preach among the Protestants of Poitou. From 1689 to 1699 he was tutor to **Louis XIV**'s grandson, the young Duke of Burgundy, and as such he wrote the *Fables*, the *Dialogues of the Dead*, the *History of the Ancient Philosophers*, and *Adventures of Télémaque* (1699). He had been presented by the king to the abbey of St Valéry (1694) and to the archbishopric of Cambrai (1695). He had formed in 1687 the acquaintance of the celebrated quietist mystic, **Madame Guyon**, and, convinced of the unfairness of the outcry against her, he advised her to submit her book to **Bossuet**, who condemned it. Fénelon acquiesced, but refused to join in any personal condemnation. Fénelon composed his own *Explication des maximes des saints sur la vie intérieure* in defence of certain of Madame Guyon's doctrines. A fierce controversy ensued, and in the end the pope condemned the *Maximes des saints*. Fénelon's *Télémaque* was considered by the king a disguised satire upon his court and from then on Fénelon was strictly restrained within his diocese. From this date he lived almost exclusively for his flock, but in the revived Jansenistic dispute he engaged earnestly on the side of orthodoxy. His works are voluminous, and on a variety of subjects.

FENG YOULAN (1895–) Chinese philosopher, born in Tanghe County, Henan Province. He is best known for his *History of Chinese Philosophy* (2 vols, 1931–33, with a supplement in 1936). He has held academic posts in many universities, including Pennsylvania (1946–47). Denounced in 1968 during the Cultural Revolution as a counter-revolutionary, he did not reappear until 1973. He has also been a leader in the movement to revive Neo-Confucianism.

FENLEY, Molissa (1954–) American dancer-choreographer, born in Las Vegas. Raised in Nigeria, she studied dance at Mills College, California, before moving to New York, where she made her choreographic début in 1978. Although she has created ensemble pieces for her own now-defunct group and other companies, her reputation rests on physically demanding, high-energy solos like *Eureka* (1982) and *State of Darkness* (1988).

FENNING, Frederick William (1919–88) British nuclear physicist and pioneer of nuclear reactor technology. He was educated at Clacton County High School before graduating in the physics tripos at Cambridge University in 1940, when he joined the team (part of the Tube Alloys programme) at the Cavendish Laboratory which was following up neutron diffusion problems associated with the possibilities for an atomic bomb; later in the war he was sent to Canada, where he played a major role in starting up the ZEEP reactor at Chalk River. After the war he returned to the new research establishment at Harwell as an experimental scientist, and was closely concerned with the design of early nuclear reactors in Britain. As chief physicist and then director of reactor technology at Risley he was particularly associated with work on the Advanced Gas-Cooled Reactor (AGR) which led to the operation of the Windscale (now Sellafield) AGR. He returned to Harwell as deputy director in 1966; from 1979 to 1984 he was deputy director of the Atomic Energy Research Establishment.

FENTON, Roger (1819–69) English photographer, born in Lancashire. He studied painting in Paris and exhibited at the Royal Academy 1849–51. He photographed in Russia in 1852 and was a founder and the first honorary secretary of the Photographic Society (later the Royal) in 1853; Queen **Victoria** became its patron, and Fenton photographed the royal family at Balmoral and Windsor. In 1855 he went to the Crimea as the world's first accredited war-photographer, using the large cameras and wet-plates of the period to record the serving officers and men and the conditions of the campaign. It is for this work that he is best known, although little action could be depicted. He subsequently travelled widely throughout Britain, producing fine architectural and landscape studies, but gave up photography in 1862 to follow law.

FENWICK, Sir John (c.1645–1697) English conspirator, born in Northumberland. After serving in the army in 1688 he became Tory MP for the county of his birth. He took part in the assassination plot, and in 1696, being committed to the Tower, made an artful confession involving several Whig leaders in the Jacobite intrigues. The only witness against him had been spirited out of the country, but the Whig party secured the passing of a bill of attainder under which he was beheaded.

FERBER, Edna (1887–1968) American writer, born in Kalamazoo, Michigan. She was the author of numerous novels and short stories, including *Dawn O'Hara* (1911), *Gigolo* (1922), *So Big* (1924, Pulitzer prize), *Cimarron* (1929) and *Saratoga Trunk* (1941). She is probably best remembered as the writer of *Show Boat* (1926), which inspired the musical play of that name. She also wrote plays with **Kaufman**, such as *Dinner at Eight* (1932) and *Stage Door* (1936).

FERDAUSI See **FIRDAUSI**

FERDINAND I (1793–1875) emperor of Austria from 1835 to 1848, born in Vienna. He was the eldest son of **Francis I** by his second marriage with **Maria Theresa**, princess of the Two Sicilies. When he succeeded his father in 1835 it was expected that he would inaugurate a liberal policy, but he was a ruler of limited intelligence, content to maintain the absolute principles of **Metternich**. When the revolutionary movement broke out in 1847–48, Ferdinand consented to Metternich's dismissal and the appointment of a responsible ministry. But after the October insurrection in Vienna he abdicated in favour of **Francis Joseph**. He retired to Prague, where he died.

FERDINAND I (1861–1948) ex-king of Bulgaria, born in Vienna. The youngest son of Prince Augustus of Saxe-Coburg and Princess Clementine of Orléans, he served in the Austrian army. On the abdication of Prince Alexander of Bulgaria, Ferdinand was offered, and accepted, the crown in 1887. In 1908 he proclaimed Bulgaria independent, and took the title of king or tsar. Joining the Balkan League against Turkey (1912), Bulgaria gained part of Thrace and access to the Aegean; but, breaking the league, she lost her gains in Macedonia and Adrianople, and had to cede part of the Dobrudja to Rumania (1913). Allying himself with the Central Powers, he invaded Serbia in October 1915. His armies routed, 'Foxy Ferdinand' abdicated on 4 October 1918, his son **Boris III** (1894–1943), succeeding him.

FERDINAND I (1503–64) Holy Roman Emperor from 1558, the second son of **Philip I, the Handsome** (briefly king of Castile), and younger brother of the emperor **Charles V**. In 1521 Charles recognized Ferdinand as ruler of the family's hereditary possessions in Austria and in the same year Ferdinand married Anna, daughter of Ladislas II of Bohemia. He was elected king of Bohemia in 1526, but failed to secure the crown of Hungary, where **John Zápolya** was elected in 1527, although an eventual compromise maintained the integrity of the **Habsburg** possessions in both nations. Left by Charles V to conduct the affairs of the empire during the emperor's frequent absences, Ferdinand was elected king of the Romans in 1531 and recognized as Charles' heir to the imperial throne in 1551. The main threats to the empire were twofold: the external threat posed by the expansionist policy of the Ottoman sultan **Süleyman II, the Magnificent**, and the internal threat from the religious divisions between Catholic and Lutheran. Unable to prevent Süleyman's incursions into Hungary, the imperial forces under Charles V successfully relieved Vienna in 1529, but the Austrian lands were again threatened by the Turks in 1532 and 1541. In 1534 Philip of Hesse, the political leader of the Lutheran princes, wrested Württemberg from Habsburg control, and Ferdinand supported the emperor in 1546–47 in his campaign to crush the protestant Schmalkaldic League. But his appraisal of the religious situation was more realistic than his brother's and it was Ferdinand who was principally responsible for the religious compromise at Augsburg in 1555 that brought the religious wars to an end. An admirer of **Erasmus** (the second edition of *Handbook of the Christian Prince* was dedicated to Ferdinand) he strove to emulate the Erasmian virtues of compromise and reconciliation.

FERDINAND II (1578–1637) Holy Roman Emperor from 1619, grandson of **Ferdinand I**. Born in Graz, Austria he received his education at the Jesuit University of Ingolstadt (1590–95). The pattern of a counter-Reformation prince, he instigated the Thirty Years War (1618–48). He compelled the Protestant subjects on his Austrian lands to choose between conversion or exile and, upon his election as emperor in 1619, strove to extend the policy of 'one church, one king' throughout the empire. Threatened on two fronts, by the election of the Protestant Elector of the Palatinate, **Frederick V**, as king of Bohemia, and by that of the Protestant prince of Transylvania, **Bethlen Gabor**, as king of Hungary, he responded by assembling a formidable pan-Catholic force. Troops from Spain and Bavaria overran the Palatinate, while the forces of the Catholic League routed the Bohemian Protestants at the White Mountain near Prague in 1620, and Polish forces under **Sigismund III** forced Gabor to renounce the throne of Hungary. An alliance of Protestant nations under Danish hegemony was defeated by the army of the Catholic League and the imperial army under **Albert von Wallenstein**, resulting in the peace of Lübeck in 1629. In **Gustav II Adolf** of Sweden the Protestants found a more effective champion, while vital financial support for the German Protestants was provided by Catholic France under the pragmatic aegis of Cardinal **Richelieu**. Although the battle of Lützen (1632) was a Protestant victory, Gustav Adolf himself was killed and the Swedish army was defeated at Nördlingen in 1634. On the face of it Ferdinand had in the 1620s been supremely successful in his religious aims, banning Protestant worship in Bohemia and by the Edict of Restitution of 1629 decreeing the restoration of all secularized church lands within the empire, but he was in the final analysis unable to extirpate Protestantism. This fact was accepted by the compromise peace of Prague (1634), which was primarily effected by his son, the future **Ferdinand III**.

FERDINAND III (1608–57) Holy Roman Emperor from 1637, the son of the emperor **Ferdinand II**. Born in Graz, in Austria, he became king of Hungary in 1625 and of Bohemia in 1627. Less warlike by nature than his father, he nonetheless conspired in the overthrow of **Albert von Wallenstein** and succeeded him as commander of the imperial armies. He was the leader of a peace party in the imperial court, and after succeeding to the imperial crown in 1637, he continued the struggle against the Protestants but opened negotiations at Münster in 1644, and in 1648 signed the Peace of Westphalia that ended the Thirty Years' War. An accomplished musician, he was a notable patron of the arts.

FERDINAND I (1751–1825) king of the Two Sicilies, third son of **Charles III** of Spain. When Charles ascended the Spanish throne in 1759 Ferdinand succeeded him in Naples, under a regency, as Ferdinand IV. After his marriage, in 1768, with Maria Carolina (d.1814), daughter of **Maria Theresa**, he fell completely under her influence, and lost his popularity. He joined England and Austria against France in 1793, but in 1801 he was forced to make a treaty with

Napoleon. A violation of this treaty compelled him in 1806 to take refuge in Sicily, under English protection. The French took possession of Naples, but Ferdinand was reinstated by the Congress of Vienna in 1815, and the following year united his two states into the Kingdom of the Two Sicilies. A popular movement in 1820 compelled him to introduce a constitution, but with Austrian help he established a rigorous despotism. He was succeeded by his son, Francis I.

FERDINAND II (1810–59) king of the Two Sicilies, son of **Francis I**, whom he succeeded in 1830. On the death of his first wife, a daughter of **Victor Emmanuel I**, in 1836, he married and gave himself up to Austrian counsels. From this time on Naples became the scene of incessant conspiracy, insurrection and political persecutions. Ferdinand yielded to the storm of 1848 and granted a constitution, but the Sicilians mistrusted his pledges and declared that he had forfeited the Sicilian crown. He subdued the revolt in Sicily by bombarding its chief cities, thus earning himself the epithet of 'Bomba'. He then set aside the constitution, while all who had taken part in reforms were subjected to those persecutions which were brought to international light by **William Gladstone**. On his death he was succeeded by his son Francis II (1836–94), the weak and cowardly 'Bombino', who fell in 1860–61 before **Garibaldi** and the attainment of Italian unity.

FERDINAND III (1200–52) king of Castile from 1217 and of Leon from 1230. From 1224 he devoted himself to a series of offensives against the weakened Almohad caliphate in Andalusia. After achieving a major breakthrough with the capture of Cordoba (1236), he went on to take Jaen, Seville, Cadiz and the surrounding territories, settling his conquests with Christian inhabitants. By his death he had annexed more Muslim territory that any other Spanish king, and reduced the remaining Muslim states to vassal kingdoms of Castile. He was canonized in 1671.

FERDINAND VI (1711–59) king of Spain, son of **Philip V**, succeeded his father in 1746. Timid and indolent on the one hand but good-natured and peace-loving on the other, he did his best to keep Spain neutral in European conflicts following the disadvantageous treaty of Aix-la-Chapelle in 1747. He went violently insane during the last years of his life.

FERDINAND VII (1788–1833) king of Spain, eldest son of **Charles IV** and Queen Luisa. He intrigued against his parents and was banished from Madrid in 1807. When **Napoleon** invaded Spain in 1808, Charles abdicated in favour of his son, but Ferdinand was brushed aside by the French emperor and replaced as king by Napoleon's brother **Joseph Bonaparte**. For six years Ferdinand lived in exile on the estate of the French foreign minister, **Talleyrand**, at Valençay, where the treaty was signed with Napoleon in 1813 that restored him to the throne. He refused to accept Napoleon's liberal Constitution of Cadiz (1812) and inaugurated a period of counter-revolutionary terror. A revolution in 1820 obliged Ferdinand briefly to recognize the 1812 constitution but repressive absolutism was reinstated three years later with the aid of French troops. The second terror lasted until his death in 1833, which signalled the outbreak of the first Carlist war (1833–39).

FERDINAND III (1769–1824) Grand Duke of Tuscany and Archduke of Austria, born in Florence. He inaugurated many reforms, encouraged commerce, opened up good roads, and was the first to recognize the French Republic, in 1792. Next year Russia and Britain constrained him to become a passive member of the coalition against France, but on the French occupation of Piedmont in 1795 he resumed friendly relations with France. In 1797, to save his states from annexation, Ferdinand concluded a very unfavourable treaty with **Napoleon**. French intrigues drove him into an Austrian alliance, and Bonaparte declared war against Austria and Tuscany. In 1799 Ferdinand retired to Vienna, and at the Peace of Lunéville (1801) renounced all claim on Tuscany; he was reinstated by the Peace of Paris (1814).

FERDINAND 'THE CATHOLIC' (Ferdinand II of Aragon) (1452–1516) the first monarch of all Spain: as Ferdinand V of Castile, Ferdinand II of Aragon and Sicily, and Ferdinand III of Naples. The son of John II of Navarre and Aragon, he was born at Sos and married (1469) **Isabella of Castile**, sister of Henry IV of Castile; after Henry's death in 1474, Ferdinand led Isabella's successful campaign for the throne of Castile, and when his own father, John of Aragon, died in 1479, the crowns of Aragon and Castile were united through their marriage to form the basis of modern Spain. Ferdinand suppressed local bandits by forming a *santa hermandad*, or 'holy brotherhood', of militia police, and established the Inquisition (1478–80). He campaigned vigorously against the Moors in Spain, and finally conquered Granada in 1492. In that same year he expelled the Jews from the kingdom, and financed the expedition of **Christopher Columbus** to the Americas. The discovery of the New World gave Spain the resources for foreign expansionism; in 1465 he formed a Holy League to help the pope drive the French from Naples, and was granted the title of 'the Catholic', and a few years later, in 1503, Naples became a Spanish possession. In 1504 Isabella died, and Ferdinand promptly had their insane daughter the Infanta Joanna (married to **Philip I, 'the Handsome'**) proclaimed queen of Castile, with himself as regent. In 1505 he married Germaine de Foix, a niece of **Louis XIII** of France. Ferdinand and Isabella's fourth daughter, **Catherine of Aragon**, was briefly married to **Arthur**, prince of Wales, and later to his brother, **Henry VIII**. Ferdinand conquered Oran in 1509 and Navarre in 1512, thus becoming monarch of all Spain from the Pyrenees to Gibraltar. He was succeeded by his grandson, the Holy Roman Emperor **Charles V** (son of Joanna and Philip I).

FERDUSI See **FIRDAUSI**

FERGUSON, Adam (1723–1816) Scottish philosopher and historian, born in Logierait, Perthshire. He became professor first of natural philosophy (1759) then of moral philosophy (1764) at Edinburgh, and was a member of the Scottish 'common sense' school of philosophy along with **Thomas Reid** and **Dugald Stewart**. He travelled to Philadelphia as secretary to the commission sent out by Lord **North** to negotiate with the American colonists in 1778–79. His works include an *Essay on the History of Civil Society* (1767), *The History of the Progress and Termination of the Roman Republic* (1783) and *Principles of Moral and Political Science* (1792).

FERGUSON, Harry George (1884–1960) Irish engineer and inventor, born in Hillsborough, County Down. He started his own garage business in Belfast at the age of 16, and while working with his brother on the repair of cars and cycles he built his own aeroplane, which made the first flight from Irish soil in December 1909. Over many years he developed the famous Ferguson farm tractor with a hydraulic linkage which controlled the depth of ploughing, and made the tractor itself more stable and efficient. These machines played a large part in the mechanization of British agriculture during and after World War II.

FERGUSON, James (1710–76) Scottish astronomer, born in Rothiemay, Banffshire, the son of a farm labourer. While keeping sheep he was constantly busy in making mechanical models, and mapping the stars at which he developed considerable skill. In 1748 he began lecturing on astronomy and mechanics, and wrote assiduously. His principal works are *Astronomy Explained upon Newton's Principles* (1756) and *Lectures on Mechanics, Hydrostatics, Pneumatics, and Optics* (1760).

FERGUSON, Sir John (1832–1907) Scottish statesman, born in Edinburgh, was Conservative MP for Ayrshire (1854–57; 1859–68), under-secretary of state (1867–68), governor of South Australia (1868–73), governor of New Zealand (1873–74) and governor of Bombay (1880–85). In 1885 elected for Manchester, he was foreign under-secretary in 1886–91, and postmaster general in 1891–92. He perished in the earthquake of 1907 at Kingston, Jamaica.

FERGUSON, Patrick (1744–80) Scottish soldier and inventor, born in Pitfour, Aberdeenshire. He served in the army in Germany and Tobago. In 1776 he invented a breech-loading rifle, firing seven shots a minute, and sighted for ranges of from 100 to 500 yards; and with it he armed a corps of loyalists, who helped at the battle of Brandywine (1777) to defeat the Americans. He was killed at the battle of King's Mountain, South Carolina.

FERGUSON, Robert (c.1637–1714) known as the 'Plotter', Scottish conspirator, born near Alford, in Aberdeenshire. In 1662 he was ousted as a Presbyterian from the vicarage of Godmersham in Kent. For ten years he played a leading part in every treasonable scheme against the last two Stuart kings, and twice had to flee the kingdom. But after the Revolution of 1688, of which in 1706 he published a history, he conspired as busily for the Jacobite cause. He was arrested for treason in 1704, but not tried. His younger brother, James (d.1705), commanded a brigade at Blenheim, and died at Bois-le-Duc.

FERGUSON, Sir Samuel (1810–86) Irish poet and Celtic scholar, born in Belfast. Called to the Irish bar in 1838, he was appointed in 1867 the first deputy keeper of Irish Records. As president of the Royal Irish Academy he gave a powerful impetus to the study of early Irish art. His spirited poems were published as *Lays of the Western Gael* (1865), *Congal* (1872), *Poems* (1880), and *The Forging of the Anchor* (1883). His edition of the *Leabhar Breac* appeared in 1876; his *Ogham Inscriptions* in 1887.

FERGUSSON, John Duncan (1874–1961) Scottish painter, born in Perthshire. He took up painting after a medical training. One of the group of Scottish Colourists, along with **Samuel John Peploe** and **Francis Cadell**, he acknowledged a debt to the Glasgow School of painting which emphasized colour rather than line. Trips to North Africa, Spain (1897) and Paris (which he made his home before and after World War I) brought him into contact with Mediterranean light and landscape, and with the painting of the Post Impressionists and Fauves. He is best known for his series of World War I paintings of naval dockyards and his portraits of the female nude, which reveal an understanding of **Cézanne**, Cubism and Fauve colour, as well as an interest in new ideas about dance, movement and rhythm.

FERGUSSON, Robert (1750–74) Scottish poet, born in Edinburgh, the son of a solicitor's clerk. He was educated at the High School of Edinburgh and of Dundee, and at St Andrews University, and was employed in the commissary office in Edinburgh, contributing poems to **Ruddiman**'s *Weekly Magazine*, from 1771, which gained him local fame. His company was much sought and convivial excesses permanently injured his health. Following an awakening of religious interest, inspired by a meeting with **John Brown**, he fell into deep depression, and was reduced to insanity by a fall downstairs. He died in a public asylum. He was a major influence and inspiration for **Robert Burns**, who placed a headstone on his grave in 1789. He left 33 poems in Scots, and 50 in English. Essentially an Edinburgh poet, his most famous poem is *Auld Reekie* (1773), tracing a day in the life of the city. Other major and familiar poems are *Elegy on the Death of Scots Music*, *The Daft Days* (his first published poem), *Hallow Fair*, *To the Tron Kirk Bell*, *Leith Races* and the satirical *The Rising of the Session*.

FERISHTAH, or **Firishtah** (c.1550–c.1615) Persian historian, born in Astrabad. He went as a child to India, became captain in the bodyguard of the prince of Ahmednagar, and on his deposition went to Bijapur (1589). He wrote a great History of the Muhammadan power in India (1609, trans 1831–32).

FERMAT, Pierre de (1601–65) French mathematician, born in Beaumont. He studied law at Toulouse, where he became a councillor of parliament. His passion was mathematics, most of his work being communicated in letters to friends containing results without proof. His correspondence with **Pascal** marks the foundation of probability theory. He studied maximum and minimum values of functions in advance of the differential calculus, but is best known for his work in number theory, the proofs of many of his discoveries being first published by **Leonhard Euler** a hundred years later. His 'last theorem' is the most famous unsolved problem in mathematics: it states that there are no integers positive x, y, and z with $x^n + y^n = z^n$ if n is greater than 2. In optics Fermat's principle was the first statement of a variational principle in physics; it says that the path taken by a ray of light between two given points is the one in which the light takes the least time compared with any other possible path.

FERMI, Enrico (1901–54) Italian-born American nuclear physicist, born in Rome. He studied at Pisa, at Göttingen under **Max Born**, and at Leiden, and became professor of theoretical physics at Rome in 1927. Between 1927 and 1933 he published his semi-quantitative method of calculating atomic particles and in 1934 he and his colleagues split the nuclei of uranium atoms by bombarding them with neutrons, thus producing artificial radioactive substances. He was awarded the 1938 Nobel prize for physics. Fearing for the safety of his Jewish wife in the light of Italy's anti-semitic legislation, he went straight from the prize presentation in Stockholm to the USA, where he became professor at Columbia University (1939). He played a prominent part in interesting the American government in atomic energy and constructed the first American nuclear reactor at Chicago (1942). The element fermium was named after him.

FERMOR, Patrick Michael Leigh (1915–) English travel writer of English and Irish descent. Expelled from King's School, Canterbury, he set out in 1933 on a leisurely walk from Rotterdam to Constantinople. *A Time of Gifts* (1977) recounted the journey as far as Hungary; *Between the Woods and the Water* (1986) took it to its terminus. Both have been praised for their incisive grasp of the mood of pre-war Europe, and few doubted the veracity of his account despite its being more than 40 years in gestation. Later he spent an adventurous war in Albania, Greece and Crete where, disguised as a shepherd, he lived for two years organizing the Resistance and the capture and evacuation of the German commander, General Kreipe. Among his other books are *The Traveller's Tree*, about the West Indies, which won the Heinemann Foundation prize in 1950, and *Mani* (1958), which was awarded the Duff Cooper Memorial prize.

FERN, Fanny See **WILLIS, Nathaniel Parker**

FERNANDEL, stage-name of **Fernand Joseph Désiré Contandin** (1903–71) French film comedian, born in Marseille. He worked in a bank and soap factory before his début on the stage in 1922, and from 1930 appeared in over a hundred films, interrupted only temporarily by military service and Nazi occupation. He established himself internationally with his moving portrayal of the naïve country priest of *The Little World of Don Camillo* (1953), and with his versatile handling of six separate roles in *The Sheep has Five Legs* (1953), which gave full rein to his extraordinary facial mobility.

FERNANDEZ, Juan (c.1536–c.1604) Spanish navigator. In 1563 he discovered the Pacific island named after him; he also discovered San Felix and San Ambrosio Islands.

FERNEL, Jean François (?1497–1558) French physician. The son of an innkeeper at Montdidier, he turned to medicine only after some years studying philosophy, mathematics and astrology. He soon became a popular medical teacher and his reputation as a physician soared when he saved the life of the Dauphin's (later **Henri II**) mistress. He preferred his teaching and scholarship to court life, however, and despite his essential adherence to Galenism. he was an astute observer whose many writings synthesized 16th-century medical orthodoxy. He coined the Latin words which became 'physiology' and 'pathology'. His *magnum opus*, the *Universa medicina* (1567), was edited by a disciple after his death.

FERRABOSCO, Alfonso (1543–88) Italian composer, son of **Domenico Maria Ferrabosco**, born in Bologna. He came to England before 1562, and was for some time in the service of Queen **Elizabeth**. He left England in 1578 and entered the service of the Duke of Savoy. His compositions include madrigals, motets, and music for viols.

FERRABOSCO, Alfonso (c.1575–1628) English composer of Italian extraction, son of **Alfonso Ferrabosco** (1543–88), born in Greenwich. In the service of **James I** and **Charles I**, he wrote music for masques, songs and, most notably, music for viol consorts, showing his mastery of counterpoint and invention.

FERRABOSCO, Domenico Maria (1513–74) Italian composer, father of **Alfonso Ferrabosco** (1543–88), born in Bologna. He composed madrigals and motets. Other members of the family include the three sons of **Alfonso Ferrabosco** (c.1575–1628), Alfonso (c.1620–c.1660), Henry (c.1623–c.1658) and John (1626–82), all of whom held court appointments: Henry was killed in Jamaica and John was appointed organist of Ely Cathedral in 1662.

FERRANTI, Sebastian Ziani de (1864–1930) English electrical engineer and inventor, born in Liverpool of Italian extraction. He was educated in a Roman Catholic college at Ramsgate and at evening classes at University College London. From his early experiments with dynamos and alternators he conceived the idea of the large-scale generation and distribution of electricity at high voltages, and in 1887 he was appointed chief electrician to the London Electric Supply Corporation which planned to provide power to the whole of London north of the Thames from a power-station at Deptford. This scheme was temporarily frustrated by the Electricity Lighting Act of 1888, but it nevertheless contained all the elements of the national electricity grid system which came into being some 40 years later. From 1882 to 1927 he took out 176 patents, and the firm of Ferranti Ltd which he founded in 1905 is still in the forefront of electrical and electronic engineering.

FERRAR, Nicholas (1592–1637) English theologian and mystic. An Anglican deacon, in 1625 he founded a Utopian religious community at Little Gidding in Huntingdonshire (now Cambridgeshire). The community numbered 30 people, who with constant services and perpetual prayer engaged in the occupation of fine bookbinding. The community printed and published the first edition of **George Herbert**'s *The Temple* (1633). It was not broken up by the Puritans till 1647.

FERRARA, Andrea (fl.16th century) Italian broadsword maker, probably born in Ferrara. With his brother he was in great repute as an armourer in Belluno in 1585. It is said that he tempered sword blades by the method employed by the smiths of Damascus.

FERRARI, Enzo (1898–1988) Italian racing-car designer, born in Modena. He became a racing driver in 1920 (with Alfa-Romeo), and founded the company which bears his name in 1929. He was president until 1977. In 1940 he started to design his own cars and, since 1951, the marque has won nearly 100 of the over 400 Grand Prix races in which they have competed.

FERRARI, Gaudenzio (c.1471–1546) Italian painter, most of whose works are in the Lombard galleries.

FERRARI, Paolo (1822–89) Italian dramatist, born in Modena. He wrote many excellent comedies, including *Goldoni* (1852) and *Parini e la satira* (1857). In 1860 he became professor of history at Modena, and afterwards at Milan.

FERRARO, Geraldine Anne (1935–) American Democrat politician, born in Newburgh, New York. The daughter of Italian Roman Catholic immigrants, she was educated at Marymount College, Fordham University and New York Law School and, after marrying wealthy businessman John Zaccaro in 1960, established a successful law practice (1961–74). She served as assistant district attorney for the Queens district of New York between 1974 and 1978 and worked at the Supreme Court from 1978, heading a special bureau for victims of violent crime, before being elected to the House of Representatives in 1981. In Congress, she gained a reputation as an effective, liberal-minded politician and was selected in 1984 by **Walter Mondale** to be the first female vice-presidential candidate of a major party, in an effort to add sparkle to the Democrat 'ticket'. After the Democrats' convincing defeat she retired from politics.

FERREIRA, Antonio (1528–69) Portuguese poet, born in Lisbon. He introduced a classical style into Portuguese verse and drama, earning the title 'The Portuguese Horace'.

FERREL, William (1817–91) American meteorologist, born in Fulton County, Pennsylvania. He studied the effects of the earth's rotation on wind and marine currents, and invented a tide-predicting machine.

FERRERS, Laurence Shirley, 4th Earl (1720–60) English criminal, the last nobleman to die a felon's death in England. In a paroxysm of passion he killed his old land steward. Tried by his peers in Westminster Hall, he was hanged at Tyburn.

FERRIER, Sir David (1843–1928) Scottish neurologist, born in Aberdeen. He graduated there in 1863 and took his MD at Edinburgh in 1868. In 1871 he joined the staff of King's College, London, where he was appointed to the specially created chair of neuropathology in 1889. He is known for his work on the localization of brain functions.

FERRIER, James Frederick (1808–64) Scottish philosopher, born in Edinburgh. He became professor of history at Edinburgh in 1842 and professor of moral philosophy at St Andrews in 1845. His book *The Institutes of Metaphysics* (1854) was the first important work of the British Idealist (neo-Hegelian) movement. He introduced the term 'epistemology' into English and propounded also an 'agnoiology', or theory of ignorance.

FERRIER, Kathleen (1912–53) English contralto singer, born in Higher Walton, Lancashire. An accomplished amateur pianist, she won a prize for singing at a local music festival and was encouraged by this to undertake serious studies in 1940. The range and richness of her voice, together with her remarkable technical control, rapidly won her a great reputation. In 1946 she sang Lucrezia in **Britten**'s *The Rape of Lucrezia*, and Orpheus in **Gluck**'s *Orfeo* at Glyndebourne; from then onwards, she was in great demand throughout Europe and America. Her greatest success, perhaps, was in **Mahler**'s *The Song of the Earth*, at the first Edinburgh Festival (1947) and at Salzburg (1949).

FERRIER, Susan Edmonstone (1782–1854) Scottish novelist, born in Edinburgh, the daughter of a lawyer who became principal clerk to the Court of Session with Sir **Walter Scott**. Her first work, *Marriage* (1818), a novel of provincial social manners, was followed by *The Inheritance* (1824) and *Destiny* (1831), a Highland romance. She enjoyed a close friendship with Scott, who was by some for a time credited with the authorship of her books.

FERRY, Jules François Camille (1832–93) French statesman, born at Saint Dié in the Vosges. Admitted to the Paris bar in 1854, he identified himself with the opponents of the Empire. In 1869 he was elected to the Corps Législatif, where he voted against the war with Prussia; and during the siege of Paris (1870–71) he was mayor of the city. As minister of public instruction (1879) he brought forward a bill excluding Jesuits from the schools. It was rejected, but the expulsion of the Jesuits was effected by decrees founded on obsolete laws, and brought about the dissolution of the ministry in September 1880. Ferry then formed a cabinet, which lasted till November 1881. His last ministry (1883–85) fell through his policy of 'colonial expansion', involving war in Madagascar and Indo-China.

FERSEN, Frederik Axel, Count von (1719–94) Swedish soldier and statesman, born in Stockholm. A descendant of the Scottish Macphersons, he served successively in the French and Swedish armies, and was made a field-marshal in 1770. He became leader of the anti-Royalist opposition and was ultimately assassinated in Stockholm.

FERSEN, Hans Axel, Comte de (1755–1810) Swedish soldier and statesman, son of count **Frederik Axel Fersen**. He served in the French court at Versailles, and in 1791, disguised as a coachman, drove the royal family in their abortive flight to Varennes. In 1801 he was appointed earl marshall of Sweden. He was murdered by a Stockholm mob on the false charge of having poisoned the crown prince.

FESCH, Joseph (1763–1839) French prelate, born in Ajaccio, the half-brother of Letizia Ramolino, **Napoleon**'s mother. Ordained priest, he helped on the concordat with Pope **Pius VII** in 1801, and was raised to be archbishop of Lyons (1802) and cardinal (1803). At a conference of clergy in Paris in 1810 he expressed views which lost him the favour of Napoleon, who was further exasperated by his letter to the pope, then in captivity at Fontainebleau (1812). At the approach of the Austrians in 1814 he fled to Rome, where he died.

FESSENDEN, Reginald Aubrey (1866–1932) Canadian-born American radio engineer and inventor, born in East Bolton, Quebec. Educated in Canada, he moved first to Bermuda where he developed an interest in science, and then to New York (1886) where he met **Thomas Edison** and became the chief chemist in his research laboratories in New Jersey. By 1892 he had returned to academic life, first at Purdue University and then as professor of electrical engineering at the University of Pittsburgh (1893–1900) where he began to pursue his major research interest in radio communication. Of his more than 500 patents the one of most fundamental importance was his invention of amplitude modulation, through which on Christmas Eve, 1906, he was able to broadcast what was probably the first American radio programme from the transmitter he had built at Brant Rock, Massachusetts.

FESSENDEN, William Pitt (1806–69) American Republican politician, born in Boscawen, New Hampshire. Athough illegitimate, he was educated at Bowdoin College and started in professional life by his father's support. Admitted to the Maine bar in 1827, he rose in the Whig party and had some anti-slavery sympathies which won him his election to the US Senate as a Republican in 1854, his maiden speech being an attack on the Kansas-Nebraska bill which sought to make slavery optional for those territories. He was a sound, orthodox politician, a close ally and friend of Senator James W Grimes of Iowa, who made his mark on the Finance Committee, and marshalled opposition to the **Buchanan** administration (1857–61) while being overshadowed by more flamboyant figures. **Lincoln** made him secretary of the Treasury in 1864; he returned to the senate in 1865. Lincoln's successor, **Andrew Johnson**, a Democrat, convinced Fessenden that the Republican party was being endangered by a judicious presidential amnesty to former Confederates who would then swamp the House of Representatives and perhaps imperil the Union war debt or legalize the Confederate debt. Thus Fessenden, as chairman of the Joint House and Senate Committee of Fifteen, framed in the Fourteenth Amendment to the US Constitution (adopted 1868) a measure which would specifically avert either, and protect the rights of emancipated slaves. Historians now realize that it was Fessenden and Grimes and not more radical figures, who set the tone.

FESTINGER, Leon (1919–) American psychologist, born in New York City, one of the most influential figures in postwar social psychology. He was educated at the State University of Iowa (PhD 1942). Between 1943 and 1955 he taught successively at Rochester University, MIT, and Michigan and Minnesota Universities; he then moved to Stanford University (1955–68) and later to the New School for Social Research in New York (from 1968). His contribution has centred on the introduction and development of the deceptively simple concept of 'cognitive dissonance'. According to the theory, people are unable to tolerate conflicting cognitions (beliefs, thoughts, perceptions) for any length of time, and have to resolve such internal conflicts by rejecting or devaluing one or more of the cognitions. The theory has proved useful in the understanding of a variety of psychological phenomena, and led to certain counter-intuitive predictions that were successfully borne out experimentally. He received the Distinguished Scientist award of the American Psychological Association in 1959.

FESTUS, Porcius (d.c.62 AD) Roman procurator of Judaea, who succeeded **Felix** in 60 AD. In 62 the apostle **Paul** defended himself before him (Acts xxv).

FÉTIS, François Joseph (1784–1871) Belgian writer on music, professor at the Paris Conservatory (1821) and director of the Brussels Conservatory (1833). He produced a *Universal Biography of Musicians* (1835–44) and *General History of Music* (1868–76).

FETTES, Sir William (1750–1836) Scottish merchant and philanthropist. He made a fortune from tea and wine, was twice lord provost of Edinburgh and left £166000 to found Fettes College (1870), designed by **David Bryce**.

FEUCHTWANGER, Lion (1889–1958) German writer, born in Munich. He won a European reputation with the 18th-century historical novel presenting an elaborately detailed picture of the lives, sufferings and weaknesses of central European Jewry in *Jud Süss* (1925), as well as the 14th-century tale *Die hässliche Herzogin* (1923), which as *The Ugly Duchess* (1927) was a great success in Britain. During World War I he was interned in Tunis. His thinly disguised satire on **Hitler**'s Munich putsch, *Erfolg* (1930), earned him the hatred of the Nazis. In 1933 he fled to France, where in 1940 he was interned by the German army, but escaped to the USA. He also wrote numerous dramas, and collaborated with **Brecht** in a translation of **Marlowe**'s *Edward II*. His later works included detailed part-biographies of **Goya** (1952) and **Rousseau** (1954).

FEUERBACH, Anselm (1829–80) German painter, born in Speyer. He lived after 1855 chiefly in Rome and died in Venice. He produced landscape and genre paintings and large subject pieces which had considerable influence in the revival of the classical ideal in German art.

FEUERBACH, Ludwig Andreas (1804–72) German philosopher, son of **Paul Feuerbach**, born in Landshut, Bavaria. He was a pupil of **Hegel** at Berlin but reacted against his Idealism. His most famous work, *Das Wesen des Christentums* (1841), which was translated by Mary Ann Evans (**George Eliot**) as *The Essence of Christianity*, attacked conventional Christianity and agreed that religion is 'the dream of the human mind', projecting on to an illusory God our own human ideals and nature. His naturalistic materialism was a strong influence on **Marx** and **Engels**.

FEUERBACH, Paul Johann Anselm von (1775–1833) German jurist, born in Jena. He made a brilliant reputation by his *Kritik des natürlichen Rechts* (1796) and his *Anti-Hobbes* (1798). His *Lehrbuch des gemeinen peinlichen Rechts* (1801) placed him at the head of the new school of Rigorists and his penal code for Bavaria (1813) was taken as a basis for amending the criminal law of several other countries. In 1808–11 he published a great collection of criminal cases. In his *Geschworenengericht* (1813–25) he maintained that the verdict of a jury is not adequate legal proof of a crime. He was appointed a judge at Bamberg (1814) and at Anspach (1817).

FEUILLET, Octave (1821–90) French novelist, born in Saint Lô. He was one of **Dumas**' literary assistants, and began his own career with *Le Fruit défendu*. From 1848 he published in the *Revue des deux mondes* a series collected in *Scènes et proverbes* and *Scènes et comédies* (1853–56). He wrote many popular novels and plays.

FÉVAL, Paul Henri Corentin (1817–87) French novelist, born in Rennes. His many novels include *Les Mystères de Londres* (1844) and *Le Bossu* (1858); some of his novels had an extraordinary success when dramatized.

FEYDEAU, Ernest Aimé (1821–73) French novelist. His stories depict the worst features of society in the time of the Empire. *Sylvie* is a novel of more than ordinary power.

FEYDEAU, Georges Léon Jules Marie (1862–1921) French dramatist, the son of **Ernest Aimé Feydeau** and a prostitute. His name is synonymous with French bedroom farce. He wrote his first play, *La Tailleur pour Dames* (Ladies' Tailor), when he was 24 and subsequently maintained a prolific output. His characters are Parisian bourgeois couples seeking diversion from each other; his farces, therefore, rely on the twin themes of adultery and the chase. Among his plays are such enduring (and rather endearing), classics as *Le Dindon* (1896), *La Dame de chez Maxim* (1899), *L'Hôtel du libre Échange* (1899) and *Une Puce à l'oreille* (1907), produced as *A Flea in Her Ear* at the National Theatre in 1965.

FEYNMAN, Richard (1918–88) American physicist, born in New York. During World War II he worked with the Los Alamos team in New Mexico building the first atomic bomb. Thereafter he taught at Cornell University (1945–50) and was professor at the California Institute of Technology (from 1950). He made considerable theoretical advances in quantum electrodynamics, for which he was awarded the Nobel prize for physics in 1965, jointly with **Shinichiro Tomonaga** and **Julian Schwinger**.

FIACRE, or **Fiachrach, St** (d.670) Irish hermit, who founded a monastery in France, on the site of the village of Saint-Fiacre-en-Brie, near Paris. In 1640 one Nicholas Sauvage, a hirer of hackney carriages, lived at the Hôtel St Fiacre in the Rue St Martin, Paris; hence the name 'fiacre'. He is the patron saint of cab drivers and gardeners.

FIBICH, Zdenko (Zdeněk) (1850–1900) Czech composer, born at Sěbořic. He wrote operas, symphonies, and works for solo piano and was kapellmeister in Prague from 1878. One of his melodies, *Poème*, has remained a popular favourite.

FIBIGER, Johannes Andreas Grib (1867–1928) Danish pathologist, born in Silkeborg. He became professor and head of the Institute of Pathological Anatomy at Copenhagen in 1900. The first to induce cancer experimentally, feeding rats with cockroaches carrying the parasite *spiroptera neoplastica*, he won the Nobel prize for physiology or medicine in 1926.

FIBONACCI, Leonardo (c.1170–c.1250) Italian mathematician, also known as **Leonardo of Pisa**. The first outstanding mathematician of the middle ages, he was responsible for popularizing the modern decimal system of numerals, which originated in India. His main work *Liber abaci* (The Book of Calculations 1202) illustrates the virtues of the new numeric system, showing how it can be used to simplify highly complex calculations; the book also includes work on geometry, the theory of proportion and techniques for determining the roots of equations. His greatest work, the *Liber quadratorum* (The Book of Square Numbers, 1225) contains remarkably advanced contributions to number theory and is dedicated to his patron, the Holy Roman Emperor **Frederick II**. He discovered the 'Fibonacci sequence' of integers in which each number is equal to the sum of the preceding two (1,1,2,3,5,8,...)

FICHTE, Johann Gottlieb (1762–1814) German philosopher, born in Rammenau, Saxony. He studied at Jena, made a precarious living for some years as an itinerant tutor in philosophy, in the course of which he met **Kant** at Königsberg and became a devoted disciple. He was eventually appointed professor at Jena in 1794. His *Wissenschaftslehre* of 1785 modified the Kantian system and posited the Ego as the basic reality, affirming itself in the act of consciousness and constructing the external world (the 'non-ego') as its field of action. The *Grundlage des Naturrechts* (1796) and *System der Sittenlehre* (1798) elaborate his system of thought. He went on to teach at Berlin (1799), after an accusation of atheism, and at Erlangen (1805), where he published more popular versions of his philosophy in *Grundzüge des gegenwärtigen Zeitalters* (1806) and *Anweisung zum seligen Leben und Religionslehre* (1806). In 1807–08 he delivered a famous series of patriotic lectures, *Reden an die Deutsche Nation*, in which he tried to foster German nationalism in resistance to **Napoleon I**. In this context Fichte's metaphysical 'Ego' became the German nation, an idea that was later perverted into the Nazi concept of the *Herrenvolk*. In 1810 he became the first rector of the new University of Berlin, whose constitution he had drawn up. His son Immanuel Hermann von Fichte (1797–1879) also became a professor of philosophy (at Bonn, then Tübingen) and was ennobled in 1867.

FICINO, Marsilio (1433–99) Italian philosopher, born in Figline, Florence. **Cosimo de' Medici** appointed him head of the Platonic Academy in Florence and commissioned from him translations (into Latin) from and commentaries on **Plato**, **Plotinus** and the *Corpus Hermeticum*. He was ordained a priest in 1473, and became rector of two churches and canon of the cathedral in Florence. He retired to the country when the Medici were expelled from Florence in 1494. He was a major influence in the Renaissance revival of Platonism and his own rather eclectic system was largely an attempt to reconcile Platonism with Christianity.

FICK, Adolph Eugen (1829–1901) German physiologist, professor at Zürich and Würzburg. A law of diffusion in liquids was named after him, when he discovered that the mass of solute diffusing through unit area per second is proportional to the concentration gradient.

FICK, August (1833–1916) German philologist, born in Petershagen. Professor at Göttingen (1876) and Breslau (1887), he pioneered the comparative study of Indo-European vocabulary with his Indo-Germanic dictionary (1870). He also wrote works on Greek personal names, and the original language of the *Iliad*.

FIELD, Cyrus West (1819–92) American financier, born in Stockbridge, Massachusetts, brother of **David Dudley Field** and **Stephen Johnson Field**. After a career as a paper manufacturer, he helped to finance the first telegraph cable across the Atlantic, achieved after several attempts in 1866. He organized the New York, Newfoundland, and London Telegraph Company in 1854, and the Atlantic Telegraph Company in 1856, but he suffered severe financial losses and died poor.

FIELD, David Dudley (1805–94) American jurist, born in Haddam, Connecticut, brother of **Cyrus West Field** and **Stephen Johnson Field**. He was admitted to the New York bar in 1828, and laboured to reform the judiciary system. A great advocate of codification, in 1857 he was appointed by the state to prepare penal, political and civil codes, of which the first has been adopted by New York, and all have been accepted by some other states. He did much for international law and for law reform generally. His *Outlines of an International Code* (1872) were translated into various languages.

FIELD, Eugene (1850–95) American writer, born in St Louis, Missouri. He became a journalist at 23, and from 1883 was a columnist with the *Chicago Morning News*, achieving a reputation as humorist and poet with his column 'Sharps and Flats'. He wrote the well-known nursery lullaby 'Wynken, Blynken, and Nod', and published several books of children's verse.

FIELD, John (1782–1837) Irish pianist and composer, born in Dublin. An infant prodigy, he was apprenticed to **Clementi**, who used him to demonstrate the capabilities of his pianos. In 1802 he accompanied Clementi to Paris, Vienna and St Petersburg, where he settled in 1804 as a music teacher, returning to London in 1832. His 19 *Nocturnes* and other important keyboard music influenced **Chopin**.

FIELD, Marshall (1834–1906) American merchant, born in Conway, Massachusetts. He started as a clerk in Pittsfield, Massachusetts, moving to Chicago in 1856, where he became founder of the Chicago department store known from 1881 as Marshall Field and Company, one of the world's largest and most progressive emporia.

FIELD, Nathan (1587–?1633) English actor and dramatist, born in London. He was educated at St Paul's school and in 1600 became one of the children of the Queen's Chapel. He was one of the comedians of the Queen's Revels (1604–13) and various other troupes. As a playwright he collaborated with **Beaumont** and **Fletcher** and with **Massinger** in the latter's *The Fatal Dowry* (1632) and wrote two comedies, *A Woman is a Weathercocke* (1612) and *Amends for Ladies* (1618).

FIELD, Stephen Johnson (1816–99) American judge, born in Haddam, Connecticut, brother of **Cyrus West Field** and **David Dudley Field**. He helped to draw up the California state codes and became chief justice there in 1859. He served as a judge of the US Supreme Court from 1863 to 1897.

FIELDING, Anthony Vandyke Copley (1787–1855) English watercolour painter, born near Halifax. A pupil of **John Varley**, his landscapes show technical excellence and atmosphere, but are often deficient in design. He lived for some years at Worthing, where he produced many of his well-known downland paintings and marine pieces.

FIELDING, Henry (1707–54) English novelist, born at Sharpham Park, near Glastonbury in Somerset, the son of an army lieutenant and a judge's daughter. He was educated privately, then at Eton. He fell in love with a young heiress at Lyme Regis, attempted to abduct her and was bound over to keep the peace. He went to London and in 1728 published a satirical poem, *The Masquerade*, and a comedy, *Love in Several Masques*. Thereafter he studied at the University of Leiden (1728–29), before returning to London, and in the space of eight years he wrote 25 dramatic pieces: light comedies, adaptations of **Molière**, farces, ballad operas, burlesques (including *Tom Thumb*), and a series of satires attacking Sir **Robert Walpole** and his government. This last prompted the introduction of the Theatrical Licensing Act of 1737 and effectively ended Fielding's career as a playwright and as a theatre manager (he had formed his own company, and was running the Little Theatre, Haymarket). He now turned to the law and was admitted as a student at the Middle Temple; he was called to the bar in 1740, but did not shine on the circuit on account of disabling gout. While still a student he turned to journalism and became editor of *The Champion* (1739–41). Incensed by the publication of **Richardson**'s prudish *Pamela*, in 1740 he ridiculed it in a pseudonymous parody, *An Apology for the Life of Mrs Shamela Andrews* (1741). In 1742 came *The Adventures of Joseph Andrews and his Friend, Mr Abraham Adams*. Three volumes of *Miscellanies* (including *The Life of Jonathan Wild the Great*) followed in 1743. *The History of Tom Jones, a Foundling* was probably begun in the summer of 1746 and was completed towards the end of 1748. In the interim he caused a scandal by marrying Mary Daniel, the maid of his first wife, Mary Craddock (d.1744). He was made a justice of the peace for Westminster and Middlesex in 1748 and campaigned vigorously against legal corruption, and helped his half-brother, Sir John

Fielding (1721–80) to found the Bow Street Runners as an embryo detective force. In 1749 *The History of Tom Jones, a Foundling* was published to public acclaim, though its reception by some literary luminaries was unenthusiastic. **Samuel Johnson** called it vicious and there were those who held it responsible for two earth tremors that shook London shortly after its publication. But it endures as one of the great comic and picaresque novels in the English language, and **Coleridge** thought the plot one of the three most perfect ever planned. He followed it with *Amelia* in 1751. In 1752 he was heavily involved with *The Covent Garden Journal*, which contains some of his most acerbic satire. During his last years, however, illness overtook him. He was still ardent in his fight against corruption but at the age of 45 he could not move without the help of crutches. He died in Lisbon where he had gone in search of better health.

FIELDS, Dame Gracie, originally **Grace Stansfield** (1898–1979) English comedienne and singer, born in Rochdale, Lancashire. A child performer, she progressed, via revues and pantomime, to become one of the country's premier music-hall attractions, affectionately known as 'Our Gracie'. A chirpy, natural talent, she was adept at both comic songs and plaintive ballads. Her long career encompassed radio, recordings, television and films like *Sally in Our Alley* (1931), *Sing As We Go* (1934) and *Holy Matrimony* (1943). In semi-retirement from the 1950s, she won a Silvania TV award for her performance in *The Old Lady Shows Her Medals* (1956) and, in 1960, published her autobiography *Sing As We Go*. A royal favourite, she appeared in ten command performances between 1928 and 1978, the year she was created a DBE.

FIELDS, James Thomas (1817–81) American writer and publisher, born in Portsmouth, New Hampshire. He edited the *Atlantic Monthly* from 1862 to 1870, and lectured on literary subjects. He also wrote books on verse, and volumes on **Hawthorne** and **Dickens**.

FIELDS, W C, originally **William Claude Dukenfield** (1879–1946) American comedian, born in Philadelphia, Pennsylvania. A carnival juggler as a teenager, he moved on to vaudeville, appearing all over America and Europe before settling as the star attraction at the *Ziegfeld Follies* from 1915 to 1921. He made his film début in *Pool Sharks* (1915) and appeared in many short comedies during the silent era. A bulbous nose and gravelly voice enhanced his creation of a bibulous, child-hating misanthrope, continually at odds with the world, an image that was said to be not unlike his own personality. The writer and performer of several classic comedies like *It's a Gift* (1934), *The Bank Dick* (1940), *My Little Chickadee* (1940) and *Never Give a Sucker an Even Break* (1941), he also played Micawber in *David Copperfield* (1935). Illness and a legendary reputation for being difficult restricted later creative opportunities, and his final appearance was as a guest artist in *Sensations of 1945*.

FIENNES, Sir Ranulph Twisleton-Wykeham (1945–) English polar explorer, born in Windsor, Berkshire. Educated at Eton, he served with the Royal Scots Greys and the SAS, and fought with the sultan of Oman's armed forces. He was the leader of six major expeditions between 1969 and 1986, including a journey up the White Nile by hovercraft, parachuting onto the Jostedal glacier in Norway (1970), travelling 4000 miles up rivers in northern Canada and Alaska (1971), and overland towards the North Pole (1976–78). Between 1979 and 1982 he organized the Transglobe expedition which traced the Greenwich Meridian crossing both Poles. Since then he has made several attempts to reach the North Pole unsupported.

FIESCHI, Count Giovanni Luigi de' (c.1523–1547) Italian nobleman of an illustrious Genoese house. He belonged to a line hereditarily at feud with that of the famous admiral, **Andrea Doria**, who had restored republican government in Genoa. Fieschi with his three brothers and others organized a plot for the overthrow of Doria and the establishment of an oligarchy. The gates of the city were forced, on 2 January 1547, the fleet captured, and Doria put to flight. But Fieschi, stepping from one galley to another at night, fell overboard, and was drowned in the harbour. The scheme ended there, and Doria returned to wreak merciless vengeance on the other plotters.

FIESCHI, Joseph (1790–1836) Corsican conspirator. Dismissed from a minor government post for fraud, with several accomplices he constructed and fired an infernal machine of 25 guns at King **Louis-Philippe** in 1835. Eighteen people were killed, but the king escaped almost unhurt, and Fieschi was executed after trial.

FIESOLE, Giovanni da See **ANGELICO, Fra**

FIGG, James (d.1736) English fencer and pugilist, born in Thame. He gave displays of quarterstaff, fencing and boxing in Marylebone, and ran a booth at Southwark. He is regarded as one of the greatest of 18th-century sporting figures, and is portrayed in **Hogarth**'s *Rake's Progress* and *Southwark Fair*.

FIGUERAS, Estanislao (1819–82) Spanish statesman, born in Barcelona. For taking part in republican plots in 1866 he was imprisoned; but after the expulsion of **Isabella II** he became a member of the republican government. On the abdication of King Amadeus I in 1873 he became president of the Spanish republic, but soon resigned.

FIGUEROA, Leonardo de (c.1650–1730) Spanish architect, born in Seville. An innovative exponent of Hispanic baroque, he was interested in surface complexity and was the first to use exposed brickwork in Seville at the Hospital de Venerables Sacerdote (1687–97). In the Magdalena Church in Seville (1691–1709) he used the undulant cornice for the first time in Spain in this rebuilding of a mudéjar building. His most influential and important work which presents a glittering assembly of Figueroa's most distinctive forms is the San Tolemo doorway, Seville (1724–34) where balcony walls part in many layers to reveal a Borrominesque window beneath an oval medallion.

FIGUIER, Louis (1819–94) French writer, born in Montpellier. He became professor at the École de Pharmacie in Paris, and wrote on modern science and industry, alchemy and in defence of immortality. Many of these have been translated, including *The Ocean World*, *The World Before the Deluge*, and *The Day after Death*. His wife, Juliette Bouscaren (1829–79), wrote several novels.

FILARETE, Antonio, originally **Antonio di Pietro Averlino** (c.1400–c.1469) Florentine sculptor, architect and theorist, whose nickname means 'lover of virtue'. He may have trained with **Ghiberti**, though the bronze doors of Old St Peter's, Rome (c.1433–1445), his earliest surviving work, are more archaic in style than those of the Florentine Baptistry. Banished from Rome for the alleged theft of a relic, he travelled north and in 1450 settled in Milan, where he worked for **Francesco Sforza** from 1451 to 1465. His major project there was the Ospedale Maggiore (begun 1457), a vast enterprise never completed to his design, which introduced the concept of the centrally-planned building and other Renaissance ideas to Lombardy. His remarkable *Trattato d'Architettura* (1460–64) includes a scheme for an ideal city built to a symmetrical plan, called Sforzinda.

FILCHNER, Wilhelm (1877–1957) German geographer and explorer, born in Munich. He studied cartography and geography at Munich University and then joined the Trigonometrical division in Prussia, and later worked with the Berlin Earth-Magnetic Institute and the Potsdam Astrophysics Institute. In 1910 he led the Second German Antarctic Expedition, and during a preparatory trip crossed and mapped Vestspitsbergen. In the ship *Deutschland* (1910–12), the expedition made surveys of South Georgia, before travelling to Vahsel Bay, the furthest south yet reached in that sector of the antarctic. There they became stuck in the ice of the Weddell Sea, drifting for 700 miles northwards before escaping nine months later having carried out useful observations of ice drift and disproving the theory of a second antarctic continent. A return trip to Antarctica was frustrated by the outbreak of war. In 1900 he had ridden on horseback from Russia across the Pamirs to Samarkand, which inspired further expeditions to Tibet (1903–05, 1926–28 and 1934–38), during which he traversed the length of Tibet and explored the upper Hwang Ho. With Professor Erich Przybyllok, his companion on earlier trips, he undertook a magnetic survey of Nepal (1939–40) and established magnetic stations in China and Tibet. He lived in India during World War II as his anti-Nazi feelings were well known, and then returned to Zürich to write.

FILDES, Sir Luke (1844–1927) English painter, born in Liverpool. He became known as a woodcut designer for magazines, and illustrated **Dickens**' *Edwin Drood* (1870). He also painted many subject pictures.

FILICAIA, Vincenzo da (1642–1707) Italian lyric poet, born in Florence. He studied there and at Pisa, and held a post under the Grand-Duke of Tuscany. He is remembered for his patriotic sonnets, and his ode on the liberation of Vienna from the Turks (1684).

FILLAN, St (d.777) Irish churchman, the son of a Munster prince. He became abbot of the monastery on the Holy Loch in Argyll, but withdrew to Upper Glendochart (Strathfillan), where he died. In 1318 **Robert Bruce** re-established an Augustinian priory there. His square-shaped bronze bell, and the Quigrich, or bronze head of his pastoral staff, are in the Antiquarian Museum in Edinburgh. St Fillans, on Loch Earn, is associated with an earlier saint called 'the leper'.

FILLMORE, Millard (1800–74) from 1850 to 1853 13th president of the United States, born in Summer Hill, New York. A farmer's son, and bred a wool-carder, he educated himself, and became a lawyer, comptroller of New York State (1847), and vice-president (1848). On the slavery question he was a supporter of 'compromise'.

FILMER, Sir Robert (c.1590–1653) English writer, born in East Sutton, Kent. He was an extreme advocate of the divine right of kings, in his *Patriarcha* (1680). He also strenuously opposed witch hunting.

FINCH, Alfred William (1854–1930) Anglo-Finnish painter and ceramic artist, born in Brussels. He lived in Finland from 1897, and was an exponent of Pointillism.

FINCH, Heneage, 1st Earl of Nottingham (1621–82) lord chancellor, born in Kent. He was the son of a cousin of Sir John Finch, Baron Finch (1584–1660), speaker and lord-keeper. Educated at Westminster and Christ Church, Oxford, he was called to the bar in 1645. After the Restoration, as solicitor-general he took part in the trial of the regicides, and became attorney-general (1670) and lord chancellor (1674). As high steward he presided at the trial of **Stafford** in 1680. He died on 18 December 1682. His son Daniel (1647–1730), a Tory, but not a Jacobite, statesman, succeeded him as 2nd Earl of Nottingham, and in 1729 became also 6th Earl of Winchelsea.

FINCH, Peter, originally **William Mitchell** (1916–77) British actor, of Australian origin, born in London. Australia became a permanent base during the Depression when he worked in vaudeville and the newly-established indigenous film industry. A popular radio actor who formed his own theatre group, he was encouraged to resume his career in Britain by a visit from **Laurence Olivier**. Rugged and authoritative, with an off-screen reputation as a hellraiser, his renown spread internationally, giving him the opportunity to portray a wide variety of film roles, as in *The Nun's Story* (1959), *Far From the Madding Crowd* (1967), *Sunday, Bloody Sunday* (1971) and *Network* (1976), for which he received the first-ever posthumous Academy Award.

FINCK, Heinrich (1445–1527) German composer. From c.1490 he was court musician at Cracow in Poland, and later at Stuttgart, Augsburg and Salzburg. He wrote church music, mostly *cantus firmus*, and influenced the development of 16th-century choral style.

FINDLATER, Andrew (1810–85) Scottish editor, born near New Aberdour in Aberdeenshire. He graduated from Aberdeen, and from 1842 to 1849 was headmaster of Gordon's Hospital there. He came to Edinburgh (1853) to supervise for Messrs **Chambers** a new edition of the *Information for the People* (1857). He also edited the first edition of *Chambers' Encyclopaedia* (1860–68), and wrote manuals on astronomy, philology, and physical geography.

FINDLATER, Jane (1866–1946) Scottish novelist, born in Lochearnhead, Perthshire, daughter of a Free Church minister, and sister of **Mary Findlater**. She had a great success with her first novel, *The Green Graves of Balgowrie* (1896), an 18th-century fiction based on family papers. It was followed by *A Daughter of Strife* (1897), *Rachel* (1899), *The Story of a Mother* (1902) and *The Ladder to the Stars* (1906). In collaboration with her sister she wrote the novel *Crossriggs* (1908) and others.

FINDLATER, Mary (1865–1963) Scottish novelist, born in Lochearnhead, Perthshire, daughter of a Free Church minister, and sister of **Jane Findlater**. She wrote several novels of her own, and collaborated with her sister in *Crossriggs* (1908) and others.

FINGER, Godfrey, originally **Gottfried** (fl.1685–1717) Czech composer, born in Olomuc. He came to England c.1685 where he became a musician at the court of **James II**. He wrote a number of instrumental works for flutes and violins, and composed incidental music for the plays of **Congreve** and others. He left England in 1701, because, we are told, of xenophobic prejudice against his work, and he became chamber musician to the queen of Prussia.

FINI, Tommaso See **MASOLINO DA PANICALE**

FINK, Albert (1827–97) German-born American structural engineer, born in Lauterbach. Educated in engineering and architecture at Darmstadt, he emigrated to the USA in 1849. He invented (1852) the Fink truss bridge which became widely used on American and other railways, and also carried out pioneering studies of transportation costs which inaugurated the science of railway economics.

FINLAY, George (1799–1875) Scottish classical historian, born of Scottish parents in Faversham in Kent. After studying at Glasgow and Göttingen, he joined **Byron** in the Greek War of Independence in 1823, and settled in Attica. He wrote several works on Greek history, published in composite form as *History* *of Greece*, from the Roman conquest to the Greek revolution (1844–61, new ed 7 vols, 1877).

FINLAY, Ian Hamilton (1925–) Scottish artist, poet and writer, born in the Bahamas to Scottish parents who returned to their native country when he was a child. He spent a brief period at Glasgow School of Art before World War II. In the 1950s he began his career as a writer, and became increasingly concerned with the formal qualities of individual words; his writings of the early 1960s played a leading part in the foundation of the 'concrete poetry' movement. Since then the major theme of his art has been the relationship between words and images. In 1966 he moved, with his wife Sue, to a farmhouse near Dunsyre in the Pentland Hills, later named 'Little Sparta', and began to transform the grounds into an original modern conception of a classical garden, with sculptures and stone inscriptions carefully placed within the landscape. Like his prints, posters and other works, these are produced in collaboration with a number of skilled craftsmen.

FINLAY, Robert Bannatyne, Viscount (1842–1929) Scottish jurist and statesman, born in Edinburgh. He studied medicine there, was called to the English bar in 1867, and was Unionist MP for Inverness Burghs (1885–92, 1895–1906), and Edinburgh University (1910–16). Solicitor-general (1895-1900) and attorney-general (1900–06), he was lord chancellor from 1916 to 1919, in 1920 member of the Hague Permanent Court of Arbitration and in 1921 a judge of the Permanent Court of International Justice. He was created a viscount in 1919.

FINLEY, James (1762–1828) American civil engineer, born in Pennsylvania. He was a judge and justice of the peace when he conceived the idea of building a bridge on the suspension principle with masonry towers and wrought-iron chains. His first bridge of 70 ft span was completed in 1801, one of the earliest of its type anywhere in the world, and in 1810 a similar bridge of 244 ft span was built at Newburyport on the Merrimack river. His bridges had particularly substantial decks and unlike those of some other builders, there is no record of a Finley bridge having been blown down by strong winds.

FINNBOGADÓTTIR, Vigdís (1930–) president of Iceland, the first woman in world history to be elected head of state. She was born in Reykjavík, and went to France to study French language and literature, specializing in drama at the University of Grenoble and the Sorbonne in Paris (1949–53). She returned to Iceland to work for the National Theatre, while pursuing further studies at the University of Iceland. For ten years (1962–72) she taught French in senior school in Reykjavík and French drama and theatre history at the university, presented arts programmes on television, and worked as a cultural hostess for the Icelandic Tourist Bureau during the summer vacations. From 1972 to 1980 she was the director of the Reykjavík City Theatre. In 1980 she was persuaded to stand for the non-political office of president of Iceland, winning a narrow victory against three male candidates; she was returned unopposed in 1984 and re-elected in 1988. Known as 'President Vigdís', she was married in 1954 and divorced in 1963. She adopted a baby daughter in 1972, one of the first instances in Iceland of a single person adopting a child.

FINNEY, Albert (1936–) English actor, born in Salford, Lancashire. A student at RADA, he made his stage début at Birmingham in *Julius Caesar* (1956) and his London début in *The Party* (1958). At Stratford in 1959 he appeared in *King Lear*, *Othello* and *A Midsummer Night's Dream*. He made his film début in *The Entertainer* (1960) but it was his definitive portrayal of the working-class rebel in *Saturday Night and Sunday Morning* (1960) that established him as a star. On stage he appeared in *Billy Liar* (1960) and *Luther* (1961), joining the National Theatre in 1965 and serving as associate artistic director of the Royal Court Theatre from 1972 to 1975. Recent stage work includes *The Biko Inquest* (1984) and *Orphans* (1986). On film he directed *Charlie Bubbles* (1967) and received Academy Award nominations for *Tom Jones* (1963), *Murder on the Orient Express* (1974), *The Dresser* (1983) and *Under the Volcano* (1984).

FINNEY, Tom (1921–) English footballer, born in Preston. One of the greatest wingers ever to play football, he was a contemporary of the great **Stanley Matthews**. More direct than the latter and capable of playing either flank, his mazy dribbling, good finishing and excellent deportment earned him 76 England caps. He was a Preston North End player all his footballing life and the modest integrity which kept him with a comparatively small club prevented him from winning any major domestic honours in English football.

FINNIAN, St Irish churchman. He is said to have taught 3000 pupils at the monastery of Clonard, in Meath, where he died.

FINSCH, Friedrich Hermann Otto (1839–1917) German naturalist and traveller, born in Silesia, one of the greatest ornithological explorers of his age. Apprenticed as a painter on glass, he became assistant curator at the Dutch National Museum in Leiden, before becoming curator of the Bremen Museum (1864–78). He travelled all over the world and published accounts of the birds in every quarter of the globe, particularly East Africa and Polynesia (*Beiträge zur Fauna Central Polynesiens*, 1867, and *Die Vögel Ost-Afrikas*, 1870), but is best remembered as an expert on the parrots of the world (*Die Papageien*, 1867). In 1884 he was appointed **Bismarck**'s imperial commissioner to New Guinea, which led to the formation of German protectorates in the area (Kaiser Wilhelm's Land and the Bismarck Archipelago). From 1905 he was head of the ethnographical department of the Municipal Museum in Brunswick. Finsch's Wheatear was named in his honour.

FINSEN, Niels Ryberg (1860–1904) Danish physician and scientist, born in the Faroe Islands, the founder of phototherapy. He discovered the curative power of the chemical rays of light (sunlight, electric light, Röntgen rays, etc), and taught anatomy at the University of Copenhagen, where he had studied. He accomplished his epoch-making work in spite of chronic illness. He was awarded the Nobel prize for physiology or medicine in 1903.

FINZI, Gerald Raphael (1901–56) British composer, born in London. He studied under Ernest Farrar and Edward Bairstow. The death of Farrar in World War I—his father had died when he was eight, and he also lost his three elder brothers—had a profound effect on him. Introspective by nature, he was attracted to the countryside and the folk idiom, and in 1922–25 lived and worked in isolation in Gloucestershire. He then settled in London, however, took a course in counterpoint, met other contemporary musicians including **Holst** and **Vaughan Williams**, and from 1930–33 taught composition at the Royal Academy of Music. In 1937 he returned to the country, building a house in Wiltshire, and during the war worked at the ministry of war transport. A lover of literature, he is best known for his songs; he set to music many poems by **Thomas Hardy** and the metaphysical poets, sonnets by **Milton**, and **Wordsworth**'s ode on the *Intimations of Immortality*, which was first performed at the 1950

Three Choirs Festival. Among his orchestral compositions are the *Grand Fantasia and Toccata* (1953), and his church music includes the *Dies Natalis*. He did considerable research into 18th-century English music, and his fine collection of music of this period is housed at St Andrews University.

FIORELLI, Giuseppe (1823–96) Italian archaeologist, born in Naples, whose excavations at Pompeii helped preserve the ancient city. As professor of archaeology at Naples University and director of excavations (1860–75), he dug for the first time layer by layer and on a large scale so that completed buildings and blocks of the city could be explored and displayed. He also devised a method for making casts of humans and animals overwhelmed when volcanic ash covered Pompeii in AD 79, pouring plaster into the voids left when they decayed to recreate their external appearance in minute detail. He founded a training school where foreigners as well as Italians could learn archaeological technique, and made a particular study of the materials and building methods used in the city. Director of the National Museum at Naples from 1863, he was director general of Italian Antiquities and Fine Arts (1875–96).

FIRBANK, (Arthur Annesley) Ronald (1886–1926) English novelist, born in London, the son of a wealthy company director. Educated at Uppingham and Cambridge, where he was converted to Roman Catholicism, in 1909 he left university without taking a degree and travelled extensively in Spain, Italy, the Middle East and North Africa. Sunstroke as a child left him delicate and although he acquired friends he was by nature solitary, invariably unaccompanied on his frequent visits to the theatre. A homosexual, he cultivated eccentricity such as the palm tree in his apartment which he employed a gardener to water twice a day. His novels (written on piles of blue postcards) are slight but innovative and anticipate **Evelyn Waugh**, **Anthony Powell**, **Ivy Compton-Burnett** and others. In 1905 he published a volume containing two short stories, *Odette d'Antrevernes*, and several novels followed, among them *Vainglory* (1915), *Valmouth* (1919) and *Prancing Nigger* (1924), inspired by a visit to Haiti. None made much of an impact though the **Sitwells** championed him. His last complete work before his premature death from a disease of the lungs, *Concerning the Eccentricities of Cardinal Pirelli* (1926), is quintessential Firbank, the dialogue witty and inconsequential, the hero meeting his end while in ardent pursuit of a choir boy.

FIRDAUSI, or **Ferd(a)usi,** pen-name of **Abu-'l Kasim Mansur** (c.935–c.1020) Persian poet, born near Tús in Khorasan. When he was about 60 he spent some years at the court of **Mahmud of Ghazni**, where he wrote his masterpiece the *Shah Náma* (Book of Kings). When this was finished in 1008, the poet, receiving 60000 silver dirhams instead of the promised 60000 gold dinars, fled from Ghazni, leaving behind him a scathing satire on the sultan. Mahmud at length sent the 60000 gold dinars to Firdausi at Tus, just as his remains were being carried to the grave. The *Shah Nama*, based on actual events from the annals of Persia, is for the most part composed of mythological and fanciful incidents. He also wrote a number of shorter pieces, kasidas and ghazals. His *Yusuf u Zulaykha* is based on the story of Joseph and Potiphar's wife.

FIRENZUOLA, Agnolo (1493–1548) Italian author, born in Florence. He became abbot of Prato, paraphrased the *Golden Ass* of **Apuleius**, and wrote a couple of comedies and some licentious poems.

FIRESTONE, Harvey Samuel (1868–1938) American industrialist, born in Columbiana, Ohio. He started by selling solid rubber carriage tyres in Chicago and in 1900 he founded the Firestone Tire and Rubber Company in Akron, Ohio, with a $10000 investment which gave him half interest. The company grew to be one of the biggest industrial corporations in the USA. He pioneered the pneumatic tyre for the Ford model T, non-skid treads, and tyres for farm tractors and motor trucks. To break the monopolistic power of rubber growers in SE Asia he started rubber plantations in Liberia in 1924.

FIRISHTA See **FERISHTAH**

FIRTH, Sir Charles Harding (1857–1936) English historian, born in Sheffield. He was professor of modern history at Oxford, 1904–25, and wrote much on the 17th century, particularly on such themes as *Oliver Cromwell and the Rule of the Puritans in England* (1953).

FIRTH, Francis (1822–98) English topographical photographer, born in Chesterfield. He became interested in photography while working with a printing firm and between 1856 and 1859 travelled extensively in Egypt and the near east, using the large 40x50 cm cameras and complicated wet-plate process of the period to produce the first photographic traveller's records to be seen in Britain. From 1864 he toured throughout Britain and established a nation-wide service of photographs of local scenes as prints and postcards, a business which by the end of his life had extended into Europe and survived commercially until 1971.

FIRTH, John Rupert (1890–1960) English linguist, born in Keighley, Yorkshire. Professor of English at the University of the Punjab, Lahore, from 1919 to 1928, he was senior lecturer in phonetics at University College, London between 1928 and 1938; he became a senior lecturer in the School of Oriental and African Studies in 1938, and head of the department of phonetics and linguistics in the School in 1941. In 1944 he was appointed professor of general linguistics at London University, the first such chair in Great Britain. In contrast to, for example, **Bloomfield**, Firth insisted that meaning was central to the study of language. He is particularly remembered for his development of prosodic phonology and the contextual theory of meaning. He wrote many articles but only two books, *Speech* (1930) and *The Tongues of Men* (1937), both deliberately written as popular works.

FIRTH, Mark (1819–80) English industrialist and philanthropist, born in Sheffield. In 1849 with his father and brother he established there the great Norfolk steelworks. He was a munificent benefactor to Sheffield, his gifts including almshouses, a park and the Firth College (1879), now part of the university.

FIRTH, Sir Raymond William (1901–) English social anthropologist, born and educated in Auckland, New Zealand. He studied under **Bronislaw Malinowski** at the London School of Economics and carried out fieldwork (1928–29) on the island of Tikopia in the Solomon Islands. He spent two years at Sydney University before returning to England in 1932 to take up a lectureship at the London School of Economics, becoming reader in 1935 and professor from 1944 to 1968. His major contributions have been in the fields of economic anthropology, social change, and anthropological theory (especially social organization). His major monographs include *We, the Tikopia* (1936), *Primitive Polynesian Economy* (1939) and *Social Change in Tikopia* (1959). Other significant contributions include studies of Malay peasant fishermen, kinship in London, and a major work on symbolism, *Symbols Public and Private* (1973).

FISCHART, Johann (c.1545–1590) German satirist whose Rabelaisian works lash with inexhaustible humour the corruptions of the clergy, the astrological fancies and other follies of the time. *Flöhhatz, Weibertratz* (1573) is outrageously comic and original. Essentially different are *Das glückhafft Schiff von Zürich* (in verse, 1576) and his spiritual songs.

FISCHER, Bobby (Robert James) (1943–) American chess player, born in Chicago, world champion (1972–75). Brought up by his mother in Brooklyn after the divorce of his parents in 1945, he won both the US junior and senior chess titles at the age of 14. From the earliest stages of his career he dictated terms of finance and playing conditions to tournament organizers, and his threats of withdrawal were not always idle. He entertained a plethora of phobias over hidden cameras, shiny chess pieces, glaring lights, restless opponents and bugged seating, but his brilliance over the board led to his achieving the highest results rating, Elo 2785, in the history of chess. In 1972 he won the world championship title with an acrimonious win over **Boris Spassky** in Reykjavík, Iceland, and thereafter withdrew from competitive chess. Failure to agree terms and conditions in 1975 for a defence of his title against **Anatoly Karpov** resulted in FIDÉ (Fédération Internationale des Échecs) stripping him of it by default. Numerous subsequent attempts failed to lure him back to the board, and he has lived in virtual seclusion since then in and around Los Angeles.

FISCHER, Emil Hermann (1852–1919) German chemist, born in Euskirchen, Rhenish Prussia. Professor of chemistry at Berlin from 1892, he won the Nobel prize for chemistry in 1902. Hydrazine, rosaniline, synthetic sugar, fermentation, the purine group, synthetic peptides, and veronal were among his studies and discoveries.

FISCHER, Ernst Otto (1918–) German inorganic chemist, born in Munich, the son of a professor of physics. He was educated at the Technical College, and spent his career there. In 1951, and independently of Sir **Geoffrey Wilkinson**, he deduced the structure of the remarkable synthetic compound, ferrocene, concluding that its molecule consisted of a sandwich of two carbon rings with an iron atom centrally placed between them. He confirmed this idea by X-ray crystal diffraction analysis. This novel and peculiar class of organometallic sandwich compounds now numbers thousands. Fischer and Wilkinson shared the Nobel prize for chemistry in 1973.

FISCHER, Hans (1881–1945) German scientist. From 1921 he was professor of organic chemistry and director of the Institute at Munich. His researches on haemin, the porphyrins, chlorophyll and other related compounds won him the Nobel prize for chemistry in 1930. He died by his own hand after his laboratories had been destroyed in the bombing of Munich.

FISCHER VON ERLACH, Johann Bernard (1656–1723) Austrian architect, born in Graz. The founder and outstanding exponent of the Austrian Baroque style, he trained in Rome under **Bernini** and moved to Vienna as architect to the Habsburg court in 1687. His major works there are the Kariskirche (1716) and Hofbibliotek (1723); he also designed the Kollegienkirche in Salzburg (1707), and several palaces like the Schönbrunn palace in Vienna (1711). He wrote a history of architecture in 1721.

FISCHER-DIESKAU, Dietrich (1925–) German baritone, born in Berlin. He studied under Georg Walter and Weissenborn, and soon after making his professional début at Freiburg in 1947 joined the Berlin Municipal Opera as a principal baritone, but he soon became one of the foremost interpreters of German Lieder, particularly the song-cycles of **Schubert**.

FISH, Hamilton (1808–93) American politician, born in New York. As secretary of state under **Grant** (1869–77) he signed the Washington Treaty of 1871, and completed the settlement of the Alabama Question.

FISHBEIN, Morris (1889–1976) American physician, writer and journal editor, born in St Louis, Missouri. Soon after receiving his MD from Rush Medical College in Chicago, he joined the staff of the *Journal of the American Medical Association* where as assistant editor (1913–24) and editor (1924–49) he gradually acquired enormous influence in American medical politics. For decades he was known as the 'voice of the AMA', where he campaigned against government involvement in medical practice and in favour of the traditional contractual fee-for-service structure. He castigated unorthodox medical practitioners and sought to increase health consciousness among lay people through his syndicated newspaper column and his *Modern Home Medical Adviser* (1935) and many other popular books. Appearing as a reactionary in his later years, he did at least improve the standards and reputation of *JAMA*.

FISHER, Andrew (1862–1928) Scottish-born Australian politician. A coal-miner from the age of twelve, he emigrated to Queensland in 1885. From mining, he gradually moved into trade union activity and politics, entering the Queensland state assembly in 1893 and the first federal parliament in 1901. He became Australian Labor party (ALP) leader in 1907 and then prime minister (1908–09, 1910–13 and 1914–15). At the start of World War I he made the dramatic promise to support the war effort 'to the last man and the last shilling'. He was Australian high commissioner in London (1916–21).

FISHER, Bud, originally **Harry Conway** (1885–1954) American strip cartoonist, born in Chicago, the creator of the world-famous *Mutt and Jeff* comic strip. Leaving university early to become staff cartoonist of the *San Francisco Chronicle* (1905), he introduced a regular strip, *A.Mutt*, illustrating the racing tips of a gambler named Mr A Mutt and involving Mutt's family, cat included (1907). Fisher soon moved to the *San Francisco Examiner*, where Jeff, Mutt's partner, was introduced in 1908, but the title did not change to *Mutt and Jeff* until 1915. In the 1920s he was the highest-paid cartoonist in the world. Fisher later set up an animation studio and produced a weekly *Mutt and Jeff* cartoon.

FISHER, Geoffrey Francis, Baron Fisher of Lambeth (1887–1972) English prelate, archbishop of Canterbury, 1945–61. Born in Higham-on-the-Hill, near Nuneaton, Warwick and educated at Marlborough and Oxford, he was ordained in 1912 and was from 1914 to 1932 headmaster of Repton School. He was 45 when he took up his first ecclesiastical appointment as bishop of Chester in 1932. In 1939 he became bishop of London. As archbishop of Canterbury he crowned Queen **Elizabeth** in Westminster Abbey in June 1953. He was created a life peer in 1961.

FISHER, Herbert Albert Laurens (1865–1940) English historian, born in London. He was a fellow, tutor and warden (1925) of New College, Oxford, and vice-chancellor of Sheffield University (1912). As education minister (1916–22) he sponsored notable acts, including the Fisher Act (1918). He wrote on **Napoleon**, but is best known for his *History of Europe* (1936).

FISHER, John Arbuthnot, 1st Baron Fisher of Kilverstone (1841–1920) English naval commander, born in Ceylon. He entered the navy in 1854, and saw service in the China Wars (1859–60) and the Egyptian War (1882). A lord of the admiralty from 1892–97, he was commander-in-chief on the North American and West Indies station (1897–99). In 1904 he was appointed First Sea Lord; he effected great improvements in naval training, and introduced Dreadnought battleships and 'Invincible' battle cruisers in preparation for war against Germany. He resigned in 1915 in protest against the Dardanelles expedition.

FISHER, John, St (1469–1535) English prelate and humanist, born in Beverley. Educated at Michaelhouse, Cambridge, of which he became master (1497), he was made chaplain to Margaret, Countess of Richmond, **Henry VII**'s mother, in 1502. In 1503 he was appointed first Lady Margaret professor of divinity, and in 1504 chancellor of Cambridge University and bishop of Rochester. He zealously promoted the New Learning, and advocated reformation from within. He resisted the Lutheran schism, and in 1527 he firmly pronounced against **Henry VIII**'s divorce from **Catherine of Aragon**.In 1534 he was accused of treason and, for refusing the oath of succession, was sent with Sir **Thomas More** to the Tower. In May 1535 Pope **Paul III** made him a cardinal; on 17 June, now an old man, he was tried for refusing to recognize Henry as head of the Church of England; on 22 June he was beheaded on Tower Hill. He was canonized in 1935. His feast day is 9 July.

FISHER, Sir Ronald Aylmer (1890–1962) English statistician and geneticist, the leading figure in biological and agricultural statistics in the first half of the 20th century, born in East Finchley, London. Educated at Harrow, he graduated in mathematics at Cambridge. In 1919 he became statistician at the Rothamsted agricultural research institute. There he developed his techniques for the design and analysis of experiments which he expounded in his classic work *Statistical methods for research workers* (1925), and which have become standard in medical and biological research. He also worked on genetics and evolution, and studied the genetics of human blood groups, elucidating the rhesus factor. He became professor of eugenics at University College, London (1933–43) and of genetics at Cambridge (1943–57). After his retirement, he moved to Australia.

FISK, Sir Ernest Thomas (1886–1965) English pioneer of radio, born in Sunbury-on-Thames, Middlesex. Trained by the Marconi company as a ship's radio operator, he arrived in Australia in 1910 to demonstrate the company's equipment and became resident engineer in the following year. In 1918 he successfully received in Sydney a morse signal from **Marconi**'s transmitter at Caernarvon, North Wales, the first direct radio signal between the two countries. In 1924 he made the first human voice contact between Australia and England when he spoke to Marconi in England. He had already established the Amalgamated Wireless (Australasia) Company, becoming its managing director in 1916 and chairman in 1932. He was knighted in 1937, and in 1944 resigned from AWA to return to England as managing director of EMI. He returned to Sydney on his retirement in 1951.

FISKE, John, originally **Edmund Fisk Green** (1842–1901) American historian, born in Hartford, Connecticut. He studied at Harvard, where he became tutor and librarian. He wrote numerous popular books on American history, especially the colonial period; also works on Spencerian philosophy and Darwinism.

FITCH, John (1743–98) American inventor, born in Windsor, Connecticut, gunsmith to the American troops in the War of Independence (1775–83). In 1785 he completed a model steamboat and in 1786–90 built four steam-ships up to 60 ft in length propelled by sets of reciprocating paddles. About 1796 he experimented with screw propulsion. None of his projects achieved commercial success; disillusioned, he poisoned himself.

FITCH, Sir Joshua Girling (1824–1903) English educationist and writer, born in Southwark. Educated in elementary schools and London University, he taught at Borough Road School and was head at Kingsland before becoming tutor (1852), and principal (1856), at Borough Road College, Southwark. He became an inspector of schools in 1863, assistant commissioner of schools in Yorkshire (1865–67), of elementary schools in the large northern towns (1869), and of endowed schools (1870–77). He was chief inspector for Eastern Division (1883–85) and inspector of elementary training colleges for women in England and Wales (1885–94). His *Lectures on Teaching* (1881) were based on the first course of lectures on the art of teaching specifically addressed to the members of an English University—Cambridge (Lent Term, 1880). He visited America and reported on American education (1888); his *The Chautauqua Reading Circles* (1888) suggested the National Home Reading Union. He helped to found Girton College, Cambridge, and the Girls' Public Day School Company. He was one of the few inspectors to have been educated at, and to have taught in, an elementary school.

FITCH, Val Logsdon (1923–) American physicist, born in Merriman, Nebraska. He was educated at McGill University and Columbia, and in 1954 he moved to Princeton. Together with **James Cronin** he demonstrated the non-conservation of parity and charge conjugation in certain particle reactions, for which they received the Nobel prize for physics in 1980.

FITT, Gerry (Gerard), Baron Fitt (1926–) Northern Irish politician, born in Belfast. He was a merchant seaman for twelve years before entering local politics. He represented (1962–72) the Dock Division of Belfast as an Eire Labour MP in the Northern Ireland parliament, then founded and led the Social Democratic and Labour party. He was an SDLP member of parliament for nine years, resigning the leadership in 1979 to sit as a socialist. Fitt, an opponent of violence who has had to endure the animosity of both Republican and Loyalist extremists, lost his Belfast seat in the 1983 general election and the same year was made a life peer.

FITTIG, Rudolf (1835–1910) German scientist. Professor of organic chemistry at Tübingen (1869) and at Strasbourg (1876), he was famous for his work on organic compounds. His name is associated with the 'Wurtz-Fittig reaction' (with **Charles Adolphe Wurtz**).

FITTON, Mary (c.1578–1647) English courtier, maid of honour to Queen **Elizabeth**. She was the mistress in 1600 of William Herbert, Earl of Pembroke, and has been identified by some commentators as the 'dark lady' of **Shakespeare**'s Sonnets cxxvii–clvii.

FITZBALL, Edward, originally **Ball** (1792–1873). English popular dramatist. He won outstanding popularity in the 1820s for his countless fantastically staged and highly intricate melodramas. He looted his material where he chose and took wild liberties with originals, such as his *The Flying Dutchman* (1827), derived from John Howison's haunting story, *The Pilot*, from **James Fenimore Cooper**'s *The Red Rover* (1829) and from **Edward Bulwer-Lytton**'s *Paul Clifford* (1835). His *Jonathan Bradford* (1833), based on a famous murder case, ran for 260 nights at the Surrey Theatre. He wrote a vivid autobiography, *Thirty-Five Years of a Dramatic Author's Life* (1859), which is an invaluable source for 19th-century English theatre history.

FITZGERALD, Barry, stage name of **William Joseph Shields** (1888–1961) Irish actor, born in Dublin.

Educated at Merchant Taylor's (Protestant) school, he joined the Irish civil service in 1911 and, after a spell in extra-mural amateur acting, played in the Abbey Theatre out of office hours (1916–29) under a stage name in conformity with civil service requirements. He became a full-time actor, toured the USA and won distinction as Fluther Good and Captain Boyle in **Sean O'Casey**'s *The Plough and the Stars* and *Juno and the Paycock* respectively, both on stage and screen. He went to Hollywood in 1937 and broadened his repertoire to include outstanding successes in **Eugene O'Neill**'s *The Long Voyage Home* (1940), and **Agatha Christie**'s *And Then There Were None* (1945), as well as the phenomenally successful *Going My Way* (1944) and the police thriller *Naked City* (1948), returning to Irish locations for *The Quiet Man* (1952) and *Happy Ever After* (1954). He starred in over 40 films, and returned to Ireland in 1959.

FITZGERALD, Lord Edward (1763–98) Irish nationalist politician, born in Carton House, County Kildare, a younger son of the Duke of Leinster. He served with distinction in the American War of Independence (1775–83), was MP for Athy in the Irish parliament and was drawn to Paris in 1792 by the revolution. There he renounced his title, married, and returned to Ireland in 1793, to plunge into political conspiracy. He joined the United Irishmen in 1796, and went to France to arrange for a French invasion of Ireland. The plot was betrayed and Fitzgerald, with a price of £1000 on his head, was seized in Dublin: in the desperate scuffle that ensued he received mortal wounds.

FITZGERALD, Edward (1809–83) English scholar and poet, born near Woodbridge, Suffolk, the translator of **Omar Khayyám**. A country gentleman by birth and inclination, he was educated at King Edward VI School in Bury St Edmunds and Trinity College, Cambridge, where he developed close literary friendships with **Thackeray**, **Carlisle** and **Tennyson** (who dedicated his poem *Tiresias* to him). He had a brief and unsuccessful marriage, wrote poetry, and in 1851 published *Euphranor*: *A Dialogue on Youth* (a comment on English education), followed by a book of aphorisms, *Polonius*: *A Collection of Wise Saws and Modern Instances* (1852). After studying Spanish privately, he published blank-verse translations of six plays by **Calderón** in 1853. An interest in Persian poetry led him to publish, anonymously, a translation of *Salámán and Absál*, an allegory by Kami (1856). In 1859 he published, anonymously at first, his free poetic translation of quatrains from the *Rubáiyát of Omar Khayyám* (4th revised edition, 1879). He also translated **Aeschylus** and **Sophocles**, and two more plays by Calderón, and left a host of delightful letters, edited and published after his death.

FITZGERALD, Ella (1918–) American jazz singer, born in Newport News, Virginia and raised in New York. She was 'discovered' at the age of 16 during an amateur night at the Apollo Theatre, Harlem, and went on to become one of the most celebrated performers in her field. She began her professional career with the Tiny Bradshaw Band, moving to the Chick Webb Orchestra and taking over the leadership when Webb died in 1939. Since 1940, she has worked mainly as a featured artiste with her own trio, but there have been notable engagements and recordings with **Louis Armstrong**, **Duke Ellington**, **Count Basie** and Jazz at the Philharmonic. Fitzgerald's range and clarity in her earlier years, and her understanding of jazz interpretation, have made her a consistent influence.

FITZGERALD, Francis Scott Key (1896–1940) American novelist, born in St Paul, Minnesota. He was educated at Newman School, New Jersey, and Princeton, where one of his contemporaries was **Edmund Wilson**. He enlisted in the US army in World War I but never left America. He married Zelda Sayre (1900–47), and in 1920 published his first novel, *This Side of Paradise*, based on his experience at Princeton. He captured the spirit of the 1920s ('The Jazz Age'), especially in *The Great Gatsby* (1925), his best-known book. Other novels include *The Beautiful and Damned* (1922), and *Tender is the Night* (1934). His short stories were equally notable, published in *Flappers and Philosophers* (1920), *Tales of the Jazz Age* (1922), *All the Sad Young Men* (1926), and *Taps at Reveille* (1936). Living the strenuous life of a playboy in Europe and America, his wife grew increasingly mentally unstable. Driven by debts and alcoholism, he went to Hollywood in 1937 to work as a scriptwriter, where he wrote a final, unfinished novel about a Hollywood producer, *The Last Tycoon* (1941).

FITZGERALD, Dr Garrett (1926–) Irish politician. The son of Desmond Fitzgerald, minister for external affairs in the Irish Free State 1922–7, and for defence 1927–32, he was born in Dublin and educated at Belvedere College, University College and King's Inns, Dublin. He was a lecturer in political economy at University College, Dublin, 1959–73, and was elected Fine Gael member of the Irish parliament for Dublin South-East in 1969. Minister for foreign affairs 1973–77, he then became leader of the Fine Gael party, and was prime minister of the 1981–82 government, and again from 1983 until 1987. In 1985 he participated in the formulation and signing of the Anglo-Irish Agreement. He relinquished his leadership of Fine Gael in 1987.

FITZGERALD, George Francis (1851–1901) Irish physicist. Professor of natural philosophy at Dublin (1881–1901), he made important discoveries in the fields of electrolysis and electromagnetic radiation. His name is associated, with **Hendrik Antoon Lorentz**, with the 'Fitzgerald-Lorentz contraction' in the phenomenon of change in moving bodies as observed in the **Michelson-Morley** experiment.

FITZGERALD, Gerald See **DESMOND, Earl of**

FITZGERALD, Gerald, 8th Earl of Kildare (d.1513) Irish leader, known as the 'Great Earl'. He succeeded to the title in 1477, and was appointed lord deputy by **Edward IV** in 1481, and retained by **Richard III** and, for a time, by **Henry VII**. He was suspected of plotting against the crown and was ousted from his command, convicted of treason before a parliament in Drogheda in 1494, and sent to the Tower while Sir **Edward Poynings** was deputy. He was pardoned two years later and made deputy again, and presided over the first Irish parliament held under Poynings's Act in 1498. He defeated Southern chieftains at Knockdoe, County Galway, in 1505, was retained in office by **Henry VII**, but died of wounds during a campaign against Gaelic rebels.

FITZGERALD, Gerald, 9th Earl of Kildare (1487–1534) Irish leader, son of **Gerald Fitzgerald**, 8th Earl, and known as 'the Young'. He was educated in England as a hostage for his father, whose return to full trust was symbolized by his own return to Ireland in 1504, and appointment as lord high treasurer. He succeeded his father as earl and lord deputy in 1513. He fell foul of **Wolsey** who had him examined in London in 1515, but he survived this and other similar attempts at his overthrow in 1519 and 1526 (at the cost of a spell in the Tower, with his reinstatement as deputy coming only in 1532). He was wounded in battle and now became vulnerable also to a second group of enemies, the Butlers of Ormond, connections of the new Queen

Anne Boleyn. On their instance he was summoned once more to London, and died in the Tower.

FITZGERALD, Thomas, 10th Earl of Kildare (1513–37) Irish leader, son of **Gerald Fitzgerald**, 9th Earl, and known as 'Silken Thomas'. Educated in England, he was made acting deputy by his father on the latter's final summons to England in 1534. On hearing rumours that his father had been executed in London, Thomas summoned the council to St Mary's Abbey in Dublin, renounced his allegiance to **Henry VIII**, attacked Dublin Castle unsucessfully, lost his base at Maynooth and surrendered on a guarantee of personal safety from the English commander. He was imprisoned in the Tower and hanged, drawn and quartered with his five uncles at Tyburn.

FITZGIBBON, John, 1st Earl of Clare (1749–1802) Irish Unionist statesman, born near Donnybrook, Dublin. He studied at Trinity College, Dublin, and Christ Church, Oxford, and was called to the Irish bar in 1772. He entered the Irish House of Commons in 1778 and became Irish attorney-general in 1783. Such was his brilliance and his political reliability that in 1789 he was appointed the first native to be lord chancellor of Ireland for almost a century, raised to the peerage as Baron Fitzgibbon and later promoted, receiving his earldom in 1795 and a British peerage as Lord Fitzgibbon of Sidbury (Devonshire) in 1799. He resisted any concessions to Irish Catholic sentiment, played a part in the ousting of Lord-Lieutenant Fitzwilliam in 1795, and was a prominent supporter of the Act of Union of the British and Irish Parliaments (1800). On his death in Dublin his coffin was pelted with dead cats.

FITZHERBERT, Mrs Maria Anne, née **Smythe** (1756–1837) wife of King **George IV**. A Roman Catholic widow, she secretly married the Prince of Wales in 1785. This marriage, contracted without the king's consent, was invalid under the Royal Marriage Act of 1772; the prince afterwards denied that there had been a marriage at all. On his marriage to Princess **Caroline of Brunswick** in 1795 the connection was interrupted, resumed with the pope's consent, and finally broken off in 1803.

FITZJAMES, James See **BERWICK**

FITZROY, Sir Charles Augustus (1796–1858) English administrator, born in Shipley Hall, Derbyshire, the second son of the 3rd Duke of Grafton. He married a daughter of the 4th Duke of Richmond and his wife, daughter of the 4th Duke of Gordon. This multiplicity of ducal connections secured for FitzRoy rapid preferment, first in 1837 as lieutenant-governor of Prince Edward Island and then from 1841 to 1845 as lieutenant-governor of the Leeward Islands in the Caribbean. In 1846 he was appointed governor-in-chief of New South Wales. He was soon faced with disputes between the various Australian colonies and he recommended to the British parliament that some superior post should be established in Australia to which such matters could be referred. In 1851 FitzRoy did in fact receive the commission of 'Governor-General of All Her Majesty's Australian Possessions', thus paving the way for the federation of Australian colonies 50 years later. His period of office was marked by a number of key constitutional innovations: the separation from New South Wales of the new colony of Victoria, the establishment of legislative councils there, in Tasmania, and in South and Western Australia, and a constitution conferring responsible government upon New South Wales.

FITZROY, Robert (1805–65) English naval officer and meteorologist, grandson of the Duke of **Grafton**, born at Ampton Hall near Bury St Edmunds. In command of the *Beagle* he surveyed the coasts of Patagonia and Tierra del Fuego (1828–30). In 1831, accompanied by **Charles Darwin** as scientific observer, he circumnavigated the globe in the *Beagle*, and collaborated with Darwin in publishing in 1839 a *Narrative of the Surveying Voyages of HMS 'Adventure' and 'Beagle'*. Governor of New Zealand (1843–45), he was promoted rear-admiral (1857) and vice-admiral (1863) on the retired list. In 1854 he was attached to the meteorological department of the board of trade. The 'Fitzroy barometer' was invented by him; and he instituted the storm warnings that developed into daily weather forecasts.

FITZSIMMONS, Bob (Robert Prometheus) (1862–1917) English-born American pugilist and world champion, born in Helston, Cornwall, and reared in New Zealand. After emigrating to the USA in 1890 he won the world middleweight championship from 'Nonpareil' **Jack Dempsey** at New Orleans in 1891, and the world heavyweight championship from **'Gentleman Jim' Corbett** at Carson City in 1897. He lost his heavyweight title to **James J Jeffries** at Coney Island in 1899, but won the world light-heavyweight championship in 1903. He lost it in 1905, and retired from the ring in 1914.

FITZWILLIAM, Richard, 7th Viscount Fitzwilliam of Meryon (1745–1816) Irish peer, founder by bequest of the Fitzwilliam Museum in Cambridge.

FITZWILLIAM, William, 2nd Earl Fitzwilliam (1748–1833) British statesman, lord-lieutenant for three months of Ireland (1794–95), where his warm support of Catholic emancipation aroused enthusiastic hopes. **Pitt** thought him too liberal; and his recall was followed by the Rebellion of 1798. He was president of the council in the **Grenville** ministry in 1806.

FIZEAU, Armand Hippolyte Louis (1819–96) French physicist. In 1849 he was the first to measure the velocity of light by an experiment confined to the earth's surface, in which field he later collaborated with **Jean Bernard Léon Foucault**. Fizeau demonstrated also the use of the **Doppler** principle in determining star velocity in the line of sight.

FLACIUS, or **Vlacich, Matthias** (1520–75) Lutheran theologian, born in Albona in Illyria. Professor of Hebrew at Wittenberg in 1544, he was deprived of his chair for his attacks upon **Melanchthon**'s compromise, known as the Leipzig Interim. From 1557 to 1562 he was professor of theology at Jena, but was again deprived for teaching that original sin was inherent in man's nature. After this he led a wandering life. His principal works are *Clavis Scripturae Sacrae* (1567), *Catalogus Testium Veritatis* (1556), and *Ecclesiastica Historia* (1559–74). The church history called *Magdeburg Centuries* was only partly his.

FLAGSTAD, Kirsten (1895–1962) Norwegian soprano, born in Hamar. She studied in Stockholm and Oslo, where she made her operatic début in 1913. She excelled in Wagnerian roles such as Sieglinde at Bayreuth (1934) and Isolde in New York (1935), and was acclaimed in most of the world's major opera houses. In 1958 she was made director of the Norwegian State Opera.

FLAHAUT DE LA BILLARDERIE, Auguste Charles Joseph, Comte de (1785–1870) French soldier and diplomat, believed to be the illegitimate son of **Talleyrand**. He fought under **Napoleon**, and was the paramour of **Caroline Murat** (Napoleon's sister) and of **Hortense de Beauharnais** (Napoleon's step-daughter), whose son by him became Duke of Morny. An exile after Waterloo, he married the Baroness Keith and Nairne (1788–1867). After 1830 he returned to France, was ambassador at Vienna (1842–48) and London

(1860–62), and was grand chancellor of the Legion of Honour.

FLAHERTY, Robert Joseph (1884–1951) American film producer and explorer, born in Iron Mountain, Michigan. Brought up in Canada, he brought documentary films to the fore with *Nanook of the North* (1922, the story of an Eskimo family) and *Moana* (1926, a documentary about the South Seas). His last great success was *Louisiana Story* (1948). He also produced *Man of Aran* in Ireland (1932–34) and *Elephant Boy* (1937).

FLAMBARD, Rannulf, or **Ralph** (d.1128) Norman ecclesiastic, justiciar of England under **William II**. Bishop of Durham in 1099, he ministered to the king's vices and extravagances by oppressive extortion of the people.

FLAMINIUS, Gaius (d.217 BC) Roman soldier and statesman, of plebeian origin. Consul in 223 BC, he distributed the Ager Gallicus tribal lands left uninhabited since 283. He was the first Roman commander to cross the Po when he defeated the Insubres at the Addua (223). He extended his road, the Via Flamina, from Rome to Ariminum (Rimini) in 220, and built the Circus Flaminius. Consul again in 217, he tried to stem **Hannibal**'s invasion of Etruria but was defeated and killed at Lake Trasimene.

FLAMMARION, Camille (1842–1925) French astronomer, born in Montigny-le-Roi. He entered the Paris Observatory in 1858, and wrote books on astronomy, ballooning, physical research, etc, and founded the observatory of Juvisy (1883).

FLAMSTEED, John (1646–1719) English astronomer and clergyman, born in Denby near Derby, the first astronomer-royal of England. In 1676 Greenwich Observatory was built and Flamsteed (appointed astronomer-royal the previous year) began the observations that initiated modern practical astronomy. He formed the first trustworthy catalogue of the fixed stars, and furnished those observations by which **Isaac Newton** verified his lunar theory. His great work is *Historia Coelestis Britannica*, an account of astronomical observation (3 vols, 1725). He took holy orders, and from 1684 held the Surrey living of Burstow.

FLANAGAN, Barry (1941–) English 'environmental' sculptor, born in Prestatyn, Flintshire. He studied at Birmingham College of Art (1957–58) and attended evening classes under Sir **Anthony Caro** in 1961 before enrolling at St Martin's School of Art (1964–66). His early sculptures were made of cloth or hessian filled with shavings or Dunlopillo®; others consisted simply of piles of sand and pieces of rope. Since 1973 he has returned to more traditional materials such as stone and bronze.

FLANDERS, Michael (1922–75) English entertainer and writer, born in London. Confined to a wheelchair by polio from 1943, he contributed words and lyrics to a number of London revues during the 1950s, including *Penny Plain* (1951), and *Airs on a Shoestring* (1953). In 1954 he co-translated **Stravinsky**'s *The Soldier's Tale* for the Edinburgh Festival. In 1956, he wrote the words and lyrics, and **Donald Swann** the music, for *At the Drop of a Hat* in which they both made their names. It was followed by *At the Drop of Another Hat* in 1963.

FLANDIN, Pierre Étienne (1889–1958) French politician, born in Paris. A member of the Chamber from 1914, he held office in several governments and was prime minister in 1934–35.

FLANDRIN, Jean Hippolyte (1809–64) French painter, born in Lyon. In 1830 he won the *Prix de Rome*, and in 1842 began his great frescoes in the church of St Germain-des-Prés, Paris. After this he was mainly engaged in fresco painting, although he executed many fine portraits.

FLATMAN, Thomas (1635–88) English miniaturist and poet, born in London. He was educated at Winchester and New College, Oxford, and was called to the bar in 1662. He executed many miniature portraits in the style of **Samuel Cooper**, eg, his self-portrait (1673) in the Victoria and Albert Museum. In the following year he published *Poems and Songs*.

FLAUBERT, Gustave (1821–80) French novelist, born in Rouen, the son of a doctor. He studied law reluctantly at Paris, where his friendship with **Victor Hugo**, **Maxime du Camp**, and the poet Louise Colet (1808–76), his lover from 1846 to 1854, stimulated his already apparent talent for writing. When barely past his student days he was afflicted by an obscure form of nervous disease, which may have been to some extent responsible for the morbidity and pessimism which characterized his work from the very beginning. These traits, together with a violent hatred and contempt for bourgeois society, are revealed in his first masterpiece, *Madame Bovary* (1857), a painful but powerful tragedy of an unhappy bourgeois wife who has an affair. The book achieved a *succès de scandale* after it had been condemned as immoral and its author prosecuted, albeit unsuccessfully, but it has held its place among the classics. His second work, *Salammbô* (1862), dealt with the struggle between Rome and Carthage and is rather overweighted with archaeological detail. *L'Éducation sentimentale* (1869) was less effective, but in 1874 appeared the splendid *La Tentation de St Antoine*, the masterpiece of its kind. *Trois contes* (1877) reveals his mastery of the short story and foreshadows **Maupassant**, whom he influenced. After his death appeared *Bouvard et Pécuchet* which had not received his final revision. His correspondence with **George Sand** was published in 1884.

FLAVIN, Dan (1933–) American artist, born in New York. He attended the US Air Force Meteorological Technician Training School, Maryland University and the New York School of Social Research, but had no art education. He began to make his 'electric light icons' in 1961, consisting of fluorescent tubes hung on walls or set up as free-standing 'proposals' (he prefers this term to 'sculptures'), an activity some critics have called Luminism, and which has obvious links with Minimalism.

FLAXMAN, John (1755–1826) English sculptor, born in York, the son of a moulder of plaster figures. A delicate and slightly-deformed child, he displayed an early talent for drawing and modelling, and in 1769 became a student at the Royal Academy. He worked for twelve years, from 1775, as a designer for **Josiah Wedgwood**, and thereafter directed the Wedgwood studio in Rome (1787–94), where he also executed several classical groups and began his drawings for the *Iliad* and *Odyssey* (published in 1793), the tragedies of **Aeschylus** (1795) and **Dante**'s *Divine Comedy* (1787). In 1810 he was appointed the first professor of sculpture at the Royal Academy of Art. His sculptures include the monument to the Earl of Mansfield in Westminster Abbey, to the poet **William Collins** in Chichester Cathedral, to the poet **Thomas Chatterton** in St Mary Redcliffe, Bristol, and to Lord **Nelson** in St Paul's Cathedral, and his statues of **Robert Burns** and **John Kemble** in Westminster Abbey.

FLECK, Sir Alexander, Baron Fleck (1889–1968) Scottish industrial chemist, born in Glasgow. Educated at Glasgow University, he lectured there for two years, before working as a physical chemist on radium and later on the manufacture of sodium. He became chairman of ICI in 1953 and was chairman of the committee which investigated the nationalized coal industry.

FLECKER, James Elroy (1884–1915) English poet, born in Lewisham. Educated at Uppingham, he studied Oriental languages at Trinity College, Cambridge, then entered the consular service. He was posted first to Constantinople and then to Beirut. He wrote *Hassan* (staged 1923) and published several volumes of rich verse, *The Bridge of Fire* (1907), *The Golden Journey to Samarkand* (1913), and *Old Ships* (1915).

FLECKNOE, Richard (c.1600–c.1678) Irish poet, and probably a priest. After travelling (1640–50) in Europe, Asia, Africa and Brazil, he went to London, where he took part in the wars of the wits, wrote five plays, and published *Short Discourse on the English Stage* (1664), which provoked **Dryden** to caricature him as 'MacFlecknoe' in his satire on **Shadwell**, and inspired a good-humoured lampoon by **Marvell**.

FLEETWOOD, Charles (c.1618–1692) English parliamentary soldier, of good Northamptonshire stock. He commanded a cavalry regiment at Naseby (1645), was elected MP for Marlborough in 1646, was commander of the parliamentary forces in England before the battle of Worcester (1651), and commander-in-chief in Ireland (1652–55). In 1652 he married **Cromwell**'s daughter, Bridget, the widow of **Henry Ireton**. He was commander-in-chief in 1659, but had to give way before **Monk**, and was deprived of office at the Restoration.

FLEISCHER, Max (1883–1972) Austrian-born American cartoonist, inventor and animated film producer, born in Vienna and taken to New York at the age of four. Joining the staff of *Brooklyn Eagle* (1900) as errand boy, he soon moved to the art department. As art editor of *Popular Science* (1914) he developed an inventive talent, patenting his rotoscope in 1917, a device still used for transferring live action film into animated cartoon via tracing. With his brother Dave (1894–1979) he produced many *Out Of The Inkwell* films, which combined live action with animation. The brothers also created the 'bouncing-ball' singalong cartoons, silent but synchronized to the cinema orchestras. Having made the first experimental sound-on-film cartoons in the mid-1920s, Max went on to produce the *Betty Boop Talkartoons* (1930) and his best-remembered series, *Popeye the Sailor* (1933) from the strips by **E C Segar**, followed by the feature-length cartoons, *Gulliver's Travels* (1939) and *Mr Bug Goes to Town* (1941).

FLÉMALLE, Master of See **CAMPIN, Robert**

FLEMING, Sir Alexander (1881–1955) Scottish bacteriologist, and the discoverer in 1928 of penicillin, born in Loudoun, Ayrshire. He was educated at Kilmarnock, and became a shipping clerk in London for five years before matriculating (1902) and embarking on a brilliant medical studentship, qualifying as a surgeon at St Mary's Hospital, Paddington, where he spent the rest of his career. It was only by his expert marksmanship in the college rifle team, however, that he managed to find a place in Sir **Almroth Wright**'s bacteriological laboratory there. As a researcher he became the first to use anti-typhoid vaccines on human beings, and pioneered the use of salvarsan against syphilis (see **Paul Ehrlich**), and while a medical officer in France during World War 1, discovered the antiseptic powers of lysozyme, present in tears and mucus. In 1928 by chance exposure of a culture of *staphylococci* he noticed a curious mould, penicillin, which he found to have unsurpassed antibiotic powers. Unheeded by colleagues and without sufficient chemical knowledge, he had to wait eleven years before two brilliant experimentalists, **Howard Florey** and Sir **Ernst Chain**, with whom he shared the 1945 Nobel prize for physiology or medicine, perfected a method of producing the volatile drug. Fleming was appointed professor of bacteriology at London in 1938.

FLEMING, Ian Lancaster (1908–64) English novelist, born in London, brother of **Peter Fleming**. Educated at Eton and Sandhurst, he studied languages at Munich and Geneva universities, worked as a foreign correspondent with Reuters in Moscow (1929–33), and then as a banker and stockbroker (1933–39). During World War II he was a senior naval intelligence officer, and was then the foreign manager of *The Sunday Times* (1945–59). His varied career gave him the background for a series of twelve novels and seven short stories featuring Commander James Bond, the archetypal, suave British secret service agent 007, starting with *Casino Royale* (1953) and including *From Russia with Love* (1957), *Dr No* (1958), *Goldfinger* (1959), *Thunderball* (1961) and *The Man with the Golden Gun* (1965). They sold millions of copies worldwide, and have been turned into highly successful films.

FLEMING, Sir John Ambrose (1849–1945) English physicist and electrical engineer, born in Lancaster. Professor of electrical engineering at University College, London (1885–1926), he invented the thermionic valve and was a pioneer in the application of electricity to lighting and heating on a large scale.

FLEMING, Margaret (1803–11) Scottish child author, born in Kirkcaldy, Fife. She was distantly related to Sir **Walter Scott**, who referred to her as 'Pet Marjorie', and she was the theme of an exquisite essay by Dr **John Brown**. She wrote poems and a 3-volume Diary.

FLEMING, Paul (1609–40) German lyric poet, born in Hartenstein. The first German to use the sonnet form, he is best known for his lyrical and religious poetry in *Geistliche und weltliche Poemata* (1642).

FLEMING, (Robert) Peter (1907–71) English travel writer and journalist, born in London, the brother of **Ian Fleming**. Educated at Eton and Christ Church, Oxford, he took a stop-gap job in the Economic Advisory Council before being appointed assistant literary editor of *The Spectator*. In 1932 he read an advert in *The Times* for members to make up an expedition to explore rivers in Central Brazil and ascertain the fate of Colonel **Percy Fawcett** who had disappeared without trace in 1925. It provided the colourful copy which surfaced in *Brazilian Adventure* (1933), a landmark in travel literature and an immediate bestseller. In a similar vein are *One's Company* (1934) and *News From Tartary* (1936), an account of 'an undeservedly successful attempt' to travel overland from Peking to Kashmir.

FLEMING, Sir Sandford (1827–1915) Scots-born Canadian railway engineer, born in Kirkcaldy. He went to Canada in 1845, and became chief engineer of the Inter-colonial Railway (1867–76) and of the Canadian Pacific Railway (1872–80). He surveyed several famous routes, including Yellowhead and Kicking Horse passes.

FLEMING, Tom (1927–) Scottish actor, director and poet, born in Edinburgh. He made his first speaking appearance as Bruce McRae in **Emlyn Williams**' *The Late Christopher Bean* during a tour of India in 1945. He co-founded the Gateway Theatre, Edinburgh, in 1953, and until 1962 appeared in and directed many productions there. He joined the Royal Shakespeare Company in 1962, appearing in the title role in *Cymbeline*, and the following year returned to Stratford to play Prospero in *The Tempest*. In 1965 he was appointed the first director of the Edinburgh Civic Theatre Trust, and founded a new company at the

Royal Lyceum Theatre in the city. He has subsequently appeared as an actor and director in many Scottish theatres. His books of poetry include *So That Was Spring* (1954), and *Sax Roses for a Luve Frae Hame* (1961). He has also been a radio and television commentator since 1952, specializing in state and royal events.

FLEMMING, Walther (1843–1915) German biologist, born in Sachsenberg. He is best known for his research on cell division, to which he gave the name mitosis. He also did important work on the splitting of chromosomes, and on microscope technique.

FLETCHER, Andrew, of Saltoun (1655–1716), Scottish patriot. He sat in the Scots parliament in 1681, and so consistently opposed Stuart policy latterly that twice he had to flee to Holland. He returned to Scotland at the revolution. He was the first patron of **William Paterson**, the projector of the Darien expedition, and the bitterness caused in Scotland by the treatment of the Darien colonists gave Fletcher and the nationalist party their strength in the struggle against the inevitable union with England. His famous 'limitations' aimed at constructing a federative instead of an incorporating union. After the Union, Fletcher retired in disgust from public life, devoting himself to promoting agriculture; he introduced fanners and the mill for pot-barley. He died in London. His writings were reprinted in London in 1732.

FLETCHER, Giles (?1588–1623) English poet, brother of **Phineas Fletcher**, and cousin of **John Fletcher**. He was educated at Westminster School and Trinity College, Cambridge. A classical scholar, he became reader in Greek language at Cambridge, and in 1619 became rector of Alderton in Suffolk. His chief work is his long Spenserian allegorical poem *Christ's Victory and Triumph* (1610).

FLETCHER, John (1579–1625) English dramatist, closely associated with **Francis Beaumont**, born in Rye, Sussex, the third son of that dean of Peterborough who disturbed the last moments of **Mary, Queen of Scots**. He came of a literary family, being the nephew of Giles Fletcher the elder and cousin of the Spenserian poets **Giles** and **Phineas Fletcher**. All that we know of him, apart from his work for the theatre, is that he entered Benet (now Corpus) College, Cambridge, and that he died of the plague in 1625. The problem of disentangling his own plays from those on which he collaborated with Beaumont, **Massinger**, **Rowley** and **Shakespeare** is very difficult but three or four certainly of his own devising are outstanding and the collaboration with Beaumont yielded some memorable plays. The best of his own plays are *The Faithful Shepherdess*, which ranks as a pastoral with **Ben Jonson**'s *Sad Shepherd* and **Milton**'s *Comus*; *The Humorous Lieutenant*, acted in 1619, and *Rule a Wife and Have a Wife* (1624), on the favourite theme of conjugal mastery. Of the ten or so plays on which he collaborated with Beaumont the best known are *The Knight of the Burning Pestle* (attributed mainly or possibly solely to Beaumont), *Philaster* (1610), a romantic comedy, *A King and No King* (1611) and *The Maid's Tragedy* (1611), generally accounted their best work. Collaboration with Shakespeare probably resulted in *Two Noble Kinsmen*, a melodramatic version of **Chaucer**'s *Knight's Tale*, and *Henry VIII* (or insertions therein). A vein of tender poetry in Fletcher and his relaxed type of versification are useful evidence in disentangling his various collaborations.

FLETCHER, John Gould (1886–1950) American poet and essayist, born in Little Rock, Arkansas. He followed the Imagists while living in London and Paris (1908–33), but later turned to American subjects. He won the Pulitzer prize in 1939 for his *Selected Poems*. He published his autobiographical *Life is my Song* in 1937.

FLETCHER, Phineas (1582–1650) English poet, brother of **Giles Fletcher**, cousin of **John Fletcher**, and son of Giles Fletcher, LLD (1549–1611), Queen **Elizabeth**'s minister in Germany and Russia. He was educated at Eton and Cambridge, and in 1621 became rector of Hilgay in Norfolk. His *Purple Island, or the Isle of Man* (1633), contains an elaborate description of the human body viewed as an island, the bones being its foundations, and the veins its rivers.

FLEURY, André Hercule de (1653–1743) French prelate, born in Lodève. As bishop of Fréjus, he became tutor to the young **Louis XV** at his accession in 1715. From the outset he subtly exerted his influence on policy. His opposition to the duke of Bourbon was restrained and effectively led to his acquisition of the premiership and a cardinal's hat (1726). Temporarily, his moderation endowed France with the tranquillity her tangled finances demanded, but he needlessly prolonged Louis' constitutional minority, and with France committed to the War of the Austrian Succession, he was cast aside.

FLEURY, Claude (1640–1725) French church historian, born in Paris. He was tutor to various princes, prior of Argenteuil and confessor to young **Louis XV**. Among his numerous works were *Moeurs des Israélites* (1681); *Moeurs des Chrétiens* (1662); *Droit ecclésiastique* (1687); and the great *Histoire ecclésiastique* (20 vols, 1691–1720)—the first complete church history, on which he laboured 30 years. Fleury's own work only reached to 1414; it was continued to 1778 by others.

FLEXNER, Simon (1863–1946) American microbiologist and medical administrator, born in Louisville, Kentucky. He studied medicine in the local medical school, but had his passion for medical research awakened by William Henry Welch at Johns Hopkins. After another year's study in Europe he joined Welch's department of pathology before moving to Pennsylvania University (1899–1903), and then to become director of laboratories at the newly-established Rockefeller Institute for Medical Research (1903–35). He did important research in bacteriology, virology and immunology; he isolated the dysentery bacillus (1900), developed a serum for cerebrospinal meningitis (1907), and led the team that determined the cause of poliomyelitis. Equally importantly, he shaped the Rockefeller Institute into a powerful and productive centre of medical research. He encouraged both **John Rockefeller Sr** and **Jr** to establish research fellowships in the natural sciences, and edited for many years (1905–46) the outstanding American periodical of medical research, *Journal of Experimental Medicine*.

FLIEDNER, Theodor (1800–64) German clergyman and humanitarian, born in Eppstein. In 1822 he became pastor of Kaiserwerth near Düsseldorf, where he founded in 1826 a society for prison reform, in 1833 a refuge for discharged women convicts, and in 1836 the first Protestant deaconesses' home in Germany. He went on to found numerous other charity establishments all over the country. His son Fritz (1845–1901) worked as a Protestant evangelist in Spain and wrote *Iglesia Evangélica Española*.

FLINCK, Govaert (1615–60) Dutch portrait and religious painter, born in Cleves. A pupil of **Rembrandt**, he painted biblical and genre pictures.

FLINDERS, Matthew (1774–1814) English explorer, born in Donington, Lincolnshire. A naval officer and hydrographer, in 1795–1800 he surveyed the coast of New South Wales with **George Bass**, and in 1801–03 was commissioned to circumnavigate Australia. On his way home he was wrecked, and detained by the French governor of Mauritius until 1810. The Flinders river in Queensland, and the Flinders range in South Australia are named after him.

FLINT, Frank Stewart (1885–1960) English poet and translator, born in London. A civil servant in the ministry of labour, he joined the Imagist movement and published lyric poetry, *In the Net of the Stars* (1909), *Cadences* (1915) and *Otherworld* (1920). A brilliant linguist, he also produced many translations.

FLINT, Sir William Russell (1880–1969) Scottish artist and illustrator, born in Edinburgh. He settled in London in 1900, where he painted many watercolours to illustrate books (eg, **Chaucer**, **Matthew Arnold**) and paintings of Scottish and foreign subjects. He wrote *Models of Propriety* (1951).

FLITCROFT, Henry (1679–1769) English architect, born in Hampton Court, where his father was the king's gardener. The Earl of **Burlington** became his patron, and he held various official appointments, becoming comptroller of the works in 1758. He designed the London churches of St Giles in the Fields and St John at Hampstead, and he rebuilt parts of Wentworth House in Yorkshire and Woburn Abbey.

FLOOD, Henry (1723–91) Irish politician, educated at Trinity College, Dublin, and Oxford. He became a leader in the popular party in the Irish parliament after his election in 1759. In 1775 he became vice-treasurer of Ireland, but was removed in 1781 as a strong Nationalist. Considering **Grattan**'s reform bills inadequate, Flood strove without success to carry a more sweeping measure, and became involved in a bitter quarrel with his former friend. In 1783 he was returned as MP for Winchester, and in 1785 for Seaford, but he failed to make a great mark at Westminster.

FLOQUET, Charles Thomas (1828–96) French radical politician, born in St Jean de Luz. He strenuously opposed **Napoleon III**'s régime, edited the *République française*, and was elected to the Chamber of Deputies in 1876. President of the Chamber from 1885 to 1888 and 1889–93, he belonged to the anti-Boulangist faction and wounded its leader in a duel in 1888. His political influence waned after his implication in the Panama scandal of 1893.

FLORENCE OF WORCESTER (d.1118) English chronicler, a monk of Worcester. He wrote a *Chronicon* which comes down to 1116, and which, about 1030, becomes of some value as an independent authority. It was edited by **Thorpe** in 1848, and translated by Forester (1847) and Stevenson (1853).

FLORES, Juan José (1801–64) South American statesman, born in Puerto Cabello in Venezuela. He fought with distinction in the war of independence, and became first president of the republic of Ecuador 1830–35 and 1839–43.

FLOREY, Sir Howard Walter, Baron Florey of Adelaide (1898–1968) Australian pathologist, born and educated in Adelaide. He studied physiology as a Rhodes scholar at Oxford and pathology in Cambridge, and was professor of pathology at Sheffield (1931) and Oxford (1935-62), where he headed the Sir William Dunn school of pathology. With **Ernst Chain** as head of the biochemistry department he succeeded in isolating and purifying for clinical use the antibacterial enzyme penicillin, which had been accidentally discovered by **Alexander Fleming** in 1928. By 1941 they had carried out successful tests on nine human patients, and quickly arranged for its manufacture and large-scale production in the USA as an antibiotic. It was ready in time to treat casualties in the D-Day battles in Normandy, where it proved highly successful in combating bacterial infections. For this vital work, Florey shared the 1945 Nobel prize for physiology or medicine with Fleming and Chain. He was provost of Queen's College, Oxford, from 1962, and was made a life peer in 1965. He never lost touch with his Australian roots, and did much to found the Australian National University at Canberra.

FLORIO, John (c.1533–1625) the translator of **Montaigne**, born of Italian Protestant parentage in London. About 1576 he was a tutor in foreign languages at Oxford, and in 1578 published his *First Fruits*, accompanied by *A Perfect Induction to the Italian and English Tongues*. His next work was *Second Fruits*, with 6000 Italian proverbs (1591). His Italian and English dictionary, entitled *A World of Words*, was published in 1598. In 1603 Florio was appointed reader in Italian to Queen **Anne** and in 1604 groom of the privy-chamber. His famous translation of Montaigne (1603) has appeared in several modern editions.

FLORIS, or DE VRIENDT, Cornelis (c.1514 or 1520–1575) Dutch sculptor, ornamentalist and architect, a native of Antwerp. He studied sculpture under Giambologna, visiting Rome c.1538. He brought Italian and French Renaissance details to Flanders and diffused his style through a book of engravings, *Veedlderleijniuwe inventien van Antychsche* (1556–57); his works were published later in Vredeman de Vries's *Architectura*. Most remarkable among his works were the Town Hall, Antwerp (1561–66) and the marble reredos at Tournai Cathedral (1572).

FLORY See **FLEURY**

FLORY, Paul John (1910–85) American polymer chemist, born in Sterling, Illinois. He graduated at Ohio State University and afterwards worked on polymers in industry, and at Stanford University from 1961. His major contributions to theory and experiment in the chemistry of polymers led to him receiving the Nobel prize for chemistry in 1974.

FLOTOW, Friedrich, Freiherr von (1812–83) German composer, born in Teutendorf in Mecklenburg. He made his reputation with *Le Naufrage de la Méduse* (1839), *Stradella* (1844), and *Martha* (1847), the last two characterized by pleasing melody. From 1856 to 1863 he was director of the theatre at Schwerin.

FLOURENS, Gustave (1838–71) French communard, son of **Pierre Flourens**. He distinguished himself by his book, *La Science de l'homme* (1865), as an ardent republican took part in the Cretan insurrection against the Turks (1866), and fell fighting for the Paris Commune.

FLOURENS, Pierre Jean Marie (1794–1867) French physiologist, father of **Gustave Flourens**. He became secretary of the Academy of Sciences (1833) and professor at the Collège de France (1835). He was elected to the Chamber of Deputies in 1838 and made a peer of France in 1846. He wrote on neurophysiology and on animal instinct, and was the first to demonstrate the functions of the different parts of the brain.

FLOWER, Sir William Henry (1831–99) English zoologist, born in Stratford-upon-Avon. After serving as a surgeon in the Crimean War, he was appointed conservator of the Hunterian Museum in Glasgow (1861), and in 1869 Hunterian professor of comparative anatomy and physiology. From 1884 to 1898 he was director of natural history at the British Museum. He revolutionized museum displays.

FLUDD, Robert (1574–1637) English physician, mystic and pantheistic theosophist, born in Milgate. Influenced by **Paracelsus**, he recognized three cosmic elements—God (archetypus), world (macrocosmos) and man (microcosmos). He wrote a treatise in defence of Rosicrucians, *Apologia Compendiaria Fraternitatem de Rosea Croce* (1616).

FLYNN, Errol (1909–59) Australian-born American actor, born in Hobart, Tasmania. His father was a distinguished zoologist and marine biologist, and after attending various Australian and English schools he worked briefly as a shipping-clerk, tobacco-plantation manager and journalist before setting out to search for gold in New Guinea. Having played the role of **Fletcher Christian** in the Australian-made film, *In the Wake of the Bounty* (1933), he came to England to gain acting experience, joined the Northampton Repertory Company, and after a part in a film made by the London branch of Warner's studios, was offered a Hollywood contract. His first American film, *Captain Blood* (1935), established him as a hero of historical swashbucklers, confirmed in films such as *The Charge of the Light Brigade* (1936), *The Adventures of Robin Hood* (1938) and *The Sea Hawk* (1940). During the 1940s his off-screen reputation for drinking, drug-taking and womanizing became legendary and eventually affected his career, which was briefly revived by his acclaimed performance as a drunken wastrel in *The Sun Also Rises* (1957). After two more films, his final venture was a disastrous semi-documentary, *The Cuban Rebel Girls* (1959), which he wrote, co-produced and narrated, in tribute to **Fidel Castro**.

FO, Dario (1926–) Italian dramatist. He began his career as a stage designer and author of comic monologues, and from 1959 to 1968 ran a small theatre company in Milan with his wife, the actress Franca Rame. He has written many plays, based on traditional comic forms, but after 1962 and the abolition of official censorship, his plays took on far more explicitly political themes. The best-known plays, *Accidental Death of an Anarchist* (1970), and the frenetic *Can't Pay, Won't Pay* (1974), use traditional techniques of farce in order to score political points.

FOCH, Ferdinand (1851–1929) French soldier, and marshal of France, born in Tarbes. Educated at the École Supérieure de la Guerre he became professor of strategy there (1894) and commandant (1897). He proved himself a great strategist at the Marne (September 1914) and at the 1st battle of Ypres (November 1914), where he supported British defence against a renewed German thrust. He commanded the French Army Group of the North during the Somme battles (1916). As generalissimo of the Allied armies from March 1918 he directed the hammerstrokes which drove back the Germans and won the war. He wrote *Principles of War* (trans 1919), and his *Memoirs* (1931).

FOIX, Gaston (1489–1512) French nobleman and soldier, nephew of **Louis XII** of France. He became Duke of Nemours in 1505. In the Italian wars he displayed such genius and bravery as to earn the title of 'Thunderbolt of Italy'. He twice overthrew the Swiss, at Como and Milan (1511); chased the papal troops from Bologna; seized Brescia from the Venetians (1512); and defeated the Spaniards at Ravenna, where, however, he was killed.

FOKINE, Michel (1880–1942) Russian-born American dancer and choreographer, born in St Petersburg and trained at the Imperial Ballet there. After teaching at his old school, he joined **Diaghilev**'s Ballet Russe in 1909 as choreographer. On leaving the company he worked in Europe, teaching and choreographing for both theatre and ballet. He is credited with the creation of a more expressive approach to the ballet than the artificial, stylized mode prevalent at the turn of the century.

FOKKER, Anthony (Anton Herman Gerard) (1890–1939) Dutch-born American aircraft engineer, born in Kediri in Java. He taught himself to fly and built his first plane in 1911, and in 1913 founded the Fokker aircraft factory at Schwerin in Germany, which made warplanes for the German air force in World War I. He also developed the apparatus allowing machine guns to shoot through revolving propeller blades. After the war he set up a factory in the Netherlands. He emigrated to the USA in 1922, and became president of the Fokker Aircraft Corporation of America.

FOLEY, John Henry (1818–74) Irish sculptor, born in Dublin. He went to London in 1834, and executed many statues of public figures, including that of **Albert**, Prince Consort for the Albert Memorial. Other major commissions were statues of **Edmund Burke** and **Goldsmith** at Trinity College, Dublin, and **Henry Grattan** on College Green, Dublin. He also made the design for the **O'Connell** Monument in Dublin.

FOLKERS, Karl August (1906–) American biochemist, born in Decatur, Illinois. He studied at Illinois, Wisconsin and Yale and afterwards directed research at Merck and Co, at the Stanford Research Institute, and at Texas University. His work on antibiotics and vitamins included, notably, the first isolation of the antipernicious anaemia factor, cyanocobalamin (Vitamin B12), by a Merck team in 1948.

FOLKES, Martin (1690–1754) English numismatist, born in London. He published *A Table of English Gold Coins* (1736) and *A Table of English Silver Coins* (1745).

FONBLANQUE, Albany William (1793–1872) English journalist, born in London. From 1830 he was editor of the *Examiner*. His best articles were reprinted as *England under Seven Administrations* (1837). In 1847 he became statistical secretary to the Board of Trade.

FONDA, Henry James (1905–82) American film and stage actor, born in Grand Island, Nebraska. A chance involvement with the Omaha Community Playhouse led to his professional association with the theatre and a long and distinguished career in which his self-effacing manner and dry, flat tones were effectively used to project honesty and decency. His film début in *A Farmer Takes A Wife* (1935) was followed by over 100 screen appearances, notable amongst them *Young Mr Lincoln* (1939), *The Grapes of Wrath* (1940), *The Lady Eve* (1941), *The Oxbow Incident* (1943), *Twelve Angry Men* (1957) and *On Golden Pond* (1981), for which he received an Academy Award. A frequent stage performer, he enjoyed long runs with *Mister Roberts* (1948–51), *Two for the Seesaw* (1958) and *Clarence Darrow* (1974–75). Married five times, his children include actors **Jane Fonda** and Peter (1939–).

FONDA, Jane Seymour (1937–) American actress, born in New York City. She made her stage début, with her father **Henry Fonda**, in *The Country Girl* (1955). A student at the Actor's Studio and part-time model, she made her film début in *Tall Story* (1960). Work in Europe and marriage to director Roger Vadim labelled her as a 'sex kitten', an image further encouraged by her appearance as comic strip heroine *Barbarella* (1968). Later she established a new career as a versatile dramatic actress of considerable emotional depth and sensitivity, winning Academy Awards for *Klute* (1971) and *Coming Home* (1978) and an Emmy for *The Dollmaker* (1983). Courting disfavour with her outspoken criticisms of the Vietnam War, she is now a powerful film executive and energetic proselytizer for physical health through bestselling videos and books.

FONSECA, Eleonora Pimentel, Marchesa di (1758–99) Neapolitan noblewoman. She was lady-in-waiting to Queen **Maria Carolina**, wife of **Ferdinand I** of the Two Sicilies, until she forfeited her mistress's favour by remarking on her intimacy with Sir **John Acton**. An active French partisan, on the fall of the

Parthenopean republic (1798–99) she was hanged at the queen's instigation.

FONSECA, Manoel Deodoro da (1827–92) Brazilian statesman, born in Alagoas. He was first president of Brazil, 1889–91.

FONTAINE, Just (1933–) French footballer and manager, born in Morocco. He established an enduring record when in the final stages of the 1958 World Cup in Sweden he scored 13 goals, including four against West Germany in the play-off match to determine third place. He formed a prolific partnership with Raymond Kopa of Reims, whom he later joined from Nice. A brief period as manager of the French international squad was comparatively unsuccessful.

FONTANA, Carlo (1634 or 1638–1714) Swiss-born Italian architect. A pupil of **Bernini**, he worked as papal architect in Rome, where he designed many major works including the fountain in the Piazza di San Pietro, and the tombs of Popes **Clement XI** and Innocent XII, and Queen **Kristina** of Sweden, in St Peter's. He designed Loyola College in Spain and the Palazzo Durazzo at Genoa.

FONTANA, Domenico (1543–1607) Swiss-born Italian architect, born in Melide near Lugano. He was papal architect in Rome, and worked on the Lateran Palace and the Vatican Library. He was afterwards royal architect in Naples.

FONTANA, Lucio (1899–1968) Italian artist, born in Rosario, Argentina. Brought up in Milan, he studied at the Accademia di Brera (1928–30), and in 1935 signed the First Manifesto of Italian Abstract Artists. After World War II (which he spent in Argentina) he made his name as the inventor of *Spazialismo* (Spatialism) and as a pioneer of 'environmental art'. He is best-known for his bare or monochrome canvases holed or slashed to create what he called *Attese*. These in turn looked forward to the 'gesture' or 'performance' art of the 1960s.

FONTANE, Theodor (1819–98) German poet and novelist, born in Neuruppin. He worked in the family chemist's business until in 1849 he took to literature in Berlin. Periods of residence in Britain between 1855 and 1859 as a newspaper correspondent led to ballads such as *Archibald Douglas* and *Die Brück am Tay* and other British-flavoured pieces. His later realistic novels influenced **Thomas Mann**; the first of them, *Vor dem Sturm* (1878), an account of Prussian nobility, was followed by *L'Adultera* (1882) and *Effi Briest* (1898).

FONTANES, Louis, Marquis de (1757–1821) French writer and politican, born in Niort. In 1777 he went to Paris, where he acquired a reputation by his poems, among which are *Le Cri de mon coeur* (1778), *Le Verger* (1788), a metrical translation of **Pope**'s *Essay on Man* (1783), and an imitation of **Gray**'s *Elegy*. He supported the Revolution, but later criticized it, and founded the *Mercure de France* in 1799. In 1804 he was made president of the Corps Législatif. In 1810 he entered the senate, and was raised to the peerage by **Louis XVIII**.

FONTENELLE, Bernard le Bovier de (1657–1757) French author, born in Rouen. A nephew of **Corneille**, he began his literary career in Paris. In the great quarrel of Moderns versus Ancients, he sided with the Moderns, assailing the Greeks and their French imitators, and receiving in return the satiric shafts of **Boileau**, **Racine**, **Jean Baptiste Rousseau** and **La Bruyère**. After the failure on the stage of his *Aspar*, he produced an imitation of **Lucian**, *Dialogues des morts*, and the 'precious' *Lettres du Chevalier d'Her*.... In 1697 he was made secretary to the Académie des Sciences, of which he later was president. He died in Paris in his hundredth year. He had attempted almost every form of literature—idylls, satires, dialogues, critical essays, histories and tragedies. His *Entretiens sur la pluralité des mondes* (1868), and *Histoire des oracles* (1867), are considered his best works.

FONTEYN, Dame Margot, stage name of **Margaret Hookham** (1919–) English ballerina, considered one of the finest technicians of this century. Born in Reigate, she studied under **Nicholai Legat** and **Ninette de Valois** among others, then joined the Vic-Wells Ballet, which became Sadler's Wells Ballet and finally the Royal Ballet, with whom she spent her entire career. She created many roles with the choreographers Ninette de Valois and Sir **Frederick Ashton**, among them *The Haunted Ballroom* (1939), *Symphonic Variations* (1946) and *The Fairy Queen* (1946). She rose in the Royal Ballet to become its queen ballerina, partnering **Rudolph Nureyev** and performing work by **Roland Petit** and **Kenneth MacMillan**.

FOOT, Sir Dingle Mackintosh (1905–78) English lawyer and politician. He was educated at Oxford, where he was president of the Liberal club (1927) and of the Union (1928). He was Liberal MP for Dundee (1931–45), joined the Labour party in 1956 and was Labour MP for Ipswich (1957–70), and solicitor-general (1964–67). He took silk in 1954, and was knighted in 1964. See his *British Political Crises* (1976).

FOOT, Hugh Mackintosh, Baron Caradon (1907–) English administrator. He was educated at Cambridge (president of the Union, 1929). He has held many government administrative posts abroad, in Palestine, Transjordan, Cyprus, Jamaica and Nigeria. Since 1961 his work has been mainly in connection with the United Nations (permanent representative 1964–70) and as a consultant to the UN development programme. He was awarded a life peerage in 1964. He published *A Start in Freedom* in 1964.

FOOT, Isaac (1880–1960) English politician, father of **Dingle**, **Hugh**, **John** and **Michael Foot**. He was a solicitor in Plymouth and Liberal MP for Bodmin (1922–24 and 1929–35).

FOOT, John Mackintosh, Baron Foot (1909–) English lawyer and politician. He took his degree in law at Oxford. He was president of the Liberal club and of the Union in 1931. He stood unsuccessfully as a Liberal for Basingstoke (1934 and 1935) and for Bodmin (1945 and 1950). He is senior partner of the family legal firm in Plymouth, and was awarded a life peerage in 1967.

FOOT, Michael Mackintosh (1913–) English politician, son of **Isaac Foot**. He was educated at Oxford, where he was president of the Union (1933). He was assistant editor of *Tribune* (1937–38), joint editor (1948–52) and editor (1955–60). He was also acting editor of the *Evening Standard* (1942–44) and a political columnist on the *Daily Herald* (1945–55), and represented Ebbw Vale from 1960. He was secretary of state for employment (1974–76), and was deputy leader of the Labour party (1976–80) and leader of the House of Commons (1976–79). In 1980 he became leader of the Labour party, resigning in 1983 after his party's heavy defeat in the general election of that year. A pacifist, he has long been a supporter of the Campaign for Nuclear Disarmament. He is a distinguished journalist and author. His books include the influential *Guilty Men*, written with colleagues and published in 1940, and a life of **Aneurin Bevan**.

FOOTE, Andrew Hull (1806–63) American naval officer, born in New Haven, Connecticut. He entered the navy in 1822, and was promoted captain in 1849. He helped to abolish the liquor ration in the US navy (1862). In 1856 he stormed four Chinese forts at Canton, which had fired on him. In the Civil War he organized the western flotilla, and in February 1862 stormed Fort Henry. Shortly afterwards he was wounded and resigned as rear admiral.

FOOTE, Arthur William (1853–1937) American composer, born in Salem, Massachusetts. A noted organist, he taught at the New York Conservatory from 1920 to 1937; he wrote church and chamber music as well as books on harmony and keyboard technique.

FOOTE, Samuel (1720–77) English wit, playwright and actor, born in Truro. His brilliant mimicry of prominent people led to legal proceedings being taken against him on several occasions. His plays, which include *Taste* (1752) and *The Minor* (1760), were mainly political satire, and have not stood the test of time.

FOPPA, Vincenzo (c.1427–c.1515) Italian painter. He was the leader of the Lombard school of painting which lasted till the time of **Leonardo da Vinci**.

FORBES, Alexander Penrose (1817–75) Scottish prelate, born in Edinburgh, the son of a law lord. In 1848 he was consecrated bishop of Brechin. He laboured to further Tractarian principles, but his charge (1857) on the manner of the Eucharistic Presence led to his trial before the other Scottish bishops in 1860, and a censure and admonition. He edited the *Arbuthnot Missal* (1864), and published *Kalendars of Scottish Saints* (1872).

FORBES, Duncan, of Culloden (1685–1747) Scottish judge, born in Bunchrew near Inverness. After studying at Edinburgh and Leyden, he was called to the bar, and appointed sheriff of Midlothian. He rose rapidly in practice and political influence through the 2nd Duke of **Argyll**. In 1715 he was in the north, actively opposing the rebels; afterwards he protested against trying the prisoners in England, and resisted the forfeitures. In 1725 he became lord advocate, in 1737 lord president of the Court of Session; in 1734 he succeeded his brother in the family estates. For a long time he largely ruled the destinies of Scotland and contributed to her dawning prosperity by developing her internal resources, by winning over the Jacobites, and by forming Highland regiments under loyal colonels. The 1745 Jacobite rebellion rather took him by surprise. He hastened to the north, and did much to check the rebels, beating off the Frasers' attack on Culloden House. But he had to take refuge in Skye, and after his return was regarded with disfavour by the government, because he advocated treating the rebels with mercy.

FORBES, Edward (1815–54) Manx naturalist, born in Douglas, Isle of Man. He studied medicine at Edinburgh, but from 1836 devoted himself to the natural sciences. In 1841 he was naturalist on the *Beacon* during the survey of a part of Asia Minor. In 1843 he became professor of botany at King's College, London; in 1844 palaeontologist to the Museum of Geology; in 1851 professor of natural history to the School of Mines; and in 1853 professor of natural history at Edinburgh. He did much to advance and systematize several disciplines in natural history. He made formative observations in oceanography and was one of the founders of the science of biogeography.

FORBES, George (1849–1936) Scottish electrical engineer, born in Edinburgh, son of **James David Forbes**. He was the inventor of the carbon brush for dynamos. He made improvements in the method of measuring the velocity of light (with **James Young**), and in the field of range-finding. In 1880 he forecast the existence of Pluto.

FORBES, James David (1809–68) Scottish physicist, born in Edinburgh, grandson of Sir **William Forbes of Pitsligo**. Professor at Edinburgh (1833–60) and principal of St Andrews College (1860–68), he is known for his work on glaciers. He wrote *Travelling through the Alps* (1843) and *Theory of Glaciers* (1859).

FORBES, (Joan) Rosita (1893–1967) English writer and traveller, born in Swinderby, Lincolnshire. Having visited almost every country in the world and particularly Arabia and North Africa, she used her experiences as the raw material for exciting travel books, including *The Secret of the Sahara-Kufara* (1922), *From Red Sea to Blue Nile* (1928), *The Prodigious Caribbean* (1940), *Appointment in the Sun* (1949), and *Islands in the Sun* (1950).

FORBES, Malcolm Stevenson (1919–90) American publisher, born in Brooklyn, New York City, where his father, a Scot, founded *Forbes* in 1917, then the only business magazine in America. For the first dozen years the magazine prospered but in the 1930s its circumstances—and the family's—changed when rivals like *Fortune* and *Business Week* appeared on the scene. It was nevertheless kept alive and Malcolm Forbes became its editor-in-chief and publisher in 1957, since when circulation and profits escalated, making its owner the talk of gossip columns and a multi-millionaire. Notorious for his extravagance, he had a passionate interest in ballooning as well as **Fabergé** eggs, of which he had one of the world's foremost collections.

FORBES, Robert (1708–75) Scottish Episcopalian churchman. He was a minister in Leith from 1735, and in 1745 was imprisoned as a Jacobite. He collected the Jacobite material for *The Lyon in Mourning* (1747–75). In 1762 he was appointed bishop of Ross and Cromarty.

FORBES, Sir William of Pitsligo (1739–1806) Scottish banker, born in Edinburgh. He worked with, and in 1761 became a partner in, the Edinburgh bank of Coutts & Co, which changed its name to Forbes, Hunter & Co in 1763 (later the Union Bank, 1830). He was a founder member of the Society of Antiquaries of Scotland (1780) and the Royal Society of Edinburgh (1783). His second son, John Hay (1776–1854), was the judge, Lord Medwyn.

FORBES MACKENZIE See **MACKENZIE, William Forbes**

FORBES-ROBERTSON, Sir Johnston (1853–1937) English actor, born in London. He made his début in 1874 and soon established himself as a West End favourite. In 1895, he became actor-manager of the London Lyceum and crowned his productions there with *Hamlet* in 1897. His later years were marked by success in *The Passing of the Third Floor Back* (1913). In 1900 he married Gertrude Elliot, an American actress who often partnered him. A daughter, Jean (1905–62), carried on the tradition and became actress-manager in *The Lady of the Camellias* in 1934.

FORCELLINI, Egidio See **FACCIOLATI, Jacopo**

FORCHAMMER, Peter Wilhelm (1801–94) German classical antiquary, professor of philology at Kiel and director of the archaeological museum founded by himself and **Otto John**. His brother, geologist Johann George (1794–1865), born in Husum, wrote on the geology of Denmark.

FORD, Ford Madox, originally **Ford Hermann Hueffer** (1873–1939) English novelist, editor and poet, born in Merton, Surrey, the son of **Francis Hueffer**, the music critic of *The Times* and grandson, on his mother's side, of **Ford Madox Brown**. Brought up in pre-Raphaelite circles, he published his first book when he was only 18, a fairy story entitled *The Brown Owl* (1891), and a novel, *The Shifting of the Fire*, appeared the following year. In 1894 he eloped with and married

Elsie Martindale, presaging a life of emotional upheaval. He met **Joseph Conrad** in 1898 and they co-authored various works including *The Inheritors* (1901) and *Romance* (1903). He founded the *English Review* in 1908, which he edited for 15 months and in which he published **Hardy**, **Wells**, **D H Lawrence** and **Wyndham Lewis** among others. In 1924, while living in Paris, he was founder-editor of the *Transatlantic Review* which gave space to **Joyce**, **Pound**, **Gertrude Stein** and the young **Hemingway**. He wrote almost 80 books in a hectic career but is best remembered for three novels: *The Fifth Queen* (1906), *The Good Soldier* (1915), and *Parade's End*, the title he gave to what is often known as the Tietjens war tetralogy: *Some Do Not* (1924), *No More Parades* (1925), *A Man Could Stand Up* (1926) and *Last Post* (1928).

FORD, Gerald Rudolph (1913–) 38th president of the USA, born in Omaha, Nebraska. After going with a football scholarship to the University of Michigan, he studied law at Yale and served in the US navy during World War II. From 1949 to 1973 he was a Republican member of the House of Representatives, becoming minority leader in 1965. On the resignation of **Spiro Agnew** in October 1973 he was appointed vice-president, becoming president in August 1974 when President **Nixon** resigned because of the Watergate scandal. Ford assumed the presidency during a time of economic difficulties and was faced with a resurgent, Democrat-dominated congress which firmly resisted his domestic and external policy initiatives. His relations with congress were made worse by his controversial decision to grant a full pardon to former president Nixon in September 1974. In the November 1976 presidential election he was defeated by **Jimmy Carter**.

FORD, Harrison (1942–) American actor, born in Chicago. After appearances in summer stock theatre, he made his film début in *Dead Heat on a Merry-Go-Round* (1966). He served a long apprenticeship in film and television, interspersed with employment as a carpenter, before achieving stardom in *Star Wars* (1977) and its two sequels. Cast as resourceful, swashbuckling heroes, he found great popularity as an archaeologist/adventurer in *Raiders of the Lost Ark* (1981) and its sequels *Indiana Jones and the Temple of Doom* (1984) and *Indiana Jones and the Last Crusade* (1989). He enhanced his reputation with testing characterizations in *Witness* (1985, Academy Award nomination) and *The Mosquito Coast* (1986). His second wife is the screenwriter Melissa Matheson.

FORD, Henry (1863–1947) American automobile engineer and manufacturer, born in Greenfield, Michigan. Apprenticed to a machinist in Detroit at the age of 15, he produced his first petrol-driven motor car in 1893. In 1899 he became chief engineer of the Detroit Automobile Company and in 1903 founded the Ford Motor Company. He pioneered the modern 'assembly line' mass-production techniques for his famous Model T (1908–09), 15 million of which were produced up to 1928. He also branched out into aircraft and tractor manufacture. A fervent pacifist who thought that 'history is bunk', he tried to negotiate a European peace in 1915 by chartering a 'Peace Ship' to Europe. His policy of paying his employees more than a normal rate led to violent disagreements with the code laid down in the **Roosevelt** recovery programme in 1931. In 1919 he was succeeded by his son Edsel Bryant (1893–1943), and in 1945 by his grandson **Henry II Ford**, after Henry senior had tried hard to resume absolute control of the ailing company.

FORD, Henry II (1917–87) American automobile maker, and grandson of **Henry Ford**. After the death of his father, Edsel Bryant Ford (1893–1943), he seized control of the Ford Motor Company from his grandfather in 1945. The company was in difficulties, but he reorganized it and rebuilt the management teams. He stepped down as chief executive officer in 1979 and as chairman in 1980, but stayed as member of the board of directors.

FORD, John (c.1586–c.1640) English dramatist, born in Ilsington, Devon. He studied for a year at Oxford and entered the Middle Temple in 1602. He was expelled for debt but readmitted. He was greatly influenced by **Robert Burton**, whose *Anatomy of Melancholy* (1621) turned Ford's dramatic gifts towards stage presentation of the melancholy, the unnatural and the horrible in *The Lover's Melancholy* (1629), *'Tis Pity She's a Whore* (1633), *The Lady's Trial* (1639), etc. He also wrote a masterful chronicle play, *Perkin Warbeck* (1634). Ford often collaborated with **Dekker**, **Rowley** and **Webster**.

FORD, John, originally **Sean Aloysius O'Fearna** (1895–1973) American film director, born in Cape Elizabeth, Maine, of Irish immigrant parents. He made his directorial début with a western, *The Tornado* (1917). An affectionate chronicler of American history in films like *The Iron Horse* (1924), *Young Mr. Lincoln* (1939) and *My Darling Clementine* (1946), he enjoyed a long association with actor **John Wayne** which resulted in such classics as *Stagecoach* (1939), *The Searchers* (1956) and *The Man Who Shot Liberty Valance* (1962). Adept at all genres, he frequently explored his Irish roots, as in *The Informer* (1935, Academy Award), but achieved his greatest renown for poetic visions of the American West: its rugged heroes, pioneering families and sense of male camaraderie. His other Academy Awards were for *The Grapes of Wrath* (1940), *How Green Was My Valley* (1941) and *The Quiet Man* (1952); and he received the first American Film Institute Life Achievement Award in 1973. He also co-directed the first film in Cinerama, *How the West Was Won* (1962).

FORD, Richard (1796–1858) English travel writer, born in Winchester. After studying at Trinity College, Oxford, he was called to the bar, but never practised. He spent the years 1830–34 in riding tours in Spain, and wrote *Handbook for Travellers in Spain* (1845) and *Gatherings from Spain* (1846). He introduced the British public to the works of **Velazquez**.

FORDE, Daryll (1902–73) English anthropologist. He studied geography at University College London, and taught there (1923–28) and later at the University of Wales (1930–45), before becoming professor of anthropology at University College London, from 1945 to 1969. He carried out anthropological fieldwork in Arizona and New Mexico (1928–29), Nigeria (1935 and 1939) and the Gambia (1945). He made extensive contributions to the anthropology of Africa, and was director of the African Institute from the end of World War II until his death. In his major works, which include *Habitat, Economy and Society* (1934), *Marriage and the Family among the Yakö* (1941) and *The Context of Belief* (1958), he explored patterns of kinship and marriage, relations between environment, economy and social organization, and the role of anthropology as practised by indigenous scholars.

FORDE, Francis Michael (1890–1983) Australian politician, born in Mitchell, Queensland. Originally a teacher and an electrical engineer, he became a Labor member of the Queensland legislature in 1917. From 1922 to 1946 he sat in the federal parliament, and was deputy prime minister during World War II, forming a caretaker government on **Curtin**'s death in 1945 before joining the Australian delegation to the San Francisco

Conference. From 1946 to 1953 he was high commissioner in Canada.

FORDHAM, George (1837–87) English jockey, born in Cambridge. He won the Derby on Sir Bevys in 1879, and the Oaks and Ascot Cup five times.

FORDUN, John of (d.c.1384) Scottish chronicler, probably born in Fordoun, in Kincardineshire. He may have been a chantry priest in Aberdeen. He was the compiler of *Chronica gentis Scotorum*, the chief authority for the history of Scotland prior to the 15th century. He brought his history down to 1153, but he left collections extending to 1383. **Walter Bower** in 1441 resumed and enlarged the unfinished work as the *Scotichronicon*, but many of his alterations corrupted Fordun's narrative.

FOREL, Auguste Henri (1848–1931) Swiss psychologist and entomologist, and a pioneer in sex hygiene. An authority on the psychology of ants, he was professor of psychiatry at Zürich (1879–98) and made notable contributions in the fields of the anatomy of the brain and nerves, hypnotism, and forensic psychiatry.

FOREST, John (c.1474–1538) English friar, burnt in Smithfield by **Henry VIII** for upholding the papal supremacy.

FOREST, Lee de See **DE FOREST**

FORESTER, Cecil Scott (1899–1966) British writer, born in Cairo. He studied medicine, but turned to writing full-time after the success of his first novel, *Payment Deferred* (1926). He also wrote *The African Queen* (1935, which was made into a successful film), *The General* (1936) and *The Ship* (1943). He is best known for his creation of Horatio Hornblower, a British naval officer in the Napoleonic era whose career he chronicled in a series of popular novels, starting with *The Happy Return* (1937) and *Ship of the Line* (1938, James Tait Black Memorial Prize). He also wrote biographical and travel books and collaborated with C E Bechofer Roberts on a play about Nurse **Edith Cavell**.

FORMAN, Simon (1552–1611) English astrologer and quack doctor, born in Quidhampton, Wiltshire. He studied at Magdalen College, Oxford, and set up a lucrative practice in 1583 in London, particularly in love potions for ladies of the Court, and was constantly prosecuted by the church and the College of Physicians. He left in manuscript form a *Booke of Plaies* containing the earliest accounts of the performances of some of **Shakespeare**'s plays.

FORMBY, George (1904–61) English entertainer, born in Wigan. The son of a North Country comedian, he briefly pursued a career as a jockey before following in his father's footsteps. He developed an act in music halls throughout England that was subsequently transferred to film. In a series of low-budget, slapstick comedies he portrayed a shy young man with an irrepressible grin and ever-ready ukelele to accompany his risqué songs. From *Boots Boots* (1934) to *George in Civvy Street* (1946) he was one of Britain's most popular film stars. Falling out of favour with post-war cinema audiences, he returned to the stage. Latterly dogged by ill-health he was long dominated by his formidable wife Beryl, who died in 1960.

FORREST, Edwin (1806–72) American actor, born in Philadelphia, where he made his début in 1820. At twenty he appeared as Othello in New York with great success. He had successful seasons in London (1836–37), but in 1845 his Macbeth was hissed by the audience. His implacable rivalry with **Macready** created a feeling of resentment that prompted him to hiss the latter's performance in Edinburgh and destroyed his reputation in England and Scotland. The hissing of Macready's Macbeth by Forrest's sympathizers in New York in 1849 led to a riot which cost 22 lives. He retired temporarily in 1853, but returned to the stage in 1860 and made his last appearance as **Richelieu** in Boston in 1871.

FORREST, John, 1st Baron Forrest of Bunbury (1847–1918) Australian explorer and politician, born in Bunbury in Western Australia. From 1864 he was a colonial surveyor. In 1869 he penetrated inland from Perth to 123° E long, and next year reached South Australia from the west along the south coast. With his brother Alexander (1849–1901) he made an eastward journey in 1874. Surveyor-general for the colony from 1883, he was the first premier of Western Australia (1890–1901), and later minister for defence, for home affairs and treasurer. He died on his return from London in 1918 where he had been granted a peerage, the first to an Australian.

FORRESTAL, James (1892–1949) US politician, born in Beacon, New York. After a business career he entered US government service in 1940. From 1944 to 1947 he was secretary of the navy and, till his suicide in 1949, secretary of defense.

FORRESTER, Alfred Henry (1804–72), and his brother **Charles Robert** (1803–50) English artists, born in London. They wrote and illustrated verse, burlesques, children's stories, etc, under the joint pseudonym of Alfred Crowquill.

FORRESTER, Jay Wright (1918–) American computer engineer, born in Anselmo, Nebraska. Educated at Nebraska University, he became a pioneer in the development of computer storage devices. From 1944 to 1951 he supervised the building of the Whirlwind computer at the Massachusetts Institute of Technology, during the course of which (1949) he devised the first magnetic core store (memory) for an electronic digital computer. From 1951 to 1956 he was a founder and director of the Digital Computer Laboratory. He has written several books, including *Industrial Dynamics* (1961), *Principles of Systems* (1968) and *World Dynamics* (1971).

FORSSMAN, Werner (1904–76) German physician, born in Berlin. He graduated at Berlin University and was an army doctor until 1945, then practised at various places including Bad Kreuznach and Düsseldorf. He became known for his development of new techniques in heart surgery, including cardiac catheterization, in which he carried out dangerous experiments on himself. He was awarded the 1956 Nobel prize for physiology or medicine jointly with **André Cournand** and **Dickenson Richards**.

FORSTER, E M (Edward Morgan) (1879–1970) English novelist and critic, born in London. He was educated at Tonbridge School, where he was miserable, and King's College, Cambridge, where he revelled in the 'Bloomsbury circle' of **G E Moore**, **G M Trevelyan** and **Lowes Dickinson**, whose biography he wrote in 1934, and with whom he founded the *Independent Review* in 1903. In his novels he examined with subtle insight the pre-1914 English middle-class ethos and its custodians the civil service, the church and the public schools. An indictment of the latter is embodied in *The Longest Journey* (1907), and a period in Italy provided the background for *Where Angels Fear to Tread* (1905) and *A Room with a View* (1908). *Howards End* (1910) was written after he had been tutor in Nassenheide (1905). But it is in his masterpiece, *A Passage to India* (1924), that he puts English values and Indian susceptibilities to his finest scrutiny. The spiritual tensions of two clashing civilizations are resolved in the strange symbolism of the Malabar Cave. He was awarded the Tait Black Memorial and Femina Vie

Heureuse prizes for the latter in 1925. His Indian experiences as secretary to the Maharajah of Dewas Senior (1921) he described in *The Hill of Devi* (1953). Collections of short stories include *The Celestial Omnibus* (1914) and *The Eternal Moment* (1928); collections of essays, *Abinger Harvest* (1936) and *Two Cheers for Democracy* (1951). His Cambridge Clark lectures, *Aspects of the Novel* (1927), expressed his literary aesthetics as firmly opposed to **Aristotle**. He was elected a fellow of King's College, Cambridge in 1946. *Marianne Thornton* (1958) is a domestic biography. In 1951 he collaborated with Eric Crozier on the libretto of **Britten**'s opera, *Billy Budd*. His novel *Maurice* (written 1913–14), on the theme of homosexuality, was published posthumously in 1971.

FORSTER, John (1812–76) English biographer, historian and journalist, born in Newcastle. He was educated for the bar, but in 1833 began to write political articles in the *Examiner*; he edited successively the *Foreign Quarterly Review*, the *Daily News* and (1847–56) the *Examiner*. He was the author of many biographical and historical essays and an admirable series dealing with the Commonwealth—*Lives of the Statesmen of the Commonwealth* (1836–39); *Debates on the Grand Remonstrance* (1860); *Arrest of the Five Members* (1860); and *Sir John Eliot, a Biography* (1864). He is, however, best remembered for his *Life and Times of Goldsmith* (1848), *Landor* (1868), *Life of Dickens* (1871–74), and vol 1 of a *Life of Swift* (1875).

FORSTER, William Edward (1819–86) English Liberal statesman, born of Quaker parentage in Bradpole, Dorset. He abandoned the bar for the wool industry. During the Irish famine of 1845 he visited the distressed districts as almoner of a Quaker relief fund; in 1850 he married Jane, daughter of Dr **Thomas Arnold** of Rugby. In 1861 he became Liberal MP for Bradford. He rose to cabinet rank and in 1870 carried the Elementary Education Act. Under the **Gladstone** administration of 1880 he was chief secretary for Ireland. He was attacked unceasingly in Parliament by the Irish members, and his life was threatened by the 'Invincibles' for his measures of coercion. He was a severe critic of **Parnell** and, determined to re-establish law and order, had him and other Irish leaders arrested. When in April 1882 a majority of the cabinet determined to release the 'suspects', Forster and Lord Cowper (the lord-lieutenant) resigned. A strong opponent of Home Rule, he died in London.

FÖRSTER, Johann Georg Adam (1754–94) German traveller and writer. With his father, **Johann Reinhold Förster**, he accompanied Captain **James Cook** on his second voyage (1772–75), and published an account in *A Voyage Round the World* (1777). He became professor at Kassel (1778) and Vilna (1784), and librarian at Mainz (1788).

FÖRSTER, Johann Reinhold (1729–98) German naturalist and clergyman, born in Dirschau (Tczew) of parents of Scottish extraction (Forrester). He studied theology at Halle and became a country minister near Danzig. He left the church in 1765 and undertook a survey of new German colonies on the Volga, in south-west Russia. He taught at the Dissenter's Academy in Warrington, Lancashire (1766–69), and published a *Catalogue of the Animals of North America* (1771), although he never went there. With his son, **Johann Georg Adam Förster**, he accompanied **Cook** as naturalist on his second world voyage on the *Resolution* (1772–75). A pioneer ornithologist of Antarctica, New Zealand and the Pacific, he wrote *Observations made during a Voyage Around the World* (1778). In 1780 he was appointed professor of natural history at Halle. Förster's Tern is named after him.

FORSYTH, Alexander John (1769–1843) Scottish inventor and clergyman. Minister from 1791 of Belhelvie, Aberdeenshire, in 1807 he patented his improved detonating mechanism for firearms, which resulted in the adoption of the percussion-cap by the British forces. **Napoleon** offered him £20000 for the secret of his invention, but he patriotically refused. The first instalment of the pension tardily awarded to him by the British Government arrived on the day of his death.

FORSYTH, Bill (1946–) Scottish filmmaker, born in Glasgow. He entered the film industry in 1963 and started making his own documentaries after the death of his employer. He was a first-year drop-out from the National Film School in 1971, but his *That Sinking Feeling* ('a fairytale for the workless') was warmly received at the 1979 Edinburgh Film Festival. Particularly interested in exploring the lives of characters on the edge of society, he enjoyed considerable commercial success with the adolescent romance *Gregory's Girl* (1980) and *Local Hero* (1983), which focused on the impact of the oil business on a remote Scottish community. He has since explored the more fragile melancholy of dislocated individuals: a love-struck radio DJ in *Comfort and Joy* (1984), and an eccentric hobo in *Housekeeping* (1987), his first American film.

FORSYTH, Bruce, originally **Bruce Joseph Forsyth-Johnson** (1928–) English entertainer, born in Edmonton, London. Trained as a dancer, he made his professional début as 'Boy Bruce–The Mighty Atom' at the Theatre Royal, Bilston in 1942. An all-round song'n'dance man and comic, his vast showbusiness experience includes a spell as the resident comedian at the Windmill Theatre (1949–51) as well as innumerable appearances in cabaret and music-hall. He made his television début in *Music Hall* (1954) but gained national popularity as the compère of *Sunday Night at the London Palladium* (1958–60). His jaunty manner, catchphrases, deftness at audience participation and ability for quick-witted ad-libbing have won him enduring affection as the host of such game shows as *The Generation Game* (1971–78) and *Play Your Cards Right* (1980–87). His musical talents have been seen in television specials and on stage in one-man shows and productions like *Little Me* (1964), *Birds on the Wing* (1969), *The Travelling Music Show* (1978) and *Bruce Forsyth on Broadway* (1979). A perennial Royal Command Performer and charity golfer, his few film appearances include *Star!* (1968) and *Bedknobs and Broomsticks* (1971).

FORSYTH, Frederick (1938–) English author of suspense thrillers, born in Ashford, Kent. Educated at Tonbridge School, Kent, he served in the Royal Air Force and later became a journalist. His reputation rests on three taut thrillers, *The Day of the Jackal* (1971), *The Odessa File* (1972) and *The Dogs of War* (1974), meticulously researched, precisely plotted nail-biters.

FORSYTH, Gordon Mitchell (1879–1953) Scottish ceramic designer and teacher, born in Fraserburgh, Aberdeenshire. He trained in Aberdeen and at the Royal College of Art, winning a travelling scholarship to Italy in 1902. From 1902 to 1905 he was art director to Minton, Hollins & Co and moved to Pilkington Tile & Pottery Co in 1906 where he specialized in lustre ware. He frequently made use of lettering and mottoes as a title to his work. He encouraged throwers to produce individual decorative designs and to sign and date their own work. He served as a designer to the Royal Air Force (1916–19), before his appointment as superintendent of art instruction at the Stoke-on-Trent

School of Art. His influence on the period was enormous and among his many pupils were **Clarice Cliff** and **Susie Cooper**. He was art adviser to the British Pottery Manufacturers Federation and was noted for the breadth of his knowledge in artistic education, aspects of design and his awareness of the demands of industry. His publications include *The Art and Craft of the Potter* (1934) and *20th Century Ceramics* (1936).

FORSYTH, Peter Taylor (1848–1921) Scottish Congregational theologian and preacher, born in Aberdeen. As principal of Hackney Theological College, Hampstead (1901–21), he championed a high doctrine of church, ministry, sacrament, and preaching in the Congregational Church. Influenced in his student days by **Albrecht Ritschl** at Göttingen, he rejected theological liberalism in the early 1880s, and came to a deep belief in God's holiness and the realities of sin and grace. His *The Cruciality of the Cross* (1909), *The Person and the Place of Jesus Christ* (1909), and *The Work of Christ* (1910), in some ways anticipating the neo-orthodoxy of **Barth** and **Brunner**, have enjoyed renewed popularity since World War II.

FORSYTH, Sir Thomas Douglas (1827–86) British administrator in India, born in Birkenhead. He entered the East India Company in 1848 and was created CB for his services after the Mutiny. In 1870 he conducted a mission to Yarkand, and in 1874 concluded a commercial treaty with Kashgar. He succeeded in averting war with Burma in 1875.

FORSYTHE, William (1949–) American dancer, choreographer and artistic director, born in New York City. He trained at the Joffrey Ballet School before dancing with the company (1971–73). **John Cranko** invited him to the Stuttgart Ballet in 1973. His first ballet, *Urlicht* (1976), led to an appointment as resident choreographer. He became artistic director of Frankfurt Ballet in 1984, establishing himself as a leading figure of European contemporary dance theatre by extending the classical ballet vocabulary into a language all his own. His controversial, rule-bending works—including *Say Bye Bye* (1980), *Artifact* (1984) and *Impressing the Czar* (1988)—frequently use spoken text and stage mechanics to enhance the steps.

FORT, Paul (1872–1960) French poet, born in Reims. He settled in Paris, where in 1890 he founded the 'Théâtre des Arts' for presenting a wide range of European drama and recitals of symbolist poetry. He is best known for his popular *Ballades françaises* (1st vol 1897), in which he brought poetry closer to the rhythms of everyday speech. He also wrote several plays, founded and edited the literary magazine *Vers et Prose* (1905–14), and wrote *Histoire de la poésie française depuis 1850* (1927).

FORTEBRACCIO See **BRACCIO DA MONTONE**

FORTES, Meyer (1906–83) British social anthropologist, born in South Africa. Educated in Cape Town, he trained in psychology before coming to study anthropology at the London School of Economics under **Charles Seligman**, **Bronislaw Malinowski** and **Raymond Firth**. In 1946 he became reader at Oxford and from 1950 to 1973 he was professor of social anthropology at Cambridge. During the 1930s, he carried out fieldwork in West Africa among the Tallensi and the Ashanti, which resulted in several classic monographs including *The Dynamics of Clanship among the Tallensi* (1945), *The Web of Kinship among the Tallensi* (1949) and *Time and Social Structure* (1970). These studies laid the foundations for the theory of descent, a cornerstone of the 'structural-functionalism' dominating the social anthropology of the 1950s and 1960s. His most complete theoretical statement is in *Kinship and the Social Order* (1969), where he argues that kinship relations have an irreducible moral content. His early and enduring interest in psychology is particularly apparent in his work on ancestor worship, as in *Oedipus and Job in West African Religion* (1959). His last work, *Rules and the Emergence of Society* (1983), a critique of sociobiological theories of human kinship and social organization, was left incomplete at his death.

FORTESCUE, Sir John (c.1385–1476) English jurist, born in Somerset and educated at Exeter College, Oxford. Called to the bar, he was in 1441 made serjeant-at-law, and in 1442 lord chief-justice of the King's Bench. In the struggle between York and Lancaster he was loyal to the latter and fled with **Margaret of Anjou** and her son to Scotland, and there was probably appointed lord chancellor by **Henry VI**. In 1463 he embarked with them for Holland. During exile he wrote his *De Laudibus Legum Angliae* (printed in 1537) for the instruction of Prince **Edward**, and of immense value to later jurists. After the final defeat of the House of Lancaster at Tewkesbury (1471) he submitted to Edward IV. He also wrote *The Governance of England* (1714).

FORTESCUE, Sir John William (1859–1933) English military historian, born in Madeira and brought up near Barnstaple. He became private secretary to the governor of the Windward Islands and from 1886 to 1890 was private secretary to the governor of New Zealand. He was librarian of Windsor Castle (1905–26). As well as his monumental 13-volume *History of the British Army* (1899–1930), his writings include *Statesmen of the Great War 1793–1814* (1911), *County Lieutenancies and the Army, 1803–1814* (1925), *Wellington* (1925) and, in a different vein, *The Story of a Red Deer* (1897).

FORTIGUERRA, Niccolo (1674–1735) Italian poet and prelate. He was bishop and papal chamberlain to **Clement XI**, and is remembered for his satirical epic, *Il Ricciardetto* (1738).

FORTIN, Jean Nicolas (1750–1831) French scientific instrument-maker, born in Mouchy-la-Ville. He worked for many eminent scientists including **Lavoisier**, **Gay-Lussac**, **Arago**, and **Dulong**. He was notable for precision-balances, comparators and dividing-engines, but especially for an improved barometer to which his name is given. Though he did not invent the leather bag, the ivory point or the glass tube in the cistern, he appears to have been the first to use all three together in 1797 in a sensitive portable barometer.

FORTUNE, Robert (1813–80) Scottish horticulturist, born in Edrom, Berwickshire. He was at first employed as a gardener in the Royal Botanic Garden, Edinburgh, and at the Horticultural Society, Chiswick. From 1843 he travelled extensively in the East for the London Botanical Society, introducing many oriental plants into Britain (including the double yellow rose, the Japanese anemone, and the fan-palm *Chamaerops Fortuneii*), and planted tea successfully in India's North West Provinces. He published accounts of his travels, including *Yeddo and Peking* (1863).

FORTUNY Y CARBO, Mariano (1839–74) Spanish painter, born in Reus in Tarragona. When Spain declared war against Morocco, Fortuny followed the army, and filled his portfolios with studies of Eastern life. The best of his rococo pictures are *The Spanish Marriage*, *Book-Lover in the Library of Richelieu*, and *Academicians Choosing a Model*.

FOSBURY, Dick (Richard) (1947–) American athlete, born in Portland, Oregon. He pioneered a new technique in high jumping which revolutionized this event after he won the Olympic Gold Medal at Mexico City in 1968 with a jump of 2.24 metres (7′4¼″), using what came to be known as the 'Fosbury Flop'. This cut across conventional athletics coaching in that the bar was jumped head-first and backwards.

FOSCARI, Francesco (c.1370–1457) doge of Venice from 1423. By his great military skill carried a conflict with Milan to a successful conclusion in the Treaty of Férrara (1433). His last years were embittered by the unjust torturing and banishment of his son Giacopo.

FOSCOLO, Ugo (1778–1827) Italian author, born in Zante. He was educated at Spalato and Venice. His bitter disappointment when Venice was ceded to Austria found vent in the *Lettere di Jacopo Ortis* (1802). Believing that France was destined to liberate Italy, he served in the French armies, but, no longer fooled by **Napoleon**'s intentions, he returned to Milan, and published in 1807 his best poem, *I Sepolcri*. He translated **Sterne**'s *Sentimental Journey*, and wrote two tragedies, *Ajace* and *Ricciarda*. In 1809 he was for a few months professor of eloquence in Pavia. After 1814, when the Austrians entered Milan, he finally sought refuge in London. There he published his *Saggi sul Petrarca*, *Discorso sul testo del Decamerone*, *Discorso sul testo di Dante*, and various papers in the *Quarterly Review* and *Edinburgh Review*. His last years were embittered by poverty and neglect.

FOSDICK, Harry Emerson (1878–1969) American Baptist minister, born in Buffalo, New York. Ordained in 1903, he was a professor at Union Theological Seminary, New York, from 1915, and pastor of the interdenominational Riverside Church in New York from 1926 to 1946. An outstanding preacher, he was a leading 'modernist' in the controversy on Fundamentalism in the 1920s. He wrote a number of popular books.

FOSS, Lukas (1922–) German-born American composer, born in Berlin. He settled in America in 1937. He studied under **Paul Hindemith** and first attracted attention with his cantata, *The Prairie* (1941). His largest work to date is *A Parable of Death*, for soloist, narrator, choir and orchestra, but he has also written a symphony, concertos, chamber music and an opera on **Mark Twain**'s story *The Jumping Frog of Calaveras County*. His later music is in aleatory style and also includes radical re-workings of baroque music. He was professor of music at the University of California at Los Angeles (1951–62), and has been guest conductor with many American and European orchestras.

FOSSE, Bob (Robert Louis) (1927–87) American theatre and film choreographer and director, born in Chicago, Illinois. The son of a vaudeville entertainer, he started performing on stage at the age of 13. In 1950 he made his Broadway début in the revue *Dance Me a Song*. It was his contribution to the musical *The Pajama Game*, a witty number called *Steam Heat*, which established him as a choreographer. During his long career he choreographed eleven Broadway shows, including *Damn Yankees* (1955), *Red Head* (1959), *Little Me* (1963), *Sweet Charity* (1966), *Pippin* (1973) and *Dancin'* (1978), and won six Tony Awards. Moving into film, he was both director and choreographer of *Cabaret* (1972). In 1979 he continued that success with *All That Jazz*, which he not only directed and choreographed but for which he also supplied the screenplay.

FOSTER, (Myles) Birket (1825–99) English artist, born in North Shields. From 1841 to 1846 he produced a large number of subjects for wood-engravings, many of them for the *Illustrated London News*. After 1859 he devoted himself primarily to watercolours, mainly of rustic scenes.

FOSTER, Sir Michael (1689–1763) English judge and text-writer, born in Marlborough, Wiltshire and educated at Exeter College, Oxford. Justice of the King's Bench (1745), he was a judge of high reputation and held a deep concern for personal liberty. He published *Examination of the Scheme of Church Power* (1735) setting out the superiority of parliament and the common law over the extravagant claims propounded by the high church wing of the Church of England. His major work was *Crown Cases and Discourses upon a Few Branches of the Crown Law* (1762); a collection of reports, largely of his own criminal cases, and of commentaries on major problems of legal principle such as treason and homicide, it was a great influence on the development of modern criminal law.

FOSTER, Sir Michael (1836–1907) English physiologist, born in Huntingdon. He was educated there and at University College, London. He taught physiology there until 1870, then moved to Cambridge, where he became professor in 1883. He was MP for London University (1900–06). His *Textbook of Physiology* (1877) became a standard work.

FOSTER, Norman (1935–) English architect, born in Manchester. A leading exponent of the technological approach to architecture, he trained in Manchester and was a founder member with **Richard Rogers** and their wives of Team 4, producing in 1966 Reliant Controls Factory, Swindon. In the 1970s he experimented with simplicity and with pushing technology to the limits, as seen in Willis Faber Dumas Building, Ipswich (1975) and Sainsbury Centre, the University of East Anglia (1978) which won international acclaim as a highly-serviced single pure space. His Hong Kong and Shanghai Bank, Hong Kong (1979–85), with boldly expressive structure and immaculate detailing, was highly praised. His technological innovation continued with the ongoing cultural centre at Nîmes in France.

FOSTER, Stephen Collins (1826–64) American song writer, born in Pittsburgh. Of his 125 compositions the best-known are 'The Old Folks at Home', 'Nelly Bly', 'Camptown Races', 'Beautiful Dreamer', 'Jeannie with the Light Brown Hair', 'Old Kentucky Home', and 'Come where my Love lies dreaming'. The music and words are his own composition. Despite his immense success, he died in poverty and obscurity.

FOU TS'ONG (1934–) Chinese concert pianist, born in Shanghai. Internationally acclaimed as an interpreter of **Mozart** and **Chopin**, he studied under the Italian pianist and founder of the Shanghai Symphony Orchestra, Mario Paci. He won third prize in the International Chopin Competition in Warsaw (1955). Since 1958 he has made his base in London and performed extensively on the international circuit.

FOUCAULD, Charles Eugène de, Vicomte (Brother Charles of Jesus) (1858–1916) French soldier, explorer, missionary-monk and mystic, born in Strasbourg. Achieving fame through his exploration of Morocco (1883–84), he returned to Catholicism in 1886 and embarked on a life-long spiritual journey. A Trappist in France and Syria, a hermit in Nazareth, a garrison priest at Beni-Abbès Algeria, and a nomadic hermit among the Tuareg around Tamanrasset—he felt called to imitate **Christ** in a life of personal poverty in small contemplative communities financed solely by their own manual labour. Though murdered, his ideals survived in the foundation of the Little Brothers (1933–) and Little Sisters (1939–) of Jesus, now active worldwide.

FOUCAULT, Jean Bernard Léon (1819–68) French physicist, born in Paris. He determined the velocity of light by the revolving mirror method and proved that light travels more slowly in water than in air (1850). In 1851, by means of a freely suspended pendulum, he proved that the earth rotates. In 1852 he constructed the gyroscope, in 1857 the Foucault prism and in 1858 he improved the mirrors of reflecting telescopes.

FOUCAULT, Michel (1926–84) French philosopher and historian of ideas, born in Poitiers. A student of the Marxist philosopher **Louis Althusser**, in 1970 he became professor in history of systems of thought at the Collège de France, Paris. He wrote a series of very influential and provocative books including *Histoire de la Folie* (1961), translated as *Madness and Civilization* (1971); *Les Mots et les Choses* (1966), translated as *The Order of Things* (1970); *L'Archéologie du savoir* (1969), translated as *The Archaeology of Knowledge* (1972); and *Histoire de la Sexualité* (1976), translated as *The History of Sexuality* (1984). His basic thesis in tracing the changing historical assumptions about what counts as 'knowledge' at any one time was both relativistic and cynical. Prevailing social attitudes are manipulated by those in power, both to define such categories as insanity, illness, sexuality and criminality, and to use these in turn to identify and oppress the 'deviants'.

FOUCHÉ, Joseph, Duke of Otranto (1763–1829) French revolutionary and statesman, born in Nantes. A priest and a teacher, at the revolution he was elected to the National Convention in 1792, and voted for the execution of **Louis XVI**. Commissioned to castigate Lyon (1794), he rivalled his associates in blood-thirstiness. In 1794 he was expelled from the Convention as a terrorist. Yet in September 1799 he was appointed minister of police; and this post he held with interruptions till 1815, having made terms with the Bourbons when he foresaw **Napoleon**'s downfall. But he had scarcely been appointed ambassador to Dresden when decree of banishment was pronounced against the regicides (1816), and he thereafter lived in exile. He died at Trieste. Unscrupulous, politic and sagacious, he made an admirable head of police, and helped to save France from anarchy.

FOUCQUET See **FOUQUET**

FOULD, Achille (1800–67) French financier and politician, born in Paris of Jewish parents and trained in his father's bank. Elected in 1842 to the Chamber of Deputies, after the revolution of 1848 he rendered service to the provisional government, and during the presidency of **Louis Napoleon** was four times minister of finance. He stabilized the country's finances. He resigned (1852) on the confiscation of the property of the Orléans family was again appointed minister of finance (1861–67).

FOULDS, John (1880–1939) English composer, born in Manchester and largely self-taught. He played cello in the Halle Orchestra under **Richter**, who premiered his *Cello Concerto* (1911). A tone poem, *Epithalamium*, was heard under **Wood** in London (1906). Known mainly for light music during his lifetime, Foulds forged an eclectic and innovative style, the value of which was long overlooked. From 1915 he became fascinated with oriental, especially Indian, music, and absorbed eastern and western styles in a remarkable fusion. In 1935 he emigrated to India where he died from cholera. His major works include *A World Requiem* (1921), a tone poem, *April-England* (1926–32), *Mantras* for orchestra (1930), *Quartetto Intimo* (1932; his 9th string quartet) and other chamber, orchestral, vocal and piano pieces.

FOULIS, Robert (1707–76) Scottish bookseller and printer. He set up shop in Glasgow in 1741, and in 1743 became printer to the university and produced the well-known editions of the classics, including the 'immaculate' *Horace* (with only six misprints). In 1744 he took his brother Andrew (1712–75) into partnership. In 1753 Robert established an academy of art in Glasgow which produced many prints, oil-paintings, etc. But the printing business declined with Andrew's death and Robert was compelled to sell off the pictures in London.

FOUQUÉ, Friedrich Heinrich Karl, Baron de la Motte (1777–1843) German writer and soldier, of Huguenot ancestry. He served as a Prussian cavalry officer in 1794 and 1813. The interval between these campaigns was devoted to literary pursuits, and the rest of his life was spent in Paris and on his estate at Nennhausen, and after 1830 in Halle. He published a long series of romances, based on Norse legend and old French poetry, his masterpiece being the fairy-tale *Undine* (1811).

FOUQUET, Jean (c.1420–c.1480) French painter, born in Tours. Nothing is known of his early life, but he visited Rome between 1445 and 1448 when pope **Eugenius IV** commissioned a portrait from him. Returning to Tours, he opened a prosperous workshop. In 1475 he received the official title of king's painter. In a copy of the *Antiquities of the Jews* of **Josephus**, there are paintings which have been attributed to him; similarly the *Hours of Étienne Chevalier* at Chantilly, and several panel portraits, including that of **Charles VII**, and **Agnes Sorel** as the Virgin. In his miniatures Fouquet combines Italian influences, such as architectural perspectives and ornamental detail, with the more northern traits of realistic and unidealized portrayal.

FOUQUET, Nicolas, Vicomte de Melun et de Vaux and Marquis de Belle-Isle (1615–80) French statesman, born in Paris. **Mazarin** made him *procureur-général* to the parlement of Paris (1650) and superintendent of finance (1653). He now became ambitious to succeed Mazarin, and to secure himself friends he distributed money lavishly. But **Louis XIV** himself took up the reins of power on Mazarin's death, and, instigated by **Colbert**, arrested Fouquet in September 1661. After a three years' trial he was sentenced to life imprisonment in the fortress of Pignerol, where he died. He has been falsely identified with the Man with the Iron Mask, who lived until 1703.

FOUQUIER-TINVILLE, Antoine Quentin (1747–95) French revolutionary politician, born in Hérouelles, public prosecutor to the revolutionary Tribunal from 1793. He superintended all the political executions during the Reign of Terror until July 1794, sending his friends, among them **Robespierre**, **Danton** and **Hébert**, to execution as cheerfully as he sent their enemies; at last he himself was guillotined.

FOURCROY, Antoine François de (1755–1809) French chemist, born in Paris. He qualified in medicine in 1780, became a professor at the Jardin des Plantes in 1784, and worked with **Lavoisier** and with **Vauquelin**. He became a leader in the active scientific life of France, and was minister of public instruction under **Napoleon** (1802–08). An able writer and lecturer, he did much to popularize Lavoisier's new theory of chemistry.

FOURDRINIER, Henry (1766–1854) and his brother **Sealy** (d.1847) English paper-makers and inventors. With the assistance of **Bryan Donkin** they patented in 1806 an improved design of a paper-making machine capable of producing a continuous sheet of paper. The liquid pulp is fed on to a wire mesh belt through which the water drains away, and the resulting damp web of paper is first heated and then passed between heavy rollers which give it the required smooth finish. The same basic type of machine, with further improvements, is still in use today.

FOURIER, (François Marie) Charles (1772–1837) French social theorist, born in Besançon. He worked for some years as a commercial traveller but became repelled and obsessed by the abuses of 'civilization'. After the revolution (in which he was imprisoned, and only just survived the guillotine) he published a number of utopian socialist works: *Théorie des quatre mouvements et des destinées générales* (1808), *Traité d'association domestique agricole* (1822) and *Le Nouveau Monde industriel et sociétaire* (1829); in these he advocated a reorganization of society into self-sufficient units (*phalanstères*) which would be scientifically planned to offer a maximum of both co-operation and self-fulfilment to their members; conventional living arrangements, property ownership and marriage would all be radically redesigned. Several experimental 'phalanxes' were founded in France and the USA, and though these failed, his ideas attracted great popular interest and many adherents.

FOURIER, Jean Baptiste Joseph, Baron de (1768–1830) French mathematician. He accompanied **Napoleon** to Egypt in 1798, and on his return in 1802 was made prefect of the department of Grenoble and created baron in 1808. In 1822 he published *Théorie analytique de la chaleur* in which he formulated and solved the partial differential equations for heat flow in a solid body. To do this he introduced the expansion of functions in trigonometric series, now called Fourier series, which have become an essential tool in mathematical physics and a major theme of analysis ever since. He also discovered an important theorem on the roots of algebraic equations.

FOURNEYRON, Benoît (1802–67) French engineer and inventor, born in St-Étienne, Loire, where he was educated at the École des Mines. In the early 19th century traditional water-wheels were still an important source of power in many industries, and Fourneyron determined to improve on their very low efficiency, of the order of 20 per cent. His prototype outward-flow radial turbine of 1827 developed about five horsepower at an efficiency of 65 per cent, and by 1833 he had built a larger 50 hp turbine with an efficiency of about 75 per cent. In 1895 Fourneyron turbines were installed in the Niagara Falls hydro-electric generating station, but their inherent drawback of a poor part-load performance led to their being replaced after a few years.

FOURNIER, Henri Alain See **ALAIN-FOURNIER**

FOURNIER D'ALBE, Edmund Edward (1868–1933) English physicist and inventor, born in London. In 1903 he produced an English–Irish dictionary. He invented the optophone (whereby blind people can read by ear), and among other things was the first to transmit a portrait from London by telephotography (1923).

FOWKE, Captain Francis (1823–65) Anglo-Irish engineer and architect, designer of the original plans for several major museums in Britain. Born in Belfast, he obtained a commission in the Royal Engineers on the strength of his drawing; in 1856 he was appointed architect and engineer to the government department of science and art. He planned the Albert Hall in London, produced the original designs for the Victoria and Albert Museum in London (completed by Sir **Aston Webb**), and planned the Royal Scottish Museum in Edinburgh.

FOWLER, Henry Watson (1858–1933) English lexicographer, born in Tonbridge, Kent, the compiler of *Modern English Usage*. Educated at Rugby School and Balliol College, Oxford, he became a schoolmaster at Sedbergh (1882–99), then went to London to try journalism. After the failure of his *Collected Essays*, published in 1903 at his own expense, he went to Guernsey (Channel Islands) where his brother Frank George (1871–1918) was a tomato-grower. Together they produced *The King's English* (1906) and the *Concise Oxford Dictionary* (1911). After his brother's death, Fowler produced the *Pocket Oxford Dictionary* (1924), and his immensely successful, if mannered, *Dictionary of Modern English Usage* (1926). The American counterpart is Margaret Nicholson's *A Dictionary of American English Usage, Based on Fowler*.

FOWLER, Sir John (1817–98) English civil engineer, born in Wadsley Hall, Sheffield. From an early age he engaged in railway construction, including the London Metropolitan Railway and the original Underground in London, and Victoria Station. River improvement and dock construction also occupied his attention. He was consulting engineer to **Ismail Pasha**, khedive of Egypt (1871–79). He designed the Pimlico Railway Bridge (1860), and, with Sir **Benjamin Baker**, the Forth Railway Bridge (1882–90).

FOWLER, William Alfred (1911–) American physicist, born in Pittsburgh. He studied at the California Institute of Technology and spent his entire working career there. In the 1950s with **Hoyle** and others he contributed to new theories of energy formation by nuclear reactions in stars; this and his later work in cosmology led to him sharing the Nobel prize for physics in 1983 with **Subrahmanyan Chandrasekhar**.

FOWLES, John Robert (1926–) English novelist, born in Leigh-on-Sea. Educated at Bedford School, Edinburgh University and New College, Oxford, where he studied French, he served in the Royal Marines (1945–46). Thereafter he taught in schools in France, and in Greece (1951–52), and London. An allusive and richly descriptive writer, his first novel was *The Collector* (1963), still perhaps his most sensational, in which he probes the reasons why a young man of one class 'collected', incarcerated and dissected the girl, from another class, whom he thought he loved. *The Magus* (1965; revised 1977) is the book which made his name. Drawing on his own experience, it is set in the 1960s on a remote Greek island. It is a disturbing and much-imitated yarn about an English school-teacher, his bizarre experiences, and his involvement with a master trickster. *The French Lieutenant's Woman* (1969), however, exceeded it in popularity, in large part due to the film version with **Meryl Streep** in the title role. Later books—*Daniel Martin* (1977), *Mantissa* (1982) and *A Maggot* (1985)—suffered a critical backlash but underlined his willingness to experiment, as well as the fecundity of his imagination. He also published a collection of short stories in *The Ebony Tower* (1974).

FOX, Sir Charles (1810–74) English civil engineer, born in Derby. He built the Crystal Palace, which housed the Great Exhibition (1851). He also did much railway construction with his two sons, Sir Charles Douglas (1840–1921) and Sir Francis (1844–1927), both eminent engineers.

FOX, Charles James (1749–1806) English Liberal statesman, third son of the 1st Lord Holland, born in London and educated at Eton and Hertford College, Oxford. At 19 he became MP for Midhurst. He later became a supporter of Lord **North**, and was made a Lord of Admiralty. In 1772 he resigned, but next year was named a commissioner of the Treasury. North dismissed him in 1775 after a quarrel. During the American war Fox was the most formidable opponent of the coercive measures of government. After the downfall of North (1782), he was one of the secretaries of state. In 1783 the North and Fox coalition was formed, and Fox resumed his former office; but the rejection of his India Bill by the Lords led to the resignation of his government. Now **Pitt** came into power, and the long contest between him and Fox began. The regency, the trial of **Warren Hastings** and the French Revolution gave ample scope to the talents and energies of Fox, who employed his influence to modify, if not to counteract, the policy of his great rival. He was a strenuous opponent of the war with France, and an advocate of non-intervention. After Pitt's death in January 1806, Fox, recalled to office, set in train negotiations for a peace with France. He was on the point of introducing a bill for the abolition of the slave trade when he died at. He was buried, near Pitt, in Westminster Abbey. Fox was a fast liver, addicted to gambling and drinking; his bearing towards his opponents was generous. **Burke** called him 'the greatest debater the world ever saw'.

FOX, George (1624–91) English religious leader, and founder of the Society of Friends, or 'Quakers', born in Fenny Drayton, Leicestershire. Apprenticed to a Nottingham shoemaker, and a Puritan by upbringing, at the age of 19 he rebelled against the formalism of the established church, and the state's control of it. Bible in hand he wandered about the country, often interrupting services, especially when conducted by formalist 'professors'. The 'inner light' was the central idea of his teaching. He inveighed against sacerdotalism and formalism, and was equally vehement against social convention. Priests, lawyers and soldiers were all obnoxious to him. The Lord forbade him to put off his hat to any, high or low. He denounced amusements. In 1646 he had a divine revelation that inspired him to preach a gospel of brotherly love, and call his society the 'Friends of Truth'. His life is a record of insults, persecutions and imprisonments. In 1656, the year after he and his followers refused to take the oath of abjuration, they had so increased that nearly one thousand of them were in jail. He visited Wales and Scotland, and having married Margaret Fell, widow of a judge and one of his followers, went to Barbados, Jamaica, America, Holland, and Germany, latterly accompanied by **William Penn**, **Robert Barclay**, and other Quaker leaders. His preaching and writings were often turgid, incoherent and mystical, but as a writer he will be remembered by his *Journal* (1874).

FOX, Henry Richard, 3rd Baron See **HOLLAND**

FOX, William Johnson (1786–1864) English orator and political writer, born in Wrentham near Southwold. Trained for the Independent ministry, he became a Unitarian, and delivered a series of rationalist addresses at his chapel in Finsbury. He aroused public feeling in favour of the Anti-Corn-Law League; and his *Letters of a Norwich Weaver Boy* on the necessity of free trade were widely quoted and read. From 1847 till 1863 he sat as an advanced Liberal for Oldham. His best parliamentary speeches were upon education.

FOXE, John (1516–87) English martyrologist, born in Boston in Lincolnshire. At 16 he entered Brasenose College, Oxford, and was fellow of Magdalen 1538–45. During the reign of **Mary I** he lived on the Continent, where he met **Knox**, **Grindal** and Whittingham. On **Elizabeth**'s accession he received a pension and a prebend of Salisbury (1563), but lived chiefly in London and was debarred from further preferment because of his objection to wearing the surplice. He published numerous controversial treatises and sermons, besides an apocalyptic Latin mystery play called *Christus Triumphans* (1556). His best known work is his *History of the Acts and Monuments of the Church*, popularly known as *Foxe's Book of Martyrs*, the first part of which was published in Latin at Strasbourg in 1554 (trans 1563). Written in vivid English prose, it is a history of the English Protestant martyrs from the 14th century to his own day.

FOXE, or Fox, Richard (c.1448–1528) English prelate, the founder of Corpus Christi College, Oxford. Born in Ropesley near Grantham, he studied at Oxford, Cambridge and Paris, and latterly became bishop successively of Exeter, Bath and Wells, Durham and Winchester. He founded Corpus Christi in 1517.

FOY, Maximilien Sébastien (1775–1825) French soldier, born in Ham. He entered the army in 1791, and held commands in the Italian (1801) and the Austrian (1805) campaigns. In 1807 **Napoleon** sent him to Turkey to assist Sultan **Selim III** against the Russians and British and hold the Dardanelles. From 1808 to 1812 he commanded in Portugal and Spain; he was wounded at Bussaco (1810), was impressed by **Wellington**'s manoeuvres at Salamanca, and was present at all the battles of the Pyrenees. He was wounded again at Waterloo (1815), where he commanded under **Ney**. Elected a deputy in 1819, he was a constant advocate of constitutional liberty. He wrote *Histoire de la guerre de la Péninsule* (1827).

FOYT, A J (Anthony Joseph Jr) (1935–) American motor-racing driver, born in Houston, Texas. He was the most successful driver ever in the Indianapolis 500 (the 500-mile, 200-lap race in the USA, started in 1911), winning it four times, in 1961, 1964, 1967 and 1977. He also won the equally famous Le Mans 24-hour race in 1967. He is the only racing driver to have won seven national championships. His 1983 biography was called *A.J.: The Life of America's Race Car Driver*. He also breeds and trains racehorses.

FRA ANGELICO See **ANGELICO**

FRA BARTOLOMMEO See **BARTOLOMMEO**

FRACASTORO, Girolamo (1483–1553) Italian scholar and physician, born in Verona. In 1502 he became professor of philosophy at Padua, but also practised successfully as a physician at Verona. He excelled as geographer, astronomer and mathematician. He wrote on the theory of music and wrote a Latin poem on the 'new' venereal disease, *Syphilis sive morbus Gallicus* (1530), from which the word *syphilis* is derived. His works on contagion contained an early version of the germ theory of disease.

FRA DIAVOLO, properly **Michele Pezza** (1760–1806) Italian brigand and renegade monk, born in Itri. For years he headed a band of desperados in the Calabrian mountains and evaded capture by skilful guerrilla warfare. In 1806 he attempted to excite Calabria against France, but was taken prisoner and executed at Naples.

FRAENKEL-CONRAT, Heinz (1910–) German-born American biochemist, born in Breslau. He studied medicine there and biochemistry in Edinburgh before moving to the USA in 1936 and joining the staff of the University of California at Berkeley in 1951. His work with viruses showed by 1955 that some could be split reversibly into a protein component and a nucleic acid, and that the latter alone was an infective agent; it was a 'living chemical' and a basic unit in the new science of molecular biology.

FRAGONARD, Jean Honoré (1732–1806) French painter and engraver, born in Grasse. He studied under **Boucher** and **Chardin** in Paris and gained the 'Prix de Rome' in 1752. A brilliant technician, he painted, with a loose touch and luscious colouring, genre pictures of contemporary life, the amours of the French court (notably *The Progress of Love* for Madame **du Barry**), and landscapes foreshadowing Impressionism. His *Bacchante endormie*, *La Chemise enlevée* and other works are in the Louvre and he is also represented in the Wallace Collection, London. The French Revolution ruined his career.

FRAME, Janet Paterson (1924–) New Zealand novelist and short story writer, born in Dunedin. She was educated at Otago University Teachers Training College. Her first book was a collection of short stories, *The Lagoon: Stories* (1952), which she followed five years later with a novel, *Owls Do Cry*. Having spent much time in psychiatric hospitals after severe mental breakdowns, her novels walk a tight-rope between danger and safety, where the looming threat of disorder attracts those it frightens. Honoured in her homeland but only belatedly receiving international recognition, key books are *Scented Gardens for the Blind* (1963), *A State of Siege* (1966), *Intensive Care* (1970) and *Living in the Maniototo* (1979).

FRAMPTON, Sir George James (1860–1928) English sculptor, born in London. He studied under **Frith**. Among his works are *Peter Pan* in Kensington Gardens, the Lions at the British Museum, and the **Edith Cavell** memorial, London.

FRAMPTON, Tregonwell (1641–1727) English racehorse trainer, the 'father of the turf'. He was born in Moreton near Dorchester, and from 1695 was royal trainer at Newmarket.

FRANCE, Anatole, pseud of **Anatole François Thibault** (1844–1924) French writer, the son of a Parisian bookseller. He began his literary career as a publisher's reader, 'blurb' writer and critic and in 1879 published his first volume of stories, *Jocaste et le chat maigre* and his first novel, *Le Crime de Sylvestre Bonnard* (1881). He had married in 1877 after being appointed keeper at the Senate Library, a position he was to lose in 1891 because of a literary quarrel with Leconte de Lisle. Under the literary patronage of Madame de Caillavet, whose love affair with him brought about his divorce (1893), he poured out a number of graceful, lively novels, critical studies and the like, such as the Parnassian *Le Livre de mon ami* (1885), a picture of childhood happiness, which stands in strong contrast to the later satirical, solipsistic and sceptical works such as *Les Opinions de Jérôme Coignard* (1893). Another remarkable collection of short stories was published under the title *Balthasar* (1889), and his vast classical knowledge found expression in *Thaïs* (1890). The **Dreyfus** case (1896) stirred him into politics as an opponent of church and state and champion of internationalism. His *L'Isle des pingouins* (1908), a fable of modern French history, was followed in 1912 by *Les Dieux ont soif*. He was awarded the Nobel prize for literature in 1921.

FRANCE, Celia (1921–) English dancer, born in London. Trained under **Marie Rambert**, **Antony Tudor** and Vera Volkova, she performed with Ballet Rambert from 1937 to 1940, moving to Sadler's Wells Royal Ballet in 1941 where she created roles in **Robert Helpmann**'s *Hamlet* (1942) and *Miracle in the Gorbals* (1944). Only months after returning to Ballet Rambert in 1950 she was invited by a group of dance patrons in Toronto to set up a new ballet company for Canada. In 1951 the National Ballet of Canada was founded under her directorship, and until her retirement in 1974 she built up a repertoire strong on Russian classics and work from British choreographers like **Frederick Ashton** and **Antony Tudor**.

FRANCESCA, Piero della or **Franceschi Piero de'** See **PIERO DELLA FRANCESCA**

FRANCESCA DA RIMINI (d.1285) Italian noblewoman, daughter of Giovanni da Polenta, lord of Ravenna. She was married to Giovanni the Lame, son of Malatesta, lord of Rimini, but she already loved Paolo, Giovanni's brother; and Giovanni, surprising the lovers together, slew them both. Her story was immortalized in **Dante**'s *Inferno*.

FRANCESCO DI GIORGIO (1439–1501/2) Italian painter, sculptor and architect, born in Siena. Most of his paintings were executed in his early career and now he is best known as an architect and architectural theorist. By 1477 he was working in Urbino where, as a military engineer, he designed the city's fortifications and, it is generally accepted, exploded the first land-mine in 1495 at a siege of Naples. He wrote a treatise on architecture and town planning, and **Leonardo da Vinci**, who knew him, owned one of his architectural manuscripts. He was appointed chief architect of Siena Cathedral in 1498.

FRANCESCO DI PAULA See **FRANCIS, St, of Paola**

FRANCHET D'ESPEREY, Louis Félix Marie François (1856–1942) French soldier, born in Algeria to a Royalist Catholic family. He graduated from St Cyr, followed by cavalry service in Algeria, Tunis, Indo-China, Morocco and Peking after the Boxer Rising. He was made commanding general of the French Fifth Army in 1914, gaining success at the Marne, but failed in 1918 to check the German offensive. **Clemenceau** made him commander-in-chief of allied armies in Macedonia, where from Salonika he overthrew Bulgaria and advanced as far as Budapest; only the end of the war prevented his dash for Berlin. He was made marshal of France in 1922, served in North Africa, had some links to the French extreme Right but refused to support **Pétain** in the replacement of France by the Vichy State.

FRANCHEVILLE, or **Franqueville, Pierre** (1548–1616) French sculptor, painter and architect, born in Cambrai. He was long domiciled in Italy, where he studied under **Bologna**. He executed the two colossal statues of Jupiter and Janus in the courtyard of the **Grimaldi** palace, Genoa, and five statues in the Nicolini Chapel in Florence. Recalled to France by **Henri IV** in 1604, he made the marble statue of David in the Louvre, Paris, and *Saturn carrying off Cybele* in the Tuileries Gardens.

FRANCIA, José Gaspar Rodriguez (1756–1840) dictator of Paraguay, born near Asunción. He studied theology, took his degree as a DD, and was a professor of divinity. Next he practised law for 30 years with a high reputation. He was past 50 when the revolution which shattered the Spanish yoke in South America broke out. Francia took a leading part in the movement in Paraguay, and on the declaration of independence in 1811 became secretary of the national junta, in 1813 one of the two consuls, and in 1814 dictator—first for three years, and then for life. Under his firm rule, which excluded all foreign intercourse, Paraguay rapidly improved. He was an unscrupulous despot, and yet he improved agriculture, promoted education, repressed superstition, and enforced strict justice in his law-courts, however little he regarded it for himself.

FRANCIA, or **Francesco Raibolini** (1450–1517) Italian goldsmith and painter, born in Bologna. He achieved fame as a craftsman in metal, in niello, and designed the first italic type for **Aldus Manutius**. As a painter in oils or in fresco he is particularly noted for his madonnas. His sons, Giacomo (c.1486–1557) and Giulio (1487–1543), were also painters.

FRANCIABIGIO, or **Francesco di Cristofano** (1482–1525) Florentine painter. He worked in collaboration with **Andrea del Sarto** on the church of the Annunziata and the Chiostro dello Scalzo and was much influenced by him and by **Raphael**. His *Madonna del Pozzo* was long thought to be by Raphael.

FRANCIS OF ASSISI, St, originally **Giovanni Bernadone** (1181–1226) Italian religious, founder of the Franciscan Order, born in Assisi, the son of a wealthy merchant. From his familiarity in his youth with the language of the troubadours, he acquired the name of *Il Francesco* ('the little Frenchman'). He was remarkable for his love of gaiety, of knightly exercises and ostentatious living. A serious illness was the first stage in his conversion, but in c.1205 he joined a military expedition. Halted by a dream, he returned and devoted himself to the care of the poor and the sick. In 1206 he was inspired to rebuild the ruined church of San Damiano. He renounced his patrimony, even his clothes, and lived as a hermit. His zeal became infectious and by 1210 he had a brotherhood of eleven for which he drew up a rule which was originally approved by Pope Innocent II. In 1212 he also founded the Poor Clares, a Franciscan order for women. Like the older forms of monastic life, the Franciscan system is founded on chastity, poverty and obedience, with the emphasis on the second. He repudiated all idea of property, even in those things for personal use. The order increased rapidly in membership; at the first general assembly in 1219, 5000 members were present; 500 more were claimants for admission. Francis himself went to Egypt (1223) and preached in the presence of the sultan, who promised better treatment for his Christian prisoners, and for the Franciscan order the privilege they have since enjoyed as guardians of the Holy Sepulchre. It is after his return to Italy that his biographers place the legend of his receiving, while in an ecstasy of prayer, the marks (*stigmata*) of the wounds of **Jesus Christ** (1224). He was canonized by Pope **Gregory IX** in 1228, and in 1980 was designated patron saint of ecology. His works consist of letters, sermons, ascetic treatises, proverbs and hymns, including the well-known *Canticle of the Sun*.

FRANCIS, of Paola, or **St Francesco di Paula** (1416–1507) Italian Franciscan monk, founder of Minim friars, born in Paola in Calabria. Of poor parents, he retired to a cave at 19 and was soon joined by others. He founded his order in 1436. Communities were established throughout Europe, but not in the British Isles. **Louis XI** of France summoned Francesco to his death-bed, and **Charles VIII** and **Louis XII** built him convents at Plessis-les-Tours and Amboise. He died at Plessis on Good Friday, and was canonized in 1519. His feast day is 2 April.

FRANCIS, of Sales (1567–1622) French Roman Catholic prelate and devotional writer, born in the family *château* of Sales in Savoy. Educated by the Jesuits in Paris, he studied civil law at Padua, took orders and became a distinguished preacher. He was successfully employed in a mission for the conversion of the Calvinistic population of Chablais, and in 1599 was appointed bishop of Nicopolis. In 1602 in Paris he was invited to preach the Lent at the Louvre and his lectures had so much influence in converting several Huguenot nobles that the king offered him a French bishopric, which he declined. Soon afterwards, on the death of his colleague, he became sole bishop of Geneva. His administration of his diocese was exemplary. His *Introduction to a Devout Life* (1608), immediately a classic, was the first manual of piety addressed to those living in society. He established a congregation of nuns of the order of the Visitation under the direction of Madame de Chantal, with whom he long maintained a correspondence, published in 1660. In 1665 he was canonized by **Alexander VII**.

FRANCIS, Xavier, St (1506–52) Spanish missionary, the 'Apostle of the Indies', born at his mother's castle of Xavero or Xavier near Sanguesa, in the Basque country. He was the youngest son of Juan de Jasso, privy-councillor to the king of Navarre. He studied, then lectured, at Paris, becoming acquainted with **Ignatius Loyola** with whom he founded the Jesuit Society (1534). Ordained priest in 1537, he lived in Rome in the service of the society, and was sent by John III of Portugal as a missionary to the Portuguese colonies of the east. He arrived at Goa in 1542 and worked with great energy and enthusiasm among the native population and the Europeans also. A year later he visited Travancore where he baptized 10000 natives. He then visited Malacca, the Banda Islands, Amboyna, the Moluccas and Ceylon, where he converted the king of Kandy and many of his people. In 1548 he founded a mission in Japan which flourished for 100 years. In 1552 he returned to Goa to organize a mission to China, but the intrigues of the Portuguese merchants and difficulties caused by the governor of Malacca wore out his strength and he died soon after reaching the island of San-chian near Canton. He was buried, finally, in Goa and was canonized in 1622. His only literary remains are Letters (1631) and a Catechism, with some short ascetic treatises.

FRANCIS I (1494–1547) king of France from 1515 to 1547 and notable patron of the Renaissance. Born in Cognac, he was the son of Charles, Count of Angoulême, and nephew and son-in-law of **Louis XII**, whom he succeeded at a time when France's rivalry with the Austrian Habsburg dynasty was at its most intense. Within a few months of his accession he crossed the Alps and gained control of Milan by the victory of Marignano. On the death of the emperor **Maximilian I** in 1519 he became a candidate for Holy Roman Emperor, but lost the election to the Habsburg **Charles I** of Spain (the emperor **Charles V**). In 1520 he met **Henry VIII** of England at the Field of Cloth of Gold, near Guînes, a costly and portentous occasion that underlined the power and prosperity of France. From then on, Francis waged intermittent war against the emperor Charles. In 1525 he was taken prisoner at the battle of Pavia, and only released the following year in return for renouncing Flanders, Artois, Burgundy, and all his Italian possessions. Two years later he was in a Holy League with the pope, England and Venice to check Charles' growing power, but once again lost Italy in the ensuing Treaty of Cambrai (1529). In a final war with Charles, Francis was victorious at Cérisolles (1544), but later that year was compelled to make a peace at Crespy in which he abandoned all his Italian claims. In religious affairs he won control over the French church through the concordat of Bologna (1516) and in general he tried to act the part of a peacemaker; but in the later years of his reign, he allowed the persecution of heretics in 1534, and was involved in the massacre of the Vaudois (Provençal peasants) in 1554. But he extended protection to humanist scholars like **Erasmus** and the French humanists of the Cercle de Meaux. Brilliant, flamboyant and cultured, he fostered learning and the arts, and created the palace of Fontainebleu.

FRANCIS II (1544–60) king of France from 1559 to 1560, eldest son of **Henri II** and **Catherine de' Medici**. A weak and sickly child, he was betrothed in 1548 to the five-year-old **Mary, Queen of Scots** and married to her in 1558. In 1559 he succeeded to the throne on the death of his father, but died the following year.

FRANCIS I (1708–65) Holy Roman Emperor from 1745, was the eldest son of Leopold, Duke of Lorraine and Grand Duke of Tuscany. In 1736 he married **Maria Theresa** of Austria.

FRANCIS II, of the Holy Roman Empire, I of Austria (1768–1835) in 1792 succeeded his father, **Leopold II** as Holy Roman Emperor. His first war with **Napoleon** ended with the Peace of Campo Formio (1797), when Austria lost the Netherlands and Lombardy and received in return Venice, Dalmatia and Istria; the second ended with the Treaty of Lunéville (1801) after defeats at Marengo and Hohenlinden. Then followed the campaign of 1805, when the French victories of Ulm and Austerlitz and the capture of Vienna compelled Austria to purchase peace at Pressburg by the truce of Venetia, Tyrol and Vorarlberg. On the foundation of the Confederation of the Rhine (1806), Francis renounced the title of German-Roman emperor, and retained that of emperor of Austria (Francis I), which he had assumed in 1804. In 1809 another attempt ended in the Treaty of Vienna with the loss of Salzburg, Carinthia, Trieste, part of Croatia, Dalmatia and Galicia. After a short alliance with France the emperor, in conjunction with the Russians and Prussians, assailed Napoleon and won the battle of Leipzig (1813). By the Treaty of Vienna (1815) Francis recovered, thanks to **Metternich**, Lombardy, Venetia and Galacia. His policy was conservative and anti-liberal, but personally he was an urbane and popular ruler.

FRANCIS JOSEF See **FRANZ JOSEPH**

FRANCIS, Dick (Richard Stanley) (1920–) English jockey and author, born in Surrey, a highly successful example of a top-class sportsman who became a writer on his own subject. Starting as an amateur National Hunt jockey he turned professional comparatively late, at the age of 28. As a rider he is best remembered for the Grand National of 1956 when, on the Queen Mother's (see **Elizabeth**) Devon Loch, he was on the point of winning when the horse collapsed 50 yards from the winning post. He retired the following year and became a racing correspondent with the *Daily Express*. He also began writing popular thrillers with a racing background which won him the Golden Dagger award of the American Crime Writers' Association in 1980. His autobiography, *The Sport of Queens*, was published in 1957.

FRANCIS, James Bicheno (1815–92) English-born American engineer and inventor, born in South Leigh, Oxfordshire. He emigrated to the USA in 1833, working first on railroad construction. By 1837 he had been appointed chief engineer to the 'Proprietors of the Locks and Canals on the Merrimack River', and when they decided in 1845 to develop the river's power potential he began to work on the design of an inward-flow turbine that now bears his name. He is also remembered by the Francis formula for the flow of water over weirs.

FRANCIS, John (1811–82) English journalist, born in Bermondsey. He was publisher of the *Athenaeum* from 1831, and did much for the repeal of fiscal restrictions on the press.

FRANCIS, Sir Philip (1740–1818) British civil servant, born in Dublin and educated at St Paul's School, London. After serving in many minor government posts he became in 1773 a member of the Council of Bengal; in 1780 he fought a duel with **Warren Hastings** (with whom he was always quarrelling), and was seriously wounded. In 1781 he returned home with a fortune gained at whist. He entered parliament in 1784. He was energetic in the proceedings against Hastings, wrote many pamphlets, and was made a KCB in 1806. He was devoted to the prince-regent, supported **Wilberforce** against the slave trade and founded the 'Friends of the People'. In 1814 he married a second wife whom he encouraged in her belief that he was the author of the Letters of Junius, printed in the *Public Advertiser* (1769–72).

FRANCIS, Sam (1923–) American abstract painter, born in San Mateo, California. He began as a medical student but turned to painting in 1945, studying at the California School of Fine Arts, San Francisco. He visited Paris in 1950 and had his first one-man show there in 1952. He also visited Japan, and his technique, applying thinned paint in small irregular blots which he allowed to trickle down the surface to create an all-over pattern, reflects both American Action Painting of the late 1940s and early 1950s, and traditional oriental calligraphy.

FRANCK, César Auguste (1822–90) Belgian-born French composer, born in Liège of German family. He studied at Liège Conservatoire at an early age, and later at Paris, where he acquired French nationality. A student of great promise, he was in the running for the Prix de Rome when his father, who wanted him to be virtuoso pianist, withdrew him from the conservatoire and started him on a round of concerts. He was fond of composition, but his ideas were somewhat outlandish in the eyes of his teachers, and it was not until his three piano trios (1842–43) had been subscribed by a number of eminent musicians that he received any recognition as a composer, and even these pieces were hardly heard in France, being better known in Germany, where they were sponsored by **Liszt**. In 1848 he married, and settled in Paris as a teacher and organist, composing in his spare time. In 1872 he was made organ professor at the conservatoire, and devoted more time to composition, finishing in 1879 his tone-poem *Les Béatitudes*, which met with no success until three years after his death. Much of his considerable output was undistinguished; his reputation rests on a few masterpieces all written after the age of 50, the best-known being his string quartet (composed in the year of his death, yet the first of his works to win real public acclaim), his symphony in D minor, his violin sonata, his *Variations symphoniques* for piano and orchestra, and his tone poem *Le Chasseur maudit*. Some of his organ music is also often performed. Though fame came late, his death after a street accident was untimely, for he was in robust health and might have gone on to consolidate his newly-found reputation.

FRANCK, James (1882–1964) German-born American physicist, born in Hamburg. Professor of physics at Göttingen (1920), he worked on research with **Gustav Hertz** into the laws governing the transfer of energy between molecules, for which they were jointly awarded the Nobel prize for physics in 1925. He emigrated to the USA in 1935 and was professor of physical chemistry at Chicago (1938–49). He worked on the development of the atomic bomb in World War II, but headed the Franck Committee of scientists who urged that the bomb should not be used.

FRANCK, Sebastian (1499–1542) German humanist, born in Donauwörth. After being ordained a priest he was converted to Protestantism, but his insistence upon moral reform rather than dogma caused him to drift away from **Luther**. In 1528 he published a treatise against drunkenness, followed in 1531 by his *Chronica*, perhaps the first attempt at a universal German history. Its advocacy of religious tolerance led to his banishment from Strasbourg and in 1539 he was expelled from Ulm for his *Paradoxa* (1534). He also published one of the earliest collections of German proverbs (1541).

FRANCKE, August Hermann (1663–1727) German pietist and educationist, born in Lübeck. In 1692 he became professor of oriental languages at Halle, in 1698 of theology. A pupil of **Philipp Spener**, he became widely known for his philanthropic activities, founding schools and orphanages which were later combined into the Francke Institute.

FRANCO (BAHAMONDE), Francisco (1892–1975) Spanish military dictator, born in El Ferrol, Galicia. He commanded the Spanish Foreign Legion in Morocco, became chief of staff in 1935, and in 1936, deemed politically dangerous, was sent to govern the Canaries. From there he flew to Morocco, and, landing troops in Spain, from 1936 to 1939 overthrew the republican government in a bitter civil war, with bodily aid from **Hitler** and **Mussolini** and with himself as head (*Caudillo*) of the régime. During World War II he skilfully kept Spain neutral, although his speeches were markedly pro-German. In 1947 he intimated that after his death Spain would again become a monarchy. Despite economic difficulties and quarrels with his own party, Franco managed to remain firmly in control, and his pact with the USA for military bases in Spain in return for economic aid helped to foster tacit acceptance of his undemocratic régime by other western powers. He was succeeded as Spanish leader by King **Juan Carlos I**.

FRANGIPANI a noble Roman family which figured in the **Guelf** and Ghibelline quarrels of the 12th and 13th centuries causing a schism in the church and the election of an antipope, Gregory VIII.

FRANK, Anne (1929–45) German Jewish concentration-camp victim, born in Frankfurt-am-Main. She fled from the Nazis to Holland in 1933 with her family, and after the Nazi occupation of Holland hid with her family and four others in a sealed-off office back-room in Amsterdam from 1942 until they were betrayed in August 1944. She died in Belsen concentration camp. The lively, moving diary she kept during her concealment was published in 1947 (trans 1952), was dramatized and filmed, and Anne Frank became a symbol of suffering under the Nazis. Her name was given to villages and schools for refugee children throughout western Europe.

FRANK, Bruno (1887–1945) German author, born in Stuttgart. He wrote historical novels, such as *Die Fürstin* (1915), *Aus vielen Jahren* (1937) and *Die Tochter* (1943), in a style reminiscent of **Thomas Mann**. His lyric poetry is also noteworthy. Of Jewish descent, he fled the Nazi régime and went to Beverly Hills in California. His *Der Reisepass* (1937) was directed against National Socialism.

FRANK, Hans (1900–46) German Nazi politician, born in Karlsruhe. He was minister of justice in Bavaria (1933), president of the German Law Academy (1934) and governor-general in 1939 of Poland, where he established concentration camps and conducted a policy of persecution and extermination. He was condemned as a war criminal and hanged.

FRANK, Ilya Mikhailovich (1908–) Soviet physicist, born in St Petersburg (now Leningrad). He was educated at Moscow State University, and in 1944 he was appointed professor of physics there, after working for four years at the State Optical Institute. By 1937, working with **P A Cherenkov** and **I Y Tamm**, they were able to explain the 'Cherenkov effect'. They showed that the effect arises when a charged particle traverses a medium when moving at a speed greater than the speed of light in that medium. The effect is dramatically visible in the blue glow in a uranium reactor core containing heavy water. Cherenkov, Frank and Tamm shared the Nobel prize for physics in 1958.

FRANK, Johann Peter (1745–1821) German physician, medical reformer and author, born in Rotalben, in the Palatinate. He studied medicine at several German and French universities (MD Heidelberg University). His active, peripatetic career took him throughout eastern Europe, as he held various university, hospital, court and administrative positions in Italy, Austria, Germany and Russia. One of his patrons was the 'enlightened despot' **Joseph II** of Austria. He wrote many medical works, but his major achievement was the multi-volume *System of a Complete Medical Police*, published between 1779 and 1825, in which he described a comprehensive system of medical care which, in combining preventative and curative medical services, was an early vision of the welfare state.

FRANK, Leonhard (1882–1961) German poet and novelist, born in Würzburg. He fought in World War I and conceived a horror of war which led to his strongly pacifist *Der Mensch ist gut* (1917). His *Karl und Anna* (1928), also a war story, was successfully turned into a play. He left Germany and went to live in Hollywood, where he wrote several books, including *Von drei Millionen drei* (1932).

FRANK, Waldo David (1889–1967) American novelist and journalist, born in Long Branch, New Jersey. He wrote novels and other works coloured by mysticism and expressionism, including *City Block* (1922), *The Unwelcome Man* (1917), *The Rediscovery of America* (1929) and the play *New Year's Eve* (1939).

FRANKAU, Gilbert (1884–1953) English novelist, born in London. A son of Julia Frankau, who wrote under the name of 'Frank Danby', writing came easily to him. His early works were great successes and he continued to write best-sellers, for he was, above everything, a professional writer, with a flair for anticipating popular taste. Of his many best-sellers, the following are notable: *One of Us* (1912), *Peter Jackson, Cigar Merchant* (1919), *Men, Maids and Mustard-Pots* (1923), *World without End* (1943).

FRANKAU, Pamela (1908–67) English novelist, daughter of **Gilbert Frankau**. She epitomized in her early novels such as in *The Marriage of Harlequin*, her first novel, the era of the 'bright young things'. Like her father, a true professional, she outgrew this phase and her later novels were serious in intent. Typical are *The Willow Cabin* (1949) and *A Wreath for The Enemy* (1954). *The Offshore Light* (1952) was written under the pseudonym Eliot Naylor.

FRANKENTHALER, Helen (1928–) American abstract painter, born in New York. She studied under the Mexican painter **Rufino Tamayo** and at Bennington College, Vermont. Influenced by **Hans Hofmann**, with whom she studied briefly at the Art Students' League in New York in 1950, and **Jackson Pollock**, she developed a technique of applying very thin paint to unprimed canvas, allowing it to soak in and create atmospheric stains and blots on the surface. Her best-known picture is *Mountains and Sea* (1952). She married the artist **Robert Motherwell** in 1955, and has taught at various universities in the USA.

FRANKFURTER, Felix (1882–1965) American law teacher and judge, born in Vienna. Educated at the College of the City of New York and at Harvard, he taught at the Harvard Law School (1914–39) and served as an associate justice of the US Supreme Court (1939–62). He was a noted supporter of civil liberties and founded the American Civil Liberties Union, though in court he advocated judicial restraint in opposing legislative and executive policy. In constitutional cases he claimed that judges should consider whether legislators could reasonably have enacted such a law. His major works are *The Business of the Supreme Court* (with JM Landis, 1927) and *The Public and its Government* (1930).

FRANKL, Ludwig, Ritter von Hochwart (1810–93) Austrian poet of Jewish origin, a professor of aesthetics at the Vienna Conservatory (1851). He established the first Jewish school in Jerusalem (1856). He wrote epics, ballads, satirical poems, many of which have been translated.

FRANKLAND, Sir Edward (1825–99) English organic chemist, born in Churchtown, Lancashire, became professor at the Royal Institution, London, in 1863. He propounded the theory of valency (1852–60) and with **Lockyer** discovered helium in the sun's atmosphere in 1868. He was an expert on sanitation. He was awarded the Copley medal in 1894.

FRANKLIN, Aretha (1942–) American soul singer and pianist, born in Memphis, Tennessee. Variously known as 'Lady Soul' and the 'Queen Of Soul', she has had more million-selling singles than any other female recording artist. The daughter of a well-known Detroit preacher and gospel singer, she had established her name on the gospel circuit with his New Bethel Baptist Church and his gospelling tours before she signed a recording contract with Columbia Records in 1960. Although she spent six years with that label and recorded several successful albums, it was only after moving to Atlantic Records in 1967 that her full potential was realized. Producer Jerry Wexler capitalized on both her piano-playing skills and her gospel roots, most notably on *I Never Loved A Man The Way I Love You* (1967) and on *Lady Soul* (1968). In 1972 she returned to the church with her album *Amazing Grace*, a two-record set of gospel songs recorded live in Los Angeles. Subsequent albums have included *Everything I Feel in Me* (1974), *Almighty Fire* (1978), *Love All The Hurt Away* (1981), *Get It Right* (1983) and *Aretha* (1986). In 1987 she recorded *One Lord, One Faith, One Baptism* in her father's Detroit church.

FRANKLIN, Benjamin (1706–90) American statesman and scientist, youngest son and 15th child of a family of 17, born in Boston, Massachusetts. He was apprenticed at twelve to his brother James, a printer, who started a newspaper, the *New England Courant*, in 1709. When James was imprisoned by the speaker of the Assembly for his outspoken criticism, Benjamin assumed the paper's management. The two brothers later fell out and Benjamin drifted to Philadelphia, where he secured work as a printer. During 1724–26 he worked for 18 months in London, before returning to Philadelphia to establish his own successful printing house, and in 1729 he purchased the *Pennsylvania Gazette*. A year later, he married Deborah Read, by whom he had two children, a son who died in his youth, and a daughter, Sally. He also had an illegitimate son, William. In 1732 he commenced the publication of *Poor Richard's Almanac*, which attained an unprecedented circulation. In 1736 Franklin was appointed clerk of the Assembly, in 1737 postmaster of Philadelphia, and in 1754 deputy postmaster-general for the colonies, being elected and re-elected a member of the Assembly almost uninterruptedly until his first mission to England. In 1746 he commenced his famous researches in electricity which made him an FRS. He brought out fully the distinction between positive and negative electricity; he proved that lightning and electricity are identical; and he suggested the protecting of buildings by lightning-conductors. Further, he discovered the course of storms over the North-American continent; the course of the Gulf Stream, its high temperature, and the use of the thermometer in navigating it; and the various powers of different colours to absorb solar heat. In 1757 he was sent to England to insist upon the right of the province to tax the proprietors of land held under the **Penn** charter for the cost of defending it from the French and Indians, succeeded in his mission, and during his five years' absence received honorary degrees from Oxford and Edinburgh. In 1764 he was again sent to England to contest the pretensions of parliament to tax the American colonies without representation. The differences, however, between the British government and the colonies became too grave to be reconciled by negotiation, and in 1775 Franklin returned to the USA, where he participated actively in the deliberations which resulted in the Declaration of Independence on 4 July 1776. To secure foreign assistance in the war Franklin was sent to Paris in 1776. His skill as a negotiator and his personal popularity, reinforced by the antipathy of French and English, favoured his mission, and on 6 February 1778, a treaty of alliance was signed, while munitions of war and money were sent from France. On 3 September 1783, his mission was crowned with success through England's recognition of the independence of the United States. Franklin was US minister in Paris till 1785, when he returned to Philadelphia, and was elected president of the state of Pennsylvania, a post to which he was twice re-elected. He was also a delegate to the convention which framed the constitution of the USA. In 1788 he retired from public life.

FRANKLIN, Frederic (1914–) English dancer, ballet director and teacher, born in Liverpool. His musical-comedy training led to stints in cabarets and casinos in London and Paris, until **Anton Dolin** invited him to join the Markova-Dolin Ballet (1935–37). He consolidated his international stardom as a member of Ballet Russe de Monte Carlo (1938–49 and 1954–56), originating roles in such ballets as **Leonide Massine**'s *Gaite Parisienne* (1938) and **Agnes De Mille**'s *Rodeo* (1942, as the Champion Roper). He became company ballet master in 1944. Later he worked with various companies including his own Slavenska-Franklin Ballet (founded 1951), National Ballet of Washington (artistic director, 1962–74), Pittsburgh Ballet Theatre (co-director) and Chicago Ballet.

FRANKLIN, Sir John (1786–1847) English arctic explorer, born in Spilsby, Lincolnshire. He entered the navy at 14 and was present at the battles of Copenhagen (1801) and Trafalgar (1805). In 1818 he was in a fruitless expedition to Spitsbergen, and made extensive land journeys along the Coppermine river and the Canadian arctic coast, including the Mackenzie River (1819–22, 1825–29). He was governor of Van Diemen's Land (Tasmania) from 1834 to 1845. In 1845 he commanded the *Erebus* and *Terror* in an attempt to discover the Northwest passage. Leaving Baffin Bay via Lancaster Sound, they wintered at Beechey Island, then, following their instructions to turn south at 98° long and work along the coast of the North American mainland, they were beleaguered by thick ice in the Victoria Strait (1846). Franklin died on 11 June, 1847. The 105 survivors under Captain Crozier attempted to walk to one of the Hudson's Bay Company's posts on Back's River, but died of starvation and scurvy. Numerous relief expeditions were sent out, and one of them, organized by Franklin's widow, found a record of the expedition to April 1848 with definite proof that Franklin had discovered the Northwest passage. He was commemorated in Westminster Abbey (1875). Franklin's Gull is named after him.

FRANKLIN, John Hope (1915–) American historian, born in Rentiesville, Oklahoma, the son of a black attorney. Educated at Fisk University and Harvard, he taught at several black institutions, joining Howard University in 1947 when he published his fine survey of the American black historical experience,

From Slavery to Freedom: A History of American Negroes (1947). In 1956 he became chairman of the department of history at Brooklyn College, and published *The Militant South*. His moderate *Reconstruction after the Civil War* (1961) laid a judicious foundation for a reappraisal of the post-Civil War era from the black standpoint, which was where work was most urgently needed. His remarkable blend of generosity to whites and understanding of blacks showed itself characteristically in *The Emancipation Proclamation* (1963). He became professor of American history at Chicago University in 1964, and was the first black president of the American Historical Association (1978–79). He also wrote *Racial Equality in America* (1976).

FRANKLIN, (Stella Marian Sarah) Miles, pseud **'Brent of Bin Bin'** (1879–1954) Australian novelist, born in Talbingo, near Tamut, New South Wales. Known to her family as Stella, she was a fifth-generation Australian, her great-great-grandfather having been a convict in the First Fleet. She was the eldest of seven children and spent her first ten years at Brindabella, a farm in the bush country. Later the family moved downmarket to a district fictionalized in *My Brilliant Career* (1901) as Possum Gully. Eventually they settled in a Sydney suburb. Having flirted with nursing she turned to journalism, became involved in the feminist movement, wrote *My Brilliant Career*, and emigrated in 1906 to the USA, where she worked as secretary to the Women's Trade Union League. Moving to England in 1915, despite a deep aversion to war, she helped with the war effort, serving with the Scottish Women's Hospital at Ostrovo, in Macedonia. In 1927 she returned permanently to Australia, where the 'Brent of Bin' series, starting with *Up the Country* (1928), made the pseudonymous author the subject of much speculation. Her best work appeared under her own name, including the autobiographical novels *All That Swagger* (1936) and *My Career Goes Bung* (1946), and a collection of essays on Australian literature, *Laughter, Not for a Cage* (1956). The annual Miles Franklin awards are now among Australia's most prestigious literary prizes.

FRANKLIN, Rosalind Elsie (1920–58) English X-ray crystallographer, born in London. She studied chemistry at Cambridge and worked in research associations in Britain and in Paris (1947–50) before joining a research group at King's College, London (1951–53). There she extended the X-ray diffraction studies by **Maurice Wilkins** on DNA, and obtained exceptionally good diffraction photographs using a hydrated form of DNA; these were of great value to **James Dewey Watson** and **Francis Crick** in their deduction of the full structure of DNA which effectively created modern molecular biology in 1953.

FRANQUEVILLE, Pierre See **FRANCHEVILLE**

FRANZ, Robert (1815–92) German composer, born in Halle. He published over 250 songs, a Kyrie, chorales, and arrangements of the vocal masterpieces of **J S Bach** and **Handel**.

FRANZ FERDINAND (1863–1914) archduke of Austria, nephew and heir-apparent (from 1896) to the emperor **Franz Joseph**. On a visit to Sarajevo (in modern Yugoslavia) in June 1914 he and his wife Sophie were assassinated by a group of young Serbian nationalists led by **Gavrilo Princip**. Austria used the incident as a pretext for attacking Serbia, which precipitated World War I.

FRANZ JOSEPH, properly **Franz Joseph I** (1830–1916) emperor of Austria (1848), king of Hungary (1867), son of the archduke Francis (Emperor **Francis I**'s son), and nephew of **Ferdinand I**, whom he succeeded. His first task was to subdue the Hungarian revolt and pacify Lombardy. Having accomplished this, the aspirations of the various nationalities of the empire were rigorously suppressed, and a determined effort made to fuse them into one state; the emperor reasserted his claim to rule as an absolute sovereign; the policy of bureaucratic centralization was again reverted to; and a close alliance was entered into with the church to combat liberal progress. In 1859 Lombardy was wrested from Austria by Sardinia; and by the war with Prussia in 1866 Austria was excluded from Germany, and compelled to surrender Venetia to Sardinia, Prussia's ally. The emperor then adopted a more conciliatory policy towards the various national groups within the empire. His annexation of Bosnia-Herzegovina in 1908 agitated Europe; his attack on Serbia in 1914 precipitated World War I. By the suicide of his son Rudolf (1858–89), and the murder at Sarajevo of his heir-apparent, **Franz Ferdinand**, eldest son of the emperor's brother Charles Louis (1833–96), the crown passed to **Charles I**. Elizabeth of Bavaria (1837–98), Franz Joseph's wife, was fatally stabbed in Geneva by an anarchist.

FRANZOS, Karl Emil (1848–1904) Austrian novelist, born of Jewish parentage in Podolia on the Austro-Russian border. His themes and settings were taken from Galicia, the Bukovina, south Russia and Romania; his novels, which contain vivid pictures of life among Jews and peasants, include *Aus Halbasien* (1876), *Die Juden von Barnow* (1877), *Ein Kampf ums Recht* (1882) and *Der Pojaz* (1905).

FRASCH, Hermann (1851–1914) German-born American industrial chemist, born in Gailsdorf, Württemberg. He emigrated to the USA in 1868 and worked there and in Canada as a chemist and oil man. He is best known for the Frasch process of extracting sulphur from deep underground deposits by the use of superheated steam.

FRASER, Sir Alexander (c.1537–1623) Scottish land-owner and entrepreneur, the 7th laird of Philorth in Aberdeenshire. He founded the harbour-town of Fraserburgh on his estates in 1576. In 1592 he founded a short-lived University of Fraserburgh, which closed down in 1597 from lack of funds.

FRASER, Bruce Austin, 1st Baron Fraser of North Cape (1888–1981) English naval officer. Educated at Bradfield College, he entered the Royal Navy in 1902 and became a gunnery specialist. He served at sea in World War I and was chief of staff Mediterranean Fleet (1938–39). In World War II he was controller of the navy (1939–42), commander-in-chief Home Fleet (1943–44), Eastern Fleet (1944) and British Pacific Fleet (1945–46). He was a British signatory at the Tokyo Bay Peace Ceremony (1945). He was first sea lord from 1948 to 1951.

FRASER, Dawn (1937–) Australian swimmer, born in Balmain, Sydney. Her talent was discovered as a schoolgirl, while swimming in the harbourside pool in Birchgrove which now bears her name. In her swimming career she broke 27 world records and won 29 Australian championships. Her outstanding achievement was in winning gold medals at three successive Olympic Games—Melbourne (1956), Rome (1960) and Tokyo (1964), in each case setting a new Olympic record. At the Rome games she broke three world records within one hour. In 1964 she became the first woman to break the 'magic minute' for the 100 metres with a time of 58.9 seconds, a record which was to stand for 20 years. Although her rebellious spirit often brought her into conflict with the swimming authorities, she was awarded the MBE in 1967.

FRASER, John Malcolm (1930–) Australian political leader, born in Melbourne, educated at Melbourne Grammar School and Oxford University. In 1955 he became the youngest MP in the House of Representatives and was minister for the army (1966–68), minister for defence (1969–71), and minister for education and science (1968–9 and 1971–2). He stands to the right of his party, the Liberals, and succeeded Bill Snedden as their leader in March 1975. After the constitutional crisis of November 1975 he was asked to lead a caretaker government until the elections in December, in which the Liberal-National Country coalition he was leading was returned to power. He remained prime minister until his party's defeat in the elections of 1983 by the Labor party, for which it was only the second victory in 33 years; soon after, he resigned his parliamentary seat. He is a farmer, owning a large estate at Nareen, W Victoria.

FRASER, Marjory Kennedy (1857–1930) Scottish singer and folk-song collector, born in Perth. One of a large musical family, she trained in Paris as a concert singer. In 1882 she started studying Gaelic music, took lessons in Gaelic, and started collecting Hebridean folk-songs, to which she gave modern harmonic settings. In 1909 she published *Songs of the Hebrides*. She also wrote the libretto of **Granville Bantock**'s opera *The Seal Woman*.

FRASER, Peter (1884–1950) Scots-born New Zealand politician, born in Fearn, Ross and Cromarty. In 1910 he emigrated to New Zealand, and was Labour prime minister from 1940 to 1949.

FRASER, Simon See **LOVAT, Lord**

FRASER, Simon (1776–1862) Canadian fur trader, and discoverer of the Fraser River, born in Bennington, New York (now Vermont). He settled in Cornwall, Ontario, after the death of his Scottish father who was killed fighting in the American War of Independence. Working as a clerk in the North-West Company he was promoted to partner in 1801, and was sent in 1805 to establish the first trading posts in the Rocky Mountains. Following **Mackenzie**'s route he opened up a vast area which he called New Caledonia between the plains and the Pacific, and in 1808 followed the Fraser River, named after him, to its mouth. He headed the Red River Department of the North-West Company during conflict with settlers of the rival Hudson's Bay Company, before his retirement in 1818.

FRASER, Sir William (1816–98) Scottish archivist. A deputy keeper of records of Scotland (1880–92), he issued a series of sumptuous family histories with original charters, valuable as sources for Scottish history. By his will he endowed the Edinburgh chair of Scottish history, financed the *Scottish Peerage*, and founded the Fraser Homes.

FRAUNHOFER, Joseph von (1787–1826) German physicist, born in Straubing in Bavaria. In 1807 he founded an optical institute at Munich, and improved prisms and telescopes, which enabled him to discover the dark lines in the sun's spectrum, called Fraunhofer's lines. In 1823 he became professor and academician at Munich.

FRAYN, Michael (1933–) English dramatist, journalist and humorist, born in London. A journalist by training, he has published a number of comic novels, among them *The Tin Men* (1965), and *Towards the End of the Morning* (1967), about the newspaper business. His stage plays include *Alphabetical Order* (1975), set in the library of a provincial newspaper; *Clouds* (1976), about two rival journalists in Cuba; *Noises Off* (1982), a frenetic farce about putting on a frenetic farce; and *Benefactors* (1984), a piece about middle class mores. His finest play is *Make and Break* (1980), a satirical look at the lives of salesmen at a foreign trade fair. He is also a translator of **Chekhov**.

FRAZER, Sir James George (1854–1941) Scottish anthropologist and folklorist, born in Glasgow. Educated at Larchfield Academy, Helensburgh, at Glasgow University and Trinity College, Cambridge, he became a classics fellow there. He studied law and was called to the English bar in 1879, but never practised, and turned his attention to anthropology which, in combination with his classical studies, produced his monumental work, *The Golden Bough: A Study in Comparative Religion* (12 vols, 1890–1915), named after the golden bough in the sacred grove at Nemi, near Rome. His other anthropological works included *Totemism* (1884), *Totemism and Exogamy* (1911), *The Belief in Immortality and the Worship of the Dead* (1913–22), and *Magic and Religion* (1944). He also published an edition of **Sallust** (1884), and a translation of **Pausanias**'s *Description of Greece* (1898). He was professor of social anthropology at Liverpool (1907–08) and Cambridge (from 1908).

FRÉCHETTE, Louis Honoré (1839–1908) 'Canadian laureate', born in Levis, Quebec. He was called to the bar, and elected to the Dominion parliament in 1874. He published prose works and plays, and his poems *Mes Loisirs* (1863), *La Voix d'un Exilé* (1867) and others, were 'crowned' by the French Academy.

FREDEGOND (d.597) Frankish queen, first mistress, then wife, of Chilperic, king of Neustria. She waged a relentless feud with **Brunhilda**, wife of Sigbert, king of Austrasia, and sister of Chilperic of Neustria's first wife, a feud intensified by the rivalry between the two kingdoms.

FREDERIC, Harold (1856–96) American novelist, born in Utica, New York. After a poverty-stricken youth, he became a journalist and was in 1884 appointed European correspondent of *The New York Times*. He wrote *Seth's Brother's Wife* (1887), *The Return of the O'Mahony* (1892) and others, novels depicting his own background, but his best work is *The Damnation of Theron Ware* (1896).

FREDERICK I, Barbarossa (Redbeard) (c.1123–1190) Holy Roman Emperor, of the **Hohenstaufen** family, considered one of the greatest German monarchs. He succeeded his father, Duke Frederick of Swabia, in 1147, and his uncle **Conrad III**, as emperor in 1152. His reign was one long struggle against refractory vassals at home and the turbulent civic republics of Lombardy and the pope in Italy. The capture in 1162 of Milan brought all the recalcitrant states of Italy to submission. Five years later he even seemed on the point of subduing the pope; he had taken Rome by storm, when his army was suddenly overwhelmed by a terrible plague. This was the signal for revolt in Lombardy; but it was not until 1174 that Frederick was able to undertake the reduction of his Italian subjects. He incurred a severe defeat at Legnano (1176), but this proved to be more valuable to him than his previous successes. It led him to change his previous policy to one of clemency and concession, whereby the Lombards were converted into contented subjects. In 1177 he acknowledged **Alexander III** as pope, and thus paved the way for the final pacification of 1183. In Germany, Frederick conciliated his strongest vassals by giving them new fiefs or by raising their titular dignities, whilst the weaker he kept in check by conferring additional rights upon the municipal communities. Thus, he elevated Austria to the rank of a duchy, created Duke Ladislaus of Bohemia king, and granted Brunswick and Lüneberg to the **Guelf** princes. He also quelled the rebellious spirit of **Henry the Lion** of Bavaria, and asserted his feudal superiority over Poland, Hungary, Denmark and Burgundy. When at the height of his power he led the Third Crusade against **Saladin** in 1189. He defeated the Muslims at Philomelium and Iconium, but drowned in the following year while crossing the river Saleph in Cilicia. He was buried in the church of St Peter at Antioch. He was succeeded by his son, **Henry VI**.

FREDERICK II, of Germany (1194–1250) Holy Roman Emperor, called 'The Wonder of the World', the last great ruler of the **Hohenstaufen** dynasty. Born in Jesi, near Ancona, he was the grandson of **Frederick I, 'Barbarossa'** and the son of the emperor **Henry VI** and of Constance, heiress of Sicily, of which he became king in 1198. In 1212 he wrested the imperial crown from **Otto IV**, and on his promising to undertake a crusade to the Holy Land, Pope **Innocent III** (who had been his guardian) sanctioned his coronation in 1215 (he was crowned in 1220). Frederick's first priority was the consolidation of imperial power in Italy by reducing the pontificate to a mere archiepiscopal dignity. To that end he devoted himself to organizing his Italian territories: he founded the University of Naples, encouraged the medical school of Salerno, patronized art and literature, and commissioned his chancellor to draw up a code of laws to suit his German and Italian subjects. His departure to the Holy Land was originally fixed for 1223, but difficulties in Italy led to five years' delay. Through his second marriage to Isabella of Brienne (1225) he had a claim to the throne of Jerusalem; when he eventually embarked on his crusade (1228–29) he captured Bethlehem and Nazareth, and crowned himself king of Jerusalem. On his return to Italy he had to reconquer his Neapolitan dominions from papal troops, and the rest of his reign was troubled by constant struggles with the papacy, during which he was excommunicated by Pope Innocent IV and deposed for a while. In 1235 he married, as his third wife, Isabella, daughter of King **John** of England and sister of **Henry III**. Intellectually, Frederick was perhaps one of the most enlightened men of his age, in his toleration of Jews and Muslims, in his free-trade policy, in his recognition of popular representation by parliaments, and in his anticipation of the later humanistic movement; but at the same time he was a persecutor of heretics, an upholder of absolute sovereignty, and a supporter of the power of princes against the cities. He not only spoke all the principal languages of his extensive empire, but was one of the first to write Italian poems, took a great interest in the arts, and was a diligent student of natural science.

FREDERICK III, of Germany (1415–93) Holy Roman Emperor, the fifth Duke of Austria of that name, was born in Innsbruck. Elected king of Germany in 1440 because of his lack of power and love of peace, he occupied the imperial throne for 53 years. In 1452 he became the last Holy Roman Emperor to be crowned by a pope in Rome. His reign was one of anarchy, wars raging on the frontiers of the empire, and disorders within. During its course Frederick lost his hold upon Switzerland; purchased peace from his brother Albert in Upper Austria; allowed **Francesca Sforza** to take Milan, **George Podiebrad** to seat himself on the throne of Bohemia, and **Matthias Corvinus** on that of Hungary; and remained apathetic under two Turkish invasions (1469 and 1475). Nevertheless, by the marriage of his son, **Maximilian I**, to Mary, daughter of **Charles the Bold** of Burgundy, he laid the foundation of the subsequent greatness of the Habsburgs. Though he neglected the interests of the empire for alchemy, astrology and botany, he lost no opportunity to aggrandize his own family. From his time the imperial dignity continued almost hereditary in the House of Austria.

FREDERICK I (1657–1713) first king of Prussia from 1701 and elector of Brandenberg as Frederick III from 1588, the second son of **Frederick-William**, the 'Great Elector'. Born in Königsberg, in 1584 he married (as his second wife) **Sophia Charlotte**, sister of **George I** of Britain. He succeeded his father as Elector of Brandenberg in 1688. In return for military aid to the emperor **Leopold I** in the War of the Spanish Succession (1701–14), he was allowed to crown himself as king of Prussia in 1701. A weak man who delighted in an outward show of pomp and magnificence, he was dubbed the 'ape of **Louis XIV**'; he attempted to make Berlin a city of culture and splendour on the model of Paris. He patronized engineers, architects, painters, musicians and scholars (especially **Leibniz**), and during his reign the Academy of Sciences at Berlin and the University of Halle were founded.

FREDERICK II, the Great (1712–86) king of Prussia, born in Berlin, the son of **Frederick-William I**, and of Sophia-Dorothea, daughter of **George I** of Great Britain. His early years were spent under military training and a rigid system of education, against which he rebelled fiercely but in vain. At 18 he made an attempt to excape to the court of Great Britain. His father saw in this an act both of political rebellion and of military insubordination, and would have punished it with death but for the intercession of the emperor. As it was, the prince was closely confined at Küstrin, while his confidant, Lieutenant Katte, was beheaded before his eyes. Frederick recognized that submission was inevitable, and threw himself with nervous alacrity into the military and civil duties with which he was after a time entrusted. He won his final restoration to favour when in 1733 he dutifully accepted as his bride the Princess Elizabeth of Brunswick-Wolfenbüttel (1715–97). From 1734 Frederick resided at Rheinsberg, where he devoted his leisure to the study of music and French literature, for which he had a keen and lasting admiration. He achieved almost professional skill on the flute, for which he composed many pieces, some of which are still played. He corresponded with **Voltaire** (who in 1750 visited Berlin), and studied the 'philosophical' doctrines. On 31 May 1740, Frederick became king; and in October the accession of **Maria Theresa** separated the crown of Austria from the imperial diadem. Frederick, in possession of a fine army and a well-filled treasury, seized the opportunity. Reviving an antiquated claim to Silesia, he entered that province (December 1740), defeated the Austrians at Mollwitz (1741) and Chotusitz (1742), and, having concluded an alliance for 15 years with France, forced Maria Theresa to yield him Upper and Lower Silesia by the Treaty of Breslau (1742). The second Silesian War (1744–45) left Frederick with still further augmented territories and the reputation of being one of the first military commanders of the day. The next 11 years were years of peace; but Frederick's energetic internal reforms were coloured by the expectation of renewed war. In 1756 the third Silesian War, the 'Seven Years' War', began. Frederick anticipated attack by himself becoming the aggressor, and during all this momentous struggle displayed a courage, a military genius, and a resource in victory and defeat which entitle him to the name of 'the Great'. At the Peace of Hubertsburg (15 February 1763), he had added a tenfold prestige to the Prussian army. Jealousy of Austrian aggrandizement continued to influence his policy. In 1772 it induced him to share in the first partition of Poland, by which he acquired Polish Prussia and a portion of

Great Poland. In 1778 it led him to take arms in a brief campaign, which ended in the acquisiton of the Franconian duchies. One of his last political actions was the formation of the 'Fürstenbund', which was the first definite appearance of Prussia as a rival to Austria for the lead in Germany. Frederick was an able administrator, and contrived to carry on his wars without incurring a penny of debt. He regarded himself as the first servant of the state; he was his own prime minister in a very literal sense. His conviction of the immaturity of his country explains the discrepancy between his theoretical writings on government and the scant liberty he granted to his people; he justified his arbitrary actions by his good intentions and his keener insight. Prussia under him was governed as one huge camp. With a view to providing treasure for future wars he fostered woollen and other manufactures by a high protective tariff; but he made himself unpopular by the introduction of the French excise system. During Frederick's reign, however, the country rapidly recovered from the ravages of war, while the army was raised to a strength of 200 000 men. By his death the area of Prussia had doubled, and, notwithstanding the temporary eclipse under **Napoleon**, the foundation of Prussia's greatness was laid. Frederick was essentially a just, if somewhat austere man, and the administration of justice under his rule was pure; the press enjoyed comparative freedom; and freedom of conscience was promoted. Frederick was a voluminous writer on political, historical and military subjects. His works, written wholly in French, were published by the Berlin Academy (31 vols, 1846–57), as also his *Political Correspondence* (1879 *et seq*).

FREDERICK III (1831–88) German emperor and eighth king of Prussia, only son of **William I**, born in Potsdam. In 1858 he married **Victoria**, princess royal of England. As crown prince of Prussia (from 1861) he protested against **Bismarck**'s reactionary policy in relation to constitutional questions and the press. In the Franco-German War he commanded the third army; he was at Wissembourg, Wörth and Sedan, and was made field marshal (1870). In 1871 he became crown prince of the German Empire. In 1878, when the emperor William was wounded by an assassin, the crown prince was appointed provisional regent. When, in 1888, Emperor William I died, Frederick was already ill, with cancer of the throat. He was proclaimed emperor as Frederick III, but he died at Potsdam. His son, William II, succeeded him. Frederick had a great horror of war, intensely disliked autocratic ideas, and sought to liberalize German institutions.

FREDERICK V (1596–1632) elector of the Palatinate from 1610 to 1623 and king of Bohemia from 1619–20, son of the elector Frederick IV (1574–1610). He was educated at the Huguenot academy at Sedan, and in 1613 married **Elizabeth**, daughter of **James VI and I** of Scotland and England. Their daughter **Sophia** became the mother of **George I** of Britain. The capital of the Palatinate, Heidelberg, already an intellectual centre of German calvinism, became known, under the refined young couple, for its artistic and cultural life. During his father's reign, the Protestant Union had been formed under Palatinate leadership (1608), and when in 1619 the crown of Bohemia was offered to Frederick his calvinist ministers urged him to accept. His exercise of regal power lasted only one winter (hence the derisive nickname, 'the Winter King') and the Bohemian Protestants were routed by imperial forces at the White Mountain near Prague in November 1620. The adventure also cost Frederick his hereditary lands, which were overrun by Spanish and Bavarian troops during his absence and passed into the possession of his Catholic cousin, Maximilian of Bavaria. In exile in the Hague with his wife and growing young family, Frederick was obliged to wait on events, but he died in 1632, a fortnight after the death in battle of the most effective champion of the Protestant cause, the Swedish king, **Gustav II Adolf**. His son, Charles Louis, was eventually restored to his electoral dignity by the Peace of Westphalia in 1648.

FREDERICK (AUGUSTUS), Duke of York (1763–1827) second son of King **George III** of Great Britain. A soldier by profession, he was unsuccessful both in the field in the Netherlands (1793–99) and as British commander-in-chief (1798–1809), and earned the nickname of the 'grand old Duke of York' in the nursery rhyme. But his painstaking reform of the army proved of lasting benefit, especially to **Wellington**. In 1809 he resigned because of the traffic in appointments conducted by his mistress, **Mary Anne Clarke**, but was exonerated and reinstated in 1811. He founded the Duke of York's School in London, and is commemorated by the Duke of York's column in Waterloo Place, London.

FREDERICK CHARLES, Prince (1828–85) Prussian soldier, nicknamed the 'Iron Prince', or the 'Red Prince' from his favourite hussar uniform, born in Berlin, nephew of the emperor **William I**. He served in the Schleswig-Holstein war (1848), commanded the right wing in the Danish war (1864), and in the Seven Weeks' War of 1866 against Austria helped to win the victory of Königgrätz. In the Franco-German war (1870–71) he commanded the second army, drove **Bazaine** into Metz, which capitulated, and, promoted to field marshal, captured Orléans, broke up the army of the Loire, and scattered **Chanzy**'s portion of it at Le Mans. In 1879 his daughter, Princess Louise Marguerite, married the Duke of **Connaught**.

FREDERICK LOUIS, Prince of Wales (1707–51) son of **George II** and **Caroline of Aspach** and father of **George III**. He quarrelled with his father over his allowance. In 1736 he married the Princess Augusta of Saxe-Gotha, in 1737 joined the parliamentary opposition, and was banished from court.

FREDERICK WILLIAM (1620–88) elector of Brandenburg from 1640, known as the Great Elector, born in Berlin. He was greatly affected during his childhood by the chaos and destruction of the Thirty Years' War (1620–48). He lived for some time in Holland (1634–38), where he studied briefly at the University of Leiden, the centre of calvinist learning, and gained an appreciation of Dutch art, architecture and technology. He was responsible for rebuilding the war-ravaged electorate after his succession in 1640, adding to the Hohenzollern territories, establishing an effective standing army, and reorganizing the privy council and civil service. In foreign, affairs he pursued a policy of shifting alliances, supporting both parties in turn during the First Northern War (1655–60) between Sweden and Poland and switching from the anti-French alliance of 1674 to support for **Louis XIV** in 1679, but returning to his anti-French stance in the 1680s. He granted asylum by the Edict of Potsdam (1685) to all French Huguenots expelled from France following Louis' revocation of the Edict of Nantes. A discriminating patron of the arts and education, he established the royal Library and Art Gallery in Berlin, founded the University of Duisberg and reorganized those at Königsberg and Frankfurt-am-Oder. Despite his own deep calvinist faith, he pursued an official policy of religious toleration which he regarded as of signal economic benefit to his under-developed and sparsely populated dominions.

FREDERICK-WILLIAM I (1688–1740) king of Prussia, succeeded his father, **Frederick I**, in 1713.

Boorishly contemptuous of art, poetry, philosophy and letters, he had a passion for soldiering which brought him Pomerania, with Stettin. He possessed fierce energy and great administrative ability and established a centralized hierarchy of administrative offices that gave Prussia the most professional bureaucracy in Europe, as well as a formidable army. He encouraged native industries, particularly wool, did away with vestiges of the old feudal system and pursued a policy of religious toleration. He laid the foundation of the future power of Prussia. He was succeeded by his son **Frederick II, the Great**.

FREDERICK-WILLIAM II (1744–97) king of Prussia, nephew and successor of **Frederick II, the Great**. The abolition of some of his predecessor's oppressive measures, including the coffee and tobacco duties, made him very popular at his accession in 1786, but he soon lost the regard of his subjects by his predilection for unworthy favourites, and by the abrogation of the freedom of the press and religion (1788). He dissipated the fortune his uncle left in the treasury in a useless war with Holland. His foreign policy was weak, while he oppressed his subjects with debt and increased taxation. He acquired large areas of Polish Prussia and Silesia by the partitions of Poland in 1793 and 1795, as also Ansbach and Bayreuth.

FREDERICK-WILLIAM III (1770–1840) king of Prussia, succeeded his father, **Frederick-William II**, in 1797. At first he was neutral towards **Napoleon**; but eventually his truculent policy so exasperated the Prussians that, instigated by their idolized Queen **Louisa**, they forced the king to declare war (1806). After the disastrous defeats of Jena and Auerstädt, Frederick-William fled into East Prussia, while Napoleon entered Berlin. By the Treaty of Tilsit (1807) Prussia was deprived of all her territories west of the Elbe, and all that she had acquired by the partition of Poland. For the next five years Frederick-William laboured to reorganize his enfeebled government. Napoleon's disastrous termination of the Russian campaign was the beginning of the war of liberation. Although the Prussians were defeated at Lützen and Bautzen, Prussia was finally delivered by the decisive victory of Leipzig (1813). By the Treaty of Vienna (1815) Prussia recovered her possessions west of the Elbe, and acquired Berg and Jülich, parts of Saxony and Westphalia, and the whole of Pomerania; but she gave up her Polish acquisitions save Posen to Russia, Friesland to Holland, and Ansbach and Bayreuth to Bavaria. The latter part of his reign was one of reaction. The democratic movements of 1819 and 1830 were rigorously suppressed, and the freedom of the press curtailed. Nevertheless, provincial diets were established (1823); the finances were put on a better footing; education was encouraged, and the *Zollverein* or customs union was established.

FREDERICK-WILLIAM IV (1795–1861) king of Prussia, succeeded his father, **Frederick-William III**, in 1840. He began his reign by granting minor reforms and promising radical changes, but always evaded the fulfilment of these pledges. He was possessed by vague ideas of the divine right of kings, and by a mystic pietism. He refused the imperial crown offered him by the Liberal Frankfurt Diet in 1849, and opposed the popular movement of 1848; but when the people stormed the arsenal and seized the palace of the Prince of Prussia (afterwards **William I**), the king granted a representative parliament (1850). In 1857, afflicted with insanity, he resigned the administration to his brother, who from 1858 acted as regent till his accession, as William I, on the death of Frederick-William.

FREDERICK WILLIAM, Duke of Brunswick (1771–1815) Prussian soldier. He fought for Prussia against France in 1792 and 1806, when he was taken prisoner and **Napoleon** vetoed his accession to the duchy. He raised a free corps in Bohemia, and in 1809, with his 700 'black hussars' and 800 infantry, achieved a masterly retreat to Brunswick, Elsfleth and England. He subsequently took part in the Peninsular War, and received from the British government £6000 a year, which he retained until his accession to his duchy in 1813. He joined the allied army after the return of Napoleon from Elba, and fell while leading his Black Brunswickers at Quatre Bras.

FREDERIK I (1471–1533) king of Denmark and Norway from 1523, son of **Kristian I** and uncle of **Kristian II**. As Duke of Holstein, he was chosen king when Kristian II, who had just lost Sweden to **Gustav I Vasa**, was dethroned in 1523 by a rebellion in Denmark. In 1531–32 he fended off an invasion of Norway by the ex-king; he then tricked him into accepting safe-conduct for a parley in Copenhagen, and imprisoned him for life instead. Frederik died soon afterwards, on the verge of accepting Lutheranism, and was succeeded by his son **Kristian III**.

FREDERIK II (1534–88) king of Denmark from 1559, son and successor of **Kristian III**. In the early years of his reign he was engaged in a seven-year war against the Sweden of the deranged **Erik XIV**, which was brought to an inconclusive ending with the Treaty of Stettin (1370). The remainder of his reign was a period of peace and prosperity. A pleasure-loving monarch, he built the magnificent Renaissance castle of Kronborg at Elsinore, to which he brought English musicians to provide entertainment, and was a patron of the astronomer **Tycho Brahe** and other scientists. He was succeeded by his young son, **Kristian IV**. His daughter, **Anne of Denmark**, married King **James VI and I** of Scotland and England.

FREDERIK III (1609–70) king of Denmark and Norway from 1648, son and successor of **Kristian IV**. The first half of his reign was taken up with costly wars against Sweden; but after the peace settlement of 1660 he established absolute hereditary monarchy over Denmark, Norway and Iceland, embodied in the Royal Law (*Kongelov*) of 1655. He was an enlightened patron of scientific and antiquarian studies, and founded the Royal Library in Copenhagen.

FREDERIK VI (1768–1839) king of Denmark from 1808, and of Norway, 1808–14. The son of **Kristian VII**, he was appointed regent in 1784 when his father was declared insane. During his regency, with the help of outstandingly able ministers, he abolished feudal serfdom, amended the criminal code, prohibited the slave trade in Danish colonies, and promoted free trade and industrial development. During the Napoleonic Wars, the Danish fleet was destroyed off Copenhagen by a British naval force under **Nelson** (1801), and in 1807, despite Danish neutrality, Copenhagen was bombarded for three days and battered into submission by Lord **Cathcart**. This forced Denmark into the arms of **Napoleon**; and with the overthrow of Napoleon's empire in 1814, Denmark lost Norway to Sweden. Under Frederik's paternalistic rule the economy recovered from bankruptcy. In 1834 he granted a new constitution with four consultative provincial assemblies—the start of parliamentary democracy in Denmark. He was succeeded by his son, **Kristian VIII**.

FREDERIK VII (1808–63) king of Denmark from 1848, son and successor of **Kristian VIII**, and the last of the Oldenburg line. In 1849 he promulgated a new and liberal constitution abolishing monarchical absolutism. He died childless, and was succeeded by **Kristian IX**.

FREDERIK VIII (1843–1912) king of Denmark from 1906, son and successor of **Kristian IX**, and brother of Queen **Alexandra** of Britain. In 1907 he made a state visit to Iceland to celebrate the granting of home rule there (1904). He married Princess Louise of Sweden, and was well-liked for his simple lifestyle. His second son, Prince Carl, became King **Haakon VII** of Norway. He was succeeded by his eldest son, **Kristian X**.

FREDERIK IX (1899–1972) king of Denmark from 1947, son and successor of **Kristian X**. A naval officer (rising to rear admiral in 1946), he was crown prince from 1912. During World War II he assisted his father in resistance to the German occupation, and was held under house arrest (1943–45). He granted home rule to the Faeroes in 1948, and in 1953 a new constitution provided for female succession to the throne. In 1935 he had married Ingrid, daughter of King **Gustav VI Adolf** of Sweden; their eldest daughter now became crown princess and succeeded him as Queen **Margrethe II** in 1972. Their youngest daughter, Anne-Marie, married ex-King **Constantine II** of Greece.

FREDRIK I (1675–1751) king of Sweden from 1720. Born in Kassel, in Hesse, he fought for England in the War of the Spanish Succession, and as Prince Frederick of Hesse-Kassel he married, in 1715, **Ulrika Eleonora**, the younger sister of King **Karl XII** and future queen of Sweden. In 1720 his wife abdicated the throne in his favour, under a new constitution which deprived the crown of most of its authority. He spent most of his time in hunting and love affairs, leaving the conduct of government to his chancellor, Arvid Horn. He died childless, and was succeeded by **Adolf Fredrik**.

FREEDMAN, Barnet (1901–58) English painter and lithographer, born in Stepney, London, the son of Russian Jewish immigrants. As a boy he was bedridden through illness. He attended evening classes at St Martin's School of Art (1917–22), and won a scholarship to the Royal College of Art (1922–25). A pioneer in the revival of colour lithography, his first one-man show was held at the Literary Bookshop in 1929. He designed posters, book illustrations and book covers. He was visiting instructor at the Royal College of Art from 1928, and at the Ruskin School, Oxford. He worked for London Transport, Shell-Mex, BP Ltd, the BBC and the General Post Office. In 1935 his design was selected for the **George V** jubilee stamp. In 1940 he was appointed official war artist to the Admiralty and painted coastal defences, naval portraits and studies on battleships and submarines.

FREEMAN, Edward Augustus (1823–92) English historian, born in Harborne, Staffordshire. Educated at Trinity College, Oxford, he succeeded **William Stubbs** as Regius professor of modern history. Among his prolific output were his *History of Federal Government* (1863) and *History of the Norman Conquest* (1867–76).

FREEMAN, John (1880–1929) English poet, born in London. He rose from clerk to become secretary and director of an insurance company (1927). His *Stone Trees* (1916) and other volumes of poetry made his reputation. He won the Hawthornden Prize with *Poems New and Old* in 1920 and wrote studies of *George Moore* (1922) and *Herman Melville* (1926).

FREEMAN, Sir Ralph (1880–1950) English civil engineer, born in London, educated at the City and Guilds of London Institute. In 1901 he joined the firm of consulting engineers which in 1938 became Freeman, Fox & Partners, specializing in the design of steel bridges. His first notable design was for Sydney Harbour Bridge, a construction of 1670ft span (1932). He was later involved with his partner Sir **Gilbert Roberts** in the design of the long-span suspension bridges over the estuaries of the Forth, Severn and Humber rivers, though he did not live to see any of them built.

FREEMAN, Walter (1895–1972) American neurologist, born in Philadelphia. He was a leading expert on neurosurgery, and developed the operation of prefrontal lobotomy, used in certain mental illnesses but now largely discredited.

FREEMAN-THOMAS, Freeman See **WILLINGDON**

FREGE, Friedrich Ludwig Gottlob (1848–1925) German logician, mathematician and philosopher, born in Wismar. He was educated at Jena, where he spent his whole professional career, becoming professor in 1879. He worked in comparative obscurity in his lifetime, though both **Bertrand Russell** and **Wittgenstein** noticed his originality and he is now regarded as the founding father of modern mathematical logic and the philosophy of language. A particular technical contribution to logic was his theory of quantification. His main works are *Begriffschrift* (1879), *Die Grundlagen der Arithmetik* (1884), and *Die Grundgesetze der Arithmetik* (2 vols, 1893,1903). These have all been translated into English, as has a collection of his still influential philosophical essays analyzing such basic logical concepts as meaning, sense and reference. In 1902 he abandoned his ambitious attempt to derive the whole of arithmetic from logic after Russell produced a devasting paradox which undermined it. He became generally depressed by the poor reception of his ideas and wrote little in his last 20 years.

FREILIGRATH, Ferdinand (1810–76) German poet and democrat, born in Detmold. He abandoned commerce for literature, but became a protagonist of German democracy and his writings became more and more political. He was obliged to seek refuge in Belgium and Britain for his *Glaubensbekenntnis* (1844). He returned to Germany in 1848 and became leader of the democratic party. He was again expelled after a trial for his poem *Die Toten an die Lebenden* (1848). He translated many English classics into German.

FRELENG, Friz (Isadore) (1906–) American animated cartoon director/producer, born in Kansas City. After winning a cartoon contest he joined **Disney** and then moved to Hollywood to animate *Oswald the Rabbit*. He made a trial sound cartoon, *Bosko the Talk-Ink Kid* (1929), and then made *Looney Tunes*, starting with *Sinkin' in the Bathtub* (1930). He directed the first Cinecolor *Merrie Melodies* cartoon, *Beauty and the Beast* (1934), and the first Porky Pig, *I Haven't Got a Hat* (1935), *Katzenjammer Kids* cartoons (1938), and *Rhapsody in Rivets* (1943). He then created the irascible Yosemite Sam (*Hare Trigger*, 1945), Sylvester the lisping cat (*Tweety Pie*, 1946, for which he won his first Oscar), and the Mexican mouse, *Speedy Gonzalez* (1955, his second Oscar). His third was for *Knighty-Knight Bugs* (1957).

FRELINGHUYSEN, Frederick (1753–1804) American statesman, father of Theodore Frelinghuysen and uncle of F T Frelinghuysen. He raised a corps of artillery, and fought in the War of Independence, and was a member of the Continental congress in 1778 and 1782–83, and a US senator from 1793 to 1796.

FRÉMONT, John Charles (1813–90) American explorer and politician, born in Savannah, Georgia. He became a teacher of mathematics in the navy and in 1838 started surveying. In 1842 he crossed the Rocky Mountains (where a peak is named after him), and demonstrated the feasibility of an overland route across the continent. In 1843 he explored the Great Salt Lake, advancing to the mouth of the Columbia River; and in 1845 examined the continental watershed. After participating in the annexation of Upper California in 1847, he started in 1848 upon a fourth expedition along the upper Rio Grande. In 1849 he crossed over to California, where he settled, and next year became senator of the new state. In 1853 he conducted a fifth expedition. In 1856 he was the Republican and anti-slavery candidate for the presidency but was defeated by **James Buchanan**; nominated again in 1864, he withdrew in favour of **Abraham Lincoln**. He served in the regular army as major-general (1861–62), but resigned rather than serve under General **John Pope**. In 1873 the French authorities sentenced him in absence to imprisonment for fraud in connection with the Southern Pacific railway scheme. Frémont was governor of Arizona from 1878 to 1882, and died in New York.

FRÉMY, Edmond (1814–94) French chemist. He prepared anhydrous hydrogen fluoride, wrote on the synthesis of rubies, and worked on the ferrates, the colouring of flower and saponification of fats.

FRENCH, Daniel Chester (1850–1931) American sculptor, born in Exeter, New Hampshire. He studied sculpture in New York and in 1873–74 produced *The Minute Man* for the town of Concorde, Massachusetts. Following a period in Florence, he studied at the École des Beaux Arts in Paris from 1886 to 1888. He produced a 60-foot high *Statue of The Republic* for the 1893 Chicago world's fair and the seated figure of **Abraham Lincoln** for the Washington Lincoln Memorial (1918–22).

FRENCH, Sir John, Earl of Ypres (1852–1925) English soldier, born in Ripple, Kent. He joined the navy (like his father) in 1866, but transferred to the army in 1874 and was with the 19th Hussars in Sudan 1884–85, and cavalry commander in South Africa in the 2nd Boer War (1899–1901). Chief of Imperial General Staff 1911–14, he took command of the British Expeditionary Force in France in August 1914. He was superseded by General **Haig** and became commander-in-chief home forces in December, 1915. He was lord-lieutenant of Ireland (1918–21) during the Anglo-Irish War, and got a grant of £50000 in 1919.

FRENEAU, Philip (1752–1832) American sailor and poet, born in New York. He commanded a privateer in the American War of Independence, was captured by the British, and wrote *The British Prison Ship* (1781). He also wrote a number of shorter poems, including 'The Indian Burying Ground' and 'The Wild Honeysuckle'.

FRENSSEN, Gustav (1863–1945) German novelist, born a carpenter's son in Barlt in Holstein. He studied for the church but turned to writing and attracted attention by his *Jörn Uhl* (1901), a novel of peasant life. *Hilligenlei* (1906), a life of **Jesus Christ** set in a Germanic background, aroused much controversy.

FRERE, Sir Henry Bartle Edward (1815–84) Welsh colonial administrator, born in Clybach in Brecknock. He studied at Haileybury. As chief-commissioner of Sind he kept order during the Mutiny. He was governor of Bombay (1862–67). In 1872 he signed a treaty with the sultan of Zanzibar abolishing the slave trade. In 1877 he was appointed governor of the Cape and High Commissioner in South Africa, where his treatment of the Zulus caused his recall in 1880.

FRERE, John Hookham (1769–1841) English diplomat, wit and translator, born in London, and educated at Eton and Caius College, Cambridge. He entered the Foreign Office, in 1796 was returned for Looe, supported **Pitt**'s government, and contributed to the *Anti-Jacobin*; among his verse are 'The Loves of the Triangles', a parody on **Darwin**'s *Loves of the Plants*, and 'The Needy Knife-grinder', written in collaboration with his school friend, **Canning**. Under-secretary for foreign affairs (1799), he was appointed envoy to Lisbon (1800), and twice minister to Spain (1802 and 1808). Recalled after the retreat to La Coruña, he retired in 1821 to Malta, where he devoted himself to Greek, Hebrew and Maltese. Frere's clever mock-heroic *Specimen of an intended National Work by William and Robert Whistlecraft* (1817) suggested its ottava rima to **Byron** for his *Beppo*: but his fame rests on his admirable translations of the *Archarnians*, *Knights*, *Birds*, and *Frogs* of Aristophanes, published in 1907.

FRÉRON, Élie Catherine (1718–76) French critic. He was a professor in the Collège Louis le Grand, and wrote in defence of church and king against **Voltaire** and the Encyclopédistes.

FRESCOBALDI, Girolamo (1583–1643) Italian composer, born in Rome. He studied the organ at Ferrara Cathedral, became organist at S Maria in Trastevere, Rome, and travelled much in the Low Countries. From 1608 until his death he was organist at St Peter's in Rome. He composed chiefly organ works and madrigals.

FRESENIUS, Karl Remigius (1818–97) German chemist. Professor at the Agricultural Institute from 1845, his revised tables for qualitative and quantitative analysis are still in use.

FRESNAYE, Roger de la (1885–1925) French artist, born in Le Mans. He studied in Paris and was influenced by **Cézanne**; he associated with **Jacques Villon** in the Section d'Or group.

FRESNEL, Augustin Jean (1788–1827) French physicist, born in Broglie. Head of the department of public works in Paris, his optical investigations contributed materially to the establishment of the undulatory theory of light; he invented the well-known compound lighthouse lens and produced circularly polarized light by means of a special prism (Fresnel's rhomb).

FREUD, Anna (1895–1982) Viennese-born British psychoanalyst, youngest daughter of **Sigmund Freud** and pioneer of child psychoanalysis. She taught at the Cottage Lyceum in Vienna, and emigrated with her father to London in 1938, where she organized (1940–45) a residential war nursery for homeless children. In 1947 she founded the Hampstead Child Therapy Clinic. She made important contributions to child psychology; her works include *The Ego and the Mechanism of Defence* (1937), and *Beyond the Best Interests of the Child* (1973).

FREUD, Lucian (1922–) German-born British painter, born in Berlin, the grandson of **Sigmund Freud**. He moved to Britain in 1933. Largely self-taught, he later studied at the Central School of Arts and Crafts in London (1938–39) and the East Anglican School of Painting and Drawing, Dedham. In his early years he was one of the Neo-Romantic group of English painters along with **Minton**, Craxton, **Sutherland** and **Piper**, but since the 1950s he has developed a realistic style. This is seen to the best advantage in his highly modelled and acutely observed portraits and nude studies. The peculiar angles from which he paints the human form give his pictures an unsettling air. He is the only consistently representational painter to achieve high standing in British art since World War II.

FREUD, Sigmund (1856–1939) Austrian neurologist and founder of psychoanalysis. Born in Freiburg, Moravia, of Jewish parentage, he studied medicine at Vienna and joined the staff of the Vienna General Hospital in 1882, specializing in neurology. He collaborated with the Austrian neurologist Joseph Breuer in the treatment of hysteria by the recall of painful experiences under hypnosis, then moved to Paris in

1885 to study under **Jean Martin Charcot**; it was there that he changed from neurology to psychopathology. Returning to Vienna he developed the technique of conversational 'free association' in place of hypnosis and refined psychoanalysis as a method of treatment. In 1895 he published, with Breuer, *Studien über Hysterie*, but two years later their friendship ended as a result of Freud's theories of infantile sexuality. Despite opposition from friends, patients and medical colleagues he developed his revolutionary thinking, and in 1900 published his seminal work, *Die Traumdeutung* (The Interpretation of Dreams), arguing that dreams, like neuroses, are disguised manifestations of repressed sexual desires. Appointed extraordinary professor of neuropathology at the University of Vienna in 1902, he started weekly seminars in his home with kindred minds like **Alfred Adler** (the original 'Psychological Wednesday Society'), and produced further crucial works, *The Psychopathology of Everyday Life* (1904), and *Three Essays on the Theory of Sexuality* (1905), which met with intense and uncomprehending opposition. In 1908 these weekly meetings became the Vienna Psychoanalytical Society, and, in 1910, the international Psychoanalytical Association, with **Carl Jung** as the first president. Both Adler (1911) and Jung (1913) broke with Freud to develop their own theories. Undeterred, Freud produced *Totem and Tabu* (1913), *Beyond the Pleasure Principle* (1919–20), and *Ego and Id* (1923), elaborating his theories of the division of the unconscious mind into the 'Id', the 'Ego', and the 'Super-Ego'. In 1927 he published a controversial view of religion, *The Future of an Illusion*. He was awarded the prestigious **Goethe** prize in 1930, and in 1933 published *Why War?*, written in collaboration with **Albert Einstein**. Under the Nazi régime psychoanalysis was banned, and in 1938, after the annexation of Austria, Freud was extricated from Vienna and brought to London with his family. He made his home in Hampstead, but died of cancer the following year.

FREUND, Wilhelm (1806–94) German philologist and lexicographer, born in Kempen in Posen. He compiled the *Wörterbuch der lateinischen Sprache* (1834–45), on which most English-Latin dictionaries are based.

FREY-WYSSLING, Albert Friedrich (1900–) Swiss botanist, born in Küsnacht. He studied in Zürich, Jena and Paris and became professor of botany in Zürich in 1938. He did much to establish ultrastructural studies on plant cells by the use of polarization microscopy, in the period before about 1940; thereafter X-ray diffraction and electron microscopy techniques became available to confirm and extend his results by these more direct methods.

FREYBERG, Bernard, 1st Baron Freyberg (1889–1963) New Zealand soldier, born in London. Educated at Wellington College, New Zealand, at the outbreak of World War I he came to England to enlist and served with the Royal Naval Division in Gallipoli and France, winning the VC at Beaumont Hamel. After experience in the Southern Command and at the war office, in World War II he was given command of the New Zealand forces in the middle east. He commanded commonwealth forces in ill-fated operations in Greece and Crete (1941) and in the Sahara Desert. He commanded the New Zealand Corps in Italy (1944–45), including operations at Monte Cassino. He was governor-general of New Zealand (1946–52) and lieutenant-governor of Windsor Castle (1956–63).

FREYCINET, Charles Louis de Saulces de (1818–1923) French statesman, born at Foix, Ariège. Originally an engineer, in 1870 he was called by **Gambetta** to the war department; his conduct there he described in *La Guerre en province* (1871). Four times premier, he wrote on engineering, sanitation, etc and was admitted to the Academy of Sciences and to the French Academy (1890).

FREYSSINET, Marie Eugène Léon (1879–1962) French civil engineer, born in Objat, Corrèze. He graduated from both the École Polytechnique and the École des Ponts et Chaussées in Paris. His intuitive rather than analytical approach to reinforced concrete design reached its height in his airship hangars at Orly (1916–24, destroyed 1944) where he used corrugated parabolic arches over 200 ft high yet only $3\frac{1}{2}$ in thick. Realizing that concrete's great weakness is its lack of strength in tension, he sought ways of putting concrete structures into a state of permanent compression even under load, and succeeded in developing practical techniques for prestressing concrete by the use of stretched steel tendons. From 1930 he was one of the leading exponents of this virtually new structural material, employing it to full advantage in bridges, foundations, a dam in Algeria, the airport runway at Orly and a water tower at Orléans.

FREYTAG, Georg Wilhelm Friedrich (1788–1861) German orientalist, born in Lüneberg. He became professor of oriental languages at Bonn in 1819. His reputation rests on his *Lexicon Arabico-Latinum* (1830–37), and works on Arabic literature and history.

FREYTAG, Gustav (1816–95) German novelist and playwright, born in Kreuzburg in Silesia. From 1839 to 1847 he was *Privatdozent* of German at Breslau University. A deputy to the North German Diet, he attended the Prussian crown prince in the Franco-German campaign (1870). His comedies and other plays, such as *Die Valentine* (1846) and *Die Journalisten* (1853) proved brilliant successes, but his greatest achievement is *Soll und Haben* (1855), a realistic novel of German commercial life (trans *Debit and Credit*, 1858). It was followed by *Die Verlorene Handschrift* (1864; trans *The Lost Manuscript*, 1865), and the series (1872–81) called *Die Ahnen*.

FRICK, Henry Clay (1849–1919) American industrialist, born in West Overton, Pennsylvania. He had little education, but grasped at post-Civil War expansion by forming a company to supply the Pittsburgh steel mills with coke, and was a millionaire at 30. **Andrew Carnegie** was associated with him from 1884, and invited him to become chairman of the Carnegie steel company in 1889. He reorganized the company and made a highly profitable investment for the firm in iron ore at Lake Superior. He was a hard and ruthless employer, unsuccessfully using 200 hired Pinkerton guards in pitched battle, to dislodge strikers at the Carnegie Steel Plant at Homestead, Pennsylvania (1892), and on their failure, called in the Pennsylvania National Guard. The strike was broken, but Frick was shot and stabbed by Alexander Berkman, an associate of the anarchist **Emma Goldman**, although ultimately recovering. He broke with Carnegie in 1900, and became director of **J Pierpont Morgan**'s United States Steel (1901). He built up the distinguished Frick Collection of fine art, now a museum in New York City; he also endowed hospitals, schools and a large park in Pittsburgh.

FRICK, Wilhelm (1877–1946) German politician, born in Alsenz. He participated in **Hitler**'s Munich putsch (1923), led the Nazi faction in the *Reichstag* from 1924 and as minister of the interior from 1933 banned trade unionism and freedom of the press, and encouraged anti-Semitism. Ousted by **Himmler** in 1943, he became 'Protector' of Bohemia and Moravia. He was found guilty of war crimes at Nuremberg and executed.

FRICKER, Peter Racine (1920–90) English composer, born in London. He studied at the Royal College of Music, was musical director of Morley College, London, 1952–64, and then moved to the University of California, Santa Barbara. The influence of **Bartók** and **Schoenberg** is apparent in such works as the *String Quartet in One Movement* (1948), the *First Symphony* (1948–49) and the *Sonata for Violin and Piano* (1950). Later works include symphonies, the *Cello Sonata* (1956), an oratorio, *The Vision of Judgement* (1957–58), and other chamber, choral and keyboard works.

FRIDA, Emil See **VRCHLICKY, Jaroslav**

FRIDESWIDE, St (d.c.735) Anglo-Saxon abbess and patron saint of Oxford. The daughter of Didanus, an ealdorman, she founded a nunnery at Oxford on the site of what is now Christ Church College. She was canonized in 1481. Her feast day is 19 October.

FRIEDAN, Betty (Elizabeth), née **Goldstein** (1921–) American feminist and writer, born in Peoria, Illinois. Educated at Smith College, she became a housewife in New York and then wrote a best-seller, *The Feminine Mystique* (1963), which analyzed the role of women in American society and articulated their frustrations. She was founder and first president of the National Organization for Women (1966), and headed the National Women's Strike for Equality (1970). She warned against the dangers of competing against men by adopting undesirable male qualities, and wrote *It Changed My Life* (1977) and *The Second Stage* (1981).

FRIEDEL, Charles (1832–99) French chemist. Latterly professor of organic chemistry at the Sorbonne, he worked on the production of artificial minerals (diamonds); he and the American chemist James Mason Crafts (1839–1917) gave their names to the Friedel-Crafts reaction for the synthesis of benzene homologues.

FRIEDLAND, Valentin (1490–1556) German educationist, more commonly known as Trotzendorf from his birthplace near Görlitz. He studied under **Luther** and **Melanchthon** at Wittenberg. Settling at Goldberg in Silesia, he founded a school in 1531 which was run entirely by the boys themselves.

FRIEDMAN, Herbert (1916–) American astrophysicist, born in New York City. Educated at Brooklyn College and Johns Hopkins University, he spent his career at the US Naval Research Laboratory in Washington. He did pioneering work in the use of rockets in astronomy, and in the study of astronomical X-ray sources. From the 1940s he used rockets carrying X-ray detectors to study the Sun's X-rays; and following **B Rossi**'s discovery in 1962 of the first non-solar X-ray source, Friedman showed in 1964 that one such source coincided with the remnant of a luminous supernova in the Crab nebula. After this early work, X-ray astronomy developed as an important area of astrophysics: so also has the use of rockets, to carry astronomical instruments above the absorbing layer of the Earth's atmosphere.

FRIEDMAN, Milton (1912–) United States economist, born in New York and educated in Chicago and New York. After eight years at the National Bureau of Economic Research (1937–45) he was professor of economics at Chicago University (1946–83), where he became the foremost exponent of monetarism. In such works as *A Monetary History of the United States, 1867–1960* (1963) and *Inflation: Causes and Consequences* (1963) he argued that a country's economy can be controlled through its money supply. He was awarded the 1976 Nobel prize for economics, and was a policy adviser to the **Reagan** administration (1981–88). His ideas were applied in Britain, with almost messianic zeal by the Conservative government of **Margaret Thatcher** after the 1979 general election.

FRIEDRICH, Caspar David (1774–1840) German painter, born in Pomerania. He studied at the Academy of Copenhagen from 1794 to 1798 and then, despite his classical training, did not visit Rome but spent the rest of his life in Dresden. His work won the approval of **Goethe**, and in 1805 he won a Weimar Art Society prize. His paintings from c.1808 were highly controversial in their treatment of landscape as vast and desolate expanses in which man—often a solitary figure—is depicted as a melancholy spectator of Nature's awesome power. Such works helped to establish the notion of the sublime as a central concern of the Romantic movement. He taught at the Dresden Academy from 1816 and became a professor in 1824.

FRIES, Elias Magnus (1794–1878) Swedish botanist. He was professor at Uppsala, and keeper of the botanic garden there. He wrote on fungi, lichens and the flora of Scandinavia, and introduced a new classificatory system. The genus *Freesia* is named after him.

FRIESE-GREENE, William (1855–1921) English pioneer of the motion-picture, born in Bristol. His first successful picture, using celluloid film, was shown in public in 1890, in which year his invention was patented. His experiments included three-dimensional and colour cinematography. He died almost penniless.

FRIESZ, (Émile) Othon (1879–1949) French painter, born in Le Havre. He attended the École des Beaux Arts, and studied with **Bonnat** and **Dufy**. At first an enthusiastic impressionist, he was later influenced by **Cèzanne**.

FRIML, (Charles) Rudolf (1879–1972) Hungarian-born American pianist and composer, born in Prague. He studied at the Prague Conservatory under Dvořák, and settled in the USA in 1906. He wrote a piano concerto, film music for Hollywood (where he died), piano pieces and many operettas, including the popular *Rose Marie* (1924) and *The Vagabond King* (1925). His songs include *The Donkey Serenade* (1937).

FRISCH, Karl von (1886–1982) Austrian ethologist and zoologist, born in Vienna. He studied medicine there before abandoning it for zoology which he studied at Munich and Trieste and afterwards taught at four universities, with much of his career spent at Munich, founding the Zoological Institute there in 1932. He was a key figure in developing ethology using field observation of animals combined with ingenious experiments. His 40-year study of the honey bee showed that forager bees communicate information (on the location of food sources) in part by use of coded dances. In 1973 he shared the Nobel prize for physiology or medicine with those other pioneers of ethology, **Konrad Lorenz** and **Nikolaas Tinbergen**. His books included *The Dancing Bees* (1927, trans 1954) and *Animal Architecture* (1974).

FRISCH, Max Rudolph (1911–) Swiss novelist and playwright, born in Zürich. In 1933, forced by economic circumstances to abandon the study of German literature at Zürich University, he became a journalist. Later he trained as an architect but not before publishing *Leaves from a Knapsack* (1942), while serving with the Swiss frontier guard. In 1958 he became the first foreigner to be awarded the Buchner prize of the German Academy for language and poetry. His bibliography is extensive but as a novelist he is known outside German-speaking Europe chiefly for two novels, *I'm Not Stiller* (1954) and *Homo Faber* (1957). He has had international success as a playwright after being a disciple of **Brecht** in the 1940s, *The*

Fire Raisers (1953) and *Andorra* (1961) having become modern stage classics.

FRISCH, Otto Robert (1904–79) Austrian physicist, born in Vienna. In 1939 he became head of the nuclear physics division at Harwell in England, and in 1947 professor of natural philosophy at Cambridge. He and **Lise Meitner** first used the term 'nuclear fission' (1939). He wrote *Meet the Atoms* (1947).

FRISCH, Ragnar Anton Kittil (1895–1973) Norwegian economist. He studied at Oslo, and was professor of economics there from 1931 to 1965, and editor of *Econometrica* (1933–55). He was a pioneer of econometrics, the application of statistics to economic planning. He shared the first Nobel prize for economics in 1969 with **Jan Tinbergen**.

FRITH, John (1503–33) English Protestant martyr, born in Westerham, Kent. From Eton he went to King's College, Cambridge, from where in 1525 **Wolsey** summoned him to his new foundation at Oxford. A year later suspicion of heresy drove him to Marburg, where he saw much of **William Tyndale** and **Patrick Hamilton**, and wrote several Protestant treatises. Venturing back in 1532, he was burned at Smithfield.

FRITH, William Powell (1819–1909) English painter, born in Aldfield. By selling both paintings and their copyright, he made himself the wealthiest artist of his time. The Pre-Raphaelites criticized the vulgarity of his historical and genre works, but he took a new direction with his huge canvases of Victorian scenes, *Ramsgate Sands* (1854, bought by Queen **Victoria** for Buckingham Palace), *Derby Day* (1858, National Gallery) and *The Railway Station* (1862, Holloway College), which achieved huge popular success and were hailed by **Ruskin** as the art of the future.

FRITSCH, Elizabeth (1940–) English potter, born in Shropshire. She studied harp and piano at the Royal Academy of Music prior to attending the Royal College of Art (1968–71). One of the most talented contemporary potters of her generation, her work is sometimes inspired by music using coiling spires and geometric patterns in coloured slips with a matt texture akin to ivory frescoes. Her vessels, like those of **Hans Coper** and **Lucie Rie**, who were both influential in her development, are regarded on equal terms with the important painters and sculptors of today.

FROBENIUS, Ferdinand Georg (1849–1917) German mathematician, born in Berlin, the son of a parson. He studied at Göttingen and Berlin, where he took his doctorate in 1870, and from 1875 to 1892 taught at Zürich, before returning to Berlin as professor. He founded the theory of group representations, which was later to become essential in quantum mechanics, and a major theme of 20th-century mathematics.

FROBENIUS, Joannes (1460–1527) German printer. He founded a printing office in Basel (1491), and issued 300 works, including a Vulgate, **Erasmus**, **Tertullian**, **Ambrose**, and Greek New Testament (1496).

FROBERGER, Johann Jakob (1616–67) German composer, born in Stuttgart. A pupil of **Girolamo Frescobaldi**, he was court organist at Vienna (1637–57), and made concert tours to Italy, Paris, London and Brussels. Of his many compositions, the best remembered are his suites for harpsichord.

FROBISHER, Sir Martin (c.1535–1594) English sailor, born in Altofts near Wakefield, Yorkshire. Sent to sea as a boy, he traded to Guinea and elsewhere. In 1576, with the *Gabriel* and the *Michael* and a complement of 35 men, he set off in search of a Northwest Passage to Cathay. The *Michael* was abandoned, but Frobisher, almost lost off the coast of Greenland, reached Labrador and discovered Frobisher Bay. From two subsequent expeditions (1571 and 1578) he brought back 'black earth' which was supposed to be gold from Frobisher Bay. In 1585 he commanded a vessel in **Francis Drake**'s expedition to the West Indies, and was knighted for his services against the Armada in command of the *Triumph*. He was mortally wounded at the siege of Crozon, near Brest.

FRÖDING, Gustav (1860–1911) Swedish poet, born near Karlstad. He studied at Uppsala and became a schoolmaster and journalist, but suffered bouts of mental illness. He is considered the greatest Swedish lyric poet, often compared to **Robert Burns**, combining dialect and folksong and homespun philosophy in his portrayal of local characters, as in *Guitarr och dragharmonika* (Guitar and Harmonica, 1891), *Nya dikter* (New Poems, 1894), and *Räggler å paschaser* (Drops and Fragments, 1896). The gentle humour of his earlier poems later turned to a tragic quest for the Holy Grail.

FROEBEL, Friedrich Wilhelm August (1782–1852) German educationist and founder of the kindergarten system, born in Oberweissbach. He studied at Jena, Göttingen and Berlin, and in 1805 began teaching at Frankfurt-am-Main. In 1816 he put into practice his educational system at a school he founded at Griesheim, whose aim (to help the child's mind to grow naturally and spontaneously) he expounded in *Die Menschenerziehung* (1826). Catholic opposition foiled his attempts to establish a school near Lucerne (1831). After starting an orphanage at Burgdorf in Bern, where he began to train teachers for educational work, in 1836 he opened his first kindergarten school at Blankenburg. The rest of his life was spent in organizing kindergarten schools.

FRÖLICH, Alfred See **BABINSKI, Joseph**

FROHSCHAMMER, Jakob (1821–93) German Catholic theologian and philosopher, born near Ratisbon. He became widely known for his history of dogma (1850) which was banned by the pope. In another work he championed freedom of science from the church. He founded the first Liberal Catholic paper, *Athenä*, in which he gave an account of **Darwin**'s theory. He was excommunicated in 1871.

FROISSART, Jean (c.1333–c.1404) French chronicler and poet, born in Valenciennes, Hainault. He was educated for the church, but at 19 began to write the history of the wars of his time. In 1360 he went to England, where he received a gracious welcome from **Philippa of Hainault**, wife of **Edward III**, who appointed him clerk of her chamber. In 1364 he travelled in Scotland, where he was the guest of King **David II** and of the Earl of **Douglas**. In 1366 he went to Aquitaine with **Edward the Black Prince** (the son of Edward III); in 1368 he was in Italy, possibly with **Chaucer** and **Petrarch**, at the marriage of the Duke of **Clarence**. For a time he was curate at Lestines in the diocese of Liège; and was afterwards at various continental courts. About 1390 he settled in Flanders, and resumed work on his *Chroniques*. In 1395 he revisited England, and was cordially welcomed by **Richard II**. He then returned to Chimay, where he had obtained a canonry, and where he may have died. Froissart's famous book deals with the period 1326–1400. Mainly occupied with the affairs of France, England, Scotland and Flanders during the Hundred Years' War (1337–1453), he supplies valuable information about Germany, Italy and Spain, and even touches occasionally on Hungary and the Balkan peninsula. His is the most vivid and entertaining of all medieval chroniclers, accurate and impartial in his statements. The main defects in his work are the frequent repetitions and the negligent arrangement. He likewise wrote a considerable number of verses—*ballades*, *rondeaux* and *virelais*; his Round Table metrical romance *Méliador*, was discovered in 1894.

FROMENT, Nicolas (fl.1450–90) French painter, who has left some fine examples of the late Gothic style containing features surprisingly Flemish in appearance. He was court painter to King René, whose portrait is incorporated in his masterpiece, a triptych in the cathedral of Aix-en-Provence, having as its centrepiece **Moses** and the burning bush.

FROMENTIN, Eugène (1820–76) French painter and author, born in La Rochelle. Visits to Algeria and the near east provided him with abundant material *Chasse au faucon en Algérie* and *Halte de cavaliers arabes* (both in the Louvre) are painted in almost scientific detail, their colour and composition betraying the influence of **Delacroix**. His three travel books also provide vivid pictures of the Algerian scene. But he is best known as the author of *Dominique* (1862), a nostalgic autobiographical novel and *Les Maîtres d'autrefois* (1876), written during a tour of Belgian and Dutch art galleries, which contains some brilliant art criticism.

FROMM, Erich (1900–80) German-born American psychoanalyst and social philosopher, born in Frankfurt. He was educated at the universities of Frankfurt, Heidelberg, and Munich, and at the Berlin Institute of Psychoanalysis. In 1934, he emigrated to the USA and after holding various university appointments became professor at New York in 1962. He emphasised social and economic and cultural factors on human behaviour. His works include *Escape from Freedom* (in Britain, *The Fear of Freedom*, 1941), *Man for Himself* (1947), *Psychoanalysis and Religion* (1951), *The Sane Society* (1955), *Sigmund Freud's Mission* (1959), *The Dogma of Christ* (1963) and *The Heart of Man* (1964).

FRONTENAC, Louis de Buade, Comte de (1620–98) French-Canadian statesman. He served in the army, and in 1672 was appointed governor of the French possessions in North America. He was recalled after ten years of quarrelling with the Jesuits, but he had gained the confidence of the settlers and the respect of the Indians; and in 1689, when a war with England was added to constant attacks from the Iroquois he was sent out again. He set the Indians on New England villages, repulsed a British attack on Quebec, and completely broke the power of the Iroquois. He died in Quebec.

FRONTINUS, Sextus Julius (c.40–103) Roman soldier and writer. He was appointed Roman governor of Britain in 75, and established the legionary fortress at Isca (Caerleon on the Usk). In 97 he was made superintendent of the waterworks at Rome. He wrote the *Strategematica*, a treatise on war in four volumes, and the *De Aquis Urbis Romae*, on the Roman water-system.

FRONTO, Marcus Cornelius (c.100–c.176) Roman orator, born in Cirta in Numidia (North Africa). He was entrusted by **Antoninus Pius** with the education of **Marcus Aurelius** and Lucius Verus. In 143 he was consul with **Herodes Atticus**. Two series of his letters to Marcus Aurelius were discovered in 1815. He was a champion of the early Latin stylists.

FROST, David Paradine (1939–) English broadcaster and businessman, born in Tenterden, Kent. Educated at Cambridge he participated in The Footlights revue and edited *Granta* before moving into television in 1961. He hosted *That Was The Week That Was* (1962–63), a popular, late-night revue show whose topical satire and irreverent attitude to authority were innovations in television light entertainment. Subsequent shows, in Britain and America, include *The Frost Report* (1966–67), *Frost on Friday* (1968–70), *The David Frost Show* (1969–72) and many others. His trans-Atlantic television career divides into two areas: as anchorman and satirist in shows like *The Guinness Book of World Records* (1981–) and *The Spitting Image Movie Awards* (1987), and as a diligent interviewer of world leaders in such programmes as *The Nixon Interviews* (1976–77) and *The Shah Speaks* (1980). A producer of films like *The Slipper and the Rose* (1976), he was also a co-founder and presenter of Britain's *TV-am* (1983–). His many international honours include the Golden Rose of Montreux (1967) and the Emmy (1970 and 1971). His publications include *How to Live Under Labour* (1964), *I Gave Them A Sword* (1978) and *The World's Shortest Books* (1987).

FROST, John (d.1877) Welsh Chartist leader, born in Newport. A prosperous tailor and draper, he became mayor of Newport (1836–37). On 4 November 1839 he led a Chartist insurrection designed to seize control of Newport, which was repulsed by troops with heavy loss of Chartist lives. He was sentenced to be hanged, drawn and quartered, but the sentence was commuted to transportation for life to Tasmania. In 1856, given an unconditional pardon, he returned to a triumphant welcome in Newport. He died in Bristol, where he was buried.

FROST, Robert Lee (1874–1963) American lyric poet, 'the voice of New England', born in San Francisco, the son of a New England father and Scottish mother. He studied at Harvard, but did not graduate and was teacher, cobbler and New Hampshire farmer, before going to Britain (1912–15), where, under the encouragement of **Rupert Brooke**, **Abercrombie** and **Wilfred Gibson**, he published *A Boy's Will* (1913) and *North of Boston* (1914), which brought him an international reputation. Returning in glory to the USA, he became professor of English at Amherst (1916), and continued to write poetry which in character, background and situation is essentially New England. He was awarded the Pulitzer prize in 1924, 1931 and 1937, and received a US senate citation of honour in 1950. He was professor of poetry at Harvard from 1939 to 1943 before returning to Amherst (1949–63).

FROST, Terry (1915–) English painter, born in Leamington Spa, Warwickshire. Taken prisoner in Crete in 1941 he spent World War II in prisoner-of-war camps. After the war he attended evening classes at Birmingham Art College, then moved to St Ives, Cornwall. His first abstract paintings date from 1949. He has held various teaching posts, including a readership in the department of fine art at Newcastle University, but has constantly returned to Cornwall. In 1960 he visited the USA and met **Mark Rothko**, **Barnet Newman**, **Franz Kline** and other leading Abstract Expressionists. Since 1952 he has had over 30 one-man shows in Britain, Europe and America.

FROUDE, James Anthony (1818–94) English historian, brother of **Richard Hurrell Froude** and **William Froude**, born in Dartington, Devon. Educated at Westminster and Oriel College, Oxford, in 1842 he was elected a fellow of Exeter College, Oxford. He received deacon's orders in 1844, and was some time under **Newman**'s influence; but a change was revealed in *Shadows of the Clouds* by 'Zeta', a psychological novel (1847, suppressed), and still more in *The Nemesis of Faith* (1848), which cost Froude both his fellowship and an educational post in Tasmania. For the next few years he wrote for *Fraser's Magazine* (which for a while he edited) and the *Westminster Review*, and in 1856 issued volumes i–ii of his *History of England from the Fall of Wolsey to the Spanish Armada*, completed in twelve volumes in 1869. In this work Froude shows supreme literary ability; but, like **Macaulay**, he is a man of letters first and a historian second. His views of men and motives are those of the 19th century, distorted by his own highly individualistic judgment. His brilliant essays *English in Ireland in the Eighteenth Century* (1871–74) and *Caesar* (1879) provide further evidence for this criticism. In 1874, and again in 1875, he visited the South African colonies on a mission from the home government, and published his impressions in *Two Lectures on South Africa* (1880). As **Carlyle**'s literary executor he edited his *Reminiscences* (1881), **Jane Carlyle**'s *Letters* (1882) and wrote Carlyle's own *Life* (1882–84). Later works are *Oceana* (1886), a delightful account of an Australasian voyage; *The English in the West Indies* (1888); *The Two Chiefs of Dunboy* (1889), an Irish historical romance; *The Earl of Beaconsfield* (1890); *The Divorce of Catharine of Aragon* (1891); *The Spanish Story of the Armada* (1892); *Life and Letters of Erasmus* (1894); and *Lectures on the Council of Trent* (1896). In 1892 he succeeded **Freeman** as professor of modern history at Oxford.

FROUDE, Richard Hurrell (1803–36) English tractarian, brother of **James Anthony Froude** and **William Froude**. He became fellow and tutor of Oriel College, Oxford, in 1827. With **Newman** and **Keble** he helped to initiate the 'Oxford Movement', and wrote Tracts 9 and 63. His diaries, posthumously published as *Remains* (1838–39), betrayed hostility to the leaders of the Reformation and encouraged the development of Anglo-Catholicism.

FROUDE, William (1810–79) English engineer and applied mathematician, brother of **James Anthony Froude** and **Richard Hurrell Froude**. In 1827 he became an assistant to **Isambard Kingdom Brunel**. Retiring from professional work in 1846, he devoted himself to investigating the conditions of naval construction.

FRUMENTIUS, St (4th century) the apostle of Ethiopia, born in Phoenicia. He was captured while on a voyage by Ethiopians, became the king's secretary, and gradually secured the introduction of Christianity. In 326 he was consecrated bishop of Axum by **Athanasius** in Alexandria.

FRUNDSBERG, Georg von (1473–1528) German soldier, founder and leader of German *Landsknechte* during the Italian wars of **Maximilian I** and **Charles V**. He fought in 20 pitched battles, and Pavia (1525) was largely won by him.

FRY, Charles Burgess (1872–1956) English sportsman, born in Croydon. An outstanding all-rounder who has been considered by some as the greatest ever all-round British sportsman, he gained his Blue at Oxford for athletics, cricket and soccer, and later represented his country in all three. Best remembered as a cricketer, he played 26 Tests for England. In his early days he bowled and batted, but in 1900 was called for throwing and thereafter concentrated on batting. In 1912 he captained England in the Triangular Test series. With **Don Bradman** he holds the record of six consecutive centuries in first-class cricket. After World War I he acted as India's delegate to the League of Nations on the suggestion of **K S Ranjitsinjhi**. He was offered the throne of Albania, but declined. Later in his career he commanded the training ship *Mercury*, and became a journalist. A man of prodigious versatility, he once lamented never having been involved in the Derby, drawing from a friend the remark, 'What as Charles? Trainer, jockey or horse?'

FRY, Christopher Harris (1907–) English dramatist, born in Bristol, educated at Bedford Modern School. He combined being a schoolmaster with a love of the stage, which became a full-time occupation on his appointment as director of Tunbridge Wells Repertory Players (1932–36). In 1940 he became director of the Playhouse at Oxford, having in the meantime written two pageant-plays, *Thursday's Child* and *The Tower*, also *The Boy with a Cart*, a charming rustic play on the subject of the Sussex saint, Cuthman. After service in World War II he began a series of outstanding plays in free verse, often with undertones of religion and mysticism, including *A Phoenix too Frequent* (1946), *The Firstborn* (1946), *The Lady's not for Burning* (1949), *Thor, with Angels* (1949), *Venus Observed* (1950), *A Sleep of Prisoners* (1951), *The Dark is Light Enough* (1954), *Curtmantle* (1962) and *A Yard of Sun* (1970). He has also produced highly successful translations of **Anouilh** and **Giraudoux**.

FRY, Elizabeth, née **Gurney** (1780–1845) English Quaker prison reformer, daughter of a rich Quaker banker, John Gurney, and sister of **Joseph John Gurney**. In 1800 she married Joseph Fry, a London Quaker merchant, and in 1810 became a preacher for the Society of Friends. She visited Newgate Prison for women in 1813 and found 300 women, with their children, in appalling conditions, and thereafter devoted her life to prison and asylum reform at home and abroad. She also founded hostels for the homeless, as well as charity organizations, despite her husband's bankruptcy in 1828.

FRY, Joseph (1728–87) English Quaker businessman and type-founder, born in Sutton Benger in Wiltshire. He settled in Bristol as a doctor, but went into a pottery enterprise; founded the well-known chocolate business; and from 1764 onwards became eminent as a type-founder.

FRY, Roger Eliot (1866–1934) English artist and art critic, born in London. A landscape painter himself, he became a champion of modern artists, particularly **Cézanne**, and organized the first London exhibition of Post-Impressionists in 1910. He wrote extensively on art and aesthetics, propounding a theory of 'significant form' and colour, rather than content, as the only criteria for great art. He founded the Omega Workshops in London (1913–21), in association with **Vanessa Bell** and **Duncan Grant** and others of the Bloomsbury group, to design textiles, pottery and furniture. His writings include *Vision and Design* (1920), *Transformations* (1926), *Cézanne* (1927), *Henri Matisse* (1930), *French Art* (1932) and *Reflections on British Painting* (1934).

FRYXELL, Anders (1795–1881) Swedish historian. He was a parish priest from 1835 to 1847, but therafter gave himself entirely to literary work at Stockholm. His *Narratives from Swedish History* (46 vols, 1832–80) have been translated into English (1844).

FUAD I (1868–1936) Egyptian ruler, son of Khedive **Ismail Pasha** and father of **Farouk I**. He was sultan of Egypt from 1917 and king from 1922, when the British protectorate was terminated.

FUAD PASHA, Mehmed (1814–69) Turkish statesman and littérateur. He was the son of the poet, Izzet-Mollah, became an Admiralty physician, but in 1835 took up history and politics. After diplomatic service in London and Madrid, he became grand interpreter to the Porte, minister of foreign affairs (1852 and 1855), and Grand Vizier (1861–66). To him Turkey owed the hatti-sherif of 1856.

FUCHS, Klaus Emil Julius (1911–88) German-born British physicist and spy, born in Russelsheim near Frankfurt. The son of a Protestant pacifist pastor, he was taught a creed called 'Christian communism', and was educated at Kiel and Leipzig universities. Escaping from Nazi persecution to Britain in 1933, he was interned on the outbreak of World War II, but released and naturalized in 1942. From 1943 he was one of the most brilliant of a group of British scientists sent to America to work on the atom bomb. In 1946 he became head of the theoretical physics division at Harwell. In March 1950 he was sentenced to 14 years' imprisonment for disclosing nuclear secrets to the Russians over a six-year period; in 1951 he was formally deprived of British citizenship. On his release in June 1959 he became an East German citizen and worked at East Germany's nuclear research centre until his retirement in 1979.

FUCHS, Leonhard (1501–66) German botanist. He was professor at Tübingen, a pioneer of German botany, and wrote *Historia stirpium* (1542). The genus *Fuchsia* was named after him.

FUCHS, Sir Vivian Ernest (1908–) English Antarctic explorer and scientist, leader of the Commonwealth Antarctic Expedition (1956–58), born in Kent. The son of a farmer of German origin, he was educated at Brighton College and St John's, Cambridge. After four geological expeditions in East Africa (1929–38), he served in West Africa and Germany during World War II. As director of the Falkland Islands Dependencies Survey (1947) he set up scientific bases on Graham Land peninsula, and while marooned there for a year, conceived the plan for an overland crossing of Antarctica, which materialized in 1955 when he was appointed leader of the Commonwealth expedition. With a party of ten he set out by snow tractor from Shackleton Base, Weddell Sea, on 24 November 1957, reached the South Pole on 19 January 1958, and continuing via Depot 700 with the assistance of Sir **Edmund Hillary** and his New Zealand party, reached Scott Base, Victoria Land, on 2 March. He was awarded the gold medal of the Royal Geographical Society (1951), and its Polar medal (1953) and clasp (1958).

FUCINI, Renato, pseud **Neri Tanfucio** (1843–1921) Italian writer, born in Monterotondo, near Pisa, the son of a country doctor. He studied agriculture and engineering in Pisa, and became city engineer in Florence. He had a bright wit which found outlet in dialect verse, published as *Centi Sonetti* (1872). When Florence ceased to be a capital city he lost his post and retired to the country. *Le veglie di Neri* (1884), a collection of tales, is his best-known work. *All' aria aperta* (1897) is reckoned the best modern collection of Italian humorous novellas. He also wrote books for children and personal anecdotes.

FUENTES, Carlos (1928–) Mexican novelist and playwright, born in Panama City. While very young he travelled extensively as his father changed diplomatic posts. Educated at the Colegio Frances Morelos, his graduate studies took him to the National University of Mexico and the Institut des Hautes Études Internationales in Geneva, which led to a career in international affairs. A secretary of the Mexican delegation to the International Labor Organization, he eventually became cultural attaché to the Mexican Embassy in Geneva (1950–52) and press secretary to the United Nations Information Centre, Mexico City. He served as the Mexican ambassador to France (1975–77), and has held a variety of teaching posts. An energetic cultural promoter, writer of articles and reviewer, he has published prolifically since his first collection of fantastic, myth-inspired short-stories, *Los dias enmascarados* (The Masked Days) in 1954. Many of his novels have been published in English, among them *Terra Nostra* (1975), regarded as his masterpiece, the culmination and synthesis of his novel-writing practice and thought on the identity and destiny of Spain and Latin America.

FUGARD, Athol (1932–) South African dramatist and theatre director, born in Middleburg, Cape Province, and educated at Port Elizabeth Technical College and Cape Town University. After leaving university in 1953 he worked as a seaman and journalist before becoming a stage manager and settling firmly into a theatrical career in 1959 as actor, director and playwright. Since 1965 he has been director of the Serpent Players in Port Elizabeth, and in 1972 co-founded the Space Experimental Theatre, Cape Town. His plays are set in contemporary South Africa, but his presentation of the bleakness and frustration of life for those especially on the fringes of society raises their political and social deprivation to the level of universal human tragedy. His work has met with official opposition; *Blood Knot* (1960), portraying two coloured brothers, one light- and one dark-skinned, was censored, and some of his work has only been published and produced abroad. His plays include *Boesman and Lena* (1969), *Statements after an arrest under the Immorality Act* (1972), *Sizwe Banzi is Dead* (1973), *Dimetos* (1976) and *A Lesson from Aloes* (1979). He has also written film scripts and a novel, *Tsotsi* (1980). Fugard has become increasingly popular in Britain, and later plays, *Master Harold and the Boys* (1982), *The Road to Mecca* (1984), and *A Place with the Pigs* (1987), have been staged at the National Theatre. The latter play veers away from the South African themes of his earlier work, being inspired by a newspaper story about a Red Army deserter who hid in a pigsty for over 40 years.

FUGGER name of a South German family of bankers and merchants in the early 16th century which founded lines of counts and princes. Johannes (1348–1409), was a master-weaver, who was born near Schwabmünchen, and settled at Augsburg in 1368. His second son, Jacob (d.1469), carried on an extensive business. Three of his sons extended their business to an extraordinary degree, married into the noblest houses, and were ennobled by the emperor **Maximilian I**, who mortgaged to them for 10 000 gold gulden the county of Kirchberg and the lordship of Weissenhorn. The house attained the height of its prosperity and influence under **Charles V**, when its fortunes came to rest on the sons of George (d.1506), founders of the two chief lines of the house of Fugger. The brothers were zealous Catholics, opponents of **Luther**. Charles V made them counts, invested them with the still mortgaged properties of Kirchberg and Weissenhorn, and gave them the rights of princes. The Fuggers continued still to carry on their commerce, increased their immense wealth, and attained the highest posts in the empire. They possessed great libraries and art collections, maintained painters and musicians, and encouraged art and science.

FÜHRICH, Joseph von (1800–76) Viennese religious painter, born in Kratzau in Bohemia. His work can be seen in churches throughout Austria.

FUKUDA, Takeo (1905–) Japanese politician and financier. He worked at the ministry of finance (1929–50) and was deputy vice-minister (1945–46), director of the banking bureau (1946–47), and director of the budget bureau (1947–50). He has been a member of the house of representatives since 1952 and served as minister of finance (1965–66, 1968–71 and 1973–74). In 1974 he became deputy prime minister and director of the Economic Planning Agency, until his appointment as prime minister from 1976 to 1978. He was president of the Liberal-Democratic party from 1966 to 1968 and from 1976 to 1978.

FUKUI, Kenichi (1918–) Japanese chemist, born in Nara. He became professor of physical chemistry at Kyoto Imperial University in 1951. His work on the theory of chemical reactions, and perhaps especially his development of the frontier orbital method for predicting the path of pericyclic organic reactions, led to him sharing the Nobel prize for chemistry in 1981 with **Roald Hoffmann**.

FULBECKE, William (1560–c.1603) English jurist, born in Lincoln. He was the author of *Direction or Preparative to the Study of the Law* (1600), one of the oldest English legal text-books, which was still in use in the 19th century, and of other legal works.

FULBRIGHT, James William (1905–) American Democrat politician and lawyer, born in Sumner, Missouri. Educated in Arkansas, at Oxford (Rhodes scholar), and at George Washington University law school, he was elected to the House of Representatives in 1942, where he introduced a resolution in 1943 advocating the creation of, and US participation in, the United Nations. In 1944 he entered the senate and was responsible for the Fulbright Act of 1946 establishing an exchange scholarship system for students and teachers between the USA and other countries. He distinguished himself in 1954 by his opposition to **Joseph McCarthy**. He advocated a more liberal US foreign policy particularly in relation to communist China and Cuba, and criticized the escalation of the war in Vietnam. He wrote *Old Myths and New Realities* (1965) and *The Arrogance of Power* (1967).

FULGENTIUS (468–533) African Christian prelate, bishop from 507 of Ruspe in Numidia. He wrote Latin treatises against the Arians and semi-Pelagians.

FULLER, Andrew (1754–1815) English Baptist pastor, born in Wicken, Cambridgeshire. His treatise *The Gospel worthy of all Acceptance* (1784), involved him in a controversy with the ultra-calvinists. In 1792 he became the first secretary of the newly-founded Baptist Missionary Society. His other writings include *Calvanistic and Socinian Systems Compared* (1793) and *Socinianism Indefensible* (1797).

FULLER, (Richard) Buckminster (1895–1983) American engineer, born in Milton. He studied at Harvard and the US Naval Academy, commencing practice in 1922. In 1917 he discovered energetic/synergetic geometry, and later devised a structural system known as Tensegrity Structures. Following the machine aesthetic, he experimented with structural designs, aimed at economical, efficent, trouble-free living (developed from systems of aircraft and chassis construction), intended for mass-production. Dymaxion House (1927) embodied these practical ideas. After 1945 he designed geodesic domes, great space-frame enclosures, based on polyhedra; the largest design was realized at the Union Tank Car Repair Shop, Louisiana (1958), and the best-known at the US Pavilion, Montreal Exhibition (1967).

FULLER, George (1822–84) American artist, born in Deerfield, Massachusetts. He is best known for his haunting landscape and figure paintings, especially *Romany Girl*, *The Tomato Patch*, and *Winifred Dysart*.

FULLER, John Frederick Charles (1878–1966) English soldier, born in Chichester. Commissioned in the Oxfordshire and Buckinghamshire Light Infantry in 1898, he served in the 2nd Boer War (1899–1902). In World War I he served with the Royal Tank Corps, and became an advocate of the armour-cum-fighter-plane war of movement as subsequently exploited by **Hitler**'s *Reichswehr*. He retired in 1933 and became renowned for his writings on theory of war, particularly relating to mobile and armoured forces, including *Reformation of War* (1923), *Foundations of the Science of War* (1926), *Memoirs of an Unconventional Soldier* (1936) and *Decisive Battles* (3 vols, 1956).

FULLER, Loie, originally **Marie Louise Fuller** (1862–1928) American dancer, choreographer and producer, born in Illinois. A pioneer in the field of performance art, she began her career in vaudeville and as a circus artist (1865–91). In 1891 her exotic solo skirt-dance, using multi-directional coloured lights on the yards of swirling silk she wore, created a sensation, especially in Europe. Her Paris début in 1892 was met with overwhelming acclaim. In 1900 she appeared at the Paris World Fair. Group pieces also figured among her (more than 100) dances. She founded a school in 1908, and was a model for **Toulouse-Lautrec, Auguste Rodin** and many other prominent artists.

FULLER, (Sarah) Margaret, Marchioness Ossoli (1810–50) American feminist and critic, born in Cambridgeport, Massachusetts. Rigorously educated by her father before attending the local school at the age of 14, she went on to teach in Boston (1836–37) and Providence (1837–39). There, joining the intellectual élite, she held her celebrated 'conversations', cultural discussions with a circle of Boston ladies, which attracted several prominent reformers and transcendentalists. From 1840 to 1842 she was editor of *The Dial*, the transcendentalist journal, and in 1844 went to New York where she became literary critic for the *New York Tribune*. Moving to Italy in 1847, she married Marquis Giovanni Ossoli, and with him became involved in the Revolution of 1848. She was drowned in a shipwreck on her way back to New York, along with her husband and young son. Her publications include *Summer on the Lakes* (1844), and *Woman in the 19th Century* (1855).

FULLER, Roy Broadbent (1912–) English poet and novelist, born in Oldham. He went to school in Blackpool, trained as a solicitor, and spent his professional career as a solicitor with building societies. His first collection of poetry, *Poems*, appeared in 1939 and was, he fully admitted, very strongly influenced by **Auden**. His war-time experiences in the Royal Navy (1941–45) prompted *The Middle of a War* (1942) and *A Lost Season* (1944). This saw the development of the note of self-criticism, the idea that the experience of collective responsibility cannot support the view of the poet as an infallible intelligence, which was to become an integral part of his later poetry. His traditionalist attitude kept him apart from the strong current of neo-Romantic revival initiated by **Dylan Thomas** after the war, but his *Brutus's Orchard* (1957) and *Collected Poems* (1962) established him as a major poet, and his later works include *Buff* (1965), *Song Cycle from a Record Sleeve* (1972), *An Old War* (1974), *From the Joke Shop* (1975) and *Retreads* (1979). His novels show great skill in observation and intricacy of plot, and include *Second Curtain* (1953), *The Ruined Boys* (1959), *The Perfect Fool* (1963) and *The Carnal Island* (1970). He was professor of poetry at Oxford 1968–73, and *Owl and Artificers* (1971) is a stimulating and entertaining collection of his lectures. He has also published the autobiographical *Souvenirs* (1980) and *Vamp Till Ready* (1982).

FULLER, Thomas (1608–61) English clergyman and antiquary, born in Aldwinkle St Peter's, Northamptonshire, and author of *History of the Worthies of Britain*. He studied at Sidney Sussex College, Cambridge, and became prebendary of Salisbury in 1631 and rector of Broadwindsor, Dorset, in 1634. His first ambitious work was about the Crusades, *The History of the Holy War* (1639). Just before the outbreak of the Civil War he was appointed preacher to the Chapel Royal at the Savoy, in London, and during the war he was chaplain to the royalist commander, **Ralph Hopton**. He compiled a collection of miscellanies in *The Holy State and The Profane State* (1642), and wrote tracts to comfort the troops: *Good Thoughts in Bad Times* (1645), *Good Thoughts in Worse Times* (1647), and *The Cause and Cure of a Troubled Conscience* (1647), and a satire directed at **Cromwell** (*Andronicus or the Unfortunate Politician*). After the war he was allowed to preach, on sufferance, and in 1649 he was given the curacy of Waltham Abbey. In 1655 he brought out his long-projected *Church History of Britain*, to which was appended his *History of Cambridge University*. With the Restoration he published *Mixt Contemplations in Better Times* (1660) and was appointed chaplain-extraordinary to **Charles II**. He did not live to complete his most famous work, *History of the Worthies of Britain*, an encyclopaedic miscellany about the counties of Britain and their notable men. It was published by his son the year after his death.

FULTON, Rikki (1924–) Scottish actor and comedian, born in Glasgow. He began his career as a broadcaster at the BBC in Glasgow, performing in drama, features, children's and religious programmes, and appeared at several Scottish repertory theatres before moving to London. From 1951 to 1955 he presented various weekly programmes. Returning to Scotland he starred in the *Five past Eight* variety shows in Edinburgh and Glasgow, and since the 1950s has regularly appeared in pantomime in both cities, and is recognized as one of the great pantomime dames. He also has a stage double-act with Jack Milroy in which they appear as the teddy boys Francie and Josie. On television, *Scotch and Wry*, his own series composed of comic sketches, began in 1978 and remains hugely popular. In 1985 he adapted and starred in *A Wee Touch of Class*, a successful transposition of **Molière**'s *Le Bourgeois Gentilhomme* from 17th-century France to 19th-century Edinburgh.

FULTON, Robert (1765–1815) American engineer, born of Irish parents in what is now Fulton township, Pennsylvania. He painted miniature portraits and landscapes in Philadelphia from 1782, but in 1786 he went to London and studied under the painter **Benjamin West**, but gradually applied his energies wholly to mechanical engineering. In 1794 he obtained from the British government a patent for a double-inclined plane to supersede locks, and invented a mill for sawing and polishing marble. In 1797 he went to Paris, where he devoted himself to new projects and inventions, among them a submarine torpedo boat, but neither the French nor the British government would take it up. In 1803 he made two experiments on the Seine with small steamboats. In 1806 he returned to New York and in 1807 launched a steam vessel, the *Clermont*, on the Hudson, which accomplished the voyage (nearly 150 miles) to Albany in 32 hours. Although he was not the first to apply steam to inland navigation, he was the first to do so successfully. He was employed by the US government on canals and other works, and in constructing (1814) the world's first steam warship, *Fulton the First*.

FUNK, Casimir (1884–1967) Polish-born American biochemist, born in Warsaw. He studied in Berlin and Bern and worked as a research assistant at the Lister Institute, London (1910–13), becoming head of the biochemical department at the Cancer Hospital Research Institute (1913–15). He emigrated to the USA in 1915, and later headed a research institute in Warsaw (1923–27) and Paris (1928–39). He was best known for his work on vitamins, which he identified and named 'vitamines' in 1912.

FUNK, Walther (1890–1960) German Nazi politician. One of **Hitler**'s chief advisers, he succeeded **Schacht** as minister of economics and president of the Reichsbank, and played a leading part in planning the economic aspects of the attack on Russia, and in the exploitation of occupied territories. Captured in 1945, he was sentenced to life imprisonment as a war criminal, but was released in 1957 on account of illness.

FURETIÈRE, Antoine (1619–88) French scholar and lexicographer, Abbé of Chalivoy. A writer of comic verse and fables, he compiled a massive *Dictionnaire Universel*, only to be expelled from the Académie, which claimed a monopoly on its collections (1674). It was eventually published in Rotterdam in 1690.

FURNESS, Christopher Furness, 1st Baron (1852–1912) English shipowner, born in West Hartlepool. He became a shipbroker in 1876 and soon afterwards established the Furness line. He went into partnership with Edward Withy in 1885, which marked the beginning of a huge shipbuilding and engineering business. A Liberal MP, he was one of the first to start a co-partnership scheme among his employees. He was knighted in 1895 and was created baron in 1910. He was succeeded by his son, Marmaduke (1883–1940), who was created a viscount in 1918.

FURNESS, Horace Howard (1833–1912) American Shakespearean scholar, born in Philadelphia. A lawyer by profession, he devoted his life to his *Variorum* edition of **Shakespeare**, starting with *Romeo and Juliet* in 1871. The work was continued by his son Horace Howard II (1865–1930).

FURNISS, Harry (1854–1925) Irish caricaturist, born in Wexford, the son of an English engineer. In 1873 he went to London and worked as a caricaturist on the *Illustrated London News* (1876–84) and *Punch* (1884–94). He made the illustrations for **Lewis Carroll**'s *Sylvie and Bruno*, and editions of **Dickens** and **Thackeray**. He edited and published his own cartoon magazine, *Like Joka* (1894), and wrote *Confessions of a Caricaturist*. He also worked in the film industry with **Thomas Alva Edison** (1912–13), acted in films, and was a pioneer of the animated cartoon film (1914).

FURNIVALL, Frederick James (1825–1910) English philologist, son of a doctor at Egham. He studied at London and Cambridge universities, won fame as an oarsman and racing-boat designer, was called to the bar, and, influenced by **J F D Maurice** and Christian socialism, helped to found the Working Men's College in London. But it was as a philologist and editor of English texts that he became famous, giving a great impulse to Early English scholarship. He founded the Early English Text Society, the **Chaucer**, Ballad, New **Shakespeare**, **Wycliffe** and **Shelley** Societies, and edited some score of texts, including **Chaucer** and the **Percy** *Ballads*, **Brunne**'s *Handlying Synne*, **William Harrison**'s *Description of England*, **Stubbes**' *Anatomy of Abuses*, and **Hoccleve**, besides writing the introduction to the 'Leopold' Shakespeare. He also edited the Philological Society's dictionary (from 1861) that became the *Oxford English Dictionary*.

FURPHY, Joseph (1843–1912) Australian writer, born in Yering, Yarra Glen, Victoria, of Irish emigrant parents. Born into a hard-working and well-read family, he worked as a farmer and a bullock-driver before moving to Shepparton, Victoria, in 1883. There he worked at the iron-foundry which had been established by his elder brother. This security enabled him to contribute, under the name 'Tom Collins', a series of articles to the *Bulletin* magazine, and to write a 1220-page manuscript of his novel, *Such is Life*. After much revision and abridgment, this work was published in 1903. An edition of the deleted sections of Furphy's book was published after his death, as *Rigby's Romance* (1921), but his reputation rests on his one major work with its credo 'Temper, democratic; bias, offensively Australian', a credo which encapsulated his hard-working philosophy and marked a move away from literature's romantic concept of Australia's pioneering days.

FURSE, Charles Wellington (1868–1904) English painter. He studied at the Slade School under **Legros**, and in Paris. An active member of the New English Art Club, his portrait and subject paintings are noted for easy, fluent brushwork.

FÜRST, Julius (1805–73) German orientalist, born in Zerkowo in Posen. In 1864 he became professor at Leipzig. His works include books on the Jewish medieval philosophers (1845) and the biblical and Jewish-Hellenic literature, and his great *Hebrew and Chaldee Lexicon* (1851–54).

FURTWÄNGLER, Wilhelm (1886–1954) German conductor, born in Berlin, son of Adolf Furtwängler (1853–1907), the celebrated classical archaeologist. He succeeded **Arthur Nikisch** in 1922 as conductor of the Gewandhaus concerts in Leipzig and of the Berlin Philharmonic. International tours established him as one of the leading musical personalities of his age, though his highly subjective and romantic interpretations of the German masters aroused controversy. His ambivalent attitude to the **Hitler** régime cost him some popularity outside Germany, but after the war he quickly re-established himself.

FUSELI, Henry, real name **Johann Heinrich Füssli** (1741–1825) Swiss-born British painter and art-critic, born in Zürich. In England in 1763, he was encouraged by Sir **Joshua Reynolds** to go to Italy (1770–78). He became professor of painting at the Royal Academy, and keeper in 1804. His 200 paintings include *The Nightmare* (1781) and two series to illustrate **Shakespeare**'s and **Milton**'s works, by which he is chiefly known. His literary works, with life, were published by **Knowles** (1831).

FUST, Johann (c.1400–1466) German printer and goldsmith, born in Mainz. In 1450 and 1452 he made loans to the printer **Gutenberg**, to help complete the printing of his bible. When the loans were not repaid he sued for the debt, receiving, in lieu of payment, Gutenberg's printing plant, with which he started his own business, taking **Peter Schöffer**, his son-in-law, as partner. They published the Gutenberg Bible in 1465.

FUSTEL DE COULANGES, Numa Denis (1830–89) French historian, born in Paris. He was professor at Amiens, Paris, Strasbourg, and from 1875 at the École Normale, Paris. His *Chio* (1857) and *Polybe* (1858) preceded his *La Cité antique* (1864), which threw fresh light on the social and religious institutions of antiquity. His *Histoire des institutions politiques de l'ancienne France* (1875–92) attacked racial theories in political history. Both are literary masterpieces.

FYFE, Sir David Patrick Maxwell See **KILMUIR, 1st Earl of**

FYFFE, Charles Alan (1845–92) English historian, born in Blackheath. Educated at Balliol College, Oxford, he was elected a fellow of University College, and published *A History of Modern Europe* (1880–90).

FYSH, Sir (Wilmot) Hudson (1895–1974) Australian civil aviation pioneer, born in Launceston, Tasmania. He served with the Australian Imperial Forces at Gallipoli in World War I and later, having transferred to the Australian Flying Corps, was awarded the DFC. With another returned ex-war pilot, he surveyed a route between Darwin and Longreach, Queensland, for the 1919 Britain-Australia air race, and in the following year, with the backing of local pastoralists, he established the Queensland and Northern Territory Aerial Services Limited, now known as QANTAS. In 1931 he was involved in the pioneering Australia-England airmail flights, which led to the formation of Qantas Empire Airways as a joint venture with Imperial Airways of the UK. In 1947 Qantas was acquired by the Australian government. Fysh became managing director, was knighted in 1953, and retired as chairman in 1966. He was a notable aviation historian, and wrote a number of books on the early days of civil aviation.

G

GABELENTZ, Hans Conon von der (1807–74) German linguist, born in Altenburg. He knew 80 languages, and is remembered for his great work on the Melanesian languages (1860–73). His son, Georg (1840–93), in 1878 became oriental professor at Leipzig, in 1889 at Berlin.

GABELSBERGER, Franz Xaver (1789–1848) German bureaucrat, born in Munich. He was the inventor of the chief German system of shorthand, having in 1809 entered the Bavarian civil service.

GABIN, Jean, originally **Jean Alexis Moncorgé** (1904–76) French actor, born in Paris. Part of a showbusiness family, he built his reputation in cabaret, revues, the Folies Bergères and the Moulin Rouge, before making his film début in *Chacun sa Chance* (1930). His performances as world-weary, fatalistic anti-heroes in films like *Pépé le Moko* (1937), *La Grande Illusion* (1937), *Quai des Brumes* (1938) and *Le Jour se Lève* (1939) were seen to embody the pessimistic spirit of pre-war France. He escaped to America during World War II, later joining the Free French navy, participating in the Normandy invasion and receiving the Croix de Guerre and Medaille Militaire. In the 1950s he re-established his dominance of the French film scene with his portraits of mature, wise professionals. Active until his death, he received the Venice Festival Best Actor prize for *La Nuit est Mon Royaume* (1951) and *Touchez Pas au Grisbi* (1954), and similar awards at the Berlin Festival for *Archimede le Clochard* (1958) and *Le Chat* (1971).

GABIROL, ibn See **AVICEBRÓN**

GABLE, Christopher (1940–) English dancer, born in London. He studied at the Royal Ballet School, and was soon dancing solo roles as a principal and partner to **Lynn Seymour**. After six years he retired as a dancer in 1967, having created roles in **Kenneth MacMillan**'s *Images of Love* (1964) and **Frederick Ashton**'s *The Two Pigeons* (1961). He was chosen to play the lead in MacMillan's new *Romeo and Juliet* with Lynn Seymour, but they were replaced in the première at the last minute by **Nureyev** and **Fonteyn**. As an actor in the 1970s he landed roles in films like **Ken Russell**'s *The Boy Friend* (1972). In 1986 he became director of the Manchester-based Northern Ballet Theatre and in 1987 he choreographed *A Simple Man*, based on the life of the artist **L S Lowry**, for television.

GABLE, (William) Clark (1901–60) American film actor, born in Cadiz, Ohio. Early stage experience was intermingled with casual labour and work as an extra in silent films. A concentrated assault on Hollywood stardom resulted in twelve film appearances in 1931. Embodying rugged male virtues, he also evinced an impudent sense of humour, and at the peak of his popularity won an Academy Award for *It Happened One Night* (1934). He was voted King of Hollywood in 1937 and was judged the perfect Rhett Butler in *Gone With the Wind* (1939). He returned to the cinema after World War II army service and remained in demand as a sparring partner in films like *Mogambo* (1953), *Teacher's Pet* (1958) and *The Misfits* (1960). Married five times, his third wife was actress **Carole Lombard**, who was killed in a 1942 air crash.

GABO, Naum, originally **Naum Neevia Pevsner** (1890–1977) Russian-born American constructivist sculptor, born in Bryansk, Russia. He first studied medicine and engineering, then art in Munich (1911–12). With his brother, **Antoine Pevsner**, and **Tatlin** and **Malevich**, he was associated with the Moscow Suprematist Group (1913), and in 1920 broke away with his brother and Tatlin to form the group of Russian Constructivists, who have had considerable influence on 20th-century architecture and design. In 1920 they published their *Realistic Manifesto*. As their theories did not coincide with those of Russian official art circles, he was forced into exile, and lived in Berlin (1923–33), Paris (1933–35) and England (1936-45). In 1946 he went to the USA. There are several examples of his completely non-figurative geometrical 'constructions in space', mainly made in transparent plastics, in the Museum of Modern Art, New York.

GABOR, Dennis (1900–79) Hungarian-born British physicist, born in Budapest. After obtaining a doctorate in engineering in Berlin (1927) he worked as a research engineer, but left Germany in 1933. In 1948 he joined Imperial College, London, and was appointed professor of applied electron physics (1958–67). He is credited with the invention in 1947 of the technique of (and the name) holography, a method of photographically recording and reproducing three-dimensional images, for which he was awarded the Nobel prize for physics in 1971. The invention came out of his work on improving the resolution of the electron microscope.

GABORIAU, Émile (1835–73) French writer of detective fiction, born in Saujon in Charente-Inférieure. He had already contributed to some of the smaller Parisian papers, when he leapt to fame with *L'Affaire Lerouge* (1866), featuring his detective Lecoq. It was followed by *Le Dossier 113* (1867), *Monsieur Lecoq* (1869), *Les Esclaves de Paris* (1869), *La Corde au cou* (1873), and several others.

GABRIEL, Jacques Ange (1698–1782) French architect, born in Paris. As court architect to **Louis XV** he planned a number of additions to Versailles and other palaces, and designed the Petit Trianon (1768). He also laid out the Place de la Concorde (1753).

GABRIELI, Andrea (c.1533–1586) Italian composer, born in Venice. After studying under **Adrian Willaert**, he became organist of St Mark's Church. He wrote masses and other choral works; his organ pieces include toccatas and ricercare, the latter foreshadowing the fugue.

GABRIELI, Giovanni (c.1555–1612) Italian composer, nephew and pupil of **Andrea Gabrieli**. He composed choral and instrumental works in which he exploited the acoustics of St Mark's in Venice with brilliant antiphonal and echo effects, using double choirs, double ensembles of wind instruments and other devices, as in his well-known *Sonata pian e forte*. He published much of his uncle's music, and became a renowned teacher.

GADAMER, Hans-Georg (1900–) German philosopher, born in Marburg, Hesse. A pupil of **Heidegger**, he became rector at Leipzig and held chairs at Frankfurt (1947) and Heidelberg (1949–68). His major work is *Wahrheit und Methode* (1960), translated as

Truth and Method (1975), and he is known particularly for his theory of hermeneutics, which has been useful both in philosophy and in related subjects in explaining the nature of understanding and interpretation.

GADDAFI, Colonel Muammar (1942–) Libyan political and military leader. Born into a nomadic family, he abandoned university studies to attend military academy in 1963. He formed the Free Officers Movement which overthrew the régime of King Idris in 1969. Gaddafi became chairman of the revolutionary command council, promoted himself to colonel (the highest rank in the revolutionary army) and became commander-in-chief of the Libyan armed forces. As *de facto* head of state, he set about eradicating colonialism by expelling foreigners and closing down British and US bases. He also encouraged a religious revival and return to the fundamental principles of Islam. A somewhat unpredictable figure, Gaddafi has openly supported violent revolutionaries in other parts of the world while following a unique blend of democratic and autocratic government at home.

GADDI, Agnolo (c.1333–1396) Florentine painter and architect, son of **Taddeo Gaddi**. He painted the frescoes of the *Discovery of the Cross* in S Croce at Florence and of the *Legends of the Holy Girdle* in the cathedral at Prato. His work shows the influence of **Giotto**.

GADDI, Gaddo (c.1260–1332) Florentine painter, founder of the Gaddi family. He worked in mosaic in Rome and Florence.

GADDI, Taddeo (c.1300–1366) Florentine painter, son of **Gaddo Gaddi**. He was **Giotto**'s best pupil and also his godson. His finest work is seen in the frescoes of the *Life of the Virgin* in the Baroncelli chapel of S Croce. Though the best-known of Giotto's followers, his style deviated from that of his master, whom he does not match in figure painting, but whom he excels in architectural perspective.

GADDIS, William (1922–) American novelist, born in New York City. He was educated at Harvard University, worked for the *New Yorker* (1946–47), lived and travelled abroad, and freelanced as a speech and filmscript writer from 1956 into the 1970s. He has written three novels: *The Recognitions* (1955), the complex story of a forger; *JR* (1976), about an eleven-year-old ragged capitalist operating from pay phones and post office money orders; and *Carpenter's Gothic* (1985), in which a Vietnam War veteran works as a media consultant for a fundamentalist preacher. An ambitious satirist, he is one of America's most prominent contemporary novelists. He won a National Book award in 1976.

GADE, Niels Wilhelm (1817–90) Danish composer, born in Copenhagen. He began as violinist, but on a royal grant studied at Leipzig and became a friend of **Schumann** and **Mendelssohn**, from whom he took over the Gewandhaus orchestra in 1847, but next year returned to Copenhagen. He composed eight symphonies, a violin concerto, several choral works and smaller pieces. The Scandinavian element in his music distinguishes him from the Leipzig school.

GADES, Antonio (1936–) Spanish dancer, choreographer and teacher, born in Alicante. As a teenager he made his début in cabaret, then joined Pilar Lopez's company for nine years. In the early 1960s he worked mainly in Italy, collaborating with **Anton Dolin** and staging dances at La Scala, Milan. The company he formed for the New York World's Fair of 1964 has since toured the world. He has appeared in various films, the most acclaimed being the flamenco trilogy directed by Carlos Saura: *Blood Wedding* (1981), *Carmen* (1983) and *El Amor Brujo* (1986).

GADOLIN, Johan (1760–1852) Finnish chemist, born in Abo, where he became professor of chemistry. He isolated the oxide of the rare element, gadolinium, named after him.

GADSDEN, Christopher (1724–1805) American Revolutionary leader, born in Charleston, South Carolina. He was a member of the first Continental Congress (1774), became a brigadier-general in the Continental army during the Revolution, and was lieutenant-governor of South Carolina.

GADSDEN, James (1788–1858) American soldier and diplomat. He served in the war of 1812 and against the Seminoles. In 1853 he was appointed minister to Mexico, and negotiated the purchase (Gadsden purchase) of part of Arizona and New Mexico for railway construction.

GAFFKY, Georg Theodor August (1850–1918) German bacteriologist, born in Hanover. He isolated and cultivated the typhoid bacillus (1884).

GAGARIN, Yuri (1934–68) Russian cosmonaut, born in the Smolensk district, joined the Soviet Air Force in 1957, and in 1961 became the first man to travel in space, completing a circuit of the earth in the *Vostok* spaceship satellite. A Hero of the Soviet Union, he shared the Galabert Astronautical prize with **John Glenn** in 1963. He was killed in a plane accident in training.

GAGE, Thomas (1721–87) English soldier, second son of the first Viscount Gage. He accompanied Braddock's ill-fated expedition against Duguesue (1755), and became military governor of Montreal in 1760. From 1763 to 1772 he was commander-in-chief of the British forces in America, and in 1774 governor of Massachusetts. In April 1775 he sent a force to seize arms from the colonists at Concord; and next day the skirmish at Lexington took place which began the American Revolution. After the battle of Bunker Hill (June 1775) he was relieved by **Howe**.

GAGERN, Heinrich Wilhelm August, Freiherr von (1799–1880) German statesman, born in Bayreuth. A founder of the student movement (*Burschenschaft*) of 1815–19, he held office in Hesse-Darmstadt, and was president of the Frankfurt parliament (1848–49). From 1859 he again took part in grand-ducal politics, as a partisan of Austria against Prussia.

GAHN, Johan Gottlieb (1745–1818) Swedish chemist and mineralogist, born at Voxna, Gävleborg. Originally a miner, he later studied mineralogy and invented a method for preparing metallic manganese on a larger scale. He shared the discovery of phosphoric acid in the bones with **Carl Wilhelm Scheele** in 1770. The mineral gahnite is named after him.

GAINSBOROUGH, Thomas (1727–88) English landscape and portrait painter, one of the great English masters and founder of the English school, born in Sudbury, Suffolk. In his youth he copied Dutch landscapes and at 14 was sent to London where he learnt the art of rococo decoration under Gravelot and Hayman. *The Charterhouse* (1748) marks the end of his apprenticeship. In 1745 he married one of his subjects, Margaret Burr, the illegitimate daughter of the 4th Duke of Beaufort, and settled as portrait painter at Ipswich. *Mr and Mrs Andrews* (1748) and several 'chimney-piece' paintings belong to this, his Suffolk period. In 1760 he moved to Bath, where he established himself with his portrait of *Earl Nugent* (1760). His portraits combine the elegance of **Van Dyck** with his own characteristic informality, although in his later work he increasingly tends towards fashionable artificialities. There are such early masterpieces as *Lord and Lady Howe*, *Mrs Portman* (Tate) and *Blue Boy* (Huntington Collection, Pasadena), and the great landscapes, *The Harvest Wagon* (1767; Barber Institute, Birmingham) and *The Watering Place* (1777; Tate) in which **Rubens'** influence is discernible. In 1768 he became a foundation member of the Royal Academy, at which he exhibited annually, until, somewhat discontented with the place assigned to *The King's Daughters* in 1784, he retired. In 1774 he moved to London. To this last great period belong the superb character study *Mr Truman*, the luxuriant *Mrs Graham* (1777; Edinburgh), *George III* and *Queen Charlotte* (1781; Windsor Castle), and his serene rendering of *Mrs Siddons*, the actress (1785), without the theatricality of other artists' rendering of her. Landscapes include *Cottage Door* (1780; Pasadena), *The Morning Walk* (1780), which is closer to his 'fancy pieces' based on **Murillo**'s paintings than to nature, and *Cattle crossing a Bridge* (1781), the most rococo of all his work.

GAIRDNER, James (1828–1912) Scottish historian, born in Edinburgh. He entered the Public Record Office in London, where he became assistant-keeper in 1859. He showed erudition, accuracy, and good judgment in editing historical documents, as also in his own works—*The Houses of Lancaster and York* (1874); *Life of Richard III* (1878); *Lollardy and the Reformation in England* (1908–13), and others.

GAIRDNER, William Henry Temple (1873–1928) Scottish missionary and Islamic scholar, born in Ardrossan, Ayrshire. He graduated from Cambridge, and in 1898 went to work with the Church Missionary Society in Cairo. A master of colloquial Arabic and Islamic literature, and a writer of hymns and poems, he sought to train indigenous Christian leaders, and was convinced that Muslims could be won to Christianity by personal testimony and by seeing how Christians lived their faith. He wrote *The Reproach of Islam* (1909) and (with W A Eddy) *The Values of Christianity and Islam* (1927).

GAIRY, Sir Eric Matthew (1922–) Grenadian politician. In 1950 he founded the country's first political party, the left-of-centre Grenada United Labour party (GULP) and was soon a dominant figure in Caribbean politics. He held the posts of chief minister in the Federation of the West Indies (1957–62), premier of Grenada (1967–74) and, at independence, in 1974, prime minister. He was ousted by the left-wing leader Maurice Bishop in 1979.

GAISERIC, or **Genseric** (c.390–477) king of the Vandals and Alans, illegitimate son of Godigisel who led the Vandals in their invasion of Gaul. In 427 he succeeded his half-brother Gunderic. Invited by Bonifacius, the Roman governor of Africa, Gaiseric crossed over from Spain to Numidia in 429, captured and sacked Hippo (430), seized Carthage (439), and made it the capital of his new dominions. He quickly built up a formidable maritime power, and his fleets carried the terror of his name as far as the Peloponnesus. An Arian, he persecuted orthodox Catholics with ferocious cruelty. Eudoxia, the widow of **Valentinian III**, eager for revenge upon her husband's murderer Maximus, invited Gaiseric to Rome. The Vandal fleet sailed for the Tiber; the city was taken (455), and given up to a 14 days' sack. Gaiseric carried off the empress Eudoxia and her two daughters, one of whom became the wife of his eldest son Huneric, who succeeded him. Fleets sent against the Vandals in 457 and 468 were defeated. Gaiseric died in 477, in the possession of all his conquests, the greatest of the Vandal kings.

GAISFORD, Thomas (1780–1855) English Greek scholar. He became regius professor of Greek at Oxford in 1812 and in 1831 dean of Christ Church. He produced editions of **Herodotus**, Hephaestion, **Stobaeus** and **Suidas**. The Gaisford prizes were founded in his memory.

GAITSKELL, Hugh Todd Naylor (1906–63) English Labour politician, born in London. He was educated at Winchester and at New College, Oxford, becoming a Socialist during the 1926 general strike. On leaving Oxford he became a Workers' Educational Association lecturer in economics in the Nottinghamshire coalfield. In 1938 he became reader in political economy in the University of London. Elected MP for Leeds South in 1945, he became parliamentary secretary to the ministry of fuel and power in 1946 and minister in 1947. Appointed minister of state for economic affairs in 1950, he became in 1950–51 the youngest Chancellor of the Exchequer since **Balfour**. His introduction of national health service charges led to the resignation of **Aneurin Bevan** as minister of health and to a long 'personality' feud with Bevan and the hostile left wing of the Labour party. But his ascendancy in the party grew steadily and in December 1955 he was elected leader of the opposition by a large majority over Bevan. He bitterly opposed **Eden**'s Suez action (1956), attempted to modify Labour policy from total nationalization to the 'shareholder state', and refused to accept a narrow conference vote for unilateral disarmament (1960). This caused a crisis of leadership in which he retained the loyalty of most Labour MPs. He wrote *Money and Everyday Life* (1939).

GAIUS (fl.130–180) Roman jurist, on whose *Institutes* were based **Justinian**'s. They are the only substantial text of classical Roman law that have survived. His other works were largely used in the compilation of the *Digest*. The *Institutes*, lost until **Barthold Niebuhr** discovered a manuscript at Verona in 1816, have been repeatedly edited; and a fragment of an older manuscript was printed in *Oxyrhynchus Papyri*, vol. xvii (1928).

GAIUS See **CALIGULA**

GAJDUSEK, Daniel Carleton (1923–) American virologist and man of science, joint winner of the 1976 Nobel prize for physiology or medicine. He studied physics at Rochester and medicine at Harvard. He spent much time in Papua New Guinea, studying the origin and dissemination of infectious diseases amongst the Fore people, especially a slowly developing lethal viral disease called *kuru*. He shared the Nobel prize with **Baruch Blumberg**.

GÁL, Hans (1890–1987) Austrian composer and writer on music, born in Brunn near Vienna. He studied at Vienna University, subsequently taught there himself (1919–29) and in Mainz (1933). He returned as a conductor to Vienna, but the Anschluss drove him out and, at **Tovey**'s suggestion, he settled in Edinburgh where he became a university lecturer (1945), remaining in Scotland for the rest of his life. A writer and lecturer of wit and perception and a composer of exquisite craftsmanship, his musical style remained that of late Romanticism. He wrote five operas, four symphonies, other orchestral music, many part-songs, four string quartets and many other chamber and piano works.

GALAWDEWOS (d.1559) emperor of Ethiopia from 1540. With Portuguese aid he defeated the Muslims who, under **Ahmad Gran, (Ahmad Ibn Ibrahim Al-Ghazi)** had dominated Ethiopia in the early years of the century. He strengthened the authority of the monarchy and reformed the cultural and religious institutions of the empire. Towards the end of his reign he was preoccupied with the migration of Galla tribesmen but, despite various successes in battle (1554–55), was unable permanently to check their advance.

GALBA, Servius Sulpicius (3 BC–69 AD) Roman emperor. He became consul in 33, and administered Aquitania, Germany, Africa and Hispania Tarraconensis with competence and integrity. In 68 the Gallic legions rose against **Nero**, and in June proclaimed Galba emperor. But he soon made himself unpopular by favouritism, ill-timed severity, and avarice, and was assassinated by the praetorians in Rome.

GALBRAITH, John Kenneth (1908–) Canadian-born American economist, born in Ontario. Educated at the Universities of Toronto, California and Cambridge, he emigrated to the USA in 1931. In 1939 he became assistant professor of economics at Princeton University and held various administrative posts before becoming Paul M Warburg professor of economics at Harvard from 1949 to 1975. In 1961–63 he was US Ambassador to India. His written works include *American Capitalism: The Concept of Countervailing Power* (1952) *The Great Crash* (1955), *The Affluent Society* (1958), *The Liberal Hour* (1960), *Made to Last* (1964), *The Age of Uncertainty* (1977) (which was made into a BBC television series), *A History of Economics* (1987) and *The New Industrial State* (1967). He also wrote his autobiography, *A Life In Our Times* (1981).

GALDÓS See **PÉREZ GALDÓS**

GALEN, or **Claudius Galenus** (c.130–c.201) Greek physician, born in Pergamum in Mysia, Asia Minor. He studied medicine there and at Smyrna, Corinth and Alexandria. He was chief physician to the gladiators in Pergamum from 157, then moved to Rome and became friend and physician to the emperor **Marcus Aurelius**. He was also physician to emperors **Commodus** and **Severus**. Galen was a voluminous writer on medical and philosophical subjects. The work extant under his name consists of 83 genuine treatises and 15 commentaries on **Hippocrates**. He was a careful dissector of animals, a somewhat too theoretical physiologist, and was the first to diagnose by the pulse. For many centuries he was considered the standard authority on medical matters.

GALERIUS, Galerius Valerius Maximianus (d.311) Roman emperor, born near Serdica in Dacia. He rose high in the army, was made Caesar by **Diocletian** (292), and on Diocletian's abdication (305) became with **Constantius Chlorus** joint ruler of the Roman empire, Galerius taking the eastern half. When Constantius died at York (306) the troops in Britain and Gaul transferred their allegiance to his son, **Constantine**; but Galerius retained the east till his death. Christian tradition presented him as a persecutor of their faith.

GALGACUS, See **CALGACUS**

GALIANI, Ferdinando (1728–87) Italian economist, born in Chieti. He lived in Paris (1760–69) as a Neapolitan secretary of legation on close terms with the Encyclopédistes, and then was a minister of the King of Naples, working on economic policy. He wrote against both extreme protection and complete free trade, in *Della moneta* (1750) and *Dialogues sur le commerce des blé* (1770).

GALIGNANI, John Anthony (1796–1873) and **William** (1798–1882), Parisian publishers, born in London. They greatly improved *Galignani's Messenger*, started in Paris by their father in 1814, and made it a medium for advocating cordiality between England and France. The brothers founded at Corbeil a hospital for Englishmen; and in 1889 the Galignani Home for aged printers and booksellers was opened at Neuilly.

GALILEI, Galileo, known as **Galileo** (1564–1642) Italian astronomer, mathematician and natural philosopher, born in Pisa. As a student of medicine he came to disbelieve and despise the prevailing Aristotelian philosophy. Entering Pisa University in 1581, he inferred in 1583 from the oscillations of a suspended lamp in the cathedral (equal in time whatever their range) the value of a pendulum for the exact measurement of time. The study of mathematics led him to invent a hydrostatic balance and write a treatise on specific gravity; and, appointed professor of mathematics in the university, he propounded and proved the theorem that all falling bodies, great or small, descend with equal velocity. The hostility of the Aristotelians led him to resign his chair (1591) and retire to Florence. When he became professor of mathematics at Padua (1592–1610), his lectures attracted pupils from all parts of Europe. Among his discoveries were a species of thermometer and a proportional compass or sector; and he perfected the refracting telescope (a Dutch invention of 1608). Galileo pursued a series of astronomical investigations, which convinced him of the correctness of the Copernican theory. He concluded that the Moon owed her illumination to reflection, and that its surface was diversified by valleys and mountains. The Milky Way he pronounced a track of countless stars. Another series of observations led to the discovery of four satellites of Jupiter (1610). He also noticed spots on the Sun, from whose movement he inferred its rotation. In this year he was recalled to Florence by the Grand Duke of Tuscany. In 1611 he was received with great distinction at Rome. Yet the publication, two years later, of his dissertation on the solar spots in which he boldly advocated the Copernican system, provoked the censure of the ecclesiastical authorities. He promised (1616) to abstain from all future advocacy of the condemned doctrines. But in 1632 he published the *Dialogo sopra i due massimi sistemi del mondo*, in favour of the Copernican system. Pope **Urban VIII** was led to believe that Galileo had here satirized him as a timid and blind traditionalist; and Galileo, summoned before the Inquisition, after a wearisome trial and imprisonment, was condemned to abjure his scientific creed. He was further sentenced to indefinite imprisonment by the Inquisition—a sentence commuted by Pope Urban, at the request of the Duke of Tuscany, to permission to reside at Siena, and finally at Florence. Under home arrest at Arcetri, near Florence, he continued his researches, even after his hearing and sight were much impaired. Other discoveries of his were the law of uniformly accelerated motion towards the Earth, the parabolic path of projectiles, virtual velocities, and the law that all bodies have weight. Just before he became totally blind (1637) he made yet another discovery, that of the Moon's monthly and annual librations.

GALL, St (c.550–645) Irish monk, one of the twelve who followed St **Columban** to the Continent in c.585. In 614 he fixed his cell at a point on the Steinach river in Switzerland, round which grew up a great Benedictine abbey and the town of St Gall. His feast day is 16 October.

GALL, Franz Joseph (1758–1828) German physician and founder of phrenology, born in Tiefenbrunn in Baden. In 1785 he settled in Vienna as a physician. He gradually evolved theories by which he traced talents and other qualities to the functions of particular areas of the brain, and the shape of the skull. His lectures on phrenology were a popular success, but suppressed in 1802 as being subversive of religion.

GALLAND, Antoine (1646–1715) French orientalist, born in Rollot, Picardy. He travelled in Syria and the Levant, and became professor in Arabic at the Collège de France. His translation of the *Arabian Nights* (1704–08) was the first in any western language.

GALLANT, Mavis (1922–) Canadian short-story writer and novelist, born in Montreal. Her father was English, her mother German-Russian-Breton, and she spent her childhood going from school to school, 17 in all, which made education 'virtually impossible'. Living entirely by writing, she contributes mainly to the *New Yorker* from her home in Paris. She has written two novels, *Green Water, Green Sky* (1959) and *A Fairly Good Time* (1970), several collections of short stories, and a diary of the 1968 street troubles in Paris.

GALLAS, Matthias von, Count of Campo and Duke of Lucera (1584–1647) Austrian soldier, born in Trient. He became one of **Wallenstein**'s chief commanders in the Thirty Years' War and succeeded Wallenstein after the latter's murder (1634), in which he was implicated. He was beaten at Breitenach (1631), but won a decisive victory over the Swedes at Nördlingen (1634). After a disastrous series of campaigns he was dismissed in 1645.

GALLATIN, Albert (1761–1849) Swiss-born American financier and statesman, born in Geneva, a cousin of Mme **de Staël**. He graduated at Geneva in 1779 and went in 1780 to the USA. He taught French at Harvard, bought land in Virginia and Pennyslvania, in 1793 was elected a senator, in 1795 a member of the House of Representatives, and from 1801 to 1813 was US secretary of the Treasury. He took an important part in the peace negotiations with Britain in 1814, and signed the Treaty of Ghent. From 1815 to 1823 he was minister at Paris, in 1826 at London. He wrote on finance, politics, and the Indian tribes.

GALLÉ, Émile (1846–1904) French designer and glass maker, born in Nancy. His study of botany influenced much of his work, inluding the decoration of his father's ceramics. His own interests turned towards glass. By 1874 he was settled in Nancy running a glass workshop, which grew to employ 300 workers, as well as managing what had been his father's pottery. His distinctive designs for glass, reflecting his experiments with materials and techniques, were broadly within Art Nouveau, as was his furniture. He exhibited work at several major exhibitions including those in Paris in 1889 and 1900. With Victor Prouvé and Louis Majorelle he formed the École de Nancy in 1901.

GALLE, Johann Gottfried (1812–1910) German astronomer, born in Pabsthaus, near Wittenberg. In 1846 he discovered the planet Neptune, whose existence had been already postulated in the calculations of **Urbain Leverrier**. From 1851 to 1857 he was director of Breslau observatory.

GALLÉN-KALLELA, Akseli Valdemar (1865–1931) Finnish painter, born in Pori. A pioneer of the national romantic style, he chose his themes mainly from Finnish mythology, particularly the folk epic, *Kalevala*.

GALLI-CURCI, Amelita (1882–1963) Italian soprano, born in Milan. Although a prize-winning piano student at Milan Conservatory, as a singer she was self-taught, and first appeared in opera in 1909. Her brilliance of style was attractive enough to compensate for deficiencies of technique, and in 1916 she joined Chicago Opera Company. From 1919 onwards, she worked principally at the Metropolitan Opera, New York, and was first heard in Britain in 1924. She was forced to retire early, following a throat injury.

GALLIÉNI, Joseph Simon (1849–1916) French soldier, born in St Béat, Haute Garonne. He served in the war of 1870–71, also in West Africa and Tonkin, was governor of Upper Senegal from 1886, and governor-general of Madagascar 1897–1905. As minister for war, and military governor of Paris from 1914, he saw to its fortifications and contributed to the victory of the Marne (1914) by his foresight and planning. He was posthumously created marshal of France in 1921.

GALLIENNE, Richard Le See **LE GALLIENNE**

GALLIENUS, Publius Licinius (c.218–68) Roman emperor, from 253 colleague and from 260 successor to his father, Valerian. But his authority was limited to Italy, for in the provinces the legions frequently revolted, and proclaimed their commanders Caesars. In 268, while besieging one of his rivals in Milan, he was murdered by some of his officers. A hostile tradition perhaps misrepresents his achievements.

GALLIO, Junius Annaeus (1st century AD) Roman proconsul of Achaia under **Claudius I** and brother of **Seneca**. He dismissed the charge brought by the Jews against St **Paul** at Corinth in AD 52.

GALLITZIN, Dimitri Augustine (1770–1841) originally **Galitzin**, Russian-born American priest, born in The Hague, Netherlands. He was a member of the boyar Galitzin family, son of a Russian ambassador and a Prussian-born Catholic mother, the pious and learned Princess Amalie Galitzin. In 1787 he entered the Roman Catholic church, emigrated to the USA in 1792 and was ordained a priest in 1795. He was sent as a missionary to Cambria County, Pennsylvania, where he founded the town of Loretto (1799) and became known as 'Father Smith' and the 'Apostle of the Alleghanies'. He was vicar-general for western Pennsylvania, and wrote several tracts, including *Defence of Catholic Principles* (1816), *Letter to a Protestant Friend* (1820), and *Appeal to the Protestant Public* (1834).

GALLUP, George Horace (1901–84) American public opinion pollster, born in Jefferson, Iowa. He became professor of journalism in Drake University (1929–31) and Northwestern University (1931–32). He was director of research for the Young & Rubicam advertising agency in New York (1932–47). In 1935 he founded the American Institute of Public Opinion, and evolved the Gallup Polls for testing the state of public opinion, which made its name by correctly predicting the outcome of the 1936 US presidential elections. He wrote *Public Opinion in a Democracy* (1939), and *Guide to Public Opinion Polls* (1944 and 1948).

GALLUS, Gaius Cornelius (c.70–26 BC) Roman poet, born in Forum Julii (Fréjus) in Gaul. He lived in Rome in intimate friendship with **Virgil** and **Ovid** and was appointed prefect of Egypt by **Augustus**; but, having fallen into disfavour and been banished, committed suicide. He was considered the founder of the Roman elegy, from his four books of elegies upon his mistress 'Lycoris' (in reality the actress Cyntheris). Only a few fragments are extant.

GALOIS, Évariste (1811–32) French mathematician, born in Bourg-la-Reine. He entered the École Normale Supérieure in 1829, but was expelled in 1830 for republican sympathies. He engaged in political agitation, was imprisoned twice, and was killed in a duel. His mathematical reputation rests on fewer than 100 pages of posthumously published work of original genius: a memoir on the solubility of equations by radicals, and a mathematical testament written the night before his death giving the essentials of his discoveries on the theory of algebraic equations and abelian integrals. Some of his results had been independently obtained by **Niels Henrik Abel**. The brevity and obscurity of his writing delayed the understanding of his work, but it is now seen as a cornerstone of modern algebra in which the concept of a group first became of central importance.

GALSWORTHY, John (1867–1933) English novelist and playwright, born in Combe, Surrey. Educated at Harrow and New College, Oxford, he was called to the bar in 1890, but chose to travel and set up as a writer. He met **Joseph Conrad** and they became lifelong friends. He published his first book, a collection of short stories, *From the Four Winds*, in 1897, under the pseudonym John Sinjohn. In 1906 he had a success with his first play, *The Silver Box*, and in the same year published *The Man of Property*, the first in his celebrated *Forsyte Saga* series (the others were *In Chancery* (1920) and *To Let* (1921). In these novels is recorded a departed way of life, that of the affluent middle class which ruled England before the 1914 war. The class is criticized on account of its possessiveness, but there is also nostalgia, for Galsworthy as a man born into the class could appreciate its virtues. This nostalgia deepens in what was collectively entitled *A Modern Comedy* (1929) which includes *The White Monkey* (1924), *The Silver Spoon* and *Swan Song* (1928). In this second cycle of the Saga the post-war generation is under scrutiny, but not without the author's appreciation of their plight in an age in which their world had crashed. Among his other novels are *The Island Pharisees* (1904), *The Country House* (1907), *Fraternity* (1909), and *The Patrician* (1911). He was also a prolific playwright, and produced more than 30 plays for the London stage. They best illustrate his reforming zeal, and also his sentimentality. *Strife* (1909) shows employers and men locked in a four-month struggle, which ends through the death of the strike-leader's wife. *Justice* (1910) helped to achieve its object of humanizing the penal code. *The Skin Game* (1920) attempts to hold the scales between the aristocratic Mr Hillcrist and the rich parvenu Hornblower, but the latter is so vulgar that sympathies are tipped against him. Technically these plays are first-rate theatre but are marred, especially in the later ones, *A Bit o' Love* and *Loyalties* (1922), by the parsimony of the language in dialogue which did well enough in the novels but makes the plays appear rather bare. He won the Nobel prize for literature in 1932.

GALT, Sir Alexander Tilloch (1817–93) English-born Canadian statesman, son of **John Galt**, born in Chelsea, London. He emigrated to Canada in 1835. He entered the Canadian parliament in 1849, and was finance minister 1858–62 and 1864–66, high commissioner in Britain 1880–83.

GALT, John (1779–1839) Scottish novelist and Canadian pioneer, born in Irvine, the son of a sea-captain. He was educated at Greenock Grammar School and became a junior clerk in a local merchant's firm in 1796. After contributing to local journals, he moved to London in 1804 and set up in business as a merchant. The venture was not a success, and from 1809 to 1811 he travelled for his health's sake in the Levant, where he met **Byron**. On his return he published *Letters from the Levant* and other accounts of his travels. He busied himself in various business posts, and wrote a number of school textbooks under the pseudonym 'Rev T Clark'. He then started writing novels for *Blackwood's Magazine*. *The Ayrshire Legatees* appeared in 1820, followed by *The Steam-Boat* in 1821. Its successor, *The Annals of the Parish* (1821), is his masterpiece, in which the description of events in the life of a parish minister throws interesting light on contemporary social history. He produced in quick succession *Sir Andrew Wylie* (1822), *The Provost* (1822) and *The Entail* (1823). His historical romances were less successful. He went to Canada in 1826, founded the town of Guelph, and played a prominent part in organizing immigration, but returned ruined in 1829, and produced a new novel *Lawrie Todd* (1830), and *The Member* (1832), on corruption in politics. He also wrote a Life of **Byron** (1830) and an autobiography (1834). In depicting life in small towns and villages Galt has few rivals. He possesses rich humour, genuine pathos and a rare mastery of Scottish dialect.

GALTIERI, Leopoldo Fortunato (1926–) Argentinian soldier and politician, born in Caseras, in the province of Buenos Aires. After training at the National Military College he was commissioned in 1945 and progressed steadily to the rank of lieutenant-general in 1979, when he joined the junta which had been in power since the military coup which ousted **Isabelita Peron** in 1976. In 1981 the leader of the junta, General Viola, died of a heart attack and Galtieri succeeded him as president. The state of the Argentinian economy worsened and, to counter mounting domestic criticism, in April 1982 Galtieri ordered the invasion of the long-disputed Malvinas (Falkland) Islands. Their recovery by Britain, after a brief and humiliating war, brought about his downfall. He was court-martialled in 1983 and sentenced to twelve years' imprisonment for negligence in starting and losing the Falklands War.

GALTON, Sir Francis (1822–1911) English scientist, cousin of **Charles Darwin**, born in Birmingham. Educated at King Edward's School, he studied medicine at the Birmingham Hospital and King's College, London, and graduated from Trinity College, Cambridge. In 1846 he travelled in North Africa, and in 1850 explored unknown territory in South Africa, publishing *Narrative of an Explorer in Tropical South Africa* and *Art of Travel* (1855). His investigations in meteorology in *Meteorographica* (1863) were the basis for modern weather maps. Latterly he devoted himself to heredity, founding and endowing the study of eugenics, and publishing *Hereditary Genius* (1869), *English Men of Science: their Nature and Nurture* (1874) and *Natural Inheritance* (1889). He also devised the system of fingerprint identification with *Finger Prints* (1892). His researches into colour blindness and mental imagery were also of great value.

GALUPPI, Baldassaro (1706–85) Italian light-operatic composer, born near Venice. He lived in London from 1741 to 1744 and wrote the popular *I filosofo di campagna*, as well as sacred music and sonatas.

GALVANI, Luigi (1737–98) Italian physiologist, born in Bologna. He studied there, and in 1768 became lecturer in anatomy and professor of obstetrics from 1782. He discovered animal electricity by connecting the leg muscle of a frog to its corresponding nerve (hence 'to galvanize'), wrongly believing the source of the current to be in the material of muscle and nerve.

GAMA, Vasco da (c.1469–1525) Portuguese navigator, the first westerner to sail round the Cape of Good Hope to Asia, born in Sines in Alemtejo. He early distinguished himself as a mariner, and was selected by King **Emanuel I** to discover a route to India round the Cape. The expedition of three vessels with 168 men left Lisbon in 1497, but was four months in reaching St Helena. After rounding the Cape, despite hurricanes and mutinies, he made Malindi early in the following year. Here he found a skilful Indian pilot, crossed the Indian Ocean, and arrived at Calicut in 1498. The ruler of Calicut soon became actively hostile, and da Gama had to fight his way out of the harbour. In 1499 he arrived back in Lisbon, and was ennobled. But the 40 Portuguese left were murdered, and to avenge them the king fitted out a squadron of 20 ships under da Gama (1502), which founded the colonies of Mozambique and Sofala, bombarded Calicut, and reached the Tagus with 13 richly-laden vessels in 1503. In 1524 da Gama became viceroy to India. He died in Cochin and his body was brought home to Portugal.

GAMAGE, Albert Walter (1855–1930) English merchant, born in Hereford. He became a draper's apprentice in London, and in 1878 founded the famous store in Holborn which bore his name.

GAMALIEL (d.c.50) Palestinian rabbi, the teacher of St **Paul**. A prominent Pharisee, he taught 'the law' early in the 1st century. Tolerant and peaceful, he seems to have placed Christianity on a par with other sects and encouraged long-suffering on all sides.

GAMBETTA, Léon Michel (1838–82) French politician, born in Cahors, of Genoese-Jewish extraction. He became a member of the Paris bar in 1859, attracted attention by his advanced liberal views, and in 1869 was elected deputy. After the surrender of **Napoleon III** Gambetta was one of the proclaimers of the Republic, on 4 September 1870. As minister of the interior in the Government of National Defence, he escaped from Paris under siege by balloon to Tours, and for five months was dictator of France. In spite of the surrender of Metz he called up army after army, and sent them against the Germans; even when Paris capitulated, he demanded that the war should be carried on to the end. His colleagues in Paris having repudiated his decree from Bordeaux disfranchising all members of royal dynasties, he resigned, and retired into Spain (1871). Elected again, he took no part in the suppression of the Commune. After its fall he became the chief of the advanced Republicans. When the Duke **de Broglie** took office (May 1877) in the hope of restoring the monarchy, a civil war seemed imminent, but was averted by Gambetta, and Marshal **MacMahon**, the president, refrained from pushing matters to an extremity. Gambetta was imprisoned and fined for having declared respecting MacMahon 'Il faudra ou se soumettre, ou se démettre', but two months later he was re-elected for Belleville, and in 1879 MacMahon resigned. In November 1880, on the resignation of the **Ferry** ministry, Gambetta, from 1879 president of the chamber, succeeded in forming a cabinet, but when in January 1882 the chamber rejected his *scrutin de liste* proposal he immediately resigned. He died from the effects of 'an accidental wound in the hand from a revolver'.

GAMBIER, James Gambier, 1st Baron (1756–1833) English naval commander, born in the Bahamas. He fought with distinction in Howes's action off Ushant (1794), was promoted rear admiral (1795) and served as lord commissioner of the Admiralty (1795–1801, 1804–06). He was governor of Newfoundland (1802–04). As admiral he commanded the British fleet at the bombardment of Copenhagen in 1807. At the battle of Aix Roads in 1809 he disregarded signals from **Thomas Cochrane Dundonald**, but was acquitted by a court martial. He was made admiral of the fleet in 1830.

GAMBLE, Josias Christopher (1776–1848) Scottish industrialist born in Enniskillen. He was a founder with **James Muspratt** of the British chemical industry based in the St Helens area near Liverpool. A graduate in theology from Glasgow, he spent a period as a cleric before manufacturing chemicals in Dublin and then in Glasgow, and most profitably in partnership with Muspratt in St Helens, making bleaching powder, soda ash, and sulphuric acid.

GAMBON, Michael (1940–) Irish actor, born in Dublin, now resident in England. He joined the National Theatre for its inaugural season in 1963, and subsequently appeared in repertory at Birmingham and elsewhere, and, in 1974, in London in **Alan Ayckbourn**'s *The Norman Conquests*, and *Just Between Ourselves* in 1977. His performance in the title role of **John Dexter**'s 1980 production of **Brech**'s *The Life of Galileo* consolidated his reputation. He became the leading actor in the National Theatre company which Ayckbourn directed from 1986 to 1987. He has made several television appearances, notably in the title role of **Dennis Potter**'s BBC serial, *The Singing Detective* (1986). His films include *Paris by Night* (1989).

GAMELIN, Maurice Gustave (1872–1958) French soldier, educated at the Military Academy of St Cyr. Commissioned in the *Tirailleurs Algériens* he was appointed *aide-de-camp* to General **Joffre** in 1906, and became his *chef de cabinet* in 1911. He attained lieutenant-colonel's rank in 1914, but no divisional command until 1925. In 1935 seniority brought him the post of chief of staff of the army and membership of the *Conseil Supérieur de la Guerre*; but his fitness for overall command was exposed in his pronouncement that 'To attack is to lose'. In 1940, blind to the lessons of the 1939 Polish campaign, he refused to re-think his outmoded defensive strategy of 'solid fronts', which crumbled under the German *blitzkrieg*. He was hurriedly replaced by General **Weygand**, tried, and imprisoned (1943–45).

GAMOW, George (1904–68) Russian-born American physicist, born in Odessa, the son of a teacher. He made important advances in both cosmology and molecular biology. He was educated at Leningrad University, where later he was professor of physics (1931–34). He did research at Göttingen, Copenhagen and Cambridge before he moved to the USA as professor of physics at George Washington University (1934–55) and at Colorado (1956–68). In 1948, with **Ralph Alpher** and **Hans Bethe**, he suggested an explanation for the observed abundance of chemical elements in the universe based on thermonuclear processes in the early stages of a hot evolving universe. He showed that the heavier elements could only have been formed in the hot interiors of stars, and that our Sun is not cooling down, and he was a major expounder of the 'big bang' theory of the origin of the universe. In molecular biology he made a major contribution to the problem: how does the order of the four different kinds of nucleic acid bases in DNA chains govern the synthesis of proteins from amino acids? He realized that short sequences of the bases could form a 'code' capable of carrying information directing the synthesis of proteins, a proposal shown by the mid-1950s to be correct.

GANDHI, Indira (1917–84) Indian politician, daughter of **Nehru**, born in Allahabad. Her education included a year at Somerville College, Oxford. She was deeply involved in the independence issue, and spent a year in prison. She married Feroze Gandhi (d.1960) in 1942 and had two sons, **Rajiv** (1944–) and Sanjay (1946–80), who died in an aircrash. Member of central committee of Indian Congress (1950), president of party (1959–60), and minister of information (1964), she took over as prime minister in 1966 after the death of **Shastri**. In June 1975, after her conviction for election malpractices, she declared a 'state of emergency' in India. Civil liberties were curtailed and strict censorship imposed. These restrictions were lifted in 1977 during the campaign for a general election, in which the Congress party was defeated and Mrs Gandhi lost her seat. Acquitted after her arrest on charges of corruption, in 1978 she resigned from the Congress Parliamentary party, and became leader of the new Indian National Congress (I). She returned to power as prime minister following the 1980 general election, but was assassinated in October 1984 by members of her Sikh bodyguard, resentful of her employment of troops to storm the Golden Temple at Amritsar and dislodge malcontents. This murder provoked a Hindu backlash in Delhi, involving the massacre of 3000 Sikhs.

GANDHI, Mohandâs Karamchand, known as **Mahatma** (1869–1948) Indian leader, born in Porbandar, Kathiawar. He studied law in London, and in 1893 he gave up a Bombay legal practice worth £5000 a year to live on £1 a week in South Africa, where he spent 21 years opposing discriminatory legislation against Indians. In 1914 he returned to India. While supporting the British in World War I, he took an increasing interest in the Home Rule movement (*Swaraj*), over which he soon obtained a personal dominance, becoming master of the congress organization. His civil disobedience campaign of 1920 involved violent disorders. From 1922 to 1924 he was in jail for conspiracy and in 1930 he led a 200-mile march to the sea to collect salt in symbolic defiance of the government monopoly. He was rearrested and on his release in 1931 negotiated a truce between congress and the government and attended the London Round Table Conference on Indian constitutional reform. Back in India, he renewed the civil disobedience campaign and was arrested again—the pattern, along with his 'fasts unto death', of his political activity for the next six years. He assisted in the adoption of the constitutional compromise of 1937 under which Congress ministers accepted office in the new provincial legislatures. When war broke out, Gandhi, convinced that only a free India could give Britain effective moral support, urged 'complete independence' more and more strongly. He described the **Cripps** proposal in 1942 for a constituent assembly with the promise of a new Constitution after the war as 'a post-dated cheque on a crashing bank'. In August 1942 he was arrested for concurring in civil disobedience action to obstruct the war effort, and was released in May 1944. In 1946 Gandhi negotiated with the British Cabinet Mission which recommended the new constitutional structure. In May 1947 he hailed Britain's decision to grant India independence as 'the noblest act of the British nation'. His last months were darkened by communal strife between Hindu and Muslim; but his fasts to shame the instigators helped to avert deeper tragedy. He was assassinated in Delhi by a Hindu fanatic, on 30 January 1948—ten days after a previous attempt on his life. In his lifetime Mahatma ('a great soul') Gandhi was venerated as a moral teacher, a reformer who sought an India as free from caste as from materialism, a dedicated patriot who gave the Swaraj movement a new quality. Critics, however, thought him the victim of a power of self-delusion which blinded him to the disaster and bloodshed his 'nonviolent' campaigns invoked. But in Asia particularly he has been regarded as a great influence for peace whose teaching had a message not only for India—of whose nationhood he became the almost mystical incarnation—but for the world. His publications include the autobiographical *The Story of My Experiment with Truth* (republished 1949).

GANDHI, Rajiv (1944–) Indian politician, the eldest son of **Indira Gandhi** and the grandson of **Nehru**. Born into a Kashmiri-Brahmin family which had governed India for all but four years since 1947, he was educated at Doon School (Dehra Dun) and Cambridge University, where he failed his engineering degree. He married an Italian, Sonia Maino, in 1968. In contrast to his younger brother Sanjay (1946–80), he exhibited little interest in politics and became a pilot with Indian Airlines. Following Sanjay's death in an air crash he assumed the family's political mantle, being elected to his brother's Amethi parliamentary seat in 1981 and appointed a general-secretary of the Congress (I) party in 1983. After the assassination of Indira Gandhi in 1984 he became prime minister and secured a record majority in the parliamentary elections later that year. He attempted to cleanse and rejuvenate the Congress (I), inducting new technocrats, and introducing a freer market economic programme. Congress (I) suffered heavy losses under his leadership in the 1989 general election, and he was forced to resign as premier after his party was defeated in the general election of November 1989.

GANGEŚA (c.1200) Indian philosopher, and founder of the *Navya-nyāya* or new *Nyāya* school of Hindu philosophy, in Mithila, Bihar. His approach emphasizing philosophical logic rather than knowledge of the external world claimed in *Nyāya* philosophy stemming from **Gautama**, was continued by his son Vardhamāna. Later eminent exponents included Pakshadhara (1400–95) and Raghunātha (1477–1547).

GANSFORT, Wessel Harmens See **WESSEL, Johan**

GARAVANI, Valentino (1933–) Italian fashion designer, born in Rome. He studied fashion in Milan and Paris, then worked for Dessès and **Guy Laroche** in Paris. He opened his own house in Rome in 1959, but achieved world-wide recognition with his 1962 show in Florence.

GARBAREK, Jan (1947–) Norwegian saxophonist and composer, born in Mysen, who became interested in jazz through the recordings of **John Coltrane**. Self-taught at first, he was playing at European jazz festivals by 1966 and one year later joined the Scandinavian orchestra led by American avant garde composer George Russell. Garbarek worked in America for a while in 1970 under experimental leaders such as Keith Jarrett and Don Cherry. Since returning to Europe he has formed successive small bands which have explored influences from India, South America and Scandinavian folk roots, often using electronics. He is one of the rare European jazz musicians whose work has influenced his American contemporaries.

GARBETT, Cyril Foster (1875–1955) English prelate, born in Tongham, near Aldershot. Educated at Portsmouth Grammar School, Keble College and Cuddesdon College, Oxford, he was bishop of Southwark from 1919 to 1932 and of Winchester from 1932, until he was appointed archbishop of York in 1942. He was one of the most outspoken leaders of the Church, a prelate of great pastoral gifts and a humanitarian remembered for his warmth of personality and strength of character. Publications include *The Church and Social Problems* (1939) and a trilogy on Church and State (1947–52).

GARBO, Greta, professional name of **Greta Lovisa Gustafsson** (1905–90) Swedish-born American film actress, born in Stockholm. A shop-girl who won a bathing beauty competition at 16, she won a scholarship to the Royal Theatre Dramatic School in Stockholm, and starred in Mauritz Stiller's *Gösta Berling's Saga* (1924); he gave his star the name Garbo, chosen before he met her. She went to the USA in 1925, and her greatest successes, following *Anna Christie* (1930), her first talking picture, were *Queen Christina* (1933), *Anna Karenina* (1935), *Camille* (1936), and *Ninotchka* (1939). She retired from films in 1941, after the failure of *Two-Faced Woman*. She became an American citizen in 1951 but remained a total recluse for the rest of her life.

GARBORG, Arne Evenson (1851–1924) Norwegian writer, born in Jaeren. He was a leader in the movement to establish a new Norwegian literary language (*Landsmål*, 'national languages) based on western country dialects (later called *Nynorsk*, New Norwegian), and from 1877 edited the periodical *Fedra-*

heimen. He wrote a cycle of lyric poems, *Haugtussa* (The Hill Innocent, 1895), and a series of realistic novels, such as *Bondestudenter* (Peasant Students, 1883), *Fred* (Peace, 1890) and *Trette Men* (Tired Men, 1891). He also wrote a drama on religious problems, *Laereren* (The Teacher, 1896), and later attacked Lutheran theology in two controversial works.

GARCÍA, Manuel (1775–1832) Spanish tenor and composer, born in Seville. After making a reputation as a tenor in Cadiz and Madrid, he won great success from 1808 onward in Paris, Italy and London. In 1825 he visited New York and Mexico, where he was robbed of all his money; and after his return to Paris was compelled to teach singing. Several of his compositions, such as *Il Califo di Bagdad*, were much admired.

GARĆIA, Manuel (1805–1906) Spanish singing teacher, son of **Manuel García**, born in Zafra in Catalonia. He taught singing in Paris and London, wrote on the art, and invented the laryngoscope.

GARCÍA, Maria See **MALIBRAN, Marie Felicita**

GARCÍA, Paulina Viardot-Garcia (1821–1910) Spanish mezzo-soprano singer, daughter of **Manuel García**. As well as singing, she also composed operettas and songs.

GARCÍA, Perez Alan (1949–) Peruvian politician, born in Lima. After studying law at the Catholic University, Lima, he continued his education in Guatemala, Spain and France before returning to Peru in 1978 for election to the National Congress, for the moderate, left-wing APRA party, which he had joined as a youth. Four years later he became secretary-general of the party and in 1985 succeeded **Fernando Belaúnde** as president, becoming the first civilian to do so in democratic elections. He inherited an ailing economy which forced him to trim his socialist programme.

GARCÍA GUTIÉRREZ, Antonio (1813–84) Spanish poet and scientist, born in Chiclana de la Frontero, Cadiz. He worked in the consular service from 1864, and was director of the Archaeological Museum in Madrid from 1872. An exponent of 19th-century romanticism, he scored an early success with *El Trovador* (1836), the play which inspired **Verdi**'s opera. He is noted for his versification. Of his other plays the last two, *Venganza catalana* (1864) and *Juan Lorenzo* (1865), were most noteworthy. He published two volumes of lyric poetry, *Luz y Tinieblas*.

GARCÍA LORCA See **LORCA**

GARCÍA ROBLES, Alfonso (1911–) Mexican diplomat. After studying law, at Mexico and Paris universities and at the Academy of International Law in the Netherlands, he became a member of the Mexican foreign service. From 1964 to 1971 he was under-secretary for foreign affairs. In this capacity he furthered his interest in international nuclear disarmament, and was instrumental in forming the Treaty of Tlateloco (1967), which aimed to abolish nuclear weapons in Latin America. Since 1977 he has been Mexican delegate on the UN Disarmament Committee. His publications include *338 Days of Tlateloco* (1977). He was awarded the 1982 Nobel prize for peace, jointly with **Alva Myrdal**.

GARCILASO DE LA VEGA (1503–36) Spanish poet and soldier, born in Toledo. He fought bravely in the wars of **Charles V**, and died of a wound received near Fréjus. Although he was not a prolific writer he is known because he introduced the Petrarchian sonnet into Spain and wrote odes in imitation of **Virgil**.

GARCILASO DE LA VEGA, called **El Inca** (c.1540–c.1616) Spanish writer, born in Cuzco, son of one of the conquerors of Peru by an Inca princess. At 20, he went to Spain, where he spent the rest of his life. His account of the conquest of Florida by Fernando de Soto (1605) was followed in 1609–17 by his great *Comentarios*, in which he movingly describes the legends and beliefs of his mother's people (trans Markham, 1869).

GARDEN, Mary, originally **Mary Davidson** (1874–1967) Scottish soprano, born in Aberdeen. Taken to America as a child, she studied singing in Chicago and then in Paris. Her career began sensationally when she took over in mid-performance the title role in **Charpentier**'s new *Louise* at the Opéra-Comique in 1900, when the singer was taken ill. In 1902 she created the role of Mélisande in **Debussy**'s *Pelléas et Mélisande* at the composer's request, and in 1903 recorded songs with Debussy. **Massenet** and Erlanger also wrote leading roles for her. She sang at Covent Garden (1902–03), and she was a legendary Manon, Thaïs, Violetta, Salomé, Carmen, and Juliet (**Gounod**). Her American début was in 1907 and in 1910 she began a 20-year association with Chicago Grand Opera, which she also briefly directed (1921–22). She returned to Scotland in 1939.

GARDINER, Samuel Rawson (1829–1902) English historian, born in Ropley, Hampshire, and educated at Winchester and Christ Church, Oxford. For some years he filled the chair of modern history at King's College, London, but resigned it in 1885 to continue his *History* at Oxford on an All Souls' fellowship. In 1882 he was granted a pension. The first instalment of his great *History of England from the accession of James I to the Restoration* appeared in 1863; and at his death he had brought the work down to 1656. He had also published *The Thirty Years' War* (1874), *Introduction to the Study of English History* (1881), written in conjunction with J Bass Mullinger, and *The Student's History of England* (1890–1892).

GARDINER, Stephen (c.1483–1555) English prelate, born in Bury St Edmunds. Master of Trinity Hall, Cambridge, he became **Wolsey**'s secretary in 1525. Between 1527 and 1533 he was sent to Rome to further **Henry VIII**'s divorce from **Catherine of Aragon**, having been made bishop of Winchester in 1531. He supported the royal supremacy in his *De Vera Obedientia* (1535), helped to encompass **Thomas Cromwell**'s downfall and to frame the Six Articles. He was appointed chancellor of Cambridge in 1540. He opposed doctrinal reformation, and for this he was imprisoned and deprived on **Edward VI**'s accession. Released and restored by **Mary I** in 1553, he became an arch-persecutor of Protestants.

GARDNER, Ava, originally **Lucy Johnson** (1922–90) American film actress, born in North Carolina. Signed by MGM as a teenager, she emerged from the ranks of decorative starlets with her portrayal of a ravishing femme fatale in *The Killers* (1946). A green-eyed brunette, once voted the world's most beautiful woman, she remained a leading lady for two decades, portraying an earthy combination of sensuality and cynicism in films like *Mogambo* (1953), *The Barefoot Contessa* (1954) and *Night of the Iguana* (1964). She continued to work as a character actress in films and on television, and was married to Mickey Rooney, Artie Shaw and **Frank Sinatra**.

GARDNER, Erle Stanley (1889–1970) American crime novelist, born in Malden, Massachusetts. He was educated at Palo Alto High School, California, studied in law offices and was admitted to the Californian bar, where he became an ingenious lawyer for the defence (1922–38). A prolific, often pseudonymous, writer of stories and novels, his name is synonymous with that of Perry Mason, his fictional lawyer-sleuth and the hero of 82 courtroom dramas, who first appeared in *The Case* *of the Velvet Claws* (1933). With a little help from Della Street, his faithful secretary, and private eye Paul Drake, Mason frequently defied the rulebook in his quest to clear his client's name. With Raymond Burr playing Perry Mason, the books enjoyed enhanced popularity when they were made into a long-running television series. He also wrote a series of detective novels featuring the District Attorney Doug Selby ('the DA').

GARFIELD, James Abram (1831–81) 20th president of the United States, born in Orange. At ten he already added to his widowed mother's income by farm work. A graduate of Williams College, he taught in a school, served as a lay preacher, became a lawyer and was elected to the state senate in 1859. On the outbreak of the Civil War, he commanded a regiment of volunteers. His brigade gained the battle of Middle Creek, 10 January, 1862, and he was promoted brigadier-general. He had been made major-general for gallantry at Chickamauga (1863), when he resigned his command to enter congress, where he sat until 1880, acting as leader of the Republican party. In 1880, now a US senator, he was adopted as presidential candidate by the Republicans. After his election to the presidency (March 1881) he identified himself with the cause of civil service reform, thereby irritating a powerful section of his own party. On the morning of 2 July he was shot by a disappointed office-seeker, Charles Guiteau, and died on 19 September. His speeches were published in 1882.

GARFINKEL, Harold (1917–) American sociologist, born in Newark, New Jersey. Educated at Harvard University, where he was a student of **Talcott Parsons**, he taught briefly at Ohio State University before moving in 1954 to the department of sociology at the University of California, Los Angeles, where he remained until he retired in 1988. He is the founder of the sociological tradition of ethnomethodology, an approach to social science which focuses on the practical reasoning processes that ordinary people use in order to understand and act within the social world.

GARIBALDI, Giuseppe (1807–82) Italian patriot, born a sailor's son in Nice. He himself went early to sea. In 1834 he became involved in the 'Young Italy' movement of **Mazzini**, and was condemned to death for taking part in an attempt to seize Genoa. He escaped ultimately to South America, where in the rebellion of Rio Grande against Brazil he distinguished himself as a guerrilla fighter and privateer, was taken prisoner, and eloped with and married the beautiful Creole, Anita Riveira de Silva, the mother of his children Menotti, Ricciotti and Teresa. Returning to Italy during the 1848 revolution, he served with the Sardinian army against the Austrians and commanded the Roman republic army in its defence of the city against the French. He lived in exile until 1854 when he returned to settle down to a life of farming, but was fighting the Austrians again in the war of liberation of 1859. In 1860, at the head of 1000 'Red Shirts', he conquered Sicily and Naples for the new unified kingdom of Italy. In 1862 and 1867 he led two unsuccessful expeditions to liberate Rome from papal rule. He was a good commander of irregulars but his ignorance of politics sometimes harmed his cause. Nevertheless, he remains the central figure in the story of Italian independence.

GARIOCH, Robert, pen-name of **Robert Garioch Sutherland** (1909–81) Scottish poet, born in Edinburgh. Educated at the Royal High School, Edinburgh, and Edinburgh University, he spent most of his professional career as a teacher in Scotland and England. He made his literary début in 1933 with the surrealistic verse play *The Masque of Edinburgh* (published in expanded form in 1954). His first publications, *Seventeen Poems for Sixpence* (1940), in which he collaborated with **Sorley MacLean**, and *Chuckies on the Cairn* (1949), were hand-printed. His later work included *Selected Poems* (1966), *The Big Music* (1971), *Dr Faust in Rose Street* (1973) and *Collected Poems* (1977). He favoured the Scots language, in which he wrote in various styles and moods, from the colloquial to the literary. He translated into Scots works as diverse as **Pindar**, **Hesiod**, **George Buchanan**'s Latin plays *Jeptha* and *Baptistes*, Anglo-Saxon elegies, and the poems of the 19th-century Italian dialect poet Giuseppe Giacchino Belli. His prose works included *Two Men and a Blanket* (1975), an account of his experience in prisoner-of-war camps during World War II. Garioch particularly acknowledged the influence of **Robert Fergusson** on his poetry, perhaps most clearly seen in his sonnet on Fergusson's grave, his *To Robert Fergusson* and *The Muir*. He was writer in residence at Edinburgh University from 1971 to 1973.

GARLAND, (Hamilton) Hamlin (1860–1940) American writer, born in West Salem, Wisconsin. He often interrupted his schooling to help his father farm in Iowa, but in 1884 went to Boston to teach and finally to write. In short stories such as the collections, *Main Travelled Roads* (1887) and *Prairie Folks* (1892), in verse and in novels, he vividly, often grimly, described the farmlife of the Midwest. *A Daughter of the Middle Border* (1921), the sequel to his autobiographical novel *A Son of the Middle Border* (1917), won the Pulitzer prize.

GARLAND, Judy, originally **Frances Gumm** (1922–69) American entertainer, born in Grand Rapids, Minnesota. Part of a showbusiness family, she partnered two sisters in a vaudeville act that led to a film contract. Bright and vivacious, with a vibrant singing voice, she appeared in several of the finest film musicals ever made, among them *The Wizard of Oz* (1939), *Meet Me in St Louis* (1944) and *Easter Parade* (1948). Personal appearances confirmed the emotional power of her voice, and in *A Star is Born* (1954) she gave an outstanding dramatic performance. Despite emotional and medical difficulties and a reputation for unreliability, she achieved the status of a legendary performer and actress. Married five times, her daughters **Liza Minnelli** and Lorna Luft have followed in her footsteps.

GARNERIN, André Jacques (1769–1823) French aeronaut. A former balloon inspector in the French army, he gave the first public demonstration of a descent by parachute from a free-flying balloon at Paris in 1797, and thereafter made exhibition jumps in many countries including one of 8000 feet in England in 1802. He was assisted in making improvements to the design of his parachutes by his brother, Jean Baptiste Olivier (1766 –1849).

GARNETT, David (1892–1981) English novelist, son of **Edward Garnett**, born in Brighton. He studied botany at the Royal College of Science. His first book, *Lady into Fox* (1922), won both the Hawthornden and the Tait Black Memorial prize. *A Man in the Zoo* (1924) and *The Sailor's Return* (1925) were also successful, as were several other novels. Literary adviser to the Nonesuch Press (1923–32) and literary editor of the *New Statesman* (1932–34), he joined the RAF in 1939, and used his experience to write *War in the Air* (1941).

GARNETT, Edward (1868–1937) English writer and critic, son of **Richard Garnett**. As a publisher's reader he fostered the careers of many literary figures, including **Conrad**, **Galsworthy** and **D H Lawrence**. He was the author of the set of critical essays *Friday Nights* (1922). He also wrote plays, including *The Breaking Point* (1907) and *The Trial of Jeanne d'Arc* (1912). His wife, Constance, née Black (1862–1946), was a distinguished translator of Russian novels.

GARNETT, Richard (1835–1906) English writer and bibliographer, born in Lichfield. He was keeper of printed books at the British Museum (1890–99), and author of verse, critical works and biographies including *Shelley* (1862), *Carlyle* (1883), *Twilight of the Gods* (1888) and *The Age of Dryden* (1895).

GARNETT, Tony (1936–) English television and film producer, born in Birmingham. After studying psychology at London University he became an actor, appearing in numerous television plays and the film *The Boys* (1962). He joined the BBC Drama Department in 1964 as a script editor working on the Wednesday Play series. As a producer he has tackled a variety of political topics and social ills and enjoyed a long association with director **Kenneth Loach** on such influential television work as *Cathy Come Home* (1966), *Days of Hope* (1975) and *The Price of Coal* (1976). His films, also in collaboration with Loach, include *Kes* (1969), *Family Life* (1971) and *Black Jack* (1979). He made his directorial début with *Prostitute* (1980). Now resident in Los Angeles, he has directed *Handgun* (1982), and returned to production on Roland Joffé's *Fat Man and Little Boy* (1989).

GARNIER, Francis, properly **Marie Joseph François** (1839–73) French explorer, born in St Étienne. As a naval officer, he fought in the Chinese war (1860–62). Appointed to a post in Cochin-China, he was second-in-command of the Mekong River Expedition (1866–68) during which he mapped 3100 miles of unknown territory in Cambodia and Yunnan. He aided in the defence of Paris (1870–71), and in the Tonkin war (1873) took Hanoi, but was killed in a fight.

GARNIER, Robert (1534–90) French poet and playwright, born in Maine. He was the most distinguished of the predecessors of **Corneille**. His *Oeuvres complètes* (2 vols) include eight masterly tragedies, of which perhaps the best are *Antigone* (1580) and *Les Juives* (1583).

GARNIER, Tony (Antoine) (1869–1948) French architect, born in Lyon. He studied at the École des Beaux Arts in Paris. As architect of Lyon he made a major contribution to the forming of 20th-century architectural and urban planning through his utopian ideal *Une Cité Industrielle*, exhibited in 1904 and published in 1917. It combined functionalism with political and social reform, using the latest technology and materials. Through it he produced sophisticated reinforced concrete buildings at Lyon, including the Grange Blanche hospital (1911–27) and the Stadium (1913–18), and the Hôtel de Ville at Boulogne-Bilancourt (1931–33). His early designs were published in *Les grands travaux de la ville de Lyons* (1920).

GARNIER-PAGÈS, Louis Antoine (1803–78) French politician. A member of the chamber of deputies (1842–48), he led the extreme Left. Mayor of Paris (1848) and finance minister of the provisional government, he was a member of the Corps Législatif in 1864, and of the provisional government in 1871. He wrote *Histoire de la Révolution de* 1848 (1861–62) and *L'Opposition et l'Empire* (1872).

GAROFALO, originally **Benvenuto Tisi** (1481–1559) Italian painter, born in Ferrara, the last and foremost artist of the Ferrarese school. He worked chiefly in the churches and palaces of his native city, in Bologna and in Rome. The church of San Lorenzo, Ferrara, contains his *Adoration of the Magi*, and his *Sarifice to Ceres* is in the National Gallery, London.

GARRETT, João See **ALMEIDA-GARRETT**

GARRETT, Misses See **ANDERSON, Elizabeth Garrett**

GARRICK, David (1717–79) English actor, manager and dramatist, born in Hereford. He was educated at Lichfield grammar school. In 1736 he was sent to study Latin and Greek under **Samuel Johnson** at Edial, and in March 1737 he set off for London to study for the bar. But circumstances brought Garrick's legal studies to nothing, and in 1738 he became a wine-merchant with his eldest brother—a partnership dissolved in 1740. Garrick now devoted his mind to preparing for the stage, and in 1741 he made his successful début at Ipswich as Aboan in **Southerne**'s *Oroonoko*. On 19 October he appeared in London at Goodman's Fields; and his success as Richard III was so great that within a few weeks the two patent theatres were deserted, and crowds flocked to the unfashionable East End playhouse. But, as Goodman's Fields had no licence, the managers of Drury Lane and Covent Garden had it closed. Garrick played at both the patent theatres, and ultimately settled at Drury Lane, of which he became joint-patentee in 1747. He retired from the stage and from management in 1776. During this period Garrick was himself the great attraction and played continually, his only long rest being a trip to the Continent in 1763–65, when he fancied that his popularity was in danger of diminishing. He was buried in Westminster Abbey. He was equally at home in tragedy, comedy or farce. In 1749 he married Eva Marie Violetti (1724–1822), a Catholic Viennese dancer.

GARRISON, William Lloyd (1805–79) American journalist and anti-slavery campaigner, born in Newburyport, Massachusetts. A printer to trade, he became editor of the *Newburyport Herald* (1824) and the *National Philanthropist* (1828). Encouraged by **Benjamin Lundy** he denounced slavery so vigorously that he was imprisoned. He was founder-editor of *The Liberator* (1831–65), visited Britain on lecture tours, and in 1833 founded the American Anti-Slavery Society. After the abolition of slavery, he turned his crusading attention to women's suffrage and the plight of the American Indian.

GARROD, Sir Archibald Edward (1857–1936) English physician, born in London. He studied at Oxford and became Regius professor of medicine there in 1920. He did research on rheumatism, urinary pigments, and rare metabolic diseases.

GARROD, Dorothy Annie Elizabeth (1892–1968) English archaeologist, daughter of Sir **Archibald Garrod**. She studied at Newnham College, Cambridge, directed expeditions to Kurdistan (1928) and Palestine (1929–34), and took part in the excavations in the Lebanon (1958–64). An expert on the Palaeolithic or Old Stone Age, she became the first woman to hold a professorial chair at Cambridge in 1939.

GARROD, Heathcote William (1878–1960) English scholar, born in Wells. Educated at Oxford, he won the Gaisford Prize (1900) and the Newdigate (1901), and became a fellow of Merton College. He edited classical texts and the *Oxford Book of Latin Verse* (1912) and was professor of poetry (1923–28). He wrote much on the art of poetry and on poets, and published essays of considerable charm and humour.

GARSHIN, Vsevolod Mikhailovich (1855–88) Russian author, born in Bachmut. He wrote short stories, greatly influenced by **Tolstoy**, including *The Red Flower* (1883), and *The Signal* (1912). He served in the Turkish war, and was wounded and invalided home in 1878.

GARSTIN, Sir William Edmund (1849–1925) English engineer, born in India. Educated at Cheltenham and King's College, London, he became an official in the Indian Public Works Department (1872). Transferred to Egypt in 1885, he was responsible for the plans and building of the Aswan dam and the barrages of Asyut and Esna, compiled two valuable reports on the hydrography of the Upper Nile, erected the new buildings of the National Museum of Egyptian Antiquities (1902) and initiated the geological survey of Egypt (1896).

GARTH, Sir Samuel (1661–1719) English physician and poet, born in Bowland Forest, Yorkshire. He was physician in ordinary to **George I**, and physician-general to the army. A member of the Kit-Cat Club, he is remembered for his burlesque poem, 'The Dispensary' (1699), a satire on uncharitable apothecaries and physicians. 'Claremont' (1715) is a topographical poem in the manner of **Pope**'s 'Windsor Forest'. He also edited a composite translation of **Ovid**'s *Metamorphoses*, published in 1717.

GARVIN, James Louis (1868–1947) English journalist, born in Birmingham. He became, after a spell as leader-writer for *The Daily Telegraph*, editor of *The Observer* (1908–42). He also edited the *Encyclopaedia Britannica* (14th ed) and wrote a biography of **Joseph Chamberlain** (1932–34).

GASCOIGNE, George (c.1525–1577) English poet and dramatist, born in Cardington in Bedfordshire. He studied at Trinity College, Cambridge, entered Gray's Inn, wrote poems, and sat in parliament for Bedford (1557–59), but was disinherited for his extravagance. He married **Nicholas Breton**'s widowed mother (to improve his finances), but, still persecuted by creditors, served in Holland under the Prince of Orange (1573–75). Surprised by a Spanish force and taken prisoner, he was detained four months. He then settled in Walthamstow, where he collected and published his poems. He translated in prose and verse, from Greek, Latin and Italian. *The Complaynt of Phylomene*, a verse narrative in the style of **Ovid**, was begun in 1563. *The Supposes* is from *I Suppositi* of **Ariosto**; *Jocasta* (1566, with Francis Kinwelmersh), practically a translation from Dolce's *Giocasta* (based on the *Phoenissae* of **Euripides**), is the second tragedy in English blank verse; *The Glasse of Government* (1575) is an original comedy. *The Steele Glas* is the earliest blank-verse satire; and in the *Certayne Notes of Instruction on Making of Verse* (1575) there is the first considerable English essay on the subject. To this zealous experimenter English literature owes a deep debt, though much of his work is hopelessly tedious.

GASKELL, Mrs Elizabeth Cleghorn, née **Stevenson** (1810–65) English novelist, born in Cheyne Row, Chelsea, London. Her father was in succession teacher, preacher, farmer, boarding-house keeper, writer and keeper of the records to the Treasury. She was brought up by an aunt in Knutsford—the Cranford of her stories—and grew up well-adjusted and beautiful. She married in 1832 William Gaskell (1805–84), a Unitarian minister in Manchester. Here she studied working men and women. In 1848 she published anonymously *Mary Barton*, followed by *The Moorland Cottage* (1850), *Cranford* (1853), *Ruth* (1853), *North and South* (1855), *Round the Sofa* (1859), *Right at Last* (1860), *Sylvia's Lovers* (1863), *Cousin Phillis* (1865), and *Wives and Daughters* (1865). As well as her novels she wrote *The Life of Charlotte Brontë* (1857).

GASPERI, Alcide de (1881–1954) Italian statesman, born in Trentino. He studied at Innsbruck and Vienna, entered parliament in 1911, was imprisoned by **Mussolini** as an anti-Fascist, and thereafter worked in the Vatican library until 1946, when he became prime minister of the new republic and remained in office until his death.

GASQUET, Francis Aidan (1846–1929) English prelate, born in London of French ancestry. Educated at Downside, he became a Benedictine and was made prior of Downside Abbey in 1878. Created a cardinal in 1914, he became prefect of the Vatican archives in 1918. He helped in the revision of the Vulgate and wrote *Henry VIII and the English Monasteries* (1888–89), and *Monastic Life in the Middle Ages* (1922), both from a strongly pro-Roman standpoint.

GASS, William Howard (1924–) American novelist, born in Fargo, North Dakota. He was educated at Ohio Wesleyan University, Delaware, and Cornell University. A philosopher and literary critic, as well as novelist, he derives from and is allied with the *symbolistes*, New Critics and the structuralists. His novels are *Omensetter's Luck* (1966) and *Willie Masters' Lonesome Wife* (1971), an essay-novella.

GASSENDI, Pierre (1592–1655) French philosopher and scientist, born in Champtercier, Provence. Ordained priest in 1616, he became professor of philosophy at Aix in 1617 and professor of mathematics at the Collège Royal in Paris in 1645. **Kepler** and **Galileo** were among his friends. He was a strong advocate of the experimental approach to science and tried to reconcile an atomic theory of matter (based on the Epicurean model) with Christian doctrine. He may be best known as an early critic of **Descartes** in the Fifth of the *Objections* (1642) to the *Meditations*, but he also wrote on **Epicurus**, **Tycho Brahe** and **Copernicus**. His other works include *Exercitationes Paradoxicae adversus Aristoteleos* (1624), *Institutio Astronomica* (1647) and the *Syntagma Philosophicum* (published posthumously in 1658).

GASSER, Herbert Spencer (1888–1963) American physiologist, born in Platteville, Wisconsin. He became professor at Washington University in St Louis in 1916 and at Cornell in 1931. From 1935 he was director of the Rockefeller Institute for Medical Research. He shared the 1944 Nobel prize for physiology or medicine with **Joseph Erlanger** for their joint work on nerve fibres and nerve impulse transmission.

GASSETT See **ORTEGA Y GASSET**

GASTON DE FOIX See **FOIX**

GATAKER, Thomas (1574–1654) English Puritan churchman, born in London. He studied at St John's College, Cambridge, and in 1611 became rector of Rotherhithe. As a member of the Westminster Assembly he opposed the imposition of the Covenant, and condemned the trial of **Charles I**. His 25 works include the once-controversial *Of the Nature and use of Lots* (1616).

GATES, Horatio (1728–1806) English-born American revolutionary soldier, born in Maldon, Essex. He entered the English army, served in America under **Braddock**, and escaped with difficulty from the disaster of the Duguesne expedition (1755) and on the peace of 1763 purchased an estate in Virginia. In the War of Independence he sided with his adoptive country, and in 1775 was made adjutant-general, and in 1776 commander of the army which had just retreated from Canada. In August 1777 he took command of the northern department, and compelled the surrender of the British army under **Burgoyne** at Saratoga in October. This success gained him a great reputation, and he sought to supplant **Washington**, the commander-in-chief. In 1780 he commanded the army of the South, but was routed by **Cornwallis** near Camden, South Carolina, and was superseded. He retired to

Virginia till 1790, emancipated his slaves and settled in New York, where he died.

GATHORNE-HARDY See **CRANBROOK**

GATLING, Richard Jordan (1818–1903) American inventor, born in Money's Neck, North Carolina. He studied medicine but never practised, and is known for his invention of the rapid-fire Gatling gun (1861–62), a revolving battery gun, with ten parallel barrels, firing 1200 shots a minute.

GATTING, Michael William (1957–) English cricketer, born in Kingsbury, Middlesex. He made his mark as a forceful batsman with Middlesex; at the beginning of the 1988 season he had played 58 Tests and made nine Test hundreds, including 241 against India at Madras in 1984–85. As captain, he was involved in a dispute with a Pakistan umpire during the 1987–88 tour of that country and lost the captaincy after the first Test against West Indies in England in 1988.

GATTY, Harold Charles (1903–57) Australian aviator and naturalist, born in Campbell Town, Tasmania. He trained for a naval career but went to California in 1927. His interest in navigation led him to open a laboratory making and repairing instruments, and preparing maps. He devised a ground-speed-and-drift indicator which still forms the basis of automatic pilots used in modern aircraft. In 1929 he flew as navigator on a non-stop flight from Los Angeles to New York. In 1930, on a cross-Pacific flight between Japan and the USA, fuel trouble forced him to turn back the plane 1200 miles out. Gatty navigated a safe return entirely by 'dead-reckoning'. The American stuntman **Wiley Post** obtained Gatty's services as navigator in a round-the-world flight in 1931 which covered 15000 miles in under nine days, an achievement which owed much to Gatty's expert navigation. He served with the US and Australian forces in the Pacific during World War II and in 1943 published *The Raft Book*, on star navigation, which became standard equipment in all USAAF life rafts. After the war he settled in Fiji and founded Fiji Airways. His best-selling book *Nature is your Guide* was published shortly after his death.

GATTY, Margaret See **EWING, Juliana Horatia**

GAUDEN, John (1605–62) English prelate, born at Mayland vicarage, Essex. Educated at Bury St Edmund's school and St John's College, Cambridge, he also studied at Oxford. He became master of the Temple in 1659, bishop of Exeter in 1660, and bishop of Worcester in 1662. He edited **Hooker**'s works (1662), and claimed authorship of *Eikon Basilike* which purported to be the meditations of **Charles I**. He published a number of works against the Puritans including the monumental *Ecclesiae Anglicannae Suspiria* (1659).

GAUDÍ, I CORNET, Antonio (1852–1926) Spanish architect, born in Riudoms, Catalonia. After an apprenticeship to a blacksmith, he studied architecture at the Escuela Superior de Arquitectura in Barcelona, and became the leading exponent of Catalan 'Modernism' (a branch of the Art Nouveau movement in architecture) inspired by a nationalistic search for a romantic medieval past. Strikingly original and ingenious, he designed a number of highly individualistic and unconventional buildings, such as the Palacio Güell (1886–89) and its adjoining Park Güell (1900–14), for his chief patron, Don Basilio Güell; the Casa Batlló (1904–17); and the Casa Milá (1905–09). His most celebrated work was on the extravagant and ornate church of the Sagrada Familia in Barcelona, which occupied him from 1884 until his death. It is still under construction.

GAUDIER-BRZESKA, Henri, originally **Henri Gaudier** (1891–1915) French sculptor, born in St Jean de Braye, near Orléans. In Paris in 1910 he met the Polish artist Sophie Brzeska and from 1911 they both used the hyphenated name. In 1911 they settled in London and met leading members of the British avant-garde. He became a founder member of the London Group in 1913, and the following year signed the Vorticist Manifesto. He drew upon African tribal art but rapidly developed a personal abstract style exemplified in both carvings and drawings. He was killed in action at Neuville-Saint-Vaast.

GAUGUIN, Eugène Henri Paul (1848–1903) French post-Impressionist painter, born in Paris, the son of a journalist and a half-Peruvian Creole mother. He went to sea at seventeen, but settled down in Paris in 1871 and became a successful stockbroker with a predilection for painting and for collecting Impressionist paintings. By 1883, however, he had already exhibited his own work with the help of **Camille Pissarro** and, determined to give up all for art, left his Danish wife and five children, went to Pont Aven, Brittany, where he became the leader of a group of painters and met the painter and theorist, Emile Bernard (1868–1941). He made a voyage to Martinique (1887–88), and quarrelled with **Van Gogh** at Arles (1888), and moved in the Symbolists' circle in Paris. He gradually evolved his own style, *synthesism*, in accordance with his heartfelt hatred of civilization and identification with the emotional directness of primitive peoples. He moved to Tahiti in 1891–1901, and thence to the Marquesas Islands. Thus from his Brittany seascapes, the *Still Life with Three Puppies* (1888; Modern Art, New York), the stained-glass effects of *The Vision after the Sermon* (1888; National Gallery, Edinburgh) with its echoes of Romanesque, Japanese and Breton folk art, there is a conscious development to the tapestrylike canvases, painted in purples, greens, dark-reds and browns of native subjects on Tahiti and at Dominiha on the Marquesas Islands, eg *No Te Aha De Riri*, *Why are you angry?* (1896; Chicago), and *Faa Iheihe*, *decorated with ornaments* (1898; Tate Gallery, London), which echoes his great allegorical painting dashed off prior to an unsuccessful arsenic suicide attempt in January 1898, *D'où venons-nous? Que sommes-nous? Où allons-nous?* (Boston). Gauguin also excelled in wood carvings of pagan idols and wrote an autobiographical novel, *Noa-Noa* (1894–1900). He is remembered not only because of the tragic choices he made, and as the subject of many popular novels, particularly **Somerset Maugham**'s *The Moon and Sixpence*, but because he directed attention to primitive art as a valid field of aesthetic exploration and consequently influenced almost every school of 20th-century art.

GAULLE See **DE GAULLE**

GAUMONT, Léon Ernest (1864–1946) French cinema inventor. He synchronized a projected film with a phonograph in 1901 and was responsible for the first talking pictures, demonstrated at the Académie des Sciences at Paris in 1910 and at the Royal Institute in 1912. He also introduced an early form of coloured cinema-film, using a three -colour separation method with special lenses and projectors.

GAUNT, John of See **JOHN OF GAUNT**

GAUSS, Carl Friedrich (1777–1855) German mathematician, astronomer and physicist, born in Brunswick to poor parents. His great mathematical precocity came to the notice of the Duke of Brunswick who paid for his education at the Collegium Carolinum at Brunswick and the university of Göttingen. In 1807 he became director of the Göttingen observatory where he remained for the rest of his life. He is generally regarded as one of the greatest mathematicians of all time. A notebook kept in Latin by him as a youth was discovered in 1898 showing that, from the age of 15, he had conjectured many remarkable results, including the prime number theorem and ideas of non-Euclidean geometry. In 1796 he announced that he had found a ruler and compass construction for the 17-sided polygon, and in 1801 published his *Disquisitiones arithmeticae*, containing wholly new advances in number theory. The discovery of the asteroid Ceres by **Piazzi** in 1801 led him to the study of celestial mechanics, on which he published a treatise in 1809. From 1818 to 1825 he directed the geodetic survey of Hanover, and this and his astronomical work involved him in much heavy routine calculation, and led to his study of the theory of errors of observation, and the method of least squares. Nevertheless he found time for much work on pure mathematics, including differential equations, the hypergeometric function, the curvature of surfaces, four different proofs of the fundamental theorem of algebra, quadratic reciprocity and much else in number theory. In physics he studied the Earth's magnetism and developed the magnetometer in conjunction with **Wilhelm Eduard Weber**, and gave a mathematical theory of optical systems of lenses. Manuscripts unpublished until long after his death show that he had made many other discoveries including the theory of elliptic functions that had been published independently by **Niels Henrik Abel** and **Carl Gustav Jacobi**.

GAUTAMA, (Gotama) Indian philosopher, born in Bihar. The founder of *Nyāya*, one of the six classical systems of Hindu philosophy, his *Nyāya Sūtras* are principally concerned with ways of knowing and of reaching valid logical conclusions. Their claim that one can obtain real knowledge of the external world was disputed by Śrīharsha and the *Navya-nyāya* school founded by **Gangeśa**.

GAUTIER, Hubert (1660–1737) French civil engineer, born in Nîmes. He was one of the first to recognize the importance of applying scientific principles to the design and execution of engineering works. After nearly 30 years as chief government engineer of the Province of Languedoc, in 1716 he was appointed inspector of the newly-created Corps des Ponts et Chaussées, responsible for virtually all public works throughout France. At the time he had just published the two classic textbooks, the *Traité des Chemins* (1715) and the *Traité des Ponts* (1716), in which he summarised ancient and contemporary engineering practice, emphasizing the importance of strict supervision, careful testing of materials, and observance of the principles of structural mechanics.

GAUTIER, Théophile (1811–72) French poet and novelist, born in Tarbes. From painting he turned to literature, and became an extreme 'romanticist'. In 1830 he published his first long poem, *Albertus*, in 1832 the striking *Comédie de la mort*. His poetry reached its highest in *Émaux et camées* (1856). In 1835 appeared his celebrated novel, *Mademoiselle de Maupin*, with its defiant preface. He wrote many other novels and masterly short stories—*Les Jeunes-France* (1833), *Fortunio* (1838), *Une Larme du diable* (1839), *Militona* (1847), *La Peau de tigre* (1852), *Jettatura* (1857), *Le Capitaine Fracasse* (1863), *La Belle Jenny* (1865), *Spirite* (1866), and others. His theatrical criticisms were collected as *L'Histoire de l'art dramatique en France* (1859); his articles on the Salon form perhaps the best history of the French art of his day. *Caprices et zigzags*, *Constantinople*, *Voyage en Russie* and *Voyage en Espagne* contain delightful travel sketches. Other works were an enlarged edition of his *Émaux et camées* (1872); *Les Grotesques* (1844), on 16th- and 17th-century writers; *Honoré de Balzac* (1858); *Ménagerie intime* (1869), a kind of informal autobiography; *Histoire du romantisme* (1872); and the posthumous works, *Portraits et souvenirs littéraires* (1875) and *L'Orient* (1877). His daughter Judith Gautier (1845–1917) wrote novels, plays, poems and translations.

GAVARNI, Paul, pseud of **Sulpice Guillaume Chevalier** (1801–66) French illustrator and caricaturist, born in Paris. He started his career as a mechanical engineer, but became a caricaturist for *Les Gens du Monde* and *Le Charivari*. At first he ridiculed the follies of the Parisians with good-humoured irony; but later a deep earnestness showed itself in his productions. After a visit to London in 1849, he reproduced in *L'Illustration* the scenes of misery he had witnessed there. He also illustrated several books, including those of **Eugène Sue**, **Balzac** and **Ernst Theodor Hoffmann**. Two collections of his drawings, *Oeuvres choisies* (1848) and *Perles et parures* (1850), were published in Paris.

GAVASKAR, Sunil Manohar (1949–) Indian cricketer, born in Bombay. Educated at St Xavier's College and Bombay University, he has become the most prolific run-scorer in Test cricket history. Known as the 'Little Master' for the severe perfection of his style as well as his short stature, he has played in 125 Test matches for India since 1971, and scored 10122 runs, including 34 test centuries.

GAVAZZI, Allesandro (1809–89) Italian priest and social reformer, born in Bologna. He became a Barnabite monk and supported the liberal policy of **Pius IX**, and on the fall of Rome in 1849 escaped to England, where he joined the Evangelical Church and founded the (Protestant) Italian Free Church (1850–60). He was a chaplain with **Garibaldi** at Palermo in 1860, and in 1870 organized the Free Church of Italy. He established a theological school in Rome in 1875.

GAVESTON, Piers de See **EDWARD II**

GAY, Delphine de See **GIRARDIN**

GAY, John (1685–1732) English poet, born in Barnstaple, Devon, into a prosperous Nonconformist family. Educated at Barnstaple Grammar School, he was apprenticed to a silk-mercer in London, but soon returned home and became a writer. In 1708 he published his first poem, *Wine*, and in 1711 a pamphlet on the *Present State of Wit*. Appointed secretary to the duchess of **Monmouth** (1712), in 1713 he dedicated to **Pope** the georgic *Rural Sports*. In 1714 he published *The Fan* and *The Shepherd's Week*, and accompanied Lord Clarendon, envoy to Hanover, as secretary. When the duchess died he wrote a poem on the newly-arrived Princess of Wales. *What d'ye Call It?* (1715) was called 'a tragi-comi-pastoral farce'. *Trivia*, a clever picture of town life, came next; and later he bore the blame of *Three Hours after Marriage* (1717), a play which he had written with Pope and **Arbuthnot**. In 1720 he published his poems by subscription, clearing £1000; but this and some South Sea stock vanished in the crash of 1720. In 1724 he produced *The Captives*, a tragedy, and in 1727 the first series of his popular *Fables*. But his greatest success was *The Beggar's Opera* (1728), set to music by **Pepusch**, the outcome of a suggestion made by **Swift** in 1716. Its popularity was extraordinary; it ran 62 nights, and by the 36th, Gay had netted over £700; forthwith he set about a sequel, *Polly*, which was prohibited, but which in book form brought in £1200. After this he lived chiefly with the Duke and Duchess of Queensberry, the kindest of his many patrons. He wrote another opera, *Achilles* (produced posthumously in 1733). He was buried in Westminster Abbey.

GAY-LUSSAC, Joseph Louis (1778–1850) French chemist and physicist, born in St Léonard in Haute Vienne. With **Jean Baptiste Biot**, and later alone, he made balloon ascents for investigating the laws of terrestrial magnetism, and for collecting samples of air for analysis, which resulted in his famous memoir to the Academy of Sciences (1805) with **Alexander von Humboldt**, stating that oxygen and hydrogen combine at the ratio of one to two volumes respectively to form water. This led to the discovery of the law of volumes (1808). In 1809 he became professor of physics at the Sorbonne, and from 1832 of chemistry in the Jardin des Plantes. He was the first to prepare hydriodic and iodic acids; and in 1815 he succeeded in isolating cyanogen. His investigations regarding the manufacture of sulphuric acid led to the introduction of the Gay-Lussac tower; those on the manufacture of the bleaching chlorides, the centesimal alcoholometer and the assaying of silver are also important. In 1818 he became superintendent of the government manufactory of gunpowder, and in 1829 chief assayer to the mint. In 1839 he was made a peer of France.

GAYE, Marvin (1939–84) American soul singer, born in Washington DC, the son of a clergyman. He started singing and playing the organ in church and at 15 joined the 'doo-wop' group, The Rainbows. Moving to Detroit, he signed a recording contract with the Tamla/Motown company in 1961 after the company's founder Berry Gordy had heard him singing at an informal party. Most of his early recordings were in the 'beat ballad' idiom although there were notable exceptions including the dance-oriented 'Hitch Hike', and the twelve-bar blues of 'Can I Get A Witness'. 'I Heard It Through The Grapevine' (1968) was his last standard Motown recording and from 1970, despite arguments with the company management, he adopted a more independent attitude towards recording. *What's Going On* (1971) was a concept album that showed a fluidity and intelligence far removed from his previous teen ballad hits. Subsequent albums included *Here My Dear* (1979), *In Our Lifetime* (1981) and *Midnight Love* (1982). He was killed by a gunshot during a quarrel with his father.

GAYOOM, Maumoon Abdul (1937–) Maldivian politician. Educated at the Al-Azhar ur Cairo, he lectured in Islamic studies at the American University, Cairo (1967–69) and Nigeria University (1969–71). He returned to the Maldives in 1972 to head the government shipping (1972–73) and telephone (1974) departments, before being appointed special undersecretary to Prime Minister Ahmed Zaki in 1974. Between 1975 and 1978 he held a variety of diplomatic and ministerial posts, before succeeding Ibrahim Nasir as executive president and minister of defence in 1978. He was re-elected president in 1983 and 1988. Soon after the 1988 re-election a coup led by the exiled businessman Abdullah Luthufi was foiled by Indian paratroops. Gayoom then continued his programme of rural development and non-alignment.

GAZA, Theodorus (1398–1478) Byzantine scholar, born in Thessalonica. He fled before the Turks to Italy (c.1444), and taught Greek at Ferrara and later philosophy at Rome. Cardinal **Bessarion** obtained for him a small benefice in Calabria. His principal work was a Greek grammar (1495) and he translated into Latin portions of **Aristotle**, **Theophrastus**, and St **Chrysostom**.

GEBER (14th century) Spanish alchemist who took the name of Geber (Latin for **Jabir**) to trade on the reputation of Jabir ibn Hayyan, a celebrated Arabic alchemist. His principal writings include *Summa Perfectionis Magisterii*, and tractates in geometry.

GED, William (1690–1749) Scottish printer. He began as a goldsmith in Edinburgh, and in 1725 patented a process of stereotyping. He was commissioned by Cambridge University to stereotype prayer books and bibles, but his partner's unfairness and workmen's opposition compelled him to return to Edinburgh (1733).

GEDDES, Alexander (1737–1802) Scottish biblical scholar, born in Rathven parish, Banff. Educated for the priesthood at Paris (1758–64), in 1769 he took a cure of souls at Auchinhalrig, Banff, where his sympathy with local Protestants led to his dismissal (1780). Going to London, he made a new translation of the Bible for English Catholics (1792–1800).

GEDDES, Andrew (1783–1844) Scottish painter and etcher, born in Edinburgh. He worked with his father in the Excise office, but in 1806 went to London to study painting as a fellow pupil of Sir **David Wilkie**. He worked in London for most of his life.

GEDDES, Auckland Campbell, 1st Baron (1879–1954) British politician and surgeon, brother of Sir **Eric Geddes**. Educated at George Watson's College, Edinburgh, he studied medicine at the university, and after service in the South African war, became assistant professor of anatomy at Edinburgh, at McGill University, Montreal, where he was president (1919–20), and at the Royal College of Surgeons, Dublin. During World War I he attained the rank of brigadier-general, was appointed director of recruiting (1916) and minister of national service in 1917, after entering parliament as a Unionist and being knighted. He became minister of reconstruction (1919), president of the board of trade (1919–20) and British ambassador to the USA (1920–24). He then retired from politics, except to preside over the royal commission on food prices (1924–25).

GEDDES, Sir Eric Campbell (1875–1937) British politician, brother of **Auckland Geddes**, born in India and educated in Edinburgh. He engaged in lumbering and railway work in America, India and England, was director-general of military railways 1916–17, First Lord of the Admiralty 1917, a member of the war cabinet 1918, and first minister of transport in 1919–21. He presided over the 'Geddes Axe' committee on national expenditure in 1922.

GEDDES, Jenny (c.1600–c.1660) Scottish vegetable-seller, traditionally reputed to have started the riots in St Giles' cathedral, Edinburgh, when **Laud**'s prayer book was introduced on Sunday, 23 July 1637. According to the popular legend she threw her folding-stool at Bishop Lindsay, shouting: 'Thou false thief, dost thou say mass at my lug?'. There is no historical evidence of her exploit. Sydserf in 1661 mentions 'the immortal Jenet Geddes' as having burned 'her leather chair of state' in a Restoration bonfire, and the story appears in full detail in Phillips's continuation of Baker's *Chronicle* (1660).

GEDDES, Sir Patrick (1854–1932) Scottish biologist, sociologist and pioneer of town planning, born in Perth. Educated at Perth Academy and University College, London (under **T H Huxley**), he was a demonstrator in botany at Edinburgh before becoming professor of botany at Dunne (1889–1914). Taking the theory of evolution as a basis for ethics, history and sociology, he wrote *The Evolution of Sex* (1889). In 1892 he established the 'world's first sociological laboratory' in the Outlook Tower on Castlehill, Edinburgh, to demonstrate regional differentiation. Increasingly involved in town and regional renovation, he wrote *City Development* (1904) and *Cities in Evolution* (1915), in which he coined the terms 'megalopolis' and 'kaktopia'. After World War I he was professor of civics and sociology at Bombay University (1920–23), and in 1924 moved to France and established an unofficial 'Scots College' at Montpellier.

GEER, Baron Gerhard Jacob de (1858–1943) Swedish quaternary geologist, born in Stockholm, the son of a prime minister of Sweden. He achieved a major advance in geological dating. Educated at Uppsala, he was professor of geology there from 1897. He devised a novel and valuable method for dating by the study of varves (the annual deposits of sediment under glacial meltwater), which greatly advanced knowledge of the later geological history of the last Ice Age. The method was eventually displaced by the use of radioisotope methods.

GEERAERTS See **GHEERAERTS**

GEERTGEN TOT SINT JANS (c.1460–c.1490) Dutch painter, born in Leiden. Little is known about his life; his name means 'little Gerard of the Brethren of St John' and he worked for this religious Order in Haarlem. Only about 15 paintings are now attributed to him. These works, mostly fragments of larger altarpieces, and all religious in subject, are characterized by strong colours, convincing landscape and, perhaps most notably, very individual figures.

GEERTZ, Clifford James (1923–) American cultural anthropologist, born in San Francisco. He studied at Antioch College and Harvard, became professor of anthropology at the University of California (1958–60) and at Chicago (1960–70), and professor of social science at Princeton's Institute of Advanced Study in 1970. He carried out fieldwork in Java (1952–54) and Bali (1957–58), resulting in a series of works on environment and economy, social change and religion. These include *The Religion of Java* (1960), *Agricultural Involution* (1963), *Peddlers and Princes* (1963), and *Person, Time and Conflict in Bali* (1966). In the 1960s and 1970s he made several field trips to Morocco, from which he developed a comparative approach to religion, as in *Islam Observed* (1968), and to processes of social change. His eloquent theoretical essays on topics ranging from art and ideology to politics and nationalism, collected in *The Interpretation of Cultures* (1973) and *Local Knowledge* (1983) were particularly influential. In these he advocates an interpretative stance, in which cultures are compared to literary texts.

GEGENBAUR, Karl (1826–1903) German comparative anatomist and apostle of evolution theory, born in Würzburg. He became professor at Jena in 1855, and at Heidelberg in 1873. His chief work, *Comparative Anatomy* (trans 1878), threw much light on the evolution of the skull from his study of cartilaginous fishes.

GEHLEN, Arnold (1904–76) German philosopher and sociologist, born in Leipzig. He is particularly associated with 'philosophical anthropology', which tried to connect coherently biological, cultural and philosophical aspects of human nature. His most important works are *Der Mensch: seine Natur und seine Stellung in der Welt* (1940), *Urmensch und Spätkultur* (1956), *Die Seele in technischen Zeitalter* (1960) and *Moral und Hypermoral* (1965).

GEHRIG, Lou (Henry Louis) (1903–41) American baseball player, born in New York. Known as the 'Iron Horse' for his remarkable endurance, he played a record number of 2130 consecutive major-league games for the New York Yankees (1925–39). He was voted Most Valuable Player (MVP) four times (1927, 1931, 1934 and 1936). His career was cut short by motor neurone disease, now known in the USA as 'Lou Gehrig's disease'. In 1939 he was elected to the National Baseball Hall of Fame. The story of his life was told in the film *Pride of the Yankees* (1942), with **Gary Cooper** in the title role.

GEIBEL, Emmanuel von (1815–84) German poet, born in Lübeck. He studied at Bonn, and was tutor (1838–39) in Athens to the family of the Russian ambassador. He made many translations from the Greek, Spanish and Italian authors, and with **Heyse** founded the Munich school of poetry, which emphasized harmony and form.

GEIGER, Abraham (1810–74) German-Jewish scholar, born in Frankfurt. He studied at Heidelberg and Bonn, and was rabbi successively at Wiesbaden, Breslau, Frankfurt and Berlin. He wrote on biblical criticism; but his principal work is *Das Judenthum und seine Geschichte*.

GEIGER, Hans Wilhelm (1882–1945) German physicist, born in Neustadt-an-der-Haardt. He worked under **Ernest Rutherford** at Manchester (1906–12), investigated beta-ray radioactivity and, with Walther Müller, devised a counter to measure it. He was professor at Kiel (1925) and at Tübingen (1929).

GEIJER, Erik Gustav (1783–1877) Swedish poet and historian, born in Ransäter in Värmland. He studied at Uppsala and was appointed professor of history there in 1817. A founder of the Gothic Society and its journal, *Iduna*, in 1811, in which he published much of his best poetry, he had a profound influence on both literature and historiography in Sweden. His works included *Impressions of England* (1809–10, trans 1932), and a *History of the Swedish People* (1832–36).

GEIKIE, Sir Archibald (1835–1924) Scottish geologist, brother of **James Geikie**, born in Edinburgh. Educated at the Royal High School and Edinburgh University, in 1855 he was appointed to the Geological Survey; in 1867 became director of the Geological Survey in Scotland; from 1870 to 1881 was professor of geology at Edinburgh; and was (1882–1901) director-general of the survey of the United Kingdom, and head of the Geological Museum, London. He did much to encourage microscopic petrography and volcanic geology and wrote several notable textbooks as well as biographical works.

GEIKIE, James (1839–1915) Scottish geologist, brother of Sir **Archibald Geikie**, born in Edinburgh. He served on the Geological Survey of Scotland from 1861, and was professor of geology at Edinburgh (1882–1914). Besides verse translations from **Heinrich Heine**, a large number of geological maps, sections and memoirs published by the Geological Survey, he wrote a standard work on the glacial period (1874) and several other geological books.

GEILER VON KAISERSBERG, Johann (1445–1510) German priest, born in Schaffhausen. In 1478 he became a preacher in Strasbourg Cathedral. He left many earnest, witty and original works, mainly devotional, and had a reputation as the greatest pulpit orator of his age.

GEISSLER, Heinrich (1814–79) German inventor, born in Saxony. He became a glass-blower and settled in Bonn in 1854. The Geissler tube, by which the passage of electricity through rarefied gases can be seen, and the Geissler mercury pump, are among his inventions.

GEITEL, Hans Friedrich (1855–1923) German physicist, born in Brunswick. With **Julius Elster**, he invented the first practical photoelectric cell, a photometer and a **Tesla** transformer.

GELASIUS I, St (pope 492–96), an African by birth, he was one of the earliest bishops of Rome to assert the supremacy of the papal chair. He repressed Pelagianism, renewed the ban against the oriental patriarch, drove out the Manichaeans from Rome, and wrote against the Eutychians and Nestorians.

GELASIUS II pope (1118–19), formerly John of Gaeta, cardinal and chancellor under **Urban II** and Paschal II. On the death of the latter in 1118 was chosen pope by the party hostile to the emperor **Henry V**. Gelasius fled to Gaeta to escape the advancing imperialists, and excommunicated Henry and **Gregory VIII**, the antipope he had set up. Shortly after he was able to return to Rome, but in the same autumn had to flee to France, where he died in the monastery at Cluny.

GELDOF, Bob (1954–) Irish rock musician and philanthropist, born in Dublin. Educated at Black Rock College, he worked in Canada as a pop journalist then returned home in 1975 to form the successful rock group, the Boomtown Rats (1975–86). Moved by television pictures of widespread suffering in famine-stricken Ethiopia, he established the pop charity 'Bandaid' trust in 1984. This raised £8 million for African famine relief through the release of the record 'Do they know it's Christmas ?'. In 1985, simultaneous 'Live Aid' charity concerts were held in London and Philadelphia, which, transmitted by satellite throughout the world, raised a further £48 million. Further charitable events followed and the bluntly outspoken Geldof was awarded an honorary KBE in 1986, as well as a variety of international honours.

GELÉE See **CLAUDE LORRAINE**

GELFAND, Izrail Moiseevich (1913–) Russian mathematician, born in Krasnye Okny. He studied in Moscow, where he became professor in 1943. The leader of an important school of Soviet mathematicians, he has worked mainly in **Banach** algebras, the representation theory of **Lie** groups, important in quantum mechanics, and in generalized functions, used in solving the differential equations that arise in mathematical physics.

GELLERT, Christian Fürchtegott (1715–69) German poet and moralist, born in Hainichen, Saxony. He was educated at Leipzig, and in 1751 became a professor there. He was a prolific writer of stories and fables, and two of his comedies, *Das Loos in der Lotterei* and *Die kranke Frau*, were popular favourites. His moralistic novel *Leben der schwedischen Gräfin von G-* (1747–48) shows the influence of **Samuel Richardson**.

GELLIUS, Aulus (2nd century) Latin author, supposed to have been born in Rome. He is said to have practised law there, after studying philosophy in Athens. He wrote *Noctes Atticae*, a medley of language, antiquities, history and literature. It contains many extracts from lost authors.

GELL-MANN, Murray (1929–) American theoretical physicist, born in New York City, the originator of the quark hypothesis. He entered Yale University when he was only 15 years old, and graduated in 1948. He gained his PhD from the Massachusetts Institute of Technology, spent a year at the Institute of Advanced Studies in Princeton, then joined the Institute for Nuclear Studies at Chicago University, where he worked with **Enrico Fermi**. He became professor of theoretical physics at the California Institute of Technology in 1956. When he was 24 he made a major contribution to the theory of elementary particles by introducing the concept of 'strangeness', a new quantum number which must be conserved in any so-called 'strong' nuclear interaction event. Gell-Mann and Y Ne'eman (independently) used 'strangeness' to group mesons, nucleons (neutrons and protons) and hyperons, and thus they were able to form predictions in the same way that **Mendeleyev** had about chemical elements. The omega-minus particle was predicted by this theory and observed in 1964. Their book on this work was entitled *The Eightfold Way* (1964), a pun on the Buddhist eightfold route to nirvana. Gell-Mann and G Zweig introduced the concept of quarks which have one-third integral charge and baryon number. From these the other nuclear particles (hadrons) can be made. The name is an invented word, associated with a line in **Joyce**'s *Finnegans Wake*. Six quarks have been predicted, and five have so far been indirectly detected: the six are named as Up, Down, Strange, Charm, Bottom and Top. For this work he was awarded the Nobel prize for physics in 1969.

GELON (d.478 BC) tyrant of Gela from 485 BC. He later made himself master of Syracuse, and extended his influence over half of Sicily. A powerful military ruler, he refused to aid the Greeks against **Xerxes I**, and defeated the Carthaginians at Himera (480).

GEMAYEL, Amin (1942–) Lebanese politician, brother of **Bachir Gemayel**. Trained as a lawyer, he supported Bachir in the 1975–76 civil war, and was his successor to the presidency in September 1982. More moderate, his policies initially proved no more successful in determining a peaceful settlement of the problems of Lebanese government. In 1988 his presidency came to an end and no obvious Christian successor, as required by the constitution, was apparent, resulting in continuing disorder within Lebanon.

GEMAYEL, Bachir (1947–82) Lebanese army officer and politician, brother of **Amin Gemayel** and son of **Pierre Gemayel**. He joined the militia of his father's Phalangist party at the age of 11, and on his return after a brief period in the USA working in a Washington law office, he was appointed the party's political director in the Ashrefieh sector of East Beirut, and was an active leader of the Christian militia in the civil war of 1975–76. By the systematic elimination of possible rivals he arrived at uncontested leadership of the military forces of East Beirut. His evident distancing of his party from Israeli support, and wish to expel all foreign influence from Lebanese affairs, effected his election as president in 1982. Having twice escaped assassination, he was killed in a bomb explosion while still president-elect.

GEMAYEL, Sheikh Pierre (1905–) Lebanese politician, father of **Amin** and **Bachir Gemayel**. A member of the Maronite Christian community of Lebanon, he was educated at the University of St Joseph, Beirut, and Cochin Hospital, Paris, where he trained as a pharmacist. In 1936 he founded the Kataeb or Phalangist party, modelled on the Spanish and German Fascist organizations, and in 1937 became its leader. He was twice imprisoned, in 1937 and in 1943, the year in which he organized a general strike. He held various ministerial posts (1960–67), and led the Phalangist Militia in the 1975–76 civil war.

GEMS, Pam (1925–) English dramatist. Among her best-known plays are *Piaf* (1978), and *Camille* (1984), portraying women as victims in worlds ruled by men. Although she had written several radio, television scripts and stage plays before the mid 1970s, it was her *Dusa, Stas, Fish and Vi* which brought her widespread recognition when it was staged in London in 1975. A look at the lives of four contemporary women, it was a courageous piece of feminist drama. She also wrote *The Danton Affair* (1986), dealing with the conflict between **Danton** and **Robespierre**.

GENEEN, Harold Sydney (1910–) English-born American accountant and industrialist, born in Bournemouth. He worked as a clerk for a firm of Wall St stockbrokers (1926–32) while studying at night to obtain a degree from New York University. He became a director of International Telephone and Telegraph (ITT) in 1959, taking on the role of chairman in 1964. He stepped down as chief executive in 1977, having seen the annual sales of the company rise from $766m to $22000m in a 17-year period. He published his views on management in his book *Managing* (1984).

GENET, Jean (1910–86) French author, born in Paris. At the age of seven months his mother gave him to the Hospice des Enfants Assistés in Paris and two days later he went to foster parents. He showed a religious temperament as a child and served as an altar boy in the local church, but later turned to crime and spent many years in reformatories and prisons, in France and abroad, for theft, male prostitution, etc. He began to write in 1942 in Fresnes prison where he was serving a life sentence after ten convictions for theft. His first novel, *Notre-Dame des Fleurs* (1944, trans *Our Lady of the Flowers*, 1964) created a sensation. In it he first portrayed his world of homosexuals and criminals, evoking in a characteristically ceremonial and religious language his view of a universe of violence and betrayal, prison and inevitable death. Later novels include *Miracle de la Rose* (1946, trans 1965), *Pompes Funèbres* (1947) and *Querelle de Brest* (1947, trans 1966). In 1948 he was granted a pardon by the president after a petition by French intellectuals. The book *Saint Genet* (1952, trans 1963), by **Sartre**, widened his fame among the French intelligentsia. Several plays, including *Les Bonnes* (1947), *Les Nègres* (1959) and *Les Paravents* (1961), and poems such as *Les Condamnés à mort* (1942), *Chants Secrets* (1945) and *La Galère, La parade, un chant d'amour* (1948), share the criminal underworld setting and profoundly pessimistic outlook of the novels, expressed in ritualistic and mystical style. On release from prison he was associated with revolutionary movements in many countries. He wrote an autobiography, *Le Journal du voleur* (1949, trans *Thief's Journal*, 1964).

GENEVIÈVE, St (c.422–512) patron saint of Paris, born at Nanterre near Paris. After taking the veil from St **Germanus**, she acquired an extraordinary reputation for sanctity, increased by her assurance that **Attila** and his Huns would not touch Paris in 451, and by her expedition for the relief of the starving city during Childeric's Frankish invasion. In 460 she built a church over the tomb of St **Denis**, where she herself was buried. Her feast day is 3 January.

GENGA, Girolamo (c.1476–1551) Italian architect and religious painter, born in Urbino, where he designed the duke's palace.

GENGHIS KHAN (c.1162–1227) Mongol conqueror, born in Deligun Bulduk on the river Onon, the son of a Mongol chief. Called at 13 to succeed his father, he had to struggle hard for years against hostile tribes. His ambition awakening with his continued success, he spent six years in subjugating the Naimans, between Lake Balkhash and the Irtysh, and in conquering Tangut, south of the Gobi Desert. From the Turkish Uigurs, who voluntarily submitted, the Mongols derived their civilization, alphabet and laws. In 1206 he dropped his name Temujin for that of Genghis (Jingis or Chingis) Khan, 'Universal Ruler', in 1211, he overran the empire of North China, and in 1217 conquered and annexed the Kara-Khitai Khanate empire from Lake Balkhash to Tibet. In 1218 he attacked the powerful empire of Khwarezm, bounded by the Jaxartes, Indus, Persian Gulf and Caspian, took Bokhara, Samarkand, Khwarezm and other chief cities, and returned home in 1225. Two of Genghis' lieutenants penetrated northwards from the southern shore of the Caspian through Georgia into southern Russian and the Crimea, everywhere routing and slaying, and returned by way of the Volga. Meanwhile in the far east another of his generals had completed the conquest of all northern China (1217–23) except Honan. After a few months' rest Genghis set out to chastise the king of Tangut; and, after thoroughly subduing the country, died on 18 August. Genghis was not only a warrior and conqueror, but a skilful administrator and ruler; he not only conquered empires stretching from the Black Sea to the Pacific, but organized them into states which outlasted the short span that usually measures the life of Asiatic sovereignties.

GENLIS, Stéphanie Felicité Ducrest de St Aubin, Comtesse de (1746–1830) French writer, born in Champcéri near Autun. At the age of 16 she married the Comte de Genlis, and in 1770 was made lady-in-waiting to the Duchess of Chartres, to whose husband, Orléans 'Égalité', she became mistress. She wrote four volumes of short plays entitled *Théâtre d'education* (1779) for her charges, the royal children, including the future King **Louis-Philippe**, and nearly a hundred volumes of historical romances and 'improving' works. Her *Mémoires* (1825) contain interesting social comments on the period.

GENNARO See **JANUARIUS**

GENNEP, Charles-Arnold Kurr van (1873–1957) French ethnographer and folklorist, born in Württemberg, Germany, of a Dutch father and French mother. He grew up in France, where his career was not primarily academic. He worked for the French government in various cultural organizations from 1903 to 10, and again from 1919 to 1921. He also held brief academic appointments at Neuchâtel, Oxford and Cambridge. He became an energetic collector and publisher of folklore materials, including the *Manuel de Folklore Français Contemporaine* (1937–58). However he is principally known for his earlier work, *Les Rites de Passage* (1909), a comparative study of rituals marking transitions of social status. He discovered that such rituals have a regular tripartite structure, in which a stage of separation is followed by stages of transition and reincorporation. His other publications include *Religions, Mœurs et légendes* (1908–14).

GENSCHER, Hans-Dietrich (1927–) West German politician, born in Halle (now in East Germany). Like many other children of the period he was briefly a member of the **Hitler** Youth and fought in the army during World War II. After the war he remained in the German Democratic Republic (GDR), studying law at Leipzig and joining the Liberal-Democratic party, before fleeing to West Germany in 1952 as a result of the increasing repression of the GDR's Communist régime. He became secretary-general of the Free Democratic party (FDP) in 1959 and served as interior minister (1969–74), before being appointed FDP chairman, vice-chancellor and foreign minister in 1974 when the party's leader, **Walter Scheel**, was elected federal president. Genscher has served as foreign minister ever since, emerging as a committed supporter of Ostpolitik and advocate of European co-operation. As FDP leader, he masterminded the party's switch of allegiance from the Social Democratic party to the Christian Democratic Union which resulted in the downfall of the **Schmidt** government in 1982. He resigned as FDP chairman in 1985, but, as foreign minister, has remained an influential force, seeking to pursue a new 'second phase' of détente in a quiet, but energetic, manner.

GENSERIC See **GAISERIC**

GENTH, Frederick Augustus (1820–93) German-born American mineralogist, born in Wächtersbach near Hanau. Educated at Giessen and Marburg, he went to the USA in 1848 and became professor of chemistry and mineralogy at Pennsylvania (1872). He investigated the cobalt-ammonium compounds, and discovered 24 new minerals, one of which is named genthite.

GENTILE, Giovanni (1875–1944) Italian philosopher, educationist and politician, born in Castelvetrano, Sicily. He was professor of philosophy successively at Naples (1898–1906), Palermo (1906–14), Pisa (1914–17) and Rome (1917–44). He collaborated with **Benedetto Croce** in editing the periodical *La Critica* (1903-22) and in developing a distinctive strain of Italian idealism. But they came to disagree both philosophically and politically. Gentile propounded a theory of 'actualism', in which nothing is real except the pure act of thought, the distinctions between theory and practice, subject and object, and past and present being mere mental constructs. He also became an apologist for Fascism and an ideological mouthpiece for **Mussolini**. He was the Fascist minister of public instruction (1922–24), and presided over two commissions on constitutional reform and over the Supreme Council for Public Education (1926–28). Perhaps his most important achievement was to plan the new *Enciclopedia Italiana* (35 vols, 1929–36), which became the main cultural monument of the régime. He was assassinated by Communist partisans in Florence after Mussolini's overthrow. His main philosophical work was the *Theory of Mind as Pure Act* (1916), and he also wrote a number of works on education.

GENTILE DA FABRIANO See **FABRIANO**

GENTILESCHI, Artemisia (1590–c.1642) Italian painter, daughter of **Orazio Gentileschi**. She lived in Naples, but visited England (1638–39) and left a self-portrait at Hampton Court. Her chief work is a *Judith and Holophernes* in the Uffizi, Florence.

GENTILESCHI, Orazio (1563–1647) Italian painter born in Pisa. He settled in England in 1626, the first Italian painter called to England by **Charles I**, having been patronized by the Vatican and the **Medicis** in Genoa. He was responsible for the decoration of the Queen's House at Greenwich (partly transferred to Marlborough House), and painted *Discovery of Moses* in Madrid, *Flight into Egypt* in the Louvre and *Joseph and Potiphar's Wife* at Hampton Court. His attempt to introduce the Italian style of decoration into England was unsuccessful, although his reputation stood very high for a time.

GENTILI, Alberico (1552–1608) Italian jurist and writer on international law and politics, born in Sangenesio in the March of Ancona. Exiled as a Protestant, in 1580 he settled in England and lectured at Oxford. He was the first true scholar in international law and his works, especially *De Jure Belli* (1598), are fundamental.

GENTZ, Friedrich von (1764–1832) German publicist and diplomat, born in Breslau. In 1786 he entered the public service of Prussia, but in 1802 exchanged into that of Austria; he wrote bitterly against **Napoleon**. An adherent from 1810 of **Metternich**, at the Congress of Vienna in 1814 he was first secretary, as also in subsequent conferences. His writings are distinguished for elegance. The theorist and practical exponent of 'Balance of Power' in Europe, he received liberal *douceurs* from various foreign governments.

GÉNY, François (1861–1959) French legal theorist, professor of law at Nancy. His major work is *Méthodes d'interprétation et sources en droit privé positif* (1899), in which he contended that lawyers must supplement the norms derived from the codes, case-law and doctrine by objective factors such as social data, history and reason, so as to arrive at a decision which takes account of surrounding circumstances. His approach influenced legal thinking in many countries.

GEOFFREY OF MONMOUTH (c.1100–c.1154) Welsh chronicler and ecclesiastic, thought to be the son of Breton parents. He studied at Oxford, and was archdeacon of Llandarff or Monmouth (c.1140) and was appointed bishop of St Asaph in 1152. He compiled a totally fictitious history of Britain (*Historia Regum Britanniae*) which traced the descent of British kings back to the Trojans, and claimed to have based it on old Welsh chronicles that he alone had seen. Although worthless as history, it brought enduring romance by introducing the figure of King **Arthur** to European literature.

GEOFFRIN, Marie Thérèse, née **Rodet** (1699–1777) French patron of literature, born in Paris. She married a rich man at the age of 15 and when he died soon after, he left her an immense fortune. She had a genuine love of learning and art, and her *salon* became a rendezvous of the men of letters and artists of Paris, especially the *philosophes*.

GEOFFROY SAINT-HILAIRE, Étienne (1772–1844) French zoologist, born in Étampes. In 1793 he became professor of zoology in the Museum of Natural History at Paris, and began the great zoological collection. In 1798 he was one of the scientific commission that accompanied Bonaparte to Egypt; in 1809 he was appointed professor of zoology in the Faculty of Sciences. He endeavoured to establish the unity of plan in organic structure; and he raised teratology to a science, principally in his *Philosophie anatomique* (1818–20). He also wrote *L'Histoire naturelle des mammifères* (1820–42), *Philosophie zoologique* (1830), and *Études progressives d'un naturaliste* (1835).

GEOFFROY SAINT-HILAIRE, Isidore (1805–61) French zoologist, born in Paris, son of **Étienne Geoffroy Saint-Hilaire**. He became assistant-naturalist at the museum in 1824, and professor of zoology in the Faculty of Sciences in 1850. He made a special study of teratology, publishing in 1832–37 a work on monstrous forms. The results of his investigations on the domestication of foreign animals in France appeared in *Domestication et naturalisation des animaux utiles* (1854). In 1852 he published the first volume of his *Histoire naturelle générale des règnes organiques*, but died before completing the third volume. He was a strong advocate of the use of horse flesh as human food.

GEORGE, St patron of chivalry and guardian saint of England and Portugal. He may have been tortured and put to death by **Diocletian** at Nicomedia, 23 April 303. Or he may have suffered (c.250) at Lydda in Palestine where his alleged tomb is exhibited. By many writers, for example **Gibbon**, he has been confused with the Arian George of Cappadocia (d. 361), who after a troubled life as army contractor and tax gatherer became archbishop of Alexandria, and five years later was torn in pieces by a furious mob. St George of the Eastern Church was no doubt a real personage of an earlier date than George of Cappadocia, but beyond this nothing is known of him, and his name was early obscured by fable. The famous story of his fight with the dragon cannot be traced much earlier than **Voragine**'s *Legenda Aurea*. The Crusades gave a great impetus to his cult; many chivalrous orders assumed him as their patron; and he was adopted as guardian saint by England, Aragon and Portugal. In 1348 **Edward III** founded St George's Chapel, Windsor, and in 1344 the Order of the Garter was instituted.

GEORGE I (1660–1727) king of Great Britain and Ireland from 1717, elector of Hanover (1698–1727), and the first Hanoverian king of Great Britain and Ireland (1714–27), the eldest son of Ernest August, elector of Hanover, and **Sophia**, daughter of **Elizabeth** of Bohemia. A great-grandson of **James VI and I** of Scotland and England, he succeeded to the British throne on the death of Queen **Anne** in accordance with the Act of Settlement (1701). As a young man he held a military command in the War of Succession against **Louis XIV** of France. He married his cousin, Sophia Dorothea of Zell (1666–1726), in 1682, but divorced her in 1694 for adultery with a Swedish nobleman, and although he lived openly with his own mistresses, kept his ex-wife imprisoned in the castle of Ahlden until her death. The Hanoverian succession was unpopular in England, with widespread demonstrations against the new king on his accession, but Whig support for him was strengthened by the unsuccessful Jacobite rising in 1715 to restore the exiled **Stewart**, who were debarred from the throne on account of their Roman Catholicism. The '15' was exploited by the Whigs to discredit the Tories in the light of their lukewarm support for the Hanoverian king, while George's own preference for the Whigs served to give them a monopoly of power which was to last for another 50 years. The Septennial Act of 1716 extended the period between parliamentary elections to seven years and further reduced the level of popular participation in the political affairs of the nation. He never learned English, and although he preferred whenever possible to spend time in Hanover, he was far from being a mere figurehead in the government of Britain. His reign saw an unprecedented dominance of the court party over parliament, intensified during the premiership of Sir **Robert Walpole**, from 1721 onwards. George's relatively low political profile is a tribute to the power and cohesion of the alliance between monarch and ruling oligarchy, rather than any evidence of weakness or indifference on the part of the king.

GEORGE II (1683–1760) king of Great Britain and Ireland and elector of Hanover (1727–60), the son of **George I**. In 1705 he married Caroline of Anspach. Despite the personal antipathy that had existed between father and son during most of George's adult life and his opposition to his father's government, the new king was soon persuaded to maintain his father's principal minister in power. Sir **Robert Walpole** continued to dominate British politics until his fall in 1742, and thereafter the system that he had established continued to operate, little altered, under his successors. The peace policy pursued by Walpole was, however, breached by war with Spain in 1737 and British participation in the War of Austrian Succession (1742–48). The king took the field as commander of the British army at the battle of Dettingen (1743), which he won—the last British monarch to take part in a battle. In 1745 a Jacobite rising in Scotland under the Young Pretender, **Charles Edward Stewart**, was at first alarmingly successful, but, without the hoped-for aid from France, the Scots had little real chance against the British army and were savagely cut down at Culloden by George's second son, William Augustus, the Duke of **Cumberland**. British involvement in the Seven Years' War in 1756–57 was largely undertaken in defence of Hanover, but, while Britain suffered reverses in Europe, this was more than offset by successes further afield. **Robert Clive**'s victory at Plassey in 1757 helped to lay the foundations of British India and the capture of Quebec by General **Wolfe** in 1759 established British supremacy in North America. George died suddenly at Kensington the following year, before the conclusion of the Seven Years' War (1756–63).

GEORGE III (1738–1820) king of Great Britain, the eldest son of Frederick Louis, Prince of Wales (1707–51), born in London. His father having predeceased him, in 1760 he succeeded his grandfather, **George II**, as king of Great Britain and Ireland and Elector of Hanover (king from 1815). He was the first of the House of Hanover to command general respect on becoming sovereign, and at the outset he conciliated all classes of his subjects. In 1761, he married **Charlotte Sophia**, princess of Mecklenburg-Strelitz. Four or five years before he is said to have had a daughter by Hannah Lightfoot, (c.1740–c.1840), a Quaker, and to have married her; it is less open to doubt that, after ascending the throne, he wished to marry Lady Sarah Lennox. Eager to govern as well as reign, George felt certain that his own way was the right one, and that were it followed all would go well; hence friction soon arose between him and his people. **Pitt** was the popular idol; but the king disliked Pitt and his policy, and George's former tutor the Earl of **Bute** became prime minister in May 1762 in the place of **Thomas Pelham** Duke of Newcastle. If Bute had been a strong man he might have justified his promotion, but, timid and incompetent, he succumbed in April 1763 to the clamour evoked by the unpopular treaty of peace with France and Spain. During the two years' administration of **Grenville**, his successor, the first attempt to tax the American colonies was made. The repeal of the unpopular Stamp Act, but accompanied by a declaration of the right of Great Britain to tax the colonists, took place during the premiership of **Rockingham**, who held office for 11 months. The Earl of **Chatham**, who followed him, held office for 14 months, and the Duke of **Grafton** for three years. In Lord **North** George III found a minister after his own heart, and North remained at the head of the government from 1770 till 1782. During his administration the American colonies, exasperated at renewed attempts at taxation, proclaimed (4 July 1776) and eventually achieved their independence, the treaty of peace with Great Britain being signed in February 1783. The determination of the king not to grant any concessions to those whom he deemed rebels caused the struggle to be much protracted. Lord North was succeeded by Rockingham, who died after three months in office. Among his colleagues were **Fox**, **Burke** and **Sheridan**, whom George detested, and who, when Lord **Shelburne** took Rockingham's place, refused to serve with him; but he secured William Pitt as Chancellor of the Exchequer. The friends of Fox and the followers of Lord North overthrew Shelburne in ten months; and the Duke of Portland's coalition ministry lasted only eight months (1783). In the interval the king compelled his ministers to resign, called Pitt to office in December 1783, and dissolved parliament. Pitt remained in office for 18 years. The complete victory of his party at the general election in 1784 was a triumph for the king as much as for Pitt; there was now an end to the supremacy of the old Whig families. The Tory party had been consolidated and was prepared to give effect to the policy of George III. The struggle had been long and severe. **John Wilkes** had taken part in it; and 'Junius' had denounced the ministers whom the king trusted. Popular feeling ran high against the sovereign for a time, but he gradually regained the affections of his subjects. When the union between Ireland and Great Britain was proposed George III wrote to Pitt characterizing it as one of the most useful measures of his reign; but when the union was effected (1 January 1801), and Pitt proposed carrying out his pledges as to

Catholic emancipation, the king refused his assent. Pitt resigned; the king rejected his advice to form a strong administration, including Fox, and entrusted **Addington** with the task of forming a ministry, which held office till war with France was renewed. Pitt then resumed office, but died in 1806. A ministry was formed in which Fox and **Sidmouth** held ofice, and of which Lord Grenville was the head; it was reconstituted after Fox's death, and was succeeded in 1807 by one under the Duke of Portland. In 1809 **Perceval** succeeded to the premiership. In 1810 the Princess Amelia, George's favourite child, fell dangerously ill; this preyed on the king's mind, and hastened an attack of mental derangement, not the first he had had. In 1811 the Prince of Wales was appointed regent; and till his death, on 29 January 1820, George was hopelessly insane; he also lost his sight (his ailment is now believed to have been caused by porphyria). George III was well-meaning and intensely patriotic; pious and a pattern of the domestic virtues. During his reign were fought decisive battles in America, India and Europe, and many great conquests made. Great statesmen, such as Chatham, Pitt and Fox, adorned it; as did great captains, such as **Nelson** and **Wellington**; and many great names in modern English literature—**Johnson**, **Gibbon**, **Burns**, **Cowper**, **Crabbe**, **Scott**, **Byron**, **Coleridge**, **Wordsworth**, **Southey**, **Shelley** and **Keats**. When George III ascended the throne the national debt was £138 000 000 sterling; before his death it was more than £800 000 000. On the other hand, trade and commerce made gigantic strides; during his reign both imports and exports had increased more than fourfold in money value.

GEORGE IV (1762–1830) king of Great Britain, the eldest son of **George III**. Owing to his father's derangement, he became Prince Regent in 1811, and succeeded in 1820. Until the age of 19 the Prince had been kept under strict discipline, against which he sometimes rebelled. At 18 he had an intrigue with an actress, Mrs Robinson, and at 20 he went through the ceremony of marriage with Mrs **Fitzherbert**, a Roman Catholic; this union was canonically valid, but not acceptable in English law. Out of antagonism to his father he affected to be a Whig, and much of the king's aversion to **Fox**, **Burke** and **Sheridan** was due to their associating with him. In 1795 he married Princess **Caroline** of Brunswick, parliament agreeing to pay his debts, £650 000. As king he sought to divorce her; but her death in 1821 ended a struggle and scandal in which the people sympathized with the queen. In 1821 George IV visited Ireland and Hanover; and in 1822 Scotland, where a magnificent reception was organized by Sir **Walter Scott**. Though a professed Whig when Prince of Wales, George IV governed as his father had done with the aid of the Tories. **Perceval**, **Liverpool**, **Canning**, **Ripon** and **Wellington** successively held office while he was regent and king. He was a man of culture and wit, who left to the nation a valuable collection of books and paintings. His patronage of the arts may be appreciated at Windsor and Brighton, and he also recognized the genius of **John Nash** as an architect and town planner.

GEORGE V (1865–1936) king of Great Britain, born at Marlborough House. He served in the navy, travelled in many parts of the empire, and was created Prince of Wales in 1901. He had five sons, the youngest Prince John (1905–19), and one daughter (Victoria Alexandra Alice Mary, Princess Royal, 1897–1965, married the 6th Earl of Harewood, d.1947) and succeeded his father, **Edward VII**, in 1910. His reign was marked, among other things, by the Union of South Africa (1910), his visit to India for the Coronation Durbar (1911), World War I (1914–18), the adoption of the surname Windsor (1917), Sinn Fein Rebellion (1916), Irish Free State settlement (1922), the first Labour governments (1924–25, 1929–31), the General Strike (1926), Scottish church union (1929), economic crisis and 'national' government (1931), Statute of Westminster (1931), and the Government of India Act (1935). He originated the famous Christmas Day broadcasts to the nation in 1932. In 1893 he married **Mary**, formerly Princess Victoria Mary Augusta Louise Olga Pauline Claudine Agnes of Teck (1867–1953). She was born in Kensington Palace, London, and married Prince **George** in 1893. She organized women's war work (1914–18), devoted her time to the interests of women and children, continuing with many public and philanthropic activities after the death of her husband. She was known and loved as a regal and in many ways highly individual figure with a keen sense of duty. She was a keen and discerning collector of antiques and *objets d'art*.

GEORGE VI (1895–1952) king of Great Britain, second son of **George V**, father of **Elizabeth II** and Princess **Margaret Rose**, born at Sandringham. Educated at Dartmouth Naval College and at Trinity College, Cambridge, he served in the Grand Fleet at the battle of Jutland (1916), was an air cadet at Cranwell and in 1918 on the staff of the Independent Force, RAF. Keenly interested in the human problems of industry, he became president of the Boys' Welfare Association and originated the summer camps for public school and working-class boys. In 1920 he was created Duke of York and married Lady **Elizabeth Bowes-Lyon** in 1923. An outstanding tennis player, he played at Wimbledon in the All-England championships in 1926. The following year, he and the duchess toured Australia. On the abdication of his elder brother, **Edward VIII**, he ascended the throne in 1936. During World War II he set a personal example in wartime restrictions, continued to reside in bomb-damaged Buckingham Palace, visited all theatres of war and delivered many broadcasts, for which he overcame a speech impediment. In 1947 he toured South Africa and substituted the title of head of the Commonwealth for that of Emperor of India, when that subcontinent was granted independence by the Labour government. Unnoticed by the public, his health was rapidly declining, yet he persevered with his duties, his last great public occasion being the opening of the Festival of Britain in 1951. He died suddenly of coronary thrombosis.

GEORGE I (1845–1913) king of Greece from 1863, second son of King **Kristian IX** of Denmark. Born in Copenhagen, he served in the Danish Navy. On the deposition of Otto (king of Greece 1832–62) he was elected king in 1863 by the Greek national assembly, and married in 1867 the Grand Duchess Olga, niece of Tsar **Alexander II** of Russia. His reign saw the consolidation of Greek territory in Thessaly and Epirus, and the suppression of a Cretan insurrection in 1896–7. Involved in the Balkan War of 1912–13, he was assassinated at Salonika, and succeeded by his son **Constantine I**.

GEORGE II (1890–1947) king of Greece 1922–23 and 1935–47, son of **Constantine I** and grandson of **George I**. He succeeded to the throne on his father's second abdication in 1922, but was deposed in 1923 by a military junta. Restored to the throne by plebiscite in 1935, he worked closely with his dictatorial prime minister, **Yanni Metaxas**. When Greece was overrun by the Germans after successfully resisting the Italian invasion of 1940–41, he withdrew to Crete and then

England. In 1946 he was restored to the throne, again by plebiscite. He was succeeded by his brother **Paul I**.

GEORGE V (1819–78) last king of Hanover (1851–66), was born in Berlin. Blind from 1833 and a complete absolutist, by siding with Austria he lost Hanover to Prussia and died an exile in Paris. His son, **Ernest Augustus** (1845–1923), Duke of Cumberland (removed from British peerage 1917), maintained his Hanoverian claim till 1913; his son, Ernest Augustus (b. 1887; deposed 1918), Duke of Brunswick, married **William II**'s daughter, Victoria Louisa.

GEORGE, Prince, of Denmark See **ANNE**

GEORGE, David Lloyd See **LLOYD GEORGE OF DWYFOR**

GEORGE, Henry (1839–97) American economist, born in Philadelphia. He went to sea, and in 1858 arrived in California, where he became a printer and married. He wrote for several newspapers, and became the owner of the *San Francisco Daily Evening Post* (1871–75) and took an active part in public questions. He published *Our Land and Land Policy* in 1870 and, *Progress and Poverty* (1877–79). His fundamental remedy for poverty was a 'single tax' levied on the value of land exclusive of improvements, and the abolition of all taxes which fall upon industry and thrift.

GEORGE, Mlle, stage name of **Marguerite Joséphine Weimar** (1787–1867) French tragedienne, born in Bayeux. She was famed at the Comédie Française for her playing in both classical tragedy and the early romantic dramas. In her *Mémoirs* she left an account of her liaison with **Napoleon**.

GEORGE, Stefan (1868–1933) German poet, born in Büdeshein near Bingen. He edited (1892–1919) *Blätter für die Kunst*, a journal devoted to the work of a group of advanced poets and writers to which he belonged, and wrote lyric verse in *Hymnen* (1890), *Der siebente Ring* (1907) and *Der Stern des Bundes* (1914), which shows the influence of the French Symbolists and the English pre-Raphaelites. He also translated the works of **Baudelaire**, **Shakespeare** and **Dante**. His poems, dispensing with punctuation and capitals, are an expression of mood, conveying an impression rather than a meaning. In *Das neue Reich* (1928) he advocated a new German culture, not in accord with that of the Nazis.

GEORGE-BROWN, Baron George Alfred (1914–85) English Labour politician, born in Southwark, London. He left school at 15, attended further education classes, was an official of the Transport and General Workers Union before entering parliament as MP for Belper division in 1945. After holding minor posts in the Labour government of 1945–51, he became opposition spokesman on defence (1958–61), when he supported **Gaitskell** in opposing unilateral disarmament. He unsuccessfully contested **Wilson** for party leadership in 1963. Vice-chairman and deputy leader of the Labour party from 1960, he was first secretary of state and secretary of state for economic affairs (1964–66), when he instigated a prices and incomes policy, which fell victim to the later freeze on wages and prices. He resigned in July 1966, but resumed his post, becoming foreign secretary in August. A flamboyant, impetuous and controversial figure, Brown finally resigned and returned to the back benches in March 1968 during the gold crisis. Having lost his seat in the 1970 general election he was created a life peer.

GEORGE OF PODIEBRAD See **PODIEBRAD**

GÉRANDO, Joseph Marie, Baron de (1772–1842) French philosopher, statesman and philanthropist, born of Italian ancestry in Lyon. He held high administrative posts under **Napoleon I**, and from 1811 was a councillor of state. His works include *Des signes et de l'art de penser* (1800), *Histoire de philosophie* (1803), *Visiteur du pauvre* (1820) and *Du perfectionnement moral* (1824).

GÉRARD, Étienne Maurice, Comte (1773–1852) French soldier, and marshal of France, born in Damvilliers. He served on the Rhine, in Italy, La Vendée, Germany and Spain. For his services at Austerlitz (1805) he was appointed general of brigade. He fought at Jena, Erfurt and Wagram, in the Russian Campaign, and at Ligny and Wavre. In 1831 he drove the Dutch out of Flanders, and in 1832 compelled Antwerp to capitulate. Under **Louis-Philippe** he was twice war minister.

GÉRARD, François Pascal Simon, Baron (1770–1837) French painter, born in Rome, but brought up in Paris. He became a pupil of **Jaques Louis David** and a member of the Revolutionary Tribunal in 1793. His full-length portrait of **Isabey** the miniaturist (1796) and his *Cupid and Psyche* (1798), both in the Louvre, established his reputation, and leading men and women of the empire and the Restoration sat to him. He also painted historical mythological and battle scenes. After the fall of **Napoleon** in 1815 he became court painter to **Louis XVIII**.

GERARD, John (1545–1612) English herbalist and barber-surgeon, born in Nantwich. His London garden became famous for its rare plants, and for 20 years (1577–98) he was superintendent of Lord **Burghley**'s gardens. He wrote *The Herball, or general histoire of plantes* (1597).

GERARDS See **GHEERAERTS**

GERBERT See **SYLVERSTER II**

GERHARD, Roberto (1896–1970) Catalan-born British composer of Swiss parentage, born in Valls near Tarragona. He studied piano with **Granados y Campiña** (1915–16), and composition with **Pedrell** (1916–22) and **Schoenberg** (1923–28). After the Republican collapse in the Civil War he left Barcelona to settle in England in 1939, becoming a British subject (1960). There he wrote most of his music, which was characterized by virtuosic orchestral, rhythmic and melodic inventiveness. He composed ballets, an opera *The Duenna* (1945–47), five symphonies, concertos for violin and piano, chamber music, incidental music and some electronic music.

GERHARDIE, William Alexander (1895–1977) English novelist, born of English parents in St Petersburg where he was educated. He served in the British embassy at Petrograd (1917–18), later with the military mission in Siberia, before going to Worcester College, Oxford, where he wrote a lively study of **Anton Chekhov** (1923) and *Futility: A Novel on Russian Themes* (1922). In 1925 came *The Polyglots*, his most celebrated novel, described by **Anthony Powell** as 'outstanding...particularly in the rare gift of making child characters come alive'. Among his later novels only *Of Mortal Love* (1936), a love story blending humour, pathos and tenderness, and admired by **Edwin Muir** and others, stands comparison with his early fiction. *Memoirs of a Polyglot*, his autobiography, was published in 1931, a biographical history of *The Romanoffs* in 1940, and *God's Fifth Column* (1981), an idiosyncratic account of the years 1890–1940.

GERHARDT, Charles Frédéric (1816–56) French chemist, born in Strasbourg. He studied chemistry at Leipzig and Giessen, and in 1848 settled in Paris. Between 1849 and 1855 he published his views of homologous and heterologous series and the theory of types with which his name is associated, and researched into anhydrous acids and oxides. In 1855 he became professor of chemistry at Strasbourg.

GERHARDT, Paul (1607–76) German hymnwriter, born in Gräfenhainichen in Saxony. He became assistant pastor at St Nicholas in Berlin in 1657, but for opposing the elector's attempted union of the Lutheran and Reformed Churches was banished in 1666. From 1669 he was pastor of Lübben. One of the greatest German Lutheran hymnists, his hymns were unique in their sincerity and simplicity in the age of baroque.

GÉRICAULT, Theodore (1791–1824) French painter, born in Rouen. In 1810 he became a pupil of **Guérin**, in whose studio he met and befriended **Delacroix**. A great admirer of the 17th-century Dutch and Flemish schools, he revolted against the current classicism, and his unorthodox approach and bold use of colour incurred the disapproval of his teacher, who advised him to give up painting. His first important exhibition piece was *Officer of Light Horse* at the Salon of 1812, which was followed by other canvases noteworthy for their realism. In his quest for authenticity he spent much time studying the raw material of his pictures, thus achieving the great effectiveness of his masterpiece *The Raft of the Medusa* (1819, Louvre), based on a shipwreck which had shortly before caused a sensation in France. It impressed Delacroix but was harshly criticized and Géricault withdrew to England, where he did a number of paintings of racing scenes and landscapes and conceived an admiration for **Constable** and **Bonington**, whose work he brought to the notice of the French. Towards the end of his life he made five portraits of the insane (1822–23).

GERMAIN, Lord George See **SACKVILLE, Lord George**

GERMAN, Sir Edward, originally **Edward German Jones** (1862–1936) English composer, born in Whitchurch, Shropshire. He studied at the Royal Academy of Music; in 1888 he was made musical director of the Globe Theatre, London, and became known for his incidental music to **Shakespeare**. In 1901 he emerged as a light opera composer, when he completed **Sullivan**'s *Emerald Isle* after the composer's death. His own works include *Merrie England* (1902), *Tom Jones* (1907), *Fallen Fairies* (1909), several symphonies, suites, chamber music and songs and the *Welsh Rhapsody* (1904).

GERMANICUS CAESAR (15 BC–9 AD) Roman soldier, son of Nero Claudius **Drusus**, and of Antonia, daughter of **Antonius Marcus** and niece of **Augustus**. Adopted by the emperor **Tiberius**, he was consul in AD 12, and in 13 was appointed to the command of the eight legions on the Rhine, and in 14 quelled a great mutiny. Next year he marched to meet **Arminius**, whom he overthrew in two desperate battles, the second near Minden. Tiberius, jealous of his popularity, recalled him in 17, and sent him to the East, at the same time appointing as viceroy of Syria, in order secretly to counteract him, the envious Calpurnius Piso. Germanicus died at Ephidaphnae near Antioch, probably of poison. His wife, **Agrippina the Elder**, and two of her sons were eventually put to death; the third son, **Caligula**, was spared to be emperor. A daughter, **Agrippina the Younger**, became as remarkable for her vices as her mother had been for her virtues.

GERMANUS, St (c.378–448) bishop of Auxerre. He was invited over to Britain to combat Pelagianism in 429. Under him the Christian Britons won the bloodless 'Alleluia Victory' over the Picts and Saxons at Maes Garmon (Germanus' field) in Flintshire.

GERMER, Lester Halbert (1896–1971) American physicist, born in Chicago. While on the research staff of the Western Electric Co (1917–53), he worked with **Clinton Davisson** on experiments that demonstrated the diffraction of electrons by crystals (1927), confirming the theories of **Louis-Victor de Broglie**.

GÉRÔME, Jean Léon (1824–1904) French historical genre painter, born in Vesoul. He began to exhibit in 1847; and in 1863 he became professor of painting in the École des Beaux-Arts, where he taught **Redon** and **Eakins**. His *Polytechnic Student* is in the Tate. A first-rate draughtsman, he achieved distinction as a sculptor and a decorative painter of anecdotal and erotic subjects.

GERONIMO, Indian name **Goyathlay** (1829–1909) American Apache chief, born in Arizona. In 1885-86, in a spectacular uprising, he led the Chiricahua Apaches in a series of raids against the whites, but was eventually captured by General **George Crook**. He escaped, but later surrendered, and became a farmer in Oklahoma with his people. He dictated his autobiography, *Geronimo: His Own Story*, in 1906.

GERRY, Elbridge (1744–1814) American statesman, born in Marblehead, Massachusetts. He was sent to the first National Congress. Elected governor of Massachusetts in 1810, he rearranged the electoral districts so as to secure the advantage to the Republican party— whence (from a joke on *salamander*) the word *gerrymander*. He was vice-president of the USA (1813–14).

GERSHWIN, George (1898–1937) American composer, born in New York. He studied music in the traditional way, but published his first popular song at the age of 14, and became famous as a composer of Broadway musicals, bringing unusual skill and originality to the genre. His most famous works of this style are perhaps *Lady Be Good* (1924) and *Of Thee I sing* (1931), written, as were several of his works, in collaboration with his brother Ira (1896–1983). In 1924 a commission from the conductor **Paul Whiteman** led to his composition of the *Rhapsody in Blue*, a concert work combining romantic emotionalism with the jazz idiom with unusual success; he followed this by the *Concerto in F*, and *An American in Paris*, exploiting the same forces. His and Ira's black opera, *Porgy and Bess* (1935), has won worldwide popularity. Gershwin, who described jazz as 'a very powerful American folk-music', brought skill and sincerity not only to 'symphonic jazz', but to the modern popular song and musical comedy, which are no less important in his hands than the more ambitious (in a traditional sense) forms he handled.

GERSON, Jean le Charlier de (1363–1429) French theologian and mystic, born in the village of Gerson, in the diocese of Reims, and educated in Paris. 'Doctor Christianissimus', as he was called, was a nominalist, opposed to scholasticism, but a Christian mystic. As chancellor of the University of Paris from 1395 he supported the proposal for putting an end to the Great Schism between Rome and Avignon by the resignation of both the contending pontiffs, especially at the councils of Pisa and Constance (1414). But his own fortunes were marred by the animosity of the Duke of Burgundy, for denouncing the murder of the Duke of Orléans. Gerson prudently retired to Rattenburg in Tirol, where he composed his *De Consolatione Theologiae*. It was only after several years that he was able to return to France and settle in a monastery in Lyon.

GERSTÄCKER, Friedrich (1816–72) German writer and traveller, born in Hamburg. He worked his way through the United States, South America, Polynesia and Australia, and wrote colourful adventure stories, including *Mississippi River Pirates* (1848).

GERTRUDE, St (626–59) Frankish religious. The daughter of **Pepin** the Elder, she became abbess of the monastery at Nivelles, Brabant, on the death of her mother, and after refusing to marry **Dagobert I**. Her feast day is 17 March.

GERTRUDE OF HELFTA, sometimes called **the Great, St** (1256–c.1302) Germany mystic. She entered the convent of Helfta near Eisleben at the age of five, and when 15 began to have visions which she described in Latin treatises. She was never formally canonized.

GERVASE OF CANTERBURY (c.1141–c.1210) English monk and chronicler of the reigns of **Stephen**, **Henry II** and **Richard I**, and author of a history of the archbishops of Canterbury.

GERVASE OF TILBURY (c.1150–c.1220) English historical writer, born probably in Tilbury. He lectured on canon law at Bologna, and was marshal of the kingdom of Arles, perhaps provost of the nunnery at Ebsdorf. Of his *Otia Imperialia*, composed about 1212 for the entertainment of the emperor **Otto IV**, the first two books consist of an abstract of geography and history, the third contains a collection of curious beliefs about the 'Veronica', British sirens, the magnet, etc. He also prepared a *Liber Facetiarum* or book of anecdotes for **Henry II**'s son Henry, which is no longer in existence.

GERVINUS, Georg Gottfried (1805–71) German critic and historian, born in Darmstadt. In 1836 he became a professor at Göttengen, one of the seven who protested in 1837 against the suspension of the Hanoverian constitution. Among his works are commentaries on **Shakespeare** (1849–52) and *Geschichte des 19. Jahrhunderts* (1856–66). He was elected to the National Assembly in 1848.

GESELL, Arnold Lucius (1880–1961) American psychologist, born in Alma, Wisconsin, a pioneer in the study of child psychology. Educated at Clark (PhD 1906, ScD 1930) and Yale (MD 1915) universities, he was professor of child hygiene at Yale School of Medicine (1915–48) and established the Yale Psychological Clinic (now the Clinic of Child Development of the Yale School of Medicine), of which he was director (1911–48). He was research consultant to the Gesell Institute of Child Development (1950-58). Particularly concerned with early infant development, he devised standard scales for measuring its progress. His writings were supplemented by an original and extensive use of the medium of film for purposes of scientific and educational communication. His books included *An Atlas of Infant Behavior* (1934), *Infant and Child in the Culture of Today* (1943), *The Child from Five to Ten* (1946) and *Child Development* (1949).

GESENIUS, Heinrich Friedrich Wilhelm (1786–1842) German biblical scholar, born in Nordhausen. He became professor of theology at Halle in 1811. His first great work was *Hebräisches u. Chaldäisches Handwörterbuch* (1810–12). His *Hebr. Elementarbuch*, consisting of the *Hebräische Grammatik* (1813) and the *Hebräisches Lesebuch* (1814), has contributed enormously to the knowledge of the Hebrew language. His greatest work is *Thesaurus philologico -criticus Linguae Hebraicae et Chaldaicae* (part I 1829; completed by Rödiger, 1858).

GESNER, Conrad, or **Conradus Gesnerus** (1516–65) Swiss naturalist and physician, born in Zürich, the most many-sided and industrious scholar of the 16th century. In 1537 he became professor of Greek at Lausanne and published a Greek-Latin Dictionary, in 1541 he was professor of philosophy and then natural history at Zürich. He published 72 works, and left 18 others in progress. His *Bibliotheca Universalis* (1545–49) contained the titles of all the books then known in Hebrew, Greek and Latin, with criticisms and summaries of each. His *Historia Animalium* (1551–58) attempted to bring together all that was known in his time of every animal. But probably botany was his forte. He collected over 500 plants undescribed by the ancients, and was preparing a third magnum opus at his death from plague; the beautiful and accurate coloured drawings of plants for this work have been published in eight volumes (1973–80). He also wrote on medicine, mineralogy and philology. His works were immensely influential in natural history.

GESSLER, Hermann See **TELL, William**

GESSNER, Salomon (1730–88) Swiss pastoral poet, who also painted and engraved landscapes, born in Zürich, where he was a bookseller. *Daphnis* (1754), a sentimental bucolic, was followed two years later by a volume of *Idyls* and by *Inkel und Yariko*. His *Tod Abels* (1758), a type of idyllic heroic prose poem, had the greatest success. His landscape paintings are all in the conventional classic style, but his engravings are of real merit. In 1772 he published a second volume of *Idyls* and a series of letters on landscape painting.

GESUALDO, Carlo, Prince of Venosa (c.1561–1613) Italian lutenist and composer, born in Naples. He achieved notoriety for ordering the murder of his unfaithful wife and her lover in 1590. He wrote many sacred vocal works and published six books of madrigals, remarkable for bold homophonic progressions and telling use of dissonance.

GETTY, Jean Paul (1892–1976) American oil executive, multi-millionaire and art collector, born in Minneapolis. After studying at Berkeley and Oxford, Getty entered the oil business in his early twenties and made a quarter of a million dollars in his first two years. His father (also a successful oil man) died in 1930, leaving him $15 million. He merged his father's interests with his own, and went on to acquire and control more than 100 companies, and to become one of the richest men in the world. Despite the size of his business empire, Getty reputedly made most of the major policy decisions himself, and his image was that of a colourful, individualistic entrepreneur rather than a faceless corporation executive. His personal wealth was estimated in 1968 at over one billion dollars, and over the years he acquired a huge and extremely valuable art collection. He was married and divorced five times, and developed a legendary reputation for miserliness, installing a pay-telephone for guests in his English mansion. He wrote several books, including a history of the family oil business and two autobiographies, *My Life and Fortunes* (1963) and *As I see It* (1976).

GETZ, Stan (Stanley) (1927–) American jazz saxophonist, born in Philadelphia and educated in New York, where he started playing professionally at 15. Before the age of 20 he was working under such important bandleaders as **Stan Kenton** and **Benny Goodman**. With the **Woody Herman** Orchestra from 1947 to 1949, he was a member of the 'Four Brothers' saxophone section which gave the band a unique ensemble sound. He has since led his own small groups, and during the 1960s he helped to popularize the bossa nova jazz style. With his light tone and articulate phrasing, he is one of the most copied of tenor saxophone stylists.

GEULINCX, Arnold (1624–69) Belgian philosopher, born in Antwerp. He taught at the Catholic University of Louvain but was expelled for his anti-scholasticism; he converted to Calvinism and became professor of philosophy at Leyden in 1665. He was a leading exponent of **Descartes**' philosophy and is best known for his doctrine of 'Occasionalism': God himself 'occasions' every mental or physical process, while body and mind operate separately, without causal interaction, like two clocks which are perfectly synchronized. His main works are *Quaestiones Quedlibeticae* (1653) re-edited by him as *Saturnalia* (1665), *Logica Restituta* (1662) and *De Virtute* (1665). After his death further works were published under his pseudonym, Philaretus, including six treatises on ethics under the title *Gnothi Seauton* ('Know Thysdg', (1675) and *Metaphysica Vera* (1691).

GEYL, Pieter (1887–1966) Dutch historian and patriot, born in Dordrecht. He was educated in The Hague, at Leiden and in Italy. After serving as London correspondent of the *Nieuwe Rotterdamsche Courant* (1913–19), he was appointed the first professor of Dutch studies in London University (1919–36) and professor of modern history at Utrecht (1936–58). During World War II, he was imprisoned in Buchenwald and other Nazi concentration camps. He was a believer in a 'greater Netherlands', always mourning the loss of Flanders and Brabant during the Dutch wars of independence in the late 16th century. As a historian, however, he was a climatologist and environmentalist, arguing that the outcome of the Dutch revolt against **Habsburg** Spain was dictated by movements of rivers and water-currents rather than religion or economics. His multi-volume history of the revolt and its sequels were published in the 1930s, translated into English as *The Revolt of the Netherlands* and *The Netherlands Divided*, while his struggle against Hitlerian domination of Europe is reflected in his *Napoleon, For and Against*, originally written in 1944. He was also a poet and essayist, debating with numerous living and dead historians, and was the leading interpreter of the Dutch past to his country and the world.

GEZELLE, Guido (1830–99) Flemish poet, born in Bruges. Ordained in 1854, he was for 28 years a curé in Courtrai. He published many volumes of verse, wrote on philology and folklore, founded literary magazines, and is regarded as the founder of the West Flemish school.

GHAZALI, Abu Hamid Mohammed al- (1058–1111) Islamic philosopher, theologian and jurist, born and died in Tus in Persia (near the modern Meshed). In 1091 he was appointed to the prestigious position of professor of philosophy at Nizamiyah College, Baghdad, where he exercised great academic and political influence; but in 1095 he suffered a spiritual crisis which led to a nervous breakdown and a speech impediment that prevented him from lecturing. He abandoned his position for the ascetic life of a mendicant sufi (mystic), spending his time in meditation and spiritual exercises. Although he did teach again briefly he eventually retired to Tus to found a monastic community. His doctrines represent a reaction against Aristotelianism and an attempt to reconcile philosophy and Islamic dogma. He was a prolific author, and some of his main works are: *The Intentions of the Philosophers*, *The Incoherence of the Philosophers*, *The Deliverance from Error* and the monumental *The Revival of the Religious Sciences*.

GHEERAERTS, Marcus (c.1510–1590) Flemish-born religious and animal painter and engraver. He was driven out of Bruges for his Protestantism and settled in London (c.1568).

GHEERAERTS, Marcus (1561–1635) Flemish born artist, son of **Marcus Gheeraerts** the elder. He was court painter to **James I**, and specialized in portraits. Many pictures attributed to him are of doubtful authenticity, but among the best of those certainly his are *Lady Russell* (1625, Woburn), and *William Camden* and *Sir Henry Savile* (both 1621, Bodleian).

GHEORGIU-DEJ, Gheorghe (1901–65) Romanian communist politician. He joined the Romanian Communist party (RCP) in 1930 and was imprisoned in 1933 for his role in the Grivita railway strike. On his release in 1944 he became secretary-general of the RCP and minister of communications (1944–46) and in 1945 was instrumental in the ousting of the coalition government of Nicolae Radescu (1874–1953) and the establishment of a communist régime. He then served in a variety of economic posts (1946–52) and as prime minister (1952–55), before becoming state president in 1961. Although retaining the support of Moscow, he adopted increasingly independent policies during the 1960s.

GHERARDESCA See **UGOLINO, Count**

GHIBERTI, Lorenzo (1378–1455) Florentine goldsmith, bronze-caster and sculptor, born in Florence. In 1400 he executed frescoes in the palace of Pandolfo Malatesta at Rimini and in 1402 won the competition to make a pair of bronze doors for the Florence Baptistery. His chief competitor was **Brunelleschi** and both the panels they entered for this prestigious competition can be seen today in the Bargello Museum. Much of Ghiberti's life was spent completing this set of doors. No sooner were they completed in 1424 when Ghiberti was entrusted with the execution of another set, made to emulate the first pair, and dubbed by **Michelangelo** the 'Gates of Paradise' (1425–52). Ghiberti was also responsible for the three bronze figures of the saints **Matthew**, **Stephen** and **John the Baptist** which adorn the exterior of Or San Michele. His large and flourishing workshop was a training ground for a distinguished generation of Florentine artists, including **Donatello**, **Michelozzi** and **Uccello**. In true Renaissance fashion, he was also a humanist and scholar, and wrote *I commentarii*, a wide ranging history of art.

GHIKA, Helena, pseud **Dora d'Istria** (1829–88) Romanian author and traveller, a daughter of Prince Michael Ghika, born in Bucharest. She married Prince Koltzoff-Massalsky, of St Petersburg, but from 1855 lived mainly in Florence. Her works include *La Vie monastique dans l'Église orientale* (1855), *La Suisse allemande* (1856), *Les Femmes en orient* (1860), and a family history.

GHIRLANDAIO, Domenico, properly **Domenico di Tommaso Bigordi** (1449–94) Florentine painter, born in Florence. Apprenticed to a goldsmith, probably his father, a metal garland-maker or 'Ghirlandaio', he became a painter when he was 31. He painted principally frescoes, and in his native city. Among these are six subjects from the life of St **Francis** (1485) and an altarpiece, the *Adoration of the Shepherds* (now in the Florentine Academy), for the church of S Trinità; and in the choir of S Maria Novella a series illustrating the lives of the Virgin and the Baptist (1490). Between 1482 and 1484 he painted for Pope **Sixtus IV**, in the Sistine Chapel, the fresco *Christ calling Peter and Andrew*. His easel pictures include the *Adoration of the Magi* (1488), in the church of the Innocenti at Florence, and the *Visitation of the Virgin* (1491), in the Louvre; and mosaics the *Annunciation* in the cathedral of Florence. The many figures in his religious scenes are beautifully characterized, the faces full of expression and feeling, but his composition tends to be unimaginative and the grouping formal and repetitive. His work is of great historical value for its detailed portrayal of costume, domestic features etc. He was assisted by his brothers David (1452–1525) and Benedetto (1458–97).

GIACOMETTI, Alberto (1901–66) Swiss sculptor and painter, born in Stampa, the son of an artist. He studied at Geneva and worked mainly in Paris, at first under **Bourdelle**. He joined the Surrealists in 1930, producing many abstract constructions of a symbolic kind, arriving finally at the characteristic 'thin man' bronzes, long spidery statuettes, rigid in posture yet trembling on the verge of movement, suggesting transience, change and decay, eg *Pointing Man* (1947, Tate).

GIACOMO, Salvator di (1860–1934) Neapolitan writer. He wrote novels and plays, and songs and lyrics in dialect. He was librarian in the National Library in Naples and also compiled several historical and bibliographical works.

GIACOSA, Giuseppe (1847–1906) Italian dramatist, born in Colleretto-Parella, Piedmont. He was a successful practitioner of various types of play, ranging from historical dramas and comedies in verse to contemporary social problem pieces. Representative of the former are *Il Conte Rosso* (1880), *La Contessa di Challant* (1891). His social problem plays include *Resa a discrezione* (1888), *Tristi amori* (1887), *Diritti dell' anima* (1894), *Come le foglie* (1900) and *Il piu forte* (1904). He was not a radical, but emphasized bourgeois ideals of decency, homely virtues and established institutions. Consequently, his plays are not performed in modern repertory, though *Come le foglie*, his best piece, dealing with the disintegration of a wealthy family, has been filmed. With Luigi Illica he also collaborated on the libretti for *La Bohème*, *Madame Butterfly* and *Tosca*.

GIAEVER, Ivar (1929–) Norwegian-born American physicist, born in Bergen. He studied electrical engineering in Oslo and emigrated to Canada in 1954. After moving in 1956 to the General Electric Research and Development Center in Schenectady, New York, he examined tunnelling effects in superconductors; this field of work, of great value in microelectronics, had previously been the subject of related work by **Leo Esaki** and was later further developed by **Brian Josephson**, and all three men shared the Nobel prize for physics in 1973 for their contributions.

GIANIBELLI, Federigo (fl.1530–88) Italian military engineer, born in Mantua. He entered the service of Queen **Elizabeth** of England, and during the siege of Antwerp (1585) destroyed with an explosive ship a Spanish bridge over the Scheldt. He rendered great service in the preparations for resisting the Armada of 1588, and died in London.

GIANNONE, Pietro (1676–1748) Italian antipapal historian, born in Ischitella in Naples. A barrister, his *Storia civile del regno di Napoli* (1723) led to his excommunication and banishment from Naples; at Geneva he published *Il Triregno*, a bitter attack upon the papal pretensions. Decoyed into Savoy in 1736, he was kidnapped by secret agents and imprisoned in Turin until his death.

GIAP, Vo Nguyen (1912–) Vietnamese military leader, born in Quang Binh Province. He studied law at Hanoi University, and joined the Vietnamese Communist party, and trained in China. He led the Viet Minh army in revolt against the French, leading to the decisive defeat of their garrison at Dien Bien Phu in 1954. As vice-premier and defence minister of North Vietnam, he masterminded the military strategy that forced the US forces to leave South Vietnam (1973) and led to the reunification of Vietnam in 1975. He was a member of the politburo from 1976 to 1982. He wrote *People's War, People's Army* (1961), which became a textbook for revolutionaries, and *Military Art of People's War* (1970).

GIAUQUE, William Francis (1895–1982) Canadian-born American chemist, born at Niagara Falls, Ontario. He became professor in the University of California in 1934. In 1929 he took part in the discovery of the existence of isotopes of oxygen, and he later developed the adiabatic demagnetization method for the production of very low temperatures. He was awarded the Nobel prize for chemistry in 1949.

GIBB, Sir Alexander (1872–1958) Scottish civil engineer, born near Dundee, fifth generation in a line of civil engineers begun by his great-great-grandfather William (1736–91), who was a master mason and what would now be called a civil engineering contractor. His son John (1776–1850) became **Thomas Telford**'s trusted deputy on bridges and harbour works in Scotland, then turned to contracting like his father before him; his son Alexander (1804–67) was apprenticed to Telford, worked with **Robert Stevenson**, and built railways in Scotland and England; his son Easton (1841–1916) built reservoirs, railways, and the bridge over the Thames at Kew. His son Alexander joined the firm of Easton Gibb & Son in 1900, and from 1909 to 1916 worked on the construction of Rosyth naval dockyard, then after five years in government posts set up in practice as a consulting engineer. His firm became one of the world's largest, their work at home and abroad including hydro-electric schemes, bridges, docks and harbours, and many other kinds of civil engineering project.

GIBB, Andrew Dewar (1888–1974) Scottish jurist, born in Paisley, He studied at Glasgow, was called to the Scottish (1914) and English (1917) bar, and after lecturing at Edinburgh and Cambridge became Regius professor of law at Glasgow (1934–58). He wrote several works on Scots law and on the case for Scottish home rule, and he was chairman of the Scottish National Party (1936–40), of the Saltire Society (1955-57), and president of the Covenant Association from 1957.

GIBBINGS, Robert John (1889–1958) Irish illustrator and writer, born in Cork. He is famous for the engravings and woodcuts with which he illustrated most of his own river-exploration books, like *Sweet Thames Run Softly* (1940), *Lovely is The Lee* (1945) and *Sweet Cork of Thee* (1951). He was director of the Golden Cockerel Press from 1924 to 1933, and through it was instrumental in reviving the art of wood engraving. He travelled widely and was perhaps the first artist to use diving equipment to make underwater drawings.

GIBBON, Edward (1737–94) English historian, born in Putney, the son of a country gentleman. Educated at Westminster and Magdalen College, Oxford, he derived little benefit from either; his *Autobiography* contains a scathing attack on the Oxford of his time. Becoming a Roman Catholic at the age of sixteen, he was sent to Lausanne, where for five years he boarded with a Calvanist pastor who by a judicious course of reading wooed him back to the Protestant faith. Full details of all this are given in the *Autobiography*, as also of the one romance in his life—his love for the minister's daughter, Suzanne Curchod who afterwards became Madame **Neckar** and the mother of Mme **de Staël**. In classic form he acquiesced in his father's veto on the marriage—'I sighed as a lover, I obeyed as a son'. Having returned to England in 1758, he employed his leisure in his father's house on an *Essai sur l'étude de la littérature*, but his bookish solitude was interrupted for four years (1759–63) by service in the Hampshire militia, a useful preparation for the historian, as he acknowledges. It was in Rome the following year (1764) that 'musing among the ruins of the Capitol' he was seized with the ambition of writing *The Decline and Fall of the Roman Empire*. His father had left him the means to settle in London in 1772 and so devote himself to his great task. He entered parliament in 1774, and as a devoted follower of Lord

North was made commissioner of trade and plantations. This employment also he regarded as a 'school of civil prudense' and therefore experience for the great History, the first volume of which appeared in 1776. The general acclamation was disturbed by the scandal of the famous chapters 15–16, which showed Gibbon in the role of a 5th-century pagan philosopher deriding Christianity with gentle irony. His *Vindication* (1779) did not reassure the learned public as the relatively cold reception of the second and third volumes (1781) proved. The last three volumes were written in Lausanne though published in London (1788). He returned to England and spent much of the remainder of his days with Lord Sheffield, who published his *Miscellaneous Works* (1796), which contains the *Autobiography* pieced together from fragments left by Gibbon. The chief concept of his great work is the continuity of the Roman Empire down to the fall of Constantinople. His limitations or positive errors—his blending of sources of different periods and his consistently pessimistic view of the unrelieved bleakness and misery of the later Empire in no way detract from the greatness of his achievement. His idea of history, too, as 'little more than the register of the crimes, follies and misfortunes of mankind' might be regarded by the objective historian as a limitation, but the *Decline and Fall* is literature as well as history and his pessimism sets the tone for the work. His detestation of enthusiasm is a mark of his age, and he is no less severe on pagan than on Christian superstition. Here again his cynicism adds a spice to the work which relates it to literature rather than history.

GIBBON, Lewis Grassic, pseud of **James Leslie Mitchell** (1901–35) Scottish novelist, born on the farm of Hillhead of Seggat, Auchterless, Aberdeenshire. His father was a farmer and he was educated at the local school before attending Mackie Academy, Stonehaven, which he left after a year to become a newspaper reporter. Stirred by the promise of the Russian Revolution he became a member of the Communist party. In 1919 he moved to Glasgow where he was employed on the *Scottish Farmer*, but his career in journalism was curtailed when he was dismissed for fiddling expenses. He attempted suicide, returned home and decided to enlist. He spent three and a half years with the Royal Army Service Corps in Persia, India and Egypt. In 1923 he left the army but poverty drove him to join up again, this time in the Royal Air Force, where he served as a clerk until 1929. His first published book was *Hanno, or the Future of Exploration* (1928) and others followed rapidly: *Stained Radiance* (1930), *The Thirteenth Disciple* (1931), *Three go Back* (1932) and *The Lost Trumpet* (1932). *Sunset Song*, his greatest achievement, was published in 1932, the first of his books to appear under his pseudonym. Written in less than two months it was published under his mother's name as the first in a projected trilogy of novels, *A Scots Quair*, on the life of a young girl called Chris Guthrie. The second volume, *Cloud Howe* appeared in 1933 and the third part, *Grey Granite*, in 1934. An unfinished novel, *The Speak of the Mearns*, was published in 1982. He also wrote a life of the Scottish explorer, **Mungo Park** (1934), and published *The Conquest of the Maya* (1934).

GIBBONS, Grinling (1648–1721) Dutch-born English sculptor and woodcarver, born in Rotterdam. He had for some time practised his art in England, when, discovered by **Evelyn** carving a crucifix (1671), he was appointed by **Charles II** to a place in the board of works, and employed in the chapel at Windsor; here and in the choir stalls and organ screen in St Paul's Cathedral, his work displays great taste and delicacy of finish. At Chatsworth, Burghley, Southwick and other mansions he executed an immense quantity of carved embellishment; the ceiling of a room at Petworth is his *chef-d'œuvre*. His favourite nature motifs were used indiscriminately but always with an eye for design. He produced several fine pieces in marble and bronze, including the statue of **James II** at Whitehall.

GIBBONS, James (1834–1921) American prelate, born in Baltimore. He became archbishop of that city in 1877, and a cardinal in 1886. He was largely responsible for the growth of the Roman Catholic Church in America. He wrote *The Faith of Our Fathers* (1876), *Our Christian Heritage* (1889), and many other books.

GIBBONS, Orlando (1583–1625) English composer, son of a professional Cambridge musician, probably born in Oxford. In 1604 he was appointed organist of the Chapel Royal, London. He studied at Cambridge and Oxford, and in 1623 he became organist of Westminster Abbey. In 1625 he went with the king and court to Canterbury, where he died. He did not write much but some compositions are masterpieces. The best known are his Morning and Evening Service in F; among his anthems, 'O Clap your Hands' and 'God is gone up', 'Hosanna', 'Lift up your Heads', and 'Almighty and everlasting God'; and of his madrigals, 'The Silver Swan', 'O that the learned Poets', and 'Dainty, fine sweet Bird'. Besides these he left hymns, fantasies for viols, and virginal pieces.

GIBBONS, Stella Dorothea (1902–89) English writer, born in London. She worked as a journalist and later began a series of successful novels. She also wrote poetry and short stories. Her *Cold Comfort Farm* (1933), a light-hearted satire on the melodramatic rural novels such as those written by **Mary Webb**, won the Femina Vie Heureuse prize, and established itself as a classic of parody.

GIBBS, James (1682–1754) Scottish architect, born in Aberdeen. He studied in Holland as a protégé of the exiled Earl of Mar, and then, under **Carlo Fontana**, in Italy. A friend and disciple of **Wren**, he became in 1713 one of the commissioners for building new churches in London, but was dismissed in 1715 for his Roman Catholicism. He designed St Mary-le-Strand (1717), the steeple of St Clement Danes (1719), St Peter's, Vere Street (1724), and St Martin-in-the-Fields (1726), the latter being perhaps his most influential and attractive work. He was also responsible for St Bartholomew's Hospital (1730), the circular Radcliffe Camera at Oxford (1737–47) and the Senate House at Cambridge (1730). His *Book of Architecture* (1728) helped to spread the Palladian style and influenced the design of many churches of the colonial period in America.

GIBBS, Josiah Willard (1839–1903) American mathematical physicist, born in New Haven, Connecticut. He graduated at Yale, and after studying in Europe for a few years, returned there in 1869, where he became professor in 1871. He contributed to the study of thermodynamics, and his most important work, first published as *On the Equilibrium of Heterogeneous Substances* (1876 and 1878), and including his 'phase rule', established him as a founder of physical chemistry.

GIBBS, Sir Vicary (1751–1820) English judge, born in Exeter. He became solicitor-general, attorney-general, lord chief-baron, and chief justice of the common pleas, having made his reputation for his defence of **John Horne Tooke** in 1794. His bitter sarcasm and lack of humour gained him the nickname of 'Vinegar Gibbs'.

GIBBS, William Francis (1886–1967) American naval architect, born in Philadelphia. He was educated at Harvard and Columbia where he studied law, but became increasingly interested in the design of ships, especially from the point of view of safety in the event of a collision. In partnership with his brother Frederick he designed yachts, luxury liners and, from 1933, US naval vessels and the 'Liberty Ships' of World War II. His most famous design was the 53 330 ton *United States* which regained the Blue Riband of the North Atlantic for the USA in 1952, making the crossing at an average speed of 35.6 knots, still unbeaten by a passenger liner.

GIBBS-SMITH, Charles Harvard (1909–81) English aeronautical historian, born in Teddington. Educated at Westminster School and Harvard, in 1947 he joined the Victoria and Albert Museum as keeper responsible for the photographic collection (director, 1939). He became instructor in aircraft recognition at the ministry of information during World War II and developed a keen interest in the history of aeronautics. He wrote the definitive *Aviation—an Historical Survey From its Origins to the End of World War II* (1960) for the Science Museum, the masterly *Sir George Cayley's Aeronautics, 1796–1855* (1962) and *The Rebirth of European Aviation* (1974). He took up a research fellowship at the Science Museum in 1976 and in 1978 he was appointed as the Smithsonian Institution's first Lindbergh professor of aerospace history at the Aerospace Museum, Washington DC. His staunch championing of the pre-eminence of the **Wright** brothers led to controversy but he brought new standards of accuracy and insight to a subject much covered by hearsay and myth.

GIBSON, Sir Alexander Drummond (1926–) Scottish conductor, born in Motherwell. He studied the piano at the Royal Scottish Academy of Music and read music at Glasgow University. In 1948, after military service, he won a scholarship to the Royal College of Music in London, where he studied the piano and conducting, and formed and conducted a student orchestra. After studying in Salzburg with Markevich and in Siena with van Kempen, he joined Sadler's Wells Opera as a répétiteur. From 1952 to 1954 he was associate conductor of the BBC Scottish Symphony Orchestra, then returned to Sadler's Wells, becoming, in 1957, the company's youngest musical director. In 1959 he moved to Scotland as the first native-born principal conductor and artistic director of the Scottish National Orchestra, bringing many new works to Scotland, often well in advance of their London performances. In 1962 he helped to form Scottish Opera and as its artistic director was responsible for many notable successes, such as the first complete performance of **Berlioz**'s *Les Troyens* in 1969, and in 1971, the first production in Scotland of **Wagner**'s *Ring* cycle in German. He retired from the Scottish National Orchestra in 1984.

GIBSON, Althea (1927–) American tennis player, born in Silver City, South Carolina, the first black player to achieve success at the highest levels of the game. Tall and elegant, she won the French and Italian singles championships in 1956, and the British and American titles in both 1957 and 1958. She turned professional in 1959 and won the professional singles title in 1960. Later she appeared in some films, and played professional golf.

GIBSON, Cameron Michael Henderson (1947–) Irish rugby player, born in Belfast. A brilliant centre-threequarter, he established a world-wide reputation while still at Cambridge. He was a stalwart of Irish international rugby in the 1960s and early 1970s and took part in two Lions tours of New Zealand and one of South Africa.

GIBSON, Charles Dana (1867–1944) American illustrator and cartoonist, born in Roxbury, Massachusetts. A brilliant black-and-white artist, he drew society cartoons for various periodicals like *Life*, *Scribner's*, *Century*, and *Harper's*. In his celebrated 'Gibson Girl' drawings, he created the idealized prototype of the beautiful, well-bred American woman.

GIBSON, Edmund (1669–1748) English church jurist, born in Westmorland. He became bishop of Lincoln (1716), then of London (1720). He edited the *Anglo-Saxon Chronicle* and translated Camden's *Britannia*, but he is best known for his great *Codex iuris ecclesiastici Anglicani* (1713). His aim was to reconcile the clergy and universities to the Hanoverian dynasty.

GIBSON, Edward See **ASHBOURNE**

GIBSON, Guy (1918–44) English airman. As a wing-commander in the RAF he led the famous 'dambusters' raid on the Möhne and Eder dams in 1943, an exploit for which he received the VC. He was killed on a later operation. See his *Enemy Coast Ahead* (1946).

GIBSON, James Jerome (1904–79) American psychologist, born in McConnelsville, Ohio. Educated at Princeton and Edinburgh Universities, he taught psychology at Smith College (1928–49), and at Cornell University (1949–72). During World War II he served as director of the Research Unit in Aviation Psychology for the US Air Force. Partly as a result of his warime studies of such visual skills as those needed to land an aeroplane, he became convinced that an understanding of perception could emerge from research that divorced it from its behavioural context. He rejected the traditional reductionist approach of the psychological laboratory as inappropriate, and developed the concept of 'direct perception' of 'invariant' attributes of the visual world, transcending the sensory processes that might be involved. His emphasis on the role of vision as the handmaiden for bodily action rather than as a means of achieving awareness of our surroundings has proved increasingly influential in the psychology of perception. He gained the Distinguished Scientist award of the American Psychological Association in 1961, and was elected to the National Academy of Sciences in 1967.

GIBSON, John (1790–1866) English sculptor, born in Gyffin, near Conway, the son of a market -gardener. He found a patron in **Roscoe**, and proceeding to Rome in 1817, studied under **Canova** and **Thorvaldsen**, and lived there permanently. His best works are *Psyche borne by Zephyrs*, *Hylas surprised by Nymphs* and *Venus with the Turtle*. The innovation of tinting his figures (eg his Venus), he defended by reference to Greek precedents.

GIBSON, Josh (1911–47) American baseball player, born in Buena Vista, Georgia, known as the 'Negro Babe Ruth'. A legendary hitter, he was barred from major-league baseball because he was black, and could play only in the negro league. Playing for the Pittsburgh Homestead Grays and the Pittsburgh Crawfords, it is estimated that he hit more than 950 home runs in his career. In 1972 he was elected to the National Baseball Hall of Fame.

GIBSON, Richard (1615–90) English court dwarf and painter of miniatures. He was a page to **Charles I** and **Henrietta Maria**, and the king gave away the bride when he married Anne Shepherd (1620–1709), like himself only 3 feet 10 inches high. He later made several portraits of **Cromwell** and was himself painted by **Lely**.

GIBSON, Robert (1935–) American baseball player, born in Omaha. A noted pitcher with the St Louis

Cardinals, with whom he started in 1959, he was twice named best pitcher in the National League and in 1968 became Most Valuable Player in the league on the strength of his exceptionally low earned-run average of 1.12. He set a World Series record of strike-outs against the Detroit Tigers in 1968.

GIBSON, Thomas Milner (1806–84) British politician, born in Trinidad. Returned MP for Manchester (1841), he was a leading Anti-Corn-Law orator. While sitting for Ashton-under-Lyne (1857–68) he was president of the board of trade (1859–60), and also *ad-interim* president of the Poor Law Commission. It was mainly owing to him that the advertisement duty was repealed (1853), then the newspaper stamp duty (1855) and the paper duty (1861).

GIBSON, Wilfrid Wilson (1878–1962) English poet and playwright, born in Hexham. He was educated privately, and from 1902 wrote numerous volumes of verse, starting with *Urlyn the Harper and Other Songs*, on the plight of ordinary people faced with industrial change. Later volumes included *The Island Stag* (1947). He also wrote plays, including *Daily Bread* (1910) and a collection of verse plays, *Within Four Walls* (1950). A realist, he was concerned with everyday matters, particularly industrial poverty.

GIDDINGS, Joshua Reed (1795–1864) American politician and anti-slavery campaigner, born in Athens, Pennsylvania. He sat in congress (1838–59); in 1861 he was appointed consul-general in Canada.

GIDE, André Paul Guillaume (1869–1951) French novelist, diarist and man-of-letters, born in Paris. His father, who died when he was eleven, was professor of law at the Sorbonne. An only, lonely child, he had an irregular upbringing and was educated in a Protestant secondary school in Paris and privately. A devotee of literature and music, he embarked on his career by writing essays, then poetry, biography, fiction, drama, criticism, memoirs and translation. He wrote more than 50 books in all, and came to be regarded as the grand old man of French literature. By 1917 he had emerged as the prophet of French youth and his unorthodox views were the subject of much debate. Though he married his cousin in 1892, he was bisexual with a strong physical attraction towards men. His international reputation rests largely on his stylish novels in which there is a sharp conflict between the spiritual and the physical. Significant titles are *L'Immoraliste* (1902), trans *The Immoralist*, 1930), *La Porte étroite* (1909, trans *Strait is the Gate*, 1924), *Les Caves du Vatican* (1914, trans *The Vatican Cellars*, 1952), *La Symphonie Pastorale* (1919, trans *Two Symphonies*, 1931) and *Les Faux Monnayeurs* (1925, trans *The Coiners*, 1927, revised 1950, *The Counterfeiters*). He was a founder of the magazine *La Nouvelle Française*, and kept up a voluminous correspondence, as well as being a critic of French bureaucracy at home and in the African colonies. His *Journals*, covering the years from 1889–1949, are trenchant, witty and self-revealing, and an essential supplement to his autobiography, *Si le Grain ne meurt* (1926, trans *If It Die...*, 1935). In 1947 he was awarded the Nobel prize for literature.

GIDE, Charles (1847–1932) French economist, born in Uzès (Gard). He was professor in turn at Bordeaux, Montpellier and Paris. His *Principes d'économie politique* (1883) became a standard work.

GIDEON greatest of the judges of Israel, son of Joash. He suppressed Baal-worship, and put an end to the seven years' domination of the Midianites by routing them near Mount Gilboa.

GIELGUD, Sir (Arthur) John (1904–) English actor and producer, a grand-nephew of **Ellen Terry**. He made his name in *The Constant Nymph* (1926) and *The Good Companions* (1931), became a leading Shakespearian actor of the British theatre and directed many of the Shakespeare Memorial Theatre productions, as well as *The Cherry Orchard* (1954) and *The Chalk Garden* (1956) in London. He has also appeared in many films, notably as Disraeli in *The Prime Minister* (1940) and as Cassius in *Julius Caesar* (1952). He played Othello at Stratford in 1961 and Prospero at the National Theatre in 1974. Like **Olivier**, he adapted to changing dramatic styles and to the new wave of plays popularized by the Royal Court Theatre, appearing during the 1960s and 70s in plays by **David Storey**, **Edward Bond** and **Harold Pinter**. He now appears increasingly in cameo roles in films, although he returned to the stage in 1988, playing in Hugh Whitemore's *Sir Sydney Cockerell: The Best of Friends* (1988). He published his autobiography, *An Actor in his Time*, in 1979.

GIELGUD, Maina (1945–) English dancer, artistic director and teacher, born in London. The niece of actor Sir **John Gielgud**, she studied with many distinguished teachers prior to her 1961 début with **Roland Petit**'s company. She was either a member of or a guest artist with such companies as Ballet of the 20th Century (1967–71) and London Festival Ballet (1972–75). In 1983 she was appointed artistic director of the Australian Ballet.

GIEREK, Edward (1913–) Polish politician, born in Porabka (Bedzin district), the son of a miner. He lived in France (1923–34) during the Pilsudski dictatorship, and joined the French Communist party in 1931. He was deported to Poland in 1934, and lived in Belgium (1937–48), becoming a member of the Belgian resistance. On his return to Poland in 1948, he joined the ruling Polish United Workers' party (PUWP), being inducted into its politburo in 1956 and appointed party boss of Silesia. He became PUWP leader in 1970 when **Gomulka** resigned after strikes and riots in Gdansk, Gdynia and Szczecin. Head of the party's 'technocrat faction', he embarked on an ambitious industrialization programme. This plunged the country heavily into debt and, following a wave of strikes in Warsaw and Gdansk, spearheaded by the 'Solidarity' free trade union movement, he was forced to resign in 1980.

GIERKE, Otto Friedrich von (1841–1921) German legal theorist, professor of law in and rector of Berlin University. His interest in the history, theory and law of associations resulted in *Das deutsche Genossenschaftrecht* (1886–1913, unfinished), and led him to seek to ensure that the German Civil Code of 1896–1900 was influenced by Germanic ideas of social groups. He also published a *Deutsches Privatrecht* (1895–1917) which interprets the Civil Code in this way, in opposition to those who approached German law from a Roman standpoint.

GIESEBRECHT, Wilhelm von (1814–89) German historian, born in Berlin. He became professor of history at Königsberg in 1857, in 1862 at Munich. His chief works are a history of the Germanic Empire to 1181 (1855–88). It was the first history of the middle ages based upon a critical study of primary sources.

GIESEKING, Walter (1895–1956) German pianist, born in Lyons, France. He studied in Hanover and made his first public appearance in 1915 and, after World War I, he established an international reputation, especially in the works of **Debussy** and **Ravel**. At his death he was engaged in recording the complete piano works of **Mozart**, and **Beethoven**'s piano sonatas.

GIFFARD, Henri (1825–82) French engineer and inventor, born in Paris. He studied at the Collège Bourbon and the École Centrale. In 1852 he built a light 3 hp steam engine, fitted it with an 11 ft propeller and succeeded in piloting a balloon, steered by a rudder, over a distance of 17 miles. This can be considered as the first powered and controlled flight ever achieved, in a craft which was a primitive example of the dirigible or semi-rigid airship. In 1858 he patented a steam injector which became widely used in locomotives and other types of steam engine, and made him a fortune. He continued with his aeronautical experiments, and left his money to the state for humanitarian and scientific purposes.

GIFFEN, Sir Robert (1837–1910) Scottish economist and statistician, born in Strathaven. At first a journalist, he eventually became comptroller-general of the commercial, labour and statistical department of the board of trade. His works include *Essays in Finance* (1879–1886), *The Growth of Capital* (1890) and *Case against Bimetallism* (1892).

GIFFORD, Adam (1820–87) Scottish judge, born in Edinburgh. He was called to the Scottish bar in 1849, and was raised to the bench as Lord Gifford in 1870. In his will he left endowments to Edinburgh, Glasgow, Aberdeen and St Andrews Universities for regular series of undogmatic lectures in natural theology.

GIFFORD, Robert Swain (1840–1905) American landscape painter, born in Naushon, Massachusetts. He travelled and painted in Europe and the Near East and settled in New York. He is best known for his sombre treatment of moorlands and seascapes.

GIFFORD, William (1756–1826) English editor and critic, born in Ashburton in Devon, the son of a glazier. Left an orphan at the age of twelve, he was enabled to resume school by a local surgeon who liked his verses. He went to Exeter College, Oxford, and after graduating in 1782, travelled on the Continent with Lord Grosvenor's son. His first production, the *Baviad* (1794), was a satire on the Della Cruscan school of poetry; the *Maeviad* (1796), against corrupt drama. The titles were based on two minor Roman poets, **Bavius** and **Maevius**. Gifford's editorship of the *Anti-Jacobin* (1797–98) gained him favour with the Tory magnates. In 1802 appeared his translation of **Juvenal**, with his autobiography. He edited **Massinger**, **Ford**, **Shirley** and **Ben Jonson**, and was the first editor of **Scott**'s *Quarterly Review* (1809–24). He possessed much satirical acerbity, but little merit as a poet, and as a critic was unduly biased.

GIGLI, Beniamino (1890–1957) Italian tenor, born in Recanati. The son of a shoemaker, he won a scholarship to the Accademia di Santa Cecilia. He made his operatic début in **Ponchielli**'s *La Gioconda* in 1914, and by 1929 had won a worldwide reputation. A lyric-dramatic tenor of superb natural gifts, he compensated for technical deficiencies and weakness as an actor by the vitality of his singing and was at his best in the works of **Verdi** and **Puccini**.

GIL POLO, Gaspar (c.1535–1591) Spanish poet, born in Valencia. He continued **Montemayor**'s *Diana* in his *Diana enamorada* (1564), which was very popular throughout Europe and was used by both **Cervantes** and **Shakespeare** as a basis for a plot. It marks a stage in the history of the novel.

GIL VICENTE See **VICENTE, Gil**

GILBERT AND GEORGE, (Gilbert Proesch and **George Passmore)** ((1943– and 1944–)) English avant-garde artists. Gilbert studied at the Academy of Art in Munich, George at Dartington Hall and at the Oxford School of Art. They made their name in the late 1960s as performance artists (the 'singing sculptures'), with faces and hands painted gold, holding their poses for hours at a time. More recently they have concentrated on photopieces, assembled from a number of separately framed photographs which key together to make a single whole.

GILBERT OF SEMPRINGHAM, St (c.1083–1189) English priest. In 1148 he founded at his birthplace, Sempringham, Lincolnshire, the order of Gilbertines for both monks and nuns, and lay sisters and brothers. It was dissolved at the Reformation. His feast day is 4 February.

GILBERT, Sir Alfred (1854–1934) English sculptor, born in London. He studied in France and Italy and executed work of remarkable simplicity and grace, including his statue of *Eros* in Piccadilly Circus, London, and *Comedy and Tragedy* (1892). He was also a considerable goldsmith. He was professor at the Royal Academy from 1900 to 1909.

GILBERT, Cass (1859–1934) American architect, born in Zanesville, Ohio. Educated at the Massachusetts Institute of Technology, he is remembered as the designer of the first tower skyscraper, the flamboyant 66 storey Woolworth Building in New York (1912), then the tallest building in the world (not counting the Eiffel Tower). He designed many equally outstanding public buildings, including the US Customs House in New York City (1907) and the Supreme Court Building in Washington DC (1935), and the campuses of the Universities of Minnesota (Minneapolis) and Texas (Austin).

GILBERT, Grove Karl (1843–1918) American geologist, born in Rochester, New York. He became chief geologist of the US geological survey (1889). He formulated many of the laws of geological processes. His report on the Henry mountains became the foundation of many modern theories of denudation and river-development. He also published a history of the Niagara river and introduced technical terms such as 'laccolith' and 'hanging valley'.

GILBERT, Sir (Joseph) Henry (1817–1901) English agricultural chemist, born in Hull. Educated at Glasgow and London, from 1843 he was associated with Sir John Bennet Lawes in the Rothamsted Agricultural Laboratory and in 1884 became professor of rural economy at Oxford. He is particularly noted for his work on nitrogen fertilizers.

GILBERT, Sir Humphrey (1537–83) English navigator, born in Buxham, half brother of Sir **Walter Raleigh**. He served under Sir **Henry Sidney** in Ireland (1566–70) and was made governor of Munster; he then campaigned in the Netherlands (1570–75). In 1578 he led an unsuccessful colonizing expedition to the New World; in a second attempt in 1583 he landed in Newfoundland, of which he took possession for the crown, and established a colony at St John's. He was drowned on the homeward journey.

GILBERT, Sir John (1817–97) English painter and illustrator, born in Blackheath. Mainly self-taught, he began to exhibit in oil and watercolour in 1836. Known as 'The Scott of painting' he is remembered for his illustrations of **Shakespeare**, **Scott**, **Cervantes**, etc, and for his wood-carvings in the *Illustrated London News*.

GILBERT, Walter (1932–) American molecular biologist, born in Boston, Massachusetts. He studied physics and mathematics at Harvard and Cambridge and taught physics at Harvard from 1959 before moving to biophysics and then to molecular biology; he became professor of biophysics at Harvard in 1968. By 1966 he had done ingenious work in isolating a sample of the elusive repressor substances, which **Jacques Monod** and **François Jacob** had hypothesized in 1961 to be centrally involved in controlling gene action. He went on to devise an elegant method for finding the sequence of bases in nucleic acids, for which he shared the 1980 Nobel prize for chemistry with **Frederick Sanger** and **Paul Berg**.

GILBERT, William (1540–1603) English physician, the 'father of electricity', born in Colchester. In 1561 he was elected fellow of St John's College, Cambridge, and in 1573 settled in London, where he was appointed physician to Queen **Elizabeth** (1601), and King **James VI and I** (1603). In his *De Magnete* (1600) he established the magnetic nature of the earth; and he conjectured that terrestrial magnetism and electricity were two allied emanations of a single force. He was the first to use the terms 'electricity', 'electric force' and 'electric attraction', and to point out that amber is not the only substance which when rubbed attracts light objects. The *gilbert* unit of magnetomotive power is named after him.

GILBERT, William (1804–89) English novelist, born in Bishopstoke. He abandoned the East India Company's service for the study of surgery, and that in turn for literature. His 30 works, published from 1858 onwards, include the delightful *King George's Middy*, a Life of **Lucrezia Borgia**, and several **Defoe**-like novels—*Dives and Lazarus*, *Shirley Hall Asylum* and *De Profundis*.

GILBERT, Sir William Schwenck (1836–1911) English parodist and librettist of the 'Gilbert and Sullivan' light operas, born in London. He studied at King's College, London, and became a clerk in the privy-council office (1857–62). Called to the bar in 1864, he failed to attract lucrative briefs and made his living from magazine contributions to *Punch* and *Fun*, for which he wrote much humorous verse under his boyhood nickname 'Bab', which was collected in 1869 as the *Bab Ballads*. He also wrote a Christmas burlesque, *Dulcemara, or The Little Duck and The Great Quack* (1866) and *The Palace of Truth* (1870), which both made a hit on the stage, followed by *Pygmalion and Galatea* (1871). But it is as the librettist of Sir **Arthur Sullivan's** light operas that he is best remembered. Their famous partnership, begun in 1871, scored its first success with *Trial by Jury* under **D'Oyly Carte**'s able management at the Royalty Theatre, London, in 1875. The same jibing, ludicrously topsy-turvy wit, beautifully accentuated by Sullivan's scores, pervaded the procession of light operas that followed, from *The Sorcerer* (1877), *HMS Pinafore* (1878) and *The Pirates of Penzance* (1879) to *The Gondoliers* (1889) and *The Grand Duke* (1896), which played first at the Opéra Comique and from 1881 in the newly-built Savoy Theatre. It was a carpet in the Savoy, considered too costly by the ever-argumentative Gilbert, that touched off a quarrel between him and Sullivan. They created only three more pieces before Sullivan's death and **Edward German**'s efforts to fill the gap in *Fallen Fairies* (1909) proved unsuccessful.

GILBEY, Sir Walter (1831–1914) English wine merchant, born in Bishop's Stortford. He was founder of the well-known wine company, horse-breeder and agriculturist.

GILBRETH, Frank Bunker (1868–1924) American engineer and efficiency expert, born in Fairfield, Maine. He began work as an apprentice bricklayer in 1885, and from that time devoted himself to developing time-and-motion studies of industrial processes as a means of increasing efficiency. Later he and his wife Lillian Evelyn (née Molder, 1879–1972) made detailed laboratory studies of the basic elements involved in manual work which they called 'therbligs', such as search, find, select, grasp, assemble, and so on. Together with **Frederick W Taylor** they were the founders of scientific management as it is universally practised today. The Gilbreths had twelve children, two of whom collaborated in writing the popular book and film *Cheaper by the Dozen* in 1949–50.

GILCHRIST, Alexander (1828–61) English biographer, husband of **Anne Gilchrist**, born in Newington Green. He was the author of *Life of Etty* (1855), and a *Life of Blake*, completed by his wife (1863).

GILCHRIST, Anne, née **Burrows** (1828–85) English writer, wife of **Alexander Gilchrist**, born in London. They married in 1851. She completed her husband's *Life of Blake*, wrote on **Whitman**, and on New England village life, and published a *Life of Mary Lamb* (1883).

GILCHRIST, Percy Carlyle (1851–1935) English metallurgist, born in Lyme Regis. He developed, with his cousin **Sydney Gilchrist Thomas**, a new process for smelting iron ore, which removed phosphorus containing impurities. Gilchrist studied at the Royal School of Mines, becoming a Murchison Medallist. He took a post as chemist first at Cwm Avon ironworks in South Wales, and then at Blaenavon ironworks. Here, in his spare time, he carried out tests for smelting phosphoric iron ores using a furnace lined with a basic material, such as magnesium oxide, which would combine with and remove the phosphate impurities in the iron ore. The Gilchrist-Thomas process doubled the potential steel production of the world by making possible the use of the large European phosphoric iron ore fields.

GILDAS, St (c.493–570) Romano-British historian and monk, born in Strathclyde. He fled the strife that raged in his neighbourhood and went to Wales, where he married; after his wife died he became a monk. His famous treatise, *De Excidio et Conquestu Britanniae*, probably written between 516 and 547, is the only extant history of the Celts, and the only contemporary British version of events from the invasion of the Romans to his own time.

GILES, Latin **Aegidius, St** (d.c.700) according to legend an Athenian of royal descent, devoted from his cradle to good works. After giving away his patrimony, he lived two years with St Caesarius at Arles, and then retired to a hermitage, where he lived on herbs and the milk of a hind. The Frankish king, hunting the hind, discovered him and was so impressed with his holiness that he built a monastery on the spot and made him its abbot. Here he died. He is the patron of lepers, beggars and cripples.

GILES, Carl Ronald (1916–) British cartoonist and animator, born in London. A self-taught artist, he worked his way up from film company office boy (1930) to animator on advertising films, then worked on the *Come On Steve* cartoons (1935). He joined *Reynolds News* in 1938 to draw weekly topical cartoons and a strip, *Young Ernie*, before transferring to the *Daily Express* and *Sunday Express* (1943) where he developed his 'Giles Family' cartoons, dominated by Grandma.

GILES, Herbert Allen (1845–1935) English scholar and linguist, born in Oxford. After a career in the diplomatic service in China between 1867 and 1892, he returned to Britain and from 1897 to 1932 was professor of Chinese at Cambridge University. Although interest in the Chinese language was initially small and Giles had few pupils, he published a great number of books on Chinese language and civilization which did much to arouse in Britain a serious interest in Chinese culture. He modified the romanization system of Sir **Thomas Wade**, his predecessor at Cambridge, and his use of this Wade-Giles system (as it came to be known) in his *Chinese-English Dictionary* (1892 and 1912) established it as the preferred transliteration system in English-speaking countries for most of this century. Among his other works are a

Chinese Biographical Dictionary (1898), *A History of Chinese Literature* (1901 and 1923) and *An Introduction to the History of Chinese Pictorial Art* (1905 and 1918).

GILES, William Ernest Powell (1835–97) English-born Australian explorer, born in Bristol. Educated at Christ's Hospital, London, he emigrated to Adelaide in 1850 where he worked in the Victoria goldfields. From 1861 to 1865 he searched for pastures inland from the Darling River. Under the sponsorship of Sir **Ferdinand Müller**, he was sent to explore areas to the west of the Central Overland telegraph between Adelaide and Darwin, first in 1872 when he discovered Lake Amadeus and again in 1874 when he penetrated the Gibson Desert, named after a companion who died there. He tried again (1875–76), and managed to cross from Port Augusta to Perth, a distance of 2500 miles in five months and back along a line just south of the Tropic of Capricorn; this extraordinary feat of endurance is described in his *Australia Twice Traversed* (1889). However, he had failed to find good grazing and died in obscurity.

GILL, (Louis) André, pseud of **Louise André Gosset de Guines** (1840–85) French caricaturist. He lampooned the famous of the day by drawing them with outsized heads and dwarfish bodies.

GILL, Sir David (1843–1914) Scottish astronomer, born in Aberdeen and educated there. He was HM Astronomer at the Cape Observatory (1879–1907) and pioneered the use of photography for charting the heavens.

GILL, Eric in full, **Arthur Eric Rowton Gill** (1882–1940) English sculptor, engraver, writer and typographer, born in Brighton, the son of a clergyman. At the age of 21 he abandoned an apprenticeship in architecture and took up letter-cutting and masonry and later engraving. In 1909 he carved his first stone figure, *The Madonna and Child.* Through the influence of **Augustus John** he exhibited at the Chenil Galleries, Chelsea, in 1911, and thereafter, for the rest of his life, maintained a steady output of stone and wood carvings, engravings (for his own press, St Dominic, and also for the Golden Cockerel Press), type designs, such as Perpetua, Bunyan and Gill Sans-serif, subsequently adopted by Monotype and used all over the world; as also was a stream of books dealing with his various crafts, his thoughts and religious beliefs. Devotion, of a starkly sincere quality, is the sign manual of all his art; works include the *Stations of the Cross*, executed in Hoptonwood stone in Westminster Cathedral (1913), war memorials up and down the country after World War I, the gigantic figure *Mankind* (1928), now in the Tate Gallery, the fine altarpiece at Rossall School Chapel, the sculptures at Broadcasting House, London, and many more. He joined the Fabian movement, but later found the socialist ethic limited and joined the Catholic Church. He founded an ideal community at Ditchling.

GILLESPIE, Dizzy (John Birks) (1917–) American jazz trumpeter, composer and bandleader, born in Cheraw, South Carolina, who emerged as a leading exponent of bebop in the 1940s. After studying musical theory and harmony at Laurinburg Institute, North Carolina, he began his career in swing bands led by Teddy Hill, Cab Calloway, **Benny Carter** and Charlie Barnet. Along with **Charlie Parker**, **Thelonious Monk**, and others, he was involved in informal jam session experiments in New York that produced the bebop style. In 1945 Gillespie formed the first of his several big bands working in the new idiom; in 1956 he led an orchestra on two international tours as cultural missions for the US State Department. Although Gillespie has worked intermittently with large orchestras since, he is best-known as a leader of small combos and as a virtuoso who extended the working range of the trumpet.

GILLESPIE, George (1613–48) Scottish clergyman, born in Kirkcaldy. He studied at St Andrews and in 1638 was ordained minister of Wemyss. A leader of Scottish church opposition to **Charles I**'s innovations in worship, he published *English Popish Ceremonies* in 1637. He became minister of Greyfriars, Edinburgh, in 1642, and in 1643 was sent to the Westminster Assembly, where he took a great part in the debates on discipline and dogma. His *Aaron's Rod Blossoming* (1646) is a masterly statement of the high presbyterian claim for spiritual independence. In 1648 he became minister at the High Church, Edinburgh, and was moderator of the General Assembly.

GILLESPIE, James (1726–97) Scottish snuff and tobacco merchant in Edinburgh. He bought the estate of Spylaw, and left money to found a hospital (designed by William Bush) in 1801–03 which became a school run by the Merchant Taylors' Company.

GILLESPIE, Thomas (1708–74) Scottish clergyman, born in Duddingston. From 1741 he was minister of Carnock near Dunfermline, where in 1749 he opposed the ordination of a minister, was deposed by the General Assembly in 1752 and founded in 1761 the Relief Church, which was later absorbed into the United Presbyterian Church.

GILLETTE, King Camp (1855–1932) American inventor and businessman, born in Fond du Lac, Wisconsin. After working for years as a travelling salesman, he invented a safety razor and disposable blade, which he started marketing in 1901. A Utopian socialist, he set up a 'World Corporation' in Arizona in 1910 to advocate a world planned economy. He wrote on social theories in various publications like *Gillette's Industrial Solution* (1900) and *The People's Corporation* (1924).

GILLIÉRON, Jules (1854–1926) Swiss linguist, born in Neuveville. He studied under **Gaston Paris** at the École des hautes études in Paris, where he himself was professor of Romance dialectology from 1883 until his death. His *Atlas linguistiques de la France*, produced in collaboration with Edmond Edmont and published between 1902 and 1912, was a stimulus to, and provided a basic model for, further studies in linguistic geography. Among Gilliéron's other works are *La Généalogie des mots qui désignent l''abeille'* (1918) and *Pathologie et thérapeutique verbales* (1915–21).

GILLIES, Sir Harold Delf (1882–1960) New Zealand plastic surgeon, born in Dunedin and educated at Wanganui College and Cambridge. In 1920 he published his *Plastic Surgery of the Face*, which established this art as a recognized branch of medicine. During World War II he was responsible for setting up plastic surgery units throughout the country and was personally in charge of the largest one at Park Prewett Hospital, Basingstoke. In 1957 he published *The Principles and Art of Plastic Surgery*, the standard work on this subject.

GILLIES, John (1747–1836) Scottish historian, born near Brechin. Educated at Glasgow University, he worked as a tutor in Europe before moving to London (from 1784). He published a translation (1778) of **Isocrates** and **Lysias**, *History of Ancient Greece* (1786), *Frederick II of Prussia* (1789), and *History of the World from Alexander to Augustus* (1807–10). In 1793 he was appointed royal historiographer for Scotland.

GILLIES, Sir William George (1898–1973) Scottish artist, born in Haddington. He studied at the Edinburgh College of Art, in Italy, and under André Lhote in France. His finely organized interpretations of

Scottish landscape (many in watercolour) are well known, and his work is represented in the Tate Gallery. He was principal of Edinburgh College of Art from 1961 to 1966.

GILLOTT, Joseph (1799–1873) English inventor, born in Sheffield. He shares with Sir **Josiah Mason** the credit for having perfected the manufacture of steel pen-nibs.

GILLRAY, James (1757–1815) English caricaturist, born in Chelsea, the son of a Lanark trooper. He first became known as a successful engraver about 1784, and between 1779 and 1811 issued 1500 caricatures. They are full of broad humour and keen satire aimed against the French, **Napoleon**, **George III**, the leading politicians and the social follies of his day. For the last four years of his life he was insane.

GILLY, Friedrich (1772–1800) German architect, born in Berlin, the son of an architect. His work displayed considerable geometric control, evidently inspired by that of the French visionary architects in Paris. After a travelling scholarship in 1797, he became professor of optics and perspective at the Academy of Architecture in Berlin in 1798. His designs include the Funerary Precinct and Temple to **Frederick II, the Great** of Prussia (1796), and the Prussian National Theatre, Berlin (1798), both severe, classical designs.

GILMAN, Charlotte Anna, née **Perkins** (1860–1935) American feminist and writer, born in Hartford, Connecticut. Brought up by her mother, she was educated at Rhode Island School of Design. She married a painter, Charles Stetson, in 1884, but separated in 1888, divorcing in 1894. Moving to California, she published her first stories, most memorably 'The Yellow Wall-Paper' (1892) and a collection of poetry, *In This Our World* (1893). She lectured on women's issues, as well as wider social concerns, and in 1898 wrote *Women and Economics*, now recognized as a feminist landmark. In 1902 she married her cousin George Gilman, a New York lawyer. She founded, edited and wrote for the journal *Forerunner* (1909–16). Her later works include *The Man-made World* (1911) and *His Religion and Hers* (1923). She commited suicide on being told that she was suffering from incurable cancer.

GILMAN, Harold (1878–1919) English artist, born in Rode, Somerset. He studied at the Slade School and in Spain. He was associated with the Camden Town Group (1910), and was later the first president of the London Group. Influenced by **Pissarro** and **Van Gogh**, he used 'fauve' colouring to paint interiors and portraits, eg his *Mrs Mounter* in the Tate Gallery, London.

GILMORE, Dame Mary Jane (1865–1962) Australian poet and author, born in Cotta Walla, near Goulburn, New South Wales. She moved with her family to Wagga Wagga, New South Wales, at the age of ten, and later taught at schools in the area. In 1896 she left to join William Lane's Utopian 'New Australia' settlement in Paraguay, South America. There she met and married a shearer, William Gilmore, and they returned to Australia in 1902, to settle in Sydney from 1912 onwards. Her socialist sympathies were now harnessed to campaigning for the betterment of the sick and the helpless, through the women's column which she edited for over 20 years in the Sydney *Worker* newspaper, but also in her six volumes of poetry published between 1910 and 1954. Three books of recollections illustrate her lifelong efforts to preserve early Australian traditions and folklore. She was created DBE in 1937, and **William Dobell**'s controversial portrait of her was unveiled on her 92nd birthday in 1957. A collection of tributes to Dame Mary was published in 1965, and an edition of her letters in 1980.

GILMOUR, John Scott Lennox (1906–86) English botanist, born in London. He was director of the Royal Horticultural Society Gardens, Wisley (1946–51) and director of the Cambridge University Botanic Garden (1951–73). His name has been given to the 'Gilmourian' concept of multiple classifications.

GILPIN, Bernard (1517–83) Anglican clergyman, born in Kentmere Hall, Westmorland. He studied at Queen's College, Oxford, and at Louvain and Paris, and became archdeacon of Durham in 1556. His fearless honesty against pluralites brought accusations of heresy which, however, were unsuccessful, and on Queen **Elizabeth**'s succession in 1558 he was appointed rector of Houghton le Spring. He turned down many lucrative offers, preferring to minister to his parish and to make preaching excursions into the remotest parts of northern England, which earned him the nickname 'Apostle of the North'.

GILPIN, John (1930–) English dancer, born in Southsea. A child actor, he studied at the Rambert School, joining Ballet Rambert in 1945. In 1949 he was a principal with **Petit**'s Ballets de Paris, returning to Britain in 1950 to join London Festival Ballet, where he became artistic director 1962–65. Known for his faultless technique, he created roles in Robin Howard's *The Sailor's Return* (1947), **Frederick Ashton**'s *Le Reve de Leonor* (1949) and **Anton Dolin**'s *Variations for Four* (1957). He returned to dancing in the late 1960s and now combines teaching and acting.

GILPIN, William (1724–1804) English clergyman, writer and artist, born in Scaleby, Carlisle. Educated at Oxford, in 1777 he became vicar of Boldre in Hampshire. A leader of the 18th-century cult of the picturesque, he was the author of works on the scenery of Britain, illustrated by his own aquatint engravings. He is satirized by **Combe** in *Dr Syntax*. His brother Sawrey (1733–1807) was a highly successful animal painter, especially of horses.

GILRUTH, Robert Rowe (1913–) American engineer, born in Nashwauk, Minnesota. He graduated at the University of Minnesota in aeronautical engineering in 1935, and has ever since been associated with the design and operation of high speed and supersonic aircraft, guided missiles, and space vehicles. In 1958 he was appointed head of the NASA man-in-space programme which put the first American, **John Glenn**, into earth orbit in 1962. The next objective, known as the Apollo lunar landing project, was achieved under his direction on 20 July 1969 when **Neil Armstrong**, on the Apollo 11 mission, became the first man to set foot on the moon.

GILSON, Étienne (1884–1978) French historian and philosopher. Professor at the Sorbonne (1921–32) and the Collège de France (1932–51), he was founder of the Pontifical Institute of Medieval Studies at Toronto University (1929). He is known especially for his works on medieval Christian philosophy.

GIMSON, Ernest William (1864–1919) English architect and furniture designer, born in Leicester. He was recommended by **William Morris** to take up articles with J D Sedding in London, where he met Ernest Barnsley (1863–1926) and his brother Sydney (1865–1926). Gimson designed, within the Arts and Crafts 'vernacular' idiom, a number of houses around Leicester, and other buildings. However, he is mainly associated with the design of furniture. After a short-lived furniture-making enterprise, Kenton and Company (1890–92), he and the Barnsley brothers moved in 1895 to the Cotswolds where they all designed or made furniture. Gimson's own designs included ladder-back chairs and fine examples of cabinet-making, mostly in untreated native timbers, as well as metalwork such as sconces and fire-dogs.

GINCKELL, or **Ginkel, Godert de, 1st Earl of Athlone** (1630–1703) Dutch-born British soldier, born in Utrecht. He accompanied **William III** to England in 1688. He commanded a body of horse at the battle of the Boyne (1690), and on the king's return to England was left as commander-in-chief in Ireland. He reduced Ballymore and Athlone, defeated St Ruth at Aghrim, and finally captured Limerick (1691). In 1692 he was created Earl of Athlone. He afterwards commanded the Dutch troops under **Marlborough** (1702).

GINER DE LOS RIOS, Francisco (1839–1915), Spanish educationist, born in Ronda, Malaga, Spain's leading 20th-century educational philosopher and reformer. After his career as professor of philosophy had twice been interrupted, the second time by imprisonment because of his refusal to kow-tow to reactionary authority, he founded, with a group of intellectuals, the *Instituto Libre de Enseñanza* in Madrid (1876). This was a kind of free university through which three generations of distinguished writers and artists passed, such as **Garcia Lorca**, whose generation enjoyed a brief flowering in the Republic (1931–36). Pedagogically ahead of his time, Giner saw education as primarily 'making man' (*formar hombres*). His Instituto rejected text-books and examinations, and students were encouraged to go to primary sources. Essential activities included visits to factories, farms, and the mountains, and workshop discussions. His educational ideas, which owe much to the philosophers **Krause** and **Locke**, are set out in *Ensayos sobre educación* (1902).

GINSBERG, Allen (1926–) American poet, born in Newark, New Jersey. Brought up in a Jewish community, his father was also a poet and his mother was a left-wing Russian emigrant. He was educated at Columbia University. A homosexual and drug experimentalist, he was born of the 'Beat' movement and was friendly with **Jack Kerouac**, **William Burroughs** and others. *Howl and Other Poems* (1956), his first book, was a *succès de scandale*. The title poem was named by Kerouac because it seemed to him to let out from some primal level of human consciousness 'the pent-up rage and frustrations of the inner being'. Whether this was so or not, it launched Ginsberg on a high profile career as proficient public performer. Numerous collections have appeared including *Kaddish and Other Poems* (1961), *The Gates of Wrath*: *Rhymed Poems*, 1948–52, and *First Blues*: *Rags & Harmonium Songs* 1971–74 (1975). Despite his initial anti-establishment stance, he has won honours and awards. His *Journals* were published in 1977.

GINSBURG, Christian David (1831–1914) Polish-born English Biblical scholar, born in Warsaw. He came early to England and converted to Christianity in 1846. He established himself as an authority on the Hebrew scriptures, and published many editions and commentaries.

GIOBERTI, Vicenzo (1801–52) Italian philosopher and politician, born in Turin. He was ordained in 1825 and became chaplain to the court of Sardinia, but fell from favour through his radical republican views. He was in exile from 1833, and from Brussels published works advocating a united Italy and extolling the papacy as its divinely appointed agency. He returned to Italy in 1848 to great popularity and held a succession of posts culminating in that of premier of Sardinia-Piedmont in 1848–49, but his fortunes changed rapidly and he moved to Paris where he died. His works include an *Introduction to Philosophy* (1839), *On the Moral and Civil Primacy of the Italian Race* (1843) and *On the Civic Renewal of Italy* (1851). His philosophy centred on the concept of being and is usually described as 'ontologism'. The philosophical and the political theories were linked through a process of 'palingenesis', the actualization in human life of the ideal.

GIOLITTI, Giovanni (1842–1928) Italian statesman, born in Mondovi. Trained as a lawyer, he was five times prime minister from 1892 to 1921. He introduced universal suffrage and tried unsuccessfully to keep Italy neutral during World War I. After it, he introduced vast schemes of social reforms. He was a near socialist in his political persuasions.

GIORDANO, Luca (1632–1705) Italian painter, born in Naples. He acquired the power of working with extreme rapidity (whence his nickname Luca Fa Presto, 'Luca works quickly'), and of imitating the great masters. In Florence he painted the ceiling frescoes in the Ballroom of the Palazzo Medici-Riccardi. From 1692 to 1702 he was in Madrid, as court painter to **Charles II** of Spain, and embellished the Escorial. His oils and frescoes are in most European collections.

GIORDANO, Umberto (1867–1948) Italian operatic composer, born in Foggia. He is remembered especially for *Andrea Chenier* (1896) and *Fedora* (1898). There followed *Siberia* (1903) and other operas, the last being *Il Re* (1929).

GIORGIONE, or **Giorgio Barbarelli** (c.1478–1511) Italian painter, born near Castelfranco. He probably studied at Venice under **Giovanni Bellini**, and soon developed a freer and larger manner, characterized by intense poetic feeling and by great beauty and richness of colouring. Several early portraits by him have disappeared, but an *Enthroned Madonna* is an altarpiece at Castelfranco. In Venice he was extensively employed in fresco painting, but some fragments in the Fondaco de'Tedeschi are all that now remain of this work. *The Tempest* at Venice, with its lovely landscape, is attributed to him. *The Family of Giorgione* in Venice, *The Three Philosophers* in Vienna, and the *Sleeping Venus* in the Dresden Gallery are admittedly genuine. Many of his pictures were completed by other painters, including the *Sleeping Venus* and *The Three Philosophers*. Giorgione was a great innovator, he created a new type, the small intimate easel picture with a new treatment of figures in landscape. He was the first great romantic artist.

GIOTTO (DI BONDONE) (c.1266–1337) Italian painter and architect, born in Vespignano, near Florence. The most innovative artist of his time, he is generally credited with being the artist in whose style the seeds of the Renaissance are to be found. At the age of ten, he was supposedly found by **Cimabue** tending sheep and drawing a lamb on flat stone and was taken by him to study art in Florence. His earliest work may have been connected with the making of mosaics for the Florence Baptistery. As a painter he worked in all the major artistic centres of Italy but his most important works are the frescoes in the Arena Chapel, Padua; the Navicella mosaic in Saint Peter's, Rome; the cycle of frescoes depicting scenes from the life of Saint **Francis**, at Assisi; frescoes in the Peruzzi Chapel in the church of S Croce in Florence; and the Ognissanti Madonna, now in the Uffizi, Florence. In terms of style he broke with the rigid conventions of Byzantine art, typified by the work of Cimabue, and composed simplified and moving dramatic narratives peopled by realistically observed and believable figures. Irrelevant detail is absent and the figures are left to tell the stories for themselves. The repercussions of Giotto's innovations can be seen in the work of **Masaccio** a century later and ultimately in the work of **Michelangelo**

himself, who studied and made copies of Giotto's compositions. In 1334 Giotto was appointed master of works for the cathedral and city of Florence. Aided by **Andrea Pisano**, he decorated the façade of the cathedral with statues and designed the campanile himself. It still bears his name but is much altered.

GIOVANNI, di Paolo also known as **Giovanni dal Poggio** (c.1403–1482/83) Italian painter, born in Siena. He may have trained with **Taddeo di Bartoli**; and was certainly influenced by **Gentile da Fabriano**, who was in Siena from 1424 to 1426. Though little is known of his life, many documented works by him have survived, dating from 1426 to c.1475. Like his contemporary **Sassetta**, he worked in a style which is essentially archaizing, continuing the tradition of Sienese Trecento masters rather than looking to new developments elsewhere. Nevertheless, his narrative abilities and highly personal vision give his paintings considerable charm and appeal.

GIPPS, Sir George (1791–1847) English colonial administrator, governor of New South Wales (1838–46). Born in Ringwould, Deal, he served in the Royal Engineers. His policy of land selling by auction instead of the colonial office policy of a fixed price showed him to be an unpopular but farsighted opponent of land monopoly. Gippsland in Victoria is named after him.

GIRALDI, Giambattista, surnamed **Cynthius, Cinthio, Centeo,** or **Cinzio** (1504–73) Italian writer, born in Ferrara. He was professor of natural philosophy at Florence and then of *belles lettres*. Later, he held the chair of rhetoric at Pavia. He is the author of nine plays in imitation of **Seneca**, of which *Orbecche* (1541) is regarded as the first modern tragedy on classical lines to be performed in Italy. His *Ecatommiti* (published in 1565) is a collection of tales that was translated into French and Spanish and gave **Shakespeare** his plots for *Measure for Measure* and *Othello*.

GIRALDUS CAMBRENSIS, or **Girald de Barri** or **Gerald of Wales** (c.1146–c.1223) Norman-Welsh chronicler and ecclesiastic of noble birth, born in Manorbier Castle, Dyfed. The nephew of David, bishop of St David's, he was educated at the abbey of St Peter, Gloucester, and later studied in Paris. He became archdeacon of St David's, and when his uncle died (1176) was expected to be elected bishop there, but his nomination was rejected because he was a Welshman by King **Henry II** of England. Reconciled with the king, he was appointed royal chaplain from 1184 to 1189, and in 1185–86 accompanied Prince (later King) **John** on a military expedition to Ireland. He wrote *Topographia Hibernica* (c.1188), a record of the natural history, inhabitants and folk-tales of Ireland, and collected material for his *Expugnatio Hibernica* (c.1189), an account of the conquest of Ireland by Henry II. In 1188 he accompanied archbishop **Baldwin** of Canterbury on a preaching tour of Wales to recruit support for the Third Crusade, and wrote up his impressions in the vivid and invaluable *Itinierarium Cambriae* (1191). When the see of St David's fell vacant again in 1198 his nomination was once again rejected, this time by the new archbishop of Canterbury, **Hubert Walter**. For five years he challenged the decision, travelling three times to Rome to plead his cause before Pope **Innocent III**, but in 1203 he admitted defeat and devoted the rest of his life to his studies and to writing. He wrote an autobiography, *De Rebus a se Gestis*: *Gemma Ecclesiastica*, a handbook for the instruction of the clergy; and *De Principis Instructione*, a manual on the upbringing of a prince.

GIRARD, Stephen (1750–1831) French-born American businessman and philanthropist, born near Bordeaux. He was successively cabin-boy, mate, captain and part-owner of an American coasting vessel. In 1769 he settled as a trader in Philadelphia, where he established a bank which became the mainstay of the US government during the war of 1812. He was a sceptic, a miser and an exacting master, yet in the yellow fever epidemic in 1793 he nursed many of the sick in the hospitals, and in public matters his generosity was remarkable. Among other bequests he left $2 000 000 for founding Girard College in Philadelphia for male white orphans; no minister of any sect was to be allowed on its board or to visit it.

GIRARDIN, Delphine de, née **Gay** (1804–55) French writer, born in Aix-la-Chapelle, first wife of **Émile de Girardin**. A fashionable figure, graced by beauty, charm and wit, she was acclaimed by the outstanding literary men of the period. She contributed *feuilletons* to her husband's paper under the pseudonym of the Vicomte Charles de Launay, elegant sketches of society life, and wrote some poetry, plays and novels, of which *Le Lorgnon* (1831) is the best.

GIRARDIN, Émile de (1806–81) French journalist, born in Paris, the illegitimate son of General Alexandre de Girardin. In 1827 he published an autobiographical novel, *Émile* and founded his first periodical *Le Voleur* (1828). After the July revolution (1830) he started the *Journal des Connaissances Utiles*, and in 1831 married **Delphine de Girardin**. In 1836 he inaugurated low-price journalism in France with the halfpenny Orléanist *La Presse*. A charge that *La Presse* was subsidized by government led to a fatal duel with Armand Carrel (1800–36), editor of the *National*. From this time he gradually became a confirmed republican. He promoted **Louis Napoleon**'s election to the presidency, but was exiled for disapproving of the *coup d'état*. He next threw himself into the arms of the socialists, and during the Commune proposed a scheme for splitting France into 15 federal states. In 1874, however, he founded *La France*, in which he supported the republic. He also wrote some plays.

GIRARDIN, François Saint-Marc (1801–73) French literary critic and politician, born in Paris. In 1834 he became professor of literature at the Sorbonne, and as a leader writer for the *Journal des Débats* combated the democratic opposition, and was elected to the National Assembly in 1871. He published several large works, among them *Cours de Littérature Dramatique* (1843) and *Souvenirs et réflexions* (1859).

GIRARDON, François (1630–1715) French sculptor, born in Troyes. He studied in Rome, and after 1650 settled in Paris and joined the Le Brun group. He worked on decorative sculpture in **Louis XIV**'s galleries, gardens and palaces, mostly at Versailles, where he is noted for the fountain figures, and designed the tomb of **Richelieu** in the Sorbonne.

GIRAUD, Henri Honoré (1879–1949) French soldier. Trained at St Cyr, he joined the Zouaves. In World War I after his capture and escape, he rose to become chief of staff of the Moroccan Division. Following service as military governor of Metz, in early 1940 he commanded in turn the French 7th and 9th Armies, again suffering capture and internment by the Germans. Escaping his captors, in 1942 he was picked up by a British submarine and landed in North Africa. Much diplomacy was required to win his support for the Allied cause as a subordinate of General **Eisenhower**, and to secure his collaboration, as joint chairman of the French Committee of National Liberation, with General **de Gaulle**. On the abolition of his post of commander-in-chief of the French forces, he refused the appointment of inspector-general of the forces to become a highly critical right-wing deputy in the 2nd Provisional Assembly of 1946.

GIRAUDOUX, (Hippolyte) Jean (1882–1944) French writer, born in Bellac in Limousin. After a brilliant academic career and extensive travel, he joined the diplomatic service and became head of the French ministry of information during World War II, until his affiliations became suspect. As a poet and novelist, steeped in symbolism, much affected by psychoanalytic theories, he pioneered an Impressionistic technique in literature, exemplified particularly in *Provinciales* (1909), *Simon le Pathétique* (1918), and the reflection of his war experiences, *Retour d'Alsace* (1917). His plays, for which he is chiefly remembered and in which he remains essentially a poet, are mainly fantasies based on Greek myths and biblical lore, satirically treated as commentary on modern life. They include *La Folle de Chaillot* (1945), *La Guerre de Troie n'aura pas Lieu* (1935) and *Pour Lucrèce*. The last two were translated as *Tiger at the Gates* (1955) and *Duel of Angels* (1958) by **Christopher Fry**.

GIRTIN, Thomas (1775–1802) English painter, one of the greatest of the earlier landscape painters in watercolours. He was a close friend and a contemporary of **Turner**, with whom he worked in the studio of **John Raphael Smith**, colouring prints. He painted some of his best landscapes in the north of England and in France, which he visited from 1801 to 1802 for his health. His paintings were among the first in which watercolour was exploited as a true medium as distinct from a tint for colouring drawings, as in *The White House at Chelsea* (1800, Tate Gallery). His breadth of vision and noble simplicity were in sharp contrast to the detailed fussiness of the majority of early watercolourists. He influenced **Constable** considerably.

GISCARD D'ESTAING, Valéry (1926–) French conservative politician, born in Koblenz, Germany, the son of a wealthy Auvergne-based inspector of finance with distant connections to **Louis XV**. He gained a Croix de Guerre for his activities in the liberation movement. After the war, he graduated from the prestigious École Nationale d'Administration and worked in the ministry of finance, before being inducted into the private 'cabinet' of prime minister **Edgar Faure** in 1953. He entered the National Assembly, representing the Puy-de-dome, in 1956 as an Independent Republican and became finance minister to President **de Gaulle** in 1962. Giscard fell out with de Gaulle in 1966, but returned as finance minister during the **Pompidou** presidency (1969–74). Following Pompidou's death he was narrowly elected president in May 1974 and proceeded to introduce a series of liberalizing reforms. However, faced with deteriorating external economic conditions, he was defeated by the socialist, **François Mitterrand**, in the presidential election of 1981. Giscard was re-elected to the National Assembly in 1984 and remains an influential figure within the Union pour la Democratie Francaise (Union for French Democracy), a centre-right grouping which he formed in 1978. In November 1989 he resigned from the French National Assembly to play, instead, a leading role in the European parliament.

GISH, Lillian Diana, originally **Lillian de Guiche** (1896–) American actress, born in Springfield, Ohio. Making her stage début at the age of five, she acted in touring theatre companies with her sister Dorothy (1898–1968), with whom she made a joint film début in *An Unseen Enemy* (1912). A long association with **D W Griffith** brought her leading roles in *Birth of a Nation* (1915), *Intolerance* (1916) and *Broken Blossoms* (1919) and created a gallery of waif-like heroines with indomitable spirits. Ill-served by talking pictures, she returned to the stage in 1930 where her many credits include *The Trip to Bountiful* (1953), *Romeo and Juliet* (1965) and *Uncle Vanya* (1973). She has continued to play supporting roles in television and on film, including *Duel in the Sun* (1946) and *The Night of the Hunter* (1955), and returned to a major screen role in *The Whales of August* (1987). She has directed one film, *Remodelling Her Husband* (1920), and written several volumes of autobiography. She received an honorary Academy Award in 1971.

GISSING, George Robert (1857–1903) English novelist, born in Wakefield, Yorkshire, the son of a pharmacist who imbued him with a love of literature. On his father's death Gissing was sent to boarding school where he earned a scholarship to Owens College (now the University of Manchester). From there he won another scholarship to the University of London but before he could take it up he became enamoured of Marianne ('Nell') Harrison, thought to have been a prostitute, from whom he contracted venereal disease. Intent on transforming her into a seamstress, he stole from coat-pockets in his college, for which he was sentenced to a month's hard labour and expelled from college. He was packed off to America in disgrace where he came close to starvation, but while in Chicago he wrote a melodramtic tale of English life which was bought by the *Chicago Tribune*. He subsisted by writing for a spell but he returned to England in 1877, met up again with Harrison in London and started his first novel, *Workers in the Dawn* (1880), which predicts disaster when two such people marry. Ignoring his own sound advice he married Nell in 1879. Doggedly productive, he fed the circulating libraries with three-decker novels which appeared with almost annual regularity: *The Unclassed* (1884), *Isabel Clarendon* (1886), *Demos* (1886), *Thyrza* (1887), *A Life's Morning* (1888) and *The Nether World* (1889), one of the most graphic accounts of Victorian poverty ever written. His industry, however, was not financially rewarding and the couple struggled until Nell died in 1888. Now better off, he travelled on the continent and turned his thoughts to more middle-class matters. The result was his finest fiction: *The Emancipated* (1890), *New Grub Street* (1891), a grim rebuke to all aspiring authors, *Denzil Quarrier* and *Born in Exile* (both 1892), *The Odd Women* (1893), *In the Year of the Jubilee* (1894), *Eve's Ransom* and *Sleeping Fires* (both 1895), *The Paying Guest* (1896) and *The Whirlpool* (1897). Late in 1890 he met Edith Underwood, of a similar background to Nell, and they married in 1891. They had two sons and many rows and separated in 1897. His latter years were slightly more prosperous and happy than his earlier ones. In Paris in 1898 he met a Frenchwoman, Gabrielle Fleury, with whom he moved to the south of France for the sake of his lungs. He wrote several books in his final five years: a notable critical biography of **Dickens** (1898), a travel book, *By the Ionian Sea* (1900) and *The Private Papers of Henry Ryecroft* (1902), a spoof autobiography that was instantly successful. Few writers have stuck at their vocation with Gissing's single-mindedness. He lacked the sense of humour that made **Dickens** a favourite but he never shirked from depicting the unpalatable and few have caught so memorably the drudgery of day-to-day existence. His *Commonplace Book* was published in 1962 and *The Diary of George Gissing, Novelist* appeared in 1982.

GIUGIARO, Giorgio (1938–) Italian automobile and industrial designer, born in Garessio, near Cuneo. After working in the 1960s for the bodywork designers Bertone and Ghia, he established his own firm, Ital Design, in 1969. While he has designed for such makers as Alfa-Romeo and Lancia, the models have mostly been those aimed at a popular market. He is especially associated with outstanding small cars such as the first Volkswagen 'Golf' (1974) and the Fiat 'Panda' (1980) and 'Uno'(1983). Since the late 1970s Ital has extended its scope to product design including cameras for Nikon, sewing machines for Necchi and watches for Seiko.

GIULIO ROMANO, properly **Giulio Pippi de' Giannuzzi** (c.1492–1546) Italian painter and architect, born in Rome. He assisted **Raphael** in the execution of several of his finest works, and at his death in 1520 completed the *Transfiguration* in the Vatican. In 1524 he went to Mantua on the invitation of the Duke. The drainage of the marshes and the protection of the city from the floods of the Po and Mincio attest his skill as an engineer; while his genius as an architect found scope in the restoration and adornment of the Palazzo del Tè, the cathedral, and a ducal palace. In Bologna he designed the façade of the church of S Petronio. Among his oil paintings are the *Martyrdom of St Stephen* (at Genoa), a *Holy Family* (Dresden), and the *Madonna della Gatta* (Naples).

GIUSTI, Giuseppe (1809–50) Italian poet and political satirist, born near Pistoia. In a brilliant series of poems he mercilessly denounced the enemies of Italy and the vices of the age. He was elected to the Tuscan chamber of deputies in 1848.

GIVENCHY, Hubert James Marcel Taffin de (1927–) French fashion designer, born in Beauvais. He was two years old when his father died, and his grandfather, who had at one time studied painting, was an early influence. He attended the École des Beaux-Arts and the Faculté de Droit in Paris. He obtained a job with Fath in 1944, then worked with Piguet, Lelong and **Elsa Schiaparelli**. He opened his own house in 1952. His Bettina blouse in white cotton became internationally famous. In the early 1950s he met **Balenciaga**, who influenced and encouraged him. His clothes are noted for their elegance and quality. He produces ready-to-wear clothes under his Nouvelle Boutique label.

GLADSTONE, Herbert John Gladstone, 1st Viscount (1854–1930) English statesman, youngest son of **W E Gladstone**. He was Liberal MP for Leeds (1880–1910), was criticized for 'revealing' his father's intentions as to the Irish question (1885), became Liberal chief whip in 1899, home secretary from 1905 to 1910, when he was appointed first governor-general of the Union of South Africa and raised to the peerage. He was head of the War Refugees Association (1914–19) and published his political reminiscences, *After Thirty Years* in 1928.

GLADSTONE, William Ewart (1809–98) English Liberal statesman, born in Liverpool, the fourth son of Sir John Gladstone (1764–1851), a well-known Liverpool merchant and MP of Scottish ancestry. He was educated at Eton and at Christ Church, Oxford. He had distinguished himself greatly in the Union debating society, and in 1832 was returned by Newark as a Conservative to the reformed parliament. In December 1834 **Peel** appointed him a junior lord of the Treasury, and next year under-secretary for the colonies. When Lord **John Russell** brought forward his motions on the Irish Church, Peel was defeated and resigned, and Gladstone went with him. When Peel returned to office in 1841, Gladstone became vice-president of the board of trade and master of the Mint, and in 1843 president of the board of trade. In February 1845 he resigned because he could not approve of the Maynooth grant; but in December in thorough sympathy with Peel, who had adopted free-trade principles, he rejoined the government as colonial secretary. No longer, however, in political sympathy with the Duke of Newcastle, whose influence had obtained for him the representation of Newark, he gave up his seat, and did not re-enter parliament until the corn-law struggle was over; then, at the general election of 1847 he, still as a Tory, was elected by the University of Oxford. Hitherto he had been the traditional Tory; but the corn-law agitation set him thinking over the defects of the social system. He startled Europe by the terrible description which he gave in 1851 of the condition of the prisons of Naples under King 'Bomba', and the cruelties inflicted on political prisoners. By the death of Peel in July 1850 Gladstone was brought more directly to the front; and he compelled the House of Commons and the country to recognize in him a supreme master of parliamentary debate. His first really great speech in parliament was made in the debate on **Disraeli**'s budget in 1852. On the fall of the short-lived Tory administration, Lord **Aberdeen** formed the famous Coalition Ministry, with **Palmerston** for home secretary, Lord John Russell for foreign secretary and Gladstone for Chancellor of the Exchequer. His speech on the introduction of his first budget was again masterly. The Crimean War broke up the Coalition Ministry; Palmerston became prime minister, and Gladstone retained his office for a short time; but when Palmerston gave way to the demand for the appointment of the Sebastopol committee, Gladstone felt bound to resign. However, he returned as Chancellor in 1850 when Palmerston was again in office. In 1865 South Lancashire returned Gladstone, who, on Lord Palmerston's death and Lord Russell's accession to the premiership, became leader of the House of Commons. A minor reform bill was introduced enlarging the franchise in boroughs and counties. The Conservative party opposed it, and were supported by a considerable section of the Liberals. The bill was defeated: the Liberals went out of office (1866). The serious condition of Ireland, however, and the Fenian insurrection brought the Liberals to power with Gladstone as prime minister in 1868. In his first session he disestablished and disendowed the Irish church; and in the next session he passed a measure recognizing the right of the Irish tenant to compensation for improvements. For the first time in English history a system of national education was established. The Ballot Act was passed for the protection of voters. The system of purchase in the army was abolished by a kind of *coup d'état*. Then Gladstone introduced a measure to improve university education in Ireland. This bill was intended for the benefit of Irish Catholics; but it did not satisfy Catholic demands, Catholic members voted against it, and with that help the Conservatives threw out the bill (1873). Gladstone tendered his resignation, but Disraeli declined to undertake any responsibility, and Gladstone had to remain at the head of affairs. But the by-elections began to tell against the Liberals, Gladstone suddenly dissolved parliament and Disraeli came back to power (1874). For some time Gladstone occupied himself with his literary studies, but the Bulgarian atrocities (1876) aroused his generous anger against the Ottoman power in Europe. Parliament was dissolved in 1880, the Liberals came in with an overwhelming majority, and Gladstone (now member for Midlothian) became prime minister once more. He succeeded in carrying out a scheme of parliamentary reform, which went a long way towards universal male suffrage. But he found himself drawn into a series of wars in North and South Africa; and had to pass coercive measures for Ireland. After Gladstone's government had suffered defeat (June), Lord **Salisbury** came back into office for a few months; but at the general election, the first for the newly-made voters under the Reform Act, Gladstone was returned to office (1886). He made up his mind that the Irish people were in favour of Home Rule, but a split was caused in his party, his bill was rejected and after an appeal to the country he was defeated at the polls. But the general election of 1892 returned him again to office. In 1893 his Home Rule Bill was carried in the Commons, but was thrown out by the Lords. His advanced age made him resign in March 1894. He died at Hawarden, and was buried in Westminster Abbey.

GLAISHER, James (1809–1903) English meteorologist, born in London. He joined the ordnance survey in 1829, and later became chief meteorologist at Greenwich. He made a large number of balloon ascents, once reaching a height of over seven miles to study the higher strata of the atmosphere. He compiled dew-point tables and wrote on several scientific subjects.

GLANVILL, Joseph (1636–80) English philosopher and clergyman, born in Plymouth. After studying at Oxford, he served as vicar of Frome (1662), rector of the Abbey Church in Bath (1666) and prebendary of Worcester (1678). He was a sympathizer with the Cambridge Platonists against the rigid Aristotelianism current in Oxford, and in his famous work *The Vanity of Dogmatising* (2nd edition, 1665) he attacked scholastic philosophy, supported experimental science and appealed for freedom of thought. He dedicated the work to the newly-established Royal Society, of which he had become a fellow in 1664. After his death **Henry More** edited and published his *Sadducismus Triumphatus* (1681) which, surprisingly perhaps, attacked the rationalizing scepticism of those who denied the existence of ghosts, witches and other apparitions of the spirit.

GLANVILL, Ranulf de (d.1190) English jurist, born in Stratford St Andrew, near Saxmundam, chief justiciary of England (1180–89). He was an adviser to **Henry II** and reputed author of the earliest treatise on the laws of England, the *Tractatus de Legibus et Consuetudinibus Angliae* (c.1187), which describes the procedure of the king's courts. In 1174 he raised a body of knights and captured at Alnwick King **William the Lion** of Scotland. He joined the crusade and died at the siege of Acre (1190).The *Tractus* is a brief but lucid exposition of the law, based on the writs which initiated actions, and it is historically very important.

GLANVILLE-HICKS, Peggy (1912–) Australian composer, born in Melbourne, Victoria. She studied at the Conservatorium of Music, Melbourne, at the Royal College of Music, London, and with **Vaughan Williams**, **Nadia Boulanger**, Arthur Benjamin and **Egon Wellesz**. Between 1948 and 1958 she was music critic of the *New York Herald Tribune* and in 1959 she went to Greece where her opera *Nausicaa*, (to a text by **Robert Graves**), was produced for the 1961 Athens Festival. Much of her output has been for theatre and ballet. Other major works include the operas *The Transposed Heads* (story by **Thomas Mann**) and *Sappho* (by **Lawrence Durrell**), an *Etruscan Concerto*, *Letters from Morocco* and *Concerto Romantico*. From 1975 she has been director of Asian studies at Australia Music Centre, Sydney.

GLAPTHORNE, Henry (1610–c.1644) English dramatist, born in Whittlesey. Between 1629 and 1643, he wrote a few poems and some plays, including *Albertus Wallenstein*; *Argalus and Parthenia*, a poetical dramatization of part of the *Arcadia*; *The Hollander* and *Wit in a Constable* (comedies); and *The Ladies Priviledge*. *The Lady Mother* was also attributed to him.

GLAS, John (1695–1773) Scottish sectarian, born in Auchtermuchty, the founder about 1730 of the small religious sect of Glassites or Sandemanians. From 1719 he was minister of Tealing near Dundee. Deposed in 1728, he formed a congregation based on simple apostolic practice. The name Sandemanians was from his son-in-law Robert Sandeman (1718–71). They held that church establishments were unscriptural and that congregations should be self-governing.

GLASER, Donald Arthur (1926–) American physicist, born in Cleveland, Ohio. While working at the University of Michigan (1949–60) he developed the 'bubble chamber' for observing the paths of atomic particles, an achievement which won him the Nobel prize for physics in 1960, the year in which he became professor at the University of California.

GLASGOW, Ellen Anderson Gholson (1874–1945) American novelist, born in Richmond, Virginia. She was best known for her stories of the South, including *The Descendant* (1897), *The Voice of the People* (1900), *Virginia* (1913), and *In This Our Life* (1941, Pulitzer prize).

GLASHOW, Sheldon Lee (1932–) American physicist, born in New York City. He studied at Cornell, Harvard, Copenhagen and Geneva, and became professor of physics at Harvard in 1967. He was a major contributor to theories explaining electromagnetic and nuclear forces, and to the theory of nuclear particles using quarks as fundamental components of nuclei and now known as quantum chromodynamics (QCD). He shared the Nobel prize for physics in 1979, with **Abdus Salam** and **Steven Weinberg**.

GLASPELL, Susan (1882–1948) American writer, born in Davenport, Iowa. She was the author of novels, including *Fidelity* (1915), *Brook Evans* (1928) and *The Fugitive's Return* (1929), also of plays, among them *Trifles* (1917) and *Alison's House* (1930), based on the life of **Emily Dickinson**, which won a Pulitzer prize.

GLASS, Philip (1937–) American composer, born in Baltimore. He studied with **Nadia Boulanger** (1964–66), and the Indian musician **Ravi Shankar**. He was much influenced by Far Eastern music with its static harmonies, the melodic repetition found in North African music, and by rock music. The resulting 'minimalist' style, often cast over long periods with unremitting rhythmic patterns and simple diatonic chords, gained him a huge cult following, especially in such stage works as *Einstein on the Beach* (1976), *Satyagraha* (1980), *Akhnaton* (1984) and *The Making of the Representative for Planet* 8 (1988).

GLAUBER, Johann Rudolph (1604–70) German physician, born in Karlstadt. In 1648 he discovered hydrochloric acid; he was probably the first to produce nitric acid; and he discovered Glauber's salt (sodium sulphate), the therapeutic virtues of which he greatly exaggerated; also acetone, benzine and alkaloids.

GLAZEBROOK, Sir Richard Tetley (1854–1935) English physicist, born in Liverpool. Director of the National Physical Laboratory from 1900, he is known for his work on electrical standards.

GLAZUNOV, Aleksandr Konstantinovich (1865–1936) Russian composer, born in St Petersburg. He studied under **Rimsky-Korsakov**, and was director of the Petersburg Conservatory from 1906 until the revolution of 1917, when the Soviet government gave him the title of People's Artist of the Republic. In 1927 he emigrated to Paris. Among his compositions are eight symphonies and works in every branch except opera.

GLEIG, George Robert (1796–1888) Scottish novelist and historian, born in Stirling, the son of the bishop of Brechin. He studied at Glasgow and Balliol College, Oxford, joined the army, and served in the Peninsular War (1813) and in North America (1814). He took orders (1820), and became chaplain-general of the army (1844) and inspector-general of military schools (1846). He wrote *The Subaltern* (1825) and other novels, and books on military history and biography, especially a Life of **Wellington** (1862).

GLEIM, Johann Wilhelm Ludwig (1719–1803) German poet, born in Ermsleben near Halberstadt. His *Lieder eines Preussischen Grenadiers* contributed to the war poetry of the age of **Frederick II, the Great**.

GLEMP, Jozef (1929–) Polish ecclesiastic. He became bishop of Warmia in 1979 and succeeded Cardinal Stefan Wyszinski as archbishop of Gniezno and Warsaw and primate of Poland after the latter's death in 1981. A specialist in civil and canonical law, Glemp was a prominent figure during Poland's internal political unrest. He was made a cardinal early in 1983.

GLEN, William (1789–1826) Scottish poet, born in Glasgow. He spent most of his life in the West Indies. His only volume of poems and songs, *Poems Chiefly Lyrical*, published posthumously in 1815, contains the popular Jacobite lament, 'Wae's me for Prince Charlie'.

GLENDOWER, or **Glyndwr, Owen** (c.1350–c.1416) Welsh rebel, born in Montgomeryshire, who claimed descent from **Llywelyn ap Gruffudd**. He studied law at Westminster, and became esquire to the Earl of Arundel, but in 1401 fell into dispute with Lord Grey over some lands, and, unable to obtain redress from **Henry IV**, carried on a guerrilla warfare against the English lords of the Marches which became a national war of independence. He proclaimed himself Prince of Wales, and in 1402 captured Lord Grey and Sir Edmund Mortimer, both of whom married Glendower's daughters and joined him in the coalition with **Henry Percy** (Hotspur). That coalition ended in the battle of Shrewsbury (1403), won by King Henry. In 1404 Glendower entered into a treaty with **Charles VI** of France, who in 1405 sent a force to Wales; and the Welsh prince, though often defeated, kept up a desultory warfare till his death about 1416.

GLENN, John Herschel (1921–) American astronaut, born in Cambridge, Ohio, the first American to orbit the Earth. Educated at Maryland University, he joined the US Marine Corps in 1943, and served in the Pacific during World War II, and later in Korea. In 1957 he completed a record-breaking supersonic flight from Los Angeles to New York. He became an astronaut in 1959, and in 1962 made a three-orbit flight in the 'Friendship 7' space capsule. He resigned from the Marine Corps in 1965, and became a senator for Ohio in 1975. He sought the Democratic nomination for the presidency in 1984.

GLEYRE, Charles (1806–74) Swiss painter, born in Chevilly in the Swiss canton Vaud. He studied in Italy, travelled in Greece and Egypt and took over **Delaroche**'s teaching school in Paris. **Monet**, **Renoir** and **Sisley** numbered among his pupils. Much of his work is at Lausanne.

GLINKA, Mikhail Ivanovich (1804–57) Russian composer, born in Novopasskoi, Smolensk. He began life as a civil servant, but a visit to Italy made him eager to study music, which he did in Berlin, returning to Russia to produce his famous opera *A Life for the Tsar* (1836). His *Russlan and Ludmilla* (1847), based on a poem by **Pushkin**, pioneered the style of the Russian national school of composers.

GLISSON, Francis (c.1597–1677) English physician and anatomist. The place and exact date of his birth are unknown, but he matriculated at Gonville and Caius College, Cambridge, in 1617. He remained in Cambridge as a fellow and teacher of Greek, then turned to medicine, obtaining his MD in 1634. He became Regius professor of physic in Cambridge in 1636, though he spent most of his time in London, where he was an early fellow of the Royal Society and president of the Royal College of Physicians of London. Glisson had a successful practice and in addition wrote several substantial monographs, including one on the anatomy and physiology of the liver, and one on rickets, then thought to be a new disease in Britain. He also used the term 'irritability', and **Haller**, when he defined it more precisely, credited Glisson with originating the term.

GLISTRUP, Mogens (1926–) Danish politician. From 1956 to 1963 he was a member of the faculty of law at Copenhagen University. In 1972 he founded the anti-tax Progress party (*Fremskridtspartiet*), which after the general election in 1973 became a right-wing force in Danish politics. Since 1973 he has been a member of the Danish parliament (*Folketinget*).

GLOUCESTER, Gilbert de Clare, 6th Earl of (d.1230) English nobleman, father of the 7th Earl of **Gloucester** also **7th Earl of Clare** and **5th Earl of Hertford**. He brought the house of Clare to the peak of its fortunes, and was one of the 25 barons entrusted with carrying out Magna Carta.

GLOUCESTER, Gilbert de Clare, 8th Earl of (1243–95) also 9th Earl of **Clare** and 7th Earl of **Hertford**, English nobleman, son of Richard de Clare, 7th Earl of **Gloucester** and known as the 'Red Earl'. He sided with **Simon de Montfort** and helped him win the battle of Lewes (1264) against the king's forces; but after quarrelling with de Montfort, he made common cause with Prince Edward (later **Edward I**), and won the battle of Evesham (1265). He married Joan, daughter of Edward 1, and built Caerphilly Castle in Wales.

GLOUCESTER, Gilbert de Clare, 9th Earl of (1291–1314) also 10th Earl of **Clare** and 8th Earl of **Hertford**, English nobleman, the son of Gilbert de Clare, 8th Earl of **Gloucester**. His younger sister, Margaret, was married to **Piers de Gaveston**, the favourite of **Edward II**, and after Gaveston's execution he acted as mediator for the barons with the king. He was killed in the English defeat by the Scots at Bannockburn (1314). Another sister, Lady Elizabeth de Clare (c.1291–1360), endowed Clare College, Cambridge (1336).

GLOUCESTER, Humphrey, Duke of, and **Earl of Pembroke** (1391–1447) English prince and literary patron, the youngest son of King **Henry IV** and protector during the minority of **Henry VI**. He had a distinguished career as a soldier, and also cultivated friendships with literary figures like **Lydgate** and the Italian humanists who supplied him with manuscript books. He later presented these to Oxford University to form the nucleus of a university library. As regent of England (1420-21) and protector (1422-29) he was overshadowed by his younger brother, the Duke of **Bedford**. He was involved in bitter quarrels with his uncle, Cardinal **Henry Beaufort**, whom he tried to deprive of his see. In 1447 he was arrested for high treason on suspicion of plotting against the king's life, and died five days later in custody.

GLOUCESTER, Prince Henry, Duke of (1900–74) prince of the UK, third son of **George V**. Educated privately and at Eton College, he became a captain in the 10th Hussars and was created duke in 1928. In 1935 he married Lady Alice Montagu-Douglas-Scott, and they had two children: Prince William (1941–72) and

Prince **Richard**, who succeeded him. He was governor-general of Australia (1945–47).

GLOUCESTER, Prince Richard (Alexander Walter George), Duke of (1944–) prince of the UK, younger son of Prince Henry, Duke of **Gloucester** and grandson of **George V**. An architect by training, in 1972 he married Brigitte Eva van Deurs, the daughter of a Danish lawyer; they have one son, Alexander, Earl of Ulster (b.1974), and two daughters, Lady Davina Windsor (b.1977) and Lady Rose Windsor (b.1980).

GLOUCESTER, Prince Richard, Duke of See **RICHARD III**

GLOUCESTER, Richard de Clare, 7th Earl of (1222–62) also 8th Earl of **Clare** and 6th Earl of **Hertford**, English nobleman, son of Gilbert de Clare, 6th Earl of **Gloucester**. He was envoy to Scotland (1255) and to Germany (1256); he was twice defeated by the Welsh (1244 and 1257). A supporter of **Simon de Montfort**, he later quarrelled with him.

GLOUCESTER, Robert, Earl of (d.1147) English prince. An illegitimate son of **Henry I**, he was the principle supporter of his half-sister **Matilda**, the 'Empress Maud', in her civil war against **Stephen**.

GLOVER, Julia, née **Betterton** (1779–1850) Irish comic actress, born in Newry. She made her début in 1789, and was sold by her father to Samuel Glover in 1798. In 1802 she appeared at Drury Lane, London, and became a leading lady of the London stage, a successful Mrs Malaprop. Her second son, William Howard (1819–75), was a composer and conductor.

GLOVICHISCH See **CLOVIO, Giulio**

GLUBB, Sir John Bagot (1897–1986) English soldier, known as 'Glubb Pasha', born in Preston, Lancashire. He was educated at Cheltenham College and the Royal Military Academy, Woolwich. After service in the Royal Engineers in World War I, he was the first organizer of the native police force in the new State of Iraq, in 1920. In 1926 he became an administrative inspector in the Iraqi government. In 1930 he was transferred to British-mandated Transjordan, organizing her Arab Legion's Desert Patrol. In 1939 he became commandant of the legion, making it the most efficient Arab army in the middle east (the Jordanian army). He was abruptly dismissed from his post in 1956 following Arab criticism. With immense prestige among the Bedouin, 'Glubb Pasha' was one of the most influential figures in Arabia in the period of British paramountcy. His publications include *The Story of the Arab Legion* (1948), *A Soldier with the Arabs* (1957), *Britain and the Arabs* (1959), *The Course of Empire* (1963), *The Middle East Crisis: A Personal Interpretation* (1967). He also wrote *Into Battle: A soldier's diary of the Great War* (1977).

GLUCK, Christoph Wilibald (1714–87) Austro-German composer, born in Bavaria. After teaching music at Prague, in 1736 he went to Vienna, then in 1738 to Milan, where he studied for four years under San-Martini. In 1741 he wrote his first opera, *Artaserse*, and seven others followed in the next four years. Having achieved some reputation, he was invited in 1745 to London, where a new opera, *La Caduta de' giganti*, was performed, and where his study of **Handel**'s work proved to be the turning point in his career. His next opera shows signs of this new tendency, while some of the music in *Telemacco* (Rome 1750) and *La Clemanza di Tito* (Naples 1751) he afterwards considered good enough to be incorporated in *Armide* and *Iphigénie*. But his style did not mature until in Florence he found Calzabigi, a librettist worthy of his music. In 1762 he produced *Orfeo*, which struck the keynote of modern music drama. *Alceste* followed (1766), and *Paride ed Elena* (1769), the last work written for Vienna before he went to Paris. There his *Iphigénie en Aulide* (1774), and *Orphée*, an adaptation of his earlier *Orfeo*, met with enormous success. The famous Gluck and **Piccinni** war divided Paris into Gluckists and Piccinnists, representing French and Italian opera styles respectively. Gluck finally conquered with his *Iphigénie en Tauride* (1779), and retired from Paris full of honour.

GLUCKMAN, Max Herman (1911–75) South African-born British social anthropologist, born in Johannesburg. He studied at Witwatersrand and Oxford, then carried out field research in southern and central Africa among the Zulu (1936–38), Barotse (1939–47) and Tonga (1944). He was director of the Rhodes-Livingstone Institute, Northern Rhodesia (1941–47), then was a lecturer at Oxford (1947–49) and in 1949 was appointed to the chair of social anthropology at Manchester, becoming research professor in 1971. During this period he built up a distinctive school of social anthropological research with a strong regional focus on central African societies, stressing the role of conflict in the maintenance of social cohesion. His major works were in the anthropology of law, politics and ritual, and included *Custom and Conflict in Africa* (1955), *The Judicial Process among the Barotse of Northern Rhodesia* (1955) and *Politics, Law and Ritual in Tribal Society* (1965).

GLYN, Elinor, née **Sutherland** (1864–1943) British popular novelist, born in Jersey, Channel Islands. She married in 1892. Starting with *The Visits of Elizabeth* (1900), she found fame with *Three Weeks* (1907), a book which gained a reputation for being risqué. *Man and Maid* (1922), *Did She?* (1934), *The Third Eye* (1940)—with such titles she kept her public enthralled. Nonsensical, faulty in construction and ungrammatical, her novels were nevertheless read with avidity. She went to Hollywood (1922–27), where 'it' (her version of sex appeal) was glamorized on the screen. She also wrote an autobiography, *Romance Adventure* (1936).

GLYNDWR, Owen See **GLENDOWER**

GMELIN, Johann Friedrich (1748–1804) German naturalist and physician, nephew of **Johann Georg Gmelin**. He was professor at Tübingen, then Göttingen. He compiled *Onomatologia Botanica* (10 vols, 1772–78), and edited **Linnaeus**'s *Systema Naturae* (1788–93).

GMELIN, Johann Georg (1709–55) German botanist, born in Tübingen. He was professor of chemistry and botany at St Petersburg, then Tübingen. He travelled in Siberia (1733–43), and wrote *Flora Sibirica* (1748–1749), and *Reisen durch Sibirien* (1751–52).

GMELIN, Leopold (1788–1853) German chemist, son of **Johann Friedrich Gmelin**, born in Göttingen. From 1817 to 1850 he was professor of medicine and chemistry at Heidelberg. He discovered potassium ferricyanide, known as *Gmelin's salt*, in 1822, introduced the terms *ester* and *ketone* into organic chemistry and published a textbook of inorganic chemistry (trans 1849). *Gmelin's test* is for the presence of bile pigments.

GMELIN, Samuel Gottlieb (1744–74) German botanist, born in Tübingen, nephew of **Johann Georg Gmelin**. He became professor of botany at St Petersburg (1767), explored the Don, the Volga and the Caspian Sea. He wrote *Historia Fucurum* (1768) and *Reise durch Russland* (1774). He died in the Crimea as a Tartar prisoner.

GNEISENAU, August Wilhelm Anton, Graf Neithardt von (1760–1831) Prussian soldier, born in Schildau in Prussian Saxony. In 1782 he accompanied the German auxiliaries of England to America, in 1786 joined the Prussian army, and in 1806 fought against

Napoleon at Saalfeld and Jena. His gallant defence of Colberg (1807) led to his appointment on the commission with **Scharnhorst** for the reorganization of the Prussian army. In the War of Liberation (1813–14) he rendered distinguished service at Leipzig (1813); in the Waterloo campaign as chief of **Blücher**'s staff he directed the strategy of the Prussian army. In 1831, on the outbreak of the Polish rebellion, he had been made field-marshal and commander of the Prussian army on the Polish frontier, when he died of cholera at Posen.

GÖBBELS, Joseph See **GOEBBELS**

GOBELIN a French family of dyers, probably from Reims, who, about 1450, founded on the outskirts of Paris a factory which later became famous for its tapestry.

GOBINEAU, Joseph Arthur, Comte de (1816–82) French orientalist and diplomat, born in Bordeaux. Secretary to de Toqueville, he was a member of the French diplomatic service (1849–77). He wrote several romances and a history of Persia, but is best known for his essay *The Inequality of Human Races*, and has been called the 'intellectual parent' of **Nietzsche** and the real inventor of the super-man and super-morality.

GODARD, Benjamin Louis Paul (1849–95) French composer and violinist, born in Paris. He studied under **Henri Vieuxtemps**, and is now remembered chiefly for the 'Berceuse' from his opera *Jocelyn*.

GODARD, Jean-Luc (1930–) French film director, born and educated in Paris. He began his career as a cinema critic in 1950, and contributed to *Cahiers du Cinema* from 1952 to 1965. He started making his own short films in 1954 and his first feature film *A Bout de Souffle* (*Breathless*) (1959), established him as one of the leaders of the 'New Wave' of film-making. His elliptical narrative style and original use of jump cuts, freeze frames, and so on, gained him much critical attention, enthusiastic and otherwise. His most notable work from the 1960s includes *Pierrot Le Fou* (1965), *Alphaville* (1965) and *Week-end* (1967). After an unsuccessful trip to America, he submerged himself in 'revolutionary anti-capitalist' films, although he returned to more mainstream concerns in the 80s with *Sauve Qui Peut La Vie* (1980), *Hail Mary* (1985) and the highly idiosyncratic *King Lear* (1987).

GODDARD, Rayner Goddard, Baron (1877–1971) lord chief justice of England (1946–1958). Educated at Marlborough and Trinity College, Oxford, he was called to the bar in 1899, appointed a High Court judge in the King's Bench division in 1932 and became a lord justice of appeal and a privy councillor in 1938. In 1944 he was made a life peer and became a lord-of-appeal-in-ordinary and in 1946 lord chief justice. A strong traditionalist and a believer in both capital and corporal punishment, he stressed that punishment must punish.

GODDARD, Robert Hutchings (1882–1945) American physicist and rocket pioneer, born in Worcester, Massachusetts. Of both scientific and artistic inclinations he developed a strong fascination with the possibilities of flight to Mars when only 17. He studied at Clark University and Princeton, where he published theoretical rocket calculations, and was appointed professor of physics at Clark University (1914–43). He began designing and testing rocket motors in 1914 assisted by funds from the Smithsonian Institution and the US army, and in 1918 demonstrated a tube-launched rocket—later termed the Bazooka. In 1919 his paper, *A Method of Reaching Extreme Altitudes*, included moonflight. In 1926 he launched the first liquid-propelled rocket (9 lb thrust), and in 1927 one of 200 lb thrust. Receiving $50 000 from the Guggenheim Foundation in 1930 he launched rockets at 500 mph to 2000 ft. In 1935 he exceeded the speed of sound. He developed jet vanes and gyroscopic control ten years before the Germans and described the prospects for electric propulsion, a solar-powered generator and electrostatically accelerated jets of ionized gas.

GÖDEL, Kurt (1906–78) Austrian-born American logician and mathematician, born in Brno, Czechoslovakia. He studied and taught in Vienna, then emigrated to the USA in 1940 and joined the Institute for Advanced Study at Princeton. He stimulated a great deal of significant work in mathematical logic and propounded one of the most important proofs in modern mathematics: Gödel's theorem, published in 1931, demonstrated the existence of formally undecidable elements in any formal system of arithmetic (like **Russell**'s in the *Principia Mathematica*).

GODERICH, Viscount See **RIPON, Earl of**

GODFREY, Bob (Robert) (1921–) Australian-born British animated cartoon producer/director, born in New South Wales and brought to England as a baby. After training in animation as a background artist, he made *Watch the Birdie* (1954), a Goonish cartoon which won the *Amateur Cine World* award, and a contract to make television commercials. His first solo short, *Polygamous Polonius* was selected for the 1960 Royal Film Performance; it brought a new bawdy humour to British cartoons, as in his *Henry 9 till 5* (1965), *Kama Sutra Rides Again* (1971), and others which received 'X' (adult) ratings. His musical cartoon, *Great*, the life of **Isambard Kingdom Brunel**, won the Academy Award (1975).

GODFREY, Sir Dan (1868–1939) English conductor, born in London. He conducted opera and symphony concerts throughout Britain and from 1893 to 1934 was director of music to the corporation of Bournemouth and its symphony orchestra. His father, Daniel (1831–1903), was bandmaster of the Grenadier Guards (1856–96). His uncle, Charles (1839–1904), was bandmaster of the Scots Fusiliers and the Royal Horse Guards and professor of military music at the Royal College of Music. Another uncle, Adolphus Frederick (1837–82), was bandmaster of the Coldstream Guards, as was Charles (1790–1863), Sir Dan's grandfather, who founded *Jullien's Journal*, devoted to military music, and was appointed musician-in-ordinary to the king (1831).

GODFREY, Sir Edmund Berry (1622–78) English politician and London woodmonger and JP, knighted in 1666. His unsolved murder, one of the most celebrated of historical mysteries, was made by **Titus Oates** the coping-stone of his 'Popish Plot'.

GODFREY OF BOUILLON (c.1060–1100) French crusader, eldest son of Count Eustace II of Boulogne and Ida of Bouillon. In 1076 he became Count of Verdun and Lord of Bouillon in the Ardennes as heir to his maternal uncle Godfrey (the Hunchback). He had to fight to maintain this inheritance against rival claimants and other local enemies, even after his appointment as Duke of Lower Lotharingia by the emperor **Henry IV** (1089), and in 1096 he sold or mortgaged all of his lands and joined the First Crusade. In July 1099 he was elected ruler of Jerusalem, taking the title of 'Advocate' or Defender of the Holy Sepulchre, and in August defeated an Egyptian invasion at Ascalon. He had begun to extend the territory held by the Christians when he died after a reign of only a year.

GODFREY OF STRASBURG See **GOTTFRIED VON STRASSBURG**

GODIVA, Lady (d.1080) English noblewoman and religious benefactor, wife of Leofric, Earl of Chester (d.1057). According to the 13th-century chronicler

Roger of Wendover, she rode naked through the market-place of Coventry in order to persuade her husband to reduce the taxes he had imposed. A later embellishment of the legend suggests that she requested the townspeople to remain indoors, which they all did except for 'Peeping Tom', who was struck blind. Godiva built and endowed monasteries at Coventry and Stow.

GODLEE, Sir Rickman John (1859–1925) English surgeon, born in London. In 1884 he became the first to remove a tumour of the brain surgically. A nephew of **Joseph Lister**, and his biographer, he was appointed surgeon (1885) and professor (1892) at University College Hospital, London.

GODOLPHIN, Sidney Godolphin, 1st Earl of (1645–1712) English statesman, born in Godolphin Hall near Helston, Cornwall. He became a royal page in 1662, entered parliament in 1668, visited Holland in 1678, and in 1684 was made head of the treasury and Baron Godolphin. On **William III**'s landing in 1688 Godolphin stood by **James II**, and was sent with Halifax and Nottingham to negotiate with William; when James's flight was known, he voted for a regency. Yet in February 1689 William reinstated him as first commissioner of the Treasury. Godolphin was a Tory; and, when William began to replace his Tory ministers by Whigs, Godolphin's turn to go came in 1696. **Anne** on her accession made him her sole lord high treasurer (1702); in 1706 he was created earl. In 1698 he married Henrietta, daughter of the Duke of **Marlborough**. His able management of the finances furnished Marlborough the supplies needed for his campaigns without increasing the public debt by more than one million annually. To prevent his own overthrow, he constrained Anne to dismiss **Harley** (1708); but the influence of Harley's friend and relative, Mrs **Masham**, continuing to increase, and the power of Harley to grow, Godolphin in 1710 was himself dismissed.

GODOWSKY, Leopold (1870–1938) Lithuanian-born American pianist and composer, born in Soshly near Vilna. He toured in Russia as a boy, studied briefly in Berlin when aged 14, and then went to the USA where he spent much of his subsequent life, although often touring to Europe. He became an American citizen in 1891. He worked at the Chicago Conservatory of Music (1895–1900) and was professor at Vienna (1909–14). He was a supremely skilful master of the keyboard, developing the possibilities of the instrument (and left hand technique in particular) to the utmost. However difficult and complex his compositions and many transcriptions may appear to be, they remain innately pianistic.

GODOY, Manuel de, Duke of Alcudia (1767–1851) Spanish statesman, born in Badajoz. A member of **Charles IV**'s bodyguard, he became the royal favourite and was made prime minister in 1792, having encompassed the deposing of **Aranda**. He led Spain into a series of disasters which culminated in the French invasion of 1808, when the king was obliged to imprison him as a protection from popular fury. He subsequently intrigued with **Napoleon** and spent the rest of his life in exile in Rome and Paris, where he died.

GODRIC, St (c.1065–1170) English hermit, born in Norfolk. He worked as a pedlar, mariner (possibly pirate), pilgrim and seer. From 1110, and for the rest of his long life, he lived as a hermit in a hut at Finchale, on the river Wear near Durham.

GODWIN-AUSTEN, Henry Haversham (1834–1923) English soldier and surveyor, son of the geologist Robert Alfred Cloyne (1808–84). A lieutenant-colonel, he was attached to the trigonometrical survey of India (1856–77). The second highest mountain in the world, the Himalayan 'K2', was named after him in 1888.

GODWIN (d.1053) Anglo-Saxon nobleman and warrior, father of King **Harold Godwinsson**. He was probably son of the South Saxon Wulfnoth but later stories make his father a churl. He became a favourite of King **Knut** (Canute), who made him an earl in 1018, and in 1019 became Earl of the West Saxons. In 1042 he helped to raise **Edward 'the Confessor'** to the throne, and married him to his daughter Edith. He led the struggle against the king's foreign favourites, and Edward revenged himself by heaping insults upon Queen Edith, confining her in the monastery of Wherwell, and banishing Godwin and his sons in 1051. But in 1052 they landed in the south of England; the royal troops, the navy and vast numbers of burghers and peasants went over to Godwin; and the king was forced to grant his demands, and reinstate his family. Godwin died at Winchester. His son Harold was for a few months Edward's successor.

GODWIN, Edward William (1833–86) English architect and designer, born in Bristol where he trained and, from 1854, practised as an architect. Northampton Town Hall (1861) dates from his early Gothicist period. In 1865 he moved his practice to London. His mainly domestic architecture included the White House (1877), a studio house in Chelsea for his friend **Whistler**. A central figure in the 'Aesthetic Movement', his furniture designs after 1875 were much influenced by the Japanese taste which that movement made fashionable. Much of it, in ebonized pine, was remarkably advanced in its simple unornamented structure. He was also a theatrical designer, dress reformer and journalist. He was the lover of **Ellen Terry**; their son was **Edward Gordon Craig**.

GODWIN, Fay Simmonds (1931–) English photographer, born in Berlin, the daughter of a diplomat. Educated in numerous schools worldwide, she began by taking photographs of her two young sons but has become best known for her landscapes, including Welsh and Scottish scenes. Since 1970 she has worked as a freelance photographer, based in London. Her many publications include *The Oldest Road* (1975, co-authored with J R C Anderson).

GODWIN, Francis (1562–1633) English prelate and author, born in Hannington, Northamptonshire, the son of bishop Thomas Godwin (1517–90). Educated at Oxford, he became rector of Sampford, bishop of Llandaff (1601) and of Hereford (1617). His eight works include *A Catalogue of the Bishops of England* (1601), but he is best known for his science-fiction romance, *Man in the Moon or a Voyage Thither, by Domingo Gonsales* (1638), used as a source by Bishop **John Wilkins**, **Cyrano de Bergerac** and **Swift**.

GODWIN, Sir Harry (1901–85) English botanist/ecologist. A pioneer of British pollen analysis, he was professor of botany at Cambridge, 1960- -68. His works include *Plant Biology* (1930) and *The History of the British Flora* (1975).

GODWIN, Mary Wollstonecraft See **Wollstonecraft, Mary**

GODWIN, William (1756–1836) English political writer and novelist. Born at Wisbech, he passed his boyhood at Guestwick in Norfolk. After three years at Hindolveston day school, three more with a tutor at Norwich, and one as usher in his former school, in 1773 he entered Hoxton Presbyterian College; in 1778 left it as pure a Sandemanian and Tory as he had gone in. But during a five years' ministry at Ware, Stowmarket and Beaconsfield, he turned Socinian and republican, and by 1787 was a 'complete unbeliever'.

Meanwhile he had taken up writing. The French Revolution gave him an opening, and his *Enquiry Concerning Political Justice* (1793) brought him fame and a thousand guineas, and captivated **Coleridge**, **Wordsworth**, **Southey**, and later and above all **Shelley**, who became his disciple, son-in-law and subsidizer. It was calmly subversive of everything (law and 'marriage, the worst of all laws'), but it deprecated violence, and was deemed caviare for the multitude, so its author escaped prosecution. His masterpiece, *The Adventures of Caleb Williams* (1794), was designed to give 'a general review of the modes of domestic and unrecorded despotism'; unlike most novels with a purpose, it is really a strong book. In 1897 he married **Mary Wollstonecraft**, who was pregnant by him; but she died soon after the baby was born. Four years later he married Mrs Clairmont, who had two children already, and a third was born of the marriage. So there were poor Fanny Imlay (1794–1816), who died by her own hand; Mary Wollstonecraft Godwin (1797–1851), who in 1816 married Shelley; Charles Clairmont; 'Claire' Clairmont (1797–1879), the mother by **Byron** of Allegra; and William Godwin (1803–32). A bookselling business long involved Godwin in difficulties, and in 1833 he was glad to accept the sinecure post of yeoman-usher of the Exchequer. His tragedy, *Antonio* (1800), was hopelessly damned. The best of his later prose works are *The Enquirer* (1797) and *St Leon* (1799).

GOEBBELS, Joseph (1897–1945) German Nazi politician. The son of a Rhenish factory foreman, he was educated at a Catholic school and the Gymnasium. A deformed foot absolving him from military service, his attainment of a number of scholarships enabled him to attend eight universities. Indigent and adrift, he became **Hitler**'s enthusiastic supporter, and was appointed editor of the Nazi sheet *Voelkische Freiheit*. With the Führer's accession to power 'Jupp' was made head of the ministry of public enlightenment and propaganda, an assignment he fulfilled with conspicuous ability. Vain and ruthlessly ambitious, he was a less ostentatious spendthrift than **Goering**, while his numerous amours did nothing to impoverish his infinite capacity for work. A bitter anti-Semite, his undoubted gift of mob oratory made him a powerful exponent of the more radical aspects of the Nazi philosophy. Wartime conditions greatly expanded his responsibilities and power, and by 1943, while Hitler was running the war, Goebbels was virtually running the country. A schizophrenic, alternating wishful thinking with hard-headed realism, he retained Hitler's confidence to the last, and like his Führer chose immolation for himself and his family rather than surrender.

GOEBEL, Karl von (1855–1932) German botanist, born in Billigheim, Baden. A distinguished plant morphologist, he was successively professor in Rostock, Marburg and Munich. He wrote *Organographie der Pflanzen* (1898–1901), and founded the botanical institute and gardens at Munich.

GOEHR, (Peter) Alexander (1932–) German-born English composer, born in Berlin, the son of a conductor. Brought to England in 1933, he studied at the Royal Manchester College (1952–55) and in Paris. He was professor of music at Leeds University (from 1971) and at Cambridge (since 1976). His compositions include the operas *Arden Must Die* (1967) and *Behold the Sun* (1985), concertos, choral, orchestral and chamber music.

GOEPPERT-MAYER, Maria née **Goeppert** (1906–72) German-born American physicist, born in Kattowitz (now Katowice in Poland). She graduated at Göttingen in 1930, emigrated to the USA and taught at Johns Hopkins University, where her husband, Joseph Mayer, was professor of chemical physics. From 1960 she held a chair at the University of California. She was awarded (with **Eugene Paul Wigner** and **Hans Jensen**) the Nobel prize for physics in 1963 for research on nuclear shell structure.

GOERDELER, Carl (1884–1945) German politician, born in Schneidemühl. He served under **Hitler** as commissar for price control (1934), but resigned from his mayoralty of Leipzig in 1937 and became one of the leaders of opposition to Hitler, culminating in **Stauffenburg**'s unsuccessful bomb plot of 20 July 1944, for which Goerdeler was executed together with a number of generals.

GOERING, Hermann Wilhelm (1893–1946) German politico-military leader, born in Rosenheim, Bavaria. In World War I he was one of the first infantry officers to fight on the western front. In 1915 he transferred to the air force, became an ace pilot and later commanded the famous 'Death Squadron'. In 1922 he joined the Nazi party and next year commanded the **Hitler** storm troopers, but had to go into exile for five years after the failure of the November Munich putsch. In 1928 he became one of the twelve Nazi deputies to the Reichstag. In the troubled economic crisis years his influence increased and in 1932 he became president of the Reichstag. When Hitler assumed power in 1933 Goering entered the Nazi government, his several posts including that of Reich commissioner for air. An early exploit of his as Hitler's chief lieutenant was the instigation of the Reichstag fire, his pretext for outlawing his communist opponents. The evil genius of Nazism, he founded the Gestapo, set up the concentration camps for political, racial and religious suspects, and, in the great purge of 30 June 1934, had his comrades murdered. Two years later the international phase of his career opened when he mobilized Germany for total war under the slogan 'Guns Before Butter'. When the Munich ('peace in our time') Agreement was made in 1938, he thoughtfully announced a five-fold extension of the Luftwaffe. Early in 1940 he became economic dictator of Germany and in June reached the pinnacle of his power when Hitler made him marshal of the Reich, the first and only holder of the rank. But the Battle of Britain, the failure of the 1941 Nazi bombing attacks to disrupt the British ports and cities, and the mounting Allied air attacks on Germany in 1942 and 1943 led to a decline in his prestige. By the time of the Allied liberation of Normandy in 1944 he was in disgrace. As the war drew to a close, he attempted a palace revolution. Hitler condemned him to death, but he escaped and was captured by US troops. In 1946 he was the principal defendant at the Nuremberg War Crimes Trial when his record of unscrupulous intrigue and merciless oppression was laid bare. He was condemned for guilt 'unique in its enormity', but committed suicide by poison on 15 October a few hours prior to his intended execution.

GOETHALS, George Washington (1858–1928) American engineer, born in Brooklyn, New York. He was chief engineer of the Panama Canal (1907–1914), and civil governor of the Canal Zone (1914–16).

GOETHE, Johann Wolfgang von (1749–1832) German poet, dramatist, scientist and court official, born in Frankfurt-am-Main. He was educated privately and studied reluctantly for his father's profession, law, at Leipzig (1765–68), but a love affair with Käthchen Schönkopf inspired his first two plays, *Die Laune des Verliebten* (1767) and *Die Mitschuldigen*, which was, however, not staged until 1787. After a protracted illness he continued his law studies at Strasbourg from 1770 where he came under the influence of **Herder**, the pioneer of German Romanticism. He read **Goldsmith**'s *Vicar of Wakefield* and dabbled in alchemy, anatomy and the antiquities. Another love affair, with Friedericke Brion, inspired 'Röslein auf der Heide' and several fine lyrics. In 1771 he qualified, returned to Frankfurt, became a newspaper critic and captured the thwarted spirit of German nationalism in that early masterpiece of *Sturm und Drang* drama, *Götz von Berlichingen*, which in the person of the chivalrous robber-knight whose values had outlived his age, epitomized the man of genius at odds with society. *Faust* was begun, and Goethe followed up his first triumph with his self-revelatory cautionary novel, *Leiden des jungen Werthers* (1774), which mirrored his hopeless affair with Charlotte Buff, a friend's fiancée. Werther is made to solve the problem of clashing obligations by nobly and romantically committing suicide. Goethe himself, however, 'saved himself by flight'. *Clavigo*, a Hamlet-like drama followed in the same vein, based on **Beaumarchais**' *Mémoires*. Lili Schönemann inspired the love lyrics of 1775. In the autumn he surprisingly accepted the post of court-official and privy councillor (1776) to the young Duke of Weimar. He conscientiously carried out all his state duties, interested himself in a geological survey, and taken in hand, emotionally, by the young widow, **Charlotte von Stein**, exerted a steadying influence on the inexperienced duke. His ten-year relationship with Charlotte did little to help his development as a creative writer, valuable as his 'anchor' might have seemed to him psychologically. In 1782 he extended his scientific researches to comparative anatomy, discovered the intermaxillary bone in man (1784), and formulated a vertebral theory of the skull. In botany he developed a theory that the leaf represented the characteristic form of which all the other parts of a plant are variations, and made foolish attempts to refute **Newton**'s theory of light. He wrote a novel on theatrical life, *Wilhelm Meisters Theatralische Sendung*, not discovered until 1910, which contains the enigmatic poetry of Mignon's songs, epitomizing the best in German romantic poetry, including the famous 'Nur wer die Sehnsucht kennt'. His visits to Italy (1786–88 and 1790) cured him of his emotional dependence on Charlotte von Stein and contributed to a greater preoccupation with poetical form, as in the severely classical verse version of his drama, *Iphigenie* (1789), and the more modern subjects *Egmont* (1788) and *Tasso* (1790). His love for classical Italy, coupled with his passion for Christiane Vulpius, whom he married in 1806, found full expression in *Römische Elegien* (1795). From 1794 dates his friendship with **Schiller**, with whom he conducted an interesting correspondence on aesthetics (1794–1805) and carried on a friendly contest in the writing of ballads which resulted on Schiller's part in *Die Glocke* and on Goethe's in the epic idyll *Hermann und Dorothea* (1798). They wrote against philistinism in the literary magazine *Horen*. Goethe's last great period saw the prototype of the favourite German literary composition, the *Bildungsroman* in *Wilhelm Meisters Lehrjahre* (1796) continued as *Wilhelm Meisters Wanderjahre* (1821–29). *Wilhelm Meister* became the idol of the German Romantics, of whom Goethe increasingly disapproved. He disliked their enthusiasm for the French Revolution, which he satirized in a number of works, including the epic poem *Reineke Fuchs* (1794), based on a medieval theme, and the drama *Die natürliche Tochter* (1803), and their disregard for style, which he attempted to correct by example in his novel *Die Wahlverwandtschaften* (1809) and the collection of lyrics, inspired by Marianne von Willemer, *West-östlicher Divan* (1819). But his masterpiece is his version of **Marlowe**'s drama of *Faust*, on which he worked for most of his life. Begun in 1775, the first part was published after much revision and Schiller's advice in 1808, and the second part in 1832. The disillusioned scholar, Faust, deserts his 'ivory tower' to seek happiness in real life, makes a pact with Satan, who brings about the love-affair, seduction and death of Gretchen, an ordinary village girl, and subtly brings Faust by other such escapades to the brink of moral degradation. Part one is generally regarded as one of the classics of world literature. Goethe took little part in the political upheavals of his time. Yet **Napoleon** made a point of meeting Goethe at the congress of Erfurt (1803), and Goethe in 1813 kept aloof from the *Befreiungskriege*, having identified Napoleon with the salvation of European civilization. Goethe was buried near Schiller in the ducal vault at Weimar, a towering influence on German literature.

GOETZ VON BERLICHINGEN See **GÖTZ**

GOFFE, William (c.1605–1679) English regicide, born at Stanmer rectory, Sussex. He became major-general in the parliamentary army, sat in the House of Commons, and signed **Charles I**'s death-warrant. In 1660 he fled to America, lived for many years in seclusion at Hadley, Massachusetts, and died at Hartford.

GOFFMAN, Erving (1922–82) Canadian-born American sociologist, born in Alberta. He was educated at the universities of Toronto and Chicago, and from 1949 to 1951 he carried out research at Edinburgh University. He then returned to Chicago, before serving as a visiting scientist at the National Institute for Mental Health from 1954 to 1957. In 1958 he joined the department of sociology at the University of California, Berkeley, remaining there until 1968, when he moved to Pennsylvania University. Renowned for his work on patterns of human communication, he was particularly interested in the way in which people present themselves to each other, and what happens when they deviate from accepted norms. His later work was concerned with language. His books include *Asylums* (1961), *Stigma* (1963), *Behavior in Public Places* (1963), *Relations in Public* (1972) and *Forms of Talk* (1981).

GOGOL, Nikolai Vasilievich (1809–52) Russian novelist and dramatist, born in Sorochinstsi in Poltava. In 1829 he settled in St Petersburg, and in 1831–32 published his first major work, *Evenings on a Farm near Dikanka*, followed by two collections of short stories, *Mirgorod* and *Arabesques* (1835) which contained some of his finest stories, like *The Overcoat*, *Nevsky Prospect*, and *The Diary of a Madman*, which introduce a nightmarish world of Gogol's fantastic imagination, exemplifying his irrational fears, frustrations and obsessions. In 1836 he brought out his play, *The Inspector-General*, the best of Russian comedies, a wild and boisterous satire exposing the corruption, ignorance and vanity of provincial officials. He left Russia for Italy in 1836, and in Rome wrote the first part of *Dead Souls* (1842), one of the great novels in world literature. It deals with an attempt by small landowners to swindle the government by the purchase of dead serfs whose names should have been struck off the register. His later work shows increasing obsession with his own sinfulness and he burnt many of his remaining manuscripts, including the second part of *Dead Souls*. He returned to Russia in 1846.

GOKHALE, Gopal Krishna (1866–1915) Indian politician, born in Kolhapur. He became professor of history at Fergusson College, Poona, resigning in 1904, when he was selected representative of the Bombay legislative council at the supreme council, eventually becoming president of congress in 1905. He was a leading protagonist of Indian self-government within the empire and influenced **Gandhi**.

GOLD, Thomas (1920–) Austrian-born American astronomer, born in Vienna. He studied at Cambridge and worked in the UK before moving to the USA in 1956. While in England he worked with Hermann Bondi and **Fred Hoyle** on the steady-state theory of the origin of the universe (1948); the theory was later to be displaced through new evidence, but it was a valuable contribution to cosmology. In 1959 he became director of the Center for Radiophysics and Space Research at Cornell University, and in 1968 he suggested that pulsars (discovered by **Bell**, **Burnell** and **Hewish** in that year) are rapidly rotating neutron stars, as was later confirmed. He also offered an individualistic theory of the origin of petroleum and natural gas on Earth, arguing that some major deposits are of non-biological origin, and arise from gas trapped in the Earth's interior from the time of the planet's formation.

GOLDBERGER, Joseph (1874–1929) Hungarian-born American physician and epidemiologist, born in Girált. He went to the USA as a child and qualified in medicine (1895) at the Bellevue Hospital Medical College in New York City. After private medical practice he joined the United States Public Health Service (1899), where he investigated the mechanisms of the spread of a number of infectious diseases, including measles, typhus and yellow fever. His brilliant epidemiological studies of pellagra within institutions in the southern USA demonstrated that pellagra is a nutritional disorder caused by an imbalanced diet and cured by the addition of fresh milk, meat or yeast. The deficiency was later shown to be niacin, one of the vitamin B complex.

GOLDING, Louis (1895–1958) English novelist and essayist. His best-known work is *Magnolia Street* (1932), the story of a typical street in a provincial city whose inhabitants were Jews on one side, Gentiles on the other.

GOLDING, William Gerald (1911–) English novelist, born in St Columb Minor, Cornwall. He was educated at Marlborough Grammar School and Brasenose College, Oxford, where—after first taking examinations in botany, zoology, chemistry and physics—he revolted against science and transferred to English literature, devoting himself to Anglo-Saxon. After five years at Oxford he published his first book, *Poems* (1934), a rarity which he now disowns. He spent the next five years working in small theatre companies, as an actor, director and writer, and in 1958 he adapted the short story 'Envoy Extraordinary' for the stage as *The Brass Butterfly*. He married in 1939 and spent the war years in the Royal Navy. From 1945 to 1961 he was a teacher of English and philosophy at Bishop Wordsworth's School, Salisbury, a career he detested. He gained international celebrity with *The Lord of the Flies* (1954), which has become a classroom classic. A chronicle of the increasingly tribal and primitive activities of a group of schoolboys wrecked on a desert island in the wake of a nuclear war, Golding has said that it arose from his five years' war service, and ten years of teaching small boys. *The Inheritors* (1955) was his second novel and in theme and tone it is the blood-brother of its predecessor, human malevolence surfacing through mob-atrocity and in the arena of power. Next came *Pincher Martin* (1956), *Free Fall* (1959), *The Spire* (1964) and *The Pyramid* (1967). There was a gap of twelve years before *Darkness Visible* (1979), during which he wrote short stories, a film script and aborted novels. In recent years he has returned to his old productivity. With *Rites of Passage* (1980), the first of a trilogy about a 19th-century voyage from England to Australia, he won the Booker prize. *Close Quarter* (1987) was its sequel and the trilogy closed with *Fire Down Below* (1989). His only other novel is *The Paper Men* (1984). In 1983 he was awarded the Nobel prize for literature.

GOLDMAN, Emma, known as **Red Emma** (1869–1940) Lithuanian-born American anarchist, born in Kaunas, of Jewish parents. She was brought up in East Prussia, but moved in 1882 to St Petersburg (Leningrad), where she worked in a glove factory and absorbed prevailing nihilist ideas. She emigrated to the USA in 1885, where she worked in the garment industry and joined the anarchists in New York who were protesting against the unjust executions of four of their number for the Haymarket bomb-throwing on 4 May 1886 in Chicago. She was active in anarchist agitation against tyrannical employers, and was jailed in 1893 for incitement to riot in New York. She founded and edited the anarchist monthly *Mother Earth* (1906–17) in partnership with Alexander Berkman, who had in 1892 attempted to assassinate **Henry Clay Frick**. Winning international celebrity through her stirring speeches and her visits to anarchist congresses in Paris (1899) and Amsterdam (1907), she worked extensively in American urban slums, but in 1917 was fined $10 000 and sentenced to two years imprisonment for opposing registration of military recruits, and in 1919 was deported to the USSR (to which she was ideologically opposed). She returned to the USA in 1924, supported the anarchists in the Spanish Civil War, and published an autobiography *Living My Life* (1931) and several other works, including *Anarchism and Other Essays* (1910) and *My Disillusionment in Russia* (1923).

GOLDMARK, Carl (1830–1915) Hungarian composer, born in Keszthely. He studied in Vienna and composed *Die Königin von Saba* (1875), *Merlin* (1886) and other lavishly colourful operas, two symphonies, two violin concertos and other works. His nephew Rubin (1872–1936), the American composer, taught **Copland** and **Gershwin**.

GOLDMARK, Peter Carl (1906–77) Hungarian-born American engineer and inventor, born in Budapest. He studied at the Universities of Vienna and Berlin, then emigrated to the USA in 1933 and found employment in the laboratories of the Columbia Broadcasting System, where he developed the first practical colour television system, used for experimental transmissions in New York in 1940. He led the team that invented the long-playing microgroove record in 1948, and later built a special type of camera for the lunar orbiting space vehicle which transmitted very high definition pictures of the moon's surface back to the earth.

GOLDONI, Carlo (1707–93) Italian dramatist, born in Venice. He studied for the law, but his heart was set on writing plays. A tragedy, *Belisario* (1732), proved a success; but he soon discovered that his forte was comedy, and he decided to write for the Italian comic stage. He spent several years in wandering over north Italy, until in 1740 he settled in his birthplace, where for 20 years he poured out comedy after comedy. He wrote no fewer than 250 plays in Italian, French and the Venetian dialect. He was greatly influenced by **Molière** and the *commedia dell' arte*, although many of his subjects are derived from direct observation of daily life. His best-known plays are *La Locandiera* (1753), *I Rusteghi* (1760), which provided the plot for *The*

School for Fathers produced in London in 1946, and *Le Baruffe Chiozzotte* (1762). In 1762 he undertook to write for the Italian theatre in Paris, and was attached to the French court until the revolution. He published his *Mémoires* in 1787.

GOLDSCHMIDT, Berthold (1903–) German-born composer, he fled from Nazi Germany to London in 1935. A younger contemporary of many avant-garde composers, he had a promising career in Germany, and became artistic adviser to **Karl Ebert** at the Berlin City Opera. In 1932 his first opera was premiered at Mannheim: *Der gewaltige Hahnrei* (The Magnificent Cuckold). After his escape to London he composed his 2nd String Quartet in 1936, expressing the sorrow of his race. In 1951 he was one of four winners in a competition for a new opera sponsored by the Arts Council for the Festival of Britain, but neither his opera (*Beatrice Cenci*) nor any of the others was performed. An expert on the music of **Gustav Mahler**, in 1960 he helped to complete Mahler's unfinished 10th symphony, and conducted its first performance in London in 1988.

GOLDSCHMIDT, Hans (1861–1923) German chemist, born in Berlin. He invented the highly inflammable mixture of finely divided aluminium powder and magnesium ribbon (thermite). The high temperatures attained make this useful for welding (Thermit process) and incendiary bombs.

GOLDSCHMIDT, Madame See **LIND, Jenny**

GOLDSCHMIDT, Meier Aaron (1819–87) Danish journalist and novelist, born in Vordingborg of Jewish parentage. He founded a satirical peridical, *Corsaren*, in 1840. His best-known novels are *En Jöde* (1845, translated as *The Jew of Denmark*), and *Hjemlös* (*Homeless*, 1853–57). He also wrote his autobiography (1877).

GOLDSCHMIDT, Richard Benedikt (1878–1958) German biologist, born in Frankfurt-am-Main. He was appointed biological director of the Kaiser-Wilhelm Institute, Berlin, in 1921, and in 1935 went to the USA where he became professor of zoology at California University (1936–58). He conducted experiments on X-chromosomes, using butterflies, and was the author of the theory that it is not the qualities of the individual genes, but the serial pattern of the chromosomes and the chemical configuration of the chromosome molecule that are decisive factors in heredity. Among his books are *Die Lehre von der Vererbung* (1927), *Die sexuellen Zwischenstufen* (1931), *Physiological Genetics* (1938), *The Material Basis of Evolution* (1940), and *Theoretical Genetics* (1955).

GOLDSCHMIDT, Victor Moritz (1888–1947) Swiss-born Norwegian chemist, born in Zürich, regarded as the founder of modern geochemistry. The son of a physical chemist, he graduated from Christiania (now Oslo) University in 1911, and stayed to become the director of the Mineralogical Institute there when he was 26. In 1929 he moved to Göttingen, but returned six years later when the Nazis came to power. In Norway he was imprisoned by the Germans as a Jew, but escaped to Sweden in a haycart and went to England in 1943. His success was in applying physical chemistry to mineralogy. Using X-ray techniques he worked out the crystal structure of over 200 compounds and 75 elements, and made the first tables of ionic radii. In 1929 he postulated what is now known as Goldschmidt's law: that the structure of a crystal is determined by the ratio of the numbers of ions, the ratio of their sizes, and polarization properties. This work enabled him to predict in which minerals and rocks various elements could be found.

GOLDSMITH, Oliver (1728–74) Irish playwright, novelist and poet, born in Pallasmore, County Longford, Ireland, the son of the curate of Kilkenny West. Educated at local schools and Trinity College, Dublin, he was rejected for the church, and thereupon started for America, but got no farther than Cork. He was next equipped with £50 to study law in London: this disappeared at a Dublin gaming-table. In 1752 he went to Edinburgh to study medicine, and stayed there nearly two years, but was more noted for his social gifts than his professional acquirements. He drifted to Leiden, again lost at play what money he had, and finally set out to make the 'grand tour' on foot, living on his wits and as a flute-playing 'busker', returning penniless in 1756. For a time he practised as a poor physician in Southwark, then was proof reader to **Richardson**, and next an usher in Dr Milner's 'classical academy' at Peckham. Ralph Griffiths of the *Monthly Review* retained him for a few months and in February 1758 appeared his first definite work, a translation of the Memoirs of Jean Marteilhe, a persecuted French Protestant. He next wrote an *Enquiry into the Present State of Polite Learning in Europe* (1759), which attracted some notice, and better days dawned for Goldsmith. He started and edited a weekly, *The Bee* (1759), and contributed to *The Busy Body* and *The Lady's Magazine*. Then came overtures from **Smollett** and **John Newbery** the bookseller. For Smollett's *British Magazine* he wrote some of his best essays; for Newbery's *Public Ledger* he wrote the *Chinese Letters* (1760–71; republished as *The Citizen of the World*). In 1764 the 'Literary Club' was founded, and he was one of its nine original members. His anonymous *History of England* was followed by *The Traveller*, a poem which gave him a foremost place among the poets of the day. *The Vicar of Wakefield* (1766) secured his reputation as a novelist. *The Good Natur'd Man*, a comedy (1768), was a moderate success. But he again escaped from enforced compilation of histories with his best poetical effort, *The Deserted Village* (1770). Three years afterwards he achieved high dramatic honours with *She Stoops to Conquer*. A year later he died of a fever. He was buried in the Temple Churchyard, and the club erected a monument to him in Westminster Abbey. In the year of his death were published the unfinished rhymed sketches called *Retaliation*, and in 1776 *The Haunch of Venison*.

GOLDSTEIN, Eugen (1850–1930) German physicist, born in Gleiwitz, Silesia. He worked at the Berlin Observatory, discovered in 1876 the shadows cast at right angles to cathode rays and in 1886 the 'canal rays' — which were later shown to be positively charged particles of atomic mass.

GOLDSTEIN, Joseph Leonard (1940–) American molecular geneticist, winner of the 1985 Nobel prize for physiology or medicine. Educated at Texas University in Dallas, he researched biomedical genetics at the National Heart Institute (1968–70) and Washington University, Seattle (1970–72), and was appointed professor at Texas in 1972. His researches, with **Michael Brown**, into cholesterol metabolism and the discovery of low-density LDL receptors brought their joint award of the Nobel prize in 1985.

GOLDWATER, Barry Morris (1909–) American Republican politician, born in Phoenix, Arizona, the son of a Jewish father of Polish descent and a Protestant Episcopalian mother. He was educated at Arizona University and served as a ferry pilot during World War II. He worked at Goldwater's Stores in Phoenix, Alabama, becoming president 1937–53, marketing a popular brand of men's undergarments, before representing his home state in the senate (1953–65). A conservative 'main street' Republican, he supported **Joseph McCarthy** and opposed President **Eisenhower** and state intervention in economic affairs. He contested the 1964 presidential election for the Republicans, but was heavily defeated by **Lyndon B Johnson**. Returning to the senate in 1969, he chaired the Armed Services Commission, before retiring in 1986. Many of his ideas were later adopted by the Republican 'New Right' and implemented by the **Reagan** administration.

GOLDWYN, Samuel, originally **Goldfish** (1882–1974) Polish-born American film producer, born of Jewish parents in Warsaw. At the age of eleven, an orphan, he ran away to relatives in England, and again at thirteen to the USA. After working as a glove-salesman, he founded a film company with a depressed playwright, **Cecil B de Mille**, as director and produced *The Squaw Man* (1913). In 1917 he founded the Goldwyn Pictures Corporation, in 1919 the Eminent Authors Pictures and finally in 1925 the Metro-Goldwyn-Mayer Company, allying himself with the United Artists from 1926. His 'film-of-the-book' policy included such films as *Bulldog Drummond* (1929), *All Quiet on the Western Front* (1930), *Stella Dallas* (1937) and *Wuthering Heights* (1939). He also produced *Little Foxes* (1941), *The Best Years of Our Lives* (1946, Academy Award), *The Secret Life of Walter Mitty* (1947), *Guys and Dolls* (1955) and *Porgy and Bess* (1959). His Goldwynisms are celebrated, such as 'include me out'.

GOLGI, Camillo (1843–1926) Italian cytologist, born in Corteno, Lombardy. Professor of pathology at Pavia (1876–1918), he discovered the 'Golgi bodies' in animal cells which, through their affinity for metallic salts, are readily visible under the microscope, and opened up a new field of research into the central nervous system, sense organs, muscles and glands. He shared with **Ramón y Cajal** the 1906 Nobel prize for physiology or medicine.

GOLITSYN See **GALLITZIN**

GOLLANCZ, Sir Hermann (1852–1930) German-born British rabbi and scholar, brother of Sir **Israel Gollancz**, born in Bremen. An authority on Hebrew language and literature, he became professor at University College London (1902–24), and was preacher at the Bayswater synagogue (1892–1923). He was the first British rabbi to be knighted (1923), sat on several government commissions and did much philanthropic work.

GOLLANCZ, Sir Israel (1864–1930) English scholar, brother of Sir **Hermann Gollancz**, born in London. In 1906 he was appointed professor of English literature at University College, London. An authority on early English texts, he was a founder and first secretary of the British Academy.

GOLLANCZ, Sir Victor (1893–1967) English publisher, author and philanthropist, born in London into a family of Jewish businessmen. He was educated at St Paul's School and New College, Oxford, where he won the Chancellor's prize for Latin prose. As a young man he was in revolt against his home and against orthodox Judaism, which he eventually rejected. He was for a time a master and military instructor at Repton School, but went into publishing in 1920 and in 1928 founded his own firm. But he was best known for his innumerable campaigns and pressure group activities. In 1919 he was secretary of the Radical Research Group and in 1936 he founded the Left Book Club which was to have an enormous influence on the growth of the Labour party. During World War II he helped to get Jewish refugees out of Germany, but as soon as the war ended he worked hard to relieve starvation in Germany and tried to oppose the view that the Germans should share in the collective guilt for the crimes committed by the Nazis. In the same spirit he founded the Jewish Society for Human Service which had Arab relief as the first of its aims. He also vigorously launched national campaigns for the abolition of capital punishment and for nuclear disarmament.

GOLTZ, Colmar, Freiherr von der (1843–1916) German soldier, known as 'Goltz Pasha', born in Bielkenfeld. He reorganized the Ottoman army (1883–95), then returned to Germany, where he became a field marshal (1911). In World War I he was military governor of Belgium after its conquest (1914), then took command of the Turkish army in Mesopotamia, and despite his age, repulsed the Allied forces seeking to relieve Kut-el-Mara. He died of cholera shortly before the British surrender at Kut under Sir **Charles Townshend**. He wrote *Nation in Arms* (1883).

GOMARUS, or **Gommer, Francis** (1563–1641) Dutch Calvinist theologian, born in Bruges. As divinity professor at Leiden (1594) he became known for his hostility to his colleague, **Arminius**. At the synod of Dort (1618) he secured the Arminians' expulsion from the Reformed Church. From then until his death he was professor at Groningen.

GOMBERG, Moses (1866–1947) Russian-born American chemist, born in Elisabetgrad, in the Ukraine. In 1884 he emigrated to the USA and was educated at Michigan, Munich and Heidelberg, and became professor at Michigan (1904–36). He is famous for his discovery of organic free radicals.

GOMBRICH, Sir Ernst Hans Josef (1909–) Austrian-born British art historian, born in Vienna, the son of a lawyer father and a pianist mother. He studied at the university of Vienna (PhD, 1933), then emigrated to Britain, where he joined the staff of the Warburg Institute, London, in 1936, becoming its director and professor of the history of the classical tradition from 1959 until he retired in 1976. During World War II he worked for the BBC Monitoring Service. His books include *The Story of Art* (1950), *Art & Illusion* (1960)—a most influential study of the psychology of pictorial representation—and *The Sense of Order* (1979).

GOMPERS, Samuel (1850–1924) English-born American labour leader, born in London. He went to USA in 1863, and helped to found the American Federation of Labor, of which he was long president.

GOMULKA, Wladyslaw (1905–) Polish Communist leader, born in Krosno, South East Poland. A local trade union leader, he organized during World War II underground resistance to the Germans and took an active part in the defence of Warsaw. In 1943 he became secretary of the outlawed underground Communist party. He became vice-president of the first postwar Polish government, but from 1948 was gradually relieved of all his posts for 'non-appreciation of the decisive role of the Soviet Union' and arrested in 1951. But for **Stalin**'s death in 1953, he would have been executed. Later in 1954 he was released from solitary confinement. He was rehabilitated in August 1956 and returned to power as party first secretary in October—thus preparing the way for a new course for Polish society. He was re-elected to this post in 1959. Braving the risk of a 'Stalinist' military putsch, Gomulka sought to put Poland on the road to a measure of freedom and independence, allowing freer discussion within a Marxist framework. In 1971, following a political crisis, he resigned office.

GONÇALVES, Nuno (fl.1450–72) Portuguese painter. He is recorded, in 1463, as court painter to **Alfonso V**. He was virtually forgotten until the discovery of his only extant work, an altarpiece for the convent of St Vincent (the patron saint of Portugal) in 1882. This work was exhibited in Paris in 1931 and established him as the most important Portuguese painter of the 15th century. The altarpiece—comprising six panels—contains many portraits of the court and nobles and, in style, shows the influence of contemporary Flemish painting, most notably that of **Bouts**.

GONCHAROV, Ivan Alexandrovich (1812–91) Russian novelist, born in Simbirsk. He graduated from Moscow University (1834), led an uneventful life in the civil service and wrote *Oblomov* (1857; trans 1915), one of the greatest and most typical works of Russian realism. His other two novels fail to attain the same heights.

GONCHAROVA, Natalia Sergeyevna (1881–1962) Russian-born French painter and designer, born in Ladyzhino, Tula province, south of Moscow. She began as a science student but turned to sculpture c.1898, studying at the Moscow Academy of Art. She began painting in 1904 and, like **Mikhail Larionov** (whom she lived with and eventually married on her 74th birthday) and **Kasimir Malevich**, liked the flat colours and primitive forms of Russian folk art, combining these with the new influences of Cubism and Fauvism with an original flair. She moved to Geneva in 1915 with Larionov to design for **Diaghilev**'s ballets, and went to Paris in 1921. She took French nationality in 1938.

GONCOURT, Edmond de and **Jules de** (1822–96) (1830–70), French novelists, born in Nanay and Paris respectively. Primarily artists, in 1849 they travelled across France making watercolour sketches and taking notes of everything they saw. Their important work began when, after collaborating in studies of history and art, especially Japanese art, they turned to writing novels. Their subject was not the passions but the manners of the 19th century combined with a sense of the enormous influence of environment and habit upon man. The first of their novels, *Les Hommes de Lettres* (1860; new ed as *Charles Demailly*), was followed by *Soeur Philomème* (1861), *René Mauperin* (1864), *Germinie Lacerteux* (1865), *Manetts Salomon* (1867), and *Madame Gervaisais* (1869), their greatest novel. After Jules's death, Edmond published the extraordinarily popular *La Fille Élisa* (1878), *La Faustin* (1882), and *Chérie* (1885). The interesting *Idées et Sensations* (1886) had already revealed their morbid acuteness of sensation, and *La Maison d'un artiste* (1881) had shown their love for *bric-à-brac*. In the *Lettres de Jules de Goncourt* (1885) and in the *Journal des Goncourt* (9 vols, 1888–96) they revealed their methods and their conception of fiction. Edmond, in his will, founded the Goncourt Academy to foster fiction with the annual Prix Goncourt.

GÓNGORA Y ARGOTE, Don Luis de (1561–1627) Spanish lyric poet, born in Córdoba. He studied law, but in 1606 took orders and became a prebendary of Córdoba, and eventually chaplain to **Philip III**. His earlier writings are elegant and stylish. His later works, consisting for the most part of longer poems, such as *Solidades*, *Polifemo*, *Piramo y Tisbe*, are written in an entirely novel style, which his followers designated the *stilo culto*.

GONNE, Maud See **MacBRIDE**

GONVILLE, Edmund See **CAIUS, John**

GONZAGA a princely north Italian family named from a small town in the province of Mantua, who ruled Mantua for three centuries, and from 1432 were marquises, from 1530 dukes of Mantua. They were the champions of the imperial interests, and were always at war with the Visconti Dukes of Milan. The tenth and last Duke of Mantua, who had sided with the French, was deprived by the emperor **Joseph I** of his estates, and died in exile in 1708. The Dukes of Montferrat were a branch of the Gonzagas.

GONZAGA, Luigi, known as **St Aloysius** (1568–91) Italian Jesuit, and the patron saint of youth. The eldest son of the Marquis of Castiglione, near Brescia, he renounced his title to become a missionary and entered the Society of Jesus in 1585. When Rome was stricken with plague in 1591 he devoted himself to the care of the sick, but was himself infected and died. He was canonized in 1726, and in 1926 was declared the patron saint of Christian youth by Pope **Pius XI**. His feast day is 21 June.

GONZAGA, Tomás António, pseud **Dirceu** (1744–1809) Portuguese poet, born in Oporto of an English mother and a Brazilian father. He studied for the law, and was sent to Vila-Rica in 1782 where he met the 'Marilia' of his verses. He was exiled to Mozambique for his revolutionary activities. There he married a rich mulatta and became a leading citizen of Mozambique. His *Marilia de Dirceu* (1792) contains the best verses in the Arcadian tradition apart from **Bocage**, and they are considered masterpieces of the Mineiro school.

GONZALES, Pancho (Ricardo Alonzo) (1928–) American tennis player, born in Los Angeles. He won the US singles in 1948 and 1949, and the doubles at both Wimbledon and France in 1949, when he turned professional. As tennis was still predominantly amateur, this effectively sidelined him, but, with an elegance of touch complemented by a very strong service, he was indisputably the world's leading player for most of the 1950s. In 1969 he took part in the longest-ever men's singles match at Wimbledon, playing 112 games to defeat fellow-American, Charlie Pasarell.

GONZÁLEZ, Felipe (1942–) Spanish politician, prime minister since December 1982. Born in Seville, he studied law and practised as a lawyer, joining the Spanish Socialist Workers' party (PSOE), then an illegal organization, in 1962. The party regained legal status in 1977, three years after González became secretary-general. González persuaded the PSOE to adopt a more moderate, less overtly Marxist line, and in the general elections of 1982, they won a substantial overall majority to become the first left-wing administration since the Socialist-led coalition of 1936. In 1986 he and his party were re-elected for another term.

GONZÁLEZ, Julio (1876–1942) Spanish sculptor, born in Barcelona, where he studied. In 1900 he went to Paris, joining the avant-garde circle around **Picasso**. He began as a painter, but in 1927 turned to sculpture, mainly in wrought and welded iron. Like Picasso he was inspired initially by African masks, and worked in a Cubist style, but also had links with Surrealism. He made a life-size figure of a peasant mother (1936–37), a symbol of popular resistance in the Spanish Civil War, for the Paris Exposition Universelle.

GONZALVO DE CÓRDOBA, Hernández (1453–1515) Spanish soldier, known as 'the Great Captain', born in Montilla near Córdoba. He served with distinction against the Moors of Granada, and afterwards in Portugal. Sent to assist **Ferdinand 'the Catholic'** (Ferdinand III of Naples) in his Holy League against the French (1495), he conquered the greater part of the kingdom of Naples, and expelled the French. When the partition of Naples was determined upon in 1500, Gonzalvo again set out for Italy, but first took Zante and Cephalonia from the Turks, and restored them to the Venetians. He then landed in Sicily, occupied Naples and Calabria, and demanded from the French that they should keep the compact. This demand being rejected, war was waged with varied success; but ultimately Gonzalvo won a great battle (1503) at the Garigliano river, which by careful planning and tactics he crossed five miles above Minturno, at a spot where in 1943 the 56th British Division found a crossing. His victory secured Naples for Spain. Recalled in 1506, and treated by the king with neglect, Gonzalvo withdrew to his estates in Granada.

GOOCH, Sir Daniel (1816–89) English engineer, born in Bedlington, Northumberland. He was early associated with the **Stephensons** in railway construction, became locomotive superintendent of the Great Western Railway (1837–64), and then distinguished himself in submarine telegraphy by laying the first Atlantic cable (1865–66). His three brothers, Thomas Longridge (1808–82), John Veret (1812–1900) and William Frederick (b.1825) were also civil or locomotive engineers.

GOOCH, George Peabody (1873–1968) English historian, born in London. Liberal MP for Bath (1906–10), and editor of the *Contemporary Review* (1911–60), he was the author of *English Democratic Ideas in the 17th century* (1898), *Germany and the French Revolution* (1920), *Studies in Diplomacy and Statecraft* (1942) and other works on political and diplomatic history.

GOODALL, Frederick (1822–1904) English artist, born in London, son of the engraver Edward Goodall (1795–1870). He is remembered for his subject pictures *Raising the Maypole* (1851), *Cranmer at the Traitors' Gate* (1856), etc.

GOODE, George Brown (1851–96) American ichthyologist, born in New Albany, Indiana. On the staff of the Smithsonian Institute in Washington from 1827, he was US fish commissioner (1887–1888) and author of *American Fishes* (1888) and *Oceanic Ichthyology* (1895).

GOODHART, Arthur Lehman (1891–1978) American jurist, born in New York, and educated at the Hotchkiss School and Yale University. He lived most of his life in England, becoming professor of jurisprudence at Oxford and master of University College there (1951–63). His major scholarly work was his editorship of the *Law Quarterly Review* (1926–75) to which he contributed many valuable articles and a stream of perceptive case notes examining recent decisions analytically and critically but constructively. He also published a few small books on legal theory.

GOODMAN, Benny (Benjamin David) (1909–86) American clarinettist and bandleader, born in Chicago to a poor immigrant family. A musical prodigy, he was working in dance bands by the age of 13, joining the Ben Pollack Orchestra at 15. Goodman formed his own orchestra in New York in 1934 and, thanks to media exposure became one of the best-known leaders of the era with the soubriquet 'King of Swing'. Hiring top black musicians such as pianist Teddy Wilson and vibraphone-player **Lionel Hampton**, Goodman successfully defied racial taboos of the time. He led a succession of large and small bands for three decades, occasionally performing as a classical player, and was noted for his technical facility and clean tone.

GOODMAN, Isador (1909–82) South African-born Australian pianist and composer, born in Cape Town. He studied at the Royal College of Music, London, and appeared in concerts in England and Europe before emigrating to Australia in 1930 where he taught at the New South Wales Conservatorium of Music. For the next 50 years he performed in recital and as a soloist with leading orchestras, in concert and for television and radio. In 1944 he wrote his *New Guinean Fantasy* on that island at the height of the battle there. Goodman was a renowned exponent of the romantic repertoire, and especially of **Rachmaninov** and **Liszt**. He played Liszt's first piano concerto in London at the age of 14 with Sir **Malcolm Sargent** and made his Australian début with the same work in 1930.

GOODRICH, Samuel Griswold, pseud **Peter Parley** (1793–1860) American publisher, born in Ridgefield, Connecticut. He edited in Boston *The Token* (1828–42) to which he contributed moralistic poems, tales and essays for children and in which the best of **Hawthorne**'s 'Twice-told Tales' appeared. He published some 200 volumes, mostly for the young as 'Peter Parley' books, starting with *The Tales of Peter Parley about America* (1827).

GOODRICKE, John (1764–86) English astronomer, born in Groningen. Despite being deaf and mute from an early age, he first accounted for variable stars. He was awarded the Copley Medal of the Royal Society in 1783.

GOODSIR, John (1814–67) Scottish anatomist, born in Anstruther. He studied at St Andrews and Edinburgh, where he became professor of anatomy in 1846. He is best known for his work in cellular theory.

GOODYEAR, Charles (1800–60) American inventor, born in New Haven, Connecticut. Having failed as an iron-manufacturer, in 1834 he began research into the properties of rubber. Amid poverty and ridicule he pursued the experiments which ended, in 1844, in the invention of vulcanized rubber, which led to the development of the rubber-manufacturing industry and the production of the well-known tyres named after him.

GOOGE, Barnabe (1540–94) English poet, born in Alvingham in Lincolnshire. He studied both at Cambridge and Oxford, travelled on the Continent, and became one of the gentlemen-pensioners of Queen **Elizabeth**. His best works are a series of eight *Eclogues* (1563) and his *Cupido Conquered*.

GOOSSENS, Eugène (1845–1906) Belgian conductor, born in Bruges. He studied at the Brussels Conservatoire and became a conductor of several opera companies in Belgium, France and Italy before making his name in comic opera with the Carl Rosa Company in Britain from 1873. He founded the Goossens Male Voice Choir in Liverpool in 1894.

GOOSSENS, Eugène (1867–1958) Belgian violinist and conductor, son of **Eugène Goossens** (1845–1906), born in Bordeaux. He studied at the Brussels Conservatoire and at the Royal Academy of Music, London, played with the Carl Rosa Company under his father (1884–86) and with the orchestra at Covent Garden (1893–94). He was principal conductor of the Carl Rosa Company (1899–1915).

GOOSSENS, Sir Eugene (1893–1962) English composer and conductor, son of **Eugène Goossens** (1867–1958), born in London. He studied in Bruges and London, and became associate conductor to Sir **Thomas Beecham** in his opera seasons. In 1921 he gave a highly successful series of orchestral concerts, in which he brought out some of his own music. From 1923 to 1945 he worked in America, as conductor of the Rochester (New York) Philharmonic Orchestra and of the Cincinnati Symphony Orchestra. Appointed conductor of the Sydney Symphony Orchestra and director of the New South Wales Conservatory in 1947, he had a profound influence in Australia both on standards of performance and the training of musicians. His own music, which includes the operas *Judith* (1929) and *Don Juan de Mañara* (1937), a large-scale oratorio *The Apocalypse*, and two symphonies, was critically acclaimed.

GOOSSENS, Léon (1897–1988) English oboist, brother of Sir **Eugene Goossens**, born in Liverpool. He studied at the Royal College of Music and, after 1913, held leading posts in most of the major London orchestras, retiring from orchestral work to devote himself to solo playing and teaching. His sisters Marie (1894–) and Sidonie (1899–) were well-known harpists.

GÖRANSSON, Göran Fredrik (1819–1900) Swedish industrialist and engineer. He made the Bessemer process of producing steel a practical possibility in 1858. He was one of the founders of the Sandviken Iron Works company in 1868 and under his leadership it achieved international repute. His son Henrik and grandson Fredrik succeeded him in turn as directors of the company.

GORBACHEV, Mikhail Sergeevich (1931–) Soviet communist politician, born in Privolnoye village in the North Caucasus region, the son of an agricultural mechanic. After distinguishing himself at school, he was sent to Moscow University to study law in 1950. Here he met and married a philosophy student, Raisa (1933–), before returning to Stavropol to work for the Communist party (CPSU), which he had joined in 1952. He was appointed regional agriculture secretary in 1962 and, after taking an external degree at the Stavropol Institute of Agriculture, emerged as an imaginative reformer, but strict disciplinarian. He became Stavropol party leader in 1970 and, having impressed his influential fellow countryman, **Yuri Andropov**, was brought into the CPSU secretariat as agriculture secretary in 1978. He was promoted to full membership of the politburo in 1980 and in 1983, following Andropov's election as party general-secretary, took broader charge of the Soviet economy. During the **Chernenko** administration (1984–85) he established himself as the second-ranking figure in what was a 'dual key' administration and was swiftly appointed party general-secretary after Chernenko's death. He soon made his presence felt as party leader, forcing the retirement of obstructive colleagues and bringing into the politburo and secretariat a new group of younger technocrats, more supportive of his vision of reform. He also introduced a major campaign against alcoholism and corruption during 1985–86 and, after strongly criticizing the **Brezhnev** era, unveiled, under the slogans *glasnost* ('openness') and *perestroika* ('restructuring'), a series of 'liberalizing' economic, political and cultural reforms with the aim of making the Soviet economy and society more efficient and open. Overseas he launched a new 'detente offensive', meeting the US president **Ronald Reagan** in a series of summits (1985-88) and signing an Intermediate Nuclear Forces (INF) abolition treaty in 1987, and in 1989 sanctioned the USSR's military withdrawal from Afghanistan, and its progressive disengagement from eastern Europe. He was elected head of state in 1988, and became an executive president, with increased powers, in 1990. He has sought to transform the USSR into a new 'socialist pluralist' democracy, but has encountered internal opposition from party conservatives, radicals, and successionist-minded nationalists, particularly in the Baltic republics.

GORCHAKOV, Prince Alexander Michaelovich (1798–1883) Russian statesman, cousin of Prince **Michale Gorchakov**, born in St Petersburg in 1798, ambassador at Vienna (1854–56), succeeded **Nesselrode** as foreign minister. As chancellor of the empire (1863) he was, till **Bismarck**'s rise, the most powerful minister in Europe. He secured Austrian neutrality in the Franco-German war of 1870, and in 1871 absolved Russia from the treaty of Paris (1856). After the conclusion of the Russo-Turkish war, the repudiation of the treaty of San Stefano, and the signing of the treaty of Berlin his influence began to wane, and he retired in 1882. He died at Baden-Baden.

GORCHAKOV, Prince Michael (1795–1861) Russian soldier, cousin of Prince **Alexander Gorchakov**. He served against the French in the Napoleonic campaign of 1812–14, and in the Russo-Turkish war of 1828–29. He helped to suppress the Polish revolution of 1831 and took part in the capture of Warsaw, and helped suppress the Hungarian insurrection in 1849. On the outbreak of the Crimean war (1853–56) he commanded in the Danubian Principalities, and, now commander-in-chief in the Crimea (1855), was defeated on the Tchernaya, but recovered his laurels by his gallant defence of Sebastopol. He was military governor of Poland from 1856 to 1861.

GORDIAN I, properly **Marcus Antonius Gordianus** (158–238) roman emperor in 238, grandfather of **Gordian III**, was twice consul, and next proconsul of Africa. During a rebellion in Africa against the emperor Maximinus, Gordian, then in his 80th year, was proclaimed emperor conjointly with his son Gordian II (238) but committed suicide a month later when the latter was slain in a battle near Carthage by Capellianus, governor of Numidia.

GORDIAN III, known as **Gordianus Pius** (c.224–244) Roman emperor, grandson of **Gordian I**. He was elevated by the Praetorians to the rank of Augustus in 238. In 242 he marched against the Persians and relieved Antioch, but was assassinated by his own soldiers.

GORDIMER, Nadine (1923–) South African novelist, born in Springs, Transvaal. She was educated at a convent school, and at the University of the Witersrand, Johannesburg. One of the world's premier novelists in English, her work is rooted in South Africa, where she has continued to live. Her first book was a collecton of short stories, *Face to Face* (1949), followed by another collection, *The Soft Voice of the Serpent* (1952). In 1954 she married, as her second husband, Reinhold Cassirer, a Jewish refugee from Nazi Germany. In 1953 had come her first novel, *The Lying Days* in which a white girl triumphs over the provincial narrowness and racial bigotry of her parents' mining village existence, though she too has to come to terms with the limitations of her social background. This recurrent theme dominated Gordimer's early books, such as *Occasion for Loving* (1963) and *The Late Bourgeois World* (1966). Apartheid, and her character's reaction to it, is ever present in her fiction, most powerfully in *The Conservationist* (1974), joint winner of the Booker prize. Other important titles are *A Guest of Honour* (1970), *Burger's Daughter* (1979), *July's People* (1981), and *A Sport of Nature* (1987), in which a self-possessed white girl is transformed into a political activist intent on returning Africa to the rule of the Africans. Much fêted, she has received many awards, including the Malaparte prize from Italy, the Nelly Sachs prize from Germany, the Scottish Arts Council's Neil Gunn Fellowship and the French international award, the Grand Aigle d'Or.

GORDON-CUMMING, Roualeyn George (1820–66) British lion hunter. He undertook those famous hunting exploits narrated in his *Five Years of a Hunter's Life* (1850).

GORDON name of a Scottish family which takes its origin and name from the lands of Gordon in Berwickshire and whose members became Lords of Strathbogie from 1357, Earls of Huntly from 1445,

Marquesses of Huntly from 1599 and Dukes of Gordon from 1684 until 1836, when the title became extinct. Its 157 branches include the Lochinvar line (Viscounts Kenmure from 1633, extinct in 1847), the Earlston branch, a cadet branch of the latter, and according to tradition the Earls of **Aberdeen** are descended from an illegitimate brother of Sir Adam of Gordon, killed at Homildon in 1402.

GORDON, Alexander, 4th Duke of Gordon (c.1745–1827) Scottish nobleman. He was the author of the well-known song, 'Cauld Kail in Aberdeen'. His wife, the sprightly Jane Maxwell (c.1749–1812), was known as the 'beautiful Duchess of Gordon'.

GORDON, George, 2nd Earl of Huntly (d.c.1502) Scottish nobleman, and high chancellor of Scotland (1498–1501). He married Princess Annabella, daughter of **James I** of Scotland. Their second son married the Countess of Sutherland and was progenitor of the Earls of Sutherland. Their third son was progenitor of the turbulent Gordons of Gight, from whom **Byron**'s maternal ancestors were descended.

GORDON, George, 4th Earl of Huntly (1514–62) Scottish nobleman and high chancellor of Scotland. He supported Cardinal **Beaton** against Arran (1543), but when stripped by the crown of his new earldom of Moray rushed into revolt and was killed at Corrichie.

GORDON, George, 6th Earl, and **1st Marquis of Huntly** (1562–1636) Scottish nobleman, head of the Roman Catholics in Scotland. He defeated at Glenlivet a royal force under the Earl of Argyll in 1594, but, submitting to the king, was pardoned and made Marquis in 1599.

GORDON, Lord George (1751–93) English anti-Catholic agitator, born in London. He was educated at Eton, entered the navy and retired as lieutenant in 1772. Elected MP in 1774, he attacked both sides. An act of 1778 having brought Roman Catholics relief from certain disabilities, Lord George, as president of a Protestant association, headed (2 June 1780) a mob of 50000 persons, who marched in procession to the House of Commons to present a petition for its repeal. For five days, serious rioting took place during which many Catholic chapels and private houses, Newgate, and the house of the chief-justice, Lord Mansfield, were destroyed. On the 7th the troops were called out, and 285 of the rioters were reported killed, 173 wounded and 139 arrested, 21 being executed. Property to the value of £180000 was destroyed in the riots. Lord George was tried for high treason; but Erskine's defence got him off. He subsequently turned Jew, calling himself Israel Abraham George Gordon. In 1787 he was convicted for a libel on **Marie Antoinette**, fled to Holland, was extradited and taken to Newgate, where he died of gaol fever.

GORDON, Adam Lindsay (1833–70) popular Australian poet, born in Fayal in the Azores where his mother's father had a plantation. He completed his education in England but vanished to Australia after a series of reckless adventures and joined the mounted police. He bought a cottage called Dingly Dell, married, but continued to pursue his equestrian exploits. However, a series of mishaps—a riding accident causing severe head injuries, a fire that precipitated bankruptcy and the death of his infant daughter—caused him to move to Melbourne where he committed suicide. He is remembered for ballads that reflect his interest in horses: 'The Sick Stockrider', 'How We Beat the Favourite' and 'The Ride From the Wreck'. Much of his best work is collected in *Sea Spray and Smoke Drift* (1867) and *Bush Ballads and Galloping Rhymes* (1870). He is the only Australian poet honoured in the poets' corner of Westminster Abbey.

GORDON, Charles George (1833–85) English soldier, known as 'Chinese Gordon' born in Woolwich. He entered the Royal Military Academy, Woolwich, in 1847, and the Royal Engineers in 1852. He served before Sebastopol from January 1855 to the end of the siege; and was engaged in surveying the new frontiers between Turkey and Russia (1856–57). In 1860 he went to China and took part in the capture of Peking and the destruction of the Summer Palace. In command of a Chinese force (1863–64), he fought 33 actions against the Taipings and took numerous walled towns, effectually crushing the formidable rebellion—a feat that placed 'Chinese Gordon' in the foremost rank of the soldiers of his day. From 1865 he was for six years engaged in ordinary engineering duties at Gravesend, devoting his spare moments to relieving the want and misery of the poor, visiting the sick, teaching, feeding and clothing the waifs and strays. He was on the Danube Navigation Commission (1871–72). In 1873 he accepted employment under **Ismail Pasha**, Khedive of Egypt, and took up Sir **Samuel White Baker**'s work of opening up the vast regions of the equatorial Nile. A chain of posts was established along the Nile, steamers were placed above the last of the rapids, and the navigation of Lake Albert was successfully accomplished; but realizing that his efforts to suppress the slave trade must remain unsuccessful unless his power extended to the vast plain countries lying west of the Nile basin, Gordon returned to England in 1876. Going out again in 1877, he was appointed governor of the Sudan, from the Second Cataract of the Nile to the Great Lakes, and from the Red Sea to the head-waters of the streams that fall into Lake Chad. During the next three years, fever-wracked and surrounded by enemies, he reconnoitred this vast territory; his feats of government and engineering astounded the world. But in 1880, his health undermined, he resigned; he made a short visit to India and China, and the close of 1880 found him in Ireland propounding a scheme of land-law improvement. For a year he volunteered to take another officer's duty in Mauritius, and from Mauritius proceeded to the Cape in colonial employment, finally returning to England at the close of 1882. Almost the whole of 1883 was spent in Palestine in quiet and reflection. Early in 1884 he was asked by the British government to proceed once more to the Sudan to relieve the garrisons in Egypt which were in rebel territory. A month after he reached Khartoum it was invested by the troops of the Mahdi (Mohammed Ahmed). The siege had lasted five months when a relief expedition was organized in England. In September the advance up the Nile began, and early in November the troops entered the Sudan and the advance guard arrived on 28 January 1885, in the neighbourhood of Khartoum. It was too late. The palace had been taken two days earlier, and Gordon had been murdered on the palace steps. The national memorial is the Gordon Boys' School at Woking. There are memorials of him in St Paul's Cathedral and elsewhere.

GORDON, Cyrus Herzl (1908–) American Hebrew scholar, born in Philadelphia. He graduated at the University of Pennsylvania and taught Hebrew there before becoming field archaeologist in Bible lands with the American Schools of Oriental Research (1931–35). Thereafter he taught at Johns Hopkins University, Princeton, Dropsie College and Brandeis University before retirement in 1973. He said his life was motivated by 'transmitting the growing historic tradition along with the spirit of scientific enlightenment'. His books include *The Living Past* (1941), *Adventures in the Near East* (1957), and various technical handbooks on Ugaritic.

GORDON, David (1936–) American dance-choreographer, born in Brooklyn, New York and noted for his often humorous experimentation. He studied painting before he began dancing with James Waring's company in New York (1958–62). He was a founding member (1962) of the seminal Judson Dance Theatre and, in the following decade, the improvisational dance-theatre collective Grand Union. In 1974 he formed his own Pick-Up Company. Several of his works are in the repertories of major American and British classical and modern dance companies. He is married to the English-born ex-**Cunningham** dancer, Valda Setterfield.

GORDON, James See **GORDON, Robert**

GORDON, Sir John Watson (1788–1864) Scottish painter, born in Edinburgh. A pupil of **Raeburn**, he succeeded him in 1823 as the leading portrait painter of Scotland. His portraits of **Macaulay**, the Prince of Wales and many others are in the Scottish National Gallery and **De Quincey** in the National Portrait Gallery, London.

GORDON, Noele (1922–85) English actress, born in East Ham, London. She made her first stage appearance at the age of two in a concert staged by the Maud Wells Dancing Academy. After studying at RADA she worked in repertory and pantomime before such London successes as *Diamond Lil* (1948) and *Brigadoon* (1949–51). She assisted **John Logie Baird** with his early experiments in colour television and first appeared on that medium in *Ah, Wilderness* (1938). She later studied television techniques in the USA, and returned to Britain as an adviser to ATV and host of such series as *Lunch Box* (1955) and *Fancy That* (1956). She became a household name as the owner of the motel in the television soap-opera *Crossroads* (1964–81). Unceremoniously dismissed from the series, she returned to the stage in barnstorming musicals like *Gypsy* (1981), *Call Me Madam* (1982–83) and *No, No Nanette* (1983).

GORDON, Patrick (1635–99) Scottish soldier of fortune, born in Easter Auchleuchries, Aberdeenshire. A Catholic, at 16 he entered the Jesuit College of Braunsberg, but absconded in 1653, eventually joining the Swedish army during the war with Poland in 1655. During the next six years he was repeatedly captured and every time fought for his captors until retaken. In 1661 he joined the Russian army and rose to high rank. Although he was sent on missions to Britain in 1665 and 1685, he did not succeed in his desire to return to Scotland permanently. Under Tsar **Peter the Great** he was made general in 1688, crushed a conspiracy in 1689 and a serious revolt in 1698.

GORDON, Robert (1580–1661) Scottish cartographer, of Straloch. Along with his son, James (c.1615–1686), who was minister of Rothiemay, Banffshire, he revised and edited **Timothy Pont**'s Scottish maps for **Willem Blaeu's** *Atlas*. The son also wrote *Scots Affairs* 1624–51 (Spalding Club, 1841). A grandson, Robert Gordon (1665–1732), founded a boys' school, Robert Gordon's College, in Aberdeen.

GORE, Catherine Grace Frances, née **Moody** (1799–1861) English novelist, born in East Retford, Nottinghamshire. She was a prolific and immensely popular writer of novels, mainly of fashionable life, such as *Mothers and Daughters* (1831), *Mrs Armytage* (1836) and *The Banker's Wife* (1843). She also wrote three plays.

GORE, Charles (1853–1932) Anglican prelate and theologian, and nephew of the 4th Earl of Arran. Educated at Harrow and Oxford, he became fellow of Trinity College, Oxford in 1875 and first principal of Pusey House in 1884. His contribution to *Lux Mundi* (1889) abandoned the strict tractarian view of biblical inspiration, and his Bampton Lectures (1891) were equally controversial. He founded at Pusey House in 1892 the Community of the Resurrection, and became bishop successively of Worcester (1901), Birmingham (1904) and Oxford (1911–19).

GORE, Spencer Frederick (1878–1914) English painter, born in Epsom, Surrey. He studied at the Slade School of Art during its most creative period, (1896–99), and joined the New English Art Club in 1909. He was a founder member and first president of the Camden Town Group (1911), and became a member of the London Group in 1913. He met **Sickert** in Dieppe in 1904 and was inspired to paint theatre and music hall subjects, using a quasi-Pointilliste technique learnt from **Lucien Pissarro**. In 1912 he contributed to **Roger Fry**'s Second Post-Impressionist exhibition.

GOREN, Charles Henry (1901–) American contract bridge expert and author, born in Philadelphia. He practised law in Philadelphia until 1936, when he abandoned law to concentrate on bridge. As a masterful player, he put his knowledge into print with numerous books, including *Winning Bridge Made Easy* (1936) and *Contract Bridge in a Nutshell* (1946). He also wrote on backgammon (*Goren's Modern Backgammon Complete*, 1974), and contributed a daily newspaper column, syndicated in the USA.

GORGAS, William Crawford (1854–1920) American military doctor, born near Mobile, Alabama. He established a great reputation as an epidemiologist by his extermination of yellow fever in Havana in 1898, and in the Panama Canal Zone before and during construction of the waterway.

GÖRGEI, Arthur (1818–1916) Hungarian rebel soldier, born in Toporcz, North Hungary. During the revolt of 1848 he compelled Jellachich and his 10000 Croats to capitulate at Ozora. As Hungarian commander-in-chief he relieved Komorn by inflicting a series of severe defeats on the Austrians, practically driving them out of the country. In 1849 he was repeatedly defeated and in August surrendered with his army of 24000 men to the Russians at Világos near Arad. Görgei was imprisoned at Klagenfurt, but was eventually set free and returned to Hungary in 1868.

GORGES, Sir Ferdinando (c.1566–1647) English colonist in America, born in Ashton in Somerset. He founded two Plymouth companies (1606–19 and 1620–35) for planting lands in New England. In 1639 he received a charter constituting him proprietor of Maine. His grandson sold his rights to Massachusetts in 1677.

GORGIAS (c.490–c.385 BC) Greek philosopher and rhetorician, born in Sicily, one of the 'sophists' who were professional itinerant teachers of oratory and political skills. He came to Athens as ambassador in 427 and quickly became a celebrity for his public performances. His philosophy was an extreme form of scepticism or nihilism: that nothing exists, that if it did it would be unknowable, that if it were knowable it would be incommunicable to others; we live in a world of opinion, manipulated by persuasion. He is memorably portrayed in **Plato**'s dialogue, the *Gorgias*, where he and **Socrates** debate the morality implicit in his teachings and activities.

GORIA, Giovanni (1943–) Italian politician, born in Asti, in the Piemonte region, where he became provincial secretary of the Christian Democratic party (DC). He was elected to the Chamber of Deputies in 1976 and held a number of ministerial posts in DC-led coalition governments before being made Treasury minister in 1982. In 1987, after a near constitutional crisis had been averted, when the socialists withdrew their support for the Christian Democrats, Goria accepted the challenge of forming another coalition which he led until it collapsed in March 1988.

GÖRING, Hermann Wilhelm See **GOERING**

GORKY, Arshile, originally **Vosdanig Manoog Adoian** (1905–48) Armenian-born American painter, born in Khorkom Vari in Turkish Armenia. Emigrating to the USA in 1920, he studied at the Rhode Island School of Design and in Boston, moving to New York in 1925. His art combined ideas from the European Surrealists who had fled to New York in the early 1940s and from biomorphic abstraction (eg, **Joan Miró**), and he played a key role in the emergence of the New York school of Action Painters in the 1940s.

GORKY, Maxim, pen-name of **Aleksei Maksimovich Peshkov** (1868–1936) Russian novelist, born in Nizhni Novgorod (now Gorky). He was successively pedlar, scullery boy, gardener, dock hand, tramp and writer, a restless nomadic life he described brilliantly in his autobiographical trilogy, *Childhood* (1913–14), *In the World* (1915–16) and *My Universities* (1923). He first achieved fame with his story *Chelkash* (1895), followed by others in a romantic vein, glorifying the unusual, with vividly drawn characters, mostly tramps and down-and-outs. *Foma Gordeyev* (1899) marks his transition from romanticism to realism. In 1902 he produced his best-known play, *The Lower Depths*. Involved in strikes and imprisoned in 1905, he lived abroad until 1914 and then engaged in revolutionary propaganda. From 1922 to 1928 he lived abroad again on account of his health, but then returned, a wholehearted supporter of the Soviet régime. He sponsored 'social realism' as the official school in Soviet literature and art.

GÖRRES, Johann Joseph von (1776–1848) German writer, born in Koblenz. In 1812 Koblenz became the literary centre of the national movement. Denouncing absolutism with great vigour, he angered the Prussian government, and had to flee the country (1820). In 1827 he was made professor of literature at Munich, where he devoted himself to literature and controversial theology. His chief work was his *Christliche Mystik* (1842).

GORSHKOV, Sergei Georgievich (1910–88) Soviet admiral, born in Podolsk in the Ukraine. He joined the navy in 1927 and was given command of surface boats in the Black Sea from 1932 onwards, ending World War II in charge of a destroyer squadron. He was appointed commander-in-chief of the Soviet navy by **Khrushchev** in 1956, with the brief to cut back expenditure. However, after the Cuban missile crisis (1962) and Khrushchev's ousting, the new Soviet leader, **Leonid Brezhnev**, pressed for naval expansion to enable the USSR to project itself globally. Gorshkov supported this view and oversaw a massive naval build-up, both surface and underwater, creating a force capable of challenging the West's by the 1970s. He remained in command of the navy until his death.

GORST, Sir John Eldon (1835–1916) English politician, born in Preston. He became a popular civil commissioner in the Maori country in New Zealand, was called to the bar in 1865 and entered parliament, a staunch supporter of **Disraeli**. He later joined the Fourth Party led by **Randolph Churchill**, was knighted in 1885 and ultimately joined the Liberal party. He held several ministerial offices, including that of solicitor-general (1885–86).

GORT, John Standish Surtees Prendergast Vereker, 6th Viscount (1886–1946) English soldier, son of the 5th Viscount. Educated at Harrow and the Royal Military College, Woolwich, he served with the Grenadier Guards in World War I and won the VC in 1918. He was appointed chief of the imperial general staff in 1938. In World War II he was commander-in-chief of the British forces overwhelmed in the initial German victories of 1940. Afterwards he was governor of Gibraltar (1941–42) and of Malta from 1942 to 1944, and was promoted field marshal in 1943. He was high commissioner for Palestine and Transjordan (1944–45).

GORTON, Sir John Grey (1911–) Australian politician. Educated at Geelong Grammar School and Brasenose College, Oxford, in 1940 he joined the RAAF, serving in Europe, Malaya and Australia. Seriously wounded, he was discharged in 1944. He was a Liberal senator for Victoria (1949–68) and a member of the House of Representatives (1968–75). He served in the governments of Sir **Robert Menzies** and **Harold Holt** and, when Holt died while swimming near Melbourne in 1967, succeeded him as prime minister. In 1971 he was defeated on a vote of confidence and resigned in favour of **William McMahon**, becoming deputy leader of his party.

GORTON, Samuel (1592–1677) English colonist and religious leader, founder of the sect of 'Gortonites', born in Gorton, Lancashire. He emigrated in 1637 to Massachusetts Colony in New England. He denied the doctrine of the Trinity and the existence of heaven and hell, and in 1637–38 he was tried for heresy and banished. He fell foul of other authorities before returning to London in 1644, where he was given a letter of safe conduct by John Rich, the 2nd Earl of **Warwick**, to settle in Rhode Island (1648). He gave the township Shawomet a new name, Warwick, and lived there peacefully with a few faithful Gortonite adherents.

GORTSCHAKOFF See **GORCHAKOV**

GOSCHEN, George Joachim Goschen, 1st Viscount (1831–1907) British statesman, the son of a London merchant of German extraction. In 1863 he published *The Theory of Foreign Exchanges*, and became Liberal MP for the City of London, holding office as vice-president of the board of trade (1865), chancellor of the Duchy of Lancaster (1866), president of the Poor-Law board (1868), and head of the Admiralty (1871–74). He regulated Egyptian finances (1876), and as ambassador extraordinary to the Porte (1880) induced Turkey to fulfil her treaty obligations to Greece. Opposing Home Rule, he was Unionist Chancellor of the Exchequer (1887–92), and in 1888 converted part of the national debt; he was First Lord of the Admiralty (1895–99). His brother, Sir William Edward Goschen (1847–1924), was British ambassador at Berlin (1908–14).

GOSS, Sir John (1800–80) English composer of anthems and glees, born in Fareham, Hampshire, the son of an organist. He became organist of St Paul's from 1838 to 1872, and composer to the English Chapel Royal.

GOSSE, Sir Edmund William (1845–1928) English poet and critic, born in London, son of **Philip Henry Gosse**. He was educated privately, and became assistant librarian in the British Museum (1867–75), then translator to the Board of Trade (1875–1904) and finally librarian to the House of Lords (1904–14). He published two volumes of poems, *On Viol and Flute* (1873) and *Collected Poems* (1911). His *Studies in the Literature of Northern Europe* (1879), and other critical works, first introduced **Ibsen** to English-speaking readers. He also wrote on **Congreve** (1888), **Donne** (1899), **Jeremy Taylor** (1904), Sir **Thomas Browne** (1905), **Swinburne** (1917), and **Malherbe** (1920), although his special field was *Seventeenth-century Studies* (1897). He described his father's character and beliefs in *Father and Son* (1907).

GOSSE, Philip Henry (1810–88) English naturalist, born in Worcester. He went to North America in 1827 and became a professional naturalist in Jamaica, with a particular interest in coastal marine biology. His *Manual of Marine Zoology* (1855–56) and *History of British Sea-anemones and Corals* (1860), written on his return to England, greatly expanded interest in marine organisms. He published *Omphalos* (1857) in opposition to evolutionary theory. His best-known work was the *Romance of Natural History* (1860–62).

GOSSE, William Christie (1842–81) English-born Australian explorer, born in Hoddesden, Hertfordshire. His family emigrated to Adelaide, South Australia, in 1850 where he was educated privately and where he joined the South Australian surveyor-general's department. In 1873 he led an expedition from Alice Springs in the Northern Territory (which was at that time administered by South Australia), in search of an overland route to Perth on the west coast of the continent. Gosse discovered, and named, Ayers Rock after Sir **Henry Ayers**, a massive sandstone monolith, which had been sighted by **Ernest Giles** in the previous year. Although his group was forced to turn back, his maps proved invaluable to Sir **John Forrest**'s successful 1874 expedition from Perth.

GOT, Edmond François Jules (1822–1901) French actor, born in Lignerolles (Orne). In 1844 he made his début. From 1850 to 1866 he was a member of the Comédie Française. He received the cross of the Légion d'Honneur in 1881.

GOTHARDT, Matthias See **GRUNEWALD**

GOTTFRIED VON STRASSBURG (fl.1200) German poet. He wrote the masterly German version of the legend of *Tristan and Isolde*, based on the Anglo-Norman poem by **Thomas**. He is also noteworthy as an early exponent of literary criticism, having left appraisals of the work of poets of the period.

GOTTHELF, Jeremias See **BITZIUS, Albert**

GOTTLIEB, Adolph (1903–74) American painter, born in New York. He attended the Art Students' League in New York, and from 1921 to 1923 studied in Paris. In 1935 he joined the New York avant-garde group The Ten, whose membership included **Mark Rothko**. From 1941 he painted an unusual series of pictographs in which a grid system is drawn onto the canvas and a primitive symbol inserted in each space. His strong interest in African and American Indian art informed these works. After 1950 his paintings became radically simplified, consisting of gestural marks of bright colour which evoke imaginary landscapes. He stands as one of the most original of the Abstract Expressionist school of painters.

GOTTLIEB, Robert Adams (1931–) American publisher and editor, born in New York City. Educated at Columbia University and at Cambridge, he was editor-in-chief at Simon & Schuster (1955–68) and at Alfred Knopf (1968–87). He has been editor of the *New Yorker* since 1987.

GOTTSCHALK See **HINCMAR**

GOTTSCHALK, Louis Moreau (1829–69) American pianist-composer, born in New Orleans. He studied in Paris (1842–46), winning the admiration of **Chopin** and **Berlioz**. After touring in France, Switzerland and Spain, he returned to the USA (1853) and enjoyed success with his piano and piano-orchestral compositions, many of which explore Creole, African and Spanish idioms.

GOTTSCHALL, Rudolf von (1823–1909) German writer, born in Breslau. A keen Liberal, he produced two volumes of political verse (1842–43). From 1864 he lived in Leipzig and edited *Brockhaus'sche Blätter* and *Unsere Zeit*. He also wrote a comedy entitled *Pitt und Fox* (1854), tragedies and historical novels.

GOTTSCHED, Johann Christoph (1700–66) German man of letters, born in Judithenkirch near Königsberg. In 1730 he became professor of philosophy and poetry at Leipzig, and in 1734 of logic and metaphysics. He laboured to improve his mother-tongue as a literary vehicle, and to reform the German drama by banishing buffoonery and raising the style and tone. He founded the Leipzig school of acting and criticism, introducing French classical principles. But he became pedantic and vain, and showed a petty jealousy of all literary authority save his own, opposing **Bodmer** and **Lessing**. His drama, *The Dying Cato* (1732), notwithstanding its immense success, is sadly barren.

GOTTWALD, Klement (1896–1953) Czech politician, born in Dedice, Moravia. In World War I he fought with the Austro-Hungarian army. He then joined the Communist party, whose secretary-general he became in 1927. He opposed the Munich Agreement of 1938 and later went to Moscow, where he was trained for eventual office. In 1945 he became, as a Communist leader, vice-premier in the Czech provisional government. Prime minister in 1946, he carried out in February 1948 the Communist *coup d'état* which averted a defeat for his party at the polls. In June he became president. Strong in the support of Moscow, whose line he followed closely, he established a complete dictatorship in Czechoslovakia.

GÖTZ VON BERLICHINGEN (1480–1562) German condottiere born in Jaxthausen in Württemberg, nicknamed 'of the iron-hand' because of a steel replacement for his right hand lost in the siege of Landshut (1505). From 1497 onwards he was involved in continual feuds, in which he displayed both lawless daring and chivalrous magnanimity. Twice he was placed under the ban of the empire. He fought for Duke Ulrich of Württemberg (1519) against the Swabian league, and after his heroic defence of Möckmühl was taken prisoner. In the Peasants' War of 1525 he led a section of the insurgents, was captured by the Swabian league, kept a prisoner at Augsburg for two years, and sentenced to perpetual imprisonment. He was only freed on the dissolution of the league in 1540. In 1542 he was fighting in Hungary against the Turks, and in 1544 in France. He died in his castle of Hornberg. He wrote an autobiography, published in 1731, on which **Goethe** grounded his drama *Götz von Berlichingen*.

GOUDIMEL, Claude (c.1514–1572) French composer of masses, motets, chansons and psalm tunes, born in Besançon. He taught music at Rome, and died at Lyons as a Huguenot just after the massacre of St Bartholomew.

GOUDSMIT, Samuel Abraham (1902–78) Dutch-born American physicist, born in The Hague. He studied in Amsterdam and Leiden and emigrated in 1927 to the USA, where he was professor at Michigan (1932–46) and later worked at the Brookhaven National Laboratory, Long Island (1948–70). Aged 23, he and his fellow-student George Uhlenbeck (b.1900) had proposed the idea that electrons in atoms can show an effect which they described as electron spin, a novel and important concept which soon proved to be correct. In World War II he headed the secret Alsos mission charged (1944) with following German progress in atomic bomb research; this led to the award of the US Medal of Freedom, and to his book *Alsos* (1947).

GOUGH, Sir Hubert de la Poer (1870–1963) Irish soldier and mutineer, born in Gurteen, County Waterford, into an Irish military and political family. Educated at Eton and Sandhurst, he served in the Boer war, relieving Ladysmith against orders. After an instructorship at Staff College (1903–06) and command of the 16th Lancers, he returned to Ireland as brigadier-general commanding the 3rd Cavalry Brigade at the Curragh. In 1914, he and 57 other officers threatened to resign rather than take arms in Ulster to impose Home Rule against Sir **Edward Carson**'s Ulster Volunteers, and won the day; the episode convinced extreme Irish nationalist elements that reliance on government home rule promises was hopeless and only force would be respected. Gough was rapidly promoted in World War I, becoming major-general for the first battle of Ypres and lieutenant-general for Loos, but his command of the Fifth Army at the third Ypres campaign impaired his reputation. He was made a scapegoat for British military failure during the German advance of March 1918. In 1922 he was retired as a full general. He wrote a self-vindication in his *Fifth Army* (1931). His memoirs, *Soldiering On*, appeared in 1954.

GOUGH, Hugh Gough, 1st Viscount (1779–1869) Anglo-Irish soldier, born in Woodstown, County Limerick. Entering the army in 1793, he served in the West Indies (1797–1800), through the Peninsular War, and in India; and in 1838 was made commander-in-chief of the forces sent against China during the Opium War. After storming Canton and forcing the Yangtze-Kiang, he compelled the Chinese to sign the Treaty of Nanking (1842), and in 1843 he defeated the Mahrattas in India. In the Sikh War in 1845 he worsted the enemy in the battles of Mudki, Ferozeshah and Sobraon, for which he was given a peerage. In 1848 the Sikhs renewed the war, but were again defeated by Gough at Ramnagar, Chillianwalla, and Gujerat, victories which resulted in the annexation of the Punjab.

GOUJON, Jean (c.1510–1568) French Renaissance sculptor. His finest work includes *Diana reclining by a Stag*, in the Louvre; the reliefs for the Fountain of the Innocents, also in the Louvre; the monument to the Duke of Brézé in Rouen Cathedral; and several reliefs in the Louvre, where he worked (1555–1562). He was a Huguenot, but seems to have died before the St Bartholomew massacre in 1572.

GOULD, Benjamin Apthorp (1824–96) American astronomer, born in Boston, Massachusetts. Educated at Harvard and Göttingen, he founded the *Astronomical Journal* (1849–61), was director of the Dudley Observatory at Albany (1856–59) and in 1866 determined, by aid of the submarine cable, the difference in longitude between Europe and America. He helped to found and was director from 1868 of the national observatory at Cordoba, Argentina. His *Uranometry of the Southern Heavens* complemented **Friedrich Argelander**'s *Atlas* of the Northern Heavens.

GOULD, Bryan Charles (1939–) British politician. Born in New Zealand, the son of a bank official, he distinguished himself at his state school by winning a university scholarship at the unprecedented age of 15, entering Auckland University two years later. A Rhodes Scholarship took him to Balliol College, Oxford and, in 1964, instead of returning to New Zealand, he joined the British diplomatic service. He was, however, now more interested in a political career and in 1968 left the civil service to become a don at Worcester College, Oxford (1968–74). His own background and distaste for the British class system made the Labour party his natural choice and, after experience in local politics, he entered the House of Commons, representing Southampton Test (1974–79). He lost his seat in the 1979 general election but returned in 1983 to represent Dagenham, having spent the intervening four years as a television journalist. His rise in the Labour party was rapid and in 1986 he was elected to the shadow cabinet. His communication skills and varied experience soon made him a nationally known figure.

GOULD, Chester (1900–85) American strip cartoonist, born in Pawnee, Oklahoma,the creator of *Dick Tracey*, the first 'tough detective' in comics. He won a cartoon contest in *American Boy* magazine (1916), and drew sports cartoons for *Daily Oklahoma* whilst at college. After a year at the Zuckerman Art Studio in Chicago (1921), he joined the art staff of the *Chicago American*, creating his first strip, *Fillum Fables* (1924), then moving to the *Chicago Tribune* to draw *Girl Friends* (1929). He submitted a new idea in continuity strips, *Plainclothes Tracy*, to the *New York Daily News*, who rechristened it *Dick Tracy*. It kept Gould busy until his retirement in 1977, when his former assistant took it over.

GOULD, Sir Francis Carruthers (1881–1925) English cartoonist, born in Barnstaple. As 'FCG' of the *Westminster Gazette* he was a pioneer of what he called 'picture politics', and was the sole illustrator of *Picture Politics* magazine.

GOULD, Glenn (1932–82) Canadian pianist and composer, born in Toronto. Starting to play the piano at the age of three, he studied at the Royal Conservatory of Music before making his début, at fourteen, as a soloist with the Toronto Symphony orchestra. Since then he has toured extensively in the USA and Europe and has made many recordings particularly of works by **Bach** and **Beethoven**. In 1956 saw the world première of his own work, *A String Quartet*. In 1964 he retired from the concert platform, believing concerts were doomed to be a thing of the past, and devoted himself to recording and broadcasting. His writings were collected together as *The Glenn Gould Reader* (1987).

GOULD, Jay (Jason) (1836–92) American financier, born in Roxbury, New York. He made a survey of parts of the state, engaged in lumbering, and in 1857 became the principal shareholder in a Pennsylvania bank. He began to buy up railroad bonds, started as a broker in New York (1859), and manipulated shares to seize the presidency of the Erie railway company (1868–72). He tried to corner the gold market, causing the 'Black Friday' stock market crash of September 1869. He bought up huge areas of railroad companies, and died unlamented, worth some $100000000.

GOULD, John (1804–81) English ornithologist and publisher, born in Lyme Regis. In 1827 he became curator and preserver (taxidermist) to the new Zoological Society's museum in London. An accomplished artist, he travelled widely, drawing birds whose skins he collected for the museum. Working with the newly developed technique of lithography, and assisted by his talented wife Elizabeth, he produced 18 monumental books of sumptuous bird illustrations, including *Birds of Europe* (5 vols, 1832–37), *Birds of Australia* (7 vols, 1840–48), *Birds of Asia* (1849–83) and *Birds of Great Britain* (5 vols, 1862–73). One of his assistant draughtsmen at the Zoological Society was **Edward Lear**.

GOULD, Morton (1913–) American composer, born in New York. Gould's music is national in style and exploits the various aspects of popular music from both North and South America. He has composed symphonies and a variety of works in more popular style, including a *Concerto for Tapdancer*.

GOULD, Nat (Nathaniel) (1857–1919) English sporting journalist and novelist, born in Manchester. He became a sports columnist for a newspaper in Sydney, Australia, and achieved great success with his first novel about the turf, *The Double Event*. He subsequently wrote some 130 thrillers about horse-racing, and an autobiography, *The Magic of Sport* (1909).

GOULD, Sabine Baring- See **BARING-GOULD**

GOULD, Stephen Jay (1941–) American palaeontologist, born in New York. Educated at Antioch College and Columbia, he was professor of geology at Harvard from 1973. His forceful support for modern views on evolution has been expressed in many articles and books, including *Ever Since Darwin* (1977), *The Panda's Thumb* (1980), *Hen's Teeth and Horses' Toes* (1983), and *The Flamingo's Smile* (1985).

GOULED APTIDON, Hassan (1916–) Djiboutian politican, born in Djibouti city. He was a representative of French Somaliland in France while becoming increasingly active in the independence movement. He joined the African People's League for Independence (LPAI) in 1967 and when independence was achieved, in 1977, became the country's first president. Later LPAI was amalgamated with other parties to become the People's Progress party (RPP) and Djibouti's sole political party. He pursued a largely successful policy of amicable neutralism in a war-torn region and was re -elected in 1987 for a final six-year term.

GOUNOD, Charles François (1818–93) French composer, born in Paris. He studied at the Conservatoire, and in Rome. On his return to Paris he was for a time organist of the church of the Missions Etrangères where his earliest compositions, chiefly polyphonic in style, were performed; one of them, a *Messe solennelle*, attracted attention. His first opera, *Sapho*, was produced in 1851, and *La Nonne sanglante* in 1854. His comic opera, *Le Médecin maigré lui* (1858), was a great success; in 1859 *Faust* raised its composer to the foremost rank. *Philémon et Baucis* followed in 1860; in 1862, *La Reine de Saba* (or *Irène*); in 1864, *Mireille*; in 1867, *Roméo et Juliette*. He also published masses, hymns and anthems, and was popular as a songwriter, his oratorio *The Redemption* was produced at the Birmingham Festival in 1882; its sequel, *Mors et Vita*, at Brussels in 1886. He fled to England during the Franco-Prussian war (1870). He was a member of the Institute (1866) and a commander of the Legion of Honour (1877).

GOURMONT, Rémy de (1858–1915) French poet, novelist and critic, born in Bazoches-en-Houlme, Normandy. Having been dismissed from his post at the Bibliothèque Nationale Paris, because of an allegedy pro-German article in *Mercure de France*, of which he was a co-founder, he lived the life of a recluse. His creative work—poetry and novels in the symbolist vogue—is cerebral and stylistic, betraying a 'fin de siècle' obsession with words as sound more than as sense. But his evaluative work, which includes *Le Livre des masques* (1896–1898) and *Promenades philosophiques* (1905–09), is clear-sighted and individualistic exhibiting scholarship and intellectual curiosity. His novels include *Sixtine* (1890) and *Un Cœur virginal* (1907).

GOW, Niel (1727–1807) Scottish violinist and songwriter, born near Dunkeld. He composed nearly a hundred tunes; and from his singular skill with the bow his name is still a household word in Scotland. His youngest son, Nathaniel (1766–1831), became king's trumpeter for Scotland, bandleader, and music publisher of Scottish airs including his own, of which there are over 200.

GOWARD, Mary See **KEELEY, Robert**

GOWER, David Ivon (1957–) English cricketer and Test captain, born in Tunbridge Wells. He came to the fore quickly chiefly because of the elegance of his left-handed stroke play. A consistent rather than heavy scorer he had by 1988 accumulated 7000 runs in Test cricket, including 14 centuries. At his best he appeared to play fast bowling with ample time to spare; out of form he could appear languid and detached. He was captain of England in the mid 1980s though without particular success, but was recalled as captain in 1989, only to lose the captaincy and his place in the team after a crushing defeat in the Test series against Australia.

GOWER, John (c.1325–1408) English poet, born into a wealthy family in Kent. He spent most of his life in London, and had contacts with the court in the service of **Richard II** and **Henry IV**. He was a personal friend of **Chaucer**, and wrote *Speculum Meditantis*, in French verse, which was discovered at Cambridge only in 1898. Other works include the *Vox Clamantis*, elegiacs in Latin (1382–84), describing the rising under **Wat Tyler**; and the long poem entitled *Confessio Amantis*, written in English, perhaps in 1383. There are extant also 50French ballads, written by Gower in his youth. The *Confessio Amantis* comprises a prologue and eight books, and largely consists of over a hundred stories taken from **Ovid**'s *Metamorphoses*, the *Gesta Romanorum*, and medieval histories of Troy. He was blind from about 1400.

GOWERS, Sir Ernest Arthur (1880–1966) English civil servant, son of the neurologist Sir William Richard (1845–1915). Educated at Rugby and Clare College, Cambridge, he was called to the bar in 1906. After a distinguished career in the civil service he emerged as the champion of *Plain Words* (1948) and *ABC of Plain Words* (1951), designed to rescue the English language from slipshod use, not least from jargon.

GOWING, Sir Lawrence Burnett (1918–) English painter and writer on art, born in Stoke Newington. He studied at the Euston Road School under **William Coldstream**, and his impressionist style is often applied to portraits, eg *Mrs Roberts* in the Tate Gallery, London. He was professor of fine art in the University of Durham from 1948–58, principal of Chelsea School of Art (1958–65), professor of fine art at Leeds (1967–75), and Slade professor of fine art at University College, London (1975–85). He has written studies of *Renoir* (1947) and *Vermeer* (1952). Among his other publications are works on **Constable** (1961), **Goya** (1965) and **Matisse** (1979).

GOWON, Yakubu (1934–) Nigerian soldier and politician, born in Garam in Plateau state, a Christian in a Muslim area. After military training in Nigeria and Britain (Sandhurst), he joined the Nigerian army, becoming adjutant-general in 1963 and commander-in-chief in 1966. Ethnic and tribal differences had been recognized by Nigeria's federal structure after independence but conflicts between the north and south threatened anarchy, prompting a military takeover in 1966, led by General Gowon, who became president. He could not, however, prevent a costly civil war which lasted until 1970. In 1975 he was ousted in a bloodless coup while in Kampala. After pursuing academic studies in Britain, he eventually settled in Togo.

GOWRIE, Earl of See **RUTHVEN**

GOYA Y LUCIENTES, Francisco José de (1746–1828) Spanish artist, born in Fuendetodos, near Saragossa. After travelling in Italy he returned to Spain in 1775 to design for the Royal Tapestry Works. At first he worked quite conventionally, painting scenes of court pastorals strongly influenced by **Tiepolo** and the Neapolitans. However, he soon began introducing scenes from everyday Spanish life — *Stilt Walkers*, *Blind Guitarist* — which show his passion for reality.

At the same time he studied **Velasquez** in the Royal Collections, and this prompted him to begin painting portraits. In 1786 he was appointed court painter to **Charles IV** (chief painter in 1799). The portraits, particularly those done of the Spanish Royal Family, for example *The Family of Charles IV* are painted in an unflattering and uncompromising style which makes one wonder how acceptable they were to their subjects. In a series of 82 satirical etchings called *Los Caprichos*, Goya castigated the follies of the court. After the Napoleonic occupation he produced an equally sardonic series entitled *The Disasters of War*. His religious paintings, particularly those for the church of San Antonio de la Florida, Madrid, are extremely freely painted. After 1792 Goya became increasingly deaf and in later life retired first to the outskirts of Madrid where he painted some extraordinary decorations for his own house (House of the Deaf Man, now in the Prado Madrid), and in 1824, on the accession of Ferdinand VII, went into voluntary exile in France where he continued to work. His originality and timelessness have resulted in his enormous reputation and popularity, and his work has influenced virtually every major painter from **Delacroix** to **Picasso**.

GOZZI, Count Carlo (1720–1806) Italian dramatist, born in Venice. He wrote *Tartana* (1757), a satirical poem against **Goldoni**; a very popular comedy, *Fiaba dell' amore delle tre Melarance* (1761); and several similar 'dramatic fairy-tales', the best-known, from **Schiller**'s translation of it, being *Turandot*. His brother, Count Gasparo (1713–86), edited two journals in Venice, and was press censor there. Among his works are *Il mondo morale* (1760) and *Lettere famigliari* (1755).

GOZZOLI, Benozzo, properly **Benozzo di Lese** (c.1420–97) Italian painter, born in Florence. A pupil of **Fra Angelico**, in Florence (1456–64) he adorned the Palazzo Medici-Riccardi with scriptural subjects, including his famous *Journey of the Magi* in which Florentine councillors accompanied by members of the **Medici** family appear, and painted similar frescoes at San Gimignano (1464–67), and in the Campo Santo at Pisa (1468–84).

GRAAF, Regnier de (1641–73) Dutch physician and anatomist, born in Schoonhoven. He practised at Delft, and in 1663 wrote a famous treatise on the pancreatic juice. In 1672 discovered the Graafian vesicles of the female ovary.

GRABBE, Christian Dietrich (1801–36) German dramatist, born in Detmold. A precursor of Realism, he wrote powerful tragedies on the lives of *Don Juan und Faust* (1822), *Kaiser Friedrich Barbarossa* (1829) and *Napoleon* (1831).

GRACCHUS a famous Roman family to which belonged Tiberius Sempronius (slain 212 BC), a distinguished opponent of **Hannibal** in the second Punic War; and another Tiberius Sempronius (born about 210 BC), who conquered the Celtiberians and pacified Spain. His wife, Cornelia, daughter of **Scipio Africanus**, bore him the two famous brothers, the Gracchi.

GRACCHUS, Caius Sempronius (c.159–121 BC) Roman statesman. At the time of the death of his brother Tiberius Gracchus, he was serving in Spain under **Scipio Africanus**. He was elected to the tribuneship in 123 and 122. His first measure was to renew his brother's agrarian law; and to relieve the immediate misery of the poor, he employed them upon new roads throughout Italy. But by a senatorial intrigue his colleague Livius Drusus was bribed to undermine his influence by surpassing him in the liberality of his measures, Caius was rejected from a third tribuneship, and the senate began to repeal his enactments. Caius appearing in the Forum to make opposition, a fearful riot ensued, in which 3000 of his partisans were slain; he himself held aloof from the fight, but was compelled to flee with a single slave, who first slew his master and then himself. The commons saw their folly too late, and endeavoured to atone for their crime by erecting statues to the brothers. Their mother survived them by many years, and on her tomb the Roman people inscribed 'Cornelia, mother of the Gracchi'.

GRACCHUS, Tiberius Sempronius (168–133 BC) Roman statesman. In 137 he served as quaestor in Spain, where the kindly remembrance of his father enabled him to gain better terms from the Numantines for 20000 conquered Roman soldiers. The hopeless poverty of thousands of the Roman citizens weighed on his mind, and he began an agitation for reform. Elected tribune in 133, he reimposed the agrarian law of Licinius Stolo, requisitioned all land held in excess and distributed it in allotments to the poor. His deposition of his fellow tribune Marcus Octavius, who had vetoed his proposal, threatened to undermine the authority of the senate. When Attalus, king of Pergamus, died and bequeathed his wealth to the Roman people, Gracchus proposed that it should be divided among the poor, to enable them to stock their newly-acquired farms. But he was accused of having violated the sacred character of the tribuneship by the deposition of his colleague Caecina; thousands of the fickle mob deserted him; and during the next election for the tribuneship he, with 300 of his friends, was murdered.

GRACE, William Gilbert ('W G') (1848–1915) English cricketer and physician, born in Downend near Bristol. The first genuinely great cricketer of modern times, and one of the earliest practitioners of gamesmanship, he quickly became a national hero. He started playing first-class cricket for Gloucestershire in 1864, and was immediately picked for the Gentlemen Players match. In 1871 he scored 2739 runs in a season; in 1876 he scored 344 runs in an innings for MCC. He took his medical degree in 1879 and had a practice in Bristol, but devoted most of his time to cricket. He toured Canada and the USA, and twice captained the Test team against Australia, in 1880 and 1882. By 1895 he had scored 100 first-class centuries. In his long career in first-class cricket, from 1864 to 1908, he made 126 centuries, scored 54896 runs and took 2864 wickets. Two of his brothers also played Test cricket for England and appeared with him in the Gloucestershire side.

GRACIAN, (y Morales) Baltasar (1601–58) Spanish philosopher and writer, born in Belmonte, Aragon. He entered the Jesuit order in 1619 and later became head of the College at Tarragona. His early works like *The Hero* (1637), *The Politician* (1640), *The Man of Discretion* (1646) and *The Manual Oracle and the Art of Prudence* (1647) are all heavily didactic guides to life. He set out his literary ideas on *conceptismo*, the art of conceited writing, in *Subtlety and the Art of Genius* (1642). He is best known, however, for his three-part allegorical novel, *The Critic* (1651, 1653, 1657), in which civilization and society are portrayed through the eyes of a savage.

GRADE, Lew (Louis Winogradsky), Baron (1906–) Russian-born British television producer, born near Odessa, the eldest of three brothers who were to dominate British showbusiness for over 40 years. He arrived in Britain in 1912, accompanied by his parents and younger brother Boris, who became Bernard Delfont (1909–). The brothers both became dancers (semi-professional at first) winning competitions during the 'Charleston' craze of the 1920s but both gave up to become theatrical agents, booking variety acts into theatres. Lew joined forces with his youngest brother Leslie Grade and was joint managing director of their theatrical agency until 1955. Bernard and Lew became impresarios as well as agents, assembling and financing groups of acts and putting on whole shows. Bernard entered theatrical management in 1941, and during the next 20 years acquired many theatrical properties, notably the London Hippodrome which he converted into the Talk of the Town restaurant in 1958. He acquired control of more than 30 companies—embracing theatre, film, television, music and property interests—and presented the annual Royal Variety Performance from 1958 to 1978. He has presented a record number of West End shows. He was made a life peer (Baron Delfont of Stepney) in 1976. Lew was an early entrant to the world of commercial television and became managing director of ATV in 1962. He has headed several large film entertainment and communications companies. He was made a life peer (Baron Grade of Elstree) in 1976.

GRAEBE, Karl (1841–1927) German organic chemist, born in Frankfurt-am-Main. Professor at Königsberg (1870) and Geneva (1878–1906), with **Carl Theodore Liebermann** (1842–1914) he first synthesized alizarin from anthraquinone (1869), a process of great importance to the German dyestuffs industry.

GRAEBNER, (Robert) Fritz (1877–1934) German ethnologist, born in Berlin. He studied history at Berlin, joined the staff of the Royal Museum of Ethnology in Berlin in 1899, but moved to the Rautenstrauch-Joest Museum in Cologne in 1906 (director in 1925), and became honorary professor at Cologne University in 1926. He is principally known for developing the theory of *Kulturkreise*, clusters of diffusing cultural traits which he used to explain cultural similarities and differences. His most important work, *Methode der Ethnologie* (1911), became the cornerstone for the German culture-historical school of ethnology.

GRAELLS, Mariano de la Paz (1809–98) Spanish naturalist, born in Tricio, Lograno, and known as the 'father of Spanish Natural History'. He studied at Barcelona and became curator of the Natural History Museum at the Academy of Science and Arts there. He was professor of zoology at Madrid (from 1837) and later professor of comparative anatomy, and director of the National Museum of Natural Sciences and of the Botanical Gardens. An outstanding entomologist, he discovered the Spanish Moon Moth. He also published a *Flora of Catalonia* (1831).

GRAF, Steffi (1969–) West German tennis player, born in Bruehl. She first came to prominence in 1984 when she won the Olympic demonstration event and reached the last 16 at Wimbledon. In 1988, she won the Grand Slam of singles titles—the US, French, Australian and Wimbledon—as well as the gold medal at the Seoul Olympics. She was surprisingly defeated, by Arantxa Sanchez, in the 1989 French final, but the retention the same year of her Wimbledon title confirmed her position as world number one.

GRAFTON, Augustus Henry Fitzroy, 3rd Duke of (1735–1811) English statesman, a descendant of **Charles II**. He came into notice in 1763 in the opposition to **Bute**, and was secretary of state under **Rockingham** (1765–66). In July 1766 **Pitt** became premier and Earl of Chatham, making Grafton first lord of the Treasury; but owing to Chatham's illness Grafton had to undertake the duties of premier from September 1767. He resigned in 1770, but was lord privy seal under **North** (1771–75) and in the new Rockingham ministry (1782–83). Though possessed of more honesty of purpose than the invectives of 'Junius' would have us believe, he had a weakness for the fair sex and for the turf which often distracted him from more urgent business.

GRAFTON, Richard (c.1513–c.1572) English printer and historian. A grocer by trade, he went to Antwerp in 1537 and there printed the Matthews Bible, the revised **Coverdale** New Testament and the 'Great' (folio) Bible. He became printer to **Edward VI**, produced the Book of Common Prayer (1549), but fell into disfavour for printing Lady **Jane Grey**'s proclamation. He also wrote three histories of England, and sat in parliament.

GRAHAM, Billy (William Franklin) (1918–) American evangelist, born in Charlotte, North Carolina. After studying at Florida Bible Institute (now Trinity College), 1938–40, he was ordained a minister of the Southern Baptist Church (1940). In 1943 he graduated in anthropology from Wheaton College, Illinois, and in the same year married Ruth Bell. He made his first high-profile preaching crusade in Los Angeles in 1949 and has since conducted his crusades on all continents, and has preached in the Soviet Union and other East European countries. Through his crusades and the subsidiary ministries of broadcasting, films and the printed word it is claimed that millions have been won to Christianity. A charismatic figure who has been the friend and counsellor of many in high office, including **Richard Nixon**, Graham has consistently emerged from investigative reporting as a person of high integrity, and his Billy Graham Evangelistic Association as a model of financial accountability. His books include *Peace with God* (1952), *World Aflame* (1965), *Angels* (1975), and *A Biblical Standard for Evangelists*.

GRAHAM, Dougal (c.1724–1779) Scottish ballad and chap-book writer, born in Raploch near Stirling. He followed Prince **Charles Stewart**'s army in 1745–46 and wrote a metrical eyewitness account of the campaign. He was appointed bellman of Glasgow about 1770. Of his rambling ballads, the best known are *John Hielandman's Remarks on Glasgow* and *Turnimspike*.

GRAHAM, Ennis See **MOLESWORTH, Mary Louisa**

GRAHAM, James (1745–94) Scottish quack-doctor, born and died in Edinburgh. He studied medicine there, but did not graduate although he styled himself 'Dr Graham'. After several years abroad he set up practice, first in Bristol (1774) then Bath (1775) and finally also in London, where he established 'temples of Health and hymen' and prescribed remedies and lectured. He put his patients on a 'magnetic throne', into electrically charged baths or into 'celestial beds'. Although denounced as a quack and frequently imprisoned, he became fashionable, his clientele including the Prince of Wales and the Duchess of Devonshire. In 1781, it is alleged, he exhibited Emma Lyon, later Lady **Hamilton**, as the 'Goddess of Health'. In 1783 he was arrested in Edinburgh after writing articles in support of his lectures, which had been prohibited, under a forged eminent name. In 1790 he indulged in 'earth bathing', turned religious and styled himself 'the servant of the Lord O.W.L.' (Oh wonderful love). His pamphlets and extravagant advertisements reveal him as an 'admass' man born two centuries before his time.

GRAHAM, Sir James Robert George, Bart (1792–1861) British statesman, born in Netherby in Cumberland, and educated at Westminster and Christ Church, Oxford. In 1813 he became private secretary to the British minister in Sicily. He entered parliament as a Whig in 1826, and supported Catholic emancipation and the Reform Bill. Earl **Grey** made him (1830) First Lord of the Admiralty; but in 1834 he resigned over the Irish church question, and in 1841 became home secretary under **Peel**. In 1844 he issued a warrant for opening the letters of **Mazzini**, and the information thus obtained was communicated to the Austrian minister. His high-handed dealing with the Scottish church increased the troubles which ended in the Disruption of 1843. He gave Peel warm support in carrying the Corn-Law Repeal Bill, and resigned (1846) as soon as it was carried. On Peel's death in 1850 he became leader of the Peelites, and from 1852 to 1855 was First Lord of the Admiralty in the Coalition ministry.

GRAHAM, John, of Claverhouse See **DUNDEE**

GRAHAM, Martha (1894–) American dancer, teacher, choreographer and pioneer of modern dance, born in Pittsburgh. She trained in Los Angeles with the Denishawn School and appeared on stage first in vaudeville and revue. In 1926, after a period performing with the Ruth St Denis and Ted Shawn companies, she made her independent début in Manhattan. Influenced greatly by the composer Louis Horst, her early work constitutes a remarkable contribution to the American Constructavist movement and to the development of modern dance. *Lamentation* (1930) and *Frontier* (1935) are among her better-known early works. In 1930 she founded the Dance Repertory Theatre, in which she trained the company in her own method, which was to use every aspect of the body and the mind to dramatic purpose—movement, breathing and muscular control. Her ballets are based on the same idea of unity, in décor, choreography and music and, frequently, spoken dialogue. One of her best-known ballets, *Appalachian Spring* (1958), was a product of her great interest in Red Indian life and mythology and the early American pioneer spirit, and much of her work has been based on the reinterpretation of ancient myths and historical characters. Director and teacher of dancing at the Martha Graham School of Contemporary Dance in New York, her method of dance training has been widely adopted in schools and colleges around the world.

GRAHAM, Otto Everett, Jr (1921–) American football quarter-back with the Cleveland Browns, the most successful team in the American Football Conference (formed in 1946 in opposition to the already established National Football League). In 1950, the Browns went into the NFL and he led them to championship victories in 1950, 1954 and 1955. He was head coach of the Washington Redskins from 1966 to 1968.

GRAHAM, Robert Bontine Cunninghame See **CUNNINGHAME GRAHAM, Robert**

GRAHAM, Stephen (1884–1975) English traveller and writer. He travelled widely in Scandinavia, Russia, Central Asia, the Middle and Near East. He served in World War I and returned to a life of travel in South America and Russia, contributing to *The Times* and publishing numerous books of his travels, particularly on Russia, including lives of **Peter I, the Great** (1929), **Stalin** (1931) and **Ivan IV, the Terrible** (1932), *Summing up on Russia* (1951) and *Pay as You Run* (1955).

GRAHAM, Thomas (1805–69) Scottish chemist and physicist, born in Glasgow. In 1830 he became professor of chemistry at Glasgow, and in 1837 at University College London. In 1855 he was appointed master of the Mint. He was one of the founders of physical chemistry. His researches on the molecular diffusion of gases led him to formulate the law 'that the diffusion rate of gases is inversely as the square root of their density'. He discovered the properties of colloids and their separation by dialysis.

GRAHAM, Thomas See **LYNEDOCH**

GRAHAME, James (1765–1811) Scottish poet, born in Glasgow. He studied law at Glasgow University and was called to the bar, but was forced to give up his career through ill-health. He took Anglican orders in 1809 and became a curate in Shipton, Gloucestershire and, later, Sedgefield, Durham. He wrote a dramatic poem, *Mary, Queen of Scots* (1801), but most of his poetry was evocative of the quiet Scottish countryside, especially *The Sabbath* (1804) and *The Birds of Scotland* (1806), with an introduction that made it 'popular ornithology'.

GRAHAME, Kenneth (1859–1932) Scottish children's writer, born in Edinburgh, the son of an advocate. He was brought up in Inverary, Argyll, until 1864, and then by his grandmother in Cookham Dene, in Berkshire. He was educated at St Edward's School, Oxford, and in 1876 entered the Bank of England as a gentleman clerk. He became its secretary in 1898 and retired for health reasons in 1908. His early work consisted of collected essays and country tales, *Pagan Papers* (1893), *The Golden Age* (1895) and *Dream Days* (1898), which revealed a remarkably subtle, delicate and humorous sympathy with the child mind. In 1908 he published his best-known work, *The Wind in the Willows* (1908), with its quaint riverside characters, Rat, Mole, Badger and Toad, which has become a children's classic.

GRAHAME-WHITE, Claude (1879–1959) English aviator and engineer. He was the first Englishman to be granted a British certificate of proficiency in aviation (1910). In 1909 he founded the first British flying school at Paris, in France, and in 1910 founded his own company to build aircraft. He helped to establish London Aerodrome at Hendon (1911) and published books on the aeroplane and flying.

GRAHN, Lucile (1819–1907) Danish ballerina, born in Copenhagen. Making her official début at only seven, she subsequently studied and worked in the Royal Danish Ballet with **Auguste Bournonville**, creating Astrid in his *Valdemar* (1835) and then becoming his first *La Sylphide* in 1836. To escape his influence she based herself in Paris, also dancing in Hamburg, St Petersburg and London. Retiring from dancing in 1856, she was ballet mistress at the Leipzig State Theatre (1858–61) and then with the Munich Court Opera (1869–75), where she assisted **Richard Wagner** in the production of *Das Rheingold* and *Die Meistersinger von Nürnberg*. A street in Munich is named after her.

GRAINGER, Percy (1882–1961) Australian composer and pianist, born in Melbourne. He studied under Pabst and **Busoni**, and settled in the USA in 1915. A friend and admirer of **Grieg**, he followed his example in championing the revival of folk-music, and this forms a basis of much of his work. His *Molly on the Shore*, *Mock Morris* and *Shepherds Hey* are examples of his skilful use of traditional dance themes.

GRAM, Hans Christian Joachim (1853–1938) Danish bacteriologist, born in Copenhagen. Professor at Copenhagen, he established in 1884 a microbiological staining method for bacteria, distinguishing the *Gram-positive* from the *Gram-negative*.

GRAMME, Zénobe Théophile (1876–1941) Belgian electrical engineer, born in Jehay-Bodegnée. In 1869 he built the first successful direct-current dynamo, incorporating a ring-wound armature (the 'Gramme ring'), which after various improvements he manufactured from 1871; it was the first electric generator to be used commercially, for electro-plating as well as electric lighting. In 1873 he showed that a dynamo could function in reverse as an electric motor.

GRAMONT, or **Grammont, Philibert, Comte de** (1621–1707) French courtier. He served under **Condé** and **Turenne**, and became a favourite at the court of **Louis XIV**, but his gallantries brought him exile from France in 1662. He found congenial society among the merry profligates of the court of **Charles II** of Great Britain. Here, after many adventures, he married, but not without compulsion, Elizabeth Hamilton (1641–1708), with whom he afterwards returned to France. At 80 he inspired his Mémoires of the 'amorous intrigues' at Charles's court, or revised them when written by his brother-in-law, Count **Anthony Hamilton**. The book is a singular revelation of a world of villainy, written with grace and vigour. It was first printed anonymously in 1713.

GRAMSCI, Antonio (1891–1937) Italian political leader and theoretician, born in Ales, Sardinia. Brought up in poverty, he was a brilliant student at Turin University and was soon drawn into political activity in the Socialist party. He helped found a left-wing paper, *L'Ordine Nuovo* (1919), and was active in promoting workers' councils in factories. But he became dissatisfied with moderate, reformist socialism and helped to establish the separate Italian Communist party in 1921. He was the Italian representative at the Third International in Moscow in 1922, and in 1924 he became leader of the party in parliament. **Mussolini** had by now come to power; in 1926 the Communist party was banned by the Fascists and Gramsci himself was arrested and spent the rest of his life in prison. His great reputation derives, ironically, from the time when his active political career ended, for while in prison he completed some 30 notebooks (over 2000 printed pages) of reflections, which were published posthumously (*Lettere del carcere*, 1947) and are now regarded as one of the most important political texts of this century.

GRANADOS Y CAMPIÑA, Enrique (1868–1916) Spanish composer and pianist, born in Lérida. He studied at Barcelona and at Paris. A composer of Spanish dances, his *Goyescas* for piano are his most accomplished works. He was drowned when the *Sussex* was torpedoed by the Germans in the English Channel.

GRANBY, John Manners, Marquis of (1721–70) English soldier, eldest son of the Duke of Rutland. MP for Grantham in 1742, he was hastily commissioned at the time of the 1745 Jacobite rebellion, and subsequently served on the Duke of **Cumberland**'s staff, reaching substantive major-general's rank in 1755. As colonel of 'The Blues' and second-in-command of the British Horse at Minden (1759), he was a furious but impotent witness of Lord **George Sackville**'s failure to lead the cavalry into action, which earned his commander the contemptuous title of 'The Great Incompetent'. In 1760 Granby, at the head of his cheering squadrons, triumphantly redeemed the cavalry's tarnished reputation with the spectacular victory of Warburg. 'The mob's hero', in **Walpole**'s sneering phrase, was everywhere acclaimed, and in 1763 was appointed master-general of the ordnance, succeeding the aged **Ligonier** as commander-in-chief in 1766.

GRAND, Sarah, née **Frances Elizabeth Clarke** (1854–1943) British novelist, born of English parentage in Donaghadee, Ireland. At the age of 16 she married an army doctor, D C McFall (d.1898). In 1923 and from 1925 to 1929 she was mayoress of Bath. Her reputation rests on *The Heavenly Twins* (1893) and *The Beth Book* (1898), in which she skilfully handles sex problems. Her later works, including *The Winged Victory* (1916), are advocacies of feminine emancipation.

GRANDI, Dino, Count (1895–1988) Italian politician and diplomat, one of the closest lieutenants of the Fascist dictator **Benito Mussolini**. Born at Mordano, near Bologna, he studied law and joined the Fascist quadrumvirate during the 1922 march on Rome. He became Mussolini's foreign minister (1929–32), then Italian ambassador in London (1932–39), during which time he unsuccessfully warned the *duce* of British opposition to the Abyssinian invasion (1935). He was created count in 1937, but recalled in 1939 after the formation of the Berlin-Rome Axis, and appointed minister of justice. In July 1943 he moved the motion in the Fascist grand council which brought about Mussolini's resignation, then fled to Portugal before being sentenced to death in absentia by a Fascist Republican court at Verona. For many years he lived in exile in Brazil, then returned to Italy in 1973 and wrote two acclaimed books, *The Foreign Policy of Italy, 1929–32*, and *My Country*.

GRANDVILLE, pseud of **Jean Ignace Isidore Gérard** (1803–47) French caricaturist and book illustrator, born in Nancy. As a contributor to periodicals such as *Le Charivari* and *La Caricature*, he made his reputation with satirical lithographs of public figures in animal forms, and fantastic humorous sketches. He also illustrated editions of **La Fontaine** and **Swift**. He died in a lunatic asylum near Paris.

GRANGE, Kenneth Henry (1929–) English industrial designer, born in London. He studied at Willesdon School of Arts and Crafts (1944–47) before working as a technical illustrator. After some years working in architectural and design practices, he ran his own design consultancy from 1958 to 1971. In 1971 he co-founded the multi-disciplinary practice Pentagram. His product designs are among the most familiar even to those who do not know his name. They include food mixers for Kenwood, cameras for Kodak, a sewing machine for 'Frister-Rossmann', pens for Parker, locomotives for British Rail and the unloved parking meter for Venner. His designs possess an elegance and appeal that attest to the thoroughness of his attention to every detail. He became a royal designer for industry in 1969.

GRANGE, Lady, née **Rachel Chiesley** (d.1745) wife of the Lord Justice Clerk of Scotland, James Erskine, Lord Grange (1679–1754), who kept her a prisoner on St Kilda for seven years. She was a bad-tempered woman, opposed to her husband's Jacobite views (he was the brother of the 6th Earl of **Mar**, who had been the leader of the 1715 Jacobite rising). On threatening to expose her husband's conspiratorial views one night in 1731, she was spirited away to the Hebrides, while her death was announced in Edinburgh and a mock funeral held. After three years of captivity on a lonely island off North Uist, she was sent to the remote island group of St Kilda, where she was held incommunicado on the island of Hirta for eight years (1734–42). She was then taken back to the Western Isles, where she managed to smuggle a letter to her cousin, the Lord Advocate, who sent a gunboat to look for her, but failed to trace her whereabouts. She died on the Vaternish peninsula.

GRANGE, (Howard Edward) Red (1903–) American football player and coach, born in Forksville, Pennsylvania. His achievements as a running back in the 1920s earned him the nickname 'the Galloping Ghost'. He played for Illinois University from 1923 to 1925, where he gained 4280 yards and was described as the 'greatest broken-field runner in the history of the game'. When he signed for the Chicago Bears in 1925 it caused a great row in the sport over the registration of student players. He was the first man to earn $100000 in a season. He went on to play in New York before returning to the Bears (1929–35).

GRANGER, James (1723–76) English biographer, born in Shaftesbury. He died vicar of Shiplake, Oxfordshire. He published a *Biographical History of England...adapted to a Methodical Catalogue of Engraved British Heads* (1769) and insisted 'on the utility of a collection of engraved portraits', by publishing later editions with blank interleaved paper for inserting extra illustrations. This led to extraordinary zeal in collecting portraits, and 'grangerized copies' were embellished with engravings clipped from every conceivable source, even the most valuable early books. He himself is said to have cut some 14000 engraved portraits from other books.

GRANIER DE CASSAGNAC See **CASSAGNAC, Adolphe Granier de**

GRANIT, Ragnar Arthur (1900–) Finnish-born Swedish physiologist, joint winner of the 1987 Nobel prize for physiology or medicine. Educated at Helsinki University, he worked under Sir **Charles Sherrington** at Oxford (1928–31), and became professor of neurophysiology at the Karolinska Institute in Stockholm (1940–67). He pioneered the study of the neurophysiology of vision by the use of microelectrodes, and was awarded the 1987 Nobel prize jointly with **George Wald** and **Haldan Hartline**.

GRANT, Sir Alexander (1826–84) British educationist, born in New York. Educated at Harrow and Balliol College, Oxford, he was elected a fellow of Oriel in 1849 and edited **Aristotle**'s *Ethics* (1857). He succeeded as tenth baronet in 1856, became inspector of schools at Madras in 1858, professor of history in Elphinstone College, Bombay, and vice-chancellor of Bombay University. In 1868 he was appointed principal of Edinburgh University, where he helped to found the medical school.

GRANT, Alexander (1925–) New Zealand dancer and director, born in Wellington. A scholarship took him to London and the Royal Ballet, Covent Garden, where he was to spend his entire dancing career. A soloist by 1949, he became best known for character roles like Bottom in **Frederick Ashton**'s *The Dream* (1964). From 1971 to 1975 he was director of the Royal Ballet's off-shoot, Ballet For All. From 1976 to 1983 he was director of the National Ballet of Canada.

GRANT, Anne, née **MacVicar** (1755–1838) Scottish poet and essayist, born in Glasgow, the daughter of an army officer. She lived in North America as a child (1758–68). In 1779 she married the Rev James Grant, minister of nearby Laggan. Left a widow in 1801, she turned to writing and published *Poems* (1803), *Letters from the Mountains* (1806), *Memoirs of an American Lady* (1808), and *Superstitions of the Highlanders* (1811). In 1810 she moved to Edinburgh, and in 1825 she received a pension of £50 through the influence of Sir **Walter Scott**.

GRANT, Cary, originally **Archibald Leach** (1904–86) British-born American film actor, born in Bristol. An acrobat and juggler, he travelled to America in 1920 and stayed to pursue a stage career before making his film début in *This is the Night* (1932). He developed a reputation as a suave, debonair performer in sophisticated light comedy, displaying metronomic timing and a sense of the ridiculous in films like *Bringing Up Baby* (1938), *His Girl Friday* (1940) and *Arsenic and Old Lace* (1944). He was also notable as a romantic adventurer in **Hitchcock** thrillers like *Notorious* (1946) and *North By Northwest* (1959). Married five times, he retired from the screen in 1966 and received a special Academy Award in 1970 for his 'unique mastery of the art of screen acting'.

GRANT, Duncan James Corrowr (1885–1978) Scottish painter, born in Rothiemurchus, Inverness. He studied at the Westminster and Slade Schools, in Italy and Paris, and was associated with **Roger Fry**'s Omega Workshops, and later with the London Group. His works, mainly landscapes, portraits and still-life, owe something to the influence of Roger Fry and **Cézanne**, but he also designed textiles, pottery, etc. His *Girl at the piano* is in the Tate Gallery, London.

GRANT, Sir Francis (1803–78) Scottish painter, born in Edinburgh, brother of Sir **James Hope Grant**. He painted sporting scenes, and his portrait groups were in great demand, such as the *Meet of HM Staghounds* and the *Melton Hunt* executed for the Duke of **Wellington**. He was president of the Royal Academy in 1866.

GRANT, James (1822–87) Scottish novelist, born in Edinburgh. After a childhood in Newfoundland and military service he published a long series of novels and histories, illustrative mainly of the achievements of Scottish arms abroad. Among his works are *Adventures of an Aide-de-Camp*; *Frank Hilton, or the Queen's Own*; *Bothwell*; *The Yellow Frigate*, etc.

GRANT, James Augustus (1827–92) Scottish soldier and explorer, born in Nairn. Educated at Marischal College, Aberdeen, he joined the Indian army, eventually reaching the rank of colonel, and seeing service in the battle of Gujerat, the Indian Mutiny, and in the Abyssinian campaign of 1868. With **John Hanning Speke** he explored the sources of the Nile (1860–63) and made important botanical collections. On Speke's death he became the main spokesman for the expedition, becoming a leading African specialist. He wrote *A Walk Across Africa* (1864).

GRANT, Sir James Hope (1808–75) Scottish soldier, born in Kilgraston, Perthshire, brother of Sir **Francis Grant**. He distinguished himself in the two Sikh wars (1845–49), the Indian Mutiny (1857) and the 1860 expedition against China. He commanded the army of Madras (1861–65).

GRANT, Sir William (1755–1832) Scottish-born English judge, born near Elgin. Educated at Elgin Grammar School, King's College, Aberdeen, and Leiden, he was called to the English bar, served as attorney-general of Quebec (1776), as MP for Shrewsbury (1790) and then Banff (1796). A Welsh judge in 1793, and chief justice of Chester (1798), he was appointed master of the rolls (1801–17). In this office he achieved a very high reputation as an equity judge, while in the privy council he contributed substantially to the development of prize law during the Napoleonic wars.

GRANT, Ulysses Simpson (1822–85) American soldier and 18th president of the USA, born in Point Pleasant, Ohio. After graduating from West Point in 1843, he fought in an undistinguished manner in the Mexican War (1846–48), slowly gaining promotion to the position of captain in 1853. He resigned from the army in 1854 and settled on a farm near St Louis, Missouri. However, on the outbreak of the Civil War in 1861 he returned to the army, swiftly becoming a brigadier-general, and secured a series of military successes in the western theatre, culminating in the capture of Vicksburg, Mississippi, in 1863. Having driven the enemy out of Tennessee, he was made a lieutenant-general and given command of the Union forces in 1864. His plan of campaign was to concentrate all the national forces into several distinct armies, which should operate simultaneously against the enemy, **William Sherman** moving toward Atlanta, while

Grant accompanied the army of the Potomac against Richmond. On 4 May he crossed the Rapidan, encountered General **Lee** in the wilderness, and fought a desperate three days' battle, and pursuing the offensive, he drove the enemy within the lines of Richmond. On 29 March 1865, a week's hard fighting began, after which Lee surrendered his entire army on 9 April. The fall of Richmond substantially ended the war. In July 1866 Grant was appointed full general; in 1868 and 1872 he was elected president by the Republicans. Among the events of his administration were the guaranteeing of the right of suffrage without regard to race, colour or previous servitude, and the peaceful settlement of the 'Alabama Claims'. The proposal of a third term of presidency not having been approved, Grant became a sleeping partner in a banking-house. In May 1884 the house suspended, and it was discovered that two of the partners had robbed the general of all he possessed. In the hope of providing for his family, he had begun his autobiography, when in 1884 a sore throat proved to be cancer at the root of the tongue. The sympathies of the nation were aroused, and in March 1885 congress restored him to his rank of general, which he had lost on accepting the presidency.

GRANT, William (1863–1946) Scottish lexicographer, born in Elgin. He studied in France, Belgium and Germany, and became a lecturer in English, modern languages and phonetics at Aberdeen University. He was until his death editor of the *Scottish National Dictionary*, and published various works on Scottish dialects.

GRANVELLE, Antoine Perrenot (1517–86) French-born Spanish prelate and diplomat, son of the jurist and diplomat, Nicholas (1484–1550). Born in Besançon, in 1540 he was appointed bishop of Arras and secretary of state to the emperor, **Charles V**. On the latter's abdication in 1535, he transferred his services to **Philip II** of Spain. In 1559 he became prime minister to **Margaret of Parma** in the Netherlands, in 1560 archbishop of Malinies, and the following year cardinal. His policy of repressing the Protestants provoked such hostility in the Low Countries, however, that at the king's advice he retired in 1564 to Franche-Comte. In 1570 he represented Spain in Rome in drawing up a treaty of alliance with Venice and the papal see against the Turks. From 1570 to 1575 he was viceroy of Naples. He died in Madrid.

GRANVILLE See **GRENVILLE, Sir Bevil**

GRANVILLE, Earl See **CARTERET** and **LEVESON-GOWER**

GRANVILLE-BARKER, Harley (1877–1946) English actor, playwright and producer, born in London. As an actor, he was distinguished by his appearance in **Shaw** plays—he played Marchbanks in *Candida* in 1900. In 1904 he became co-manager of the Court Theatre with Vedrenne, and there followed a four-year season that was a landmark in the history of the British theatre. First performances in England of plays by **Maeterlinck**, **Schnitzler**, **Hauptmann**, **Yeats**, **Galsworthy**, **Masefield** and **Shaw** were performed in circumstances that set new standards of acting and design. In 1907 he left the Court and continued his success with a series of **Shakespeare** plays at the Savoy. He retired from the stage in the early 1920s. Barker wrote several plays, including *The Marrying of Ann Leete* (1902), *The Voysey Inheritance* (1905), *Waste* (performed privately in 1907, publicly in 1936) and *The Madras House* (1910). With William Archer he devised a scheme for a national theatre. He was married first to Lillah McCarthy and then to Helen Huntington Gates, with whom he made the standard translations of plays by **Martínez Sierra** and the **Quintero** brothers. His prefaces to Shakespeare's plays (4 vols, 1927–45) are valuable for their original criticism and ideas on production.

GRAPPELLI, Stephane (1908–) French jazz violinist, born in Paris. Classically trained on violin and other instruments, he was a founder-member of the Quintette du Hot Club de France which brought a European influence into jazz from the mid 1930s. The Belgian gipsy guitarist, **Django Reinhardt**, was his co-leader. Grappelli worked as a solo artist in London during World War II, returning later to France. Since then he has performed prolifically throughout the world, usually leading a quartet and adhering to the bright swing-based style of which he is a recognized master.

GRASS, Günter Wilhelm (1927–) German novelist, born in Danzig (Gdansk, Poland). He was educated at Danzig Volksschule and Gymnasium. Having trained as a stone mason and sculptor, he attended the Academy of Art, Düsseldorf, and the State Academy of Fine Arts, Berlin. He served in World War II and was held as a prisoner-of-war. He has worked as a farm labourer, miner, apprentice stonecutter and jazz musician, and was a speech-writer for **Willy Brandt** when he was mayor of West Berlin. *Die Blechtrommel* (1959, trans *The Tin Drum*, 1962) was the first of the novels that have made him Germany's greatest living novelist. Ostensibly the autobiography of Oska Matzerath, detained in a mental hospital for a murder he did not commit, it caused a furore in Germany because of its depiction of the Nazis. Intellectual and experimental, in form, theme and language, his books consistently challenge the status quo and question our reading of the past. A prolific playwright and poet, he excels in fiction. Important books are *Katz und Maus* (1961, trans *Cat and Mouse*, 1963), *Hundejahre* (1963, trans *Dog Years*, 1965), *Ortlich betäubt* (1969, trans *Local Anaesthetic*, 1970) and *Der Butt* (1977, trans *The Flounder*, 1978).

GRASSI, Giovanni Battista (1854–1925) Italian zoologist, born in Rovellasca. He became professor of comparative anatomy at Rome in 1895, and did important work on worms, eels, termites, and on establishing the role of the anopheles mosquito in the transmission of malaria.

GRASSMANN, Hermann Günther (1809–77) German mathematician and philologist, born in Stettin. He came from a scholarly family and studied theology and classics at Berlin (1827–30), then became a schoolmaster in Berlin and Stettin. His book *Ausdehnungslehre* (1844, 2nd ed 1862) set out a new theory of *n*-dimensional geometry expressed in a novel language and notation. Its obscurity led to its almost complete neglect by mathematicians of the time and it is only since his death that its importance has gradually been recognized; it anticipated much later work in quaternions, vectors, tensors, matrices and differential forms. From 1849 he studied Sanskrit and other ancient Indo-European languages and, unlike his mathematics, his work in Indo-European and Germanic philology met with immediate acceptance.

GRATIAN, (Augustus Gratianus) (359–83) Roman emperor from 375, son of the **Valentinian**. In 367 his father made him Augustus in Gaul. On Valentinian's death he was elevated to the throne, with his half-brother Valentinian II as colleague. Gaul, Spain and Britain fell to Gratian's share, but as his brother was only four years old he virtually ruled the whole western empire; and in 378, on the death of his uncle Valens, he suddenly became sovereign also of the eastern empire. Thereupon he recalled **Theodosius** from Spain, and appointed him his colleague in 379. He was much influenced by St **Ambrose**, and persecuted pagans and heretics. He was eventually overthrown by the usurper Maximus, and was murdered at Lyon.

GRATIAN, (Franciscus Gratianus) (12th century) Italian jurist and Carmaldulensian monk of Bologna. Between 1139 and 1150 he compiled the collection of canon law known as the *Decretum Gratiani*, which became the basic text for all studies of canon law.

GRATTAN, Henry (1746–1820) Irish statesman, born in Dublin. Educated at Trinity College, Dublin and at the Middle Temple, he became such a fervent supporter of **Henry Flood** that his father disinherited him. He deserted law for politics in 1775 when he entered the Irish parliament for Charlemont. When Flood, who had been leading the fight for Irish independence, accepted a government post, Grattan immediately took his place, attempting to secure the removal of the restrictions imposed on Irish trade. When the concessions he won were revoked in 1779, he began the struggle for legislative independence. In 1782 he secured the abolition of all claims by the British parliament to legislate for Ireland, but could not prevent the Act of Union and sat in the parliament at Westminster until his death.

GRAUN, Karl Heinrich (1703/4–1759) German composer, born near Torgau. A singer as well as a composer, he became kapellmeister to **Frederick II, the Great** (1740), and remained with him throughout his career. His works include 32 operas and a 'Passion piece'. His brother Johann Gottlieb (1699–1771), also a composer, was a pupil of **Guiseppe Tartini**.

GRAVENEY, Thomas William (1927–) English cricketer and television commentator, born in Riding Mill, Northumberland. A tall, graceful batsman, he had a patchy Test career; nevertheless, he made eleven Test centuries in the course of compiling 4882 runs, recording double centuries against West Indies at Nottingham in 1957. His career revived in the early 1960s when he moved from Gloucestershire to Worcestershire.

GRAVES, Alfred Perceval (1846–1931) Irish writer and educationist, born in Dublin. An inspector of schools in England, he wrote much Irish folk verse and songs, including 'Father O'Flynn' and an autobiography, *To Return to All That* (1930). A leader of the Celtic revival, he helped to found the Irish Literary Society in London.

GRAVES, Richard (1715–1804) English author, born in Mickleton. Educated at Pembroke College, Oxford, he became a fellow of All Souls, Oxford, in 1736, and also rector of Claverton, near Bath. Of his great output, only his novel *The Spirtual Quixote* (1772), which satirizes **George Whitefield**, is remembered.

GRAVES, Robert James (1796–1853) Irish physician, born in Dublin, the son of a clergyman and biblical scholar. He studied medicine in Edinburgh but took his MB in 1818 from Dublin. After three years' travel in Europe (several months of it with the painter **Turner**), he returned to Dublin when he was appointed physician to the Meath Hospital. There he reorganized medical teaching along the lines advocated in France, with emphasis on physical examination and systematic note-taking and autopsies. He was an excellent diagnostician, best remembered today for his description of a form of hyperthyroidism (Graves' Disease), and his *Clinical Lectures on the Practice of Medicine* (1843) won an international reputation.

GRAVES, Robert von Ranke (1895–1985) English poet, novelist, essayist and critic, born in London and educated at Charterhouse. He joined up in 1914 and his first poetry—*Over the Brazier* (1916), *Fairies and Fusiliers* (1917)—was published during the conflict. Poems by him also appeared in the popular anthology *Georgian Poetry*, but he did not discover his distinctive voice until 1924, when his war-shattered nerves had experienced the delights and disillusions of married love. A year later he met **Laura Riding** with whom he absconded to Majorca on the proceeds of his autobiography, *Goodbye to All That* (1929), and a hack Life of **T E Lawrence**. He lived, travelled and collaborated with Riding until 1939, returned to England for World War II, but returned to settle permanently in Majorca with his second wife, Beryl Hodge, in 1946. His best poetry, written between about 1928 and 1943, is pellucid, tender and evocative, far closer to the metaphysicals than the Victorians. Generally regarded as the best love poet of his generation, he has a broad-based bibliography. His historical novels, eg *I, Claudius* (1934), *Claudius the God* (1934), are confident and imaginative reconstructions. *The White Goddess* (1948) is his most significant non-fiction title, its credo being that real poets get their gift from the Muse. His interest in myth prompted *Greek Myths* (1955) and *Hebrew Myths* (1963).

GRAY, Asa (1810–88) American botanist, born in Sauquoit, New York. He took his MD in 1831, but relinquished medicine for botany, and from 1842 to 1873 was professor of natural history at Harvard, becoming meanwhile a strong Darwinian. From 1838 to 1842 he published the *Flora of North America*. His other works include *Genera Florae Americae Boreali-Orientalis Illustrata* (1845–50), *A Free Examination of Darwin's Treatise* (1861), and *Manual of the Botany of the Northern United States* (1848, known as *Gray's Manual*).

GRAY, David (1838–61) Scottish poet, born in Merkland, near Kirkintilloch, the son of a handloom weaver. He studied divinity at Glasgow University, but took to poetry and in 1860 moved to London with **Robert Buchanan**, but died of consumption the following year. His only collection of poetry, *The Luggie and Other Poems*, a lyrical poem in praise of the stream near his birthplace, was published posthumously in 1874. It also contained *In the Shadows*.

GRAY, Edward Whitaker (1748–1806) English botanist and physician, brother of **Samuel Frederick Gray**. In 1773 he was appointed librarian to the College of Physicians, and in 1787 became keeper of the natural history collections at the British Museum, which he arranged on the Linnaean system, and was much criticized for this.

GRAY, Elisha (1835–1901) American inventor, born in Barnesville, Ohio. A manufacturer of telegraphic apparatus, his firm became the Western Electric Co. His 60 patents included a multiplex telegraph. He also claimed the invention of the telephone, but lost the patent rights to **Alexander Graham Bell** after a long legal battle in the US Supreme Court.

GRAY, George Robert (1808–72) English ornithologist and entomologist, born in London, son of **Samuel Frederick Gray** and brother of **John Edward Gray**. Educated at Merchant Taylor's School, he became zoological assistant at the British Museum in 1831. His first task was cataloguing insects, and he published *Entomology of Australia* (1833). He soon took over the ornithological section of the museum (1831–72), where he produced his most important work, *Genera of Birds* (3 vols, 1844–49). Gray's Grasshopper Warbler is named after him.

GRAY, John Edward (1800–75) English zoologist and botanist, born in Walsall, Staffordshire, son of **Samuel Frederick Gray** and brother of **George Robert Gray**. He studied medicine in London, but was much more interested in botany, and was co-author with his father of *The Natural Arrangement of British Plants* (1821). In 1824 he joined the British Museum as assistant keeper of zoology (keeper, 1840–74) and increased its collections enormously. He published 1162 books, memoirs and notes, mostly zoological but including *Handbook of British Waterweeds* (1864).

GRAY, Milner Connorton (1899–) English graphic designer, born in London, where he studied at Goldsmith's College. He has always been associated with multi-disciplinary design practices. In 1922 he formed probably the first such in Britain with Charles Bassett (Bassett-Gray), and later co-founded with **Misha Black** the Industrial Design Partnership (1935) and the Design Research Unit (1945). He was also, in 1930, one of the founders of the designers' professional body, The Society of Industrial Artists (now Chartered Society of Designers). He worked for the ministry of information during World War II and was involved in two major exhibitions, 'Britain Can Make It' (1946) and the 'Festival of Britain' (1951). Although he designed in other fields, such as ceramics and furniture, he is best known for his co-ordinated 'corporate identity' schemes for such organizations as Ilford, Austin Reed, ICI, Gilbey and British Rail. He became a royal designer for industry in 1937.

GRAY, Robert (1809–72) English prelate. The son of Robert Gray (1762–1834), bishop of Bristol from 1827, he became the first Anglican bishop of Cape Town in 1847 (metropolitan in 1853). He pronounced the deposition of Bishop **John William Colenso** in 1863.

GRAY, Robert (1825–87) Scottish ornithologist, and founder of the Glasgow Natural History Society (1851). A cashier with the Bank of Scotland, he was co-author of *Birds of Ayrshire and Wigtownshire* (1869) and wrote *Birds of the West of Scotland* (1871).

GRAY, Samuel Frederick (1766–1828) English botanist and pharmacologist, brother of **Edward Whitaker Gray**. He published *Supplement to the Pharmacopoeia* (1821), became a lecturer in botany, and wrote *Natural Arrangement of British Plants* (1821) with his son **John Edward Gray**.

GRAY, Simon (1936–) English dramatist, director and novelist, born on Hayling Island. He has written novels and several television plays, but is best known as a stage dramatist. His first play, *Wise Child*, was produced in 1967. Subsequent plays include *Butley* (1971); *Otherwise Engaged* (1975); *The Rear Column* (1978); *Quartermaine's Terms* (1981); *The Common Pursuit* (1984); and *Melon* (1987). A lecturer in English literature at Queen Mary College, London, for 20 years, many of his plays are set in the world of academics, publishers, or academics who publish. His best television play is *After Pilkington* (1987), a wry thriller set in Oxford. He has also published books about the process of staging a play, *An Unnatural Pursuit* (1985) and *How's That for Telling 'Em, Fat Lady?* (1988).

GRAY, Stephen (?–1736) English physicist. He was one of the first experimenters in static electricity, using frictional methods to prove conduction.

GRAY, Thomas (1716–71) English poet, born in London. His father, Philip Gray, was of so violent and jealous a temper that his wife, Dorothy Antrobus, was obliged to separate from him. It was mainly through her efforts that Gray was sent to Eton (1727) and afterwards to Peterhouse, Cambridge (1734). At Eton he met **Horace Walpole**, whom in 1739 he accompanied on the grand tour. They spent two and a half years in France and Italy, but quarrelled at Reggio and parted. Walpole afterwards returned to blame himself, and the breach was healed within three years. Gray returned to England in September 1741. In 1742 he wrote his *Ode on a Distant Prospect of Eton College*, and had begun the *Elegy Written in a Country Churchyard* in Stoke Poges, Buckinghamshire. In the winter he went back to Cambridge, took his bachelorship in civil law, and took up residence in Peterhouse. This was perhaps the happiest period of his life; he wrote letters and enjoyed the company of his friends. The *Ode on Eton College* was printed in 1747 and the *Elegy* was printed in February 1751. His mother died in 1753, and was buried at Stoke Poges, with an epitaph from her son's pen on her tombstone. In 1750 he began the *Pindaric Odes*; the *Progress of Poesy* was finished in 1754; *The Bard*, begun at the same time, in 1757. He moved to Pembroke College, where he spent the remainder of his life quietly in scholarly seclusion. His two Pindaric odes were printed in 1757, and put their author at the head of living English poets. The laureateship was offered to him in 1757, but he declined. From 1760 he devoted himself to early English poetry; later he made studies in Icelandic and Celtic verse, which bore fruit in his Eddaic poems, *The Fatal Sisters* and *The Descent of Odin*—genuine precursors of Romanticism. In 1765 he visited Glamis Castle in Scotland, in 1769 the English Lakes. In 1768 he collected his poems in the first general edition, and accepted the professorship of history and modern languages at Cambridge. He was now comparatively rich, and enjoyed an enviable reputation. He was buried beside his mother at Stoke Poges.

GRAYSON, David See **BAKER, Dame Jane (Abbott)**

GRAZIANI, Rodolfo, Marquis of Neghelli (1882–1955) Italian soldier and administrator, born near Frosinone. He served in World War I, and thereafter in Tripolitania and Cyrenaica. As governor of Somaliland from 1934, he conducted the conquest of Abyssinia from the south (1935–36), and from 1936 to 1937 was a ruthless viceroy of (modern) Ethiopia. In World War II, as governor of Libya, he was ejected from Egypt by British and imperial troops under **Wavell** (1940–41) and resigned, but after the fall of **Mussolini** in 1943 re-emerged as minister of defence and head of continuing Fascist armed resistance. He was captured by his own countrymen on the eve of final capitulation in Italy (1945), tried for war-crimes and sentenced in 1950, but released the same year.

GREATHEAD, James Henry (1844–96) South African-born British inventor, born in Grahamstown, Cape Colony. He went to England in 1859 and after studying civil engineering as an apprentice, at the age of 24 he undertook to build a subway under the Thames in London (1869). To penetrate the very difficult water-bearing strata he devised the Greathead shield, a cylindrical wrought-iron tube pushed forward by powerful screws as material was excavated in front of it. He engaged in various other surface and underground railway contracts and in 1884 patented further improvements to his shield, incorporating the use of compressed air and forward propulsion by hydraulic jacks instead of screws, with which he built the City and South London railway tunnels (1886).

GREATRAKES, or **Greatorex, Valentine** (1629–83) Irish physician, known as the 'touch doctor', was born and died in Affane, County Waterford. From 1649 to 1656 he was an officer in the parliamentary army in Ireland, and from 1662 became famous for curing king's evil and all manner of diseases by 'touching' or 'stroking'. He failed at Whitehall before the king in 1666, but his gratuitous cures were attested by **Robert Boyle**, **Ralph Cudworth**, **Henry More**, and others. To scepticism he replied in his *Brief Account* (1666).

GREAVES, James (1940–) English footballer and television commentator, born in London. Possibly the most deadly finisher to have played Association football, he scored 357 goals in 517 league matches with Chelsea, Tottenham Hotspur and West Ham United. A brief spell with A C Milan in Italy was spectacularly unsuccessful. Greaves possessed to an incredible extent the poacher's 'nose' for a goal and he had the ability to change pace almost undetected. For all that, his highly individual style of play made him difficult to fit into a team pattern and **Alf Ramsey** felt able to do without him in the World Cup Final of 1966. After his retirement he made a new career as a television sports commentator.

GRECO, El, properly **Domenico Theotocopoulos** (1541–1614) Spanish painter, born in Candia, Crete. He studied in Italy, possibly as a pupil of **Titian**, and he is known to have settled in Toledo about 1577, when he was commissioned to execute the decorations for the new church of S Domingo el Antiguo, the centrepiece being the *Assumption of the Virgin* (now at Chicago). He became a portrait painter whose reputation fluctuated because of the suspicion which greeted his characteristic distortions. His painting is a curious blend of Italian Mannerism and Baroque rhythm, with elongated flame-like figures, arbitrary lighting and colour, and, in his later pictures, almost Impressionist brushwork. The most famous of his paintings is probably the *Burial of Count Orgaz* (1586) in the Church of S Tomé, Toledo. Many of his works are to be seen in Toledo, where there is also the Museo del Greco; his *Crucifixion* and *Resurrection* are held in the Prado, Madrid; in New York are, among others, his *Self-portrait* and *View of Toledo*; and the National Gallery, London, has a version of the *Purification of the Temple* and *Christ's Agony in Gethsemane*.

GREELEY, Horace (1811–72) American editor and politician, born in Amherst, New Hampshire. He worked as a printer, came to New York in 1831, started the weekly *New Yorker* in 1834 and in 1841 the daily New York *Tribune*, of which he was the leading editor till his death, exerting, without concern for popularity, a supreme influence on American opinion. The *Tribune* was at first Whig, then antislavery Whig, and finally extreme Republican; it advocated to some extent the social theories of **Fourier**. Greeley at first upheld the constitutional right of the southern states to secede; but when the war began he became one of its most zealous advocates. He published in the *Tribune* the impressive 'Prayer of Twenty Millions', and within a month the emancipation proclamation was issued. After **Lee**'s surrender he warmly advocated a universal amnesty; and his going to Richmond and signing the bail-bond of **Jefferson Davis** awakened a storm of public indignation. In religious faith he was a Universalist. An unsuccessful candidate in 1872 for the presidency, he died in New York.

GREELY, Adolphus Washington (1844–1935) American Arctic explorer, born in Newburyport, Massachusetts. A volunteer in the Civil War, he later entered the regular army as lieutenant. In 1881 he conducted an American expedition to Smith Sound to set up a meteorological station; one of the team travelled to within 396 miles of the pole, the farthest point reached till then. The relief boat failed to turn up in 1883, and when rescue came in 1884, only six of the party of 25 were still alive. In 1887 Greely became chief of the signal service. Major-general in 1906, he retired in 1908 and was awarded the Congressional Medal of Honour in 1931.

GREEN, Charles (1785–1870) English balloonist, born in London. From 1821 to 1852 he made 527 balloon ascents—one, in 1838, to 27 146 feet.

GREEN, George (1793–1841) English mathematician and physicist, born in Sneinton near Nottingham. The son of a baker and miller, he was largely self-taught. In 1828 he published a pamphlet, *An essay on the application of mathematical analysis to the theories of electricity and magnetism*, containing what are now known as Green's theorem and Green's functions. He entered Caius College, Cambridge, in 1833, published several papers on wave motion and optics, and was elected a fellow in 1839.

GREEN, Henry, pseud of **Henry Vincent Yorke** (1905–73) English novelist, born in Tewkesbury, Gloucestershire, and brought up in his family home in the West Country. Educated at Eton and Oxford, he became managing director in his father's engineering company in Birmingham, but pursued a parallel career as a novelist. While still an undergraduate he published *Blindness* (1926), the story of a clever and artistic boy who, blinded in a senseless train accident, turns to writing with powers extraordinarily heightened by his affliction. A contemporary of **Anthony Powell** and **Evelyn Waugh**, his second novel, *Living* (1929), gave a unique insight into life on the factory floor in Birmingham. An elliptical writer and highly stylized, like **Ivy Compton Burnett** he relies heavily on dialogue, plot being conspicuous by its absence. Partial to terse and sophisticated titles such as *Party Going* (1939), *Caught* (1943), *Loving* (1945), *Back* (1946), *Concluding* (1948), *Nothing* (1950) and *Doting* (1952), his influence and reputation extended far beyond the literary cognoscenti, and his writing was much admired in Europe. *Pack My Bag: A Self Portrait* (1940) is autobiographical.

GREEN, John Richard (1837–83) English historian, born in Oxford, and educated at Magdalen School and Jesus College there. He took orders and was in succession curate and vicar of two east-end London parishes, yet snatched time to contribute historical articles to the *Saturday Review*. In 1868 he became librarian at Lambeth, but next year developed tuberculosis, and this made all active work impossible. Thus began his *Short History of the English People* (1874), the first complete history of England from the social side related to geography and the antiquities with superb literary skill. Its instant success encouraged a larger edition, *A History of the English People* (1877–80). His *Making of England* (1881) and the *Conquest of England* (1883) are fragments of an intended history of early England.

GREEN, Julien (1900–) French novelist, born of American parents in Paris. Educated partly in the USA, he was bilingual, and became a convert to Catholicism. He began a successful series of psychological studies in a melancholy vein, written in French but later translated, with *Mont-Cinère* (1925, trans as *Avarice House*). His other works include *The Closed Garden* (1927), *Léviathan* (The Dark Journey), written in 1929, which won the Harper Prize Novel contest, and *Moira* (1950). See his *Journals* I, II, and III (1938–46), *Memories of Happy Days* (1942) and *Memories of Evil Days* (1976).

GREEN, Mary Anne Everett, née **Wood** (1818–95) English historian, born in Sheffield. She calendared the papers of the reigns of **James I** (1857–58) and **Charles II** (1860–68); completed the calendar of the state papers of Queen **Elizabeth I**, with addenda (1869–74); and edited the Commonwealth papers (1875–88).

GREEN, Thomas Hill (1836–82) English philosopher, born in Birkin Rectory, Yorkshire. He was educated at Rugby School and Oxford, where he was an influential teacher and became professor of philosophy in 1878. One of the British school of idealists, influenced by **Kant** and **Hegel**, which included **William Wallace**, **F H Bradley** and **Edward Caird**, his own special interests were in social and political questions. His most important works were the critical Introduction to his edition of **Hume** (1874) and the posthumous *Prolegomena to Ethics* (1883) and *Lectures on the Principles of Political Obligation* (1885).

GREENAWAY, Catherine, known as **Kate** (1846–1901) English artist and book-illustrator, the daughter of a London wood-engraver. She started publishing her immensely popular portrayals of child life in 1879 with *Under the Windows*, followed by *Kate Greenaway's Birthday Book* (1880) and *Mother Goose* (1881). The Greenaway medal is awarded annually for the best British children's book artist.

GREENAWAY, Peter (1942–) English filmmaker and painter, born in London. Trained as a painter, he first exhibited at the Lord's Gallery in 1964. Employed at the Central Office of Information (1965–76), he worked as an editor and began making his own short films. He later gained a reputation for originality and invention on the international festival circuit with such works as *A Walk Through H* (1978) and *The Falls* (1980) before *The Draughtsman's Contract* (1982) won him critical acclaim and a wider audience. He has subsequently pursued a prolific career utilizing ravishing visual composition, a painterly sense of colour and the distinctive music of Michael Nyman to explore such preoccupations as sex, death, decay and gamesmanship in films like *The Belly of An Architect* (1987), *Drowning By Numbers* (1988) and *The Cook, The Thief, His Wife and Her Lover* (1989).

GREENE, (Henry) Graham (1904–) English novelist, short-story writer, essayist, playwright and biographer, born in Berkhamsted. He was educated at Berkhamsted School where his father was headmaster, a factor which made his schooldays difficult. In *A Sort of Life* (1971), the first of two autobiographies (*Ways of Escape*, the second volume, appeared in 1980), he recounts how he played Russian roulette and of how, aged 13, he tried to cut open his leg with a penknife. He went to Balliol College, Oxford, and while there published *Bubbling April* (1925), a collection of verse. He became a Roman Catholic in 1926 and took up journalism as a career with *The Times*. He married in 1927 but it was dissolved. *The Man Within* (1925), like its two immediate successors—*The Name of Action* (1930), *Rumour at Nightfall* (1932)—made little impression and he subsequently disowned them though he later allowed the first to be included in the Collected Edition. *Stamboul Train* (1932) was his first fully successful novel. Like many of his subsequent novels it is sombrely romantic, fusing tragedy and comedy in a peculiar no-man's land that critics christened 'Greeneland'. *It's a Battlefield* (1934) and *England Made Me* (1935) are likewise 'Entertainments', an almost derogatory epithet that Greene first fastened to *Stamboul Train*. A prolific writer, he has written a great number of novels, stories, plays and biographies as well as film criticism. He was the film critic for *Night and Day*, and was partly responsible for its demise when the magazine was successfully sued after he had accused Twentieth Century Fox of 'procuring' **Shirley Temple** 'for immoral purposes'. His career as 'a Catholic novelist' began with *Brighton Rock* (1938), a thriller which asserts that human justice is inadequate and irrelevant to the real struggle against evil. A recurring theme in his work, this is explored in other of the 'Catholic' novels—*The Power and the Glory* (1940), *The Heart of the Matter* (1948) and *The Quiet American* (1955)—whose unorthodoxy has often led him into controversy with the church's hierarchy. Other notable novels include *The Third Man* (1950, filmed by **Carol Reed**), *The End of the Affair* (1951), *Our Man in Havanna* (1958), *A Burnt-Out Case* (1961), *The Comedians* (1965), *Travels With My Aunt* (1969), *The Honorary Consul* (1973), *The Human Factor* (1978), *Doctor Fischer of Geneva* (1980), *Monsignor Quixote* (1982), and *The Captain and the Enemy* (1988). The multifarious settings reflect his wanderlust and his fascination with uncomfortable countries—Argentina, the Congo, Mexico, Vietnam—as well as his seeming disregard for his personal safety. He has also published travel books: *Journey Without Maps* (1936), *The Lawless Roads* (1939) and *In Search of a Character: Two African Journals* (1961). The *Collected Essays* appeared in 1969; the *Collected Stories* in 1972. His plays include *The Living Room* (1953), *The Potting Shed* (1957) and *The Complaisant Lover* (1959). Few modern writers have his range and power, critical acclaim and popular success; he is cited often by his peers as the greatest living novelist.

GREENE, Nathanael (1742–86) American soldier, born in Warwick, Rhode Island, a Quaker's son. A major general in the Continental army he distinguished himself at Trenton (December 1776) and Princeton (January 1777). At the Brandywine (September 1777) he commanded a division and saved the American army from complete destruction; and at Germantown (October 1777) he commanded the left wing, skilfully covering the retreat. From 1778 to 1780 he was quartermaster-general of the army. In 1780 he succeeded **Gates** in command of the army of the south, which had just been defeated by **Cornwallis**, and was without discipline, clothing, arms or spirit. By great activity he got his army into better condition, and though defeated by Cornwallis at Guilford Courthouse (March 1781) he conducted a masterly retreat into South Carolina which, with Georgia, was rapidly retaken, till at Eutaw Springs (September 1781) the war in the south was ended in what was virtually an American victory. A general second perhaps only to **Washington**, he died at Mulberry Grove, Georgia.

GREENE, Robert (1558–92) English dramatist, born in Norwich and educated at Cambridge. He wrote a stream of plays and romances. The latter are often tedious and insipid, but they abound in beautiful poetry. One of them, *Pandosto*, supplied **Shakespeare** with hints for the plot of *The Winter's Tale*. The most popular of his plays was *Friar Bacon and Friar Bungay*. As Greene helped to lay the foundations of the English drama, even his worst plays are valuable historically. After his death appeared the pamphlet entitled *The Repentance of Robert Greene, Master of Arts*, in which he lays bare the wickedness of his former life. His *Groat's Worth of Wit bought with a Million of Repentance* contains one of the few authentic contemporary allusions to Shakespeare.

GREENE, Sir Hugh Carleton (1910–87) English journalist and television executive, brother of **Graham Greene**, born in Berkhamsted, Hertfordshire. After studying at Merton College, Oxford, he moved to Germany, working as a foreign correspondent for the *Daily Herald* and later *The Daily Telegraph* (1934–39). In 1940 he joined the BBC to work on propaganda broadcasts to Germany. In 1946 he became controller of broadcasting in the British zone of Germany and rebuilt the country's peacetime radio service. He worked with the BBC's Overseas Service from 1952 to 1956 and was also the BBC's first director of news and current affairs (1958–60) before being chosen as director-general (1960–69). He injected fresh vigour into the BBC, encouraging it to compete with Independent Television and creating a liberal climate in which programme-makers flourished.

GREENIDGE, Cuthbert Gordon (1951–) West Indian cricketer, born in St Peter, Barbados. An explosive opening batsman, he spent a long time as an English county player with Hampshire, and he averaged 82.23 for the English season of 1984. He scored a century on his Test début, and has since scored twelve others. He holds five West Indian Test partnership records.

GREENOUGH, Horatio (1805–52) American sculptor and writer, born in Boston, Massachusetts. After two years at Harvard he moved to Italy in 1825, where he became a leading member of the American artistic colony there. His principal work is a colossal statue in classical style of **George Washington** as Zeus, commissioned for the Capitol rotunda but now in the Smithsonian Institution, Washington. His advanced views on functionalism and freedom from ornament in design, as expressed in his *Travels, Observations and Experience of a Yankee Stonecutter* (1852), probably influenced the architectural ideas of **Louis Sullivan** and **Frank Lloyd Wright**.

GREENSPAN, Alan (1926–) American businessman and financier. He was president and chief executive officer, Townsend-Greenspan and Co Inc, New York City (1954–74 and 1977–). He was consultant to the US Treasury and to the federal reserve board (1971–74). He has been a consultant to the congressional budget office since 1977, and was a member of the president's economic policy advisory board from 1981 to 1989. He was appointed chairman of the board of governors of the Federal Reserve Bank in 1987.

GREENWAY, Francis Howard (1777–1837) English-born Australian architect, born in Mangotsfield, Gloucestershire, of a West Country family of builders and stonemasons. A student of **John Nash**, he set up his own architecture firm but went bankrupt. In 1812 he was transported for forgery, arriving in Sydney two years later. He was soon given 'ticket-of-leave' and established himself in practice as an architect in the town. Governor **Macquarie** appointed him civil architect, and Greenway designed most of the early colony's public buildings. He made effective use of local material and the best remaining examples of his work, including St James's Church, Sydney, and St Matthew's Church, Windsor, New South Wales, are elegant examples of the Georgian style. Later, his abrasive manner caused him to lose his influential supporters, but he is depicted today on the Australian $10 note, a considerable distinction for a convicted forger.

GREENWOOD, Arthur (1880–1954) English politician, born in Leeds and educated at Leeds University. A wartime member of **Lloyd George**'s secretariat, he became an MP in 1922 and deputy leader of the parliamentary Labour party in 1935, showing himself an outspoken critic of 'appeasement'. In the 1940 government he was minister without portfolio, in 1945 he became lord privy seal, and he resigned from the government in 1947. He remained treasurer of the Labour party, of whose national executive he became chairman in 1953. He did much to shape Labour's social policies. His son, Anthony (1911–82), also a Labour politician, entered parliament in 1946, holding various parliamentary appointments from 1964, minister of housing from 1966; he was made a life peer in 1970.

GREENWOOD, Joan (1921–87) English actress, born in Chelsea. She studied at RADA before making her stage début in *Le Malade Imaginaire* (1938). Her film début came in *John Smith Wakes Up* (1940) and her early theatre work included *The Women* (1939) and *Peter Pan* (1941–42). A woman of distinctive style, her husky tones and feline grace allowed her to be witty and sensual in the portrayal of classical roles and contemporary femmes fatales. She toured with ENSA during the war and appeared with **Donald Wolfit**'s company thereafter. Her film credits include the influential and enduring Ealing comedies *Whisky Galore* (1948), *Kind Hearts and Coronets* (1949) and *The Man in the White Suit* (1951). Later stage successes numbered *Lysistrata* (1957), *Hedda Gabler* (1960) and *Oblomov* (1964). Her film roles included *Tom Jones* (1963) and *Little Dorrit* (1987). She married actor André Morell in 1960.

GREENWOOD, Walter (1903–74) English writer, born in Salford. His novel *Love on the Dole* (1933), inspired by his experiences of unemployment and depression in the early 1930s, made a considerable impact as a document of the times and was subsequently dramatized. He also wrote other novels with a social slant, and several plays.

GREER, Germaine (1939–) Australian feminist, author and lecturer. After attending the universities of Melbourne, Sydney and Cambridge (PhD) she became a lecturer in English at Warwick University (1968–73). Her controversial and highly successful book *The Female Eunuch* (1970) portrayed marriage as a legalized form of slavery for women, and attacked the systematic denial and misrepresentation of female sexuality by male-dominated society. A regular contributor to newspapers and periodicals, and a frequent television panellist, she became (1979) director of the Tulsa Centre for the Study of Women's Literature. Her later works include *Sex and Destiny: the Politics of Human Fertility* (1984).

GREG, William Rathbone (1809–81) English essayist, born in Manchester. He became the manager of mills at Bury and then a commissioner of customs in 1856, and was comptroller of HM Stationery Office (1864–77). His numerous essays on political and social history were collected in *Essays on Political and Social Science* (1854), *Literary and Social Judgments* (1869), and *Miscellaneous Essays* (1884). His *Rocks Ahead* (1874) took a highly pessimistic view of the future of Britain, anticipating with foreboding the political supremacy of the lower classes, industrial decline and the divorce of intelligence from religion.

GREGG, John Robert (1867–1948) Irish-born American publisher, and inventor of a shorthand system named after him, born in Shantonagh, County Monaghan. While working in Liverpool he invented a new shorthand system, published in *Light Line Phonography* and *Gregg Shorthand Manual* (1888). He emigrated to the USA in 1893 and established the Gregg Publishing Company. He published *Gregg Phrase Book* (1901) and *Gregg Speed Studies* (1917), and also founded the *American Shorthand Teacher* in 1920 (later renamed *American Business World*).

GREGG, Sir Norman McAlister (1892–1966) Australian ophthalmologist, born in Burwood, Sydney. Educated at Sydney University, he served with the Royal Australian Medical Corps in World War I and won the MC in France. He later studied ophthalmology in London before returning to Sydney. After an epidemic of German measles there in 1939, his research proved the link between the incidence of that illness in pregnancy and cataracts or blindness in children.

GRÉGOIRE, Henri (1750–1831) French prelate and revolutionary, born near Lunéville. He took orders, and lectured at the Jesuit College of Pont-á-Mousson.

His *Essai sur la régénération des juifs* (1778) became widely popular. Curé of Embermênil in Lorraine, and an ardent democrat, he was sent to the states-general of 1789 as a deputy of the clergy, where he attached himself to the Tiers-état party, and took a prominent part throughout the revolution. He was the first of his order to take the oaths, and was elected 'constitutional bishop' of Loir-et-Cher. He exercised a stern democracy which he identified with the Christian brotherhood of the gospel. At the blasphemous Feast of Reason he refused, in front of the infuriated people, to renounce Christianity. After the 18th Brumaire he became a member of the Corps Législatif, and the Concordat forced him to resign his bishopric. He died in Paris, unreconciled with the church. Among his works are *Histoire des sectes religieuses* (1814) and *L'Église gallicane* (1818).

GREGOR, William (1761–1817) English chemist and clergyman, born in Trewarthenick, Cornwall. A minister in Devonshire and Cornwall, he analysed local minerals, particularly the sand known as *ilmenite*, in which he discovered titanium.

GREGOROVIUS, Ferdinand (1821–91) German historian, born in Neidenburg, East Prussia. He studied theology, but devoted himself to poetry and literature and settled in Rome in 1852. His great standard work is the *History of Rome in the Middle Ages* (trans 1895–1902). Among his numerous other works are *Tombs of the Popes* (trans 1903), *Lucrezia Borgia* (1874), and histories of Athens and Corsica.

GREGORY, St (c.240–332) 'the Illuminator', the apostle of Armenia, said to have been of the royal Persian race of the **Arsacidae**. Brought up a Christian in Cappadocia, he was kept a prisoner for 14 years by Tiridates III for refusing to condone idolatry but, after converting the king (301), he was made patriarch of Armenia.

GREGORY I, the Great (c.540–604) pope (590) and saint, a father of the church. Born in Rome, he was appointed by **Justin II** praetor of Rome, but about 575 relinquished this office. He distributed his wealth among the poor and withdrew into a monastery at Rome, one of seven he had founded. It was while he was here that he saw one day some Anglo-Saxon youths in the slave-market, and was seized with a longing to convert their country to Christianity. He set out on his journey but Pope Benedict compelled him to return due to his popularity. **Pelagius II** sent Gregory as nuncio to Constantinople for aid against the Lombards. He stayed there three years, writing his *Moralia*, an exposition of **Job**. On the death of Pelagius Gregory was unanimously called by the clergy, senate, and people to succeed him. He tried to evade the dignity, but was forced to give in. It is doubtful whether any pope has surpassed Gregory I as an administrator. The Roman church is indebted to him for the complete organization of their public services and ritual and for the systematization of her sacred chants. The mission to England he entrusted to **Augustine** and the Gothic kingdom of Spain, long Arian, was reconciled with the church. His zeal for the reformation of the church was not inferior to his ardour for its growth. Towards heathens and Jews he was most tolerant, and he used all his efforts to repress slave-dealing and to mitigate slavery. When Rome was threatened by the Lombards, he showed himself virtually a temporal sovereign; he rejected the assumption by John, patriarch of Constantinople, of the title of oecumenical or universal bishop. In his writings the whole dogmatical system of the modern church is fully developed. He left homilies on **Ezekiel** and on the gospels, the *Regula* (or *Cura Pastoralis*), and the *Sacramentarium* and *Antiphonarium*. In exegesis he is a fearless allegorist; his Letters and Dialogues abound with miraculous and legendary narratives. His feast day is 12 March.

GREGORY II (669–731) pope (715), and saint, by birth a Roman. The authority of the eastern emperors had sunk in the west into little more than a name and the tyrannical measures of the emperor Leo the Isaurian against image-worship weakened the tie even more. Gregory protested strongly against the imperial policy, the result being a notable aggrandizement of the political authority and influence of the popes in Italy. Under Gregory's auspices **Boniface** began his missionary work in Germany.

GREGORY III (d.741) pope (731–741) and saint, born in Syria. He succeeded **Gregory II**, and excommunicated the Iconoclasts. The threat of the Lombards became so formidable that, the eastern emperors being powerless to help, the Romans compelled Gregory to send a deputation to **Charles Martel**, soliciting his aid, and offering to make him consul of Rome. This offer is of great historical importance: it failed to enlist the aid of Charles but it was a step towards the independence of the west.

GREGORY VII, Hildebrand, St (c.1020–1085) pope (1073), the great representative of the temporal claims of the medieval papacy. Born near Soana in Tuscany, his original name was Hildebrand. He passed his youth in Rome, in the monastery of St Maria. On the death of Gregory VI, whose chaplain he was, he is reported (doubtfully) to have spent some time at Cluny, from where he was recalled by the new and zealous pope **Leo IX**, whom he accompanied to Rome in 1049, and who made him a cardinal. During the four following pontificates Hildebrand continued to exercise great influence and was himself elected pope three days after the death of **Alexander II**. He addressed himself to amending the secularized condition of the church. The feudal standing of the higher clergy, the claims of sovereigns upon temporalities, and the consequent temptation to simony were, he held, the cause of all the evils present in Europe. While he tried to enforce all the details of discipline, it was against investiture that his main efforts were directed. In 1074 he prohibited this practice, under pain of excommunication, and in 1075 he actually issued that sentence against several bishops and councillors of the empire. The emperor **Henry IV**, disregarding these menaces, was cited to Rome to answer for his conduct. Henry's sole reply was defiance and in a diet in Worms in 1076 he declared Gregory deposed. The pontiff retaliated by excommunication, which, unless removed by absolution in twelve months, involved (according also to imperial law) the forfeiture of all civil rights and deposition from every civil and political office. Henry's Saxon subjects appealing over this law against him, compelled him to yield, and by a humiliating penance at Canossa in January 1077 he obtained absolution from the pope in person. But in 1080 Henry resumed hostilities, again declaring Gregory deposed, and appointed an antipope as Clement III. After a siege of three years, Henry took possession of Rome in 1084. Just, however, as Gregory was on the point of falling into his hands, **Robert Guiscard**, the Norman Duke of Apulia, entered the city, set Gregory free, and compelled Henry to return to Germany. But the wretched condition to which Rome was reduced obliged Gregory to withdraw ultimately to Salerno, where he died.

GREGORY VIII, Alberto di Morra (d.1187) pope (1187), died within two months of his election. In 1118 there had already been an antipope who assumed the style of Gregory VIII, but who was expelled and humiliated in 1123.

GREGORY IX (1148–1241) pope (1227), constantly feuded with the emperor **Frederick II**, and asserted the highest view of papal power.

GREGORY XIII, Ugo Buoncompagni (1502–85) pope (1572), born in Bologna, where he was professor of law for several years. He settled at Rome in 1539, was one of the theologians of the Council of Trent, became cardinal in 1565, and was sent as legate to Spain. On the death of **Pius V**, Gregory was elected pope. He displayed extraordinary zeal for the promotion of education; many of the colleges in Rome were wholly or in part endowed by him. The most interesting event of his pontificate was the correction of the calendar and the introduction of the Gregorian computation in 1582. A grievous imputation rests on Gregory's memory from his having ordered a *Te Deum* in Rome on occasion of the massacre of St Bartholomew—on the report of the French ambassador, which represented that infamous episode as the suppression of a Huguenot conspiracy. Gregory published a valuable edition of the *Decretum Gratiani*.

GREGORY XV (1554–1623) pope (1621). He established the still-used procedure for papal elections, set up the congregation of the Propagation of the Faith, regained Moravia and Bohemia to the Roman faith, and canonized **Francis Xavier**, **Ignatius Loyola** and **Teresa of Avila**, among others.

GREGORY XVI (1765–1846) pope (1831), represented reaction and ultramontanism in a revolutionary period. He favoured the Jesuits, and increased the papal debt by spending on buildings and museums.

GREGORY, Augustus Charles (1819–1905) English-born Australian surveyor and explorer, born in Farnsfield, Nottingham. He went to Australia in 1829, joining the Western Australian Survey Department in 1841. In 1846, together with his brothers Frank and Henry, he set out to explore a large area north of Perth and discovered coal on the Irwin River. In 1848 he travelled inland from Shark Bay and found lead in the Murchison River. He then headed the Northern Australian Expedition (1855–56), instigated by the Royal Geographical Society and financed by the British government, which discovered new pastures along the reverse of the route of **Ludwig Leichhardt** in a third of the time. In 1858 his explorations showed that many rivers drained into Lake Eyre and so solved the mystery of the South Australian Lakes. He was surveyor general of the new state of Queensland (1859).

GREGORY, David (1659–1708) Scottish mathematician, nephew of **James Gregory**, born in Aberdeen. He became professor of mathematics at Edinburgh in 1683, and Savilian professor of astronomy at Oxford in 1692. He lacked the originality of his uncle but published textbooks on geometry, astronomy (promoting **Newton**'s gravitational theories) and optics, in which he suggested the possibility of an achromatic lens.

GREGORY, Isabella Augusta, Lady, née **Persse** (1852–1932) Irish playwright. After her marriage to Sir William Henry Gregory (1817–92), governor of Ceylon (1872–77), in 1880, she became an associate of **W B Yeats** in the foundation of the Abbey Theatre in Dublin and the Irish players. For these she wrote a number of short plays; her best, *Spreading the News* (1904) and *The Rising of the Moon* (1907). She also wrote Irish legends in dialect and translated **Molière**.

GREGORY, James (1638–75) Scottish mathematician, born in Drumoak, Aberdeenshire. He graduated from Aberdeen University and went to London in 1662, and the following year published *Optica promota*, containing a description of the Gregorian reflecting telescope that he had invented in 1661. From 1664 to 1667 he was in Padua, where he published a book on the quadrature of the circle and hyperbola, giving convergent infinite sequences for the areas of these curves. In 1668 he became professor of mathematics at St Andrews University. However, he considered himself badly treated there and moved to the chair at Edinburgh in 1674 at double the salary, but died a year later. Much of his later work was concerned with infinite series, a term which he introduced into the language.

GREGORY, James (1753–1821) Scottish physician, born in Aberdeen. He was professor at Edinburgh (1776) and gave his name to 'Gregory's Mixture'.

GREGORY OF NAZIANZUS, St (c.330–c.389) Greek prelate and theologian, born in Cappadocia. Educated at Caesarea, Alexandria and Athens he became a close friend of **Basil the Great**, was made bishop of Sasima, but withdrew to a life of religious study at Nazianzus near his birthplace. The emperor **Theodosius I, the Great** made him patriarch of Constantinople (380), but this dignity also he resigned in the following year. His theological works were largely concerned with upholding Nicene orthodoxy and include discourses, letters and hymns.

GREGORY OF NYSSA (331–95) Christian theologian, was by his brother **Basil the Great** consecrated bishop of Nyssa in Cappadocia about 371. During the persecution of the adherents of the Nicene Creed in the reign of **Valens**, Gregory was deposed, but on the death of Valens was welcomed back (378). He was present at the Council of Constantinople in 381, and was appointed to share in the oversight of the diocese of Pontus. He travelled to Arabia and Jerusalem to set in order the churches there, and was again at a synod in Constantinople in 394. His chief works are his *Twelve Books against Eunomius*, a treatise on the Trinity, several ascetic treatises, many sermons, 23 epistles, and his great *Cathechetical Oration* (1903).

GREGORY OF TOURS (c.538–594) Frankish prelate and historian, born in Arverna (now Clermont), to a distinguished Roman family of Gaul. His recovery from sickness, through a pilgrimage to the grave of St **Martin** of Tours, led Gregory to devote himself to the church, and he was elected bishop of Tours in 573. As a supporter of Sigbert of Austrasia and his wife **Brunhilda** against Chilperic and his wife **Fredegond**, he had to suffer much persecution. His *Historia Francorum* is the chief authority for the history of Gaul in the 6th century. His *Miraculorum libri vii* is a hagiographical compilation.

GREGORY THAUMATURGUS (c.213–c.270) ie, 'wonder-worker', the apostle of Pontus, born in Neocaesarea in Pontus. He became a disciple of **Origen**, and was consecrated bishop of Neocaesarea. His *Ekthesis*, or *Confession of Faith*, is a summary of Origen's theology. The genuineness of two other treatises is doubtful. His *Panegyricus* (which contains an autobiography) is printed among the works of Origen.

GREIG, Sir Samuel (1735–88) Scottish naval commander in the Russian navy, born in Inverkeithing. He transferred to the Russian navy in 1763, just after the assumption of power by the empress **Catherine II, the Great**, and fought in the war with the Turks (1768–72) and the victory at Česme (1770). Promoted rear admiral (1770) and vice admiral (1773), he reformed the fleet and led it in the Baltic war against Sweden (1788–90). His son, Alexis Samuelovich (1775–1845), also became an admiral in the Russian navy and fought in the Russo-Turkish wars of 1807 and 1828–29.

GREIG, Tony (Antony) (1946–) South African cricketer, born in Queenstown. A good all-rounder, he captained England in Test matches, scoring 3599 runs and eight centuries. His great height enabled him to bowl sharp medium pace and he took 141 Test wickets, twice taking ten in a match. He played a leading part in recruiting players from all Test countries to join the rival organization, World Series Cricket, being assembled by the Australian entrepreneur **Kerry Packer** in 1977, and was stripped of the England captaincy. He later became a commentator with Packer's Channel Nine television station in Australia.

GRENFELL, Joyce (1910–75) English entertainer, born in London. She made her début in *The Little Revue* in 1939 and, after touring hospitals with concert parties during World War II, appeared in revue until the early 1950s, delivering comic monologues. She later appeared in her own one-woman shows, such as *Joyce Grenfell Requests The Pleasure*. Her monologues exploited the foibles and manners of middle-class, home counties schoolmistresses and ageing spinster daughters. She wrote her autobiography, *Joyce Grenfell Requests the Pleasure* (1976), and *George, Don't Do That* (1977).

GRENFELL, Julian Henry Francis (1888–1915) English poet. Educated at Eton and Balliol College, Oxford, he was killed in World War I. He is remembered for his fine war poem 'Into Battle' which was published in *The Times* in 1915 and is much favoured by anthologists.

GRENFELL, Sir Wilfred Thomason (1865–1940) English physician and missionary. An Oxford rugby blue and house surgeon to the London Hospital, he took a master mariner's certificate and became a medical missionary in the North Sea fisheries. In 1892 he went to Labrador and founded hospitals, orphanages and other social services as well as fitting out hospital ships for the fishing grounds.

GRENVILLE, Sir Bevil (1596–1643) English royalist soldier, born in Brinn, Cornwall, and hero of **Hawker**'s ballad, *Song of the Western Men*. He studied at Exeter College, Oxford, entered parliament in 1621, and sided for some years with the popular party. From 1639 he warmly espoused the king's cause, helped defeat the parliamentarians at Bradock Down (1643), but fell at the head of the Cornish Infantry in the royalist victory of Landsdowne.

GRENVILLE, George (1712–70) English statesman, younger brother of Richard Grenville, Earl Temple, and father of **William Grenville**, entered parliament in 1741, in 1762 became secretary of state and First Lord of the Admiralty, and in 1763 prime minister. The prosecution of **Wilkes** and the passing of the American Stamp Act took place during his ministry. He resigned in 1765.

GRENVILLE, Sir Richard (c.1541–1591) English naval commander and landowner, born in Buckland Abbey, Devon of ancient Cornish stock. He distinguished himself early by his courage on land and sea in campaigns in Ireland and against the Turks in Hungary. Knighted about 1577 he was member of parliament for Cornwall in 1571 and 1584, and sheriff in 1577. In 1585 he commanded the seven ships carrying **Raleigh**'s first colony to Virginia (the present North Carolina). He fought and despoiled the Spaniards like others of his time. He contributed three ships to the English fleet against the Spanish Armada (1588). In 1591 he was second-in-command of Lord **Thomas Howard**'s squadron of six vessels to the Azores. On board the *Revenge* he was cut off from the main body of the fleet off Flores by a huge Spanish fleet, and sunk after an epic battle against overwhelming odds. **Tennyson** wrote of it in his ballad, *The Revenge*.

GRENVILLE, William Wyndham Grenville, 1st Baron (1759–1834) English statesman, third surviving son of **George Grenville**, studied at Eton and Oxford, became in 1782 a member of parliament, in 1783 paymaster-general, in 1789 speaker; and while home secretary (1790) was created baron. He became foreign secretary in 1791, and resigned, along with **Pitt**, in 1801 on the refusal of **George III** to assent to Catholic emancipation, of which Grenville was a chief supporter. In 1806 he formed the government of 'All the Talent', which, before its dissolution in 1807, abolished the slave-trade. From 1809 to 1815 he acted along with Earl **Grey**, and generally supported **Canning**.

GRESHAM, Sir Thomas (1519–79) English financier and philanthropist, founder of the Royal Exchange, probably born in London, son of Sir Richard Gresham (c.1485–1549), a Lord Mayor of London (1537). From Cambridge in 1543 he passed into the Mercers' Company, and in 1551 was employed as 'king's merchant' at Antwerp. In two years he paid off a heavy loan and restored the king's credit. As a Protestant he was dismissed by Queen **Mary I**, but soon reinstated by Queen **Elizabeth**, who made him ambassador to Netherlands (1559–61). In 1569, on his advice, the state borrowed money from London merchants instead of from foreigners. He made the observation, known as 'Gresham's Law', that of two coins of equal legal exchange value, that of the lower intrinsic value would tend to drive the other out of use. Having in 1564 lost his only son, Richard, from 1566 to 1568 he devoted a portion of his great wealth to building an Exchange, in imitation of that of Antwerp; he made provision for founding Gresham College, London, and he left money for eight alms-houses.

GRESLEY, Sir (Herbert) Nigel (1876–1941) Scottish locomotive engineer, born in Edinburgh. For 30 years from 1911 he was the foremost British locomotive designer of such classic trains as the streamlined 'Silver Jubilee' and 'Coronation' in the mid-1930s. His A4 class Pacific 4-6-2 'Mallard' achieved a world record speed for a steam locomotive of 126 mph in July 1938 which has never been exceeded.

GRÉTRY, André Ernest Modeste (1741–1813) French composer of Belgian birth, born in Liège. He settled in Paris, and composed over 40 comic operas, of which *Le Huron* (1768) and *Lucile* (1769) were the earliest; among the best known are *Raoul* and *Richard Coeur-de-Lion*. He became inspector of the Conservatoire and a member of the Institute. He published his *Mémoires* in 1796.

GRETZKY, Wayne (1961–) Canadian ice-hockey player and holder of numerous records in the sport, born in Bradford, Ontario. He joined the Edmonton Oilers in 1979 and has scored more goals in a season than any other player (92 in 1981–82). He was voted the Most Valuable Player in the National Hockey League from 1980 through to 1987, going on to play for the Los Angeles Kings but carrying with him his nickname, 'The Great One'.

GREUZE, Jean Baptiste (1725–1805) French genre and portrait painter, born in Tournus near Mâcon. His first notable works were historical; after a visit to Italy (1755) he painted Italian subjects; but he is seen at his best in such studies of girls as *The Broken Pitcher* in the Louvre and *Girl with Doves* in the Wallace Collection, London. He died in poverty.

GREVILLE, Charles Cavendish Fulke (1794–1865) English diarist. He was educated at Eton and Christ Church, Oxford, and became private secretary to Earl Bathurst, and was clerk of the privy council (1821–59).

His position gave him peculiar facilities for studying court and public life, as witnessed in his noted *Memoirs* (1875–87); see also his *Letters* (1924), *The Greville Diary* (1927).

GRÉVILLE, Henry, pseud of **Alice Durand,** née **Fleury** (1842–1902) French novelist, born in Paris. She accompanied her father to St Petersburg in 1857, and wrote Russian society novels.

GREVILLE, Sir Fulke, 1st Baron Brooke (1554–1628) English poet and courtier, born in Beauchamp Court, Warwickshire. He was educated at Shrewsbury and Jesus College, Cambridge. A friend of Sir **Philip Sidney** and a favourite of Queen **Elizabeth**, he held many important offices, including secretary for Wales (1583–1628) and Chancellor of the Exchequer (1614–21). He was created baron in 1620. He wrote several didactic poems, over a hundred sonnets, and two tragedies, including *The Tragedy of Mustapha* (1609), printed in 1633. His best-remembered work is his *Life of the Renowned Sir Philip Sidney* (published 1652) with its vivid pictures of contemporary figures. He died a tragic death, murdered by an old retainer who thought himself cut out of his master's will.

GRÉVY, François Paul Jules (1807–91) French statesman, born in Mont-sous-Vaudrey, Jura. As an advocate he acquired distinction in the defence of republican political prisoners. Vice-president of the constituent assembly, he opposed **Louis Napoleon**, and after the *coup d'état* retired from politics; but in 1869 he was again returned for Jura. In February 1871 he became president of the National Assembly, and was re-elected in 1876, 1877 and 1879. The monarchist schemes were attacked by Grévy (1873–76); in 1879 he was elected president of the Republic for seven years. In 1885 he was again elected for seven years, but, hampered by ministerial difficulties, resigned in December 1887. He died at Mont-sous-Vaudrey.

GREW, Nehemiah (1641–1712) English botanist and physician, born in Atherstone. Educated at Cambridge and Leiden, he practised at Coventry and London, and was the author of the pioneering *Anatomy of Plants*, and of *Comparative Anatomy of the Stomach and Guts* (1681).

GREY OF FALLODON, Edward Grey, 1st Viscount (1862–1933) British statesman. Educated at Winchester and Balliol College, Oxford, he succeeded his grandfather in 1882, and was Liberal MP for Berwick-on-Tweed 1885–1916, secretary for foreign affairs 1905–1916, and distinguished himself in the Balkan peace negotiations 1913, and on the outbreak of World War I in 1914. Ambassador at Washington, 1919–20, chancellor of Oxford University from 1928, he issued *Memoirs* in 1925, and wrote on birds (1927) and fly-fishing (1889).

GREY, Albert Henry George Grey, 4th Earl (1851–1917) English colonial administrator, nephew of the 3rd Earl **Grey**. He was an MP (1880–86), administrator of Rhodesia (1896–97), then a BSA company director, and governor-general of Canada (1904–11).

GREY, Dame Beryl, stage name of **Mrs Beryl Svenson** (1927–) English ballerina, born in London. She won a scholarship to Sadler's Wells Ballet School at the age of nine, and her first solo appearance at Sadler's Wells Theatre was in the part of Sabrina, in *Comus*, in 1941. The youngest Giselle ever, at the age of 16 she was prima ballerina of the Sadler's Wells Ballet 1942–57, and has also appeared with the Bolshoi Ballet in Russia (1957–58) and the Chinese Ballet in Peking (1964). She was artistic director of the London Festival Ballet, 1968–79.

GREY, Charles Grey, 2nd Earl (1764–1845) English statesman, born in Fallodon, Northumberland, and educated at Eton and King's College, Cambridge. Whig MP for Northumberland (1786), he was one of the managers of the impeachment of **Warren Hastings**, and in 1792 helped to found the Society of the Friends of the People. He introduced the motion for the impeachment of **Pitt**, and took a prominent part in the temporary 'secession' of the Whigs from parliament; he also denounced the union between England and Ireland. In 1806 Grey, now Lord Howick, became First Lord of the Admiralty, and on the death of **Fox** foreign secretary and leader of the House of Commons. He carried through the act abolishing the African slave-trade. In 1807 he succeeded his father as second Earl Grey. He opposed the renewal of the war in 1815, denounced the coercive measures of the government, condemned the bill against Queen **Caroline**, defended the right of public meeting, and supported the enlightened commercial policy of **Huskisson**. In 1830 he formed a government whose policy, he said, would be one of peace, retrenchment, and reform. The first Reform Bill was produced in March 1831; its defeat led to a dissolution and the return of a parliament still more devoted to reform. A second bill was carried, which the Lords threw out in October, and riots ensued. Early in 1832 a third bill was carried in the Commons, and it weathered the second reading in the Upper House; but when a motion to postpone the disfranchising clauses was adopted, ministers resigned. The Duke of **Wellington** failed to form an administration, and Grey returned to office with power to create a sufficent number of peers to carry the measure. Wellington now withdrew his oppositon, and in June the Reform Bill passed the House of Lords. Grey was the chief of a powerful party in the first reformed parliament, he carried the act for the abolition of slavery in the colonies, as well as a number of minor reforms; but dissensions sprang up, and in consequence of his Irish difficulties he resigned in July 1834.

GREY, Sir George (1799–1882) English statesman, nephew of Charles, 2nd Earl **Grey**, born in Gibraltar. He took a first-class degree from Oriel College, Oxford, and relinquished the law after succeeding his father in the baronetcy in 1828. MP for Devonport (1832–47), under-secretary for the colonies (1834–35), he ably defended against **Roebuck** Lord **John Russell**'s bill for the temporary suspension of the Lower Canadian constitution. In 1839 Grey became judge-advocate, in 1841 chancellor of the duchy of Lancaster, and in 1846 home secretary. During the Chartist disturbances he discharged his duties with vigour and discrimination. He carried the Crown and Government Security Bill, the Alien Bill, and a measure for the further suspension in Ireland of the Habeas Corpus Act (1849). In 1854 he became colonial secretary, and in 1855, under **Palmerston**, took his old post of home secretary. From 1859 he was chancellor of the duchy of Lancaster, and home secretary again (1861–66).

GREY, Sir George (1812–98) British explorer and administrator, born in Lisbon, Portugal. He made two expeditions, in 1837 and 1839, to the north-west of Western Australia, and was later appointed resident magistrate at King George Sound, on the south coast, where he produced a vocabulary of local aboriginal dialects. In 1840 he was appointed governor of South Australia in succession to Gawler, whose administration he criticized in an anonymous memorandum to the Colonial Office. Grey set about a stringent reform of the colony's finances, and although resented, his autocratic and often duplicitous methods ensured the economic success of the colony, but his unfortunate style of leadership led to his transfer to New Zealand as lieutenant-governor in 1845. He was moved in 1854 to become governor of Cape Colony and high commissioner of South Africa, and in 1861 was sent back to New Zealand for a second term, before being dismissed in 1868. He was a member of the New Zealand House of Representatives from 1874 to 1894, with a short term as premier from 1877 to 1879, before retiring to England.

GREY, Henry Grey, 3rd Earl (1802–94) English statesman, son of Charles, 2nd Earl **Grey**. He entered parliament in 1826 as Lord Howick, he became under-secretary for the colonies in his father's ministry, retired in 1833, but was subsequently under-secretary in the home department, and in 1835 secretary for war. In 1841 he opposed **Peel**'s policy, in 1845 succeeded to the peerage, in 1846 became colonial secretary, and in 1852 published his *Defence of Lord John Russell's Colonial Policy*. He opposed the Crimean war, and condemned Beaconsfield's (**Disraeli**'s) Eastern policy. In 1858 he issued his *Essay on Parliamentary Government as to Reform*, and in 1867 his father's *Correspondence with William IV*.

GREY, Lady Jane (1537–54) queen of England for ten days in 1553, the eldest daughter of Henry Grey, Marquess of Dorset and Frances Brandon, daughter of the Duke of Suffolk. Born in Broadstairs, and well educated under the tutorship of **John Aylmer** (later bishop of London), she proved a ready pupil and was especially proficient at languages. During the final illness of **Edward VI**, she was married against her will to Lord **Guildford Dudley**, fourth son of the lord protector, John Dudley, the Earl of **Warwick**, as part of the latter's schemes to ensure a Protestant succession. Declared queen on Edward's death in July, she was rapidly superceded by Edward's sister, **Mary I**, and made prisoner in the Tower. Following a rebellion in her favour under Sir **Thomas Wyatt**, in which her father (now Duke of Suffolk) also took part, she was beheaded with her husband on Tower Hill on 12 February.

GREY, Maria Georgina, née **Shirreff** (1816–1906) English pioneer of women's education, sister of **Emily Shirreff**. She married her cousin William Thomas Grey in 1841. She helped to found the National Union for Promoting the Higher Education of Women (1871), which created the Girls' Public Day School Company, later Trust, in 1872 to establish 'good and cheap Day Schools for Girls of all classes above those attending the Public Elementary Schools', and eventually had some 38 schools which set new academic standards for girls' education. One of the first schools, Croydon, had a kindergarten; with her sister she revived interest in the work of the German educationist **Froebel** and promoted the Froebel Society. The Women's Educational Union opened what was later called Maria Grey College in 1878 as a training college for teachers in higher grade girls' schools. She also published a novel and works on women's enfranchisement and education.

GREY, Zane (1875–1939) American novelist, born in Zanesville, Ohio. He began his working life as a dentist, but after a trip out west in 1904 turned out 'westerns' with machine-like regularity, totalling 54 novels. His best known, *Riders of the Purple Sage*, sold nearly two million copies. His hobby of big-game fishing off the coasts of Australia and New Zealand was utilized in such books as *Tales of Fishing* (1919). His success was due to the 'escapist' lure of his simple adventure plots and attractive, authentic settings.

GRIBOYEDOV, Aleksander Sergeyevich (1795–1829) Russian writer and diplomat, born in Moscow. He wrote *Gore ot Uma* (1824; trans *The Mischief of Being Clever*), a comedy in rhymed iambics, which satirizes the contemporary Moscow society so aptly that it has provided household phrases for the Russian people. Involved in the Decembrist Revolt, he was, however, cleared, and in 1828 became Russian ambassador to Persia. He was killed in an anti-Russian demonstration at the embassy in Teheran.

GRIEG, Edvard Hagerup (1843–1907) Norwegian composer, born in Bergen of Scots descent, his forebear Alexander Greig having emigrated from Aberdeen during the post-1745 depression. On the recommendation of the famous violin virtuoso, **Ole Bull**, he studied at the Leipzig Conservatory, where he came strongly under the influence of **Schumann**'s music. The lack of openings in Norway led to his making Copenhagen his main base between 1863 and 1867. In 1867 he married his cousin, Nina Hagerup, a well-known singer. There he was in close contact with **Niels Gade**, **H C Andersen** and the young Norwegian poet-composer Nordraak. Under their stimulus, he evolved from a German-trained romanticist into a strongly national Norwegian composer. After some years teaching and conducting in Christiania, the success of his incidental music for **Ibsen**'s *Peer Gynt* (1876) on top of the award of a state pension in 1874 enabled him to settle near Bergen. Apart from his A minor piano concerto, some orchestral suites, and three violin sonatas and one quartet, his output included little in the larger forms. In his incidental music to *Peer Gynt* and **Björnson**'s *Sigurd Jorsalfar* and his choral music, and especially in his numerous songs and piano pieces, in which his fastidious taste, sense of the picturesque and intense awareness of his folk heritage synthesized, he expressed himself most individually and successfully.

GRIEG, (Johan) Nordahl Brun (1902–43) Norwegian poet and dramatist, born in Bergen. He studied at Oslo and Oxford, and spent much of his youth travelling, mirrored in his volumes of early poetry such as *Rundt Kap det Gode Haab* (Round the Cape of Good Hope, 1922) and *Norge i våre hjerter* (Norway in our Hearts, 1925). His novel, *Skibet gaar videre* (The Ship Sails On, 1924), crystallized his experiences on a voyage to Australia as an ordinary seaman. A committed anti-Fascist, he wrote dramas about national freedom, as in *Vår aere og vår makt* (Our Honour and our Might, 1935) and *Nederlaget* (Defeat, 1937, about the Paris Commune of 1871). During World War II he joined the Resistance, escaped to London, and broadcast his patriotic verses back to his homeland. His plane was shot down over Berlin in 1943.

GRIERSON, Sir Herbert John Clifford (1866–1960) Scottish critic and scholar, born in Lerwick, Shetland. He was educated at King's College, Aberdeen, where he became professor (1894–1915), and Christ Church, Oxford. He was appointed Regius professor of rhetoric and English literature at Edinburgh (1915–35) and elected rector (1936–39). He edited the poems of **Donne** (1912), and his studies include *Metaphysical Poets* (1921), *Cross Currents in the Literature of the 17th Century* (1929), *Milton and Wordsworth* (1937), *Essays and Addresses* (1940).

GRIERSON, John (1898–1972) Scottish documentary film producer, born in Kilmadock, Stirlingshire, the 'father of British documentary'. After studying communications in the USA he joined the Empire Marketing Board in 1928, with whom he made his reputation with *Drifters* (1929), a film about herring fishermen. He headed the British GPO unit from 1933, inspiring hundreds of short films (including *Night Mail*, with a verse commentary by **W H Auden**). During World War II he set up the National Film

Board of Canada, and was then appointed director of mass communications for UNESCO (1946–48) and film controller at the Central Office of Information in London (1948–50). From 1957 to 1965 he presented an anthology of international documentary films on television.

GRIERSON, Sir Robert, of Lag (c.1655–1733) Scottish Jacobite laird, born about 1655. He succeeded his cousin in the Dumfriesshire estates in 1669. He was for some years steward of Kirkcudbright, and so harried the Covenanters as to leave his name a byword for cruelty; he was one of the judges of the Wigtown martyrs. He received a Nova Scotia baronetcy in 1685, with a pension of £200. After the revolution he was fined and imprisoned as a Jacobite, and in 1696 was arraigned on a false charge of coining.

GRIESBACH, Johann Jakob (1745–1812) German New Testament scholar, born in Butzbach. He studied theology at Tübingen, Halle and Leipzig, lectured at Halle, and in 1775 became a professor at Jena and devoted himself to critical revision of the New Testament text, reclassifying the MSS into three recensions, Alexandrian, Western and Byzantine. See his *Commentarius Criticus* (1811), in which he coined the term 'synoptic' for the first three Gospels.

GRIEVE, Christopher Murray See **MACDIARMID, Hugh**

GRIFFIN, Bernard (1899–1956) English prelate, born in Birmingham. Educated at the English and Beda Colleges, Rome, he became archbishop of Westminster in 1943 and cardinal in 1946. He toured postwar Europe and America and in 1950 was papal legate for the centenary celebrations of the reconstitution of the English hierarchy.

GRIFFIN, Gerald (1803–40) Irish novelist, born in Limerick. He wrote for local journals and went to London in 1823 to make a career in literature. He failed as a dramatist, but was more successful with collections of short stories of southern Irish life like *Holland Tide* (1826) and *Tales of the Munster Festivals* (1827). His novel, *The Collegians*, on which **Boucicault**'s drama *Colleen Bawn* is founded, was published anonymously in 1829. In 1838 he burned his manuscripts and entered a monastery.

GRIFFIN, Walter Burley (1876–1937) American architect and town planner, born in Maywood, Illinois. He graduated from Illinois State University and was for some years an associate of **Frank Lloyd Wright** before establishing his own practice in 1905. In 1912 he won an international competition for the design of the new federal capital of Australia, Canberra, which was to be built on a virgin site in the south of New South Wales. His original design was set aside but Griffin was invited to Melbourne in 1913 and became director of design and construction for the new city. Various disputes led to a royal commission which, in 1917, found in favour of Griffin. He remained as director until the end of 1920 but refused to serve on the committee which superseded him, although his final grandiose and geometric plan was adopted officially in 1925. He then went into private practice in Australia, designing a number of notable buildings and the eccentric Castlecrag estate in north Sydney. He developed something of a speciality in municipal incinerators, designing twelve such buildings, one of which is now preserved. In 1935 he went to India following an invitation to design a library for Lucknow University, and died there two years later.

GRIFFITH, Arthur (1872–1922) Irish political leader, born in Dublin. He was a compositor for a time, and joined the Gaelic League; from 1896 to 1898 he lived in South Africa and worked as a gold-miner in the Rand. Back in Ireland he edited a new weekly paper, *The United Irishman*. In 1905 he founded a new political party, Sinn Fein ('We Ourselves'), and a paper of that name in 1906. A supporter of the Irish volunteers, he took no part in the Easter Rising of 1916, but was imprisoned. He was elected vice-president when a republic was declared in 1918. During the Troubles he was imprisoned again, but signed the Anglo-Irish treaty of 1921 that gave Eire independence.

GRIFFITH, David Lewelyn Wark ('DW') (1875–1948) American film director, born in Kentucky. He started as an actor and short-story writer, before entering the infant film industry, learning his trade in hundreds of short films. After experimenting with new techniques in photography and production he brought out two masterpieces, *The Birth of a Nation* (1915) and *Intolerance* (1916). His *Hearts of the World* (1918) incorporated war scenes actually filmed at the front. Other classic examples are *Broken Blossoms* (1919), and *Orphans of the Storm* (1922).

GRIFFITH, Sir Richard John (1784–1878) Irish geologist and civil engineer, born in Dublin. He became an army officer in the royal Irish Artillery in 1799, but later studied civil engineering in London and Edinburgh. He returned to Ireland in 1808, surveyed the coalfields of Leinster, and examined the Irish bogs for a government commission. As commissioner of valuations after the Irish Valuation Act of 1827 he created 'Griffith's Valuations' for country rate assessments. He published his *Geological Map of Ireland* in 1855, and was consulted in all major Irish building projects, including the National Gallery and Museum of Natural History, Dublin.

GRIFFITH, Samuel Walker (1845–1920) Welsh-born Australian judge, born in Merthyr Tydfil, Glamorgan. Emigrating to Australia in 1854, he studied at Sydney University. From 1867 he practised law in Queensland, and became prime minister of that state three times. He was an active proponent of federation and as chairman of the Constitutional Committee of the National Australian Convention in 1891 had a major role in drafting what became in 1900 the Australian Commonwealth Constitution. Chief justice of Queensland from 1893, he was first chief justice of the High Court of Australia from 1900 to 1919. As such he had considerable responsibility for the Court's assumption of authority to rule on the legislative validity of Commonwealth and State legislation. In non-constitutional cases also, many of his judgments were of importance and retain high authority.

GRIFFITHS, James (1890–1975) Welsh miners' leader and statesman, born in Bettws, Ammanford, Carmarthenshire. A leading official in the miners' union in South Wales, he was elected Labour MP for Llanelli, 1936–70. In the Labour governments 1945–51, he was minister of National Insurance and secretary of state for the colonies. A strong believer in a measure of devolution for Wales, he argued for a separate Welsh Office, and became the first secretary of state for Wales, from 1964 to 1966. He was a moderating influence in Labour party politics during the tensions of the **Gaitskell-Bevan** disputes in the 1950s.

GRIFFITHS, Trevor (1935–) English dramatist, born in Manchester. His first plays, *The Wages of Thin* (1969) and *Occupations* (1970) were staged in his native Manchester. In 1973, *The Party* was staged by the National Theatre; set in May 1968, the play revolves around a discussion of left-wing politics, with **Laurence Olivier**, in his last stage role, playing the central character of John Tagg, an eloquent Glaswegian Trotskyist. *Comedians* (1975) is the story of a group of young apprentice comedians learning their craft under the guidance of an ageing comic. Other plays include *Real Dreams* (1986), a typically angry political piece.

GRIGNARD, (François Auguste) Victor (1871–1935) French organic chemist, born in Cherbourg. Educated at Cherbourg and Lyons, he became professor at Nancy (1910) and at Lyons (1919–35). He discovered the organo-magnesium compounds, which led to the introduction of the 'Grignard reaction', as a method of synthesis. He shared the Nobel prize for chemistry with **Paul Sabatier** in 1912.

GRIGOROVICH, Yuri (1927–) Soviet dancer, artistic director, teacher and choreographer, born in Leningrad. He trained at the Leningrad Choreographic School before joining the Kirov Ballet as a soloist in 1946. His first major ballet, *The Stone Flower* (1957), marked a new stage for Soviet choreography. He followed it with *Legend of Love* (1961). In 1964 he switched allegiance from the Kirov, where he was ballet master, to become chief choreographer and artistic director of the Bolshoi Ballet. His concept of a 'total theatre' for ballet means the dancing springs more purely from the music and is freer from mime than was previously the case in Russia. Functioning as his own librettist, he has brought a fleet elegance to the Bolshoi's celebrated muscular style in ballets like *Spartacus* (1968), for which he was awarded the Lenin prize in 1970, and *Ivan the Terrible* (1975). He has also staged new versions of the classics. A People's Artist of the RSFSR, he is married to Bolshoi dancer **Natalia Bessmertnova**.

GRIGSON, Geoffrey Edward Harvey (1905–85) English poet, critic and editor, born in Pelynt, Cornwall. The founder of the influential magazine *New Verse* (1933–39), he published volumes of verse—*Collected Poems*, 1924–62 (1963)—essays, and anthologies. Erudite, eclectic and idiosyncratic, his was a refreshing anti-establishment voice.

GRILLO See **RISTORI, Adelaide**

GRILLPARZER, Franz (1791–1872) Austrian dramatic poet, born in Vienna. He was in the imperial civil service from 1813 to 1856. He first attracted notice in 1817 with a tragedy, *Die Ahnfrau*, followed by *Sappho* (1818), *Das goldene Vlies* (1820), *Des Meeres und der Liebe Wellen* (1831), *Der Traum ein Leben* (1834), and others. He produced lyric poetry and one excellent prose novel, *Der arme Spielmann*.

GRIMALD, Nicholas (1519–62) English poet and playwright, born of Genoese ancestry in Huntingdonshire. He studied at Christ's College, Cambridge, and became **Ridley**'s chaplain, but recanted under Queen **Mary I**. He contributed 40 poems to **Tottel**'s *Songes and Sonettes* (1557), known as *Tottel's Miscellany*, and translated **Virgil** and **Cicero**. He also wrote two Latin verse tragedies on religious subjects.

GRIMALDI a noble Genoese house, from 1419 lords of the principality of Monaco.

GRIMALDI, Francesco Maria (1618–63) Italian physicist, born in Bologna, where he became professor of mathematics (1638). A Jesuit, he discovered diffraction of light and researched into interference and prismatic dispersion. He was one of the first to postulate a wave theory of light.

GRIMALDI, Joseph (1779–1837) English pantomime clown, born in London. His first appearance was at Sadler's Wells on 16 April 1781 as an infant dancer. He regularly performed there until his retirement from the stage in 1828. He took part in the pantomime of 1781, or that of 1782, at Drury Lane.

GRIMBALD, St (c.820–903) prior of a Flemish monastery near St Omer. About 893 **Alfred the Great** invited him to England. He died abbot of the New Minster in Winchester.

GRIMBERG, Carl (1875–1941) Swedish historian. His huge and romantic popularizing work *Svenska folkets underbara öden 1–11* (The Wonderful Fortunes of the Swedish People, 1913–39) has moulded the popular view of national history.

GRIMKÉ, Angelina Emily (1805–79) American feminist and social reformer, sister of **Sarah Grimké**, born in Charleston, South Carolina. In 1829 she moved to join her sister in Philadelphia, where she vigorously appealed to the women of American to support their fight against slavery (*Appeal to the Christian Women of the South* (1836) and *Appeal to Women of the Nominally Free States* (1837). In 1838 she married and her sister joined her and her husband. With Sarah she continued to agitate for reform until their joint retirement in 1867. Their most significant work was *American Slavery as it is: Testimony of a Thousand Witnesses* (1838).

GRIMKÉ, Sarah Moore (1792–1873) American feminist and social reformer, sister of **Angelina Grimké**, born in Charleston, South Carolina, the daughter of a slave-owning judge. Revolted by the practice of slavery she moved to Philadelphia in 1821, becoming a Quaker, and was soon joined by her sister. Together they set out to eradicate slavery. They moved to New York, where they lectured for the American Anti-Slavery Society (the first women to do so), and broadened their concern to include women's emancipation. They both lectured and taught until their retirement in 1867. Sarah's works include *Epistle to the Clergy of the Southern States* (1836), aimed at changing their views on slavery, and *The Condition of Women* (1838).

GRIMM, Friedrich Melchior, Baron von (1723–1807) German critic and journalist, born in Ratisbon. After studying at Leipzig he accompanied a nobleman to Paris, and became reader to the crown prince of Saxe-Gotha. He became acquainted with **Rousseau** in 1749, and through him with **Diderot**, **Holbach** and Madame d'Epinay. His connection with the Encyclopédistes opened up a brilliant career. He became secretary to the Duke of Orléans, and began to write for several German princes a series of fortnightly private newsletters on Parisian life (1757–73) which gave the most trenchant criticism of all important French books. They were collected as *Correspondance Littéraire* (1812). In 1776 he was made a baron by the Duke of Gotha, and appointed minister-plenipotentiary at the French court. At the revolution he withdrew to Gotha, and afterwards to the court of **Catherine II** of Russia, from where he was sent in 1795 as Russian minister to Hamburg.

GRIMM, Jacob Ludwig Carl (1785–1863) and his brother **Wilhelm Carl** (1786–1859), German folklorists and philologists, born in Hanau in Hesse-Kassel. They both studied at Marburg. In 1808 Jacob became librarian to **Jérôme Bonaparte**, king of Westphalia, and published a work on the Meistersingers (1811). In 1812 the brothers published the first volume of the famous *Kinder und Hausmärchen* (*Grimm's Fairy Tales*)—a work which formed a foundation for the science of comparative folklore. The second volume followed in 1815; the third in 1822. In 1829 the two removed to Göttingen, where Jacob became professor and librarian, and Wilhelm under-librarian (professor 1835). They were among the seven professors dismissed in 1837 for refusing to take the oath of allegiance to the King of Prussia. In 1841 the brothers received professorships in Berlin, where they commenced the compilation of the massive *Deutsches Wörterbuch* (1854–1961). As a philologist, Jacob Grimm published

Deutsche Grammatik (1819), perhaps the greatest philological work of the age. His *Deutsche Rechtsalterthümer* (1828) and *Deutsche Mythologie* (1835) dealt with German usages in the Middle Ages and the old Teutonic superstitions. He also published *Geschichte der deutschen Sprache* (1848) and *Reinhart Fuchs* (1834). He also formulated 'Grimm's Law' of sound changes, an elaboration of earlier findings by the Swedish philologist **Ihre** and the Danish scholar **Rask**, but an important contribution to the study of philology. Wilhelm's chief independent work was *Die Deutsche Heldensage* (1829).

GRIMMELSHAUSEN, Hans Jacob Christoffel von (c.1622–1676) German novelist, born in Gelnhausen in Hesse-Kassel. He served on the imperial side in the Thirty Years' War (1618–48), led a wandering life, but ultimately settled down in Renchen near Kehl, where he became a senior civil servant of the town. In later life he produced a series of remarkable novels. His best works are on the model of the Spanish picaresque romances. The sufferings of the German peasantry at the hands of the lawless troopers who overran the country have never been more powerfully pictured than in *Simplicissimus* (1669, trans 1924), It was followed by *Trutz Simplex* (1669), *Springinsfeld* (1670), *Das wunderbarliche Vogelnest* (1672), and others.

GRIMOND, Jo (Joseph), Baron Grimond (1913–) British Liberal politician, educated at Eton and Balliol College, Oxford. He was called to the bar in 1937, and served during World War II with the Fife and Forfar Yeomanry. In 1945 he contested the Orkney and Shetland seat, which he ultimately won in 1950. He was secretary of the National Trust for Scotland (1947–49) and rector of Edinburgh University (1960–64). From 1956 to 1967 he was leader of the Liberal Party, during which time Liberal representation in Parliament was doubled. His aim of making the Liberal party the real radical alternative to Conservatism was only partially realized in the creation of the Social Democratic party, and later the (Social and) Liberal Democrats. He retired from Parliament in 1983. He published his *A Personal Manifesto* in 1983. He was made a life peer in 1983.

GRIMTHORPE, Edmund Beckett Grimthorpe, 1st Baron (1816–1905) English lawyer, and authority on architecture and horology, born in Carlton Hall, near Newark. Educated at Doncaster, Eton, and Trinity College, Cambridge, he made a fortune at the bar, and then turned his attention to church architecture and clock-making. He designed a new casement for Big Ben in the Palace of Westminster, and restored St Albans Abbey.

GRINDAL, Edmund (1519–83) English prelate and archbishop of Canterbury from 1575, born in St Bees and educated at Cambridge, where he was in turn scholar, fellow and master of Pembroke Hall. A prebendary of Westminster under **Edward VI**, he lived abroad during **Mary I**'s reign, and there studied the doctrines of Geneva, returning to England on the accession of Queen **Elizabeth** (1558). In 1559 he became bishop of London, in 1570 archbishop of York, and in 1575 archbishop of Canterbury. His Puritan sympathies soon estranged him from the court, and his refusal to put down 'prophesyings' or private meetings of the clergy for the study of scripture led to his five years' sequestration in 1577.

GRINGORE, or **Gringoire, Pierre** (c.1475–1538) French poet and dramatist, born in Caen. While taking the chief roles in a theatrical society he was active in the production of pantomime farces, and is one of the creators of the French political comedy. He attacked the enemies of **Louis XII** and thus found cover for his comments on the vices of the nobility, the clergy and even the pope himself. In later life he was a herald to the Duke of Lorraine, and wrote religious poetry. His works include the famous *Mystère de Monseigneur Saint Loys* (c.1524). Gringore figures in **Victor Hugo**'s *Notre Dame*, and in a play by **Banville**.

GRINNELL, Henry (1799–1874) American shipping merchant, born in New Bedford, Massachusetts. He financed an Arctic expedition to search for Sir **John Franklin** in 1850, and another in 1853–55 under **Elisha Kent Kane**. Grinnell Land was named after him.

GRIS, Juan, pseud of **José Victoriano González** (1887–1927) Spanish painter, born in Madrid. He studied in Madrid, and went in 1906 to Paris, where he associated with **Picasso** and **Matisse** and became one of the most logical and consistent exponents of synthetic Cubism. In 1912 he exhibited with the Cubists in the Section d'Or exhibition in Paris, and in 1920 at the Salon des Indépendants. He settled at Boulogne and in 1923 designed the décor for three **Diaghilev** productions. He also worked as a book illustrator. In most of his paintings, the composition of the picture dictates the deliberate distortion and rhythmic rearrangement of the subjects, eg, the *Still Life with Dice* (1922) in the Musée d'Art Moderne, Paris.

GRISEBACH, August Heinrich Rudolph (1814–79) German plant-geographer and taxonomist, born in Hanover. He studied medicine and natural history in Göttingen and Berlin, and made an important collecting journey in north-west Turkey and Central Balkan Peninsula in 1835. Professor of botany at Göttingen from 1841, his publications included *Flora of British West Indian Islands* (1859–1864) and *Vegetation der Erde* (2 vols, 1872).

GRISI, Carlotta (1819–99) Italian ballet-dancer, cousin of the Italian sopranos **Giuditta** and **Giulia Grisi**. She studied under **Jules Perrot**, who became her husband, and was the original 'Giselle' in 1841 at Paris.

GRISI, Giuditta (1805–40) Italian mezzo-soprano, born in Milan, sister of **Giulia Grisi** whom she taught. She was the original Romeo in **Bellini**'s *I Capuleti ed i Montecchi*, but retired on marrying Count Barni in 1833.

GRISI, Giulia (1811–69) Italian soprano, born in Milan, sister of **Giuditta Grisi**. She was renowned for her roles in **Bellini**'s operas, especialy *I Puritani*, which was written for her, and *Norma*.

GRIVAS, George Theodorou (1898–1974) leader of 'EOKA', the Cypriot terrorist organization in the 1950s, born in Cyprus. He commanded a Greek Army division in the Albanian campaign of 1940–41 and was leader of a secret organization called 'X' during the German occupation of Greece. In December 1945 he headed an extreme nationalist movement against the communists. Some nine years later he became head of the underground campaign against British rule in Cyprus, calling himself 'Dighenis' after a legendary Greek hero. His secret diaries were found in 1956 when he had a price of £10000 on his head. After the Cyprus settlement, February 1959, Grivas left Cyprus and, acclaimed a national hero by the Greeks, was promoted general in the Greek army. In 1964 he returned to Cyprus until 1967, when he was recalled to Athens. He returned secretly to Cyprus in 1971 and directed a terrorist campaign for *Enosis* till his death.

GROCK, stage name of **Adrien Wettach** (1880–1959) Swiss clown, world-famous for his virtuosity in both circus and theatre. He wrote *Ich lebe gern* (1930) and *Grock, King of Clowns* (1956, trans Creighton).

GROCYN, William (c.1446–1519) English scholar and humanist, born in Colerne, Wiltshire, the first to teach Greek publicly at Oxford. He was educated at Winchester, and went to New College, Oxford in 1465. He studied in Italy (1488–91), acquiring a knowledge of Greek from the Greek exile **Chalkondylas**; and then settled again at Oxford, where Sir **Thomas More** was his pupil. **Erasmus** lived at Oxford in Grocyn's house, and speaks of him as his 'patronus et praeceptor'. In 1506 he became master of All Hallows' College near Maidstone.

GROEN VAN PRINSTERER, Guilaumme (1801–76) Dutch historian and statesman, born in Voorburg. After studying law and classics at Leiden university, he became secretary to the king's cabinet and archivist to the Dutch royal family, and edited the massive *Archives de la maison d'Orange-Nassau* (1835–61). Converted to evangelical faith in 1830, he advocated a Christian approach to political affairs, rejecting both reactionary conservatism and secular liberalism. In 1847 he published a seminal critique of the French Revolution, *Ongeloof en Revolutie* (Unbelief and Revolution); it became the classic statement of a renascent calvinist political movement in the Netherlands that gave rise to the Anti-Revolutionary party in defense of constitutional monarchy and parliamentary rights, which later joined with the Christian Historical Union to form the Dutch Christian Democratic Party (CDA). He was a member of the Second Chamber of government from 1949 to 1965. His spiritual and intellectual political heir was **Abraham Kuyper**.

GROFÉ, Ferde (1892–1972) American composer, born in New York. He is known for a number of orchestral suites—all named after American places—which are descriptive of the American scene. He orchestrated the *Rhapsody in Blue* for **Gershwin**, and the modern-style orchestra based upon saxophones rather than strings is attributed to him.

GROLIER, Jean Vicomte d'Aguisy (1479–1565) French bibliophile, born in Lyons. He was attached to the court of **Francis I**, went to Italy as intendant-general of the army, was long employed in diplomacy at Milan and Rome, and then became treasurer general of France (1547). He built up a magnificent library of 3000 volumes, dispersed in 1675. He acquired choice copies of the best works, and had them magnificiently bound, with the inscription *Io. Grolierii et Amicorum*. About 350 of his books have come to light.

GROMYKO, Andrei Andreevich (1909–89) Russian statesman, born near Minsk of peasant stock. He studied agriculture and economics and became a research scientist at the Soviet Academy of Sciences. In 1939 he joined the staff of the Russian embassy in Washington, becoming ambassador in 1943 and attending the famous 'big three' conferences at Teheran, Yalta and Potsdam. In 1946 he was elected a deputy of the Supreme Soviet, and in the same year became deputy foreign minister and was made permanent delegate to the UN Security Council, achieving an unenviable reputation through his use of the power of veto no fewer than 25 times. For a few months (1952–53) he was ambassador to the United Kingdom. He succeeded **Shepilov** as foreign minister in 1957, holding this post until 1985. Initially, he relentlessly pursued the 'cold war' against the West, showing no relaxation of the austere and humourless demeanour for which he had become notorious in western diplomatic circles. During the 1970s, however, he adapted to the new détente line. Between July 1985 and October 1988 he held the ceremonial post of head of state and remained a member of the politburo.

GRONCHI, Giovanni (1887–1978) Italian politician, born in Pisa. He played an important part in the organization of trade unionism in Italy, and was one of the founders of the Italian Popular party. He held various political posts until 1923, when he retired from public life for the duration of Fascism. In 1942 he again became a political figure, and was president of the Chamber of Deputies from its foundation in 1948. He was president of Italy from 1955 until 1962.

GRONOVIUS, Jacobus (1645–1716) Dutch classical scholar, son of **Johann Friedrich Gronovius**, born in Deventer. He studied there and at Leiden, became professor at Pisa and in 1679 was appointed to his father's chair at Leiden. His works were *Thesaurus Antiquitatum Graecorum* (1697–1702), and editions of **Polybius**, **Herodotus**, **Cicero**, and **Ammianus Marcellinus**. His elder son, Johann Friedrich (1690–1760), became an eminent botanist; the younger son Abraham (1694–1775) became librarian at Leiden University.

GRONOVIUS, Johann Friedrich (1611–71) Dutch classical scholar, father of **Jacobus Gronovius**, born in Hamburg. In 1643 he became professor at Deventer, and in 1658 at Leiden. He edited **Livy**, **Statius**, **Tacitus**, **Phaedrus**, **Seneca**, **Sallust**, **Pliny** and **Plautus**, and published many learned works, among them *De Sestertiis*.

GROOT, Huig van See **GROTIUS**

GROOTE, Geert de, or **Gerardus Magnus** (1340–84) Dutch religious reformer. Under the influence of the Flemish mystic **Johannes Ruysbroek** he entered a Carthusian monastery in 1375. About 1376 he founded at Deventer the 'Brethren of Common Life', and the houses of Augustinian canons.

GROPIUS, Walter Adolph (1883–1969) German-born American architect, born in Berlin. He studied in Munich and worked in the office of **Peter Behrens** in Berlin; after World War I he was appointed director of the Grand Ducal group of schools in art in Weimar, which he amalgamated and reorganized to form the Bauhaus, which aimed at a new functional interpretation of the applied arts, utilizing glass, metals and textiles. His revolutionary methods and bold use of unusual building materials were condemned as 'architectural socialism' in Weimar, and the Bauhaus was transferred (in 1925) to Dessau, housed in a building which Gropius had designed for it. When the Nazis came to power the Bauhaus became a Nazi training school, and Gropius went to London (1934–37), where he worked on factory designs and housing estates for the Home Counties, including a revolutionary adjunct to Christ Church College, Oxford, which was never built. In 1937 he emigrated to the US, where he became professor of architecture at Harvard University (1938–52), and designed the Harvard Graduate Center (1949) and the American Embassy in Athens (1960). His other major constructions include the Fagus shoe factory at Alfeld (1911), a model factory and office for the Cologne Exhibition (1914), and large housing estates in Germany. He also designed Adler car bodies (1929–33).

GROS, Antoine Jean, Baron (1771–1835) French historical painter, born in Paris. He studied under **Jaques Louis David** and later travelled with **Napoleon**'s armies and acquired celebrity by his great pictures of his battles (1797–1811); *Charles V and Francis I* (1812); *Departure of Louis XVIII for Ghent* (1815); and *Embarkation of the Duchess of Angoulême* (1815). These works combine Classicism and Romanticism. Later Gros attempted a return to Classicism, found his work ignored and drowned himself in the Seine.

GROSE, Francis (1731–91) English antiquary, born in Greenford, Middlesex, of Swiss extraction. He squandered the family fortune, but applied himself to his *Antiquities of England and Wales* (1773–1787). He toured Scotland and Ireland for antiquarian material but died suddenly in Dublin. Other works include *A Classical Dictionary of the Vulgar Tongue* (1785) and *Treatise on Ancient Armour and Weapons* (1785–1789).

GROSS, Hans (1847–1915) Austrian criminologist and lawyer, born in Graz. A pioneer in the application of science to the detection of crime, from 1905 he was professor of criminal law at Graz, where he established the first criminal museum. His *Handbuch für Untersuchungsrichter* (1893; Eng trans 1907) is a standard work.

GROSSETESTE, Robert (c.1175–1253) English prelate, born in Stradbroke in Suffolk, and educated at Lincoln, Oxford and Paris. He had for some years been the first teacher of theology in the Franciscan school at Oxford, and had held many preferments, including the chancellorship of Oxford. But he resigned them all when in 1235 he became bishop of Lincoln and undertook the reformation of abuses, involving himself with his own chapter and with Pope **Innocent IV**. The pope granted English benefices to Romans who drew the revenues of their office, but seldom appeared in the country. Grosseteste set himself strongly against this, incurring a temporary suspension from his bishopric and a continual menace of excommunication. In the last year of the bishop's life he refused the pope's request to promote his nephew, an Italian, to a canonry and the pope is said to have excommunicated him. Even so his clergy went on obeying him till his death in Buckden near Huntingdon. Pegge's catalogue of his works included 'treatises on sound, motion, heat, colour form, angles, atmospheric pressure, poison, the rainbow, comets, light, the astrolabe, necromancy and witchcraft'.

GROSSI, Tommaso (1791–1853) Italian poet, born in Bellano on Lake Como. He studied law at Padua and practised at Milan. His first poem, *La Prineide* (1814), was a battle poem in the Milanese dialect. There followed several historical romances, and the epic poem for which he is best known, *I Lombardi alla prima crociata* (1826).

GROSSMITH, George (1847–1912) English comedian and entertainer. From 1877 to 1889 he took leading parts in **Gilbert** and **Sullivan**'s operas. With his brother, Weedon (1853–1919), he wrote *Diary of a Nobody* in *Punch* (1892). His son George (1874–1935) was a well-known musical-comedy actor (*Our Miss Gibbs*, *Sally*, *No, No, Nanette*, etc), songwriter and manager of the Gaiety Theatre.

GROSZ, George (1893–1959) German-born American artist, born in Berlin. He studied at Dresden and Berlin, and was associated with the Berlin Dadaists in 1917 and 1918. While in Germany he produced a series of bitter, ironical drawings attacking German militarism and the middle classes. He fled to the USA in 1932 (becoming naturalized in 1938) and subsequently produced many oil-paintings of a symbolic nature. He returned to Berlin in 1959, where he died.

GROSZ, Karoly (1930–) Hungarian communist politician. Born in Miskolc, the son of a steel worker, he began his career as a printer and then a newspaper editor. He joined the ruling Hungarian Socialist Workers' party (HSWP) in 1945 and moved to Budapest in 1961 to work in the agitprop department, becoming its deputy head in 1968 and its head in 1974. Grosz served as Budapest party chief (1984–87) and was inducted into the HSWP politburo in 1985. He became prime minister in 1987 and succeeded **Janos Kadar** as HSWP leader in 1988, giving up his position as prime minister six months later. He pragmatically moved with the times and, following the lead given by **Mikhail Gorbachev** in Moscow, became a committed and frank-speaking reformer in both the economic and political spheres, seeking to establish in Hungary a new system of 'socialist pluralism'. However, when, in October 1989, the HSWP reconstituted itself as the new Hungarian Socialist party (HSP), he was replaced as party leader by Rezso Nyers, a radical social democrat.

GROTE, George (1794–1871) English historian and politician, born in Clay Hill, Beckenham, Kent. Educated at Charterhouse, in 1810 he became a clerk in the bank founded in 1766 by his grandfather (a native of Bremen) in Threadneedle Street, of which he became governor (1830–43). From 1832 to 1841 he was MP for the City of London. During his first session he brought forward a motion for the adoption of the ballot; it was lost, but Grote continued to advocate the measure until he retired from parliamentary life and the banking-house to devote himself exclusively to literature, mainly to his great *History of Greece* (1846–1856). In 1865 he concluded an elaborate work on *Plato and the other Companions of Socrates*, which, with his (unfinished) *Aristotle*, was supplementary to the *History*. He also wrote *Fragments on Ethical Subjects* (1876). He was buried in Westminster Abbey. His wife, née Harriet Lewin (1792–1878), wrote a *Memoir of Ary Scheffer* (1860), *Collected Papers in Prose and Verse* (1862), and *The Personal Life of George Grote* (1873).

GROTEFEND, Georg Friedrich (1775–1853) German scholar and epigraphist, born in Münden in Hanover. A schoolteacher at Göttingen, Frankfurt and Hanover, he wrote on Latin, Umbrian and Oscan philology. He achieved fame in 1802 by deciphering several symbols in the Persian cuneiform alphabet for a bet.

GROTH, Klaus (1819–99) German poet, born in Heide in Holstein. A schoolteacher, in 1866 he became professor of German language and literature at Kiel. His masterpiece, *Quickborn* (1852), is a series of poems in Low German (Plattdeutsch) dealing with life in Ditmarsh. Some of his work is in High German, and he published children's tales and short stories.

GROTIUS, Hugo, or **Huig de Groot** (1583–1645) Dutch jurist and theologian, born in Delft. He studied at Leiden, and accompanied an embassy to France. On his return he practised as a lawyer in the Hague; in 1613 he was appointed pensionary of Rotterdam. The religious disputes between the Remonstrants or Arminians and their opponents were now at their height. Grotius, like his patron the grand-pensionary **Barneveldt**, supported the Remonstrants. In 1618 both were arrested, tried, and condemned by the dominant party under Prince **Maurice**: Barneveldt to death, and Grotius to imprisonment for life. He escaped, however, with the aid of his wife, and found refuge in Paris in 1621, when **Louis XIII** for a time gave him a pension. In 1625 he published his great work on International Law, *De Jura Belli et Pacis* in which he appealed to 'natural Law' and the social contract as a basis for rational principles on which a system of laws could be formulated. His influence was profound. In 1634 he entered the Swedish service as ambassador at the French court. On his retirement in 1645 he proceeded to Stockholm, but, disliking court and climate, was on his way back to Holland when he died. Grotius also wrote Latin and Dutch verse. His tragedy, *Adamus Exsul*, was one of **Milton**'s sources. His best historical work is *Annales de Rebus Belgicis* (1657). He annotated the Bible (1641–46), and wrote the famous *De Veritate Religionis Christianae* (1627).

GROTOWSKI, Jerzy (1933–) Polish stage director and avant-gardist. He trained at the Cracow Theatre School, and moved to Wroclaw in 1965, where he established the Theatre Laboratory. In 1968 the

Theatre Laboratory visited the Edinburgh Festival, and went on to London and New York. In 1968 he published *Towards a Poor Theatre*, detailing many of his ideas about theatre and performance. In 1976 he disbanded his Theatre Laboratory, and embarked on a new direction, working with actors and students on shows of his own devising to which no audiences are admitted.

GROUCHY, Emmanuel, Marquis de (1766–1847) French Napoleonic soldier, born in Paris. He threw in his lot with the Revolution, and had his first taste of war during the Vendean revolt, was second to **Hoche** in the abortive expedition to Ireland (1796), and greatly distinguished himself in Italy (1798). Later he fought at Hohenlinden, Eylau, Friedland, Wagram, and in the Russian campaign of 1812; and after Leipzig covered the retreat of the French. On **Napoleon**'s escape from Elba, he destroyed the Bourbon opposition in the south of France, and helped to rout **Blücher** at Ligny, but failed to play an effective part at Waterloo due to misleading orders (1815). After Waterloo, as commander-in-chief of the broken armies of France, he led them skilfully back towards the capital; then, resigning, retired to the USA. He returned in 1819, and was reinstated as marshal in 1831.

GROVE, Sir George (1820–1900) English musicologist, biblical scholar and civil engineer, born in Clapham. Trained as a civil engineer, he erected in the West Indies the first two cast-iron lighthouses, and assisted in the Britannia tubular bridge. He was secretary to the Society of Arts (1849–52), and then secretary and director of the Crystal Palace Company. He was editor of *Macmillan's Magazine*, a major contributor to Sir **William Smith**'s *Dictionary of the Bible*, and editor of the great *Dictionary of Music and Musicians* (1878–89; 5th ed 1954). On a journey with Sir **Arthur Sullivan** to Vienna in 1867 he participated in the discovery of compositions by **Schubert**. His *Beethoven and his Nine Symphonies* (1896; new ed 1956) remained a standard work for years. He was knighted in 1883 on the opening of the Royal College of Music, of which he was director till 1895.

GROVE, Sir William Robert (1811–96) Welsh physicist and jurist, born in Swansea. Educated at Oxford, he invented a new type of voltaic cell named after him (1839). As professor of physics at the London Institution (1841–64), he studied electrolytic decomposition and demonstrated the dissociation of water. Thereafter he turned to the law, was raised to the bench (1871), and became a judge in the High Court of Justice (1875–87).

GRUB, George (1812–92) Scottish church historian, born in Aberdeen. He was librarian to the Society of Advocates in Aberdeen (1841), and lecturer in Scots Law at Marischal College, Aberdeen (1842), and professor from 1881. He was the author of an *Ecclesiastical History of Scotland* (1861) from the Episcopalian standpoint.

GRUBB, Sir Kenneth George (1900–80) English missionary, ecumenist, and Anglican lay churchman, born in Oxton, Nottinghamshire. Following extensive research on religious and social conditions in South America in the 1930s and wartime service with the ministry of information, he became president of the Church Missionary Society (1944–69), chairman of the Churches Committee on International Affairs (1946–68), and chairman of the House of Laity in the Church Assembly (1959–70). Author of several studies on South America and successive editions of the *World Christian Handbook* (1949–68), he revealed his waspish assessments of himself and others in *A Layman Looks at the Church* (1964) and his autobiography *Crypts of Power* (1971).

GRUENBERG, Louis (1884–1964) American composer of Russian birth, born near Brest-Litovsk. He was taken to the USA at the age of two. A pupil of **Busoni**, he worked as a concert pianist until 1919, and then retired to devote himself to composition. He wrote extensively for orchestra, chamber music combinations and voices, but is best known for his opera *The Emperor Jones*, based on **Eugene O'Neill**'s play.

GRUMMAN, Leroy Randle (1895–1982) American engineer and aircraft pioneer, born in Huntington, New York. He studied engineering at Cornell University, and served as a navy pilot in World War I. From 1921 to 1929 he was general manager of the Loening Aeronautical Corporation, thereafter forming the Grumman Aircraft Engineering Corporation at Bethpage, Long Island. He produced a series of successful navy aircraft—Wildcat, Hellcat, Bearcat and Tiger Cat—which played vital roles in the naval wars in the Pacific and the Atlantic in World War II. These were followed by jet fighters Panther, Cougar and Tiger, and several attack and search aircraft. Grumman built the Lunar Excursion Module (LEM) for the Apollo flights to the Moon.

GRÜN, Anastasius See **AUERSPERG**

GRÜN, Hans See **BALDUNG**

GRUNDTVIG, Nikolai Frederik Severin (1783–1872) Danish theologian and poet, born in Udby in Zealand. He studied theology at Copenhagen, but turned to writing after a broken love affair. He wrote *Northern Mythology* (1801) and *The Decline of the Heroic Age in the North* (1809), and some volumes of patriotic poetry. He became a curate in his father's church in 1815, but was soon embroiled in controversy over his criticisms of the rationalist tendency in the Danish church, and was suspended from preaching in 1825. His antiquarian interests had continued with translations of **Snorri Sturluson**'s *Heimskringla* and **Saxo Grammaticus**, followed by a translation of *Beowulf* (1820). During three study tours to England he formed the ideas which led to the creation of Folk High Schools, which had a tremendous effect on rural life and education. In 1862 he was made titular 'bishop' of Zealand.

GRUNER, Elioth (1882–1939) New Zealand-born Australian painter of Norwegian and Irish parentage, born in Gisborne, New Zealand. Having arrived in Sydney as an infant, he was accepted by **Julian Ashton** as a pupil in 1894, and later became an assistant at Ashton's Sydney Art School. He won his first Wynne prize, for landscape painting, in 1916 and was to win six more in the next twenty years. Although sometimes criticized for a primness and lack of vitality, his best work captures the special quality of the Australian light, and he is regarded as one of Australia's leading landscape artists. He organized the exhibition of Australian art shown at the Royal Academy in 1923, and his work was exhibited at the Royal Academy and the Paris Salon.

GRÜNEWALD, Isaak (1889–1946) Swedish painter, born in Stockholm, a leader of Scandinavian Expressionism. His wife, Sigrid Grünewald-Hjerten (1885–1946), was also a painter.

GRÜNEWALD, Matthias, real name **Mathis Nithardt,** otherwise **Gothardt** (1480?–1528) German artist, architect, and engineer, probably born in Würzburg. Very little is known of his life, but he was court painter to the archbishop of Mainz from 1508 to 1514 and to Cardinal Albrecht of Brandenburg from 1515 to 1525, and he designed waterworks for Magdeburg about 1526. In 1516 he completed the great

Isenheim altarpiece (Colmar Museum), the nine paintings of which exhibit his rare, livid colours and his use of distortion to portray passion and suffering. Grünewald is the *Mathis der Maler* of **Hindemith**'s opera.

GRYPHIUS, or **GREIF, Andreas** (1616–64) German lyric poet and dramatist, born in Glogau, Silesia. He travelled in Holland, France and Italy, studying medicine and astronomy, and returned to his native town. His early misfortunes led him to the 'all is vanity' theme of his lyrics, expressed in deep gloom, collected under the title *Sonn-und-Feiertagssonette* (1639). His dramas mainly concern martyrdom and include *Leo Armenius* (1650), *Catharina von Georgien* (1657) and *Papinianus* (1659). But he also wrote the charming pastoral, *Die geliebte Dornrose* (1660), the comedies *Herr Peter Squentz* (1663), which resembles the Bottom scenes in **Shakespeare**'s *A Midsummer Night's Dream*, and *Horribilicribrifax* (1663), satirizing the Thirty Years' War. He was indirectly influenced by Shakespeare and **Vondel**.

GRYPHIUS, Sebastian (1493–1556) German printer, born in Reutlingen in Swabia. In 1528 he came to Lyons and there between 1528 and 1547 printed more than 300 works, notable for their accuracy and clear type. Among the more noted are the fine Latin Bible of 1550 and **Étienne Dolet**'s *Commentaria Linguae Latinae* (1536). Gryphius's sons, Antoine and François, were also famous French printers.

GUARDI, Francesco (1712–93) Italian painter, born in Pinzolo. He was a pupil of **Canaletto**, and was noted for his views of Venice, full of sparkling colour, with an impressionist's eye for effects of light. His *View of the Church and Piazza of S Marco* is in the National Gallery. His brothers, Giovanni Antonio (1669–1760) and Nicolò (1715–86), often collaborated with him.

GUARESCHI, Giovanni (1908–68) Italian journalist and writer, born in Parma. He became editor of the Milan magazine *Bertoldo*. After World War II, in which he was a prisoner, he returned to Milan and journalism, but it was *The Little World of Don Camillo* (1950) which brought him fame. These stories of the village priest and the communist mayor with their broad humour and rich humanity have been translated into many languages, and have been followed by *Don Camillo and the Prodigal Son* (1952) and others. He illustrated his books with his own drawings.

GUARINI, Giovanni Battista (1538–1612) Italian poet, born in Ferrara. He was entrusted by Duke Alfonso II with diplomatic missions to the pope, the emperor, and was sent to Venice and Poland. His chief work was the famous pastoral play, *Il Pastor Fido* (1585), really an imitation of **Tasso**'s *Aminta*.

GUARINI, Guarino, originally **Camillo** (1624–83) Italian Baroque architect, philosopher and mathematician, born in Modena. At the age of 15 he became a Theatine monk. In Rome he studied **Borromini**, from whom he developed his own style. A love of complexity and movement in all dimensions is the keynote of his work. He designed several churches in Turin, of which the only two survivors are San Lorenzo (1668–80) and Capella della SS Sindone (1668), and the Palazzo Carignano (1679), as well as palaces for Bavaria and Baden. He also published books on mathematics, astronomy, and architecture. His influential *Architectura Civile* (published posthumously in 1737), concerning the relationship of geometry and architecture, also included a defence of Gothic architecture.

GUARINO DA VERONA (1370–1460) Italian humanist, born in Verona. In 1388 he went to Constantinople to learn Greek under **Chrysoloras**; after his return (1410), he taught Greek in Verona, Padua, Bologna and Ferrara. He wrote Greek and Latin grammars, translated parts of **Strabo** and **Plutarch**, and helped to establish the text of **Livy**, **Plautus**, **Catullus** and **Pliny**.

GUARNIERI, or **Guarneri** a celebrated Italian family of violin-makers of Cremona, of whom the most important were Andrea (fl.1650–1695), his sons Giuseppe (fl.1690–1730) and Pietro (fl.1690–1725), and Giuseppe's son Giuseppe (fl.1725–45), the last especially famous, and commonly known as Giuseppe del Gesù because he signed his violins with IHS after his name.

GUBERNATIS, Angelo de (1840–1913) Italian orientalist, born in Turin. In 1863 he became professor of Sanskrit at Florence, but resigned his chair that same year to follow the socialistic dreams of **Bakunin**, whose cousin he married, but soon had himself re-elected professor (1867); in 1891 he accepted a call to Rome. His works on zoological mythology, birth and funeral customs, Vedic mythology, plant lore and comparative mythology are marred by fantastic solar interpretation; he also published reminiscences, a French dictionary of contemporary authors, histories of Indian and of universal literature, and other works.

GUDERIAN, Heinz (1888–1954) German soldier. A leading tank expert and exponent of the *Blitzkrieg* theory, he created the panzer armies which overran Poland in 1939 and France in 1940. He commanded the 2nd Panzer Group in Army Group Centre under **Bock** in the attack on the USSR in June, 1941. Recalled after the failure to take Moscow, he was chief of general staff in 1944, and after the anti-Hitler plot in the same year was made commander on the eastern front. He wrote *Panzer Leader* (1952).

GUEDALLA, Philip (1889–1944) English writer, born in London. Educated at Rugby and Oxford, he was a barrister (1913–1923). Sometimes described as the most distinguished and certainly the most popular historian of his time, he was the author of *Second Empire* (1922), *Palmerston* (1926), *The Hundred Days* (1934), *The Hundredth Year* (1940), *Two Marshals* (**Bazaine** and **Pétain**) (1943) and *Middle East* (1944).

GUELF (c.825–1866) more properly Welf, a German dynasty. The first known Welf was a member of the Frankish aristocracy who held lands in Bavaria and Swabia around 825. The elder line died out with Welf III (1047), whose sister Kunigunde married Azzo II, Marquis of Este. Their son Welf IV became Duke of Bavaria in 1070, and the family reached the height of its power under **Henry the Lion**, Duke of Saxony and Bavaria. After his struggle with **Frederick I, Barbarossa** Henry was deprived of both duchies but was permitted to retain his allodial possessions in north Germany which were formed into the duchy of Braunschweig-Lüneburg (1235) for his grandson Otto (1204–52), from whom all subsequent branches descend. The elder, Lüneburg branch became electors (1692) and later kings (1814) of Hanover, and in 1714 the elector George Ludwig ascended the British throne as **George I**. The union of the crowns of Britain and Hanover under the Guelfs continued until the death of **William IV** (1837); on the accession of **Victoria**, Hanover (which under the Salic Law could only be ruled by males) passed to her uncle Ernest Augustus III (1771–1851), Duke of Cumberland, whose son **George V** of Hanover lost his throne when Hanover was annexed by Prussia in 1866. In medieval Italy, the term Guelfs came to be applied to political factions, represented especially in the cities of Lombardy and Tuscany, which were at least nominally allies of the papacy and the Angevin rulers of Naples. Their opponents were the imperialist Ghibellines, originally supporters of the **Hohenstaufen** dynasty.

GUERCINO, 'the squint-eyed', properly **Gian-Francesco Barbieri** (1590–1666) Italian painter of the Bolognese school, born in Cento. He painted the famous *Aurora* at the Villa Ludovisi in Rome for Pope **Gregory XV**. In 1642, after the death of **Guido Reni**, he became the dominant painter of Bologna, combining in his work the liveliness and movement of the **Carracci** with a warmer, more Venetian colouring.

GUERICKE, Otto von (1602–86) German engineer and physicist, inventor of the vacuum pump, born in Magdeburg (now in East Germany). He worked in Leipzig, Helmstadt, Jena and Leiden, studying law and mathematics, mechanics and fortifications. An engineer in the Swedish army, he became one of the four burgomasters of Magdeburg from 1646 to 1681, elected for his service to the town as an engineer and diplomat during its siege in the Thirty Years' War. His interest in the possibility of a vacuum led him to modify a water pump so that it would remove most of the air from a container. His most dramatic demonstration of atmospheric pressure took place at Regensburg before the emperor **Ferdinand III**. Two large metal hemispheres were placed together and the air within pumped out; they could not be separated by two teams of eight horses, but fell apart when the air re-entered. Such pumps allowed new areas of physics to be studied.

GUÉRIN, Charles (1873–1907) French symbolist poet, born in Lunéville. He travelled in Germany and Italy and periodically stayed in Paris. His work is confined to a few collections, including *Le Cœur solitaire* (1898) and *L'Éros funèbre* (1900). A later series, *L'Homme intérieur* (1906), echoed his late conversion to the Catholic faith.

GUÉRIN, Eugénie de (1805–48) French writer, born in the château of Le Cayla (Tarn), sister of **Georges Guerin**, to whom she was devoted. She is chiefly known for her *Journal* (1855), which is imbued with mysticism, but she also wrote poems and edited her brother's papers.

GUÉRIN, Georges Maurice de (1810–39) French poet, born in the château of Le Cayla (Tarn), brother of **Eugénie de Guárin**. He entered the community of **Lamennais** at Le Chesnay in Brittany. He followed his master in his estrangement from Rome, and, going like him to Paris (1833) to try journalism, became a teacher at the Collège Stanislas. He married a rich Creole lady in November 1838, and died of consumption. His *Reliquiae*, including the *Centaur* (a kind of prose poem), letters and poems, were published in 1860.

GUÉRIN, Pierre Narcisse, Baron (1774–1833) historical painter, born in Paris. A skilful painter of classical subjects but inclined to melodrama, he was appointed professor at the École des Beaux-Arts (1814), where he counted among his pupils Géricault and **Delacroix**. From 1822 to 1829 he was director of the French Academy of Painting in Rome.

GUERRA See **JUNQUEIRO**

GUERRAZZI, Francesco Domenico (1804–73) Italian writer and politician, born in Leghorn. He had won a great reputation by his patriotic and political fictions when, on the Grand Duke of Tuscany's flight (1849), he was proclaimed dictator in spite of his disinclination for a republic. On the duke's restoration he was condemned to the galleys, but ultimately permitted to select Corsica as his place of banishment. Restored to liberty by later events, he sat in the parliament of Turin (1862–65). His chief works of fiction are *La Battaglia di Benevento* (1827), *L'Assedio di Firenze* (1836) and *Isabella Orsini* (1844).

GUERRERO, José Gustavo (1876–1958) El Salvadorian lawyer and statesman. He practised in San Salvador and was the author of many books on international law. A judge of the Permanent Court of International Justice from 1930, he became its president (1937–39), and a judge of the International Court of Justice (1946–55) and president, (1946–49).

GUESCLIN, Bertrand du (c.1320–1380) French soldier, and constable of France, born near Dinan. He early took part in the contests for the dukedom of Brittany. After King **John**'s capture at Poitiers in 1356, du Guesclin fought splendidly against the English, his military skill being especially shown at Rennes (1356) and Dinan (1357); he took Melun (1359) and other fortified towns, and freed the Seine from the English. He won the battle of Cocherel against Charles the Bad of Navarre, but was defeated and taken prisoner by the English at Auray, and ransomed only for 100000 livres. He next supported Henry of Trastamare against **Pedro the Cruel**, king of Castile, but was defeated and taken prisoner by **Edward the Black Prince** (1367). Again ransomed, he defeated and captured Pedro in 1309, and placed the crown of Castile on the head of Henry of Trastamare; but was recalled by **Charles V** of France, hard pressed by the English, to be made Constable of France. In 1370 he opened his campaigns against the English, and soon nearly all their possessions were in the hands of the French. He died during the siege of Châteauneuf de Randon.

GUESS, George See **SEQUOYAH**

GUEST, Lady Charlotte See **SCHREIBER, Lady Charlotte Elizabeth**

GUEST, Sir Josiah John (1785–1852) Welsh industrialist, born in Dowlais. He inherited the Dowlais Iron Company founded by his grandfather, John Guest, and made it the leading iron producer in South Wales. Guest was interested in the welfare of his workers and in Welsh culture. In 1833 he married Lady Charlotte Bertie, later **Charlotte Schrieber**, and she participated fully in his industrial and cultural concerns.

GUETTARD, Jean Étienne (1715–86) French geologist, born in Étampes. Keeper of the natural history collections of the Duke of Orléans, he studied 'weathering' and prepared the first geological map of France.

GUEVARA, Antonio de (1490–1545) Spanish prelate and writer. A Dominican, he became bishop of Mondoñedo and confessor of **Charles V**. He used in his book on **Marcus Aurelius** the exalted style which anticipated the euphuism of **Lyly**. His 'Familiar Letters' were also very popular in an English version.

GUEVARA, Ernesto Che, properly **Ernesto Guevera de la Serna** (1928–67) Argentinian Communist revolutionary leader. He graduated in medicine at the university of Buenos Aires (1953), then joined **Fidel Castro**'s revolutionary movement in Mexico (1955) and played an important part in the Cuban revolution (1956–59) and afterwards held government posts under Castro. An activist of revolution elsewhere, he left Cuba in 1965 to become a guerrilla leader in South America, and was captured and executed by goverment troops while trying to foment a revolt. He became a hero of left-wing youth in the 1960s. He wrote *Guerrilla Warfare* (1961) and *Reminiscences of the Cuban Revolutionary War* (1968).

GUEVARA, Luiz Vélez de (1570–1644) Spanish dramatist. He wrote many plays in the style of **Lope de Vega**. His novel *El Diablo cojuelo* (1641) was used as the model for **Le Sage**'s *Diable boiteux*.

GUICCIARDINI, Francesco (1483–1540) Italian historian, born in Florence. He became professor of law there, and also practised as an advocate; but his real field was diplomacy. His apprenticeship served in Spain (1512–14), he became papal governor of Modena and Reggio (1515), Parma (1521), the Romagna (1523) and Bologna (1531). Retiring from the papal service in 1534, he secured the election of **Cosimo de' Medici** as Duke of Florence; but, disappointed of the post of mayor of the palace, withdrew to Arcetri, and busied himself with his great *Storia d'Italia*, a dispassionate analytical history of Italy from 1494 to 1532.

GUICCIOLI, Teresa Gamba Ghiselli, Countess (1801–73) Italian noblewoman, and mistress (1819-23) of Lord **Byron**. The daughter of a Ravenna noblewoman, in 1817 she was married to the 60-year-old Count Alessandro Guiccioli. In 1851 she married the French Marquis de Boissy (1798–1866). She later wrote *Lord Byron jugé par les témoins de sa vie* (1868).

GUIDI, Tommaso See **MASACCIO**

GUIDO D'AREZZO, or **Guido Aretino** (c.990–1050) Benedictine monk and musical theorist. A monk at Pomposa near Ferrara, he is supposed to have died prior of the Camaldolite monastery of Avellana. He contributed a great deal to musical science; the invention of the staff is ascribed to him; and he seems to have been the first to adopt in naming the notes of the scale the initial syllables of the hemistichs of a hymn in honour of St **John the Baptist** (*ut, re, mi*, etc).

GUIGNES, Joseph de (1721–1800) French orientalist, born in Pontoise. His great work is *L'Histoire générale des Huns, Turcs, et Mogols* (1756–58). His son, Chrétien Louis Joseph (1759–1845), published a Chinese dictionary (1813).

GUILBERT, Yvette (c.1869–1944) French comedienne, born in Paris. She was a penniless seamstress before she turned to acting and won fame for her songs and sketches of all facets of Parisian life. After 1890 she became known for her revivals of old French ballads. She visited America and founded a school of acting in New York. She wrote two novels, and *La Chanson de ma vie* (1919).

GUILLAUME, Charles Édouard (1861–1938) Swiss physicist, born in Fleurier. Educated at Neuchâtel, he became director of the Bureau of International Weights and Measures at Sèvres. He discovered a nickel-steel alloy, 'Invar', which does not expand significantly and can therefore be used in precision instruments and standard measures, and was awarded the Nobel prize for physics in 1920.

GUILLAUME DE MACHAUT (c.1300–1377) French poet and musician, born in Machault, Champagne. He worked successively under the patronage of John of Luxemburg and **John II** of France. *Le Livre du voir-dit*, written in the form of letters from the elderly poet to a girl, influenced **Chaucer**. He was one of the creators of the harmonic art, and wrote masses, songs, ballades and organ music.

GUILLEMIN, Roger (Charles Louis) (1924–) French-born American physiologist, joint winner of the 1977 Nobel prize for physiology or medicine. A Resistance fighter during World War II, he studied medicine and was research professor at Montreal, Baylor University and the Salk Institute. For his work on the hormones produced by the hypothalamus which regulate the pituitary gland he shared the 1977 Nobel prize with **Andrew Schally** and **Rosalyn Yalow**.

GUILLOTIN, Joseph Ignace (1738–1814) French physician and Revolutionary, born in Saintes. As a deputy in the Estates General in 1789, he proposed to the Constituent Assembly the use of a decapitating instrument, which was adopted in 1791 and was named after him though similar apparatus had been used earlier in Scotland, Germany and Italy.

GUIMARD, Hector Germain (1867–1942) French architect, born in Lyon. He was the most important Art Nouveau architect active in Paris between 1890 and World War I. For his outstanding architectural scheme, the *Castel Béranger* apartment block (1894–98), he designed every aspect of the building and its interiors. He is best known for the famous Paris Métro entrances of the early 1900s, many of which are still in place.

GUIMERÁ, Ángel (1849–1924) Catalan poet and dramatist, born in Santa Cruz, Tenerife. His work falls into three periods, of which the first and third—for the most part, historical plays—show the influence of the French Romantics. His middle period owes its preoccupation with contemporary life to **Ibsen**. He is regarded as the greatest Catalan dramatist. His most famous play is *Terra Baixa* (1896), on which **D'Albert** based his opera *Tiefland*.

GUINNESS, Sir Alec (1914–) English actor, born in London. After training for the stage while he worked as an advertising copywriter he joined the Old Vic company in 1936; he rejoined the company in 1946 after serving in the Royal Navy throughout World War II. His extraordinary versatility is seen in parts ranging from the most controversial of Hamlets to outstanding success in films both comic and serious. In 1958 he was awarded an Oscar for his part in the film *The Bridge on the River Kwai*, and the following year he was knighted. Like other theatrical knights, Guinness now appears infrequently on the stage, although he gave an acclaimed performance as a Soviet diplomat in *A Walk in the Woods*, a two-hander by American Lee Blessing, in 1989. He has continued his extraordinary success in films, among the most recent being the six-hour-long *Little Dorrit*, and *A Handful of Dust* (1988), adapted from the **Evelyn Waugh** novel. On television during the 1970s he was seen as the inscrutable spycatcher George Smiley in the adaptations of **John le Carré**'s *Tinker, Tailor, Soldier Spy*, and *Smiley's People*.

GUINNESS, Sir Benjamin Lee (1798–1868) Irish brewer, born in Dublin, grandson of Arthur Guinness (1725–1803), founder of Guinness's Brewery (1759). He joined the firm at an early age, and became sole owner at his father's death in 1855. Under him the brand of stout became famous and the business grew into the largest of its kind in the world. He was the first lord mayor of Dublin in 1851 and MP from 1865 to 1868. He restored St Patrick's Cathedral (1860–65) at his own expense.

GUINNESS, Edward Cecil, 1st Earl of Iveagh (1847–1927) Irish brewer, third son of Sir **Benjamin Lee Guinness**. He spent much of his huge fortune on philanthropic projects including housing in Dublin and London, and gave the mansion of Kenwood at Highgate, London with its collection of paintings, to the nation.

GUISCARD, Robert (c.1015–1085) Norman soldier, Duke of Apulia and Calabria, the sixth of the twelve sons of Tancred de Hauteville, born near Coutances in Normandy. He won great renown in South Italy as a soldier, captured Reggio and Cosenza (1060), and conquered Calabria. As the champion of Pope **Nicholas II** he, along with his younger brother **Roger I** of Sicily, waged incessant war against Greeks and Saracens in South Italy and Sicily; later he fought against the Byzantine emperor, **Alexius Comnenus**, gaining a great victory over him at Durazzo (1081). Marching towards Constantinople, he learned that the Emperor **Henri IV** had invaded Italy; he hastened back, compelled Henri to retreat, and liberated Pope **Gregory VII** who was besieged in the castle of St

Angelo (1084). Then, having returned to Epirus, he repeatedly defeated the Greeks, and was advancing a second time to Constantinople when he died suddenly during the siege of Cephalonia.

GUISE name of a ducal family of Lorraine, taken from the town of that name. The direct line became extinct on the death (1675) of François Joseph, the 7th Duke.

GUISE, Charles (1525–74) French prelate and archbishop of Reims, created cardinal of Guise in 1547. He was the son of **Claude of Lorraine, 1st Duke of Guise** and brother of **Mary of Lorraine Guise** and **Francis, 2nd Duke of Guise**, with whom he became all-powerful in the reign of **Francis II**. He introduced the Inquisition into France and exerted a great influence at the Council of Trent.

GUISE, Claude of Lorraine, 1st Duke (1496–1550) French nobleman and soldier, born in the château of Condé, the fifth son of René II, Duke of Lorraine. He fought under **Francis I** at Marignano in Italy in 1515, but after that campaign remained at home to defend France against the English and Germans, and defeated the imperial army at Neufchâteau. He was regent during the captivity of Francis by **Charles V** (1525–27). For suppressing the peasant revolt in Lorraine (1527) Francis created him Duke of Guise. He was the father of **Mary of Lorraine Guise**, who married **James V** of Scotland and became mother of **Mary, Queen of Scots**.

GUISE, Francis, 2nd Duke (1519–63) French soldier and statesman, known as 'Le Balafré' (the Scarred), son of Claude, 1st Duke of **Guise**. He fought at Montmédy (1542) and the siege of Landercies (1543) and Boulogne (1545). In 1552–53 he held Metz against **Charles V** of Germany, and added to his reputation at Renti (1554), and in 1556 commanded the expedition against Naples. Recalled in 1557 to defend the northern frontier against the English, he took Calais (1558) and other towns, and brought about the treaty of Château Cambrésis (1559). He and his brother, Cardinal **Charles of Guise**, shared the chief power in the state during the reign of **Francis II**. Heading the Roman Catholic party, they sternly repressed Protestantism. Guise and **Montmorency** won a victory over the Huguenots at Dreux (1562), and Guise was besieging Orléans when he was assassinated by a Huguenot.

GUISE, Henri, 3rd Duke (1550–88) French soldier and statesman, also known as 'Le Balafré' (the Scarred), son of Francis, 2nd Duke of **Guise**. He fought fiercely against the Protestants at Jarnac and Moncontour (1569), and forced **Coligny** to raise the siege of Poitiers. He was one of the contrivers of the massacre on St Bartholomew's Day (1572), and was the head of the Holy League against the Bourbons (1576). He was, however, ambitious to succeed to the throne of France, when **Henri III** procured his assassination at Blois.

GUISE, Henri, 5th Duke (1614–64) French prelate and soldier, grand-nephew of Henri, 3rd Duke of **Guise**. At the age of 15 he became archbishop of Reims, but in 1640 succeeded to the dukedom. Having joined the league against **Richelieu**, he was condemned to death, but fled to Flanders. He put himself at the head of **Masaniello**'s revolt in Naples as the representative of the Anjou family, but was taken by the Spanish (1647) and carried to Madrid, where he remained five years. After another attempt to win Naples (1654) he settled in Paris. He published his Mémoires in 1669.

GUISE, Mary of Lorraine (1515–60) daughter of Claude of Lorraine, 1st Duke of **Guise**. In 1534 she married Louis of Orléans, Duke of Longueville, and in 1538 **James V** of Scotland, at whose death (1542) she was left with one child, **Mary, Queen of Scots**. During the troubled years that followed, the queen mother acted with wisdom and moderation: but after her accession to the regency in 1554 she allowed the Guises so much influence that the Protestant nobles raised a rebellion (1559), which continued to her death in Edinburgh Castle.

GUITRY, Sacha (1885–1957) French actor and dramatist, born in St Petersburg. He wrote nearly a hundred plays, mostly light comedies, many of which have been successfully performed in English. The son of the actor-manager Lucien Guitry (1860–1925), he first appeared on the stage in Russia with his father's company. His first appearance in Paris was in 1902, still under his father's management. He came to London in 1920 with *Nono*, a play written when he was 16. It starred the second of his five wives, the enchanting Yvonne Printemps. He also wrote and directed several delightful films, including *Le Roman d'un tricheur* (1936) and *Les Perles de la couronne* (1937).

GUIZOT, François Pierre Guillaume (1787–1874) French historian and statesman, born in Nîmes, of Huguenot stock. In 1805 he went to Paris to study law, but soon drifted into literature, and in 1812 became professor of modern history at the Sorbonne. After the fall of **Napoleon** he held various official posts, but as a Liberal was deprived of his appointments in 1821, and in 1825 was interdicted from lecturing. With some friends he then published *Mémoires relatifs à l'histoire de France jusqu'au* 13 *siècle* (31 vols) and *Mémoires relatifs à la Révolution d'Angleterre* (25 vols), and edited translations of **Shakespeare** and **Hallam**. Restored to his chair in 1828, he began his famous lectures, later published, on the history of civilization. Elected to the Chamber (1830), he became minister first of the interior, and then of public instruction, establishing a system of primary education. In 1840 he came to London as ambassador, but was recalled to replace **Thiers** as the king's chief adviser. To checkmate **Palmerston** he plunged into the indefensible 'Spanish Marriages' and relapsed into reactionary methods of government which were partly responsible for the Revolution of 1848 and the fall of **Louis-Philippe**, with whom he escaped to London. In November 1849 he returned to Paris and made efforts to rally the monarchists, but after the *coup d'état* of 1851 gave himself up entirely to his historical publications.

GULBENKIAN, Calouste Sarkis (1869–1955) British financier, industrialist, and diplomat, born in Scutari, of Ottoman-Turkish nationality. In 1888 he entered his father's oil business in Baku. After becoming a naturalized British subject in 1902 he brought the Russians into the new Royal Dutch-Shell merger and in 1907 he arranged for the latter to break into the American market, thus laying the foundations of an important British dollar asset. In 1916 he organized French entry into the Turkish Petroleum Company, instead of the Germans, and between 1921 and 1928 he did the same for the Americans. In 1940 in 'Vichy' France the 5 per cent Iraq Petroleum Company interest was confiscated by Britain, and he was declared an 'Enemy under the Act', whereupon he assumed Persian citizenship. From 1948 to 1954 he negotiated oil concessions between America and Saudi Arabia. He left $70 000 000 and vast art collections to finance an international Gulbenkian Foundation. His son Nubar Sarkis (1896–1972), philanthropist and *bon vivant*, was commercial attaché to the Iranian embassy, 1926–51 and 1956–65, and until his father's death worked with him.

GULDBERG, Cato Maximilian (1836–1902) Norwegian chemist and mathematician, born in Christiania (now Oslo), where he became professor of applied mathematics. With his brother-in-law, **Peter Waage**, he formulated the chemical law of mass action (1864) governing the speed of reaction and the relative concentrations of the reactants.

GULLY, John (1783–1863) English sportsman, born in Wick near Bristol. A butcher to trade, he was the British heavyweight boxing champion (1806–08) and then became a publican. In the 1830s he took up horse-racing and won the Derby thrice (1832, 1846 and 1854) and other classic races. He was MP for Pontefract (1832–37), and later became a colliery owner. He was the father of 24 children.

GUMILEV, Nikolai Stepanovich (1886–1921) Russian poet, a leader of the Acmeist school which revolted against Symbolism. His exotic and vivid poems include *The Quiver* (1915) with some fine verses of war and adventure, and *The Pyre* and *The Pillar of Fire*, which contain his best pieces. He also wrote criticism and translated French and English poetry. He was shot as a counter-revolutionary. His wife was the poet **Anna Akhmatova**.

GUNDELACH, Finn Olav (1925–81) Danish diplomat and European commissioner, born in Vejle. He attended the University of Aarhus, gaining a degree in economics. He had a distinguished career in the Danish diplomatic service, culminating in his appointment as ambassador to the European Economic Community in 1967. He directed the negotiations for Denmark's entry into the Community on 1 January, 1973, and became his country's first European Commissioner. He took temporary charge of the fisheries policy in 1976 during Sir **Christopher Soames**' illness, in the period of delicate negotiations with Iceland. In 1977 he was promoted to vice-president of the new European Commission under **Roy Jenkins** and was given charge of the EEC's common agricultural policy, in which he attempted to maintain a better balance between farmers and consumers than had previously been the case.

GUNDICARIUS (c.385–437) first recorded king of the Burgundians, also known as **Gunther** and **Gunnar**. He is said to have crossed the middle Rhine and established a new kingdom with his capital in the region of Worms. He was an ally of the Romans, but was killed when his army was annihilated by the Huns. In later Germanic and Norse heroic legend he was cast as the brother-in-law of **Attila the Hun**, who had not, in fact, taken part in the war against the Burgundians, but who was said to covet their gold, for which he put Gunnar/Gundicarius to death in a snake pit.

GUNDOLF, Friedrich, properly **Gundelfinger** (1880–1931) German scholar and literary critic, born in Darmstadt. He was a brilliant disciple of **Stefan George**, and his studies, based on George's theories of history and art, combined with his own sensitive and imaginative style, had a marked influence on literature and literary criticism. His works include *Shakespeare und der deutsche Geist* (1911), the biographies *Goethe* (1916) and *George* (1920), and a translation of **Shakespeare** (1908–14). From 1920 he was professor at Heidelberg.

GUNDULF (1024–1108) Norman prelate, and bishop of Rochester from 1077. A monk at Bec and Caen, in 1070 he followed **Lanfranc** to England. He built the Tower of London, rebuilt Rochester cathedral and founded St Bartholomew's hospital in Chatham. The great keep of Rochester castle is also attributed to him.

GUNN, Neil Miller (1891–1973) Scottish novelist, born in Dunbeath, Caithness, the son of a fisherman. Educated at the village school, and privately in Galloway, he passed the Civil Service examination in 1907, and moved to London. He was in the Civil Service until 1937, from 1911 as an officer of customs and excise in Inverness and elsewhere in Scotland. After writing a number of short stories, his first novel, *Grey Coast* (1926), was immediately acclaimed, and was followed by *The Lost Glen* (serialized in 1928) and a historical novel on the Viking Age, the even more successful *Morning Tide* (1931). Other works include *Sun Circle* (1933), *Butcher's Broom* (1934), *Highland River* (1937, Tait Black Memorial Prize), *Wild Geese Overhead* (1939) and *The Silver Darlings* (1941). Gunn was at his best when describing the ordinary life and background of a Highland fishing or crofting community, and when interpreting in simple prose the complex character of the Celt. His last novels were *The Well at the World's End* (1951), *Bloodhunt* (1952) and *The Other Landscape* (1954).

GUNN, Thom (Thomson) William (1929–) English poet, born in Gravesend. He attended University College School, London, and, following national service, read English at Trinity College, Cambridge. His first collection, *Fighting Terms* (1954), labelled him a 'Movement' poet. He moved to the USA in 1954 where he has lived ever since. His second book, *The Sense of Movement* (1957), is overtly existentialist; his third, *My Sad Captains* (1961), is more contemplative. Subsequent volumes—*Touch* (1967), *Moly* (1971), and *Jack Straw's Castle* (1976)—were not universally well-received but he is undoubtedly one of the major poets of the second half of the century. *Selected Poems 1950–1975* were published in 1979; in 1982 appeared *The Passages of Joy*, in which he writes frankly about his homosexuality.

GUNNARSSON, Gunnar (1889–1975) Icelandic novelist, born at Valthjófsstaðir, who wrote all his major works in Danish before re-writing them in Icelandic. At the age of 18 he went to Denmark to seek fame and fortune. His first novel, *Af Borgslægtens Historie* (From the Annals of the House of Borg, 1920, translated into English as *Guest the One-Eyed*, 1920), was the first Icelandic work to be turned into a feature film. A prolific writer, his acknowledged masterpiece was the autobiographical novel, *Kirken paa Bjerget* (The Church on the Mountain, 5 vols, 1923–28, translated into English in two volumes as *Ships in the Sky* and *The Night and the Dream*).

GUNNING, Elizabeth (1734–90) Irish socialite, born near St Ives, Cambridgeshire, and sister of **Maria Gunning**. She married the Duke of Hamilton in 1752 and, on his death in 1759, the future Duke of Argyll. She was created Baroness Hamilton in 1770.

GUNNING, Maria (1733–60) Irish socialite, born near St Ives, Cambridgeshire, and sister of **Elizabeth Gunning**. She came to London with her sister in 1751 and married the Earl of Coventry in 1752 and was so popular that she was mobbed in Hyde Park.

GUNTER, Edmund (1581–1626) English mathematician and astronomer, born in Hertfordshire and educated at Westminster and Christ Church, Oxford. He got a Southwark living in 1615, but in 1619 became professor of astronomy in Gresham College, London, and invented many measuring instruments that bear his name; Gunter's Chain, the 22-yard-long, 100-link chain used by surveyors; Gunter's Line, the forerunner of the modern slide-rule; Gunter's Scale, a two-foot rule with scales of chords, tangents and logarithmic lines for solving navigational problems; and the portable Gunter's Quadrant. He made the first observation of the variation of the magnetic compass, and introduced the words 'cosine' and 'cotangent' into the language of trigonometry. His reliability gave rise to the familiar American expression 'according to Gunter'.

GUNTHER, John (1901–70) American author and journalist, born in Chicago. He was a foreign correspondent for the *Chicago Daily News* and for NBC. He established his reputation with the bestselling *Inside Europe* (1939), followed by a series of similar works, in which firsthand material is blended with documentary information to present penetrating social and political studies. Other books include *Death Be Not Proud* (1949), and *A Fragment of Autobiography* (1962).

GÜNTHER, Albert Charles Ludwig Gothenhilf (1830–1914) German-born British zoologist, born in Esslingen. He studied at Tübingen, Berlin, and Bonn, and from 1857 was on the British Museum staff. He became a naturalized Briton in 1862 and was appointed keeper in 1885. He worked on fishes, reptiles and amphibians.

GÜNTHER, Johann Christian (1695–1723) German poet, born in Strugan in Silesia. He wrote love lyrics notable for their sensitivity and their lack of affectation.

GUREVICH, Mikhail Iosifovich (1893–1976) Soviet aircraft designer, born in Rubanshchina, near Kursk. He graduated in 1925 from the aviation faculty of Kharkov Technological Institute. He was best known for the fighter aircraft produced by the design bureau he headed with **Artem Ivanovich Mikoyan**, the MiG (M̄ikoyan 'ī' (= 'and') Ḡurevich) series.

GURNEY, Sir Goldsworthy (1793–1875) English inventor, born in Treator near Padstow. He devised an improved limelight known as the Drummond Light, and built a series of steam carriages, one of which in 1829 ran from London to Bath and back at the rate of 15 miles an hour.

GURNEY, Ivor (1890–1937) English composer and poet, born in Gloucester. In 1900 he became a chorister in Gloucester Cathedral, and then a pupil of the organist, Sir Herbert Brewer. At the Royal College of Music he studied compositon under **Stanford**. On military service in France during World War I he was wounded and gassed and, after spending much time in hospital, published two collections of poems: *Severn and Somme* (1917) and *War's Embers* (1919). After the war he returned to the Royal College of Music to study with **Vaughan Williams** and in 1920 published his first songs, 5 *Elizabethan Songs*, before returning to Gloucester. He suffered increasingly from depression, eventually entering a mental hospital from which he was transferred to a London hospital where he died of tuberculosis. An instinctual writer of both music and poetry rather than a skilled craftsman, his songs are considered his most important work; he remained largely uninfluenced by the contemporary folk-song movement, looking rather to Elizabethan music and the German classics for inspiration.

GURNEY, Joseph John (1788–1847) English Quaker banker and reformer, brother of **Elizabeth Fry**, born at Earlham Hall. He became a minister for the Society of Friends in 1818, visited North America and the West Indies (1837–40), and campaigned actively for Negro emancipation, prison reform and the abolition of capital punishment.

GUSTAFSSON, Lars (1936–) Swedish novelist and philosopher. His doctoral thesis, published in 1978 as *Language and Lies*, explored the problem of language as a barrier between experience and understanding, much influenced by **Wittgenstein**. His major literary work is a series of five novels under the general title of *Cracks in the Wall* (1971–78).

GUSTAV I VASA, (Gustav Eriksson) (1496–1560) king of Sweden from 1523, the first Swedish king of the House of Vasa. He was born into the Swedish nobility at Lindholmen in Uppland. In 1518, during the patriotic struggle against King **Kristian II** of Denmark and Norway, he was carried off to Denmark as a hostage; after a year he escaped to Lübeck and thence back to Sweden, where he wandered for months with a price on his head, trying to raise resistance against the Danes. In November 1520, immediately after his coronation in Stockholm as king of Sweden, Kristian II carried out a mass execution of the Swedish nobility, including Gustav's father and many relatives (the infamous 'Blood-Bath of Stockholm'); this roused the Swedes to rebellion, and in 1523 Gustav captured Stockholm and drove the Danes from Sweden, thus ending the triple-crown Kalmar Union of 1397. Gustav was elected king in 1523. An orator of impressive presence and a hard worker, Gustav imposed order and peace on the demoralized kingdom. He introduced the Lutheran Reformation, made himself head of the Swedish church, and confiscated Catholic church properties, using the revenues to build up a well-organized standing army and navy. He fostered schools, promoted trade, and built roads, bridges and canals. He was married three times: to Katarina of Saxony-Lauenburg; to Margareta Leijonhufvud; and to Katarina Stenbock (his second and third wife both belonged to the Swedish aristocracy). In 1544 he persuaded the Riksdag (parliament) to declare the monarchy hereditary, and was succeeded by his son of the first marriage, **Erik XIV**, followed by the sons of his second marriage, **Johan III**, and, later, **Karl IX**.

GUSTAV II ADOLF, (Gustavus Adolphus) (1594–1632) king of Sweden from 1611, champion of Protestantism and known as 'the Lion of the North'. Born in Stockholm, he was the son and successor of **Karl IX** and grandson of **Gustav I Vasa**. When he came to the throne at the age of 17 he found the country deeply involved in wars and disorder, but he quickly conciliated the nobility, reorganized the government, and revitalized the army. When Denmark, under **Kristian IV**, invaded Sweden in 1611, he fought off the attack and made a favourable peace at Knäred (1613). He waged successful war against Russia (1613–17) and received a large part of Finland and Livonia through the Treaty of Stolbova (1617). He fought a long war against King **Sigismund III Vasa** of Poland (1621–29), who still had designs on the Swedish throne, and took Livonia and forced a favourable six-year truce with the Treaty of Altmark. This left him free to intervene directly in the Thirty Years' War (1618–48), on behalf of the Protestants against the Catholic League of the Habsburg Holy Roman Emperor, **Ferdinand II**, and his victorious general **Albrecht Wallenstein**. Leaving the government in the care of his able chancellor, **Axel Oxenstierna**, he crossed to Pomerania in 1630 with 15000 men and took Stettino but in 1631 failed to save the citizenry of Magdeburg, on the Elbeg from being massacred by Count von Tilley, who had supplanted Wallenstein. But in September of that year he decisively defeated Tilly at Breitenfeld, near Leipzig, and took the Palatinate and Mainz. In the spring of 1632 he advanced into Bavaria, defeated and killed Tilly and captured Augsburg and Munich. The emperor Ferdinand now recalled Wallenstein, and in November 1632 the two armies met in a furious battle at Lützen, near Leipzig. The Swedes won, but Gustav Adolf was mortally wounded. His heart was taken back to Stockholm in his blood-stained silken shirt. A compelling leader of dazzling abilities and military achievement, he left Sweden the strongest power in Europe. Married to Maria Eleanora of Brandenburg, he was succeeded by their only child, his six-year-old daughter, Queen **Kristina**.

GUSTAV III (1746–92) king of Sweden from 1771, son and successor of King **Adolf Frederik**, and Louisa Ulrika, sister of King **Frederick II, the Great** of Prussia. Reared by his mother in the new spirit of the Enlightenment, he was at home with the most celebrated thinkers and artists of his day. A brilliant and captivating figure, he ascended the throne at a low ebb in Swedish affairs, and set himself to break the power of the oligarchy of nobles. He arrested the council in a body and declared a new form of government (1772), purged the bureaucracy and encouraged agriculture, commerce and science. He granted religious toleration, but also created a secret police system and introduced censorship. His court became a northern Versailles, with the foundation of the Royal Opera House (1782), the Swedish Academy (1786) after the French pattern, and the Royal Dramatic Theatre (1788). But poor harvests and a failing economy created discontent, and as a diversion he launched into a war against Russia (1788–90) that proved unpopular and inconclusive. In 1789 he assumed new royal prerogatives as absolute monarch. When the French Revolution got under way he encouraged one of his household officers, Count **Hans Axel Fersen**, to attempt to rescue the French royal family in the abortive 'Flight to Varennes' (June 1791), and planned to use his army to go to the help of **Louis XVI**, but in March 1792 he was shot by a former army officer, **Johan Jakob Anckarström**, during a masked ball at the Royal Opera House, and died a lingering death of gangrene. Married to Sofia Magdalena of Denmark, he was succeeded by his young son, **Gustav IV Adolf**.

GUSTAV IV ADOLF (1778–1837) king of Sweden 1792–1809, son and successor of **Gustav III**. During his minority, the regent was his uncle Karl (Charles), Duke of Sudermania. In the first years of his reign as an absolute monarch, he did much to improve Swedish agriculture with a General Enclosure Act (1803). But his aversion to **Napoleon** induced him to abandon Swedish neutrality and declare war on France in 1805. When Russia changed sides as a result of the treaty of Tilsit (1807) and became an ally of Napoleon, the Swedes were driven from Pomerania and lost their last German possessions. In 1808 Sweden was attacked by Denmark, under **Frederik VI**, and Finland was simultaneously invaded by Russia under Tsar **Alexander I**. Tactless and autocratic by nature, Gustav Adolf spurned an offer of help by a British force under Sir **John Moore** off Gothenburg, and Finland was accordingly annexed by Russia in 1809. He was arrested in a military coup and forced to abdicate. He was exiled with his family (Queen Frederika of Baden and their children), and after divorcing his wife in 1812 spent 25 years wandering alone in Europe before he died in Switzerland. He was succeeded by his uncle as King **Karl XIII** under a new constitution that limited the absolute power of the monarchy.

GUSTAV V (1858–1950) king of Sweden from 1907, the longest-reigning king in Swedish history, the son and successor of **Oscar II**. Shy and reserved by nature, he disliked pomp and spectacle and refused a coronation ceremony, thus becoming the first 'uncrowned king' on the Swedish throne. Nevertheless, he sought to assert the personal power of the monarchy, and in 1914, in his famous 'Courtyard Speech' to a farmers' rally in the courtyard of the Royal Palace in Stockholm, he challenged the government with a call for greater spending on defence. Demands for his abdication were stilled by the outbreak of World War I, when Sweden mobilized but remained neutral. Thereafter he reigned as a popular constitutional monarch, and in World War II came to symbolize the unity of the nation. In 1881 he married Princess Viktoria, daughter of the Grand Duke of Baden and grand-daughter of Sofia of Sweden (**Gustav IV Adolf**'s daughter), thus uniting the reigning Bernadotte dynasty with the former royal house of Vasa. His nephew was Count **Folke Bernadotte**. He was succeeded by his son, **Gustav VI Adolf**.

GUSTAV VI (1882–1973) king of Sweden from 1950, son and successor of **Gustav V**. He was a respected scholar and archaeologist, and an authority on Chinese art; he organized several archaeological excavations, and was called in as an expert for the 1936 exhibition of Chinese art in London. In 1905 he married Princess Margaret (1882–1920), daughter of Prince Arthur, Duke of Connaught and grand-daughter of Queen **Victoria**, by whom he had four sons and a daughter, Ingrid, who married King **Frederik IX** of Denmark; and in 1923 he married Lady Louise Mountbatten (1889–1965), sister of Earl **Mountbatten** of Burma. On Gustav Adolf's accession in 1950 Lady Louise became the first British-born queen in Swedish history. During his reign a new constitution was under preparation, and the king worked to transform the crown into a democratic monarchy, which helped to preserve it against political demands for a republic. His eldest son, Gustav Adolf (1906–47), having been killed in an air-crash, he was succeeded by his grandson, **Carl XVI Gustaf**.

GUSTON, Philip (1913–80) Canadian-born American painter, born in Montreal. His family moved to the USA in 1916 and he settled in New York in 1936 where he was involved with the Federal Works of Art Project (1935–40). His work of the 1950s was in the Abstract Expressionist style, but from the late 1960s he introduced brightly coloured and crudely drawn comic-strip characters into his painting. A major series depicted the Ku Klux Klan group.

GUTENBERG, Beno (1889–1960) German-born American geophysicist, born in Darmstadt. He studied at Darmstadt and Göttingen, and taught at Freiberg from 1926. In 1930 he moved to the USA, to the California Institute of Technology. In 1913 he had proposed that data on earthquake shock waves can be interpreted as showing that the Earth's core is liquid, a novel idea now fully accepted. The existence of some type of core had been deduced by **Richard Oldham** in 1906, and Inge Lehmann later showed this to contain a solid inner core.

GUTENBERG, Johannes Gensfleisch (1400–68) German printer, regarded as the inventor of printing, born in Mainz, son of a patrician, Friele Gensfleisch or Gutenberg. Between 1430 and 1444 he was in Strasbourg, where he was probably a goldsmith and here (by 1439) he may have begun printing. In Mainz again by 1448 he entered into partnership c.1450 with **Johannes Fust** who financed a printing press. This partnership ended in 1455; Fust sued him for the debt when the loan was not repaid, and received the printing plant in lieu of payment. He carried on the concern with the assistance of **Peter Schöffer** his son-in-law and completed the famous bible which Gutenberg had begun, while Gutenberg, aided by Konrad Humery, set up another printing press. Although Gutenberg is credited with the invention of printing, it is probable that rudimentary printing, whether invented by **Laurens Janszoon (Coster)** or not, was practised before Gutenberg's development of the art. Apart from his 42-line bible, Gutenberg is credited with the *Fragment of the Last Judgment* (c.1445), and editions of **Aelius Donatus**' Latin school grammar.

GUTHLAC, St (c.673–714) English monk at Repton in 697, and a hermit at Crowland Abbey in 699, where he lived a life of severe asceticism.

GUTHORM, or **Guthrum** (d.890) Danish king of East Anglia, and opponent of King **Alfred the Great**. He led a major Viking invasion of Anglo-Saxon England in 871 (the 'Great Summer Army'), seized East Anglia and conquered Northumbria and Mercia. He attacked Wessex early in 878 and drove Alfred into hiding in Somerset. By May of that year Alfred had recovered sufficiently to defeat the Danes at the crucial battle of Edington in Wiltshire; in the ensuing treaty, Guthorm agreed to leave Wessex and accept baptism as a Christian, and he and his army settled down peacefully in East Anglia.

GUTHRIE, Sir James (1859–1930) Scottish painter, born in Greenock. He studied law, which he abandoned to study art in Paris and London. A follower of the Glasgow School, he turned from genre to portraiture, of which he became a notable exponent.

GUTHRIE, Samuel (1782–1848) American chemist, born in Brimfield, Massachusetts. He was one of the discoverers in 1831 of chloroform, invented percussion priming powder and devised a process of rapid conversion of potato starch into sugar.

GUTHRIE, Thomas (1803–73) Scottish clergyman and social reformer, born in Brechin. He studied at Edinburgh, and was minister at Arbirlot (1830), Old Greyfriar's, Edinburgh (1837), and St John's, Edinburgh (1840). At the Disruption of 1843 he helped to found the Free Church, and until 1864 ministered to Free St John's, Castlehill, Edinburgh. In eleven months (1845–46) he raised £116000 for providing Free Church manses; in 1847 he published his first *Plea for Ragged Schools*, and became an authority on the case of juvenile delinquents. He also used his gifts of oratory in the cause of temperance and other social reforms, and in favour of compulsory education. He was the first editor of the *Sunday Magazine* from 1864. He also wrote *The City: its sins and sorrows* (1857).

GUTHRIE, Thomas Anstey See **ANSTEY, F**

GUTHRIE, Sir William Tyrone (1900–71) English theatrical producer, born in Tunbridge Wells and educated at Wellington College and Oxford. He worked for the BBC but made his reputation as a producer at the Westminster theatre (1930–31). He was administrator of the Old Vic and Sadler's Wells (1939–45), director of the former (1950–51) and produced extensively abroad and at the Edinburgh Festival. He was knighted in 1961, and founded the Tyrone Guthrie Theatre in Minneapolis in 1963. He wrote *A Life in the Theatre* (1960).

GUTHRIE, Woody (Woodrow Wilson) (1912–67) American folk-singer, songwriter and author, born in Okemah, Oklahoma. A folk-poet in the true sense, he travelled the length and breadth of the USA and wrote hundreds of songs about his experiences, using mostly traditional country-music and blues themes. His deep concern about the plight of the poor people of America hardened into active campaigning for trade unions and racial equality in the 1930s and 1940s, and, with **Pete Seeger**, he formed the influential radical group, the Almanac Singers. At the same time he wrote many much-loved songs for children, but it is for classic folk-song statements like 'This Land is Your Land', 'So Long It's Been Good to Know You', and 'Pastures of Plenty' that he is best remembered. His colourful autobiography, *Bound for Glory*, was published in 1943. His career came to an end in the 1950s when he contracted Huntington's disease.

GUTIÉRREZ, Gustavo (1928–) Peruvian liberation theologian, born in Lima. Abandoning medical studies for the Roman Catholic priesthood, he studied philosophy and psychology at Louvain (1951–55) and theology at Lyon (1955–59) before ordination in Lima, becoming professor of theology at the Cathoic university there in 1960. His seminal and classic *A Theology of Liberation* (1971, English trans, 1973) is dedicated to 'doing' theology. This is defined as 'critical reflection on historical praxis': and is based on responding to the needs of the poor and oppressed rather than on imposing solutions from the outside. This has challenged supporters of the *status quo* in Latin America and practitioners of academic theology elsewhere. He explores the biblical and spiritual roots of liberation theology more deeply in *The Power of the Poor in History* (1984), *We Drink from Our Own Wells* (1984), and *On Job* (1987).

GUTS MUTHS, Johann Christoph Friedrich (1759–1839) German physical educationist, born in Quedlinburg. From 1785 to 1837 he taught gymnastics and geography at Schnepfenthal. He made gymnastics a branch of German education, and wrote several educational works.

GUTTUSO, Renato (1912–87) Italian artist, born in Palermo. He worked for some time in Milan and settled in Rome in 1937. He was associated with various anti-Fascist groups from 1942 to 1945, and much of his work reflects this experience. After the war he began to paint dramatic Realist pictures of the lives of the Italian peasants.

GUTZKOW, Karl Ferdinand (1811–78) German author, born in Berlin. He was influenced by the French Revolution of 1830, and for his *Wally die Zweiflerin* (1835) got three months' imprisonment as a champion of the 'Young Germany' movement. He next became a journalist, and in 1847 director of the Court Theatre at Dresden, having meanwhile written many dramas, the most successful being *Richard Savage* (1839) and *Zopf und Schwert* (1844). Among his romances is *Die Ritter vom Geiste* (1850–52).

GÜTZLAFF, Karl Friedrich August (1803–51) German missionary, born in Pyritz in Pomerania. In Bangkok he translated the Bible into Siamese (1828–30), and after 1831 lived and worked in China, where he translated the Bible into Chinese.

GUY, Thomas (c.1644–1724) English bookseller and philanthropist, founder of Guy's Hospital, born in Horselydown, Southwark, the son of a lighterman. He began business in 1668 importing English bibles from Holland; later he contracted with Oxford University for the privilege of printing bibles. By this means, and by selling out South Sea shares, he amassed a fortune. He was MP from 1695 to 1707. In 1707 he built and furnished three wards of St Thomas's Hospital. In 1722 he founded the hospital in Southwark which bears his name, and built and endowed almshouses.

GUY, William (1859–1950) pioneer English dentist and dean of Edinburgh Dental Hospital and School, born in Kent, the son of a doctor. He studied medicine at Edinburgh, was a general physician in Cumberland, returned to Edinburgh to learn dentistry and became partner to the Dental School's founder, **John Smith**, whose daughter Helen he married. He was dean of the school from 1899 to 1933. He put Scotland in the forefront of the drive for professionalization in dentistry, lobbying for the 1921 Act to outlaw amateur and untrained dentists from practice, and pressurizing other scientific bodies to accept dentistry as a respectable science. He published *Mostly Memories—. Some Digressions* (1948).

GUY OF AREZZO See **GUIDO D'AREZZO**

GUY OF LUSIGNAN (d.1194) French crusader. He became king of Jerusalem in 1186 as consort of

Sibylla, daughter of Amalric I, but was defeated and captured at Hattin (1187) by **Saladin**, who overran most of the kingdom. On the death of his wife in 1190 the throne passed to **Conrad of Montferrat**, but as compensation Guy received Cyprus, where his family ruled until 1474.

GUYON, Jeanne Marie de la Mothe, née **Bouvier** (1648–1717) French mystic, born in Montargis. She had destined herself for the cloister, but was married at 16 to the wealthy and elderly Jacques de la Motte Guyon. A widow at 28, she determined to devote her life to the poor and needy, and to the cultivation of spiritual perfection. The former part of her plan she began to carry out in 1681 in Geneva, but three years later she was forced to leave on the grounds that her Quietist doctrines were heretical. In Turin, Grenoble, Nice, Genoa, Vercelli and Paris, where she finally settled in 1686, she became the centre of a movement for the promotion of 'holy living'. In January 1688 she was arrested for heretical opinions, and for having been in correspondence with **Molinos**, the leader of Quietism in Spain. Released by the intervention of Madame de **Maintenon**, she was, after a nine-month detention, again imprisoned in 1695, and not released from the Bastille until 1702. She died in Blois. Her works include *Les Torrens spirituels*, *Moyen court de faire oraison*, a mystical interpretation of the Song of Solomon, an autobiography, letters, and some spiritual poetry.

GUYON, Richard Debaufre (1803–56) English soldier of fortune, born in Walcot, Bath, the son of a naval commander of Huguenot ancestry. He entered the Austrian service in 1823, and married the daughter of a Hungarian field-marshal in 1838. During the Hungarian uprising of 1848 he played a prominent part in the struggle for independence. During the retreat of **Görgei**'s army he re-established communication with the government at Debreczin; he did brilliant service at Kapolya, Komorn and elsewhere; and after the war, escaping to Turkey and entering the service of the sultan, he was governor of Damascus as Kurshid Pasha. In the Crimean War he organized the army of Kars. He died in Constantinople.

GUYOT, Arnold (1807–84) Swiss-born American geographer, born in Boudevilliers. In 1839 he became professor of geology at Neuchâtel, and studied glaciers in Switzerland with **Jean Louis Agassiz**. In 1848 he followed Agassiz to America, where he lectured at the Lowell Institute on *Earth and Man* (1853), and in 1854 became professor of physical geography and geology at Princeton. In charge of the meteorological department of the Smithsonian Institution, he published *Meteorological and Physical Tables*. He wrote *Earth and Man* (1849), and was joint editor of *Johnson's Cyclopaedia* (1874–77).

GUYS, Constantin (1805–92) Dutch-born French artist. He is known for his sketches of the Crimean War for the *Illustrated London News*, and for his penetrating character studies after he settled in Paris in 1865.

GUYTON DE MORVEAU, Baron Louis Bernard (1737–1816) French chemist, born in Dijon. He began a career as a lawyer but became a chemist and parliamentarian. He worked with **Lavoisier** to reform chemical nomenclature; studied chemical affinity; showed that metals gain in weight on heating in air; and helped found the École Polytechnique. Although he was an influential member of the National Assembly and the Convention, he did little to reduce the revolutionary Terror or to save Lavoisier. He was master of the Mint from 1800 to 1814.

GUZMAN, Dominic de See **DOMINIC, St**

GUZMÁN BLANCO, Antonio (1829–99) Venezuelan dictator, born in Carácas. After being banished and taking part in two invasions, he became vice-president of Venezuela in 1863. Driven from office (1868), he headed a revolution which restored him to power (1870), and till 1889 was virtual dictator, himself holding the presidency (1873–77), (1879–84) and (1886–87).

GWYER, Sir Maurice Linford (1878–1952) English lawyer, born in London. Educated at Westminster School and Christ Church, Oxford, he taught law at Oxford and worked in the civil service, eventually becoming Treasury solicitor and in 1934 first parliamentary counsel to the Treasury. In 1937 he became chief justice of India but was also able to act as vice-chancellor of the University of Delhi (1938–50). He edited some editions of Sir **William Anson** on *Contract* and Anson's *Law and Custom of the Constitution*.

GWYN, Eleanor, known as **Nell** (c.1650–1687) English actress, and mistress of **Charles II**. Born presumably in Hereford, of humble parentage, she lived precariously as an orange girl before going on the boards at Drury Lane. She quickly established herself as a comedienne, especially in 'breeches parts'. 'Pretty, witty Nellie's' first protector was Lord Buckhurst; but the transfer of her affections to Charles II was genuine. She had at least one son by the king—Charles Beauclerk, Duke of St Albans—and James Beauclerk is often held to have been a second. She is said to have urged Charles to found Chelsea Hospital.

GWYNN, Stephen Lucius (1864–1950) Irish biographer and literary historian, born in Dublin into a scholarly family, grandson of **William Smith O'Brien**. Educated in Dublin and at Brasenose College, Oxford, he became a schoolmaster and then a journalist in London (1896–1904). He moved into Irish nationalist politics as MP for Galway (1906–18), and later wrote a fine memoir of his leader, *John Redmond's Last Years*. His wife became a Roman Catholic and their sons prominent Roman Catholic intellectuals. His literary output was prodigious, his *Masters of English Literature* (1904) proving one of the great best-sellers of all time. Perhaps his most remarkable work is *Experiences of a Literary Man* (1926), a great record of the meaning of life in the midst of literature.

GWYNNE-VAUGHAN, Dame Helen Charlotte Isabella, née **Fraser** (1879–1967) English botanist and servicewoman. Educated at Cheltenham Ladies' College and King's College, London, she became head and later professor of botany at Birkbeck College, London, in 1909. She became an authority on fungi. In World War I she was organizer (1917) and later controller of the Women's Army Auxiliary Air Force in France, and commandant of the Women's Royal Auxiliary Air Force (1918–19). In World War II she was chief controller of the Women's Auxiliary Territorial Service (1939–41). She retired from Birkbeck in 1944.

GYGES (d.c.648 BC) king of Lydia, and founder of the Mermnad dynasty. He came to power in c.685 BC when he murdered his predecessor Candaules, married his wife, and became king of Lydia. It was under him that Lydian power and wealth began to grow, and close relations developed with the Greek world. He initiated an aggressive policy towards the Greek cities of Asia Minor which his successors continued down to **Croesus**, but also cultivated good relations with the Oracle of Apollo at Delphi, and with Ashurbanipal (**Sardanapalus**) of Assyria. He died fighting an invasion of the Cimmerians.

GYLLENHAMMAR, Pehr Gustaf (1935–) Swedish industrialist, born in Gothenburg. He was educated at Lund University and studied international law in England, the USA and Switzerland. He joined the

Volvo motor company in 1970, was managing director (1971–83), and became chairman in 1983. He has written numerous articles and a number of books, including *I Believe in Sweden* (1973) and *Industrial Policy for Human Beings* (1979).

GYP, pseud of the **Comtesse de Mirabeau de Martel** (1849–1932) French novelist, born in the château of Koëtsal in Brittany. She wrote a series of humorous novels, describing fashionable society, of which the best known are *Petit Bob* (1882) and *Mariage de Chiffon* (1894).

H

HAAKON I HARALDSSON, 'the Good' (?914–961) king of Norway from c.945. The youngest son of **Harald I Halfdanarson**, he was reared in England at the Christian court of King **Athelstan** and became known as 'Haakon Athelstan's-fosterling'. When news came that his father had died in 945, he returned to Norway to dispute the right to the crown with his half-brother, **Erik 'Blood-Axe'**, and seized the throne himself. He proved to be an able legislator and administrator. He brought missionaries from England and built some churches, but his attempts to convert Norway to Christianity met stubborn resistance. He had to fight off several attempts on the throne by the sons of Erik Blood-Axe, led by **Harald 'Grey-Cloak'**, and eventually died in battle against them.

HAAKON IV HAAKONSSON, 'the Old' (1204–63) king of Norway from 1217. The illegitimate grandson of the 'usurper' **Sverrir Sigurdsson**, he was placed on the throne as a boy of 13 by his powerful and ambitious uncle, Duke Skúli, who acted as regent. Eventually Skúli tried to rebel against his nephew, but was defeated and killed in 1240. Haakon strengthened relationships with the church, and was ceremoniously crowned in 1247. A great empire-builder, he annexed Iceland and Greenland to the Norwegian crown (1262), but in the following year, on an expedition to the Western Isles of Scotland to reassert Norwegian power there, he suffered a setback at the Battle of Largs against **Alexander III** of Scotland and died at Kirkwall in the Orkneys on his way back to Norway.

HAAKON VII (1872–1957) king of Norway from 1905. Born at Charlottenlund as Prince Carl of Denmark, second son of King **Frederik VIII**, he was elected king of Norway when Norway voted for independence from Sweden. In 1896 he married Princess Maud (1869–1938), youngest daughter of King **Edward VII** of Britain. Known as the 'people's king', he dispensed with much of the pomp of royalty. When Germany invaded Norway in 1940 he refused to abdicate, and when further armed resistance was impossible, carried on the resistance from England, returning in triumph in 1945. He was succeeded by his son, **Olav V**.

HAASE, Hugo (1863–1919) German socialist leader (Independent from 1916), born at Allenstein (East Prussia). He studied law, entered the Reichstag in 1897, took a leading part in the revolution in November 1918, and a year later was assassinated.

HABA, Alois (1893–1972) Czech composer, born in Vyzovice. He studied in Prague, Vienna and Berlin and was made professor at Prague Conservatory in 1924. He composed prolifically, and showed interest in the division of the scale into quarter-tones. His works include an opera, *The Mother*, and orchestral, chamber and pianoforte music. His brother Karel (1898–1972) was a violinist, teacher and composer.

HABER, Fritz (1868–1934) German chemist, born in Breslau. He became professor of chemistry at Karlsruhe (1898) and director of Kaiser Whilhelm Institute in Berlin (1911–33). With his brother-in-law **Carl Bosch** he invented the process for the synthesis of ammonia from hydrogen and atmospheric nitrogen in the air, thus overcoming the shortage of natural nitrate deposits open to the German explosives industry during World War I. He was awarded the Nobel prize for chemistry in 1918.

HABERL, Franz Xaver (1840–1910) German musicologist, born in Ober Ellenbach. He was kapellmeister at Passans Cathedral (1862–67), and is known for his researches on 16th-century music, especially that of **Palestrina**, whose great 33-volume edition of works he completed from volume X onwards.

HABERMAS, Jürgen (1929–) German philosopher and sociologist, born in Düsseldorf. He was educated at Göttingen, Zürich and Bonn, and from 1955 to 1959 was a research assistant at the Institute of Social Research, Frankfurt. He studied for his doctorate at Marburg (1959–61) and in 1961 became professor of philosophy at Heidelberg. He later became professor of philosophy and sociology at Frankfurt (1964) and from 1971 to 1980 was director of the **Max Planck** Institute, Starnberg. The central theme of his work is the possibility of a rational political commitment to socialism in societies in which science and technology are dominant. His books include *Theory and Practice* (1963, trans 1973), *Towards a Rational Society* (1968, trans 1970), *Knowledge and Human Interests* (1968, trans 1971) and *The Theory of Communicative Action* (1981, trans 1984).

HABINGTON, William (1605–54) English poet, born in Hindlip, Worcestershire. His father, Thomas (1560–1647), an antiquary, was imprisoned, and his uncle, Edward (?1553–1586) executed, for complicity in **Babington**'s plot. He was educated at St Omer and Paris, and married Lucy Herbert, daughter of the first lord Powis. He immortalized her in his *Castara* (1634), a collection of metaphysical lyrics which are uneven in quality but contain some pieces of considerable charm. He also wrote *The Historie of Edward the Fourth* (1640), and a play, *The Queen of Aragon* (1640).

HABSBURG, or **Hapsburg** major European royal dynasty and former imperial house of Austria-Hungary. The name comes from the castle of Habsburg, or Habichtsburg ('Hawk's Castle') on the river Aar in Switzerland, first built in the 11th century. The first Count of Habsburg was Werner I (d.1096); his descendant, Count Rudolf IV, was elected king of Germany in 1273 as **Rudolf I**, *de facto* the first Habsburg emperor although he was never anointed by the pope. The first 'proper' emperor was **Frederick III** (Frederick III of Germany), who was crowned in 1452. From that time the Habsburgs wore the imperial crown almost without break as a family possession until the Empire was dissolved in 1806. After the death of Emperor **Charles V** (Charles I of Spain) the House of Habsburg divided into two lines; the Spanish line died with **Charles II** of Spain, but the Austrian line continued until the abdication of **Charles**, the last Habsburg-Lorraine emperor of Austria and Hungary, in 1918.

HABYARIMANA, Juvenal (1937–) Rwandan soldier and politician, born in Gasiza, in Gisenji prefecture. Educated at a military school, he joined the National Guard and rose rapidly to the rank of major-general, and head of the Guard, by 1973. In the same year, as fighting between the Tutsi and Hutu tribes restarted, he led a bloodless coup against President Gregoire Kayibanda and established a military régime. He founded the National Revolutionary Development Movement (MRND) as the only legal party and promised an eventual return to constitutional government.

HACHA, Emil (1872–1945) Czech politician, born in Trhové Sviny, Bohemia. He became president of Czechoslovakia in 1938 on **Beneš**' resignation following the German annexation of Sudetenland; as such, under duress, he made over the state to **Hitler** (1939). He was puppet president of the subsequent German protectorate of Bohemia and Moravia (1939–45).

HÄCKEL, Ernst See **HAECKEL**

HACKETT, Sir John Winthrop (1910–) English soldier and academic. Educated at Geelong Grammar School (Australia) and New College, Oxford, he was commissioned in the 8th Hussars in 1931. In World War II he served with distinction in the Middle East, Sicily, Italy and notably with the 4th Parachute Brigade at Arnhem in 1944. He commanded the 7th Armoured Division as major general (1956), and was commandant of the Royal Military College of Science (1958). He was commander-in-chief, Northern Ireland, in 1961 and of the British Army of the Rhine and of the Northern Army Group in 1966. He was principal of King's College, University of London from 1968 to 1975. His publications include *I was a Stranger* (1977), *The Untold Story* (1982), and *The Profession of Arms* (1983).

HACKWORTH, Green Haywood (1883–1973) American lawyer, legal adviser of the State Department (1925–46) and author of a great *Digest of International Law* (1940–43). He became a judge of the International Court of Justice (1946–61) and was its president (1955–58).

HACKWORTH, Timothy (1786–1850) English locomotive engineer, born in Wylam, Northumberland. He was manager of the Stockton-Darlington railway (1825–40), and builder of a number of famous engines, including the *Royal George* and the *Sans Pareil*, rival of **George Stephenson**'s *Rocket*.

HADAMARD, Jacques (Salomon) (1865–1963) French mathematician, born in Versailles. Educated in Paris, he became lecturer in Bordeaux (1893–97), the Sorbonne (1897–1909), and then professor at the Collège de France and the École Polytechnique until his retirement in 1937. He was a leading figure in French mathematics throughout his career, working in complex function theory, differential geometry and partial differential equations. In 1896 he and de la Vallée Poussin independently proved the definitive form of the prime number theorem, previously conjectured in cruder forms by **Adrien Marie Legendre** and **Carl Friedrich Gauss**, and proved in a weaker form by **Pafnutii Chebyshev**. He lived to an exceptional age, and was still publishing mathematical work in his eighties.

HADDINGTON, Earls of See **HAMILTON** family

HADDON, Alfred Cort (1855–1940) English anthropologist, born in London. He studied at Cambridge. In 1880 he was appointed professor of zoology at Dublin. A visit to the Torres Straits, ostensibly to study coral reefs, led to his interest in the native culture of the region, and he went on to organize the Cambridge Anthropological Expedition to the Torres Straits (1898–99), many of whose members—including **Rivers**, Myers and **Seligman**—were to become leading figures in the developing science of anthropology. The reports of the expedition were published in six volumes (1901–35). From 1904 to 1925, Haddon was reader in ethnology at Cambridge University.

HADEN, Sir Francis Seymour (1818–1910) English etcher, born in London. The founder of the Royal Hospital for Incurables, he pursued his career as a surgeon alongside that of etching. His work, which was largely concentrated in the period 1859–63, revived the art of creative printing, and in 1880 he founded the Royal Society of Painter-Etchers and Engravers.

HADFIELD, Sir Robert Abbot (1858–1940) English metallurgist and industrialist, born in Sheffield. He discovered valuable new steel alloys. The son of a Sheffield steel manufacturer who was a pioneer of steel casting, Hadfield was educated locally, taking an interest in science. Due to his father's ill-health he took over the firm at 24, but continued his research into steel alloys. **Mushet**'s attempted improvement of the Bessemer process of steel making had resulted in brittle metal. Hadfield found that by adding 12–14% of manganese and subsequent heating to 1000° and quenching in water produced a steel alloy hard and strong, suitable for metal working. With Sir William Barrett he worked on the important silicon alloys and the magnetic properties of this alloy were recognized. Hadfield worked on armour-piercing and heat-resisting steels.

HADLEE, Richard John (1951–) New Zealand cricketer, born in Christchurch. Undoubtedly the greatest all-round cricketer his country has ever produced, his father Walter and brother Dayle also represented New Zealand at Test level. In 1989 he became the first bowler to take more than 400 Test wickets, several times taking ten or more wickets in a match. A strong hitter, he has made over 2622 runs, including two centuries. Hard-working, courteous, a model professional cricketer, his unstinting endeavours took Nottinghamshire to the county championship during his spell with them in the 1980s.

HADLEY, John (1682–1744) English mathematician. He invented a reflecting telescope (1720) and the reflecting (Hadley's) quadrant (1730).

HADLEY, Patrick Arthur Sheldon (1899–1973) English composer, born in Cambridge, known for his choral work. Educated at King's College School, Cambridge and Winchester College (1912–17), he became a second lieutenant in the Royal Field Artillery during World War I, losing a leg within weeks of going into action. In 1922 he took a music degree from Cambridge, and from 1922 to 1925 he studied at the Royal College of Music, learning composition under **Vaughan Williams** and conducting from **Adrian Boult**. In 1925 he became a staff member of the RCM and met **Delius**, whose work had a considerable influence upon him. He became professor of music at Cambridge (1946–62), where he established excellent male-voice chapel and secular choirs. He wrote his most significant work, a choral symphony entitled *The Hills*, in 1946.

HADOW, Sir William Henry (1859–1937) English scholar, educational administrator and musicologist, born in Ebrington, Gloucestershire. A minister's son, he was educated at Malvern and Worcester College, Oxford, where he was successively scholar, lecturer (1884), fellow, tutor and dean (1889) and honorary fellow (1909). He lectured brilliantly and without notes in classics and music. His *Studies in Modern Music* (1892 and 1895) are widely held to have marked a milestone in musical criticism. His *Sonata Form* (1896) epitomized his grace of style, while his *The Viennese Period* in the *Oxford History of Music* is held to be his masterpiece. He was principal of Armstrong College, Newcastle upon Tyne, 1909–19, and vice-chancellor of Sheffield University, 1919–30. He was chairman of the Consultative Committee, (set up by the Education Act of 1918), and of the board of education 1920–34. Under his chairmanship no less than six reports were published. The most famous and influential was *The Education of the Adolescent* (1926) which called for the re-organization of elementary education, the abandonment of all-age schools and the creation of secondary modern schools. Economic stringency delayed its implementation but it was a major breakthrough in educational thinking. Other reports include those of 1931 (Primary School) and 1933 (Infant and Nursery Schools). He was a leading influence in English education at all levels in the 1920s and 1930s.

HADRIAN, Publius Aelius Hadrianus (76–138) Roman emperor from 117, born in Rome, or, according to some sources, in Italica, in Spain. After his father's death in 86, he accompanied the emperor **Trajan**, his kinsman and guardian, on his wars. He became prefect of Syria, and after Trajan's death was proclaimed emperor by the army (117). Insurrections had broken out in Egypt, Palestine and Syria; Moesia and Mauretania were invaded by barbarians; and the Parthians had once more asserted their independence. Hadrian concluded a peace with the last, having resolved to limit the boundaries of the empire in the East, and after appeasing the invaders of Moesia, he established his authority at Rome, and suppressed a conspiracy against his life. About 120 he began his long tour of the empire He visited Gaul, Germany, Britain (where he built the wall from the Solway to the Tyne), Spain, Mauretania, Egypt, Asia Minor and Greece, returning to Rome at the end of 126. He wintered twice in Athens (125–26, 129–30). After crushing a major revolt in Judaea (132–134), he returned to Italy, where he died. He reorganized the army, ruled justly and was a patron of the arts. Among his buildings were his mausoleum (now part of the castle of St Angelo); the magnificent villa at Tibur; and he founded Adrianopolis.

HAECKEL, Ernst Heinrich Philipp August (1834–1919) German naturalist, born in Potsdam. He studied at Würzburg, Berlin and Vienna, and was professor of zoology at Jena (1862–1909), making expeditions to the North Sea shores, the Mediterranean, Madeira, the Canaries, Arabia, India, etc. He wrote on the radiolarians (1862), calcareous sponges (1872), and jellyfishes (1879), and *Challenger* Reports on *Deep-sea Medusae* (1882), *Siphonophora* (1888), and *Radiolaria* (1887). One of the first to sketch the genealogical tree of animals, Haeckel explained that the life history of the individual is a recapitulation of its historic evolution.

HAFFKINE, Waldemar Mordecai Wolff (1860–1930) Russian-born British bacteriologist, born in Odessa. He assisted **Pasteur** (1889–93), and as bacteriologist to the government of India (1893–1915) introduced his method of protective inoculation against cholera. He became a British subject in 1899.

HÁFIZ, pseud of **Shams ed-Dín Muhammed** (d.c.1388) Persian lyrical poet, born in Shíráz. From the charming sweetness of his poetry he was named by his contemporaries *Chagarlab*, or 'Sugar-lip'. His ghazals are all on sensuous subjects—wine, flowers, beautiful damsels—but they also possess an esoteric significance to the initiated, and his name is a household word throughout Iran. Háfiz, like nearly all the great poets of Persia, was of the sect of Súfi philosophers, the mystics of Islam. His tomb, two miles northeast of Shíráz, has been magnificently adorned by princes, and is visited by pilgrims from all parts of Iran.

HAFSTEIN, Hannes (Pétursson) (1861–1922) Icelandic politician and poet, born at Möðruvellir in the north of Iceland, the first Icelandic premier under Home Rule (1904–07, 1912–14). He studied at Reykjavík and Copenhagen university, where he became a brilliant lawyer. He returned to Iceland in 1887 a fervent nationalist with a growing reputation as a lyric poet, and became leader of the independence party in the campaign for Home Rule from Denmark. In his premiership he brought about large improvements in education, health care and commerce, and inaugurated a telephone and telegraph system. In his poetry he was one of the early proponents of realism in Icelandic literature.

HAGEDORN, Friedrich von (1708–54) German poet, born in Hamburg. In 1733 he became secretary to the 'English Court' trading company at Hamburg, and wrote satirical, narrative and 'society' verses.

HAGENBECK, Carl (1844–1913) German animal tamer, born in Hamburg. He toured the USA, and in 1907 founded the famous circus and zoological park at Stellingen, near Hamburg. He wrote *Beasts and Men* (1909).

HÄGERSTRAND, Torsten (1916–) Swedish geographer, born in Moheda. Educated at Lund University, he taught there until 1971 (professor from 1957). He was then appointed a research professor at the State Council for Social Research (1971–). Indications of his international experience and recognition have been his vice-presidency of the International Geographical Union, the American Geographical Society medal (1966) and the 'outstanding achievement award' of the Association of American Geographers (1968). An instigator of the quantitative revolution in Europe, he made Lund a major centre of innovation in geographical studies. He developed theoretical probability models of information diffusion and established a new economic theory in which time and space are regarded as scarce resources.

HAGGARD, Sir (Henry) Rider (1856–1925) English novelist, born in Bradenham Hall, Norfolk, the son of a lawyer. Educated at Ipswich grammar school, he went to Natal in 1875 as secretary to Sir Henry Bulwer, and next year accompanied Sir Theophilus Shepstone to the Transvaal. He returned in 1879 (finally in 1881) to England, married, and settled down to a literary life. His *Cetewayo and his White Neighbours* (1882) pleased the Cape politicians, but attracted no attention elsewhere. *King Solomon's Mines* (1885) made him famous, and was followed by *She* (1887), *Allan Quatermain* (1887), *Eric Bright-eyes* (1891), *The Pearl Maiden* (1903), *Agesha* (1905) and many other stories. Other publications include *Rural England* (1902) and *The Days of My Life* (1926).

HAGGART, David (1801–21) Scottish criminal. A fairground pickpocket and thief, he frequented racecourses and was imprisoned for theft six times, but escaped from jail on most occasions. On the last occasion he killed a warder at Dumfries in 1820 and fled to Ireland, where he was captured, sent back to Edinburgh for trial, and hanged. He compiled an autobiography in Scottish thieves' slang, which was published by the phrenologist **George Combe**.

HAGGETT, Peter (1933–) English geographer, born in Pawlett, Somerset. He studied at Dr Morgan's School, Bridgewater, and St Catharine's College, Cambridge. After various university appointments at home and abroad, he became professor of urban and regional geography at Bristol University in 1966. He was a leading exponent in the advance towards a unifying philosophical and methodological basis for human geography, as exemplified in his book, *Locational Analysis in Human Geography* (1965). Focusing on the 'region' as an open system, this work presented a new framework for human geography. It emphasized the critical association of the earth sciences, social sciences and geometrical sciences, and led to fundamental debate in the subject.

HAHN, Kurt Matthias Robert Martin (1886–1974) German educationist, born in Berlin. He was educated at Wilhelm Gymnasium, Berlin, and Christ Church, Oxford, and the universities of Berlin, Heidelberg, Freiburg and Göttingen. He founded a school at Castle Salem in Germany, based on his ideas of what an English public school was supposed to be. In 1933 he fled from Nazi Germany to Britain, and founded Gordonstoun in Morayshire (Scotland) in 1934 on similar lines, emphasizing physical rather than intellectual activities in education, giving boys opportunities for self-discovery through practical tasks and allowing them to move up academically at their own pace. A man of overpowering and autocratic personality, he dominated his school and imposed his obsessions with sex and aesthetics on his pupils. His ideas were probably more influential than they deserved to be, attracting the attention of the Admiralty and the War Office, and greatly affecting the development of such establishments as the Outward Bound Schools (1941) and the Atlantic Colleges (1957).

HAHN, Otto (1879–1968) German physical chemist, born in Frankfurt. After studies at Frankfurt, Marburg and Munich, he conducted researches into radioactivity under Sir **William Ramsay** in London and Lord **Rutherford** at Montreal. With **Lisa Meitner** in Berlin in 1917 he discovered the radioactive protactinium. In 1928 he became director of the Kaiser Wilhelm Institute in Berlin. In 1938, following the researches of the **Joliot-Curies**, he bombarded uranium with neutrons to find the first chemical evidence of nuclear fission products. The Nazi government did not grasp the potentialities of this discovery and Hahn spent the war-years doing small-scale experiments for the industrial use of nuclear energy. After the war he was interned in Cambridge, but from 1946 to 1960 he was president of the **Max Planck** Society in Göttingen, and signed the 'Göttingen Declaration' in April 1957 refusing to co-operate in the contemplated West German manufacture of nuclear weapons. He was awarded the Nobel prize for chemistry in 1944.

HAHN, Reynaldo (1874–1947) Venezualan-born, French composer, singer, pianist, conductor and writer on music, born in Caracas. At the age of three he was taken to Paris, studied composition with **Massenet**, and soon showed precocious musical gifts, especially in his early songs. He became the darling of the salons and the intimate friend of **Proust**. As conductor he was a noted Mozartian. His compositions included ballets, musical comedies (*Ciboulette*, 1923; *Mozart*, 1925) and instrumental works.

HAHN-HAHN, Ida, Countess (1805–80) German novelist, born in Tressow in Mecklenburg-Schwerin. She wrote society novels influenced by the 'Young Germany' movement, before turning Catholic and founding a convent in Mainz (1854).

HAHNEMANN, Christian Friedrich Samuel (1755–1843) German physician and founder of homeopathy, born in Meissen. He studied at Leipzig, and for ten years practised medicine. After six years of experiments on the curative power of bark, he came to the conclusion that medicine produces a very similar condition in healthy persons to that which it relieves in the sick. His own infinitesimal doses of medicine provoked the apothecaries, who refused to dispense them; accordingly he illegally gave his medicines to his patients, free of charge, and was prosecuted in every town in which he tried to settle from 1798 until 1810. He then returned to Leipzig, where he taught his system until 1821, when he was again driven out. He retired first to Köthen, and then in 1835 to Paris.

HAIDAR ALI (1728–82) Indian soldier and ruler. By his bravery he attracted the notice of the Maharaja of Mysore's minister, and soon rose to power, ousting both prime minister and raja. He conquered Calicut, Bednor and Cannanore, and by 1766 his dominions included more than 84000 sq m. He withheld the customary tribute from the Mahrattas, and carried on war against them. He waged two wars against the British, in the first of which (1767–69) he was almost successful. Defeated by the Mahrattas in 1772 he claimed British support; but when this was refused he became their bitter enemy. Taking advantage of the war between Britain and the French (1778), he and his son **Tippoo Sahib**, descended upon the Carnatic, routed the British, and ravaged the country to within 40 miles of Madras, but were ultimately defeated in three battles by Sir **Eyre Coote**.

HAIG, Alexander Meigs, Jr (1924–) United States soldier and public official, born in Philadelphia, Pennsylvania. Educated at the US Military Academy, West Point, Naval War College and Georgetown University he joined the US Army in 1947. He served in Korea (1950–51) and the Vietnam War (1966–67) and was made a general in 1973. During the **Nixon** presidency he was deputy to **Henry Kissinger** in the National Security Council and became White House chief of staff (1973–74), at the height of the Watergate scandal. Returning to military duty in 1974, he was NATO's supreme allied commander, Europe (1974–79). He was President **Reagan**'s secretary of state (1981–82), but resigned as a result of policy differences. He unsuccessfully sought the Republican party's presidential nomination in 1988.

HAIG, Douglas, 1st Earl Haig of Bemersyde (1861–1928) Scottish soldier and field-marshal, born in Edinburgh. Educated at Clifton, Oxford University and the Royal Military College, Sandhurst, he was commissioned in the 7th Hussars. Active service in Egypt and South Africa, followed by staff and command assignments in India, led to his appointment in 1911 as GOC Aldershot. In August 1914 he took the 1st Corps of the British Expeditionary Force to France, and succeeded Sir **John French** as c-in-c in December 1915. With the flanks of the battle zone sealed by the sea and the Swiss Border and the Germans operating on interior lines, Haig was forced to forgo war of movement and wage a costly and exhausting war of attrition; a difficult task appreciably aggravated by the progressive deterioration of the French after the failure of the Nivelle offensive of 1917, and **Lloyd George**'s hampering distrust and irresponsible attempts to control strategy. Under the overall command of **Foch**, Haig's reward came with his army's successful offensive of August 1918, leading to the German plea for an armistice. After the war, he organized the Royal British Legion for the care of ex-servicemen.

HAIGH, John George (1909–49) English murderer, born in Stamford. A company director, he shot a widow (1949) and subsequently disposed of her body by reducing it in sulphuric acid. A vital clue leading to his conviction and execution was a plastic denture which had resisted the acid. He probably murdered five others in the same way and although the motive was money it is possible that he drank his victims' blood.

HAILE SELASSIE (1891–1975) emperor of Ethiopia from 1930, previously Prince Ras Tafari, son of Ras Makonnen. He led the revolution in 1916 against Lij Yasu and became regent and heir to the throne. He westernized the institutions of his country. He settled in England after the Italian conquest of

Abyssinia (1935–36), but in 1941 was restored after the liberation by British forces. In the early 1960s he played a crucial part in the establishment of the Organisation of African Unity (OAU). Opposition to his reign had existed since 1960, and the disastrous famine of 1973 led to economic chaos, industrial strikes and mutiny among the armed forces, and the emperor was deposed in 1974 in favour of the Crown Prince, though he was allowed to return to his palace at Addis Ababa. Accusations of corruption levelled against him and his family have not destroyed the unique prestige and reverence in which he is held by certain groups, notably the Rastafarians.

HAILES, Sir David Dalrymple, Lord (1726–92) Scottish jurist and historian, born in Edinburgh, a great grandson of the 1st Viscount Stair. He became a judge of the Court of Session in 1766 and a judge of the High Court of Justiciary also in 1776, but is best known for historical writings, the chronological *Annals of Scotland* (1776–79), still a valuable work.

HAILEY, Arthur (1920–) English-born Canadian popular novelist, born in Luton. He became a naturalized Canadian in 1947. He has written many best-selling blockbusters about disasters, several of which enjoyed a new lease of life when filmed. Indicative titles include *Hotel* (1965), *Airport* (1968) and *Wheels* (1971).

HAILSHAM, Douglas McGarel Hogg, 1st Viscount (1872–1950) English jurist and statesman, father of Quintin Hogg, 2nd Viscount **Hailsham**. He entered parliament in 1922, was attorney-general from 1922 to 1924, and 1924 to 1928, lord chancellor in 1928-29 and from 1935 to 1938 and secretary for war 1931–35. He was made a baron in 1928 and a viscount in 1929.

HAILSHAM, Quintin McGarel Hogg, 2nd Viscount (1907–) English jurist and statesman, born in London, son of **Douglas Hailsham**, 1st Viscount. Educated at Eton College Christ Church College, Oxford (president of the Union, 1929) he became a fellow of All Souls in 1931. In 1932 he was called to the bar and from 1938 to 1950 he was MP for Oxford City. He succeeded to the title in 1950, and, among several political posts, was First Lord of the Admiralty (1956–57), minister of education (1957), lord president of the Council (1957–59; 1960–64), and chairman of the Conservative party (1957–59). He was minister for science and technology (1959–64), and secretary of state for education and science (1964). In the Conservative leadership crisis of November 1963, he renounced his peerage for life, and was re-elected to the House of Commons in the St Marylebone by-election. He was opposition minister for the home office from 1966. In 1970 he was created a life peer (Baron Hailsham of Saint Marylebone) and became lord chancellor (1970–74, 1979–87). His several publications include *The Case for Conservatism* (1947), *The Conservative Case* (1959), and *The Door Wherein I Went* (1975).

HAITINK, Bernard (1929–) Dutch conductor, born in Amsterdam. His first appearance with the Concertgebouw Orchestra was in 1956; in 1961 he became its principal conductor and in 1964 its chief conductor. He was appointed principal conductor of the London Philharmonic (1967), and its artistic director from 1969 to 1978. He then became music director of the Glyndebourne Festival, and in 1987 music director of the Royal Opera House, Covent Garden. He has toured internationally and, in addition to opera, is an acclaimed interpreter of **Bruckner** and **Mahler**. He was created an honorary KBE in 1977.

HĀKIM, al- (985–1021) sixth Fatimide caliph of Egypt from 996, succeeding his father at the age of eleven. The early part of his reign was characterized by the persecution of the Christian and Jewish minorities and the destruction of thousands of churches including the Holy Sepulchre in Jerusalem (1003–13), although many of the civil penalties and confiscations were later reversed, while his extreme Shi'ite policies in Muslim affairs aroused the antagonism of the predominantly Sunni population. From 1017 al-Hākim became convinced of his own divinity, which was publicly preached by his followers Hamza and al-Darazī, and in the midst of a growing crisis the caliph disappeared in mysterious circumstances. His cult became the basis of the Druze religion which took root in the Lebanon, Syria and Galilee.

HAKLUYT, Richard (c.1552–1616) English geographer, cleric and historian, born in Hertfordshire. From Westminster School he went in 1570 to Christ Church College, Oxford, where he afterwards became the first ordained lecturer on geography. He introduced the use of globes into English schools. The publication of *Divers Voyages touching the Discovery of America* (1582) commissioned by **Walter Raleigh** advocating colonization of North America as a base for exploration via the Northwest Passage to the East seems to have procured for him in 1584 the chaplaincy of the English embassy to Paris; there he wrote *Discourse concerning Western Discoveries* (1584). On his return to England in 1588 he began to collect materials for his *Principal Navigations, Voyages, and Discoveries of the English Nation* (1598–1600; a major 3-volume work on the history of exploration which drew on first hand accounts in many languages). Made a prebendary of Westminster in 1602, he was buried there. The *Hakluyt Society* was instituted in 1846 to promote an interest in geography and the maintaining of records of expeditions and geographical writings.

HAKON See **HAAKON**

HALAS, George Stanley (1895–1983) American football coach with the Chicago Bears and team owner, born in Chicago. A co-founder of the National Football League (1920), he helped shape the modern professional game, bringing large crowds in to watch the sport for the first time. In 1968 he retired as head coach to the Bears for the fourth and last time. After more than 40 years of coaching his record showed 320 wins, 147 defeats and 30 draws. As player, coach and owner, he earned the nickname 'Papa Bear'.

HALAS, John, originally **Halasz** (1912–) Hungarian-born British animated cartoon producer, born in Budapest. He started as a magazine joke cartoonist in 1930, then turned to animation and moved to London, where he met and married **Joy Batchelor** and formed the Halas-Batchelor animation unit.

HALDANE, Elizabeth Sanderson (1862–1937) Scottish author, sister of **John Scott Haldane** and **Richard Burdon Haldane**. She studied nursing, for a while managed the Royal Infirmary, Edinburgh, and became the first woman justice of the peace in Scotland (1920). She wrote a Life of **Descartes** (1905) and with Ross edited his philosophical works, translated **Hegel** and wrote commentaries on **George Eliot** (1927) and Mrs **Gaskell** (1930).

HALDANE, James Alexander (1768–1851) Scottish minister, born in Dundee, brother of **Robert Haldane**. Educated there and at Edinburgh, he served with the East India Company (1785–94). With **Charles Simeon** of Cambridge he made an evangelistic tour of Scotland in 1797, from which Congregational Churches developed. With his brother Robert he opened a tabernacle in Edinburgh in 1801, where he preached gratuitously for 50 years, and which in 1808 he led into the Baptist fold. His pamphlets were widely read.

HALDANE, John Burdon Sanderson (1892–1964) Anglo-Indian biologist of Scottish descent, born in Oxford, the son of physiologist **John Scott Haldane**. Educated at Eton, he went to Oxford to study mathematics and biology, but graduated in classics and philosophy, switching later to genetics. Eccentric and wilful, he became an atheist during World War I, and later reader in biochemistry at Cambridge (1922–32), conducting research on enzymes. He switched to population genetics and the mathematics of natural selection, and became professor of genetics at London University (1933–37), but again switched to the chair of biometry at University College, London (1937–57), and studied underwater conditions and submarine deaths. A committed Marxist, he was chairman of the editorial board of the communist *Daily Worker* (1940–49), but left the Communist party in 1956 over the **Lysenko** controversy and 'Soviet interference in science'. In 1957 he emigrated to India (appartently in protest over Suez) and adopted Indian nationality, and became professor of the Indian Statistical Institute in Calcutta, but resigned in 1961 after quarrelling with his colleagues. He became head of the Orissa State Genetics and Biometry Laboratory in 1962. His numerous popular works included *Animal Biology* (with **J S Huxley**, 1927), *Possible Worlds* (1927), *Science and Ethics* (1928), *The Inequality of Man* (1932), *Fact and Faith* (1934), *Heredity and Politics* (1938), and *Science in Everyday Life* (1939).

HALDANE, John Scott (1860–1936) Scottish physiologist, brother of Richard Burdon, 1st Viscount **Haldane**, grand-nephew of **Robert Haldane**, father of **J B S Haldane** and **Naomi Mitchison**. Born in Edinburgh, he became demonstrator and reader in medicine at Oxford (1887–1913) and was elected fellow of New College, Oxford. He became an authority on the effects of industrial occupations upon respiration and served as a director of a mining research laboratory at Birmingham from 1912.

HALDANE, Richard Burdon, 1st Viscount Haldane (1856–1928) Scottish jurist, philosopher and and Liberal statesman, grandson of **James Alexander Haldane**. Educated at Edinburgh and Göttingen, he was called to the bar in 1879, entered parliament in 1879 as a Liberal, supported the Boer war and as secretary of state for war (1905–12) remodelled the army and founded the Territorials. He was lord chancellor (1912–15 and, under Labour, in 1924), and ranked high as a judge. He gave the Gifford Lectures at St Andrews (1902–04) and published three philosophical treatises.

HALDANE, Robert (1764–1842) Scottish evangelist and writer, born in London, brother of **James Haldane**. He was in the navy during the relief of Gibraltar, but settled on his estates at Airthrey, near Stirling, in 1783. The French Revolution brought about a spiritual revolution within him, and he with his brother James founded the Society for Propagating the Gospel at Home (1797), built tabernacles for itinerant preachers (the first Congregational Churches) and lectured to theological students in Geneva and Montauban (1817).

HALDIMAND, Sir Frederick (1718–91) Swiss-born British soldier, born in the canton of Neuchâtel. From 1756 he commanded British regiments or garrisons in the American colonial wars with the French and the Indians, including **Amherst**'s expedition against Montreal in 1760. He was commander of the British army in North America at Boston (1773–74), and from 1778 to 1784 was governor of Canada.

HALE, Edward Everett (1822–1909) American Unitarian clergyman and writer, born in Boston, Massachusetts where he became pastor of the South Congregational Church in 1856. He did much philanthropic work and his book *Ten Times One is Ten* (1870) inspired numerous 'Lend a Hand' clubs. He edited religious and other journals, and documents on the founding of Virginia, and wrote short stories. He was the grand-nephew of **Nathan Hale**.

HALE, George Ellery (1868–1938) American astronomer, born in Chicago. A graduate of Massachusetts Institute of Technology, he was director at the Yerkes Observatory (1895–1905), and at Mount Wilson (1904–23). He earned fame by his brilliant researches on sunspots, and invented the spectroheliograph.

HALE, Sir Matthew (1609–76) English judge, born in Alderley in Gloucestershire. He studied at Oxford, entered Lincoln's Inn in 1628, and in 1637 was called to the bar. A justice of the common pleas from 1654 until **Cromwell**'s death in 1658, after the Restoration (which he zealously promoted) he was made chief-baron of the Exchequer, and in 1671 chief justice of the King's Bench. Devout, acute, learned and sensible, although a believer in witchcraft, he wrote a *History of the Common Law* (1713), a *History of the Pleas of the Crown* (1736), both still important, and the *Prerogatives of the King* (printed 1776), besides religious works.

HALE, Nathan (1755–76) American revolutionary soldier, now considered the 'patron saint' of American espionage agencies. Born in Coventry, Connecticut, he became a captain in the Continental army. In 1776 he volunteered to penetrate the British lines on Long Island and procure intelligence for **Washington**, but was detected, and hanged as a spy in New York City. His statue stands at the HQ of the CIA at Langley, Virginia.

HALE, Sarah Josepha, née **Buell** (1788–1879) American writer, born in Newport, New Hampshire. In 1828 she became editor of the *Ladies' Magazine*, Boston. She wrote a novel, *Northwood* (1827), and a book of *Poems for Our Children* (1830), which contained 'Mary had a Little Lamb'.

HALES See **ALEXANDER OF HALES**

HALES, John (1584–1656) English clergyman, known as the 'Ever-memorable', born in Bath. Educated at Corpus Christi College, Oxford he became a fellow and lecturer at Merton College. In 1616 he went to The Hague as chaplain to the ambassador, Sir Dudley Carleton, for whom he made a report of the famous synod of Dort which convinced him of the futility of extreme dogma, and so inspiring him to reject calvinism. In 1619 he returned to Eton to study. His too-liberal *Tract concerning Schism and Schismatics* displeased **Laud**, who was, however, satisfied after a personal conference and an apologetic letter, and appointed him to a canonry at Windsor (1639).

HALES, Stephen (1677–1761) English botanist and chemist, the 'father of plant physiology', born in Beaksbourn, Canterbury. He entered Corpus Christi College, Cambridge, in 1696, was elected fellow in 1702, and became in 1709 perpetual curate of Teddington. His *Vegetable Staticks* (1727) was the foundation of vegetable physiology. In *Haemastaticks* (1733) he discussed the circulation of the blood and blood pressure.. Besides a work on dissolving stones in the bladder, he wrote in the *Philosophical Transactions* on ventilation, electricity, analysis of air, etc. He also invented machines for ventilating, distilling sea water, preserving meat, etc.

HALEVI, Jehuda (1075–1141) Spanish Jewish poet, philosopher and a prominent physician, born in Toledo. His experience of anti-semitism in Cordova led him to expound and celebrate the superiority of

Judaism against **Aristotle**'s philosophy, Christianity and Islam in various highly-wrought prose and poetic works. He encouraged a vision of the Jewish people and the land of Israel which has endeared him to modern Zionists. His main philosophical work (in Arabic) is the *Book of the Khazars* (in full, the 'Book of Argument and Proof in Defence of the Despised Faith'), and there is a collection of his poems entitled *Diwan*, including *Zionide* ('Ode to Zion'), the most widely translated Hebrew poem of the middle ages. He reputedly died in Egypt on his way to Jerusalem.

HALÉVY, Daniel (1872–1962) French historian, born in Paris, the younger son of **Ludovic Halévy**. An authority on the history of the 3rd Republic, he wrote Lives of **Nietzsche** (1909), **Vauban** (1923), **Michelet** (1928) and numerous historical works.

HALÉVY, Élie (1870–1937) French historian, born in Étretat, son of Ludovic Halévy. He became professor of political science at Paris in 1898 and wrote *La Formation du radicalism philosophique* (1901–04), *Histoire du peuple anglais au XIXe siècle* (1912 ff) and *L'Ère des tyrannies* (1938).

HALÉVY, Jacques (Fromental Elié) originally **Elias Lévy** (1799–1862) French composer, brother of **Léon Halévy**, born in Paris. His first successful opera was *Clari* (1828), followed by the comic opera *Le Dilettante d'Avignon* (1829). His masterpiece, *La Juive* (1835), made him famous across Europe. His next best work is the comic opera, *L'Éclair* (1835), but he produced about a dozen other operatic works. He worthily carried on the succession of the great school of French opera, midway between **Maria Cherubini** and **Giacomo Meyerbeer**. Admitted to the Academy of Fine Arts in 1846, he became perpetual secretary in 1854. His *éloges* were collected as *Souvenirs et Portraits* (1861–63). Among his pupils were **Bizet** and **Charles Gounod**.

HALÉVY, Joseph (1827–1917) French orientalist, born in Adrianople. In 1868 he travelled in northern Abyssinia, and in 1869–70 crossed Yemen in quest of Sabaean inscriptions for the French Academy. His books describe his journeys or deal with the dialects of the Falashas, Sabaean and cuneiform inscriptions.

HALÉVY, Léon (1802–83) French writer, brother of **Jacques Halévy**, born in Paris. He became professor of literature at the Polytechnic School. He wrote the introduction to **Saint-Simon**'s *Opinions* (1825), also histories, poetry, fables, novels, dramatic poems, and translations of *Macbeth*, *Clavigo*, and other works. His most important books are *Résumé de l'histoire des juifs* (1827–28), *Poésies européennes* (1837), and *La Grèce tragique* (1845–61).

HALÉVY, Ludovic (1834–1908) French playwright and novelist, son of **Léon Halévy**, born in Paris. In 1861 he became secretary to the Corps Législatif. With **Meilhac** he wrote libretti for the best-known operettas of **Offenbach**, and for **Bizet**'s *Carmen*, and produced vaudevilles and comedies. His *Madame et Monsieur Cardinal* (1873) and *Les petites Cardinal* (1880) are delightful sketches of Parisian theatrical life. *L'Invasion* (1872) contained his personal recollections of the war. His charming *L'Abbé Constantin* (1882) was followed by *Criquette*, *Deux Mariages*, *Princesse*, and *Mariette* (1893).

HALIBURTON, Hugh, pseud of **James Logie Robertson** (1846–1922) Scottish poet, born in Milnathort, Kinross. He became a student-teacher in Haddington, and later he studied at Edinburgh. He became the first English master at Edinburgh Ladies' College, later Mary Erskine's School (1876–1913) In the guise of a shepherd in the Ochil Hills, 'Hugh Haliburton', he published *Horace in Homespun: A Series of Scottish Pastorals* (1886) and *Ochil Idylls* (1891). He also wrote essays, and edited **James Thomson**.

HALIBURTON, Thomas Chandler (1796–1865) Canadian writer and jurist, born in Windsor, Nova Scotia. He was called to the bar in 1820, and became a member of the House of Assembly, chief justice of the common pleas (1828), and judge of the supreme court (1842). In 1856 he retired to England, and from 1859 to 1863 was Conservative MP for Launceston. He is best known as the creator of Sam Slick, a sort of American Sam Weller, in newspaper sketches collected between 1837 and 1840 as *The Clockmaker, or Sayings and Doings of Samuel Slick of Slickville*, continued as *The Attaché, or Sam Slick in England* (1843–44). Other works include *Traits of American Humour* (1843) and *Rule and Misrule of the English in America* (1850).

HALIFAX, Charles Montagu, 1st Earl of (1661–1715) English statesman and poet, a nephew of the Parliamentary general, the Earl of **Manchester**, born in Horton, Northamptonshire. From Westminster he passed in 1679 to Trinity College, Cambridge. His most notable poetical achievement was a parody on **Dryden**'s *The Hind and the Panther*, entitled *The Town and Country Mouse* (1687), of which he was joint author with **Matthew Prior**. MP for Maldon (1688) and a lord of the Treasury (1692), he in that year proposed to raise a million sterling by way of loan—establishing the national debt. In 1694 money was again wanted, and Halifax supplied it by originating the Bank of England, as proposed by **William Paterson** three years earlier. For this service he was appointed Chancellor of the Exchequer. He was responsible for the recoinage in 1695, the appointment of his friend **Isaac Newton** as warden of the mint, and of raising a tax on windows to pay the expense; he first introduced exchequer bills. In 1697 he became premier, but his arrogance and vanity soon made him unpopular, and on the Tories coming into power in 1699 he was obliged to accept the auditorship of the Exchequer and withdraw from the Commons as Baron Halifax. He was unsuccessfully impeached in 1701, and again in 1703. He strongly supported the union with Scotland and the Hanoverian succession. On Queen **Anne**'s death he was appointed a member of the council of regency, and on **George I**'s arrival became an earl and prime minister.

HALIFAX, Sir Charles Wood, 1st Viscount (1800–85) English Liberal statesman, grandson of **Charles Montagu Halifax** and grandfather of **Edward Halifax**, was Chancellor of the Exchequer (1846–52) and secretary for India (1859–66).

HALIFAX, Edward Frederick Lindley Wood, 1st Earl of (2nd creation) (1881–1959) English Conservative statesman, grandson of **Charles Montagu Halifax**. He was (as Baron Irwin 1925) viceroy of India (1926–31), foreign secretary (1938–40) under **Neville Chamberlain**, whose 'appeasement' policy he implemented, and ambassador to the USA (1941–46). He was created earl in 1944.

HALIFAX, George Savile, 1st Marquis of (1633–95) English statesman. He was created viscount (1668) for his share in the Restoration. In 1675 he opposed **Danby**'s Test Bill, and in 1679 by a display of extraordinary oratory procured the rejection of the Exclusion Bill. Three years later he was created a marquis and made lord privy seal. On the accession of **James II** he became president of the council, but was dismissed in 1685 for his opposition to the repeal of the Test and Habeas Corpus Acts. One of the three commissioners appointed by James II to treat with William of Orange (**William III**) after he landed in England, on James's flight he tendered his allegiance to

William and resumed the office of lord privy seal; but, joining the Opposition, he resigned his post in 1689. His defence is to be read in his *Character of a Trimmer*. His *Miscellanies* show him a witty epigrammatist.

HALKETT, Hugh, Baron von (1783–1863) Hanoverian soldier, born in Musselburgh, Scotland. He served with distinction in the British army in the Napoleonic wars, fought in the Peninsula and commanded the Hanoverian militia at Waterloo (1815).

HALKETT, Samuel (1814–71) Scottish scholar. He was librarian to the Advocates' Library in Edinburgh (from 1848), and compiled the *Dictionary of Anonymous Literature* (4 vols, 1882–88) completed by the Rev. John Laing (1809–80). From 1850 he was librarian of New College, Edinburgh.

HALL, Anna Maria See **HALL, Samuel Carter**.

HALL, Asaph (1829–1907) American astronomer, born at Goshen, Connecticut. From 1862 to 1891 he was on the staff of the naval observatory at Washington. In 1877 he discovered the two satellites of Mars which he named Deimos and Phobos.

HALL, Basil (1788–1844) Scottish travel writer, born in Edinburgh. A naval officer (1802–23) he wrote popular works on Korea (1818), Chile, Peru and Mexico (1824) and *Travels in North America* (1829). He also wrote novels and short stories.

HALL, Ben (Benjamin) (1837–65) Australian bushranger, born in New South Wales, son of an English convict. At 16 he married the daughter of a wealthy cattleman and settled down to farming. In 1862 he was arrested in connection with a recent robbery but was acquitted and freed but on returning home found that his young wife had left him, taking their young son. In anger Hall joined the gang led by Frank Gardiner, and in the following month they held up a gold coach carrying £28000 of bullion. Again arrested, and again released, Hall returned to his farm to find it burned down by the police and all his cattle killed. He was now committed to a life of outlawry and a series of audacious exploits followed, which engaged the sympathies of the locals. However, after the needless shooting of a constable by one of the gang, he decided to change his ways. He retired to a secluded camp but was betrayed by a companion and died in a hail of police bullets at the age of 28.

HALL, Charles Francis (1821–71) American Arctic explorer, born in Rochester, New Hampshire. Successively blacksmith, journalist, stationer and engraver, he became interested in the fate of Sir **John Franklin** whose expedition had been lost in 1847. He made two search expeditions (1860–62 and 1864-69), living alone among the Eskimos, and bringing back relics and the bones of one of Franklin's men. In 1871 he sailed in command of the *Polaris* on an 'expedition to the North Pole', and on 29 August reached, via Smith's Sound, 82° 16′ N, then the highest latitude reached; next turning southward, he went into winter quarters at Thank God Harbour, Greenland (81° 38′ N), where he was taken ill, and died. His companions reached home in the autumn of 1873.

HALL, Charles Martin (1863–1914) American chemist, born in Thompson, Ohio. In 1886 he discovered (independently of **Paul Héroult**) the first economic method of obtaining aluminium from bauxite electrolytically. He helped to found the Aluminum Company of America, of which he became vice-president in 1890.

HALL, Chester Moor (1703–71) English inventor, from Essex. In 1733 he anticipated **Dollond** in the invention of the achromatic telescope.

HALL, or **Halle, Edward** (c.1499–1547) English historian, born in London. He was educated at Eton and King's College, Cambridge, where he was elected fellow, and at Gray's Inn. He became a common serjeant in 1532. His *Union of the Noble Famelies of Lancastre and Yorke* (1542, commonly called *Hall's Chronicle*) was only brought down to 1532; the rest, down to 1546, was completed by the editor, **Richard Grafton**. Hall's stately dignity and the reality of his figures had a charm for **Shakespeare**; and to the student of **Henry VIII**'s reign the work is really valuable as the intelligent evidence of an eye witness, though too eulogistic of the king.

HALL, Sir Edward Marshall (1858–1927) English lawyer, born in Brighton. He was called to the bar in 1888 after an unpromising career at Rugby and Cambridge. Although the victim of bitter hostility in the Harmsworth press, he built up his reputation through a series of spectacular victories in murder cases such as Robert Wood (1903), Edward Lawrence (1909), Ronald Light (1920) and Harold Greenwood (1920), where his supreme powers of classical advocacy offset his legal ignorance (a propensity for wrangling with the judiciary probably cut both ways). His notable failures included **Frederick Henry Seddon** and **George Joseph Smith**, but not through any errors of his. His greatest civil triumph was *Russell* v *Russell* (1923). Despite (or possibly because of) his oratorical powers he made little mark as MP (Conservative) for Southport (1900–06) and East Toxteth (1910–16), while his legendary reputation owed much to his biographer Edward Marjoribanks.

HALL, Granville Stanley (1844–1924) American psychologist and educationist, born in Ashfield, Massachusetts. Having studied at Leipzig under **Wilhelm Wundt**, he became professor at Antioch College, and in 1876–81 was lecturer at Harvard. In 1882, as professor at Johns Hopkins, he introduced experimental psychology on a laboratory scale. In 1887 he founded the *American Journal of Psychology*. He exercised a profound influence on the development of educational psychology and child psychology in the USA, and became the first president of Clark University (1889–1920). His works include *The Contents of Children's Minds* (1883), *Educational Problems* (1911) and *Life and Confessions of a Psychologist* (1923).

HALL, Sir James, (1761–1832) Scottish geologist, of Dunglass, a Haddingtonshire baronet. He sought to prove in the laboratory the geological theories of his friend and mentor **James Hutton** and so founded experimental geology.

HALL, James (1811–98) American geologist and palaeontologist, born in Hingham, Massachussetts. He directed the New York State survey (1834–43) and pioneered the study of US geology. He was director of the New York Museum of Natural History (1871–98), and wrote *New York State Natural History Survey*.

HALL, Joseph (1574–1656) English prelate and writer, born in Ashby-de-la-Zouch. He became a fellow of Emmanuel College, Cambridge, in 1595 and in 1617 he was made dean of Worcester and accompanied **James VI and I** to Scotland to help establish episcopacy. As bishop of Exeter (from 1627) he was suspected by **Laud** of Puritanism, and after being translated to Norwich in 1641 protested with other prelates against the validity of laws passed during their enforced absence from parliament, and spent seven months in the Tower. Soon after, he was deprived of his living, and in 1647 retired to a small farm in Higham. Among his works are *Contemplations*, *Christian Meditations*, *Episcopacy*, and *Mundus Alter et Idem*. His poetical satires *Virgidemiarum* (1597–98) **Pope** called 'the best poetry and the truest satire in the English language'.

HALL, Marguerite Radclyffe (1886–1943) English writer, born in Bournemouth. She began as a lyric poet with several volumes of verse, some of which have become songs, but turned to novel writing in 1924 with *The Forge* and *The Unlit Lamp*. Her *Adam's Breed* (1926) won the Femina Vie Heureuse and the Tait Black Memorial prizes, but *The Well of Loneliness* (1928), which embodies a sympathetic approach to female homosexuality, caused a prolonged furore and was banned in Britain for many years.

HALL, Marshall (1790–1857) English physician and physiologist, born in Basford, Nottinghamshire. After studying at Edinburgh, Paris, Göttingen and Berlin, he settled at Nottingham in 1817, and practised in London from 1826 until 1853. He did important work on reflex action of the spinal system (1833–37); his name is also associated with a standard method of restoring suspended respiration. He wrote on diagnosis (1817), the circulation (1831), *Respiration and Irritability* (1832), and other subjects.

HALL, Sir Peter Reginald Frederick (1930–) British theatre, opera and film director. Born in Bury St Edmunds, he was educated at the Perse School and St Catherine's College, Cambridge. While at university he produced and acted in more than 20 plays; his first professional production was at Windsor in 1953. After working in repertory and for the Arts Council, he was artistic director of the Elizabethan Theatre Company in 1953, assistant director of the London Arts Theatre in 1954 and Director 1955–56, and formed his own producing company, The International Playwrights' Theatre, in 1957. In the previous year as well as directing his first wife, Leslie Caron, in *Gigi*, he had done *Love's Labour's Lost* at the Stratford Memorial Theatre, and after several productions there, he became director of what was now the Royal Shakespeare Company, and remained as managing director of the company's theatres in Stratford and London until 1968. Among his many productions during this period were the *Wars of the Roses* trilogy (*Henry VI* parts 1, 2 and 3 and *Richard III* in 1963), Pinter's *The Homecoming* (1965) and Gogol's *The Government Inspector* (1966). Continuing to direct for the RSC, he was from 1969 to 1971 director of the Covent Garden Opera; his operatic productions there and at Glyndebourne include *The Magic Flute* (1966), *The Knot Garden* (1970), *Tristan and Isolde* (1971), *The Marriage of Figaro* (1973), *Fidelio* (1979) and *A Midsummer Night's Dream* (1981). In 1873 he was appointed successor to **Olivier** as director of the National Theatre; his notable productions there include *No Man's Land* (1975), *Tamburlaine the Great* (1976), *Amadeus* (1979), *Othello* (1980), and *The Oresteia* (1981). In 1983 he became artistic director of the Glyndebourne Festival. Among his films are *Work is a Four Letter Word* (1968), *Perfect Friday* (1971) and *Akenfield* (1974). He was made a CBE in 1963 and knighted in 1977. Hall left the National Theatre in 1988, ending his directorship with a sequence of three late Shakespearian plays: *The Winter's Tale*, *Cymbeline* and *The Tempest*. He still directs opera, but in 1988 set up the Peter Hall Company, the inaugural project being his own production of **Tennessee Williams**' *Orpheus Descending*. That was followed in 1989 by Hall's production of *The Merchant of Venice*, with **Dustin Hoffman** as Shylock.

HALL, Robert (1764–1831) English Baptist clergyman, born in Arnsby near Leicester. Educated at a Baptist academy in Bristol and in Aberdeen he was appointed assistant minister and tutor at the Bristol Academy. There and at Cambridge from 1790, his preaching drew huge congregations. In 1806 he settled in Leicester. He wrote *Apology for the Freedom of the Press* (1793).

HALL, Wesley (1937–) West Indian cricketer, born in Barbados. One of the game's greatest fast bowlers, with Charlie Griffith he formed a dreaded opening attack; and although playing in only 48 Test matches he took 192 Test wickets including that rarity, a Test hat-trick (against Pakistan at Lahore in 1958–59). A lusty tail-end batsman, he took part in a record West Indian stand for the 10th wicket of 98 (unbroken) with **Frank Worrell** against India at Port of Spain in 1961–62. He now occupies an official position with the department of tourism in the government of Barbados.

HALLAM, Henry (1777–1859) English historian, born in Windsor. Educated at Eton and Christ Church College, Oxford, he was called to the bar in 1802. A private income, however, as well as various appointments found for him by his Whig friends, permitted him the pursuit of his literary interests. His three main works, written with painstaking accuracy, if lacking in colour, were: *Europe during the Middle Ages* (1818), *The Constitutional History of England from Henry VII to George II* (1827) and the *Introduction to the Literature of Europe in the 15th, 16th and 17th Centuries* (1837–39), and these established his reputation, despite his Whig prejudices. He edited the *Remains in Prose and Verse* (1834) of his son Arthur Henry Hallam (1811–33), who died abroad and was the subject of **Tennyson**'s *In Memoriam*.

HALLE, Adam de la (c.1235–1287) French poet and composer, born in Arras, nicknamed 'le bossu d'Arras', 'the Hunchback' (although he was not misshapen). He followed Robert II of Artois to Naples in 1283. He was the originator of French comic opera, with *Le Jeu de Robin et de Marion*, and the modern comedy of the half-autobiographic composition called *Le Jeu Adan ou de la fuellie*. He also wrote poems in medieval verse forms.

HALLE, Edward See **HALL, Edward**

HALLÉ, Sir Charles (1819–95) German-born British pianist and conductor, born in Hagen, Westphalia. He studied first at Darmstadt, and from 1840 at Paris, where his reputation was established by his concerts of classical music. Driven to England by the Revolution of 1848, he settled in Manchester, where in 1858 he founded his famous orchestra. This did much to raise the standard of musical taste by familiarizing the British public with the great classical masters, and he was knighted in 1888. In the same year he married the violinist Wilhelmine Neruda (1839–1911).

HALLECK, Fitz-Greene (1790–1867) American poet, born in Guilford, Connecticut. He became a clerk in New York, and in 1832 private secretary to **John Jacob Astor**; in 1849 he retired on an annuity left him by Astor, to Guilford. He published numerous poems, including the long mock-Byronic poem, *Fanny* (1819), a satire on the literature, fashions and politics of the time.

HALLECK, Henry Wager (1815–72) American soldier, born in Westernville, New York. He served in the Mexican war and having taken a leading part in organizing the state of California, in the Civil War (1861) he was appointed commander of the Missouri. In May 1862 he captured Corinth; in July became general-in-chief; but in March 1864 he was superseded by General **Grant**. Chief of staff until 1865, he commanded the military division of the Pacific until 1869, and that of the South until his death. He published *Elements of Military Science* (1846), and books on mining laws.

HALLER, Albrecht von (1708–77) Swiss anatomist, botanist, physiologist and poet, born in Bern. He studied anatomy and botany in Tübingen and Leiden, and started practice in 1729, but in 1736 became professor of anatomy, surgery and medicine in the new university of Göttingen. Here he organized a botanical garden, an anatomical museum and theatre, and an obstetrical school, helped to found the Academy of Sciences, wrote anatomical and physiological works, and took an active part in the literary movement. In 1753 he resigned and returned to Bern, where he became magistrate and director of a saltworks. After this he wrote three political romances, and prepared four large bibliographies of botany, anatomy, surgery and medicine. His poems were descriptive, didactic and (the best of them) lyrical.

HALLESBY, Ole Kristian (1879–1961) Norwegian theologian and preacher. Professor of the Free Faculty of Theology, Oslo (1909–52), he wrote several theological textbooks, but is best-known outside Norway for translations of his devotional and apologetic writings, *Prayer* (1948), *Why I am a Christian* (1950), and *Under His Wings* (1978). Imprisoned like other religious leaders during World War II for opposing Nazi control of the church, he had great influence on lay Christians through his chairmanship of the Norwegian Lutheran Home Mission, and on students as first president of the International Federation of Evangelical Students (1947).

HALLEY, Edmond (1656–1742) English astronomer and mathematician, born in London. Educated at St Paul's School and Queen's College, Oxford, he published three papers on the orbits of the planets, on a sunspot, and on the occultation of Mars while still an undergraduate at Queen's. In 1676 he left for St Helena to make the first catalogue of the stars in the southern hemisphere (*Catalogus Stellarum Australium*, 1679). In 1680 he was in Paris with **Giovanni Cassini**, observing comets. It was in cometary astronomy that he made his greatest mark; he predicted correctly the return (in 1758, 1835 and 1910) of a comet that had been observed in 1583, and is now named after him. He was the first to make a complete observation of the transit of Mercury; he was the first to recommend the observation of the transits of Venus with a view to determining the sun's parallax. He established the mathematical law connecting barometric pressure with heights above sea-level (on the basis of **Boyle**'s law). He published studies on magnetic variations (1683), trade winds and monsoons (1686), investigated diving and underwater activites, and voyaged in the Atlantic to test his theory of the magnetic variation of the compass, which he embodied in a magnetic sea-chart (1701). He encouraged **Isaac Newton** to write his celebrated *Principia* (1687) and paid for the publication out of his own pocket. With his *Breslau Table of Mortality* (1693), he laid the actuarial foundations for life insurance and annuities. In 1703 he was appointed Savilian professor at Oxford, where he built an observatory on the roof of his house which is still to be seen; and in 1720 he succeeded **John Flamsteed** as astronomer-royal of England.

HALLGRÍMSSON, Jónas (1807–45) Icelandic lyric poet, born in Hraun in the north of Iceland, the most important innovator in modern Icelandic poetry. He attended the Latin School at Bessastaðir, where he read deeply in classical and Old Icelandic literature, and then studied law at Copenhagen University before turning to natural history and literature. As a student he and his friends founded the periodical *Fjölnir* (1835–47), which added inspiration to the independence movement led by **Jón Sigurðsson**. His poetry brilliantly combined fervent nationalism and intensely lyrical romanticism, and he is still the best loved of all Icelandic poets. His collected poems were first published in 1847.

HALLIWELL-PHILLIPPS, James Orchard (1820–89) English Shakespearean scholar and antiquary, born in Chelsea. He studied at Jesus College, Cambridge, and contributed much to Shakespearean studies by his *Outlines of the Life of Shakespeare* (1848) and a Folio edition of Shakespeare (1863–65). He also published *Nursery Rhymes and Tales of England* (1845), *Dictionary of Archaic and Provincial Words* (1847), and *Popular Rhymes and Nursery Tales* (1849).

HALLSTROM, Sir Edward John Lees (1886–1970) Australian pioneer of refrigeration, born in Coonamble, New South Wales. He left school at 13 and worked in a furniture factory, later opening his own works to make first ice-chests and then wooden cabinets for refrigerators. Eventually he started making the units themselves, to his own design, and marketed the first popular domestic Australian refrigerator. With the expansion of demand after World War II he was able to channel his wealth into philanthropic acts, particularly towards medical research and children's hospitals. He had a keen practical interest in zoology and was an active collector, preserver and breeder of wild animals. He made many gifts to the Taronga zoo in Sydney, in 1947 alone giving more than 1500 birds and animals, and he held a number of trustee positions at the zoo from 1941, culminating in honorary life directorship.

HALS, Frans (c.1580–1666) Dutch portrait and genre painter, born in Mechlin, known as 'the Elder' to differentiate him from his son, 'the Younger' (1637–69), also an artist. Little is known of his early life except that he studied under **Karel van Mander** and settled permanently in Haarlem c.1603. He was twice married, led a ramshackle domestic life with many children, but, despite many commissions, was constantly overshadowed by poverty. Among his early conventional portraits are those of *Paulus von Berestyn* and his wife *Catherine* (1620), *Jacob Pietersz Olyean* and *Aletta Hanemans* (1625), and the dignified, sumptuously costumed *Portrait of a Man* (1622). But it is by his studies of every nuance of smile from the vague, arrogant amusement of the *Laughing Cavalier* (Wallace Collection, London) to the broad grins and outright vulgar leers of the low life sketches, the *Gypsy Girl* (Louvre), the *Hille Bobbe* (Berlin), the *Jolly Toper* (Amsterdam) which belong to the period 1625–35 that Hals achieved his perennial popularity. Another formal masterpiece is *Pieter van den Broecke* (1633; Kenwood, London). But from 1640 onwards, the virile, swaggering colours give way to more contemplative, sombre blacks and greys. His own struggles and disappointments no doubt contributed to the bitter psychological study of old age, *The Seated Man* (Kassell), as well as the last of the eight magnificent portrait groups in the Franz Hals Museum at Haarlem, *The Women Guardians of the Haarlem Almshouse* (1664), who sat for him out of charity and whom he portrays with bitter irony in all their prim, cold, starchy 'do-gooderdom'. They are a world apart from an earlier group, the *Banquet of the Company of St Adrian* (1627), in which the mood of robust merrymaking is symbolized by the upturned glass in the hand of one of the officers, the whole assembly a feast of many-splendoured colour.

HALSBURY, Hardinge Stanley Giffard, 1st Earl of (1823–1921) English lawyer and politician, born in London. Called to the bar in 1850, he became solicitor-general (1875), Conservative MP (1877), and lord chancellor (1885, 1886–92, 1895–1905). He was a sound rather than distinguished judge, and conservative in politics and temperament; he led the 'Die-Hards' in defence of the Lords' Veto (1911); and he supervised the enclyclopaedia, *The Laws of England* (1905–16).

HALSEY, William Frederick, Jr, known as **'Bull'** (1884–1959) American naval officer, born in Elizabeth, New Jersey. Educated at the US Naval Academy, Annapolis (1904), he served in White Fleet (1908–09), and held destroyer commands in World War I and thereafter (1919–25). He qualified as a naval pilot in 1934 and commanded the USS *Saratoga* and Naval Air Station Pensacola. He commanded the Carrier Division as rear admiral (1938) and vice-admiral (1940), and distinguished himself in carrier battles and amphibious operations throughout the Pacific War (1941–45), latterly as commander 3rd Fleet in the battles for the Caroline and Philippine islands, and for the carrier attacks on the Japanese mainland. In October 1944 he defeated the Japaese navy at the Battle of Leyte Gulf. He retired as fleet admiral in 1949.

HALSTED, William Stewart (1852–1922) American surgeon, born in New York. In 1881 he administered what is thought to be the first blood transfusion in the USA. Professor at Johns Hopkins University from 1886, he first used cocaine injection for local anaesthesia, and devised successful operative techniques for cancer of the breast and inguinal hernia. He pioneered the use of rubber gloves in surgery.

HAMADA, Shoji (1894–1978) Japanese potter, widely recognized as one of the great modern potters. He studied and held a professorship at the Institute of Pottery in Kyoto. He worked primarily in stoneware using ash or iron glazes producing utilitarian wares in strong, simple shapes brushed with abstract design. He visited England in 1920 with **Bernard Leach** and took part in experiments with lead-glazed slipware. On his return to Japan in 1923, he joined a pottery community in Okinawa and later lived and worked in Mashiko alongside the simple country potters, epitomizing his belief in a direct approach and the simplistic beauty of the hand-made as opposed to the dehumanizing influences of industrialization. He became director of the Folk Art Museum in 1962.

HAMANN, Johann Georg (1730–88) German philosopher and theologian, born in Königsberg, and a friend of **Kant**. He seems to have had a desultory early career as private tutor, merchant, commercial traveller and secretary, but he settled down eventually in 1767 as a government employee in Königsberg in the excise office and custom house, and he remained there till 1784 when private patronage ensured him a more comfortable income. He was concerned in his writings to reconcile Christianity and philosophy, and his impatient distrust of rationalism and abstraction led him to emphasize the role of faith and develop an original form of fideism. His style is notoriously cryptic and opaque, but he was an important influence on **Herder**, **Goethe**, **Hegel** and **Kierkegaard**, and there has been a revival of interest in his work.

HAMAYUN (1508–56) Mughal emperor. He succeeded his father, **Babar**, in 1530 and spent most of his reign contesting the lordship of India with the Afghan ruler, **Sher Shah**, by whom he was decisively defeated at Chausa on the Ganges in 1539. Driven into exile, Hamayun was not able to regain his throne until 1555 and he died the following year.

HAMERTON, Philip Gilbert (1834–94) English writer on art, born in Laneside, Oldham. He began as an art critic by contributing to the *Saturday Review*, and later was founder-editor of the art periodical, *The Portfolio*. He wrote several books, including *The Intellectual Life* (1873, letters of advice addressed to literary aspirants and others), *Human Intercourse*, *The Graphic Arts* (1882), and *Landscape* (1885).

HAMILCAR (c.270–228 BC) Carthaginian soldier, next to his son **Hannibal** the greatest of the Carthaginians, was surnamed Barca (Hebrew *Barak*) or 'Lightning'. When a young man, he came into prominence in the 16th year of the First Punic War (247 BC). After ravaging the Italian coast, he landed in Sicily near Panormus, and, seizing the stronghold of Ercte with a small band of mercenaries, waged war for three years against Rome. He occupied Mount Eryx (244–42) and stood at bay against a Roman army. When at the close of the First Punic war (241) Sicily was yielded to Rome, the Carthaginian mercenaries revolted; but Hamilcar crushed the rebellion after a terrible struggle in 238. His master conception was to redress the loss of Sicily by creating in Spain an infantry capable of coping with Roman legionaries. He entered Spain in 237, and before his death in the winter (229–28) he had built up a new dominion. The conceptions of the great Hamilcar were carried out by his even mightier son Hannibal.

HAMILTON name of a Scottish noble family, believed to be of English origin, which can be traced back to Walter FitzGilbert, called Hamilton, who in 1296 held lands in Lanarkshire, swore fealty to **Edward I**, and in 1314 held Bothwell Castle for the English. His surrender of it, with the English knights who had fled there from Bannockburn, was rewarded by **Robert Bruce** with a knighthood and grants of lands in Clydesdale, West Lothian and elsewhere. His grandson, Sir David of Hamilton of Cadzow, was the first to assume the surname of Hamilton. The Earls of Haddington are descended from a younger son of Sir David. Other titles apart from those appearing below conferred on members of the house were those of Lord Belhaven, Viscount Boyne, Baron Brancepeth, Viscount Clanboy and Earl of Clanbrassil.

HAMILTON, Sir James, 1st Baron (d.1479) great-grandson of Sir David of Hamilton of Cadzow, created baron in 1445. Allied by marriage and descent to the **Douglas**es, he followed them in the beginning of their struggle with the crown, but forsook them in 1454, and for reward got large grants of their forfeited lands. After the death of his first wife, he married in 1469 Princess Mary Stewart, eldest daughter of **James II** of Scotland, formerly the wife of the attainted Earl of Arran. His son James (c.1477–1529) was created earl of Arran in 1503.

HAMILTON, James, 2nd Earl of Arran, 3rd Baron (?1515–1575) Scottish nobleman, grandson of Sir James, 1st Baron **Hamilton** by the niece of Cardinal **Beaton**, and was a young man when the death of **James V** in 1542 left only an infant, the future **Mary, Queen of Scots** between him and the throne. He was chosen regent and tutor to the young queen, and held these offices till 1554. He received a grant of the duchy of Châtelherault in 1548, from **Henri II** of France.

HAMILTON, James, 3rd Earl of Arran, 4th Baron (1530–1609) Scottish nobleman, eldest son of the 2nd Earl. He was proposed as the husband both of **Mary, Queen of Scots** and of Queen **Elizabeth** of England, but went mad in 1562.

HAMILTON, James, 3rd Marquis and 1st Duke of (1606–49) Scottish nobleman. He led an army of 6000 men to the support of King **Gustav II Adolf** of Sweden in 1631-32, and later played a conspicuous part in the contest between **Charles I** and the Covenanters. Created duke in 1643, he led a Scottish army into England (1643) but was defeated by **Cromwell** at Preston, and beheaded.

HAMILTON, James Douglas, 4th Duke of (1658–1712) Scottish nobleman, was created 1st Duke of Brandon in 1771, a title challenged by the House of Lords. He fought against **Monmouth**, led Scottish opposition to the Union, but discouraged bloodshed. He helped to negotiate the Treaty of Utrecht (1713) and was killed, as described in **Thackeray**'s *Henry Esmond*, in a duel with Lord **Mohun**.

HAMILTON, John, 1st Marquis of (?1532–1604) Scottish nobleman, brother of the insane **James Hamilton**, 3rd Earl of Arran. A devoted adherent of **Mary, Queen of Scots**, he helped to rescue her from captivity on Loch Leven and reinstate her on the throne (1568). He fled to France in 1579, but was reconciled with King **James VI** of Scotland (later **James I** of England) in 1585. In 1588 he was sent to negotiate the king's marriage to **Anne of Denmark**, and was created Marquis in 1599.

HAMILTON, Alexander (1757–1804) American statesman, born in the West Indian island of Nevis. When a student in New York he wrote a series of papers in defence of the rights of the colonies against Great Britain; and on the outbreak of the war, as captain of artillery, he served in New York and New Jersey, and in 1777 became **Washington**'s aide-de-camp. In 1781, after a quarrel, Hamilton resigned his appointment, but he continued with the army and distinguished himself at Yorktown. After the war, he studied law and became one of the most eminent lawyers in New York; in 1782 he was returned to congress. In 1786 he took the leading part in the convention at Annapolis, which prepared the way for the great convention that met at Philadelphia in 1787. In the same year he conceived the series of essays afterwards collected as *The Federalist*, and himself wrote 51 out of the 85. On the establishment of the new government in 1789, Hamilton was appointed secretary of the treasury and restored the country's finances to a firm footing. In 1795 he resigned his office, but remained the actual leader of the Federal party until his death, and was foremost in the party strife of 1801. His successful effort to thwart the ambition of his rival, **Aaron Burr**, involved him in a mortal duel with him.

HAMILTON, Anthony (c.1646–1720) Irish soldier and writer, born in Roscrea Castle, County Tipperary. At the age of 21 he went to France after the Cromwellian invasion of 1651, and there got a captain's commission. He returned to Ireland after the Restoration (1660) and raised Irish troops for service in France. In 1685 he was appointed governor of Limerick, and fought against **William III** at the Boyne (1690), and after that he lived at the exiled court of St Germain-en-Laye. His writings are full of wit and talent, particularly his *Contes de féerie* (1730–49; English trans 1760). His principal work is his *Mémoires du Comte de Gramont*, an account of the court of **Charles II** between 1662 and 1664).

HAMILTON, Emma, Lady, née **Emily Lyon** (c.1765–1815) mistress of Lord **Nelson**, born in Cheshire. Her girlhood was passed at Hawarden. She had had three places in London, had borne two children to a navy captain and a baronet, and had posed as Hygieia in the 'Temple of Health' of **James Graham** the famous quack, when in 1782 she accepted the protection of the Hon Charles Greville (1749–1809), to exchange it in 1786 for that of his uncle, Sir **William Hamilton** (1730–1803). After five years at Naples, in 1791 she married him and was admitted to the closest intimacy by Maria Caroline, queen of **Ferdinand I**. Nelson first met her in 1793; they became lovers, and in 1801 she gave birth to a daughter, Horatia (d.1881), later acknowledged by Nelson as his child. After Nelson's death she squandered her inheritance from her husband, and in 1813 was arrested for debt.

HAMILTON, Hamish (1900–88) British publisher, and founder of the London publishing house of Hamish Hamilton Ltd. Born in Indianapolis, USA, of a Scottish father and an American mother of Dutch stock, he spent his childhood in Scotland and was educated at Rugby School and Caius College, Cambridge, studying medicine (briefly) and then modern languages, and becoming an accomplished Olympic oarsman. He joined Harper & Brothers, the New York publishers, as London manager in 1926; in 1931 he founded his own firm, with the support of Harpers, who helped him build up a particularly strong list of American writers. In 1965 he sold his company to Thomson Publications Ltd, who later sold it to Viking-Penguin. He retired as chairman in 1981.

HAMILTON, Iain Ellis (1922–) Scottish composer, born in Glasgow. Originally trained as an engineer, in 1947 he entered the Royal College of Music, first attracting attention when his clarinet quintet was played at a concert of the Society for the Promotion of New Music. In 1951, he won the Royal Philharmonic Society's prize for his clarinet concerto, and an award from the Koussevitsky Foundation for his second symphony, which was followed by the symphonic variations (1953). He emigrated to the USA in 1962 and has produced many orchestral and chamber works as well as operas including *The Royal Hunt of the Sun* and *The Cataline Conspiracy*.

HAMILTON, Sir Ian Standish Monteith (1853–1947) English soldier, born in Corfu. He entered the army (1873), and served with distinction in Afghanistan (1878) and the Boer wars (1881, 1899–1901). In World War I, as a general, he led the disastrous Gallipoli expedition (1915). Relieved of his command, he later became lieutenant of the Tower (1918–20).

HAMILTON, James See **MORAY, James Stuart**

HAMILTON, James (1769–1829) English educationist, born in London. He introduced a new system of learning languages in America (1815) and England discarding grammar, and using instead a literal word for word translation of the Gospel of St **John**. His system resembled that of **Jacotot**.

HAMILTON, Patrick (1503–28) 'the protomartyr of the Scottish Reformation', son of Sir Patrick Hamilton and Catherine Stewart, the illegitimate daughter of the Duke of Albany, second son of **James II**. Born in the diocese of Glasgow, he took his MA at Paris in 1520, then proceeded to Louvain, and in 1523 was at St Andrews, whence he returned to the Continent (1527) to escape troubles on account of his Lutheranism. After a brief stay in Wittenberg, where he met **Luther** and **Melanchthon**, he settled for some months in Marburg, where he wrote (in Latin) a series of theological propositions known as 'Patrick's Places', propounding the doctrines of the Lutherans. He returned that same autumn to Scotland, and married. Next year he was summoned to St Andrews by Archbishop **James Beaton**, and on a renewed charge of heresy was burned before St Salvator's College. His death did more to extend the Reformation in Scotland than ever his life could have done.

HAMILTON, Richard (1922–) English painter, born in London. He studied painting (1938–40) at the Royal Academy Schools; during World War II he was trained as an engineering draughtsman. In 1948 he entered a further period of study, at the Slade School of Art, and subsequently taught at the Central School of Art and Crafts, London, and Durham University. During the 1950s he devised and participated in several influential exhibitions, notably 'This is Tomorrow' (1956, London, Whitechapel Art Gallery), which introduced the concept of Pop Art, of which he became a leading pioneer. His work in this vein subtly and skilfully fuses painting with printed imagery derived from advertisements, pin-up photographs and the like to comment ironically on contemporary life, politics and popular culture. He is an articulate exponent of his art and ideas; his publications include *Collected Words* (1953–82).

HAMILTON, Terrick (1781–1876) Scottish linguist and orientalist. He was the translator (1820) of the first four volumes of *Sirat Antarah*, narrative of the poet **Antar**. After service with the East India Company he became secretary of the British embassy at Constantinople.

HAMILTON, Thomas (1784–1858) Scottish architect, born in Glasgow. He studied as a mason with his father, beginning independent practice in Edinburgh before 1817. He was a leading figure in the international Greek Revival, together with his contemporary in Edinburgh, **William Henry Playfair**. In 1826 he was among the founders of the Royal Scottish Academy. His Grecian designs include the Burns Monument, Galloway (1820), the Royal High School, Edinburgh (1825–29), and the Royal College of Physicians Hall (1844–45), in Edinburgh. Cumston (Compstone) House, Kirkcudbright (1828), in a Tudor style, and a handful of gothic church designs, demonstrate his versatility. As a prime mover of the Edinburgh Improvement Act (1827) to create the New Town, he designed the George IV and King's Bridges which followed.

HAMILTON, Walter Kerr (1808–69) English prelate, born in London. Educated at Eton, Laleham (under **Thomas Arnold**), and Christ Church College, Oxford, in 1854 he became bishop of Salisbury, the first Tractarian to become a diocesan bishop in England. A member of the Oxford Movement, he founded Salisbury Theological College (1860) and advocated cathedral reform.

HAMILTON, William (c.1665–1751) Scottish poet, of Gilbertfield near Glasgow, born in Ladyford, Ayrshire. An army officer, like his father, he turned to writing and collecting verse. He was the friend and correspondent of **Allan Ramsay**, with whom he exchanged a series of *Familiar Epistles*. His most notable poem is the mock heroic *Last Dying Words of Bonny Heck*, about a greyhound. In 1772 he published an English translation of **Blind Harry**'s *Wallace*.

HAMILTON, William (1704–54) Scottish poet, born in Bangour, West Lothian. Educated at the High School of Edinburgh, and Edinburgh University, he contributed romantic songs and ballads to **Ramsay**'s *Tea-table Miscellany* (1724). He joined in the Jacobite Rising of 1745, and on its collapse escaped to Rouen, but was permitted to return in 1749 and to succeed to the family estate of Bangour. The first collection of his poems was edited by **Adam Smith** in 1748. He is best known for his ballad, 'The Braes of Yarrow'.

HAMILTON, Sir William (1730–1803) Scottish diplomat and antiquary, husband of Lady **Emma Hamilton**. He was British ambassador at Naples (1764–1800), and in 1791 he married Emma there. He took an active part in the excavation of Herculaneum and Pompeii, and formed rare collections of antiquities, one of them purchased in 1772 for the British Museum. He wrote several works on Greek and Roman antiquities. He may have condoned his wife's intimacy with **Nelson**, for the latter was present at his death.

HAMILTON, Sir William (1788–1856) Scottish philosopher, born in Glasgow. Educated at Glasgow and Balliol College, Oxford, he became professor of civil history in Edinburgh in 1821 and of logic and metaphysics in 1836. His main work was published posthumously as *Lectures on Metaphysics and Logic* (1859–60), presenting views on perception and knowledge that were later criticized in **J S Mill**'s *An Examination of Sir William Hamilton's Philosophy* (1865). He published many important articles, mostly in *The Edinburgh Review*, which were collected in 1852 under the title *Discussions on Philosophy and Literature, Education and University Reform*, and he edited a major edition of the works of **Thomas Reid** (1846). He was in his day a figure of great importance in the revival of philosophy in Britain.

HAMILTON, Sir William Rowan (1805–65) Irish mathematician, the inventor of quaternions, born in Dublin. At the age of nine he knew 13 languages, at 15 he had read **Newton's** *Principia*, and began original investigations. In 1827, while still an undergraduate, he was appointed professor of astronomy at Dublin and Irish astronomer-royal; in 1835 he was knighted. His first published work was on optics, and he then developed a new approach to dynamics which became of importance in the 20th-century development of quantum mechanics. He introduced quanternions as a new algebraic approach to three-dimensional geometry, and they have proved to be the seed of much modern algebra.

HAMLEY, Sir Edward Bruce (1824–93) English soldier, born in Bodmin. He served in Ireland, Canada and the Crimea, and was commandant of the Staff College (1870–77). He commanded the second division in the Egyptian campaign of 1882. Conservative MP for Birkenhead from 1885 to 1892, he wrote on *The War in the Crimea* (1855), *The Operations of War* (1866), *Voltaire* (1877), etc.

HAMLIN, Hannibal (1809–91) American statesman, born in Paris, Maine. He practised law (1833–48), was speaker of the Maine house of representatives, and was returned to Congress in 1842 and 1844. He sat in the US senate as a Democrat (1848–57), when he was elected governor by the Republicans, having separated from his party over his anti-slavery opinions. In the same year, 1857, he resigned to return to the senate; and in 1861 became vice-president under **Lincoln**. He was in the senate again (1869–81); and was minister to Spain (1881–82).

HAMMARSKJÖLD, Dag Hjalmar Agne Carl (1905–61) Swedish statesman, secretary-general of the United Nations from 1953, born in Jönköping. In 1933 he became an assistant professor at Stockholm University, in 1935 secretary and from 1941 to 1948, chairman of the Bank of Sweden. He was Swedish foreign minister (1951–53), a delegate to OEEC, UNISAN, the Council of Europe and the UN General Assembly. Hammarskjöld, who once described himself as 'the curator of the secrets of 82 nations', played a leading part in the setting up of the UN Emergency Force in Sinai and Gaza in 1956, in conciliation moves in the Middle East in 1957–58 and in sending observers to the Lebanon in 1958. He was awarded the Nobel peace prize for 1961 after his death in an air crash near Ndola in Zambia in September 1961, while he was engaged in negotiations over the Congo crisis.

HAMMER, Armand (1899–) American business executive, born in New York. He trained as a physician at Columbia, and served with the US Army Medical Corps (1918–19). In 1921, soon after taking his medical degree, he went to Russia to help with an influenza epidemic, but turned to business, and exported grain to the USSR in exchange for furs, dealing face to face with **Lenin** and subsequent Soviet leaders. He founded the A Hammer Pencil Company in 1925, operating in New York, London and Moscow, and has maintained strong trading and political connections with the USSR since, acting as intermediary between them and the US government on a number of occasions, including the Soviet troop withdrawal from Afghanistan (1987). In 1957 he bought the small Occidental Petroleum Corporation of California, and turned it into a giant. He founded Hammer Galleries Inc (New York) in 1930.

HAMMERSTEIN, Oscar (c.1847–1919) German-born American theatre manager, born in Stettin. He emigrated to the United States in 1863, made a fortune by inventing a machine for spreading tobacco leaves, and founded and edited the *United States Tobacco Journal*. He leased, built or opened numerous theatres in New York, Philadelphia and London.

HAMMERSTEIN, Oscar II (1895–1960) American librettist, nephew of **Oscar Hammerstein** (c.1847–1919). He was the author of a large number of musical plays, often in collaboration with the composer Richard Rodgers (1902–79), of which the most popular were *Rose Marie* (1924), *Desert Song* (1926), *Music in the Air* (1932), *Oklahoma!* (1943), *Carmen Jones* (1943), *South Pacific* (1949), *The King and I* (1951), and *The Sound of Music* (1959).

HAMMETT, (Samuel) Dashiell (1894–1961) American crime writer, born in St Mary's County, Maryland. He grew up in Philadelphia and Baltimore and left school at 14. He was a messenger boy, newsboy, clerk, time keeper, yardman, machine operator, and stevedore before joining the Pinkerton Detective Agency as an operator. World War I ruined his health, and interrupted his sleuthing but he took it up again on his discharge. He served his literary apprenticeship in magazines like *Black Mask*, writing stories as hard as diamonds. His four best novels—*Red Harvest* (1929), *The Dain Curse* (1929), *The Maltese Falcon* (1930) and *The Glass Menagerie* (1931)—made the scarred ex-detective a celebrity in Hollywood and New York, where he met **Lillian Hellman**, with whom he lived for the rest of his life; but he had already taken to the bottle and never equalled his first literary successes. *The Thin Man* (1934), written in a brief period of sobriety in **Nathanael West**'s mismanaged hotel, has an inflated reputation largely because it was made into a popular film, as were all of Hammett's novels. Drinking and gambling excessively, he made a living script-writing. He enlisted during World War II but was discharged with emphysema, but he continued to drink immoderately until 1948 when an attack of delirium tremens turned him to temperance. Politically a radical, he was anti-**McCarthy** and served a six-month jail sentence for his sympathies. A collection of short stories, *The Big Knockover and Other Stories* (1966), appeared posthumously. Original, unsentimental and an acute social observer, he is the father of the hard-boiled school of detective fiction.

HAMMOND, Eric Albert Barratt (1929–) English trade union leader. He became active in trade union affairs in his early twenties and rose from shop steward in 1953 to general secretary of the Electrical, Electronics, Telecommunications and Plumbing Union (EETPU) in 1984. He was a long-time outspoken critic of what he saw as old-fashioned unionism and concluded a number of single-union, 'no strike', agreements with employers, in defiance of Trades Union Congress (TUC) policy. Criticism of him and his union came to a head in 1988 when the EETPU was dismissed from the TUC.

HAMMOND, Henry (1605–60) English clergyman, born in Chertsey. Educated at Eton and Magdalen College, Oxford, in 1633 he became rector of Penshurst, and in 1643 archdeacon of Chichester. His loyalty to **Charles I** cost him his living but he officiated as chaplain to the king till 1647, when he returned to Oxford, and was chosen sub-dean of Christ Church. Deprived and imprisoned by the parliamentary commissioners in 1648, he retired to Westwood in Worcestershire, where he died. He published *Paraphrase and Annotations on the New Testament* in 1653.

HAMMOND, Dame Joan Hood (1912–) New Zealand-born Australian operatic soprano, born in Christchurch. She studied at the Sydney Conservatorium of Music, originally as a violinist. An active sportswoman, she won a number of golf and swimming championships up to 1935. When an arm injury forced her to give up the violin, she turned to singing, performing **Handel**'s *Messiah* in London in 1938 and making her operatic début the following year in Vienna. From 1945 she sang leading roles in some 30 operas, and made many recordings; her *Turandot* was the first classical record to win a gold disc for sales of over one million. She retired from singing in 1971 to become artistic director of the Victoria Opera, and was head of vocal studies at the Victorian College of the Arts. In 1970 she received the Sir Charles Santley award (for musician of the year) from the Worshipful Company of Musicians in London and was made a DBE in 1974.

HAMMOND, John Lawrence Le Breton (1872–1949) English reforming journalist and social historian, born in Yorkshire, the son of a vicar. Educated at Bradford Grammar School and Oxford, his politics were Liberal-Labour, shown in his early editorship of the *Speaker* (1899–1906), but he went to the Civil Service Commission and then (after armed service) to the ministry of reconstruction until 1918. He later became a major figure on the *Manchester Guardian*. Married from 1901 to Lucy Barbara Bradby (1873–1961), they formed a team remorselessly revealing the harshness of English social conditions from 1760 to 1832, in *The Village Labourer* (1911), *The Town Labourer* (1917), and *The Skilled Labourer* (1919). *Lord Shaftesbury* (1923) brought them into the next stages of social injustice as they showed in *The Age of the Chartists* (1930), reworked as *The Bleak Age* (1934). Hammond also wrote lives of **Charles James Fox** (1903) and the *Guardian*'s editor **C P Scott** (1934), but his *magnum opus* was *Gladstone and the Irish Nation* (1938), an appreciative but not uncritical study based on the **Gladstone** MSS.

HAMMOND, Walter (1903–65) English cricketer, born in Dover. In his long career as a Gloucestershire player he scored over 50000 runs, of which 7249 were obtained in 85 Tests at an average of 58.45 (almost 3000 of them against Australia). He was a fine bowler and wonderful fielder, taking ten catches in a match against Surrey in 1928 in which he also scored two centuries. He reverted to amateur status in 1938, but although he captained England in Australia in 1946–47, he was not considered a success and retired from top-class cricket soon afterwards.

HAMMURABI (18th century BC) Babylonian king, the 6th of the Amorite 1st dynasty. He extended the Babylonian empire and set up a remarkably efficient administration, as his letter to his governors testifies. A tablet inscribed with the code of Hammurabian Law, surprisingly advanced for one of the earliest known legal codes, is in the Louvre.

HAMNETT, Katherine (1952–) English fashion designer, born in Gravesend, Kent, the daughter of a diplomat. Educated at Cheltenham Ladies College, she studied fashion at St Martin's School of Art in London, then worked as a freelance designer, setting up a short-lived company (1969–74) and then her own business in 1979. She draws inspiration for designs from workwear, and from movements such as the peace movement which she supports.

HAMP, Pierre, pseud of **Pierre Bourillon** (1876–1962) French author, born in Nice of humble parentage. He was in every sense a self-made and self-educated man, and brought to bear in his novels a realism bred of firsthand experience. Among his works are *Marée fraîche* (1908), *Le Rail* (1912), *Les Métiers blessés* (1919), *Le Lin* (1924) and *La Laine* (1931), his novels of industrial life forming a cycle which he called *La Peine des hommes*.

HAMPDEN, John (1594–1643) English parliamentarian and patriot, the eldest son of William Hampden of Hampden, Buckinghamshire. He was educated at Magdalen College, Oxford, and in 1613 at the Inner Temple, London. In 1621 he was returned by Grampound to parliament, and subsequently he sat for Wendover. Although he was no orator, his judgment, veracity and high character secured for him a leading position in the opposition party. In 1626 he helped to prepare the charges against **Buckingham**; next year, having refused to pay his proportion of the general loan which **Charles I** attempted to raise on his own authority, he was imprisoned. His leading associates were **Pym** and **Eliot**. When Charles dissolved parliament in 1629, Hampden retired to his seat in Buckinghamshire, and gave himself up to the life of a country gentleman. In 1634 Charles resorted to the import of ship-money, and in 1636 he extended it to inland places. Hampden refused to pay his share, and in 1637 he was prosecuted before the Court of Exchequer. Seven of the twelve judges sided against him, but the prosecution made Hampden the most popular man in England. He was member for Buckinghamshire both in the Short Parliament and the Long Parliament, where he took part in almost all its leading transactions, especially those which ended in **Strafford**'s death. He had never any faith in the king, and when it seemed not impossible that Charles would be able to crush the liberties of his country, Hampden, like **Cromwell**, meditated self exile to New England. He was one of the five members whose attempted seizure by Charles (1642) precipitated the Civil War. When hostilities broke out, Hampden subscribed £2000 to the public service, took a colonel's commission, and raised a regiment of infantry for the Parliamentary army; at Edgehill and Reading he exhibited personal bravery and generalship. On 18 June 1643, while endeavouring, on Chalgrove Field, to check a marauding force under Prince **Rupert**, he was wounded in the shoulder and died at Thame. He was the most moderate, tactical, urbane and single-minded of the leaders of the Long Parliament.

HAMPDEN, Renn Dickson (1793–1868) English clergyman, born in Barbados. He took a double first at Oxford in 1813, and became a fellow and tutor of Oriel College. His Bampton lectures on the *Scholastic Philosophy* (1832) raised a controversy that threatened to break up the Church of England. His appointments to the principalship of St Mary's Hall (1833), and to the chairs of moral philosophy (1834) and divinity (1836), were denounced by the High Church party and his elevation to the see of Hereford in 1847 was regarded as a death blow to Trinitarian religion.

HAMPOLE, Richard Rolle de (c.1290–1349) English hermit and poet, the 'Hermit of Hampole', near Doncaster, born in Thornton in Yorkshire. He was sent to Oxford, but at 19 became a hermit. He wrote English lyrics and religious books in Latin and English, and translated and expounded the Psalms in prose. However, *The Pricke of Conscience* (*Stimulus Conscientiae*) is no longer thought to be by him.

HAMPSON, Frank (1918–84) English strip cartoonist, born in Audenshaw, Manchester, the creator of *Dan Dare, Pilot of the Future*, considered the finest science-fiction strip ever drawn. He became a Post Office telegraph boy and after studying art at Southport contributed his first strip to the Post Office staff magazine in 1937. In 1950 he designed a Christian comic for boys which eventually became *Eagle*, the most successful comic ever, thanks to his two-page weekly serial, *Dan Dare*, a painted strip which introduced a unique authenticity through Hampson's use of human models and carefully modelled spaceships.

HAMPTON, Christopher (1946–) English dramatist, born in the Azores and educated at Oxford. His first play, *When Did You Last See My Mother?* (1964), led to his appointment as the Royal Court Theatre's first resident dramatist. The Court produced all his earlier plays, including *Total Eclipse* (1968), *The Philanthropist* (1970), *Savages* (1973), set in Brazil, and *Treats* (1976). His finest play is considered to be *Tales From Hollywood* (1982), but his most commercial success has been *Les Liaisons Dangereuses*, a penetrating study of sexual manners, morality and responsibility, adapted from the novel by **Laclos**.

HAMPTON, Lionel (1909–) American jazz musician and bandleader, born in Louisville, Kentucky. Originally a drummer, he was given xylophone tuition while a young man in Chicago. He later introduced the vibraphone into jazz, recording with **Louis Armstrong** in 1930. Hampton was a member of **Benny Goodman**'s small groups in the late 1930s. He first formed a permanent big band in 1940, continuing as a leader until the 1980s and taking his entertaining brand of musicianship and showmanship on many overseas tours.

HAMPTON, Wade (c.1751–1835) American soldier, born in Halifax County, Virginia. He served in the American War of Independence (1775–83), and became a member of the US House of Representatives. He rejoined the army in 1808, and in 1813, now a major-general, made an unsuccessful attempt to invade Canada.

HAMPTON, Wade (1818–1902) American soldier, born in Columbia, South Carolina, grandson of **Wade Hampton**. In 1861 he raised 'Hampton's Legion'. As brigadier-general he commanded a cavalry force in 1862–63, was wounded at Gettysburg, received the command of **Lee**'s cavalry in 1864, and in 1865 served in South Carolina against **Sherman**. He became state governor (1876), and was US senator (1878–91).

HAMSUN, Knut, pseud of **Knut Pedersen** (1859–1952) Norwegian novelist, born in Lom in Gudbrandsdal. He had no formal education, and spent his boyhood with his uncle, a fisherman on the Lofoten Islands. He worked at various odd jobs, including shoemaking, coal-mining and teaching, and twice visited the USA (1882–84, 1886–88), where he worked as a streetcar attendant in Chicago and a farmhand in North Dakota. He sprang to fame with his novel *Sult* (Hunger, 1890), followed by *Mysterier* (Mysteries, 1892) and the lyrical *Pan* (1894). His masterpiece is considered *Markens grøde* (Growth of the Soil, 1917), which was instrumental in his award of the 1920 Nobel prize for literature. A recluse during the inter-war years, he lost popularity during World War II for his Nazi sympathies and support of the **Quisling** regime, for which he was imprisoned in 1948, but his reputation has been largely rehabilitated.

HAN DYNASTY (206 BC–220 AD) the name of a major Chinese dynasty, successor to the **Ch'in** dynasty, founded by general Liu Pang (256–195 BC) with its capital at Ch'ang-an. The empire was consolidated by conquest by the sixth emperor, Wu Di ('Martial Emperor', 157–87 BC), who reigned from 140–87 BC. Under the Han emperors, Confucianism was recognized as the state religion, the production and export of silk was expanded, and paper was invented. A huge state bureaucracy was developed, and the building of an extensive canal system begun. The earlier period, known as the Western, or Former, Han (206 BC–9 AD), was interrupted by a usurper, Wang Mang (45 BC–23 AD), who was regent for two child emperors and seized power from 9 to 23 AD, when he was killed by rebels. The Han dynasty was restored for a second period, known as the Eastern, or Later, Han (23–220). Buddhism was introduced under the emperor Ming Di ('Enlightened Emperor', 26–76), who reigned from 58 to 76.

HAN SUYIN (1917–) Chinese-born English novelist, born Elizabeth Chow in Peking, the daughter of a Belgian mother and a Chinese railway engineer. She studied medicine at Yenching, Brussels and London, where after the death in the civil war of her husband, General Tang, she completed her studies. She then practised in Hong Kong, which with its undercurrents of pro-Western and anti-Western loyalties, Old China versus the New, White versus Yellow, provided the background for her first partly-autobiographical novel *A Many-splendoured Thing* (1952), which in the love affair of an emancipated Chinese girl and an English journalist symbolizes the political and ideological climate of the British colony. It was made into a film in 1955. In 1952 she married an English police officer in Singapore, where she practised in an anti-tuberculosis clinic. Her other novels include *Destination Chungking* (1953), *And the Rain my Drink* (1954), *The Mountain is Young* (1958) and *Four Faces* (1963). She also wrote a semi-autobiographical and historical trilogy, *The Crippled Tree* (1965), *A Mortal Flower* (1966) and *Birdless Summer* (1968), and two volumes of contemporary Chinese history, *The Morning Deluge* and *The Wind in the Tower* (1972).

HANBURY-TENISON, Robin Airling (1936–) British explorer, author and broadcaster. Brought up in Ireland, and educated at Eton and Oxford, in 1958 he achieved the first land crossing of South America at its widest point, and during the 1960s crossed the Sahara many times by camel in search of prehistoric paintings. In 1964, with Sebastian Snow, who fell ill during the journey, he travelled from the Caribbean to the South Atlantic (6000 miles) through South America, in 3 months. His concern for Indian tribes led to him being one of the founding members of Survival International, of which he is now president. He took part in both British Hovercraft expeditions in Amazonas (1968) and trans-Africa (1969). In 1971 he was invited by the Brazilian government to undertake a three-month expedition, and subsequently visited 33 tribes, publishing a report on their plight. He took part in the British Trans-Americas expedition of 1972, crossing the Darien gap and writing a report on the impact of the road on the Cuna Indians. In 1973 he and his wife, Marika, travelled through the Outer Islands of Indonesia and the following year returned to travel 200 miles through the interior of Sulawesi. He led the Royal Geographical Society's Gunung Mulu (Sarawak) Expedition 1977/78, a multi-disciplinary survey of a tropical forest ecosystem in a newly-created national park involving 115 scientists over 15 months. His wife died in 1982, and he has since remarried. With Louella, he has ridden on horseback from Cornwall to Carmargue, along the Great Wall of China, and South to North through New Zealand.

HANCOCK, John (1737–93) American statesman, born in Quincy, Massachusetts. As president (1775–77) of the Continental Congress, he first signed the Declaration of Independence.

HANCOCK, Sir (William) Keith (1898–1988) Australian historian and writer, born in Fitzroy, Victoria. Educated at Melbourne University, he became a Rhodes scholar in 1922 and was the first Australian to be elected a fellow of All Souls, Oxford. From 1924 he held professorships at Adelaide, Birmingham and Oxford universities, before becoming director of the Institute of Commonwealth Studies in London from 1939 to 1957. Hancock returned to Australia in 1957 as foundation director of research studies and later professor of history at the Australian National University, Canberra, Author of many important works including the classic *Australia* (1930) and a life of **Jan Smuts** (1962–68), he gave the ABC's Boyer Lectures entitled 'Today, Yesterday and Tomorrow' in 1973.

HANCOCK, Lang (Langley George) (1909–) Australian mining industrialist, born in Perth, Western Australia. In 1934 he leased claims for the mining of 'blue' asbestos at Wittenoom, Western Australia, and developed a processing plant in partnership with Peter Wright. Hancock pioneered the use of light aircraft for prospecting, after having fortuitously discovered substantial iron ore deposits in the Pilbara region. Having established his claim, he concluded mining agreements with a number of companies, thus initiating the growth of Australian extractive industries. He went on to discover further deposits between 1963 to 1969, including Rhodes Ridge, the largest deposit in the world, of an estimated ten million tonnes. He held controversial views on politics and aboriginal affairs and in 1974 formed a secessionist movement in Western Australia with the aim of better political representation.

HANCOCK, Thomas (1786–1865) English inventor and manufacturer, born in Marlborough, the son of a timber merchant and cabinetmaker. In 1820 he obtained a patent for the 'application of a certain material (rubber) to render various parts of dress and other articles more elastic'. In experimenting with the preparation of rubber for water-proofing and other purposes he built what was intended to be a shredding machine but found that the end product was a solid homogeneous block of rubber, in a form that was much more suitable for manufacturing purposes. He patented his 'masticator' and a number of other devices and processes, including (in 1843) the first English patent for vulcanization of rubber. For a time he was in partnership with **Charles Macintosh**.

HANCOCK, Tony (Anthony John) (1924–68) English comedian, born in Birmingham. The son of an amateur entertainer, he overcame extreme stage-fright to try his hand as a stand-up comic in RAF concert parties and touring gang shows before making his professional stage début in *Wings* (1946). Pantomimes, cabaret and radio appearances in *Educating Archie* (1951) contributed to his growing popularity and he made his film début in *Orders is Orders* (1954). The radio series *Hancock's Half Hour* (1954), written by Alan Simpson and Ray Galton, allowed him to refine a lugubrious comic persona as a pompous, belligerent misfit whose capricious social aspirations and blinkered patriotism are frequently thwarted or belittled. The series transferred to television from 1956 to 1961, gaining record-breaking viewing figures and rare public affection. Dispensing with his regular co-stars and writers, he made ill-advised attempts at solo projects and serious 'artistic' endeavours in films like *The Rebel* (1960) and *The Punch and Judy Man* (1963). A chronic alcoholic beset by self-doubt and unable to reconcile his ambition with his talent, he spent his final years in a self-destructive round of aborted projects and unsatisfactory performances, and committed suicide while attempting a further comeback on Australian television.

HANCOCK, Winfield Scott (1824–86) American soldier, born in Montgomery County, Pennsylvania. He studied at West Point, served through the Mexican war, and was captain when the Civil War broke out. In 1861 he organized the army of the Potomac, was prominent at South Mountain, Antietam and Fredericksburg, and in 1863 took command of the 2nd corps. At Gettysburg he was in command until **Meade**'s arrival; and on 3 July was severely wounded. In 1864 he was conspicuous in the battles of the Wilderness, Spottsylvania and Cold Harbor, and in 1864 was created brigadier-general, but was disabled for active service by a wound. Democratic candidate for the presidency in 1880, he was defeated by **Garfield**.

HAND, (Billings) Learned (1872–1961) American jurist, born in Albany, New York, into a dynasty of New York judges. He graduated from Harvard University (1893) and its Law School (1896), and practised law in New York City and at the state capital Albany, until he was appointed US judge for the Southern District of New York from 1908 to 1924; subsequently he was appointed judge of the Federal Court of Appeals for the Second Circuit (1924–51). His legal judgments were profound and extended into all branches of law, having so much influence on the US Supreme Court that although never appointed to it, he was sometimes called the Supreme Court's 'tenth man'. He was hostile to judicial 'legislation' and held that judges should not go beyond the immediate case in hand, but also opposed Congressional attempts to limit judicial discretion. From 1951 to 1961 he continued to hear special cases. He published *The Bill of Rights* (1958) and *The Spirit of Liberty* (1952, 1960), and had more influence than any other judge of his time outside the Supreme Court (and more than most judges in it).

HANDEL, properly **Händel, George Friederic** (1685–1759) German-English composer, born in Halle. Persisting in studying music against the wishes of his barber-surgeon father, he became organist of Halle Cathedral at the age of 17 whilst also studying law at the university. From 1703 to 1706 he gained invaluable experience as a violinist and keyboard player in the Hamburg opera orchestra, during which time he tried his hand at writing Italian operas, such as *Almira*. The next four years were spent in Italy, where as 'il caro Sassone' he established a great reputation as a keyboard virtuoso and had considerable success as an operatic composer. Appointed in 1710 to the court of the Elector of Hanover, he took frequent leaves of absence to try his fortune in London, introducing himself with the opera *Rinaldo* (1711). This persistent absenteeism displeased his master, and the succession of the Elector to the English throne as **George I** led at first to some awkwardness; the *Water Music*, composed for a river procession, is said to have been a peace offering. Attached to the households of the Earl of Burlington and subsequently to that of the Duke of Chandos between 1713 and 1720, he then went into opera promotion at the King's Theatre, Haymarket, under the auspices of the newly founded Royal Academy of Music 'to secure a constant supply of operas by Handel to be performed under his direction'. Attempting to satisfy the fickle taste of the fashionable London world with Italian opera was difficult, and his success varied (the Royal Academy of Music came to an end in 1728, was resuscitated temporarily, but collapsed again, after which Handel went into partnership with John Rich at his theatre in Covent Garden). Artistic and political intrigues, and opposition to composers and companies, not to mention the success of the parodistic *Beggar's Opera*, induced him to experiment with a new form, the English oratorio. Though leaning on operatic models, and performed in theatres usually during Lent, this venture proved enormously popular. In 1735, Handel conducted 15 oratorio concerts in London. Despite a stroke in 1737, in the next five years he produced *Saul* (1739), *Israel in Egypt* (1739) and *The Messiah* (1742), the latter having been first performed in Dublin. *Samson* followed in 1743, succeeded by *Joseph*, *Semele*, *Judas Maccabeus*, *Solomon*, and others, his last *Jephthah*, appearing in 1750. He was buried in Poet's Corner, Westminster Abbey. A sociable, cultivated, cosmopolitan figure, and a very prolific composer like his exact contemporary **J S Bach**, he wrote for the most part in the current Italianate style, though in his settings of English words there are reflections of **Purcell**. His output included 46 operas, 32 oratorios, large numbers of cantatas, sacred music, concerti grossi and other orchestral, instrumental and vocal music.

HANDKE, Peter (1942–) Austrian dramatist and novelist. Trained as a lawyer, his plays are obscure and the subject of some controversy. His first play, *Offending the Audience* (1966) presents four people who speak randomly and insult the audience. The titles of his other plays are intriguing, such as *My Foot My Tutor* (1969), *A Ride Across Lake Constance* (1971), *A Sorrow Beyond Dreams* (1977).

HANDLEY, Tommy (Thomas Reginald) (1892–1949) English comedian, born in Liverpool. He served in World War I, working in variety and concert parties, and in the infancy of radio became known as a regular broadcaster. In 1939 he achieved nationwide fame through his weekly programme ITMA (It's That Man Again), which, with its endearing mixture of satire, parody, slapstick, and wit became a major factor in the boosting of wartime morale and continued as a prime favourite until brought to an untimely end by his sudden death.

HANDLIN, Oscar (1915–) American historian, born in Brooklyn, New York, the son of Russian immigrants. After graduating from Brooklyn College (1934) and teaching there (1936–38), he was given a junior teaching post at Harvard, took his doctorate there in 1940, and remained on its staff in chairs of increasing honour. His doctoral thesis and first book, *Boston's Immigrants* 1790–1865 (1941) is, artistically, still his masterpiece: updated as *The Uprooted* (1951, Pulitzer prize), a comprehensive survey of all American immigration. With his sociologist wife, Mary Flug Handlin, he published *Commonwealth* (1947), a history of Massachusetts, and some of her work and influence are also present in his instructive essays, *Race and Nationality in American Life* (1957). He has also written *The Americans* (1963), *Truth in History* (1979) and *The Distortion of America* (1981).

HANDS, Terry (Terence) (1941–) English stage director, born in Aldershot, and co-founder of the Everyman Theatre, Liverpool (1964). He joined the Royal Shakespeare Company in 1966, became an associate director in 1967, joint artistic director with **Trevor Nunn** in 1978, and sole artistic director and chief executive in 1987. He was consultant director at the Comedie Française 1975–77, and has directed Shakespeare at the Burgtheater in Vienna. Among his more recent RSC productions are *Othello* (1985), with Ben Kingsley in the title role, and *Romeo and Juliet* (1989). He attracted much criticism in 1988 by producing at Stratford a pop opera, *Carrie*, based on a horror novel. It received profoundly hostile reviews and subsequently crashed on Broadway.

HANDY, Charles Brian (1932–) Irish management teacher, born in Dublin. Educated at Oxford, he was a manager in Shell Petroleum and an economist in the City of London. In 1982 he became professor of management development at the London Graduate School of Business and, in 1977, was appointed warden of St George's House, Windsor (the Church of England's 'staff college'). His comparative study of managers in Britain, America, Europe and Japan, *The Making of Managers* published in 1988, has helped to shape current management education.

HANDY, William Christopher (1873–1958) American black composer, born in Florence, Alabama. Overcoming the opposition of his father, a Methodist preacher, to his choice of a musical career, Handy joined a minstrel show as a cornet player, and in 1903 formed his own band in Memphis, subsequently moving to Chicago and to New York, where he formed his own publishing company. He was the first to introduce the Negro 'blues' style to printed music, his most famous work being the *Saint Louis Blues* (1914). He wrote *Father of the Blues* (1958).

HANIF, Mohammed (1934–) Pakistan cricketer, born in Junagadh. A member of the great cricketing family which produced two other Test players (his brothers Mushtaq and Sadiq), he made the first of his 55 appearances when only 17. In his Test appearances he scored twelve centuries, including two in the match against England at Dacca in 1961–62. A natural stroke-maker, he holds the world's highest individual score, 499 for Karachi against Bahawalpur in 1958–59.

HANKEY, Sir Maurice Pascal Alers, 1st Baron Hankey (1877–1963) English soldier and public official, born in Biarritz. Educated at Rugby School, he was commissioned in the Royal Marine Artillery (1895), and served in naval intelligence from 1902 to 1906. He became naval assistant secretary, Committee of Imperial Defence in 1908, and succeeded as secretary in 1912. In World War I he served as secretary of the Imperial War Cabinet until its dissolution (1919). He was appointed secretary of the cabinet (1919), of the Committee of Imperial Defence (1920) and clerk of the privy council (1923), and held these appointments concurrently until his retirement (1938). At the outbreak of World War II he became minister without portfolio in the war cabinet, and thereafter successively chancellor of the Duchy of Lancaster (1940) and paymaster general (1941-1942).

HANNA, Mark (Marcus Alonzo) (1837–1904) American businessman and politician, born in New Lisbon, Ohio. His family moved to Cleveland, where he worked in his father's wholesale grocery. He served in the Union army (1864) and, starting in partnership with his father in coal and iron, made the most of the great post-war expansion. He helped organize the Union National Bank, bought the Cleveland Opera House, invested in Cleveland street-railways, and moved into politics to protect business interests, backing Ohio candidates for the presidency successfully (**Garfield**, 1880), unsuccessfully (John Sherman, 1888), and very successfully (**McKinley**, 1896). He transformed local and state Republican boss systems into a massively-organized national fighting force for the 1896 election, carrying campaign finance to unprecedented lengths and exploiting business terror of the Democratic and Populist campaign of **William Jennings Bryan** against the gold standard. He refused cabinet office, but accepted an Ohio Senate seat in 1897. He was heartbroken by McKinley's assassination in 1901, and while feared by President **Theodore Roosevelt** as rival for the 1904 Republican nomination, supported Roosevelt's pro-Labor 'Square Deal' intervention in the Pennsylvania coal strike, believing that employers must have decent standards to avert socialism.

HANNA, William Denby (1910–) American animated cartoonist, born in New Mexico, and creator with **Joseph Roland Barbera** of the immortal cat-and-mouse duo, *Tom and Jerry*. A structural engineer by training, he turned to cartooning and became one of the first directors at the new MGM animation studio in 1937, making **Rudolph Dirks**'s *Captain and the Kids*, before teaming up with Barbera.

HANNIBAL, 'the grace of Baal' (247–182 BC) Carthaginian soldier, the son of **Hamilcar**. In his ninth year his father bade him swear eternal enmity to Rome. He served in Spain under Hamilcar and **Hasdrubal**; elected general after the assassination of Hasdrubal he reduced all southern Spain up to the Ebro (221–219), with the exception of the Iberian town of Saguntum. Saguntum fell in 218, and the Second Punic war began. In 218 he left New Carthage, crossed the Pyrenees, gained the Rhone, defeated the Gauls, and crossed the Alps in 15 days, in the face of almost insuperable obstacles. His troops, used to the African and Spanish climate, perished in thousands amid ice and snow; but he overcame the Taurini, forced Ligurian and Celtic tribes to serve in his army, and at the river Ticinus drove back the Romans under **Publius Cornelius Scipio** (218). The first great battle was then fought in the plain of the Trebia, when the men of the Roman consular army were either cut to pieces or scattered in flight. Wintering in the valley of the Po, in spring 217 Hannibal crossed the Apennines, wasted Etruria with fire and sword, and marched towards Rome. He awaited the consul **Gaius Flaminius** by Lake Trasimene, where he inflicted on him a crushing defeat; the Roman army was annihilated. Passing through Apulia and Campania, he wintered at Gerunium, and in the spring at Cannae (216) on the Aufidus utterly destroyed another Roman army under **Quintus Fabius** ('Cunctator'). But after Cannae the tide turned. His niggardly countrymen denied him necessary support. As his veterans were lost to him he had no means of filling their places, while the Romans could put army after army into the field. But through the long years during which he maintained a hopeless struggle in Italy he was never defeated. He spent the winter of 216–215 at Capua. When he again took the field the Romans wisely avoided a pitched battle, though the Carthaginians overran Italy, took towns, and gained minor victories. But Capua fell in 210. In 207 his brother **Hasdrubal (Barca)**, marching from Spain to his aid, was defeated and slain at the Metaurus by the consul Nero. For four years Hannibal stood at bay in the hill-country of Bruttium, till in 203 he was recalled to Africa to repel a Roman invasion by Scipio. In the next year he met Scipio at Zama; his raw levies fled, his veterans were cut to pieces, and Carthage was at the mercy of Rome. So ended the Second Punic war. Peace being made, Hannibal turned his genius to political reforms, but aroused such virulent opposition that he went into exile at the court of **Antiochus III** at Ephesus, then to that of Prusias, king of Bithynia. When the Romans demanded his surrender, he escaped to Bithynia, but took poison.

HANNINGTON, James (1847–85) English missionary, born in Hurstpierpoint. He studied at Oxford, and in 1882, after a seven years' curacy in his native parish, he went out to Uganda under the Church Missionary Society. Fever and dysentry forced him to return to England but in June 1884 he was consecrated first bishop of Eastern Equatorial Africa, and in January 1885 went to Mombasa. In July he travelled to Uganda, where he was slain by King Mwanga.

HANNO (5th century BC) Carthaginian navigator. He undertook a voyage of exploration along the west coast of Africa. He founded colonies, and reached Cape Nun or the Bight of Benin. His *Periplus* survives in a Greek translation.

HANOTAUX, Gabriel (1853–1944) French historian and statesman, born in Beaurevoir, Aisne. He held minor government offices, and was twice foreign minister (1892–98). He wrote on **Richelieu**, **Joan of Arc**, and **Foch** and a great history of *Contemporary France* (1903–08).

HANRATTY, James (c.1936–62) convicted English murderer. He was found guilty of the murder of Michael Gregsten, who was shot while in his car with his lover, Valerie Storie, in a layby on the A6 on 22 August 1962. The case proved controversial and has been shadowed with doubt ever since the verdict and death-penalty sentence. Hanratty was arrested on 11 October. Storie, who survived, despite being raped, and paralysed by several bullets, picked out Hanratty from an identity parade. Hanratty, who was reportedly a feeble-minded petty criminal, was charged on 14 October. He denied the charge but refused to name his alibis, saying that to do so would be to betray his friends' trust. He then changed the location of his alibi from Liverpool to Rhyl. The jury found him guilty. After he was hanged on 4 April, 1962, several witnesses came forward who said that they believed they had seen him in Rhyl. Many still argue that Hanratty was innocent.

HANSARD, Luke (1752–1828) English printer, born in Norwich. After joining the office of Hughes, printer to the House of Commons, he became acting manager in 1774, in 1798 succeeding as sole proprietor of the business. He and his descendants printed the parliamentary reports from 1774 to 1889 and the official reports of proceedings in Parliament are still called 'Hansard' in his honour. **William Cobbett**'s *Parliamentary Debates* was continued from 1806 by his son, Thomas, and successors.

HANSEN, Christian Frederik (1746–1845) Danish neo-classical architect, born in Copenhagen. He studied in Rome and was influenced by **Palladio**, **Ledoux** and geometry. The most important architect of his day, he was responsible for the rebuilding of Copenhagen after the 1807 British bombardment. Roman models inspired the strong simple masses of the Court House (1803–16) linked by bridges to its forbidding detention block. Only the chapel remains of his rebuilding of the Christenborg Palace, a porticoed rectangle surmounted by a saucerdome. In the cathedral (1811–29) he reused the old walls but introduced a bold geometrical interplay.

HANSEN, Gerhard Henrik Armauer (1841–1912) Norwegian physician and bacteriologist, born in Bergen. In 1869 he discovered the leprosy bacillus.

HANSEN, Marcus Lee (1892–1938) American historian, born in Neenah, Wisconsin, the son of a Baptist minister. Educated in Michigan, Minnesota and Iowa, he then studied at Harvard under **Frederick Turner**. He became convinced of the necessity to study the European background, and toured Europe inspecting archives and newspapers (1925–27), and made a special study of the ethnic composition of the USA in 1790 for the American Council of Learned Societies. He taught at Illinois University from 1892 to 1938. All his books were published posthumously in 1940: *The Mingling of the Canadian and American Peoples*, *The Immigrant in American History* and *The Atlantic Migration 1607–1860*.

HANSEN, Martin Alfred (1909–55) Danish novelist. He came from farming stock, worked on the land and as a teacher, but after 1945 devoted himself to writing. His early novels deal with social problems in the 1930s (*Nu opgiver han*, 'Surrender', 1935; *Kolonien*; 'The Colony', 1937). Later he developed a more profound style in *Jonathans Rejse* ('Jonathan's Journey', 1941) and *Lykkelige Kristoffer* ('Lucky Christopher' 1945), outwardly picaresque novels but in reality closely related to his work for the Danish underground press during the Occupation. With *Løgneren* ('The Liar' 1950), a psychological novel intended first for broadcasting as a serial, he reached a wider public than ever. In 1952 appeared his most original work, the metaphysical *Orm og Tyr* ('The Serpent and the Bull'). Other writings include *Torne-busken* ('The Thorn Bush', 1946, short stories) and *Tanker i en Skorsten*, ('Thoughts up a Chimney' 1948 essays).

HANSLICK, Eduard (1825–1904) Austrian music critic and writer on aesthetics, professor from 1861 at Vienna. He supported **Schumann** and **Brahms** against **Wagner** in his critical writings and propounded a form theory of aesthetics in his *Vom Musikalisch-Schönen* (1854; trans 1891), which did for music what the Bell-Fry theories later did for painting.

HANSOM, Joseph Aloysius (1803–82) English inventor and architect, born in York. He invented the 'Patent Safety (Hansom) Cab' in 1834 and designed Birmingham town hall and the RC cathedral at Plymouth.

HANSON, Duane (1925–) American sculptor, born in Alexandria, Minnesota. He studied at the Cranbrook Academy of Art, Bloomfield, Michigan, before going to Germany where he lived from 1953 to 1961. He specializes in life-size figures made from polyester resin stiffened with fibre-glass; once assembled these are painted realistically and adorned with hats, wristwatches, etc. His earlier work was violent (eg *Abortion*, 1966), but more recently he has made mildly satirical pieces like *Woman with Shopping Trolley* (1969) and *Tourists* (1970).

HANSON, Howard (1896–1981) American composer of Swedish descent, born in Wahoo, Nebraska. He was awarded the American Prix de Rome in 1921, and after three years' study in Italy was director of the Eastman School of Music until 1964, which, under his leadership, became one of the most important centres of American musical life. His compositions, firmly in the tradition of 19th-century romanticism, include an opera, *The Merry Mount*, and seven symphonies.

HANSON, Raymond (1913–76) Australian composer and teacher, born in Sydney. He studied at the New South Wales Conservatorium of Music, to which he returned to lecture from 1948 until his death. Hanson had a considerable formative influence on the new generation of Australian composers and also, through his teaching, on the future of music education in Australia. Of Hanson's own work, his *Trumpet Concerto* is well known and was one of the first Australian recordings to be released internationally. Other works include operas, a ballet, a symphony, four concertos, chamber music and film scores, and music for piano including his bitter piano sonata written between 1938 and 1940, which was his protest against war.

HANSON-DYER, Louise Berta Mosson (1884–1962) Australian music publisher and patron, born in Melbourne. She was an accomplished pianist, studying in Edinburgh and at the Royal College of Music, London. After marrying James Dyer she became the centre of Melbourne's musical life, helping establish the British Music Society there in 1921. In 1927 the Dyers left for London, and then Paris, where Louise established Editions du Oiseau-Lyre, a music publishing business and in 1933 brought out a complete edition of the works of **Couperin**, followed by works of **Purcell** and **Blow**. The press set a new standard of music printing, and she became a leader in the revival of early music. In the 1950s the press was among the first to issue on LP some of the works of **Monteverdi**, Purcell and **Handel**. Now Mrs Hanson-Dyer, as she had remarried in 1939 after the death of her first husband, she was permanently resident in France and, after the war, in Monaco, but she maintained her links with Australia, and published the works of leading Australian composers **Peggy Glanville-Hicks** and **Margaret Sutherland**. Her considerable Australian estate was left to Melbourne University for music research.

HANSSON, Ola (1860–1925) Swedish poet and novelist, born in Hönsinge. Having acquired a name with his naturalistic lyric poetry, he left Sweden for Germany in 1890 in the face of negative criticism and public apathy on the publication of his erotic volume, *Sensitiva amorosa*. Thereafter he wrote mostly in German, much influenced by **Nietzsche**.

HANSTEEN, Kristoph (1784–1873) Norwegian astronomer, born in Christiania (later Oslo), where he became professor of mathematics in 1814. He investigated terrestrial magnetism, discovered the 'law of magnetic force' (1821) and made a scientific journey to Eastern Siberia (1828–30).

HANTZSCH, Arthur (1857–1935) German organic chemist, born in Dresden. Professor at Zurich, Wurzburg and Leipzig, he investigated the arrangement of atoms in the molecules of nitrogen compounds and the electrical conductivity of organic compounds.

HANWAY, Jonas (1712–86) English traveller and philanthropist, born in Portsmouth. Apprenticed at 17 to a Lisbon merchant, he afterwards traded at St Petersburg, and travelled through Russia and Persia (1743–50). He published an account of his travels in 1753, and spent the rest of his life mostly in London as a navy victualling commissioner (1762–83). He was an unwearying friend to chimney sweeps, waifs and down-and-outs, and advocated solitary confinement for prisoners and milder punishments. The author of 74 works, he wrote against the practice of giving gratuities, and was the first Englishman to carry an umbrella.

HAPSBURG See **HABSBURG**

HARALD GORMSSON, 'Blue-Tooth' (c.910–985) king of Denmark from c.950. The son of Gorm the Old and father of **Svein Fork-Beard**, he was the first king to unify all the provinces of Denmark under a single crown. He was converted to Christianity by a German missionary, Poppo, in c.960, and made Christianity the state religion of Denmark. He erected the massive Jelling Stone at Jelling to proclaim his conversion of Denmark ('and made the Danes Christian'), and exhumed for proper Christian burial the bodies of his father Gorm and his mother Thyri from the great burial mounds at Jelling in which they had been laid. He is also now thought to have built the fortified military barracks at Trelleborg and elsewhere in Denmark; he strengthened the unity and central administration of the country, and repelled attacks from Norway and Germany. Harald Blue-Tooth was eventually deposed by his son Svein Fork-Beard in 985, and died in exile soon afterwards.

HARALD I HALFDANARSON, 'Fine-Hair' (c.865–942) king of Norway from c.890 to 942, the first ruler to claim sovereignty over all Norway. The son of Halfdan the Black (king of Vestfold), he fought his way to power with a crushing defeat of his opponents at the naval battle of Hafursfjord, off Stavanger, in c.890. His authoritarian rule caused many of the old aristocratic families to emigrate west to the Orkneys, Hebrides and Ireland, and to newly-settled Iceland. Harald made several punitive expeditions across the North Sea to subdue his former subjects and impose Norwegian rule over the Northern and Western Isles of Scotland. When he was nearly 80 years old, in 942, he abdicated in favour of his eldest son, **Erik 'Blood-Axe'** and died three years later, in 945.

HARALD II ERIKSSON, 'Greycloak' (d.970) king of Norway from c.965. The eldest son of **Erik 'Blood-Axe'**, after his father's death in England in 954 he took refuge at the Danish court with his mother, Gunnhild, the sister of king **Harald Gormsson, 'Blue-Tooth'**. With Danish support he and his four brothers made several assaults on Norway from 960 onwards against their uncle, King **Haakon I Haraldsson**, and eventually killed him in battle off Hardangerfjord. Harald Greycloak's reign was unpopular, especially when he tried to impose Christianity on his subjects. When he tried to break free of his alliance with Denmark one of his enemies, Earl Haakon of Lade, enlisted Harald Blue-Tooth's help for another invasion, and Greycloak was caught and killed at Limfjord in 970.

HARALD III SIGURDSSON, 'Hardraade' (1015–66) King of Norway from 1045. The half-brother of **Olaf II Haraldsson** (St Olaf), he was present at the battle of Stiklestad in 1030 where St Olaf was killed, and sought refuge in Kiev at the court of his kinsman, Prince Yaroslav the Wise, in Kiev with his nephew, **Magnus Olafsson, 'the Good'**. He had a lurid career as a Viking mercenary with the Varangian Guard in Constantinople, and returned to Norway in 1045 to demand, and receive, a half-share in the kingdom from his nephew. He became sole king on his nephew's death in 1047, and earned the nickname Hardraade ('Hard-Ruler'). After long and unrelenting wars against king **Svein II Ulfsson** of Denmark, he invaded England in 1066 to claim the throne after the death of **Edward, 'the Confessor'**, but was defeated and killed by **Harold II** at Stamford Bridge.

HARCOURT, Sir William Venables Vernon (1789–1871) English chemist and clergyman, born in Sudbury, Derbyshire, the son of the archbishop of York. He was privately educated at home, then spent five years in the Royal Navy before going to Christchurch College, Oxford, in 1807, intending to become a clergyman. At Christchurch he met John Kidd, who interested him in the sciences. After graduation he moved to clerical duties at Bishopsthorpe, and also set up his own chemical laboratory there, taking advice from **William Wollaston** and **Humphry Davy**. He was an amateur scientist whose importance lay in his influence and the stimulation he gave to others. He became the first president of the Yorkshire Philosophical Society and he played an essential role in the establishment of the British Association for the Advancement of Science, which was to be open to all interested in science, at a time when the Royal Society was becoming more restrictive and professional in its membership.

HARCOURT, Sir William Vernon (1827–1904) English Liberal statesman, born in York. He graduated from Trinity College, Cambridge, in 1851. Called to the bar in 1854, QC in 1866, he acquired distinction by his contributions to the *Saturday Review*, and by his letters in *The Times* signed 'Historicus', and collected in 1863. Liberal MP for the city of Oxford (1868), in 1869 he was elected professor of international law at Cambridge; he was solicitor-general (1873–74); in 1880 he became home secretary. In 1885 he went out of office with **Gladstone**, but returned with him for six months in 1886, when he was Chancellor of the Exchequer—an office he resumed in 1892. On Gladstone's retirement in 1893 Sir William became leader of the Lower House. His principal work was the revision of the death duties and his 1894 budget. His lukewarm support of his chief led to Lord **Rosebery**'s resignation in 1896. After a crusade against Ritualism in 1898, he resigned the Liberal leadership, remaining a private member of the party. His second wife (1876) was Motley's daughter Elizabeth (1841–1928). His son, Lewis Vernon (1863–1922), Viscount (1916), was first commissioner of works 1905–10, 1915–16; colonial secretary, 1910–15.

HARDAKNUT KNUTSSON (1018–42) king of Denmark from 1035 and of England from 1040. He was the son of **Knut Sveinsson** (Canute the Great) and Emma (the widow of King **Ethelred, 'the Unready'**), and was Knut's only legitimate heir. He inherited Denmark on his father's death in 1035, but was unable to come to England immediately to claim the throne there. The English elected his half-brother, **Harold I Knutsson** ('Harefoot') regent in his stead, and then confirmed Harold as king in 1037. Hardaknut mounted an expedition to invade England to claim the crown, but Harold died in March, 1040, before he arrived. Hardaknut was thereupon elected king, and promptly punished the English by imposing a savage fleet-tax to pay for his expedition. His reign was universally disliked, and he died in June 1042 of convulsions at a drinking party.

HARDEN, Sir Arthur (1865–1940) English chemist, born in Manchester. He worked in the Jenner (now Lister) Institute from 1897 and became professor of biochemistry at London in 1912. In 1929 he was awarded the Nobel prize for chemistry (with **Hans von Euler-Chelpin**) for his work on alcoholic fermentation and enzymes.

HARDEN, Maximilian (1861–1927) German journalist, born in Berlin. He founded and edited the weekly *Die Zukunft* (1892–1922) in which he exposed court scandals. A fearless critic with a powerful pen, he was silenced and called up as an army clerk in 1917.

HARDENBERG, Friedrich von See **NOVALIS**

HARDENBERG, Karl August, Fürst von (1750–1822) Prussian statesman, born in Essenrode in Hanover. After holding appointments in Hanover, Brunswick, Ansbach and Bayreuth, he became a Prussian minister on Bayreuth's union with Prussia in 1791, and in 1803 first Prussian minister. His policy was to preserve neutrality in the war between France and Britain; but in 1806, under **Napoleon**'s influence, he was dismissed. In 1810 he was appointed chancellor, and addressed himself to the task of completing the reforms begun by **Heinrich Stein**. In the war of liberation he played a prominent part, and after the treaty of Paris (June 1814) was made a prince. He took part in the congress of Vienna, and in the treaties of Paris (1815). He reorganized the council of state (1817), of which he was appointed president, and drew up the new Prussian system of imposts. To Hardenberg (with Stein), Prussia owed the improvements in her army system, abolition of serfdom and the privileges of the nobles, encouragement of municipalities, and the reform of education.

HARDIE, James Keir (1856–1915) Scottish Labour leader, one of the founders of the Labour party, born near Holytown, Lanarkshire. He worked in a coalpit from childhood. Victimized as champion of the miners (whom he organized) he moved to Cumnock and became a journalist. The first of all Labour candidates, he was defeated (1888) in Mid-Lanark, sat for West Ham, South (1892–95), and Merthyr Tydfil (1900–15), and in and out of parliament worked strenuously for socialism and the unemployed. He started and edited *The Labour Leader*, handed it over in 1903 to the Independent Labour party, of which, founded in 1893, he was chairman till 1900 and again in 1913–14. He strenuously opposed Liberal influence on the trade unions and strongly advocated the formation of a separate political party, as distinct from the existing Labour Representation League. A strong pacifist, he lost his seat through opposing the Boer War.

HARDING, John See **HARDYNG**

HARDING, Sir John, 1st Baron of Petherton (1896–1989) English soldier and field-marshal, born in South Petherton, Somerset. A subaltern in World War I, he rose to chief of staff of the Allied Army in Italy in 1944. From 1955 to 1957, as governor-general of Cyprus during the political and terrorist campaign against Britain, he re-organized the security forces to combat terrorism, re-established order through the imposition of martial law and press control, banished Archbishop **Makarios**, and, although he failed to bring about a political settlement, was widely respected for his straightforward, soldierly approach.

HARDING, Stephen, St (d.1134) English churchman, born in Sherborne in Dorset. He was the co-founder and from 1109 to 1033 third abbot of the monastery of Cîteaux, south of Dijon and endeavoured to restore the Cistercian rule to its original simplicity.

HARDING, Warren Gamaliel (1865–1923) American statesman, born in Corsica, Ohio, a doctor's son. He became a journalist, a newspaper owner (the *Marion Star*), state senator (1899–1903) and lieutenant-governor (1904–06) of the Ohio, Repulican senator (1915–20) and was elected 29th president of the USA in 1920. During his administration, peace treaties were concluded with Germany, Austria and Hungary in 1921, and the Washington Conference convened. However, following a series of scandals involving corruption among members of his cabinet, Harding fell ill and unexpectedly died while in San Francisco.

HARDINGE OF LAHORE, Henry Hardinge, 1st Viscount (1785–1856) English soldier and colonial administrator, born in Wrotham, Kent. Twice wounded in the Peninsular War, from 1809 to 1813 he was deputy quartermaster-general of the Portuguese army. After **Napoleon**'s escape from Elba, Hardinge was appointed commissioner at the Prussian headquarters, and lost an arm at Ligny. From 1820 to 1844 he was an MP, secretary of war under **Wellington** (1828–30 and 1841–44) and chief secretary for Ireland (1830 and 1834–35). In 1844 he was appointed governor-general of India. During the 1st Sikh War he was present at the battles of Mudki, Firozshah and Sobraon as second in command to Lord **Gough** and negotiated the peace of Lahore (1845). Returning to England in 1848 he succeeded Wellington as commander-in-chief (1852), but was demoted in 1855 during the Crimean War. His grandson, Charles, 1st Baron Hardinge of Penshurst (1858–1944), was viceroy of India (1910–16), permanent under-secretary for foreign affairs and ambassador in Paris (1920–22).

HARDOUIN, Jean (1646–1729) French classical scholar, born in Quimper. He entered the Jesuit order, and from 1683 was librarian of the Collège de Louis le

Grand in Paris. He maintained that the entire body of classical literature, with very few exceptions, had been written by the monks of the 13th century. He rejected all the reputed remains of ancient art, as well as the Septuagint and the Greek New Testament. His works include an edition of **Pliny, 'the Elder'** (1689), *Collectio Conciliorum* (1715), a commentary on the New Testament, and several volumes on numismatics and chronology.

HARDWICK, Philip (1792–1870) English architect, born in London. Son of the architect Thomas Hardwick (1752–1929), he designed Euston railway station, the hall and library of Lincoln's Inn, Goldsmiths' Hall and Limerick Cathedral.

HARDWICKE, Philip Yorke, 1st Earl of (1690–1764) English judge, the son of a Dover attorney. He became attorney- general (1725), chief justice of the King's Bench (1733) and lord chancellor (1737). He supported Sir **Robert Walpole**, and held office under **Thomas Pelham**, Duke of Newcastle; presided at the trial of the rebel lords in 1745, and promoted the laws that proscribed tartan and abolished heritable jurisdiction in Scotland. His Marriage Act of 1754 abolished Fleet marriages. He did much to settle the doctrine of equity in their modern form and systematize its principles. His son, Philip, 2nd Earl (1720–90) held public offices, wrote *Athenian Letters* and edited *Walpoliana*, and his second son, Charles (1722–70) became lord chancellor, but died three days later.

HARDWICKE, Sir Cedric Webster (1893–1964) English actor, born in Lye, Worcestershire. He served in World War I and made his name in Birmingham repertory company's productions of **Shaw's** plays and in *The Barretts of Wimpole Street* (1934). He also played leading roles in a number of films, including *Dreyfus*, *Things to Come*, *The Winslow Boy*, etc. He was knighted in 1934 and was Cambridge Rede Lecturer in 1936.

HARDY, Alexandre (c.1570–c.1631) French dramatist, born in Paris. His over 500 melodramatic pieces are largely lifted from Spanish authors, but he reduced the role of the chorus in French drama.

HARDY, Sir Alister Clavering (1896–1985) English marine biologist, born in Nottingham. From 1924 to 1928 he served on the *Discovery* expedition in the Antarctic, and in 1928 founded the oceanographic department at Hull University where he was professor of zoology. Later he became professor of zoology and comparative anatomy at Oxford (1946–61). He made quantitative researches into marine plankton and invented the continuous plankton recorder which permitted the detailed study of surface life in the oceans. He also pioneered the study of the diet of the herring.

HARDY, Bert (1913–) English photo-journalist, born in London. He started as a messenger and laboratory assistant in a photographic agency and although self-taught was, in 1938, one of the first to use a Leica 35 mm camera. He was on the staff of *Picture Post* until 1957, except for service as an Army photographer from 1942 to 1946, during which he recorded the horrors of the concentration camps, and his later assignments took him to the Korean and Vietnam Wars. After the closure of *Picture Post* he was in much demand for advertizing until his retirement in 1967. In both war and peace his portrayal of ordinary people was outstanding, and his records of London under the Blitz rank among the finest of the period.

HARDY, Gathorne See **CRANBROOK**

HARDY, Godfrey Harold (1877–1947) English mathematician, born in Cranleigh. Educated at Winchester and Cambridge, he became a fellow of Trinity College in 1900. In 1920 he became Savilian professor at Oxford, but returned to Cambridge as Sadleirian professor (1931–42). He was an internationally important figure in mathematical analysis, and was chiefly responsible for introducing English mathematicians to the great advances in function theory that had been made abroad. In much of his work in analytic number theory, the **Riemann** zeta-function, **Fourier** series and divergent series, he collaborated with **John Littlewood**. He brought the self-taught Indian genius **Srinivasa Ramanujan** to Cambridge and introduced his work to the mathematical world. His mathematical philosophy was described for the layman in his book *A Mathematician's Apology* (1940), in which he claimed that one of the attractions of pure mathematics was its lack of practical use. Cricket was the other great passion of his life.

HARDY, Oliver See **LAUREL, Stan**

HARDY, Sir Thomas Duffus (1804–78) English archivist, born in Port Royal, Jamaica. In 1819 he entered the Record Office in the Tower, and quickly became an expert in reading ancient MSS. His earliest writings—illustrating the reign of King **John**—appeared in *Archaeologia* and the *Excerpta Historica*. In 1861 he became deputy keeper of the Public Records. He edited *Close Rolls*, *Patent Rolls*, *Norman Rolls*, and *Charter Rolls* (1833–44); *William of Malmesbury* (1840); *Catalogue* of lord chancellors, keepers of great seal, etc (1843); *Modus tenendi Parliamentum* (1846); *Syllabus* of Rymer's *Foedera* (1869–85), etc. His brother, Sir William Hardy (1807–87), succeeded him as deputy keeper, edited Jehan de Waurin's *Chroniques et Anchiennes Istories de la Grant Bretaigne* (1864–84), and translated vols, i and ii.

HARDY, Sir Thomas Masterman, (1769–1839) English naval officer, born in Portisham, Dorset. He was closely associated with **Nelson**, whom he served as flag-captain at the battle of Trafalgar (1805). He was First Sea Lord (1830), and from 1834 was governor of Greenwich Hospital. He was promoted vice admiral in 1837.

HARDY, Thomas (1840–1928) English novelist, poet and dramatist, born in Upper Bockhampton, near Dorchester, the son of a stonemason. As a boy he learned to play the fiddle and was bookish. He was educated locally and at 16 was articled to an architect. At 22 he went to London to train as an architect, and returned home in 1867 to pursue his chosen profession, but he had already begun his first novel, *The Poor Man and the Lady*, which was never published. There is speculation that around this time he met and fell in love with Tryphena Sparks, to whom he was related. The nature of their relationship is unclear but in 1868 he was sent to St Juliot, Cornwall, where he met Emma Gifford, whom he married in 1874. By then he had published four novels—*Desperate Remedies* (1871), *Under the Greenwood Tree*, *A Pair of Blue Eyes* (1873), and *Far From the Madding Crowd* (1874). The marriage was not idyllic but, ironically, when Emma died in 1912 Hardy was moved to write some of the most moving love poems in the language. A flood of novels continued to appear, vibrant, brooding descriptive passages providing the backdrop to potent tragi-comedies. Among the most durable are *The Return of the Native* (1878), *The Mayor of Casterbridge* (1886) and *Tess of the D'Urbervilles* (1891). Though Hardy was held in high esteem, critics carped at his seemingly inbred pessimism, and both *Tess* and *Jude the Obscure* (1895) were attacked virulently; thereafter Hardy turned his attention to poetry which he had always regarded as superior to fiction. His first collection, *Wessex Poems*, appeared in 1898; his last, *Winter Words*, in 1928, the year of his death. After Emma's death he married Florence Dugdale and lived in Dorset, much visited by aficionados and the literati. *The Dynasts*, a gargantuan drama in blank verse, occupied him for many years and was published in three instalments between 1904 and 1908. A biography published initially in two parts in 1928 and 1930 is thought to have been largely dictated by Hardy to Florence though it appeared under her name.

HARDYNG, John (1378–c.1465) English chronicler. In 1390 he entered the household of Henry **Percy**, 'Hotspur', whom he saw fall on Shrewsbury Field in 1403. Pardoned for his treason, he became constable of Warkworth Castle, and fought at Agincourt (1415). He served the crown in confidential missions to Scotland. His chronicle, composed in limping stanzas, deals with the history of England from the earliest times down to **Henry VI**'s flight into Scotland. He extended it and presented it to **Edward IV** just after his accession. Its interest lies more in its eye-witness account of the Agincourt campaign than as a historical record or work of poetry. **Richard Grafton** continued it down to **Henry VIII**.

HARE, David (1947–) English dramatist, director and filmmaker, born in Bexhill, and one of the finest playwrights of his generation. He graduated from Cambridge and was active in fringe theatre for many years, co-founding Portable Theatre in 1968 and Joint Stock in 1974. He succeeded **Christopher Hampton** as resident dramatist and literary manager of the Royal Court Theatre, London, 1967–71, and at Nottingham Playhouse in 1973. *Slag* was staged in 1970, *The Great Exhibition* in 1972, and *Knuckle* in 1974, but the best of his early works is *Teeth 'n' Smiles* (1975), a commentary on the state of modern Britain. His plays often have linked films, such as *Plenty* (1978), with the complementary television film *Licking Hitler* (1978) and *The Secret Rapture* (his major play to date) and the complementary political film *Paris by Night* (1989). His other television films are *Dreams of Leaving* (1980), and *Saigon... Year of the Cat* (1983). He wrote and directed his first feature film, *Wetherby*, in 1985.

HARE, Sir John (1844–1921) English comedian and manager, born in Giggleswick in Yorkshire. He acted at the Prince of Wales (1865–74) and co-managed the Court (1874–79). Later he managed the St James's (1879–88) and Garrick (1889–95) theatres. He was knighted in 1907.

HARE, Julius Charles (1795–1855) English theologian, born near Vincenza in Italy. Educated at Charterhouse and Trinity College, Cambridge, he became a fellow in 1818, ordained in 1826, and in 1853 chaplain to the Queen. His annual charge encouraged the study of German theology. Among his works are *Guesses at Truth* (with A W Hare, 1827), *Vindication of Niebuhr's History* (1829), *Victory of Faith* (1840), and others. His *Life* and *Essays and Tales of John Sterling* (1848) prompted **Carlyle**'s corrective biography.

HARE, Robert (1781–1858) American chemist, born in Philadelphia. Professor of chemistry at the University of Pennsylvania (1818–47), he devised an oxyhydrogen blowpipe, and in 1816 the calorimeter and the apparatus for measuring the relative density of liquids. He published *Spiritualism Demonstrated* (1855).

HARE, Robertson (1891–1979) English actor, born in London. He built up his reputation as a comedian in the famous 'Aldwych farces', such as *Thark*, *Plunder*, *Rookery Nook* and *Cuckoo in the Nest*, cast invariably in 'henpecked little man' parts in which his ultimate 'debagging' became proverbial. He also featured in many other stage comedies and films.

HARE, William See **BURKE, William**

HARE, William Henry (Dusty) (1952–) English rugby union player, born in Newark. A Nottinghamshire sheep farmer, he holds the all-time points-scoring record. When he retired in 1989 he had scored more than 7000 points (1800 for Nottingham, 4503 for Leicester, 240 for England, 88 for the British Lions and 596 in other representative matches). His phenomenal accuracy as a place kicker never deserted him through an 18-year career during which he won 23 full caps for England.

HAREWOOD, George Henry Hubert Lascelles, 7th Earl of (1923–) English nobleman and arts patron, the elder son of the Princess Royal, and cousin of Queen **Elizabeth**, born at Harewood near Leeds. Educated at Eton and King's College, Cambridge, he served as captain in the Grenadier Guards in World War II, and was a prisoner of war. Keenly interested in music and drama, he was artistic director of the Edinburgh International Festival (1960-65) and of Leeds Festival from 1958, and Managing Director of English Opera North 1978-81.

HARGRAVE, Lawrence (1850–1915) English-born Australian aeronautical pioneer, born in Greenwich, London. He arrived in Sydney in 1865, and spent five years exploring in New Guinea before, in 1878, being appointed to a post at the Sydney Observatory. He resigned five years later to devote his time to aeronautical experiments. In 1893 he developed the box-kite to produce a wing form used in early aircraft. In November 1894, four tethered kites successfully lifted Hargraves five metres from the ground. His later work on curved wing surfaces presaged the wing shape of the **Wright** brothers' aeroplane of 1903. He also designed a radial rotary engine in 1899, the predecessor of the engine which drove most aircraft in the early days of aviation. His other projects included wave-driven ships and a one-wheel gyroscopic car.

HARGRAVES, Edward Hammond (1815–91) English gold prospector, born in Gosport, Hampshire. He went out as a youth to Australia, then to the Californian gold diggings in 1849. From similarity in geological formation he suspected that gold would be found in Australia also. Finding gold in the Blue Hills, New South Wales, in 1851, he was appointed commissioner of crown lands, and received a government reward of £10000. In 1855, a year after his return to England, he published *Australia and its Goldfields*.

HARGREAVES, James (c.1720–1778) English inventor, born probably in Blackburn, an illiterate weaver and carpenter of Standhill. About 1764 he invented the spinning-jenny, but his fellow spinners broke into his house and destroyed his frame (1768). He removed to Nottingham, where he erected a spinning mill, but his patent proved invalid, as he had disclosed his invention. He continued to manufacture yarn till his death.

HÄRING, Georg Wilhelm Heinrich, pseud **Wilibald Alexis** (1798–1871) German writer, born in Breslau. He wrote the historical romance *Walladmor* (1823–24), professedly as by Sir **Walter Scott**, a fraud that led to its translation into several languages (into English, very freely, by **De Quincey**, 1824). It was followed by *Die Geächteten* (1825), *Schloss Avalon* (1827), and books of travel, sketches and dramas.

HARINGTON, Sir Charles Robert (1897–1972) English chemist, professor of pathological chemistry at University College, London (1931–42), and director of the National Institute of Medical Research (1942–62). He synthesized thyroxine and published *The Thyroid Gland* (1933).

HARINGTON, Sir John (1561–1612) English courtier and writer, born in Kelston near Bath. From Cambridge he went to the court of his godmother, Queen **Elizabeth**. His wit brought him into much favour, which he endangered by the freedom of his satires. In 1599 he served under **Essex** in Ireland, and was knighted by him on the field, much to the queen's displeasure. To strengthen his amazing application to King **James VI and I** for the office of chancellor and archbishop of Ireland he composed in 1605 *A Short View of the State of Ireland*, an interesting and singularly modern essay. He is remembered as the metrical translator of **Ariosto**'s *Orlando Furioso* (1591): his other writings include Rabelaisian pamphlets, epigrams *The Metamorphosis of Ajax* (1596), containing the earliest design for a water closet, and a *Tract on the Succession to the Crown*.

HARIRI, Abu Mohammed al Kasim ibn Ali (1054–1122) Arabic writer, known as 'the silk merchant', born in Basra. As well as works on Arabic grammar and syntax, he wrote *Makamat* (Literary Gatherings), a collection of witty rhymed tales of adventure.

HARLAN, John Marshall (1833–1911) American jurist, born in Boyle County, Kentucky, into a slaveholding family. He graduated from Central College, Kentucky, in 1850, and was admitted to the bar in 1853 after reading law at Transylvania University. He was an unsuccessful candidate for the House of Representatives in 1858, and a presidential elector on the Bell-Everett (Constitutional Union) ticket in 1860. He supported the Union in the Civil War, Kentucky having declared its neutrality, and commanded a volunteer Union regiment, resigning in 1863 to be elected Kentucky attorney-general (re-elected 1865). He practised law from 1867, moved to the Republican party and contested the governorship unsuccessfully in 1871 and 1875. By now a Radical Republican, he supported the successful candidate for party nomination, **Rutherford B Hayes**, who appointed him to a commission to decide between rival state governments in Louisiana and then appointed him to the Supreme Court. He served 34 years (1877–1911), invariably and often solely defending the Thirteenth and Fourteenth Amendments as upholders of black civil rights, specifically (in a minority of one) denouncing the Court's acceptance of 'separate but equal' schools and stating that the Constitution was 'colour-blind'. His grandson, John Marshall Harlan (1899–1971), was also a distinguished jurist, and a Supreme Court judge from 1955 to 1971.

HARLAND, Sir Edward James (1831–96) British shipbuilder, founder in Belfast in 1858 of the firm which became Harland and Wolff, in whose yard have been built many famous Atlantic liners and warships. Gustav William Wolff (1834–1913), his partner from 1860, was born in Hamburg, but learned engineering at Liverpool and Manchester.

HARLEY, Robert, 1st Earl of Oxford (1661–1724) English statesman, born in London. He entered the Inner Temple in 1682, and the House of Commons, as a Whig, in 1689. In 1701 he was elected speaker, and in 1704 also became secretary of state. He soon joined the Tories, however, and was chief minister to Queen **Anne** from 1711 to 1714, when he was dismissed for alleged treasonable acts and sent to the Tower. Two years later he was acquitted by the Peers but spent the remainder of his life in retirement.

HARLOW, Harry Frederick (1905–81) American psychologist, born in Fairfield, Iowa. Educated at Stanford University (PhD 1930), he taught at Wisconsin University (1930–50) and (1952–74), and was director of the Regional Primate Center there from 1961 to 1971. He became research professor at Arizona University in 1974. His two major contributions to psychology both derived from his research on the behaviour of captive monkeys at Wisconsin University, and both constituted a departure from the traditional methods of laboratory investigations of animal behaviour. The first was the discovery and analysis of 'learning sets': he argued that 'learning to learn' a particular type of problem was a much more appropriate index of animal intelligence than any individual test. Secondly, he performed experiments on social development, in which he studied the effects of a number of early manipulations upon an infant monkey's behaviour then and in later life. He also contributed to the growing field of neuropsychology, particularly to the vexed question of the putatively differential effects of brain damage sustained in infancy and in adulthood. He received the National Medal of Science in 1967.

HARLOW, Jean, originally **Harlean Carpentier** (1911–37) American actress, born in Kansas City, Missouri. After attending the Hollywood School for Girls in Los Angeles, she eloped with a local business tycoon at the age of 16 and moved to Los Angeles, where she made her film début in *Moran of the Marines* (1928) and appeared as an extra before being signed to a contract by **Howard Hughes** and featuring in *Hell's Angels* (1930). Roles in *Platinum Blonde* (1931), *Red-Headed Woman* (1932) and *Red Dust* (1932) established her screen image as a fast-talking, wisecracking blonde who gave as good as she got and brazenly flaunted her sexuality. Under contract to M-G-M from 1932 she proved a memorable sparring partner for the studio's top male stars and developed into a deft comedienne in films like *Dinner at Eight* (1933), *Bombshell* (1933) and *Libelled Lady* (1936). Her death at the age of 26 from cerebral oedema followed a life blighted by ill-health and personal problems, including three failed marriages.

HARMENSEN, Jacob See **ARMINIUS, Jacobus**

HARMODIUS (d.514BC) Athenian murderer, who with Aristogeiton in 514 BC murdered **Hipparchus**, younger brother of the 'tyrant' Hippias. They meant to kill Hippias also, but Harmodius was cut down, whilst Aristogeiton, who fled, was taken and executed. Subsequently they were regarded as patriotic martyrs, and received divine honours.

HARMSWORTH, Alfred Charles William, 1st Viscount Northcliffe (1865–1922) Irish journalist and newspaper magnate, born in Chapelizod, County Dublin. One of the pioneers of mass circulation journalism, he was brought up in London and already at school edited the school magazine, complete with gossip column, and during the holidays reported for the local newspaper. Soon after leaving school, he became editor of *Youth* and with his brother **Harold Sydney Harmsworth** (later Lord Rothermere) started *Answers to Correspondents* (1888), a rather flimsy imitation of the famous *Tit Bits*. He founded *Comic Cuts* (1890) under the motto 'amusing without being vulgar' and an imitation *Chips* to discourage further competitors. In 1894 he absorbed the *London Evening News* and sponsored the Jackson Arctic expedition. He also published a number of Sunday magazine papers and in 1896 revolutionized Fleet Street with his *Daily Mail*, with its snappy American-style make-up and news presentation. The brothers Harmsworth also bought up the *Sunday Dispatch* and many provincial papers, in 1903 pioneered the first newspaper for women, the *Daily Mirror*, founded the Amalgamated Press for periodical and popular educational literature and acquired vast forests in Newfoundland for newsprint. In 1908, after secret negotiations, Northcliffe became proprietor of *The Times*, took a gamble by lowering its price to one penny in 1914 to restore its sagging circulation and made its editorial policy a vehicle for his political ambitions. But like **Beaverbrook**, he found that success in journalism was not an asset to the aspiring politician. His controversies with **Lloyd George** raged throughout World War I, and his attack on Lord **Kitchener** in the *Daily Mail* reduced its circulation by nearly 300000. But in 1917 he led a war mission to the USA and in 1918 directed British propaganda. Suffering from ill-health and nervous strain, he made a world tour in 1921 but died soon after his return.

HARMSWORTH, Cecil Bishopp Harmsworth, 1st Baron (1869–1948) British Liberal politician. He was under-secretary at the home office (1912), at the foreign office (1919–22) and minister of blockade. He was created baron in 1939.

HARMSWORTH, Harold Sydney, 1st Viscount Rothermere (1868–1940) Irish newspaper magnate, born in London. He was closely associated with his brother **Alfred Charles William Harmsworth** (Lord Northcliffe), and in addition founded the *Glasgow Daily Record*. In 1910 he established the King Edward chair of English literature at Cambridge and received a baronetcy. He dissociated himself from his brother in 1914 and concentrated on the *Daily Mirror*, which reached a circulation of three million by 1922. He also founded the *Sunday Pictorial* (1915), was air minister (1917–18), and after his brother's death acquired control of the *Daily Mail* and *Sunday Dispatch*.

HARNACK, Adolf von (1851–1930) German theologian, born in Dorpat, son of the Lutheran dogmatic theologian Theodosius Harnack (1817–89). He became a professor at Leipzig (1876), Giessen (1879), Marburg (1886) and Berlin (1889). His writings are on Gnosticism (1873), **Ignatius of Antioch** (1878), Monasticism (2nd ed 1882), the history of dogma, of old Christian literature, and a history of the Berlin Academy. From 1893 the orthodox suspected him of heresy on account of his critism of the Apostles' Creed. From 1905 to 1921 he was keeper of the Royal (later State) Library, Berlin. His brother Otto (1857–1914) was professor of literature and history at Darmstadt, then at Stuttgart, and wrote on **Goethe**, **Schiller**, and **Humboldt**.

HAROLD II (c.1022–1066) king of England, son of Earl **Godwin**. By 1045 he was Earl of East Anglia, and in 1053 succeeded to his father's earldom of Essex. Henceforward he was the right hand of King **Edward the Confessor**, and he directed the affairs of the kingdom with unusual vigour. His brother Tostig became Earl of the Northumbrians in 1055, and two years later two other brothers were raised to earldoms. Meantime Harold drove back the Welsh marauders, and added Herefordshire to his earldom. The death in 1057 of **Edward the Ætheling**, son of **Edmund Ironside**, son and heir of **Edward the Confessor**, opened up the path for Harold's ambitious hopes of the crown. He made a pilgrimage to Rome in 1058, and after his return completed his church at Waltham. In 1063, provoked by the fresh incursions of the Welsh king Gruffyd, he marched against him, traversed the country, beat the enemy at every point, and gave the government to the dead king's brothers. In c.1064 he made a celebrated visit to the court of **William**, Duke of Normandy, when he seems to have made some kind of oath to William. It is, however, certain that Harold helped William in a war with the Bretons. On his return he married Ealdgyth, Gruffyd's widow, though Ealdgyth Swan-neck, who had borne his five children, was still alive. In 1065 the Northumbrians rebelled against Tostig, and Harold acquiesced in his replacement by Morcar and to Tostig's banishment. In January 1066 King Edward died; and Harold, his nominee, was chosen king, and crowned in Westminster Abbey. Duke William lost no time in preparing for the invasion of England, and Tostig, after making overtures to the Normans and the Scots, succeeded in drawing to his side **Harald Hardraade**, king of Norway. In September their army reached the Humber and took York, and Harold marched to meet them. At Stamford Bridge he won a complete victory on 25 September 1066, Tostig and Harald Hardraade being among the slain. But four days later William landed in the south of England at Pevensey. Harold marched southwards with the utmost dispatch, and the two armies met at Senlac, about nine miles from Hastings. On 14 October 1066, from nine in the morning until nightfall, the English fought stubbornly, but the pretended flight of the Normans drew them from their impregnable position and gave the Normans the victory. Harold himself fell, probably pierced through the eye with an arrow. His body was identified by Ealdgyth Swan-neck, and was buried at Waltham.

HAROLD I KNUTSSON, 'Harefoot' (d.1040) king of England from 1037, younger son of **Knut Sveinsson** (Canute the Great) and his English mistress Ælfgifu of Northampton. On Knut's death the English elected Harold Harefoot regent for his half-brother **Hardaknut**, King of Denmark, the legitimate heir to the throne, who could not leave Denmark to claim the crown. In 1037 Harold was elected king, but died in March 1040 just as Hardaknut was poised to invade England.

HARPE, LA See **LA HARPE**

HARPER, Edward (1941–) English composer, born in Taunton. A lecturer in music at Edinburgh University, he directs the New Music Group of Scotland. Early works owed much to serial and aleatoric styles, but with the orchestral *Bartók Games* (1972) and a one-act opera *Fanny Rodin* (1975) he evolved a more tonally-based style. Other works include the operas *Hedda Gabler* (1985), *The Mellstock Quire* (1988), a symphony, concertos, choral works, two string quartets and other chamber and vocal pieces.

HARPER and BROTHERS a firm of New York publishers, consisted originally of James (1795–1869), John (1797–1875), Joseph Wesley (1801–70) and Fletcher (1806–77). James and John began publishing in 1818. The firm of Harper and Brothers, established in 1833, is carried on by descendants, and issues *Harper's Magazine* (monthly since 1850), and other publications.

HARPIGNIES, Henri (1819–1916) French landscape painter, born in Valenciennes. He went to Italy and later became associated with the Barbizon school.

HARRIMAN, William Averell (1891–1986) American statesman. A close friend of President **Franklin Roosevelt**, he was prominent in the National Recovery Administration in 1934. In 1941 he was his special war-aid representative in Britain. In 1943 he was appointed ambassador to the USSR and in 1946 to Britain. He was secretary of commerce (1946–48) and special assistant to President **Truman** (1950–51), helping to organize NATO. From 1951 to 1953 he was director of foreign aid under the Mutual Secutity Act and was governor of New York (1955–58). He was ambassador-at-large (1961) and from 1965 to 1969, and held minor political appointments from 1961 to 1964. In 1968 he was US representative at the Vietnam peace talks in Paris.

HARRINGTON, James (1611–77) English political theorist, born in Upton, Northants. He studied at Trinity College, Oxford, travelled to Rome, and, though a republican, became in 1646 a personal attendant of **Charles I**, and attended him to the scaffold. His semi-romance *Oceana* (1656) sets forth a commonwealth, maintaining that the real basis of power is property, especially landed property, from which no one person should derive more than £3000 a year; and that the rulers should be changed every three years and their successors elected by ballot. In 1661 he was arrested for attempting to change the constitution, and went temporarily insane in prison.

HARRINGTON, Sir John See **HARINGTON**

HARRIOT, or **Hariot, Thomas** (c.1560–1621) English mathematician and scientist, born in Oxford, where he graduated in 1580. In 1584–85 he was mathematical tutor to Sir **Walter Raleigh** and was sent to survey Virginia, on which he published *A Briefe and True Report of the New Found Land of Virginia* (1588). He corresponded with **Johannes Kepler** on astronomical matters, observed **Halley**'s comet in 1607 and made observations with the newly-discovered telescope from 1609, as early as **Galileo**. His map of the moon, and drawings of sunspots and the satellites of Jupiter survive. He studied optics, refraction by prisms, and the formation of rainbows. Most of his work was never published and remains in manuscript, although his *Artis analyticae praxis*, a treatise on algebra, was published posthumously in 1631, showing that he had developed an effective algebraic notation for the solution of equations.

HARRIS, Sir, Arthur Travers, known as **'Bomber Harris'** (1892–1984) English air force officer, born in Cheltenham, Gloucestershire. Educated at Allhallows School, he emigrated to Rhodesia in 1910, and saw active service with the 1st Rhodesian Regiment in SW Africa (1914–15) and with the Royal Flying Corps in France and in defence of London. On the formation of the Royal Air Force (April 1918) he received a permanent commission with the rank of squadron leader. Promoted air commodore in 1937, he commanded No.4 Group Bomber Command (1937–38), and RAF Palestine and Transjordan (1938–39). He was deputy chief of Air Staff (1940–41), and head of the RAF Delegation in the USA (1941). As commander-in-chief Bomber Command RAF (1942–45) he earned the nickname of 'Bomber Harris'. After the war he was managing director of the South African Marine Corporation (1946–53).

HARRIS, Frank (1856–1931) Irish writer and journalist, born, according to his autobiography, in Galway, but according to his own later statement, in Tenby. He ran away to New York at the age of 15, became a bootblack, a labourer building Brooklyn Bridge, and a worker in a Chicago hotel, but in 1874 embarked upon the study of law at the University of Kansas. About 1876 he returned to England and entered the newspaper world. Perhaps the most colourful figure in contemporary journalistic circles, an incorrigible liar, a vociferous boaster, an unscrupulous adventurer and philanderer, with an obsession with sex which got his autobiography *My Life and Loves* (1923–27) banned for pornography, he nevertheless had a considerable impact on Fleet Street as editor of the *Fortnightly Review*, *Saturday Review*, *Vanity Fair* and of the *Evening News*, which became under his aegis a pioneer in the new cult of provocative headlines and suggestive sensationalism. He is also remembered for his *Contemporary Portraits* (1915–30), a series of profiles, interesting but distorted by personal prejudice, as well as lives of **Oscar Wilde** (1920) and **Shaw** (1931), some novels, short stories and plays, and two original but not particularly scholarly works on **Shakespeare**.

HARRIS, George, 1st Baron Harris (1746–1829) English soldier. Educated at Westminster School and Royal Military Academy, he served in Ireland, America and the West Indies, and from 1790 to 1792 fought against **Tippoo Sahib** in India. Made a general in 1794, he won renown and the thanks of parliament as commander-in-chief of the campaign which ended in the victory of Seringapatam and the annexation of Mysore in 1799.

HARRIS, George Robert Canning, 4th Baron Harris (1851–1932) English statesman. Under-secretary for India (1885–86), for war (1886–89) and governor of Bombay (1890–95), he is remembered also as a great figure in the cricket world, an Oxford blue, captain of Kent and of England, and president of the MCC in 1895.

HARRIS, Howel (1714–73) Welsh clergyman, born in Treveca in Brecon, the founder of Welsh Calvinistic Methodism. He became a Methodist preacher in 1735, and in 1752 went back to Trevaca and founded a kind of Protestant monastery, whose members he referred to as the 'family'. His autobiography was published in 1791.

HARRIS, James (1709–80) English scholar, born in Salisbury. He studied at Wadham College, Oxford, and Lincoln's Inn. On his father's death (1733), left master of an ample fortune, he devoted himself to the classics, but in 1761 entered parliament, and in 1763 became a lord of the Admiralty and of the Treasury, in 1764 secretary and comptroller to Queen **Charlotte Sophia**. In 1744 he published *Art and Happinness*; in 1751 *Hermes*, an inquiry into universal grammar. His works were edited by his son, James, 1st Earl of **Malmesbury** (1746–1820).

HARRIS, James Rendel (1852–1941) English Quaker scholar, born in Plymouth. After graduating from Cambridge, where he became fellow of Clare College, he taught New Testament Greek at Johns Hopkins University (1882–85) and at Haverford College (1886–92), and paleography at Cambridge (1892–1903). He was director of studies at the Friends' Settlement at Woodbrooke (1904–18), and then curator of manuscripts at the John Rylands Library, Manchester (1918–25), whence he travelled extensively in the Near and Middle East. His numerous books include *New Testament Autographs* (1882), *Biblical Fragments from Mount Sinai* (1890), *The Guiding Hand of God* (1905), *Leyden Documents Relating to the Pilgrim Fathers* (1920), and *The Migration of Culture* (1936).

HARRIS, Joel Chandler (1848–1908) American author, born in Eatonton, Georgia. He was in turn printer, lawyer, and journalist on the staff of the Atlanta *Constitution* (1876–1900). His *Uncle Remus* (1880) made him internationally famous, at once to children and to students of folklore. Later works are *Nights with Uncle Remus* (1883), *Mingo*, *Daddy Jake*, *Aaron in the Wildwoods*, *Sister Jane*, *Tales of the Home Folks*, *Plantation Pageants*, *Minervy Ann* (1899), and a history of Georgia (1899).

HARRIS, Julie (Julia) (1925–) American actress, born in Michigan. She made her New York début in 1945 as a student at Yale School of Drama, and in 1946 won critical acclaim as a member of the Old Vic New York company for her roles in *Henry IV Part Two* and **Sophocles**' *Oedipus*. She established her reputation as a leading actress with her performance as Frankie Adams in **Carson McCullers**' *The Member of the Wedding* in 1950, following this with an appearance as Sally Bowles in *I am a Camera* in 1951. She played Juliet at

Stratford Ontario in 1960 and Ophelia in **Joseph Papp**'s production of *Hamlet* in New York in 1964. She has appeared since in several notable American plays, and is renowned for her solo performance as **Emily Dickinson** in *The Belle of Amherst* in 1976.

HARRIS, Paul (1868–1947) American lawyer, born in Racine, Wisconsin. He was the founder in 1905 of the Rotary movement in Chicago which began as a young business men's luncheon club and expanded in 1912 into Rotary International, now a worldwide organization dedicated to the maintenance of high standards of service and integrity in commercial and professional life.

HARRIS, Reg (Reginald Hargreaves) (1920–) English track cyclist born in Bury, Lancashire. He came to prominence in 1947 when he won the world amateur sprint championship, and followed this with silver medals in sprint and tandem in the 1948 Olympic Games in London. That same year he turned professional and was world sprint champion from 1949 to 1951 and again in 1954, setting records in the process which stood for 20 years.

HARRIS, Renatus or **René,** known as **'the Elder'** (c.1640–c.1715) French-born British organ builder. He moved to England from France around 1660 with his father, whom he assisted in building organs for Salisbury, Gloucester and Worcester cathedrals. In 1684 he engaged in a contest with his great rival, **Bernard Smith**, over a commission for the Temple Church, London. Both constructed organs, challenging the other to make improvements. In this way the vox humana, cromorna and double bassoon stops were heard for the first time. **Henry Purcell** and **John Blow** performed on Smith's organ, and **Giovanni Draghi** on Harris's; Harris lost the contest. He built 39 organs in all, many for London churches as well as for **James II**'s private chapels, and for several cathedrals including Chichester (1678), Winchester (1681), Bristol (1685) and Hereford (1686), as well as King's College, Cambridge (1686). His two sons were both organ-builders: John (fl.1737) and Renatus the Younger (d.1727).

HARRIS, Rolf (1930–) Australian entertainer and artist, born in Bassendean, Perth, Western Australia. He won a radio 'Amateur Hour' competition at the age of 18, and after graduating from the University of Western Australia, went to London in 1952 where he studied art. While there he performed at the 'Down Under Club' and in 1954 started working for the BBC children's department. He returned to Perth in 1960 to present a children's television programme and then had commercial success with his recordings. He has since appeared widely on stage and television, and has written popular books.

HARRIS, Rosemary (1930–) English actress. She made her début in New York in 1952, and in London a year later, in *The Seven Year Itch*. She appeared with the Bristol Old Vic and the Old Vic in London, before visiting New York again in 1956, this time with the Old Vic Company, as Cressida in **Tyrone Guthrie**'s modern dress version of *Troilus and Cressida*. She appeared in many plays in the USA before returning to Britain, joining the Chichester Festival Theatre for its inaugural 1962 season. She won huge acclaim in London in 1969, playing three characters in **Neil Simon**'s *Plaza Suite*. She has continued to alternate between Britain and America, playing the British and American classics.

HARRIS, Roy (1898–1979) American composer, born in Oklahoma and brought up in California. Until the age of 24, he had no specialized musical training, but studies in Los Angeles led to a Guggenheim Scholarship which enabled him to study in Paris under **Nadia Boulanger**. His music is ruggedly American in character and includes 15 symphonies.

HARRIS, Theodore Wilson (1921–) British novelist, born in New Amsterdam, British Guiana (now Guyana). He was educated at Queen's College, Georgetown and worked as a surveyor. In 1959 he moved to London. One of the pre-eminent Caribbean writers, *The Guyana Quartet* (1960–63) is his masterpiece; starting with a poetic exploration, it evolves into a composite picture of Guyana, its various landscapes and racial communities.

HARRIS, Thomas Lake (1823–1906) English-born American spiritualist, born in Fenny Stratford, Buckinghamshire. At the age of three he was taken to America, and in 1843 became a Universalist pastor. In 1850 he set up as a spiritualistic medium and founded the 'Church of the Good Shepherd' about 1858 on doctrines compounded of **Swedenborg** and **Fourier**. His followers included **Laurence Oliphant**.

HARRISON, Benjamin (1833–1901) 23rd president of the USA, born in North Bend, Ohio, the grandson of **William Henry Harrison**. Benjamin graduated at Miami University, Oxford, Ohio, in 1852, and in 1854 settled as a lawyer in Indianapolis. Entering the Union army in 1862, he was first lieutenant and then colonel of the 70th Regiment Indiana Volunteers. He served in **Sherman**'s Atlanta campaign, distinguishing himself in the battles of Resaca, Peach Tree Creek, and Nashville, and in 1865 he became brevet-brigadier-general. He took an active part in the **Grant** presidential campaigns of 1868 and 1872, and was nominated by the Republicans for the state governship in 1876, but defeated. In 1878 he presided over the State Convention, in 1880 was chairman of his state delegation, and was elected US senator for Indiana. In 1888 he was nominated for president, **Cleveland** being put forward by the Democrats for re-election. Contest turned on protection or free trade, and Harrison's election was a triumph for protection; but in 1892 he was defeated by Cleveland. In 1893 he became a professor at San Francisco.

HARRISON, Frederic (1831–1923) English jurist and philosopher, born in London. Educated at King's College School, London, and Wadham College, Oxford, he became fellow and tutor of his college, but was called to the bar in 1858, and practised conveyancing and in the courts of Equity. He sat on the Royal Commission upon Trade Unions (1867–69), was secretary to the commission for the Digest of the Law (1869–70), professor of jurisprudence and international law at Lincoln's Inn Hall (1877–89), and an alderman, London County Council (1889–93). A Positivist and an advanced Liberal, he wrote *The Meaning of History* (1862), *The Philosophy of Common Sense* (1908), *On Society* (1918) and other works.

HARRISON, George See **BEATLES, The**

HARRISON, Jane Ellen (1850–1928) English classical scholar, born in Cottingham, Yorkshire. Lecturer in classical archaeology at Newnham College, Cambridge (1898–22), her most important works are the *Prolegomena to the Study of Greek Religion* (1903), *Themis, a study of the social origins of Greek Religion* (1912) and *Ancient Art and Ritual* (new ed 1948).

HARRISON, John (1693–1776) English inventor and horologist, born in Foulby, near Pontefract. By 1726 he had constructed a timekeeper with compensating apparatus for correcting errors due to variations of climate. In 1713 the government had offered three prizes for the discovery of a method to determine longitude accurately. After long perseverance he developed a marine chronometer which, in a voyage to Jamaica (1761–62) determined the longitude within 18 geographical miles. After further trials, he was awarded the first prize (1765–73). He also invented the gridiron pendulum (1726), the going fusee, and the remontoir escapement.

HARRISON, Sir Rex, originally **Reginald Carey Harrison** (1908–90) English actor, born in Huyton, Lancashire. On leaving school he joined the Liverpool Playhouse and later toured before making his West End début in *Getting Gertie Married* (1930) and his film début in *The Great Game* (1930). Film and stage roles followed, including his Broadway début in *Sweet Aloes* (1936) and the long-running *French Without Tears* (1936–38). An urbane light-comedian and roguish leading man, his films include *Major Barbara* (1940), *Blithe Spirit* (1945), *Anna and the King of Siam* (1946), *Cleopatra* (1962) and *Dr. Dolittle* (1967). He was first to take the role of Professor Higgins in *My Fair Lady* (1956–58), which he repeated on film in 1964, winning an Academy Award. More recent stage work includes *The Kingfisher* (1978), *Heartbreak House* (1983) and *The Admirable Crichton* (1988). He has been married six times; his autobiography, *Rex*, was published in 1974. He was knighted in 1989.

HARRISON, Ross Granville (1870–1959) American biologist, born in Germantown, Pennsylvania. He was professor of biology at Johns Hopkins (1899–1907) and Yale (1907–38), and introduced the hanging-drop culture method (1907) for the study of living tissues.

HARRISON, Thomas (1606–60) English parliamentary soldier and regicide, born in Newcastle-under-Lyme. He joined the parliamentary army and fought at Edgehill (1642), Marston Moor (1644) and the decisive battle of Naseby (1645). He commanded the guard which took **Charles I** from Hurst Castle to London, sat among his judges, and signed his death warrant (1649). He did good service at Worcester (1951), but was too uncompromising in religion and politics alike to favour **Cromwell**'s tolerant ideas, and was deprived of his commission, and later imprisoned for his share in plots hatched by the more irreconcilable bigots. He refused to go into exile at the Restoration and was executed.

HARRISON, William (1534–93) English topographer and clergyman, born in London. He studied at Cambridge and Oxford, and in 1586 became canon of Windsor. His studies, and his use of **John Leland**'s MSS resulted in his *Description of England*, as well as *Description of Britain*, written for **Holinshed**'s *Chronicles*.

HARRISON, William Henry (1773–1841) 9th president of the USA, grandfather of **Benjamin Harrison**, born in Charles City county, Virginia. Harrison joined the army **Anthony Wayne** led against the Indians, and distinguished himself at the battle on the Miami (1794). When Indiana Territory was formed (1800) he was appointed governor. He attempted to avoid war with the Indians, but was compelled to quell **Tecumseh**'s outbreak, ending in the battle of Tippecanoe (7 November 1811). In the war of 1812–14 he received the command in the northwest, repulsed the British under Proctor, and by the victory of **Oliver Perry** on Lake Erie was enabled to pursue the invaders into Canada, where, on 5 October 1813, he routed them in the battle of the Thames. In 1816 he was elected to congress, and in 1824 became US senator. In 1840 he was elected president by an overwhelming majority, but died in Washington a month after his inauguration on 4 April having caught pneumonia.

HARRISSON, Tom (1911–76) English ethnologist and sociologist. Educated at Harrow and Pembroke College, Cambridge, he was curator of Sarawak museum from 1947, known especially for his exploration and research in Borneo, where he organized guerilla activities against the Japanese invaders in World War II, and for his application of the techniques of social anthropology to the study of British urban communities by 'Mass Observation'. Among his books are *Borneo Jungle* (1938), *Mass Observation* (1937), *Living among Cannibals* (1942), and *World Within* (1959), the last-named describing his war experiences.

HARROD, Sir Henry Roy Forbes (1900–78) English economist, born in London. He was educated at Oxford, where he became a don in 1922. He was Nuffield Professor of International Economics at Oxford from 1952 to 1967. He wrote widely, as a biographer, and on philosophy and logic, besides economics. His major contributions to economic theory are dynamic concepts of conditions of economic growth, particularly the Harrod-Domar model of economic growth. The Polish-born American economist Evsey Domar (1914–) developed a similar insight independently at about the same time.

HARRY, Blind (fl.1470–92) Scottish poet, blind from birth. He lived by telling tales, and from 1490 to 1492 was at the court of **James IV**, receiving occasional small gratuities. His major known work is the *Wallace*, on the life of the Scottish patriot **William Wallace**, written in rhyming couplets. The language is frequently obscure, but the work is written with vigour, and breaks sometimes into poetry. The author seems to have been familiar with the metrical romances, and represents himself as indebted to the Latin Life of Wallace by Master John Blair, Wallace's chaplain, and to another by Sir Thomas Gray, parson of Liberton. The poem transfers to its hero some of the achievements of **Robert the Bruce**, and contains many mistakes or misrepresentations, but much of the narrative can bear the test of historical criticism.

HART, Gary, originally **Hartpence** (1936–) American Democrat politician, born in Ottawa, Kansas. He was educated at Yale University where he became immersed in Democratic party politics, working as a volunteer during **J F Kennedy**'s 1960 presidential campaign. He moved to Denver, Colorado, where he established a law practice and, after managing **George McGovern**'s presidential campaign between 1970 and 1972, entered the US senate in 1974. He acquired a reputation as a 'neo-liberal', seeking to combine social and environmental reform with enhanced economic efficiency. He contested the Democrats' presidential nomination in 1980 and almost defeated the 'party insider', **Walter Mondale**. He retired from the senate in 1986 to concentrate on a bid for the presidency which proved unsuccessful.

HART, Herbert Lionel Adolphus (1907–) English jurist, educated at Cheltenham College and New College, Oxford. He practised at the Chancery bar and taught philosophy at Oxford, becoming professor of jurisprudence (1952–68), and later principal of Brasenose College (1973–78). He wrote extensively, his most significant works including *Causation in the Law* (with AM Honore, 1959), *Law, Liberty and Morality* (1963), *Essays on Bentham* (1982). He also edited some of **Bentham**'s works, notably *Of Laws in General* (1970). Particularly important is his *The Concept of Law* (1961) in which he contends that a defining characteristic of a legal system is that it should include a fundamental rule for the identification of the other rules of the system. Rules of law, he claims, fall into two categories: those which are primary, being prescriptive of behaviour, and those whch are secondary, and which relate to the identification, creation, change and application of the primary rules. This has been a most influential book, widely studied and discussed in English-speaking countries.

HART, Dame Judith Constance Mary, Lady Hart (1924–) English politician, born in Burnley, Lancashire. Educated at the London School of Economics, and a life-time Labour party member, she entered the House of Commons, representing Lanark, in 1959, and joined **Harold Wilson**'s government in 1964, reaching cabinet rank as paymaster-general in 1968. She then had three successful terms as minister of overseas development (1969–70, 1974–75 and 1977–79). She was a popular and influential left -winger, with a strong concern for the needs of Third World countries. She was made a Dame of the British Empire in 1979 and a life peer in 1988.

HART, Moss (1904–61) American dramatist and director, born in the Bronx, New York. In his teens, he worked in a theatrical office, where he wrote his first play, *Beloved Bandit*, and as an actor and a social organizer at summer camps. Many of his satirical plays were written in collaboration, especially with **George S Kaufman**, including *Once in a Lifetime* (1930), *Merrily We Roll Along* (1934), *You Can't Take It With You* (1936), *The Man Who Came to Dinner* (1939), and *George Washington Slept Here* (1940). He wrote books for musicals, including *Lady In The Dark* (1941) with **Kurt Weill** and Ira Gershwin. His own plays include *Winged Victory* (1943), and *Climate of Eden* (1952), and the screenplay for the film *A Star is Born* (1954). He directed many plays and musicals, including *My Fair Lady* (1956), and *Camelot* (1961).

HART, William Surrey (1862/65–1946) American actor and filmmaker, born in Newburgh, New York. An employee of the New York City post office, he studied acting and toured the country with numerous troupes before Broadway successes in *Ben Hur* (1899), *The Squaw Man* (1905) and *The Virginian* (1907–08). He made his film début in *The Fugitive* (1913) and went on to enjoy great popularity in a series of westerns as a mature, solemn-faced defender of truth, justice and the honour of good women. He often devised the original story and directed his moralistic adventures, including *Wild Bill Hickok* (1923), *Singer Jim McKee* (1924) and *Tumbleweeds* (1925). He published several volumes of sagebrush yarns and an autobiography, *My Life East and West* (1929). His last years were spent in retirement on a ranch in California.

HARTE, Francis Brett (1836–1902) American author, born in Albany, New York. He went to California in 1854, and became a compositor in San Francisco. Sketches of his experiences among the miners attracted much attention. He was secretary of the US Mint in San Francisco (1864–70) and during this period wrote some of his most famous poems, among them 'John Burns of Gettysburg' and 'The Society upon the Stanislau'. In 1868 he founded and edited the *Overland Monthly*, to which he contributed, among others, *The Luck of Roaring Camp* and *The Outcasts of Poker Flat* (1870). He was American consul at Krefeld (1878–80) and at Glasgow (1880–85), and then lived in London until his death.

HARTHACNUT See **HARDAKNUT KNUTSSON**

HARTINGTON, Lord See **CAVENDISH, Spencer Compton**

HARTLEY, David (1705–57) English philosopher, physician and psychologist, born in Luddenden, Halifax. Educated at Cambridge, he first studied for the Church but changed direction and became a successful medical practitioner. His *Observations on Man, His Frame, His Duty and His Expectations* (1749) relates psychology closely to physiology and develops a theory of the association of sensations with sets of ideas which forms part of an associationist tradition running from **Hume** through to **J S Mill** and **Herbert Spencer**.

HARTLEY, David (1732–1813) English inventor, son of the philosopher **David Hartley**. He was a fellow of Merton College, Oxford, and MP from 1774 to 1784. With **Benjamin Franklin**, he drafted the Treaty of Paris between Britain and the USA in 1783 that ended the American War of Independence. But his main claim to fame is that he invented a system of fireproofing houses.

HARTLEY, Leslie Poles (1895–1972) English writer, born near Peterborough. His early short stories, *Night Fears* (1924) and *The Killing Bottle* (1932), established his reputation as a master of the macabre. Later he transferred his Jamesian power of 'turning the screw' to psychological relationships and made a new success with such novels as his trilogy *The Shrimp and the Anemone* (1944), *The Sixth Heaven* (1946) and *Eustace and Hilda* (1947), and also *The Boat* (1950)—among his finest work—and *The Go-Between* (1953). Later novels include *A Perfect Woman* (1955), *The Hireling* (1957) and *My Sister's Keeper* (1970).

HARTLEY, Marsden (1877–1943) American painter and writer, one of the pioneers of American modern art, born in Lewiston, Maine. In 1892 he won a scholarship to the Cleveland School of Art and in 1898 moved to New York. He visited France and Germany (1912–15), experimenting with the latest styles. Inspired by **Kandinsky** and **Franz Marc** his work became abstract, and he exhibited with the Blaue Reiter group; but landscapes—especially mountains—always attracted him. He travelled widely in the 1920s and did not settle finally in Maine until 1934.

HARTLIB, Samuel (c.1600–70) German-born English educationist, born in Elbing in Prussia, son of a Polish refugee and an English mother. Coming to England about 1628, he busied himself in trade, in agriculture, and on a school to be conducted on new principles, which inspired his friend **Milton**'s *Tractate on Education* (1644), as well as Sir **William Petty**'s *Two Letters* (1647–48). **Cromwell** gave him a pension. He wrote on education and husbandry, and a Utopian essay, *Macaria* (1641).

HARTLINE, Haldan Keffer (1903–83) American physiologist, born in Bloomsburg, Pennsylavnia. He was educated at Johns Hopkins, taught at Cornell (1931–49) and Johns Hopkins (1949–53), and from 1954 to 1974 was professor of physiology at the Rockefeller University, New York. By the use of very small electrodes applied to cells in the eyes of frogs and crabs, he was able to show how an eye distinguishes shapes; he shared the 1967 Nobel prize for physiology or medicine for his work on the neurophysiology of vision with **George Wald** and **Ragnar Granit**.

HARTLING, Poul (1914–) Danish politician, who represented the Liberal party (*Venstre*). He was Danish foreign minister (1968–71) and prime minister from 1973 to 1975. From 1978 to 1985 he was the UN high commissioner for refugees.

HARTMANN, (Karl Robert) Eduard von (1842–1906) German philosopher, born in Berlin. After service as an artillery officer (1858–65), he settled in Berlin and developed a comprehensive philosophical system, designed to supersede and reconcile all previous systems and sciences, which seems in fact to be an eclectic synthesis from **Hegel**, **Schelling** and **Schopenhauer** and is based on a doctrine of evolutionary history in which the 'unconscious' has a central and creative role. This is set out in his massive work *Die Philosophie des Unbewussten* (Philosophy of the Unconscious, 1869); he also wrote on ethics and aesthetics.

HARTMANN, Nicolai (1882–1950) German philosopher, born in Riga (Latvia). He studied at St Petersburg and Marburg, and was professor successively at Marburg (1920), Cologne (1925), Berlin (1931) and Göttingen (from 1945). He was initially much influenced by **Kant** but came to be sceptical of systematic metaphysics. His main works are *Die Philosophie der Deutschen Idealismus* (1923–29), *Ethik* (1926), *Neue Wege der Ontologie* (1942) and *Philosophie der Natur* (1950), and he was one of Germany's most respected philosophers in the immediate post-war years.

HARTMANN VON AUE (c.1170–1215) German poet of the Middle High German period, who took part in the Crusade of 1197. The most popular of his narrative poems is *Der arme Heinrich*, which, based on a Swabian tradition, is utilized in **Longfellow**'s *Golden Legend*. *Erec* and *Iwein* are both drawn from the Arthurian cycle, and closely follow **Chrétien de Troyes**. In *Gregor vom Steine*, he relates how worldly passion is expiated by religious faith. The songs are mainly love songs.

HARTNELL, Sir Norman (1901–78) English couturier and court dressmaker. Educated at Magdalene College, Cambridge, he started his own business in 1923, receiving the Royal Warrant in 1940. Costumes for leading actresses, wartime 'utility' dresses, the WRAC uniform and Princess **Elizabeth**'s wedding and coronation gowns all formed part of his work. He published his autobiography, *Silver and Gold* in 1955.

HARTNETT, Sir Laurence John (1898–1986) English-born Australian automotive engineer, born in Woking, Surrey. He was head of General Motors' English subsidiary, Vauxhall, and went to Australia in 1934 to take over GM-Holden, formed to take over the company established by Sir **Edward Wheewall Holden** in 1917. His enthusiasm for a locally-built mass production car, despite the opposition of his New York bosses, won over the Australian government. War production intervened and the first 'Holden' car appeared in 1946, by which time Hartnett had resigned from the company to produce his own small car. This project, and a later joint venture with a Japanese motor company, foundered due to government opposition.

HARTREE, Douglas Rayner (1897–1958) English mathematician and physicist, born in Cambridge, where he graduated after working on the science of anti-aircraft gunnery during World War I. From 1929 to 1945 he was professor of applied mathematics and theoretical physics at Manchester, returning to Cambridge as professor of mathematical physics in 1946. His work was mainly on computational methods applied to a wide variety of problems ranging from atomic physics, where he invented the method of the self-consistent field in quantum mechanics, to the automated control of chemical plants. At Manchester he developed the differential analyser, an analogue computer, and was deeply involved in the early days of the electronic digital computer.

HARTSHORNE, Richard (1899–) American geographer, born in Kittanning. Educated at Chicago University, he taught at Minnesota University (1924–40) and at Wisconsin University as professor of geography (1940–70). Following distinguished research in North America in the 1920s and 1930s and in Europe (1938–39) he published what has become a major milestone in the history of geographical ideas, *The Nature of Geography: a critical survey of current thought in the light of the past* (1939). In this he argued for regional geography as the core of a non-theoretical discipline. A retrospective view, *Perspective on the Nature of Geography*, appeared in 1959.

HARTUNG, Hans (1904–89) German-born French artist, born in Leipzig. He studied in Basel, Leipzig, Dresden and Munich; although in his earlier years he was influenced by the German Impressionists and Expressionists, from 1928 onwards he produced mainly abstract work. During World War II he served in the Foreign Legion and gained French citizenship in 1945. His later paintings, which have made him one of the most famous French abstract painters, show a free calligraphy allied to that of Chinese brushwork.

HARTY, Sir (Herbert) Hamilton (1880–1941) Irish composer, conductor and pianist, born in Hillsborough, County Down. He conducted the Hallé (1920–33) and other orchestras. His compositions include an *Irish Symphony*, many songs, and he made well-known arrangements of **Handel**'s *Fireworks* and *Water Music* suites.

HARTZENBUSCH, Juan Eugenio (1806–80) Spanish dramatic poet, born in Madrid. He was director of the national library (1862), and wrote mostly plays, of which the medieval *The Lovers of Teruel* (1837) is the best.

HĀRŪN AL-RASCHĪD (766–809) fifth Abbasid caliph, known to posterity especially from the *Arabian Nights*. He came to the throne on the death of his brother al-Hādī with the help of the influential Barmakid family which he permitted to dominate his early reign, but gradually removed from power. He was a great patron of the arts, enthusiastic in waging war against the Byzantines, but less interested in the detail of central government, he weakened the empire through his attempts to divide it among his three sons.

HARVARD, John (1607–38) English-born American colonial clergyman, born in Southwark. He studied at Emmanuel College, Cambridge, and in 1637, having married, went out to Charlestown, Massachusetts, where he preached a while, but soon died of consumption. He bequeathed £779 and over 300 volumes to the newly-founded college at Cambridge that was later named in his honour.

HARVEY-JONES, Sir John Henry (1924–) English industrial executive, born in Kent. He was educated at Dartmouth and served in the navy until 1956, when he joined ICI. As chairman (1982–87) he was largely responsible for reshaping the company.

HARVEY, David (1935–) English geographer, born in Gillingham, Kent, and educated at St John's College, Cambridge. Following various research and teaching posts, including Lund (with **Hägherstrand**, 1960–61), Pennsylvania State (1965–66) and Johns Hopkins (1966–69), he was appointed Halford Mackinder professor of geography at Oxford in 1987. He was a founder member of the so-called 'positivist' school, and his book, *Explanation in Geography* (1969), was regarded by adherents of that school as the fundamental reference. He has subsequently become one of its major critics, and his advocacy of 'radical' geography (in which the subject is viewed as a tool of social revolution) crystallized in his book *Social Justice and the City* (1973). His other works include *The Limits to Capital* (1982), *The Urbanisation of Capital* (1985) and *Consciousness and the Urban Experience* (1985).

HARVEY, Gabriel (c.1550–1630) English poet, born in Saffron Walden, the son of a rope-maker. Educated at Christ Church, Cambridge, he became a fellow of Pembroke Hall. Although he was cantankerous and arrogant, he became **Spenser**'s friend. He published some satirical verses in 1579, and attacked both **Robert Greene** and **Thomas Nashe**. He claimed to be the father of the English hexameter.

HARVEY, Sir George (1806–76) Scottish painter, born in St Ninians near Stirling. He settled in Edinburgh in 1823, and studied at the Trustees' Academy. He painted celebrated pictures like *The*

Covenanters' Covenant, *The Curlers*, *Battle of Drumclog*, *A Highland Funeral*, and *Bunyan in Bedford Gaol*.

HARVEY, Sir John Martin (1863–1944) English actor-manager. He intended to follow in his father's footsteps as a naval architect, but soon developed a preference for the stage and from 1882 to 1896 he was with **Irving** at the Lyceum. He also toured the provinces in **Shakespeare**, and in 1899 under his own management produced at the Lyceum *The Only Way*, adapted from *A Tale of Two Cities*, in which he played Sydney Carton, his most successful role. He became world-famous as a romantic actor and manager. He married Angelita da Silva, who was his leading lady for many years.

HARVEY, (Robert) Neil (1928–) Australian cricketer, born in Melbourne. One of the great left-handed batsmen, he made four Test tours of England, making a century in his first Test, at Headingley in 1948, while only 19 years old. In all Test cricket he scored 6149 runs and 21 centuries, and with C C McDonald he holds the record for an Australian third wicket Test partnership with an unbroken 295 against West Indies at Kingston in 1954–55.

HARVEY, William (1578–1657) English physician, and discoverer of the circulation of the blood, born in Folkestone. He went to school at King's School, Canterbury, and studied medicine at Caius College, Cambridge, and at Padua, under **Hieronymus Fabricius**. In 1602 he set up practice as a physician in London. In 1609 he was appointed physician to St Bartholomew's Hospital, and in 1615 Lumleian lecturer at the College of Physicians. In 1628 he published his celebrated treatise, *Exercitatio Anatomica de Motu Cordis et Sanguinis*, in which he expounded his views of the circulation of the blood. Successively physician to **James I** and **Charles I**, he accompanied the Earl of **Arundel** in his embassy to the emperor in 1636, and publicly demonstrated his theory at Nuremberg. He was present at the battle of Edgehill in 1642 in attendance on Charles I, then accompanied the king to Oxford, as warden of Merton College. On the surrender of Oxford to the parliamentary forces in July 1646, he returned to London. His book on animal reproduction *Exercitationes de Generatione Animalium*, appeared in 1651. He was buried at Hempstead near Saffron Walden, and in 1833 reburied in the Harvey Chapel there. Harvey's works in Latin were published in 1766; a translation by Dr Willis appeared in 1847.

HARVEY, William Henry (1811–66) Irish botanist, born in Limerick of Quaker parents. He was colonial treasurer at Cape Town (1836–42), where he made a large herbarium collection of South African plants. He published *Genera of South African Plants* (1838) and *Manual of British Algae* (1840) before his appointment as keeper of the Herbarium, Trinity College, Dublin. He travelled extensively, to Ceylon, Australia, Fiji etc, between 1853 and 1856, to collect seaweeds, and was the author of important works on them.

HARWOOD, Harold Marsh (1874–1959) English dramatist, born in Eccles, Lancashire. He served as an army physician during World War I, and married in 1918 Fryn Tennyson Jesse, the author with whom he collaborated on many light plays. He was best known for his political play, *The Grain of Mustard Seed* (1920). He managed the Ambassadors Theatre, London (1920–32).

HARWOOD, Sir Henry (1888–1959) English naval commander. As commander of the South American division, he commanded the British ships at the battle of the River Plate in which the German pocket battleship *Graf Spee* was sunk in December 1939. He was commander-in-chief of the Mediterranean fleet in 1942.

HASDRUBAL name of several Carthaginian soldiers, including a son-in-law (murdered 221 BC), and a son (killed at the Metaurus, 207 BC) of **Hamilcar**.

HASDRUBAL (d.221) Carthaginian general, son-in-law of **Hamilcar**, whom he succeeded as commander in Spain in 229. He extended the Carthaginian empire in Spain to the boundary of the river Ebro, and founded Cartagena. He was murdered by a Celtic slave, and succeeded by **Hannibal**.

HASDRUBAL (BARCA) (d.207) Carthaginian general, son of **Hamilcar** and brother of **Hannibal**. He was left in command of the Carthaginian army in 218 when Hannibal invaded Italy at the start of the 2nd Punic War. From 218 to 208 he fought successfully against the Roman general **Publius Cornelius Scipio** and his son Gnaeus Scipio Africanus. In 207 he marched across the Alps to Italy to bring help to his brother, but was intercepted at the river Metaurus and killed.

HAŠEK, Jaroslav (1883–1923) Czechoslovakian novelist and short-story writer, born in Bohemia. A compulsive and accomplished hoaxer and practical joker who despised pomposity and authority, he is best known for the novel *The Good Soldier Schweyk*, a brilliantly incisive satire on military life. The character of Schweyk, an irresponsible and undisciplined drunkard, liar, scrounger and Philistine, is widely thought to be at least partly autobiographical in inspiration. In 1915 he deserted the Austrian Army (Austria ruled Czechoslovakia at the time) and crossed over to the Russian side. Characteristically, however, he managed to make satirical attacks on both régimes.

HASELRIG, Sir Arthur (d.1661) English parliamentarian, one of the Five Members (see **John Hampden**). He sat in the Long and Short Parliaments for his native county, Leicestershire, commanded a parliamentary regiment of cuirassiers, and in 1647 became governor of Newcastle. In 1660 he half acquiesced in the Restoration, but died a prisoner in the Tower.

HASENCLEVER, Walter (1890–1940) German dramatist and poet, born in Aachen. He wrote the lyrical poems *Der Jüngling* (1913) and *Tod und Auferstehung* (1916), and pioneered German Expressionism with his father-son drama *Der Sohn* (1914). *Ein besserer Herr* (1927) is one of his comedies. A pacifist, he committed suicide in a French internment camp.

HASLUCK, Sir Paul Meernaa Caedwalla (1905–) Australian statesman and historian, born in Freemantle, Western Australia. Educated at the University of Western Australia, he was seconded during World War II to the Australian department of external affairs, becoming head of the Australian mission to the United Nations from which position he resigned in 1947. He returned to the university as reader, before winning a seat in the House of Representatives in 1949. Minister for territories (1951–63), for defence (1963–64), and for external affairs (1964–69), he was defeated in his bid for the leadership of his party and his country after the drowning of **Harold Holt**, but was nominated by the successful **John Gorton** as governor-general of Australia, a position which he filled with distinction from 1969 to 1974. As an historian, he has published a number of major studies on Australia's colour problem, foreign affairs, and welfare, as well as his two-volume *The Government and the People* in the Australian Official War History.

HASSALL, John (1868–1948) English artist and cartoonist, born in Walmer, Kent. He studied art at

Antwerp and Paris, and in 1895 entered the advertising field, becoming the acknowledged pioneer of modern poster design. Among railway posters, his 'Skegness is so bracing' holds the record for longevity and ubiquity. He also illustrated children's books and drew cartoons for many magazines.

HASSAN II (1929–) king of Morocco, born in Rabat, the eldest son of Sultan Mulay Mohammed Bin Yusuf, who was proclaimed king as Mohammed V in 1957. Educated in France at Bordeaux University, Crown Prince Hassan served his father as head of the army and, on his accession as king in 1961, also became prime minister. He suspended parliament and established a royal dictatorship in 1965 after riots in Casablanca. Despite constitutional reforms in 1970 and 1972, he retained supreme religious and political authority. His forces occupied Spanish (Western) Sahara in 1957. He mobilized a large army to check the incursion of Polisario guerrillas across his western Saharan frontier from 1976 to 1988. Unrest in the larger towns led Hassan to appoint a coalition 'government of national unity' under a civilian prime minister in 1984.

HASSE, Johann Adolf (1699–1783) German composer, born near Hamburg. He became famous as 'Il Sassone' through his opera *Sesostrate* (Naples 1725); he was kapellmeister at Dresden, and in 1733 was brought to London to head an Italian opposition to **Handel**. Here *Artaserse* was produced with success, but Hasse soon returned to Dresden, and retired to Vienna and Venice. He married the Venetian singer, Faustina Bordoni (1700-81). In all he produced 70 stageworks, about 100 cantatas and countless other vocal works.

HASSELL, Odd (1897–) Norwegian physical chemist, born in Oslo. Educated there and in Berlin, he spent his career in Oslo, as professor of chemistry from 1934. In 1943, and independently of Sir **Derek Barton**, he developed the basic ideas of chemical conformational analysis, for which he shared with Barton the Nobel prize for chemistry in 1969.

HASSLER, Hans Leo (1562–1612) German composer, born in Nuremberg. He studied under **Andrea Gabrieli** in Venice, and after 1595 was organist at Augsburg, Ulm and Dresden, as well as in his native city. He wrote choral, chamber and keyboard works, often strongly redolent of the Venetian school.

HASTINGS, Francis Rawdon-Hastings, 1st Marquis of (1754–1826) English soldier and colonial administrator, governor-general of Bengal, born in Dublin, and educated at Harrow. He fought with distinction in the American War of Independence (1775–81), in 1794 led reinforcements to Frederick, Duke of **York** at Malines, became active in politics, and in 1813 was made governor-general of India. Here he warred successfully against the Gurkhas (1814–16) and the Pindaris and Mahrattas (1817–18), purchased Singapore island (1819), encouraged Indian education and the freedom of the press, reformed the law system, and elevated the civil service; but in 1821 he resigned after apparently unfounded charges of corruption had been made against him, and from 1824 till his death off Naples he was governor of Malta.

HASTINGS, James (1852–1922) Scottish clergyman and editor, born in Huntly. Educated at the University and Free Church College, Aberdeen, he became minister at Kinneff (1884), Dundee (1897) and St Cyrus (1901–11). He founded the *Expository Times* (1889), and compiled Bible dictionaries and the notable *Encyclopaedia of Religion and Ethics* (12 vols, 1908–21).

HASTINGS, Sir Patrick (1880–1952) English lawyer. He served in the Boer War, was called to the bar in 1904, and became a KC in 1919. He made a great reputation in criminal cases, notably the trials for murder of Vaquier (1924) and Rouse (1931). MP for Wallsend (1922-26), he was attorney-general in the 1924 Labour government. He also wrote plays, of which *Scotch Mist* (1926) and *The Blind Goddess* (1947), were successfully staged in London.

HASTINGS, Warren (1732–1818) English administrator in India, born in Churchill, Oxfordshire. Educated at Westminster, in 1750 he went out to Calcutta as a writer in the service of the East India Company, was British resident at Murshidabad (1758–61) and then a member of council at Calcutta. He came home in 1764, in 1769 returned to India as second in council at Madras, and in 1772 became governor of Bengal and president of the council. A year later he was created governor-general, with a council of four members, three appointed from home. The majority in council led by Sir **Philip Francis** was opposed to Hastings from the first; the finances were in disorder. One of Hastings' first tasks was to bring to trial the two chief fiscal ministers of Bengal on charges of embezzlement; but the case broke down. A corrupt official, Nuncomar (Nand Kumar), who had been employed in conducting it, and who had subsequently brought charges of corruption against Hastings, in 1775 was tried and executed on an old charge of forgery, a proceeding which threw obloquy on Hastings and on the chief justice, Sir **Elijah Impey**. Hastings made an appraisement of the landed estates, revised the assessment, improved the administration of justice, organized the opium revenue, waged vigorous war with the Mahrattas, and made the Company's power paramount in many parts of India. In 1777 an attempt was made to depose him, which was only frustrated by the action of the Supreme Court; that same year, his first wife having died 18 years before, he married the divorced wife of Baron Imhoff, a German officer. In 1780 he was freed from embarrassment in the council by the retirement of Philip Francis, whom he wounded in a duel; he himself resigned office in 1784 and sailed for England, where he soon became subject to a parliamentary inquiry with a view to impeachment. Among the charges preferred against him by the Whig opposition were the aid given to the Nawáb of Oudh against the Rohilla Afghans, his punishment of the Zemindar of Benares for noncompliance with a demand for aid in the first Mahratta war, and his connivance in the forfeiture of property belonging to the Begums or dowager-princesses of Oudh. On these grounds he was impeached at the bar of the House of Lords, and the trial began on 13 February 1788, in Westminster Hall, among the managers for the Commons being **Edmund Burke**, **Charles Fox**, **Richard Sheridan**, the future Lord **Minto** and **Charles Grey**. It occupied more than seven years and 145 sittings. Finally, on 23 April 1795, Hastings was acquitted on all the charges, unanimously on all that affected his personal honour. But he left the court a ruined man, the £80000 that he brought from India having been all but consumed in expenses. The East India Company, however, made generous provision for his declining years; and, at the ancestral seat of Daylesford, Worcestershire, which in 1788 he had bought back in pursuance of his boyhood's ambition, he passed the rest of his life as a country gentleman.

HATCH, Edwin (1835–89) English theologian, born in Derby. He became professor of classics at Toronto (1859–62), vice-principal of St Mary Hall, Oxford (1867–85) and reader in ecclesiastical history at Oxford (1884). His Bampton Lectures (1880), on *The Organisation of the Early Christian Churches*, were hostile to High Church claims and established his reputation in England and Germany. Besides theological works he published a collection of religious poetry.

HATHAWAY, Anne See **SHAKESPEARE, William**

HATRY, Clarence Charles (1888–1965) English forger. He established himself as an insurance broker in 1911 and went on to register several companies, including his Commercial Bank of London in 1920. A committed gambler, he frequently sustained huge losses. In 1929 one of his companies, Corporation and General Securities, failed in its attempt to take over United Steel. This led to substantial losses for his investors, and he was prosecuted. He confessed to forgery and was sentenced in 1930 to 14 years of penal servitude. He was released in 1939. Despite his past record, he continued to operate as a financier until his death.

HATSHEPSUT (?1540–?1481BC) queen of Egypt of the 18th dynasty. She was the daughter of Tuthmosis I who associated her with him on the throne (or was forced to do so), since she was the only one of the family of royal birth, and married her to Tuthmosis II, his son by another wife. On Tuthmosis II's accession in 1516, she became the real ruler; and, on his death in 1503, she acted as regent for her nephew, Tuthmosis III. Pursuing a peaceful policy, thereby perhaps endangering Egypt's Asian possessions, she built up the economy of the country. She opened the turquoise mines at the Wadi Maghareh, built the great mortuary temple at Deir-el-Bahri, sent a marine expedition to Punt (Somaliland?), and erected (1485) two obelisks at Karnak. The fiction was maintained that she was a male ruler, and she is represented with a beard.

HATTERSLEY, Roy Sydney George (1932–) English Labour politician. Educated at Hull University, he was a journalist and Health Service executive as well as a member of Sheffield City Council before first becoming a Labour MP in 1964. A supporter of Britain's membership of the EEC, he was minister of state at the foreign office for two years, then secretary of state for prices and consumer protection in the **Callaghan** government (1976–79). He has since been opposition spokesman on the environment and on home affairs. Regarded as being on the 'right wing' of the party, Hattersley was elected Deputy Leader of the Labour party in 1983, constituting, with **Neil Kinnock** as leader, Labour's 'dream ticket'. Both were convincingly re-elected in 1988. He is a regular contributor to newspapers and periodicals.

HATTON, Sir Christopher (1540–91) English courtier, born in Holdenby in Northamptonshire. From Oxford he proceeded to the Inner Temple, and by 1564 had won the favour of Queen **Elizabeth** by his dancing. He entered parliament, and in 1587 was appointed Lord Chancellor.

HATTON, John Liptrot (1809–86) English composer, born in Liverpool. Settling in London in 1832, he soon made his name as a composer of numerous operas, cantatas, overtures and entr'actes, but is remembered chiefly for his songs, such as 'Good-bye, Sweetheart', 'To Anthea', and 'Simon the Cellarer'.

HAUCH, Johannes Carsten (1790–1872) Danish writer, born in Fredrikshald (Halden). He was lecturer in natural sciences at Sorø (1824–46), and in 1846 was appointed professor of northern literature at Kiel. The Holstein revolution (1848) drove him to Copenhagen, where he became professor of aesthetics. He wrote historical tragedies, lyrical poems, tales and romances.

HAUFF, Wilhelm (1802–27) German novelist, born in Stuttgart. He studied at Tübingen, was a tutor, then editor of a paper. His fairy tales and short stories are admirable for their simplicity and playful fancy—*Die Bettlerin vom Pont des Arts* and *Phantasien im Bremer Ratskeller* in particular. *Lichtenstein* is an imitation of **Scott**.

HAUGHEY, Charles James (1925–) Irish politician. Educated at University College, Dublin, he was called to the Irish bar in 1949. A former chartered accountant, Haughey has been a Fianna Fáil MP since 1957, and he is a former minister of justice, agriculture, and finance. In 1970 he was dismissed from the ministry because of a political disagreement with the prime minister **Jack Lynch**, and he was subsequently tried and acquitted on a charge of conspiracy illegally to import arms. He succeeded Lynch as PM in 1979 and leader of Fianna Fáil and governed for two years. Haughey again came to power in 1982 but was defeated nine months later on a motion of confidence proposed by Haughey. In February 1987 Haughey was re-elected for another term.

HAUKE, von See **BATTENBERG** family

HAUKSBEE, Francis See **HAWKSBEE**

HAUPTMAN, Herbert Aaron (1917–) American mathematical physicist, born in New York City. Educated at the City College of New York and Maryland University, he worked in the US Naval Research Laboratories in Washington until 1970, and afterwards at the Medical Foundation of Buffalo Inc. With **Jerome Karle** he devised novel direct methods for computing molecular structures from X-ray crystal diffraction data; the major advances made led to them sharing the Nobel prize for chemistry in 1985.

HAUPTMANN, Gerhart (1862–1946) German dramatist and novelist, born in Obersalzbrunn, Silesia. He studied sculpture in Breslau and Rome before settling down in Berlin in 1885. His first play, *Vor Sonnenaufgang* (Before Sunrise, 1889), introduced the new social drama of **Ibsen**, **Zola** and **Strindberg** to Germany, but Hauptmann alleviated the extreme naturalism with a note of compassion. *Einsame Menschen* (Lonely People, 1891), for example, in which a man is torn between his love for two women, a young girl student and his plain, self-effacing wife, portrays the latter, not the former, as the heroine. *Die Weber* (1892) deals with the broader setting of the Silesian weavers' revolt of 1844 and introduces a new theatrical phenomenon, the collective hero. *Florian Gayer*, an historical play, marks a transition to a strange mixture of fantasy and naturalism maintained in other such outstanding works as *Hanneles Himmelfahrt* (Little Hanne's Journey to Heaven, 1893), *Die Versunkene Glocke* (The Submerged Bell, 1896), *Fuhrmann Herschel* (1899), and *Rose Bernd* (1903). His later plays in a variety of styles offer no advance, although the comedies *Der Biberpelz* (The Beaverskin, 1893), and *Der rote Hahn* (The Red Cock, 1901), were later adapted and revised by **Brecht** to suit the East German Communist censorship. His novels include *Der Narr im Christo: Emmanuel Quint* (The Fool in Christ: Emmanuel Quint, 1910), and *Atlantis* (1912). He was awarded the Nobel prize for literature in 1912.

HAUSDORFF, Felix (1868–1942) German mathematician, born in Breslau. He studied at Leipzig and Berlin, and taught at Leipzig (1896–1910). In 1910 he moved to Bonn, where he stayed until, as a Jew, he was forced by the Nazis to resign his chair in 1935; ultimately he committed suicide with his family to avoid the concentration camps. He is regarded as the founder of point set topology, and his book *Grundzüge der Mengenlehre* (1914) introduced the basic concepts of topological spaces and metric spaces which have since become part of the standard equipment of analysis and topology. His work on set theory continued that of **Georg Cantor** and **Ernst Zermelo**.

HAUSER, Gayelord (Helmut Eugene Benjamin Gellert) (1895–1984) German-born American popular nutritionist. He emigrated to the USA after World War I and set up business in California in 1927 advocating special vegetable diets featuring 'wonder foods' like brewer's yeast, skim milk, wheat germ and blackstrap molasses. He made a fortune with best-selling books such as *Look Younger, Live Longer* (1950) and *Be Happier, be Healthier* (1952).

HAUSER, Kaspar (?1812–1833) German foundling, the 'wild boy', was found in the marketplace of Nuremberg on 26 May 1828. Though apparently 16 years old, his mind was a blank, his behaviour that of a little child. Afterwards he was able to give some account of himself. So long as he could remember he had been in a hole; he was attended by a 'man', who had at last taught him to stand and walk, and who had brought him to the place where he was found. At first he showed a wonderful quickness of apprehension, but his moral character began to deteriorate, and he was being gradually forgotten, when on 14 December 1833, he was found with a wound in the side, dealt he said, by 'the man'. Three days later he died. Many have regarded him as an imposter who committed suicide: others, as of noble birth and the victim of a hideous crime.

HAUSSMANN, Georges Eugène (1809–91) French financier and town-planner, born in Paris. He entered the public service, and under **Napoleon III** became prefect of the Seine (1853). He then began his task of improving Paris by widening streets, laying out boulevards and parks, building bridges, etc. For these services he was made baron and senator; but the heavy tax burden laid upon the citizens led to his dismissal in 1870. In 1871 he was appointed director of the *Crédit Mobilier*, and in 1881 was elected to the Chamber of Deputies. He died in comparative poverty.

HAÜY, René Just (1743–1822) French mineralogist, born in St Just, dep Oise. He discovered the geometrical law of crystallization. His brother Valentin (1746–1822) devoted his life to the education of the blind.

HAVEL, Vaclav (1936) Czech dramatist and statesman, born in Prague where he was educated at the Academy of Dramatic Art. He began work as a stagehand at the Prague 'Theatre on the Balustrade', becoming resident writer there from 1960 to 1969. His work includes *Zahradni Slavnost* (The Garden Party, 1963), *Spiklenci* (The Conspirators, 1970) and *Temptation* (1987). Deemed subversive, he was frequently arrested, and in 1979 was imprisoned for four and a half years. He was again imprisoned in February 1989, but was released three months later. In December 1989, after the overthrow of the Czechoslovakian Communist party, he was elected president by direct popular vote.

HAVELOCK, Sir Henry (1795–1857) English soldier, born in Bishop-Wearmouth, Sunderland. He was educated at Charterhouse and the Middle Temple, but entered the army a month after Waterloo, and went out to India in 1823, his interest in religion being stimulated during the voyage. He distinguished himself in the Afghan and Sikh wars, and in 1856 commanded a division in Persia. On the outbreak of the Indian mutiny he organized a column of a 1000 Higlanders and others at Allahabad with which to relieve Cawnpore and Lucknow, engaged and broke the rebels at Fatehpur, and, driving them before him, entered Cawnpore. Next crossing the Ganges, he fought eight victorious battles, but through sickness in his little army had to retire to Cawnpore. In September **Outram** arrived with reinforcements, and Havelock again advanced, Outram waiving his superior rank, and serving under Havelock as a volunteer. The relieving force engaged the enemy at the Alum Bagh, three miles from Lucknow; they next fought their way to the Residency, where they in turn were besieged until November when Sir **Colin Campbell** forced his way to their rescue. A week after the relief Havelock, now a KCB, died of dysentry. The rank of a baronet's widow and a pension were given to his widow, daughter of the Baptist missionary Dr Marshman, whose church Havelock joined in 1829. The baronetcy was conferred on his son, Sir Henry Havelock Allan, VC (1830–97), who from 1874 was a Liberal and Unionist MP for Sunderland and SE Durham, took the name Allan in 1880, and was killed by Afridis in the Khyber Pass.

HAVERGAL, William Henry (1793–1870) English hymn writer, born in High Wycombe, Buckinghamshire. He took holy orders at Oxford, and composed hymn tunes, chants and songs, and wrote *History of the Old 100th tune*. He also published sermons and pamphlets.

HAVERS, Robert Michael Oldfield, Baron Havers (1923–) English lawyer and politician. Educated at Westminster School and Cambridge, he saw wartime service in the Royal Navy, was called to the bar in 1948 and made a QC in 1964. He enjoyed a successful career as advocate and judge before entering the House of Commons, as Conservative member for Wimbledon, in 1970. He was solicitor-general under **Edward Heath** (1972–74) and attorney-general under **Margaret Thatcher** (1979–87). He was made a life peer in 1987 and then had a brief period as lord chancellor before retiring, after a mild heart attack, in 1988.

HAVILLAND, Geoffrey de See **DE HAVILLAND**

HAVLICEK, John (1940–) American professional basketball player, born in Lansing, Ohio. He joined the Boston Celtics in the National Basketball Association after graduating from Ohio State University. During his career with Boston he played in eight NBA championship teams, averaging 20.8 points per game. He stayed with Boston from 1963 to 1978 and was voted Most Valuable Player in the NBA in 1974.

HAWES, Stephen (c.1475–1525) English allegorical poet, born probably in Aldeburgh, Suffolk. He was attached to the court from 1502 as groom of the chamber to **Henry VII**. His chief work is the allegory, *The Passetyme of Pleasure* (1509), dedicated to the king. He also wrote *The Example of Virtue* (1504).

HAWKE, Edward Hawke, 1st Baron (1705–81) English naval commander, born in London. He entered the navy in 1720, and by 1747 was a rear admiral of the white; in that year he defeated a French squadron guarding a convoy from La Rochelle off Cape Finisterre. In the Anglo-French Seven Years' War of 1756–63, he destroyed the French fleet in Quiberon Bay in November, 1759, thus preventing an invasion of Britain. He was First Lord of the Admiralty from 1766 to 1771, and Admiral of the Fleet in 1768.

HAWKE, Robert James Lee (1929–) Australian trade union executive and politician, prime minister since March 1983. Born in Bordertown, South Australia, he was educated at the University of Western Australia and Brasenose College, Oxford (Rhodes Scholar 1953). He worked for the Australian Council of Trade Unions for over 20 years (President, 1970–80) before becoming an MP in 1980. His Labor party defeated the ruling Liberals in the 1983 general election only one month after adopting him as leader. In the 1987 general election the Labor party narrowly increased its majority in the House of Representatives although it failed to control the senate. Frequently described as a colourful figure, he is a skilled orator who has won praise for his handling and settling of industrial disputes.

HAWKER, Robert Stephen (1803–75) English poet, born in Plymouth. He was educated at Pembroke College, Oxford, and won the Newdigate prize for poetry in 1827. In 1834 he became vicar of Morwenstow, on the Cornish coast, where he shared many of the superstitions of his people as to apparitions and the evil eye. His poetry includes *Tendrils* (1821), the Cornish ballads in *Records of the Western Shore* (1832–36), *Reeds Shaken with the Wind* (1843), *The Quest of the Sangraal* (1864). His best-known ballad is *The Song of the Western Men*, with its refrain 'And shall Trelawny die?', based on an old Cornish refrain. Twelve hours before his death he was admitted to the Roman Catholic Communion.

HAWKESWORTH, John (c.1715–1773) English author, born in London. In 1744 he succeeded Dr **Johnson** on the *Gentleman's Magazine*. In 1752 he started, with Johnson and others, *The Adventurer*, half of whose 140 numbers were from Hawkesworth's pen. He published a volume of fairy tales (1761), wrote a play, *Edgar and Emmeline* (1761), edited **Swift**, and prepared the account of Captain **Cook**'s first voyage, which formed volumes ii–iii of Hawkesworth's *Voyages* (3 vols, 1773).

HAWKING, Stephen William (1942–) English theoretical physicist, born in Oxford. He studied at Oxford and at Cambridge, where he was appointed Lucasian professor of mathematics in 1979. His early research on relativity led him to study gravitational singularities such as the 'big bang' when the universe originated, and the 'black holes' where space-time is curved. The theory of black holes, which result from the death of stars, owes much to his mathematical work. His book *A Brief History of Time* (1988) is a notably successful popular account of modern cosmology. His achievements are especially remarkable because from the 1960s he has suffered from a highly disabling and progressive neuromotor disease.

HAWKINS, Sir Anthony Hope See **HOPE, Anthony**

HAWKINS, Coleman (1904–69) American tenor saxophonist, born in St Joseph, Missouri. He received piano lessons as a child and studied music at Washburn College, Topeka. In 1923 he joined the **Fletcher Henderson** Orchestra, where he laid the foundations of the tenor saxophone's future pre-eminence as a jazz solo instrument. During the 1930s he worked in Europe for five years, becoming the most influential jazz 'exile' of that period. Returning to America in 1939, his recording of the ballad 'Body and Soul' became a benchmark for jazz saxophonists in the swing style. Renowned for his full tone and well-constructed improvisations, Hawkins later embraced the bebop movement and was also a member of the touring Jazz at the Philharmonic groups.

HAWKINS, Erick (1909–) American dancer, choreographer and teacher, born in Colorado. He read Greek at Harvard and studied at the School of American Ballet and with Harald Kreutzberg, a pupil of **Mary Wigman**. He joined American Ballet (1935–37) and Ballet Caravan (1936–39), creating his first choreography for the latter group. In 1938 he became the first man to dance with the **Martha Graham** company, creating roles in many of her most famous dances until 1951. They were married from 1948 to 1954. He formed his own company in the mid 1950s in association with composer Lucia Dlugoszewski and sculptor Ralph Dorazio. Influenced by Greek and Asian philosophy, his mainly abstract dances reflect his unforced, natural approach to movement.

HAWKINS, Henry, 1st Baron Brampton (1817–1907) English judge, born in Hitchin. He became QC in 1858, was counsel for the defence and later for the crown in the **Tichborne** case (1871-74), and became judge in 1876. In civil cases, fearing possible reversal of his decisions on appeal, he employed various tricks to avoid passing judgments. In the numerous murder cases which came before him, his fairness, however, did not warrant the nickname 'Hanging Hawkins' which was given him.

HAWKINS, Sir John (1532–95) English navigator and naval commander, born in Plymouth. He became the first Englishman to traffic in slaves (1562), taking slaves from west Africa to the Spanish West Indies; his 'commercial' career closed with a disastrous third voyage (1567), when he and **Drake** were intercepted by a Spanish fleet. He became navy treasurer in 1573, and reorganised the fleet to get it into shape for the confrontation with the Spanish Armada. Thereafter he made havoc of the Spanish West India Trade. In 1595, with his kinsman Drake, he commanded an expedition to the Spanish Main, but died at Porto Rico. His only son, Sir Richard (c.1562–1622), was also a naval commander and fought against the Armada. He went on a round-the-world plundering expedition (1593) but was captured in Peru and held prisoner in Spain until 1602. He wrote *Observations on His Voyage into the South Seas* (1622).

HAWKINS, Sir John (1719–89) English musicologist, born in London. He became an attorney, and as magistrate was knighted in 1772 for his services in the riots of 1768–69. He collected a valuable musical library, and in 1776 produced his *General History of the Science and Practice of Music*, which was unfortunately overshadowed by that of **Charles Burney**. He was **Samuel Johnson**'s literary executor, and published (1787–89) an inaccurate Life and an edition of Johnson's works. His daughter, Laetitia, published her own *Memoirs* 1822, which included a great deal about Dr Johnson.

HAWKSBEE, or **Hauksbee, Francis** (d.c.1713) English physicist. He carried further the observations by the physician **William Gilbert** on electricity and **Robert Boyle** on air, inventing the first glass electrical machine, and improved the air pump. Francis Hawksbee, the younger (1687–1763), apparently his son, was also an electrician, and was in 1723 appointed clerk and housekeeper to the Royal Society.

HAWKSHAW, Sir John (1811–91) English engineer, born in Leeds. He was a mining engineer in Venezuela (1831–34) and consulting engineer in the construction of Charing Cross and Cannon Street stations and bridges and the Inner Circle underground railway in London. He also constructed the Severn Tunnel and the Amsterdam ship canal, and in 1872–86 was one of the engineers of the original Channel Tunnel project.

HAWKSMOOR, Nicholas (1661–1736) English architect, born in Nottinghamshire. He became a clerk to **Wren** and also assisted **Vanbrugh** at Blenheim Palace and Castle Howard. His most individual contributions are the London churches, St Mary Woolnoth, St George's, Bloomsbury, St Anne's, Lunehouse and Christ Church, Spitalfields, as well as parts of Queen's College and All Souls, Oxford.

HAWKWOOD, Sir John de, Ital **'Giovanni' Acuto** (d. 1394) English soldier of fortune, born in Hedingham, Essex. He is said to have distinguished himself at Crécy (1346) and Poitiers (1356), was knighted by **Edward III**, and in 1360 led a band of mercenaries to Italy, where he at first took service with Pisa against

Florence, and fought in various causes, but at last agreed to fight the battles of Florence for an annual pension.

HAWORTH, Adrian Hardy (1766–1833) English botanist and entomologist. He published important works on British Lepidoptera and succulent plants, including *Lepidoptera Britannica* (3 vols, 1803–12) and *Synopsis Plantorum Succulentorum* (1812).

HAWORTH, Sir Walter Norman (1883–1950) English chemist, born in Chorley, Lancashire. Educated at Manchester and Göttingen, he was professor of organic chemistry at Newcastle (1920–25) and Birmingham (1925–48). He determined the constitution of vitamin C and various carbohydrates, for which he shared the Nobel prize with **Paul Karrer** in 1937.

HAWTHORNE, Nathaniel (1804–64) American novelist and short-story writer, born in Salem, Massachusetts, the son of a merchant captain, who died when the boy was only four years old. He and his mother lived in straitened circumstances. At the age of 14 he went with her to a lonely farm in the woods of Raymond, Maine, and there became accustomed to solitude. He began his first novel at Bowdon College, graduating in 1825, but progress was slow. After his return to Salem he shut himself away for twelve years 'in a heavy seclusion', writing tales and verses. In 1828 he published anonymously his first novel, *Fanshawe*, which was unsuccessful. Continuing to contribute to annuals and magazines, he edited in 1836 a short-lived periodical. Meanwhile some of his short stories had gained such favourable notice from the London *Athenaeum* that in 1837 *Twice-told Tales*, a volume of them, was published. His genius, however, was not yet appreciated in his own country. In 1839 the historian **George Bancroft**, then collector of the port of Boston, appointed him weigher and gauger in the custom-house, a post he held until 1841. He then joined for a year the Brook Farm idyllic, semi-socialistic community near Boston. Meanwhile he wrote and published a series of simple stories for children from New England history *Grandfather's Chair*, *Famous Old People* and *Liberty Tree* (1841). Moving to Concord, Massachusetts, he issued *Biographical Stories* (1842) for children, and brought out an enlarged edition of the *Twice-told Tales* (1842). He wrote sketches and studies for the *Democratic Review*, which formed the *Mosses from an Old Manse* (1846). The *Review* failed; and, as he lost all his savings at Brook Farm, he was forced to accept a place in the custom-house again—this time as surveyor in Salem. By the time his contract had finished he had completed (1850) *The Scarlet Letter*, still the best-known of his works. At Lenox, Massachusetts, he then entered upon a phase of remarkable productiveness, writing *The House of the Seven Gables* (1851), *Wonder Book* (1851), *The Snow Image* (1852), and *The Blithedale Romance* (1852), which drew upon the Brook Farm episode. He settled in Concord in 1852, and wrote a campaign biography of his old schoolfriend, President **Franklin Pierce**, and on Pierce's inauguration became consul at Liverpool (1853–57). He completed *Tanglewood Tales* in 1853, as a continuation of *Wonder Book*. A year and half spent in Rome and Florence, beginning in 1858, supplied him with the materials for *The Marble Faun* (1860), published in England as *Transformation*. Returning to Concord, he wrote for the *Atlantic Monthly* the brilliant papers on England collected as *Our Old Home* (1863). He began a new romance, based on the idea of an elixir of immortality, which remained unfinished at his death. With little faculty for poetry, Hawthorne had a singular command over the musical qualities of prose. Although exceptionally fitted for conveying subtleties of thought and fantasy, his style is invariably clear and strongly marked by common sense. Hawthorne was only gradually recognized in his own country.

HAXO, François Nicholas Benoit (1774–1838) French military engineer, born in Lunéville. He became a general under **Napoleon** and won fame for his reconstructions of **Vauban**'s fortifications and for his brilliant direction of the siege of Antwerp citadel in 1832.

HAY, Ian, pseud of Major-General John Hay Beith (1876–1952) Scottish novelist and dramatist, born in Manchester, the son of a cotton merchant. He was educated at Fettes College, Edinburgh and St John's College, Cambridge and became a language master at his old school. He served in World War I, and was awarded the Military Cross. His light popular novels, *Pip* (1907), *A Safety Match* (1911), *A Knight on Wheels* (1914), were followed by the war books *The First Hundred Thousand* (1915), *Carrying On* (1917) and *The Last Million* (1918). Many novels and comedies followed, best known of the latter being *Tilly of Bloomsbury* (1919) and *Housemaster* (1936). He was director of public relations at the War Office (1938–41).

HAY, John (1838–1905) American statesman, born in Salem, Indiana. Admitted to the Illinois bar in 1861, he was assistant private secretary to President **Lincoln**, and during the war served for some months. He was secretary of legation at Paris (1865–67) and Madrid (1868–70), and *chargé d'affaires* at Vienna (1867–68); on the staff of the *New York Tribune* (1870–75), and first assistant-secretary of state (1879–81). His *Pike County Ballads* (1871) include 'Little Breeches' and 'Jim Bludso'; he also published *Castilian Days* (1871), *The Bread-winner* (anon 1883), and, with Nicolay, a Life of Lincoln (1891). In 1897 he became ambassador to Britain; in 1898 secretary of state to President **McKinley**.

HAY, Lucy See **CARLISLE, Lucy, Countess of**

HAYDEE, Marcia (1939–) Brazilian dancer and director, born in Niteroi. After studying with Vaslav Veltchek she made an early début with the Rio de Janeiro Teatro Municipal. Further study with the Sadler's Wells Ballet School led to her joining the Grand Ballet of Marquis de Cuevas in 1957 and then Stuttgart Ballet in 1961. Her talents blossomed under the direction of Stuttgart's **John Cranko**, for whom she created roles in *Romeo and Juliet* (1962), *Onegin* (1965), *Carmen* (1971) and *Initials R.B.M.E.* (1972). As one of the greatest dramatic ballerinas of her time, she guested frequently around the world and worked for major choreographers like **Kenneth MacMillan** and **Glen Tetley**. In 1976 she was appointed artistic director of Stuttgart Ballet.

HAYDEN, Bill (William George) (1933–) Australian politician, born in Brisbane, the son of a working-class Californian who had settled in Australia during World War I and an Irish mother. He served in the state civil and police services before acquiring a late thirst for education, joining the Australian Labor party and entering the federal parliament in 1961. He served under **Gough Whitlam** and replaced him as party leader in 1977. In 1983 he surrendered the leadership to the more charismatic **Bob Hawke** and was foreign minister in his government (1983–88). In 1989 he became governor-general of Australia, characteristically refusing the customary knighthood which accompanies the post.

HAYDEN, Ferdinand Vandeveer (1829–87) American geologist, born in Westfield, Massachusetts. After working on surveys in the northwest (1853–62), he became professor of geology at Pennsylvania University (1865–72) and was subsequently head of the US geological survey. He was influential in securing the establishment of Yellowstone National Park.

HAYDN, Franz Joseph (1732–1809) Austrian composer, born in Rohrau, Lower Austria, the son of a wheelwright. Educated at the Cathedral Choir School of St Stephen's, Vienna, he earned his living initially by playing in street orchestras and teaching, but gained valuable experience from acting as accompanist and part-time valet to the famous Italian opera composer and singing teacher, **Niccola Porpora**, and as musical director (1759–60) for Count von Morzin, who kept a small company of court musicians for whom he wrote his earliest symphonies. His marriage in 1760 to the sharp-tempered Maria Anna Keller was unhappy. Entering the service of the Esterházy family in 1761, he remained with them on and off, first at Eisenstadt and later at Esterháza until 1790. As musical director of a princely establishment his duties included the performance and composition of chamber and orchestral music, sacred music and opera for domestic consumption. These favourable conditions led to a vast output, notable, technically, for his development and near-standardization of the four-movement string quartet and the 'classical' symphony, with sonata or 'first movement' form as a basic structural ingredient. This was to influence the whole course of European music. Though he himself rarely travelled during his Esterházy period, his compositions gained an international reputation and were in demand in France, Germany, England, Spain and Italy. Retiring in fact though not in name from Esterháza in 1790, he subsequently paid two visits to London, sponsored by the violinist and impresario J P Salomon (1745–1815), during which he directed performances of the specially commissioned 'Salomon' or 'London' Symphonies (Nos 93–104). He was made a Doctor of Music of Oxford in 1791. During the closing years of his life in Vienna, his main works were *The Creation*, *The Seasons* and his final quartets. Though the most famous composer of his day, he was quick to recognize the genius of the young **Mozart**, but was slower to appreciate the turbulent, questing spirit of **Beethoven**, who was his pupil in 1792. His spontaneity, melodiousness, faultless craftsmanship and a gift for the expression of both high spirits and gravity were strongly tinged in the 1770s by the prevailing *Sturm und Drang* atmosphere as well as by personal problems. His output includes 104 symphonies, about 50 concertos, 84 string quartets, 24 stage works, 12 masses, orchestral divertimenti, keyboard sonatas, and diverse chamber, choral, instrumental, and vocal pieces.

HAYDN, Michael (1737–1806) Austrian composer, brother of **Franz Joseph Haydn**, born in Rohrau. He was a cathedral chorister with Joseph in Vienna and ultimately became musical director and concert master to the Archbishop in Salzburg, where he remained until his death, having declined an offer of the post of assistant to his brother at Esterháza. Some of his compositions are of considerable merit and charm; and several of his church pieces and instrumental works are still performed. **Carl Weber** was among his pupils.

HAYDON, Benjamin Robert (1786–1846) English historical painter, born in Plymouth. He studied at the Royal Academy but later became a severe critic of that body. While he was painting *The Raising of Lazarus* (1823; Tate), he was arrested for debt. His *Mock Election* was purchased by **George IV**, and he had some success with other large paintings like *The Reform Banquet* (1832) and *Cassandra* (1834). But poverty continued to dog him, and he shot himself in his studio.

HAYEK, Friedrich August von (1899–) Austrian-born British political economist, born in Vienna. Director of the Austrian Institute for Economic Research (1927–31), he lectured at Vienna (1929–31), when he was appointed Tooke professor of economic science at London (1931–50). His *Prices and Production* (1931), *Monetary Theory and the Trade Cycle* (1933), and *The Pure Theory of Capital* (1941) dealt with important problems arising out of industrial fluctuations. He was appointed to a professorship at Chicago in 1950 and was at the University of Freiburg. from 1962 to 1969. Strongly opposed to Keynesianism, his later works, *The Road to Serfdom* (1944), *Individualism and Economic Order* (1948) and *The Constitution of Liberty* (1960) show an increasing concern for the problems posed for individual values by increased economic controls. Works published during the same period on theoretical psychology and the history of ideas indicate a further broadening of interests, manifested by his *Studies in Philosophy, Politics and Economics* (1967) and *The Political Order of a Free People* (1979). He was awarded the Nobel prize in economic science in 1974, jointly with **Gunnar Myrdal**.

HAYEM, Georges (1841–1920) French physician and pioneer of the study of diseases of the blood. Born in Paris, he studied medicine there, receiving his MD in 1868. He became professor of therapy and materia medica in 1879, working for much of his long career at the Hôpital Tenon. He first described the platelets in the blood, and did classic work on the formation and diseases of the red and white blood cells. He also published important accounts of diseases of several organs, including the stomach, liver, heart and brain. His work was notable for the way he attempted to apply the results of experimental physiology or pathology to the clinical setting.

HAYES, Helen (1900–) American actress, born in Washington. She won fame in a wide variety of stage productions, such as *Pollyanna* (1917–18), *Dear Brutus* (1919), and *The Wisteria Trees* (1951). She appeared in several films, including *A Farewell to Arms* (1932), *My Son John* (1951), and *The Sin of Madelon Claudet* (1931) for which she won an Academy Award in 1932. Other films she has appeared in include *Airport* (1970) and *Candleshoe* (1978).

HAYES, Isaac Israel (1832–81) American Arctic explorer, born in Chester County, Pennsylvania. He sailed as surgeon in the **Elisha Kent Kane** expedition (1853–54) and wrote *An Arctic Boat-journey* (1860). He led a second Arctic expedition (1860–61), and in 1869 a third one described in *The Land of Desolation* (1871).

HAYES, Rutherford Birchard (1822–93) 19th president of the USA, born in Delaware, Ohio. He graduated at Kenyon College, Ohio, in 1842, and practised as a lawyer at Cincinnati (1849–61). In the Civil War he served with distinction, retiring as major-general. He was returned to congress from Ohio in 1865 and 1866, and governor in 1867, 1869 and 1875. In 1876 he was Republican candidate for the presidency, the Democratic candidate being **Samuel J Tilden**. Some of the electoral votes being disputed, a commission gave them to Hayes, thus securing him a majority. Under the Hayes administration the country recovered commercial prosperity. His policy included reform of the civil service, conciliation of the southern states, and resumption of specie payments; but the bill for the monetization of silver was carried against his veto.

HAYLEY, William (1745–1820) English poet and writer, born in Chichester. He wrote verse, essays, plays, lives of **Milton** and **Romney**. His best biography was *The Life of Cowper* (1803).

HAYM, Rudolf (1821–1901) German scholar and author, born in Grünberg in Silesia. In 1848 he sat in the Frankfurt national assembly and became professor at Halle in 1860. He wrote biographies of **Humboldt** (1856), **Hegel** (1857), **Schopenhauer** (1864), **Herder** (1877–85) and **Duncker** (1891), and a monograph, *Die romantische Schule* (1870).

HAYMAN, Francis (1708–76) English painter and illustrator, born in Exeter. His most ambitious work was the decoration of the boxes and pavilions at Vauxhall Gardens. He also painted portrait groups which influenced **Gainsborough** who, for a time, worked under him. As a designer and illustrator he worked in the London studio of Hubert Gravelot, the most important link between French and English art of the time and, amongst other work, illustrated the books of **Samuel Richardson**. From 1760 he was president of the Society of Artists and, in 1768, a founder member and the first librarian of the Royal Academy.

HAYNAU, Julius Jakob, Baron von (1786–1853) Austrian soldier, born in Cassel. He entered the Austrian service in 1801, and gained notoriety during the Italian campaigns (1848–49) for his ruthless severity, especially at the capture of Brescia, where his flogging of women gained him the name of the 'Hyena of Brescia'. From the siege of Venice he was summoned to the supreme military command in Hungary in 1849; and his successes at Raab, Komorn and Szegedin did much to secure Austrian supremacy. Appointed dictator of Hungary in 1849 after its pacification, he was dismissed in 1850 for excessive violence, and that same year in London was assaulted by Barclay and Perkins's draymen.

HAYNE, Robert Young (1791–1839) American statesman, born in South Carolina. He was admitted to the bar in 1812, and served in the war with Great Britain. He became speaker of the state legislature and attorney-general of the state, and sat in the US senate (1823–32). He opposed protection, and in 1832 supported the doctrine of nullification. South Carolina in 1832 adopted an ordinance of nullification, Hayne was elected governor, and the state prepared to resist the federal power by force of arms. A compromise, however, was agreed to, and the ordinance was repealed. His nephew, Paul Hamilton (1830–86), the 'Laureate of the South', wrote war songs, sonnets, etc which were collected in 1882.

HAYNES, Elwood (1857–1925) American inventor, born in Portland, Indiana. In 1893 he constructed what is claimed to be the first American automobile, preserved in the Smithsonian Institution. He also patented a number of alloys, including a type of stainless steel (1919).

HAYNES, John (1934–) English footballer, born in London, where he spent all his career with the comparatively unfashionable Fulham. The club's director and later chairman, the comedian **Tommy Trinder** persuaded Haynes to stay with Fulham by making him the first £100 per week footballer in the history of the British game. A highly gifted and creative inside-forward, he won 56 caps and captained his country 22 times.

HAYS, Will (William Harrison) (1879–1954) American politician and film censor, born in Sullivan, Indiana. A lawyer by training, he was Republican national chairman (1918–20) and engineered **Warren Harding**'s presidential campaign. He became US Postmaster General (1921–22), and from 1922 to 1945 served as the first president of the Motion Picture Producers and Distributors of America. In 1930 he formulated the Production Code, known as the Hays Code, which enforced a rigorous code of morality on American films, and was not superseded until 1966.

HAYTER, Stanley William (1901–88) English artist and engraver, and founder of the celebrated Atelier 17 in Paris. He was born in Hackney, London, of a long line of artists, and studied chemistry and geology at King's College, London, for a career in the oil industry. He worked for the Anglo-Iranian Oil Company in Abadan for three years, from 1922 to 1925, then returned to London in 1926 to exhibit the portraits and landscapes he had painted in Iran. He moved to Paris to study art at the Académie Julian, where he learned printmaking and line-engraving. In 1927 he founded a studio in which artists of all nationalities could work together; in 1933 it moved to No. 17, Rue Campagne Première, where it became internationally known as Atelier 17. In World War II it was moved to New York from 1940 to 1950, when it returned to Paris. As a painter, Hayter became one of the earliest members of the Surrealist movement under the influence of **André Breton** (1896–1966); but it is as a master innovator in printmaking that he made his greatest mark. His publications include *New Ways of Gravure* (1949) and *About Prints* (1962).

HAYWARD, Abraham (1802–84) English essayist, born in Wishford, Wiltshire. Called to the bar in 1832, he founded and edited the *Law Magazine*, and was made a QC in 1845. Many of his best articles, including 'The Art of Dining', were reprinted in his *Biographical and Critical Essays* (1858–73) and *Eminent Statesmen and Writers* (1880).

HAYWOOD, Eliza, née **Fowler** (c.1693–1756) English novelist, born in London. After being deserted by her husband, she became an actress and wrote a number of scandalous society novels, in which the characters resembled living persons so closely, the names being thinly concealed by the use of asterisks, as to be libellous. **Pope** denounced her in the *Dunciad*. She issued the periodical *The Female Spectator* (1744–46) and *The Parrot* (1747). Her works include *Memoirs of a Certain Island adjacent to Utopia* (1725), and two 'straight' novels, *The History of Betsy Thoughtless* (1751) and *The History of Jemmy and Jenny Hessamy* (1753).

HAYWORTH, Rita, originally **Margarita Carmen Cansino** (1918–87) American film actress and dancer, born into a showbusiness family in New York. A cousin of **Ginger Rogers**, her nightclub appearances led to a succession of small roles in B-pictures. Blossoming into an international beauty, she was both an enigmatic temptress, as in *Blood and Sand* (1941) and *Gilda* (1946), and a vivacious leading lady in musicals such as *Cover Girl* (1944). Her allure dimmed in middle-age and later roles were lacklustre, although she was effective as the faded beauty in *Separate Tables* (1958). Her five husbands included **Orson Welles** and Prince Aly Khan. She suffered from Alzheimer's disease for many years prior to her death.

HAZELIUS, Artur Immanuel (1833–1901) Swedish ethnologist and museum curator. His collection of artefacts illustrative of the old folk and peasant culture of Sweden led him to found, in 1873, the ethnographic museum in Stockholm that became the Nordic Museum. His greatest achievement, however, was the foundation in 1891 of Skansen in Stockholm, the world's first major open-air museum and a monument to his belief in popular education.

HAZLITT, William (1778–1830) English essayist, born in Maidstone, Kent, the son of a Unitarian minister, who moved to Boston, Massachusetts, in 1783, and to Wem in Shropshire in 1787. At the age of 15 the boy was sent to Hackney College to study for the ministry, but had abandoned the notion when in 1796 he met **Coleridge**, and by him was encouraged to write *Principles of Human Action* (1805). Having tried portrait painting, he published in 1806 his *Free Thoughts on Public Affairs*, in 1807 his *Reply to Malthus*, and in 1812 he found employment in London on the *Morning Chronicle* and *Examiner*. From 1814 to 1830 he contributed to the *Edinburgh Review* and his *Round Table* essays and *Characters of Shakespeare's Plays* appeared in 1817. Between 1818 and 1821 he delivered at the Surrey Institute his lectures on *The English Poets*, *English Comic Writers*, and *Dramatic Literature of the Age of Elizabeth*. His marriage with Sarah Stoddart in 1808 proved a failure and they were divorced in Edinburgh in 1822. His essays in the *London Magazine* were later republished in his *Table Talk* (1821) and *Plain Speaker* (1826). A passion for Sarah Walker, the daughter of a tailor with whom he lodged, found expression in the frantic *Liber Amoris* (1823). In 1824 he married a charming widow with £300 a year, who travelled with him to Italy, but left him for ever on the return journey. His *Spirit of the Age, or Contemporary Portraits* appeared in 1825; his *Life of Napoleon Bonaparte* between 1828 and 1830. His last years darkened by ill-health and money difficulties, he died with the words, 'Well, I've had a happy life'. He was a deadly controversialist, a master of epigram, invective and withering irony. His style ranges from lively gossip to glowing rhapsody; the best of his work is in his later collections of essays.

HAZZARD, Shirley (1931–) Australian-born American novelist, born and educated in Sydney. She has published numerous short stories, often in the *New Yorker* magazine, and four novels. Her novel, *The Transit of Venus* (1980) established her as a major contemporary writer. *People in Glass Houses* (1967) satirizes monumental organizations such as the United Nations, for which she worked for ten years in the 1950s and later criticized in her *Defeat of an Ideal* (1973).

HEAD, Sir Edmund Walker, 8th Baronet (1805–68) English administrator, born near Maidstone. He was educated at Oriel College, Oxford, and became a fellow of Merton. After serving as poor-law commissioner, he was lieutenant-governor of New Brunswick (1847–54), then governor-general of Canada till 1861. He wrote on *Spanish and French Painting* (1847), *Ballads* (1868), etc.

HEAD, Sir Francis Bond (1793–1875) English administrator, born in the Hermitage near Rochester. He entered the Royal Engineers, served at Waterloo, and as major retired in 1825. He was lieutenant-governor of Upper Canada (1835–37), where he suppressed an insurrection led by **William Lyon Mackenzie**, which heralded Lord **Durham**'s mission to Canada.

HEAD, Sir Henry (1861–1940) English neurologist, born in Stamford Hill, London. He studied natural sciences at Trinity College, Cambridge, and clinical medicine at University College Hospital, London. His interest in the functions and diseases of the nervous system dated from his student days, and his famous observations on the sensory changes in his own arm after cutting some of the nerves to it, reinforced his reputation as a leading scientifically-inclined neurologist. He wrote widely on disorders of speech (aphasias) and other neurological disorders, and edited the journal *Brain* from 1910 to 1925. Among his patients was **Virginia Woolf**.

HEAD, Richard (c.1637–86) English hack-writer, born in Ireland. He is best known as the author of part one of *The English Rogue* (1665–71), the other three parts being by the bookseller Francis Kirkman.

HEAL, Sir Ambrose (1872–1959) English furniture designer, born in London. Educated at Marlborough and the Slade School of Art, he served an apprenticeship as a cabinet maker before joining the family firm in 1893, and began designing furniture influenced by the Arts and Crafts Movement. From the 1930s, the firm adopted a fashionable modern manner providing homes with an inexpensive alternative to reproduction furniture and costly Arts and Crafts pieces.

HEALEY, Denis Winston (1917–) English politician, born in Keighley, Yorkshire. Educated at Oxford, he served with the Royal Engineers in North Africa and Italy (1940–45), attaining the rank of major. For seven years after World War II he was secretary of the Labour party's international department before becoming MP for Leeds in 1952. He was a member of the shadow cabinet for five years before becoming secretary of state for defence in the **Wilson** government of 1964, a post which he held for six years. His five years (1974–79) as Chancellor of the Exchequer were a rather stormy period marked by a sterling crisis and subsequent intervention by the International Monetary Fund. Healey unsuccessfully contested the Labour party leadership in 1976 and again in 1980 when he was somewhat unexpectedly defeated by **Michael Foot**. He was however elected deputy leader ahead of his left-wing opponent **Tony Benn**. In 1987 he resigned from the shadow cabinet.

HEALY, Timothy Michael (1855–1931) Irish Nationalist leader, born in Bantry. He sat in parliament (1880–1918), headed in 1890 the revolt against **Parnell**, and became an Independent Nationalist. First governor-general of the Irish Free State (1922–28).

HEANEY, Seamus Justin (1939–) Irish poet and critic, born in Castledawson, County Derry, in Northern Ireland. Educated at St Columba's College, Londonderry, and Queen's College, Belfast, he lectured there (1966–72) before becoming a full-time writer. An Ulster Catholic, the violence in the North so disturbed him that he moved to the Republic in 1972, and taught at Caryfort College, Dublin, from 1975. He made his début as a poet with *Eleven Poems* (1965). Redolent of the rural Ireland in which he grew up, his work seems nurtured by the landscape, lush, peaty and, to an extent, menacing. One of the greatest modern poets writing in English, he is regarded as a worthy successor to **W B Yeats**. Significant collectons are *Death of a Naturalist* (1966), *Wintering Out* (1972), *North* (1975), *Bog Poems* (1975), *Stations* (1975), *Field Work* (1979) and *Station Island* (1984). *Selected Poems* 1965–75 appeared in 1980.

HEARN, Lafcadio (1850–1904) American journalist of Greek-Irish parentage, born on the island of Leucadia. He was trained as a journalist in the USA and worked on the Cincinnati *Commerical* (1873–77) and New Orleans *Times-Democrat* (1881–87). He went to Japan in 1890 and became a naturalized Japanese under the name Koisumi Yakumo and wrote enthusiastically on things Japanese.

HEARNE, Samuel (1745–92) English explorer of northern Canada, born in London. He served in the Royal Navy and then joined the Hudson's Bay Company, who sent him to Canada to Fort Prince of Wales (Churchill) in 1769. During a journey in search of copper in 1770 he became the first European to travel overland by canoe and sled to the Arctic Ocean by following the Coppermine River north of the Great Slave Lake. He clearly reported details of the frozen wastes and the Indian-Inuit (Eskimo) conflicts he observed. In 1774 he set up the first interior trading post for the company at Cumberland House, and then became governor of Fort Prince of Wales, where he was captured and taken to France in 1782. There his release was negotiated on condition he published an account of his travels. He returned to re-establish Churchill as a trading post in 1783, but ill health forced him to return to England in 1787.

HEARNE, Thomas (1678–1735) English antiquary, born in White Waltham, Berkshire. He graduated from St Edmund Hall, Oxford, and in 1712 became second keeper to the Bodleian Library—a post he had to resign as a Jacobite in 1716. Among his 41 works were *Reliquiae Bodleianae* (1703), **Leland**'s *Itinerary* (1710–12) and *Collectanea* (1715), editions of **William Camden**'s *Annals* (1717), **Fordun**'s *Scotichronicon* (1722), etc.

HEARST, William Randolph (1863–1951) American newspaper owner, born in San Francisco, the son of a newspaper proprietor. After studying at Harvard he took over the *San Francisco Examiner* in 1887 from his father. He acquired the *New York Morning Journal* (1895) and launched the *Evening Journal* in 1896. He revolutionized journalism by the introduction of banner headlines, lavish illustrations and other sensational methods, nicknamed by critics 'the yellow press'. He made himself the head of a national chain of newspapers and periodicals, including the *Chicago Examiner*, *Boston American*, *Cosmopolitan*, and *Harper's Bazaar*. He was a member of the US House of Representatives (1903–07), but failed in attempts to become mayor and governor of New York. He built a spectacular residence at San Simeon, California. His career inspired the **Orson Welles** film *Citizen Kane* (1941).

HEARTFIELD, John, originally **Helmut Herzfelde** (1891–1968) German photomonteur and painter, the son of the poet Franz Held. Together with **George Grosz**, he was a leading member of the Berlin Dada group in the aftermath of World War I, producing satirical collages from pasted, superimposed photographs cut from magazines. A lifelong pacifist and staunch communist, he moved to East Berlin in 1950, and anglicized his name as a gesture of sympathy with America.

HEATH, Edward Richard George (1916–) English Conservative politician, born in Broadstairs. He was a scholar of Balliol College, Oxford, served in World War II and entered Parliament in 1950, one of **R A Butler**'s 'One Nation' new Tory intellectuals. He was an assistant (1953–55) and chief whip (1955–59), minister of labour (1959–60) when he became lord privy seal and the chief negotiator for Britain's entry into the European Common Market, abortive because of the French, yet earning him the German Charlemagne prize (1963). In the **Douglas-Home** administration (1963) he became secretary of state for industry and president of the board of trade (1963). Elected leader of the Conservative party in July 1965, he was opposition leader until, on the Conservative victory in the 1970 general election, he became prime minister. After a confrontation with the miners' union in 1973 the Conservatives narrowly lost the general election of February 1974, the loss being confirmed by another election in October 1974. In 1975 he was replaced as leader by **Margaret Thatcher**. Since 1979 he has become an increasingly outspoken critic of what he has regarded as the extreme policies of 'Thatcherism'.

HEATH, Neville George (1917–46) English murderer, born in Ilford, Essex. He was thrice cashiered, from the RAF, RASC and South African Air Force, before committing two notoriously brutal sexual murders in the summer of 1946 for which he was tried and executed.

HEATHCOAT, John (1783–1861) English inventor, born near Derby. In 1808 he designed a machine for making lace, and set up a factory in Nottingham which was destroyed in 1816 by the Luddites. He then moved his business to Tiverton in Devon. He also invented ribbon- and net-making machinery.

HEATHCOAT-AMORY See **AMORY**

HEATHFIELD, George Augustus Eliott, 1st Baron (1717–90) Scottish soldier, born in Stobs in Roxburghshire. Educated at Leiden, the French military college of La Fère, and Woolwich, he served in the War of the Austrian Succession, the Seven Years' War and in Cuba (1762), returning as lieutenant-general. When Britain became involved in hostilities with Spain in 1775, Eliott was sent out to Gibraltar. His heroic defence, from June 1779 to February 1783, ranks as one of the most memorable achievements of British arms.

HEATON, Sir John Henniker (1848–1914) English politician, born in Rochester. He was MP (1885–1910), and championed successfully the penny postage rate within the British Empire and including the USA

HEAVISIDE, Oliver (1850–1925) English physicist, born in London. A telegrapher by training, he spent much of his life living like a hermit in Devon. There he made various important advances in the study of electrical communications; and in 1902, independently of Arthur Edwin Kennelly (1861–1939), he predicted the existence of an ionized gaseous layer capable of reflecting radio waves, the Heaviside layer (now known as the ionosphere), which was verified 20 years later.

HEBB, Donald Olding (1904–85) Canadian psychologist, born in Chester, Nova Scotia. Educated at Dalhousie and McGill Universities, he subsequently studied with **Karl Lashley** at Harvard (PhD 1936) and also worked with him later at the Yerkes Laboratories of Primate Biology in Florida (1942–47). In 1947 he rejoined McGill University where he remained until his retirement, becoming chairman of the Psychology Department (1948–58) and later chancellor of the university (1970–74). He was the first non-American to become president of the American Psychological Association. His best-remembered, theoretical contributions to psychology were embodied in his book *The Organization of Behaviour* (1949), in which he argued that long-term memories could be encoded in the brain by means of changes occurring at the synapse (the point at which one nerve cell can communicate chemically with another), and that repeated use would itself strengthen such a synapse. There is now good physiological evidence for such ' Hebb synapses'. He also introduced and developed the concept of the 'cell assembly', a diffuse network of nerve cells which could be activated for relatively short periods and which would be the physical embodiment of transient thoughts and perceptions. His ideas are currently enjoying a renaissance in the new field of 'computational neuroscience'.

HEBBEL, Friedrich (1813–63) German dramatist, born in Wesselburen in Ditmarsh. He studied in Hamburg from 1835 and after stays in Heidelberg, Munich, Copenhagen, settled in Vienna (1846). His only contemporary play is *Maria Magdalena* (1842), his favourite settings being of a legendary, historical or biblical character, as *Herodes und Marianne* (1852) and his masterpiece, the *Nibelungen* trilogy (1855–60). Hebbel constantly portrayed the inherent Hegelian conflict between individuality and humanity as a whole.

HEBER, Reginald (1783–1826) English prelate and hymnwriter, born in Malpas, Cheshire. He wrote his prize poem *Palestine* at Oxford (1803). Inducted into the family living of Hodnet in Shropshire (1807), he was a frequent contributor to the *Quarterly Review*, and in 1812 published a volume of *Hymns*. He was appointed Bampton lecturer in 1815, a prebendary of St Asaph in 1817, and preacher of Lincoln's Inn in 1822. In 1823 he was appointed bishop of Calcutta, but his episcopate was terminated by his sudden death at Trichinopoly. He published sermons, *A Journey through India*, and other works, and edited **Jeremy Taylor**'s *Works* (1822). As a poet, his fame rests upon *Palestine* and his *Hymns*, which include 'From Greenland's Icy Mountains' and 'Holy, Holy, Holy'. His half-brother, Richard (1774–1833), was a famous bibliomaniac with a collection estimated at 146827 volumes.

HEBERDEN, William (1710–1801) English physician, born in London. He studied and practised in Cambridge, but in 1748 set up in London. He distinguished chickenpox from smallpox, described *angina pectoris* and prescribed treatment for it. He attended Dr **Samuel Johnson**, and was the last to write medical papers in Latin.

HÉBERT, Jacques René (1755–94) French revolutionary, nicknamed 'Père Duchesne', born in Alençon. A servant in Paris, he was dismissed more than once for embezzlement, but soon after the outbreak of the Revolution became a prominent Jacobin and editor of *Le Père Duchesne*, established to crush a constitutional newspaper of the same title. As a member of the revolutionary council, he played a conspicuous part in the September massacres. He was on the commission appointed to examine **Marie Antoinette** and brought up the trumped-up charge of incestuous practices with the dauphin. He and his fellows were mainly instrumental in converting Notre Dame into a temple of Reason. But he went too fast for **Robespierre**, who had him guillotined.

HECATAEUS OF MILETUS (c.550–476 BC) pioneer Greek historian and geographer. He attempted to demythologize Greek history in his prose *Genealogies* (or *Histories*) by giving the poetic fables about the divine or heroic ancestries of leading Milesian families a pseudo-chronological framework. He travelled widely, visiting Greece, Thrace, Persia, and parts of Italy, Spain and Africa, and wrote a *Tour of the World* (of which only fragments remain) describing local customs and curiosities, and which he published with an improved version of the map made by **Anaximander** of Miletus.

HECHT, Ben (1894–1964) American writer, born in New York. Starting as a journalist in Chicago, he wrote novels, plays and filmscripts. From 1946 he was dedicated to the Zionist cause and vilification of Britain as in *A Flag is Born* (1946). His plays include *The Front Page* (1928), and his screenplays include *Wuthering Heights* (1939), *Spellbound* (1945) and *Notorious* (1946).

HECKEL, Erich (1883–1970) German painter, a founder of the Expressionist school, the *Brücke* (c. 1905). He studied architecture at Dresden before turning to painting. He excelled in lithography and the woodcut, eg, *Self-portrait* (1917; Munich). Vilified by the Nazis, he stayed in Berlin and was professor at Karlsruhe (1949–56).

HECKEL, Johann Adam (?1812–1877) German woodwind instrument-maker. In 1831 he established his own workshop in Biebrich near Wiesbaden, and with the guidance of a bassoon player, Carl Almenraeder (1786–1843), introduced improvements in the structure and key-system of bassoons, which, when standardized, marked off the German from the French type. His son, Wilhelm (1856–1909), and grandsons, Wilhelm Hermann (1879–1952) and August (1880–1914), carried on the business, which introduced several instrumental novelties such as the Heckelphone (1903).

HECKER, Friedrich Karl Franz (1811–81) German political agitator, born in Eichtersheim, Baden. He became an advocate, headed the republican movement of 1848, with a band of revolutionists invaded Baden, but was defeated and fled to America. In the Civil War he commanded a brigade.

HECKER, Isaac Thomas (1819–88) American clergyman, born in New York of German parentage, and founder of the Paulists. He passed from Brook Farm socialism to Behmenite mysticism, became a Catholic (1844) and, after studies in England, a Redemptorist Father. Claiming new freedom, he was extruded from that order, but founded 'the Missionary Priests of St Paul', and greatly extended Catholicism in America. His 'Americanism' or tendency to democratize Catholicism created much controversy. His works included *Questions of the Soul* (1850) and *The Church and the Age* (1888).

HEDIN, Sven Anders (1865–1952) Swedish explorer and geographer, born in Stockholm. A lifelong explorer of uncharted regions of central Asia, Tibet and China, he first went to Persia in 1885 as a tutor, and was attached to a Swedish-Norwegian embassy to the Shah in 1890. From then until 1908 he was constantly on his travels, particularly in the Himalayas, the Gobi desert, and Tibet, of which he made the first detailed map (1908). On his return to Sweden he was accorded a hero's welcome. After World War I he organized and led the Sino-Swedish Scientific Expedition to the northwest provinces of China (1927–33). The Sven Hedin Foundation in Stockholm contains some 8000 geological specimens and artefacts collected by Hedin. He was a gifted writer and his accounts of his journeys achieved much popularity. He was vocal on a number of issues in Swedish politics, arguing for increased national defence, warning of Russian expansionism and advocating a strongly pro-German stance even during the 1930s and World War II.

HEDLEY, William (1779–1843) English inventor, born in Newburn near Newcastle-upon-Tyne. A colliery 'viewer' and lessee, in 1813 he improved on Trevithick's locomotive, proving that loads could be moved by the traction of smooth wheels in smooth rails. His locomotive was known as *Puffing Billy*.

HEDWIG, Johannes (1730–99) Transylvanian-born German botanist and physician born in Kronstadt (now Brasov, Romania). He studied medicine at Leipzig and after practising as a physician became professor of botany there (1789). He gave special attention to cryptogams; his posthumous *Species Muscotum* (1801) is the internationally accepted starting point for the scientific naming of mosses.

HEEM, Jan Davidsz de (c.1606–1684) Dutch artist, born in Utrecht and arguably the greatest Dutch still-life painter. He settled in Antwerp. His paintings are in most European galleries and in the United States. His son Cornelis (1631–95) was also a painter.

HEEMSKERCK, Maerten van (1498–1574) Dutch portrait and religious painter, born in Heemskerck. By c.1528 he was working in Haarlem with the Italianate painter **Jan van Scorel**. Following his lead, van Heemskerck also travelled to Italy and spent the period 1532 to 1535 in Rome where he was greatly attracted to the work of **Michelangelo** and **Raphael**. While in Rome he also studied antiquities, and his surviving sketchbooks supply us with a vivid account of the ancient monuments of the city as they appeared in the 16th century. He spent the remainder of his life in Haarlem.

HEENAN See **SAYERS, Tom** and **MENKEN, Adah Isaacs**

HEENAN, John Carmel, Cardinal (1905–75) Roman Catholic archbishop of Westminster (1963–75). Born in Ilford, Essex, and educated at Ushaw and the English College, Rome, he was ordained in 1930. He became a parish priest in east London and during the war worked with the BBC, becoming well-known as the Radio Priest. He became bishop of Leeds in 1951, archbishop of Liverpool in 1957, and archbishop of Westminster in 1963. A convinced ecumenical, he supported the causes of religious liberty and reconciliation with the Jews at the Second Vatican Council, and was created cardinal in 1965. He wrote several doctrinal and autobiographical works.

HEEREN, Arnold Hermann Ludwig (1760–1842) German historian, born near Bremen. In 1787 he became professor of philosophy, and in 1801 of history, at Göttingen. His first great work was an economic history of the ancient world (1793–96). He also wrote on the study of the classics since the Renaissance (1797–1802), a history of the states of the ancient world (1799) and *Political System of Europe and its Colonies* (1800). His economic interpretation of history foreshadowed **Marx** and **Engels**.

HEEZEN, Bruce Charles (1924–77) American oceanographer, born in Vinton, Iowa. He first showed the existence and importance of ocean turbidity currents. Educated at Iowa and at Columbia, where he worked from 1948, he used in 1952 the records of failure of the many Atlantic communications cables during the earthquake of 1929. He was able to deduce the existence of a rapid sediment slump, or turbidity current, which had moved massive quantities of undersea sediment. In 1957, with **William Ewing** he went on to demonstrate that mid-ocean ridges have a central rift.

HEFELE, Karl Joseph von (1800–93) German Roman Catholic prelate and historian, born in Unterkochen in Württemberg. In 1840 he became Catholic professor of church history at Tübingen. He became a dangerous enemy of the dogma of papal infallibility, even after consecration as bishop of Rottenburg in 1869, by contributions to the Honorius Controversy (1870). But in 1871 he submitted an explanation on the dogma. He wrote on the conversion of southwest Germany (1837), Ximenes (1844), church history (1864–65), etc; his great work is the *Konziliengeschichte* (1855–74).

HEFFER, Eric Samuel (1922–) English Labour politician. Apprenticed as a carpenter-joiner at the age of 14, he worked in the trade, apart from war service in the RAF, until he entered the House of Commons, representing Liverpool, Walton, in 1964. He had joined the Labour party as a youth and was Liverpool president (1959–60) and Liverpool city councillor (1960–66). A traditional socialist, favouring public ownership and strongly unilateralist, he distrusted centrist tendencies and had a brief, uncomfortable period as a junior minister (1974–75). He unsuccessfully challenged **Roy Hattersley** for the deputy leadership in 1988.

HEFNER, Hugh Marston (1926–) American editor and publisher, born in Chicago. His parents were Methodists; smoking, drinking and attending the cinema were forbidden. He attended Illinois University, did postgraduate work in psychology, and worked as a personnel manager, advertising copywriter and in the subscriptons department of *Esquire* magazine until 1952, when he resigned to start a new magazine. Investing $10000, he published *Playboy* in December 1953 with the then unknown **Marilyn Monroe** posing nude. 'Girly' photographs, practical advice on sexual problems, men's talk and articles of high literary standard combined to make the magazine a notorious success and Hefner a conspicuously wealthy man (he is photographed frequently at his mansion surrounded by a bevy of 'playmates'). The *Playboy* empire extended into real estate, clubs (with the ludicrous 'bunnies') and sundry products.

HEGEL, Georg Wilhelm Friedrich (1770–1831) German philosopher, the last and perhaps the most important of the great German idealist philosophers in the line from **Kant**, **Fichte** and **Schelling**. Born in Stuttgart, he studied theology at Tübingen, and was a tutor in Berne (1793) and Frankfurt-am-Main (1796); in 1801 he became a lecturer at Jena but his academic career was interrupted in 1806 by the closure of the university after **Napoleon**'s victory at Jena. He was temporarily a newspaper editor at Bamberg and then headmaster of the gymnasium at Nuremberg from 1808–16. He had published in 1807 his first great work *Phänomenologie des Geistes* (The Phenomenology of Mind), describing how the human mind has progressed from mere consciousness through self-consciousness, reason, spirit and religion to absolute knowledge. His seond great work was *Wissenschaft der Logik* (Science of Logic, 2 volumes, 1812 and 1816) in which he set out his famous dialectic, a triadic process whereby thesis generates antithesis and both are superseded by a higher synthesis which incorporates what is rational in them and rejects the irrational. This dialectical progression is not applied narrowly just to logical argument but to the evolution of ideas and to historical movements on the largest possible scale. The work gained him the chair at Heidelberg in 1816, and he now resumed his university career and produced in 1817 a compendium of his entire system: *Encyclopädie der philosophischen Wissenschaften in Grundrisse* (Encyclopedia of the Philosophical Sciences, comprising logic, philosophy of nature and of mind). In 1818 he succeeded **Fichte** as professor in Berlin and remained there until his death from a cholera epidemic. His later works include the *Grundlinien der Philosophie des Rechts* (Philosophy of Right, 1821), which contains his political philosophy, and his important lectures on the history of philosophy, art and the philosophy of history. Hegel was a system-builder of the most ambitious and thorough kind, and though his philosophy is difficult and obscure it has been a great influence on such different groups as Marxists, Positivists, British Idealists, and Existentialists. In this century his importance declined after attacks by **Moore**, **Russell** and the analytic philosophers, but he is now experiencing a modest revival of interest.

HEGESIPPUS, St (d.180) Greek Christian church historian, almost certainly a Jewish convert. He made a journey by way of Corinth to Rome, and there compiled a list of the bishops of Rome to Anicetus (156–167), so that he must have written his history about that period. It was entitled *Five Memorials of Ecclesiastical Affairs*, and unfortunately survives only in a few fragments which **Eusebius of Caesarea** embodied in his own history.

HEIBERG, Gunnar Edvard Rode (1857–1929) Norwegian dramatist, born in Christiania (now Oslo). He wrote expressionist plays in the radical and rational tradition of Norwegian literature, such as *Balkonen* (The Balcony, 1894) and *Kjaerlighetens Tragedie* (the Tragedy of Love, 1904).

HEIBERG, Johan Ludvig (1791–1860) Danish playwright, son of **Peter Andreas Heiberg**, and the creator of vaudeville in Denmark. He wrote a series of enormously popular musical comedies, of which his masterpiece was *Nej!* (No!, 1836). His romantic play *Elverhøj* (Hills of the Elves, 1828), is considered a classic. He was married to the actress Johanne Luise Heiberg, and later became director of the Theatre Royal in Copenhagen (1849–56). He also wrote on philosophy.

HEIBERG, Johan Ludvig (1854–1928) Danish classical scholar, born in Aalborg. He was simultaneously schoolmaster and professor of classical philology at Copenhagen (1896–1925). He edited a vast amount of Greek literature, especially the Greek mathematicians and medical writers.

HEIBERG, Peter Andreas (1758–1841) Danish writer and diplomat. A biting social satirist, he published comic songs and pamphlets, and founded a periodical, *Rigsdalerseddelens haendelser* (Money Matters, 1787–93), which so infuriated the government that he was eventually exiled. He moved to Paris, where he joined the French foreign ministry and accompanied **Talleyrand** on diplomatic missions.

HEIDEGGER, Martin (1889–1976) German philosopher, born in Messkirch in Baden, the son of a Catholic sexton. He joined the Jesuits as a novice and went on to teach philosophy at Freiburg, where he did a dissertation on **Duns Scotus**. He became professor at Marburg (1923–28) and then succeeded **Husserl** as professor at Freiburg (1929–45), where he was appointed rector in 1933. In a notorious inaugural address he declared his support for **Hitler**. He was officially retired in 1945 but continued to be an influential teacher and lecturer. He succeeded Husserl as a leading figure in the phenomenological movement, but was also much influenced by **Kierkegaard**, and though he disclaimed the label of 'existentialist' he was a key influence on **Sartre** through his writings on the nature and predicament of human existence, the search for 'authenticity' and the distractions of *Angst* (dread). His major work is the highly original but almost unreadable *Sein und Zeit* (Being and Time, 1927), which presents a classification of the modes of 'Being' and an examination of the distinctively human mode of existence (*Dasein*) characterized by participation and involvement in the world of objects. His deliberate obscurity and riddling style partly account for his poor reception in the Anglo-Saxon world, but he is a continuing influence on continental European intellectuals.

HEIDENSTAM, (Karl Gustav) Verner von (1859–1940) Swedish writer, born in Olshammer. He lived in southern Europe and the Middle East (1876–87), and published his impressions in a volume of poetry, *Vallfart och Vandringsår* (Pilgrimage and Years of Wandering, 1888), which together with his programmatic work, *Renässans*, inspired a literary renaissance in Sweden and established him as the leader of the new romantic movement of the 1890s. He published several further volumes of poetry, including *Endymion* (1889), the epic *Hans Alienus* (1892), *Dikter* (Poems, 1895), and *Ett folk* (One People, 1899). Later he turned to historical fiction, as in *Karolinerna* (The Carlists, 1897–98) and *Folkungaträdet* (The Tree of the Folkungs, 1905–07). He was awarded the 1916 Nobel prize for literature.

HEIFETZ, Jascha (1901–87) American violinist of Russo-Polish birth, born in Vilna. In 1910 he began studies at St Petersburg Conservatory, touring Russia, Germany and Scandinavia at the age of twelve. After the Russian Revolution he settled in the USA, becoming an American citizen in 1924. He first appeared in Britain in 1920. Among works commissioned by him from leading composers is **William Walton**'s violin concerto.

HEIJN, or **Heyn, Piet** (1578–1629) Dutch naval commander, born in Delfshaven. After an adventurous career as a galley-slave of the Spanish and a merchant captain, in 1623 he became vice admiral under the Dutch East India Company. In 1624 he defeated the Spaniards near San Salvador in Brazil, and again in 1626 off Bahia, returning with an immense booty. In 1626 he captured the Spanish silver flotilla, valued at 12000000 guilders; in 1629 was made Admiral of Holland. He died in a sea-fight against the privateers of Dunkirk.

HEIN, Piet, pseudonym **Kumbel** (1905–) Danish poet, designer and inventor. His poems include several collections of aphoristic *Grooks*. He defined the 'super -ellipse' (a special curve) and used it for architectural and design purposes. From 1969 to 1976 he lived in Britain.

HEINE, Heinrich (1797–1856) German poet and essayist, born of Jewish parents in Düsseldorf. At the age of 17 he was sent to Frankfurt to learn banking, and next tried trading on his own account in Hamburg, but soon failed. In 1819 he went to Bonn; there, and at Berlin and Göttingen, he studied law, taking his doctor's degree in 1825. But his mind was fixed on poetry. In Berlin in 1821 he published *Gedichte*, which at once was a great success. A second collection, *Lyrisches Intermezzo*, appeared in 1823. The first and second volumes of the prose *Reisebilder* were published (1826–27) and *Das Buch der Lieder* created excitement throughout Germany. In 1825 he became a Christian to secure the rights of German citizenship, but only alienated the esteem of his own people. His revolutionary opinions remained insuperable hindrances to his official employment in Germany. When his enthusiasm was roused by the July revolution in Paris, he went there in 1831, going into a voluntary exile from which he never returned. After 1825 he travelled in England and Italy; he worked on newspapers in Bavaria; and he wrote two more volumes of *Reisebilder* (1830–31). The July revolution seems to have awakened a seriousness in Heine. He turned from poetry to politics, and assumed the role of leader of the cosmopolitan democratic movement. One of his chief aims was to make the French and the Germans acquainted with one another's intellectual and artistic achievements. From this came the *Französische Zustände* (1833), first printed in the *Allgemeine Zeitung*; *De l'Allemagne* (1835), the French version of *Die Romantische Schule* (1836); and *Philosophie und Literatur in Deutschland*, part of the miscellaneous writings entitled *Der Salon* (4 vols, 1835–40). His ambiguous attitude and his attack on **Ludwig Börne** brought down upon him the emnity of his revolutionary compatriots. On the eve of a duel, which his book on Börne (1840) ultimately cost him, he married Eugénie Mirat ('Mathilde', d.1883), a Paris grisette, with whom he had been living for seven years. From 1848 he was confined to bed by spinal paralysis. He lingered on in excruciating pain, borne with heroic patience. During these years he published *Neue Gedichte* and *Deutschland*, a satirical poem (1844); *Atta Troll: Ein Sommernachtstraum*, the 'swansong of romanticism' (1847); a collection of poems, *Romancero* (1851); and three volumes of *Vermischte Schriften* (1854).

HEINECCIUS, Johann Gottlieb (1681–1741) German jurist. He was professor at Halle (from 1713, and again from 1733). He published in Latin a *Syntagma* of Roman legal antiquities (1718), a history of the Civil Law (1733), the elements of German law (1735), and a *Jus Naturae et Gentium* (1737). His brother, **Johann Michaelis** (1674–1722), a famous preacher in Halle, was the first to study seals scientifically.

HEINEMANN, Gustav (1899–1976) West German statesman, born in Schwelm, in the Ruhr district, and educated at Marburg and Münster. He practised as an advocate from 1926 and lectured on law at Cologne (1933–39). After the war he was a founder of the Christian Democratic Union, and was minister of the Interior in Adenauer's government (1949–50), resigning over a fundamental difference over defence policy. Heinemann, a pacifist, opposing Germany's re-armament. He formed his own neutralist party, but later joined the Social Democratic party, was elected to the Bundestag (1957) and was minister of Justice in Kiesinger's 'Grand Coalition' government from 1966. In 1969 he was elected president but resigned in 1974.

HEINEMANN, William (1863–1920) English publisher, born in Surbiton. He founded his publishing house in London in 1890 and established its reputation with the works of **Stevenson**, **Kipling**, **H G Wells**, **Galsworthy**, **Somerset Maugham**, **Priestley**, and others.

HEINICHEN, Johann David (1683–1729) German composer, born in Krössuln, near Weissenfels. From 1719 until his death he was kapellmeister there. He wrote many choral and chamber works as well as operas and a manual on continuo-playing.

HEINKEL, Ernst Heinrich (1888–1958) German aircraft engineer, born in Grunbach. He founded in 1922 the Heinkel-Flugzeugwerke at Warnemünde, making at first seaplanes, and later bombers and fighters which achieved fame in World War II. He built the first jet plane, the HE-178, in 1939, and also the first rocket powered aircraft, the HE-176.

HEINSE, Johann (1749–1803) German romance writer and poet, born in Thuringia. He wrote several novels, including *Ardinghello* (1787).

HEINSIUS, Anthony (1641–1720) Dutch statesman, born in Delft. In 1688 he became Grand Pensionary of Holland, and was the close friend of **William III** (of Great Britain).

HEINSIUS, Daniel (1580–1655) Dutch classical scholar, born in Ghent. Professor at Leiden from 1605, he edited many Latin classics, and published Latin poems and orations. His son, Nicolaas (1620–81), obtained distinction as a diplomatic agent and classical scholar.

HEINZ, Henry John (1844–1919) American food manufacturer and packer, born of German parents in Pittsburgh, Pennsylvania. At the age of eight he peddled produce from the family garden, and in 1876 became co-founder, with his brother and cousin, of F & J Heinz. The business was reorganized as H J Heinz Co. in 1888, and he was its president from 1905 to 1919. He invented the advertising slogan '57 Varieties' in 1896, promoted the pure food movement in the US, and was a pioneer in staff welfare work.

HEINZE, Sir Bernard Thomas (1894–1982) Australian conductor and teacher, born in Shepparton, Victoria. Educated at Melbourne University, he studied at the Royal College of Music, London and, after World War I, in Paris and Berlin. He then became Ormond professor of music at Melbourne University in 1925, a post which he held until 1956 when he was appointed director of the New South Wales State Conservatorium of Music, retiring in 1966. From 1933 to 1956 he was conductor of the Victorian Symphony Orchestra, and also recorded with the Melbourne and Sydney orchestras. He pioneered the introduction of good music to schools from 1924 with his 'Young People's Concerts', which he continued with the Australian Broadcasting Corporation as its music adviser from 1932. With the ABC, Heinze was instrumental in founding symphony orchestras in each Australian state.

HEISENBERG, Werner Karl (1901–76) German theoretical physicist, born in Würzburg. Educated at Munich and Göttingen, he became professor of physics at Leipzig (1927–41) and professor at Berlin and director of the Kaiser Wilhelm Institute (1941–45). From 1945 to 1958 he was director of the **Max Planck** Institute at Göttingen (and from 1958 at Munich). With **Max Born** he developed quantum mechanics and formulated the revolutionary principle of indeterminacy (uncertainty principle), in nuclear physics (1925). He won the 1932 Nobel prize for physics. In 1958, he and **Wolfgang Pauli** announced the formulation of a unified field theory, which if established would remove the indeterminacy principle and re-instate **Einstein**.

HEKMATYAR, Gulbuddin (1949–) Afghan guerrilla leader. Formerly an engineer, in the 1970s he opposed the republican government of General Mohammad Daud Khan, and rose to prominence during the 1980s in the fight to oust the Soviet-installed communist régime in Afghanistan. As leader of one of the two factions of the Hizb-i Islami (Islamic party), he was seen as the most intransigently fundamentalist, refusing to join an interim 'national unity' government with Afghan communists as the Soviet Union began to wind down its military commitment. He was injured in a car bomb attack on his group's headquarters in Peshawar in 1987, and in 1988 briefly served as president of the seven-party mujahadeen alliance.

HELD, Al (1928–) American painter, born in Brooklyn, New York. He studied at the Art Students' League in New York from 1948 to 1949 and in Paris from 1950 to 1952. He returned to New York and during the 1950s painted in the Abstract Expressionist manner. From 1960 he adopted a more geometric style, painting complex cube-like structures with heavy impasto paint. In the 1980s he turned to acrylic paints, rendering precise and brightly coloured geometric forms in a deep perspectival space.

HELENA, St (c.255–330) Roman Empress, wife of the emperor **Constantius Chlorus** and mother of **Constantine I, the Great**. Traditionally she came from Bithynia, the daughter of an innkeeper. For political reasons Constantius divorced her in 292; but when Constantine was declared emperor by his army in York in 306, he made her Empress Dowager. In 312, when toleration was extended to Christianity, she was baptized. In 326, according to tradition, she visited Jerusalem, and founded the basilicas on the Mount of Olives and at Bethlehem. Her feast day is 18 August.

HELIODORUS (fl.3rd and 4th century AD) Greek romance writer and Sophist, born in Emesa in Syria. One of the earliest Greek novelists, he was the author of *Aethiopica*, which narrates in poetic prose, at times with almost epic beauty and simplicity, the loves of Theagenes and Chariclea.

HELIOGABALUS (204–22) Roman emperor, born in Emesa. His real name was Varius Avitus Bassianus, but having, when a child, been appointed high priest of the Syro -Phoenician sun god Elagabal, he assumed the name of that deity. In 218, Heliogabalus was proclaimed emperor by the soldiers; he defeated his rival Macrinus on the borders of Syria and Phoenicia. His brief reign was marked by extravagant personal behaviour and intolerant promotion of the God Elagabal. He was murdered by the praetorians in a palace revolution.

HELLER, Joseph (1923–) American novelist, born in Brooklyn, New York. He served in the US army air force in World War II, drawing on the experience for his black comedy, *Catch* 22, based on the simple premise that a fighter-pilot who wants to be excused duty need only ask, but by asking proves that he is sane and fit to fly. After selling slowly for some years it became an international bestseller and a byword for war's absurdity. Later books—*Something Happened* (1974), *Good as Gold* (1979), *God Knows* (1984) and *Picture This* (1988)—tended to receive churlish notices but are no less satiric and are often at least as accomplished as their more celebrated predecessor.

HELLER, Stephen (1813–88) Hungarian pianist and composer, born in Budapest. He made his début as a pianist at nine. From 1830, settling in Augsburg, he studied composition; in 1838 he moved to Paris, where he composed and taught until his death.

HELLMAN, Lillian Florence (1907–84) American playwright, born into a Jewish family in New Orleans. Educated at New York University and Columbia University, she worked for the New York *Herald Tribune* as a reviewer (1925–28) and for M-G-M in Hollywood as reader of plays (1927–32). She lived for many years with the detective writer **Dashiell Hammett**, who encouraged her writing. She had her first stage success with *The Children's Hour* (1934), which ran on Broadway for 86 weeks. This was followed by *Days to Come* (1936) and *The Little Foxes* (1939), which was later adapted into a film starring **Bette Davis**. During World War II she also wrote the anti-Fascist plays *Watch on the Rhine* (1941, winner of the Critics Circle Award), and *The Searching Wind* (1944). When she came before the Un-American Activities committee in 1952 during the **Joseph McCarthy** era she coined the famous phrase 'I can't cut my conscience to fit this year's fashions'. This period was described in her *Scoundrel Time* (1976). Her other plays included *The Autumn Garden* (1951) and *Toys in the Attic* (1960). Her autobiographical works included *An Unfinished Woman* (1969) and *Pentimento* (1973). A left-wing activist, and sensitive to social injustice and personal suffering, her voice was one of the most persuasive in the modern American theatre. Mercurial, she nurtured her animosities, and sued for libel when **Mary McCarthy** said of her that 'every word she writes is a lie, including "and" and "the"', a reference to the misrepresentations in her memoir *Scoundrel Time*. But Hellman died before the case came to court.

HELMHOLTZ, Hermann von (1821–94) German physiologist and physicist, born in Potsdam. He was successively professor of physiology at Königsberg (1849), Bonn (1855), and Heidelberg (1858). In 1871 he became professor of physics in Berlin. He was equally distinguished in physiology, mathematics, and experimental and mathematical physics. His physiological works are principally connected with the eye, the ear, and the nervous system. His work on vision (eg on the perception of colour) is regarded as fundamental to modern visual science. He invented an ophthalmoscope (1850) independently of **Charles Babbage**. He is also important for his analysis of the spectrum, his explanation of vowel sounds, his papers on the conservation of energy with reference to muscular action, his paper on *Conservation of Energy* (1847), his two memoirs in Crelle's *Journal*, on vortex motion in fluids, and on the vibrations of air in open pipes; and for researches into the development of electric current within a galvanic battery.

HELMONT, Jean Baptiste van (1579–1644) Flemish chemist, born in Brussels. He studied medicine, mysticism and finally chemistry under the influence of **Paracelsus**. He first emphasized the use of the balance in chemistry, and by its means showed the indestructibility of matter in chemical changes. He devoted much study to gases, and invented the word *gas*. He was also the first to take the melting-point of ice and the boiling-point of water as standards for temperature. He first employed the term *saturation* to signify the combination of an acid with a base; and he was one of the earliest investigators of the chemistry of the fluids of the human body. His works, entitled *Ortus Medicinae*, were often reprinted. His youngest son, Franciscus Mercurius (1614–99), was a teacher of deaf-mutes.

HELMS, Richard McGarrah (1913–) American intelligence officer, born in Pennsylvania. Educated in Switzerland and at Williams College, USA, he was a journalist before joining the US navy in 1942. After World War II he was inducted into the newly-formed Central Intelligence Agency (CIA) and rose to become the organization's director in 1966. He was dismissed by President **Nixon** in 1973 and appointed ambassador to Iran (1973–76). In 1977 he was convicted of lying before a congressional committee, arguing that his oath as head of the intelligence service required him to keep secrets from the public.

HÉLOÏSE See **ABELARD**

HELPMANN, Sir Robert (1909–86) Australian dancer, actor and choreographer, born in Mount Gambier. He made his début in Adelaide in 1923, joined **Pavlova**'s touring company in 1929 and in 1931 came to Britain to study under **Ninette de Valois**. He was the first dancer of the newly founded Sadler's Wells Ballet (1933–50). A master of mime, he created with distinction the role of 'Master of Tregennis' in the *Haunted Ballroom* (1934). His choreographic work includes *Hamlet* (1942), *Miracle in the Gorbals* (1944), a modern parable set in Glasgow, and *Yugen* (1965), created in Australia. His acting roles were mainly Shakespearean with the occasional part in a **George Bernard Shaw**. He also danced in the ballet films *The Red Shoes* (1948) and *The Tales of Hoffman* (1950). He was joint artistic director of Australian ballet (1965–76).

HELST, Bartholomaeus van der (1611–70) Dutch painter, born in Haarlem. He was joint founder in 1653 of the painters' guild of **St Luke** at Amsterdam, where he flourished as a portrait painter in the manner of **Frans Hals**.

HELVÉTIUS, Claude-Adrien (1715–71) French philosopher of Swiss origin, born in Paris. He trained for a financial career and in 1738 was appointed to the lucrative office of farmer-general. From there he moved to become chamberlain to the queen's household where he associated with French philosophers of the day such as **Diderot** and **D'Alembert** with whom he was later to collaborate on the *Encyclopédie*. In 1751 he withdrew from public life to the family estate at Voré where he spent the rest of his life in philosophy, philanthropic work and educating his family. In 1758 he published the controversial *De l'esprit*, advancing the view that sensation is the source of all intellectual activity and that self-interest is the motive force of all human action. The book was promptly denounced by the Sorbonne and condemned by the parliament of Paris to be publicly burnt. As a result it was widely read, was translated into all the main European languages, and together with his posthumous *De l'homme* (1772) greatly influenced **Bentham** and the British utilitarians.

HEMANS, Felicia Dorothea, née **Browne** (1793–1835) English poet, born in Liverpool, the daughter of a merchant. Bertween 1808 and 1812 she published three volumes of poems, and in 1812 married an Irishman, Captain Alfred Hemans. He deserted her in 1818, and she turned to writing for a living. She produced a large number of books of verse of all kinds, love lyrics, classical, mythological, sentimental, including *The Siege of Valencia* (1823) and *Records of Women* (1828). She is perhaps best remembered for the poem *Casabianca*, better known as 'The boy stood on the burning deck', and 'The stately homes of England'.

HEMINGWAY, Ernest Millar (1899–1961) American novelist and short story writer, born in Oak Park, a respectable suburb of Chicago. His father was a doctor and a keen sportsman, an enthusiasm his son was to share. He was educated at grammar school and the palatial Oak Park and River Forest Township High School, where he distinguished himself only in English. His mother wanted him to become a violinist but, modelling himself on **Ring Lardner**, he was determined to become a journalist and a writer. He got a job on the *Kansas City Star* as a cub reporter where he was paid 15 dollars a week and was given a copy of the style book which told him to write in the manner of the mature Hemingway. In April 1918 he resigned and joined the Red Cross, to be hurled into World War I as an ambulance driver on the Italian front, where he was badly wounded. Returning to America he began to write features for the Toronto *Star Weekly* in 1919 and married Hadley Richardson, the first of four wives, in 1921. That same year he came to Europe as a roving correspondent and covered several large conferences. In Paris he moved easily and conspicuously among other émigré artists and came into contact with **Gertrude Stein**, **Ezra Pound**, **James Joyce** and **Scott Fitzgerald**. *A Moveable Feast* records this time, reliving the struggle he and his new wife had to make ends meet. *Three Stories and Ten Poems* was given a limited circulation in Paris in 1923 and in 1924 he published *In Our Time* which met with critical approval in America a year later. *The Sun Also Rises* (1926) and a volume of short stories, *Men Without Women* (1927), confirmed his reputation, and in 1928, divorced from Hadley and re-married to Pauline Pfeiffer, he moved to Key West in Florida. Disentangling fact from myth in the years that followed is not easy. Drinking, brawling, posturing, big-game hunting, deep-sea fishing and bull-fighting, all competed with writing. Nevertheless the body of work is impressive, if uneven. In 1929, he published *A Farewell to Arms*, and the bull-fighting classic, *Death in the Afternoon*, in 1932. *Green Hills in Africa* tells of tension-filled big-game hunts. Perhaps his most popular book is *For Whom the Bell Tolls*, published in 1940, about the Civil War in Spain to which Hemingway went as a journalist. Significant later titles are *Across the River and Into the Trees* (1950) and *The Old Man and the Sea* (1952). He won the Pulitzer prize in 1953 and the Nobel prize for literature in 1954. Having cheated death on more than one occasion and given to numbing depressions, he shot himself in the mouth in Ketchum, Idaho, after having lived for years in Cuba.

HEMSTERHUIS, Tiberius (1685–1766) Dutch philologist, born in Groningen. He became professor of Greek at Amsterdam in 1704, Franeker in 1720, and of Greek history at Leyden in 1750. He created a new school of Greek scholarship. His editions of the *Onomasticon* of Pollux (1706), of **Lucian**'s *Select Dialogues* (1708–32), and of **Aristophanes**' *Plutus* (1744) are his chief works.

HENCH, Philip Showalter (1896–1965) American physician, born in Pittsburgh, where he took his medical degree. Head of the department of rheumatics at the Mayo Clinic (Rochester) from 1926, and professor of medicine at Minnesota University from 1947, he discovered cortisone, and shared the 1950 Nobel prize for physiology or medicine with **Edward Kendall** and **Tadeuse Reichstein** for their work on rheumatoid arthritis.

HENDERSON, Alexander (c.1583–1646) Scottish Covenanter, born in Creich in Fife, and educated at St Andrews. In 1610, as an Episcopalian, he was made a professor there of rhetoric and philosophy, and in 1611 or 1612 was appointed to the parish of Leuchars. He was one of the authors of the National Covenant, and was moderator of the General Assembly at Glasgow in 1638 which restored all its liberties to the Kirk of Scotland. Moderator again in 1641 and in 1643, he drafted the Solemn League and Covenant, and was a commissioner for three years to the Westminster Assembly. He was the author of *Bishop's Doom* (1638).

HENDERSON, Arthur (1863–1935) Scottish Labour politician, born in Glasgow. He was brought up in Newcastle, where he worked as an iron-moulder and became a lay preacher. He helped to build up the Labour party, of which he was chairman (1908–10, 1914–17, 1931–32), served in the Coalition cabinets (1915–17), was home secretary (1924), foreign secretary (1929–31), when he refused, with the majority of the Labour party, to enter **Ramsay MacDonald**'s National Government (1931). A crusader for disarmament, he was president of the World Disarmament Conference (1932).

HENDERSON, Fletcher (1897–1952) American pianist, arranger and bandleader, born in Cuthbert, Georgia. He graduated in chemistry from the all-black Atlanta University, but moving to New York in 1920 to continue his studies, he became diverted into a musical career, starting as house pianist for publishing and recording companies. In 1924 he put together a big band for what was supposed to be a temporary engagement, but stayed at the head of an orchestra until the mid 1930s, attracting the finest instrumentalists and arrangers of the time. His own orchestrations, and those of **Don Redman**, set the standard for the swing era; but lacking business acumen, Henderson lost the initiative and, until he suffered a stroke in 1950, continued to perform in relative obscurity.

HENDERSON, Hamish (1919–) Scottish folklorist, composer and poet, born in Blairgowrie. One of his early poetic works, 'Ninth Elegy for the Dead in Cyrenaica' (1948), won him the **Somerset Maugham** award, but his considerable literary output has been overshadowed by his outstanding contributions to folk-song. Through his researches in the field for the School of Scottish Studies, he was largely responsible for bringing great but unknown traditional singers, like **Jeannie Robertson**, to the fore, thereby ensuring the survival of the Scots ballad tradition. Many of his own compositions—notably 'Freedom Come All Ye', 'Farewell to Sicily' and 'The John Maclean March'—have themselves become part of the traditional singer's repertoire.

HENDERSON, Sir Nevile Meyrick (1882–1942) English diplomat, born in Sedgwick, Sussex. He was minister to Yugoslavia (1929–35), ambassador to Argentina (1935–37), and to Germany until the outbreak of World War II. He wrote *Failure of a Mission* (1940).

HENDERSON, Thomas (1798–1844) Scottish astronomer, born in Dundee. Although intended for a law career, he devoted his leisure hours to astronomical calculations, and in 1831 was appointed director of the Royal Observatory at the Cape of Good Hope. In 1832 he measured the parallax of the star, alpha Centauri. In 1834 he became first astronomer royal for Scotland.

HENDRIX, Jimi (James Marshall) (1942–70) American black rock guitarist and singer, born in Seattle, Washington. Born in a poor black neighbourhood, he taught himself guitar and went on to become one of rock music's most innovative and influential instrumentalists. After being invalided out of the army in

1962 he moved to Nashville and played in numerous groups, including a period with **Little Richard**'s road band. However it was not until he moved to Britain in 1966 and formed the Jimi Hendrix Experience (with Noel Redding and Mitch Mitchell) that his true potential was realized. The band's first single 'Hey Joe' was an immediate British success and his adventurous first album, *Are You Experienced?* was an unexpected international success which paved the way for other psychedelic and experimental rock acts. The two subsequent albums—*Axis: Bold As Love* and *Electric Ladyland* —helped make 1968 his most commercially successful year. However the pressures of success also helped to destroy him both professionally and personally. The Jimi Hendrix Experience broke up in 1969 and a subsequent group, The Band Of Gypsies, disbanded after recording only one album. He died from suffocation on his own vomit as a result of mixing drugs and alcohol.

HENG SAMRIN (1934–) Cambodian (Kampuchean) politician. He served as a political commissar and commander in **Pol Pot**'s Khmer Rouge (1976–78) but, alienated by his brutal tactics, led an abortive coup against him, then fled to Vietnam. Here he established the Kampuchean People's Revolutionary party (KPRP) and became head of the new Vietnamese-installed government. He has remained in 'de facto' control of Cambodia since 1979 but following Vietnam's withdrawal of its troops from Cambodia in 1979, his influence has begun to wane, with the country's more accommodating prime minister, Hun Sen, growing in stature as a peace settlement is sought.

HENGHAM, Ralph de (?1250–1311) English judge and legal writer, a judge of the King's Bench, then of the Common Pleas (1273–74), and chief justice of the King's Bench (1274–89). He was removed and fined for false judgment and false imprisonment, but later, possibly considered less guilty than others involved in the same offence, may have been pardoned, and became (1301–08) chief justice of the Common Pleas. He wrote two Latin tracts on procedure, *Hengham Magna* and *Hengham Parva*, and may also have written the texts called *Fet Asaver*, *Judicium Essoniorum* and *Modus Componendi Brevium*.

HENGIST (d.488) and **HORSA** (d.455), two semi-legendary Jutish brothers, said by **Nennius** and the *Anglo-Saxon Chronicle* to have led the first band of Germanic invaders to Britain. They landed from Jutland at Ebbsfleet in the Isle of Thanet in 449 to help King **Vortigern** against the Picts, and were rewarded with the gift of Thanet. Soon after they turned against Vortigern, but were defeated at Aylesford, where Horsa was slain. Hengist, however, is said to have conquered Kent. Both names mean 'horse'.

HENGSTENBERG, Ernst Wilhelm (1802–69) German Protestant theologian, born in Fröndenberg, Westphalia, and educated at Bonn. At first a rationalist, at Basel (1823) he passed to the opposite extreme, and thereafter as teacher, editor and author of many books, combated rationalism in every form, and sought to restore the orthodoxy of the 16th century.

HENIE, Sonja (1912–69) Norwegian ice-skater, born in Oslo. After winning the gold medal in figure-skating at the Olympics of 1928, 1932 and 1936, she turned professional and starred in touring ice-shows, and later went to Hollywood where she made several films.

HENLE, Friedrich Gustav Jakob (1809–85) German anatomist, born in Fürth. He held professorships at Zürich, Heidelberg and Göttingen, discovered the tubules in the kidney which are named after him and wrote treatises on systematic anatomy.

HENLEIN, Konrad (1898–1945) Sudeten German politician. He was the leader in the agitation on the eve of World War II leading in 1938 to Germany's seizure of Sudetenland from Czechoslovakia, and in 1939 to the institution of the German protectorate of Bohemia and Moravia and the dissolution of Czechoslovakia. Gauleiter of Sudetenland in 1938 and from 1939 civil commissioner for Bohemia, on Germany's subsequent defeat in the war he committed suicide when in American hands.

HENLEY, John (1692–1756) English clergyman, known as 'Orator Henley', born in Melton-Mowbray. He studied at St John's College, Cambridge, taught in the school of his native town, compiled a grammar of seven languages, *The Complete Linguist* (1719–21), and was ordained in 1716. In 1726, he set up an 'oratory', to teach universal knowledge in weekday lectures and primitive Christianity in Sunday sermons, but his addresses were a medley of ribaldry and solemnity, wit and absurdity. His *Oratory Transactions* contain a life of himself. He was ridiculed by **Pope** in his *Dunciad*.

HENLEY, William Ernest (1849–1903) English poet, playwright, critic and editor, born in Gloucester. Crippled by tuberculosis as a boy, he spent nearly two years in Edinburgh Infirmary (1873–75), where he wrote *A Book of Verses* (1888) which won him the friendship of **R L Stevenson**, with whom he collaborated in four plays, *Deacon Brodie* (1880), *Beau Austin* (1884), *Admiral Guinea* (1884) and *Macaire* (1885). Other volumes of his verse, with its unusual rhymes and esoteric words, followed: *The Song of the Sword* (1892), *Collected Poems* (1898), *For England's Sake* (1900), *Hawthorn and Lavender* (1901), *A Song of Speed* (1903) and *In Hospital* (1903), which contains his best-known poem, 'Invictus'. A pungent critic, he successfully edited the *Magazine of Art*, (1882–86) and the *Scots Observer* (1889), which he renamed *The National Observer*. He was joint compiler of a dictionary of slang (1894–1904).

HENNEBIQUE, François (1842–1921) French structural engineer, one of the first to make extensive use of ferro-concrete (as reinforced concrete was then known). He built the first reinforced concrete bridge at Viggen in Switzerland in 1894, the first grain elevator at Roubaix in 1895, and the first multi-storey reinforced concrete framed building in Britain, Weaver's Mill at Swansea, in 1898. The popularity of his system was so great that by 1910 over 40000 structures of various kinds had been completed, one of the most notable being the fifteen-storey Royal Liver Building in Liverpool (1909).

HENNER, Jean Jacques (1829–1905) French painter, born in Alsace. He is best known for his religious subjects, portraits and nudes somewhat in the manner of **Correggio**, including *Girl Reading* in the Luxembourg gardens.

HENNINGSEN, Charles Frederick (1815–77) Anglo-Swedish soldier of fortune, born in England of Swedish parentage. He served with the Carlists in Spain, with the Russians in Circassia, with **Lajos Kossuth** in Hungary, and with **William Walker** in Nicaragua. In the American Civil War (1861–65) he commanded a Confederate brigade, and afterwards superintended the manufacture of Minié rifles. He wrote books, including *The White Slave* (1845) and *The Past and Future of Hungary* (1852).

HENRI I (1008–60) king of France, son of Robert II. He ascended the throne in 1031 and was involved in struggles with Normandy and with Burgundy, which he had unwisely granted to his rival brother, Robert.

HENRI II (1519–59) king of France from 1547, the son of **Francis I**. In 1533, as Duke of Orléans, he married the 14-year-old **Catherine de' Medici**, by whom he had seven surviving children, three of whom became kings of France (**Francis II**, **Charles IX** and **Henri III**). He became heir apparent in 1536 at the death of his brother, the dauphin Francis. Dominated by his mistress, Diane of Poitiers, and by Anne de Montmorency, constable of France, he succeeded his father in 1547, and introduced reforms at court to curb extravagance and regularize the country's disordered finances. In alliance with Scotland he declared war on England, and captured Boulogne (1550) and Calais (1558). War against the Holy Roman Emperor, **Charles V**, also gained for France the French-speaking bishoprics of Metz, Toul and Verdun, but the king's ambitions in Italy were thwarted when his army was annihilated at St Quentin in 1557. At home he was alarmed at the rapid spread of Protestantism and initiated the persecution of Huguenots that would lead to the Wars of Religion (1562–98). He died of accidental wounds received in a tournament, and was succeeded by the first of his sons, the ailing boy-king Francis II, husband of **Mary Queen of Scots**.

HENRI III (1551–89) king of France from 1574, the third son of **Henri II** and **Catherine de'Medici**; he succeeded his brother, **Charles IX**. As Duke of Anjou he was in command of the royal army during Charles's reign, and won victories over the Huguenots at the battles of Jarnac and Monconteur in 1569. With his mother he was responsible for instigating the slaughter of Parisian Huguenots at the St Bartholomew Day Massacre in 1572. At his mother's insistence he was elected king of Poland in 1573, but had to return to France soon after his coronation in 1574 to ascend the French throne at his brother's death. In 1575 he was deposed by his Polish subjects. His reign in France was a period of incessant civil war between Huguenots and Catholics, and between the sons of Catherine de'Medici. His brother François, Duke of Alençon, placed himself at the head of the Huguenots and won the favourable Treaty of Etigny in 1576, while Henri aligned himself with the extreme Catholic League headed by Henri, Duke of **Guise**. After the death of François in 1584, Henri joined the Huguenots, now that his brother-in-law, the Protestant Henri of Navarre (the future **Henri IV**), was heir-presumptive to the throne, but was obliged to capitulate to the Catholic rebels at Nemours in 1585. From now on, Henri was caught amid the rivalry between Henri of Guise and Henri of Navarre. In 1588 he was beseiged in Paris by Henri of Guise (the Day of the Barricades), but managed to escape, and in the following year had Guise imprisoned and put to death. In 1589, soon after the death of his mother, he was assassinated by a Catholic friar incensed at the king's opposition to the Catholic League. With his death the Valois line of kings ended.

HENRI IV, known as **Henri of Navarre** (1553–1610) king of France from 1589 in succession to **Henri III**. The first of the **Bourbon** monarchy, he was the third son of Antoine de Bourbon and **Jeanne d'Albret**, heiress of Henri d'Albret (Henri II) of Navarre. Brought up by his mother as a Calvinist, he headed the Protestant forces in the Third Huguenot War (1569–72), but was worsted at the battle of Jarnac (1569). In 1572 he succeeded his mother to the throne of Navarre as Henri III. After the peace of St Germain in 1572 he married **Margaret of Valois**, sister of **Charles IX** and **Henri III** of France, and was spared in the St Bartholomew Day Massacre (1572) on condition that he professed himself a Catholic. For three years he was virtually a prisoner at the French court, but in 1576 he escaped to Alençon, revoked his forced confession, and by the 1580s had established himself as the leader of the French Protestants. The death in 1584 of the king's brother (François, Duke of Alençon) made him heir-presumptive to the French throne, and the last years of the reign were characterized by a struggle for power, known as the War of the Three Henris (1585–89) between himself and Henri, Duke of **Guise**, leader of the Catholic League. In 1588 Henri of Guise was murdered by Henri III, and when Henri III was himself assassinated in 1589, Henri of Navarre claimed the throne and marched on Paris, which was in the hands of the Catholic League. In the war that followed, Henri won the decisive battles; and in 1593 he formally renounced Protestantism and declared himself a Catholic, and was crowned at Chartres in the following year. With the Edict of Nantes of 1598, guaranteeing the rights of the Huguenot minority, he brought an end to more than 40 years of religious wars in France. In the same year, the Treaty of Vervins ended nine years of war with **Philip II** of Spain. A great conciliator, he was able to restore to France strong monarchy and stable government, and restore the country's shattered economy. He built up an efficient centralized bureaucracy, while his leading minister, the Duke of **Sully**, was responsible for a ruthless overhaul of French finances, drastically reducing the national debt. Although Henri showed favour to the Huguenots, he also patronized the Jesuits, and gave a positive lead to the revival in learning and the arts. In 1599 he divorced Margaret de Valois (the union was childless), and in 1600 married his second wife, **Marie de'Medici**; their children included the future **Louis XIII** and **Henrietta Maria**, queen consort of **Charles I** of Great Britain. In May 1610, with war threatening with Spain and the Empire, Marie was crowned formally to give more authority to her regency during Henry's absence on campaign. Three days before the king was due to leave Paris he was assassinated by a Catholic religious fanatic, **François Ravaillac**.

HENRI, Robert (1865–1929) American painter, born in Cincinnati, Ohio and brought up in Nebraska. He first studied at the Pennsylvania Academy and, in 1888, went to Paris to study at the École des Beaux Arts. On his return to Philadelphia he taught at the Women's School of Design (1891–96) and became an ardent advocate of realism in art and, as such, began a movement which, in the first decade of the 20th century, came to be known as the 'Ash-can School'. In 1898 he began teaching at the New York School of Art. He enjoyed considerable success but, as a juror for the National Academy in 1907, he was enraged when his own work and that of his followers failed to gain recognition and, in protest, he mounted his own exhibition under the title of *The Eight*. He continued to teach the importance of a popular and democratic type of art within his own art school which he established in New York in 1908. He also wrote a book, *The Art Spirit* (1923) which influenced many younger artists.

HENRIETTA ANNE, Duchess of Orléans (1644–70) the youngest daughter of **Charles I** of Great Britain and **Henrietta Maria**, and sister of **Charles II**. She was born in Exeter while the English civil wars were still at their height. Brought up by her mother in France, she married **Louis XIV**'s homosexual brother Philippe, but was also rumoured to have been for a time the mistress of the French king himself. Known as 'Minette', she was the favourite sister of Charles II and played an important part in the negotiations of the Secret Treaty of Dover (1670) between Charles and Louis. There were strong rumours that her subsequent death was caused by poison, although it was more probably a case of a ruptured appendix.

HENRIETTA MARIA (1609–69) queen consort of **Charles I** of Britain, born in the Louvre, Paris, the youngest child of **Henri IV** of France. Her father's assassination six months afterwards left her to the upbringing of her mother, **Marie de' Medici**. She was married in 1625 to Charles I. Her French attendants and Roman Catholic beliefs made her extremely unpopular. In February 1642, under the threat of impeachment, she fled to Holland and raised funds for the royalist cause. A year later she landed at Bridlington, and met Charles near Edgehill. On 3 April 1644, they separated at Abingdon for the last time. At Exeter, on 16 June, she gave birth to **Henrietta Anne** and a fortnight later she was compelled to flee to France. The war of the Fronde (1648) reduced her temporarily to destitution, despite the liberal allowance assigned to her. She paid two visits to England after the Restoration (1660–61 and 1662–65).

HENRY I (1068–1135) king of England from 1100, youngest and only English-born son of **William I, the Conqueror**, born, traditionally, in Selby. When war broke out between his brothers, **William II, Rufus** and Robert of Normandy, Henry helped the latter to defend Normandy; yet in the treaty which followed (1091) he was excluded from the succession. Immediately after William's death, Henry seized the royal treasure, and was elected king by the witan. He issued a charter restoring the laws of **Edward the Confessor** and the Conqueror, recalled **Anselm**, and set about great and popular reforms in the administration of justice. He strengthened his position by a marriage with Eadgyth (Matilda), daughter of King **Malcolm III, Canmore** of Scotland and Queen **Margaret**, who was descended from the old English royal house. Robert had been granted a pension of 3000 marks to resign his claim to the English crown and concentrate his attentions on Normandy, but in 1105–06 Henry made war against his badly-governed duchy; Robert was defeated at Tinchebrai (1106), and was kept a prisoner for life (28 years). To hold Normandy, Henry was obliged to wage nearly constant warfare. King **Louis VI** of France took part with William, Robert's youthful son; but the first war ended in the favourable peace of Gisors (1113); and in 1114 Henry's daughter **Matilda** was married to the emperor Henry V. The second war (1116–20) was marked by the defeat of the French king at Noyon in 1119, and Henry was able to satisfy the pope, who succeeded in bringing about a peace. In 1120 Henry's only legitimate son, William, was drowned on his way from Normandy to England. Consequently, in 1126 Matilda, now a widow, came back from Germany; Henry made the barons swear to receive her as Lady of England; and the same year she was married to Geoffrey **Plantagenet**, son of the Count of Anjou. Henry died near Rouen, and the crown was seized by his sister Adela's son, **Stephen** of Blois. Henry I was posthumously styled Beauclerc, or the Scholar, in honour of his learning, which was, in fact, limited. Able he was, and crafty, consistent, passionless in his policy, but often guilty of acts of cold-blooded cruelty. His reign marks a milestone in the development of governmental institutions such as the Exchequer and the itinerant justices.

HENRY II (1133–89) king of England from 1154, the son of **Matilda**, **Henry I**'s daughter, and her second husband, Geoffrey **Plantagenet**, was born in Le Mans. At 18 he was invested with the duchy of Normandy, his mother's heritage, and within a year became also, by his father's death, Count of Anjou; while in 1152 his marriage with **Eleanor of Aquitaine**, the divorced wife of **Louis VII**, added Poitou and Guienne to his dominions. In January 1153 he landed in England, and in November a treaty was agreed to whereby Henry was declared the successor of **Stephen**; he was crowned in 1154. He confirmed his grandfather's laws, re-established the Exchequer, banished the foreign mercenaries, demolished the adulterine castles erected in Stephen's reign, and recovered the royal estates. Much of the early part of his reign was spent dealing with problems arising from his continental possessions. When he turned to concentrate on English affairs, Henry was determined to increase royal control over justice. From the barons his reforms met with little serious opposition: with the clergy he was less successful. To aid him in reducing the authority of the church he appointed his chancellor, **Thomas à Becket** to the see of Canterbury. Henry compelled him and the other prelates to agree to the 'Constitutions of Clarendon', but Becket proved a sturdy churchman, and the struggle between him and his monarch was terminated only by his murder (1170). In 1174 Henry did penance at Becket's tomb, but in many respects he succeeded in bringing the church to subordination in civil matters. Meanwhile he organized an expedition to Ireland. The English pope, **Adrian IV**, had in 1155 given Henry authority over the entire island; and a number of Norman-Welsh knights had gained a footing in the country—among them Richard de Clare, Earl of Pembroke, nicknamed **Strongbow**, who in 1170 married the heiress of Leinster and assumed rule as the Earl of Leinster. Henry was jealous at the rise of a powerful feudal baronage in Ireland, and during his stay there (1171–72) he broke the power of Strongbow and the other nobles. By 1185 Prince John (the future King **John**) had been given some sort of responsibility for Ireland, but before the end of 1186 he was driven from the country, and all was left in confusion. The eldest of Henry's sons had died in childhood; the second, Henry, born in 1155, was crowned as his father's associate and successor in 1170. In 1173, incited by their jealous mother, Queen Eleanor, the prince John and his brother **Richard Coeur de Lion** rebelled against their father, and their cause was espoused by the kings of France and Scotland. The latter, **William the Lion**, was ravaging the north of England when he was taken prisoner at Alnwick in 1174, and to obtain his liberty he agreed to the Treaty of Falaise. In a few months Henry had re-established his authority in all his dominions. During a second, more limited, rebellion Henry the Younger died (1183); and in 1185 Geoffrey, the next son, was killed in a tournament at Paris. In 1188, while Henry was engaged in a war with **Philip II** of France, Richard joined the French king; and in 1189, Henry, having lost Le Mans and the chief castles of Maine, agreed to a treaty of peace granting an indemnity to the followers of Richard. Soon afterwards Henry died at Chinon, and was succeeded by Richard I, Coeur de Lion. On the whole, Henry was an able and enlightened sovereign, a clear-headed, unprincipled politician, and an able general; his reign was one of great legal and financial reforms. His success can be judged by the fact that he kept an empire, stretching from the Scottish border to the Pyrenees, intact until the very last month of his life. His mistress, fair Rosamond, daughter of Walter Clifford, was said to have borne him two sons, William Longsword, Earl of Salisbury, and Geoffrey, archbishop of York, but this is improbable.

HENRY III (1207–72) king of England from 1216, born in Winchester, son of King **John**. In 1227 he declared himself of age; in 1232 he deprived **Hubert de Burgh**, who had ruled as regent and justiciary, of all his offices; and in 1234 he took the administration into his own hands. A war with France cost him Poitou, and might have cost him all his continental possessions but for the generosity of **Louis IX**. He reissued the Great Charter, with omissions; and he confirmed it more than once as a condition of a money grant. He was beset with favourites; his misrule and extortion roused all classes, and in 1258 he was forced to agree to the Provisions of Oxford, transferring his power to a commission of barons. Disunion among the barons, partly caused by the ambition of **Simon de Montfort**, enabled Henry to repudiate his oath, and after a brief war (1263) the matter was referred to Louis IX of France, who annulled the Provisions. De Montfort and his party took up arms against the king, defeated him, made him prisoner at Lewes (1264), and forced him to the humiliating agreement called the Mise of Lewes. But within a year Gilbert de Clare, 9th Earl of **Gloucester**, deserted de Montfort, and, with Prince Edward (later **Edward I**), defeated and slew him at Evesham (1265).

HENRY IV (1367–1413) king of England from 1399, the first king of the House of Lancaster, son of **John of Gaunt**. He was surnamed Bolingbroke, from his birthplace in Lincolnshire. His father was fourth son of **Edward III**, his mother a daughter of Duke Henry of Lancaster. In 1386 Henry married a rich heiress, Mary de Bohun. In 1397 he supported **Richard II** against the Duke of Gloucester, and was created Duke of Hereford; in 1398 he was banished, and in 1399, when his father died, his estates were declared forfeit to Richard. In July Henry landed at Ravenspur in Yorkshire; on 29 September he induced Richard, deserted and betrayed, to sign a renunciation of his claims; thereupon he had himself crowned; and four months later Richard died, of starvation probably, in Pontefract Castle (1400). During Henry's reign rebellion and lawlessness were rife, and frequent descents were made upon the coast by expeditions from France. The king's movements were constantly hampered for want of money, and 'war treasurers' were ultimately appointed by the impatient Commons to watch the disbursement of the sums voted. Under **Owen Glendower** the Welsh maintained a large degree of independence throughout this reign. Henry invaded Scotland in 1400, besieging Edinburgh Castle until compelled by famine to retire. In 1402, while the king was engaged against the Welsh, the Scots invaded Northumberland; but they were encountered by Henry **Percy**, Earl of Northumberland and his son Harry **Percy** (Hotspur), and were defeated (14 September) at Humbleton (or Homildon), where Archibald, 4th Earl of **Douglas**, was taken prisoner. Harry Percy and his house shortly after allied with Douglas and Glendower against Henry; but the king met the Percies at Shrewsbury (21 July 1403), where they were utterly defeated, Hotspur slain, and Douglas again taken prisoner. In 1406 Prince James of Scotland (afterwards **James I**) was captured on his way to France, and was detained and educated in England. The civil wars in France gave Henry an opportunity to send two expeditions (1411–12) there; but in his later years he was a chronic invalid, afflicted with epileptic fits. He died in the Jerusalem Chamber at Westminster.

HENRY V (1387–1422) king of England from 1413, the eldest of the six children of **Henry IV** by Mary de Bohun, and in 1399 created Prince of Wales. From 1401 to 1408 he was engaged against **Owen Glendower** and the Welsh rebels; in 1409 he became constable of Dover, and in 1410 captain of Calais. To this time belong the exaggerated stories of his wild youth. He was crowned on 10 April, 1413, and at the outset of his reign liberated the young Earl of March, the true heir to the crown, restored Henry **Percy**'s (Hotspur) son to his father's lands and honours, and had **Richard II**'s body buried in Westminster. The great effort of his reign was an attempted conquest of France; and in 1414 he demanded the French crown, to which he seems to have believed that he had a valid claim through his great-grandfather, **Edward III**. In August 1415 he sailed with a great army, and on 22 September took Harfleur. On 25 October, at Agincourt, he gained a battle against such odds as to make his victory one of the most notable in history. Two years after he again invaded France, and by the end of 1418 Normandy was once more subject to the English crown. In 1420 was concluded the 'perpetual peace' of Troyes, under which Henry was recognized as regent and 'heir of France', and married the French king's daughter, **Catherine of Valois**. In February 1421 he took his young queen to England to be crowned; but in a month he was recalled to France by news of the defeat of his brother, Thomas, the Duke of **Clarence**. Henry was seized with illness, and died at Vincennes, leaving an infant (**Henry VI**) to succeed him. Henry was devout, just, and pure of life; yet his religion did not make him merciful to a conquered enemy; and he persecuted the Lollards, who had become the first group of English heretics to represent a political threat.

HENRY VI (1421–71) king of England from 1422 to 1461 and 1470 to 1471, only child of **Henry V** and **Catharine of Valois**, born in Windsor. During his minority his uncle, John, the Duke of **Bedford**, was appointed to govern France, and another uncle, Humphrey, Duke of **Gloucester**, to be protector of England, with a council appointed by parliament. In France, the incapable Charles VI having died, the dauphin assumed the title of **Charles VII**, but his army was almost annihilated by the English at Verneuil (1424). In 1429 the siege of Orléans was raised by the French, inspired by **Joan of Arc**, and after this the English power declined steadily. Henry was crowned king of England in 1429, and king of France at Paris in 1431. Bedford, the only English leader of note, died in 1435; Paris was recovered by the dauphin in 1436, Normandy was lost in 1450; and in 1453 the English were expelled from all France (Calais excepted). In 1455 Henry married the strong-minded **Margaret of Anjou**; in 1447 the Beaufort party and she had Gloucester arrested for treason; and five days later he was found dead in his bed, but there is no proof that he was murdered. **Jack Cade** obtained temporary possession of London, but was soon captured and executed. As a descendant of Lionel, Duke of Clarence, **Edward III**'s third son, Richard, Duke of **York**, had a better title to the crown than Henry; in 1454, during the latter's mental lapse, he was appointed protector by parliament. On the king's recovery York levied an army to maintain his power, and at St Albans (1455) the Yorkists were victors and the king taken prisoner. This was the first of many battles between the Houses of York and Lancaster in the Wars of the Roses. A return of Henry's disorder made York again protector in 1455–56; and on his recovery Henry vainly strove to maintain peace between the factions. Margaret of Anjou headed the Lancastrian forces; but in 1461 **Edward IV** was proclaimed king, and in 1465 Henry was captured and committed to the Tower. In 1470 Richard Neville, Earl of **Warwick** restored him to the throne, but six months later he was again in Edward's hands; and at Tewkesbury (4 May 1471) his son was slain and Margaret taken prisoner. Edward returned to London on 21 May; and that night Henry was murdered. Henry, the 'royal saint', founded Eton and King's College, Cambridge. It was probably his inability to govern rather than the advent of bastard feudalism which was responsible for the civil disturbances known as the Wars of the Roses.

HENRY VII (1457–1509) first Tudor king of England from 1485, the son of Edmund Tudor, Earl of Richmond, and Margaret Beaufort, father of **Henry VIII**, born in Pembroke Castle. He was the grandson of that Owen Tudor who married Queen **Catherine of Valois**, widow of **Henry V**. His mother, a great-granddaughter of **John of Gaunt**, ranked as the lineal descendant of the House of Lancaster. After the Lancastrian defeat at Tewkesbury (1471), Henry was whisked away to Brittany, where all the Yorkist attempts on his life and liberty were frustrated. On 1 August 1485, Henry landed, unopposed, at Milford Haven. After the death of **Richard III** on Bosworth Field, parliament assented to Henry's assumption of the regal title. As monarch, his undeviating policy was to restore peace and prosperity to a warworn and impoverished land; an aim which his marriage of reconciliation with Elizabeth of York (eldest daughter of **Edward IV**) materially advanced. Minor Yorkist revolts, like the pretensions of such pinchbeck claimants to the throne as **Lambert Simnel** and **Perkin Warbeck**, were firmly dealt with; but Henry's policy in general was mercantilist and pacific, as was demonstrated by his readiness to conclude peace with France for a promised indemnity of £149000. With the self-immolation of the feudal aristocracy in the recent war, the matrix of power had shifted from the castle to the bourse; and Henry's shipbuilding subsidies expanded his mercantile marine while giving him first call on craft speedily convertible into warships. The marriage of Henry's heir, the future **Henry VIII** to **Catherine of Aragon** cemented an alliance with Spain that largely nullified the soaring aspirations of France; while long-nursed Caledonian enmity was undermined when **James IV** of Scotland married his daughter **Margaret Tudor**. A widower after 1503, Henry's design to further his policy by remarriage was cut short by his death in 1509. His personal fortune of over a million and a half pounds reflected the commercial prosperity his prudent policy had restored to the realm. He had adopted the policies of **Edward IV** and had created a situation in which they could succeed.

HENRY VIII (1491–1547) king of England from 1509, second son of **Henry VII**, born in Greenwich. During the first years of his reign he held a place in the hearts of his people. In his earlier manhood he was accounted the handsomest and most accomplished prince of his time; and his accession to the throne was hailed by such men as **Colet**, **Erasmus** and **More**. Seven weeks later Henry married **Catherine of Aragon**, his brother Prince **Arthur**'s widow—a step of tremendous consequence. As a member of the Holy League, formed by the pope and Spain against **Louis XII**, in 1512 he invaded France, and next year won the so-called Battle of Spurs, and captured Terouenne and Tournay. During his absence a greater triumph was gained in the defeat of the Scots at Flodden (1513). It was in this French war that **Wolsey** became prominent. As early as 1514 he was, after the king, the first man in the country. The chief aim of Wolsey and his master was to hold in equipoise France and Spain, and to win for England as arbiter an importance to which her own resources hardly entitled her. The support of England was accordingly till 1525 given to Spain against France. The struggle between **Charles V** and **Francis I** proceeded with varying success till, in 1525, Francis was brought to the verge of ruin by his defeat and capture at Pavia. As the ascendancy thus gained by the emperor endangered the balance of power, England was now thrown into alliance with France. In 1521 the Duke of Buckingham, a descendant of **Edward III**, was executed on an almost groundless charge of treason. The same year Henry published his famous book on the Sacraments in reply to **Luther**, and received from Pope **Leo X** the title borne by all Henry's successors, 'Defender of the Faith'. To enable him to play his part in Continental affairs, Henry had frequent need of heavy supplies; and Wolsey took on himself all the odium of excessive taxation. Wolsey made himself still further odious by the suppression of all monasteries with less than seven inmates, devoting the revenues to educational purposes. In 1525 Henry's expensive foreign policy again brought him into straits, and Wolsey proposed an illegal tax, the Amicable Loan; it met with the strongest opposition, and Wolsey was forced to abandon it. The turning-point in Henry's reign is the moment when he determined that his marriage with Catherine of Aragon must be nullified. All her children, except **Mary Tudor**, had died in infancy, and Henry professed to see in this the judgment of Heaven on an unnatural alliance; any doubt of the legitimacy of Mary might lead to a renewal of the civil wars; further, Henry had set his affections on **Anne Boleyn**, a niece of **Thomas Howard**, 3rd Duke of Norfolk. Pope **Clement VII** was at first disposed to humour Henry, and in 1528 sent Cardinal **Campeggio** to England to try the validity of the marriage. The visit settled nothing; and the pope, under pressure from the emperor, revoked the case to the Roman curia. This proved the ruin of Wolsey, who now found himself without a friend at home or abroad. In 1529 he was stripped of his goods and honours, and dismissed in disgrace; next year he was summoned to London on a charge of high treason, but died on the way. Despite the coldness of the pope, Henry was determined as ever on the divorce, and by humbling the clergy he thought he could bring the pope to terms. In 1531 the whole body of the clergy, on the same grounds as Wolsey, were declared guilty of treason under the law of *praemunire*, and purchased pardon only by paying £118840. He extorted from them his recognition as 'protector and supreme head of the church and clergy of England', and in 1532 abolished the annates paid to the pope. Sir Thomas More, who had succeeded to the chancellorship, and who saw the inevitable end of Henry's policy, prayed to be relieved of the Great Seal. In further defiance of Rome, Henry (1533) was privately married to Anne Boleyn. In 1534 it was enacted that all bishops should be appointed by a *congé d'élire* from the crown, and that all recourse to the bishop of Rome should be illegal. It was also enacted that the king's marriage with Catherine was invalid, that the succession to the crown should lie with the issue of Henry's marriage with Anne Boleyn, and that the king was the sole supreme head of the Church of England. To this last act Bishop **Fisher** and Sir Thomas More refused to swear, and both were executed next year. The supporters of Luther were treated with the same severity as those of the church who refused to acknowledge the king in the place of the pope. To show that his quarrel was with the pope and not the church, and to proclaim his soundness in doctrine, Henry ordered (1537) the publication of the *Bishops' Book* or the *Institution of a Christian Man*, strictly orthodox save on the headship of the pope. In the famous *Statue of the Six Articles*, known as the 'Bloody Statute', all the fundamental doctrines of the church of Rome are insisted on, with the severest penalties, as necessary articles of belief (1539). In 1535 Henry appointed a commission under **Thomas Cromwell** to report on the state of the monasteries for the guidance of parliament; and the document seemed to justify the most drastic dealing. An act was passed for the suppression of all monasteries with a revenue under £200 a year—a high-handed and unpopular step. This, together with the fact that everywhere there was much misery by reason of the land being extensively converted from agricultural to pastoral purposes, caused, the year after the suppression of the smaller monasteries, a formidable insurrection in the northern counties, known as the 'Pilgrimage of Grace'. The revolt was crushed, and Henry next (1536) suppressed all the remaining monasteries. The bulk of the revenues passed to the crown and to those who had made themselves useful to the king. In 1536 Queen Catherine died, and the same year Anne Boleyn herself was executed for infidelity. The day after her execution Henry was betrothed to **Jane Seymour** who died leaving a son, afterwards **Edward VI**. **Anne of Cleves** was chosen as the king's fourth wife, in the hope of attaching the Protestant interest of Germany. Anne's personal appearance proved so little to Henry's taste that he consented to the marriage only on the condition that a divorce should follow speedily. Cromwell had made himself as generally detested as Wolsey. It was mainly through his action that Anne had been brought forward, and his enemies used Henry's indignation to effect his ruin. Accused of high treason by the Duke of Norfolk, he was executed on a bill of attainder, without a trial (1540); and Henry married **Catherine Howard**, another niece of the Catholic Duke of Norfolk. Before two years had passed Catherine suffered the same fate as Anne Boleyn, on the same charge, and in July 1543 Henry married his sixth wife, **Catherine Parr**, widow of Lord Latimer, who was happy enough to survive him. During all these years Henry's interest in the struggle between Francis I and the emperor had been kept alive by the intrigues of France in Scotland. At length Henry and Francis concluded a peace (1546), of which Scotland also had the benefit. The execution of the **Henry Howard**, Earl of Surrey, son of the Duke of Norfolk, on a charge of high treason, completes the long list of the judicial murders of Henry's reign. Norfolk himself was saved from the same fate only by the death of Henry himself. Henry is apt to be judged simply as an unnatural monster, influenced by motives of cruelty and lust. Yet from first to last he was popular with his people, and he inspired the most devoted affection of those in immediate contact with him. In point of personal morals he was pure compared with Francis or **James V** of Scotland; even in the shedding of blood he was merciful compared with Francis. Only a prince of the most imperious will could have effected the great ecclesiastical revolution.

HENRY (1594–1612) Prince of Wales, the eldest son of **James VI and I** and **Anne of Denmark**. Notable for the strict morality of his way of life, in marked contrast to his father, and known to support a vigorously Protestant and anti-Spanish foreign policy, Henry became the focus for the hopes of those at court with puritan sympathies. His death, loudly rumoured to be a result of poison, brought nationwide regret while the hopes of forward Protestants centred increasingly upon Henry's sister, **Elizabeth**, and her husband, **Frederick V** of the Palatinate.

HENRI V, of France so-called See **CHAMBORD, Henri**

HENRY III (1017–56) Holy Roman Emperor, son of **Conrad II**, father of **Henry IV**, became king of the Germans in 1026, Duke of Bavaria in 1027, Duke of Swabia in 1038, and emperor in 1039. He resolutely maintained the imperial prerogatives of power, and encouraged the efforts of the Cluniac monks to reform the ecclesiastical system of Europe. In 1046 he put an end to the intrigues of the three rival popes by deposing all three and electing Clement II in their stead. In 1042 he compelled the Duke of Bohemia to acknowledge himself a vassal of the empire. By repeated campaigns in Hungary he established the supremacy of the empire in 1044. Henry also stretched his authority over the Norman conquerors of Apulia and Calabria. He promoted learning and the arts, founded numerous monastic schools, and built many great churches.

HENRY IV (1050–1106) Holy Roman Emperor from 1056, elected king of the Germans in 1053, succeeded his father, **Henry III** in 1056, under the regency of his mother Agnes of Poitou. About 1070 he began to act for himself. His first task was to break the power of the nobles; but his measures provoked a rising of the Saxons, who in 1074 forced upon Henry humiliating terms. In 1075 he defeated them at Hohenburg, and then proceeded to take vengeance upon the princes, secular and ecclesiastical, who had opposed him. The case of the latter gave Pope **Gregory VII** a pretext to interfere in the affairs of Germany. This was the beginning of the great duel between pope and emperor. In 1076 Henry declared the pontiff deposed. Gregory retaliated by excommunicating Henry. The king, seeing his vassals and princes falling away from him, hastened to Italy to make submission at Canossa as a humble penitent, and in January 1077 the ban of excommunication was removed. Having found adherents among the Lombards, Henry renewed the conflict, but was again excommunicated. He thereupon appointed a new pope, Clement III, hastened over the Alps and besieged Rome, and in 1084 caused himself to be crowned emperor by the antipope. In Germany, during Henry's absence, three rival kings of the Germans successively found support. But Henry managed to triumph over them all. He had crossed the Alps for the third time (1090) to support Clement III, when he learned that his son Conrad had joined his enemies and been crowned king at Monza. Disheartened, he retired to Lombardy in despair, but at length returned (1097) to Germany. His second son, Henry (the future emperor Henry V), was elected king of the Germans and heir to the empire. This prince, however, was induced to rebel by Pope Pascal II (1099–1118); he took the emperor prisoner in 1105, and compelled him to abdicate. The emperor escaped and found safety at Liége, where he died. He was succeeded by Prince Henry (1081–1125) as Henry V.

HENRY VI (1165–97) Holy Roman Emperor from 1190, the son of **Frederick I Barbarossa**. He married Constance, aunt and heiress of William II of Sicily (1186) and succeeded his father in 1190. He was opposed by the papacy, the **Guelfs**, **Richard I** of England and Constance's illegitimate brother **Tancred** who had been elected king by the Sicilian barons on the death of William. This hostile coalition collapsed when Richard fell into the hands of **Leopold V** of Austria, who turned his captive over to Henry. On the death of Tancred (1194) he overran Sicily, where Constance bore him a son, **Frederick II**. Emperor since 1191 and now king of Sicily, he was regarded by contemporaries as the most powerful man on earth, although he was unsuccessful in his plans to make the empire hereditary. Still a young man, he died at Messina, probably of malaria, while engaged in preparations for a crusade.

HENRY VII (1274–1313) Holy Roman Emperor from 1308, and king of Germany, originally Count of Luxembourg, a French-speaking minor prince from the extreme west of the empire. He was elected emperor in 1308 as an alternative candidate to Charles of Valois mainly due to the skilful diplomacy of his brother Baldwin, archbishop of Trier. His family soon rose to great power with the marriage of his son John to Elizabeth, heiress of Bohemia (1311). In 1310 Henry led an army to Italy where he remained with the aim of restoring imperial authority, but made little progress against the opposition of King Robert of Naples and the **Guelf** cities, and the imperialist cause collapsed when he died near Siena, probably of malaria.

HENRY, known as **The Navigator** (1394–1460) Portuguese prince, third son of John I, king of Portugal, and Philippa, daughter of **John of Gaunt**. He distinguished himself at the capture of Ceuta, in North Africa, in 1415. He was made governor of the Algarve in 1419, and took up his residence at Sagres; and during the war against the Moors his sailors reached parts of the ocean before unknown. He erected an observatory and a school for navigation, and dispatched some of his pupils on voyages of discovery, resulting in the discovery of the Madeira Islands in 1418 the Azores and the Cape Verde Islands. His pupils also explored the west coast of Africa, as far as Sierra Leone, and established many trading posts.

HENRY, Carl Ferdinand Howard (1913–) American Protestant theologian, born in New York City, the son of German immigrants. In 1933, after conversion, he turned from journalism, studied and taught theology, and was the founding editor of *Christianity Today* magazine (1956–68). Through it he became widely recognized as a leading spokesman for conservative evangelicals. His many books include *The Uneasy Conscience of Modern Fundamentalism* (1948), which spurred evangelicals out of cultural isolation into social engagement, *Christian Personal Ethics* (1957), and *God, Revelation and Authority* (6 vols, 1976–82), available also in Korean and Mandarin.

HENRY, Joseph (1797–1878) American physicist, born in Albany, New York. In 1832 he became professor of natural philosophy at Princeton, and in 1846 first secretary of the Smithsonian Institution. He discovered electrical induction independently of **Michael Faraday** and constructed the first electromagnetic motor (1829), demonstrated the oscillatory nature of electric discharges (1842), and introduced a system of weather forecasting. The 'henry' unit of inductance is named after him.

HENRY, O, pen-name of **William Sydney Porter** (1862–1910) American writer, master of the short story, born in Greenboro, North Carolina. Brought up during the depression in the South, he settled in Austin, Texas, where he became a bank-teller. In 1894 he 'borrowed' money from the bank to help his consumptive wife and to start a literary magazine, the *Rolling Stone*, but ran away at the height of the scandal. He returned, however, in 1897 to his wife's deathbed. He was found technically guilty of embezzlement, spent three years in jail (1898–1901), where he adopted his pseudonym and began to write short stories. His second marriage came to nothing and he roamed about the New York back streets from 1902, where he found ample material for his tales. His list of many collections was *Cabbages and Kings* (1904). His use of coincidence and trick endings, his purple phraseology and caricature have been criticized, but nothing can detract from the technical brilliance and boldness of his comic writing.

HENRY, Patrick (1736–99) American statesman, born in Hanover county, Virginia. He failed in storekeeping and in farming, so turned lawyer in 1760, and first displayed his great eloquence in pleading the cause of the people against an unpopular tax (1763). A great patriot in the War of Independence, he delivered the first speech in the Continental congress (1774). In 1776 he carried the vote of the Virginia convention for independence, and became governor of the new state. He was four times re-elected. In 1791 he retired from public life.

HENRY, William (1774–1836) English chemist, born in Manchester. He studied medicine at Edinburgh, practised in Manchester, but soon devoted himself to chemistry. He formulated the law named after him that the amount of gas absorbed by a liquid varies directly as the pressure.

HENRY OF BLOIS (1101–71) English prelate, younger brother of King **Stephen**. He was bishop of Winchester from 1129, and papal legate in England from 1139. He supported Stephen against the empress **Matilda** (Maud), and went to France after Stephen's death (1154).

HENRY OF HUNTINGDON (c.1084–1155) English chronicler, archdeacon of Huntingdon from 1109. In 1139 he visited Rome. He compiled a *Historia Anglorum* down to 1154.

HENRY THE FOWLER (c.876–936) king of Germany as Henry I from 919. The founder of the Saxon dynasty, he was Duke of Saxony from 912. He brought Swabia and Bavaria into the German confederation, regained Lotharingia (925), defeated the Wends in 928 and the Hungarians in 933 and seized Schleswig from Denmark in 934. He was about to claim the imperial crown as Holy Roman Emperor in 936 when he died. He was succeeded by his son, **Otto I the Great**. Another son was St **Bruno** (925–65).

HENRY THE LION (1129–95) duke of Saxony and Bavaria, was the head of the **Guelf** family. After Bavaria (taken from his father Henry the Proud) was restored to him by the Emperor **Frederick I Barbarossa** (1156) he was the most powerful prince in Germany, whose domains stretched from the Baltic to the Adriatic. He expanded the frontiers of Saxony to the east against the Slavs, and did much to encourage the commerce of his lands, developing the towns of Lüneburg, Breman, Lübeck and Brunswick, but his ambitions and growing might aroused the opposition of a league of Saxon princes (1166) and of Frederick I, who defeated him and deprived him of his lands (1180). His vast concentration of power having been broken up, Henry went into exile at the court of **Henry II** of England, whose daughter Mathilda he had married in 1168. He returned to Germany in 1184 and was reconciled to the emperor **Henry VI** in 1194.

HENRY THE MINSTREL See **HARRY, Blind**

HENRYSON, Robert (c.1425–c.1508) Scottish poet. He is usually designated 'schoolmaster of Dunfermline', and was certainly a notary in 1478. His best-known work was the *Testament of Cresseid*, a kind of supplement to **Chaucer**'s poem on the same subject. Of his 14 extant poems, *Robene and Makyne* is the earliest Scottish specimen of pastoral poetry. Other works include a metrical version of thirteen *Morall Fabels of Esope the Phrygian*, possibly his masterpiece.

HENSCHEL, Sir George (1850–1934) German-born British composer, conductor, singer and pianist, born in Breslau. He came to England in 1877, was naturalized in 1890, and knighted 1914. He composed operas, a Requiem and chamber music, conducted the Boston Symphony Orchestra and became the first conductor of the Scottish Symphony Orchestra (1893–95).

HENSEN, Christian Andreas Viktor (1835–1924) German physiologist, born in Kiel. He did research work on embryology, and the anatomy of the organs of sense (the Hensen duct in the ear), and investigated the production of marine fauna which he named *plankton*.

HENSLOWE, Philip (d.1616) English stage-manager. He was originally a dyer and starch-maker, but became in 1584 lessee of the Rose theatre on the Bankside. From 1591 till his death in 1616 he was in partnership with **Edward Alleyn**, who married his step-daughter in 1592. Henslowe's business diary from 1593 to 1609, preserved at Dulwich College, contains invaluable information about the stage of **Shakespeare**'s day.

HENSON, Herbert Hensley (1863–1947) English prelate. Educated at Oxford, he was ordained and ministered in Essex, and in 1900 became canon of Westminster Abbey, and rector of St Margaret's Westminster. He was subsequently dean of Durham (1912–18), bishop of Hereford (1918–20, an appointment that caused an outcry because of his radical views), and bishop of Durham (1920–39). His many publications included *Apostolic Christianity* (1898), *Christian Marriage* (1907), *Anglicanism* (1921), *Notes on Spiritual Healing* (1925), *Disestablishment* (1929), and *Retrospect of an Unimportant Life* (3 vols, 1942–50).

HENSON, Jim (James Maury) (1936–90) American puppeteer and fantasy filmmaker, born in Greenville, Mississippi. A commercial art student, he secured a job on local television in Washington DC and was later host of his own show entitled *Sam and Friends* (1955–61). After graduating from Maryland University, his creations began to appear on national television series including *The Jimmy Dean Show* (1963–66). Intrigued by television technology and the potential of the medium, he continued to refine his endearing characters and, in 1969, launched *Sesame Street*, a series that entertained and educated pre-school children. Many of his long-established puppets, like Kermit the Frog and Miss Piggy, gained phenomenal popularity in the series *The Muppet Show* (1976–81) which reached an estimated 235 million viewers in more than 100 countries. The characters were subsequently utilized in a string of films and a Grammy-winning album of the same title (1979). The recipient of numerous Emmy awards, he has continued to make innovative television programmes combining live action and increasingly sophisticated puppetry, including *Fraggle Rock* (1983–) and *The Storyteller* (1987–). He has also diversified into special-effects adventure films like *The Dark Crystal* (1982), *Labyrinth* (1986) and *The Witches* (1989).

HENSON, Leslie (1891–1957) English comedian, remembered for his facial elasticity. He took leading roles in *Lady Luck* (1927), *Funny Face* (1928), *It's a Boy* (1930), *Harvey* (1950), etc, and produced the famous Aldwych farces and many other plays. He published an autobiography, *Yours Faithfully* (1948).

HENTY, George Alfred (1832–1902) English novelist and journalist, born in Trumpington. Educated at Westminster and Caius College, Cambridge, he became a special correspondent for the *Morning Advertiser* during the Crimean war and for the *Standard* in the Franco-Prussian war. He was best known, however, for his 80 historical adventure stories for boys, including *With Clive in India* (1884) and *With Moore at Corunna* (1898).

HENZE, Hans Werner (1926–) German composer, born in Gütersloh. He studied with Fortner at Heidelberg, and with René Leibowitz in Darmstadt and Paris. After early absorption of serial techniques he later reacted against the strictness and exclusiveness of the 'Darmstadt school' and sought, in symphonic and theatre music, to communicate his aesthetic and social views directly with the public, without compromising either the personal or the contemporary qualities of his style. His political awareness was stimulated particularly by the Vietnam War and the student movements of 1967–68, and his subsequent music reflects his socialist commitment to movements in Germany, Italy and Cuba. His stage works include nine full-length and three one-act operas (notably *Das Wundertheater*, 1948, rev 1964, *Boulevard Solitude*—based on the theme of *Manon Lescaut*, 1951, *König Hirsch*, 1955, *Elegy for Young Lovers*, 1961, *The Bassarids*, 1965, *We Come to the River*, 1975, *The English Cat*, 1983), six full-length and five chamber ballets, and other music-theatre works. He has composed seven symphonies, five string quartets, concertos, and other orchestral, chamber, vocal and piano music. His collected writings from 1953 to 1981 were published as *Music and Politics* (1982).

HEPBURN, James See **BOTHWELL, Earl of**

HEPBURN, Katharine (1909–) American film and stage actress, born in Hartford, Connecticut and educated at Bryn Mawr College. She made her professional stage début in *The Czarina* (1928) in Baltimore, but attained international fame as a film actress where her distinctive New England diction and fine bone structure complemented a versatile talent capable of all shades of drama and farce. She won Academy Awards for *Morning Glory* (1933), *Guess Who's Coming to Dinner?* (1967), *The Lion in Winter* (1968) and *On Golden Pond* (1981). On stage she has continued to tackle the classics and enjoyed enormous success in the musical *Coco* (1970). Among many of her outstanding films were *Bringing Up Baby* (1938), *The Philadelphia Story* (1940), *Woman of the Year* (1942), which saw the beginning of a 25-year professional and personal relationship with co-star **Spencer Tracy**, *The African Queen* (1951) and *Long Day's Journey Into Night* (1962). She continues to act despite suffering from Parkinson's Disease. Television work includes *The Glass Menagerie* (1973), *Love Among the Ruins* (1975) and *Mrs Delafield Wants to Marry* (1986).

HEPPLEWHITE, George (d.1786) English furniture designer. He seems to have trained as a cabinet-maker with the Lancaster firm of Gillow, and then set up a workshop at St Giles, Cripplegate, in London; but not a single piece of extant furniture is attributable to him. His simple and elegant designs, characterized by the free use of inlaid ornament and the use of shield or heart shapes in chair backs, only became famous with the posthumous publication of his *Cabinet-Maker and Upholsterer's Guide* by his widow in 1788.

HEPWORTH, Dame (Jocelyn) Barbara (1903–75) English sculptor, born in Wakefield. She studied at the Leeds School of Art, the Royal College of Art and in Italy. She married, first, the sculptor John Skeaping (1901–80), and then the painter **Ben Nicholson**. She was one of the foremost nonfigurative sculptors of her time, notable for the strength and formal discipline of her carving (eg, the *Contrapuntal Forms* exhibited at the Festival of Britain, 1951). Her representational paintings and drawings are of equal power.

HERACLITUS (fl.500 BC) Greek philosopher, born in Ephesus of an old aristocratic family. He was known as 'the obscure' and 'the riddler' in legitimate criticism of his oracular style. He wrote a book, *On Nature*, of which only fragments remain and we are more than usually reliant on conjecture in interpreting his thought. His most famous doctrine is that everything is in a state of flux ('you can never step into the same river twice'); the apparent unity and stability of the world conceals a dynamic tension between opposites, which is somehow measured and controlled by reason (*Logos*) or its physical manifestation, fire; fire is the ultimate constituent of the world, and the fire of the human soul is thus linked to the cosmic fire which virtuous souls eventually join. His vivid, suggestive style has tended either to fascinate or to repel, but philosophers as eminent as **Hegel** have claimed to have taken inspiration from him.

HERACLIUS (c.575–641) Byzantine emperor. Born in Cappadocia, he revolted against **Phocas**, slew him, and took his throne (610). The empire was threatened to the north by the Avars, and to the east by the Persians under **Chosroes II** who overran Syria, Egypt and Asia Minor. Heraclius carried out far-reaching reoganizations of the army, the provincial government, and the empire's finances, and made Greek its official language. These reforms enabled him to defeat the Persians in a series of campaigns which restored the lost territories (628–33). However, he failed to resolve the differences between the orthodox and monphysite parties in the church, and from 634 the recent gains in the East were almost completely lost to the followers of **Muhammad** under the caliph 'Umar.

HERBART, Johann Friedrich (1776–1841) German philosopher and educational theorist, born in Oldenburg. He was a teacher in Switzerland from 1797–1800, when he became interested in **Pestalozzi**'s educational methods, was professor of philosophy at Göttingen from 1805 to 1808, and at Königsberg (as **Kant**'s successor) from 1809 to 1833, returning to Göttingen 1833–41. His metaphysics posited a multiplicity of 'reals' (things which in themselves possess absolute existence independently of being perceived), and led to a psychology which rejected the notions of faculties and innate ideas and formed a basis for his pedagogical theories. His main publications were: *Psychologie als Wissenschaft neu gegrundet auf Erfahrung*, *Metaphysik und Mathematik* (2 vols, 1824–25), and *Allgemeine Pädagogik* (1806).

HERBELOT, Barthélemy d' (1625–95) French orientalist, born in Paris. In 1692 he became professor of Syriac in the Collège de France. His *Bibliothèque Orientale* (1697) is a universal dictionary of oriental knowledge.

HERBERT name of an English noble family, descended from 'Herbertus Camerarius' who came over from France with **William I, the Conqueror**; seven or eight generations later the Herberts diverged into the Earls of Powis, the Lords Herbert of Cherbury, the Herberts of Muckross, and several untitled branches in England, Wales, and Ireland. Sir William Herbert of Raglan Castle, Monmouth, was knighted in 1415 by **Henry V** for his valour in the French wars. His descendants were Earls of Pembroke and Huntingdon, the Earls of Carnarvon descending from the 8th Earl of Pembroke.

HERBERT, Sir William, 1st Earl of Pembroke (d.1469) son of Sir William Herbert of Raglan Castle. An adherent of the House of York in the Wars of the Roses, he was created Earl of Pembroke by **Edward IV** in 1468, but was captured by the Lancastrians and beheaded.

HERBERT, Sir William, 1st Earl of Pembroke (2nd creation) (c.1501–1570) English soldier and diplomat. He married Anne Parr, the sister of **Catherine Parr**, **Henry VIII**'s sixth wife. He supported **Mary I** against Lady **Jane Grey** and put down Sir **Thomas Wyatt**'s rebellion (1554).

HERBERT, Henry, 2nd Earl of Pembroke (c.1534–1601) English courtier, prominent at the trial of **Mary, Queen of Scots**. He married first Lady Catherine Grey (1553), sister of Lady **Jane Grey**, and in 1577 Mary Sidney, sister of the poet Sir **Philip Sidney**, who dedicated his *Arcadia* to her.

HERBERT, William, 3rd Earl of Pembroke (1580–1630) English poet. He was a patron of **Ben Jonson**, **Massinger** and **Inigo Jones**, and a lord chamberlain of the court (1615–30). He became chancellor of Oxford University in 1617 and had Pembroke College named after him. **Shakespeare**'s 'W H', the 'onlie begetter' of the *Sonnets* has been taken by some to refer to him.

HERBERT, Philip, 4th Earl of Pembroke (1584–1650) English statesman, brother of the poet **William Herbert**. A favourite of **James VI and I**, he was created 1st Earl of Montgomery in 1605. He married Anne **Clifford**, who restored several churches and castles in England. He strove to promote peace between **Charles I** and the Scots, but left the king and joined the Parliamentarians (1641), and became vice-chancellor of Oxford (1641–50).

HERBERT, Sir A P (Alan Patrick) (1890–1971) English writer and politician. He was called to the bar but never practised, having established himself in his twenties as a witty writer of verses, joining *Punch* in 1924. His first theatrical success with **Nigel Playfair** in the revue *Riverside Nights* (1926) was followed by a series of brilliant libretti for comic operas, including *Tantivy Towers* (1930), a version of **Offenbach**'s *Helen* (1932), *Derby Day* (1932) and *Bless the Bride* (1947). He was also the author of several successful novels, notably *The Secret Battle* (1919), *The Water Gipsies* (1930) and *Holy Deadlock* (1934). In *What a Word* (1935) and many humorous articles he campaigned against jargon and officialese. From 1935 to 1950 he was Independent member of parliament for Oxford University, and introduced a marriage bill in the House of Commons that became law as the Matrimonial Causes Act 1938, and did much to improve divorce conditions.

HERBERT, George (1593–1633) English metaphysical poet and clergyman, member of a distinguished Anglo-Welsh family, the son of Lady Magdalen Herbert (to whom **Donne** addressed his *Holy Sonnets*) and brother of Lord **Herbert of Cherbury**. Educated at Westminster and Trinity College, Cambridge, he was elected a fellow there at the age of 22 in 1614, and Public Orator in 1619. He was MP for Montgomery in 1624–25. His connection with the court, and particularly the favour of King **James VI and I**, seemed to point to a worldly career, and his poems, 'Affliction' and 'The Collar', indicate the sharpness of the decision which finally directed him to the Church. In 1630, under the influence of **Laud**, he took orders and spent his few remaining years as the zealous parish priest of Bemerton in Wiltshire. Like his friend **Nicholas Ferrar**, but without Ferrar's mystical piety, he represents both in his life and works the counter-challenge of the Laudian party to the Puritans. The Church was Christ's comely bride to be decked with seemly ornament and 'The mean thy praise and glory is'. This twofold conception, along with his ideal of Christian humility and unwearying service, pervades all his writing, verse and prose alike. Practically all his religious lyrics are included in *The Temple, Sacred Poems and Private Ejaculations*, posthumously published in 1633. His chief prose work, *A Priest in the Temple*, containing guidance for the country parson, was published in his *Remains* (1652).

HERBERT, Victor (1859–1924) Irish-born American composer, born in Dublin. A cellist by training, he played in the orchestras of **Johann Strauss** and the Stuttgart Court before settling in New York as leading cellist of the Metropolitan Opera Company's Orchestra. His successful comic opera, *Prince Ananias* (1893), was followed by a long series of similar works containing such enduringly popular songs as 'Ah, sweet mystery of life' and 'Kiss me again'. His ambition to succeed as a composer of serious opera resulted in *Natoma* (1911) and *Madeleine* (1914).

HERBERT, Wally (Walter William) (1934–) British Arctic explorer. Brought up in South Africa and trained at the School of Military Survey, he spent two years in Egypt before joining the Falkland Islands Dependencies Survey in 1955 for two and a half years in Antarctica, travelling long distances by dog-sled. This was followed by expeditions to Lapland, Svalbard, and Greenland. He participated in the New Zealand Antarctic Expedition (1960–62) which surveyed 26000 square miles of Queen Maud Range, and commemorated the 50th anniversary of **Amundsen**'s attainment of the Pole by following his return journey. He achieved the first surface crossing of the Arctic Ocean (1968–69), a journey of 3620 miles in 464 days, the longest sustained sledge journey in history. He lived in the Arctic, with his wife and daughter, and filmed for long periods with the Inuit (Eskimos), and between 1978 and 1982 he made several attempts to circumnavigate Greenland. He has written a number of books, including *The Noose of Laurels* (1989) on the **Cook-Peary** controversy.

HERBERT OF CHERBURY, Edward Herbert, 1st Baron (1583–1648) English soldier, statesman and philosopher, brother of **George Herbert**, born in Eyton, Shropshire. He was made a knight of the Bath in 1603 and as a member of the privy council was sent as ambassador to France in 1619, when he tried to negotiate between **Louis XIII** and his Protestant subjects. In 1624 he was made a peer of Ireland, and in 1629 of England. When the Civil War broke out he at first sided half-heartedly with the royalists, but in 1644 surrendered to the parliamentarians. Considered one of the finest deistical writers, his works include *De Religione Gentilium* (1645), in which he proves that all religions recognize five main articles, from the acknowledgement of a supreme God to the concept that there are rewards and punishments in a future state. He also wrote poetry, contemporary histories and an autobiography.

HERBERT OF LEA, Sidney Herbert, 1st Baron (1810–61) English statesman, son of the 11th earl of Pembroke, born in Richmond. He was educated at Harrow and Oriel College, Oxford. In 1832 he was elected Conservative MP for South Wiltshire, and was **Peel**'s secretary to the Admiralty from 1841 to 1845, when he became secretary-at-war. He opposed **Cobden**'s motion for a select committee on the corn-laws. In 1852 he was again secretary-at-war under **Aberdeen**, was largely blamed for the hardships of the army before Sebastopol, but sent **Florence Nightingale** to the Crimea. He was for a few weeks **Palmerston**'s colonial secretary in 1855, and his secretary-at-war in 1859. Great improvements in the sanitary conditions and education of the forces, the amalgamation of the Indian with the imperial army, and the organization of the volunteer movement were results of his army administration. After his resignation, he was called (1861) to the House of Lords as Baron Herbert of Lea.

HERBERTSON, Andrew John (1865–1915) Scottish geographer, born in Galashiels and educated at Edinburgh University. After a period at the Ben Nevis and Fort William observatories (1892–93) and an assistantship with **Patrick Geddes** at Dundee (1892), he taught at Manchester (1894–96), Heriot-Watt college, Edinburgh (1896–99) and, finally, at Oxford (1899–1915), where he became head of the department of geography after **Halford John Mackinder** (1905). There he introduced what was to become a distinctive interest in human and regional geography, and developed his scheme of world natural regions, based on the association of physical features, vegetation and climate.

HERD, David (1732–1810) Scottish anthologist, born in Marykirk in Kincardine, the son of a farmer. He worked for most of his life as an accountant in Edinburgh, collecting songs and ballads in his spare time. He was the editor of *Ancient Scottish Ballads* (2 vols, 1776).

HERDER, Johann Gottfried (1744–1803) German critic and poet, born in Mohrungen in East Prussia. He studied at Königsberg, and there made the acquaintance of **Kant** and **Hamann**. In 1764 he became teacher in a school and assistant pastor in a church in Riga. Between 1766 and 1769 he wrote two works, in which he maintained that the truest poetry is the poetry of the people. In 1769 he met **Goethe** in Strasbourg. In 1770 he was appointed court preacher at Bückeburg, and in 1776 first preacher in Weimar. Herder's love for the songs of the people, for unsophisticated human nature, found expression in an admirable collection of folksongs, *Stimmen der Völker in Liedern* (1778–79), a work on the spirit of Hebrew poetry (1782–83; trans 1833), a treatise on the influence of poetry on manners (1778), in oriental mythological tales, in parables and legends, in his version of the *Cid* (1805), and other works. The supreme importance of the historical method is fully recognized in these and a book on the origin of language (1772), and especially in his masterpiece, *Ideen zur Geschichte der Menschheit* (1784–91; trans 1800), which is remarkable for its anticipations of evolutionary theories. He is best remembered for the influence he exerted on Goethe and the growing German Romanticism.

HEREDIA, José María (1803–39) Cuban poet, born in Santiago, de Cuba, cousin of the French poet **José María de Heredia**. He was exiled to the USA for anti-government activities in 1823. He is remembered for his patriotic verse and for his ode to Niagara.

HEREDIA, José María de (1842–1905) French poet, born in Santiago, Cuba, cousin of the Cuban poet **José María Heredia**. He went at an early age to France, where he was educated. One of the Parnassians, he achieved a great reputation with a comparatively small output, his finest work being found in his sonnets, which appeared in the collection *La Trophée* (1893).

HEREFORD, Earls of See **BOHUN** family

HEREWARD, 'the Wake' (11th century) Anglo-Saxon thane and rebel. A Lincolnshire squire, he led a raid on Peterborough Abbey in 1070 as a protest against the appointment of a Norman abbot by **William I, the Conqueror**. He took refuge on the Isle of Ely with other rebels. When William succeeded in penetrating to the English camp of refuge in 1071, Hereward cut his way through to the fastnesses of the swampy fens northwards and escaped. He was the hero of **Charles Kingsley**'s romance, *Hereward the Wake* (1866).

HERGÉ, (Georges Rémi) (1907–83) Belgian strip cartoonist, born in Etterbeek, near Brussels, the creator of *Tin-Tin* the boy detective. He drew his first strip, *Totor*, for a boy scouts' weekly in 1926. He created the Tin-Tin strip for the children's supplement of the newspaper *Le Vingtième Siècle*, using the pen-name Hergé, a phonetic version of his initials, RG. *Tin-Tin in the Land of the Soviets* was quickly republished in album format (1930), as were all the adventures of the young detective: 22 volumes in all.

HERGESHEIMER, Joseph (1880–1954) American novelist, born in Philadelphia. He studied art, but made his name with *Mountain Blood* (1915), *The Three Black Pennys* (1917), *Tubal Cain* (1918), *Java Head* (1919), *The Bright Shawl* (1922), *The Foolscap Rose* (1934) and other novels and short stories.

HERIOT, George (1563–1624) Scottish goldsmith and philanthropist, born in Edinburgh. He started business in 1586, and in 1597 was appointed goldsmith to **Anne of Denmark**, and then to her husband King **James VI** in 1603. Heriot followed the King to London, where, as court jeweller and banker, he amassed considerable wealth. He bequeathed £23 625 to found a hospital or school in Edinburgh for sons of poor burgesses. As 'Jingling Geordie' he figures in **Scott**'s *Fortunes of Nigel*.

HERKOMER, Sir Hubert von (1849–1914) German-born British artist and film pioneer, born in Waal, Bavaria. He studied art at Southampton, Munich and the College of Art in South Kensington, and in 1870 settled in London. As well as painting, he worked as an engraver, wood-carver, ironsmith, architect, journalist, playwright, composer, singer and actor. He was also a pioneer producer/director of British silent films, with his own studio at Bushey. He was Slade professor of fine art at Oxford (1889–94). His portrait paintings included those of **Wagner**, **Ruskin** and Lord **Kelvin**. An enthusiast for 'colour music', in which different colours instead of sounds are produced by a keyboard, he was knighted in 1907.

HERMAN, Woody (Woodrow Charles) (1913–87) American bandleader, alto saxophonist and clarinettist, born in Milwaukee, Wisconsin. Having learned to play saxophone at the age of nine, he left home at 17 to begin his professional career. He was a member of the band led by Isham Jones, but when this broke up in 1936, Herman took certain key members as the nucleus of his own first band, which established itself by the mid 1940s as a stylistic leader, particularly in its saxophone voicings. The Herman Orchestra was one of the very few to survive intact beyond the 1950s.

HERMANDSZOON See **ARMINIUS**

HERMANN, Johann Gottfried Jakob (1772–1848) German classical scholar, born in Leipzig. From 1803 he was professor of eloquence and poetry at Leipzig. He wrote on classical metre and Greek grammar, stressing the importance of linguistic over antiquarian evidence in historical research, and left *Opuscula* (1827–77).

HERMANNSSON, Steingrímur (1928–) Icelandic politician. He trained as an electrical engineer in the USA, returning to pursue an industrial career. He was director of Iceland's National Research Council (1957–78) and then made the transition into politics, becoming chairman of the Progressive party (PP) in 1979. He became a minister in 1978 and then prime minister, heading a PP-Independence party (IP) coalition (1983–87) after which he accepted the foreign affairs portfolio in the government of Thorsteinn Pálsson. He became prime minister again in 1988.

HERMAS (1st century) one of the Apostolic fathers. He was the author of the early Christian treatise called the *Shepherd*. He is sometimes identified as the brother of Pius I, bishop of Rome from 142 to 157.

HERMES, Georg (1775–1831) German Roman Catholic theologian, born in Dreyerwalde in Westphalia. He became theological professor at Münster in 1807, and in 1819 at Bonn. In his works, eg, his *Philosophische Einleitung in die Christkatholische Theologie* (1819), he sought to combine the Catholic faith and doctrines with Kantian philosophy. The Hermesian method became influential in the Rhineland, but his doctrines were condemned by a papal brief in 1835 as heretical, and his followers were deprived of their professorships.

HERMITE, Charles (1822–1901) French mathematician. Professor at the École Polytechnique, he proved that the base, *e*, of natural logarithms is transcendental. He published works on the theory of numbers, elliptic functions, and invariant theory.

HERNÁNDEZ, José (1854–86) Argentinian poet, born near Buenos Aires. He is known for his *gaucho* poetry of life on the pampas, where he had spent his early life among the cattlemen. His masterpiece is the epic *El gaucho Martín Fierro* (1872–79).

HERO OF ALEXANDRIA (1st century AD) Greek mathematician. He invented many pneumatic machines and toys, among them Hero's fountain, the aeolipile, and a double forcing-pump suitable for a fire engine. He wrote on pneumatics, mechanics and mensuration, including the formula for expressing the area of a triangle in terms of its sides.

HEROD, the Great (74–4 BC) ruler of Palestine in Roman times. The second son of **Antipater**, procurator of Judaea, in 47 BC he was made governor of Galilee; ultimately he and his elder brother were made joint tetrarchs of Judaea. Displaced by Antigonus of the Hasmonean dynasty, he fled to Rome, where he obtained, through **Marcus Antonius**, a full recognition of his claims, and became tetrarch of Judaea in 40 BC. On Antony's fall he secured the favour of **Augustus**, and obtained the title of king of Judaea in 31 BC; his reign was stained with cruelties and atrocities. Every member of the Hasmonean family, and even those of his own blood, fell a sacrifice to his jealous fears; and latterly the lightest suspicion sufficed as the ground for wholesale butcheries. The slaughter of the innocents at Bethlehem is quite in keeping with his character, but is not alluded to by **Josephus**; so was his ordering the death of his wife Mariamne and his two sons by her. Herod's one eminent quality was his love of magnificence in architecture. He married ten wives, by whom he had 14 children.

HEROD, Antipas (22 BC–c.40 AD) ruler of Palestine in Roman times, son of **Herod the Great**, by whose will he was named tetrarch of Galilee and Peraea. He divorced his first wife in order to marry Herodias, the wife of his half-brother Philip—a union against which **John the Baptist** remonstrated at the cost of his life. It was when Herod Antipas was at Jerusalem for the Passover that **Jesus** was sent before him by **Pilate** for examination. In 39 he made a journey to Rome in the hope of obtaining from **Caligula** the title of king; he not only failed, but, through the intrigues of **Herod Agrippa**, was banished to Lugdunum (Lyon), where he died.

HEROD, Agrippa I (10 BC–44 AD) son of Aristobulus and Berenice and grandson of **Herod the Great**, was educated and lived at Rome until his debts compelled him to take refuge in Idumea. From this period almost to the death of **Tiberius** he suffered a variety of misfortunes, but, having formed a friendship with **Caligula**, he received from him four tetrarchies, and after the banishment of **Herod Antipas** that of Galilee and Peraea. **Claudius** added to his dominions Judaea and Samaria.

HEROD, Agrippa II (27–100) ruler of Palestine in Roman times, son of **Herod Agrippa I**. He was in Rome when his father died. **Claudius** detained him, and changed the kingdom back into a Roman province. In 53 he received nearly all his paternal possessions, which were subsequently enlarged by **Nero**. Agrippa spent great sums in adorning Jerusalem, and did all in his power to dissuade the Jews from rebelling. When Jerusalem was taken by the Jews he went with his sister to Rome, where he became praetor. It was before him that **Paul** made his defence.

HERODAS See **HERONDAS**

HERODES ATTICUS (101–77) Greek orator and sophist, born in Marathon. A friend of the emperor

Hadrian, he was summoned to Rome in 140 by **Antoninus Pius**. He was consul in 143 with **Marcus Cornelius Fronto**, and a tutor to **Marcus Aurelius**. He is remembered as a prodigious benefactor of public buildings, including the Stadium and Odeum in Athens, a theatre in Corinth, a race-course at Delphi and a hospital at Thermopylae.

HERODIAN (170–240) Greek historian, born in Syria. He lived in Rome, and wrote a history of the Roman emperors in eight books, from the death of **Marcus Aurelius** (180) to the accession of **Gordian III** (238).

HERODOTUS (c.485–425 BC) Greek historian, born in Halicarnassus, a Greek colony on the coast of Asia Minor. When the colonies were freed from the Persian yoke, he left his native town, and travelled in Asia Minor, the Aegean islands, Greece, Macedonia, Thrace, the coasts of the Black Sea, Persia, Tyre, Egypt, and Cyrene. In 443 BC the colony of Thurii was founded by Athens on the Tarentine Gulf, and Herodotus joined it. From Thurii he visited Sicily and Lower Italy. On his travels, he collected historical, geographical, ethnological, mythological and archaeological material for his history which was designed to record not only the wars but the causes of the wars between Greece and the barbarians. Beginning with the conquest of the Greek colonies in Asia Minor by the Lydian king **Croesus**, he gives a history of Lydia, and then passes to Persia, Babylon and Egypt. In books v to ix we have the history of the two Persian wars (500–479 BC). **Cicero** called him 'the father of history'.

HÉROLD, Louis Joseph Ferdinand (1791–1833) French composer, born in Paris. He wrote many operas, and is best remembered for his comic operas, such as *Zampa* (1831) and *Le Pré aux clercs* (1832). He also wrote several ballets and piano music.

HERON, Patrick (1920–) English painter, writer and textile designer, born in Headingley, Leeds. From 1937 to 1939 he studied at the Slade School of Art, London. A conscientious objector during the war, he worked as a farm labourer. At St Ives (1944–45) he met **Ben Nicholson, Barbara Hepworth** and Adrian Stokes. From 1947 to 1950 he was art critic for the *New Statesman & Nation*, and from 1953 to 1956 taught at the Central School of Art, London. He has travelled and lectured in Australia, Brazil and the USA, and has held numerous one-man exhibitions worldwide.

HERONDAS, or **Herodas** (3rd century BC) Greek poet, a native of Cos or Miletus. His work *Mimiambi*, pictures of Greek life in dialogue, comprising some 700 verses, was discovered on an Egyptian papyrus in the British Museum in 1891.

HEROPHILUS (fl.300 BC) Greek anatomist, born in Chalcedon, founder of the school of anatomy in Alexandria. He was the first to dissect the human body to compare it with that of other animals. He described the brain, liver, spleen, sexual organs and nervous system, dividing the latter into sensory and motor.

HÉROULT, Paul Louis Toussaint (1863–1914) French metallurgist, invented the method of extracting aluminium by the electrolysis of cryolite, and a furnace for producing electric steel.

HERRERA, Antonio de (1549–1625) Spanish historian, born in Cuellar near Segovia. He wrote a history of *Castilian Exploits in the Pacific* (1601–15), a description of the West Indies, and a history of England and Scotland in the time of **Mary, Queen of Scots**.

HERRERA, Fernando de (c.1534–1597) Spanish lyric poet, born in Seville. He took holy orders. Many of his love poems are remarkable for tender feeling, while his odes sometimes attain the grandeur of **Milton**. He wrote a prose history of the war in Cyprus (1572), and translated **Stapleton**'s life of Sir **Thomas More** from Latin.

HERRERA, Francisco, 'El Mozo' (the younger) (1622–85) Spanish painter, son and pupil of **Francisco** 'the Elder'. He worked in Rome, and in 1656 moved back to Seville, where he helped to found the Academy. In 1661 he went to Spain, and became painter to **Philip IV** in Madrid. His best works are a fresco, *The Ascension*, in the Atocha church in Madrid, and *St Francis*, in Seville Cathedral.

HERRERA, Francisco, 'El Viejo' (the elder) (1576–1656) Spanish painter, born in Seville. He painted historical pieces, wine shops, fairs, carnivals, and the like.

HERRICK, Robert (1591–1674) English poet, born in London, the son of a goldsmith. He was apprenticed to his uncle, also a goldsmith, but went to Trinity Hall, Cambridge, at the age of 22. After graduating in 1620 he took holy orders and was presented with a living in Devon (1629), of which he was deprived as a royalist in 1647. The following year, he published *Hesperides: or the Works both Humane and Divine of Robert Herrick Esq*, with a separate section of religious verse entitled *Noble Numbers*. Despite *Noble Numbers* he is the most pagan of English poets, vying with his Latin models in the celebration of imagined mistresses—Julia, Anthea, Corinna, and others. He was at his best when describing rural rites as in *The Hock Cart* and *Twelfth Night*, and in lyrical gems such as 'Gather ye rosebuds while ye may' and 'Cherry Ripe'. Youth and love and the pagan fields were his themes at a time when the west country was devastated by the Civil War. He resumed his living in his Devon parish in 1662 after the Restoration.

HERRIMAN, George (1880–1944) American strip cartoonist, born in New Orleans, the creator of *Krazy Kat*, the first comic strip to achieve intellectual acclaim with its originality of language and weird scenes. Starting as office boy on the *Los Angeles Herald*, he migrated to the *New York World* in 1901, drawing a strip, *Lariat Pete* (1903). Becoming a sports cartoonist on the *New York Journal* (1904), he launched a daily strip, *Baron Mooch* (1907), replacing it with *The Dingbat Family* in 1910. The family cat, lurking in bottom corners, eventually evolved into *Krazy Kat* (1913), about an apparently bisexual feline and its love for a mouse named Ignatz.

HERRING, John Frederick (1795–1865) English stagecoach driver turned painter. He was the most popular painter of sporting scenes in his day.

HERRIOT, Édouard (1872–1957) French radical-socialist statesman, born in Troyes, became professor at the Lycée Ampère, Lyon, and was mayor there from 1905 until his death. He was minister of transport during World War I, premier 1924–25, 1926 (for two days) and 1932, was several times president of the Chamber of Deputies, a post which he was holding in 1942 when he became a prisoner of Vichy and of the Nazis, after renouncing his Legion of Honour, when that honour was conferred on collaborators with the Germans. After the Liberation, he was reinvested with the decoration and was president of the national assembly (1947–53), and was then elected life president. A keen supporter of the League of Nations, he opposed, however, the whole concept of the European Defence Community, especially German rearmament. He wrote a number of literary and biographical studies, the best known of which are *Madame Récamier* (1904) and *Beethoven* (1932).

HERSCHEL, Caroline Lucretia (1750–1848) German astronomer, sister of Sir **William Herschel**, born in Hanover. In 1772 she joined her brother in

Bath. Acting as his assistant she made independent observations, and discovered eight comets and several nebulae and clusters of stars. In 1798 she published a star catalogue. She returned to Germany in 1822.

HERSCHEL, Sir John Frederick William (1792–1871) English astronomer, son of Sir **William Herschel**, born in Slough. He was educated at Eton and St John's College, Cambridge, where in 1813 he was senior wrangler and first Smith's prizeman. He continued and augmented his father's researches, discovering 525 nebulae and clusters. In 1848 he was president of the Royal Astronomical Society and from 1850 to 1855 master of the Mint. He pioneered celestial photography, carried out research on photo-active chemicals and the wave theory of light, and translated from **Johann Schiller** and the *Iliad*. He was buried in Westminster Abbey.

HERSCHEL, Sir (Frederick) William (1738–1822) German-born British astronomer, brother of **Caroline Herschel**, born in Hanover. He visited England in 1755 as oboist in the Hanoverian Guards band; in 1766 he became an organist and teacher of music at Bath. Taking up astronomy, he made (1773–74) a reflecting telescope, with which in 1781 he discovered the planet Uranus, called by him 'Georgium Sidus'. In 1782 he was appointed private astronomer to **George III**; and at Slough near Windsor, assisted by his sister, he continued his researches. He was knighted in 1816. He greatly added to knowledge of the solar system, of the Milky Way, and of the nebulae; he discovered, besides Uranus and two of its satellites, two satellites of Saturn, the rotation of Saturn's rings, the period of rotation of Saturn, and the motions of binary stars; and made a famous catalogue of double stars. In 1789 he erected a telescope 40 feet long.

HERSCHELL, Farrer, Lord (1837–99) English politician and judge, born in Brampton, Hampshire. Educated at University College, London, he served as a Liberal MP (1874–86), solicitor-general (1880–85) and Lord Chancellor in 1886 and 1892–95. A vigorous supporter of **William Gladstone**, he was less distinguished as a judge than as a politician.

HERSEY, John Richard (1914–) American author, born in Tientsin, China. He was educated at Yale, and was correspondent in the far east for the magazine *Time*. His novels include *A Bell for Adano* (1944), which was dramatized and filmed, *Hiroshima* (1946), the first on-the-spot description of the effects of a nuclear explosion, *The War Lover* (1959), *The Child Buyer* (1960), *Under the Eye of the Storm* (1967) and *The Walnut Door* (1977).

HERSHEY, Alfred Day (1908–) American biologist, born in Owosso, Michigan. He studied at Michigan State College and from 1950 to 1974 worked in the Carnegie Institution, Washington. He became an expert on bacteriophage ('phage') and in the early 1950s, working with Martha Chase, proved that the DNA of this organism is its genetic information-carrying component. This possibility had been tentatively suggested by **Oswald Avery** in 1944, but Hershey and Chase provided firm evidence for the idea, and they and others showed that the DNA of other organisms fulfils the same key genetic role. Hershey shared the 1969 Nobel prize for physiology or medicine with **Salvador Luria** and **Max Delbrück**.

HERSKOVITS, Melville Jean (1895–1963) American cultural anthropologist, born in Bellefontaine, Ohio. He studied at Columbia University under **Franz Boas** and taught at Northwestern University, Illinois, from 1927 to 1963, where he founded the first US university programme in African studies (1951). He was an uncompromising advocate of cultural relativism, the view that all standards of judgment are culture-bound, and his most complete presentation of this is in *Man and His Works* (1948). His major interest in African cultures and his great knowledge of the continent gave rise to *The Human Factor in Changing Africa* (1962). He was also a pioneer in the field of economic anthropology, and published *The Economic Life of Primitive Peoples* in 1940. His other works include *American Negro* (1928), *Myth of the Negro Past* (1941), *Economic Anthropology* (1952) and *Cultural Dynamics* (1964).

HERTER, Christian Archibald (1895–1966) American politician, educated at Harvard, was governor of Massachusetts (1953–57), and under-secretary of state to **John Foster Dulles**, whom he succeeded as secretary (1959–61). His background of diplomatic experience included being acting minister to Belgium at the age of 21, and personal assistant to **Herbert Hoover** (1921–24). A sincere if reticent internationalist, he tended to be overshadowed by Dulles.

HERTWIG, Oscar Wilhelm August (1849–1922) German zoologist, born in Friedberg, Hessen. Professor at Jena and Berlin, he demonstrated that only one sperm enters the egg in fertilization (1879).

HERTZ, Gustav Ludwig (1887–1975) German physicist, nephew of **Heinrich Hertz**, born in Hamburg. Professor of physics at Berlin, and director of the Siemens Research Laboratory, he shared the 1925 Nobel prize for physics with **James Franck** for confirming the quantum theory by their experiments on the effects produced by bombarding atoms with electrons. After World War II he went to the USSR to become head of a research laboratory (1945–54), and returned to East Germany to be director of Karl Marx University, Leipzig (1954–61).

HERTZ, Heinrich Rudolf (1857–94) German physicist, born in Hamburg. He studied under **Gustav Robert Kirchhoff** and **Hermann von Helmholtz**, and became professor at Bonn in 1889. In 1887 he realized **James Clerk-Maxwell**'s predictions, by his fundamental discovery of electromagnetic waves, which, excepting wavelength, behave like light waves.

HERTZ, Henrik, originally **Heyman** (1798–1870) Danish poet, born in Copenhagen. He published a collection of rhymed satirical letters, *Gjengangerbreve* (Letters of a Ghost, 1830), and several dramas, including *Svend Dyrings Hus* (1837) and *Kong Renés Datter* (1845).

HERTZ, Joseph Herman (1872–1946) British Zionist leader and writer, born in Rebrin, Czechoslovakia (then in Hungary). He studied at Columbia University, New York, and became rabbi at Johannesburg from 1898 to 1911 (with a temporary expulsion by president **Kruger** for his pro-British attitude during the 2nd Boer War). He was appointed professor of philosophy at Transvaal University College in 1906. In 1913 he became chief rabbi of the Hebrew Congregations of the British Empire. He wrote *The Jew in South Africa* (1905) and other works.

HERTZOG, James Barry Munnik (1866–1942) Dutch South African statesman, born in Wellington, Cape Colony. He was a Boer general (1899–1902) and in 1910 became minister of justice in the first Union government. In 1913 he founded the Nationalist party, advocating complete South African independence, and in World War I opposed co-operation with Britain. As premier (1924–39), in coalition with Labour (1924–29), and with **Smuts** in a United party (1933–39), he renounced his earlier secessionism, but on the outbreak of World War II declared for neutrality, was defeated, lost office, and in 1940 retired.

HERTZSPRUNG, Ejnar (1873–1967) Danish astronomer, born in Frederiksberg. He trained as a chemical engineer at the Copenhagen Polytechnic, and he worked as a chemist for ten years before appointment as an astronomer at the Potsdam Observatory (1909–19). He had then already shown that for most stars, colour and brightness are related; all later work on the evolution of stars begins with Hertzsprung's work on this relationship. He also did much to develop **Henrietta Leavitt**'s methods for finding stellar distances, and used it to find the first distances outside our own galaxy. He worked at Leiden University observatory from 1919 to 1945, and remained an active researcher until he was over 90.

HERVIEU, Paul Ernest (1857–1915) French dramatist and novelist, born in Neuilly. His plays included *L'Énigme* (1901), *Le Dédale* (1903) and other powerful pieces.

HERWARTH VON BITTENFELD, Karl Eberhard (1796–1884) Prussian general. He served in the war of liberation against **Napoleon**, in 1864 captured Alsen, and in the Seven Week's War of 1866 contributed to the victories ending with Königgrätz. In 1870 he was made governor of the Rhine provinces, in 1871 a field-marshal.

HERWEGH, Georg (1817–75) German revolutionary poet, born in Stuttgart. In 1836 he took up journalism, but in 1839, under threat of being court-martialled for insubordination during his military service, he fled to Switzerland. There he published *Gedichte eines Lebendigen* (1841), establishing him as a revolutionary poet. He was well received in Germany, but his popularity came to and end when he led an invasion of Baden (1848), his behaviour earning him criticism from all sides, and he returned to Switzerland, publishing very little before his death.

HERZ, Henri (1806–88) Jewish pianist and composer, born in Vienna. A professor of music (1842–74) at the Conservatoire in Paris—he founded a piano-manufacturing company there, which produced prize-winning instruments.

HERZ, Henriette, née **de Lemos** (1764–1847) German-Jewish socialite in Berlin, wife of Markus Herz (1747–1803), doctor and philosopher. A woman of outstanding beauty and culture, she held a brilliant *salon* for the greatest intellectual figures of the day. She became a Christian in 1817.

HERZBERG, Gerhard (1904–) German-born Canadian physical chemist, a dominant figure in modern spectroscopy, born in Hamburg. Educated in Göttingen and Berlin, he taught at Darmstadt before emigrating to Canada in 1935, where he taught at the University of Saskatchewan (1935–45). From 1949 to 1969 he directed the division of pure physics at the National Research Council in Ottawa. He greatly developed and used spectroscopic methods for a variety of purposes, including the detailed study of energy levels in atoms and molecules, and the detection of unusual molecules both in laboratory work and in interstellar space. He was awarded the Nobel prize for chemistry in 1971.

HERZEN, Alexander (1812–70) Russian political thinker and writer, born in Moscow, the illegitimate son of a nobleman. He was imprisoned in 1834 for his revolutionary socialism and exiled to the provinces. In 1847 he left Russia for Paris, and in 1851 settled in London, becoming a powerful propagandist by his novels and treatises, and by the smuggling into Russia of his journal *Kolokol* ('The Bell', 1857–67). His memoirs were published in *My Past and Thoughts* (1861–67).

HERZL, Theodor (1860–1904) Zionist leader, born in Budapest. He graduated in law at Vienna, but wrote essays and plays until the **Dreyfus** trial (1894) and the anti-Semitism it aroused, which he reported for a Viennese newspaper, possessed him. In the pamphlet *Judenstaat* (1896) he advocated the remedy in the formation of a Jewish state, convened the first Zionist Congress at Basel (1897) and negotiated with the kaiser, **Wilhelm I, Abd-ul-Hamid II**, the Russian premier, **Joseph Chamberlain** and Baron Rothschild.

HERZOG, Johann Jakob (1805–82) Swiss theologian, born in Basel. He became professor at Lausanne (1830), Halle (1847), and Erlangen (1854), and edited the great *Realencyklopädie für protestantische Theologie und Kirche* (22 vols, 1854–68).

HERZOG, Maurice (1919–) French engineer and mountaineer, born in Lyon. As a youngster he climbed the Alps, and, during World War II, served in the Artillery and the Chasseurs Alpins, receiving the Croix de Guerre. He was chosen to lead the French Himalayan expedition in 1950, and climbed Annapurna (26926 ft) the first 8000-metre peak to be scaled. On the descent, he lost several fingers and toes through frostbite.

HESELRIGE, Sir Arthur See **HASELRIG**

HESELTINE, Michael (Ray Dibdin) (1933–) English politician. Educated at Shrewsbury School and Pembroke College, Oxford, after national service he established a successful publishing business, Haymarket Press, before entering the House of Commons in 1966, representing Tavistock, and, from 1974, Henley-on-Thames. After holding junior posts under **Edward Heath**, he joined **Margaret Thatcher**'s cabinet in 1979 with the environment portfolio, but resigned dramatically as defence secretary in 1986, claiming that he had been calumnied over the Westland Affair. Always popular at party conferences, he has long been seen as a potential Conservative leader.

HESELTINE, Philip Arnold See **WARLOCK, Peter**

HESIOD (c.8th century BC) Greek poet, born in Ascra, at the foot of Mount Helicon, the son of a sea captain. One of the earliest known Greek poets, he is best known for two works, *Works and Days* and *Theogony*. The *Works and Days* is generally considered to consist of two originally distinct poems, one exalting honest labour and denouncing corrupt and unjust judges; the other containing advice as to the days, lucky or unlucky, for the farmer's work. The *Theogony* teaches the origin of the universe out of Chaos and the history of the gods. Hesiod's poetry is didactic. *Works and Days* gives an invaluable picture of the Greek village community in the 8th century BC, and the *Theogony* is of importance to the comparative mythologist.

HESS, Germain Henri (1802–50) Swiss-born Russian chemist, born in Geneva. As professor of chemistry at St Petersburg, he formulated Hess's law (1840), which states that the net heat evolved or absorbed in any chemical reaction depends only on the initial and final stages.

HESS, Dame Myra (1890–1966) English pianist, born in London. She studied under **Tobias Matthay** at the Royal Academy of Music, and was an immediate success on her first public appearance in 1907. She worked as a chamber musician, recitalist and virtuoso, achieving fame in North America as well as Britain. During World War II she organized the lunchtime concerts in the National Gallery, for which she was awarded the DBE in 1941.

HESS, Rudolf (Walter Richard) (1894–1987) German politician, born in Alexandria, Egypt. Educated at Godesberg, he fought in World War I, after which he studied at Munich University, where he fell under **Hitler**'s spell. He joined the Nazi party in 1920, took part in the abortive Munich rising (1923) and, having shared Hitler's imprisonment and, it is said, taken down from him *Mein Kampf*, became in 1934 his deputy as party leader and in 1939 his successor-designate, after **Goering**, as *Führer*. In May 1941, on the eve of Germany's attack on Russia, he flew alone to Scotland (Eaglesham), to plead the cause of a negotiated Anglo-German peace, which prompted **Churchill**'s comment: 'The maggot is in the apple'. He was temporarily imprisoned in the Tower of London, then under psychiatric care near Aldershot. He was sentenced at the Nuremberg Trials (1946) to life imprisonment. At Spandau jail, where he became in 1966 the sole remaining prisoner, he was nicknamed 'Mad Rudi' for his eccentricities.

HESS, Victor Francis (1883–1964) Austrian-born American physicist, born in Waldstein. On the staff at Vienna University he realized during balloon ascents that high-energy radiation in the earth's atmosphere originated from outer space. He also helped to determine the number of alpha-particles given off by a gram of radium (1918). For his work on 'cosmic radiation' he was awarded the 1936 Nobel prize for physics, jointly with **Carl Anderson**. In 1938 he emigrated to the USA to become professor of physics at Fordham University, New York (1938–56).

HESS, Walter Rudolf (1881–1973) Swiss physiologist, born in Frauenfeld. As professor of physiology at Zürich (1917–51) he did much important research on the nervous system, and developed methods of stimulating localized areas of the brain by means of needle electrodes. He was awarded the 1949 Nobel prize for physiology or medicine with **Antonio Egas Moniz**.

HESSE, Eva (1936–70) German-born American sculptor, born in Hamburg into a Jewish family. Her family emigrated to the USA in 1939 and settled in New York, where she remained until her death. She attended the Pratt Institute, New York, from 1952 to 1953, and Cooper Union from 1954 to 1957. From 1965 she worked in a variety of unusual materials, including rubber, plastic, string and polythene. These were made into hauntingly bizarre objects designed to rest on the floor or against a wall or even be suspended from the ceiling. Her unconventional techniques and imaginative work exerted a strong influence on later sculptors.

HESSE, Hermann (1877–1962) German-born Swiss novelist and poet, born in Calw in Württemberg. He was a bookseller and antiquarian in Basel from 1895 to 1902, and published his first novel, *Peter Camenzind*, in 1904. From then on he devoted himself to writing, living in Switzerland from 1911, becoming a naturalized citizen in 1923. *Rosshalde* (1914) examines the problem of the artist. *Knulp* (1915) is a tribute to vagabondage. *Demian* (1919, trans 1958) is a psychoanalytic study of incest, while *Narziss und Goldmund* (1930, trans 1958) portrays the two sides of man's nature by contrasting a monk and a voluptuary. *Steppenwolf* (1927, trans 1929) mirrors the confusion of modern existence, and *Das Glasperlenspiel* (1945, trans as *Magister Ludi* in 1949 and as *The Glass Bead Game* in 1970) is a Utopian fantasy on the theme of withdrawal from the world. Hesse was awarded both the Goethe prize and the Nobel prize for literature in 1946. His poetry was collected in *Die Gedichte* in 1942, and his letters, *Briefe*, appeared in 1951. *Beschwörungen* (Affirmations, 1955), confirmed that his powers were not diminished by age. Though he disclaimed any ruling purpose, the theme of his work might be stated as a musing on the difficulties put in the way of the individual in his efforts to build up an integrated, harmonious self. All this is expressed in sensitive and sensuous language rising to the majestic and visionary.

HESTON, Charlton, originally **John Charlton Carter** (1923–) American actor, born in Evanston, Illinois. He made his film début in an amateur production of *Peer Gynt* (1941) and, after air force war service and further theatre experience, made his Broadway début in *Antony and Cleopatra* (1947). In Hollywood from 1950, with his strapping physique and aquiline profile, he portrayed historical personages or larger-than-life heroes in epics such as *The Ten Commandments* (1956), *Ben Hur* (1959, Academy Award) and *El Cid* (1961). He displayed his potential as a character actor in *Touch of Evil* (1958), *The War Lord* (1965) and *Will Penny* (1967). He has frequently returned to the stage, and also directs: *Antony and Cleopatra* (1972) on film and, for television, *A Man for All Seasons* (1988). His autobiography, *The Actor's Life*, was published in 1978.

HESYCHIUS (fl.5th or 6th century) Alexandrian Greek scholar. He compiled a Greek lexicon in which are preserved many words and phrases found nowhere else; of particular importance are the original rare words used by Greek poets which have later been replaced by commoner synonyms.

HETTNER, Alfred (1859–1941) German geographer, born in Dresden. He travelled and explored in Europe, Asia, Africa and the Americas, and was a pioneer of modern methods of systematic geography. Among his books are geographies of Russia and England, also *Die Geographie* (1927) and *Der Gang der Kultur über die Erde* (1929).

HEUGLIN, Theodor von (1824–76) German naturalist and traveller. A mining engineer by training, he turned to ornithology and made several expeditions to north-east Africa between 1852 and 1875, and wrote the classic *Ornithologie Nord-Ost Afrikas* (2 vols, 1869–74). He also made expeditions to Spitzbergen and the Arctic (1870–71), and wrote popular accounts of his travels.

HEUSLER, Andreas (1865–1940) German philologist. Professor at Berlin (1894–1919) and Basel (1919–40), he was one of the greatest scholars of Old Icelandic and Old Germanic literature of his time. His many works included *Lied und Epos in germanischen Sagendichtung* (1905), *Das Strafrecht der Isländersagas* (1914), and *Die altgermanische Dichtung* (1924).

HEUSS, Theodor (1884–1963) German statesman and Federal president, born in Brackenheim, Württemberg. He studied at Munich and Berlin and became editor of the political magazine *Hilfe* (1905–12), professor at the Berlin College of Political Science (1920–33), and MP (1924–28, 1930–32). A prolific author and journalist, he wrote two books denouncing **Hitler**, and when the latter came to power in 1933, Heuss was dismissed from his professorship and his books were publicly burnt. Nevertheless, he continued to write them in retirement at Heidelberg under the pseudonym of 'Brackenheim' until 1946, when he became founder member of the Free Democratic party, professor at Stuttgart, and helped to draft the new federal constitution. He was president (1949–59) and in that capacity paid a state visit to Britain in October 1958, the first German head of state to do so since 1907. **Albert Schweitzer** officiated when Heuss in 1907 married Elly Knapp (1881–1951), social scientist and author. He published his autobiographical *Vorspiele* in 1954.

HEVELIUS, Johannes (1611–87) German astronomer, born in Danzig. He established the foremost observatory there in 1641 and built another when the first was burnt down in 1679. He catalogued 1500 stars, discovered four comets and was one of the first to observe the transit of Mercury. He gave names to many lunar features in *Selenographia* (1647).

HEVESY, George Karl von (1885–1966) Hungarian-born Swedish chemist, born in Budapest. In 1923 he discovered, with **Dirk Coster**, the element hafnium at Copenhagen (Hafnium being the Latin name for the city). He was a professor of Freiburg University from 1926, but during World War II went to Sweden, where he became professor at Stockholm. He was awarded the 1943 Nobel prize for physics for his work on radioisotope indicators.

HEWISH, Antony (1924–) English radio astronomer, born in Fowey. He studied at Cambridge and spent his career there, as professor of radio astronomy from 1971. In 1967 he began studies using a radio telescope of novel design, on the scintillation ('twinkling') of quasars (a class of radio stars). This led him and his student **Joycelyn Bell Burnell** to discover the first radio stars emitting radio signals in regular pulses; named as pulsars, many others have since been discovered. They are believed to be very small and dense rotating neutron stars. Hewish shared the Nobel prize for physics in 1974 with his former teacher, Sir **Martin Ryle**.

HEWLETT, Maurice Henry (1861–1923) English novelist, poet and essayist, born in London, the son of a civil servant. He was the keeper of land revenue records (1896–1900), and made his name with his historical romance *The Forest Lovers* (1898); but his poem *The Song of the Plow* (1916) is perhaps his best work.

HEYDEN, Jan van der (1637–1712) Dutch painter, born in Gorinchem. Although he produced still life paintings both at the beginning and end of his career, he is best remembered for his novel and meticulously detailed townscapes of Amsterdam, executed in the 1660s. In that city, where he lived from 1650 until his death, his financial success was mostly due to his mechanical inventions, especially of fire-fighting equipment and street lighting. These inventions were depicted in a series of engravings executed by him and published in book form in 1690 under the title of *Brandspuiten-boek* (Fire Engine Book).

HEYDRICH, Reinhard, 'the hangman' (1904–42) Nazi politician and deputy-chief of the Gestapo, born in Halle, as a youth joined the violent anti-Weimar 'Free Corps', in 1931 had to quit the navy, and, turning Nazi, rose to be second-in-command of the secret police, and presently was charged with subduing **Hitler**'s war-occupied countries. In 1941 he was made deputy-protector of Bohemia and Moravia, but next year was struck down in his terror career by Czech assassins. In the murderous reprisals, Lidice village was razed and every man put to death.

HEYER, Georgette (1902–74) English historical and detective novelist, born in London of partly South Slav descent. She studied at Westminster College, London, and after marriage in 1925 travelled in East Africa and Yugoslavia until 1929. By that time she had produced several well-researched historical novels from various periods, including *The Black Moth* (1921) and *Beauvallet* (1929). She risked fictional studies of real figures in crisis with books on **William I, The Conqueror, Charles II**, and the battle of Waterloo. It was not until *Regency Buck* (1935) and later novels that she really came into her own with the Regency period, on which she made herself an outstanding authority. *My Lord John* (1976), on **Henry V**'s brother, was unfinished at her death. She also wrote modern comedy detective novels with dexterity, such as *Death in the Stocks* (1935) and *Behold, Here's Poison* (1936), and used detective and thriller plots with pace and irony in historical fiction such as *The Talisman Ring* (1936), *The Reluctant Widow* (1946) and *The Quiet Gentleman* (1951).

HEYERDAHL, Thor (1914–) Norwegian anthropologist. Educated at the University of Oslo, he served with the free Norwegian military forces from 1940 to 1945. In 1937 he had led his first expedition to Fatu Hiva in the Marquesas Islands of the Pacific and during this year-long stay with his wife suspected that certain aspects of the Polynesian culture owed their origins to settlers from the Americas, possibly the pre-Inca inhabitants of Peru. To prove this, in 1947 he and five colleagues sailed a balsa-wood raft, *Kon-Tiki*, from Callao, Peru 4300 nautical miles to Tuamotu Island in the South Pacific, spending 101 days adrift. Although the academic community was initially slow to acknowledge his work, his success in this venture and subsequent archaeological expeditions on the Galapagos in 1953 and Easter Island in 1955, won him popular fame and several distinguished awards. In 1969 he wished to test the theory that ancient Mediterranean people could have crossed the Atlantic to Central America before **Columbus**, and sailed from Morocco to the West Indies in the papyrus-reed boats of the Ra expeditions. The first of these in 1969 broke up just short of its objective, but the 1970 voyage succeeded in reaching Barbados in 57 days. His subsequent journey (1977–78) in the reed-ship *Tigris*, was to show that these craft could not only sail before the wind but could be manoeuvred against the wind and so complete two-way journeys through the ancient world via the Persian Gulf and Arabian Sea. The political conflict in Ethiopia, Somalia and the Yemen and the appalling pollution, especially from oil, led them to burn the *Tigris* in protest at Djibouti, their journey's end.

HEYLIN, Peter (1599–1662) English clergyman and historian, born in Burford, Oxfordshire. A royalist, he was deprived of his preferments under the Commonwealth, but after the Restoration became subdean of Westminster. He wrote a Life of **Laud**, cosmographies, histories of England, of the Reformation, and of the Presbyterians, and anti-Puritan pamphlets.

HEYMANS, Corneille Jean François (1892–1968) French-Belgian physiologist, born in Ghent, where he became professor of pharmaco-dynamics. He developed the technique of 'cross circulation' of blood, and was awarded the 1938 Nobel prize for physiology or medicine for his work on the sinus aorta. In 1950 he discovered that pressoreceptors (special nerve endings) monitor blood pressure.

HEYN, Piet See **HEIJN**

HEYNE, Christian Gottlob (1729–1812) German classical philologist, born in Chemnitz. In 1763 he became professor of eloquence at Göttingen, which he established as an important centre for classical studies. He edited **Virgil**, **Pindar**, **Apollodorus** and **Homer**'s *Iliad* (1802).

HEYROVSY, Jaroslav (1890–1967) Czech chemist, born in Prague. At Charles University in Prague he discovered in 1922 polarographic analysis and developed the method for application to high-purity substances. For this he won the Nobel prize for chemistry in 1959, the first Czech national to gain a Nobel award.

HEYSE, Paul Johann von (1830–1914) German writer, born in Berlin. He settled in Munich in 1854. He excelled as a short-story teller, his *novellen* being marked by a graceful style, sly humour and often sensuality. These were collected in *Das Buch der Freundschaft* (1883–84) and other volumes. He also wrote novels, plays and epic poems, and translations of

Italian poets. He was awarded the 1910 Nobel prize for literature.

HEYSEN, Sir (Wilhelm Ernst) Hans (Franz) (1877–1968) German-born Australian landscape painter, born in Hamburg. Emigrating to Adelaide with his parents in 1884, he sold his first painting at the age of 16 for ten shillings. A local businessman paid for his tuition at the Adelaide School of Design, and other businessmen sponsored his trip to Europe in 1899, where he studied in Paris and painted in Italy, Holland and the UK. Returning to Adelaide in 1903 to teach, the following year he won the Wynne prize for landscape painting. Primarily a water-colourist, his first important exhibition was in Melbourne, in 1908, and his success grew during the following 20 years. Heysen won the Wynne prize nine times between 1904 and 1932, received the OBE in 1951 and was knighted in 1959. His daughter Nora Heysen (1911–) is a noted Impressionist painter of still-life and portraits, and won the Archibald prize in 1938.

HEYWOOD, John (c.1497–c.1580) English epigrammatist, playwright and musician, born perhaps in London. After studying at Oxford, he was introduced at Court by Sir **Thomas More**, who was a distant cousin by marriage, and made himself, by his wit and his skill in singing and playing on the virginals, a favourite with **Henry VIII** and with Queen **Mary I**, to whom he had been music teacher in her youth. He was a devout Catholic, and after the accession of **Elizabeth** went to Belgium. He wrote several short plays or interludes, whose individual characters represent classes, such as the Pedlar, the Pardoner, and the like. They thus form a link between the old moralities and the modern drama. He is remembered above all, however, for his collections of proverbs and epigrams. His wearisome allegorical poem, *The Spider and the Flie*, contrasts Catholicism and Protestantism. He was the grandfather of **John Donne**.

HEYWOOD, Thomas (c.1574–1641) English dramatist, poet and actor, born in Lincolnshire, the son of a clergyman. He was educated at Cambridge, and was writing plays by 1596. In 1598 he was engaged by **Philip Henslowe** as an actor with the Lord Admiral's Men. Up to 1633 he had a large share in the composition of 220 plays. He was also the author of a historical poem, *Troja Britannica* (1609); an *Apology for Actors* (1612); *Nine Bookes of Various History concerning Women* (1624); a long poem, *The Hierarchie of the Blessed Angells* (1635); a volume of rhymed translations from **Lucian**, **Erasmus**, and **Ovid**; various pageants, tracts and treatises; and *The Life of Ambrosius Merlin* (1641). 24 of Heywood's plays have survived. The best is *A Woman Kilde with Kindnesse* (1607), a domestic tragedy; and with this may be coupled *The English Traveller* (1633). His work is usually distinguished by naturalness and simplicity. In the two parts of *The Fair Maid of the West* (1631), and in *Fortune by Land and Sea* (1655), partly written by **William Rowley**, he gives some spirited descriptions of sea fights. *The Rape of Lucreece* (1608) is chiefly noticeable for its songs; *Love's Maistresse* (1636) is fanciful and ingenious; and there is much tenderness in *A Challenge for Beautie* (1636). In *The Royall King and Loyall Subject* (1637) the doctrine of passive obedience to kingly authority is stressed.

HIBBERT, Robert (1770–1849) British merchant and philanthropist, born in Jamaica. A slave-owner in Jamaica, he moved to England, and in 1847 founded the Hibbert Trust, whose funds, in 1878 applied to the Hibbert Lectures, also aided the *Hibbert Journal* (1920–70).

HICHENS, Robert Smythe (1864–1950) English novelist. He studied music, but made his name as a novelist with books such as *The Green Carnation* (1894), *The Garden of Allah* (1905), *The Call of the Blood* (1906), *The Paradine Case* (1933) and *That Which is Hidden* (1939).

HICK, John Harwood (1922–) English theologian and philosopher of religion, born in Scarborough. During a long teaching career in the USA and Cambridge, followed by professorships in Birmingham (1967–82) and at Claremont Graduate School, California (1979–), Hick has produced several standard textbooks and anthologies in the philosophy of religion, as well as studies such as *Faith and Knowledge* (1966), *Evil and the God of Love* (1966), and *Death and Eternal Life* (1976). His concern with questions about the status of Christianity among the world religions, raised in *God and the Universe of Faiths* (1973) and *The Myth of God Incarnate* (1977), is developed in *Problems of Religious Pluralism* (1985) and the expanded Gifford lectures, *An Interpretation of Religion* (1989).

HICKES, George (1642–1715) English nonjuror and philologist, born in Newsham, near Thirsk. Educated at Oxford, in 1683 he became Dean of Worcester, but as a nonjuror was deprived of his deanery in 1690, and in 1694 was consecrated nonjuring bishop of Thetford. He published works in controversial and practical divinity, a *Thesaurus Linguarum Veterum Septentrionalium* (1705), and a grammar of Anglo-Saxon and Moeso-Gothic (1689).

HICKS, Sir Edward Seymour (1871–1949) British actor-manager and author, born in Jersey. He made his début at Islington in 1887 and built up a reputation as a light comedian, appearing in many successful plays written by himself, including *The Man in Dress Clothes*, *The Gay Gordons*, and *Vintage Wine*. He wrote several books of reminiscences.

HICKS, Elias (1748–1830) American clergyman, born in Hempstead, Long Island. A carpenter to trade, he became a Quaker preacher in 1775. By his Unitarianism he was held responsible for the split in the American Society into Orthodox and 'Hicksite' Friends in 1827.

HICKS, Sir John Richard (1904–89) English economist, born in Leamington Spa. Educated at Clifton College and Balliol College, Oxford, he taught at the London School of Economics (1926–35), and was professor of political economy at Manchester (1938–46) and Oxford (1952–65). He wrote a classic book on the conflict between business-cycle theory and equilibrium theory (*Value and Capital*, 1939), and other works include *A Theory of Economic History* (1969) and *Causality in Economics* (1979). He shared the 1972 Nobel prize for economics with **Kenneth Arrow**.

HICKS, William, known as **'Hicks Pasha'** (1830–83) English soldier. After long service in India (1848–80), he was in command of the Egyptian forces in the Sudan annihilated by the Mahdi (**Mohammed Ahmed**) at El Obeid.

HIERO I (d.467 or 466 BC) king of Syracuse, won a great naval victory over the Etruscans in 474. Though reputedly violent and rapacious, in contrast with his idealized brother and predecessor **Gelon**, he had a keen interest in poetry, and was the patron of **Simonides of Ceos**, **Aeschylus**, Bacchylides, and **Pindar**.

HIERO II (?308–215 BC) king of Syracuse, son of a noble Syracusan. He came to the fore during the troubles in Sicily after the retreat of **Pyrrhus** (275 BC), and in 269 was hailed as king. He joined the Carthaginians in besieging Messana, which had surrendered to the Romans; but was beaten by **Appius Claudius**. In 263 he concluded a 15-year peace with

Rome, and in 258 a permanent one. In the second Punic war Hiero supported the Romans with money and troops. He was a patron of the arts, and was a relative and friend of **Archimedes**.

HIGDEN, Ralph or **Ranulf** (d.1364) English chronicler, a Benedictine monk of St Werburgh's monastery in Chester. He wrote a Latin *Polychronicon*, a general history from the creation to about 1342, which was continued by others to 1377. An English translation of the *Polychronicon* by **John of Trevisa** was printed by **Caxton** in 1482.

HIGGINS, Alex ('Hurricane') (1949–) Irish snooker player, born in Belfast. Playing at great speed, hence his nickname, he won the world championship in 1972 and 1982, and in the Coral UK Tournament of the latter year achieved one of the greatest snooker victories ever when he defeated **Steve Davis** over 31 frames, having trailed 0–7. With Dennis Taylor and Eugene Hughes he won the Guinness World Cup for Ireland in 1986 and 1987. Volatile and unpredictable, he contributed to the remarkable resurrection of the sport through television.

HIGGINS, George Vincent (1939–) American novelist, born in Brockton, Massachusetts. He was admitted to the Massachusetts bar in 1967, but worked in newspapers before becoming a successful attorney. He has used his experience of low-life and his observation of criminals at close quarters to telling effect in a spate of acclaimed literary thrillers. *The Friends of Eddie Coyle* (1972) was his first book and he has published many since, invariably told almost entirely in dialogue and using Boston as a backdrop. Titles include *Cogan's Trade* (1974), *Kennedy for the Defence* (1980), *Imposters* (1986), *Outlaws* (1987) and *Wonderful Years, Wonderful Years* (1988).

HIGGINS, Jack, pseud of **Harry Patterson** (1929–) English thriller writer, born in Newcastle-upon-Tyne. He also writes as Martin Fallon, Hugh Marlowe and James Graham. He was educated at Roundhay School, Leeds, Beckett Park College for Teachers, and the London School of Economics. He was a teacher and college lecturer before becoming a bestselling author with the success of *The Eagle Has Landed* (1975), a tale of derring-do set during World War II in which the Germans plot to kidnap **Winston Churchill**.

HIGGINS, Matthew James, known as **'Jacob Omnium'** (1810–68) Irish controversialist, born in Benown Castle, County Meath. He earned his nickname from the title of his first published article. A prominent journalist, his intellectual force, his humour and irony, were directed against the abuses and minor evils of social and public life by means of letters and articles to the press. He stood 6 feet 8 inches high. His *Essays on Social Subjects* was published in 1875.

HIGGINSON, Thomas Wentworth (1823–1911) American writer, born in Cambridge, Massachusetts. He was ordained to the ministry, from which he retired in 1858. Meanwhile he had been active in the anti-slavery agitation, and, with others, was indicted for the murder of a man killed during an attempt to rescue a fugitive slave, but escaped through a flaw in the indictment. In the Civil War he commanded the first regiment in the Union army raised from among former slaves. In 1880–81 he was a member of the Massachusetts legislature. His books include, as well as histories of the USA, *Outdoor Papers* (1863), *Army Life in a Black Regiment* (1870), *Oldport Days* (1873), *Common-Sense about Women* (1881), *Hints on Writing and Speech-making* (1887) and *Concerning All of Us* (1892).

HIGHSMITH, Patricia (1921–) American thriller writer, born in Fort Worth, Texas. Her first novel, *Strangers on a Train* (1950), was filmed by **Alfred Hitchcock**. Her third, *The Talented Mr Ripley* (1955), was awarded the Edgar Allan Poe Scroll by the Mystery Writers of America. She creates a world which **Graham Greene** has characterized as claustrophobic and irrational, one 'we enter each time with a sense of personal danger'.

HIGHTOWER, Rosella (1920–) American dancer and teacher, born in Ardmore, Oklahoma. A dazzling technician, she studied in Kansas City, Missouri before beginning her long career as a leading ballerina with Ballet Russe de Monte Carlo (1938–41), American Ballet Theatre (1941–45), **Léonide Massine**'s Ballet Russe Highlights and the Original Ballet Russe (both 1945–46). She joined Nouveau Ballet de Monte Carlo in 1947 and, later, the Grand Ballet du Marquis de Cuevas (until 1961), touring the world and making guest appearances with various companies. In 1962 she became director of the Centre de Danse Classique in Cannes, ballet director of the Marseilles Opéra (1967–71), Ballet de Nancy (1973–74), and her own company in Cannes in 1976.

HIJIKATA, Tatsumi (1928–86) Japanese performance artist, born in Akita province. He was a key figure in the Japanese avant-garde of the 1950s and 1960s, closely linked with artists in many disciplines. His 1959 performance *Kinjiki* (Forbidden Colours), a rejection of both traditional Japanese and modern dance, shocked audiences because of its explicit sexuality. With Kazuo Ohno he is credited with the founding of the butoh dance-theatre movement, that draws on and yet refutes traditional Japanese Kabuki and Noh theatre and such Western art forms as modern dance, German expressionism and pop art. His company Ankoku Butoh (Dance of Total Darkness) gave performances from 1963 to 1966. His 1968 piece *Nikutai No Hanran* (Rebellion of the Body) is acknowledged as one of the most important productions in the development of butoh.

HILARION, St (c.291–371) Palestinian hermit, and founder of the monastic system in Palestine (329). Educated at Alexandria, he lived as a hermit in the desert between Gaza and Egypt from 306, and died in Cyprus.

HILARY, St (c.315–c.368) French prelate, and one of the Doctors of the Church, born of pagan parents in Limonum (Poitiers). He did not become a Christian till he was advanced in life. About 350 he was elected bishop of Poitiers, and immediately rose to the first place as an opponent of Arianism. His principal work is that on the Trinity, but his three addresses to the emperor **Constantius** are remarkable for the boldness of their language. His feast day is 13 January, which also marks the beginning of an Oxford term and English law sittings to which his name is consequently applied.

HILARY OF ARLES, St (c.403–49) French prelate. Educated in Lerins, he became bishop of Arles in 429. He presided at several synods, especially that of Orange in 441, whose proceedings involved him in a serious controversy with Pope **Leo the Great**. His feast day is 5 May.

HILBERT, David (1862–1943) German mathematician, born in Königsberg. He studied and taught at the university there until he became professor at Göttingen (1895–1930). His definitive work on invariant theory, published in 1890, removed the need for further work on a subject that had occupied so many 19th-century mathematicians, at the same time laying the foundations for modern algebraic geometry; and in 1897 he published a report on algebraic number theory which was the basis of much later work. He studied the axiomatic foundations of geometry, integral equations, the calculus of variations, theoretical physics (which he claimed was too difficult to be left to physicists), and mathematical logic. At the International Congress of Mathematicians in 1900 he listed 23 problems which he regarded as important for contemporary mathematics; the solutions of many of these have led to interesting advances, while others are still unsolved.

HILDA, St (614–80) Anglo-Saxon abbess, the daughter of a nephew of St **Edwin** of Northumbria. Baptized at 13 by **Paulinus**, in 649 she became abbess of Hartlepool and in 657 founded the monastery at Streaneshalch or Whitby, a double house for nuns and monks, over which she ruled wisely for 22 years.

HILDEBRAND See **BEETS, Nicholas**

HILDEBRAND See **GREGORY VII**

HILDEBRAND, Adolf (1847–1921) German sculptor, born in Harburg. He sought a renaissance of classical realism in his public monuments to **Brahms** at Meiningen, **Bismarck** at Bremen, **Schiller** at Nuremberg, etc, and founded a new school of art criticism by his *Das Problem der Form* (1893).

HILDEBRANDT, Johann Lukas von (1668–1745) Austrian architect, born in Genoa. A fortifications engineer in the Austrian army from 1695 to 1701, he trained in Genoa and then in Rome, and became court engineer in Vienna in 1701. A master of the Late Baroque, he was influenced by the work of **Palladio**, **Vignoa**, **Borromini**, **Guarini** and **Carlo Fontana**. His earlier works were heavily influenced by the Italian school, as at the Mansfield Fondi garden palace (1697–1715) but he gradually developed a more mature style which was less classical and more intuitive, as seen in the Starhemborg-Schönberg garden palace (1705–06), where his mastery of the relationship between house and garden is clear.

HILL, Aaron (1685–1750) English poet, dramatist and speculator, born in London. He wrote *Zaire* (1736) and *Mérope* (1749, adapted from **Voltaire**), and wrote the scenario for **Handel**'s opera *Rinaldo* (1711). He was one of **Pope**'s victims in the *Dunciad*, and replied with *Progress of Wit* (1730).

HILL, Alfred Francis (1870–1960) Australian composer, born in Melbourne, Victoria. His family went to Wellington, New Zealand, and at the age of 14 Hill was appearing with the New Zealand Opera Orchestra. He studied at Leipzig Conservatorium from 1887. Returning to New Zealand in 1891 he became conductor of the Wellington Orchestral Society, and collected and recorded much Maori music, which influenced his music of the period. Returning to Australia in 1897, he worked in Sydney, where he conducted for the **J C Williamson** Company. For twenty years from 1915 he was professor of composition and harmony at the New South Wales Conservatorium of Music. His work includes 13 symphonies, many of which are orchestrations of his earlier string quartets, ten operas, a *Maori Rhapsody*, five concertos, and a considerable body of chamber music, keyboard and vocal music. His wife, Mirrie Irma Hill, (1892–) was a noted composer, pianist and teacher.

HILL, Archibald Vivian (1886–1977) English physiologist, born in Bristol. He was professor at Manchester (1920), University College, London (1923), and from 1926 to 1951 Foulerton research professor of the Royal Society. He shared the 1922 Nobel prize for physiology or medicine with **Otto Meyerhof** for his researches into heat production in muscle contraction. He organized air defence in World War II and was MP for Cambridge (1940–45). His works include *Muscular Movement in Man* (1927).

HILL, Benny, originally **Alfred Hawthorne** (1925–) English comedian, born in Southampton. An enthusiastic performer in school shows, he was a milkman, drummer and driver before finding employment as an assistant stage manager. During World War II he appeared in *Stars in Battledress* and later followed the traditional comic's route of working men's clubs, revues and end-of-the-pier shows. An early convert to the potential of television, he appeared in *Hi There* (1949) and was named TV personality of the year in 1954. He made his film début in *Who Done It?* (1956) but gained national popularity with the saucy *The Benny Hill Show* (1957–66). His few film appearances include *Chitty,Chitty,Bang,Bang* (1968) and *The Italian Job* (1969). He enjoyed a hit record with 'Ernie, The Fastest Milkman in the West' (1971), and has spent over two decades writing and performing in top-rated television specials that have been seen around the world.

HILL, David Octavius (1802–70) Scottish photographer and painter, pioneer in the use of the calotype process in photographic portraiture. In 1843 he was commissioned to portray the founders of the Free Church of Scotland, and with the help of the Edinburgh chemist, **Robert Adamson**, applied the calotype process of making photographic prints on silver chloride paper, newly invented by **William Henry Fox Talbot**. In the five years from 1843 Hill and Adamson produced some 2500 calotypes, mostly portraits but also landscapes, the paper negatives of the process giving an exceptional texture and character to their work.

HILL, Geoffrey William (1932–) English poet, born in Bromsgrove, Worcestershire. Educated at Keble College, Oxford, he made his career in academia. A deep, dark and densely allusive writer, brooding on death, sex and religion, his first collection of *Poems* was published by a small press in 1952. *For the Unfallen: Poems 1952–1958* (1959) marked his true emergence, since when he has become appreciated by the cognoscenti. His later collections, *Preghiere* (1964), *King Log* (1968), *Mercian Hymns* (1971), *Somewhere is Such a Kingdom: 1952–1971* (1975), *Tenebrae* (1978) and *The Mystery of the Charity of Charles Péguy* (1983), all won prestigious literary prizes.

HILL, George Birkbeck Norman (1835–1903) English educationist and writer, nephew of Sir **Rowland Hill**. He was until 1876 headmaster of Bruce Castle School, Tottenham, and was an authority on the life and works of Dr **Samuel Johnson**. He also edited letters of **Boswell** and **Hume**, and wrote on General **Gordon** in Africa.

HILL, (Norman) Graham (1929–75) English racing driver and world champion, born in Hampstead, London. He won the world championship in 1962 in a BRM, and was runner-up twice in the following three years. In 1967 he rejoined Lotus and won the world championship for a second time (1968). Cool, resourceful and daring, he survived several bad crashes, including one which left him with two broken legs. He was killed in a private plane crash.

HILL, James Jerome (1838–1916) Canadian-born American railway magnate, born in Guelph, Ontario. He moved to St Paul, Minnesota, in 1856, where he entered the transportation business. He took over the St Paul-Pacific line and extended it to link with the Canadian system, later gaining control of the Northern Pacific Railroad after a stock exchange battle with Edward H Harriman. He was also active in the construction of the Canadian Pacific Railroad.

HILL, Matthew Davenport (1792–1872) English legal reformer, born in Birmingham. In his practice at the English bar, he was particularly notable for his defence of radicals. He also sat in parliament, but was renowned mainly for his efforts towards the reform of the criminal law and of penal methods; he advocated the establishment of reformatories for young offenders, the release of offenders on licence and other measures, and was instrumental in having many of them adopted.

HILL, Octavia (1838–1912) English reformer and founder of the National Trust, born in London, the granddaughter of **Thomas Southwood Smith**. Influenced by the Christian socialism of **Frederick Denison Maurice**, and tutored in art by **John Ruskin**, she became an active promoter of improved housing conditions for the poor in London. From 1864, with Ruskin's financial help, she bought slum houses for improvement projects. With Denison she founded the Charity Organization Society (1869). Her books included *Homes of the London Poor* (1875) and *Our Common Land* (1878). A leader of the open-space movement, she was a co-founder in 1895 of the National Trust for Places of Historic Interest or Natural Beauty.

HILL, Rowland (1744–1833) English popular preacher, son of a Shropshire baronet. At St John's College, Cambridge, he was influenced by the evangelist **George Whitefield**, and from his ordination in 1773 till 1783 he was an itinerant preacher, afterwards making his headquarters at Surrey Chapel, Blackfriars Road, London, which he built himself. He helped to found the Religious Tract Society and the London Missionary Society, and it is said that the first London Sunday school was his. His *Village Dialogues* (1801) was immensely popular.

HILL, Sir Rowland (1795–1879) English originator of penny postage, born in Kidderminster. Until 1833 he was a teacher, noted for his system of school self-discipline. He was one of the founders of the Society for the Diffusion of Useful Knowledge (1826). He interested himself in the socialistic schemes of **Robert Owen**, and took an active share in the colonization of South Australia. In his *Post-office Reform* (1837) he advocated a low and uniform rate of postage, to be prepaid by stamps, between places in the British Isles; and in January 1840 a uniform penny rate was introduced. In 1846 the Liberals made him secretary to the postmaster general and in 1854 secretary to the Post Office. He established the book-post (1848), and reformed the money order office (1848) and the packet service. In 1864 he resigned and was given a pension and a parliamentary grant. In a report of 1867 he advocated national ownership of railways. He was buried in Westminster Abbey.

HILL, Rowland, 1st Viscount (1772–1842) English soldier, born in Prees Hall, Shropshire. He distinguished himself under **Abercromby** in Egypt and under **Wellington** in the Peninsular War. At Waterloo (1815) he swept the Old Guard from the field, and in 1828 succeeded Wellington as commander-in-chief at home, but resigned in 1842.

HILLARY, Sir Edmund (1919–) New Zealand mountaineer and explorer, educated at Auckland Grammar School. After specializing as an apiarist, he took part in Himalayan climbs and as a member of **John Hunt**'s Everest expedition he attained, with Sherpa **Tenzing**, the summit of Mount Everest on 29 May 1953, for which achievement he was knighted. He subsequently established a medical and educational charity, the Himalayan Trust, for the Sherpa peoples of Nepal. As part of the Commonwealth Trans-Antarctic Expedition 1955–58 led by Sir **Vivian Fuchs**, whilst laying depots for the crossing of the continent, he and a New Zealand expeditionary party reached the South Pole on 3 January 1958, the first people to do this overland since **Scott** and **Amundsen**. In 1974 he navigated the Ganges upstream using jet boats, and latterly became New Zealand High Commissioner to India (1984).

HILLEL, surnamed **Hababli 'the Babylonian'** and **Hazaken, 'the Elder'** (c.60 BC–?) Jewish sage, born in Babylonia, and one of the greatest doctors of the Jewish law. At the age of 40 he came to Palestine, where he was chosen president of the Sanhedrin as an authority on biblical law.

HILLER, Ferdinand (1811–85) German pianist and composer, born in Frankfurt-am-Main. His compositions include operas, symphonies and cantatas; he also wrote books on harmony, **Beethoven** (1871) and **Mendelssohn** (1874).

HILLER, Johann Adam (1728–1804) German composer, born near Görlitz, Prussia. He studied law at Leipzig University, where he also performed as a singer and flautist. From 1763 he concentrated on composing, and wrote over 30 comic operas, practically creating this genre in Germany. He was also a noted conductor and teacher.

HILLER, Dame Wendy (1912–) English actress, born in Bramhall, Cheshire. Interested in dramatics as a child, she joined the Manchester Repertory Theatre straight from school in 1930. She made her London début in *Love on the Dole* (1935) and her film début in *Lancashire Luck* (1937). At the 1936 Malvern Festival she played Saint Joan and Eliza Dolittle, a role she recreated at the behest of **George Bernard Shaw** in the 1938 film of *Pygmalion*. Her clarity of diction and spirited personality made her one of Britain's leading stage performers, while her sporadic film career includes performances of distinction in *Major Barbara* (1940), *I Know Where I'm Going* (1945), *Sons and Lovers* (1960), *A Man for All Seasons* (1966) and *Separate Tables* (1958), for which she received an Academy Award. She married the dramatist Ronald Gow in 1937.

HILLIARD, Nicholas (1537–1619) English court goldsmith and miniaturist, born in Exeter. He worked for Queen **Elizabeth** and **James VI and I** and founded the English school of miniature painting.

HILLIER, James (1915–) Canadian-born American physicist, born in Brantford, Ontario. He was a major contributor to the development of the electron microscope. Educated in Toronto, he moved to the USA in 1940 and made his career with RCA (the Radio Corporation of America). There he led the group which made the first successful high-resolution electron microscope, in 1940; unknown to them, a similar device had been made in 1938 by Ernest Ruska (1906–88) and M Knoll in Berlin for the Siemens and Halske Co. Hillier continued to supervise improvements in RCA's electron microscopes, whose commercial availability after World War II revolutionized biology.

HILLIER, Tristram Paul (1905–) British artist, born in Peking. He studied at the Slade School, London, and under **André Lhote** in Paris. Many of his paintings are of ships and beaches, the earlier ones of a Surrealist character; he has lived much in France, particularly in Dieppe, and his craftmanship and smooth handling of paint are such that his oil paintings are often mistaken for tempera.

HILTON, Conrad Nicholson (1887–1979) American hotelier, born in San Antonio, New Mexico. He became a cashier in New Mexico State Bank in 1913, and became president and partner in A H Hilton and Son, General Store. After World War I he took over the family inn on the death of his father in 1918, and bought his first hotel in Cisco, Texas, in 1919, and built up a chain of hotels in the major cities in the USA.

After World War II he formed Hilton Hotels Corporation in 1946, and Hilton International in 1948. He continued to expand the company until his son, Barron Hilton, took over as president in 1966. He published his autobiography, *Be My Guest*, in 1957.

HILTON, James (1900–54) English novelist, born in Leigh, Lancashire. He quickly established himself as a writer, his first novel, *Catherine Herself*, being published in 1920. Many of his successful novels were filmed—*Knight without Armour* (1933), *Lost Horizon* (1933, awarded the Hawthornden prize in 1934), *Goodbye Mr Chips* (1934) and *Random Harvest* (1941).

HILTON, Roger (1911–75) English painter, born in Northwood, Middlesex. He studied at the Slade School of Art, London (1929–31), and was awarded a bursary which he did not take up. After spending some time in Paris in the 1930s, he was captured at Dieppe in 1942 and was a prisoner-of-war till 1945. He produced his first abstract paintings in 1950. From 1954 to 1956 he taught at the Central School of Art. He won first prize in the John Moores Liverpool Exhibition in 1963 and the UNESCO prize at the Venice Biennale, 1964.

HILTON, Walter (d.1396) English mystic and writer. An Augustinian canon of Thurgarton, Nottinghamshire, he was the author of *The Ladder of Perfection* and possibly *The Cloud of Unknowing*, two books important in the history of English prose.

HIMMLER, Heinrich (1900–45) German Nazi leader and chief of police, born in Munich. Educated at the Landshut High School, he joined the army. In 1919 he studied at the Munich Technical College, found employment in a nitrate works and turned to poultry farming. An early Nazi, he was flag bearer in the Munich putsch (1923). In 1929 **Hitler** made him head of the SS (*Schutzstaffel*, protective force), which he developed from Hitler's personal bodyguard into a powerful party weapon. With **Heydrich**, he used it to carry out the assassination of **Röhm** (1934) and other Nazis opposed to Hitler. Inside Germany and later in Nazi war-occupied countries, he unleashed through his secret police (*Gestapo*) an unmatched political and anti-Semitic terror of espionage, wholesale detention, mass deportation, torture, execution, massacre, and by his systematic 'liquidation' of whole national and racial groups initiated the barbarous crime of genocide. In 1943 he was given the post of minister of the interior to curb any defeatism. After the attempt on Hitler's life by the army in July 1944, he was made commander-in-chief of the home forces, into which he henceforth recruited mere boys. His offer of unconditional surrender to the Allies (but excluding Russia) having failed, he disappeared but was captured by the British near Bremen. By swallowing a cyanide phial concealed in his mouth, he escaped justice as the pioneer of the horror of the gas oven and the concentration camp, and as the butcher of over seven million people.

HINAULT, Bernard (1954–) French cyclist, born in Yffiniac. He won the Tour de France a record five times between 1978 and 1985. (Only two other men have ever won the race five times: **Jacques Anquetil** and **Eddy Merckx**). Known as 'Le Blaireau' or 'The Badger', he led a protest during the 1978 Tour in which all the riders walked across the finishing line pushing their bikes, complaining about the long days in the saddle. In 1985 he won his last Tour despite a fall midway through in which he broke his nose. He retired on his 32nd birthday and became technical adviser to the Tour de France.

HINCMAR (c.806–882) French prelate of the family of the counts of Toulouse. Educated in the monastery of St Denis, he was abbot of Compiègne and St Germain, and in 845 was elected archbishop of Reims. He helped to degrade and imprison the German theologian Gottschalk (who died in 868 after 18 years' captivity) for his predestinarian views, and strenuously opposed Adrian II's attempts by church censures to compel obedience in imperial politics; he also resisted the emperor's intruding unworthy favourites into benefices.

HINDEMITH, Paul (1895–1963) German composer, born in Hanau. He ran away from home aged eleven because of his parents' opposition to a musical career, and earned a living by playing all sorts of instruments in cafés, cinemas and dance halls. He studied at Hoch's Conservatory in Frankfurt, and from 1915 to 1923 was leader of the Frankfurt Opera Orchestra, which he often conducted. He also played the viola in the famous Amar quartet (1922–29), with which he toured Europe. His early *Kammermusik*, notably his concerto for piano and five solo instruments (1925), reveals a trend towards neoclassicism, continued in the operas *Cardillac* (1926), based on a story by **E T A Hoffmann**, in which he contrives a complete separation between music and action, and *Neues vom Tage* (1929), an operatic satire on the modern press, which inverts all the romantic association of Wagnerian opera. One scene, set in a lady's bathroom, particularly shocked Nazi sensibilities. In 1927 he was appointed professor at the Berlin High School for music, and in 1929 gave the first performance in London of **William Walton**'s Viola Concerto, which profoundly influenced Hindemith's own *Philharmonic Concerto* (1932). With the *Konzertmusik*, comprising the violin concerto (1930), and *Das Unaufhörliche*, 'perpetual' second string trio (1933), Hindemith's work passed into a transitional phase. He based his tonality on the chromatic scale, relating the notes acoustically around one key note. He also launched out into *Gebrauchsmusik*—pieces written with specific utilitarian aims such as for children's entertainment, newsreels and community singing. The Nazis banned his politically-pointed *Mathis der Maler* symphony (1934; opera 1938) despite **Wilhelm Furtwängler**'s defence, and Hindemith went to live in Turkey, and then in Britain, where he composed the *Trauermusik* for viola and strings (1936) on **George V**'s death, and the ballet *Nobelissima Visione* (1938). From 1939 he taught in the USA. His later, mellower, compositions include the *Symphonic metamorphosis of Themes by Weber* (1944) and the requiem based on **Walt Whitman**'s commemorative *For Those We Love* (1944). In 1947 he was appointed professor at Yale and in 1953 at Zürich, where he composed his opera on **Johann Kepler**'s Life, *Die Harmonie der Welt* (1957). In 1945 he published *The Craft of Musical Composition*.

HINDENBURG, Paul von Beneckendorff und von (1847–1934) German soldier and president, born in Posen of a Prussian Junker family. He was educated at the cadet schools at Wahlstatt and Berlin, fought at the battle of Königgrätz (1866) and in the Franco-Prussian war (1870–71) rose to the rank of general (1903) and retired in 1911. Recalled at the outbreak of World War I, he and **Ludendorff** won decisive victories over the Russians at Tannenberg (1914) and at the Masurian Lakes (1915). His successes against the Russians were not, however, repeated on the western front, and in the summer of 1918 he was obliged to supervise the retreat of the German armies. A national hero and 'father figure', he was president of Germany (1925–34). He did not oppose **Stresemann**'s enlightened foreign policy, but neither did he oppose the rise of Hitler, whom he defeated in the presidential election (1932) and who became chancellor in 1933. But such was his influence that **Hitler** was unable to overthrow constitutional government until his death.

HINDLEY, Myra (1942–) convicted English murderer, born in Gorton. While working as a typist she met **Ian Brady**. They became lovers and soon embarked on a series of murders which were to horrify the public. The couple lured children back to their house in Manchester and tortured them before killing them. David Smith, Hindley's brother-in-law, contacted the police on 7 October 1965 about the murders. Hindley and Brady were arrested, the body of 17-year-old Edward Evans was found at their house, and a huge search for other victims' bodies began on the Pennine moors. The graves and remains of 10-year-old Lesley Ann Downey and 12-year-old John Kilbride were found on Saddleworth Moor. Hindley and Brady became known as the 'Moors Murderers'. Hindley was convicted on two counts of murder and was sentenced to life imprisonment. Her claims in recent years that she has reformed have not led to her release. She made a private confession to two other murders in 1986 and the body of Pauline Reade was found in August 1987, 24 years after her disappearance. The body of 12-year-old Keith Bennett has never been found.

HINDLIP, Lord See **ALLSOPP, Samuel**

HINDMARSH, Sir John (c.1782–1860) British naval officer and administrator, born probably in Chatham, Kent, the son of a naval gunner. He joined the HMS *Bellerophon* at the age of 14 and fought with the Channel fleet under Admiral **Richard Howe**, and later in the Mediterranean under **Nelson** at the Battle of the Nile in 1798 (when he was commended for action which saved his ship) and at Trafalgar in 1805. After the war he became the first governor of South Australia. Hindmarsh objected strongly to the plan for the site for the new town of Adelaide in the middle of a plain six miles from the sea, drawn up by **William Light**, and tried to veto this, but met with strong objections from the settlers. The vagueness of Hindmarsh's powers led him into conflict with the resident commissioners, which set the tone for his period of office, and he was recalled to London in 1838. He was restored to favour two years later as lieutenant-governor of Heligoland, a small rocky island in the North Sea.

HINE, Lewis Wickes (1874–1940) American photographer, born in Oshkosh, Wisconsin. He studied sociology in Chicago and New York (1900–07), making a photographic study of Ellis Island immigrants as an expression of his social concern; a similar record of child labour took him far afield in the United States between 1908 and 1915. During World War I he documented the plight of refugees for the American Red Cross and in 1930–31 recorded the construction of the Empire State Building with a survey entitled *Men at Work* (1932). In the later 1930s he registered the effects of the Depression for a US government project, leaving a detailed picture of the social life of industrial America which spanned some three decades.

HINES, Earl Kenneth ('Fatha') (1903–83) American jazz pianist and bandleader, born in Duquesne, Pennsylvania. He received his first piano lessons from his mother and began to play professionally while a teenager. Moving to Chicago in 1923, he worked under such important leaders as Erskine Tate and Carroll Dickerson, then in association with trumpeter **Louis Armstrong**. His 1928 recording of 'Weather Bird' with Armstrong was a highly influential duet performance. Hines formed his own band in 1928, expanding it to a large orchestra; a twelve-year residency at the Grand Terrace Ballroom, Chicago, with national tours and recording engagements, led to fame as one of the masters of the swing era. He led big bands until 1948, working thereafter in small groups including a period (1948–51) with Louis Armstrong's All-Stars, and touring abroad. His economical, linear approach to solo improvisation, known as 'trumpet-style piano', began a significant development among jazz pianists.

HINKLER, Bert (Herbert John Louis) (1892–1933) Australian pioneer aviator, born in Bundaberg, Queensland. He went to England in 1913 and joined the Sopwith company, then enlisted in the Royal Naval Air Service in World War I, during which he won the DSM and was commissioned. After the war he bought an Avro 'Baby', and flew non-stop to Turin, on what was intended to be the first leg of a flight back to Australia, but wars in the Near East prevented this. In 1921, having shipped his plane to Sydney, he flew it non-stop 700 miles to his home town. In 1928 he created a new England-Australia record, arriving in Darwin, Northern Territory, 16 days after leaving England. He went to the USA in 1931 and bought a **de Havilland** 'Puss Moth', but, unable to find work, he decided to fly it back to England, which he did by way of Jamaica, Brazil and West Africa, creating another three records on the journey. Later he set out on another solo flight to Australia and he left England in his 'Puss Moth' in January 1933, but crashed in the Italian Alps and was buried in Florence with full military honours.

HINKSON, Mrs See **TYNAN, Katharine**

HINSHELWOOD, Sir Cyril Norman (1897–1967) English chemist, born in London. He was Dr Lee's professor of chemistry at Oxford (1937–64), and senior research fellow at Imperial College from 1964. Simultaneously with **Nikolai Semenov** he investigated chemical reaction kinetics in the interwar years, for which they shared the Nobel prize for chemistry in 1956. A considerable linguist and classical scholar, he had the unique distinction of being president of both the Royal Society (from 1955) and of the Classical Association in 1960.

HINSLEY, Arthur (1865–1943) English prelate, born in Selby, Yorkshire. Rector of the English College at Rome from 1917 to 1928, and archbishop of Westminster from 1935, he was made a cardinal in 1937. He was outspoken in his opposition to the Fascist powers in Germany and Italy.

HINTON, Christopher, Baron Hinton of Bankside (1901–83) English nuclear engineer, born in Tisbury, Wiltshire. As an apprentice in a railway workshop he won a scholarship to Cambridge and rose to chief engineer of the alkali division of ICI at Norwich (1931–40). During World War II he supervised explosives filling stations. From 1946 as deputy director of atomic energy production, he constructed the world's first large-scale commercial atomic power station at Calder Hall, opened in 1956, which successfully combined the production of electricity with that of radioactive plutonium at the neighbouring gas-cooled atomic reactor at Windscale (now Sellafield), Cumberland.

HIOUEN-THSANG See **HWEN-T'SIANG**

HIPPARCHUS (fl.160–125 BC) Greek astonomer, born in Nicaea in Bithynia. He carried out observations at Rhodes, discovered the precession of the equinoxes and the eccentricity of the sun's path, determined the length of the solar year, estimated the distances of the sun and moon from the earth, drew up a catalogue of 1080 stars, fixed the geographical position of places by latitude and longitude, and invented trigonometry.

HIPPAS OF ELIS (5th century BC) Greek sophist, a contemporary of **Socrates**. He was vividly portrayed in **Plato**'s dialogues as a virtuoso performer as teacher, orator, memory-man and polymath. He is also credited with a mathematical discovery.

HIPPER, Franz von (1863–1932) German naval officer. He commanded the German scouting groups at the battles of Dogger Bank (1915) and Jutland (1916). He succeeded as commander-in-chief of the German High Seas fleet in 1918.

HIPPIAS and **HIPPARCHUS** See **PISISTRATUS**

HIPPOCRATES (d.c.485BC) tyrant of Gela, which he made it the dominant city of Sicily.

HIPPOCRATES (?c.460–377 or 359 BC) Greek physician, known as the 'father of medicine', and associated with the medical profession's 'Hippocratic Oath'. The most celebrated physician of antiquity, he was born and practised on the island of Cos, but little is known of him except that he taught for money. The so-called 'Hippocratic Corpus' is a collection of 72 medical and surgical treatises written over two centuries by his followers, and only one or two can be fairly ascribed to him. He seems to have tried to distinguish medicine proper from the traditional wisdom and magic of early societies, and laid the early foundations of scientific medicine; he was said to be good at diagnosis and prognosis, and believed that the four fluids or humours of the body (blood, phlegm, yellow bile and black bile) are the primary seats of disease.

HIPPOLYTUS, St (170–235) Christian leader and antipope in Rome. He defended the doctrine of the *Logos* and attacked the Gnostics. He was with **Irenaeus** in Gaul in 194, was a presbyter at Rome, and in 218 was elected antipope in opposition to the heretical (Monarchian) **Calixtus I**. The schism lasted till 235, when Hippolytus and the successor of Calixtus were both deported to work in the Roman mines in Sardinia, where Hippolytus died. He is generally believed to be the author of a *Refutation of all Heresies* in ten books, discovered in 1842 in a 14th-century manuscript at Mount Athos. He also wrote a smaller work against heretics extant in a Latin translation. The so-called *Canons of Hippolytus* are more probably Graeco-Egyptian in origin.

HIRE, Philippe de la (1640–1718) French engineer, born in Paris. A mathematician as well as a keen experimenter, he was employed for some years on geodesic work. In 1682 he joined the Collège Royal where he taught mathematics, and five years later he became professor at the Royal Academy of Architecture. His most notable work is the *Traité de Méchanique* (1695) in which he correctly analysed the forces acting at various points in an arch, making use of geometrical techniques now generally known as graphic statics.

HIROHITO (1901–89) emperor of Japan, the 124th in direct lineage, and the first Japanese prince to visit the west (1921). He acceded in 1926, and his reign was marked by rapid militarization and the aggressive wars against China (1931–32 and 1937–45) and against the USA (1941–45), which ended with the two atomic bombs on Hiroshima and Nagasaki. Under American occupation, Hirohito in 1946 renounced his legendary divinity and most of his powers to become a democratic constitutional monarch.

HIROSHIGE, Ando (1797–1858) Japanese *Ukiyoye* painter, celebrated for his impressive landscape colour prints, executed in a freer but less austere manner than his greater contemporary, **Hokusai**. His *Fifty-three Stages of the Tokaido* had a great influence on western Impressionist painters, but heralded the decline of *Ukiyoye* (wood block print design, literally 'passing world' art).

HIRSCH, Moritz von, Baron (1831–96) German financier and philanthropist, born in Munich. He amassed a fortune in Balkan railroad contracts, and devoted his wealth to improving the lot of the Jews. He financed the Jewish Colonization Association to assist Jewish emigration to the USA.

HIRSCH, Samson Raphael (1808–88) German Jewish theologian, born in Hamburg. He was leader of the modern revival of orthodox Judaism.

HIS, Wilhelm (1831–1904) Swiss biologist, born in Basel. Professor of anatomy at Basel and Leipzig, he introduced the microtome (1865) and pioneered developmental mechanics. His son Wilhelm (1863–1934) discovered the bundle of nerve fibres of the heart.

HISLOP, Joseph (1884–1977) Scottish operatic tenor, born in Edinburgh but closely associated with Scandinavia. He trained as a photoprocessor engraver and went to work in Gothenburg, Sweden, where his fine tenor voice was noticed in a male voice choir. After tuition in Stockholm he made his debut at the Royal Swedish Opera in 1914 as Faust in **Gounod**'s opera. He subsequently appeared at the San Carlo Opera, Naples (1920), Covent Garden, London (in *La Bohème*), Chicago and New York Opera, Turin, Venice, Milan and Buenos Aires. In 1927 and 1931 he made an Empire concert tour of Australia, New Zealand and South Africa, and in 1928 sang Faust in a controversial production at Covent Garden opposite **Chaliapin**. In the 1930s he appeared in a film, *The Loves of Robert Burns* (directed by Herbert Wilcox), created the role of **Goethe** in the British première of **Franz Lehar**'s musical play *Frederica*, and sang Sir Walter Raleigh in a revival of **Edward German**'s *Merrie England*. From 1937 to 1947 he taught at the Royal Academy and the Opera School in Stockholm, where his pupils included **Birgit Nilsson** and **Jussi Björling**, and later coached singers in London. From 1947 he was an adviser at the Royal Opera House, Covent Garden, and at Sadler's Wells, and later became a professor at the Guildhall School of Music.

HISS, Alger (1904–) American state department official, born in Baltimore, a former secretary to Justice **Wendell Holmes** and adviser at the Yalta conference (1945). He stood trial twice (1949, 1950) on a charge of perjury, having denied before a Congressional Un-American Activities Committee that he had passed 200 secret state documents to Whittaker Chambers, an editor of *Time*, in 1938 an agent for an international communist spy ring. Many eminent Americans, including two supreme court judges, and **Adlai Stevenson** and **John Foster Dulles**, testified to Hiss's character, but he was convicted on a majority verdict at his second trial and sentenced to five years' imprisonment. The suspicions of the public, intensified by the subsequent **Klaus Fuchs** case in Britain, were fully exploited politically, not least by Senator **Joseph McCarthy**.

HITCHCOCK, Sir Alfred Joseph (1899–1980) English filmmaker, born in Leytonstone, London. He began as a junior film technician in 1920, and by 1925 had graduated to motion picture director. An unexcelled master of suspense, he directed such films in Britain as *The Thirty-Nine Steps* (1935) and *The Lady Vanishes* (1938). In Hollywood he made *Rebecca* (1940, Academy Award), *Dial M for Murder* (1954) and *Rear Window* (1955), all of which exemplify the famous 'Hitchcock touch'. Later films include *Psycho* (1960), *The Birds* (1963), and *Frenzy* (1972).

HITCHCOCK, Edward (1793–1864) American geologist, born in Deerfield, Massachusetts. Professor of chemistry at Amherst (1825–45), he conducted geological surveys of Massachussetts, and explored dinosaur tracks in Connecticut Valley.

HITCHCOCK, Lambert (1795–1852) American furniture designer, born in Cheshire, Connecticut. In 1818 he established a furniture factory in Barkhamsted (now Riverton), employing 100 workers for mass production of Hitchcock chairs, now considered collectors' items. He also made the first designer rocking-chair.

HITCHENS, Ivon (1893–1979) English painter, born in London. He studied at St John's Wood School of Art and at the Royal Academy, joining the Seven and Five Society (1922), the London Group (1931), and the Society of Mural Painters. Painting in a semi-abstract style with obvious roots in Cubism, he always retained a strongly expressive feeling for natural forms, especially in the wide, horizontal landscapes which he painted from 1936. His first retrospective exhibition was in Leeds in 1945, since when he has had many one-man shows in Europe and America.

HITLER, Adolf (1889–1945) German dictator, born in Braunau in Upper Austria, the son of a minor customs official, originally called Schicklgrüber. He was educated at the secondary schools of Linz and Steyr, and destined by his father for the civil service. Hitler, however, saw himself as a great artist and perhaps purposely disgraced himself in his school leaving examinations. After his father's death he attended a private art school in Munich, but failed twice to pass into the Vienna Academy. Advised to try architecture, he was debarred for lack of a school leaving certificate. He lived on his wits in Vienna (1904–13), making a precarious living by selling bad postcard sketches, beating carpets, and doing odd jobs. He worked only fitfully and spent his time in passionate political arguments directed at the money-lending Jews and the trade unions, which he thought were the tools of the former. He dodged military service, and in 1913 emigrated to Munich, where he found employment as a draughtsman. In 1914 he volunteered for war service in a Bavarian regiment, rose to the rank of corporal, and was recommended for the award of the Iron Cross for service as a runner on the western front. At the time of the German surrender in 1918 he was lying wounded, and temporarily blinded by gas, in hospital. In 1919, while acting as an informer for the army, spying on the activities of small political parties, he became the seventh member of one of them, the name of which he changed to National Socialist German Workers' party (NSDAP) in 1920. Its programme was a convenient mixture of mild radicalism, bitter hatred of the politicians who had 'dishonoured Germany' by signing the Versailles *Diktat*, and clever exploitation of provincial grievances against the weak federal government. By 1923 Hitler was strong enough to attempt with General **Ludendorff**'s and other extreme right-wing factions the overthrow of the Bavarian government. On 9 November, the Nazis marched through the streets of Munich, **Mussolini**-style. But the police, with whom they had a tacit agreement, machine-gunned the Nazi column. Hitler narrowly escaped serious injury, **Goering** was badly wounded, and 16 storm troopers were killed. After nine months' imprisonment in Landsberg jail, during which he dictated his autobiography and political testament, *Mein Kampf* (1925, trans 1939), to **Rudolf Hess**, he began, with **Goebbels**, to woo the Ruhr industrialists, **Krupp** and others, and, although unsuccessful in the presidential elections of 1932 when he stood against **Hindenburg**, Hitler was made chancellor in January 1933 on the advice of **von Papen**, who thought that he could best be brought to heel inside the Cabinet. Hitler, however, soon dispensed with constitutional restraints. He silenced all opposition, and, engineering successfully the burning of the *Reichstag* building (February 1933), advertising it as a communist plot, called for a general election, in which the police, under Goering, allowed the Nazis full play to break up the meetings of their opponents. Only under these conditions did the Nazi party achieve a bare majority, Hitler arrogating to himself absolute power through the Enabling Acts. Opposition inside his own party he ruthlessly crushed by the purge of June 1934 in which his rival **Röhm** and hundreds of influential Nazis were murdered at the hands of Hitler's bodyguard, the SS, under **Himmler** and **Heydrich**. Hindenburg's convenient demise in August left Hitler sole master in Germany. Under the pretext of undoing the wrongs of the Versailles treaty and of uniting the German peoples and extending their living-space (*Lebensraum*) he openly rearmed (1935), sent troops into the demilitarized Rhineland zone, established the Rome-Berlin 'axis' (October 1936) with Mussolini's Italy, created 'Greater Germany' by the invasion of Austria (1938), and, by systematic infiltration and engineered incidents, engendered a favourable situation for an easy absorption of the Sudeten or German-populated border lands of Czechoslovakia, to which Britain and France acquiesced at Munich (September 1938). Renouncing further territorial claims, Hitler nevertheless seized Bohemia and Moravia, took Memel from Lithuania and demanded from Poland the return of Danzig and free access to East Prussia through the 'Corridor'. Poland's refusal, backed by Britain and France, precipitated World War II, on 3 September 1939. Meanwhile Hitler's domestic policy was one of thorough nazification of all aspects of German life, enforced by the Secret State Police (*Gestapo*), and the establishment of concentration camps for political opponents and Jews, who were sytematically persecuted. Strategic roads or *Autobahnen* were built, **Schacht**'s economic policy expanded German exports up to 1936, and then Goering's 'Guns before Butter' four-year plan boosted armaments and the construction of the Siegfried Line. Hitler entered the war with the grave misgivings of the German High Command, but as his 'intuitions' scored massive triumphs in the first two years, he more and more ignored the advice of military experts. Peace with Russia having been secured by the Molotov-Ribbentrop pact (August 1939), Poland was invaded, and after three weeks' *Blitzkrieg* (lightning war) was divided between Russia and Germany. In 1940 Denmark, Norway, Holland, Belgium and France were occupied and the British expelled at Dunkirk. But Goering's invincible *Luftwaffe* was routed in the Battle of Britain (August–September 1940) and Hitler turned eastwards, entered Romania (October 1940), invaded Yugoslavia and Greece (April 1941), and, ignoring his pact of convenience with **Stalin**, attacked Russia and, as ally of Japan, found himself at war with the United States (December 1941). The *Wehrmacht* penetrated to the gates of Moscow and Leningrad, to the Volga, into the Caucasus and, with Italy as an ally from 1940, to North Africa as far as Alexandria. But there the tide turned. **Montgomery**'s victory over **Rommel** at El Alamein (October 1942), and **Paulus**'s grave defeat, through Hitler's misdirection, at Stalingrad (November 1942), heralded the Nazi withdrawal from North Africa pursued by the British and Americans (November 1942–May 1943). The Allied invasion of Sicily, Italian capitulation (September 1943) and engulfing Russian victories (1943–44) followed. The Anglo-American invasion of Normandy and the breaching of Rommel's 'Atlantic Wall' (June 1944) were not countered by Hitler's V1 and V2 guided missile attacks on southern England. He miraculously survived the explosion of the bomb placed at his feet by Colonel **Stauffenberg**, 19

July 1944, and purged the army of all suspects, including Rommel, who was given Hobson's choice to commit suicide. **Rundstedt**'s counter-offensive against the Allies, in the Ardennes, December 1944, under Hitler's direction failed and the invasion of Germany followed. Hitler lived out his fantasies, commanding nonexistent armies from his *Bunker*, the air-raid shelter under the chancellory building in Berlin. With the Russians only several hundred yards away, he went through a grotesque marriage ceremony with his mistress, **Eva Braun**, in the presence of the Goebbels family, who then poisoned themselves. All available evidence suggests that Hitler and his wife committed suicide and had their bodies cremated on 30 April 1945. His much-vaunted *Third Reich*, which was to have endured for ever, ended ingloriously after twelve years of unparalleled barbarity, in which 30 million people lost their lives, 12 million of them far away from the battlefields, by mass shootings, in forced labour camps and in the gas ovens of Belsen, Dachau, Auschwitz, Ravensbrück and other concentration camps in accordance with Nazi racial theories and the 'New Order', not forgetting the indiscriminate torture and murder of many prisoners-of-war, or the uprooting and extermination of entire village communities in Poland, France and Russia. Such horror prompted the international trial at Nuremberg (1945–46), at which 21 of the leading living Nazis were tried and eleven executed for war crimes.

HITOMARO, Kakinomoto no See **AKAHITO, Yamabe no**

HITTORF, Johann Wilhelm (1824–1914) German chemist, born in Bonn. He became professor at Münster, did research on electrolytes, and studied the discharge of rarefied gases with the Hittorf tube.

HJARTARSON, Snorri (1906–86) Icelandic poet, born in Borgarfjöroður. He studied art in Copenhagen and Oslo, but soon turned to writing and published a novel written in Norwegian, *Höjt flyver ravnen* (High Soars the Raven, 1934). He returned to Iceland in 1936 to become one of the most influential poets of his day, combining traditional and modern poetry with musical and painterly images. He published only four volumes of poetry, and was awarded the Nordic Council's literary award for 1981.

HJELMSLEV, Louis Trolle (1899–1965) Danish linguist, born in Copenhagen. He founded the Linguistic Circle of Copenhagen in 1931, and was a co-founder of the journal *Acta Linguistica* in 1939. With associates in Copenhagen, he devised a system of linguistic analysis known as glossematics, based on the study of the distribution of, and the relationships between, the smallest meaningful units of a language (glossemes). This is outlined in his *Prolegomena to a Theory of Language* (1943, trans 1953, 1961).

HO CHI-MINH, Nguyen Van Thann (1892–1969) Vietnamese political leader, born in Central Vietnam. From 1912 he visited London and the USA and lived in France from 1918, where he was a founder member of the Communist party. From 1922 he was often in Moscow. He placed himself at the head of the Vietminh independence movement in 1941, and between 1946 and 1954 directed the successful military operations against the French, becoming prime minister (1954–55) and president (1954) of North Vietnam. Re-elected in 1960, 'Uncle Ho' was a leading force in the war between North (Viet Cong) and South (with American support) Vietnam during the 1960s.

HOAD, Lewis Alan (1934–) Australian tennis player, born in Sydney. With his doubles partner, **Ken Rosewall**, he had a meteoric rise to fame, winning the Wimbledon doubles titles and a Davis Cup challenge match against the U S A before he was 20 years old. He defeated Rosewall in the Wimbledon final of 1956, and won again the following year, but thereafter turned professional and was ineligible by the rules of the time to compete for the game's major honours.

HOADLY, Benjamin (1676–1761) English prelate, born in Westerham, Kent. Bishop successively of Bangor (1715), Hereford (1721), Salisbury (1723) and Winchester (1734), and controversial writer, he defended the cause of civil and religious liberty against both crown and clergy, and carried on a controversy with **Francis Atterbury** on the obedience due to the civil power by ecclesiastics. A sermon before the king in 1717 sought to show that Christ had not delegated His powers to any ecclesiastical authorities. It led to the fierce Bangorian Controversy and incidentally to the indefinite prorogation of Convocation.

HOAGLAND, Mahlon Bush (1921–) American biochemist, born in Boston, Massachusetts. He studied medicine at Harvard, taught there (1960–67), and was scientific director of the Worcester Foundation for Experimental Biology from 1970 to 1985. In the 1950s he isolated transfer RNA (t-RNA) and went on to show, in some detail, how cells use it to synthesize proteins from amino acids.

HOARE, Sir Richard (1648–1718) English banker, born in London. He became a Lombard Street goldsmith (c.1673) and moved (c.1693) to Fleet Street, where he founded the bank which still bears his name. He was lord mayor of London in 1713.

HOARE, Sir Samuel See **TEMPLEWOOD**

HOBART PASHA, properly **August Charles Hobart-Hampden** (1822–86) English naval commander and adventurer, third son of the 6th Earl of Buckinghamshire, born in Waltham-on-the-Wolds, Leicestershire. He served in the Royal Navy from 1835 to 1863 during the American Civil War as 'Captain Roberts', repeatedly ran the blockade of the Southern ports, and afterwards became naval adviser to Turkey (1867) and was made pasha and admiral. In the Russo-Turkish war (1878) he commanded the Turkish Black Sea fleet. He wrote *Never Caught* (1867), on his blockade-running exploits, and *Sketches from My Life*.

HOBBEMA, Meindert (1638–1709) Dutch landscape painter, born probably in Amsterdam. He studied under **Ruisdael**, but lacked his master's genius and range, contenting himself with florid, placid and charming watermill scenes. Nevertheless his masterpiece, *The Avenue, Middelharnis* (1689), in the National Gallery, London is a striking exception and has greatly influenced modern landscape artists. Through marriage, he became collector of the city's wine customs.

HOBBES, Thomas (1588–1679) English political philosopher, born in Malmesbury, prematurely, as he liked to explain, when his mother heard news of the approaching Armada. He was the son of a wayward country vicar, brought up by an uncle, and was educated at Magdalen Hall, Oxford (1603–08). He was supported over a long life by the patronage of the great, in particular that of the **Cavendish** family, the Earls of Devonshire, with whom he travelled widely as family tutor, thereby making the acquaintance of many leading intellectual figures of his day: **Bacon**, **Selden** and **Ben Jonson** in England, **Galileo** in Florence, and the circle of **Mersenne** in Paris, including **Descartes** and **Gassendi**. But the first real intellectual turning-point of his life was his introduction at the age of 40 to Euclidean geometry, and he conceived the ambition of extending this compelling deductive certainty to a comprehensive science of man and society. His interest in political theory had already been indicated in his first published work, a translation of **Thucydides**' *History* (1629); and, becoming increasingly concerned with the civil disorders of the time, he wrote the *Elements of Law Natural and Politic* (completed in 1640 but not properly published until 1650), in which he attempted to set out in mathematical fashion the rules of a political science, and went on to argue in favour of monarchical government. When the Long Parliament assembled later in 1640 he quickly departed for France, 'the first of those that fled', to be followed by other royalists who in 1646 helped him to the position of tutor in mathematics to the exiled Prince of Wales (the future **Charles II**) in Paris. By then he had completed a set of 'Objections' (1641) to Descartes' *Meditations*, which Mersenne had commissioned from him (as from other scholars), and the *De Cive* (1642), a fuller statement of his new science of the state or 'civil philosophy'. His next work was his masterpiece, *Leviathan* (1651), which presented and connected his mature thoughts on metaphysics, psychology and political philosophy. He was a thorough-going materialist. The world was conceived as a mechanical system consisting wholly of bodies in motion, driven by the forces of attraction and repulsion, which could be seen also to govern human psychology and to determine what we call 'good' and 'evil'. Human beings are wholly selfish, and in a state of nature there would be 'a war of every man against every man . . . and the life of man solitary, poor, nasty, brutish and short'. Hence enlightened self-interest explains the nature and function of the sovereign state: we are forced to establish a social contract in which we surrender the right of aggression to an absolute ruler, whose commands are the law. The *Leviathan* offended the royal exiles at Paris and the French government by its hostility to Church power and religious obedience, and in 1652 Hobbes returned to England, made his peace with **Cromwell** and the parliamentary régime, and settled in London. But he continued for the rest of his long life to write and to arouse controversy. *De Corpore* appeared in 1655, *De Homine* in 1658. At the Restoration Charles II gave his old tutor a pension and helped quash a bill aimed at Hobbes, whose enemies in the clergy claimed that the Plague and the Great Fire of London of 1665–66 revealed God's wrath against England for harbouring such an atheist. He was banned from publishing in England in 1666 and his later books were published in Holland in the first instance. He wrote on tirelessly in his 80s, and amongst other things published *Behemoth: a history of the causes of the Civil Wars of England* (completed 1668, published 1682), an autobiography in Latin verse (1672), and verse translations of the *Iliad* (1675) and *Odyssey* (1676).

HOBBS, Sir John Berry ('Jack') (1882–1963) English cricketer, born in Cambridge and one of England's greatest batsmen. He first played first-class cricket for Cambridgeshire in 1904, but joined Surrey the following year and played for them for 30 years (1905–35). He played in 61 Test matches between 1907 and 1930, when he and **Bert Sutcliffe** (1894–1937) established themselves as an unrivalled pair of opening batsmen, and he captained England in 1926. In his first-class career he made 197 centuries, and scored 61 237 runs (including the highest score at Lord's with 316 in 1926). He also made the highest ever score in the Gentlemen v. Players match, 266 not out; 98 of his 197 centuries were made after he attained the age of 40. An immensely popular figure, he was the first cricketer to be knighted, in 1953. After his retirement from cricket he ran a sports shop. Modest and pleasant in demeanour he is regarded, with Bert Sutcliffe and **Frank Woolley**, as one of the great exponents of classical English batsmanship.

HOBHOUSE, John Cam, 1st Baron Broughton (1786–1869) British statesman and friend of **Byron**, was educated at Westminster and Trinity College, Cambridge. His *Journey through Albania with Lord Byron* he published in 1813. He entered parliament as a Radical in 1820, succeeded as baronet in 1831, and in 1832–52 held various cabinet Offices. He coined the term 'His Majesty's opposition'.

HOBHOUSE, Leonard Trelawney (1864–1929) English social philosopher and journalist, born in St Ives, Cornwall. A fellow of Merton College, Oxford (1894), he joined the editorial staff of the *Manchester Guardian* in 1897 and transferred to the editorship of the *Sociological Review* in 1903. For the same period, 1903–05, he was secretary of the Free Trade Union, and became political editor of *Tribune* (1906–07). From 1907 he was professor of sociology at London University. His best known works are *Labour Movement* (1893), *Theory of Knowledge* (1896), *Morals in Evolution* (1906), and *Development and Purpose* (1913). He thought the key to evolution lay in 'conditioned teleology'.

HOBSON, John Atkinson (1858–1940) English economist, born in Derby. He graduated at Oxford. An opponent of orthodox economic theories, he believed 'under-consumption' to be the main cause of unemployment. He wrote *The Science of Wealth* (1911), and an autobiography, *Confessions of an Economic Heretic* (1938).

HOBSON, Sir Harold (1904–) English dramatic critic, born into a mining family in Rotherham. Paralyzed in the right leg when he was seven, he was unable to attend school until he was sixteen. He won a scholarship to Sheffield University, but chose instead to go to Oxford. He was drama critic of the *Sunday Times* (1947–76) and became one of the most influential critics in Britain. He was also drama critic of the Christian Science Monitor (1931–74). An authority on French theatre and the French avant-garde, he hailed *Waiting for Godot* by **Samuel Beckett** on its London première in 1955. He wrote a number of books on British and French theatre, an autobiography (*Indirect Journey*, 1978), and a personal history, *Theatre in Britain* (1984).

HOBSON, Thomas (c.1544–1631) English carrier and inn-keeper of Cambridge. For some 50 years he drove a stagecoach the 60 miles from Cambridge to London at breakneck speed. He kept a stable of horses to rent out to students at the university, and required each customer to take the horse nearest the stable door, whatever its quality; hence the expression 'Hobson's choice', meaning no choice at all.

HOBY, Sir Thomas (1530–66) English courtier and diplomat. He was half-brother to the Protestant diplomatist, Sir Philip Hoby (1505–58). He is best known for his translation of **Castiglione**'s *Il cortegiano* as *The Courtyer of Count Baldesser Castilio* (1561).

HOCCLEVE, or **Occleve, Thomas** (c.1368–1426) English poet. He spent his life as a clerk in the privy seal office in London (1378–1425). His chief work is a free but tedious version of the *De Regimine Principum* of Aegidius Romanus, in **Chaucer**'s seven-line stanza. He also wrote *Ars Secondi Mori*; an autobiographical poem, *La Male Regla* (1406); and *Regiment of Princes* (1412).

HOCHE, Lazare (1768–97) French revolutionary soldier, born in Montreuil. Promoted from corporal to general, he defended Dunkirk against **Frederick Augustus**, the Duke of York, and drove the Austrians out of Alsace (1793), ended the civil war in La Vendée

(1795), commanded the attempted invasion of Ireland (1796), and defeated the Austrians at Neuwied (1797).

HOCHHUTH, Rolf (1931–) German dramatist, born in Eschwege Werran. He studied history and philosophy at Munich and Heidelberg, and worked as an editor before turning to documentary drama. His main claim to fame is the controversial subject matter of his plays. *The Representative* (1963) accused Pope **Pius XII** of not intervening to stop the Nazi persecution of the Jews. It caused a furore, as did the implication in his second play, *Soldiers* (1967), that **Winston Churchill** was involved in the assassination of the Polish war-time leader, General **Sikorski**. He also wrote a novel, *German Love Story* (1978), about Nazi atrocities.

HOCKING, Joseph (1855–1937) English clergyman and writer, born in St Stephens, Cornwall. He was from 1878 a land surveyor and from 1884 to 1910 a Nonconformist minister. He wrote many novels of a religious tendency. His elder brother, Silas Kitto (1850–1935), from 1870 to 1896 also a minister, wrote many similar novels.

HOCKNEY, David (1937–) English artist, born in Bradford. After a traditional training at Bradford College of Art his paintings began to attract interest while he was studying at the Royal College of Art. Associated with the Pop art movement from his earliest work, he experimented with different styles with an originality and innocence that was to become the characteristic of all his work. His early paintings are a vital and witty juxtaposition of artistic styles and fashions, with graffiti-like figures and words, or lines of the poems that often influenced him, and a technique ranging from the broad use of heavy colour to a minute delicacy of line. A visit to the USA inspired his series of etchings, *The Rake's Progress* (1963), based on his adventures in New York. He taught at the University of California from 1965 to 1967, and it was a visit to California that inspired his well-known 'swimming-pool' paintings, prompted by his fascination with the representation of water. He edited and illustrated 14 *Poems of C V Cavafy*, the Greek poet, and in 1970 a series of etchings illustrating fairy-tales by the brothers **Grimm** was published. His later work, often portraits, though with the same directness and innocence, has become less 'primitive', more representational. He also designed the stage-setting for several operas, including **Mozart**'s *Magic Flute* at Glyndebourne (1978), and costumes and sets for the Metropolitan Opera House, New York.

HODGE, Charles (1797–1878) American theologian, born in Philadelphia. In 1822 he became professor at Princeton Theological Seminary. He founded and edited the *Princeton Review*, and wrote a history of the Presbyterian Church in America (1840), and the well-known *Systematic Theology* (1871–1872). His son, Archibald Alexander (1823–1886), who succeeded his father at Princeton in 1878, wrote *Outlines of Theology* (1860).

HODGKIN, Sir Alan Lloyd (1914–) English physiologist. He was a fellow of Trinity College, Cambridge, and lecturer at Cambridge (1945–52), becoming Royal Society research professor (1952–69), and professor of biophysics (1970–81). During World War II he worked on radar, and with Sir **Andrew Huxley** explained nerve transmissions in physico-chemical terms. He was awarded the 1963 Nobel prize for physiology or medicine jointly with Huxley and Sir **John Carew Eccles** for research on nerve impulses.

HODGKIN, Dorothy Mary, née **Crowfoot** (1910–) English chemist, born in Cairo. Educated at Oxford and Cambridge, she became a research fellow at Somerville College, Oxford (1936–77) and Wolfson research professor at the Royal Society (1960–77). A crystallographer of distinction, she was awarded the Nobel prize for chemistry in 1964 for discoveries, by the use of X-ray techniques, of the structure of molecules, including penicillin, vitamin B 12 and insulin.

HODGKIN, Howard (1932–) English painter, born in London. He trained chiefly at Bath Academy of Art and subsequently taught for many years, latterly at Chelsea School of Art. His highly personal style has not followed any of the major art movements of recent decades; though at first sight apparently abstract, his paintings are in fact representational, usually of interiors with people captured at a particular moment in time. He has spent some time in India, and his interest in the traditional painting of that country is reflected in the decorative features of his compositions and his use of brilliant colour as well as his preference for working on a small scale. In 1985 he won the Turner prize for contemporary British art.

HODGKIN, Thomas (1798–1866) English physician and pathologist, born in Tottenham. He held various posts at Guy's Hospital and described the glandular disease, *lymphadenoma*, which is named after him.

HODGKIN, Thomas (1831–1913) English historian, born of Quaker stock in Tottenham. He became a banker in Newcastle, and was the author of *Italy and her Invaders* (8 vols, 1880–99). His son, Robert Howard (1877–1951), born in Newcastle, wrote *A History of the Anglo-Saxons* (1935).

HODGKINS, Frances Mary (1869–1947) New Zealand artist, born and educated in Dunedin. She travelled extensively in Europe with long sojourns in Paris and England. Her paintings, examples of which are in the Tate Gallery and the Victoria and Albert museum, are characterized by a harmonious use of flat colour somewhat reminiscent of **Matisse**, and though older than most of her circle she was ranked as a leader of contemporary romanticism.

HODGKINSON, Eaton (1789–1861) English engineer, born in Anderton, Cheshire. He had little formal higher education, but became one of the foremost authorities on the strength of materials. As a result of tests carried out in the engineering works of Sir **William Fairbairn**, he proposed in 1830 the famous 'Hodgkinson's beam' as the most efficient form of cast-iron beam, and after a further series of experiments he published in 1840 a paper *On the Strength of Pillars of Cast Iron and other Materials*. Hodgkinson also collaborated with Fairbairn and **Robert Stephenson** on the design of the rectangular wrought-iron tubes within which trains crossed the Menai Strait in four continuous spans, two of 460 ft and two of 230 ft. The Britannia Bridge, opened in 1850, constituted a significant advance in the theory and practice of structural engineering at the time.

HODGSON, Brian Houghton (1800–95) English orientalist, born near Macclesfield. He entered the East India Company's service in 1818, was resident in Nepal (1820–43), and settled in England in 1858. He wrote some 170 very valuable papers on the technology, languages and zoology of Nepal and Tibet, sent home 354 MSS, on which our knowledge of northern Buddhism is mainly based, and made a collection of 10 500 birds.

HODGSON, Leonard (1889–1969) English Anglican theologian, born in London. Teaching at Magdalen College, Oxford, and the General Theological Seminary, New York, before returning to Oxford as professor of moral and pastoral theology (1938–54) and then professor of divinity (1944–58), he was also theological secretary to the Commission on Faith and Order of the World Council of Churches, Geneva (1933–52), and warden of William Temple College, Rugby (1954–66). He wrote some 20 books, including *The Doctrine of the Trinity* (1943) and *The Doctrine of the Atonement* (1951). His Gifford lectures, *For Faith and Freedom* (2 vols, 1956–57), aimed to show that 'the Christian faith, while it forbids us to claim knowledge we have not got, gives us light enough to walk in the way that leads to knowing more'.

HODGSON, Ralph (1871–1962) English poet, born in Yorkshire. He became a journalist in London and published three volumes of Georgian poems with the recurring theme of nature and England: *The Last Blackbird* (1907), *Eve* (1913), and *Poems* (1917) containing 'The Song of Honour', 'The Moor', 'The Journeyman', and the polemic against the destruction of animals for feminine vanity in 'To Deck a Woman'. He lectured in Japan (1924–38), and made his home in Ohio, USA. An anthology of his works appeared as *The Skylark and Other Poems* (1958). He was awarded the Order of the Rising Sun (1938) and the Queen's Gold Medal (1954).

HODLER, Ferdinand (1853–1918) Swiss painter, born in Bern. He developed a highly decorative style of landscape, historical and genre painting with strong colouring and outline, sometimes using parallel *motifs* for effect. His works include the *Battle of Marignano*, *William Tell*, *Night*, *Day*, and many others at Bern, Zürich and elsewhere.

HODSON, William Stephen Raikes (1821–58) English soldier, born in Maisemore Court near Gloucester. He joined the Indian army in 1845, served in the 1st Sikh War (1845–46), and in 1852–55, as commandant of the Guides Corps, did excellent service on the Northwest Frontier. In 1856 he was deprived of his command for irregularities in the regimental accounts and unjust treatment of the natives. Restored to rank in 1857, he was head of the intelligence department before Delhi during the Indian Mutiny (1857–58), and raised the irregular cavalry known as Hodson's Horse. On the fall of Delhi in 1857 he discovered the mughal, and shot the two princes with his own hand. He himself was killed at Lucknow.

HOE, Richard Marsh (1812–86) American inventor and industrialist, born in New York, the eldest son of Robert Hoe (1784–1833), a British-born American manufacturer of printing presses. He joined his father's firm when he was 15 years old and took over the business with his cousin Matthew three years later when his father retired. Like **Augustus Applegath** in London, he saw the advantages of printing on a cylinder instead of a flat plate, and the Hoe rotary press was first used by the *Philadelphia Public Ledger* in 1847. In 1865 William Bullock installed for the *Philadelphia Inquirer* a rotary press that printed on a continuous roll of newsprint, but by 1871 Hoe had produced a new design incorporating all the main features introduced by his rivals.

HOFER, Andreas (1767–1810) Tyrolese patriot leader and innkeeper, born in St Leonhard. In 1808 he called the Tyrolese to arms to expel the French and Bavarians, and defeated the Bavarians at the battle of Iusel Berg (1809). The Treaty of Schönbrunn between Austria and France after the battle of Wagram (July 1809) left Tyrol unsupported. The French again invaded them; but in eight days Hofer routed them and retook Innsbruck, and for the next two months was ruler of his native land. By the peace of Vienna (October) Austria again left Tyrol at the mercy of her enemies. Hofer once more took up arms; but this time the French and Bavarians were too strong for him; Hofer had to disband his followers and take refuge in the mountains. Two months later he was betrayed, captured and taken to Mantua, where he was tried by court martial and shot.

HOFER, Karl (1878–1955) German artist, born in Karlsruhe, where he studied. He spent many years in France and Italy and his work was much influenced by his war experiences; his severe style and harsh, brilliant colours express the bitterness of the times in symbolic terms.

HOFF, Jacobus Henricus van't (1852–1911) Dutch chemist, born in Amsterdam, a founder of physical chemistry and stereochemistry. Educated at the University of Leiden, he became professor of chemistry at Amsterdam (1877), Leipzig (1887) and Berlin (1895). He postulated the asymmetrical carbon atom, first applied thermodynamics to chemical reactions, discovered that osmotic pressure varies directly with the absolute temperature, and investigated the formation of double salts. He won the first Nobel prize for chemistry in 1901.

HOFFA, Jimmy (James Riddle) (1913–75) American labour leader, born in Brazil, Indiana. He was a grocery warehouseman when he joined the International Brotherhood of Teamsters, Chauffeurs, Warehousemen and Helpers of America (the Teamsters' Union) in 1931. He proceeded to re-organize it, strengthening central control, and was elected president in 1957. In the same year the Teamsters were expelled from the American Federation of Labor and Congress of Industrial Organizations (AFL-CIO) for repudiating its ethics code. Hoffa negotiated the Teamsters' first national contract in 1964, but, following corruption investigations by the attorney general, **Robert F Kennedy**, was imprisoned in 1967 for attempted bribery of a federal court jury. His sentence was commuted by President **Nixon** and he was given parole in 1971, on condition that he resigned as Teamsters leader. In 1975 he disappeared and is believed to have been murdered.

HOFFMAN, Dustin (1937–) American actor, born in Los Angeles. A student at the Pasadena Playhouse (1956–58), he then pursued a career on stage and television in New York, interspersed with a variety of odd jobs. He made his Broadway début in *A Cook for Mr. General* (1961) and came to prominence with his performance in *Journey of the Fifth Horse* (1966). Following a modest film début in *The Tiger Makes Out* (1967), he gained attention and an Oscar nomination for *The Graduate* (1967). A notoriously exacting perfectionist, he has consistently displayed his versatility and mastery of detailed characterization, winning an Academy Award for *Kramer vs. Kramer* (1979) and *Rainman* (1989), and earning nominations for *Midnight Cowboy* (1969), *Lenny* (1974) and *Tootsie* (1982). He returned to Broadway in *Death of a Salesman* (1984), winning an Emmy for the television reprise of that role the following year. He tackled his first Shakespearian role on the London stage as Shylock in *The Merchant of Venice* in 1989.

HOFFMAN, Samuel Kurtz (1902–) American rocket propulsion engineer, born in Williamsport, Pennsylvania. He graduated in mechanical engineering at Pennsylvania State University (1925), and after working in the aviation industry returned there from 1945 to 1949 as professor of aeronautical engineering. From 1949 he led the team developing rocket engines at North American Aviation, raising their power from an initial 75000 pounds of thrust to 1.5 million pounds by the mid 1960s. Eight of these engines powered the multi-stage Saturn 5 launching vehicle which ultimately, in July 1969, took American astronauts on the first stage of their journey to the moon.

HOFFMANN, August Heinrich, called **'Hoffmann von Fallersleben'** (1798–1874) German poet and philologist, and composer of the German national anthem, born at Fallersleben in Lüneburg. He was keeper of the university library of Breslau (1823–38), and professor of German there (1830–42). A popular writer of light lyrics, he published *Lieder und Romanzen* in 1841; but the publication of his *Unpolitische Lieder* in 1842 cost him his chair. In 1860 he became librarian to the Duke of Ratibor at Korvei, where he died. He is best known for his popular and patriotic *Volkslieder*, including 'Alle Vögel sind schon da' and the song 'Deutschland, Deutschland über Alles' (1841), which became the German national anthem in 1922. He also published several works on philology and antiquities, including *Horae Belgicae* (1830–62).

HOFFMANN, Ernst Theodor Wilhelm, called **'Amadeus'** (1776–1822) German writer, music critic and caricaturist, born in Königsberg. Trained as a lawyer, he had an unsettled career until 1816, when he attained a high position in the Supreme Court in Berlin. A remarkable essay on **Mozart**'s *Don Giovanni*, the composition of an opera (*Undine* 1816) and the direction of the Bamberg theatre for two months (1808), testify to his real interests. He was the archpriest of ultra-German romanticism. His wit bubbled over in irony, ridicule and sarcasm, and his imagination was inexhaustible, but utterly undisciplined, wild and fantastic. His shorter tales were mostly published in the collections *Phantasiestücke* (1814), *Nachtstücke* (1817) and *Die Serapionsbrüder* (1819–25). His longer works include *Elixiere des Teufels* (1816; trans 1824), *Seltsame Leiden eines Theaterdirektors* (1818), *Klein Zaches* (1819) and *Lebensansichten des Katers Murr* (1821–22, partly autobiographical). Three of his stories provided the basis for **Offenbach**'s opera, *Tales of Hoffmann* (1881), and another for **Delibes**'s *Coppelia*. As a composer his most important opera was *Undine*, a precursor of the scores of **Weber** and **Wagner**. He also composed vocal, chamber, orchestral and piano works. He was an influential writer on music, notably in his reviews of **Beethoven**'s works.

HOFFMANN, Friedrich (1660–1742) German physician. He was professor of medicine at Halle, and physician to **Frederick I** of Prussia; he introduced various medicines, including Hoffmann's drops and anodyne.

HOFFMANN, Josef (1870–1956) Austrian architect, born in Pirnitz. He was a leader of the Vienna 'Secession' group (1899—seceding from the traditional Viennese style), and in 1903 founded the *Wiener Werkstätte* (Vienna Workshops), devoted to arts and crafts. He himself designed metalwork, glass and furniture. His main architectural achievements were the white-stuccoed Purkersdorf Sanatorium (1903–05) and Stociet House in Brussels (1905–11). He was city architect of Vienna from 1920, and designed the Austrian pavilion for the 1934 Venice Bienniale.

HOFFMANN, Roald (1937–) Polish-born American chemist, born in Zloczow. He moved to the USA in 1949 and studied at Columbia and Harvard, and worked at Cornell University from 1965. With **R B Woodward** he developed the Woodward-Hoffmann rules, which enable the path of an important class of organic reactions to be predicted. Hoffmann shared the Nobel prize for chemistry in 1981 with **Kenichi Fukui**, who had worked independently in related areas.

HOFFNUNG, Gerard (1925–59) German-born British cartoonist and musician, born in Berlin and brought to England as a boy. His first cartoon was published in *Lilliput* magazine while he was still at school (1941). After studying art at Highgate School of Arts, he became art master at Stamford School (1945) and Harrow (1948). He was staff cartoonist on the London *Evening News* (1947) and after a brief time in New York (1950) returned in 1951 to freelance for *Punch* and others. His interest in music led to his creation of the Hoffnung Music Festivals at the Royal Festival Hall in which his caricatures came to life and sound. They were also animated by Halas-Batchelor in the television series, *Tales From Hoffnung* (1965).

HOFMANN, August Wilhelm von (1818–92) German chemist, born in Giessen. He became first director of the Royal College of Chemistry in London in 1845, and from 1856 to 1865 he was chemist to the Royal Mint. He went to Berlin as professor of chemistry in 1865, and was ennobled in 1888. He obtained aniline from coal products, discovered many other organic compounds, including formaldehyde (1867), and devoted much labour to the theory of chemical types.

HOFMANN, Hans (1880–1966) German-born American painter, born in Weissenberg. He studied painting in Munich and from 1904 to 1914 lived in Paris, where he met **Matisse** and the Cubists. He returned to Germany in 1914, opening an art school in Munich. In 1932 he emigrated to the USA, settling in New York where, again, he opened an art school. He took American nationality in 1941. Around 1940 he developed a painterly abstract style, dripping paint on to the canvas and applying bright colour in broad strokes. These works had a significant impact on the development of abstract painting in the USA.

HOFMANNSTHAL, Hugo von (1874–1929) Austrian poet and dramatist, born in Vienna into a banking family of Austro-Jewish-Italian origins. While still at school he attracted attention by his symbolic, neo-romantic poems or 'lyrical dramas' such as *Gestern*, *Der Tod des Tizian* and *Leben*, in which the transitory and elusive nature of life and its short-lived pleasures compel the quest for the world of the spirit. An emotional and intellectual crisis, a sudden awareness of the drying-up of his lyrical gifts, precipitated the 'Chandos Letters' (1902), an imaginary correspondence between Lord **Bacon** and a young Elizabethan nobleman, in which Hofmannsthal, in the guise of the latter, gives his reasons for abandoning poetry, his new hatred for abstract terms, his doubts of the possibility of successful communication. Thenceforth he devoted himself to drama, most of his works being based on that of other dramatists: *Electra* (1903), *Das geretete Venedig* (1905), and the morality plays *Jedermann* (1912) and *Das Salzburger grosse Welttheater* (1923). One of his major works is the comedy, *Der Schwierige* (1921). Having renounced **Stefan George** and his circle, Hofmannsthal turned to the composer **Richard Strauss**, for whom he wrote the libretti for *Der Rosenkavalier* (1911), *Ariadne auf Naxos* (1912), *Die Frau ohne Schatten* (1919) and others. With Strauss and **Max Reinhardt**, he was instrumental in founding the Salzburg Festival after World War I. His statue there was demolished by the Nazis in 1938.

HOFMEISTER, Wilhelm Friedrich Benedikt (1824–77) German botanist. Originally a music publisher and bookseller in Leipzig, he became expert in microscopes and was appointed professor of botany at Heidelberg (1863) and in 1872 at Tübingen. He did fundamental work on plant embryology, and discovered the alternation of generations and cryptograms, so epoch-making that he is considered one of the greatest botanists of all time.

HOFMEYR, Jan Hendrik (1845–1909) South African statesman, born in Cape Town. He took to journalism, as 'Onze Jan' rose to be political leader of the Cape Dutch and dominated the Afrikaner Bond. He represented the Cape at the Colonial Conferences of 1887 and 1894. After the **Jameson** Raid (1895) he parted from **Rhodes**, and thereafter worked outside parliament. His nephew, Jan Hendrik (1894–1948), was deputy premier to **Smuts** and advocated a liberal policy towards the African natives.

HOFSTADTER, Richard (1916–70) American historian, born in Buffalo, New York. He was educated at Buffalo University and Columbia, where he taught from 1946 to 1970. His doctoral thesis, published as *Social Darwinism in American Thought 1860–1915* (1944), discussed the use of a philosophy of natural selection as rationale and as impetus for the unfettered development of American capitalism. *The American Political Tradition and the Men Who Made It* (1948) similarly examined ideological rationale and disguise in studying the impulses behind the careers and movements of major American politicians and statesmen. In his *The Age of Reform* (1955) he offered sociological rather than economic explanations of political behaviour. Like many other American-Jewish scholars, he anxiously questioned American society for fear that forms of Hitlerism might yet emerge, and his *Anti-Intellectualism in American Life* (1963), *The Development of Academic Freedom in the United States* (1955) and *The Paranoid Style in American Politics* (1965) all reflected his sense of the liberal mind and its enemies. But he was too lively ever to remain on any track for any length, and in such work as *The Idea of a Party System* (1969) he brilliantly worked out how late party politics was in receiving American endorsement.

HOFSTADTER, Robert (1915–) American physicist, born in New York. He taught at Pennsylvania University and Stanford University, where he became professor of physics in 1954. He studied the atomic structure of protons and neutrons on the large linear accelerator there and determined their electromagnetic form factors. He shared the 1961 Nobel prize for physics with **Rudolph Mössbauer**.

HOGAN, ('Ben') William Benjamin (1912–) American golfer, born in Stephenville, Texas. One of the world greats, he began his career at the age of 11 as a caddie. A professional at various country clubs, he fought his way to the top despite financial difficulties. He won the US Open four times, the US Masters twice, the US PGA twice, and the British Open once; in 1948 he won all three major US titles in the one season. In 1949 he was critically injured in a car accident, but went on to win 11 major tournaments in 1951; and in 1953 he won every major world championship. A Hollywood film, *Follow the Sun* (1951), was based on his life-story.

HOGARTH, David George (1862–1929) English archaeologist, keeper of the Ashmolean Museum, Oxford (1909–27). He excavated in Asia Minor, Syria and Egypt. In 1915 he was involved in organizing Arab revolt against Turks.

HOGARTH, William (1697–1764) English painter and engraver, born in Smithfield, London, the son of a teacher. Early apprenticed to a silverplate engraver, he studied painting under Sir **James Thornhill**, whose daughter he married, after eloping with her, in 1729. By 1720 he already had his own business, engraving coats-of-arms, shop-bills and book plates, and painting conversation pieces and portraits, including that of *Sarah Malcolm*, the triple murderess (1732–33). But tiring of conventional art forms, he resurrected the 'pictured morality' of medieval art by his 'modern moral subjects', often comprising several pictures in a series, but, unlike the modern strip cartoon, each artistically and representationally self-sufficient. The first of these was *A Harlot's Progress* (1730–31), destroyed by fire (1755). With an unerring eye for human foibles, he was often forthright to the point of coarseness, but although his didactic purpose was unmistakable, seldom indulged in melodrama. Single works such as *Southwark Fair* and the superbly captured atmosphere of a stag party entitled *A Midnight Modern Conversation* (both 1733) precede his eight pictures of *A Rake's Progress* (1733–35). In 1735 he opened his own academy in St Martin's Lane. Two pictures in the conventional style, *The Pool of Bethesda* and *The Good Samaritan* (1735), he presented to St Bartholomew's Hospital in the hope of attracting commissions. He later returned to moral narrative, of which his masterpiece is the *Marriage à la mode* series (1743–45), and then extended his social commentaries to 'men of the lowest rank' by drawing attention to their typical vices in prints such as the *Industry and Idleness* series (1747), *Gin Lane*, and *Beer Street* (1751). He later ventured into politics with a cartoon of **Wilkes, Pitt** and **Temple** as warmongers (1762). His liberating influence upon the art of portraiture may be gathered from the informal treatment of *Captain Coram* (1740), his *Self-Portrait* (c. 1758) and that early undated study in impressionism, *The Shrimp Girl*. He explained his artistic theories in *Analysis of Beauty* (1753) and was buried in Chiswick cemetery.

HOGBEN, Lancelot (1895–1975) English physiologist and writer, born in Southsea and educated at Cambridge. He held academic appointments in zoology in England, Scotland, Canada and South Africa before becoming Mason professor of zoology at Birmingham (1941–47), and professor of medical statistics (1947–61). He wrote several popular books on scientific subjects, including *Mathematics for the Million* (1936) and *Science for the Citizen* (1938), as well as many specialist publications, such as *The Loom of Language* (1943) in which he set out his version of an international auxiliary language *Interglossa*.

HOGG, James (1770–1835) Scottish poet and novelist, known as the 'Ettrick Shepherd', born on Ettrickhall farm in the Ettrick Forest, Selkirkshire. He tended sheep in his youth and had only a spasmodic education. He inherited, however, a rich store of ballads from his mother. In 1790 he became shepherd to **William Laidlaw** at Blackhouse in Selkirkshire, who encouraged him to write. On a visit to Edinburgh in 1801 to sell his employer's sheep, he had his *Scottish Pastorals, Poems, Songs, &c*, printed, but without success. He was fortunate, however, in making the acquaintance of Sir **Walter Scott**, then sheriff of Selkirkshire, who published in the second volume of his *Border Minstrelsy* (1803) several of Hogg's mother's ballads. With the proceeds of *The Mountain Bard* (1803), Hogg dabbled unsuccessfully in farming, but eventually settled in Edinburgh. Another volume of poems, *The Forest Minstrel* (1810), failed, but *The Queen's Wake* (1813) at once gained him cordial recognition. A bequest of a farm at Altrive Lake (now Edinhope) from the Duchess of Buccleuch enabled him to marry in 1820 and to produce in rapid succession a number of works both in verse and prose. He ended his days a well-known figure of Edinburgh society, a regular contributor to *Blackwood's Magazine*, and was the 'Ettrick Shepherd' of **John Wilson**'s *Noctes Ambrosianae*. He described himself as 'the king of the Mountain and Fairy School'. His poems of the supernatural are best when he avoids gothic elaboration and relies on the suggestive understatement of the ballad style, as in his 'Kilmeny' and 'The Witch of Fife'. 'The Aged Widow's Lament' shows the influence of the Scottish vernacular tradition. His debt to **Burns** is apparent in 'The Author's Address to his Auld Dog Hector' and in the riotous 'Village of Balmaquhapple'. Of his prose works, the most remarkable is *Private Memoirs and Confessions of a Justified Sinner* (1824), a macabre novel which anticipates **Stevenson**'s *Dr Jekyll and Mr Hyde* with its haunting 'split personality' theme. In 1834 he published his *Domestic Manners and Private Life of Sir Walter Scott*, against the wishes of Scott's family.

HOGG, Quintin See **HAILSHAM, 2nd Viscount**

HOGG, Quintin (1845–1903) English philanthropist, born in London. Educated at Eton, he joined first tea merchants, then sugar merchants in the City of London, where he became prominent and, until 1882 when bounties for the protection of lime-grown sugar affected the East India trade, very prosperous. In 1864 he founded a ragged school at Charing Cross, then a Youths' Christian Institute, and in 1882 opened Regent Street Polytechnic to permit the members to gratify, as he wrote, 'any reasonable taste, whether athletic, intellectual, spiritual, or social'. This initiated the Polytechnic movement in London, but the intensity of voluntary work affected his health and he actually died in the Polytechnic.

HOGG, Thomas Jefferson See **SHELLEY, Percy Bysshe**

HOHENHEIM, Theophrastus Bombastus von See **PARACELSUS**

HOHENLOHE-SCHILLINGSFÜRST, Chlodwic, prince of (1819–1901) Prussian statesman, born in Rothenburg in Bavaria. In 1894 he succeeded **Caprivi** as chancellor of the German empire and prime minister of Prussia.

HOHENSTAUFEN German royal dynasty named after the castle of Staufen in north-eastern Swabia. From 1138 to 1254 its members wore the crown of the Holy Roman Empire, starting with **Conrad III** and ending with Conrad IV, and including **Frederick I Barbarossa** and **Frederick II**. They were also kings of Germany and of Sicily. The Hohenstaufen period is associated with a flowering of German courtly culture.

HOHENZOLLERN German dynastic family which ruled in Brandenburg-Prussia from 1415 to 1918. It derived its name from the ancestral 9th-century castle of Zollern in Swabia. In 1415 a member of the family was made Elector of Brandenburg by the emperor **Sigismund**, thus founding the Prussian dynasty; the last elector, Frederick III (1688–1713) became the first king of Prussia as **Frederick I** in 1701. The kings of Prussia were German emperors from 1872 to 1918 (**William I, Frederick III**, and **William II**). Another branch of the family were kings of Rumania from 1881 to 1947 (**Carol I**, Ferdinand I and **Carol II**).

HOHFELD, Wesley Newcomb (1879–1918) American jurist and law teacher at Yale. Interested in the analysis of the legal concept of a 'right', he sought to develop a theory of law based on legal relations, and his work, though never fully developed, stimulated much later thinking on the subject.

HOHNER, Matthias (1833–1902) German mouth-organ manufacturer. In 1857 he established his firm at Trossingen, Württemberg. His five sons added music publishing (1931), the manufacture of accordions, harmonicas, saxophones and (from 1945) electrical musical instruments, established an accordion school at Trossingen in 1931, and made the family business the biggest of its kind.

HOKUSAI, Katsushika (1760–1849) Japanese artist and wood-engraver, born in Tokyo. He was early apprenticed to a wood-engraver under whom he mastered the conventional *surimono* or commemorative paintings and book illustrations. But he soon abandoned the traditional style and academic subjects for the coloured woodcut designs of the *avant garde* Ukiyoye ('the passing world') school, which treated in forceful expressionist manner commonplace subjects of the everyday world. From 1814 to 1819 he worked on the ten volumes of the famous *Mangwa* or 'Sketches at Random', in which he depicts most facets of Japanese life. Hokusai delighted the passerby by feats of artistic versatility, eg, dashing off the outline of a sparrow on a grain of corn. Living exclusively to improve his art, *Gwakiôjn* or 'Old Man mad on drawings', studied Dutch paintings and entered his great period (1823–30) with the wonderful *Hundred Views of Mount Fuji* published in 1835, the *Waterfalls, Famous Bridges, Large Flowers* and the *Ghost Stories*.

HOLBACH, Paul Heinrich Dietrich, Baron d' (1723–89) German-born French philosopher, born in Heidelsheim. Having settled in Paris, he contributed 376 articles to the *Encyclopédie* (edited by **Diderot** and others), mostly on chemistry and related scientific topics, and was a leading materialist and atheist. His other writings, which were sometimes pseudonymous, include *Le Christianisme dévoilé* (1761), *Système de la nature* (1770) and *Système Sociale* (1773).

HOLBEIN, Hans, 'the younger' (1497–1543) German painter, born in Augsburg, the son of Hans Holbein the elder (c.1460–1524), also a painter of merit. He studied under his father, and was influenced by the work of **Burgkmair**. About 1516 he was at work in Basel, but did not settle there till 1520; during the interval he was painting at Zürich and Lucerne. Among works executed during this period are the portraits of the Burgomaster Meier and his wife, two portraits of **Erasmus**, and one of **Melanchthon**. During his residence at Basel he was largely employed upon designs for woodcuts, including illustrations for various editions of **Luther**'s Old and New Testaments (1522 and 1523). His most important woodcuts, however—the series of *The Dance of Death* and the *Old Testament Cuts*—were not issued till 1538. About the end of 1526 he visited England, where he was introduced by Erasmus to Sir **Thomas More**, and began his great series of portraits of eminent Englishmen of his time, the studies for many of which exist in the royal collection at Windsor. On his return to Basel (1529) he painted the group of his wife and two children now in the museum there; and in 1530 resumed work in the council hall, executing pictures that are now destroyed. Probably in 1532 he again visited London, where he painted many portraits for the German merchants of the Hanseatic League. To this period are also due the great portrait group known as *The Ambassadors* (National Gallery, London), the portraits of **Thomas Cromwell**, and the miniatures of Henry and **Charles Brandon**, sons of the Duke of Suffolk, in the royal collection at Windsor. In 1536 he was appointed painter to **Henry VIII**, and as such executed at Whitehall Palace a mural painting of the monarch and Queen **Jane Seymour** with **Henry VII** and Elizabeth of York, destroyed in the fire of 1698. In 1538 he was dispatched to the Netherlands to paint a likeness of **Kristina** of Denmark (a prospective wife for Henry), and in 1539 he painted **Anne of Cleves**, at Cleves. Miniatures of his period, now in the Victoria and Albert Museum, are outstanding in quality. His last work was *Henry VIII granting a Charter to the Barber-Surgeons*, still in their guildhall. He died of the plague in London. A master of portraiture, Holbein had a genius for subordinating the interest in garments and accessories to heighten facial characteristics.

HOLBERG, Ludvig, Baron (1684–1754) Norwegian man of letters, born in Bergen, and considered the founder of both Norwegian and Danish modern literature. He was educated in Copenhagen and wrote a book on the history of Europe (1711), then settled in Denmark after travelling widely in Europe, largely on foot (1714–16). He published various historical and legal works, and in 1717 was appointed professor of metaphysics at Copenhagen University, then of eloquence (1720), and history (1730). His career as a satirist began with a comic epic, *Peder Paars* (1719), followed by a series of more than 30 classic comedies for the newly-opened Danish theatre in Copenhagen (1722–27). Thereafter he concentrated on historical books, including biographies and histories of Denmark, the Church, and the Jews. After one more satirical classic, *Niels Klims underjordiske reise* (Niels Klim's Subterranean Journey, 1741), he wrote only reflective and philosophical works.

HOLBOØLL, Einar (1855–1927) Danish postmaster who originated the idea of special stamp issues for charitable purposes by his *Julemaerket* stamp (1904) for a tuberculosis prevention fund. The idea has since been adopted by countries all over the world.

HOLBORNE, Anthony (d.c.1602) English composer, known chiefly for a collection of pavanes, galliards and other dance movements for five instruments (1599). With his brother William he wrote a manual for the cittern containing a number of compositions for that instrument.

HOLBROOKE, Josef (Charles) (1878–1958) English composer of chamber music and opera, born in Croydon. He studied at the Royal Academy, was an accomplished pianist, and composed the symphonic poems *Queen Mab* (1904), *The Bells*, (1906) and *Apollo and the Seaman* (1908). He also wrote a trilogy of operas based on Welsh legends, the first of which, *The Children of Don* (1912), was performed at Salzburg in 1923. His variation of 'Three Blind Mice' formed his most popular composition.

HOLCROFT, Thomas (1745–1809) English playwright and novelist, born in London, the son of a shoemaker. After three years as a Newmarket stable boy, then eight as a shoemaker, schoolmaster, and servant-secretary to **Granville Sharp**, in 1770 he became a strolling player. But settling in London (1778), where he became a friend of **William Godwin**, **Thomas Paine** and **Charles Lamb**, he took to writing. *Alwyn, or the Gentleman Comedian* (1780) was the first of four novels. He also wrote nearly 30 plays, mostly melodramas, of which *The Follies of a Day* (1784) and *The Road to Ruin* (1792) were the best. His eldest son, William (1773–89), robbed his father of £40 and having been found by him on an American-bound vessel, shot himself. An ardent democrat, in 1794 Holcroft was tried for high treason with Sir **Thomas Masterman Hardy**, **John Horne Tooke** and others and acquitted, but the adverse publicity reduced him to poverty and made him go abroad to Hamburg and Paris (1799–1801). His entertaining Memoirs were continued by **Hazlitt** (1816).

HOLDEN, Sir Edward Wheewall (1896–1978) Australian pioneer motor manufacturer, born in Adelaide, South Australia. His father's business was firstly as a saddler, later expanded to carriage-building and car body trimming, producing body panels and motorcycle sidecar bodies. He joined his father and eventually Holdens became the major Australian producer of bodies for imported chassis, especially from General Motors in the USA. He had studied automation methods in the USA and rapidly expanded the productivity of the company; by 1929 Holdens was the biggest body-builder in the British Empire. However, through a downturn in demand during the Depression, General Motors acquired Holdens, and Edward became chairman in 1931.

HOLDEN, Sir Isaac (1807–97) Scottish inventor, born in Hurlet, Renfrewshire. He worked in a Paisley cotton mill, studied chemistry in his leisure hours, and became an assistant teacher in Reading in 1829. He invented the Lucifer match, but was anticipated by **John Walker** of Stockton-on-Tees. In 1846 he joined with **Lister**, who had done much to improve woolcombing, in starting a mill near Paris. Lister retired, the firm became Isaac Holden & Sons in 1859, and the Alston works near Bradford were founded. After he had spent some £50000 in experiments, Holden's woolcombing machinery brought him fame and fortune. He was a Liberal MP from 1865 to 1895.

HÖLDERLIN, Johann Christian Friedrich (1770–1843) German poet, born in Lauffen on the Neckar. He studied theology at Tübingen, and philosophy with **Schelling** and **Hegel** under **Fichte** at Jena. With a growing enthusiasm for poetry, he developed an aversion to the 'snug parsonage' for which he was intended. As family tutor in Frankfurt-am-Main (1796–98) he found in the wife of his banker-employer, Susette Gontard (the 'Diotima' of his works), the feminine embodiment of all he venerated in Hellenism. His early poetry owed far too much to **Klopstock** and to **Schiller**, who published Hölderlin's efforts in his literary magazines, but the inspiration provided by 'Diotima' helped him to discover his true poetical self. However the commercial philistinism, which Hölderlin roundly condemned in his philosophical novel, *Hyperion* (1797–99), and the understandable jealousy of the banker, made his stay in Frankfurt-am-Main finally impossible. During a temporary refuge at Hamburg he wrote splendid fragments for a verse drama on the death of **Empedocles**, elegiac odes and the magnificent elegy 'Menon's Laments for Diotima', which examines the discrepancy between the actual and the ideally possible. For a short time he tutored in Switzerland (1801), but returned to his mother at Nuertingen where he wrote 'Brot und Wein' and 'Der Rhein'. In July 1802, after a spell of employment by the German Consul at Bordeaux, he returned in an advanced state of schizophrenia, aggravated by the news of 'Diotima's' death. For a short time he enjoyed the sinecure of court librarian to the Landgrave of Hesse-Homburg, procured for him and paid by his friend von Sinclair. After a period in an asylum (1806–07), he lived out his life in the charge of a Tübingen carpenter. It was the admiration of **Rilke** and **Stefan George** which first established Hölderlin as one of Germany's greatest poets, 80 years after his death.

HOLDING, Michael (1954–) West Indian cricketer, born in Jamaica. Widely regarded as having one of the most beautiful and fluent fast-bowling actions of all time, he played in 60 Tests for the West Indies, taking 249 wickets, twice taking eight wickets in an innings, and twice taking 14 wickets in a match. Against England at The Oval in 1974 his match analysis was 14–149. After his retiral from Test cricket in 1984 he continued to play county cricket with Derbyshire.

HOLDSWORTH, Sir William Searle (1871–1944) English jurist, born in Beckenham, Kent. Educated at Dulwich College and New College, Oxford, he was Vinerian professor of English law at Oxford (1922–44). He wrote a magisterial *History of English Law*, surveying its development from its beginnings to 1875 (17 vols, 1903–72), which is a classic of scholarship, as well as numerous other works on facets of English legal history. He served on the Indian States Committee in 1928, and the Committee on Ministers' Powers (1929–32).

HOLIDAY, Billie (Eleanora) also known as **'Lady Day'** (1915–59) American jazz singer, born in Baltimore. One of the most influential but tragic singers in jazz, she had an insecure childhood and was jailed for prostitution while a teenager. In the early 1930s, however, she was working as a singer in New York clubs and her wistful voice and remarkable jazz interpretation of popular songs led to work with **Benny Goodman** and recording sessions with such leading soloists as Teddy Wilson and **Lester Young**. In the late 1930s she worked with the big bands of **Count Basie** and Artie Shaw. During the 1940s she appeared in several films (including *New Orleans*, with **Louis Armstrong**) but by the end of that decade she was falling victim to drug addiction. Despite the deterioration of her voice from that period, the melodic and rhythmic subtlety of her singing has inspired many followers.

HOLINSHED, Raphael (d.c.1580) English chronicler, born apparently of a Cheshire family. He went to London early in **Elizabeth**'s reign, and became a translator in Reginald Wolfe's printing office. For Wolfe and his successors he undertook the compilation of *The Chronicles of England, Scotland, and Ireland* (2 vols, fol 1577). This, together with its predecessor, **Edward Hall**'s *Chronicle*, was the direct source from which **Shakespeare** drew materials for legendary and historical plays. Holinshed was not the only writer of the work which bears his name. He was assisted by **William Harrison**; by Richard Stanyhurst, who contributed the description of Ireland; and by John Hooker (1525–1601), who wrote most of the history of Ireland. Holinshed had access to the manuscripts of **John Leland**.

HOLKERI, Harri (1937–) Finnish politician, born in Oripaa. He became politically active as a young man and was secretary of the Youth League of the centrist National Coalition party (KOK) in 1959. He then served as the party's information secretary (1962–64), research secretary (1964–65) and national secretary (1975–71). He was elected to Helsinki City Council in 1969 and to parliament (Eduskunta) in 1970. He became prime minister in 1987.

HOLLAND, Henry (1746–1806) English architect. Pupil and son-in-law of **Lancelot ('Capability') Brown**, he designed old Carlton House in London, the original Brighton Pavilion, Brook's Club and many other buildings.

HOLLAND, Sir Henry Rich, 1st Earl of (1590–1649) English courtier and soldier, brother of John Rich, 2nd Earl of **Warwick**. A favourite of **James VI and I** of Scotland and England, in 1624 he negotiated the marriage between the future **Charles I** and **Henrietta Maria**. Before the outbreak of the Civil War (1642–51) he deserted Charles and joined the parliamentarians, but eventually attempted a royalist rising in 1648, and was captured and executed.

HOLLAND, Henry Richard Fox, 3rd Baron (1773–1840) English Liberal statesman, nephew of **Charles James Fox**, born at Winterslow house, Wiltshire. He succeeded to the title at the age of one. Educated at Eton and Christ Church, Oxford, he was lord privy seal in the **Grenville** ministry (1806–07) and then shared the long banishment of the Whigs from office. He worked for reform of the criminal code, attacked the slave trade, although he was himself a West Indian planter, and threw himself wholeheartedly into the the corn-law struggle. Chancellor of the duchy of Lancaster (1830–34), he died at Holland House, Kensington. He wrote biographies of **Guillén de Castro** and **Lope de Vega**, translated Spanish comedies, prepared a Life of his uncle, and edited the memoirs of Lord Waldegrave. His wife, Elizabeth Vassall (1770–1845), daughter of a wealthy Jamaica planter, married in 1786 Sir Godfrey Webster, but the marriage was dissolved in 1797 for her adultery with Lord Holland, who immediately married her. She was distinguished for beauty, conversational gifts and autocratic ways; and till the end of her life Holland House was the meeting place of the most brilliant wits and distinguished statemen of the time.

HOLLAND, Henry Scott (1847–1918) English clergyman and theologian, born in Ledbury. Tutor at Christ Church (1870–84), he became a canon of Truro in 1882, of St Paul's in 1884 and of Christ Church in 1910 when he was appointed Regius professor of divinity at Oxford. He led the High Church *Lux Mundi* group of theologians, influenced by neo-Hegelianism, who were devoted to social reform according to Christian principles.

HOLLAND, John Philip (1840–1914) Irish-born American inventor, born in Liscannor, County Clare. He was a school teacher in Ireland (1852–72), and, after emigrating to the USA in 1873, in Paterson, New Jersey. He offered a submarine design to the US navy which was rejected in 1875 as impracticable, but he continued his experiments with a practical submarine, the *Fenian Ram* (financed by the Fenian Society), which was launched on the Hudson River in 1881. In 1898 he launched the *Holland VI* and successfully demonstrated it on and under the Potomac river; it had almost all the features of a modern non-nuclear submarine, including an internal-combustion engine on the surface and an electric motor when submerged, hydroplanes and ballast tanks to regulate the depth, torpedo tubes, and a retractable periscope. It finally convinced the navies of the world that the submarine must be taken seriously as a weapon of war.

HOLLAND, Josiah Gilbert (1819–81) American editor and novelist, born in Belchertown, Massachusetts. He became assistant editor of the Springfield *Republican* and part proprietor in 1851. In 1870, with Roswell Smith and the **Scribners**, he founded *Scribner's Monthly*, which he edited, and in which appeared some of his novels, including *Arthur Bonnicastle* (1873), *The Story of Sevenoaks* (1875), and *Nicholas Minturn* (1876).

HOLLAND, Philemon (1552–1637) English scholar, 'the translator-general in his age', born in Chelmsford. Educated at Trinity College, Cambridge, from about 1595 he practised medicine in Coventry, and in 1628 became headmaster of the free school there. He translated **Livy**, **Pliny**'s *Natural History*, **Suetonius**, **Plutarch**'s *Morals*, **Ammianus Marcellinus**, **Xenophon**'s *Cyropaedia* and **William Camden**'s *Britannia*. His son, Henry (1583–c.1650), a bookseller in London, published *Baziliologia* (1618) and *Heroologia Anglica* (1620).

HOLLAND, Sir Sidney George (1893–1961) New Zealand politican, born in Greendale, Canterbury. He was managing director of an engineering company before taking up politics. Entering parliament as a member of the National party in 1935, he was leader of the opposition (1940–49), and then premier (1949–1957), resigning to become minister without portfolio.

HOLLAND, Sir Thomas Erskine (1835–1926) English jurist, born in Brighton, great-grandson of Lord Chancellor **Thomas Erskine**. Educated at Brighton College and Magdalen College, Oxford, he was Chichele professor of international law and diplomacy at Oxford (1874–1910). Author of *Elements of Jurisprudence* (1880), long a standard work, he was the editor of several classical works in the history of international law by **Alberico Gentili** and **Richard**

Zouche, and wrote War Office and Admiralty manuals of military and prize law.

HOLLAR, Wenceslaus (1607–77) Bohemian engraver and etcher, born in Prague. He came to London with the Earl of **Arundel and Surrey** in 1637, served in a royalist regiment, and was taken prisoner at Basing House. From 1645 to 1652 he lived in Antwerp. Returning to London at the Restoration he was appointed 'His Majesty's designer'. He produced two magnificent plates of costume, entitled *Severall Habits of English Women* (1640) and *Theatrum Mulierum* (1643), as well as maps, panoramas, etc, preserved in the British Museum and the Royal Library, Windsor. His panoramic view of London from Southwark after the Great Fire is one of the most valuable topographical records of the 17th century.

HOLLERITH, Herman (1860–1929) American inventor and computer scientist, born in Buffalo, New York. He graduated in 1879 from the School of Mines at Columbia University, and worked as a statistician on the processing of data relating to the manufacturing industries for the US census of 1880. Realizing the need for automation in the recording and processing of such a mass of data, he devised a system based initially on cards with holes punched in them (similar to that invented by **Jacquard** in 1801 to produce a variety of complicated patterns on his loom). Hollerith used electrical contacts made through the holes in his cards to actuate electromechanical counters, and he worked on the development of his system while employed first at the Massachusetts Institute of Technology, and then in the US Patent Office (1884–90). He won a competition for the most efficient data-processing equipment to be used in the 1890 US census, established his own company in 1896, and later merged with two others to become the International Business Machines Corporation (IBM) in 1924.

HOLLES, Denzil, 1st Baron (1599–1680) English statesman, the second son of the 1st Earl of Clare. He entered parliament in 1624. In 1629 he was one of the members who held the Speaker in his chair whilst resolutions were passed against Arminianism and tonnage and poundage. For this he was fined a thousand marks, and lived seven or eight years in exile. He was one of the five members whom **Charles I** attempted to arrest in 1642, and was a leader of the Presbyterians. In the Civil War, dreading the supremacy of the army more than the pretensions of the king, he was an advocate of peace. For proposing in 1647 to disband the army he was accused of treason, but fled to Normandy. In 1660 he was the spokesman of the commission delegated to recall **Charles II** at Breda; in 1661 hc was created Baron Holles of Ifield in Sussex. His last important public duty was the negotiation of the treaty of Breda in 1667. As Charles became more autocratic, Holles leaned more to the opposition.

HOLLEY, Robert William (1922–) American biochemist, born in Urbana, Illinois. Working mainly in the Cornell Medical School and at the Salk Institute in California (from 1968), he was a member of the team which first synthesized penicillin in the 1940s; and it was there, in the 1960s, that he secured the first pure sample of a transfer RNA (1 gram from 90 kilos of yeast) and elucidated the full molecular structure of this nucleic acid, which has a central place in the cellular synthesis of proteins. He shared the 1968 Nobel prize for physiology or medicine with **Har Gobind Khorana** and **Marshall Nirenberg**.

HOLLIS, Sir Roger Henry (1905–73) British civil servant. Educated at Clifton public school and Worcester College, Oxford, he travelled extensively in China before joining the British counter-intelligence service MI5 in the late 1930s. He was appointed deputy director general in 1953 and director-general (1956–65). In his memoirs *Spycatcher* (1987), **Peter Wright** argued that Hollis, with **Blunt**, **Burgess**, **MacLean** and **Philby**, was a Soviet spy.

HOLLOWAY, Stanley (1890–1982) English entertainer, born in London. A diverse background as an office boy, choir soloist and World War I army lieutenant preceded his London stage début in *Kissing Time* (1920) and first film appearance in *The Rotters* (1921). He was an original member of *The Co-Optimists* revue group which performed from 1921 to 1930. Popular on radio and in pantomime, he created the monologue characters of Sam Small and the Ramsbottom family, while his hearty, down-to-earth manner and booming tones made him a genial comedy actor in Ealing film classics like *Passport to Pimlico* (1948), *The Lavender Hill Mob* (1951) and *The Titfield Thunderbolt* (1952). He made his New York début in *A Midsummer Night's Dream* (1954) and created the role of Alfred Dolittle in *My Fair Lady* on Broadway (1956–58) and later on film (1964). An active performer until his death, he also had his own television series *Our Man Higgins* (1962) and published an autobiography, *Wiv a Little Bit of Luck* (1969).

HOLLOWAY, Thomas (1800–83) English manufacturer and philanthropist, born in Devonport. He produced patent medicines which made him a fortune. In 1885 he founded an asylum for the insane, and in 1886 a women's college at Egham, near Virginia Water.

HOLLY, Buddy (Charles Hardin) (1936–59) American rock singer, songwriter and guitarist, born in Lubbock, Texas. Despite the fact that his recording career lasted less than two years, he is one of the most influential pioneers of rock-and-roll. Originally from a country and western background, he was also influenced by hill-billy, Mexican and black music. He was the first to add drums and a rhythm-and-blues beat to the basic country style. With his band The Crickets he was the first to use what was to become the standard rock-and-roll line-up of two guitars, bass and drums, and he was also the first to use double-tracking and over-dubbing on his recordings. Splitting from The Crickets in 1958, financial commitments forced him to undertake an arduous touring schedule, and he died when a plane carrying him between concerts crashed. At the time he had released only three American albums. Only after his death was the full significance of his contribution to rock music realized. He became an important cult figure and much of his material was released posthumously. His most popular records include 'That'll Be The Day', 'Not Fade Away', 'Peggy Sue', and 'Oh Boy'.

HOLM, Hanya, originally **Johanna Eckert** (1893–) German-born American dancer, choreographer and teacher, born in Worms. A pupil of **Émile Jacques-Dalcroze**, starting in 1921 she worked as both teacher and dancer with **Mary Wigman**, who sent her to New York in 1931 to establish the American branch of her school. In 1936 she founded her own studio, developing a technique that fused the disciplines of Wigman's approach to movement with a more American emphasis on speed and rhythm. She became a key figure in the field of modern dance, dividing her time between concert work and the staging of dances for such Broadway muscials as *Kiss Me Kate* (1948), *My Fair Lady* (1956) and *Camelot* (1960).

HOLM, Ian (1931–) English actor, born in Ilford. He was a member of the Shakespeare Memorial Theatre company at Stratford in 1954–55, and, after touring Europe with **Laurence Olivier** in *Titus And-*

ronicus, returned to Stratford in 1957, playing many roles. His greatest achievement at Stratford was in 1963–64, when he played Prince Hal, Henry V, and Richard III in *The Wars of The Roses*. He has appeared in some modern work, including **Pinter**'s *The Homecoming* in 1965, and **Bond**'s *The Sea*. He has made occasional television appearances, including a memorable performance as Bernard Samson in the adaptation of **Len Deighton**'s *Game, Set and Match* trilogy (1988).

HOLMAN, James (1786–1857) 'the Blind Traveller', born in Exeter. As a lieutenant in the navy he lost his sight in 1810. Yet he travelled through France and Italy to the Rhineland (1819–21). He next started on a journey (1822–24) around the world, but at Irkutsk in Siberia was arrested as a spy and sent back to Britain. He again set off in 1827, and this time accomplished his purpose. Finally, he visited south-east Europe. He published accounts of his travels (1822, 1825, 1834–35).

HOLMES, Arthur (1890–1965) English geologist, born in Hebburn-on-Tyne, a pioneer of geochronology. Professor of geology at Durham (1924–43) and Edinburgh (1943–56), he determined the ages of rocks by measuring their radioactive constituents, and was an early scientific supporter of **Alfred Wegener**'s continental drift theory. He wrote *The Age of the Earth* (1913) and *Principles of Physical Geology* (1944).

HOLMES, Oliver Wendell (1809–94) American physician and writer, born in Cambridge, Massachusetts. He graduated at Harvard College in 1829, and, giving up law for medicine, spent two years in the hospitals of Europe. From 1839 to 1840 he was professor of anatomy and physiology at Dartmouth College, and in 1842 made the discovery that puerperal fever was contagious. From 1847 to 1882 he was professor of anatomy at Harvard. He began writing verse while an undergraduate, but 20 years passed with desultory efforts, before *The Autocrat of the Breakfast Table* (1857–58) made him famous by its fresh unconventional tone. This was followed by *The Professor at the Breakfast Table* (1858–59) and *The Poet at the Breakfast Table* (1872). *Elsie Venner* (1859–60), was the first of three novels, foreshadowing modern 'Freudian' fiction. He published several volumes of poetry, starting with *Songs in Many Keys* (1862). He also wrote *Our Hundred Days in Europe* (1887), an account of a visit made in 1886.

HOLMES, Oliver Wendell (1841–1935) American judge, born in Boston, son of **Oliver Wendell Holmes** (1809–94). Educated at Harvard Law School, he served in the Union army as captain in the Civil War. From 1867 he practised law in Boston, edited Kent's *Commentaries* (1873), became editor of the *American Law Review*, and Weld professor of law at Harvard (1873–82). He made his reputation with a fundamental book on *The Common Law* (1881). He was then associate justice (1882) and chief justice (1899–1902) of the Supreme Court of Massachusetts, and associate justice of the US Supreme Court (1902–32). He was one of the great judicial figures of his time, and many of his judgments on common law and equity, as well as his dissent on the interpretation of the 14th amendment, have become famous. His opinions are famous for their knowledge and the depth of thought underlying them.

HOLMES, William Henry (1846–1933) American archaeologist and museum director, born near Cadiz, Ohio. Trained as an artist, his interests turned to archaeology in 1875 when exploring ancient cliff dwellings in the arid Southwest with the US Geological Survey. A visit to the Yucatán while he was curator of anthropology at the Field Museum of Natural History, Chicago, stimulated a major contribution to Mesoamerican archaeology, his magnificently illustrated *Archaeological studies among the ancient cities of Mexico* (1895–97). Outstanding too were his classificatory studies of prehistoric ceramics and stone technology in North America, notably *Aboriginal pottery of the eastern United States* (1903) and the *Handbook of aboriginal American antiquities* (1919). He worked at the Smithsonian Institution, Washington DC, for much of his career, acting as chief of the Bureau of American Ethnology (1902–09) and director of the National Gallery of Art (1920–32).

HOLROYD, Michael de Courcy Fraser (1935–) English biographer, born in London. He studied sciences at Eton, and literature at Maidenhead Public Library. His first book was *Hugh Kingsmill: a critical biography* (1964). His two-volume life of **Lytton Strachey**, *The Unknown Years* (1967) and *The Year of Achievement* (1968), is recognized as a landmark in biographical writing. The official biographer of **George Bernard Shaw**, two volumes have appeared to date: *The Search for Love* (1988) and *The Pursuit of Power* (1989). He is married to novelist **Margaret Drabble**.

HOLST, Gustav Theodore, originally **von Holst** (1874–1934) English composer, born of Swedish origin in Cheltenham. He conducted village choirs before entering the Royal College of Music, London, on a scholarship in 1893. He studied under **Charles Stanford**, but neuritis in his hand prevented him from becoming a concert pianist. Instead he played first trombone in the Carl Rosa Opera Company and later joined the Scottish Orchestra. In 1905 he became music master at St Paul's Girls' School, in 1907 musical director at Morley College, London, and in 1919 was appointed to a similar post at Reading College. It took him some time to find his own personal style as composer, and to shake off the influence of **Grieg** and **Wagner**. His early enthusiasm for Hindu literature is reflected in the opera, *Sida*, the *opera di camera*, *Savitri*, and the *Hymns from the Rig-Veda*. He shared **Vaughan Williams**' interest in the English folksong tradition, which inspired his *St Paul's Suite for Strings* (1913). Economy and clarity became his hallmark. The seven-movement suite *The Planets* (1914–17), in which each planet's astrological associations are treated in musical terms, marked his emergence as a major composer. Sublime conceptions also pervade *The Hymn of Jesus* (1917) and his choral setting of **Walt Whitman**'s *Ode to Death* (1919). Two comic operas followed: *The Perfect Fool* (1921) and the Falstaffian *At the Boar's Head* (1924). An abrupt change to stark austerity marked his extraordinary orchestral piece, inspired by **Thomas Hardy**'s *Return of the Native*, *Egdon Heath* (1927). His dexterous experiment in polytonality, the *Concerto for Two Violins* (1929), earned him the gold medal of the Royal Philharmonic Society. He was buried in Chichester Cathedral. His daughter Imogen (1907–1984), like her father, was a musical educationist, conductor and composer of folksong arrangements, and was associated with **Benjamin Britten** in the Aldeburgh Festivals.

HOLT, Harold (1908–67) Australian politician, born in Sydney, the son of an impresario. He studied law at Melbourne University, joined the United Australia party, which was to be replaced by the Liberal party of Australia, and entered the House of Representatives in 1935. He became deputy leader of his party in 1956, and leader and prime minister, when **Robert Menzies** retired, in 1966. During the Vietnam War he strongly supported the USA with the slogan 'all the way with LBJ'. He died in office while swimming at Portsea, near Melbourne.

HOLT, Sir John (1642–1710) English judge, born in Thame. Educated at Winchester and Oriel College, Oxford, he was called to the bar in 1663. He figured as counsel in most of the state trials of that period, and in 1686 was made recorder of London and king's serjeant. In 1689 he became lord chief justice of the King's Bench. He was a Whig, but his judicial career was entirely free from party bias or intrigue, and he was noteworthy for his recognition of the rights of accused persons and the liberties of the subject.

HOLTBY, Winifred (1898–1935) English novelist and feminist, born in Rudston, Yorkshire. She was educated at Oxford, was a director from 1926 of *Time and Tide*, and wrote a number of novels, but is chiefy remembered for *South Riding* (1935).

HOLTEI, Karl von (1798–1880) German actor and dramatic poet, born in Breslau. He wrote musical plays, such as *Der alte Freiherr* (1825) and *Lenore* (1829), as well as novels and the autobiographical *Vierzig Jahre* (8 vols, 1843–50).

HÖLTY, Ludwig Christoph Heinrich (1748–76) German poet, born in Mariensee, Hanover. He was a co-founder of the *Göttigen Hain*, a literary coterie dedicated to promoting the national spirit in German verse. Some of his poetry is based on the Minnesänger.

HOLTZMANN, Adolf (1810–70) German philologist, born in Karlsruhe. In 1852 he became professor of German at Heidelberg. He wrote on the connection between Greek and Indian fables (1844–47); on Celts and Germans (1855), maintaining that the two races were originally identical; and on the *Nibelungenlied* (1854). His son, Heinrich Julius (1832–1910), German theologian, became professor of theology at Heidelberg (1861) and at Strasburg (1874), and was ultimately a leading representative of modern New Testament criticism.

HOLUB, Miroslav (1923–) Czech poet and scientist, born in Plzen. He took a PhD in immunology and has had a distinguished career in medicine, doing much to popularize science through his editing of the magazine *Vesmir*. His verse is informed with analytical scepticism, wryly humorous but admirably concise and cutting. *Day Duty* (1958) was his first published collection, since when several have appeared, many being translated into English. His *Selected Poems* were published in 1967; recent collections include *Sagittal Section* (1980) and *On the Contrary* (1982).

HOLYOAKE, George Jacob (1817–1906) English social reformer, the founder of Secularism, born in Birmingham. He taught mathematics for some years at the Mechanics' Institution in Birmingham, lectured on **Robert Owen**'s socialist system, was secretary to **Garibaldi**'s British contingent, edited the *Reasoner*, and promoted the bill legalizing secular affirmations. He was the last person imprisoned in England on a charge of atheism (1842). His work included histories of the Co-operative movement, writings on secularism, *Sixty Years of an Agitator's Life* (1892), and *Public Speaking and Debate* (1895).

HOLYOAKE, Sir Keith Jacka (1904–83) New Zealand politician, the son of a shopkeeper and farmer. He worked on the family farm at Scarborough, near Pahiatua, on North Island, and then bought and successfully expanded it. He joined the Reform party, which was to be superseded by the New Zealand National party, and entered the House of Representatives from 1932 to 1938 as its youngest member. Re-elected in 1943, he became deputy leader of the National party in 1946, deputy prime minister in 1949, and party leader and prime minister, on the retirement of Sir **Sydney Holland**, in 1957. He was prime minister again from 1960 to 1972, and later served as governor-general of New Zealand (1977–80).

HOLYWOOD See **SACROBOSCO**

HOLZ, Arno (1863–1929) German author and critic, born in Rastenburg, East Prussia. He first produced lyric poetry, but he is best known for his criticism. *Die Kunst, ihr Wesen und ihre Gesetze* (1890–92) inaugurated the German Impressionist school. *Revolution der Lyrik* (1899) rejected all metrical devices, and *Phantasus* (1898–89) was written on this theory. *Papa Hamlet* (1899) and the drama *Familie Selicke* (1890), both written in collaboration with Johannes Aschaf, are influenced by **Zola**.

HOME, Anne See **HUNTER, John**

HOME, Daniel Dunglas (1833–86) Scottish spiritualist, born near Edinburgh. He went to the USA in the 1840s to live with an aunt, who became so alarmed at the unexplained noises and other phenomena associated with his presence that she turned him out of her house. He soon won fame as a medium, and as an exponent of table-turning and levitation, and went to London in 1855 where his séances were attended by high society there and on the Continent. He published an autobiography, *Incidents of My Life* (2 vols, 1863 and 1872). He was the subject of **Browning**'s sceptical poem, *Mr Sludge, the Medium* (1864), but persuaded scientists like Sir **William Crookes**, in the full glare of electricity, that he was genuine.

HOME, Henry See **KAMES, Lord**

HOME, John (1722–1808) Scottish clergyman and dramatist, born in Leith. He graduated at Edinburgh in 1742. He fought on the government side in the 1745 Rising and was taken prisoner at Falkirk (1746), but made a daring escape from Doune Castle. The next year he became minister of Athelstaneford, where he wrote the tragedy *Agis*, and, in 1754, *Douglas*, founded on a Scots ballad. Each of these was rejected in London by **David Garrick**, but *Douglas*, produced in the Canongate Theatre, Edinburgh (1756), met with brilliant success, and evoked the oft-quoted and possibly apocryphal 'whaur's yer Wullie Shakespeare noo?' from an over-enthusiastic member of the audience. It also won great popularity in London, but it gave such offence to the Edinburgh Presbytery that Home resigned his ministry (1757), and became private secretary to the Earl of Bute and tutor to the Prince of Wales, who on his accession as **George III** gave him a pension of £300 a year, to which a sinecure of equal value was added in 1763. The success of *Douglas* induced Garrick to bring out *Agis*, and to accept Home's next play, *The Siege of Aquileia* (1760). His other works are *The Fatal Discovery* (1769), *Alonzo* (1773), *Alfred* (1778), occasional poems, and, in prose, *A History of the Rebellion of 1745* (1802). He married in 1770, and in 1779 settled in Edinburgh.

HOME OF THE HIRSEL, Baron Alexander Frederick Douglas-Home (1903–) Scottish Conservative politician, born in London, heir to the Scottish earldom of Home. He was educated at Eton and Christchurch, Oxford, entered Parliament in 1931 and was **Chamberlain**'s secretary during the latter's abortive negotiations with **Hitler** and **Mussolini** (1937–39). Out of parliament (1945–51), he became minister of state, Scottish office (1951–55), succeeded to the peerage as 14th Earl (1951), was Commonwealth-relations secretary (1955–60), leader of the House of Lords and lord president of the council (1957–60), and foreign secretary (1960–63). After **Macmillan**'s resignation, he astonished everyone by emerging as premier (November 1963). He made history by renouncing his peerage and fighting a by-election at Kinross, during which, although premier, he was technically a member of neither House. A similar situation was depicted in the play, *The Reluctant Peer* (1963), by his brother, **William Douglas-Home**. After defeat by the Labour party in the general election of 1964 he was leader of the opposition until replaced in the following year by **Edward Heath**, in whose 1970–74 government he was foreign secretary. In 1974 he was made a life peer.

HOMER (8th century BC) Greek epic poet, to whom are attributed two distinct but complementary epics, the *Iliad* (telling of the fall of Troy) and the *Odyssey* (telling of the wanderings of Odysseus on his adventurous way back to Ithaca). Nothing is known about Homer for certain (indeed, some scholars think that no 'Homer' ever existed, or that two or more poets may have been involved). The Homer of tradition seems to have lived in Ionia, directly across the Aegean from mainland Greece; and four city-states have claims to have been his birthplace: the Ionian mainland cities of Smyrna, Colophon and Ephesus, and the island of Chios. His most likely date is the second half of the 8th century BC, with the later poem, the *Odyssey*, being written about 700 BC, half a millennium after the fall of the city of Troy to an invading Myceanean host around 1200 BC. The method of composition of the epics is also in dispute. Some scholars believe that shorter lays by earlier anonymous poets were simply combined and amended by Homer; other believe that the amalgamation of these shorter works into the majestic structure of the two great epics was an act of individual and supreme literary genius. Homer's lifetime seems to have coincided with the introduction of writing into the Greek world, and he may have utilised this new technique and committed his verses to writing, or dictated them to others. The tradition that he was blind may have little basis in fact. On Chios there is an open-air archaic sanctuary at Vrontados, originally dedicated to Cybele, now called the 'Stone of Homer', where, according to a relatively young tradition, he is alleged to have sat and passed on his poems to his pupils, the so-called 'Homeridae', a guild of professional reciters.

HOMER, Winslow (1836–1910) American painter, born in Boston. After apprenticeship to a lithographer (1855–57), he began his career as an illustrator for magazines such as *Harper's Weekly* (1859–67), and specialized in water-colours of outdoor life painted in a naturalistic style which, in their clear outline and firm structure, were opposed to contemporary French Impressionism. He spent two years (1881–83) at Tynemouth, England, and on his return to America continued to depict the sea at Protus Neck, an isolated fishing village on the eastern seaboard, where he spent the rest of his life. His work was highly original and is often regarded as a reflection of the American pioneering spirit.

HONDA, Soichiro (1906–) Japanese motor cycle and car manufacturer, born in Iwata Gun. He started as a garage apprentice in 1922 and opened his own garage in 1928. By 1934 he had started a piston-ring production factory. He began producing motor cycles in 1948, and became president of Honda Corporation in the same year, until 1973. He stayed on as a director, and was appointed 'supreme adviser' in 1983.

HONDIUS, Jodocus (Joost de Hondt) (1563–1612) Flemish cartographer. He emigrated to London c.1584 and moved from there to Amsterdam c.1593. In addition to his own maps of the world and the hemispheres, he engraved much of **John Speed**'s work.

HONE, William (1780–1842) English writer and bookseller, born in Bath. At the age of ten he became a London lawyer's clerk, and at 20 started a book and print shop, which, however, soon failed. He struggled to make a living by writing for various papers, then started the *Traveller* (1815), and the *Reformist's Register* (1817). In December 1817 he was acquitted in three separate trials for publishing things calculated to injure public morals and bring the Prayer Book into contempt, an historic landmark in the freedom of the press. Among his later satires, illustrated by **Cruikshank**, were *The Political House that Jack built*, *The Queen's Matrimonial Ladder*, *The Man in the Moon*, and *The Political Showman*. His obscure antiquarian interests were reflected in *Apocryphal New Testament* (1820), *Every-day Book* (1826), *Table-book* (1827–28) and *Year-book* (1829). Nonetheless, he landed in a debtor's jail, from which his friends extricated him to start him in a coffee house— also a failure. In his last years, growing devout, he became a preacher.

HONECKER, Erich (1912–) East German politician, born in Neunkirchen in the Saarland (now in West Germany). The son of a miner, Honecker joined the German Communist party in 1929 and was imprisoned for anti-Fascist activity between 1935 and 1945. After the war, he was elected to the East German parliament (Volkskammer) in 1949, and served as a 'candidate' member of the Socialist Unity party (SED) politburo and security force worker during the 1950s. In 1958 Honecker became a full member of the SED politburo and secretariat, and during the 1960s was secretary of the national defence council, before being appointed head (first secretary) of the SED in 1971. Following **Walter Ulbricht**'s death in 1973, Honecker became the country's effective leader, and was elected chairman of the council of state (head of state) in October 1976. He proceeded to govern in an outwardly austere and efficient manner and, while favouring east-west détente, closely followed the lead given by the Soviet Union. Following a wave of pro-democracy demonstrations he was replaced in 1989 as SED leader and head of state by Egon Krenz who, himself, was forced to resign two months later. Despite suffering from kidney cancer, he was arrested in 1990 and faced trial on charges of treason, corruption, and abuse of power.

HONEGGER, Arthur (1892–1955) French composer of Swiss parentage, born in Le Havre. He studied in Zürich and at the Paris Conservatoire, and after World War I became one of the group of Parisian composers known as *Les Six*. His dramatic oratorio *King David* established his reputation in 1921, and amongst his subsequent works, *Pacific 231* (1923), his musical picture of a locomotive, won considerable popularity. He composed five symphonies, and these, like a second dramatic oratorio, *Joan of Arc at the Stake* (1936), are works of considerable depth and power.

HONORIUS, Flavius (384–423) western Roman emperor. He was the second son of **Theodosius I, the Great**, at whose death the empire was divided between his sons **Arcadius** and Honorius, the latter (only ten years old) receiving the western half. **Stilicho** was the *de facto* ruler of the western empire until 408; and after his death **Alaric I, the Goth** overran Italy, and took Rome (410). Honorius died at Ravenna, which he had made his capital in 403.

HONORIUS I (d.638) pope from 625 to 638. He was involved with the paschal controversy in Ireland and with the Anglo-Saxon Church. In the Monothelite controversy he abstained from condemning the new doctrines, and for so doing was stigmatized as a heretic at the Council of Constantinople (680). The three other popes of that name, all Italians, were Honorius II (1124–30, an anti-pope), III (1216–27) and IV (1285–87).

HONTHEIM, Johann Nikolaus von (1701–90) German ecclesiastic, born in Trier, where he became bishop. He wrote two works on the history of Trier (1750-57), but is remembered chiefly for a theological essay (1763) under the pseudonym 'Justinius Febronius', in which he propounded a system of church government combining an exaggerated Gallicanism with the democratic element of congregationalism ('Febronianism').

HONTHORST, Gerard van (1590–1656) Dutch painter, born in Utrecht. He worked in Rome and Utrecht, and twice visited England (1620 and 1628), where he painted portraits of **Charles I** and **Henrietta Maria**. He was fond of painting interiors, dimly illumined. His brother William (1604–1666), a historical and portrait painter, worked for the court of Berlin (1650–64).

HOOCH, or **Hoogh, Pieter de** (c.1629–c.1684) Dutch genre painter, born in Rotterdam. By 1654 he was living in Delft and probably came under the influence of **Carel Fabritius** and the latter's pupil, **Vermeer**. His *Interior of a Dutch House* (National Gallery, London) and the *Card Players* in the royal collection are among the outstanding examples of the Dutch school of the 17th century, with their characteristically serene domestic interior or courtyard scenes, warm colouring and delicate light effects. About 1665 he moved to Amsterdam, but his later work became increasingly artificial.

HOOD, Alexander, 1st Viscount Bridport (1727–1814) English naval commander, brother of **Samuel, 1st Viscount Hood**. He entered the navy in 1741. In 1761 he recaptured from the French the *Warwick*, a 60-gun ship, and during the French revolutionary war he served under Richard, 1st Earl **Howe** in the Channel and the Strait of Gibraltar, and took part in the 'Glorious First of June' engagement off Ushant in 1794. He was commander-in-chief of the Channel fleet (1797–1800).

HOOD, John Bell (1831–79) American soldier, born in Owingsville, Kentucky. He commanded the 'Texas Brigade' in the Confederate army, and was wounded at Gaines's Mill, Gettysburg, and Chickamauga. He commanded a corps in the retreat to Atlanta, and in July 1864 succeeded **Joseph Johnston** in command. On 1 September he had to evacuate the city, and leave the road free for **Sherman**'s march to the sea. He afterwards pushed as far north as Nashville; but, defeated by **George Henry Thomas**, was relieved of command in January 1865 at his own request.

HOOD, Raymond Mathewson (1881–1934) American architect, born in Pawtucket, Rhode Island. Educated in Massachusetts, he trained at the Institute of Technology before moving to the École des Beaux Arts, Paris, in 1905. In 1922, with John Mead Howells (1868–1959), he won the competition for the Chicago Tribune Tower, designed with Gothic details. He became the leading designer of skyscrapers in North America in the following decade. The American Radiator Building, New York (completed 1924), again demonstrated his focus on historicist styles. Later works in New York City were designed in a modern, rationalist style, such as the Daily News Building (1929–30), the Rockefeller Center (1930–40) and the McGraw-Hill Building (1931).

HOOD, Samuel, 1st Viscount Hood (1724–1816) English naval commander, brother of **Alexander Hood**, born in Thorncombe, Dorset. He entered the navy in 1741, and became post-captain in 1756. In command of the *Vestal* frigate, he took the French frigate *Bellona* after a fiercely-contested action (1759); in 1778 he was made commissioner of Portsmouth dockyard. In 1780, promoted to flag rank, he was sent to reinforce **Rodney** on the North American and West Indian stations; in 1781 he was engaged in the battle in Chesapeake Bay which failed to get through to the English forces at Yorktown. In the West Indies in 1782 he outmanoeuvred the French off St Kitts, and he had a conspicuous share in the decisive victory off Dominica later that year. In 1784 he stood against **Fox** for Westminster, and was elected; in 1788 he became a lord of the Admiralty. In the French revolutionary wars he captured Toulon (1793) and Corsica (1794).

HOOD, Thomas (1799–1845) English poet and humorist, born in London, the son of a Scottish bookseller from Errol. At the age of 13 he was placed in a merchant's counting-house in the City, but, his health failing, was sent in 1815 to Dundee, to his father's relations, where he wrote for the local newspapers and magazines. In 1818 he returned to London, and entered the studio of his uncle, an engraver. After a short apprenticeship he worked for a while for himself. In 1821 he was appointed sub-editor of the *London Magazine*, and found himself in daily companionship with such men as **Procter**, **John Cary**, **Allan Cunningham**, **De Quincey**, **Hazlitt** and **Charles Lamb**. It was, however, the intimacy with John Hamilton Reynolds, whose sister he married in 1825, that chiefly encouraged and trained Hood's poetic faculty. Between July 1821 and July 1823 he published in the magazine some of his finest poems— 'Lycus the Centaur', 'Two Peacocks of Bedfont' and 'Ode to Autumn'. But these, issued anonymously, failed to attract notice when in 1827 he produced them and others in book form. In 1825 he published (anonymously) a volume of *Odes and Addresses to Great People* which was an instant success. In the first series of *Whims and Oddities* (1826) he exhibited his graphic talent in those 'picture-puns' of which he seems to have been the inventor. A second series appeared in 1827, followed by *National Tales*. In 1829 he edited *The Gem*, a remarkable little 'annual', in which his *Eugene Aram* appeared. He left London in 1829 for Winchmore Hill, where he began the first of the *Comic Annuals* which he produced yearly and single-handedly from 1830 to 1839. In 1834 the failure of a publisher plunged Hood into serious difficulties; and in 1835 the family went for five years to Koblenz and Ostend. During these years, struggling against tuberculosis, he wrote *Up the Rhine* (1839). He returned to England in 1840. In 1841 he became editor of the *New Monthly Magazine*, and in 1844 started a periodical of his own, *Hood's Monthly Magazine*. Meantime in the Christmas number of *Punch* (1843) had appeared 'The Song of the Shirt', and in *Hood's Magazine* there followed the 'Haunted House', the 'Lay of the Labourer', and the 'Bridge of Sighs'. His only surviving son, Tom (1835–74), published poems and humorous novels, and in 1865 became editor of *Fun*.

HOOK, James (1746–1827) English composer and organist, born in Norwich. In 1769 he became organist and composer at Marylebone Gardens, and held the equivalent post at Vauxhall Gardens (1774–1820). He wrote the music for a large number of plays, notably those of his wife, Miss Madden, and his son, **Theodore Edward Hook**, as well as cantatas, odes and a vast number of popular songs, including 'The Lass of Richmond Hill'.

HOOK, Sidney (1902–89) American philosopher and educationist, born in New York. An expositor of the work of **John Dewey** and **Marx**, he was professor at New York University (1932–72), and politically active, first as a spokesman for Marxism, but latterly as a leading social democrat. Among his many books are *Towards* *an Understanding of Karl Marx* (1933), *From Hegel to Marx* (1936), *John Dewey: an intellectual portrait* (1936), *Heresy, yes. Conspiracy, no* (1953) and *Revolution, Reform and Social Justice* (1976).

HOOK, Theodore Edward (1788–1841) English man of letters, son of **James Hook**, born in London. Educated at Harrow School, he achieved early fame as the author of 13 successful comic operas and melodramas (1805–11). He was well known as a maker of puns and as a practical joker—his greatest performance was the Berners Street Hoax (1809). In 1812 he was appointed accountant general of Mauritius. In 1817 he was dismissed after a large deficiency was discovered in the accounts, and was later imprisoned (1823–25). Meanwhile, in 1820, he had started the Tory journal *John Bull.* He wrote a number of short stories and fashionable novels, such as *Maxwell* (1830), *Gilbert Gurney* (1936) and *Jack Brag* (1837).

HOOK, Walter Farquhar (1798–1875) English clergyman and church historian, born in London. Educated at Winchester and Christ Church, Oxford, he became vicar of Leeds in 1837. Mainly by his energy and enthusiasm 21 churches were built in Leeds, as well as 23 parsonages and 27 schools. He became dean of Chichester in 1859. Among his works are *A Church Dictionary* (1842), *Ecclesiastical Biography* (1845–52) and *Lives of the Archbishops of Canterbury* (1860–76).

HOOKE, Robert (1635–1703) English chemist, physicist and architect, born in Freshwater, Isle of Wight. Educated at Westminster School and Christ Church College, Oxford, he worked as an assistant to **John Wilkins** on flying machines, John Willis on chemical research, and **Robert Boyle** on air pumps. In 1662 he was appointed the first curator of experiments at the newly-founded Royal Society (secretary, 1667), and in 1665 became professor of physics at Gresham College, London. In that year he published his *Micrographia*, an account of his microscopic investigations in botany, chemistry, etc. One of the most brilliant scientists of his age, he anticipated the invention of the steam-engine, formulated Hooke's Law of the extension and compression of elastic bodies, and formulated the simplest theory of the arch, the balance-spring of watches, and the anchor-escapement for clocks. He anticipated **Isaac Newton** with his law of the inverse square in gravitation (1678). He constructed the first Gregorian telescope, with which he discovered the fifth star in Orion and inferred the rotation of Jupiter. He materially invented the microscope, the quadrant, and a marine barometer. After the Great Fire of London (1666) he was appointed city surveyor, and designed the new Bethlehem Hospital (Moorfields) and Montague House.

HOOKER, John See **HOOKER, Richard**

HOOKER, Joseph (1814–79) American soldier, born in Hadley, Massachusetts. He served in the Mexican war (1846–48), commanded a division of the 3rd corps in the Peninsular campaign of 1862, and compelled the enemy to evacuate Manassas. During the Civil War (1861–65), in command of the 1st corps he opened the battle at Antietam. At Williamsburg (1862) he earned the nickname of 'Fighting Joe'. In January 1863 he succeeded **Burnside** in the command of the army of the Potomac. In April, crossing the Rappahannock, he marched through the wilderness to near Chancellorsville, where he awaited **Lee**'s attack. But the Confederates turned the National flank, and, attacking the rear, threw part of Hooker's army into confusion. Next day the Confederates drove Hooker to the north side of the river, and he was superseded by **Meade** in June. In November he carried Lookout Mountain, and took part in the attack on Missionary Ridge. He accompanied Sherman in his invasion of Georgia, and served until the fall of Atlanta in 1864. He died in New York.

HOOKER, Sir Joseph Dalton (1817–1911) English botanist and traveller, son of Sir **William Jackson Hooker**, born in Halesworth, Suffolk, and educated at Glasgow High School and University. In 1865 he succeeded his father as director of the Royal Botanic Gardens at Kew. He went on several expeditions which resulted in works on the flora of New Zealand, Antarctica and India, as well as his *Himalayan Journals* (1854), and his monumental *Genera Plantarum*.

HOOKER, Richard (1554–1600) English theologian, born near Exeter. At an early age he showed a sharp intellect, and through his uncle, the antiquary, John Hooker or Vowell (1525–1601), chamberlain of the city, was brought under the notice of **John Jewel**, bishop of Salisbury, and sent to Corpus College, Oxford, where he became a fellow in 1577. In 1581 he took orders, and preached at Paul's Cross. He was led into a marriage with Joan Churchman, the shrewish unlovely daughter of his landlady in London, and in 1584 he became rector of Drayton-Beauchamp near Tring. Next year he obtained, through **John Whitgift**, the mastership of the Temple, against a strong effort made to promote the Temple reader Travers, a prominent Calvinist and Puritan. Travers' sermons soon became attacks upon the latitudinarianism of Hooker. and when Whitgift silenced Travers, the latter appealed to the Council with charges against Hooker's doctrine which Hooker answered in masterly fashion. But having been drawn into controversy against his inclination, he felt it his duty to set down the real basis of church government and in order to achieve this he asked Whitgift to move him to a quieter living. In 1591 he accepted the living of Boscombe near Salisbury and became subdean and prebendary of Sarum. Here he finished four of the proposed eight books of the *Laws of Ecclesiastical Polity* (1594), the earliest great work of the kind in the English language. It is mainly to Hooker's work that Anglican theology owes its tone and direction. The fifth book appeared in 1597 and the last three posthumously (1648, 1662, 1648). He died in Bishopsbourne, near Canterbury, where he had lived since 1595.

HOOKER, Sir Stanley George (1907–84) English aero-engine designer, born in the Isle of Sheppey, Kent. After studying mathematics and aeronautics at Imperial College, London, and gaining the Busk Studentship (1928), he went to Oxford where he published several papers for the Royal Society on compressible fluid flow. After a spell as a scientific civil servant he joined Rolls-Royce (1938), investigating the performance and design of superchargers for the Merlin aero-engine. He led Rolls-Royce into the jet engine in 1943, and as chief engineer produced the Welland, Nene, Derwent, Avon and Trent engines. In 1949 he moved to the Bristol Aero-Engine Division of the Bristol Aeroplane Company working on Proteus, Olympus (for Concorde), Orpheus, and Pegasus (Harrier) jet engines. He returned from retirement in 1970 to resolve the problems of the RB-211. His autobiography *Not Much of an Engineer* was published in 1984.

HOOKER, Thomas (c.1586–1647) English Nonconformist preacher, born in Markfield, Leicester. He became a fellow of Emmanuel College, Cambridge, and was for three years a Puritan lecturer at Chelmsford. In 1630 he went to Holland, but was ejected for his Nonconformity; in 1633 he sailed for Massachusetts, and received a charge at Cambridge. In 1636 he moved with his congregation to Connecticut, and founded the town of Hartford.

HOOKER, Sir Willam Jackson (1785–1865) English botanist, born in Norwich. He collected specimens in Scotland (1806) and Iceland (1809), writing his *Recollections of Iceland* (1811). He became professor at Glasgow (1820), and the first director of the Royal Botanic Gardens at Kew in 1841.

HOOPER, John (1495–1555) English prelate and martyr, born in Somerset. Educated at Oxford, he entered a Cistercian monastery at Gloucester in 1518. The reading of **Zwingli** made him a Reformer. He went in 1539 for safety's sake to the Continent, married in 1546, and settled in Zürich. After his return in 1549 he became a popular preacher in London, and in 1550 was appointed bishop of Gloucester, but was imprisoned for some weeks in the Fleet prison for his scruples over the oath and the episcopal habit. In 1552 he received the bishopric of Worcester *in commendam*. In 1553, under **Mary I**, he was again committed to the Fleet, and was burned for heresy at Gloucester.

HOOTON, Ernest Albert (1887–1954) American physical anthropologist, born in Clemansville, Wisconsin. He studied classics at Lawrence College and Wisconsin University, but his interests turned to anthropology while holding a scholarship at Oxford. From 1913 to 1954 he taught anthropology at Harvard, and his laboratory became the main US centre for training physical anthropology specialists. In his many popular writings, including *Up From the Ape* (1931) and *Apes, Men and Morons* (1937), he introduced the subject to a wide readership. In his research he concentrated on the racial classification of the human species, and on relationships between body build and behaviour, as in *The American Criminal* (1939) and *Crime and Man* (1939).

HOOVER, Herbert Clark (1874–1964) 31st president of the USA, born of Quaker parentage in West Branch, Iowa. He was trained in mining engineering, and gathered experience in the States, Australia, China (in the Boxer rising) and elsewhere. Both during and after Wold War I he was closely associated with relief of distress in Europe. He was secretary of commerce under **Harding**. As the Republican candidate he defeated **'Al' Smith** in the presidential election of 1928, but his opposition to direct governmental assistance for the unemployed after the world slump of 1929 made him unpopular and he was beaten by **F D Roosevelt** in 1932. He assisted President **Truman** with the various American European economic relief programmes which followed World War II.

HOOVER, John Edgar (1895–1972) United States public servant, born in Washington DC. Following the premature death of his father, he was forced to support his family at an early age, graduating in law at George Washington University in 1917, after taking evening classes. He then entered the Justice Department, becoming special assistant to the attorney-general in 1919 and assistant director of the Federal Bureau of Investigation (FBI) in 1921. He became FBI director in 1924 and remained in charge of the Bureau until his death, remodelling it to make it more efficient, and campaigning against city gangster rackets in the inter-war years and communist sympathisers in the post-war period. He was later criticized for abusing his position by engaging in vendettas against liberal activists.

HOOVER, William Henry (1849–1932) American industrialist, born in Ohio. After running a tannery business (1870–1907), he bought the patent of an electric cleaning machine from a janitor, James Murray Spangler, and formed the Electric Suction Sweeper Co in 1908 (renamed Hoover in 1910) to manufacture and market it throughout the world.

HOPE name of a Scottish noble family descended from John de Hope, 1500–60, who probably came to Scotland from France with Magdalen de Valois, queen of **James V**, in 1537, and set up as a merchant in Edinburgh.

HOPE, Sir Charles, 1st Earl of Hopetoun (1681–1742) Scottish nobleman. He was elected privy councillor and a peer in 1702. A supporter of the Union (1707) with England, he became lord-lieutenant of Linlithgow in 1715 and in 1723 lord high commissioner to the general assembly of the Church of Scotland. He commissioned William Bruce in 1699 to build Hopetoun House on his estates, near Queensferry, and the building was considerably altered and completed in 1753 by the famous Scottish architects, William, and his son **Robert, Adam**.

HOPE, Sir John, 4th Earl of Hopetoun (1765–1823) Scottish soldier. He served at the battle of Alexandria (1801), under Sir **John Moore** in Spain where he distinguished himself in the retreat to Corunna (1808), and finally under **Wellington** throughout the Peninsular War.

HOPE, John Adrian Louis, 7th Earl and 1st Marquis of Linlithgow (1860–1908) Scottish administrator, father of the 8th Earl of **Hope**, was appointed first governor-general of Australia (1900–02) and was created marquis in 1902.

HOPE, Victor Alexander John, 8th Earl and 2nd Marquis (1887–1952) Scottish administrator, viceroy of India (1936–43) and chancellor of Edinburgh University from 1944. His twin sons were, Charles William, 3rd Marquis (1912–), who won the MC and was taken prisoner with the 51st Highland Division in 1940, and John Adrian, 1st Baron Glendevon (1912–), who served in Italy during World War II, was a Conservative MP from 1950 to 1964, when he became a peer, and was minister of works (1959–62).

HOPE, A D (Alec Derwent) (1907–) Australian poet and critic, born in Cooma, New South Wales, the son of a Presbyterian minister. Most of his childhood was spent in New South Wales and Tasmania. He graduated from Sydney University and took up a scholarship at Oxford. He returned to Australia in 1931 and was a distinguished academic, teaching English at several Australian colleges, before retiring in 1972 to concentrate on poetry. Regarded by some critics as austere, intellectual and lacking any identifiable Australian experience, he is a richly allusive poet, pre-eminent among his contemporaries. Few awards have passed him by since the appearance of his first collection. *The Wandering Isles*, in 1955. Subsequent volumes include *Poems* (1960), *A D Hope* (1963), *Collected Poems 1930–1965* (1966, expanded 1972), *Selected Poems* (1973), *A Late Picking* (1975), *A Book of Answers* (1978), *The Drifting Continent* (1979), *Antechinus* (1981) and *The Tragical History of Dr Faustus* (1982).

HOPE, Anthony, pseud of **Sir Anthony Hope Hawkins** (1863–1933) English novelist, born in London, the son of a clergyman in Clapton. Educated at Balliol College, Oxford, he was called to the bar in 1887. He wrote several plays and novels in his spare time, and made his name as writer with a collection of sketches, *The Dolly Dialogues* (1894). But he is chiefly remembered for his 'Ruritanian' romances, *The Prisoner of Zenda* (1894; dramatized 1896) and its sequel, *Rupert of Hentzau* (1898).

HOPE, Bob, originally **Leslie Townes Hope** (1903–) English-born American comedian, born in Eltham, London, and raised in Ohio from 1907. He became a naturalized American citizen in 1920. Working in vaudeville as a master of 'songs, patter and eccentric dancing', he made his Broadway début in *The Sidewalks of New York* (1927). Featured prominently in *Roberta* (1933), he made his film début in the short *Going Spanish* (1934), and gained a growing following as a radio comic. The film *The Big Broadcast of 1938* gave him his lifelong theme tune 'Thanks for the Memory', and the popularity of *The Cat and the Canary* (1939) firmly established his screen persona of the cowardly braggart. Famed for his ski-slope nose, lop-sided grin and impeccable timing, he was one of the most popular performers of the 1940s with the radio programme *The Bob Hope Pepsodent Show* (1939–48) and a string of hit films including *The Ghost Breakers* (1940), *My Favourite Blonde* (1942), *Paleface* (1948) and the enduring *Road to . . .* series with **Bing Crosby** and Dorothy Lamour that ran from *Singapore* (1940) to *Hong Kong* (1961). A star of television, a court jester to various US presidents, an indefatigable entertainer of American troops, a noted golfer and humanitarian, he has become a showbusiness institution and one of its wealthiest success stories. The recipient of countless international honours, he has written several humorous books including *I Never Left Home* (1944), *I Owe Russia $1200* (1963) and *Confessions of a Hooker* (1985).

HOPE, Laurence, pseud of **Adela Florence Nicolson,** née **Cory** (1865–1904) English poet, born in Stoke Bishop, Gloucestershire. She lived in India and wrote poems, influenced by **Swinburne** and coloured by the Orient, among them the *Indian Love Lyrics*, some of which are best known in their musical settings by Amy Woodford Finden.

HOPE, Thomas (1769–1831) English connoisseur and antiquarian, born in London. A man of considerable wealth, he travelled widely in Europe and the near east in his youth, collecting marbles and making drawings of buildings and sculptures. He pioneered a Neoclassical Regency style, and introduced the vogue of Egyptian and Roman decoration in his mansion in Duchess Street, London. He wrote *House Furniture and Interior Decoration* (1807), and a novel, *Anastasius, or Memoirs of a Modern Greek* (1819), a picaresque tale of an unscrupulous Greek adventurer, which enjoyed great popularity in its time.

HOPE, Thomas Charles (1766–1844) Scottish chemist, born in Edinburgh. He studied medicine there, and afterwards taught chemistry in Glasgow and from 1795 in Edinburgh, where he taught with, and then succeeded, **Joseph Black**. Hope confirmed the earlier but neglected observations that water has a maximum density close to 4°C, an important result in biology, climatology and physics. He recognized and described in 1793 a new mineral from Strontian in Scotland; he even described the characteristic red flame colour of the new element present in it (strontium) which was isolated by Sir **Humphrey Davy** in 1808. Hope was a highly successful teacher (his lectures were attended by 575 students in 1825) and was probably the first in Britain to teach the new ideas due to **Lavoisier**.

HOPE, Sir Thomas, of Craighall (1580–1646) Scottish judge and jurist. Lord Advocate of Scotland (1626–46), he wrote *Minor Practicks* (1726), a short treatise on Scots law, and *Major Practicks* (1937–38), a substantial collection of notes of statutes, cases and practical points distributed under eight major and many subsidiary headings. It is a valuable source for understanding early 17th-century law.

HOPETOUN See **HOPE**

HOPF, Heinz (1894–1971) German mathematician, born in Breslau. After war service he studied at Berlin and Göttingen, where he met the Russian topologist **Pavel Aleksandrov** with whom he wrote the influential *Topologie* (1935). In 1931 he became professor at Zürich. One of Europe's leading topologists, he worked on many aspects of combinatorial topology, including homotopy theory and vector fields.

HOPKINS, Anthony (1937–) Welsh actor, born in Port Talbot. A graduate of RADA, he made his stage début in *The Quare Fellow* (1960) at Manchester, and appeared extensively in regional repertory prior to his London début in *Julius Caesar* (1964). A member of the National Theatre from 1966 to 1973, he made his film début in *The White Bus* (1967). Stockily built, his mastery of timing and technique have allowed him to portray a vast variety of characters from the saturnine to the heroic. His film appearances include *The Lion in Winter* (1968), *Magic* (1978), *The Elephant Man* (1980) and *The Bounty* (1984). On television he won a BAFTA award for *War and Peace* (1972) and Emmys for *The Lindbergh Kidnapping Case* (1976) and *The Bunker* (1981). Long dominant on stage, his brooding intensity has been cast to memorable effect in *Equus* (1974) and a triumphant National Theatre hat trick of *Pravda* (1985), *King Lear* (1986) and *Antony and Cleopatra* (1987).

HOPKINS, Sir Frederick Gowland (1861–1947) English biochemist, born in Eastbourne. Professor at Cambridge from 1914, he was a pioneer in the study of accessory food factors, now called vitamins. He was awarded the Copley Medal in 1926, and shared with **Christiaan Eijkman** the 1929 Nobel prize for physiology or medicine.

HOPKINS, Gerard Manley (1844–89) English poet, born in Stratford, London, the son of a prosperous marine insurance agent. He was educated at Highgate School and Balliol College, Oxford, where he was a pupil of **Jowett** and **Pater** and a disciple of **Pusey**, and met his lifelong friend **Robert Bridges**. The religious ferment of the times absorbed him and finally he followed **John Henry Newman** into the Roman Catholic church in 1866. In 1868 he became a Jesuit novice, was ordained a priest in 1877, and taught at Stoneyhurst School (1882–84). In 1884 he was appointed to the chair of Greek at University College, Dublin. None of his poems was published in his lifetime, but his friend Bridges brought out a full edition in 1918. His first and most famous poem, 'The Wreck of the *Deutschland*' (1876) used what he called 'sprung rhythm', which gave an extraordinary freshness to his best-loved poetry, such as 'The Windhover' and 'Pied Beauty'. The *Letters to Robert Bridges*, *The Correspondence of Gerard Manley Hopkins and Richard Watson Dixon* (1935), and the *Notebooks* (1937), set forth his ideals for poetry, and gave explanations of his experiments in prosody.

HOPKINS, Harry Lloyd (1890–1946) American administrator, born in Sioux City, Iowa. He was Federal emergency relief administrator in the depression of 1933, and under President **Franklin D Roosevelt** headed the New Deal projects in the Works Progress Administration (1935–38). He became secretary of commerce 1938–40, and supervised the lend-lease programme in 1941. As Roosevelt's closest confidante and special assistant, he undertook several important missions to Russia, Britain, etc, during World War II.

HOPKINS, John See **STERNHOLD, Thomas**

HOPKINS, Johns (1795–1873) American businessman, born in Anne Arundel Country, Maryland. A grocer in Baltimore, he retired in 1847 with a large fortune. Besides a public park for Baltimore, he gave

$4 500 000 to found a free hospital, and over $3 000 000 to found the Johns Hopkins University.

HOPKINS, Mark (1802–87) American educationist, born in Stockbridge, Massachusetts. President (1836–72) of Williams Congregational College, Williamstown, Massachusetts, he published many essays, sermons and religious books, and was made a member of the Hall of Fame. His brother Albert (1807–72) was an astronomer.

HOPKINS, Matthew (d.1647) English witchfinder-general, appointed in 1644. He caused the deaths of scores of victims, and discharged his duties so conscientiously that he himself became suspect, and, being found guilty by his own test in that he floated, bound, in water, was hanged.

HOPKINS, Samuel (1721–1803) American Congregational theologian, born in Waterbury, Connecticut. He studied at Yale, and was pastor (1743–69) of Housatonick (now Great Barrington), Massachusetts, and then of Newport. A close friend of **Jonathan Edwards** (1745–1801), his *System of Doctrines* (1793) maintains that all virtue consists in disinterested benevolence, and that all sin is selfishness (Hopkinsianism).

HOPMAN, Harry (Henry Christian) (1906–85) Australian lawn tennis player and team captain, born in Sydney. Despite being a talented singles player, he specialized almost exclusively in doubles. He is, however, best known for his captaincy of the Australian Davis Cup side. He was briefly in charge before World War II and his return to the post in 1950 saw Australia dominate world men's tennis. In the next 17 years Australians were to win Wimbledon 10 times and the Davis Cup 15 times as Hopman produced a stream of talented players, from **Rosewall** and **Hoad** to **Laver** and Newcombe. A strict disciplinarian, he demanded total commitment. Willing to take a chance with young players, he often had players representing Australia in the Davis Cup before they were 20 years old. His wife Nell was also a noted legislator in women's tennis.

HOPPE-SEYLER, Felix, in full **Ernst Felix Immanuel** (1825–95) German physiological chemist, born in Freiburg-im-Breisgau, the son of a clergyman. A pioneer in the application of chemical methods to understand physiological processes, he showed how the haemoglobin in the red blood cells binds oxygen, subsequently delivered to the tissues, and investigated the chemical composition and functions of chlorophyll as well as the chemistry of putrefaction. He taught in Berlin, Tübingen and Strasbourg and founded, in 1877, the *Zeitschrift für physiologische chemie*.

HOPPER, Edward (1882–1967) American painter, born in Nyack, New York. He studied under **Robert Henri** from 1900 to 1906, and between 1906 and 1910 made several trips to Europe. His style of painting, however, owed little to the various contemporary European art movements and, in later years, was similarly unaffected by American abstraction. His paintings of commonplace urban scenes are characterized by a pervasive sense of stillness and isolation in which figures are anonymous and uncommunicative. Although he gave up painting for a time (1913–23) in order to work as a commercial illustrator, he received official recognition with a retrospective exhibition at the New York Museum of Modern Art in 1933.

HOPPNER, John (c.1758–1810) English portrait painter, born in Whitechapel of German parents. At first a chorister in the Chapel Royal, he entered the Royal Academy schools in 1775 and was Sir **Thomas Lawrence**'s only rival as a fashionable portrait painter. *The Countess of Oxford* is his masterpiece.

HOPTON, Ralph Hopton, 1st Baron (1598–1652) English royalist soldier from Somerset. An MP from 1624, he was expelled in 1642 for royalist leanings. As commander for the king in the south-west of England (1642–46) he won some victories and was created Lord Hopton in 1643. He surrendered at Truro (1646) and died in exile in Bruges.

HORACE, Quintus Horatius Flaccus (65–8 BC) Roman poet and satirist, born near Venusia in southern Italy. His father was a manumitted slave, who as collector of taxes or auctioneer had saved enough money to buy a small estate. Horace was taken to Rome and taught by the best masters. About eighteen he went to Athens to complete his education; and he was still there when the murder of **Julius Caesar** (44 BC) rekindled civil war. The same year he joined **Brutus**, who visited Athens while levying troops. He was present as an officer at the battle of Philippi (42 BC), and joined in the flight that followed the Republican defeat, but found his way back to Italy. His property having been confiscated, he found employment in the civil service; but poverty, he said, drove him to make verses. His earliest were chiefly satires and lampoons; but some of his first lyrical pieces made him known to **Virgil**, who about 38 BC introduced him to **Maecenas**, minister of **Augustus** and a munificent patron of art and letters. To his liberality Horace owed release from business and the gift of the farm among the Sabine Hills. From then on his springs and summers were generally spent in Rome, his autumns at the Sabine farm or a small villa at Tubur. As the unrivalled lyric poet of the time he had become poet laureate, a position he retained until his death. The first book of *Satires*, ten in number, appeared in 35 BC; a second volume of eight satires in 30 BC; and about the same time the small collection of lyrics known as the *Epodes*. In 19 BC he produced his greatest work, three books of *Odes*. To about the same date belong his *Epistles*. The remainder of his writings are the *Carmen Seculare*; a fourth book of *Odes*; and three more epistles, one of which, known as the *Ars Poetica*, was perhaps left unfinished at his death. From his own lifetime till now Horace has had a popularity unequalled in literature.

HORATIUS the name of three legendary brothers chosen by King Tullus Hostilius in the 7th century BC to fight for Rome against the three Curiatii brothers of Alba Longa. Two of the Horatii were speedily slain; the third, feigning flight, engaged each of his wounded opponents singly, and overcame them all. It was a descendant of the survivor, Publius Horatius Cocles, (530–500 BC) who in 505 BC held the bridge over the Tiber against the army of Lars Porsena in **Macaulay**'s *Lays of Ancient Rome*.

HORDERN, Sir Michael (1911–) English actor, born in Berkhampsted. He was an amateur actor with the St Pancras People's Theatre before making his first professional appearance as Lodovico in *Othello* at the People's Palace in 1937. After World War II, he appeared at Stratford-upon-Avon as Mr Toad in *Toad of Toad Hall*. In 1952 he joined the Stratford Memorial Theatre company to play a number of roles, and the Old Vic in 1953–54 as Polonius in *Hamlet*, King John, Prospero in *The Tempest*, and a much-acclaimed Malvolio in *Twelfth Night*. He has had outstanding success in both classical and modern roles, such as the philosopher in **Tom Stoppard**'s *Jumpers* (1972) and the judge in **Howard Barker**'s *Stripwell* (1975). He has made numerous film and television appearances, notably in the television adaptation of **John Mortimer**'s *Paradise Postponed* (1986). A formidable classical actor, he has also cornered the market in amiable, elderly eccentrics.

HORE-BELISHA, Leslie, 1st Baron Hore-Belisha (1893–1957) English barrister and politician, born in Devonport and educated at Clifton College and Oxford. After war service, he became a London journalist and in 1923, the year he was called to the bar, Liberal MP for Devonport. In 1931 he became first chairman of the National Liberal party. In 1934, as minister of transport, he gave his name to the 'Belisha' beacons, drafted a new highway code and inaugurated driving tests for motorists. As secretary of state for war (1937–40) he carried out several far-ranging and controversial reforms to modernize and democratize the Army. He was minister of national insurance in the 1945 'caretaker' government, but lost his seat at the July election. In 1954 he received a peerage.

HORKHEIMER, Max (1895–1973) German philosopher and social theorist, born in Stuttgart. He studied at Frankfurt, and became a leading figure in the Frankfurt School, together with **Adorno** and **Marcuse**, and was director of the Institut für Sozialforschung there in 1930. He moved with the school to New York City when the Nazis came to power in 1933, and returned to Frankfurt in 1950 as professor at the university. He published a series of influential articles in the 1930s, collected in two volumes under the title *Kritische Theorie* (1968), which expound the basic principles of the school in their critique of industrial civilization and epistemology and the key tenets of their 'critical theory'. His other major works include *Dialektik der Aufklärung* (with Adorno, 1947) and *Eclipse of Reason* (1947).

HORMAYR, Joseph, Freiherr von (1782–1848) Austrian historian, born in Innsbruck. In 1803 he became keeper of the Austrian archives, and in 1816 imperial historiographer. But, having been imprisoned by **Metternich** for suspected complicity in a Tirolese revolt, in 1828 he entered the service of Bavaria, and became director of the Munich royal archives. He published several works on the history of Tyrol, an 'Austrian **Plutarch**', and a general history of modern times.

HORN, Charles Edward (1786–1849) English singer and composer, born in London of German parentage. His works include the songs 'Cherry Ripe' and 'I know a bank', as well as glees and piano-pieces.

HORN, Count See **EGMONT, Lamoral**

HORNBLOWER, Jonathan Carter (1753–1815) English engineer, born in Chacewater, Cornwall, the son of Jonathan Hornblower (1717–80), also an engineer. As a young man he was employed with his father and three brothers by **Boulton** and **James Watt** to build one of their engines. He determined to improve Watt's design and by 1781 had obtained a patent for a single-acting compound engine with two cylinders, in which the steam acted expansively and hence much more efficiently. He was judged, however, to have infringed Watt's patent of the separate condenser, and had to abandon further development of his engine. He later patented a rotary type of steam engine which was never built.

HORNBY, Albert Sidney (1898–1978) English teacher, grammarian and lexicographer, born in Chester. It has been said of Hornby that 'no man has ever done more to further the use of English as an international language'. In 1923 he went to Japan to teach English, and in the 1930s became involved in the preparation of an English dictionary for Japanese students of English, published in Japan in 1942, and printed in 1948 by Oxford University Press as *A Learner's Dictionary of Current English* (retitled in 1952 *The Advanced Learner's Dictionary of Current English*) Although he wrote many other books—textbooks, grammars and dictionaries—it is for this dictionary that he is best known.

HORNBY, Sir Geoffrey Thomas Phipps (1825–95) English naval commander, son of Sir **Phipps Hornby**. He was present at the bombardment of Acre (1840), and became commander-in-chief in the Mediterranean (1877–80). In the Russo-Turkish war of 1878 he took the fleet through the Dardanelles to Constantinople. In 1888 he was promoted Admiral of the Fleet.

HORNBY, Sir Phipps (1785–1867) English naval commander, born in Winwick, Lancashire, he entered the navy in 1797, and commanded a frigate in **Hoste**'s victory of Lissa (1811). He was commander-in-chief in the Pacific (1847–50), and was appointed a lord of the Admiralty (1851–52). He was promoted Admiral in 1858.

HORNE, Donald Richmond (1921–) Australian writer, born in New South Wales, one of Australia's most original and influential writers. The author of *The Lucky Country* (1964), he became associate professor of political studies at the University of New South Wales. His other books have included *The Permit* (1965), *Money Made Us* (1976), *Death of The Lucky Country* (1976), *His Excellency's Pleasure* (1977), *Right Way, Don't Go Back* (1978), *In Search of Billy Hughes* (1979), *Time of Hope* (1980), *Winner Takes All* (1981), *The Great Museum* (1984), *Confessions of a New Boy* (1985), *A History of the Australian People* (1985), *The Public Culture* (1986) and *The Lucky Country We Visited* (1987).

HORNE, Marilyn Bernice (1934–) American mezzo-soprano opera singer, born in Bradford, Pennsylvania. She made her début in *The Bartered Bride*, Los Angeles (1954), at Covent Garden as Marie in *Wozzeck* (1964), and at the New York Metropolitan as Adalgisa in *Norma* (1970). She is also a noted recitalist.

HORNE, Richard Henry 'Hengist' (1803–84) English writer. He was educated at Sandhurst, and served in the Mexican navy and did his share of fighting at Vera Cruz, San Juan Ulloa and elsewhere. Having survived yellow fever, sharks, broken ribs, shipwreck, mutiny and fire, he returned to England and took up writing. He was the author of the epic *Orion* (1843) which he published at the price of one farthing to show his contempt for a public that would not buy poetry. In 1852 he went to Australia as commissioner for crown lands, and became a person of consequence in Victoria and published *Australian Facts and Prospects* and *Australian Autobiography* (1859). He returned to England in 1869. Among his books are *A New Spirit of the Age* (1844), in which **Elizabeth Barrett Browning** helped him, and two tragedies, *Cosmo de' Medici* (1837) and *The Death of Marlowe* (1837).

HORNE-TOOKE See **TOOKE, John Horne**

HORNER, Arthur Lewis (1894–1968) Welsh politician and trade unionist, born in Merthyr Tydfil, Glamorgan. He abandoned his studies at a Baptist College to enter politics and work in a Rhondda coalmine. A founder-member of the British Communist party, he stood unsuccessfully for parliament a number of times. He was elected president of the South Wales miners' union in 1936 and general secretary of the National Union in 1946. He was a likeable character, with friends who had little sympathy with his communist views.

HORNER, Francis (1778–1817) Scottish economist and politician, born in Edinburgh, the son of a merchant. Educated at Edinburgh University, he was called to the Scottish bar in 1797 and the English bar in 1802. He entered parliament in 1806, initiated several committees on economic matters, especially the convertibility of bullion, and opposed agricultural protection and the slave trade. He helped to found, and contributed to, the *Edinburgh Review* in 1802. He died of tuberculosis in Pisa.

HORNIMAN, Annie Elizabeth Fredericka (1860–1937) English theatre manager and patron, born in Forest Hall, London, the daughter of a wealthy Quaker tea-merchant. She developed a secret passion for the theatre in her teens, studied at the Slade School of Art, and travelled widely, especially in Germany. She failed with a play on the London stage in 1894, and went to Ireland in 1903. She later financed the first staging of **Yeats**'s *The Land of Heart's Desire* and **Shaw**'s *Arms and the Man*. She even acted a little, eg as the Gipsy Woman in Shaw's *The Gadfly* (a curtain-raiser) in 1898. In 1904 she sponsored the building of the Abbey Theatre in Dublin. She later quarrelled with Yeats, but Shaw never failed to pay her tribute. In 1908 she purchased the Gaiety Theatre in Manchester, which she called 'the first theatre with a catholic repertoire in England'. Until the company disbanded in 1917 for want of financial success, she put on over 100 new plays by the so-called 'Manchester School', mostly directed by **Lewis Casson** who married a member of the company, **Sybil Thorndike**. In Britain, the Repertory Theatre Movement and many reputations among playwrights and actors are her legacy: in Ireland, perhaps Irish national theatre itself.

HORNUNG, Ernest William (1866–1921) English novelist, born in Middlesbrough. Brother-in-law of **Arthur Conan Doyle**, he was the creator of Raffles the gentleman burglar, hero of *The Amateur Cracksman* (1899), *Mr Justice Raffles* (1909) and many other adventure stories.

HOROWITZ, Vladimir, originally **Vladimir Gorowicz** (1904–89) Russian pianist, born in Kiev. He studied at the conservatory there and with Sergei Tarnowsky and Felix Blumenfeld. He made his début at Kharkov, 1921, was heard in Berlin, 1925, and made his US début, under **Beecham**, in 1928. In 1933 he married Wanda Toscanini, daughter of **Arturo Toscanini**. He settled in the USA in 1940. His concert career was interrupted several times: by illness from 1936 to 1939; again after 1952 when he only recorded; he emerged from retirement to rapturous acclaim in 1965; again retired, but re-emerged in 1974 and played in Russia in 1986. One of the most accomplished players of the century, his technical and interpretative mastery was consummate in music ranging from **Scarlatti** to **Liszt**, **Scriabin**, and **Prokofiev**.

HORROCKS, Sir Brian Gwynne (1895–1985) English soldier. Educated at Uppingham and the Royal Military College, he joined the Middlesex Regiment in 1914. He served in France from 1914 to 1918 and in Russia in 1919. Command and staff assignments led to his appointment to command the 9th Armoured Division and then the 13th and 10th Corps in North Africa. His 30th Corps struggled gamely but unavailingly to link up with the airborne troops in Arnhem. On retirement Horrocks was made Gentleman Usher of the Black Rod. He later made a reputation as a military journalist and broadcaster, and wrote *A Full Life* (1960) and *Corps Commander* (1977).

HORROCKS, Jeremiah (1619–41) English astronomer, born in Toxteth, Liverpool. In 1632 he entered Emmanuel College, Cambridge, and in 1639 became curate of Hoole, Lancashire, where he made his first observation of the transit of Venus (24 November 1639, old style), deduced the solar parallax, corrected the solar diameter, and made tidal observations.

HORSA See **HENGIST**

HORSLEY, Samuel (1733–1806) English prelate, born in London. Educated at Westminster and Trinity Hall, Cambridge, in 1759 he succeeded his father as rector of Newington in Surrey. He published several scientific works and proposed a complete edition of **Newton**'s works, which was published in 1785. But the chief event in his career was the controversy (1783–89) with **Joseph Priestley**, who in his *History of the Corruptions of Christianity* included the orthodox doctrine of Christ's uncreated divinity. His services were rewarded with the bishopric of St Davids in 1788, Rochester in 1793, and St Asaph in 1802.

HORSLEY, Sir Victor Alexander Haden (1857–1916) English physiologist and surgeon, born in Kensington. He was Fullerian professor at the Royal Institution (1891–93) and professor of pathology at University College London (1893–96). He distinguished himself by his work on the localization of brain function, brain surgery, and the treatment of myxoedema. He died on active service in Mesopotamia. His father, John Callcott Horsley (1817–1903), was a genre painter, and his grandfather, William Horsley (1774–1858), a London organist and glee composer.

HORTA, Victor, Baron (1861–1947) Belgian architect, born in Ghent, regarded as the originator of Art Nouveau. Heavily influenced by the 1878 Paris World's Fair, he wanted to create a true modern western architecture. His works in Brussels included Maison Tassel (1892–93), which was at the same time individual and contemporary but conscious of tradition; Maison Solray (1894–1900), a luxurious design full of light and movement; and Maison du Peuple (1895–99), a masterpiece in metal, glass and stone (demolished in 1964). He also designed the first department store, l'Innovation (1901), in Brussels. His popularity declined after 1900 but he is now recognized as a master.

HORTENSE, Queen See **BONAPARTE, Louis**

HORTHY DE NAGYBÁNYA, Nikolaus (1868–1957) regent of Hungary (1920–44), born in Kenderes. He rose to the post of naval ADC to Francis Joseph, and after his victory at Otranto (1917) became commander-in-chief of the Austro-Hungarian fleet (1918). He was minister of war in the counter-revolutionary 'white' government (1919), opposing **Bela Kun**'s communist régime in Budapest and suppressing it with Romanian help (1920). His aim of restoring the Habsburg monarchy proved unpopular and so he allowed himself to be proclaimed regent. He ruled virtually as dictator, but allowed some parliamentary forms. He supported the Axis powers in World War II, supporting Germany's invasion of Yugoslavia and Russia until Hungary itself was overrun in March 1944. In October 1944 Horthy defied **Hitler** in broadcasting an appeal to the Allied powers for an armistice, and was imprisoned in the castle of Weilheim, Bavaria, where he fell into American hands (1945), and was set free the following year. He died in Estoril, Portugal, where he had lived since 1949.

HORTON, Lester (1906–53) American dancer, choreographer and teacher, born in Indianapolis, Indiana. He studied ballet with **Adolph Bolm** and was greatly influenced by Japanese movement theatre and Native American dancing. He left the American Midwest for California, where he was based until his death. He formed a dance company in the early 1930s, designing sets and costumes as well as devising dances, and opened his own theatre in 1948. He also worked in films and nightclubs. A neck injury forced him to retire from performing in 1944, but he continued to choreograph and, most importantly, teach.

HORVÁTH, Mihály (1809–78) Hungarian prelate and revolutionary. Professor of Hungarian at Vienna

(1844), and bishop of Csanad (1848), he took an active part in the revolution of 1848 and became minister of education. After the revolution was crushed (1849) he lived in exile, but returned under the amnesty of 1867. He was the author of a history of Hungary.

HOSKINS, Bob (Robert William) (1942–) English actor, born in Bury St Edmunds, Suffolk. A market porter, circus fire-eater, steeplejack and seaman, he sampled numerous other occupations before alighting on acting and making his début in *Romeo and Juliet* (1969) at Stoke-on-Trent. Avidly learning his craft, his notable stage performances include *Richard III* (1971), *King Lear* (1971), *Veterans* (1972), *The Iceman Cometh* (1976) and *Guys and Dolls* (1981). His ebullient personality and bullet-sized frame lend themselves to exuberant comedy or hardhitting drama, and he achieved widespread public recognition with the television series *Pennies From Heaven* (1978) and as the menacing hoodlum in the film *The Long Good Friday* (1980). After several years as a reliable and much-employed supporting actor in films he acquired international stardom with his award-winning performances in *Mona Lisa* (1986) and *Who Framed Roger Rabbit* (1988). He then made his directorial début with *The Raggedy Rawney* (1988).

HOSTE, Sir William (1780–1828) English naval commander, born in Ingoldisthorpe, Norfolk. He served under **Nelson**, and in 1811, off Lissa in the Adriatic with four frigates, destroyed a Franco-Venetian squadron of eleven. He also captured Cattaro (now Kotor) and Ragusa (now Dubrovnik) (1813–14).

HOSTIENSIS, originally **Enrico Bartolomei,** or **Henricus de Segusio** (c.1200–1271) Italian canonist, diplomat and cardinal bishop of Ostia. He taught canon law, possibly at Bologna and certainly at Paris, and became a papal diplomat. He wrote a famous *Summa* sometimes called *Summa Copiosa* (1253), which was an influential synthesis of Roman and canon law. He also wrote *Lectura in Novellas Innocentii IV* (1253) and *Lectura in Quinque Libros Decretalium* (c.1239).

HOSTILIUS, Tullus (7th century BC) third of the legendary kings of Rome. He succeeded **Numa Pompilius** in c.673 BC. He destroyed Alba, and removed the inhabitants to Rome; the other wars credited to him may be unhistorical.

HOTCHKISS, Benjamin Berkeley (1826–85) American inventor, born in Watertown, Connecticut. He devised an improved type of cannon shell, the Hotchkiss revolving-barrel machine gun (1872), and a magazine rifle (1875) widely used in the USA, France and Britain.

HOTHAM, Sir John (d.1645) English parliamentarian soldier. In 1642 he held Hull against **Charles I**, but in January 1645 was beheaded by parliament for his negotiations with the Earl of Newcastle, as was also his eldest son, John.

HOTMAN or **HOTOMAN, François** (1524–90) French jurist. He taught at Bourges and engaged in legal, political and religious controversies. He wrote on Roman law, feudal law and French public law, notably *Anti-Tribonian* (1567) and *Franco-gallia* (1573), in which he contended that there was no historical basis for the growth of royal absolutism in France, and argued for representative government and an elective monarchy. In *Anti-Tribonian* he argued for unity of legislation and a union of practice, with historical and synthetic treatment of law, and for a French code which did not borrow exclusively from Roman law.

HOTSPUR, Harry See **PERCY** family

HOUBRAKEN, Arnold (1660–1719) Dutch portrait and historical painter and also art historian, born in Dordrecht. His son, Jakob (1698–1780), was a copper-engraver.

HOUDIN, Robert (1805–71) French conjurer, born in Blois, and considered the father of modern conjuring. He employed himself in Paris for some years in making mechanical toys and automata, and gave magical soirées at the Palais Royal (1845–55). In 1856 he was sent by the government to Algiers to destroy the influence of the dervishes by exposing their pretended miracles.

HOUDINI, Harry, real name **Erich Weiss** (1874–1926) Hungarian-born American magician and escape artist, born in Budapest, the son of a rabbi. He could escape from any kind of bonds or container, from prison cells to padlocked underwater boxes. He was a vigorous campaigner against fraudulent mediums, and was president of the Society of American Magicians.

HOUDON, Jean Antoine (1741–1828) French classical sculptor, born in Versailles. He won the *prix de Rome* in 1761. He spent ten years in Rome, and there executed the colossal figure of *St Bruno* in Sta Maria degli Angeli. In 1785 he visited America to execute a monument to Washington, a copy of which stands outside the National Gallery, London. His most famous busts are those of **Diderot**, **Voltaire** (foyer of the Théâtre Français, Paris), **Napoleon**, **Catherine the Great** and **Rousseau** (Louvre). He was appointed professor at the École des Beaux-Arts in 1805.

HOUGHTON, Lord See **MILNES, Richard Monckton**

HOUGHTON, William Stanley (1881–1913) English dramatist and critic, born in Ashton-upon-Mersey. After amateur dramatics in Manchester he wrote *The Dear Departed* (1908), *The Younger Generation* (1910), *Hindle Wakes* (1912), etc.

HOUNSFIELD, Sir Godfrey Newbold (1919–) English electrical engineer, born in Newark. He studied at the City and Guilds College and Faraday House College in London, worked as a radar lecturer in the RAF during World War II, joined Thorn/EMI in 1951 and became head of medical systems research in 1972. He headed the team which, independently of **Allan MacLeod Cormack**, developed the technique of computer-assisted tomography (CAT), which enables detailed X-ray pictures of 'slices' of the human body to be produced. He shared the 1979 Nobel prize for physiology or medicine with Cormack.

HOUPHOUËT-BOIGNY, Felix (1905–) Ivory Coast politician, born in Yamoussoukro, the country's new capital. He studied medicine in Dakar, Senegal, and practised as a doctor (1925–40). He then entered politics, sitting in the French Constitutional Assembly (1945–46) and the National Assembly (1946–59). During this period he served in the cabinets of Pflimlin, **de Gaulle** and Debré. When the Ivory Coast achieved full independence in 1960, he became its first president. Very much a political pragmatist, he has been criticized for maintaining links with South Africa but, despite this, has been applauded for the stability and strength of his country's economy.

HOUSE, Edward Mandell (1858–1938) American diplomat, born in Houston, Texas. During and after World War I he represented America in many conferences, and was long a close associate of President **Wilson**.

HOUSEMAN, John, originally **Jaques Haussman** (1902–89) Hungarian-born American stage director, producer, teacher and actor, born in Bucharest. Educated in England, he first worked as a producer in New York in 1934. He joined the Federal Theater Project in 1935. With **Orson Welles**, he founded the

Mercury Theater in New York in 1937. He became editor of the Mercury Theater of the Air, producing Welles's famous adaptation of **H G Wells**' *The War of the Worlds* in 1938. He was artistic director from 1956 to 1959 of the American Shakespeare Festival at Stratford, Connecticut. From 1959 to 1964 he was artistic director of the University of California Professional Theater Group and became producing director of APA Phoenix, New York (1967–68), director of the drama division of the Juilliard School of the Performing Arts, New York (1968–76), and artistic director of the City Center Acting Company, New York (1972–75). He made many film appearances, notably in *The Paper Chase* (1973). He wrote three volumes of autobiography: *Run-Through* (1972), *Front and Center* (1981), and *Final Dress* (1983).

HOUSMAN, Alfred Edward (1859–1936) English scholar and poet, born in Fockbury, Worcestershire, brother of **Laurence Housman**. Educated at Bromsgrove School, he won a scholarship to St John's College, Oxford, where he failed in Greats finals and entered the Patent Office. Nevertheless he became a distinguished classical scholar, and in 1892 he was appointed professor of Latin at University College, London, and professor of Latin at Cambridge from 1911. He published critical editions of Maniluis (1903–30), **Juvenal** (1905) and **Lucan** (1926). He is known primarily by his poetry—*A Shropshire Lad* (1896), *Last Poems* (1922), and *More Poems*, published posthumously in 1936. The lyrics in *A Shropshire Lad* are arranged roughly to form a cyclical poem in which an uprooted country lad recalls the innocence and pleasures but also, and more poignantly, the frustrations and local tragedies of a countryside which is only an imagined Shropshire and indeed hardly pastoral in the old sense at all.

HOUSMAN, Laurence (1865–1959) English novelist and dramatist, younger brother of **A E Housman**, born in Bromsgrove. He studied art at Lambeth and South Kensington, and attracted attention by his illustrations of **Meredith**'s poem 'Jump-to-Glory Jane'. He is best known for his *Little Plays of St Francis* (1922) and his Victorian biographical 'chamber plays', *Angels and Ministers* (1921), *Victoria Regina* (1937), etc. His autobiography, *The Unexpected Years* (1937), reveals a romantic Victorian figure, a Conservative radical who espoused pacificism and votes for women.

HOUSSAY, Bernardo Alberto (1887–1971) Argentine physiologist, born in Buenos Aires. He was professor at Buenos Aires until dismissed by president **Juan Perón** in 1943, and thereafter founded the Institute of Biology and Experimental Medicine, in 1944. He investigated pituitary hormones and shared the 1947 Nobel prize for physiology or medicine with **Carl** and Gerty **Cori.**

HOUSTON, Edwin James (1847–1914) American electrical engineer, born in Alexandria, Virginia. With **Elihu Thomson** he invented the Thomson-Houston arc lighting, patented in 1881.

HOUSTON, Samuel (1793–1863) American soldier and statesman, born in Lexington, Virginia. He enlisted in the army in 1813, but resigned in 1818 and studied law. In 1823 and 1825 he was elected a member of congress, and in 1827 governor of Tennessee. From 1829 he spent three years among the Cherokees in what is now Oklahoma. In the Texan war, as commander-in-chief, he defeated the Mexicans on the San Jacinto in April 1836, and achieved Texan independence. He was elected president of the republic, re-elected in 1841, and on the annexation of Texas, in 1845, returned to the US senate. Elected governor of Texas in 1859, he opposed secession, was deposed in 1861, and retired to private life. Houston, Texas is named after him.

HOVEDEN, Roger of See **ROGER OF HOVEDON**

HOWARD the name of the house which stands at the head of the English Catholic nobility, was founded by Sir William Howard, chief-justice of the Common Pleas (d.1308). His grandson, Sir John Howard, was a captain of the king's navy and sheriff of Norfolk; and *his* grandson married the daughter of the 1st Duke of Norfolk and coheiress of the house of Mowbray. In one or other of their widespead branches, the Howards have enjoyed, or still enjoy, the earldoms of Carlisle, Suffolk, Berkshire, Northampton, Arundel, Wicklow, Norwich, and Effingham, and the baronies of Bindon, Howard de Walden, Howard of Castle Rising, and Howard of Effingham.

HOWARD, Catherine (d.1542) queen of England from 1540, the fifth wife of **Henry VIII**. She was the grand-daughter of **Thomas Howard**, 2nd Duke of Norfolk, and niece of **Thomas Howard**, 3rd Duke of Norfolk. In 1540 she married Henry VIII immediately after his divorce from **Anne of Cleves**. In November 1541, after clandestine meetings with a musician (Henry Mannock) and a kinsman (Thomas Culpepper), whom she had known before her marriage, she was charged by **Cranmer** with sexual intercourse before her marriage. On her confession, both men were executed, and Catherine was attainted by parliament and beheaded in February 1542.

HOWARD, Charles, Lord Howard of Effingham, Earl of Nottingham (1536–1624) English naval commander, son of Sir **John Howard**, 1st Duke of Norfolk and Lord High Admiral of England. He succeeded his father in 1573 and in 1585 was himself appointed Lord High Admiral. He was commander-in -chief of the English fleet against the Spanish Armada (1588). In 1596 he commanded the expedition (with **Essex**) that sacked Cadiz. He was a commissioner at the trial of **Mary Queen of Scots** (1586), and in 1601 quelled Essex's rebellion.

HOWARD, Henry, Earl of Surrey See **SURREY**

HOWARD, Sir John, known as **Jack of Norfolk, 1st Duke of Norfolk** (c.1430–1485) English nobleman. **Edward IV** made him constable of Norwich Castle, sheriff of Norfolk and Suffolk, treasurer of the royal household, Lord Howard and duke of Norfolk, earl marshal of England (a distinction still borne by his descendants), and lord admiral of England, Ireland and Aquitaine. He was slain on Bosworth field and his honours were attainted.

HOWARD, Thomas, 2nd Duke of Norfolk, 1st Earl of Surrey (1443–1524) English nobleman, son of Sir **John Howard**, 1st Duke of Norfolk. Wounded at Bosworth Field (1485), he was captured, and after three years imprisonment in the Tower, obtained a reversal of his own and his father's attainders, and was restored to his honours. As lieutenant general of the North, he defeated the Scots at Flodden (1513).

HOWARD, Thomas, 3rd Duke of Norfolk, Earl of Surrey (1473–1554) English statesman, son of **Thomas Howard**, 2nd Duke of Norfolk. His first wife, in 1495, was Anne (d.1512), the daughter of **Edward IV** and sister of **Henry VII**; his second wife, 1513, was Elizabeth (d.1558), the duaghter of Edward Stafford, 3rd Duke of Buckingham, who was executed by **Henry VIII** in 1521. Howard was lord high admiral (1513), and lord lieutenant of Ireland (1520). He was uncle to **Anne Boleyn**, Henry VIII's second wife, but as lord steward presided over her trial for adultery (1536). He lost influence at court when another niece, **Catherine Howard**, Henry VIII's fifth wife, was beheaded for adultery in 1542. Throughout the reign of **Edward VI** he was imprisoned on suspicion of the treason for which Henry VIII had executed his eldest son, **Henry Howard, Earl of Surrey**, in 1547. He was released on the accession of Queen **Mary I** (Mary Tudor) in 1553.

HOWARD, Thomas, 4th Duke of Norfolk, 1st Earl of Northampton (1536–72) son of **Henry Howard**, Earl of Surrey. He succeeded his grandfather, the 3rd Duke, as duke and earl marshal in 1554. As a commissioner appointed to inquire into Scottish affairs, he was imprisoned (1569-70) for attempting to marry **Mary, Queen of Scots**; later he was involved in a plot with **Philip II** of Spain to free Mary, and was executed.

HOWARD, Thomas, 2nd Earl of Arundel and Surrey (1586–1646) English statesman and connoisseur. He was prominent in the court and public life of his day, but is remembered for his art collections, particularly for the Arundel Marbles (statues, inscribed marbles, etc), gifted by his grandson to Oxford University (1667).

HOWARD, Sir Ebenezer (1850–1928) English town planner and reformer, and founder of the garden city movement. He emigrated to Nebraska in 1872, but returned to England in 1877 and became a parliamentary shorthand-writer. His *Tomorrow* (1898), later republished as *Garden Cities of Tomorrow* (1902), envisaged self-contained communities with both rural and urban amenities and green belts, and led to the formation in 1899 of the Garden City Association and to the laying out of Letchworth (1903) and Welwyn Garden City (1919) as prototypes.

HOWARD, Edward (d.1841) English novelist, a navy lieutenant. On his retirement he wrote sea stories, including *Rattlin the Reefer* (1836) and, *Outward Bound* (1838).

HOWARD, Elizabeth Jane See **AMIS, Kingsley**

HOWARD, John (1726–90) English prison reformer, born in Hackney, London, the son of a wealthy upholsterer. On his travels in 1756 he was captured by a French privateer and imprisoned in Brest as a prisoner of war. In 1773, as high sheriff of Bedfordshire, he was appalled by conditions in Bedford gaol and undertook a tour of British prisons that led to two acts of Parliament in 1774, which provided for sanitary standards and replaced prisoners' fees for jailers with official salaries. Thereafter he travelled widely, and wrote *The State of Prisons in England and Wales, with an Account of some Foreign Prisons* (1777), and *An Account of the Principal Lazarettos in Europe* (1780). He died of typhus contracted while visiting a Russian military hospital at Kherson in the Crimea. The Howard League for Penal Reform, founded in 1866, was named after him.

HOWARD, Leslie, originally **Leslie Howard Stainer** (1893–1943) English actor, of Hungarian origin, born in London. A bank employee who made his film début in *The Heroine of Mons* (1914), he turned to dramatics after being invalided home from the Western Front during World War I. He made his stage début in *Peg o' My Heart* (1917), and concentrated on theatre work over the next decade, appearing on Broadway in *Just Suppose* (1922), *The Green Hat* (1925) and *Her Cardboard Lover* (1928, with **Tallulah Bankhead**). From 1930 he turned to the screen where he grew to personify an archetypically tweedy Englishman: scholarly, idealistic, witty and courageous. His many film successes include *Of Human Bondage* (1934), *The Scarlet Pimpernel* (1934), *The Petrified Forest* (1936) and *Pygmalion* (1938), which he co-directed. After reluctantly portraying the effete Ashley Wilkes in *Gone With the Wind* (1939), he returned to Britain to assist in the war effort by producing and directing such patriotic fare as *Pimpernel Smith* (1941) and *The First of the Few* (1942). Returning from a lecture trip to Lisbon in 1943 his plane was shot down by the Nazis, who had believed **Winston Churchill** to be on board. His son, Ronald Howard (1918–), also became an actor.

HOWARD, Oliver Otis (1830–1909) American soldier, born in Leeds, Maine. He graduated from West Point in 1854. At the outbreak of the Civil War he took command of a regiment of Maine volunteers in 1861. In 1864 he commanded the army of Tennessee, and led the right wing of **Sherman**'s army on the march to the sea. He was commissioner of the Freedmen's Bureau (1865–74). From 1869 to 1874 he was first president of Howard University at Washington, named after him. Later he conducted two campaigns against the Indians (1877–78).

HOWARD, Sir Robert (1626–98) English Restoration dramatist, son of the 1st Earl of Berkshire. He wrote *The Committee* (1663) and the *Indian Queen*, the latter assisted by his brother-in-law, **John Dryden**. His brothers Edward and James were also dramatists.

HOWARD, Trevor Wallace (1916–88) English actor, born in Cliftonville, Kent. A student at RADA, he made his stage début in *Revolt in a Reformatory* (1934) and acted exclusively in the theatre until World War II. Invalided out of the Royal Artillery, he enjoyed West End success in *A Soldier for Christmas*, (1944) and made his film début in *The Way Ahead* (1944). *Brief Encounter* (1945) brought him to the forefront of British performers, a position he held for some years as a dependable, trustworthy leading man, occasionally asked to depict cynicism or weakness, as in *The Third Man* (1949) and *The Heart of the Matter* (1953). Developing into a character actor of international stature, he was nominated for an Academy Award in *Sons and Lovers* (1960), but spent his later years largely in secondary cameos, including *Mutiny on the Bounty* (1962), *Ryan's Daughter* (1970), *Conduct Unbecoming* (1975) and *White Mischief* (1987). He also reminded audiences of his under-used talents in television work like *Catholics* (1973).

HOWARD OF EFFINGHAM See **HOWARD** family

HOWE, Elias (1819–67) American inventor, born in Spencer, Massachusetts. He worked as a mechanic in Lowell and Boston, where he constructed and patented (1846) the first sewing machine. He made an unsuccessful visit to England to introduce his invention, and, returning in 1847 to Boston, found his patent had been infringed. Harassed by poverty, he entered on a seven years' war of litigation to protect his rights, was ultimately successful (1854), and amassed a fortune.

HOWE, Sir (Richard Edward) Geoffrey (1926–) English politician. He was called to the bar in 1952 and first elected to parliament as a Conservative MP in 1964. Knighted in 1970, he was solicitor-general from 1970 to 1972. In his four years as Chancellor of the Exchequer (1979–83) he successfully engineered a reduction in the rate of inflation. He became foreign secretary after the 1983 general election. In 1989, in a major cabinet reshuffle, he was moved from the foreign office to the leadership of the House of Commons, but insisted on retaining an official country residence, with the title of deputy prime minister.

HOWE, Gordon (Gordie) (1928–) Canadian ice-hockey player, born in Floral, Saskatchewan, the holder of the all-time goals-scoring record. Playing mainly for the Detroit Red Wings (1946–71), he scored 1071 goals (801 in the National Hockey League). He was named Canada's Athlete of the Year in 1963. After retiring he stayed in the game, working with the Hartford Whalers.

HOWE, John (1630–1705) English Puritan clergyman, born in Loughborough. He studied at Cambridge and Oxford, and, after preaching for some time at Winwick and Great Torrington, was appointed domestic chaplain to **Cromwell** in 1656. In 1659 he returned to Torrington, but the Act of Uniformity ejected him in 1662, and he wandered about preaching in secret till 1671. In 1668 he published *The Blessedness of the Righteous*; in 1671 became domestic chaplain to Lord Massereene of Antrim Castle in Ireland. Here he wrote his *Vanity of Man as Mortal*, and began his greatest work, *The Good Man the Living Temple of God* (1676–1702). In 1676 he became pastor of the dissenting congregation in Silver Street, London. In 1685 he travelled with Lord Wharton on the Contintent, and settled in Utrecht, till in 1687 the Declaration of Indulgence recalled him to England, where he died.

HOWE, Joseph (1804–73) Canadian statesman, born in Nova Scotia. Proprietor and editor of the Halifax *Nova Scotian*, he became premier of Nova Scotia (1863–1870), and after federation entered the first Canadian government at Ottawa.

HOWE, Julia, née **Ward** (1819–1910) American feminist, reformer and writer, born in New York, wife of **Samuel Gridley Howe**. A wealthy banker's daughter, she became a prominent suffragette and abolitionist, and founded the New England Woman Suffrage Association (1868) and the New England Women's Club (1868). She published several volumes of poetry, including *Passion Flowers* (1854) and *Words for the Hour* (1857), as well as travel books and a play. She also wrote the 'Battle Hymn of the Republic' (published in *Atlantic Monthly*, 1862), and edited *Woman's Journal* (1870–90). In 1908 she became the first woman to be elected to the American Academy of Arts and Letters.

HOWE, Richard, 1st Earl (1726–99) English naval officer, born in London, son of the second Viscount Howe, and brother of **William 5th Viscount Howe**. He left Eton at 13 and entered the navy, and served under **Anson** against the Spaniards in the Pacific. Made post-captain at 20, he drove from the coast of Scotland two French ships conveying troops and ammunition to Prince **Charles Stewart**, the Young Pretender, in 1746. After serving off the coast of Africa, he distinguished himself in the naval operations of the Seven Years' War (1756–63). In 1758 he succeeded to the Irish title of viscount on the death of his brother, brigadier George Augustus (1724–58). Appointed a Lord of the Admiralty in 1763, he became in 1765 treasurer of the Navy. In 1776 he was appointed commander of the British fleet during the American War of Independence. In 1778 he defended the American coast against a superior French force. In 1882 he was sent out to relieve Gibraltar, disembarked troops and supplies, and then offered battle to the combined fleets of France and Spain, which declined an engagement. He was made First Lord of the Admiralty in 1783. When war with France broke out in 1793 he took command of the Channel Fleet, and next year gained a great victory off Ushant on 'the Glorious First of June'. His last service was to recall to their duty the mutinous seamen at Spithead and Portsmouth in 1797.

HOWE, Samuel Gridley (1801–76) American reformer and philanthropist, born in Boston, husband of **Julia Ward Howe**. In the Greek War of Independence (1821–31) he organized the medical staff of the Greek army (1824–27), went to America to raise contributions, and, returning with supplies, formed a colony on the isthmus of Corinth. Swamp-fever drove him from the country in 1830. In 1831 he went to Paris to study the methods of educating the blind, and, becoming mixed up in the Polish insurrection, spent six weeks in a Prussian prison. On his return to Boston he established the Perkins School for the Blind, and taught **Laura Bridgman**, among others. Also concerned with the education of the feeble-minded, he was a prison reformer and an abolitionist, and from 1851 to 1853 he edited the antislavery *Commonwealth*. In 1867 he revisited Greece with supplies for the Cretans.

HOWE, William, 5th Viscount Howe (1729–1814) English soldier, brother of **Richard, 1st Earl Howe**. He joined the army in 1746, served under **Wolfe** at Louisburg (1758) and at Quebec (1759), where he led the famous advance to the Heights of Abraham. He became MP in 1758. In the American War of Independence (1775–83) he won the victory at Bunker Hill (1775) and became commander-in-chief. Supported by his sailor-brother from the sea, in 1776 he captured Brooklyn, New York, and, after the victory of White Plains, Washington, the following year he defeated the Americans at Brandywine Creek. His subsequent lethargy marred his military career, and he was superseded by Sir **Henry Clinton** in 1778 after failure at Valley Forge.

HOWELL, James (c.1593–1666) English writer. He studied at Oxford and travelled abroad on business and in 1627 entered parliament. From 1632 to 1642 he was mainly employed as a royalist spy, and during the Civil War was imprisoned by parliament (1642–50). At the Restoration the office of royal historian was created for him. As well as translations from Italian, French and Spanish, Howell wrote 41 works on history, politics and philosophy, as well as *Instructions for Forreine Travell* (1642), a supplement to **Cotgrave**'s dictionary and the witty and entertaining *Epistolae Ho-Elianae; or Familiar Letters* (1645–55).

HOWELLS, Herbert (1892–1983) English composer, born in Lydney, Gloucestershire. He studied under **Charles Stanford** at the Royal College of Music, where he became professor of composition (1920) after a short time as sub-organist of Salisbury Cathedral. In 1936 he followed **Gustav Holst** as director of music at St Paul's Girls' School, and in 1952 became professor of music at London University, retiring in 1962, though he continued to teach there until well into his eighties. He is best known for his choral works, especially the *Hymnus Paradisi*, which combine an alert sense of 20th-century musical developments with a firm foundation in the English choral tradition.

HOWELLS, William Dean (1837–1920) American novelist and critic, born in Martin's Ferry, Ohio. He became a compositor in a printing office from 1856 to 1861 on the staff of the *Ohio State Journal*. Stimulated by the works of **Cervantes**, **Pope** and **Heine**, he began to write poetry which was published in the *Atlantic Monthly* (1860–61), which he later edited (1871–81). His biography of **Lincoln** (1860) managed to procure for him the post of US consul in Venice (1861–65). His association with *Harper's Magazine* (1886–91) made him the king of critics in America, writing an *Easy Chair* column for *Harper's* from 1900 to 1920. The 'reticent realism' of his early novels, as in the slight *Their Wedding Journey* (1872), matured in depth of feeling in *The Lady of the Aroostook* (1879) and finally gave way to Tolstoyan humanitarian naturalism in *A Hazard of New Fortunes* (1890). His theories of fiction, which influenced **Mark Twain**, **Henry James** and **Wendell Holmes**, were expounded in *Criticism and Fiction* (1891). He also wrote the autobiographical *Years of my Youth* (1915) and *Literary Friends* (1900).

HOWERD, Frankie, originally **Francis Alick Howard** (1922–) English comedian and actor. He made his début at the Stage Door Canteen, Piccadilly,

London, in 1946, and appeared in revues in London during the 1950s, including *Out of This World* (1950), *Pardon My French* (1953), and *Way Out In Piccadilly* (1960). He has acted occasionally in plays. He gave a notable performance in **Sondheim**'s musical, *A Funny Thing Happened on the Way to the Forum*, in 1963. He has appeared regularly on television and in films, his most famous role being that of a Roman slave in the television series *Up Pompeii* (1970–71), a series drenched in sexual innuendo. His films include *The Ladykillers* (1956), *Carry On Doctor* (1968), *Up Pompeii* (1971), and *Up the Chastity Belt* (1972).

HOXHA, Enver (1908–85) Albanian politician, born in Gjinokaster. Educated in France and once a schoolteacher, he founded and led the Albanian Communist party (1941) in the fight for national independence (the country was overrun by Germans and Italians during the war), adopting a guerrilla warfare strategy. In 1946 he deposed King **Zog** (who had fled in 1939) and became effective head of state, holding the positions of prime minister (1944–54), foreign minister (1946–53) and supreme commander of the armed forces (1946–54). From 1954, Hoxha controlled the political scene through his position as first secretary of the Albanian Party of Labour (Communist party), and instituted a rigid Stalinist programme of thorough nationalization and collectivization which left Albania with the lowest per capita income in Europe on his death. A major secularization drive was also launched, while, in its external relations, an isolationist policy, independent of both Soviet and Chinese communism, was pursued.

HOYLAND, John (1934–) English painter, born in Sheffield. He studied at Sheffield College of Art (1951–56) and at the Royal Academy Schools (1956–60), and has held numerous teaching posts, including principal lecturer at the Chelsea School of Art. He won an international Young Artists prize in Tokyo in 1964. In America in the same year he met 'Colour Field' painters like **Morris Louis** and turned to hard-edge abstraction using broad, freely-painted rectangles of rich colour.

HOYLE, Edmond (1672–1769) English authority on card games, called the 'Father of Whist'. His popular *A Short Treatise on the Game of Whist* (1742) systematized the rules of the game and remained the standard until the rules were changed in 1864. In 1748 he added manuals on backgammon, brag, quadrille, piquet and chess into an omnibus volume, *Hoyle's Standard Games*. The weight of his authority gave rise to the expression 'according to Hoyle' as an idiom for correct usage.

HOYLE, Sir Fred (1915–) English astronomer and mathematician, born in Bingley, Yorkshire. Educated at Bingley Grammar School and Emmanuel College, Cambridge, he taught mathematics at Cambridge (1945–58), was Plumian professor of astronomy and experimental philosophy there (1958–72). and professor-at-large at Cornell University (1972–78). In 1948, with Hermann Bondi and Thomas Gold, he propounded the 'steady state' theory of the universe, and wrote *Nature of the Universe* (1952) and *Frontiers of Astronomy* (1955). He also wrote science fiction, including *The Black Cloud* (1957).

HOYTE, (Hugh) Desmond (1929–) Guyanese politician, born in Georgetown. After studies at London University and the Middle Temple, he taught in a boys' school in Grenada (1955–57) and then practised as a lawyer in Guyana. He joined the socialist People's National Congress (PNC), party and in 1968, two years after Guyana achieved full independence, was elected to the National Assembly. He held a number of ministerial posts before becoming prime minister under **Forbes Burnham**. On Burnham's death, in 1985, he succeeded him as president.

HRDLIČKA, Ales (1869–1943) Bohemian-born American physical anthropologist, born in Humpolec. He studied in America and was on the staff of the Natural History Museum, New York, and the National Museum, Washington. His anthropological studies inclined him to the view that American Indians were of Asiatic origin.

HROMADKA, Josef Luki (1889–1969) Czech Reformed theologian, born in Hodslavice, Moravia. He studied at Basel, Heidelberg, Vienna, Prague, and at the United Free Church College, Aberdeen, and was theological professor at Prague (1920–39) and at Princeton Theological Seminary (1939–47). Thereafter in what was hailed as a courageous decision he returned to Czechoslovakia and became dean of the Comenius faculty, Prague, in 1950. Active in the World Council of Churches from its inception, he contributed much to Christian-Marxist dialogue, and received the Lenin peace prize in 1958. He died a few months after the Russians invaded his homeland, an act against which he protested, causing his resignation from the Christian Peace Conference which he had founded. His major writings in English include *Masaryk* (1930), *Christianity in Thought and Life* (1931), *Luther* (1935), *Calvin* (1936), *The Gospel for Atheists* (1958), and *My Life between East and West* (1969).

HROSWITHA (c.932–1002) German poet and Benedictine nun of Gandersheim near Göttingen. She wrote Latin poems and six prose Terentian comedies, with a religious slant. She is regarded as the first German woman poet.

HROZNY, Bedřich (1879–1952) Czech orientalist and archaelogist, born in Lissa. Professor at Vienna (1905–19) and Prague (1919–52), he was the first to decipher the Hittite language. He excavated Hittite sites, and wrote *Die Sprache der Hethiter* (1917).

HSIA KUEI See **XIA GUIA**

HSUAN T'UNG See **PU-YI**

HSÜAN TSANG (c.600–664) Chinese Buddhist traveller, born in Honan. He became a Buddhist monk in 620 and made a long pilgrimage through China and India during which he travelled 40000 miles in 16 years. His books graphically describe the Buddhist world in the Middle Ages.

HUA GUOFENG (1920–) Chinese politician, born in Shanxi province into a poor peasant family. He fought under Zhu De during the liberation war of 1937–49, before later rising up the official ranks of the Communist party (CCP) during the 1950s and 1960s in **Mao Zedong**'s home province of Hunan; eventually becoming local first secretary in 1970. An agronomist by training and a skilled organizer, Hua was inducted into the CCP Central Committee in 1969 and the politburo in August 1973, and was appointed minister for public security in 1975. Viewed as an orthodox and loyal Maoist, Hua, despite his relative inexperience, was selected to succeed **Zhou Enlai** as prime minister in January 1976, and succeeded Mao as party leader on the latter's death in September 1976. He dominated Chinese politics during 1976–77, seeking economic modernization along traditional 'extensivist' lines, although also aiming at a greater opening-up of the country to external Western contacts. From 1978, however, he was gradually eclipsed by the reformist **Deng Xiaoping**, being replaced as prime minister and CCP Chairman by the latter's protégés, **Zhao Ziyang** and **Hu Yaobang**, in September 1980 and June 1981 respectively. Hua was ousted from the politbureau in

September 1982, but retained his position in the CCP Central Committee.

HUANG-TI See **SHIH HUANG TI**

HUBBARD, Lafayette Ronald (1911–86) American scientologist and science-fiction writer, born in Tilden, Nebraska, and the inspiration behind the Church of Scientology. From the age of 16 he travelled extensively in the Far East before completing his education at Woodward Preparatory School and George Washington University. He became a professional writer of adventure stories, turning to science fiction in 1938, with such classics as *Slave of Sleep* (1939), *Fear* (1940), *Final Blackout* (1940), *Death's Deputy* (1940) and *Typewriter in the Sky* (1940). He served in the US navy during World War II, and in 1950 published *Dianetics: The Modern Science of Mental Health*, which claimed to be pioneering in its exploration of the human mind and its detailed description of how the mind works. This was followed by *Science of Survival* (1951), which formed the basis of the Scientology philosophy. The first Church of Scientology was founded by a group of adherents in Los Angeles in 1954; in 1955 Hubbard became the executive director of the Founding Church Washington. From 1959 to 1966 he made his base in East Grinstead in England, and resigned his position as executive director of the church in 1966. In 1982 he returned to science fiction with an epic bestseller, *Battlefield Earth: A Saga of the Year 3000*, followed by a ten-volume series under the composite title *Mission Earth* (1985–87).

HUBBLE, Edwin Powell (1889–1953) American astronomer, born in Marshfield, Missouri. He was astronomer at the Mt Wilson Observatory at Pasadena, California (1919–48), and Mt Palomar (1948–53). He demonstrated that some nebulae are independent galaxies, and in 1929 he discovered 'red shift' and announced 'Hubble's constant' for the expansion of the universe, showing that the more distant the galaxy, the greater the speed with which it is receding.

HUBEL, David Hunter (1926–) Canadian-born American neurophysiologist, and joint winner of the 1981 Nobel prize for physiology or medicine. He studied medicine at McGill University in Montreal, then did research at Johns Hopkins (1954–59) and worked at Harvard from 1959. With **Torsten Wiesel** at Harvard Medical School he investigated the mechanics of visual perception at the cortical level, and shared the Nobel prize with him and **Roger Sperry**.

HUBER, Eugen (1849–1923) Swiss jurist, professor of law at Basel from 1880 and at Bern from 1892. He wrote *System und Geschichte des schweizerische Privatrechts* (1886–93) and other works on law, and was draftsman of the Swiss Civil Code which came into force in 1912.

HUBER, Ulricus (1636–94) Dutch jurist. Professor at Franeker, Utrecht and Leiden, and a judge in Friesland, he was author of *De jure civitatis* (1682), *Heedendaagse Rechtsgeleertheyt* (1686, translated as *Jurisprudence of My Time*, 1939), *Praelectiones juris civilis* (1687) and other works, many of which have been influential in South Africa.

HUBERT, St (656–727) Frankish prelate, son of the Duke of Guienne, and patron saint of hunting. He lived a luxurious life, but was converted to Christianity and in 708 became bishop of Liège. In art he is a hunter converted by the apparition of a crucifix between the horns of a stag. This story may have been borrowed from St Eustace. His festival is November 3.

HUC, Evariste Régis (1813–60) French missionary, born in Toulouse. In 1839 he joined the mission of the Lazarist Fathers to China. In 1844, with Père Gabet and a single native convert, he set out for Tibet, and in January 1846 reached Lhasa; but scarcely had they started a mission there when an order for their expulsion was obtained by the Chinese resident, and they were conveyed back to Canton. Huc's health having broken down, he returned to France in 1852. He wrote *Souvenirs d'un voyage dans la Tartarie, le Tibet et le Chine*.

HUC, Philippe See **DERÈME, Tristan**

HUCH, Ricarda (1864–1947) German novelist, historian and feminist, born in Brunswick into a wealthy Protestant merchant family. She studied history at Zürich, taught at a girls' school there, travelled extensively in Italy, married (unhappily) twice, and finally settled in Munich in 1910. A neo-romantic, she rejected naturalism, and wrote novels including the semi-autobiographical *Erinnerungen von Ludolf Ursleu dem Jüngeren* (1893) and *Aus der Triumphgasse* (1902), criticism including *Die Blütezeit, Ausbreitung und Verfall der Romantik* (1899–1902), and social and political works including *Der Grosse Krieg in Deutschland* (1912–14). She also wrote on religious themes, in *Luther's Glaube* (1915) and *Das Zeitalter der Glaubenspaltung* (1937). The first woman to be admitted to the Prussian Academy of Literature in 1931, she resigned in 1933 over the expulsion of Jewish writers. She lived in Jena in World War II.

HUDDLESTON, John (1608–98) English Benedictine monk, born in Faringdon Hall near Preston. In 1651 he aided **Charles II** in his escape from Worcester, and in 1685 he reconciled him on his deathbed to Catholicism.

HUDDLESTON, (Ernest Urban) Trevor (1913–) English Anglican missionary, educated at Christ Church, Oxford, and ordained in 1937. He entered the Community of the Resurrection and in 1943 went to Johannesburg, where he ultimately became provincial of the order (1949–55). From 1956 to 1958 he was novice-master of the Community in Mirfield Yorkshire, and from 1958 to 1960 prior of its London House. From 1960 to 1968 he was bishop of Masasi, Tanzania, then bishop suffragan of Stepney until 1978, and bishop of Mauritius and archbishop of the Indian Ocean (1978–83). He is distinguished by a passionate belief that the doctrine of the universal brotherhood of men in Christ should be universally applied. His book, *Naught for your Comfort* (1956), reflects this conviction in the light of his experiences in South Africa and its racial problems and policies. He also wrote *God's World* (1966) and *I Believe; Reflections on the Apostles' Creed*

HUDSON, George (1800–71) English 'Railway King', born near York. He was a linen-draper there, when, inheriting £30000 in 1828, he went into local politics and invested heavily in the North Midland Railway. He bought large estates, was thrice lord mayor of York, and was elected MP for Sunderland (1845). But the railway mania of 1847–48 plunged him into ruin. He was accused of having 'cooked' accounts, and of having paid dividends out of capital. Legal proceedings were instituted and his suddenly-acquired gains were swept away. Sunderland, however, continued to elect him until 1859.

HUDSON, Henry (c.1550–1611) English navigator, associated with the search for the North-West Passage. In April 1607 he set sail with eleven sailors in a small vessel, the *Hopewell*, on his first voyage for the English Muscovy Company to seek a north-east passage across the pole to China and the Far East. He reached Spitsbergen and (probably) Jan Mayen Island. On his second voyage (1608) he reached Novaya Zemlya. He undertook a third voyage in 1609 for the Dutch East India Company, on the *Half Moon*, heading northwest this time. He sailed for Davis Strait, then steered southwards and discovered the Hudson River, and ascended it for 150 miles, to Albany. In April 1610 he set out on his fourth voyage on the *Discovery* (70 tons) with a crew of 20 and his twelve-year-old son; he reached Greenland in June, arrived at Hudson Strait and entered the great bay which now bears his name. In November his ship was trapped in the ice in James Bay, on the south of Hudson Bay. During the winter he was accused of distributing the food unfairly, and when the ice began to break up, the men mutinied. On 23 June, Hudson and his son, with seven others, were cast adrift in an open boat, and never seen again. Of the 13 mutineers, eight eventually reached England, but all seem to have escaped punishment.

HUDSON, Manley Ottmer (1886–1960) American jurist, born in St Peters, Missouri. Educated at West Jewell College and Harvard, he became professor at Harvard. A member of the Permanent Court of Arbitration at The Hague (1933–45), and a judge of the Permanent Court of International Justice (1936–46), he became chairman of the International Law Commission. His works include *The Permanent Court of International Justice* (2nd ed 1943), and he edited many volumes of cases and legislation on international law, including the *American Journal of International Law* (1924–60).

HUDSON, 'Sir' Jeffery (1619–82) English dwarf, 3 feet 9 inches high, born a butcher's son in Oakham. He was court dwarf to Queen **Henrietta Maria**, and served as captain of horse at the start of the Civil War. He was imprisoned in 1679 as a Catholic over the 'Popish Plot'.

HUDSON, Thomas (1701–79) English portrait painter, born in London. He studied under Jonathan Richardson, whose daughter he married. Although a fashionable and accomplished (though undistinguished) artist, he is now best known as the teacher of Sir **Joshua Reynolds**. Hudson was the busiest portrait painter in London from c.1745 until 1755, when he retired, probably due to the competition provided by his former pupil.

HUDSON, William (1734–93) English botanist and apothecary, born in Kendal. He came to London to train as an apothecary, and from 1765 to 1771 was demonstrator at the Chelsea Physic Garden of the Apothecaries' Company; his *Flora Anglica* (1762) was the first British work to adopt the classification and binomial nomenclature of **Linnaeus** for British plants, and contained much original material.

HUDSON, Sir William (1896–1978) New Zealand-born hydro-electric engineer, born in Nelson, South Island. After service in World War I, he joined the Armstrong Whitworth company and worked for five years on hydro-electric schemes in New Zealand, then worked in Australia until 1930. Between 1931 and 1937 he was in charge of the Galloway hydro-electric scheme in Scotland before returning to Sydney, eventually to head the Metropolitan Water Board. In 1949 he was appointed commissioner of the Snowy Mountains Hydro-Electric Authority in southern New South Wales, one of the 'seven engineering wonders of the world'. This scheme involved the construction of 16 dams, seven power stations, and 150 kilometres of tunnels. That the project was completed ahead of time in 1973 was due to Hudson's leadership, although he had retired six years previously.

HUDSON, William Henry (1841–1922) American-born British author and naturalist, of Argentine extraction, born near Buenos Aires. He came to England in 1869 and became a British subject in 1900. His early writings concerned the natural history of South America, but he is best known for his delightful account of his rambles in the New Forest in *Hampshire Days* (1903) and his romantic novel *Green Mansions* (1904). His ornithological works include *Birds in London* (1898), *Birds of La Plata* (1920), *The Book of a Naturalist* (1919), and *Rare, vanishing and lost British Birds* (1923). A bird sanctuary, containing Sir **Jacob Epstein**'s 'Rima' sculpture, was erected to his memory in Hyde Park, London (1925).

HUEFFER, Francis (1845–89) German-born British music critic, son-in-law of **Ford Madox Brown**, born in Westphalia. He settled in London in 1869 and as music critic of *The Times* championed *Richard Wagner and the Music of the Future* (1874).

HUERTA, Vicente García de la (1730–87) Spanish poet and critic, born in Zafra. He was head of the Royal Library in Madrid. His famous tragedy of *Raquel* (1778) was based upon the story of Alfonso VIII's love for the beautiful Jewess, Rachel.

HUET, Pierre Daniel (1630–1721) French prelate and scholar, born in Caen. In 1652 he visited the court of Queen **Kristina** in Sweden, and discovered in Stockholm the manuscript of **Origen** which he edited (1668). In 1670 he was appointed with **Bossuet** tutor of the dauphin. Having in 1676 taken orders, he was successively Abbot of Aunay (1678), bishop of Soissons (1685) and Avranches (1692), and abbot of Fontenay (1699). In 1679 his *Demonstratio Evangelica* appeared. In 1701 he withdrew to the Jesuits' house in Paris. He also wrote a critique of Cartesian philosophy and *Faiblesse de l'esprit humain*.

HÜGEL, Baron Friedrich von (1852–1925) Austrian-born British theologian and biblical critic, born in Florence, son of the Austrian ambassador. He settled in England in 1871. The founder of the London Society for the Study of Religion (1905), he wrote *The Mystical Element in Religion* (1908–09), *Eternal Life* (1912) and *The Reality of God* (published posthumously in 1931).

HUGGINS, Charles Brenton (1901–) Canadian-born American surgeon, born in Halifax, Nova Scotia. He worked at Chicago University from 1927, where he became professor of surgery in 1936 and was head of the Ben May Laboratory for Cancer Research from 1951 to 1969. He shared the 1966 Nobel prize for physiology or medicine with **Francis Peyton Rous** for work on cancer research, notably his discovery of hormonal treatment for cancer of the prostate gland.

HUGGINS, Godfrey Martin, 1st Viscount Malvern of Rhodesia and Bexley (1883–1971) Rhodesian statesman. He practised medicine in London and in Rhodesia (1911–21) before entering politics in 1923, was premier of Southern Rhodesia (1933–53) and of the Federation of Rhodesia and Nyasaland (1953–56). He was created viscount in 1955.

HUGGINS, Sir William (1824–1910) English astronomer, born in London. For some years he studied physiology with the microscope. In 1855 he built an observatory near London, where he invented the stellar spectroscope and began the study of the physical constitution of stars, planets, comets and nebulae. By researches on the spectra of the sun and certain comets, he ascertained that their luminous properties are not the same. He determined the amount of heat that reaches the earth from some of the fixed stars. His wife, Margaret Lindsay, née Murray (1848–1915), shared his work.

HUGH, St, of Avalon, also called **St Hugh of Lincoln** (c.1135–1200) French-born English prelate, born of a noble family at Avalon in Burgundy. Priest at the Grande Chartreuse (1160–70), he was called to England by **Henry II** to found a Carthusian monastery at Witham, Somerset (1178). He became bishop of Lincoln (1186), where he fought against the savage forestry laws in the royal forests and defended the Jews against rioting mobs. He also began the rebuilding of Lincoln cathedral. He refused to pay taxes to finance French wars (money grant), and was canonized in 1220. His feast day is 17 November.

HUGH CAPET See **CAPET**

HUGHES, Arthur (1830–1915) English painter, born in London. He entered the Royal Academy Schools in 1847, and, by 1852, was associated with the Pre-Raphaelite Brotherhood and its principal members **W H Hunt**, **J E Millais** and **D G Rossetti**. Although he never formally joined the Brotherhood, he produced several paintings during the 1850s that rank as some of the finest of works executed in its typically precise and richly coloured style. He also, from c.1855, pursued a successful career as an illustrator of the works of, amongst others, Alexander Munro and **Christina Rossetti**. He visited Italy in 1862 but, in later life, lived a reclusive life and exhibited for the last time at the Academy in 1908.

HUGHES, Charles Evans (1862–1948) American jurist and politician, born in Glens Falls, New York. Admitted to the bar in 1884, he became governor of New York (1907–10) and an associate justice, US Supreme Court (1910). He ran against **Woodrow Wilson** as Republican candidate for the presidency in 1916, became secretary of state (1921–25) in the **Warren Harding** administration, and was appointed chief justice (1930–41). He presided at the Washington Arms Limitation Conference (1921–25) and was a judge of the Permanent Court of International Justice, 1928–30. He wrote also *The Supreme Court of the United States* (1928).

HUGHES, David Edward (1831–1900) English inventor, born in London. He was brought up in Virginia and became professor of music at Bardston College, Kentucky (1850–53). In 1855 he invented a telegraph typewriter which was widely adopted, and in 1878 a microphone and an induction balance. He left a large fortune to London hospitals.

HUGHES, Howard Robard (1905–76) American millionaire businessman, film producer and director, and aviator, born in Houston, Texas. He inherited his father's oil-drilling equipment company at the age of eighteen, and two years later in 1926 began to involve himself and his profits in Hollywood films. During the next six years he made several films, including *Hell's Angels* (1930) and *Scarface* (1932). Already known as an eccentric, he suddenly left Hollywood in 1932, and, after working for a short while as a pilot under an assumed name, turned his entire attention to designing, building and flying aircraft. Between 1935 and 1938 he broke most of the world's air speed records, was awarded a congressional medal from Washington, and then abruptly returned to filmmaking, producing and directing his most controversial film, *The Outlaw* (1943), starring Jane Russell. He continued his involvement in aviation by designing and building the Hercules, an oversized wooden sea-plane that was completed in 1947, flew only once, but yielded valuable technical knowledge to the aviation industry. After severe injuries sustained in an air-crash in 1946 his eccentricity increased, and he eventually became a recluse, from 1966 living in complete seclusion while still controlling his vast business interests from sealed-off hotel suites, and giving rise to endless rumour and speculation. In 1971 an 'authorized' biography was announced, but the authors were imprisoned for fraud, and the mystery surrounding him continued until his death.

HUGHES, Hugh Price (1847–1902) Welsh Wesleyan minister, born in Carmarthen. He founded the *Methodist Times* (1885), and in 1886 he was chosen to pioneer the West London mission. In his preaching he combined methodism and socialism, and turned public opinion against **Parnell**.

HUGHES, (James Mercer) Langston (1902–67) American poet, short-story writer and dramatist, born in Joplin, Missouri, and educated at Lincoln University, Pennsylvannia. Throughout the 1920s he was a leading figure in the black renaissance, but his influence was belatedly recognized. *Weary Blues* (1926) was his first of several collections of verse, culminating in *Selected Poems* (1959). His memorable character, 'Jesse B Simple', first made his entrance in racy newspaper sketches and thereafter in several volumes before the publication in 1957 of *The Best of Simple*. His lyrical verse, resonant of his vast knowledge of folk culture, jazz, the blues and colloquial speech, was highly popular and made him famous, but critics were slow to take him seriously. *The Big Sea* (1940) and *I Wonder as I Wander* (1956) are autobiographical.

HUGHES, Richard Arthur Warren (1900–76) English novelist, born in Weybridge, Surrey, of Welsh descent. He was educated at Charterhouse and Oriel College, Oxford. He wrote poetry and plays from an early age, co-founded and directed the Portmadoc (Caernarvonshire) Players (1922–25), wrote a one-act play, *The Sister's Tragedy* (1922), and a volume of verse, *Gypsy Night and Other Poems*, in the same year, followed by *Confessio Juvenis* (1925). He travelled widely in Europe, America and the West Indies, and eventually settled in Wales. He is best known for *A High Wind in Jamacia* (1929, entitled *The Innocent Voyage* in the USA), a superior adventure yarn about a family of children captured by pirates while sailing to England. In *Hazard: A Sea Story* (1938) he also drew on his experience of the sea. Of his later work, *The Fox in the Attic* (1961), and *The Wooden Shepherdess* (1972), the first of an unfinished series covering the period from World War I to the rise of the Nazis and their aftermath, were significant.

HUGHES, Ted (Edward James) (1930–) English poet, born in Mytholmroyd, a mill town in West Yorkshire. When he was seven his family moved to Mexborough, Yorkshire, where his parents opened a stationery and tobacco shop. At the local grammar school he began to write poetry—bloodcurdling verses about Zulus and cowboys. He won a scholarship to Pembroke College, Cambridge, where he opted for English literature, but switched to archaeology and anthropology, which was to have a profound effect on his poetry. After graduating he had a number of colourful jobs—zookeeper, gardener, nightwatchman—and occasionally published poems in university poetry magazines. He married the American writer **Sylvia Plath** in 1956 and they settled in Cambridge where Hughes taught while Plath studied. That same year he won an American poetry competition, judged by **W H Auden**, Sir **Stephen Spender** and **Marianne Moore**, with the poems that were to form *The Hawk in the Rain* (1957). For the next few years he lived in America where he taught and was supported by a Guggenheim Foundation grant. *Lupercal* (1960), his second collection, won the Somerset Maugham Award and the Hawthornden prize. In 1963 Sylvia Plath committed suicide and for the next few years no new book of adult verse emerged, though he did complete books of prose and poetry for children. *Wodwo* (1967) was his next major work, and in 1970 came *Crow*, an evocation of a mythical, symbolic bird and witness to the history of man and his destruction. Among later volumes are *Cave Birds* (1975), *Season Songs* (1976), *Gaudete* (1977), *Moortown* (1979) and *The Remains of*

Elmet (1979), on which he collaborated with the photographer **Fay Godwin**. Of his books for children, the most remarkable is *The Iron Man* (1968). Drawn magnetically towards the primitive, he is a writer at one with nature, mesmerised by its beauty but not blind to its cruelty and violence. Much acclaimed and imitated, he was appointed poet laureate in 1984.

HUGHES, Thomas (1822–96) English reformer and novelist, born in Uffington, Berkshire. He was educated at Rugby and Oriel College, Oxford, was called to the bar in 1848, and became a county court judge in 1882. He was Liberal MP (1865–74) and closely associated with **John Frederick Denison Maurice** and the Christian Socialists, supported trade unionism and helped to found the Working Men's College, of which he was principal from 1872 to 1883, and a model settlement in Tennessee, USA. He is primarily remembered as the author of the semi-autobiographical public school classic, *Tom Brown's Schooldays* (1856), based on his school experiences at Rugby under the headmastership of Dr **Thomas Arnold**. The sequel, *Tom Brown at Oxford* (1861), was less successful. He also wrote a number of biographies and social studies.

HUGHES, William Morris (1864–1952) Welsh-born Australian statesman, born in Llandudno, Wales. He went to Australia (1884), entered New South Wales and Commonwealth parliaments, and in 1915–23 was federal prime minister and attorney-general in Labour and Coalition governments, founding the United Australian party in the early 1930s.

HUGO, Victor Marie (1802–85) French poet and author, and leader of the French Romantic movement, born in Besançon, the son of a general. He was educated in Paris at the Feuillantines, in Madrid, and at the École Polytechnique. At the age of 14 he produced a tragedy; and at 20, when he published his first set of *Odes et Ballades* (1822), he had been victor three times at the Floral Games of Toulouse. In 1823 he published *Han d'Islande*, a wild romance of an impossible Iceland; and followed it with *Bug-Jargal* (1824), a second set of *Odes et ballades* (1826), and *Cromwell* (1827), whose preface set out Hugo's poetical creed. In 1828 his *Orientales* revealed him as a master of rhythms. In 1830 came *Hernani*—the first of those 'five-act lyrics' of which Hugo's drama is composed. In 1831 he produced one of his best-known novels, *Notre Dame de Paris*, an outstanding historical romance, and *Les Feuilles d'automne*, which includes some of his best poetry and his best play, *Marion Delorme*. *Le Roi s'amuse* (1832), which was banned, is superbly written, and as *Rigoletto* has become universally popular. *Lucrèce Borgia* and *Marie Tudor* followed in 1832. In 1834 came *Claude Gueux*, which is pure humanitarian sentimentalism, and the *Littérature et philosophie mêlées*, a collection of his youthful writings in prose. In 1835 came *Angelo*, a third melodrama in prose, and the admirable *Chants du crépuscule*, and in 1836 the opera of *La Esmeralda*. In 1837 *Les Voix intérieures* appeared, in which the poet's diction is held by some to have found its noblest expression, and in 1838 *Ruy Blas*, after *Hernani* the most famous of his dramatic works. In 1840 *Les Rayons et les ombres*, yet another collection of sonorous verse, came out. He failed at the Théâtre Français in 1843 with the ponderous trilogy of *Les Burgraves*. During the 1840s he became involved with republican politics, and was elected to the Constituent Assembly in 1848. After the *coup d'état* he was exiled by **Napoleon III**, and went to Guernsey in the Channel Islands (1851–70) where he issued his satirical *Napoléon le petit* (1852). His next book of poetry, *Les Châtiments* (1853), was followed by *Les Contemplations*, the best of his earlier poems, and perhaps his greatest poetic achievement, the *Légende des siècles* (1859). His greatest novel, *Les Misérables*, a panoramic piece of social history, came out in 1862. This was followed by the extraordinary rhapsody called *William Shakespeare* (1864), *Les Chansons des rues et des bois* (1865), the novel *Les Travailleurs de la mer*, an idyll of passion, adventure and self-sacrifice, set in Guernsey (1866), and *L'Homme qui rit* (1869), a piece of fiction meant to be historical. He returned from Guernsey to Paris in 1870, and stayed through the Commune, but then departed for Brussels, protesting publicly against the action of the Belgian government in respect of the beaten Communists, in consequence of which he was again expelled. In 1872 he published *L'Année terrible*, a series of pictures of the war, and in 1874 his last romance in prose appeared, *Quatre-vingt-treize*. In 1876 he was made a senator, and published the second part of the *Légende*. *L'Histoire d'un crime* (1877) has been described as 'the apotheosis of the Special Correspondent', and *L'Art d'être grand-père* (1877) contains much charming verse. His declining years produced *Le Pape* (a piece humanitarian, anticlerical, and above all theatrical), *La Pitié suprême*, *L'Âne* (1880), *Les Quatre Vents de l'esprit* (1881), and *Torquemada* (1882). He was buried in the Panthéon.

HULL, Cordell (1871–1955) American statesman, born in Overton, Tennessee. He was educated at Cumberland University, Tennessee. Under **Franklin Roosevelt**, he became secretary of state in 1933 and served for the longest term in that office until he retired in 1944, having attended most of the great wartime conferences. He was a strong advocate of maximum aid to the Allies. One of the architects of 'bipartisanship', he received the Nobel peace prize in 1944.

HULL, Isaac (1773–1843) American naval officer, born in Derby, Connecticut, the nephew of **William Hull**. He entered the navy in 1798 after commanding a ship in the West Indian trade. He served in the war against Tripoli (1803–04), and in 1806 he was appointed to the *Constitution* frigate, popularly known as 'Old Ironsides'. In 1812 he captured the British frigate *Guerrière*. He afterwards commanded Mediterranean and Pacific squadrons.

HULL, William (1753–1825) American soldier, born in Derby, Connecticut. He fought in the American War of Independence (1775–83), and was governor of Michigan territory (1805–12). In the war with Britain (1812) he was sent with 1500 men to defend Detroit, was compelled to surrender, and was afterwards court-martialled for cowardice and sentenced to be shot—a sentence not carried out.

HULLAH, John Pyke (1812–84) English composer and music teacher, born in Worcester. In 1836 he composed *The Village Coquettes* to **Charles Dickens**' libretto; in 1841 he began popular singing classes in Exeter Hall; and from 1872 to 1882 was musical inspector of training schools. He opposed the 'Tonic Sol-fa' method. Among his works are a *History of Modern Music* (1862). Of his songs, 'The Three Fishers' and 'The Storm' achieved wide popularity.

HULME, Thomas Ernest (1883–1917) English critic, poet and philosopher, born in Endon, Staffordshire. Educated at Newcastle-under-Lyme High School, he was sent down from St John's College, Cambridge, for brawling, and after a stay in Canada he taught in Brussels and developed an interest in philosophy. He joined **Pound**, **Wyndham Lewis** and **Epstein** as a champion of modern abstract art, of the poetic movement known as 'Imagism' and of the anti-liberal political writings of **Georges Sorel**, which he translated. Killed in action in France, he left a massive collection of notes, edited under the titles *Speculation* (1924) and *More Specu-*

lation (1956), which expose philistinism and attack what he considered to be weak and outworn liberalism.

HULSE, John (1708–90) English clergyman, born in Middlewich. He studied at St John's, Cambridge, took orders, and bequeathed his property to found the Hulsean divinity professorship and lectures at Cambridge.

HULTON, Sir Edward George Warris (1906–88) English magazine proprietor and journalist, born in Harrogate. He was educated at Harrow and Brasenose College, Oxford, and was called to the bar, Inner Temple. He succeeded to his father's newspaper interests and became chairman of Hulton Press Ltd. He was founder of *Picture Post*, a brilliant experiment in journalism which ceased in 1957.

HUMBOLDT, (Friedrich Heinrich) Alexander, Baron von (1769–1859) German naturalist and traveller, brother of **Karl Wilhelm von Humboldt**, born in Berlin. He studied at Frankfurt-an-der-Oder, Berlin, Göttingen, and under **Abraham Werner** in the Mining Academy at Freiberg, where he published *Flora Subterranea Fribergensis* (1793). He then held a post in the mining department in Upper Franconia, and produced a work on muscular irritability (1799). For five years (1799–1804) he and **Aimé Bonpland** explored unknown territory in South America, which led to his monumental *Voyage de Humboldt et Bonpland aux Regions Equinoxiales* (23 vols, 1805–34). In Paris he made, with **Joseph Louis Gay-Lussac**, experiments on the chemical constitution of the atmosphere; and in 1807, after a visit to Italy, he came back to Paris with Prince Wilhelm of Prussia on a political mission, and remained in France till 1827. In 1829, he explored Central Asia with **Christian Ehrenberg** and Gustav Rose (1798–1873), the mineralogist, and their examination of the strata which produce gold and platinum, magnetic obeservations, and geological and botanical collections are described in a work by Rose (1837–42) and in Humboldt's *Asie Centrale* (1843). The political changes of the year 1830 led to his employment in political services; and during the ensuing twelve years he was frequently in Paris, where he published his *Géographie du nouveau continent* (1835–38). His work of popular science, *Kosmos* (1845–62), endeavoured to provide a comprehensive physical picture of the universe.

HUMBOLDT, Karl Wilhelm von (1767–1835) German statesman and philologist, elder brother of **Alexander von Humboldt**, born in Potsdam. After travelling in Europe, he became a diplomat, but without official employment. In 1791 he married, and for some years lived in retirement, associating with **Schiller** and devoting himself to literature. In 1801 he became Prussian minister at Rome, and was a most generous patron of young artists and men of science. He returned to Prussia (1808) to fill the post of first minister of education, and founded the Friedrich Wilhelm (now Humboldt) University of Berlin. In 1810 he went to Vienna as minister-plenipotentiary, and to London in 1817. He was the first to study the Basque language scientifically, and also worked on the languages of the east and of the South Sea Islands.

HUME, Allan Octavian (1829–1912) Scottish colonialist and naturalist, son of **Joseph Hume**. Educated at Haileybury Training College, he studied medicine at University College Hospital in London and joined the Bengal Civil Service in 1849. He became commissioner of customs for the North West Provinces, and director-general of agriculture. He built a huge library and museum for his vast collection of Asiatic birds at Simla, and in 1872 founded a quarterly journal on Indian ornithology. He retired in 1882, but in 1883 the manuscript of his projected book on Indian birds was stolen and sold as waste paper. In despair he presented his whole collection to the British Museum. In 1885 he was founder and first secretary (until 1908) of the first National Congress in Bombay. Hume's Tawny Owl, Lesser Whitethroat and Wheatear are named after him.

HUME, (George) Basil (1923–) English Benedictine monk and cardinal, born in Newcastle-upon-Tyne. Educated at Ampleforth College, St Benet's Hall, Oxford, and Fribourg University, Switzerland, he was ordained a priest in 1950, and returned to Ampleforth College as senior modern language master two years later. From 1957 to 1963 he was magister scholarum of the English Benedictine Congregation, and in 1963 became abbot of Ampleforth, where he remained until created archbishop of Westminster and a cardinal in 1976. He published *Searching for God* (1977), *In Praise of Benedict* (1981) and *To Be a Pilgrim* (1984).

HUME, David (1711–76) Scottish philosopher and historian, born in Edinburgh. His early years were unsettled: he studied but did not graduate at Edinburgh University; he took up law, but suffered from bouts of depression, and tried his hand instead at commerce as a counting-house clerk in Bristol. In 1734 he went to La Flèche in Anjou where he stayed for three years studying and working on his first and most important work, *A Treatise of Human Nature*, which he had published anonymously in London (1739–40) when he had returned to Scotland to stay on the family estate at Ninewells in Berwickshire (1739–45). The subtitle is 'an attempt to introduce the experimental method of reasoning into moral subjects' and the book is in many ways the culmination of the empiricist tradition from **John Locke** and **George Berkeley**, with major, and still influential, discussions of perception, causation, personal identity and what became known as 'the naturalistic fallacy' in ethics. In political theory he argued for the 'artificiality' of the principles of justice and political obligation, and challenged the rationalistic 'natural law' and 'social contract' theories of **Thomas Hobbes**, **Richard Hooker**, Locke and **Rousseau**. Hume was bitterly disappointed at the initial reception of the *Treatise* ('it fell dead-born from the press') and put out the more popular *Essays Moral and Political* (1741, 1742), which were immediately successful and helped gratify his literary ambitions. His efforts to secure an independent income still proceeded by fits and starts: his atheism doomed his applications for the professorships of moral philosophy at Edinburgh (1744) and logic at Glasgow (1751); he became tutor for a year in 1745 to an insane nobleman, the Marquis of Annandale, then became secretary to General St Clair on an expedition to France in 1746 and secret missions to Vienna and Turin in 1748. In 1748 he published a simplified version of the *Treatise* entitled *Enquiry concerning Human Understanding*, its translation was said to wake **Immanuel Kant** from his 'dogmatic slumbers' and provoked the Idealists to counter Hume's scepticism. The brilliant *Dialogues concerning Natural Religion* were written in 1750 but were prudently left unpublished until 1759. He became keeper of the Advocates' Library in Edinburgh in 1752 and achieved real fame and recognition with his *Political Discourses* (1752) and his monumental *History of England* in five volumes (1754–62). From 1763 to 1765 he acted as secretary to the ambassador in Paris, and was received with great enthusiasm by the French court and literary society ('Here I feed on ambrosia, drink nothing but nectar, breathe incense only, and walk on flowers'). He returned to London in 1766 with

Rousseau, whom he had befriended but who was to provoke a bitter and famous quarrel with him, became under-secretary of state for the Northern Department in 1767, returning finally to Scotland in 1768 to settle in Edinburgh where he died and was widely mourned, the equal in intellectual reputation to his contemporary **Adam Smith**. He has been a dominant influence on empiricist philosophers of the twentieth century.

HUME, David (1757–1838) Scottish jurist, nephew of **David Hume** the philosopher, born in Ninewells, Berwickshire. Educated at Edinburgh High School, and Edinburgh and Glasgow Universities, he was professor of Scots law at Edinburgh (1786–1822), and baron of the Scottish Court of Exchequer (1822–34). He wrote the classic text on Scottish criminal law, *Commentaries on the Law of Scotland respecting the Description and Punishment of Crimes* (2 vols, 1797), and *Commentaries on the Law of Scotland respecting the Trial for Crimes* (2 vols, 1800) later combined into one work. These were based on exhaustive investigation of court records. His *Lectures on Scots Law*, published posthumously, are also highly regarded.

HUME, David of Godscroft (c.1560–c.1630) Scottish genealogist, born in Dunbar, the historian of the **Douglas** family. He probably studied at St Andrews, Paris and Geneva, before returning to Scotland to become secretary to the Douglases. At the time of the Union of crowns between England and Scotland he wrote *De unione insulae Britanniae* (1605); but his main work, the eulogistic *Origin and Descent of the Family of Douglas*, was published posthumously in 1633, and extended as *History of the House and Race of Douglas and Angus* in 1644. In rural retirement at Godscroft, in Berwickshire, he turned his hand to writing Latin verses in the style of **Ovid**.

HUME, Fergus (1859–1932) English writer. Brought up in Dunedin, New Zealand, he was called to the New Zealand bar and practised as a lawyer. He was a pioneer of the detective story in *The Mystery of a Hansom Cab* (1887), and returned to England in 1888, where he published other detective novels including *The Bishop's Secret* (1900) and *The Caravan Mystery* (1926).

HUME, Hamilton (1797–1873) Australian explorer, born in Parramatta, New South Wales. At the age of 17 he made the first of many expeditions, and in the next eight years explored the Goulburn and Yass plains and Lake Bathurst in southern New South Wales, reached the Clyde river, and received grants of land as reward. In 1824 he was encouraged by Governor **Brisbane** to find an overland passage from Lake George to the southern sea. The expedition followed the route to Western Port, which proved horrendously difficult, but following this course they discovered part of the Murray river, and made the first sighting of Australia's highest mountain, Mount Kosciusko. That the party ended up on the wrong side of Port Phillip Bay, instead of the intended objective, later provoked a pamphlet war between Hume and his navigator which continued for many years. In 1828 Hume joined **Charles Sturt**'s expedition which discovered the Darling river, but poor health prevented his continuing, and he settled down to farm his land grants near Yass.

HUME, John (1937–) Northern Ireland politician, born in Londonderry. Educated at the National University of Ireland, he was a founder member of the Credit Union party, which was a forerunner to the Social Democratic Labour party (SDLP). He sat in the Northern Ireland parliament (1969 –72) and the Northern Ireland assembly (1972–73) and became widely respected as a moderate, non-violent member of the Catholic community. He became SDLP leader in 1979 and in the same year was elected to the European parliament. He has represented Foyle in the House of Commons since 1983.

HUME, Joseph (1777–1855) Scottish radical politician, born in Montrose. He studied medicine at Edinburgh, and in 1797 became assistant surgeon under the East India Company. He acquired several native languages, and in the Mahratta war (1802–07) filled important offices. On the conclusion of peace he returned to England (1808), his fortune made. A political philosopher of the school of **James Mill** and **Jeremy Bentham**, he sat in parliament (1812, 1819–55). He advocated savings banks, freedom of trade with India, abolition of flogging in the army, of naval impressment and of imprisonment for debt, repeal of the act prohibiting export of machinery, and many other reforms. He denounced the Orange lodges' design to make the Duke of Cumberland king on the death of **William IV**.

HUME, Sir Patrick (1641–1724) Scottish statesman and Covenanter, Lord Chancellor of Scotland. In 1690 he was created Lord Polwarth, and in 1679 Earl of Marchmont . He was the father of Lady **Grizel Baillie**.

HUMMEL, Johann Nepomuk (1778–1837) Austrian pianist and composer, born in Pressburg. He was taught by his father, the director of the School of Military Music at Pressburg, and when the family moved to Vienna his playing impressed **Mozart**, who gave him lessons. He began playing in public in 1787, and after a tour of Germany, Denmark, Britain and Holland he studied composition under **Johann Albrechtsberger** and also received instruction from **Haydn**, **Salieri** and **Clementi**. In 1804 he became kapellmeister to Prince Esterházy, Haydn's former master, and later held similar appointments at Stuttgart (1816) and Weimar (1819–37). He wrote several ballets and operas, but was best known for his piano and chamber works, and wrote a manual of piano technique (1828) which had considerable influence.

HUMPERDINCK, Engelbert (1854–1921) German composer, born in Siegburg near Bonn. He studied music at Cologne, Frankfurt, Munich and Berlin, and travelled in France, Spain and Italy. He taught at Barcelona, Cologne, Frankfurt and Berlin, and became famous as the composer of the musical fairy play, *Hänsel und Gretel* (1893), which was phenomenally successful. *Schneewittchen, Königskinder* (opera, 1910), *The Miracle* (pantomime, 1912) and others followed.

HUMPHREY, Doris (1895–1958) American dancer, choreographer, teacher and one of the founders of modern dance, born in Oak Park, Illinois. She started dancing at the age of eight, and in 1913 began a career as a teacher of ballroom dancing in Chicago. From 1917 to 1927 she was with the Denishawn Company as a dancer, beginning to choreograph in 1920 with *Tragica*. With her partner **Charles Weidman**, also ex-Denishawn, she founded her own company in 1928, which thrived in New York City until the early 1940s. She originated the Juilliard Dance Theatre (1935), and ran the Bennington College Summer School of Dance (1934–42). She choreographed highly original work including *The Shakers* (1931), the trilogy *New Dance* (1935), *Theatre Piece* (1935) and *With My Red Fires* (1936), building the foundations for the future vocabulary and philosophy of modern dance. Disabled by arthritis, she gave up dancing in 1944 but choreographed for the company set up by one of her most talented students, **José Limón**. She was artistic director of the Limón company from 1946 to 1958. She left a legacy rivalled only by her contemporary **Martha Graham** in its influence on modern dance. She wrote *The Art of Making Dances* (1959).

HUMPHREY, Duke See **GLOUCESTER**

HUMPHREY, Hubert Horatio (1911–78) American politician, born in Wallace, South Dakota. Educated at Minnesota and Louisiana Universities, he entered politics as mayor of Minneapolis in 1945, being elected as Democratic senator in 1948. He built up a strong reputation as a liberal, particularly on the civil rights issue, but, as vice-president from 1964 under the **Lyndon B Johnson** administration, alienated many former supporters by his apparent support of the increasingly-unpopular policy of continuation of the war in Vietnam. Although he won the Democratic presidential nomination in 1968 at the first ballot, a substantial minority of Democrats opposed his choice, and the general mood of disillusion with Democratic policies and a compromise candidate led to **Nixon**'s election victory.

HUMPHREYS, Cecil Frances See **ALEXANDER**

HUMPHREYS, Emyr (1919–) Welsh novelist, poet and dramatist, born in Prestatyn, Clwyd, and educated at University College, Aberystwyth, where he read history, learned Welsh and became a nationalist. He has worked as a teacher and a BBC Wales drama producer. The author of 16 novels, he won the Somerset Maugham Award for *Hear and Forgive* (1952), and the Hawthornden prize for *A Toy Epic* (1958). He has also published a collection of short stories and four volumes of verse.

HUMPHRIES, (John) Barry (1934–) Australian comic performer and writer, and creator of 'Dame Edna Everage', born in Camberwell, Melbourne. A student at Melbourne University, he made his theatrical début at the Union Theatre, Melbourne (1953–54), and also appeared with the Phillip Street Revue (1956). In Britain from 1959, he made his London début in *The Demon Barber* (1959) and subsequently appeared in *Oliver!* (1960, 1963 and 1968). He created the Barry MacKenzie comic strip in *Private Eye* (1964–73). His many stage shows include *A Nice Night's Entertainment* (1962), *A Load of Olde Stuffe* (1971), *An Evening's Intercourse with the Widely Liked Barry Humphries* (1981–82) and *Back With a Vengeance* (1987–89). His characters, including the repellent cultural attaché Sir Les Patterson and the acid-tongued superstar housewife Dame Edna Everage, have been frequent visitors to television screens and *The Dame Edna Experience* (1987–89) was a particularly popular celebrity chat show. His films include *Bedazzled!* (1967), *Barry MacKenzie Holds His Own* (1975), a rare dramatic role in *The Getting of Wisdom* (1977), and *Les Patterson Saves the World* (1987). His many humorous books include *Treasury of Australian Kitsch* (1980) and *The Traveller's Tool* (1985).

HUNT, Henry, called **'Orator Hunt'** (1773–1835) English radical, born in Upavon, Wiltshire. He became a well-to-do farmer, but in 1800 his quick temper brought him six weeks in jail. He came out a hot radical, and spent the rest of his life advocating the repeal of the corn-laws and parliamentary reform. In 1819 he presided over the demonstration that ended in the Peterloo Massacre, and delivered a speech which cost him three years' imprisonment (1820–23). He was subsequently MP for Preston (1831–33).

HUNT, (William) Holman (1827–1910) English painter, born in London. In 1845 he was admitted a student of the Royal Academy. He shared a studio with **Dante Gabriel Rossetti**, and the pair, along with **Millais** and a few others, inaugurated the 'Pre-Raphaelite Brotherhood', which aimed at detailed and uncompromising truth to nature. The first of his Pre-Raphaelite works was *Rienze* (1849); others which followed include *The Hireling Shepherd* (1852), *Claudio and Isabella* (1853), *Strayed Sheep* (1853) and *The Light of the World* (1854, now in Keble College, Oxford). The result of several visits to the East appeared in *The Scapegoat* (1856) and *The Finding of Christ in the Temple* (1860). Among the world-famous canvases are *Isabella and the Pot of Basil* (1867), *May Day, Magdalen Tower* (1891) and *The Lady of Shalott*. His *Pre-Raphaelitism and the Pre-Raphaelite Brotherhood* (1905) is a valuable record of the movement.

HUNT, (Henry Cecil) John, Baron Hunt of Lanfair Waterdine (1910–) English mountaineer and social reformer. He was educated at Marlborough and Sandhurst. After a distinguished military career in India and Europe, he led the first successful expedition to climb Mount Everest (see Sir **Edmund Hillary**), and was knighted. He has since been involved in mountaineering expeditions in western europe, the middle east, Himalayas, Caucasus, Greenland, Russia, Greece and Poland. From its inception in 1956, he was director of the Duke of **Edinburgh**'s Award Scheme and was created a life peer for services to youth on his retirement in 1966. He then became Chairman of the Parole Board of England and Wales (1967–1974) and the National Association of Probation Officers (1974–1980). He became a Knight of the Garter in 1979.

HUNT, (James Henry) Leigh (1784–1859) English poet and essayist, born in Southgate, Middlesex, the son of an immigrant US preacher. Educated at Christ's Hospital, his first collection of poetry was privately printed as *Juvenilia* in 1801. With his brother, a printer, he edited, from 1808 to 1821, *The Examiner*, which became a focus of liberal opinion and so attracted leading men of letters, including **Byron**, **Moore**, **Shelley** and **Lamb**. He was imprisoned with his brother for two years (1813–15) for a libel on the Prince Regent. *The Examiner*, however, was more a literary and social than a political forum. It introduced Shelley and **Keats** to the public—Keats' sonnet *On First Looking into Chapman's Homer* first appeared there in 1816, the year in which Hunt issued his own romance, *The Story of Rimini*. He founded and edited *The Indicator* (1819–21). In 1822 he joined Shelley in Italy with his wife and seven children to found a new quarterly, *The Liberal*. Shelley's tragic death by drowning that year forced Hunt to accept the hospitality of Lord Byron at his palace in Pisa. The association with Byron was unhappy and *The Liberal* (1822–23) was short-lived. After Byron's death in 1824, Hunt returned to England in 1825 to carry on a busy life of literary journalism, liberal politics and poetry. His house at Hampstead attracted all that was notable in the literary world, not without envy or ridicule, however, as **Dickens**' caricature of him as Harold Skimpole in *Bleak House* shows. His importance is less in his works, poetic or critical, than in his being one of those invaluable people who introduce authors to each other, but his *Examiner* is not to be dismissed, and his autobiography is a valuable picture of the times.

HUNT, William Henry (1790–1864) English painter, born in London, a creator of the English school of watercolour painting. The son of a tinplate worker, he was ranked by **Ruskin** with the greatest colourists of the school. He chose very simple subjects, like *Peaches and Grapes*, *Old Pollard* and *Wild Flowers*.

HUNTER, Evan, originally **Salvatore A Lambino** (1926–) American novelist, born in New York City. Writing under the name 'Ed McBain', he is renowned for his '87th Precinct' thrillers. He was educated in New York, served in the US navy and taught before concentrating on his career as a novelist. As Evan Hunter he is best known for *The Blackboard Jungle*

(1954), about a young teacher in an inner city high school confronted with recalcitrant students and sundry social problems. It was acclaimed for its realism and topicality.

HUNTER, John (1728–93) Scottish physiologist and surgeon, born in Long Calderwood, East Kilbride, the 'founder of scientific surgery,' and brother of **William Hunter**. His father was a younger son of the ancient house of Hunterston, in Ayrshire. He worked as assistant in the dissecting room to his brother (1748–59), studied surgery at Chelsea Hospital and St Bartholomew's, and in 1754 entered St George's Hospital, becoming house-surgeon in 1756 and lecturer for his brother in the anatomical school. In 1760 he entered the army as staff-surgeon, and served in the expedition to Belleisle and Portugal. At the peace in 1763 he started the practice of surgery in London, and devoted much time and money to comparative anatomy. One of his pupils was **Edward Jenner**. In 1768 he was appointed surgeon at St George's Hospital, in 1776 surgeon-extraordinary to King **George III**, and in 1790 surgeon-general to the army. In 1785 he built his museum, with lecture-rooms, and performed his first artery ligature for the cure of aneurysm. His collection, containing 10 563 specimens, was bought by the government in 1795 and presented to the Royal College of Surgeons, but was destroyed in an air raid in World War II. His *Natural History of Human Teeth* (1771–78) revolutionized dentistry. He investigated a large number of subjects, from venereal disease and embryology to blood, inflammation and gunshot wounds. He married in 1771 Anne Home (1742–1821), author of 'My mother bids me bind my hair' and other songs set to music by **Haydn**. He was buried in the church of St Martin-in-the-Fields, and transferred to Westminster Abbey in 1859.

HUNTER, John (1737–1821) Scottish naval captain and administrator, born in Leith. He studied for the ministry at Aberdeen University, but left at the age of 17 to join the navy. In 1786 he was appointed second captain on the *Sirius*, flagship of the first fleet, which was to sail for Australia under the command of Captain **Arthur Phillip**. Hunter arrived in New South Wales in 1788, and then sailed round the Horn to Cape Town for desperately needed supplies. He continued eastward, eventually circumnavigating the globe, and on return to Sydney set off for Norfolk Island, where the ship was wrecked and the crew were marooned for eleven months. In 1792 he returned to England, but went back to New South Wales as its second governor in 1795. Here he found the military had effectively taken over the running of the colony, and Hunter had great difficulty in restoring civil government, making such powerful enemies that he was recalled to London in 1800. During his governorship he greatly encouraged the exploratory voyages of **George Bass** and **Matthew Flinders**, and as a keen natural scientist he promoted many valuable expeditions in search of botanical and zoological specimens.

HUNTER, William (1718–83) Scottish anatomist and obstetrician, brother of **John Hunter**, born in Long Calderwood, East Kilbride. He studied divinity for five years at Glasgow University, but in 1737 took up medicine with **William Cullen**, and was trained in anatomy at St George's Hospital in London. From about 1748 he confined his practice to midwifery; in 1764 was appointed physician-extraordinary to Queen **Charlotte Sophia**; and in 1768 became the first professor of anatomy to the Royal Academy. In 1770 he built a house with an amphitheatre for lectures, a dissecting-room, a museum, and a cabinet of medals and coins. His Hunterian museum was bequeathed finally, with an endowment of £8000, to Glasgow University. His chief work was on the uterus.

HUNTER, Sir William Wilson (1840–1900) Scottish statistician, born in Glasgow. He studied there, at Paris and Bonn, and in 1862 entered the civil service of India. His post as superintendent of public instruction in Orissa (1866–69) gave him the opportunity to write the *Annals of Rural Bengal* (1868) and *A Comparative Dictionary of the Non-Aryan Languages of India* (1868). Then, after being secretary to the Bengal government and the government of India, he in 1871 became director-general of the statistical department of India; the Indian census of 1872 was his first work. In 1887 he retired and returned home to write books mostly on Indian subjects.

HUNTINGDON, Selina, née **Shirley, Countess of** (1707–91) English Methodist leader, the daughter of Earl Ferrers. In 1728 she married the Earl of Huntingdon (d.1746). Joining the Methodists in 1739, she made **George Whitefield** her chaplain in 1748, and assumed a leadership among his followers, who became known as 'The Countess of Huntingdon's Connection'. For the education of ministers she established in 1768 a college at Trevecca in Brecknockshire (removed in 1792 to Cheshunt, Herts), and built or bought numerous chapels, the principal one at Bath. She died in London, bequeathing to four persons her 64 chapels, most of which became identical with the Congregational churches.

HUNTINGTON, Collis Porter (1821–1900) American railway pioneer, born in Harwinton, Connecticut. A pedlar and shopkeeper, he went to California in 1849 and pioneered the Central Pacific Railway, which was completed in 1869, as well as the Southern Pacific (1881), of which he became president, together with the allied steamship companies. His nephew, Henry Edwards Huntington (1850–1927), also a railroad executive, acquired an immense art collection and library, which he presented to the nation in 1922, together with his estate at Pasadena, California.

HUNTINGTON, Ellsworth (1876–1943) American geographer and explorer, born in Galesburg, Illinois. After teaching at Euphrates College, Turkey, he went on expeditions to Central Asia (1903–06), and became a teacher of geography and research associate at Yale University. He wrote on Asiatic subjects and carried out research on the relations between climate and anthropology. His books include *The Pulse of Progress* (1926), *The Human Habitat* (1927) and *Mainsprings of Circulation* (1945).

HUNTSMAN, Benjamin (1704–76) English inventor, born in Barton-on-Humber, the son of Dutch immigrants. He was apprenticed to a clockmaker and in 1725 established a business in Doncaster making clocks, locks and scientific instruments. The high cost and variable quality of the steel he had to import from Germany and Sweden prompted him to experiment in an effort to improve on the cementation process then in use; by 1742 he had developed the crucible process, which produced a better and more uniform steel with less expenditure of labour and fuel, at a foundry he opened in Sheffield. The drawback was that crucible steel could be made only in relatively small quantities, and it required the advances of **Kelly**, **Bessemer**, **Siemens** and **Martin** in the mid 19th century before steel could become a major structural material.

HUNYADY, János Corvinus (c.1387–1456) Hungarian warrior and statesman, the national hero of Hungary. Apparently a Wallach by birth, he was knighted and in 1409 presented by the emperor **Sigismund** with the Castle of Hunyad in Transylvania. His life was dedicated to crusades against the Turks.

He led a campaign against them in 1437–38 and again from 1441 to 1443, when he expelled them from Transylvania in 1442 and scored brilliant victories south of the Danube in 1443. He was defeated at Varna in 1444, and became regent from 1446 to 1452. He fought the Turks again but was defeated at Kossovo (1448). In 1456 he routed the Turkish armies besieging Belgrade, thus securing a 70-year peace, but died of dysentery soon afterwards. He left two sons, Ladislaus, who was beheaded on a charge of conspiracy, and **Matthias Corvinus**.

HURD, Douglas Richard (1930–) English politician. The son of Baron Hurd, he was educated at Eton and Trinity College, Cambridge before joining the diplomatic service in 1952. After posts in Peking (Beijing), New York and Rome, he joined the Conservative party research department in 1966. Moving into active politics he became private and then political secretary to **Edward Heath** (1968–74) and then held a number of junior posts in **Margaret Thatcher**'s government (1979–84). Resignations by senior cabinet ministers from 1984 fortuitously made Hurd's progress suddenly rapid, from Northern Ireland secretary (1984–85) to home secretary in 1985 and, unexpectedly, foreign secretary in 1989. Regarded as a 'non-Thatcherite' moderate, he also writes political thrillers.

HURD, Richard (1720–1808) English prelate and writer, named the 'Beauty of Holiness' on account of his comeliness and piety. Born in Congreve, Staffordshire, he became a fellow of Emmanuel College, Cambridge, in 1742. In 1750 he became a Whitehall preacher, in 1774 bishop of Lichfield and Coventry, and in 1781 of Worcester. Among his works are *Commentary on Horace's Ars Poetica* (1749); *Dissertations on Poetry* (1755–57); *Dialogues on Sincerity* (1759); and *Letters on Chivalry and Romance* (1762). He also edited **William Warburton** (1788).

HURST, Sir Cecil James Barrington (1870–1963) English lawyer, born in Horsham Park, Sussex. Educated at Westminster and Trinity College, Cambridge, in 1902 he became assistant legal adviser to the Foreign Office and legal adviser in 1918. He worked on the Paris Peace Treaties of 1919 and proposed the Permanent Court of International Justice. From 1929 to 1946 he was a judge of this court, becoming president in 1934–36, and in this capacity greatly strengthened the court's prestige and authority. He was president of the Institute of International Law and a founder of the *British Yearbook of International Law* in 1919.

HURST, Geoffrey (1941–) English footballer, born in Ashton-under-Lyne, Lancashire. He became famous as the only player ever to score three goals in a World Cup Final, against West Germany at Wembley in 1966. A composed, hard-working, unflamboyant player, he scored 24 goals for England in 49 appearances. Most of his career was spent with West Ham United before he moved on to Stoke City.

HURSTON, Zora Neale (1901–60) American black novelist, born in Eatonville, Florida. The nine secure years she spent there, described in *Dust Tracks on a Road* (1942), ended when her mother died and her father, a Baptist preacher and thrice mayor of the town, remarried. Her life from then on was 'a series of wanderings'—occasional work, interrupted education, working as a wardrobe assistant with a theatre troupe—until she enrolled as a full-time student at Baltimore's Morgan Academy. Moving to Washington DC she became a part-time student at Howard University and began to write. Influenced by her studies in cultural anthropology at Barnard College and Columbia University, she became a prominent figure in the Harlem Renaissance. A precursor of black women writers like **Alice Walker** and **Toni Morrison**, her novels include *Jonah's Gourd Vine* (1934), *Their Eyes Were Watching God* (1937), *Moses, Man of the Mountain* (1939) and *Seraph on the Suwanee* (1948). In the 1950s she withdrew from public life, and was distanced from many contemporaries by her controversial attack on the Supreme Court's ruling on school desegregation. She argued that pressure for integration denied the value of existing black institutions. Her last years were plagued by ill-health and she died in poverty.

HUS, John See **HUSS**

HUSAK, Gustav (1913–) Czechoslovakian politician, born in Bratislava in Slovakia. He trained as a lawyer at the Bratislava Law Faculty, and was a member of the resistance movement during World War II. After the war he worked for the Slovak Communist party (SCP) before being imprisoned, on political grounds, in 1951. Rehabilitated in 1960, he worked at the Academy of Sciences (1963–68) before becoming first secretary of the SCP and deputy premier in 1968. After the 'Prague Spring' and the Soviet invasion of 1968, he replaced **Dubček** as leader of the Communist party of Czechoslovakia (CCP) in 1969. His task was to restore order, 'cleanse' the CCP and introduce a new federalist constitution. He became state president in 1975 and, pursuing a policy of cautious Brezhnevite reform, remained the dominant figure in Czechoslovakia until his retirement in 1987. He was replaced as state president by **Vaclav Havel** in 1989 after the CCP regime was overthrown.

HU SHIH (1891–1962) Chinese liberal scholar and reformer, born in Chiki, Anhwei. He went to school in Shanghai, and went on to study English literature, political science and philosophy at Cornell (1910–14) and Columbia (1915–17), where he became a disciple of the American philosopher **John Dewey** and developed his ideas for the revitalization of Chinese culture and literature by the use of the vernacular. He became professor of philosophy at Beijing University (1917–26) and at Shanghai (1927–31), and dean of the college of arts and letters at Beijing (1932–37). He wrote extensively on Chinese philosophy, but is best known for his championing of *pai-hua*, the new Chinese vernacular that would make literature accessible to the masses; he wrote poetry in *pai-hua* (*Experimental Poems*, 1920). An opponent of communism, he served the Nationalist government as ambassador to the USA (1938–42) and the United Nations (1957), and was president of the Academica Sinaica on Taiwan (1958–62).

HUSKISSON, William (1770–1830) English statesman, born in Birts Morton Court, Worcestershire. He was in Paris (1783–92), and in 1795 was appointed under-secretary in the colonial department. Next year he entered parliament for Morpeth as a supporter of **Pitt**. Returned for Liskeard in 1804, he became secretary of the treasury; and held the same office under the Duke of Portland (1807–09). In 1814 he became commissioner of the woods and forests, in 1823 president of the board of trade and treasurer of the navy, and in 1827 colonial secretary, but he resigned office finally in 1828. He obtained the removal of restrictions on the trade of the colonies with foreign countries, the removal or reduction of many import duties, and relaxation of the navigation laws, and was an active pioneer of free trade. He received fatal injuries at the opening of the Liverpool and Manchester Railway.

HUSS, or **Hus, John** (c.1369–1415) Bohemian religious reformer, born in Husinetz (of which Hus is a contraction) near Prachatitz, the son of a Bohemian peasant. In 1398, two years after taking his master's degree at Prague, he began to lecture there on theology. He had come under the influence of **Wycliffe**'s writings, probably through **Anne of Bohemia**'s retinue. In 1402 he was appointed rector of the university, and began to preach at the Bethlehem chapel; in 1408 he was forbidden to exercise priestly functions within the diocese. In 1409 he was re-elected rector, but the archbishop commissioned an inquisitor to investigate the charges of heretical teaching against him. In connection with this, Pope Alexander V promulgated a bull condemning Wycliffe's teaching, ordered all his writings to be publicly burned, and forbade preaching in any except collegiate, parish and monastery churches. As Huss continued preaching, he was excommunicated (1411). Popular riots followed, and Huss, backed by the people, still maintained his position; nor did he give in even after the city was laid under papal interdict. But by 1413 matters had greatly changed, Huss having spoken out yet more boldly against the church, resulting in some of his more influential supporters, including the university, falling away from him. On the advice of King **Wenceslas** of Bohemia he left Prague and found refuge at the castles of his supporters, for nearly all the nobles were with him. He began writing his principal work, *De Ecclesia*, which, like many of his minor writings, contains numerous passages taken almost verbatim from Wycliffe. About this time a general council was summoned to meet at Constance, and Huss was called upon to present himself before it. Provided with a 'safe conduct' guarantee from the Emperor **Sigismund**, he reached Constance in November 1414. Three weeks later he was seized and thrown into prison. No precise charge had been lodged against him; but he had resumed preaching in Constance. The council condemned Wycliffe's writings in 1415 which did not bode well, and his own trial began in June 1416; but he was not permitted to speak freely in his own defence, nor allowed to have a defender. Called upon to recant unconditionally, and to pledge himself not to teach the doctrines that were put in accusation against him, Huss categorically refused, and was burned on 6 July. The rage of his followers in Bohemia led to the bloody Hussite wars, in which the two parties of Hussites under such leaders as **Ziska** and **Podiebrad** more than held their own in many battles with all the forces of the empire. They were not reduced till about the middle of the century.

HUSSEIN, ibn Talal (1935–) king of Jordan since 1952, great-grandson of **Hussein ibn Ali** and cousin of King **Faisal II** of Iraq. He was educated at Victoria College, Alexandria, and in Britain at Harrow and Sandhurst, and succeeded his father, King Talal, who was deposed because of mental illness. His marriage in 1955 to Princess Dina, a graduate of Girton College, Cambridge, was later dissolved, and in 1961 he married an English girl, given the title Princess Muna, who in 1962 gave birth to an heir, Abdullah. The young king maintained a vigorous and highly personal rule in the face of the political upheavals inside and outside his exposed country, steering a middle course, on the one side favouring the western powers, particularly Britain, on the other pacifying Arab nationalism, eg by his curt dismissal of the British general, Sir **John Glubb**, in 1956. His federation of Jordan with Iraq in 1958 came to an unexpected end with the Iraqi military *coup d'état* in July of the same year. In 1972 he divorced Princess Muna and married Alia Baha Eddin Toukan, who was killed in an air accident in 1977. The following year he married Lisa Halaby.

HUSSEIN, Saddam (1937–) Iraqi politician, born in Tikrit, near Baghdad, into a peasant family. Educated in Baghdad, he joined the Arab Ba'ath Socialist party in 1957. In 1959 he escaped to Syria and Egypt after being sentenced to death for the attempted assassination of the head of state, General Kassem. He returned to Iraq in 1963 after the downfall of Kassem, but in 1964 he was imprisoned for plotting to overthrow the new régime. After his release (1966) he took a leading part in the 1968 revolution which ousted the civilian government and established a Revolutionary Command Council (RCC). Initially behind the scenes, and then more overtly, he strengthened his position, and in 1979 became RCC chairman and state president. Ruthless in the pursuit of his objectives, he fought a bitter war against his neighbour, Iran (1980–88) and dealt harshly with Kurdish rebels seeking a degree of autonomy.

HUSSEIN IBN ALI (1856–1931) king of the Hejaz (1916–24), and founder of the modern Arab Hashemite dynasty, great-grandfather of King **Hussein** of Jordan and father of King **Faisal I**. He was emir of Mecca (1908–16), and after first siding with the Turks and Germany in World War I, on the advice of **T E Lawrence** came over to the side of the Allies, declaring for Arab independence (1916), and was chosen first king of the Hejaz. After provoking the opposition of the Wahabis and Britain, he was forced to abdicate in 1924, was exiled in Cyprus and died in Amman.

HUSSERL, Edmund Gustav Albrecht (1859–1938) German philosopher, of Jewish origin, born in Prossnitz in the Austrian empire. He studied mathematics at Berlin (under **Weierstrass**), psychology at Vienna (under **Brentano**) and taught at Halle (1887), Göttingen (1901) and Freiburg (1916). He became founder and leader of the philosophical school of phenomenology. His *Logische Untersuchungen* (1900–01) defended philosophy as fundamentally an *a priori* discipline, unlike psychology, and in his *Ideen zu einer reinen Phänomelogie und phänomenologischen Philosophie* (1913) he presented a programme for the systematic investigation of consciousness and its objects, which proceeded by 'bracketing off', or suspending belief in, the empirical world to gain an indubitable vantage-point in subjective consciousness. His approach greatly influenced philosophers in Germany and in the USA, particularly **Heidegger**, and helped give rise to Gestalt psychology.

HUSSEY, Obed (1792–1860) American inventor, born in Maine, New England. He spent his life in the invention, improvement and manufacture of machines for use in agriculture and light engineering. He achieved his greatest success with his reaping machine which he patented in 1833, the year before a very similar machine was patented by **Cyrus McCormick** based on the earliest known mechanical reaper invented in 1826 by **Patrick Bell** in Scotland. Hussey's and McCormick's machines were both exhibited at the Great Exhibition of 1851, and although Hussey won the gold medal it was eventually McCormick who became the leading manufacturer in America.

HUSTON, John Marcellus (1906–87) American-born Irish filmmaker, born in Nevada, Missouri, son of the character actor Walter Huston. His early background involved spells as a boxer in California, a competitive horseman in Mexico and a journalist in New York. In Hollywood from 1929, he acted in films like *The Storm* (1930), and contributed to a range of screenplays including *Murders in the Rue Morgue* (1932), *Juarez* (1939) and *High Sierra* (1941). He made his directorial début with *The Maltese Falcon* (1941). Particularly adept at high adventure and film noir, he showed a consistent interest in quests that proved fruitless, or in men beset by delusions of grandeur. His numerous successes include *Key Largo* (1948), *The African Queen* (1951), *Moulin Rouge* (1952), *The Misfits* (1960), *Fat City* (1972), *The Man Who Would Be King* (1975) and *The Dead* (1987). Latterly a prolific actor, he displayed reptilian patriarchal menace in *Chinatown* (1974), for which he received an Academy Award nomination; he also won directing and screeplay awards for *The Treasure of the Sierra Madre* (1947). An Irish citizen from 1964, he married five times and his sons Danny and Tony plus his daughter Anjelica have followed in his footsteps, the latter winning an Academy Award for her father's *Prizzi's Honor* (1985). His autobiography, *An Open Book*, was published in 1980.

HUTCHESON, Francis (1694–1746) British philosopher, a native of Ulster, of Scottish descent, probably born in Drumalig, County Down. He studied for the church at Glasgow (1710–16), started a successful private academy in Dublin, where he was a popular preacher, and then returned to Glasgow as professor of moral philosophy from 1729 until his death. His main works were: *An Inquiry into the Original of Our Ideas of Beauty and Virtue* (1725), *An Essay on the Nature and Conduct of the Passions and Affections, with Illustrations on the Moral Sense* (1726) and *System of Moral Philosophy* (posthumously published in 1755). He developed the theory of 'moral sense' first stated by **Shaftesbury**, by which moral distinctions are directly intuited rather than arrived at by reasoning, and he identified virtue with universal benevolence. In this he anticipated the utilitarians, and his formula 'the greatest happiness for the greatest numbers' was taken up, slightly modified, by **Bentham**.

HUTCHINSON, Anne, née **Marbury** (c.1590–1643) English religious leader and American pioneer, the daughter of a Lincolnshire clergyman. In 1634 she emigrated with her husband to Boston, Massachusetts, where she lectured and denounced the Massachusetts clergy as being 'under the covenant of works, not of grace'. Tried for heresy and sedition, and banished, she, with some friends, acquired territory from the Narragansett Indians of Rhode Island, and set up a democracy (1638). After her husband's death (1642) she removed to a new settlement in what is now Pelham Bay in New York state, where she and all but one of her family of 15 were murdered by Indians.

HUTCHINSON, John (1615–64) English Puritan, soldier and regicide, born in Nottingham. He studied at Peterhouse, Cambridge, and Lincoln's Inn. A parliamentarian, he was governor of Nottingham and successfully held the town (1643–45). Returned in 1646 to parliament for Nottingham, he was one of King **Charles I**'s judges, and signed the warrant for his execution. He sat in the first council of state, but, alarmed at the ambitious schemes of **Cromwell**, ceased to take part in politics. At the Restoration he was included in the Act of Amnesty, but was later imprisoned in the Tower and at Sandown Castle on a groundless suspicion of treasonable conspiracy, and died. The Memoirs, written by his widow for her children, and first published in 1806, revealed a delightful picture of a grave and courteous gentleman, wholly free from austerity and fanaticism.

HUTCHINSON, John (1674–1737) English theologian, born in Spennithorne, Yorkshire. In 1724 he published *Moses' Principia*, defending the Mosaic cosmogony and assailing **Newton**'s theory of gravitation. His *Thoughts concerning Religion* affirm the 'Hutchinsonian' theory that the Scriptures contain the elements not only of true religion, but of all rational philosophy.

HUTCHINSON, Sir Jonathan (1828–1913) English surgeon, born in Selby, Yorkshire. He became surgeon at the London hospital (1863–83), and Hunterian professor of surgery at the Royal College of Surgeons. 'Hutchinson's triad' are the three symptoms of congenital syphilis first described by him.

HUTCHISON, Sir William Oliphant (1889–1970) Scottish artist, born in Collessie, Fife. He studied at Edinburgh and in Paris, and is known for his portraits and landscapes. He was director of the Glasgow School of Art from 1933 to 1943.

HUTTEN, Philip von (c.1511–1546) German explorer, nephew of **Ulrich von Hutten**. In 1528 the emperor **Charles V** granted Venezuela to the Welsers, rich Augsburg merchants; Hutten sailed with one of their companies, and after various journeyings (1536–1538) set out in 1541 in search of the Golden City (El Dorado). After several years of wandering, harassed by the natives, he and his followers were routed in an attack on a large Indian city. Severely wounded, he was conveyed back to Coro and beheaded by a usurping Spanish viceroy.

HUTTEN, Ulrich von (1488–1523) German humanist, born in the castle of Steckelberg, uncle of **Philip von Hutten**, He was sent in 1499 to the neighbouring Benedictine monastery of Fulda, but his temper drove him to leave in 1504. He visited various universities, and then in 1512 passed into Italy. Returning to Germany in 1517, and crowned poet laureate by the emperor **Maximilian I**, he entered the service of Albert, archbishop of Mainz, and shared in the famous satires against the ignorance of the monks, the *Epistolae Obscurorum Virorum*. Eager to see Germany free from foreign and priestly domination, he took part in 1519, along with **Franz von Sickingen**, in the campaign of the Swabian League against Ulrich of Württemberg. He took on **Luther**'s cause with his customary impetuosity and vehemence. A set of dialogues (1520) containing a formal manifesto against Rome moved the pope to have him dismissed from the archbishop's service. He found shelter in Sickingen's castle of Ebernburg in the Palatinate, where he engaged in virulent polemics against the papal party to rouse the German emperor, nobles and people. His earliest work in German, *Aufwecker der teutschen Nation* (1520), is a satiric poem. Driven to flee to Basel in 1522, he was coldly treated by **Erasmus**. He finally found a resting place through **Zwingli**'s help on the island of Ufnau in the Lake of Zürich, the exact location of which was discovered in 1958.

HUTTER, Leonhard (1563–1616) German theologian, and champion of Lutheran orthodoxy. He taught theology at Wittenberg from 1596. His *Compendium locorum theologicorum* (1610) and *Concordia concors* (1614) were long standard works.

HUTTON, James (1726–97) Scottish geologist, born in Edinburgh. He studied medicine there, in Paris and in Leiden. In 1754 he devoted himself in Berwickshire to agriculture and chemistry, which led him to mineralogy and geology; in 1768 he moved to Edinburgh. The Huttonian theory, emphasizing the igneous origin of many rocks and deprecating the assumption of causes other than those we see still at work, was expounded before the Royal Society of Edinburgh in *A Theory of the Earth* (1785; expanded, vols i, ii 1795; iii 1899). It formed the basis of modern geology.

HUTTON, Sir Leonard (1916–) English cricketer, born in Pudsey, Yorkshire. A Yorkshire player throughout his career, he first played for England in 1937, scoring a century on his first Test against

Australia in 1938. In the Oval Test against Australia in 1938, he compiled a record Test score of 364, which stood for 20 years until it was exceeded by one run by Sir **Garfield Sobers**. Renowned for the perfection of his batting technique, he made 129 centuries in his first-class career. After the war he captained England in 23 Test matches (the first professional cricketer to do so on a regular basis); he regained the 'Ashes' from Australia in the Test series of 1953, and retained them during the Australian tour of 1954–55, thus ending 20 years for Australian supremacy. He retired in 1956 and was knighted that year for his outstanding services to cricket.

HUXLEY, Aldous Leonard (1894–1963) English novelist and essayist, son of **Leonard Huxley** and brother of **Sir Julian Sorell Huxley**, born in Godalming, Surrey. He was educated at Eton and Balliol College, Oxford, where he read English, not biology as he intended, because of an eye disease, which compelled him to settle in the warmer climate of California (1937). Some Shelleyan poetry, literary journalism and a volume of short stories *Limbo* (1920) were followed by *Crome Yellow* (1921) and *Antic Hay* (1923), satires on post-war Britain. *Those Barren Leaves* (1925) and *Point Counter Point* (1928) were written in Italy, where he associated with **D H Lawrence**, who appears as Mark Rampion in the last named. In 1932, in his most famous novel, *Brave New World*, Huxley warns of the dangers of moral anarchy in a scientific age, by depicting a repulsive Utopia, in which Platonic harmony is achieved by scientifically breeding and conditioning a society of human robots, for whom happiness is synonymous with subordination, a much more sinister prophecy than **Orwell**'s *1984*, which still required thought control and police terror. Despite the wit and satire, Huxley was in deadly earnest, as his essay *Brave New World Revisited* (1959) shows. An alternative possibility, of bestial individualism in the degeneration of the survivors of an atomic war, is explored in *Ape and Essence* (1948). From such pessimism Huxley took refuge in the exploration of mysticism. *Eyeless in Gaza* (1936) and *After Many a Summer* (1939, James Tait Black prize) pointed the way to *Time must have a Stop* (1944), in which he attempted to describe a person's state of mind at the moment of and just after death. *The Doors of Perception* (1954) describes a controversial short-cut to mysticism, the drug mescalin which reduces the 'sublime' mystical state to a mere function of the adrenal glands. In contrast, the novelette *The Genius and the Goddess* (1955) reverts to the earlier Huxley, the problems posed by the discrepancy between an extraordinary intellect and a deficiency in other human endowments. Huxley wrote numerous essays on related topics, beginning with *Proper Studies* (1927), and biographies.

HUXLEY, Sir Andrew Fielding (1917–) English physiologist, half-brother of **Aldous** and **Julian Sorrell Huxley**. He studied at Trinity College, Cambridge, becoming a fellow there in 1941 and assistant director of research in physiology at the university. He worked on operational research (1940–45) and with **Alan Hodgkin** provided a physico-chemical explanation for nerve transmission; he also gave the first satisfying outline of a theory of muscular contraction. He was Jodrell professor of physiology at University College London from 1960 to 1969, and Royal Society Research Professor from 1969. With Hodgkin and Sir **John Eccles**, he was awarded the 1963 Nobel prize for physiology or medicine.

HUXLEY, Elspeth Josceline, née **Grant** (1907–) English novelist, born in Kenya. In 1931 she married Gervas Huxley (1894–1971), grandson of **Thomas Henry Huxley**, and has written many novels and essays on her native land and its problems.

HUXLEY, Hugh Esmor (1924–) English biophysicist, born in Birkenhead. He studied at Christ's College, Cambridge, worked on radars in World War II, and turned to biophysics at the Massachusetts Institute of Technology (1952–54) and the MRC Laboratory of Molecular Biology from 1961. From the 1950s he was the central figure in developing the sliding filament model of muscle contraction, in which muscle action is seen as depending on protein filaments which are interdigitated and which slide past each other to produce contraction. He developed this concept in detail, and devised X-ray diffraction and electron microscopy techniques for this work which are also applicable in other studies in physiology. He has been professor of biology at Brandeis University since 1987.

HUXLEY, Sir Julian Sorell (1887–1975) English biologist and humanist, son of **Leonard Huxley** and brother of **Aldous Huxley**. Educated at Eton and Balliol College, Oxford, where he won the Newdigate prize (1908), he was professor at the Rice Institute, Texas (1913–16), and after World War I became professor of zoology at King's College, London (1925–27), Fullerian professor at the Royal Institution (1926–29), and secretary to the Zoological Society of London (1935–42). His writings include *Essays of a Biologist* (1923), *Religion without Revelation* (1927), *Animal Biology* (with **J B S Haldane**, 1927), *The Science of Life* (with **H G Wells**, 1931), *Evolution: The Modern Synthesis* (1942), *Evolutionary Ethics* (1943), *Biological Aspects of Cancer* (1957), and *Towards a New Humanism* (1957). He extended the application of his scientific knowledge to political and social problems, formulating a pragmatic ethical theory of 'evolutionary humanism', based on the principle of natural selection. He was the first director-general of UNESCO (1946–48).

HUXLEY, Leonard (1860–1933) English editor, son of **Thomas Henry Huxley**. He taught at Charterhouse (1884–1901), and was assistant editor (1901–16) and editor (1916–33) of the *Cornhill Magazine*. He wrote a life of Sir **Joseph Hooker** (1918), edited **Jane Welsh Carlyle**'s Letters and married a niece of **Matthew Arnold**.

HUXLEY, Thomas Henry (1825–95) English biologist, born in Ealing, Middlesex, the son of a schoolmaster. He studied medicine at Charing Cross Hospital and entered the Royal Navy medical service. As assistant surgeon on HMS *Rattlesnake* on a surveying expedition to the South Seas (1846–50), he collected and studied specimens of marine animals, particularly plankton. From 1854 to 1885 he was professor of natural history at the Royal School of Mines (later the Normal School of Science). He became the foremost scientific supporter of **Charles Darwin**'s theory of evolution by natural selection, tackling Bishop **Samuel Wilberforce** in a celebrated exchange at the British Association meeting in Oxford (1860), when he declared that he would rather be descended from an ape than a bishop, and wrote *Evidence as to Man's Place in Nature* (1863). He also studied fossils, and influenced the teaching of biology and science in schools as a member of the London Schools Board. Later he turned to theology and philosophy, and coined the term 'agnostic' for his views. He wrote *Lay Sermons* (1870), *Science and Culture* (1881), *Evolution and Ethics* (1893) and *Science and Education* (published posthumously in 1899). One of his seven children was **Leonard Huxley**.

HU YAOBANG (1915–89) Chinese politician, born into a poor peasant family in Hunan province. He joined the Red Army in 1929 and took part in the Long March (1934–36). He held a number of posts under **Deng Xiaoping** before becoming head of the Communist Youth League (1952–67). During the 1966–69 Cultural Revolution he was purged as a 'capitalist roader' and 'rusticated'. He was briefly rehabilitated (1975–76), but did not return to high office until 1978, when, through his patron Deng, he joined the Communist party's politburo. From head of the secretariat he was promoted to party leader in 1981, but dismissed in 1987 for his relaxed handling of a wave of student unrest. Popularly revered as a liberal reformer, his death triggered an unprecedented wave of pro-democracy demonstrations.

HUYGENS, Christiaan (1629–93) Dutch physicist, born at The Hague, the second son of the poet Constantyn Huygens (1596–1687), who was secretary to the Prince of Orange. Huygens studied at Leiden and Breda. His mathematical *Theoremata* was published in 1651. Next he made the pendulum clock on **Galileo**'s suggestion (1657), and developed the latter's doctrine of accelerated motion under gravity. In 1655 he discovered the rings and fourth satellite of Saturn, along with the micrometer. In 1660 he visited England, where he was elected FRS. He discovered the laws of collision of elastic bodies at the same time as **Wallis** and **Wren**, and improved the air-pump. In optics he first propounded the undulatory theory of light, and discovered polarization. The 'principle of Huygens' is a part of the wave theory. He lived in Paris, a member of the Royal Academy of Sciences (1666–81). Then as a Protestant he felt it prudent to return to The Hague.

HUYSMANN, Roelof See **AGRICOLA, Rudolphus**

HUYSMANS, Cornelius, 'the second' (1648–1727) Dutch landscape and religious painter, born in Antwerp. He was a relative of **Jacob Huysmans**. His religious paintings, a successful blend of Italian and Flemish styles, include *Christ on the Road to Emmaus*.

HUYSMANS, Jacob (c.1636–96) Dutch portrait painter, a relative of **Cornelius Huysmans**, born in Antwerp. He came to London about 1661 and became fashionable at the Restoration court.

HUYSMANS, Joris Karl (1848–1907) French novelist of Dutch origin, born in Paris. From ultrarealism, as in his *Les Soeurs Vatard* (1879), *À vau-l'eau* (1882), and *À rebours* (1884), he changed over to a devil-worshipping mysticism as in *Là-Bas* (1891), but returned to the Roman church with *En Route* (1892). His autobiography. *Art Moderne* (1882) is a superb study of Impressionist painting.

HUYSUM, Jan van (1682–1749) Dutch painter, born in Amsterdam. He studied under his father, Justus (1659–1716), a landscape painter. Jan also painted landscapes, purely conventional in style. But his fruit and flower pieces are distinguished for exquisite finish and are represented in the Louvre, Paris and Vienna. A brother, Jacob (1680–1740), also a painter, worked in London.

HWEN-T'SIANG, or **Hiouen-Thsang** (c.605–664) Chinese Buddhist monk, born near Honan. In 629 he set out on a pilgrimage to India, travelling by way of the Gobi Desert, Tashkent, Samarkand, Bamian and Peshawar. He remained in India (631–44), visiting the sacred places and studying the sacred books. His Memoirs (648) are important for the history of India and Buddhism.

HYACINTHE, Père properly **Charles Loyson**, (1827–1912) French Carmelite preacher. He taught philosophy and theology at Avignon and Nantes, gathering enthusiastic audiences to the Madeleine and Notre Dame in Paris. He boldly denounced abuses in the church and was excommunicated (1869). He married in 1872, and continued to preach, protesting against the Infallibility Dogma. In 1879 he founded a Gallican Catholic Church in Paris. His writings include *Mon Testament, ma protestation* (1873).

HYATT, John Wesley (1837–1920) American inventor, born in Starkey, New York. He was apprenticed as a printer, but soon found his real vocation as an inventor, beginning with a knife sharpener in 1861 and later including a water filter, a multiple-needle sewing-machine, an improved sugar cane mill and the Hyatt roller bearing, for the manufacture of which he established a factory in 1892. His most successful discovery was the result of his efforts to find a substitute for ivory in dominoes and billiard balls; in 1868 he added camphor to cellulose nitrate and called the resulting plastic 'celluloid', from which by 1875 he was making 'Hyatt billiard balls' and other articles. The same substance had been discovered independently in England by **Alexander Parkes** in 1862; he christened it 'Parkesine', but failed to make it a commercial success.

HYDE, Charles Cheney (1873–1952) American jurist, born in Chicago. Educated at Yale and Harvard, he taught law at Northwestern University, Illinois (1907–25), and Columbia University (1925–45). He served as solicitor for the US department of state and was a member of the Permanent Court of Arbitration at The Hague (1951–52). His major work, *International Law, Chiefly as Interpreted and Applied by the United States* (1922, revised 1945) is of high authority.

HYDE, Douglas (1860–1949) Irish scholar and writer, born in County Roscommon. Educated at Trinity College, Dublin, he was professor of modern languages at the University of New Brunswick for a time, but returned to Ireland to lead the movement to revive the Irish language and literature, using his Irish pen-name of *An Craoibhin*. He was the founder and first president of the Gaelic League (1893–1915), and translated much traditional material in *Beside the Fire* (1890), and *The Love Songs of Connacht* (1894). He also wrote a *Literary History of Ireland* (1899). He was one of the founders of the Abbey Theatre in 1904, and wrote the first play in Irish to be performed professionally, *Casadh an tSúgán* (The Twisting of the Rope, 1901). He was professor of modern Irish at University College, Dublin (1909–32). Active in political life, he was the first president of the republic of Ireland (1938–45).

HYDE, Edward See **CLARENDON, Earl of**

HYDER ALI See **HAIDAR ALI**

HYNE, Charles John Cutcliffe Wright (1865–1944) English traveller and author, born in Bibury. He is remembered above all as the creator of the fictional character 'Captain Kettle' in several adventure stories.

HYPATIA (c.375–415) Greek philosopher, the first notable female astronomer and mathematician, who taught at Alexandria and became head of the neoplatonist school there. She was renowned for her eloquence, beauty, and learning, and drew pupils from all parts of the Greek world, Christian and pagan. **Cyril**, archbishop of Alexandria, came to resent her influence, and she was brutally murdered by a Christian mob he may have incited to riot.

HYPERIDES, or **Hypereides** (389–322 BC) Athenian orator and statesman. He became a professional speech-writer, and earned large sums. From the first he opposed the party which advocated peace with **Philip II** of Macedonia, and so supported **Demosthenes** till after the death of Philip and during the early portion of **Alexander**'s career. In 324, however, in the corruption case involving Harpalus, he was one of Demosthenes' accusers. He promoted the Lamian War against Macedonia (323–22) after the death of Alexander, for which he was put to death by **Antipater**. Although Hyperides was admired and studied in Roman times, it was not until 1847 that papyri containing four of his orations were discovered by English travellers in Egypt. In his speeches Hyperides is always transparent, never monotonous, witty to a degree, refined in his raillery, and delightful in his irony.

HYRCANUS I, John (135–104 BC) Jewish high priest, son of Simon Maccabaeus (see **Maccabees**). He was at first tributary to the Syrians; but on the death of Antiochus VII he made himself independent, subdued the Samaritans and Idumaeans, concluded an alliance with the Romans, and extended his territories almost to the limits of the Davidic monarchy. Hyrcanus was a just and enlightened ruler, and the country was prosperous during his reign. He left five sons, two of whom, Aristobulus and Alexander, governed with the title of king.

HYRCANUS II (d.30 BC) Jewish high priest, grandson of **John Hyrcanus** and son of Alexander. On the death of his father (76 BC) he was appointed high priest by his mother Alexandra, who ruled Judaea till her death (67 BC). His younger brother Aristobulus and he then warred for power with varying fortune till Aristobulus was poisoned (49 BC). In 47 BC **Caesar** made **Antipater** of Idumaea procurator of Judaea with supreme power; and a son of Aristobulus, with Parthian help, captured Hyrcanus, and carried him off to Seleucia. But when **Herod, the Great**, son of Antipater, came to power, the aged Hyrcanus was invited home to Jerusalem, where he lived in peace till, suspected of intriguing against Herod, he was put to death in 30 BC.

HYRTL, Joseph (1810–94) Austrian anatomist. He was professor of anatomy at Prague (1837) and Vienna (1845–74), and researched into the anatomy of the ear and the comparative anatomy of fishes.

HYSLOP, James (1798–1827) Scottish poet, born in Kirkconnel, Dumfriesshire. While a shepherd he wrote the poem 'The Cameronian's Dream' (1821).

I

IACOCCA, Lee (Lido Anthony) (1924–) American businessman, and head of Chrysler Corporation, born in Allentown, Pennsylvania. He worked for the Ford Motor Company (1946–78), at first in sales, rising to become president in 1970. In 1978 he joined Chrysler Corporation as president and chief executive officer when the company was in serious financial difficulties, with declining market share. Since 1979 he has also been chairman of the board and has steered the company back to profitability and health. He published a best-selling autobiography (with William Kovak), *Iacocca* (1985), and a sequel, *Talking Straight* (1989).

IAMBLICHUS (2nd century) Syrian-Greek author of a lost Greek romance, *Babyloniaca*.

IBÁÑEZ, Vicente Blasco (1867–1928) Spanish novelist, born in Valentia. He dealt in realistic fashion with provincial life and social revolution. Notable works are *Blood and Sand* (trans 1913), *The Cabin* (trans 1919), and *The Four Horsemen of the Apocalypse* (trans 1919), which vividly portrays World War I and earned him world fame.

IBARRURI GOMEZ, Dolores, known as **La Pasionaria** (1895–1989) Spanish writer and politician, born in Gallarta, in Vizcaya province, the daughter of a Basque miner. She worked as a maid-servant, then joined the Socialist party in 1917 and worked as a journalist for the workers' press, using the pseudonym 'La Pasionaria' ('the passion flower'). She helped to found the Spanish Communist party in 1920, edited several communist newspapers, founded the Anti-Fascist Womens' League in 1934 and was elected to parliament in 1936. During the Civil War (1936–39) she became legendary for her passionate exhortations to the Spanish people to fight against the Fascist forces, declaring that 'It is better to die on your feet than to live on your knees'. When **Franco** came to power in 1939 she left for the Soviet Union, returning to Spain in 1977, when, at the age of 81, she was re-elected to the National Assembly.

IBERT, Jacques (1890–1962) French composer, born in Paris. He studied in Paris, winning the French Prix de Rome in 1919. In 1937 he was made director of the French Academy in Rome. Ibert's works include seven operas, ballets, cantatas and chamber music, and the orchestral *Divertissement* (1928), based upon his incidental music for **Labiche**'s play, *The Italian Straw Hat*, and *Escales* (1922) suite.

IBN 'ARABI (1165–1240) Arab mystic poet. His writings present in obscure language a form of pantheism.

IBN BAJJAH See **AVEMPACE**

IBN BATTUTAH (1304–68) Arab traveller and geographer, born in Tangiers. He spent 30 years (1325–54) in travel, covering all the Muslim countries, visiting Mecca, Persia, Mesopotamia, Asia Minor, Bokhara, India, China, Sumatra, southern Spain and Timbuktu. He then settled at Fez, and dictated the entertaining history of his journeys, published with a French translation in 1855–59. See his *Travels in Asia* (1929).

IBN DAUD, Abraham (c.1100–c.1180) Spanish-Jewish philosopher, born in Toledo, the first to draw systematically on **Aristotle**. His *Al-Aqida al Rafia* (The Exalted Faith, 1160), argues the essential harmony of philosophy and Torah, and his *Sefer hak-Kabbalah* (1161) was an influential history demonstrating the tradition of Rabbinic authority from **Moses** to his own day.

IBN GABIROL See **AVICEBRÓN**

IBN KHALDUN (1332–1406) Arab philosopher, historian and politician, born in Tunis. He held various political positions in Spain but largely abandoned politics in 1375 and in 1382 went to Cairo where he became professor and a chief judge. His major work was a monumental history of the Arabs, *Kitab al-ibar* and the influential *Maqaddimah* (Introduction to History) which outlined a cyclical theory of history by which nomadic peoples became civilized, attained a peak of culture, were then corrupted by their own success, and were in turn destroyed by another, more vigorous nomadic culture.

IBN SAUD, Abdul Aziz (1880–1953) king of Saudi Arabia, the outstanding Arab ruler of his time. Born in Riyadh, he followed his family into exile in 1890 and was brought up in Kuwait. In 1901 he succeeded his father and with a small band of followers set out to reconquer the family domains from the Rashidi rulers, an aim which he achieved with British recognition in 1927. His ambitions against King **Hussein ibn Ali** however, had been frustrated by British intervention (1921). He substituted patriarchal administration by the nationalistic *Ikwan* colonies (brotherhoods) and made pilgrimages to Mecca safe for all Muslims. He changed his title from sultan of Nejd to king of Hejaz and Nejd in 1927 and in 1932 to king of Saudi Arabia. After the discovery of oil (1938) he granted substantial concessions to American oil companies. He remained neutral but friendly to the Allies in World War II. He had over a hundred wives. His son Saud Ibn Abdul Aziz (1902–69) had been prime minister for three months when he succeeded his father in 1953. Without straining relations with **Nasser**'s Egypt, he visited the USA in March 1957. In 1964 he was peacefully deposed by the council of ministers, and his brother Faisal Ibn Abdul Aziz (1904–75) succeeded to the throne, as well as remaining prime minister and minister of foreign affairs.

IBRAHIM, Abdullah, formerly **Dollar Brand** (1934–) South African jazz pianist, born in Cape Town of Bushman and Basuto parents. He began to play the piano as a child, later forming the Jazz Epistles group which recorded the country's first black jazz album in 1960. He moved to Switzerland for political reasons and was heard there by **Duke Ellington** (1962) who invited him to work in the USA. In 1966, Brand had the unique honour of replacing Ellington at the piano when the orchestra was on tour. Since then, he has worked as a soloist and leader in America and Europe, notably in the 1980s with his septet Ekaya ('Home'). Ibrahim, who also plays cello, soprano saxophone and flute, adopted his Muslim name in the 1970s and is remarkable for his jazz interpretations of the melodies and rhythms of his African childhood.

IBRAHIM ADIL SHAH II (d.1626) sultan of Bijapur of the Adil Shah dynasty. He succeeded to the throne in 1579 while still a minor. Although a Sunni

Muslim, he was extremely tolerant of all faiths, employing Hindus as well as Muslims and permitting Christian preaching. He was a very able administrator and left his successor a full treasury and a well-equipped army. Nevertheless Bijapur survived as an independent sultanate only until 1686 when it was incorporated by **Aurangzeb** into the Mughal empire.

IBRAHIM PASHA (1789–1848) viceroy of Egypt. He was the adopted son, lieutenant and (for two months) successor of **Mehemet 'Ali**.

IBSEN, Henrik (1828–1906) Norwegian dramatist, born in Skien, the founder of modern prose drama. The son of a wealthy merchant who went bankrupt, he worked as a chemist's assistant in Grimstad (1844–50), intending to study medicine, and wrote his first play there, *Catilina*, which was rejected. He got a job in journalism in Bergen, then was given a post as stage director and resident playwright at Ole Bull's Theatre, for which he wrote five conventional romantic dramas. In 1857 he was appointed director of the Norwegian Theatre in Christiania (Oslo), having just written his first play of significance, *Kongsemnerne* (The Pretenders), on a historical theme from Norway's past, in the manner of **Schiller**. In 1862 he wrote *Kaerlighedens Komedie* (Love's Comedy), with its satirical theme of marriage as a millstone to idealism. The theatre went bankrupt the following year, and Ibsen went into voluntary exile for the next few years, to Rome, Dresden and Munich (1864–92), and it was there that he wrote the bulk of his dramas. The dramatic poem *Brand* appeared in 1865, and gave him his first major success, as well as the award of a government pension. The existentialist *Peer Gynt* followed in 1867, and a third historical drama, *Kejser og Galilaer* (Emperor and Galilean) in 1873. He then turned to his plays of realism and social issues, which revolutionized European drama and on which his towering reputation rests: *Samfundets støtter* (Pillars of Society, 1877), *En dukkehjem* (A Doll's House, 1879), *Gengangere* (Ghosts, 1881), *En folkefiende* (An Enemy of the People, 1882), *Vildanden* (The Wild Duck, 1884), *Rosmersholm* (1886), *Fruen fra havet* (The Lady from the Sea, 1888), and *Hedda Gabler* (1890). Thereafter he returned to Norway; his last plays are characterized by a strong emphasis on symbolism, with *Bygmester Solness* (The Master Builder, 1892), *Lille Eyolf* (Little Eyolf, 1894), *John Gabriel Borkman* (1896), and *Naar vi døde vaagner* (When We Dead Awaken, 1899). In 1900 he suffered a stroke which ended his literary career.

IBYCUS (fl.mid 6th century BC) Greek poet from Rhegium in Italy. He lived at the court of **Polycrates**, tyrant of Samos, and wrote choral lyrics in Doric anticipating **Pindar**. Legend has it that he was slain by robbers near Corinth, and as he was dying he called upon a flock of cranes to avenge him. The cranes then hovered over the theatre at Corinth, and one of the murderers exclaimed, 'Behold the avengers of Ibycus!' This led to their conviction. The story is told in **Schiller**'s ballad.

ICAHN, Carl (1936–) American arbitrageur and options specialist, born in New York. A post-graduate student at the New York School of Medicine, he became an apprentice broker with Dreyfus Corporation. He became an options manager in 1963 and formed his own company, Icahn and Company, in 1968, holding the posts of chairman and chief executive since then. He has been chairman and chief executive officer of ACF Industries Inc since 1984, and chairman of the airline TWA since 1986.

ICHIKAWA, Fusaye (1893–1981) Japanese feminist and politician. Starting her working life as a teacher, she moved to Tokyo as a young woman and became involved in politics and feminism, helping to found the New Women's Association (c.1920) which successfully fought for women's right to attend political meetings. During her time in the USA (1921–24) she was impressed by the US suffrage movement, and in 1924 formed the Women's Suffrage League in Japan. Following World War II she became head of the New Japan Women's League, which secured the vote for women in 1945, and went on to fight for their wider rights. She campaigned against legalized prostitution and from 1952 to 1971 served in the Japanese Diet, where she continued to press for an end to bureaucratic corruption. After defeat in 1971 she was triumphantly returned to parliament in 1975 and 1980.

ICTINUS (5th century BC) Greek architect. With Callicrates he designed the Parthenon (438 BC). He was also architect of temples at Eleusis and near Phigalia.

IDA (d.599) king of Bernicia (Northumbria). According to the Venerable **Bede** he was an Anglican king who thrust northward over the river Tees in 547, landing at Flamborough, and established a fortified stronghold on the rock of Bamburgh as the capital of his new kingdom.

IDDESLEIGH, Stafford Henry Northcote, 1st Earl of (1818–87) English Conservative statesman, born in London of an old Devonshire family. He was educated at Eton and Balliol College, Oxford, became private secretary to **Gladstone** in 1842, was called to the bar in 1847 and in 1851 succeeded his grandfather as eighth baronet. In 1855 he entered parliament, was financial secretary to the Treasury under Lord **Derby** in 1859, and in 1866 was appointed president of the board of trade. While at the India Office in 1868 he had charge of the Abyssinian Expedition. In 1871 Gladstone appointed him commissioner in the *Alabama* affair. He was Chancellor of the Exchequer in 1874, and introduced the Friendly Societies Bill (1875). Upon the death of **Disraeli** he became joint leader of the party with the Marquis of **Salisbury**. In the second Salisbury ministry he was foreign secretary, but resigned early in January 1887. He was created earl in 1885.

IDRIESS, Ion Llewellyn (1889–1979) Australian author, born in Waverley, Sydney. After a wandering life as opal miner, rabbit exterminator and crocodile hunter, he served with the Australian Imperial Forces at Gallipoli and in the near east, and then travelled widely throughout Australia and in the Pacific Islands. These experiences were later to provide colour for his books. Published in 1931, *Lasseter's Last Ride*, the story of the search for the 'lost' gold reef, was his first success. In the next 40 years Idriess wrote almost one book each year, of which the best known are *Flynn of the Inland* (1932, about Rev John Flynn, founder of the Flying Doctor Service), *The Desert Column* (1932, based on his experiences with the Australian Light Horse during World War I), *The Cattle King* (1936, the life of Sir **Sidney Kidman**), and *Onward Australia* (1944).

IDRIS ALOMA (d.c.1600) ruler of Bornu from c.1569. He was a warrior-king and the dominant figure in the central Sudan. During his reign, and those of his sons, the Karini peoples of Bornu became a distinct, unified nation.

IDRISI See **EDRISI**

IFFLAND, August Wilhelm (1759–1814) German actor, born in Hanover. He was the author of numerous popular plays, including *Die Jäger*.

IGNATIEV, Nikolai Pavlovich (1832–1908) Russian diplomat, born in St Petersburg, in 1856 entered the diplomatic service. In 1858 he induced China to give up the Amur province; and in 1860, while ambassador at

(Peking), secured another large strip of territory for the Maritime Province. With Khiva and Bokhara he concluded treaties. In 1867 he was made ambassador at Constantinople. An ardent Panslavist, he intrigued with the Balkan Slavs, and took a principal part in the diplomatic proceedings before and after the Russo-Turkish war of 1878; the treaty of San Stefano was mainly his work. Under **Alexander III** he was minister of the interior (1881), but was dismissed in June 1882.

IGNATIUS LOYOLA, St, properly **Iñigo López de Recalde** (1491–1556) Spanish soldier and founder of the Jesuits. He was born at his ancestral castle of Loyola in the Basque province of Guipúzcoa. A page in the court of **Ferdinand 'the Catholic'**, he then became a soldier. In the defence of Pampeluna he was severely wounded in the leg, which he had to have re-broken in order to be re-set. After this operation his convalescence was slow; and, his stock of romances exhausted, he turned to works on the lives of **Jesus Christ** and the saints. The result was a spiritual enthusiasm as intense as that by which he had hitherto been drawn to chivalry. Renouncing military life, he resolved to begin his new life by a pilgrimage to Jerusalem. In 1522 he set out on his pilgrimage, the first step of which was a voluntary engagement to serve the poor and sick in the hospital of Manresa. There his zeal and devotion attracted such notice that he withdrew to a cavern in the vicinity, where he pursued alone his course of self-prescribed austerity, until, utterly exhausted, he was carried back to the hospital. From Manresa he went to Rome, then proceeded on foot to Venice and there embarked for Cyprus and the Holy Land. He returned to Venice and Barcelona in 1524. He then resolved to prepare himself for the work of religious teaching, and at the age of 33 returned to the rudiments of grammar, followed up by courses at Alcalá, Salamanca and Paris. In 1534 he founded, with St **Francis Xavier** and four other associates, the Society of Jesus. The original aim was limited to a pilgrimage to the Holy Land, and the conversion of the Infidels, but as access to the Holy Land was cut off by war with the Turks, the associates sought to meet the new wants engendered by the Reformation. Loyola went to Rome in 1539, and submitted to Pope **Paul III** the rule of the proposed order, and the vow by which the members bound themselves to go as missionaries to any country the pope might choose. The rule was approved in 1540, and next year the association elected Loyola as its first general. From this time he resided in Rome. At Manresa he wrote the first draft of the *Spiritual Exercises*, a vital work in the training of Jesuits. He sent out missionaries to Japan, India and Brazil, and founded schools for training the young. He was beatified in 1609, and canonized in 1622. His feast day is 31 July.

IGNATIUS OF ANTIOCH (c.35–c.107) Christian prelate, one of the apostolic fathers, reputed to be a disciple of St **John**, and second bishop of Antioch. According to the *Chronicon* of **Eusebius of Caesarea** (c.320) he died a martyr in Rome under **Trajan**. The *Ignatian Epistles* were written on his way to Rome after being arrested. The warnings against Judaism and Docetism, as well as the high doctrine of the bishop's office reflected in these epistles, were somewhat extreme, but allowances must be made for his predicament. Two other recensions of the letters have survived, one of which, a Syriac version, is a 4th-century redraft. His feast day is 1 February.

IHRE, Johan (1707–80) Swedish philologist, born in Lund, of Scottish extraction. In 1748 he became professor of belles-lettres and political economy. His *Glossarium Suiogothicum* (1769) was the foundation of Swedish philology. He noted a number of the sound correspondences later developed by **Rask** and **Grimm** into what has become known as Grimm's Law.

I-HSING (682–727) Chinese inventor. He established a reputation as a 'holy man' and became a Buddhist monk as well as having an influential role in the Chinese court where he assumed the role of seer. He devised a new calendar which was adopted in 724, and wrote several mathematical and astronomical treatises, which led him to experiment with new devices and instruments. His masterpiece was a water-driven celestial sphere, thought to be the first regulated by an escapement, the first to use concentric gears and shafts as part of the mechanism, and the first Chinese clock to strike the hours and half-hours. Sadly, it was in use for only a short time, the bronze and iron parts corroding rapidly, after which it was consigned to a museum.

ILBERT, Sir Courtenay Peregrine (1841–1924) English parliamentary draftsman, born in Kingsbridge, Devon, and educated at Marlborough and Balliol College, Oxford. After teaching at Oxford and service as legal member of council in India (1882–86), he worked as parliamentary counsel to the Treasury (1886–1902), and clerk of the House of Commons (1902–21). He wrote *Legislative Methods and Forms* (1901), *The Mechanics of Law-making* (1914) and *Parliament, its History, Constitution and Practice* (1911).

ILLINGWORTH, Raymond (1932–) English cricketer, born in Pudsey. A natural captain, he led both Yorkshire and Leicestershire to the county championship, slowly developing into a proficient all-round Test player (batsman and spin-bowler). He won 66 Test caps for England (36 as captain), taking 122 wickets and scoring two Test centuries; as England captain he won the Ashes in Australia in 1962–63. He was manager of Yorkshire from 1979 to 1984; after his retirement he became a cricket television commentator.

ILYUSHIN, Sergei Vladimirovich (1894–1977) Russian aircraft designer, born in Vologda Oblast. After being drafted into the army in 1914, he served as an aircraft mechanic and began flight training in 1917. He graduated from the North-East Zhukovsky Air Force Academy in 1926, leading to his appointment in 1931 as director of the aircraft construction section of the Scientific and Technical Committee, Main Air Force Board. His first successful design, the TSKB-30, (1936) gained several records and was extensively used as a bomber in World War II. His other designs included the IL-2 Shturmovik dive-bomber (1939), the twin-engined passenger-carrying IL-12 (1946), the IL-28 jet bomber (1948), the IL-18 Moskva turboprop airliner (1957), the 182-passenger IL-62 jet of 1957 and its wide-bodied successor, the IL-86 airbus (350 passengers). An outstanding designer, and a leading Communist party official, he became a professor of aircraft design at the Zhukovsky Air Force Engineering Academy in 1948.

IMHOF, Eduard (1895–1986) Swiss cartographer, born in Schiers, and educated at the Swiss Federal Institute of Technology (ETH) (1914–19). He was elected to the first Swiss chair in cartography (1925) and founded the prestigious Institute of Cartography at the ETH, which he directed until his retirement in 1965. He pioneered good design as the basis of the cartographic discipline and published classic texts on relief and thematic techniques. As a cartographic artist throughout his life, he produced 50 full-colour relief maps. He edited the *Atlas der Schweiz* (1961–78).

IMHOTEP (fl.c.2980 BC) Egyptian physician and adviser to King Zoser (3rd dynasty). He was probably the architect of the so-called Step Pyramid at Sakkara, near Cairo. In time he came to be revered as a sage, and during the Saite period (500 BC) he was worshipped as the life-giving son of Ptah, god of Memphis. The Greeks identified him with their own god of healing, Asclepius, because of his reputed knowledge of medicine. Many bronze figures of him have been discovered.

IMLAY, Gilbert See **WOLLSTONECRAFT, Mary**

IMMELMANN, Max (1890–1916) German airman. He laid the foundation of German fighter tactics in World War I, and originated the 'Immelmann turn'—a half-loop followed by a half-roll. He was killed in action.

IMMERMANN, Karl Leberecht (1796–1840) German dramatist and novelist, born in Magdeburg. In 1817 he entered the public service of Prussia, and served in Münster, Magdeburg and Düsseldorf. His fame rests upon his tales (*Miscellen*, 1830) and the satirical novels *Die Epigonen* (1836) and *Münchhausen* (1839).

IMPEY, Sir Elijah (1732–1809) British judge, born in Hammersmith. He was called to the bar in 1756 and appointed chief justice to the new supreme court at Calcutta in 1774. A friend of **Warren Hastings**, he was recalled in 1783 and, charged with corruption in 1787, defended himself and was acquitted.

INA, or **Ine** (7th century) one of the most important early West Saxon kings. According to the Venerable **Bede**, he came to power in 688; during his long reign of nearly 40 years he put church organizations on a proper footing and promulgated the earliest extant code of West Saxon laws. He abdicated in 726, and died on a pilgrimage to Rome.

INCHBALD, Elizabeth, née **Simpson** (1753–1821) English novelist, playwright and actress, born in Bury St Edmunds, the daughter of a farmer. She ran away to go on the stage and in 1772 married John Inchbald, an actor in London. She made her début at Bristol as Cordelia. After the death of her husband in 1779 she appeared at Covent Garden, but from 1789 made her name as a playwright and author of 19 sentimental comedies, including *The Wedding Day* (1794) and *Lover's Vows* (1798). She also wrote the novels *A Simple Story* (1791) and *Nature and Art* (1796). She was editor of the 24-volume *The British Theatre* (1806–09).

INDIANA, Robert, originally **Robert Clarke** (1928–) American painter and graphic designer, born in New Castle, Indiana. He studied art in Indianapolis (1945–46), in Ithaca, New York, and at the Art Institute of Chicago before travelling to Britain in 1953. Settling in New York in 1956, he began making hard-edged abstract pictures and stencilled wooden constructions, which fall into the early Pop Art movement. His best-known images are based on the letters LOVE, as featured in his first one-man show in New York (1962). His other word-paintings have included HUG, ERR and EAT.

INDY, Vincent d' (1851–1931) French composer, born in Paris. An ardent student, disciple and biographer of **César Franck**, he founded the Schola Cantorum in Paris in 1894, published *Treatise of Composition* (1900) and composed operas, chamber music and, notably, the *Symphonie cévenole* (1886) in the spirit of French Romanticism.

INE See **INA**

INEZ DE CASTRO See **CASTRO**

INGE, William Motter (1913–73) American playwright and novelist, born in Independence, Kansas. He was educated at Kansas University and George Peabody College for Teachers, and taught and wrote art criticism for the St Louis *Star-Times*. Outside the mainstream of American theatre, he is nevertheless important for four plays—*Come Back, Little Sheba* (1950), *Picnic* (1953), *Bus Stop* (1955) and *The Dark at the Top of the Stairs* (first produced in 1947 and revised in 1957)—in which he transforms the lives of drab people living in drab surroundings into significant dramas of human experience. He was awarded the Pulitzer prize in 1953.

INGE, William Ralph (1860–1954) English prelate and theologian, born in Crayke, Yorkshire. Educated at Eton and King's College, Cambridge, he taught at Eton and was vicar of All Saints, Kensington, for two years before being appointed in 1907 professor of divinity at Cambridge. From 1911 to 1934 he was dean of St Paul's, earning for himself by his pessimism in sermons and newspaper articles the sobriquet of 'the Gloomy Dean'. Popular books include *Outspoken Essays* (1919, 1922) and *Lay Thoughts of a Dean* (1926, 1931); more serious works examined, among other things, Neoplatonism and Christian Mysticism.

INGEBORG See **PHILIP II** of France

INGELOW, Jean (1820–97) English poet and novelist, born in Boston, Lincolnshire. She wrote devotional poetry, lyrics and ballads, of which the short poem 'High Tide on the Coast of Lincolnshire 1571' is her best. Her tales for children include *Mopsa the Fairy* (1869), and her novels *Off the Skelligs* (1872).

INGEMANN, Bernhard Severin (1789–1862) Danish poet and novelist, born in Thorkildstrup in Falster. He is best known for his idealized romantic historical novels *Valdemar Sejer* (1826), *Kong Erik* (1833) and *Prins Otto af Danmark* (1835), and historical poems *Waldemar the Great* (1824), *Queen Margaret* (1836) and *Holger Danske* (1837). From 1822 he lectured at the Royal Academy of Sorø, near Copenhagen.

INGEN-HAUSZ, Jan (1730–99) Dutch physician and plant physiologist, born in Breda. He practised as a doctor in England and was physician to the empress **Maria Theresa**. In 1779 he discovered that carbon dioxide is absorbed by plants in the day and given out at night. He also devised a method for comparing heat conductivities.

INGERSOLL, Robert Green (1833–99) American lawyer and orator, born in Dresden, New York State, the son of a Congregational minister. In the Civil War he was colonel of a Federal cavalry regiment; in 1867 he became state attorney-general of Illinois. A successful Republican orator, he was also noted for his agnostic lectures attacking Christian beliefs, and wrote numerous books, including *The Gods, and Other Lectures* (1876) and *Why I Am An Agnostic* (1896).

INGLEBY, Clement Mansfield (1823–86) English philosopher and Shakespearian scholar, born in Edgbaston. He graduated from Trinity College, Cambridge, and practised for a while as a solicitor, but in 1859 devoted himself to literature. His earliest works were handbooks of logic (1856) and metaphysics (1869), but his life-work began with *The Shakespeare Fabrications* (1859), and included a long series of works, of which the best known was *Shakespeare: the Man and the Book* (1877–81).

INGLIS, Elsie Maud (1864–1917) Scottish surgeon and reformer, born in Naini Tal, India. One of the first women medical students at Edinburgh and Glasgow, she inaugurated the second medical school for women at Edinburgh (1892). In 1901, appalled at the lack of maternity facilities and the prejudice held against women doctors by their male colleagues, she founded a maternity hospital in Edinburgh, completely staffed by women. In 1906 she founded the Scottish Women's Suffragette Federation, which sent two women ambulance units to France and Serbia in 1915. She set up three military hospitals in Serbia (1916), fell into Austrian hands, was repatriated, but in 1917 returned to Russia with a voluntary corps, which was withdrawn after the revolution.

INGLIS, John, Baron Glencorse (1810–91) Scottish judge, born in Edinburgh. He established himself as a leading advocate by his brilliant defence of **Madeleine Smith** in 1857, and rose to be successively lord justice-clerk (1858) and lord president of the Court of Session (1867–91). As such he ranks very high as a judge and many of his judgments are classics. He also played a major role in the reform of the Scottish universities.

INGLIS, Sir John Eardley Wilmot (1814–62) British soldier, born in Nova Scotia. He joined the British army in 1833 and fought in India at Mooltan and Gujerat (1848–49). He commanded the British forces at Lucknow during the historic siege in the Indian mutiny (1857), was promoted major-general and knighted.

INGOLDSBY, Thomas See **BARHAM, Richard Harris**

INGRAHAM, Joseph Holt (1809–60) American novelist and clergyman, born in Portland, Maine. He was for some time a sailor, and then taught languages at a college in Mississippi. He published some sensational romances, such as *Pirate of the Gulf* (1836) and *Scarlet Feather* (1845); but after he was ordained to the Episcopal priesthood (1852), he wrote religious romances such as *The Prince of the House of David* (1855).

INGRAHAM, Prentiss (1843–1904) American soldier of fortune and novelist, son of **Joseph Holt Ingraham**. He served in Mexico, Austria, Africa and Cuba before settling in New York and writing some 700 'dime novels', many with Buffalo Bill (**William Cody**) as the hero. He also wrote plays, short stories and poems.

INGRAM, Collingwood, known as **'Cherry Ingram'** (1880–1981) English ornithologist, botanist, gardener and traveller, grandson of the newspaper proprietor **Herbert Ingram**. He had a garden at Bettenden, Kent, celebrated for its collection of Japanese ornamental cherries. His books include *The Birds of the Riviera* (1926), *Isles of the Seven Seas* (1936), *Ornamental Cherries* (1948), *In Search of Birds* (1966), *A Garden of Memories* (1970) and *The Migration of the Swallow* (1974).

INGRAM, Herbert (1811–60) English journalist, born in Boston, Lincolnshire. In 1842 he founded the *Illustrated London News*. He was MP for Boston from 1856. He was drowned in a boat collision on Lake Michigan in the USA.

INGRES, Jean Auguste Dominique (1780–1867) French painter, the leading exponent of the classical tradition in France in the 19th century, born in Montauban. He went to Paris in 1796 to study painting under **Jacques Louis David**. In 1801 he won the prix de Rome with *Achilles receiving the Ambassadors of Agamemnon* (École des Beaux Arts), but quarrelled with David and from 1806 to 1820 lived in Rome, where he began many of his famous nudes, including *Baigneuse* and *La Source* (begun in 1807 but not completed till 1859), both in the Louvre. Many of the paintings he sent to Paris from Rome attracted vehement criticism, especially from **Delacroix**, whose work Ingres detested. Ingres' paintings display superb draughtsmanship, but little interest in facial characteristics or colour. His motto was 'A thing well drawn is well enough painted'. He also painted historical subjects such as *Paolo and Francesca* (1819, Chantilly) and in Florence (1820–24) painted *The Oath to Louis XIII* for Montauban Cathedral, which appeased the rival schools of Classicists and Romantics in France. He returned to Paris in 1826 and was appointed professor at the Academy. His *Apotheosis of Homer* (Louvre ceiling) was well received, but not *The Martyrdom of St Symphorian* (1834, Autun Cathedral) and Ingres went off again to Italy (1834–41), becoming director of the French Academy in Rome. His *Stratonice* (Chantilly), *Vierge à l'hostie* (Louvre) and *Odalisque à l'esclave* re-established him in Paris and he returned in triumph, was awarded the Légion d'Honeur and made a senator (1862).

INMAN, William (1825–81) English ship-owner, born in Leicester. In 1857 he founded the Inman Line, which from 1860 made weekly crossings to New York from Liverpool.

INNES, Cosmo (1798–1874) Scottish jurist and historian, born in Durris. Educated at Glasgow and Oxford, he was called to the Scottish bar in 1822. He became sheriff of Moray in 1840, then an official of the Court of Session, and in 1846 professor of constitutional law and history in the University of Edinburgh. He is best known as the author of *Scotland in the Middle Ages* (1860), *Sketches of Early Scotch History* (1861) and *Lectures on Scotch Legal Antiquities* (1872). He prepared volume one of *Acts of the Parliament of Scotland*, was a member of the Bannatyne, Maitland and Spalding Clubs, and edited for them several cartularies of the old religious houses of Scotland. He also published several memoirs, including one of Dean **Edward Ramsay**.

INNES, Thomas (1663–1744) Scottish historian, born in Drumgask in Aberdeenshire. He was educated at Paris, took holy orders in 1692, and was a priest at Inveraven in Banff (1698–1701). He spent most of his life in Paris, where his brother Lewis (1651–1738) was principal of the Scots College from 1682 to 1713. He returned to Scotland (1722–25), and became vice-principal of the Scots College in Paris in 1727. In 1729 he published his *Critical Essay on the Ancient Inhabitants of Scotland*, which dismissed the existence of 40 legendary pre-Christian kings of Scotland. It served as introduction to his *Civil and Ecclesiastical History of Scotland*, which was only completed down to **Columba**'s death (831).

INNESS, George (1825–94) American landscape artist, born near Newburgh, New York. He visited Italy and France and came under the influence of the Barbizon school. Among his best-known paintings are *Delaware Valley* and *Evening, Medfield, Massachusetts*, in the Metropolitan Museum at New York, and *Rainbow after a Storm* in Chicago Art Institute.

INNOCENT I, St (360–417) pope from 402 to 417. A native of Albano, his pontificate, next to that of **Leo the Great**, is the most important for the relations of Rome to the other churches. He enforced the celibacy of the clergy; he maintained the right of the bishop of Rome to judge appeals from other churches, and his letters abound with assertions of universal jurisdiction. During his pontificate, Rome was sacked in 410 by **Alaric I**. His feast day is 28 July.

INNOCENT III (1160–1216) pope from 1198 to 1216, the greatest pope of this name. He was born Lotario de' Conti at Agnagni and succeeded Pope Celestine III. His pontificate is regarded as the culminating point of the temporal and spiritual supremacy of the Roman see; under the impulse of his zeal for the glory of the church almost every state and kingdom was brought into subjection. He judged between rival emperors in Germany and had **Otto IV** deposed. He made **Philip Augustus** of France take back his wife. He laid England under an interdict and excommunicated King **John** for refusing to recognize

Stephen Langton as archbishop of Canterbury. John's submission made England and Ireland satellites of the Holy See. In his time the Latin conquest of Constantinople in the Fourth Crusade destroyed the pretensions of his eastern rivals. He zealously repressed simony and other abuses of the time. He promoted the spiritual movement in which the Franciscan and Dominican orders had their origin. Under him the famous fourth Lateran Council was held in 1215. His works embrace sermons, a remarkable treatise on the *Misery of the Condition of Man*, a large number of letters, and perhaps the 'golden sequence' 'Veni, sancte Spiritus'.

INNOCENT XI (1611–89) pope from 1676 to 1689, born Benedetto Odescalchi in Como. As pope, he proved a vigorous and judicious reformer, and strove hard to put an end to the abuse by **Louis XIV** of the king's claim to keep sees vacant and appropriate their revenues. The conflict was regarding the right of asylum enjoyed by the foreign ambassadors in Rome, which had been extended to the district round their houses. These districts had gradually become nests of crime, and of frauds upon the revenue; and the pope gave notice that he would not thereafter receive the credentials of any new ambassador who would not renounce these claims. Louis XIV instructed a new ambassador to maintain the dignity of France, and sent a large body of officers to support him. Innocent would grant no audience. Louis seized the papal territory of Avignon, but the pope died before the dispute was settled.

INÖNÜ, Ismet, adopted name of **Ismet Paza** (1884–1973) Turkish soldier and politician, born in Izmir, Asia Minor. After a distinguished army career in the war (1914–18) he became **Kemal Atatürk**'s chief of staff in the war against the Greeks (1919–22), defeating them twice at the village of Inönü, which he adopted as his last name. As the first premier of Atatürk's new republic (1923–37) he signed the Treaty of Lausanne (1923), introduced many political reforms transforming Turkey into a modern state, and was unanimously elected president in 1938 on Atatürk's death. From 1950 he was leader of the opposition. He became premier again with General Gürsel as president in 1961, surviving repeated assassination attempts, an army *coup* and constitutional crisis in 1963, but resigned in 1965 after failing to govern effectively with minority support.

IONESCO, Eugène (1912–) Romanian-born French playwright, educated at Bucharest and Paris, where he settled in 1940. He pioneered a new style of drama with his short surrealistic plays, including *The Bald Prima Donna* (1950), *The Lesson* (1951), *The Chairs* (1952), *L'Amedée* (1954), *Victims of Duty* (1957), *The Picture* (1958) and *Le Rhinocéros* (1960), based on the highly personal material of his dreams, hidden desires and inner conflicts, on the Freudian assumption that humanity has a dream-world in common. His contempt for realism, the robot-like deficiencies of his characters, the suggestive irrationality of their outpourings, his paradoxical view that art is the attempt to communicate an incommunicable reality, have led to criticism by disciples of social realism. His later plays include *Jeux de Massacre* (1970), *Macbett* (1972) and *Voyages chez les Morts ou Thème et Variations* (1980); among many essays and other writings, he wrote the novel *The Hermit* (1975).

IONESCU, Take (1858–1922) Romanian politician. He became leader of the Conservative-Democratic party in 1907 and was foreign minister in 1917–18 and from 1920 to 1922. He was Romanian delegate at the Versailles conference.

IPATIEFF, Vladimir (1867–1952) Russian-born American chemist, born in Moscow. An officer in the Russian army, he was professor of chemistry at the Artillery Academy in St Petersburg (1898–1906). He synthesized isoprene, the basic unit of natural rubber, and made contributions to the catalytic chemistry of unsaturated carbons, of great value to the petrochemical industry. During World War I he directed Russia's chemical warfare programme. He emigrated to the USA in 1930 and became professor at Northwestern University (1931–35), where he developed a process for making high-octane petrol.

IPHICRATES (415–353 BC) Athenian soldier. He served in the Corinthian War (395–387), in Egypt (374), and against Sparta (372–371). He is known for introducing a new and more mobile kind of infantry, the 'peltasts', armed with a light shield ('pelte') and javelin, which he used with immense effect.

IQBAL, Sir Mohammed (1875–1938) Indian poet and philosopher, born in Sialkot (now in Pakistan). He taught philosophy at Lahore, studied law in England, and was knighted in 1923. He wrote poems in Urdu and Persian which are full of a compelling mysticism and nationalism which caused him to be regarded almost as a prophet by Muslims.

IRELAND, John (1879–1962) English composer, born in Cheshire. He studied composition under **Charles Stanford** at the Royal College of Music, London. His poetic feelings, inspired by ancient traditions and places, are in evidence in such works as the orchestral prelude *The Forgotten Rite* (1913) of the Channel islands, and the rhapsody *Mai-dun* (1921) of the Wessex countryside. He established his reputation with his Violin Sonata in A (1917), and between the wars was a prominent member of the English musical renaissance. The piano concerto (1930) and *These Things Shall Be* (1937) for chorus and orchestra feature strongly among his later works, which include song settings of poems by **Hardy**, **Masefield**, **Housman** and others.

IRELAND, William Henry (1777–1835) English literary forger, born in London, the son of an engraver. He was articled at the age of 17 to a London conveyancer. He was tempted by his father's enthusiasm for **Shakespeare** to forge an autograph of the poet on a carefully copied old lease. His audacity grew with the credulity of his dupes, and he produced private letters and annotated books. **Boswell**, **Warton** and hundreds more came, saw and believed; but those, like **Malone**, qualified to judge saw through the forgery and denounced it. Ireland then produced a deed of Shakespeare's bequeathing his books and papers to a William-Henrye Irelaunde, an assumed ancestor. Next a new historical play entitled *Vortigern* was announced, and produced by **Sheridan** at Drury Lane (1796)—it was damned at once. This nipped in the bud a projected series of historical plays. His father finally began to suspect and the young man was forced to confess. He published a statement in 1796, and expanded it in his *Confessions* (1805). He produced a dozen poems, four or five novels, and ten or more biographical and miscellaneous compilations, but ended his life in poverty.

IRENAEUS, St (c.130–c.200) Greek theologian, one of the Christian fathers of the Greek church, born in Asia Minor. He was a pupil of **Polycarp** who had been a disciple of **John** the Apostle. He became a priest of the Graeco-Gaulish church of Lyon under Bishop Pothinus, after whose martyrdom in 177 he was elected to the see. **Gregory of Tours** says that Irenaeus met his death in the persecution under **Severus** in 202, but this has never been substantiated. Irenaeus was a successful missionary bishop, but he is chiefly remembered for his opposition to Gnosticism (especially the Valentinians), against which he wrote his invaluable work *Against Heresies*. A masterly expositor of Christian theology, he was a key figure also in the maintenance of contact between eastern and western sections of the church. His feast day is 3 July.

IRENE (752–803) Byzantine empress, a poor orphan of Athens whose beauty and talents led the emperor Leo IV to marry her in 769. After 780 she ruled as regent for her son, Constantine VI. She imprisoned and blinded him and her husband's five brothers, and ruled in her own right from 797, but in 802 she was banished to Lesbos. For her part in the restoration of the veneration of icons she was recognized as a saint by the Greek church.

IRETON, Henry (1611–51) English soldier, born in Attenborough, Nottingham. He graduated from Trinity College, Cambridge, in 1629, and at the outbreak of the Civil War (1642–51) offered his services to parliament, fighting at Edgehill (1642), Naseby (1645) and the siege of Bristol. In 1646 he married Bridget, the daughter of **Cromwell**. In 1647 he proposed a solution to the conflict by means of a constitutional monarchy (the so called 'Heads of the Proposals'), but later he signed the warrant for the king's execution (1649). He accompanied Cromwell to Ireland, and in 1650 became lord-deputy. He died of the plague before Limerick, and was buried in Westminster Abbey until the Restoration, when his remains were transferred to Tyburn.

IRIARTE Y OROPESA, Tomas de (1750–91) Spanish poet, writer of fables, born in Orotava, Tenerife. He was the author of *Fábulas Literarias* (1782), and a translator of **Horace**.

IRIGOYEN, Hipólito (1850–1933) Argentine politician, born in Buenos Aires. He became leader of the Radical Civic Union party in 1896 and worked for electoral reform, which, when it came in 1912, ushered him into power as the first Radical president of the Argentine (1916–22). He was again elected in 1928, but deposed by a military *coup* in 1930.

IRNERIUS, the 'Lucerna Juris' (d. before 1140) Italian jurist, born in Bologna. He was one of the first to devote serious study to **Justinian I**, and was the most famous of the early teachers of the law school at Bologna. He wrote numerous texts on Roman law.

IRONSIDE, William Edmund, 1st Baron Ironside (1880–1959) Scottish soldier, born in Ironside, Aberdeenshire. He served as a secret agent disguised as a railwayman in the 2nd Boer War (1899–1902) and held several staff-appointments in World War I. He commanded the Archangel expedition against the Bolsheviks (1918) and the allied contingent in North Persia (1920). He was chief of the Imperial General Staff at the outbreak of World War II, was promoted field marshal (1940) and placed in command of the home defence forces (1940). The 'Ironsides', fast, light-armoured vehicles, were named after him.

IRVINE, Sir Alexander (c.1600–1658) laird of Drum, an Aberdeenshire royalist. He was descended from the 'gude' Sir Alexander Irvine, provost of Aberdeen, who fell in single combat at Harlaw (1411) as celebrated in the ballad of the battle.

IRVINE, Andrew (1951–) Scottish rugby player, born in Edinburgh. He played soccer until the age of 12, then attended Heriot's School and took up rugby, eventually following in the tradition whereby George Heriot's School supplied the Scottish international team with full backs (previous holders of the position being Dan Drysdale and K J F Scotland). He won 51 caps for Scotland, scored more points in South Africa than any touring Lion had previously done, and was the first player in the world to score more than 300 points in international rugby.

IRVING, Edward (1792–1834) Scottish clergyman and mystic, born in Annan. He studied at Edinburgh University, became a schoolmaster and in 1819 was appointed assistant to **Thomas Chalmers** in Glasgow. In 1822 he was asked to the Caledonian Church, Hatton Garden, London, where he enjoyed a phenomenal success as a preacher. In 1825 he began to announce the imminent second advent of **Jesus Christ**; this was followed up by the translation of *The Coming of the Messiah* (1827), supposedly written by a Christian Jew, but really by a Spanish Jesuit. By 1828, when his *Homilies on the Sacraments* appeared, he had begun to elaborate his views of the Incarnation, asserting Christ's oneness with us in all the attributes of humanity and he was charged with heresy for maintaining the sinfulness of Christ's nature. He was convicted of heresy by the London presbytery in 1830, ejected from his new church in Regent's Square in 1832, and finally deposed in 1833. The majority of his congregation adhered to him, and a new communion, the Catholic Apostolic Church, was developed, commonly known as Irvingite, though Irving had little to do with its development.

IRVING, Sir Henry, John Henry Brodribb (1838–1905) English actor, born in Keinton-Mandeville, Somerset. He was for a time a clerk in London but made his first appearance at the Sunderland Theatre in 1856. He acted in Edinburgh (1857–60), Manchester (1860–65), Liverpool, and in 1866 made his London début at the St James's Theatre. In 1871 he transferred to the Lyceum and with his *Hamlet* (1874), *Macbeth* (1875) and *Othello* (1876) gained his reputation as the greatest English actor of his time. His striking presence and flair for interpreting the subtler emotions made him more successful in the portrayal of static characters such as Shylock and Malvolio rather than in the great tragic roles of King Lear or Hamlet. In 1878 his famous theatrical partnership with **Ellen Terry** at the Lyceum, where he became actor-manager-lessee, began with her Ophelia to his Hamlet and lasted till 1902. A notable success was Wills' version of **Goethe**'s *Faust* (1885), in which Ellen Terry played Marguerite to Irving's Mephistopheles. In April 1889 they gave a command performance of *The Bells* before Queen **Victoria** at Sandringham, and in 1893 produced **Tennyson**'s play *Becket*. Irving toured the USA with his company eight times. In 1898 the failure of his son's play and the loss by fire of the Lyceum's stock of scenery compelled Irving to sell the lease of the Lyceum, which was eventually turned into a music-hall. In 1895 he became the first actor to receive a knighthood. His ashes were interred in Westminster Abbey. Irving wrote *The Drama* (1893) and published an edition of **Shakespeare**'s plays (1888). Of his sons, Laurence (1871–1914) was a novelist and playwright who was drowned in the *Empress of Ireland* disaster, and Henry Brodribb ('H B'; 1870–1919) was also an actor.

IRVING, Washington (1783–1859) American man of letters, born in New York, the son of a prosperous hardware merchant. He studied law, but on account of his delicate health was sent in 1804 to Europe. He visited Rome, Paris, the Netherlands and London, and in 1806 returned to New York, and was admitted to the bar. His first publication was *Salmagundi* (1808), a series of satirical essays in semi-monthly sheet in imitation of the *Spectator*, which ran for 20 issues. His first characteristically boisterous work was *A History of New York, by Diedrich Knickerbocker* (1809), a good-natured burlesque upon the old Dutch settlers of Manhattan Island. He served as an officer in the 1812 war, wrote biographies of American naval heroes, became a friend of Sir **Walter Scott** and under the pseudonym 'Geoffrey Crayon' wrote *The Sketch Book* (1819–20), a miscellany, containing in different styles such items as 'Rip Van Winkle', 'The Legend of Sleepy Hollow' and 'Westminster Abbey', which have something of his sadness at the loss of his betrothed and his brothers' fortune. Another sketch book, *Bracebridge Hall* (1822), was followed after three years' travel in France and Germany by another miscellany, *Tales of a Traveller* (1824). His stay in Spain (1826–29) produced such studies as *The History of the Life and Voyages of Christopher Columbus* (1828), *A Chronicle of the Conquest of Granada* (1829) and *Voyages of the Companions of Columbus* (1831). After leaving Spain, he was for a short time secretary to the United States Legation in London. On his return to his native city (1832) he was welcomed enthusiastically, but the criticisms by **Fenimore Cooper** and others that he had written only about Europe resulted in *A Tour on the Prairie* (1835) and *The Adventures of Captain Bonneville, USA* (1837). He reached the height of his career when he was appointed US ambassador to Spain (1842–46).

ISAAC I, Comnenus (d.1061) eastern Roman emperor in Constantinople from 1057 to 1059. He established the finances of the empire on a sounder footing, laid the clergy under contribution at the tax collections, and repelled the Hungarians attacking his northern frontier; and then, resigning the crown (1059), retired to a monastery, where he died. He wrote commentaries on **Homer**.

ISAAC II, Angelus (d.1204) eastern Roman emperor in Constantinople from 1185. After a reign of war and tumult he was dethroned, blinded and imprisoned by his brother Alexius in 1195. Restored in 1203, he reigned six months, was again dethroned, and died in prison.

ISAACS, Alick (1921–67) Scottish virologist, born in Glasgow, the discoverer of interferon. He studied medicine at Glasgow, did research work at Sheffield and Melbourne, and joined the virology division of the National Institute for Research in 1950 (chief, 1961). His research into the way influenza viruses interacted and impeded each other's growth led to his isolation of a substance he called interferon which can inhibit viral infection.

ISAACS, Sir Isaac Alfred (1855–1948) Australian jurist and politician, born in Melbourne, the son of a Jewish tailor. He became a barrister and, as attorney-general for the colony of Victoria, helped prepare the federal constitution (1897–99). He sat in the federal parliament (1901–06), was a justice of the high court (1906–30), and chief justice (1930–31). From 1931 to 1936 he was governor-general, the first Australian to hold that office.

ISAACS, Jeremy Israel (1932–) Scottish television executive, born in Glasgow. Educated at Merton College, Oxford, he became a producer with Granada Television in 1958 on such current affairs series as *What the Papers Say* and *All Our Yesterdays* (1960–63). He later worked on the BBC's *Panorama* (1965) and at Thames Television (1968–78) where he produced the comprehensive, clear-sighted documentary epic *The World at War* (1975). His later programmes include *Ireland: A Television History* (1981) and the brutal drama *A Sense of Freedom* (1981). He served as the first chief executive of Channel 4 (1981–87), vigorously defending its right to offer alternative programming and service minority interests. In 1988 he became general director of the Royal Opera House in Covent Garden.

ISAACS, Rufus See **READING**

ISAACS, Susan Brierley, née **Fairhurst** (1885–1948) English specialist in the education of young children, born in Bromley Cross, Lancashire. She studied philosophy and psychology at Manchester and Cambridge, and lectured in Manchester and London. A disciple of **Freud** and believer in the enduring effects of early childhood experiences, she ran an experimental progressive school, Malting House, in Cambridge (1924–27), which aimed at letting children find out for themselves rather than by direct instruction, and at allowing them emotional expression rather than imposing a restrictive discipline. She was the influential head of the department of child development at the Institute of Education, London (1933–43). She published *Intellectual Growth in Young Children* (1930) and *Social Development of Young Children* (1933). Some of her conclusions challenged the theories of **Jean Piaget** concerning the stages of children's intellectual development, before it was acceptable to question Piaget's work. She was a powerful influence on the theory and practice of the education of young children between the wars.

ISABELLA (1292–1358) queen of England, consort of **Edward II**. She was a daughter of **Philip IV** of France. After her marriage at Boulogne in 1308, she was treated with little consideration, and returned to France in 1325 when her brother, **Charles IV**, seized Edward's territories in France. In love with one of Edward's disaffected nobles, Roger de Mortimer (later Earl of March), she invaded England in 1326 and routed Edward's troops, forcing him to abdicate in favour of her young son, **Edward III**, with herself and Mortimer as regents. In September 1327, they procured the murder of Edward in Berkeley Castle. Three years later, in 1330, Edward III asserted his authority, and Isabella and Mortimer were arrested. Mortimer was hung, drawn and quartered, while Isabella withdrew to Castle Rising, near King's Lynn, for the rest of her life.

ISABELLA II (1830–1904) queen of Spain, born in Madrid. On the death of her father, **Ferdinand VII** (1833), she succeeded to the throne, with her mother, Queen **Maria Christina**, as regent. She attained her majority in 1843, and in 1846 married her cousin, Francisco de Assisi. Although popular with the Spanish people, her scandalous private life made her the tool of rival factions and in 1868 she was deposed and exiled to France, where in 1870 she abdicated in favour of her son, **Alfonso XII**.

ISABELLA OF ANGOULÊME (d.1246) queen of England, consort of King **John**, whom she married in 1200. In 1214 she was imprisoned by John at Gloucester, and after his death in 1216 she returned to France, where she married a former lover, the Comte de la Marche, in 1220. Isabella was the mother of **Henry III**; her daughter by John, Isabella (1214–41), married the emperor **Frederick II**.

ISABELLA OF CASTILE (1451–1504) queen of Spain. The daughter of King John II of Castile and Leon, she succeeded her brother to the crown in 1474. In 1469 she married **Ferdinand 'the Catholic'** of Aragon, and became joint sovereign with him, his title being Ferdinand V of Aragon and Castile.

ISABEY, Jean Baptiste (1767–1855) French portrait painter and miniaturist, born in Nancy. Trained under **Jacques Louis David**, he painted portraits of revolution notabilities, and afterwards became court painter to **Napoleon** and the **Bourbons**. His son, Eugène (1804–86), was an historical painter.

ISAEUS (4th century BC) Athenian orator. Little is known of his life. He was a professional speech writer, but barely a dozen of the 50 speeches he composed have survived.

ISAIAH, Hebrew **Jeshaiah** (8th century BC) Old Testament prophet, the son of Amoz. He was a citizen of Jerusalem, who began to prophesy about 747 BC and wielded great influence in the kingdom of Judah until the Assyrian invasion of 701 BC. According to tradition, he was later martyred. The Book of Isaiah contains his prophecies, of which the first 39 are considered authentic.

ISHERWOOD, Christopher William Bradshaw (1904–) English-born American novelist, born in Disley, Cheshire. He was educated at Repton and Corpus Christi College, Cambridge, studied medicine at King's College, London (1928–29), but gave it up to teach English in Germany (1930–33). His first two novels were *All the Conspirators* (1928) and *The Memorial* (1932). His best-known works, *Mr Norris Changes Trains* (1935) and *Goodbye to Berlin* (1939), were based on his experiences in the decadence of post-slump, pre-**Hitler** Berlin. In collaboration with **Auden**, a school friend, he wrote three prose-verse plays with political overtones in which by expressionist technique, music hall parody and ample symbolism, the unsavoury social climate was forcefully exposed against idealist remedies: *The Dog beneath the Skin* (1935), *Ascent of F6* (1937), and *On the Frontier* (1938). He travelled in China with Auden in 1938 and wrote *Journey to a War* (1939). In 1939 he emigrated to California to work as scriptwriter for Metro-Goldwyn-Mayer and in 1946 took American citizenship. He translated the Hindu epic poem, the Bhagavad-Gita, with Swami Prabhavananda (1944), who also collaborated in *Shan-Kara's Crest-Jewel of Discrimination* (1947) and *How to Know God; the Yogi Aphorisms of Patanjali* (1953). The Broadway hit *I am a Camera*, and the musical *Cabaret*, were based on his earlier Berlin stories, especially *Sally Bowles* (1937). He also translated **Baudelaire**'s *Intimate Journals* (1947). Later novels include *Prater Violet* (1945), *The World in the Evening* (1954), and *Meeting by the River* (1967). He has also written several autobiographical books.

ISHMAEL Old Testament Israelite, son of **Abraham** by Hagar, the Egyptian handmaid of his wife Sarah. He is represented as the progenitor of the Arabs. **Muhammad** asserted his descent from Ishmael.

ISIDORE OF SEVILLE, St, or **Isidorus Hispalensis** (c.560–636) Spanish prelate and scholar, born in Seville or Carthagena. A doctor of the church, and the last of the western fathers of the church, he succeeded his older brother, St **Leander**, as archbishop of Seville c.600 and was considered the most learned man of his age. His episcopate was notable for the councils at Seville in 618 or 619, and at Toledo in 633, whose canons formed the basis of the constitutional law of Spain. He also collected all the decrees of councils and other church laws before his time. A voluminous writer, he is best known for his vast encyclopaedia of knowledge, *Etymologiae*, which was a standard work for scholars throughout the middle ages. He also wrote an introduction to the Old and New Testaments; a defence of Christianity against the Jews; three books of 'Sentences'; books on ecclesiastical offices and the monastic rule; and a history of the Goths, Vandals and Suevi.

ISLA, José Francisco de (1703–81) Spanish satirist, born in Vidanes, northwest Spain. After joining the Jesuits, for some years he lectured on philosophy and theology in Segovia, Santiago and Pamplona, and became famous as a preacher, but still more as a humorist and satirist by his writings, especially his novel of *Fray Gerundio* (1758–70). The *Letters of Juan de la Encina* (1732) are a good example of his style. A more characteristic one is the *Dia Grande de Navarra*. What **Cervantes** had done with the sham chivalry and sentiment of the romances, Isla strove to do in *Fray Gerundio* with the vulgar buffooneries of the popular preachers, and especially the preaching friars of the day. It was well received by all except the friars, but the Inquisition stopped the publication of the book. In 1767 he shared the fate of the Jesuits in their expulsion from Spain, and went to Bologna. He translated **Le Sage**'s *Gil Blas*, which he humorously claimed to have restored to its native language.

ISLAM, Kazi Nazrul (1899–1976) Bengali poet, hailed as the 'Rebel Poet of Bengal' and later as the 'National Poet of Bangladesh', born into extreme poverty in the West Bengali village of Churulia. He rose to fame in the 1920s as a poet and leader of the anti-British movement in India with his poem *The Rebel*, which brought him overnight fame. He published a bi-monthly radical magazine, *Dhumketu* ('The Comet') which was virulently revolutionary and anti-British in tone, and spent 40 days on hunger-strike in jail. In the 1930s he concentrated more on composing music and songs—over 4000 songs and lyrics in all—and made a huge name also as an actor and radio personality. In 1942 he contracted a brain disease that bereft him of his faculties, including his speech; after Partition, which he had always opposed, he lived in penury until he was brought home in honour to the newly independent state of Bangladesh and installed as the national poet. A Muslim, he married a Hindu and was a lifelong advocate of Muslim-Hindu unity; he wrote more than 500 devotional Hindu songs.

ISLEBIUS, Magister See **AGRICOLA, Johann**

ISLIP, Simon (d.1366) English prelate, archbishop of Canterbury from 1349, probably born in Islip near Oxford. A fellow of Merton College, Oxford in 1307, he founded a college at Oxford for monks and secular clergy in 1361 which later, under **Wolsey**, was absorbed into Cardinal, now Christ Church, College.

ISMAIL PASHA (1830–95) khedive of Egypt, born in Cairo. He was second son of **Ibrahim Pasha**, and grandson of the famous **Mehemet 'Ali**. Educated at St Cyr, in 1863 he succeeded **Sa'id Pasha** as viceroy, and in 1867 assumed the hereditary title of khedive. In 1872 the sultan granted him also the right (withdrawn in 1879) of concluding treaties and of maintaining an army, and virtually gave him sovereign powers. Ismail began a series of vast internal reforms, and, extending his dominions southward, annexed Dar-Fûr in 1874, thereafter endeavouring, through Sir **Samuel Baker** and General **Charles Gordon**, governors of the Sudan, to suppress the slave trade. To provide funds for his vast undertakings in 1875 he sold to Great Britain 177000 shares in the Suez Canal for £4000000. The Egyptian finances, however, were almost hopelessly involved; and after several failures a dual British and French control was established, the finances being placed under European management. A promise of constitutional government ended in 1879 in the summary dismissal of Nubar Pasha's ministry, bringing with it the peremptory interference of the European governments. The khedive, who declined to abdicate, was deposed by the sultan in June 1879, and Prince **Tewfik**, his eldest son, was proclaimed khedive. Ismail ultimately retired to Constantinople, where he died.

ISMAY, Hastings Lionel Ismay, 1st Baron (1887–1965) English soldier, known as 'Pug', educated at Charterhouse and Sandhurst. He joined the 21st Cavalry, Frontier Force, in 1907. He served on India's north west Frontier in 1908 and in Somaliland in World War I. His appointment in 1926 as assistant secretary to the Committee of Imperial Defence inaugurated a long and fruitful association with politico-military organizations, which culminated in his service as chief of staff to **Winston Churchill** as both prime minister and minister of defence. Secretary of state for commonwealth relations (1951–52), he was secretary-general to NATO from 1952 to 1957.

ISMET PAZA See **INÖNÜ, Ismet**

ISOCRATES (436–338 BC) Athenian orator and pamphleteer, born in Athens. He received an excellent education; in his youth he heard the orator **Gorgias**, and joined the circle of **Socrates**, but abandoned philosophy for speech-writing, which he also gave up when he found, after six speeches, that he had not the practical gifts for winning cases in a law court. About 390 BC he set up as a teacher of oratory, though he claimed also to give a general practical education. He attracted pupils subsequently distinguished as statesmen, historians and orators. He himself composed model speeches for his pupils, such as the *Panegyricus* (c.380 BC) and the *Plataeicus* (373 BC). But he also wrote speeches intended to be practical; the *Archidamus* may actually have been composed for the Spartan king Archidamus. But the majority, for instance the *Symmachicus*, the *Areopagiticus*, the *Panathenaicus* (342–339 BC) and the letters to **Philip II** of Macedonia, were designed to be circulated and read—they are in fact the earliest political pamphlets known. As a politician, his one idea was to unite all Greeks in a joint attack upon the common foe, Persia. The outcome was the destruction of Greek freedom at Chaeronea by Philip. He was the first Athenian orator to treat rhetorical prose as a work of art.

ISRÄELS, Jozef (1824–1911) Dutch genre painter, born in Gröningen. He studied at Amsterdam and Paris, where he exhibited in 1855 a historical picture of **William the Silent**. But he soon turned to scenes from humble life, especially the portrayal of fisher folk. He also worked as an etcher.

ISSIGONIS, Sir Alec (Alexander Arnold Constantine) (1906–88) Turkish-born British automobile designer, born in Smyrna. He settled in Britain in 1923 and studied at Battersea Polytechnic, demonstrating skills as a draughtsman and leanings towards engineering. His early fascination for cars led him to use his talents in the motor industry, and a period as an enthusiastic sports driver in the 1930s and 1940s familiarized him with all aspects of car design. His greatest successes during his long association with Morris (later BMC) were the Morris 'Minor', launched in 1948 and produced until 1971, and the revolutionary 'Mini' launched in 1959. A version of the 'Mini' is still in production, and more than five million have been manufactured. He became a royal designer for industry in 1967.

ITO, Marquis Hirobumi (1838–1909) Japanese statesman, born in Choshu province. He was four times premier of Japan, visited London in 1863, 1871 and 1882–1901, drafted the Japanese constitution, and was assassinated by a Korean at Harbin.

ITTEN, Johannes (1888–1967) Swiss painter and teacher, born in Sudern-Linden. He studied art in Stuttgart (1913–16) before moving to Vienna where he started his own art school. A leading theorist at the Bauhaus (1919–23), he wrote on the theory of colour (*Kunst der Farbe*, 1961) and developed the idea of a compulsory 'preliminary course', based on research into natural forms and the laws of basic design. This has been widely adopted in art schools.

ITÚRBIDE, Agustín de (1783–1824) Mexican soldier and emperor, born in Valladolid (now Morelia). He favoured Mexican independence, but fought for the Crown because he opposed the social revolution of the independence movement of Hidalgo and **Morelos**. He defeated Morelos' army at Valladolid (1810), and was given command of the royalist army but, dissatisfied with the imposition of a constitutional monarchy in Spain, betrayed the royalists and joined with the Liberals to issue the Plan de Iguala declaring Mexico independent (1821). Then, betraying that movement, he created himself Emperor Agustín I in the style of **Napoleon** (1822). Unable to govern, his popularity plummeted, and he was forced to abdicate (1823). He went into exile in Europe, but returned the following year, and was captured.

IVAN I, called **Kalita ('Moneybag')** Grand Duke of Moscow from 1328. A sound administrator and reformer, he made Moscow the capital of Russia by transferring the metropolitan cathedral there in 1326. His son, Ivan II, reigned after him from 1353 to 1359.

IVAN III, called **'the Great'** (1440–1505) ruler of Russia and Grand Duke of Russia (1462–1505). He succeeded in shaking off entirely the yoke of the Tartars, and in subjecting a number of the Russian principalities to his own sway. In 1472 he married Sophia, a niece of **Constantine XI Palaeologus**, assumed the title of 'Ruler of all Russia', and adopted the two-headed eagle of the Byzantine empire.

IVAN IV (1530–84) tsar of Russia from 1533, known as **'Ivan the Terrible'**, although the Russian word *groznyi* more properly signifies 'awe-inspiring'. The grandson of **Ivan III 'the Great'**, he was only three years old at the death of his father, Grand Prince Vasily. Following a period when authority was in the hands first of his mother, Elena, and then, following her murder in 1537, of the Russian boyars, Ivan assumed power in 1647, becoming the first ruler of Russia to adopt the title of 'tsar'. He proceeded steadily to reduce the power of the upper nobility (princes and boyars) in favour of the minor gentry. He summoned a legislative assembly in 1549, inaugurating a period of reform in both state and church that continued for the next decade, establishing a new code of law and a system of local self-government. In 1552 he wrested Kazan from the Tartars and in 1554 captured Astrakhan. In 1558 he invaded Livonia, capturing the important Baltic port of Narva. In 1565, suspecting that a boyar rebellion was imminent, he offered to abdicate but was brought back by popular demand with sweeping powers to take drastic measures against those who had opposed him. This led to a prolonged spate of arrests and executions. In 1570 he ravaged the free city of Novgorod. In 1571 the Crimean Tartars invaded Russia and fired Moscow, but Ivan was able to inflict a punishing defeat upon them the following year. In the last years of his reign, he rehabilitated posthumously many of the victims of his middle years, but in a fit of anger in 1581 accidentally killed his own eldest son, so that the throne passed on his death to his sickly and feeble-minded second son, Fedor.

IVANOV, Lev Ivanovich (1834–1901) Russian choreographer, teacher and dancer, born in Moscow. After studying in Moscow and St Petersburg (Leningrad), he joined the Maryinsky Theater in 1850, becoming principal dancer in 1869. Appointed rehearsal director by **Marius Petipa** in 1882, he became second ballet master under Petipa in 1885, the year of his choreographic début, with a new version of *La fille mal gardée*, which, like much of his work, is now lost. His two most celebrated works have survived—**Tchaikovsky**'s *The Nutcracker* (1892), and the second and fourth acts of Tchaikovsky's *Swan Lake* (1895). His

'White Acts' are now considered among the masterpieces of classical ballet, creating the quintessential image of ballerina as swan. Despite his achievements, he lived in the shadow of Petipa and died in poverty.

IVANOV, Vyacheslav Ivanovich (1866–1949) Russian poet and critic. He studied in Berlin and lived in Greece and Italy, where he was converted to Roman Catholicism. His poetry was enriched by his philological studies, and he wrote studies on the cult of **Dionysus**, on **Dostoyevsky**, **Byron** and **Nietzsche**.

IVEAGH, Lord See **GUINNESS, Edward Cecil**

IVES, Charles Edward (1874–1954) American composer, born in Danbury, Connecticut. He studied music at Yale and worked in insurance till 1930, when he retired. His music is firmly based in the American tradition, but at the same time he experimented with dissonances, polytonal harmonies, and conflicting rhythms, anticipating modern European trends. He composed five symphonies, chamber music (including the well-known 2nd piano sonata, the *Concord Sonata*), and many songs. In 1947 he was awarded the Pulitzer prize for his 3rd symphony (composed 1911).

IVES, Frederick Eugene (1856–1937) American inventor, born in Litchfield, Connecticut. He experimented with the possibilities of photography as a means of illustration, and invented (1878) and improved (1885), the half-tone process. He later pioneered natural colours for motion pictures (1914).

IWASA MATAHEI (c.1578–1650) Japanese painter. He was founder of the Ukiyoye school.

IWERKS, U B, originally **Ubbe Iwwerks** (1901–71) American animated-cartoon director, born in Kansas City. The animator who put life into **Walt Disney**'s sketches of Mickey Mouse, he began as an apprentice to the Union Bank Note Company (1916). In 1920 in partnership, he set up the Disney-Iwerks Studio, and produced *Laugh-O-Gram* cartoons, followed by *Alice in Cartoonland* (1923). Iwerks joined Disney in California to animate *Oswald the Lucky Rabbit* (1924), then animated the first film to star Mickey Mouse, *Plane Crazy* (1928). He produced *Flip the Frog* in Cinecolor (1930), *Willie Whopper* (1933) and *Comicolor Cartoons* (1933), *Porky and Gabby* (1937) and *Gran'pop* (1939). He won Academy Awards (1959, 1964) for his technical achievements. He developed xerographic animation for *The* 101 *Dalmations* (1961) and directed special effects for **Alfred Hitchcock**'s *The Birds* (1963).

IYASU, the Great (d.1706) emperor of Ethiopia. He succeeded to the throne in 1682 and proved to be a brave and far-sighted ruler. A modernizer and patron of the arts, he made a determined effort to reunify the kingdom following the wholesale migration of Galla tribesmen into the empire, and to reform its institutions after a period of decline during the 17th century. He was assassinated by a kinsman of his wife.

J

JABIR IBN HAYYAN, Abu Musa (c.721–c.815) Arab alchemist, and court physician to caliph **Harūn al-Rashíd**. He wrote a number of works on alchemy and metaphysics which were widely circulated in the middle ages.

JACKLIN, Tony (Anthony) (1944–) English golfer, born in Scunthorpe. In 1969 at Royal Lytham he became the first Briton to win the Open Championship since Max Faulkner in 1951. In the following year he won the US Open. A successful member of successive Ryder Cup teams, in the 1980s he became an even more successful non-playing captain.

JACKSON, Andrew (1767–1845) 7th president of the USA, born in Waxhaw, South Carolina. After being admitted to the bar he became public prosecutor in Nashville in 1788. He helped to frame the constitution of Tennessee, and became its representative in congress in 1796, its senator in 1797, and a judge of its supreme court (1798–1804). When war was declared against Great Britain in 1812, as major-general of the state militia he led 2500 men to Natchez, but was ordered to disband them. Jackson, however, marched them back to Nashville, and in September 1813 took the field against the Creek Indians in Alabama, achieving a decisive victory at Horseshoe Bend in March 1814. In May 'Old Hickory' was made major-general in the regular army, and appointed to the command of the South. Pensacola in Spanish Florida being then used by the British as a base of operations, Jackson invaded Spanish soil, stormed Pensacola, and successfully defended New Orleans against Sir Edward Pakenham (January 1815), who was killed in the attack. In 1818 Jackson again invaded Florida, and severely chastised the Seminoles. After the purchase of Florida he was its first governor, but soon resigned, and in 1823 was again elected to the US senate. In 1824 as a candidate for the presidency he had the highest popular vote, but not a majority; in 1828 he was elected, having a majority of electoral votes. He was fearless, honest, prompt to decide everything for personal reasons, and swept out great numbers of minor officials to fill their places with his partisans—on the principle (as was said of him): 'To the victor belong the spoils'. Questions of tariff and 'nullification' were prominent during his presidency. The president's veto power was much more freely used by Jackson than by his predecessors. He opposed legislation for premature renewing of the charter of the Bank of the United States, believing that this centralized money power was working against him, and on this issue was re-elected president by an overwhelming majority in 1832. In his administration the national debt was fully paid in 1835, and the surplus revenue which accumulated was distributed to the several states. In 1837 he retired.

JACKSON, Cyril (1746–1819) English clergyman and scholar, born in Yorkshire. A distinguished dean of Christ Church College, Oxford (1783–1809), he tutored **George Canning** and Sir **Robert Peel**.

JACKSON, Frederick John Foakes (1855–1941) English church historian, born in Ipswich. Educated at Eton and Trinity College, Cambridge, he is known for his *History of the Christian Church* (1891), *The Beginnings of Christianity* (5 vols, 1920–33), and other works.

JACKSON, Glenda (1936–) English actress, born in Birkenhead, Cheshire. A student at RADA, she made her theatrical début in *Separate Tables* (1957) at Worthing and her London début in the same year in *All Kinds of Men*. She made her film début in *This Sporting Life* (1963) but remained primarily a stage actress in such productions as *Alfie* (1963), *Hamlet* (1965) and *Marat/Sade* (1965). Her performance in the film *Women in Love* (1969) earned her international recognition and an Academy Award. She won a second Academy Award for *A Touch of Class* (1973) and her film appearances include *Sunday, Bloody Sunday* (1971), *Hedda* (1975), *Stevie* (1978) and *Business as Usual* (1987). Her stage career has encompassed *Hedda Gabler* (1975), *Rose* (1980), *Strange Interlude* (1984), *The House of Bernarda Alba* (1986) and *Macbeth* (1988). Her television work includes the series *Elizabeth R.* (1971) and the film *The Patricia Neal Story* (1981).

JACKSON, (George) Holbrook (1874–1948) English bibliophile and literary historian, born in Liverpool. Moving to Leeds to work in lace-manufacture, he encountered a fellow-Nietzschean in A R Orage, with whom he helped establish the formidable political and literary *New Age* (1907), winning support from the subject of his book *Bernard Shaw* (1907). Jackson was active in the Fabian Society, and his life-long devotion to **William Morris** was reflected in various works from his early study to his Morris Anthology, *On Art and Socialism* (1947). His *The Eighteen Nineties* (1913) established the literary contours of the decade. He was an engaging and usually celebratory literary critic, as shown in his editorial work for *T.P.'s Weekly* and *Today*, but after World War I he supported himself by managing trade journals and giving himself up to bibliophilia such as the enormous *Anatomy of Bibliomania* (1931), the captivating anthology *Bookman's Holiday* (1945), *The Printing of Books*, *The Reading of Books* and *The Fear of Books*.

JACKSON, Jesse (1941–) American politician and clergyman, born in Greenville, North Carolina, the adopted son of a janitor. He won a football scholarship to Illinois University before entering a Chicago seminary. He was ordained a Baptist minister in 1968. As a charismatic preacher and black-activist politician, he worked with **Martin Luther King**, before establishing Operation PUSH (People United to Save Humanity, 1971) to promote black economic advancement. He contested the Democratic party's 1984 presidential nomination, constructing what he termed a 'Rainbow Coalition' of radical minority social and pressure groups, and won a fifth of the delegates' votes, but lost the nominations to **Walter Mondale**. In 1986 he successfully campaigned for American disinvestment in South Africa and came second to **Michael Dukakis** in the Democrats' 1988 presidential nomination contest, doubling his 1984 vote share.

JACKSON, John (1769–1845) English pugilist, born in London and known as 'Gentleman Jackson'. He won the English heavyweight boxing championship in 1795 and retired undefeated in 1803 after only three defences of his title. After his retirement he started a school of self-defence in London, where one of his pupils was Lord **Byron**, who celebrated him in verse.

JACKSON, John Hughlings (1835–1911) English neurologist, born in Providence Green, Yorkshire. Physician at the London Hospital (1874–94) and at the National Hospital for the Paralysed and Epileptic until 1906, he investigated unilateral epileptiform seizures and discovered that certain regions of the brain are associated with certain movements of the limbs.

JACKSON, Laura See **RIDING**

JACKSON, Marjorie (1931–) Australian sprinter, the first Australian woman athlete of undoubted world class, born in Coffs Harbour, New South Wales. She came to prominence by twice defeating the hitherto invincible **Fanny Blankers-Koen** in 1948, after she had swept the boards at the London Olympics. Her career blossomed and she won both sprints and was in the winning sprint relay team at the Commonwealth Games of 1950. The peak of her achievement came at Helsinki in 1952 when she won both Olympic sprints, crowning a two-year period in which she had set 13 world sprinting records.

JACKSON, Michael (1958–) American pop singer, born in Gary, Indiana. With his brothers, Jackie, Tito, Marlon and Jermaine in the vocal/instrumental pop group The Jacksons, he had known stardom from the age of eleven, and sang on four consecutive number-one hits. Between 1972 and 1975 he also had six solo hits on the Motown record label. In 1977 he played the scarecrow in *The Wiz*, a black remake of the film *The Wizard of Oz*. His first major solo album was *Off The Wall* (1979) and he consolidated his career with *Thriller* (1982) which sold over 35 million copies and which helped to establish him as one of the major pop superstars of the 1980s. Having been a celebrity since childhood, he developed a reclusive lifestyle in adulthood, and is often portrayed in the media as an eccentric introvert.

JACKSON, Milt (Milton) (1923–) American vibraphone player, born in Detroit. He learned the guitar and piano while at school, taking up xylophone and vibraphone in his teens. His 'discovery' by **Dizzy Gillespie** in 1945 led to his emergence as the most important vibraphone player of the bebop era. In 1952 he was a founding member of the Modern Jazz Quartet which with a change of drummer, existed until 1974 and re-formed in the 1980s. Jackson's lyrical interpretations, particularly of ballads, kept him in the forefront of jazz through periods of stylistic change.

JACKSON, Sir Stanley (1870–1947) English cricketer and politician, born near Leeds. Educated at Harrow and Trinity College, Cambridge, he played first for England against Australia while still at the university (1893), and was a regular Test player until 1905, in which year he was captain. He also played for Yorkshire. Entering parliament in 1915, he became chairman of the Conservative party (1923) and governor of Bengal (1927).

JACKSON, Sir Thomas Graham (1835–1924) English architect. He studied under Sir **George Gilbert Scott** and was responsible for many restorations of and additions to libraries, public schools and colleges at Eton, Harrow and Rugby, the Inner Temple, the Bodleian Library and the New Examination Schools at Oxford.

JACKSON, Thomas Jonathan, 'Stonewall Jackson' (1824–63) American soldier and Confederate general in the Civil War, born in Clarksburg, West Virginia. In 1851 he became professor in the Virginia Military Institute. At the outbreak of war in 1861 he took command of the Confederate troops at Harper's Ferry on the secession of Virginia, and commanded a brigade at Bull Run, where his firm stand gained him his sobriquet 'Stonewall'. Promoted major-general, in the campaign of the Shenandoah valley (1862) he outgeneralled **Nathaniel Banks** and **Frémont**, and eventually drove them back upon the Lower Shenandoah. Hastening to Richmond, he turned the scale at Gaines's Mills (27 June), and returned to defeat Banks at Cedar Run in August. He then seized **Pope**'s depot at Manassas, and his corps bore the brunt of the fighting in the victorious second battle there on 30 August. On 15 September he captured Harper's Ferry with 13000 prisoners, and next day arrived at Sharpsburg, where his presence, in the battle of Antietam, saved **Lee** from disaster. As lieutenant-general he commanded the right wing at Fredericksburg (13 December), and at Chancellorsville (1 May 1863) he repulsed **Hooker**. Next night he fell upon the right of the Federal army and drove it back on Chancellorsville. Returning from a reconnaissance, his party was accidentally fired on by his own troops and Jackson received three wounds. His left arm was amputated; but on 10 May he died.

JACKSON, Sir William Godfrey Fothergill (1917–) English soldier and historian. Educated at Shrewsbury School, Royal Military Academy, Woolwich, and King's College, Cambridge, he was commissioned in the Royal Engineers (1937). He served during World War II in Norway (1940), North Africa, Sicily and Italy (1942–43) and the far east (1945). Assistant chief of General Staff (1968–70), he was commander-in-chief Northern Command (1970–72), and quartermaster-general at the ministry of defence (1973–76). He served as military historian in the cabinet office (1977–78 and 1982–), and was governor and commander-in-chief, Gibraltar (1978–82). His publications on military historical and strategic subjects include *Attack in the West* (1953), *Seven Roads to Moscow* (1957), *The Battle for Italy* (1967) and *Overlord*: *Normandy 1944* (1978).

JACK THE RIPPER (19th century) unidentified English murderer. Between August and November 1888, six women were found murdered and mutilated in Whitechapel and the adjoining Aldgate in the east end of London. All were prostitutes; five were found in the street and the sixth in a house. The murderer was never discovered. The affair roused much public disquiet, many wild accusations, provoked a violent press campaign against the CID and the home secretary, and resulted in some reform of police methods.

JACOB, François (1920–) French biochemist, born in Nancy. Educated at the University of Paris and the Sorbonne, he worked at the Pasteur Institute in Paris (from 1950), and in 1964 was appointed professor of cellular genetics at the Collège de France. With **Lwoff** and **Jacques Monod** he conducted research into cell physiology and the structure of genes, for which they were jointly awarded the 1965 Nobel prize for physiology or medicine.

JACOB, Giles (1686–1744) English legal lexicographer, born in Romsey, Hampshire. Author of a *New Law Dictionary* (1729), he also wrote several lesser legal works, and *Poetical Register or Lives and Characters of English Dramatic Poets* (1719–20).

JACOB, P L See **LACROIX, Paul**

JACOB, Violet, née **Kennedy-Erskine** (1863–1946) Scottish poet and novelist, born in Montrose, the daughter of the laird of Dun. She married Major Arthur Otway Jacob and lived for some years in India. Although she began as a novelist, she is best known for poems in the Angus dialect, such as *Songs of Angus* (1915), *More Songs of Angus* (1918), *Bonnie Joann* (1922) and *The Northern Lights* (1927). Her *Lairds of Dun* (1931) is a standard history of her native district.

JACOBA See **JACQUELINE OF HOLLAND**

JACOBI, Carl Gustav Jacob (1804–51) German mathematician, born in Potsdam. As professor of mathematics at Königsberg (1827–42), his book *Fundamenta nova* (1829) was the first definitive study of elliptic functions, which he and **Niels Henrik Abel** had independently discovered. He also made important advances in the study of differential equations, the theory of numbers, and determinants.

JACOBI, Derek (1938–) English actor, born in London. He had acted at Cambridge University and with the National Youth Theatre before he made his professional début in N F Simpson's *One Way Pendulum* at Birmingham Repertory Theatre in 1961. Since then, Jacobi has become one of Britain's most notable classical actors. He joined the National Theatre's inaugural 1963 company, making his London début that year as Laertes in *Hamlet*. In 1972 he joined the Prospect Theatre Company and in 1980 he made his New York début in Nikolai Erdman's *The Suicide*. He joined the Royal Shakespeare Company in 1982. He made his début as director in 1988, with his production of *Hamlet* for the Renaissance Theatre Company. He has made several film and television appearances, of which the most famous is the title role in the television adaptation of *I, Claudius* in 1977.

JACOBS, Joseph (1854–1916) Australian scholar and folklorist, born in Sydney. He graduated from Cambridge (1876), and devoted himself to the collection of fables and myths. He compiled several collections, and was the editor of the *Jewish Encyclopaedia* in America (from 1900).

JACOBS, William Wymark (1863–1943) English short-story writer, born in Wapping, London. He was a post-office official (1883–99) and began writing humorous yarns of bargees and tars, most of which were illustrated by Will Owen, such as *Many Cargoes* (1896), *The Skipper's Wooing* (1897) and *Deep Waters* (1919). He also wrote macabre tales, such as his best-known story, *The Monkey's Paw* (1902).

JACOBSEN, Arne (1902–71) Danish architect and designer, born in Copenhagen. Educated at the Royal Danish Academy, he won a House of the Future competition in 1929 and became a leading exponent of Modernism. In 1956 he became a professor of architecture at the Royal Danish Academy. He designed many private houses in the Bellavista resort near Copenhagen; his main public buildings were the SAS skyscraper in Copenhagen (1955), and St Catherine's College, Oxford (1964). He also designed cutlery and textiles, and classic furniture, especially the 'Egg' and 'Swan' chairs for his Royal Hotel in Copenhagen.

JACOBSEN, Jens Peter (1847–85) Danish novelist, born in Thisted in Jutland. He studied science at Copenhagen, translated **Charles Darwin** and became, under the influence of **Brandes**, the leader of the new Danish naturalistic movement. Having contracted tuberculosis in Italy, he published some beautiful poems and short stories such as 'Mogens' (1872), and also two novels, *Fru Marie Grubbe* (1876) and *Niels Lyhne* (1880). Half-realist, half-dreamer, his deliberate impressionist style found many disciples, **Rilke** among them.

JACOBUS DE VORAGINE See **VORAGINE**

JACOPONE DA TODI See **TODI**

JACOTOT, Jean Joseph (1770–1840) French educationist, inventor of the 'universal method', born in Dijon. He was successively soldier, military secretary, and professor. His system resembles that of **James Hamilton**. He advocated (1826) the teaching of French based on a single book (Télémaque), known as the 'universal method' always starting each lesson at the beginning and going a little further each day. He postulated that the mental capacities of all men are equal and that the unequal results of education depend almost exclusively upon will. He expounded his views in *Enseignement Universel* (1823).

JACQUARD, Joseph Marie (1752–1834) French silk-weaver of Lyon. His invention (1801–08) of the Jacquard Loom enabled an ordinary workman to produce the most beautiful patterns in a style previously accomplished only with patience, skill and labour. But though **Napoleon** rewarded him with a small pension and the Légion d'Honneur, the silk weavers themselves offered such violent opposition to his machine that on one occasion he narrowly escaped with his life. At his death his machine was in almost universal use.

JACQUE, Charles Emile (1813–94) French painter and etcher, born in Paris. A prominent member of the Barbizon school, he is best known for his paintings of sheep and etchings of rural scenes, many of them in the Louvre.

JACQUELINE OF HOLLAND, or **Jacoba of Bavaria** (1401–36) Dutch noblewoman, daughter of William, Count of Zeeland, Holland and Bavaria. She made a series of marriages which caused her much trouble. She married, first (1415), Prince John, dauphin of France, who died in 1417. She waged war against John of Bavaria for the right to succeed to her father's title there, then in 1418 married her weak cousin, the Duke of Brabant, who mortgaged Holland and Zeeland to John of Bavaria. Repudiating the marriage, she went to England, where she married (illegally) Humphrey, Duke of **Gloucester**, in 1422. Deserted by him during an invasion to regain her lands in Hainault, she was captured by **Philip the Good** of Burgundy, and relinquished to him her claims to sovereignty. In 1433 she married (illegally again), Frans van Borsselen, a Zeeland noble.

JACQUES, Hattie, originally **Josephine Edwina Jacques** (1924–80) English comic actress, born in Sandgate, Kent. A factory worker and Red Cross nurse during the war, she made her stage début at the Player's Theatre in 1944 and returned there frequently in pantomime. She toured with the Young Vic in *The King Stag* (1947–48) and made the first of many film appearances in *Green for Danger* (1946). She was frequently called upon to play sturdy matrons, schoolmarms and bossy figures of authority, and was a highly respected foil to some top comedians: on radio in *ITMA* (1948–50) and *Educating Archie* (1950–54), and on television in various long-running series with **Eric Sykes** from 1959 until her death. Later stage work included *Twenty Minutes South* (1955), which she directed, *Large As Life* (1960) and *Hatful of Sykes* (1979). A stalwart of the *Carry On* ... films, she appeared in 14 of the series between *Carry on Sergeant* (1958) and *Carry on Dick* (1974).

JACUZZI, Candido (1903–86) Italian-born American inventor. He was an engineer whose infant son suffered from arthritis; in an attempt to relieve the pain by hydro-therapy he devised a pump that produced a whirlpool effect in a bath, and when his invention became generally available a bath with such a facility was known as a 'jacuzzi'.

JAGAN, Cheddi Berrat (1918–) Guyanan politician, born in Port Mourant, the son of an East Indian headman. He qualified as a dentist at Chicago University and after a spell of provincial politics was elected to the House of Assembly in 1953 when his communist-inspired People's Progressive party secured a majority. The British colonial office, fearing the subversion of the colony's government, suspended the constitution, deprived Jagan and his ministers of their portfolios and sent British forces to the territory. In 1954 Jagan was imprisoned for violating an order restricting his movements to Georgetown. In 1955 he was re-elected leader of the party, which was returned to power with a two-thirds majority in August 1957. He became minister of trade and industry in an executive over which the governor of British Guiana had extensive powers of veto and nomination. From 1961 until 1964 he was the first premier of British Guiana (now Guyana).

JAGGER, Charles Sargeant (1885–1934) English sculptor, born in Yorkshire. He studied at the Royal College of Art and at Rome, and executed mainly mythological and historical subjects. His most famous work is the *Royal Artillery Memorial* at Hyde Park Corner, London.

JAGGER, Mick See **ROLLING STONES, The**

JAGIELLON East European ruling dynasty of the 14th to 16th centuries which reigned in Lithuania, Poland, Hungary and Bohemia. It was named after Jagiello, Grand Duke of Lithuania (1351–1434), who married Jadwiga, queen of Poland, in 1386, thus uniting the two realms, and who ruled as Wladyslaw II Jagiello.

JAHANGIR, originally **Salim** (1569–1627) Mughal emperor, son of **Akbar the Great**. He took the title of Jahangir on his accession in 1605. The earlier part of his reign was a period of peace and great prosperity for the empire, with a steady growth of trade and commerce and a great flowering of the arts. The latter part of the reign was characterized by continual rebellions against his rule, principally on behalf of his various sons, and he was only able to survive as ruler by dint of the courage and vigour of the empress, Nur Jahan. He was, however, a just and tolerant man and a consistent patron of the arts.

JAHN, Frederick Ludwig (1778–1852) Prussian physical educationist, known as the 'Father of gymnastics' (*Turnvater*), born in Lanz. In 1811 he started the first gymnasium (*Turnplatz*) in Berlin and his methods soon became very popular. An ardent nationalist, he commanded a volunteer corps in the Napoleonic Wars (1813–15); and after the peace of 1815 resumed his teaching, and published *Die deutsche Turnkunst* (1816). But the gymnasia began to witness political gatherings, too liberal to please the Prussian government, and they were closed in 1818. Jahn, who had taken a prominent part in the movement, was arrested in 1819, and suffered five years' imprisonment. He was elected to the Frankfurt National Assembly in 1848.

JAHN, Johann (1750–1816) German biblical scholar, born in Tasswitz in Moravia. A Roman Catholic, he became professor of oriental languages at Olmütz, and in 1789 at Vienna; but the boldness of his criticism led in 1806 to his retirement to a canonry. Notable works were his introduction to the Old Testament (1792), *Archaeologia Biblica* (1805) and *Enchiridion Hermeneuticae* (1812).

JAHN, Otto (1813–69) German archaeologist and musicologist, born in Kiel. He lectured at Kiel, Greifswald and Leipzig. Deprived of his chair in 1851 for political activities in 1848–49, he became in 1855 professor of archaeology at Bonn. He published works on Greek art (1846), representations of ancient life on vases (1861, 1868), and the evil eye (1850), besides a Life of **Mozart** (4 vols, 1856–60) and essays on music.

JAIMINI (c.200 BC) Indian founder of the *Pūrva-Mīmāmsā* school of Hindu philosophy. The *Pūrva-Mīmāmsā* system is also known as *Vkya-śāstra*, the study of words, from its concern with correct methods of interpreting the Vedas. Little is known of Jaimini himself, but his *Mīmāmsā Sūtra* emphasizes the need for right action and performing the duties required by the Vedas. Right action presupposes understanding how to acquire valid knowledge, one of the *Mīmāmsā Sūtra*'s chief concerns.

JAKES, Milos (1922–) Czechoslovakian politician, born in Ceske Chalupy. Originally an electrical engineer, he joined the Communist party of Czechoslovakia (CCP) in 1945 and studied in Moscow (1955–58). He supported the Soviet invasion of Czechoslovakia in 1968 and later, as head of the CCP's central control commission, oversaw the purge of reformist personnel. He entered the CCP secretariat in 1977 and the politburo in 1981, and in December 1987 replaced **Gustav Husak** as party leader. Although enjoying close personal relations with the Soviet leader **Mikhail Gorbachev**, he emerged as a cautious reformer who made it clear that restructuring ('prestavba') in Czechoslovakia would be a slow and limited process. He was forced to step down as CCP leader in November 1989, following a series of pro-democracy rallies.

JAKOBSON, Roman Osipovich (1896–1982) Russian-born American linguist, born in Moscow. He was professor at the Higher Dramatic School, Moscow (1920–23) and at Brno, Czechoslovakia (1933–39). One of the principal founders of the Prague School of Linguistics, he was an important contributor to many fields of study in general linguistics and Slavonic philology. He left Europe for America in 1941, and after teaching at Columbia University (1943–49) was professor of Slavic languages and literature (1949–67) and general linguistics (1960–67) at Harvard, and Institute professor at the Massachusetts Institute of Technology (1957–67). Six volumes of his *Selected Works* were published between 1962 and 1971. Jakobson, Fant and Halle's *Preliminaries to Speech Analysis* (1952) was a pioneering work in distinctive feature analysis of speech sounds.

JALAL AD-DIN RUMI, Mohammed ibn Mohammed (1207–73) Persian lyric poet and mystic, born in Balkh. He settled at Iconium (Konya) in 1226 and founded a sect. He wrote a lot of exquisite lyrical poetry, including a long epic on the Sufi mystical doctrine, *Masnavi y ma' navi*.

JAMES, St, known as **'the Great'** (d.44 AD), one of the Twelve Apostles in the New Testament. The son of the fisherman Zebedee, he was the brother of **John**, and present at most of the major events of **Jesus Christ**'s ministry. Later he may have preached in Spain, but returned to Judaea in 44 and was put to death by **Herod Agrippa**. Later legend suggests that his remains were miraculously spirited to Santiago de Compostela in France, which became a centre of medieval pilgrimage. His feast day is 25 July.

JAMES, St, (1st century) known as **'the Just'** In the New Testament he is called 'the Lord's brother'. He was converted at the time of the Resurrection, and became head of the Christian community of Jerusalem. He was stoned to death by order of the Sanhedrin in 62 AD. Most theologians consider him the author of the *Epistle of James*, although it has been ascribed to both the others. The first of the Catholic Epistles, it was put by **Eusebius of Caesarea** among the list of controverted books (*Antilegomena*), and was finally declared canonical by the third Council of Carthage (397).

JAMES, St, known as **'the Younger'** one of the Twelve Apostles, the son of Alphaeus. His feast day is 1 May.

JAMES I (1394–1437) king of Scotland from 1424, second son of **Robert III**, born in Dunfermline. After his elder brother David, Duke of Rothesay, was murdered at Falkland (1402), allegedly by his uncle, the Duke of **Albany**, James was sent for safety to France, but was captured by the English. He remained a prisoner for 18 years, but also received a good education, exposure to the Lancastrian court of **Henry IV**, and military experience in **Henry V**'s French campaigns. Albany meanwhile ruled Scotland as governor until his death in 1420, when his son, Murdoch, assumed the regency and the country rapidly fell into disorder. Negotiations for the return of James were completed with the Treaty of London in 1423 and a ransom agreed of £33000 sterling (or £66000 Scots). In 1424 James married Joan Beaufort (d.1445), a daughter of the Earl of Somerset, niece of **Richard II**, and they soon came to Scotland. James dealt ruthlessly with potential rivals to his authority. Within eight months Murdoch, his two sons and the 80-year-old Earl of Lennox were all beheaded at Stirling, the first state executions since 1320. Descendants of **Robert II** by his second marriage were treated with suspicion: the Earl of March was deprived of some of his estates; the vast earldom of Mar was annexed to the crown on the death of the earl in 1435. Finance and law and order were the two other main domestic themes of his reign. The series of parliaments called after 1424, while encouraging attendance by lesser landowners, was dominated by the king's need for increased taxation, partly to pay off the ransom, and partly to meet increased expenditure on his court, artillery and building work at Linlithgow. In 1424 parliament agreed to an increase in customs dues and a five per cent tax on lands and goods, which in itself realized £25000; but by 1431 it was already showing reluctance to grant further taxes. James, described by the chronicler **Boece** as 'our lawgiver king', for the most part only refined, repeated or extended judicial enactments of previous kings and many of his activities, here as elsewhere, had a fiscal motive. In foreign affairs, he attempted to increase trade by renewing a commercial treaty with the Netherlands, and also concluded treaties with Denmark, Norway and Sweden. His relations with the church were abrasive and his criticisms of monastic orders pointed. His treatment of his nobility caused much resentment but his murder in the Dominican friary at Perth, the first assassination of a Scottish king for 400 years, was the work of a small, isolated group of dissidents led by Sir Robert Stewart and Sir Robert Graham, both descendants of Robert II's second marriage. The murderers failed to find support, and were brutally tortured to death. James left one surviving son (James, later **James II**), and six daughters; the eldest, Margaret (1424–45), who married the Dauphin, later **Louis XI**, of France, was a gifted poet. James was the first of many Stewart kings to act as a patron of the arts and almost certainly wrote the tender, passionate collection of poems, *Kingis Quair* ('king's quire' or book), about 1423–24.

JAMES II (1430–60) king of Scotland from 1437, son of **James I** and known as 'James of the fiery face' because of a birth mark. He was six years old at his father's murder. Thereupon the queen mother took shelter in Edinburgh Castle with her son, who was put under her charge and that of Sir Alexander Livingston. But Sir William Crichton, the Chancellor, who was governor of the castle, contested custody of the boy; a closer liaison with Livingston lasted until 1444 when the Livingstons began to monopolize offices, power and access to the king. In 1449, shortly after James's marriage to Mary, daughter of the Duke of Gueldres, the Livingstons were dismissed from office but the king had also to contend with the accumulating power of the **Douglas** family. Opinions vary as to who was aggressor and victim in the sharp tussle between them, which came to a climax in 1452 when James stabbed to death William, the eighth earl, at Stirling Castle. The king was allowed to get away with the murder and the royal campaign against the Douglases was completed by their wholesale forfeiture in 1455, which also smoothed the way for a series of grants of earldoms and lands to families such as the **Campbells**, **Gordons** and **Hamiltons**. A growing stability in domestic politics was vitiated by the king's reckless involvement in the English struggles between the houses of York and Lancaster. In 1460 he marched for England with a powerful army. He laid siege to Roxburgh Castle, which had been held by the English for over a hundred years, but was killed by the bursting of a cannon.

JAMES III (1451–88) king of Scotland from 1460, son of **James II**. He was brought up under the guardianship of Bishop **Kennedy** of St Andrews, while the Earl of Angus was made lieutenant-general. His tutor was the leading humanist scholar, Archibald Whitelaw, who held the office of royal secretary for much of the reign and inspired James with a love of culture and a sincere piety. The beginnings of the flowering of vernacular literature that marked **James IV**'s court began in this reign. His minority, although marked by the rise of the Boyds at the expense of others after 1466, did not see the degree of disturbance that had marked previous reigns. By 1469, when parliament condemned the Boyds and James married Margaret, daughter of **Kristian I** of Denmark, bringing Orkney and Shetland in pledge as part of her dowry, the king was firmly in control. Various aspects of his rule created resentment: short of finance, and with successive parliaments reluctant to grant taxes, James by the 1480s resorted to debasement of the coinage, stigmatized as 'black money'; his efforts between 1471 and 1473 to engage in campaigns in Brittany and Gueldres fell on deaf ears and his attempts between 1474 and 1479 to bring about a reconciliation with England were before their time and almost as unpopular. The breakdown of relations with England brought war in 1480, and the threat of English invasion resulted in a calculated political demonstration by his nobles, who hanged Robert Cochrane and other unpopular royal favourites at Lauder Bridge in 1482. The rebellion which brought about his downfall and death at Sauchieburn resulted from a further crisis of confidence in the king but ironically was less widespread. The eldest of his sons, James, who had appeared with the rebels in the field, succeeded as **James IV**. Much of the unpopularity of James III, however, may be the garnishing of later royal apologists.

JAMES IV (1473–1513) king of Scotland from 1488 after the murder of his father **James III**, after Sauchieburn. His confederates in the rebellion took possession of the offices of state, the royal Treasury and the late king's jewels, and even accused the loyal barons of treason and deprived them of their estates. After 1489 moderation and conciliation replaced such opportunism. Much of the early 1490s was taken up with securing recognition for the new régime at home and abroad. As a result his council was composed of a far broader, and more stable, coalition of the great magnates than under his three predecessors, and a vindication of Sauchieburn, sent around the courts of Europe, helped to win wide recognition for his rule. Athletic, warlike and pious, James has been called an ideal medieval king, for he did not resort to either the brutality or the outrageous venality of some of his predecessors. His provision of two successive royal bastards to the archbishopric of St Andrews began the treatment of the church as a mere department of state, a policy which was to reach new heights in the next reign. Yet in other aspects his reign was probably the epitome and climax of Scottish medieval kingship rather than of new monarchy (he was the last Scottish king to speak Gaelic). His rising status, as a king popular at home and respected abroad, was confirmed by his marriage in August 1503 to **Margaret Tudor**, eldest daughter of **Henry VII**—an alliance which ultimately led to the union of the crowns in 1603. The real beginnings of a Renaissance court belong to his reign, with vast sums spent on building work, as at Stirling Castle, and on military and naval ventures. James' castles were the venues for a brilliant Renaissance court, inhabited by musicians such as Robert Carver and poets such as **William Dunbar**. The king's popularity ironically increased the scale of the disaster which ended his life, at Flodden on 9 September 1513. An army of no fewer than 20000, probably the largest ever to be assembled in Scotland, which embarked on a Border raid to fulfil Scotland's obligations to its recently renewed alliance with France, was crushed. Although English claims that 10000 Scots died on the battlefield are probably exaggerated, no fewer than a dozen nobles, two bishops and two abbots died beside their king.

JAMES V (1512–42) king of Scotland from 1513, son of **James IV**, born in Linlithgow. He was only an infant when his father's death gave him the crown. The queen-dowager, **Margaret Tudor**, was appointed regent, but on her marriage (1514) with the Earl of Angus, the Duke of **Albany**, son of the younger brother of **James III** and heir presumptive, was made regent in her stead. Amid the contentions of the rival French and English factions, and the private quarrels of the nobles, the country was reduced to a state of anarchy. Albany, who was hampered by the changing priorities as much as by Scottish factional politics, retired to France in 1524. James' education was entrusted to Gavin Dunbar, who became archbishop of Glasgow in 1524. In 1525 he fell into the hands of Angus, who kept him a close prisoner until in 1528 he made his escape from Falkland to Stirling, and as an independent sovereign began to carry out a judicious policy which was largely framed by the need to increase the delapidated crown revenues. He continued and greatly extended his father's policy of making the church a virtual department of state. The church granted him six separate taxes during the 1530s; only a fraction of the tax of 1532 went towards its ostensible purpose, the financing of a College of Justice, but this marked the final and important step in the emergence of a central civil law court. The church, forced to raise cash to pay these taxes, resorted to feuing and permanent alienation of its lands, which fatally undermined its position as an institution on the eve of the Reformation. The pope, anxious to prevent a Henrician-style revolt against Rome in Scotland, acceded to the claims of the crown to make ecclesiastical appointments 'in commendam' and, as a result, some of the greatest religious houses, such as the Charterhouse at Perth, the abbeys of Coldingham and Holyrood and St Andrews Priory, were given to five of the six bastard young sons of the king. In 1537 James married Madelaine, daughter of **Francis I** of France, but within a year of her death he married **Mary of Guise**-Lorraine; each brought a substantial dowry and confirmed the Franco-Scottish alliance. He developed a certain reputation as the 'poor man's king', but his increasingly brusque treatment of the nobility revealed the unacceptable face of Stewart monarchy, seen at its worst in 1537 in the unusual burning of a noblewoman, Lady Janet Glamis, allegedly for treason. Anglo-Scottish relations, which had been deteriorating from 1536, burst into open war after he failed to attend a conference with **Henry VIII** at York in 1541. There was great reluctance to join his army to repulse an English invasion, which made the subsequent rout at Solway Moss, in November 1542, a humiliating defeat for the king rather than a national disaster like Flodden (1513). He died, less because of illness than a lack of will to live, leaving a week-old infant, **Mary, Queen of Scots**, to succeed him. Sometimes seen as the most unpleasant of all Stewart kings, who overstepped many unwritten conventions, he was also a highly talented Renaissance monarch. The monuments to his reign are the literary works produced at his glittering court, such as the poems and plays of Sir **David Lindsay**, and the ambitious, costly architectural transformation of Stirling Castle and the palaces of Holyrood, Falkland and Linlithgow.

JAMES VI, king of Scotland from 1567, **James I** of England from 1603 (1566–1625) the son of **Mary, Queen of Scots**, and Henry, Lord Darnley. Born in Edinburgh Castle, he was baptized Charles James at Stirling Castle. On his mother's forced abdication in 1567 he was proclaimed king, as James VI. He was placed in the keeping of the Earl of Mar, and taught by **George Buchanan**. A civil war between his supporters, the 'king's men', and those of his mother, the 'queen's men', lasted until 1573 and saw three successive, short-lived regencies, of **Moray**, Lennox and Mar. A measure of stability emerged after 1572 during the regency of **James Morton**, who laid down some of the foundations for James's later personal reign. Morton fell briefly from power in 1578, recovered, but was arrested and executed in 1581, largely at the instigation of Captain James Stewart, created Earl of Arran, and James' cousin, Esme Stuart, made Duke of Lennox. Suspicion of these two royal favourites combined with ultra-Protestantism to induce a coup, the Ruthven Raid (1582), when the king was seized. Although presbyterian ministers were not involved, the General Assembly, by approving 'this late work of reformation', stamped a life-long suspicion of the aims of the kirk in the young king's mind. Within ten months James had escaped and a counter-coup orchestrated by Arran was instituted. In 1584 a parliament reiterated the primacy of the crown over all estates, including the church; within days more than a score of radical ministers had fled into exile in England along with some of the Ruthven lords. The exiles returned by the end of 1585 and Arran was displaced from power, but the assertion of royal power, now under the guiding hand of the Chancellor, John Maitland of Thirlestane (1543–95), continued. The execution of Mary, Queen of Scots in 1587 drew a token protest from her son, but it was not allowed to disturb the league recently concluded with England, (the Treaty of Berwick, 1586) or James' English pension. In 1589 he went to Denmark, where he married the Princess **Anne of Denmark** (1574–1619) and she was crowned queen in May 1590. The early 1590s saw a careful playing-off of Roman Catholic and ultra-Protestant factions against each other and by 1596 a new stability resulted. A mysterious presbyterian riot in Edinburgh in December 1596 heralded the beginning of a long campaign by the crown, first to influence the General Assembly and latterly to introduce bishops into the kirk; this was completed by 1610 despite bitter opposition, especially from **Andrew Melville**, who was imprisoned in the Tower of London for five years. On the death of **Elizabeth** of England (1603), James ascended to the throne of England as great-grandson of **James IV**'s English wife, **Margaret Tudor**. Although he promised to visit Scotland once every three years, he next returned in 1617. A joint monarchy thus became absentee monarchy, although the king's political skill and knowledge allowed him to govern Scotland 'by his pen'. James, who went to England as an acknowledged, successful and learned king, was at first well received by his English subjects. But the dislike of this scheme for a 'perfect union' of his two kingdoms, distrust of some of the crown's financial devices, and resentment of royal favourites accelerated and made more acrimonious the recasting of the relationship between crown and parliament that inevitably followed the end of a long reign such as that of Elizabeth. The death of the king's eldest son, Henry, Prince of Wales (1612) devolved the succession on his second son, the future **Charles I**, who became closely attached to the king's new favourite, **Buckingham**. It was James' vision of bringing peace to a war-torn Europe as much as their escapades in Spain which brought renewed friction with the House of Commons after 1621. James died at Theobalds. His achievements as king of England are still a matter of acute dispute, but he is widely recognized as one of the most successful kings of Scotland, where politics and society were transformed during his long reign. This calculating, tough-minded and talented scholar-king ill deserves the half-truth so often ascribed to him as 'the wisest fool in Christendom'.

JAMES VII, of Scotland, II of England (both 1685–88) (1633–1701) second son of **Charles I**, and brother of **Charles II**. He was born at St James's Palace, London, and was created Duke of York. Nine months before his father's execution in 1649 he escaped to Holland, served under **Turenne** (1652–55), and in 1657 took Spanish service in Flanders. At the Restoration (1660) James was made lord high admiral of England, twice commanding the English fleet in the ensuing wars with the Dutch. In 1659 he had entered into a private marriage contract with Anne Hyde, daughter of the Earl of **Clarendon**; and the year after her death in 1671 as a professed Catholic, he himself became a convert to Catholicism. In 1673 parliament passed the Test Act, and James was obliged to resign the office of lord high admiral. Shortly after, he married **Mary of Modena**, daughter of the Duke of Modena. The national ferment occasioned by the Popish Plot became so formidable that he had to retire to the continent, and during his absence an attempt was made to exclude him from the succession. He returned at the close of 1679, and was sent to Scotland to take the management of its affairs; this period saw the beginnings of a remarkable cultural renaissance under his patronage. Meanwhile the Exclusion Bill was twice passed by the Commons, but in the first instance it was rejected by the Lords, and on the second was lost by the dissolution of parliament. During this period James spent much of his time in exile but after defeat of the bill he returned to England, and in direct violation of the law took his seat in the council, and resumed the direction of naval affairs. At the death of Charles II in 1685 James ascended the throne, and immediately proceeded to levy, on his own warrant, the customs and excise duties which had been granted to Charles only for life. He sent a mission to Rome, heard mass in public, and became, like his brother, the pensioner of the French king. In Scotland, parliament remained loyal, despite renewed persecution of the Covenanters; in England the futile rebellion of **Monmouth** was followed by the 'Bloody Assize'. The suspension of the Test Act by the king's authority, his prosecution of the seven bishops on a charge of seditious libel, his conferring ecclesiastical benefices on Roman Catholics, his violation of the rights of the universities of Oxford and Cambridge, his plan for packing parliament, and numerous other arbitrary acts showed his fixed determination to overthrow the constitution and the church. The indignation of the people was at length roused, and the interposition of William, Prince of Orange, James' son-in-law and nephew and the future **William III**, was formally solicited by seven leading politicians. William landed at Torbay, 4 November 1688, with a powerful army, and marched towards London. He was everywhere hailed as a deliverer, while James was deserted not only by his ministers and troops, but even by his daughter the Princess Anne (later Queen **Anne**). The unfortunate king, on the first appearance of danger, had sent his wife and infant son to France; and, after one futile start and his arrest at Faversham, James also escaped and joined them at St Germain. He was hospitably received by **Louis XIV**, who settled a pension on him. In 1689, aided by a small body of French troops, he invaded Ireland and made an ineffectual attempt to regain his throne. He was defeated at the battle of the Boyne (1690), and returned to St Germain, where he resided until his death. He left two daughters—Mary, married to the Prince of Orange, and Anne, afterwards queen—and one son by his second wife, **James Francis Edward Stewart**. He had several illegitimate children—one of them, Marshal **Berwick**.

JAMES, Arthur Lloyd (1884–1943) Welsh phonetician, born in Pentre. He graduated at Cardiff University and at Trinity College, Cambridge, became lecturer in phonetics at University College, London in 1920, and in 1927 head (professor, 1933) of the phonetics department at the School of Oriental and African Studies. He is chiefly remembered for his *Historical Introduction to French Phonetics* (1929) and for his work with the BBC, whose adviser he was in all matters concerning pronunciation, and whose well-known handbooks on the pronunciation of place names he edited. He committed suicide after killing his wife, as a result of a depressive psychosis brought on by the war.

JAMES, C L R (Cyril Lionel Robert) (1901–89) Trinidadian writer, lecturer, political activist and cricket enthusiast, born in Tunapuna, Trinidad. He won a scholarship to Queens Royal College. An autodidact and a useful cricketer, he was urged to leave Trinidad for England by Constantine O'Leary and it was there that *The Life of Captain Cipriani* was published in 1929 at O'Leary's expense. James repaid the kindness by acting as his mentor's amanuensis for his newspaper column and five books. James' aim was the freedom of the black races through Marxism and revolution. For his political activities he was deported from the USA, while in Trinidad his former pupil, Eric Williams, the prime minister, put him under house arrest. Perhaps his most influential book was *The Black Jacobins: Toussaint L'Ouverture and the San Domingo Revolution* (1938) which impressed **Michael Foot** among others. He wrote only one novel, *Minty Alley* (1936), a study of the relationship between education and working-class West Indians. *Beyond the Boundary* (1963), is in part autobiographical: a fusion of anecdote, report, analysis and comment, in which sport and politics are harmoniously and ingeniously conjugated.

JAMES, Eric John Francis, Baron James of Rusholme (1909–) English educational administrator. Educated at Taunton's School, Southampton, and Queen's College, Oxford, he became assistant master at Winchester (1933–45), high master at Manchester Grammar School (1945–62) and vice chancellor of York University (1962–73). He was chairman of the

Committee to Inquire into the Training of Teachers (1970–71) which reported in 1972 (*Teacher Education and Training*). The *James Report* recommended a restructuring of the pattern of teacher training and advocated an all-graduate entry to the profession. It was the first education report to emphasize the importance of systematic in-service education for teachers. Unfortunately, economic circumstances to a large extent precluded its implementation.

JAMES, George Payne Rainsford (1799–1860) English novelist, born in London. Influenced by Sir **Walter Scott** he wrote numerous historical romances, such as *Richelieu* (1829), and *Henry Masterton* (1832), parodied by **Thackeray** in *Barbazure* for his two horsemen (his stock opening).

JAMES, Henry (1843–1916) American novelist, brother of **William James**, born in New York, of Irish and Scottish stock. Until his father's death he was known as Henry James, junior; his father, Henry James (1811–82), was a well-known theological writer and lecturer, and an exponent of **Swedenborg** and Sandemanianism. After a roving youth in America and Europe (where he met **Turgenev** and **Flaubert**), and desultory law studies at Harvard, he began in 1865 to contribute brilliant literary reviews and short stories. His work as a novelist falls into three periods. To the first, in which he is mainly concerned with the 'international situation', the impact of American life on the older European civilization, belong *Roderick Hudson* (1875), *The American* (1877), *Daisy Miller* (1879), *Washington Square* (1880), *Portrait of a Lady* (1881), *Princess Casamassima* (1886), in which he probes the shadier aspects of European political life, and finally *The Bostonians* (1886). From 1876 he made his home in England, chiefly in London and in Rye, Sussex, where he struck up an oddly contrasted friendship with the brilliant pioneer of science fiction and self-conscious reformer of mankind, **H G Wells**, a friendship which lasted until the latter's savage attack on the Jamesian ethos in the novel, *Boon* (1915). His second period, devoted to purely English subjects, comprises *The Tragic Muse* (1890), *The Spoils of Poynton* (1897), *What Maisie Knew* (1897) and *The Awkward Age* (1899). James reverts to Anglo-American attitudes in his last period, which includes *The Wings of a Dove* (1902), *The Ambassadors* (1903), possibly his masterpiece, *The Golden Bowl* (1904) and two unfinished novels. Collections of his characteristic 'long short stories' include *Terminations* (1895), *The Two Magics* (1898) and *The Altar of the Dead* (1909). James is the acknowledged master of the psychological novel, which has profoundly influenced the 20th-century literary scene. Plot is sacrificed in the interests of minute delineation of character. Many seemingly insignificant incidents, however, subtly contribute allegorically or metaphorically to the author's intentions. The outbreak of World War I brought out his pro-English sympathies. He became a British subject and shortly before his death was awarded the OM. He also wrote critical studies such as *French Poets and Novelists* (1878) and the essay, 'On the Art of Fiction' (1884), travel sketches such as *The American Scene* (1906) and three volumes of memoirs, *A Small Boy and Others* (1913), *Notes of a Son and a Brother* (1914) and the unfinished *The Middle Years* (1917).

JAMES, Henry, 1st Baron James of Hereford (1828–1911) English lawyer, born in Hereford. Educated at Cheltenham College, he was called to the bar in 1852, entered parliament as a liberal in 1869 and rose to become attorney-general in 1873. He defended the case for *The Times* before the **Parnell** Commission. He opposed Home Rule for Ireland and declined the office of Lord Chancellor in 1886. From 1895 to 1902 he was chancellor of the duchy of Lancaster, with a peerage.

JAMES, Jesse Woodson (1847–82) American Wild West robber, born in Clay County, Missouri. He led numerous bank and train robberies before being murdered by one of his fellow brigands. He has been the subject of numerous Hollywood 'Westerns'.

JAMES, Montague Rhodes (1862–1936) English scholar and author, born in Goodnestone, Kent. Provost of King's College, Cambridge (1905–18), he was director of the Fitzwilliam Museum (1894–1908) and vice-chancellor of Cambridge (1913–15). In 1918 he was appointed provost of his old school, Eton. He catalogued the manuscripts of every Cambridge college, of Aberdeen University, and several London libraries, and wrote studies on the *Apocrypha*, and the art and literature of the middle ages. He was also the author of the highly popular collection of *Ghost Stories of an Antiquary* (1905–11), and *Twelve Medieval Ghost Stories* (1922) etc. He was awarded the OM in 1930. See his autobiography, *Eton and King's* (1926).

JAMES, P D (Phyliss Dorothy) (1920–) English thriller writer, born in Oxford, the eldest child of an official in the Inland Revenue. She was educated at Cambridge Girls' High School. Before World War II she worked in the theatre; during the war she was a Red Cross nurse, and also worked in the ministry of food. Later she was employed in hospital administration before working in the home office, first in the police department, where she was involved with the forensic science service, thereafter in the criminal law department. Since 1979 she has devoted herself to writing. *Cover Her Face*, published in 1966, was her first novel, a well-crafted, but slight detective story. Nine more have followed, many featuring the superior detective who is also a minor poet, Commander Adam Dalgleish, culminating in *A Taste for Death* (1986), macabre, elegant and substantial, which enjoyed an international vogue. One of the new 'queens of crime' she was awarded the Crime Writers Asociation prize in 1967.

JAMES, Robert (1705–76) English physician, born in Staffordshire. He practised in London and invented James's fever powders, which were popular in the 18th and 19th centuries. He also compiled a *Medicinal Dictionary* (1743).

JAMES, William (d.1827) English naval historian. He compiled *The Naval History* (5 vols, 1822–24), which disclosed American naval superiority. He was a Jamaican attorney, and from 1815 lived in England.

JAMES, William (1842–1910) American philosopher and psychologist, brother of **Henry James**, born in New York. He graduated in medicine at Harvard, where he taught comparative anatomy from 1872, then philosophy from 1882, becoming professor in 1885 and changing his professorial title in 1889 from philosophy to psychology. In his *Principles of Psychology* (1890) he places psychology firmly on a physiological basis and represents the mind as an instrument for coping with the world. In philosophy he developed the pragmatist ideas of **Charles Peirce** and described himself as a 'radical empiricist': metaphysical disputes can be resolved or dissolved by examining the practical consequences of competing theories—beliefs are true if and because they work, not vice versa. He expounded these ideas most famously in *The Will to Believe* (1907) and *Pragmatism* (1907); and he treated ethics and religion in the same practical, non-dogmatic way, as in *Varieties of Religious Experience* (1902), which comprises his Gifford Lectures delivered in Edinburgh, and *The Meaning of Truth* (1909).

JAMESON, Anna Brownell, née **Murphy** (1794–1860) Irish art critic and author, born in Dublin. Her writings include *Diary of an Ennuyée* (1826), *Characteristics of Shakespeare's Women* (1832), *Beauties of the Court of Charles II* (1833), and works on art.

JAMESON, Sir Leander Starr, 1st Baronet (1853–1917) South African statesman, born in Edinburgh, studied medicine there and at London, and began practice at Kimberley in 1878. Through **Cecil Rhodes** 'Dr Jim' engaged in pioneer work, was in 1891 made administrator for the South Africa Company at Fort Salisbury, and won enormous popularity. During the troubles at Johannesburg between the Uitlanders and the Boer government, Jameson, who by order of Rhodes had concentrated the military forces of Rhodesia at Mafeking on the Transvaal frontier, started with 500 troopers to support the Uitlanders, 29 December 1895. At Krugersdorp they were overpowered by an overwhelming force of Boers, and, sleepless and famishing, were after a sharp fight compelled to surrender, 2 January 1896. Handed over to the British authorities, Dr Jameson was in July condemned in London to 15 months' imprisonment, but was released in December. In 1900 he was elected to the Cape Legislative Assembly, and in 1904–08 was (Progressive) premier of Cape Colony. A baronet from 1911, he retired from politics in 1912, and became president of the BSA Company in 1913.

JAMESON, (Margaret) Storm (1891–1986) English novelist, born in Whitby. Her first success was *The Lovely Ship* (1927), which was followed by more than 30 books that maintained her reputation as storyteller and stylist. These include *The Voyage Home* (1930), *The Delicate Monster* (1937), *Cloudless May* (1943), *The Black Laurel* (1948), *The Writer's Situation* (1950), *The Hidden River* (1955), *A Cup of Tea for Mr Thorgill* (1957), *Last Score* (1961), *The Aristide Case* (1964), *The White Crow* (1968). An autobiography, *No Time Like the Present*, appeared in 1933.

JAMESONE, George (c.1588–1644) Scottish portrait painter, born in Aberdeen. In 1612 he was bound apprentice for eight years to John Anderson, a painter in Edinburgh. The earliest of the Scottish portraitists, he was painting in Aberdeen by 1620, but moved to Edinburgh in the 1630s.

JAMET, Marie (1820–93) French religious, known as Marie Augustine de la Compassion. A St Servan seamstress, she was a founder in 1840 of the Little Sisters of the Poor.

JAMI (1414–92) Persian poet, born in Jam in Khorasan. Among his poems were *Yūsuf o Zalīkhā* (trans by A Rogers, 1895) and *Salámán u Absál* which was translated by **Edward FitzGerald**. He also wrote prose works.

JAMIESON, John (1759–1838) Scottish lexicographer and philologist, born in Glasgow. He studied theology at Glasgow University, and was an Anti-Burgher secessionist minister in Forfar (1781–97) and Nicholson Street, Edinburgh (1797–1830). He wrote several scriptural treatises, but his chief work was his monumental *Etymological Dictionary of the Scottish Language* (2 vols 1808–09, supplement 1825). He also edited **Barbour**'s *The Brus* (1820) and **Blind Harry**'s *Wallace* (1820).

JAMISON, Judith (1943–) American black dancer, born in Philadelphia. She studied piano and violin in her home-town at the Judimar School before making her New York début as a guest dancer with American Ballet Theatre in 1964. She joined **Alvin Ailey**'s American Dance Theatre the following year, becoming one of his top soloists. He choreographed the solo *Cry* for her in 1971, a showcase for her statuesque physique, musical sensitivity and dramatic stage presence. She also starred in the Broadway musical *Sophisticated Ladies* (1981). She is married to the Puerto Rican dancer, Miguel Godreau.

JAMMES, Francis (1868–1938) French writer, born in Tournay in the Pyrenees. He wrote poems of nature and religion, such as *De l'angélus de l'aube à l'angélus du soir* (1898), *Deuil des primevères* (1901), *Triomphe de la vie* (1904) and *Géorgiques Chrétiennes* (1911–12), and prose romances such as *Le Roman du lièvre* (1903).

JAMNITZER, or **Jamitzer, Wenzel** (1508–85) Austrian-born German goldsmith, born in Vienna. He founded a family workshop in Nuremberg with his brother Albrecht and later worked with his sons as court goldsmith. His grandson, Christoph (1563–1618), published a book of fantastic engravings, *Grotteszkenbuch* (1610).

JANÁČEK, Leoš (1854–1928) Czech composer, born in Moravia, the son of a village schoolmaster. At 16 he was choirmaster at Brno, where he eventually settled after studying at Prague and Leipzig. Devoted to the Czech folksong tradition, he matured late as a composer, principally of operas, of which *Jenufa* (1904, first performed 1912), *Osud* (1904), and perhaps *The House of the Dead* (1938), for which he wrote his own libretto based on **Dostoyevsky**'s autobiographical novel, are the most strikingly original in terms of rhythm and subtle melodic dependence upon language. His other compositions include eight further operas, a mass, a sextet for wind instruments and the song cycle, *The Diary of One Who Has Vanished*. *Jenufa* (produced Brno, 1904) is often regarded as his masterpiece. Only after its delayed Prague première (1916) was his international reputation secured. The late flowering of masterworks which followed included the operas *The Excursions of Mr Brouček* (1917), *Kátya Kabanová* (1921), *The Cunning Little Vixen* (1924), *The Makropulos Case* (1925) and *From the House of the Dead* (1928); the *Glagolitic Mass* (1926), two string quarters (1923, 1928), *Sinfonietta* (1926), and *The Diary of One Who Disappeared* (1919–24). Janáček's scientific study of the melodic shapes and rhythmic patterns of speech give his work a strikingly original quality, enhanced by bold, idiosyncratic orchestration, his deep sense of nationalism and intimate choice of subject matter.

JANE, Frederick Thomas (1870–1916) British naval author, journalist and artist, born in Upottery, Devon. He worked first as an artist, then as a naval correspondent on various periodicals. He founded and edited *Jane's Fighting Ships* (1898) and *All the World's Aircraft* (1909), the annuals by which his name is still best known. Inventor of the naval war game, his non-fiction works include *Heresies of Sea Power* (1906) and *The World's Warships* (1915). Among his novels are *Ever Mohun* (1901) and *A Royal Bluejacket* (1908).

JANET, François See **CLOUET**

JANET, Pierre (1859–1947) French psychologist and neurologist, born in Paris. He studied under **Jean Martin Charcot**, lectured in philosophy and became the director of the psychological laboratory at La Salpêtrière hospital in Paris (1899), and professor of psychology at the Sorbonne (1898) and Collège de France (1902). His theory of hysteria, which linked 'dissociation' with a lowering of psychic energy, was described by **Sigmund Freud** as the first significant psychological theory, based as it was on sound clinical practice.

JANIN, Jules Gabriel (1804–74) French critic and novelist, born in St Etienne. He turned to journalism in his youth, and his dramatic criticisms in the *Journal des Débats* made his reputation as an opponent of

Romanticism and advocate of a Classical revival. His strange and at least half-serious story *L'Âne mort et la femme guillotinée* (1829) was followed by *Barnave* (1831), half-historical novel, half polemic against the **Orléans** family. He also compiled a *Histoire de la littérature dramatique* (1858).

JANNINGS, Emil, originally **Theodor Emil Janenz** (1885–1950) German actor, born in Rorschach in Switzerland. He made his name in **Max Reinhardt**'s company from 1906, and was introduced into moving pictures by **Ernst Lubitsch**. He worked in American films from 1926 to 1929, and won Academy Awards for his performances in *The Way of All Flesh* (1928) and *The Last Command* (1928). He then returned to Germany, where he appeared with **Marlene Dietrich** in *The Blue Angel* (1930), his most famous film. He stayed in Germany throughout the Nazi régime, contributing to many of their propaganda films. Blacklisted by the Allies after World War II, he retired to Austria.

JANSEN, Cornelius Otto (1585–1638) Dutch theologian, and founder of the Jansenist sect, born in Acquoi, near Leerdam in Holland. He studied at Utrecht, Louvain and Paris and became professor of theology at Bayonne and in 1630 at Louvain. In 1636 he was made bishop of Ypres. He died just as he had completed his great work, the *Augustinus* (4 vols published in 1640)), which sought to prove that the teaching of St **Augustine** against the Pelagians and semi-Pelagians on grace, free will and predestination was directly opposed to the teaching of the Jesuit schools. Jansen repudiated the ordinary Catholic dogma of the freedom of the will, and refused to admit merely sufficient grace, maintaining that interior grace is irresistible, and that **Jesus Christ** died for all. On its publication in 1640 the *Augustinus* caused a major outcry, especially by the Jesuits, and it was prohibited by a decree of the Inquisition in 1641. In the following year it was condemned by **Urban VIII** in the bull *In Eminenti*. Jansen was supported by **Arnauld**, **Pascal** and the Port-Royalists. The controversy raged in France for nearly a century, when a large number of Jansenists emigrated to the Netherlands. The Utrecht Jansenists are in doctrine and discipline strictly orthodox Roman Catholics, known by their countrymen as Oude Roomsch ('Old Roman').

JANSKY, Karl Guthe (1905–50) American radio engineer, born in Norman, Oklahoma. He studied at the University of Wisconsin and joined the Bell Telephone Laboratories in 1928. While investigating the sources of interference on short-wave radio telephone transmissions he detected a weak source of static which appeared to be outside the solar system altogether. He published his findings in December 1932, thus initiating the science of radio astronomy, but he did not pursue further work in this field himself, and it was left to **Grote Reber** to construct the world's first radio telescope in 1937. After the end of World War II advances in radar and other microwave techniques led to the widespread adoption of radio astronomy as a means of celestial exploration. The unit of radio emission strength, the jansky, is named after him.

JANSSEN, Cornelis, originally **Cornelius Johnson** (1593–c.1664) English-born Dutch portrait painter, born in London. He left England in 1643, and lived in Amsterdam. His portraits show the influence of **Van Dyck**, with whom he worked at the court of **Charles I**. He is represented in the National Gallery, London, and at Chatsworth.

JANSSEN, or **Johnson, Geraert** (fl.c.1616) English sculptor, born in London, the son of an immigrant Dutch sculptor and an English mother. He is best known for his portrait bust of **Shakespeare** at Stratford-on-Avon.

JANSSEN, Pierre Jules César (1824–1907) French astronomer, born in Paris. Lame from childhood, he became head of the Astrophysical Observatory at Meudon (1876), and greatly advanced spectrum analysis by his observation of the bright line spectrum of the solar atmosphere (1868). He established an observatory on Mont Blanc, and published a pioneering book of celestial photographs, *Atlas de photographies solaries* (1904).

JANSSENS, Abraham (c.1575–1632) Flemish painter of Antwerp. His most famous pictures are the *Entombment of Christ* and the *Adoration of the Magi* at Antwerp.

JANSSON, Tove (1914–) Finnish-Swedish author and artist, whose Moomintroll books for children, starting with *The Magician's Hat* (1949) and illustrated by herself, are as much appreciated by adults. Set in the fantastic yet real world of the Moomins, the books emphasize the security of family life. They have reached an international audience and she has been the recipient of many literary prizes. In later years she has written a number of books such as *Sommarboken* (The Summer Book, 1972) for adults.

JANSZOON, Laurens, often called **Coster** (c.1370–1440) Dutch official in Haarlem, credited by some with the invention of printing before **Gutenberg**. He is supposed to have made his great invention between 1420 and 1426, to have been sacristan (*Koster*) at Haarlem, and is thought to have died of the plague.

JANUARIUS, St, or **San Gennaro** (?–c.305) Italian prelate and patron saint of Naples, bishop of Benevento. According to tradition, he was martyred in Pozzuoli in 305, during the persecutions of **Diocletian**. His body is preserved in Naples cathedral, with two phials supposed to contain his dried blood, believed to liquefy on 19 September, his feast day, and other occasions.

JAQUES-DALCROZE, Émile (1865–1951) Swiss composer, born in Vienna. He was the founder of eurhythmics, a method of expressing the rhythmical aspects of music by physical movement. He taught at Dresden and Geneva, where he was professor of the conservatory, and composed operas and other works.

JARDINE, Douglas Robert (1900–58) English cricketer, born in Bombay, captain of England during the controversial 'bodyline' tour of Australia in 1932–33. In 1927 he scored five centuries and was picked for the Test team that toured Australia in 1927–28, where he scored 341 Test runs. He returned to Australia as captain for the 1932–33 tour, where he employed **Harold Larwood** to bowl extremely fast at the batsman's body (the so-called 'leg theory'), causing severe injury to the Australian batsmen. He wrote a defence of his tactics in *In Quest of the Ashes* (1933).

JARDINE, Sir William (1800–74) Scottish naturalist and physician, born in Dumfriesshire. He studied medicine at Edinburgh and Paris, but devoted himself to ornithology after inheriting the estate of Jardine Hall in Dumfries. With **Prideaux John Selby** he produced *Illustrations of Ornithology* (1825–43), and founded the *Magazine of Zoology and Botany* (1837). He also compiled the *Naturalist's Library* (1838–43) and *Contributions to Ornithology* (1848–52).

JARMAN, Derek (1942–) English painter and filmmaker, born in Northwood, Middlesex. He studied painting at the Slade School, London (1963–67) and had work exhibited at the Young Contemporaries' and John Moores exhibitions before moving into costume and set design for the Royal Ballet. Continuing to paint, he first worked in the cinema as a production designer for **Ken Russell**'s *The Devils* (1970). He directed his first feature film, *Sebastiane*, in 1976 and has transferred his painterly instincts to the cinema in a succession of often controversial works exploring the decline of modern Britain, his homosexual sensibilities and artistic idols. His films include *Jubilee* (1977), *Caravaggio* (1985) and *The Last of England* (1987). He has also directed pop videos, designed for opera and ballet and written several volumes including the autobiographical *Dancing Ledge* (1984).

JÄRNEFELT, Armas (1869–1958) Finnish-born Swedish opera composer and conductor, brother-in-law of **Sibelius**, born in Viipuri. He studied under **Busoni** and **Massenet** and conducted in Germany, Helsinki and Stockholm, taking Swedish citizenship in 1910. He is best known for his *Praeludium* and *Berceuse* for orchestra and for choral music.

JARRELL, Randall (1914–65) American poet and critic, born in Nashville, Tennessee. He served in the air force in World War II. He loved teaching and eschewed prestigious universities for unfashionable girls' colleges in the south. A potent, passionate and compassionate writer, he published several collections including *Blood for a Stranger* (1942) and *The Lost World*, published posthumously in 1966. His *Complete Poems* appeared in 1969. An uncompromising critic and merciless reviewer of bad verse, he wrote one novel, *Pictures from an Institution* (1954), an early satirical campus novel. He committed suicide, possibly as a result of his war experience.

JARRY, Alfred (1873–1907) French writer, born in Laval, Mayenne. He was educated at Rennes. His play, *Ubu roi*, an attack on bourgeois conventions, was first written when he was 15; later rewritten, it was produced in 1896. Ubu, the hero, symbolizes the crassness of the bourgeoisie pushed to absurd lengths by the lust of power. He wrote two sequels, *Ubu enchaîné* (1900) and *Ubu sur la butte* (1901), as well as short stories and poems and other plays. He invented a logic of the absurd, which he called *pataphysique* and his work is considered a precursor of the Theatre of the Absurd. He died an alcoholic.

JARUZELSKI, General Wojciech (1923–) Polish soldier and politician, born near Lublin. After a long and distinguished military career (chief of general staff 1965, minister of defence 1968) he became a member of the politburo in 1971 and was appointed prime minister and Communist party leader after the resignations of Pinkowski and Kania in 1981. Later that year, in an attempt to ease the country's crippling economic problems and to counteract the increasing political influence of the free trade union Solidarity, Jaruzelski declared a state of martial law. Solidarity was declared an illegal organization and its leaders were detained and put on trial. Martial law was suspended at the end of 1982 and lifted in July of the following year. In November 1985 Jaruzelski resigned as prime minister to become state president, but remained the dominant political figure in Poland, overseeing a transition to a new form of 'socialist pluralist' democracy in 1989.

JASMIN, pseud of **Jacques Boé** (1798–1864) Provençal poet, born in Agen. A barber by profession, he wrote homely verses in his local dialect. Among his best pieces (collected in *Las Papillôtos*) are the mock-heroic *Charivari* (1825); *The Blind Girl of Castel-Cuillé* (1835), which was translated by **Longfellow**; *Françovneto* (1840); and *The Son's Week* (1849).

JASPERS, Karl Theodor (1883–1969) German-born Swiss philosopher, one of the founders of existentialism, born in Oldenburg. He studied medicine at Berlin, Göttingen and Heidelberg, where he undertook research in a psychiatric clinic, published a textbook on psychopathology (*Allgemeine Psychopathologie*, 1913) and was professor of psychology from 1916–20. From 1921 he was professor of philosophy at Heidelberg until dismissed by the Nazis in 1937; his work was banned but he stayed in Germany and was awarded the Goethe prize in 1947 for his uncompromising stand. In 1948 he settled in Basle as a Swiss citizen, and was appointed professor. His main work was the three-volume *Philosophie* (1932). In this he developed his own brand of existentialism whereby *Existenz* (Being) necessarily transcends and eludes ordinary objective thought: at the limits of the intellect the 'authentic self' must make a leap of apprehension of a different kind.

JAURÈS, Jean (1859–1914) French socialist leader, writer and orator, born in Castres (Tarn). A deputy from 1885 to 1889, he lectured on philosophy at Toulouse, became a deputy again from 1893. He founded the French Socialist party, and in 1904 helped to found the socialist paper *L'Humanité*, which he edited until his assassination in July 1914.

JAVOLENUS PRISCUS (c.60–125) Roman jurist. He was consul, commander of several legions, governor successively of Germany, Syria and Africa, and writer of legal texts. Particularly notable is his *Epistulae* (in 15 books), from which several excerpts are included in **Justinian**'s *Digest*.

JAWARA, Alhaji Sir Dawda (Kair abu) (1924–) Gambian politician, born in Barajally. After qualifying at Glasgow University, he returned to The Gambia to work in the national veterinary service (1957–60). He entered politics in 1960 and progressed rapidly, becoming minister of education and then premier (1962–65). When full independence was achieved in 1965 he became prime minister and when it chose republican status, in 1970, president. He was re-elected in 1972, 1977, 1982 and 1987, despite an abortive coup against him in 1981. The coup was thwarted by Senegalese troops and brought the two countries closer together into a confederation of Senegambia.

JAWLENSKY, Alexei von (1864–1941) Russian painter, born in Kuslovo. He began as an officer in the Imperial Guards but turned to painting in 1889, studying at the St Petersburg Academy under **Ilya Repin**. In 1896 went to Munich where he met **Kandinsky**, and in 1905 to France where he was strongly influenced by the work of **Van Gogh**, **Gauguin** and **Matisse**, developing a personal style which combined traditional Russian icons and peasant art with the new Fauvist emphasis on strong, flat colours and harsh outlines. A founder member of the *Neue Künstlervereiningung* in Munich in 1909, he was never a pure abstractionist. In 1924, with Kandinsky, **Klee** and **Feininger**, he founded the short-lived *Der Blaue Vier* (Blue Four association).

JAY, John (1745–1829) American jurist and statesman, born in New York. Admitted to the bar in 1768, he was elected to the Continental Congress (1774–77) and drafted the constitution of New York state in 1777, of which he was appointed chief justice. He was elected president of congress in 1778, and in 1779 was sent as minister to Spain. From 1782 he was one of the most influential of the commissioners negotiating peace with Britain. He was secretary for foreign affairs (1784–89), and then became chief justice of the Supreme Court (1789–95). In 1794 he concluded with Lord **Grenville** the convention known as 'Jay's Treaty', which, though favourable to the USA, was denounced by the Democrats as a betrayal of France. He was Governor of New York, 1795–1801.

JAYAWARDENE, Junius Richard (1906–) Sri Lankan politician, born in Colombo into a well-connected, élite (goyigama) family. He studied law at

Colombo University before entering the House of Representatives in 1947 as a representative of the liberal-conservative United National party (UNP). He held a number of ministerial posts (1953–70), before becoming leader of the UNP, and of the opposition, in 1970. He so revitalized it that it returned to power in 1977. He introduced a new constitution in 1978, creating a republic, and became the country's first president. He embarked on a new, freer-market economic strategy but was confronted with mounting unrest between Tamil separatists and the indigenous Sinhalese, forcing the imposition of a state of emergency in 1983 and the postponement of new elections until 1988, when he stepped down as president.

JEANMAIRE, Zizi See **PETIT, Roland**

JEANNE D'ALBRET (1528–72) queen of Navarre and mother of King **Henri IV** of France. A Huguenot and a poet, she was the only daughter and heiress of Henri d'Albret (Henri II) of Navarre and **Margaret of Angoulême**, and succeeded in 1562. She married Antoine de Bourbon, Duc de Vendôme, in 1548, and gave birth to Henri in 1553.

JEANNE D'ARC See **JOAN OF ARC**

JEANNERET, Charles Édouard See **LE CORBUSIER**

JEANS, Sir James Hopwood (1877–1946) English physicist, astronomer and writer, born in Ormskirk, near Southport. A fellow of Trinity College, Cambridge, he taught applied mathematics at Princeton (1905–9) and Cambridge (1910–12). He made important contributions to the dynamical theory of gases, radiation, quantum theory and stellar evolution, but was best known for his popular exposition of physical and astronomical theories and their philosophical bearings, such as *The Universe around us* (1929) and *The New Background of Science* (1933). He married Susi Hock (1911–), the Australian-born organist and harpsichordist.

JEBAVÝ, Václav See **BŘEZINA, Otakar**

JEBB, Sir Richard Claverhouse (1841–1905) Scottish scholar, born in Dundee. He graduated from Trinity College, Cambridge, was elected fellow, and in 1875 appointed professor of Greek at Glasgow, and in 1889 regius professor of Greek at Cambridge. In 1891 he was elected MP (Unionist) for Cambridge University. His greatest works are his editions of **Sophocles** (with translations, 9 vols, 1883–1917).

JEEJEEBHOY See **JEJEEBHOY**

JEFFERIES, (John) Richard (1848–87) English naturalist and novelist, born near Swindon, the son of a Wiltshire farmer. He started as a provincial journalist and became known by a letter to *The Times* (1872) on the Wiltshire labourers. His first real success, *The Gamekeeper at Home* (1878), was followed by other books on rural life, including *Wild Life in a Southern County* (1879), *Hodge and his Masters* (1880), *Wood Magic* (1881), *Bevis: The Story of a Boy* (1882) and *Amaryllis at the Fair* (1887). *The Story of my Heart* (1883) is a strange autobiography of inner life; *After London, or Wild England* (1885), is a curious romance of the future.

JEFFERSON, Joseph (1829–1905) American comic actor, born in Philadelphia. He came of a theatrical stock, his great-grandfather having belonged to **Garrick's** company at Drury Lane, while his father and grandfather were well-known American actors. Jefferson appeared on the stage at three, and had for years been a strolling actor, when in 1857, in New York, he made a hit as Doctor Pangloss, and in 1858 created the part of Asa Trenchard in *Our American Cousin*. In 1865 he visited London, and at the Adelphi first played his famous part of Rip Van Winkle.

JEFFERSON, Thomas (1743–1826) 3rd president of the USA, born in Shadwell, Albemarle County, Virginia. In 1767 he was admitted to the bar, and practised with success. In 1769 he was elected to the House of Burgesses, where he joined the revolutionary party. He took a prominent part in the calling of the first Continental Congress in 1774, to which he was sent as a delegate; and it was he who drafted the celebrated Declaration of Independence, signed 4 July 1776. Jefferson now assisted the people of Virginia in forming a state constitution, and was governor (1779–81). In congress he secured (1783) the adoption of the decimal system of coinage. He was sent to France in 1784 with **Franklin** and **Samuel Adams** as pleni-potentiary; next year he succeeded Franklin as minister there; and in 1789 **Washington** appointed him secretary of state. From the origin of the Federal and Republican parties, Jefferson was the recognized head of the latter, while the other members of the cabinet and the president were Federalists. In 1794 he withdrew from public life, but in 1797 was called to the vice-presidency of the United States, and in 1801 was chosen president by the House of Representatives. The popular vote re-elected him by a large majority for the next presidental term. Among the chief events of his first term were the war with Tripoli, the admission of Ohio, and the Louisiana purchase; of his second term, the firing on the *Chesapeake* by the *Leopard*, the Embargo, the trial of **Aaron Burr** for treason, and the prohibition of the slave trade. In 1809 he retired, but continued to advise in the capacity of elder statesman, and helped to found the University of Virginia (1825).

JEFFERY, Dorothy See **PENTREATH, Dolly**

JEFFREY, Francis Jeffrey, Lord (1773–1850) Scottish jurist and critic, born in Edinburgh. He studied at Glasgow and Oxford, and in 1794 was called to the Scottish bar, but as a Whig made little progress for many years. In the trials for sedition (1817–22) he acquired a great reputation; in 1820 and again in 1823 he was elected lord rector of Glasgow University, in 1829 dean of the faculty of advocates. In 1830 he was returned as MP for Perth, and on the formation of Earl **Grey**'s ministry became lord advocate. After the passing of the Reform Bill he was returned for Edinburgh, which he represented until 1834, when he was made a judge of the Court of Session. From 1815 he lived at Craigcrook. Along with **Sydney Smith**, **Francis Horner** and a few others, he established the *Edinburgh Review*, of which he was editor until 1829. He was a prolific and brilliant—if biased—contributor, as in his strictures on **Wordsworth**, **Keats** and **Byron**. While in the USA to marry his second wife, he dined with President **Madison** during the British-American War of 1812. A selection of his articles was published in 1844.

JEFFREYS, George Jeffreys, 1st Baron, (1648–89) English judge, known as the 'infamous Jeffreys', born in Acton near Wrexham. Called to the bar in 1668, he rose rapidly, and became in 1671 common serjeant of the City of London. Previously nominally a Puritan, he began to intrigue for court favour, was made solicitor to the Duke of York, was knighted in 1677, and became recorder of London in 1678. Actively concerned in the Popish Plot prosecutions, he was made chief justice of Chester and king's serjeant in 1680, baronet in 1681 and chief justice of King's Bench in 1683. Though able and impartial in civil cases it was otherwise in criminal. His first exploit was the judicial murder of **Algernon Sidney**, but in every state trial he proved a willing tool of the crown, thus earning the favour of King **James II**, who raised him to the peerage (1685). Among his earliest trials were those of **Titus**

Oates and **Richard Baxter**; he was then sent to the west to try the followers of the Duke of **Monmouth**, and hanged, transported, whipped and fined hundreds of them, during the 'Bloody Assize'. He was Lord Chancellor from 1685 until the downfall of King James in 1688, and supported all the king's measures as president of the newly-revived Court of High Commission, and in the trial of the seven bishops. He nevertheless had rational views on witchcraft, and was too honest to turn Catholic. On James's flight he tried to follow his example, but was caught in Wapping, disguised as a sailor, and sent to the Tower to save him from the mob. There he died.

JEFFREYS, Sir Harold (1891–1989) English geophysicist, astronomer and mathematician, born in Birtley, Durham. Educated at Armstrong College (Newcastle-upon-Tyne) and St John's College, Cambridge, he became reader in geophysics at Cambridge (1931–46). In a wide-ranging scientific career, he investigated the effect of radioactivity on the cooling of the earth and postulated that the earth's core is liquid. He studied earthquakes and monsoons, and estimated anew the age of the solar system. He calculated anew the surface temperatures of the outer planets, and postulated that Mercury might once have been a satellite of Venus. In mathematics he made contributions to probability theory and operational calculus.

JEFFRIES, James Jackson (1875–1953) American pugilist and World Champion, born in Carroll, Ohio. Nicknamed 'The Boilermaker' because he worked in a boiler factory, he trained as sparring partner to **'Gentleman' Jim Corbett**. In 1899 he won the world heavyweight championship by knocking out **Bob Fitzsimmons** in 11 rounds. He retired undefeated in 1905, but in 1910 he was persuaded to return to the ring as the 'great white hope' against the new black champion, **Jack Johnson**, who knocked him out in the 15th round.

JEFFRIES, John (1744–1819) American balloonist and physician, born in Boston. A loyalist during the American revolution, he settled in England and made the first balloon crossing of the English channel with the French aeronaut, **François Blanchard**, in 1785.

JEHU, king of Israel (842–815 BC) He had been military commander under King **Ahab**, but after his death led a military coup against his son Jehoram, and slaughtered the royal family, including his mother **Jezebel**. Having seized the throne for himself, he founded a dynasty that presided over a decline in the fortunes of Israel, which was to pay tribute to Assyria.

JEJEEBHOY, Sir Jamsetjee (1783–1859) Indian Parsee merchant and philanthropist, born in Bombay. He was taken into partnership by his father-in-law, a Bombay merchant, in 1800. When peace was restored in Europe in 1815, Indian trade with Europe increased enormously. By 1822 he had amassed £2000000, with which he contributed generously to various educational and philanthropic institutions in Bombay.

JEKYLL, Gertrude (1843–1932) English horticulturalist and garden designer, born in London. She trained as an artist but was forced by failing eyesight to abandon painting and took up landscape design at her garden at Munstead Wood, Surrey. In association with the young architect **Edwin Lutyens** she designed more than 300 gardens for his buildings that had a great influence on promoting colour design in garden planning. Her books included *Wood and Garden* (1899), *Home and Garden* (1900), *Wall and Water Gardens* (1901), *Colour in the Flower Garden* (1918) and *Garden Ornament* (1918).

JELLAČIC, Josef, Count (1801–59) Hungarian politician, born in Petrovaradin. He became an officer in the Austrian army and a devoted servant of Austrian imperialism. He was appointed governor of Croatia and helped to suppress the Hungarian rising (1848), although forced to capitulate at Ozora by **Arthur Görgei**.

JELLICOE, John Rushworth Jellicoe, 1st Earl (1859–1935) English naval commander, born in Southampton, the son of a sea captain. He served in the Egyptian war of 1882, and was one of the survivors of the collision between HMS *Victoria* and HMS *Camperdown* in 1893. He was chief of staff on an international overland expedition to relieve the legations in Peking during the Boxer rising (1900), where he was severely wounded. After special courses in gunnery, he played a major part in the overdue modernization of the fleet under **Fisher**, particularly in the adoption of the new *Dreadnought* battleships, torpedo and submarine tactics, as director of naval ordnance (1905–07) and as controller of the navy (1908–10). At the outbreak of World War I he was appointed c-in-c of the Grand fleet with the acting rank of admiral. After two minor engagements at the Heligoland Bight (August 1914) and off the Dogger Bank (January 1915) he managed to catch the reluctant German fleet at sea off Jutland in the evening of 31 May 1916. The battle was never fully joined, but the German fleet beat a hasty retreat favoured by poor visibility. He served as First Sea Lord (1916–12), but was unjustly dismissed after a disagreement with Sir **Eric Geddes** of the War Cabinet. In 1919 he was promoted Admiral of the Fleet, and was governor of New Zealand (1920–24). He was buried in St Paul's Cathedral.

JENGHIZ KHAN See **GENGHIS**

JENKINS, David Edward (1925–) English theologian and prelate, born in Bromley, Kent. Appointed bishop of Durham in 1984 amidst controversy over his interpretation of the Virgin Birth and the Resurrection, his recent trilogy, *God, Miracle and the Church of England* (1987), *God, Politics and the Future* (1988), and *God, Jesus and Life in the Spirit* (1988), maintains the exploratory spirit of earlier books, which included *A Guide to the Debate About God* (1966), *Living with Questions* (1969), *The Glory of Man* (1967) and *The Contradiction of Christianity* (1976). A lecturer in Birmingham and Oxford before being appointed director of *Humanum* studies at the World Council of Churches, Geneva (1969–73), he was then director of the William Temple Foundation, Manchester (1973–78) and professor of theology at Leeds (1979–84).

JENKINS, Herbert (1876–1923) English publisher and writer, born in Norwich. His humorous books about the Cockney, Bindle (1916, 1918, etc), were amongst the first publications of the publishing house which he founded in 1912.

JENKINS, John (1592–1678) English composer, born in Maidstone, Kent. He served as musician to the royal and noble families and composed a great number of fantasies for strings, *In Nomines*, suites, catches, anthems and songs.

JENKINS, Robert (18th century) English merchant captain, engaged in trading in the West Indies. In 1731 he alleged that his sloop had been boarded by a Spanish *guarda costa*, and that, though no proof of smuggling had been found, he had been tortured, and had his ear torn off. He produced the alleged ear in 1738 in the House of Commons and so helped to force **Walpole** into the 'War of Jenkins' Ear' against Spain in 1739, which merged into the War of the Austrian Succession (1740–48). Jenkins served with the East India Company, and for a time as governor of St Helena.

JENKINS, Roy, Baron Jenkins (1920–) Welsh Labour politician and author, born in Abersychan. He was educated at the local grammar school and at Balliol College, Oxford, where he obtained first class honours in modern greats. Elected MP for Central Southwark in 1948, he was the youngest member of the House; he sat for the Stetchford division of Birmingham from 1950 to 1976. He introduced, as a Private Members' Bill, the controversial Obscene Publications Bill, strengthening the position of authors, publishers and printers *vis-à-vis* prosecutions for obscenity. After a successful spell as minister of aviation (1964–65) he was made home secretary, in which office his alleged 'softness' towards criminals provoked criticism. In 1967 he changed posts with **Callaghan** to become Chancellor of the Exchequer, introducing a notably stringent Budget in March 1968. In 1970–72 he was deputy leader of the Labour party in opposition, and was again appointed home secretary on Labour's return to power in 1974. He held this post until 1976, and was president of the European Commission (1977–81). He was a founder-member and a member of the joint leadership of the Social Democratic party 1981–2, became its first leader in 1982, but stood down the following year in favour of Dr **David Owen**. He returned to the House of Commons, representing Glasgow (Hillhead) between 1982 and 1987 and was made a life peer in that year. He was also elected chancellor of Oxford University in 1987. A successful journalist and author, his books include *Mr Balfour's Poodle* (1954), *Sir Charles Dilke* (1958), and *Asquith* (1964).

JENKINSON See **LIVERPOOL, Earl of**

JENNER, Edward (1749–1823) English physician, the discoverer of vaccination, born in Berkeley vicarage, Gloucestershire. He was apprenticed to a surgeon at Sodbury, near Bristol, in 1770 went to London to study under **John Hunter**, and in 1773 settled in Berkeley, where he acquired a large practice. In 1775 he began to examine the truth of the traditions respecting cowpox, and became convinced that it was efficacious as a protection against smallpox. Many investigations delayed the actual discovery of the prophylactic power of vaccination, and the crowning experiment was made in 1796, when he vaccinated an eight-year-old boy with cowpox matter from the hands of a milkmaid, and soon afterwards inoculated him with smallpox. Yet the practice met with violent opposition for a year, until over seventy principal physicians and surgeons in London signed a declaration of their entire confidence in it.

JENNER, Sir William (1815–98) English physician, born in Chatham. He was educated at University College London, where he was professor from 1848 to 1879. He became physician in ordinary to Queen **Victoria** in 1862, and to the Prince of Wales in 1863. He established the difference between typhus and typhoid fevers (1851). His brother, Charles (1810–93), made a fortune as an Edinburgh linen draper.

JENNINGS, Herbert Spencer (1868–1947) American zoologist, born in Tonica, Illinois. Professor of experimental zoology (1906) and zoology (1910–38) at Johns Hopkins University, he wrote the standard work *Contributions to the Study of the Behaviour of the Lower Organisms* (1919) and investigated heredity and variation of micro-organisms.

JENNINGS, Sarah See **MARLBOROUGH, John Churchill**

JENSEN, Adolf (1837–79) German songwriter and composer for the piano, born in Königsberg. From 1856 to 1868 he was a musician successively at Posen, Copenhagen and Berlin.

JENSEN, Georg (1866–1935) Danish silversmith. Having worked as a sculptor, he founded his silversmithy in Copenhagen in 1904, and revived the high artistic traditions of Danish silver.

JENSEN, (Johannes) Hans (Daniel) (1907–73) German physicist, born in Hamburg. Professor at Hamburg (1936–41) and Hanover (1941–49), in 1949 he became professor of theoretical physics at Heidelberg. With **Maria Goeppert-Mayer** and **Eugene Wigner**, he was awarded the Nobel prize for physics in 1963 for research on nuclear shell structure.

JENSEN, Johannes Vilhelm (1873–1950) Danish novelist, essayist and poet, born in Farsö, Jutland. His native land and its people are described in his *Himmerlandshistorier* (1898–1910), but many of his works, such as *The Forest* and *Madama d'Ora* (1904), are based on his extensive travels in the Far East and America. In *Den Lange Rejse* (1908–22; trans *The Long Journey*, 1922–24) the journey traced, however, is that of man through the ages, the three constitutent novels being an expression of Jensen's Darwinism. His psychological study of **Kristian II** of Denmark, *Kongens Fald* (trans *The Fall of the King*, 1933), his short prose works, *Myter* (1904–44), 14 of which were translated into English as *The Waving Rye* (1959), and his lyric poetry (1901–41), all serve to vindicate his high place in modern Scandinavian literature. He was awarded the Nobel prize for literature in 1944.

JENSEN, Wilhelm (1837–1911) German poet and novelist, born in Heiligenhafen in north east Holstein. He studied medicine and history at a variety of universities, and his main works, such as *Vom römischen Reich deutscher nation* (3 vols 1882), are concerned with German history. In 1888 he moved to Munich where he spent most of his life. His writing includes tragedies, songs, poetry, and novels such as *Flut und Ebbe* (1877) and *Aus See und Sand* (1897).

JEREMIAH (7th century BC.) Old Testament prophet, son of Hilkiah the priest. He was a native of Anathoth, near Jerusalem. He was in Jerusalem during the siege by **Nebuchadrezzar**, and is said to have died a martyr's death at Tahpanhes in Egypt. The *Book of Jeremiah* warns of the impending fall of Jerusalem to Nebuchadrezzar and the Babylonian exile, and foretold the coming of a Messiah.

JERNE, Niels Kai (1911–) Danish immunologist, born in London of Danish parents, and joint winner of the 1984 Nobel prize for physiology or medicine. He worked at the Danish State Serum Institute (1943–55) and later took a medical degree at Copenhagen. He was chief medical officer of the World Health Organization (1956–62), and founding-director of the Institute of Immunology at Basle (1969–80). For his researches into the way the immune system in the body creates antibodies against disease, he shared the Nobel prize with **César Milstein** and Georges Kōhler.

JEROBOAM I (10th century BC) first king of the divided kingdom of Israel. He was made by **Solomon** superintendent of the labours and taxes exacted from his tribe of Ephraim at the construction of the fortifications of Zion. The growing disaffection towards Solomon fostered his ambition, but he was obliged to flee to Egypt. After Solomon's death he headed the successful revolt of the northern tribes against Rehoboam, and, as their king, established idol shrines at Dan and Bethel to wean away his people from the pilgrimages to Jerusalem. He reigned 22 years.

JEROBOAM II (8th century BC) king of Israel, son of Joash. He thrust back the Syrians, and reconquered Ammon and Moab.

JEROME BONAPARTE See **BONAPARTE**

JEROME OF PRAGUE (c.1365–1416) Czech religious reformer and friend of **John Hus**, born in Prague. Educated at Oxford, he became a convert there to **Wycliffe**'s doctrines, and zealously taught them after his return home (1407). The king of Poland employed him to reorganize the University of Cracow in 1410 and the king of Hungary invited him to preach before him in Budapest. Jerome entered wholeheartedly into promoting the theology of Huss. When Huss was arrested in Constance Jerome wanted to go and defend him, but, being refused a safe-conduct, he set out to return to Prague. He was arrested in Bavaria in April 1415, and was brought back to Constance. He recanted, but withdrew his recantation, and went to the stake.

JEROME, St, properly **Eusebius Sophronius Hieronymus** (c.342–420) Italian scholar and Latin Church father, born in Stridon. He studied Greek and Latin rhetoric and philosophy at Rome, where he was also baptized. In 370 he settled in Aquileia with his friend **Rufinus**, but then went to the East, and after a dangerous illness at Antioch, retired between 374 and 378 to the desert of Chalcis. In 379, ordained priest at Antioch by St **Paulinus of Nola**, he went to Constantinople, and became intimate with **Gregory Nazianzen**. In 382 he went on a mission connected with the Meletian schism at Antioch to Rome, where he became secretary to Pope Damasus, and where he enjoyed great influence. In 385 he led a pilgrimage to the Holy Land, and settled in Bethlehem in 386. It was here that Jerome pursued or completed his great literary labours, in particular his Vulgate version of the Bible, the first Latin translation of the Bible from the Hebrew. He wrote biblical commentaries, and also fiery invectives against Jovinian, Vigilantius and the Pelagians, and even against Rufinus and St **Augustine**. St Jerome was the most learned and eloquent of the Latin Fathers. His feast day is 30 September.

JEROME, Jennie See **CHURCHILL, Lord Randolph Henry Spencer**

JEROME, Jerome K (Klapka) (1859–1927) English humorous writer, novelist and playwright, born in Walsall, Staffordshire, and brought up in London. Successively a clerk, schoolmaster, reporter, actor and journalist, he became joint editor of *The Idler* in 1892 and started his own twopenny weekly, *To-Day*. His magnificently ridiculous *Three Men in a Boat* (1889), the account of a boat trip up the Thames from Kingston to Oxford, established itself as a humorous classic of the whimsical. Other books include *The Idle Thoughts of an Idle Fellow* (1889), *Three Men on the Bummel* (1900), *Paul Kelver* (1902), the morality play, *The Passing of the Third Floor Back* (1907), and his autobiography, *My Life and Times* (1926).

JERROLD, Douglas William (1803–57) English author, dramatist and wit, born in London, the son of Samuel Jerrold, actor and manager. In 1813 he joined the navy as a midshipman, but on the close of the war he started life anew as a printer's apprentice, and in 1819 was a compositor on the *Sunday Monitor* but rose to become its dramatic critic. In 1825 he was engaged to write plays for the Coburg Theatre, and from 1829 for the Surrey Theatre. From 1841 he was one of the original contributors to the newly-launched *Punch* magazine, writing under the pseudonym 'Q', and edited the *Illuminated Magazine* (1843–44), *Douglas Jerrold's Shilling Magazine* (1845–48), and *Douglas Jerrold's Weekly Newspaper* (1846–48). In 1852 he became editor of *Lloyd's Weekly Newspaper*. He wrote several novels as well as *The Story of a Feather*, *Cakes and Ale*, *Punch's Letters to his Son*, *Punch's Complete Letter-writer*, and *Mrs Caudle's Curtain Lectures* (1846), and several plays, including *Black-ey'd Susan* (1829), and the comedies *The Bride of Ludgate* (1831), *The Prisoner of Ludgate* (1831), *Time Works Wonders* (1845) and *The Catspaw* (1850). *Other Times* (1868) is a selection from his political writings in *Lloyd's*. His son William Blanchard Jerrold (1826–84), succeeded his father as editor of *Lloyd's* and also wrote novels and plays.

JERVIS, Sir John See **ST VINCENT**

JESPERSEN, Otto (1860–1943) Danish philologist, born in Randers. Professor of English language and literature at Copenhagen University (1893–1925), he revolutionized the teaching of languages. In 1904 his *Sprogundervisning* was published in English as *How to Teach a Foreign Language*, and became perhaps the best-known statement of what is now called the 'Direct Method' reform. His other books include *Progress in Language* (1894), *Growth and Structure of the English Language* (1905), *A Modern English Grammar on Historical Principles* (1909), and *Philosophy of Grammar* (1924). He also invented an international language, 'Novial', with its own grammar and lexicon.

JESSE, Fryn (Friniwyd Tennyson) (1889–1958) English novelist, dramatist and editor of several volumes of the *Notable British Trials* series. A great-niece of **Tennyson**, she studied painting, but during World War I took up journalism and after it served on **Herbert Hoover**'s Relief Commission for Europe. In 1918 she married H M Harwood, the dramatist, and with him collaborated in a number of light plays and a series of war-time letters, *London Front* (1940) and *While London Burns* (1942). But she is best known for her novels set in Cornwall, such as *The White Riband* (1921), *Tom Fool* (1926) and *Moonraker* (1927), as well as *A Pin to See a Peepshow* (1934), based on the Thompson-Bywaters murder case. She also published collected poems, *The Happy Bride* (1920), and remarkable accounts of the trials of **Madeleine Smith** (1927), Timothy Evans and **John Christie** (1958).

JESSEL, Sir George (1824–83) English judge, born in London. Educated at University College, London, he served as a Liberal MP (1868–73) solicitor-general (1871–73), and then as master of the rolls (1873–83). Very learned, with a remarkable memory and penetrating intellect, he gave many judicial opinions of continuing value and made important contributions to legal principle by reshaping older doctrines, especially of equity. He was also active in the development of the University of London.

JESSOP, William (1745–1814) English civil engineer, born in Devonport. He became a pupil of **John Smeaton** at the age of 16 and worked with him on canals in Yorkshire and elsewhere. With others he founded the Butterley Iron Works in 1790 and began to manufacture fish-bellied cast-iron rails which marked an important advance in railway track technology. He was involved as chief engineer on the construction of the Grand Junction Canal with its mile-long tunnel at Blisworth, the Surrey Iron Railway (opened in 1802), the docks on the Avon at Bristol and the West India Docks on the Thames. His works put him alongside Smeaton, **Telford** and **Rennie** in the front rank of early British civil engineers.

JESUS CHRIST (c.6 BC–c.30 AD) the founder of Christianity, born 'the Son of God' in Bethlehem, Judaea. According to the accounts in St **Matthew**'s and St **Luke**'s gospels, he was the first-born child of the Virgin **Mary** of the tribe of Judah and descendant of **David** and wife of **Joseph**, a carpenter. The birth took place in a stable, because on their way to Joseph's home town, Nazareth, in order to comply with the regulations for a Roman population census, they found 'there was no room for them at the inn'. According to St Matthew, Jesus's birth took place just prior to the demise of **Herod the Great** (4 BC), but the Roman census referred to by St Luke did not take place before 6 AD. The only biographical sources are the four gospels of the New Testament of which St Mark, containing the recollection of **Peter**, is the oldest, and probably the most reliable, and it has been estimated that their entire compass covers only 50 days in the life of Christ. But he is also mentioned by **Tacitus**, **Suetonius** and **Josephus** and in certain anti-Christian Hebrew writings of the time. Little is written of his early boyhood and manhood. He is believed to have followed Joseph's trade of carpentry but at the age of twelve we are told how his astonished mother saw him knowledgeably discoursing with the scribes, being assured by him that he was about his 'father's business'. But nearly 18 years passed in obscurity, before his baptism at the hands of his cousin, **John the Baptist**, gave him the first divine intimation of his mission. After 40 days in the wilderness wrestling successfully with all manner of temptations, he gathered around him twelve disciples and undertook two missionary journeys through Galilee culminating in the miraculous feeding of the five thousand (Mark vi, 30–52), which, seen through the eyes of Herod, John the Baptist's executioner, had obvious dangerous political implications. Furthermore, Jesus's association with 'publicans and sinners', his apparent flouting of traditional religious practices, the performance of miracles on the Sabbath, the driving of the money-lenders from the temple and the whole tenor of his revolutionary Sermon on the Mount (Matthew v–vii), emphasizing love, humility, meekness and charity, roused the Pharisees. Christ and his disciples sought refuge for a while in the Gentile territories of Tyre and Sidon, where he secretly revealed himself to them as the promised Messiah, and hinted beyond their comprehension at his coming passion, death and resurrection. According to Mark, he returned to Jerusalem in triumph, a week before the Passover feast, and after the famous 'Last Supper' with his disciples. He was betrayed by one of them, **Judas Iscariot**, by a kiss, and after a hurried trial condemned to death by the Sanhedrin. The necessary confirmation of the sentence from **Pontius Pilate**, the Roman procurator, was obtained on the grounds of political expediency and not through any proof of treason implicit in any claim to territorial kingship by Christ. Jesus was crucified early on either the Passover or the preceding day (the 'preparation of the Passover'). The chronology of the passion is a very complicated question. Jesus was buried the same day. The instrument of crucifixion, the cross, became the symbol of Christianity. The following Sunday, according to all four gospels, the disciples hiding away in an 'upper room' suddenly took courage through receipt of the Holy Ghost and several revelations that Christ 'had risen from the dead' and would continue his leadership for ever. The history of the church begins here with the *Acts of the Apostles* in the New Testament. The apostolic succession claimed by the Catholic church begins with Christ's public declaration to Peter (Matthew xvi, 17–19) that on him he would build his church. Roman persecutions only served to strengthen it. In the 4th century in Nicaea, Christian theologians incorporated Platonic metaphysics into their theology. Roman empires in east and west became Christianized but with distinctive liturgies formally separating in the 11th century, although common elements are to be found in them. Rome until the 16th century was the hub of western Christianity when the reformatory movements of **Calvin**, **Luther** and **Zwingli**, allied to local nationalism, split the western church into an increasing number of sects, depending for their individual authority on multifarious interpretations of the New Testament but all united in their opposition to papal supremacy. But a growing movement for church reunion was initiated at the beginning of the 20th century.

JEVONS, William Stanley (1835–82) English economist and logician, born in Liverpool, the son-in-law of **John Edward Taylor**. He studied chemistry and metallurgy at University College London, and became assayer to the Mint at Sydney, Australia (1854–59). He then returned to England and studied logic under **Augustus De Morgan** at London and in 1866 became professor of logic at Owen's College, Manchester, and in 1876 professor of political economy at London. He introduced mathematical methods into economics, was one of the first to use the concept of final or marginal utility as opposed to the classical cost of production theories, and wrote *Theory of Political Economy* (1871) and the posthumous *Principles of Economics* (1905). He also wrote an important practical paper, *Investigations in Currency and Finance* (1884). In his *Pure Logic and other Minor Works* (1890) he wrongly deplored **George Boole**'s extensive use of algebraic methods in his calculus of classes, attacked **Mill**'s inductive logic and expounded alternatives in *The Principles of Science* (1874), but is also remembered for his introductory textbook, *Lessons in Logic* (1870). A professorship in political economy at Manchester was endowed in his memory.

JEWEL, John (1522–71) English prelate, a father of English Protestantism, born in Berrynarbor near Ilfracombe. Educated at Barnstaple and at Merton and Corpus Christi Colleges, Oxford, he absorbed reformed doctrines early in his career. On **Mary I**'s accession he went abroad (Frankfurt, Strasbourg, etc), but was appointed bishop of Salisbury by **Elizabeth** in 1559. His ability as a controversialist soon made him one of the foremost churchmen of his age, as in his *Apologia Ecclesiae Anglicanae* (1562) against Rome.

JEWETT, (Theodora) Sara Orne (1849–1909) American novelist, born in South Berwick, Maine. She wrote a series of sketches, *The Country of the Pointed Firs* (1896), and romantic novels and stories based on the provincial life of her state, such as *A Country Doctor* (1884) and *A White Heron* (1886), and a historical novel, *The Tory Lover* (1901). She was the first president of Vassar College (1862–64).

JEWSBURY, Geraldine (Endsor) (1812–80) English novelist, born in Measham, Derbyshire, the daughter of a businessman. From 1854 she lived in Chelsea, to be near her friend **Jane Welsh Carlyle**. She contributed articles and reviews to various journals, and wrote six novels, including *Zoë* (1845), *The Half Sisters* (1848), *Marion Withers* (1851), and *Right or Wrong* (1859). *A Selection from the Letters of Geraldine Jewsbury to Jane Carlyle* (1892) aroused controversy.

JEX-BLAKE, Sophia Louisa (1840–1912) English physician and pioneer of medical education for women, born in Hastings. She was the sister of Thomas William (1832–1915), headmaster of Rugby and dean of Wells. She studied at Queen's College for Women, London, and became a tutor in mathematics there (1859–61). From 1865 she studied medicine in New York under **Elizabeth Blackwell**, but since English medical schools were closed to women she could not continue her studies on her return. She fought her way into Edinburgh University, however, where with five other women she was allowed to matriculate in 1869, but the university authorities reversed their decision in 1873.

She waged a public campaign in London, opened the London School of Medicine for Women in 1874 and in 1876 won her campaign when medical examiners were permitted by law to examine women students. In 1886 she founded a medical school in Edinburgh, where from 1894 women were finally allowed to graduate in medicine.

JEZEBEL, Phoenician princess (d.842 BC) daughter of Ethbaal, king of Tyre and Sidon, and wife of king **Ahab** of Israel (869–850). She introduced Phoenician habits (and religion) to the capital, Samaria, thus earning the undying hatred of the prophet **Elijah** and his successors. After Ahab's death, Jezebel was the power behind the throne of her sons until the usurper **Jehu** seized power in an army coup; he had Jezebel thrown from a window, and trampled her to death under his chariot.

JHABVALA, Ruth Prawer (1927–) British novelist, short story and screenplay writer, born in Cologne, Germany, of Polish parents. Her parents emigrated to Britain in 1939. She graduated from Queen Mary College, London University, married a visiting Indian architect, and lived in Delhi (1951–75). Most of her fiction relates to India, taking the viewpoint of an outsider looking in. Significant novels include *To Whom She Will Marry* (1955), *Esmond in India* (1958), *The Householder* (1960), and *Heat and Dust* (1975) which won the Booker prize. In association with the film makers James Ivory and Ismail Merchant, she has written several accomplished screenplays, among them *Shakespeare Wallah* (1965) and *A Room with a View* (1986).

JHERING, Rudolf von (1818–92) German jurist, sometimes regarded as the father of sociological jurisprudence. He founded a school of jurisprudence based on teleological principles, and wrote extensively on Roman law and legal history.

JIANG QING, or **Chiang Ch'ing** (1914–) Chinese politician. Born in Zhucheng, Shandong Province the daughter of a carpenter, she trained in drama before studying literature at Qingdao University, and became a stage and film actress in Shanghai. Having already come into contact with left-wing ideas at university, in 1936 she went to the Chinese Communist party headquarters at Yenan to study Marxist-Leninist theory, and met the Communist leader, **Mao Zedong**; she became his third wife in 1939. She was attached to the ministry of culture in 1950–54, but it was in the 1960s that she began her attacks on bourgeois influences in the arts and literature, and she became one of the leaders of the 1965–69 'Cultural Revolution'. In 1969 she was elected to the Politburo, but after Mao's death in 1976 she was arrested with three others—the hated 'gang of four'—after having attempted to seize power through organizing militia coups in Shanghai and Beijing. She was imprisoned, expelled from the Communist party, tried in 1980 with subverting the government and wrongly arresting, detaining and torturing numbers of innocent people. She was sentenced to death, though the sentence was later suspended.

JIANG ZEMIN (1926–) Chinese politician, born in Yangzhou, in Jiangsu province, the son-in-law of former president **Li Xiannian**. After university he began his career as an electrical engineer and then trained in the Soviet Union at the Stalin Automobile Factory. He was commercial counsellor at the Chinese embassy in Moscow (1950–56) and during the 1960s and 1970s held a number of posts in the heavy and power industry ministries. He was elected to the Chinese Communist party's (CCP) central committee in 1982 and appointed mayor of Shanghai in 1985. Here he gained a reputation as a cautious reformer, loyal to the party line. He was inducted into the CCP's politburo in 1987 and in June 1989, following the Tiananmen Square pro-democracy massacre and the dismissal of Zhao Ziyang, was elected party leader. Fluent in English and Russian, Jiang has, as a compromise figure, pledged to maintain China's 'open door' economic strategy.

JIMÉNEZ, Francisco See **XIMENES**

JIMÉNEZ, Juan Ramón (1881–1958) Spanish lyric poet, born in Moguer, Huelva, which he made famous by his delightful story of the young poet and his donkey, *Platero y Yo* (1914; trans 1956), one of the classics of modern Spanish literature. He abandoned his law studies and settled in Madrid. His early poetry, impressionistic and rich in evocative imagery and sound, echoed that of **Verlaine**. *Almas de Violeta* (1901), *Arias Tristes* (1903) and *Jardines Lefanos* (1905) belong to this period. With *El Silencio de Oro* (1922) there came a mood of optimism and a zest for experimentation with styles and rhythms. In 1936 he left Spain because of the Civil War and settled in Florida. In his last period he emerges as a major poet, treating the major themes of life in novel sounds, illusions and styles in a subtly spun *vers libre*. He was awarded the Nobel prize for literature in 1956.

JINNAH, Mohammed Ali (1876–1948) Pakistani statesman, born in Karachi. He studied at Bombay and Lincoln's Inn, London, and was called to the bar in 1897. He obtained a large practice in Bombay, in 1910 was elected to the Viceroy's legislative council and, already a member of the Indian National Congress, in 1913 joined the Indian Muslim League and as its president brought about peaceful co-existence between it and the Congress party through the 'Lucknow Pact' (1916). Although he supported the efforts of Congress to boycott the Simon Commission (1928), he opposed **Gandhi**'s civil disobedience policy and, resigning from the Congress party, which he believed to be exclusively fostering Hindu interests, continued to advocate his '14 points' safeguarding Moslem minorities at the London Round Table Conference (1931). By 1940 he was strongly advocating separate statehood for the Moslems and he stubbornly resisted all British efforts, such as the **Cripps** mission (1942) and Gandhi's statesmanlike overtures (1944), to save Indian unity. Thus on 15 August 1947, the Dominion of Pakistan came into existence and Jinnah, *Quaid-i-Azam* 'Great Leader', became its first governor-general and had to contend with the consequences of the new political division, the refugee problem, the communal riots in Punjab and the fighting in Kashmir.

JOACHIM, Joseph (1831–1907) Hungarian violinist and composer, born in Kittsee near Pressburg. He first appeared in London in 1844 at the age of seven under the patronage of **Mendelssohn**, making a great impact. In 1869 he became director of the Berlin Conservatory; he founded the Joachim Quartet which was renowned for its performances of **Bach**, **Mozart** and **Beethoven**. He also composed three violin concertos and overtures to *Hamlet* and *Henry IV*.

JOACHIM OF FLORIS, or **FIORE** (c.1135–1202) Italian mystic, born in Calabria. In 1177 he became abbot of the Cistercian monastery of Corazzo and later founded a stricter order of monks, Ordo Florensis, at San Giovanni in Fiore, which was absorbed by the Cistercians in 1505. His mystical interpretation of history, based on historical parallels or 'concordances' between the history of the Jewish people and that of the church, was grouped into three ages, each corresponding to a member of the Trinity, the last, that of the Spirit, which was to bring perfect liberty, to commence in 1260. This mystical historicism was widely accepted although condemned by the Lateran council in 1215, but lost influence when its prophecies did not come to pass.

JOAD, Cyril Edwin Mitchinson (1891–1953) English philosopher and controversialist, born in Durham and educated at Blundell's School and Balliol College, Oxford. He was a civil servant from 1914 to 1930, then became head of the philosophy department at Birkbeck College, London. He was a prolific popularizer, writing 47 books in all, notably a *Guide to Philosophy* (1936) and a *Guide to the Philosophy of Morals and Politics* (1938). But he was best-known to the public at large for his appearances on the BBC 'Brains Trust' radio programme and for his catchphrase 'It all depends what you mean by ...'.

JOAN See **EDWARD THE BLACK PRINCE**

JOAN a fictitious personage long believed to have been, as John VII, pope (855–58). One legend has it that she was born in Mainz, the daughter of English parents, and so well educated by her lover that she in due time became cardinal and pope. Her reign was said to have ended abruptly when she died on giving birth to a child during a papal procession between St Peter's and the Lateran, a route since avoided on such occasions.

JOAN, or **Joanna,** of **Navarre** (c.1370–1437) queen consort of King **Henry IV** of England, and stepmother of **Henry V**. She married first the Duke of Brittany (1386), by whom she had eight children; after his death in 1399, she married Henry IV in 1402. After Henry's death in 1413, she was imprisoned for three years on specious allegations of witchcraft.

JOAN OF ARC, St, Jeanne d'Arc, known as **the Maid of Orléans** (c.1412–31) French patriot and martyr, one of the most remarkable women of all time, the daughter of well-off peasants in Domrémy on the borders of Lorraine and Champagne. The English over-ran the area in 1421 and in 1424 withdrew. Joan received no formal education but had an argumentative nature and shrewd common sense. At the age of 13 she thought she heard the voices of St Michael, St **Catherine** and St **Margaret** bidding her rescue the Paris region from English domination. She persuaded the local commander, Robert de Baudricourt, after he had had her exorcised, to take her in 1429 across English-occupied territory to the dauphin (the future **Charles VII**) at Chinon. She, according to legend, was called into a gathering of courtiers, among them the dauphin in disguise, and her success in identifying him at once was interpreted as divine confirmation of his previously doubted legitimacy and claims to the throne. She was equally successful in an ecclesiastical examination to which she was subjected in Poitiers and was consequently allowed to join the army assembled at Blois for the relief of Orléans. Clad in a suit of white armour and flying her own standard, she entered Orléans with an advance guard on 29 April and by 8 May had forced the English to raise the siege and retire in June from the principal strongholds on the Loire. To put further heart into the French resistance, she took the dauphin with an army of 12000 through English-held territory to be crowned Charles VII in Reims Cathedral. She then found it extremely difficult to persuade him to undertake further military exploits, especially the relief of Paris. At last she set out on her own to relieve Compiègne from the Burgundians, was captured in a sortie (1430) and sold to the English by John of Luxembourg for 10 000 crowns. She was put on trial (1431) for heresy and sorcery by an ecclesiastical court of the Inquisition, presided over by Pierre Cauchon, bishop of Beauvais. Most of the available facts concerning Joan's life are those preserved in the records of the trial. She was found guilty, taken out to the churchyard of St Ouen on 24 May to be burnt, but at the last moment broke down and made a wild recantation. This she later abjured and suffered her martyrdom at the stake in the market place of Rouen on 30 May, faithful to her 'voices'. In 1456, in order to strengthen the validity of Charles VII's coronation, the trial was declared irregular. Belief in her divine mission made her flout military advice—in the end disastrously, but she rallied her countrymen, halted the English ascendancy in France for ever and was one of the first in history to die for a Christian-inspired concept of nationalism. In 1904 she was designated Venerable, declared Blessed in 1908 and finally canonized in 1920. Her feast day is 30 May.

JOASH See **ATHALIAH**

JOBS, Steven (1955–) American computer inventor-entrepreneur, born in San Francisco. He was educated at Reed College, Portland, before becoming a computer hobbyist and co-founder with Stephen Wozniak of Apple Computer Company in a garage in 1976. Their brainchild, the Apple II computer (1977), helped launch the personal computer and made their company the fastest growing in US history. In 1985 Jobs left Apple and founded a new company, NeXT Inc.

JOCELIN DE BRAKELOND (c.1155–1215) English chronicler. A Benedictine monk in Bury St Edmunds from 1173, he wrote a domestic chronicle of his abbey from 1173 to 1202. The *Chronica* inspired **Carlyle**'s *Past and Present*.

JOCHUMSSON, Matthías (1835–1920) Icelandic poet and clergyman, born at Skógar in Thorskafjörður, a farmer's son. After training as a merchant in Copenhagen, he became a Lutheran pastor (1865) at various places in Iceland. Best known as a lyric poet, he drew for his inspiration on the historic traditions of the sagas, and composed the words of the choral anthem written for the millennnial celebrations of 1874 (*Ó, Guð vors lands*—God of our Land) which is now the national anthem. He was regarded as unofficial poet laureate. He also wrote plays, including a historical drama about bishop **Jón Arason** (1900), and translated **Byron**, **Ibsen**, and **Shakespeare**'s major tragedies.

JODELLE, Étienne (1532–73) French poet and dramatist. He was the only Parisian member of the Pléiade, and he wrote the first French tragedy, *Cléopatre captive* (1552), as well as two comedies.

JODL, Alfred (1890–1946) German soldier, born in Aachen. He was an artillery subaltern in World War I and rose to the rank of general of artillery in 1940. For the remainder of World War II he was the planning genius of the German High Command and Hitler's chief adviser. He condemned the anti-Hitler plot (1944), counselled the terror bombing of English cities and signed orders to shoot commandoes and prisoners of war. From January 1945 he was chief of the Operations Staff. He was found guilty of war crimes on all four counts at Nuremburg (1946) and executed. A Munich denazification court posthumously exonerated him on charges of being a 'major offender' in 1953.

JOFFRE, Joseph Jacques Césaire (1852–1931) French soldier, born in Rivesaltes. He entered the army in 1870, and rose to be French chief of staff (1914), and planned the victory in the Battle of the Marne (September 1914). Silent, patient, mathematical, he carried out a policy of attrition or 'nibbling' against the Germans. He was commander-in-chief of the French armies from 1915 to 1916, but resigned after the French failure at Verdun (1916), and was made a marshal of France. In 1917 he became president of the Allied War Council.

JOFFREY, Robert, originally **Abdullah Jaffa Anver Bey Kahn** (1930–88) American dancer, choreographer, teacher and ballet director of Afghan descent, born in Seattle, Washington. He studied at the School of American Ballet and New York's High School of Performing Arts, and made his début in **Roland Petit**'s Ballets de Paris in 1949. He choreographed his first ballet in 1952 and within a few years had formed his own school and company, which was touring America by the middle of the decade. Working closely with dancer-choreographer Gerald Arpino, he cultivated a young, trendy and energetic image for his company, helping to usher in the American ballet boom of the 1960s thanks to the topical themes, rock music and multi-media techniques deployed alongside revivals of contemporary classics.

JOHAN III (1537–92) king of Sweden from 1568, second son of King **Gustav I Vasa** and his second wife Margareta Leijonhufvud, and half-brother and successor of **Eric XIV**. Having been made Duke of Finland by his father, he was seized and imprisoned (1563–67) by his paranoiac brother Erik XIV. With his younger brother, Karl (the future **Karl IX**), he rebelled against Eric and deposed him in 1568, ascending the throne himself as Johan III. He brought the Seven-Year War with Denmark to an inconclusive end with the Treaty of Stettin in 1570; and in 1578–83 he was in alliance with Poland in a war against Russia. An avid student of theology, he tried unsuccessfully to impose on Sweden his own synthesis of Lutheranism and Catholicism and his 'Red Book' liturgy. He married Katarina Jagellonica, sister of **Sigismund II Augustus** of Poland, and had their Catholic son **Sigismund III Vasa** crowned king of Poland in 1587. After Katarina's death in 1583 he married Gunilla Bielke of an old noble family. He was succeeded on the Swedish throne by Sigismund III of Poland, who was soon deposed, however, and succeeded by Karl IX.

JOHANNES SECUNDUS, Jan Everts, or **Everaerts** (1511–36) Dutch poet, writing in Latin, born in The Hague. He studied law at Bourges, and was secretary to the archbishop of Toledo, the bishop of Utrecht, and the Emperor **Charles V**. His famous work is *Basia*.

JOHANNES VON SAAZ (c.1350–1415) German author, born in Schüttwa. He wrote *Der Ackermann aus Böhmen* (c.1400), a classic piece of German prose in which the author reproaches Death for the loss of his wife, Margarete, before the heavenly Judge.

JOHANSON, Donald Carl (1943–) American palaeoanthropologist, born in Chicago of Swedish immigrant parents. A graduate of Chicago University, he worked at the Cleveland Museum of Natural History (1972, curator for 1974). His spectacular finds of fossil hominids 3–4 million years old at Hadar in the Afar triangle of Ethiopia (1972–77) generated world-wide interest. They include 'Lucy', a unique female specimen that is half complete, and the so-called 'First Family', a scattered group containing the remains of 13 individuals. *Lucy: The Beginnings of Humankind* (with Maitland Edey, 1981) has a strong autobiographical flavour. In 1981 he was appointed director of the Institute of Human Origins, Berkeley, California.

JOHANSSEN, Wilhelm Ludwig (1857–1927) Danish botanist and geneticist, born in Copenhagen. Professor at the university there from 1905, he pioneered experimental genetics by his experiments with Princess beans which led to the pureline theory. He was the author of *Elemente der exacte Erblichkeit* (1909).

JOHN, St one of the Twelve Apostles, son of Zebedee and younger brother of **James**. He was a Galilean fisherman, probably a native of Bethsaida. Some have thought that his mother was **Salome**, who may have been the sister of the mother of **Jesus**. Early tradition represents him as having been slain by the Jews, like his brother James. But from the time of Justin (c.150) he has been identified with the author of the Apocalypse, and from that of **Irenaeus** (c. 175) he has been represented as spending his closing years in Ephesus, and dying there at an advanced age, after having written the Apocalypse, the Gospel and the three Epistles which bear his name. There are various theories of the authorship of these works.

JOHN, St, Chrysostom See **CHRYSOSTOM**

JOHN the name of twenty-one popes and two antipopes XVI or XVII (997–8) and XXIII the former included in the papal numbering, which erroneously contained a fictitious John XV who was thought to have ruled for a few weeks immediately prior to the true John XV (985–96).

JOHN XII, originally **Octavian** (?937–964) pope (955–64), the grandson of **Marozia**, was elected pope by the dominant party when he was only 18. The Emperor **Otto** in 963 in a synod of the clergy caused sentence of deposition for scandalous life to be pronounced against him, and Leo VIII to be elected instead. In the next year John drove out Leo but he died suddenly.

JOHN XXII, originally **Jacques Duèse** (c. 1245–1344) pope (1316–34), one of the most celebrated of the popes of Avignon, born in Cahors in 1244, and elected in 1316. Attempting to carry out the policy of **Gregory VII**, he interposed his authority in the contest for the imperial crown between Louis of Bavaria and Frederick of Austria, supporting the latter and excommunicating his rival. A long contest ensued both in Germany and Italy, where the Guelph or papal party was represented by Robert, king of Naples, and the Ghibelline by Frederick of Sicily. The latter was also excommunicated by John; but in 1327 Louis entered Italy, and, crowned at Milan with the crown of Lombardy, advanced upon Rome, expelled the papal legate, and was crowned emperor by two Lombard bishops. He caused the pope to be deposed on a charge of heresy and breach of fealty. When Louis returned to Germany, Guelphic predominance at Rome was restored but John died in Avignon having accumulated a vast treasure.

JOHN XXIII, originally **Baldassare Cossa** (c. 1370–1419) antipope (1410–15), a Neapolitan noble, a cardinal who was recognized throughout most of Europe as the successor of Alexander V, having been elected by the Alexandrian faction in 1410. He convened the council of Constance, but was deposed in 1415 for his excesses, yet re-appointed cardinal.

JOHN XXIII, originally **Angelo Guiseppe Roncalli** (1881–1963), pope (1958–63), the son of a peasant in Sotto il Monte near Bergamo in northern Italy, in 1881. Ordained in 1904, he served as sergeant in the medical corps and as chaplain in World War I, and subsequently as apostolic delegate to Bulgaria, Turkey and Greece. In 1944 he became the first Papal Nuncio to liberated France and championed the controversial system of worker-priests. Patriarch of Venice in 1953, he was elected pope in October 1958 on the twelfth ballot. He convened the 21st ecumenical council in order to seek unity between the various Christian sects and broke with tradition by leaving the Vatican for short visits to hospitals and prisons in Rome. In 1963 he issued the celebrated encyclical *Pacem in Terris* (Peace on Earth), advocating reconcilation between

East and West. His diary was published in 1965 as *The Journal of a Soul.*

JOHN, surnamed **Lackland** (1167–1216) king of England from 1199, youngest son of **Henry II**, born in Oxford. His father sent him to Ireland in 1185, but his misconduct soon compelled his recall. He attempted to seize the crown during King **Richard I**'s captivity in Austria; but he was pardoned and nominated his successor by his brother on his deathbed. John was crowned at Westminster (27 May 1199), although **Arthur**, son of John's elder brother Geoffrey, had a rival claim. On the Continent Arthur was acknowledged and his claims were supported by **Philip II** of France, whom, however, in May 1200 John succeeded in buying off. In the same year he obtained a divorce from his cousin Isabella of Gloucester, and married **Isabella of Angoulême**. In the war in France Arthur was taken prisoner, and before Easter 1203 was murdered. Philip at once marched against John until by March 1204 only Aquitaine and a few other small areas were left to John. In 1205 John entered on a quarrel with the church, the occasion being a disputed election to the archbishopric of Canterbury. In 1207 Pope **Innocent III** consecrated **Stephen Langton**, an English cardinal, and John declined to receive him. In 1208 the kingdom was placed under an interdict but John retaliated by confiscating the property of the clergy who obeyed the interdict. In 1209 he compelled the Scots king, **William the Lion**, who had joined his enemies, to do him homage, put down a rebellion in Ireland (1210), and subdued Llewellyn, the independent Prince of Wales (1212). Meanwhile he had been excommunicated (1209), and, in 1212, the pope issued a bull deposing him, Philip being charged with the execution of the sentence. John, finding his position untenable, was compelled to make abject submission to Rome, agreeing (May 1213) to hold his kingdom as a fief of the papacy, and to pay a thousand marks yearly as tribute. Philip, disappointed, turned his forces against Flanders; but the French fleet was surprised by the English, 300 vessels being captured, and 100 burned. In 1213 John made a campaign in Poitou, but it turned out badly, and he returned to enter on the struggle with his subjects. A demand by the barons, clergy, and people that John should keep his oath and restore the laws of **Henry I** was scornfully rejected. Preparations for war began on both sides. The army of the barons assembled at Stamford and marched to London; they met the king at Runnymede, and on 15 June 1215 the Great Charter (Magna Carta) was signed. It had little immediate effect. In August the pope annulled the charter, and the war broke out again. The first successes were all on the side of John, until the barons called over the French dauphin (the future **Louis VIII**) to be their leader. Louis landed in May 1216, and John's fortunes had become desperate, when he died at Newark, 19 October. His reign, however, saw improvements in the civil administration, the Exchequer and the law courts.

JOHN, 'the Blind' (1296–1346) king of Bohemia, son of Count **Henry III** of Luxembourg (afterwards the emperor Henry VII). Having married (1310) Elizabeth, the heiress of Bohemia, he was crowned king in 1311. In the struggle between Austria and Bavaria for the imperial crown he contributed to the Bavarian victory at Mühldorf in 1322. From 1333–35 he was warring in Italy for the Guelph party. In 1334 he married a Bourbon and became an ally of the French king. By 1340 he had become completely blind: nonetheless he fought at the battle of Crécy in 1346 with conspicuous gallantry until he fell in a last hopeless charge; his motto *Ich Dien*, 'I serve', was adopted by **Edward the Black Prince**, on the request of his father, **Edward III**, who commanded the English army in the battle.

JOHN II, 'the Good' (1319–64) king of France, succeeded his father, **Philip VI**, in 1350. In 1356 he was taken prisoner by **Edward the Black Prince** at Poitiers and taken to England. After the treaty of Bretigny (1360) he returned home, leaving his second son, the Duke of Anjou, as a hostage; and when the duke broke his parole and escaped (1363), John chivalrously returned to London, where he died.

JOHN II CASIMIR (1609–72) king of Poland, son of King **Sigismund III Vasa** of Sweden. He was elected king to succeed his brother, **Ladislas IV**, in 1648. A successful Swedish invasion forced John Casimir to take refuge in Silesia while moves were made to elect **Karl X Gustav** of Sweden in his place. John Casimir returned to Sweden in 1656 but hostilities continued until the peace of Oliwa (1660). On his return, the king had solemnly promised to alleviate the plight of the Polish serfs and the court made a strenuous effort to introduce constitutional reform (1660–61). All reformist legislation was opposed by the conservative opposition and, when the court persisted, they raised a rebellion under their leader, Jerzy Lubomirski (1665–66). Frustrated in all his efforts, John Casimir abdicated in 1668 and ended his life as a pensioner of **Louis XIV** in Paris.

JOHN II COMNENUS (1088–1143) Byzantine emperor, succeeded his father **Alexius I Comnenus** in 1118. In government he relied on trusted servants rather than his immediate family, some of whom, such as his sister Anna and brother Isaac, intrigued against him and were deprived of their positions. Apart from an abortive attempt to curtail the trading privileges of the Venetians, his energetic rule was distinguished by military and diplomatic success. In the Balkans his victory over the Patzinaks (1122) effectively ended a long-standing threat to the empire and was thereafter commemorated by a public holiday; in the east he recovered territory in Cilicia and asserted Byzantine overlordship over the Normans of Antioch (1137). He was killed in a hunting accident while on campaign.

JOHN III SOBIESKI (1624–96) king of Poland from 1674, a native Pole of noble blood, son of the senator Jacob Sobieski. A superb soldier, he fought successful campaigns from 1671 to 1673 against both Cossack and Tartar invaders and against a superior Turkish army in Moldavia. He was elected king in 1674. His queen, Mary Kazimiera, was a remarkable woman in her own right, who played an important part in directing her husband's prodigious energies and ambitions. Both monarchs were significant patrons of the arts, and though themselves pious Catholics, pursued a tolerant policy towards the non-Catholic peoples of Poland. His entire reign was spent campaigning against Tartar invaders and against the Turks. In 1683, in alliance with the Holy Roman Emperor **Leopold I**, he led the army that defeated the Turks before Vienna, a victory that made the Polish king a hero to the whole of Christian Europe. Subsequent campaigns in 1686 and 1691 were less successful and he died a disappointed man in 1696.

JOHN IV (1604–56) king of Portugal and Duke of Bragança. He was the leading aristocrat and greatest landowner in Portugal. When the country freed itself from Spanish rule in 1640, the duke became king of the newly independent Portugal. Despite alliances with France, Sweden and the Dutch and with Portugal's ancient ally, England, he was unable to secure Spanish recognition of independent Portugal during his lifetime.

JOHN, Augustus (Edwin) (1878–1961) Welsh painter, born in Tenby. He studied at the Slade School in

London (1896–99) with his sister **Gwen John**, and in Paris, and made an early reputation for himself by his etchings (1900–14). His favourite themes were gipsies, fishing folk and wild, lovely, yet naturally regal women, as in *Lyric Fantasy* (1913). In his portraits of women, including many of his wife Dorelia, he is concerned more with unique items of individual beauty or dignity than with portrayal of character, as for example the beautifully caught posture of the scarlet-gowned cellist *Madame Suggia* (1923). But he could portray character as the studies of **Shaw** (c. 1914), **Thomas Hardy** (1923) and **Dylan Thomas** amply testify.

JOHN, Barry (1945–) Welsh rugby player, born in Cefneithin. One of the greatest outside-halves that Wales has ever produced, he played 25 times for his country, scoring a record 90 points, before retiring at the early age of 27. A devastating player with Llanelli and Cardiff at club level, his elusiveness and skill at dropping goals made him equally effective at international level. On the Lions tour of New Zealand in 1971 he scored 180 points.

JOHN, Elton, real name **Reginald Kenneth Dwight** (1947–) English singer, songwriter and pianist, born in Pinner, Middlesex. One of the most successful pop-rock stars of the 1970s, he began his career as pianist with the group Bluesology, which he left after their 1967 hit 'Let The Heartaches Begin'. Teaming up with lyricist Bernie Taupin, he launched his solo career with the undistinguished album *Empty Sky* in 1969. *Elton John* (1970), which included the single 'Your Song', brought his first solo success. A self-styled 'ultimate rock fan', his music was a synthesis of current popular styles which he forged into a durable hybrid of pop and rock. In a prolific career his albums have included *Tumbleweed Connection* (1970), *Don't Shoot Me I'm Only The Piano Player* (1973), the autobiographical *Captain Fantastic And The Browndirt Cowboy* (1975), and *A Single Man* (1979). In the mid 1970s he developed a highly flamboyant stage image and an extravagant piano style. During the mid 1970s he also purchased Watford Football Club (chairman, 1976–) and formed his own record label, Rocket Records. In 1979 he became the first western rock star to play in Moscow—an event documented in the film *To Russia With Elton* (1979).

JOHN, Gwen (1876–1939) Welsh painter, born in Haverfordwest, Pembrokeshire, elder sister of **Augustus John**. She lived in Tenby, Pembrokeshire, before studying at the Slade School (1895–98). Moving to Paris in 1904, she worked as an artist's model, becoming **Rodin**'s mistress c.1906. After converting to Roman Catholicism in 1913 she lived at Meudon, where she became increasingly religious and reclusive. She exhibited with the New English Art Club from 1900–11, and her work was included in the Armory Show of 1913. Her only one-woman show during her lifetime was in London, 1926.

JOHN, Otto (1909–) West German lawyer and ex-security chief. He was defendant in the most curious postwar treason case. Originally chief legal adviser to the German civil aviation company *Lufthansa*, in 1944 he played, with his brother Hans, a prominent role in the abortive anti-**Hitler** plot of 20 July, after which he made good his escape to Britain via Spain and worked for the British Psychological Warfare Executive. At the end of the war, he joined a London legal firm and appeared as a prosecution witness in the Nuremberg and **von Manstein** trials. In 1950 he was appointed to the newly formed West German Office for the protection of the constitution. His sensitivity against former Nazi influence in postwar German political life earned him the enmity of **Adenauer** and Schröder. Attending the annual commemorative ceremony of 20 July in West Berlin in 1954, he mysteriously disappeared and later broadcast for the East German communists. In 1956 he returned to the West, was arrested, tried, and sentenced to four years' hard labour for treasonable falsification and conspiracy. John's case was that he was drugged by a friend, Wohlgemuth, a wealthy communist-sympathizing doctor in West Berlin, and driven to the communist sector where he was held a prisoner and forced to make broadcasts until he managed to escape. Released in 1958, he still protests his innocence.

JOHN, Patrick (1937–) Dominican politician. In the period before full independence he served in the government of chief minister Edward LeBlanc and succeeded him in 1974. On independence in 1978 he became the country's first prime minister. His increasingly authoritarian style of government led to the loss of his assembly seat in 1980 and his replacement as prime minister by **Eugenia Charles**. The following year he was arrested for alleged complicity in a plot to overthrow Charles but was acquitted of the charge. A subsequent trial, in 1985, found him guilty and he was given a twelve-year prison sentence.

JOHN FREDERICK, the Magnanimous (1503–54) Elector of Ernestine Saxony. He succeeded to the electoral title on the death of his father, John the Constant, in 1532. An enthusiastic supporter of **Martin Luther**, he was an influential figure in the Schmalkaldic League of Protestant princes. He favoured negotiations with the Catholic Habsburgs but his own uncompromising Lutheranism militated against their success. Following the defeat of the League at the battle of Mühlberg, he was imprisoned and stripped of his electoral title and lands. He refused to compromise his religious position and was hailed as a hero of the faith upon his release in 1552.

JOHN GEORGE I (1585–1656) Elector of Saxony. He succeeded his elder brother, Christian II, in 1611. A leading Lutheran prince, his native conservatism and his strong distaste for Calvinism made him an unsteady defender of protestantism. During the Thirty Years' War he at first supported the Catholic emperor, **Ferdinand II**, before agreeing in 1631 to head a defensive Protestant alliance. His support for the cause remained lukewarm and in 1635 he signed the separate Peace of Prague with the emperor.

JOHN OF AUSTRIA, known as **Don** (1547–78) Spanish soldier, illegitimate son of the Emperor **Charles V** and Barbara Blomberg of Ratisbon, born in Ratisbon. He was early brought to Spain, and after the death of his father was acknowledged by his half-brother, **Philip II**. In 1569–70 he was sent with an army to suppress the revolt of the Moriscos (converted Moors) in Andalusia. In October 1571, with the fleets of Spain, the pope and Venice, he defeated the Turks in the great sea fight of Lepanto. In 1573 he took Tunis, and conceived the scheme of forming a kingdom for himself. But Philip, jealous of this design, sent him to Milan, and in 1576 as viceroy to the Spanish Netherlands. He sought to win the favour of the people by mildness; hard pressed for a time by William the Silent, with the help of Parma's troops he won the victory of Gembloux in 1577. He died at Namur, perhaps poisoned.

JOHN OF BEVERLEY, St (d. 721) English prelate, born in Harpham, Humberside. After studying at Canterbury, he became a monk at St **Hilda**'s double monastery (for nuns and monks) at Whitby in Yorkshire. In 687 he became bishop of Hexham and in 705 was consecrated bishop of York. During his ministry he took an especial interest in the poor and disabled. In

717 he retired to the monastery of Beverley, which he had founded while bishop of York.

JOHN OF CAPISTRANO, properly **Giovanni da** (1386–1456) Italian prelate, born in Capistrano in the Abruzzi. He entered the Franciscan order at the age of 30, having been govenor of Perugia from 1426 and was employed as legate by several popes, and acted as inquisitor against the Fraticelli. In 1450 he preached a crusade in Germany against Turks and heretics, and opposed the Hussites in Moravia. His fanaticism led to many cruelties, such as the racking and burning of forty Jews in Breslau. When Belgrade was besieged by **Mohammed II** in 1456, he led a rabble of 60000 to its relief; but he died in Ilak, on the Danube. He was canonized in 1690. His feast day is 28 March.

JOHN OF DAMASCUS, St, or **Chrysorrhoas** (c.676–c.754) Greek theologian and hymn writer of the Eastern Church. Born in Damascus he was carefully educated by the learned Italian monk **Cosmas**. He replied to the iconoclastic measures of Leo the Isaurian with two addresses in which he vigorously defended image worship. His later years were spent in the monastery of Mar Saba near Jerusalem. There, ordained a priest, he wrote his hymns, an encyclopaedia of Christian theology (*Fount of Wisdom*), treatises against superstitions and Jacobite and Monophysite heretics, homilies, and *Barlaam and Joasaph*, now known to be a disguised version of the life of **Buddha**.

JOHN OF GAUNT, Duke of Lancaster (1340–99) English prince, fourth son of **Edward III**, born in Ghent. In 1359 he married his cousin, Blanche of Lancaster, and was created duke in 1362. She died in 1369, and in 1372 he married Constance, daughter of **Pedro the Cruel** of Castile, and assumed the title of King of Castile, though he failed by his expeditions to oust his rival, Henry of Trastamare. Before his father's death John became the most influential personage in the realm, and was thought to be aiming at the crown. He opposed the clergy and protected **Wycliffe**. Young King **Richard II**, distrusting him, sent him in 1386 on another attempt to secure a treaty for the marriage of his daughter Catherine to the future king of Castile. After his return to England (1389) he reconciled Richard to his (John's) brother, the Duke of Gloucester, and by Richard was made Duke of Aquitaine, and sent on several embassies to France. On his second wife's death he had married in 1396 his mistress, Catherine Swynford, by whom he had three sons, legitimated in 1397; from the eldest descended **Henry VIII**.

JOHN OF LEYDEN, originally **Jan Beuckelson** or **Bockhold** (1509–36) Dutch Anabaptist, born in Leiden. He wandered about for some time as a journeyman tailor, then settled in his native city as merchant and innkeeper, and became noted as an orator. Turning Anabaptist, in 1534 he went to Münster, and led a Protestant rebellion, setting up a 'kingdom of Zion', with polygamy and community of goods. In 1535 the city was taken by the bishop of Münster, and John and his followers were tortured to death.

JOHN OF NEPOMUK, St (c.1330–93) Bohemian cleric, and patron saint of Czechoslovakia, born in Pomuk near Pilsen. He studied at Prague, and became confessor to Sophia, wife of **Wenceslas IV**. For refusing to betray to the monarch the confession of the queen, John was put to the torture, then drowned in the Moldau. In 1729 he was canonized. His feast day is 16 May. By some historians two personages of the same name are enumerated—one, the martyr of the confessional; the other, a victim to the simoniacal tyranny of Wenceslas.

JOHN OF SALISBURY (c.1115–80) English prelate and scholar, born in Salisbury. He studied at Paris, under **Abelard**, was a clerk to Pope **Eugenius III** and to Archbishop **Theobald** at Canterbury, but fell into disfavour with **Henry II** and retired to Reims, where he wrote *Historia Pontificalis*. He returned to England and witnessed **Thomas à Becket**'s murder at Canterbury. In 1176 he became bishop of Chartres. A learned classical writer, he wrote lives of Becket and **Anselm**, *Polycraticus* on church and state diplomacy, *Metalogicon*, and *Entheticus*, *Historia Pontificalis* on logic and Aristotelian philosophy.

JOHN OF THE CROSS, St (1542–91) Spanish mystic and poet, born in Juan de Yepes y Álvarez in Fontiveros, Ávila. A Carmelite monk, in 1568 he founded with St **Teresa** of Ávila, the ascetic order of Discalced Carmelites. He accompanied St Teresa to Valladolid, where he lived an extremely ascetic life in a hovel until she appointed him to a convent in Ávila, where he was arrested (1577) and imprisoned at Toledo. He escaped in 1578 and lived in illness at the monastery of Úbeda. He was canonized in 1726, and declared a Doctor of the Church in 1926. His poetry includes the intensely lyrical *Cántico espiritual* (Spiritual Cantide) and *Noche oscura del alma* (Dark Night of the Soul).

JOHN OF TREVISA (1326–1412) Cornish translator of **Higden**, Glanville and Bartholomaeus Anglicus. He was a fellow of Exeter and Queen's Colleges, Oxford, and vicar of Berkeley and canon of Westbury (probably Westbury-on-Trym).

JOHN PAUL I, originally **Albino Luciani** (1912–78) pope in 1978. Born near Belluno, Italy, the son of a labourer in a Venice glass factory, he was educated at seminaries in the Venice area and at the Gregorian University in Rome, and ordained in 1935. He was a parish priest and teacher in Belluno, and also vicar general of the diocese of Vittorio Veneto from 1954 until 1958, when he became bishop of the diocese. He was nominated patriarch of Venice in 1969 and created cardinal in 1973. He was elected pope in August 1978 on the death of **Paul VI**, and died only 33 days later, being succeeded by **John Paul II**.

JOHN PAUL II, originally **Karol Jozef Wojtyla** (1920–) pope from 1978. Born and educated in Poland, he became the first non-Italian pope in 450 years. Ordained in 1946, he was professor of moral theology at the Universities of Lublin and Cracow. Archbishop and metropolitan of Cracow from 1964 to 1978, he was created cardinal in 1967. Noted for his energy and analytical ability, he has made various foreign trips, preaching to huge audiences. He is the author of a play, numerous poems and several books including *The Freedom of Renewal* (1972), *The Future of the Church* (1979) and *Collected Poems* (1982)

JOHN THE BAPTIST, St (fl.c.27) Jewish prophet, considered the forerunner of **Jesus Christ**. The son of the priest Zacharias and Elizabeth and the cousin of **Mary**, the mother of **Jesus**, he baptized and preached repentance and forgiveness of sins, denounced **Herod Antipas** for taking Herodias, his brother Philip's wife, and was imprisoned and executed at the request of **Salome**, daughter of Herodias. He baptized Jesus himself.

JOHN THE FEARLESS (1371–1419) Duke of Burgundy, the eldest son of **Philip the Bold**. He married Margaret of Bavaria (1385) and took part in the disastrous Crusade of Nicopolis (1396), when he was captured by the Turks and afterwards ransomed. His father's death in 1404 left him in possession of Burgundy, Flanders and Artois, and he soon put himself at the head of opposition to the government of Louis, Duke of **Orléans**, brother of the periodically insane Charles VI, the Foolish. His assassination of

Orléans (1407) led to civil war between the Burgundian party and Orléan's supporters, the Armagnacs. John gained, lost and regained control of Paris, the king, and the government, but was murdered during a conference at Montereau-Faut-Yonne, probably at the instigation of the Dauphin, the future **Charles VII**.

JOHNS, Jasper (1930–) American painter, sculptor and printmaker, born in Augusta, Georgia, and raised in South Carolina. He moved to New York in 1949 and worked first as a commercial artist. In the mid 1950s, after meeting **Robert Rauschenberg**, he began to create bold pictorial images such as flags, targets and numbers, using heavily-textured wax-based print in a manner derived fron the Abstract Expressionists, and often incorporating plaster casts. This work became an important source for the development of Pop Art in the USA. In the 1960s and 1970s he produced increasingly complex paintings, frequently with objects like brushes and rulers attached. His sculptures are of banal items, executed with detailed realism.

JOHNS, W E (William Earl) (1893–1968) English aviator and writer, author of the 'Biggles' stories, born in Hertford. He served in the Norfolk Yeomanry and when commissioned in 1916, transferred to the Royal Flying Corps where he served wtih some distinction. He retired from the Royal Air Force in 1930, edited *Popular Flying* and *Flying* in the 1930s, and served in the ministry of information (1939–45). His wartime marriage broke up after 1918 and he lived for many years with a lady his publishers prevented him from marrying, considering that his status as a children's author forbade his divorce. His stories are rattling good flying yarns, with his World War I experiences almost bodily transferred to later periods. In World War I he had been captured and sentenced to be shot; and the 'Biggles' series reflects unspoken anger at the expendability of airmen in bureaucratic thinking, while his World War II female pilot, 'Worrals', is savagely contemptuous of male self-satisfaction and hostility to acceptance of women as equals. He later tried his hand, less successfully, at space exploration stories.

JOHNS HOPKINS See **HOPKINS, Johns**

JOHNSON, Alexander Bryan (1786–1867) English-born American philosopher, born in Gosport of Dutch-Jewish ancestry. He settled in Utica, New York, in 1801 where he enjoyed a successful career in business. He published three philosophical works, *The Philosophy of Human Knowledge* (1828), *A Treatise on Language: or the relation which Words bear to Things* (1836) and *The Meaning of Words* (1854), which can now be seen to anticipate views familiar to the logical positivists and linguistic philosophers of the twentieth century. He also published works on politics, economics and banking.

JOHNSON, Amy (1903–41) English aviator, born in Hull, the daughter of a fish merchant. She studied economics at Sheffield University, then worked as a typist, joined the London Aeroplane Club and gained her certificate as a ground engineer (the first woman to do so) and pilot in 1929. In 1930 she flew solo from England to Australia (the first woman to do so) in her aircraft *Jason*, winning £10,000 from the London *Daily Mail*. In 1931 she flew to Japan via Moscow and back, and in 1932 made a record solo flight to Cape Town and back. She married the Scottish airman **James Mollison** (1932), and with him crossed the Atlantic in a de Havilland biplane in 39 hours (1933) and flew to India in 22 hours (1934). In 1936 she set a new record for a solo flight from London to Cape Town. Divorced in 1938, she joined the Air Transport Auxiliary as a pilot in World War II, and was lost after baling out over the Thames estuary.

JOHNSON, Andrew (1808–75) 17th president of the USA, born of humble parentage in Raleigh, North Carolina. In 1824 he went to Laurens, South Carolina, to work as a journeyman tailor, and in 1826 emigrated to Greenville, Tennessee. He served as alderman and mayor; in 1835 and 1839 became a member of the legislature; in 1841 was elected to the state senate, and in 1843 to congress. In 1853 and 1855 he was chosen governor of Tennessee, and in 1857 US senator. A moderate Jacksonian Democrat, Johnson was alone among Southern senators in standing by the Union during the Civil War and was made military governor of Tennessee (1862) and elected to the vice-presidency (March 1865). On **Lincoln**'s assassination (14 April 1865) he became president. He sought to carry out the conciliatory policy of his predecessor, but the assassination had provoked a revulsion of public feeling, and Johnson's policy was denounced as evincing disloyal sympathies. Soon a radical majority of congress were opposing his policy, and while he urged the readmission of Southern representatives, the Radical Republican majority insisted that the Southern states should be kept for a period under military government. Johnson vetoed the congressional measures; and congress passed them over his veto. Finally, his removal of secretary **Stanton** from the war department precipitated a crisis. Johnson claimed the right to change his 'constitutional advisers', and in return he was charged with violation of the 'Tenure of Office Act', in doing so without the consent of the senate. He was impeached and brought to trial, but acquitted by a single vote. He retired from office in March 1869, and was elected to the senate in January 1875.

JOHNSON, Ben (1961–) Jamaican-born Canadian runner, born in Falmouth. In the middle 1980s he was the world's fastest sprinter with **Carl Lewis**. He was unbeaten in 21 consecutive starts over 100 metres and at the 1988 Seoul Olympics set a new world 100 metres record, but was immediately deprived of his gold medal for having employed illegal substances in his preparation for the games.

JOHNSON, Dame Celia (1908–82) English actress, born in Richmond, Surrey. A student at RADA, she made her stage début in *Major Barbara* (1928) at Huddersfield and her London bow in *A Hundred Years Old* (1929). Soon cast as a leading lady, she made her first New York appearance as Ophelia in *Hamlet* (1931) and enjoyed a long run in *The Wind and the Rain* (1933–35) in London. *Dirty Work* (1934) marked the first of her rare screen appearances, although she created an unforgettable impression as the sad-eyed suburban housewife in *Brief Encounter* (1945) and won a British Film Award for *The Prime of Miss Jean Brodie* (1969). Often in well-bred roles, her career ranged from exquisitely modulated portraits of quiet despair to sophisticated high comedy and her many theatrical successes included *The Three Sisters* (1951), *The Reluctant Debutante* (1955), *The Grass is Greener* (1958), *Hay Fever* (1965) and *The Kingfisher* (1977).

JOHNSON, Earvin (Magic) (1959–) American professional basketball player with the Los Angeles Lakers since 1979, born in Lansing, Michigan. Named the National Basketball Association's Most Valuable Player in 1979, he was a member of NBA championship teams in 1980, 1982, 1985, 1987 and 1988. His autobiography, published in 1983, was called, simply, *Magic*.

JOHNSON, Esther See **SWIFT, Jonathan**

JOHNSON, Eyvind (1900–76) Swedish novelist and short-story writer, born of working-class parents in the far north of Sweden. After a number of years in mainly manual occupations he spent most of the 1920s in Paris and Berlin. His four-part *Romanen om Olof* (The Story of Olof, 1934–37) is the finest of the many working-class autobiographical novels written in Sweden in the 1930s. He was much involved in anti-Nazi causes, and produced a number of novels, especially the *Krilon* series (1941–43), castigating totalitarianism. The same humanitarian values are evident in his later historical novels, particularly *Strändernas svall* (Return to Ithaca, 1946), *Drömmar om rosor och eld* (Dreams about Roses and Fire, 1949) and *Hans nådes tid* (The Days of his Grace, 1960). He shared the 1974 Nobel prize for literature with his fellow Swede, **Harry Martinson**.

JOHNSON, Geraert See **JANSSEN**

JOHNSON, Hewlett, known as **the 'Red Dean'** (1874–1966) English prelate, born of a capitalist family in Macclesfield. Educated at Manchester and Oxford Universities, he began life as an engineering apprentice, did welfare work in the Manchester slums and joined the Independent Labour party, resolving to become 'a missionary engineer'. He was ordained in 1905. In 1924 he became dean of Manchester and from 1931 to 1963 was dean of Canterbury. In 1938 he visited Russia and with the publication of *The Socialist Sixth of the World* began his years of praise for Sovietism. In 1951 he received the **Stalin** peace prize. Though he was not a member of the Communist party, his untiring championship of the Communist states and Marxist policies involved him in continuous and vigorous controversy in Britain. His sobriquet was a self-bestowed title when, during the Spanish War, he said 'I saw red—you can call me red'. Other publications include *Christians and Communism* (1956) and the autobiographical *Searching for Light* (1968).

JOHNSON, J J (James Louis) (1924–) American jazz trombonist and composer, born in Indianapolis, Indiana. He took up the trombone at 14 after studying piano. While working professionally in New York in the 1940s, he was inspired by the bebop movement; his recordings of the period with **Charlie Parker** and others show him to be the first slide trombonist to answer the demands of the style for speed, articulation and harmonic sophistication. Although he worked from the 1960s largely as a composer for films and televison, his playing continues to influence modern jazz trombonists.

JOHNSON, Jack (John Arthur) (1878–1946) black American pugilist and world champion. Born in Galveston, Texas, he became the first black world heavyweight boxing champion by defeating the Canadian Tommy Burns at Sydney in 1908. His win provoked violent racial prejudice, despite his superb skills as a boxer. In 1910 he defeated the 'great white hope', the former champion **James J Jeffries**, with a knock-out in the 15th round. He lost his title in 1915 to the giant Jess Willard by a controversial knock-out in the 26th round. His relationship with a white woman led to a conviction under the Mann Act for transporting a white woman across state lines for immoral purposes. He died in a car accident in North Carolina in 1946. His life was the subject of a Broadway play, *The Great White Hope*, in 1968.

JOHNSON, James P (James Price) (1894–1955) American pianist and composer, born in New Brunswick, New Jersey. He was given rudimentary piano instruction by his mother. The family moved to New York in 1908 and, while still at school, Johnson was taking part in informal after-hours sessions with other pianists, mainly ragtime performers. In 1912 he began a series of piano-playing jobs in cabarets, movie-houses and dance-halls, eventually becoming the most accomplished player in the post-ragtime 'stride' style. A prolific performer in the 1920s and during the traditional jazz revival of the 1940s, he wrote more than 200 songs (including 'The Charleston') as well as several stage shows, and was a strong influence on such later pianists as **Fats Waller** and **Art Tatum**.

JOHNSON, James Weldon (1871–1938) American author, born in Jacksonville, Florida. He practised at the bar there from 1897 to 1901, and in 1906 he was American consul at Puerto Cabello, Venezuela, and at Corinto, Nicaragua (1909–12). He was secretary of the National Association for the Advancement of Colored People (1916–30) and was awarded the Spingarn medal (1925). From 1930 he was professor of creative literature at Fisk University. He wrote extensively on Black problems, and compiled collections of Black poetry.

JOHNSON, Lionel Pigot (1867–1902) English poet and critic, born in Broadstairs, Kent. The son of an army officer, he was educated at Winchester and New College, Oxford. He moved to London, surrounded himself with books, and made a living in literary journalism. He converted to Roman Catholicism in 1891 and fell under the spell of the Celtic Twilight, as *Poems* (1895) and *Ireland and Other Poems* (1897) testify. His most famous and frequently anthologized poem, however, is *By the Statue of King Charles at Charing Cross*. A friend of **Oscar Wilde** and **W B Yeats**, he was influential in his day and did much to promote an appreciation of **Thomas Hardy**. But he was an immoderate drinker and often appears tipsy and ridiculous in anecdotes. He died as a result of a fall caused by the effects of alcohol.

JOHNSON, Lyndon Baines (1908–73) 36th president of the USA, born in Stonewall, Texas, into a Baptist family which was greatly involved in local politics. He worked his way through college to become a teacher, then a congressman's secretary before being elected a strong 'New Deal' Democrat representative in 1937. He joined the US Navy immediately after Pearl Harbor, and was decorated. 'LBJ' was elected senator in 1948 and became vice-president under **Kennedy** in 1960, having earlier contested the party's nomination. A professional politician, he had been majority leader in the senate since 1955. In Kennedy's motorcade at the latter's assassination in Dallas, Texas, in 1963, he was immediately sworn in as president. He was returned as president in the 1964 election with a huge majority. Under his administration the Civil Rights Act (1964), introduced by Kennedy the previous year, and the Voting Rights Act (1965) were passed, making effective, if limited, improvements to the Black position in American society. He also introduced, under the slogan the 'Great Society', a series of important economic and social welfare reforms, including a Medicare programme for the aged and measures to improve education. The continuation and ever-increasing escalation of the war in Vietnam led to active protest and growing unpopularity for Johnson, however, and in 1968 he announced his decision not to stand for another presidental term of office and to retire from active politics.

JOHNSON, Pamela Hansford (Lady Snow) (1912–81) English novelist. She is best known for her sensitive portrayal of her native postwar London, stripped of its wartime poise and a prey to the second rate in mind and heart. Her works include *An Avenue of Stone* (1947), its sequel *A Summer to Decide* (1948), the tragi-comical *The Unspeakable Skipton* (1958), her study of **Ivy Compton Burnett** (1953), her *Six Proust Reconstructions* (1958), and the novels *An Error of Judgment* (1962), *The Honours Board* (1970), and *The Good Husband* (1978). In 1950 she married the novelist **C P Snow**.

JOHNSON, Philip Cortelyou (1906–) American architect and theorist, born in Cleveland, Ohio. A graduate of Harvard, he is renowned for his publication *The International Style* (1932) with Henry-Russell Hitchcock, which coined the popular term. From 1940 to 1943 he studied architecture under **Walter Gropius** and **Marcel Breuer**. He designed his own home, the Glass House, New Canaan, Connecticut (1949–50), on principles of space unification, derived from **Ludwig Mies van der Rohe**, with whom he designed the Seagram Building skyscraper, New York City (1945). Further works include the Amon Carter Museum of Western Art, Texas (1961), and the New York State Theater, Lincoln Center (1964). From 1964 to 1973 he entered successive partnerships with Richard Foster and John Burgee. In 1978–84 he designed the granite American Telephone and Telegraph Company building in New York City, following the structure and classical form of early skyscrapers (post-modernism).

JOHNSON, Richard Mentor (1781–1850) vice president of the USA. He was a member of congress from 1807 to 1819, of the US senate till 1829, and of congress till 1837. He was elected vice president (1837–41) by the senate, after the elections had not thrown up a majority in the electoral college for any one candidate.

JOHNSON, Samuel (1709–84) English writer, critic, lexicographer, and conversationalist, always known as Dr Johnson, born in Lichfield, Staffordshire. The son of a bookseller, he read voraciously in his father's shop. Educated at Lichfield Grammar School and Pembroke College, Oxford, he left without taking a degree in 1731. He taught briefly at a school in Market Bosworth, and then moved to Birmingham where he did some writing. In 1735 he married a widow 20 years older then himself, Elizabeth ('Tetty') Porter, and they opened a school at Edial, near Lichfield, where one of the pupils was the future actor, **David Garrick**. The school failed, and in 1737, accompanied by the young Garrick, the Johnsons moved to London where he finished writing a tragedy, *Irene* (not to be staged for 12 years), and earned a living writing parliamentary reports for *The Gentleman's Magazine*. In it he published (anonymously) his first poem, *London: A Poem in Imitation of the Third Satire of Juvenal* (1738). In 1744 he produced a topical and successful *Life* of his friend **Richard Savage**. Meanwhile he had been cataloguing the great library of Edward Harley, Earl of Oxford, and was able further to indulge his huge appetite for reading. In 1747 he issued a prospectus of a *Dictionary of the English Language*, which was to take him eight years to complete. During this time he published a long didactic poem, *The Vanity of Human Wishes* (1749), based on another of **Juvenal**'s satires. Garrick fulfilled a boyhood promise by producing his *Irene* at Drury Lane Theatre (1749), and Johnson himself wrote and edited, practically single-handedly, a bi-weekly periodical, *The Rambler*, which ran for 208 issues (1750–52), full of moral essays written (anonymously) by himself. In 1752 his wife, 'Tetty', died, plunging him into lasting depression. His great Dictionary appeared in 1755, which gave rise to a celebrated letter in which Johnson disdained an offer of patronage from Lord **Chesterfield**. Johnson was awarded an honorary degree at Oxford, but he had to continue literary hack-work to earn a living, contributing reviews for the *Literary Magazine*, and *The Idler* series of papers in *The Universal Chronicle* (1758–60). During this time his mother died, and he wrote his moral fable, *Rasselas: The Prince of Abyssinia* (1759), in a week to defray the funeral expenses. With the accession of **George III** in 1760, Johnson was granted a pension of £300 for life, which brought him financial security for the first time. In 1763 he met the young Scot, **James Boswell**, who would become his biographer, and with whom he would share a delightful tour of the Hebrides in 1773 (*A Journey to the Western Isles of Scotland*, 1775). In 1764 he founded the Literary Club with a circle of friends, including **Joshua Reynolds**, **Edmund Burke** and **Oliver Goldsmith**; later members were Boswell, Garrick and **Charles James Fox**. In 1765 he published his critical edition of **Shakespeare**'s plays (8 vols), with its classic Preface, and then set to work on his monumental *Lives of the Most Eminent English Poets* (10 vols, 1779–81). In that year his friend, the brewer Henry Thrale, died; his widow, **Hester Thrale**, who had looked after Johnson for many years, fell in love with an Italian musician, Gabriele Piozzi, and Johnson's wounded fury at their marriage in 1784 provoked a total estrangement. He died in dejection, and is buried in Westminster Abbey.

JOHNSON, Virginia E Shelman (1925–) American psychologist and sexologist, born in Springfield, Missouri. Educated at Missouri University, she joined with **William Masters**' group in 1957, and achieved fame through their investigations of the physiology of sexual intercourse, using volunteer subjects under laboratory conditions at their Reproductive Biology Research Foundation in St Louis. She and Masters (who were married in 1971), co-authored *Human Sexual Response* in 1966. They also wrote *On Sex and Human Loving* (1986).

JOHNSON, Sir William (1715–74) Irish merchant and colonial administrator, born in County Meath. In 1737 he emigrated to America, and became a fur-trader in the Mohawk Valley (now in New York State). By his fairness he acquired great influence with the Red Indians. In the Anglo-French Wars he often led the 'Six Nations' against the French, especially at Lake George. He was appointed Superintendent of Indian Affairs (1756–64) and built himself a fine residence (Johnson Hall) on the Mohawk River. After the death of his wife he took into his house Molly Brant, a sister of the Mohawk chief **Joseph Brant**, and had eight children with her. She was known as 'the Indian Lady Johnson'.

JOHNSON, William Eugene, nicknamed **Pussyfoot** (1862–1945) American reformer and temperance propagandist, born in Coventry, New York. He became a journalist, and later a special officer in the US Indian Service 1908–11, where he received his nickname from his methods in raiding gambling saloons in Indian Territory. He was prominent during the prohibitionist movement in America and lectured for the cause all over Europe. In 1919 he lost an eye when he was struck and dragged from a lecture platform in London by medical students.

JOHNSTON, Albert Sidney (1803–62) American soldier, born in Kentucky. He served in the US army until 1834; in 1836 he joined the army of Texas, and became its head, and in 1838 was secretary of Texas. He served in the Mexican war under General **Zachary Taylor**, who in 1849 appointed him paymaster in the US army. From 1857 to 1859 he was sent to 'pacify' the Mormons in Utah, and as brigadier-general commanded in Utah and on the Pacific. In 1861 he resigned to become a Confederate general in the Civil War (1861–65). Appointed to the command of Kentucky and Tennessee, he fortified Bowling Green, and held the Northern army in check until February 1862, when he retreated to Nashville and later to Corinth, Mississippi. Here he concentrated 50000 men and attacked **Grant** at Shiloh on 6 April 1862. The Union army was surprised, and the advantage lay with the

Confederates until Johnston was mortally wounded. Next day Grant's supports came up and the Confederates, now under **Beauregard**, were driven back to Corinth.

JOHNSTON, Alexander Keith (1804–71) Scottish cartographer, born near Penicuik. With his brother he founded the Edinburgh map-making firm of W and A K Johnston (1826). His *National Atlas* (1843) procured him the appointment of geographer royal for Scotland. Other works are a *Physical Atlas* (1848) and the famous *Royal Atlas* (1861), besides atlases of astronomy etc, a physical globe, and a gazatteer.

JOHNSTON, or **Jonston, Arthur** (1587–1641) Scottish physician, poet and humanist, born in Caskieben, Aberdeenshire. He graduated MD at Padua in 1610, and visited many seats of learning. He practised medicine in France, and his fame as a Latin poet spread over Europe. In about 1625 he was appointed physician to King **Charles I**. His famous translation of the Psalms of David into Latin verse was published at Aberdeen in 1637. He edited the *Deliciae Poetarum Scotorum hujus Aevi* (1637), an anthology of Latin poetry from Scotland, to which he also contributed notable poems. In 1637 he became rector of King's College, Aberdeen.

JOHNSTON, (William) Denis (1901–84) Irish playwright, born in Dublin, the son of a Protestant liberal judge. Educated at St Andrew's School, Dublin, Merchiston Castle School, Edinburgh, Cambridge and Harvard, he joined the English (1925) and Northern Ireland (1926) bars. His impressionist play, *Shadowdance*, was rejected by Lady **Gregory** for the Abbey Theatre, then retitled *The Old Lady Says 'No'* and became a major success at the Gate Theatre in 1929, followed by a further triumph with *The Moon on the Yellow River* (1931) and several others for the next three decades. His autobiographical *Nine Rivers from Jordan* (1953) recounted his experiences as a war correspondent. His *In Search of Swift* (1959) was an impressive argument for **Swift**'s inability to marry Esther Johnson ('Stella') having been caused by an illegitimate half-sibling relationship. He wrote a later autobiographical work, *The Brazen Head* (1977). His daughter, Jennifer Johnston (1930–), is a successful novelist.

JOHNSTON, Edward (1872–1944) English calligrapher, born in Uruguay. He virtually taught himself the art of calligraphy by studying medieval manuscripts and discovering how to prepare and use reeds and quills. From 1899 to 1912 he taught, at W R Lethaby's invitation, at the Central School of Fine Arts and Crafts, London, where one of his students was **Eric Gill**; he also taught at the Royal College of Art. His books, *Writing and Illuminating, and Lettering* (1906) and *Manuscript and Inscription Letters* (1909), were landmarks in the revival and development of calligraphy. When, in 1913, **Frank Pick** required a clear standard letter form for London Transport, Johnston produced his classic sans-serif alphabet which is still in use. It demonstrates his meticulous craftsmanship in which the spacing was as important as the letter form itself.

JOHNSTON, George Henry (1912–70) Australian author and journalist, born in Malvern, Victoria. After studying commercial art, he worked as a journalist and during World War II his syndicated dispatches from New Guinea, India and Burma, Italy and the North Atlantic as a war correspondent were widely read. He also wrote five books on his experiences, published between 1941 and 1944. Returning to journalism after the war, he worked in London before making a new home in the Greek islands with his wife and fellow-author, Charmian Clift (1923–69). With her he wrote three novels, and she described their life in the islands in short stories and essays. He wrote a number of novels, short stories and plays, and achieved distinction with his semi-autobiographical trilogy *My Brother Jack* (1964), *Clean Straw for Nothing* (1969) and the unfinished *A Cartload of Clay* (1971).

JOHNSTON, Sir Harry Hamilton (1858–1927) English explorer and writer, born in Kennington, London. From 1879 he travelled in Africa, led the Royal Society's expedition to Kilimanjaro in 1884, and as commissioner for South Central Africa made possible British acquisition of Northern Rhodesia and Nyasaland. He wrote books on the Congo and zoology, five novels and *The Story of My Life* (1923).

JOHNSTON, Joseph Eggleston (1807–91) American soldier, born near Farnville, Virginia. He graduated at West Point, fought in the Seminole war, became captain of engineers in 1846, served in the war with Mexico, and in 1860 was quartermaster-general. At the outbreak of the Civil War (1861–65) he resigned to enter the Confederate service, and as brigadier-general took command of the army of the Shenandoah. He supported **Beauregard** at the first battle of Bull Run, in 1862 was disabled by a wound, in 1863 failed to relieve Vicksburg, and in 1864 stubbornly contested **Sherman**'s progress towards Atlanta, but, being steadily driven back, was relieved of his command. In February 1865 he was restored, and Lee ordered him to 'drive back Sherman'; but he had only a fourth of the Northern general's strength, and surrendered to Sherman on 26 April 1865. He later engaged in railway and insurance business, was elected to congress in 1877, was a US commissioner of railroads and died in Washington.

JOHNSTONE name of a Scottish noble family taken from the lordship of Johnstone in Annandale, Dumfriesshire. In former days it was one of the most powerful and turbulent clans of the west Border, and was at constant feud with its neighbours, especially the Maxwells. Of three branches, Johnstone of Annandale, Johnstone of Westerhall, and Johnston of Hilton and Caskieben in Aberdeenshire, the first, which retained the ancient patrimony, was ennobled by **Charles I**, and became successively Lords Johnstone of Lochwood, Earls of Hartfell, and Earls and Marquises of Annandale.

JOHNSTONE, Jimmy (James) (1944–) Scottish footballer, born in Viewpark, Lanarkshire. Tiny and speedy, he was a member of the Glasgow Celtic side which won the European Cup in 1967 and he played a leading part in Celtic's virtual monopoly of domestic competition in the five years from 1965. He epitomized the classic Scots tradition of the small, gifted individualist but was not always amenable to discipline and he merited many more caps than the 23 he received. Unable to settle away from Scotland, his spells of playing in England, Ireland and the USA were not particularly productive.

JOHNSTONE, James, 'Chevalier de' (1719–c.1800) Scottish soldier, born in Edinburgh, the son of a merchant. As Prince **Charles Edward Stewart**'s aide-de-camp he fought at Culloden in 1746, and, then taking service with the French, was present at the capture of Louisbourg and the capitulation of Quebec (1759). He wrote his *Memoirs* (of the 1745 Rising).

JOHNSTONE, William (1897–1981) Scottish painter, born in Denholm, Roxburghshire; he studied at Edinburgh College of Art and subsequently in Paris. His work in the late 1920s and 1930s shows the influence of Surrealism, in its use of rounded semi-abstract images suggestive of dream-like landscapes and human forms. He held a series of teaching posts in London, latterly as principal of the Central School of

Arts and Crafts (1947–60). It was in the last decade of his life that he produced what is arguably his best work: large, free abstract paintings and ink drawings which have something of the feeling of Eastern calligraphy, but are still evocative of the natural world.

JOINVILLE, François Ferdinand d'Orléans, Prince de (1818–1900) French naval officer and author, born in Neuilly, the third son of **Louis Philippe**. He served in the French navy from 1834–48, and was on **McClellan**'s staff during the Virginian campaign in the American Civil War (1862). Exiled from France in 1870, he returned incognito in 1871 and served in the war against Prussia. From 1871–75 he sat in the National Assembly. His works included *Essais sur la marine française* (1852) and *Vieux Souvenirs* (1894).

JOINVILLE, Jean, Sire de (c.1224–1319) French historian, born in Champagne. He became seneschal to the count of Champagne and king of Navarre, took part in the unfortunate Seventh Crusade of **Louis IX** (1248–54), returned with him to France, and lived partly at court, partly on his estates. At Acre in 1250 he composed a Christian manual, his *Credo*; and throughout the crusade he took notes of events and wrote down his impressions, which he fashioned at the age of almost 80 into his delightful *Vie de Saint Louis* (1309).

JÓKAI, Maurus, or **Mór** (1825–1904) Hungarian novelist, born in Komaróm. He was an active partisan of the Hungarian struggle in 1848. As well as dramas, humorous essays and poems, he wrote many novels and romances, including *The Turks in Hungary* (1852), *The Magyar Nabob* (1853) and its continuation *Zoltan Karpathy* (1854), *The New Landlord* (1862), *Black Diamonds* (1870), *The Romance of the Coming Century* (1873), *The Modern Midas* (1875), *The Comedians of Life* (1876), *God is One* (1877), *The White Woman of Leutschau* (1884) and *The Gipsy Baron* (1885). He was editor of several newspapers, and conspicuous as a Liberal parliamentarian.

JOLIOT-CURIE, Irène, née **Curie** (1897–1956) French physicist, born in Paris, daughter of **Pierre** and **Marie Curie** and wife of **Jean Frédéric Joliot-Curie**. She worked as her mother's assistant at the Radium Institute in Paris, taking charge of the work in 1932. In that year she discovered, with her mother, the projection of atomic nuclei by neutrons, and in 1934 she and her husband succeeded in producing radioactive elements artifically, for which they received the 1935 Nobel prize for chemistry. She died of cancer, probably caused by lifelong exposure to radioactivity.

JOLIOT-CURIE, Jean Frédéric, original surname **Joliot** (1900–58) French physicist, husband (1926) of **Irène Joliot-Curie**, born in Paris. He studied under **Paul Langevin** at the Sorbonne where in 1925 he became assistant to **Marie Curie**, mother of Irène. In 1935 he shared with his wife the Nobel prize for their discovery of artificial radioactivity. Professor at the Collège de France (1937), he became a strong supporter of the Resistance movement during World War II, and a member of the Communist party. After the liberation he became director of scientific research and (1946–50) high commissioner for atomic energy, a position from which he was dismissed for his political activites. President of the Communist-sponsored World Peace Council, he was awarded the Stalin peace prize (1951). Commander of the *Légion d'honneur*, he was given a state funeral by the Gaullist government when he died from cancer, caused by lifelong exposure to radioactivity.

JOLSON, Al, stage-name of **Asa Yoelson** (1886–1950) Russian-born American actor and singer, born in St Petersburg. The son of a rabbi, he emigrated to the USA in 1893 and made his stage début in *The Children of the Ghetto* (1899). He toured with circus and minstrel shows and became famous for his characteristic imitations of Negro singers in such hits as 'Mammy' (1909), 'Sonny Boy', etc. He was the star of the first talking picture *The Jazz Singer* in 1927. His recorded voice featured in the commemorative films *The Jolson Story* and *Jolson Sings Again*.

JOLY, John (1857–1933) Irish geologist and physicist, born in Offaly. He studied at Trinity College, Dublin, where he became professor of geology and mineralogy in 1897. He invented a photometer in 1888, calculated the age of the earth (as 100 million years) by measuring the sodium content of the sea (1899) and formulated the theory of thermal cycles based on the radioactive elements in the earth's crust. With Walter Stevenson he evolved the 'Dublin method' in radiotherapy, pioneered colour photography and the radium treatment of cancer.

JOMINI, Henri Baron (1779–1869) Swiss soldier and strategist, born in Payerne in Vaud. After commanding a Swiss battalion he attached himself to Marshall **Ney**, to whom he became chief of staff; he was created baron after the peace of Tilsit (1807). He attracted **Napoleon**'s notice by his *Traité des grandes opérations militaires* (1804). He distinguished himself at Jena (1806), in the Spanish campaigns (1808) and during the retreat from Russia; but, offended at his treatment by Napoleon, he entered the Russian service (1813), and fought against Turkey (1828). He wrote a great history of the wars of the Revolution (1806), a Life of Napoleon (1827) and a *Précis de l'art de guerre* (1830).

JOMMELLI, Niccoló (1714–74) Italian composer of more than 50 operas, born in Aversa. He unfortunately germanized his style and lost his popularity after a spell as kapellmeister to the Duke of Württemberg.

JONES, Allen (1937–) English painter, sculptor and printmaker, born in Southampton. He studied at Hornsey Art School (1955–59), and at the Royal College of Art (1959–60), and his first one-man show was held in London, in 1962. An early Pop artist, he won several prizes (eg Paris Biennale, 1963) and from c.1965 specialized in slick, fetishistic images (high-heeled shoes, stockings, etc) taken from pornographic or glossy fashion magazines.

JONES, Bob (Robert Reynolds) (1883–1968) American evangelist, born in Dale County, Alabama. He conducted revival meetings from the age of 13, and was licensed by the Methodist Church to preach at the age of 15. Educated at Southern University, Greensboro, South Carolina, he began full-time evangelistic work in 1902, and is estimated to have preached more than 12000 'down-to-earth gospel messages'. In 1939 he left the Methodist Church, which he charged with theological liberalism, and broke also with other evangelists, notably **Billy Graham**, who displayed ecumenical tendencies. To further his brand of fundamentalism, in 1927 he founded Bob Jones University which from small beginnings in Florida eventually (1947) settled in Greenville, South Carolina with several thousand students. The school is known for its biblical theology, its Puritanical code which is binding on its students, and tends towards right-wing politics. He once drew unwelcome attention on himself by a pamphlet entitled 'Is Segregation Scriptural?', to which he answered yes. His son, Bob Jones Jr (b.1911), succeeded him as president of Bob Jones University.

JONES, Bobby (Robert Tyre) (1902–71) American amateur golfer, one of the greatest golfers in the history of the game. Born in Atlanta, Georgia, he studied law and was called to the Georgia bar in 1928. He won the

US Open four times (1923, 1926, 1929, 1930), the British Open three times (1926, 1927, 1930), the US Amateur championships five times and the British Amateur championship once. In 1930 he achieved the staggering feat of winning the 'Grand Slam' of the American and British Open and Amateur championships in the same year. Thereafter, at the age of 28, he retired from competitive golf, having no major golfing challenges left.

JONES, Chuck (Charles) (1912–) American animated cartoon director, born in Spokane, Washington. His early work included *Daffy and the Dinosaur* (1939), the Inki series (*Inki and the Minah Bird*, 1943, etc) and fast-paced duels between Wile E Coyote and the Road Runner (*Fast and Furry-ous*, 1949, etc). Pepe le Pew, the amorous skunk, won him his first Oscar with *For Scentimental Reasons* (1951). His Bugs Bunny cartoons include the classic *What's Opera Doc* (1957) and the stereoscopic *Lumber Jack Rabbit* (1954). He won another Oscar with *The Dot and the Line* (1965). For television he created many specials including **Kipling**'s *Rikki-Tikki-Tavi*, winning another Oscar for *A Christmas Carol* (1972).

JONES, Daniel (1881–1967) English phonetician. He was called to the bar in 1907, when he was also appointed lecturer in phonetics at University College, London (professor 1921–49). He collaborated with others in compiling Cantonese (1912), Sechuana (1916) and Sinhalese (1919) phonetic readers. He wrote *Outline of English Phonetics* (1916), and compiled an *English Pronouncing Dictionary* (1917, 14th ed 1977). His other works included *The Phoneme* (1950), and *Cardinal Vowels* (1956). He was secretary (1928–49) and president (1950–67) of the International Phonetic Association.

JONES, David Michael (1895–1974) English poet and artist, born in Kent. His father was Welsh and though he only lived there briefly he identified himself strongly with Wales. After art school he served in World War I and had an abiding interest in martial matters. His war experience is central to *In Parenthesis* (1937), the first of his two major literary works. *The Anathemata* (1952) is likewise personal but draws heavily on his religious influences. He became a Roman Catholic in 1921. In 1922 he met **Eric Gill**, the beginning of a long association. As an artist he is less well known but his paintings, water-colours, drawings and inscriptions have a lucidity that some of his literary work lacks.

JONES, Ebenezer (1820–60) English poet, born in Islington, London. He was brought up a strict Calvinist and despite long hours as a clerk completed *Studies of Sensation and Event* (1843), which were admired by **Browning** and **Rossetti**. In his *Land Monopoly* (1849) he anticipated the economic theory of **Henry George** by 30 years.

JONES, Edward Burne See **BURNE-JONES**

JONES, Eli Stanley (1884–1973) American missionary to India, born in Baltimore, Maryland. Going to India as a missionary of the Methodist Episcopal Church in 1907, he later became an itinerant evangelist, declining a bishopric in 1928. Concerned equally for social justice and spirituality, he supported Indian aspirations for independence and was sensitive to Indian religious traditions, founding two Christian *ashrams*, one at Sat Tal and the other in Lucknow (where he also founded a psychiatric centre). He worked outside India for part of each year and wrote nearly 30 books, although none became better-known than *The Christ of the Indian Road* (1925). *Christ at the Round Table* (1928) and *Mahatma Ghandhi: An Interpretation* (1948) were also significant in their day.

JONES, Ernest (1819–69) English Chartist poet and leader, born in Berlin. He was the son of the equerry to **William Duke of Cumberland**, and came to England in 1838. In 1841 he published his romance, *The Wood Spirit*, was called to the bar in 1844, and next year became leader of the Chartist movement, issuing *The Labourer*, *Notes of the People* and *The People's Paper*, and rejecting nearly £2000 per annum, left to him on condition that he should abandon the Chartist cause. For his part in the Chartist proceedings at Manchester in 1848 he got two years' solitary confinement, and in prison composed an epic, *The Revolt of Hindostan*. After his release he wrote *The Battleday* (1855), *The Painter of Florence* and *The Emperor's Vigil* (1856), and *Beldagon Church* and *Corayda* (1860). He made several unsuccessful efforts to enter parliament.

JONES, Ernest (1879–1958) Welsh psychoanalyst, born in Llwchwr, Glamorgan. He studied at Cardiff University College and qualified as physician in London. Medical journalism and neurological research brought him into contact with the work of **Sigmund Freud** and his new approach to neurosis. He learnt German in order to study Freud's work more closely and in 1908 became his lifelong disciple and personal friend. He introduced psychoanalysis into Britain and North America, and in 1912 formed a committee of Freud's closest collaborators to uphold the Freudian theory. He founded the British Psycho-Analytical Society in 1913, and in 1920 the *International Journal of Psycho-Analysis* which he edited (1920–33). He was professor of psychiatry at Toronto (1909–12) and director of the London Clinic for Psycho-Analysis. Among his numerous works and translations is a psychoanalytical study of *Hamlet and Oedipus* and an authoritative biography of Freud (1953–57).

JONES, Gwyn (1907–) Welsh scholar and writer, born in Blackwood, Gwent. Educated at Tredegar Grammar School and the University of Wales, he was a schoolmaster and lecturer before becoming professor of English language and literature at the University College of Wales, Aberystwyth (1940–64). His works on Norse history and literature include *The Norse Atlantic Saga* (1964) and *A History of the Vikings* (1968), and various translations including *The Vatnsdalers' Saga* (1942) and *Egil's Saga* (1960). His Welsh studies include a translation of the *Mabinogion* (1948), *Welsh Legends and Folk-Tales* (1955), and editing *Welsh Short Stories* (1956) and *The Oxford Book of Welsh Verse in English* (1977). He has also published several novels and collections of short stories.

JONES, Dame Gwyneth (1936–) Welsh dramatic soprano, born in Pontnewyndd. She studied at the Royal College of Music and elsewhere. She made her Covent Garden début in 1963, first sang at the Vienna State Opera, 1966, and subsequently at Bayreuth, Munich, La Scala Milan, and other great houses of the world. She is renowned as an interpreter of the heroines of **Wagner** and **Strauss** operas.

JONES, Sir Harold Spencer (1890–1960) English astronomer, born in London. He graduated at Cambridge reading mathematics, and became chief assistant to the Astronomer Royal at Greenwich (1913–23). He then served as astronomer at the Royal Observatory at the Cape of Good Hope (1923–33), before returning to Greenwich to become Astronomer Royal in 1933–55. At the Cape he organized an international project to determine accurately the Earth-Sun distance (the astronomical unit), utilizing a close approach of the asteroid Eros, improving previous values. In 1939, using the new quartz-crystal clocks, he discovered that the Earth's rotation was slowing down by about a second a year. A new system of measuring time, ephemeris time, independent of the Earth's rotation rate, was introduced. In 1948 he began the move of the Royal Observatory from Greenwich, where the atmospheric pollution of London, and sodium lighting, was making observational difficulties. The move to Herstmonceux was completed in 1958 after his retirement. The Royal Greenwich Observatory is now to be moved to Cambridge.

JONES, Henry (1831–99) English physician and writer. Under the pseudonym 'Cavendish' he published many books on whist and other games.

JONES, Henry Arthur (1851–1929) English dramatist, together with **Pinero** the founder of the 'realist problem' drama in Britain, born in Grandborough, Buckinghamshire. He was in business till 1878, when *Only Round the Corner* was produced at Exeter. His first great hit was a melodrama, *The Silver King* (1882). This was followed by *Saints and Sinners* (1884), *Rebellious Susan* (1894), *The Philistines* (1895), *The Liars* (1897), *The Manoeuvres of Jane* (1898), *Mrs Dane's Defence* (1900), *Mary Goes First* (1913) and other social comedies.

JONES, Sir Henry Stuart (1867–1939) English classical scholar, born in Hunslet, Leeds. He studied at Balliol College, Oxford, and in Greece and Italy, became Camden professor of ancient history at Oxford and principal of University College, Aberystwyth, in 1927. He contributed to archaeological studies and ancient history, edited **Thucydides** (1898–1900) and edited the Greek lexicon of **Liddell** and Scott (9th ed 1925–40).

JONES, Inigo (1573–1652) English architect, born in London. The founder of classical English architecture, he studied landscape painting in Italy, and from Venice introduced the Palladian style into England. In Denmark, he is said to have designed the palaces of Rosenborg and Frederiksborg. In 1606 **James VI and I** employed him in arranging the masques of **Ben Jonson**. He introduced the proscenium arch and movable scenery to the English stage. From 1613 to 1614 he revisited Italy and on his return in 1615 was appointed surveyor-general of the royal buildings. In 1616 he designed the Queen's House at Greenwich, completed in the 1630s. Other commissions included the rebuilding of the Banqueting Hall at Whitehall, the nave and transepts and a large Corinthian portico of old St Paul's, Marlborough Chapel, the Double-Cube room at Wilton and possibly the York Water Gate. He laid out Covent Garden and Lincoln's Inn Fields.

JONES, James (1921–77) American novelist, born in Robinson, Illinois, the son of a dentist. Educated at the University of Hawaii, he served in the US army as a sergeant (1939–44), boxed as a welterweight in Golden Gloves tournaments, and was awarded a Purple Heart. His wartime experience in Hawaii led to *From Here to Eternity* (1951), a classic war novel for which he received a National Book award. Later work was dissappointing, with the exception of *The Thin Red Line* (1962).

JONES, John (c.1597–1660) Welsh soldier and politician, born in Maes-y-garnedd, Merionethshire. He fought for Parliament during the Civil War and became member for Merioneth in 1646. He was one of the signatories of the death warrant of **Charles I**. During the Interregnum, he was a vigorous member of the government with responsibilities in Wales and Ireland. He was executed as a regicide.

JONES, John Paul, originally **John Paul** (1747–92) Scottish-born American naval officer, born in Kirkbean, Galloway, the son of a gardener, John Paul. Apprenticed as sailor boy, he made several voyages to America, and in 1773 inherited a property in Fredericksburg, Virginia, having been mate on a slaver for five years; about the same date he assumed the name of Jones. At the outbreak of the American War of Independence in 1775 he was commissioned as a senior lieutenant. In 1778 he cruised into British waters in the *Ranger* and made a daring descent on the Solway Firth in Scotland. In 1779, as commodore of a small French squadron displaying American colours, he threatened Leith, off Flamborough Head won a hard fought engagement on the *Bon Homme Richard* against the British Frigate *Serapis*. In 1788 he entered the Russian service, and as rear admiral of the Black Sea fleet fought in the Russo-Turkish war of 1788–89. He died in Paris, and his remains were taken to the USA in 1905.

JONES, Owen (1741–1814) Welsh antiquary. A prominent figure in the literary life of Wales for more than half a century, and a chief benefactor of Welsh scholarship, he went to London as a young man as an apprentice to a skinner. Later he bought the business for himself and became a wealthy man. His *Myvyrian Archaeology of Wales* (1801–07) is a collection of poetic pieces dating from the 6th to the 14th centuries.

JONES, Owen (1809–74) Welsh architect and designer, son of the antiquary **Owen Jones** (1741–1814), born in London. He was superintendent of works for the Great Exhibition of 1851 in London, and director of decoration for the Crystal Palace when it was re-erected at Sydenham. He also designed St James's Hall in London. He wrote a monumental *Grammar of Ornament* (1856), magnificently illustrated with decorative patterns and motifs from many cultures and periods.

JONES, Philip (1618–74) Welsh soldier and politician, born in Swansea. He fought for Parliament during the Civil War, and played an important part in the government of Wales during the Interregnum. He was high in **Cromwell**'s favour during the Protectorate. After the Restoration, he retired to his Welsh estate in the Vale of Glamorgan.

JONES, Robert (fl.1600) English lutenist and composer. He graduated at Oxford (1597), composed madrigals, including a six-part one in **Thomas Morley**'s *The Triumphes of Oriana* as well as five books of 'ayres', with lute accompaniments.

JONES, Thomas (1870–1955) Welsh administrator and writer, born in Rhymney, Monmouthshire. An academic economist at Glasgow and Belfast, he was special investigator for the Royal Commission on the Poor Law (1903–09), assistant (later deputy) secretary of the cabinet from 1916 to 1930, and played an important role in the negotiation of the Irish Treaty (1922) and the General Strike (1926). Appointed by **Lloyd George**, he served under four prime ministers. In 1930 he was appointed the first secretary of the Pilgrim Trust, from which he promoted CEMA (Council for the Encouragement of Music and Arts) in 1939 which became the Arts Council of Great Britain. In 1927 he founded the only adult residential college in Wales, Coleg Harlech. He was chairman of Gregynog Press (fine printed books), and wrote an account of his work as a civil servant in *Whitehall Diaries*.

JONES, Sir William (1746–94) English jurist and Orientalist, born in London. Educated at Harrow and University College, Oxford, he was called to the bar in 1774 and in 1776 became commissioner of bankrupts. He published a *Persian Grammar* (1772), Latin Commentaries on Asiatic Poetry (1774), and a translation of seven ancient Arabic poems (1780). In 1783 he obtained a judgeship in the Supreme Court of Judicature in Bengal. He devoted himself to Sanskrit, and in 1787 was the first to point out its startling resemblance to Latin and Greek. He established the Asiatic Society of Bengal (1784), and was its first president. He completed a translation of *Sakuntala*, the *Hitopadesa*, parts of the Vedas, and Manu, and wrote some important legal works.

JONGEN, Joseph (1873–1953) Belgian composer. He won the Belgian *Prix de Rome* and was professor at Liège Conservatoire until the outbreak of World War I when he went to England. He became director of the Brussels Conservatoire (1920–39). He composed piano, violin and organ works, the symphonic poem *Lalla Roukh*, an opera and a ballet.

JONSON, Ben (1572–1637) English dramatist, born in Westminster, probably of Border descent. He was educated at Westminster School under **Camden**, to whom he paid the tribute 'Camden most reverend head to whom I owe/All that I am in arts, all that I know'. After working for a while with his stepfather, a bricklayer, he volunteered for military service in Flanders before joining **Henslowe**'s company of players. He killed a fellow player in a duel, became a Catholic in prison, but later recanted. His *Every Man in his Humour*, with **Shakespeare** in the cast, was performed at the Curtain in 1598 to be followed not so successfully by *Every Man Out of His Humour* in 1599. The equally tiresome *Cynthia's Revels*, largely allegorical, was succeeded by *The Poetaster* which at least was salted by a personal attack on **Dekker** and **Marston**. He now tried Roman tragedy, but his *Sejanus* (1603) and his later venture, *Catiline* (1611), are so larded with classical references as to be merely closet plays. If he was trying to show Shakespeare how to write a Roman tragedy he failed badly, but his larger intent of discarding romantic comedy and writing realistically (though his theory of 'humours' was hardly comparable with genuine realism) helped to produce his four masterpieces—*Volpone* (1606), *The Silent Woman* (1609), *The Alchemist* (1610) and *Bartholomew Fair* (1614). *Volpone* is an unpleasant satire on senile sensuality and greedy legacy hunters. *The Silent Woman* is farcical comedy involving a heartless hoax. **Dryden** praised it for its construction, but *The Alchemist* is better with its single plot and strict adherence to the unities. *Bartholomew Fair* has indeed all the fun of the fair, salted by Ben's anti-Puritan prejudices, though the plot gets lost in the motley of eccentrics. After the much poorer *The Devil is an Ass* (1616), Jonson turned or rather returned to the masque—he had collaborated with **Inigo Jones** in *The Masque of Blacknesse*, 1605—and produced a number of those glittering displays down to 1625 when **James VI and I**'s death terminated his period of Court favour. His renewed attempt to attract theatre audiences left him in the angry mood of the ode 'Come leave the loathed stage' (1632). Only his unfinished pastoral play *The Sad Shepherd* survives of his declining years. Ben attracted the learned and courtly, to several of whom his superb verse letters are addressed. His lyric genius was second only to Shakespeare's. 'Drink to me only with thine Eyes' in *Volpone* (of all places) and 'Queen and Huntress chaste and fair' and 'Slow, slow fresh Fount' in the dreary stretches of *Cynthia's Revels* are but a few of these gemlike lyrics. His *Timber; or Discoveries*, printed in the folio of 1640, prove him a considerable critic with a bent towards the neo-classicism which Cowley and Dryden inaugurated.

JÓNSSON, Arngrímur known as 'the Learned' (1568–1648), Icelandic scholar, born in Víðidalur. After university in Denmark he returned to Iceland to become headmaster of the Latin school at the bishopric of Hólar. He collected old Icelandic manuscripts and wrote a number of important Latin works on the language, literature and history of Iceland, including *Brevis commentarius de Islandia* (1593), *Crymogaea* (a general description of the country, 1609), and *Specimen Islandiae historicum et magna ex parte chorographicum* (1643). He was a pioneer in the renaissance of scholarly interest in northern antiquity.

JÓNSSON, Ásgrímur (1876–1958) Icelandic landscape painter, born on the farm of Rútsstaða-Suðurkot, and the Grand Old Man of the modern arts in Iceland. He was the first artist to portray the Icelandic landscapes in all its vivid variety and ethereal colour. In 1907 he was given a generous state grant to travel and study abroad, where he came into contact with the Impressionists. Back home in Iceland he travelled all over the country, seeking fresh landscapes and subject-matter to paint. He also turned to water-colours, and to interpreting Icelandic folk-tales. His home in Reykjavík and his private collection of 500 of his own paintings, which he bequeathed to the nation, are now an art gallery.

JÓNSSON, Bólu-Hjálmar (1796–1875) Icelandic folk-poet, born in Eyjafjörður. A man of fierce pride and temper, he lived on a peasant croft and struggled with poverty all his life, making a meagre living from wood-carving. He was also one of the most eloquent and natural of poets; his verses, whether railing against the church and authority or revelling in marvellous poetic imagery, circulated orally all over the country, and were only collected and published after his death.

JÓNSSON, Einar (1874–1954) Icelandic sculptor, born on the farm of Galtafell. He went to Copenhagen to study art, and after exhibiting his powerful realistic work *Outlaws* (1901, now in Reykjavík), was given a grant by the Icelandic government to study in Rome. In 1903 he was given the Grand Grant of the Copenhagen Academy. After extensive travel, he settled in Copenhagen in 1905, but in 1909 offered all his works to the Icelandic nation on condition that they were housed properly. The offer was accepted, and in 1914 he returned to Iceland, hailed as its national sculptor. He spent two years in the USA making a statue of the first European settler in North America, Thorfinn Karlsefni, for a new sculpture park in Philadelphia. Thereafter he lived in increasing isolation in his home-cum-museum in Reykjavík, withdrawing into a private world of fantasy and religious mysticism, heavy with allegory and symbolism, like *Evolution* and *New Life*. The temple -like studio home built for him by the state in Reykjavík is now the Einar Jónsson Museum.

JÓNSSON, Finnur (1858–1934) Icelandic scholar and philologist, born in Akureyri. Educated in Reykjavík and at Copenhagen, he was appointed professor of Old Icelandic studies there in 1898. He published a host of critical editions of sagas and histories, including *Hauksbók* (1892–96), *Heimskringla* (4 vols, 1893–1901), and *Egils saga* (1886–88); he also compiled a monumental History of Old Norse Literature (*Den oldnorske og oldislenske litteraturs historie*, 1894–1902), and a pioneering edition of all known Old Icelandic skaldic poetry, *Den norsk-islandske skjaldedigtning*, 4 vols, 1908–15).

JÓNSSON, Finnur (1892–1989) Icelandic Modernist painter, born on the farm of Strýta, younger brother of the sculptor Ríkarður Jónsson (1888–1977). He worked first as a seaman, then became an apprentice goldsmith and went to study in Copenhagen, where he discovered a vocation for painting in 1921. He went to Berlin, where he joined the Modernist group at Der Sturm gallery, and Dresden, where he was much influenced by **Oskar Kokoschka**. Back in Iceland he held the first-ever exhibition of abstract art in Reykjavík in 1925, causing something of a scandal, and thereafter worked in more traditional styles, painting landscapes and scenes from fishing life. His later paintings showed a return towards abstraction.

JONSTON, Arthur See **JOHNSTON, Arthur**

JOOS VAN CLEVE See **CLEVE**

JOOSS, Kurt (1901–79) German dancer, choreographer, teacher and director, born in Wasseralfingen. A student at the Stuttgart Academy of Music, he became star pupil of the theoretician **Rudolf von Laban**. While working as ballet master in Münster, he co-founded the Neue Tanzbühne for which he choreographed his first works. In 1927 he was appointed director of the dance department at the Essen Folkwang School where he founded the Folkwang Tanztheatre in 1928 which finally became the Folkwang Tanzbühne. *Le Bal* (1930), *The Prodigal Son* (1931), *Pulcinella* (1932), and two of his most memorable works, *The Green Table* (1932) and *The Big City* (1932), were made during this productive period. He left Germany during the Nazi years and toured the world, basing his company in Britain. He returned to Essen in 1949, and was ballet master of Düsseldorf Opera from 1954 to 1956. He was one of the first choreographers to blend classical technique with modern theatrical ideas to create dance for 'the common man'.

JOPLIN, Scott (1868–1917) American Negro pianist and composer, born in Texas, one of the originators of 'Ragtime' music and one of its foremost exponents. Largely self-taught, he became a professional musician in his teens, but later studied music at George Smith College, Sedalia. In the 1890s he formed and led a travelling vocal ensemble, and began to compose. His first major published work—the *Maple Leaf Rag*, named after a club in which he had played—proved to be the turning point in his career, and the resulting prosperity enabled him to concentrate on composing and teaching rather than playing. Although he was responsible for several famous and popular tunes, he was disheartened by the lack of commercial success of his two operas. Ragtime experienced a revival in the 1970s, and his music became more widely known.

JOPLIN, Thomas (c.1790–1847) English economist, born in Newcastle-upon-Tyne. He wrote a number of works on joint-stock banking in Scotland, and advocated a merger of small provincial banks. He became a director of such a scheme with the founding of the National Provincial Bank (1833) and opposed the monopoly of the Bank of England.

JORDAENS, Jakob (1593–1678) Flemish painter, born in Antwerp. He became a member of an Antwerp guild in 1616 and from 1630 came under the influence of **Rubens**, who obtained for him the patronage of the kings of Spain and Sweden. His early paintings such as the *Four Evangelists* (1632) show him to be deficient in the handling of chiaroscuro effects and colour generally, but he improved vastly in such later canvases as *The Triumph of Frederick Henry* (1652) although he never achieved the delicacy of Rubens. He also designed tapestries, and painted portraits.

JORDAN, Camille (1771–1821) French Liberal politician, born in Lyon. He supported the royalists during the Revolution and fled (1793). He subsequently became a member of the council of The Five Hundred (1797), opposed **Napoleon** and became a deputy in 1816.

JORDAN, (Marie-Ennemond) Camille (1838–1922) French mathematician, born in Lyons. Professor at the École Polytechnique and at the Collège de France, he was the leading group theorist of his day, and his *Traité de substitutions* (1870) remained a standard work for many years. He applied group theory to geometry and linear differential equations, and his *Cours d'analyse* was an influential textbook for the French school of analysts.

JORDAN, Dorothy, née **Bland** (1761–1816) Irish actress, born near Waterford. She made her début in Dublin (1777) and soon became popular, obtaining in 1782 an engagement from Tate Wilkinson at Leeds. She appeared with phenomenal success at Drury Lane in *The Country Girl* in October 1785. In 1790 she began a liaison with the Duke of Clarence, later **William IV**, which lasted until 1811 and she bore him ten children. After playing in London and in the provinces until 1814, she is said to have been compelled to retire to France for a debt of £2000. In 1831 King William made their eldest son Earl of Munster.

JORDAN, Michael Jeffrey (1963–) American professional basketball player with the Chicago Bulls since 1984, born in Brooklyn, New York. Named as the National Basketball Association's Most Valuable Player in 1988, he had already earned himself a glowing reputation as a college player. A member of the USA Olympic winning team in 1984, he holds the record for most points in an NBA play-off game (63).

JORDAN, Neil (1950–) Irish filmmaker and writer, born in Sligo. After reading history and literature at University College, Dublin, he worked at various jobs in London before returning home and helping to form the Irish Writers Co-operative (1974). His first collection of stories, *Night in Tunisia* (1976), earned the Guardian Fiction Prize and was followed by the acclaimed novels *The Past* (1980) and *The Dreams of the Beast* (1983). Interested in exploring cinema as a visual means of story-telling, he was given the opportunity to work as a script consultant on *Excalibur* (1981). He made his directorial début with the thriller *Angel* (1982) and has boldly emphasized the fairy-tale and fantasy elements of such challenging works as *The Company of Wolves* (1984) and *Mona Lisa* (1986). Recently, he has turned his hand to comedy with *High Spirits* (1988) and *We're No Angels* (1989).

JORDANES (fl.6th century) Gothic monk and historian. His chief work was a history of the Goths (*De origine actibusque Getarum*), believed to have been written in the middle of the 6th century, condensed from a lost book by **Cassiodorus**.

JORDANUS DE NEMORE (fl.c.1220) medieval French physicist. He did valuable work in mechanics, but almost nothing is known of his life, except that he lived and wrote in the first half of the 13th century; even the meaning of 'de Nemore' is unknown. Some twelve books in Latin allegedly written by him were recorded by 1260, dealing with 'the science of weights', ie statics. Here he invented the idea of component forces, studied inclined planes, made the principle of mechanical work less vague, and moved towards (but did not reach) the concept of static moment. His approach linked **Aristotle**'s ideas in physics with the more exact mathematical approach of **Archimedes**. His ideas in mechanics must have influenced **Galileo**; he also wrote (or at least has ascribed to him) treatises on geometry, algebra and arithmetic, but the significance of these on later thought is unclear.

JØRGENSEN, Anker (1922–) Danish politician. He worked his way up through the organizations of the Danish labour movement and has been a member of the Danish parliament (*Folketinget*) since 1964. From 1973 to 1987 he was leader of the Social Democratic party and was prime minister from 1972 to 1973 and again from 1975 to 1982. Since 1982 he has been chairman of the Danish delegation in the Nordic Council.

JÖRGENSEN, Johannes (1866–1956) Danish novelist and poet, born in Svendborg. He lived most of his life in Italy, in Assisi, where he became a Roman Catholic (1896), but returned to Svendborg, his birthplace, shortly before his death. He published several volumes of poetry, as well as biographies of St **Francis of Assisi** (1907), St **Catherine of Siena** (1915), and St Birgitta of Sweden (1941–43), as well as an autobiography, *Mit livs Legende* (Legend of my Life, 1916–28).

JÖRGENSEN, Jörgen, 'King of Iceland' (1779–1844) Danish adventurer, known as the 'Dog-Days King'. The son of a watchmaker, he was born in Copenhagen. An able student, he was expelled from Copenhagen University for reckless conduct, and spent several years working on a whaler in the Pacific. In 1806 he returned to Denmark and in 1807 became captain of a Danish privateer in the war against England. Captured and imprisoned, he was soon released in London on parole, and was employed by an English merchant, Samuel Phelps, as an interpreter on a trading voyage to Iceland, which was then a Danish colony. Arriving in Reykjavík on 21 June 1809, he decided to free Iceland from the imperial Danish yoke; with a small group of armed men he seized the governor, declared Iceland's independence, and proclaimed himself Protector. On 9 August 1809, at the end of the Dog-Days, a British armed sloop, the *Talbot*, arrived in Reykjavík and removed him in irons. He lived in London on his wits for some years, but was convicted of robbery in 1820 and transported to Tasmania, where he worked as a policeman and took part in expeditions of exploration.

JORN, Asger Oluf, original surname **Jørgensen** (1914–73) Danish painter, born in Vejrum, West Jutland. He studied art in Paris from 1936 with **Léger** and **Le Corbusier**, and in 1948–50 founded the 'Cobra' group (Co[penhagen], Br[ussels], A[msterdam]) which aimed to exploit fantastic imagery derived from the unconscious, undirected by reason.

JOSEPH Old Testament Hebrew figure, the elder of the two sons of **Jacob** by Rachel. His being sold into Egypt and his ultimate rise to power there are recorded in Genesis.

JOSEPH husband of the Virgin **Mary**. A carpenter in Nazareth, he appears last in the gospel history when **Jesus Christ** is twelve years old (Luke, ii. 43); he is never mentioned during **Jesus**' ministry, and may be assumed to have been already dead.

JOSEPH I (1678–1711) Holy Roman Emperor from 1705, the eldest son of **Leopold I**. He defeated the Hungarian rebels under Francis II **Rákóczi** in 1711 while Prince **Eugene** of Savoy led the imperial army in alliance with the British forces under the Duke of **Marlborough** in the continuing struggle against **Louis XIV** of France.

JOSEPH II (1741–90) emperor of Germany, son of **Francis I** and **Maria Theresa**. In 1764 he was elected king of the Romans, and after his father's death (1765) emperor of Germany; but until his mother's death (1780) his power was limited to the command of the army and the direction of foreign affairs. Although he failed to add Bavaria to the Austrian dominions (1777–79 and again in 1785), he acquired Galicia, Lodomeria, and Zips, at the first partition of Poland in 1772; and in 1780 he appropriated a great part of Passau and Salzburg. As soon as he found himself in full possession of the government of Austria he declared himself independent of the pope, and prohibited the publication of any new papal bulls without his *placet*. He suppressed 700 convents, reduced the number of the regular clergy from 63000 to 27000, prohibited papal dispensations as to marriage, and in 1781 published the Edict of Toleration for Protestants and Greeks. He also abolished serfdom, reorganized taxation, and curtailed the feudal privileges of the nobles. In 1788 he engaged in an unsuccessful war with Turkey, and in the same year there were outbreaks of insurrection within his non-German territories.

JOSEPH, king of Naples See **BONAPARTE**.

JOSEPH, Sir Keith (Sinjohn), Baron Joseph (1918–) English politician, born in London. He was a barrister before becoming a Conservative MP in 1956. A former secretary of state for social services (1970–74) and industry (1979–81), he held the education and science portfolio from 1981 to 1986. He was given an overall responsibility for Conservative policy and research in 1975 and was a close political adviser to **Margaret Thatcher**. He succeeded to the baronetcy in 1944, and was made a life peer in 1987 when he retired from active politics.

JOSEPH, Père, originally **François Joseph le Clerc du Tremblay** (1577–1638) French priest and diplomat, born in Paris. A soldier by trade, he became a member of the Capuchin order in 1599, and went on several diplomatic missions for **Richelieu**. He became known as the 'Éminence Grise' (the 'Grey Eminence') in contrast to Richelieu, the 'Éminence Rouge'.

JOSEPH OF ARIMATHEA (1st century AD) New Testament figure described as a 'councillor'. A wealthy Samaritan he went to **Pontius Pilate** and asked for the body of **Jesus** after the Crucifixion, and buried it in his own rock-hewn tomb. According to legend he visited England after the Crucifixion, bringing the Holy Grail, and built a church at Glastonbury.

JOSÉPHINE de Beauharnais, née **Marie Joséphine Rose Tascher de la Pagerie** (1763–1814) wife of **Napoleon** and French empress, born in Martinique. In 1779 she married there the Vicomte **de Beauharnais**. In 1796, two years after his execution, she married Napoleon, and accompanied him in his Italian campaign, but soon returned to Paris. At Malmaison, and afterwards at the Luxembourg and the Tuileries, she attracted round her the most brilliant society of France, and contributed considerably to the establishment of her husband's power. But the marriage, being childless, was dissolved in 1809. Joséphine retained the title of empress, and continues to lie at Malmaison where she died while Napoleon was sovereign of Elba.

JOSEPHSON, Brian David (1940–) Welsh physicist, born in Cardiff, the discoverer of tunnelling between superconductors. He studied at Cambridge and has spent his career there, as professor of physics from 1974. In 1962, while a research student, he deduced theoretically the possibility of the 'Josephson effect' on electric currents in superconductors separated by a very thin insulator. He showed theoretically that a current can flow between the superconductors with no applied voltage, and that when a DC voltage is applied an AC current of frequency proportional to the voltage is produced. The effect was soon observed experimentally by **Philip Warren Anderson**, and such *Josephson junctions* have since been much used in research and in fast switches for computers. Josephson shared the 1973 Nobel prize for physics, with **Leo Esaki** and **Ivar Giaever**.

JOSEPHUS, Flavius (c.37–c.100) Jewish historian and soldier, born in Jerusalem. He was the son of a priest, while his mother was descended from the Asmonean princes. His acquirements in Hebrew and Greek literature soon drew public attention upon him, and he became conspicuous amongst the Pharisees, the national party, at 26 being chosen delegate to **Nero** in Rome. When the Jews rose in their last and fatal insurrection against the Romans (66), Josephus, as governor of Galilee, displayed great valour and prudence; but the advance of **Vespasian** (67) made resistance hopeless, although he held out in Jotapata against a siege for 47 days. Josephus was kept in a sort of easy imprisonment for three years, and was present in the Roman army at the siege of Jerusalem by **Titus** (70). After this he appears to have resided in Rome. He survived **Herod Agrippa II**, who died in 100. His works are *History of the Jewish War*, written both in Hebrew and Greek (the Hebrew version is no longer extant); *Jewish Antiquities*, containing the history of his countrymen from the earliest times to the end of the reign of Nero; a treatise on the *Antiquity of the Jews*, against the Alexandrian Greek scholar Apion; and an *Autobiography* (37–90 AD).

JOSHUA Old Testament figure, the son of Nun, of the tribe of Ephraim, and successor to **Moses** as leader of the Israelites. He was one of the twelve spies sent to collect information about the Canaanites, and during the 40 years' wanderings acted as 'minister' or personal attendant of Moses. After 'the Lord was angry with Moses' Joshua was expressly designated to lead the people into Canaan. *The Book of Joshua* is a narrative of the conquest and settlement of Canaan under his leadership.

JOSIAH (649–609 BC) king of Judah. He succeeded his father Amon at the age of eight. He re-established the worship of Jehovah, and instituted the rites in the newly-discovered 'Book of the Law'. He fell at Megiddo attempting to check Pharaoh Necho's advance against the Assyrians.

JOSIKA, Baron Miklós von (1794–1865) Hungarian novelist in the romantic tradition of Sir **Walter Scott**. He was involved in the revolution of 1848, and had to live in exile in Brussels and Dresden.

JOSQUIN See **DES PRÉS**

JOUBERT, Joseph (1754–1824) French writer and moralist, born in Montignac in Périgord. He studied and taught at the college of Toulouse. He then went to Paris, and lived through all the fever of the Revolution. In 1809 he was nominated by **Napoleon** to the council of the new university. His friend **Chateaubriand** edited a small volume from his papers, and Joubert found fame with his *Pensées* (1838) which are in the best French tradition of **La Rochefoucauld**, **Pascal**, **La Bruyère** and **Vauvenargues**.

JOUBERT, Piet (Petrus Jacobus) (1834–1900) Afrikaanes soldier and statesman, born in Cango, Cape Colony. A farmer in the Transvaal from 1840, he studied law and was elected to parliament in 1860, becoming attorney-general (1870) and acting president (1875). In the 1st Boer War (1880–81) he commanded the Transvaal's forces, and defeated Colley in 1881. He negotiated the Pretoria Convention (1881), and became vice-president in 1883, and opposed **Kruger** for the presidency. In the 2nd Boer War (1899–1902) he held command at the outset, but resigned from ill-health and died soon afterwards.

JOUFFROY, Théodore Simon (1796–1842) French philosopher, born in Pontets in the Jura. Professor of philosophy at Paris (1817), in 1838 he became university librarian. He wrote lucid commentaries on **Thomas Reid** and **Dugald Stewart**, translated their works and wrote *Mélanges philosophiques* (1833), *Cours de droit naturel* (1835), and other works.

JOUFFROY D'ABBANS, Claude, Marquis de (1751–1832) French engineer and pioneer of steam-navigation. He served in the army, and in 1783 made a small paddle-wheel steamboat, the *Pyroscaphe*. Compelled to emigrate and ruined by the revolution, he failed to float a company till after **Robert Fulton** had made his successful experiments on the Seine in 1803.

JOULE, James Prescott (1818–89) English physicist, born in Salford, famous for his experiments in heat (the joule, a unit of work or energy is named after him). He studied chemistry under **John Dalton** and in a series of notable researches (1843–78) showed experimentally that heat is a form of energy, determined quantitatively the amount of mechanical (and later electrical) energy to be expended in the propagation of heat energy and established the mechanical equivalent of heat. This became the basis of the theory of the conservation of energy. With Lord **Kelvin**, he measured the fall in temperature when a gas expands without doing external work and formulated the absolute scale of temperature. He was also the first to describe the phenomenon of magnetostriction.

JOURDAN, Jean-Baptiste, Comte (1762–1833) French soldier, and marshal of France, born in Limoges. He joined the Revolutionary army and defeated the Austrians at Wattignies (October 1793), gained the victory of Fleurus (June 1794), and then drove the Austrians across the Rhine, took Luxembourg, and besieged Mainz. But in October, 1795, he was defeated at Höchst, and four times from 1796 to 1799 by the Archduke **Charles** of Austria. **Napoleon** employed him in 1800 in Piedmont; in 1804 he was made marshal, and in 1806 governor of Naples. In 1813 he was defeated by **Wellington** at Vitoria, and in 1814 transferred his allegiance to **Louis XVIII**, who made him a count. He supported the Revolution of 1830.

JOUVENEL, Henri de (1876–1935) French politician and journalist, husband (1910–35) of the writer **Colette**, born in Paris. He attained a high position in the ministry of justice before editing *Le Matin*. Elected senator in 1921, he was delegate to the League of Nations (1922 and 1924) and was high commissioner in Syria (1925–26).

JOUVET, Louis (1887–1951) French theatre and film director and actor, born in Finistère. He graduated as a pharmacist but took to the stage. After World War I he toured the USA with **Jacques Copeau**'s company (1918–19). He became stage-manager (1922) and director (1924) of the Comédie des Champs Élysées. Equally at home in modern as in classical French drama, he was the first to recognize **Jean Giraudoux**, all but one of whose plays (1928–46) he produced, as well as **Cocteau**'s *La Machine infernale* (1931). His company transferred to the Théâtre de l'Athénée (1934–51), but in 1936–37 he directed at the Comédiè Française outstanding productions of **Molière's** *L'École des femmes* and **Corneille**'s *L'Illusion*. He was equally outstanding as an actor in such films as *Carnival in Flanders* (1935), *Un Carnet de bal* (1937), *La Fin du jour* (1939), *Volpone* (1940) and *Retour à la vie* (1949).

JOUY, Victor Joseph Étienne de (1764–1846) French playwright, librettist, and author, born in Jouy near Versailles. Till 1797 he served as a soldier in India and at home. He wrote *L'Hermite de la Chansée d' Antin* (1812–14) and other prose works.

JOWETT, Benjamin (1817–93) English scholar, born in Camberwell. Educated at St Paul's School and Balliol College, Oxford, he was elected a fellow there in 1838, and tutor from 1840. He was elected master of Balliol in 1870; from 1855 to 1893 he was regius professor of Greek, from 1882 till 1886 vice-chancellor of Oxford University. As master of Balliol his Liberal influence permeated the college to a degree almost unexampled. Jowett belonged to the Broad Church party. For his article 'On the Interpretation of Scripture' in *Essays and Reviews* (1860) he was tried but acquitted by the vice-chancellor's court. He is best known for his fine translations of the *Dialogues* of **Plato** (1871), **Thucydides** (1881), the *Politics* of **Aristotle** (1885), and Plato's *Republic* (1894).

JOWITT, William Allen, 1st Earl Jowitt, Viscount Stevenage, (1885–1957) English judge and politician, born in Stevenage, Hertfordshire. Educated at Marlborough and Oxford, he was called to the bar in 1909 and took silk in 1922. He was Liberal MP for the Hartlepools (1922–24) and for five months for a Preston constituency (1929), which he resigned on joining the Labour party and becoming attorney-general; he was returned with an increased majority as a Socialist. In 1931 he joined the National Government, and was expelled from the Labour party, but returned to it in 1936, and became MP for Ashton-under-Lyne in 1939. In 1945 he became Lord Chancellor, and piloted through the Conservative House of Lords a mass of Socialist legislation. His publications include *The Strange Case of Alger Hiss* (1953) and *Some Were Spies* (1954).

JOYCE, Eileen Alannah (1912–) Australian concert pianist, born in Zeehan, Tasmania. Her talent was discovered by **Percy Grainger** when she was a child and she was sent at the age of 15 to study at Leipzig conservatorium under Teichmuller and **Schnabel**. In 1930 she was introduced to Sir **Henry Wood**, who immediately arranged her début at one of the famous promenade concerts under his baton. She became a prolific broadcaster and during the war frequently visited the blitzed towns of Britain with **Malcolm Sargent** and the London Philharmonic. She has toured every continent and played with many major orchestras, having a repertoire of over 50 piano concertos and numerous recital programmes. She is particularly known for her work on film soundtracks, especially of *Brief Encounter* and *The Seventh Veil* and the film of her childhood, *Wherever She Goes*. She retired prematurely in 1960 but returned to the concert platform in 1967.

JOYCE, James Augustine Aloysius (1882–1941) Irish writer, born in Dublin, which despite his long exile provides the setting for most of his work. Educated by Jesuits at Clongowes Wood College and Belvedere College, he went to University College, Dublin. A linguist and voracious reader, he corresponded with **Ibsen**. Among other influences were **Dante**, **George Moore** and **Yeats**. Catholicism's bigotry distressed him and in 1902 he went to Paris for a year, living in poverty and writing poetry. His mother's death prompted his return to Ireland, when he stayed briefly in the Martello Tower which features in the early part of *Ulysses*; he then left Ireland with Nora Barnacle, who was to be his companion for the rest of his life. He taught English for a spell in Trieste, but had to scrounge to make ends meet. After a war spent mainly in Switzerland the couple settled in Paris. By now Joyce was the author of two books: *Chamber Music* (1907) and *Dubliners* (1914), a collection of short stories that includes among other celebrated items, 'The Dead'. The stories were greeted enthusiastically, and Joyce was championed by **Pound**. The autobiographical *A Portrait of the Artist as a Young Man* appeared in instalments in *The Egoist* (1914–15). Petitioned by Yeats and Pound on his behalf, the Royal Literary Fund in 1915 made him a grant and shortly afterwards the civil list followed suit. But his health was failing, his eyesight deteriorating and he was deeply disturbed by his daughter's mental illness. In 1922 his seminal novel, *Ulysses*, was published in Paris on 2 February. It immediately provoked violent reactions, but the story of Leopold Bloom's day-long perambulation through Dublin is now regarded as epochal, a great leap forward for fiction. It was not published in the United Kingdom until 1936. Plagued by worsening glaucoma, Joyce supervised publication of *Finnegan's Wake*, in 1939. Much critical energy has been spent trying to analyze Joyce's work, but readers continue to delight in his word play, comedy and irrepressible power of invention.

JOYCE, William (1906–46) American-born British traitor, born in Brooklyn, New York, of Irish parentage. As a child he lived in Ireland and in 1922 his family emigrated to England. In 1933 he joined Sir **Oswald Mosley**'s British Union of Fascists and secured a British passport by falsely claiming to have been born in Galway. Expelled from Mosley's party in 1937, he founded his own fanatical, **Hitler**-worshipping, British National Socialist party. He fled to Germany before war broke out and from September 1939 to April 1945 broadcast from Radio Hamburg a propaganda stream of falsehood, abuse and threats against Britain. Each broadcast was heralded by the characteristic 'Chairmanny Calling', in a pretentious voice, the title 'Lord Haw-Haw' having been inherited from a previous broadcaster with an upper-class drawl. He was captured by the British at Flensburg, was tried at the Old Bailey, London, in 1945, convicted and executed. His defence was his American birth, but his British passport, valid until July 1940, established nine months of treason.

JOYNER-KERSEE, Jackie (Jacqueline) (1962–) American athlete, born in East St Louis, Illinois. At the Los Angeles Olympics of 1984, she won the heptathlon silver medal. Four years later, at Seoul, she won gold in both heptathlon and long jump. She is the sister of triple jumper Al Joyner, and sister-in-law of the sprinter Florence Griffith Joyner.

JOYNSON-HICKS, William, 1st Viscount Brentford (1865–1932) English Conservative politician. He entered parliament in 1908 and was successively postmaster-general, minister of health and home secretary (1924–29). He played a leading part in defeating the Prayer Book Measure (1927). His second son, Lancelot William, 3rd Viscount (1902–), was also a Conservative politician.

JUAN, Don See **JOHN OF AUSTRIA**

JUAN CARLOS I (1938–) king of Spain from 1975, born in Rome, the grandson of **Alfonso XIII**. He spent his childhood in Rome and Spain. In 1954 Don Juan de Borbón (his father, 3rd son of Alfonso) and General **Franco** agreed that Juan Carlos should take precedence over his father as pretender. He trained in the armed forces (1957–59) and was formally named by Franco as the future king in 1969. He became king in November 1975, on Franco's death, and has presided over a gradual return to democracy in Spain, despite internal political difficulties reflected in two attempted coups. In 1962 he married Sofia (1938–), elder daughter of King **Paul** of the Hellenes; their son, the Prince of the Artemis, was born in 1978 after their two daughters Elena (1963–) and Cristina (1965–).

JUAN DE LA CRUZ See **JOHN OF THE CROSS, St**

JUANA, 'the mad' ('la loca') (1479–1555) countess of Flanders and queen of Castile, daughter of **Ferdinand** and **Isabella** of Spain. She became the wife of Philip the Handsome of Flanders in 1495. The couple settled in Ghent and had several children, of whom the eldest was the future emperor, **Charles V**. On her mother's death in 1505, she became queen of Castile and she and Philip moved to Spain in 1506. Philip died the same year and Juana, who suffered from severe melancholia, was declared unfit to govern and was shut away under close watch in Tordesillas while her father assumed the regency of Castile. Although Ferdinand died in 1516, her son, Charles, now king of Spain, did not release her and Juana remained incarcerated, along with her youngest daughter, Catalina, until her death.

JUÁREZ, Benito Pablo (1806–72) president of Mexico, born of Zapotec Indian parents in San Pablo Guelatao, Oaxaca. He worked his way through law school, entered politics, and was elected governor of Oaxaco in 1848, winning a reputation for honesty and efficiency. In 1853, with the return of **Santa Anna** he was imprisoned then exiled to New Orleans, where he supported the Ayutla Revolution which overthrew the dictator. In 1856 Juárez, as head of the Supreme Court, oversaw a series of Liberal reform laws abolishing special military and ecclesiastical courts and restricting the ownership of real property by church and other corporate groups. Conservatives forced the resignation of President Comonfort (1858), leaving Juárez as self-proclaimed president to retreat from Mexico City to Vera Cruz, where he issued decrees abolishing religious orders, and confiscating all church property. In 1861 he entered Mexico City victorious and was elected president in his own right. But European demands for the repayment of government debts led to the occupation of the Mexican customs house at Vera Cruz, which the French emperor, **Napoleon III**, used as an excuse to occupy Mexico. Mexican Conservatives took advantage of the French presence to make **Maximilian** of Habsburg the emperor of Mexico. At the close of the US Civil War (1865), American diplomatic pressure and the threat of military force brought about the withdrawal of French troops which, combined with a series of military victories by **Porfirio Díaz**, resulted in the fall of Maximilian, who was captured and executed at Queretaro in 1867. Juárez's election to a third term as president (1867–71) was unconstitutional yet popular. His fourth election in 1871 led to revolts, which only ceased with his death. Juárez remains the embodiment of republican Mexico.

JUDAH Old Testament figure, fourth son of **Jacob** and Leah, was founder of the greatest of the twelve tribes of Israel.

JUDAS, called **Iscariot** one of the Twelve Apostles, and the betrayer of **Jesus** for 30 pieces of silver. He was probably a native of Kerioth in the tribe of Judah. He is traditionally said to have hanged himself in remorse.

JUDAS MACCABAEUS See **MACCABEES**

JUDD, Donald (1928–) American Minimalist artist, born in Excelsior Springs, Missouri. He studied at the College of William and Mary (1948-49), Columbia University (1949–53), and at the Art Student's League, (1947–48 and 1950–53). Judd, who had his first one-man show in New York in 1964, has metal boxes manufactured to his specification, spray-painted one colour and stood on the floor. He has therefore only 'minimal' contact with his work, which is deliberately non-imitative, non-expressive and not 'composed' in any traditional sense.

JUDE, St One of the Twelve Apostles, probably the Judas who was one of the 'brethran of the Lord' (Matt. xiii 55; Mark vi 3), perhaps a brother of St **James 'the Just'**. According to tradition he was martyred in Persia. His feast day is 28 October. The *Epistle of Jude* in the New Testament was placed among the *Antilegomena*, or disputed books, by the primitive Church. Many critics hold that it is directed against the Gnostics of the 2nd century.

JUDITH Old Testament Jewish heroine. In the Apocryphal *Book of Judith*, she is portrayed as a widow who made her way into the tent of Holofernes, general of **Nebuchadrezzar**, cut off his head, and so saved her native town of Bethulia.

JUDSON, Adoniram (1788–1850) American missionary, born in Malden, Massachusetts. He thought of turning playwright, but in 1812, having married, went to Burma as a Baptist missionary, and was a prisoner during the Anglo-Burmese war (1824–26). His Burmese translation of the Bible (1833) was followed by a Burmese-English dictionary (1849). He died at sea.

JUGNAUTH, Sir Aneerood (1930–) Mauritian politician. After qualifying as a barrister in London in 1954, he returned to Mauritius and was elected to the legislative council in the period before full independence in 1968. In 1970 he co-founded the socialist Mauritius Militant Movement (MMM), from which he later broke away to form his own Mauritius Socialist party (PSM), and in 1982 he became prime minister at the head of a PSM-MMM alliance. In 1983 his party was reconstituted as the Mauritius Socialist Movement (MSM) with a pledge to make the country a republic within the Commonwealth. He failed to obtain legislative approval for this constitutional change but retained his control of a MSM-led coalition in elections in 1983 and 1987.

JUGURTHA (d.104 BC) king of Numidia. By the murder of one cousin he secured a part of the kingdom of his grandfather **Masinissa**, and bribed the Roman senate to support him (116). But in spite of Roman warnings, he soon invaded his surviving cousin Adherbal's part of the kingdom, besieged him in Cirta (112), and put him and the Romans who were with him to death. Thereupon war was declared by the Romans; but, by bribery, Jugurtha contrived to baffle their power, until in 106 he had to flee to the king of Mauretania, whom **Sulla** persuaded to deliver him up. He was left to die in prison in Rome.

JUIN, Alphonse Pierre (1888–1967) French soldier, born in Bône, Algeria. He passed out top of his class, which included **Charles de Gaulle**, at the St Cyr Military Academy, fought in the Moroccan campaigns (1912–14) and World War I, and in 1938 became chief of staff in North Africa. As divisional commander in the First French Army he fought and was captured by the Germans in 1940, but was released in June 1941. He became military governor of Morocco, having declined the post of Vichy minister of war. After the Allied invasion of Tunisia, he changed sides, helped to defeat **von Arnim**'s Afrika Corps remnants and distinguished himself in the subsequent Italian campaign. He became chief of staff of the National Defence Committee in Liberated France (1944–47), was resident-general in Morocco (1947–51) and served in senior NATO commands GCB (1944). Promoted field-marshal in 1952 he broke with De Gaulle in 1960 over his Algerian policy, and retired. He wrote *La France en Algérie* (1963).

JULIA (36 BC–14 AD) Roman noblewoman, daughter of the Emperor **Augustus** and Scribonia. She was married at the age of 14 to her cousin Marcellus, a nephew of Augustus; after his death in 23 BC she married in 21 BC **Marcus Vipsanius Agrippa**, to whom she bore three sons and two daughters. He died in 12 BC, whereupon Julia was married to **Tiberius** (11 BC). The marriage was unhappy and her conduct far from irreproachable. In 2 BC her father Augustus learned of her adulteries and banished her to the isle of Pandataria, and from there to Reggio, where she died voluntarily of starvation. Her mother shared her exile.

JULIAN, Flavius Claudius Julianus, 'the Apostate' (c.331–363) Roman emperor (361–366), born in Constantinople, the youngest son of **Constantius**, and half-brother of **Constantine the Great**. On Constantine's death in 337, and the accession of his three sons, there was a general massacre of the males of the younger line of the Flavian family. Only Julian and his elder half-brother Gallus were spared, considered too young to be dangerous, while their father, brother, uncle and cousins perished. Embittered by this tragedy he lost all belief in Christianity, now an established religion. In 355 he spent a few happy months at Athens in studying Greek philosophy, and the same year was summoned to Milan to assume the rank of Caesar, and marry Helena, the sister of the emperor Constantius II (his cousin). For the next five years he served as soldier, overthrowing the Alemanni near Strasbourg, and subduing the Frankish tribes along the Rhine. He endeared himself to the soldiers by his personal courage, his success in war, and the severe simplicity of his life. The emperor became alarmed at his growing popularity and in 360 demanded that he should send some of his best troops to serve against the Persians; his soldiers, however, rose in insurrection and proclaimed him Augustus. Next, he set out with his army for Constantinople. At Sirmium on the Danube he openly declared himself a pagan. There he learnt of the opportune death of his cousin (361), which opened up to him the government of the world. The first winter he spent at Constantinople in a course of public reforms. Towards Christians and Jews he adopted a policy of toleration, but none the less he devoted himself to restoring the dignity of the old religion. He stripped the church of its privileges by every means short of persecution. He spent 362–363 at Antioch, and made himself somewhat unpopular by fixing an arbitrary price on corn in order to stave off a threatened famine. In 363 he set out against the Persians. He crossed the Tigris, advanced to Ctesiphon, was enticed farther by a Persian traitor, and was at length forced to retreat through barren country, harassed by swarms of Persian cavalry. The enemy were repeatedly beaten off, but in one of the attacks the emperor was mortally wounded by a spearthrust. Julian's extant writings are a series of *Epistles*; nine *Orations*; *Caesares*, satires on past Caesars; and the *Misopōgōn*. His chief work, *Kata Christianōn*, is lost.

JULIAN or **JULIANA OF NORWICH** (c.1342–after 1413) English mystic. Named possibly after the Norwich church outside which she became an anchoress at some stage of her life, Julian received a series of visions on 8 May 1373. Her account of these visions, written shortly afterwards, and meditations on their significanace, made 20 years later (almost the only information we have about her) have survived in mid 15th- and mid 16th-century manuscript copies, published in modern versions as the *Showings* or *Revelations of Divine Love*. Her prayers, her assurance that everything is held in being by the love of God so 'all will be well', and her characterization of the Trinity as Father, Mother, and Lord, speak to many in search of a contemporary spirituality.

JULIANA, Louise Emma Marie Wilhelmina (1909–) queen of the Netherlands (1948–80), born in The Hague and educated at Leiden University where she took a law degree. She married in 1937 Prince Bernhard zur Lippe-Biesterfeld, and they have four daughters: Queen **Beatrix Wilhelmina Armgard**; Princess Irene Emma Elizabeth (1939–), married Prince Hugo of Bourbon-Parma (1939–), son of the Carlist pretender to the Spanish throne, Prince Xavier, in 1964 (against her parents' wishes, and forfeiting her right of succession); Princess Margriet Francisca (1943–), married Pieter van Vollenhoven in 1967; and Princess Maria Christina (1947–), married Jorge Giullermo in 1975. On the German invasion of Holland in 1940 Juliana escaped to Britain and later resided in Canada. She returned to Holland in 1945, and in 1948, on the abdication of her mother Queen Wilhemina, became queen. She herself abdicated in favour of her eldest daughter, Beatrix, in 1980.

JULIUS II (1443–1513) pope from 1503, born Giuliano della Rovere in Albizuola, the nephew of **Sixtus IV**. His public career was mainly devoted to political and military enterprises for the re-establishment of papal sovereignty in its ancient territory, and for the extinction of foreign domination in Italy. To compel Venice to restore the papal provinces on the Adriatic, he entered into the league of Cambrai with the Emperor **Maximilian**, **Ferdinand of Aragon** and **Louis XII** of France, and placed the republic under the ban of the church. On the submission of Venice, suspecting the designs of Louis, he entered into a 'Holy League' with Spain and England. Louis XII ineffectually attempted to enlist the church against the pope. The Council of Pisa, convened under Louis's influence, was a failure; and the fifth Lateran Council, assembled by Julius, completely frustrated the designs of the French king. A liberal patron of the arts, he employed **Bramante** for the design of St Peter's begun in 1506, had **Raphael** brought to Rome to decorate his private apartments and commissioned **Michelangelo** for the frescoes on the ceiling of the Sistine chapel and for his own tomb. His military exploits inspired **Erasmus'** satire *Julius Exclusus*.

JULIUS III (1487–1555) pope from 1550, born Gianmaria del Monte in Rome. He was one of the three delegates to the Council of Trent, which he reopened after his election. He sent Cardinal **Reginald Pole** to organize with **Mary I, Tudor** the reunion of England with the Church of Rome.

JUMIÈGES See **ROBERT** and **WILLIAM**

JUNG, Carl Gustav (1875–1961) Swiss psychiatrist, born in Basel. He studied medicine there and worked under **Eugen Bleuler** at the Burghölzli mental clinic at Zürich (1900–09). His early *Studies in Word Association* (1904–09, in which he coined the term 'complex') and *The Psychology of Dementia Praecox* (1906–97) led to his meeting **Sigmund Freud** in Vienna in 1907. He became Freud's leading collaborator and was elected president of the International Psychoanalytical Association (1910). His independent researches, making him increasingly critical of Freud's insistence on the psychosexual origins of the neuroses, which he published in *The Psychology of the Unconscious* (1911–12), caused a break in 1913. From then onwards he went on to devolop his own school of 'analytical psychology'. He introduced the concepts of 'introvert' and 'extrovert' personalities, and developed the theory of the 'collective unconscious' with its archetypes of man's basic psychic nature. He held professorships at Zürich (1933–41) and Basel (1944–61). His other main works were: *On Psychic Energy* (1928), *Psychology and Religion* (1937), *Psychology and Alchemy* (1944), *Aion* (1951), *The Undiscovered Self* (1957) and his autobiographical *Memories, Dreams, Reflections* (1962).

JUNG, Johann Heinrich, pseud **Jung Stilling** (1740–1817) German mystic and writer. Though qualified in medicine, he became professor of political economy at Marburg (1787–1804), then at Heidelberg, and wrote semi-mystical romances and works on political economy, as well as a charming autobiography including *Heinrich Stillings Jugend*, edited by **Goethe** (1777–1804).

JUNG BAHADUR, Sir (1816–77) prime minister of Nepal. He assisted the British with a body of Gurkhas during the Indian Mutiny.

JÜNGEL, Eberhard (1934–) German Protestant theologian, born in Magdeburg. A student in Naumberg, Berlin, Zürich and Basle, he lectured in East Berlin before becoming professor of systematic theology in Zürich (1966–69), and then at Tübingen (1969–). He has written widely in German on the death of **Jesus Christ** and the doctrine of justification, on problems of religious language, and on natural theology. His works available in English include *Death* (1975), *The Doctrine of the Trinity* (1976), *God as the Mystery of the World* (1983), and *Theological Essays* (1987).

JUNIUS, Franciscus, properly **François du Jon** (1591–1677) German-born Dutch philologist, born in Heidelberg. He was brought up in Holland by his brother-in-law **Isaak Vossius**. From 1621 to 1651 he was tutor in England to the family of **Thomas Howard**, Earl of **Arundel**. He collected and edited Anglo-Saxon MSS now in the Bodleian Library, and edited works associated with **Caedmon**. He later came back to England in 1674, and died near Windsor.

JUNKER, Wilhelm Johann (1840–92) German traveller, born in Moscow. He studied medicine in Germany. In 1869 he travelled in Iceland, and in North Africa in 1873. In 1876–78 he explored the western tributaries of the Upper Nile; in 1879 he set off again and after four years among the Monbuttu and Niam-Niam, and some time with **Emin Pasha**, he returned in 1887.

JUNKERS, Hugo (1859–1935) German aircraft engineer, born in Rheydt. He was professor of mechanical engineering at Aachen (1897–1912). After World War I he founded aircraft factories at Dessau, Magdeburg and Stassfurt, which produced many famous planes, both civil and military.

JUNOT, Andoche (1771–1813) French soldier, born in Bussy-le-Grand. He entered the Revolutionary army in 1792 and distinguished himself in the early wars of the republic. He was adjutant under **Napoleon** in Egypt. In 1806 he was made governor of Paris, and in 1807 was appointed to the command of the army for Portugal. He quickly made himself master of all the strong places in the kingdom, was created Duc d'Abrantés, and appointed governor of Portugal; but, defeated by **Wellington** at Vimeiro (1808), was obliged to conclude the Convention of Cintra and retire from Portugal. He served in Germany and Russia, and after defeat at Smolensk (1812) was sent to govern Illyria. Mentally deranged, he threw himself from a window of his father's house near Dijon. His wife, the extravagant Duchesse d'Abrantès (1784–1838), gained a reputation by her *Mémoires* (1831–35).

JUNQUEIRO, Abilio Guerra (1850–1923) Portuguese lyric poet and satirist, born in Freixo. He became a deputy in 1872, opposed the Braganzas (the ruling Portuguese dynasty) and was tried for *lèse majesté* in 1907. After the revolution he was minister to Switzerland. His poetry shows the influence of **Victor Hugo**.

JUSSERAND, Jean (Adrien Antoine) Jules (1855–1932) French writer and diplomat, born in Lyon. He served in the French embassy in London from 1887 to 1890, and from 1902 to 1925 was ambassador to the USA. He wrote (in French and in English) on the English theatre (1878), an early novel (1887), a literary history of the English people (1895–1909), and *America then and now* (1916, Pulitzer prize).

JUSSIEU, Antoine Laurent de (1748–1836) French botanist, nephew of **Bernard Jussieu**. He studied at Paris under his uncle and became professor at the Jardin des Plantes (1793–1826), which he reorganized as the Muséum National d'Histoire Naturelle. He elaborated in his *Genera Plantarum* (1778–89) his uncle's system of classification.

JUSSIEU, Bernard (c.1699–1777) French botanist. A demonstrator at the Jardin des Plantes (1722), he created a botanical garden at Trianon for **Louis XV** and adopted a system which has become the basis of modern natural botanical classification. He first suggested that polyps were animals. His brother Antoine (1686–1758), a physician and professor of the Jardin des Plantes, edited **Tournefort**'s *Institutiones Rei Herbariae* (1719).

JUSTIN, St, known as **the Martyr** (c.100–c.165) Greek theologian, and one of the Fathers of the Church. Born in Sichem in Samaria, he was successively a Stoic and a Platonist; after his conversion to Christianity in Ephesus (c.130) he travelled about on foot defending its truths. At Rome between 150 and 160 he wrote the *Apologia* of Christianity addressed to the emperor **Marcus Aurelius**, followed by a second one, and a *Dialogue with Trypho*, defending Christianity against Judaism. He is said to have been martyred. His feast day is 14 April.

JUSTIN I (450–527) Byzantine emperor from 518, born in Illyria of peasant stock. He became commander in the imperial bodyguard, and in 518 was raised to the Byzantine throne by the army. Owing to his total want of learning he wisely resigned the civil administration to the quaestor Proclus. In 519 he entered into an arrangement with the pope; in 523 resigned to Theodoric, king of Italy, the right of appointing 'consuls' in Rome; and in the same year became involved in a war with the Persians. He was succeeded by his nephew **Justinian I**.

JUSTIN II (d.578) Byzantine emperor from 565. He succeeded his uncle, **Justinian I**, and married and was ruled by Sophia, the unscrupulous niece of the Empress **Theodora**. He yielded part of Italy to the Lombards, was unsuccessful against the Persians and Avars, and became insane.

JUSTINIAN I, (Flavius Petrus Sabbatius Justinianus) (c.482–565) emperor of the East Roman Empire from 527, born in Tauresium in Illyria, the son of a Slavonic peasant. The nephew of **Justin I**, he was educated at Constantinople, in 521 was named consul, and in 527 was proclaimed by Justin his colleague in the empire. Justin died the same year, and Justinian, proclaimed sole emperor, was crowned along with his wife **Theodora**, a former actress. His reign is the most brilliant in the history of the late empire. He selected the ablest generals; and under **Narses** and **Belisarius** his reign may be said to have largely restored the Roman empire to its ancient limits, and to have reunited the East and West. His first war—that with Persia—ended in a favourable treaty. But the conflict of the Blue and Green factions in 532 was an outburst of political discontent which went so far as to elect a rival emperor. Justinian had thought of flight, when Narses, Belisarius and Theodora repressed the tumults relentlessly; 35 000 victims fell in a single day. Through Belisarius's generalship, the Vandal kingdom of Africa was reannexed to the empire; and Belisarius and Narses restored the imperial authority in Rome, Northern Italy and Spain. Justinian constructed or renewed a vast line of fortifications along the eastern and south-eastern frontier of his empire which, with his great public buildings, involved a heavy expenditure. It was as a legislator that Justinian gained his most enduring renown. He set himself to collect and codify the principal imperial *constitutiones* or statutes in force at his accession. The *Codex*, by which all previous imperial enactments were repealed, was published in 529. The writings of the jurists or commentators on the

Roman law were next harmonized, and published under the title *Digesta* or *Pandectae* in 533. The direction of this work was entrusted to **Tribonianus** with a committee of professors and advocates, who also prepared a systematic and elementary treatise on the law—the *Institutiones* (533), based on the *Institutiones* of **Gaius**. A new edition of the *Codex* was issued in 534. During the subsequent years of his reign Justinian promulgated many new laws or constitutions, known as *Novellae*. The Institutes, Digest, Code and Novels together make up what is known as the *Corpus Juris Civilis*, a work which was immensely influential on the law of nearly all European countries down to modern times.

JUSTUS, of Ghent, originally **Joos van Wassenhove** (fl.c.1460–c.1480) Netherlandish painter. He became a member of the painters' guild in Antwerp in 1460, and in 1464 was a master in Ghent. There he was an associate of **Hugo van der Goes**. He left Ghent some time after 1469, and in the mid 1470s is recorded at the court of Federigo da Montefeltro, Duke of Urbino. His only surviving documented work is *The Institution of the Eucharist* (1472–74), though he is also thought to have painted a series of 28 *Famous Men* for the Ducal Palace (c.1476). His work was an important source of knowledge of the Netherlandish oil technique for contemporary Italian painters.

JUVARRA, or **Juvara, Filippo** (1678–1736) Italian architect, a supreme exponent of rococo design, born in Sicily. He studied under **Carlo Fontana** in Rome. Influenced by the Roman Baroque, **Bernini** and French planning, his major works include the Palazzo Madama in Turin (1718–21), of which only the staircase block was built, of proportions and magnificence hitherto unknown in Italy. Other works include the hunting lodge at Stupinigi, outside Turin (1729), a country palace with wings radiating from and encompassing a central grande salone, a masterpiece in which he briefly eclipsed even the splendours of **Guarini**.

JUVENAL, Decimus Junius Juvenalis (c.55–c.140) Roman lawyer and satirist, born in Aquinum in the Volscian country. He received the usual rhetorical education, and served as tribune in the army, fulfilled some local functions at Aquinum, was in Britain, and returned home in safety. He was also for a time in Egypt. His 16 brilliant satires in verse of Roman times and vices (c.100–c.128), written from the viewpoint of an angry Stoic moralist, range from exposures of unnatural vices, the misery of poverty, the extravagance of the ruling classes and the precarious makeshift life of their hangers-on, to his hatred of Jews and women. The last was the subject of his sixth satire, of which a part was not discovered until 1899. **Dryden**'s versions of five of Juvenal's satires are amongst the best of his works. **Dr Johnson** imitated two of the most famous in his *London* and *Vanity of Human Wishes*.

JUXON, William (1582–1663) English prelate, born in Chichester. Educated at Merchant Taylor's School and St John's College, Oxford, he succeeded **Laud** as its president in 1621, and became a prebendary of Chichester and dean of Worcester (1627), bishop of London (1633), and lord high treasurer (1635). In **Charles I**'s vacillation about the fate of **Strafford**, Juxon advised him to refuse his assent to the bill. He ministered to the king in his last moments and the king gave him his insignia of the Order of the Garter with the word 'Remember' before putting his head on the execution block. During the Commonwealth Juxon retired to his Gloucestershire seat, and after the Restoration was appointed archbishop of Canterbury.

K

KABALEVSKY, Dmitry Borisovich (1904–87) Russian composer and pedagogue, born in St Petersburg (Leningrad). In 1925 he entered Moscow Conservatory, studied composition with **Nikolai Miaskovsky**, and taught there himself from 1932. His prolific output included four symphonies, operas, concertos, film scores, and much chamber and piano music.

KADAR, Janos (1912–89) Hungarian politician, born in Kapoly in south west Hungary. He began life as an instrument-maker and was early attracted to the Communist party. During World War II he was a member of the central committee of the underground party, escaping from capture by the Gestapo. He emerged after the war as first party secretary and one of the leading figures of the Communist régime. In 1950, as minister of the interior, he was arrested for 'Titoist' sympathies. He was freed in 1953, was rehabilitated in 1954 and became secretary of the party committee for Budapest in 1955. When the Hungarian anti-Soviet revolution broke out in October 1956 he was a member of the 'national' anti-Stalinist government of **Imre Nagy**. On 1 November he declared that the Communist party had been dissolved as it had 'degenerated into perpetuating despotism and national slavery'. But as Soviet tanks crushed the revolution, he formed a puppet government which in the closing months of 1956 held Hungary in a ruthless reign of terror. The majority of his countrymen regarded him as a traitor, but a few saw him as a victim of forces beyond his control. He resigned in 1958, but became premier and first secretary of the central committee in 1961. In 1965 he lost the premiership, but remained first secretary. He proceeded to introduce a series of 'market socialist' economic reforms which helped raise living standards, while continuing to retain cordial political relations with the Soviet Union. In 1988 he stepped down as Communist party leader, moving to the new titular post of party president. He was stripped from this position and removed from the Communist party's central committee in 1989, shortly before his death.

KAEL, Pauline (1919–) American film critic, born in Petaluma, California. She was educated at the University of California at Berkeley. A waspish, insightful reviewer, she has been movie critic of the *New Yorker* since 1968. She has published several anthologies of her articles: *Kiss Kiss Bang Bang* (1968), *When the Lights Go Down* (1980), *5001 Nights at the Movies* (1982) and *State of the Art* (1985).

KAFKA, Franz (1883–1924) Austrian novelist, born of German Jewish parents in Prague.He graduated in law from Prague, and although overwhelmed by a desire to write, found employment (1907–23) as an official in the accident prevention department of the government-sponsored Worker's Accident Insurance Institution. A hypersensitive, almost exclusively introspective person with an extraordinary attachment to his father, he eventually moved to Berlin to live with Dora Dymant in 1923, his only brief spell of happiness before succumbing to a lung disease. His short stories and essays, including, 'Der Heizer' ('The Boilerman', 1913), 'Betrachtungen' ('Meditations', 1913) and 'Die Verwandlung' ('Metamorphosis', 1916), were published in his lifetime, but he refused to do the same for his three unfinished novels, which, through his friend **Max Brod**, were published posthumously and translated by **Edwin** and Willa **Muir**. They are *Prozess* (1925, trans The Trial, 1937), *Das Schloss* (1926, trans The Castle, 1937) and *Amerika* (1927, trans 1938). Literary critics have interpreted *Das Schloss* variously, as a modern *Pilgrim's Progress* (but there is literally no progress), as a literary exercise in Kierkegaardian existentialist theology, as an allegory of the Jew in a Gentile world, or psychoanalytically as a monstrous expression of Kafka's Oedipus complex, but his solipsism primarily portrays society as a pointless, schizophrenically rational organization into which the bewildered but unshocked individual has strayed. Kafka has exerted a tremendous influence on Western literature, not least on such writers as **Albert Camus**, **Rex Warner** and **Samuel Beckett**.

KAGANOVICH, Lazar Moiseyevich (1893–) Russian politician, born in Gomel. He joined the Communist party in 1911 and after the Revolution became secretary of the Ukrainian central committee. In 1928 he became Moscow party secretary and during the 1930s played a prominent role in the brutal, forced collectivization programme, and in the great purges of 1936–38. He also served as commissar for railways and was made a deputy chairman of the council of ministers in 1947. He survived the death of his brother-in-law, **Stalin**, in 1953, but was dismissed in 1957, being posted to a managerial position in a Siberian cement works. He retired into obscurity in Moscow, the last prominent survivor of the Stalin era.

KAGAWA, Toyohiko (1888–1960) Japanese social reformer and evangelist. A convert to Christianity, he was educated at the Presbyterian College in Tokyo, and Princeton Theological Seminary in the USA. Returning to Japan, he became an evangelist and social worker in the slums of Kobe. He became a leader in the Japanese labour movement, helping found the Federation of Labour (1918) and Farmer's Union (1921). He helped to establish agricultural collectives. He founded the Anti-War League in 1928; after World War II he was a leader in the woman suffrage movement, and helped with the process of democratization. He wrote numerous books, including the autobiographical novel *Before the Dawn* (1920).

KAGEL, Mauricio Raúl (1931–) Argentinian composer, born in Buenos Aires. Prominent in the avant-garde movement, he evolved a fantastically complex serial organization of the elements of music combined with aleatory elements drawn from random visual patterns, linguistic permutations, electronic sounds and unconventional percussion instruments. His work often had a strong visual or theatrical aspect. Since 1957 he has lived mainly in Cologne.

KAHLO, Frida (1907–54) Mexican artist, born in Coyoicoán, Mexico City, the daughter of a Jewish German immigrant photographer and a Catholic Mexican mother. A serious road accident at the age of 15 destroyed her dreams of a career as a doctor, but during her convalescence she started painting, and sent her work to the painter **Diego Rivera**, whom she married in 1928; it was a colourful but tortured marriage, in which they divorced, but ultimately remarried. Characterized by vibrant imagery, many of her pictures were striking self-portraits. Pain, which dogged her all her life, and the suffering of women are recurring and indelible themes in her surrealistic and often shocking pictures. She and Rivera mixed in a well-known circle of artists, photographers and politically controversial figures such as **Trotsky**. The surrealist poet and essayist **André Breton** likened her paintings to 'a ribbon around a bomb' (1938). In 1940 she participated in the International Exhibition of Surrealism in Mexico City, and in 1946 won a prize at the Annual National Exhibition at the Palace of Fine Arts. The Frida Kahlo Museum was opened in her house in Coyoicoán in 1958.

KAHN, Louis Isadore (1901–74) Estonian-born American architect, born in Osel (now Saaremaa). He moved to the USA in 1905 (naturalized 1917). A graduate of Pennsylvania, he taught at Yale (1947–57) and Pennsylvania (1957–74). He was a pioneer of Functionalist architecture, expressed in a New Brutalist vein, clearly demonstrated in the Richards Medical Research Building, Pennsylvania (1957–61). **Buckminster Fuller**'s geodesic designs influenced his City Tower Municipal Building, Philadelphia (with Anne Tyng, 1952–57). Further works include the Yale University Art Gallery (with Douglas Orr, 1953), the Salk Institute in La Jolla, California (1959–65), the Indian Institute of Management, Ahmedabad (with **Doshi**, 1962–74), and the Paul Mellon Center, Yale (1969–72).

KAIN, Karen (1951–) Canadian dancer, born in Hamilton, Ontario. After training with the Canadian National Ballet School she joined the company in 1969, becoming principal dancer in 1970. Canada's most popular ballerina, she has danced the major classical leads as well as interpreting roles in works by contemporary choreographers. She partnered **Rudolf Nureyev** in New York, and as guest artist at the Ballet de Marseille she created a leading role in **Roland Petit**'s *Les Intermittences du Coeur* (1974).

KAISER, Henry John (1882–1967) American industrialist, born in New York State. From 1914 to 1933 he worked on major civil engineering projects in the United States, Canada and the West Indies. As manager of seven highly productive shipyards on the Pacific coast of the United States during World War II, he developed revolutionary methods of prefabrication and assembly in shipbuilding—enabling his ships to be constructed and lauched within six days. His vast industrial empire included a motor, a steel, and an aluminium and chemical corporation.

KALAU See **CALOVIUS**

KALDOR, Nicholas, Baron Kaldor of Newnham (1908–86) Hungarian-born British economist, born in Budapest. Educated in Budapest and at the London School of Economics, he taught at LSE from 1932 to 1947. During World War II he served on both the British and US Strategic Bombing Surveys. In 1947 he became director of the research and planning commission of the Economic Commission for Europe, and was professor of economics at Cambridge from 1966 to 1975. He held a number of senior United Nations appointments, and was fiscal adviser to the Treasury and to several overseas governments. He wrote *An Expenditure Tax* (1955), advocating expenditure taxes as opposed to income tax, and *The Scourge of Monetarism* (1982).

KALECKI, Michal (1899–1970) Polish economist and economic journalist, born in Lodz. He studied engineering in Warsaw and Gdansk, and taught himself economics. He worked in Oxford at the Institute of Statistics from 1940 to 1945, was a United Nations economist from 1946 to 1954, and a government economist and teacher of economics in Poland from 1955 to 1967. A Marxist, he was critical of both capitalism and socialism. He developed a theory of macroeconomic dynamics and introduced the new western methods in economics to the Soviet bloc. His books include *Essays in the Theory of Economic Fluctuations* (1939) and *Studies in Economic Dynamics* (1943).

KÁLIDÁSA (fl. 450) India's greatest dramatist, is best known through his drama *Sákuntala*.

KALININ, Mikhail Ivanovich (1875–1946) Soviet politician, born in Tver (which was renamed after him in 1932). In early life he was a peasant and a metal-worker. Entering politics as a champion of the peasant class, he won great popularity, becoming president of the Soviet central executive committee (1919–38), and of the Presidium of the Supreme Soviet (1938–46).

KALONGA (mid 17th century–18th century) the dynastic title of the paramount chiefs of the Maravi kingdoms of central southern Africa. *Kalonga* **Muzura** in the mid 17th century allied himself with the Portuguese. A formidable warrior, he was able to subjugate the lesser kingdoms of the area but, by the beginning of the 18th century, the empire was collapsing from fragmentation amongst the ruling group and competition from the subject-peoples, particularly the Chewa kingdom whose rulers, the **Undi** replaced the *kalonga* as the dominant political authority in the area during the 18th century.

KALTENBRUNNER, Ernst (1902–46) Austrian Nazi leader, head of the SS at the time of the Anschluss. He became head of the security police in 1943, sent millions of Jews and political suspects to their deaths in concentration camps, and was responsible for orders sanctioning the murder of prisoners of war and baled-out airmen. He was condemned by the Nuremberg Tribunal and hanged.

KAMEN, Martin David (1913–) Canadian-born American biochemist, born in Toronto. He studied in Chicago and afterwards held posts in a number of US universities. He worked on a variety of topics; he showed that the oxygen formed in plants by photosynthesis is derived from water (and not from CO_2); he discovered the carbon isotope ^{14}C, afterwards much used as a biochemical tracer; he studied photosynthetic bacteria and nitrogen-fixing bacteria; and contributed to the discovery of messenger-RNA.

KAMENEV, originally **Rosenfeld, Lev Borisovich** (1883–1936) Soviet politician, born of Jewish parentage in Moscow. He was an active revolutionary from 1901 and was exiled to Siberia in 1915. Liberated during the revolution in 1917, he became a member of the Communist central committee. Expelled as a Trotskyist in 1927, he was readmitted next year but again expelled in 1932. He was shot after being arrested with **Zinoviev** for conspiring against **Stalin**. In 1988 he was posthumously rehabilitated by the new Soviet leadership, after the Supreme Court found him innocent of his alleged 1930s crimes. His wife, Tatyana, who was similarly shot after a 'show trial' in 1937, has also been rehabilitated.

KAMERLINGH ONNES See **ONNES**

KAMES, Henry Home, Lord (1696–1782) Scottish jurist, legal historian and philosopher, born in Kames, Berwickshire. Called to the bar in 1723, he was raised to the bench as Lord Kames in 1752. He was a leading figure in the Scottish Enlightenment. Besides many books on Scots law he published *Essays on Morality* (1751), *An Introduction to the Art of Thinking* (1761),

Elements of Criticism (his best-known work, 1762), and *Sketches of the History of Man* (1774).

KAMMERER, Paul (1880–1926) Austrian zoologist. Born and educated in Vienna, he joined the Institute of Experimental Biology there. His experimental work was skilful, and he claimed results in support of **Lamarck**'s view that characteristics acquired in life can be inherited by later generations. The best-known of these results concerned the development of the midwife toad, and Kammerer successfully debated his results on this when he visited Britain in 1923. However, in 1926 G K Noble of the American Museum of Natural History examined material preserved from Kammerer's work in Vienna, and showed that dark swellings which had been claimed to be nuptial pads, induced in the toads and inherited through three generations, were due to injections of ink. Kammerer shot himself a few months later. Attempts to replicate other results claimed by him were unsuccessful.

KÄMPFER, Engelbert (1651–1716) German traveller and physician. After visiting India, Java and Siam, he spent two years in Japan (1692–94). His *History of Japan and Siam* appeared in English in 1727.

KAMPRAD, Ingvar (1926–) Swedish businessman, born in Pjätteryd, reputed to be the third richest man in Sweden. He is the founder (1943) and owner of the IKEA furniture company, whose products have established themselves as a life-style for many Swedes. Even though the company now has 64 outlets worldwide and has diversified into the financial and insurance sectors, its centre remains the Småland village of Ämhult.

KANĀDA (c.300 BC) Indian founder of the *Vaiśeshika* school of Hindu philosophy, sometimes identified with the legendary sage Kāśyapa. Kanāda, meaning 'eater of atoms', may just be a descriptive name for the otherwise unknown author of the *Vaiśeshika Sūtra*, a work which holds that things are made of invisible eternal atoms of earth, water, light or air. Although Kanāda himself does not mention God, later commentators saw a need for a supreme being to regulate the atoms and account for the existence of the world.

KANARIS, Constantine (1790–1877) Greek naval officer and statesman, born on the Isle of Ipsara. A merchant-captain, he was one of those who provided their own ships for service in the struggle for Greek independence. He used fireships to blow up the Turkish flagship in the Strait of Chios (1822), repeated the feat in the harbour of Tenedos, and in 1824 burnt a Turkish frigate and some transport ships. He was appointed to important commands, and was made a senator in 1847. He was prime minister of Greece on three occasions between 1848 and 1877, and took part in the revolution that put **George I** on the throne in 1863.

KANDINSKY, Vasily (1866–1944) Russian-born French painter, born in Moscow, the originator of Abstract Painting. After studying law in Munich, he went to Paris where, at the age of 30, he began painting. A watercolour produced as early as 1910 can be called 'abstract', but in fact all representational elements were not banished from his work until the 1920s. In Paris he absorbed the influence of the Nabis and the Fauves, but Russian icon painting and folk-art were equal influences on him. In this he was at one with his Russian contemporaries. He moved to Munich in 1896. In 1912 he published his famous book, *On the Spiritual in Art* and in the same year was a co-founder with **Franz Marc** and **Paul Klee** of the Blaue Reiter ('Blue Rider') Group. He returned to Russia to teach in 1914, and after the Russian Revolution became head of the Museum of Modern Art (1919) and founded the Russian Academy (1921). In 1922 he left Russia and was eventually put in charge of the Weimar Bauhaus School. From 1920 his paintings are predominantly geometric, in line with the Suprematist and Constructivist work he had left behind in Moscow, which was eventually to fall out of favour there. In 1933 he moved to France (he became a naturalized citizen in 1939), and came under the influence of **Miró**. As a theoretician he has exerted considerable influence.

KANE, Bob (Robert) (1916–) American cartoonist and animator, born in New York, the creator of *Batman*. He studied art at Cooper Union, joined the **Max Fleischer** Studio as a trainee animator in 1934, and entered the comicbook field with *Hiram Hick* in *Wow* (1936). His early strips were humorous, but mystery and menace entered his serial, *Peter Pupp*, in *Wags* (1937), where a cartoon hero battled a one-eyed super-villain. Working to scripts by his partner, Bill Finger (1917–74), he created *The Batman* for No.27 of *Detective Comics* (May 1939), which caught on rapidly. Kane returned to animation to create *Courageous Cat* (1958) and *Cool McCool* (1969) for television.

KANE, Elisha Kent (1820–57) American arctic explorer, born in Philadelphia. Entering the US navy as surgeon, he visited China, the East Indies, Arabia, Egypt, Europe, the west coast of Africa, and Mexico. In 1850 he sailed as surgeon and naturalist with the first expedition financed by **Henry Grinnell** in search of Sir **John Franklin** (1850–51). His account of it appeared in 1854. In 1853 he again set out as commander of a second arctic expedition (1853–55).

KANHAI, Rohan Babulal (1935–) West Indian cricketer, born in Berbice, Guyana. Small in stature but immensely powerful, he was one of the West Indies' leading batsmen in the 1960s and 1970s. He played in 79 Tests, including 61 consecutive appearances, scoring 6277 runs and 15 centuries (two in the match against Australia at Adelaide in 1960–61). His fiery temper sometimes brought him into confrontation with umpires, but he rendered great service to his country and to Warwickshire, where he played for several seasons.

KANO, Motonobu (1476–1559) Japanese painter, born in Kyoto. He was the son of the painter Kano Masanobu (1434–1530), who had introduced the Kano style of painting which was directed at the feudal lords and warriors and not, as before, at the monks and priests. Borrowing from Buddhist and Chinese sources, the new style nevertheless had a nationalistic character. The latter was exemplified by Motonobu, who achieved a synthesis of Kanga (ink painting in the Chinese style) with the lively colours of Yamato-e (the Japanese style) and arrived at the decorative art of a dynamism hitherto unknown. Under him the Kano School established itself, artistically as well as socially, and became a virtual academy. His most famous works, originally in various sanctuaries and monasteries in Kyoto, now preserved in its National Museum, show the decorative treatment of nature, which became standard for the Kano school.

KANT, Immanuel (1724–1804) German philosopher, one of the great figures in the history of western thought. The son of a saddler, he was born in Königsberg, Prussia (now Kaliningrad in the USSR), and stayed there all his life. He studied and then taught at the university, becoming professor of logic and metaphysics in 1770. He lived a quiet, orderly life and local people were said to set their watches by the time of his daily walk. His early publications were in the natural sciences, particularly geophysics and astronomy, and in an essay on Newtonian cosmology

(*Allgemeine Naturgeschichte und Theorie des Himmels*, 1755) he anticipated the nebular theory of **Laplace** and predicted the existence of the planet Uranus before its actual discovery by **William Herschel** in 1781. He published extensively, but his most important works were produced relatively late in his life: the *Kritik der reinen Vernunft* (Critique of Pure Reason, 1781), *Kritik der praktischen Vernunft* (Critique of Practical Reason, 1788), and *Kritik der Urteilskraft* (Critique of Judgement, 1790). The first of these is a philosophical classic, though a very difficult one, which he himself described as 'dry, obscure, contrary to all ordinary ideas, and prolix to boot'. In it he responds to **Hume**'s empiricism and argues that the immediate objects of perception depend not only on our sensations but also on our perceptual equipment, which orders and structures those sensations into intelligible unities. He likened his conclusions to a Copernican revolution in philosophy, whereby some of the properties we observe in objects are due to the nature of the observer, rather than the objects themselves. There are basic concepts (or 'categories'), like cause and effect, which are not learnt from experience but constitute our basic conceptual apparatus for making sense of experience and the world. The second *Critique* deals with ethics, and his views are developed in the *Grundlagen zur Metaphysik der Sitten* (Groundwork to a Metaphysic of Morals, 1785) where he presents the famous Categorical Imperative, 'Act only on that maxim which you can at the same time will to become a universal law'. The third *Critique* deals with aesthetics or judgments of 'taste', for which he tries to provide an objective basis and which he connects with our ability to recognize 'purposiveness' in nature. He also wrote on political topics, and his *Perpetual Peace* (1795) advocates a world system of free states. Kant described his philosophy as 'transcendental' or 'critical' idealism, and he exerted an enormous influence on subsequent philosophy, especially the idealism of **Fichte**, **Hegel** and **Schelling**.

KANTOR, Tadeusz (1915–) Polish stage director and designer. He designed stage sets for the Stary Theatre, Cracow, from 1945 to 1955 before founding his own experimental theatre company, Cricot 2. The world tour of his own play, *Dead Class* (1975), a largely silent piece involving the actors portraying corpses in a school classroom, brought him international acclaim. Another of his plays, *Wielopole, Wielopole*, was seen in Italy in 1979, and at the Edinburgh Festival and London a year later.

KANTOROVICH, Leonid Vitaliyevich (1912–86) Soviet economist and mathematician, born in St Petersburg (Leningrad), and educated there. He was a professor at Leningrad State University (1934–60) and, later, was director of the mathematical economics laboratory at the Moscow Institute of National Economic Management (1971–76) and the Institute of System Studies at the Moscow Academy of Sciences (from 1976). He shared the 1975 Nobel prize for economics with **Tjalling Koopmans**.

KAPILA (7th century BC) Indian founder of the Sāmkhya school of Hindu philosophy. An almost legendary figure, said to have spent the latter half of his life on Sagar Island at the mouth of the Ganges, he is held to be the originator of the philosophical system presently expounded in the 3rd–5th century AD commentary of Iśvarakrishna and the *Sāmkhya Sūtra* (c. 1400 AD). It is notable for parallels with Buddhist thought and a theory of evolution or constant 'becoming' of the world.

KAPITZA, Peter, Russ **Pyotr Leonidovich Kapitsa** (1894–1984) Russian physicist, born in Kronstadt. He studied at Petrograd and under **Ernest Rutherford** at Cambridge, where he became assistant director of magnetic research at the Cavendish laboratory (1924–32). In 1934 he returned to Russia, where he was appointed director of the Institute of Physical Problems. He was dismissed in 1946 for refusing to work on the atomic bomb, but reinstated in 1955. He is known for his work on high-intensity magnetism, on low temperature, and on the liquefaction of hydrogen and helium, and was awarded the 1978 Nobel prize for physics, jointly with **Arno Penzias** and **Robert Wilson**.

KAPLAN, Viktor (1876–1934) Austrian inventor, born in Murz. Educated as a mechanical engineer at the Technische Hochschule in Vienna, from 1903 he taught at the equivalent institution in Brunn. In his research he experimented with a propeller turbine working at very low heads of water, and found that its efficiency was greatly improved if the angle of the blades could be varied to suit the operating conditions. He patented the Kaplan turbine in 1920 and it has since been used in most of the world's low-head (less than about 30 metres) hydro power schemes, as well as in the world's first major tidal power scheme on the estuary of the river Rance in Brittany.

KAPP, Friedrich (1824–84) German politician. He went to New York after the 1848 revolution, returned to Berlin in 1870, wrote a number of histories, including *Aus und über Amerika* (1876), and was a member of the Reichstag from 1871 to 1878 and 1881 to 1884.

KAPP, Wolfgang (1858–1922) German revolutionary, son of **Friedrich Kapp**, born in New York. A civil servant and director of the Prussian agricultural banks, he founded the German Fatherland party in 1917. A member of the Reichstag from 1918, in 1920 he led a monarchist putsch against the Weimar republic. He seized Berlin and declared himself chancellor, but was baulked by a general strike. He fled to Sweden, but returning to Germany in 1922 he was arrested, and died while awaiting trial.

KAPROW, Allen (1927–) American avant-garde artist and theorist, born in Atlantic City. He studied art under the influential painter and theorist **Hans Hofmann** (1947–48), and music under **John Cage** (1956–58). Rejecting such traditional values as craftsmanship and permanence, he instead promotes 'happenings', involving spectator participation, and welcoming unplanned, chance developments. He has had many exhibitions, at Amsterdam and Stockholm 1961, Paris 1963, Boston and New York 1966, and elsewhere.

KAPTEYN, Jacobus Cornelius (1851–1922) Dutch astronomer, born in Barnevelt. Professor at Groningen from 1878, he plotted the stars of the southern hemisphere from the photographic survey of Sir **David Gill**, and is celebrated for his discovery that all stars whose proper motion can be detected are part of one of two streams moving in different directions at different speeds.

KARA MUSTAFA (d.1683) Turkish grand vizier. He was brought up in the family of grand vizier Mehmet **Köprülü**, whose daughter he married. On the death of Fazil Ahmed **Köprülü** in 1676, Kara Mustafa became grand vizier and in 1682 conquered the whole of upper Hungary while gathering a huge army for an assault upon Vienna. The Austrians, reinforced by the Polish king **John Sobieski**, forced the Ottomans to retreat, and Kara Mustafa was dismissed and executed in Belgrade.

KARADJORDJEVIĆ ruling dynasty of Serbia and Yugoslavia, descended from Kara Djordje Petrović ('Black George' c.1752–1817), a pig-dealer from Topola, who, after rebelling against Serbia's Turkish overlords, was accepted as supreme leader of the Serbs from 1804 to 1813. His son, Alexander Karadjordjević (1806–85), reigned as sovereign prince of Serbia (1842–59).

KARADŽIĆ, Vuk Stefanović (1787–1864) Serbian poet and philologist, born in Tršić. He published collections of national songs and tales, and evolved the simplified Cyrillic alphabet in order to produce literature in the vernacular. He translated the New Testament into Serbian.

KARAJAN, Herbert von (1908–89) Austrian conductor, born in Salzburg. After studying in Salzburg and Vienna, his career began at the opera houses of Ulm (1927–33) and Aachen (1933–42). He conducted at the Berlin Staatsoper (1937–45) with growing fame. He joined the Nazi party in 1933 and was 'denazified' by the Allied occupation forces in 1946. After the war he was associated principally with the Berlin Philharmonic Orchestra, the Salzburg Festival (director 1964–88), the Vienna State Opera and the Vienna Gesellschaft der Musikfreunde. He conducted at Bayreuth, Edinburgh and other major festivals. His passion for the theatre and for acoustical research was evident in his work as an opera producer, in his idiosyncratic casting, the refined, brilliant (yet often controversial) quality of his recordings, and in the films he directed and conducted.

KARAMANLIS, Konstantinos (1907–) Greek politician. A former lawyer, he held several government posts before being called upon by King **Paul I** to form a government in 1955. He remained prime minister almost continuously for eight years, during which time Greece signed a treaty of alliance with Cyprus and Turkey. After his party's election defeat in 1963 he left politics and lived abroad, but he returned to become prime minister in 1974, supervising the restoration of civilian rule after the collapse of the military government. He was president 1980–85.

KARAMZIN, Nikolai Mikhailovich (1766–1826) Russian historian and novelist, born in Mikhailovka in Orenburg. Among his writings are *Letters of a Russian Traveller* (1790–92), an account of his travels in western Europe, several novels, including *Poor Lisa* (1792) and *Natalia, the Boyar's Daughter* (1792), and a great unfinished *History of Russia* (1816–29) down to 1613. His influence on the literature of Russia and its development was considerable. He modernized the literary language by his introduction of western idioms and his writing as a whole reflected western thought.

KARL, emperor of Austria See **CHARLES**

KARL, (Charles) fifteen kings of Sweden, of whom the first six are legendary or fictitious:

KARL VIII (Charles VIII) (1408–70) also known as Karl Knutsson, king of Sweden 1448–57, 1464–65, and 1467–70, and of Norway, 1449–50. A powerful Swedish magnate, he was appointed guardian of the realm, 1438–40. During the reign of Kristofer of Bavaria he was given large fiefs in Finland, but was brought back and elected king as Karl VIII on Kristofer's death in 1448, and elected king of Norway in 1449. He lost the Norwegian throne immediately to **Kristian I** of Denmark, and in 1457 was driven from Sweden by an insurrection in favour of Kristian. He was twice recalled to the throne by warring factions of the nobility before his death in 1470.

KARL IX (Charles IX) (1550–1611) king of Sweden from 1604, youngest son of **Gustav I Vasa** and his second wife Margareta Leijonhufvud, half-brother of **Erik XIV** and uncle of King **Sigismund III Vasa** of Poland and Sweden. In 1568, as Duke Karl, he led a rebellion against Erik XIV which deposed him and brought their brother **Johann III**, the second son of Gustav I Vasa, to the throne (1568–92). A champion of Lutheranism, he resisted the Counter-Reformation promoted by Johan III and his son and successor Sigismund III; he called the Convention of Uppsala in 1593 which renounced Catholicism before the Catholic Sigismund arrived from Poland for his coronation, then took over as regent during his renewed absence. When Sigismund returned in 1598 to reclaim his kingdom, Duke Karl defeated and deposed him, declaring himself 'administrator of the realm' in 1599. He was formally proclaimed king as Karl IX in 1604. He fought a long and inconclusive war with Poland (1600–10), and in the last year of his reign Sweden was invaded by Denmark under **Kristian IV** in the Kalmar War (1611–13). He married first Maria of the Palatinate, then Kristina of Holstein-Gottorp, and was succeeded by his young son, **Gustav II Adolf**.

KARL X GUSTAV (Charles X) (1622–60) king of Sweden from 1654, cousin and successor of Queen **Kristina**. The son of John Casimir, Count Palatine, and Catherine, daughter of **Karl IX** and sister of **Gustav II Adolf**, he was trained at the military academy in Sorö (Denmark). An outstanding soldier, he took part in the Thirty Years' War as generalissimo of the Swedish forces in Germany, and was appointed crown prince in 1650. He succeeded to the throne on Kristina's abdication. He overran Poland in 1655 and forced the elector of Brandenburg to acknowledge his lordship over Prussia, and in 1656 crushed the Polish forces anew in a terrible three-day battle at Warsaw (28–30 July 1656). His next war was with the Danes (1657–58), when he crossed the Little and Great Belt on the ice in one of the most daring exploits in military history and seized Zealand, and extorted from the Danes through the treaty of Roskilde (1658) the southern parts of the Scandinavian peninsula which had been Danish-held territory for centuries. Later in the year he launched a new attack on Denmark, but with Dutch help the Swedes were repulsed at the gates of Copenhagen by King **Frederik III** on the ramparts with his troops. He died suddenly the following year at Gothenburg and was succeeded by his four-year-old son, **Karl XI**. He was married to Hedvig Eleonora of Holstein-Gottorp (d.1715).

KARL XI (Charles XI) (1655–97) king of Sweden from 1660, son and successor of **Karl X Gustav**. After twelve years of regency rule by the nobility, he assumed power in 1672, and in 1675 helped to staunch a Danish invasion by his gallantry in the field at Lund, and won favourable terms in the ensuing peace treaty (1679). In the aftermath of the war he severely trimmed the power of the nobility (the so-called 'Reduction' in which the lands of the nobles were reduced) and reorganized the armed forces and the administration. In 1693 he was granted almost absolute monarchical power, with which he carried out far-reaching reforms in the administration of the country. He was married to Ulrika Eleonar 'the Elder' of Denmark (1656–93), and was succeeded by his adolescent son, **Karl XII**.

KARL XII (Charles XII) (1682–1718) king of Sweden from 1697, son and successor of **Karl XI** and Ulrika Eleonora 'the Elder' of Denmark, and one of Sweden's greatest warrior kings. He assumed the throne at the age of 15, having been declared of age. In 1700 the Great Northern War broke out, with a joint invasion of Swedish territory by Denmark and Saxony. Karl initially had no desire for war himself, but when Russia joined the alliance later in the year he counter-attacked by invading Denmark, and with the help of an Anglo-Dutch squadron commanded by Sir **George Rooke** forced the Danes, under his great rival Frederik IV, to sue for peace. In November 1700 he force-marched his army of 8000 men into Estonia and routed a huge Russian army besieging Narva, and in the following year gained a costly victory over the Saxons on the river Dvina. Next he defeated the Saxons at Kliszow in 1702, and in 1704 dethroned King **Augustus II** of Poland in favour of his ally **Stanislaw Leszczynski**. His victories were consolidated at the Peace of Altansträdt in 1706. In furtherance of his grand design of total Swedish dominion of the Baltic, in 1707 he launched a surprise invasion of Russia, and almost captured the tsar, **Peter I, the Great**, at Grodno. But his plan for a direct march on Moscow failed and after a terrible winter the Swedes were heavily defeated at Poltava in June 1709. The Swedish army surrendered at Prevolotjna, and Karl escaped with difficulty to Bender in the Crimea, where he spent the next five years in virtual internment but constantly importuning the Turks to make war on Russia, until he was eventually arrested after a bloody fracas at Bender. Later that year he made an astonishing incognito journey across half of Europe, covering 1250 miles on horseback in 15 days to the Baltic port of Stralsund. Cornered there by a ring of enemies for a year, he escaped in December 1715 to Lund in Sweden, 15 years after he had left his homeland. Undaunted, he raised a new army to keep the Russians at bay, and in 1716 launched a preliminary attack on Norway. He now formed an ambitious plan: he would be given freedom by Russia to conquer Norway in exchange for the Baltic provinces of Sweden, and then land in Scotland to put the Jacobite **James Stewart**, the 'Old Pretender', on the British throne. But having made his treaty with the Russians and invaded Norway again in 1718, he was shot dead at the siege of the border fortress of Fredriksten, near Frederikshald. A man of great ability, circumstances had made him a military adventurer, and by the end of his life he had become a futile victim of his own glittering legend. He died unmarried, and was succeeded by his younger sister, Queen **Ulrika Eleonora**.

KARL XIII (1748–1818) king of Sweden from 1809 and of Norway from 1814, younger brother of **Gustav III**, and uncle and successor to his nephew **Gustav IV Adolf**. As Duke of Sudermania he commanded the Swedish fleet against Russia (1788–90), and after his brother's assassination in 1792 was made regent during the minority of his nephew (1792–96). When Gustav IV Adolf was deposed in 1809, Karl was elected king, and signed a new constitution limiting the powers of the monarchy. In the following year, the French marshal **Bernadotte** was elected crown prince and adopted by the king as **Karl Johan** (Charles John); he soon took over the reins of power, and in 1814 secured the crown of Norway for Sweden. Karl XIII was married to Charlotte of Oldenburg (d.1818), whose diary is an important source for the history of her time.

KARL XIV JOHAN (Charles John, originally **Jean Baptiste Jules Bernadotte)** (1763–1844) king of Sweden and Norway from 1818. Born a lawyer's son in Pau in France, he joined the French army as a common soldier in 1780, became an ardent partisan of the Revolution and found rapid promotion to brigadier-general in 1794 and then marshal in 1804. For his gallantry at the battle of Austerlitz in 1805 he was created prince and Duke of Pontecorvo. But he was never liked nor fully trusted by **Napoleon**. In 1810 he was elected crown prince of Sweden and Norway and heir to the elderly, childless **Karl XIII**; he turned Protestant, and assumed the name of Karl Johan. When the king's health failed in the following year, Bernadotte took command of affairs. Swedish interests now came first. Instead of supporting Napoleon he made alliance with Russia, helped defeat Napoleon in the battle of Nations in 1813, and in 1814 attacked Denmark and secured a union between Norway and Sweden which lasted until 1905. He succeeded to the throne on the king's death in 1818, and throughout his reign tried to resist the growing tide of liberalism which wanted to curtail the autocratic powers of the crown; in this he was only partially successful. He became the founder of the present royal dynasty of Sweden; in 1798 he had married Desirée (Desideria) Clary, daughter of a wealthy Marseilles merchant, and was succeeded on his death by his son **Oskar I**.

KARL XV (Charles XV) (1826–72) king of Sweden and Norway from 1859, son and successor of **Oskar I**. As crown prince he was an enthusiastic supporter of the idea of a united Scandinavia; but after his accession in 1859 the dream died. He promised to support Denmark in her border disputes with Germany, but when Denmark declared war on Germany in 1864 over Schleswig-Holstein the Swedish government refused to honour the king's pledge. During his reign the old Riksdag of the four Estates was replaced in 1865–66 by a Riksdag of two chambers with equal rights. A cheerful and flamboyant character, he was also a poet and artist of ability. Married to Lovisa of the Netherlands, he left no son and was succeeded by his younger brother, **Oskar II**.

KARLE, Jerome (1918–) American physicist, born in New York City. He studied at the City College of New York, at Harvard, and Michigan University. He made his career in the US Naval Research Laboratories in Washington, specializing in diffraction methods for studying the fine structure of crystalline matter. For his major contribution in this important field, he shared the Nobel prize for chemistry in 1985 with **Herbert Hauptman**.

KARLFELDT, Erik Axel (1864–1931) Swedish lyric poet, born in Folkärna, Dalarna. He published several volumes of highly individual nature poetry reflecting the traditional language and customs of peasant life in his native province. Critics have not been kind to his poetry, but it has proved enduringly popular with the public. He was secretary of the Swedish Academy from 1912. He was posthumously awarded the 1931 Nobel prize for literature.

KARLOFF, Boris, originally **William Henry Pratt** (1887–1969) English-born American film star, born in London. The youngest child of a civil servant, he was educated at Uppingham, Merchant Taylor's School, London, and London University. Originally aiming for a diplomatic career, he went to Canada and the USA at the age of 21 and became involved in acting. He spent ten years in repertory companies, then went to Hollywood, and after several silent films made his name as the monster in *Frankenstein* (1931). Apart from a notable performance in a World War I story, *The Lost Patrol* (1934), his career was mostly spent in popular horror films, though his performances frequently transcended the crudity of the genre, bringing, as in *Frankenstein*, a depth and pathos to the characterization of monsters, ghosts, resurrected Egyptian mummies, etc. He made a successful return to the stage in *Arsenic and Old Lace* (1941), and was a particularly effective Captain Hook in *Peter Pan* (1951). He continued to appear in films and on television and the stage until his death.

KARMAL, Babrak (1929–) Afghan politician, the son of an army officer. Educated at Kabul University, where he studied law and political science, he was imprisoned for anti-government activity during the early 1950s. In 1965 he formed the Khalq ('masses') party and, in 1967, the breakaway Parcham ('banner') party. These two groups merged in 1977 to form the banned People's Democratic party of Afghanistan (PDPA), with Karmal as deputy leader. After briefly holding office as president and prime minister in 1978, he was forced into exile in eastern Europe, returning in 1979, after the Soviet military invasion, to become head of state. Karmal's rule was fiercely opposed by the mujahadeen guerrillas and in 1986 he was replaced as president and PDPA leader by **Najibullah Ahmadzai**.

KÁRMÁN, Theodore von (1881–1963) Hungarian-born American physicist and aeronautical engineer, born in Budapest, sometimes called the father of modern aerodynamics. He graduated as an engineer from Budapest Technical University (1902), gained a PhD under **Ludwig Prandtl** at Göttingen (1908), and in 1912 became professor of aeronautics and mechanics at the University of Aachen and head of the Aeronautical Institute there. After visits to the USA in 1926, he became director of the Guggenheim Aeronautical Laboratories (1930–49) and the Jet Propulsion Laboratory (1942–45) at the California Institute of Technology. He founded the Aerojet Engineering Corporation in the early 1940s. In 1951 he founded the major international aerospace research organization AGARD (Advisory Group for Aeronautical Research and Development) as part of NATO. He was the first recipient of the National Medal of Science in 1963, and published major works in many fields. Several theories bear his name, such as the Kármán vortex street (1911).

KÁROLY See **CHARLES, emperor of Austria**

KARP, David (1922–) American author, born in New York of Russian-Jewish descent. He served in the American army, worked as a journalist, as a radio, TV and paperback writer, and emerged as a serious novelist with *One* (1953), an Orwellian condemnation of totalitarianism. Other works include *The Day of the Monkey* (1955), on British colonialism, *All Honourable Men* (1956), *The Sleepwalkers* (1960), and *Last Believers* (1964).

KARPOV, Anatoly Yevgenyevich (1951–) Russian chess player and world champion (1975–85). Born in Zlatoust, in the Urals, he received early chess tuition from former world champion **Mikhail Botvinnik**, winning the 1969 world junior championship. After **Bobby Fischer** refused to defend his title, he became world champion by default in 1975, defending his title successfully against Viktor Korchnoi in 1978 and 1982, in acrimonious matches. His 1984–85 defence against **Gary Kasparov** was controversially halted by FIDÉ (Fédération Internationale des Échecs) when he led but showed signs of cracking under the physical and psychological pressure. Kasparov won the title when the match was resumed from scratch in 1985. Karpov made unsuccessful attempts to regain his title from Kasparov in 1986 and 1987.

KARR, (Jean Baptiste) Alphonse (1808–90) French writer, born in Paris. His *Sous les tilleuls* (1832) by its originality and wit found its author an audience for a long series of novels, of which *Geneviève* (1838) is the best. In 1839 he became editor of *Le Figaro*, and started the issue of the bitterly satirical *Les Guêpes*. His *Voyage autour de mon jardin* (1845) is his best-known book. He wrote his reminiscences, *Livre de bord* (4 vols, 1879–80). His daughter, Thérèse (1835–87), published tales and historical books.

KARRER, Paul (1889–1971) Swiss chemist, born in Moscow. Educated at Zürich, where he became professor of organic chemistry (1919), he was the first to isolate vitamins A and K, and he produced synthetically vitamins B_2 and E. He shared the Nobel prize for chemistry with Sir **Walter Haworth** in 1937.

KARSAVINA, Tamara Platonovna (1885–1978) Russian-born British dancer, born St Petersburg (Leningrad). She trained at the Imperial Ballet School at the time **Cecchetti** was teaching, and joined the Maryinsky Theatre in 1902. In 1909 she also became one of the original members of **Diaghilev**'s company for which she created roles in ballets by **Michel Fokine** and **Nijinsky**. She moved to London in 1918 with her husband, an English diplomat, though always remained associated with the Russian ballet, guesting with Diaghilev's Ballet Russes and later advising on recreating Diaghilev productions. She was vice-president of the Royal Academy of Dancing until 1955 and wrote several books, including the autobiographical *Theatre Street* (1930), *Ballet Technique* (1956), and *Classical Ballet* (1962).

KARSH, Yousef (1908–) Turkish-born Canadian photographer, born in Mardin, Turkey, who emigrated to Canada in 1924. He was apprenticed to a Boston portraitist (1928–31), and in 1932 opened his own studio in Ottawa, being appointed official portrait photographer to the Canadian government in 1935. His wartime studies of **Winston Churchill** and other national leaders were widely reproduced, and he has continued to portray statesmen, artists and writers throughout the world.

KARTINI, Raden Adjeng (1879–1904) Javanese aristocrat, one of the first to advocate equal opportunities for Indonesian women. Her ideas and aspirations, as expressed in letters to a Dutch penfriend, were published as *Door duisternis tot licht* (1911). She set up a school in her house in 1903, with the blessing of the country's education minister. She later started another school with her husband, the regent of Renbang, but died soon after giving birth to her first child.

KASPAROV, Gary Kimovich originally **Gary Weinstein** (1963–) Russian chess player, born in Baku, and world champion since 1985. His surname was changed by the authorities after the death of his father in a road accident. He won the USSR under-18 championship at the age of twelve and became world junior champion at 16. His 1984–85 match with **Anatoly Karpov** for the world title was the longest in the history of chess—after 48 games, played over six months in Moscow, he had recovered from 0–5 to 3–5, with Karpov requiring only one more win, but showing signs of cracking under the physical and psychological pressure. In one of the most controversial decisions ever made in chess history, the match was abandoned by FIDÉ, and the players were given six months to recuperate. On resumption from scratch he won the title, which he defended successfully against Karpov in 1986 and 1987. Long-term friction between him and FIDÉ resulted in his establishing the Grandmasters' Association in 1987. In an autobiography, *Child Of Change* (1987), he portrayed himself as a chess product of the revolution of Soviet life instituted under **Gorbachov**'s policy of *glasnost*.

KASSAI See **THEODORE**

KASSEM, Abdul Karim (1914–63) Iraqi soldier and revolutionary, born in Baghdad, the son of a carpenter. He joined the army and by 1955 had risen to the rank of brigadier. In 1958 he led the coup which resulted in the overthrow of the monarchy and the deaths of King **Faisal II**, his uncle Prince Abdul Ilah, and the pro-western prime minister General **Nuri Es-Sa'id**. Kassem suspended the constitution and established a left-wing military régime with himself as prime minister and head of state, but soon found himself increasingly isolated in the Arab world. He survived one assassination attempt, but failed to crush a Kurdish rebellion (1961–63) and was killed in a coup led by

Colonel Salem Aref, who reinstated constitutional government.

KASTLER, Alfred (1902–) French scientist. As laboratory director of the École Normale Supérieure in Paris (1941–72), he was awarded the Nobel prize for physics in 1966 for his work on the development of lasers.

KÄSTNER, Erich (1899–1974) German writer, born in Dresden. He is best known for his books for children. His writing career, however, began with two volumes of verse, *Herz auf Taille* (1928) and *Lärm im Spiegel* (1929), both cleverly satirical. His novels include *Fabian* (1931, trans 1932), and *Three Men in the Snow* (1934, trans 1935). His delightful children's books, which include *Emil and the Detectives* (1928), *Annaluise and Anton* (1929), and *The Flying Classroom* (1933), gained him worldwide fame. Among his later writings is the autobiographical *When I was a Little Boy* (1957, trans 1959).

KATHARINE See **CATHERINE**

KATKOV, Mikhail Nikiforovich (1818–87) Russian journalist. He was professor of philosophy at Moscow, and after 1861 editor of the *Moscow Gazette*. He was at first an advocate of reform, but was converted by the Polish rising of 1863 into a Panslavist leader and a supporter of reactionary government.

KATZ, Alex (1927–) American painter, born in New York. He studied painting at Cooper Union, New York, from 1946 to 1949 and at Skowhegan School, Maine, from 1949 to 1950. He has since lived in New York. From 1959 he began making portraits of his friends in a deliberately gauche, naïve style, simplifying forms and using a limited palette. These large-scale portraits, which have a directness bordering on kitsch, have been likened to cinematic images of film idols.

KATZ, Sir Bernard (1911–) German-born British biophysicist, born in Leipzig. He studied at Leipzig, but left Nazi Germany in 1935 and continued his research at University College, London, where he spent most of his research and teaching career (professor, 1952–78). He discovered how the neural transmitter acetylcholine is released by neural impulses, and shared the 1970 Nobel prize for physiology or medicine with **Julius Axelrod** and Ulf von Euler.

KAUFFMANN, Angelica (1741–1807) Swiss painter, born in Chur in the Grisons. At eleven she was painting portraits of notables in Italy, and in 1766 was persuaded by **Reynolds** to go to London. There she soon became famous as a painter of classical and mythological pictures, and as a portrait-painter, and was nominated one of the first batch of Royal Academicians (1769). In the 1770s she executed decorative wall-paintings for houses built by the **Adam** brothers. After an unhappy first marriage in 1781 she married the Venetian painter, **Antonio Zucchi**, and returned to Italy. Her rather pretty paintings are well known from engravings by **Bartolozzi**.

KAUFMAN, George Simon (1889–1961) American playwright, born in Pittsburgh. In collaboration with **Moss Hart** he wrote *You Can't Take it with You* (Pulitzer prize, 1939) and *The Man Who Came to Dinner* (1939). Other works include *The Solid Gold Cadillac* (with Howard Teichmann, 1953) and many musicals, some of which have been filmed.

KAUFMAN, Henry (1927–) German-born American economist and banker, born in Wenings. He moved to the USA in 1937. From 1957 to 1961 he was assistant chief economist in the research department of the Federal Reserve Bank, New York. He joined Salomon Bros in 1962, became a partner in 1967 and managing director in 1981. He is chief economist in charge of (among other interests) bond market research and bond portfolio analysis, and a member of the board of governors of Tel Aviv University. He published *Interest Rates, the Markets, and the New Financial World* in 1986.

KAUFMANN, Constantine Petrovich von (1818–82) Russian soldier. He distinguished himself at Kars (1855) and from 1867 to 1882 was governor of Turkestan. In 1868 he occupied Samarkand, and in 1873 conducted the campaign against Khiva. He died at Tashkent.

KAULBACH, Wilhelm von (1805–74) German painter, born in Arolsen. From 1849 he was director of the Munich Academy of Painting, and painted grandiose historical subjects, especially the murals in the Neuer Museum. His son Hermann (1846–1909), nephew Friedrich (1822–1903), and the latter's son Friedrich August (1850–1920) were also painters.

KAUNDA, Kenneth David (1924–) Zambian politician, born in Lubwa. He became a teacher and founded the Zambian African National Congress (1958); subsequently he was imprisoned and the movement banned. In 1960 elected president of the United National Independent Party, he played a leading part in his country's independence negotiations, and became premier in January 1964, the country obtaining independence in October that year, since when he has been Zambia's president. He has written *Zambia Shall Be Free* (1962), *A Humanist in Africa* (1966), and *Letter to My Children* (1980). He was elected chairman of the Organization of African Unity (OAU) in 1970 and 1987.

KAUNITZ-RIETBERG, Wenzel Anton, Prince von (1711–94) Austrian statesman. He distinguished himself in 1748 at the congress of Aix-la-Chapelle, and as Austrian ambassador at the French court from 1750 to 1752 converted old enmity into friendship. In 1753 he was appointed chancellor, and for almost 40 years directed Austrian politics. Active in the ecclesiastical reforms of **Joseph II**, he was a liberal patron of arts and sciences.

KAUTSKY, Karl Johann (1854–1938) German socialist leader, born in Prague. In 1883 he founded and edited *Die Neue Zeit*. A disciple of **Marx**, he wrote a study of Marxist economic theory (1887), and of Sir **Thomas More** and his *Utopia* (1888). He also wrote against Bolshevism in *Die Diktatur des Proleteriats* (1918, trans 1931).

KAVANAGH, Patrick Joseph (1905–67) Irish poet and novelist, born in County Monaghan. The son of a cobbler and smallholder he farmed before leaving for Dublin in 1939 to pursue a career as a writer and journalist. A caricature of the roistering Irish poet, perhaps his greatest achievement is *The Great Hunger* (1942), a long, angry and passionate poem which does not gloss the harsh reality of life for a frustrated Irish farmer and his sister. In *Tarry Flynn* (1948), an autobiographical novel, he depicts sensitively and convincingly the countryside where he was brought up. Kavanagh's unorthodox and virtually antisocial lifestyle in Dublin led to a savage anonymous profile (actually by another poet, Valentin Iremonger). In his libel action, *Kavanagh* v *The Leader* (1953), he was the victim of a brutal cross-examination by opposing counsel **John A Costello**, from which he never really recovered. Poems written in the last decade of his life when his health was failing are generally thought to be inferior, but the best are admirably direct, intelligently and wittily contemplating his sexual isolation and his attempts to overcome his academic stage-Irishness. The *Collected Poems* was published in 1964.

KAWABATA, Yasunari (1899–1972) Japanese writer, born in Osaka. He was educated at Tokyo

University (1920–24), reading English and then Japanese literature. In 1922 he published some short stories, *Tales to hold in the Palm of your Hand*. His first novel, *The Dancer of Izu Province*, was published in 1925. He experimented with various Western novel forms, but by the mid-1930s returned to traditional Japanese ones. Later novels include *Red Group of Asakusa* (1930), *Snow Country* (1935–47, trans 1957), *Thousand Cranes* (1949, trans 1959), *Kyoto* (1962) and *The Sound of the Mountain* (1949–54, trans 1971). He won the 1968 Nobel prize for literature, the first Japanese writer to do so. He committed suicide.

KAY-SHUTTLEWORTH, Sir James Phillips (1804–77) English physician and educationist, born in Rochdale. He studied and practised medicine. As secretary to the committee of the privy council on education he was instrumental in establishing a system of government school inspection. The pupil-teacher system originated with him and he founded his own training college which later became St John's College, Battersea. In 1842 he married the heiress of the Shuttleworths of Gawthorpe, and assumed her surname.

KAY, John See **ARKWRIGHT, Sir Richard**

KAY, John (1704–c1780) English inventor, born near Bury in Lancashire. He may have been educated in France, but many details of his life are hazy. He was certainly back in Bury by 1730 when he patented an 'engine' for twisting and cording mohair and worsted. Then three years later he patented his flying shuttle, one of the most important inventions in the history of textile machinery. Output and quality were both substantially improved, and Kay's new shuttle was eagerly adopted by the Yorkshire woollen manufacturers, but they were reluctant to pay the royalties due to him and the cost of court actions against defaulters nearly ruined him. In 1753 his house at Bury was ransacked by a mob of textile workers who feared that his machines would destroy their livelihood; he left England soon after for France, where he is believed to have died a pauper.

KAY, John (1742–1826) Scottish artist, born near Dalkeith. He was a prosperous Edinburgh barber, acquainted with Edinburgh society, and in 1785 opened a print shop for caricatures of local celebrities etched by himself. His *Original Portraits, with Biographical Sketches* is an invaluable record of Edinburgh.

KAYE, Danny, professional name of **David Daniel Kominski** (1913–87) American stage, film and television entertainer, born in Brooklyn, New York. A singer and dancer at school and summer camps, he toured extensively in the 1930, and made his film début in the short *Dime a Dance* (1937). He made his New York début in *The Straw Hat Revue* (1939) and followed this with stage successes in *Lady in The Dark* and *Let's Face It*. His first feature film, *Up in Arms* (1944), was an instant success and launched a career as an international 'stuntman of humour', noted for his mimicry, slapstick antics and tongue-twisting speciality songs. His best loved films include *The Secret Life of Walter Mitty* (1947), *Hans Christian Anderson* (1952) and *The Court Jester* (1956). As a straight dramatic actor his most accomplished performance was as a concentration-camp survivor fighting anti-Semitism in the television film *Skokie* (1981). A tireless fundraiser for UNICEF, he received a special Academy Award in 1954 for his 'unique talents, his service to the Academy, the motion picture industry and the American people'.

KAYE, Nora, originally **Nora Koreff** (1920–87) American dancer, born in New York. She studied at the School of American Ballet and the New York Metropolitan Opera Ballet School, dancing as a child with the latter company and also at Radio City Music Hall. She joined American Ballet Theatre at its inception in 1939 and soon became the leading dramatic ballerina of her generation, creating the role of Hagar in Antony Tudor's *Pillar of Fire* (1942), and appearing in other modern ballets as well as the classics. She was a member of New York City Ballet (1951–54), and then returned to ABT until her retirement in 1961. She co-founded Ballet of Two Worlds with her choreographer-husband Herbert Ross, and assisted him in his stage and film work, including *The Turning Point* (1977), until her death.

KAYE-SMITH, Sheila (1887–1956) English novelist, born in St Leonards. She wrote novels mainly of fate and Sussex soil. In 1924 she married T P Fry, a clergyman and heir to a baronetcy, and in 1929 became a Roman Catholic. Her writings include *Sussex Gorse* (1916), *Tamarisk Town* (1919), *Joanna Godden* (1921), and *The End of the House of Alard* (1923). She was satirized by **Stella Gibbons** in *Cold Comfort Farm*.

KAZAN, Elia, originally **Kazanjoglous** (1909–) Turkish-born American stage and film director, born in Constantinople. He studied at Williams College and Yale, then acted in minor roles on Broadway and in Hollywood before becoming a director of plays and films. He founded (with **Lee Strasberg**) the Actors Studio (1947) with its emphasis on 'Method Acting'. His Broadway productions include the works of **Wilder**, **Arthur Miller**, and **Tennessee Williams**. Many of his films have a social or political theme, eg, *Gentleman's Agreement* (Academy Award, 1948), on anti-Semitism, *Pinky* (1949), on the colour problem, *Viva Zapata* (1952), *On the Waterfront* (1954, Oscar winner), and *Face in the Crowd* (1957). The latter three deal with megalomania, the revolutionary figure without statecraft, the trades union boss turned gangster, and the TV demagogue. Other notable films include Tennessee Williams' *A Streetcar Named Desire* (1951) and *Baby Doll* (1956), **Steinbeck**'s *East of Eden* (1954), **Inge**'s *Splendour in the Grass* (1962), *America, America* (1964) and *The Arrangement* (1969), based on his autobiographical novels (1963 and 1967), *The Visitors* (1972) and *The Last Tycoon* (1976).

KAZANTZAKIS, Nikos (1883–1957) Greek novelist, poet and dramatist, born in Heraklion, Crete. After studying law at Athens University, he spent some years travelling in Europe and Asia. He published his first novel *Toda Raba* in 1929, but is best known for the novel *Zorba the Greek* (1946) and the epic autobiographical narrative poem, *The Odyssey, a Modern Sequel* (1938). He also wrote *Christ Recrucified* (1948), a novel, and translated many literary classics into modern Greek.

KAZINCZY, Ferenc (1759–1831) Hungarian writer, born in Érsemlyén. He was a leading figure in the Hungarian literary revival and a strong advocate of the reform of the language. He translated many European classics and wrote poetry; there are 22 volumes of his letters. He died of cholera.

KEAN, Charles John (1811–68) English actor, born in Waterford. He was the son of **Edmund**, educated at Eton. To support his mother and himself he became an actor. He appeared at Drury Lane in 1827 as Young Norval, with little success, but developed and improved his performance in the provinces. In 1850 he became joint-lessee of the Princess's Theatre, and produced a long series of 'revivals'. In 1859 he virtually retired, though he played in America and the provinces to within seven months of his death. In 1842 he married the actress, Ellen Tree (1805-80).

KEAN, Edmund (1789–1833) English actor, born in London. It is likely he was the illegitimate son of Anne

Carey, an actress and entertainer, and grand-daughter of **Henry Carey**, the composer of 'Sally in Our Alley'. His father is thought to have been Edmund Kean, a thespian and drunk, who committed suicide when his son was an infant. He was taken into care by Charlotte Tidswell, a member of the company, and formerly a mistress of Edmund's uncle, Moses, a ventriloquist. He was taught singing, dancing, fencing and elocution, and by eight had made several appearances on the Drury Lane stage. But his real mother reclaimed him and exploited his precocity at fairs round the country, and he played Hamlet before **Nelson** and Lady **Hamilton** in Carmarthen. However, he broke free of his mother in 1804 and set up on his own in the provinces. For nine years he was an itinerant player and married a bad actress, Mary Chalmers, by whom he had two sons. He finally appeared at Drury Lane in a major role in 1814, playing Shylock in *The Merchant of Venice*. A delighted audience acclaimed his unconventional interpretation as a dark, desperate, bitter rogue brandishing a cleaver. Villainous parts suited him best and he continued to meet approval from the crowd, but the tide turned with a number of poor performances: as Lear, a leaden Romeo, and Hamlet. But his Macbeth was magnificent, and he excelled himself as Richard III and Iago. Unable to cope with his fame, he led a debauched and profligate life, drinking intemperately and philandering outrageously. The final straw came when his affair with the wife of Alderman Cox—a member of the Drury Lane bureaucracy—was discovered. The audience was not amused, but he charmed back their favour, only to lose it repeatedly. In America, where he first went in 1820, there was a similar pattern. He returned to England but was no longer the force he was. In 1831 he burdened himself with the management of the King's Theatre at Richmond and toured intermittently; but his health was poor and his last performance was at Drury Lane on 25 March 1833, playing Othello to his son Charles' Iago.

KEANE, Molly (1904–) Irish novelist, born in County Kildare into 'a rather serious Hunting and Fishing and Church-going family'. Her father originally came from a Somerset family and her mother, a poet, was the author of 'The Songs of the Glens of Antrim'. When young she wrote only to supplement her dress allowance, adopting the pseudonym M J Farrell. *The Knight of the Cheerful Countenance*, her first book, was written when she was 17. Between 1928 and 1952 she wrote ten novels, including *The Rising Tide* (1937), *Two Days in Aragon* (1941) and *Loving Without Tears* (1951), drawing her material from the foibles of her own class. A spirited, impish writer, she also wrote plays, such as *Spring Meeting* (1938), *Ducks and Drakes* (1942), *Treasure Hunt* (1949) and *Dazzling Prospect* (1961). When her husband died at 36 she stopped writing for many years, but *Good Behaviour* (1981), short-listed for the Booker prize, led to the reprinting of many of her books and a revival of critical appreciation. *Loving and Giving* (1988) is a bleak comedy seen through the eyes of an eight-year-old girl who is a witness to the break-up of her parents' marriage and the desuetude of the family mansion.

KEATE, John (1773–1852) English clergyman and teacher, born in Wells, and headmaster of Eton (1809–34). A diminutive man, he was a stern disciplinarian and once flogged 80 boys together.

KEATING, Geoffrey (?1570–?1645) Irish historian, writing in his Gaelic name of **Seathrún Céitinn**, born in Burges, County Tipperary, of Norman-Irish stock. He was educated for the priesthood at Bordeaux, and returned to Ireland as a doctor of theology in 1610. He served as Tipperary parish priest, apparently causing offence to local landowners for reproof of their living in concubinage, was nomadic and for a time fugitive, and his chief work *Foras Feasa ar Éirinn* (History of Ireland) was alleged to have been written in a cave. At this time he also wrote many songs, hymns and poems, and a spiritual essay translated as *The Three Shafts of Death*. He had once more obtained a parish in 1634, at Cappoquin, County Waterford. He was ultimately caught up in the Irish phase of the civil wars of 1640. According to legend, he was killed in a church in Clonmel, County Tipperary, by Cromwellian soldiers.

KEATING, Tom (1917–84) English art restorer and celebrated forger of paintings, born in London to a poor family. The scandal about his fakes of the works of the great masters broke in 1976, when an art expert writing in *The Times* suggested that a work by **Samuel Palmer**, which sold at an auction for £9400, was not genuine. Keating admitted that a series of nine pictures, bearing imitations of Samuel Palmer's signature, were in fact drawn by himself, and estimated that there were some 2500 of his fakes in circulation. Drawing on his Cockney roots, he dubbed his works 'Sexton Blakes' in true rhyming slang fashion. In 1979 he was put on trial at the Old Bailey for forgery, but charges were eventually dropped because of his deteriorating health. Keating and his work became very popular with the public who enjoyed the way in which he had fooled high-brow art-dealers. He went on to do art programmes for television.

KEATON, 'Buster' (Joseph Francis) (1895–1966) American film comedian, born in Pickway, the son of vaudeville artists of Scots and Irish descent. He joined their act 'The Three Keatons' at the age of three, developing great acrobatic skill, until 1917 when he went to Hollywood and made his film début in *The Butcher Boy* (1917). Renowned for his inimitable 'deadpan' expression, he starred in and directed such silent classics as *Our Hospitality* (1923), *The Navigator* (1924) and *The General* (1926). His reputation went into eclipse with the advent of talking films until in the 1950s and 1960s many of his silent masterpieces were re-released, and he himself began to appear in character roles in films like *Sunset Boulevard* (1950) and *Limelight* (1952). He received a special Academy Award in 1959 for his 'unique talents'.

KEATS, Ezra Jack (1916–) American illustrator of children's books, born in Brooklyn, New York City. *My Dog is Lost* (1960) was his first book, but *The Snowy Day* (1962), about a small black boy's adventure in the snow, is the one for which he is best known. Among later books, *Peter's Chair* (1967), a typically simple story, boldly and vividly perceived, was a notable success.

KEATS, John (1795–1821) English poet, born in London, the son of a livery-stable keeper. He went to school at Enfield. In 1811 he was apprenticed to a surgeon at Edmonton, and later (1815–17) was a medical student in the London hospitals, but took to writing poetry. **Leigh Hunt**, his neighbour in Hampstead, introduced him to other young romantics, including **Shelley**, and published his first sonnets in *The Examiner* (1816). His first volume of poems (1817) combined 'Hymn to Pan' and the 'Bacchic procession' which anticipate the great odes to come. In 1818 he published the long mythological poem *Endymion*. He returned from a walking tour in Scotland (1818), which exhausted him, to find the savage reviews of *Endymion* in *Blackwood's Magazine* and the *Quarterly*. To add to his troubles his younger brother Tom was dying of consumption, and his love affair with Fanny Brawne seems to have brought him more vexation than comfort. It was under these circumstances that he published the volume of 1820, *Lamia and Other Poems*, a landmark in English poetry. Except for the romantic poem 'Isabella or The Pot of Basil', a romance based on **Boccaccio**'s *Decameron*, and the first version of his epical poem, 'Hyperion', all the significant verse in this famous volume is the work of 1819, such as the two splendid romances 'The Eve of St Agnes' and 'Lamia', and the great odes—'On a Grecian Urn', 'To a Nightingale', 'To Autumn', 'On Melancholy' and 'To Psyche'. In particular, 'The Eve of St Agnes' displays a wealth of sensuous imagery almost unequalled in English poetry. In 'Lamia', the best told of the tales, he turns from stanza form to the couplet as used by **Dryden** in his romantic *Fables*. Keats' letters are regarded as equally important as his poems, and throw light on his poetical development no less than on his unhappy love affair with Fanny Brawne. It is clear that he was both attracted and repelled by the notion of the poet as teacher or prophet. Having prepared the 1820 volume for the press, Keats, now seriously ill with consumption, sailed for Italy in September 1820, reached Rome and died there attended only by his artist friend **Joseph Severn**. The house in which he died (26 Piazza di Spagna), at the foot of the Spanish steps, is now known as the Keats-Shelley house, a place of literary pilgrimage with an outstanding library of English romantic literature.

KEBLE, John (1792–1866) English churchman and religious poet, inspirer of the 'Oxford Movement', born in Fairford, Gloucestershire, near his father's living of Coln St Aldwins. At 15 he was elected a scholar at Corpus Christi College, Oxford, and in 1810 took a double first. In 1811 he was elected a fellow of Oriel and in 1812 won the Latin and English essay prizes. In 1815 he was ordained deacon, beginning active work as curate of East Leach, while continuing to live in Oxford, where he was college tutor (1818–23). In 1827 he published his first book of poems, *The Christian Year*. His theory of poetry, explained in the *British Critic* in 1838, was worked out at length in his Latin lectures delivered as Oxford professor of poetry (1831–41). Meanwhile Keble had gathered round him a small band of pupils, of whom the most striking was **Hurrell Froude**, and in this circle originated the Tractarian movement. In his sermon on national apostasy (1833) Keble gave the signal for action, and for the next eight years was engaged with **Newman**, **Pusey**, **Isaac Williams** and others in the issue of *Tracts for the Times*, brought to an end by Tract No. 90 in 1841. Keble had in 1835 married, and had moved to the Hampshire living of Hursely, where he remained until his death. With Pusey he was the steadying influence which supported the party under the shock caused by Newman's conversion to Catholicism. Other works are a Life of Bishop Wilson, an edition of **Richard Hooker**, the *Lyra Innocentium* (1846), a poetical translation of the Psalter, *Letters of Spiritual Counsel*, twelve volumes of parochial sermons, and *Studia Sacra*. Keble College, Oxford, was founded in his memory (1870).

KEE, Robert (1919–) English broadcaster and writer. After reading history at Magdalen College, Oxford, he joined the RAF and was shot down over Holland, spending four years in a p.o.w. camp. His first novel, *A Crowd is Not Company* (1947), reflected this experience and won him the Atlantic Award for literature. Other novels include *The Impossible Shore* (1949) and *A Sign of the Times* (1955). As a print journalist, he worked for *Picture Post* (1948–51) and was a special correspondent for *The Observer* (1956–57) and *The Sunday Times* (1957–58). Joining the BBC, he worked on *Panorama* from 1958 to 1962. The recipient of the **Richard Dimbleby** BAFTA Award (1976), his other major television work includes the series *Ireland* (1981), co-founding the breakfast programme TV-am (1983), and *Seven Days* (1984–88). His non-fiction books include *The Green Flag* (1972), *Ireland: A History* (1980) and *Trial and Error* (1986).

KEELER, Christine (1942–) English former model and show girl. After an unhappy childhood spent mainly in the Thames Valley, at Wraysbury, she left home at 16 and migrated to London, where she obtained work at Murray's Cabaret Club. Here she met **Mandy Rice-Davies**, a girl who had arrived in similar circumstances, and was to become a close friend. Stephen Ward, an osteopath, was a frequent visitor to the club and he and Keeler formed a relationship whereby she eventually lived with him, although there were frequent rifts between them. Ward introduced her and Rice-Davies into his circle of influential friends, including the Conservative cabinet minister, **John Profumo**, with whom she had an affair; this led to Profumo's resignation from politics, the prosecution of Ward for living on immoral earnings, and Ward's eventual suicide. Keeler herself served a prison sentence for related offences. In the late 1980s, her autobiography, studies of the Ward trial and its aftermath, and the film *Scandal*, in which she collaborated, revived interest in the events and raised doubts about the validity of the charges made against her and Ward.

KEELER, James Edward (1857–1900) American astronomer, born in La Salle, Illinois. Educated at the Johns Hopkins University, Heidelberg and Berlin, he was director of the Allegheny Observatory (1891–98) and the Lick Observatory from 1898. He established the composition of Saturn's rings (as **James Clerk Maxwell** had postulated), and carried out important spectroscopic work on nebulae, discovering 120000 of them.

KEELEY, Robert (1793–1869) English comedian, born in London. He married Mary Goward (1806–99), who, born in Ipswich, made her début at the Lyceum in 1825. Their daughters were both actresses.

KEENE, Charles Samuel (1823–91) English illustrator and cartoonist, born in Hornsey. Having tried both law and architecture, he was apprenticed to a wood engraver. He worked for the *Illustrated London News*, and from 1851 until his death he contributed gentle satires of lower-class society to *Punch*. He also illustrated books, including *Robinson Crusoe* and *The Cloister and the Hearth*.

KEIGHTLEY, Thomas (1789–1872) Irish writer, born in Dublin. In 1824 he settled in London. His histories of Rome, Greece and England long held their place as school manuals, and his *Fairy Mythology* (1850) and his life and annotated edition of **Milton** (1855–59) are among his best works.

KEILIN, David (1887–1963) British biochemist, born in Moscow, the son of a Polish businessman. Educated in Warsaw, Liège, and Paris, his career thereafter was spent in Cambridge, where he was director of the Molteno Institute from 1931 and Quick professor of biology. His ingenious studies of enzymes and animal pigments led to his major discovery, the pigment cytochrome, which occurs in plant and animal cells and has a key role in biochemical oxidation. A keen entomologist, he used insects in many of his experiments in animal biochemistry.

KEILLOR, Garrison (1942–) American humorous writer and radio performer, born in Minnesota. He graduated from Minnesota University in 1966, already writing for the *New Yorker*. In 1974 he first hosted the live radio show, 'A Prairie Home Companion', delivering a weekly monologue set in the quiet, fictional mid-western town of Lake Wobegon, 'where all the women are strong, all the men are good looking, and all the children are above average'. When the show closed in 1987 he was celebrated for his wry, deliberate, hypnotic storytelling. Most of his written work appears first in the *New Yorker*. Described as 'the best humorous writer to have come out of America since **Thurber**', his four books are *Happy to be Here* (1981), *Lake Wobegon Days* (1985), *Leaving Home* (1987), and *We Are Still Married* (1989).

KEINO, Kipchoge (1940–) African athlete, born in Kipsamo, Kenya, one of Africa's outstanding athletes. Concentrating on middle-distance events, his most effective range lay between 1500 and 5000 metres. At the 1968 Mexico City Olympics he won the 1500 metres, and at Munich in 1972 he won the gold medal for the 3000 metres steeplechase. In 1965 he established new world records for the 3000 and 5000 metres.

KEIR, James (1735–1820) Scottish chemist and industrialist, born in Edinburgh, the youngest of 18 children of a prosperous family. He was educated at the Edinburgh High School and University, where he studied medicine, and met **Erasmus Darwin**, who was to become a lifelong friend. He then joined the army, and served in the West Indies, resigning in 1768. He married and settled in West Bromwich and remained there; he joined Darwin's circle of friends and became a member of the Lunar Society of Birmingham, an organization founded to promote interest in science and technology. He assisted **Joseph Priestley** in Birmingham, and was a friend of **Josiah Wedgwood** (both fellow-members). Becoming interested in chemistry and geology, he set up a glass -making business at Stourbridge, but gave it up in 1778 to manage **Boulton** and **Watt**'s engineering works, and then in 1780 began to make alkalies (soda and potash) and soap. He wrote widely on science; his most valuable contribution was probably a translation of Macquer's *Dictionary of Chemistry* (1776) with additions.

KEITEL, Wilhelm (1882–1946) German soldier. He joined the army in 1901 and was an artillery staff officer in World War I. In the 1930s he became an ardent Nazi, and in 1938 was appointed chief of the supreme command of the armed forces. In 1940 he signed the Compiègne armistice with France and was **Hitler**'s chief military adviser throughout the war. In May 1945, he was one of the German signatories of unconditional surrender to Russia and the Allies in Berlin. He was executed in October 1946 for war crimes.

KEITH-FALCONER See **FALCONER, Ion Keith**

KEITH, Sir Arthur (1866–1955) Scottish physical anthropologist, born in Aberdeen. He wrote *Introduction to the Study of Anthropoid Apes* (1896), *Human Embryology and Morphology* (1901) and works on ancient man, including *Concerning Man's Origin* (1927) and *New Theory of Human Evolution* (1948).

KEITH, James (1696–1758) Scottish soldier and field marshal in the Prussian army, born in the castle of Inverugie near Peterhead. He came of an ancient family (represented now by the Earl of Kintore), which had for centuries held the hereditary office of Great Marischal of Scotland. He was destined for the law, but in 1715 he engaged with his brother in the Jacobite Rising, and in 1719 in **Alberoni**'s futile expedition to the West Highlands, which ended in the 'battle' of Glenshiel. Both times the brothers escaped to the Continent. James held for nine years a Spanish colonelcy and took part in the siege of Gibraltar (1726–27). But his Episcopal creed was against him and in 1728 he entered the Russian service as a major-general. He distinguished himself in the wars with Turkey and Sweden, particularly at the siege of Otchakoff (1737) and the reduction of the Åland Islands (1743). He next visited Paris and London, where he made his peace with the Hanoverian government. In 1747, finding the Russian service disagreeable, he exchanged it for that of Prussia, and **Frederick II, the Great** gave him at once the rank of field marshal. From this time his name is associated with that of Frederick, who relied as much on Keith's military genius as he did on the diplomatic ability of his brother, the Earl Marischal. His military talents became still more conspicuous upon the breaking out of the Seven Years' War (1756). He shared Frederick's doubtful fortunes before Prague, was present at the victories of Lobositz and Rossbach, and conducted the masterly retreat from Olmütz. At Hochkirch he was shot dead while for the third time charging the enemy. He died poor and unmarried, but he left children by his mistress, the Swede, Eve Merthens (d.1811).

KEITH, Viscount See **ELPHINSTONE, George Keith**

KEKKONEN, Urho Kaleva (1900–86) Finnish statesman, born in Pielavesi. After studying law at Helsinki University and fighting against the Bolsheviks in 1918, he entered the Finnish parliament as an Agrarian party deputy, holding ministerial office from 1936 to 1939 and in 1944. He was prime minister on four occasions in the early 1950s before being elected president in 1956, in succession to **Juo Paasikivi**. Although Kekkonen had always been hostile to Stalinist Russia, as president he encouraged a policy of cautious friendship with the Soviet Union. At the same time his strict neutrality ensured that he retained the confidence of his Scandinavian neighbours. He supported Finland's membership of the European Free Trade Association (1961) and in 1975 was host to the 35-nation European Security Conference in Helsinki. Five years later he accepted a Lenin peace prize. His popularity in Finland led to the passage of special legislation enabling him to remain in office until 1984, but his health gave way and he resigned in 1981.

KEKULÉ VON STRADONITZ, Friedrich August (1829–96) German chemist, born in Darmstadt. He became professor at Ghent and at Bonn (1867). He made a major contribution to organic chemistry by developing structural theories, including the cyclic structure of benzene.

KELLER, Gottfried (1819–90) Swiss poet and novelist, born near Zürich. He studied landscape painting at Munich (1840–42), but turned to literature. From 1861 to 1876 he was state secretary of his native canton. His chief works are *Der grüne Heinrich* (1854), *Die Leute von Seldwyla* (1856; which includes *A Village Romeo and Juliet*), *Sieben Legenden* (1872), *Züricher Novellen* (1878), and *Martin Salander* (1886). He excelled as a writer of short stories, and his powers of characterization and description and his sense of humour are best illustrated in his volumes of *Novellen*.

KELLER, Hans (1919–85) Austrian-born British musicologist, born in Vienna; he emigrated to England in 1938. His musical journalism and analytical criticism bespoke a mind of exceptional logic, individuality and linguistic dexterity. He co-founded the magazine *Music Survey*, wrote for many other journals, served on the BBC staff from 1959 and broadcast frequently. He was influentially erudite upon contemporary music, chamber music and football.

KELLER, Helen Adams (1880–1968) American writer, born in Tuscumbia, Alabama. She became deaf and blind at 19 months, but, educated by Anne M Sullivan (Mrs Macy), she later learned to speak, graduated in 1904, and attained high distinction as a lecturer, writer and scholar.

KELLERMANN, François Étienne Christophe, Duke of Valmy (1735–1820) French soldier born in Wolfsbuchweiler in Alsace. He entered the army in 1752 and served in the Seven Years' War (1756–63). In the French Revolution he was a major-general. In 1792 he repelled the Duke of Brunswick, and helped **Dumouriez** deliver France by the famous 'cannonade of Valmy'. Yet on allegation of treason he was imprisoned by **Robespierre**. He afterwards served in Italy, and under the Empire was made a marshal and duke. In 1809 and 1812 he commanded the reserves on the Rhine. At the Restoration he attached himself to the Bourbons. His son, François Étienne (1770–1835), led the charge at the battle of Marengo (1800).

KELLEY, Florence (1859–1932) American feminist and social reformer, born into a middle-class family in Philadelphia. Educated at Cornell University and at Zürich, where she became a socialist, from 1891 to 1899 she worked at **Jane Addams**'s Hull House Settlement and subsequently became the first woman factory inspector in Illinois, successfully fighting to reduce working hours and improve methods and conditions of production. Gaining a law degree from Northwestern University (1895), she moved to New York in 1899, becoming general secretary of the National Consumers' League, and in 1910 was one of the founders of the National Association for the Advancement of Colored People. She helped establish the Women's International League for Peace and Freedom (1919). Her works include *Some Ethical Gains Through Legislation* (1905) and a translation of **Engels**'s *Condition of the Working Class in England in 1844* (1887).

KELLGREN, Johan Henric (1751–95) Swedish poet and journalist, born in Floby. He was editor from 1780 of the journal *Stockholmsposten*, where he made a reputation as a satirist. He was librarian (1780) and later secretary and literary adviser to King **Gustav III**, with whom he collaborated on a tragedy, *Gustav Wasa* (1782), and became a member of the newly-founded Swedish Academy in 1786. As a poet he excelled in patriotic and lyrical verse, and, although a representative of the Enlightenment, was not unsympathetic to the new ideas of Romanticism.

KELLOGG, Frank Billings (1856–1937) American jurist and statesman, born in Potsdam, New York. After law practice in Minnesota, he became senator (1917–23), ambassador in London (1923–25), and secretary of state (1925–29). With **Aristide Briand** he drew up the Briand-Kellogg Pact (1928) outlawing war, which became the legal basis for the Nuremberg trials (1945–46). He was a judge of the Permanent Court of Justice at the Hague (1930–35), and was awarded the 1929 Nobel prize for peace.

KELLOGG, John Harvey (1852–1943) and his brother **Will Keith** (1860–1951) American inventors, born in Tyrone and Battle Creek, Michigan. They joined forces, as physician and industrialist respectively, at Battle Creek Sanitarium to develop a process of cooking, rolling and toasting wheat and corn into crisp flakes that made a nourishing breakfast cereal for their patients. Soon their corn flakes were being sold through the mail, and in 1906 the W K Kellogg Company was founded. The new product was extensively advertised and resulted in a revolution in the breakfast eating habits of the Americans, and before long the rest of the western world. In 1930 the W K Kellogg Foundation took its place as one of the leading philanthropic institutions in America.

KELLY, or **Kelley, Edward** See **DEE, John**

KELLY, Ellsworth (1923–) American artist, born in Newburgh, New York. He studied in Boston and at the Académie des Beaux-Arts in Paris, and lived in France until 1954. From the late 1950s he made his name as a 'hard-edge' abstract painter with his wide, flat areas of strong colour ('post-painterly abstraction'). He is also a sculptor, and made a screen for the Philadelphia Transport Building in 1956.

KELLY, Gene (Eugene Curran) (1912–) American dancer, born in Pittsburgh, Pennsylvania. A dance instructor with a degree in economics, he journeyed to New York and found employment in the chorus of *Leave it to Me* (1938). Several stage roles followed before he was cast in *Pal Joey* (1939) and signed to a film contract, making his début in *For Me and My Girl* (1942). An athletic dancer and choreographer with a perennially breezy disposition, he brought many innovations in style and technique to film musicals like *Anchors Aweigh* (1945), *On The Town* (1949), *An American in Paris* (1951) and *Singin' in the Rain* (1952). When the screen musical passed from favour, he worked as a dramatic actor in such films as *Marjorie Morningstar* (1958) and *Inherit the Wind* (1960), and as a director, most notably on the screen version of *Hello Dolly* (1969). He has also directed on Broadway, devised a ballet for the Paris opera and worked frequently on television, recently in mini-series like *Sins* (1987). He received an honorary Academy Award in 1951.

KELLY, George A (1905–66) American psychologist, born in Kansas. He studied at several universities, including Edinburgh (BEd 1930) and Iowa (PhD 1931), and taught at Fort Hays Kansas State College prior to World War II, during which he was an aviation psychologist with the US Navy. From 1946 he worked at the Ohio State University, leaving to take up a post at Brandeis University in 1965. Best known for his novel approach to the understanding of personality, he devised the repertory grid test, an open-ended method for exploring an individual's 'personal constructs' (categories in terms of which one perceives and construes others). The inter-relations of these constructs can then be used in psychotherapy to help infer (and change) the ways in which subjective 'theories' are used by the individual in dealing with others.

KELLY, Grace Patricia (1929–82) American film actress, born in Philadelphia, the daughter of a wealthy self-made Irish businessman. After studying at the American Academy of Dramatic Art she acted in television and on Broadway, and made her film début in *Fourteen Hours* (1951). Her short but highly successful film career as a coolly elegant beauty included such classics as the Western *High Noon* (1952, with **Gary Cooper**), *Rear Window* (1954), *The Country Girl* (1954, Academy Award), *To Catch a Thief* (1955, with **Cary Grant**), and *High Society* (1956). In 1956 she married Prince **Rainier III** of Monaco, and retired from the screen. She was killed in a car accident.

KELLY, Howard Atwood (1858–1943) American surgeon and gynaecologist, born in Camden, New Jersey, the son of a businessman. He practised surgery and gynaecology for several years before accepting a post at Pennsylvania University. In 1889 he became one of four original professors at the Johns Hopkins Medical School, where he remained until his retirement in 1919. He pioneered the use of cocaine anaesthesia, developed a number of operations for the kidney and bladder, and played an important role in the development of gynaecology as a surgical speciality separate from obstetrics. His textbooks (*Operative Gynecology*, 1898, and *Medical Gynecology*, 1908) dominated the field and described many of his technical innovations. During his long retirement he wrote on botany and medical history.

KELLY, Ned (1855–80) Australian outlaw, the son of a transported Irish criminal. He became a horse-thief, and from 1878, a bushranger in Victoria and New South Wales. He was hanged in Melbourne and became a popular mythical figure.

KELLY, Walt (Walter Crawford) (1913–73) American animator and strip cartoonist, born in Philadelphia, the creator of the opossum Pogo. The son of a scenic painter, he joined the **Walt Disney** studio in Hollywood as an animator in 1935. He moved to comic books in 1941, creating his most famous characters, Albert Alligator and Pogo Possum of Okefenokee Swamp. He became art editor of the *New York Star* (1948), introducing *Pogo* as a daily strip. The serial uniquely embraced slapstick, fantasy and influential political comment.

KELLY, William (1811–88) American inventor, born in Pittsburgh, the son of a wealthy landowner. He developed an early interest in metallurgy, and at the age of 35, when he and his brother acquired an interest in iron-ore deposits and a nearby furnace, he became involved in the manufacture of wrought iron articles. He soon discovered that an air blast directed on to, or blown through, molten cast iron can remove much of the carbon in it, so that the resulting metal becomes a mild steel, strong and ductile, suitable for a much wider range of applications than relatively brittle cast iron. He built seven of his 'converters' between 1851 and 1856, when he heard that **Henry Bessemer** had been granted an American patent for the same process; he managed to convince the patent office of his prior claim, but was almost immediately bankrupted in the 1857 financial panic. He continued to improve his process and made it in every way as effective as that of Bessemer, but he never achieved commercial success, and his invention has come to be known as the Bessemer converter.

KELSEN, Hans (1881–1973) Austrian-born American jurist and legal theorist. Professor at Vienna (1911–30) and at Cologne (1930–33), he moved to Prague (1933–38) and then to the USA, ultimately to Berkeley. His early work was on constitutional law and he worked on the Austrian constitution of 1920 and was a judge of the Austrian constitutional court until 1929; he also worked on international law. He is mainly known as a legal theorist and creator of the 'pure theory of law' (*Reine Rechtslehre*, 1934), in which the science of law had to be exclusively normative and pure, not practical. His work has been powerfully influential and he is probably the greatest legal theorist of the twentieth century. Important translated works are *General Theory of Law and the State* (1949) and *Pure Theory of Law* (1967).

KELVIN, William Thomson, 1st Baron (1824–1907) Irish-born Scottish physicist and mathematician, born in Belfast. He was brought to Glasgow in 1832 when his father was appointed professor of mathematics there. He entered Glasgow University at the age of ten, went to Cambridge at 16, graduated second wrangler and was elected a fellow of Porterhouse. After studying in Paris under **Henri Victor Regnault**, at the age of 22 he was appointed professor of mathematics and natural philosphy (1846–99), and turned his mind to physics. In a career of astonishing versatility, he brilliantly combined pure and applied science. In an early paper (1842) he solved important problems in electrostatics. He proposed the absolute, or Kelvin, temperature scale (1848). Simultaneously with **Rudolf Clausius** he established the second law of thermodynamics. He investigated geomagnetism, and hydrodynamics (particularly wave-motion and vortex-motion). He was chief consultant on the laying of the first submarine Atlantic cable (1857–58), and grew wealthy by patenting a mirror galvanometer for speeding telegraphic transmission. He improved ships' compasses, and invented innumerable electrical instruments (his house in Glasgow was the first to be lit by electric light); these instruments were manufactured by his own company, Kelvin & White. He invented a tide predictor, a harmonic analyzer, a siphon recorder and numerous other devices. He was created 1st Baron Kelvin of Largs in 1892. He is buried in Westminster Abbey, beside Sir **Isaac Newton**.

KEMAL PASHA See **MUSTAFA KEMAL ATATURK**

KEMBLE, Charles (1775–1854) English actor, brother of **John Philip Kemble**, born in Brecon. He made his first appearance at Sheffield in 1792 and in 1794 played Malcolm to his brother's Macbeth. He retired from the stage in 1840, when he was appointed examiner of plays. He chiefly excelled in characters of the second rank, and he specially distinguished himself in comedy.

KEMBLE, Frances Anne, 'Fanny Kemble' (1809–93) English actress, daughter of **Charles Kemble**. She made her début at Covent Garden in October 1829, when her Juliet created a great sensation. For three years she played leading parts in London, then in 1832 went with her father to America, where in 1834 she married Pierce Butler, a Southern planter. They were divorced in 1848 and, resuming her maiden name, she gave Shakespearian readings for twenty years. She published dramas, poems, and eight volumes of autobiography.

KEMBLE, John Mitchell (1807–57) Anglo-Saxon scholar, son of **Charles Kemble**. He studied at Trinity College, Cambridge, and at Göttingen under **Jakob Grimm**. His edition of *Beowulf* (1833–37) and *Codex Diplomaticus Aevi Saxonici* (1839–48) were valuable, but less important than his unfinished *History of the Saxons in England* (1849). He edited the *British and Foreign Review* (1835–44) and in 1840 succeeded his father as examiner of plays.

KEMBLE, John Philip (1757–1823) English actor, brother of **Charles Kemble**, eldest son of **Roger**, was born in Prescot. His father intended him for the Catholic priesthood, and sent him to a seminary at Sedgley Park, Staffordshire, and to the English college at Douai. But the life of a priest did not appeal to him and he became an actor. His first appearance was at Wolverhampton in 1776. He joined the York circuit under Tate Wilkinson and he played in Ireland. The success of his sister, Mrs **Sarah Siddons**, gave him the opportunity, and in September 1783 he played Hamlet at Drury Lane, and aroused the keenest interest. He continued to play leading tragic characters at Drury Lane for many years, and in 1788 became **Sheridan**'s manager. In 1802 he purchased a share in Covent Garden Theatre, became manager, and made his first appearance there in 1803 as Hamlet. In 1808 the theatre was burned, and on the opening of the new building (1809) the notorious OP (ie, 'Old Price') Riots broke out. Kemble retired in 1817, and afterwards settled in Lausanne.

KEMBLE, Roger (1721–1802) travelling English theatre manager. He was the father of **Charles**, **John Philip**, and **Stephen Kemble** and **Sarah Siddons**.

KEMBLE, Stephen (1758–1822) brother of **John Philip**, born in Kington, Herefordshire. He was chiefly remarkable for his enormous bulk, which enabled him to play Falstaff without stuffing. He was manager of the Edinburgh Theatre (1792–1800), where he was always involved in lawsuits and other troubles.

KEMP, George Meikle (1795–1844) Scottish draughtsman, born in Hillriggs near Biggar, the son of a shepherd. A carpenter by trade, he worked in England and France and made a study of Gothic architecture there. In 1838 his second design for the **Scott** Monument in Edinburgh was accepted, but before its completion he was accidentally drowned in an Edinburgh canal.

KEMP, John (c.1380–1454) English prelate, born in Olantigh near Ashford, Kent. He became a fellow of Merton College, Oxford, bishop of Rochester (1419), and of Chichester and London (1421), chancellor and archbishop of York (1426), a cardinal (1439), and archbishop of Canterbury (1452).

KEMP, Lindsay (1939–) Scottish mime artist, actor, dancer, teacher and director, born on the Isle of Lewis in the Hebrides. After studying at Bradford Art College, he began his dance training with Ballet Rambert. His teachers included **Marie Rambert**, **Charles Weidman** and mime artist **Marcel Marceau**. His colourful career was launched at the 1964 Edinburgh Festival. He has had his own company in various forms since the early 1960s and has created his own work in camp, extravagant style since then, including *The Parade's Gone By* (1975) and *Cruel Garden* (1977, in collaboration with **Christopher Bruce**), both for Ballet Rambert, and *Flowers* (based on the writings of **Jean Genet**, 1973), *Midsummer Night's Dream* (1979) and *The Big Parade* for his own company. He taught rock star **David Bowie** mime (which he used memorably on his Ziggy Stardust concerts in the early 1970s), and appeared in **Ken Russell**'s films *Savage Messiah* and *Valentino* (1977) and **Derek Jarman's** *Sebastiane* (1975) and *Jubilee* (1977).

KEMPE, Margery, née **Brunham** (b.1364) English mystic, daughter of a mayor of Lynn. She was the wife of a burgess in Lynn and the mother of 14 children. After a period of insanity she experienced a conversion and undertook numerous pilgrimages. Between 1432 and 1436 she dictated her spiritual autobiography, *The Book of Margery Kempe*, which recounts her persecution by devils and men, repeated accusations of Lollardism (see **John Wycliffe**), her copious weepings, and her journeys to Jerusalem and to Germany, and has been hailed as a classic.

KEMPE, William (d.1603) a comedian who in 1599 danced from London to Norwich. He wrote *Nine Daies Wonder* (ed by Dyce, Camden Society).

KEMPENFELT, Richard (1718–82) English naval officer. He served in command of HM Ships in the West Indies (1739) and in the East Indies in the Seven Years' War (1756–63). Promoted rear admiral in 1780, he won a brilliant action against a French convoy off Ushant in 1781. He was drowned when his flagship, HMS *Royal George*, capsized off Spithead. He is remembered for his progressive ideas on signalling, health at sea (about which he gave support to the findings of **James Lind**), and organization. His recommended divisional system survived in the Royal Navy in modern times.

KEMPIS, Thomas á (1379–1471) German religious writer, so called from his birthplace, Kempen. In 1400 he entered the Augustinian convent of Agnietenberg near Zwolle in the Netherlands, took holy orders in 1413, was chosen sub-prior in 1429, and died as superior. He wrote sermons, ascetical treatises, pious biographies, letters and hymns, and in particular the famous treatise *On the Following* (or *Imitation*) *of Christ*. Its theology is almost purely ascetical, and (excepting the fourth book, which is based on the doctrine of the real presence) the work has been used by Christians of all denominations.

KEMSLEY, James Gomer Berry, 1st Viscount (1883–1968) Welsh newspaper proprietor, born in Merthyr Tydfil. He became chairman of Kemsley Newspapers Ltd in 1937, controlling *The Sunday Times* and other newspapers. He was created a baronet in 1928, raised to the peerage in 1936, and received a viscountcy in 1945. In 1950 he published *The Kemsley Manual of Journalism*. His brothers, Henry Seymour, Lord Buckland (1877–1928) and William Ewert, 1st Viscount **Camrose**, also owned newspapers.

KEN, Thomas (1631–1711) English prelate and hymn-writer, born in Little Berkhampstead, Hertfordshire. He held several livings and in 1666 was elected a fellow of Winchester where he prepared his *Manual of Prayers for Scholars of Winchester College* (1674), and wrote his morning, evening, and midnight hymns, the first two of which, 'Awake, my soul', and 'Glory to Thee, my God, this night', are among the best known. In 1679 he was appointed by **Charles II** chaplain to Princess **Mary**, wife of William of Orange (**William III**), but offended William, and returned home in 1680, when he became a royal chaplain. In 1683, on Charles II's visit to Winchester, Ken refused to give up his house for the accommodation of **Nell Gwynne**. In the same year he went to Tangiers as a chaplain, and in 1685 was consecrated bishop of Bath and Wells. The chief event of his bishopric was his trial and acquittal among the 'Seven Bishops' in 1688 for refusing to read the Declaration of Indulgence. At the 'Glorious Revolution' of 1688 he refused to take the oath of allegiance to William, and was deprived of his bishopric in 1691.

KENDAL, Dame Madge, stage name of **Margaret Brunton Grimston,** *née* Margaret Shafto Robertson (1849–1935) English actress, born in Cleethorpes, sister of **T W Robertson**. She appeared in Shakespearean roles and by the 1870s was leading lady at the Haymarket Theatre. In 1869 she married the actor William Hunter Kendal, properly Grimston (1843–1917), with whom she appeared in many productions, particularly Shakespearean. She was created a DBE in 1926.

KENDALL, Edward Calvin (1886–1972) American chemist, born in South Norwalk, Connecticut. At the Mayo Clinic, Rochester, he isolated the hormone of the thyroid gland, thyroxin (1915), and adrenal hormones like cortisone. With **Philip Hench** and **Tadens Reichstein**, he was awarded the Nobel prize for medicine in 1950.

KENDREW, Sir John Cowdery (1917–) English biochemist, born in Oxford. Educated at the Dragon School, Oxford, Clifton College, Bristol, and Trinity College, Cambridge, he was elected a fellow of Peterhouse College, Cambridge (1947–75), and was co-founder (with **Max Perutz**) and deputy chairman of the Medical Research Council unit for molecular biology at Cambridge (1946–75). He carried out researches in the chemistry of the blood and discovered the structure of the muscle protein myoglobin (1957), and was awarded the 1962 Nobel prize for chemistry jointly with Perutz. He wrote *The Thread of Life* (1966), and was president of St John's College, Oxford (1981–87).

KENEALLY, Thomas Michael (1935–) Australian novelist, born in Sydney, New South Wales. He studied for the priesthood and the law and served in the Australian Citizens' Military Forces. He has taught and lectured in drama. He would like, he has said, to disown his first two novels—*The Place at Whitton* (1964) and *The Fear* (1965). His third novel, *Bring Larks and Heroes* (1967) was 'an attempt to follow out an epic theme in terms of a young soldier's exile to Australia'. *Three Cheers for a Paraclete* (1968) and *The Survivor* (1969) were 'character' studies in the English tradition, but it was the publication of *The Chant of Jimmy Blacksmith* (1972), based on the slaughter of a white family by a hitherto docile Aboriginal employee, that marked the beginning of his mature fiction. As gifted as he is prolific, he is a born storytelller whose sympathies lie with the oppressed and the outcast. His reputation grew steadily until he published *Schindler's Ark* (1982), which tells how a German industrialist helped over 1000 Jews survive the Nazis. It was a controversial winner of the Booker prize because it blurred the boundary between fact and fiction. Recent books include *A Family Madness* (1985) and *The Playmaker* (1987), in which a group of young convicts in a remote penal colony stage the first-ever play in that part of the universe.

KENILOREA, Sir Peter (Kauona Keninarais'ona) (1943–) Solomon Islands politician, born in Takataka on Malaita Island. After training in New Zealand, he worked as a teacher before entering the Solomon Islands' civil service in 1971. He then moved into politics, eventually leading the Solomon Islands United party (SIUPA). He became chief minister in 1976 and prime minister after independence in 1978. His opposition to decentralization led to his departure in 1981, but he returned in 1984, leading a coalition government. He resigned the premiership in 1986, but remained foreign minister and deputy premier until the SIUPA coalition was defeated in the 1989 general election.

KENNAN, George Frost (1904–) American diplomat and historian, born in Milwaukee, Wisconsin. After graduating from Princeton in 1925 he joined the US foreign service and worked in 'listening posts' around the USSR. During World War II he served in the US legations in Berlin, Lisbon and Moscow, and in 1947 was appointed director of policy planning by secretary of state **George C Marshall**. He advocated the policy of 'containment' of the Soviet Union, a strategy which was adopted by secretary of state **Dean Acheson**, whom he served as principal adviser (1949–52), and **John Foster Dulles**. Kennan subsequently served as US ambassador in Moscow (1952–53) and Yugoslavia (1961–63). From 1956 to 1974, as professor of history at the Institute for Advanced Study in Princeton, he revised his strategic views and called for US 'disengagement' from Europe, and wrote *The Nuclear Delusion* (1982). His other books include *Realities of American Foreign Policy* (1954) and *Russia Leaves the War* (1956).

KENNAWAY, James (1928–68) Scottish novelist, born in Auchterarder, Perthshire, the son of a solicitor and a doctor. From a quiet, middle-class background, he went to public school at Glenalmond. He did national service before going to Trinity College, Oxford, following this by working for a London publisher and beginning to write in earnest. He married in 1951, and *The Kennaway Papers* (1981), edited by his wife Susan, gives an insight into his mercurial character and their turbulent relationship. *Tunes of Glory* (1956) was his first novel and remains his best known. The author himself wrote the screenplay to what was a successful film starring **Alec Guinness** and **John Mills** in a classic class confrontation set in a military barracks in Scotland. *Household Ghosts* (1961) was equally powerful and was made into a stage-play (1967) and a film (1969) under the title *Country Dance*. Later books of note are *The Bells of Shoreditch* (1967), *Some Gorgeous Accident* (1967) and *The Cost of Living Like This* (1969). *Silence*, a novel, was published posthumously in 1972.

KENNEDY, Edward Moore (1932–) American politician, youngest son of **Joseph Kennedy**, born in Brookline, Massachusetts. Educated at Harvard and Virginia University Law School, he was admitted to the Massachusetts bar in 1959, and was elected as Democratic senator for his brother **John F Kennedy**'s Massachusetts seat in 1962. In 1969 he became the youngest-ever majority whip in the US senate, but his involvement the same year in a car accident at Chappaquidick in which a girl was drowned dogged his subsequent political career, and caused his withdrawal as a presidential candidate in 1979.

KENNEDY, James (c.1408–65) Scottish prelate, son of James Kennedy of Dunure, grandson of King **Robert III** of Scotland and nephew of King **James I**. A graduate of St Andrews University and Louvain, he became bishop of Dunkeld in 1437, then bishop of St Andrews in 1440. As advisor to **James II**, he opposed the growing dominance of the **Douglases** in Scotland. During the minority of **James III**, he led the 'old lords' party in support of the Lancastrians. He founded St Salvator's College at St Andrews.

KENNEDY, John Fitzgerald (1917–63) 35th president of the US, son of **Joseph Kennedy**, born in Brookline, Massachusetts. He studied at Harvard and under **Laski** in London, and after service at the embassy there (1938), wrote a thesis on Britain's unpreparedness for war. His *Profiles of Courage* (1956) won the Pulitzer prize. As a torpedo boat commander in the Pacific, he was awarded the navy medal and the Purple Heart. Elected Democrat representative (1947) and senator (1952) for Massachusetts, in 1960 he was the first Catholic, and the youngest person, to be elected president, on the smallest majority of the popular vote. The conservatism of Congress stalled his bid for a 'new frontier' in social legislation. Through his brother **Robert Kennedy** he supported federal desegregation policy in schools and universities, and prepared further civil rights legislation. He displayed firmness and moderation in foreign policy, and in October 1962, at the risk of nuclear war, induced the Soviet Union to withdraw its missiles from Cuba, and achieved a partial nuclear test ban treaty with the Soviet Union in 1963. This followed the unsuccessful Bay of Pigs invasion of **Castro**'s Cuba (April 1961). On 22 November 1963, he was assassinated by rifle fire while being driven in an open car through Dallas, Texas. The alleged assassin, **Lee Harvey Oswald**, was himself shot and killed at point-blank range by Jack Ruby two days later while under heavy police escort on a jail transfer.

KENNEDY, Joseph Patrick (1888–1969) American multi-millionaire, born in Boston, grandson of an Irish Catholic immigrant, son of a Boston publican. Educated at Harvard, he made a large fortune in the 1920s, and during the 1930s was a strong supporter of **Roosevelt** and the 'New Deal', being rewarded with minor administrative posts, and the ambassadorship to Britain (1938–40). After World War II he concentrated on fulfilling his ambitions of a political dynasty through his sons. He had married in 1914 Rose Fitzgerald, daughter of a local politician, John F Fitzgerald, also of Irish immigrant descent. They had nine children, including **John F**, **Robert** and **Edward Kennedy**, at whose political disposal he placed his fortune. The eldest son, Joseph Patrick (1915–44), was killed in a flying accident while on naval service in World War II. For the careers of **John** and **Robert Kennedy** see separate entries.

KENNEDY, Ludovic Henry Coverley (1919–) Scottish broadcaster and writer, born in Edinburgh. Educated at Christ Church, Oxford, he served in the Royal Navy (1939–46) before becoming a librarian, lecturer and later editor of the BBC's *First Reading*

(1953–54). In 1950 he married the ballerina Moira Shearer. On television, he introduced *Profile* (1955–56), was an ITN newscaster (1956–58), hosted *This Week* (1958–60) and contributed to the BBC's *Panorama* (1960–63). He contested the Rochdale by-election as a Liberal in 1958 and the general election of 1959. He has devoted himself to defending victims of alleged injustice, helping to set the record straight on the falsely accused and wrongly convicted. His many notable series include *Your Verdict* (1962), *Your Witness* (1967–70) and *A Life With Crime* (1979). He has also acted as host on *Face the Press* (1968–72), *Tonight* (1976–78) and *Did You See?* (1980–88), among many others. His books include *Ten Rillington Place* (1961), *The Trial of Stephen Ward* (1964) and *A Presumption of Innocence: The Amazing Case of Patrick Meehan* (1975). He published an autobiography, *On My Way To The Club*, in 1989.

KENNEDY, Margaret (1896–1967) English novelist, journalist, and playwright, born in London, the daughter of a barrister. She was educated at Cheltenham College and Somerville College, Oxford. A historian by training, her first book was *A Century of Revolution* (1922). Thereafter she wrote novels, all of which gained a fair measure of success, particularly her second, *The Constant Nymph* (1924), and its sequel, *The Fool of the Family* (1930). She also wrote plays, notably *Escape Me Never* (1933).

KENNEDY, Robert Francis (1925–68) American politician, third son of **Joseph Kennedy**, born in Brookline, Massachusetts. Educated at Harvard and Virginia University Law School, he served at sea (1944–46) in World War II, was admitted to the Massachusetts bar (1951) and served on the Select Committee on Improper Activities (1957–59), when he prosecuted several top union leaders. An efficient manager of his brother **John F Kennedy**'s presidential campaign, he was an energetic attorney-general (1961–64) under the latter's administration, notable in his dealings with civil rights problems. Senator for New York from 1965, his tardy decision to stand as a Democratic presidential candidate in 1968 branded him as an opportunist to some, as an idealist reformer, closely identified with the struggles of America's underprivileged minorities, to others. On 5 June 1968, after winning the Californian primary election, he was shot, and died the following day. His assassin, **Sirhan Sirhan**, a 24-year-old Jordanian-born immigrant, was sentenced to the gas chamber in 1969.

KENNEDY, William Joseph (1928–) American novelist and screenwriter, born in Albany, New York. Educated at Siena College, Loudonville, New York, he served in the US army (1950–52) before becoming a journalist and eventually a full-time writer. *The Ink Truck* (1969) is distinct from subsequent novels for it does not use the locale of his hometown as a backdrop. *Legs* (1975) is the first of the 'Albany' novels, a mixture of fact and fiction which retells the story of Legs Diamond, the notorious gangster. In *Billy Phelan's Greatest Game* (1978), Albany is as important as the two main characters, the gamester Billy Phelan and journalist Martin Daugherty. *Ironweed* (1983), his best-known novel, describes the homecoming of a fallen baseball star, now down-and-out, drunk and maudlin. **Jack Nicholson** made an accurate film portrayal and the book won a Pulitzer prize. *Quinns's Book* was published in 1988.

KENNELLY, Arthur Edwin (1861–1939) Irish American engineer, born in Bombay. He went to the USA in 1887, and worked as assistant to **Edison**. He became a professor at Harvard from 1902 to 1930, and in 1902 suggested, almost simultaneously with **Oliver Heaviside**, the existence of an ionized E-layer in the atmosphere known as the Kennelly-Heaviside layer, or Heaviside layer.

KENNETH I, called **Macalpin** (9th century) king of the Scots. He seems to have succeeded his father Alpin as king in 841, and to have won acceptance by the Picts by 843. His reign marked a decisive step in the making of a united kingdom and also saw the shift of the centre of the church from Iona to the court at Dunkeld.

KENNINGTON, Eric Henri (1888–1960) English painter and sculptor, born in London. He was an official war artist in both world wars, and in the field of sculpture and designed many memorials.

KENNY, Elizabeth (1886–1952) Australian nurse, renowned as 'Sister Kenny'. She began practising as a nurse in the bush-country in Australia (1912), and then joined the Australian army nursing corps (1915–19). She developed a new technique for treating poliomyelitis by muscle therapy rather than immobilization with casts and splints. She established clinics in Australia (1933), Britain (1937) and America (Minneapolis, 1940), and travelled widely to demonstrate her methods. She published her autobiography, *And They Shall Walk*, in 1943.

KENT, Bruce (1929–) British cleric and peace campaigner. After education in Canada and at Oxford University, he was ordained in 1958 and then served as a curate in Kensington, London (1958–63). He was subsequently secretary in the Archbishop's House, Westminster, Catholic chaplain to London University and a parish priest. He became increasingly involved in the Campaign for Nuclear Disarmament (CND), becoming its general secretary in 1980, its vice-chairman in 1985 and its chairman in 1987. In that year he resigned his ministry.

KENT, Edward, Duke of(1767–1820) fourth son of **George III**, born in Buckingham Palace. At Gibraltar, first (1790–91) as colonel, and then (1802) as governor, his martinet discipline caused continual mutinies. These culminated in an encounter in which blood was shed, after which he was recalled. In 1818 he married Victoria Mary Louisa (1786–1861), daughter of the Duke of Saxe-Saalfeld-Coburg, and widow of the Prince of Leiningen. For the sake of economy they lived at Leiningen, and came to England for the birth (24 May 1819) of their child, the Princess **Victoria**. The duke died eight months later. Owing to the deaths without issue of his three elder brothers, **George IV**, the Duke of York, and **William IV**, the crown came to the Princess Victoria in 1837.

KENT, Edward (George Nicholas Patrick) Duke of Kent, (1935–) son of George, Duke of **Kent**. He was commissioned in the army in 1955. In 1961 he married Katharine Worsley (b.1933), and they have three children, George Philip Nicholas, Earl of St Andrews (b.1962), Helen Marina Lucy (b.1964) and Nicholas Charles Edward Jonathan (b.1970). He retired from the army in 1976.

KENT, George Edward Alexander Edmund, Duke of Kent, (1902–42) son of King **George V** and Queen Mary. He passed out of Dartmouth Naval College in 1920, but because of delicate health served in the foreign office and inspected factories for the home office, the first member of the British royal family to work in the civil service. In 1934 he was created duke, and married Princess Marina of Greece and Denmark (1906–68), a first cousin of King **George I** of Greece and a great-niece of Queen **Alexandra**. He was killed on active service, as chief welfare officer of the RAF Home Command, when his Sunderland flying-boat on its way to Iceland crashed in the north of Scotland. Their three children are Edward Duke of **Kent**, Princess **Alexandra**

and Prince Michael of Kent (1942–), who married in 1978 Baroness Marie-Christine von Reibniz, and whose children are Lord Frederick Windsor (1979–) and Lady Gabriella Windsor (1981–).

KENT, James (1763–1847) American lawyer, born in Fredericksburgh, New York. After serving in the New York legislature he became professor of law in Columbia College 1794–98, and then a justice of the supreme court of New York. In 1804 he became chief justice, and from 1814 to 1823 was state chancellor. His *Commentaries on American Law* (1826–30), modelled on Sir **William Blackstone**, was America's first legal classic and immensely influential for many years.

KENT, Rockwell (1882–1971) American artist, born in Tarrytown, New York. He studied with **William Merritt Chase** in 1900 and became well known as a painter, book designer and illustrator, explorer, writer, sailor and political activist. His output of wood engravings, lithographs, textiles, oils and watercolours was inspired by the great outdoors, his rugged lifestyle and experience of travel. He was involved in the organization of the 1910 Exhibition of Independent Artists and was awarded the Lenin Peace prize in Moscow in 1967. He travelled to Alaska, Latin America, Europe and Greenland.

KENT, William (1684–1748) English architect and landscape designer, born in Yorkshire. He studied painting in Rome (1709–19), and played a leading part in introducing the Palladian style of architecture into Britain. He designed many public buildings in London, including the Royal Mews in Trafalgar Square, the Treasury buildings and the Horse Guards block in Whitehall. As an interior designer he decorated Burlington House and Chiswick House in London. As a landscape designer he liberated gardens from strict formality and introduced romantic settings, as at Stowe House in Buckinghamshire. An artist of immense versatility, he also designed the Gothic screens in Westminster Hall and Gloucester Cathedral.

KENTIGERN, St, also called **Mungo** (c.518–603) Celtic churchman, the apostle of Cumbria. According to legend he was the son of a Princess Thenew, who was cast from Traprain Law, then exposed on the Firth of Forth in a coracle. It carried her to Culross, where she bore a son (about 518). Mother and child were baptized (an anachronism) by St **Serf**, who reared the boy in his monastery, where he was so beloved that his name Kentigern ('chief lord') was often exchanged for Mungo ('dear friend'). He founded a monastery at Cathures (now Glasgow), and in 543 was consecrated bishop of Cumbria. In 553 he was driven to seek refuge in Wales, where he visited St **David**, and where he founded another monastery and a bishopric, which still bears the name of his disciple, St Asaph. In 573 he was recalled by a new king, Rederech Hael, and about 584 was visited by **Columba**. He was buried in Glasgow Cathedral, which is named after him as St Mungo's. A fragment of a Life, and the *Vita Kentigerni* by Joceline of Furness both belong to the 12th century.

KENTNER, Louis Philip (1905–87) Hungarian-born British pianist, born in Karwin, Silesia. He studied from the age of six at the Budapest Royal Academy and made his début in Budapest in 1916. An acclaimed interpreter of **Chopin** and **Liszt**, he also gave first performances of works by **Bartók**, **Kodály**, **Tippett**, **Walton** and others. He settled in England in 1935 and was a frequent chamber-music partner of his brother-in-law, **Yehudui Menuhin**.

KENTON, Stan (Stanley Newcomb) (1912–79) American pianist, composer and bandleader, born in Wichita, Kansas. Brought up in Los Angeles, he studied piano privately before beginning his professional career in 1934 with a succession of lesser-known big bands. He first formed his own orchestra in 1941, but is more immediately associated with the big band 'progressive' jazz style of the 1950s, using dissonant ensemble writing. His later orchestras were unusual for their five-member trombone sections; and although some aspects of progressive jazz were dismissed as pretentious, Kenton's innovations, employing adventurous arrangers and outstanding soloists, have stood the test of time.

KENYATTA, Jomo (c.1889–1978) Kenyan politician, born an orphan in Mitumi, Kenya. Educated at a Scots mission school, he began as a herd boy. He joined the Kikuyu Central Association (1922), and became its president. He visited Britain in 1929 and from 1931 to 1944, and studied for a year at London University under **Malinowski**, who wrote the preface to his book *Facing Mount Kenya* (1938). He visited Russia thrice, and was president of the Pan African Federation with **Nkrumah** as secretary. He worked on the land during the war and married an Englishwoman in 1942. On returning to Kenya in 1946 his Kenya African Union advocated extreme nationalism, and he led the Mau Mau guerrilla group. Sentenced to seven years' hard labour in 1952, he was released in 1958, but exiled first to a remote northern area, then to his native village. Elected president of the dominant KANU party, and MP in 1961, he became prime minister in June 1963, retaining the post after Kenya's independence in December 1963, and becoming president of the republic of Kenya in December 1964.

KENYON, Dame Kathleen Mary (1906–78) English archaeologist of biblical sites, particularly Jerusalem and Jericho. The daughter of a director of the British Museum, she was educated at St Paul's Girls' School and Somerville College, Oxford. She was lecturer in Palestinian archaeology at London University (1948–62) and principal of St Hugh's College, Oxford (1962–73). She was also director of the British School of Archaeology in Jerusalem from 1951 to 1966. Her most notable books are *Digging up Jericho* (1957), *Archaeology in the Holy Land* (1965), and *Digging up Jerusalem* (1974).

KENZO, Takada (1940–) Japanese fashion designer, born in Kyoto. After studying art and graduating in Japan, he worked there for a time, but produced freelance collections in Paris from 1964. He started a shop called Jungle Jap in 1970, and is known for his innovative ideas and use of traditional designs. He creates clothes with both oriental and western influences and is a trendsetter in the field of knitwear.

KEPLER, Johann (1571–1630) German astronomer, born in Weil der Stadt in Württemberg. He studied at Tübingen, and in 1593 was appointed professor of mathematics at Graz. In 1600 he went to Prague as assistant to **Tycho Brahe**, and succeeded him in 1601 as court astonomer to the emperor **Rudolf II**. In 1612 he became a mathematics teacher at Linz, and in 1628 became astrologer to **Albrecht Wallenstein** at Sagan in Silesia. In his *Mysterium cosmographicum* (1596) he proclaimed that five kinds of regular polyhedral bodies govern the five planetary orbits. He announced his First and Second Laws in *Astronomia nova* (1909) which formed the groundwork of **Isaac Newton**'s discoveries, and are the starting point of modern astronomy. His Third Law was promulgated in *Harmonice mundi* (1619), stating that 'the square of a planet's periodic time is proportional to the cube of its mean distance from the sun'. He also made many discoveries in optics, general physics, and geometry.

KEPPEL, Augustus, 1st Viscount (1725–86) English naval commander, second son of the 2nd Earl of

Albemarle. He served under **Hawke** in the Seven Years' War (1756–63), captured Gorée in 1758, commanded a ship in the battle of Quiberon Bay in 1759, and in the capture of Belleisle in 1761, and was second in command at the capture of Havana in 1762. In 1778, as commander-in-chief of the grand fleet, he encountered the French fleet off Ushant, but the French escaped. He was tried by court martial for neglect of duty, but was acquitted. He became First Lord of the Admiralty in 1782–83.

KEPPEL, Sir Henry (1809–1904) English naval commander, son of the 4th Earl of Albemarle. He saw service during the war against China (1842), in the naval brigades before Sebastopol in the Crimea (1854), and in Chinese waters (1857). He also commanded a seven-nation force against pirates in the area from 1867 to 1869. He was promoted admiral in 1869, and admiral of the fleet in 1877. He wrote *A Sailor's Life under Four Sovereigns* (3 vols, 1899).

KER, William Paton (1855–1923) Scottish scholar, born in Glasgow. Educated at Glasgow and at Balliol College, Oxford, he was professor of English at Cardiff (1883), University College, London (1889), and of poetry at Oxford (1920). A talker, lecturer, and writer of prodigious learning and vitality, he wrote *Epic and Romance* (1897), *The Dark Ages* (1904), *Essays on Medieval Literature* (1905), and *The Art of Poetry* (1923).

KEREKOU, Mathieu Ahmed (1933–) Benin soldier and politician, born in Natitingou. Trained in France, he served in the French army before joining the army of what was Dahomey, where he took part in a coup which removed the civilian government in 1967. He returned to military matters the following year and rose to the position of army deputy chief. In 1972 he led the coup which removed the government of Justin Ahomadegbe, establishing a National Council of the Revolution (CNR), intended to lead the country towards 'scientific socialism'. To mark this new direction, the name of Benin was adopted. Gradually social and economic stability returned, the CNR was dissolved and a civilian administration installed. Kerekou was elected president in 1980 and re-elected in 1984. In 1987 he resigned from the army as a gesture of his commitment to genuine democracy.

KERENSKY, Alexander Feodorovich (1881–1970) Russian revolutionary leader, born in Simbirsk (now Ulyanovsk), the son of a high school principal. He studied law at Leningrad, and defended in some celebrated political trials. He was a member of the Socialist Revolutionary party from 1905, and a member of the Duma (1912–17). He took a leading part in the revolution of 1917, becoming minister of justice (March), for war (May), and premier (July). He insisted on Russia remaining a combatant in World War I, and crushed **Kornilov**'s military revolt (September), but was deposed (November) by the Bolsheviks and fled to France. In 1940 he went to Australia and in 1946 to the USA, where he taught at Stanford University from 1956. His writings include *The Prelude to Bolshevism* (1919), *The Catastrophe* (1927), *The Road to Tragedy* (1935), and *The Kerensky Memoirs* (1966).

KERGUÉLEN-TRÉMAREC, Yves Joseph de (1745–97) French aristocrat and naval officer, born in Quimper in Brittany. On an unsuccessful voyage of exploration seeking Terra Australis he discovered a group of islands in the South Indian Ocean to which he gave his name as Kerguélen's Islands (1772).

KERN, Jerome (1885–1945) American composer, born in New York. He wrote a vast quantity of music for musical comedy and films. His scores include *The Red Petticoat* (which first brought a 'western' setting to Broadway in 1912) *Sally*, *Roberta*, and *Very Warm for May*, and contain such evergreen songs as 'Look for the Silver Lining' and 'Smoke Gets in your Eyes'. His greatest success came with the operetta *Show Boat* (1927), a work which has had a lasting influence upon American light entertainment.

KERNER, Andreas Justinus (1786–1862) German poet, born in Ludwigsburg in Württemberg. He became a physician at Wildbad, and settled finally in Weinsberg in 1818. He published several volumes of poetry between 1811 and 1852. He studied animal magnetism, believed in occultism, and wrote *Die Seherin von Prevorst* (1829).

KERNER VON MARILAUN, Anton Joseph (1831–98) Austrian botanist, born in Mautern. He studied medicine at Vienna, and was professor at Innsbruck (1860–78) and Vienna (1878–98). He was the author of pioneering ecological works such as *Das Pflanzenleben der Donauländer* (1863), *Die Schutzmittel der Blüthen* (1876), *Monographia Pulmonariarum* (1878) and the highly influential and popular *Pflanzenleben* (The Natural History of Plants, 1886–91).

KEROUAC, Jack (John) (1922–69) American novelist, born in Lowell, Massachusetts. His parents, devout Roman Catholics, came from rural communities in the French-speaking part of Quebec, and French was spoken in the home. He did not begin to learn to speak English until he was six. His childhood was happy, but various disasters struck the stability of the family, including the death of an older brother and floods which destroyed his father's print shop and press. He was educated at Lowell High School before accepting a football scholarship at Columbia University, but he turned his back on both and spent the early years of World War II working as a grease monkey in Hartford before returning to Lowell where he got a job as a sports journalist on the *Lowell Sun*. His major energies, however, were spent working on an autobiographical novel that was never published. In 1942 he went to Washington where he worked briefly on the construction of the Pentagon before joining the US merchant marines, subsequently enlisting in the US navy (1943). After only a month he was discharged and branded an 'indifferent character', having discarded his rifle in favour of **Boswell**'s *Life of Johnson*. His life is frequently seen as a rebellion against authority but his various scrapes and outbreaks of outrageous behaviour were less the actions of a subversive than of a weak-willed conservative influenced by persuasive friends like **Allen Ginsberg**, **Gary Snyder** and Neal Cassady, whom Kerouac portrayed as Dean Moriarty in his most famous novel, *On the Road* (1957). Collectively, he called the group 'the Beat Generation', a label he came to regret and repudiate. *The Town and the City* (1950), his first novel, showed the scars of his reading of **Thomas Wolfe**. *On the Road* was his second. Loose, apparently structureless and episodic, it follows two friends as they weave their way across America. It has been much imitated (on film as well as in fiction) and made Kerouac a cult-hero. Later books—*The Dharma Bums* (1958), *Doctor Sax* (1959), *Big Sur* (1962)—were even more self-indulgent as he flirted with Zen Buddhism.

KÉROUALLE, Louise de See **PORTSMOUTH**

KERR, or **Ker** an Anglo-Norman family, first recorded in Scotland at the end of the 12th century. Sir Andrew Ker of Cessford (d.1526), whose younger brother, George, was ancestor of the Kers of Faudonside, had two sons—Sir Walter, whose grandson, Robert Ker, was created Earl of Roxburghe in 1616, and Mark, commendator of Newbattle, whose son,

Mark Kerr, was created Earl of Lothian in 1606. The second Earl of Roxburghe was only a Ker by his mother. His grandson, the 5th Earl, was created duke in 1707. John, 3rd Duke (1740–1804), was a renowned book-collector.

KERR, Deborah, originally **Deborah Jane Kerr-Trimmer** (1921–) Scottish actress, born in Helensburgh. Trained as a dancer, she made her stage début in the corps-de-ballet of a Sadler's Wells production of *Prometheus* (1938). Choosing instead to act, she appeared in repertory in Oxford before making her film début in *Contraband* (1940). British successes in *The Life and Death of Colonel Blimp* (1943) and *Black Narcissus* (1947) brought her a Hollywood contract. Invariably cast in well-bred, ladylike roles, she played numerous governesses and nuns, sensationally straying from her established image to play a nymphomaniac in *From Here to Eternity* (1953). Nominated six times for an Academy Award, she retired from the screen in 1969, returning to the theatre in works such as *Seascape* (1975), *Long Day's Journey Into Night* (1977) and *Overheard* (1981). Active on stage and television, she returned to the cinema in *The Assam Garden* (1985).

KERR, John (1824–1907) Scottish physicist, born in Ardrossan. Educated at Glasgow University in theology, he became a lecturer in mathematics. In 1876 he discovered the magneto-optic effect which was then named after him. He was the author of *An Elementary Treatise on Rational Mechanics* (1867).

KERR, Sir John Robert (1914–) Australian lawyer and administrator, born in Sydney, the son of a boilermaker. He graduated from Sydney University with first class honours and the university medal. He was admitted to the New South Wales bar in 1938 and, following war service, became a QC in 1953. After a number of senior legal and judicial appointments, he became chief justice of New South Wales in 1972, and lieutenant-governor in the following year. He was sworn in as governor-general of the Commonwealth of Australia in 1974, and the next year made constitutional history. The coalition opposition had refused to pass the government's budget bill unless a federal election was called. The private banks declined to release funds to enable the business of government to be conducted. To resolve this impasse he exercised his vice-regal 'reserve powers' and withdrew the commission of the prime minister, **Gough Whitlam**, requesting the leader of the opposition, **Malcolm Fraser**, to form a caretaker government and to call an immediate election. At that election, Kerr's actions were endorsed by the voters, who elected a new coalition government, led by Fraser. Stepping down as governor-general in 1977, he was named Australian ambassador to UNESCO in 1978, but the ensuing controversy obliged him to resign without taking up the appointment.

KERTÉSZ, André (1894–1985) Hungarian-born American photographer, born in Budapest. He started as a photographer in 1912, using glass plates, served as a photographer with the Hungarian army in World War I, emigrated to France in 1925 and then to the USA in 1936, and became an American citizen in 1944. He was acclaimed in Paris as a freelance photo-reporter of the 'human condition', and he strongly influenced **Brassai** and **Cartier-Bresson**; he was one of the first serious users of the Leica miniature camera in 1928. His work in New York in the 1940s and 1950s for Condé-Nast publications and similar magazines became more glossily conventional, and he did not return to a more individual creative style until 1962. A major retrospective exhibition at the New York Museum of Modern Art in 1964 was followed by numerous international presentations which brought him awards and belated official recognition in the 1970s.

KESEY, Ken Elton (1935–) American author, born in La Junta, Colorado. Associated with the 'Beat' movement, he worked as a ward attendant in a mental hospital, an experience he used to telling effect in *One Flew Over the Cuckoo's Nest* (1963), narrated by an Indian named Chief Bromden whose father was the last chief of the tribe. Filmed in 1975 by Milos Forman it won five Oscars, including that for Best Film. *Sometimes a Great Notion* (1966) sunk like lead and he relinquished 'literature' for 'life'. He served a prison sentence for marijuana possession and formed the 'Merry Pranksters', whose weird exploits are described at length in *The Electric Kool-Aid Acid Test* (1967) by **Tom Wolfe**.

KET, Robert (d.1549) English rebel, a landowner of Wymondham in Norfolk. In July 1549 he headed 16000 insurgents in an uprising against common land enclosures. Norwich was twice captured by the rebels; on the second occasion they held it until they were driven out by John Dudley, Earl of **Warwick**. Kett was captured and hanged.

KETCH, Jack (d.1686) English hangman and headsman from about 1663. He was notorious for his barbarity and bungling, particularly the executions of William, Lord **Russell** (1683) and the Duke of **Monmouth** (1685). His name became synonymous with the hangman's job.

KETÈLBEY, Albert William, pseudonym of **Anton Vodorinski** (1875–1959) English composer and conductor, born in Birmingham. Success came early with, for example, a piano sonata written at the age of eleven. His light, colourful and tuneful orchestral pieces had enormous popularity, and included *In a Monastery Garden*, *In a Persian Market* and *Sanctuary of the Heart* and many others.

KETTLEWELL, Henry Bernard David (1907–79) English geneticist and entomologist, born in Howden, Yorkshire. Educated at Charterhouse School and in Paris, he studied medicine at Gonville and Caius College, Cambridge, and St Bartholomew's Hospital, London. From 1952 he held various posts in the genetics unit of the zoology department, Oxford. His best known research was concerned with the industrial melanism of the peppered moth (*Bison Betularia*). This common moth developed a dark-coloured morph in areas where industry and dense populations caused atmospheric carbon pollution. He demonstrated the survival value of the dark coloration in industrial regions and the original light coloration in rural areas, thus demonstrating the effectiveness of natural selection as an evolutionary process.

KEULEN, Ludolph van See **CEULEN**

KEY, Ellen Karolina Sophia (1849–1926) Swedish reformer and educationist, born in Sundsholm, Småland. She became a teacher in Stockholm (1880–99) when her father lost his fortune. She made her name as a writer on the feminist movement, child welfare, sex, love, and marriage, in *Barnets århundrade* (1900) and *Lifslinjer* (1903–36).

KEY, Francis Scott (1780–1843) American lawyer and poet, born in Maryland, author of *The Star-Spangled Banner*. During the British bombardment of Fort McHenry, Baltimore, in September, 1814, which he witnessed from a British man-of-war, he wrote a poem about the lone American flag seen flying over the fort as dawn broke. It was published as *The Defence of Fort McHenry*, and later set to a tune by the English composer, **John Stafford Smith** (*To Anacreon in*

Heaven). In 1931 it was adopted as the American national anthem as *The Star-Spangled Banner*.

KEY, Thomas Hewitt (1799–1875) English classical scholar, born in London. Educated at St John's and Trinity College, Cambridge, he was appointed professor of Latin in the University of London (1828), and of comparative grammar (1842). He was the author of a *Latin Grammar* (1846) and a *Latin Dictionary* (1888).

KEYES, Roger John Brownlow, 1st Baron Keyes (1872–1945) English naval commander. He entered the navy in 1885, served at Witu (1890) and in the Boxer Rebellion (1900). He was inspecting captain of submarines (1912–15) and commodore Harwich in 1914. In World War I he was chief of staff Eastern Mediterranean (1915–16) and in 1918 commanded the Dover Patrol, leading the raids on German U-boat bases at Zeebrugge and Ostend (1918). He was commander-in-chief Mediterranean (1925–29), and commander Portsmouth (1929–31). MP for Portsmouth (1934–43), he was recalled in 1940, and appointed director of combined operations (1940–41), subsequently becoming liaison officer to the Belgians. He wrote *Naval Memoirs* (2 vols, 1934–35), *Adventures Ashore and Afloat* (1939) and *Amphibious Warfare and Combined Operations* (1943). His son, Lieut-Colonel Geoffrey Keyes, MC and posthumous VC, was killed in the historic commando raid on Rommel's HQ in 1941.

KEYES, Sydney Arthur Kilworth (1922–43) English poet, born in Dartford, Kent. His first book of poems, *The Iron Laurel*, was published in 1942, and his second, *The Cruel Solstice*, in 1944 (Hawthornden prize), after his death in action in Libya.

KEYNES, John Maynard, 1st Baron (1883–1946) English economist, pioneer of the theory of full employment, born in Cambridge. The son of John Neville (1852–1949) the Cambridge logician and political economist, he was educated at Eton and King's College, Cambridge, where he became one of the 'Bloomsbury group' and where, from 1908, he lectured sporadically in economics. He was at the India Office (1906–08) and in 1913, as a member of the royal commission on Indian finance and currency, published his first book on this subject. In both world wars he was an adviser to the Treasury, which he represented at the Versailles Peace Conference but resigned in strong opposition to the terms of the draft treaty. He set out his views against the harsh economic terms imposed on Germany in the Versailles Treaty in *The Economic Consequences of the Peace* (1919), written with the encouragement of **Jan Smuts**. In 1921 *Treatise of Probability* appeared, in which he explored the logical relationships between calling something 'highly probable' and a 'justifiable induction'. In 1923 he became chairman of the Liberal periodical, *Nation*, and pamphleteered his controversial views on European reconstruction, strongly attacking **Churchill**'s restoration of the gold standard (1925). The unemployment crises inspired his two great works, *A Treatise on Money* (1930) and the revolutionary *General Theory of Employment, Interest and Money* (1936). He argued that full employment was not an automatic condition, expounded a new theory of the rate of interest, and set out the principles underlying the flows of income and expenditure. He also fought the Treasury view that unemployment was incurable. His views on a planned economy influenced **Roosevelt**'s 'New Deal' administration. He married a **Diaghilev** ballerina, Lydia Lopokova, and with her helped to found the Vic-Wells ballet. He financed the establishment of the Arts Theatre, Cambridge. In 1943 he proposed the international clearing union, played a leading part (1944–46) in the formulation of the Bretton Woods agreements, the establishment of the International Monetary Fund, and the troublesome, abortive negotiations for a continuation of American Lend-lease. He died just prior to being awarded the OM. He also wrote *Essays in Persuasion* (1931) and *Essays in Biography* (1933).

KEYSER, Hendrik de (1565–1621) Dutch architect and sculptor. He trained with the sculptor **Abraham Bloemaert** in 1591. His designs in a Mannerist vein were often tempered with traditional Dutch details. He engineered an opening bridge (1596), and from 1612 he produced an imitation marble. Notable sculptural commissions were the Tomb of the Silent Delft (1614–21) and the bronze statue of **Erasmus** in Rotterdam (1621). His three Amsterdam churches form a group: Zuiderkerk (1603–14), Westerkerk (1620–38) and Noorderkerk (1620–22). Between 1608 and 1611, with Cornelis Danckerts, he designed the Amsterdam Exchange (derived from the London Royal Exchange). In 1615 he produced designs for Haarlemmerpoort gates. Certain later works were published in *Architectura Moderna* (1631), which served as a pattern book for succeeding generations.

KHALID, ibn Abdul Aziz (1913–82) King of Saudi Arabia from 1975, fourth son of the founder of the Saudi dynasty, and king of Saudi Arabia from 1975 till his death. A quiet and unspectacular monarch who had been troubled by ill-health for many years, he ascended the throne after the assassination of his brother King **Faisal**. Khalid's caution and moderation served as a stabilizing factor in the volatile Middle East and won international respect. His personal influence was in evidence at the halting of the Lebanese civil war (1975–76) and in Saudi Arabia's disagreement with the other members of the Organisation of Petroleum Exporting Countries over oil price increases. Khalid was especially esteemed by the Bedouin tribesmen, who shared with him a religious outlook and a fondness for the traditional pursuits of falconry and hunting.

KHAMA, Sir Seretse (1921–80) African politician, born at Serowe, Bechuanaland (now Botswana). He was nephew of Tshekedi Khama (1905–59), who was chief regent of the Bamangwato from 1925. Seretse was educated in Africa and Balliol College, Oxford. While a student at the Inner Temple in 1948 he married an Englishwoman, and in 1950, with his uncle, was banned from the chieftainship and the territory of the Bamangwato. Allowed to return in 1956, he became active in politics, and was restored to the chieftainship in 1963. He became first prime minister of Bechuanaland in 1965 and president of Botswana in 1966, having received a knighthood.

KHATCHATURIAN, Aram (1903–78) Russian composer, born in Tbilisi, Georgia, of Armenian descent. A student of folksong, and an authority on oriental music, his compositions include symphonies, concertos, ballets, film and instrumental music.

KHAYYAM, Omar See **OMAR KHAYYAM**

KHINCHIN, Aleksandr Yakovlevich (1894–1959) Russian mathematician, born in Kondrovo. He studied at Moscow University, and became professor there in 1927. With **Andrei Kolmogorov** he founded the Soviet school of probability theory; he also worked in analysis, number theory, statistical mechanics and information theory.

KHOMEINI, Ayatollah Ruhollah (1900–89) Iranian religious and political leader. A Shiite Muslim who was bitterly opposed to the pro-western régime of Shah of Persia Mohammed Reza Pahlavi, Khomeini was exiled to Turkey, Iraq and France from 1964. He returned to Iran amid great popular acclaim in 1979 after the collapse of the Shah's government, and became virtual head of state. Under his leadership, Iran underwent a turbulent 'Islamic Revolution' in which a return was made to the strict observance of Muslim principles and traditions, many of which had been abandoned during the previous régime. In 1989 he provoked international controversy by publicly commanding the killing of **Salman Rushdie**, author of the novel *The Satanic Verses*.

KHORANA, Har Gobind (1922–) Indian-born American molecular chemist, born in Raipur (now in Pakistan). He studied at Punjab University, Liverpool, Zürich and Cambridge, and moved to Vancouver in 1952. His work on nucleotide synthesis at Wisconsin (1960–70) was a major contribution to the elucidation of the genetic code whereby a sequence of nucleotide triplets ('codons') within DNA molecules transfer genetic information between generations in living cells. Then, in 1970, he achieved a historic synthesis, that of the first artificial gene; he moved to the Massachusetts Institute of Technology in the same year. He shared the 1968 Nobel prize for physiology or medicine with **Marshall Nirenberg** and **Robert Holley**.

KHOSRU See **CHOSROES**

KHRUSHCHEV, Nikita Sergeyevich (1894–1971) Soviet politician, born in Kalinovka near Kursk. He was a shepherd boy and a locksmith and is said to have been almost illiterate until the age of 25. Joining the Communist party in 1918, he fought in the Civil War and rose rapidly in the party organization. In 1939 he was made a full member of the Politburo and of the Praesidium of the Supreme Soviet. In World War II he organized guerrilla warfare in the Ukraine against the invading Germans and took charge of the reconstruction of devastated territory. In 1949 he launched a drastic reorganization of Soviet agriculture. In 1953 on the death of **Stalin** he became first secetary of the All Union party and three years later, at the 20th congress of the Communist party, denounced Stalinism and the 'personality cult'. The following year he demoted **Molotov**, **Kaganovich** and **Malenkov**—all possible rivals. Khrushchev, who did much to enhance the ambitions and status of the Soviet Union abroad, was nevertheless deposed in 1964 and forced into retirement. Opposition to his decentralization, economic reforms, and attacks on the entrenched party bureaucracy, coupled with concern amongst conservative colleagues at his forceful and personalized leadership style and at the destablilizing impact of de-Stalinization in the cultural and political spheres, were the prime factors behind Khrushchev's ousting. He has been substantially rehabilitated during recent years, with the text of his 'secret speech' to the 20th Communist party congress (1956, in which he formally denounced Stalinism) being officially published for the first time in 1989.

KIDD, Michael (1919–) American dancer, choreographer and director, born in Brooklyn, New York. Having studied privately and at the School of American Ballet, he appeared on Broadway in 1937 and danced with American Ballet the same year. He later danced with Ballet Caravan (1937–40), Dance Players (1941–42) and American Ballet Theatre (1942–47), for whom he choreographed *On Stage I* (1945). He then became a successful choreographer of Broadway and Hollywood musicals, including *Finian's Rainbow* (1947), *Guys and Dolls* (1951), *Can-Can* (1953), *Seven Brides for Seven Brothers* (1954) and *Hello, Dolly!* (1969). He also appeared in the 1955 film *It's Always Fair Weather* with **Gene Kelly**.

KIDD, William, known as **Captain Kidd** (c.1645–1701) Scottish merchant and privateer, born in Greenock. His early life is unknown; but in the 1680s he was operating as a successful sea-captain with a small fleet of trading vessels, based in New York. During the War of the League of Augsburg against France (1688–97) he fought as a privateer to protect Anglo-American trade routes in the West Indies; and in 1691 was given a reward by New York City for his exploits. In 1695 he went to London and was given command of an expedition against pirates in the Indian Ocean. He reached Madagascar early in 1697, but instead of attacking pirates began to sanction attacks on merchant ships as well, including the *Quedagh Maiden*, an Armenian merchantman. After a two-year cruise he returned to the West Indies to find that he had been proclaimed a pirate. He sailed to Boston, where he surrendered on promise of a pardon in 1699. Instead he was sent as a prisoner to London, where he was convicted of piracy and hanged.

KIDDER, Alfred Vincent (1885–1963) American archaeologist, born in Marquette, Michigan, and pioneer of stratigraphic methods on a large scale in the USA. He was educated at Harvard, where he came under the influence of the Egyptologist **George A Reisner**, whose systematic approach to fieldwork he adopted with notable success in Utah, Colorado, and New Mexico (1907–14). His extensive excavations (1915–29) at Pecos, New Mexico, an Indian pueblo inhabited from 1000 AD to the 19th century, revolutionized American settlement archaeology and allowed him to develop a chronological sequence for the cultures of the region, promulgated in his *Introduction to the Study of Southwestern Archaeology* (1924), which, with modifications, still endures. He subsequently became involved in Maya archaeology, from 1929 undertaking major work for the Carnegie Institution of Washington, at Kaminaljuyu and at Uaxactun in Guatemala. He later joined the faculty of the Peabody Museum at Harvard (1939–50).

KIDMAN, Sir Sidney (1857–1935) Australian pastoralist, born near Adelaide, South Australia. He left home at the age of 13, with five shillings in his pocket and riding a one-eyed horse. In 1886 he bought his first grazing station and 30 years later he controlled lands greater in area than the whole of England. By judicious dealing in horses and cattle he gradually built up sufficient capital to purchase vast numbers of stations. This ability to move stock to well-watered areas in times of drought, and selling in the best markets, enabled Kidman to withstand the depression years of the 1890s and the Great Drought of 1902. During World War I he gave fighter planes to the forces and made substantial gifts to charities and the government.

KIEFER, Anselm (1945–) German avant-garde artist, born in Donaueschingen, Bavaria. He held his first one-man show in Karlsruhe, in 1969. A pupil of **Joseph Beuys** in Düsseldorf (1970–72), he lives and works in Hornbach/Odenwald, making 'books' from photographs or woodcuts, sometimes cut or worked over. Some critics have seen 'Fascist', others medieval or Nordic, symbolism in his work.

KIELLAND, Alexander Lange (1849–1906) Norwegian novelist, born in Stavanger, where he became burgomaster in 1891. A follower of **Georg Brandes**, he was an exponent of the realist school. His stylish novels of social satire included *Garman og Worse* (1880), *Skipper Worse* (1882) and *Tales of Two Countries* (1891). He also wrote plays and short stories.

KIENHOLZ, Edward (1927–) American avant-garde artist, born in Fairfield, Washington. Self-taught, he opened the Now Gallery in Los Angeles in 1956, and co-founded the city's first avante-garde gallery, the Ferus Gallery, in 1957. He makes 'assemblages' which are typically room-size and incorporate dummies, furniture, bones, rugs, household objects, and quantities of 'blood' arranged to create shockingly violent tableaux, eg *State Hospital* (1966). He held a major exhibition in Los Angeles in 1968.

KIENZL, Wilhelm (1857–1941) Austrian composer, born in Waizenkirchen, Austria. He became kapellmeister at Amsterdam, Krefeld, Graz, Hamburg and Munich. His third opera, *Der Evangelimann* (Berlin 1895, London 1897), was his first and greatest success.

KIERKEGAARD, Sören Aabye (1813–55) Danish philosopher and religious thinker, regarded as one of the founders of Existentialism. He was born in Copenhagen and read theology at the university there, though in fact he interested himself more in literature and philosophy. He periodically suffered emotional disturbances and anguish which his later writings sometimes reflect: he was particularly oppressed by his father's death in 1838 and by the burden of guilt he felt he had thereby inherited. He became engaged after leaving university in 1840, but after great heart-searching broke that off because he felt domestic responsibilities were incompatible with his personal mission from God to be a writer. His philosophy represents a strong reaction against the dominant German traditions of the day, and in particular against **Hegel**'s system. Kierkegaard tried to reinstate the central importance of the individual and of the deliberate, significant choices each of us makes in forming our future selves. His philosophical works tend to be unorthodox and entertaining in a literary and determinedly unacademic style: *The Concept of Irony* (1841), *Either—Or* (2 vols, 1843), *Philosophical Fragments* (1844) and *Concluding Unscientific Postscript* (1846). He was also opposed to much in organized Christianity, again stressing the necessity for individual choice against prescribed dogma and ritual in such works as *Fear and Trembling* (1843), *Works of Love* (1847), *Christian Discourses* (1848) and *The Sickness unto Death* (1849). He achieved real recognition only in this century and has been a great influence on such thinkers as **Barth**, **Heidegger**, **Jaspers** and **Buber**.

KIESINGER, Kurt Georg (1904–88) West German politician, born in Ebingen. He practised as a lawyer (1935–40), and, having joined the Nazi party in 1933, although not an active member in the following years, served during World War II at the foreign office on radio propaganda. Interned after the war until 1947, he was released by the Allies as a 'fellow traveller' and completely exonerated by a German court in 1948. The next year he became a member of the Bundestag until 1958, when he became a minister-president of his native Baden-Württemberg until 1966. He was president of the Bundesrat (1962–63), and in 1966 succeeded **Erhard** as chancellor after economic crisis had forced the latter's resignation. Long a convinced supporter of **Adenauer**'s plans for European unity, he formed with **Willy Brandt** a 'grand coalition' government combining the Christian Democratic Union and the Social Democrats, until in 1969 he was succeeded as chancellor by Brandt. He remained in the Bundestag until 1980.

KILBURN, Tom (1921–) English computer scientist, born in Dewsbury. Educated at Wheelwright Grammar School, Dewsbury, and Sidney Sussex College, Cambridge, he became professor of computer science at Manchester (1964–81) and one of the dominant figures in British computer design. After working with Sir **Frederic Calland Williams** to build the world's first operational stored-program computer in 1948, he directed a series of collaborative ventures with Ferranti Ltd. His design for the ATLAS computer (1962) pioneered many modern concepts in paging, virtual memory and multiprogramming.

KILIAN, St See **CILIAN**

KILLIGREW, Thomas (1612–83) English dramatist, brother of Sir **William Killigrew**, page in the household of **Charles I**, and afterwards a companion of **Charles II** in exile and his groom of the bedchamber after the Restoration. He published in 1664 nine indifferent plays, written, he claimed, in nine different cities. He was for some time manager of the king's company, and obtained permission to give female parts to women.

KILLIGREW, Sir William (1606–95) English dramatist, brother of **Thomas Killigrew**. He fought in the Civil War, and wrote a comedy, *Pandora*, and tragicomedies, such as *Selindra*, *Ormasdes*, and *The Siege of Urbin*.

KILLY, Jean-Claude (1944–) French ski racer, born in Val d'Isère. He won the downhill and combined gold medals at the world championship in Chile in 1966; in 1968, when the Winter Olympics were held almost on his own ground at Grenoble, he won three gold medals for slalom, giant slalom and downhill. He turned professional immediately afterwards and pursued a highly profitable career as an endorser and later manufacturer of winter sports equipment.

KILMUIR, David Patrick Maxwell Fyfe, 1st Earl of (1900–67) Scottish jurist and statesman, born in Aberdeen. Educated at George Watson's College, Edinburgh, and Balliol College, Oxford, he took silk in 1934, the youngest KC since the time of **Charles II**. He was MP for West Derby (Liverpool) (1935–54), when he became Lord Chancellor. He was deputy chief prosecutor at the Nuremberg trial of the principal Nazi war criminals. Home secretary and minister for Welsh affairs in the 1951 government, he advised on a heavy programme of controversial legislation. He was knighted in 1942, created Viscount 1954, and Earl and Baron Fyfe of Dornoch in 1962. He wrote *Monopoly* (1948) and *Political Adventure* (1964).

KILVERT, (Robert) Francis (1840–79) English clergyman and diarist. He was a curate at Clyro in Radnorshire and later vicar of Bredwardine on the Wye. His *Diary* (1870–79), giving a vivid picture of rural life in the Welsh marches, was discovered in 1937 and published in three volumes (1938–40).

KILWARDBY, Robert (d.1279) English prelate, a Dominican. In 1273 he was made archbishop of Canterbury, and in 1278 a cardinal. He died at Viterbo.

KIM DAE JUNG (1924–) South Korean politician born in Mokpo, near Kwangju, the poor south-western province of Cholla. A Roman Catholic, he was imprisoned by communist troops during the Korean War. He challenged General **Park Chung-Hee** for the presidency in 1971 and was imprisoned (1976–78 and 1980–82) for alleged 'anti-government activities'. He lived in exile in the United States (1982–85) and on his return successfully spearheaded an opposition campaign for democratization. Although popular among blue-collar workers and fellow Chollans, Kim is distrusted by the business and military élite and in the 1987 presidential election was defeated by the government nominee, **Roh Tae Woo**.

KIM IL SUNG, Marshal (1912–) North Korean soldier and political leader, born near Pyongyang in April 1912. He founded the Korean People's Revolutionary Army in 1932 and led a long struggle against the Japanese. He proclaimed the Republic in 1948, three years after founding the Workers' Party of Korea, and he has effectively been head of state ever since, as premier until 1972, then as president. Kim was re-elected president in 1982 and 1986, and has established a unique personality cult welded to an isolationist, Stalinist political-economic system. He has sought to establish his son, Kim Jong Il (1942–), as his designated successor.

KIM YOUNG SAM (1927–) South Korean politician, born in Geoje District, in South Kyongsang province, and educated at Seoul National University. After election to the National Assembly in 1954, he was a founder member of the opposition New Democratic party (NDP), becoming its president in 1974. His opposition to the **Park Chung-Hee** régime resulted in his being banned from all political activity. In 1983 he staged a 23-day pro-democracy hunger strike and in 1985 his political ban was formally lifted. In that year he helped form the New Korea Democratic party (NKDP) and in 1987 the centrist Reunification Democratic party (RDP). In his 1987 bid for the presidency he came second, behind the governing party's candidate, **Roh Tae Woo**. In 1990 he merged the RDP with the ruling party to form the new Democratic Liberal party (DLP).

KIMBERLEY, John Wodehouse, 1st Earl of (1826–1902) English Liberal statesman. He was Lord Privy-Seal 1868–70, colonial secretary 1870–74 and 1880–82, secretary for India 1882–85 and 1886, secretary for India and lord president of the council 1892–94, and then foreign secretary till 1895. Kimberley in South Africa was named after him.

KIMHI, or **Kimchi, David** (c.1160–1235) French Jewish grammarian and lexicographer, born in Narbonne. His chief work is the *Book of Completeness*, which comprises a Hebrew grammar and a lexicon; subsequent Hebrew grammars and lexicons are based on this. He also wrote biblical commentaries, the most interesting of which is his work on the *Psalms* with its polemics against the Christian interpretation of them, and his commentary on *Genesis* in which biblical stories are explained as visions. His father Joseph Kimhi (c.1105–1170) and brother Moses (d.c.1190) are also noted for their work on the Hebrew language and their biblical commentaries.

KINCK, Hans Ernst (1865–1926) Norwegian novelist and dramatist, born in Öksfjord. His works illustrate his deep love of nature and his interest in the lives of peasants, and include *Sneskavlen brast* (1918–19) and *Driftekaren* (1908), a verse play.

KING, B B, real name **Riley B King** (1928–) American blues singer and guitarist, born into a black sharecropping family in Itta Bena, Mississippi. One of the best-known blues performers and an important consolidator of blues styles, he has had a considerable influence on rock as well as blues players with his economical guitar style. As a disc-jockey on the radio station WDIA in the 1940s he became known as the 'Beale Street Blues Boy', later shortened to B B. In 1950 he signed a recording contract wih Modern Records which led to a string of rhythm-and-blues hits over the next ten years. In 1961 he moved to ABC Records, who released what is probably his finest album, *Live At The Regal* (1965). His reputation grew considerably in the late 1960s as the blues influence on rock music came to be acknowledged by white audiences. In the late 1970s he became the first blues artist to tour the USSR. Albums released during his prolific recording career have included *Confessin' The Blues* (1966), *Indianola Mississippi Seeds* (1970), the Grammy award-winning *There Must Be A Better World Somewhere* (1981) and *Six Silver Strings* (1985).

KING, Billy Jean, née **Moffat** (1943–) American tennis player, born in California. Between 1965 and 1980 she was one of the dominant players in women's tennis and won a record twenty titles at Wimbledon, consisting of six singles titles, ten women's doubles and four mixed doubles. Towards the end of her playing career she became involved in the administration of tennis, and as president of the Women's Tennis Association (1980–81) she played a prominent role in working for the improvement of remuneration and playing conditions for women in professional tennis. She has written several books, including *Tennis to Win* (1970), *Billie Jean* (1974), *Secrets of Winning Tennis* (1975), and *Billie Jean King* (1982).

KING, Cecil (Harmsworth) (1901–87) British newspaper proprietor, nephew of the **Harmsworth** brothers. He joined the *Daily Mirror* in 1926. Appointed a director in 1929, he was chairman of Daily Mirror Newspapers Ltd and Sunday Pictorial Newspapers Ltd (1951–63) and chairman of the International Publishing Corporation (1963–68).

KING, Edward (1829–1910) English bishop and son of the archdeacon of Rochester. He graduated from Oriel College, Oxford in 1851, was principal of Cuddesdon 1863–73, Regius professor of pastoral theology 1873–85, and then bishop of Lincoln. He was tried in 1890 for ritualistic practices, but was condemned on only two charges.

KING, Ernest Joseph (1878–1956) American naval officer, born in Lorain, Ohio, of British parents. A graduate of the US Naval Academy, Annapolis, he was commissioned in 1903. During World War I he served on the staff of commander-in-chief US Atlantic Fleet (1916–19). He qualified in submarines, and commanded the submarine base at New London (1923–25). He also qualified in naval aviation (1927). He was commander-in-chief, Atlantic Fleet, with the rank of admiral (January–December 1941), and commander-in-chief of the US fleet (December 1941). As chief of Naval Operations (March 1942–December 1945) he masterminded the carrier-bases campaign against the Japanese.

KING, Jessie Marion (1875–1949) Scottish designer and illustrator, born in New Kilpatrick (now Bearsden), the daughter of a minister. She studied at Glasgow School of Art (1895–99), and won a travelling scholarship to Italy and Germany. She was an internationally renowned and much sought-after book illustrator who also designed jewellery, wallpaper and was greatly involved with batik and pottery. In 1908 she married the designer **Ernest Archibald Taylor**. She participated in the decoration of **Mackintosh**'s Scottish Pavilion at the Exposizione Nazionale in Turin, and won a gold medal for the design of a book cover. She also worked with Liberty's, designing fabrics and part of the Cymric silver range. With her husband, she moved to Paris in 1911 and returned to Scotland at the outbreak of World War I. She lived in Kirkcudbright and exhibited up to the time of her death.

KING, John (1838–72) Irish-born Australian traveller, born in Moy, County Tyrone, the first white man to cross the Australian continent and survive. He was a member of the **Burke** and **Wills** expedition which set out from Melbourne in 1860; four members of the expedition reached the tidal marshes of the Flinders River at the edge of the Gulf of Carpentaria. On the way back, three of them, including Burke and Wills, died of starvation; the fourth man, John King, was given succour by the Aborigines and eventually found by a relief party six months later emaciated but alive. He married in 1871 but died the following year from tuberculosis

KING, Martin Luther, Jr (1929–68) American black clergyman and civil rights campaigner, born in Atlanta, Georgia. The son of a Baptist pastor, he studied systematic theology at Crozier Theological Seminary in Chester, Pennsylvania, and Boston University, and set up the first black ministry at Montgomery, Alabama, in 1955. He came to national prominence as leader of the Alabama bus boycott, and founded the Southern Christian Leadership Conference in 1957, which organized civil rights activities throughout the country. A brilliant orator, he galvanized the movement, based on the principle of non-violence, and led the great march on Washington in 1963, where he delivered his memorable 'I have a dream' speech. In 1964 he received an honorary doctorate from Yale, the Kennedy peace prize, and the Nobel peace prize. He was assassinated in Memphis, Tennessee, while on a civil rights mission. His white assassin, James Earl Ray, was apprehended in London, and in 1969 was sentenced in Memphis to 99 years. His widow, Coretta Scott King (1927–) has carried on his work through the Martin Luther King, Jr, Centre for Social Changes in Alabama. The third Monday in January is celebrated as Martin Luther King day in the USA.

KING, William Lyon Mackenzie (1874–1950) Canadian Liberal statesman, born in Kitchener, Ontario. He studied law at Toronto, and won a fellowship in political science at Ontario. He accepted the newly created post of deputy minister of labour (1900–08), when he left the civil service and became an MP, being appointed minister of labour (1909–14). In 1914 he became director of industrial relations in the Rockefeller Foundation for industrial problems, publishing an important study on the subject, *Industry and Humanity*, in 1918. In 1919 he became Liberal leader and was prime minister 1921–26, 1926–30, and 1935–48. His view that the dominions should be autonomous communities within the British Empire and not form a single entity as **Smuts** advocated, materialized in the Statute of Westminster (1931). He opposed sanctions against Italy over Ethiopia and on the eve of World War II wrote to **Hitler**, **Mussolini** and President Mosicki of Poland urging them to preserve the peace, but promptly declared war on Germany with the other dominions once Poland was attacked. He opposed conscription, except eventually for overseas service, signed agreements with **Roosevelt** (1940–41) integrating the economies of the two countries, and represented Canada at the London and San Francisco foundation conferences of the United Nations (1945).

KING, William Rufus (1786–1853) American statesman, born in North Carolina. A member of the state legislature for three years, he entered congress in 1810, was senator for Alabama 1820–1844, minister to France 1844–46, senator again 1846–53, and, just before his death, became vice-president of the USA.

KINGDON-WARD, Frank (1885–1958) English botanist, plant explorer and writer, son of the botanist Harry Marshall Ward (1854–1906). He made important botanical journeys in China, Tibet, Burma, Thailand etc, and wrote on his travels and on his associated plant discoveries. His publications include *The Land of the Blue Poppy* (1913) and *In Farthest Burma* (1921).

KINGLAKE, Alexander William (1809–91) English historian, born in Wilton House, near Taunton. Educated at Eton and Trinity College, Cambridge, he was called to the bar in 1837, and made a fair practice, but retired in 1856 to devote himself to literature and politics. A tour about 1835 had already given birth to *Eōthen* (1844), one of the most brilliant and popular books of eastern travel. In 1854 he went out to the Crimea. He was returned for Bridgwater as a Liberal in 1857, took a prominent part against Lord **Palmerston**'s Conspiracy Bill, and denounced the French annexation of Savoy. His *History of the War in the Crimea* (8 vols, 1863–87) is one of the finest historical works of its century.

KINGO, Thomas Hansen (1634–1703) Danish poet and prelate, born in Slangerup, of Scottish descent. The greatest Baroque poet in Denmark's literary history, he was bishop of Fyn from 1677. He wrote collections of hymns (*Aandeligt sjungekor*, 1674 and 1681) and much secular and religious poetry.

KINGSFORD, Anna, née **Bonus** (1846–88) English doctor and religious writer, born in Stratford, Essex. In 1867 she married a Shropshire clergyman, Algernon Kingsford, and became a convert to Catholicism (1870). An antivivisectionist, MD of Paris (1880), a vegetarian, a Theosophist, and much else, in 1884 she founded the Hermetic Society to reconcile Christianity with eastern religions.

KINGSFORD SMITH, Sir Charles Edward (1897–1935) Australian pioneer aviator, born in Hamilton, Queensland. On his 18th birthday he enlisted in the Australian Imperial Force, later transferring to the Royal Flying Corps with whom he won the Military Cross in 1918. After the war he was involved in popular stunt-flying and joy-riding, before returning to Australia in 1921 and joining the pioneering West Australian Airways, flying a mail route to the north of the state. In 1926 he met **Charles Ulm**, with whom in the following year he made a record-breaking flight round Australia. In the USA they bought a Fokker Tri-motor, which they named *Southern Cross*, and flew it back to Australia in ten days, making the first air crossing of the Pacific. They set up an impressive list of aviation 'firsts' and records, culminating in the first aerial circumnavigation of the globe in 1929–30. With Ulm he started an airline to set up mail flights between the state capitals, but this enterprise failed through lack of government support. He was knighted in 1932. In November 1935 he set off with another pilot from Allahabad, India, on the second leg of an attempt at the England–Australia record, but the plane went missing over the Bay of Bengal.

KINGSLEY, Charles (1819–75) English author, born at Holne vicarage, Dartmoor. In 1838 he entered Magdalene College, Cambridge, and took a classical first in 1842. As curate and then (1844) rector, he spent the rest of his life at Eversley in Hampshire. His dramatic poem, *The Saint's Tragedy, or The True Story of Elizabeth of Hungary* (1848), was followed by *Alton Locke* (1850) and *Yeast* (1851), brilliant social novels which had enormous influence at the time. He had thrown himself into various schemes for the improvement of the working classes, and like **J F D Maurice** was a 'Christian Socialist'. As 'Parson Lot' he published an immense number of articles on current topics, especially in the *Christian Socialist* and *Politics for the People*. *Hypatia* (1853) is a brilliant picture of early Christianity in conflict with Greek philosophy at Alexandria. *Westward Ho!* (1855) is a lifelike representation of Elizabethan England and the Spanish Main. *Two Years Ago* (1857) and *Hereward the Wake* (1866) were his later novels. In 1860 he was appointed professor of modern history at Cambridge, *The Roman and the Teuton* (1864) being based on his Cambridge lectures. In 1869 he resigned his professorship and was appointed canon of Chester. In 1869–70 he made a voyage to the West Indies, and on his return issued the charming account *At Last*. In 1873 he was appointed canon of Westminster and chaplain to Queen **Victoria**. The collected works of this combative, enthusiastic and sympathetic apostle of what was called (*not* by him) 'muscular Christianity' fill 28 volumes (1879–81), and include *Glaucus* (1855), *The Heroes* (1856), *The Water*

Babies (1863), *Town Geology* (1872), *Prose Idylls* (1873) and *Health and Education* (1874).

KINGSLEY, Henry (1830–76) English novelist, brother of **Charles Kingsley**. He was educated at King's College School, London, and Worcester College, Oxford. From 1853 to 1858 he worked as a gold prospector in Australia, and on his return published a vigorous picture of colonial life in *Recollections of Geoffry Hamlyn* (1859). After this came *Ravenshoe* (1861), his masterpiece, followed by *Austin Elliot* (1863) and *The Hillyars and the Burtons*, another novel of Australian life (1865). In 1869–70 he edited the *Edinburgh Daily Review*.

KINGSLEY, Mary Henrietta (1862–1900) English traveller and writer, born in Islington, London. Her father was George Kingsley, also a traveller, and she was the niece of **Charles Kingsley**. She was not formally educated, but was a voracious reader in her father's scientific library. When her parents became invalids Mary took over the running of the household; when they died she planned the first of two remarkable journeys to West Africa in 1893, living among and bartering with the natives while retaining European dress. Returning from her second journey in 1895, she wrote *Travels in West Africa* (1899), which was based on her diaries. *West African Studies* also appeared in 1899. Latterly she was consulted by colonial administrators, for her expertise was wide and her understanding of African culture broad-based. Serving as a nurse in the second Boer War, she died of enteric fever.

KINGSLEY, Mary St Leger (1852–1931) English novelist, daughter of **Charles Kingsley**. In 1876 she married the Rev W Harrison, rector of Clovelly, and as 'Lucas Malet' completed her father's *Tutor's Story* (1916) and wrote powerful novels, including *Mrs Lorimer* (1882), *Colonel Enderby's Wife* (1885), *The Wages of Sin* (1890), *The Carissima* (1896) and *Sir Richard Calmady* (1901). She became a Roman Catholic in 1899.

KINGSMILL, Hugh, originally **Hugh Kingsmill Lunn** (1889–1949) English biographer and anthologist, younger brother of **Arnold Lunn** and Brian Lunn. Educated at Harrow, Oxford and Dublin, he became a writer, initially winning odium for iconoclasm degenerating into idleness. But after the failure of his *Matthew Arnold* (1928), he recovered himself with the satirical fantasy *The Return of William Shakespeare* (1929), produced works of art in his *Frank Harris* (1932) and his elegant essays *The Table of Truth* and *The Progress of a Biographer* (1949). He produced excellent anthologies, such as *Invective and Abuse* (1944), *Johnson Without Boswell* (1940) and *The Worst of Love* (1931), while with **Hesketh Pearson** he established a delightful art-form in conversational literary journeys such as *Skye High* (1937), *This Blessed Plot* (1942) and *Talking of Dick Whittington* (1947).

KINGSTON, Duchess of See **CHUDLEIGH, Elizabeth**

KINGSTON, William Henry Giles (1814–80) English author, son of a merchant in Oporto, where he spent much of his youth. He wrote over 150 boys' adventure stories including such favourites as *Peter the Whaler* (1851) and *The Three Midshipmen* (1862).

KINKEL, Gottfried (1815–82) German poet, born in Oberkassel near Bonn. He lectured at Bonn on theology, poetry and the history of art. Involved in the revolutionary movement of 1848, he was imprisoned in Spandau (1850), from where he escaped. He taught German in London until 1866, when he was appointed professor of archaeology and art at Zürich. As a poet his fame rests upon *Otto der Schütz* (1846), *Der Grobschmied von Antwerpen* (1872), *Tanagra* (1883), *Gedichte* (1843–68), and a drama, *Nimrod* (1857). He also wrote a history of art (1845) and monographs on **Freiligrath** (1867), and **Rubens** (1874). His first wife, Johanna (1810–58), a distinguished musician, wrote a novel, *Hans Ibeles in London* (1860), and, with her husband, *Erzählungen* (1849), a collection of tales.

KINMONT WILLIE See **ARMSTRONG, Sir Walter**

KINNOCK, Neil Gordon (1942–) Welsh politician. Educated at University College Cardiff, he has been Labour MP for Bedwellty since 1970, and leader of the British Labour party since 1983. He was a member of the Labour party's National Executive Committee from 1978 and chief opposition spokesman on education from 1979. He was at the centre of a controversy in 1981 when he headed a group of left-wing MPs who refused support to **Tony Benn** during elections for the deputy leadership of the party. A skilful orator, Kinnock was the left's obvious choice in the Labour leadership contest of 1983, being regarded by many as the favoured candidate of the outgoing leader, **Michael Foot** (he was former parliamentary private secretary to Foot). He was elected party leader by a large majority and re-elected in 1988. Since assuming the leadership he has succeeded in isolating the extreme elements within the party and persuaded it to adopt more moderate policies, better attuned to contemporary conditions.

KINSEY, Alfred Charles (1894–1956) American sexologist and zoologist, born in Hoboken, New Jersey. He was professor of zoology at Indiana from 1920, and in 1942 was the founder-director of the Institute for Sex Research there for the scientific study of human sexual behaviour. He published two controversial studies, *Sexual Behaviour in the Human Male* (1948, the so-called 'Kinsey Report'), and *Sexual Behaviour in the Human Female* (1953).

KIPLING, Rudyard (1865–1936) English writer, born in Bombay, the son of John Lockwood Kipling (1837–1911), principal of the School of Art in Lahore. He was educated at the United Services College, Westward Ho!, in Devon, in England, but returned in 1880 to India, where he worked as a journalist on the Lahore *Civil and Military Gazette*. His mildly satirical verses *Departmental Ditties* (1886), and the short stories *Plain Tales from the Hills* (1888) and *Soldiers Three* (1889), won him a reputation in England. He returned in 1889 and settled in London, where *The Light that Failed* (1890), his first attempt at a full-length novel, was not altogether successful. In London he met Wolcott Balestier, the American author-publisher, with whom he collaborated in *The Naulakha* (1892), and whose sister Caroline he married (1892). A spell of residence in his wife's native state of Vermont ended abruptly in 1899 through incompatibility with in-laws and locals, and the remainder of Kipling's career was spent in England. Meanwhile he had written the brilliantly successful *Barrack Room Ballads* (1892) and *The Seven Seas* (1896), both collections of verse, and further short stories published as *Many Inventions* (1893) and *The Day's Work* (1899). The two *Jungle Books* (1894–95) have won a place among the classic animal stories, and *Stalky and Co* (1899) presents semi-autobiographical but delighfully uninhibited episodes based on the author's schooldays. *Kim* appeared in 1901, and the children's classic *Just So Stories* in 1902. The verse collection *The Five Nations* (1903) included the highly successful 'Recessional', written for Queen **Victoria**'s diamond jubilee in 1897. Later works include *Puck of Pook's Hill* (1906), *Rewards and Fairies* (1910), *Debits and Credits* (1926), and the autobiographical

Something of Myself (1937). Kipling's real merit as a writer has tended to become obscured in recent years and he has been accused of imperialism and jingoism, but this ignores not only the great body of his work which was far removed from this sphere, but also his own criticisms and satire on some of the less admirable aspects of colonialism. He was awarded the Nobel prize for literature in 1907.

KIPP, Petrus Jacobus (1808–64) Dutch chemist, was born in Utrecht. He started a business in laboratory apparatus in Delft in 1830. He invented the apparatus called after him for the continuous and automatic production of gases such as carbon dioxide, hydrogen and hydrogen sulphide. A representation of it appears in the arms of the Dutch Chemical Society. He also invented a method of fixing carbon and pastel drawings.

KIPPING, Frederick Stanley (1863–1949) English chemist, born in Manchester. Professor of chemistry at Nottingham, he investigated silicon compounds and was responsible for their development and use in the production of plastics capable of resisting higher temperatures.

KIRCHHOFF, Gustav Robert (1824–87) German physicist, born in Königsberg. Professor at Heidelberg (1854–75) and Berlin (1875–86), he distinguished himself in electricity, heat, optics and especially (with **Robert Wilhelm Bunsen**) spectrum analysis, which led to the discovery of caesium and rubidium (1859).

KIRCHNER, Ernst Ludwig (1880–1938) German artist, born in Aschaffenburg. He studied architecture at Dresden, but became the leading spirit in the formation in Dresden, with **Erich Heckel** and Karl Schmidt-Rottluff, of 'Die Brücke' ('The Bridge', 1905–13), the first group of German Expressionists, whose work was much influenced by primitive German woodcuts. His work was characterized by erotic, vibrant colours and angular outlines. He moved to Switzerland in 1914. Many of his works were confiscated as degenerate by the Nazis in 1937, and he committed suicide in 1938.

KIRK, Alan Goodrich (1888–1963) American naval officer and diplomat, born in Philadelphia. Educated at the US Naval Academy, Annapolis, he was commissioned in the US navy in 1909. He served as naval attaché London (1939–41) and was promoted rear admiral in 1941. He commanded the amphibious forces in the invasion of Sicily (1943) and the Western Task Force in the Normandy landing in 1944. He was ambassador to Belgium (1946–49), the USSR (1949–52), and Taiwan (1962).

KIRK, Norman Eric (1923–74) New Zealand politician, born on South Island at Waimate, Canterbury. He began his career as a driver of stationary engines, joined the Labour party and moved from local into national politics, becoming president of the party in 1964. He was leader of the opposition in the House of Representatives (1965–72) and became prime minister in 1972, at a time when his country's economy was in difficulties and, with Britain's entry into the Economic Community, New Zealand's external relations had to be reassessed. He died in office in 1974 and was succeeded by the finance minister, **Wallace Rowling**.

KIRKCALDY, Sir William, of Grange (c.1520–1573) Scottish politician. As one of **Beaton**'s murderers (1546) he was imprisoned at Mont St Michel (1547–50). He took service with France, but in 1559 was opposing the French cause in Scotland. He figured at Carberry Hill, was made governor of Edinburgh Castle, and did much to win Langside; but, going over to **Mary, Queen of Scots**' party, he held Edinburgh Castle for her till May 1573. He was hanged on 3 August.

KIRKE, Percy (c.1646–91) English soldier of fortune. He served under **James, Duke of Monmouth**, in France in 1673, under **Turenne** on the Rhine and **Luxembourg** in the Netherlands. He was governor of Tangier from 1682 to 1684. He transferred to the colonelcy of the old Tangier regiment, whose badge was a paschal lamb—hence the nickname 'Kirke's Lambs' for his men. They fought at Sedgemoor in 1685, and became notorious for the atrocities committed there.

KIRKEBY, Per (1938–) Danish painter. Professor at the Staatliche Hochschule für Bildende Künste, Frankfurt, since 1988, for several years he has been a prominent representative of new, experimental Danish painting. He has also published poetry, essays and novels, directed several documentary films, and took part in two Greenland expeditions in the 1960s. He was awarded the Thorvaldsen medal in 1987.

KIRKLAND, Gelsey (1952–) American dancer, born in Bethlehem, Pennsylvania. After studying at the School of American Ballet, she joined New York City Ballet in 1968, becoming a principal in 1972. Roles were created for her by **George Balanchine** (*The Firebird*, 1970) and **Jerome Robbins** (*The Goldberg Variations*, 1971, and *An Evening Walze* 1973), and by **Antony Tudor** in his last two ballets, *The Leaves Are Fading* (1975) and *The Tillers in the Fields* (1978). She moved to American Ballet Theatre Ballet in 1975 where she partnered **Baryshnikov**, the couple becoming one of the decade's most celebrated partnerships. A troubled personal life curtailed her career in the early 1980s, but she made a dramatic and successful comeback in *Swan Lake* with the Royal Ballet in London where she has settled. Her flawed but dazzling career is documented in her controversial autobiography, *Dancing on My Grave* (1986).

KIRKPATRICK, Jeane Duane Jordan (1926–) American academic and stateswoman, born in Duncan, Oklahoma. Educated at Columbia University and Paris University, she became a research analyst for the state department (1951–53). She then concentrated on a career as an academic, at Trinity College and Georgetown University, Washington DC, becoming Georgetown's professor of government in 1978. Noted for her 'hawkish', anti-communist defence stance and advocacy of a new Latin-American and Pacific-orientated diplomatic strategy, she was appointed permanent representative to the United Nations by President **Reagan** in 1981, remaining there until 1985. Formerly a Democrat, she joined the Republican party in 1985.

KIRKUP, Seymour Stocker (1788–1880) English artist, born in London. A **Dante** scholar, and a spiritualist, he was the friend of **Haydon**, **Landor**, **Trelawny**, and the **Brownings**. From 1816 he lived in Italy, chiefly in Florence, where in 1840 he discovered **Giotto**'s portrait of Dante.

KIRKWOOD, Daniel (1814–95) American astronomer, born in Harford, Maryland. He became professor of mathematics at Delaware (1851) and at Indiana (1856). He explained the unequal distribution of asteroids in the ring system of Saturn in terms of the 'Kirkwood gaps' and subjected the theories of the **Marquis de Laplace** to penetrating criticism. His works include *Comets and Meteors* (1873) and *The Asteroids* (1887).

KIRSTEIN, Lincoln (1907–) American writer, impresario and ballet director, born in Rochester, New York. Educated at Harvard, he was an influential force in the ballet world, best known for recognizing the talents of **George Balanchine** and taking him to the USA to co-found the School of American Ballet in

1934, the organization which led to the creation of New York City Ballet. Their American Ballet became attached to the Metropolitan Opera in 1935 and at the same time Kirstein ran the touring company Ballet Caravan. In 1946 they founded the Ballet Society and in 1948 moved to New York's new City Centre as the directors of what has become one of America's top-ranking companies, New York City Ballet. He was founder editor of *Dance Index Magazine* (1942–48), and has written many books, including *Dance* (1935) and *Movement and Metaphor* (1970), and some poetry, including *Low Ceiling* (1935) and *Rhymes of a PFC* (1964).

KIRWAN, Richard (1733–1812) Irish chemist, born in Galway. He published (1784) the first systematic English treatise on mineralogy, and was a leading exponent of the phlogiston theory.

KISFALUDY, Karoly (1788–1830) Hungarian dramatist, brother of the poet Sandor Kisfaludy (1772–1844). He was the regenerator of the national drama, and became famous for his *Tartars in Hungary* (1819).

KISSINGER, Henry Alfred (1923–) American politician, born in Fürth, Germany. He settled in America in 1938. He was professor of government at Harvard (1962–71) and in 1968 he became President **Nixon**'s adviser on national security affairs. He was awarded the 1973 Nobel peace prize with the Vietnamese statesman **Le Duc Tho**, and became secretary of state. He played a major role in the improvement of relations (détente) with both China and the Soviet Union during the early 1970s and in the peace negotiations between the Arabs and Israelis (1973–75) which continued during the **Ford** administration, emerging as the arch exponent of 'shuttle diplomacy'. He ceased to be secretary of state in 1977 when **Jimmy Carter** became president, but later, in 1983, was appointed by President **Reagan** to head a bipartisan commission on Central America.

KITAJ, R B (Ronald Brooks) (1932–) American painter, born in Cleveland, Ohio. He was a sailor from 1951 to 1955 and travelled extensively. Following army service, he went to Oxford, where he studied art. In 1960 he entered the Royal College of Art, London and formed a close friendship with fellow student **David Hockney**. Since 1960, apart from brief periods of residency in France, Spain and the USA, he has lived in London. His oil paintings and pastels demonstrate a mastery of figure drawing, while his economic use of line and the flattened colour recall oriental art.

KITASATO, Shibasaburo (1852–1931) Japanese bacteriologist. He studied in Berlin under **Robert Koch** and later founded in Japan an Institute for Infectious Diseases. He discovered the bacillus of bubonic plague (1894), isolated the bacilli of symptomatic anthrax, dysentery and tetanus, and prepared a diphtheria antitoxin.

KITCHENER, Horatio Herbert, 1st Earl Kitchener of Khartoum (1850–1916) Irish soldier and statesman, born near Ballylongford, County Kerry. Educated in Switzerland and the Royal Military Academy, Woolwich, he entered the Royal Engineers in 1871. On the Palestine survey (1874–78), and then on that of Cyprus till 1882, he served in the Sudan campaign (1883–85). He was sirdar of the Egyptian army from 1890, and, by the final rout of the dervishes at Omdurman in September, 1898, won back the Sudan for Egypt, and was made a peer. Successively chief of the staff and commander-in-chief in South Africa (1900–02), he finished the 2nd Boer War. He was made a viscount in 1902, and appointed commander-in-chief in India (1902–09), and agent and consul-general in Egypt (1911). He was appointed secretary for war on 7 August 1914, and had recruited a great army before he was lost with HMS *Hampshire* (mined off Orkney) on 5 June 1916.

KITT, Eartha Mae (c.1928–) Creole American entertainer, born in North, South Carolina. A graduate of the New York School of the Performing Arts, she made her New York début as a member of Katherine Dunham's dance troupe in *Blue Holiday* (1945). She toured throughout Europe and was subsequently cast by **Orson Welles** in his production of *Dr. Faustus* (1951). Her theatrical credits include *New Faces of 1952*, *Shinbone Alley* (1957) and *The Owl and the Pussycat* (1965–66). A figure of sinuous grace and vocal vibrancy, her fiery personality and cat-like singing voice made her a prime cabaret attraction across the world and a top recording artiste. Since her début in *Casbah* (1948), her film appearances have included *New Faces* (1954), *St. Louis Blues* (1957) *Anna Lucasta* (1958) and the documentary *All By Myself* (1982). On television from 1953, she received the Golden Rose of Montreux for *Kaskade* (1962) and was appropriately cast as Catwoman in the series *Batman* (1966). Recent theatre work includes *Timbuktu!* (1978–80), *Blues in the Night* (1985), a show-stopping appearance in *Follies* (1988–89) and a one-woman show. Her autobiographies include *Thursday's Child* (1956), *Alone With Me* (1976), and *I'm Still Here* (1989).

KIVI, Aleksis, originally **Stenvall** (1834–72) Finnish playwright and novelist, born in Nurmijärvi. He wrote in Finnish not Swedish, establishing the western dialect as the modern literary language of Finland, and is considered the father of the Finnish theatre and novel. He wrote the first Finnish novel, *Seitsemän veljestä* (Seven Brothers, 1870), and a collection of Finnish poems, *Kanervala* (1866). As a dramatist he wrote rural comedies like *Nummisuutarit* (The Cobblers on the Heath, 1864), and a tragedy, *Kullervo* (1864), based on one of the central figures in the *Kalevala*.

KJARVAL, Jóhannes (Sveinsson) (1885–1972) Icelandic Symbolist painter, born on the remote farm of Efri-Ey, one of the pioneers of modern Icelandic art. He worked as a farm labourer and a deck-hand for some years, then went to Reykjavík where he was taught by **Ásgrímur Jónsson** and held a one-man show in 1908. Eventually he realized his dream of becoming a professional painter when his friends held a lottery to raise funds for his schooling abroad. He went to London in 1911, where he was refused admission to the Royal Academy schools but came under the influence of the works of **Turner**, and studied instead at the Royal Academy in Copenhagen (1912–18). From 1918 he lived in Iceland but travelled widely. Essentially an eccentric romantic with strong mystical and symbolist tendencies, he had a powerful sense of historical nationalism, and often featured the 'hidden people' of Icelandic folklore. His output was astonishing in its range and eclecticism; long before his death he had become the best-loved painter in Iceland.

KJELDAHL, Johan Gustav Christoffer Thorsager (1849–1900) Danish chemist. Director of the Carlsberg Laboratory in Copenhagen (1876–1900), he was noted for his analytical methods and especially for the method of nitrogen determination named after him.

KJELLAND, Alexander See **KIELLAND**

KLAPKA, George (1820–92) Hungarian soldier and patriot, born in Temesvár. He became a lieutenant general in the Austrian army, but in the Hungarian uprising of 1848 fought valiantly against the Austrians, holding Komorn for eight weeks after the rest of Hungary had submitted. The amnesty of 1867 let him return from exile, and he died at Budapest. He wrote a history of the war (1851) and Memoirs (1850–87).

KLAPROTH, Heinrich Julius von (1783–1835) German orientalist, born in Berlin, the son of **Martin Klaproth**. In 1805 he accompanied a Russian embassy to China, and when it was stopped at the frontier, he took the opportunity to explore Siberia. In 1807–08 he carried out ethnographic and linguistic studies in Georgia and the Caucasus. In 1815 he moved to Paris, and was appointed professor of Asiatic languages and literature by the king of Prussia the following year, with permission to remain in Paris, where he died.

KLAPROTH, Martin Heinrich (1743–1817) German chemist, born in Wernigerode. He became the first professor of chemistry at Berlin University (1810), devised new analytical methods, discovered zirconium and uranium, and named tellurium.

KLÉBER, Jean Baptiste (1753–1800) French soldier, born in Strasbourg. In 1776 he obtained a commission in the Austrian army. Inspector for a time of public buildings at Belfort, in 1792 he enlisted as a volunteer in the French Revolutionary army, and by 1793 had risen to a general of brigade. As such he commanded in the Vendéean war, but was recalled for leniency. In 1794 he led the left wing at Fleurus, and captured Maastricht; in June 1796 he gained the victory of Altenkirchen. He accompanied **Napoleon** to Egypt, was wounded at Alexandria, and won the battle of Mount Tabor (1799). When Napoleon left Egypt he entrusted the chief command to Kléber, who concluded a convention with Sir **Sidney Smith** for its evacuation; but on Admiral **Keith**'s refusal to ratify it, Kléber resolved to reconquer Egypt, and destroyed the Turkish army at Helipolis and took Cairo. In the course of an attempt to conclude a treaty with the Turks, he was assassinated by an Egyptian fanatic in Cairo.

KLEE, Paul (1879–1940) Swiss artist, born in Münchenbuchsee near Bern. He studied at Munich and settled there, and was associated with **Marc** and **Kandinsky** in the Blaue Reiter ('Blue Rider') group (1911–12). From 1920 to 1931 he taught at the Bauhaus in Weimar and Dessau, his *Pädagogisches Skizzenbuch* being published in 1925, and then in Düsseldorf (1931–33). After he had returned to Bern in 1933, many of his works were confiscated by the Nazis in Germany as degenerate. Klee's work has been called Surrealist, but in his fantastic, small-scale, mainly abstract pictures he created, with supreme technical skill in many media, a very personal world of free fancy, expressed with a sly wit and subtle colouring and giving the effect of inspired doodling, eg, the well-known *Twittering Machine* in the Museum of Modern Art, New York.

KLEIBER, Erich (1890–1956) Austrian conductor, born in Vienna. At the age of 33 he became director of the Berlin State Opera, holding this post for twelve years until forced by the Nazis to leave Germany. In 1938 he became a citizen of the Argentine. After the war he was again appointed director of the Berlin State Opera, until his resignation in 1955. He gave the first performance of **Alban Berg**'s *Wozzeck*.

KLEIN, Anne Hannah, née **Hannah Golofski** (?1921–1974) American fashion designer, born in New York. In 1938 she started as a sketcher on Seventh Avenue. In 1948, Junior Sophisticates was launched, and Anne Klein & Co was established in 1968. She was a noted leader in designing sophisticated, practical sportswear for young women. She recognized early a need for blazers, trousers, and separates, and her designs were popular in America.

KLEIN, Calvin Richard (1942–) American fashion designer, born in New York. He graduated from New York's Fashion Institute of Technology in 1962, and after gaining experience in New York, he set up his own firm in 1968. He quickly achieved recognition and is known for understatement and the simple but sophisticated style of his clothes, including 'designer jeans'.

KLEIN, Christian Felix (1849–1925) German mathematician, born in Düsseldorf. He studied at Bonn (1865–68), and held chairs at Erlangen (1872–75), Munich (1875–80), Leipzig (1880–86), and Göttingen (1886–1913), where he spent the rest of his life. He worked on geometry, including non-Euclidean geometry, function theory (in which he developed **Bernhard Riemann**'s ideas) and elliptic modular and automorphic functions. His 'Erlanger Programm' showed how different geometries could be classified in terms of group theory. He also wrote on the history of mathematics, encouraged links between pure and applied mathematics and engineering, and promoted general mathematical education.

KLEIN, Lawrence Robert (1920–) American economist, born in Omaha. Educated in California, at the Massachusetts Institute of Technology, and at Oxford, he has been professor at the universities of Chicago (1944–47), Michigan (1949–54) and Pennsylvania (from 1958). He was economic adviser to President **Carter** (1976–81), and was awarded the 1980 Nobel prize for economics for his work on forecasting business fluctuations and portraying economic interrelationships.

KLEIN, Yves (1928–62) French artist, born in Nice. A judo expert (he lived in Japan 1952–53), musician and leader of the post-war European neo-Dada movement, his monochrome (usually blue) canvases date from 1946. His *Anthropométries* involved girls covered with blue paint being dragged across canvases to the accompaniment of his *Symphonie monotone* (one-note symphony, composed in 1947).

KLEIST, Heinrich von (1777–1811) German dramatist and poet, born in Frankfurt-am-Oder. He left the army in 1799 to study, and soon devoted himself to literature. His best plays are still popular, notably *Prinz Friedrich von Homburg* (1811), and his finest tale is *Michael Kohlhaas*. He committed suicide.

KLEMPERER, Otto (1885–1973) German conductor, born in Breslau. He studied at Frankfurt and Berlin and first appeared as a conductor in 1907. He made a name as a champion of modern music and in 1927 was appointed director of the Kroll Opera in Berlin, until it was closed down in 1931. Nazism drove him to the USA in 1933, where he was director of the Los Angeles Symphony Orchestra till 1939. In spite of continuing ill-health, he was musical director of Budapest Opera from 1947 to 1950. In his later years he concentrated mainly on the German classical and romantic composers, and was particularly known for his interpretation of **Beethoven**. His compositions included a mass and lieder.

KLIMT, Gustav (1862–1918) Austrian painter and designer, born in Vienna. He studied at the Vienna School of Arts and Crafts. From 1883 to 1892 he worked in collaboration with his brother and another artist as a painter of grandiose decorative schemes. Under the influence of contemporary movements such as Impressionism, Symbolism and Art Nouveau, he became a founder and the first president (1898–1903) of the Vienna Secession, dedicated to furthering the avant-garde. His murals for Vienna University (1900–03) were considered pornographic, and aroused official condemnation. He produced a number of portraits, mainly of women, as well as large allegorical and mythological paintings; typically, these combine a naturalistic though highly mannered delineation of the figure with an elaborately patterned, richly decorative treatment of the background or clothing, creating a luxuriant, languidly decadent effect.

KLINE, Franz Joseph (1910–62) American artist, born in Wilkes-Barre, Pennsylvania. He studied at Boston University (1931–35) before going to London where he studied at Hetherley School of Art (1937–38). Throughout the 1940s he worked in a traditional style, painting urban scenery, but after c.1950 he went abstract, using black, irregular shapes on white canvases. He taught at Black Mountain College in 1952.

KLINGENSTIERNA, Samuel (1698–1765) Swedish mathematician and scientist, born in Linköping. His father, who died when the boy was nine, had been a major in **Karl XII**'s army, and his son's education was supervised by the bishop of Linköping. He studied law at Uppsala, but turned to mathematics and physics. He was appointed secretary to the Swedish Treasury, and given a scholarship to travel and study. He studied under **Christian Wolff** at Marburg, and **Jean Bernoulli** at Basle. He was appointed professor of mathematics at Uppsala, and in 1750 professor of physics there; he was appointed tutor to the crown prince (later **Gustav III**) in 1756. He showed that some of **Newton**'s views on the refraction of light were incorrect, and designed lenses free from chromatic and spherical aberration. By communicating his findings to **John Dollond** he contributed also to Dollond's success in constructing achromatic compound lenses, valuable in both telescope and microscope construction.

KLINGER, Friedrich Maximilian von (1752–1831) German playwright and novelist, born in Frankfurt-am-Main. He was an officer in the Russian army from 1780 to 1811, and curator of Dorpat University from 1803 to 1817. The 'Sturm-und-Drang' school was named after one of his tragedies, *Der Wirrwarr, oder Sturm und Drang* (1776). He wrote several other plays and some novels.

KLINGER, Max (1857–77) German painter and sculptor, born in Leipzig. He studied in Karlsruhe, Brussels and Paris, and excited hostility as well as admiration by his pen drawings and etchings, which were audaciously original in concept and often imbued with macabre realism. Later, he turned to painting, and did much work in coloured sculpture, including **Beethoven** (1902).

KLINT, Kaare (1888–1954) Danish architect and furniture designer, born in Copenhagen. His father was P V Jensen Klint (1853–1930), the architect of Gruntvig's Church in Copenhagen, which Kaare Klint completed in 1940. His furniture was based upon dimensional and anthropometric research as exemplified by his standardized, modular storage units. His admiration for furniture of the great English 18th-century designers and his respect for tradition, together with his analytical approach, led him to design in a rational, modern idiom. He was one of the initiators of Denmark's prominence in the field of design, partly through his teaching at the Royal Danish Academy of Fine Arts, which he helped to found in 1924. He was made an honorary royal designer for industry in Britain in 1949.

KLOPSTOCK, Friedrich Gottlieb (1724–1803) German poet, born in Quedlinburg. Inspired by **Virgil** and **Milton**, he began *The Messiah* as a student at Jena (1745), continued it at Leipzig (1748), and completed it in 1773. He settled in Hamburg in 1771 with a sinecure appointment, and pensions from **Frederik V** of Denmark (from 1751) and the Margrave of Baden. Regarded in his day as a great religious poet, he helped inaugurate the golden age of German literature.

KLUCK, Alexander von (1846–1934) Prussian soldier, born in Münster. In August 1914 he drove the Anglo-French forces almost to Paris, but, defeated at the Marne (6 September), had to retreat. Wounded in 1915, he retired in 1916. He wrote *Der Marsch auf Paris und die Marneschlacht* (1920).

KLUCKHOHN, Clyde Kay Maben (1905–60) American cultural anthropologist, born in Le Mars, Iowa. He studied at Princeton, Wisconsin, Vienna and Oxford, and in 1935 was appointed to the faculty of Harvard, where he remained for the rest of his career. His abiding research interest was in the culture of the Navaho Indians, and his classic monograph *Navaho Witchcraft* (1944) was outstanding both for its ethnographic depth and for its combination of social structural and psychoanalytical approaches. He was a major contributor to culture theory, in which he collaborated closely with **Alfred Louis Kroeber**. He set out his views on culture patterns and value systems in the popular work *Mirror for Man* (1949).

KLUG, Sir Aaron (1926–) Lithuanian-born British biophysicist. He moved to South Africa at three years old and later studied at Johannesburg and Cape Town. He moved to Britain in 1949. Mainly working in Cambridge, he became director there of the Medical Research Council Laboratory of Molecular Biology in 1986. A physicist by training, his interest in viruses began during a period spent in **Bernal**'s laboratory in London from 1954 to 1961, where he worked with **Rosalind Franklin**. Later he began to bring together X-ray diffraction methods, electron microscopy, structural modelling, and symmetry arguments to elucidate the structure of viruses such as tomato bushy stunt virus and polio virus. From the 1970s he also applied these methods to the study of chromosomes, and other biological macromolecules such as muscle filaments. He was awarded the Nobel prize for chemistry in 1982.

KLUGE, Günther von (1882–1944) German soldier. In 1939 he carried out the Nazi occupation of the Polish Corridor, commanded the German armies on the central Russian front (1942) and in July 1944 replaced **Rundstedt** as commander-in-chief of the Nazi armies in France confronting the Allied invasion, but was himself replaced after the Falaise gap débâcle. He committed suicide after the plot to kill **Hitler**.

KNEALE, Nigel (1922–) Manx writer and dramatist, born on the Isle of Man. After working in a lawyer's office, he first gained attention with a collection of short stories, *Tomato Cain* (1949), which won the Somerset Maugham prize. After a spell at RADA he joined the drama department of the BBC in a general capacity and progressed to writing the serial *The Quatermass Experiment* (1953): an imaginative science-fiction drama, reflecting the paranoia of the day, its immense popularity led to *Quatermass II* (1955), *Quatermass and the Pit* (1959), *Quatermass* (1978) and three feature films. His early television adaptations also include *Curtain Down* (1952), *Wuthering Heights* (1953) and *1984* (1954). His film scripts include *The Abominable Snowman* (1957), *First Men in the Moon* (1964), *The Witches* (1966) and *Halloween III* (1983). His television plays include *The Year of the Sex Olympics* (1968), *Bam! Pow! Zap!* (1969), *Beasts* (1975) and *Kinvig* (1981).

KNELLER, Sir Godfrey (1646–1723) German-born portrait painter, born in Lübeck. He studied at Amsterdam and in Italy, in 1676 went to London, and in 1680 was appointed court painter. In 1691 **William III** knighted him, and in 1715 **George I** made him a baronet. His best-known works are the *Beauties of Hampton Court* (painted for William III), his 48 portraits of the 'Kit-Cat Club', and of ten reigning monarchs (**Charles II** to **George I**, **Louis XIV**, **Peter the Great**, and the emperor Charles VI). His brother, John Zacharias (1644–1702), architectural and portrait painter, also settled in England.

KNICKERBOCKER, Harmen Jansen (c.1650–c.1716) Dutch colonist, from Friesland, one of the earliest settlers of New Amsterdam (New York). He went to New Amsterdam in 1674 and settled near Albany (1682). A descendant, Johannes (1749–1827), was a friend of **Washington Irving**, who immortalized the name through his *History of New York* by 'Diedrich Knickerbocker' (1809).

KNIGHT, Charles (1791–1873) English author and publisher, born in Windsor. From journalism, as proprietor of the *Windsor and Eton Express* (1811–21), he turned to publishing popular editions of serious literature such as *Pictorial Shakespeare* (1838–41) and *Popular History of England* (1862), and cheap reference books such as the *Penny Cyclopaedia* (1833–44). From 1860 he published *The London Gazette*.

KNIGHT, Dame Laura, née **Johnson** (1877–1970) English artist, born in Long Eaton. She studied at Nottingham, married her fellow-student, the portrait painter Harold Knight (1874–1961), in 1903, and travelled in many parts of the world. She produced a long series of oil paintings of the ballet, the circus and gipsy life, in a lively and forceful style, and also executed a number of watercolour landscapes.

KNOLLES, Richard (1550–1610) English historian. A schoolmaster at Sandwich, he wrote a *Generall Historie of the Turkes* (1603).

KNOLLYS, Sir Francis (1514–96) English statesman. From 1572 he was treasurer of Queen **Elizabeth**'s household. In 1568–69 he had charge of **Mary, Queen of Scots**.

KNOTT, Alan Philip Eric (1946–) English cricketer, born in Belvedere. One of a great trio of Kent wicketkeepers (with Leslie Ames and **Godfrey Evans**), he played in 95 Test matches, and his 269 dismissals are exceeded only by Rodney Marsh of Australia. He was a genuine wicketkeeper-batsman whose 4389 runs included five centuries. He kept wicket for England in 65 consecutive Test matches.

KNOWLES, Sir James (1831–1908) English architect and editor, born in London. Educated at University College, London, he designed many important churches and edifices. In 1869 he founded the Metaphysical Society, became editor of the *Contemporary Review* in 1870, and in 1877 founded the *Nineteenth Century*.

KNOWLES, James Sheridan (1784–1862) Irish dramatist, born in Cork, the son of a schoolmaster and a cousin of **Richard Brinsley Sheridan**. After serving in the militia he studied medicine at Aberdeen, but took to the stage. He did not achieve distinction and subsequently opened a school in Belfast and (1816–28) in Glasgow. His tragedy, *Caius Gracchus* (1815), was first performed in Belfast. *Virginius*, his most effective play, had been a success in Glasgow before **William Macready** produced it at Covent Garden in 1820. As well as *William Tell* (1825), his most successful plays were *Love*, *The Hunchback* (1832), *The Wife* (1833), and *The Love Chase* (1837). He appeared with fair success in many of his own pieces. About 1844 he became a Baptist preacher, drew large audiences to Exeter Hall, and published two anti-Roman Catholic works.

KNOX, Archibald (1864–1933) Manx designer, born on the Isle of Man. He studied at Douglas School of Art, and worked part-time in an architectural office. In 1899 he designed silverwork and metalwork for Liberty & Co. By 1900 he was their main designer and the inspiration behind the Celtic revival. Apart from the Cymric (silver) and Tudric (pewter) ranges he also designed carpets, textiles, jewellery and pottery as well as teaching for Liberty's.

KNOX, Edmund George Valpy, pen-name **Evoe** (1881–1971) English humorous writer and parodist, brother of **Ronald Arbuthnott Knox**. He joined the staff of *Punch* in 1921 and became editor from 1932 to 1949, contributing articles under his pen-name. His best work was republished in book form and includes *Parodies Regained*, *Fiction as She is Wrote*, *It Occurs to Me*, *Awful Occasions*, *Here's Misery* and *Folly Calling*.

KNOX, John (c.1513–1572) Scottish Protestant reformer, born in or near Haddington. He was educated there and probably at the University of St Andrews. From 1540 to 1543 he acted as notary in Haddington, and must till the latter year have been in Catholic orders. In 1544 he was acting as tutor to the sons of two families, by whom he was brought into contact with **George Wishart**, now full of zeal for the Lutheran reformation; and from then on Knox identified with him. Wishart was burned by Cardinal **David Beaton** in March 1546, and Beaton was murdered in May. The cardinal's murderers held the castle of St Andrews and here Knox joined them with his pupils (1547). Here he was formally called to the ministry. A few months later the castle surrendered to the French and for 18 months Knox remained a prisoner on the French galleys. In February 1549, on the intercession of **Edward VI**, Knox regained his liberty, and for four years made his home in England. In 1551 he was appointed one of six chaplains to Edward VI, and in 1552 was offered, but refused, the bishopric of Rochester. Knox, with five others, was consulted by **Cranmer** regarding his forty-two articles, and largely on Knox's representation the thirty-eighth article was so couched as to commit the Church of England to the Genevan doctrine of the eucharist. On **Mary I**'s accession Knox fled to the continent, then ministered briefly to the English congregation at Frankfurt-am-Main. In Geneva he found a congregation of his own way of thinking, but ventured into Scotland in September 1555, making preaching journeys to Kyle, Castle Campbell, etc, and returned to Geneva in July 1556. For the next two years he remained chiefly in Geneva, and was much influenced by **Calvin**. To 1558 belongs his *First Blast of the Trumpet against the Monstrous Regiment of Women*. In 1557 the advocates of reform in Scotland bound themselves to religious revolution by the *First Covenant*; and by 1558 they felt themselves strong enough to summon Knox to their aid. From May 1559 Knox, again in Scotland, was preaching at Perth and St Andrews. He gained these important towns to his cause, and by his labours in Edinburgh he also won a strong party. But the Reformers could not hold their ground against the regent, **Mary of Guise**, subsidized by France with money and soldiers. Mainly through the efforts of Knox, the assistance of England was obtained against the French invasion; and by the treaty of Leith and the death of the regent (1560) the insurgent party became masters of the country. Parliament ordered the ministers to draw up a *Confession of Faith* and Protestantism was established (1560). Now the ministers drew up the *First Book of Discipline* (1561), with its suggestions for the religious and educational organization of the country. The return of **Mary, Queen of Scots** (August 1561) introduced new elements into the strife of parties; and during the six years of her reign Knox's attitude towards her was that of uncompromising antagonism. The celebration of mass in Holyrood Chapel first roused his wrath; and a sermon delivered by him in St

Giles High Kirk led to the first of his famous interviews with Mary. He went so far as to alienate the most powerful noble of his own party—Lord James Stuart, afterwards the Regent **Moray**; but the marriage of Mary with Lord Darnley (1565) brought them together again. After the murder of **David Rizzio** he withdrew to Ayrshire, where he wrote part of his *History of the Reformation in Scotland.* The murder of Darnley, Mary's marriage with **Bothwell**, and her flight into England again threw the management of affairs into the hands of the Protestant party; and under Moray as regent the acts of 1560 in favour of the Reformed religion were duly ratified by the Estates. The assassination of Moray in 1570, and the formation of a strong party in favour of Mary, once more endangered the cause, and Knox removed to St Andrews for safety. In November 1572, at the induction of his successor, he made his last public appearance at St Giles. He was buried in the churchyard then attached to St Giles. His first wife, Marjory Bowes, died in 1560, leaving him two sons. By his second wife, Margaret Stewart, daughter of Lord Ochiltree, whom (then not above 16) he married in 1564, he had three daughters. Knox is the pre-eminent type of the religious Reformer—single-minded of purpose, and indifferent or hostile to every interest of life that did not advance his cause. The term fanatic is hardly applicable to one who combined in such degree the shrewdest worldly sense with ever-ready wit and native humour. The impress of his individuality, stamped on every page of his *History of the Reformation in Scotland*, renders his work unique.

KNOX, Robert (1791–1862) Scottish anatomist, born in Edinburgh. He became conservator of the newly-established museum of Edinburgh's Royal College of Surgeons in 1824, and from 1826 to 1840 ran an anatomy school. He won fame as a teacher but aroused considerable dislike through having obtained subjects for dissection from **William Burke** and **William Hare**. He wrote extensively on anatomy and anthropology. He is the subject of **James Bridie**'s play *The Anatomist*.

KNOX, Ronald Arbuthnott (1888–1957) English theologian and writer, born in Birmingham, the son of an Anglican bishop, brother of **Edmund George Knox**. Educated at Eton and Balliol College, Oxford, he became a fellow and lecturer at Trinity College, Oxford, in 1910, but resigned in 1917 on his reception into the Church of Rome. He was Catholic chaplain at Oxford from 1926 to 1939. Author of numerous works of apologetics, his modern translation of the Bible, widely used by Roman Catholics, is specially noteworthy. His essays are distinguished by their satirical wit and trenchant criticism of some contemporary modes and manners. He published his autobiographical *A Spiritual Aeneid* in 1918. He also wrote several detective novels, such as *Still Dead* (1934).

KNUSSEN, (Stuart) Oliver (1952–) English composer and conductor, born in Glasgow. He showed early flair for composition, conducting the London Symphony Orchestra in his first symphony in 1968. Two symphonies have followed, together with numerous orchestral, chamber and vocal works, and operas (including *Where the Wild Things Are*, 1979–83). He became a co-director of the Aldeburgh Festival in 1983.

KNUT, Sveinsson (Canute the Great) (d.1035) king of England from 1016, Denmark from 1018 and Norway from 1030. One of the most effective of the early kings of England, he was the son of **Svein I Haraldsson**, **'Fork-Beard'**. He accompanied his father on his attempted conquest of England (1013–14), but on his father's death withdrew to Denmark where his elder brother Harald had inherited the throne. The English recalled **Æthelred II**, **the 'Unready'** from refuge in Normandy to be their king again, but Knut returned with an army in 1015 and soon made himself master of all England except London. Æthelred died in April 1016, and the English elected his son, **Edmund Ironside**, to the throne. Knut defeated Edmund at the battle of Ashington in Essex, and then concluded a treaty sharing the kingdom between them. Edmund died a month later, and Knut became undisputed king of England. To strengthen his position he banished or executed all possible claimants to the throne from the royal dynasty of Wessex; he discarded his English mistress, Ælgifu of Northampton, and summoned Æthelred's widow, Emma, from Normandy to be his wife (their son was **Hardaknut**, king of Denmark and also, briefly, of England). He inherited the throne of Denmark from his brother in 1018 and went to Denmark the following year to consolidate his power there; later he helped to overthrow **Olaf II Haraldsson** (St Olaf) of Norway, and seized the throne there in 1030, installing his son Svein (by Ælgifu) as a puppet ruler. As king of England he brought firm government, justice and security from external threat, and showed reverence and generosity to the church and its native saints. The story of his apparent attempt to turn back the tide has been totally misconstrued in folklore: in fact, he was trying to demonstrate to his courtiers that only God could control the tide, not man. He died in Shaftesbury and was interred in Winchester Cathedral. With his death, his Anglo-Scandinavian empire quickly disintegrated. He was succeeded in England by **Harald I Knutsson**, **'Harefoot'**, his younger son by Ælgifu, and then (1040–42) by Hardaknut. In Norway the unpopular Svein was immediately deposed by **Magnus I Olafsson** ('the Good'), who also inherited Denmark on the death of Hardaknut.

KOCH, Johannes See **COCCEIUS**

KOCH, Ludwig (1881–1974) German naturalist, author, and lecturer. He followed a musical career in Paris and Milan, first as a violinist, then as a lieder and oratorio singer. He organized the 'Music in the Life of the Nations' exhibition (1927), and in 1928 joined the staff of a recording company. He made the first outdoor recordings of songs of wild birds, and, coming to England in 1936, became known as a pioneer collector of bird and animal sounds. His joint publications include *Songs of Wild Birds* (1936) and *Animal Language* (1938).

KOCH, Robert (1843–1910) German physician and pioneer bacteriologist, born in Klausthal in the Harz. He practised medicine at Hanover and elsewhere, but his work on wounds, septicaemia and splenic fever gained him a seat on the imperial board of health in 1880. Further researches in microscopy and bacteriology led to his discovery in 1882 of the tubercle bacillus. In 1883 he was leader of the German expedition sent to Egypt and India in quest of the cholera germ. For his discovery of the cholera bacillus he received a gift of £5000 from the government. In 1890 he produced tuberculin as a lymph-inoculation cure for tuberculosis, but it did not prove effective as a cure. He became professor at Berlin and director of the Institute of Hygiene in 1885, and first director of the Berlin Institute for Infectious Diseases in 1891. In 1896 and 1903 he was summoned to South Africa to study rinderpest and other cattle plagues. He won the Nobel prize for physiology or medicine in 1905.

KOCHBAS See **BAR COCHBA**

KÖCHEL, Ludwig Ritter von (1800–77) Austrian musicologist, born in Stein. He compiled the famous catalogue of **Mozart**'s works, arranging them in chronological order, and giving them the 'K' numbers now commonly used to identify them.

KOCHER, Emil Theodor (1841–1917) Swiss surgeon, born and educated in Bern where he became a professor in 1872. He was noted for his work on the physiology, pathology and surgery of the thyroid gland, and was the first to excise it in an operation for goitre. In 1909 he was awarded the Nobel prize for physiology or medicine.

KOCK, Paul de (1794–1871) French novelist, born in Passy. He produced an endless series of novels about Parisian life, vivacious, piquant and very readable.

KODÁLY, Zoltán (1882–1967) Hungarian composer, born in Kecskemét. He studied in Budapest Conservatory where he became professor. Among his best known works are his *Háry János* suite, *Dances of Galanta*, and his many choral compositions, especially his *Psalmus Hungaricus* and *Te Deum*. In 1913 he and **Bartók** drafted a plan for a Hungarian folk-music collection, but the first volume was not published until 1951. He carried out important reforms in the field of musical education and developed an evolutionary system of training and sight-singing.

KOECHLIN, Charles Louis Eugène (1867–1950) French composer and writer on music, born in Paris, where he studied under **Massenet** and **Fauré** at the conservatoire. He excelled in colourful and inventive orchestration in his symphonies, symphonic poems, choral-orchestral works (including seven based on **Kipling**'s *Jungle Book*), film music and works inspired by Hollywood, such as the *Seven Stars Symphony*, and wrote prolifically and eclectically for a wide range of vocal and chamber combinations. His writings included studies of recent French music and treatises on music theory.

KOESTLER, Arthur (1905–83) Hungarian-born British author and journalist, political refugee and prisoner, born in Budapest. He studied pure science at Vienna and, embracing the cause of Zionism as described in *Promise and Fulfilment* (1949), worked on a collective farm in Palestine (1926). However, his idealism modified by his experiences, he became a political correspondent and later scientific editor for a German newspaper group. Dismissed as a communist, he travelled in Russia (1932–33), but became disillusioned, breaking with the party finally in 1938, as described in *The God that Failed* (1950). He reported the Spanish Civil War (1936–37) for the London *News Chronicle*, was imprisoned under sentence of death by **Franco**, as retold in *Spanish Testament* (1938) and *Dialogue with Death* (1942), and again by the French (1940). He escaped from German-occupied France via the French Foreign Legion, and, after a short imprisonment in London, joined the Pioneer Corps. These experiences, described in *Scum of the Earth* (1941), provided the background of his first novel in English, *Arrival and Departure* (1943). The degeneration of revolutionary idealism in Roman times under **Spartacus** he portrayed in *The Gladiators* (1939), which was followed in 1940 by the striking modern equivalent, *Darkness at Noon*, Koestler's masterpiece and one of the great political novels of the century. Intelligent humanism and anti-communism provide the themes for such essays as *The Yogi and the Commissar* (1945), *The Trail of the Dinosaur* (1955), *Reflections on Hanging* (1956) and *The Sleepwalkers* (1959), on the theories, lives and struggles with religious orthodoxy of **Copernicus**, **Kepler** and **Galileo**. *The Act of Creation* (1964), *The Ghost in the Machine* (1967), and *The Case of the Midwife Toad* (1971) were among his later works; *Bricks to Babel* (1980) is a selection from his non-fiction writings. He and his wife committed suicide together when he became terminally ill.

KOETSU, Hon Ami (1558–1637) Japanese calligrapher and designer born in Kyoto. Adopted into one of the rich merchant families, a family of sword connoisseurs, he started his career as a tea-master, and was to be famous for his raku and lacquer ware; but his numerous interests made him both one of the most creative figures in the history of Japanese art and an artist of tremendously wide achievement. He collaborated with the great master of the later decorative style, Sotatsu (1576–1643). In 1615 he founded Takagamine, a community of artists and craftsmen in northern Kyoto which infused the Japanese art world with new vigour.

KOFFKA, Kurt (1886–1941) German psychologist, and co-founder of the Gestalt school of psychology. At the University of Geissen he took part in experiments in perception with **Wolfgang Köhler**, conducted by **Max Wertheimer**. He later taught at Oxford and at Smith College, USA. He was the author of *Principles of Gestalt Psychology* (1935).

KOHL, Helmut (1930–) West German politician. Son of a Catholic tax official, he was born in Ludwigshafen on the Rhine and studied law, attending the universities of Frankfurt and Heidelberg, after a brief career in the chemical industry. He joined the Christian Democrats as a boy after the war, and became chairman for the Rhineland-Palatinate in 1956, and minister-president of the state in 1969. In 1976 he moved to Bonn as a member of the federal parliament and was chosen to run as Christian Democrat and Christian Social Union candidate for the chancellorship; although **Helmut Schmidt** retained power through his coalition with the Free Democratic party, Kohl made the CDU/CSU the largest party in parliament. In 1980 he was replaced as chancellor candidate by **Franz-Josef Strauss**; Schmidt again won, but the sudden collapse of his coalition in 1982 led to Kohl's installation as interim Chancellor, and in the elections of 1983 the CDU/CSU increased its number of seats, and formed a government. Thoroughly conservative, yet not in favour of an economy uncontrolled by state intervention, and anti-Soviet though by no means unquestioningly pro-American, Kohl holds an essentially central course between political extremes. From 1984 to 1986 Kohl was implicated in the 'Flick bribes scandal' concerned with the illegal business funding of political parties, but he was cleared of all charges of perjury and deception by the Bonn public prosecutor in May 1986 and was re-elected as chancellor in the Bundestag elections of January 1987.

KÖHLER, Wolfgang (1887–1967) German psychologist, born in Estonia, and co-founder with **Kurt Koffka** of the Gestalt school of psychology. He was director of the anthropoid research station in the Canary Islands (1913–20), where he became an authority on problem-solving in animals. He later held chairs of psychology at Berlin, Swathmore College, Pennsylvania, and Dartmouth College.

KOHLRAUSCH, Friedrich Wilhelm Georg (1840–1910) German physicist. Professor of physics at Berlin (1895), he was noted for his researches on magnetism and electricity. He wrote *Leitfaden der praktischen Physik* (1870).

KOKOSCHKA, Oskar (1886–1980) Austrian-born British artist and writer, born in Pöchlarn. He studied from 1904 to 1908 in Vienna, and taught at the Dresden Academy of Art (1919–24); thereafter he travelled widely, and painted many Expressionist landscapes in Spain, France, England etc. In 1938 he fled to England for political reasons, becoming naturalized in 1947, and painted a number of politically symbolic works, as well as portraits and landscapes. In the 1920s he also wrote a number of Expressionist dramas, including *Orpheus und Eurydike*. From 1953 he lived in Switzerland.

KOLBE, Hermann (1818–84) German scientist, born near Göttingen. He was professor at Marburg (1851–65) and Leipzig (1865–84). An outstanding teacher and experimenter, he did much in the development of organic chemical theory.

KOLCHAK, Aleksandr Vasilievich (1874–1920) Russian naval commander. In World War I he was in command of the Black Sea fleet. After the Russian revolution of 1917, he went to Omsk as war minister in the anti-Bolshevik government, and cleared Siberia, in co-operation with **Denikin**, as leader of the White Army. In 1919 Omsk fell to the Bolsheviks; and Kolchak was betrayed, and shot.

KOLFF, Willem Johan (1911–) Dutch-born American physician, developer of the artificial kidney, born in Leiden. A medical student in Leiden, he received his MD in 1946 from Groningen University. Kolff constructed his first rotating drum artificial kidney in wartime Holland and treated his first patient with it in 1943. Since 1950, when he moved to the USA, he has worked primarily at the Cleveland Clinic and Utah University, developing the artificial kidney further; he was also involved in research on the heart-lung machine used during open-heart surgery.

KOLLÁR, Jan (1793–1852) Czech poet and Slavonic scholar, a Hungarian Slovak. He was Protestant pastor at Pest (1813–49), and then professor of archaeology at Vienna. He wrote a cycle of sonnets, and compiled an edition of Slovakian folk-songs.

KÖLLIKER, Rudolph Albert von (1817–1905) Swiss anatomist and embryologist, famous for his microscopic work. He was born in Zürich, and became professor there (1845) and at Würzburg (1847). His chief works include *Manual of Human Histology* (1852) and *Entwicklungs geschichte des Menschen* (1861).

KOLLONTAI, Alexandra Mikhaylovna (1872–1952) Russian feminist and revolutionary, the world's first female ambassador. Born in St Petersburg into an upper-class family, she rejected her privileged upbringing and became interested in socialism. Married to an army officer, she nevertheless joined the Russian Social Democratic party, and for her revolutionary behaviour was exiled to Germany in 1908. In 1915 she travelled widely in the USA, begging the nation not to join World War I, and urging the acceptance of socialism. In 1917, following the Revolution, she returned to Russia, becoming commissar for public welfare. In this post she agitated for domestic and social reforms, including collective childcare and easier divorce proceedings. Although her private liaisons shocked the party, she was appointed minister to Norway (1923–25, 1927–30), Mexico (1926–27) and Sweden (1930–45), becoming ambassador in 1943. She played a vital part in negotiating the termination of the Soviet-Finnish war (1944). Her works, such as *The New Morality and the Working Class* (1918), and her collection of short stories, *Love of Worker Bees* (1923), aroused considerable controversy because of their open discussion of subjects like sexuality and women's place in society and the economy. Her autobiography, written in 1926, was not published in Russia.

KOLLWITZ, Käthe, née **Schmidt** (1867–1945) German graphic artist and sculptor, born in East Prussia, the daughter of a Free Congregation pastor. She studied in Königsberg, then Berlin, where she studied drawing and married a medical student, Karl Kollwitz, who went on to work in a poor quarter of the city. Although she has been called an Expressionist, she was uninterested in the fashions of modern art. Influenced by **Max Klinger**'s prints she chose serious, tragic subjects, with strong social or political content, eg her early etchings: the *Weaver's Revolt* (1897–98) and the *Peasants' War* (1902–08). From c.1910 she preferred lithography, and after being expelled by the Nazis in 1933 from the Prussian Academy (its first woman member) she made a moving series of eight prints on the theme of *Death* (1934–35).

KOLMOGOROV, Andrei Nikolaevich (1903–87) Russian mathematician, born in Tambov. He studied at Moscow University and in Paris, returning to Moscow in 1931 where he remained for the rest of his life. He worked on the theory of functions of a real variable, functional analysis, mathematical logic, and topology, but is particularly remembered for his creation of the axiomatic theory of probability in his book *Grundbegriffe der Wahrscheinlichkeitsrechnung* (1933), and his work with **Aleksandr Khinchin** on Markov processes. He also worked in applied mathematics on the theory of turbulence, information theory and cybernetics.

KOMENSKÝ, Ian See **COMENIUS, John Amos**

KOMOROWSKI, Tadeusz Bór (1895–1966) Polish soldier, born in Lwów. As 'General Bór' he led the heroic but unsuccessful Warsaw rising against the occupying Germans in 1944, and settled in England after World War II.

KÖNIG, Friedrich (1774–1833) German printer, inventor of the steam printing-press, born in Eisleben. In 1810 through the support of a printer in London, he obtained a patent for a press. A second patent was obtained in 1811 for a cylinder-press, improved and in 1814 adopted by *The Times*. He also made steam printing-presses near Würzburg.

KÖNIGSMARK, Count Philipp Christoph von (1665–c.1694) Swedish nobleman. After entering the service of the Elector of Hanover, he was accused of an intrigue with Sophia Dorothea (1666–1726), wife of the future **George I** of Britain, and suddenly disappeared (probably murdered) in 1694.

KÖNIGSMARK, Marie Aurora, Countess of Königsmark (?1668–1728) sister of Count **Philipp Königsmark**. In 1694 she became the mistress of **Augustus II 'the Strong'** of Saxony, and by him mother of Maurice of Saxony. After falling from favour, she was pensioned off as prioress of Quedlinburg.

KONINCK, Philips de (1619–88) Dutch painter, born in Amsterdam. He was possibly a pupil of **Rembrandt**, and certainly a member of the same artistic circle. He painted portraits, religious subjects and scenes of everyday life, but his best paintings by far were panoramic landscapes with large areas of sky. (He was also the captain of a barge which crossed from Leiden to Rotterdam). He had a cousin, Salomon, who painted large, historical scenes in the style of Rembrandt.

KONRAD, kings of Germany See **CONRAD**

KONRAD, John (1942–) Australian swimmer, born in Riga, Latvia. Despite having suffered from polio, he represented Australia at the Olympiads of 1956, 1960 and 1964, and at the Rome Olympics of 1960 he won the gold medal in the 1500 metres and bronze medals in the 400 metres and the 4 x 200 metres freestyle relay. His sister, Ilsa (1944–) was also a noted swimmer and won a silver medal in the Olympic relay at Rome in 1960. Between them the Konrads established 37 world records in the years between 1958 and 1960.

KONWICKI, Tadeusz (1926–) Lithuanian-born dissident writer and filmmaker. After fighting with guerrilla forces in Lithuania against both German and Russian occupation in World War II he moved to Poland, where he has made his home. His book *A Minor Apocalypse* was banned. In the 1950s, *At the Construction Site* was a much prized novel about the party as an engineer of souls. He was denounced in 1968. His latest book, *Moonrise, Moonrise* (1988), is about the early struggles of the Solidarity movement. His films include *Salto* and *The Last Day*.

KOO, Vi Kyuin Wellington (1888–1985) Chinese statesman. Educated at Columbia University, USA, he was Chinese ambassador to Britain (1941–46) and to the USA (1946–56). In 1964 he was vice president of the International Court of Justice.

KOOPMANS, Tjalling Charles (1910–85) Dutch-born American economist, born in 'sGraveland. Educated at Utrecht and Leiden universities, he emigrated to the USA in 1940, and worked for a shipping firm, devising a system to optimize transport costs. He was professor of economics at Chicago (1948–55) and Yale (1955–81). He shared the 1975 Nobel prize for economics (with **Leonid Kantorovich**) for his contributions to the theory of optimal allocation of resources.

KOPP, Hermann Franz Moritz (1817–92) German chemist. Professor of chemistry at Giessen (1843–63) and Heidelberg (1863–90), he was one of the founders of physical chemistry and a historian of the subject.

KOPPEL, Herman (1908–) Danish composer and pianist. Educated at the Royal Danish Academy of Music, he has been a professor at the Academy since 1955. He made his début as a composer in 1929 and as a pianist in 1930. His compositions include seven symphonies, four piano concertos, six string quartets, an opera (*Macbeth*, 1970), a ballet and music for theatre, film and radio. He has been awarded several prizes, among them the Ove Christensen honorary prize in 1952 and the Carl Nielsen prize in 1958.

KÖPRÜLÜ (late 17th century) the name of three Turkish grand viziers who effectively controlled the Ottoman government for most of the late 17th century. Mehmet Köprülü (d.1661) was an Albanian by birth who rose from working in the imperial kitchen to become grand vizier in 1656 when he was in his seventies. He ruthlessly consolidated his power and rebuilt the Ottoman fleet for service against the Venetians. He retired shortly before his death in 1661 in favour of his son, Fazil Ahmed Köprülü (c.1676), who, during his 15 years as grand vizier, built upon the foundation laid down by his father. He personally led the army against Austria, securing advantageous terms at the peace of Vasvar (Eisenberg) in 1664, and against Crete which was taken in 1669. He died of dropsy and his place was taken by his foster-brother Kara Mustafa, who brought the Ottomans to the gates of Venice. Fazil Ahmed's younger brother, Fazil Mustafa Köprülü (d.1691), became grand vizier in 1689. Like his predecessors, he reformed the administration and reorganized the army. He showed particular concern for non-Muslim subjects in the Balkans. He was killed in battle near Karlowitz.

KORBUT, Olga (1956–) Russian gymnast, born in Grodno, Byelorussia. A tiny slip of a girl, she captivated the world at the 1972 Olympics at Munich with her lithe grace, and gave gymnastics a new lease of life as a sport. She won a gold medal as a member of the winning Russian team, as well as individual golds in the beam and floor exercises and silver for the parallel bars. After retiring, she became a coach.

KORDA, Sir Alexander (1893–1956) Hungarian-born British film producer, born in Turkeye, Hungary. Starting as a newspaperman in Budapest, he became a film producer there, then in Vienna, Berlin and Hollywood, where he was director of United Artists Corporations of America and Paris. He came to Britain and in 1932 founded London Film Productions and Denham studios. His films include *The Private Life of Henry VIII* (1932), *Rembrandt* (1936), *The Third Man* (1949) and *The Red Shoes* (1948). He was knighted in 1942, the first filmmaker to be so honoured.

KORIN, Ogata (1658–1716) Japanese calligrapher and designer of pottery and lacquer ware, born in Kyoto. A relative of **Koetsu**, he first trained in the Kano school; he later followed the style initiated by Sotatsu. His artistic career only fully started in 1697 when he went virtually bankrupt; he first made designs for the pottery of his younger brother Kenzan, but eventually devoted himself entirely to painting. He became the greatest master of the decorative style of painting of his generation, a style which is associated with the new wealthy and cultured merchant class of the Tokugawa period, into which he was born. His work is characterized by simplified composition, an emphasis on decorative power in spacing and patterning of forms, and the use of dramatic colour contrast.

KORNBERG, Arthur (1918–) American biochemist, born in Brooklyn, New York. A graduate in medicine from Rochester University, he was director of enzyme research at the National Institutes of Health (1947–52) and head of the department of microbiology at Washington University from 1953 to 1959. He discovered the DNA enzyme polymerase, for which he shared the 1959 Nobel prize for physiology or medicine with **Severo Ochoa**. In 1959 he was appointed professor at Stanford University, and became the first to synthesize viral DNA (1967). He wrote *DNA Replication* (1980).

KÖRNER, Karl Theodor (1791–1813) German lyric poet, born in Dresden. He wrote plays and fiery patriotic songs such as *Leier und Schwert* (1814), which contained the *Schwert-Lied*, written shortly before his death in battle.

KORNGOLD, Erich Wolfgang (1897–1957) Austrian-born American composer, born in Brünn (now Brno), the son of the eminent music critic Julius Korngold (1860–1945). His teachers included **Zemlinsky** in Vienna and, from the age of twelve, he had spectacular success there and throughout Germany as a composer of chamber, orchestral and stage works in lush late-Romantic vein. His finest operas were *Violanta* (1916) and *Die tote Stadt* (1920). He was professor at the Vienna State Academy of Music (1930), but in 1934 he emigrated to Hollywood and composed a series of magnificent film scores, two of which, *Robin Hood* and *Anthony Adverse*, received Oscars. His post-war works included a violin and a cello concerto and a symphony.

KORNILOV, Lavr Georgyevich (1870–1918) Russian soldier, a Cossack born in western Siberia. In World War I he took command of all troops in August 1917, marched on St Petersburg, and tried to set up a military directory, but was forced to surrender by **Kerensky**. He organised a Cossack force, but fell in battle.

KOROLENKO, Vladimir (1853–1921) Russian novelist, born in Zhitomir. Returning from exile in Siberia (1879–85), he published *Makar's Dream*, and made his name by stories and articles.

KOROLEV, Sergei Pavlovich (1906–66) Russian aircraft engineer and rocket designer, born in Zhitomir. Graduating from the Moscow Higher Technical School in 1929, he became a pilot and designed successful gliders and a light plane (SK-4) in 1930. In 1931 he formed the Moscow Group for Investigating Jet Propulsion, which launched the Soviet Union's first liquid-propelled rocket in 1933. By 1949 he was engaged in high-altitude sounding flights employing rockets. As chief designer of Soviet spacecraft he directed the Soviet Union's space programme with such historic 'firsts' as the first orbiting Sputniks in 1957 and the first manned space flight of **Yuri Gagarin** in 1961, the *Vostok* and *Voskhod* manned spacecraft, and the *Cosmos* series of satellites.

KORZYBSKI, Alfred Habdank Skarbek (1879–1950) Polish-born American scholar and philosopher of language, born in Warsaw. Sent by the Russian army on a military mission to North America during World War I, he remained in the USA after the fall of the tsar, becoming a US citizen in 1940. He is best known as the originator of general semantics, a system of linguistic philosophy concerned with the study of language as a representation of reality, which aims to increase people's ability to analyze the meanings and uses of words in order to promote mutual understanding between individuals and the accurate transmission of ideas from one generation to another. He was founder and director of the Institute of General Semantics in Chicago. His major work on general semantics is *Science and Sanity: An Introduction to Non-Aristotelian Systems and General Semantics* (1933). He also wrote *Manhood of Humanity: the Science and Art of Human Engineering* (1921).

KOSCIUSZKO, Tadeusz Andrezei Bonawentura (1746–1817) Polish soldier and patriot, born near Slonim in Lithuania. He chose the career of arms, and was trained in France. In 1777 he went to the United States, where he fought for the colonists in the War of Independence (1775–83) and became brigadier-general. He returned to Poland in 1784; and when Russia attacked his country in 1792, with 4000 men he held Dubienka for five days against 18000. In 1794, after the second partition of Poland, he headed the national movement in Cracow, and was appointed dictator and commander-in-chief. His defeat of a greatly superior force of Russians at Raclawice was followed by a rising in Warsaw. He established a provisional government and took the field, but, defeated, fell back upon Warsaw and maintained himself there, until, overpowered by superior numbers in the battle of Maciejowice, 10 October 1794, and wounded, he was taken prisoner. Two years later the emperor **Paul** of Russia restored him to liberty. He went first to England, then in 1797 to America, and finally in 1798 to France, where he farmed near Fontainebleau. In 1806 he refused to support **Napoleon**'s plan for the restoration of Poland. He settled at Soleure in Switzerland in 1816, and died by the fall of his horse over a precipice.

KOSINSKI, Jerzy Nikodem (1933–) Polish-born American novelist, born in Lodz. Educated in political science at Lodz University, he taught there (1955–57) before emigrating to the USA in 1957. He has had a distinguished academic career. His novels espouse a belief in survival at all costs, his characters machinating to make the most of a given situation. The best known are *The Painted Bird* (1965), a classic of Holocaust literature, *Steps* (1968), *Being There* (1971), *Blind Date* (1977), and *Passion Play* (1979).

KOSSEL, Albrecht (1853–1927) German physiological chemist. Professor at Heidelberg (1901–23), he investigated the chemistry of cells and of proteins, and was awarded the 1910 Nobel prize for physiology or medicine.

KOSSEL, Walther (1888–1956) German physicist, son of **Albrecht Kossel**. Professor of physics at Kiel (1921) and Danzig (1932), he did much research on atomic physics, especially on **Röntgen** spectra, and was known for his physical theory of chemical valency.

KOSSOFF, Leon (1926–) English painter, born in London. He studied at the St Martin's School of Art, at the Borough Polytechnic (under David Bomberg, 1949–53), and at the Royal College of Art (1953–56). Painting figures in interiors and city views, he follows Bomberg and **Soutine** in his expressive style, using very thick impasto. His colours were originally sombre, but brightened after c.1975. He held an exhibition at the Whitechapel Gallery, London, in 1972.

KOSSUTH, Lajos (1802–94) Hungarian revolutionary, born in Monok near Zemplin, of a poor but noble family. He practised law for a time, in 1832 was a deputy at the diet of Pressburg, and edited a journal which, owing to the law, was not printed, but transcribed. The issue of a lithographed paper led, in 1837, to imprisonment. Liberated in 1840, he became editor of the *Pesti Hirlap*, advocating extreme Liberal views. In 1847, sent by Pest to the diet, he became leader of the opposition; and after the French Revolution of 1848 he demanded an independent government for Hungary. In September 1848, at the head of the Committee of National Defence, he prosecuted with extraordinary energy the measures necessary for carrying on war; and in April 1849 he induced the National Assembly at Debrecen to declare that the Habsburg dynasty had forfeited the throne. Appointed provisional governor of Hungary, he sought in vain to secure the intervention of the Western Powers; and finding that the dissensions between himself and **Görgei** were damaging the national cause, he resigned his dictatorship in favour of Görgei. After the defeat at Temesvár on 9 August 1849, he fled to Turkey, where he was made a prisoner, but not extradited. In September 1851, liberated by British and American influence, he came to England, where, as subsequently in the USA, he was received with respect and sympathy. From 1852 he resided mainly in England till, on the Franco-Italian war with Austria in 1859, he proposed to **Napoleon III** to arrange a Hungarian rising against Austria. The peace of Villafranca bitterly disappointed Kossuth; and in 1861 and in 1866 he tried in vain to bring about a rising against Austria. When in 1867 **Deák** effected the reconciliation of Hungary with the dynasty, Kossuth retired from active political life, and afterwards lived mostly in Turin. In 1867 he refused to avail himself of the general amnesty. Between 1880 and 1882 he published three volumes of *Memories of my Exile*; others followed in 1890; and at his death he had completed a work on Hungarian history.

KOSTER See **JANSZOON, Laurens**

KOSYGIN, Alexei Nikolayevich (1904–80) Soviet politician, born and educated in Leningrad. Elected to the Supreme Soviet (1938), he held a variety of industrial posts, being a member of the Central Committee (1939–60) and of the Politburo (1946–52). Chairman of state economic planning commission (1959–60) and first deputy prime minister (with **Mikoyan**) from 1960, in 1964 he succeeded **Khrushchev** as chairman of the Council of Ministers (prime minister). He attempted modest, decentralizing reforms, but was blocked by the party machine and the caution of **Brezhnev**. He resigned in 1980 because of ill health, and died soon after.

KOTELAWALA, Sir John (1896–1980) Sinhalese statesman. Educated at Colombo and Cambridge University, he became leader of the House of Representatives in 1952, and was prime minister of Ceylon (now Sri Lanka) (1953–56). He was created KBE in 1948.

KOTZÉ, Sir John Gilbert (1849–1940) South African judge, born in Cape Town. After studying law in London, he practised at the Cape bar. In 1877 when the South African Republic was annexed by Britain he was appointed first judge of the new Supreme Court of the Transvaal, and became chief justice in 1881 after the first Anglo-Boer War. He strove to improve the standard of the administration of justice and tried to apply Roman-Dutch legal principles to circumstances which were radically different from those for which they were originally devised. In 1897 he held that laws of the Volksraad conflicting with the constitution would be invalid, and was consequently dismissed by President **Kruger**. After 1901 he continued to serve as a judge, although not in the Transvaal, and was a judge of appeal from 1922 to 1927. He was an outstanding judge with a thorough knowledge of Roman-Dutch law, and was a vigorous advocate of codification.

KOTZEBUE, August Friedrich Ferdinand von (1761–1819) German dramatist, born in Weimar. He filled various offices in the service of Russia, and was a facile writer of plays, tales, satires, historical works, etc; he was stabbed to death by a Jena student, because he had ridiculed the *Burschenschaft* movement. Besides quarreling with **Goethe**, Kotzebue satirized the leaders of the Romantic school. Among his 200 lively but superficial dramas are *Menschenhass und Reue* (known on the English stage as *The Stranger*), *Die Hussiten vor Naumburg* and *Die beiden Klingsberge*.

KOTZEBUE, Otto (1787–1846) German explorer and naval officer, son of **August von Kotzebue**, born in Tallin, Estonia. He accompanied Baron **von Krusenstern** round the world in 1803–06. In 1815–18 he tried to find a passage across the Arctic Ocean, and discovered Kotzebue Sound near Bering Strait. He later made two voyages of exploration in the Pacific, and commanded another round-the-world voyage (1823–26).

KOUFAX, Sanford (Sandy) (1935–) American baseball player, considered to be one of the greatest pitchers ever, born in Brooklyn, New York. He played in his home town, then in Los Angeles with the Dodgers. His short career reached its peak in the 1960s. In 1963 he was named Most Valuable Player as the Dodgers beat the New York Yankees in the World Series. In 1965 he again helped the Dodgers to a World Series victory over Minnesota with two consecutive 'shut-outs' (where the opposition fail to score a single run). But in 1966, at only 31, he had to retire from the game with arthritis of the left elbow, which impeded his throwing.

KOUNTCHE, Seyni (1931–87) Niger soldier and politician. He underwent military training in France and served in the French army before Niger achieved full independence in 1960, with **Hamani Diori** as its first president. Opposition to Diori grew during the severe drought of 1968–74 and Kountche, as army chief-of-staff, was the natural, if reluctant, leader of the coup which overthrew him. He established a military government and set about restoring the country's economy, with the eventual prospect of a return to civilian rule, but died while undergoing surgery in a Paris hospital.

KOUSSEVITZKY, Serge (1874–1951) Russian-born American conductor, composer and double-bass player, born in Vishny-Volotchok. He founded his own orchestra in Moscow in 1909, and after the revolution was director of the State Symphony Orchestra in Petrograd. He left Russia in 1920, worked in Paris, and settled in Boston in 1924, remaining conductor of its symphony orchestra for 25 years. Throughout his life he championed new music; in Russia he performed and published **Medtner**, **Prokofiev**, **Rachmaninov**, **Scriabin**, and **Stravinsky**; in the US he commissioned and premiered many works which became 20th-century classics. He founded the Berkshire Symphonic Festivals (1934) and the Berkshire Music Centre (1940) at Tanglewood, Massachusetts.

KOUWENHOVEN, William Bennett (1886–1975) American electrical engineer, born in New York City. He studied at the Brooklyn Polytechnic, where he later taught physics. He moved to Washington University in 1913 and the following year to Johns Hopkins where he became professor of electrical engineering in 1930. In the 1930s he developed the first practical electrical defibrillator which has come into general use for the treatment of heart-beat irregularities; in 1959 he introduced the first-aid technique of external heart massage.

KOVALEVSKAYA, Sofya Vasilyevna (1850–91) Russian mathematician and novelist, daughter of a Moscow artillery officer. Married to a brother of **Alexander Kovalevsky**, she made a distinguished name for herself throughout Europe as a mathematician. As a woman she found it impossible to obtain an academic post in Europe until finally she obtained a lectureship at Stockholm and then a professorship in 1889. She worked on Abelian integrals, partial differential equations and the form of Saturn's rings. She also made a name as a novelist, her works including *Vera Brantzova* (1895).

KOVALEVSKY, Alexander (1840–1901) Russian embryologist, born in Dünaburg. Professor at St Petersburg, Kassan, Kiev and Odessa, he is known for his researches on the embryology of invertebrates which led to **Haeckel**'s Gastraea theory; for his discovery of the life history and true position of the Ascidians; and for investigations of the development of the amphioxus, Balanoglossus, Sagitta, and Brachiopods.

KOZLOV, Ivan Ivanovich (1779–1840) Russian poet. He translated **Byron** and **Thomas Moore**. He turned to poetry after going blind at the age of 30.

KOZLOV, Peter (1863–1935) Russian traveller and archaeologist. He explored the Altai, the Gobi desert, and the head-waters of the great Chinese rivers. In 1909 he discovered the ancient city of Khara Khoto in the Gobi, with its library.

KRAEPELIN, Emil (1856–1926) German psychiatrist. Professor at Dorpat, Heidelberg and Munich, he was a pioneer in the psychological study of serious mental diseases (psychoses), which he divided into two groups, manic-depressive and dementia-praecox. He did research on brain fatigue and on the mental effects of alcohol.

KRAFFT-EBING, Richard, Freiherr von (1840–1902) German psychiatrist, born in Mannheim. He was professor at Strasbourg and at Vienna. Much of his work was on forensic psychiatry and on sexual pathology (*Psychopathia Sexualis* 1876).

KRAG, Jens Otto (1914–78) Danish politician. He was minister of foreign affairs from 1958 to 1962, when he became leader of the Social Democratic party, which he led until 1972. During this time he had two periods as prime minister (1962–68 and 1971–72). In 1972 he led Denmark into the Common Market, but after the EEC referendum (October 1972), which showed 63.3% of the votes in favour of membership and 36.7% against, he surprisingly decided to resign and was succeeded by **Anker Jorgensen**.

KRAMER, Dame Leonie Judith (1924–) Australian academic, writer and administrator, born in Melbourne. Educated at Melbourne University and at St Hugh's College, Oxford, in 1968 she was appointed professor of Australian literature at Sydney University, the first ever to hold such a post. As a scholar and critic she has held positions on a number of influential bodies, being a member of the board of the Australian Broadcasting Commission since 1947 (chairman 1981–83), member of the Universities Council (1977–86), and council member of the Australian National University, Canberra, from 1984. Her published works include three critical volumes on the Australian author **Henry Handel Richardson**. She has co-authored two books on language and literature, edited the *Oxford History of Australian Literature* (1981) and co-edited the companion *Oxford Anthology of Australian Literature* (1985). She was created a DBE in 1983.

KRAPOTKIN, Prince Peter See **KROPOTKIN**

KRASZEWSKI, Józef Ignacy (1812–87) Polish historical novelist and poet, born in Warsaw. He was one of the most prolific of all Polish authors, his works exceeding 300. His best-known novel is *Jermola the Potter* (1857). In 1884 he was imprisoned at Magdeburg for treason.

KRAUS, Karl (1874–1936) Austrian critic and dramatist, and publisher and sole writer of the radical satirical magazine *Die Fackel* (The Torch), from 1899 to 1936. He was among the first to champion the work of the German playwright, **Frank Wedekind**. He himself wrote the apocalyptic and satirical plays, *The Last Days of Mankind* (1919) and *The Unconquerable Ones* (1928), both savage portraits of politics and social morality.

KRAY, Ronald and **Reginald** (1933–) convicted English murderers who ran a criminal Mafia-style operation in the East End of London in the 1960s. Their gang or 'firm' collected protection money, organized illegal gambling and drinking clubs and participated in gang warfare. Ronnie Kray, nicknamed 'Colonel', was the dominant twin, who modelled himself on Chicago gangsters. An early attempt to convict the brothers of murder failed. Their activities became increasingly violent, and in the late 1960s, Ronnie Kray shot dead a member of a rival gang and Reggie stabbed another to death because he had threatened his brother. The twins were tried at the Old Bailey in 1969, were found guilty and were sentenced to life imprisonment of not less than 30 years. A campaign to free them in 1987 failed.

KREBS, Sir Hans Adolf (1900–81) German-born British biochemist, born in Hildesheim. In 1932 he discovered the series of chemical reactions called the urea cycle. He emigrated to Britain in 1934, and became lecturer (1935) and professor (1945) at Sheffield, and professor at Oxford (1954–67). In 1953 he won the Nobel prize for physiology or medicine (with **Fritz Lipmann**) for researches into metabolic processes, particularly the 'Krebs cycle'.

KREISKY, Bruno (1911–) Austrian politician, born in Vienna. Educated at Vienna University, he joined the Social Democratic party of Austria (SPO) as a young man and was imprisoned for his political activities from 1935 until he escaped to Sweden in 1938. He returned to Austria and served in the foreign service (1946–51) and the prime minister's office (1951–53). He was increasingly active in party politics and in 1970 became prime minister in a minority SPO government. He steadily increased his majority in subsequent elections but in 1983, when that majority disappeared, he refused to serve in a coalition and resigned.

KREISLER, Fritz (1875–1962) Austrian-born American violinist, born in Vienna. He studied medicine and became an Uhlan officer. He composed violin pieces, a string quartet and an operetta, *Apple Blossoms* (1919), which was a Broadway success. He became an American citizen in 1943.

KREITMAN, Esther See **SINGER**

KŘENEK, Ernst (1900–) American composer, born in Vienna. He worked with various German theatres as a conductor-director, and eventually became professor at Vassar College, New York. He has written two symphonies, and his style ranges from jazz (as in his opera *Jonny spielt auf*, 1927, which made his name), to serialism (as in *Karl V*, 1930–3). Since the mid 1950s he has adopted various avant-garde idioms.

KRETZER, Marx (1854–1941) German novelist, born in Posen. Essentially a writer on social problems and working people, he has, on account of his realism, been called the German **Zola**. His books include *Die Betrogenen* (1882, concerning poverty and prostitution), *Die Verkommenen* (1883), *Meister Timpe* (1888), and *Das Gesicht Christi* (1897).

KREUGER, Ivar (1880–1932) Swedish industrialist and financier, born in Kalmar. Trained as a civil engineer, he emigrated to America where he worked as real-estate salesman and building contractor. He went to South Africa before returning to Sweden in 1907. In 1913 he founded the United Swedish Match Company and began a series of acquisitions and combinations which brought him control of three-quarters of the world's match trade. He lent large sums to governments in return for monopolistic concessions. In 1931 he was in difficulties and in March 1932, unable to meet a bank demand, he committed suicide. Huge irregularities in his financial dealings over seven years were revealed after his death.

KRILOF, Ivan Andreevich See **KRYLOV**

KRIPKE, Saul (1940–) American philosopher and logician, born in Bay Shore, New York. He was educated at Harvard and has taught at Rockefeller University (1968–76) and Princeton (since 1976). As a youthful prodigy he made remarkable technical advances in modal logic, whose wider philosophical implications were later explored in such famous papers as 'Naming and Necessity' (1972).

KRISHNA MENON, Vengalil Krishnan (1896–1974) Indian politician, born in Calicut, Malabar. He was educated at the Presidency College, Madras, and at London University. He came to Britain in 1924 and became a history teacher and a London barrister. In 1929 he became secretary of the India League and the mouthpiece of Indian nationalism in Britain. When India became a Dominion in 1947 he became India's high commissioner in London. In 1952 he became leader of the Indian delegation to the United Nations, bringing **Jawaharlal Nehru**'s influence to bear on international problems as leader of the Asian 'uncommitted' and 'neutralist' bloc. During the first 1956 Suez crisis on the nationalization of the Canal he formulated a plan to deal with it. As defence minister (1957–62) he came into conflict at the United Nations with Britain over Kashmir. He was minister of defence production for a short time in 1962.

KRISHNA RAYA (fl.16th century) ruler of the Hindu empire of Vijayanagar. A warrior king, he spent much of his reign at war with the sultan of Bijapur, inflicting a severe defeat upon the Muslims at the battle of Raichur in 1520. A poet himself, he was a liberal patron of writers in the Telugu language of the region.

KRISHNAMURTI, Jiddu (1895–1986) Indian theosophist, born in Madras. He was educated in England by **Annie Besant**, who in 1925 proclaimed him the Messiah. Later he dissolved The Order of the Star in the East (founded by Besant), and travelled the world teaching and advocating a way of life and thought unconditioned by the narrowness of nationality, race and religion.

KRISTIAN, (Christian) ten kings of Denmark and other Scandinavian countries.

KRISTIAN I (1426–81) king of Denmark from 1448, Norway from 1450, and Sweden from 1457 to 1464, the founder of the Oldenburg royal line. The son of Dietrich, Count of Oldenburg, and Hedvig, heiress of Schleswig and Holstein, he was elected king of Denmark in succession to Kristopher III. In 1540 he was accepted as king of Norway, ousting **Karl VIII** (Karl Knutsson) of Sweden, and in 1457 he ousted Karl from the throne of Sweden as well (although he lost the crown to Karl again in 1464). In 1460 he was elected sovereign ruler of Schleswig and Holstein. Improvident and spendthrift, he maintained a splendid court in Copenhagen, but was always chronically short of money; to provide a dowry of 60 000 guilders for the marriage of his daughter Margaret to **James III** of Scotland, he mortgaged the Orkneys and Shetland for 8000 guilders to make up the balance—a pledge that was never redeemed. In Denmark, however, he founded the University of Copenhagen in 1478. He was succeeded by his son, John (Hans) I.

KRISTIAN II (1481–1559) king of Denmark, Norway and Sweden. He mounted the throne of Norway and Denmark in 1513. His marriage in 1515 to Elisabeth of Habsburg, sister of the emperor **Charles V** did not extinguish his love for his mistress **Dyveke**. In 1520 he overthrew **Sten Sture**, the regent of Sweden, and thereafter was crowned king. But his treacherous massacre in the Stockholm 'blood-bath' of the foremost men in Sweden (8–10 November 1520) roused such opposition that he was driven out by **Gustav I Vasa** in 1523, marking the end of the Kalmar Union between the three kingdoms. In Denmark a popular revolt drove him for refuge to the Netherlands, and placed his uncle, **Frederik I**, on the throne. Assisted, however, by Charles V, Kristian landed in Norway in 1531, but at Akershus next year was totally defeated, and spent his remaining years in imprisonment.

KRISTIAN III (1503–59) king of Denmark and Norway from 1534, elder son and successor of **Frederik I**. An ardent Lutheran, he imposed the Reformation on Denmark, Norway and Iceland, and established the Lutheran state church. He acceded to the throne in the midst of a civil war, the so-called 'Count's War' (1533–36) between Catholic supporters of the ex-king **Kristian II** and the Protestant son of Frederik. It ended only with the capitulation of Copenhagen in August 1536. Six days later, Kristian arrested all the Catholic bishops who had opposed him, and confiscated church lands. He then encouraged agriculture and trade, brought out a Danish translation of the German Bible (1550), and hugely strengthened the monarchy. He was succeeded by his son, **Frederik II**.

KRISTIAN IV (1577–1648) king of Denmark and Norway from 1588, and one of the best-remembered monarchs of Scandinavia. The son of **Frederik II**, whom he succeeded, he ruled under regents until 1596. A man of action and heroic stature, he strengthened the Danish navy and army, and enhanced the city of Copenhagen with magnificent new buildings. He also founded the city of Kristiania (Christiania) on the site of medieval Oslo after it was burnt down in 1624. He invaded the Sweden of the young **Gustav II Adolf** in 1611, but failed to capture Stockholm and made peace in 1613 with the treaty of Knǎed. In the Thirty Years' War (1618–48) he joined the Protestant Union in 1625 to help his niece, **Elizabeth of Bohemia**, but retired from the fray after a catastrophic defeat at Lutter am Barenberge, near Hamelin, by Graf von Tilley and **Wallenstein** in 1626. Denmark's power and prestige were now shattered, and the rest of Kristian's reign was a story of steady decline. In 1628 he formed a defensive Baltic alliance with Gustav II Adolf against Wallenstein; but in a second war with the Sweden of Queen **Kristina** from 1643 to 1645, he lost the dominion of the Baltic he had previously gained. He was succeeded by his son, **Frederik III**.

KRISTIAN VII (1749–1808) king of Denmark and Norway from 1766, son and successor of Frederik V. From an early age he suffered from dementia praecox, aggravated by the harshness of his tutor. He married in 1766 his English cousin, Caroline Matilda, sister of King **George III** of Britain, and in 1768 made a glittering tour of Europe, accompanied by his court physician, Count **Johann Struensee**, whom he soon appointed privy councillor. Struensee became the queen's lover and seized effective power, but in 1772 was charged with treason and executed, while the queen was divorced and exiled to Hanover. In 1784 the king was adjudged insane, and relinquished control to his son, Crown Prince Frederik, who eventually succeeded to the throne as **Frederik VI**.

KRISTIAN VIII (1786–1848) king of Denmark from 1839, son and successor of **Frederik VI**. As crown prince of Denmark he was elected king of Norway in 1814 to go with a new constitution (17 May), but was promptly ousted when Norway was taken by **Karl XIV Johan** (Bernadotte) of Sweden. As king of Denmark he revived the ancient Althing (parliament) of Iceland as a consultative assembly in 1843, and allowed freedom of trade with Iceland. Early in 1848 he signed an order abolishing monarchical absolutism, which was implemented by his son and successor, **Frederik VII**, the following year.

KRISTIAN IX (1818–1906) king of Denmark from 1863, in succession to the childless **Frederik VII**. A prince of Glücksburg, he was confirmed as crown prince of Denmark by the Protocol of London, signed by all the great powers in 1852 when it became clear that the old Oldenburg line would become extinct. On succeeding to the throne in 1863, he was immediately obliged to sign the 'November Constitution' of 1863 incorporating Schleswig into the Danish kingdom; this led to war with Prussia and Austria and the loss of both Schleswig and Holstein. In 1874, on the 1000th anniversary of the settlement of Iceland, he paid the first royal visit by a reigning monarch, and granted Iceland's first constitution, of limited autonomy under a governor. He was succeeded in 1906 by his elder son as **Frederik VIII**, while his younger son became King **George I** of Greece. His elder daughter, **Alexandra**, married the future King **Edward VII** of Britain, and his younger daughter, Mari Dagmar, married the future Tsar **Alexander III** of Russia.

KRISTIAN X (1870–1947) king of Denmark from 1912 and of Iceland 1888–1944. The son of **Frederick VIII**, he was revered as a symbol of resistance during the German occupation in World War II. In 1915 he signed a new constitution granting the vote to women, and in 1918 signed the Act of Union with Iceland which granted Iceland full independence in personal union with the Danish sovereign (this ended in 1944). During World War II he elected to stay on in Denmark; he would ride on horseback through the streets as a defiant reminder of his presence, until he was put under house arrest by the Germans (1943–45). He married Alexandrine, Duchess of Mecklenburg-Schwerin, and was succeeded by their son, **Frederik IX**.

KRISTINA (1626–89) queen of Sweden from 1632 to 1654, daughter and successor of **Gustav II Adolf**. Clever and beautiful, she was educated like a boy during her minority, when the affairs of the kingdom were ably managed by her father's chancellor, **Axel Oxenstierna**. Oxenstierna continued Swedish military involvement in the Thirty Years' War and planted the Swedish flag in the New World by building Fort Carolina at Wilmington on the Delaware. In 1644 Kristina came of age, and quickly brought to an end the costly war against the Denmark of **Kristian IV** with the peace of Westphalia in 1648. She was crowned 'king' in 1650. She gave dazzling brilliance to the Swedish court, patronizing the arts and attracting some of the best minds in Europe, like **Hugh Grotius**, **Salamatius** and **Descartes**, who died there in 1650. Bisexual by nature, she was strongly averse to marriage and found child-bearing repugnant. She refused to marry her cousin, **Karl X Gustav**, but instead proclaimed him crown prince; then, having secretly embraced Catholicism, and impatient of the personal restraints imposed on her as a ruler, she abdicated in 1654. She went into well-endowed exile, was received into the Catholic Church at Innsbruck, and entered Rome on horseback dressed as an Amazon. At Fontainebleau in 1657 she had her Italian equerry executed for treason, for betraying her plans to obtain the throne of Naples. When Karl X Gustav died in 1660 she hastened back to Sweden, but failed to get herself reinstated. In 1667 she aspired to the throne of Poland. For the rest of her life she lived in Rome as a pensioner of the pope, and was a generous and discerning patron of the arts, sponsoring the sculptor **Bernini** and the composers **Corelli** and **Scarlatti**.

KROEBER, Alfred Louis (1876–1960) American cultural anthropologist, born in Hoboken, New Jersey. He studied under **Franz Boas** at Columbia University, and went on to build up the anthropology department at the University of California at Berkeley (1901–46, professor from 1919). His extensive studies of the Californian Indians were compiled in his *Handbook of the Indians of California* (1925). However his primary influence lies in his concept of cultures as patterned wholes, each with its own 'configuration' or 'style', and undergoing a process of growth or development analogous to that of an organism. His view of culture-history was replete with biological metaphor, as in *Cultural and Natural Areas of Native North America* (1939), which correlates cultural areas, defined by complexes of traits, with ecological areas defined by associations of species, and *Configurations of Culture Growth* (1944) which documents the rise, flourishing and eventual decay of civilizations in terms of cultural life-cycles. His most influential work, *Anthropology* (1923), is a monument to the establishment of anthropology as a professional academic discipline. Many of his most influential papers are collected in *The Nature of Culture* (1952).

KROGH, Schack August Steenberg (1874–1949) Danish physiologist, professor of zoophysiology at Copenhagen (1916–45). He won the Nobel prize for physiology or medicine in 1920 for his discovery of the regulation of the motor mechanism of capillaries.

KRONECKER, Leopold (1823–91) German mathematician, born in Liegnitz, the son of a wealthy businessman. He obtained his doctorate at Berlin in 1845, where he was taught by **P Lejeune Dirichlet** and **Ernst Kummer**, returned home to manage the family estate, and then returned to Berlin in 1855 to live as a private scholar. He worked in algebraic number theory, elliptic functions and the foundations of analysis. He fell out with **Karl Weierstrass** and **Georg Cantor** over the use of the infinite in mathematics, as he believed that mathematics should be essentially based on the arithmetic of the whole numbers. He once said 'God made the integers; all the rest is the work of man.'

KROPOTKIN, Prince Peter (1842–1921) Russian geographer, savant, revolutionary and nihilist, born in Moscow. In 1857 he entered the corps of pages. After five years' service and exploration in Siberia, he returned to the capital to study mathematics, while acting as secretary to the Geographical Society. In 1871 he explored the glacial deposits of Finland and Sweden; in 1872 he associated himself with the extremist section of the International Workingman's Association. Arrested (1874) and imprisoned in Russia, he escaped to England in 1876. At Lyon he was condemned in 1883 to five years' imprisonment for anarchism; but, released in 1886, he settled in England till the revolution of 1917 took him back to Russia. He wrote on anarchism, the French Revolution, Russian literature, Asia, mutual aid in evolution, and *Memoirs of a Revolutionist* (1900).

KRÜDENER, Barbara Juliana von (1764–1824) Russian mystic, born in Riga, the daughter of Baron von Vietinghoff. She married in 1782 Baron von Krüdener, Russian ambassador at Venice, but separated in 1785. From 1789 she lived in Riga, St Petersburg and Paris. In 1803 she published a remarkable novel, *Valérie*, supposed to be autobiographical, and presently gave herself up to an exaggerated mysticism. Expelled in 1817–18 from Switzerland and Germany, and repulsed by her former admirer, the emperor **Alexander**, she retired to her paternal estates near Riga, where she entered into relations with the Moravian Brethren. She died in Karasu-Bazar in the Crimea.

KRUGER, Paul (Stephanus Johannes Paulus) (1825–1904) South African politician, born in Colesberg in Cape Colony. With his fellow-Boers he trekked to Natal, the Orange Free State, and the Transvaal, and won such a reputation for cleverness, coolness, and courage that in the war against Britain (1881), he was appointed head of the provisional government. In 1883 he was elected president of the Transvaal or South African Republic, and again in 1888, 1893 and 1898. 'Oom Paul' was the soul of the policy that issued in the war of 1899–1902; he showed consummate resolution and energy, but after the tide had turned against the Boers, came to Europe to seek (in vain) alliances against Britain. He made his headquarters at Utrecht, and thence issued *The Memoirs of Paul Kruger, told by Himself* (1902).

KRUPP, Alfred (1812–87) German arms manufacturer, born in Essen. He succeeded his father **Friedrich** (1787–1826), who had founded a small iron forge there in 1810, and began manufacturing arms in 1837. At the Great Exhibition in London (1851) he exhibited a solid flawless ingot of cast steel weighing 4000 kg. He established the first **Bessemer** steel plant and became the foremost arms supplier not only to Germany but to any country in the world, his first steel gun being manufactured in 1847. He acquired large mines, collieries and docks, and became a dominating force in the development of the Ruhr territories.

KRUPP, Alfried Alwin Felix (1907–67) German industrialist, son of **Gustav Krupp**, born in Essen. He graduated from Aachen Technical College, became an honorary member of **Hitler**'s SS, and in 1943 succeeded his father to the Krupp empire. He was arrested (1945) and convicted (1947) with eleven fellow-directors by an American military tribunal for plunder in Nazi-occupied territories and for employing slave labour under inhuman concentration camp conditions. He was sentenced to twelve years' imprisonment and his property was to be confiscated. By an amnesty (1951) he was released and his property restored with the proviso, under the Mehlem agreement (1953, negotiated with the three allied powers and incorporated in the Federal German Constitution), that he should sell his iron and steel assets for a reasonable offer within five years. This, however, was extended yearly from 1958 with diminishing prospect of fulfilment. Meanwhile he actually increased these assets by the acquisition of the Bochumer Verein (1958). Krupp played a prominent part in the West German 'economic miracle', building factories in Turkey, Pakistan, India and the Soviet Union. In 1959 he belatedly agreed to pay some compensation to former victims of forced labour, but only to those of Jewish origin. His son Arndt succeeded him.

KRUPP, Bertha See **KRUPP, Gustav**

KRUPP, Friedrich Alfred (1854–1902) German arms manufacturer, son of **Alfred Krupp**. He incorporated shipbuilding, armour-plate manufacture (1890) and chrome nickel steel production into the Krupp empire and became a personal friend of the Prussian emperor.

KRUPP, Gustav originally **Gustav von Bohlen und Halbach** (1870–1950), German industrialist. In 1906 he married Bertha Krupp (1886–1957), daughter of **Friedrich Alfred Krupp** and granddaughter of **Alfred Krupp**, and by special imperial edict he was allowed to adopt the name 'Krupp' (inserted before the 'von'). He took over the firm, gained the monopoly of German arms manufacture during World War I and manufactured the long-range gun for the shelling of Paris, nicknamed 'Big Bertha'. He turned to agricultural machinery and steam engines after the war, backed first **Hindenburg** against **Hitler**, but then supported the latter's party financially and connived in secret re-armament, contrary to the Versailles Treaty, after the latter's rise to power in 1933. Hitler's *Lex-Krupp* (1943) confirmed exclusive family ownership for the firm. After World War II, the Krupp empire was split up by the Allies, but Gustav was too senile to stand trial as a war criminal at Nuremberg.

KRUSENSTERN, Adam Johann, Baron von (1770–1846) Russian admiral, born in Haggud in Estonia. He served (1793–99) in the British navy, and was commissioned by Tsar **Alexander I** to command a Russian exploring expedition in the North Pacific, which ultimately became a voyage round the world (1803–06), the first by a Russian.

KRYLOV, Ivan Andreevich (1768–1844) Russian writer of fables, born in Moscow. He started writing from the age of 20. Secretary to a prince, and then aimless traveller through Russia, he obtained a government post in 1806, and, settling down, wrote nine collections of fables which appeared between 1809 and 1843. He also translated **La Fontaine**'s *Fables*.

KUBELIK, Jeronym Rafael (1914–) Czech conductor, son of the violin virtuoso Jan Kubelik (1880–1940), born in Bychory. He studied at Prague Conservatory, and first conducted the Czech Philharmonic Orchestra before he was 20. By 1939 he had established an international reputation, and in 1948 settled in England. He was conductor of the Chicago Symphony Orchestra (1950–53), at Covent Garden (1955–58) and from 1961 with the Bavarian Radio Orchestra. He has composed two operas, *Veronika* (staged 1947) and *Cornelia Faroli* (staged 1972), symphonies, concerts, and other works.

KUBIN, Alfred (1877–1959) Austrian painter and engraver, born in Leitmeritz. He exhibited in Munich with the Blaue Reiter group in 1911. He was also influenced by **Goya** and **Odilon Redon** in his drawings and engravings of dreamlike subjects, and he illustrated many books in this vein.

KUBLAI KHAN (1214–94) great khan of the Mongols from 1260 and emperor of China from 1271, grandson of **Genghis Khan**. He completed the conquest of northern China. An energetic prince, he suppressed his rivals, adopted the Chinese mode of civilization, encouraged men of letters, and made Buddhism the state religion. An attempt to invade Japan ended in disaster. He established himself at Cambaluc (the modern Beijing), the first foreigner ever to rule in China. His dominions extended from the Arctic Ocean to the Straits of Malacca, and from Korea to Asia Minor and the confines of Hungary. The splendour of his court inspired the graphic pages of **Marco Polo**, who spent 17 years in the service of Kublai—and at a later date fired the imagination of **Coleridge**.

KUBRICK, Stanley (1928–) American film director, born in the Bronx, New York. A staff photographer with *Look* magazine, he made his directorial début with the documentary *Day of the Fight* (1950), moving into features with *Fear and Desire* (1953) and establishing his reputation with the thriller *The Killing* (1956) and the anti-war drama *Paths of Glory* (1957). He has tackled a wide variety of subjects, painstakingly preparing each new film and shrouding his work in secrecy. Noted for his mastery of technique and visual composition, he is frequently criticized for an increasingly grandiose approach to his material and a lack of humanity. Resident in England from 1961, his notable successes include *Lolita* (1962), *Dr. Strangelove* (1963), *2001: A Space Odyssey* (1968) and *A Clockwork Orange* (1971).

KUGLER, Franz (1808–58) German art historian, who influenced the revival of Prussian art, born in Stettin. In 1833 he became professor in the Academy of Art and *dozent* at the University of Berlin. Part of his history of painting from the time of **Constantine the Great** (*Geschichte der Malerei*, 1837) was translated by the **Eastlakes** and others.

KUHN, (Franz Felix) Adalbert (1812–81) German philologist and folklorist, born in Königsberg. A teacher and director (from 1870) of the Kollnisches Gymnasium in Berlin, he founded a new school of comparative mythology based on comparative philology. He published collections of German folk-tales, but is best known for his work on the Indo-European languages. He was founder and editor (from 1851) of the *Zeitschrift für vergleichende Sprachforschung*, now entitled *Historische Sprachforschung*.

KUHN, Richard (1900–67) Austrian-born German chemist. A graduate of Munich University, he was director of the Kaiser Wilhelm Institute and professor at Heidelberg Unviersity from 1929. He was noted for his work on the structure and synthesis of vitamins A and B, and on carotinoids. He was awarded the 1938 Nobel prize for chemistry, but was forbidden to accept it by the Nazi government (he received the prize after World War II).

KUHN, Thomas Samuel (1922–) American philosopher and historian of science, born in Cincinnati, Ohio. He studied physics at Harvard and worked first as a physicist, but became interested in the historical development of science and published an original, and soon celebrated, work, *The Structure of Scientific Revolutions* (1962), which challenged the idea of cumulative, unidirectional scientific progress. His theory of 'paradigms', as sets of related concepts which compete for acceptance in times of rapid scientific change or revolution, has been influential in many other fields of enquiry. His other works include *The Copernican Revolution* (1957) and *Sources for the History of Quantum Physics* (1967). He has held positions at Harvard, Boston, Berkeley (1958–64),

Princeton (1964–79), and the Massachusetts Institute of Technology (from 1979).

KÜHNE, Wilhelm (1837–1900) German physiologist, professor at Heidelberg from 1871, noted for his study of the chemistry of digestive processes. He introduced the term *enzyme* to describe organic substances which activate chemical changes.

KUIPER, Gerard Peter (1905–73) Dutch-born American astronomer, born in Harenkarspel. Educated in Leiden, he moved to the USA in 1933. He took an appointment at the Lick Observatory in California, then taught at Harvard (1935–36), and joined the Yerkes Observatory before moving to the McDonald Observatory in Texas in 1939. He discovered two new satellites: Miranda, the fifth satellite of Uranus; and Nereid, the second satellite of Neptune (1948–49). His study of the planetary atmospheres detected carbon dioxide on Mars and methane on Titan, the largest Saturnian satellite. He was involved with the early American space flights, including the Ranger and Mariner missions.

KUMMER, Ernst Eduard (1810–93) German mathematician, born in Sorau. He studied theology, mathematics and philosophy at the University of Halle, and then taught at the Gymnasium in Liegnitz (1832–42), where **Leopold Kronecker** was among his students. He became known to **Karl Jacobi** and **P Lejeune Dirichlet** through his work on the hypergeometric series, and was elected a member of the Berlin Academy of Sciences in 1839. He was professor of mathematics at Breslau from 1842 to 1855, and at Berlin from 1855. He worked in number theory, where, in trying to prove **Pierre de Fermat**'s last theorem, he introduced 'ideal numbers', later developed by **Richard Dedekind** and Kronecker into one of the fundamental tools of modern algebra, and in geometry, where he discovered the quartic surface named after him.

KUN, Béla (1886–c.1937) Hungarian political leader and revolutionary, born in Transylvania. He was a journalist, soldier and prisoner in Russia, and in 1918 founded the Hungarian Communist party. In March 1919 he organised a communist revolution in Budapest and set up a Soviet republic which succeeded Karolyi's government. It failed to gain popular support, and he was forced to flee for his life in August of that year. After escaping to Vienna he returned to Russia. He is believed to have been killed in a Stalinist purge.

KUNDERA, Milan (1929–) Czechoslovakian-born French novelist, born in Brno, the son of a pianist. He was educated in Prague at Charles University and the Academy of Music and Dramatic Arts Film Faculty. He worked as a labourer and as a jazz musician before devoting himself to literature. For several years he was a professor at the Prague Institute for Advanced Cinematographic Studies. *The Joke*, his first novel, was published in 1967. After the Russian invasion in 1968 he lost his post and his books were proscribed. In 1975 he settled in France and took French citizenship. *The Joke* and the stories in *Laughable Loves* (1970; trans 1974) are his only books to have been published in his homeland; the publication in 1979 of *The Book of Laughter and Forgetting* (trans 1980) prompted the revocation of his Czech citizenship. Once described as 'a healthy sceptic whose novels are all anti-something', in exile he has emerged as one of the major world writers of the late 20th century. Other novels are *Life is Elsewhere* (1973; trans 1974), *The Farewell Party* (1976) and *The Unbearable Lightness of Being* (1984).

KÜNG, Hans (1928–) Swiss Roman Catholic theologian, born in Sursee, Lucerne. A professor at Tübingen (1960–), he has written extensively for fellow theologians and for lay people. His questioning of received interpretations of Catholic doctrine, as in *Justification* (1965), *The Church* (1967), and *Infallible? An Inquiry* (1971), and his presentations of the Christian faith, as in *On Being a Christian* (1977), *Does God Exist?* (1980), and *Eternal Life?* (1984), aroused controversy both in Germany and with the Vatican authorities, who withdrew his licence to teach as a Catholic theologian in 1979. He defended himself in *Why I am still a Christian* (1987).

KUNIGUNDE, St (d.1030) German empress, the daughter of Count Siegfried of Luxemburg, and wife of Emperor **Henry II** of Germany. According to legend, when her virtue was impugned she vindicated herself by walking barefoot over hot ploughshares. After the emperor's death in 1024 she retired into the convent of Kaufungen near Cassel, and died there. She was canonized in 1200.

KUNITZ, Stanley Jasspon (1905–) American poet, born in Worcester, Massachusetts and educated at Harvard University. A literature academic, he taught poetry at the New School for Social Research in New York City (1950–57) and Columbia University (from 1963). His first collection of verse was *Intellectual Things* (1930). *Selected Poems 1928–1958* was awarded a Pulitzer prize in 1959. Subsequent books include *The Testing-Tree* (1971) and *The Terrible Threshold: Selected Poems 1940–1970* (1974). He has also published literary reference books.

KUPKA, Frank (František) (1871–1957) Czech painter, born in Opočno, East Bohemia. He studied art at the Kunstgewerbeschule at Jaromer (1888), and in 1889 entered the Academy of Prague. In 1892 he went to Vienna, at that time a centre of the European avant-garde. Moving to Paris in 1895, he worked as an illustrator and pursued his interest in theosophy and the occult, before meeting the Cubists. With **Kandinsky**, he was one of the pioneers of pure abstraction, a style called Orphism.

KUPRIN, Alexander (1870–1938) Russian novelist. He gave up the army for literature. As a teller of short tales he ranks next to **Chekhov**. Those translated include *The Duel*, *The River of Life*, *A Slav Soul*, *The Bracelet of Garnets* and *Sasha*.

KURCHATOV, Igor Vasilevich (1903–60) Russian physicist, born in Eastern Russia. He was appointed director of nuclear physics at the Leningrad Institute (1938) and, before the end of World War II, of the Soviet Atomic Energy Institute. He carried out important studies of neutron reactions and was the leading figure in the building of Russia's first atomic (1949) and thermonuclear (1953) bombs, and the world's first industrial nuclear power plant (1954). He became a member of the Supreme Soviet in 1949.

KUROPATKIN, Alexei Nikolaievich (1848–1925) Russian soldier, born a noble of Pskov. He was Russian chief of staff under **Skobeleff** in the Turkish war (1877–78), commander-in-chief in Caucasia (1897), minister of war (1898), and commander-in-chief in Manchuria (1904–05) against the victorious Japanese. He commanded the Russian armies on the northern front February–August 1916, and then was governor of Turkestan until the Revolution in 1917.

KUROSAWA, Akira (1910–) Japanese film director, born in Tokyo. He brilliantly adapted the techniques of the No theatre to filmmaking in such films as *Rashomon* (1950), which won the Venice Film Festival prize, *Living* (1952) and *The Seven Samurai* (1955), an uncompromisingly savage view of the samurai code. Also characteristic are his vigorous adaptations of **Shakespeare**'s *Macbeth* (*The Throne of Blood*, 1957) and a samurai version of *King Lear* (*Ran*, 1985). More versatile than the popularity of his samurai films may suggest, he has also adapted **Dostoevsky** (*The Idiot*, 1951) and **Maxim Gorky** (*The Lower Depths*, 1957) for the screen. His Siberian epic *Dersu Uzala* (1975) won an Academy Award as Best Foreign Film.

KURTZMAN, Harvey (1924–) American strip cartoonist and scriptwriter, born in Brooklyn, New York. Creator of *Mad*, the world's most popular humour magazine, he studied art at Cooper Union, and entered comic books drawing *Magno* (1943). He created *Silver Linings* for the *Herald-Tribune*, then *Hey Look* one-pagers for Marvel comic. He became editor of *Frontline Combat* and *Two-Fisted Tales*, and in 1952 created *Mad* as a parody of comic books and characters, later converting it to magazine format. He also created the humour magazines *Trump*, *Humbug* and *Help*, then the colour strip *Little Annie Fanny* for *Playboy* (1962).

KUSCH, Polykarp (1911–) German-born American physicist, born in Blankenburg. Taken to the USA as a baby, he became a naturalized US citizen in 1922. A graduate of Illinois University, he became professor of physics at Columbia (1937–72) and Texas (from 1972). He shared (with **Willis Lamb**) the 1955 Nobel prize for physics for his precise determination of the magnetic moment of the electron.

KUTS, Vladimir Petrovich (1927–75) Russian athlete and middle-distance runner, born in Aleksino, Sumy Oblast. At one time holder of the world record for the 10 000 metres (28 minutes 30.4 seconds) and the 5000 metres (13 minutes 35 seconds), he won two gold medals in the 1956 Olympics in Melbourne for 5000 and 10 000 metres, where he was voted the best athlete of the Games.

KUTUZOV, Mikhail Harionovich, Prince of Smolensk (1745–1813) Russian soldier. He distinguished himself in Poland and in the Turkish wars, and from 1805 to 1812 commanded against the French. In 1812, as commander-in-chief, he fought **Napoleon** obstinately at Borodino, and later obtained a great victory over **Davout** and **Ney** at Smolensk. His army pursued the retreating French out of Russia into Prussia, where he died.

KUYP See **CUYP**

KUYPER, Abraham (1837–1920) Dutch theologian and politician, born in Massluis. As a pastor, founder of the Free University of Amsterdam (1880), member of the Dutch parliament, and prime minister (1900–05), Kuyper sought to develop a Christian world-view of society. He founded two newspapers and wrote numerous books, few of which have been translated into English, apart from *Lectures on Calvinism* (1898), *Principles of Sacred Theology* (1898), and *The Work of the Holy Spirit* (1900). His theology of common grace, the kingdom of God, and the 'sphere-sovereignty' of the church and other social institutions, offered a Calvinistic version of Christian Socialism.

KUZNETS, Simon Smith (1901–85) Russian-born American economist and statistician, born in Pinsk, Ukraine. He emigrated to the USA in 1922, studied at Columbia, and studied business cycles for the National Bureau of Economic Research from 1927. He was professor of economics at Pennsylvania (1930–54), Johns Hopkins (1954–60) and Harvard (1960–71). In his work he combined a concern for facts and measurement with creative and original ideas on economic growth and social change, such as the 20-year 'Kuznets cycle' of economic growth. His major publication was *National Income and its Composition, 1919–1938* (2 vols, 1941). He was awarded the Nobel prize for economics in 1971.

KYAN, John Howard (1774–1850) Irish inventor, born in Dublin. He worked in a brewery in England, and in 1832 invented a patent method of preserving wood, known as the 'kyanizing' process. He died in New York, where he was planning the filtering of the water supply.

KYD, Thomas (1558–94) English dramatist, born in London. He was probably educated at Merchant Taylors' School, and was most likely brought up as a scrivener under his father. His tragedies early brought him reputation, especially *The Spanish Tragedy*. Kyd translated from the French (1594) a tedious tragedy on **Pompey**'s daughter Cornelia, perhaps produced *Solyman and Perseda* (1592) and *Arden of Faversham*. He has been credited with a share in other plays, and probably wrote the lost original *Hamlet*. Between 1590 and 1593 he was in the service of an unknown lord. Imprisoned in 1593 on a charge of atheism (Unitarianism), which he tried to shift on to **Marlowe**'s shoulders, **Jonson**'s 'sporting Kyd' died in poverty.

KYLIAN, Jiri (1947–) Czech dancer and choreographer, born in Prague. After training at the Prague Conservatory, he was given a scholarship in 1967 to study in London at the Royal Ballet School. A year later he joined Stuttgart Ballet, making a start on his prolific choreographic output in 1970. After a short period as assistant artistic director at Netherlands Dance Theatre, he became sole director of the company in 1978 and has been associated with it ever since. His many works include *Sinfonietta* with music by **Janáček** (1979), *Symphony of Psalms* (1978), the all-male *Soldiers' Mass* (1980), *Return to the Strange Land* (1975), *L'Enfant et les Sortileges* (1984), *Kaguya-Hine* (1988) and three based on aboriginal culture, *Nomads* (1981), *Stamping Ground* (1982) and *Dreamtime* (1983).

KYPRIANOU, Spyros (1932–) Cypriot politician, born in Limassol, where he attended the Greek Gymnasium. He continued his education at the City of London College, and was called to the bar in 1954. During that period he founded the Cypriot Students' Union and became its first president. He became secretary to Archbishbop **Makarios** in London in 1952, and returned with him to Cyprus in 1959. He was foreign minister (1961–72), and in 1976 founded the Democratic Front (DIKO). On Makarios' death in 1977 he became acting president, and then president. He was re-elected in 1978 and 1983, but was defeated by the independent candidate **Georgios Vassilou** in 1988. Despite efforts to find a peaceful solution to the divisions in Cyprus, success always eluded him.

KYRLE, John (1637–1724) English philanthropist, known as the 'Man of Ross'. Educated at Ross grammar school and Balliol College, Oxford, he passed most of his life on his estates at Ross-on-Wye in Herefordshire. He spent his fortune on building churches and hospitals. **Alexander Pope** sang his praises in his third *Moral Epistle*. The Kyrle Society for improving the lot of the poor was founded in his memory (1877).

L

LAAR, Pieter van, known as **I Bamboccio ('the Cripple')** (c.1590–c.1658) Dutch artist, born in Haarlem. He is noted for his paintings of country scenes, weddings, wakes, and fairs. He gave his name to the term 'bambochades' for genre paintings of bucolic themes.

LABADIE, Jean de (1610–74) French ex-Jesuit Protestant reformer, born in Bourg near Bordeaux. A former member of the Jesuits, he became a pietist and a Calvinist convert in 1650. He preached a return to primitive Christianity in the Netherlands, and was excommunicated from the Reformed Church in 1670, whereupon he moved his Labadist colony to Germany. He died at Altona.

LABAN, Rudolf von (1879–1958) Hungarian dancer, choreographer, dance theorist and notator, born in Bratislava, originally Pozsony. He studied ballet, acting and painting in Paris and later danced in Vienna and many German cities. From 1910 he founded numerous European schools, theatres and institutions as well as heading an organization of amateur 'movement choirs' throughout Germany. He was ballet director of Berlin State Opera (1930–34) and created dances for the Berlin Olympic Games in 1936. He moved to England two years later, where he furthered his ideas about modern educational dance and movement in industrial settings. He established the Art of Movement Studio in 1946, now known as the Laban Centre and part of Goldsmiths College, London University. As early as 1920 he published the first of several volumes detailing his influential system of dance notation, now known as Labanotation.

LABÉ, or **Charlieu, Louise** (c.1520–1566) French poet, born in Parcieux, Ain. Educated in the Renaissance manner, she learned Latin and music, and was a skilled rider. In 1542 she fought, disguised as a knight, at the siege of Perpignan. In 1550 she married a wealthy rope manufacturer, Ennemond Perrin, at Lyon and was then called 'la Belle Cordière' (the Lovely Ropemaker). In 1555 she published her *Oeuvres*, including many Petrachan sonnets. She was also noted for her love affairs.

LABICHE, Eugène (1815–88) French playwright, born in Paris. He wrote one novel, *La Clef des Champs* (1838), and was the author of over a hundred comedies, farces and vaudevilles. His *Frisette* (1846) was the original of **John Maddison Morton**'s *Cox and Box*, and his *Le Voyage de M. Perrichon* (1860) is a perennial favourite.

LABLACHE, Luigi (1794–1858) Italian operatic singer, born in Naples, the son of a French émigré and an Irish mother. Although he studied violin and cello at the Conservatorio della Pietra de' Turchini, he concentrated on singing, and became the most famous bass of his time, his magnificent voice ranging from E flat to e' flat. He sang in Milan, Vienna, London and Paris, and had songs especially written for him, notably by **Schubert**. He was also a talented actor, equally at ease in tragedy or comedy.

LABOUCHÈRE, Henry Du Pré, known as **'Labby'** (1831–1912) English radical journalist and politician. Educated at Eton and Trinity College, Cambridge, he was in the diplomatic service from 1854 to 1864. A Liberal MP from 1865 to 1868 and 1880 to 1906, he made his reputation as a journalist on *The Daily News* during the Franco-Prussian war in 1870 and *The World* under **Edmund Yates**. In 1876 he became founder-editor and owner of the weekly journal *Truth*, which exposed sham and corruption, including the fraudulent papers forged by **Richard Piggot** to incriminate **Charles Parnell** in the Phoenix Park tragedy in 1886.

LABOULAYE, Edouard René de (1811–83) French jurist and politician, born in Paris. In 1849 he became professor of comparative jurisprudence in the Collège de France. His chief works are on French law, and a *Histoire politique des États-Unis* (1855–66). He edited a historical review and some of his tales, including *Paris en Amérique*, have been translated. He entered the National Assembly in 1871, and in 1876 became a life senator.

LA BOURDONNAIS, Bertrand François Mahé de (1699–1753) French naval officer, born in St-Malo. By 1723 he had distinguished himself as captain in the naval service of the French Indies. In 1734 he became governor of Île de France and Bourbon (Mauritius) and was featured in the novel *Paul et Virginie* by **Jacques Henri Bernardin de Saint-Pierre**. In 1740 he inflicted great loss upon England; in 1746 he compelled Madras to capitulate, but granted terms on payment of 9000000 livres. Accused by **Joseph Dupleix** of betraying the French East Indies Company's interests, he returned to Paris in 1748 and languished in the Bastille until 1752, when he was declared guiltless.

LABROUSTE, (Pierre François) Henri (1801–75) French architect, born in Paris. Described as a romantic rationalist he was able to balance functional and imaginative forces to produce effective buildings. He studied at both the École des Beaux Arts and in Rome. His two most influential works are Bibliothèque Sainte Geneviève (1838–50) and Bibliothèque Nationale reading room (1860–67), both in Paris. The former consists of a monumental stone rectangle encasing the closed book stacks supporting an iron-work structure for the reading rooms above; the latter is a fantasy shoe-horned into a restricted site in the old Palais Nazarin, where an innovatory tightly-fitted cage of iron and glass, topped with skylit domes, creates a delicate feeling of movement and light.

LA BRUYÈRE, Jean de (1645–96) French writer, born in Paris. He was educated by the Oratorians, and was chosen to aid **Jacques Bossuet** in educating the Dauphin. For a time he was treasurer at Caen. He became tutor to the Duc de Bourbon, grandson of the great **Condé**, and received a pension from the Condés until his death. His *Caractères* (1688), which gained him a host of implacable enemies as well as an immense reputation, consists of two parts, the one a translation of **Theophrastus**, the other a collection of maxims, reflections and character portraits of men and women of the time. He found a powerful protecter in the Duchesse de Bourbon, a daughter of **Louis XIV**. His *Dialogues sur le quiétisme* (1699) were directed against **Fénelon**. A great writer rather than a great thinker, his insight into character is shrewd rather than profound.

LACAILLE, Nicolas Louis de (1713–62) French astronomer. From 1750 to 1754 he visited the Cape of

Good Hope, where he was the first to measure a South African arc of the meridian, and compiled an extensive catalogue of southern stars.

LA CALPRENÈDE See **CALPRENÈDE**

LACÉPÈDE, Bernard de Laville, Comte de (1756–1825) French naturalist, born in Agen. He became curator in the Royal Gardens at Paris in 1785, and at the revolution he became professor of natural history in the Jardin des Plantes. He was made senator in 1799, minister of state in 1809, and in 1814 a peer of France. Besides continuing **Buffon**'s *Histoire Naturelle*, he wrote most of *Histoire naturelle des poissons* (1798–1803), *Les Âges de la nature* (1830), and other works.

LACHAISE, Francois d'Aix (1624–1709) French Jesuit, born at the castle of Aix in Forez. **Louis XIV** selected him for his confessor in 1675—a post he retained till his death in spite of the difficulties of his position. The cemetery Pére Lachaise was called after him.

LACHAISE, Gaston (1882–1935) French-born American painter, born in Paris, the son of a cabinet maker. He studied at the École des Beaux Arts in Paris from 1898 to 1903. With Isabel Nagel, an American who later became his wife, he left for Boston, arriving in January 1906. He never returned to France. He worked initially for the jeweller **René Lalique** and from 1912 as an assistant to the sculptor **Paul Manship** in New York. He became a naturalized American citizen in 1916. Lachaise is chiefly known for his curvaceous bronze statues of women in which the breasts and hips are massively enlarged; his wife was the model for many of these works.

LA CHAUSSÉE, Pierre Claude Nivelle de (1692–1754) French playwright, born in Paris. He began writing plays after he was 40 and produced several of a sentimental nature which enjoyed great popularity. *La Comédie larmoyante*, as his work was named by critics, did however have a certain influence on later writers, including **Voltaire**. Among his plays were *Préjuge à la mode* (1735), *Mélanide* (1741), and *L'École des mères* (1744).

LACHMANN, Karl Konrad Friedrich Wilhelm (1793–1851) German philologist, born in Brunswick. He was professor successively at Königsberg and Berlin. A founder of modern textual criticism, he edited the *Nibelungenlied*, **Walther von der Vogelweide**, **Propertius**, **Lucretius**, and others. In his *Betrachtungen* (1837–41) he maintained that the *Iliad* consisted of 16 independent lays enlarged and interpolated. The smaller edition of his New Testament appeared in 1831; the larger in 1842–50—both based mainly on uncial MSS.

LACLOS, Pierre Ambroise François Choderlos de (1741–1803) French novelist and politician, born in Amiens. Romantic and frustrated, he spent nearly all his life in the army but saw no active service until he was 60 and ended his career as a general. He is remembered by his one masterpiece, *Les Liaisons dangereuses* (1782). This epistolary novel reveals the influence of **Rousseau** and **Richardson** and is a cynical, detached analysis of personal and sexual relationships. He also wrote *De l'éducation des femmes* (1785).

LACONDAMINE, Charles Marie de (1701–74) French mathematician and scientist, born in Paris. He served in the army, travelled extensively, and was sent to Peru (1735–43) to measure a degree of the meridian. He explored the Amazon, brought back the poison curare and definite information on India rubber and platinum. He wrote in favour of inoculation.

LACORDAIRE, Jean Baptiste Henri (1802–61) French prelate and theologian, born in Recey-sur-Ource. He studied law in Paris. A convert from Deism, he was ordained in 1827. He attracted attention by his sermons (*Conférences*) at Notre Dame (1835–36) but withdrew to Rome at the height of his fame, entering the Dominican order in 1839. Next year he reappeared at Notre Dame, where he renewed his success, and in 1854 he delivered his last and most eloquent *Conférences* at Toulouse, thereafter becoming director of the Collège de Sorèze.

LACOSTE, Robert (1898–1989) French socialist politician, born in Azerat. He began his career as a tax-collector. Later he became editor of the civil servants' journal and a member of the administrative committee of the CGT. In World War II he began the first trade union Resistance group. In 1944 he was minister of industrial production, and was minister for industry and commerce in 1946–47 and again in 1948. From 1956 to 1958 he was resident minister in Algeria, and his at times ruthless campaign against the rebels there served to underline one controversial aspect of French post-war politics. He was senator for the Dordogne, 1971–80.

LACRETELLE, Jean Charles Dominique de (1766–1855) French journalist and historian, born in Metz. He was attracted to Paris on the outbreak of the revolution in 1789. He helped to edit the *Débats* and the *Journal de Paris*, was a member of the French Academy from 1811 and its president in 1816. Of his works the best known are *Histoire du dix-huitième siècle* (1808), *Précis historique de la révolution* (1801–06), and *Histoire de France pendant les guerres de religion* (1814–16).

LACROIX, Christian (1951–) French couturier, born in Arles, Provence, the son of an engineer who sketched women and their clothes. He himself started sketching as a child. He studied classics in Montpellier, specializing in French and Italian painting and the history of costume. He studied fashion history, from 1973, intending to become a museum curator, but obtained employment at Hermès, the leather firm, and with Guy Paulin, the ready-to-wear designer. In 1981 he joined **Jean Patou**, who showed his first collection in 1982. In 1987 he left Patou and, with other partners, opened The House of Lacroix in Paris. He made his name with ornate and frivolous clothes.

LACROIX, Paul (1806–84) French scholar, better known as P L Jacob, Bibliophile, born in Paris. While still at school he began to edit the old French classics, such as **Marot**, **Rabelais**, and others. He wrote an immense number of romances, plays, histories, biographies, and a great series on the manners, customs, costumes, arts and sciences of France from the middle ages. He also wrote two elaborate works on the *History of Prostitution* under the name 'Pierre Dufour'. From 1855 he was keeper of the Arsenal library.

LACTANTIUS, Lucius Caelius or **Caecilius, Firmianus** (4th century) Christian apologist, brought up in North Africa. He settled as a teacher of rhetoric in Nicomedia in Bithynia, where he was converted probably by witnessing the constancy of the Christian martyrs under the persecution of **Diocletian**. About 313 he was invited to Gaul by **Constantine** to act as tutor to his son Crispus. His principal work is his *Divinarum Institutionum libri vii*, a systematic account of Christian attitudes to life.

LACY, Peter, Count (1678–1751) Irish soldier, and field marshal in Russia, born in Kelledy, County Limerick. In 1691 he joined the Irish Brigade in the service of France and in Italy. About 1698 he entered the service of **Peter the Great** of Russia, and was placed in command of the Grand Musketeers. He fought in the Swedish war and was wounded at Poltava (1709).

In 1728 he was made Governor of Livonia (Latvia). From 1733 to 1735 he led a Russian expedition to Poland to put Augustus III on the throne, and was promoted field marshal in 1736. In 1743 he retired to his estates in Livonia.

LADISLAS IV, or **WLADYSLAW** (1595–1648) king of Poland, son of **Sigismund III Vasa** of Sweden. He was elected to the Polish throne in 1632. His reign was a peaceful one, since Poland, despite attempts to draw the country into the conflict, remained neutral during the Thirty Years' War. At home, he crushed the Cossack rebellions from 1637 to 1638, initiating ten years of 'golden peace' in the Ukraine. Although he harboured grandiose plans to gain the Swedish throne and to drive the Turks from the Balkans, he lacked sufficient support amongst the Polish gentry.

LAËNNEC, René Théophile Hyacinthe (1781–1826) French physician, the 'father of thoracic medicine', born in Quimper in Brittany. An army doctor from 1799, in 1814 he became editor of the *Journal de Médecine* and physician to the Salpêtrère and in 1816 chief physician to the Hôpital Necker, where he invented the stethoscope in the same year. His work on tuberculosis, pleuritis and chest diseases was valuable. In 1819 he published his *Traité de l'auscultation médiate*.

LAESTADIUS, Lars Levi (1800–61) Swedish priest and botanist, born in Arjeplog. He became the parson in Karesuando in 1826 where he continued his botanical work. He underwent a profound spiritual crisis in the early 1840s and began the ecstatic revivalist preaching that had great influence among the Lapps. Today there are some 300000 Laestadians in Finland and 20000 in Sweden.

LA FARGE, John (1835–1910) American landscape and ecclesiastical painter, born in New York. He travelled widely in Europe, and painted pre-Impressionist landscapes and flowers from 1860 to 1876. Thereafter he concentrated on murals and stained-glass work in churches, especially *The Ascension* in the Church of the Ascension in New York (1857). He wrote *Considerations on Painting* (1895) and *An Artist's Letters from Japan* (1897).

LA FARINA, Giuseppe (1815–63) Italian historian and statesman, born in Messina. He was an early advocate of Italian unity and wrote a history of Italy.

LAFAYETTE, Marie Joseph Paul Yves Roch Gilbert Motier, Marquis de (1757–1834) French reformer, born in the castle of Chavagnac in Auvergne. He entered the army, sailed for America in 1777 to aid the colonists, and was given a division by **Washington**. He was home for a few months in 1779, crossed the Atlantic again, was charged with the defence of Virginia, and shared in the battle of Yorktown. On a third visit to America in 1784 he had an enthusiastic reception. Now a pronounced reformer, he was called to the Assembly of Notables in 1787, sat in the States-General, and in the National Assembly of 1789. He laid on its table a declaration of rights based on the American Declaration of Independence and, appointed to command the armed citizens, formed the National Guard. He struggled incessantly for order and humanity, but the Jacobins hated his moderation, and the court abhorred his reforming zeal. He supported the abolition of titles and all class privileges. He won the first victories at Philippeville, Maubeuge and Florennes, but the hatred of the Jacobins increased, and at length he rode over the frontier to Liège and was imprisoned by the Austrians till **Napoleon** obtained his liberation in 1797. He sat in the Chamber of Deputies in 1818–24 as one of the extreme Left, and from 1825 to 1830 was again a leader of the opposition. In 1830 he took part in the revolution, and commanded the National Guard. In 1824 he revisited America, by invitation of congress, who voted him $200000 and a township.

LA FAYETTE, Marie Madeleine Pioche de Lavergne, Comtesse de (1634–93) French novelist and reformer of French romance-writing, born in Paris, daughter of the governor of Le Havre. She married the Comte de La Fayette in 1655, and in her 33rd year formed a liaison with **La Rochefoucauld** which lasted until his death in 1680. Down to her own death she still played a leading part at the French court, as was proved by her *Lettere inedite* (1880); prior to their publication it was believed that her last years were given to devotion. Her novels are *Zaïde* (1670) and *La Princesse de Clèves* (1678), a study in conflict between love and marriage in the court-life of her day, which led to reaction against the long-winded romances of **Calprenède** and **Scudéry**.

LAFERTÉ, Victor See **DOLGORUKOVA, Katharina**

LAFFITTE, Jacques (1767–1844) French financier and statesman, born in Bayonne. He acquired great wealth as a Paris banker, and in 1814 became governor of the Bank of France. He was elected to the Chamber of Deputies in 1817. In 1830 his house was the headquarters of the revolution, and he supplied a great part of the funds needed. In November he formed a Cabinet, but he only held power until March. From the ruins of his fortune he founded a Discount Bank in 1837. In 1843 he was elected president of the Chamber of Deputies.

LAFFITTE, Pierre (1823–1903) French philosopher, born in Béguey (Gironde). He was a friend and disciple of **Auguste Comte**, whom he succeeded as head of the Comité Positiviste in 1857. He became professor at the Collège de France in 1892 and among his works are: *Leçons de cosmographie* (1853), *Cours philosophique sur l'histoire générale de l'humanité* (1859), *Les grands types de l'humanité* (1874) and *De la morale positive* (1880).

LA FOLLETTE, Robert Marion (1855–1925) American politician, born in Primrose, Wisconsin. He was a senator from 1905, and as 'Progressive' candidate for the presidency was defeated in 1924, having gained nearly five million votes.

LA FONTAINE, Jean de (1621–95) French poet, born in Château-Thierry in Champagne. He assisted his father, a superintendent of woods and forests. He soon devoted himself to the study of the old writers and to verse writing. In 1654 he published a verse translation of the *Eunuchus* of **Terence**, and then went to Paris, where **Fouquet** became his patron. His *Contes et nouvelles en vers* appeared in 1665, his *Fables choisies mises en vers* in 1668, and his *Amours de Psyché et de Cupidon* in 1669. For nearly 20 years he was maintained in the household of Mme de la Sablière. In 1684 he presented an admirable *Discours en vers* on his reception by the Academy. La Fontaine was a brilliant writer and his verse, especially as found in the *Contes* and *Fables*, is lively and original.

LAFONTAINE, Oskar (1943–) West German politician, born in Saarlois. Educated at Bonn University, he became leader of the Saar regional branch of the Social Democratic party (SPD) in 1977 and served as mayor of Saarbrucken (1976–85). He gained a reputation for radicalism and was variously dubbed 'Red Oskar' and the 'Ayatollah of the Saarland'. He began to mellow, however, after his election as minister-president of the Saarland state assembly in 1985. In 1987 he was appointed a deputy chairman of the SPD's federal organization and he is viewed as a likely future SPD chancellor-candidate.

LAGERKVIST, Pär Fabian (1891–1974) Swedish novelist, poet and playwright, winner of the 1951 Nobel prize for literature. He studied at Uppsala and began his literary career first as a prose writer and then as an expressionist poet with *Ångest* (Angst, 1916), and *Kaos* (Chaos, 1918), in which he emphasizes the catastrophe of war. Later, in the face of extremist creeds and slogans, he adopted a critical humanism with the (later dramatized) novel *Bödeln* (The Hangman, 1933) and the novel *Dvärgen* (The Dwarf, 1944), which explored the problems of evil and human brutality. His novel *Barabbas* (1950), which won him the Nobel prize, concerns the thief in whose place Christ was crucified. Man's search for God was also explored in the play *Mannen utan själ* (The Man without a Soul, 1936). An ideological play, *Lät människan leva* (Let Man Live, 1949), was a study of political terrorism in which **Jesus Christ, Socrates, Bruno, Joan of Arc** and an American negro appear as victims.

LAGERLÖF, Selma Ottiliana Lovisa (1858–1940) Swedish novelist, the first woman winner of the Nobel prize for literature (1909), and the first woman member of the Swedish Academy (1914). She taught at Landskrona (1885–95), and first sprang to fame with her novel *Gösta Berlings saga* (The Story of Gösta Berling, 1891), based on the traditions and legends of her native Värmland, as were many of her later books, such as her trilogy on the Löwensköld family (1925–28, trans 'The Rings of the Lowenskolds', 1931). She also wrote the children's classic, *Nils Holgerssons underbara resa genom Sverige* (The Wonderful Adventures of Nils, 1906–07). Although a member of the neo-romantic generation of the 1890s, her work is characterized by a social and moral seriousness, as in *Antikrists Mirakler* (The Miracles of Anti-Christ, 1897) and *Bannlyst* (The Outcast, 1918).

LAGRANGE, Joseph Louis de, Comte (1736–1813) French mathematician, born in Turin. In 1766 he succeeded **Leonhard Euler** as director of the mathematical section of the Berlin Academy, having gained a European reputation by his work on the calculus of variations, celestial mechanics and the nature of sound. While in Prussia he read before the Berlin Academy some 60 dissertations on celestial mechanics, number theory, algebraic and differential equations. He returned to Paris in 1787 at the invitation of **Louis XVI**. Under **Napoleon** he became a senator and a count and taught at the École Normale and the École Polytechnique. In 1788 he published *Traité de mécanique analytique*, one of his most important works. His work on the theory of algebraic equations was one of the important steps in the early development of group theory. He was buried in the Panthéon.

LA GUARDIA, Fiorello Henry (1882–1947) American lawyer and politician, born in New York of Italian-Jewish origin. He became deputy attorney-general of New York (1915–17), served with the American air force in Italy and sat in congress (1917–21, 1923–33) as a Republican. As a popular mayor of New York (thrice re-elected, 1933–45) he initiated housing and labour safeguards schemes, was one of the early opponents of **Hitler**'s anti-Semitic policies—he had his ears boxed in public by enraged American Fascists—and was civil administrator of allied-occupied Italy. In 1946 he was appointed director-general of UNRRA. New York's airport is named after him.

LAGUERRE, Louis (1663–1721) French artist, born in Paris. In 1683 he went to London, where he carried out schemes of elaborate, allegorical decoration at Chatsworth, Petworth, Blenheim and elsewhere.

LAHARPE, Frédéric César (1754–1838) Swiss politician, born in Rolle in Vaud. President of the Helvetic Republic in 1798–1800, he lived a good deal in Russia as tutor and as guest of **Alexander I**. He died in Lausanne.

LA HARPE, Jean François de (1739–1803) French poet and critic, born in Paris. In 1763 he produced a successful tragedy, *Warwick*, followed by others. His best-known works are, however, his critical lectures *Lycée, ou Cours de littérature* (1799–1805). His *Correspondance littéraire* (1801), by the bitterness of its criticisms, rekindled fierce controversies. He supported the revolution at first, but after five months' imprisonment (1794) became a firm supporter of church and crown.

LAIDLAW, William (1780–1845) Scottish poet, born in Blackhouse, Selkirkshire. He wrote lyrics, but is best known as the friend and copying secretary of Sir **Walter Scott**. His shepherd for ten years was **James Hogg**, and together they helped Scott prepare his *Minstrelsy of the Scottish Border*. Laidlaw became factor at Abbotsford, 1817–26.

LAING, Alexander Gordon (1793–1826) Scottish explorer, born in Edinburgh. Having served seven years as an officer in the West Indies, in 1825 he was sent to explore the Niger's source, which he found. He was murdered after leaving Timbuktu.

LAING, David (1793–1878) Scottish antiquary, born in Edinburgh, the son of a bookseller. He cut short his studies at Edinburgh University to join his father as a partner. In 1837 he was appointed librarian of the Signet Library. He was honorary secretary of the Bannatyne Club, and edited many of its issues. He left behind him a private library of unusual value, and bequeathed many rare MSS to Edinburgh University. His more important works were his editions of **Robert Baillie**'s *Letters and Journals* (1841–42), of **John Knox** (4 vols, 1846–64), Sir **David Lyndsay**, **Dunbar** and **Henryson**.

LAING, John See **HALKETT, Samuel**

LAING, Malcolm (1762–1818) Scottish historian, born in Orkney, brother of **Samuel Laing**. Educated in Kirkwall and at Edinburgh University, he graduated in law and was called to the bar, but hardly practised as an advocate, turning to historical studies instead. He completed the last volume of Robert Henry's *History of Great Britain* (1783), and in 1802 published his own *History of Scotland 1604–1707*. This contained an onslaught on the authenticity of the **Ossian** poems translated by **James Macpherson**. He also published *The Life and Histories of James VI* (1804). He returned to Orkney in 1808 and was MP until 1812.

LAING, Ronald David (1927–89) Scottish psychiatrist, born in Glasgow of working-class parents. A medical graduate of Glasgow University (1951), he practised as a psychiatrist in Glasgow (1953–56). He joined the Tavistock Clinic in London in 1957 and the Tavistock Institute for Human Relations in 1960, and was chairman of the Philadelphia Association (1964–82). He sprang to prominence with his revolutionary ideas about mental disorder with the publication of *The Divided Self* (1960). His principal thesis was that psychiatrists should not attempt to cure or ameliorate the symptoms of mental illness (itself a term which he repudiated) but rather should encourage patients to view themselves as going through an enriching experience. In expounding this doctrine of 'anti-psychiatry', he implied in his writings that the primary responsibility for psychiatric breakdown lies with society and/or with the patient's immediate family. His writings extended from psychiatry into existential philosophy, and later into poetry. His other books included *The Politics of Experience* (1967), *Knots* (1970), *The Politics of the Family* (1976), *Sonnets* (1980) and *The Voice of Experience* (1982).

LAING, Samuel (1780–1868) Scottish writer, born in Orkney, brother of **Malcolm Laing**. He travelled and wrote on Norway, Sweden, Russia and France. His major achievement was his monumental translation of *Heimskringla* by **Snorri Sturluson** (History of the Kings of Norway).

LAIRD, Macgregor (1808–61) Scottish explorer and merchant, born in Greenock. He first travelled to the lower Niger with **Richard Lander**'s last expedition (1832–34), and was the first European to ascend the Benue River. In 1837 he started a transatlantic steamship company, for which the *Sirius* became the first ship to cross entirely under steam in 1854. In 1854 he financed a second expedition to the Niger, led by **William Balfour Baikie**.

LAIRESSE, Gérard de (1641–1711) Dutch painter and etcher. After he became blind in 1690, he wrote *The Art of Painting* (trans 1738).

LAÏS the name of two Corinthian courtesans, famous for their beauty. The elder flourished during the Peloponnesian war; the younger, born in Sicily, came as a child to Corinth, and sat as a model to **Apelles**.

LAITHWAITE, Eric Roberts (1921–) English electrical engineer and inventor, born in Atherton, Yorkshire. He studied at Regent Street Polytechnic and Manchester University, where after war service in the RAF he remained until 1964, when he was appointed professor of heavy electrical engineering at the Imperial College of Science and Technology in the University of London. His principal research interest is in the linear motor, a means of propulsion utilizing electro-magnetic forces acting along linear tracks; by incorporating magnetic levitation or air cushion suspension, high speed experimental vehicles have been constructed without either wheels or conventional rotating electric motors. A gifted lecturer and writer on scientific and engineering subjects, especially to young and non-technical audiences, his Royal Institution Christmas Lectures in 1966 and 1974 were particularly memorable. He was a professor of the Royal Institution (1967–76), and received the Nikola Tesla Award from the Institution of Electrical and Electronic Engineers in 1986.

LAKATOS, Imre (1922–74) Hungarian philosopher of mathematics and science, born in Debrecen. He came to England in 1956 after the Hungarian uprising. He taught at the London School of Economics from 1960 and became professor there in 1969. His best-known work is *Proofs and Refutations* (1976), a collection of articles in dialogue form demonstrating the creative and informal nature of real mathematical discovery. In philosophy of science he propounded a 'methodology of scientific research programmes' as an alternative to the theories of **Popper** and **Thomas Kuhn** to explain scientific change and revolutions. Two volumes of *Philosophical Papers* were published in 1978.

LAKE, Gerard, Viscount (1744–1808) English soldier, nephew of **George Colman** (the elder). He served in Germany (1760–62), America (1781), and the Low Countries (1793–94), where his most brilliant exploit was the capture of some forts near Lille. In 1798 he routed the Irish rebels at Vinegar Hill, and received the surrender of the French near Cloone. Commander-in-chief North West India (1801–07), against **Sindhia** and Holkar he won several battles and took Aligarh, Delhi and Agra.

LAKER, Sir Freddie (Frederick Alfred) (1922–) English business executive, born in Kent. Educated at Simon Langton School, Canterbury, he started his career in aviation with Short Brothers. From 1941 to 1946 he was a member of the Air Transport Auxiliary and, from 1960 to 1965, was a manager with British United Airways. In 1966 he became chairman and managing director of Laker Airways Ltd. His career was severely set back by the failure of the 'Skytrain' project in 1982.

LAKER, James Charles (1922–86) English cricketer and broadcaster, born in Bradford. He was discovered by Surrey immediately after World War II and was a member of the county side which won seven consecutive championships between 1952 and 1958. His off-spinners were a large factor in England's domination of the late 1950s international scene. His great season was 1956, when he took 19 of the 20 Australian wickets to fall in the Test match at Old Trafford. Earlier in that season he had taken all ten Australian wickets in the match with Surrey at the Oval. In harness with **Tony Lock**, he could be unplayable on a pitch which offered the slightest assistance. His book, *Over to Me* (1960), offended the cricket establishment and temporarily cost him his membership of Surrey and the MCC. In later years he became a television commentator.

LALANDE, Joseph Jérôme Le Français de (1732–1807) French astronomer, born in Bourg-en-Bresse. In 1751 he was sent to Berlin by the French Academy to determine the moon's parallax. He was from 1762 professor of astronomy in the Collège de France, from 1768 director of the Paris Observatory. His chief work is *Traité d'astronomie* (1764).

LALANNE, Maxine (1827–86) French etcher and lithographer, born in Bordeaux. He arrived in Paris in 1852 where he executed his first lithograph in 1853. From 1853 to 1863 he worked mainly with charcoal drawings, prior to his début as an engraver when he exhibited 32 works for the Society of Engravers. In 1866 he began a highly successful collaboration with the 'House of Cadart' who published his treatise on acid engraving which ran to seven editions. A prolific artist whose brilliantly executed plates of town and landscape were drawn from life, he transcribed his impressions of the troubles of 1870–71 in a series of plates such as 'The Siege of Paris' and 'Bastion '66'.

LALIQUE, René (1860–1945) French jeweller and designer, born in Ay. In 1885 he established a jewellery firm in Paris, producing Art Nouveau styles. He was also an artist-craftsman in glass, which he decorated with relief figures, animals and flowers.

LALLY, Thomas Arthur, Comte de, Baron de Tollendal (1702–66) French soldier, born in Romans in Dauphiné. He was the son of Sir Gerard O'Lally, an Irish Jacobite in the French service. He distinguished himself with the Jacobite Irish Brigade in Flanders, accompanied Prince **Charles Edward Stewart** to Scotland in 1745, and in 1756 became commander-in-chief in the French East Indies. He started offensive operations against the British, and besieged Madras; but being defeated, retreated to Pondicherry, which was attacked in March 1760 by a superior British force. Lally capitulated in January 1761, and was taken to England. Accused of cowardice, he returned to France and was thrown into the Bastille. The parliament of Paris at last condemned him, and he was executed. But his son, supported by **Voltaire**, procured a royal decree in 1778, declaring the condemnation unjust, and restoring all the forfeited honours.

LALLY, Trophime Gérard, Marquis de Lally-Tollendal (1751–1830) French aristocrat, son of **Thomas Lally**. He was one of those nobles who acted in the

States-General in 1789 with the Third Estate, but soon allied himself with the court. He advocated a constitution with two chambers, and sought to protect the king, but had to flee to England. **Louis XVIII** made him a peer. He wrote *Defence of the French Emigrants* (1794), and *Life of Wentworth, Earl of Strafford* (2nd ed 1814).

LALO, (Victor Antoine) Édouard (1823–92) French composer and viola player, born in Lille of a military family. His musical compositions include *Symphonie espagnole* and other violin works, and operas, the best known being *Le Roi d'Ys*, and the ballet *Namouna*.

LAM, Wilfredo (1902–82) Cuban painter, born in Sagua la Grande. He studied at the San Alejandro Academy in Havana and at the San Fernando Academy in Madrid, holding his first one-man show in Madrid, 1928. In 1938, in Paris, he met **Picasso**, who became his friend, and the Surrealist **André Breton** in 1940. Lam fused Latin-American, African, and Oceanic elements with the forms and conventions of the European modern movement, eg *The Jungle*, 1943. His numerous exhibitions included one in New York (with Picasso, 1939), Havana (1951), and Caracas (1955). He won the Guggenheim International award in 1964.

LAMARCK, Jean (Baptiste Pierre Antoine de Monet) Chevalier de (1744–1829) French naturalist and pre-Darwinian evolutionist, born in Bazentin. As an army officer at Toulon and Monaco he became interested in the Mediterranean flora; and resigning after an injury, he held a post in a Paris bank, and meanwhile began to study medicine and botany. In 1773 he published a *Flore française*. In 1774 he became keeper of the royal garden (afterwards the nucleus of the Jardin des plantes), where he lectured on zoology. He made the basic distinction between vertebrates and invertebrates. About 1801 he had begun to think about the relations and origin of species, expressing his conclusions in his famous *Philosophie zoologique* (1809) in which he postulated that acquired characters can be inherited by later generations. His *Histoire des animaux sans vertèbres* appeared in 1815–22. Hard work and illness enfeebled his sight and left him blind and poor. Lamarck broke with the old notion of immutable species, sought to explain their transformation and the evolution of the animal world, and prepared the way for the now accepted theory of descent.

LA MARMORA, Alfonso Ferrero, Marquis de (1804–78) Italian soldier and statesman, born in Turin. He distinguished himself in the war of independence of 1848, and was minister of war from 1848 to 1859. He commanded the Sardinian troops in the Crimea (1855), took part in the war of 1859, was prime minister of Sardinia from 1860 to 1866, was commander-in-chief in 1861, and prime minister again from 1864 to 1866. In the campaign against Austria in 1866 he lost the battle of Custozza. His publication (1873) of the secret negotiations between Prussia and Italy incurred the censure of **Bismarck**.

LAMARTINE, Alphonse Marie Louis de (1790–1869) French poet, statesman and historian, born in Mâcon. He was brought up on ultraroyalist principles, spent much of his youth in Italy, and on the fall of **Napoleon** entered the garde royale. His first volume of poems, probably his best known and most successful, the *Méditations*, was published in 1820. He was successively secretary of legation at Naples and *chargé d'affaires* at Florence. In 1829 he declined the post of foreign secretary in the Bourbon ministry of **Auguste Polignac**, and with another series of poems, *Harmonies poétiques et religieuses*, achieved his unanimous election to the Academy. Lamartine, still a royalist, disapproved of the revolution of 1830. A tour to the East produced his *Souvenirs d'Orient*. Recalled to France in 1833, he became deputy for Mâcon. Between 1834 and 1848 he published his poems, *Jocelyn* and *La Chute d'un ange*, and the celebrated *Histoire des Girondins*. He did not support the Orléanist régime and he became a member of the Provisional Government (1848), and, as minister of foreign affairs, the ruling spirit. After two risings of the extreme party of **Louis Blanc** and **Ledru Rollin**, the executive committee resigned, and conferred the command of the forces on **Cavaignac**. After a terrible conflict the insurrection was suppressed. When **Napoleon III** came to power Lamartine devoted himself to literature, publishing *Confidences*, *Raphaël* (both autobiographical), *Geneviève*, the *Tailleur de pierres de St-Point* (a prose tale), and *Histoire de la restauration*. He wrote on **Joan of Arc**, **Cromwell**, Madame de **Sévigné**, and others, and issued monthly *Entretiens familiers*.

LAMB, Lady Caroline See **MELBOURNE, William Lamb**

LAMB, Charles (1775–1834) English essayist, born in the Temple, London, where his father was a clerk to Samuel Salt, a wealthy bencher. Educated at Christ's Hospital (1782–89), where he formed a lasting friendship with **Coleridge**, he obtained a position in the South Sea House, but in 1792 was promoted to the India House, where he remained for more than 30 years. In 1792, also, Samuel Salt died, and with a legacy from him, his own salary, and whatever his elder sister Mary (1764–1847) could earn by needlework, the family retired to humble lodgings. In 1796 the terrible disaster occurred which was destined to mould the future life of Charles Lamb. The strain of insanity inherited from the mother began to show itself in Mary, and in an attack of mania she stabbed her invalid mother to death. Her brother's guardianship was accepted by the authorities and to this trust Lamb from that moment devoted his life. In the meantime he had fallen in love, but renounced all hope of marriage when the duty of tending his sister appeared to him paramount. Lamb's earliest poems (1795), first printed with Coleridge's in 1796–97, were prompted by this deep attachment. In 1798 Lamb and Charles Lloyd attempted a slight volume of their own (*Blank Verse*) and here for the first time Lamb's individuality made itself felt in the 'Old Familiar Faces'. In 1797 he also published his little prose romance, *The Tale of Rosamund Gray and Old Blind Margaret*; and in 1801 *John Woodvil*—the fruit of that study of the dramatic poetry of the Elizabethan period, in whose revival he was to play so large a part. Meantime, Lamb and his sister were wandering from lodging to lodging, and in 1801 they moved to Lamb's old familiar neighbourhood, where they stayed for 16 years. Charles's experiments in literature had as yet brought him neither money nor reputation and so he wrote a farce, *Mr H* (1806), which failed. For **William Godwin**'s 'Juvenile Library', Charles and Mary wrote in 1807 their *Tales from Shakespeare*—Mary taking the comedies, Charles the tragedies. This was Lamb's first success. The brother and sister next composed jointly *Mrs Leicester's School* (1807) and *Poetry for Children* (1809). Charles also made a prose version of the *Adventures of Ulysses*, and a volume of selections from the Elizabethan dramatists showed him as one of the most subtle and original of critics. Three years later his unsigned articles in **Leigh Hunt**'s *Reflector* on **Hogarth** and the tragedies of **Shakespeare** proved him a prose writer of new and unique quality. In 1818 Lamb collected his scattered verse and prose in two volumes as the *Works of Charles Lamb*, and this paved the way for his being invited to join the staff of the new *London Magazine*. His first essay, in August 1820, 'Recollections of the old South Sea House', was signed 'Elia', the name of a foreigner who had been a fellow-clerk. The first collection of the *Essays of Elia* was published in 1823; *The Last Essays of Elia* were collected in 1833. In 1825 Lamb, who had been failing in health, resigned his post in the India House. The brother and sister were now free to wander and finally they moved to Edmonton. The absence of settled occupation had not brought Lamb the comfort he had looked for: the separation from his friends and the now almost continuous mental alienation of his sister left him companionless, and with the death of Coleridge in 1834 the chief attractions of his life were gone. In December of that year, he too died and was buried in Edmonton churchyard. His sister survived him nearly 13 years, and was buried by his side. Lamb's place in literature is unique and unchallengeable. He is familiar through his works, which are composed in the form of personal confidences; through his many friends, who have made known his every mood and trait; and through his letters, the most fascinating correspondence in the English language.

LAMB, William See **MELBOURNE**

LAMB, Willis Eugene (1913–) American physicist. He was professor of physics at Columbia (1948), Stanford (1951), Oxford (1956), Yale (1962), and Arizona (1974). In 1955 he shared with **Polykarp Kusch** the Nobel prize for physics for his researches into the hydrogen spectrum.

LAMBALLE, Marie Thérèse Louise de Savoie-Carignan, Princesse de (1749–92) French aristocrat, born in Turin, daughter of the Prince de Carignan. In 1767 she married Louis de **Bourbon**, Prince de Lamballe, but next year was left a widow. Beautiful and charming, she was made by **Marie Antoinette** superintendent of the household (1774), and her own intimate companion. She escaped to England in 1791, but returned to share the queen's imprisonment in the Temple, and refused to take the oath of detestation of the king, queen and monarchy. As she left the courtroom she was torn to pieces by the mob.

LAMBARDE, William (1536–1601) English lawyer, born in London. He made a collection and translation of the Anglo-Saxon laws, *Archaeonomia* (1568); published a *Perambulation of Kent* (1576); wrote *Eirenarcha or the Office of Justices of Peace* (1581), which for some time was the standard authority on that subject, and *Archeion, or a Commentary upon the High Courts of Justice in England* (1635). He became a master in Chancery in 1592, and shortly before his death was made keeper of the records in the Tower of London.

LAMBERT, Constant (1905–51) English composer, conductor and critic, the son of **George Washington Lambert**, born in London. His first success came when, as a student at the Royal College of Music, he was commissioned by **Diaghilev** to write a ballet, *Romeo and Juliet*, first performed in 1926. For several years he worked as conductor for the Camargo Society and later of Sadler's Wells Ballet, upon which company his outstanding musicianship and understanding of the problems of ballet had a lasting influence; he was also active as a concert conductor and music critic. His book *Music Ho!* (1934) is enlivened by his understanding of painting, his appreciation of jazz, his devotion to Elizabethan music and the works of such composers as **Liszt** and **Berlioz**, and by its acidly witty, polished style. Of his compositions, *The Rio Grande* (1929), one of the most successful concert works in jazz idiom, is perhaps the most famous, but his lyrical gifts show themselves in the ballets *Pomona* (1927) and *Horoscope* (1938) as well as the cantata *Summer's Last Will and Testament* (1936). His concerto for piano and chamber orchestra was composed in memory of **Philip Heseltine**.

LAMBERT, George Washington Thomas (1873–1930) Australian painter and sculptor, born in St Petersburg, Russia, where his American father was a railway engineer. His mother took him to Warren, New South Wales in 1887 and in 1889 he was working in Sydney and attending art classes run by **Julian Ashton**, to which he returned two years later after a time working as a station-hand in the country. He was soon contributing drawings to magazines and illustrating books. From 1894 he was exhibiting paintings, and in 1899 he won the Wynne prize for landscape painting. The next year Lambert went to England, then studied briefly in Paris, and returned to live in Chelsea where his principal work was in portraiture. His portrait subjects included Sir **George Reid** and an equestrian King **Edward VII**. In World War I he was an official war artist for Australia, and went to the Near East front, later visiting Gallipoli to make sketches with **C E W Bean**, the war historian. He returned to Australia in 1921, was involved in the contemporary arts movement, and took up sculpture.

LAMBERT, Johann Heinrich (1728–77) German mathematician, born in Mulhouse in Alsace. He first showed how to measure scientifically the intensity of light, in his *Photometria* (1760). A work of his on analytical logic (1764) was greatly valued by **Immanuel Kant**. In mathematics he proved that the numbers π and e are irrational, and studied the mathematics of map projections. He also wrote on cosmology.

LAMBERT, John (1619–84) English parliamentary soldier, born in Calton near Settle, Yorkshire. He studied at the Inns of Court, but on the outbreak of the Civil War in 1641 became a captain under **Thomas Fairfax**, and at Marston Moor led Fairfax's cavalry. Commissary-general of the army in the north (1645), and major-general of the northern counties (1647), he helped **Cromwell** to crush the Scots under **James, 3rd Marquis of Hamilton** at Preston (1648), and captured Pontefract Castle in March 1649. In 1650 he went with Cromwell to Scotland as major-general, led the van at Dunbar, won the victory of Inverkeithing, pursued **Charles II** to Worcester in 1651, and at the battle commanded the troops on the eastern bank of the Severn. He helped to install Cromwell as protector, but opposed the proposition to declare him king. He headed the cabal which overthrew **Richard Cromwell** in 1659. He was now looked upon as the leader of the Fifth Monarchy or extreme republican party; he suppressed the Royalist insurrection in Cheshire in August 1659 and virtually governed the country with his officers as the 'committee of safety'. **Monk**'s counter-plot frustrated his designs. He was sent to the Tower, tried in 1662, and kept prisoner on Drake's Island till his death.

LAMBTON, John George See **DURHAM**

LAMENNAIS, Félicité Robert de (1782–1854) French priest and writer, born in St-Malo. With his brother, Jean Marie Robert (1780–1860), also a priest, he retired to their estate at La Chesnaie near Dinan, where he wrote *Réflexions sur l'état de l'église* (1808) which was suppressed by **Napoleon**. On returning from London, where he had fled during the Hundred Days, he was ordained priest, and began in 1816 his famous *Essai sur l'indifférence en mattière de religion* (1818–24), a magnificent, if paradoxical denunciation of private judgment and toleration, which was favourably received at Rome. But notions of popular liberty, fanned by the revolution of 1830, began to change his outlook, and *L'Avenir*, a journal founded by him in 1830 with **Montalembert** and others, was suspended in 1831 and officially condemned by the pope in 1832. The *Paroles d'un croyant* (1834) brought about complete rupture with the church, and revolutionary doctrines in his later work got him a year's imprisonment. Active in the 1848 revolution, he sat in the Assembly until the *coup d'état*. At his death he refused to make peace with the church. His works include the remarkable *Esquisse d'une philosophie* (1840–46).

LA METTRIE, Julien Offray de (1709–51) French philosopher and physician, born in St-Malo. He first studied theology, then switched to medicine and in 1742 became surgeon to the Guards in Paris. He expounded a materialistic philosophy in which all psychical phenomena were to be explained as the effects of organic changes in the brain and nervous system. His first exposition of this in *L'histoire naturelle de l'âme* in 1745 provoked such hostility that the book was publicly burned and he was forced to flee to Leiden. He further developed these theories in *L'Homme machine* (1747) and had to move on again to escape arrest, finding refuge in Berlin under the protection of **Frederick II the Great** of Prussia. He worked out the ethical implications of his materialism in such works as *Discours sur le bonheur* (1748), *Le Petit Homme à longue queue* (1751) and *L'Art de jouir* (1751) where he argued that the only real pleasures are those of the senses, that the enjoyment of pleasure is the only goal of life, that virtue is just enlightened self-interest and that the soul perished with the body ('*la farce est jouée*'). He seems to have lived a life of carefree hedonism according to these precepts, and died of food poisoning. Frederick himself wrote a memoir of his life.

LAMMING, George Eric (1927–) Barbadian novelist, born in Carrington Village. He was a teacher in Trinidad and in Venezuela before going to England in 1950, where he worked as a factory labourer and hosted a book programme for the BBC West Indian Service. His first novels, with their unfamiliar background and argot, received a lukewarm reception. Beginning with *In the Castle of My Skin* (1953), he has explored the West Indian experience in a complex and highly textured way. Of his novels, *The Emigrants* (1954) is the saddest; *Season of Adventure* (1960) articulates hs own dilemma as an artist; *Natives of My Person* (1972), with its archaic vocabulary and mythic roots, is perhaps his *tour de force*.

LAMOND, Frederic (1868–1948) Scottish pianist and composer, born in Glasgow. A pupil of **Bülow** and **Liszt**, he made his début at Berlin in 1885 and followed this by touring in Europe and America. He excelled in playing **Beethoven**. Among his compositions are an overture *Aus dem schottischem Hochlande*, a symphony, and several piano works.

LAMONT, Johann von (1805–79) Scots-born German astronomer, born in Braemar. He went in 1817 to the Scottish seminary at Ratisbon, and became in 1835 director of Bogenhausen Observatory. In 1852 he became professor of astronomy at Munich where his work included cataloguing over 34000 stars. His best work, however, was on terrestrial magnetism. In 1840 he set up a magnetic observatory at Boghausen, and in 1849 published *Handbuch des Erdmagnetismus*.

LAMORCIÈRE, Christophe Léon Louis Juchault de (1806–65) French soldier, born in Nantes. He entered the army in 1826, and served in Algeria from 1833 to 1847. Through his energy chiefly the war was brought to an end by the capture of **Abd-el-Kader** in 1847. In June 1848 he carried the Paris barricades and quelled the Socialists. He was war minister under **Cavaignac**, but was banished after the *coup d'état* of 1851. He went to Rome in 1860, commanded the papal troops, but, defeated by **Cialdini** at Castelfidardo (September), capitulated at Ancona.

LA MOTTE, Antoine Houdar de (1672–1731) French poet and playwright, born in Paris. He was translator of the *Iliad* into French verse. Of his other writings, perhaps the best known is the play *Inès de Castro*.

LA MOTTE, Jeanne de Valois, Comtesse de (1756–91) French adventuress. Having become the mistress of Cardinal **Rohan-Guéménée**, she duped him into standing security for the acquisition of a diamond necklace, allegedly at the request of **Marie Antoinette**. When the plot was revealed she was branded and imprisoned (1786), but escaped from gaol the following year and joined her husband in London, where she died as a result of a drunken fall from a three-storey window.

LA MOTTE FOUQUÉ See **FOUQUÉ**

L'AMOUR, Louis (1908–88) American writer of Wild West novels. Born in Jamestown, North Dakota, he grew up riding and hunting in the West, and earned his living in a variety of ways—prize-fighter, tugboat deckhand, lumberjack, gold prospector and deputy sheriff. His first novel about the Wild West, *Hondo* (1953), was an instant success, and he followed it with another 80 novels, including, *The Iron Marshall*, *The Quick and the Dead*, *Ride the Dark Trail*, and *How the West Was Won*, of which several were made into successful films. In 1984 he was awarded the Presidential Medal of Freedom.

LAMPEDUSA, Giuseppe Tomsasi di (1896–1957) Italian novelist, born in Palermo, Sicily, son of the Duke of Parma and grandson of the Prince of Lampedusa. His family had once been rich but indolence, divided inheritance and apathy had reduced its circumstances. As a youth he was wild but he turned bookish and scholarly and, despite familial disapproval, buried himself in his library where he read voraciously and eclectically in several languages. His mother, born Beatrice Mastrogiovanni Tasca, was the dominant influence in his life and it was not until she died that he felt free to embark on the novel that is his memorial, his only book, *Il Gattopardo* (1958; trans *The Leopard*, 1960). Set in Sicily in the latter half of the 19th century it is a historical novel, violent, decadent and nostalgic. It was rapturously received then vilified by the Italian literary establishment, including **Moravia**, but has subsequently come to be regarded as the greatest Italian novel of the 20th century.

LANCASTER, Burt (Stephen Burton) (1913–) American film actor, born in New York City. A former circus acrobat, he performed in army shows before turning professional and making his Broadway début in *A Sound of Hunting* (1945). Signed to a Hollywood contract his film début followed in *The Killers* (1946). Tall and muscular, he was cast in a succession of tough-guy roles, proving himself an athletic swashbuckler with a lithe manner and a ready grin. One of the first actors to form his own production company, he increasingly sought opportunities to test his dramatic abilities, earning Academy Award nominations for *From Here to Eternity* (1953), for his winning role as *Elmer Gantry* (1960), and for *Birdman of Alcatraz* (1962) and *Atlantic City* (1980).

LANCASTER, Duke of See **JOHN OF GAUNT**

LANCASTER, Sir James (c.1554–1618) English navigator. A soldier and merchant, he served under **Francis Drake** in the Armada battle (1588), went on the first English trading expedition to the East Indies in 1591–94, and in 1595 captured Pernambuco. In 1600–03 he commanded the first fleet of the East India

Company that visited the East Indies, and on his return was knighted. He later promoted voyages in search of the Northwest Passage.

LANCASTER, Joseph (1778–1838) English educationist and Quaker. In 1798 he opened a school in London based on a monitorial system which was taken up by the Nonconformists, while **Andrew Bell** and his rival system were supported by the Church of England. The Lancasterian schools were undenominational, and the bible formed a large part of the teaching. The Royal Lancasterian Society, afterwards known as the British and Foreign School Society, was formed in 1808. Lancaster left the Society in anger in 1818, and went to the USA, where he gave lectures and founded several schools.

LANCASTER, Sir Osbert (1908–86) English cartoonist and creator of the 'pocket cartoon', born in London. He studied art at Byam Shaw and the Slade School of Art, and worked on *Architectural Review* (1932), writing and illustrating humorous articles. For some time he designed posters for London Transport, book jackets, hotel murals, etc, before joining the *Daily Express* (1939) for a long series of front page *Pocket Cartoons*, witty comments for which he invented Lady Maudie Littlehampton and friends. He also designed sets and costumes for ballet (*Pineapple Poll*, etc) and opera (*Rake's Progress*, etc) and wrote many books, including his autobiography, *All Done From Memory* (1953).

LANCHESTER, Frederick William (1868–1946) English engineer, inventor and designer, born in Lewisham, London. A pioneer of automobile design and manufacture, he built the first experimental motor car in Britain (1895) and founded the Lanchester Engine Company in 1899, which produced the first Lanchester car in 1901. Turning his attention to aeronautics, he laid the foundations of aircraft design in *Aerial flight* (2 vols, 1907–08), which was ahead of its time in describing boundary layers, induced drag and the dynamics of flight. Another of his original contributions was *Aircraft in Warfare* (1914); quantifying numerical strength in contending military forces, this was an early essay in operational analysis.

LANCRET, Nicolas (1690–1743) French painter, born in Paris. He was renowned for his *fête-galante* paintings of balls, fairs and village weddings in the style of **Watteau**.

LAND, Edwin Herbert (1909–) American inventor and physicist, born in Bridgeport, Connecticut. He is known especially for his discoveries relating to light polarization, for his invention of the 'Polaroid' camera, which takes and processes photographs on the spot, and for research on the nature of colour vision.

LANDAU, Lev Davidovich (1908–68) Russian scientist, born in Baku. He graduated at Leningrad, studied with **Niels Bohr** in Copenhagen, and became professor of physics at Moscow (1937). Known for his important quantum theory researches, he received the Nobel prize for physics in 1962 for work on theories of condensed matter, particularly helium.

LANDELLS, Ebenezer (1808–60) English wood-engraver, born in Newcastle-on-Tyne. In 1841 he originated the humorous magazine *Punch*, worked under **Thomas Bewick**, and in 1829 settled in London. He contributed wood engravings to both *Punch* and the *Illustrated London News*.

LANDER, Harald, originally **Alfred Bernhardt Stevnsborg** (1905–71) Danish-born French dancer, choreographer and teacher, born in Copenhagen. He trained at the Royal Danish Ballet School and then joined the company (1923) to become one of its best character soloists. He studied and danced in the USA, South America and the USSR (1926–29), returning to the RDB as ballet master and, in 1932, director. Under him the company flourished. He preserved the works of **August Bournonville** while developing a new repertoire (including some 30 ballets of his own) of contemporary European works and nurturing new dancers. From 1950 to 1966 he was married to the Danish dancer Toni Pihl Petersen (1931–). They moved to Paris in the early 1950s, where he became ballet master and director of the Opéra's school. He became a French citizen in 1956, but continued to stage his works—the most famous is *Études* (1948), based on a ballet class—all over the world. Toni, a teacher as well as a ballerina with the RDB (1947–50 and 1971–76), also danced with London Festival Ballet (1954–59) and American Ballet Theatre (1961–71).

LANDER, Richard (1803–34) English explorer, born in Truro. In 1825 he accompanied **Hugh Clapperton** as his servant to Sokoto. There Clapperton died, and Lander published an account of the expedition. The British government sent him and his brother John (1807–39) to make further researches along the lower Niger. In 1830 they proved that the Niger flows through many channels into the Bight of Benin. During a third expedition, organized by **Macgregor Laird**, Richard Lander was wounded by Niger natives, and died in Fernando Pó.

LANDIS, Kenesaw Mountain (1866–1944) American jurist and baseball commissioner, born in Millville, Ohio. As a district judge in Illinois in 1907 he imposed a huge fine of $29 000 000 on the Standard Oil Company over rebate cases (the decision was reversed on appeal). After the bribery scandal in the World Series of 1919, when the Chicago White Sox were accused of deliberately losing a game to the Cincinnati Reds, he was appointed first commissioner of organized baseball in 1920. He drove eight Chicago players out of the game, although they had been acquitted in court, and his autocratic rule undoubtedly helped to restore the credibility of the game.

LANDOR, Walter Savage (1775–1864) English writer, born in Warwick, the son of a doctor. At ten he was sent to Rugby, but was removed for insubordination; he was also sent down from Trinity College, Oxford, which he entered in 1793. Soon after publishing *Poems* in 1795 (which he soon withdrew), he quarrelled with his father, but was reconciled, and retired to South Wales on an allowance of £150 a year. The exotic *Gebir* (1798), a poem showing the influence of **Milton** and **Pindar**, was the occasion of his lifelong friendship with **Southey**; but it was a failure. On his father's death in 1805 Landor had a considerable income, but much of it went in equipping volunteers to fight **Napoleon** in Spain (1808). Next year he purchased Llanthony Abbey in Monmouthshire, but soon quarrelled with neighbours and tenantry alike, and had ruin staring him in the face. In 1811 he married Julia Thuillier, but the marriage was not a success and in 1814 he left her in Jersey and crossed to France. Rejoined by his wife in Tours, he went in 1815 to Italy, where he remained in Como, Pisa and Florence until 1835, with the exception of a short visit to England. *Count Julian*, lacking in all the qualities of a successful tragedy, had appeared in 1812; and to this period belongs his best-known work, *Imaginary Conversations* (i and ii, 1824–29). A second quarrel with his wife in 1835 led to his return to Bath until 1858. During these years he wrote the *Examination of Shakespeare* (1834), *Pericles and Aspasia* (1836), *Pentameron* (1837), *Hellenics* (1847), and *Poemata et Inscriptiones* (1847). In 1858 an unhappy scandal (see his *Dry Sticks Fagoted*), which involved him in an action for libel, again drove him to Italy and he lived in Florence until his death.

LANDOWSKA, Wanda (1879–1959) Polish pianist, harpsichordist, and musical scholar, born in Warsaw. In 1900 she went to Paris, and in 1912 became professor of the harpsichord at the Berlin Hochshule. After World War I, in which she was detained, she undertook many extensive concert tours. At Saint-Leu-la-Forêt near Paris she established in 1927 her École de Musique Ancienne, where she gave specialized training in the performance of old works. In 1940 she had to flee first to the south of France, then to Switzerland, and finally in 1941 to the USA. Excelling as a player of **J S Bach** and **Handel**, she renewed interest in the harpsichord, and **Manuel de Falla** wrote his harpsichord concerto for her. She herself composed songs and piano and orchestral pieces. She made a profound study of old music and on this subject wrote *La Musique ancienne* (1908, trans. 1927). Among her other writings were *Bach et ses Interprètes* (1906) and many articles.

LANDRU, Henri Desiré (1869–1922) French murderer, born in Paris. He served in the army, then worked in garages and in the furniture trade. Between 1904 and 1915 he was imprisoned four times for swindling. His career as a mass murderer began in 1915 and lasted for four years. He was arrested in 1919, tried in 1921, convicted of the murders of ten women and a boy, and executed.

LANDSEER, Sir Edwin Henry (1802–73) English animal painter, born in London, the son of the engraver John Landseer (1769–1852). Trained by his father to sketch animals from life, he began exhibiting at the Royal Academy when only 13. His animal pieces were generally made subservient to some sentiment or idea, without, however, losing their correctness and force of draughtsmanship. The scene of several fine pictures is laid in the highlands of Scotland, which he first visited in 1824. His *Monarch of the Glen* was exhibited in 1851; the bronze lions at the foot of **Nelson**'s Monument in Trafalgar Square were modelled by him (1859–66). He was buried in St Paul's. Most of Landseer's pictures are well known from the excellent engravings of them by his elder brother Thomas (1796–1800).

LANDSTEINER, Karl (1868–1943) Austrian-born American pathologist, the discoverer of blood groups. Born in Vienna, he was a research assistant at the Pathological Institute there, and professor of pathological anatomy from 1909. He went to the USA to work in the Rockefeller Institute for Medical Research (1922–39). He won the 1930 Nobel prize for physiology or medicine, especially for his valuable discovery of the four major human blood groups (A,O,B,AB) which he discovered in 1901, and the M and N groups (discovered in 1927). In 1940 he also discovered the rhesus (Rh) factor.

LANE, Sir Allen (Lane Williams) (1902–70) English publisher, born in Bristol, and pioneer of paperback books. Educated at Bristol, he was apprenticed in 1919 to The Bodley Head publishing house under its founder and his relative John Lane (1854–1925). He resigned as managing director in 1935 in order to form Penguin Books Ltd, a revolutionary step in the publishing trade. He began by reprinting novels in paper covers at sixpence each, expanding to other series such as non-fictional Pelicans and children's Puffins, establishing a highly successful publishing concern.

LANE, (William) Arbuthnot (1856–1943) Scottish surgeon, born in Fort George, Inverness-shire. He was the first to join fractures with metal plates instead of wires. Other important contributions to medicine were his treatment of the cleft palate and of 'chronic intestinal stasis'. In 1925 he founded the New Health Society.

LANE, Edward William (1801–76) English Arabic scholar, born in Hereford, the son of a cleric. He trained as an engraver in London, but went to Egypt for his health, where he was given a Greek slave, Anastasia, whom he later married. He wrote *Manners and Customs of the Modern Egyptians* (1836), followed by the annotated translation of the *Thousand and One Nights* (1838–40), which was the first accurate rendering, and by *Selections from the Koran* (1843). The great work of his life was the *Arabic-English Lexicon* (8 vols, 1863–93), of which the last three volumes were completed by his grand-nephew, Stanley Lane-Poole (1854–1931).

LANE, Geoffrey Dawson, Lord, of St Ippollitts (1918–) English judge. Appointed a judge in 1966, he became a lord justice of appeal in 1974, a lord of appeal in ordinary in 1979 and lord chief justice of England in 1980, in which capacity he proved a vigorous leader of the courts.

LANE, Sir Hugh Percy (1875–1915) Irish art collector and critic, born in Ballybrack, Cork. He was responsible for founding a gallery of modern art in Dublin at the beginning of the 20th century by his encouragement of contemporary artists, such as **Jack Butler Yeats** and **William Orpen**, and by his own gifts of pictures. Director of the National Gallery of Ireland in 1914, he was drowned the following year when the *Lusitania* was torpedoed. The disposition of his collection of French Impressionists caused a dispute between London and Dublin that was only settled in 1959 by a decision to share them.

LANE, Richard James (1800–82) English engraver, brother of **Edward William Lane**, born in Berkeley Castle. An associate-engraver of the Royal Academy (1827), he turned to lithography, reproducing with unsurpassed delicacy and precision works by Sir **Thomas Lawrence**, **Gainsborough**, **Charles Robert Leslie**, **Landseer** and George Richmond. He was also a sculptor.

LANFRANC (c.1005–1089) Italian prelate and archbishop of Canterbury, born in Pavia. Educated for the law, about 1039 he founded a school at Avranches, in 1041 became a Benedictine at Bec, and in 1046 was chosen prior. He contended against **Berengar of Tours** in the controversy over transubstantiation. He at first condemned the marriage of William of Normandy (**William I**) with his cousin, but in 1059 went to Rome to procure the papal dispensation; and in 1062 William made him prior of St Stephen's Abbey at Caen, and in 1070 archbishop of Canterbury. His chief writings are Commentaries on the Epistles of St Paul, a Treatise against Berengar's *De Corpore et sanguine Domini* (1079), and Sermons.

LANFRANCO, Giovanni (c.1581–1647) Italian religious painter, born in Parma. One of the first Italian Baroque painters, his work, the best of which can be seen on the dome of S Andrea della Valle in Rome and in his paintings for the cathedral at Naples, was widely copied by later painters.

LANFREY, Pierre (1828–77) French historian and republican politician, born in Chambéry. His great work was his (hostile) *Histoire de Napoléon I* (5 vols, 1867–75).

LANG, Andrew (1844–1912) Scottish man of letters, born in Selkirk, nephew of **William Young Sellar**. Educated at The Edinburgh Academy, St Andrews, Glasgow and Balliol College, Oxford, he was a fellow of Merton College, Oxford (1868–74), studying myth, ritual and totemism. He moved to London in 1875 to take up journalism, and became one of the most versatile and famous writers of his day. He specialized in mythology, and took part in a celebrated controversy with **Friedrich Max Müller** over the interpretation of folktales, arguing that folklore was the foundation of literary mythology. He wrote *Custom and Myth* (1884), *Myth, Ritual and Religion* (1887), *Modern Mythology* (1897) and *The Making of Religion* (1898). He wrote a *History of Scotland* (3 vols, 1899–1904) and a *History of English Literature* (1912), and published a number of fairy books which enjoyed great popularity. He also produced studies of many literary figures, including *Books and Bookmen* (1886) and *Letters to Dead Authors* (1886), a translation of **Homer**, and several volumes of verse.

LANG, Cosmo Gordon (1864–1945) Scottish Anglican prelate, and archbishop of Canterbury, born in Fyvie, Aberdeenshire. He was the third son of John Marshall Lang (1834–1909), principal of Aberdeen University. Entering the Church of England in 1890, he was a curate at Leeds, became dean of divinity at Magdalen College, Oxford, bishop of Stepney (1901–08) and canon of St Paul's. In 1908 he was appointed archbishop of York and in 1928 archbishop of Canterbury until he retired in 1942. A man of wide interests, he was accepted by all parties in the Church of England and was both counsellor and friend to the royal family.

LANG, Fritz (1890–1976) Austrian-born American film director, born in Vienna and educated there at the College of Technical Sciences and the Academy of Graphic Arts. He wanted to become a painter but in 1919 joined the Decla Film Company. In 1926 in Berlin he directed two *Dr Mebuse* films, and *Metropolis* (1926), a nightmare of the future where a large section of the population is reduced to slavery. When **Hitler** came to power in 1933, **Goebbels** offered him the post of head of the German film industry. Lang refused and the same night fled to Paris and later to the USA. Among his many films of this period, *Fury* (1936) was acclaimed as a masterpiece for its nightmare qualities in portraying mob rule. His many other films include: *Halbblut* (The Half Caste 1919), *Liliom* (1933), *You Only Live Once* (1937), *The Return of Frank James* (1940), *Hangmen Also Die* (1943), *Secret Beyond the Door* (1948), *The House By the River* (1949), *Clash by Night* (1951), *Human Desire* (1954), *While the City Sleeps* (1955), and *Beyond a Reasonable Doubt* (1956). Back in Germany in 1960 he directed a third *Dr Mebuse* film.

LANG, John Dunmore (1799–1878) Scottish-born Australian clergyman and politician, born in Greenock, near Glasgow. Educated at Glasgow University, he arrived in New South Wales in 1823 with a mission to establish Presbyterianism in the new colony. The foundation stone of Scots Church, Sydney, was laid in the following year. With the support of Lord Bathurst, secretary of state for the colonies, a grant was made from the treasury, Lang was paid a salary, and the church opened in 1826. He started a weekly newspaper in 1835 and was soon involved in lawsuits as a result of his outspoken comments, being imprisoned on four occasions either for debt or libel. He was concerned about education, and energetic in assisting the emigration of skilled workers. He was elected member of the legislative council for three periods and of the legislative assembly from 1859 to 1869.

LANGDELL, Christopher Columbus (1826–1906) American legal scholar, born in Hillsborough, New Hampshire, and educated at Harvard. As Dane professor (1870–75) and dean of the Harvard Law School (1875–95), he raised the School's standards and exercised a powerful influence on legal education throughout the USA. Initiating the 'case method' of teaching, he compiled the first *Casebook on Contracts* (1871) which established a national trend.

LANGDON, Harry Philmore (1884–1944) American comedian, born in Council Bluffs, Iowa. As a child he appeared in amateur shows and joined *Dr. Belcher's Kickapoo Indian Medicine Show* in 1897. Gaining experience in minstrel shows, circuses, vaudeville and burlesque, he perfected his pantomine skills and developed the character of a baby-faced little-boy-lost: an innocent, handicapped by indecisiveness and bemused by the wider world. He made his film début in the serial *The Master Mystery* (1918) and was signed by **Mack Sennett** for a series of short comedies, beginning with *Picking Peaches* (1924). He moved on to features and the very popular trio of *Tramp Tramp Tramp* (1926), *The Strong Man* (1926) and *Long Pants* (1927). Then he unwisely decided to direct himself; the films failed and he earned a reputation for being difficult. An inexpert businessman, he filed for bankruptcy in 1931. He continued to appear in comedy shorts and was seen in supporting roles in films like *Hallelujah, I'm a Bum* (1933) and *Zenobia* (1939) and worked behind the scenes on such **Laurel** and **Hardy** films as *Blockheads* (1938) and *Saps at Sea* (1940).

LANGE, Carl Georg (1834–1900) Danish physician and psychologist. As professor of pathological anatomy at Copenhagen University, he advanced a theory of emotion which was independently developed by **William James** and is now known as the James-Lange theory. He also wrote a history of materialism.

LANGE, David Russell (1942–) New Zealand politician. After studying law at Auckland University and qualifying as a solicitor and barrister, he worked as a crusading lawyer for the underprivileged in Auckland. His election to the House of Representatives in 1977 changed the direction of his life and he rose rapidly to become deputy leader of the Labour party in 1979 and leader in 1983. He won a decisive victory in the 1984 general election on a non-nuclear defence policy, which he immediately put into effect, despite criticism from other Western countries, particularly the USA. He and his party were re-elected in 1987, but, following bouts of ill-health and disagreements within his party, he resigned the premiership in 1989.

LANGE, Dorothea, originally **Nutzhorn** (1895–1965) American photographer. Born in Hoboken, New Jersey, she studied at Columbia and established a studio in San Francisco in 1919, but became dissatisfied with the role of a society photographer. She is best known for her social records of migrant workers, share-croppers and tenant farmers throughout the south and west of the USA in the depression years from 1935, especially for her celebrated study, 'Migrant Mother' (1936). With her husband, economist Paul Taylor, she collaborated on a book, *An American Exodus: A Record of Human Erosion* (1939). After World War II she worked as a free-lance photo-reporter in Asia, South America and the Middle East (1958–63), and died in California.

LANGE, Johann Peter (1802–84) German theologian, born in Sonnborn near Elberfeld. In 1841 he became professor of theology at Zürich, and in 1854 at Bonn. His best-known works are a *Life of Jesus Christ* (1839) and his great *Bibelwerk* (1857 et seq).

LANGER, Susanne (Knauth) (1895–1985) American philosopher, born in New York. She was a graduate of Radcliffe College, where she taught from 1927 to 1942, holding positions subsequently at the University of Delaware, Columbia University and Connecticut College. She was much influenced by **Ernst Cassirer** and published important works in linguistic analysis and, more especially, aesthetics, such as *Philosophy in a New Key* (1942), *Feeling and Form* (1953), *Problems of Art* (1957), and *Mind: An Essay on Human Feeling* (3 vols, 1967–82).

LANGEVIN, Sir Hector Louis (1826–1906) Canadian statesman, born in Quebec. He was called to the bar in 1850 and became mayor of Quebec (1858–60). Thereafter he held many government posts, including solicitor-general (1864–66), postmaster-general (1860–67) and secretary of state (1867–69).

LANGEVIN, Paul (1872–1946) French physicist. Professor at the Sorbonne (1909), he was noted for his work on the molecular structure of gases, and for his theory of magnetism. Imprisoned by the Nazis after the occupation of France, he was later released and, though kept under surveillance at Troyes, managed to escape to Switzerland. After the liberation he returned to Paris.

LANGHAM, Simon (d.1376) English prelate, born in Langham in Rutland. He became prior and abbot of Westminster (1349), treasurer of England (1360), bishop of Ely (1362), chancellor (1363), archbishop of Canterbury (1366) and a cardinal (1368).

LANGHORNE, John (1735–79) English poet, born in Winton, Kirkby Stephen. From 1766 he was rector of Blagdon, Somerset. He wrote poems and, with his brother, the Rev William Langhorne (1721–72), translated **Plutarch**'s Lives (6 vols, 1770).

LANGLAND, or **Langley, William** (c.1332–c.1400) English poet, born possibly in Ledbury in Herefordshire, thought to have been the illegitimate son of the rector of Shipton-under-Wychwood in Oxfordshire. Educated at the Benedictine school at Malvern, he became a clerk, but, having married early, could not take more than minor orders, and possibly earned a poor living in London from 1362 by singing in a chantry and by copying legal documents. In that year he began the composition of his famous *Vision of William concerning Piers the Plowman*, which has great defects as a work of art; but the moral earnestness and energy of the author (or authors as has been theorized) sometimes glow into really noble poetry brightened by vivid glimpses of the life of the poorer classes.

LANGLEY, John Newport (1852–1925) English physiologist. Professor at Cambridge from 1903, he was noted for his research on the sympathetic nervous system. He owned and edited the *Journal of Physiology*.

LANGLEY, Samuel Pierpont (1834–1906) American astronomer and aeronautical pioneer, born in Roxbury, Massachusetts. In 1867 he was appointed professor of astronomy at Western University of Pennsylvania and director of the Allegheny Observatory. He greatly advanced solar physics and invented the bolometer for measuring radiant heat. A pioneer of heavier-than-air mechanically-propelled flying machines, he built models that flew in the 1890s. His first full-size machine failed to fly in 1903, but flew well in 1914.

LANGLEY, William See **LANGLAND**

LANGMUIR, Irving (1881–1957) American chemist, born in Brooklyn, New York. Educated at Columbia and Göttingen, he was associated with the General Electric Company (1909–50), being from 1932 associate director of the research laboratory. He won the Nobel prize for chemistry in 1932 for work on surface chemistry. His many inventions include the gas-filled tungsten lamp, and the atomic hydrogen welding torch.

LANGTON, Stephen (c.1150–1228) English prelate, and archbishop of Canterbury. He was educated at the University of Paris. His friend and fellow-student Pope **Innocent III** in 1206 gave him a post in his household and made him a cardinal. On the disputed election to the see of Canterbury in 1205–07, Langton was recommended by the pope and, having been elected, was consecrated by Innocent himself at Viterbo in 1207. His appointment was resisted by King **John**, and Langton was kept out of the see until 1213, living mostly at Pontigny. He sided warmly with the barons against John and his name is the first of the subscribing witnesses of Magna Carta. Although the pope excommunicated the barons, Langton refused to publish the excommunication, and was suspended from his functions in 1215. He was reinstated in 1218.

LANGTRY, Lillie, properly **Emilie Charlotte,** née **Le Breton** (1853–1929) British actress, born in Jersey. Daughter of the dean of the island, she was one of the most noted beauties of her time. She married Edward Langtry in 1874, and made her first important stage appearance in 1881. Her nickname, *The Jersey Lily*, originated in the title of **Millais**'s portrait of her. Her beauty brought her to the attention of the Prince of Wales, later **Edward VII**, and she became his mistress. She managed the Imperial Theatre which was never successful. Widowed in 1897, she married in 1899 Hugo Gerald de Bathe, and became well known as a racehorse owner. She died in Monte Carlo. She wrote *All at Sea* (as Lillie de Bathe) in 1909, and her reminiscences, *The Days I Knew* (1925).

LANIER, Sidney (1842–81) American poet, born in Macon, Georgia. He was a Confederate private in Virginia, an advocate in Macon, a flute player with the Peabody Orchestra, Baltimore, and lecturer in English literature at Johns Hopkins University (1879). Among his writings are a novel, *Tiger Lilies* (1867), critical studies such as *The Science of English Verse* (1880) and *The English Novel* (1883), as well as poetry. He believed in a scientific approach towards poetry-writing, breaking away from the traditional metrical techniques and making it more akin to musical composition, illustrated in later poems such as 'Corn' and 'The Symphony'.

LANJUINAIS, Jean Denis (1753–1827) French statesman, born in Rennes. A Girondist, he was made a count by **Napoleon**, and a peer by **Louis XVIII**.

LANKESTER, Sir Edwin Ray (1847–1929) English zoologist, born in London, the son of the scientific writer, Dr Edwin Lankester (1814–74). He was fellow and tutor of Exeter College, Oxford, professor at London University and at Oxford, and in 1898–1907 director of the British Museum (Natural History). His contributions to zoology included important work in embryology and protozoology. Largely responsible for the founding of the Marine Biological Association in 1884, he became its president in 1892. Among his many books are *Comparative Longevity* (1871), *Degeneration* (1880), *Advancement of Science* (1890), and *Science from an Easy Chair* (1910–12), and he edited a great *Treatise on Zoology* (1900–09).

LANNES, Jean, Duke de Montebello (1769–1809) French soldier, born in Lectoure (Gers), the son of a livery stable keeper. He entered the army in 1792, and by his conspicuous bravery in the Italian campaign fought his way up to be general of brigade by 1796. He rendered important service on the 18th Brumaire in 1799 that brought **Napoleon** to power. In 1800 he won the battle of Montebello, and had a distinguished share at Marengo, Austerlitz (1805), Jena (1806), Eylau and Friedland (1807), and took Saragossa (1809). He commanded the centre at the battle of Aspern and Esslung, where he was mortally wounded and died in Vienna.

LANSBURY, Angela (1925–) American actress, born in London. She was under contract to the Metro-

Goldwyn-Meyer film studios from 1943 to 1950, appearing in such films as *Gaslight* (1944), *National Velvet* (1944), and *Samson and Delilah* (1949). She became a naturalized American citizen in 1951. After she became freelance she made many more films, including *The Reluctant Debutante* (1958); *The Manchurian Candidate* (1963); *Bedknobs and Broomsticks* (1972); and *Death on the Nile* (1978). She made her Broadway stage début in **Feydeau**'s *Hotel Paradiso* in 1957, and became noted as an actress in such musicals as **Sondheim**'s *Anyone Can Whistle* (1964) and *Sweeney Todd* (1979). She played Gertrude in *Hamlet* at the National Theatre, London, in 1975. She has appeared frequently in American television series.

LANSBURY, George (1859–1940) English politician, born near Lowestoft. For many years before entering parliament he worked for the reform of the conditions of the poor. He was first elected Labour member of parliament for Bow and Bromely in 1910, resigning in 1912 to stand again as a supporter of women's suffrage. He was defeated and was not re-elected until 1922. Meanwhile he founded the *Daily Herald*, which he edited until 1922, when it became the official paper of the Labour party. In 1929 he became first commissioner of works and a very able leader of the Labour party (1931–35). Besides his help to the poor, he opened up London's parks for games and provided a bathing place on the Serpentine. He wrote *My Life* (1928).

LANSDOWNE, Henry Charles Keith Petty-Fitzmaurice, 5th Marquis of (1845–1927) English statesman, great grandson of Sir **William Petty**. He became marquis in 1866, and from 1868 held minor offices in the Liberal administration. From 1872 to 1874 he was under-secretary for war, in 1880 for India, joining the Liberal Unionists. Governor-general of Canada (1883–88) and of India (1888–94), he was war secretary from 1895 to 1900. From 1900 to 1905 as foreign secretary he promoted arbitration treaties with the USA, the *Entente Cordiale*, and the Japanese alliance. Unionist leader in the Lords from 1903, he sat (without portfolio) in **Asquith**'s coalition cabinet (1915–16), advocating peace by negotiation in 1917.

LANSDOWNE, Henry Petty-Fitzmaurice, 3rd Marquis of (1780–1863) English statesman, son of the 1st marquis, better known as the Earl of Shelburne. He graduated at Cambridge in 1801, and became MP for Calne next year. He led in the attack on Lord **Melville** (1805), and succeeded **Pitt** as member for Cambridge University (1806), and also as Chancellor of the Exchequer in the **Grenville** administration. In 1809, by the death of his half-brother, he became marquis. A cautious Liberal, in 1826 he entered the **Canning** Cabinet, and in the **Goderich** administration (1827–28) presided at the foreign office. Under Lord **Grey** (1830) Lansdowne became president of the council, and helped to pass the Reform Bill of 1832. He held office, with a short interval, until 1841. In 1846, under **Russell**, he resumed his post, taking with it the leadership of the Lords. Requested to form an administration in 1852, he preferred to serve without office in the **Aberdeen** coalition and in 1855 again declined the premiership. He formed a great library and art collection.

LANSING, Robert (1864–1928) American lawyer and statesman, born in Watertown, New York. He became an attorney in 1889, and made a name as US counsel in arbitration cases (eg Bering Sea, N Atlantic coast fisheries). An authority on international law, he became counsellor for the Department of State in 1914, and succeeded **William Jennings Bryan** as President **Woodrow Wilson**'s secretary of state in June 1915. He supported the president during World War I, attended the Peace Conference in Paris, (1919), but resigned in 1920 over the League of Nations. He was author of *The Peace Negotiations* (1921) and *The Big Four and others of the Peace Conference* (1921).

LANSON, Gustave (1857–1934) French critic and historian, born in Orleans. He became professor of French literature at the Sorbonne in 1900, and director of the École Normale Supérieure, 1919–27. Among his scholarly works are a standard history of French literature (1894), *Manuel bibliographique de la littérature française moderne* (1913), and critical studies of French authors and their works, including **Voltaire**, **Corneille** and **Lamartine**.

LANSTON, Tolbert (1844–1913) American inventor, born in Troy, Ohio. He patented the Monotype, 'a type-forming and composing machine', in 1887. It was first used commercially in 1897 and revolutionized printing processes.

LANTZ, Walter (1900–) American cartoonist and film animator, born in New Rochelle, New York, the creator of the *Woody Woodpecker* character. An office boy on the *New York American* (1914), he studied cartooning by correspondence course and got his start with **William Randolph Hearst**'s animation studio in 1916. He rose to be writer/director/'star' of his own *Dinky Doodle* cartoons, then went to Hollywood, where he took over *Oswald the Lucky Rabbit* (1928) after **Walt Disney** left Universal Pictures, and remained with that studio for over 50 years. Of the many characters he created the most popular is *Woody Woodpecker*, who first burst on the screen in *Knock Knock* (1940), and whose characteristic laugh is supplied by Mrs Lantz (actress Grace Stafford).

LAO-TZU (6th century BC) Chinese philosopher and sage, literally 'the old master'. Little is known of his life but he is regarded as the inspiration for Taoism and for one of its principal works, the *Tao-te-Ching* (The Way of Power), compiled some 300 years after his death, which teaches self-sufficiency, simplicity and detachment. Taoism venerates the 'feminine' qualities which promote longevity, equanimity and an instinctive unity with nature.

LA PASIONARA See **BARRURI GOMEZ, Dolores**

LA PÉROUSE, Jean François de Galaup, Comte de (1741–88) French navigator, born in Guo near Albi. He distinguished himself in the naval war against Britain (1778–83) by destroying the forts of the Hudson's Bay Company. In 1785, in command of an expedition of discovery, he visited the north-west coast of America, explored the north-eastern coasts of Asia, and sailed through La Pérouse Strait between Sakhalin and Yezo. In 1788 he sailed from Botany Bay, and his two ships were wrecked north of the New Hebrides.

LAPLACE, Pierre Simon, Marquis de (1749–1827) French mathematician and astronomer, born in Beaumont-en-Auge, Normandy, the son of a farmer. He studied at Caen, went to Paris and became professor of mathematics at the École Militaire where he gained fame by his researches on the inequalities in the motion of Jupiter and Saturn, and the theory of the satellites of Jupiter. In 1799 he entered the senate, becoming its vice-president in 1803, and minister of the interior for six weeks, after which he was replaced because of an incapacity for administration. He was created marquis by **Louis XVIII** in 1817. His astronomical work culminated in the publication of the five monumental volumes of *Mécanique céleste* (1799–1825), the greatest work on celestial mechanics since **Newton**'s *Principia*. His *Système du monde* (1796) is a non-mathematical exposition, of masterly clarity, of all his astronomical theories, and his famous nebular hypothesis of planetary origin occurs as a note in later editions. In his study of the gravitational attraction of spheroids he formulated the fundamental differential equation in physics which bears his name. He also made important contributions to the theory of probability.

LAPWORTH, Arthur (1872–1941) Scottish chemist, born in Galashiels, the son of **Charles Lapworth**. He was educated at Birmingham University and the City and Guilds College, London. After holding a number of senior academic posts, he was appointed professor of organic chemistry at Manchester in 1913. He became professor of physical and inorganic chemistry in 1922. He had early ideas on an electronic theory of organic chemical reactions. He classified reagents by charge type, and suggested the existence of alternating electrical polarity along a chain of atoms, and alternating positive and negative centres at which reactions occurred. These ideas, developed in discussion with his friend **Robert Robinson**, were expanded by the latter in the 1930s to dominate organic chemical theory, with notable success.

LAPWORTH, Charles (1842–1920) English geologist, born in Faringdon. A school-teacher in Galashiels, he did important work in elucidating the geology of the south of Scotland and the northwest Highlands. He was professor of geology at Birmingham (1881–1913) and wrote especially on graptolites. The term Ordovician was introduced by him.

LA RAMÉE, Louise See **OUIDA**

LARDNER, Dionysius (1793–1859) Irish scientific writer, born in Dublin. He attracted attention by his works on algebraic geometry (1823) and the calculus (1825) and was elected professor of natural philosophy and astronomy at London University (1827), but is best known as the originator and editor of *Lardner's Cabinet Cyclopaedia* (133 vols, 1829–49), followed by the historical *Dr Lardner's Cabinet Library* (9 vols, 1830–32), the *Edinburgh Cabinet Library* (38 vols, 1830–44) and *Museum of Science and Art* (12 vols, 1854–56). From 1840 to 1845 he lectured in the USA and Cuba; after his return to Europe he settled in Paris.

LARDNER, Nathaniel (1684–1768) English Nonconformist clergyman and biblical scholar, born in Kent. He pioneered critical research into early Christian literature, and wrote *The Credibility of Gospel History* (1727).

LARGILLIÈRE, Nicolas (1656–1746) French portrait painter, born in Paris. He lived for some years in England where he was **Lely**'s assistant. He was one of the most popular portraitists of his day.

LARIONOV, Mikhail Fyodorovich (1881–1964) Russian painter, born in Tiraspol in the Ukraine. He studied sculpture and architecture at the Moscow Institute of Painting until 1908. Beginning as a Russian Post-Impressionist, influenced by **Pierre Bonnard** and the Fauves, he gradually took to a more 'primitive' approach based on Russian folk art. He worked closely with his future wife, Natalia Goncharova, and together they developed Rayonism (1912–14), a style akin to Italian Futurism. They held a joint exhibition in Paris 1914. From 1915 they worked on ballet designs for **Diaghilev**.

LARIVEY, Pierre (c.1550–1612) French dramatist of Italian descent. As the introducer of Italian-style comedy to the French stage he foreshadowed **Molière** and **Regnard**. His licentious *Comédies facétieuses* (2 vols, 1579, 1611) were adaptations of existing Italian pieces.

LARKIN, James (1876–1947) Irish Labour leader, born in Liverpool. He was organizer of the Irish Transport and General Workers' Union. Deported from the USA in 1923 for his anarchistic activities, he continued at the head of the IT and GWU, organizing strikes and fostering strife until expelled in 1924. He was Ireland's representative at the Third International, but later gave up Communism, continuing as an extreme Labour leader.

LARKIN, Philip Arthur (1922–85) English poet, librarian and jazz critic, born in Coventry, Warwickshire, where his father was city treasurer. He was educated at King Henry VIII School, Coventry, and at St John's College, Oxford. The Oxford of the time is evoked in the novel, *Jill* (1946). After leaving Oxford, he took up librarianship and *A Girl in Winter* (1947), his only other novel, tells of a day in the life of a refugee librarian employed in a drab English provincial town. He eventually became librarian at the University of Hull in 1955. His early poems appeared in the anthology, *Poetry from Oxford in Wartime* (1944), and in a collection, *The North Ship* (1945). **Yeats**, **Hardy** and **Dylan Thomas** were then his presiding influences. He was friendly with **Kingsley Amis** who made the hero of his novel *Lucky Jim* (1954), Jim Dixon, share Larkin's antipathy towards **Mozart**. *XX Poems* was published privately in 1950 when he was in Belfast and marked the emergence of an individual 'voice'. Further collections appeared at measured intervals: *The Less Deceived* (1955), *The Whitson Weddings* (1964) and *High Windows* (1974). The *Collected Poems* were published posthumously in 1988 and became a bestseller. He also edited *The Oxford Book of Twentieth Century English Verse* (1937). The self he projected to the world from his fastness in Hull was of a xenophobic, reactionary old fogey, downcast and ill at ease in the modern world. But much of the time his tongue was firmly in his cheek and his poetry reveals a considerable talent for technique and a sure grasp of modern idiom. His articles on jazz were collected in *All What Jazz?* (1970), and his essays in *Required Writing* (1983).

LAROCHE, Guy (1923–89) French fashion designer, born in La Rochelle, near Bordeaux, into a cattle-farming family. He worked in millinery, first in Paris, then on Seventh Avenue, New York, before returning to Paris where he worked for Dessès for eight years. In 1957 he started his own business and showed a small collection. By 1961 he was producing both couture and ready-to-wear clothes, achieving a reputation for skilful cutting. From 1966 his designs included menswear.

LA ROCHEFOUCAULD, François, 6th Duc de (1613–80) French writer, born in Paris. He devoted himself to the cause of the queen, **Marie de' Medici**, in opposition to **Richelieu**, and became entangled in a series of love adventures and political intrigues, the result being that he was forced to live in exile from 1639 to 1642. About 1645 he formed a liaison wth Mme **de Longueville**. He then joined the Frondeurs and was wounded at the siege of Paris. In 1652, wounded again, he retired to the country. On **Mazarin**'s death in 1661 he returned to the court of **Louis XIV**, and about the same time began a liaison with Mme de Sablé. A surreptitious edition of his *Mémoires*, written in retirement, was published in 1662, but as it gave wide offence he denied its authorship. His *Réflexions, ou sentences et maximes morales*, appeared in 1665. His last years were brightened by his liaison with Mme **de La Fayette**, which lasted until he died. For brevity, clearness and style the *Maxims* could hardly be excelled. Their author was a remorseless analyst of man's character, and tracks out self-love in its most elusive forms and under its most cunning disguises.

LA ROCHEJAQUELEIN, Louis du Verger, Marquis de (1777–1815) French soldier. He emigrated at the French Revolution, returned to France in 1801, and in 1813 headed the Royalists in the revolt at La Vendée. **Louis XVIII** gave him in 1814 the command of the army of La Vendée, where, during the Hundred Days, he maintained the Royalist cause, supported by the British. He fell at Pont-des-Mathis.

LA ROCHEJAQUELEIN, Marie Louise Victoire (1772–1857) French writer, wife of **Louis du Verger de Larochejaquelein**. She published valuable *Mémoires* of the Napoleonic war (1815).

LAROUSSE, Pierre Athanase (1817–75) French publisher and lexicographer, born in Toucy in Yonne. He founded a publishing house and bookshop in Paris in 1852 and issued educational textbooks. He also founded a journal for teachers, *École Normale*, in 1859. His major work was his *Grand dictionnaire universel du XIXe siècle* (17 vols, 1866–76).

LARRA, Mariano José de (1809–37) Spanish poet, satirist and political writer, born in Madrid. As a journalist he was unequalled and he published two periodicals between 1828 and 1833, but it was as a satirist that he became well known. His masterly prose writings include *El Doncel de Don Enrique el Doliente* (1834), a novel, *Macías* (1834), a play and adaptations of French plays.

LARREY, Jean Dominique, Baron (1766–1842) French military surgeon, born in Beaudéan, near Bagnères-de-Bigorre. He served first as a naval surgeon, and in 1793 joined the army, where he introduced the field hospitals and ambulance services. From 1797 he accompanied **Napoleon** on his campaigns, became head of the army medical departments, and a baron. He wrote on army surgery and the treatment of wounds.

LARRIEU, Daniel (1957–) French dancer and choreographer, born in Marseilles. He began performing professionally in 1978, and formed in 1982 a three-person company called Astrakan that won the Bagnolet international choreographic competition that year. His biggest success to date is the underwater modern ballet *Waterproof* (1986), commissioned by Centre National de Danse Contemporaine in Angers and performed in swimming pools to video accompaniment. A witty choreographer interested in challenging audience expectations of what dance and theatre can be, he has received commissions from London Contemporary Dance Theatre, Netherlands Dance Theatre and the Frankfurt Ballet.

LARSEN, Henning (1925–) Danish architect. Educated at the Royal Danish Academy, Copenhagen, the Architectural Association, London and Massachusetts Institute of Technology, Boston, he became a lecturer at the Royal Danish Academy in 1959 and has been professor of architecture since 1968. He was a visiting professor at Yale University in 1964 and at Princeton University in 1965. His buildings include the University of Trondheim (Norway), university institutes at Freie Universität (Berlin), houses at Milton Keynes (England), and the Foreign Ministry and the Danish Embassy in Riyadh (Saudi Arabia). The Foreign Ministry in Riyadh has been described as one of the first buildings successfully to combine eastern and western architectural traditions. Larsen was chosen as architect of the 1100-seat Compton Verney opera house, near Stratford-upon-Avon, in England.

LARSSON, Carl (1853–1919) Swedish artist, born in Stockholm. A talented draughtsman, he financed his studies at the Academy of Arts (1869–76) by illustrating newspapers and magazines. He visited Paris in 1877 and lived from 1882 to 1884 in Grez-sur-Loing where he was the centre of the Scandinavian artists' colony. He abandoned oils for impressionistic water-colours of rural life. In 1885 he returned to Sweden and, after some years teaching in Gothenburg, he settled in the idyllic province of Dalarna in 1898. It is the series of 26 watercolours entitled *A Home* (1894–99), which gaily depict his own home at Sundborn, that won him international renown and enormous popularity in Sweden. He also produced monumental historical paintings and was an outstanding illustrator of books.

LARTIGUE, Jacques-Henri (1894–1986) French photographer and painter, born in Curbvoie. He was given his first plate-camera in 1901 and from the age of eight used a Brownie No2 hand-camera for candid family snapshots. He continued to adopt an informal approach to the photography of everyday subjects, including experiences in World War I, and can be said to have elevated the snapshot into a creative art form. He was an early user of Autochrome, the Lumière system of colour photography, especially to record the life of the leisured classes of the 1920s. Subsequently more interested in painting, he continued with some creative photography throughout his life and a one-man show at the New York Museum of Modern Art in 1963 aroused wide interest. His 1970 collection, *Diary of a Century* is particularly evocative of the elegance of the *belle epoque* and the inter-war years in France.

LARWOOD, Harold (1904–) English cricketer, born in Nuncargate. His career was comparatively brief and he played in only 21 Test matches, but with his Nottinghamshire colleague Bill Voce he constituted an opening attack of blistering speed. He was employed by **D R Jardine** to bowl 'Bodyline' in the controversial 1932–33 tour of Australia when several of the home batsmen were seriously hurt, and diplomatic relations between the two countries were imperilled. On his return, feeling that he had not been supported in official quarters, he retired from Test cricket and in later life, somewhat ironically, settled happily in Australia. He published two memoirs, *Bodyline* (1933) and *The Larwood Story* (1965).

LA SALLE, Antoine de (c.1398–1470) French writer, born in Burgundy or Touraine. He lived at the courts of Provence and Flanders, and wrote *Chronique du petit Jehan de Saintré* (1456), and a knightly romance *Quinze joyes de mariage*, and was the reputed author of *Cent nouvelles nouvelles*.

LA SALLE, Jean Baptiste Abbé de, St (1651–1719) French educational reformer, born in Reims. He set up schools for the poor, reformatories, and training colleges for teachers, and was the founder in 1684 (with twelve companions) of the Brothers of the Christian Schools, known as Christian Brothers. He was canonized in 1900.

LA SALLE, René Robert Cavalier, Sieur de (1643–87) French explorer and pioneer of Canada, born in Rouen. Having settled as a trader near Montreal, he descended the Ohio and Mississippi to the sea (1682), claiming Louisiana for France and naming it after **Louis XIV**. In 1684 an expedition was fitted out to establish a French settlement on the Gulf of Mexico, but La Salle spent two years in fruitless journeys searching for the Mississippi Delta. His followers mutinied, and he was murdered.

LASCARIS, Constantine (d.1493 or 1501) Greek grammarian, brother of **John Lascaris**. After the fall of Constantinople to the Turks in 1453 he fled to Italy, where he was taken into the patronage of Duke **Francesco Sforza**. He taught Greek in Rome, Naples and Messina, and revived classical studies there. His Greek grammar, *Erotemata* (1476), was the first Greek book to be printed in Italy. His library in now in the Escorial.

LASCARIS, John, or **Janipus,** known as **Rhyndacenus** (c.1435–c.1535) Greek scholar, brother of **Constantine Lascaris**. He lived in Florence and worked as librarian to Lorenzo **de' Medici**, collecting MSS and teaching. On his patron's death he went to Paris, where he served in various diplomatic posts. He taught Greek, and edited a number of Greek classics from manuscript, and wrote grammars, letters and epigrams.

LAS CASAS, Bartolomé de (1474–1566) Spanish missionary, known as the 'Apostle of the Indians', born in Seville. He sailed in the third voyage of **Columbus** (1498), and in 1502 went to Hispaniola as a planter. Eight years later he was ordained to the priesthood. In 1511 he accompanied **Diego Velázquez** to Cuba, assisted in the pacification of the island, and was rewarded by a commandery of Indians. But soon a desire to protect and defend the natives made him give up his own slaves; in 1515 he went to Spain, where he prevailed on Cardinal **Ximenes** to send a commission of inquiry to the West Indies. He revisited Spain to secure stronger measures; and finally, to prevent the extirpation of the natives, he proposed that the colonists should be permitted to import black slaves —a proposal only too readily acceded to. He also attempted to take Castilian peasants as colonists in a model settlement in Venezuela, but failed, and spent eight years (1522–30) in a convent in Hispaniola. In 1530 he again visited Spain, and, after missionary travels in Mexico, Nicaragua, Peru and Guatemala, returned to devote four years to the cause of the Indians, writing his *Veynte Razones* and *Brevísima Relación de la destrucción de las Indias* (1552). Appointed bishop of Chiapa, he was received (1544) with hostility by the colonists, returned to Spain, and resigned his see (1547). He still contended with the authorities in favour of the Indians until his death in Madrid. His most important work is the unfinished *Historia de las Indias* (1875–76).

LAS CASES, Emmanuel Dieudonné, Comte de (1766–1842) French historian, born in Las Cases, Haute Garonne. A lieutenant in the navy, he fled to England at the revolution. His *Atlas historique* (1803–04) gave him a European reputation. Though a royalist by birth, he was so fascinated by **Napoleon**'s genius that he insisted on sharing his exile on St Helena. Deported to the Cape by Sir **Hudson Lowe** in 1816, he returned to Europe, and published (1821–23) the *Mémorial de Sainte Hélène*, which caused an immense sensation.

LASCO, Johannes a, or **Jan Łaski** (c.1499–1560) Polish reformer, born in Łask, Piotrkow, of a noble family. He was ordained priest in 1521, and in 1523 in Basel came into contact with **Erasmus** and **Farel**. Caught in the current of the Reformation, he left home in 1538 and about 1540 moved to East Friesland, where he established a presbyterian form of church government as superintendent at Emden. In 1550, on **Cranmer**'s invitation, he became head of a congregation of Protestant refugees in London. **Mary I**'s accession in 1553 drove him back to Emden, and he finally returned to Poland in 1556.

LASDUN, Sir Denys Louis (1914–) English architect, born in London. Educated at Rugby School and trained at the Architectural Association School, he worked with **Wells Coates** (1935–37), joining the Tecton partnership (1938–40). He partnered Lindsey Drake (1949–50), and in 1960 began the Denys Lasdun partnership. He was professor at Leeds from 1962 to 1963. His architecture follows the modern tradition, with horizontal emphasis, forceful articulation of mass and respect for urban context; the occasional reference to the works of **Le Corbusier** is apparent. His early works include flats on the Paddington Estate, London, and the flats at St James's Place, London. He is renowned particularly for the Royal College of Musicians (1958–64) in London, the University of East Anglia, Norwich (1962–68), the National Theatre, London (1965–76), European Investment Bank, Luxembourg (1975), and the Institute of Education (1970–78) in London. He was awarded the Royal Gold Medal of the RIBA in 1977. His publications include *A Language and a Theme* (1976) and *Architecture in an Age of Scepticism* (1984).

LASHLEY, Karl Spencer (1890–1958) American psychologist, born in Davis, Virginia and known as the 'father of neuropsychology'. He was professor at the universities of Minnesota (1920–26) and Chicago (1929–35), and research professor of neuropsychology at Harvard (1935–55). In 1942 he also became director of the Yerkes Laboratory for primate biology at Orange Park, Florida. He made valuable contributions to the study of localization of brain function.

LASKER, Eduard (1829–84) Prussian Liberal politician, born of Jewish parentage in Posen. He was one of the founders of the National Liberal party and is important chiefly for the codification of the laws of Germany, for which he was largely responsible. He died in New York on a visit to America.

LASKER, Emanuel (1868–1941) German chess player, born in Berlinchen (now Barliner) in Brandenburg, world champion from 1894 to 1921. He defeated **Wilhelm Steinitz** in 1894 for the world title before he reached his chess prime. Consequently, his tournament record as champion was greater than any other until **Anatoly Karpov**, and his reign was the longest in the history of chess. He was the first chess master to treat the game as a war of psychological attrition. His tenure was extended by the intervention of World War I, and he lost the championship in 1921 to **José Raúl Capablanca**. His doctorate in mathematics was gained at Erlangen University, and his theorem of vector spaces is still known by his name. Driven out of Germany and his property confiscated in 1933 because of his Jewish birth, he lived the remainder of his life in England, the USSR and the USA.

LASKI, Harold Joseph (1893–1950) English political scientist and socialist, born in Manchester. He was educated at Manchester Grammar School and New College, Oxford, and lectured at McGill University (1914–16), Harvard (1916–20), Amherst (1917) and Yale (1919–20, 1931). In 1920 he joined the staff of the London School of Economics, and became professor of political science in 1926. He was chairman of the Labour party (1945–46). Laski was a brilliant talker, and as lecturer at the London School of Economics had a great influence over his students, who revered him. His political philosophy was a modified Marxism. He had a strong belief in individual freedom, but the downfall of the Labour government in 1931 forced him to feel that some revolution in Britain was necessary. His works include *Authority in the Modern State* (1919), *A Grammar of Politics* (1925), *Liberty in the Modern State* (1930) and *The American Presidency* (1940).

LASKI, Jan See **LASCO**

LASKI, Marghanita (1915–88) English novelist and critic, born in Manchester, niece of **Harold Joseph Laski**. Educated at Oxford, her first novel, *Love on the Supertax*, appeared in 1944. She wrote extensively for newspapers and reviews. Her later novels include *Little Boy Lost* (1949) and *The Victorian Chaise-longue* (1953). She also wrote a play, *The Offshore Island* (1959), as well as editing and writing various studies and critical works. She married John E Howard in 1937.

LASSALLE, Ferdinand (1825–64) German social democrat, born, the son of a rich Jewish merchant, in Breslau. A disciple of **Hegel**, he wrote a work on

Heraclitus (published 1858), and in Paris made the acquaintance of **Heine**. On his return to Berlin he met in 1844–45 the Countess Sophie Hatzfeld (1805–81), a lady at variance with her husband, prosecuted her cause before 36 tribunals, and after eight years of litigation forced the husband to a compromise favourable to the countess. He took part in the revolution of 1848, during which he met **Marx**, and for an inflammatory speech got six months in prison. He lived in the Rhine country until 1857, when he returned to Berlin and wrote his *System der erworbenen Rechte* (1861). At Leipzig he founded the Universal German Working-men's Association (the forerunner of the Social Democratic party) to agitate for universal suffrage. In 1863–64 he tried to win the Rhineland and Berlin to his cause; in his *Bastiat-Schulze, or Capital and Labour*, he attacked **Schulze-Delitzsch**, the representative of Liberalism. He died shortly after a duel with Count Racowitza of Wallachia over the hand of Helene von Domiges. In his political writings he taught that Europe's historical development is to culminate in a democracy of labour, in which political interests shall be subservient to social considerations—the social democracy.

LASSELL, William (1799–1880) English astronomer, born in Bolton. He built an observatory at Starfield near Liverpool, where he constructed and mounted equatorial reflecting telescopes. He discovered several planetary satellites, including Triton (1846) and Hyperion (1848, simultaneously with the **Bonds** at Harvard). He also discovered Ariel and Umbriel, satellites of Uranus (1851).

LASSEN, Christian (1800–76) Norwegian orientalist, born in Bergen. He assisted **Schlegel** and **Eugène Burnouf**, and was professor of ancient Indian languages at Bonn from 1830 until he became blind in 1864. Amongst his most important books are works on Persian cuneiforms (1836–45), the Greek kings in Bactria (1838), Prakrit (1837), and Indian civilization (1844–61).

LASSUS, Orlandus, or **Orlando di Lasso** (c.1532–1594) Netherlandish musician and composer, born in Mons. He wrote many masses, motets and other works, and travelled widely, visiting Italy, England and France. In 1570 he was ennobled by **Maximilian II**. Unlike his contemporary, **Palestrina**, he wrote not only church music but also a vast number of secular works, and ranks as one of the greatest composers of early times.

LÁSZLÓ, Sir Philip, properly **Philip Alexius László de Lombos** (1869–1937) Hungarian-born British portrait painter, born in Budapest. He worked in England and gained an international reputation as a painter of royalty and heads of state.

LATHAM, John (1740–1837) English ornithologist, born in Eltham. One of the founders of the Linnean Society, he wrote *A General History of Birds* in eleven volumes (1821–28), for which he designed, etched and coloured all the illustrations. He lived from 1796 at Romsey.

LATHAM, Sir John Greig (1877–1964) Australian politician and judge. He taught at Melbourne University, practised at the bar and served in World War I. From 1922 he became attorney-general of the Commonwealth, leader of the Opposition, deputy prime minister (1931–34), and chief justice of the High Court of Australia (1935–52). In this office he enhanced the standing of the High Court, keeping it distinct from politics, and favoured Commonwealth power against state power.

LATHROP, Julia Clifford (1858–1932) American social reformer, born in Rockford, Illinois. Educated at Vassar College, in 1880 she joined **Jane Addams**'s Hull House Settlement in Chicago. She was active in promoting welfare for children and the mentally ill. One of the founders of the Chicago Institute of Social Science (1903–04), she was associated with the Chicago School of Philanthropy from 1908 to 1920, and was first head of the Federal Children's Bureau (1912). She was a member of the Child Welfare Committee of the League of Nations from 1925 to 1931.

LATIMER, Hugh (c.1485–1555) English Protestant martyr, born in Thurcaston, near Leicester, the son of a yeoman. He was sent to Cambridge, in 1510 was elected a fellow of Clare College, and in 1522 was appointed a university preacher. In 1524 for his BD thesis he delivered a philippic against **Melanchthon**, for he was, in his own words, 'as obstinate a papist as any in England'. Next year, however, through **Bilney**, he 'began to smell the Word of God, forsaking the school doctors and such fooleries', and soon becoming noted as a zealous preacher of the reformed doctrines. One of the Cambridge divines appointed to examine the lawfulness of **Henry VIII**'s marriage to **Catherine of Aragon** he declared on the king's side; and he was made chaplain to **Anne Boleyn** and rector of West Kington in Wiltshire. In 1535 he was consecrated as bishop of Worcester and at the opening of Convocation in June 1536 he preached two powerful sermons urging on the Reformation. Consequently falling out of favour at court he retired to his diocese, and laboured there in a continual round of 'teaching, preaching, exhorting, writing, correcting and reforming'. Twice during Henry's reign he was sent to the Tower, in 1539 and 1546, on the former occasion resigning his bishopric. At **Edward VI**'s accession he declined to resume his episcopal functions, but devoted himself to preaching and practical works of benevolence. Under **Mary I** he was examined at Oxford (1554), and committed to jail. In September 1555, with **Ridley** and **Cranmer**, he was found guilty of heresy, and on 16 October was burned with Ridley opposite Balliol College.

LATINI, Brunetto (c.1210–c.1295) Florentine writer and statesman. A member of the **Guelf** party, he was exiled to France from 1260 to 1266, and there wrote the encyclopaedic *Li Livres dou Trésor*.

LA TOUR, Georges de (1593–1652) French artist, born in Vic-sur-Seille in Lorraine. From 1620 he worked at Lunéville in the same province and achieved a high reputation. The Duke of Lorraine became his patron and later the king himself accepted a painting by him, liking it so much he had all works by other masters removed from his chambers. Unfortunately, La Tour was entirely forgotten until his rediscovery in 1915 and in the meantime works by him were attributed to **Le Nain** and followers of **Caravaggio**. He specialized in candlelit scenes, using a palette of warm, glowing reds and browns to obtain eerie effects. Of the 40 works by him which have been positively identified, most are of religious subjects, such as *St Joseph the Carpenter* (Louvre) and *The Lamentation over St Sebastian* (Berlin).

LA TOUR, Maurice Quentin de (1704–88) French pastellist and portrait painter, born in St Quentin. He settled in Paris, where he became immensely popular. His best works include portraits of Madame **de Pompadour**, **Voltaire** and **Rousseau**.

LA TOUR D'AUVERGNE, Théophile Malo Corret de (1743–1800) French soldier, born in Carhaix in Finistère. He enlisted in 1767, distinguished himself at Port Mahon in 1782, steadily refused advancement and was killed, a simple captain, at Oberhausen in Bavaria. His remains were interred in the Panthéon in 1889. French biographies are full of instances of his valour,

Spartan simplicity and chivalrous affection. He was known as the 'First Grenadier of France'. He wrote a book on the Breton language and antiquities.

LATREILLE, Pierre Andrezac (1762–1833) French entomologist, born in Brives in Corrèze, and known as the father of modern entomology. An ordained priest, he became professor of natural history at Paris. He is best known for his pioneering work on the classification of insects and crustaceans.

LATROBE, Benjamin Henry (1764–1820) English-born American civil engineer, born in Fulneck, Yorkshire, the son of a Moravian minister. He was trained as both an architect and a civil engineer before emigrating to the USA in 1796. He introduced the Greek Revival style to America and was surveyor of public buildings in Washington, DC, from 1803 to 1817, his work including parts of the Capitol and the White House. As an engineer he designed waterworks for the city of Philadelphia (1801), worked on the Washington navy yard, and joined with **Robert Fulton** in a scheme to build steamboats (1813–15). When this project failed he was ruined financially and suffered a nervous breakdown, but soon returned to Washington to make good the damage sustained by the Capitol and the White House, burned by the British in 1814. In 1817 his son Henry died of yellow fever while building the New Orleans waterworks; Latrobe went there in 1820 to complete the works but soon died of the same cause. Another son, Benjamin Henry (1806–78), and a grandson Charles Hazlehurst (1834–1902), were both noted American railway civil engineers.

LATTIMORE, Owen (1900–89) American sinologist and defender of civil liberties, born in Washington, DC, the son of an American trader in China. He spent his early childhood in China, was educated in England and Lausanne, and worked in China in business and journalism in the 1920s, travelling in Mongolia and Manchuria and returning to the USA to study at Harvard, where his proficiency led to his being sent back for research work: hence, although later an eminent academic, he never took a university degree. He published outstanding narratives of his journeys and observations in central Asia such as *The Desert Road to Turkestan* (1928), *High Tartary* (1930), *Mongol Journeys* (1941), and his masterpiece, *Inner Asian Frontiers of China* (1940). He was made political adviser to **Chiang Kai-Shek** by President **Franklin D Roosevelt** in 1941–42, but resigned because of his inability to persuade Chiang to follow a programme of social justice. He was director of Pacific operations in the office of war information, edited *Pacific Affairs* (1934–41), published important syndicated columns on Far Eastern questions (summed up in his *Solution in Asia*, 1945, and *The Situation in Asia*, 1949), and held major academic posts in Johns Hopkins University and in Leeds. While on a UN mission to Afghanistan in 1950 he was named as the top Russian agent in the USA by Senator **Joseph McCarthy**: the five-year struggle to clear his name of this utterly baseless charge was carried out with great courage by himself and his wife Eleanor (1895–1970), and its initial phase was brilliantly described in his *Ordeal by Slander* (1950). However, he suffered from the treachery of frightened academics and ultimately settled in England, and later in Paris, playing a major part in the development of Chinese studies in Europe, stressing a Chinese rather than a Western perspective.

LATTRE DE TASSIGNY, Jean de (1889–1952) French soldier, born in Mouilleron-en-Pareds. Educated at the Jesuit College at Poitiers and at St Cyr, he commanded an infantry battalion during World War I, was wounded four times and decorated with the Croix de Guerre. By 1940 he commanded the 14th division in rearguard actions against the advancing Germans, and was then sent by the Vichy government to command in Tunisia. He was recalled for sympathy with the Allies and arrested in 1942 for resisting the German occupation of the neutral zone. He escaped from Rion prison to North Africa in 1943, was secretly flown by an RAF plane to London, and later as commander of the French 1st army took a brilliant part in the Allied liberation of France (1944–45), signing the German surrender. He was responsible for the reorganization of the French army and was appointed c-in-c of Western Union Land Forces under **Montgomery** in 1948. In 1950 as c-in-c in French Indo-China, he successfully turned the tide against the Vietminh rebels, by introducing novel tactics. He was posthumously made a marshal of France in 1952.

LATUDE, Henri Masers de (1725–1805) French artillery officer. He sought to secure Madame de **Pompadour**'s favour by revealing a plot to poison her. The plot was of his own contriving, and he was sent without trial to the Bastille in 1749. He made three daring but futile escapes from prison, and was at last released in 1777, on condition that he lived in his native village of Montagnac in Languedoc. Lingering in Paris, he was reimprisoned till 1784. At the revolution he was treated as a victim of despotism and voted a pension.

LAUBACH, Frank Charles (1884–1970) American missionary and pioneer of adult basic education, born in Benton, Pennsylvania. Discovering that the Moror tribespeople of the Philippines (whom he had been sent to evangelize in 1915) were unable to read or write, he devised a simple way to combat illiteracy. His method and its application in Southern Asia, India, and Latin America are described in *India shall be Literate* (1940), *Teaching the World to Read* (1948), and *Thirty Years with the Silent Billion* (1961); and his spiritual motivation in *Letters by a Modern Mystic* (1937) and *Channels of Spiritual Power* (1955).

LAUBE, Heinrich (1806–84) German playwright and manager, born in Sprottau in Silesia. He was one of the leaders of the 'Young Germany' movement and editor of *Die elegante Welt*, its literary organ. He was director of Vienna's Burgtheater (1850–67), and among his writings are works on the theatre, on historical themes, novels such as *Das junge Europa* (1833–37), *Die Karlsschüler* (1847), a drama of the young **Schiller**, and a biography of **Grillparzer**.

LAUD, William (1573–1645) English prelate, and archbishop of Canterbury, born in Reading, a well-to-do clothier's son. From Reading Free School he passed at 16 to St John's College, Oxford, becoming a fellow four years later. Ordained in 1601, he made himself obnoxious to the university authorities by his open antipathy to the dominant Puritanism; but his solid learning, his amazing industry, his administrative capacity, his sincere and unselfish churchmanship, soon won him friends and patrons. One of these was Charles Blount, Earl of Devonshire, whom in 1605 Laud married to the divorced Lady Rich (an offence that always was heavy on his conscience); another was **Buckingham**, to whom he became confessor in 1622. Meanwhile he rose steadily from preferment to preferment—incumbent of five livings (1607–10), president of his old college and king's chaplain (1611), prebendary of Lincoln (1614), archdeacon of Huntingdon (1615), dean of Gloucester (1616), prebendary of Westminster and bishop of St Davids (1621), bishop of Bath and Wells, dean of the Chapel Royal, and a privy councillor (1626), bishop of London (1628), chancellor of Oxford (1630), and finally archbishop of Canterbury

(1633), in the very week that he received two offers of a cardinal's hat. Already, after Buckingham's assassination, he had virtually become the first minister of the crown, one with **Strafford** and **Charles I** in the triumvirate whose aim was absolutism in church and state. Laud's task was to raise the Church of England to its rightful position as a branch of the Church Catholic, to root out Calvinism in England and Presbyterianism in Scotland. In England he drew up a list of 'Orthodox' and 'Puritan' ministers, whom he proceeded to separate by scolding, suspending and depriving. Freedom of worship was withdrawn from Walloon and French refugees; Englishmen abroad were forbidden to attend Calvinistic services; and at home 'gospel preaching', justification by faith, and Sabbatarianism were to be superseded by an elaborate ritual, by the doctrine of the real presence, celibacy and confession, and by the Book of Sports—changes rigorously enforced by the court of High Commission and the Star Chamber. In Scotland, Laud's attempt (1635–37) to Anglicize the church gave birth to the riot in St Giles', Edinburgh; the riot led to the Covenant, the Covenant to the 'Bishops' war', and this to the meeting of the Long Parliament, which in 1640 impeached the archbishop of treason, and ten weeks later sent him to the Tower. He would not escape (**Grotius** urged him to do so); and at last, after a tedious and complicated trial before a handful of peers, in December 1644, he was voted 'guilty of endeavouring to subvert the laws, to overthrow the Protestant religion, and to act as an enemy to Parliament'. The judges declared that this was not treason; but under an unconstitutional ordinance of attainder, he was beheaded on Tower Hill.

LAUDA, Niki (Nikolas Andreas) (1949–) Austrian racing driver, born in Vienna. World champion racing driver in 1975, 1977 and 1984, his last two wins involved astonishing feats of physical and mental bravery. In 1976 he suffered horrific burns and injuries in the German Grand Prix at the Nürburgring. Despite a series of operations he remained a contender for the 1976 Japanese Grand Prix, but finally declined to race because of adverse weather conditions. He then refuted rumours that he had lost his nerve by winning again in 1977. Going on to drive for Brabham meant a two-year absence from Grand Prix racing, before he crowned his come-back with McLaren by winning his third and last Grand Prix championship in 1984. He retired in 1985.

LAUDER, Estée, née **Mentzer** (1908–) American businesswoman and beautician, born in New York City, the daughter of poor Hungarian immigrants. She worked her way up in the cosmetics industry by selling a face cream made by her uncle. She founded Estée Lauder Inc in 1946, and had great success with Youth Dew bath oil in the 1950s. She was named one of 100 women of achievement by *Harpers Bazaar* in 1967, and named one of the Top Ten outstanding women in business in 1970. Her husband and partner, Joe Lauder, died in 1982. She published her autobiography, *Estée: A Success Story*, in 1985.

LAUDER, Sir Harry (1870–1950) Scottish comic singer, born in Portobello. He started his career on the music-hall stage as an Irish comedian, but made his name as a singer of Scots songs, many of which were of his own composition, such as 'Roamin' in the Gloamin'. He was knighted in 1919 for his work in organizing entertainments for the troops during World War I. His appeal was by no means confined to Scottish audiences; some of his biggest successes were on the stages of London's famous music halls and his popularity abroad was immense, especially in the USA and the Commonwealth countries, which he toured almost annually after 1907. He wrote volumes of memoirs, the best known of which is *Roamin' in the Gloamin'* (1928).

LAUDER, Robert Scott (1803–69) Scottish painter, born in Silvermills, Edinburgh. He lived in Italy and in Munich from 1833 to 1838, then in London until 1849, when he returned to Edinburgh. Sir **Walter Scott**'s novels provided him with subjects for his most successful historical paintings.

LAUDER, Sir Thomas Dick (1784–1848) Scottish writer, born in Fountainhall, Midlothian. He served in the Cameron Highlanders and married in 1808 the heiress of Relugas in Morayshire. He succeeded to the baronetcy in 1820, and lived at the Grange, Edinburgh, from 1832 until his death. He was secretary to the Board of Scottish Manufacturers (1839–48). Lauder wrote two romances, *Lochindhu* (1825) and *The Wolf of Badenoch* (1827), but his best works are his *An Account of the Great Morayshire Floods* (1830) and the unfinished *Scottish Rivers*, which appeared in *Tait's Magazine* (1847–49). He also compiled *Highland Rambles and Legends to Shorten the Way* (1837) and *Legends and Tales of the Highlands* (1841).

LAUDER, William (c.1680–1771) Scottish scholar and charlatan. In 1747–50 he sought to prove, by blatant forgeries, that **Milton**'s *Paradise Lost* had plagiarized various 17th-century poets writing in Latin. He was exposed by Bishop **John Douglas**, and died poor in Barbados.

LAUDERDALE, John Maitland, Duke of (1616–82) Scottish statesman, born at Lethington (now Lennoxlove) near Haddington. He succeeded his father as second Earl of Lauderdale in 1645, was taken prisoner at Worcester in 1651, and spent nine years in the Tower, at Windsor and at Portland. At the Restoration, he became Scottish secretary of state and then made it his main object to bring about the absolute power of the crown in church and state. A member of the privy council, he had a seat in the so-called Cabal ministry and was created a duke in 1672. He made numerous enemies and in 1678 a vote was carried in the Commons praying for his removal from the royal presence forever, but it was thrown out, in dubious circumstances, by a single vote. It seems probable that many of Lauderdale's harsher measures, especially against the Episcopal Church in Scotland, were the result not so much of personal ambition but of an inability to tolerate the follies of less astute contemporaries. His dukedom died with him in 1682, while his earldom passed to his brother.

LAUE, Max von (1879–1960) German physicist, born near Koblenz. He was professor at Zürich, Frankfurt and Berlin. He did good work in relativity, predicted that X-rays would be diffracted by a crystal, and won the Nobel prize for physics in 1914. He was later appointed director of the Kaiser Wilhelm Institute for Theoretical Physics (1951).

LAUGHTON, Charles (1899–1962) English-born American actor, born in Scarborough. After working in his family's hotel business, he first appeared on stage in 1926 and his parts included Ephikhodov in *The Cherry Orchard*, Mr Crispin in *A Man with Red Hair*, Poirot in *Alibi* and William Marble in *Payment Deferred*. He appeared with the Old Vic Company in 1933, played in and produced **Shaw**'s *Don Juan in Hell* and *Major Barbara*, and as a Shakespearean actor gave fine performances in, amongst others, *Macbeth*, *Measure for Measure* and *King Lear*. He began to act in films in 1932 and his great dramatic sense and technique made memorable such roles as **Henry VIII** in *The Private Life of Henry VIII* (1932, Academy

Award), Mr Barrett in *The Barretts of Wimpole Street* (1934), Captain **Bligh** in *Mutiny on the Bounty* (1935) and Quasimodo in *The Hunchback of Notre Dame* (1939). He was married to the actress Elsa Lanchester (1902–86), and became an American citizen in 1950.

LAUGHTON, Sir John Knox (1830–1915) English naval historian, born in Liverpool. He became professor of modern history at King's College, Cambridge in 1883. His books include *Studies in Naval History* (1887), *Defeat of the Spanish Armada* (1894) and *Nelson* (1895).

LAURANA, Luciano da (c.1420–1479) Italian architect, born in Dalmatia. He was working in Urbino c.1465, and by 1468 had been appointed architect in chief at the Ducal Palace, a member of the humanist court of Federigo da Montefeltro. The design of the palace courtyard evidenced his familiarity with recent Renaissance masterpieces in the field, particularly **Brunelleschi**'s Foundling Hospital, Florence.

LAUREL, Stan, originally **Arthur Stanley Jefferson** (1890–1965), born in Ulverston, Lancashire and **Hardy, Oliver** (1892–1957), born near Atlanta, Georgia, stage and screen comedians. Laurel, a teenage member of Fred Karno's touring company and sometime understudy to **Charlie Chaplin**, first went to the USA in 1910. After gaining his first film part in 1917, he appeared in many of the early silent comedies and had tried producing and directing before his partnership with Hardy began in 1926. Hardy had been destined for a military career, but left college to join a troupe of minstrels before drifting into the film industry. Though Laurel is usually described as the more creative partner, the team was much funnier and more successful than its individual parts. They made many full-length feature films, but their best efforts are generally reckoned to be their early (1927–31) shorts. They survived the advent of the 'talkies' better than many others, though their style was basically silent. Purveying good honest slapstick, they deliberately avoided any attempt at subtlety. Ollie—fat, pretentious and blustering—fiddled with his tie and appealed to the camera for help, while Stan—thin, bullied and confused— scratched his head, looked blank and dissolved into tears. Their contrasting personalities, their general clumsiness and stupidity, and their disaster-packed predicaments made them a universally popular comedy duo.

LAUREN, Ralph, originally **Ralph Lipschitz** (1939–) American fashion designer, born in the Bronx, New York City. He attended night school for business studies and worked as a salesman in Bloomingdales. In 1967 he joined Beau Brummel Neckwear and created the Polo range for men, later including womenswear. He is famous for his American styles, such as the 'prairie look' and 'frontier fashions'.

LAURENCE, Margaret, originally **Jean Margaret Wemyss** (1926–87) Canadian novelist of Scots-Irish descent, born in the prairie town of Neepawa, Manitoba. Her first stories appeared in the high school paper. Aged 18, she left home to study at United College (now Winnipeg University) from which she graduated in 1947—the same year she married John Laurence, a civil engineer. His job took them to England, Somaliland and, in 1952, to Ghana, where they spent five years. *A Tree for Poverty* (1954), a collection of translated Somali poetry and folk-tales, and the travel book *The Prophet's Camel Bell* (1963), came from her East African experience. *This Side Jordan* (1960), her first novel, was set in Ghana. She moved to England in 1962 and a year later a collection of stories, *The Tomorrow-Tamer*, set in West Africa, appeared. In Penn, Buckinghamshire, she wrote her famous Manawaka series based on her home town: *The Stone Angel* (1964), *A Jest of God* (1966), *The Fire-Dwellers* (1969), *A Bird in the House* (1970), and *The Diviners* (1974). One of Canada's most potent novelists, she received Governor General Awards in 1967 and 1975, and in 1972 was made a Companion of the Order of Canada.

LAURENCIN, Marie (1885–1957) French artist, born in Paris. She exhibited in the Salon des Indépendents in 1907. Best known for her portraits of women in misty pastel colours, she also illustrated many books with water colours and lithographs.

LAURENS, Henri (1885–1954) French graphic artist and sculptor, born in Paris. He was a leading exponent of three-dimensional Cubism.

LAURENT, Auguste (1807–53) French chemist, born in La Folie, Haute Marne. After eight years as professor in Bordeaux (1838–45) he went to Paris to work with **Charles Frédéric Gerhardt**. Ignored by his fellow-scientists, he was forced by financial difficulties to become assayer at the Mint. He propounded the nucleus theory of organic radicals, discovered anthracine, worked on the classification of organic compounds and gave his name to 'Laurent's Acid'. His very valuable *Méthode de chimie* was published posthumously in 1854.

LAURIER, Sir Wilfrid (1841–1919) Canadian statesman, born in St Lin, Quebec. He shone at the Canadian bar and in 1877 was minister of inland revenue in the Liberal ministry. In 1891 he became leader of the Liberal party and prime minister in 1896. He was the first French-Canadian and also the first Roman Catholic to be premier of Canada. In 1911 his government was defeated on the question of commercial reciprocity with the United States, but he remained Liberal leader. Though he had a strong feeling for Empire, Laurier was a firm supporter of self-government for Canada. During World War I his party was divided on the conscription question, Laurier being against conscription though entirely in agreement with Canada's entering the war. In his home policy he was an advocate of free trade, passed many reforms to benefit the working classes and helped to plan a transcontinental railway, the Grand Trunk.

LAURISTON, Alexandre Jacques Bernard Law, Marquis de (1768–1828) French soldier, born in Pondicherry, grand-nephew of the financier, **John Law** of Lauriston. He was **Napoleon**'s comrade at the Artillery School, filled diplomatic appointments at Copenhagen and London, held high commands at Wagram (1809) and in the retreat from Moscow (1812) fought at Bautzen (1813) and Katzbach, and was taken prisoner at Leipzig. Already ennobled, he was made a peer by **Louis XVIII**, became marquis in 1817 and marshal in 1821.

LAUTERPACHT, Sir Hersch (1897–1960) Polish-born English lawyer, born near Lemberg and educated in Vienna. He came to England in 1923 and became a law teacher in London, and Whewell professor of International Law at Cambridge (1938–55). He acted for Britain in many international disputes and ultimately became a judge of the International Court of Justice (1954–60). He wrote extensively on international law, his works including *The Function of Law in the International Community* (1933), *Recognition in International Law* (1947) and *International Law and Human Rights* (1950); he also edited **LFL Oppenheim**'s *International Law*.

LAUZUN, Antonin Nompar de Gaumont, Duc De (1633–1723) French soldier from Gascony. Captain of **Louis XIV**'s bodyguard, he was imprisoned by Louis for his affair with his niece, the **Duchesse de Mont-**

pensier, whom he may have wed secretly. In 1688 he conducted **Mary of Modena**, wife of **James II**, on her flight from London to Paris. He commanded a French force on behalf of James in Ireland in 1690. Armand Louis de Gontaut, **Duc de Biron**, also bore the title of Duc de Lauzun.

LAVAL, Carl Gustaf Patrik de (1845–1913) Swedish engineer, born in Orsa. He invented a centrifugal cream separator in 1878 and made important contributions to the development of the steam turbine and many other devices.

LAVAL, Pierre (1883–1945) French politician, born in Châteldon (Puy-de-Dôme). He became an advocate, deputy (1914), senator (1926) and premier (1931–32, 1935–36). From Socialism he moved to the Right, and in the Vichy government was **Pétain**'s deputy (1940), rival and prime minister (1942–44), when he openly collaborated with the Germans. Fleeing after the liberation, from France to Germany and Spain, he was brought back, condemned to death as a collaborationist and executed.

LAVAL-MONTMORENCY, François Xavier (1622–1708) French prelate and missionary. He was sent as vicar apostolic to Quebec in 1659, and became the first bishop of Quebec from 1674 to 1688. In 1663 he founded the seminary of Quebec, which in 1852 was named Laval University after him.

LAVALETTE, Antoine Marie Chamans, Comte de (1769–1830) French politician and Napoleonic general. He served in the Alps, was aide-de-camp to **Napoleon** and, after the war, French minister to Saxony, postmaster-general and a councillor of state. After the second **Bourbon** restoration (1815) he was condemned to death, but escaped by changing clothes with his wife, a niece of Empress **Joséphine**.

LA VALLIÈRE, Louise Françoise de Labaume Leblanc, Duchesse de (1644–1710) French aristocrat, born in Tours. Brought to court by her mother, she became **Louis XIV**'s mistress in 1661 and bore him four children. When the Marquise de **Montespan** superseded her she retired to a Carmelite nunnery in Paris (1647). *Réflexions sur la miséricorde de Dieu par une dame pénitente* (1680) is attributed to her.

LAVATER, Johann Kaspar (1741–1801) Swiss physiognomist, theologian and poet, born in Zürich. In 1769 he received Protestant orders. He made himself known by a volume of poems, *Schweizerlieder* (1767). His *Aussichten in die Ewigkeit* (1768–78) is characterized by religious enthusiasm and mysticism. He attempted to elevate physiognomy into a science in his *Physiognomische Fragmente* (1775–78, trans 1793). While tending the wounded at the capture of Zürich by **Masséna** (September 1799) he received a wound, of which he later died.

LAVELEYE, Émile Louis Victor de (1822–92) Belgian economist, born in Bruges. In 1864 he became professor of political economy at Liège. His works include *De la propriété* (1874); *Le Socialisme contemporain* (1881) and *Éléments d'économie politique* (1882).

LAVER, James (1899–1975) English writer and art critic, born in Liverpool. He won the Newdigate prize for verse at Oxford in 1921, and later books of verse included *His Last Sebastian* (1922) and *Ladies' Mistakes* (1933). He was assistant keeper, later keeper at the Victoria and Albert Museum from 1922 to 1959. He wrote several books of art criticism, including *French Painting and the 19th century* (1937) and *Fragonard* (1956), and made a substantial contribution to the history of English costume with such books as *Taste and Fashion* (1937), *Fashions and Fashion Plates* (1943) and *Children's Costume in the 19th Century* (1951).

LAVER, Rod (Rodney George) (1938–) Australian tennis player, born in Rockhampton, Queensland. A powerful and swift left-handed player, he won the Wimbledon singles title both as an amateur and as a professional. He first won the Wimbledon title in 1961, and won it again in 1962 in the course of a Grand Slam of all the major titles (British, American, French and Australian). He turned professional in 1962 and won the professional world singles title five times between 1964 and 1970. When it allowed professionals to participate in 1968, he won Wimbledon in that year, and won again in the course of another Grand Slam the following year.

LAVERAN, Charles Louis Alphonse (1845–1922) French physician and parasitologist, born and educated in Paris. He became professor of military medicine and epidemic diseases at the military college of Val de Grâce (1874–78 and 1884–94). He studied malaria in Algeria (1878–83), discovering in 1880 the blood parasite which caused the disease. He also did important work on other diseases including sleeping-sickness and kala-azar. From 1896 until his death he was at the Pasteur Institute at Paris. In 1907 he was awarded the Nobel prize for physiology or medicine.

LAVERY, Sir John (1856–1941) Irish painter, born in Belfast, the son of a publican. He studied in Glasgow, London and Paris. A portrait painter of the Glasgow school, his work enjoyed great popularity, especially his conversation pieces and paintings of women.

LAVIGERIE, Charles Martial Allemand (1825–92) French prelate, born in Bayonne. In 1863 he was made bishop of Nancy, in 1867 archbishop of Algiers, and cardinal in 1882. As primate of Africa and archbishop of Algiers (1884) he became well-known for his missionary work, and founded the order of the White Fathers (1868). In 1888 he founded the Anti-Slavery Society.

LAVIN, Mary (1912–) Irish short-story writer and novelist, born in East Walpole, Massachusetts. Her parents returned to Ireland when she was nine and she has lived there ever since. 'Miss Holland', her first short story, was published in the *Dublin Magazine* where it was admired by Lord **Dunsany** who encouraged her and later wrote an introduction to her first collection, *Tales from Bective Bridge* (1942), which was awarded the James Tait Black Memorial prize. Notwithstanding two early novels—*The House in Clewe Street* (1945) and *Mary O'Grady* (1950)—she has concentrated on the short story. She has published many collections and her stories were collected in 1971. Further collections are *A Memory and Other Stories* (1972), *The Shrine and Other Stories* (1977), and *A Family Likeness* (1985). Her laurels include the Katherine Mansfield prize and the Gregory Medal, founded by **W B Yeats** to be 'the supreme award of the Irish nation'.

LAVISSE, Ernest (1842–1922) French historian, born in Nouvion-en-Thiérache, Aisne. He taught history to the son of **Napoleon III** and was professor of history at the Sorbonne, where he completely changed the teaching methods. He edited the *Revue de Paris* (1894) and became director of the École Normale Supérieure (1902–20). He wrote works on Prussian history after visiting Germany, but is perhaps best known for the immense history which he published in collaboration with **Rambaud**, *Histoire générale du IVᵉ siècle à nos jours* (1893–1900). Then came *Histoire de France depuis les origines jusqu'à la Révolution* (9 vols, 1903–11) and *Histoire contemporaine* (10 vols, completed 1922).

LAVOISIER, Antoine Laurent (1743–94) French chemist, born in Paris, known as the founder of modern chemistry. To finance his investigations, he accepted in 1768 the office of farmer-general of taxes. As director of the government powder mills (1776), he greatly improved gunpowder, its supply and manufacture, and successfully applied chemistry to agriculture. He discovered oxygen, by rightly interpreting **Joseph Priestley**'s facts, its importance in respiration, combustion and as a compound with metals. His *Traité élémentaire de chimie* (1789) was a masterpiece. Politically Liberal, he saw the great necessity for reform in France but was against revolutionary methods. But despite a lifetime of work for the state, inquiring into the problems of taxation (which he helped to reform), hospitals and prisons, he was guillotined as a farmer of taxes.

LA VOISIN, real name **Catherine Monvoisin** (d.1680) French poisoner, who grew wealthy by concocting potions and selling them to the ladies at the court of **Louis XIV**. When the poison plots were discovered in 1679, involving such well-known figures as the Duchess **Mancini** and the Marquise **de Montespan**, La Voisin was found to be responsible after an examination by a secret tribunal. She was burned in 1680.

LAW, Andrew Bonar (1858–1923) Canadian-born Scottish statesman, born in Kingston, New Brunswick. He was an iron merchant in Glasgow, and Unionist MP from 1900. In 1911 he succeeded **Balfour** as Unionist leader in the House of Commons. He was colonial secretary in 1915–16, then a member of the War Cabinet, Chancellor of the Exchequer (1916–18), lord privy seal (1919), and from 1916 leader of the House of Commons. He retired in March 1921, but despite ill-health was premier from October 1922 to May 1923.

LAW, Denis (1940–) Scottish footballer, born in Aberdeen. One of the greatest of Scottish footballers, he never played at senior level in his own country, all his career being spent in England with the exception of a brief and unsuccessful spell in Italy. He made his international début when only 18 years old and shortly afterwards moved to Manchester City. After the Italian failure with Turin, he returned to Manchester United, the club with which he is indelibly associated. With them he won every major domestic honour, although injury excluded him from the European Cup success of 1968. Needle-sharp in the penalty area and very powerful in the air, Law shares with **Kenny Dalglish** the record of 30 goals scored for Scotland.

LAW, Edward See **ELLENBOROUGH**

LAW, John of Lauriston (1671–1729) Scottish financier, born in Edinburgh, son of a goldsmith and banker. Educated at the Royal High School, he became a successful gambler and speculator. He went to London to make his fortune, but in 1694 was imprisoned for killing a man in a duel over a lady. In 1695 he escaped from prison and fled to the Continent. In Amsterdam he made a study of the credit operations of the bank, and later settled in Genoa after eloping with the wife of a Frenchman. He made a fortune there and in Venice. In 1703 he returned to Edinburgh, a zealous advocate of a paper currency; but his proposals to the Scottish parliament on this subject, outlined in his *Money and Trade Considered* (1705), were unfavourably received. Back on the Continent, he won and lost vast sums in gambling and speculation, but at last settling in Paris, he and his brother William (1675–1752) set up in 1716 a private bank. This prospered so that the regent, Philippe, Duc **d'Orléans**, adopted in 1718 Law's plan of a national bank. In 1719 he originated a joint-stock company for reclaiming and settling lands in the Mississippi valley, called the *Mississippi scheme*, which made him a paper millionaire. He became a French citizen and a Roman Catholic, and in 1720 was made comptroller-general of finance for France. When the bubble burst he became an object of popular hatred, left France, and spent four years in England. He finally settled in Venice, where he died.

LAW, William (1686–1761) English churchman and writer, born in Kingscliffe, Northamptonshire, the son of a grocer. He entered Emmanuel College, Cambridge, in 1705, becoming a fellow in 1711. Unable to subscribe to the oath of allegiance to **George I**, he forfeited his fellowship. About 1727 he became tutor to the father of **Edward Gibbon**, and for ten years was 'the much-honoured friend and spiritual director of the whole family'. The elder Gibbon died in 1737, and three years later Law retired to Kingscliffe. About 1733 he had begun to study **Jakob Böhme**, and most of his later books are expositions of his mysticism. Law won his first triumphs against controversy with his *Three Letters* (1717). His *Remarks on Mandeville's Fable of the Bees* (1723) is a masterpiece of caustic wit. Only less admirable is the *Case of Reason* (1732), in answer to **Tindal** the Deist. But his most famous work remains the *Serious Call to a Devout and Holy Life* (1729), which profoundly influenced Dr **Johnson** and the **Wesleys**.

LAWES, Henry (1596–1662) English composer, born in Dinton, Wiltshire. He set **Milton**'s *Comus* to music and also **Robert Herrick**'s verses. Highly regarded by Milton, who sang his praises in a sonnet, his adaptation of music to verse and rhythm was masterly. His half-brother, William (d.1645), was also a composer, one of **Charles I**'s court musicians; he was killed at Chester during the Civil War.

LAWES, Sir John Bennet (1814–1900) English agriculturist, born in Rothamsted, St Albans. He carried out a long series of experiments with plants and then with crops on his estate there, and from these grew the artificial fertilizer industry. For the manufacture of his 'super-phosphates' he set up a factory at Deptford Creek in 1842. Even more important than this commercial enterprise were his purely scientific researches into agriculture. With him, aided by his partner Sir **Henry Gilbert**, agriculture became a science and the Rothamsted Experimental Station which he founded in 1843, is world famous.

LAWLER, Ray (1911–) Australian playwright, born in Melbourne. He was a factory-hand at the age of 13 but soon gravitated to the stage. His *Summer of the Seventeenth Doll*, a play of the 'outback', with its down-to-earth realism and with Lawler himself in a leading role, brought him fame outside Australia.

LAWRENCE, St (Laurentius) (d.258) Christian Martyr, said to have been born in Huesca in Spain. He became a deacon at Rome. In the persecution of **Valerianus** he was condemned to be broiled. His feast day is 10 August.

LAWRENCE, D H (David Herbert) (1885–1930) English novelist, poet and essayist, born in Eastwood, Nottinghamshire, the son of a miner. With tubercular tendencies, of which he eventually died, he became, through his mother's devotion, a schoolmaster and began to write, encouraged by the notice taken of his work by **Ford Madox Ford** and **Edward Garnett**. In 1911, after the success of his first novel, *The White Peacock*, he decided to live by writing. In 1912 he eloped with Frieda von Richthofen, a cousin of the German war ace Baron **Mannfred von Richthofen** and wife of Ernest Weekley, a professor at Nottingham University. They travelled in Germany, Austria and Italy from 1912 to 1913, and married in 1914 after her divorce. Lawrence had made his reputation with the semi-autobiographical *Sons and Lovers* (1913). They returned to England at the outbreak of World War I and lived in an atmosphere of suspicion and persecution in a cottage in Cornwall. In 1915 he published *The Rainbow*, an exploration of marital and sexual relations, and was horrified to find himself prosecuted for obscenity. He left England in 1919, and after three years' residence in Italy, where he produced another exploration of sex and marriage, *Women in Love* (1921), he went to America, settling in Mexico until the progress of his disease drove him back to Italy where his last years were spent. His sensitive spirit was again shocked by his further prosecutions for obscenity over the private publication in Florence of *Lady Chatterley's Lover* in 1928 and over an exhibition of his paintings in London in 1929. *Lady Chatterley's Lover* was not published in the UK in unexpurgated form until after a sensational obscenity trial in 1961. Opinion is still divided over Lawrence's worth as a writer but there can be no doubt about his effect on the younger intellectuals of his period. He challenged them by his attempt to interpret human emotion on a deeper level of consciousness than that handled by his contemporaries. This provoked either sharp criticism or an almost idolatrous respect. His descriptive passages are sometimes superb, but he had little humour, and this occasionally produced unintentionally comic effects. His finest writing occurs in his poems, where all but essentials have been pared away, but most of his novels have an enduring strength. His other major novels include *Aaron's Rod* (1922), *Kangaroo* (1923, reflecting a visit to Australia) and *The Plumed Serpent* (1926, set in Mexico). His collected poems were published in 1928.

LAWRENCE, Ernest Orlando (1901–58) American physicist, born in Canton, South Dakota. A graduate of South Dakota, Minnesota and Yale, in 1929 he constructed the first cyclotron for the production of artificial radioactivity, fundamental to the development of the atomic bomb. He was professor at Berkeley, California, from 1930, and in 1936 was appointed first director of the radiation laboratory there. He was awarded the Nobel prize for physics in 1939.

LAWRENCE, Geoffrey, 3rd Baron Trevithin and **1st Baron Oaksey** (1880–1971) English lawyer. He graduated at Oxford and was called to the bar in 1906. He became a judge of the high court of justice (King's Bench Division) in 1932, a lord justice of appeal in 1944 and was a lord of appeal in ordinary 1947–57. He was president of the International Tribunal for the trial of war criminals at Nuremberg in 1945 and was distinguished for his fair and impartial conduct of the proceedings. Created Baron Oaksey in 1947, he succeeded his brother in the title of Trevithin in 1959.

LAWRENCE, Sir Henry Montgomery (1806–57) English soldier and colonial administrator, born in Matara, Ceylon. Educated at Derry, Bristol and Addiscombe, in 1823 he joined the Bengal Artillery. He took part in the first Burmese war (1828), in the first Afghan war (1838), and in the Sikh Wars (1845 and 1848). In 1856 he pointed out the danger of reducing the British army, and the latent germs of rebellion. In 1857 he was appointed to Lucknow, and did all he could to restore contentment there, but the Indian Mutiny broke out in May. It was owing to his foresight that it was made possible for a thousand Europeans and eight hundred Indians to defend the Residency for nearly four months against 7000 rebels. He was mortally injured by a shell.

LAWRENCE, John Laird Mair, 1st Baron (1811–79) English administrator, brother of Sir **Henry Lawrence**, born in Richmond, Yorkshire. In 1827 he obtained a presentation to Haileybury College. His first years in the Indian civil service were spent at Delhi. Successively commissioner and lieutenant-governor of the Punjab, he used every effort to curb the oppression of the people by their chiefs, devised a system of land tenure, and devoted his whole energy to restoring peace and prosperity. The once restless Sikhs had become so attached to his rule that Lawrence was enabled to disarm the mutineers in the Punjab, to raise an army of 59000 men, and to capture Delhi from the rebels after a siege of over three months. In 1863 he succeeded Lord **Elgin** as governor-general of India. He did not believe in British interference in Asia beyond the frontier of India, and was especially opposed to intriguing in Afghanistan. Created Baron Lawrence on his return home in 1869, he was chairman of the London School Board, 1870–73. He devoted the last days of his life in parliament (1878) to an exposure of the policy which led up to the disastrous Afghan war.

LAWRENCE, Marjorie Florence (1908–79) Australian operatic soprano, born in Deans Marsh, Victoria. She won a singing competition in nearby Geelong in 1928, and her parents were persuaded by the operatic singer **John Brownlee** to let her study overseas. She made her operatic début in 1932 with the Monte Carlo Opera, and the following year appeared in Paris. She became a member of the Metropolitan Opera, New York, in 1935 where for four years she was a leading Wagnerian soprano. In 1941, while touring in Mexico, she contracted poliomyelitis. Returning to the USA she was treated there by Sister **Elizabeth Kenny**, and by the end of the following year was making guest appearances at 'The Met' in a wheelchair. During World War II she travelled extensively to entertain the troops, including visits to the Pacific and to Europe. Her autobiography was filmed as *Interrupted Melody*. Later she took up teaching at the University of Southern Illinois.

LAWRENCE, T E (Thomas Edward) known as **'Lawrence of Arabia'** (1888–1935) Anglo-Irish soldier and Arabist, born in Tremadoc, Caernarvonshire, in North Wales and brought up in Oxford. Educated at Oxford City High School and Jesus College, Oxford, he became a junior member of the British Museum archaeological team under Sir **Flinders Petrie** at Carchemish, on the Euphrates (1911–14) and thus made his first intimate acquaintance with the desert dwellers. In World War I he worked for army intelligence in North Africa (1914–16); in 1916 he joined the Arab revolt against the Turks. Operating in command of the levies of the Emir Faisal (later **Faisal I**), he co-operated with General **Allenby**'s triumphal advance and entered Damascus in October 1918. As a delegate to the Peace Conference and, later, as adviser on Arab affairs to the Colonial Office (1921–22), his inability to secure all he had set out to achieve for the Arab cause he had espoused led to his withdrawal from what he termed 'the shallow grave of public duty'. He turned his back on his legendary fame in 1922 and joined the RAF as an aircraftman under the assumed name of 'John Hume Ross'. When his identity was discovered he joined the Royal Tank Corps in 1923 as 'T E Shaw'. In 1925 he transferred back to the RAF. He was discharged in 1935, and was killed in a motorcycling accident in Dorset. His major works were *The Seven Pillars of Wisdom* (for private circulation, 1926), *Revolt in the Desert* (1927), *Crusader Castles* (1936), *Oriental Assembly* (1929) and *The Mint* (1955).

LAWRENCE, Sir Thomas (1769–1830) English painter, born in Bristol, the son of an innkeeper. As a child he was famed for his portraits and at the age of twelve he had his own studio in Bath. His full-length portrait of Queen **Charlotte**, now in the National Gallery, which he painted at the age of twenty, was remarkable for its maturity and is one of his best works. In 1792 he was appointed limner to **George III** and in 1820 he succeeded **Benjamin West** as president of the Royal Academy. He was buried in St Paul's. Lawrence was the favourite portrait painter of his time, and had an immense European practice.

LAWRY, William Morris (1937–) Australian cricketer, born in Melbourne. He made a reputation as a studious left-handed batsman who was difficult to dislodge, and as a wary captain. He took part in several mammoth stands, notably one of 382 with **R B Simpson** at Bridgetown in 1964–65; but his value was most often seen in adversity, as when he scored 60 not out in Australia's meagre total of 116 against England in 1970–71. In all he played 67 times for Australia, scoring 5234 runs and recording 13 centuries.

LAWSON, Henry Hertzberg (1867–1922) Australian writer, born in New South Wales of Scandinavian ancestry. He published short stories and narrative verse of the Australian scene, collected in *Short Stories in Prose and Verse* (1894) and *While the Billy Boils* (1896).

LAWSON, Nigel (1932–) English Conservative politician, educated at Westminster and Christ Church College, Oxford, where he graduated with 1st class honours. He embarked on a journalistic career after completing Royal Navy national service (1954–56). From *The Financial Times* he moved to the *Daily Telegraph*, where he was city editor, and then gradually entered politics, unsuccessfully fighting the Slough seat for the Conservatives in 1970 and then becoming MP for Blaby, Leicestershire, in 1974. **Margaret Thatcher** appointed him financial secretary to the Treasury in 1979, from where he rose to energy secretary (1981–83) and Chancellor of the Exchequer in 1983, from which post he dramatically resigned in 1989.

LAWTON, Tommy (1919–) English footballer, born in Lancashire. Tall, rangy, and a fine header of the ball, he epitomized the ideal English centre-forward. His most famous days were with Everton and Arsenal but he also served Burnley, Chelsea, Notts County and Brentford. Like most of his generation he lost almost seven years to World War II, otherwise his full international record would have been even more remarkable than his 22 goals in 23 matches.

LAXNESS, Halldór, pseud of **Halldór Guðjónsson** (1902–) Icelandic novelist, born in Reykjavík, winner of the Nobel prize for literature in 1955. Brought up on the farm of Laxnes, near Reykjavík, he travelled widely to seek experience. After World War I he steeped himself in Expressionism in Germany, Catholicism in a monastery in Luxembourg, and Surrealism in France, before going to Canada and the USA (1927–30), where he was converted to Socialism. In his fiction he explored the reality of Iceland, past and present, and rejuvenated Icelandic prose, in a series of incomparable epic novels like *Salka Valka* (1931–32), *Sjálfstætt fólk* (1934–35, trans *Independent People*), *Heimsljós* (1937–40, *World Light*), and *Íslandsklukkan* (1943–49, *Iceland's Bell*). After World War II he continued to turn out a stream of brilliantly executed novels on Icelandic life: *Atómstöðin* (1948, *The Atom Station*), *Gerpla* (1952, *The Happy Warriors*), *Brekkukotsannáll* (1957, *The Fish Can Sing*), *Paradisarheimt* (1960, *Paradise Reclaimed*), and *Kristnihald undir Jökli* (1968, *Christianity at Glacier*). He has also written a number of plays, and adapted some of his own novels for the stage.

LAYAMON (fl. early 13th century) English poet and priest at Ernley (now Areley Regis), on the Severn near Bewdley. In c.1200 he wrote an alliterative verse chronicle, the *Brut*, a history of England which was an amplified imitation of **Wace**'s *Brut d'Angleterre*. It is important in the history of English versification as the first poem written in Middle English.

LAYARD, Sir Austen Henry (1817–94) English archaeologist and politician, born in Paris. In 1845–47 and 1849–51 he excavated at Nimrud, near Mosul in Iraq, identifying it as the ancient city of Nineveh and finding the remains of four palaces of the 7th–9th centuries BC. He brought several large sculptures to London in 1848, and wrote books on Assyrian civilization. He became an MP in 1852, under-secretary of foreign affairs (1861–66), chief commissioner of works (1868–69), and British ambassador in Spain (1869) and Istanbul (1877–80).

LAZARSFELD, Paul Felix (1901–76) Austrian-born American sociologist, born in Vienna. After studying mathematics and law at Vienna University, he taught mathematics and physics in a Viennese secondary school. He also taught statistics in the university department of psychology, and in 1927 he set up a social psychology research centre at the university. In 1933 the Rockefeller Foundation awarded him a scholarship to the USA, where he settled, working first at Newark University, then at Princeton. In 1940 he joined the department of sociology at Columbia, where in 1945 he established the Bureau of Applied Social Research. He retired in 1969. It is as a quantitative methodologist that his influence has been greatest, but he also wrote about popular culture in mass communications, political sociology and applied sociology.

LAZARUS, Emma (1849–87) American poet and essayist, born in New York. She published striking volumes of poems and translations, including *Admetus and other poems* (1871), *Songs of a Semite* (1882) and *By the Waters of Babylon* (1887). She also wrote a prose romance, *Alide: An Episode of Goethe's Life* (1874), and a verse tragedy, *The Spagnaletto* (1876). A champion of oppressed Jewry, she is best known for her sonnet, 'The New Colossus' (1883), inscribed on the Statue of Liberty in New York harbour.

LEACH, Bernard Howell (1887–1979) English potter, born in Hong Kong, the leading figure in the development of Studio Pottery in Britain. He studied at the Slade School of Art and returned to Japan at the age of 21 to teach. He soon found the urge to study pottery and became the sole pupil of Ogata Kenzan. He returned to England with his family in 1920 and, together with **Shoji Hamada**, established the pottery at St Ives in Cornwall. He produced stoneware and raku-ware using local materials and also turned to the 17th century as inspiration to produce English slipware. One of his aims was to provide sound hand-made pots sufficiently inexpensive for people of moderate means to take into daily use. From 1922 to 1924 he began to take on student apprentices, among whom were **Michael Cardew** and **Katherine Pleydell-Bouverie**. He had regular exhibitions of his work and began teaching at Dartington Hall, Devon, in 1932. His written works include *A Potter's Book* (1940).

LEACH, Sir Edmund Ronald (1910–89) English social anthropologist. Educated at Marlborough he studied mathematics and engineering at Clare College, Cambridge, then travelled in China before returning to England in 1937 to study anthropology under **Bronislaw Malinowski** at the London School of Economics. Soon after leaving to carry out fieldwork among the Kachin of Burma he was overtaken by World War II, which he spent serving in Burma. After the war he took up a post in anthropology at the London School of Economics (1947–53), and published his first major monograph, *Political Systems of Highland Burma*, in 1954. This overturned orthodox notions of social structural equilibrium, demonstrating the complex and fluctuating relationship between ideal models and political conduct. Leach's attack on structural-functional theory continued with *Pul Eliya* (1961), a study of a village in Ceylon. He was university reader in social anthropology at Cambridge from 1957 to 1972, and professor from 1972 to 1978. In later years his major interest shifted to structuralism. His analyses of myth and ritual, as in *Genesis as Myth and other essays* (1969), were always grounded in the pragmatic context of social and political action. His considerable influence both within and outside anthropology was mainly as a provocative and polemical critic of prevailing orthodoxies. He was Provost of King's College, Cambridge, from 1966 to 1979. His other publications include *Rethinking Anthropology* (1961), *Lévi-Strauss* (1970), *Culture and Communication* (1976), and *Social Anthropology* (1982).

LEACH, William Elford (1790–1836) English naturalist, born in Plymouth. He studied medicine at St Bartholomew's Hospital, London, Edinburgh University and St Andrew's, but turned to zoology and joined the British Museum. As an assistant keeper he collected specimens and published numerous catalogues. He died of cholera on holiday in Italy. Leach's Storm-Petrel is named after him.

LEACOCK, Stephen Butler (1869–1944) English-born Canadian humorist and economist, born in Swanmore, Hampshire. Educated at the University of Toronto, he became first a teacher, later a lecturer at McGill University, and in 1908 head of the economics department there. He wrote several books on his subject, including *Elements of Political Science* (1906), *Practical Political Economy* (1910) and *The Economic Prosperity of the British Empire* (1931). But it is as a humorist that he became widely known. Among his popular short stories, essays and parodies are *Literary Lapses* (1910), *Nonsense Novels* (1911), *Behind the Beyond* (1913), *Winsome Winnie* (1920) and *The Garden of Folly* (1924). He also wrote biographies of **Mark Twain** (1932) and **Dickens** (1933). *The Boy I Left Behind Me*, an autobiography, appeared in 1946.

LEADE, Jane, née **Ward** See **BOHME, Jakob**

LEAKE, William Martin (1777–1860) English antiquarian topographer of Greece, born in London. Joining the army in 1794, he served in Turkey and other parts of the Levant. He helped in the survey of the valley of the Nile and retired from the army with the rank of lieutenant-colonel in 1823. He presented his collections to the British Museum, and wrote learned works on Greece and Greek antiquities, including *Topography of Athens* (1821) and *Numismata Hellenica* (1854).

LEAKEY, Louis Seymour Bazett (1903–72) African-born British archaeologist and physical anthropologist, born in Kabete, Kenya, of missionary parents, where he grew up with the Kikuyu tribe. Educated at Weymouth College and St John's College, Cambridge, he took part in several archaeological expeditions in East Africa, made a study of the Kikuyu and wrote widely on African anthropology. He was curator of the Coryndon Memorial Museum at Nairobi (1945–61). His great discoveries of early hominid fossils took place at Olduvai Gorge in East Africa, where in 1959, together with his wife **Mary Leakey**, he unearthed the skull of *Zinjanthropus*, subsequently reclassified as *Australopithecus robustus* and now thought to be about 1.7 million years old. In 1964 he found remains of *Homo habilis*, a smaller species some 2 million years old, which led him to postulate the simultaneous evolution of two different species, of which *Homo habilis* was the true ancestor of man, while *Australopithecus* became extinct; in 1967 he discovered *Kenyapithecus africanus*, fossilized remains of a Miocene ape, c.14 million years old. He also unearthed evidence of human habitation in California more than 50000 years old.

LEAKEY, Mary Douglas, née **Nicol** (1913–) English archaeologist, born in London, and wife of **Louis Leakey**, whose excavations and fossil finds in East Africa revolutionized ideas about human origins. Her interest in prehistory was roused during childhood trips to south-west France where she collected stone tools and visited the painted caves around Les Eyzies. She met Leakey while preparing drawings for his book *Adam's Ancestors* (1934), became his second wife in 1936, and moved shortly afterwards to Kenya where she undertook pioneer archaeological research (1937–42) at sites such as Olorgesailie and Rusinga Island. In 1948, at Rusinga, in Lake Victoria, she discovered *Proconsul africanus*, a 1.7 million-year-old dryopithecine (primitive ape) that brought the Leakeys international attention and financial sponsorship for the first time. From 1951 she worked at Olduvai Gorge in Tanzania, initially on a modest scale, but more extensively from 1959 when her discovery of the 1.75 million-year-old hominid *Zinjanthropus* (*Australopithecus boisei*), filmed as it happened, captured the public imagination and drew vastly increased funding. *Homo habilis*, a new species contemporary with, but more advanced than, *Zinjanthropus* was found in 1960 and published amidst much controversy in 1964. Perhaps most remarkable of all was her excavation in 1976 at Laetoli, 30 miles south of Olduvai, of three trails of fossilized hominid footprints which demonstrated unequivocally that our ancestors already walked upright 3.6 million years ago. Her books include *Olduvai Gorge: My Search for Early Man* (1979) and an autobiography, *Disclosing the Past* (1984).

LEAKEY, Richard Erskine Frere (1944–) Kenyan palaeoanthropologist, second son of **Louis** and **Mary Leakey**, born and educated in Nairobi. From an early age he worked in the field with his parents, finding his first fossil bone at the age of six. He left school at 16 and trapped animals for zoos, collected animal skeletons for zoologists, and ran a safari company before organizing his first research expedition, to Peninj on Lake Natron (1964), Lake Baringo (1966), and the Omo valley in Ethiopia (1967). From 1969 to 1975 he worked with the archaeologist Glynn Isaac at Koobi Fora, part of a vast fossil site covering 500 square miles on the eastern shores of Lake Turkana, discovering well-preserved hominid remains that drew worldwide publicity. Of particular note are crania of *Australopithecus boisei* (KNM-ER 406/7, found 1969), of *Homo habilis* dated 1.9 million years (KNM-ER 1470, found 1972), and of *Homo erectus* dated 1.5 million years (KNM-ER 3733, found 1975). He was appointed administrative director of the National Museum of Kenya in 1968 (director in 1974). His publications include *Origins* (1977) and *The Making of Mankind* (1981), both with Roger Lewin, and an autobiography stimulated by the kidney transplant he underwent in 1979, *One Life* (1983).

LEAN, Sir David (1908–) English film director, born in Croydon. Beginning as a clapperboard boy, he gradually progressed within the industry from camera assistant to assistant editor to editor. He was an editor for *Gaumont Sound News* (1930) and *British Movietone News* (1931–32) before moving on to fictional features like *Escape Me Never* (1936) and

Pygmalion (1938). His co-direction, with **Noël Coward**, of *In Which We Serve* (1942), and *Blithe Spirit* (1945), led to a full-scale directorial career in which his craftsmanship and compositional acumen have been combined with a strong sense of narrative in films like *Brief Encounter* (1945), *Great Expectations* (1946) and *Oliver Twist* (1948). Increasingly drawn towards works of an epic and grandiose scale, he won Academy Awards for *Bridge on the River Kwai* (1957) and *Lawrence of Arabia* (1962). In 1965 he made *Dr. Zhivago*, followed by *Ryan's Daughter* (1970). His sparse output has been attributed to exacting artistic standards and *A Passage to India* (1984) marked his first film in 14 years.

LEANDER, St (d.c.600) Spanish prelate, elder brother of **Isidore of Seville** and his predecessor as archbishop of Seville (c.577–c.600). A friend of Pope **Gregory I the Great**, he laid the foundations of church organization in Spain, and converted the Visigoths from Arianism.

LEAR, Edward (1812–88) English artist, humorist and traveller, born in London. In 1832 he was engaged by the 13th Earl of Derby to make coloured drawings of the rare birds and animals in the menagerie at Knowsley Hall (Merseyside). Under the earl's patronage he travelled widely in Italy and Greece, making landscape sketches and oil paintings which he published in several travel books, including *Sketches of Rome* (1842) and *Illustrated Excursions in Italy* (1846). He became a friend of his patron's grandchildren, whom he entertained with nonsense limericks and other verse which he illustrated with his own sketches and first published (anonymously) as *A Book of Nonsense* in 1846. Later he published *Nonsense Songs, Stories, Botany, and Alphabets* (1870), *More Nonsense Rhymes* (1871), and *Laughable Lyrics* (1876). He spent most of his latter years in Italy.

LEAR, William Powell (1902–78) American inventor and electronic engineer, born in Hannibal, Missouri. He joined the US navy at 16 and studied radio and electronics. His inventive genius resulted in more than 150 patents in the fields of radio, electronics, aviation and automobile engineering, including the first practical car radio, the first commercial radio compass for aircraft, and an automatic pilot for jet aircraft. In 1962 he founded Lear Jet Corp. which developed and became the largest manufacturer of small private jet planes; another, Lear Motors Corp. (1967) tried unsuccessfully to introduce steam-powered cars and buses.

LEARMONT, Thomas See **THOMAS THE RHYMER**

LEAVIS, Frank Raymond (1895–1978) English literary critic. He fought against literary dilettantism in the quarterly, *Scrutiny* (1932–53), which he founded and edited, as well as in his *New Bearings in English Poetry* (1932). From 1936 to 1962 he was a fellow of Downing College, Cambridge. His sociological study, *Culture and Environment* (1933; with D Thomson), deploring the separation of culture and environment in modern times and stressing the importance of impressing critical standards upon the young, has become a classic. Other works include *Revaluation* (1936), *The Great Tradition* (1948), *The Common Pursuit* (1952), *D H Lawrence* (1955), *Two Cultures?* (1962), in which he challenged the theories of **C P Snow** on literature and science, *Anna Karenina and Other Essays* (1967) and *Dickens the Novelist* (1970). His wife, Queenie Dorothy (1906–81), was a scholar in her own right as well as a collaborator in much of her husband's work, and published, among other works, *Fiction and the Reading Public* in 1932.

LEAVITT, Henrietta Swan (1868–1921) American astronomer, born in Lancaster, Massachusetts. She discovered the period-luminosity relationship of Cepheid variable stars. The daughter of a Congregational Minister, she attended Radcliffe College where she gained an interest in astronomy. She became a volunteer research assistant at Harvard College Observatory and joined the staff there in 1902, quickly becoming head of the department of photographic photometry. Like **Annie Cannon**, her colleague, she was very deaf. Whilst studying Cepheid variable stars she noticed that the brighter they were the longer their period of light variation. By 1912 she had succeeded in showing that the apparent magnitude decreased linearly with the logarithm of the period. This simple relationship proved invaluable as the basis for a method of measuring the distance of stars.

LEBEDEV, Pëtr Nikolajevich (1866–1912) Russian physicist, born in Moscow. He studied at Strasbourg and became professor of physics at Moscow (1900–12). He proved that light exerts a pressure on bodies, and investigated the earth's magnetism.

LE BEL, Joseph Achille (1847–1930) French chemist, born in Pechelbronn, Alsace, one of the founders of stereochemistry. His family owned an oil well and refinery at Pechelbronn. He was educated at the École Polytechnique before managing the family business for some years. He then sold his share of the oil business and studied chemistry at the Sorbonne. He held no academic post but became an industrial consultant, and continued research on his private estate. In 1874 he published his account of the asymmetric carbon atom (a carbon atom bound to four different groups, and resulting in a molecule capable of existing in two forms, related as object and mirror image) two months after **van't Hoff**'s identical but independent work was published, giving van't Hoff the priority in this fundamental stereochemical concept.

LEBESGUE, Henri (Léon) (1875–1941) French mathematician, born in Beauvais. He studied at the École Normale Supérieure, and taught at Rennes, Poitiers, the Sorbonne and the Collège de France. Following the work of **Émile Borel** and René Baire (1874–1932), he developed the theory of measure and integration which bears his name, and applied it to many problems of analysis, in particular to the theory of **Fourier** series. Overcoming the defects of the **Riemann** integral, this theory has proved indispensable in all subsequent modern analysis.

LEBLANC, Nicolas (1742–1806) French industrial chemist and physician, born in Issoudun, and a founder of the modern chemical industry based on salt. He trained as a physician and became surgeon to the future Duc **d'Orléans (Phillippe Égalité)** in 1780. Soda ash, which was essential for the industries of the late 18th century, was made from wood, seaweed etc, which was in short supply and expensive to transport. The duke was interested in chemistry, and probably through him Leblanc learned that the French Academy of Sciences offered a prize in 1775 for a new process for making soda (sodium carbonate). He devised a cheap, simple process, based on salt and sulphuric acid, but never received the prize. In 1791 he was granted a patent for his invention, and with finance from the Duc d'Orléans built a factory for its production. The duke was guillotined in 1793 and the factory confiscated. When the factory was returned to Leblanc in 1802 by **Napoleon**, he had no money to continue, and committed suicide. Leblanc's process was operated on a large scale for a century, despite its environmental offensiveness. Soda is essential for making glass, soap, and many chemicals; it is now made by the method due to **Ernest Solvay**.

LEBRUN, Albert (1871–1950) French statesman, born in Mercy-le-Haut (Meurthe-et-Moselle). He studied mining engineering, became a deputy (Left Republican) in 1900, was minister for the colonies (1911–14), for blockade and liberated regions (1917–19), senator (1920), and president of the Senate (1931). The last president of the Third Republic, he surrendered his powers to **Pétain** in 1940, and went into retirement from which he did not re-emerge, although consulted by General **de Gaulle** in 1944. His health was affected by a period of internment after arrest by the Gestapo in 1943.

LE BRUN, Charles (1619–90) French historical painter, born in Paris. He studied in Rome for four years under **Poussin**, and for nearly 40 years (1647–83) exercised a despotic influence over French art and artists, being usually considered the founder of the French school of painting. He helped to found the Academy of Painting and Sculpture in 1648 and was the first director of the Gobelins tapestry works (1662). From 1668 to 1683 he was employed by **Louis XIV** in the decoration of Versailles.

LE CARRÉ, John, pseud **of David John Moore Cornwell** (1931–) English novelist, born in Poole, Dorset. He was educated at Sherborne School, Berne University, and, after military service in Austria, at Oxford. He taught French and German for two years at Eton before going into the British Foreign Service as second secretary in Bonn, and consul in Hamburg, from which post he resigned in 1964 to become a full-time writer. His novels present the unglamorous side of diplomacy and espionage, a world of boredom, squalor and shabby deceit in complete contrast to the popular spy fiction of **Ian Fleming**. His settings and characters have a compelling authenticity and he questions the morality of present-day diplomacy and traditional patriotic attitudes. His first published novel, *Call for The Dead* (1961) introduced his 'anti-hero' George Smiley, who appears in most of his stories. *A Murder of Quality* appeared in 1962, followed the next year by the very successful *The Spy Who Came In From The Cold*. After *The Looking-Glass War* (1965) and *A Small Town in Germany* (1968), a departure from his usual subject and style entitled *A Naive and Sentimental Lover* (1971) was not well received, and he returned to his former world with *Tinker, Tailor, Soldier, Spy* (1974), *The Honourable Schoolboy* (1977), *Smiley's People* (1980), *The Little Drummer Girl* (1983), and *A Perfect Spy* (1986). Many of his novels have been successfully filmed or televised.

LE CHATELIER, Henry See **CHATELIER**

LECKY, William Edward Hartpole (1838–1903) Irish historian and philosopher, born near Dublin. Educated at Trinity College, Dublin, in 1861 he published anonymously *The Leaders of Public Opinion in Ireland*, four brilliant essays on **Swift**, **Flood**, **Grattan** and **O'Connell**. One of the greatest and most unbiased historians, his works include *History of Rationalism* (1865), *History of England in the 18th Century* (1878–90), *Democracy and Liberty* (1896) and *The Map of Life* (1899). A decided Unionist but having a real sympathy with Irish problems, he became MP for Dublin University in 1895, and a privy councillor in 1897.

LECLAIR, Jean Marie (1697–1764) French composer and violinist, born in Lyon. He wrote many fine sonatas for the violin, and also the opera *Scylla et Glaucus* (1746). He was murdered in a suburb of Paris.

LECLANCHÉ, Georges (1839–82) French chemist, born in Paris. An engineer by training, he is remembered for the galvanic cell invented by him and given his name.

LE CLERC, Jean, or **Johannes Clericus** (1657–1736) Swiss theologian and Biblical scholar, born in Geneva. A champion of Arminianism, in 1684 he became professor of philosophy in the Remonstrant seminary at Amsterdam. He wrote over 70 works and revealed what were then startling opinions on the authorship of the Pentateuch and on inspiration generally. His Bible commentaries were completed in 1731. Serial publications were *Bibliothèque universelle et historique* (25 vols, 1686–93), *Bibliothèque choisie* (28 vols, 1703–13), and *Bibliothèque ancienne et moderne* (29 vols, 1714–26).

LE CLERC (de HAUTECLOCQUE), Jacques Philippe (1902–47) French soldier, born into an aristocratic family. He graduated from St Cyr (1924) and served in Morocco before returning as an instructor. In World War II he served with the French army in France (1939–40), was captured twice during the German invasion, but escaped on both occasions, and joined the Free French forces under **Charles De Gaulle** in England. He became military commander in French Equatorial Africa, and led a force across the desert to join the British 8th Army, in 1942. He commanded the French 2nd Armoured Division in Normandy, and received the surrender of Paris in 1944.

LÉCLUSE, Charles de (1525–1609) French botanist known as 'Carolus Clusius', born in Arras. He travelled in Spain, England, Hungary, and the New World, and from 1593 was a professor at Leiden. He published *Rariorum plantarium historia* (1601).

LECOCQ, Alexandre Charles (1832–1918) French composer of comic operas, born in Paris. He studied at the Paris Conservatoire (1849–54), where he took many prizes, and won a reputation as an excellent organist. His many operettas, in the style of **Offenbach**, include *Le Docteur Miracle* (1857), *Giroflé-Girofla* (1874) and *L'Égyptienne* (1890), but although he dominated the French stage in this genre, his more serious music was never appreciated.

LECONTE DE LISLE, Charles Marie (1818–94) French poet, born in Réunion. After some years of travel he settled down to a literary life in Paris. He exercised a profound influence on all the younger poets, headed the school called *Parnassiens*, and succeeded to **Victor Hugo**'s chair at the Academy in 1886. His early poems appeared as *Poésies complètes* (1858). Other volumes are *Poèmes barbares* (1862) and *Poèmes tragiques* (1884); and he translated many classics. His verse is marked by regularity and faultlessness of form.

LECOQ, Jacques (1921–) French mime artist, teacher and director, born in Paris. He began in 1945 as an actor with the Compagnie des Comédiens in Grenoble, becoming responsible for the group's physical training. In 1948, he joined the Padua University Theatre, Italy, as a teacher and director, where he produced his first pantomimes. He became a member of the Piccolo Theatre in Milan in 1951. In 1956 he returned to Paris and established his own school: the École Internationale de Mime et de Théâtre. He formed his own company in 1959, and began his research into the various theatrical disciplines of the clown, the buffoon, commedia, tragedy and melodrama, in terms of the actor's physical movement on the stage.

LE CORBUSIER, pseud of **Charles Édouard Jeanneret** (1887–1965) Swiss-born French architect, born in La Chaux-de-Fonds. After working in Paris with the architect **Auguste Perret**, he associated with **Peter Behrens** in Germany (1910–11). In 1919 he published in Paris (with **Amédée Ozenfant**) the Purist manifesto and began to work on his theory of the interrelation between modern machine forms and the techniques of contemporary architecture. His books, *Vers une architecture* (1923), *Le Modulor* (1948) and *Le Modulor 2* (1955), have had worldwide influence on town planning and building design. His first building, based on the technique of the Modulor (a system using standard-sized units, the proportions of which are calculated according to those of the human figure), was the *Unité d'habitation*, Marseilles (1945–50), which was conceived as one of a number of tall buildings which, when the overall scheme ('la Ville radieuse') had been completed, would form a pattern projecting from the 'carpet' of low buildings and open spaces. This was his favourite type of town-planning concept, used again in designing Chandigarh, the new capital of the Punjab. Some of his buildings are raised on stilts or *piloti*, an innovation first used by him in the Swiss Pavilion in the Cité Universitaire in Paris. In the 1920s, in collaboration with Charlotte Perriand, he designed furniture, especially chairs, which used tubular metal in their construction.

LECOUVREUR, Adrienne (1692–1730) French actress, born near Chalons. She made her début at the Comédie Française in 1717, and soon became famous for her acting, and her admirers, amongst whom were Marshal **de Saxe**, **Voltaire** and Lord **Peterborough**. Some ascribed her death to poisoning by a rival, the Duchesse de Bouillon. This is the plot of the play by **Scribe** and Legouvé.

LEDERBERG, Joshua (1925–) American biologist and geneticist, born in New York, and joint winner of the 1958 Nobel prize for physiology or medicine. He studied biology at Columbia and became professor at Wisconsin (1947–59) and Stanford (1959–78), and president of Rockefeller University from 1978. With **Edward Tatum** he demonstrated that bacteria can reproduce by a sexual process, thus founding the science of bacterial genetics. He also discovered the process of transduction for the transmission of genes, allowing the possibility of genetic engineering. He shared the Nobel prize with Tatum and **George Beadle**.

LEDOUX, Claude Nicolas (1736–1806) French architect, one of the great artists of neo-classicism. As architect to **Louis XVI**, his major works include the Château at Louveciennes for Madame **du Barry** (1771–73), acclaimed by **Fragnonard**. The Saltworks at Arc-et-Senans (1775–80) expressed his **Rousseau**-inspired philosophy that human happiness is found in the rational exploitation of nature and the healthy organization of labour. His theatre at Bresançon (1771–73) also reflects the social order. In 1785 he was employed by the Fermes-Général to erect 60 tax buildings around Paris; of the few that were built, La Vilette, a rotunda, is the best. In 1804 he published *L'Architecture Considérée sous le rapport de l'art des mœurs et de Législation.*

LEDRU-ROLLIN, Alexandre Auguste (1807–74) French politician, born in Fontenay. Admitted to the bar in 1830, he made a name as defender of Republicans and as a democratic agitator. In 1841 he was elected deputy for Le Mans, and visited Ireland during **O'Connell**'s agitation. His *Appel aux travailleurs* (1846) declared universal suffrage the panacea for the miseries of the working classes. At the Revolution of 1848 he became minister of the interior in the provisional government, and in May was elected one of the interim government. But he gave offence by his arbitrary conduct, and resigned. As candidate for the presidency against Louis Napoleon (**Napoleon III**) he was beaten, and an unsuccessful attempt to provoke an insurrection in June 1849 drove him to England. He was amnestied in 1870, and after his return was elected to the Assembly.

LE DUC THO, (Phan Dinh Khai) (1911–) Vietnamese politician, born in Ninh Province. He joined the Communist party of Indo-China in 1929 and was exiled to Con Dia by the French in 1930. Released in 1937, he became head of the Nam Dinh revolutionary movement but was re-arrested and imprisoned (1939–44). After World War II, he worked for the Communist party of Vietnam (CPV), entering its politburo in 1955. For his actions as leader of the Vietnamese delegation to the Paris Conference on Indo-China (1968–73), he was awarded the 1973 Nobel peace prize, jointly with **Henry Kissinger**, but declined to accept it. He retired from the politburo in 1986.

LEE, Ann, known as **Mother Ann** (1736–1884) English-born American mystic, the illiterate daughter of a Manchester blacksmith. In 1762 she married Abraham Stanley, also a blacksmith. In 1758 she had joined the 'Shaking Quakers', or 'Shakers', who saw in her the second coming of Christ. Imprisoned in 1770 for street-preaching, she emigrated with her followers to the USA in 1774, and in 1776 founded at Niskayuna, 7 miles northwest of Albany, New York, the parent Shaker settlement.

LEE, Charles (1731–82) English-born American Revolutionary soldier, born in Dernhall, Cheshire. He went to America in 1793, and joined the Continental army as a major-general at the outbreak of the War of Independence in 1775. Captured by the British in 1776, he proposed to them a secret plan for defeating the Americans. Released in an exchange of prisoners in 1778, his intemperance and incompetence earned his dismissal in 1780.

LEE, Harriet (1757–1851) English novelist, born in London. She wrote with her sister, **Sophia Lee**, *The Canterbury Tales*, one of which was dramatized by Byron and called *Werner, or, The Inheritance*.

LEE, James Paris (1831–1904) Scots-born American inventor, born in Hawick. He emigrated with his parents to Canada, later going from Ontario to Hartford, Connecticut. The Lee-Enfield and Lee-**Metford** rifles are based in part on his designs.

LEE, Jennie, Baroness Lee of Ashridge (1904–88), Scottish Labour politician, born in Lochgelly, Fife, the daughter of a miner. She graduated from Edinburgh University with degrees in education and law and at the age of 24, as a Labour MP for North Lanark, became the youngest member of the House of Commons. A dedicated socialist, she campaigned with great wit and intelligence. In 1934 she married **Aneurin Bevan** and, despite her feminist principles, consciously stepped to one side as he rose within the Labour party. Appointed Britain's first arts minister in 1964, she doubled government funding for the arts and was instrumental in setting up the Open University. She published two autobiographies, *Tomorrow is a New Day* (1939) and *My Life with Nye* (1980).

LEE, Laurie (1914–) English poet and author, born in Slad. He was educated at the village school and in Stroud, Gloucestershire. He worked as a scriptwriter for documentary films during the 1940s and his travels in many parts of the world are the subject of much of his writing. A nature-poet of great simplicity, his works include *The Sun My Monument* (1944), *The Bloom of Candles* (1947), *My Many-Coated Man* (1955). *A Rose For Winter* (1955) describes his travels in Spain, and his three autobiographical books, *Cider With Rosie* (1959), *As I Walked Out One Midsummer Morning* (1969) and *I Can't Stay Long* (1975) are widely acclaimed for their evocation of a rural childhood and of life in the many countries he has visited.

LEE, Nathaniel (1649–92) English dramatist. From Westminster he passed to Trinity College, Cambridge. He failed as an actor through nervousness (1672), produced nine or ten tragedies between 1675 and 1682, and spent five years in Bedlam (1684–89). His best play is *The Rival Queens* (1677). He wrote with **Dryden** two plays, *Oedipus* and *The Duke of Guise*.

LEE, Richard Henry See **LEE, Robert Edward**

LEE, Robert (1804–68) Scottish theologian, born in Tweedmouth. He was educated at Berwick (where he was also for a time a boat-builder) and St Andrews. He was minister of Inverbrothock in 1833, and Campsie in 1836. In 1843 he became minister at Old Greyfriars, Edinburgh, and in 1846 was appointed professor of biblical criticism at Edinburgh University and a Queen's chaplain. In 1857 he began his reform of the Presbyterian church service. He restored the reading of prayers, kneeling at prayer and standing during the singing and in 1863 he introduced a harmonium, in 1865 an organ, into his church. These 'innovations' brought down upon him bitter attacks. His works include a *Handbook of Devotion* (1845) and *Prayers for Public Worship* (1857).

LEE, Robert E (Edward) (1807–70) American soldier, born in Westmoreland County, Virginia, one of the greatest of the Confederate generals in the American Civil War (1861–65). He was fifth in descent from Richard Lee of Shropshire, who emigrated to Virginia in the reign of **Charles I**, received large grants of land between the Potomac and Rappahannock rivers, and built the original Stratford House. In a later house, erected by his grandson, Thomas Lee, were born the distinguished brothers, Richard Henry Lee (1732–1794), mover of the resolution in favour of American Independence and a signer of the Declaration; Francis Lightfoot Lee (1734–1797), a signer of the Declaration; and William Lee (1737–95) and Arthur Lee (1740–92), diplomatists. Robert E was the son of General Henry Lee. At 18 he entered West Point, graduated second in his class in 1829, and received a commission in the engineers. In the Mexican war (1846) he was chief engineer of the central army in Mexico, and at the storming of Chapultepec was severely wounded. From 1852 to 1855 he commanded the US Military Academy, and greatly improved its efficiency. His next service was as a cavalry officer on the Texan border (1855–59). At the **John Brown** raid he was ordered to Harper's Ferry to capture the insurgents. He was in command in Texas in 1860, but was recalled to Washington in March 1861 when seven states had formed the Southern Confederacy. Virginia seceded on 17 April, and Colonel Lee, believing that his allegiance was due to his state, sent in his resignation. Within two days he was made commander-in-chief of the forces of Virginia. At Richmond he superintended the defences of the city till the autumn, when he was sent to oppose General Rosecrans in West Virginia. In the spring of 1862 he was working at the coast defences of Georgia and South Carolina, but on **McClellan**'s advance was summoned to the capital. General **J E Johnston**, chief in command, was wounded at Seven Pines in May, and Lee was put in command of the army around Richmond. His masterly strategy in the seven days' battles around Richmond defeated McClellan's purpose; his battles and strategy in opposing General **Pope**, his invasion of Maryland and Pennsylvania, and other achievements were cardinal to the history of the war. The increasing resources of the North and the decreasing resources of the South could only result in the final success of the former. On 9 April 1865, Lee surrendered his army of 28 231 men to General **Grant** at Appomattox Courthouse, Virginia, and the war was practically ended. After the close of the war he frankly accepted the result, and although deprived of his former property at Arlington on the Potomac, and the White House on the Pamunky, he declined offers of pecuniary aid, and accepted the presidency of what came to be called the Washington and Lee University at Lexington, Virginia. He married in 1832 Mary Randolph Custis (1806–73). Their eldest son, George Washington Custis Lee, resigned as first-lieutenant in the US army in 1861, was aide-de-camp to **Jefferson Davis** (1861–63), major-general of a division in 1864, and successor to his father as president of the Washington and Lee University. William Henry Fitzhugh Lee, his second son, was major-general of Confederate cavalry, and was elected to congress. Captain Robert E Lee of the Confederate cavalry was the third son.

LEE, Sir Sidney (1859–1926) English scholar and critic, born in London. Educated at the City of London School and Balliol College, Oxford, he became assistant editor of the *Dictionary of National Biography* in 1883, editor in 1891, and professor of English at East London College in 1913. He wrote a standard *Life of Shakespeare* (1898) and other works on Shakespeare. He also wrote Lives of Queen **Victoria** (1902) and **Edward VII** (1925–27).

LEE, Sophia (1750–1824) English writer, sister of **Harriet Lee**. She wrote plays and novels, including *The Chapter of Accidents* (1780), the success of which enabled her to open a girls' school in Bath.

LEE, Spike, originally **Shelton Jackson Lee** (1957–) American filmmaker, born in Atlanta, Georgia. He developed an interest in super 8 filmmaking while at Morehouse College (1975–79) and his early amateur efforts include *Last Hustle to Brooklyn* (1977). At New York University's Institute of Film and Television he gained artistic recognition and a student Academy Award for his graduation film *Joe's Bed-Stuy Barbershop: We Cut Heads* (1982). Struggling to support himself, he sank his energies into the low-budget independent feature *She's Gotta Have It* (1986) which established him internationally as a commercially viable young talent of great promise. Declaring that his intention is to express the vast richness of black culture, he has enjoyed continued box-office favour and sparked some controversy with *School Daze* (1988) and *Do The Right Thing* (1989), a blistering assault on racism. An engaging actor in his own productions, he has also directed music videos and assisted in the 1988 presidential campaign of **Jesse Jackson**.

LEE, Tsung-Dao (1926–) Chinese-born American physicist, born in Shanghai. Educated at Kiangsi and at Chekiang University, he won a scholarship to Chicago in 1946, became a lecturer at the University of California, and from 1956 was professor at Columbia University, as well as a member of the Institute for Advanced Study (1960–63). With **Chen Ning Yang** he disproved the parity principle, till then considered a fundamental physical law, and they were awarded the Nobel prize for physics in 1957.

LEE, Vernon, pen name of **Violet Paget** (1856–1935) English aesthetic philosopher, critic and novelist, born in Boulogne of English parentage. She travelled widely in her youth and settled in Florence. Studies of Italian and Renaissance art were followed by her philosophical study, *The Beautiful* (1913), one of the best expositions of the empathy theory of art. She also wrote two novels and a dramatic trilogy, *Satan the Waster* (1920), giving full rein to her pacifism.

LEE KUAN YEW (1923–) Singaporean politician, born in Singapore into a wealthy Chinese family. He studied law at Cambridge and qualified as a barrister in London before returning to Singapore in 1951 to practise. He founded the moderate, anti-communist People's Action party (PAP) in 1954 and entered the Singapore Legislative Assembly in 1955. He became the country's first prime minister in 1959 and has remained in power ever since. He has acquired a reputation for probity and industry and has overseen the implementation of a successful programme of economic development. His son, Brigadier-General Lee Hsien Loong (1952–), is viewed as his possible successor.

LEE TENG-HUI (1923–) Taiwanese politician, born in Tamsui, Taiwan. Educated at universities in the USA and Japan, he taught economics at the National Taiwan University before becoming mayor of Taipei in 1979. A member of the ruling Kuomintang party and a protégé of **Chiang Ching-Kuo**, he became vice president of Taiwan in 1984 and state president and Kuomintang leader on Chiang's death in 1988. The country's first island-born leader, he is a reforming technocrat who has significantly accelerated the pace of liberalization and 'Taiwanization'.

LEECH, John (1817–64) English caricaturist, born in London of Irish descent, the son of a coffee-house proprietor. He was educated at Charterhouse with **Thackeray** (with whom he enjoyed a lifelong friendship) and then studied medicine, but turned to art after publishing, at the age of 18, *Etchings and Sketchings, by A. Pen, Esq.* (1835). From 1841 he contributed hundreds of sketches of middle-class life and political cartoons to *Punch*, and also woodcuts to the *Illustrated London News* (1856) and *Once a Week* (1859–62). He illustrated several books, including **Dickens**' *Christmas Carol* and the sporting novels of **R S Surtees**. He also drew several lithographed series, particularly *Portraits of the Children of the Mobility* (1841). He was buried close to Thackeray at Kensal Green in London.

LEEDS, Thomas Osborne, Duke of (1632–1712) English statesman, better known as the Earl of Danby. He was the son of a Yorkshire baronet. He entered parliament for York in 1661, and in 1667 became a treasury auditor, in 1671 treasurer of the Navy, in 1673 Viscount Latimer and Baron Danby, and in 1674 lord high treasurer and Earl of Danby. He sought to enforce the laws against Roman Catholics and Dissenters, used his influence to get Princess **Mary** married to William of Orange (**William III**) in 1677, and negotiated with **Louis XIV** for bribes to **Charles II**. Louis, however, intrigued for Danby's downfall, and the Commons impeached him in 1678 for treating with foreign powers. He was kept in the Tower until 1684, although Charles at once gave him a full pardon, as the Commons persisted in the impeachment. When **James II** began to threaten the established Church, Danby signed the invitation to William of Orange. His reward was the marquisate of Carmarthen and the presidency of the council, and he resumed his old methods of government. He was created Duke of Leeds in 1694. In 1695, again impeached for accepting 5000 guineas from the East India Company, he staved off condemnation. But his power was gone, and in 1699 he retired.

LEEGHWATER, Jan Adrianszoon (1575–1650) Dutch hydraulic engineer and millwright, born in De Rijp near Amsterdam. He was largely self-educated in many fields including mechanics, building, linguistics and sculpture. In 1608 he contracted to drain the largest lake in the north of the Netherlands, 17000 acres in extent and up to 10 ft in depth. After four years' work he was successful, having made extensive use of multi-stage scoop-wheel water-lifting systems, and thereafter he was involved in many drainage projects in Holland, France, Germany, Denmark and Poland. He also devised a modified type of windmill sail which was better able to cope with sudden changes in the wind direction.

LEESE, Sir Oliver William Hargreaves (1894–1978) English soldier. He won the DSO in World War I, and in 1939 became deputy chief of staff of the British Expeditionary Force in France. In 1942 he was promoted lieutenant-general and commanded an army corps from El Alamein to Sicily, where he succeeded **Montgomery** to the command of the Eighth Army during the Italian campaign. In November 1944 he commanded an army group in Burma. He was appointed lieutenant of the Tower of London in 1954.

LEEUWENHOEK, Anton van (1632–1723) Dutch scientist, born in Delft. A clerk in an Amsterdam cloth warehouse until 1650, he moved to Delft where he became a famous microscopist, conducting a series of epoch-making discoveries in support of the circulation of the blood, and in connection with blood corpuscles, spermatozoa, etc. He first detected the fibres of the crystalline lens, the fibrils and striping of muscle, the structure of ivory and hair, the scales of the epidermis, and the distinctive characters of rotifers.

LE FANU, Joseph Sheridan (1814–73) Irish novelist and journalist, born in Dublin, a grand-nephew of **Richard Sheridan**. Called to the bar in 1839, he soon abandoned law for journalism. He began writing for the *Dublin University Magazine*, of which he became editor and proprietor (1869), and later bought three Dublin newspapers. His novels include *The House by the Churchyard* (1863), *Uncle Silas* (1864, his best known), a collection of stories, *In a Glass Darkly* (1872), and 14 other works, remarkable for their preoccupation with the supernatural. His *Poems* were edited by **Alfred Percival Graves** (1896).

LEFEBVRE, Pierre François Joseph, Duke of Danzig (1755–1820) French soldier and marshal of France, born in Ruffach in Alsace. He entered the French Guards in 1773, and by 1793 was a general, having fought at Fleurus (1690), Altenkirchen (1796) and Stockach (1799). In 1799, as governor of Paris, he supported the *coup d'état* of 18th Brumaire that overthrew the Directory and brought **Napoleon** to power, and in 1804 he was made a marshal. He took Danzig, and was created Duke of Danzig (1807), distinguished himself in the early part of the Peninsular War, and suppressed the insurrection in the Tyrol. During the Russian campaign he had the command of the Imperial Guard, and in 1814 of the left wing of the French army. Submitting to the **Bourbons**, he was made a peer, a dignity restored to him in 1819 though he had sided with his old master during the Hundred Days.

LEFEVBRE, Marcel (1905–) French schismatic Roman Catholic prelate, born in Tourcoing. He studied at the French Seminary in Rome and was ordained in 1929. In the 1930s he was a missionary in Gabon and became archbishop of Dakar, Senegal (1948–62). As a clerical traditionalist he opposed the liberalizing liturgical and spiritual reforms of the Second Vatican Council (1962–65), and in 1970 formed the 'Priestly Cofraternity of **Pius X**' to oppose them. He was suspended 'a divinis' in 1976 by Pope **Paul VI** for his refusal to stop the ordination of priests at his headquarters in Switzerland without papal permission. He defied the suspension and continued to ordain a further 216 priests before being formally excommunicated by Pope **John Paul II** in 1988, thus producing the first formal schism within the Roman Catholic Church since 1870.

LEFORT, François Jacob (1653–99) Swiss diplomat, born in Geneva of Scottish extraction. He served in the Swiss Guard at Paris, but entered the Russian service in 1675. Heading the intrigues which made **Peter I, the Great** sole ruler, he became his first favourite. An able diplomat and administrator, he backed up the tsar's reforms, and in 1694 was made admiral and generalissimo.

LEFROY, Sir John Henry (1817–90) English soldier, born in Ashe, Hampshire. He became an artillery officer, director-general of ordnance and governor of Bermuda (1870–77). He was appointed governor of Tasmania in 1880. He wrote on the Bermudas, antiquities and on ordnance, his *Handbook of Field Ordnance* (1854) being the first of this type of textbook.

LEFSCHETZ, Solomon (1884–1972) Russian-born American mathematician, born in Moscow. He studied engineering in Paris before emigrating to the USA, where he worked as an engineer. After losing both his hands in an industrial accident (1910), he was forced to abandon engineering, and turned to mathematics. He took his doctorate in 1911, and taught at Kansas (1913–25), where he soon made a reputation by his work in algebraic geometry. This led him to the study of topology and in 1925 he went to Princeton where he stayed until his retiral in 1953. He became the leading topologist of his generation in the USA. His work during World War II roused his interest in differential equations, and he continued to work on their qualitative theory, becoming visiting professor at Brown University after his retirement.

LE GALLIENNE, Eva (1899–) English actress on American stage, daughter of **Richard Le Gallienne**. She was the founder (1926) and director of the Civic Repertory Theater of New York.

LE GALLIENNE, Richard (1866–1947) English writer, born of Guernsey ancestry in Liverpool. In 1891 he became a London journalist but later lived in New York. He published many volumes of prose and verse from 1887. His style, that of the later 19th century, is old-fashioned, but his best books are *Quest of the Golden Girl* (1896), *The Romantic Nineties* (1926) and *From a Paris Garret* (1936).

LEGAT, Nicolai (1869–1937) Russian dancer, teacher, ballet master and choreographer, born in St Petersburg (Leningrad). He studied with his father at the Imperial Ballet School, graduating in 1888 and joining the Maryinsky Theatre, where he spent 20 years as a principal, dancing in major works including the first performance of **Lev Ivanov**'s *The Nutcracker* (1892). He took over the directorship of the company in 1905, dropping choreography for teaching. His pupils there included **Tamara Karsavina**, **Michel Fokine**, **Nijinsky** and Bohn. In 1923 he moved to the USA to become ballet master of **Diaghilev**'s company, but finally settled in London where he opened his own school and taught **Alexandra Danilova**, **Margot Fonteyn**, **Ninette de Valois**, **Anton Dolin** and **Serge Lifar**. His school continues to function at Mark Cross, Sussex.

LEGENDRE, Adrien-Marie (1752–1833) French mathematician, born in Paris. He studied at the Collège Mazarin, became professor of mathematics at the École Militaire and a member of the Académie des Sciences (1783). In 1787 he was appointed one of the commissioners to relate the Paris and Greenwich meridians by triangulation and in 1813 he succeeded **Joseph Louis de Lagrange** at the Bureau des Longitudes. He proposed the method of least squares in 1806 (independently of **Carl Friedrich Gauss**). His classic work *Essai sur la théorie des nombres* (1798) includes his discovery of the law of quadratic reciprocity, and his *Traité des fonctions elliptiques* (1825) became the definitive account of elliptic integrals prior to **Carl Gustav Jacobi**'s work. His *Eléments de géométrie* (1794) was translated into English by **Thomas Carlyle**.

LÉGER, Fernand (1881–1955) French painter, born in Argentan, a major force in the Cubist movement. Between 1903 and 1907 he studied at various Paris studios and initially painted in a diffuse Neo-Impressionist manner. However, like many others, he then discovered **Cézanne** and began 'constructing' his pictures with volumetric shapes. His pictures differ from those of the fellow members of the avant-garde in being more 'tubist' than 'cubist'. By 1912, in pictures like *La Femme en Bleu*, Leger was nearing pure abstraction, but after World War I he returned to primarily figurative work in which the working man is combined with machinery in monumental patterns made up of heavy black outlines and primary colour infill. He also designed theatre sets, taught at Yale University, and executed murals for the United Nations building in New York (1952). He collaborated on the first 'art-film', *Le Ballet mécanique*, in 1923. There is a museum dedicated to his work at Biot on the Côte d'Azur in the south of France.

LEGGE, James (1815–97) Scottish missionary and sinologist, born in Huntly. After graduating at Aberdeen (1835), he ran the Anglo-Chinese missionary college in Malacca, followed by 30 years in Hong Kong. In 1876 he became the first professor of Chinese at Oxford. His greatest work was a monumental edition of *Chinese Classics* (28 vols, 1861–86).

LEGRENZI, Giovanni (1626–90) Venetian composer, born in Clusone near Bergamo. He wrote church music for St Mark's, much chamber music, and 18 operas.

LEGROS, Alphonse (1837–1911) French-born British painter, born in Dijon, who adopted England as his home. On the advice of **Whistler**, he arrived in London in 1863 and by 1875 was in charge of the etching class at the Royal College. Appointed Slade professor to the University College in 1875–76, he exercised a strong traditional influence. He produced over 750 etchings and was noted for his revival of original portraiture which had been in decline for many years. His landscape and figure studies particularly mark him as an influential figure in the British etching movement.

LE GUIN, Ursula, née **Kroeber** (1929–) American science fiction writer, born in Berkeley, California, the daughter of the anthropologist **Alfred Louis Kroeber**. She was educated at Radcliffe College and Columbia University. A prolific writer both for adults and children, she has illustrated that it is possible to work in genre and be taken seriously as a writer. Much of her work focuses on subjective views of a universe incorporating numerous habitable worlds, each spawned by beings from the Hain. 'Hain' novels include *Rocannon's World* (1966), *Plant of Exile* (1966), *The Left Hand of Darkness* (1969) and *The Word for World is Forest* (1976). In a prodigious oeuvre, the 'Earth Sea' trilogy—*A Wizard of Earthsea* (1968), *The Tombs of Atuan* (1971) and *The Farthest Shore* (1972)—is another major work, its magical world where every village has its small-time sorcerer appealing to adults and children alike.

LEHÁR, Franz (1870–1948) Hungarian composer, born in Komárom. He became a conductor in Vienna and wrote a violin concerto but is best known for his operettas which include his most popular *The*

Merry Widow (1905), *The Count of Luxembourg* (1909), *Frederica* (1928) and *The Land of Smiles* (1929).

LEHMANN, Beatrix (1903–79) English actress, daughter of **Rudolph Lehmann** and sister of **John** and **Rosamond Lehmann**, born in Bourne End, Buckinghamshire. She first appeared on the stage in 1924 at the Lyric, Hammersmith, and since then has appeared in many successful plays, including, in recent years, *Family Reunion*, **Ustinov**'s *No Sign of the Dove*, and *Waltz of the Toreadors*. In 1946 she became director-producer of the Arts Council Midland Theatre Company. She has also appeared in films and written two novels and several short stories.

LEHMANN, John Frederick (1907–89) English poet and man of letters, born in Bourne End, Buckinghamshire, son of **Rudolph Lehmann**. He was educated at Eton and Trinity College, Cambridge, and founded the periodical in book format, *New Writing* (1936–41). He was managing director of the Hogarth Press with **Leonard** and **Virginia Woolf** (1938–46), and ran his own firm, John Lehmann Ltd, with his sister, **Rosamond Lehmann**, as co-director from 1946 to 1953. In 1954 he inaugurated *The London Magazine*, which he edited until 1961. His first publications were volumes of poetry, including *A Garden Revisited* (1931) and *Forty Poems* (1942). He also wrote a novel, *Evil was Abroad* (1938), and studies of *Edith Sitwell* (1952), *Virginia Woolf and her World* (1975) and *Rupert Brooke* (1980). He wrote his autobiography in three volumes, *The Whispering Gallery* (1955), *I am my Brother* (1960) and *The Ample Proposition* (1966).

LEHMANN, Liza, properly **Elizabeth Nina Mary Frederika** (1862–1918) English soprano and composer, daughter of **Rudolph Lehmann**, born in London. Very popular as a concert singer, she also composed ballads, a light opera *The Vicar of Wakefield* (1906) and a song-cycle *In a Persian Garden* (1896).

LEHMANN, Rosamond Nina (1903–90) English novelist, daughter of **Rudolph Lehmann** and sister of **Beatrix** and **John Lehmann**, born in London. Educated at Girton College, Cambridge, it provided the background for her first novel, *Dusty Answer* (1927). Her novels show a fine sensitive insight into character and her women especially are brilliantly drawn. Among her other books are *A Note in Music* (1930), *An Invitation to the Waltz* (1932) and its sequel *The Weather in the Streets* (1936), and *The Echoing Grove* (1953). Her last novel was *A Sea-Grape Tree* (1970). She also wrote a play, *No More Music* (1939), and a volume of short stories *The Gypsy's Baby* (1946). She produced the autobiographical *The Swan in the Evening* in 1967. She later developed a belief in spiritualism, and became president of the College of Psychic Studies.

LEHMANN, Rudolph Chambers (1856–1929) English journalist, born in Sheffield. He was a journalist on *Punch* (1890–1919), editor of the *Daily News* (1901), and Liberal MP for Harborough (1906–10). A well-known oarsman and coach, he published *The Complete Oarsman* in 1908.

LEHMBRUCK, Wilhelm (1881–1919) German sculptor and illustrator, born in Meidensich near Duisberg. He was early influenced by **Maillol**, and later produced Expressionist sculpture, specializing in elongated and exaggerated female torsos.

LEIBL, Wilhelm (1844–1900) German artist, born in Cologne. He studied in Paris, being much influenced by **Courbet**'s realism, and later worked in Munich. Most of his paintings are genre scenes of Bavaria and the lower Alps, although he painted a number of portraits.

LEIBNIZ, Gottfried Wilhelm (1646–1716) German philosopher and mathematician, remarkable also for his encyclopaedic knowledge and diverse accomplishments outside these fields. He was born in Leipzig, the son of a professor of moral philosophy, studied there and at Altdorf, showing great precocity of learning, and in 1667 obtained a position at the court of the Elector of Mainz on the strength of an essay on legal education. There he codified laws, drafted schemes for the unification of the churches, and was variously required to act as courtier, civil servant and international lawyer, while at the same time he absorbed the philosophy, science and mathematics of the day, especially the work of **Descartes**, **Newton**, **Pascal** and **Robert Boyle**. In 1672 he was sent on a diplomatic mission to Paris, where he met **Malebranche**, **Arnauld** and **Huygens**, and went on in 1676 to London where his discussions with mathematicians of Newton's circle led later to an unseemly controversy as to whether he or Newton was the inventor of the infinitesimal calculus. Leibniz published his system in 1684; Newton published his in 1687, though he could relate this to earlier work. The Royal Society formally declared for Newton in 1711, but the controversy was never really settled. In 1676 Leibniz visited **Spinoza** in the Hague on his way to take up a new, and his last, post as librarian to the Duke of Brunswick at Hanover. Here he continued to elaborate, without publishing, his mathematical and philosophical theories and maintained a huge learned correspondence. He also travelled in Austria and Italy in the years 1687–90 to gather materials for a large-scale history of the House of Brunswick, and went in 1700 to persuade **Frederick I** of Prussia to found the Prussian Academy of Sciences in Berlin, of which he became the first president. He was unpopular with George of Hanover and was left behind in 1714 when the Elector moved the court to London to become king of Britain (as **George I**). He died in Hanover two years later, without real recognition and with almost all his work unpublished. Leibniz was perhaps the last universal genius, spanning the whole of contemporary knowledge. He made original contributions to optics, mechanics, statistics, logic and probability theory; he conceived the idea of calculating machines, and of a universal language; he wrote on history, law and political theory; and his philosophy was the foundation of 18th-century rationalism. His *Essais de théodicée sur la Donté de Dieu, la liberté de l'homme et l'origine du mal* (the *Theodicy* 1710), was a relatively popular work in theology, expressing his optimism and faith in enlightenment and reason, which **Voltaire** satirized brilliantly in *Candide* ('all is for the best in this best of all possible worlds'). The metaphysics and more technical philosophy are to be found in his response to **Locke**, the *New Essays on Human Understanding* (completed in 1704 but not published until 1765), the *Discours de Metaphysique* (1846), the correspondence with Arnauld and with **Samuel Clarke**, and numerous short papers. His best known doctrine is that the world is composed of an infinity of simple, indivisible, immaterial, mutually isolated 'monads' which form a hierarchy, the highest of which is God; the monads do not interact causally but constitute a synchronized harmony with material phenomena. Leibniz is recognized as one of the great rationalist philosophers but he had perhaps his greatest influence (for example, on **Bertrand Russell**) as a mathematician and a pioneer of modern symbolic logic.

LEICESTER, Robert Dudley, Earl of (c.1532–1588) English statesman, the fifth son of John Dudley, Duke of **Northumberland**, and grandson of the notorious **Edmund Dudley** beheaded by **Henry VIII**. His father was executed for his support of Lady **Jane Grey**. He too was sentenced to death, but, liberated in 1554, became a favourite of Queen **Elizabeth**, who made him master of the horse, Knight of the Garter, a privy councillor, high steward of the University of Cambridge, Baron Dudley, and finally, in 1564, Earl of Leicester. In 1550 he had married Amy Robsart; in 1560 she died, apparently of poison, and rumour had it that he had killed her in order to be free to marry the queen. In 1563 Elizabeth suggested him as a husband for **Mary, Queen of Scots**; but in 1573 he made a secret marriage to the Dowager Lady Sheffield. In 1575 Elizabeth was magnificently entertained by him at his castle of Kenilworth. In 1578 he bigamously married the widow of **Walter Devereux**, Earl of **Essex**; yet Elizabeth was only temporarily greatly offended. In 1585 he commanded the expedition to the Low Countries in which Sir **Philip Sidney**, his nephew, met with his death at Zutphen. In 1587 he again showed his military incapacity in the same field, and had to be recalled. In 1588 he was appointed to command the forces assembled at Tilbury against the Spanish Armada. He died suddenly on 4 September of the same year at Cornbury, in Oxfordshire, of poison rumoured to have been intended for his wife.

LEICESTER OF HOLKHAM, Thomas William Coke, Earl of (1752–1842) English agriculturist, a descendant of the jurist Sir **Edward Coke**. One of the first agriculturists of England, by his efforts northwest Norfolk was converted from a rye-growing into a wheat-growing district, and more stock and better breeds of sheep, cattle and pigs were kept on the farms. He represented Norfolk as a Whig MP most of the period 1776–1833, and in 1837 was created Earl of Leicester of Holkham.

LEICHHARDT, (Friedrich Wilhelm) Ludwig (1813–c.1848) Prussian-born Australian naturalist and explorer, born in Trebasch. He studied at the universities of Berlin and Göttingen but obtained no formal qualifications. His interest aroused in natural history, he arrived in Sydney with an introduction to Sir **Thomas Mitchell**, surveyor-general for the colony. However, Leichhardt eventually had to mount his own expedition and, with the backing of businessmen, he set out from Brisbane north-west for Port Essington, a settlement on the coast of Arnhem Land, Northern Territory. This was reached 15 months later after extreme privation. The party's arrival back in Sydney in March 1846, when they had been presumed lost, caused great excitement. In December of the same year he set out again, attempting an east-west crossing of the northern part of the continent, to the coast of Western Australia, but was forced to turn back. On his return to Sydney he learnt that he had been awarded gold medals by the Geographical Societies of Paris and London. In February 1848 he assembled another party and set off on a trans-continental journey but nothing was heard of him or the expedition after April 1848. The mystery prompted a number of searches to be mounted, without result, the last as recently as 1953. Although unsuccessful, the searches themselves proved valuable explorations.

LEIF THE LUCKY, (Leifur heppni Eiríksson) (fl.1000) Icelandic explorer and son of **Erik the Red**. Just before the year 1000 he set sail from Greenland to explore lands which had been accidentally discovered to the west by a storm-driven compatriot; he explored Baffin Land, Labrador, and an area he called 'Vínland' (Wineland) because of the wild grapes he found growing there. The location of Vínland has defied precise identification, but incontrovertible remains of a Norse settlement have been found on Newfoundland. Other would-be Icelandic settlers, led by **Thorfinn Karlsefni**, tried to establish a colony in 'Vínland', but withdrew in the face of hostility from the native Indians. Two Icelandic sagas, *Eiríks saga rauða* and *Grænlendinga* saga, tell the story of the Norse discovery and attempted colonization of North America, 500 years before **Christopher Columbus** discovered the New World.

LEIGH, Vivien, originally **Vivian Hartley** (1913–67) English actress, born in Darjeeling, India. After studying at RADA she made her professional début in the film *Things Are Looking Up* (1934). Her stage début followed in *The Green Sash* (1935) and in the same year she was an overnight sensation in the comedy *The Mask of Virtue*. A charming, vixenish actress of great beauty, she was married to **Laurence Olivier** from 1940 to 1961 and appeared opposite him in numerous classical plays including *Romeo and Juliet* (1940, New York), *Antony and Cleopatra* (1951, New York) and *Macbeth* (1955, Stratford). Persistent ill-health and frequent bouts of manic depression curtailed her career, but she did give two electrifying Academy Award-winning performances in *Gone With the Wind* (1939) and *A Streetcar Named Desire* (1951). After her divorce from Olivier she worked on stage and made a final film appearance in *Ship of Fools* (1965). She died from tuberculosis.

LEIGH-MALLORY, Sir Trafford (1892–1944) English air force officer, born in Cheshire. Educated at Haileybury and Magdalen College, Oxford, he served with the Royal Flying Corps in World War I. In World War II he commanded Groups in Fighter Command in the Battle of Britain. He was commander-in-chief of Fighter Command (1942–44) and of Allied Expeditionary Air Forces for the Normandy landings (1944). Appointed commander-in-chief of Allied air forces in South East Asia, he was killed in an aircraft accident en route.

LEIGH-PEMBERTON, Robin (Robert) (1927–) English banker, born in Sittingbourne, Kent, and governor of the Bank of England since 1983. He practised at the bar from 1954 to 1960. In 1965 he qualified as a chartered accountant. He was chairman of Kent County Council from 1975 to 1977 and chairman of the National Westminster Bank from 1977 to 1983.

LEIGHTON, Frederic, 1st Baron Leighton of Stretton (1830–96) English painter, born in Scarborough, a doctor's son. He studied and travelled extensively in Europe and had immediate success in 1855 with his *Cimabue's Madonna carried in Procession through Florence*—a picture purchased by Queen **Victoria**. Among his later works were *Paolo and Francesca* (1861), *The Daphnephoria* (1876) and *The Bath of Psyche* (1890). He also won distinction as a sculptor, and in 1877 his *Athlete struggling with a Python* was purchased out of the **Chantrey** Bequest. Several of his paintings, as for example *Wedded* (1882), became mass bestsellers in photogravure reproduction. His *Addresses* were published in 1896. He died unmarried, and was buried in St Paul's Cathedral. His splendid house in Kensington is now a war museum.

LEIGHTON, Kenneth (1929–88) English composer and pianist, born in Wakefield. After graduating from Oxford, he studied composition with Goffredo Petrassi in Rome. He in turn taught composition at Edinburgh University from 1956, and from 1970 was Reid professor of music there. His compositions showed vigorous and individual mastery of traditional forms and contrapuntal disciplines. He was a skilful and rewarding composer of choral music, and also wrote much for his own instrument (including three concertos) as well as three symphonies, other concertos, an opera *Columba* (1981), organ and chamber music.

LEIGHTON, Robert (1611–84) Scottish prelate, born probably in London. His father was Alexander Leighton (c.1568–c.1649), Presbyterian minister in London and Utrecht, author of *Sion's Plea against the Prelacie* (1628), which earned him from **Laud** scourging, the pillory, branding and mutilation, a heavy fine and imprisonment. Robert studied at Edinburgh University and spent some years in France. He was ordained minister of Newbattle in 1641, signed the Covenant two years later (but with reservations about its possible excesses), and took part in all the Presbyterian policy of the time; most of the *Sermons* and the *Commentary on the First Epistle of Peter* were the work of the Newbattle period. In 1653 he was appointed principal of Edinburgh University. Soon after the Restoration he was induced by **Charles II** himself to become one of the new bishops, and chose Dunblane, the poorest of all the dioceses; and for the next ten years he laboured to build up the shattered walls of the church. His aim was to preserve what was best in Episcopacy and Presbytery as a basis for comprehensive union; but he succeeded only in being misunderstood by both sides. The continued persecution of the Covenanters drove him to London in 1665 to resign his see, but Charles persuaded him to return. Again in 1669 he went to London to advocate his scheme of 'accommodation' and became archbishop of Glasgow in the same year. Next followed his fruitless conferences at Edinburgh (1670–71) with leading Presbyterians. Despairing of success he was allowed to retire in 1674. His last ten years he spent at Broadhurst Manor, Sussex often preaching in the church of Horsted Keynes, where he lies. He died in a London inn.

LEININGEN See **KENT, Edward, Duke of**

LEINO, Eino, pseud of **Armas Eino Leopold Lōnnbohm** (1878–1926) Finnish poet and novelist. He developed the *Kalevala* metre into a distinctive, sombrely lyrical style of his own, best exemplified in *Helkavirsiä* (Whitsongs, 1903–16). He also wrote novels, and made fine translations of **Dante**, **Racine**, **Corneille**, **Goethe** and **Schiller**.

LEIRIS, Michel (1901–) French anthropologist, writer and poet, born in Paris. After an early involvement with the Surrealist movement (1925–29), he joined the trans-African Dakar-Djibouti expedition of 1931 to 1933. He returned to study and take up anthropology as a profession, and went on to travel widely in Africa and the Caribbean. His writings, many of them autobiographical, as in *Manhood* (1939, trans 1984) and *Rules of the Game* (4 vols, 1948–76), are marked by a consuming interest in poetry, and he has combined anthropology with a distinguished career as a literary and art critic. His major works include *L'Afrique Fantôme* (1934), *L'âge d'homme* (1939), and *Afrique Noire: la création plastique* (1967).

LEISHMAN, Sir William Boog (1865–1926) Scottish bacteriologist, born in Glasgow. He became professor of pathology in the Army Medical College, and director-general, Army Medical Service (1923). He discovered an effective vaccine for inoculation against typhoid and was first to discover the parasite of the disease kala-azar.

LELAND, Charles Godfrey, pseud **Hans Breitmann** (1825–1903) American author, born in Philadelphia. He graduated at Princeton in 1845, and afterwards studied at Heidelberg, Munich and Paris. He was admitted to the Philadelphia bar in 1851, but turned to journalism. From 1869 he resided chiefly in England and Italy, and investigated the gypsies, a subject on which between 1873 and 1891 he published four valuable works. He is best known for his poems in 'Pennsylvania Dutch', the famous *Hans Breitmann Ballads* (1871; continued in 1895). Other similar volumes gained him great popularity during his lifetime. He also translated the works of **Heine**.

LELAND, John (c.1506–1552) English antiquary, born in London. He was educated at St Paul's School under **William Lilye**, then at Christ's College, Cambridge, and All Souls College, Oxford. After a stay in Paris he became chaplain to **Henry VIII**, who in 1533 made him 'king's antiquary', with power to search for records of antiquity in the cathedrals, colleges, abbeys and priories of England. In six years he collected 'a whole world of things very memorable'. His church preferments were the rectories of Peuplingues near Calais and Haseley in Oxfordshire, a canonry of King's College (now Christ Church), Oxford, and a prebend of Salisbury. Most of his papers are in the Bodleian and British Museums. Besides his *Commentarii de Scriptoribus Britannicis*, his chief works are *The Itinerary* and *De Rebus Britannicis Collectanea*.

LELAND, John (1691–1766) English Presbyterian minister, born in Wigan. He was educated at Dublin, where from 1716 he was minister. He wrote against **Matthew Tindal** (1733) and Thomas Morgan (1739–40). His chief work is an attack on deists in *A View of the Principal Deistical Writers* (1754–56).

LELOIR, Luis Frederico (1906–) French-born Argentinian biochemist, born in Paris. Educated in Buenos Aires and at Cambridge, he worked mainly in Argentina where he set up his own Research Institute in 1947. There, away from mainstream researchers and with little equipment, he and his co-workers in 1957 discovered in some detail how the energy storage material glycogen is synthesized in the body. For this work he was awarded the Nobel prize for chemistry in 1970, being the first Argentinian to be so honoured.

LELY, Sir Peter, originally **Pieter van der Faes** (1618–80) Dutch-born British painter, born probably in Soest, Westphalia. He worked in Haarlem before he settled in London in 1641 as a portrait painter. He was patronized by **Charles I** and **Cromwell**, and in 1661 was appointed court painter to **Charles II**, for whom he changed his style of painting. His *Windsor Beauties* series is collected at Hampton Court. The 13 Greenwich portraits of *Admirals* are among his best works; these, the English admirals who fought in the 2nd Dutch War, are outstanding for depth and sincerity of characterization. They present a marked contrast to his very popular and often highly sensuous court portraits which sometimes have a hasty, superficial appearance.

LE MAIRE DE BELGES, Jean (c.1473–1524) French humanist poet. He served the Duc de **Bourbon**, **Margaret of Austria**, to whom he dedicated his *Épîtres de l'amant vert*, and **Louis XII**.

LEMAÎTRE, François Élie Jules (1853–1914) French playwright and critic, born in Vennecy, Loiret. His articles, written first for the *Journal des débats*, were issued in book form as *Impressions de théâtre* (1888–98), and those written for *Revue bleue* on modern French literature became *Les Contemporains* (1886–99). A masterly critic with a charming, lucid style, he also wrote *Rousseau* (1907), *Racine* (1908), *Fenélon* (1910) and *Chateaubriand* (1912).

LEMAÎTRE, Frédérick (1800–76) French actor, born in Le Havre. His first success was in *Richard Darlington*, a play based on Sir **Walter Scott**'s *The Surgeon's Daughter*, and this was followed by a succession of triumphs including *Hamlet*, *Kean ou Désordre et Genie*, *Ruy Blas*, and the greatest of all, *L'Auberge des Adrets*. This last was in fact Lemaître's own play. Based on an inferior melodrama, he made the character Robert Macaire a villain of genius.

Writers of the day acclaimed him; **Dumas** called him the French **Kean**, **Flaubert** called his Macaire the greatest symbol of the age and **Hugo** wrote *Ruy Blas* for him. He visited London four times and on one occasion shocked Queen **Victoria** by his Ruy Blas. He suffered ill health in his later years and died in great poverty.

LEMAÎTRE, Georges Henri (1894–1966) Belgian astrophysicist. An ordained priest, he became professor of the theory of relativity at Louvain (1927). Inspired by the work of Sir **Arthur Eddington**, he developed the 'Big Bang' theory of the origin of the Universe.

LEMERY, Nicolas (1645–1715) French chemist, born in Rouen. He studied as an apothecary there and in Paris, where about 1672 he began to make and sell chemicals and to give lectures on the subject; the latter proved highly popular. His book *Cours de chymie* (1675) had 31 editions by 1756 and had been translated into most European languages; it gave a lucid account of chemical methods and especially of pharmaceutical compounds known at the time; and on the theoretical side, it classified compounds as animal, vegetable or mineral in origin, and adopted ideas akin to those of **Boyle** on atoms, supposing for example that 'spiky atoms' were associated with acidity. He discovered little that was new, but his influence as a teacher was considerable.

LEMMON, Jack (John Uhler) (1925–) American film and stage actor, born in Boston, Massachusetts. A graduate of Harvard, he served in the navy in World War II, and got a job as a singing waiter before appearing in summer stock and numerous television plays. A Broadway revival of *Room Service* in 1953 brought him to the attention of Hollywood. Following his film début in *It Should Happen to You* (1954) he was soon established as one of the screen's most dynamic comedy performers. *Some Like It Hot* (1959) began a seven-film collaboration with director **Billy Wilder** that further illustrated his deft, bittersweet touch as a contemporary underdog caught in moral dilemmas. He has subsequently received great acclaim for his performances in *Days of Wine and Roses* (1962), *The China Syndrome* (1979) and *Missing* (1981), and has periodically returned to the stage in classics like *Long Day's Journey Into Night* (1986) and directed one film, *Kotch* (1971). Nominated eight times for an Academy Award, he won Oscars for *Mister Roberts* (1955) and *Save the Tiger* (1973).

LEMNIUS, Simon, properly **Margadant** (c.1505–1550) German humanist and poet. He was a student of **Melanchthon** at Wittenberg. Antagonistic to **Luther** and his teaching, he wrote against him in two books of Latin *Epigrams* (1538) and was expelled from the University. His other works included *Monachopornomachia* (a satirical poem, 1540), *Amores* (love poems, 1542) and a Latin translation of the *Odyssey* (1549).

LEMOINE, Sir James MacPherson (1825–1912) Canadian naturalist and writer, born in Quebec. He became superintendent of inland revenue at Quebec in 1858. He studied archaeology, ornithology and other sciences, wrote on Canadian history and was the first Canadian author to receive a knighthood.

LEMON, Mark (1809–70) English author and journalist, born in London. In 1835 he wrote a farce, followed by several melodramas, operettas, novels (the best of which is, perhaps, *Falkner Lyle*, 1866), children's stories, a *Jest Book* (1864) and essays. In 1841 he helped to establish *Punch*, becoming first joint editor (with **Henry Mayhew**), then sole editor from 1843.

LEMONNIER, Antoine Louis Camille (1844–1913) Belgian writer, born in Ixelles near Brussels. He took up art criticism in 1863, and by his novels *Un Mâle* (1881), *Happe-Chair* (1888) and other works, in French, but full of strong Flemish realism and mysticism, won fame as one of Belgium's leading prose writers. He wrote books on art, including *Gustave Courbet* (1878), *Alfred Stevens et son oeuvre* (1906), and *L'École Belge de la peinture* (1906).

LEMONNIER, Pierre Charles (1715–99) French astronomer, born in Paris. Professor at the Collège Royale from 1746, he greatly advanced astronomical measurement in France, and made twelve observations of Uranus before it was recognized as a planet.

LE MOYNE, François (1688–1737) French painter, born in Paris. He specialized in mythological subjects, especially for the Salon d'Hercule at Versailles. **Boucher** was his pupil.

LEMPRIÈRE, John (c.1765–1824) British scholar, born in Jersey. He was headmaster of Abingdon and Exeter grammar schools, and rector of Meeth and Newton-Petrock in Devon. His *Classical Dictionary* (1788) was long a standard work. Another book was *Universal Biography* (1808).

LE NAIN, Antoine; Louis and **Mathieu** (c.1588–1648, c.1593–1648, c.1607–1677) French painters and brothers, born in Laon. All three were resident in Paris by 1630. Mathieu became painter to the city in 1633, and they all became founder members of the French Académie. They each painted scenes of peasant life but, as they tended to sign their work without initials, any individual attribution has to be made on purely stylistic grounds.

LENARD, Philipp Eduard Anton (1862–1947) Hungarian-born German physicist, born in Pozsony (Bratislava) in Hungary. Professor of physics at Heidelberg (1896–98 and 1907–31), he was awarded the Nobel prize for physics in 1905. His main research concerned cathode rays, on which he wrote several books. He was an enthusiastic believer in Nazi doctrines.

LENAU, Nikolaus, in full **Nikolaus Niembsch von Strehlenau** (1802–50) German poet, born in Czatad in Hungary. He studied law and medicine at Vienna. He suffered from extreme melancholy and in 1844 he became insane, dying in an asylum near Vienna. His poetic power is best shown in his short lyrics; his longer pieces include *Faust* (1836), *Savonarola* (1837) and *Die Albigenser* (1842).

LENBACH, Franz (1836–1904) German portrait painter, born in Schrobenhausen, Bavaria. He worked mostly in Munich. For some time he copied the great masters, including **Titian**, **Rubens** and **Velazquez**, before becoming one of the greatest 19th-century German portrait painters. His portraits of **Bismarck** are specially famous.

LENCLOS, Anne, called **Ninon de** (1616–1706) French courtesan, born of a good family in Paris. She started her long career at the age of 16. Among her lovers were two marquises, two marshals, the great **Condé**, the Duc de **La Rochefoucauld**, **Sévigné** and an abbé or two. She had two sons, but never showed the slightest maternal feeling. One of them, brought up in ignorance of his mother, conceived a passion for her. Informed of their relationship, he blew out his brains. Ninon was nearly as celebrated for her manners as for her beauty. The most respectable women sent their children to her to acquire taste, style, and politeness.

LENDL, Ivan (1960–) Czech tennis player, born in Ostrawa. Following wins in the US Open (1985–86) and French Open (1986–87), he became the first official world champion in 1987. His powerful service and clinically efficient execution of shots make him a formidable clay-court player. He has, however, never won a major title on grass.

LENGLEN, Suzanne (1899–1938) French tennis player, born in Compiègne. Trained by her father, she became famous in 1914 by winning the women's world hard-court singles championship at Paris at the age of 15. She was the woman champion of France (1919–23, 1925–26), and her Wimbledon championships were the women's singles and doubles (1919–23, 1925), and the mixed doubles (1920, 1922, 1925). She won the singles and doubles gold medals at the 1920 Olympic Games. She became a professional in 1926, toured the USA, and retired in 1927 to found the Lenglen School of Tennis in Paris. Perhaps the greatest woman player of all time, she set a new fashion in female tennis dress. She published *Lawn Tennis, the Game of Nations* (1925) and a novel, *The Love-Game* (1925).

LENIN, (formerly **Ulyanov), Vladimir Ilyich** (1870–1924) Russian revolutionary, born into a middle-class family in Simbirsk (Ulyanov). He was educated at Kazan University and in 1892 began to practise law in Samara (Kuibyshev). In 1894, after five years' intensive study of **Marx**, he moved to St Petersburg (Leningrad), organizing the illegal 'Union for the Liberation of the Working Class'. Arrested for his opinions, he was exiled to Siberia for three years. During his Western exile, which began in 1900 in Switzerland, he edited the political newspaper *Iskra* (The Spark) and developed, with **Plekhanov**, an underground Social Democratic party, to assume leadership of the working classes in a revolution against Tsarism. His evolving ideas were set out in *What is to be done?* (1902), in which he advocated a professional core of party activists to spearhead the revolution. This suggestion was adopted by the party's majority, Bolshevik wing at the congress in London in 1903, but was opposed by the 'bourgeois reformism' Mensheviks (minority wing). Lenin returned to Russia in 1905, ascribing the failure of the rising of that year to lack of support for his own programme. He determined that when the time came Soviets (councils of workers, soldiers and peasants) should be the instruments of total revolution. Lenin left Russia in 1907 and spent the next decade strengthening the Bolsheviks against the Mensheviks, interpreting the gospel of Marx and **Engels** and organizing underground work in Russia. In April 1917, a few days after the deposition of Tsar **Nicholas II**, Lenin, with German connivance, made his fateful journey in a sealed train from Switzerland to Petrograd (formerly St Petersburg, later renamed Leningrad). He told his followers to prepare for the overthrow of the shaky provisional government and the remaking of Russia on a Soviet basis. In the October revolution the provisional government collapsed and the dominating Bolshevik 'rump' in the second Congress of Soviets declared that supreme power rested in them. Lenin inaugurated the 'dictatorship of the proletariat' with the formal dissolution of the Constituent Assembly. For three years he grappled with war and anarchy. In 1922 he began his 'new economic policy' of limited free enterprise to give Russia respite before entering the era of giant state planning. His health having been in progressive decline since an assassination attempt in 1918, he died on 21 January 1924, and his body was embalmed for veneration in a crystal casket in a mausoleum in Red Square, Moscow. He left a testament in which he proposed the removal of the ambitious **Stalin** as secretary of the Communist party. Shrewd, dynamic, implacable, pedantic, opportunist, ice-cold in his economic reasoning, Lenin lived only for the furtherance of Marxism. Despite his faults, he was a charismatic figure and is still today revered in the Soviet Union as the nation's guiding force.

LENNEP, Jacob van (1802–62) Dutch writer and lawyer, born in Amsterdam. He achieved a great reputation for legal knowledge. His most popular works were comedies, *Het Dorp aan die Grenzen* and *Het Dorp over die Grenzen*. Of his novels, several such as *The Rose of Dekama* and *The Adopted Son* have been translated.

LENNON, John See **BEATLES, The**

LENO, Dan, stage name of **George Galvin** (1860–1904) English comedian. He began his career at the age of four, singing and dancing in public houses, and by eighteen had become a champion clog-dancer and was invited to appear in the Surrey pantomime. Ten years later he joined the Augustus Harris management at Drury Lane, where he appeared for many years in the annual pantomime. Leno was a thin, small man and his foil was the huge, bulky Herbert Campbell. When Campbell died in 1904 as the result of an accident, Leno pined and died six months later. He will be remembered for his realistic 'dames' with their inimitable blend of Cockney humour and sentiment.

LENOIR, Jean Joseph Étienne (1822–1900) French inventor and engineer, born in Luxembourg. He invented the first practical internal combustion gas engine (c.1859) and later built the first car to use it (1860). He also constructed a boat driven by his engine (1886).

LENORMAND, Henri René (1882–1951) French dramatist, born in Paris. He was the author of *Les Possédés* (1909), *Le Mangeur de rêves* (1922), a modern equivalent of *Oedipus Rex*, *L'Homme et ses fantômes* (1924), and other plays in which **Freud**'s theory of subconscious motivation is adapted to dramatic purposes.

LENORMANT, François (1837–83) French archaeologist, born in Paris, the son of Charles Lenormant (1802–59), who was also profoundly learned in Egyptology, numismatics and archaeology. At 20 François carried off the prize in numismatics of the Académie des Inscriptions, and at 23 was digging at Eleusis. He continued his explorations, in the intervals of his work as sub-librarian at the Institute (1862–72) and professor of archaeology at the Bibliothèque Nationale (1874–83), until his health broke down from overwork and a wound received during the siege of Paris. Just before his death he was converted from scepticism to Catholicism. His chief work was *Les Origines de l'histoire d'après la Bible* (1880–84).

LENÔTRE, André (1613–1700) French landscape architect, born in Paris. The creator of French landscape-gardening, he designed many celebrated European gardens, including the gardens at Versailles and Fontainebleau, and St James's Park and Kensington Gardens in London.

LENTHALL, William (1591–1662) English lawyer and parliamentarian, born in Henley. He was speaker of the Long Parliament (1640–53), and master of the rolls from 1643. He was again made speaker in 1654, and in 1659. In 1657 he became one of **Cromwell**'s peers.

LENYA, Lotte, originally **Karoline Wilhelmine Blamauer** (1898–1981) Austrian actress and cabaret singer, born in Hitzing, Vienna. She made her public bow in a local circus at the age of six and was tightrope-walking two years later. In 1914 she moved to Switzerland and studied ballet at the Stadt Theatre in Zürich. A talented, all-round performer, she lived in Berlin from 1920 and came to represent the spirit of that decadent era. In 1926 she married **Kurt Weill** and starred in many of his works including *The Little Mahagonny* (1927) and *The Threepenny Opera* (1928). In 1933 the couple fled to Paris and in 1935 settled in the USA. Her

New York stage appearances include *The Eternal Road* (1937), *Candle in the Wind* (1941) and *The Firebrand of Florence* (1945). After Weill's death she became the public custodian of his legacy. Her husky voice (described as 'an octave below laryngitis') and emotional power won her universal recognition as the supreme interpreter of his work. Later stage appearances included *The Threepenny Opera* (1954), *Brecht on Brecht* (1962), *Cabaret* (1966) and *Mother Courage* (1972). Her rare film roles include *The Threepenny Opera* (1931), *From Russia With Love* (1963) and *Semi-Tough* (1977).

LENZ, Heinrich Friedrich Emil (1804–65) Russian-born German physicist, born in Dorpat in Russia. He first studied theology, but became professor of physics at St Petersburg (1836) and a member of the Russian Academy of Sciences. He was the first to state Lenz's law governing induced current, and is credited with discovering the dependence of electrical resistance on temperature (**Joule**'s law).

LENZ, Jakob Michael Reinhold (1751–92) German author, born in Livonia. He was one of the young authors who surrounded **Goethe** in Strasbourg. He first wrote two plays which were well received, *Der Hofmeister* (1774) and *Die Soldaten* (1776). Like all the 'Sturm und Drang' poets he was a fervent admirer of **Shakespeare**, and this was expressed in his *Anmerkungen übers Theater* (1774). He was a gifted writer of lyrics, some of them being at first attributed to Goethe. He suffered a mental breakdown while still young and died in poverty.

LEO I, St, The Great (c.390–461) pope from 440, one of the most eminent of the Latin Fathers, he is thought to have been born in Tuscany. He was the champion of orthodoxy in pronouncing against **Eutyches** who had refused to recognize the two natures of **Christ**, and was instrumental in convening in 451 the significant Council of Chalcedon in which his legates successfully pressed what has been called 'the Catholic doctrine of the Incarnation'. He stoutly resisted also the deviations of Manichaeans and Pelagians, persuaded threatening Huns (452) and Vandals (455) not to destroy Rome or its people, and consolidated the primacy of the Roman see.

LEO III (c.750–816) pope from 795. He saw during his pontificate (795–816) the formal establishment of the Empire of the West. In the 8th century the popes, through the practical withdrawal of the Eastern emperors, had exercised a temporal supremacy in Rome, under the protectorate of the Frankish sovereigns. Leo was in 799 obliged to flee to Spoleto, whence he repaired to Paderborn to confer with **Charlemagne**. On his return to Rome he was received with honour. In 800 Charlemagne, having come to Rome, was crowned emperor by the pope, and the temporal sovereignty of the pope over the Roman city and state was formally established, under the suzerainty of the emperor.

LEO X, Giovanni de' Medici (1475–1521) pope from 1513, second son of **Lorenzo de' Medici, the Magnificent**. He was created cardinal at the age of 13. In the expulsion of the **Medici** from Florence the young cardinal was included. He was employed as legate by **Julius II**, on whose death in 1513 he was chosen pope as Leo X. He brought to a successful conclusion the fifth Lateran Council. He concluded a concordat with **Francis I** of France; he consolidated and extended the reconquests of his warlike predecessor, Julius II. His desertion of Francis I for the emperor Charles V was dictated by the interests of Italy. But it is as a patron of learning and art that he is best-remembered. He founded a Greek college in Rome and established a Greek press. His vast project for the rebuilding of St Peter's, and his permitting the preaching of an indulgence in order to raise funds, provoked **Luther**'s Reformation. He regarded the movement as of little importance; and though he condemned the propositions of Luther, his measures were not marked by severity. In his moral conduct he maintained a strict propriety, and, although not free from nepotism, he was an enlightened prince.

LEO XIII Roman pontiff, originally Vincenzo Gioacchino Pecci (1810–1903), pope from 1878, born in Carpineto, son of Count Ludovico Pecci. After taking a degree in law he was appointed by **Gregory XVI** a domestic prelate in 1837, received the title of prothonotary apostolic, and was a vigorous apostolic delegate at Benevento, Perugia and Spoleto. He was made archbishop of Damietta *in partibus* and sent to Belgium as nuncio in 1843, nominated archbishop of Perugia in 1846, and in 1853 created a cardinal by **Pius IX**, soon holding the important office of camerlengo. Upon the death of Pius IX in 1878 he was elected to the papacy under the title of Leo XIII. He restored the hierarchy in Scotland and resolved the difficulty with Germany. In 1888 he denounced the Irish Plan of Campaign. He manifested enlightened views, but on questions affecting the church and his own status held staunchly to his rights. He regarded himself as the despoiled sovereign of Rome, and as a prisoner at the Vatican; and persistently declined to recognize the law of guarantees. He protested against heresy and 'godless' schools, and in his encyclicals affirmed that the only solution to the socialistic problem was the influence of the papacy. In 1894 he constrained the French clergy and the monarchists to accept the republic. In 1883 he opened the archives of the Vatican for historical investigations, and he made himself known as a poet, chiefly in the Latin tongue. The 25th anniversary of his episcopate in 1893 was marked by pilgrimages, addresses and gifts, as was the 50th anniversary of his priesthood in 1887. In 1896 he issued an encyclical pronouncing Anglican orders invalid.

LEO III (c.680–741) Byzantine emperor from 717, called 'the Isaurian' from the region of his birth in Anatolia. He raised the Byzantine Empire from a very low condition, having, as a general in the east, seized the crown in 717. He reorganized the army and financial system, and in 718 repelled a formidable attack by the Saracens. In 726 he by an edict prohibited the use of images (ie, pictures or mosaics; statues were hardly known as yet in churches) in public worship. In Italy, however, the appearance of the Iconoclasts or 'Image-Breakers' roused an enthusiastic resistance on the part of the people, and the controversy raised by the edict rent the empire for over a century. In 728 the exarchate of Ravenna was lost, and the eastern provinces became the prey of the Saracens, over whom, however, Leo won a great victory in Phrygia.

LEO AFRICANUS, properly **Alhassan ibn Mohammed Alwazzan** (c.1494–c.1552) Arab traveller and geographer, born in Cordoba. From c.1512 he travelled in northern Africa and Asia Minor. Falling into the hands of Venetian corsairs, he was sent to Pope **Leo X** in Rome, where he lived for 20 years, and accepted Christianity, but later returned to Africa and (perhaps) his old faith, and died in Tunis. He wrote *Africae Descriptio* (1526), an account of his African travels in Italian and for long the chief source of information about the Sudan.

LEOCHARES (c.370 BC) Greek sculptor. With his master **Scopas**, he decorated the Mausoleum of Halicarnassus.

LEÓN, Ponce de See **PONCE DE LEÓN**

LEONARD, Elmore John (1925–) American thriller writer, born in New Orleans. He lived in Dallas, Oklahoma City and Memphis before his family settled in Detroit in 1935. During World War II he served in the US navy and afterwards studied English literature at Detroit University. Throughout the 1950s he worked in advertising as a copywriter but since 1967 he has concentrated on screenplays and novels, remarkable for their relentless pace and vivid dialogue. Regarded as the foremost crime writer in America, his books include *Unknown Man No. 89* (1977), *The Switch* (1978), *Gold Coast* (1980), *Stick* (1983), *La Brava* (1983), *Glitz* (1985), and *Touch* (1987).

LEONARD, Graham Douglas (1921–) English prelate, born in London. Appointed bishop of Willesden in 1964 and bishop of Truro in 1973, he has been bishop of London since 1981. He is known more for his traditional Anglo-Catholic theological position than for his longstanding concern for the Church's role in education or his chairmanship of the Church of England Board for Social Responsiblility (1976–83). He opposed the 1970s Anglican-Methodist unity scheme (see *Growing into Union*, 1970), and as bishop of London became the focus of theological opposition to the ordination of women to the priesthood. His offer of pastoral support to a congregation in Tulsa, Oklahoma, in 1986 caused controversy over the role of bishops outside their own dioceses.

LEONARDO DA VINCI (1452–1519) Italian painter, sculptor, architect and engineer, born in Vinci, between Pisa and Florence, the illegitimate son of a Florentine notary. About 1470 he entered the studio of **Andrea del Verrocchio**. In 1482 he settled in Milan, and attached himself to **Ludovico Sforza**. His famous *Last Supper* (1498), commissioned jointly by Lodovico and the monks of S Maria delle Grazie, was painted on a wall of the refectory of the convent. Owing to dampness, and to the method of tempera painting—not oil, nor fresco—upon plaster, it soon showed signs of deterioration, and it has been often 'restored'; yet still it is one of the world's masterpieces. Among other paintings in Milan were portraits of two mistresses of the duke — one of them perhaps *La Belle Ferronnière* of the Louvre. He also devised a system of hydraulic irrigation of the plains of Lombardy and directed the court pageants. After the fall of Duke Ludovico in 1500 Leonardo retired to Florence, and entered the service of **Cesare Borgia**, then Duke of Romagna, as architect and engineer. In 1503 he returned to Florence, and commenced a *Madonna and Child with St Anne*, of which only the cartoon now in the Royal Academy, London, was completed. Both he and **Michelangelo** received commissions to decorate the Sala del Consiglio in the Palazzo della Signoria with historical compositions. Leonardo dealt with *The Battle of Anghiari*, a Florentine victory over Milan, and finished his cartoon; but, having employed a method of painting upon the plaster which proved a failure, he abandoned the work in 1506. About 1504 he completed his most celebrated easel picture, *Mona Lisa*. Another work portrayed the celebrated beauty Ginevra Benci; and Pacioli's *De divina Proportione* (1509) contained 60 geometrical figures from Leonardo's hand. In 1506 he was employed by **Louis XII** of France. **Francis I** bestowed on him in 1516 a yearly allowance, and assigned to his use the Château Cloux, near Amboise, where he lived until his death. Among his later works are *The Virgin of the Rocks*, now in the National Gallery, London, a figure of *St John the Baptist*, and a *Saint Anne*. There is in existence no sculpture which can positively be attributed to him, but he may well have designed or been closely associated with three works—the three figures over the north door of the Baptistery at Florence, a bronze statuette of horse and rider in the Budapest Museum and the wax bust of Flora. In his art Leonardo was hardly at all influenced by the antique; his practice was founded upon the most patient and searching study of nature and in particular the study of light and shade. He occupies a supreme place as an artist, but so few in number are the works by his hand that have reached us that he may be most fully studied in his drawings, of which there are rich collections in Milan, Paris, Florence and Vienna, as well as in the British Museum and in Windsor. His celebrated *Trattato della Pittura* was published in 1651; but a more complete manuscript, discovered by Manzi in the Vatican, was published in 1817. Voluminous MSS by him in Milan (*Codice-Atlantico*), Paris, Windsor, and elsewhere have been reproduced in facsimile. The outstanding all-round genius of the Renaissance, he had a wide knowledge and understanding far beyond his times of most of the sciences, including biology, anatomy, physiology, hydrodynamics, mechanics and aeronautics, and his notebooks, written in mirror writing contain original remarks on all of these.

LEONARDO OF PISA See **FIBONACCI**

LEONCAVALLO, Ruggiero (1858–1919) Italian composer, born in Naples. He studied at Naples Conservatory and, while touring Europe as a pianist, is thought to have been encouraged in his career by **Wagner**. He produced *I Pagliacci* (1892) followed by other less successful operas, including a *La Bohème* which failed where **Puccini**'s, on the same theme, was a success.

LEONI, Leone (1509–90) Italian goldsmith, medallist and sculptor, born in Arezzo. He worked in Milan, Genoa, Brussels and Madrid, and was the rival of **Benvenuto Cellini** in talent, vice and violence. His fine medals often depicted well-known artists, like **Titian** and **Michelangelo**, and his sculpture which was mostly in bronze included busts of **Charles V** and **Philip II**, both of whom he served for some time.

LEONIDAS, (d.c.480 BC) king of Sparta. He succeeded his half-brother, Cleomenes, in 491 BC. When the Persian king **Xerxes** approached with a large army, Leonidas opposed him at the narrow pass of Thermopylae (480) with his 300 Spartans and 700 Thespians; there all of them found a heroic death.

LEONOV, Alexei Arkhipovich (1934–) Russian astronaut, born in Listvyanka, the first man to walk in space. In 1955 he entered the Chuguyev Air Force Flying School in the Ukraine, graduating with honours in 1957, thereafter serving with air force units. He specialized in parachute training and joined the astronaut corps in 1959. On 18 March 1965 he made the first 'extra-vehicular-activity' (EVA) from the spacecraft Voskhod 2 in orbit round the earth, 'walking' in space for ten minutes. In 1975 he took part in the joint US-USSR Apollo-Soynz space mission.

LEONTIEF, Wassily (1906–) Russian-born American economist, born in St Petersburg (Leningrad). Educated at Leningrad and Berlin universities, he went to the USA in 1930. He taught at Harvard from 1931 to 1975 (professor from 1946), and from 1975 to 1984 he was director of the Institute of Economic Analysis at New York University. His most important work was an analysis of American industry, *The Structure of the American Economy, 1919–29* (1941). He was awarded the 1973 Nobel prize for economics for developing the input-output method of economic analysis, used in more than 50 industrialized countries for planning and forecasting.

LEOPARDI, Giacomo (1798–1837) Italian poet, born of poor but noble parentage in Recanati. At the age of 16 he had read all the Latin and Greek classics, could write French, Spanish, English, and Hebrew, and wrote a commentary on **Plotinus**. After a short stay in Rome, he devoted himself at home to literature, but finding his home increasingly unbearable he began to travel and, an invalid, lived successively in Bologna, Florence, Milan and Pisa. In 1833 he accompanied his friend Ranieri to Naples, and there in constant bodily anguish and hopeless despondency he lived until his death. His pessimism was unquestionably the genuine expression of Leopardi's deepest nature as well as of his reasoned conviction. He was specially gifted as a writer of lyrics, which were collected under the title *I Canti* (1831) and are among the most beautiful in Italian literature. His prose works include the dialogues and essays classed as *Operette Morali* (1827), and his *Pensieri* and letters.

LEOPOLD V (1157–94) Duke of Austria from 1177 and Styria from 1192, and captor of King **Richard I** of England. A crusader, he became a bitter enemy of Richard on the Third Crusade (1189–92), and took him prisoner in his dominions as he made his way home to England in 1192.

LEOPOLD I (1790–1865) king of Belgium from 1831, son of Francis, Duke of Saxe-Coburg, and uncle of Queen **Victoria**. A general in the Russian army, he served at Lützen, Bautzen and Leipzig. He married in 1816 the Princess **Charlotte** of Britain; in 1832 Louise, daughter of **Louis-Philippe.** After hesitation he declined the crown of Greece (1830) and in 1831 he was elected king of the Belgians. He conducted himself with prudence and moderation, with constant regard to the principles of the Belgian constitution and by his policy did much to prevent Belgium becoming too involved in the revolutions which were raging in other European countries in 1848.

LEOPOLD II (1835–1909) king of Belgium from 1865, son of **Leopold I**, born in Brussels. His chief interest was the expansion of Belgium abroad. In 1885 he became king of the independent state of the Congo, which was annexed to Belgium in 1908. At home he strengthened his country by military reforms and established a system of fortifications. He was not popular as a king, but under him Belgium flourished, developing commercially and industrially, especially during the later part of his reign. He was succeeded by his nephew, **Albert**.

LEOPOLD III (1901–83) king of Belgium from 1934 to 1951, son of **Albert**. On his own authority he ordered the capitulation of his army to the Nazis (1940), and remained a prisoner in his own palace at Laeken. He refused to abdicate until July 1951, in favour of his son **Baudouin**.

LEOPOLD I (1640–1705) Holy Roman emperor from 1658, born in Austria. The second son of the Habsburg emperor **Ferdinand III** and the Infanta Maria Anna of Spain (daughter of **Philip III**), he became king of Hungary (1655) and Bohemia (1656), and was elected emperor in 1658 in succession to his father. For most of his reign he was at war either with the Ottoman Turks over Hungary, or with the France of **Louis XIV**. The first war with Turkey (1661–64) ended with a victory by the imperial general, **Montecucculi**, at the battle of St Gotthard; the second war (1682–99) involved the siege of Vienna in 1683, relieved by **John III Sobieski** of Poland, and ended with the Treaty of Karlowitz that gave Leopold control of virtually all of Hungary. In 1686 he had combined with England and the Dutch stadtholder William of Orange (later **William III** of Great Britain) to resist French expansionism in Europe, culminating in the War of the Spanish Succession (1701–13) that attempted to prevent the succession of the **Bourbon** house in Spain. Within the empire Leopold strove to extend Habsburg power, the imperial crown being declared hereditary in the family at the Diet of Pressburg in 1687, and made Vienna a great European centre. He attempted to repress Protestantism. In 1703 his refusal to respect the traditional rights and privileges of the Hungarian nobles led to an uprising under Francis II **Rákóczi** that was still not suppressed at Leopold's death. By his third wife, Eleanora of Neuburg, he had two sons who both succeeded him as emperor, **Joseph I** and Charles VI.

LEOPOLD II (1747–92) Holy Roman Emperor from 1790, third son of **Francis I** and **Maria Theresa**. He succeeded his father as Grand-duke of Tuscany in 1765, and his brother, **Joseph I**, as emperor in 1790. He succeeded in pacifying the Netherlands and Hungary; was led by the downfall of his sister, **Marie Antoinette**, to form an alliance with Prussia against France; but died before the war broke out.

LEOPOLD, Prince See **ALBANY, Duke of**

LEPAGE See **BASTIEN-LEPAGE**

LE PARC, Julio (1928–) Argentinian artist, born in Mendoza. After training in Buenos Aires he moved to Paris in 1958 and embarked on a career which placed him at the forefront of experimental art. He was associated, for a time, with **Viktor Vasarely**, and helped found the Groupe de Recherche D'art Visuel. He became particularly interested in the artistic exploitation of movement and light. This led, around 1960, to the construction of coloured mobiles and the exploitation of light through transparent prisms and cubes. Considerable controversy was aroused when he was awarded the painting prize at the 1966 Venice Biennale. For a while, after 1968, his art became overtly political, involving the representation of personifications of capitalists, imperialists, military and so on, but his main importance remains in his participation in the Op and Kinetic art movements of the 1960s.

LE PEN, Jean-Marie (1928–) French politician. The son of a Breton fisherman, he graduated in law at Paris before serving in the 1950s as a paratrooper in Indochina and Algeria, where he lost an eye during a violent street battle. In 1956 he won a National Assembly seat as a right-wing Poujadist. During the 1960s he was connected with the extremist Organisation de l'Armée Sécrète (OAS), before forming the National Front in 1972. This party, with its extreme right-wing policies, emerged as a new 'fifth force' in French politics, winning ten per cent of the national vote in the 1986 Assembly elections. A controversial figure and noted demagogue, he unsuccessfully contested the presidency in 1988.

LEPIDUS, Marcus Aemilius (d.13 BC) Roman politician. He declared for **Julius Caesar** against **Pompey** (49 BC), and was by Caesar made dictator of Rome and his colleague in the consulate (46 BC). He supported **Marcus Antonius**, and became one of the triumvirate with **Octavian Augustus** and Antonius, with Africa for his province (40–39 BC). He thought he could maintain himself in Sicily against Octavianus, but his soldiers deserted him.

LE PLAY, Pierre Guillaume Frédéric (1806–82) French political economist and engineer, born in Honfleur. He lived in Paris, where he was professor in the school of mines. He was one of the first to realize the importance of sociology and its effect on economics; he stressed the need for co-operation between employer and employee without intervention from government. His works included *Les Œuvriers européens* (1855) and *Réforme sociale en France* (1864).

LEPSIUS, Karl Richard (1810–84) German Egyptologist, born in Naumburg. His first work on palaeography as an instrument of philology (1834) obtained the Volney prize of the French Institute. In 1836 at Rome he studied Egyptology, Nubian, Etruscan, and Oscan, writing numerous treatises. From 1842 to 1845 he was at the head of an antiquarian expedition sent to Egypt by the king of Prussia, and in 1846 was appointed professor in Berlin. His *Denkmäler aus Aegypten und Aethiopien* (12 vols, 1849–60) remains a masterpiece; his *Chronologie der Aegypter* laid the foundation for a scientific treatment of early Egyptian history. Other works are his letters from Egypt, Ethiopia and Sinai (1852), the *Königsbuch* (1858) and the *Todtenbuch* (1867), the Egyptian Book of the Dead. He wrote on Chinese, Arabic and Assyrian philology; and was a member of the Royal Academy, director of the Egyptian section of the Royal Museum, and chief librarian of the Royal Library at Berlin.

LERINS, Vincent of See **VINCENT OF LERINS**

LERMONTOV, Mikhail Yurevich (1814–41) Russian poet, born of Scottish extraction (Learmont) in Moscow. He attended Moscow University for a short time and then the military cavalry school of St Petersburg, where he received a commission in the guards. A poem written in 1837 on the death of **Pushkin** caused his arrest and he was sent to the Caucasus. Reinstated, he was again banished following a duel with the son of the French ambassador. Another duel was the cause of his death in 1841. He wrote from an early age, but much of his work was not published until the last years of his short life and his fame was posthumous. The sublime scenery of the Caucasus inspired his best poetic pieces, such as 'The Novice', 'The Demon', 'Ismail Bey', and others. His novel, *A Hero of our Time* (1839), is a masterpiece of prose writing. He wrote also a romantic verse play, *Masquerade* (1842).

LEROUX, Pierre (1797–1871) French humanitarian, born near Paris. He influenced **George Sand**, and with her founded *Revue Indépendente* (1841). A member of the Constituent Assembly and the Legislative Assembly, he was exiled from 1851 to 1869 after opposing Louis **Napoleon III**'s *coup d'état*. He wrote *De l'Humanité* (1840) and *De l'Egalité* (1848).

LE SAGE, Alain René (1668–1747) French novelist and dramatist, born in Sarzeau in Brittany. In 1692 he went to Paris to study law, but an early marriage drove him to seek his fortune in literature. The Abbé de Lionne, who had a good Spanish library, allowed Le Sage free access to it, with a pension of 600 livres. The first fruit was a volume (1700) containing two plays in imitation of Rojas and **Lope de Vega**. In 1702 *Le Point d'honneur*, from Rojas, failed on the stage. His next venture (1704) was a remake of Avellaneda's *Don Quixote*. In 1707 *Don César Ursin*, from **Calderón**, was played with success at court, and *Crispin rival de son maître* in the city; but more successful was the *Diable boiteux* (largely based on **Luiz Vélez de Guevara**). In 1708 the Théâtre Français accepted his work but shelved one play and rejected another, which later became his famous *Turcaret*. In 1715 *Gil Blas* (vols i and ii) came out, followed between 1717 and 1721 by an attempt at an Orlando. In 1724 came vol iii of *Gil Blas*; in 1726 a largely extended *Diable boiteux*; in 1732 *Guzman de Alfarache* and *Robert Chevalier de Beauchêne*; in 1734 *Estebanillo Gonzalez*; in 1735 vol iv of *Gil Blas* and the *Journée des Parques*; between 1736 and 1738 the *Bachelier de Salamanque*; in 1739 his plays, in two volumes; in 1740 *La Valise trouvée*, a volume of letters; and in 1743 the *Mélange amusant*, a collection of facetiae. The death of his son (1743), a promising actor, and his own increasing infirmities, made him abandon Paris and literary life, and retreat with his wife and daughter to Boulogne, where his second son held a canonry, and he lived there until his death in his 80th year. Le Sage's reputation as a dramatist and as a novelist rests in each case on one work: on *Turcaret* and *Gil Blas* respectively. Some critics deny originality to one who borrowed ideas, incidents and tales from others as Le Sage did, but he was the first to perceive the capabilities of the picaresque novel. His delightful style makes him the prince of raconteurs, and the final effect of his work is all his own.

LESCOT, Pierre (c.1510–1578) French Renaissance architect, born in Paris. One of the greatest architects of his time, among his works are the screen of St Germain l'Auxerrois, the Fontaine des Innocents and the Hôtel de Ligneris. His masterpiece was the Louvre, one wing of which he completely rebuilt.

LESKIEN, August (1840–1916) German Slavonic philologist, born in Kiel. He became one of the 'Neogrammarians' at Leipzig, where he was a professor from 1870. Of his writings on Slavonic language, most important are his *Handbuch des Altbulgarischen* (1871) and *Deklination im Slavisch-Litauischen und Germanischen* (1876).

LESLIE, Lesly, or **Lesley,** Scottish family probably of Flemish origin, first found between 1171 and 1199, in possession of the pastoral parish of Lesslyn or Leslie in Aberdeenshire, and ennobled in 1457 when George Leslie of Rothes was made Earl of Rothes and Lord Leslie. The fourth earl was father of Norman Leslie, master of Rothes, chief actor in the murder of Cardinal **David Beaton**. John, sixth earl (1600–41), was one of the ablest of the Covenanting leaders. His son John (1630–81) became Lord Chancellor of Scotland in 1667, and in 1680 was created Duke of Rothes. These honours became extinct upon his death without male issue in 1681. The earldom of Rothes went to his elder daughter, in whose family the title has continued. The Balquhain branch gave birth to several men of mark, such as the learned **John Leslie**, bishop of Ross, and champion of **Mary, Queen of Scots**; Sir Alexander Leslie of Auchintoul, a general in the Muscovite service (died 1663); and **Charles Leslie**, the non-juror. Other distinguished members of the family were:

LESLIE, Alexander, 1st Earl of Leven (c.1580–1661) Scottish soldier, the illegitimate son of the captain of Blair Atholl castle. He became a field marshal of Sweden under **Gustav II Adolf**. Recalled to Scotland in 1638, he took command of the Covenanting army and commanded it against **Charles I**. In 1641 he was made Earl of Leven and Lord Balgony but from 1644 he led the Covenanting army into England on behalf of the parliamentarians. He fought at Marston Moor (1644) and the storming of Newcastle. He accepted the surrender of **Charles I** at Newark in 1646 and handed him over to parliament in 1647. He joined the royalists in 1649, fought **Cromwell** in Scotland in 1650–51, was captured and imprisoned, but released on parole in 1654.

LESLIE, Charles (1650–1722) Irish nonjuror, born in Dublin. He became chancellor of the cathedral of Connor in 1687. Deprived at the Revolution of 1688 for declining the oath of allegiance, he retired to England and wrote against Papists, Deists, Socinians, Jews and Quakers, as well as in support of the nonjuring interests. He was mostly with **James Stewart**, the Pretender, in France and Italy (1713–21), and then returned to Ireland. His *Short and Easy Method with the Jews* appeared in 1684; his *Short and Easy Method* *with the Deists* in 1697; he issued a collected edition of his *Theological Works* in 1721.

LESLIE, Charles Robert (1794–1859) British genre painter, born in London of American parentage. Educated from 1800 in Philadelphia, in 1811 he returned to England and studied at the Royal Academy. His paintings were mostly scenes from famous plays and novels. He was professor of drawings at West Point, New York (1833), and from 1848 to 1852 was professor of painting at the Royal Academy. His lectures were published in the *Handbook for Young Painters* (1855). He wrote a Life of **Constable** (1843), and began one of **Reynolds**, completed by **Tom Taylor**, who also edited his *Autobiographical Recollections* (1860).

LESLIE, David (1601–82) Scottish soldier. He served under **Gustav II Adolf**, and, returning to Scotland in 1640, acted as lieutenant-general to **Alexander Leslie**, the Earl of Leven. He fought at Marston Moor (1644), and defeated **Montrose** at Philiphaugh (1645). Routed by **Cromwell** at Dunbar in 1650, and taken prisoner by him at Worcester in 1651, he was imprisoned in the Tower until the Restoration. He was made Lord Newark in 1661.

LESLIE, Frank, the name adopted by **Henry Carter** (1821–80) English illustrator and journalist, born in Ipswich. At 17 he entered a London mercantile house and the success of sketches sent by him to the *Illustrated London News* led him to join its staff. In 1848 he went to the United States, assumed the name of Frank Leslie, and in 1854 founded the *Gazette of Fashion* and the *New York Journal. Frank Leslie's Illustrated Newspaper* began in 1855, the *Chimney Corner* in 1865; he also started the *Boys' and Girls' Weekly*, the *Lady's Journal* and other publications.

LESLIE, John (1527–96) Scottish historian and prelate, born in Kingussie, the son of a priest. Educated at King's College, Aberdeen, and Toulouse, Poitiers and Paris, he returned to Scotland and was named by the Lords of the Congregation as one of the Catholics to debate points of belief with **John Knox**. A zealous partisan of **Mary, Queen of Scots**, he was appointed a lord of session in 1564 and bishop of Ross in 1566. After her downfall he published a popular *Defence of the Honour of the Right Highe, Mightye and Nobel Princesse Marie, Queen of Scotland and Dowager of France* (1569), and joined her during her imprisonment at Tutbury, but later gave evidence against her under torture. He went into exile on the continent, and in 1579 became suffragan bishop of Rouen and bishop of Coustances. His chief work was a Latin history of Scotland, *De orignine, moribus, et rebus gestis Scotorum* (1578), which was later translated into Scots, and contains a vivid account of the Reformation from a Catholic point of view.

LESLIE, Sir John (1766–1832) Scottish natural philosopher and physicist, born in Largo, Fife. He studied at St Andrews and Edinburgh, and travelled as tutor in America and on the Continent, meanwhile engaging in experimental research. He invented a differential thermometer, a hygrometer and a photometer, and wrote *An Experimental Inquiry into heat* (1804). In 1805 he obtained the chair of mathematics at Edinburgh. In 1810 he succeeded in creating artificial ice by freezing water under the air pump. Transferred to the chair of natural philosophy (1819), he also invented the pyroscope, atmometer and aethrioscope.

LESLIE, Sir Shane (John Randolph) (1885–1971) Irish man of letters, born in Glaslough, County Monaghan, into a conservative Irish Protestant landed family. Educated at Eton, Paris University and King's College, Cambridge, he visited Russia in 1907 and became friendly with **Tolstoy**. He was converted to Roman Catholicism in 1908 and unsuccessfully contested Londonderry in the Irish Nationalist interest in 1910. He published poems of some quality and produced a brilliant analysis of the pre-war generation in *The End of a Chapter* (1916). Under the influence of **Henry Adams** he followed it with a startling attempt at Irish geopolitics, *The Celt and the World*, intended to attract the Anglophobe Irish-Americans to the Allied cause: it influenced the young **F Scott Fitzgerald** but was otherwise forgotten and never published in Britain. He wrote impressive novels based on his boyhood and youth, *Doomsland*, *The Oppidan* and *The Cantab*, and published some useful clerical biographies, investigated the relations of **George IV** and Mrs **Fitzherbert** (from whom he was descended), and wrote cautious memoirs, as well as some good short stories with faintly chilling supernatural themes.

LESLIE, Thomas Edward Cliffe (1827–82) Irish political economist born in County Wexford. One of the founders of the historic method of political economy. He qualified for the bar, but in 1853 became professor of economics and jurisprudence at Belfast. His writings included *The Land Systems* (1870), studies on the land question in Ireland, Belgium, and France, and *Essays in Political and Moral Philosophy* (1879).

LESPINASSE, Claire Françoise, or **Jeanne Julie Eléonore de** (1732–76) French salon hostess, born in Lyon, an illegitimate daughter of the Countess d'Albon. At first a teacher, in 1754 she became companion to the ailing Marquis du **Deffand**, where she formed a deep platonic relationship with the philosopher **d'Alembert**. From 1764 she broke with the marquise and created a brilliant salon of her own for the literary figures of her day. Although not strikingly beautiful, she formed liaisons with the Marquis de More and the Comte de Guibert, to whom she wrote ardent love-letters that have since been published.

LESSEPS, Ferdinand, Vicomte de (1805–94) French diplomat and canal promoter, born in Versailles, a cousin of the Empress **Eugénie**. From 1825 he held diplomatic posts at Lisbon, Tunis, Cairo, and other cities. In 1854 he began his campaign for the construction of a Suez Canal, and in 1856 obtained a concession from the viceroy. The works were begun in 1860, and completed in August 1869. In 1881 work began on his over-ambitious scheme for a sea-level Panamá Canal; but work had to be abandoned in 1888 and in 1892–93 the management was charged with breach of trust, and five directors were condemned—Lesseps, now a broken old man, to five years' imprisonment for embezzlement, but the sentence was reversed. He wrote *Histoire du canal de Suez* (1875–79) and *Souvenirs de quarante ans* (1887).

LESSING, Doris May née **Tayler** (1919–) Rhodesian writer, born in Kermanshah, Iran, the daughter of a British army captain. Her family moved to Salisbury in Southern Rhodesia (now Zimbabwe), which she left at the age of 14. She continued her own education while living on the family farm by reading in European and American literature, and started to write novels. She lived in Salisbury from 1937 to 1949, where she became involved in politics and helped to start a non-racialist left-wing party. She was married twice while living in Rhodesia (Lessing is her second husband's name). Her experiences of life in working-class London after her arrival in 1949 are described in *In Pursuit of the English* (1960). She joined the Communist party briefly, and left it in 1956, in which year Rhodesia declared her a 'prohibited immigrant'. Her first published novel was *The Grass is Singing* (1950), a study of the sterility of white civilization in

Africa. *This was the Old Chief's Country* (1951), a collection of short studies, continued this theme. In 1952 *Martha Quest* appeared, the first novel in her sequence *The Children of Violence* (completed in *A Proper Marriage* (1954), *A Ripple from the Storm* (1958), *Landlocked* (1965) and *The Four-Gated City* (1969)). This sequence, to a certain extent autobiographical, explores through the life story of the heroine, Martha, contemporary social and psychological problems. The theme running through the whole sequence is the ideal city where there is no violence. The city is, however, unattainable, and political and personal catastrophe is seen as inevitable. Other novels include *The Golden Notebook* (1962) and *Briefing for a Descent into Hell* (1971), both studies of so-called 'mental breakdown' and return to normality, which question the conventional definitions of 'sanity' and 'insanity'. Other collections of short stories include *A Man and Two Women* (1963), *African Stories* (1964) and *The Story of a Non-marrying Man* (1972). Latterly, in *Canopus in Argos: Archives*, a quintet of novels, she has attempted science fiction but her commitment to exploring political and social undercurrents in contemporary society has never wavered and can be seen to potent effect in *The Good Terrorist* (1985) and *The Fifth Child* (1988).

LESSING, Gotthold Ephraim (1729–81) German man of letters, born in Kamenz in Saxony, the son of a pastor. In 1746 he started as a theological student at Leipzig. Soon he was writing plays in the French style; leaving Leipzig in debt, in Berlin he joined the unorthodox Mylius in publishing *Beiträge zur Historie des Theaters* (1750), and independently wrote plays, translated and did literary hack-work. His chief means of support was the *Vossische Zeitung*, to which he contributed criticisms. In 1751 he went to Wittenberg, took his Master's degree, and produced a series of *Vindications* of unjustly maligned or forgotten writers, such as Cardan, **Lemnius**, and others. Back in Berlin, in *Ein Vademecum für Herrn S.G. Lange* (1754) he displayed unrelenting hostility to pretentious ignorance and with **Moses Mendelssohn** he wrote an essay on *Pope, ein Metaphysiker* (1755). After writing a trio of comedies, in 1755 he produced his classic German tragedy *Miss Sara Sampson* (1755), based on English rather than French models. In 1758 he was assisting Mendelssohn and **Nicolai** with a new critical Berlin journal (*Briefe, die neueste Literatur betreffend*), in which he protested against the dictatorship of French taste, combated the inflated pedantry of the **Gottsched** school, and extolled **Shakespeare**. While secretary to the governor of Breslau he wrote his famous *Laokoon* (1766), a critical treatise defining the limits of poetry and the plastic arts. The comedy *Minna von Barnhelm* (1767) is the first German comedy on the grand scale. Appointed playwright to a new theatre in Hamburg in 1767, he wrote the *Hamburgische Dramaturgie* (1769), in which he finally overthrew the dictatorship of the French drama. The Hamburg theatre failed, and Lessing was soon in the thick of a controversy, this time with Klotz, a Halle professor, producing the *Briefe antiquarischen Inhalts* (1769) and *Wie die Alten den Tod gebildet* (1769). In 1769 the Duke of Brunswick appointed Lessing as Wolfenbüttel librarian; and he at once began to publish some of the less-known treasures of the library in *Zur Geschichte und Litteratur* (1773–81). In 1772 he wrote the great tragedy *Emilia Galotti*. Shortly before his marriage he spent eight months in Italy as companion to the young Prince Leopold of Brunswick. Between 1774 and 1778 he published the *Wolfenbüttelsche Fragmente eines Ungennanten*, a rationalist attack on orthodox Christianity from the pen of **Reimarus** which, universally attributed to Lessing, provoked a storm of refutations. The best of Lessing's counter-attacks were *Anti-Goeze* (1778) and the fine dramatic poem, *Nathan der Weise* (1779), one of the noblest pleas for toleration ever written. Later works were *Erziehung des Menschengeschlechts* (1780) and *Ernst und Falk* (1778–80), five dialogues on freemasonry.

L'ESTRANGE, Sir Roger (1616–1704) English journalist and pamphleteer, born in Hunstanton. He narrowly escaped hanging as a royalist spy for a plot to seize Lynn, in Norfolk, in 1644, and was imprisoned in Newgate, from where he escaped after four years. Pardoned by **Cromwell** in 1653, he lived quietly until the Restoration made him licenser of the press. He fought in all the quarrels of the time with a shower of pamphlets, vigorous but not coarser than those of his antagonists. He holds a place in the history of journalism by his papers, *The Public Intelligencer* (1663–66) and *The Observator* (1681–87). He translated **Aesop**'s Fables, **Seneca**'s *Morals*, **Cicero**'s *Offices*, the *Colloquies* of **Erasmus**, **Quevedo**'s *Visions*, and **Josephus**.

LE SUEUR, Eustache (1617–55) French painter. He was a pupil of **Simon Vouet**, whose style he imitated until, about 1645, he came under the influence of **Nicolas Poussin**'s classical style. In his early style his most important work was the decoration of two rooms in the Hôtel Lambert in Paris and in his later manner paintings of the life of St **Bruno** for the Charterhouse of Paris. The Louvre possesses 36 religious pictures by him, and 13 mythological. He was one of the founders and first professors of the French Royal Academy of Painting (1648).

LE SUEUR, Hubert (c.1580–c.1670) French sculptor, born in Paris. He moved to England about 1628. His most important work was the equestrian statue of **Charles I** at Charing Cross (1633).

LESZCZYNSKI See **STANISLAUS LESZCZYNSKI**

LETHABY, William Richard (1857–1931) English architect, designer and teacher, born in Barnstaple. After training he worked (1877–87) in the London practice of **Norman Shaw**. He was a founder of the Art Workers' Guild (1884) and the Arts and Crafts Exhibition Society (c.1886). He was associated with **Ernest Gimson** in Kenton and Company during the period when he designed his most important building, Avon Tyrrell near Salisbury, with Gimson plaster ceilings and Kenton furniture. In 1891 he became active in the Society for the Protection of Ancient Buildings, in which **Philip Webb** was a major influence. The Central School of Arts and Crafts, London, was founded in 1896 with Lethaby and the sculptor **George Frampton** as joint principals; Lethaby was sole principal from 1900 to 1912. He also taught at the Royal College of Art. His grounding in the Arts and Crafts movement allied to the thoughtful evolution of his ideas made him one of the most influential figures in his field. The emphasis he placed upon workshop practice at the Central School set a precedent for design education including that at the Bauhaus.

LETHINGTON See **MAITLAND, Sir Richard**

LETTS, Thomas (1803–73) English bookbinder, born in Stockwell, London. After his father's death in 1803 he began to manufacture diaries, and by 1839 was producing 28 varieties.

LEUCHTENBERG See **BEAUHARNAIS, Eugène**

LEUCIPPUS (5th century BC) Greek philosopher, born in Miletus (or Elea). He was the originator of the atomistic cosmology which **Democritus** later developed and which is most fully expounded in **Lucretius'** great poem *De Rerum Natura*. Leucippus is usually credited with two books, *The Great World System* and *On the Mind*, but his theories and writings are not reliably separable from those of Democritus.

LEUCKART, Karl Georg Friedrich Rudolf (1822–98) German zoologist, born in Helmstedt. He studied at Göttingen, and in 1850 became professor of zoology at Giessen, in 1869 at Leipzig. A pioneer of parasitology, his work on classification is important; especially noteworthy was his division of the Radiata into Coelenterata and Echinodermata. He distinguished himself by his study of the Entozoa, writing his great work *Parasites of Man* from 1879 to 1894 (trans 1886).

LEUTZE, Emanuel (1816–68) German-born American painter, born at Gmünd in Wüttemberg. Brought up in America, he studied in Europe from 1841 to 1859, then settled in New York in 1859. His paintings were mainly scenes from American history, the best known of which is *Washington crossing the Delaware*.

LE VAILLANT, François (1753–1824) French traveller and ornithologist, born in Paramaribo, Dutch Guiana. After studies in Paris he studied birds, and explored in South Africa (1781–84), and brought back the first giraffe to France.

LE VAU, or **LEVAU, Louis** (1612–70) French architect. He headed a large studio of artists and craftsmen, producing outstanding Baroque designs for the aristocracy. Among his early works, the Hôtel Lambert, Paris, stands out particularly for the ingenious use of site. His masterful design of Vaux-le-Vicomte (1657–61), with formal landscape by **André Lenôtre**, constituted an influential milestone in French architecture, leading to his Baroque masterpiece of Versailles (from 1661, again with Le Nôtre), designed on a palatial scale for court and government. Further works include the Collège des Quatre Nations, Paris (1661), where the Greek Cross plan of the church followed precedents in Rome.

LEVEN, Earl of See **LESLIE, Alexander**

LEVENE, Phoebus Aaron Theodor, originally **Fishel Aaronovich Lenin** (1869–1940) Russian-born American biochemist, born in Sasar. He qualified in medicine in St Petersburg (Lenningrad) in 1891 and emigrated to New York in 1892. His interest soon moved to chemistry, and in 1905 he became a founder-member of the Rockefeller Institute in New York, applying chemistry to biological problems, and spent his career there. The most important of his many biochemical studies is his pioneer research on the nucleic acids. His work established the nature of the sugar component which defines the two types of nucleic acid (RNA, ribonucleic acid; and DNA, deoxyribonucleic acid) before 1930, although it was not until 1953 that newer methods allowed **James Dewey Watson** and **Francis Crick** to deduce the complete structure of the nucleic acids.

LEVER, Charles (1806–72) Irish novelist, born of English parentage in Dublin. He graduated from Trinity College, Dublin in 1827, and then went to Göttingen to study medicine. His most popular work, *Charles O'Malley*, is a description of his own college life in Dublin. About 1829 he spent some time in the backwoods of Canada and North America, and related his experiences in *Arthur O'Leary* (1844), and *Con Cregan* (1849). He practised medicine in various Irish country towns, and in 1840 in Brussels. Returning to Dublin, he published *Jack Hinton* in 1843, and from 1842 to 1845 acted as editor of the *Dublin University Magazine*, and wrote further novels. In 1845 he again went to Brussels, Bonn, and Karlsruhe, where he published the *Knight of Gwynne* (1847), and to Florence, where he wrote *Roland Cashel* (1850). Then, completely changing his style, he wrote *The Daltons* (1852), followed by the *Fortunes of Glencore* (1857). He was appointed British vice-consul in Spezia in 1858, and continued to write, his work including *Luttrel of Arran* (1865) and three other novels in rapid succession, and some racy essays in *Blackwood's* by 'Cornelius O'Dowd'. In 1867 he was promoted to the consulship in Trieste. Lever's work contained brilliant, rollicking sketches of a phase of Irish life which was passing away, though no doubt his caricatures created a false idea of Irish society and character.

LEVERHULME, William Hesketh Lever, 1st Viscount (1851–1925) English soapmaker and philanthropist, born in Bolton. Beginning in his father's grocery business, he opened new shops and in 1886 with his brother, James, started the manufacture of soap from vegetable oils instead of tallow, and founded the model industrial new town of Port Sunlight. Among his many benefactions, he endowed at Liverpool University a school of tropical medicine and gave Lancaster House to the nation. After World War II he attempted to develop the economy of the Western Isles of Scotland by purchasing the Islands of Lewis and Harris and planning a huge fishing and fish-producing industry, but withdrew in 1923 after local opposition from the crofters of Lewis.

LEVERRIER, Urbain Jean Joseph (1811–77) French astronomer, born in St Lô, Normandy. In 1836 he became teacher of astronomy at the Polytechnique. His *Tables de Mercure* and several memoirs gained him admission to the Academy in 1846. From disturbances in the motions of planets he inferred the existence of an undiscovered planet, and calculated the point in the heavens where, a few days afterwards, Neptune was actually discovered by **Johann Gottfried Galle** at Berlin (1846). Elected in 1849 to the Legislative Assembly, he became counter-revolutionary. In 1852 **Louis Napoleon** made him a senator and in 1854 he succeeded **Dominique Arago** as director of the observatory of Paris.

LEVERTOV, Denise (1923–) English-born American poet, born in Ilford, Essex, into a literary household; she was the daughter of a Welsh mother and a Russian Jewish father who became an Anglican clergyman. Educated privately, she emigrated to the USA in 1948. She was appointed poetry editor of *The Nation* in 1961. *The Double Image* (1946) was her first collection of verse and others have appeared steadily. A 'British Romantic with almost Victorian background', she has been outspoken on many issues (Vietnam, feminism, etc) and her poetry is similarly questioning. Her attachment to the 'Black Mountain' poets like Charles Olson and William Carlos Williams is palpable but her voice is distinctive. *With Eyes at the Back of Our Heads* (1959), *Relearning the Alphabet* (1970), *To Stay Alive* (1971) and *Footprints* (1972) particularly stand out.

LEVESON-GOWER, George, 2nd Earl Granville (1815–91) English statesman. He was educated at Eton and Oxford, in 1836 became MP for Morpeth, in 1840 for Lichfield, and was for a brief period under-secretary for foreign affairs. He was a consistent Liberal and a freetrader. He succeeded to the peerage in 1846, and became foreign secretary in 1851, president of the council in 1853, and leader of the House of Lords in 1855. Having failed to form a ministry in 1859, he joined Lord **Palmerston**'s second administration. He retired with Earl **Russell** in 1866, having been made lord warden of the Cinque Ports in 1865. In December 1868 he became colonial secretary in **Gladstone**'s first ministry, and in 1870 foreign secretary, as again in 1880–85.

LEVEY, Barnett (1798–1837) English-born Australian pioneer, born in the East End of London. He arrived from Cork, Ireland, in 1821 to join his brother Solomon Levey (1794–1833) who had been transported for seven years for stealing a chest of tea. Barnett Levey was the first free Jewish settler to arrive in the new colony, and joined his brother who by that time had received his pardon and was a prosperous businessman. Soon Barnett was in business for himself, dealing in flour, liquor, general goods and books; with these last he established one of the first lending libraries in Australia. In 1827 he founded a company to operate Sydney's first theatre, which opened the following year behind his warehouse. Financial problems entailed the premises being turned into the Royal Hotel, and subsequently sold, but in 1832 he received the first theatre licence issued in the colony, and opened on Boxing Day 1832 on a temporary stage in the hotel. The next year, at the back of the hotel, he erected the first purpose-built theatre in Australia, the Theatre Royal.

LEVI See **MATTHEW, St**

LEVI, Primo (1919–87) Italian writer and chemist, born in Turin to Jewish parents. On completing his schooling he enrolled at Turin University to study chemistry for, as he wrote in *The Periodic Table* (1985), he believed that 'the nobility of Man ... lay in making himself the conqueror of matter'. During the war he fled into the mountains and formed a small guerrilla force; but he was betrayed and in December 1943 was arrested, turned over to the SS, and despatched to Auschwitz. He was one of the few to survive, partly because he contracted scarlet fever when the Germans evacuated the camp as the Russians approached. Those ten months in Auschwitz haunted him for the rest of his life and may have prompted his suicide. His first book *If This Is a Man* was completed soon after his return to Turin and was published in 1947. A graphic account of life in a concentration camp, it is written with a chemist's detached sensibility, making it all the more powerful. He continued to combine his career as a chemist with that of a writer. His best known book is *The Periodic Table*, a volume of memoirs and autobiographical reflections. One of the 20th century's most incisive commentators, other of his titles include *The Monkey's Wrench* (1978), *If Not Now, When?* (1982) and *Other People's Trades* (1985).

LEVI-CIVITA, Tullio (1873–1941) Italian mathematician, born in Padua. He studied in Padua and became professor there in 1897. From about 1900 he worked on the absolute differential calculus (or tensor calculus) which became the essential mathematical tool in **Einstein**'s general relativity theory. From 1918 to 1938 he was professor in Rome, but was forced to retire by Fascist laws against Jews.

LÉVI-STRAUSS, Claude (1908–) French social anthropologist. A graduate in law and philosophy, he became interested in anthropology while lecturing (1934–39) at São Paulo University, Brazil. He subsequently worked in the New School for Social Research in New York before becoming (1950–74) Director of Studies at the École Pratiques des Hautes Études in Paris. Since the publication of *The Elementary Structures of Kinship* (1949: trans 1969), Lévi-Strauss has exerted a considerable influence on contemporary anthropology: he established a new approach to analyzing various collective phenomena such as kinship, ritual and myth. In his extensive four-volume study *Mythologiques* (1964–72) he reveals the systematic ordering behind codes of expression and argues that myths are not 'justifications' but rather attempts to overcome 'contradictions'. He also argues that myths are not to be deciphered, but rather compared with other myths to elicit their 'meaning'. *Structural Anthropology* (Vol I, 1958: trans 1963) shows how Lévi-Strauss has been influenced by the structural linguistics of **de Saussure**, **Jakobson** and others, and confirms its author's outstanding contribution to the modern doctrine of structuralism. He also revived interest in totemism, presenting it in a new light, free from the religious and utilitarian elements that had accumulated in previous writings on the subject.

LEVITA, Elias (1465–1549) German grammarian and exegete, born in Neustadt near Nuremberg. An expulsion of Jews forced him to Italy, where he taught successively in Padua (1504), Venice, Rome (1514), and finally (1527) Venice again. He wrote on Job, the Psalms, Proverbs, Amos, and the vowel points; also producing a Hebrew grammar and a Talmudic and Targumic Dictionary.

LÉVY-BRUHL, Lucien (1857–1939) French philosopher and anthropologist, born in Paris. He studied at the École Normale Supérieure in Paris and was appointed to a chair in the history of modern philosophy at the Sorbonne in 1904. His early work was in moral philosophy, and he published *La Morale et la Science des Mœurs* in 1903. He went on to develop a theory of primitive mentality in *La Mentalité Primitive* (1922) and several later books. He believed that the mentality of primitive people was essentially mystical and prelogical, differing in kind from the rational and logical thought of the modern West. This view drew him into a sharp exchange with **Émile Durkheim**, and has few adherents today.

LEWALD, Fanny (1811–89) German novelist, born in Königsberg (now Kalingrad). Jewish by birth, she became a Lutheran convert in 1828 to marry a young theologian, who died just before the wedding. In 1845 she met Adolf Stahr (1805–76), a Berlin critic, with whom she lived until he was free to marry in 1855. She was an enthusiastic champion of women's rights, which were aired in her early novels, *Clementine* (1842), *Jenny* (1843) and *Eine Lebensfrage* (1845). Her later works were family sagas, like *Von Geschlecht zu Geschlecht* (1863–65) and *Die Familie Darner* (3 vols, 1887). She wrote records of travel in Italy (1847) and Great Britain (1852), and published an autobiography, *Meine Lebensgeschichte* (1861–63).

LEWES, George Henry (1817–78) English writer, born in London, grandson of the comedian, Charles Lee Lewes (1740–1803). Educated at Greenwich and in Jersey and Brittany, he left school at an early age to enter first a notary's office, and then the house of a Russian merchant. In 1838 he went to Germany for nearly two years, studying the life, language and literature of the country. On his return to London he started writing about anything and everything for the *Penny Encyclopaedia* and *Morning Chronicler*, later as a contributor to a dozen more journals, reviews and magazines, and as editor of the *Leader* (1851–54), and of the *Fortnightly* (1865–66), which he himself founded. He was unhappily married, with a family, when he began a lifelong affair with **George Eliot** in 1854. His works, as well as a tragedy and two novels (1841–48), include *The Spanish Drama* (1846); a *Life of Robespierre* (1848); *Comte's Philosophy of the Sciences* (1853), which is more than a translation; the admirable *Life and Works of Goethe* (1855); *Studies in Animal Life* (1862); *Aristotle* (1864); *On Actors and the Art of Acting* (1875); and *Problems of Life and Mind* (1874–79).

LEWIS, Alun (1915–44) Welsh soldier-poet and short-story writer, born in Cwmaman, near Aberdare.

He was educated at Cowbridge School, the University College of Wales, Aberystwyth and at Manchester University. A lieutenant in the army, his first work, a volume of short stories about army life, was *The Last Inspection* (1942), followed by a volume of poetry, *Raiders' Dawn*, in the same year. He died of gunshot wounds at Chittagong during the Burma campaign. Another volumes of verse, ironically entitled *Ha! Ha! Among the Trumpets*, was published posthumously in 1945, followed by a collection of short stories and letters, *In the Green Tree* (1948).

LEWIS, Sir (William) Arthur (1915–) West Indies-born British economist, born in St Lucia. From 1948 to 1958 he was professor of economics at Manchester University, then became first president of the University of the West Indies (1959–63). From 1963 until his retirement in 1983 he held a chair in economics at Princetown. In 1979 he was awarded the Nobel prize for economics, with **Theodore Schultz**, for work on economic development in the Third World.

LEWIS, Carl (1961–) American track and field athlete, born in Birmingham, Alabama. A brilliant all-round athlete at Houston University (1979–82), he won four gold medals at the 1984 Los Angeles Olympics (100m, 200m, 4 × 100m relay, and long jump), emulating the achievement of **Jesse Owens** at the 1936 Berlin Olympics. At the 1988 Seoul Olympics he was awarded the 100m gold medal after **Ben Johnson** was stripped of the title.

LEWIS, Cecil Day (1904–72) Irish poet, critic and detective-story writer, born in Ballintogher, Sligo. He was educated at Sherborne School and Wadham College, Oxford, and published his first verse in 1925, *Beechen Vigil and Other Poems*. He made his name as a lyric poet with *Transitional Poems* (1929), and during the 1930s, with **Auden** and **Spender**, became associated with left-wing causes, and also wrote literary criticism in *A Hope for Poetry* (1934). He became a member of the Communist party, which he renounced in 1939. During World War II he worked in the ministry of information, and then published *Poetry for You* (1944) and his major critical work, *The Poetic Image* (1947). He became professor of poetry at Oxford (1951–56) and at Harvard (1964–65), and published his last critical work, *The Poetic Impulse* (1965). He made notable translations of **Virgil** and St Valery, and was appointed poet laureate in 1968. Under the pseudonym of 'Nicholas Blake' he wrote a score of sophisticated detective novels. His autobiography, *The Buried Day*, was published in 1960.

LEWIS, C S (Clive Staples) (1898–1963) Irish-born academic, writer and Christian apologist, born in Belfast, the son of a solicitor. He taught at Oxford from 1925 to 1954, and was professor of medieval and Renaissance English at Cambridge from 1954. He published his first book *Dymer* (1926) under the name of 'Clive Hamilton'. It is a narrative poem in rhyme royal, at once satirical and idealistic, a flavour which characterizes most of his work. His medieval study, *Allegory of Love* was awarded the Hawthornden Prize (1936). His widest-known book is *The Screwtape Letters* (1942). Other titles include *The Problem of Pain* (1940), *Beyond Personality* (1944), and *Mere Christianity* (1952); works of scientific fiction including *Out of the Silent Planet* (1938) and *Perelandra* (1943); and books for children chronicling the magic land of Narnia, of which *The Last Battle* was awarded the Carnegie Prize in 1957. His autobiography *Surprised by Joy* (1955), described his brief but happy marriage to an American, Joy Davidson, and conversion to Catholicism.

LEWIS, Sir George Cornewall (1806–63) English statesman and author, born in London. Educated at Eton and Christ Church College, Oxford, he was called to the bar in 1831 and he became a poor-law commissioner in 1839. Liberal MP for Herefordshire (1847–52) and for the Radnor Boroughs from 1885, he was Chancellor of the Exchequer (1855–58), home secretary (1859–61), and then war secretary. He edited the *Edinburgh Review* from 1852 to 1855 and succeeded to a baronetcy in 1855. He wrote *Origin of the Romance Languages* (1835), *Inquiry into the Credibility of Ancient Roman History* (1855—against **Niebuhr**), *Astronomy of the Ancients* (1859), and *Dialogue on the Best Form of Government* (1859).

LEWIS, Gilbert Newton (1875–1946) American physical chemist, born in Weymouth, Massachusetts. He was a major contributor to the theory of chemical bonding, and probably did more to advance chemical theory this century than any other chemist. Educated at Nebraska University and Harvard, he then studied in Germany for two years before taking a post as government chemist in the Philippines. From 1905 to 1912 he taught at the Massachusetts Institute of Technology, then moved to California University (1912–45). He was a pioneer in taking ideas from physics and applying them to chemistry. His ideas focused on the arrangement of electrons around atomic nuclei. He assumed that all but the lightest elements (H and He) had a pair of electrons surounding the nucleus, with further electrons (in number to balance the nuclear charge) in groups; a group of eight being especially stable (the noble gases). Bonding between atoms of the lighter elements occurred in such a way that atoms gained or lost outer electrons to create octets, either by transfer (electrovalence) or by sharing (covalence). Noting that nearly all chemical compounds contain an even number of electrons, he concluded that the electron pair is especially important, and a shared electron pair can be equated with a covalent bond. He also defined a *base* as a substance which has a pair of electrons which can be used to complete the stable shell of another atom; and an *acid* as a substance able to accept a pair from another atom, to form a stable group of electrons; a very valuable concept.

LEWIS, Hywel David (1910–) Welsh philosopher of religion, born in Llandudno. Professor of the history and philosophy of religion at King's College, London (1955–77), after succeeding **C A Campbell** in the chair of philosophy at University College, Bangor, he has championed the subject against 'fashions' that might have eliminated it. He has been president of Mind and other learned societies, founder editor of *Religious Studies* (1965–84), and author of many studies, including *Our Experience of God* (1959), *The Self and Immortality* (1973), *Persons and Life after Death* (1978), and a trilogy based on his Gifford lectures: *The Elusive Mind* (1969), *The Elusive Self* (1982), and *Freedom and Alienation* (1985). He has also published several Welsh books, including a volume of poems.

LEWIS, Jerry Lee (1935–) American rock and country singer and pianist, born in Ferriday, Louisiana. His straightforward and powerful if primitive style helped establish him very quickly as one of the great originals of rock and roll. After working as a session musician at Sun Studios in Memphis he was invited to record by the label's founder, Sam Phillips. His 1957 recordings 'Whole Lotta Shakin' and 'Great Balls of Fire' became classics of rock, copied by successive generations of musicians. In 1958 he had further success with 'Breathless' and 'High School Confidential' (the title track to a film in which he starred). After he married his 14-year-old (some sources say 13-year-old) cousin Myra in 1958 he was effectively boycotted by television and the pop radio stations. During the 1960s he concentrated on country music, only returning to rock and roll in the 1970s.

LEWIS, John Llewellyn (1880–1969) American labour leader, born in Iowa. He was president of the United Mine Workers' Union from 1920 to 1960. In 1935 he formed a combination of unions, the Congress of Industrial Organizations, of which he was president till 1940. A skilful negotiator, he has made the miners' union one of the most powerful in the USA.

LEWIS, Matthew Gregory (1775–1818) English novelist, born in London. He was educated at Westminster School and Christ Church College, Oxford, and in Germany, where he met **Goethe**. In 1794 he was an attaché to The Hague and it was there he wrote *Ambrosio, or the Monk* (1796), a Gothic novel influenced by his formative reading of tales of witchcraft and the supernatural, and **Ann Radcliffe**'s *Mysteries of Udolpho*, and which inspired his nickname 'Monk' Lewis. Many others in a similar vein followed, including a musical drama, *The Castle Spectre* (1798). Concerned about the treatment of the slaves on the estates he had inherited in the West Indies, he went there in 1817, but died of yellow fever on the way home. His *Journal of a West Indian Proprietor* was published in 1834.

LEWIS, Meriwether (1774–1809) American explorer, born in Charlotteville, Virginia. He joined the army and in 1792 led an unsuccessful expedition up the Missouri River. In 1801 he became personal secretary to President **Thomas Jefferson**, and was invited with his long-time friend **William Clark** to lead an expedition (1804–06) to explore the vast unknown lands to the west of the Mississippi. It was to become the first overland journey across North America to the Pacific Coast, and one of the longest trans-continental journeys ever undertaken. Lewis became governor of Louisiana in 1806, but died in a shooting incident in a cabin in Tennessee.

LEWIS, Richard, known as **'Dic Penderyn'** (1807/8–1831) Welsh folk hero, born near Aberavon, Glamorganshire. He was accused of wounding a soldier during the Merthyr Tydfil riots of 1831, found guilty and publicly executed at Cardiff on 31 August 1831. Many were convinced of his innocence and he became a folk hero in South Wales.

LEWIS, Saunders (1893–1985) Welsh dramatist, poet and nationalist, born in Cheshire. He studied English and French at Liverpool University, and in 1924 published a study of English influences on classical Welsh 18th-century poetry, *A School of Welsh Augustans*, having become lecturer in Welsh in University College, Swansea, in 1922. He was co-founder of the Welsh Nationalist party (later Plaid Cymru) in 1925, and became its president in 1926. He became a Roman Catholic in 1932. Imprisoned in 1936 for a token act of arson against building materials for construction of an RAF bombing school at Penyberth, he was dismissed from Swansea and made his living by journalism, teaching and farming until his appointment as lecturer (later senior lecturer) in Welsh at University College, Cardiff, in 1952. He published many essays, 19 plays in Welsh and English, poems, novels, historical and literary criticism, chiefly in Welsh. He retired from public life in 1957, but continued publishing plays, his last being *Excelsior* (1980).

LEWIS, (Harry) Sinclair (1885–1951) American novelist, born in Sauk Center, Minnesota, the son of a doctor. Educated at Yale, he became a journalist and wrote several minor works before *Main Street* (1920), the first of a series of best-selling novels satirizing the arid materialism and intolerance of American small-town life. *Babbitt* (1922) still lends its title as a synonym for middle-class American philistinism. Other titles of this period are *Martin Arrowsmith* (1925), *Elmer Gantry* (1927) and *Dodsworth* (1929). From then on he tended to exonerate the ideologies and self-sufficiency he had previously pilloried, though he continued to be eagerly read. His later novels include *Cass Timberlane* (1945) and *Kingsblood Royal* (1947). He refused the Pulitzer prize for *Arrowsmith*, but accepted the Nobel prize for literature in 1930, being the first American writer to receive it.

LEWIS, Sir Thomas (1881–1945) Welsh cardiologist and clinical scientist, born in Cardiff. He received his preclinical training at University College, Cardiff. In 1902 he went to University College Hospital, in London, where he remained as student, teacher and consultant until his death. **E H Starling** stimulated his interest in cardiac physiology and the physician Sir James MacKenzie awakened his curiosity about diseases of the heart. He was the first completely to master the use of the electrocardiogram, and he and his pupils established the basic parameters which still govern the interpretation of electrocardiograms. During his later years he turned his attention to the physiology of cutaneous blood vessels and the mechanisms of pain. He fought for full-time clinical research posts to investigate what he called 'clinical science'. This broadening of his interests was signalled when he changed the name, in 1933, of the journal he had founded in 1909, from *Heart* to *Clinical Science*. His textbooks of cardiology went through multiple editions and translations.

LEWIS, (Percy) Wyndham (1882–1957) English novelist, painter and critic, born in Amehurst, Nova Scotia. He was educated at Rugby School and the Slade School of Art. With **Ezra Pound** he instituted the Vorticist movement and founded *Blast* (1914–15), the magazine which expounded their theories. From 1916 to 1918 he served on the Western Front, as a bombardier, then as a war artist. In the early 1930s, his right-wing sympathies were out of vogue. He emigrated to Canada at the beginning of World War II, returning to London in 1945. In 1951 he went blind. His novels, *Tarr* (1918), *The Childermass* (1928), and *The Apes of God* (1930) are powerful, vivid satires reflecting his talent as a painter. The autobiographical *Self Condemned* (1954), and *The Human Age* (1955) conclude the trilogy which was conceived with *The Childermass* and was modelled in part on **Dante** and **Milton**. As a writer he has been ranked by some critics alongside **James Joyce**; as a painter, he was both the foremost experimentalist of his time in British art, and a portraitist of the highest calibre.

LEWITT, Sol (1928–) American Minimalist and exponent of Conceptual Art, born in Hartford, Connecticut. He studied at Syracuse University, 1949, and worked for an architect before emerging as an abstract artist in the early 1960s. Given to abstract 'philosophy' in the 1970s, he made Minimalist sculptures (or 'structures' as he called them); but was already declaring that the concept was more important than the work, the planning more than the execution. His exhibited wall-drawings are therefore afterwards obliterated. He held an exhibition at the Museum of Modern Art, New York in 1978.

LEYDEN, John (1775–1811) Scottish poet and orientalist, born in Denholm, Roxburghshire, the son of a farmer. He studied medicine at Edinburgh University, and was licensed as a preacher in 1798. He wrote a book on European settlements in Africa (1799), and helped Sir **Walter Scott** to gather materials for his *Border Minstrelsy*, and his translations and poems in the *Edinburgh Magazine* attracted attention. In 1803 he sailed for India as assistant surgeon at Madras, travelled widely in the East, acquired 34 languages, and translated the gospels into five of them. He accompanied Lord Minto as interpreter to Java, and died of fever at Batavia. His ballads have taken a higher place than his longer poems, especially *Scenes of Infancy* (1803); his dissertation on Indo-Chinese languages is also well known.

LHÉVINNE, Josef (1874–1944) Russian-born American pianist, born in Orel, one of the great virtuoso interpreters of the Romantic repertoire. He studied at the Moscow Conservatory and played **Beethoven**'s Emperor Concerto with **Anton Rubinstein** conducting. After playing and teaching in Russia he made his American début in 1906. He lived in Berlin (1907–19), then emigrated to the USA, where he taught music. He often played two-piano recitals with his pianist wife Rosina, née Bessie (1880–1976).

L'HÔPITAL, Michel de (1507–73) French statesman, born in Aigueperse in Auvergne. He studied law at Toulouse and Padua and settled as an advocate in Paris at 30. In 1547–48 he represented **Henri II** at the Council of Trent, and then was in the household of the Duchess of Berri. In 1554 he became superintendent of finances, in 1560 chancellor of France. He strove to pacify the religious quarrel by staying the hand of the Catholic persecutors. After 1563 he lost ground and in 1568 resigned and retired to his estate near Étampes. His Latin poems, speeches, etc, appeared in 1824–25.

L'HOTE, André (1885–1962) French artist, teacher, and writer on art, born in Bordeaux. He associated with the Cubists and in his painting he combined classic precision of composition and a free, sensitive use of colour, but his greatest influence was exerted through his writings, such as *Treatise on Landscape* (1939) and *Treatise on the Figure* (1950), and his teaching in Paris, where he established the Académie Montparnasse in 1922.

LI, Choh Hao (1913–) Chinese-born American biochemist, born in Canton. He studied at Nanjing and from 1935 at Berkeley, where he became professor of biochemistry in 1950. His main work was on the pituitary hormones; he isolated adrenocorticotrophic hormone (ACTH) and by 1956 had established its molecular structure; ten years later he had similar success with the growth hormone, somatotropin, which he synthesized in 1970.

LIADOV, Anatol Konstantinovich (1855–1914) Russian composer, born in St Petersburg, where he studied under **Rimsky-Korsakov**. His works include music for the piano and the vivid nationalist symphonic poems *Baba-Yaga*, *Kikimora* and *The Enchanted Lake*. He also made collections of Russian folksongs, conducted, and was professor at St Petersburg.

LIAQUAT ALI KHAN (1895–1951) Pakistani statesman. After leaving Oxford he became a member of the Inner Temple. He joined the Moslem League in 1923, and became prime minister of Pakistan in 1947. He was assassinated in 1951.

LIBAU or **LIBAVIUS, Andreas** (c.1560–1616) German alchemist, born in Halle, Saxony. He studied at Jena University, taught history and poetry there, and then in the 1590s moved to Rothenberg an der Taube, where he began to teach and write (voluminously) on alchemy. His finest work was *Alchemia* (1597), a richly illustrated book which has a claim to be the first chemical textbook; it gives accounts of a range of chemical methods and substances, and vigorously attacks the ideas of **Paracelsus**. However, his philosophical, diffuse and mystical style limited its influence; his *Alchemia* was not translated out of Latin, was more quoted than used, and is more appreciated now as a step from alchemy towards chemistry than it was in his own time.

LIBBY, Willard Frank (1908–80) American chemist, born in Grand Valley, Colorado. He studied and lectured at Berkeley, California, where he became associate professor in 1945. He did atom-bomb research (1941–45) on the separation of the isotopes of uranium at Columbia, and from 1945 to 1954 was professor of chemistry at Chicago. From 1954 to 1959 he served on the US Atomic Energy Commission. He was awarded the 1960 Nobel prize in chemistry for his part in the invention of the Carbon-14 method of determining the age of an object. He was professor of chemistry at California University, 1959–76.

LIBERACE, originally **Wladziu Valentino Liberace** (1919–87) American entertainer, born in West Allis, a suburb of Milwaukee. The son of a musician, he was playing piano by ear at the age of four, appeared as a soloist with the Chicago Symphony Orchestra at fourteen and earned a living in nightclubs and at student dances using the stage name Walter Busterkeys. Over the years he developed an act of popular piano classics performed with a lavish sense of showmanship and dimple-cheeked charm that endeared him to several generations of American matrons. He made his film début in *East of Java* (1949) but his one starring role in *Yours Sincerely* (1955) was not well received. His television series, *The Liberace Show* (1952–57), won him an Emmy as Best Male Personality. His enduring career rested on his live performances and a flamboyant life of piano-shaped swimming-pools, glittering candelabra, and sartorial excess. He broke all box-office records at the massive Radio City Music Hall in New York during 1985. His books include *Liberace Cooks! Recipes From His Seven Dining Rooms* (1970) and *The Things I Love* (1976).

LIBERIUS (d. 366) Christian prelate, born in Rome. He became pope in 352, but was banished in 355 for refusing to confirm the decree against **Athanasius**. In 358 he regained the papal throne.

LICHFIELD, Patrick, 5th Earl of (1939–) English photographer. Educated at Harrow and Sandhurst, he served in the Grenadier Guards (1959–62), when he determined to become a professional photographer. After working as an assistant for many years he opened his own studio and since 1981 has achieved success in travel and publicity photography as well as in many personal royal portraits.

LICHTENSTEIN, Martin Hinrich Carl (1780–1857) German zoologist and naturalist, born in Hamburg. He travelled extensively in South Africa as a young man as physician to the Dutch governor of the Cape of Good Hope (1802–06), and published *Reisen in suedlichern Africa* (1810–12). He was appointed first professor of zoology at the new Berlin University in 1810, and from 1815 was the first director of the Berlin Zoological Museum, which he developed into one of the finest in Europe. Lichtenstein's Sandgrouse is named after him.

LICHTENSTEIN, Roy (1923–) American painter, born in New York. He studied painting at the Art Students' League, New York, and from 1940 to 1943 at Ohio State University, Columbus. He served in the US army from 1943 to 1946 before returning to Ohio, where he taught from 1946 to 1951. In the mid 1950s he worked in an Abstract Expressionist style, but by 1961 was painting enlarged versions of illustrations found in popular magazine advertisements and cartoon strips. He rendered these in a dead-pan style, duplicating the dot patterns of crude newspaper reproductions in brightly coloured, enlarged form. He is recognized as one of the major figures of the Pop Art movement.

LICK, James (1796–1876) American financier and philanthropist, born in Fredericksburg. A piano-maker by training, he went to California c.1848 and made a fortune in real estate investment. He founded the Lick Observatory on Mount Hamilton.

LIDDELL, Eric Henry (1902–45) Scottish athlete and missionary, known as 'The Flying Scotsman', born in Tientsin, China, of Scottish missionary parents. He was educated at Eltham College, London, and Edinburgh University, where his outstanding speed earned him seven caps in the Scotland rugby team as a wing threequarter. At the 1924 Olympics in Paris he would have been favourite to win the 100 metres had he not refused to take part on religious grounds because the heats were to be run on a Sunday (the gold medal was eventually won by Harold Abrahams). Instead, he won the bronze medal in the 200 metres, and then caused a sensation by winning the gold medal in the 400 metres (at which he was comparatively inexperienced) in a world record time of 47.6 seconds. In 1925, having completed his degree in science and a degree in divinity, he went to China to work as a Scottish Congregational Church missionary. During World War II he was interned by the Japanese at Weihsien camp; and there, not long before the war ended, he died of a brain tumour. The story of his athletic triumphs was told in the film *Chariots of Fire* (1981).

LIDDELL, Henry George (1811–98) English classical scholar. Educated at Charterhouse and Christ Church College, Oxford, he was ordained in 1838 and appointed professor of moral philosophy at Oxford. Headmaster of Westminster School (1846–55), he returned to Christ Church as dean, was vice-chancellor of the university (1870–74), and resigned the deanship in 1891. He is renowned for the *Greek-English Lexicon* (1843), based on **Franz Passow**'s dictionary, with Robert Scott (1811–87), master of Balliol College (1854–70). Liddell also wrote a *History of Rome* (1855). His daughter, Alice, was the little girl for whom **Charles Dodgson** (Lewis Carroll), his colleague at Christ Church, wrote *Alice in Wonderland*.

LIDDELL HART, Basil Henry (1895–1970) English military journalist and historian, born in Paris. Educated at St Paul's and Cambridge, he served in World War I and retired from the army in 1927. He was responsible for various tactical developments during the war, and wrote the post-war official manual of Infantry Training (1920). He was military correspondent to the *Daily Telegraph* (1925–35) and *The Times* (1935–39). In 1937 he relinquished his position as personal adviser to the minister of war to publicize the need for immediate development of air power and mechanized warfare. He wrote more than 30 books on warfare, as well as biographies of **Scipio**, **T E Lawrence**, and others.

LIDDON, Henry Parry (1829–90) English theologian, born in North Stoneham, Hampshire. He graduated at Oxford in 1850. Ordained in 1852, from 1854 to 1859 he was vice-principal of Cuddesdon Theological College, and in 1864 became a prebendary of Salisbury, in 1870 a canon of St Paul's, and Ireland professor of exegesis at Oxford (till 1882). In 1866 he delivered his Bampton Lectures on *The Divinity of Our Lord*. He strongly opposed the Church Discipline Act of 1874, and as warmly supported **Gladstone**'s crusade against the Bulgarian atrocities in 1876. Canon Liddon was the most able and eloquent exponent of Liberal High Church principles. His *Analysis of the Epistle to the Romans* was published in 1893.

LIDMAN, Sara (1923–) Swedish author, born in Missenträsk in the far north of the country. The area was the setting for her early novels such as *Tjärdalen* (The Tar Still, 1953) and *Hjortonlandet* (Cloudberry Land, 1955). The support for the underdog visible in these novels became more overtly political in the 1960s after her experiences of South Africa, Kenya and Vietnam. In the highly-acclaimed series of novels beginning with *Din tjänare hör* (Thy Servant Heareth, 1977), she returns to her roots and takes as her theme the building of the railways of the north. She has experimented with documentary forms of writing and has also written plays.

LIE, Jonas Lauritz Idemil (1833–1908) Norwegian novelist and poet, born in Eker near Drammen. He trained as a lawyer but abandoned law for literature. His novels, which present realistic portayals of fisher-life in Norway, include *Den fremsynte* (The Visionary, 1870), *Lodsen og hans Hustru* (Lodsen and his Wife, 1874), *Livsslaven* (One of Life's Slaves, 1883) and *Kommandørens Døtre* (The Commander's Daughters, 1886). He also wrote fairy-tales like *Trold* (Trolls, 1891–92), and some poetry and plays.

LIE, Marius Sophus (1842–99) Norwegian mathematician, born in Nordfjordeide. He studied at Oslo University, then supported himself by giving private lessons. After visiting **Felix Klein** in Berlin, a chair of mathematics was created for him in Oslo. In 1886 he succeeded Klein at Leipzig but returned to Oslo in 1898. His study of contact transformations arising from partial differential equations led him to develop an extensive theory of continuous groups of transformations, now known as Lie groups. This theory has become a central part of 20th-century mathematics and has important applications in quantum theory.

LIE, Trygve Halvdan (1896–1968) Norwegian lawyer, born in Oslo. He was a Labour member of the Norwegian parliament and held several posts, including minister of justice and minister of supply and shipping, before having to flee in 1940 with the government to Britain, where he acted as its foreign minister until 1945. He was elected secretary-general of the UN in 1946, but resigned in 1952. He was minister of industry (1963–1964) and of commerce and shipping from 1964. He wrote *In the Cause of Peace* (1954).

LIEB, Michael See **MUNKÁCSY**

LIEBER, Francis (1800–72) German-born American political scientist, born in Berlin. In 1827 he went to America for political reasons and became a naturalized American and professor of history and political economy at South Carolina College, Columbia, and Columbia Law School. His *Code for the Government of the Armies of the US* was widely accepted. He also created *Encyclopaedia Americana* (13 vols, 1829–33).

LIEBERMANN, Felix (1851–1925) German legal historian, born in Berlin. He worked for many years to settle the texts of the Anglo-Saxon legal codes and to elucidate them. His major work, *Die Gesetze der Angelsachsen* (3 vols, 1903–16), is indispensable for early English legal history.

LIEBERMANN, Max (1827–1935) German painter and etcher, born in Berlin. He studied at Weimar and in Paris, where he first won fame. In Germany from 1878 he painted open-air studies and scenes of humble life which were often sentimental. Later, however, his work became more colourful and romantic, and, influenced by the French Impressionists, he became the leading painter of that school in his own country.

LIEBIG, Justus, Freiherr von (1803–73) German chemist, born in Darmstadt. He studied at Bonn and Erlangen, and in 1822 went to Paris, where **Joseph Gay-Lussac** took him into his laboratory. In 1824 he became professor of chemistry at Giessen, and in 1852 at Munich. In 1845 he was created Baron. Liebig was one of the most illustrious chemists of his age; equally great in method and in practical application, he made his mark in organic chemistry, animal chemistry, and the doctrine of alcohols. He was the founder of agricultural chemistry, a discoverer of chloroform and chloral and, with **Friedrich Wohler**, of the benzoyl radical. An admirable chemical laboratory, practically the first, was established by him at Giessen. He vastly extended the method of organic analysis, and invented appliances for analysis by combustion and Liebig's condenser. His most important treatises were on the analysis of organic bodies (1837), *Animal Chemistry* (1842), *Organic Chemistry* (1843) and *Agricultural Chemistry* (1855).

LIEBKNECHT, Karl (1871–1919) German barrister and politician, son of **Wilhelm Liebknecht**. He was a member of the Reichstag from 1912 to 1916. During World War I he was imprisoned as an independent, anti-militarist, social democrat. He was a founder member with **Rosa Luxemburg** of the German Communist party (KPD) in 1918 and led an unsuccessful revolt in Berlin, the 'Spartacus League Revolution', in January 1919, during which he was killed by army officers.

LIEBKNECHT, Wilhelm (1826–1900) German social democrat, born in Giessen. For his part in the Baden insurrection of 1848–49 he had to take refuge in Switzerland and England. He returned to Germany in 1862 and during a two-year imprisonment was elected to the Reichstag (1867). With **Bebel** he edited *Vorwärts*.

LIEBRECHT, Felix (1812–90) German writer, born in Namslau in Silesia. He was professor of German at Liège (1849–67). He soon made himself known by articles on the origin and diffusion of folk-tales, and by translations enriched with annotations. Among these are *Basile's Pentamerone* (1846), *Barlaam und Josaphat* (1847), and Dunlop's *Geschichte der Prosadichtungen* (1851).

LIEVENSZ, or **LIEVENS, Jan** (1607–74) Dutch historical painter and etcher, born in Leiden. A friend of **Rembrandt**, he shared a studio with him in Leiden. He visited England and lived in Antwerp before returning to Holland, where his paintings of allegorical subjects and his portraits became very successful.

LIFAR, Serge (1905–86) Russian-born French dancer and choreographer, born in Kiev. He became a student and friend of **Diaghilev**, whose Ballet Russe he joined in 1923. Following his first important appearance in *La Boutique fantastique*, he danced with **Pavlova**, Karsavina and Spessirtzeva, and his many successful roles included **Nijinska**'s *Les Facheux* (1924) **Massine**'s *Ode* (1928) and **Balanchine**'s *Apollon* (1925) and *The Prodigal Son* (1929). He scored his first triumph as a choreographer in Paris with *Créatures de Promethée* in 1929, the year he became artistic director of the Paris Opera.

LIGACHEV, Yegor Kuzmich (1920–) Soviet politician. After training as an engineer, he worked in the Urals region during World War II, joining the Communist party (CPSU) in 1944. In 1957 he became party chief of the new 'science city' of Akademgorodok, where he gained a reputation as an austere opponent of corruption. He was brought to Moscow by **Khrushchev** in 1961 but, after Khrushchev's ousting in 1965, was sent to Tomsk, in Western Siberia, where he was regional party boss for 18 years. He was promoted to the CPSU secretariat by **Yuri Andropov** in 1983, becoming ideology secretary in 1984, and, with the accession to power of **Mikhail Gorbachev** in 1985, he was brought into the politburo. He initially served as Gorbachev's deputy but they became estranged and in 1988 he was demoted to the position of agriculture secretary. Heading a cautious, 'centralist' faction within the politburo, he is viewed as Gorbachev's most serious rival.

LIGETI, György Sándor (1923–) Hungarian composer, born in Dicsöszentmárton. He studied and later taught at the Budapest Academy of Music. He researched into Hungarian folk-music and wrote some folk-song arrangements, but not until he left Hungary in 1956 did he become seriously interested in composition. He worked for a time at the electronics studio in Cologne, and produced *Artikulation* (1958) for tape, but from then worked only with live performers. His first large orchestral composition, *Apparitions* (1958–59), made his name widely known. *Atmosphères* followed in 1961, demonstrating his technique of chromatic complexes, and in *Aventures* (1962) and *Nouvelles Aventures* (1962–65) he used his own invented language of speech sounds. Other works are the choral *Requiem* (1963–65) and *Lux Aeterna* (1966), the orchestral *Lontano* (1967), the *Double Concerto* for flute, oboe and orchestra (1972), the 'music theatre', *Le Grand Macabre* (1978), and music for harpsichord, organ and wind and string ensembles. He has held academic posts in Stockholm, California and Hamburg, and is a member of the Royal Academy of Arts and the Hamburg Free Academy of Arts.

LIGHT, William (1784–1839) British soldier and surveyor, born in Kuala Kedar, Malaya, where his father was the first British superintendent of the protectorate of Penang. Educated privately in England, he signed on for the navy and later served as a dragoon in the Peninsular wars, where his skills were employed in preparing battle maps. In 1824 he married and, with the aid of his wife's wealth, bought a yacht and travelled round the Mediterranean where he made sketches, some of which were later published. In 1834 he took command of the paddle-steamer *Nile* on its voyage to join the new navy of his friend the Pasha of Egypt. At this time he first met **John Hindmarsh** who later took over the vessel and who also beat Light to the vacant governorship of South Australia. Light was, however, appointed as surveyor-general to the new colony, and laid out the plan for Adelaide. The city was planned with squares and wide streets, the whole surrounded by the first 'green belt' of open spaces and parkland; an early and enduring example of town planning.

LIGHTFOOT, Hannah See **GEORGE III**

LIGHTFOOT, John (1602–75) English Hebraist, born in Stoke-upon-Trent. He studied at Christ's College, Cambridge, and in 1630 became rector of Ashley, Staffordshire, in 1643 of St Bartholomew's, London, and in 1644 of Great Munden, Hertfordshire. He was one of the most influential members of the Westminster Assembly, but, as an 'Erastian', often stood alone. In 1650 he was appointed master of Catherine Hall, Cambridge, in 1654–55 vice-chancellor, and in 1668 a prebendary of Ely, where he died. Lightfoot's works include the unfinished *Harmony of the Four Evangelists* (1644–50), *Commentary upon the Acts of the Apostles* (1645), and *Horae Hebraicae et Talmudicae* (1658–74), the great labour of his life.

LIGHTFOOT, Joseph Barber (1828–89) English prelate and theologian, born in Liverpool. From King Edward's School, Birmingham, he passed in 1847 to Trinity College, Cambridge, where he graduated in 1851. Elected fellow in 1852, and ordained in 1854, he became tutor of Trinity in 1857, Hulsean professor of divinity in 1861, canon of St Paul's in 1871, Lady Margaret professor of divinity at Cambridge in 1875, and bishop of Durham in 1879. A supreme grammarian and textual critic, he wrote admirable commentaries on the Pauline epistles, *Galatians* (1860), *Philippians* (1868), *Colossians* and *Philemon* (1875). His many other works include *On a Fresh Revision of the English New Testament* (1871), *Biblical Essays* (1893), and several volumes of sermons. The work of the Church Temperance Society and the White Cross Army was furthered by his efforts.

LIGNE, Charles Joseph, Prince de (1735–1814) Belgian soldier and man of letters, born in Brussels, son of an imperial field marshal whose seat was at Ligne near Tournai. In the Seven Years' War (1756–63) he served at Kolin, Leuthen and Hochkirch, and in the Russo-Turkish war (1787–93) at the siege of Belgrade (1789). A skilful diplomatist, the favourite of **Maria Theresa** and **Catherine the Great** of Russia, and the friend of **Frederick II, the Great**, **Voltaire** and **Rousseau**, he wrote *Mélanges* (34 vol, 1795–1811), *Oeuvres posthumes* (1817), a Life of Prince **Eugène** (1809), and *Lettres et Pensées* (1809).

LIGONIER, John, 1st Earl (1680–1770) British soldier, born in Castres of Huguenot parentage. He escaped to Dublin in 1697, and from 1702 served with high distinction under **Marlborough**. Colonel from 1720 of a splendid Irish regiment of dragoons, he commanded the foot at Fontenoy (1745), was taken prisoner at Val (1747), was made commander-in-chief and a viscount (1757), an earl and field marshal (1766). He was buried in Westminster Abbey.

LIGUORI, St Alfonso Maria de (1696–1787) Italian prelate, born in Naples. He abandoned law to take orders, and in 1732 with twelve companions founded the order of Liguorians or Redemptorists. In 1762 he became bishop of Sant' Agata de' Goti, and proved an ideal bishop; but he resigned in 1775, and returned to his order. He was canonized in 1839, and declared a Doctor of the Church in 1871. His voluminous writings embrace divinity, casuistry, exegesis, history, canon law, hagiography, asceticism, and even poetry.

LI HONG-ZHANG (1823–1901) Chinese statesman, born in Hofei in Nganhui. He took the Hanlin degree in 1849. In 1853, in the Taiping rebellion, he joined the Imperial army as secretary, was appointed a provincial judge, and in 1862 governor of Kiangsu, out of which, in conjunction with 'Chinese Gordon' (**Charles George Gordon**), he drove the rebels in 1863. Made an hereditary noble of the third class, in 1864 he was appointed governor-general of the Kiang provinces, and in 1872 of Chih-li and senior grand secretary. An advocate of 'Self Strengthening', he founded the Chinese navy and promoted a native mercantile marine. On the outbreak of the war with Japan (1894), Li, in supreme command in Korea, was thwarted by the incompetence, dishonesty and cowardice of inferior officers. The Chinese were swept out of Korea, and Li, whose policy was that of peace, was deprived of his honours and summoned to Peking. He refused to comply, and the disastrous course of events soon compelled the emperor to restore him to honour. Through his efforts the war was brought to a termination in 1895, China ceding Formosa (Taiwan) and paying a war indemnity of £35 000 000. Well aware of the value of Western culture and industry, he visited Europe and America in 1896. Intriguing with Russia, he fell in 1898.

LILBURNE, John (c.1614–1657) English pamphleteer and extreme Leveller (Puritan), born in Greenwich. From 1638 to 1640 he was whipped and imprisoned by the Star Chamber for importing Puritan literature. In the Parliamentary army in the Civil War he rose to the rank of lieutenant-colonel, but resigned in 1645 over the Covenant. He became an indefatigable agitator for the Levellers, thought **Cromwell**'s republic too aristocratic, and demanded greater liberty of conscience and numerous reforms. Repeatedly imprisoned for his treasonable pamphlets, he died in Eltham.

LILIENCRON, Detlev von (1844–1909) German poet and novelist, born in Kiel. He fought in the Prussian army in 1866 and 1870. He went to America but returned to Holstein in 1882, where for a time he held a civil service post. He is best known for his lyrics, which are fresh, lively and musical. His first volume, *Adjutantenritte*, appeared in 1883. Other volumes of verse were *Der Heidegänger* (1890), *Neue Gedichte* (1893) and *Gute Nacht* (1909). He also wrote novels and an epic poem, *Poggfred* (1896).

LILIENTHAL, Otto (1849–96) German aeronautical inventor and pioneer of gliders, born in Anklam. He studied bird-flight in order to build heavier-than-air flying machines resembling the birdman designs of **Leonardo da Vinci**. He made hundreds of short flights in his gliders, but crashed to his death near Berlin. His brother, Gustav (1849–1933), continued his experiments and also invented a weather-proofing material.

LILJEFORS, Bruno (1860–1939) Swedish painter, born in Uppsala. He specialized in painting animals in the wild. In the 1880s he was much influenced by Japanese art and by the French *plein air* movement. Later he moved to darker tones, more dramatic and atmospheric painting in the neo-romantic manner of the Scandinavian 1890s.

LILLEE, Dennis Keith (1949–) Australian cricketer, born in Perth, Western Australia, and one of the greatest fast bowlers in the history of the game. Hostile in bowling and temperament, he epitomized the move towards the more combative approach to international cricket. An automatic choice for his country when fit, he took 355 wickets in 70 Tests. Not the most amenable of personalities, his attempts to introduce a metal bat (illegal) into Test matches led to well-publicized clashes with the Australian cricketing authorities.

LILLEHEI, Clarence Walton (1918–) American thoracic and cardiovascular surgeon, born in Minneapolis, Minnesota. He received his training in medicine, physiology and surgery at Minnesota University. Most of his professional career was spent in the department of surgery of his alma mater, although he spent seven years (1967–74) at Cornell University Medical Center in New York City. His pioneering work on open-heart surgery was begun in the early 1950s, before the development of the pump oxygenator made such procedures more reliable.

LILLIE, Beatrice, by marriage **Lady Peel** (1898–1989) Canadian revue singer, born in Toronto. After an unsuccessful start as a drawing-room ballad singer she found her true talent in 1914 in music hall and the new vogue of 'intimate revue' which Charlot had brought over from Paris. An unrivalled comic singer, she made famous **Noël Coward's** 'Mad Dogs and Englishmen'. During World War II she played to the troops and was decorated by General **de Gaulle**. She married Sir Robert Peel, 5th Bart, in 1920.

LILLO, George (1693–1739) English dramatist and jeweller, born in London of mixed Dutch and English Dissenting parentage. He wrote seven plays, including *The London Merchant, or the History of George Barnwell* (1731) and *Fatal Curiosity* (1736), both tragedies. His *Arden of Feversham*, which was published posthumously in 1759, is a weak version of the anonymous play of that title (1592). Among the first to put middle-class characters on the English stage, he had a considerable influence on European drama.

LILLY, William (1602–81) English astrologer, born in Diseworth, Leicestershire. In 1620 he went to London, where for seven years he served an ancient citizen, married his widow, and on her death in 1633 inherited £1000. He took up astrology, and soon acquired a considerable fame and large profits. In 1634 he obtained permission to search for hidden treasure in the cloisters of Westminster, but was driven from his midnight work by a storm which he ascribed to demons. From 1644 till his death he annually issued his *Merlinus Anglicus, Junior*, containing vaticinations. In the Civil War he attached himself to the parliamentary party as soon as it promised to be successful, and was rewarded with a pension. After the Restoration he was imprisoned for a little, and was reapprehended on suspicion of knowing something about the Great Fire of London in 1666. He died in Hersham. He wrote nearly a score of works on astrology.

LILLYWHITE, (Frederick) William (1792–1854) English cricketer, born near Goodwood. He started as a bricklayer. Famous as a round-arm bowler, he did not become a professional cricketer until middle age. 'Me bowling, Pilch batting, and Box keeping wicket' was his definition of cricket.

LILY, John See **LYLY**

LILYE, or **LILY, William** (c.1466–1522) English grammarian, born in Odiham, Hampshire. After studies at Magdalen College, Oxford, he visited Jerusalem, Rhodes and Italy, and learned Greek from refugees from Constantinople. After teaching for a while in London he was appointed (1512) by Dean **John Colet** first headmaster of his new school of St Paul's—perhaps the first man to teach Greek in London. He had a hand in Colet's *Brevissima Institutio*, which, as corrected by **Erasmus**, and redacted by Lilye himself, was known as the *Eton Latin Grammar*. Besides this he wrote Latin poems (1518) and a volume of Latin verse against a rival schoolmaster (1521).

LIMBORCH, Philip van (1633–1712) Dutch theologian. He was preacher at Gouda and Amsterdam, and became in 1688 professor in the Remonstrant or Arminian college at Amsterdam. Of his numerous works the most valuable are *Institutiones Theologiae Christianae* (1686–1702) and *History of the Inquisition* (1731).

LIMBURG, or **LIMBOURG, Pol; Jehanequin and Hermann de** (fl. early 15th century) three brothers, Flemish miniaturists, of whom comparatively little is known. Taken prisoner as youths in Brussels in time of war, on their way home from Paris they were released by the Duke of Burgundy and attached to his household as painters. In 1411 they became court painters to the Duke of Berri and produced 39 illustrations for his celebrated manuscript *Très Riches Heures du Duc de Berri*, one of the greatest masterpieces of the international Gothic style. Other works have been attributed to Pol de Limbourg, including *Heures d'Ailly*, two pages of the Turin-Milan Hours and several in a book of **Terence**.

LIMÓN, José (1908–72) Mexican-born American dancer, choreographer and teacher, born in Culiacan, Sinalo. With the intention of becoming a painter, he moved to New York, where he decided to become a dancer. Studies with **Doris Humphrey** and **Charles Weidman** led to his joining their company as dancer from 1930 to 1940. He formed his own group in 1946, appointing his mentor, Doris Humphrey, as artistic director. In 1950, the José Limón Company was the first American modern dance group to tour Europe. Throughout the 1950s and 1960s it was one of America's most outstanding modern dance companies, and toured the world. His company survived his death and is still based in New York. His choreography includes *La Malinche* (1949), *The Moor's Pavanne* (1949 and one of his most celebrated works), *The Traitor* (1954), *There is a Time* (1956), *Missa Brevis* (1958), the all-male *The Unsung* (1970) and *Carlotta* (1972).

LIMOUSIN, or **LIMOSIN, Léonard** (c.1505–1577) French painter in enamel, born in Limoges. He was court painter to **Francis I** from 1930, and was appointed by **Francis I** head of the royal factory at Limoges.

LIN BIAO (1908–71) Chinese soldier and politician, born in Wuhan, in Hubei province, the son of a factory owner. He was educated at the Whampoa Military Academy and upon graduation, in 1926, joined up with the communists to fight the Kuomintang, becoming commander of the Northeast People's Liberation Army in 1945. He became defence minister in 1959 and emerged from the 'cultural revolution' of 1966 as second-in-command to **Mao Zedong**, being appointed a party vice-chairman and formally designated as Mao's heir and successor at the congress of 1969. However, in 1971, with his health deteriorating and fearing an imminent purge, Lin formulated 'Project 571' designed to assassinate Chairman Mao during a Shanghai-Beijing train journey and seize power in a military coup. This plot was uncovered and Lin was killed in September 1971 in a plane crash over Outer Mongolia while attempting to flee to the Soviet Union.

LIN YÜTANG (1895–1976) Chinese author and philologist, born in Changchow, Amoy. He studied at Shanghai, Harvard and Leipzig, became professor of English at Peking (1923–26), secretary of the Ministry of Foreign Affairs (1927), lived mainly in the USA from 1936, and was chancellor of Singapore University (1954–55). He is best known for his numerous novels and essays on, and anthologies of, Chinese wisdom and culture, and as co-author of the official romanization plan for the Chinese alphabet.

LINACRE, Thomas (c.1460–1524) English humanist and physician, born in Canterbury. He studied at Oxford, was elected fellow of All Souls in 1484, and went to Italy, where he learned Greek, and took his MD at Padua. **Erasmus** and Sir **Thomas More** were both taught Greek by him. About 1500 **Henry VII** made him tutor to Prince **Arthur**. As king's physician to **Henry VII** and **Henry VIII** he practised in London. In 1518 he founded the Royal College of Physicians, of which he became the first president. Late in life he took holy orders. Linacre was one of the earliest champions of the New Learning. He translated several of **Galen**'s works into Latin, and wrote grammatical treatises.

LINCOLN, Abraham (1809–65) 16th president of the USA, born near Hodgenville, Kentucky, the son of a restless pioneer. After several moves, the family settled in southwest Indiana in 1816. In 1818 Abraham's mother died and his father remarried shortly. His stepmother encouraged Abraham's education although there was little schooling in that backwoods country. In 1830 the Lincolns moved on to Illinois and Abraham went to work as a clerk in a store at New Salem, Illinois. Defeated as a candidate for the legislature, he purchased a small store, whose failure left him in debt; but, being made village postmaster and deputy county surveyor, he studied law and grammar. Elected to the legislature in 1834, he served until 1842, becoming leader of the Whigs. He began the practice of law in 1836. At Springfield, in 1842, he married Mary Todd (1818–82). In 1846 he sat in congress; but professional work was drawing him from politics when in 1854 **Stephen A Douglas** repealed the Missouri Compromise of 1820, and reopened the question of slavery in the territories. The bill roused intense feeling throughout the North, and Douglas defended his position in a speech at Springfield in October. Lincoln delivered in reply a speech which first fully revealed his power as a debater. He was then elected to the legislature. When the Republican party was organized in 1856 to oppose the extension of slavery Lincoln was its most prominent leader in Illinois, and the delegates of his state presented him for the vice-presidency. In 1858 Douglas, seeking re-election to the senate, began a canvass of Illinois in advocacy of his views of 'popular sovereignty'. Lincoln was also a candidate, and the contest, which gave Douglas the election, attracted the attention of the whole country. In May 1860 the Republican convention on the third ballot nominated Lincoln for the presidency. The Democratic party was divided between Douglas and **Breckinridge**. After an exciting campaign Lincoln received a popular vote of 1866462; Douglas 1375157; Breckinridge, 847953; and **John Bell**, 590631. Of the electors Lincoln had 180; Breckinridge, 72; Bell, 39; and Douglas, 12. South Carolina now seceded from the Union, and with the six Gulf states formed, in February 1861, the Confederate States of America. Lincoln, at his inaugural address on 4 March, declared the Union perpetual, argued the futility of secession, and expressed his determination that the laws should be faithfully executed in all the states. On 12 April 1861, the Confederates began the Civil War by attacking Fort Sumter in Charleston harbour. Lincoln called a special session of congress, summoned 75000 militia, ordered the enlistment of 65000 regulars, and proclaimed a blockade of the southern ports. The Confederacy soon had control of 11 states, and put in the field 100000 men. The first important battle was fought at Bull Run, Virginia, on 21 July 1861, and resulted in the rout of the Union army. On 22 September 1862, just after McClellan's victory at Antietam, Lincoln proclaimed that on and after 1 January, 1863 all slaves in states or parts of states then in rebellion should be free. On the following New Year's Day the final proclamation of emancipation was made. This greatest achievement of his administration, wrung from him by the exigencies of Civil War, was completed by the passage (1865) of the Thirteenth Amendment of the Constitution, which he planned and urged. In July 1863 **Grant**'s capture of Vicksburg restored to the Union full control of the Mississippi River, while Meade's defeat of **Lee** at Gettysburg destroyed the last hope of the Confederates to transfer the seat of war north of the Potomac. General Grant, called to the chief command in March 1864, entered upon that policy of persistent attrition of the Confederate forces which finally brought peace. In the Republican Convention in June, Lincoln was unanimously nominated for a second term. The Democrats nominated General **McClellan**. In November Lincoln received of the popular vote 2216000, and McClellan 1800000; of the electoral votes Lincoln had 212, McClellan 21. In his second inaugural address, in March 1865, Lincoln set forth the profound moral significance of the war. On Good Friday, 14 April, at Ford's Theatre, Washington, he was shot by **J Wilkes Booth**, an actor, and died next morning. Lincoln was fair and direct in speech and action, steadfast in principle, sympathetic and charitable, a man of strict morality, abstemious and familiar with the Bible, though not a professed member of any church. His fame is established as the saviour of his country and the liberator of a race. His *Collected Works* are to be found in several editions. These include his eloquent speeches —*Emancipation Proclamation* of 1862, the *Gettysburg Address* of 1863 when first were heard these words, 'government of the people, by the people, for the people', and the *Inaugural Address* of 1865.

LINCOLN, Benjamin (1733–1810) American Revolutionary soldier, born in Hingham, Massachusetts. Major general in the Continental Army, in 1776 he reinforced **Washington** after the defeat on Long Island. In 1777 he received command of the southern department. In 1780, besieged by **Clinton** in Charleston, he was compelled to capitulate. He took part in the siege of Yorktown (1781), and was secretary of war, 1781–83.

LIND, James (1716–94) Scottish physician, the 'father of naval hygiene', born in Edinburgh. He first served in the navy as a surgeon's mate, then, after qualifying in medicine at Edinburgh, became physician at the Gaslar naval hospital at Gosport. His work towards the cure and prevention of scurvy induced the Admiralty in 1795 at last to issue the order that the navy should be supplied with lemon juice. His *A Treatise of the Scurvy* (1753) is a medical classic. He stressed cleanliness in the prevention of fevers.

LIND, Jenny (1820–87) Swedish soprano, born of humble family in Stockholm. At the age of nine she entered the court theatre school of singing, and after lessons in Paris attained great international popularity. Her earnings were largely devoted to founding and endowing musical scholarships and charities in Sweden and England.

LINDAU, Paul (1839–1919) German writer, born in Magdeburg, brother of **Rudolf Lindau**. He founded *Die Gegenwart* and *Nord und Süd*, and wrote books of travel and works of criticism. He is better known as a writer of plays and novels; the most successful of the former was perhaps *Maria und Magdalena*. The novels include *Herr und Frau Bewer* (1882), and *Berlin* (1886–87).

LINDAU, Rudolf (1829–1910) German author and diplomat, brother of **Paul Lindau**. He wrote travel books and novels, and was an editor of *Revue des deux mondes* and *Journal des débats*.

LINDBERGH, Charles Augustus (1902–74) American aviator, born in Detroit. He worked as an airmail pilot on the St Louis-Chicago run, then in May 1927 achieved world fame when he made the first non-stop solo transatlantic flight from New York to Paris in a Ryan monoplane named *Spirit of St Louis* in 33½ hours, for which he was awarded the Congressional Medal of Honour. In 1932 his infant son was kidnapped and murdered, a sensational crime for which Bruno Richard Hauptmann was executed in 1926. During World War II he advocated American neutrality. His autobiography, *The Spirit of St Louis* (1953), won the Pulitzer prize (1954). His wife, Anne Morrow Lindbergh (1906–), has written *North to the Orient* (1935), *Listen, the Wind* (1938), *Gift from the Sea* (1955), *Earthshine* (1970) and others.

LINDEMANN, Frederick Alexander See **CHERWELL**

LINDEN, Johannes van der (1756–1835) Dutch jurist. He practised in Amsterdam, where he became a judge. He is remembered in South Africa for his *Rechtsgeleerd Practicaal en Koopmans-Handboek* (1806) in which he frequently refers to **Pothier**. Sometimes called *The Institutes of the Law of Holland*, in 1852 it was made the official law book of the South African Republic. He also wrote a supplement to Books 1–11 of **Johannes Voet**'s *Commentarius*, and prepared a code of civil law for the Netherlands in which he attempted to codify Roman-Dutch law, but which was not adopted.

LINDESAY, Ethel Florence See **RICHARDSON, Henry Handel**

LINDGREN, Astrid (1907–) Swedish children's novelist, born in Vimmerby. She established her reputation with *Pippi Longstocking* (1945), and while she wrote at least 50 more books, none has eclipsed its popularity.

LINDLEY, John (1799–1865) English botanist and horticulturalist, born in Catton, near Norwich, the son of a nursery gardener George Lindley (author of *Guide to Orchard and Kitchen Garden*, 1831). He was appointed assistant secretary to the Horticultural Society of London in 1827, and was professor of botany at University College, London (1829–60). In 1828 he prepared a report on the royal gardens at Kew which saved them from destruction and led to the creation of the Royal Botanic Gardens. The most important of his many publications were those on orchids, and *The Vegetable Kingdom* (1846).

LINDLEY, Nathaniel, Lord (1828–1921) English judge and text-writer, born in Chiswick, educated at University College School and University College, London. His book *Lindley on Partnership* has been a standard authority since 1860 and ensured his reputation. Made a judge in 1875, he became a lord justice of appeal in 1881, master of the rolls in 1897, a lord of appeal in ordinary (1900–05), and was highly regarded. He was the last survivor of the ancient order of serjeants (a senior grade of barrister).

LINDSAY, Alexander William Crawford See **CRAWFORD AND BALCARRES**

LINDSAY, Sir David See **LYNDSAY**

LINDSAY, Robert See **PITSCOTTIE**

LINDSAY, (Nicholas) Vachel (1879–1931) American poet, born in Springfield, Illinois. He studied painting in Chicago and New York, and from 1906 travelled America like a troubadour, trading and reciting his very popular ragtime rhymes for hospitality. His irrepressible spirits appear in *General Booth enters Into Heaven* (1913) and *The Congo* (1914). His later volumes of verse were less successful, and, suffering from extreme depression, he returned to Springfield and committed suicide.

LINDWALL, Raymond Russell (1921–) Australian cricketer, born in Sydney and considered by many cricket enthusiasts the most classical fast bowler of all time. With **Keith Miller** he formed an invincible Australian opening attack in the five years after World War II. He took 228 wickets in 61 Tests, and also scored more than 1500 runs, with two Test centuries to his name.

LING, Per Henrik (1776–1839) Swedish author and fencing master, born in Ljunga in Småland. He produced many now-forgotten romantic works on Norse themes but his gymnastic system, developed in Lund from 1804, achieved worldwide popularity as the 'Swedish System'. He founded the Gymnastic Institute in Stockholm in 1813 and became a member of the Swedish Academy in 1835.

LINGARD, John (1771–1851) English historian, born in Winchester of Catholic parents. He was sent in 1782 to the English College of Douai, where he remained till the revolution. In 1795 he received priest's orders, and in 1811 accepted the mission of Hornby, near Lancaster, declining the offer of a chair at Maynooth (as he declined a cardinal's hat, 14 years later) In 1821 he obtained his doctorate from **Pius VII** and in 1839 received a crown pension of £300. His *Antiquity of the Anglo-Saxon Church* (1806) was the pioneer of what became the labour of his life—a *History of England to 1688* (1819–30). This was fiercely assailed in the *Edinburgh Review*, but Lingard increased his reputation as a candid Catholic scholar.

LINGEN, Ralph Robert Wheeler, Baron Lingen (1819–1905) English civil servant, born in Birmingham. Educated at Trinity College, Oxford, he became a fellow of Balliol College, Oxford, (1841) and honorary fellow of Trinity College, Oxford (1886). He studied law at Lincoln's Inn and was called to the bar in 1847. He was secretary to the Education Office (1849–69) and permanent secretary of the Treasury (1869–85). The controlling executive force during the creation of the elementary education system, he was always a vigilant guardian of the public purse. He issued the code implementing 'payment by results' as proposed by the Newcastle Commission on Elementary Education (1858–61) and was held by contemporaries to be responsible for the revised Code of 1862. The Revised Code was considered by many to have had deleterious, restricting effects on education in this country far into the 20th century.

LINI, Walter Hadye (1942–) Vanuatuan politician and priest, born on Pentecost Island. He trained for the Anglican priesthood in the Solomon Islands and New Zealand, and then joined the New Hebrides National party, later renamed the Vanuaaku Pati (VP), campaigning for the return of land to indigenes. He became chief minister in 1979 and, on independence in 1980, prime minister of the new republic of Vanuatu. On the bases of a controversial non-aligned foreign policy and a 'Melanesian socialist' domestic programme, he was re-elected in 1983 and 1987, and survived an unconstitutional challenge to his leadership, engineered by the now imprisoned President Sokomanu, in 1988.

LINKLATER, Eric (1899–1974) Scottish novelist, born in Penarth, Wales, the son of a shipmaster. His paternal ancestors were Orcadian and he spent much of his childhood on the islands and returned there in later life. He was educated at the grammar school and university in Aberdeen, and served in World War I as a private in the Black Watch. In the mid-1920s he worked as a journalist on the *Times of India*, returning to Aberdeen as assistant to the professor of English (1927–28). A commonwealth fellowship took him to the USA from 1928 to 1930, after which he had a varied career as a broadcaster and a prolific writer of novels, popular histories, books for children (*The Wind on the Moon* was awarded the Carnegie Medal in 1944), plays and memoirs. *Juan in America* (1931), a picaresque classic, is his most enduring novel. His other novels include *White Maa's Saga* (1929), *Poet's Pub* (1929), *Laxdale Hall* (1933), *Magnus Merriman* (1934), *Juan in China* (1937), *Private Angelo* (1946), *The House of Gair* (1953), *The Ultimate Viking* (1955) and *The Voyage of the Challenger* (1972). *The Man on My Back* (1941), *A Year of Space* (1953) and *Fanfare for a Tin Hat* (1970) are autobiographical.

LINLEY, Thomas (1732–95) English composer, born in Wells, Somerset. In his early career he taught singing and conducted concerts at Bath. In 1775 his son-in-law **Sheridan** induced him to set his comic opera *The Duenna* to music. In 1776 they and Ford bought **David Garrick**'s share of Drury Lane Theatre. During the next 15 years Linley was its musical director, composing songs, operas, cantatas and madrigals. Of his sons, Thomas (1756–78), a friend of **Mozart**, possessed real musical genius, and William (1767–1835) composed glees and songs. Of his gifted daughters, Elizabeth Ann (1754–92), a singer, married Sheridan.

LINNA, Väinö (1920–) Finnish novelist. His best-known works are *Tuntematen sotilas* (The Unknown Soldier, 1954), a controversial novel about the Russo-Finnish war, and his trilogy *Tä ällä Pohjantähden alla* (Here Under the North Star, 1959–62), about Finnish independence in 1918.

LINNAEUS, Carolus (Carl von Linné) (1707–78) Swedish naturalist and physician, the founder of modern scientific nomenclature for plants and animals. Born in Råshult, the son of the parish pastor, he studied medicine briefly at Lund and then botany at Uppsala, and was appointed lecturer there in 1730. In 1732 he explored Swedish Lapland and published the results in *Flora Lapponica* (1737), then travelled in Dalecarlia in Sweden and went to Holland for his MD (1735). In Holland he published his system of botanical nomenclature in *Systema Naturae* (1735), followed by *Fundamenta Botanica* (1736), *Genera Plantarum* (1737) and *Critica Botanica* (1737), in which he used his so-called 'sexual system' of classification based on the number of flower parts, for long the dominant system. His major contribution was the introduction of binomial nomenclature of generic and specific names for animals and plants, which permitted the hierarchical organization later known as systematics. He returned to Sweden in 1738 and practised as a physician in Stockholm, and in 1741 became professor of medicine and botany at Uppsala. In 1749 he introduced binomial nomenclature, giving each plant a Latin generic name with a specific adjective. His other important publications included *Flora Suecica* and *Fauna Suecica* (1745), *Philosophia Botanica* (1750), and *Species Plantarum* (1753). His manuscripts and collections are kept at the Linnean Society in London, founded in his honour in 1788. In his time he had a uniquely influential position in natural history.

LINNELL, John (1792–1882) English artist, born in London, a disciple and patron of **Blake**. He studied at the Royal Academy. He painted portraits of Blake, **Malthus**, **Whately**, **Peel**, **Carlyle** and others. His landscapes were mostly Surrey scenes. He is also known for his sculpture and engraving.

LINOWITZ, Sol Myron (1913–) American lawyer, diplomat and businessman, born in Trenton, New Jersey. After graduating from Cornell University Law School, he worked in the Office of Price Administration in Washington from 1942 to 1944 and then in the Office of the General Council Navy Dept until 1946. He then joined the Xerox Corporation and became its chairman (1958–66). He has been a senior partner with the international law firm of Condert Brothers since 1969. In the 1970s he served as US Ambassador to the OAS, and was a co-negotiator of the Panama Canal Treaties of 1977. He was personal ambassador for President **Carter** during the Middle East negotiations (1979–81). His autobiography *The Making of a Public Man—a Memoir*, was published in 1985.

LIN PIAO See **LIN BIAO**

LINTON, Ralph (1893–1953) American cultural anthropologist, born in Philadelphia. Educated at Swarthmore College, Pennsylvania, he then studied at Pennsylvania, Columbia and Harvard. His early work was in North American archaeology, but his fieldwork in Polynesia (1920–22) turned his interest towards contemporary peoples. On his return he joined the Museum of Natural History in Chicago, and became professor of sociology at Wisconsin (1928–37), Columbia (1937–46) and Yale (1946–53). During his years at Wisconsin, he developed wide interests in the study of human behaviour, culture and social organization. He pioneered the use of the terms 'status' and 'role' in social science, and exercised an important influence on the development of the culture-and-personality school of anthropology. His major work was *The Study of Man* (1936). His other works include *The Culture of the Marquesas Islands* (1924), *The Tanala, A Hill Tribe of Madagascar* (1933), *The Cultural Background of Personality* (1945), and *The Tree of Culture* (1955).

LINTON, William James (1812–98) English-born American engraver and reformer, born in London, where he did much of his finest work for the *Illustrated London News*. A zealous Chartist, he wrote *To the Future* (1848) and *The Plaint of Freedom* (1852). In 1867 he emigrated to the USA and set up a printing press in New Haven, Connecticut, where he made engravings for several American publications, and wrote a *Life of Tom Paine* (1879). His wife was the writer Eliza Lynn (1822–98), born in Keswick, from whom he separated in 1867. Together they produced an illustrated volume on *The Lake Country* (1864). She later wrote novels, and contributed *Girl of the Period* articles to the *Saturday Review*.

LINTOT, Barnaby Bernard (1675–1736) English publisher, born in Horsham in Sussex. He was associated with many of the celebrated writers of his day. Among the works which he published were **Pope**'s translation of the *Iliad* in 6 volumes (1715–20), and his *Odyssey* (1725–56), the first complete edition of **Steele**'s *Dramatic Works* in collaboration with his rival publisher **Jacob Tonson**, and works by **Gay**, **Cibber**, **Parnell** and **Rowe**.

LIOUVILLE, Joseph (1809–82) French mathematician, born in St Omer, the son of an army captain. He was educated at the École Polytechnique and the École des Ponts et Chaussées, where he trained as an engineer. He taught at the École Polytechnique (1831–51), and then at the Collège de France and the University of Paris. In 1836 he founded the *Journal de Mathématiques*, which he edited for nearly 40 years, still one of the leading French mathematical journals. His work in analysis continued the study of algebraic function theory begun by **Niels Abel** and **Karl Jacobi**, and he studied the theory of differential equations, mathematical physics and celestial mechanics. In algebra he helped to make the work of **Évariste Galois** better known, and in number theory he introduced new methods of investigating transcendental numbers.

LIPATTI, Dinu (1917–50) Romanian pianist and composer, born in Bucharest of a musical family. He studied in Paris with **Cortot**, **Dukas**, and **Boulanger**, and after World War II established an international reputation as a player of intricate mastery, sensitive phrasing and clear, delicate tone quality, ideally heard in his **Bach** and **Chopin**. His career was cut short by a rare form of cancer, lymphogranulomatosis.

LIPCHITZ, Jacques (1891–1973) Lithuanian-born French sculptor, of Polish Jewish parents. He studied engineering and moved to Paris in 1909 where he started producing Cubist sculpture in 1914. In the 1920s he experimented with abstract forms he called 'transparent sculptures'. Later he developed a more dynamic style which he applied with telling effect to bronze figure and animal compositions. From 1941 he lived in the USA.

LI PENG (1928–) Chinese politician, born in Chengdu in Sichuan province, the son of the radical communist writer Li Shouxun who was executed by the Kuomintang in 1930. Adopted by **Zhou Enlai** on his mother's death in 1939, he trained as a hydro-electric engineer and was appointed minister of the electric power industry in 1981. He became a vice-premier in 1983, was elevated to the politburo in 1985 and made prime minister in 1987. As a cautious, orthodox reformer, he sought to retain firm control of the economy and favoured improved relations with the Soviet Union. In 1989, he took a strong line in facing down the student-led, pro-democracy movement, becoming in the process a popularly reviled figure.

LIPMANN, Fritz Albert (1899–1986) German-born American biochemist, born in Königsberg. He studied medicine at Berlin, and worked in biochemistry at the Carlsberg Institute in Copenhagen (1932–39). In 1939 he emigrated to the USA. He was on the research staff at the Massachusetts General Hospital (1941–57) and professor at Harvard Medical School (1949–57), and at Rockefeller University, New York, from 1957. He isolated and elucidated the molecular structure of 'coenzyme A', for which he shared the 1953 Nobel prize for physiology or medicine with Sir **Hans Krebs**.

LI PO (c.700–762) Chinese poet, born in the province of Szechwan. He led a dissipated life at the emperor's court and later was one of a wandering band calling themselves 'The Eight Immortals of the Wine Cup'. Regarded as the greatest poet of China, he wrote colourful verse of wine, women and nature. It is believed that he was drowned while attempting to kiss the moon's reflection.

LIPPERSHEY, Hans (c.1570–c.1619) Dutch optician, born in Wesel (now in West Germany). He is one of several spectacle-makers credited with the discovery that the combination of a convex and a concave lens can make distant objects appear nearer, and applied for a patent on his telescope in 1608.

LIPPI, Filippino (c.1458–1504) Italian painter, son of **Fra Lippo Lippi**. He was apprenticed to **Botticelli**, who almost certainly was a pupil of his father. He completed c.1484 the frescoes in the Brancacci Chapel in the Carmine, Florence, left unfinished by **Masaccio**. Other celebrated series of frescoes were painted by him between 1487 and 1502, one in the Strozzi Chapel in Sta Maria Novella and one in the Caraffa Chapel, S Maria sopra Minerva, in Rome. Easel pictures painted by him are *The Virgin and Saints*, *The Adoration of the Magi* and *The Vision of St Bernard*.

LIPPI, Fra Filippo, called **Lippo** (c.1406–1469) Italian religious painter, born in Florence. An orphan, he was sent to the monastery of S Maria del Carmine in Florence where he became a Carmelite monk. In 1424 he became a pupil of **Masaccio**, who was painting the frescoes in the Brancacci Chapel there. The style of his master can be seen in his early work, for example in the frescoes, *The Relaxation of the Carmelite Rule* (c.1432). Of his stay in Padua, (c.1434), no artistic record has survived. The *Tarquinia Madonna* (1437), his first dated painting, shows the Flemish influence. His greatest work, on the choir walls of Prato Cathedral, was begun in 1452. Between 1452 and 1464 he abducted a nun, Lucrezia Buti, and was released from his monastic vows by Pope **Pius II** in order to marry her. She was the model for many of his fine Madonnas, and the mother of his son, **Filippino Lippi**. His later works are deeply religious and include the series of *Nativities*. He was working in the cathedral at Spoleto when he died.

LIPPINCOTT, Joshua Ballinger (1813–86) American publisher, born in Juliustown, New Jersey. He had a bookseller's business in Philadelphia (1834–36), and then founded his well-known publishing firm. He founded *Lippincott's Magazine* in 1868.

LIPPMANN, Gabriel (1845–1921) French physicist. Professor of mathematical and experimental physics at the Sorbonne (1886), he invented a capillary electrometer, and produced the first coloured photograph of the spectrum. He was awarded the 1908 Nobel prize for physics.

LIPPMANN, Walter (1899–1974) American journalist, born in New York. He was educated at Harvard, was on the editorial staff of the *New York World* until 1931, then became a special writer for the New York *Herald Tribune*. His daily columns became internationally famous, and he won many awards, including the Pulitzer prize for International Reporting (1962). Among his best known books are *The Cold War* (1947) and *Western Unity and the Common Market* (1962).

LIPSCOMB, William Nunn (1919–) American inorganic chemist, born in Cleveland, Ohio. He studied at Kentucky and California Institute of Technology and was appointed professor of chemistry at Harvard in 1959. He deduced the molecular structures of a curious group of boron compounds by X-ray crystal diffraction analysis in the 1950s; and then went on to develop novel theories for the chemical bonding in these compounds. His ingenious experimental and theoretical methods were later applied by him and others to a variety of related chemical problems. He was awarded the Nobel prize for chemistry in 1976.

LIPSIUS, Justus, or Joest Lips (1547–1606) Flemish humanist, born in Issche, near Brussels. Professor of classics at Jena, Leiden and Louvain, he was successively Catholic, Lutheran, Calvinist and once more Catholic. His writings include editions of **Tacitus** and **Seneca**.

LIPSIUS, Richard Adelbert (1830–92) German theologian, born in Gera. He became professor at Vienna in 1861, at Kiel in 1865, and at Jena in 1871. A pioneer of the evangelical movement, he wrote on dogmatics. His brother Justus Hermann Lipsius (1834–1920) in 1869 became professor of classical philology at Leipzig, and edited the *De Corona* of Demosthenes (1876). Their sister Marie Lipsius (1837–1927) made valuable contributions to music and its history.

LIPTON, Seymour (1903–86) American sculptor, born in New York. He studied dentistry at Columbia University from 1923 to 1927. Entirely self-taught, he began sculpting in 1928 and first exhibited in 1933. Many of his 1930s works are figurative wood carvings, but during the 1940s he began constructing abstract sculptures from sheet lead. From the 1950s he worked primarily in silver-plated nickel on metal, producing spikey abstract forms which have a rapport with Surrealist sculpture.

LIPTON, Sir Thomas Johnstone (1850–1931) Scottish businessman and philanthropist, born in Glasgow of Irish parents. When nine years old he began work as an errand-boy, and in 1865 went to the USA, where he worked successively on a tobacco plantation, in the rice-fields and in a grocer's shop. Returning to Glasgow, in 1870 he opened his first grocer's shop (in Finnieston), which was rapidly followed by many others. They prospered and made him a millionaire at the age of 30 He bought tea plantations and rubber estates, factories and packing houses and made generous donations to various charities. A keen yachtsman, in 1899 he made his first challenge for the America's Cup with his yacht *Shamrock I*, followed at intervals by four other attempts between 1901 and 1930, all of them unsuccessful.

LI SHIH-CHEN (1518–93) Chinese pharmaceutical naturalist and biologist, regarded as the prince of pharmacists and the father of Chinese herbal medicine. He compiled the *Pen Tshao Kang Mu* (Great Pharmacopoeia), completed in 1578 and published in 1596. It gives an exhaustive description of 1000 plants and 1000 animals, and includes more than 8000 prescriptions.

LISLE, Alicia, née **Beckenshaw** (c.1614–1685) English parliamentarian. The widow of one of **Cromwell**'s lords, she was beheaded at Winchester by order of Judge **Jeffreys** for sheltering two of **Monmouth**'s rebels after the battle of Sedgemoor. At **Charles I**'s execution she said that her 'blood leaped within her to see the tyrant fall'.

LISLE, Claude Joseph See **ROUGET DE LISLE**

LISSAJOUS, Jules Antoine (1822–80) French physicist, professor at the Collège St Louis, Paris. In 1857 he invented the vibration microscope which showed visually the *Lissajous figures* obtained as the resultant of two simple harmonic motions at right angles to one another. His researches extended to acoustics and optics. His system of optical telegraphy was used during the siege of Paris (1871).

LISSAUER, Ernst (1882–1937) German poet and dramatist, born in Berlin. Much of his writings had a strong nationalist flavour. *1813* (1913), a poem cycle, is a eulogy on the Prussian people in their fight to remove **Napoleon** from their land, as is the successful drama *Yorck* (1921) about the Prussian general. The poem *Hassgesang gegen England* (1914) achieved tremendous popularity in wartime Germany with its well-known refrain 'Gott strafe England'. Other works include a play about **Goethe** called *Eckermann* (1921), poems on **Bruckner**, *Gloria Anton Bruckners* (1921) a critical work, *Von der Sendung des Dichters* (1922), and some volumes of verse.

LISSITZKY, El (Eliezer Markowich) (1890–1941) Russian painter and designer, born in Smolensk; he trained in engineering and architecture. In 1919 **Chagall** appointed him professor of architecture and graphic art at the art school in Vitebsk, where he came under the influence of his colleague **Kasimir Malevich**, then at the forefront of the avant-garde. Lissitzky produced a remarkable series of abstract works, called collectively *Proun*, in which he combined flat rectilinear forms and dramatic architectonic elements. During the 1920s he lived and travelled in Germany and Switzerland, transmitting Russian ideas to the West through exhibitions, writings, and contact with leading painters, architects and teachers, most importantly **Moholy-Nagy**.

LIST, Friedrich (1789–1846) German-born American political economist, born in Reutlingen, Württemberg, a disciple of **Adam Smith**. He vigorously opposed tariff barriers between German states, and was charged with sedition in 1824. In 1825 he went to the USA and became a naturalized citizen. He was US consul at Baden, Leipzig and Stuttgart successively. A strong advocate of protection for new industries, he did much by his writings to form German economic practice. His main work was *National System of Political Economy* (1841).

LISTER, Joseph, Lord (1827–1912) English surgeon, the 'father of antiseptic surgery', born in Upton, Essex. He was the son of the microscopist, Joseph Jackson Lister (1786–1869). After graduating from London University in arts (1847) and medicine (1852), he became house surgeon at Edinburgh Royal Infirmary to **James Syme**, whose daughter he married in 1856. He was successively lecturer on surgery, Edinburgh; regius professor of surgery, Glasgow (1859); professor of clinical surgery, Edinburgh (1869), of clinical surgery, King's College Hospital, London (1877–93), and president of the Royal Society (1895–1900). In addition to important observations on the coagulation of the blood, inflammation, etc, his great work was the introduction (1867) of the antiseptic system, which revolutionized modern surgery.

LISTER, Samuel Cunliffe, 1st Baron Masham (1815–1906) English inventor, born in Bradford. He worked for a Liverpool firm of merchants, then in 1837 his father built a worsted mill at Manningham of which he and his brother John were put in charge. Samuel applied himself to the improvement of textile machinery, inventing a wool-comber in 1845 after which, having quarrelled with his partner, he bought up all his competitors and made a fortune, at the same time bringing prosperity to Bradford and the wool trade of Australia and New Zealand. Later he spent a quarter of a million pounds developing a machine to spin waste silk and was nearly bankrupt by the time it was commercially successful, making him a second fortune. Among his 150 other inventions were his first, a swivel shuttle; a velvet loom; and in 1848, anticipating the patent of **Westinghouse** by 21 years, a compressed air brake for railways. A determined business man, he was also a generous benefactor, presenting Bradford with, amongst other gifts, Lister Park.

LISTON, John (1776–1846) English comedian, born in London. He played from 1805 to 1837 at the Haymarket, Drury Lane, and the Olympic. 'Paul Pry' (1825) was his best creation.

LISTON, Robert (1794–1847) Scottish surgeon, born in Ecclesmachan manse, Linlithgow. He studied at Edinburgh and London, and settled in Edinburgh in 1818 as lecturer on surgery and anatomy. His surgical skill soon won him a European reputation. In 1835 he became professor of clinical surgery at University College, London. It was he who first used a general anaesthetic in a public operation at University College Hospital on 21 December 1846. His chief works are *Elements of Surgery* (1831) and *Practical Surgery* (1837).

LISZT, Franz (1811–86) Hungarian composer and pianist, born in Raiding near Oedenburg. At nine he played in public, and was sent to study at Vienna. He next made a tour to Vienna, Munich, Stuttgart and Strasbourg; he settled in Paris in 1823, studied and played there; visited England thrice (1824–27); and around 1831 heard **Paganini**, and was fired by the resolve to become the Paganini of the piano. He became intimate with most of the great *littérateurs* then in Paris, and from 1835 to 1839 lived with the **Comtesse d'Agoult**, by whom he had three children, one of whom, Cosima, married **Wagner**. Between 1839 and 1847 he was at the height of his brilliance, giving concerts throughout Europe. He met Princess Carolyne zu Sayn-Wittgenstein in 1847 with whom he lived for many years. In 1848, at the height of his popularity, he retired to Weimar to direct the opera and concerts, to compose and teach. Here he brought out Wagner's *Lohengrin* and **Berlioz**'s *Benvenuto Cellini*, Weimar becoming the musical centre of Germany. In 1861 he resigned his appointment, and his life was subsequently divided mainly between Weimar, Rome and Budapest. In 1865 he received minor orders in the Church of Rome, and was known as Abbé. His visit to London in 1886 was a triumphal progress. As a pianist Liszt was unapproachable. His supreme command of technique was forgotten by hearers in admiration of the poetic qualities of his playing. His literary works on music include monographs on his friends **Chopin** and **Robert Franz**, and the music of the gypsies. All his original compositions have a very distinct, sometimes a very strange, individuality. In his twelve Weimar symphonic poems he created a new form of orchestral music. Several masses, the *Legend of St Elizabeth*, *Christus* and a few other works, embody his religious aspirations. As a teacher of a new generation of pianists and the friend and helper of many young composers he was selflessly generous. The vocal and piano works of his last years were markedly experimental and prophetic of 20th-century developments.

LI T'AI PO See **LI PO**

LITTLE RICHARD, real name **Richard Wayne Penniman** (1932–) American rock-and-roll singer and pianist, born in Macon, Georgia. His early recordings epitomized rock-and-roll and his wild piano style and manic songs were a model for many later performers.

Raised as a Seventh-day Adventist, he sang in church choirs throughout his childhood and screams and yells derived from gospel music were to become an important part of his recorded sound. Leaving home at 14, he started singing professionally with a series of itinerant medicine shows and became well known on the southern vaudeville circuit. He began his recording career with 'Every Hour' (1952) but it was 'Tutti Frutti' (1955)—a salacious drinking song with its lyrics cleaned up by writer Dorothy La Bostrie—that really launched his career. In the late 1950s he decided that religion was more important than rock, and most of his recordings from 1958 to 1964 were of gospel songs. In the mid 1960s he recorded with a succession of recording labels and 'Whole Lot Of Shaking Goin' On' and 'Lawdy Miss Clawdy' are among the better songs from this period. His real come-back came in 1970 with the release of *The Rill Thing* album.

LITTLETON, or **Lyttleton, Sir Thomas** (c.1415–1481) English jurist, born at Frankley House, Bromsgrove. He was recorder of Coventry in 1450, king's sergeant in 1455, in 1466 judge of common pleas, and in 1475 a Knight of the Bath. His reputation rests on his treatise on *Tenures*, written in law French, first printed in London (?1481), translated into English about 1500 and the first book giving an authoritative account of landholding. This was the text on which Sir **Edward Coke** commented in his *Coke upon Littleton* (1628).

LITTLEWOOD, Joan (1914–) English stage director. Having trained at RADA, she founded Theatre Union, an experimental company in Manchester in 1935, which reformed in 1945 as Theatre Workshop, and opened at the Theatre Royal, Stratford East, London, in 1953 with *Twelfth Night*. The group quickly won acclaim and was invited to represent Britain at the Théâtre des Nations in Paris in 1955 and 1956, and played at the Moscow Art Theatre. She also directed the first British production for **Brecht**'s *Mother Courage*, in Barnstaple in 1955, in which she played the title role. The ideology of Theatre Workshop company was agressively left-wing, and their artistic policy revolved around both a fresh, political approach to established plays and the staging of new, working-class plays, notably **Brendan Behan**'s *The Quare Fellow* (1956); Shelagh Delaney's *A Taste of Honey* (1958), and *Fings Ain't Wot They Used T'Be* (1959). In 1963 she directed the musical *Oh, What a Lovely War!* Since 1975 she has worked abroad.

LITTLEWOOD, John Edensor (1885–1977) English mathematician, born in Rochester. He was educated at St Paul's School and Trinity College, Cambridge. After lecturing in Manchester (1907–10) he returned to Cambridge as a fellow of Trinity and remained there for the rest of his life. At this time he started to collaborate with **Godfrey Hardy**, and a stream of joint papers on summability theory, Tiberian theorems, **Fourier** series, analytic number theory and the **Riemann** zeta-function followed over the next 35 years. He was elected to the Rouse Ball chair of mathematics at Cambridge in 1928. His retirement in 1950 did not affect his research and he was still publishing mathematical papers at the age of 85. His mathematical reminiscences, *A Mathematician's Miscellany*, were published in 1953.

LITTRÉ, Maximilien Paul Émile (1801–81) French lexicographer and philosopher, born in Paris. A doctor by training, he abandoned medicine for philology, and his translation of **Hippocrates** procured his election in 1839 to the Academy of Inscriptions. An ardent democrat, he fought on the barricades in 1830, was one of the principal editors of the *National* down to 1851, and became an enthusiastic supporter of **Auguste Comte**, after whose death in 1857 he became the leader of the positivist school. *La Poésie homérique et l'Ancienne Poésie française* (1847) was an attempt to render book i of the *Iliad* in the style of the trouvères. In 1854 he became editor of the *Journal des savants*. His splendid *Dictionnaire de la langue française* (1863–72) did not prevent the Academy in 1863 from rejecting its author, whom Bishop **Dupanloup** denounced as holding impious doctrines. In 1871 **Gambetta** appointed him professor of history and geography at the École Polytechnique; he was chosen representative of the Seine department in the National Assembly; and in December 1871 the Academy at last admitted him.

LITVINOV, Maxim (1876–1951) Soviet politician and diplomat, born, a Polish Jew, in Bielostock, in Russian Poland. He joined the Social Democratic party in 1898 but in 1903 joined in revolutionary activities with **Lenin** and was exiled to Siberia, but escaped. At the Revolution he was appointed Bolshevik ambassador in London (1917–18). He became deputy people's commissar for foreign affairs in 1921 and commissar (1930–39), achieving US recognition of Soviet Russia in 1934. He was dismissed in 1939 before the German-Soviet non-aggression pact, but reinstated after the German invasion of Russia, and from 1941 to 1943 was ambassador to the USA, and from 1943 to 1946 vice-minister of foreign affairs.

LIU SHAOQI, (old style, **Liu Shao-chi)** (1900–?c.1970) Chinese political leader, born in Yinshan, Hunan Province, into a land-owning family. He went to school with the future leader, **Mao Zedong**. Educated at Changsa and Shanghai (where he learned Russian), he went to Moscow to study in 1921–22, joined the Chinese Communist party, and returned to China to become a party labour organizer in Shanghai. He was elected to the politburo in 1934, and became its foremost expert on the theory and practice of organization and party structure, and wrote *How to be a Good Communist* (1939). In 1943 he became secretary general of the party, vice-chairman (1949), and chairman of the People's Republic of China in 1958, second only to Mao Zedong. He advocated a freer market economy and financial incentives, but during the Cultural Revolution (1966–69) he was denounced as a bourgeois renegade, stripped of all positions in 1967 and banished to Hunan province, while **Lin Biao** emerged as Mao's heir-apparent. He reportedly died in detention, but was posthumously rehabilitated in 1980.

LIUTPRAND, or **Luitprand** (c.922–972) Italian prelate and historian, born of a Longobard family in Pavia. He passed from the service of **Berengar II**, king of Italy, to that of the Emperor **Otto I**. Otto made him bishop of Cremona, and sent him on an embassy to Constantinople. His *Antapodosis* treats of history from 886 to 950. *De Rebus Gestis Ottonis* covers 960–64, and *De Legatione Constantinopolitanâ* is a satire on the Greek court.

LIVENS, Jan See **LIEVENSZ**

LIVERMORE, Mary Ashton, née **Rice** (1820–1905) American reformer, born in Boston. A teacher by training, in 1845 she married the Rev Daniel P Livermore, and became active in the women's suffrage movement. She was founder-editor of *The Agitator* (1869), which was later merged into the *Woman's Journal*.

LIVERPOOL, Robert Banks Jenkinson, Earl of (1770–1828) English statesman, son of the first Earl (1727–1808). Educated at Charterhouse and Christ Church College, Oxford, he entered parliament in 1791 as member for Rye. A Tory with Liberal ideas on trade and finance, in 1794 he became a member of the India Board, and in 1801 as foreign secretary negotiated the unpopular Treaty of Amiens. In 1803 he was created Lord Hawkesbury, and on **Pitt**'s return to power he went to the home office. On the death of Pitt he declined to form an administration. In 1807 he again took the home office, and next year succeeded his father as Earl of Liverpool. In **Perceval**'s ministry of 1809 he was secretary for war and the colonies. In 1812 he formed an administration which lasted for nearly 15 years. The attitude of the government to Poland, Austria, Italy and Naples, coercive measures at home, and an increase in the duty on corn were regarded as reactionary. Lord Liverpool himself was a Free Trader, and ultimately sought to liberalize the tariff. Notwithstanding the blunder of the sinking fund, his financial policy generally was sound, enlightened and economical. He united the old and the new Tories at a critical period. In February 1827 he was struck with apoplexy, and died the following year.

LIVIA, Drusilla, later called **Julia Augusta** (58 BC–29 AD) Roman empress, third wife of the emperor **Augustus**, whom she married in 39 BC after divorcing her first husband Tiberius Claudius Nero. From her first marriage she had two children, **Tiberius** the future emperor (who succeeded Augustus), and **Nero Claudius Drusus**; but her marriage with Augustus did not result in offspring. She was believed to have been influential with Augustus, and rumour credited her with promoting the interests of her sons at the expense of Augustus' kinsmen, by fair or foul means. She was adopted into the Julian family by Augustus at his death in 14 AD, and changed her name to Julia Augusta. Relations with her son Tiberius after his accession became strained, as she sought to exert influence, and when she died he did not execute her will or allow her to be deified.

LIVINGSTON American family, descended from the fifth Lord Livingston, guardian of **Mary, Queen of Scots**, and from his grandson, John Livingstone (1603–72), minister of Ancrum, banished for refusing the oath of allegiance to **Charles II**, and from 1663 pastor of the Scots kirk at Rotterdam. His son Robert (1654–1728) went to America in 1673, settled at Albany, and received land. Of his grandsons, Philip (1716–78) signed the Declaration of Independence; and William (1723–90) was the first, and able, Governor of New Jersey (1776–90); and his son became a justice of the Supreme Court. Robert R Livingston (1746–1813), great-grandson of the first Robert, was born in New York, and admitted to the bar in 1773. Sent to congress in 1775, he was one of the five charged with drawing up the Declaration of Independence, and till 1801 was chancellor of New York state. As minister plenipotentiary at Paris he negotiated the cession of Louisiana. He enabled **Robert Fulton** to construct his first steamer, and introduced in America the use of sulphate of lime as a manure, and the merino sheep. Edward Livingston (1764–1836), also a great-grandson of the first Robert, was born at Clermont, New York, and called to the bar in 1785. He sat in congress, 1795–1801, when he became US district attorney for New York, and mayor of New York; but in 1803, owing to a subordinate's misappropriations, he found himself in debt to the federal government. He handed over his property to his creditors, and in 1804 settled in New Orleans, where he obtained lucrative practice at the bar. During the second war with Britain he was aide-de-camp to General **Jackson**; and from 1822 to 1829 he represented New Orleans in congress. In 1823–24 he systematized the civil code of Louisiana. His criminal code was completed, but not directly adopted. Livingston was elected in 1829 to the senate, and in 1831 appointed secretary of state. In 1833 he went to France as plenipotentiary.

LIVINGSTONE, David (1813–73) Scottish missionary and traveller, born in Low Blantyre, Lanarkshire. From 10 till 24 years of age he was a worker in a cotton factory there. A pamphlet by **Karl Gutzlaff** kindled the desire to become a missionary. After studying medicine in London he was attracted to Africa by **Robert Moffat**. He was ordained under the London Missionary Society in 1840, and for several years worked in Bechuanaland. Repulsed by the Boers in an effort to plant native missionaries in the Transvaal, he travelled northward, discovered Lake Ngami, and determined to open trade routes east and west. The journey (1852–56) was accomplished with a handful of followers, amid great difficulties, but a vast amount of valuable information was gathered respecting the country, its products and the native tribes. He discovered the Victoria Falls of the Zambezi. He was welcomed home with extraordinary enthusiasm, and published his *Missionary Travels* (1857). In 1858 he was appointed by the government chief of an expedition for exploring the Zambezi and explored the Zambezi, Shiré and Rovuma; discovered Lakes Shirwa and Nyasa, and came to the conclusion that Lake Nyasa and its neighbourhood was the best field for commercial and missionary operations, though he was hampered by the Portuguese authorities, and by the discovery that the slave trade was extending in the district. His wife Mary, Robert Moffat's daughter, whom he had married in 1844, died in 1862 and was buried at Shupanga. The expedition was recalled in July 1863. At his own cost he now journeyed a hundred miles westward from Lake Nyasa; then himself navigated his little steamer to Bombay; and returned to England in 1864. His second book, *The Zambesi and its Tributaries* (1865), was designed to expose the Portuguese slave traders, and to find means of establishing a settlement for missions and commerce near the head of the Rovuma. The Royal Geographical Society asked him to return to Africa and settle a disputed question regarding the watershed of central Africa and the sources of the Nile. In March 1866 he started from Zanzibar, pressed westward amid innumerable hardships, and in 1867–68 discovered Lakes Mweru and Bangweulu. Obliged to return for rest to Ujiji, he struck westward again as far as the river Lualaba, thinking it might be the Nile, which afterwards proved to be the Congo. On his return after severe illness to Ujiji, Livingstone was found there by **Henry Morton Stanley**, sent to look for him by the *New York Herald*. Determined to solve the problem, he returned to Bangweulu, but died in Old Chitambo (now in Zambia). His faithful people embalmed his body, and carried it to the coast. It was conveyed to England, and buried in Westminster Abbey.

LIVIUS See **LIVY**

LIVIUS ANDRONICUS (fl.3rd century BC) Roman writer, known as 'the father of Roman dramatic and epic poetry', probably a Greek by birth, from Tarentum. He was taken prisoner at the Roman capture of the city and sold as a slave in Rome in 272 BC. He was afterwards freed by his master. He translated the *Odyssey* into Latin Saturnian verse, and wrote tragedies, comedies, and hymns after Greek models. Only fragments are extant.

LIVY, properly **Titus Livius** (59 BC–17 AD) Roman historian, born in Padua, of a noble and wealthy family. He settled in Rome in about 29 BC and was admitted to the court of **Augustus**. He never flattered the emperor, but avowed his preference for a republic. He praised **Brutus** and **Cassius**, sympathized with

Pompey, and stigmatized **Cicero**, an accessory to the murder of **Caesar**, as having got from **Marcus Antonius**' bravoes only his deserts. Of the great Caesar himself he doubted whether he was more of a curse or a blessing to the commonwealth. Such friendship as they had for each other Livy and Augustus never lost. Livy died in his native Patavium. His history of Rome from her foundation to the death of Nero Claudius Drusus (9 BC) comprised 142 books, of which those from the 11th to the 20th, and from the 46th to the 142nd, have been lost. Of the 35 that remain, the 41st and 43rd are imperfect. The 'periochae', or summaries of the contents of each book, composed in the wane of Roman literature, to catalogue names and events for rhetorical purposes, have all survived except those of books 136 and 137. But what has been spared is more than enough to confirm in modern days the judgment of antiquity which places Livy in the forefront of Latin writers. His impartiality is not less a note of his work than his veneration for the good, the generous, the heroic in man. His style is as nearly perfect as is compatible with his ideal of the historian. For investigation of facts he did not go far afield. Accepting history as fine art rather than as science, he was content to take his authorities as he found them, and where they differed was guided by taste or predilection.

LI XIANNIAN (1905–) Chinese politician, born into a poor peasant family in Hubei province. He worked as a carpenter before serving with the Kuomintang (Nationalist) forces (1926–27). After joining the Communist party (CCP) in 1927 he established the Oyuwan Soviet (people's republic) in Hubei, participated in the Long March (1934–36) and was a military commander in the war against Japan and in the civil war. He was inducted into the CCP politburo and secretariat in 1956 and 1958, but fell out of favour during the 1966–69 Cultural Revolution. He was rehabilitated, as finance minister, by **Zhou Enlai** in 1973, and later served as state president in the 'administration' of **Deng Xiaoping** (1983–88).

LLEWELLYN, Richard, pseud of **Richard Doyle Vivian Llewellyn Lloyd** (1907–83) Welsh author, born in St David's, Pembrokeshire. He established himself, after service with the regular army and a short spell as a film director, as a best-selling novelist with *How Green was my Valley* (1939), a novel about a Welsh mining village. Later works include *None but the Lonely Heart* (1943), *The Flame of Hercules* (1957), *Up into the Singing Mountain* (1963), *Green, Green My Valley Now* (1975) and *I Stand On A Quiet Shore* (1982).

LLORENTE, Juan Antonio (1756–1823) Spanish priest and historian, born in Rincón del Soto. He rose to be secretary to the Inquisition in 1789 and was made canon of Toledo in 1806. In 1809, when the Inquisition was suppressed, **Joseph Bonaparte** placed all its archives in his hands and he went to Paris, where the *Histoire critique de l'inquisition d'Espagne* came out in 1817–18. Its value was recognized at once, but it provoked bitter feeling, and Llorente was ordered to quit France.

LLOSA, Mario Vargas (1936–) Peruvian novelist, born in Arequipa. After studying law and literature in Peru, he spent many years abroad as a student in Paris and Madrid, building up a reputation as a writer, eventually returning to Lima shortly before the restoration of democratic government in Peru in 1980. *The Time of the Hero*, his first novel, published in 1962, is a powerful social satire and so outraged the authorities that a thousand copies were publicly burned. In 1965 came *The Green House*, a novel that brings to life the teeming society of Peru in the days of the rubber boom. Subsequent novels are *Conversation in the Cathedral* (1969) and *Pantaleon and the Visitors* (1974). *Aunt Julia and the Scriptwriter* (1977, trans 1982), his masterpiece, is an energetic, inventive comedy which was made into a television series in Colombia. He has also written *The War at the End of the World* (1981), *The Real Life of Alejandro Mayta* (1984) and *Who Killed Palomino Molero?* (1987). *The Perpetual Orgy* (1975) is an expression of his obsession with **Flaubert**'s *Madame Bovary*. A proponent of 'magic realism', he is one of the world's greatest novelists, a football commentator and a candidate for the Peruvian presidency, having declined an offer of the premiership in 1984. Formerly president of PEN (1976–79), he has won many honours, including the Ritz Paris Hemingway award.

LLOYD, Clive Hubert (1944–) West Indian cricketer, born in Georgetown, Guyana. Educated on a scholarship to Chatham High School, Georgetown, he worked as a hospital clerk until his first West Indies Test cap in 1966, then came to England to play for Haslingden in the Lancashire League before joining Lancashire (1968–86). A magnificent batsman and fielder, he played in 110 Test matches (captain 1974–85), scoring 7515 runs and making 19 centuries. He captained the West Indies sides which won the World Cup in 1975 and 1979.

LLOYD, Edward (d.c.1730) English coffee-house keeper. From 1688 until 1726 he owned a coffee house in Lombard St, London, after which is named 'Lloyd's', the London society of underwriters. His coffee house became a haunt of merchants and shipowners, and for them Lloyd started his *Lloyd's News*, later to become *Lloyd's List*.

LLOYD, George Walter Selwyn (1913–) English composer and conductor, born in St Ives, Cornwall. His 3rd symphony and two operas (*Iernin*, 1935, and *The Serf*, 1938) had received London performances before he served during World War II in the Royal Marines Band. He was severely shell-shocked in 1942. Another opera, *John Socman*, followed (1951), but owing to illness he retired to Devon as a market gardener, and composed only intermittently for a period. With improved health he has produced a large body of concertos and symphonies (No. 11, 1986) in a colourful if conventional style.

LLOYD, Harold Clayton (1893–1971) American film comedian, born in Burchard, Nebraska. Stagestruck from an early age, he worked extensively as an extra before gradually creating his own character of the shy, sincere, bespectacled boy-next-door, anxious to make good and perennially involved with hair-raising stunts from the top of tall buildings. He developed a reputation as the beloved King of Daredevil Comedy in works like *High and Dizzy* (1920) and, most famously, *Safety Last* (1923) in which he dangles perilously from the hands of a high-rise clock face. He enjoyed a remarkable run of hits from *Why Worry?* (1923) to *Speedy* (1928) but was less successful in the sound era and retired after *Mad Wednesday* (1947). He published an autobiography, *An American Comedy*, in 1928 and received an honorary Academy Award in 1952.

LLOYD, Henry Demarest (1847–1903) American journalist and reformer, born in New York City. A graduate of Columbia University, he became a school lecturer in economics, studied law (admitted to the bar in 1869) and became secretary of the American Free Trade League. He settled in Chicago from 1872 and worked on the Chicago *Tribune* as a reporter and a member of the editorial staff. He was reviled for his courage in pointing to the injustice of the trials of the

Haymarket anarchists, four of whom were hanged for supposedly throwing a bomb on 4 May 1886. He became more and more dedicated to exposure of capitalist abuses and his masterpiece, *Wealth Against Commonwealth* (1894), was a searing indictment of the methods by which **John D Rockefeller** built up Standard Oil. He was a strong advocate of co-operative methods, visited New Zealand and reported on it in *A Country without Strikes* (1900), vigorously supported the Populist party and corrosively denounced its 'fusion' with the Democrats and the one-issue 'free silver' movement under **William Jennings Bryan**.

LLOYD, Marie, born **Matilda Alice Victoria Wood** (1870–1922) English music-hall entertainer. Daughter of a waiter and eldest of eleven children, she made her first appearance at the Royal Eagle Music Hall (later The Grecian) in 1885. Her first great success was with a song called *The Boy I Love Sits Up in the Gallery*, and she became one of the most popular music-hall performers of all time with a wittily improper act that was often criticised for coarseness. She appeared in music halls throughout the country, and in America, South Africa and Australia, and continued on the stage until a few days before her death. Among her most famous songs were *Oh, Mr Porter*, *My Old Man Said Follow the Van* and *I'm One of the Ruins that Cromwell Knocked About a Bit*.

LLOYD, (John) Selwyn Brooke See **SELWYN LLOYD**

LLOYD-GEORGE OF DWYFOR, David Lloyd George, 1st Earl (1863–1945) Welsh Liberal statesman, born in Manchester. At the age of two when his father died, his family were taken to Wales to Llanystumdwy near Criccieth, the home of his uncle Richard Lloyd; and it was he who, seeing the latent brilliance in the young Lloyd George, took his education in hand. It was from his uncle that he acquired his religion, his industry, his vivid oratory, his radical views and his Welsh nationalism. He became a solicitor and in 1890 his career as a politician began when he was elected as an advanced Liberal for Carnarvon Boroughs. From 1905 to 1908 he was president of the board of trade and was responsible for the passing of three important Acts—the Merchant Shipping Act and the Census Production Act in 1906, and the Patents Act of 1907. As Chancellor of the Exchequer from 1908 to 1915, he reached the heights as a social reformer with his Old Age Pensions Act in 1908, the National Insurance Act in 1911, and the momentous budget of 1909–10, whose rejection by the Lords led to the constitutional crisis and the Parliament Act of 1911. Up to the outbreak of the war in 1914 he had been regarded as a pacifist. As a strong upholder of the national rights of a smaller country he saw the parallel between the Welsh and the Boers and his condemnation of the Boer War had been loud. The threat of invasion of Belgium by Germany dispelled all pacifist tendencies. In 1915 he was appointed minister of munitions, and in 1916 became war secretary and superseded **Asquith** as coalition prime minister, holding office from 1916 to 1922. By his forceful policy he was, as **Hitler** later said of him, 'the man who won the war'. He was one of the 'big three' at the peace negotiations, which he handled brilliantly although he was inclined to pay too much attention to the demands of the small countries. This later, as with Greece, led Britain into difficulties. At home there was a split in the Liberal party which never completely healed. In 1921 he treated with the Sinn Feiners and conceded the Irish Free State. This was very unpopular with the Conservatives in the government and led to his downfall and the downfall of the Liberals as a party at the election of 1922. He retained his seat until the year of his death, in which year he was made an earl. He wrote his *War Memoirs* (1933–36) and *The Truth about the Peace Treaties* (1938).

LLOYD-GEORGE OF DWYFOR, Gwilym, 1st Viscount Tenby (1894–1967) Welsh politician, second son of **David Lloyd-George**, born in Criccieth. He entered parliament as Liberal member for Pembrokeshire in 1922, again from 1929 to 1950, during which term he was parliamentary secretary to the board of trade (1939–41) and minister of fuel and power (1942–45). In 1951 he was returned as Liberal-Conservative member for Newcastle North and was minister of food until 1954. He was minister for Welsh affairs until 1957, when he was created Viscount Tenby of Bulford.

LLOYD-GEORGE OF DWYFOR, Lady Megan (1902–66) Welsh politician, born in Criccieth, younger daughter of **David Lloyd-George**. She was elected Liberal member of parliament for Anglesey in 1929 and Independent Liberal between 1931 and 1945. Defeated in the election of 1951, in 1955 she joined the Labour party and was MP for Carmarthen from 1957.

LLOYD-JONES, David Martyn (1899–1981) Welsh preacher and writer, born in Newcastle Emlyn. He trained in medicine at London but in 1926 forsook a promising career in Harley Street to enter the Christian ministry. After eleven years in Aberavon he became colleague and successor to G Campbell Morgan at Westminster Chapel, London, and for 30 years made it virtually the heart of English Nonconformity, with his expository preaching based on Reformed theology. He had also an extensive ministry through correspondence, and among evangelical ministers who met regularly for fellowship at the chapel. His published works include *Truth Unchanged, Unchanging* (1951), *From Fear to Faith* (1953), *Conversions: Psychological and Spiritual* (1959); and *Studies in the Sermon on the Mount* (2 vols, 1959–60).

LLOYD WEBBER, Andrew (1948–) English popular composer, born in London. He comes from a musical family (his brother Julian is a cellist, and his father, Dr William Lloyd Webber (1914–82) was a brilliant organist, a choirmaster and director of the London College of Music from 1964 till his death), but did not undergo a conventional musical education. Lloyd Webber met Tim Rice in 1965, and together they wrote a 'pop oratorio' *Joseph and the Amazing Technicolor Dreamcoat* (1968) which was extended and staged in 1973. Their greatest success was the 'rock opera' *Jesus Christ Superstar* (staged 1970, filmed 1973), the long-playing record of which achieved record-breaking sales. He has since composed music for *Jeeves* (1975), *Evita* (1978), *Tell Me on a Sunday* (1980), and *Cats* (1981). Lloyd Webber is increasingly successful and is now critic-proof, his shows being sold out for months in advance within hours of booking being opened to the public. His most recent successes include *The Phantom of the Opera* (1986), based on the novel (1911) by Gaston Leroux and *Aspects of Love* (1989), based on the novella (1955) by **David Garnett**.

LLYWELYN AP GRUFFYDD, (d.1282) prince of Gwynned in north Wales, grandson of **Llywelyn ap Iorwerth**. He worked towards reconsolidating the undivided territorial power once excercised by his grandfather, and in 1258 proclaimed himself Prince of Wales, thus inspiring the first experiment in Welsh statehood. He allied himself with **Simon de Montfort** and the English barons in 1262, and was recognized as overlord of Wales by the Treaty of Shrewsbury in 1265. When **Edward I** succeeded to the English throne in 1272, Llywelyn refused to do homage to him, but was invaded and forced to submit in 1277, although retaining the title of Prince of Wales. In 1282 he rebelled against Edward, but was killed in battle near Builth, and with him Wales lost her political independence. He was succeeded by his brother, **Dafydd ap Gruffydd**.

LLYWELYN AP IORWETH, called **'the Great'** (d.1240) prince of Gwynedd in north Wales. He seized power from his uncle in 1294, and soon had most of northern Wales under his control. In 1205 he married Joan (d. 1237), the illegitimate daughter of King **John** of England. He successfully maintained his independence against King John and **Henry III**, and extended his kingdom over most of Wales, before retiring to the Cistercian monastery at Aberconway, where he died and was buried.

LOACH, Kenneth (1936–) English filmmaker, born in Nuneaton, Warwickshire. After studying law at Oxford he spent some time as an actor before training as a television director and joining the BBC. He directed various early episodes of *Z Cars* (1962) before making his name in the Wednesday Play series, where his emphasis on realism and naturalistic performances dramatically illuminated social ills like homelessness in *Cathy Come Home* (1966). His first feature film, *Poor Cow* (1967), was followed by the popular *Kes* (1969), looking at wasted teenage lives, and *Family Life* (1971), a stark portrait of claustrophobic personal relations. He has continued to explore social issues and question socialist history in such television work as *Days of Hope* (1975) and *The Price of Coal* (1977) and the film *Looks and Smiles* (1981). A television documentary series, *Questions of Leadership* (1983), was banned on political grounds.

LOANE, Sir Marcus Lawrence (1911–) Australian prelate, born in Tasmania. He graduated from Sydney University, and was ordained in 1935. He was vice-principal (1939–53) and principal (1954–58) of Moore Theological College, bishop-coadjutor (1958–66) and archbishop (1966–82) of Sydney, later serving also as primate of the Anglican Church in Australia. A strong protestant who declined to meet Pope **Paul VI** when he visited Sydney, he was nonetheless active in public service, and a meticulous writer, usually on Reformation topics. Among his books are *Oxford and the Evangelical Succession* (1950); *Masters of the English Reformation* (1955); *Makers of Our Heritage* (1967); and *Hewn from the Rock* (1976).

LOBACHEVSKI, Nikolai (1792–1856) Russian mathematician, born in Nizhni Novgorod. He became professor at Kazan in 1814, where he spent the rest of his life. In the 1820s he developed a theory of non-Euclidean geometry in which **Euclid**'s parallel postulate did not hold. A similar theory was discovered almost simultaneously and independently by **János Bolyai**.

L'OBEL, or **Lobel, Matthias de** (1538–1616) Flemish naturalist, born in Lille. He became botanist and physician to King **James VI and I** of Scotland and England, and gave his name to the *Lobelia*.

LŎBO, Francisco Rodrigues (c.1580–1622) Portuguese writer, born in Leiria. He wrote *Primavera* (1601) and other remarkable prose pastorals and verse. He was drowned in the Tagus. His lyrics are of great beauty and his work holds a valuable place in the literature of his country.

LOCHNER, Stefan (c.1400–1451) German painter, born in Meersburg on Lake Constance. He was the principal master of the Cologne school, marking the transition from the Gothic style to naturalism. His best-known work is the great triptych in Cologne Cathedral.

LOCK, Graham Anthony Richard (1929–) English cricketer, born in Limpsfield. His penetrating slow left-arm bowling, complementing that of **Jim Laker**, made Surrey virtually unbeatable at county cricket level in the 1950s. He played 49 Tests for England and took 174 wickets, taking ten or more wickets in a match on three occasions. His career suffered a set-back when his bowling action came under suspicion, but after dropping out of the first-class game for a time he returned with a satisfactorily remodelled bowling method. A brilliant short-leg fielder, he also played for Western Australia and Leicestershire.

LOCKE, Alain LeRoy (1886–1954) American black educationist, born in Philadelphia. The first black Rhodes scholar at Oxford (1907–10), he became professor of philosophy at Howard University (1917). A leader of the Harlem Renaissance, his works include *The New Negro* (1925), *The Negro in America* (1933) and *Negro Art* (1937).

LOCKE, Bessie (1865–1952) American pioneer of kindergarten education, born in West Cambridge (now Arlington), Massachusetts. She herself attended a private kindergarten (then a recent importation from Germany), and went on to Brooklyn public schools and Columbia University, but took no degree. She is said to have been deflected from business to education by her observation of a friend's kindergarten in a slum area of New York City. She became convinced that the kindergarten was second only to the church as an agency for improvement. She founded the National Association for the Promotion of Kindergarten Education (National Kindergarten Association) in 1909, and became chief of the kindergarten division of the US bureau of education from 1913 to 1919, working to improve kindergarten teacher training. From 1917 she published home education articles for parents which became very influential. She helped to open over 3000 kindergartens, serving over 1.5 million children.

LOCKE, Bobby (Arthur D'Arcy) (1917–) South African golfer, born in Germiston. A slow, methodical player, he won four British Open championships (1949, 1950, 1952 and 1957), and between 1947 and 1950 won 11 events on the American tour circuit.

LOCKE, John (1632–1704) English philosopher, a formative influence on British empiricism and on theories of liberal democracy, born in Wrington, Somerset, he was educated at Westminster School and Christ Church College, Oxford. He reacted against the prevailing scholasticism at Oxford and involved himself instead in experimental studies of medicine and science, making the acquaintance or **Robert Boyle**, **John Wilkins** and others. In 1667 he joined the household of Anthony Ashley Cooper, later first Earl of **Shaftesbury**, as his personal physician and became his adviser in scientific and political matters generally. Through Ashley he made contact with the leading intellectual figures in London and was elected fellow of the Royal Society in 1668. When Ashley became Earl of Shaftesbury and chancellor in 1672, Locke became secretary to the Council of Trade and Plantations, but retired to France from 1675 to 1679, partly for reasons of health and perhaps partly from political prudence. In Paris he became acquainted with the circle of **Gassendi** and **Arnauld**. After Shaftesbury's fall and death in 1683 he felt threatened and fled to Holland where he joined the English supporters of William of Orange (the future **William III**) and remained until after the Glorious Revolution of 1688. His *Two Treatises of Government* had been largely written earlier but were published, anonymously, in 1690. They constitute his reply to the patriarchal, Divine Right theory of Sir **Robert Filmer** and also to the absolutism of **Hobbes**. The *Treatises* present a social contract theory which embodies a defence of natural rights and a justification for constitutional law, the liberty of the individual and the rule of the majority. If the ruling body offends against natural law it must be deposed, and this sanctioning of rebellion had a powerful influence on the American and the French revolutions. Locke returned to England in 1689, declined an ambassadorship and became commissioner of appeals until 1704. His health then declined further and he spent his remaining years at Oates, Essex, at the home of Sir Francis and Lady Masham (the daughter of **Cudworth**). His major philosophical work was the *Essay concerning Human Understanding*, published in 1690 though developed over some 20 years. The *Essay* is a systematic enquiry into the nature and scope of human reason, very much reflecting the scientific temper of the times in seeking to establish that 'all knowledge is founded on and ultimately derives from sense . . . . or sensation'. The work is regarded as the first and probably the most important statement of an empiricist theory of knowledge in the British tradition which led from Locke to **Berkeley** and **Hume**. His other main works were *A Letter concerning Toleration* (1689), *Some Thoughts concerning Education* (1693) and *The Reasonableness of Christianity* (1695), and are all characterized by the same tolerance, moderation and common-sense.

LOCKE, Joseph (1805–60) English civil engineer, born in Attercliffe, near Sheffield. He left school at the age of 13 and after various jobs became articled to **George Stephenson** in 1823 and began to learn the art of railway civil engineering with enthusiasm. After almost ten years with Stephenson he broke away and on his own built a large number of important railways in England, Scotland, France and elsewhere on the continent of Europe. His lines were noted for their straightness and avoidance of expensive tunnelling, but in so doing he was forced in some places to adopt gradients that were too steep for economical running.

LOCKE, Matthew (c.1621–1677) English composer, born in Exeter. Collaborating with **James Shirley** on the masque *Cupid and Death*, he won a reputation as a theatre composer. After composing the music for **Charles II**'s coronation procession, he became composer-in-ordinary to the king. A champion of the 'modern' French style of composition, his works include much incidental music for plays (though that for *Macbeth*, long attributed to him, is of doubtful authenticity), Latin church music, songs and chamber works.

LOCKE, William John (1863–1930) English novelist, born in Demerara, British Guiana (Guyana). He was educated in Trinidad and at Cambridge. He taught between 1890 and 1897 at Clifton and Glenalmond. Disliking teaching, he then became secretary of the Royal Institute of British Architects until 1907. In 1895 appeared the first of a long series of novels and plays which with their charmingly written sentimental themes had such a success during his life in both Britain and America. *The Morals of Marcus Ordeyne* (1905) and *The Beloved Vagabond* (1906) assured his reputation. Others of his popular romances included *Simon the Jester* (1910), *The Joyous Adventures of Aristide Pujol* (1912) and *The Wonderful Fear* (1916). His plays, some of which were dramatized versions of his novels, were produced with success on the London stage.

LOCKER-LAMPSON, Frederick (1821–95) English writer, born in London. He came of naval ancestry, and from government service passed to the Admiralty. He left government service in 1850. *London Lyrics* (1857) revealed him as a writer of bright and clever light verse dealing with society topics. Later collections of verse were *Lyra Elegantiarum* (1867) and *Patchwork* (1879).

LOCKHART, John Gibson (1794–1854) Scottish biographer, novelist and critic, born in Cambusnethan, Lanarkshire, the son of a Church of Scotland minister. He spent his boyhood in Glasgow, where at eleven he went from the high school to the college. At the age of 13, with a Snell exhibition to Balliol College, he went up to Oxford. In 1813 he took a first in classics; then, after a visit to the Continent to see **Goethe** in Weimar, he studied law at Edinburgh, and in 1816 was called to the Scottish bar. While still at Oxford he had written the article 'Heraldry' for the *Edinburgh Encyclopaedia*, and translated **Schlegel**'s *Lectures on the History of Literature*; from 1817 he turned more and more to letters, and with **John Wilson** became the chief mainstay of *Blackwood's Magazine*. In its pages he first exhibited the cruelty with which he savaged other writers and the caustic wit that made him the terror of his Whig opponents. In 1819 he published *Peter's Letters to His Kinsfolk* in 3 volumes, a clever skit on Edinburgh intellectual society. In 1820 he married Sophia, eldest daughter of Sir **Walter Scott**, and produced four novels—*Valerius* (1821), *Adam Blair* (1822), *Reginald Dalton* (1823) and *Matthew Wald* (1824). *Ancient Spanish Ballads* appeared in 1823; Lives of **Burns** and **Napoleon** in 1828 and 1829; and the *Memoirs of the Life of Scott*, his masterpiece, in 1837–38 (7 vols). In 1825 he moved to London to become editor until 1853 of the *Quarterly Review*. In 1843 he also became auditor of the duchy of Cornwall. But his closing years were clouded by illness and deep depression; by the secession to Rome of his only daughter, with her husband, J R Hope-Scott; and by the loss of his wife in 1837, of his two boys in 1831 and 1853. The elder was the 'Hugh Littlejohn' of Scott's *Tales of a Grandfather*; the younger, Walter, was in the army. Like Scott, Lockhart visited Italy in search of health and he too came back to Abbotsford to die. He is buried in Dryburgh Abbey beside Scott.

LOCKWOOD, Belva Ann, née **Bennett** (1830–1917) American lawyer and reformer, born in Royalton, Niagara County, New York. Educated at Genesee College, she graduated from the National University Law School in Washington (1873) and was admitted to the bar. In 1868 she married Ezekiel Lockwood, her second husband (her first died in 1853). A skilled and vigorous supporter of women's rights, she became the first woman to practise before the Supreme Court, and helped to promote various reforms, such as the Equal Pay Act for female civil servants (1872). In 1884 and 1888, as a member of the National Equal Rights party, she was nominated for the presidency. Holding strong pacifist views, she was a member of the nominating committee for the Nobel peace prize.

LOCKYER, Sir Joseph Norman (1836–1920) English astronomer, born in Rugby. As a clerk in the War Office (1857–75) he detected and named helium in the sun's chromosphere by daylight, in 1868, shortly before **William Ramsay**. He was in the government science and art department (1875–90), and later professor of astronomical physics at the Royal College of Science (1908–13). He headed many eclipse expeditions, started (1869) and edited *Nature*, and wrote much on solar chemistry and physics, on the meteoritic hypothesis, and on orientation of stone circles.

LODGE, Edmund (1756–1839) English biographer and writer on heraldry. He is best known by his *Portraits of Illustrious Personages* (1821–34) and *The Genealogy of the Existing British Peerage* (1832, enlarged 1859).

LODGE, Henry Cabot (1850–1924) American Republican senator, historian and biographer, born in Boston. He was assistant editor of the *North American Review*, but from 1878 his career was mainly political and he became a senator in 1893, later opposing US participation in the League of Nations. His grandson, Henry Cabot (1902–85), became a Republican senator in 1936, was American UN delegate (1953–60), and ambassador to South Vietnam (1963–64 and 1965–67).

LODGE, Sir Oliver Joseph (1851–1940) English physicist, born in Penkhull. He studied at the Royal College of Science and at University College, London, and in 1881 became professor of physics at Liverpool. In 1900 he was appointed first principal of the new university at Birmingham. Specially distinguished in electricity, he was a pioneer of wireless telegraphy. His scientific writings include *Signalling across Space without Wires* (1897), *Talks about Wireless* (1925) and *Advancing Science* (1931). He gave much time to psychical research and on this subject wrote *Raymond* (1916) and *My Philosophy* (1933). *Past Years: An Autobiography* appeared in 1931. His brother, Sir Richard Lodge (1855–1936), was the first professor of modern history at Glasgow University (1894–99) and thereafter at Edinburgh University (1899–1933). Among his works are *A History of Modern Europe* (1885) and *The Close of the Middle Ages, 1273–1494* (1901).

LODGE, Thomas (c.1558–1625) English dramatist, romance writer, and poet, born in West Ham. From Merchant Taylors' School he went to Trinity College, Oxford, and from there in 1578 to Lincoln's Inn, but led a wild life. In 1584 he wrote his first romance, *The Delectable Historie of Forbonius and Priscilla*, followed by *Scillaes Metamorphosis* in 1589. About 1588 he took part in a buccaneering expedition to the Canaries, and wrote another romance, *Rosalynde* (1590), his best-known work, which supplied **Shakespeare** with many of the chief incidents in *As You Like It*. He went on a second freebooting expedition to South America in 1591. He wrote many other works, including *The Wounds of the Civil War* (1594) and *A Looking-glass for London and England* (with **Robert Greene**, 1594). He turned Catholic and is believed to have taken a medical degree at Avignon (1600), and to have written a *History of the Plague* (1603). Among his remaining writings are *A Fig for Momus* (1595); translations of **Seneca** (1614) and **Josephus** (1602); *Life of William Longbeard* (1593); *Robin the Divell*, *Wits Miserie and Worlds Madness* (1596), and a collection of poems, *Phillis* (1593).

LOEB, Jacques (1859–1924) German-born American biologist, born in Mayen. Educated at Berlin, Munich and Strasbourg, he emigrated to the USA in 1891 and after various university appointments became head of the general physiology division at the Rockefeller Institute for Medical Research (1910–24). He did pioneer work on artificial parthenogenesis and also carried out research in comparative physiology and psychology. His writings include *Dynamics of Living Matter* (1906) and *Artificial Parthenogenesis and Fertilisation* (1913).

LOEB, James (1867–1933) American banker, born in New York City. With his fortune he founded the Institute of Musical Art in New York (1905) and a mental clinic in Munich. A classical scholar himself, in 1910 he provided funds for the publication of the famous Loeb Classical Library of Latin and Greek texts with English translations.

LOESSER, Frank Henry (1910–69) American songwriter and composer, born in New York City, best known for writing music and lyrics for *Guys and Dolls* (1950). He published his first lyric in 1931, and in 1937 went to Hollywood as a contract writer. With a succession of collaborators he turned out several hit songs including *See What the Boys in the Backroom Will Have*, *Two Sleepy People* (with Hoagy Carmichael), and *Baby, It's Cold Outside*. He branched out into writing his own music with *Where's Charley*, a musical version of *Charley's Aunt* (1948). After *Guys and Dolls* his other musicals include *The Most Happy Fella* (1956), and *How to Succeed in Business Without Really Trying* (1961).

LOEWE, (Johann) Karl Gottfried (1796–1869) German composer, born near Halle. He studied music and theology at Halle, and in 1822 became a musical teacher at Stettin. In 1847 he sang and played before the court in London. He composed operas (of which only one, *The Three Wishes*, was performed), oratorios, symphonies, concertos, duets, and other works for piano, but his ballads, his most notable bequest, are (including the *Erlkönig*) remarkable dramatic poems. He published his autobiography in 1870.

LOEWI, Otto (1873–1961) German pharmacologist, born in Frankfurt-am-Main. Educated at Strasbourg and Munich, he was professor of pharmacology at Graz (1909–38). Forced to leave Nazi Germany in 1938, he became research professor at New York University College of Medicine from 1940. In 1936 he shared with Sir **Henry Dale** the Nobel prize for physiology or medicine, for investigations on nerve impulses and their chemical transmission.

LOEWY, Raymond Fernand (1893–1987) French-born American industrial designer, born in Paris. He emigrated to the USA in 1919 and based his activities there. After a period of varied work as a ' commercial artist', he was commissioned to redesign the casing for the Gestetner duplicator, after which his considerable energies were employed in designing products and graphics for major industrial corporations worldwide. Clients included Shell and BP, Coca Cola, Studebaker, BMW, Sud Aviation and the National Aeronautics and Space Administration (NASA). Loewy was the archetypal American entrepreneurial designer. Undeniably associated with the 'stylist' school of design, and with the 'streamlined' style in particular, his work was far too intelligently considered to be so simply categorized. The functionalism of his NASA space stations, the elegance of his Alouette helicopter and the undecorated aerodynamic forms of his cars alone contradict such a view. He was the author of *Never Leave Well Enough Alone* (1951).

LÖFFLER, Friedrich August Johann (1852–1915) German bacteriologist, born in Frankfurt an der Oder. He started as a military surgeon, became professor at Greifswald (1888) and from 1913 was director of the Koch Institute for Infectious Diseases in Berlin. He first cultured the diphtheria bacillus (1884) discovered by Edwin Klebs and called the 'Klebs-Löffler bacillus', discovered the causal organism of glanders and swine erysipelas (1886), isolated an organism causing food poisoning and prepared a vaccine against foot-and-mouth disease (1899). He wrote an unfinished history of bacteriology (1887).

LOFFT, Capell (1751–1824) English writer and lawyer, born in London. He was a Whig barrister with a taste for letters, especially poetry. His best work was a translation of Spanish, Italian and other foreign verse under the title of *Laura, an Anthology of Sonnets* (5 vols, 1814). He was the patron of **Bloomfield**. His fourth son, Capell Lofft (1806–73), wrote poetry and an autobiography called *Self-Formation* (1837).

LOFTING, Hugh John (1886–1947) English children's novelist, born in Maidenhead. The 'Doctor Doolittle' books (1920–53), for which he is famous (despite slurs that they are racist and chauvinistic), had their origins in the trench warfare of World War I, of which he had first-hand experience. The idea of the doctor who learns animal languages came to him from his reflectons on the part that horses were playing in the war. There were a dozen Doolittle books, which he also illustrated, and though he tired of his eponymous hero—on one occasion attempting to abandon him on the Moon—his popularity with readers kept him alive. He was mainly resident in the USA from 1912.

LOFTUS, Cissie See **McCARTHY, Justin Huntly**

LOGAN, John (1748–88) Scottish poet and clergyman, born in Soutra, Midlothian. He was educated at Musselburgh Grammar School and Edinburgh University, and was appointed minister of South Leith in 1773. He wrote a successful play, *Runnemede*, in 1784 and moved to London. He is mainly remembered for his plagiarism of several poems of his friend Michael Bruce, including 'Ode to the Cuckoo', which he included in his own volume of poetry (1781).

LOGAN, John Alexander (1826–86) American soldier and legislator, born in Illinois. He served in the Mexican war, was called to the bar in 1852, and was elected to congress as a Democrat in 1858. He raised an Illinois regiment in the civil war, and retired at its close as major-general. Returned to congress as a Republican in 1866, he was repeatedly chosen as a US senator.

LOGAN, Sir William Edmund (1798–1875) Canadian geologist, born in Montreal. Educated at the Royal High School and Edinburgh University, he spent ten years in a London counting house, then became (1828) bookkeeper in Swansea to a copper-smelting company. There he made a map of the coal basin, which was incorporated into the geological survey. From 1842 to 1871 he was director of the Canadian Geological Survey.

LOISY, Alfred Firmin (1857–1940) French theologian, born in Ambrières, Haute-Marne. He was ordained priest in 1879 and in 1881 became professor of holy scripture at the Institut Catholique, where by his lectures and writings he incurred the disfavour of the church and was dismissed. In 1900 he was appointed lecturer at the Sorbonne, but resigned after his works on Biblical criticism were condemned by Pope **Pius X** in 1903 as too advanced. These books, which proved him to be the founder of the modernist movement, were *L'Évangile et l'Église* (1902), *Quatrième Évangile* (1903) and *Autour d'un petit livre* (1903). For subsequent works of the same kind he was excommunicated in 1908. He was professor of history of religion in the Collège de France from 1909 to 1932.

LOMBARD, Carole, originally **Jane Alice Peters** (1908–42) American actress, born in Fort Worth, Indiana. Later resident in California, she was spotted by director Allan Dwan and cast as a tomboy in the film *A Perfect Crime* (1921). After completing her studies she returned to filmmaking in 1925 where her blond hair and beauty made her a decorative addition to many comedy shorts for **Mark Sennett**. Signed to a long-term contract with Paramount in 1930, her roles gradually improved and she revealed a delicious comic flair in *Twentieth Century* (1934). A glamorous, sophisticated woman, unafraid to play for laughs, her witty, wacky effervescence made her the perfect heroine of screwball comedies like *My Man Godfrey* (1936), *Nothing Sacred* (1937) and *To Be or Not to Be* (1942) whilst her dramatic potential was glimpsed in *They Knew What They Wanted* (1940). Married to **Clark Gable** in 1939, she was one of Hollywood's most popular stars at the time of her death in an air crash.

LOMBARD, Peter (c.1100–1164) Italian theologian, born near Novara in Lombardy. He studied in Bologna, at Reims, and (under **Abelard**) in Paris, and, after holding a chair of theology there, in 1159 became bishop of Paris. He was generally styled *Magister Sententiarum* or the 'Master of Sentences', from his collection of sentences from **Augustine** and other Fathers on points of Christian doctrine, with objections and replies. The theological doctors of Paris in 1300 denounced some of his teachings as heretical; but his work was the standard textbook of Catholic theology down to the Reformation.

LOMBARDI, Vince (Vincent Thomas) (1913–70) American football coach, born in Brooklyn, New York City. Although a noted defensive guard in his playing days with Fordham University, he was better known as a coach. He started in professional leagues by coaching offence for the New York Giants (1954–59), despite having been a defender, but his best work was done with the Green Bay Packers from Michigan (1959–69). With this comparatively small-town team he lifted five league titles and took them successfully to two Super Bowls (1967–1968).

LOMBARDO, Pietro (c.1433–1515) Italian sculptor and architect, from Lombardy. After working in Padua, and probably Florence, he settled with his family in Venice c.1467 and became the head of the major sculpture workshop of the day. With the assistance of his sons, Tullio (c.1455–1532) and Antonio (c.1458–1516), he was responsible for both the architecture and sculptural decoration of Sta Maria dei Miracoli (1481–89), one of the finest Renaissance buildings in Venice. Amongst the many monuments he designed was the tomb of **Dante** in Ravenna.

LOMBROSO, Cesare (1836–1909) Italian physician and criminologist, born in Verona. After acting as an army surgeon, he became professor of mental diseases at Pavia (1862), and director of an asylum at Pesaro, became professor of forensic medicine (1876), psychiatry (1896) and criminal anthropology (1906) at Turin. His theory postulated the existence of a criminal type distinguishable from the normal man. His great work is *L'uomo delinquente* (1875).

LOMONOSOV, Mikhail Vasilievich (1711–65) Russian scientist and man of letters, born in Denisovka, near Archangel. The son of a fisherman, he ran away to Moscow in search of education, and later studied at St Petersburg and at Marburg in Germany under the philosopher **Christian von Wolff**. Turning to science, he became professor of chemistry at St Petersburg Academy of Sciences in 1745, and set up the first chemical laboratory in Russia there. In 1755 he founded Moscow University. Apart from his many works on science, he also wrote poetry on scientific subjects. His writings include works on rhetoric (1748), grammar (1755) and Russian history (1766); his greatest contribution to Russian culture was his systematization of the grammar and orthography.

LONDON, Fritz Wolfgang (1900–54) German-born American physicist, born in Breslau (now Wroclaw in Poland), brother of **Heinz London** and son of a professor of mathematics in Bonn. He discovered the London equations in superconductivity. He studied classics at the universities of Frankfurt and Munich and did research in philosophy leading to a doctorate at Bonn. Later he was attracted to theoretical physics and worked with **Schrödinger** at Zürich in 1927, and published on the quantum theory of the chemical bond with Walter Heitler. In 1930 he calculated the non-polar component of forces between molecules, now called Van de Waals or London forces. The brothers fled from Germany in 1933 to Oxford where they joined Sir **Francis Simon**'s group at the Clarendon Laboratory. Together they published major papers on conductivity giving the London equations (1935). Fritz moved to Duke University in the USA (1939–54) and continued to work on superconductivity, and on superfluidity.

LONDON, Heinz (1907–70) German-born British physicist, born in Bonn, West Germany, younger brother of **Fritz London** and son of a professor of mathematics in Bonn. He was educated at the universities of Bonn, Berlin, Munich and Breslau where he worked for his PhD with Sir **Francis Simon**. The brothers fled from Germany in 1933 and joined Simon's group at the Clarendon Laboratory, Oxford, working together on conductivity. He then moved to Bristol, was briefly interned as an enemy alien in 1940, and released to work on the development of the atomic bomb. In 1946 he joined the Atomic Energy Research Establishment at Harwell.

LONDON, Jack (John Griffith) (1876–1916) American novelist, born in San Francisco. He was successively sailor, tramp and gold miner before he took to writing. He used his knowledge of the Klondyke in the highly successful *Call of the Wild* (1903) and *White Fang* (1907), and of the sea in *Sea-Wolf* (1904), and *The Mutiny of the 'Elsinore'* (1914). As well as pure adventure tales, he also wrote the more serious political novel *The Iron Heel* (1907), and his autobiographical tale of alcoholism, *John Barleycorn* (1913).

LONDONDERRY See **PITT, Thomas,** and **CASTLEREAGH, Robert Stewart**

LONERGAN, Bernard Joseph Francis (1904–85) Canadian Jesuit theologian and philosopher, born in Buckingham, Quebec. He entered the Society of Jesus in 1922. Professor of systematic theology at the Gregorian University, Rome, from 1954 to 1965, his main concern was to discover precisely how theology is done, following an analysis of the way human understanding in general proceeds. The findings of his massive and seminal studies on *Insight: A Study of Human Understanding* (1957), and *Method in Theology* (1972) are summarized in *Philosophy of God, and Theology* (1973) and *Understanding and Being* (1980). His other interests in theology and the history of ideas were explored in occasional papers, assembled in *Collection* (1967), *A Second Collection* (1974), and *A Third Collection* (1985).

LONG, Crawford Williamson (1815–78) American physician, born in Danielsville, Georgia. He practised in Jefferson, Georgia, in 1842, operating on a neck tumour. He was the first to use ether as an anaesthetic, but did not reveal his discovery until 1849, after William Thomas Green had demonstrated it publicly in 1846.

LONG, Earl Kemp (1895–1960) American politician, brother of **Huey Long**. He continued his brother's method of corrupt administration coupled with sound social legislation, as lieutenant-governor (1936–38) and governor (1939–40, 1948–52, 1956–60) of Louisiana. Suffering from paranoiac schizophrenia, he was at his wife's request placed in a mental hospital in May 1959 and forcibly detained there with police help, until, using his powers as governor, he dismissed the mental hospitals superintendent and appointed politically favourable medical officers.

LONG, Huey Pierce (1893–1935) American politician, brother of **Earl Kemp Long**, born in Winnfield, Louisiana. A lawyer by profession he became governor of Louisiana (1928–31) and a US senator (1930–35). Nicknamed 'Kingfish', he was notorious for his corruption and demagoguery. He secured the support of the poor by his intensive 'Share the Wealth' social services and public works programmes, but also squandered public funds on extravagant personal projects, including the construction of a marble and bronze statehouse at Baton Rouge. He was assassinated.

LONG, Richard (1945–) English 'Land artist', born in Bristol. He takes country walks which he considers works of art in themselves, sometimes marking a place with a simple 'sculpture', eg a circle of stones, or a shallow trench: afterwards he exhibits photographs, maps, texts. He held his first one-man show in Dusseldorf, 1968, and has had a hundred since, worldwide. He won the 1989 Turner prize.

LONGCHAMP, William de (d.1197) English prelate. He was a lowly-born favourite of **Richard I**, who in 1189–90 made him chancellor, bishop of Ely, and joint justiciar of England. In 1191 he was likewise made papal legate; but because of his heated arrogance he had to withdraw to Normandy. He regained Richard's favour by raising his ransom, and was made chancellor again. He died in Poitiers.

LONGFELLOW, Henry Wadsworth (1807–82) American poet, born in Portland, Maine. He graduated at Bowdoin College in Brunswick, Maine, where one of his classmates was **Nathaniel Hawthorne**. In 1826 the college trustees sent him to Europe to qualify for the chair of foreign languages, and he spent three years abroad (1826–29) before taking up the chair at Bowdoin (1829–35). He married in 1831, but his wife died in 1835. *Outre Mer*, an account of his first European tour, appeared in 1835; and *Hyperion*, which is a journal of the second, in 1839. In 1836, after another visit to Europe, when he met **Carlyle**, he became professor of modern languages and literature at Harvard, and held the chair for nearly 18 years. *Voices of the Night* (1839), his first book of verse, made a favourable impression, which was strengthened by *Ballads* (1841), which included 'The Skeleton in Armour', 'The Wreck of the Hesperus', 'The Village Blacksmith', and 'Excelsior'. *Poems on Slavery* appeared in 1842. He made a third visit to Europe in 1842, and next year married his second wife, Frances Appleton, who died in a fire in 1861. *The Belfry of Bruges and other Poems* appeared in 1846. One of his most popular poems is *Evangeline* (1847), a tale (in hexameters) of the French exiles of Acadia. *The Golden Legend* (1851) is based on *Der arme Heinrich* of **Hartmann von Aue**. His most popular work, *Hiawatha* (1855), is based on the legends of the Redskins, using a metre borrowed from the Finnish epic, the *Kalevala*. *The Courtship of Miles Standish* (1858) is a story in hexameters of the early days of the Plymouth colony in Massachusetts. It was followed by *Tales of a Wayside Inn* (1863), which included 'Paul Revere's Ride', and an undistinguished translation of **Dante**'s *Divina Commedia* (1865–67). He paid a last visit to Europe in 1868–69. As a poet he was extremely popular during his lifetime and although his work lacks the depth of great poetry, his gift of simple, romantic story-telling in verse makes it still read widely with pleasure.

LONGHI, originally **Falca, Pietro** (1702–85) Venetian painter. He was a pupil of Balestra, and excelled in small-scale satiric pictures of Venetian life. Most of his work is in Venetian public collections, but the National Gallery, London, has three, of which the best known is *Rhinoceros in an Arena*. His son Alessandro (1733–1813) was also a painter. Some of his portraits are now attributed to his father.

LONGINUS (probably 1st century) Greek literary critic. Nothing certain is known of his life, but he is author of the celebrated work, *On the Sublime* (about two-thirds of which survives), which analyses the qualities of great literature and has been enormously influential, particularly among Romantic critics.

LONGMAN, Thomas (1699–1755) English publisher, and founder of the publishing firm which bears his name, born in Bristol, the son of a merchant. He bought a bookselling business in Paternoster Row, London, in 1724, and shared in publishing **Ainsworth**'s *Latin Dictionary*, **Ephraim Chambers**'s *Cyclopaedia*, and **Johnson**'s *Dictionary*. His nephew, Thomas Longman (1730–97), brought out a new edition of **Chambers**'s *Cyclopaedia*. Under Thomas Norton Longman (1771–1842) the firm had relations with **Wordsworth**, **Southey**, **Coleridge**, **Scott**, **Moore**, **Sydney Smith** and others. After **Constable**'s failure in 1826 the *Edinburgh Review* became the property of the firm, which also published *Lardner's Cabinet Cyclopaedia* (1829–46). Thomas Longman (1804–79), eldest son of T N Longman, issued under his special care a beautifully illustrated New Testament. His brother William (1813–77) wrote *Lectures on the History of England* (1859) and *History of Edward* III (1869). They are best known for their publication of **Macaulay**'s *Lays* (1842), *Essays* (1843) and *History* (1848–61).

LONGOMONTANUS, Christian Sörensen (1562–1647) Danish astronomer, born in Longberg, Jutland. In 1589 he became an assistant of **Tycho Brahe**, whom he accompanied to Germany. Returning to Denmark he became professor at Copenhagen, where he inaugurated the building of the observatory.

LONGSTREET, James (1821–1904) American soldier, born in Edgefield District, South Carolina. He fought in the Mexican war (1846–48), but resigned from the US army at the outbreak of the Civil War (1861–65) to join the Confederate army. He fought in both battles of Bull Run (1861,1862) and at Gettysburg (1863), and surrendered with **Lee** at Appomattox Courthouse (April 1865).

LONGUETT-HIGGINS, Hugh Christopher (1923–) English theoretical chemist and neurophysicist, born in Lenham. He was educated at Oxford, and after university posts in the USA and London he became professor of theoretical chemistry at Cambridge (1954–67), and then Royal Society professor at Edinburgh, and, at Sussex, at the Centre for Research in Perception and Cognition. He made contributions to theories of chemical bonding from the 1940s, but more recently has worked on problems of the mind, including language acquisition, music perception, and speech analysis.

LONGUEVILLE, Anne, Duchesse de (1619–79) French noblewoman, born in Vincennes, the 'soul of the Fronde'. She was the only daughter of the Prince de **Condé**, and in 1639 was married to the Duc de Longueville. She exerted a considerable influence on politics, in which she first began to interest herself as the mistress of the Duc de **la Rochefoucauld**. In the first war of the Fronde (1648) she sought in vain to gain over her brother, the Great **Condé**. In the second she won over both him and **Turenne**. After the death of her husband and her desertion by la Rochefoucauld, she entered a convent but continued to have influence at court.

LONGUS (3rd century) Greek writer. He was the author of the Greek prose romance *Daphnis and Chloë*, the first pastoral romance known, in the middle of the 3rd century AD.

LÖNNROT, Elias (1802–84) Finnish philologist and folklorist, born in Sammatti in Nyland. He studied medicine, and was district medical officer for 20 years in Kajana. As a result of his folklore researches, he was appointed professor of Finnish at Helsingfors (now Helsinki) (1853–62). His major achievement was the collection of oral popular lays, which he organized into a long, connected epic poem of ancient life in the far north, the *Kalevala* (the shorter *Old Kalevala* in 1835, the longer version in 1849). He also compiled a great Finnish-Swedish dictionary (1866–80), which helped to establish a literary Finnish language.

LONSDALE, Frederick, originally **Frederick Leonard** (1881–1954) British playwright, born in Jersey, the son of a tobacconist. He was known for his witty and sophisticated society comedies, among them *The Last of Mrs Cheyney* (1925), *On Approval* (1927) and *Canaries Sometimes Sing* (1929). He collaborated in operettas, including *Maid of the Mountains* (1916).

LONSDALE, Hugh Cecil Lowther, 5th Earl of (1857–1944) English sportsman. A landowner in Cumberland, he was a noted huntsman, steeplechaser, yachtsman and boxer. As president of the National Sporting Club he founded and presented the 'Lonsdale belts' for boxing.

LONSDALE, Dame Kathleen, née **Yardley** (1903–71) Irish crystallographer, born in Newbridge. She was one of the first to apply X-ray diffraction analysis to organic crystals. The tenth and youngest child of an Irish postmaster, she went to England with her family in 1908. She studied physics at Bedford College, London, and spent the next 20 years in the research team of **William Bragg** based at the Royal Institution. In 1927 she married Thomas Londsdale. From 1946 to 1968 she worked at University College, London, as professor of chemistry and head of the department of crystallography. Using the methods pioneered by the Braggs for finding molecular structure by X-ray diffraction of crystals, she worked out the structure of hexamethylbenzene in 1929, and two years later the structure of hexachlorobenzene, using for the first time **Fourier** analysis to solve the structure. The method was to become a major technique. Her work on organic structures gave reality to the concept of molecular orbitals. As a Quaker and convinced pacifist, she refused to register for civil defence or any other national service in 1939, despite the fact that as a mother of three children she would have been exempted from such service, and served a month in prison when she refused to pay the fine. In 1945 the Royal Society agreed to elect women fellows, and she became the first female FRS.

LONSDALE, William (1794–1871) English geologist, born in Bath. He served in the army but left it in 1815 and took up geology. He made a study of the fossils in north and south Devon, in 1837 placing them between the Silurian and the Carboniferous. This led to the establishment of the Devonian System by **Roderick Murchison** and **Adam Sedgwick** (1839).

LOOS, Adolf (1870–1933) Austrian architect and writer on design, born in Brno. After studying architecture in Dresden and a period of three years in the USA, he settled in Vienna in 1896. One of the major architects of the 'Modern Movement', he is particularly important for articulating in his own short-lived journal *Das Andere* (1903), and in other articles, the view that ornament is 'wasteful', 'decadent' and against modern 'civilized' design. His buildings and other designs such as furniture, glass and metalwork, reflect this view, but possess an elegance and visual interest which is derived from their functional form.

LOPE (DE VEGA) See **VEGA CARPIO**

LOPES, Francisco Higino Craveiro (1894–1964) Portuguese statesman, born in Lisbon of a distinguished military family. Educated at the Military School, Lisbon, he fought in the expeditionary force in Mozambique in World War I. As a full colonel in 1942 he entered negotiations for co-operation with the Allies and was responsible for the modernization of the Portuguese air force. In 1944 he entered parliament, in

1949 he was promoted to general, and was president of Portugal from 1951 to 1958.

LÓPEZ, Francisco Solano (1827–70) Paraguayan statesman, born in Asunción, a grand-nephew of **Francia**. He succeeded his father as president of Paraguay in 1862. In 1864 he provoked war with Brazil and was faced with an alliance of Brazil, Uruguay and Argentina. The war lasted for five years, during which Paraguay was completely devastated and López himself, having fled, was shot by a soldier.

LÓPEZ DE AYALA See **AYALA**

LOPOKOVA, Lydia See **KEYNES, John Maynard**

LOPUKHOV, Fyodor (1886–1973) Soviet dancer, choreographer and teacher, born in St Petersburg. He studied at the Imperial Ballet Academy before joining the Maryinsky Theatre, where he was one of their outstanding character dancers. He started choreographing in 1916, becoming one of the leading ballet experimentalists of his generation. He set the foundation of neo-classical and modern dance in Russia, introducing acrobatics into the academic vocabulary, and developing an interest in plotless, abstract ballets as a reaction against the literary, realist traditions of the 19th century. His most influential ballet was *Dance Symphony* (1923). He was artistic director of the Kirov (1923–30, and in the mid 1940s and 1950s), Maly Theatre and Bolshoi Ballet companies (both in the mid 1930s).

LORCA, Federigo García (1899–1936) Spanish poet, born in Fuente Vaqueros. He was killed, by design or misunderstanding, early in the Spanish Civil War at Granada. His gypsy songs—*Canciones* (1927) and *Romancero Gitano* (1928 and 1935), probably his best and most widely-read work, reveal a classical control of imagery, rhythm and emotion. He also wrote several successful plays, including *Bodas de Sangre* (1933), *Yerma* and *La Casa de Bernarda Alba*.

LORD, Thomas (1755–1832) English sportsman, founder of Lord's Cricket Ground in London. Born in Thirsk, in Yorkshire, he first opened a cricket ground in Dorset Square in London in 1787, which became the home of the Marylebone Cricket Club (MCC), the regulating body of English cricket, and also the county ground of Middlesex; it was moved to its present site in St John's Wood in 1814.

LOREBURN, Robert Threshie Reid, 1st Earl of (1846–1923) Scottish lawyer, born in Corfu. He studied at Balliol College, Oxford, was called to the bar in 1871, and became MP in 1880, solicitor-general and then attorney-general in 1894 and in 1905 Lord Chancellor and a baron, in 1911 an earl. He resigned in 1912. As Lord Chancellor he delivered many important judgments.

LOREN, Sophia, originally **Sofia Scicolone** (1934–) Italian actress, born in Rome. A teenage beauty queen and model, she entered films in 1950 as an extra in *Cuori sul Mare*. Under contract to Carlo Ponti, later her husband, she blossomed into a stunningly beautiful star with a talent for earthy drama and vivacious comedy. An international career followed and she won an Academy Award for *Two Women* (La Ciociara, 1961). Frequently seen in partnership with **Marcello Mastroianni**, she has attempted a wide range of characterizations with varying degrees of success. Her many films include *The Millionairess* (1961), *Marriage Italian Style* (1964), *Cinderella—Italian Style* (*C'Era Una Volta*, 1967) and *A Special Day* (*Una Giornata Particolare*, 1977). In 1979 she published *Sophia Loren: Living and Loving* (with A E Hotchner) which was filmed for television as *Sophia Loren: Her Own Story* (1980) with the actress playing both herself and her mother. Her career continues with television films like *Aurora* (1984) and *Courage* (1986).

LORENTE DE NO, Rafael (1902–) Spanish-born American neurophysiologist, born in Zaraguza. He received his MD from Madrid University. After several years in the Cajal Institute in Madrid, and a department of otolaryngology in Santander, he went to the USA where, from 1936, he worked at the Rockefeller Institute (now Rockefeller University) in New York City. His research covered a wide range of neurophysiological and neuroanatomical problems, including the co-ordination of eye movements and the functional anatomy of neuron networks.

LORENTZ, Hendrik Antoon (1853–1928) Dutch physicist, born in Arnhem. He studied at Leiden and became professor of mathematical physics there in 1878. He also directed research at the Taylor Institute, Haarlem, from 1923. He worked out the explanation by the '**Fitzgerald**-Lorentz Contraction' of the **Michelson-Morley** experiment, and prepared the way for **Einstein**. In 1902 he was awarded, with **Pieter Zeeman**, the Nobel prize for physics.

LORENZ, Konrad Zacharias (1903–89) Austrian zoologist and ethologist, born in Vienna, the son of a surgeon. Widely regarded as the father of the science of ethology (the study of animal behaviour under natural conditions), he studied at Vienna, and founded the ethological school of animal behaviour with **Nikolaas Tinbergen** in the late 1930s. Rather than studying animal learning in laboratories, Lorenz and his colleagues favoured the investigation of instinctive behaviour by animals in the wild. His studies have led to a deeper understanding of behaviour patterns. In 1935 he published his observations on imprinting in young birds (the discovery for which he is chiefly known), by which hatchlings 'learn' to recognize substitute parents at the earliest stages in life. In his book *On Aggression* (1963) he argued that while aggressive behaviour in man is inborn it may be modified or channelled into other forms of activity, whereas in other animals it is purely survival-motivated. *King Solomon's Ring* (1949), *Man Meets Dog* (1950), and *Evolution and Modification of Behaviour* (1961) also enjoyed wide popularity. He shared the 1973 Nobel prize for physiology or medicine with Nikolaas Tinbergen and **Karl von Frisch**.

LORENZETTI, Ambrogio (?1300–?1348) Italian painter from Siena, younger brother of **Pietro Lorenzetti**. He worked in Cortona and Florence, but is best known for his allegorical frescoes in the Palazzo Pubblico at Siena, symbolizing the effects of good and bad government. An *Annunciation* is also at Siena.

LORENZETTI, Pietro, also called **Pietro Laurati** (?1280–?1348) Italian painter from Siena, elder brother of **Ambrogio Lorenzetti**. Probably a pupil of **Duccio**, he was one of the liveliest of the early Sienese painters, and he also worked at Arezzo (the polyptych in S Maria della Pieve) and Assisi, where he painted dramatic frescoes of the *Passion* in the Lower Church of S Francis. A *Madonna* (1340) is in the Uffizi Gallery.

LORENZO, called **il Monaco,** originally **Piero di Giovanni** (c.1370–c.1425) Italian painter, born in Siena. He became a monk of the Camaldolese order in 1391, and lived and worked in Florence. He began as a miniature painter in the monastery of S Maria degli Angeli, but later executed many notable altarpieces, especially the *Coronation of the Virgin*. His charming pictures are represented in both the Uffizi and Louvre galleries.

LORIMER, James (1818–90) Scottish jurist, born in Aberdalgie, Perthshire. An eminent authority on international law, he was professor at Edinburgh from

1862. In *The Institutes of Law* he combated positivism and utilitarianism. He wrote also on international law, notably *The Institutes of the Law of Nations*.

LORIMER, Sir Robert Stodart (1864–1929) Scottish architect, born in Edinburgh, son of **James Lorimer**. Educated at The Edinburgh Academy and Edinburgh University, he left without a degree and was articled to an architect's office in Edinburgh and then in London. He set up on his own in Edinburgh in 1892, working on Scottish country houses like Hill of Tarvit in Fife (1904) and creating a distinctive Scottish form of the Arts and Crafts tradition of his English contemporary **Edwin Lutyens**. He built or totally remodelled some 50 country houses in Britain, like Rowallan in Ayrshire (1902), Ardkinglas in Argyll (1906), and the classical Marchmont in Berwickshire (1914). His most notable public works were the Thistle Chapel in St Giles, Edinburgh (1909–11), and the Scottish National War Memorial in Edinburgh Castle (1923–28). He also restored many castles, mansions and churches, including Balmanno House in Perthshire, Dunrobin Castle in Sutherland, Paisley Abbey and Dunblane Cathedral. His elder brother, John Henry (1856–1936) was a noted artist, and produced the celebrated painting *Ordination of Elders in a Scottish Kirk*.

LORJOU, Bernard (1908–) French artist, born in Blois. He was the founder of L'Homme Témoin group in 1949 and among a number of large satirical paintings is his *Atomic Age* (1951).

LORNE, Marquis of See **ARGYLL**

LORRAINE, Charles, Cardinal de See **GUISE**

LORRAINE, Claude See **CLAUDE LORRAINE**

LORRAINE, Ducal House of See **GUISE** family

LORRE, Peter, originally **Laszlo Löwenstein** (1904–64) Hungarian actor, born in Rosenberg. A student in Vienna, he acted in repertory theatre and gave one-man performances and readings. His early theatre appearances include *Die Pionere von Ingolstadt* (1928) in Berlin. Alleged to have played a few bit roles, his official film début came as the pathetic child murderer in the German silent-film classic *M* (1931), and set the seal on much of his subsequent career. A diminutive, sad-eyed figure with a diffident manner and a whispering, wheedling voice, he played smilingly sinister rogues or society's unfortunate outcasts, occasionally satirizing that image. He left Germany in 1933 making his way, via Paris and London, to Hollywood in 1934, where his many successes include *Mad Love* (1935), *Crime and Punishment* (1935), *Casablanca* (1942) and *The Beast With Five Fingers* (1946). A rare excursion to the right side of the law saw him cast as **John Marquand**'s Japanese detective Mr Moto in eight films, but he formed an unholy alliance with Sydney Greenstreet (1879–1954) that was seen to particular advantage in *The Maltese Falcon* (1941) and *The Mask of Dimitrios* (1944). Typecast throughout his career, his sense of humour was evident in *My Favourite Brunette* (1947) and *The Raven* (1963); he wrote and directed one film in Europe, *Die Verlorene* (1951).

LORRIS, Guillaume de (fl.13th century) French poet. He wrote, before 1260, the first part (c.4000 lines) of the *Roman de la Rose*, continued by **Jean de Meung**.

LORTZING, Gustav Albert (1801–51) German musician, born in Berlin. The son of an actor, he went early on the stage, where he picked up basic knowledge of the main instruments of the orchestra. In 1824 he produced his first operetta, 'Ali Pascha von Janina'. He became first tenor with the Leipzig Stadt Theatre (1833–43), conducted and composed operas such as *Zar und Zimmermann* (1837) for which he also wrote the libretti.

LOTHROP, Amy See **WARNER, Susan Bogert**

LOTI, Pierre See **VIAUD, Louis Marie Julien**

LOTTI, Antonio (c.1667–1740) Italian church and operatic composer, born in Venice. Organist of St Mark's from 1704, he wrote 27 operas, a variety of madrigals, songs and masses, and was a rival of **Niccola Porpora**, both as composer and conductor

LOTTO, Lorenzo (c.1480–1556) Italian religious painter, born in Venice. A masterly portrait painter, his subjects are alive and full of character. He worked in Treviso, Bergamo, Venice and Rome, finally becoming a lay brother in the Loreto monastery, where he died.

LOTZE, Rudolf Hermann (1817–81) German philosopher, born in Bautzen, Saxony. He studied medicine and philosophy at Leipzig and went on to become professor of philosophy at Leipzig (1842–44), Göttingen (1844–80) and Berlin (1880–81). He first became known as a physiologist, in opposing the then popular doctrine of 'vitalism'. He also helped to found the science of physiological psychology, but he is best known for his religious philosophy, called Theistic Idealism, which is most fully expounded in *Mikrokosmos* (3 vols, 1856–58).

LOUBET, Émile (1838–1929) French statesman, born in Marsanne (Drôme). He was seventh president of the Republic (1899–1906).

LOUDON, Gideon Ernst, Freiherr von (1717–90) Austrian soldier, born in Tootzen, Livonia, descendant of a 14th century Scottish immigrant from Ayrshire. In 1732 he entered the Russian service, but ten years later exchanged into that of Austria. In the Seven Years' War (1756–63) he won the battle of Kunersdorf (1759), but was defeated at Liegnitz (1760). As field marshal he commanded in the war of the Bavarian succession (1778), and against the Turks (1788–89), capturing Belgrade and Semendria. He was appointed commander-in-chief of the Austrian army in 1790.

LOUDON, John Claudius (1783–1843) Scottish horticultural writer, dendrologist and designer, born in Cambuslang. He worked in England and travelled in Europe, and founded and edited *The Gardener's Magazine* (1826–43). He compiled an *Encyclopaedia of Gardening* (1822), in which he illustrated a wrought-iron sash bar he had invented in 1816, which could be bent in any direction but still maintain its strength; it was this which paved the way for spectacular edifices like the Palm House in Kew Gardens and the Crystal Palace. In Porchester Terrace, London, he designed the prototype semi-detached house. He founded and edited the *Architectural Magazine* (1834), and published an influential *Encyclopaedia of Cottage, Farm and Villa Architecture and Furniture* (1833). His major work was *Arboretum et Fruticetum Brittanicum* (8 vols, 1838), devoted to trees and shrubs.

LOUGANIS, Greg (1960–) American diver, born in San Diego. He took a BA in drama before turning to diving, and won the gold medal in both the springboard and platform competitions at the 1984 Los Angeles Olympics. He won the World Championship at both events in 1986, and retained his Olympic titles in Seoul in 1988. His extraordinary courage was shown in the springboard event in Seoul, when, having hit his head on the board and requiring four stitches in the wound, he returned half an hour later to perform the same dive and go on to reclaim the gold.

LOUGHBOROUGH, Alexander Wedderburn, 1st Baron, later **1st Earl of Rosslyn** (1733–1805) Scottish jurist, born in Edinburgh, son of a Scottish judge. In 1757 he abruptly left the Scottish bar for the English, and entered parliament in 1762. He became chief justice of the common pleas (1780) and Lord Chancellor (1793).

LOUIS I, 'the Pious', (778–840) king of Aquitaine (781–814) and, as sole surviving son of **Charlemagne**, emperor of the Western or Carolingian Empire (814–840). In 817 he attempted to secure his succession by dividing his territories between his three sons, Lothair (d.855), Pepin (d.838) and Louis 'the German' (d.876), with Lothair to be the emperor. In 829, a further share was given to a fourth son, Charles the Bald (**Charles I** of France). Louis I's reign was marked by his reforms of the church in which he collaborated with the monk St Benedict of Aniane. It was also significant for the raids of the Norsemen in the north-west of the empire, especially the Seine and Scheldt basins. It is greatly debated how far the proliferation of hereditary countships and of the institutions of vassalage, often thought to result from these raids, caused a general decline in imperial authority. After his death the empire disintegrated as his sons fought for supremacy.

LOUIS II, 'the Stammerer', (846–79) king of France, second son of **Charles I the Bald**. King of Maine (856) and Aquitaine (867), he was often in revolt against his father, whom he succeeded with great difficulty as king of 'Francia' from 877 to 879.

LOUIS III (c.863–882) king of France, eldest son of **Louis II**, on whose death (879) he was proclaimed joint king with his brother **Carloman**. He took Francia and Neustria as his territories. After his short reign, he was succeeded by Carloman.

LOUIS IV, 'd'Outremer' (d.954) king of France from 936, son of **Charles III the Simple**, himself the posthumous son of **Louis II**. His early life was spent in exile but he was recalled from England on the death of King Raoul, by Hugh the Great (father of **Hugh Capet**) from whose political domination he sought successfully to escape. Nevertheless, during his reign (936–54) many territorial princes in France consolidated their power to the detriment of royal authority. He was succeeded by his son, Lothair IV, and his grandson **Louis V**.

LOUIS V, 'le Fainéant' (c.967–987) king of France, son of Lothair IV, with whose kingship he was associated in 978. King of France from 986 to 987, he died heirless and was thus the last Carolingian ruler of France. The throne passed to **Hugh Capet**, the first of the Capetian line.

LOUIS VI, 'the Fat' (1081–1137) king of France. He succeeded his father **Philip I** in 1108. For most of his reign he campaigned incessantly against the turbulent and unruly nobility of the Île-de-France and eventually re-established his authority over the royal demesne. Despite an inclination to gluttony and a corpulence which left him unable to mount a horse after the age of 46, he was one of the most active of the House of **Capet**, and greatly increased the power and prestige of the monarchy.

LOUIS VII (c.1120–1180) king of France, second son of **Louis VI**. He was originally educated for a church career, but became heir on the death of his brother Philip (1131). In 1137 he became king, married **Eleanor**, heiress of Aquitaine, and continued the consolidation of royal authority begun by his father. However, during his undistinguished participation in the Second Crusade (1147), Louis and his wife became increasingly estranged and he had the marriage annulled in 1152, whereupon Eleanor married Henry Plantagenet, Count of Anjou, who became king of England in 1154 as **Henry II**. Faced with a vast agglomeration of power on both sides of the Channel, Louis succeeded in staving off the Angevin threat, enlisting the aid of the papacy and fomenting discord within Henry's family.

LOUIS VIII, 'the Lion' (1187–1226) king of France from 1223, son of **Philip II** and Isabella of Hainault. During his father's reign, he participated in attacks on the English (1214, 1216) and led two brief crusades against the heretics of the County of Toulouse (1215, 1219). His short reign (1223–26) was marked chiefly by his acquisition of the Montfort claim to the County of Toulouse (1224) and the resumption of the Albigensian Crusade in the south in 1226. Despite his ill-explained death in the autumn of that year (variously attributed to poisoning, dysentery and sexual starvation) this royal crusade led to the submission of Count Raymond VII to his widow, Blanche of Castile (1229), and the eventual absorption of all Languedoc into the royal domain.

LOUIS IX, (St Louis) (1215–70) king of France. In 1226 he succeeded his father, **Louis VIII**, as a minor, with his mother, the pious Blanche of Castile, as regent (1226–34). During a dangerous illness he made a vow to go on crusade, and having appointed his mother regent again during his absence, set off on the Sixth Crusade (1248–54). He was soon defeated and captured, and ransomed for 1000000 marks in 1250. He remained in Palestine in Acre until his mother's death in 1252 compelled his return to France. In a long and peaceful reign he did much to strengthen loyalty to his Capetian dynasty; he founded the Abbey of Royamount in 1228, determined by the Pragmatic Sanction the relations between the French church and the Pope, countenanced the Sorbonne, set up in the provinces royal courts of justice or parliaments, and authorized a new code of laws. By the Treaty of Paris (1259) he made peace with England, recognizing **Henry III** as Duke of Aquitaine in exchange for French Suzerainty elsewhere. In 1270 he embarked on a new crusade, but died of plague in Tunis. He was canonized by Pope **Boniface VIII** in 1927.

LOUIS X, 'the Quarrelsome' (1289–1316), king of Navarre (1305–16) and of France (1314–16), the son of **Philip IV, the Fair.** During his brief reign, which was marked by unrest among his barons, he was guided in his policy by **Charles of Valois**.

LOUIS XI (1423–83) king of France from 1461. As Dauphin of France he married **Margaret of Scotland** (daughter of King **James I**) in 1426. He made two unsuccessful attempts to depose his father, **Charles VII**, but eventually succeeded to the throne on his father's death in 1461. During his reign, with a mixture of force and diplomatic cunning, he broke the power of the nobility, led by **Charles the Bold** of Burgundy, who was killed in 1477. By 1483 he had succeeded in uniting most of France under one crown (with the exception of Brittany), and laid the foundations for absolute monarchy in France. He cherished the arts and sciences, and founded three universities, but he spent his latter years in great misery, in superstitious terrors and excessive fear of death. He died in Plessis-lez-Tours.

LOUIS XII (1462–1515) king of France from 1498, and known as the 'Father of the People'. The son of Charles, Duc d'**Orléans**, he succeeded his cousin **Charles VIII ('the Affable')** on Charles' death after an unsuccessful attempt to overthrow him, and married his widow Anne of Brittany; he had previously been married to a daughter of **Louis XI**. Later, in 1514, he married Mary Tudor, the sister of **Henry VIII** of England. As king he indulged in ambitious military adventures in Italy which proved fruitless. He was eventually driven out of Lombardy by the Holy League of England, Spain, the Pope and the Holy Roman Empire, and defeated at the battle of the Spurs by

Henry VIII in 1513. His reign was popular at home, however, and he was responsible for many reforms.

LOUIS XIII (1601–43) king of France from 1610, son of **Henri IV** and his second wife **Marie de' Medici**. He was only nine years old when his father was assassinated. In 1615 his mother, as regent, arranged his marriage to **Anne of Austria** (daughter of **Philip III** of Spain); their eldest son, not born until 1638, succeeded him as **Louis XIV**. In 1617 he overthrew the regency of his mother, exiling her to the provinces, and assumed power himself. Strongly Catholic in outlook, he attempted with only moderate success to subdue the French Huguenots, and supported the emperor **Ferdinand II** in his struggle with the German Protestants. A timid man, and lacking confidence in his own abilities, in 1624 he appointed as his chief minister Cardinal **Richelieu**, who became the dominating influence of his reign and kept him apart from his Spanish wife. Richelieu continued the king's policy of subduing Huguenot resistance at home, with the siege and capture of the Huguenot stronghold of La Rochelle in 1628; while in Germany he supported the Protestants to prevent Habsburg domination of Europe. In 1629 Louis personally led a campaign in Italy to prevent Spanish expansion there. Despite a number of conspiracies against Richelieu, the king stood by him steadfastly. Although the centralization of administration and systematic patronage of the arts that characterize the reign were largely the work of Richelieu, the king was no cipher, playing his part not only in military and foreign affairs but also in the political and cultural renaissance that took place. On the death of Richelieu in 1642, he turned in the last year of his reign to an equally able minister, Cardinal **Jules Mazarin**, who was his widow's favourite and lover during her regency for Louis XIV.

LOUIS XIV (1638–1715) king of France from 1643, known as 'The Sun King' (Le Roi Soleil). Born in St Germain-en-Laye, he was the son of **Louis XIII** and **Anne of Austria**, and succeeded to the throne at the age of five. During his minority (1643–51), the government was carried on by his mother and her chief minister and lover, Cardinal **Jules Mazarin**. From 1648 to 1653 some of the nobles rose in the rebellion known as the Fronde, which was suppressed, and Mazarin continued to control the government until his death in 1661. In 1660 Louis married the Infanta Maria Theresa of Spain, daughter of **Philip IV**. After Mazarin's death Louis was his own chief minister, working with unremitting energy and making all the important decisions himself ('L'état c'est moi'). Pious and conservative, he was able to present himself within France and throughout Europe as the model of royal absolutism. In 1661 he arrested **Nicolas Fouquet**, the wealthy superintendent of finances, for corruption, and appointed the able **Jean Baptiste Colbert** to restore the economy, trade and industry; the maintenance of high tax levels enabled Louis to build great palaces like Versailles (1676–1708). As war minister he appointed Francois Michel le Tellier, marquis de **Louvois**, who created a navy and remodelled the French army into the most formidable fighting force in Europe. After the death of his father-in-law in 1665, Louis laid claim to part of the Spanish Netherlands and launched the War of Dutch Devolution (1667–68) under the command of **Turenne** and **Condé**, which provoked a triple alliance between Britain, Holland and Sweden and ended with the Treaty of Aix-La-Chapelle. For the Second Dutch War (1672–78), Louis had Britain as an ally, having bribed **Charles II** with the secret Treaty of Dover (1670); his assault was only halted when William of Orange (later **William III** of Britain) opened the sluices and inundated the country, but France did well out of the Peace of Nijmegen that ended the war in 1678. In the 1680s he secured Strasbourg and Luxembourg. His wife, Maria Theresa, died in 1683, and in 1685 Louis privately married one of his mistresses, the Marquise de **Maintenon**, under whose Catholic influence he passed the Revocation of the Edict of Nantes (1685) which led to a bloody persecution of Protestants and mass emigration of French Huguenots to Holland and England. In 1689 the opponents of French expansionism formed the Grand Alliance, stiffened by the addition of William III in England. The French were victorious at Mons (1691), Steenkirk (1692) and Neerwinden (1693), and defeated an Anglo-Dutch fleet off Cape St Vincent (1693); but the allies maintained a stubborn resistance, and by the Treaty of Ryswick (1697) Louis had to yield most of his territorial gains. In 1700 **Charles II** of Spain died, having willed his throne to Louis' grandson, Philip of Anjou (**Philip V** of Spain). The prospect of a union of the crowns of Spain and France so alarmed the other European powers that it gave rise to the War of the Spanish Succession (1701–14), which proved disastrous for France with crushing defeats at Blenheim (1704) and Ramilles (1706). Peace was only finally achieved with the Treaty of Utrecht (1713), two years before his death, leaving France practically bankrupt. The reign of Louis, 'The Sun King', had been the longest in European history, a reign of incomparable brilliance; it was the Augustan Age of French literature and art, the age of **Corneille**, **Molière**, **Racine**, **Lully**, **Poussin** and **Claude**. He had been the envy and admiration of Europe, but he had by now degenerated into a gloomy tyrant, whose death in 1715 came as a relief to all. His only son, Louis, died in 1711, and the Dauphin (his grandson, Louis of Burgundy) had died in 1712; so Louis XIV was succeeded by his great-grandson, the five-year-old **Louis XV**.

LOUIS XV (1710–74) king of France, succeeded his great-grandfather, **Louis XIV**, in 1715 at the age of five. The regent, Philip, Duc d'**Orléans**, was a tolerant and liberal man but created much scandal by the dissipation of his private life. Orléans died in 1723 and was replaced briefly by the Duc de **Bourbon**. Louis was now technically of age and was married to Maria Leczinska, the daughter of the deposed king of Poland, **Stanislaus**. In 1726 Louis replaced Bourbon by his own former tutor, the Cardinal de **Fleury**. Easy-going and unadventurous, Fleury governed France well, his mild rule not ending until his death in 1743 at the age of 90. In the years immediately before his death, Fleury was beginning to lose his control of affairs and in 1740 France became embroiled, against the wishes of the peace-loving cardinal, in the War of the Austrian Succession. Louis himself went on campaign, falling seriously ill while at Metz in 1744. Louis was still a popular king and the evident relief of his subjects at his recovery led to his being nicknamed 'le Bienaimé' (the well-beloved). Obliged for the first time after the death of Fleury to face up to his responsibilities as head of state, Louis was well intentioned but lacked his great-grandfather's application and industry. Largely uninterested in politics or administration, his principal tenets were the maintenance undiminished of the royal autocracy to which he had succeeded and the preservation from attack of the orthodox Catholic faith. By nature a pessimist, Louis lacked either the ideals or the ideas necessary to effect any real reform of the overburdened and inequitable system he had inherited. The king commanded in the field at the battle of Fontenoy, but the heavy losses incurred by the French left him with a marked distaste for warfare. Although his relationship with his wife was affectionate, he had, throughout his reign, a series of mistresses, of whom the most significant was Mme de **Pompadour**, who became 'reigning mistress' in 1745 and used her position to exert considerable influence over government policy. A woman of liberal views, the friend of many of the leaders of the French Enlightenment, Pompadour provided a counterbalance to the conservatism of the king himself. Liberal reformist views also made some headway amongst Louis' ministers but the attempts of comptroller-general Machault to bring in fiscal reform were blocked by vested interests. This allowed the local bureaucracies to increase in power, particularly the *Intendants* who were the king's principal representatives in the provinces. Peace in Europe had been temporarily achieved in 1748 but in 1756 renewed hostilities in Europe involved France in the Seven Years' War. In 1757 there were again fears that the king would die following an assassination attempt. Abroad a series of military disasters led to the disgrace of the foreign minister, Bernis, and brought to the fore in his stead the Duke of **Choiseul**, a liberal and a friend and ally of Mme de Pompadour, who worked to restore peace and reconstruct French power, forming by the *Pacte de Famille* of 1761 a permanent alliance with Spain and rebuilding the weakened French navy. He could not however prevent the Treaty of Paris (1763) which established British hegemony in India and North America. For Choiseul, the treaty was little more than a truce in an inevitable, continuing struggle between France and Britain, but Louis himself favoured a general European peace and worked behind his minister's back to promote diplomatic initiatives with this aim. Abroad Choiseul was able to incorporate the duchy of Lorraine into France in 1766 and effect the conquest of Corsica, a former Genoese colony, in 1770. At home, he was largely responsible, in alliance with the *Parlements*, for the suppression of the French Jesuits, despite the misgivings of Louis himself, who had always been friendly towards the order. Mme de Pompadour died in 1764 and the Dauphin the following year. Louis' queen died in 1768 and he found a new mistress and companion in Mme **du Barry**. The new dauphin, Louis' grandson, the future **Louis XVI**, was married in 1770 to **Marie Antoinette**, the youngest daughter of the empress **Maria Theresa**, in order to cement the alliance between France and the Empire. In the same year, Choiseul, who had incurred the enmity of the king's new mistress, was dismissed from office. For the remainder of Louis' reign, all projects for reform were abandoned. The *Parlements* had become increasingly vocal in their opposition to the government, and, with the king's support, an attempt was made by the new chancellor, **Maupeou**, to curb their power, replacing the powerful Paris magistracy, which was hereditary, with a new body made up of royal nominees. Even this relatively reactionary attempt to loosen the grip of vested interests proved of short duration, for the old system was reinstated after Louis' death. Louis' last years were ones of peace abroad and deceptive calm at home, but the prestige of the royal government had never been lower and the France Louis left to his grandson remained in the grip of the same antiquated autocracy he had inherited, weakened but unreformed.

LOUIS XVI (1754–93) king of France from 1774, the third son of the dauphin, Louis, only son of **Louis XV**. He became dauphin by the death of his father and his elder brothers. He was married in 1770 to **Marie Antoinette**, youngest daughter of the Empress **Maria Theresa**. When he ascended the throne (1774) the public treasury was empty, the state was burdened with a debt of 4000 million livres, and the people were crushed under the taxes. By advice of **Maurepas** the king restored to the Paris and provincial parliaments their semi-political rights. **Malesherbes** and **Turgot** proposed thoroughgoing reforms, accepted by the king, but rejected by the court, aristocracy, parliaments, and church. Turgot resigned. Yet Louis remitted some of the most odious taxes, made a few inconsiderable reforms, and was for a time extremely popular, being handsome, healthy, and moral, fond of manly exercises, and of working as a locksmith. In 1777 **Neckar** was made director-general, and succeeded in bringing the finances to a more tolerable condition; but through France's outlay in the American War of Independence he was obliged to propose the taxation of the privileged classes, and their resistance compelled him to resign. The lavish **Calonne** (1783) renewed for a while the splendour of the court, and advised the calling together of an Assembly of Notables. The noblemen, clergymen, state officials, councillors of parliaments, and municipal officers thus collected compelled him to fly to London. His successor, Brienne, obtained some new taxes, but the parliament of Paris refused to register the edict. The convening of the states-general was universally demanded. The king registered the edicts and banished the councillors of parliament, but had to recall them. In May 1788 he dissolved all the parliaments and established a *Cour plénière*. Matters became still worse when in August appeared the edict that the treasury should cease all cash payments except to the troops. Brienne resigned, and Neckar again became minister. An assembly of the states of the kingdom, in abeyance since 1614, was resolved upon; and by the advice of Neckar the Third Estate was called in double number. The states-general met in May 1789 at Versailles. The *tiers-état*, taking matters into their own hands, formed themselves into a National Assembly, thereby commencing the revolution; and undertaking to make a new constitution, they called themselves the Constituent Assembly. The resistance of Louis to the demands of the deputies for political independence, equal rights and universal freedom, led to their declaration of inviolability. The king retaliated by ordering troops under arms, dissolving the ministry and banishing Neckar. The consequence was revolutionary outbreaks in Paris on 12 July 1789. Next day the National Guard of Paris was called out, and on the 14th the people stormed the Bastille. Meanwhile the provinces repeated the acts of Paris. On 4 August feudal and manorial rights were abrogated by the Assembly, which declared the equality of human rights. The royal princes and all the nobles who could escape sought safety in flight. The royal family, having in vain attempted to follow their example, tried to conciliate the people by the feigned assumption of republican sentiments, but on 5 October the rabble attacked Versailles and compelled Louis and his family to return to Paris, where the Assembly also moved. The next two years witnessed the inauguration and the subsequent withdrawal of various constitutional schemes. Louis alternately made concessions to the republicans, and devised schemes for escaping from their surveillance (in June 1791 the king and queen got as far as Varennes, whence they were brought back), and each month added to his humiliation and to the audacity of those surrounding him. The Constituent Assembly was succeeded in 1791 by the Legislative Assembly. The king was compelled by the Girondists to a war with Austria in April 1792, and the early defeats of the French were visited on Louis, who was confined, in August, with his family in the Temple. The advance of the Prussians under the Duke of Brunswick into

Champagne threw Paris into the wildest excitement. The Assembly dissolved itself in September; the National Convention took its place, and the Republic was proclaimed. In December the king was brought to trial, and called upon to answer for repeated acts of treason against the Republic. On 20 January 1793 sentence of death was passed, and next day he was guillotined in the Place de la Révolution.

LOUIS XVII (1785–95) titular king of France from 1793. Born Charles Louis, the second son of **Louis XVI**, he became dauphin on the death of his brother in 1789. He became king (but only in name) in prison on the execution of his father in 1793. He remained in the Temple prison under the charge of a Jacobin shoemaker, Antoine Simon. He died, so it was reported, in June, 1795—rumour said by poison. Several persons subsequently claimed to be the dauphin—one of them a half-caste Indian, another a Potsdam watchmaker, Karl Wilhelm Naundorf, who, with a striking resemblance to the **Bourbons**, found his way to France in 1833, but was expelled in 1836, lived for a while in England, and died in Delft in 1845.

LOUIS XVIII (Stanislaw Xavier) (1755–1824) king of France from 1795, younger brother of **Louis XVI**. Married in 1771 to Princess Louise of Savoy, he was active in politics in the years leading up to the revolution (1789), opposing during his brother's reign every progressive measure of the government. He fled to Belgium in 1791, and proclaimed himself regent for **Louis XVII** in 1793, and king in 1795. The victories of the republic and **Napoleon**'s enmity compelled him frequently to change his place of abode, until in 1807 he found a refuge in England, in Hartwell, Buckinghamshire. On the fall of Napoleon (April 1814) he landed at Calais; and then began the ascendency of the 'legitimist' party. The Napoleonic constitution was set aside, and a new constitution granted with two chambers on the British model. The nobles and priests moved him to severe treatment of Imperialists, Republicans and Protestants. This opened the way for Napoleon's return from Elba (the Hundred Days in 1815), when the royal family fled from Paris, and remained at Ghent till after Waterloo. From Cambrai Louis issued a proclamation in which he acknowledged former errors, and promised moderation and an amnesty to all but traitors, and returned to Paris 'in the baggage of the Allies'. But he was powerless to prevent a backlash, the so-called, 'White Terror', when Royalist fanatics slew hundreds of adherents of the Revolution and of Protestants. The first parliamentary elections in August 1815 produced an ultra-Royalist majority that was so reactionary that in September 1816 Louis dissolved it. From 1816 to 1820 moderate policies prevailed under the liberal Minister **Decazes**, until he was overthrown by a Royalist plot. In 1823, Louis sent an army to Spain to help maintain absolutism there. He was succeeded by his younger brother, **Charles X**.

LOUIS IV 'The Bavarian' (c.1283–1347) Holy Roman Emperor, a younger son of Louis, Duke of Upper Bavaria. He was elected king of Germany in 1314, opposed by a rival candidate, Frederick II, Duke of Austria, whom he eventually defeated in battle at Mühldorf (1322). Pope **John XXII** however refused to recognize his title, referring to him only as 'Louis the Bavarian', a name which stuck. In 1328 he received the imperial crown from the people of Rome, but was forced to leave Italy the next year. Thereafter Louis remained mostly in Germany, maintaining his position against internal opposition with the financial support of the cities. He waged a war of propaganda against the papacy with the help of **Marsilius of Padua**, William of **Ockham**, and the Spiritual Franciscans; he invaded Italy (1327–30), captured Rome and set up an antipope, Nicholas V (1328–30), in opposition to Pope John. In 1338, at the Diet of Rense, the electoral princes precipitated a church/state division by declaring that the emperor did not require papal confirmation of his election. His energetic policy of family aggrandizement, however, cost him his alliance with the House of Luxembourg, who raised up a rival emperor. **Charles IV**, a year before Louis met his death while hunting.

LOUIS, Joe, professional name of **Joseph Louis Barrow** (1914–81) American boxer and world heavyweight champion, born in Lexington, Alabama. Known as the 'Brown Bomber', he won the US amateur light-heavyweight title in 1934 and turned professional. In 1936 he was defeated for the first time, by the German champion Max Schmeling with a knock-out in the 12th round (but he took merciless revenge with a first round knock-out in a return bout). He won the world championship by beating **James J Braddock** in 1937, and held it for a record 12 years, defending his title 25 times. He retired in 1949, but later made unsuccessful comebacks against Ezzard Charles in 1950 and **Rocky Marciano** in 1951. A boxer of legendary swiftness, power and grace, he won 68 of his 71 professional fights.

LOUIS, Morris, originally **Morris Bernstein** (1912–62) American painter, born in Baltimore. He studied at the Maryland Institute of Fine and Applied Arts (1929–33). In the early 1950s he was influenced by **Jackson Pollock** and the New York Action Painters, but more decisive was the impact of **Helen Frankenthaler**, whose *Mountains and Sea* (1952) inspired him to throw acrylic paint onto unprimed canvases to create brilliant patches of abstract colour, forms without depth.

LOUIS, Pierre-Charles-Alexandre (1787–1872) French clinician and pathologist, born in Ai, Champagne. He trained in medicine in Paris and practised for seven years in Russia, where his powerlessness in the face of a diphtheria epidemic convinced him that his medical knowledge was woefully inadequate. He returned to Paris and immersed himself in a hospital for seven years, collecting thousands of case histories and performing hundreds of autopsies. This resulted ultimately in his important monographs on tuberculosis and typhoid fever, and in his introduction of the 'numerical method' for evaluating the effects of therapy. Louis's numerical method was a forerunner of the modern drug trial. He was an outstanding teacher, and foreign students particularly valued his clinical lectures.

LOUIS NAPOLEON See **NAPOLEON**

LOUIS-PHILIPPE (1773–1850) king of the French, born in Paris, the eldest son of the Duc **d'Orléans**, and brought up by Madame de **Genlis**. He entered the National Guard, and, along with his father, renounced his titles, and assumed the surname 'Égalité'. He fought in the wars of the republic, but was included in the order for arrest issued against **Dumouriez**, and escaped with him into Austrian territory. For a time he supported himself as a teacher in Switzerland; he went in 1796 to the USA, and in 1800 moved to Twickenham near London. In 1809 he married Marie Amélie, daughter of **Ferdinand I** of the Two Sicilies. On the Restoration he recovered his estates, and though disliked by the court, was very popular in Paris. After the Revolution of 1830 he was first appointed lieutenant-general, and then accepted the crown as the elect of the sovereign people. The country prospered under the rule of the 'citizen king', and the middle classes amassed riches. The parliamentary franchise was limited to the wealth of the aristocracy and their hangers-on. The political corruption of the *bourgeoisie*, and its wholesale bribery by the king, united all extremists in a cry for electoral reform. A man of great ability but of little character, Louis-Philippe out of fear reacted violently. The newspapers were muzzled, and trial by jury was tampered with. Prince Louis Napoleon (future **Napoleon III**) seized this opportunity of acting twice the part of a pretender (1836, 1840). After the Duc d'Orléan's death in 1842, Republicans, Socialists and Communists, became increasingly threatening. Louis-Philippe attempted to provide an outlet for the military spirit of his subjects by campaigning in Algeria but did not succeed. 'Reform banquets' began to be held. Their repression led to violent debates in the Chamber. The Paris mob rose in February 1848, with the complicity of the regulars, national guards, and municipal police. Louis-Philippe dismissed **Guizot**, and promised reforms; but it was too late. He was forced to abdicate, and escaped to England as 'Mr Smith'. He died in Claremont.

LOUIS (Lajos) the Great (1326–82) king of Hungary and Poland, succeeded his father **Charles Robert** in 1342. Up to 1356 his reign was mostly devoted to campaigns against Queen Johanna of Naples, who was implicated in the murder of her husband Andrew, Louis's younger brother (1344). Louis's ultimate lack of success in Italy was compensated for by the conquest of Dalmatia, including the port of Dubrovnik, from Venice, recognized in the Peace of Zara (1358); and in 1370 he became king of Poland on the death of his uncle **Casimir III**. A notable patron of the arts, Louis founded the first Hungarian university at Pecs in 1367.

LOUISA (1776–1810) queen of Prussia, born in Hanover, where her father, Duke Karl of Mecklenburg-Strelitz, was commandant. Married to the crown prince of Prussia (afterwards **Frederick-William III**) in 1793, she was the mother of **Frederick-William IV** and **William I**, afterwards emperor. She endeared herself to her people by her spirit and energy during the period of national calamity that followed the battle of Jena, and especially by her patriotic and self-denying efforts to obtain concessions at Tilsit from **Napoleon**, though he had shamelessly slandered her.

LOUTHERBOURG, Philippe Jacques de (1740–1812) German-born British painter, stage designer and illustrator, educated at Strasbourg, one of the most colourful and versatile artists of the Romantic period. His work, exhibited at the Paris Salon, attracted the attention of **Denis Diderot**. In 1771 he moved to London and was hired by **David Garrick** as artistic adviser for his Drury Lane theatre, and became a British subject. He devised many innovatory stage design techniques, including highly dramatic transparent backdrops. These scenic designs strongly influenced contemporary English landscape painting. In 1781 he invented his celebrated *Eidophusikon*, a moving panorama complete with lighting and sound effects which fascinated many artists, including **Gainsborough**. He illustrated, among other works, an edition of **Shakespeare**. He eventually retired to Hammersmith where he took up faith healing.

LOUVEL, Pierre Louis See **BERRY, Charles Ferdinand**

L'OUVERTURE See **TOUSSAINT L'OUVERTURE**

LOUVOIS, François Michel le Tellier, Marquis de (1641–91) French statesman, war minister of **Louis XIV**, born in Paris. His father was chancellor and secretary of state in the war department; the son joined him as assistant secretary in 1662, and became an energetic war minister in 1668, reforming and strengthening the army. His labours bore fruit in the great war that ended with the peace of Nijmegen (1678). He took a leading part in the capture of Strasbourg (1681) and in the persecution of Protestants.

LOUŸS, Pierre (1870–1925) French poet and novelist, born in Ghent. He came to Paris, where in 1891 he founded a review called *Le Conque* to which **Régnier**, **Gide** and **Valéry** were contributors. In this were printed his first poems, most of which later appeared in *Astarté* (1891). His lyrics, based on the Greek form which he so much admired, are masterpieces of style. Other volumes are *Poésies de Méléagre de Gédara* (1893), *Scènes de la vie des courtisanes de Lucien* (1894) and *Les Chansons de Bilitis* (1894). In 1896 his novel *Aphrodite* was published with great success, and a psychological novel *La Femme et le pantin* appeared in 1898.

LOVAT, Simon Fraser, Lord (c.1667–1747) Scottish chief, born in Tomich in Ross-shire. He graduated from Aberdeen in 1695. In 1696 his father, on the death of his grand-nephew, Lord Lovat, assumed that title, and next year Simon, after failing to abduct the late lord's daughter and heiress, a child nine years of age, forcibly married her mother, a lady of the Atholl family—a crime for which he was found guilty of high treason and outlawed. In 1699, he succeeded his father as twelfth Lord Lovat, in 1702 he fled to France, but a year later returned to Scotland as a Jacobite agent and became involved in the abortive 'Queensberry plot', which forced him once more to escape to France. In 1715 he took the government side; his clan left the Jacobite rebels and he obtained a full pardon, with possession of the Lovat title and estates. In the 1745 Jacobite Rising Lovat sent his son and clan to fight for the Pretender (**Charles Edward Stewart**) while he protested his loyalty to the government. After Culloden he fled, but was captured and taken to London for trial. He defended himself with ability and dignity, and he met death (by beheading) with the same combination of gallantry and cynicism which had served him so well in life.

LOVECRAFT, H P (Howard Phillips) (1890–1937) American science fiction writer and poet, born in Providence, Rhode Island, where he lived all his life. Educated at local schools, he married the writer Sonia Greene in 1924 but they were divorced in 1929. A writer from 1908, he supported himself by ghost writing and as a revisionist. From 1923 he was a regular contributor to *Weird Tales*. His cult following can be traced to the 60 or so stories first published in that magazine and to what has posthumously come to be known as the 'Cthulhu Mythos', which holds that in the days before mankind the earth was inhabited by fish-like beings called the 'Old Ones' who worshipped the gelatinous Cthulhu. Not surprisingly Lovecraft had difficulty in accumulating readers but he gradually attracted a small but fanatical following in America and abroad, particularly France. In an area in which accepted literary criteria go by the board, Lovecraft was unique. Among his various collections are *The Shadow over Innsmouth* (1936), *The Outsider and Others* (1939), *Dreams and Fancies* (1962) and *Dagon and Other Macabre Tales* (1965). His novellas included *The Case of Charles Dexter Ward* (1928), and *At the Mountains of Madness* (1931).

LOVEJOY, Arthur Oncken (1873–1963) American historian of ideas and philosopher, born in Berlin, Germany. He studied at Berkeley, Harvard and the Sorbonne and after holding various teaching positions in America became professor of philosophy at Johns Hopkins University from 1910 to 1938. He was co-founder (in 1938) and first editor of the *Journal of the History of Ideas* and effectively invented the discipline under that title. His method of detailed 'philosophical semantics' investigating the history of key terms and concepts is best exemplified in *The Great Chain of Being: a Study of the History of an Idea* (1936) and *Essays in the History of Ideas* (1948).

LOVELACE, Augusta Ada, Countess of, née **Byron** (1815–52) English writer, mathematician and socialite, daughter of Lord **Byron**. She taught herself geometry, and was trained in astronomy and mathematics. Acquainted with many leading figures of the Victorian era, she owes much of her recent fame to her friendship with **Charles Babbage**, the computer pioneer. She translated and annotated an article on his Analytical Engine written by an Italian mathematician, L F Menabrea, adding many explanatory notes of her own. This 'Sketch of the Analytical Engine' (1843) is an important source on Babbage's work. The high-level universal computer programming language, ADA, was named in her honour.

LOVELACE, Richard (1618–57) English cavalier poet, born in Woolwich, or perhaps in Holland, the eldest son of a Kentish knight. He was educated at Charterhouse and Gloucester Hall, Oxford. He found his way to court and went on the Scottish expedition in 1639. In 1642 he was imprisoned for presenting to the House of Commons a petition from the royalists of Kent 'for the restoring the king to his rights', and was released on bail. He spent his estate in the king's cause, assisted the French in 1646 to capture Dunkirk from the Spaniards, and was flung into jail on returning to England in 1648. In jail he revised his poems, including 'To Althea, from Prison', and in 1649 published his collection of poems, *Lucasta*. He was set free at the end of 1649. In 1659 his brother published a second collection of his poems.

LOVELL, Sir (Alfred Charles) Bernard (1913–) English astronomer, born in Gloucestershire. A graduate of Bristol University, in 1951 he became professor of radio astronomy at Manchester University and director of Jodrell Bank experimental station (now the Nuffield Radio Astronomy Laboratories). He gave the radio Reith Lectures in 1958, taking for his subject *The Individual and the Universe*. He has written several books on radio astronomy and on its relevance to life and civilization today. His works include *Science and Civilisation* (1939), *World Power Resources and Social Development* (1945) *Radio Astronomy* (1951), *Discovering the Universe* (1963), *The Story of Jodrell Bank* (1968), *Emerging Cosmology* (1980) and *Voice of the Universe* (1987).

LOVER, Samuel (1797–1868) Irish writer, artist and songwriter, born in Dublin. In 1818 he established himself there as a marine painter and miniaturist. One of the founders of the *Dublin University Magazine*, he published *Legends and Stories of Ireland* in 1831 with his own illustrations. In 1835 he moved to London, where he wrote two popular novels, *Rory O'More* (1836) and *Handy Andy* (1842). He helped **Dickens** found *Bentley's Miscellany* and in 1844 started an entertainment, called 'Irish Evenings', which was a hit both in England and in USA (1846–48) with songs like *The Low-Backed Car* and *Molly Bawn*.

LOW, Sir David (Alexander Cecil) (1891–1963) British political cartoonist, born in Dunedin, New Zealand. After working for several newspapers in New Zealand and for the *Bulletin of Sydney*, he joined the *Star* in London in 1919. In 1927 he joined the staff of the *Evening Standard*, for which he drew some of his most successful cartoons. His art ridiculed all political parties, and some of his creations will never die, notably Colonel Blimp, who has been incorporated into the English language. From 1950 he worked for the *Daily Herald*, and from 1953 with *The (Manchester) Guardian*. He produced volumes of collected cartoons, including *Lloyd George and Co* (1922), *Low and I* (1923), *A Cartoon History of the War* (1941), *Low's Company* (1952), *Low's Autobiography* (1956) and many more.

LOWE, Arthur (1914–82) English character actor, born in Hayfield, Derbyshire. Becoming a salesman after leaving school, he served in the armed forces from 1939 to 1945, ultimately appearing with their Entertainments division. He made his first stage appearance in *Bedtime Story* (1945) at Hulme and his London début in *Larger Than Life* (1950). His film début in *London Belongs to Me* (1948) was the first of many supporting roles. His subsequent theatre work included *Call Me Madam* (1952), *Pal Joey* (1954) and *The Pajama Game* (1955), but it was television that brought him his greatest popularity, first as the irascible Mr Swindley in *Coronation Street* (1960–65), then as the bumbling Captain Mainwaring in *Dad's Army* (1968–77). A rotund, balding figure, he was particularly adept at portraying pompous officials and comic duffers and starred in many television series. His later stage work included *Inadmissible Evidence* (1964), *The Tempest* (1974) and *Bingo* (1974), while he took more substantial film roles in *The Ruling Class* (1972) and *O Lucky Man* (1973).

LOWE, Sir Hudson (1769–1844) Irish soldier, born in Galway. He entered the British army as an ensign at the age of 11 and served in many parts of the Mediterranean. In the Napoleonic wars he helped to conquer Zante and Cephalonia, and for nearly two years was governor of Santa Maura, Ithaca and Cephalonia. He was afterwards attached to the Prussian army of **Blücher**. In April 1816 he was appointed governor of St Helena, where he kept strict guard over **Napoleon**, which provoked rancorous attacks against him, especially from **Barry O'Meara**, Napoleon's surgeon. From 1825 to 1831 he was second in command in Ceylon.

LÖWE, Karl See **LOEWE**

LOWE, Robert See **SHERBROOKE**

LOWELL, Abbott Lawrence (1856–1943) American political scientist, brother of **Percival Lowell** and **Amy Lowell**, born in Boston into distinguished Massachusetts industrial and cultural dynasties. He graduated from Harvard in 1877, qualified in law in 1880, and practised law in Boston from 1880 to 1897, after which he lectured in law at Harvard and was made professor of government there in 1900. He was president of Harvard from 1909 to 1933. His publications included *Essays on Government* (1889), *Government and Parties in Continental Europe* (1897), *The Influence of Party Upon Legislation in England and America* (1902), *The Government of England* (1908), *Public Opinion and Popular Government* (1913), *Public Opinion in War and Peace* (1923), *Conflicts of Principle* (1932), *At War with Academic Traditions* (1934), and *What a College President Has Learned* (1938).

LOWELL, Amy (1874–1925) American imagist poet, born into an extremely wealthy family in Brookline, Massachusetts, sister of **Abbott Lowell** and **Percival Lowell**. She travelled extensively with her parents in Europe, and bought the parental home, 'Sevenals', in 1903. She wrote volumes of *vers libre* which she named 'unrhymed cadence', starting with the conventional *A Dome of Many-coloured Glass* (1912) and *Sword Blades and Poppy Seeds* (1914). She also wrote polyphonic prose. Her other works include *Six*

French Poets (1915), *Tendencies in Modern American Poetry* (1917) and a biography of **Keats** (1925).

LOWELL, James Russell (1819–91) American poet, essayist and diplomat, born in Cambridge, Massachusetts, the son of a minister. He graduated from Harvard in 1838. In 1841–44 he published two volumes of poetry, in 1845 *Conversations on the Old Poets*; and in 1843 he helped to edit *The Pioneer*, with **Hawthorne**, **Poe** and **Whittier** for contributors. In 1846, at the outbreak of the war with Mexico, he wrote a satiric poem in the Yankee dialect denouncing the pro-slavery party and the conduct of the government, and out of this grew the *Biglow Papers* (1848). A great many serious poems were written about 1848, and formed a third volume. *A Fable for Critics* (1848) is a series of witty and dashing sketches of American authors. In 1851–52 he visited Europe. In 1855 he was appointed professor of modern languages and literature at Harvard and went to Europe to finish his studies. He also edited the *Atlantic Monthly* from 1857, and with **Charles Eliot Norton** the *North American Review* (1863–67). His prose writings—*Among my Books* (1870) and *My Study Windows* (1871)—are of a very high quality. The second series of *Biglow Papers* appeared during the Civil War, in 1867. Lowell was an ardent abolitionist, and from the first gave himself unreservedly to the cause of freedom. Though he had never been a politician he was appointed in 1877 US minister to Spain, and was transferred in 1880 to Great Britain, where he remained until 1885.

LOWELL, Percival (1855–1916) American astronomer, born in Boston, brother of **Abbott Lowell** and **Amy Lowell**. Educated at Harvard, he established the Flagstaff (now Lowell) Observatory in Arizona (1894). He is best known for his observations of Mars which were intended to prove the existence of artificial Martian canals, and for his prediction of the existence of the planet Pluto (discovered by **Clyde William Tombaugh** in 1930). He was the author of works on astronomy and on Japan.

LOWELL, Robert Traill Spence, Jr (1917–77) American poet, born in Boston, Massachusetts, of a patrician New England family, the great-grand-nephew of **James Russell Lowell**. He attended St Mark's School, then Harvard, but left after two years to go to Kenyon College to study poetry, criticism and classics under **John Crowe Ransom** in what he called 'the heyday of the New Criticism'. He then attended Louisiana State University and afterwards worked briefly for a New York publisher. During World War II he was a conscientious objector and was imprisoned for six months (1944). In 1940 he married the writer Jean Stafford and became an ardent convert to Roman Catholicism. It was a fraught and violent liaison, Lowell being subject to periods of mental instability exacerbated by heavy drinking. His first collection was *Lands of Unlikeness* (1944), the first step towards what amounts, in the words of one critic, 'to his own exhaustive critical biography'. But it was not until the publication of his widely-acclaimed second volume, *Lord Weary's Castle* (1946), awarded the Pulitzer prize for poetry in 1947, that he was accorded the status of a major poet. Divorced from **Jean Stafford**, he married the writer Elizabeth Hardwick but that union also faltered and he married in 1973 another writer, Caroline Blackwood. *Life Studies* (1959) was again intensely 'confessional', as were *For the Union Dead* (1964) and *Near the Ocean* (1967), in what was a highly productive period during which he also wrote many plays and translations. He had a high public profile during the Vietnam years, as can be gauged from *Notebook* (1968), but his personal life began to disintegrate. Rather than shrink from his problems he faced them directly in *The Dolphin* (1973), making public personal letters and anxieties, and inviting new notoriety. Latterly his poetry became increasingly obscure and monotonous, and *Day by Day* (1977), published shortly before he died, did not enhance his reputation.

LOWER, Richard (1631–91) English physician and physiologist, born into an old Cornish family at Tremeer, near Bodmin. He studied at Oxford, where **Thomas Willis** and several others who were to be prominent in the early Royal Society of London influenced him. After acquiring a medical degree in 1665, he followed Willis to London. His medical practice was erratically successful, but he continued the anatomical and physiological researches he had begun in Oxford. With **Robert Hooke** he collaborated in a series of experiments on the role of the lungs in changing dark-red venous blood into bright red arterial blood. His *Tractatus de Corde* (Treatise on the Heart, 1669) was a major work on pulmonary and cardiovascular anatomy and physiology. With other fellows of the Royal Society, he conducted some experiments in transfusing blood from dog to dog, and, more problematically, from person to person.

LOWIE, Robert Harry (1883–1957) Austrian-born American cultural anthropologist, born in Vienna. He went to the USA in 1893 and grew up in New York City. Educated at City College, he studied anthropology at Columbia University under **Franz Boas**. From 1907 to 1917 he was on the staff of the American Museum, and was at the University of California, Berkeley, from 1917 to 1950. He made several ethnographic studies of North American Indian societies, especially the Crow, publishing his *Social Life of the Crow Indians* in 1912 and *The Crow Indians* in 1935. His most influential general works were *Primitive Society* (1920), *Primitive Religion* (1924), *History of Ethnological Theory* (1937) and *Social Organization* (1948), in which his theoretical position reflected that of the Boasian school of culture-history.

LOWNDES, William Thomas (c.1798–1843) English bookseller and bibliographer, born in London. He produced *The Bibliographer's Manual of English Literature* (1834) and *The British Librarian* (1839).

LOWRY, (Laurence) Stephen (1887–1976) English artist, born and trained in Manchester. He worked as a clerk all his life, but studied art in his spare time and produced many pictures of the Lancashire industrial scene, mainly in brilliant whites and greys, peopled with scurrying antlike men and women.

LOWTH, Robert (1710–87) English prelate and scholar, born in Winchester. In 1741 he became professor of poetry at Oxford, in 1766 bishop of St Davids and of Oxford, and in 1777 of London. He published *De Sacra Poesi Hebraeorum* (1753), a *Life of William of Wykeham* (1758) and a new translation of **Isaiah**. He was one of the first to treat the Bible poetry as literature in its own right.

LOWTHER, Hugh Cecil See **LONSDALE**

LOYOLA, Ignatius de See **IGNATIUS LOYOLA**

LOYSON, Charles See **HYACINTHE, Père**

LUBBERS, Rudolf Franz Marie (1939–) Dutch politician. After graduating from Erasmus University, Rotterdam, he joined the family engineering business of Lubbers Hollandia. He made rapid progress after entering politics, becoming minister of economic affairs in 1973 and, at the age of 43, prime minister in 1982, leading a Christian Democratic Appeal (CDA) coalition.

LUBBOCK, Sir John, 1st Baron Avebury (1834–1913) English politican, born in London, the son of the astronomer, Sir J W Lubbock (1803–65). From Eton he went at 14 into his father's banking house; in 1856 became a partner; served on several educational and currency commissions; and in 1870 was returned for Maidstone in the Liberal interest, in 1880 for London University—from 1886 to 1900 as a Liberal-Unionist. He succeeded in passing more than a dozen important measures, including the Bank Holidays Act (1871), the Bills of Exchange Act, the Ancient Monuments Act (1882), and the Shop Hours Act (1889). He was vice-chancellor of London University (1872–80), president of the British Association (1881), vice-president of the Royal Society, president of the London Chamber of Commerce, chairman of the London County Council (1890–92), and much else. Best known for his researches on primitive man and on the habits of bees and ants, he published *Prehistoric Times* (1865; revised 1913), *Origin of Civilisation* (1870) and many books on natural history.

LUBBOCK, Percy (1879–1965) English critic and biographer, born in London, the grandson of Sir **John Lubbock**. He was librarian of Magdalene College, Cambridge from 1906 to 1908, and among his writings are *The Craft of Fiction* (1921), *Earlham* (1922), a book of personal childhood memories, and studies of **Pepys** (1909) and **Edith Wharton** (1947).

LUBETHIN, Berthold (1901–) Russian-born British architect, born in Tilfis, Georgia. He studied under **Rodchenko**, and **Tatlin** in Moscow, and then at Atelier Perret in Paris, where he was influenced by **Le Corbusier**. In 1931 he emigrated to England, and set up his own firm, Tecton, with six students from the Architectural Association, London. His major works include the Penguin Pool at London Zoo (1933) and Highpoint I Hampstead (1935), a block of high-rise flats which was praised by Le Corbusier as a re-development of his own 'urbanisme' and utopian ideals, creating a new quality for high-rise housing. His Finsbury Health Centre (1938), a social experiment, is still in use as intended today. Very influential in the development and practice of high quality modernism, he largely retired from architecture in 1939.

LUBITSCH, Ernst (1892–1947) German-born American film director, born in Berlin. A teenage actor in **Max Reinhardt**'s theatre company, he then starred as 'Meyer' in a popular slapstick series before beginning his directorial career with *Fraülein Seifenschaum* (1914). A specialist in comedies, and costume epics like *Madame Dubarry* (1919), he was invited to Hollywood by **Mary Pickford**, whom he directed in *Rosita* (1923). He stayed to become an acknowledged master of light, sophisticated sex comedies graced with 'the Lubitsch touch': a mixture of wit, urbanity and elegance. His many saucy but subtle confections include *Forbidden Paradise* (1924), *The Love Parade* (1929), *Trouble in Paradise* (1932), *Ninotchka* (1939, with **Greta Garbo**) and *Heaven Can Wait* (1943). He became an American citizen in 1936.

LÜBKE, Heinrich (1894–1972) West German politician, born in Westphalia. A Christian Democrat, in 1959 he succeeded **Theodor Heuss** as president of the German Federal Republic, being himself succeeded in 1969 by **Gustav Heinemann**.

LUCA DELLA ROBIA See **ROBBIA, Luca della**

LUCAN, (Marcus Annaeus Lucanus) (39–65) Roman poet, born in Corduba (Córdoba) in Spain, the nephew of the philosopher **Seneca the Younger**. He studied in Rome and in Athens, and became proficient in rhetoric and philosophy. He was recalled to Rome by the emperor **Nero** who held him in high favour and made him quaestor and augur. In 60 he won the poetry competition in the first Neronia games. In 62 he published the first three books of his epic *Pharsalia* (on the civil war between **Pompey** and **Caesar**). Soon the emperor, perhaps jealous of Lucan's literary successes, forbade him to write poetry or plead in the courts. In 65 Lucan joined the conspiracy of Piso against Nero, but was betrayed and compelled to commit suicide. A precociously fluent writer in Silver Latin, the epic *Pharsalia* is all that has survived of his writing.

LUCAN, George Charles Bingham, Earl of (1800–88) English soldier. He accompanied the Russians as a volunteer against the Turks in 1828, succeeded as third earl in 1839. As commander of cavalry in the Crimean War (1853–56), he passed on the disastrous order for the Charge of the Light Brigade at Balaclava (1854), and later fought at Inkermann. He was promoted field marshal in 1887.

LUCAN, Richard John Bingham, Earl of (1934–) English nobleman, and alleged murderer, who disappeared following events on the evening of 7 November 1974, at the house of his estranged wife. On that night, Veronica Lucan ran into a pub close to her London home with blood on her face, claiming that she had just escaped from a murderer. Shortly after, police found the body of the Lucan family's nanny, Sandra Rivett, in a mail-bag in the basement of Lady Lucan's house. Lady Lucan told police that she had gone downstairs to find the nanny when a man, whom she identified as her husband, attacked her. He claimed that he had mistaken the nanny for her and had killed her. The police failed to trace Lucan, who had amassed large gambling debts and who had fought for and lost custody of his children. In June 1975 the coroner's jury charged Lord Lucan with the murder. Speculation about Lucan's whereabouts and about events that night continues to this day.

LUCARIS, or **Lukaris, Cyril** (1572–1638) Greek Orthodox prelate and theologian, born in Crete. He studied in Venice, Padua and Geneva, where he was influenced by Calvinism. He rose by 1621 to be patriarch of Constantinople. He opened negotiations with the Calvinists of England and Holland with a view to union and the reform of the Greek Church; he corresponded with **Gustav II Adolf** of Sweden, Archbishop Abbot and **Laud**; he presented the Alexandrian Codex to **Charles I**. The *Eastern Confession of the Orthodox Church*, of strong Calvinistic tendency, issued in 1629, may not have been written by him after all. The Jesuits five times brought about his deposition, and are supposed by the Greeks to have instigated his murder by the Turks: in June 1637 he was seized, and is believed to have been strangled.

LUCAS, Colin Anderson (1906–) English architect, born in London. He studied at Cambridge, and in 1930 designed a house at Bourne End, Buckinghamshire, which was the first English example of the domestic use of monolithic reinforced concrete. Subsequent designs (1933–39) played an important part in the development in England of the ideas of the European modern movement in architecture. He was a founder member of the MARS group of architects.

LUCAS, Edward Verrall (1868–1938) English essayist and biographer, born in Eltham, Kent. He became a bookseller's assistant, a reporter, contributor to and assistant editor of *Punch* and finally a publisher. He compiled anthologies, wrote novels (the best of which was *Over Bemerton's*, 1908), books of travel and about 30 volumes of essays in a light, charming vein. An authority on **Lamb**, he wrote a Life in 1905.

LUCAS, F L (Frank Lawrence) (1894–1967) English critic and poet, born in Hipperholme, Yorkshire. A fellow of and former reader in English at King's College, Cambridge, he wrote many scholarly works of criticism, including *Seneca and Elizabethan Tragedy* (1922), and *Eight Victorian Poets* (1930). Among his volumes of poetry are *Time and Memory* (1929) and *Ariadne* (1932). His plays include *Land's End* (1938). He also wrote novels and popular translations of Greek drama and poetry.

LUCAS VAN LEYDEN, or **Lucas Jacobsz** (1494–1533) Dutch painter and engraver, born in Leiden. He practised almost every branch of painting, and his most notable works include the triptych of *The Last Judgement* (1526) and *Blind Man of Jericho Healed by Christ* (1531). As an engraver he is believed to have been the first to etch on copper, rather than iron, and ranks almost with **Albrecht Dürer**, whom he knew and by whom he was much influenced.

LUCE, Clare Boothe (1903–87) American writer, socialite and wit, born in New York City. Married to the millionaire publisher **Henry Luce** at 20, she was made associate editor of *Vogue* (1930), American ambassador to Italy (1953–57) and was the author of several Broadway successes including *The Women* (1936) and *Kiss the Boys Goodbye* (1938).

LUCE, Henry Robinson (1898–1967) American magazine publisher and editor, born in Shantung, China. He founded *Time* (1923), *Fortune* (1930) and *Life* (1936). He also in the 1930s inaugurated the radio programme 'March of Time', which became a film feature. He married **Clare Boothe Luce** in 1935.

LUCIAN (c.117–c.180) Greek satirist and rhetorician writer, born in Samosata in Syria. Having learned Greek and studied rhetoric, he practised as an advocate in Antioch, and wrote and recited show speeches for a living, travelling through Asia Minor, Greece, Italy and Gaul. Having made a fortune and a name in this way, he settled in Athens, and there devoted himself to philosophy. There, too, he produced a new form of literature—humorous dialogue. Lucian lived at a time when the old faiths, the old philosophy, the old literature, were all rapidly dissolving. Never was there a better target for satire and Lucian revelled in it. The absurdity of retaining the old deities without the old belief is brought out in such works as the *Dialogues of the Gods*, *Dialogues of the Dead* and *Charon*. Whether philosophy was more disgraced by the shallowness or the vices of those who now professed it, is discussed in his *Symposium*, *Halieus*, *Biōn Prasis*, *Drapetae* and others. The old literature had been displaced by novels or romances of adventure of the most fantastic kind, which Lucian parodies in his *True Histories*. Apart from the purity of his Greek, his style is simple and delightful.

LUCIANO, Charles ('Lucky') (1897–1962) Sicilian-born American gangster, convicted leader of organized crime in New York. His family emigrated to the USA in 1907. Luciano, who earned his nickname by avoiding imprisonment and prosecution for many years, was a Mafia godfather who operated successfully and profitably in the 1920s and 1930s. He founded his empire on narcotics-peddling, extortion, prostitution and networks of vice dens. His luck finally ran out when three prostitutes agreed to give evidence against him. He was arrested on 1 February 1936 for compelling women to become prostitutes, and was later found guilty. Even from prison, he retained control of his Family, initiating a reorganization of crime and setting up the Crime Syndicate of Mafia families. In 1946 he was released and was then rearrested and deported to Italy as an undesirable alien. He settled briefly in Havanna, and then tried to settle in various European cities but was invariably turned out of them. He eventually found refuge in Italy. He died at Naples Airport in 1962 and was only posthumously allowed to return to the USA, where he was buried at St John's Cemetery in New York.

LUCILIUS, Gaius (c.180–102 BC) Roman satirist, born in Suessa Aurunca in Campania. He wrote 30 books of *Satires*, of which only fragments remain. Written in hexameters, they give a critical insight into his times.

LUCRETIA (6th century BC) Roman matron, the wife of L Tarquinius Collatinus. According to legend she was raped by Sextus Tarquinius (son of **Tarquinius Superbus**), summoned her husband and friends, and, making them take an oath to drive out the Tarquins, plunged a knife into her heart. The tale has formed the basis of several works, notably **Shakespeare**'s *Rape of Lucrece* and the opera *The Rape of Lucretia* by **Benjamin Britten**. The Tarquins were later expelled by **Lucius Junius Brutus**.

LUCRETIUS, (Titus Lucretius Carus) (c.99–55 BC) Roman poet and philosopher. He was said to have died mad from the effects of a love potion given to him by his wife Lucilia. His great work is his hexameter poem *De Natura Rerum*, in six books, in which he tried to popularize the philosophical theories of **Democritus** and **Epicurus** on the origin of the universe, with the special purpose of eradicating anything like religious belief, which he savagely denounces as the one great source of man's wickedness and misery. A calm and tranquil mind was his aim, the way to it being through a materialistic philosophy. His poem abounds in strikingly picturesque phrases, episodes of exquisite pathos and vivid description, rarely equalled in Latin poetry.

LUCULLUS, Lucius Licinius (c.110–57 BC) Roman soldier, born of a plebeian family. After service with **Sulla** he commanded the fleet in the 1st Mithradatic War. As consul in 74 he defeated **Mithradates** in the 3rd Mithradatic War, and introduced admirable reforms into Asia Minor. He twice defeated **Tigranes** of Armenia (69 and 68). But his legions became mutinous, and he was superseded by **Pompey** (66). He attempted to check Pompey's power, and was one of the first triumvirate, but soon withdrew from politics. He had acquired prodigious wealth and spent the rest of his life in such luxury that the term 'Lucullus' has been used as an epithet for good food. He was a notable patron of writers and artists.

LUCY, St (d.303) Christian martyr, the patron saint of the blind. According to tradition, she was a virgin denounced as a Christian by a rejected suitor, and martyred under **Diocletian** at Syracuse. Her feast day is 13 December.

LUCY, Sir Henry William (1845–1924) English journalist, born in Crosby near Liverpool. He worked as reporter on the *Shrewsbury Chronicle*, the *Pall Mall Gazette* and the *Exeter Gazette* (of which he became assistant editor), before being appointed *Daily News* parliamentary reporter. Writing as 'Toby, MP' of *Punch* from 1881 to 1916, he was also a novelist and a writer of books on parliamentary process.

LUCY, Sir Thomas (1532–1600) Warwickshire squire, MP, and justice of the peace. He is said to have prosecuted **Shakespeare** for stealing deer from Charlecote Park, and to have been the original of Justice Shallow.

LUDD, Ned (fl.1779) a Leicestershire simpleton who worked as a farm labourer. He destroyed some stocking frames about 1782 and it is from him that the Luddite rioters (1812–18) took their name.

LUDENDORFF, Erich von (1865–1937) German soldier, born near Posen. A staff-officer from 1904 to 1913, in 1914 he was appointed chief of staff in East Prussia, and masterminded the annihilation of the

Russians at Tannenberg (August 1914). When **Hindenburg** superseded **Falkenhayn** in 1916, Ludendorff as his first quartermaster sent **Mackensen** to the Dobruja. On the Western Front in 1918 he planned the major offensive that nearly won the war for Germany. In 1923 he was a leader in the **Hitler** putsch at Munich, but he was acquitted of treason. He was a Nazi member of the Reichstag from 1924 to 1928, but as a candidate for the presidency of the Reich in 1925 he polled few votes. Strongly opposed to Jews, Jesuits and freemasons, he later became a pacifist.

LUDLOW, Edmund (c.1617–1692) English parliamentarian and regicide, born in Maiden Bradley, Wiltshire. During the Civil War he served under Sir **William Waller** and **Thomas Fairfax**, and was returned for Wiltshire in 1646. Elected to the council of state, he was sent to Ireland as lieutenant-general of horse in 1651, but refused to recognize **Cromwell**'s protectorate. Member for Hindon in 1659, he urged the restoration of the Rump Parliament, commanded again for a while in Ireland, was nominated by **John Lambert** to the committee of safety, and strove in vain to reunite the republican party. After the Restoration he made his way to Vevey in Switzerland. In 1689 he came back, but, the House of Commons demanding his arrest, he returned to Vevey.

LUDLOW, John Malcolm Forbes (1821–1911) English social reformer, born in Nimach, India. A practising conveyancer, he was a founder of the Christian Socialist movement with **Frederick Dennison Maurice**, **Charles Kingsley** and **Thomas Hughes**. He founded and edited the weekly *Christian Socialist* (1850), helped to found the Working Men's College (1854), and was chief registrar of Friendly Societies (1875–91).

LUDMILLA, St (d.921) patron saint of Bohemia, the wife of its first Christian duke, she was murdered by her heathen daughter-in-law, Drahomira.

LUDWIG I (1786–1868) king of Bavaria, born in Strasbourg, he came to the throne in 1825, and by his lavish expenditure on pictures, public buildings and favourites, and by taxes and reactionary policy, provoked active discontent in 1830, and again in 1848, when he abdicated in favour of his son, **Maximilian II**.

LUDWIG II (1845–86) king of Bavaria, son of **Maximilian II,** born in Nymphenburg. He succeeded in 1864 and devoted himself to patronage of **Wagner** and his music. In 1870 he threw Bavaria on the side of Prussia, and offered the imperial crown to **Wilhelm I**, though he took no part in the war, and lived the life of a recluse. He was almost constantly at feud with his ministers and family, mainly on account of his insensate outlays on superfluous palaces, and was declared insane in 1886. A few days later he was found dr‹ ‹ned, with his physician, in the Starnberger Lake near his castle of Berg. It is not known whether his death was suicide, murder, or simply accidental.

LUDWIG III (1854–1921) king of Bavaria, the son of the Prince Regent Luitpold. He was born in Munich and reigned for only five years, 1913–18, when he abdicated. He was the last of the Wittelsbach family to be on the throne.

LUDWIG, originally **Cohn, Emil** (1861–1948) German author, born in Breslau. He wrote some novels and plays, but made his name as a biographer of the intuitive school, with lives of **Goethe**, **Napoleon**, **Wilhelm II**, **Bismarck**, **Christ**, **Lincoln**, and others. He lived in Switzerland.

LUDWIG, Karl Friedrich Wilhelm (1816–95) German physiologist, born in Witzenhausen. Professor at Leipzig (1865–95), he did pioneer research on glandular secretions, and his invention of the mercurial blood-gas pump revealed the role of oxygen and other gases in the bloodstream. He also invented the kymograph (1847).

LUGARD, Frederick John Dealtry, Baron Lugard (1858–1945) British soldier and colonial administrator, born in Fort St George, Madras, to a clerical and missionary family. In 1878 he was commissioned as an army officer, serving in the Sudan against **Mohammed Ahmed**, the Mahdi (1885), and in Burma after the fall of King Thibaw (1886), and commanded an expedition against slavers in Nyasaland (1888). His activities in rough-and-ready Uganda peacekeeping led to its being made a British protectorate in 1894, in which his *The Rise of Our East African Empire* (1893) was also influential. Appointed commissioner in the Nigerian hinterland by **Joseph Chamberlain** (1897), he kept a French challenge at bay and kept the peace. Britain having declared a protectorate over Northern and Southern Nigeria, Lugard was high commissioner for the North (1900–07), and established administrative paternalistic control with minimal force. He was governor of Hong Kong from 1907, helping to establish its University in 1911. He returned to Nigeria as governor of the two protectorates, becoming Governor-General (1914–19) on their amalgamation. His principle was one of use of existing tribal institutions as infrastructure for British rule. He served on the Permanent Mandates Commission of the League of Nations (1922–36), published another influential book in *The Dual Mandate in British Tropical Africa* (1922) and was active on a Parliamentary Select Committee on closer union in East Africa (1930–31).

LUGOSI, Bela, originally **Bela Ferenc Denzso Blasko** (1882–1956) Hungarian-born American actor, born in Lugos (now Romania). A student at the Academy of Performing Arts in Budapest, he made his stage début in *Ocskay Brigaderos* (1902) and appeared with various repertory companies before making his film début in *A Leopard* (1917). Moving to America in 1921, he enjoyed his greatest success on Broadway as *Dracula* (1927), a role he repeated on film in 1931. Heavily accented, he made a memorably menacing, aristocratic vampire but soon found himself typecast in low-budget horror films; more inspired exceptions include *Murders in the Rue Morgue* (1932), *The Black Cat* (1934), *Son of Frankenstein* (1939) and *Abbott and Costello Meet Frankenstein* (1948). After becoming a drug addict and successfully undergoing treatment, his later films were woeful bargain basement efforts and he died during the production of *Plan 9 from Outer Space* (1956), frequently voted the worst film ever made.

LU HSUN, or **Lu Hsin** (1881–1936) Chinese writer, born in Shaohsin in Chekiang, of a family of scholars. In 1909 he became dean of studies at the Shaohsin Middle School and later its principal. By 1913 he was professor of Chinese literature at the National Peking University and National Normal University for Women. In 1926 he went as professor to Amoy University and later was appointed dean of the College of Arts and Letters at Sun Yat-Sen University, Canton. His career as an author began with a short story, *Diary of a Madman* (1918). In 1921 appeared *The True Story of Ah Q*. Considered his most successful book, it has been translated into many languages. Between 1918 and 1925 he wrote 26 short stories and these appear in two volumes entitled *Cry* and *Hesitation*.

LUINI, or **Lovino, Bernardino** (c.1481–1532) Lombard painter, born in Luino on Lago Maggiore. He was trained in the school of **Leonardo da Vinci**, to whom many of his works have been attributed. He painted much at Milan. He is one of the five whose 'supremacy' Ruskin affirmed.

LUITPRAND See **LIUTPRAND**

LUKACS, György Szegedy von (Georg) (1885–1971) Hungarian Marxist philosopher and critic, born in Budapest. Born into a wealthy Jewish family, he studied in Budapest, Berlin and Heidelberg. He published two important early works on literary criticism, *Soul and Form* (1910) and *The Theory of the Novel* (1916). In 1918 he joined the Hungarian Communist party, but after the defeat of the uprising in 1919 he lived abroad in Vienna (1919–29) and Moscow (1930–44). He returned to Hungary after World War II as professor at Budapest and joined **Nagy**'s short-lived revolutionary government in 1956 as minister of culture. After the Russian suppression he was briefly deported and interned but returned to Budapest in 1957. He was a prolific writer on literature and aesthetics. His major book on Marxism, *History and Class Consciousness* (1923), was repudiated as heretical by the Russian Communist party and later, in abject public confession, by Lukacs himself.

LUKARIS, Cyril See **LUCARIS**

LUKE (1st century AD) A New Testament evangelist, and companion of **St Paul** on his journeys. Mentioned in *Colossians* IV 14 as 'the beloved physician', his name is suggestive of an Italian origin. Church tradition made him a native of Antioch in Syria, one of 'the seventy' mentioned in Luke X, a painter by profession, and a martyr. He is first named as author of the third gospel in the Muratorian canon (2nd century); and tradition has ever since ascribed to him both that work and the Acts of the Apostles. He is the patron saint of doctors and artists. His feast day is 18 October.

LUKE, Sir Samuel See **BUTLER, Samuel**

LULL, Ramón See **LULLY, Raymond**

LULLY, Giovanni Battista (1632–87) French composer of Italian parentage, born in Florence. He came as a boy to Paris, and was finally, after much ambitious intriguing, made operatic director by **Louis XIV** (1672). With Philippe Quinault as librettist, he composed many operas, in which he made the ballet an essential part; the favourites (till **Gluck**'s time) were *Thésée*, *Armide*, *Phaéton*, *Atys*, *Isis*, and *Acis et Galatée*. He also wrote church music, dance music and pastorals.

LULLY or LULL, Raymond or Ramón (c.1232–1315) Spanish theologian and mystic, known as, 'the enlightened doctor', born in Palma in Majorca. In his youth he served as a soldier and led a dissolute life, writing lyrical troubadour poetry, but from 1266 gave himself up to asceticism and resolved on a spiritual crusade for the conversion of the Muslims. To this end, after some years of study, he produced his *Ars Magna*, the 'Lullian method', a mechanical aid to the acquisition of knowledge and the solution of all possible problems by a systematic manipulation of certain fundamental notions (the Aristotelian categories, etc). He also wrote a book against the Averroists, and in 1291 went to Tunis to confute and convert the Muslims, but was imprisoned and banished. After visiting Naples, Rome, Majorca, Cyprus and Armenia, he again sailed (1305) for Bugia (Bougie) in Algeria, and was again banished; at Paris he lectured against the principles of **Averroës**; and returning to Bugia, was stoned and died a few days afterwards. The Lullists combined religious mysticism with alchemy, but it has been disproved that Lully himself ever dabbled in alchemy. Apart from his *Ars Magna*, of his works *Llibre de Contemplació en Déuf* is masterly and he was the first to use a vernacular language for religious or philosophical writings. He also wrote impressive poetry.

LUMIÈRE, Auguste Marie Louis Nicolas (1862–1954) and **Louis Jean** (1864–1948), French chemists and brothers. Manufacturers of photographic materials, they invented the first successful cine camera and projector (1895) and a process of colour photography. They also produced the first film newsreels, and the first 'movie' in history, *La Sortie des usines Lumiére* (1895).

LUMUMBA, Patrice Emergy (1925–61) Congolese politician, born in Katako Kombe. He became leader of the Congolese national movement and when the Congo became an independent republic in 1960 was made premier. Almost immediately the country was plunged into chaos by warring factions, and after being deposed in 1960, Lumumba was assassinated in 1961.

LUNARDI, Vicenzo (1759–1806) Italian aeronaut, born in Lucca. He made from Moorfields, on 15 September 1784, the first hyrdogen balloon ascent in England.

LUNDY, Benjamin (1789–1839) American abolitionist, born in Hardwick, New Jersey. A saddler to trade, he moved to Ohio where he organized one of the first anti-slavery societies, the Union Humane Society. An itinerant campaigner, he founded *The Genius of Universal Emancipation* (1831–36) and in 1836 *The National Enquirer* in Philadelphia (later called the *Pennsylvania Freeman*).

LUNN, Sir Arnold Henry Moore (1888–1974) English Roman Catholic apologist and Alpine ski pioneer, born in India, son of the travel-bureau pioneer Sir Henry Lunn (1859–1939) and brother of the writer **Hugh Kingsmill**. His first books were on the Alps and skiing, but he began studying Roman Catholicism from his father's Methodist perspective in *Roman Converts* (1924), *John Wesley* (1929), *The Flight from Reason* (1930) and, in debate with **Ronald A Knox**, *Difficulties*. Converted to Rome, he produced a classic of triumphalist Catholicism in *Now I See* (1933), and continued his dual-authorship debates, now from Knox's camp against **C E M Joad**, **J B S Haldane** and **G G Coulton**. *Spanish Rehearsal* (1937) defended **Franco**. An accomplished skier, he invented slalom gates and obtained Olympic recognition for the modern Alpine slalom race and downhill races. He founded and edited the *British Ski Year Book* in 1919.

LUNT, Alfred (1892–1977) American actor, born in Milwaukee. Educated at Carroll College, Waukesha, he abandoned an early notion to be an architect, making his stage début with the Castle Square Theatre Company in Boston during 1912. He made his New York début in *Romance and Arabella* (1917) and signalled his early promise in *Clarence* (1919–21). In 1922 he married actress Lynn Fontanne (1887–1983) and the couple seldom performed separately thereafter. A handsome man with a distinguished voice, he built a reputation as one of the finest actors of his generation in such plays as *The Guardsman* (1924), *Elizabeth, The Queen* (1930), *Design for Living* (1933), *Idiot's Delight* (1936) and *The Seagull* (1938). He made his film début in *Backbone* (1923) and also recreated *The Guardsman* (1931), but the couple restricted their appearances primarily to the stage. After spending the war years in London, their later work showed a decline in quality but a farewell performance in *The Visit* (1958–60) was an unqualified success. Broadway's Lunt Fontanne theatre, opened in 1958, was named in their honour.

LUPTON, Thomas Goff (1791–1873) English mezzotint engraver, born in London. He was one of the first to use steel in engraving. Among his works are **Turner**'s *Ports and Rivers*.

LURIA, Alexandr Romanovich (1902–77) Russian psychologist, born in Kazan, a physician's son and one of the founders of neuropsychology. He began his psychological studies at the Moscow Medical Institute under the influential child psychologist **L S Vygotsky**. From 1945 he taught at Moscow State University, and carried out extensive researches into the effects of brain injuries that had been sustained by people during the war. He established, and became head of, the neuropsychology subdepartment of the department of psychology at the university in 1967. His contributions to the field of neuropsychology (the application of the theories and methods of experimental psychology to the understanding of neurological disorders) have been both empirical and theoretical, his influence being particularly felt by researchers concerned with understanding the effects of damage to the frontal lobes, and of damage to those regions of the left hemisphere of the brain that are concerned with language. His books included *The Man with a Shattered World* (trans 1972) and *The Working Brain* (trans 1973).

LURIA, Salvador Edward (1912–) Italian-born American biologist, joint winner of the 1969 Nobel prize for physiology or medicine. He studied at the Institute of Radium in Paris, and in 1940 emigrated to the USA, where he worked with **Max Delbrück** and **Alfred Hershey** on the role of DNA in the viruses that infect bacteria, and shared the Nobel prize with them. He wrote *General Virology* (1953).

LUSIGNAN See **GUY OF LUSIGNAN**

LUSINCHI, Jaime (1924–) Venezuelan politician, born in Clarines, in Anzoategui state. He joined the Democratic Action party (AD) while a medical student but was exiled during the repressive régime of General Jimenez, spending the time in Argentina, Chile and the USA (1952–58). The revival of democratic government saw his return and he became politically active again, entering parliament and eventually becoming AD leader. In 1984 he succeeded the Christian Social party (COPEI) leader, Luis Herrera, as president but the austere policies he followed in an effort to solve his country's economic problems proved unpopular and he lost the 1988 election to his AD rival, Carlos Andres Perez.

LUTHER, Martin (1483–1546) German religious reformer, and founder of the Reformation born in Eisleben, the son of a miner. He went to school at Magdeburg and Eisenach, and entered the University of Erfurt in 1501, taking his degree in 1505. Before this, however, he was led to the study of the Scriptures, and spent three years in the Augustinian monastery at Erfurt. In 1507 he was ordained a priest, in 1508 lectured on philosophy in the University of Wittenberg, in 1509 on the Scriptures, and as a preacher produced a still more powerful influence. On a mission to Rome in 1510–11 he was appalled by the conditions there, and after his return his career as a Reformer began. Money was greatly needed in Rome; and its emissaries sought everywhere to raise funds by the sale of indulgences. Luther's indignation at the shameless traffic carried on by the Dominican **Johann Tetzel** became irrepressible. As professor of Biblical exegesis at Wittenberg (1512–46) he began to preach the doctrine of salvation by faith rather than works; and on 31 October 1517 he drew up a list of 95 theses on indulgences, denying to the pope all right to forgive sins, and nailed them on the church door at Wittenberg. Tetzel retreated from Saxony to Frankfurt an der Oder, where he published a set of counter-theses and burnt Luther's. The Wittenberg students retaliated by burning Tetzel's. In 1518 Luther was joined by **Melanchthon**. The pope, **Leo X**, at first took little notice of the disturbance, but in 1518 summoned Luther to Rome to answer for his theses. His university and the elector interfered, and ineffective negotiations were undertaken by Cardinal **Cajetan** and by Miltitz, envoy of the pope to the Saxon court. **Eck** and Luther held a memorable disputation at Leipzig (1519). Luther meantime attacked the papal system as a whole more boldly. **Erasmus** and **Hutten** now joined in the conflict. In 1520 the Reformer published his famous address to the *Christian Nobles of Germany*, followed by a treatise *On the Babylonish Captivity of the Church of God*, which works attacked also the doctrinal system of the Church of Rome. The papal bull containing 41 theses issued against him, he burned before a multitude of doctors, students, and citizens in Wittenberg. Germany was convulsed with excitement. **Charles V** had convened his first diet at Worms in 1521; an order was issued for the destruction of Luther's books, and he was summoned to appear before the diet. Finally he was put under the ban of the empire; on his return from Worms he was seized, at the instigation of the elector of Saxony, and lodged (really for his own protection) in the Wartburg. During the year he spent here he translated the Scriptures and composed various treatises. Civil unrest called Luther back to Wittenberg in 1522; he rebuked the unruly elements, and made a stand against lawlessness on the one hand and tyranny on the other. In this year he published his acrimonious reply to **Henry VIII** on the seven sacraments. Estrangement had gradually sprung up between Erasmus and Luther, and there was an open breach in 1525, when Erasmus published *De Libero Arbitrio*, and Luther followed with *De Servo Arbitrio*. In that year Luther married **Katherine von Bora**, one of nine nuns who had withdrawn from conventual life. In 1529 he engaged in his famous conference at Marburg with **Zwingli** and other Swiss theologians, obstinately maintaining his views as to the real (consubstantial) presence in the Eucharist. The drawing up of the Augsburg Confession, Melanchthon representing Luther, marks the culmination of the German Reformation (1530). Luther died in Eisleben, and was buried at Wittenberg. Endowed with broad human sympathies, massive energy, manly and affectionate simplicity, and rich, if sometimes coarse, humour, he was undoubtedly a spiritual genius. His intuitions of divine truth were bold, vivid and penetrating, if not philosophical and comprehensive; and he possessed the power of kindling other souls with the fire of his own convictions. His voluminous works include *Table-talk*, *Letters* and *Sermons*. His commentaries on Galatians and the Psalms are still read; and he was one of the great leaders of sacred song, his hymns having an enduring power.

LUTHULI, Albert John (1898–1967) South African black resistance leader, son of a Zulu Christian missionary. Educated at an American mission school near Durban, he spent 15 years as a teacher before being elected tribal chief of Groutville, Natal. Deposed for anti-apartheid activities, he became president-general of the African National Congress (1952–60), in which capacity he dedicated himself to a campaign of non-violent resistance and was a defendant in the notorious Johannesburg treason trial (1956–57). He was awarded the 1960 Nobel peace prize for his unswerving opposition to racial violence in the face of repressive measures by the South African government and impatience from extremist Africans. He was elected rector of Glasgow University (1962) but severe restrictions imposed by the South African government (in 1961, and for another five years in 1964), prevented him from leaving Natal. In 1962 he published *Let My People Go*.

LUTOSLAWSKI, Witold (1913–) Polish composer and conductor, born in Warsaw. He has travelled and taught widely in western Europe and the USA, being honoured with many awards in his homeland and abroad. From a huge, varied output, his orchestral works stand to the fore: *Symphonic Variations* (1938), three symphonies (1947, 1967, 1983), *Concerto for Orchestra* (1954), *Livre pour orchestre* (1968), *Cello Concerto* (1970), *Mi-parti* (1976), *Chain 3* (1986), *Piano Concerto* (1988). He has also composed chamber, vocal and piano music.

LÜTTEREL, or **Luttrell, Edward** (fl.1670–1710) English engraver, who probably came from Dublin to London, where he was a student of law. Abandoning this for art he became a crayon painter and one of the first mezzotint engravers. He executed portraits of **Samuel Butler**, and Archbishop **William Sancroft**.

LUTYENS, Sir Edwin Landseer (1869–1944) English architect, born in London. His designs ranged from the picturesque of his early country houses, including Marsh Court, Stockbridge, and the restoration of Lindisfarne Castle, which owed much to the Arts and Crafts movement, to those in the Renaissance style as Heathcote, Ilkley and Salutation, Sandwich. He finally evolved a classical style exhibited in the Cenotaph, Whitehall, and which reached its height in his design for Liverpool Roman Catholic Cathedral. Other prominent works were his magnificent Viceroy's House, New Delhi, a masterpiece in classical design, the British Pavilion at the Rome Exhibition of 1910 and the British Embassy in Washington.

LUTYENS, (Agnes) Elizabeth (1906–83) English composer, born in London, daughter of Sir **Edwin Lutyens**. She studied in Paris and at the Royal College of Music and had a setting of **Keats**'s poem *To Sleep* performed while still attending the College. She was one of the first British composers to adopt the 12-tone technique, and the *Chamber Concerto no. 1* (1939), composed in her own personal interpretation of this style, was a remarkably original work. Her compositions were, in general, not immediately well-received—the chamber opera *Infidelio* (1954) and cantata *De Amore* (1957) were not performed until 1973; but recently she has become accepted as a leading British composer. Her work includes *O Saisons, O chateaux* (1946), the chamber opera *The Pit* (1947), *Concertante* (1950), *Quincunx* (1959), *The Country of the Stars* (1963), *Vision of Youth* (1970) and *Echoi* (1979). She published her autobiography, *A Goldfish Bowl*, in 1972.

LÜTZOW, Ludwig Adolf Wilhelm, Freiherr von (1781–1834) Prussian soldier, born in Berlin. In the Napoleonic war he fought in the defeat at Auerstädt (1806). In the War of Liberation of 1813 he organized a renowned corps of volunteers, 'the Black Jäger', which operated behind the French lines.

LUWUM, Janani (1922–77) Ugandan prelate, born in East Acholi, son of poor Christians. He became a teacher after taking a missionary-run training course. Converted in 1948, he disturbed more quiescent Christians by his evangelical fervour. Ordained in the Anglican Church, he was theological college principal and bishop of Northern Uganda, before election in 1974 as archbishop of Uganda in a land where in 1971 **Idi Amin** had established a reign of terror. He spoke out fearlessly on behalf of victims and oppressed. At Amin's instigaton (some say by his hand) the archbishop was shot dead, and Anglicans in Kampala were forbidden to hold a memorial service for him.

LUXEMBOURG, Duc de, François Henri de Montmorency-Bouteville (1628–95) French soldier, born in Paris. He was brought up by his aunt, mother of the Great **Condé**, and adhered to Condé through the wars of the Fronde. After 1659 he was pardoned by **Louis XIV**, who created him Duc de Luxembourg (1661)—he had just married the heiress of Luxembourg-Piney. In 1667 he served under Condé in Franche-Comté; in 1672 he himself successfully invaded the Netherlands, and, driven back in 1673, conducted a masterly retreat. During the war he stormed Valenciennes and twice defeated the Prince of Orange. Made a marshal in 1675, soon after the peace (1678) he quarrelled with **Louvois**, and was not employed for twelve years. In 1690 he commanded in Flanders, and defeated the Allies at Fleurus (1690), and later twice more routed his old opponent, now King **William III** of Great Britain, at Steinkirk (1692) and Neerwinden (1693).

LUXEMBURG, Rosa (1871–1919) German left-wing revolutionary, born in Zamość in Poland. Converted to communism in 1890, she took part in underground activities in Poland and founded the Polish Social Democratic party (later the Polish Communist party). She moved to Berlin in 1898 and became a leader of the left-wing movement. She wrote tracts like *Sozialreform oder Revolution*. At the outbreak of World War I she formed, with **Karl Liebknecht**, the Spartakusbund (Spartacus League), and spent most of the war in prison. After her release in 1919 she took part in an abortive uprising, and was murdered with Liebknecht in Berlin.

LUYNES, Charles d'Albert, Duc de (1578–1621) French nobleman. The unworthy favourite of **Louis XIII** of France. He became in 1619 a peer of France, and in 1621 chancellor.

LVOV, Prince Georgi Evgenievich (1861–1925) Russian liberal politician, head of the provisional government in the revolution of 1917. Succeeded by **Kerensky**, he left Russia.

LWOFF, André (1902–) French biochemist of Russian-Polish extraction. He worked in the Pasteur Institute in Paris from 1921, was a member of the Resistance in World War II, and became professor of microbiology at the Sorbonne (1959). He researched the genetics of bacterial viruses and demonstrated the process of lysogeny, with implications for cancer research. In 1965 he was awarded the Nobel prize for physiology or medicine jointly with **François Jacob** and **Jacques Monod**.

LYAPUNOV, Aleksandr Mikhailovich (1857–1918) Russian mathematician, born in Yaroslavl, the son of an astronomer. He studied at St Petersburg where he came under the influence of **Pafnutii Chebyshev**, and then taught at Kharkov University, until he returned to St Petersburg as professor in 1901. He is principally associated with important methods in the theory of the stability of dynamical systems, related to **Henri Poincaré**'s work. He committed suicide after his wife's death from tuberculosis.

LYAUTEY, Louis Hubert Gonzalve (1854–1934) French soldier and colonial administrator, born in Nancy. He held administrative posts in Algeria, Tongking and Madagascar (under **Galliéni**), where he reformed the administration. But his most brilliant work was done in Morocco, where he was resident commissary-general from 1912 to 1925, with a break as French minister of war in 1916–17. He established firm French authority, and developed Casablanca as a seaport.

LYCURGUS traditional, possibly legendary, lawgiver of Sparta, who is said to have instigated the Spartan ideals of harsh military discipline.

LYCURGUS (c.390–c.325 BC) Athenian orator and statesman. A supporter of **Demosthenes**, as manager of the public revenue he distinguished himself by his integrity and his public architectural works. Only one speech and a fragment of his orations have survived.

LYDGATE, John (c.1370–c.1451) English monk and poet, born in Lydgate, near Newmarket. He became a Benedictine monk at Bury St Edmunds. He may have studied at Oxford and Cambridge. He travelled in France and perhaps Italy, and became prior of Hatfield Broadoak (Essex) in 1423. A court poet, he received a pension in 1439, but died in poverty. Lydgate's longer works are the *Troy Book*, the *Siege of Thebes* and the *Fall of Princes*. The *Siege of Thebes* is represented as a new Canterbury tale, and was based on a French verse romance. The versification is rough, and the poem dull and long-winded. The *Troy Book* was based on **Colonna**'s Latin prose *Historia Trojana*, and the *Fall of Princes* on **Boccaccio**. Other works include the *Daunce of Machabre*, from the French, *Temple of Glas*, a copy of **Chaucer**'s *House of Fame*, and *London Lickpenny*, a vivid description of contemporary manners in London.

LYELL, Sir Charles (1797–1875) Scottish geologist, born in Kinnordy, Forfarshire, the eldest son of the mycologist and **Dante** student, Charles Lyell (1767–1849). Educated at Ringwood, Salisbury, and Midhurst, he studied law at Exeter College, Oxford, but discovered a taste for geology. His *Principles of Geology* (1830–33) exercised a powerful influence on contemporary scientific thought. It denied the necessity of stupendous convulsions, and taught that the greatest geological changes might have been produced by forces still at work. *The Elements of Geology* (1838) was a supplement. *The Geological Evidences of the Antiquity of Man* (1863) startled the public by its unbiased attitude towards **Charles Darwin**. He also published *Travels in North America* (1845) and *A Second Visit to the United States* (1849). In 1832–33 he was professor of geology at King's College, London.

LYLE, Sandy (Alexander Walter Barr) (1958–) Scottish golfer, born in Shrewsbury of Scottish parents. He started his golfing career by representing England at Boys, Youth and full international levels. In 1980 and 1982 he was a narrowly-beaten finalist in the World Match-Play Championship. His major championship successes have been the European Open in 1979, the French Open in 1981, the British Open in 1985 and the US Masters Championship in 1988. An extremely long hitter with an admirably phlegmatic temperament, with **Nick Faldo** he has largely been responsible for the revival of British professional golf at world level.

LYLY, John (c.1554–1606) English dramatist and novelist, 'the Euphuist', born in the Weald of Kent. He took his BA at Magdalen College, Oxford, in 1573, and studied also at Cambridge. **William Cecil**, Lord Burghley, gave him some post of trust in his household, and he became vice-master of the St Paul's choristers. Having in 1589 taken part in the Marprelate controversy, he was returned to parliament for Aylesbury and Appleby (1597–1601). His *Euphues*, a romance in two parts—*Euphues*, *The Anatomie of Wit* (1579), and *Euphues and his England* (1580)—was received with great applause. One peculiarity of his 'new English' is the constant employment of similes drawn from fabulous stories about the properties of animals, plants and minerals; another is the excessive indulgence in antithesis. His earliest comedy was *The Woman in the Moone*, produced in or before 1583. *Campaspe* and *Sapho and Phao* were published in 1584, *Endimion* in 1591, *Gallathea* and *Midas* in 1592, *Mother Bombie* in 1594, and *Love's Metamorphosis* in 1601. The delightful songs (of doubtful authorship) were first printed in the edition of 1632.

LYNCH, Benny (1913–46) Scottish boxer, born in Glasgow. In 1935 he became the first Scot to hold a world title, taking the National Boxing Association/International Boxing Union version of the world flyweight title. From 1937 to 1938 he was undisputed world champion but lax training routines led to weight problems and he forfeited the title in 1938 when he failed to make the weight for a title bout against Jacky Jurich of the USA. During his career he won 82 out of 110 bouts.

LYNCH, John (Jack) (1917–) Irish politician. Educated at Cork and Dublin, he joined the civil service in the department of justice in 1936, continued his legal studies, and was called to the bar in 1945. He then entered politics and represented Cork for Fianna Fail (1948–81). He served in education, industry and commerce, and finance before assuming the Fianna Fail leadership and becoming taoiseach (prime minister) in 1966. He was replaced by the Fine Gael leader, Liam Cosgrave, in 1973 but was re-elected in 1977. He resigned in 1979, to be succeeded by **Charles Haughey**.

LYND, Robert (1879–1949) Irish essayist and critic, born in Belfast, the son of a Presbyterian minister. Educated at Queen's University, Belfast, he went to London in 1901 and was from 1912 literary editor of the *Daily News* (later the *News Chronicle*) and also contributed to the *New Statesman* (1913–45), signing himself Y Y. His essays, of which he wrote numerous volumes, are on a wide variety of topics. Of an intimate, witty and charming nature, titles include *The Art of Letters* (1920), *The Blue Lion* (1923), and *In Defence of Pink* (1939).

LYNDHURST, John Singleton Copley, Baron (1772–1863) Anglo-American lawyer, born in Boston, Massachusetts, the son of the American painter **John Singleton Copley**. His family brought him to London in 1875. Educated at Trinity College, Cambridge, he was called to the bar in 1804. In 1812, he made a hit by his ingenious defence of a Luddite rioter. In 1817 he obtained the acquittal of **Arthur Thistlewood** and Watson on their trial for high treason; but for the next state prosecution the government secured him on their side. In 1818 he entered parliament as member for Yarmouth. Henceforward he continued a fairly consistent Tory. In 1819, as Sir John Copley, he became solicitor-general, in 1824 attorney-general, and in 1826 master of the rolls. As Baron Lyndhurst he was Lord Chancellor under three administrations (1827–30), when his Whig opponents made him chief baron of the Exchequer; he exchanged that office for the woolsack as Lord Chancellor under Sir **Robert Peel** (1834–35). In 1841–46 he was for the third time Lord Chancellor. Lyndhurst's judgments have never been excelled for lucidity, method and legal acumen.

LYNDSAY, or Lindsay, Sir David of the Mount (c.1486–1555) Scottish poet, born probably at the Mount near Cupar, Fife, or at Garmylton (now Garleton), near Haddington. In 1512 he was appointed 'usher' of the newborn prince who became **James V**. In 1522 or earlier he married Janet Douglas, the king's seamstress. In 1524 (probably), during the regency of the Douglases, he lost or changed his place, but was restored to favour in 1529 when James V became king in his own right. In 1538 he seems to have been Lyon King-of-Arms. He went on embassies to the Netherlands, France, England and Denmark. He (or another David Lyndsay) represented Cupar in the parliaments of 1540–46. For two centuries he was the poet of the Scottish people. His poems, often coarse, are full of humour, good sense and knowledge of the world, and were said to have done more for the Reformation in Scotland than all the sermons of **Knox**. The earliest and most poetic of his writings is the allegorical *The Dreme* (1528), followed by *The Com-*

playnt of the King (1529) and *The Testament and Complaynt of our Soverane Lordis Papyngo* (1530). He wrote a satire on court life in *Ane Publict Confession of the Kingis auld Hound callit Bagsche* (1536). His most remarkable work was *The Satyre of the Thrie Estaitis*, a dramatic work first performed at Linlithgow in 1540, and revived with great success at the Edinburgh Festivals of 1948 and 1959; the most amusing, *The Historie of Squyer Meldrum*.

LYNDSAY OF PITSCOTTIE See **PITSCOTTIE**

LYNEDOCH, Thomas Graham, 1st Baron (1748–1843) Scottish soldier, son of the laird of Balgowan in Perthshire. In 1794 he raised the 90th Regiment of foot (the Perthshire Regiment), and served with it in Minorca (1798). He besieged Valetta in 1800. In the Peninsular War (1808–14) he was aide-de-camp to Sir **John Moore** at Coruña (1809) and fought at Walcheren (1809), defeated the French at Barrosa (1811), fought at Ciudad Rodrigo (1812), Badajoz, and Salamanca, commanded the left wing at Vitoria (1813), and captured Tolosa and San Sebastián. In Holland he conquered at Merxem, but failed to storm Bergen-op-Zoom (1814). He was created Baron Lynedoch of Balgowan (1814), and founded the Senior United Service Club (1817).

LYNEN, Feodor Felix Konrad (1911–79) German biochemist, born in Munich. Educated at Munich, he became head of biochemistry there and director of the Max Planck Institute for Cell Chemistry and Biochemistry (1945–79). He was awarded the Nobel prize for medicine with **Konrad Bloch** in 1964 for his work in lipid biochemistry on the formation of the cholesterol molecule, discovering the biochemistry of the vitamin biotin.

LYON, John (d.1592) English philanthropist, and yeoman land-owner of the estate of Preston, in Middlesex, regarded as the founder of the great public school of Harrow. Relatively prosperous but childless, he used his money for the endowment of local charities. In 1572 he obtained a royal charter from Queen **Elizabeth** for the pre-Reformation school at Harrow, which he supported with endowments to guarantee its continuation. In 1590 he drew up statutes and a course of classical education for the school.

LYONS, Edmund, 1st Baron (1790–1858) English naval commander, born near Christchurch, Hampshire. He entered the navy in 1803, saw service in the passage of Dardanelles (1807) and in the Dutch West Indies (1810–11). Promoted rear admiral in 1850, he served in the Mediterranean as commander-in-chief (1855–58).

LYONS, Francis Stuart Leland (1923–83) Irish historian, born in Derry to a Church of Ireland family. He was educated in Tunbridge Wells, at High School, Dublin, and Trinity College, Dublin, where he taught until becoming professor of history at the University of Kent in 1964. He progressed from his austerely technical doctoral thesis, subsequently published, on *The Irish Parliamentary Party 1890–1910*, to a series of highly readable though deeply professional works embodying detailed research and judicious assessment of modern scholarship, notably *The Fall of Parnell* (1960), *John Dillon* (1968), *Ireland Since the Famine* (1971), *Charles Stewart Parnell* (1977, the leading modern assessment) and *Culture and Anarchy in Ireland 1890–1939* (1978). He was provost of Trinity College, Dublin, from 1974 to 1981, and was working on a historical biography of **W B Yeats** when he died.

LYONS, Sir Joseph (1848–1917) English business man, born in London. He first studied art, and invented a stereoscope before joining with three friends to establish what was to become J Lyons and Co Ltd. Starting in Piccadilly with a teashop, he became head of one of the largest catering businesses in Britain.

LYONS, Joseph Aloysius (1879–1939) Australian statesman, born in Stanley, Tasmania. Educated at Tasmania University, he became a teacher but entered politics in 1909 as Labour member in the Tasmanian House of Assembly. He held the post of minister of education and railways (1914–16) and was premier (1923–29). In the federal parliament he was in turn postmaster-general, minister of public works and treasurer. In 1931 he broke away as a protest against the government's financial policy and led an opposition party, the United Australian party, which he himself founded. In 1932 he became prime minister, which position he held until his death.

LYOT, Bernard Ferdinand (1897–1952) French astronomer, born in Paris, the inventor of the coronagraph. The son of a surgeon, he studied engineering at the École Supérieure d'Electricité. He worked at the Paris Observatory at Meudon from 1920. In 1930 he invented the coronagraph, a device which allows the sun's corona to be observed without the necessity for a total solar eclipse. This is achieved by creating an artificial eclipse inside a telescope with very precisely aligned optics. He also pioneered the study of the polarization of light reflected from the surface of the Moon and of the planets, allowing him to infer something of their surface conditions.

LYRA, Nicolaus de (?1270–1340) French theologian, born in Lyre near Évreux. He was a lecturer at Paris, provincial of the Franciscans, and author of famous *Postillae* or commentaries on scripture, in which he insisted on the literal meanings and protested against the traditional allegorizing method.

LYSANDER (d.395 BC) Spartan naval commander. He commanded the fleet which defeated the Athenians at Aegospotami (405), and in 404 took Athens, thus ending the Peloponnesian war.

LYSENKO, Trofim Denisovich (1898–1976) Russian geneticist and agronomist, born in Karlovka, Ukraine. During the famines of the early 1930s he gained a considerable reputation as an instiller of good crop husbandry into the Russian peasantry. On the basis of a borrowed discovery that the phases of plant growth can be accelerated by short doses of low temperature, he developed a quasi-scientific doctrine, compounded of Darwinism and the work of **Michurin**, that heredity can be changed by good husbandry, but otherwise more in line with Marxism than with genuine scientific theorizing. As director of the Institute of Genetics of the Sovient Academy of Sciences (1940–65), he declared the accepted Mendelian theory erroneous and ruthlessly silenced any Soviet geneticists who opposed him. With the rise of **Khrushchev** and his agricultural policies, Lysenko faded from the limelight and was finally dismissed in 1965, having gravely hampered scientific and agricultural progress in the USSR. He was awarded the Stalin prize in 1949 for his book *Agrobiology* (1948).

LYSIAS (c.458–c.380 BC) Greek orator, the son of a rich Syracusan. Educated at Thurii in Italy, he settled in Athens about 440. The Thirty Tyrants in 404 stripped him and his brother Polemarchus of their wealth, and killed Polemarchus. The first use to which Lysias put his eloquence was, on the fall of the Thirty (403), to prosecute Eratosthenes, the tyrant chiefly to blame for his brother's murder. He then practised with success as a writer of speeches for litigants. From his surviving speeches Lysias emerges as delightfully lucid in thought and expression, and strong in character-drawing. The family home in Athens is portrayed in **Plato**'s *Republic*.

LYSIMACHUS (d.281 BC) Macedonian general of **Alexander the Great**, afterwards king in Thrace, to which he later added north-west Asia Minor and Macedonia. He was defeated and killed at Koroupedion by **Seleucus**.

LYSIPPUS OF SICYON (4th century BC) Greek sculptor. A prolific worker, he is said to have made more than 1500 bronzes and introduced a new naturalism. He made several portrait busts of **Alexander the Great**.

LYTE, Henry Francis (1793–1847) Scottish hymn-writer, born in Ednam, near Kelso. After entering Trinity College, Dublin, he took orders in 1815, and was for 25 years incumbent of Lower Brixham. His *Poems, chiefly Religious* (1833; reprinted as *Miscellaneous Poems*, 1868), are not as well known as his hymns, among which the best are 'Abide with me' and 'Pleasant are thy courts'.

LYTTELTON, George, 1st Baron (1709–73) English politician and man of letters, born in Hagley, Worcestershire. A direct descendant of Sir **Thomas Littleton**, he became brother-in-law of **William Pitt** the Elder. Educated at Eton and Christ Church College, Oxford, he entered parliament as MP for Okehampton in 1735. An opponent of **Horace Walpole**, he soon made a reputation as an orator, held several high political offices, and was raised to the peerage in 1759. A generous patron of literature, he was the friend of many writers, particularly the Scottish poet **James Thomson** (1700–48). Himself a minor poet, he is chiefly remembered for his *Monody* (1747) on the death of his wife. His prose works include *The Conversion and Apostleship of St Paul* (1747), *Dialogues of the Dead* (1760), and *The History of the Life of Henry the Second* (1767–71).

LYTTELTON, George William, 4th Baron, second creation (1817–76) English colonialist. As chairman of the Canterbury Association he sent Anglican colonists to New Zealand and so founded Canterbury there, the port of which bears his name. He was under-secretary for the Colonies (1846).

LYTTELTON, Oliver See **CHANDOS**

LYTTON, Edward George Lytton Bulwer, 1st Baron (1803–73) English novelist, playwright, essayist, poet and politician, born in London. He was the youngest son of General Earle Bulwer (1776–1807) by Elizabeth Barbara Lytton (1773–1843), the heiress of Knebworth in Hertfordshire. He took early to poetry and in 1820 published *Ismael and other Poems*. At Trinity Hall, Cambridge (1822–25) he won the chancellor's gold medal for a poem upon 'Sculpture', but left with only a pass degree. His unhappy marriage (1827), against his mother's wishes, to the Irish beauty Rosina Wheeler, ended in separation (1836), but called forth a marvellous literary activity, for the temporary estrangement from his mother threw him almost wholly on his own resources. His enormous output, vastly popular during his lifetime, but now forgotten, includes *Eugene Aram* (1832), *The Last Days of Pompeii* (1834), and *Harold* (1843). Among his plays are *The Lady of Lyons* (1838), *Richelieu* (1839) and *Money* (1840), and his poetry includes an epic, *King Arthur* (1848–49). MP for St Ives (1831–41), he was created a baronet in 1838, and in 1843 he succeeded to the Knebworth estate and assumed the surname of Lytton. He re-entered parliament as member for Hertfordshire in 1852, and in the **Derby** government (1858–59) was colonial secretary. In 1866 he was raised to the peerage.

LYTTON, Edward Robert Bulwer, 1st Earl of (1831–91) English poet, diplomatist and statesman, born in London. He was educated at Harrow school and at Bonn. In 1849 he went to Washington as attaché and private seretary to his uncle, **Henry Bulwer**; and subsequently he was appointed attaché, secretary of legation, consul or *chargé d'affaires* at Florence (1852), Paris (1854), The Hague (1856), St Petersburg and Constantinople (1858), Vienna (1859), Belgrade (1860), Constantinople again (1863), Athens (1864), Lisbon (1865), Madrid (1868), Vienna again (1869) and Paris (1873). In the last year he succeeded his father as second Lord Lytton, and in 1874 became minister at Lisbon, from 1876 to 1880 was Viceroy of India, and in 1880 was made Earl of Lytton; in 1887 he was sent as ambassador to Paris, and there he died. His works, published mostly under the pseudonym of 'Owen Meredith', include novels, poems, and translations from Serbian. His *Indian Administration* (1899) and his *Letters* (1906) were both edited by his daughter, Lady Betty Balfour.

LYTTON, Sir Henry Alfred (1867–1936) English actor, born in London. He first appeared on the stage with the D'Oyly Carte Opera Company in Glasgow in 1884. Till 1932 he played leading parts in **Gilbert** and **Sullivan** opera. He wrote *Secrets of a Savoyard* (1927) and *A Wandering Minstrel* (1933).

LYUBIMOV, Yuri (1917–) Soviet stage director. He joined the Vakhtangov Theatre Company in Moscow after World War II, and after the tremendous acclaim for his production of **Brecht**'s *The Good Woman of Setzuan*, was appointed director of the Taganka Theatre, Moscow, in 1964. At the Taganka he staged a series of provocative productions (both dramatically and politically), including an adaptation of *Ten Days That Shook The World* (1967), **Molière**'s *Tartuffe* (1969) and a modern-dress *Hamlet* in 1974. He fell from favour, and while he was in England in 1983 he was fired from his theatre, expelled from the Party and deprived of his Soviet citizenship. He subsequently worked on several productions outside the Soviet Union, but returned to his native country in 1988.

M

MAARTENS, Maarten, pen-name of **Jost Marius Willem van der Poorten Schwart** (1858–1915) Dutch novelist, born in Amsterdam. He spent part of his boyhood in England, went to school in Germany, and studied and taught law at Utrecht University. He wrote powerful novels in English, including *The Sin of Joost Avelingh* (1889) and *God's Fool* (1893). His Letters were edited by his daughter (1930).

MABILLON, Jean (1632–1707) French scholar, born in St Pierremont in Champagne. He became a Benedictine monk in 1654, and from 1664 worked in the abbey of St Germain-des-Prés in Paris. Considered the founder of Latin palaeography, he edited St **Bernard**'s works (1667), wrote a history of his order (9 vols, 1668–1702), and wrote *De re diplomatica* (1698).

MABLY, Gabriel Bonnot de (1709–85) French historian, born in Grenoble, the elder brother of **Condillac**. For a time he was secretary to the minister Cardinal Tencin, his uncle, and wrote *Entretiens de Phocion* (1763), *Parallèle des Romains et des Français* (1740) and *Observations sur l'histoire de la Grèce* (1766). His *De la manière d'écrire l'histoire* (1783) contains severe strictures on **Hume**, **Robertson**, **Gibbon** and **Voltaire**.

MABUSE, Jan, real name **Gossart** (c.1470–1532) Flemish painter, born in Maubeuge (Mabuse). In 1503 he entered the painters' guild of St Luke in Antwerp, and was influenced by **Memlinc** and **Quentin Matsys**. From 1508 to 1509 he accompanied **Philip of Burgundy** to Italy, where he became imbued with the High Renaissance style which he introduced to Holland. He lived latterly in Middelburg, and died in Antwerp.

McADAM, John Loudon (1756–1836) Scottish inventor and engineer, born in Ayr. He went to New York in 1770, where he made a fortune in his uncle's counting-house. On his return to Scotland in 1783 he bought the estate of Sauchrie, Ayrshire, and started experimenting with a revolutionary method of road construction. In 1816 he was appointed surveyor to the Bristol Turnpike Trust, and re-made the roads there with crushed stone bound with gravel, and raised to improve drainage—the 'macadamized' system. His advice was sought in all directions. Impoverished through his labours, he petitioned parliament in 1820, and in 1825 was voted £2000. In 1827 he was made surveyor-general of metropolitan roads.

McALISKEY, Bernadette Josephine, née **Devlin** (1947–) Irish political activist. Born into a poor Catholic family, she was brought up in Dungannon, County Tyrone, and educated at St Patrick's Girls' Academy, Dungannon, and Queen's University, Belfast. While at university she became the youngest MP in the House of Commons since **William Pitt** when she was elected as an Independent Unity candidate in 1969, at the age of 21. Her aggressive political style led to her arrest while leading Catholic rioters in the Bogside, and she was sentenced to nine months' imprisonment. In 1971 she lost Catholic support when she gave birth to an illegitimate child; she married two years later and did not stand in the 1974 general election. In 1979 she unsuccessfully sought a seat in the European Parliament, and in 1981 actively supported the IRA hunger strikers, making a dramatic appearance in Spain after her recovery from an attempted assassination in which she and her husband were shot. She was a co-founder of the Irish Republican Socialist party in 1975. She published her autobiography, *The Price of My Soul*, in 1969.

MACALPINE, John See **MACHABEUS, Johannes**

McANALLY, Ray (Raymond) (1926–89) Irish actor, born in Buncrana, Donegal. An enthusiastic participant in amateur dramatics, he made his professional début in *A Strange House* (1942). A member of Dublin's Abbey Theatre from 1947, he had appeared in some 150 productions there by 1963 and attributed his versatility to a philosophy of 'five lines one week, King Lear the next'. His many celebrated performances include *The Shadow of a Gunman* (1951), *Twilight of a Warrior* (1955) and *The Country Boy* (1959). He made his London début in *A Cheap Bunch of Nice Flowers* (1962) and subsequent West End appearances included *Who's Afraid of Virginia Woolf?* (1964), *Tiny Alice* (1970) and *The Best of Friends* (1988). A prodigious character actor of range and integrity, he was a master of stagecraft, frequently returning to the Abbey Theatre to direct and teach. Active in the cinema from 1957, he won international acclaim and a British Academy Award for his performance as the papal envoy in *The Mission* (1986) and was subsequently seen in numerous films, including *My Left Foot* (1989) and *Venus Peter* (1989). A veteran of over 500 television productions since his début in *Leap in the Dark* (1959), he won British Academy Awards for *A Perfect Spy* (1988) and *A Very British Coup* (1989).

MacARTHUR, Douglas (1880–1964) American soldier, born in Little Rock, Arkansas, son of lieutenant-general Arthur MacArthur (1845–1912). Educated at West Point, he was commissioned in the Corps of Engineers in 1903, and went to Tokyo in 1905 as aide to his father. In World War I he commanded the 42nd (Rainbow) Division in France, and was decorated 13 times and cited seven additional times for bravery. Promoted brigadier in August 1918, he became in November the youngest divisional commander in France. In 1919 he became the youngest-ever superintendent of West Point and in 1930 was made a general and chief of staff of the US army. In 1935 he became head of the US military mission to the Philippines. In World War II he was appointed commanding general of the US armed forces in the Far East in 1941. In March 1942, after a skilful but unsuccessful defence of the Bataan peninsula, he was ordered to evacuate from the Philippines to Australia, where he set up HQ as supreme commander of the South West Pacific Area. As the war developed he carried out a brilliant 'leap-frogging' strategy which enabled him to recapture the Philippine Archipelago from the Japanese. In 1944 he was appointed a general of the army, and completed the liberation of the Philippines in July 1945, and in September 1945, as supreme commander of the Allied powers, formally accepted the surrender of Japan on board the *Missouri*. He then exercised in the occupied Empire almost unlimited authority. He gave Japan a new constitution and carried out a programme of sweeping reform. When war broke out in Korea in June 1950 President

Truman ordered him to support the South Koreans in accordance with the appeal of the UN Security Council. In July he became c-in-c of the UN forces. After initial setbacks he pressed the war far into North Korea, but after the Chinese entered the war in November, MacArthur demanded powers to blockade the Chinese coast, bomb Manchurian bases and to use Chinese nationalist troops from Formosa against the communists. This led to acute differences with the US Democratic administration and in April 1951, President Truman relieved him of his commands. He failed to be nominated for the presidency in 1952. A brilliant military leader and a ruler of Japan imbued with a deep moral sense, MacArthur became a legend in his lifetime. Equally he inspired criticism for his imperious belief in his own mission and his strong sense of self-dramatization.

MACARTHUR, Elizabeth, née **Veale** (1766–1850) English-born Australian pioneer, born in Bridgerule, Devon. She married **John Macarthur** in 1788 and sailed with him and their son to New South Wales in 1789 on the second fleet. In 1793 Macarthur received a grant of land near Parramatta, New South Wales, which he named Elizabeth Farm. During her husband's prolonged absences from the colony, she was left, with their seven surviving children, to manage Macarthur's involved business ventures. Supported by her husband's nephew, Hannibal Hawkins Macarthur (1788–1861), Elizabeth introduced the merino sheep to Elizabeth Farm and to their new grant of land at Camden, New South Wales, and successfully carried out experiments in the breeding of sheep for fine wool which led to the establishment of the Australian wool industry. In 1816 Governor **Macquarie** gave an additional 600 acres to the Macarthurs in special recognition of Elizabeth's work for the betterment of the colony's agriculture. She is generally regarded as the first 'educated' woman in Australia.

MACARTHUR, John (1767–1834) Australian pioneer and wool merchant, born in England. In 1789, with his wife **Elizabeth Macarthur**, he emigrated to Australia, where he became leader of the settlers in New South Wales. He inspired the Rum Rebellion in 1808–10, in which the British soldiers mutinied and imprisoned the governor, **William Bligh** of *Bounty* fame. Macarthur was banished to England in 1810, but returned in 1816 and made a fortune in the wool trade. He was a member of the NSW Legislative Council (1825–32).

MACARTHUR, Robert Helmer (1930–72) Canadian-born American ecologist, born in Toronto. He moved to the USA at age 17 and studied mathematics; when working for his PhD at Yale he changed to zoology, and from 1965 was professor of biology at Princeton. His early work on birds led him to concentrate on population biology, and he devised methods for quantifying ecological factors. His ideas proved to be influential, especially his categorization of animals as 'R' species (opportunistic, with rapid reproduction and development, short lives and high mortality) or as 'K' species (larger, slowly developing, more stable); ten years before his early death he showed that natural selection principles apply to both groups.

MACARTNEY, George, 1st Earl (1737–1806) Irish diplomat, born in Lissanoure near Belfast. Educated at Trinity College, Dublin, in 1764 he was sent as an envoy to Russia, from 1769 to 1772 was chief-secretary of Ireland, and in 1775 was governor of Grenada. There (an Irish baron from 1776) he was taken prisoner by the French in 1779. Governor of Madras (1781–85), in 1792 he was made an earl and headed the first diplomatic mission to China. After a mission to **Louis XVIII** at Verona (1795–96), he went out as governor to the Cape (1796), but returned in ill health in 1798.

MACAULAY, Dame (Emilie) Rose (1881–1958) English novelist and essayist, born in Rugby, Warwickshire, the daughter of a Cambridge university lecturer in classical literature. Educated at Oxford High School and Somerville College, Oxford, where she read history, her first novel was *Abbots Verney* (1906), followed by *Views and Vagabonds* (1912) and *The Lee Shore* (1920), winner of a £1000 publishers' prize. Her later novels included *Potterism* (1920), *Dangerous Ages* (1921, which won the Femina Vie Heureuse prize), *Told by an Idiot* (1923), *Orphan Island* (1924), *Crewe Train* (1926), *Keeping Up Appearances* (1928), *They were Defeated* (1932), *I Would be a Private* (1937), and *And No Man's Wit* (1940). After World War II she wrote two further novels, *The World My Wilderness* (1950), and *The Towers of Trebizond* (1956), which won the Tait Black Memorial prize. Her travel books included *They Went to Portugal* (1946), *Fabled Shore* (1949), and *The Pleasure of Ruins* (1953).

MACAULAY, Thomas Babington, 1st Baron Macaulay (1800–59) English author, born in Rothley Temple, Leicestershire, son of Zachary Macaulay (1768–1838). In 1812 he was sent to a private school at Little Shelford near Cambridge, and moved in 1814 to Aspenden Hall in Hertfordshire, from where, an exceptionally precocious boy, he entered Trinity College, Cambridge, in 1818. He detested mathematics, but twice won the Chancellor's medal for English verse, and obtained a prize for Latin declamation. In 1821 he carried off the Craven prize, in 1822 took his BA, and in 1824 was elected to a fellowship. He was one of the most brilliant debaters in the Cambridge Union. Called to the bar in 1826 he had no liking for his profession but literature had irresistible attractions for him. In 1823 he became a contributor to *Knight's Quarterly Magazine*, in which appeared some of his best verses—*Ivry*, *The Spanish Armada* and *Naseby*. In 1825 he was discovered by **Jeffrey**, and his famous article on **Milton** in the August number of the *Edinburgh Review* secured him a position in literature. For nearly 20 years he was one of the most prolific and popular of the writers on the *Edinburgh Review*. In 1830 he entered parliament for the pocket borough of Calne, and in the Reform Bill debates his great powers as an orator were established. Commissioner, and then secretary, to the Board of Control, he still wrote steadily for the *Edinburgh Review*, and made a name as a conversationalist in society. Mainly for the sake of his family, impoverished by his devotion to philanthropy, he accepted the office of legal adviser to the Supreme Council of India, with a salary of £10 000, and sailed for Bengal in 1834, returning to England in 1838. In 1839 he was elected member of parliament for Edinburgh, and entered Lord **Melbourne**'s cabinet as secretary of war. The *Lays of Ancient Rome* (1842) won an immense popularity; so too did his collected *Essays* (3 vols, 1843). His connection with the *Edinburgh Review* ceased in 1845; he had by then begun his *History of England from the Accession of James II*. In 1846 he was re-elected for Edinburgh but was defeated at the general election of 1847. In 1852 he was again returned for Edinburgh and in 1856 he retired. The first two volumes of his *History* appeared in 1848, and at once attained greater popularity than any other purely historical work. The next two followed in 1855, and an unfinished fifth volume was published in 1861. In 1849 he was elected lord rector of Glasgow University. In 1857 he was raised to the peerage as Baron Macaulay of Rothley. He was buried in Westminster Abbey.

Macaulay has been convicted of historical inaccuracy, of sacrificing truth for the sake of epigram, of allowing personal dislike and Whig bias to distort his views of men and incidents, but as a picturesque narrator he has no rival.

McAULEY, Catherine (1787–1841) Irish religious, born in Dublin. She was left money by her adoptive parents to buy a site for a school for poor children and a residence for working women, and called House of Our Blessed Lady of Mercy; and in 1831 she founded the order of the Sisters of Mercy.

McBEAN, Angus Rowland (1904–) Welsh stage photographer, born in Newbridge, Monmouth, and educated at Newport. After a number of odd jobs, including the design of theatrical masks and scenery, he started as a full-time theatrical photographer in 1934, becoming noted for his individual approach to portraiture (where he used often elaborate settings designed for the individual sitter) and for his use of photographic montage, collage and double-exposure to achieve surrealistic interpretation of character. In later years he applied his creativity to the field of pop music, but withdrew from professional photography after 1969.

MACBETH (c.1005–1057) king of Scotland from 1040, Mormaer of Moray and a grandson of **Malcolm II**. He married Gruoch, granddaughter of Kenneth II. In 1040 he defeated and killed King Duncan and drove Duncan's sons, Malcolm and Donald Bán, into exile. He seems to have represented a Celtic reaction against English influence and he ruled for over a decade. **Malcolm III, Canmore**, Duncan's son, ultimately defeated and killed him at Lumphanan, 15 August 1057. **Shakespeare** got his story from **Holinshed**, who drew on **Boece**.

MACBETH, Ann (1875–1948) English embroideress, born in Little Bolton. She studied at Glasgow School of Art (1897–1900) and was a member of its staff from 1901 to 1920, latterly as head of the embroidery department. She was influential in advocating new methods of teaching embroidery through lecturing, teaching and through several books, including an instruction manual called *Educational Needlecraft*. She executed a number of ecclesiastical commissions and her embroidered panels decorate many Glasgow interiors. She was a member of the famous 'Glasgow School' and received the Lauder Award in 1930.

McBEY, James (1883–1959) Scottish artist and etcher, born in Newburgh, Aberdeenshire. Entirely self-taught, he became particularly well known as a master of British etching. After working in a bank he left to become an artist, producing his first etching in 1902. He travelled extensively in the British Isles, Spain, Holland, North Africa, Central and North America and as a war artist in France and with the Australian Camel Patrol in Egypt and Palestine during World War I. His etched work has a spontaneity and strength almost unequalled in the history of British printmaking.

MacBRIDE, Maud, née **Gonne** (1865–1953) Irish nationalist, the daughter of an English colonel. She became an agitator for the cause of Irish independence, edited a nationalist newspaper, *L'Irlande libre*, in Paris, and married Major John MacBride, who fought against the British in the Boer War and was executed as a rebel in 1916. After his death she became an active Sinn Feiner in Ireland. **W B Yeats** dedicated poems to her. Her son Sean (1904–) was foreign minister of the Irish Republic from 1948 to 1951.

McBRIDE, Willie John, originally **William** (1940–) Irish rugby player, born in Toomebridge. A man of virtually one club, he began with Ballymena in 1962 and within 10 years had won 45 caps and gone on 4 Lions tours. Massively-built and 6ft 3in tall, he had won 63 caps and played in 17 Tests on five Lions tours by the time he retired from top-class rugby, when he subsequently became interested in the management of international teams.

MacBRYDE, Robert (1913–66) Scottish artist, born in Ayrshire. He worked in industry for five years before studying at the Glasgow School of Art, and later worked with **Robert Colquhoun**, painting brilliantly-coloured Cubist lifes, and, later, brooding Expressionist figures.

MACCABEES a celebrated Jewish family. The founder of the dynasty, **Mattathias**, a priest, was the first to make a stand against the persecutions of the Jewish nation and creed by **Antiochus IV Epiphanes**. He was the great-great-grandson of Hasmon and the family is often known as the 'Hasmoneans'. Mattathias and his five sons, Jochanan, Simon, Jehudah, Eleazer and Jonathan, together with a handful of faithful men, rose against the national enemy, destroyed heathen worship, and fled into the wilderness of Judah. Their number soon increased and they were able to make descents into various villages and cities, where they restored the ancient worship of Jehovah. At the death of Mattathias (166 BC) his son Jehudah or Judas, now called Makkabi (*Makkab*, 'hammerer'), or Maccabaeus, took the command of the patriots, and repulsed the enemy, reconquered Jerusalem, purified the Temple, and re-inaugurated the holy service (164). Having concluded an alliance with the Romans, he fell in battle (160). His brother Jonathan renewed the Roman alliance, acquired the dignity of high priest, but was treacherously slain by the Syrians. Simon, the second brother, completely re-established the independence of the nation (141), and 'Judah prospered as of old'. But he was murdered (135) by his son-in-law, **Ptolemy**.

MacCAIG, Norman Alexander (1910–) Scottish poet, born in Edinburgh, the son of a chemist. His mother was born in Scalpay, Harris, and, as he wrote in 'Return to Scalpay', 'Half my thought and half my blood is Scalpay'. A poet of town and country, his formative years were spent in Edinburgh where he was educated at the Royal High School and the university, where he read classics. He became a primary school teacher, for which his friend **Hugh MacDiarmid** pronounced he had ' a real vocation' and for nearly 40 years it engaged his daylight hours. His first two collections—*Far Cry* (1943) and *The Inward Eye* (1946)—tarred him as a member of the New Apocalypse school and the label stuck 'long after it was contravening the Trades Description Act'. He disowned these when the *Collected Poems* were published in 1985. *Riding Lights* (1955) is the first evidence of the real MacCaig, lucid, direct and richly descriptive. His distinctive voice, witty and philosophical, is to be heard in numerous subsequent collections including *The Sinai Sort* (1957), *A Round of Applause* (1962), *Measures* (1965), *A Man In My Position* (1969), *The White Bird* (1973), *The Equal Skies* (1980), *A World of Difference* (1963) and *Voice-Over* (1988). He was the first fellow in creative writing at Edinburgh University (1967–69), and on retiring from school teaching he lectured in English studies at Stirling University (1970–79). The finest Scottish poet of his generation writing in English, he was awarded the Queen's Gold Medal for Poetry in 1986.

MacCARTHY, Denis Florence (1817–82) Irish author, born in Dublin. He trained for the priesthood, but wrote poetry, translated **Calderón**, and published *Shelley's Early Life* (1872).

MacCARTHY, Sir Desmond (1878–1952) English writer and critic, born in Plymouth. Educated at Eton and Trinity College, Cambridge, he entered journalism and was successively editor of *New Quarterly* and *Eye Witness* (later *New Witness*). By 1913 he was writing for *The New Statesman*, of which he became literary editor in 1920, and later dramatic critic. He became editor of *Life and Letters*, book reviewer for *The Sunday Times*, and a broadcaster of repute. His criticism, collected in book form, is represented by *Portraits* (1931), *Experience* (1935), *Drama* (1940), *Humanities* (1954) and *Theatre* (1955).

McCARTHY, Joseph Raymond (1909–57) American politician and inquisitor, born in Grand Chute, Wisconsin. He studied at Marquette University, Milwaukee, and in 1939 was a state circuit judge. After war service in the Marines and as an air-gunner, he was elected senator in 1945, although as a serving judge his election was contrary to the Constitution. Defying a Supreme Court ruling, he took his seat in the senate and in 1950 was re-elected by a huge majority, having exploited the general uneasiness felt after the treason trials of Nunn May, **Fuchs** and **Alger Hiss** by accusing the State Department of harbouring 205 prominent communists, a charge that he was later incapable of substantiating before a special subcommittee on foreign relations. Undaunted, he accused the **Truman** administration of being 'soft on communism' and the Democratic party of a record of '20 years of treason'. After the **Eisenhower** victory, McCarthy, in January 1953, became chairman of the powerful Permanent Subcommittee on Investigations and by hectoring cross-examination, damaging innuendo, and 'guilt by association', arraigned a great number of mostly innocent citizens and officials, often with full television publicity, overreaching himself when he came into direct conflict with the army, which he accused of 'coddling communists'. Formally condemned by the senate, again controlled by the Democrats in 1954, for financial irregularities, he was stung into attacking President Eisenhower and so lost most of his remaining Republican support. Truman rightly described him as a 'pathological character assassin'.

McCARTHY, Justin (1830–1912) Irish politician, novelist and historian, born in Cork. He joined the staff of the *Northern Times*, Liverpool, in 1853, and in 1860 entered the reporters' gallery for the *Morning Star*, becoming its chief editor in 1864. He resigned in 1868, and devoted the next three years to a tour of the USA. Soon after his return he became connected with the *Daily News*, and contributed to the *London*, *Westminster* and *Fortnightly Reviews*. He entered parliament in 1879 for Longford. He is better known, however, as a novelist than as a politician. His novels include *Dear Lady Disdain* (1875) and *Miss Misanthrope* (1877). Other works include *A History of our Own Times* (7 vols, 1879–1905) and *The Four Georges and William IV* (4 vols, 1889–1901).

McCARTHY, Justin Huntly (1860–1935) Irish Nationalist, son of **Justin McCarthy**, and MP from 1884 to 1892. In 1894 he married the clever impersonator and actress, Cissie Loftus (1876–1943; born in Glasgow), who divorced him in 1899. He wrote stories, plays, verse, *England under Gladstone* (1884), *Ireland since the Union* (1887), *The French Revolution* (4 vols, 1890–98) and others.

McCARTHY, Mary Therese (1912–89) American novelist and critic, born in Seattle, Washington, of mixed Catholic, Protestant and Jewish descent. She and her three younger brothers were orphaned as young children in 1918 and they were raised by grandparents, uncles and aunts. At the age of eight she won a state prize for an article entitled 'The Irish in American History'. She was educated at Forest Ridge Convent, Seattle, and Anne Wright Seminary, Tacoma, and graduated from Vassar College, New York, in 1933. She married an actor, Harold Johnsrud, who died in a fire. She began to write book reviews for the *Nation* and the *New Republic* and in 1936–37 was an editor for *Covici Friede*; from 1937 to 1948 she was an editor and theatre critic for the *Partisan Review*, during which period she wrote articles, stories and eventually novels. In 1938 she married the critic **Edmund Wilson**, but they divorced soon afterwards. In 1948 she married Bowden Bowater, whom she divorced in 1961 to marry James West, an information officer. Her best known fiction is *The Company She Keeps* (1942), *The Groves of Academe* (1952), and *The Group* (1963), a bestseller about eight Vassar graduates and their sex lives. She also wrote documentary denunciations of US involvement in the Vietnam war, in *Vietnam* (1967) and *Hanoi* (1968). Other works include *A Charmed Life* (1955), *Sights and Spectacles* (1956), the autobiographical *Memories of a Catholic Childhood* (1957), and *Cannibals and Missionaries* (1979).

McCARTNEY, Paul See **BEATLES, The**

McCAY, Winsor Zezic (1867–1934) American cartoonist and film animator, born in Spring Lake, Michigan. His first newspaper illustrations were for the *Times-Star* (1893), and he created his first strip, *Tales of the Jungle Imps*, in 1903. He joined the *New York Herald* to make his first successful strip, *Dreams of a Rarebit Fiend* (1904), which was filmed by **Edison**. He drew under the pen-name 'Silas', but used his own name for the explosive *Little Sammy Sneeze* (1904) and his masterpiece, *Little Nemo in Slumberland* (1905), which owed its success to McCay's mastery of perspective. From 1909 he began experimenting in animation, his films including *Gertie the Dinosaur* (1914), and *The Sinking of the Lusitania* (1918), the first dramatic/documentary cartoon.

MACCHABEUS See **MACHABEUS, Johannes**

MACCHIAVELLI See **MACHIAVELLI**

McCLELLAN, George Brinton (1826–85) American soldier, born in Philadelphia. In the Civil War in 1861, as major-general in the US army, he drove the enemy out of West Virginia, and was called to Washington to reorganize the army of the Potomac. In November he was made commander-in-chief, but held the position for only five months. His Virginian campaign ended disastrously. He advanced near to Richmond, but was compelled to retreat, fighting the Seven Days' Battles (June 25 to July 1, 1862). After the disastrous second battle of Bull Run (August 29–30), followed by a Confederate invasion of Maryland, he reorganized the army at Washington, marched north, met **Lee** at Antietam, and compelled him to recross the Potomac. He followed the Confederates into Virginia, but too slowly and cautiously for **Lincoln**, who replaced him with **Burnside**. In 1864, as Democratic candidate for the presidency, he was defeated by Lincoln, and in 1878 was elected governor of New Jersey.

McCLINTOCK, Barbara (1902–) American geneticist and biologist, winner of the 1983 Nobel prize for physiology or medicine. She studied at Cornell, and worked at the Carnegie Institution laboratory in Cold Spring Harbor, New York, where her researches on the genetics of maize led her to the novel idea that some genes can control other genes, and can move on the chromosome. Strangely, these important ideas were largely neglected for many years.

McCLINTOCK, Sir Francis Leopold (1819–1907) Irish naval officer and polar explorer, born in Dundalk, Ireland. He entered the navy in 1831, and took part in several expeditions to search for Sir **John Franklin**. He was promoted admiral in 1887.

McCLURE, Sir Robert John le Mesurier (1807–73) Irish explorer, born in Wexford, Ireland. He entered the navy in 1824, and served in Sir **George Back**'s Arctic expedition in 1836, and Sir **John Ross**'s Franklin expedition in 1848. As commander of a ship in another Franklin expedition (1850–54) he penetrated eastwards to the north coast of Banks Land. He received a parliamentary award for the discovery of the Northwest Passage which is now credited to Sir **John Franklin**. After serving in Chinese waters he died, an admiral.

MacCOLL, Dugald Sutherland (1859–1948) Scottish painter and art historian, born in Glasgow. He studied at London and Oxford, and after travelling Europe studying works of art he established a reputation as a critic and brought out his *Nineteenth Century Art* in 1902. As keeper of the Tate Gallery (1906–11) and of the Wallace Collection (1911–24) he instituted many reforms and improvements. He wrote *Confessions of a Keeper* (1931).

MacCOLL, Ewan, originally **James Miller** (1915–89) Scottish folk-singer, composer, collector, author, playwright and socialist, born in Salford, Lancashire. As a playwright, he collaborated with **Joan Littlewood** in forming the experimental Theatre Workshop in the 1940s and played an important role in reviving street theatre, but later became one of the most influential pioneers of the British folk-music revival. His series of 'Radio Ballads', begun in 1957, combining contemporary social comment with traditional musical forms, had a powerful influence on songwriting and performing in subsequent decades. As a collector of traditional folk-song, he has published several anthologies. Among his own compositions are 'The Shoals of Herring', 'Dirty Old Town', 'Freeborn Man' and 'The First Time Ever I Saw Your Face'.

McCOLLUM, Elmer Verner (1879–1967) American biochemist, born in Fort Scott, Kansas. He studied at Yale and was professor of biochemistry at Johns Hopkins, Baltimore, from 1917 to 1944. In 1913 he showed that more than one vitamin was necessary for normal animal growth, classifying them as vitamins A (fat-soluble), B (water-soluble), and in 1920 adding the rickets-preventative factor, D. McCollum's A, B, and D were later shown to consist of separable constituents (eg A_1 and A_2), and other groups (eg vitamin K_1 and K_2) also became known. His book *Newer Knowledge of Nutrition* (1918) was a standard text for some years, and he also wrote *A History of Nutrition* (1957).

McCORMACK, John Francis (1884–1945) Irish-born American tenor, born in Athlone. He studied in Milan, made his London début in 1905, and was engaged for Covent Garden opera for the 1905–06 season, appearing also in oratorio and as a lieder singer. As an Irish nationalist, he did not appear in England during World War I, but took American citizenship in 1919, and turned to popular sentimental songs. He was raised to the papal peerage as a count in 1928.

McCORMICK, Cyrus Hall (1809–84) American inventor and industrialist, born in Rockbridge, Virginia. He was the son of Robert McCormick (1780–1846) who patented several agricultural implements but abandoned in 1831 an attempt to build a mechanical reaper. Cyrus took up the challenge and within a short time was successful, though he did not patent his machine until 1834, the year after the reaper invented by **Obed Hussey** had been patented. American agriculture had entered a period of rapid expansion, and there was intense competition between the two men and with other manufacturers, but in the end the McCormick Harvesting Machine Company emerged as the leader. In 1902 it became the International Harvester Company, with his son Cyrus Hall Jun. (1859–1936) as first president and chairman of the board.

MacCORMICK, John MacDonald (1904–61) Scottish nationalist politician, born in Glasgow. A graduate of Glasgow University, he became active in the Scottish movement for self-government initially through the Independent Labour party, and, from its foundation, in the National Party of Scotland (1928). He was chairman of the Scottish National party from its foundation in 1934 until 1942 when the party refused his request that it seek all-party support for independence and cease fighting elections. He thereupon founded and became chairman of the Scottish Convention, and chairman of the National Assembly, organizing the Scottish Covenant in 1949 which ultimately attracted two million signatures but achieved nothing. He wrote *The Flag in the Wind* (1955).

McCOSH, James (1811–94) Scottish philosopher, born in Carskeoch, Ayrshire. He became a minister of the Church of Scotland at Arbroath and Brechin and later of the Free Church. He went on to take the chair of logic at Queen's College, Belfast, in 1851, and became president of Princeton in 1868 (where he gave his name to the building which now houses the English department). His main publication was *Intuitions of the Mind* (1860), defending the 'Common Sense' philosophy of the Scottish school of **Thomas Reid** and **Dugald Stewart**.

McCRACKEN, Esther Helen, née **Armstrong** (1902–71) English playwright and actress, born in Newcastle-upon-Tyne. From 1924 to 1937 she acted with the Newcastle Repertory Company. Her first play, *The Willing Spirit*, was produced in 1936, but it was with *Quiet Wedding* (1938) that her reputation was made as a writer of domestic comedy. Other successes were *Quiet Weekend* (1941) and *No Medals* (1944). Her first husband, Lt-Col Angus McCracken, died in action in 1943, and the following year she married Mungo Campbell.

McCRACKEN, James (1927–88) American singer, born in Gary, Indiana, the son of a fireman. He became one of the Metropolitan Opera's leading tenors, and was internationally acclaimed in the 1960s for his passionate performances of the title role in **Verdi**'s *Otello*. He started life as a steelworker, but his potential as a singer was spotted during service with the US navy. A large, powerfully-built man with an electrifying stage presence, he made his operatic debut as Rodolfo in **Puccini**'s *La Bohème* in 1952, but his Otello, first performed in Europe in 1959, marked a turning point in his career. In 1963 he returned to America to become the first native American to sing Otello at the Met. He wrote about his operatic experience with his wife (the mezzo soprano Sandra Warfield) in *A Star in the Family* (1971).

MacCREADY, Paul (1925–) American aeronautical engineer and inventor, designer of the ultra-light aircraft *Gossamer Condor* which in 1977 made the first man-powered flight over a one-mile course. Its successor, *Gossamer Albatross*, in 1979 crossed the 23 miles of the English Channel in just under three hours at a height of only a few feet, propelled and piloted by an American racing cyclist, Bryan Allen. In 1981 his *Solar Challenger* flew from Paris to London at an average speed of 37 mph, powered by 16000 solar cells; and in 1985 he built a powered reproduction of a pterodactyl.

McCRIE, Thomas (1772–1835) Scottish historian and divine, born in Duns, Berwickshire. He studied for the ministry at Edinburgh and became an 'Auld Lichts' minister there. He was the author of Lives of **John Knox** (1812) and **Andrew Melville** (1819) and of a *History of the Reformation in Spain* (1829). His son, Thomas (1798–1875), professor in the Presbyterian college at London, was the author of *Sketches of Scottish Church History* (1841) and *Annals of English Presbytery* (1872).

MacCRIMMON a Skye family, hereditary pipers to Macleod of Dunvegan, the greatest of whom was Patrick Mor (fl. 1650).

McCUBBIN, Frederick (1855–1917) Australian landscape painter, born in Melbourne, Victoria, where he lived and worked for most of his life. A part-time artist, working in his father's bakery until 1877, he became teacher of drawing at the National Gallery of Victoria's Art School in 1886, a position which he held until his death, exercising a strong but kindly influence on his pupils. The previous year, with other painters including **Tom Roberts**, he had established the first of the artist camps which grew into the 'Heidelberg school' of Australian painting. From his romantic depictions of bush life McCubbin turned to an Impressionistic style, and he exhibited in London and Paris in 1897. Although principally known for his landscapes, he also executed many successful portraits during his later years.

McCULLERS, (Lula) Carson, née **Smith** (1917–67) American novelist, born in Columbus, Georgia, where she was brought up and attended high school, graduating in 1933. Between 1934 and 1936 she went to classes at Columbia University, New York, and New York University. In 1937 she married Reeves McCullers, with whom she moved to Charlotte, North Carolina; in 1941 they moved to Greenwich Village and divorced, but were re-married in 1945, finally divorcing again in 1948. *The Heart is a Lonely Hunter*, her first book, about a deaf mute, appeared in 1940, distinguishing her immediately as a novelist of note. She wrote the best and the bulk of her work in a six-year burst through World War II. Along with **William Faulkner**, **Tennessee Williams** and **Truman Capote** she is credited with fashioning a type of fiction labelled by critics as Southern Gothic. Fusing, in her own words, 'anguish and farce', she peopled her work with grotesque characters who are expressionistic extensions of normal, universal human problems. *Reflections in a Golden Eye* appeared in 1941, followed by *The Member of the Wedding* (1946), *The Ballad of the Sad Cafe* (1951), and *Clock Without Hands*, a last ironic look at the South in 1961. In her latter years she was confined to a wheelchair.

McCULLOCH, John Ramsay (1789–1864) political economist, born in Whithorn. He edited *The Scotsman* (1818–19), and for 20 years provided most of the articles on economics in the *Edinburgh Review*. He lectured in London and in 1828 became professor of political economy in University College, and in 1838 comptroller of Her Majesty's Stationery Office. He wrote books on economics and commerce.

MacCUNN, Hamish (1868–1916) Scottish composer, born in Greenock. He studied at the Royal College of Music, and in 1888–94 was professor of harmony at the Royal Academy of Music. His works, largely Scottish in character and subject, include the overtures *Cior Mhor* (1887), *Land of the Mountain and the Flood* and *The Dowie Dens of Yarrow*, choral works, such as *The Lay of the Last Minstrel*, the operas *Jeanie Deans* (1894) and *Diarmid* (1897), and songs.

MACDIARMADA, Seán (ie **John MacDermott**) (1884–1916) Irish revolutionary, born in Kiltyclogher, County Leitrim. He worked as barman and tram-conductor in Glasgow and Belfast, where he became involved in the Ancient Order of Hibernians, participated in the Sinn Féin by-election defeat in 1908, but had already entered the moribund Irish Republican Brotherhood which he now regalvanized as agent for **Thomas J Clarke**. Appointed IRB organizer, he honeycombed the Gaelic Athletic Association, the Gaelic League, and later the Irish Volunteers with his agents, and edited the IRB paper *Irish Freedom*. Crippled by polio in 1912, his intransigence increased, and he ensured the hijack of the **MacNeill** wing of the Irish Volunteers in an ultimate insurrection which by deception of MacNeill was achieved in Easter 1916. He was afterwards court-martialled and shot.

MacDIARMID, Hugh, pen-name of **Christopher Murray Grieve** (1892–1978) Scottish poet, pioneer of the Scottish literary renaissance, born in Langholm, Dumfriesshire. Educated at Langholm Academy, he became a pupil-teacher at Broughton Higher Grade School in Edinburgh before turning to journalism. He served with the Royal Army Medical Corps in Greece and France during World War I and was a munitions worker in World War II. After World War I he married Peggy Skinner and settled as a journalist in Montrose, where he also became a town councillor (1922), and edited anthologies of contemporary Scottish writing, like *Northern Numbers* (1920–22) and *The Scottish Chapbook* (1922–23), in which he published his own early poetry. Beginning with such outstanding early lyrical verse as *Sangschaw* (1925) and *Penny Wheep* (1926), he established himself as the leader of a vigorous Scottish Renaissance by *A Drunk Man Looks at the Thistle* (1926), full of political, metaphysical and nationalistic reflections on the Scottish predicament. In his later works, however, this master of polemic, or 'flyting', increasingly allowed his poetical genius to be overburdened by philosophical gleanings in the service of a customized form of communism. Nevertheless items such as 'The Seamless Garment', 'Cattle Shaw' and 'At Lenin's Tomb' raise these later works to a very high level. Other works include *To Circumjack Cencrastus* (1930), the two *Hymns to Lenin* (1930; 1935), *Scots Unbound* (1932), *Stony Limits* (1934), *A Kist o' Whistles* (1947) and *In Memorian James Joyce* (1955). His numerous essays such as *Albyn* (1927) and *The Islands of Scotland* (1939) suffer from the same intellectual scrapbook tendency. Founder-member of the Scottish National party, and an active communist intermittently, he stood as a communist candidate in 1963. He dedicated his life to the regeneration of the Scottish literary language, repudiated by his fellow Scottish poet, **Edwin Muir**, in 1936. He brilliantly succeeded by employing a vocabulary drawn from all regions and periods, intellectualizing a previously parochial tradition. In 1931 he met his second wife, Valda Trevelin, and in 1933 went into self-imposed exile on the island of Whalsay, in Shetland. After World War II he lived in a cottage at Brownsbank, near Biggar. His autobiography was published in *Lucky Poet* (1943), and *The Company I've Kept* (1966).

MacDONAGH, Donagh (1912–68) Irish dramatist, born in Dublin, the son of **Thomas MacDonagh**. Orphaned by his father's execution in 1916 and the drowning of his mother in an attempt to plant the tricolour on an island in Dublin Bay in 1917, he was educated at Belvedere College and University College, Dublin, became a barrister in 1935 and was made a district justice in 1941. A hunchback, he won success as a writer of the exuberant *Happy as Larry* (1946), and other plays such as *God's Gentry* (1951, a study of tinker life) and *Step-in-the-Hollow* (1957). He was a highly acclaimed broadcaster, and edited with Lennox Robinson *The Oxford Book of Irish Verse* (1958), which drew criticism for its loose interpretation of Irishness. He published poems, *The Hungry Grass* (1947) and *A Warning to Conquerors* (1968), and a perceptive essay on his father, placing him in the context of the European intellectual death-wish in World War I.

MacDONAGH, Thomas (1878–1916) Irish poet, critic and nationalist, born to a schoolteaching family in Cloughjordan, County Tipperary. He went to Dublin, where he helped **P H Pearse** to found St Enda's College (1908), and published delicate and sardonic poems, original works and translations from the Irish. In 1914 he founded the Irish Theatre with Joseph Plunkett and Edward Martyn. He was also an outstanding critic of English literature, and his aspirations for Irish literature derived from his deep love of English and his recognition of comparable possibilities, as may be seen by his *Literature in Ireland* and *Thomas Campion* and by his articles in the *Irish Review*. He took part in the Irish Volunteers, was very belatedly drawn into preparations for the Easter Rising of 1916, commanded at Jacob's Factory in the fighting, and was executed. The poet **James Stephens** impressively introduced his *Poetical Works* after his death, and **Yeats** wrote his epitaph in 'Easter 1916'.

MacDONALD, Dwight (1906–82) American writer and film critic, born in New York City. While still a student at Yale he became a literary editor and while working for *Fortune* (1929–36), the business magazine, was a Trotskyite. A penetrating social and political commentator, he wrote regularly for *Partisan Review*. From 1951 to 1971 he was a staff writer for the *New Yorker* and was film critic for *Esquire* (1960–66). His essays were collected in several books, including *The Memoirs of a Revolutionist* (1957), *Against the American Grain* (1963) and *Discriminations: Essays and Afterthoughts* (1974).

MacDONALD, Elaine (1943–) Scottish dancer, born in Tadcaster. She trained at the Royal Ballet School, joining Western Ballet Theatre in 1964 and moving with the company to Glasgow when it became Scottish Ballet in the late 1960s. Though her career has been limited by a total loyalty to this company, she became a dancer of international standard and created many roles for the choreographer/director Peter Darrell including *Sun Into Darkness* (1966), *Beauty and Beast* (1969), *Tales of Hoffman* (1972), *Mary Queen of Scots* (1976) and *Five Ruckert Songs* (1978). She was made artistic controller of the company in 1988, and left the company to teach in 1989.

MACDONALD, Flora (1722–90) Scottish Jacobite heroine, born in South Uist in the Hebrides. She lost her father, a tacksman, at the age of 2; and at 13 was adopted by Lady Clanranald, wife of the chief of the clan. After the battle of Culloden (1746) which finally broke the 1745 Jacobite Rising, she conducted the Young Pretender, **Charles Edward Stewart**, disguised as her maid 'Betty Burke', from Benbecula to Portree. For this perilous feat she was much fêted during her year's captivity on the troopship in Leith Roads and at London. In 1750 she married the son of Macdonald of Kingsburgh, where in 1773 she entertained Dr **Johnson**. In 1774 her husband emigrated to North Carolina, and in 1776 in the War of Independence became a brigadier-general. He was made prisoner and Flora returned to Scotland in 1779. After two years she was rejoined by her husband, and they settled again at Kingsburgh.

MACDONALD, Frances See **MACKINTOSH, Margaret**

MACDONALD, George (1824–1905) Scottish poet and novelist, born in Huntly, Aberdeenshire, the son of a farmer. He was educated at King's College, Aberdeen, and Highbury Theological College. He became a Congregationalist pastor at Arundel and at Manchester, but ill-health drove him to literature in 1855, and he became a professor at Bedford College, London. He wrote poetry, including 'Within and Without' (1856) and *Poems* (1857), and novels such as the allegorical *Phantastes* (1858), *David Elginbrod* (1863) and *Lilith* (1895), but is now best known for his children's books, among them *At the Back of the North Wind* (1871), *The Princess and the Goblin* (1872) and *The Princess and Curdie* (1888).

MACDONALD, Jacques Étienne Joseph Alexandre, Duc de Tarrente (1765–1840) French soldier, born in Sedan, the son of a Scottish Jacobite schoolmaster. He entered the army in 1785, distinguished himself in the cause of the Revolution, and rapidly rose to high rank. In 1798 he was made governor of Rome, and subjugated Naples. **Suvorov** defeated him after a bloody contest on the Trebbia (1799). In 1805 he lost the favour of **Napoleon**; but, restored to command in 1809, he took Laibach (now Ljubljana), distinguished himself at Wagram, and was created marshal and Duc de Tarrente (Taranto). He held a command in Spain in 1810, and in the Russian campaign; and in 1813 he contributed to the successes of Lützen and Bautzen, but was routed by **Blücher** at the Katzbach. After Leipzig he helped to cover the French retreat. The Bourbons made him a peer, and from 1816 he was chancellor of the Legion of Honour.

MACDONALD, James Ramsay (1866–1937) Scottish politician, and first British Labour prime minister, born in Lossiemouth. Educated at a board school, he wrote on socialism and other problems. He was a leading member of the Independent Labour Party (1893–1930) and was secretary (1900–11) and leader (1911–14, 1922–31) of the Labour party. A member of the LCC (1901–04) and of parliament from 1906, he became leader of the opposition in 1922, and from January to November 1924 was prime minister and foreign secetary of the first Labour government in Britain—a minority government at the mercy of the Liberals. The election of 1924 put him out of office; that of 1929 brought him in again; but he met the financial crisis of 1931 by forming a predominantly Conservative 'National' government, the bulk of his party opposing; and in 1931 reconstructed it after a general election. From 1935 to 1937 he was lord president.

MACDONALD, Sir John Alexander (1815–91) Scottish-born Canadian statesman, born in Glasgow. He emigrated with his parents in 1820. He was called to the bar in 1836 and appointed QC. Entering politics he became leader of the Conservatives and premier in 1856, and in 1867 formed the first government for the new Dominion, Minister of justice and attorney-general of Canada until 1873, he was again in power from 1878 till his death in Ottawa. He was instrumental in bringing about the confederation of Canada and in securing the construction of the intercolonial and Pacific railways.

MACDONALD, Malcolm (1901–81) Scottish administrator, son of **James Ramsay Macdonald**, born in Lossiemouth. He studied at Oxford, was National government MP (1936–45) and held several ministerial appointments, including those of colonial secretary

(1935; 1938–40) and minister of health (1940–41). He was commissioner in Canada (1941–46), governor-general of Malaya and Borneo (1946–48), commissioner-general in South East Asia (1948–55), high commissioner in India (1955–60), governor-general (1963–64) and high commissioner (1964–65) in Kenya, and special representative in east and central Africa 1965–70. His books include *Borneo People* (1956) and *Angkor* (1958), and several on ornithology.

MACDONALD, Margaret See **MACKINTOSH, Margaret**

MacDONALD, Ross, pseud of **Kenneth Millar** (1915–83) Canadian-born American thriller writer, born in Los Gatos, California, of Canadian parentage, and raised in Ontario. He was educated at the University of Western Ontario (PhD), and became a college teacher. From the 1950s he lived in southern California. One of the finest writers in the genre, his Lew Archer series, a chip off **Chandler** and **Hammett**'s block, is sustained by tough and witty dialogue and rare intelligence. Immensely popular yet academically acceptable, many of his novels have been hijacked by Hollywood. Durable titles are *The Moving Target* (1949), *The Drowning Pool* (1950), *The Barbarous Coast* (1956), *The Galton Case* (1959), *The Underground Man* (1971) and *The Blue Hammer* (1976). He also wrote as John MacDonald and John Ross MacDonald.

MACDONELL, Alastair Ruadh (c.1724–1761) Scottish Jacobite, from Glengarry. He joined the French Scots brigade in 1743 and was sent to Scotland to support the 1745 Jacobite Rebellion, but was captured and imprisoned in the Tower of London (1745–47). He succeeded his father in 1754 as 13th chief of Glengarry, and became known as 'one of the best men in the Highlands', but **Andrew Lang** proved that he had become a government spy on his fellow Jacobites, in *Pickle the Spy* (1897).

McDONNELL, James Smith (1899–1980) American aircraft manufacturer and pioneer in space technology, born in Denver, Colorado. Graduating from Princeton in 1921, he took a master's degree in aeronautical engineering at the Massachusetts Institute of Technology (MIT) in 1925. He had a varied career as test pilot, stress analyst and chief engineer to several US companies, setting up his own company in 1928. By 1938 he had organized the McDonnell Aircraft Corporation and embarked on a series of successful military and naval aircraft, including the Banshee, Demon, Voodoo, and the famous F-4 Phantom, of which over 5000 were built. He took his company into space technology and constructed the Mercury and Gemini manned satellite capsules.

McDOUGALL, William (1871–1938) English-born American psychologist, born in Chadderton, Lancashire. After studying at Weimar, Manchester and Cambridge, he trained in medicine at St Thomas's Hospital, and in 1898 accompanied an anthropological expedition to the Torres Strait. He held academic posts at both Oxford and Cambridge, and in 1920 went to Harvard as professor of psychology. In 1927 he transferred to Duke University, North Carolina, where he conducted experiments in parapsychology. He preached purposive psychology as opposed to behaviourism and his chief works are *Physiological Psychology* (1905), *Body and Mind* (1911), *Outlines of Psychology* (1923), and *The Energies of Man* (1933).

MacDOWELL, Edward Alexander (1861–1908) American composer and pianist, born in New York. He studied in Paris, Wiesbaden and Frankfurt, and in 1881 was appointed head teacher of pianoforte at Darmstadt conservatory. At the invitation of **Liszt**, he played his First Piano Concerto in Zürich in 1882. He returned to the USA in 1888, and was head of the newly organized department of music at Columbia University from 1896 to 1904, when he suffered a mental breakdown. He composed extensively for orchestra, voices and piano, and is best remembered for some of his small-scale piano pieces, such as *Woodland Sketches* and *Sea Pieces*.

McENROE, John Patrick (1959–) American tennis player, born in Wiesbaden, West Germany. A left-hander, he won four US Open singles titles and three Wimbledon singles titles, and was also an invaluable member of the American Davis Cup team between 1978 and 1985. His incessant search for perfection led to fierce emotional outbursts on court and frequent wrangling with umpires. While still only in his late 20s he made a partial withdrawal from top-class tennis.

McEWEN, Sir John Blackwood (1868–1948) Scottish composer, born in Hawick. He taught music in Glasgow, and was principal of the Royal College of Music in London, 1924–36.

MacEWEN, Sir William (1848–1924) Scottish neurosurgeon, born and educated in Glasgow, where he worked throughout his life. His interest in surgery was stimulated by **Joseph Lister**, then Regius professor of surgery at Glasgow University. He adopted and then extended Lister's antiseptic surgical techniques and pioneered operations on the brain for tumours, abscesses and trauma. In addition, he operated on bones, introducing methods of implanting small grafts to replace missing portions of bones in the limbs. In 1892 he was appointed to the chair which Lister had held when MacEwen was a student.

McGEE, Thomas D'Arcy (1825–68) Irish-born Canadian writer and politician, born in Carlingford, County Louth. Educated at a Catholic 'hedge school', he was influenced by the mass movements of the Rev **Theobald Mathew** and **Daniel O'Connell** against drink and the Union. In 1842 he left for Quebec and Boston, where he worked on the local Catholic *Boston Pilot*. He became its editor at the age of 19, wrote fiction and supported a variety of romantic causes, returning to Ireland in 1845 where he was identified with the Young Ireland *Nation*. After the abortive rebellion of 1848 he returned to the USA, where he argued for US annexation of Canada in his New York *Nation*. He lost Catholic ecclesiastical support by sympathy for **Mazzini**'s anti-Papal Roman Republic, and started the *American Celt* in Boston, publishing high-flown Romantic poems and *A History of the Irish settlers in North America* (1851). He moved to Montreal in 1857, founded the *New Era* newspaper, took Canadian citizenship and became an MP in 1858, and was minister of agriculture (1864–68). He was a strong advocate of Canadian Confederation. He was assassinated in Ottawa for his opposition to a threatened Fenian invasion of Canada. His literary work as poet, publicist and political thinker improved as he aged; his published works included *A Popular History of Ireland* (1862–69) and *Poems* (1869).

McGILL, Donald, originally **Fraser Gould** (1875–1962) English comic postcard artist, born in Blackheath, considered the genius of this red-nosed art form. A junior to a naval architect, he studied cartooning with **John Hassall**'s correspondence course. In 1905 he drew his first comic card for Asher's Pictorial Postcards, for whom one popular card sold two million copies (McGill received six shillings). Famous for his outsize women in bathing costumes, paddling alongside weedy henpecked husbands, and for the double meanings in his captions, he did not receive critical attention until **George Orwell**'s *Horizon* article (1941). He is estimated to have drawn 500 cards a year for 50 years.

McGILL, James (1744–1813) Scots-born Canadian entrepreneur and philanthropist, born in Glasgow. He emigrated to Canada in the 1770s, and made a fortune in the northwest fur trade and in Montreal. He bequeathed land and money to found McGill College, Montreal, which became McGill University in 1821.

MacGILL, Patrick (1890–1963) Irish navvy, novelist and poet, born in the Glenties, County Donegal. Sold into servitude by his farming parents, he escaped to go to Scotland, working as a farm-labourer and a navvy. He wrote verses, hawked them round, attracted the attention of patrons and worked on the London *Daily Express* before being adopted as secretary by Canon **John Dalton** of Windsor. Eventually this resulted in his brilliant, naturalistic semi-autobiographical novel of migrant navvy life, *Children of the Dead End* (1914), to be followed by a powerful feminist parallel narrative of the forcing of female Irish labour into prostitution, *The Rat-Pit* (1915). MacGill volunteered when war broke out, gave a kaleidoscopic account of the troops before embarkation (*The Amateur Army*), and followed it up well with *The Red Horizon* and *The Great Push*, describing action in France in which he was wounded. He returned to Ireland as a theme with *Glenmornan*, an anti-clerical but self-excoriating novel of his native parish, the comedy of economic adventures *Lanty Hanlon*, the study of the impact of Sinn Féin, *Maureen*, and a somewhat romanticized return to navvy-land, *Moleskin Joe*, while *Black Bonar* looked at the self-made petty capitalist more savagely. MacGill married Margaret Gibbons (who published charming stories as Mrs Patrick MacGill), and went to the USA in 1930, where he declined into poverty and developed multiple sclerosis.

MACGILL-EAIN, Somhairle, or **MacLean, Sorley** (1911–) Scottish Gaelic poet, born on the island of Raasay, off Skye. He attended Raasay school and Portree High School on Skye before reading English at Edinburgh University (1929–33). He began to write while a student, and by the end of the 1930s was already an established figure on the Scottish literary scene. In 1940 he published *Seventeen Poems for Sixpence* which he produced with **Robert Garioch**, and in 1943, after his recovery from wounds sustained on active service at El Alamein, came *Dàin do Eimhir* (*Poems to Eimhir*), which contained, among other shorter poems, many of his love lyrics addressed to the legendary Eimhir of the early Irish sagas. Influenced by the metaphysical poets as well as the ancient and later Celtic literature and traditional Gaelic song, he reinvigorated the Gaelic literary language and tradition, creating a medium capable of expressing contemporary intellectual challenge, much as his friend **Hugh MacDiarmid** was reinstating Scots as a serious literary language. A teacher and headmaster until his retirement in 1972, his major collection of poems, *Reothairt is Contraigh* (*Spring tide and Neap tide*), appeared in 1977. His work has been translated and issued in bilingual editions, and reached a wide and appreciative public all over the world.

MacGILLIVRAY, James Pittendrigh (1856–1938) Scottish sculptor and poet, born in Inverurie, Aberdeenshire, the son of a sculptor. He studied under William Brodie and John Mossman. His major sculptures included the huge statue of **Robert Burns** in Irvine, the Scottish National Memorial to **Gladstone** in St Andrew's Square, Edinburgh, the great statue to the third Marquess of Bute in Cardiff, the **Byron** statue in Aberdeen, and the **John Knox** statue in St Giles's Cathedral, Edinburgh. His publications of note were verse (*Pro Patria*, 1915, and *Bog Myrtle and Peat Reek*, 1922) and various papers of professional significance. He was appointed the King's Sculptor in Ordinary for Scotland in 1921.

McGLEW, Derrick John (1929–) South African cricketer, born in Natal. A dour opening batsman, he scored seven Test centuries, including the second slowest ever, taking 545 minutes to reach his hundred against Australia at Durban in 1957–58. His adhesive technique and surname inevitably earned him the nickname of 'Sticky'.

McGONAGALL, William (1830–1902) Scottish poet and novelist, son of an immigrant Irish weaver. He spent some of his childhood on the island of South Ronaldsay in the Orkneys, settled with his family in Dundee at the age of eleven, and became a handloom weaver with his father. In 1846 he married Jean King. He did some acting at Dundee's Royal Theatre, and in 1878 published his first collection of poems, including 'Railway Bridge of the Silvery Tay'. From then on he travelled in central Scotland, giving readings and selling his poetry in broadsheets. In Edinburgh he was lionized by the legal and student fraternity. He visited London in 1880 and New York in 1887. His poems are uniformly bad, but possess a disarming naïveté and a calypso-like disregard for metre which still never fail to entertain. His *Poetic Gems* were published in 1890, and *More Poetic Gems* in 1962), followed by others.

McGOVERN, George Stanley (1922–) American Democrat politician, born the son of a methodist minister in Avon, South Dakota. After service with the USAAF in World War II, he became a professor of history and government at Dakota Wesleyan University, member of the House of Representatives (1956–61) and senator for South Dakota (from 1963). In July 1972, following a campaign expounding his new radicalism, he was chosen as Democratic candidate to oppose **Nixon** in the presidential election but was heavily defeated.

MACGREGOR, Douglas (?1906–1964) American industrial psychologist. He obtained a doctorate in psychology at Harvard University (1935) and taught there for several years (1935–37) before moving to the Massachusetts Institute of Technology (MIT), where he helped set up an Industrial Relations section in 1937. He was later president of Antioch College (1948–54), and then returned to MIT to become the first Sloan Fellows professor (1962). His highly regarded book *The Human Side of Enterprise* (1960) discussed two contrasting theories of motivation at work, which he called 'Theory X and Theory Y'. His book *The Professional Manager* was published posthumously and unfinished in 1969.

McGREGOR, Ian Kinloch (1912–) Scots-born American business executive, born in Kinlochleven. Educated at Glasgow University and the Royal College of Science and Technology (now Strathclyde University), he went to the USA in 1941, when he was seconded to work with the US army. He developed his career in business in the USA, but in 1977 he returned to the United Kingdom as deputy chairman of British Leyland, working with Sir **Michael Edwardes**. In 1980 he was appointed chairman of the British Steel Corporation, and then became chairman of the National Coal Board from 1983 to 1986. Both industries required drastic 'cut-backs' to survive; he faced strong trade union opposition, particularly from the miners in 1984–85.

MacGREGOR, John (1825–92) English writer and traveller, born in Gravesend. He was educated at Trinity College, Cambridge. He travelled widely in Europe, the Middle East and Russia, but is best remembered as the pioneer and popularizer of canoeing in Britain and designer of the 'Rob Roy' type canoe. His travel books include *A Thousand Miles in a Rob Roy Canoe* (1866).

MACGREGOR, Robert See **ROB ROY**

MACH, Ernst (1838–1916) Austrian physicist and philosopher, born in Turas, Moravia. He studied at Vienna University, and became professor of mathematics at Graz in 1864, of physics at Prague in 1867, and of physics again at Vienna in 1895. He carried out much experimental work on supersonic projectiles and on the flow of gases, obtaining some remarkable early photographs of shock waves and gas jets. His findings have proved of great importance in aeronautical design and the science of projectiles, and his name has been given to the ratio of the speed of flow of a gas to the speed of sound (Mach number) and to the angle of a shock wave to the direction of motion (Mach angle). In the field of epistemology he was determined to abolish idle metaphysical speculation. His writings greatly incluenced **Albert Einstein** and laid the foundations of logical positivism. He wrote *Mechanik in ihrer Entwickelung* (1883, trans 1902) and *Beiträzur Analyse der Empfindung* (Contributions to the analysis of Sensation, 1897).

MACHABEUS, Johannes (d.1557) Scottish reformer, one of the clan Macalpine. He was Dominican prior in Perth 1532–34, then fled as a heretic to England, married, went on to Germany, and from 1542 was professor of theology at Copenhagen till his death.

MACHADO, Antonio (1875–1939) Spanish writer, born in Seville. He wrote lyrics characterized by a nostalgic melancholy, among them *Soledades, Galerías y otros poemas* (1907) and *Campos de Castilla* (1912). His brother **Manuel** (1874–1947), also a poet, collaborated with him on several plays.

MACHAR, Josef Svatopluk (1864–1942) Czech poet. A bank official in Vienna, he was the author of satirical and political verse, known for the trilogy *Confiteor* (1887), the verse romance *Magdalena* (1893), and the epic *Warriors of God* (1897).

MACHAUT, Guillaume de See **GUILLAUME DE MACHAUT**

MACHEL, Samora Moises (1933–86) Mozambique politician. His education at a Roman Catholic mission school was cut short by the need to earn a living when his elder brother was killed in a mining accident in South Africa. He worked as a hospital nurse, rising to a senior position. In 1963 he joined the independence movement, Frelimo (Front for the Liberation of Mozambique), and became leader of the Frelimo troops waging war against the Portuguese power. When independence was achieved in 1975 he became Mozambique's first president. He died in a plane crash near the South African border in 1986.

MACHIAVELLI, Niccolò (1469–1527) Italian statesman, writer and political philosopher. He was born in Florence, but nothing much is known of his early life. In 1498, **Savonarola**'s régime in Florence was overthrown, and despite his lack of political experience Machiavelli was among those who rapidly rose to power. He was appointed head of the Second Chancery and secretary to the Council of Ten (the main foreign relations committee in the republic). He served on a variety of diplomatic missions over the next 14 years and met many important political leaders including **Louis XII** of France, **Cesare Borgia**, Pope **Julius II** and the emperor **Maximilian I**. His reports and correspondence demonstrate a shrewd appraisal of people and events and enabled him to try out ideas he was later to develop in his political works. In 1512 the Holy League of Pope Julius with **Ferdinand** of Spain turned against Florence; the **Medici** family, in exile since 1494, returned to run the city and the republic was dissolved. Machiavelli was dismissed from his post (the reasons are unclear) and in 1513 suffered the further disaster of arrest on the charge of conspiracy against the new régime. He was tortured, and although soon released and pardoned, was obliged to withdraw from public life and devote himself to writing. To console himself, as he explained in a famous letter to his friend Francesco Vettori, he studied ancient history, pondered the lessons to be learned from his experiences in government service, and drafted 'a little book' on the subject. That was his masterpiece, *The Prince* (not published until 1532). It was intended to be a handbook for rulers, advising them what to do and what to say to achieve political success, and its main theme is that rulers must always be prepared to do evil if they judge good will come of it. Machiavelli's admirers have praised him as a political realist, his critics (historically the more numerous and vocal) have denounced him as a dangerous cynic and amoralist. He dedicated the book to the Medici, hoping to secure their sympathetic attention, but he was never offered any further political offices and spent his last 15 years as a man of letters. He wrote a series of *Discourses* on **Livy** (a full-scale analysis of republican government, completed in about 1518), a treatise on *The Art of War* (published 1521), *Mandragola*, a comic play about a seduction (completed in about 1518), and several minor literary and historical works. He died among family and friends, and was buried in Santa Croce, Florence.

MACÍA, Francisco (1859–1933) leader of the Catalan movement and first president of Catalonia.

MacINDOE, Sir Archibald (1900–60) New Zealand plastic surgeon, born in Dunedin. Educated at Otago, the Mayo Clinic, and St Bartholomew's Hospital, he was the most eminent pupil of Sir **Harold Gillies**. He won fame during World War II as surgeon-in-charge at the Queen Victoria Hospital, East Grinstead, where the faces and limbs of injured airmen ('MacIndoe's guinea-pigs') were remodelled with unsurpassed skill.

MACINTOSH, Charles (1766–1843) Scottish manufacturing chemist, born in Glasgow. He patented (1823) and developed **James Syme**'s method of waterproofing, the resulting garments becoming known as 'mac(k)intoshes'.

McINTYRE, Duncan Ban, English name of **Donnchadh Ban Macan t-Saoir** (1724–1812) Gaelic poet, and gamekeeper of Beinnodòrain, born in Glenorchy, Argyll. He worked as a forester, fought as a Hanoverian at Falkirk in 1746, and from 1799 to 1806 was one of the City Guard of Edinburgh. He composed a great deal of nature poetry, which was written down by the minister's son at Killin, for the poet was illiterate. Some of it has been translated into English by **Hugh MacDiarmid**.

MACK, Connie, originally **Cornelius Alexander McGillicuddy** (1862–1956) American baseball player and manager, born in East Brookfield, Massachusetts. He was closely involved in the early days of American baseball. He was catcher with various teams from 1886 to 1916, and began his managerial career as player/manager at Pittsburgh (1894–96). He moved on to Philadelphia in 1901 and stayed for 50 years. He holds the record for most years managing (53), most games won (3776), and most games lost (4025). He won World Championships in 1910–11, 1913 and 1929–30, and in 1930 he was also honoured (unusually for a sportsman) with the Edward P Bok prize for distinguished service to Philadelphia. In 1937 he was elected to the Baseball Hall of Fame. A tall, quiet man, he signalled to his players from the dug-out without the histrionics found in the sport today.

MACK, Karl, Freiherr von (1752–1828) Austrian soldier, born in Nennslingen in Franconia. In 1770 he entered the Austrian service, and, after fighting the Turks and the French republicans, was created field-marshal in 1797. For the king of Naples he occupied Rome, but had to conclude an armistice with the French, and was driven by riots in Naples to seek safety with them. He was carried prisoner to Paris, but escaped in 1800. Having surrendered with his army to the French at Ulm in 1805, he was tried by court martial and condemned to death, but the sentence was commuted to 20 years' imprisonment. In 1808 he was liberated and in 1819 fully pardoned.

MACKAIL, John William (1859–1945) Scottish classical scholar, born in Kingarth, Bute. After a career in the civil service he resigned in 1919 to give his full time to scholarship and criticism. He wrote *Latin Literature* (1895), and a biography of **William Morris** (1899). He was elected professor of poetry at Oxford in 1906. He was the son-in-law of **Edward Burne-Jones**, and father of the novelist **Angela Thirkell**.

MACKAY, Alexander Murdoch (1849–90) Scottish missionary to Uganda (1878–87), born in Rhynie in Aberdeenshire. He trained as an engineer, but during a residence at Berlin in 1873 was led by the court preacher **Ferdinand Baur** to turn to missionary work.

MACKAY, Charles (1814–89) Scottish songwriter, born in Perth. He was editor of the Glasgow *Argus* (1844–47), and the *Illustrated London News* (1848–59), and New York correspondent of the *Times* during the civil war (1862–65). Two of his songs, 'There's a Good Time Coming' and 'Cheer, Boys, Cheer', had an extraordinary success. His prose works included *Popular Delusions* (1841) and *Forty Years' Recollections* (1877). His daughter was **Marie Corelli**, and his son Eric (1851–98) achieved a reputation as a poet.

MACKAY, Fulton (1922–87) Scottish actor, born in Paisley. He began his stage career in 1947, and was a member of the Citizens' Theatre, Glasgow, 1949–51, and 1953–58. From 1962 to 1963, he was a member of the Old Vic company. At the Royal Court Theatre in 1969 he appeared in **David Storey**'s *In Celebration*. He then became a director of the Scottish Actors Company, and appeared in numerous productions in Scotland and London. He made several television and film appearances, but is probably best remembered for playing the role of Mr Mackay, the officious prison warder, in the 1970s television series, *Porridge*.

MACKAY, James, Baron Mackay of Clashfern (1927–) Scottish jurist, born in the village of Scourie, in Sutherland, the son of a railway signalman. He won a bursary to George Heriot's School and from there went to Edinburgh University, where he was awarded a first in mathematics and physics. After teaching mathematics at St Andrews University and beginning a research degree at Cambridge he switched to law, being called to the bar in 1955. Ten years later he was made a QC, specializing in tax law. He was unexpectedly made Lord Advocate for Scotland, and a life peer, by **Margaret Thatcher**, in 1979, and Lord Chancellor, in succession to Lord **Havers**, in 1987. He took the title of his peerage from the name of the shepherd's cottage he knew as a boy. As Lord Chancellor he created consternation among the English Bar by proposing radical reforms of the profession. His personal affairs also aroused controversy when, in 1989, he clashed with the Calvinist elders of his church, the Free Presbyterians, because of his attendance at the funeral of a Roman Catholic colleague.

MACKAY, John Alexander (1889–1983) Scots-born American scholar and ecumenist, born into a Free Presbyterian family in Inverness. He was educated at Aberdeen, Princeton, and in Spain where he developed a lifelong love of Hispanic culture. He became the first Protestant to hold the chair of philosophy at Peru's National University (1915–25), served the YMCA in Uruguay and Mexico (1925–32), and later was appointed president of Princeton Theological Seminary (1936–59). A leader in the ecumenical movement, he was president of the World Alliance of Reformed Churches (1954–59). His works in English include *The Other Spanish Christ* (1932), *The Presbyterian Way of Life* (1960), and *Ecumenics: The Science of the Church Universal* (1964).

MACKAY, Robert, English name of **Rob Donn MacAoidh** (1714–78) Gaelic poet, born in Strathmore in Sutherland. He became a herdsman for the MacKay chief, Lord Reay. He became known as 'Rob Donn' as an oral bard, describing rural life in his area and the disintegration of clan society on Strathnaver and Strathmore after the 1745 Jacobite Rising. His poetry was later collected and written down by local ministers, and a first edition appeared in 1828.

MACKE, August (1887–1914) German painter, born in Meschede in the Rhineland. He studied at Düsseldorf and designed stage-scenery. Profoundly influenced by **Matisse**, whose work he saw in Munich in 1910, he founded the *Blaue Reiter* group together with **Franz Mark**. He was a sensitive colourist, bright but not garish, working in water-colour as well as oil, and remained attached to the kind of subject-matter favoured by the Impressionists: figures in a park, street scenes, children and animals (eg *The Zoo*, 1912). He was killed in action at Champagne, France.

McKELLEN, Ian (1939–) English actor, born in Burnley. He made his début at the Belgrade Theatre, Coventry, in 1961, and played in several repertory theatres before making his London début in 1964. He joined the National Theatre in 1965, and the touring Prospect Theatre Company in 1968. With the actor Edward Petherbridge he founded the Actors' Company in 1972, run along democratic lines. He played many notable parts for the Royal Shakespeare Company between 1974 and 1978. One of his greatest successes was in the title role of the 1976 **Trevor Nunn** production of *Macbeth* at The Other Place, the RSC's studio theatre at Stratford, in which Lady Macbeth was played by **Judi Dench**. Since then he has produced an awesome string of memorable roles. He has made occasional television appearances, including the title role in *Walter*, broadcast on the opening night of Channel 4 in 1982. His film roles include **John Profumo** in *Scandal* (1988).

MACKENSEN, August von (1849–1945) German soldier, born in Leipnitz. In World War I he commanded the invasion of Poland and swept the Russians from Galicia (1915), and the Romanians from Dobrudja (1916).

MACKENZIE, Sir Alexander (1764–1892) Scottish explorer and fur-trader, born in Stornoway, Isle of Lewis. In 1779 he joined the Northwest Fur Company, and in 1788 established Fort Chipewayan on Lake Athabasca. From there he discovered the Mackenzie River (1789), followed it to the sea, and in 1792–93 became the first European to cross the Rockies to the Pacific.

MACKENZIE, Alexander (1822–92) Scots-born Canadian statesman, born in Logierait, Perthshire. He went to Canada in 1842, where he worked as a mason and contractor. In 1852 he became editor of a Reform paper, from 1867 led the opposition in the Dominion parliament, and from 1873 to 1878 was premier. He thrice declined knighthood, and died in Toronto.

MACKENZIE, Sir Alexander Campbell (1847–1935) Scottish composer, born in Edinburgh. He studied music at Sondershausen, and from 1862 at the Royal Academy, London. In 1865–79 he was teacher, violinist, and conductor in Edinburgh, and in 1887–1924 was principal of the Royal Academy of Music. *The Rose of Sharon* (1884), an oratorio, contains some of his best work. He wrote operas, cantatas, Scottish rhapsodies, a concerto and a *pibroch* for violin, chamber music and songs. He wrote *A Musician's Narrative* (1927).

MACKENZIE, Sir (Edward Montague) Compton (1883–1972) English writer, born in West Hartlepool. Educated at St Paul's School and Magdalen College, Oxford, he studied for the English bar but gave up his law studies in 1907 to work on his first play, *The Gentleman in Grey*. His first novel, *The Passionate Elopement*, was published in 1911. There followed his story of theatre life, *Carnival* (1912), which was a huge success, followed by the autobiographical *Sinister Street* (2 vols, 1913–14) and *Guy and Pauline* (1915). In World War I he served in the Dardanelles, and in 1917 he became director of the Aegean Intelligence Service in Syria, a time he described in his book on the Secret Service, *Extremes Meet* (1928). His considerable output included *Sylvia Scarlett* (1918), *Poor Relations* (1919), *Rich Relatives* (1921), *Vestal Fire* (1927), *The Four Winds of Love* (4 vols, 1937–45), *Aegean Memories* (1940), *Whisky Galore* (1947), *Eastern Epic*, vol I (1951), and *Rockets Galore* (1957). His monumental autobiography, *My Life and Times* (1963–71), came out in ten *Octaves*.

MACKENZIE of Rosehaugh, Sir George (1636–91) Scottish lawyer, born in Dundee. After studying at St Andrews, Aberdeen and Bourges, he was called to the bar at Edinburgh in 1656, and in 1661 unsuccessfully defended **Archibald, Marquis of Argyll**. He entered parliament for Ross-shire in 1669, and in 1677 was named King's advocate. In the popular mind he is regarded only as 'Bluidy Mackenzie', the criminal prosecutor in the days of the persecution of the Covenanters. He cultivated Scottish literature, was a friend of **Dryden**, and was one of the first Scots to write English with purity. In 1682 he founded the Advocates Library in Edinburgh (now the National Library of Scotland). He retired at the Revolution of 1688 to Oxford, died in London, and was buried in Edinburgh in Greyfriars Churchyard. A prolific author, he wrote works of fiction, politics, history and law. His law writings include *Laws and Customs of Scotland in Matters Criminal* (1674), *Institutions of the Law of Scotland* (1684) and *Observations on the Acts of Parliament* (1686), which are still important. His *Memoirs of the Affairs of Scotland* was published in 1821.

MACKENZIE, Henry (1745–1831) Scottish writer, known as the 'Man of Feeling', born in Edinburgh, the son of a doctor. He was educated at the High School and Edinburgh University, He became a crown attorney in the Scottish Court of Exchequer (1765), and in 1804 comptroller of taxes. For more than half a century he was 'one of the most illustrious names connected with polite literature in Edinburgh', and a regular contributor to the *Scots Magazine and General Intelligencer*. His sentimental novel, *The Man of Feeling*, was published in 1771, followed by *The Man of the World* in 1773, and *Julia de Roubigné* in 1777. He also wrote two tragedies, *The Spanish Father* (1773, but never performed), and *The Prince of Tunis* (1773). He was one of the founders of the Royal Society of Edinburgh (1783). He is also remembered for his recognition of **Burns**, and as an early admirer of **Lessing** and of **Schiller**. His memoirs and anecdotes were published as *Anecdotes and Egotisms* (1927).

McKENZIE, Julia (1941–) English actress and singer. An outstanding interpreter of the work of musicals composer **Stephen Sondheim**, her London musical appearances include *Maggie May* (1965), *Mame* (1969), Sondheim's *Company* (1972); the anthologies *Cowardy Custard* (1973), *Cole* (1974), and *Side by Side* by Sondheim (1977); **Loesser**'s *Guys and Dolls* (1982), and Sondheim's *Follies* (1987). She has interspersed musicals with plays, notably **Brecht**'s *Schweyk in the Second World War* (1982); and three plays by **Alan Ayckbourn**: *The Norman Conquests* (1974), *Ten Times Table* (1979), and *Woman in Mind* (1986).

MACKENZIE, Sir Morell (1837–92) English throat specialist, born in Leytonstone. He was knighted in 1887 after attending the German Crown Prince (later **Frederick III**), whose throat condition proved to be malignant and ultimately fatal, contrary to Mackenzie's diagnosis. Mackenzie's apologia provoked much resentment in German medical circles and earned him the censure of the Royal College of Surgeons.

MACKENZIE, William Forbes (1801–62) Scottish politician, born in Portmore, Peeblesshire. MP for Peeblesshire (1837–52), he introduced a liquor Act for Scotland, passed in 1853, providing for Sunday closing and other controls.

MACKENZIE, William Lyon (1795–1861) Scots-born Canadian insurgent and politician, born in Dundee. He emigrated to Canada in 1820, and published the *Colonial Advocate* in Toronto from 1824 to 1834, in which he attacked the government ceaselessly. In 1828 he was elected to the provincial parliament for York, but was expelled in 1830 for libel on the assembly. He was mayor of Toronto in 1834. In 1837 he published in his paper a declaration of independence for Toronto, headed a band of 800 insurgents, and attacked the city (5 December). Driven off by a superior force, he fled across the border, and on 13 December seized Navy Island in the Niagara River, where he declared a provisional government. A Canadian force promptly crossed the river (29 December) and burned the American steamer, *Caroline*, which had been supplying the rebels, precipitating an international incident. Mackenzie fled to New York (January 1638), where he was sentenced by the US authorities to twelve months' imprisonment. He returned to Canada in 1849, was a member of parliament 1850–58, and died in Toronto. He was the grandfather of **W L Mackenzie King**.

MACKENZIE KING See **KING, William Lyon Mackenzie**

MACKENZIE STUART, Alexander John, Lord, of Dean (1924–) Scottish judge, born in Aberdeen. Educated at Fettes College, Sidney Sussex College, Cambridge, and Edinburgh University, he practised at the Scottish bar. He became a judge of the Court of Session in 1972 and then the first British judge appointed to the Court of Justice of the European Communities (1973–88), being president of that court in 1984–88. He published *The European Communities and the Rule of Law* (1977).

MACKERRAS, Sir (Alan) Charles MacLaurin (1925–) American-born Australian conductor, born in Schenectady. He played oboe with Sydney Symphony Orchestra (1943–46), was a staff conductor at Sadler's Wells Opera (1949–53), and returned there from 1970 as musical director, having in the meantime established an international reputation. Subsequent conducting posts have included the BBC Symphony Orchestra, Sydney Symphony Orchestra, Royal Liverpool Philharmonic Orchestra and Welsh National Opera (musical director since 1987). He is a noted scholar of the music of **Janáček**.

MCKILLOP, Mary Helen (1842–1909) Australian religious, known as Mother Mary of the Cross, born in Fitzroy, Victoria. With Father Tenison-Woods she founded the Society of the Sisters of St Joseph of the Sacred Heart in Penola, South Australia, in 1866. Although the Society quickly grew, diocesan rivalry caused Mother Mary to be excommunicated in 1871 but she was reinstated two years later by Pope **Pius IX**, who approved the Sisterhood in the same year. In 1875 Mother Mary was confirmed as superior-general of the order, which is popularly known as the 'Little Joeys'. Its work is highly regarded, and it is devoted to the education of poorer children and care of orphans and unmarried mothers. The case for the beatification of Mother Mary, the first step towards canonization, was made in 1925, and in 1975 her cause was formally introduced by the Vatican. when it was announced that she would become Australia's first saint.

MACKINDER, Sir Halford John (1861–1947) English geographer and politician, born in Gainsborough, Lincolnshire. Educated at Epsom College and Christ Church, Oxford, he became the first reader in geography at Oxford University (1887–1905) and established the first university school in the subject in 1899 (director, 1899–1904). He thus laid the foundations of British academic geography at Oxford and later at Reading and the London School of Economics. He held numerous senior university appointments, was an MP (1910–22) and also British high commissioner for South Russia (1919–1920). He was chairman of the Imperial Shipping Committee (1920–45) and of the Imperial Economic Committee (1926–41). In a widely-respected publication, *Democratic Ideals and Reality* (1919), he expounded his famous Eurasian 'Heartland' concept. He also wrote *Britain and the British Seas* (1902) and *The Nations of the Modern World* (1911).

McKINLEY, William (1843–1901) 25th president of the USA, born in Niles, Ohio. He served in the Civil War, retiring in 1867 as major to Canton, where he practised law. He was elected to congress in 1876, and repeatedly re-elected. In 1892, with business community support, he was made governor of Ohio, his name being identified with the high protective tariff carried in the McKinley Bill of 1890, though subsequently modified by the Democrats in 1894. Chosen Republican candidate for the presidency in 1896 and 1900, he conducted exciting contests with **W J Bryan**, who advocated the cause of free silver, denounced trusts, high tariffs, and imperialism, and was understood to favour labour at the expense of capital. Some Democrats, 'Gold Democrats' or 'Sound Money Democrats', in spite of their dislike of McKinley's policy on many points, supported him. In November 1900, as in 1896, he secured a large majority in the electoral college, as the representative of a gold standard and of capital. In his first term the war with Spain (1898) took place, with the conquest of Cuba and the Philippines. He was shot by an anarchist, Leon F Czolgosz, in Buffalo, New York, and died eight days later.

MACKINNON, Donald Mackenzie (1913–) Scottish philosopher of religion, born in Oban. Professor of moral philosophy at Aberdeen (1947–60) and of philosophy of religion at Cambridge (1960–78), he explored the relations between theology, metaphysics and moral philosophy, championing realism over idealism. His wide concerns, ranging from the theory of knowledge to moral freedom and political action, and from Marxist-Leninism to a theological basis for unilateral disarmament, are evidenced in numerous essays, some of which are collected in *Borderlands of Theology* (1968), *Explorations in Theology 5* (1979), and *Themes in Theology* (1988). His 1965–66 Gifford lectures were published as *The Problems of Metaphysics* (1974).

MACKINTOSH, Charles Rennie (1868–1928) Scottish architect, designer, water colourist and outstanding exponent of the Art Nouveau style in Scotland. Born in Glasgow, the son of a police superintendent, he was educated at Allan Glen's School before starting his architectural apprenticeship. In 1884 he began attending evening classes at Glasgow School of Art, and subsequently joined the established firm of Honeyman and Kepple in 1889. In 1900 he married **Margaret Mackintosh**. His architectural output, though not large and mostly within the Glasgow region, exercised very considerable influence on European design. It included the outstanding Glasgow School of Art (1897–1909), the famous Cranston tearooms, and houses such as Hill House in Helensburgh (1903–04, now in the care of the National Trust for Scotland). His style contrasted strong rectilinear structures and elements with subtle curved motifs; in his houses there are deliberate references to traditional Scottish architecture. His designs also included detailed interior design, textiles, furniture and metalwork. His work was exhibited at the Vienna Secession Exhibition in 1900, where it was much admired. In 1914 he left Scotland and did no further major architectural work; but in his latter years he turned to painting, and produced a series of exquisite watercolours, chiefly in France (1923–27).

MACKINTOSH, Elizabeth (1896–1952) Scottish novelist and playwright, born in Inverness. Under the pseudonym of Gordon Daviot she wrote more serious works, including the historical drama, *Richard of Bordeaux* (1932), the work for which she is most remembered, and a biography of **Claverhouse** (1937). *The Franchise Affair*, a detective story, was one of several which she wrote as Josephine Tey.

MACKINTOSH, Hugh Ross (1870–1936) Scottish theologian, born in Paisley. Professor of systematic theology at New College, Edinburgh (1904–36), and moderator of the General Assembly of the Church of Scotland (1932), he sought to spread understanding of developments in continental theology, which he had studied at Marburg. He helped produce translations of **Ritschl**'s *Justification and Reconciliation* and **Schleiermacher**'s *The Christian Faith*; his 1933 Croall lectures on trends from Schleiermacher to **Barth**, described by **John Baillie** as 'a fine mingling of generous appreciation with stern rebuke', were published posthumously as *Types of Modern Theology* (1937). Earlier books of note included *The Doctrine of the Person of Jesus Christ* (1912) and *The Christian Experience of Forgiveness* (1927).

MACKINTOSH, Sir James (1765–1832) Scottish writer, born in Aldourie in Inverness-shire. He studied medicine at Aberdeen, but settled in London as a journalist. His *Vindiciae Gallicae* (1791) was written as a defence of the French Revolution in reply to **Burke**'s *Reflections on the French Revolution*, and he became secretary of the 'Friends of the People' (he later recanted his views in *On the State of France*, 1815). He was called to the bar in 1795. In 1799 he delivered a brilliant series of lectures on the law of nature and of nations at Lincoln's Inn. In 1804 he was appointed recorder of Bombay, and in 1806 judge of its Admiralty Court. He spent seven years in Bombay, entering parliament after his return as Whig member for Nairn

(1813). He published a number of works on history and philosophy.

MACKINTOSH, John Pitcairn (1929–78) Scottish politician and educator, born in Simla, India. Educated at Edinburgh, Oxford and Princeton, he taught history at Glasgow and Edinburgh until 1961, when he became senior lecturer in government at the University of Ibadan, Nigeria, for two years, after which he taught politics at Glasgow and in 1965 became professor of politics at Strathclyde University. He published major studies of *The British Cabinet* (1962) and *Nigerian Politics and Government* (1966). In 1966, as Labour party candidate, he took the Conservative seat of Berwick and East Lothian and resigned his chair. As an MP he was impressed by the rising tide of Scottish and Welsh nationalism, but in any case considered that measures of devolution were vitally necessary to the health of the British constitution, a theme he outlined in *The Devolution of Power* (1968). Labour premier **Harold Wilson** was hostile to these views, and it became increasingly evident that Mackintosh had no hope of office in a Wilson administration. He lost his seat in the election of February 1974, but regained it in October. He maintained strong links with his subject, bringing out *British Government and Politics* (1970), and his acceptance of a part-time professorship of politics at Edinburgh University in 1977 made it clear he intended to be an inspiration in the growing struggle for devolution. His premature death removed a major force in the Labour attempt to bridge the counterpulls of unionism and nationalism.

MACKINTOSH, Margaret, née **MacDonald** (1865–1933) English artist, born in Staffordshire. She studied at the Glasgow College of Art, and married **Charles Rennie Mackintosh** in 1900. Best known for her work in watercolours and stained glass, she exhibited widely on the Continent, winning the Diploma of Honour at the Turin International Exhibition of 1902. She collaborated with her husband in much of his work.

MACKINTOSH, William (1662–1743) Scottish Jacobite, of Borlum, Inverness-shire. He held a command in the 1715 Rising and led his force south to join the English rebels. He was captured and imprisoned, but escaped from Newgate in 1716. Back in Scotland he took part in the abortive 1719 rising, but was captured again and died after long captivity in Edinburgh Castle. He was an early arboriculturist.

MACKLIN, Charles (c.1697–1797) Irish actor, born in the North of Ireland. After a wild, unsettled youth, he played in Bristol and Bath, and in 1733 was engaged at Drury Lane. He steadily rose in public favour, till in 1741 he appeared in his greatest role, Shylock. From then on he was acclaimed as one of the best actors of his day, successful in both tragedy and comedy. In 1735 he killed a brother-actor in a quarrel over a wig, and was tried for murder. He wrote a tragedy and several farces and comedies; of these *Love à la Mode* (1759) and *The Man of the World* (1781) were printed. His last performance was at Covent Garden in 1789; but he survived, with an annuity of £200.

MACKMURDO, Arthur Heygate (1851–1942) English architect and designer, born in London. After studying architecture, he came under the influence of **Ruskin**'s and **William Morris**'s friendship and became a central but very individual member of the Arts and Crafts movement. In 1875 he set up in architectural practice and in 1882 was a founder of the Century Guild, a group which designed for all aspects of interiors. He himself designed furniture, textiles, metalwork and for print. The title page of his book, *Wren's City Churches* (1883), an inexplicably free, linear design for a book on classical architecture, but which does resemble other examples of his decorative work, is often seen as a forerunner of 'Art Nouveau'.

McKNIGHT KAUFFER, Edward (1890–1954) American poster designer, illustrator and artist, born and educated in the USA where he trained as a painter. He arrived in England in 1914. In 1921 he gave up painting for commercial art and designed posters for the Underground Railway Co, London Transport Board, Shell-Mex, BP Ltd, Great Western Railway, General Post Office, The Orient Line, Gas Light and Coke Co and many others. He also illustrated a number of books including *Don Quixote* (Nonesuch Press, 1930) and **T S Eliot**'s *Triumphal March* (1931). He designed a wrapper for the Studio and a number of book jackets. In addition, he designed sets and costumes for various productions including the ballet *Checkmate* in 1937.

MACKWORTH, Sir Humphrey (1657–1727) Welsh politician and industrialist, born in Betton Grange, Shropshire. He married Mary Evans, the heiress of Gnoll, Neath, where he developed the coal reserves on her lands. He also obtained, through doubtful financing, mineral resources in Cardiganshire. He sat in parliament as a Tory (Cardiganshire, 1701, 1702–05; Totnes, 1705–07; Cardiganshire 1710–13) and was very energetic on parliamentary committees. He was devout and paid for schools in Cardiganshire and Neath, and was one of the founders of the Society for the Promotion of Christian Knowledge.

MACLAREN, Charles (1782–1866) Scottish writer and editor, born in Ormiston, East Lothian. He was the co-founder (1817) and first editor of *The Scotsman* (1820–45), editor of *The Encyclopaedia Britannica* (6th ed, 1820–23), and wrote *Geology of Fife and the Lothians* (1839).

MACLAREN, Ian, pen-name of **John Watson** (1850–1907) Scottish minister and writer, born in Manningtree in Essex. He was a Presbyterian minister in Liverpool from 1880 to 1895. His amazing success with his *Beside the Bonnie Brier Bush* (1894) gave rise to the name 'Kailyard School', and was followed by *Days of Auld Lang Syne* (1895) and others. He also wrote religious works.

McLAUGHLIN, John (1942–) English electric guitarist and composer, born in Doncaster. He played with British blues, rock and free-jazz groups before moving to the USA in 1968. The following year he played with **Miles Davis** on two influential jazz-rock albums, *Bitches Brew* and *In a Silent Way*. From 1971, McLaughlin led the Mahavishnu Orchestra, starting a movement of jazz and rock fusion with Indian rhythms. He has since developed this theme, often using acoustic guitar and working in trio settings.

MACLAURIN, Colin (1698–1746) Scottish mathematician, born in Kilmodan, Argyll. He graduated at Glasgow (1713), and became professor at Aberdeen (1717). In 1725 he was appointed to the chair of mathematics at Edinburgh on **Newton**'s recommendation. He published *Geometria organica* in 1720, and his best-known work, *Treatise on fluxions*, in 1742, which gave a systematic account of Newton's approach to the calculus, taking a geometric point of view rather than the analytical one used on the continent. This is often thought to have contributed to the neglect of analysis in 18th-century Britain. In 1745 he organized the defences of Edinburgh against the Jacobite army, but his efforts impaired his health and he died early in the following year.

MACLEAN, Alistair (1922–87) Scottish author, born in Glasgow. He was educated at Inverness Royal Academy, Hillhead High School and Glasgow University. He served in the Royal Navy from 1941 to 1946. In 1954, while a school-teacher, he won a short-story competition held by the *Glasgow Herald*, contributing a tale of adventure at sea. At the suggestion of **William Collins**, the publishers, he produced a full-length novel, *HMS Ulysses*, the next year, and this epic story of war-time bravery became an immediate best-seller. He followed it with *The Guns of Navarone* in 1957, and turned to full-time writing. He preferred the term 'adventure story' to 'novel' in describing his work. The settings are worldwide, including the China Seas (*South by Java Head*, 1958), Greenland (*Night Without End*, 1960), Florida (*Fear is the Key*, 1961), the Scottish islands (*When Eight Bells Toll*, 1966), a polar scientific station (*Ice Station Zebra*, 1963), Holland (*Puppet on a Chain*, 1969) and the Camargue (*Caravan to Vaccares*, 1970). As well as two secret service thrillers (written as Ian Stuart), *The Dark Crusader* (1961) and *The Satan Bug* (1962), he wrote a Western (*Breakheart Pass*, 1974) and biographies of **T E Lawrence** and Captain **Cook**. Other titles include *Where Eagles Dare* (1967), *Force Ten from Navarone* (1968), *Bear Island* (1971), *Sea Witch* (1977), and *Athabasca* (1980). Most of his stories made highly successful films.

MACLEAN, Donald Duart (1913–83) English traitor, son of Liberal cabinet minister, Sir Donald Maclean. Educated at Gresham's School and Trinity College, Cambridge, at the same time as **Anthony Blunt, Guy Burgess** and **Kim Philby**, he was similarly influenced by communism. He joined the Diplomatic Service in 1935, serving in Paris, Washington (1944–48) and Cairo (1948–50), and from 1944 acted as a Russian agent. After a 'nervous breakdown' in 1950, he became head of the American Department of the Foreign Office, but by 1951 was a suspected traitor, and in May of that year, after Philby's warning, disappeared with Burgess to Russia. He was joined in 1953 by his wife, Melinda (b.USA 1916) and children, but she left him to marry Philby in 1966. Maclean became a respected Soviet citizen, working for the Foreign Ministry and at the Institute of World Economic and International Relations. In 1970 he published *British Policy Since Suez, 1956–68*.

MACLEAN, Sir Fitzroy Hew (1911–) Scottish diplomat and soldier. He was educated at Eton and Cambridge, served with the Foreign Office from 1933, and in World War II distinguished himself as commander of the British military mission to the Yugoslav partisans (1943–45). MP for Lancaster from 1941, and for Bute and North Ayrshire from 1959, he was under-secretary for war from 1954 to 1957. His *Eastern Approaches* (1949) *Disputed Barricade* (1957), *A Person from England* (1958), and *Back from Bokhara* (1959) gained him a considerable reputation.

MACLEAN, Sorley See **MACGILL-EAIN**

MACLEHOSE, Agnes, née **Craig** (1759–1841) Scottish literary figure, daughter of an Edinburgh surgeon. In 1776 she married a Glasgow lawyer, from whom she separated in 1780, and who went to Jamaica in 1784. She met **Burns** at a party in Edinburgh in 1787, and subsequently carried on with him the well-known correspondence under the name 'Clarinda'. A number of Burn's poems and songs were dedicated to her.

MACLEISH, Archibald (1892–) American poet and librarian, born in Glencoe, Illinois. Educated at Yale and the Harvard Law School, he married Ada Hitchcock in 1916 and was posted to France. After the war and his graduation from law school in 1919, he taught constitutional law briefly at Harvard College but moved to France in 1923 to concentrate on writing. His first book of poems, *The Happy Marriage*, was published a year later. His many works include *The Pot of Earth* (1925), *The Hamlet of A. MacLeish* (1928), and *Conquistador* (1932), winner of that year's Pulitzer prize for poetry. For his *Collected Poems 1917–1952* he was awarded a second Pulitzer prize as well as the Bollingen prize and a National Book Award in 1953; and *J.B.*, a verse play, won both the Pulitzer prize in drama and the Antoinette Perry Award for best play in 1959. He was librarian of Congress (1939–44), assistant secretary of state (1944–45), co-founder of UNESCO, and Boylston professor of rhetoric and oratory at Harvard University.

McLENNAN, John Cunningham (1867–1935) Canadian physicist. Professor at Toronto (1907–31), he did much research on electricity and the superconductivity of metals. In 1932 he succeeded in liquefying helium.

McLENNAN, John Ferguson (1827–81) Scottish lawyer and theorist of social evolution, born in Inverness. Educated at King's College, Aberdeen, he then studied at Cambridge before being called to the Scottish bar in 1857. He became parliamentary draughtsman for Scotland in 1871. He is chiefly remembered for his theories of totemism and the evolution of familial organization. In *Primitive Marriage* (1865) he proposed an evolution from primitive promiscuity, through a stage of matriarchy, to patrilineal descent. He coined the terms 'exogamy' and 'endogamy', which are still in use today. He also wrote *The Patriarchal Theory*, published posthumously in 1885.

MACLENNAN, Robert Adam Ross (1936–) Scottish politician, born in Glasgow, the son of an eminent gynaecologist. He attended the Glasgow Academy, Balliol College, Oxford, Trinity College, Cambridge and Columbia University, New York, before being called to the bar in 1962. He entered parliament as Labour member for Caithness and Sutherland in 1966 and has represented it ever since. He held junior posts in the governments of **Harold Wilson** and **James Callaghan** and was a founder member of the Social Democratic party (SDP) in 1981. He came to prominence in 1987 when, after **David Owen** had resigned the SDP leadership because of his opposition to a merger with the Liberals, Maclennan offered himself as 'caretaker' leader until the terms of the merger had been agreed. He then became a leading member of the new party, the Social and Liberal Democrats (SLD), under **Paddy Ashdown**.

MACLEOD, Iain Norman (1913–70) Scottish politician. Regarded as one of the most gifted members of the post-war generation of Conservative politicians, he served as colonial secretary (1959–61) under **Harold Macmillan** and, in that capacity, oversaw the independence of many British territories in Africa. He became Chancellor of the Exchequer and seemed destined for the highest political office, but died prematurely at the age of 57.

MACLEOD, John James Rickard (1876–1935) Scottish physiologist, educated at Aberdeen, Leipzig and Cambridge. He became professor of physiology at Western Reserve University, Cleveland (1903), Toronto (1918) and Aberdeen (1928). In 1921, along with Sir **Frederick Grant Banting** and **Charles Best** he discovered insulin, and in 1923 shared the Nobel prize for physiology and medicine with Banting.

MACLEOD, Norman (1812–72) Scottish theologian, born, a minister's son, in Campbeltown, Argyll. He attended Glasgow University, and was minister of Loudon (1838–43), Dalkeith (1843–45) and the Barony Church, Glasgow, from 1851. From 1860 to 1872 he edited and contributed to *Good Words*. He wrote a host of books including *The Golden Thread* (1861) and *Reminiscences of a Highland Parish* (1867).

MACLEOD, Fiona See **SHARP, William**

MacLEOD, Baron George Fielden, of Fuinary (1895–) Scottish presbyterian clergyman, second son of Sir John MacLeod, 1st Baronet, a Glasgow MP. Educated at Winchester and Oriel College, Oxford, he won the MC and Croix de Guerre in World War I, and studied theology at Edinburgh, becoming minister of St Cuthbert's there (1926–30) and at Govan in Glasgow (1930–38). He founded the Iona Community, which set about restoring the ruined abbey on that historic island. The original dozen ministers and helpers soon grew in number and, working there every summer, renovated most of the monastic buildings. As moderator of the General Assembly (1957–58) he created controversy by supporting the unpopular scheme to introduce bishops into the kirk in the interests of church unity. Well known as a writer and broadcaster, he is strongly left-wing, as his *Only One Way Left* (1956) testifies. He succeeded to the baronetcy in 1924, but prefers not to use the title. In 1967 he was created a life peer, as Baron MacLeod of Fuinary.

MAC LIAMMÓIR, Mícháel (Michael Wilmore) (1899–1978) Irish actor, painter and writer, born in Cork. His family moved to London, and he became a child actor as Michael Darling in **Herbert Beerbohm Tree**'s production of *Peter Pan*, with **Noël Coward** as Lost Boy. He studied art at the Slade School, becoming a distinguished painter and designer inspired by **Beardsley**, and also became a proficient multilinguist after residence abroad. With his lifelong friend Hilton Edwards, he founded the Gate Theatre Company in Dublin (1928), having toured Ireland with the Shakespearean Company of Anew MacMaster. His company's work made the most of dramatic possibilities of Irish writing, drew in much European drama using his translations, adaptations, design and lighting, and offered classical material as bold in rethinking as anything in London or New York. He wrote distinguished fiction, plays and memoirs in Irish and in English, and in the 1960s his one-man shows crowned an outstanding international reputation. *The Importance of Being Oscar* (1960) magnificently realized the dramatic possibilities of **Wilde**'s life, while paying homage to his life-long beloved idol. *I Must Be Talking to My Friends* (1963, on Irish history and literature) and *Mostly About Yeats* (1970) were worthy successors. His most famous film appearance was as Iago in **Orson Welles**' *Othello* (1949, brilliantly described in his *Put Money in Thy Purse* 1954), and (for voice only) as the narrator in *Tom Jones* (1963).

MACLISE, Daniel (1806–70) Irish painter, born in Cork. He made pencil portraits in Cork, and went to London in 1827 where he studied at the school of the Royal Academy. His frescoes in the Royal Gallery of the House of Lords, *The Meeting of Wellington and Blücher* (1861) and *The Death of Nelson* (1864), are his most notable works. He was also known as an illustrator of books for **Tennyson** and **Dickens**. His sketches of contemporaries in *Fraser's Magazine* (1830–38) were published in 1874 and 1883.

McLUHAN, (Herbert) Marshall (1911–80) Canadian writer, born in Edmonton. He studied English literature at the universities of Manitoba and Cambridge. In 1946 he became professor at St Michael's College, Toronto. In 1963, having directed two surveys into culture and communication media, he was appointed director of the University of Toronto's Centre for Culture and Technology. He held controversial views on the effect of the communication media on the development of civilization, claiming that it is the media *per se*, not the information and ideas which they disseminate, that influence society. He sees the invention of printing, with its emphasis on the eye rather than the ear, as the destroyer of a cohesive, interdependent society, since it encouraged man to be more introspective, individualistic and self-centred. His publications include *The Mechanical Bride* (1951), *The Gutenberg Galaxy* (1962), *Understanding Media* (1964), *The Medium is the Message* (with Q Fiore, 1967), and *Counter-Blast* (1970).

MACLURE, William (1763–1840) Scots-born American geologist, born in Ayr, the 'father of American geology'. Educated privately, he soon made a substantial fortune as a merchant and entrepreneur. He travelled widely in Europe, Russia and the USA, and lived at times in London, Spain and Mexico and settled in the USA around 1800. On his travels he always studied the geology and met leading geologists, and he employed a personal cartographer-naturalist (Charles Lesueur, 1778–1846) and organized expeditions by others. His work as an observer and writer in geology made him influential, and he helped to found the Academy of Natural Sciences in Philadelphia and was its president from 1817 to 1840. His *Observations on the Geology of the United States* (1817) gives the first full account of its subject, and he went on to study the West Indies and Mexico. His later writing supported the ideas on evolution offered by **Lamarck**; and he believed that primitive rocks have diverse origins and opposed **Werner**'s theory of their exclusively sedimentary origin.

MACMAHON, Marie Edmé Patrice Maurice de (1808–93) French soldier and statesman, born in Sully near Autun, descended from an Irish Jacobite family. Entering the army, he served in Algeria, and distinguished himself at Constantine (1837), commanded at the Malakoff (1855), was again conspicuous in Algeria (1857–58), and for his services in the Italian campaign (1859) was made marshal and Duke of Magenta. He became governor-general of Algeria in 1864. In the Franco-German war (1870–71) he commanded the First Army Corps, but was defeated at Wörth, and captured at Sedan. After the war, as commander of the army of Versailles, he suppressed the Commune. In 1873 he was elected president of the Republic for seven years, and was suspected, not unjustly, of reactionary and monarchical leanings. He resigned in 1879.

McMAHON, Sir William (1908–) Australian politician, born in Sydney. He studied at the university there and then qualified and practised as a solicitor. After service in World War II he became active in the Liberal party and was elected to the House of Representatives in 1949. He held a variety of posts in the administrations of Sir **Robert Menzies**, **Harold Holt** and **John Gorton** until he took over the premiership, when Gorton lost a vote of confidence, in 1971. The following year the Liberals lost the general election to the Australian Labor party (ALP), led by **Gough Whitlam**. Sir William continued to lead his party until 1977.

MacMASTER, John Bach (1852–1932) American historian, born in Brooklyn, New York City. He studied civil engineering, but between 1883 and 1920 was professor of American history at Pennsylvania University. He wrote a *History of the People of the US* (8 vols, 1883–1913), *Franklin as a Man of Letters* (1887), and other works.

MACMILLAN, Alexander See **MACMILLAN, Daniel**

MACMILLAN, Daniel (1813–57) Scottish bookseller and publisher, born in Upper Corrie, Arran. Apprenticed to booksellers in Scotland and Cambridge, in 1843 he and his brother Alexander opened a bookship in London, and in the same year moved to

Cambridge. By 1844 he had branched out into publishing, first educational and religious works and by 1855 English classics such as **Kingsley**'s *Westward Ho!* and **Hughes**' *Tom Brown's Schooldays* in 1857. In the year after his death (1858) the firm opened a branch in London and by 1893 had become a limited liability company with Daniel's son, Frederick (1851–1936), as chairman. His other son, Maurice, father of **Harold MacMillan**, was also a partner.

MacMILLAN, Donald Baxter (1874–1970) American arctic explorer, born in Provinceton, Massachusetts. A member of the **Robert Peary** expedition of 1908–09, he later carried out anthropological research among the Eskimos of Labrador, and led expeditions to Greenland (1913–17). He also led expeditions to Baffin Island (1921–22), North Greenland (1923–24), and the North Pole (1925).

McMILLAN, Edwin Mattison (1907–) American physical chemist, born in California. Professor of physics at the University of California 1946–73, he was awarded (with **Glenn Seaborg**) the 1951 Nobel prize for chemistry for his part in the discovery of the transuranic elements.

MACMILLAN, Sir (Maurice) Harold, 1st Earl of Stockton (1894–1986) English statesman. Educated at Eton, he took a first class in classical moderations at Balliol College, Oxford, his studies having been interrupted by service with the Grenadier Guards during World War I, in which he was seriously wounded. In 1919–20 he was in Canada as ADC to the governor-general, the Duke of Devonshire, whose daughter Lady Dorothy (d.1966) he married. Returning to Britain, he partnered his brother Daniel in the family publishing firm, but preserved his interest in politics and stood successfully as Conservative MP for Stockton-on-Tees in 1924, was defeated in 1929, but was re-elected in 1931. Partly because he was not always willing to conform to the party line, and partly, no doubt, because his air of intellectual superiority irked his more senior colleagues, he remained a backbencher until 1940, when **Churchill** made him parliamentary secretary to the ministry of supply. After a brief spell as colonial under-secretary in 1942 he was sent to North Africa to fill the new cabinet post of minister resident at Allied Headquarters where he achieved distinction by his foresight and acumen and by his ability as a mediator in the many clashes of factions and personalities which bedevilled his term of office. Defeated in the Labour landslide of 1945, he was returned later the same year for Bromley, which he held until his retiral in 1964. He was minister of housing (1951–54), silencing general doubts by achieving his promised target of 300000 houses in a year. He was minister of defence from autumn to spring 1954–55, and thereafter foreign minister to the end of 1955, when he was appointed Chancellor of the Exchequer. On **Eden**'s resignation in 1957 he emerged, in **Butler**'s words, as 'the best prime minister we have', his appointment being received without enthusiasm, for as an intellectual and a dyed-in-the-wool aristocrat he was regarded with suspicion by many. Nevertheless, his economic expansionism at home, his resolution in foreign affairs, his integrity, and his infectious optimism inspired unforeseen confidence, and his popularity soared. Having piloted the Conservatives to victory in the general election, he embarked upon a new term as prime minister in 1959. His 'wind of change' speech at Cape Town (1960) acknowledged the inevitability of African independence. In 1962, after some electoral setbacks, he carried out a drastic 'purge' of his government, involving seven cabinet ministers. Further setbacks followed, however, with the Vasall spy case (1962) and the **Profumo** scandal (1963), and a prostate gland operation brought about his reluctant resignation on 10 October 1963. He wrote *Winds of Change* (1966), *The Blast of War* (1967), *Tides of Fortune* (1969), *Riding the Storm* (1971), *Pointing the Way* and *At The End of the Day* (both 1972). An earldom was bestowed upon him on his 90th birthday in 1984 and he took the title Earl of Stockton.

MACMILLAN, Hugh Pattison, Lord, of Aberfeldy (1873–1952) Scottish judge, born in Glasgow. Educated at Collegiate School, Greenock, and Edinburgh and Glasgow universities, he practised at the Scottish bar, became non-political Lord Advocate in the first Labour government of 1924, then moved to London and developed a large practice at the parliamentary bar and in the House of Lords. He served as a lord of appeal in ordinary (1930–39, 1941–47), in the interim serving unsuccessfully as minister of information. He served on many governmental, educational, cultural and other commissions and committees, and his judicial speeches are highly regarded.

MACMILLAN, John (1670–1753) Scottish churchman, born in Minnigaff, Kirkcudbrightshire. Ordained in 1701, he joined the 'Cameronians' of **Richard Cameron**, and in 1743 founded with them the Reformed Presbyterian Church ('MacMillanites').

MACMILLAN, Sir Kenneth (1929–) Scottish choreographer, born in Dunfermline. He trained in the School of Sadler's Wells Ballet, with whom he subsequently performed. In 1953 he began to choreograph with the Royal Ballet. After three years as director of ballet at the Deutsche Oper, Berlin, (1966–69), he returned to the Royal Ballet in 1970 as resident choreographer and director, and in 1977 became the company's principal choreographer. His ballets include *Romeo and Juliet* (1965), *The Seven Deadly Sins* (1973), *Élite Syncopations* (1974), *Mayerling* (1978), and *Isadora* (1981). As well as creating ballets for many of the world's foremost companies he has worked for theatre, television, and musical shows.

MACMILLAN, Kirkpatrick (1813–78) Scottish inventor, born near Thornhill in Dumfriesshire, the son of the village blacksmith. He was a farm labourer and a coachman before taking up the same trade as his father, at Keir. Having caught sight of a hobby-horse being ridden in the neighbourhood he resolved to make one himself, and did. After a while he began to experiment with pedals and cranks as a means of propulsion. He applied pedals to a tricycle in 1834, and in 1840 succeeded in building the world's first primitive bicycle, riding it as far afield as Dumfries and, in two days, to Glasgow, some 70 miles to the north. He never patented his invention and it was widely copied, to such an extent that for many years afterwards it was usually credited to one of his imitators, Gavin Dalzell of Lesmahagow.

McMILLAN, Margaret (1860–1931) American-born British educational reformer, born in New York and brought up near Inverness. She agitated ceaselessly in the industrial north of England for medical inspection and school clinics, and in 1902 joined her sister Rachel (1859–1917) in London, where they opened the first school clinic (1908), and the first open-air nursery school (1914). After Rachel's death, the Rachel McMillan Training College for nursery and infant teachers was established as a memorial.

MacMURROGH, Dermot, correctly **Diarmaid Mac Murchadha Uí; Mhurchadha,** surname usually anglicized as 'Murphy' (1110–71) Irish ruler and subject of **Henry II**. Succeeding his father (1126) as king of Leinster, he was ousted by the king of Connaught, for eloping with Devorgilla, wife of his vassal O'Rourke.

Dermot appealed to Henry II who permitted him to recruit allies among the Normans of Wales, the first of whom arrived in 1169. Their principal leader, Richard ('**Strongbow**') de Clare arrived in 1170, took Waterford, married Dermot's daughter Aoife, and with the Normans and Leinstermen captured the Norse city of Dublin. Strongbow succeeded Dermot in 1171 as ruler of Leinster by virtue of his marriage to Aoife but was forced to resubmit to Henry II. Posterity cast Dermot as archetypal traitor, as in **Yeats**'s play, *The Dreaming of the Bones*.

MACNAGHTEN, Edward, Lord (1830–1913) English judge, born in London. He was educated at Trinity College, Dublin, and Cambridge, where he was distinguished in both classics and rowing. He became MP in 1880, declined the home secretaryship and a judgeship and was then appointed direct from the bar in 1887 to be a lord of appeal in ordinary. He wrote opinions which were outstanding for their literary quality and their wit, but also for their extraction of a leading principle from a mass of authority. In his later years he was deemed the greatest living English judge. He was also a leader in reforming professional legal education.

McNAIR, Arnold Duncan, Lord, of Gleniffer (1885–1975) English legal scholar and judge, born in London. Educated at Aldenham School and Gonville and Caius Colleges, Cambridge, he taught law at London and Cambridge and served as vice-chancellor of Liverpool University. He was a judge of the International Court of Justice (1946–55), and its president (1952–55), and then was president of the European Court of Human Rights (1959–65). He was president of the Institute of International Law in 1949–50. His writings include *Law of Treaties* (1961), *International Law Opinions* (3 vols, 1956) and he edited **Oppenheim**'s *International Law*.

MACNAIR, Herbert (1868–1955) Scottish architect and designer, born in Glasgow. Articled to John Honeyman, the Glasgow architect, in 1888, he studied with **Charles Rennie Mackintosh** at evening classes at Glasgow School of Art, and opened up his own business specializing in the design of furniture, book illustration and posters. In 1897 he took up the post of Instructor in Design at Liverpool University. He also undertook a number of decorating commissions, including the design of the Writing Room for the Scottish Pavilion at the Exposizione Internazionale in Turin. He returned to Glasgow in 1909.

MACNAMARA, Dame (Annie) Jean (1899–1968) Australian physician, born in Beechworth, Victoria. Educated at Melbourne University, she worked in local hospitals where she developed a special interest in 'infantile paralysis'. In the poliomyelitis epidemic of 1925 she tested the use of immune serum and, convinced of its efficacy, she visited England, the USA and Canada with the aid of a Rockefeller scholarship. With Sir **Macfarlane Burnet**, she found that there was more than one strain of the polio virus, a discovery which led to the development of the **Salk** vaccine. She also supported the experimental treatment developed by Sister **Elizabeth Kenny**, and introduced the first artificial respirator (iron lung) into Australia. She was created a DBE in 1935, and later became involved in the controversial introduction of the disease myxomatosis as a means of controlling the rabbit population of Australia. In the early 1950s it was estimated that as a result of her efforts the wool industry had saved over £30 million.

McNAMARA, Robert Strange (1916–) American Democrat politician and businessman, born in San Francisco. After service in the US air force (1943–46) he worked his way up in the Ford Motor Company to president by 1960, and in 1961 joined the **Kennedy** administration as secretary of defense, in which post he was, by 1967, particularly concerned by the escalation of the war in Vietnam, and the cost of continuation. In 1968 he resigned to become president of the World Bank, a post he held until 1981.

McNAUGHT, William (1813–81) Scottish mechanical engineer and inventor, born in Paisley. He was apprenticed to **Robert Napier** at the age of 14 and attended classes at the Andersonian Institution in Glasgow. Eight years later he joined his father in the manufacture of steam-engine components, and became aware of the need felt by many industrialists for an increase in the power of the single-cylinder low-pressure beam engines they had already installed in their factories. He conceived the idea about 1845 of adding a second smaller cylinder operating at a higher pressure and exhausting its spent steam into the original cylinder where its remaining energy could be utilised. For many years the process of adding an extra cylinder to an existing engine was called 'McNaughting'.

McNAUGHTON, Andrew George Latta (1887–1966) Canadian soldier, born in Moosomin, Saskatchewan. Educated at McGill University, he became a lecturer in engineering while holding commission in the artillery arm of the Canadian militia. He served with great distinction in the artillery in World War I, and attained the rank of brigadier-general. Chief of General Staff (1929–35), he was president of the National Research Council from 1935 to 1939. In World War II he commanded the 1st Canadian Division (1939), Canadian Corps (1940), and 1st Canadian Army (1942–43) as lieutenant-general.

McNAUGHTON, Daniel (19th century) English murderer. He was tried in 1843 for the murder of Edward Drummond, private secretary to Sir **Robert Peel**. The question arose whether he knew the nature of his act. The House of Lords took the opinion of the judges, and the law of England, as to the criminal responsibility of the insane is now embodied in the judges' 'answers', known as the McNaughton Rules: (*a*) every man is presumed sane until the contrary is proved; (*b*) it must be clearly proved that at the time of committing the act, the accused was labouring under such a defect of reason as not to know the nature of the act, or that he was doing wrong.

MacNEICE, Louis (1907–63) Irish poet, born in Belfast, the son of a Church of Ireland clergyman who became a bishop. Educated at Marlborough and Merton College, Oxford, he became a lecturer in classics at Birmingham (1930–36) and in Greek at Bedford College, University of London (1936–40). He was closely associated with the British left-wing poets of the 1930s, especially **Auden**, with whom he wrote *Letters from Iceland* (1937). His poetry often has a biting colloquial humour and, with his writing for radio, ranges over a vast area of contemporary experience, ideas and images. His volumes of poetry include *Blind Fireworks* (1929), *Collected Poems* (1949), *Autumn Sequel* (1954), *Eighty-Five Poems* and *Solstices* (both 1961). He was the author of several memorable verse plays for radio, notably *The Dark Tower* (published with other radio scripts in 1947), as well as translations of **Aeschylus** and of **Goethe**'s *Faust*. He also produced several volumes of literary criticism.

McNEILL, Billy (William) (1940–) Scottish footballer and manager, born in Bellshill, Lanarkshire. An inspirational captain, known as 'Caesar', he was the backbone of the highly successful Glasgow Celtic side in the ten years which followed 1965. He received the

European Cup after Celtic's victory at Lisbon in 1967, and had nine championship and seven Scottish Cup medals. Surprisingly he was capped only 29 times. Appointed to succeed **Jock Stein** as manager of his old club in 1978 he left after a quarrel with the board, but following comparatively unsuccessful spells with Manchester City and Aston Villa he returned in 1987, and in his first season guided Celtic to League and Cup victory in the club's centenary year.

MacNEILL, John (1867–1945) Irish historian and nationalist, writing under the Gaelicized first name **Eoin**, born in Glenarm, County Antrim. Educated at St Malachy's College, Belfast, he made himself an authority on Old Irish. He ultimately became professor of early Irish history at University College, Dublin (1908–45). His pioneer work in Irish history strongly asserted the strength of its legal and cultural civilization, exhibited in the inspirational lectures *Phases of Irish History* (1919), and the more formal works *Celtic Ireland* (1921), and *Early Irish Laws and Institutions* (1935). In 1913 he inspired and led the Irish Volunteers as a defence force in case of Ulster Protestant resort to violence in the event of Home Rule enactment. His organization was taken over by **John Redmond**, who persuaded most of its members to support the Allied cause in 1914 after the outbreak of war. MacNeill maintained a minority who had guns run into Howth just before the war's outbreak. Irish Republican Brotherhood manipulation steered MacNeill's Volunteers towards insurrection in 1916 without his knowledge. In the end he accepted the insurrection with reluctance but countermanded it when it became clear German aid would fail. After the Dublin Rising MacNeill was interned, and played a part in organizing the new Sinn Féin party and its abstentionist body Dáil Éireann where, as MP for Derry, he was given cabinet status. He supported the Anglo-Irish Treaty and was minister for education in the first Free State government. He was delegate for his government to the Boundary Commission which shattered Irish nationalist hopes of a revision of Irish partition in the Catholics' favour: he resigned rather than accept its verdict, and the Boundary was left unchanged.

MACONCHY, Dame Elizabeth (1907–) English composer, born in Broxbourne, Hertfordshire, of Irish parentage. She studied under **Vaughan Williams** at the Royal College of Music and in 1929 went to Prague, where her first major work, a piano concerto, was performed the following year. Her suite, *The Land*, was performed at the London Proms in 1930, and her early works were often written for festivals of the International Society for Contemporary Music. Her most characteristic work is in the field of chamber music, and among her best-known compositions are her *Symphony* (1953) and overture *Proud Thames*, also written in Coronation Year, a carol cantata *A Christmas Morning* (1962), a choral and orchestral work *Samson and the Gates of Gaza* (1963), an opera for children, *The King of the Golden River* (1975), *Heloise and Abelard* (1978), and *My Dark Heart* (1981). She has also written a group of one-act operas, twelve string quartets and songs. She was made a DBE in 1987.

MACPHAIL, Agnes, née **Campbell** (1890–1954) Canadian suffragette and politician, Canada's first woman MP. She was born in Grey County, Ontario. A school-teacher, she became involved with the women's suffrage movement and was elected MP for the United Farmers of Ontario from 1921 to 1940. She was a leader of the Co-operative Commonwealth Federation of Canada, and represented Canada in the Assembly of the League of Nations.

McPHERSON, Aimée Semple, neé **Kennedy** (1890–1944) Canadian-born American Pentecostal evangelist, born near Ingersoll, Ontario, into a Salvation Army family. In 1908 she married a Pentecostal missionary, Robert Semple, but was soon widowed when her husbend died in China in 1910. She returned to North America with her daughter and subsequently embarked on an evangelistic career. She married again, in 1912 (to Harold McPherson, divorced 1921), and a third marriage, in 1931, also ended in divorce. Flamboyant and imaginative, she was hugely successful as an evangelist. In 1918 she founded the Foursquare Gospel Movement in Los Angeles, and for nearly two decades she conducted a preaching and healing ministry in the Angelus Temple, Los Angeles, which cost her followers $1.5 million to construct. She had her own radio station, Bible school, magazine, and social service work. Considerable controversy surrounded her: continuous embroilment in legal suits against her; a bizarre and unexplained five-week disappearance in 1926 (she claimed to have been kidnapped). Even her death raised questions; authorities differ on whether it came from a heart attack or from an overdose of barbiturates. Her books include *This is That* (1923), *In the Service of the King* (1927) and *Give Me My Own God* (1936).

MACPHERSON, James (1736–96) Scottish poet, renowned as the 'translator' of **Ossian**, born in Ruthven, Inverness-shire, a farmer's son. He was educated at King's College and Marischal College, Aberdeen, and studied for the ministry, but in 1756 became a village schoolmaster in Ruthven. In 1758 he published an epic poem, *The Highlander*, and two years later, encouraged by **Carlyle**, **Adam Ferguson**, **Hugh Blair**, and **John Home**, he published some fragments of Gaelic oral poetry, which he had collected and translated, as *Fragments of Ancient Poetry Collected in the Highlands of Scotland* (1870). In the introduction (by **Hugh Blair**) it was suggested that a great poetic epic relating to the legendary hero Fingal, as told by his son Ossian, was still extant. In 1760, Macpherson was commissioned by the Faculty of Advocates in Edinburgh to tour the Highlands in search of this material, which he published in 1762 as *Fingal: an ancient Epic Poem in Six Books*, followed by *Temora, an Epic Poem, in Eight Books* (1763). They were received with huge acclaim, but a storm of controversy soon arose about their authenticity. Macpherson could not or would not produce any originals, and it appears that he used only about 15 genuine pieces of original verse which he altered and amended, and invented the rest to create an epic form for them. In 1763 he was appointed surveyor-general of the Floridas, but soon returned to London and became a wealthy merchant with interests in the East India Company as agent to the Nabob of Arcot. He sat in parliament as MP for Camelford from 1780. He was buried, at his own request and expense, in Westminster Abbey.

MacQUAID, John Charles (1895–1973) Irish prelate, born in Cootehill, County Cavan. Educated in Cavan, Dublin, and Rome, he was ordained priest in the Holy Ghost Fathers in 1924, becoming dean of studies in 1925, and then president in 1931, at his order's Blackrock College. An influential commentator on social and moral questions, he was credited with strong links to **Éamon de Valera**, whose sons were his pupils, and this may have accounted for his being named archbishop of Dublin by Pope **Pius XII** in 1940, the only Irish bishop from a religious order during his papacy. He fell foul of de Valera through championing the cause of striking schoolteachers in 1947, and was reduced thereafter to negative rather than creative impact on state policy. He played the leading part in the Irish Bishops' successful opposition to a national health proposal, the Mother and Child Scheme of Dr Noel Browne, whose consequent resignation from the first **Costello** government led to its fall in 1951. He also banned attendance of Catholics at Trinity College, Dublin, from 1944, being bitterly hostile to mixed religious education. He retired in 1972.

MACQUARIE, Lachlan (1761–1824) Scottish soldier and colonial administrator, born on the isle of Ulva, off Mull. He joined the Black Watch in 1777, and after service in North America, India and Egypt, was appointed governor of New South Wales following the deposition of **Bligh**. The colony, depressed and demoralized, populated largely by convicts, and exploited by influential land-grabbers and monopolists, was raised by his energetic administration and firm rule to a state of prosperity; its population trebled, extensive surveys were carried out, and many miles of road were built. In 1821 political chicanery by the monopolists and his own ill health compelled him to return to Britain. Known as the 'Father of Australia' he has given name to the Lachlan and Macquarie rivers, and to Macquarie Island.

MACQUARRIE, John (1919–) Scottish theologian and philosopher of religion, born in Renfrew. A lecturer at Glasgow (1953–62), and professor at Union Theological Seminary, New York (1962–70), and at Oxford (1970–86), he has written extensively across the whole field of theology. While the influence of **Bultmann** and **Tillich** may be traced in *An Existentialist Theology* (1955) and *Principles of Christian Theology* (1966), his catholic interests may be discerned in *Paths in Spirituality* (1972), *In Search of Humanity* (1982), Gifford lectures *In Search of Deity* (1984), and *Theology, Church and Ministry* (1986). Students have also appreciated successive revisions of *Twentieth Century Religious Thought* (1963–88), and his editing of *A Dictionary of Christian Ethics* (1967), revised, with J F Childress, as *A New Dictionary of Christian Ethics* (1986).

McQUEEN, (Terence) Steven (1930–80) American film actor, born in Slater, Missouri. A rough and tumble background, including a spell in a reform school and a stint in the marines, brought him to New York where he studied at the Neighbourhood Playhouse and Uta Hagen School. Appearing in summer stock, on Broadway and television, he made his film début as an extra in *Somebody Up There Likes Me* (1956). *Wanted Dead or Alive* (1958), a highly-rated television western series, revealed his film potential and led to a co-starring role in *The Magnificent Seven* (1960). Creating an image as a laconic loner he became the archetypal 1960s cinema hero/rebel with his performances in *The Great Escape* (1963), *The Cincinnati Kid* (1965) and *Bullitt* (1968). Married to actress Ali McGraw from 1973 to 1978, he attempted **Ibsen** in *An Enemy of the People* (1977) before returning to action roles in two final films. He died after a long struggle with cancer.

MACQUER, Pierre Joseph (1718–84) French chemist. One of the first to study platinum, he discovered the arsenates of potassium and sodium. He was the compiler of a chemical dictionary (1766).

MACRAE, (John) Duncan (1905–67) Scottish actor. Educated at Allan Glen's School, Glasgow, and at Glasgow University, he was a teacher before becoming a full-time actor. He made his first London appearance in 1945, and his performances ranged from **Ibsen**, **Chekhov**, **Shaw** and **Shakespeare** to broad comedy in pantomime and on television, but it is especially as a Scottish actor that he is known and respected. His long association with the Citizens' Theatre in Glasgow dated from its opening production in 1943, and, in partnership with the Scottish playwright and critic T M Watson, he ran a company to present plays on tour in Scotland (1952–55). His best-known performances include **Bridie**'s *Gog and Magog*, **Tyrone Guthrie**'s Edinburgh Festival production of **Lyndsay's** *Ane Satyre of the Thrie Estaitis*, Robert McLellan's *Jamie the Saxt* and Robert Kemp's Scots translation of **Molière**'s *L'École des Femmes* (Let Wives Tak Tent). Among his many films are *Whisky Galore* (1948), *The Kidnappers* (1953), and *Tunes of Glory* (1960).

MACREADY, William Charles (1793–1873) English actor, son of W McCready, actor and provincial manager, born in London. He made his début at Birmingham in 1810; in 1816 he appeared at Covent Garden; but it was not until 1837 that he really became the leading English actor of his day. In 1837 he inaugurated his famous Covent Garden management, during which he produced **Shakespeare**. After two seasons he moved to Drury Lane (1841–43), then played in the provinces, Paris and America. His last visit to the USA was marked by terrible riots (10 May 1849) in which 22 people died arising out of the ill-feeling borne by the American actor **Edwin Forrest** to Macready. In 1851 Macready took his farewell of the stage at Drury Lane. He wrote *Reminiscences and Diaries* (1875) and *Diaries* (ed by W Toynbee, 1912).

MACROBIUS, Ambrosius Theodosius (5th century) Roman writer and neo-Platonist philosopher, born probably in Africa. He wrote a commentary on **Cicero**'s *Somnium Scipionis*, and *Saturnaliorum Conviviorum Libri Septem*, a series of historical, mythological and critical dialogues.

MacSWINEY, Terence (1879–1920) Irish nationalist, born in Cork. He trained as an accountant, and wrote poetry and plays under the influence of **Daniel Corkery**, with whom he founded the Cork Dramatic Society in 1908. He was a major influence in forming the Irish Volunteers in Cork in 1913, wrote for the IRB *Irish Freedom*, but accepted **MacNeill**'s countermand of the Easter Rising in 1916. He was elected Sinn Féin MP for West Cork in 1918, sitting in Dáil Éireann and maintaining his work as volunteer recruiter and organizer. In March 1920 he was elected lord mayor of Cork in the vacancy occasioned by the murder of Tómas Mac Curtain by irregular British forces, and was arrested the following August, being sentenced by court-martial to two years' imprisonment. He declared his intention of going on a hunger-strike, was transferred to Brixton Prison, and died after a fast of 74 days which had aroused world-wide sympathy; among others deeply influenced by his sacrifice was a Vietnamese kitchen-worker in the London Ritz hotel, the future **Ho Chi Minh**.

McTAGGART, John McTaggart Ellis (1866–1925) English philosopher, born in London. He was educated at Clifton College and at Trinity College, Cambridge, where he went on to teach from 1897 to 1923. His early works were commentaries on **Hegel**'s philosophy and were effectively preliminaries to his own systematic metaphysics set out in *The Nature of Existence* (2 vols: 1921, and posthumously 1927). He is regarded as the most important of the Anglo-Hegelian or Idealistic philosophers who dominated British and American thought in the late 19th and early 20th centuries.

McTAGGART, William (1835–1910) Scottish painter, born in Kintyre. He became the outstanding landscape painter of his time. He studied under **Robert Scott Lauder**, and lived in and near Edinburgh. His grandson Sir William MacTaggart (1903–81), also a painter, was a prominent representative of the modern Scottish school.

MADARIAGA, Salvador de (1886–1978) Spanish writer, scholar and diplomat, born in La Coruña. He was educated at the Instituto del Cardenal Cisneros, Madrid, and at the École Polytechnique, Paris. He was a London journalist from 1916 to 1921 and director of the disarmament section of the League of Nations Secretariat from 1922 to 1927. From 1928 to 1931 he was professor of Spanish studies at Oxford, and was Spanish ambassador to the USA in 1931 and to France from 1932 to 1934. A liberal opponent of the **Franco** régime, he lived in exile. His publications include *The Genius of Spain* (1923), *Theory and Practice of International Relations* (1938), *Portrait of Europe* (1952), *Democracy v. Liberty?* (1958) and *Latin America between the Eagle and the Bear* (1962).

MADDEN, Sir Frederick (1801–73) English antiquary, born in Portsmouth. Keeper of MSS in the British Museum (1837–66), he edited *Havelok the Dane* (1833), *William and the Werwolf* (1832), the early English versions of the *Gesta Romanorum* (1838), *The Wycliffite Versions of the Bible* (1850), **Layamon**'s *Brut* (1847), and the works of **Matthew Paris** (1858).

MADERNA, Bruno (1920–73) Italian composer and conductor, born in Venice. His father was a pianist and jazz-band leader, and Maderna appeared from the age of seven as an 'infant prodigy' violinist and conductor, going on to study composition and conducting. During the war he served with distinction on the Russian front, and then deserted to join the partisans. Early in his musical career he composed for films and radio and taught at the Venice Conservatory, then in 1955 began to research seriously into the techniques and possibilities of electronic music, founding, with **Luciano Berio**, the Studio di Fonologia Musicale of Italian Radio. He became music director of Milan Radio. His compositions are intellectual, based on a mathematical calculation of form rather than an emotional or inspirational approach, but much of the resulting music is surprisingly lyrical. He wrote pieces for combinations of live and taped music, such as the *Compositions in Three Tempi* and *Music in Two Dimensions* (1958) for flute and taped sounds, and a number of compositions for electronic music, such as *Dimensions II* (1960). His opera *Satyricon* appeared in 1973.

MADERNA, or **MADERNO, Carlo** (1556–1629) Italian architect, born in Capalago. He had moved to Rome by 1588, where he became assistant to his uncle, **Domenico Fontana**. He was the leading exponent of the early Baroque in Rome, producing bold and vigorous designs, divorced from the Mannerist style of the preceding generation. In 1603, he was appointed architect to St Peter's, where he lengthened the nave and added a massive facade (1606–12). Other notable works include S Susanna (1597–1603), and the Palazzo Barberini (1628–38), completed by **Borromini** and **Bernini**, in Rome, the latter in a revolutionary design, dispensing with the traditional quadrangular courtyard for an H-plan.

MADERO, Francisco Indalecio (1873–1913) Mexican president, born in San Pedro, Coahuila. The son of a wealthy land-owner, groomed in Paris, educated at the University of California at Berkeley, he was no social revolutionary although he greatly improved the peons' condition on his own estates. He unsuccessfully opposed **Porfirio Díaz**'s local candidates in 1904, and in 1908, when Díaz was quoted as saying that he would not seek another term, Madero took the dictator at his word and published *La sucesion presidencial en 1910*, which launched his presidential campaign. A spiritualist, vegetarian, and practitioner of homoeopathic medicine, he was an unlikely challenger for Díaz, and at first was not taken seriously. But his popularity grew rapidly and Díaz turned to repression, imprisoning Madero and many of his supporters. He escaped to the USA dressed as a railway worker and in October, 1910, issued the Plan de San Luis Potosi from his San Antonio headquarters. He led a military campaign that captured Ciudad Juarez, where he established his capital (May 1861), and the dictatorship crumbled. Once elected president (1911), Madero's moderate political reform programme pleased no one and he faced a succession of revolts by Emiliano Zapata and others demanding land reform, and by supporters of the old dictatorship. On the night of 23 February 1913, he and his vice-president were murdered following a military coup led by General Victoriano Huerta, planned with the assistance of US ambassador Henry L Wilson.

MADHVA, Kanarese (14th century) Brahmin philosopher, born near Udipi, north of Mangalore, South India. After study in Trivandrum, Banaras and elsewhere, he settled in Udipi and is traditionally held to have vanished in mid-lecture in 1317 and retired to the Himalayas. Taking **Rāmānuja**'s side against **Śankara**, he promoted *dvaita* or dualistic *Vedanta*, allowing for the separate existence of the Divine, human souls, and matter. His belief that some souls were eternally damned suggests Christian influence on his thinking.

MADISON, James (1751–1836) 4th president of the USA, born in Port Conway, Virginia. In 1776 he was a member of the Virginian Convention, in 1780 of the Continental Congress, and in 1784 of the legislature of Virginia. In the Convention of 1787, which framed the Federal constitution, he acted with **Jay** and **Alexander Hamilton**, and with them wrote the papers published as *The Federalist* (1787–88). He was the chief author of the 'Virginia plan', and suggested the compromise by which, for taxation, representation, etc, slaves were regarded as population and not chattels, five being reckoned as three persons, and which secured the adoption of the constitution by South Carolina and the other slave-holding states. Madison was elected to the first national congress; he now showed himself anxious to limit the powers of the central government, and became a leader of the Jeffersonian Republican party. In 1801, **Jefferson** having been elected president, Madison was made secretary of state. In 1809 he was elected president. The European wars of that period, with their blockades, etc, were destructive of American commerce, and brought on a war with Britain (1812). In 1817, at the close of his second term, Madison retired.

MÄDLER, Johann Heinrich von (1794–1874) German astronomer, born in Berlin. Director of Tartu Observatory, he produced the first map of Mars (1830) and a map of the moon (1836) and carried out research on double stars.

MADOC a legendary Welsh prince, long believed by his countrymen to have discovered America in 1170. The story is in Hakluyt's *Voyages* (1582) and Lloyd and Powell's *Cambria* (1584). The essay by Thomas Stephens written in 1858 for the Eisteddfod, and published in 1893, proved it to be baseless.

MADONNA, real name **Madonna Louise Ciccone** (1958–) American pop singer, born in Rochester, Michigan. She trained as a dancer at Michigan University before moving to New York where she began her professional career as a backing singer and then playing with a number of New York groups. She hired **Michael Jackson**'s manager prior to releasing *Madonna* (1983), an album which included five US hit singles. Subsequent albums have included *Like A Virgin* (1984), *True Blue* and *You Can Dance* (1987). She has also acted in films, including *Desperately Seeking Susan* (1985) and *Shanghai Surprise* (1986). An important role model for teenagers in the 1980s, her success has been greatly enhanced by clever promotion and image-making.

MADOX, Thomas (1666–1727) English legal antiquary. He investigated and transcribed legal records. His major publications were *Formulare Anglicanum* (1702), *History and Antiquities of the Exchequer* (1711) and *Baronia Anglica, An History of Land-honours and Baronies and of Tenure in Capite* (1736), which are all of great value to historical scholars.

MADVIG, Johan Nicolai (1804–86) Danish classical scholar and statesman. He was professor of Latin at Copenhagen (1829–70), and inspector of higher schools (from 1848). He was one of the chief speakers of the national Liberal party, was minister of religion and education (1848–51), and was repeatedly president of the Danish parliament. Among his works were *Opuscula Academica* (1834–42), a great *Latin Grammar* (1841), *Greek Syntax* (1846) and an *Autobiography* (1887).

MAECENAS, Gaius Cilnius (d.8 BC) Roman statesman and trusted counsellor of **Augustus**, whose name has become a synonym for a patron of letters.

MAERLANT, Jacob van (c.1235–c.1300) Flemish didactic poet. He was the author of verse translations of French and Latin originals, including the *Roman de Troie* (c.1264) and de Beauvais' *Speculum Majas* (1284).

MAES, Nicolaes (1634–93) Dutch painter, born in Dordrecht. From c.1648 he was a pupil of **Rembrandt** in Amsterdam. Painting in a style close to his master, he specialized in painting genre scenes, especially of single figures praying or sleeping. He travelled to Antwerp c.1665 and there became influenced by Flemish art, especially that of **van Dyck**. Upon his return to Holland in 1667 he began to paint portraits which, because of their very different style, were for a long time thought to have been by a different artist.

MAETERLINCK, Count Maurice (1862–1949) Belgian dramatist, born in Ghent. He studied law at Ghent University, but became a disciple of the Symbolist movement, and in 1889 produced his first volume of poetry, *Les Serres chaudes*. In the same year came his prose play, *La Princesse Maleine*, and in 1892 *Pelléas et Mélisande*, on which **Debussy** based his opera. Other plays include *Joyzelle* (1903) and *Mary Magdalene* (1910). *La Vie des abeilles* (1901) is one of his many popular expositions of scientific subjects, and he also wrote several philosophical works. He was awarded the Nobel prize for literature in 1911.

MAEVIUS (1st century BC) Roman minor poet. With his colleague **Bavius**, he was lampooned by **Virgil** in his Eclogues, and also by **Horace**. Their names were used by **William Gifford** for the titles of his satires on the Della Cruscan school of poets ('The Baviad' and 'The Maeviad').

MAFFEI, Francesco Scipione, Marchese di (1675–1755) Italian dramatist, born in Verona. He fought in the War of the Spanish Succession (1703–04) under his brother Alessandro, a field-marshal. A leading reformer of Italian drama, his tragedy *Merope* (1714) ran through 70 editions, and the comedy *Le Ceremonie* (1728) was also successful. He also wrote scholarly works, including *Verona illustrata* (1731–32).

MAGELLAN, Ferdinand (c.1480–1521) Portuguese navigator, leader of the first expedition to circumnavigate the globe. He was born near Villa Real in Tras os Montes, served in the East Indies, and was lamed for life in action in Morocco. Offering his services to Spain, he laid before **Charles V** a scheme for reaching the Moluccas by the west, and sailed from Seville on 10 August 1519 with five ships and 270 men. Having coasted Patagonia he threaded the strait which bears his name (21 October–28 November) and reached the ocean which he named the Pacific; but by now one ship had been wrecked and another had turned back for home. A third ship had to be burned and scuttled in the Pacific because so many men had died that only two ships could be manned. The ships became separated, and one was captured by the Portuguese. Magellan himself was killed by natives in the Philippine Islands, but his ship, the *Victoria*, was taken safely back to Spain by the last surviving Spanish captain, **Juan Sebastian del Cano**, on 6 September 1522, to complete the circumnavigation of the world. Of the 270 men who had set out three years earlier, fewer than 20 returned.

MAGENDIE, François (1783–1855) French physiologist, born in Bordeaux. He became prosector in anatomy (1804), physician to the Hôtel-Dieu in Paris, and professor of anatomy at the Collège de France (1831). He made important studies of nerve physiology, the veins and the physiology of food, and wrote numerous works, including the *Elements of Physiology*. In his *Journal de la physiologie expérimentale* are recorded the experiments on living animals which gained for him the character of an unscrupulous vivisector.

MAGINN, William (1794–1842) Irish writer, born in Cork. He was educated in his father's private school and at Trinity College, Dublin, and took his LL D. He taught in Cork for ten years, and in 1823 moved to London. He was a prolific contributor to *Blackwood's Magazine*, and the *Standard*, and was the joint founder of *Fraser's Magazine* (1830). A collection of his tales was edited by **Eric Partridge** (1933).

MAGINOT, André (1877–1932) French politician, born in Paris. He was first elected to the Chamber in 1910. As minister of war (1922–24; 1926–31) he pursued a policy of military preparedness and began the system of frontier fortifications which was named the 'Maginot Line' after him.

MAGLIABECHI, Antonio (1633–1714) Italian bibliophile, born in Florence. A goldsmith to trade, he gradually entombed himself among books. His learning and his memory were prodigious and precise. In 1673 he was appointed court-librarian by the Grand Duke of Tuscany; his vanity and intolerance involved him in bitter literary squabbles. His library of 30000 volumes, bequeathed to the Grand Duke, is now a free library named after him.

MAGNUS, Heinrich Gustav (1802–70) German physicist, and discoverer of the 'Magnus effect'. As professor of chemistry at Berlin University he made important discoveries in the fields of acids and gases, and in 1853 he described the Magnus effect—the sideways force experienced by a spinning ball which is responsible for the swerving of golf or tennis balls when hit with a slice.

MAGNUS, Olaus, properly **Olof Månsson** (1490–1557) Swedish historian and ecclesiastic. A Catholic priest, he left Sweden for Rome in 1523 as King **Gustav I Vasa**'s envoy but remained abroad as a result of the Reformation. There he published the first detailed map of Scandinavia, *Carta Marina* (1539), and wrote his celebrated if fanciful *Historia de gentibus septentrionalibus* (1555). His brother, Johannes (1488–1544), was sent to Sweden as papal legate in 1523, but was exiled by Gustav I Vasa. He was appointed the last Catholic archbishop of Uppsala in 1523, but continued to live in Rome with his brother. He was the author of a romantic History of the Goths (*Historia de omnibus gothorum sueonumque regibus*, 1554), and a more reliable *History of the Archbishopric of Uppsala* (1557). After his death, Olaus Magnus became titular archbishop of Uppsala.

MAGNUS ERIKSSON (1316–74) king of Sweden (1319–64), and king of Norway (as Magnus VII, 1319–55). The son of Duke Erik of Sweden and of Ingeborg, daughter of King Haakon V of Norway (1270–1319), he inherited the throne of Norway from his grandfather in 1319 at the age of three, and was elected to the Swedish throne the same year on the deposition of his treacherous uncle, King Birger Magnusson (1280–1321). In 1335 he married Blanche of Namur, by whom he had two sons. In 1355 he handed over the crown of Norway to his younger son, Haakon VI, and in the following year was temporarily deposed in Sweden by his elder son, Erik (XII). After Erik's death in 1359 he returned to power, and introduced useful new legislation, but in 1361 lost the strategic Baltic island of Gotland to an invasion by King Valdemar III 'Atterdag' of Denmark. In 1363 his son Haakon married **Margareta**, the ten-year-old daughter of King Valdemar; but the Swedish nobility rose against King Magnus and deposed him in 1364, giving the succession to his German nephew, Albrekt of Mecklenburg.

MAGNUS ERLENDSSON, (St Magnus) (d.1117) Earl of Orkney. Early in the 12th century, the Norse earldom of Orkney was shared by Magnus and his cousin, Earl Hakon; after years of feuding, they agreed to hold a peace-meeting on the island of Egilsay just after Easter, 1117. Hakon treacherously broke the terms of the truce and took Magnus prisoner, and had him executed. The manner of Magnus's death suggested martyrdom, and soon miracles were reported. His nephew, Earl Rognvald Kali, built St Magnus Cathedral in Kirkwall in his honour.

MAGNUS I OLAFSSON, 'the Good' (1024–47) king of Norway from 1035 and of Denmark from 1042. The illegitimate son of **King Olaf II Haraldsson** (St **Olaf**), he was named after the emperor **Charlemagne** (Carolus Magnus). After St Olaf's death at the battle of Stiklestad in 1030, the boy was given refuge at the court of Prince Jaroslav the Wise in Kiev, and was brought back by popular acclaim in 1035 to assume the Norwegian throne. In 1042 he inherited the Danish throne, and in the following year won a notable victory over the Wends at Lürschau Heath in southern Jutland. In 1045 he agreed to share the throne of Norway with his uncle **Harald III Hardraade** ('Hard-Ruler'), and died two years later during a campaign in Denmark.

MAGNUS III, Olafsson, 'Barelegs' (c.1074–1103) king of Norway from 1093, one of the last of the Norse Viking sea-kings bent on strengthening Norway's hold over her North Sea territories. He was the son of King **Olaf III Haraldsson** ('the Peaceful'). He harried the Orkneys and Shetland (1098–99), and in 1102–03 led another punitive naval expedition west to Scotland and Ireland; he took Dublin, and built new fortifications in the Isle of Man, but was killed in an ambush in Ulster. He earned his nickname because he abandoned Norse trousers in favour of the Scottish kilt.

MAGNUS V ERLINGSSON (1156–84) king of Norway from 1162. The son of Earl Erling the Crooked, he was raised to the throne as a child under his father's regency; in 1164 he was crowned by Archbishop Eystein at a church ceremony in Bergen, the first religious coronation in Denmark. After his father's death in 1179 he was engaged in a long war against a rival claimant to the throne, the Faroese-born 'usurper' **Sverrir Sigurdsson**; he was forced to flee to Denmark for safety, and lost his life in a naval battle in an attempt to regain his kingdom.

MAGNUS VI HAAKONSSON, 'the Law-Reformer' (1238–80) king of Norway from 1263. He was the son of **Haakon IV Haakonsson, 'the Old'**, and succeeded to the throne when his father died in the Orkneys on his return to Norway after the Battle of Largs in 1263. He made peace with King **Alexander III** of Scotland and ceded the Western Isles and the Isle of Man. He revised and standardized the laws of the land in a series of legal codes, from which he earned his nickname, and which were based on the 'four sisters' of Mercy, Truth, Fairness and Peace.

MAGNÚSSON, Árni (1663–1730) Icelandic antiquarian and philologist, and outstanding collector of old Icelandic manuscripts. Born on a farm in western Iceland, he proved himself a precocious scholar from childhood; after graduating with distinction from the cathedral school at Skálholt he studied theology at Copenhagen University (1683–85). He became a secretary in the Royal Archives and in 1701 was appointed to a new chair at Copenhagen University as professor of Danish antiquities. From 1702 to 1712 he was sent to Iceland as a royal commissioner to carry out a property census and study economic conditions in the country, and spent all his spare time building up a private collection of old manuscripts. This formed the basis of the Arnamagnæan Institute in Copenhagen, most of whose manuscripts have now been voluntarily returned from Denmark to Iceland.

MAGNÚSSON, Eiríkur (1833–1913) Icelandic philologist and scholar, editor and translator of many classical Icelandic texts. Born in eastern Iceland, he became librarian of Cambridge University, England. He translated **Jón Árnason**'s monumental collection of folk-tales (*Legends of Iceland*, 1864–66), and collaborated with **William Morris** in a notable series of Saga translations, including *Grettis Saga* (1869), *Volsunga Saga* (1870) and *The Saga Library* (5 vols, 1891–95).

MAGOUN, Horace Winchell (1907–) American neuroscientist, born in Philadelphia. He studied at Rhode Island State College and received his PhD from Northwestern University Medical School in 1934. He taught there and at Johns Hopkins University before moving in 1950 to the University of California at the Los Angeles School of Medicine. He did important work on many neurological and psychopharmacological topics and was one of the leaders in the creation of the multidisciplinary approach to the study of the nervous system called neuroscience.

MAGRITTE, René (1898–1967) Belgian Surrealist painter, born in Lessines, Hainault. Educated at the Académie Royale des Beaux-Arts (1916–18) in Brussels, he became a wallpaper designer and commercial artist. In 1924 he became a leading member of the newly-formed Belgian Surrealist group. After his first, badly-received, one-man show in Brussels in 1927, he lived in Paris until 1930, and there associated with **André Breton** and others. Apart from a brief Impressionist phase in the 1940s, Magritte remained constant to Surrealism, producing works of dreamlike incongruity, such as *Rape*, in which he substitutes a torso for a face. His major paintings include *The Wind and the Song* (1928–29) and *The Human Condition* (1, 1934; 2, 1935). He was acclaimed in the USA, although himself denying it, as an early innovator of the 'Pop Art' of the 1960s.

MAHAN, Alfred Thayer (1840–1914) American naval historian, born in West Point, New York. He served in the US navy (1854–1896), and in 1906 was given the rank of rear admiral retired. His many works included *The Influence of Sea Power upon History, 1600–1812* (3 vols, 1890–92), and Lives of **Farragut**, **Nelson** and other naval figures.

MAHATHIR BIN MOHAMAD (1925–) Malaysian politician, born in Alur Setar, in Kedah state. He practised as a doctor (1957–64) before being elected to the House of Representatives as a United Malays' National Organisation (UMNO) candidate. He won the support of UMNO's radical youth wing through his advocacy of 'affirmative action' in favour of bumiputras (ethnic Malays) and a more Islamic social policy. After holding several ministerial posts he was appointed UMNO leader and prime minister in 1981, immediately launching a new 'look east' economic policy, which sought to emulate Japanese industrialization. Despite internal ethnic conflicts, he was re-elected in 1982 and 1986.

MAHDI See **MOHAMMED AHMED**

MAHFOUZ, Naguib (1911–) Egyptian novelist, born in Cairo. The son of a middle-class merchant, he graduated from Cairo University in 1934 with a degree in philosophy. He worked in university administration and then for the government's Ministry of Waqfs, or religious foundations, and in journalism. He started writing as a boy and by 1939 had already written three novels, one of which, *The Struggle of Thebes* (1944), drew a parallel between the Hyksos invasion of ancient Egypt and the pre-war British occupation of modern Egypt. He later began work on *The Cairo Trilogy* (1956–57), a monumental work, which was somewhat overshadowed by the notoriety surrounding *The Children of Gebelawi* (1961), serialized in the magazine *Al-Ahram*, which portrays average Egyptians living the lives of Cain and Abel, **Moses**, **Jesus** and **Muhammad**. It was banned throughout the Arab world, except Lebanon. Described as 'a **Dickens** of the Cairo cafés' and the '**Balzac** of Egypt', he has been almost as prolific as those 19th-century masters. The winner of the Nobel prize for literature in 1988, his work is still unavailable in many Middle Eastern countries on account of his outspoken support for President **Sadat**'s Camp David peace treaty with Israel.

MAHLER, Gustav (1860–1911) Czechoslovakian-born Austrian composer, born in Kalist. In 1875 he went to Vienna Conservatory, where he studied composition and conducting. Unsuccessful in an opera competition with the work which he later turned into the cantata *Das klagende Lied*, he turned to conducting, rapidly reaching important positions in Prague, Leipzig, Budapest and Hamburg. In 1897 he became conductor and artistic director at Vienna State Opera House, where he established the high standards for which that theatre has since become famous. Disliking the intrigues of theatrical life and the frequent personal attacks upon him due to his Jewish birth (though he had become a convert to Roman Catholicism), he resigned after ten years to devote himself to composition and the concert platform, and from 1908 to 1911 he was conductor of the New York Philharmonic Society, spending his summers composing in Austria. His mature works consist entirely of songs and symphonies, in which latter form he composed nine works on a large scale, five of them requiring voices, and he is best known by the song-symphony *Das Lied von der Erde*, which is not included in the nine; he left a Tenth Symphony unfinished. One of the great masters of the orchestra, his work gained popularity in Britain and the USA, especially in the 1960s. He is an important bridge between the late romantic 19th-century style and the revolutionary works of **Schoenberg** and his followers.

MAHMUD OF GHAZNI (971–1030) Muslim Afghan conqueror of India. The son of Sebuktigin, a Turkish slave who became ruler of Ghazni (modern Afghanistan), he succeeded to the throne in 997. He invaded India 17 times between 1001 and 1026, and created an empire that included Punjab and much of Persia. A great patron of the arts, he made Ghazni a remarkable cultural centre.

MAHMUT II (1785–1839) Ottoman sultan of Turkey. He succeeded his brother Mustafa IV in 1808. His reign saw the loss to Russia of Bessarabia, the independence of Greece and Serbia, and the autonomy of Egypt under **Muhammad 'Alí**. Despite suffering numerous defeats on land and sea, Mahmut laboured to carry out a major reorganization of the state designed to strengthen the power of the sultan and the central government. He reasserted control over the provincial administration, previously in the hands of near-independent local rulers, and suppressed the corps of janissaries, often the instrument of palace revolutions, replacing it with a new regular army on the European model.

MAHOMET See **MUHAMMAD**

MAHON, Derek (1941–) Irish poet, born in Belfast. He was educated at Belfast Institute and Trinity College, Dublin, and taught before turning to journalism and other writing. A poet of place, drawn to squalid landscapes and desperate situations, his acknowledged influences are **Louis MacNeice** and **W H Auden**. *Twelve Poems* was published in 1965, since when there have been a number of others including *Poems 1962–1978* (1979), *The Hunt by Night* (1982) and *A Kensington Notebook* (1984).

MAHON, Lord See **STANHOPE, Philip Henry, 5th Earl of**

MAHONY, Francis Sylvester, pseud **Father Prout** (1804–66) Irish priest and humorous writer, born in Cork, the son of a woollen manufacturer of Blarney. He became a Jesuit priest, but was expelled from the order for a late-night frolic and was ordained a priest at Lucca in 1832. He moved to London in 1834 and forsook his calling for journalism and poetry, and contributed to *Fraser's Magazine* and *Bentley's Miscellany*. He is remembered as author of the poems 'The Bells of Shandon' and 'The Lady of Lee'.

MAI, Angelo (1782–1854) Italian prelate and antiquary, born in Schilpario in Lombardy. Educated to be a Jesuit, he became instead a secular priest in Milan, and keeper of the Ambrosian Library, where he discovered and edited MSS or fragments of several long-lost works, including **Cicero**, **Plautus**, **Eusebius of Caesaria** and Dionysius. Transferred to the Vatican Library in 1819, he edited a number of important ancient texts, and left an edition of the *Codex Vaticanus* unfinished at his death. He was made cardinal in 1838.

MAIDEN, Joseph Henry (1859–1925) British-born Australian botanist, born in London. He emigrated to New South Wales in 1880 and became director of Sydney Botanic Garden and government botanist, New South Wales (1896–1924). He published several works on Australian plants, notably *The Forest Flora of New South Wales* (8 vols, 1904–25), *A Critical Revision of the Genus Eucalyptus* (8 vols, 1903–33), and *Census of New South Wales Plants* (1916).

MAIDMENT, James (1794–1879) Scottish lawyer and editor, born in London. Called to the Scottish bar in 1817, he became a great authority on genealogical law cases. His most ambitious work was *The Dramatists of the Restoration* (14 vols, 1872–79), edited with W H Logan. His *Court of Session Garland* is a collection of light verse.

MAILER, Norman (1923–) American novelist, journalist and polemicist, born in Long Branch, New

Jersey. He was brought up in Brooklyn and educated at Harvard. During World War II he served in the Pacific and his first novel *The Naked and the Dead* (1948) draws heavily upon his own experience. An anti-war blast and social satire, it was a remarkable work for one so young and it became a bestseller, establishing him as a leading novelist of his generation. A proponent of the 'New Journalism', and one who helped define that solipsistic genre, he has created a vast body of work, impressive for its energy and its self-obsession. He has maintained his antagonism towards contemporary society and mores in *Barbary Shore* (1951) and *The Deer Park* (1955). *Advertisements for Myself* (1959), whose own blurb admitted that 'some of the pieces are mediocre', is generally regarded as one of his more successful books. As a polemicist, campaigner and protester he was prominent throughout the 1960s, publishing *An American Dream* (1965), *Why Are We In Vietnam?* (1967) and *Armies of the Night* (1968), whose subject is the 1967 protest march on the Pentagon. It won a National Book Award and the Pulitzer prize. Subsequent books include *Miami and the Siege of Chicago* (1969), *The Prisoner of Sex* (1971), *Marilyn* (a pictorial life of Marilyn Monroe, 1973), *The Executioner's Song* (1979), a documentary study of the execution of convicted killer Gary Gilmore, *Ancient Evenings* (1983), a gargantuan historical novel, and a thriller, *Tough Guys Don't Dance* (1984).

MAILLART, Ella Kini (1903–) Swiss travel writer, born in Geneva. She represented Switzerland in the 1924 Olympic Games in Paris in the single-handed sailing competition, captained the Swiss Ladies Hockey Team in 1931 and skied for her country from 1931 to 1934. She taught in Wales, and worked on an archaeological dig in Crete, before travelling to Moscow to study film production. In 1932 she crossed Russian Turkestan and wrote of her tribulations in both French and English. In 1934, working as a journalist for *Petit Parisien*, she went to Mongolia to report on the Japanese invasion and returned via Peking across Tibet and into Kashmir with **Peter Fleming**, described in *Forbidden Journey* (1937). She worked and journeyed in Iran and Afghanistan, and then spent the war years living in an ashram in southern India under the tutelage of Sri Ramama. She was one of the first travellers into Nepal when it opened in 1949, and wrote *The Land of the Sherpas* (1955). She works as a travel guide, and spends six months of each year in Switzerland.

MAILLART, Robert (1872–1940) Swiss civil engineer, born in Berne. He studied at the Zürich Polytechnic (1890–94), worked with **Hennebique**, then set up on his own in 1902. He was one of the first to realize the economic and aesthetic advantages of three-hinged reinforced concrete arch bridges in the Swiss Alps, designing some remarkable examples, from the bridge over the Inn at Zuoz (1901) to the spectacular curving Schwanback Bridge at Schwarzenburg (1933). He also designed many industrial buildings in which he employed the so-called 'mushroom' column supporting a flat two-way reinforced floor slab.

MAILLOL, Aristide Joseph Bonaventure (1861–1944) French sculptor, born in Banyuls-sur-mer. He studied at the École des Beaux-Arts, and spent some years designing tapestries. The latter half of his life was devoted to the representation of the nude female figure, such as the *Three Graces*, *Mediterranean* and *Night* in a style of monumental simplicity and classical serenity.

MAIMAN, Theodore Harold (1927–) American physicist, constructor of the first working laser, born in Los Angeles, the son of an electrical engineer. After military service in the US Navy, he studied engineering physics at Colorado and Stanford, then joined the Hughes Research Laboratories in Miami in 1955. The maser (producing coherent microwave radiation) had been devised and induced to work by **Charles Townes** in 1953 (and independently by **Nikolai Basov** and **Aleksandr Prokhorov** in the USSR in 1955). Maiman made some design improvements to the solid-state maser, and turned to the possibility of an optical maser, or laser (light amplification by simulated emission of radiation). He constructed the first working laser in the Hughes Laboratories in 1960. By this time Townes and **Schawlow** had published a theoretical description of a laser and started to build one. Lasers have found use in a variety of applications, including spectroscopy, surgical work such as repair of retinal detachment in the eye, and in compact disc (CD) players.

MAIMBOURG, Louis (1610–86) French Jesuit church-historian, born in Nancy. He was expelled in 1685 from the order for his defence of Gallicanism, but became a pensioner of **Louis XIV**. He wrote histories of Arianism, Lutheranism, Calvinism, and the prerogatives of the Church of Rome.

MAIMON, Solomon, originally **Salomon ben Joshua** (c.1754–1800) German philosopher, born of Jewish parents in Lithuania. He studied in Berlin and then lived a desultory, vagabond life, often in poverty, but attracted the attention of **Goethe** and **Kant**. He wrote a commentary on **Maimonides**, from whom he took his surname, and was an early critic of Kant in his *Versuch über die Transzendentalphilosophie* (1790). He lived from 1790 under the patronage of Count Kalckreuth.

MAIMONIDES, properly **Moses ben Maimon** (1135–1204) Jewish philosopher, and the foremost figure of medieval Judaism. Born in Cordoba, Spain (then under Moorish rule), he studied medicine and Greek philosophy, and settled eventually in Cairo about 1165 where he became physician to **Saladin**, sultan of Egypt, and head of the Jewish community. He wrote a Hebrew commentary on the Mishnah (Jewish code of law), but his other main writings are in Arabic. His greatest work is the *Guide to the Perplexed* (1190), which tries to harmonize the thought of Aristotle and Judaism. He was a very great influence on a range of philosophers and traditions, Jewish, Muslim and Christian.

MAINBOCHER, originally **Main Rousseau Bocher** (1891–1976) American fashion designer, born in Chicago. He studied and worked in Chicago, and after service in World War I, he stayed on in Paris, eventually becoming a fashion artist with *Harper's Bazaar* and, later, editor of French *Vogue* until 1929. He started his couture house in Paris in 1930. One of his creations was Mrs Wallis Simpson, the Duchess of **Windsor**'s, wedding dress (1937). He opened a salon for ready-to-wear clothes in New York in 1940, but returned to Europe in 1971.

MAINE, Sir Henry James Sumner (1822–88) English jurist and historian. Educated at Christ's Hospital and Pembroke College, Cambridge, after various teaching posts in England, and administrative appointments in India, he was elected master of Trinity Hall at Cambridge in 1877, and in 1887 Whewell professor of international law. It is by his work on the origin and growth of legal and social institutions that he will be best remembered. His books include *Ancient Law* (1861), *Early Law and Custom* (1883), and *International Law* (1888).

MAINTENON, Françoise d'Aubigné, Marquise de (1635–1719) known as 'Madame de Maintenon', second wife of **Louis XIV** and granddaughter of the

Huguenot **Théodore Agrippa d'Aubigné**. Born near the concièrgerie of Niort, where her father was a prisoner, her childhood was spent in penury. In her teens she was converted to Roman Catholicism. In 1652 she married the poet **Paul Scarron**, whose death in 1660 left her penniless again. In 1669 she was appointed governess of the two illegitimate sons of her friend the Marquise de **Montespan** by Louis XIV, and became the king's mistress; in 1674, with the king's help, she bought the estate and marquisate of Maintenon. After the death of Queen Maria Theresa in 1683, Louis married 'Madame de Maintenon' in secret. She was accused of wielding enormous influence over him, particularly over the persecution of Protestants after the revocation of the Edict of Nantes (1685). She founded a home for impoverished noblewomen, the Maison Royale de Saint-Louis at Saint Cyr, to which she retired when the king died in 1715.

MAIR, John See **MAJOR**

MAIRET, Ethel (1872–1952) English weaver. After visiting Ceylon between 1903 and 1906, she worked with **Charles Robert Ashbee** and the Guild of Handicrafts. She started weaving in Devon in 1911 and, after marrying Philip Mairet (her second husband), established 'Gospels', her workshop based at Ditchling in Sussex. 'Gospels' became a creative centre for many weavers from all over the world. She also wrote a great deal, revealing a desire for rethinking the educational approach to handweaving and a reassessment of its relationship to power loom production.

MAISTRE, Joseph Marie, Comte de (1753–1821) French political philosopher and diplomat, born in Chambéry, ancient capital of the Dukes of Savoy. He emigrated to Switzerland during the French Revolution (when Savoy was annexed), but became ambassador to St Petersburg 1803–17 for **Victor Emmanuel I** (king of Piedmont-Sardinia), and later minister of state of Sardinia. He was very hostile to all liberal and democratic thought, such as that displayed in the French and American revolutions, and defended a doctrine of the divine right of kings. His works include *Considérations sur la France* (1796), *Essai sur le principle générateur des constitutions politiques* (1814), and *Du Pape* (1819).

MAISTRE, Xavier, Comte de (1763–1852) French painter and soldier, brother of **Joseph Marie Maistre**, born in Chambéry. He joined the Russian army and became a general. He was an accomplished landscape and portrait artist, and wrote several charming novels.

MAITANI, Lorenzo (c.1275–1330) Italian sculptor and architect, probably born in Orvieto. Little is known of his life other than that he married in 1302 and was in charge of the building of Orvieto Cathedral. From 1310 he worked on the façade and was one of the more gifted sculptors responsible for its relief carvings of the life of **Jesus Christ** and the Last Judgment.

MAITLAND, Frederic William (1850–1906) English legal historian, grandson of the historian Samuel Roffey Maitland (1792–1866). Educated at Eton College and Trinity College, Cambridge, he became a barrister (1876), reader in English law at Cambridge (1884) and Downing professor (1888). He wrote a *History of English Law before Edward I* (1895, with Sir **Frederick Pollock**), *Domesday Book and Beyond* (1897), and other brilliant works on legal antiquities and history, and edited several volumes of legal records. He was one of the creators of English legal history.

MAITLAND of Lethington, Sir Richard (1496–1586) Scottish lawyer and poet. He became a lord of session in 1551, and (after losing his sight in 1561), lord privy seal in 1562. He was conspicuous for his moderation and integrity. His poems—mostly lamentations for the distracted state of his country—were published in 1830 by the Maitland Club. He made a collection of early Scottish poetry, now forming two manuscript volumes, which are in the Pepysian collection at Cambridge. He also wrote a *Historie of the Hous of Seytoun*.

MAITLAND, William (c.1528–1573) son of Sir **Richard Maitland**. Known as 'Secretary Lethington', in 1558 he became secretary of state to the queen-regent. He represented **Mary, Queen of Scots** at the court of **Elizabeth** but made her his enemy by his connivance at **Rizzio**'s murder in 1566. He was also privy to the murder of **Darnley** and was one of the commissioners who presented to Elizabeth an indictment of Mary in 1568. Accused of plotting against his colleagues, he was imprisoned in Edinburgh Castle and later died in prison at Leith.

MAJOR, or **Mair, John** (c.1470–1550) Scottish scholastic theologian and historian, born in Gleghornie, near North Berwick. He studied at Oxford, Cambridge and Paris, and lectured on scholastic logic and philosophy at Glasgow (1518), St Andrews (1522) and Paris (1525). His pupils included **George Buchanan**, **Patrick Hamilton**, and **John Knox**. He wrote commentaries on **Peter Lombard**, and a *History of Greater Britain* (1521). He was provost of St Salvator's College, St Andrews, from 1533 until his death.

MAJOR, John (1943–) English politician. The son of a trapeze performer, after conventional training he began a banking career but his interest in politics grew and he eventually won a Commons seat, as Conservative member for Huntingdonshire, in 1979. He entered **Margaret Thatcher**'s government as a junior minister in 1981 and rose to become Treasury chief secretary, under Chancellor **Nigel Lawson**, in 1987. Thereafter, having caught the eye of the prime minister, his progress was spectacular. In the summer of 1989 he replaced Sir **Geoffrey Howe** as foreign secretary, in controversial circumstances, and in the autumn of the same year, even more surprisingly, returned to the Treasury as Chancellor, when Lawson dramatically resigned.

MAKARIOS III, properly **Mihail Christodoulou Mouskos** (1913–77) Cypriot Orthodox archbishop and first president of the Republic of Cyprus, born near Paphos. Ordained priest in 1946, he was elected bishop of Kition in 1948, and became archbishop and primate in 1950. Suspected of collaborating with anti-British (EOKA) guerrilla forces, he was exiled to the Seychelles by the colonial government, later resided in Athens, but returned after a 1959 agreement that gave Cyprus independence and made Makarios head of state. He had to cope with a restive Turkish Muslim minority, extremists who sought union with Greece, fellow bishops who critized his dual role, and a small but active communist presence which Makarios was not above using for his own ends. A short-lived coup put his life in danger and removed him briefly from leadership in 1974, but he was reinstated in 1975. On his death the posts of archbishop and head of state were separated, thus closing a chapter of Byzantine history that had somehow lingered into the 20th century.

MAKAROVA, Natalia (1940–) Russian dancer, born in Leningrad. After studying in Leningrad, she joined the Kirov and became one of their star dancers. Stopping in London on tour in 1970 she defected to the West, becoming one of the most celebrated dancers of the 1970s, particularly in the title role of *Giselle*. Associating herself with American Ballet Theatre in New York, she often guested with the Royal Ballet, Covent Garden and other companies. While specializing in the classics, she also created roles for contemporary choreographers like **Antony Tudor**, **George Balanchine** and **Glen Tetley**. Her work as producer includes *La Bayadère* (1980) for American Ballet Theatre, *The Kingdom of the Shades* (1985) and *Swan Lake* (1988), both for London Festival Ballet. In 1988 in London she became the first dancer in exile to guest with her home company, the Kirov.

MAKART, Hans (1840–84) Austrian painter, born in Salzburg. He studied in Munich and in Italy, settled in Vienna in 1869, and in 1879 became professor at the academy there. He painted spectacular and historical pictures, of bold colour and gigantic size.

MAKEBA, Miriam (1932–) South African-born American singer, born in Johannesburg. Exiled from South Africa because of her political views, she settled in the USA where she became widely known in the 1960s as 'the empress of African song', making concert tours and recording several albums. She was the first African performer to gain an international following and played a vital role in introducing the sounds and rhythms of traditional African song to the West. Her marriage in the late 1960s to the militant black leader, Stokely Carmichael, effectively ended her career in the USA, as she was declared persona non grata: she moved to Guinea, and virtually disappeared from the international concert arena, emerging only occasionally to take part in special, politically-orientated events.

MAKKARI, Ahmed el- (1585–1631) Moorish historian, born in Makkara in Algeria. He wrote a *History of the Mohammedan Dynasties of Spain*.

MALACHY (Mael Maedoc), St (c.1094–1148) Irish prelate and reformer, born in Armagh. He became abbot of Bangor (1121), bishop of Connor (1125) and, in 1134, archbishop of Armagh. He substituted Roman for Celtic liturgy, and renewed the use of the sacraments. He returned to Connor in 1137. In 1139 he journeyed to Rome, visiting St **Bernard** at Clairvaux. On his return (1142) he introduced the Cistercian Order into Ireland. In 1148 he once more went to France, and died at Clairvaux in St Bernard's arms. The so-called 'Prophecies of St Malachy', first published in *Lignum Vitae* (1595) by the Flemish Benedictine, Arnold Wion, are spurious. He was canonized in 1190—the first papal canonization of an Irishman.

MALAMUD, Bernard (1914–86) American novelist, born in Brooklyn, New York, and educated at Columbia University, New York. He taught at Oregon State University (1949–61) and Bennington College (1961–86). One of the leading writers of contemporary America and among the 'urban-Jewish' Americans, he was more influenced by mainstream American writers than those ghettoized by their creed. *The Natural* (1952), his first novel, intended as an extended metaphor for life, and later made into a poor film starring **Robert Redford**, took as its starting point the all-American game of baseball and followed the fading career of the once-promising big-hitter Roy Hobbs. Hollywood made it a fairy tale. With *The Assistant* (1957), the mood is darker but the critical reception was warm. *A New Life* (1961) marked a new departure, from the compressed urban environment to mountainous western America, where Seymour Levin arrives at a small college to teach and unwrap happiness. *The Fixer* (1966), set in Tsarist Russia, was his bleakest and most potent book, streaked with self-deprecating humour. He wrote four more novels: *Pictures of Fidelman* (1969); *The Tenants* (1971); *Dubin's Lives* (1979); and *God's Grace* (1982), a prophetic, apocalyptic allegory. He was also an accomplished short story writer and *The Stories of Bernard Malamud* was published in 1983. He won the National Book award twice, in 1959 and 1967, and the Pulitzer prize in 1967.

MALAN, Daniel François (1874–1959) South African politician, born in Riebeek West, Cape Province. He was educated at Victoria College, Stellenbosch, and Utrecht University. On his return to South Africa in 1905 he became a predikant of the Dutch Reformed Church and after ten years abandoned his clerical career to become editor of *Die Burger*, the Nationalist newspaper. He became an MP in 1918, and in 1924 in the Nationalist-Labour government he held the portfolios of the interior, of education and of public health. He introduced measures strengthening the Nationalist position—in particular, that making Afrikaans an official language. He was leader of the Opposition from 1934 to 1939 and from 1940 to 1948 when, becoming prime minister and minister for external affairs, he embarked on the hotly controversial policies of apartheid with the aim of re-aligning South Africa's multi-racial society. He described as the kernel of his segregation policies the Group Areas Act, dividing the country into white, black and coloured zones. The apartheid legislation, which involved strongly-contested constitutional changes, was met by non-violent civil disobedience at home and vigorous criticism abroad. Dr Malan resigned from the premiership in 1954. Crusty, austere, a scholar of profound convictions and an uncompromising manner, Dr Malan was a back-veldt Moses to the Boers. He never wavered in his pulpiteering belief in a strict white supremacy, in a Heaven-sent Afrikaner mission and a rigidly hierarchical society.

MALATESTA, Enrico (1853–1932) Italian anarchist, born in Campania of a wealthy family. He studied medicine at Naples University but was expelled for encouraging student unrest. To demonstrate his beliefs, he gave away his personal wealth and worked as an electrician in cities around Europe, at the same time preaching anarchism and spending numerous periods in prison. He became something of a legend because of his unusually small stature and ability to escape. He settled in London in 1900, advocating peaceful opposition to authority, and survived an attempt to deport him in 1911 for alleged complicity with the Sidney Street anarchists who had killed three policemen. He returned to Italy in 1913 and died peacefully 19 years later.

MALCOLM I (943–54) king of Scotland, son of Donald II.

MALCOLM II (b.c.954) king of Scotland, son of Kenneth II.

MALCOLM III, called **Canmore**, (Gael *Ceann-mor*, 'great head') (c.1031–1093) king of Scotland from 1057, was a child when his father, King Duncan, was slain by **Macbeth** (1040). He spent his youth in Northumbria with his uncle, Earl Siward, who in 1054 established him in Cumbria and Lothian. In 1057, after Macbeth was killed, he became king of all Scotland. His first wife, Ingibjorg, widow of Thorfinn, Earl of Orkney, had died; and in 1069 Malcolm wedded **Margaret**, sister of **Edgar the Ætheling**. He invaded England five times between 1061 and 1093, when he was killed at Alnwick. He left five sons, of whom four succeeded him, Duncan, Edgar, **Alexander** and **David**.

MALCOLM IV (1141–65) Malcolm the Maiden, king of Scotland from 1153.

MALCOLM X (Malcolm Little) (1925–65) American black nationalist leader, born in Omaha, Nebraska, the son of a radical Baptist minister. He was brought up in Lansing, Michigan, and Boston. He was imprisoned for burglary in 1946 and in 1952, and while still in jail was converted to the Black Muslim sect led by Elijah Muhammad. On his release in 1953 he assumed the name Malcolm X and travelled the country promoting the sect. An opponent of the integrationist movement, he pressed for black separatism and advocated the use of violence in self-defence. In 1964, following a trip to Mecca, his views changed and he founded the Organization of Afro-American Unity, which blended elements of orthodox Islam, African socialism, anti-colonialism and racial solidarity. A factional feud ensued, culiminating in Malcolm X's assassination by Black Muslim enemies during a rally in Harlem in 1965.

MALEBRANCHE, Nicolas (1638–1715) French philosopher, born in Paris. He studied theology and joined the Catholic community of Oratorians in 1660, but was drawn to philosophy, particularly by **Descartes**' works. His own major work is *De la recherche de la verité* (1674), which espouses Descartes' dualism of mind and body but explains all causal interaction between them by a theory of 'occasionalism' (divine intervention, governing our bodily movements and all physical events), and argues as a corollary that 'we see all things in God' since external objects cannot act directly upon us. His other works include *Traité de la morale* (1684) and *Entretiens sur la métaphysique et la religion* (1688).

MALENKOV, Georgi Maksimilianovich (1901–88) Soviet politician, born in Orenburg in Central Russia. He began working for the Communist party's central committee in Moscow in 1925 and, noted for his loyalty, was quickly selected by **Stalin** to serve as his personal secretary. From 1934 he headed the party's personnel department and during World War II was part of the five-man defence council which managed the Soviet war effort, being placed in charge of armaments. After the war, he was appointed deputy prime minister in 1946 and made a full member of the presidium (politburo) and on Stalin's death in March 1953 initially took over as de facto party leader. This post, however, was soon assumed by **Nikita Khrushchev** and a power-struggle ensued. In February 1955 Malenkov was forced to resign as prime minister, pleading inadequate experience and admitting responsiblity for the failure of Soviet agricultural policy. He was succeeded by Marshal **Bulganin** and relegated to the office of minister for electric power stations, but in July 1957, having been accused, with **Molotov** and **Kaganovich**, of setting up an 'anti-party' group, he was dismissed both from the government and the party's presidium and central committee, and was rusticated to remotest Kazakhstan as manager of a hydro-electric plant. He retired in 1968 and died in obscurity.

MALESHERBES, Chrétien Guillaume de Lamoignon de (1721–94) French pre-revolutionary statesman, born in Paris. In 1750 he became president of the *Cour des Aides*. A determined opponent of government rapacity and tyranny, as censor of the press (1750–63) he showed himself tolerant, and was instrumental in arranging the publication of the *Encyclopédie*. In 1771 his remonstrances against royal abuses of law led to his banishment to his country-seat of Ste Lucie; at **Louis XVI**'s accession (1774) he was recalled, and took office, but retired on the dismissal of **Turgot**, and, save for a short spell in office in 1787, spent his time in travel or in the improvement of his estates. Under the Convention he went to Paris to conduct the king's defence. He was arrested in December 1793, and guillotined the following April along with his daughter and her husband.

MALET, David See **MALLET**

MALET, Lucas See **KINGSLEY, Mary St Leger**

MALEVICH, Kasimir Severinovich (1878–1935) Russian painter and designer, born and trained near Kiev. He worked in Moscow from c.1904. Around 1910 his work began to show Cubist and Futurist influence; however, he was above all interested in developing a totally non-objective art, and in 1915 he launched Suprematism, a movement dedicated to the expression in painting of the absolute purity of geometrical forms. The austerity of the earliest Suprematist works had given way by 1917 to less rigid compositions, with a greater colour range and a suggestion of three-dimensional space; however in 1918 he returned to his original ideals with the *White on White* series, the culmination of the Suprematist ethic. After this he virtually ceased to produce abstract paintings, and concentrated on exounding his theories through writing and teaching, first at Vitebsk, where he was highly influential, and later in Leningrad, where he lived from 1922. In 1926 he published *Die gegenstandlose Welt* (The Non-Objective World), in which he outlined his theories.

MALHERBE, François de (1555–1628) French poet, born in Caen. He ingratiated himself with **Henri IV**, and received a pension. He was an industrious writer, producing odes, songs, epigrams, epistles, translations and criticisms. He founded a literary tradition—'Enfin Malherbe vint'—and led his countrymen to disdain the richly-coloured and full-sounding verses of **Ronsard**, and to adopt a style clear, correct and refined, but cold and prosaic.

MALIBRAN, Marie Felicita (1808–36) Spanish mezzo-soprano singer, born in Paris. She was the daughter of the Spanish singer **Manuel Garcia**, who was her most important teacher. She made her operatic début in London in 1825. A spirited singer, she became the most famous female singer of her time. Divorcing her first husband in 1836, she remarried, but was killed the same year following a fall from a horse.

MALIK, Jacob Alexandrovich (1906–80) Soviet politician, born in the Ukraine. Said to be one of **Stalin**'s favourite 'juniors', he was ambassador to Japan from 1942 to 1945 and deputy foreign minister in 1946. In 1948 he succeeded **Andrei Gromyko** as Soviet spokesman at UNO and was ambassador to Britain (1953–60). From 1960 he was again deputy foreign minister, serving a second term as ambassador to the United Nations (1968–76).

MALINOVSKY, Rodion Yakovlevich (1898–1967) Russian soldier, born in Odessa. He was a corporal in World War I, when, after the Russian collapse, he escaped via Siberia and Singapore to fight in a Russian brigade in France. He joined the Red Army after the Revolution (1917) and was major-general at the time of the Nazi invasion in 1941. He commanded the forces which liberated Rostov, Kharkov and the Dnieper basin and led the Russian advance on Budapest and into Austria (1944–45). When Russia declared war on Japan, he took a leading part in the Manchurian campaign. In October 1957 he succeeded **Zhukov** as **Khrushchev**'s minister of defence.

MALINOWSKI, Bronislaw (1884–1942) Polish-born British anthropologist, born in Cracow, a founder of modern social anthropology. He studied physics and mathematics at the Jagellonian University, and went on to study psychology under **Wilhelm Max Wundt** at Leipzig, and sociology under **Edvard Westermarck** at London. In 1914 he left on a research assignment to Australia, but with the outbreak of war was partially confined to the Trobriand Islands, off the eastern tip of New Guinea. Returning to London in 1920, he was appointed in 1927 to the first chair in social anthropology at the London School of Economics. In 1938 he moved to the United States, where he taught at Yale

University and undertook field research in Mexico. Malinowski is remembered as the originator of modern methods of ethnographic fieldwork, involving long periods of intensive participant observation. His works on the Trobriand Islanders, especially *Argonauts of the Western Pacific* (1922) and *Coral Gardens and their Magic* (2 vols, 1935), set new standards for ethnographic description that were emulated by his many students. His better-known writings on the Trobriands include *Crime and Custom in Savage Society* (1926) and *Sex and Repression in Savage Society* (1927). Malinowski was also a strong advocate of the theory of functionalism, as set out in *A Scientific Theory of Culture* (1944), according to which social and cultural institutions exist to satisfy basic human physiological and psychological needs.

MALIPIERO, Francesco (1882–1973) Italian composer, born in Venice. He became a professor at Venice Conservatory (1932) and director there in 1939–52. He wrote much chamber and symphonic music in a highly characteristic style and edited **Monteverdi** and **Vivaldi**. He wrote *Claudio Monteverdi* (1930), *Igor Stravinsky* (1945) and the autobiographical *Cosi va lo mondo, 1922–45* (1946).

MALLARMÉ, Stéphane (1842–98) French Symbolist poet, born in Paris. He taught English in various schools in Paris and elsewhere and visited England on several occasions. He translated **Poe**'s 'The Raven' (1875). In prose and verse he was a leader of the Symbolist school, revelling in allegory, obscurity, bizarre works and constructions, *vers libre* and word-music. *L'Après-midi d'un faune*, illustrated by **Manet** (1876), is his best-known poem and made the wilful obscurity of his style famous. His *Les Dieux antiques* (1880), *Poésies* (1899), and *Vers et prose* (1893) were other works admired by the 'decadents'.

MALLET, David, originally **Malloch** (c.1705–1765) Scottish poet, born near Crieff, the son of a schoolmaster. After a period working as the janitor at Edinburgh High School in 1717–18, he then studied at the university. In 1720 he became a tutor, from 1723 to 1731, in the family of the Duke of Montrose, living mostly in London, and changed his name 'from Scots Malloch to English Mallet'. *William and Margaret* (1723), developed from the fragment of an old ballad, gained him a reputation as a poet, which he enhanced by *The Excursion* (1728). He also tried his hand at playwriting. *Mustapha* pleased for a while in 1739; *Eurydice* (1731) and *Elvira* (1763), both tragedies, were failures. *Alfred, a Masque* (1740), was written in conjunction with **James Thomson**, and one of its songs, 'Rule Britannia', was claimed for both.

MALLOWAN, Sir Max Edgar Lucien (1904–78) English archaeologist, born in London of Austrian-French extraction. He was educated at Lancing, where he was a contemporary of **Evelyn Waugh**, and at New College, Oxford (1921–25), where he studied classics. His apprenticeship in field archaeology was served with **Leonard Woolley** at Ur (1925–31), and it was at Ur that he met the novelist **Agatha Christie**, whom he married in 1930. He excavated for the British Museum at Arpachiyah near Nineveh (1932–33), and in Syria at Chagar Bazar (1935–36) and Tell Brak (1937–38). After service in the RAF in World War II he became professor of western Asiatic archaeology at London University (1947–60). From this base he continued to excavate in the Near East for several months each year, principally at Nimrud, the ancient capital of Assyria (1949–60), with striking results described in detail in *Nimrud and its remains* (1970). Agatha Christie's *Come, tell me how you live* (1946) is a wry account of Mallowan's five seasons' digging in Syria (1934–38). His own autobiography, *Mallowan's memoirs*, appeared in 1977.

MALMESBURY, James Harris, 1st Earl of (1746–1820) English diplomat. Educated at Winchester and Merton College, Oxford, he also studied at Leiden. He was an attaché in Madrid (1778–89), Berlin (1772–76), St Petersburg, now Leningrad (1777–82), and the Hague (1784–88). In 1795 he negotiated the marriage between the Prince of Wales (the future **George IV**) and **Caroline of Brunswick**. His *Diaries and Correspondence* was published in 1844.

MALMESBURY, William of See **WILLIAM OF MALMESBURY**

MALONE, Edmund (1741–1812) Irish editor of **Shakespeare**, born in Dublin. He graduated from Trinity College, was called to the Irish bar in 1767, but from 1777 devoted himself to literary work in London, his first work being a 'supplement' to **Steevens**' edition of Shakespeare (1778). His own eleven-volume edition of the great dramatist (1790) was warmly received. He had been one of the first to express his disbelief in **Chatterton**'s Rowley poems, and in 1796 he denounced the Shakespeare forgeries of **William Henry Ireland**. He left behind a large mass of materials for 'The Variorum Shakespeare', edited in 1821 by James Boswell the younger. The Malone Society was founded in his honour (1907).

MALORY, Sir Thomas (d.1471) English writer. **Caxton**'s preface to Malory's masterpiece, the *Morte d'Arthur*, states that Malory was a knight, that he finished his work in the ninth year of the reign of **Edward IV** (1469–70), and that he 'reduced' it from some French book. It is probable that he was the Sir Thomas Malory of Newbold Revel, Warwickshire, whose quarrels with a neighbouring priory and (probably) Lancastrian politics brought him imprisonment. Of Caxton's black-letter folio only two copies now exist. An independent manuscript was discovered at Winchester in 1934. *Morte d'Arthur* is the best prose romance in English and was a happy attempt to give epic unity to the whole mass of French Arthurian romance. **Tennyson**, **Swinburne** and many others took their inspiration from Malory.

MALOUF, David (1934–) Australian novelist, born in Brisbane. His father's family came to Australia in the 1880s from Lebanon and his mother's from London just before World War I. He was educated at Brisbane Grammar School and Queensland University, where he subsequently taught for two years. He went abroad for a decade and returned to Australia, tutoring at Sydney University before leaving for Italy. A full-time writer since 1978, an early project was the libretto for an opera of **Patrick White**'s *Voss*. Previously concentrating on poetry, his first novel was *Johnno* (1975) and in 1979 he was awarded the New South Wales Premier's Literary Award for *An Imaginary Life* (1978). Other novels are *Fly Away Peter* (1982) and *Harland's Half Acre* (1984). *Antipodes*, a collection of stories, appeared in 1985.

MALPIGHI, Marcello (1628–94) Italian anatomist, born near Bologna, where he studied medicine. He was professor at Pisa, Messina and Bologna, and from 1691 chief physician to Pope Innocent XII. A pioneer in microscopic anatomy, animal and vegetable, he made many pioneering discoveries.

MALRAUX, André (1901–76) French writer, born in Paris. He studied oriental languages and spent much time in China, where he worked for the Kuomintang and was active in the 1927 revolution. He also fought as a pilot with the Republican forces in the Spanish Civil War, and in World War II he escaped from a prisoner-of-war camp to join the French resistance movement. He was minister of information in **de Gaulle**'s government (1945–46), minister delegate from 1958 and minister of cultural affairs (1960–69). He is best known for his novels, which are a dramatic meditation on human destiny and are highly coloured by his personal experience of war, revolution and resistance to tyranny. Among them are *Les Conquérants* (1928), *La Condition humaine* (1933, winner of the Goncourt prize) and *L'Espoir* (1937). He also wrote *La Psychologie de l'art* (1947) and other books on art and museums.

MALTHUS, Thomas Robert (1766–1834) English economist and clergyman, born in The Rookery, near Dorking. He was ninth wrangler at Cambridge in 1788, was elected fellow of his college (Jesus) in 1793, and in 1797 became curate at Albury, Surrey. In 1798 he published anonymously his *Essay on the Principle of Population*, with a greatly enlarged and altered edition in 1807. In it he maintained that the optimistic hopes of **Rousseau** and **William Godwin** are rendered baseless by the natural tendency of population to increase faster than the means of subsistence. Malthus gives no sanction to the theories and practices currently known as Malthusianism. An amiable and benevolent man, he suffered much misrepresentation and abuse at the hands of both revolutionaries and conservatives. The problem had been handled by **Franklin**, **Hume** and many other writers, but Malthus crystallized the views of those writers, and presented them in systematic form with elaborate proofs derived from history, and he called for positive action to cut the birth-rate, by sexual abstinence or birth control. **Darwin** saw 'on reading Malthus *On Population* that natural selection was the inevitable result of the rapid increase of all organic beings', for such rapid increase necessarily leads to the struggle for existence. In 1805 he was appointed professor of political economy at the East India College at Haileybury. His other works included *An Inquiry into the Nature and Progress of Rent* (1815), largely anticipating **David Ricardo**, and *Principles of Political Economy* (1820).

MALUS, Étienne Louis (1775–1812) French physicist, born in Paris. A military engineer in **Napoleon**'s army (1796–1801), he carried out research in optics and discovered the polarization of light by reflection. His paper explaining the theory of double refraction in crystals won him the Institute's prize in 1810.

MALVERN, 1st Viscount See **HUGGINS, Godfrey Martin**

MALYNES or **DE MALINES, Gerard** (c.1586–1641) Belgian-born English merchant, and writer on law and economics, born in Antwerp. Frequently consulted by the privy council on problems of currency and exchange rates, he was the first English writer on the law applicable to commerce. His *Lex Mercatoria or the Ancient Law Merchant* (1622) shows an extensive acquaintance with natural law theory, Roman law, the works of Continental jurists and with the practical issues of commercial practice and the relevant law.

MAMELI, Goffredo (1827–49) Italian poet and patriot, born in Genoa. He was a volunteer in **Garibaldi**'s forces and wrote the Italian national anthem *Fratelli d'Italia*. He died in the defence of Rome against the French.

MAMET, David (1947–) American dramatist, screenplay writer and film director, born in Chicago. He graduated from Goddard College in Vermont and studied acting in New York. His plays, such as *American Buffalo* (1975), *Glengarry Glen Ross* (1983), and *Speed-the-Plow* (1988), address the psychological and ethical issues that confront modern, urban society, its professional superstructure and near-criminal substructure. His other plays include *Sexual Perversity in Chicago*, and *Duck Variations* (1976); *Reunion*, and *The Water Engine* (1977); *A Life in the Theater* (1978); *Edmond* (1982); and *The Shawl* (1985). He has translated plays by **Chekhov**, and his screenplays include a new adaptation of *The Postman Always Rings Twice* (1981), and *The Untouchables* (1987). He wrote and directed *House of Games* (1987), a look at seedy professional gambling, and, with Shel Silverstein, *Things Change* (1988). He published a book of essays, *Writing in Restaurants*, in 1986.

MAMLUKS a series of sultans in Egypt, commonly divided into two lines of Kipchak (Bahrīs, 1250–1382) and Circassian (Burjīs, 1382–1517) origin. Their name derives from that originally applied to the group from which they were drawn, a privileged caste of military slaves recruited from various non-Muslim peoples (especially Turks and Caucasians) and who, as converts, served in the armies of most Islamic powers from the 9th century onwards. In 1250 the Ayyūbid sultan of Egypt, Tūrān-Shāh, was murdered by a group of Turkish Kipchak mamluks belonging to his military household, who later enthroned one of their number, thus inaugurating the *dawlat al-Atrāk* ('state of the Turks'). The Mamluk leadership proved its worth by defeating the Mongol invaders of Syria at 'Ayn Jālūt and Hims (1260). One of the successful commanders in these campaigns was Baybars (1233–77), who murdered his predecessor to become sultan in 1260 and went on to consolidate Mamluk rule, capturing Caesarea, Jaffa and Antioch from the Franks and reducing the crusader states to a coastal strip based around Acre. Although he secured religious legitimation by installing various members of the **'Abbasid** family as caliphs in Cairo, Baybars was unable to establish a dynasty. In 1279 the throne was seized by al-Mansūr Qalāwūn (d.1290) whose son al-Ashraf Khalīl (d.1293) captured Acre, crushing the crusaders' kingdom (1291). Khalīl's murder by a rival led to a period of turbulence from which his brother, al-Nāsir Muhammad (d.1341), emerged victorious in 1310 after having been deposed twice. The sultanate remained in this family until 1382, when the last Qalawunid was dethroned by Barqūq (d.1399), the representative of the Circassian element whose influence had come to outweigh that of the Kipchaks. After the deposition and death of Barqūq's son Faraj (1389–1412), the succession ceased to be hereditary, but tended to be determined by the strongest Mamluk faction. In the 15th century the Mamluks failed to keep pace with developments in warfare, and consequently were no match for the technically superior Ottoman army. They were decisively defeated by **Selim I**, who incorporated Egypt into the Ottoman empire (1516–17); while the sultanate thus ended with his execution of the last Burjī, Tūmān-Bāy, the Mamluk class retained a privileged status under Ottoman rule until it was finally suppressed by **Muhammad 'Alī** in 1812.

MANASSEH biblical king of Judah, and eldest son of **Joseph**. He was the eponymous ancestor of one of the twelve tribes of Israel.

MANASSEH biblical king of Judah, son of Hezekiah whom he succeeded as king (697–42 BC). He earned an evil name for idolatry and wickedness till, as a captive in Babylon, he repented. *The Prayer of Manasseh* is apocryphal.

MANASSEH BEN ISRAEL (1604–57) Dutch Jewish scholar, born in Lisbon. He was taken early to Amsterdam, where he became chief rabbi at the age of 18 in 1622, and set up the first printing press in Holland (1626). In 1655–57 he was in England, securing from

Cromwell the readmission of the Jews. He wrote important works in Hebrew, Spanish and Latin, and in English a *Humble Address* to Cromwell, *A Declaration*, and *Vindiciae Judaeorum* (1656).

MANBY, George William (1765–1854) English inventor. He was barrack-master at Yarmouth from 1803. In 1807 he showed how to save shipwrecked persons by firing a rope to the ship from a mortar on shore. He wrote on this method, on lifeboats, criminal law and other subjects.

MANCHESTER, Edward Montagu, 2nd Earl of (1602–71) English parliamentary soldier, educated at Sidney Sussex College, Cambridge. In 1623 he accompanied Prince Charles (**Charles I**) to Spain on his abortive mission to woo the Infanta Maria, and in 1626 was raised to the House of Lords as Baron Montagu of Kimbolton, but was better known by his courtesy title of Viscount Mandeville. Siding with the popular party, and an acknowledged leader of the Puritans in the Upper House, in 1642 he was impeached by the king for entertaining traitorous designs, along with the five members of the House of Commons, and acquitted. He succeeded his father as 2nd earl in the same year. At the outbreak of the Civil War he fought for the parliament. He served under Essex at Edgehill, then held the associated (eastern) counties against **William Cavendish**, Duke of Newcastle, took Lincoln (1644), and routed Prince **Rupert** at Marston Moor (1644)—that is to say, he nominally commanded; the real fighting was done by Cromwell and his Ironsides. He then marched to oppose the royalists in the southwest, and defeated them at Newbury (the second battle). But after this battle he again showed slackness in following up the victory, a fault that had been noticed after Marston Moor. In consequence Cromwell accused him of military incompetency in the House of Commons. The Self-denying Ordinance deprived Manchester of his command (1645), and this did not allay his bitterness against Cromwell. He opposed the trial of the king, and protested against the Commonwealth. Afterwards, having been active in promoting the Restoration, he was made lord chamberlain (1660), a step designed to conciliate the Presbyterians.

MANCHESTER, William (1922–) American novelist, foreign correspondent and contemporary historian, born in Attleboro, Massachusetts. His magnum opus is *The Death of the President* (1967), written at the behest of the **Kennedy** family. A landmark in reportage, it received mixed reviews and sold in millions but has subsequently been superseded as new evidence on the assassination of President Kennedy has emerged.

MANCINI, Hortense, Duchesse de Mazarin (1646–99) Italian beauty. She was married off by Cardinal **Mazarin** to Armand Charles de la Porte, who assumed the Mazarin title, but she separated from him and became famous for her beauty at the court of **Charles II** in London.

MANCINI, Laura, Duchesse de Mercoeur (1636–57) Italian beauty, sister of **Hortense Mancini**. She came to the French court and was married to Louis de Vendôme. The famous **Duc de Vendôme** was their son.

MANCINI, Marie Anne, Duchess de Bouillon (1649–1714) Italian beauty, sister of **Hortense** and **Laura Mancini**. She became renowned for her literary salon and for her patronage of **La Fontaine**. She was banished in 1680, having been involved in the *cause célèbre* of the notorious sorceress **La Voisin** known as the 'Affair of the Poisons'.

MANCINI, Marie, Princess de Colonna (1640–1715) Italian beauty, sister of **Hortense, Marie** and **Laura Mancini**. She was a mistress of **Louis XIV**, who was prevented from marrying her only by the machinations of Cardinal **Mazarin**. She lived in Spain for most of her life.

MANCINI, Olympe, Comtesse de Soissons (1639–1708) Italian beauty, sister of **Hortense, Marie Anne, Laura** and **Marie Mancini**. She was also a mistress of **Louis XIV**, was involved with her sister, **Marie Anne** in the **La Voisin** intrigues and, accused of poisoning her husband and the Queen of Spain, fled to the Netherlands. Her son was Prince **Eugene of Savoy**.

MANDELA, Nelson Rolihlahla (1918–) African nationalist leader, born in Transkei, South Africa. He became a successful lawyer in Joahnnesburg before joining the African National Congress in 1944. For the next 20 years he directed a campaign of defiance against the South African government and its racist policies, orchestrating in 1961 a three-day national strike. Despite his memorable four-hour defence speech at his trial in 1964, he was sentenced to life imprisonment for political offences. He continued to be such a potent symbol of black resistance that a co-ordinated international campaign for his release was launched. His wife Winnie was also frequently subjected to restrictions on her personal freedom. In 1990 he was released to world-wide rejoicing and, at the age of 71, made a dignified return to the political arena, in anticipation of fundamental changes in the South African social and political system.

MANDELSTAM, Osip (1892–1941) Russian poet, critic and translator, born in Warsaw. He grew up in Leningrad and attended Heidelberg University. A classicist whose Russian 'sounds like Latin', he had a fierce love of Greek poetry. Four books of poems appeared during his lifetime: *Kamen* (1913); *Stone*; *Tristia* (1922); and *Stikhotvoreniya* (1928). *The Complete Poetry* was published in 1973. Regarded by some as the greatest Russian poet of the century, his life after the revolution was filled with pessimism for the future of Russia. Arrested, exiled and rearrested, he died of a heart attack on his way to one of **Stalin**'s camps.

MANDER, Karel van (1548–1606) Flemish portrait painter and writer, born in Meulebeke. He lived mostly in Haarlem, and is chiefly remembered for his *Schilderbouck* (1604), a collection of biographical profiles of painters, important as a source for the art history of the Low Countries.

MANDEVILLE, Bernard (1670–1733) Dutch-born British satirist, born in Dort in Holland. He took his MD at Leiden in 1691, and immediately settled in London in medical practice. He is known as the author of a short work in doggerel verse originally entitled *The Grumbling Hive* (1705), and finally *The Fable of the Bees* (1723). Writing in a vein of acute paradox, he affirms that 'private vices are public benefits', and that every species of virtue is basically some form of gross selfishness, more or less modified. The book was condemned by the grand jury of Middlesex, and was attacked by **William Law** the nonjuror, by **Berkeley**, **Warburton**, **Hutcheson** and others. Other works in an unpleasant tone are *The Virgin Unmasked* and *Free Thoughts on Religion*.

MANDEVILLE, Geoffrey de, Earl of Essex (d.1144) English baron. He succeeded his father as constable of the Tower about 1130, proved a traitor alternately to King **Stephen** and the empress **Matilda**, and taking finally to open brigandage, was besieged in the Cambridgeshire fens and slain.

MANDEVILLE, Jehan de, or **Sir John** (14th century) the name assigned to the unknown compiler of a famous book of travels (*The Voyage and Travels of Sir John Mandeville, Knight*), published apparently in 1366, and soon translated from the French into all European tongues. It may have been written by a physician, Jehan de Bourgogne, otherwise Jehan á la Barbe, who died in Liège in 1372, and who is said to have revealed on his death-bed his real name of Mandeville (or Maundevylle), explaining that he had had to flee from his native England for a homicide. Some scholars, however, attribute it to Jean d'Outremeuse, a Frenchman. 'Mandeville' claims to have travelled through Turkey, Persia, Syria, Arabia, North Africa and India, but much of the book is a compilation from various literary sources.

MANDEVILLE, Viscount See **MANCHESTER, Edward Montagu, 2nd Earl of**

MANEN, Hans van (1932–) Dutch dancer, choreographer and director, born in Nieuwer, Amstel. He joined Ballet Recital in 1952, moving to Amsterdam Opera Ballet in 1959. Later that year he became one of the founding members of Netherlands Dance Theatre, for whom he was appointed artistic director. In 1973 he left to join the Dutch National Ballet as choreographer and ballet master but has recently rekindled his relationship with NDT. His work for NDT includes *Symphony in Three Movements* (1963), *Essay in Silence* (1965), *Five Sketches* (1966), *Squares* (1969), *Septet Extra* (1973) and *Songs Without Words* (1977).

MÁNES, Josef (1820–71) Czech artist, born in Prague. He was the pupil of his father, the landscape artist Antonin (1784–1843), and he was well known for his genre and historical paintings and portraits.

MANET, Édouard (1832–83) French painter, born in Paris. Originally intended for a legal career, he was sent on a voyage to Rio to distract his thoughts from art. Nevertheless, between 1850 and 1856 he studied under Thomas Couture (1815–79), and his *Spanish Guitar Player* was awarded an honourable mention at the 1861 Salon. Pursuing official recognition, he entered his *Déjeuner sur l'herbe* for the Salon of 1863 but it scandalized the jury with its portrayal of a nude female with clothed male companions, and was rejected. This was followed by the acceptance of his *Olympia* in 1865, but, a stark depiction of a female obviously modelled by a prostitute, it elicited a similar outcry from the public. Manet was nevertheless influenced by conventional artists: *Olympia* owes a great deal to the Old Master nudes of **Giorgione**, **Titian** and **Raphael**. But the strong contrasts he learnt from the Spanish masters—he was an ardent admirer of **Velazquez**—and his adherence to the advice of **Courbet** in always selecting subjects from contemporary life, marked him out from the older Salon artists. In the 1870s he came under the influence of the Impressionists and, in particular, of **Monet** while painting at Argenteuil, and his technique became free and more spontaneous. He never exhibited with the group but became rather a father-figure to them because of his stand against the conventions of the salon. His last major work was *A Bar at the Foliès-Bergère* (1882). In that year, official recognition finally arrived—he was appointed Chevalier de la Légion d'Honneur—but he died an embittered man.

MANETHO Egyptian historian. He was high-priest of Heliopolis in the 3rd century BC. He wrote in Greek a history of the 30 dynasties from mythical times to 323 BC, of which only portions have been preserved in the works of Julius Africanus (AD 300), **Eusebius of Caesarea**, and George Syncellus (AD 800).

MANFRED (1232–66) king of Sicily from 1258. He was a natural son of the emperor **Frederick II**, and was made Prince of Tarentum. For his half-brother, Conrad IV, he acted as regent in Italy (especially Apulia), and subsequently for his nephew **Conradin of Swabia** bravely defended the interests of the empire against the aggression of Pope Innocent IV, who, however, compelled Manfred to flee for shelter to the Saracens. With their aid he defeated the papal troops, and became, in 1257, master of the whole kingdom of Naples and Sicily. On the (false) rumour of Conradin's death (1258) he was crowned king at Palermo, and, in spite of excommunication by Pope **Alexander VI**, occupied Tuscany. His brief government was mild yet vigorous; but Pope **Urban IV** renewed the excommunication, and bestowed his dominions on **Charles of Anjou**, brother of **Louis IX** of France. Manfred fell in battle at Benevento.

MANGAN, James Clarence (1803–49) Irish poet, born in Dublin, the son of a grocer. His life was a tragedy of hapless love, poverty and intemperance. He worked as a lawyer's clerk, and later found employment in the library of Trinity College, Dublin. There is fine quality in his original verse. Although he knew no Irish, he published English versions of Irish poems in *The Poets and Poetry of Munster* (1849), notably 'My Dark Rosaleen', 'The Nameless One' and 'The Woman of Three Cows'. He also published translations from German poets in *Anthologia Germanica* (1845).

MANICHAEUS, or **Mani** (c.215–276) Persian religious leader, born in Ecbatana, and founder of the heretical sect of Manichaeism. About 245 he began to proclaim his new religion at the court of the Persian king, Sapor (Shahpur) I. He travelled widely, but eventually King Bahram I abandoned him to his Zoroastrian enemies, who crucified him.

MANIKONGO (16th to 17th century) the dynastic title of the paramount chiefs of the African kingdom of Kongo. Nzinga a Nkuwa, *manikongo* in 1491, converted, under Portuguese influence, to Christianity. Although he subsequently reverted to paganism, his son, who ruled 1506–45, remained a Christian and took the name of Alfonso I. He became, however, increasingly alienated from his own people while the Portuguese profited from the connection to pursue a constant traffic in slaves that decimated the population, destroyed the country's political unity and corrupted the ruling group within Kongo. Diogo I, who ruled 1545–61, attempted to curtail Portuguese privileges but Ngola (Angola) became independent of Kongo with Portuguese aid and encouragement in 1556. Alvaro II (ruled 1587–1614) and his son, Alvaro III (ruled 1614–22) provided strong, stable government and attempted to prevent some of the cruelties of the slave trade, but tensions mounted between Kongo and the Portuguese and war broke out in 1622. Thenceforward the Portuguese increasingly transferred their attention to Angola, a colony from 1571, while the war, and subsequent disputes, left Kongo permanently weakened with power passing from the rulers to native entrepreneurs with interests in the European slave-trade.

MANIN, Daniele (1804–57) Venetian statesman, born of Jewish ancestry in Venice. He practised at the bar, and became a leader of liberal opinion; made president of the Venetian republic (1848), he was the soul of the heroic five months' defence against the Austrians. When Venice capitulated (24 August 1849), Manin, with 39 others, was excluded from the amnesty, but escaped to Paris, where he taught Italian, and died of heart disease. His bones were taken to Venice in 1868.

MANKOWITZ, (Cyril) Wolf (1924–) English author, playwright and antique dealer, born in Bethnal Green, London. An authority on **Wedgwood**, he published *Wedgwood* (1953), and *The Portland Vase* (1953), and was an editor of *The Concise Encyclopedia of English Pottery and Porcelain* (1957). Other publications include the novels *Make Me an Offer* (1952) and *A Kid for Two Farthings* (1953), and a collection of short stories, *The Mendelman Fire* (1957). Among his plays is *The Bespoke Overcoat* (1954), and his films, *The Millionairess* (1960), *The Long, The Short, and the Tall* (1961), *Casino Royale* (1967) and *The Hebrew Lesson* (1972).

MANLEY, Mary de la Riviere (c.1672–1724) British writer, born in Jersey, the daughter of a future governor of Jersey. After her father's death (1688), she was lured into a bigamous marriage with her cousin, John Manley of Truro, MP, who soon deserted her. She went to England, where she had a success with the publication of her letters. In 1696 she wrote two plays, *The Lost Lover* and *The Royal Mischief*. She wrote gossipy chronicles disguised as fiction, especially the scandalous anti-Whig *The New Atalantis* (1709). In 1711 she succeeded **Swift** as editor of *The Examiner*. She wrote a fictional account of her own early struggles in *The Adventures of Rivella* (1714). Her last work was *The Power of Love, in Seven Novels*.

MANLEY, Michael Norman (1923–) Jamaican politician, born in Kingston, the son of **Norman Manley**. Educated in Jamaica, he served in the Royal Canadian air force in World War II, and then studied at the London School of Economics (1945–49). He spent some time in journalism in Britain before returning to Jamaica. He became a leader of the National Workers' Union in the 1950s, sat in the Senate (1962–67) and was then elected to the House of Representatives. In 1969 he became leader of the People's National party (PNP) and prime minister in 1972. He embarked on a radical, socialist programme, cooling relations with the USA, and despite rising unemployment was re-elected in 1976. He was decisively defeated in 1980 and 1983 but returned to power in 1989, with a much more moderate policy stance.

MANLEY, Norman Washington (1893–) Jamaican politician, born in Kingston. He studied law, was called to the bar and then became a respected QC. In 1938 he won fame by successfully defending his cousin, and political opponent, **Alexander Bustamente**, who was then an active trade unionist, on a charge of sedition. In the same year Manley founded the People's National party (PNP) and in 1955, seven years before Jamaica achieved full independence, became prime minister. He handed over leadership of the PNP to his son **Michael** in 1969.

MANN, Heinrich (1871–1950) German novelist, brother of **Thomas Mann**, born in Lübeck. He began to be described as the German **Zola** for his ruthless exposure of pre-1914 German society in *Im Schlaraffenland* (1901, trans *Berlin, the Land of Cockaigne*, 1925), and the trilogy describing the three classes of Kaiser **Wilhelm II**'s empire, *Die Armen* (1917 the proletariat), *Der Untertan* (1918, the underling or bourgeois) and *Der Kopf* (1929, the head or governing class). He is best known for the macabre, Expressionist novel, *Professor Unrat* (1904), describing the moral degradation of a once outwardly respectable schoolmaster, which was translated and filmed as *The Blue Angel* (1932). He lived in France (1933–40) and then escaped to the USA. Other works include *Die kleine Stadt* (1901), set in a small Italian town, and a remarkable autobiography, *Ein Zeitalter wird besichtigt* (1945–46). His influence is noticeable in **Wassermann** and **Feuchtwanger**.

MANN, Horace (1796–1859) American educationist, born in Franklin, Massachusetts, the 'father of American public education'. He entered the Massachusetts legislature in 1827, and was president of the state senate. As secretary of the board of education (1837–48), he reorganized public school teachings and was responsible for setting up the first normal school in the USA (1839). He became a member of the House of Representatives (1848–53), and president of Antioch College, Ohio (1852–59).

MANN, Thomas (1875–1955) German novelist, brother of **Heinrich Mann**, born into a patrician family of merchants and senators of the Hanseatic city of Lübeck. His mother was a talented musician of mixed German and Portuguese West Indian blood. The opposition between a conservative business outlook and artistic inclinations, the clash between Nordic and Latin temperaments inherent in his own personality, and the Schopenhauerian doctrine of art being the self-abnegation of the will as the end product of decay, were to form his subject matter. At the age of 19, without completing school, he settled with his mother in Munich, and after dabbling at the university, he joined his brother in Italy, where he wrote his early masterpiece, *Buddenbrooks* (1901), the saga of a family like his own, tracing its decline through four generations, as business acumen gives way to artistic sensibilities. At the age of 25 he thus became a leading German writer. On his return to Munich he became reader for the satirical literary magazine, *Simplicissimus*, which published many of his early, remarkable short stories. The novelettes *Tonio Kröger* (1902), *Tristan* (1903) and *Der Tod in Venedig* (Death in Venice, 1913), all deal with the problem of the artist's salvation, positively in the case of the first, who resembles **Goethe**'s Werther, negatively in the last in which a successful writer dies on the brink of perverted eroticism. World War I precipitated a quarrel between the two novelist brothers, Thomas's *Betrachtungen eines Unpolitischen* (Meditations of an Unpolitical Person, 1918), revealing his militant German patriotism, already a feature of his essay on **Frederick the Great** (1915) and a distrust of political ideologies, including the radicalism of his brother. *Der Zauberberg* (The Magic Mountain, 1924), won him the Nobel prize for literature in 1929. It was inspired by a visit to his wife at a sanatorium for consumptives in Davos in 1913 and tells the story of such a patient, Hans Castorp, with the sanatorium representing Europe in its moral and intellectual disintegration. The same year, Mann delivered a speech against the rising Nazis and in 1930 exposed Italian fascism in *Mario und der Zauberer* (Mario and the Magician, 1930). He left Germany for Switzerland after 1933 and in 1936 delivered an address for **Freud**'s eightieth birthday. Both shared an enthusiasm for the biblical patriarch, **Joseph**, and Mann wrote a tetralogy on his life (1933–43). He settled in the USA in 1936 and wrote a novel on a visit to Goethe by an old love, Charlotte Buff, *Lotte in Weimar* (1939). His anti-**Hitler** broadcasts to Germany were collected under the titles *Achtung Europa!* and *Deutsche Hörer* (1945). In 1947 he returned to Switzerland and was the only returning exile to be fêted by both West and East Germany. His greatest work, a modern version of the medieval legend, *Doktor Faustus* (1947), combines art and politics in the simultaneous treatment of the life and catastrophic end of a composer, Adrian Leverkühn, and German disintegration in two world wars. His last unfinished work, hailed as Germany's greatest comic novel, *Bekenntnisse des Hochstaplers Felix Krull*, Part I (Confessions of the Confidence Trickster Felix Krull, 1954), written with astonishing wit, irony and humour and without the tortuous stylistic complexities of the *Bildungsroman*, commended itself most to English translators. Essentially a 19th-century German conservative, whose cultural landmarks vanished in World War I, he was compelled towards a critique of the artistic. Ambivalently the artist and the bourgeois fearer of Bohemianism, the unpolitical man with political duties, he was the brilliant story-teller in the classical German tradition, whose subject matter was paradoxically the end of that tradition. Other later works include *Der Erwählte* (1951), on the life of the incestuous Pope **Gregory**, *Die Betrogene* (1953) and *Last Essays*, on **Schiller**, Goethe, **Nietzsche** and **Chekhov**.

MANNERHEIM, Carl Gustav Emil, Freiherr von (1867–1951) Finnish soldier and statesman, born in Askainen. He became an officer in the Russian army in 1889. He fought in the Russo-Japanese War of 1904–05 and in World War I. When Finland declared her independence in 1917 (after the Russian Revolution), he became supreme commander and regent, and suppressed the Finnish Bolsheviks. Defeated in the presidential election of 1919, he retired into private life. In 1939, at the outbreak of the Russo-Finnish Winter War, he returned as commander-in-chief, and organized the Mannerheim Line of defence. Marshal of Finland in 1942, he was president of Finland from 1944 to 1946.

MANNERS See **RUTLAND, John James** and **GRANBY, John Manners**

MANNHEIM, Karl (1893–1947) Hungarian-born German sociologist, born in Budapest. He was educated at the universities of Budapest and Strasbourg. In 1919, following the Hungarian revolution, he emigrated to Heidelberg, where he worked as a private scholar. In 1925 he became a lecturer at Heidelberg University, remaining there until 1930, when he was appointed professor of sociology and political economy at Frankfurt University. In 1933 he was expelled from Germany by the Nazis, and fled to England, where he joined the London School of Economics. In 1945 he became professor of sociology and philosophy of education at the London University Institute of Education. He is known primarily for his contribution to the sociology of knowledge, of which he was one of the founders, but he also wrote about political planning and education. His books include *Ideology and Utopia* (1929, trans 1936), *Man and Society in an Age of Reconstruction* (1935, trans 1940), *Freedom, Power and Democratic Planning* (1950) and *Diagnosis of Our Time* (1943).

MANNING, Henry Edward (1808–92) English Roman Catholic prelate, born in Totteridge, Hertfordshire. From Harrow he passed in 1827 to Balliol College, Oxford, and, after taking a classical first in 1830, was in 1832 elected a fellow of Merton. An eloquent preacher and a High Churchman, in 1833 he became rector of Woollavington and Graffham, Sussex, and in 1840 archdeacon of Chichester. In 1851, he joined the Church of Rome, and in 1865 succeeded Cardinal **Wiseman** as archbishop of Westminster. At the Ecumenical Council of 1870 Manning was one of the most zealous supporters of the infallibility dogma; and, named cardinal in 1875, he continued a leader of the Ultramontanes. He was a member of the royal commissions on the housing of the poor (1885) and on education (1886), and took a prominent part in temperance and benevolent movements.

MANNING, Olivia (1908–80) English novelist, born in Portsmouth, the daughter of a naval officer. Much of her youth was spent in Ireland and she had 'the usual Anglo-Irish sense of belonging to nowhere'. She trained at art school, and then went to London, and published her first novel, *The Wind Changes*, in 1937. She married in 1939 and went abroad with her husband, Reggie Smith, a British Council lecturer in Bucharest. Her experiences there formed the basis of her Balkan trilogy, comprising *The Great Fortune* (1960), *The Spoilt City* (1962) and *Friends and Heroes* (1965). As the Germans approached Athens, she and her husband evacuated to Egypt and ended up in Jerusalem. She returned to London in 1946, where she resided until her death. A prolific author, her publications include *Artist Among the Missing* (1949), *School for Love* (1951), *A Different Face* (1953), and her Levant Trilogy, comprising *The Danger Tree* (1977), *The Battle Lost and Won* (1978) and *The Sum of Things* (1980). The Balkan Trilogy and the Levant Trilogy form a single narrative entitled *Fortunes of War* which **Anthony Burgess** described as 'the finest fictional record of the war produced by a British writer'.

MANNING, Thomas (1772–1840) English traveller, born at Broome rectory, Suffolk. In 1790 he entered Caius College, Cambridge, to study Chinese; and in 1806 went out as a doctor to Canton. In 1811–12 he visited Lhasa in Tibet, the first Englishman ever there. He returned in 1817 to England, visited Italy, 1827–29, and died in Bath.

MANNION, Wilfred (1918–) English footballer, born in Yorkshire. Although his career was spent with two unfashionable clubs (Middlesbrough and Hull City), he was an integral part of the great English national side of the late 1940s. Small, stocky, and master of the telling pass, he scored one goal for every four league matches he played.

MANNIX, Daniel (1864–1963) Irish-born Australian Catholic cleric, born in Deerpark, Rathluirc, County Cork. Ordained at Maynooth in 1890, he became president of the college in 1903. He went to Australia in 1913 as coadjutor in Melbourne, succeeding as archbishop in 1917. He immediately embroiled himself in controversy, opposing conscription and attacking the government for lack of aid to church schools. Vehemently anti-British in sentiment, he nonetheless was critical of the new Irish Free State. While attacking the Australian Labor party for its left-wing leanings he still championed the cause of the workers. He supported **Franco** and praised **Mussolini**, while regarding **Stalin** only as a useful ally against fascism. Censured privately for his outspokenness by the Vatican he still exhorted his clergy to obey Rome without question. Despite his extensive personal library, he was politically unread, but was acclaimed on all sides for his devout pastoral work.

MANNS, Sir August (1825–1907) German musician, born in Prussia. In 1855 he became musical director at the Crystal Palace, and from 1883 to 1902 conducted the Handel Festivals.

MANNY, Sir Walter de (d.1372) English knight, born in Hainault. He followed **Philippa of Hainault** to England in 1327 for her marriage to **Edward III**, and fought splendidly for Edward III by land and sea against the Scots, Flemings and French. He was knighted and made Lord de Manny, received large grants of land, and founded the Charterhouse monastery in London (1371).

MANNYNG, Robert (d.c.1338) also known as **Robert of Brunne**, English chronicler and poet, born in Bourne in Lincolnshire. In 1288 he entered the nearby Gilbertine monastery of Sempringham. His chief work is *Handlynge Synne* (c.1303), a free and amplified translation into English rhyming couplets of the *Manuel des Pechiez* of William of Wadington. It is a landmark in the transition from early to later Middle English, and a colourful picture of contemporary life. He also composed a rhyming translation of **Wace**'s *Brut d'Angleterre*, with a translation from French of a rhyming chronicle, *The Story of Ingeland*, by the Augustinian canon, Peter Langtoft.

MANOEL I See **EMANUEL I**

MANOEL II See **MANUEL II**

MANRIQUE, Jorge (1440–79) Spanish poet, born in Paredes de la Nava. He is best remembered for his fine elegy on his father's death, *Coplas por la muerte de su padre*.

MANSARD, or **Mansart, François** (1598–1666) French architect, born in Paris. He was apprenticed to **Salomon de Brosse**, and brought a simplified adaptation of the Baroque style into use in France. His first major work, the north wing of the Château de Blois, featured the double-angled high-pitched roof which bears his name. He designed churches like Sainte-Marie de Chaillot, the Visitation de Sainte-Marie and Val-de-Grâce, and built or remodelled several notable buildings in Paris and elsewhere, such as the Hôtel de la Vrillière and Maisons Laffitte.

MANSARD, or **Mansart, Jules Hardouin** (1645–1708) French architect, born in Paris, great-nephew of **François Mansard**. He became chief architect to **Louis XIV** and designed many notable buildings, especially part of the Palace of Versailles, including the Grand Trianon.

MANSBRIDGE, Albert (1876–1952) English adult educator, born in Gloucester and educated at Board Schools and Battersea Grammar School. He left school aged 14, and became a clerk and then cashier of the Co-operative Permanent Building Society. After attending extension classes at King's College, London, he became an evening-class teacher under the London School Board. He proposed a scheme in 1903 which led to the formation of the Association to Promote the Higher Education of Working Men, later known as the Workers' Educational Association. In 1905 he became general secretary, encouraging the development of branches and setting great store by the three-year university tutorial classes which an Oxford conference on the WEA and the university advocated in 1907. By 1914 there were 145 such classes in England and Wales. After visits to the Commonwealth in 1913–14 he became seriously ill but was instrumental in founding the National Central Library (1916), and was a member of the adult education committee of the ministry of reconstruction which produced an important report in 1919. Among his publications is a biography of **Margaret McMillan**. His life epitomizes the aspirations of the many respectable working men who sought education for self-improvement in the early 20th century.

MANSEL, Henry Longueville (1820–71) English philosopher and clergyman, born at Cosgrove rectory, Northamptonshire. Educated at St John's College, Oxford, he became the first Wayneflete professor of moral and metaphysical philosophy at Oxford in 1855, professor of ecclesiastical history there in 1866, and dean of St Paul's in 1868. He was the philosophical successor to Sir **Alexander Hamilton** whose work he expanded and developed in his *Metaphysics* (1860, originally a contribution to the *Encyclopedia Britannica*) and *The Philosophy of the Conditioned* (1866). His emphasis on the relativity of knowledge was applied also to Christian apologetics in his celebrated *The Limits of Religious Thought* (1858), which provoked an indignant rebuttal from **John Stuart Mill**.

MANSFELD, Count Ernst (1580–1626) German soldier of fortune in the Thirty Years' War, illegitimate son of **Peter Ernst Mansfeld**. Refused his father's possessions, the promised reward for his brilliant services in Hungary and elsewhere, he went over to the Protestant princes. After defending the Count-Palatine Frederick for a time (1618–20), he was driven by the disaster of the Weissenberg to retreat to the Palatinate, from which he carried on for two years a predatory war on the imperialists, defeating **Tilly** in 1622. He afterwards took service with the United Netherlands, beating the Spaniards at Fleurus (1622). At **Richelieu**'s solicitation he raised an army of 12000 men (mostly in England), but in 1626 he was crushed by **Wallenstein** at Dessau. Later, when marching to join **Gabriel Bethlen** of Translyvania, he died near Sarajevo in Bosnia.

MANSFELD, Count Peter Ernst I, later **Prince** (1517–1604) German soldier. He took part in **Charles V**'s expedition against Tunis, and was made governor of Luxembourg. In the service of **Philip II** of Spain he fought against the French, made a name as one of the most brilliant Spanish generals in the Low Countries, was sent by **Alva** to the assistance of the French king against the Protestants (1569), and acted as governor of the Spanish Low Countries.

MANSFIELD, Katherine, pseud of **Kathleen Mansfield Beauchamp** (1888–1923) New Zealand short-story writer, born in Wellington, the daughter of a successful businessman. Educated at Queen's College, London, she returned to New Zealand for two years to study music, and left again for London in 1908, determined to pursue a literary career. She lived on the breadline and like a bohemian and met, married and left her first husband, George Bowden, in the space of three weeks. Finding herself pregnant (not by her husband) she was installed by her mother in a hotel in Bavaria, but she miscarried. The experience bore fruit in the stories collected in *In A German Pension* in 1911, most of which had previously appeared in *The New Age*. That same year she met **John Middleton Murry**, and thereafter her work began to surface in Murry's *Rhythm*. From 1912 the couple lived together (they did not marry until 1918), mingling with the literati, particularly **D H Lawrence**, who portrayed them as Gudrun and Gerald in *Women in Love*. In 1916, she and Murry founded the short-lived magazine *Signature*, but she began to suffer from tuberculosis which precipitated her premature death. Her first major work was *Prelude* (1917), a recreation of the New Zealand of her childhood. *Bliss, and other stories* (1920), containing the classic stories 'Je ne parle pas francais' and 'Prelude', confirmed her standing as an original and innovative writer, named in company with **Chekhov** despite the backstabbing of her near-contemporary, **Virginia Woolf**. The only other collection published before her death at Fontainebleau was *The Garden Party, and other stories* (1922). Posthumous works include *Poems* (1923), and *Something Childish, and other stories* (1924). *The Letters of Katherine Mansfield*, edited by Murry, appeared in 1928 and *Katherine Mansfield's Letters to John Middleton Murry 1913–1922*, detailing the couple's stormy but tender relationship punctuated by lengthy separations, in 1951.

MANSFIELD, William Murray, 1st Earl (1705–93) English judge, born in Perth, the fourth son of Viscount Stormont. Educated at Westminster and Christ Church, Oxford, he was called to the bar and soon acquired an extensive practice. He was appointed solicitor-general in 1742, entered the House of Commons as member for Boroughbridge, was appointed attorney-general in 1754, and became chief-justice of the King's Bench in 1756, a member of the cabinet, and Baron Mansfield. His judgments were very influential, particularly by incorporating many principles of mercantile custom in rules of law; he thus greatly developed the law of maritime contracts, insurance and bills. He also made important contributions to international law. He was impartial as a judge, but his opinions were unpopular; 'Junius' (Sir **Philip Francis**) bitterly attacked him, and during the Gordon riots of 1780 his house was burned. Made earl in 1776, he resigned office in 1788.

MANSHIP, Paul Howard (1885–1966) American sculptor, born in St Paul, Minnesota. He studied in New York and Philadelphia and from 1908 to 1912 attended the American Academy in Rome where he was greatly influenced by antique sculpture. He returned to New York and became renowned for his bronze figurative sculptures which drew heavily on Roman and Greek sources. His subject-matter is taken principally from classical mythology and treated in the stylized, decorative manner of the Art Deco period. From 1921 to 1927 he worked in Paris. His many important commissions include the gilded *Prometheus Fountain* (1934) for the Rockefeller Center, New York City. In the 1930s he was widely regarded as America's greatest sculptor but his mannered classical style became unfashionable in the 1960s and 1970s.

MANSION, Colard (d.1484) Flemish calligrapher and illuminator, of French extraction. In the early 1470s he set up a press at Bruges with **William Caxton**.

MANSON, Sir Patrick (1844–1922) Scottish doctor, born in Aberdeenshire, known as 'Mosquito Manson' from his pioneer work with Sir **Ronald Ross** in malaria research. He practised medicine in the East in China (1871) and Hong Kong, 1883, where he started a school of medicine that became the University of Hong Kong. He became medical adviser to the Colonial Office, and in 1899 helped to found the London School of Tropical Medicine. He was the first to argue that the mosquito was host to the malaria parasite (1877).

MANSTEIN, Fritz Erich von (1887–1973) German soldier. At the outset of World War II he became chief of staff to **Rundstedt** in the Polish campaign and later in France, where he was the architect of **Hitler**'s *Blitzkrieg* invasion plan. In 1941 he was given command of an army corps on the Eastern Front and though not trained in armoured warfare handled his panzers with great resource in the Crimea. After the disaster of Stalingrad, he contrived to extricate the right wing in sufficient strength to stage a successful counter-attack at Kharkov, though he failed to relieve **Paulus**' Sixth Army. After being captured in 1945 he was imprisoned as a war criminal but released in 1953. A strong advocate of fluid defence for preventing the enemy from exploiting an advantage, he embodied his theories and an account of his military career in his *Lost victories* (trans 1959).

MANSŪR, al—'the victorious' the name adopted by the second 'Abbasid caliph Abū Ja'far 'Abd Allah b Muhammad (c.710–775). He held important military commands during the struggle against the Umayyads under his brother al-Saffāh, whom he succeeded in 754. An astute politician, he defeated several revolts, establishing a firm government dominated by the Abbasid family, and founded a new capital for the empire, Baghdad (762). He overcame considerable opposition to ensure the succession of his own son Mahdī, and died while leading his fifth pilgrimage to Mecca.

MANTEGAZZA, Paolo (1831–1910) Italian physiologist, born in Monza. He practised medicine in Argentina and at Milan, and became professor in 1860 of pathology at Pavia, in 1870 of anthropology at Florence. He wrote largely on the physiology of pleasure, pain and love, on spontaneous generation, and on physiognomy, as well as books of travel and novels.

MANTEGNA, Andrea (1431–1506) Italian painter, born in Vicenza. He was apprenticed to the tailor-painter Francesco Squarcione (1396–c.1468) in Padua, and seems to have been adopted by him. In 1453 he married a daughter of **Jacopo Bellini** and quarrelled with his master. In 1459 he was persuaded by Ludovico **Gonzaga**, Duke of Mantua, to work for him, and remained in Mantua in his service for the rest of his life with the exception of a two-year stay in Rome (1488–90) when he painted a fresco cycle for the private chapel of Pope Innocent VIII (now destroyed). In Padua he had come under the influence of **Donatello** and his debt to the master is evident in works such as his Saint Zeno Altarpiece and his *Saint Sebastian*. His style is very sculptural and ostentatious in his use of foreshortening. At Mantua his most important works were nine tempera pictures of *The Triumph of Caesar* which were acquired by **Charles I** and are now at Hampton Court, and his decoration of the ceiling of the Camera degli Sposi. The latter is an illusionistic tour-de-force in which the ceiling is opened up to the heavens and 'putti' look down from the painted balustrade. This is the first example of an effect which became common during the Baroque era. The other chief feature of his art was his incorporation of antique motifs into his compositions. In this he strove for accuracy, and with this aim he built up a collection of classical statuary which was the envy of the pope.

MANTELL, Gideon Algernon (1790–1852) English palaeontologist, born in Lewes, Sussex. He practised as a doctor there and studied the Mesozoic era. He discovered several dinosaur types, and did important work on Wealden fossils. He wrote *The Fossils of the South Downs* (1822) and *The Wonders of Geology* (1838).

MANTEUFFEL, Edwin Hans Karl, Freiherr von (1809–85) Prussian soldier, born in Dresden of an old Pomeranian family. He was colonel of the Prussian guards by 1854. As commander of the Prussian troops in Sleswick he began the war with Austria in 1866, helped to reduce the Hanoverians to capitulation, and defeated the Bavarians in four battles. In 1870–71 he first commanded the army of the north, then in command of the army of the south drove **Bourbaki** and 80000 men into Switzerland. As viceroy of Alsace-Lorraine (from 1879) he was very unpopular.

MANTLE, Mickey Charles (1931–) American professional baseball player with the New York Yankees, born in Stavinaw, Oklahoma. Between 1951 and 1968 he appeared in numerous World Series. Although he was a fast powerful hitter, an old football injury hampered his running between the bases. A 'switch hitter', he was able to bat either left- or right-handed. Accident-prone throughout his career, experts believe that if he had remained injury-free he would have broken many of the game's records. He was elected to the Baseball Hall of Fame in 1974.

MANUCCI, Aldo See **ALDUS MANUTIUS**

MANUEL, Nikolaus, called **Deutsch** (1484–1530) Swiss painter, poet and reformer, born in Berne. Beginning as a painter of stained glass, he changed over to orthodox media and produced biblical and mythological pictures in the Renaissance style, often showing the influence of **Baldung** in his tendency toward the macabre. He held several government offices, was a member of the Great Council, and wrote satirical verse.

MANUEL, Peter (1931–58) Scottish criminal, perpetrator of at least eight of the most callous murders in Scottish criminal annals. Between September 1956 and January 1958, in addition to committing a number of burglaries, he broke into the home of a Mr William Watt in Rutherglen and shot the three occupants dead, strangled and robbed a girl at Mount Vernon, robbed a house in Uddingston, killing all three of the family who lived there, and shot dead a Newcastle taxi driver. He was also accused of battering to death Ann Kneilands of East Kilbride, but was acquitted through lack of evidence. His trial at Glasgow High Court was one of the most sensational in legal history. Having already successfully defended himself against a former charge, he clearly considered himself more than a match for the conventional forces of law and order, and dismissed the counsel appearing on his behalf. Conducting his case with considerable skill, he brought in a special defence plea giving alibis and attributing the Rutherglen murders to William Watt himself, who had already suffered 67 days of imprisonment as a suspect. But he overreached himself, was found guilty of seven of the murders, and was hanged. The Newcastle shooting was later officially attributed to him by an inquest jury.

MANUEL I, Comnenus (c.1122–1180) Byzantine emperor, the youngest son of John II, whom he succeeded in 1143. His initial successes against the Turks and the Normans were halted by the massive defeat of his army at the hands of the Seljuks at Myriokephalon (1176), which marked the beginning of the downfall of the empire.

MANUEL II, Palaeologus (1350–1423) Byzantine emperor from 1391, son of Johannes V. For much of his reign he was besieged in Constantinople by the Turks. At one point he was relieved by Tamur the Tartar advancing into Asia Minor, but he failed to profit from this diversion and was overwhelmed.

MANUEL II, also **Manoel** (1889–1932) king of Portugal, born in Lisbon. On the assassination of his father King Carlos I and the Crown Prince Luis on 1 February 1908, he became king, but was forced to abdicate at the revolution of 3 October 1910. He subsequently settled in England. .

MANUZIO See **ALDUS MANUTIUS**

MANZONI, Alessandro (1785–1873) Italian novelist and poet, born in Milan of a noble family. He went to Paris from 1805 to 1807, published his first poems in 1806, married happily in 1810, and spent the next few years in writing sacred lyrics and a treatise on the religious basis of morality. But the work which gave him European fame is his historical novel, *I Promessi Sposi* (The Betrothed), a Milanese story of the 17th century (1825–27), the most notable novel in Italian literature. Despite his Catholic devoutness, he was a strong advocate of a united Italy, and became a senator of the kingdom in 1860.

MANZÙ, Giacomo (1908–) Italian sculptor, born in Bergamo. Apprenticed to various craftsmen, including a woodcarver and a stuccoist, before studying at the Fantoni Trade School, in 1930 he was commissioned to make religious reliefs and saints for the Catholic University of Milan. In 1936 he admired Greek sculpture in the Louvre, and **Rodin**'s work. He held his first one-man exhibition in Rome, 1937. Manzú, who taught sculpture in Milan (1940) and Turin (c.1940–45), revived classical techniques of relief sculpture in bronze, including the bronze doors of St Peter's in Rome (1950) and Salzburg Cathedral in Austria (1955). He also made a commissioned portrait bust of Pope **John XXIII** for the Vatican (1963). He likes to make variations on a theme, eg his nude girls seated on kitchen chairs (1933 onwards) and the series of cardinals in their tall mitres (more than 50 made since 1936) which are executed in various sizes.

MAO DUN, pseud of **Shen Yanbing** (1896–1981) Chinese writer, born in Wuzhen, Zhejiang Province. Educated at Beijing University, he became one of the foremost left-wing intellectuals and writers in China. In 1920 he was a founder-member of the Literary Research Society, and was editor of the *Short Story Monthly* (1921–23). Moving to Shanghai, he taught a course of fiction at Shanghai College, and became editor of the Hankow National Daily. In 1926 he joined the Northern Expedition as a propagandist, but had to go underground in Shanghai as a communist activist. He wrote a trilogy of novellas, published as *Shih* (Eclipse, 1930), and a bestselling novel, *Ziye* (Midnight, 1932), about financial exploiters in the decadent Shanghai of the time. His other major works were *Hong* (Rainbow), and a collection of short stories in *Spring Silkworms*. In 1930 he helped to organize the influential League of Left-Wing Writers. After the communists came to power in 1949 he was China's first minister of culture (1949–65), and was founder-editor of the literary journal *People's Literature* (1949–53). During the Cultural Revolution he was kept under house arrest in Beijing (1966–78).

MAO ZEDONG (Mao Tse-tung) (1893–1976) Chinese communist leader, first chairman (1949) of the People's Republic, born in the village of Shaoshan in Hunan province, the son of a peasant farmer. Educated at Changsha, he went in 1918 to the University of Peking (Beijing), where as a library assistant he studied the works of **Marx** and others and helped found the Chinese Communist party (CCP) in 1921. Seeing the need to adapt communism to Chinese conditions, seeking a rural, rather than urban-based, revolution, he set up a communist 'people's republic' (soviet) at Jiangxi in south-east China between 1931 and 1934. The soviet defied the attacks of **Chiang Kai-shek**'s forces until 1934, when Mao and his followers were obliged to uproot themselves and undertake an arduous and circuitous 'Long March' (1934–36) to Shaanxi province in north-west China. During this march, Mao was elected CCP chairman at the Zunyi conference of February 1935. At the new headquarters of Yanan, he set about formulating a unique communist philosophy which stressed the importance of ideology, re-education and 'rectification', and, in 1939, he married his third wife, **Jiang Qing**. By employing the tactic of mobile, rural-based guerrilla warfare, Mao's communists successfully resisted the Japanese between 1937 and 1945, and on their collapse issued forth to shatter the Nationalist régime of Chiang Kai-shek and proclaim the People's Republic of China in Beijing in 1949. Mao resigned the chairmanship of the Republic in 1959, but remained chairman of the CCP's politburo until his death. During the early 1960s, an ideological rift developed between Mao and **Khrushchev**, with Mao opposing the latter's policy of peaceful co-existence with the west and the USSR's volte face during the Cuban missiles crisis (1962). This developed into a formal split in 1962 when the Soviet Union supplied fighter aircraft to India during the brief Sino-Indian border war of that year. Domestically, Mao's influence waned during the early 1960s as a result of the failure of the 1958–60 'Great Leap Forward' experiment of rapid agricultural and industrial advance through the establishment of giant communes. However, the 'Great Helmsman' re-established his dominance during the 1966–69 'Cultural Revolution', a 'rectification' campaign directed against liberal, 'revisionist' forces. Concerned with the anarchic 'Red Guard' excesses, he then, working closely with **Zhou Enlai**, oversaw a period of reconstruction from 1970. During his final years, however, when beset by deteriorating health, his political grip weakened. Mao's writings and thoughts, set out in 'New Democracy' (1940) and, most popularly, in his 'Little Red Book', dominated the functioning of the People's Republic between 1949 and 1976. He stressed the need for reducing rural–urban differences and for 'perpetual revolution' to prevent the emergence of new elites. Overseas, Mao, after precipitating the Sino-Soviet split of 1960–62, became a firm advocate of a non-aligned 'Third World' strategy. Since 1978, the new Chinese leadership of **Deng Xiaoping** has begun to re-interpret Maoism and has criticized its policy excesses. However, many of Mao's ideas remain influential in contemporary China.

MAP, or **Mahap** or **Mapes, Walter** (c.1137–1209) ecclesiastic and writer, sometimes said to have been a Welshman, probably a native of Herefordshire. Of noble stock, he studied at Paris, became a clerk to **Henry II** of England, went on a mission to Rome, and became canon of St Paul's and archdeacon of Oxford (1197). Although famous in his day as a writer and wit, the only work which can be attributed to him with certainty is the satirical miscellany *De Nugis Curialum* (Of Courtier's Trifles) a collection of anecdotes and reflections, and tales gleaned from history, romance and gossip.

MAR, John Erskine, 6th or 11th Earl of (1675–1732) Scottish Jacobite, born in Alloa. He began life as a Whig, and by his frequent change of sides earned the nickname of 'Bobbing Joan'. He headed the Jacobite rebellion of 1715, was defeated at Sheriffmuir, and died in exile at Aix-la-Chapelle. His *Legacy* was published by the Scottish History Society in 1896.

MARADONA, Diego (1960–) Argentinian footballer, born in Lanús. He played in the 1982 World Cup in Spain, but was sent off in the match against Brazil. Almost immediately he joined Barcelona from his home country club, Boca Juniors, but injury and illness kept him out of top-class football for two seasons. Restored to health, he captained the Argentine side to World Cup victory in Mexico in 1986, earning fame for apparently fisting his first goal against England, an action which he later described as 'the hand of God'. Never happy at Barcelona, he moved for £5000000 to Napoli and helped them (1987) to their first-ever Italian championship. With his speed, phenomenal strength and balance he is one of the greatest players of his generation.

MARAIS, Marin (1656–1728) French composer and viol player, born in Paris. As a boy he was in the Sainte Chapelle choir, later becoming a bass violist in the Royal Band and in the orchestra of the Opera, of which he later became joint conductor. A pupil of **Giovanni Lully**, he wrote several operas, the most famous of which was *Alcyone* (1705), but his posthumous and growing reputation is based on his music for the viol.

MARAT, Jean Paul (1743–93) French revolutionary, physician and journalist, born in Boudry near Neuchâtel, Switzerland. He studied medicine at Bordeaux, went to Paris, Holland and London, and practised in London in the 1770s and in Paris from 1777. He was made brevet-physician to his guards by the Comte d'Artois (afterwards **Charles X**), an office which he held till 1786. Meantime he continued work in optics and electricity, and wrote several scientific works. But revolution was in the air, and Marat became a member of the Cordelier Club. In September 1789 he started issuing his radical paper, *L'ami du peuple*, inciting the 'sans-culottes' to violence. Twice at least he had to flee to London, and once he was forced to hide in the sewers of Paris. His misadventures increased his hatred of constituted authority, and on his head rests in great measure the guilt of the September massacres. In 1792 he was elected to the Convention as one of the deputies for Paris, and in April 1793 was arrested at the instigation of the Girondins, but acquitted. With **Robespierre** and **Danton** he overthrew the Girondins, but he was dying fast of a disease contracted in the sewers, and could only write sitting in his bath. On the evening of 13 July he was assassinated in his bath by **Charlotte Corday**, a member of the Girondins. His body was committed to the Panthéon with the greatest public honours, to be cast out 15 months later amid popular execration.

MARATTI, Carlo (1625–1713) Italian painter, born in Camerano. A leader of the 17th-century Baroque school, he painted many notable canvasses and frescoes in Rome, and several portraits.

MARBECK, or **Merbecke, John** (d.c.1585) English musician and theologian, organist of St George's Chapel, Windsor. He was condemned to the stake in 1544 as a Reformer, but pardoned by Bishop **Gardiner**. In 1550 he published his famous *Boke of Common Praier Noted*, an adaptation of the plain chant to the first prayer-book of **Edward VI**. He prepared the earliest concordance to the whole English Bible, and wrote several theological works.

MARC, Franz (1880–1916) German artist, born in Munich. He studied in Munich, Italy and France, and with **Kandinsky** founded the Blaue Reiter ('Blue Rider') Expressionist group in Munich in 1911. Most of his paintings were of animals (eg the famous *Tower of the Blue Horses*) portrayed in forceful colours, with a well-defined pictorial rhythm. He was killed in World War I at Verdun.

MARCANTONIO, in full **Marcantonio Raimondi** (c.1488–1534) Italian engraver, born in Bologna. At first a goldsmith, he moved to Rome in 1510 and became an engraver of other artists' works, especially **Raphael** and **Michelangelo**. The capture of Rome by **Charles Bourbon** ('Constable') in 1527 drove him back to Bologna.

MARCEAU, Marcel (1923–) French mime artist. Born in Strasbourg, he studied at the École des Beaux Arts in Paris, and in 1948 founded the Compagnie de Mime Marcel Marceau, of which he was the director until 1964, specializing in and developing the art of mime, of which he has become the leading exponent. His white-faced character, Bip, is famous from his appearances on stage and television throughout the world and among the many original performances he has devised are the mime-drama *Don Juan* (1964) and the ballet *Candide* (1971). Since 1978 he has been head of the École de Mimodrame Marcel Marceau.

MARCEAU-DESGRAVIERS, François Séverin (1769–96) French soldier, born in Chartres. He took part in the storming of the Bastille (1789). In 1792 he helped to defend Verdun with a body of volunteers, and for his services with the republican army in La Vendée was made general of division. He commanded the right wing at Fleurus, and in 1796 the first division of Jourdan's army, investing Mainz, Mannheim and Coblenz. He was mortally wounded while covering the French retreat at Altenkirchen. His body was committed to the Panthéon in 1889.

MARCEL, Gabriel Honoré (1889–1973) French existentialist philosopher and dramatist, born in Paris. He was a Red Cross Worker in World War I but made his living thereafter as a freelance writer, teacher, editor and critic. In 1929 he became a Catholic and came reluctantly to accept the label 'Christian existentialist', partly in order to contrast his views with those of **Sartre**. He emphasized the importance and possibility of 'communication' between individual people, as well as between themselves and God, but was suspicious of all philosophical abstractions and generalizations which misrepresented the freedom, uniqueness and particularity of human individuals. He was not himself a system-builder and his philosophical works tend to have a personal, meditative character, as in *Journal métaphysique* (1927), *Être et avoir* (1935), *Le Mystère de l'être* (1951), *Les Hommes contra l'humain* (1951), and *L'Homme problématique* (1955). His plays include *Un Homme de Dieu* (1925), *Le Monde Cassé* (1933), *Ariadne: Le Chemin de Crête* (1936) and *La Dimension Florestan* (1956).

MARCELLO, Benedetto (1686–1739) Italian composer, born in Venice. He was a judge of the Venetian republic, and a member of the Council of Forty, and afterwards held offices at Pola and Brescia. As a composer he is remembered for his *Estro poetico armonico* (1724–27), an eight-volume collection of settings for 50 of the Psalms of David, for his oratorio *Le Quattro Stagioni* (1731), and for his keyboard and instrumental sonatas. He wrote the satirical *Il Teatro alla moda* (1720). His brother Alessandro (c.1684–c.1750), philosopher and mathematician as well as composer, published a number of cantatas, sonatas and concertos under the pseudonym 'Eterico Stinfalico'.

MARCELLUS the name of two popes, the first martyred in 310; the second, as Cardinal Marcello Cervini presided over the Council of Trent, was elected pope in 1555, but survived his elevation only three weeks.

MARCELLUS, Marcus Claudius (c.268–c.208 BC) Roman soldier. In his first consulship (222 BC) he defeated the Insubrian Gauls, and slew their chief in single combat, claiming his spoils as *spolia opima*—the third and last time in Roman history. In the 2nd Punic war he checked **Hannibal** at Nola (216). Again consul in 214, he conducted the siege of Syracuse, which yielded only in 212. In his fifth consulship, 208, he fell in a skirmish against Hannibal.

MARCH, Auziàs (1397–1459) Catalan poet, born in Valencia. He was pioneer of the trend away from the lyricism of the troubadours towards a more metaphysical approach. Influenced by Italian models, he wrote chiefly on the themes of love and death.

MARCH, Francis Andrew (1825–1911) American philologist, born in Millbury, Massachusetts, and regarded as the founder of comparative Anglo-Saxon linguistics. Educated at Amherst College, he studied law in New York and was admitted to the bar in 1850. After some years of teaching, he became professor of English language and comparative philology at Lafayette College, Easton, Pennsylvania (1857–1906). Among his publications were the monumental *Comparative Grammar of the Anglo-Saxon Language* (1870) and *An Anglo-Saxon Reader* (1870). From 1879 to 1882 he was director of the American readers for the *New English Dictionary* (later named the *Oxford English Dictionary*).

MARCHAIS, Georges (1920–) French communist politician, the son of a miner. A former metal-worker, he joined the French Communist party (PCF) in 1947, becoming its general-secretary in 1972. Under his leadership the PCF pledged its commitment to the 'transition to socialism' by democratic means, and joined the Socialist party (PS) in a new 'Union of the Left'. This union was, however, severed by Marchais in 1977 and the party returned to an orthodox 'Moscow line', although PCF ministers participated in the Mitterrand government (1981–84). He unsuccessfully contested the 1981 presidential election.

MARCHAND, Jean Baptiste (1863–1934) French soldier and explorer. He joined the army at 20, explored the Niger, western Sudan and the Ivory Coast, and caused a Franco-British crisis by hoisting the tricolor at Fashoda in 1898. As a general he distinguished himself in World War I.

MARCHMONT See **HUME, Joseph**

MARCIANO, Rocky, originally **Rocco Francis Marchegiano** (1923–69) American heavyweight boxing champion, born in Brockton, Massachusetts. He first took up boxing as a serviceman in Britain during World War II, turned professional in 1947, and made his name when he defeated the former world champion, **Joe Louis**, in 1951, who had been beaten only once. A bruising, brawling heavyweight boxer, he won the world title from Jersey Joe Walcott the following year, and when he retired in 1956 was undefeated as world champion with a professional record of 49 bouts and 49 victories. He resisted all attempts to talk him into a come-back, and died in an air-crash the day before his birthday.

MARCION (c.100–c.165) Christian Gnostic. A wealthy shipowner of Sinope in Pontus, in about 140 he went to Rome, and founded the quasi-Gnostic Marcionites (144), which soon had churches in many eastern countries.

MARCO POLO See **POLO**

MARCONI, Guglielmo, Marchese (1874–1937) Italian physicist and inventor, born in Bologna of an Italian father and Irish mother. Educated at the Technical Institute of Livorno, he became fascinated by the discovery of electromagnetic waves by **Heinrich Hertz** and started experimenting with a device to convert them into electricity. His first successful experiments in wireless telegraphy were made at Bologna in 1895, and in 1899 he erected a wireless station at La Spezia, and formed the Marconi Telegraph Co. in London. In 1898 he transmitted signals across the English Channel and in 1901 succeeded in sending signals in Morse code across the Atlantic. He shared the 1909 Nobel prize for physics with **Karl Ferdinand Braun**. He later developed short-wave radio equipment, and established a worldwide radio telegraph network for the British government. From 1921 he lived on his yacht, the *Elettra*. In the 1930s he was a strong supporter of the Fascist leader **Mussolini**.

MARCOS, Ferdinand Edralin (1917–89) Filipino politician. Educated at the University of the Philippines, he was accused, in 1939, while a law student, of murdering a political opponent of his father, but secured his own acquittal. During World War II he led a Philippines army unit in anti-Japanese resistance and, after being captured, survived the notorious Bataan prison camp. After the war he sat in the Philippines' House of Representatives (1949–59) and Senate (1959–66) for the Liberal party and then the Nationalist party. Promising a new programme of industrial development, he was elected president in 1965 and re-elected in 1969. With a declining economy, and faced with a growing communist insurgency, he declared martial law in 1972 and began to rule by decree. After governing in an increasingly repressive and corrupt fashion, the 'Marcos régime' was eventually overthrown in 1986 by a popular 'People's Power' campaign, led by **Corazon Aquino**. The ailing Marcos and his influential wife, Imelda, fled into exile in Hawaii. On his death he left his wife to face charges of fraud and corruption.

MARCUS AURELIUS ANTONINUS (121–80) See **AURELIUS**

MARCUS AURELIUS ANTONINUS (176–217) See **CARACALLA**

MARCUSE, Herbert (1898–1979) German-born American philosopher and radical political theorist, born in Berlin. Educated at the universities of Berlin and Freiburg, he became an influential figure in the Frankfurt Institute of Social Research (the so-called 'Frankfurt School') along with **Adorno** and **Hork-**

heimer. The Nazis closed the Institute in 1933 and he fled to Geneva and thence in 1934 to the USA where the Institute was re-established in New York. He served as an intelligence officer for the US army during World War II, and when the Institute moved back to Europe in the early 1950s he remained in America as a naturalized citizen, holding a series of teaching positions at Harvard (from 1952), Brandeis (from 1954) and San Diego, California (from 1965). He had published *Eros and Civilization* in 1955, offering a Freudian analysis of the repressions imposed by the unconscious mind, but became a celebrity at the age of 66 with the publication in 1964 of *One Dimensional Man*, condemning the 'repressive tolerance' of modern industrial society which both stimulated and satisfied the superficial material desires of the masses at the cost of more fundamental needs and freedoms. He looked to students as the alienated élite who would initiate revolutionary change, but his hopes did not really survive the student riots of the 1960s at Berkeley and Paris. He expressed an equal hostility to bureaucratic communism in his *Soviet Marxism* (1958).

MARDEN, Brice (1938–) American painter, born in Bronxville, New York. He studied in Boston and Yale before settling in New York in 1963. By 1965 he was producing uniformly coloured canvases of horizontal and vertical formats. From 1968 he made two- and three-panel canvases, each of contrasting monochromatic colour. His paintings of the 1980s involved crossing diagonal and vertical lines.

MARE, De La, Walter See **DE LA MARE**

MARENZIO, Luca (c.1553–1599) Italian composer, born in Coccaglio near Brescia. Court musician to **Sigismund III** of Poland, he was a prolific writer of madrigals. He became a singer at the papal chapel in Rome, and is said to have died of unrequited love.

MAREY, Étienne Jules (1830–1903) French physiologist, born in Beaune. Professor at the Collège de France (from 1868), he pioneered scientific cinematography with his studies (1887–1900) of animal movement. He invented a number of improvements in camera design and succeeded in reducing exposure time to the region of $\frac{1}{25000}$ of a second for the purpose of photographing the flight of insects.

MARGARET, 'Maid of Norway' (1283–90) infant queen of Scotland from 1286. The grand-daughter of **Alexander III** of Scotland, she was the only child of Alexander's daughter, Margaret (who died in childbirth) and King Erik II of Norway. When Alexander III died in 1286, Margaret was the only direct survivor of the Scottish royal line. In 1289 she was betrothed to the infant Prince Edward (the future **Edward II** of England), son of **Edward I**; but she died at sea the following year on her way from Norway to the Orkneys.

MARGARET, St (c.1046–1093) Scottish queen, born in Hungary. She later came to England, but after the Norman Conquest with her mother, sister and her boy brother, **Edgar the Ætheling**, she fled from Northumberland to Scotland. Young, lovely, learned and pious, she won the heart of the Scottish king, **Malcolm Canmore**, who married her at Dunfermline in 1069. Much of her reputation comes from her confessor and biographer, Turgot. She brought Benedictine monks to Dunfermline, stimulated a certain amount of change in usages in the Celtic church, but institutional change and the real influx of new orders belong to the reigns of her sons. Canonized by Innocent IV in 1251, she remains the only Scottish royal saint.

MARGARET (ROSE), Princess (1930–) only sister of Queen **Elizabeth** of Britain, born at Glamis Castle, Scotland, the younger daughter of King **George VI**. She was the first scion of the Royal House in the direct line of succession to be born in Scotland for more than three centuries. In 1955 she rejected a possible marriage to Group-Captain Peter Townsend, whose previous marriage had been dissolved. In 1960 she married Antony Armstrong-Jones (1930–), a photographer, who was later created Earl of Snowdon. Their children are David, Viscount Linley (b.1961), and Lady Sarah Armstrong-Jones (b.1964). The marriage was dissolved in 1978.

MARGARET OF ANGOULÊME, also known as **Margaret of Navarre** (1492–1549) queen of Navarre, and one of the most brilliant women of her age. The sister of **Francis I** of France, she married first the Duke of Alençon (d.1525) and then, in 1527, Henry d'Albret (titular king of Navarre), to whom she bore **Jeanne d'Albret**, mother of **Henri IV** of France. Margaret had from her youth a strong interest in Renaissance learning, and was much influenced by **Erasmus** and the religious reformers of the Meaux circle, who looked to her for patronage and protection. Although she remained a Roman Catholic, she was also influenced by the writings of **Luther**, with which she had a certain sympathy. She encouraged agriculture, learning and the arts, and her court was the most intellectual in Europe. The patron of men of letters, including the heretical poet **Clément Marot**, she herself was a prolific writer. Her works included long devotional poems published as *Le Miroir de l'âme Pécheresse* (1531) and *Les Marguerites de la Marguerite des princesses* (1547), the shorter *Chansons religieuses*, dramas, and the secular poem *La Coche*; her last works, written at the end of her life in some mental anguish, were found and published in 1895 as *Les Dernières poésies*. Her most celebrated work was *Heptaméron*, a collection of stories on the theme of love, modelled upon the *Decameron* of **Boccaccio**.

MARGARET OF ANJOU (1429–82) queen of England, daughter of René of Anjou. In 1445 she was married to **Henry IV** of England. Owing to his weak intellect she was the virtual sovereign; and the war of 1449, in which Normandy was lost, was laid by the English to her charge. In the Wars of the Roses, Margaret, after a brave struggle of nearly 20 years, was finally defeated at Tewkesbury (1471), and lay in the Tower four years, until she was ransomed by **Louis XI**. She then retired to France, and died at the castle of Dampierre near Saumur.

MARGARET OF AUSTRIA (1480–1530) Duchess of Savoy and regent of the Netherlands. The daughter of the emperor **Maximilian I** and Mary of Burgundy, in 1497 she married, first, the Infante Juan of Spain, who died within a few months, then in 1501, Philibert II, Duke of Savoy. In 1507 her father appointed her regent of the Netherlands and guardian of her nephew, the future emperor **Charles V**. In 1519 she was appointed regent again, by Charles V, and proved herself a wise and capable stateswoman.

MARGARET OF PARMA (1522–86) regent of the Netherlands. The illegitimate daughter of the emperor **Charles V**, she married first Alessandro **de' Medici** (1536) and second Ottavio Farnese, Duke of Parma (1538), to whom she bore **Alessandro Farnese** (later Duke of Parma) in 1546. From 1559 to 1567 she was regent of the Netherlands, masterful, able, and a staunch Catholic. In 1567 she suppressed a Calvinist revolt, but was replaced by the duke of **Alva**. When her son Alessandro became governor of the Netherlands (1578–86), ruling as regent for **Philip II** of Spain, Margaret returned with him as head of the civil administration for a time.

MARGARET OF SCOTLAND (1425–45) queen of France. A poet, and the eldest daughter of **James I**, in 1436 she married at Tours the Dauphin (**Louis XI**), who hated and neglected her. She died without issue.

MARGARET OF VALOIS (1553–1615) queen of Navarre, the daughter of **Henri II** of France and **Catherine de' Medici**, and sister of **Francis II**, Charles IX and **Henri III**. Noted for her beauty and learning, in 1572 she married Henri of Navarre (later **Henri IV**). The marriage was childless, and was dissolved by the pope in 1599 in order to allow Henri to marry **Marie de' Medici**. She became famous for her *Memoires*, published in 1628.

MARGARET TUDOR (1489–1541) queen of Scotland, the eldest daughter of **Henry VII**. In 1503 she married **James IV** of Scotland, in 1514 Archibald Douglas, Earl of **Angus**, and, having divorced him, in 1527 Henry Stewart, later Lord Methven. She was a significant, but shifting, enigma in the politics of the minority of **James V**.

MARGARETA (1353–1412) queen of Denmark, Norway and Sweden, one of the greatest of the Scandinavian monarchs, and daughter of King Valdemar III 'Atterdag' of Denmark. She was married to King Haakon VI of Norway in 1363 at the age of ten. On the death of her father without male heirs in 1375 the Danish nobles offered her the crown of Denmark in trust for her five-year-old son Olav, for whom she acted as regent. By Haakon's death in 1380, Margareta became regent of Norway for Olav too. Olav died suddenly in 1387 at the age of 17, leaving her sole ruler of Denmark-Norway. In 1388 the Swedish nobles, affronted by their German king, Albrekt of Mecklenburg, offered her his crown, whereupon she invaded Sweden, took Albrekt prisoner, and took over the rule of Sweden. In 1389 she had her seven-year-old great-nephew, **Erik of Pomerania**, adopted as her successor to the three Scandinavian kingdoms. In 1397 she effected the Union of Kalmar, whereby the three kingdoms should remain for ever under one ruler, each retaining its separate laws. Erik was thereupon crowned king of the triple monarchy (as Erik VIII), but Margareta retained all real power in her own hands until her death.

MARGGRAF, Andreas Sigismund (1709–82) German chemist. He studied at Berlin, Strasbourg, Halle and Freiberg. In 1747 he discovered the sugar in sugar-beet and so prepared the way for the sugar-beet industry.

MARGRETHE II (1940–) queen of Denmark. Daughter of **Frederik IX**, whom she succeeded in 1972, she is an archaeologist, and was educated at the universities of Copenhagen, Aarhus and Cambridge, the Sorbonne, Paris, and the London School of Economics. In 1967 she married a French diplomat, Count Henri de Laborde de Monpezat, now Prince Henrik of Denmark. Their children are the heir-apparent, Prince Frederik André Henrik Christian (1968–) and Prince Joachim Holger Waldemar Christian (1969–).

MARGUERITE D'ANGOULÊME See **MARGARET OF ANGOULÊME**

MARGUERITTE, Paul (1860–1918) and his brother **Victor** (1866–1942), French novelists, born in Algeria. They wrote in collaboration or separately novels and histories, many dealing with the Franco-German war period, such as the series *Une Époque* (1898–1904).

MARIA CAROLINA (1752–1814) queen of Naples, the daughter of the emperor **Francis I** and **Maria Theresa** of Austria. In 1768 she married Ferdinand IV of Naples (**Ferdinand I** of the Two Sicilies), who fell completely under her influence. She appointed as prime minister her lover, the English naval officer, Sir **John Acton**, and joined an Austrian-British coalition against France. She was forced to flee during the uprising that led to the brief Parthenopean republic (1798–99), and again in 1806 when the French invaded Naples. She died in exile in Austria.

MARIA CHRISTINA (1806–78) queen of Spain, the daughter of **Francis I**, king of the Two Sicilies, and fourth wife of Ferdinand VII of Spain. On his death, she was left regent for their daughter **Isabella II**. A Carlist war broke out, and in 1836 she was forced to grant a constitution; in 1840 she was driven to France, but returned in 1843. Her share in the schemes of **Louis-Philippe** over the marriage of her daughters in 1846, and her reactionary policy, made her unpopular and in 1854 a revolution again drove her to France, where, except for a time in Spain (1864–68), she afterwards lived.

MARIA THERESA (1717–80) Holy Roman Empress, archduchess of Austria, queen of Hungary and Bohemia, daughter of the emperor Charles VI, born in Vienna. By the 'Pragmatic Sanction', for which the principal European powers became sureties, her father appointed her heir to his hereditary thrones. In 1736 she married Francis of Lorraine, afterwards Grand Duke of Tuscany and Holy Roman Emperor as **Francis I**; and at her father's death in 1740 she became queen of Hungary and of Bohemia, and Archduchess of Austria. At her accession the chief European powers put forward claims to her dominions. The young queen was saved by the chivalrous fidelity of the Hungarians, supported by Britain. The War of the Austrian Succession (1741–48) was terminated by the Peace of Aix-la-Chapelle. She lost Silesia to Prussia, and some lands in Italy, but her rights were admitted and her husband was recognized as Emperor Francis I. Maria Theresa instituted financial reforms, fostered agriculture, manufactures and commerce, and nearly doubled the national revenues, while decreasing taxation. Marshal Daun reorganized her armies; **Kaunitz-Rietberg** took charge of foreign affairs. But the loss of Silesia rankled in her mind and, with France as an ally, she renewed the contest with the Prussian king, **Frederick II, the Great**. The issue of the Seven Years' War (1756–63), however was to confirm Frederick in the possession of Silesia. After the peace she carried out a series of reforms; after the death of her husband in 1765, her son Joseph (Emperor **Joseph II**) was associated with her in the government. She joined with Russia and Prussia in the first partition of Poland (1772), securing Galicia and Lodomeria; while from the Porte she obtained Bukovina (1777), and from Bavaria several districts. A woman of majestic figure and an undaunted spirit, she combined tact with energy and won not merely the affection and even enthusiastic admiration of her subjects, but raised Austria from a wretched condition to a position of assured power. Although a zealous Roman Catholic, she sought to correct some of the worst abuses in the church. Of her ten surviving children, the eldest son, Joseph II, succeeded her; **Leopold**, Grand-Duke of Tuscany, succeeded him as **Leopold II**; **Ferdinand** became Duke of Modena; and **Marie Antoinette** was married to **Louis XVI** of France.

MARIANA, Juan de (1536–1624) Spanish Jesuit historian, born in Talavera. He taught in Jesuit colleges in Rome, Sicily and Paris. His last years of ill-health he spent in literary labour at Toledo. His invaluable *Historiae de Rebus Hispaniae* (1592) he afterwards continued down to the accession of **Charles V** in 1605; and his own Spanish translation (1601–09) is a classic. His *Tractatus VII Theologici et Historici* (1609) roused the suspicion of the Inquisition. But his most celebrated work is the *De Rege et Regis Institutione* (1599), which answers affirmatively the question whether it is lawful to overthrow a tyrant, even if he is a lawful king.

MARIANUS SCOTUS (c.1028–1083) Irish chronicler. Banished from Ireland, he was a Benedictine monk at Cologne (1052–58) and then a recluse at Fulda and at Mainz. He wrote *Chronicon Universale*, the story of the world from the Creation to 1082.

MARIANUS SCOTUS (d.c.1088) Irish abbot and calligrapher. He went to Bamberg in 1067, became a Benedictine, and was founder and abbot of the monastery of St Peter's in Ratisbon. He was a great calligraphist, copied the whole bible repeatedly, and left commentaries on **Paul**'s Epistles and on the Psalms.

MARIE AMÉLIE (1782–1866) queen of **Louis-Philippe**, born in Caserta. The daughter of Ferdinand IV of Naples, she married Louis-Philippe in 1809. After the revolution of 1848 she lived with her husband in Claremont.

MARIE ANTOINETTE, Josephe Jeanne (1755–93) queen of France, the fourth daughter of the empress **Maria Theresa** and the emperor **Francis I**; she was married to the Dauphin, afterwards **Louis XVI**, 1770. Young and inexperienced, she aroused criticism by her extravagance and disregard for conventions, and on becoming queen (1774) she soon deepened the dislike of her subjects by her devotion to the interests of Austria, as well as by her opposition to all the measures devised by **Turgot** and **Necker** for relieving the financial distress of the country. The miseries of France became identified with her extravagance, and in the affair of the Diamond Necklace (1784–86, see **Louis Rohan-Guéménée** and **Jeanne de Valois, Contesse de La Motte**) her guilt was taken for granted. She made herself a centre of opposition to all new ideas, and prompted the poor vacillating king into a retrograde policy to his own undoing. She was capable of strength rising to the heroic, and she possessed the power of inspiring enthusiasm. Amid the horrors of the march of women on Versailles (1789) she alone maintained her courage. But to the last she failed to understand the troubled times; and the indecision of Louis and his dread of civil war hampered her plans. She had an instinctive abhorrence of the liberal nobles like **Lafayette** and **Mirabeau**, but was at length prevailed on to make terms with Mirabeau (July 1790). But she was too independent to follow his advice, and his death in April 1791 removed the last hope of saving the monarchy. Less than three months later occurred the fatal flight to the frontier, intercepted at Varennes. The storming of the Tuileries and slaughter of the brave Swiss guards, and the trial and execution of the king (21 January 1793) quickly followed, and soon she herself was sent to the Conciergerie like a common criminal (2 August 1793). After eight weeks more of insult and brutality, the 'Widow Capet' was herself arraigned before the Revolutionary Tribunal. She bore herself with dignity and resignation. Her answers were short with the simplicity of truth. After two days and nights of questioning came the inevitable sentence, and on the same day, 16 October 1793, she died by the guillotine.

MARIE DE FRANCE (fl.c.1160–90) French poet, born in Normandy. She spent much of her life in England, where she wrote her *Lais* sometime before 1167 and her *Fables* sometime after 1170. She translated into French the *Tractatus de Purgatorio Sancti Patricii* (c.1190) and her works contain many classical allusions. The *Lais*, her most important work, dedicated to 'a noble king', probably **Henry II** of England, comprises 14 romantic narratives in octosyllabic verse based on Celtic material. A landmark in French literature, they influenced a number of later writers.

MARIE DE' MEDICI (1573–1642) queen of France from 1600 to 1610, daughter of **Francis I** and second wife of **Henri IV**, and mother of **Louis XIII**. She became regent (1610–17) for her nine-year-old son in 1610 when her husband was assassinated. Unwise in her choice of counsellors, she dismissed her husband's able minister, the Duke of **Sully**, and relied instead on a coterie of unscrupulous favourites, especially her Italian lover Concino Concini. The disaffected nobles obliged her to convoke the Estates General in 1614, where the queen received support from the young **Richelieu**, bishop of Luçon, who was given charge of foreign affairs in 1616. In 1615 she had arranged a marriage for her son Louis with the Infanta **Anne of Austria** (daughter of **Philip III** of Spain), and for her eldest daughter Elizabeth to the heir to the Spanish throne (the future **Philip IV**), thus bringing an end to the war with the Habsburgs. In 1617 young Louis assumed royal power; he arranged for the assassination of Concini, and exiled his mother and her supporters to the provinces. Thanks to the mediation of Richelieu she was reconciled to her son in 1620 and was readmitted to the council in 1622. When Richelieu was again given office in 1624 her influence as figurehead of the strongly Catholic *dévot* party remained important. When the king was absent on campaign in Italy in 1629 she acted as regent once again. She plotted tirelessly against her former protégé, Richelieu, but Richelieu broke her power and she went into exile in Brussels. Her lasting achievement was the building of the Luxembourg Palace in Paris, whose galleries were decorated by **Rubens**.

MARIE LOUISE (1791–1847) empress of the French, daughter of Francis I of Austria. She was married to **Napoleon** in 1810 (after the divorce of **Joséphine**), and in 1811 bore him a son, who was created king of Rome and who became **Napoleon II**. On Napoleon's abdication she returned to Austria, and was awarded the duchy of Parma. In 1822 she contracted a morganatic marriage with Count von Neipperg.

MARIETTE, Auguste Édouard (1821–81) French Egyptologist, born in Boulogne, where he was made professor in 1841. In 1849 he joined the staff of the Louvre, and in 1850 was dispatched to Egypt, where he brought to light important monuments and inscriptions in Memphis, Sakkara and Gizeh. In 1858 he was appointed keeper of monuments to the Egyptian government, and excavated the Sphinx, the temples of Dendera and Edfu, and made many other discoveries. He was made a pasha in 1879. He died of diabetes and was buried at the door of his museum at Bulâg, Cairo.

MARIN, John (1872–1953) American artist, born in Rutherford, New Jersey. He trained and worked as an architect before studying art at Pennsylvania Academy under Thomas Pollock Anshutz and at the Art Students League. From 1905 to 1910 he travelled to Europe. When he returned to America he came into contact with the Steiglitz circle, an avant garde movement. Well known for his watercolours and etchings executed in an extremely individual style, his early work was in the manner of **Whistler** but his later works are more expressive in style and were adapted from Cubist concepts.

MARIN, Maguy (1951–) French dancer and choreographer, born in Toulouse. Having studied dance as a child, she secured her first job with the Strasbourg Opera Ballet before continuing to train at the Mudra school in Brussels. This led to her joining **Maurice Béjart**'s Ballet of the 20th Century in the mid 1970s. In 1978 she won first prize at the Bagnolet international choreographic competition outside Paris. That same year she founded her own troupe, which in 1981 became the resident company of Creteil, a Paris suburb. She has choreographed for major European companies including Paris Opéra Ballet, Dutch National Ballet and, most notably, a 1985 version of *Cinderella* for Lyon Opéra Ballet, in a style that is as much about theatre as about dance.

MARINETTI, Emilio Filippo Tommaso (1876–1944) Italian writer, born in Alexandria, one of the founders of Futurism. He studied in Paris and Genoa, and published the original Futurist manifesto in *Figaro* in 1909. In his writings he glorified war, the machine age, speed and 'dynamism', and in 1919 he became a Fascist. His publications include *Le Futurisme* (1911), *Teatro sintetico futuristo* (1916) and *Manifesti del Futurismo* (4 vols, 1920). He condemned all traditional forms of literature and art, and his ideas were applied to painting by **Boccioni**, **Balla** and others.

MARINI, Giambattista (1569–1625) Italian poet, born in Naples. He was ducal secretary at Turin, and wrote his best work, the *Adone* (1622), at the court of France. His florid hyperbole and overstrained imagery were copied by the Marinist school.

MARINI, Marino (1901–80) Italian sculptor and painter, born in Pistoia. He studied in Florence, and from 1929 to 1940 taught at the Scuola d'Arte di Villa Reale, Monza, before moving to Milan, where he was professor at Brera Academy, 1940–70. He was never part of any modern movement, but remained an individual; his work was figurative and his best-known theme the horse and rider, which he explored in many versions over many years. He liked to combine different techniques, including colour, eg *Dancer* (1949–54). He also executed portraits of **Stravinsky**, **Chagall**, **Henry Miller** and others. He won many prizes, including the Venice Biennale (1952).

MARIO, Guiseppe, originally **Don Giovanni de Candia** (1810–83) Italian tenor, the son of a general, born in Cagliari. He achieved a long series of operatic triumphs in Paris, London, St Petersburg and America. His wife was the famous singer Giulia Grisi. After his retirement he lost his fortune through disastrous speculations.

MARIOTTE, Edme (1620–84) French physicist and priest, born in Burgundy. One of the earliest members of the Academy of Sciences, he wrote on percussion, air and its pressure, the movements of fluid bodies and of pendulums, colours, and coined the word 'barometer'. In his *Discours de la nature de l'air* (1676) he independently stated **Boyle**'s law of 1662, which was for long known in France as Mariotte's Law.

MARIS Dutch family of three brothers, all painters, especially Jacob (1837–99), painter of landscape and genre, born in The Hague. He studied there, in Antwerp, and (1866–71) in Paris, coming under the influence of **Diaz**, **Corot** and **Millet**. Matthijs (1839–1917) and Willem (1843–1910), were also famous and worked chiefly in London.

MARISCHAL See **KEITH, James**

MARITAIN, Jacques (1882–1973) French philosopher, born in Paris. Brought up a Protestant, he was educated in Paris and Heidelberg and converted to Catholicism in 1906. He was professor at the Institut Catholique in Paris from 1914 to 1940 and then taught mainly in North America, at Toronto, Columbia, Chicago and Princeton (1948–60). He was also French ambassador to the Vatican from 1945 to 1948 and later a strong opponent of the Vatican Council and the neo-modernist movement. His main works were *Les Degrés du savoir* (1932), in which he applied **Aquinas**' thought to contemporary philosophical canons in the theory of knowledge, and various writings on art and politics including *Art et scolastique* (1920) and *Humanisme intégral* (1936), which were better known abroad than in France.

MARIUS, Gaius (157–86 BC) Roman soldier. He served at the siege of Numantia (134), and in 119 was tribune. He served in Africa during the war against **Jugurtha**, and as consul ended it in 106. Meanwhile an immense horde of Cimbri and Teutons had burst into Gaul, and repeatedly defeated the Roman forces. Marius, consul for the second, third, fourth and fifth times (104–101), annihilated them after two years' fighting in a terrible two days' battle at Aquae Sextiae (Aix), in Provence, where 100000 Teutons were slain; and turning on the Cimbri in north Italy, crushed them also at Vercellae (Borgo Vercelli) (101). Marius was declared the saviour of the state, the third founder of Rome, and was made consul for the sixth time in 100. When **Sulla** as consul in 88 was entrusted with the conduct of the Mithridatic war, Marius, insanely jealous of his patrician rival, attempted to deprive him of the command, and a civil war began. Marius was soon forced to flee, and made his way to Africa. There he remained until a rising of his friends took place under **Cinna**. He then hurried back to Italy, and with Cinna marched against Rome, which had to yield. Marius was delirious in his revenge upon the aristocracy: 4000 slaves carried on the work of murder for five days and nights. Marius and Cinna were elected consuls for the year 86, but Marius died a fortnight afterwards.

MARIUS, (German **Mayr), Simon** (1570–1624) German astronomer, a pupil of **Tycho Brahe**. In 1609 he claimed to have discovered the four satellites of Jupiter independently of **Galilei**. He named them Io, Europa, Ganymede and Callisto, but other astronomers merely numbered them, as they did not recognize his claim to discovery. He was one of the earliest users of a telescope and the first to observe by this means the Andromeda nebula (1612).

MARIVAUX, Pierre Carlet de Chamblain de (1688–1763) French playwright and novelist, born in Paris of a good Norman family. He published *L'Homére travesti*, a burlesque of the *Iliad*, in 1716, and from then on wrote several comedies, of which his best is *Le Jeu de l'amour et du hasard* (1730). His best-known novel, *La Vie de Marianne* (1731–41), was never finished; it is marked by an affected 'precious' style—'Marivaudage'. His numerous comedies are the work of a clever analyst rather than a dramatist. His other romances, *Pharamond* and *Le Paysan parvenu*, are greatly inferior to *Marianne*.

MARJORIBANKS, Edward (1900–32) English politician and biographer. Educated at Eton College and Oxford, he was president of the Union (1922) and became a barrister. He turned to legal biography and his *Life of Sir Edward Marshall Hall, K.C.* (1929) was acclaimed for its enthralling style, its memorable powers of trial description and its rescue of a controversial reputation without ignoring the case against it. He became Unionist MP in 1929, published *Poems* in 1931 and was working on the life of **Edward Carson** when he shot himself in depression.

MARK (1st century AD) New Testament evangelist, more fully, 'John, whose surname was Mark', traditionally the author of the second canonical Gospel. Mark accompanied St **Paul** and Barnabas on their first missionary journey, but left them at Perga. He was later reconciled with Paul, and, according to tradition, was the 'disciple and interpreter' of **Peter** in Rome. He is also said to have gone to Alexandria as preacher. In medieval art Mark is symbolized by the lion. His feast day is 25 April.

MARK ANTONY See **ANTONIUS**

MARKHAM, Sir Clements Robert (1830–1916) English geographer, born in Stillingfleet near York. Educated at Westminster, he served in the navy (1844–51), and served in the expedition that located the records of Sir **John Franklin**. He explored Peru (1852–54), introduced cinchona-bark culture from South America into India (1860), and was geographer to the Abyssinian expedition (1867–68). As president of the Royal Geographical Society (1893–1905), he appointed Captain **Robert Scott** to lead his first Antarctic expedition. He wrote travel books and biographies and edited the *Geographical Magazine* (1872–78).

MARKIEWICZ, Constance Georgine, Countess (1868–1927) Irish nationalist, daughter of Sir Henry Gore-Booth of County Sligo, born in London. A society beauty, she studied art at the Slade School in London and in Paris, where she met and married (1900) Count Casimir Markiewicz. They settled in Dublin in 1903, and in 1908 she joined Sinn Fein and became a friend of **Maud Gonne MacBride**. Her husband left in 1913 for the Ukraine and never returned. She fought in the Easter Rising in Dublin (1916) and was sentenced to death, but reprieved in the general amnesty of 1917. In 1918 she was elected Sinn Fein MP for the St Patrick's division of Dublin—the first British woman MP—but refused to take her seat. She was elected to the first Dail Eireann in 1919 and became minister for labour, but was imprisoned twice. After the Civil War she was a member of the Dail from 1923.

MARKOV, Andrei Andreevich (1856–1922) Russian mathematician, born in Ryazan. He studied at St Petersburg (Leningrad), where he was professor from 1893 to 1905, before going into self-imposed exile in the town of Zaraisk. A student of **Pafnutii Chebyshev**, he worked on number theory, continued fractions, the moment problem, and the law of large numbers in probability theory, but his name is best known for the concept of Markov chain, a series of events in which the probability of a given event occurring depends only on the immediately previous event; this has since found many applications in physics and biology.

MARKOVA, Dame Alicia, professional name of **Lilian Alicia Marks** (1910–) English ballerina, born in London. She joined **Diaghilev**'s Ballet Russe in 1924, and on her return to Britain appeared for the Camargo Society and the Vic-Wells Ballet. There followed a period of partnership with **Anton Dolin** which led to their establishment of The Mavkova-Dolin Company in 1935. As well as performing Dolin's choreography in the joint company they also made guest appearances together around the world and were famed for their interpretation of *Giselle*. She was created DBE in 1963, was a director of the Metropolitan Opera Ballet 1963–69, and a governor of the Royal Ballet from 1973.

MARKS, Simon, 1st Baron Marks of Broughton (1888–1964) English businessman, born in Leeds, the son of a Jewish immigrant from Poland. In 1907 he inherited the 60 Marks and Spencer 'penny bazaars', which his father, Michael Marks, and Thomas Spencer, had built up from 1884. In collaboration with Israel (later Lord) Seiff, his schoolfriend and brother-in-law, Marks took Marks and Spencer from a policy of 'Don't ask the price—it's a penny' to become a major retail chain. 'Marks and Sparks' used their considerable purchasing power to encourage British clothing manufacturers to achieve demanding standards. The 'St Michael' brand label became a guarantee of high quality at a reasonable price. Marks' special ability was in employing able staff; the company retains an excellent reputation for its 'people policies'.

MARLBOROUGH, John Churchill, 1st Duke of (1650–1722) English soldier, the son of Sir Winston Churchill, an impoverished Devonshire royalist. Young Churchill's first post was as page to the Duke of York. Handsome and attractive, the favour of the voluptuous **Barbara Villiers** (Duchess of Cleveland) enriched him, and secured him an ensigncy in the Guards. Meritorious service in Tangier and with the British contingent under James, Duke of **Monmouth** and Marshal **Turenne** in Holland, together with the influence of his cousin Arabella Churchill as mistress of the Duke of York (later **James VII and II**), combined to bring Churchill promotion to colonel. His prospects were even further enhanced by his clandestine marriage, in 1677, to the beautiful Sarah Jennings, an attendant to, and already a close friend of, the Princess, later Queen **Anne**. In 1678 his discreet handling of a confidential mission to William of Orange (**William III**) led to his ennoblement as Baron Churchill of Eyemouth in Scotland (1682), and his wife was made Lady of the Bedchamber to Anne. In 1685 he faithfully completed the task of quelling the rebellion raised by his old comrade-in-arms, Monmouth, his reward being an English barony. But with the landing of the prince of Orange he pledged his support to William's cause. The value of his defection was recognized by his elevation to the earldom of Marlborough. Yet by 1692, despite his brilliant service in William's Irish campaign, the suspicion that he was still sympathetic to the Jacobites brought him into temporary disfavour, though Sarah maintained her close friendship with Anne, on whose accession (1702) she was made Groom of the Stole, Mistress of the Robes and Keeper of the Privy Purse. It was not until the War of the Spanish Succession (1701–14) that the supreme command of the British and Dutch forces was conferred on him by Queen Anne. His march to the Danube brought him the invaluable co-operation of Prince **Eugène** of Savoy, and led to the victory of Donauworth and the costly but unequivocal triumph of Blenheim (1704), which earned him a palatial residence at Woodstock. In the campaign of 1706 the military pretensions of **Louis XIV** were sharply rebuffed at Ramillies; while in 1708 **Vendôme**'s attempt to recover Flanders led to his shattering defeat at Oudenarde and the surrender of Lille and Ghent. With superior man-power to call upon, the French recovered from their failure at Malplaquet of 1709; but in 1711 the manoeuvre by which Marlborough forced **Villars**' 'impregnable' *ne plus ultra* lines and went on to capture Bouchain, exhibited the hallmark of consummate generalship. But in England **Harley** and the Tories had been conspiring for a compromise peace—the Treaty of Utrecht, which sacrificed virtually all the objects for which the war had been fought—and for Marlborough's public overthrow, while Queen Anne tired of the duchess and transferred her friendship to **Abigail Masham**. In 1711, the duke was charged with embezzlement of public monies and dismissed from office, and went abroad. With the accession of **George I** he was restored to his honours; his advice being freely sought at the time of the Jacobite uprising of 1715. After her husband's death, Sarah spent the rest of her life completing the palace at Blenheim, frequently in litigation with the architect, Sir **John Vanbrugh**, and editing her own and her husband's papers for publication.

MARLEY, Bob, (Robert Nesta) (1945–81) Jamaican singer, guitarist and composer of reggae music, born in the rural parish of St Ann. After moving to Kingston at the age of 14, he made his first record at 19 and in 1965 formed the vocal trio the Wailers with Peter Tosh and 'Bunny' Livingstone. Together they became the first reggae artists to achieve international success; Marley continued to build on this through a series of world tours after the departure of his original collaborators. By the 1970s both through his music and his religious and political views (which made him, at one point, the victim of an assassination attempt) he became a national hero. A devout Rastafarian, Marley made reggae popular with white audiences through a warm, expressive voice, memorable compositions—from the lyrical 'No Woman, No Cry' to the fiercely political 'I Shot the Sheriff' and 'Exodus'—and a willingness to embrace rock styles and techniques. Though suffering from cancer in his last years, his output was undiminished and he remained a major force in black popular music. His albums include *Catch a Fire* (1972), *Rastaman Vibration* (1976) and *Uprising* (1980).

MARLOWE, Christopher (1564–93) English dramatist, born in Canterbury, a shoemaker's son. From the King's School there he was sent to Benet (now Corpus Christi) College, Cambridge. He graduated BA in 1583 and MA in 1587. His *Tamburlaine the Great*, in two parts, was first printed in 1590, and probably produced in 1587. In spite of its bombast and violence it was infinitely superior to any tragedy that had yet appeared on the English stage. Earlier dramatists had used blank verse, but it had been stiff and ungainly, and Marlowe was the first to discover its strength and variety. *The Tragical History of Dr Faustus* was probably produced soon after *Tamburlaine*; the earliest edition is dated 1604. *Faustus* is rather a series of detached scenes than a finished drama and some of these scenes are evidently not by Marlowe. *The Jew of Malta*, produced after 1588 and first published in 1633, is a very uneven play. *Edward II*, produced about 1590, is the most mature of Marlowe's plays. It has not the magnificent poetry of *Faustus* and the first two acts of *The Jew of Malta*, but it is planned and executed with more firmness and solidity. *The Massacre at Paris*, the weakest of Marlowe's plays, has descended in a mutilated state. It was written after the assassination of **Henri III** of France (1589) and was probably one of the latest plays. *The Tragedy of Dido* (1594), left probably in a fragmentary state by Marlowe and finished by **Nash**, is of slight value. Marlowe had doubtless a hand in the three parts of *Henry VI*, and probably in *Titus Andronicus*. A wild, shapeless tragedy, *Lust's Dominion* (1657), may have been adapted from one of Marlowe's lost plays. The unfinished poem, *Hero and Leander*, composed in heroic couplets, was first published in 1598; a second edition, with Chapman's continuation, followed the same year. Marlowe's translations of **Ovid**'s *Amores* and of the first book of **Lucan**'s *Pharsalia* add nothing to his fame. The pastoral ditty, 'Come, live with me and be my love', to which Sir **Walter Raleigh** wrote an Answer, was imitated, but not equalled, by **Herrick**, **Donne** and others. It was first printed in *The Passionate Pilgrim* (1599), without the fourth and sixth stanzas, with the author's name, 'C. Marlowe', written below. Another anthology, Allot's *England's Parnassus* (1600), preserves a fragment by Marlowe, beginning 'I walked along a stream for pureness rare'. Marlowe led an irregular life, mingled with the rabble, and was on the point of being arrested for disseminating atheistic opinions when he was fatally stabbed in a tavern brawl. In tragedy he prepared the way for **Shakespeare**, on whose early work his influence is firmly stamped.

MARMION, of Scrivelsby the family which long provided the hereditary champions at English coronations. It came in with **William I** (the Conqueror), but became extinct under **Edward I**.

MARMION, Shackerley (1603–39) English dramatist, born in Aynho, Northamptonshire. He squandered a fortune, and fought in the Low Countries. He was the author of an allegorical epic, *Cupid and Psyche* (1637), and three comedies, *Holland's Leaguer* (1632), *A Fine Companion* (1633) and *The Antiquary* (1635).

MARMION, Simon (1425–89) French manuscript illuminator and painter, born probably in Amiens. He worked there, and in Tournai and Valenciennes. His illuminations are among the finest in 15th-century manuscript art.

MARMONT, Auguste Frédéric Louis Viesse de (1774–1852) French soldier, born in Châtillon-sur-Seine. He joined the artillery in 1792 and went with **Napoleon** to Italy, and fought at Lodi, in Egypt, and at Marengo (1800). He was sent to Dalmatia in 1805, defeated the Russians there, and was made Duke of Ragusa. In 1809 he was entrusted at Wagram with the pursuit of the enemy, won the battle of Znaim, and earned a marshal's baton. He was next governor of the Illyrian provinces, and in 1811 succeeded **Massena** in Portugal. A severe wound at Salamanca compelled him to retire to France. In 1813 he fought at Lützen, Bautzen and Dresden, and maintained the contest in France in 1814 till further resistance was hopeless, when he surrendered Paris and deserted the Allies, which compelled Napoleon to abdicate, and earned Marmont from the Bonapartists the title of traitor. The Bourbons loaded him with honours. At the Revolution of 1830 he endeavoured to reduce Paris to submission, and finally retreating with a few faithful battalions, conducted **Charles X** across the frontier. From then on he lived chiefly in Vienna or in Venice, where he died.

MARMONTEL, Jean François (1723–99) French author, born in Bort in the Limousin. He studied in a Jesuit college. Settling in Paris in 1745 on the advice of **Voltaire**, he wrote successful tragedies and operas, and in 1753 got a secretaryship at Versailles through Madame **de Pompadour**. In the official journal, *Le Mercure*, by then under his charge, he began his *Contes moraux* (1761). Elected to the Academy in 1763, he became its secretary in 1783, as well as royal historian of France. His most celebrated work was *Bélisaire*, a dull and wordy political romance, containing a chapter on toleration which excited furious hostility. His uncritical *Éléments de littérature* (1787) consists of his contributions to the *Encyclopédie*.

MARMORA, La See **LA MARMORA**

MARNIX, Philippe de, Baron de St Aldegonde (1538–98) Flemish statesman, born in Brussels. He studied under **Calvin** and **Beza** at Geneva, and at home was active in the Reformation, and in 1566 in the revolt against Spain. An intimate friend of **William the Silent** of Orange, he represented him at the first meeting of the Estates of the United Provinces, held at Dort in 1572, and was sent on special missions to the courts of France and England. As burgomaster of Antwerp, he defended the city for 13 months against the Spaniards; but having then capitulated, he incurred so much ill-will that he retired from public life. He wrote the patriotic 'Wilhelmus' song; the prose satire, *The Roman Beehive* (1569); a metrical translation of the Psalms (1580); and part of a prose translation of the Bible.

MARO See **VIRGIL**

MAROCHETTI, Carlo, Baron (1805–67) Italian sculptor, born in Turin. He trained in Paris and in

Rome, settled in Paris, and at the revolution of 1848 came to London, where he produced many fine statues (Queen **Victoria, Richard I, Coeur-de-Lion**, and others). He died in Passy.

MAROT, Clément (c.1497–1544) French poet, born in Cahors. He entered the service of **Margaret of Angoulême**, queen of Navarre. He was wounded at the battle of Pavia in 1525, and soon after imprisoned on a charge of heresy, but liberated next spring. He made many enemies by his witty satires, and in 1535 fled first to the court of the queen of Navarre, and later to that of the Duchess of Ferrara. He returned to Paris in 1536, and in 1538 began to translate the Psalms into French, which, when sung to secular airs, helped to make the new views fashionable; but accused of heresy by the Sorbonne, he had again to flee in 1543. He made his way to Geneva, where **Calvin** was devoting himself to the Reformation. Marot decided not to stay there because of this and went on to Turin. His poems consist of elegies, epistles, rondeaux, ballads, sonnets, madrigals, epigrams, nonsense verses and longer pieces; his special gift lay in badinage and graceful satire.

MAROZIA (d.938) Roman lady of noble birth. Of infamous reputation, she was thrice married, the mistress of Pope Sergius III, and mother of Pope John XI and grandmother of Pope **John XII**. She had influence enough to secure the deposition of Pope John X, her mother's lover, and the election of her own son, John XI. She died in prison in Rome.

MARQUAND, John Phillips (1893–1960) American novelist, born in Wilmingon, Delaware. He was educated at Newbury Port High School, Massachusetts, and Harvard University. He served with the military, was a war correspondent and wrote advertizing copy. He started as a writer of popular stories for magazines, featuring the Japanese detective Mr Moto, and later gently satirized affluent middle-class American life in a vein similar to **Sinclair Lewis**, whom he admired, in a series of notable novels. Key titles are *The Late George Apley* (1937), *Wickford Point* (1939) and *Point of No Return* (1949).

MARQUET, (Pierre) Albert (1875–1947) French artist, born in Bordeaux. He studied under **Gustave Moreau** and was one of the original Fauves. After initial hardships, he became primarily an Impressionist landscape painter and travelled widely, painting many pictures of the Seine (eg, the *Pont neuf*), Le Havre and Algiers in a cool restrained style. In his swift sketches he showed himself a master of line.

MARQUETTE, Jacques (1637–75) French Jesuit missionary and explorer, born in Laon. He was sent in 1666 to North America, where he brought Christianity to the Ottawa Indians around Lake Superior, and went on the expedition which discovered and explored the Mississippi (1673). He wrote an account of the journey.

MÁRQUEZ, Gabriel García (1928–) Colombian novelist, born in Aracataca. Educated at a Jesuit school, he studied law and journalism at the National University of Colombia, Bogotá. He was a journalist from 1950 to 1965, when he devoted himself to writing. One of Latin America's most formative and formidable writers, celebrated for his craft as well as his rhetorical exuberance and fecund imagination, he is a master of 'magic realism', the practice of rendering possible events as if they were wonders and rendering impossible events as if they were commonplace. Spinning from one fantastic, hyperbolic happening to another, his fictions are carried along in a torrent of narrative. *Cien años de soledad* (1967, trans *One Hundred Years of Solitude*, 1970) is the novel by which he is best known in the western world, a vast, referential 'total' novel charting the history of a family, a house, a town, from edenic, mythic genesis through the descent into history of war, politics, and economic exploitation to annihilation at a moment of apocalyptic revelation. It is one of the great novels of the 20th century. Many others have subsequently been translated including *El otono del patriarca* (1975, trans *The Autumn of the Patriarch*, 1976) and *Crónica de una muerte anunciada* (1981, trans *Chronicle of a Death Foretold*, 1982). He was awarded the Nobel prize for literature in 1982.

MARQUIS, Donald Robert Perry (1878–1937) American novelist, playwright and poet, born in Walnut, Illinois. His formal education was aborted at 15 and he worked at various jobs before studying art for a spell. He had a varied career as a journalist and wrote serious plays and poems, but he became a celebrity as a comic writer with *The Old Soak's History of the World* (1924). *archy and mehitabel* (1927) and *archys life of mehitabel* (1933) follow the fortunes of Archy the cockroach who cannot reach the typewriter's shift key (hence the lower case titles) and Mehitabel, an alley cat.

MARRYAT, Florence (1838–99) English novelist, daughter of **Frederick Marryat**, born in Brighton. She was successively Mrs Ross Church and Mrs Lean, and from 1865 published about 80 novels, as well as a drama and many articles in periodicals. She edited *London Society* (1872–76).

MARRYAT, Frederick (1792–1848) English naval officer and novelist, the son of an MP. In 1806 he sailed as midshipman under Lord **Cochrane**. After service in the West Indies, he had command of a sloop cruising off St Helena to guard against the escape of **Napoleon** (1820–21). He also did good work in suppressing the Channel smugglers, and some hard fighting in Burmese rivers. On his return to England (1826) he was given the command of the *Ariadne* (1828). He resigned in 1830, and from then on led the life of a man of letters. He was the author of a series of novels on sea life of which the best known are *Frank Mildmay* (1829), *Peter Simple* (1833), *Jacob Faithful* (1834) and *Mr Midshipman Easy* (1834). In 1837 he set out for a tour through the USA, where he wrote *The Phantom Ship* (1839) and a drama, *The Ocean Waif*. He received £1200 for *Mr Midshipman Easy* and £1600 for his *Diary in America* (1839), but was extravagant and unlucky in his money matters, and eventually was financially embarrassed. *Poor Jack*, *Masterman Ready*, *The Poacher* and *Percival Keene* appeared before he settled (1843) on his small farm of Langham, Norfolk, where he spent his days in farming and in writing stories for children.

MARS, Anne Françoise Boutet Monvel (1779–1847) French actress. She starred at the Comédie Française from 1799, excelling in the plays of **Molière** and **Beaumarchais**. She retired in 1841. She wrote *Mémoires* (2 vols, 1849) and *Confidences* (3 vols, 1855).

MARSALIS, Wynton (1961–) American trumpeter and composer, born in New Orleans to a musical family. Learning to play from the age of eight, he is unusual in his dual achievement as classical soloist and jazz performer. At fourteen, he performed **Haydn**'s Trumpet Concerto with the New Orleans Philharmonic Orchestra—the first of many engagements as a classical virtuoso—and went on to study at the Berkshire Music Center, Massachusetts, and Juilliard School, New York. Recruited in 1980 to **Art Blakey**'s Jazz Messengers (along with a brother, Branford Marsalis, tenor and soprano saxophones) he left in 1982 to lead the first of a succession of small groups. He won Grammy awards in 1984 for both a jazz and a classical recording.

MARSCHNER, Heinrich (1795–1861) German operatic composer, born in Zittau. He was successively music director at Dresden, Leipzig and Hanover, and is remembered mainly for his opera *Hans Heiling*.

MARSDEN, Samuel (1764–1838) English-born Australian clergyman, magistrate and farmer, born in Farsley, Yorkshire. He arrived in New South Wales as assistant chaplain in 1794. The chaplain to the colony, **Richard Johnson**, was at that time the only minister in the colony. Marsden farmed land at Parramatta, New South Wales, where he was also appointed magistrate. His harsh measures as magistrate, particularly in regard to the rising by Irish convicts in 1800, earned him the title 'The Flogging Parson'. However, he received high praise for his farming skills and was a pioneer breeder of sheep for wool production and in 1807 took to England the first commercial consignment of Australian wool. He made seven missionary journeys to New Zealand on behalf of the Church Missionary Society, and conducted the first Christian service in that country at Rangihoua, Bay of Islands, in 1814.

MARSH, George Perkins (1801–82) American diplomat and philologist, born in Woodstock, Vermont. He studied and practised law, was elected to Congress in 1842, and was US minister to Turkey (1849–53) and to Italy (1861–82), where he died. His chief linguistic works are *A Compendious Grammar of the Old Northern or Icelandic Language* (1838), *Lectures on the English Language* (1861) and *The Origin and History of the English Language* (1862). Among his other writings are a treatise on the camel, one on saints and miracles, and *Man and Nature* (1864; rewritten and reissued as *The Earth as Modified by Human Action*, 1874).

MARSH, James (1789–1846) English chemist. An expert on poisons, he worked at the Royal Arsenal, Woolwich, and assisted **Michael Faraday** at the Military Academy for a payment of thirty shillings a week. He invented the standard test for arsenic which has been given his name.

MARSH, Othniel Charles (1831–99) American palaeontologist, born in Lockport, New York. He studied at Yale, at New Haven, and in Germany, and became first professor of palaeontology at Yale in 1866. He discovered (mainly in the Rocky Mountains) over a thousand species of extinct American vertebrates.

MARSHAL, William, 1st Earl of Pembroke and Strigul (c.1146–1219) English knight, regent of England (1216–19), a nephew of the Earl of Salisbury. He won a military reputation fighting the French. After displaying his knightly prowess in Europe, he supported **Henry II** against **Richard I, Coeur de Lion** and at his dying behest went on a crusade to the Holy Land. Pardoned by Richard, who recognized his worth, he was given in 1189 the hand of the heiress of **Strongbow**, which brought him his earldom. He was appointed a justiciar and shared the marshalcy of England with his brother John until the latter's death gave him full office. He saw further fighting in Normandy (1196–99), and after Richard had been mortally wounded he supported the new king, **John**, but was shabbily treated by him and spent the years 1207–12 in Ireland. When John's troubles with the pope and with his barons began to mount, however, his loyalty asserted itself, and he returned to become the king's chief adviser. After John's death in 1216 he was by common consent appointed regent for the nine-year-old **Henry III**, and as such concluded a peace treaty with the French. He died at Caversham, having served in the reigns of four monarchs with unswerving fidelity.

MARSHALL, Alfred (1842–1924) English economist, born in London. Educated at Merchant Taylors' and St John's, Cambridge, he became a fellow there (1865), principal of University College, Bristol (1877), lecturer on political economy at Balliol College, Oxford (1883), and professor of political economy at Cambridge (1885–1908). Of his works, his *Principles of Economics* (1890) is still a standard text-book, containing his concept of 'time analysis' and other contributions to the science.

MARSHALL, George Catlett (1880–1959) American soldier and statesman, born in Uniontown, Pennsylvania. He was educated at the Virginia Military Institute, and commissioned in 1901. He rose to the highest rank and as chief of staff (1939–45) he directed the US army throughout World War II. After two years in China as special representative of the president he became secretary of state (1947–49) and originated the Marshall Aid plan for the post-war reconstruction of Europe (ERP). He was awarded the Nobel peace prize in 1953.

MARSHALL, John (1755–1835) American jurist, born in Virginia. He studied law, but served (1775–79) in the Continental army in the American Revolution. In 1788 he was elected to the state convention and in 1799 to congress. From 1801 to 1835 he was chief-justice of the USA. He established the doctrine of judicial review and the practice of the majority of the court speaking as a body and placed the Supreme Court in a position of power and independence. His decisions are a standard authority on constitutional law; a selection was published at Boston in 1839. He also wrote a Life of **Washington** (1807)

MARSHALL, Sir John Hubert (1876–1958) English archaeologist and administrator, born in Chester. He studied classics at Cambridge and excavated in Greece before being appointed director-general of archaeology in India (1902–31). He reorganized the Indian Archaeological Survey, recruiting Indians for the first time, established an ambitious programme for the listing and preservation of monuments, expanded museum services, and excavated widely on early historic sites. The city of Taxila in the Himalayan foothills (occupied 420 BC–500 AD) was the subject of a 20-year campaign (1913–33), and he worked also at the Buddhist religious centres of Sanchi in Madhya Pradesh and Sarnath near Benares. Prehistoric research was established on an equal footing in the 1920s with extensive excavation at Mohenjo Daro and Harappa, the chief cities of the Indus civilization which flourished in the north-west of the subcontinent c.2300–1750 BC. This revealed for the first time the unsuspected antiquity of Indian civilization. His publications included *Mohenjo Daro and the Indus Valley Civilization* (3 vols, 1931), *The Monuments of Sanchi* (3 vols, 1939) and *Taxila* (1951).

MARSHALL, Paule (1929–) American author, born in Brooklyn, New York City. Her parents emigrated from Barbados during World War I and she grew up in Brooklyn during the Depression. In 1948 she studied at Hunter College, New York City, but left prematurely because of illness. Later she graduated from Brooklyn College and worked for *Our World Magazine*. *Brown Girl, Brownstones* (1959), her first novel, is regarded as a classic of Black American literature, telling the story of the coming of age of Seling Boyce, the daughter of Barbadian immigrants living through the Depression and World War I. Later novels are *The Chosen Place* (1969), *The Timeless People* (1969) and *Praisesong for the Widow* (1983).

MARSHALL, Peter (1902–49) Scottish-born American Presbyterian clergyman, born in Coatbridge. Educated at the technical school and mining college there, he served in the navy before finding himself called to the ministry. Entry to a regular course of training in Scotland seemed barred because of his inadequate qualifications, so he went to the USA, graduated from Columbia Theological Seminary, Decatur, Georgia, and served pastorates in the South before his appointment in 1937 to the historic New York Avenue Presbyterian Church in Washington, DC. In 1948 he became chaplain to the US senate, where his brief prayers were especially memorable. Much in demand as a speaker, he also wrote *Mr Jones, Meet the Master* (1949), and after his premature death was himself the subject of a film, *A Man Called Peter*, based on his wife's biography of him.

MARSHALL, William (1748–1833) Scottish fiddler and composer, born in Fochabers. Hailed by **Robert Burns** as 'the first composer of strathspeys of the age', he set new standards of technical accomplishment in fiddle music and proudly claimed that he did not write for 'bunglers'. His two principal collections of compositions were published in 1781 and 1822, and among the many Marshall tunes that are still played are 'The Marquis of Huntly's Farewell' and 'Craigellachie Brig'.

MARSHALL, William Calder (1813–94) Scottish sculptor, born in Edinburgh, and trained under **Chantrey**. As well as memorial statues, busts, etc, he did the group *Agriculture* on the Albert Memorial.

MARSHMAN, Joshua (1768–1837) English missionary and orientalist, born in Westbury, Wiltshire. He had been a bookseller's apprentice, a weaver and a schoolmaster, when in 1799 he went as a Baptist missionary to Serampur, where he founded a college and translated the bible into various dialects. His son, John Clark (1794–1877), assisted his father in his work and later made much by publishing, and spent much on native education, returning to England in 1852. He wrote *History of India* (1842), and *Life and Times of the Serampore Missionaries* (1859).

MARSILIUS OF PADUA (c.1275–c.1342) Italian political theorist and philosopher, born in Padua. He was rector of the University of Paris from 1313, where he lectured on natural philosophy, engaged in medical research, and involved himself actively in Italian politics. In 1324 he completed *Defensor Pacis*, a political treatise much influenced by **Aristotle**'s *Politics*, which argued against the temporal power of clergy and pope and developed a thoroughgoing, secular theory of the state based on popular consultation and consent and on natural rights. When the authorship of the work became known he was forced to flee Paris (1326). Excommunicated by Pope **John XXII**, he took refuge at the court of Louis of Bavaria in Munich, and remained under his protection till his death.

MARSTON, John (1576–1634) English dramatist and satirist, born in Wardington, Oxfordshire, the son of a Shropshire lawyer and an Italian mother. He studied at Brasenose College, Oxford, and then studied law at the Middle Temple. Apart from *The Insatiate Countess* (which is of doubtful authorship), all his plays were published between 1602 and 1607. He then gave up play-writing, took orders in 1609, and (1616–31) was a clergyman at Christchurch, Hampshire. His first work was *The Metamorphosis of Pygmalion's Image: and Certain Satires* (1598), a licentious poem which was condemned by Archbishop **Whitgift**. Another series of uncouth and obscure satires, *The Scourge of Villany*, appeared in the same year. He began to write for the theatre in 1599. Two gloomy and ill-constructed tragedies, *Antonio and Mellida* and *Antonio's Revenge*, were published in 1602; in them passages of striking power stand out above the general mediocrity. A comedy, *The Malcontent* (1604), more skilfully constructed, was dedicated to **Ben Jonson**, with whom there were many quarrels and reconciliations. *Eastward Ho* (1605), written in conjunction with **Chapman** and Jonson, is far more genial than any comedy that Marston wrote single-handed. For some reflections on the Scots the authors were imprisoned (1604). Other plays include a comedy, *The Dutch Courtesan* (1605), *Parasitaster, or the Fawn* (1606), *Sophonisba* (1606, a tragedy), and *What You Will* (1607). The rich and graceful poetry scattered through his last play *The Insatiate Countess* (1613) is unlike anything that occurs in Marston's undoubted works, and it may have been completed by another hand.

MARSTON, John Westland (1819–90) English dramatic poet, father of **Philip Bourke Marston**, born in Boston, Lincolnshire. He gave up law for literature; and in 1842 his *Patrician's Daughter* was brought out at Drury Lane by **Macready**. It was the most successful of more than a dozen plays, all Sheridan-Knowlesian, and all forgotten. He wrote a novel (1860), a good book on *Our Recent Actors* (1888), and a mass of poetic criticism.

MARSTON, Philip Bourke (1850–87) English poet, son of **John Westland Marston**, born in London. He became blind at the age of three. He was grief-stricken at the death of his fiancée and then of his sisters, and his friends, **Oliver Madox Brown** and **Rossetti**. He is remembered for his friendship with Rossetti, **Watts-Dunton** and **Swinburne** rather than for his sonnets and lyrics—although a few of these are exquisite. *Songtide*, *All in All* and *Wind Voices* were the three volumes of poetry he published between 1870 and 1883. A collection of his short stories was published posthumously (1887).

MARTEL, Charles See **CHARLES MARTEL**

MARTEL, Sir Giffard Le Quesne (1889–1958) English soldier. During World War I he aided in the development of the first tanks, and in 1925 was responsible for the construction of the first one-man tank. In 1940 he commanded the Royal Armoured Corps and in 1943 headed the British military mission in Moscow.

MARTEL DE JANVILLE, Comtesse de See **GYP**

MARTEN, Harry (1602–80) English regicide, elder son of Sir Henry Marten (c.1562–1641), born and educated at Oxford. He was a prominent member of the Long Parliament, but was expelled from it (1643–46) as an extremist, and fought meantime in the parliamentary army. He sat on **Charles I**'s trial, fell into debt, had his life spared at the Restoration, but died still a prisoner at Chepstow.

MARTENS, Conrad (1801–78) Australian landscape painter, born in Crutched Friars, London, where his father was consul for Austria. He studied in London under the celebrated water-colourist **Copley Fielding**, and in 1833 was appointed by the commander of *The Beagle*, Robert FitzRoy, as a topographer for the voyage with **Charles Darwin** from Rio de Janeiro to Valparaiso. The scientific interests of these two men greatly influenced Marten's future work, especially in the accurate depiction of natural detail. In 1835 he arrived, by way of Tahiti, in Sydney where he set up a studio and began teaching. He travelled widely through New South Wales and southern Queensland, but his favourite subject was Sydney harbour, and a set of lithographs, 'Sketches of Sydney', was published in 1850 and 1851. In 1863 he obtained a post in the parliamentary library where he remained for the rest of his life.

MARTENS, Wilfried (1936–) Belgian politician. Educated at Louvain University, he was adviser to two governments, in 1965 and 1966, before becoming minister for community problems in 1968. He was president of the Dutch-speaking Social Christian party (CVP) from 1972 to 1979, when be became prime minister at the head of a coalition. He continued in office, apart from a brief break in 1981, heading no fewer than six coalition governments.

MARTENSEN, Hans Lassen (1808–84) Danish theologian, metropolitan of Denmark. He became professor of philosophy in Copenhagen, and in 1845 court-preacher also. In 1840 he published a monograph on Meister **Eckhart**, and in 1849 the conservative Lutheran *Christian Dogmatics* (trans 1866). This gained him in 1854 the primacy, but provoked a powerful attack by **Kierkegaard**. His *Christian Ethics* (1871–78) made his influence more dominant than ever.

MARTIAL, Marcus Valerius Martialis (c.40–c.104) Roman poet and epigrammatist, born in Bilbilis in Spain. He went to Rome in 64 AD and became a client of the influential Spanish house of the **Senecas**, through which he found a patron in L Calpurnius Piso. The failure of the Pisonian plot to assassinate **Cicero** lost Martial his warmest friends—**Lucan** and Seneca. He courted imperial and senatorial patronage by his verses for particular events. When the emperor **Titus** dedicated the Colosseum in 80 AD, Martial's epigrams in *Liber Spectacolorum* brought him equestrian rank; his flattery of **Domitianus** was gross and venal. The first 12 books of the *Epigrams* began to appear in 86–98. Advancing years having bereft him of Domitianus and his friends of the palace, in a fit of homesickness he borrowed from his admirer, the younger **Pliny**, the means of returning to Bilbilis, where he spent the rest of his life. His best work is often his most scurrilous.

MARTIN, St (c.316–c.400) French churchman, and a patron saint of France, born in Savaria (in Pannonia), the son of a military tribune. Educated at Pavia, he served in the army under **Constantine** and **Julian**. He became a disciple of St **Hilary** of Poitiers, and, returning to Pannonia, was so persecuted by the Arian party that he removed first to Italy, then to Gaul, where about 360 he founded a monastery at Ligugé near Poitiers, the first in France; but in 371–72 he was drawn by force from his retreat, and made Bishop of Tours. The fame of his sanctity and his repute as a worker of miracles attracted crowds of visitants; and to avoid distraction he established the monastery of Marmoutier near Tours, in which he himself resided. His military cloak, which he gave to a beggar, has become the symbol of charity, and he is the patron saint of publicans and inn-keepers.

MARTIN I, St (d.655) pope from 649. A Tuscan, he held the first Lateran Council (against the Monothelites) in 649, and was banished by **Constans II** in 654 to the Crimea, where he died.

MARTIN II, properly **Marinus I** (d.884) born in Gallese, pope from 883.

MARTIN III, properly **Marinus II** (d.946) pope from 942.

MARTIN IV, originally **Simon de Brie** (c.1210–1285) pope from 1281, born in Montpensier in Touraine. He was a mere tool of **Charles of Anjou**.

MARTIN V, originally **Oddone Colonna** (1368–1431) pope from 1417. He was elected in 1417 during the Council of Constance, over whose remaining sessions he presided. With his election the western schism was finally extinguished. He died suddenly in 1431, just after the opening of the Council of Basel.

MARTIN, Agnes (1912–) Canadian painter, born in Maklin, Saskatchewan. After studying at Columbia University in the 1940s she began painting in a style called Biomorphic Abstraction. She lived in New Mexico from 1956 to 1957. In 1959 she began painting the repetitive abstract grids of vertical and horizontal lines which have preoccupied her ever since. She held an exhibition at the Institute of Contemporary Art, Pennsylvania University, in 1973.

MARTIN, Archer (John Porter) (1910–) English biochemist, born in London. Educated at Bedford School and Peterhouse, Cambridge, he worked for the Wool Industry Research Association in Leeds (1938–46), the Medical Research Council (1948–59), the Abbotsbury Laboratories (1959–70), and the Wellcome Research Laboratories (1970–73). His work on nutrition led him to the study of protein structure and the developmemnt of partition chromatography to separate and analyze proteins, for which he shared the 1952 Nobel prize for chemistry with **Richard Synge**. From 1953 he worked on gas-liquid chromatography as another analytical technique. The widespread use of chromatographic methods revolutionized analytical chemistry.

MARTIN, Bon Louis Henri (1810–83) French historian, born in St Quentin, and educated as a notary. He joined **Paul Lacroix**, the 'Bibliophile Jacob', in his vast project for a history of France in 48 volumes of extracts from old histories and chronicles, published the first volume in 1833, and thenceforward toiled alone at the work, which was completed on a reduced scale in 1836, as the great *Histoire de France* (15 volumes). He was chosen deputy for Aisne in 1871, and senator in 1876.

MARTIN, Frank (1890–1974) Swiss composer and pianist, born in Geneva. He studied at Geneva Conservatory and in 1928 was appointed professor at the Jaques-Dalcroze Institute in Geneva. His works are marked by refinement and precision of style, and include the oratorios *Golgotha* and *In Terra Pax*, a Mass and the cantata *Le Vin herbé*, based upon the legend of Tristan and Isolde, as well as incidental music and works for orchestra and chamber combinations.

MARTIN, Glenn Luther (1886–1955) American aircraft manufacturer, born in Macksburg, Iowa. Influenced as a boy by the flights of the **Wright** brothers, he was educated at Kansas Wesleyan University in Salina. He built his first glider in California in 1905, and by 1909 had built and flown his first powered aircraft. In 1912 he flew a Martin-built seaplane from near Los Angeles to Catalina Island and back (32 miles). He invented a bomb sight and a free-fall parachute in 1913 and produced his MB-1 bomber at a factory at Cleveland in 1918. In 1929 he moved to Baltimore, producing such famous aircraft as the B-10 bomber and the China Clipper flying boat. In World War II his factory created the B-26 Marauder, Mariner and Mars flying boats.

MARTIN, John (1789–1854) English painter, born in Haydon Bridge near Hexham. After a struggling youth in London (from 1806) as an heraldic and enamel painter, in 1812 he exhibited at the Royal Academy the first of his 16 grandiose Biblical paintings, such as *The Fall of Babylon* (1819), *Belshazzar's Feast* (1821) and *The Deluge* (1826).

MARTIN, (Basil) Kingsley (1897–1969) English journalist, born in London, the son of a unitarian minister. Educated at Mill Hill School and Cambridge, he also studied at Princeton, and taught at the London School of Economics (1923–27), after which he entered journalism, serving on the *Manchester Guardian* (1927–31). As editor of the *New Statesman and Nation* (1932–62), he transformed it into a strongly self-assured weekly journal of socialist opinion. He kept up socialist pressure on Labour under **Attlee** and in the late 1950s the stature of his journal was acknowledged when **Khrushchev** and **John Foster Dulles** replied in its columns to an open letter it had published from **Bertrand Russell** on the Cold War. His books included

The Triumph of Lord Palmerston (1924), *French Liberal Thought in the Eighteenth Century* (1929), a memoir of **Harold Laski**, *Critic's London Diary* (a selection from his *New Statesman* column of vigorous personal comment) and two autobiographical works, *Father Figures* (1966) and *Editor* (1968).

MARTIN, Martin (d.1719) Scottish author and traveller. He was a Skye factor, who took his MD at Leiden. He wrote *Voyage to St Kilda* (1698) and *A Description of the Western Isles of Scotland* (1703) which aroused Dr **Johnson**'s interest in the country.

MARTIN, Paul (1864–1942) Anglo-French photographer, born in Herbenville, France. He went to England in 1872 but remained a French citizen throughout his life. First employed as a wood-engraver on magazine illustrations, he was an amateur photographer who made exceptional use of a disguised camera (with glass plates) to record working people in the streets of London and on holiday at the seaside over the decade 1888–98, perhaps the first use of 'candid camera' as a long-term social record. He turned professional in 1899 but produced no further work of significance. His *London by Gaslight* (1896) was recognized by the Royal Photographic Society and by **Stieglitz**, and his records have been much used in this century to represent the realities of late-Victorian everyday life.

MARTIN, Pierre Émile (1824–1915) French metallurgist, born in Bourges, the son of the owner of an iron and steel works. He devised an improved method of producing high-quality steel in an open-hearth furnace using the heat-regeneration process introduced by **Siemens**. The products of the Siemens-Martin process won a gold medal at the Paris Exhibition of 1867, and the open-hearth furnace in time overtook the **Bessemer** converter as the major source of the world's steel. Martin himself was crippled financially by unsuccessful litigation and spent his later years in poverty while others profited from his process, until in 1907 an international benefit fund restored his finances to a level of modest comfort.

MARTIN, Richard (1754–1834) Irish lawyer and humanitarian, born in Dublin. He was dubbed 'Humanity Martin' by **George IV**, who was his friend. He was educated at Harrow and Trinity, Cambridge. As MP for Galway (1801–26) in 1822 he sponsored a bill to make the cruel treatment of cattle illegal, the first legislation of its kind. Through his efforts the Royal Society for the Prevention of Cruelty to Animals was formed.

MARTIN, Sir Theodore (1816–1909) Scottish man of letters, born in Edinburgh. The well-known *Bon Gaultier Ballads* (1855), written in conjunction with **Aytoun**, was followed by verse translations from **Goethe**, **Horace**, **Catullus**, **Dante** and **Heine**. He was requested by Queen **Victoria** to write the life of Prince **Albert** (5 vols, 1874–80), and also wrote Lives of Aytoun (1867), Lord **Lyndhurst** (1883), and the Princess **Alice** (1885). His wife, Helen Faucit (1820–98), was a well-known actress, noted for her interpretations of **Shakespeare**'s heroines.

MARTIN, Violet Florence, pseud **Martin Ross** (1862–1915) Irish writer, born in County Galway. She is known chiefly for a series of novels written in collaboration with her cousin **Edith Somerville**, including *An Irish Cousin* (1889), and *Some Experiences of an Irish R.M.* (1908). She also wrote travel books about the Irish countryside, and two autobiographical works, *Some Irish Yesterdays* (1906) and *Strayaways* (1920).

MARTIN DU GARD, Roger (1881–1958) French novelist, born in Neuilly. He is best known for his eight-novel series *Les Thibault* (1922–40) dealing with family life during the first decades of the present century. Author also of several plays, he was awarded the Nobel prize for literature in 1937.

MARTINEAU, Harriet (1802–76) English writer, sister of **James Martineau**, born in Norwich, the daughter of a textile manufacturer of Huguenot descent. In 1821 she wrote her first article for the (Unitarian) *Monthly Repository*, and then produced *Devotional Exercises for the Use of Young Persons* (1826), and short stories about machinery and wages. Her next book was *Addresses for the Use of Families* (1826). In 1829 the failure of the house in which she, her mother and sisters had placed their money obliged her to earn her living. In 1832 she became a successful author through writing tales based on economic or legal ideas, in *Illustrations of Political Economy*, followed by *Poor Laws and Paupers Illustrated* (1833–34), and settled in London. After a visit to the USA (1834–36) she published *Society in America* and a novel, *Deerbrook*, in 1839, and a second novel, *The Hour and the Man*, about **Toussaint l'Overture**. From 1839 to 1844 she was an invalid at Tynemouth but recovered through mesmerism (her subsequent belief in which alienated many friends), and made her home at Ambleside in 1845, the year of *Forest and Game-law Tales*. After visiting Egypt and Palestine she issued *Eastern Life* (1848). In 1851, in conjunction with H G Atkinson, she published *Letters on the Laws of Man's Social Nature* which was so agnostic that it gave much offence, and in 1853 she translated and condensed **Comte**'s *Philosophie positive*. She also wrote much for the daily and weekly press and the larger reviews.

MARTINEAU, James (1805–1900) English Unitarian theologian, born in Norwich, brother of **Harriet Martineau**. Educated at the grammar school there and under Dr Lant Carpenter at Bristol, he became a Unitarian minister at Dublin and Liverpool, until 1841, when he was appointed professor of mental and moral philosophy at Manchester New College. He left for London in 1857, after that institution had been transferred there, becoming also a pastor in Little Portland Street Chapel. He was principal of the college there (1869–85). One of the profoundest thinkers and most effective writers of his day, his works include *Endeavours after the Christian Life* (1843–47), *A Study of Spinoza* (1882), *Types of Ethical Theory* (1885), *A Study of Religion* (1888), and *The Seat of Authority in Religion* (1890).

MARTINET, Jean (d.1672) French army officer. He won renown as a military engineer and tactician, devising forms of battle manoeuvre, pontoon bridges, and a type of copper assault boat used in **Louis XIV**'s Dutch campaign. He also achieved notoriety for his stringent and brutal forms of discipline, and was 'accidentally' killed by his troops at the siege of Duisberg.

MARTÍNEZ RUIZ, José See **AZORÍN**

MARTÍNEZ SIERRA, Gregorio (1881–1947) Spanish novelist and dramatist. A theatre manager and an original and creative producer as well as publisher, he was also a prolific writer. His plays *The Cradle Song* (trans 1917), *The Kingdom of God* (trans 1923) and *The Romantic Young Lady* (trans 1923) were also popular in Britain and America. Much of his writing was done in collaboration with his wife Maria, whose feminist opinions find expression in some of the plays.

MARTINI, or **Memmi, Simone** (c.1284–1344) Italian painter, born in Siena. A pupil of **Duccio**, he was the most important artist of the 14th-century Sienese school, notable for his grace of line and exquisite colour. He worked in Assisi from 1333 to 1339 and at the papal court at Avignon from 1339 to 1344. His *Annunciation* is in the Uffizi Gallery.

MARTINS, Peter (1946–) Danish dancer, born in Copenhagen. He trained at the Royal Danish Ballet School from the age of eight. Unusually tall at 6ft 2in, he made his début in Edinburgh with New York City Ballet. He joined the company two years later and created roles for **George Balanchine**. His partnership with NYCB's Kay Mezzo was to prove a dazzling and popular one. In the late 1970s he returned to the Royal Danish Ballet, retiring from performance in 1983. In the same year, Balanchine died and Martins stepped into his place, sharing the directorship of New York City Ballet with **Jerome Robbins**.

MARTINSON, Harry Edmund (1904–78) Swedish poet and novelist, born in Jäshög in Blekinge. After a harsh childhood as parish orphan he went to sea as a stoker in 1919 and travelled worldwide in the following decade. He made his poetic début in 1929 along with a number of young vitalist poets but soon found an individual and quickly acclaimed voice, particularly as a nature poet with such volumes as *Nomad* (1931) and *Natur* (1934); these established his reputation as a renewer of the poetic language. During the 1930s he was married to the writer Moa Martinson who was 14 years his senior. He came increasingly to question man's ethical maturity to control his own technological inventions and this led to his masterpiece, the poetic space epic *Aniara* (1956), which deals with the evacuation by rocket of a radiation-damaged earth; it was set to music as an opera by **Karl-Birger Blomdahl**. His account of his childhood and youth in *Nässlorna blomma* (Flowering Nettle, 1935) and *Vägen ut* (The Way Out, 1936) is his moving contribution to the many working-class autobiographical novels of the Swedish 1930s. His tramp novel *Vägen till Klockrike* (The Road to Klockrike, 1948) is a worthy addition to that genre. He shared the 1974 Nobel prize for literature with the Swedish novelist **Eyvind Johnson**. A Harry Martinson Society was founded in 1984.

MARTINU, Bohuslav (1890–1959) Czech composer, born at Polička. The son of a cobbler, he began to compose at the age of ten, and in 1906 he was sent by a group of fellow-townsmen to Prague Conservatory, where disciplinary regulations and the routine course of studies irritated him. Expelled from the Conservatory, he played the violin in the Czech Philharmonic Orchestra, and in 1920 attracted attention with his ballet *Ishtar*. Readmitted to the Conservatory, he studied under **Suk** until interest in the French Impressionist composers led him to work in Paris until 1941, when he escaped from Occupied France to America, where he produced a number of important works, including his first symphony, commissioned by **Koussevitsky** for the Boston Symphony Orchestra in 1942. A prolific composer, he ranges from orchestral works in 18th-century style, including a harpsichord concerto, to modern programme pieces evoked by unusual stimuli such as football (*Half Time*) or aeroplanes (*Thunderbolt P.47*). His operas include the miniature *Comedy on a Bridge*, written for radio and successfully adapted for television and stage.

MARTY, Martin Emil (1928–) American church historian, born in West Point, Nebraska. He had an extensive theological training before taking a Ph D at Chicago University. Ordained in the Lutheran church in 1952, he ministered in Illinois, then was appointed professor of the history of modern Christianity at Chicago in 1963. A versatile scholar, he was also one of the editors of the liberal *Christian Century* (1956–85), and a welcome lecturer in Roman Catholic and moderate evangelical circles. Among his many books are *A Short History of Christianity* (1959), *Second Chance for American Protestants* (1963), *Righteous Empire* (1970), *Health and Medicine in the Lutheran Tradition* (1983), and *Protestantism in the United States* (1985).

MARTYN, Henry (1781–1812) English missionary, born in Truro. He graduated from St John's College, Cambridge, as senior wrangler and first Smith's prizeman in 1801, and in 1802 became a fellow. Through the influence of **Charles Simeon** he sailed in 1805 for India as a chaplain with the East India Company. He translated the New Testament into Hindustani, Hindi and Persian, as well as the Prayer-book into Hindustani and the Psalms into Persian. After a missionary journey in Persia, he died of fever at Tokat in Asia Minor.

MARTYR, Peter See **PETER MARTYR**

MARVELL, Andrew (1621–78) English poet, born in Winestead rectory, south east Yorkshire, the son of a clergyman. He was educated at Hull Grammar School and Trinity College, Cambridge. He travelled (1642–46) in Holland, France, Italy and Spain. After a period as tutor to Lord **Fairfax**'s daughter, when he wrote his pastoral and garden poems, he was appointed tutor to **Cromwell**'s ward, William Dutton. In 1650 he wrote his *Horatian Ode upon Cromwell's Return from Ireland*, which also reflected the warmest sympathy for **Charles I**. In 1657 he became **Milton**'s assistant. In January 1659 he took his seat in parliament as member for Hull, for which he was returned again in 1660 and 1661. From 1663 to 1665 he accompanied Lord Carlisle as secretary to the embassy to Muscovy, Sweden and Denmark, but the rest of his life was devoted to his parliamentary duties, fighting against intolerance and arbitrary government. His republicanism was less the outcome of abstract theory than of experience. He accepted the Restoration while still admiring Cromwell. His writings show him willing to give **Charles II** a fair chance, but convinced at last that the Stewarts must go. His last satires are a call to arms against monarchy. Though circulated in manuscript only, they were believed to endanger his life. He died due to the stubborn ignorance of his physician—a baseless rumour suggested poison. Marvell's works are divided by the Restoration into two very distinct groups. After 1660 he concentrated on politics, except when his friendship for Milton drew from him the lines prefixed to the second edition of *Paradise Lost*. In 1672–73 he wrote *The Rehearsal Transpros'd* against religious intolerance; and in 1677 his most important tract, the *Account of the Growth of Popery and Arbitrary Government*, was published anonymously. As a poet, Marvell belongs to the pre-Restoration period, although most of his poetry was not published until 1681.

MARX, Karl (1818–83) German social, political and economic theorist, the inspiration of modern, international communism. He was born and brought up in Trier in a Jewish family which the father converted to Protestantism to escape anti-Semitism. He studied at the universities of Bonn (1835–36) and Berlin (1836–41), where he associated with the radical followers of **Hegel**, 'the young Hegelians', who were concerned particularly with the critique of religion. His own doctoral dissertation was on 'The Difference between the Philosophies of Nature in **Democritus** and **Epicurus**'. In 1842 he worked as a journalist and then editor of the liberal Cologne paper *Rheinische Zeitung*, but in 1843 the paper was suppressed by the government (which it regularly and virulently attacked) and Marx emigrated to Paris where he became a communist and first stated his belief that the proletariat must itself be the agent of revolutionary change in society. He wrote here his first long critique of capitalism, usually called *Economic and Philosophical Manuscripts of 1844* (not published until 1932), which develops the important Marxist notion of the alienation of man under capitalism. He also began in Paris his lifelong friendship with **Friedrich Engels**. Under political pressure he moved on to Brussels in 1845, and in collaboration with Engels wrote the posthumously published *German Ideology*, a full statement of his materialist conception of history, and the famous *Communist Manifesto* (1848), a masterpiece of political propaganda which ends with the celebrated rallying-cry 'The workers have nothing to lose but their chains. They have a world to win. Workers of all lands, unite!' After the 1848 revolution in Paris he returned to Cologne as editor of the radical *Neue Rheinische Zeitung*, but when that folded in 1849 he temporarily abandoned his political activism and took refuge with his family in London. They lived in some poverty, but in the reading room of the British Museum he began the researches which led to the publication of his major works of economic and political analysis: *Grundrisse der Kritik der politischen Ökonomie* (1857–58, published in Moscow 1939–41), *Zur Kritik der politischen Ökonomie* (1859), and most notably *Das Kapital* (Volume 1, 1867). This last was his magnum opus (two further volumes were added in 1884 and 1894) and one of the most influential works of the 19th century, in which he develops his mature doctrines of the theory of surplus value, class conflict and the exploitation of working class, and predicted the supersession of capitalism by socialism and the ultimate 'withering away' of the state as the classless society of communism was achieved. The role of the communist was to ease the birth-pangs of this historical evolution: 'Philosophers have previously tried to explain the world, our task is to change it'. Marx was supported in his research over these years by his collaborator, Engels, and he eked out his income by journalistic work from 1825 to 1862 as European correspondent for the *New York Daily Tribune*. He later revived his political involvement and was a leading figure in the First International (Workingmen's Association) from 1864 until its effective demise in 1872 when the anarchist followers of **Bakunin** split off. The last decade of his life was marked by increasing ill-health. He died in 1883 and was buried in Highgate cemetery, London. Many of his specific predictions and doctrines have been falsified by history, and 'Marxism' has been shown in practice often to have abhorrent social and political implications; but his general theories still exert an enormous influence on social science, and the secular adherents of 'Marxism' continue to outnumber the followers of almost any other religious or political creed.

MARX BROTHERS, American comedy team, the sons of German immigrants to New York, consisting of Julius Henry (Groucho) (1895–1977), Leonard (Chico) (1891–1961), Adolf (Harpo) (1893–1961) and Herbert (Zeppo) (1901–1979). They began their stage career in vaudeville in a team called the Six Musical Mascots that included their mother, Minnie (d.1929), and an aunt; another brother, Milton (Gummo) (1894–1977), left the act early on. Later, the brothers appeared as the Four Nightingales and finally as the Marx Brothers. They appeared in musical comedy, but their main reputation was made in a series of films including *Animal Crackers*, *Monkey Business* (both 1932), *Horse Feathers* and *Duck Soup* (both 1933). Herbert retired from films in 1935 and the remaining trio scored further successes in *A Night at the Opera*, *A Day at the Races* (1937), *A Day at the Circus* (1939), *Go West* (1940) and *The Big Store* (1941). The team then broke up and the brothers led individual careers. Each had a well-defined stencil: Groucho with his wisecracks, Chico, the pianist with his own technique, and Harpo, the dumb clown and harp maestro. Groucho Marx is the author of *Many Happy Returns*, his autobiography, *Groucho and Me* (1959) and a serious study of American income tax. Harpo's autobiography, *Harpo Speaks!* was published in 1961.

MARY, (1st century BC–1st century AD) Hebrew **Miriam**, Greek **Mariam** in the New Testament, the Blessed Virgin, the mother of **Jesus Christ**. The genealogy of Jesus in St Matthew is traced through **Joseph**; and it is assumed that Mary was of the same family. The Gospels record the Annunciation, her betrothal to **Joseph**, and her meeting with her cousin Elizabeth. **John** reports that she was present at the Crucifixion. The date of her death is often given as AD 63; the tradition of her having been assumed into heaven was defined as doctrine in 1950, and is celebrated in the festival of the Assumption.

MARY, Queen of Scots (1542–87) the daughter of **James V** of Scotland by his second wife, **Mary of Guise**, born at Linlithgow, while her father lay on his deathbed at Falkland. A queen when she was a week old, she was promised in marriage by the regent Arran to Prince **Edward** of England, but the Scottish parliament declared the promise null. War with England followed, and the disastrous defeat of Pinkie (1547); but Mary was offered in marriage to the eldest son of **Henri II** of France and **Catherine de' Medici**. The offer was accepted; and in 1548 Mary sailed from Dumbarton to Roscoff, and was affianced to the Dauphin at St Germain. Her next ten years were spent at the glittering French court, where she was carefully educated. She was brought up as a member of the large, young family of Henri II; her special friend was Elizabeth of Valois, later wife of **Philip II** of Spain. In 1558 she was married to the Dauphin, who was a year younger than her. The marriage treaty contained a secret clause, by which, if she died childless, both her Scottish realm and her right of succession to the English crown (she was the great-grandaughter of **Henry VII**) would be conveyed to France, for Henry II had laid claim to the English throne since the French victories of 1550. The death of Henri II (1559) brought the Dauphin to the throne as **Francis II**, and government passed into the hands of the **Guises**. When Francis died (1560), power shifted towards Catherine de' Medici, acting as regent for her next son **Charles IX**. Mary, like Catherine, became a dowager queen of France, with her own estates and income amounting to some £30 000 Scots, but her presence was increasingly needed in Scotland; the death of her mother in 1560 had left it in a highly fluid and dangerous state, with effective power in the hands of the Protestant Lords of the Congregation, who had held an illegal parliament in 1560 to implement a Reformation, ban the Catholic mass and the authority of the pope. Mary sailed from Calais on 14 August 1561, and arrived at Leith on the 19th. A Protestant riot threatened the first mass held in her private chapel at Holyrood and within days a proclamation, issued by her privy council, imposed a religious standstill, which in effect banned the mass to all but the queen and her household. Her chief advisers were Protestant, the talented diplomat, **William Maitland** of Lethington, and her illegitimate brother, James Stewart, Earl of **Moray**. The first of her many progresses around her realm was made in the autumn of 1562; it saw the defeat and death of the Earl of **Huntly**, the greatest Catholic magnate in Scotland. A series of candidates were proposed (1562–65) for Mary's hand, including the archduke Charles of

Austria (the pope's choice), and **Don Carlos** of Spain (Mary's own preference for a time); **Elizabeth** of England's proposal of the newly ennobled Earl of **Leicester** produced negotiations which dragged on for 18 months but were brought to a sudden end by Mary's unexpected bethrothal and marriage in 1565 to her cousin, Henry Stewart, Lord Darnley, son of the Earl of Lennox and Lady Margaret Douglas, a granddaughter of **Henry VII** of England. He, one of the most enigmatic figures in Scottish history, was three years younger than Mary, had been born and brought up in England, and inherited a family tradition of flexibility in religion and dynastic ambition. The immediate effect of the marriage was to end the 'amity' with England of 1560–65, to undermine the position of **Moray** and the **Hamilton** family, and put an end to the dangerous isolation of the young queen, who had no legitimate kin in Scotland. By the end of 1565 both Darnley and his father attended the mass and were in process of rebuilding the Lennox Stewart power base. Darnley was too young to be granted the crown matrimonial and, unsatisfied with the title of king or the award of the French Order of St Michael, became involved with **William Ruthven**, **James Morton** and other Protestant lords in a conspiracy against the queen's Italian private secretary, **David Rizzio**. The Rizzio murder (1566) in the queen's antechamber at Holyrood Palace had almost as many motives as conspirators, for it helped forestall a parliament and acted as a Protestant demonstration against the Catholic drift of Mary's policy. Within weeks Mary had succeeded in detaching Darnley from the conspirators, and escaped with him to Dunbar; Ruthven and Morton fled to England. Moray was later reinstated by the queen, but Darnley, who had betrayed both sides, became an object of mingled abhorrence and contempt. Shortly before the birth of their son, the future **James VI and I** (June 1566), the queen's affection for her husband seemed briefly to revive. In October 1566, while on progress through the Borders, she fell ill at Jedburgh, seriously enough to make her last will and testament. During her recovery their estrangement continued and Darnley refused to attend the elaborate baptism of their son, christened Charles James by Catholic rites at Stirling Castle. Their divorce was openly discussed, and Darnley spoke of leaving the country, but fell ill of the smallpox at Glasgow in January 1567. Mary went to see him, and brought him to Edinburgh. He was lodged in a small mansion beside the Kirk o' Field, just outside the southern walls. There Mary visited him daily, slept for two nights in a room below his bedchamber, and passed the evening of Sunday, 9 February, by his bedside in kindly conversation. She left him between ten and eleven o'clock to take part in a masque at Holyrood, at the marriage of a favourite valet; and about two hours after midnight the house in which Darnley slept was blown up by gunpowder, and his lifeless body was found in the garden. The chief actor in this tragedy was undoubtedly the Earl of **Bothwell**, who had recently enjoyed the queen's favour; but there were suspicions that the queen herself was not wholly ignorant of the plot. On 12 April Bothwell was brought to a mock-trial, and acquitted; on the 24th he intercepted the queen on her way from Linlithgow to Edinburgh, and carried her, with scarcely a show of resistance, to Dunbar. On 7 May he was divorced from his newly-married wife; on the 12th Mary publicly pardoned his seizure of her person, and created him Duke of Orkney; and on the 15th, three months after her husband's murder, she married the man most regarded as his murderer. This fatal step united her nobles in arms against her. Her army melted away without striking a blow on the field of Carberry (15 June), when nothing was left but to surrender to the confederate lords. They led her to Edinburgh, and the insults of the mob. Hurried next to Lochleven, she was constrained by a minority of the most radical of the nobles to sign an act of abdication in favour of her son, who, five days afterwards, was crowned James VI at Stirling. Escaping from her island-prison, she found herself in a few days at the head of an army of 6000 men, which was defeated (13 May) by the regent Moray at Langside near Glasgow. Three days afterwards Mary crossed the Solway, and threw herself on the protection of Queen Elizabeth, only to find herself a prisoner for life—first at Carlisle, then at Bolton, Tutbury, Wingfield, Coventry, Chatsworth, Sheffield, Buxton, Chartley and Fotheringay. The presence of Mary in England was a constant source of uneasiness to Elizabeth and her advisers. A large Catholic minority naturally looked to Mary as the likely restorer of the old faith. Yet her position, as guest or prisoner, was always ambiguous. The so-called first trial, at York and Westminster in 1568, did not resolve the complex dilemma in which English policy found itself. Plot followed plot in England, but after that of Ridolfi (1571), few if any posed any real threat. The last, of **Anthony Babington** in 1586, was known to **Walsingham**'s agents from the onset, and letters from Mary seemingly approving Elizabeth's death passed along a postal route opened by Walsingham himself. Mainly on the evidence of copies of these letters, Mary was brought to trial in September 1586. Sentence of death was pronounced against her in October but it was not until 1 February 1587 that Elizabeth signed the warrant of execution. It was carried into effect on the 8th, and she was buried at Peterborough; in 1612 her body was moved to **Henry VII**'s chapel at Westminster where it still lies. Her beauty and personal accomplishments have never been disputed, though often undervalued. She spoke or read in six languages, including Greek; sang well, played various musical instruments, and had by 1567 a library of over 300 books, which included the largest collection of Italian and French poetry in Scotland. Her own poetry is less important than the revival of vernacular poetry which has now been traced to the court during her personal reign, including the important collection, *The Bannatyne Miscellany*. The portraits and defences of her after 1571 largely fall into one of two moulds: Catholic martyr or papist plotter, making all the more difficult a proper assessment of Mary as Queen of Scots.

MARY I, Tudor (1516–58) queen of England from 1583, daughter of **Henry VIII** by his first wife, **Catherine of Aragon**, born in Greenwich. She was well educated, a good linguist, fond of music, devoted to her mother, and devoted to her church. Her troubles began with her mother's divorce, Henry forcing her to sign a declaration that her mother's marriage had been unlawful. During the reign of her half-brother **Edward VI** she lived in retirement, and no threats could induce her to conform to the new religion. On his death (1553) she became entitled to the crown by her father's testament and the parliamentary settlement. The Duke of **Northumberland** had, however, induced Edward and his council to set Henry's will aside in favour of his daughter-in-law Lady **Jane Grey**, but the whole country favoured Mary, who entered London on 3 August in triumph. Northumberland and two others were executed, but Lady Jane and her husband were, for the present, spared. The queen proceeded very cautiously to bring back the old religion. She reinstated the Catholic bishops and imprisoned some of the leading reformers, but dared not restore the pope's supremacy. The question upon which all turned was the queen's marriage; and she, in spite of national protests, obstinately set her heart on **Philip II**, king of Spain. The unpopularity of the proposal brought about **Wyatt**'s rebellion, quelled mainly through the queen's courage and coolness. Lady Jane was then, with her husband and father, executed; the Princess **Elizabeth**, suspected of complicity, was committed to the Tower. Injunctions were sent to the bishops to restore ecclesiastical laws to their state under Henry VIII. In 1554 Philip was married to Mary, remaining in England for over a year. Later that year **Pole** entered England as papal legate, parliament petitioned for reconciliation to the Holy See, and the realm was solemnly absolved from the papal censures. Soon after, the persecution which gave the queen the name of 'Bloody Mary' began. In 1555 **Ridley** and **Latimer** were brought to the stake; **Cranmer** followed in March 1556; and Pole, now archbishop of Canterbury, was left supreme in the councils of the queen. How far Mary herself was responsible for the cruelties practised is doubtful; but during the last three years of her reign 300 victims were burned. Broken down with sickness, with grief at her husband's heartlessness, and with disappointment at her childlessness, Mary died.

MARY II (1662–94) Stuart queen of Great Britain and Ireland from 1689; born in St James's Palace, London, the daughter of the Duke of York (later **James VII and II**) and his first wife, née Anne Hyde (1638–71). She was married in 1677 to her first cousin, William, Stadtholder of the United Netherlands, who in November 1688 landed in Torbay with an Anglo-Dutch army in response to an invitation from seven Whig peers hostile to the arbitrary rule of James II. When James fled to France, Mary came to London from Holland and was proclaimed queen on 13 February 1689. She shared the throne with her husband, who became King **William III**. Both sovereigns accepted the constitutional revolution implicit in the Declaration of Rights. Mary was content to leave executive authority with William (except when he was abroad or campaigning in Ireland) but she was largely responsible for raising the moral standard of court life and enjoyed a popularity in the kingdom which her husband never attained. She died of smallpox in Kensington Palace. Mary suffered several miscarriages, and the marriage was childless.

MARY OF GUELDRES See **JAMES II** of Scotland

MARY OF GUISE OR LORRAINE See **GUISE**

MARY OF MEDICI See **MARIE DE' MEDICI**

MARY OF MODENA, née **d'Este** (1658–1718) queen of Great Britain and Ireland (1685–88), second wife of **James VII and II**. The only daughter of Alfonso IV, Duke of Modena, she married James in 1673 when he was Duke of York. They lost five daughters and a son in infancy, but in 1688 she gave birth to **James Francis Edward Stewart** (the future 'Old Pretender'). When William of Orange (the future **William III**) landed in England later that year at the start of the 'Glorious Revolution', she escaped to France with her infant son, to be joined there later by her deposed husband. She spent the rest of her life at St Germain.

MARY OF TECK (1867–1953) queen-consort of Great Britain, wife of **George V**, born in Kensington Palace, London, the only daughter of Francis, Duke of Teck, and Princess Mary Adelaide of Cambridge, a grand-daughter of **George III**. In December 1891 Princess May (as she was known) accepted a marriage proposal from the eldest son of the Prince of Wales, the Duke of Clarence, who within six weeks died from pneumonia. The Princess then became engaged to his brother, the Duke of York, marrying him in 1893. After his accession (as George V) in 1910, Queen Mary accompanied him to Delhi as Empress of India for the historically unique Coronation Durbar of December 1911. Although by nature stiff and reserved, Queen Mary was more sympathetic to changing habits than her husband, whom she helped to mould into a 'people's king'. After the abdication of her eldest son, **Edward VIII**, she applied her wide experience to strengthening once again the popular appeal of the monarchy throughout the reign of her second son, **George VI**, whom she survived by 13 months. She died at Marlborough House, London, less than three months before the coronation of her grand-daughter, **Elizabeth**.

MASACCIO, real name **Tomasso de Giovanni di Simone Guidi** (1401–?1428) Florentine painter and pioneer of the Renaissance. In his short life he brought about a revolution in the dramatic and realistic representation of biblical events which was recognized by his contemporaries and had a great influence on **Michelangelo** and, through him, on the entire 16th century. In many ways Masaccio begins where **Giotto** left off. He strips away all the decorative affectations of the International Gothic style and concentrates on the drama of the situations. Line is not allowed to meander into graceful arabesques; instead, the gestures and groupings of the figures are used to describe the action. His greatest work is the fresco cycle in the Brancacci Chapel of the church of S Maria del Carmine in Florence (1424–27). **Masolino**, an inferior painter with whom Masaccio is associated, also worked there, as did **Filippino Lippi**. As a result, there is some difficulty with precise attributions.

MASANIELLO, properly **Tommaso Aniello** (1623–47) Neapolitan patriot, a fisherman of Amalfi. He led the successful revolt of the Neapolitans against their Spanish oppressors in July 1647, but the revolt deteriorated into murder and massacre, and he was assassinated by agents of the Spanish viceroy.

MASARYK, Jan (1886–1948) Czechoslovak diplomat and statesman, born in Prague, the son of **Thomas Masaryk**. He entered the diplomatic service and from 1925 to 1938 was Czechoslovak envoy in London, where his fluent English and personal charm won him many friends; he became a popular broadcaster during the war. In July 1941 he was appointed foreign minister of the Czechoslovak government in exile, returning with President **Benes** to Prague in 1945 and remaining in office in the hope of curbing the mounting communist predominance in Czechoslovakia's coalition governments. On 10 March 1948 his body was found beneath the open window of the foreign ministry in Prague, and it was assumed he had killed himself in protest at the Stalinization of his homeland.

MASARYK, Thomas Garrigue (1850–1937) founder-president of Czechoslovakia, born in Hodonin in Moravia, the son of a coachman. He was a professor of philosophy in Prague (1882–1914), marrying an American from Boston, Charlotte Garrigue, whose surname he took as his own second name. He supported Czech national causes in parliament in Vienna (1891–93 and 1907–14), achieving European fame for his exposure as forgeries documents intended by the Habsburg authorities to discredit the political leaders of the Slav minorities. After the coming of war in 1914, he escaped to London where he became chairman of the Czech National Council and headed a powerful pressure group of exiles who sought to convince the Allied governments of the need to create a 'new Europe' based on national self-determination. Masaryk went to Russia in 1917 to form a Czech Legion among prisoners-of-war, later travelling to the USA. Support for Masaryk from Slovak and Czech exiles in America, together with the backing of President **Woodrow Wilson**, secured US recognition of Masaryk as leader of an allied country (September 1918). In December 1918 he was welcomed back to Prague as president-elect of an independent Czechoslovakia. He took little part in active politics after his return to Europe, although he was among the first statesmen to perceive the menace of **Hitler**'s policies. In 1935 he retired in favour of his right-hand man, **Beneš**.

MASCAGNI, Pietro (1863–1945) Italian composer, born a baker's son in Leghorn (Livorno). In 1890 he produced the brilliantly successful one-act opera, *Cavalleria Rusticana*. His many later operas failed to repeat this success, though arias and intermezzi from them are still performed. These include *L'Amico Fritz* (1891), *Guglielmo Ratcliffe* (1895), *Le Maschere* (1901) and *Londoletta* (1917).

MASCALL, Eric Lionel (1905–) English Anglo-Catholic theologian, and author. He read mathematics for four years at Cambridge with the intention of making his career as an applied mathematician. An interest in philosophy led to another in theology, however, and he was ordained priest in 1932. After a few years in parish work he became sub-warden of Lincoln Theological College where he remained for eight years. From 1946 to 1962 he was tutor in theology and university lecturer in the philosophy of religion at Christ Church, Oxford, and (1962–73) professor of historical theology at London University. His books *He Who Is* (1943) and *Existence and Analogy* (1949) have acquired the character of text-books on natural theology. His other works include *Christian Theology and Natural Science* (Oxford Bampton Lectures, 1956) on the relations of theology and science, the ecumenical *The Recovery of Unity* (1958), *The Christian Universe* (1966), *Nature and Supernature* (1976), *Whatever Happened to the Human Mind* (1980) and *The Triune God* (1986).

MASEFIELD, John (1878–1967) English poet and novelist, born in Ledbury, Herefordshire. Educated at the King's School, Warwickshire, and schooled for the merchant service, he served his apprenticeship on a windjammer and acquired that intimate knowledge of the sea which gives atmosphere and authenticity to his work. Ill-health drove him ashore, and after three years in New York he returned to England to become a writer in 1897, first making his mark as a journalist. His earliest poetical work, *Salt Water Ballads*, appeared in 1902; *Dauber* (1913) confirmed his reputation as a poet of the sea. *Nan* (1909) is a tragedy of merit. His finest narrative poem is *Reynard the Fox* (1919). Other works are *The Everlasting Mercy* (1911); *The Widow in the Bye-Street* (1912); *Shakespeare* (1911); *Gallipoli* (1916); and the novels *Sard Harker* (1924), *Odtaa* (1926) and *The Hawbucks* (1929). His plays are *The Trial of Jesus* (1925) and *The Coming of Christ* (1928). He became poet laureate in 1930.

MASHAM, Abigail, Lady, née **Hill** (d.1734) English courtier, and cousin to Sarah Churchill, Duchess of **Marlborough**, through whose influence she entered the household of Queen **Anne**. In 1707 she married Samuel (later Baron) Masham. A subtle intriguer and strongly Tory, she gradually turned the queen against the Marlboroughs and in 1710 superseded her cousin as the queen's confidante and the power behind the throne.

MASINISSA (238–149 BC) king of the Eastern Numidians. He helped the Carthaginians to subdue the Massylii or Western Numidians. He accompanied his allies to Spain, and fought valiantly against the Romans, but going over to them (206 BC), he received as his reward Western Numidia and large portions of Carthaginian territory.

MASIRE, Quett Ketumile Joni (1925–) Botswana politician. He began a journalistic career before entering politics, through the Bangwaketse Tribal Council and then the Legislative Council. In 1962, with **Seretse Khama**, he was a founder member of the Botswana Democratic party (BDP) and in 1965 became deputy prime minister. When full independence was achieved in 1966 he became vice-president and, on Seretse Khama's death in 1980, president. He continued his predecessor's policy of non-alignment and helped Botswana become one of the most politically stable nations in Africa.

MASKELYNE, John Nevil (1839–1917) English magician, born in Wiltshire. Of farming stock, he became a watchmaker, which directed his interest towards the devices which he used in his entertainments. He joined forces with George Cooke (d.1904) and they appeared together, first at Cheltenham and then at the Crystal Palace, in 1865. In 1873 they leased the Egyptian Hall for three months, but their tenancy lasted for 31 years. Maskelyne then moved his 'Home of Magic' to the St George's Hall in 1905 with David Devant as his partner. He devoted much energy to exposing spiritualistic frauds.

MASKELYNE, Nevil (1732–1811) English astronomer. Educated at Westminster and Trinity College, Cambridge, in 1763 he produced the *British Mariner's Guide* and went to Barbados to test the chronometers, and in 1765 was appointed astronomer-royal. He improved methods and instruments of observation, invented the prismatic micrometer, and made important observations. In 1774 he measured the earth's density from the deflection of the plumb-line at Schiehallion in Perthshire. An ordained minister, he was rector from 1775 of Shrawardine, Salop, and from 1782 of North Runcton, Norfolk.

MASO DI BANCO (fl.1325–50) Italian painter who is recorded as working in Florence between 1343 and 1350. Although few works are ascribed to him, he was held in great esteem by later Italian artists, due to his realistic style in the manner of his famous predecessor **Giotto**. His best-known work is a fresco, in S Croce, Florence, of the legend of St Silvester who quelled a dragon which, by its foul breath, had terrorized Rome.

MASODI, Abu al Hassan Ali (d.957) Arab traveller, born in Bagdad, and one of the most important writers on history and geography in the medieval world. He travelled extensively in Egypt, Palestine, the Caspian, India, Ceylon, Madagascar, and perhaps even China. He wrote a (lost) 30-volume work, *Reports of the Age*.

MASOLINO DA PANICALE, properly **Thommaso di Cristoforo Fini** (c.1383–1447) Florentine painter, usually associated with **Masaccio** because of his work with him in the Brancacci Chapel of the church of S Maria del Carmine in Florence. 16th-century sources say that he was Masaccio's master but this seems unlikely (in the Brancacci Chapel the influence seems to be the other way around). Masolino was, however, a much older artist, trained in the International Gothic style in the **Ghiberti** and Starnina workshops. The strongest early influence on him was **Gentile da Fabriano**. Masolino's greatest work is the fresco cycle in the Baptistery and Collegiata of Castiglione d'Olona near Como (1430s). His influence is quite clear in the work of **Domenico Veneziano** and **Uccello**.

MASON, Alfred Edward Woodley (1865–1948) English novelist, born in Dulwich. He was educated at Oxford, became a successful actor, and subsequently combined writing with politics, as Liberal MP for Coventry (1906–10). His first published novel was *A*

Romance of Wastdale (1895). *Four Feathers* (1902) captured the popular imagination and *The Broken Road* (1907) cemented his success. With *At the Villa Rose* (1910) he started writing detective novels and introduced his ingenious Inspector Hanaud. From then on he alternated historical adventure and detective fiction. Several of his books have been filmed.

MASON, Charles (1730–87) English astronomer, known for the 'Mason and Dixon Line' in the USA. As an assistant at Greenwich Observatory, with the English surveyor Jeremiah Dixon (of whom little is known except that he is reputed to have been born in a coalmine and that he died in 1777), he observed the transit of Venus at the Cape of Good Hope in 1761. From 1763 to 1767 Mason and Dixon were engaged to survey the boundary between Maryland and Pennsylvania and end an 80-year-old dispute. They reached a point 224 miles west of the Delaware River, but were prevented from further work by Indians. The survey was completed by others, but the boundary was given the name Mason and Dixon Line.

MASON, Daniel Gregory (1873–1953) American composer, grandson of **Lowell Mason**, born in Brookline, Massachusetts. He studied under **Vincent D'Indy** in Paris, and became a leading exponent of neo-classical composition in America. He wrote books on American musical conditions and a study of **Beethoven**'s String Quartets. He composed three symphonies, the last of which is a study of **Abraham Lincoln**, and a considerable amount of chamber music.

MASON, James (1909–84) English actor, born in Huddersfield. He made his stage début in *The Rascal* (1931) at Aldershot and appeared at the Old Vic and with the Gate Company in Dublin before making his film début in the 'quota quickie' *Late Extra* (1935). He attained stardom with his suave, saturnine villainy in costume dramas like *The Man in Grey* (1943), *Fanny By Gaslight* (1944) and *The Seventh Veil* (1945). Moving to Hollywood in 1947 he became one of the most prolific, distinguished and reliable of cinema actors. He was nominated for the Academy Award for *A Star is Born* (1954), *Georgy Girl* (1966) and *The Verdict* (1982). Other respected performances from more than 100 films include *Odd Man Out* (1946), *Lolita* (1962) and *The Shooting Party* (1984). His autobiography, *Before I Forget*, was published in 1982.

MASON, Sir Josiah (1795–1881) English philanthropist and pen manufacturer, born in Kidderminster. He began life as a hawker, but after 1822 manufactured split-rings, and in 1829 began to make pens for Perry & Co., and soon became the greatest pen-maker in the world. He was a partner with his cousin **George Elkington** in electroplating (1842–65), and had smelting-works for copper and nickel. He endowed almshouses and an orphanage at Erdington at a cost of £260000, and gave £180000 to found the Mason College (now Birmingham University).

MASON, Lowell (1792–1872) American musician, born in Medfield, Massachusetts. As organist of a Presbyterian church in Savannah, he compiled a book of hymns, taking melodies from the works of **Handel**, **Mozart** and **Beethoven**. The success of this work led him to produce similar volumes for school use, and additional hymn books. In 1832 he founded the Boston Academy of Music, with the aim of giving free instruction to children, and was compelled by its success to organize classes for adults. The most famous of his compositions is probably the hymn tune 'From Greenland's icy mountains'.

MASON, William (1725–97) English poet and clergyman. He was a friend of **Gray**, who had been attracted to him by his *Musaeus* (1747), a lament for **Pope** in imitation of **Milton**'s *Lycidas*. He published two poor tragedies, *Elfrida* and *Caractacus*; the *English Garden* (1772–82), a tedious poem in blank verse; and, as Gray's executor, the *Memoirs of Gray* in 1775. He became vicar of Aston, Yorkshire, in 1754, and canon of York in 1762.

MASON, William (1829–1908) American musician, son of **Lowell Mason**, born in Boston. He studied the piano under **Liszt** and, in the course of a successful concert career, organized influential chamber music concerts in Boston. He wrote *Memoirs of a Musical Life* (1901).

MASPERO, Sir Gaston (1846–1916) French Egyptologist, born in Paris of Italian parents. In 1874 he became professor of Egyptology at the Collège de France, and was in 1881–86 and 1899–1914 keeper of the Bulak Museum and director of explorations in Egypt, making valuable discoveries at Sakkara, Dahshûr, and Ekhmim. He wrote many works on Egyptology.

MASSÉNA, André (1758–1817) French soldier, the greatest of **Napoleon**'s marshals. He served for 14 years in the Sardinian army, and in the French Revolution rose rapidly in rank, becoming in 1793 a general of division. He distinguished himself greatly in the campaigns in Upper Italy, gained his crushing victory over **Suvorov**'s Russians at Zürich (1799), and became marshal of the empire in 1804. In Italy he kept the archduke Charles in check, crushed him at Caldiero, and overran Naples. In 1807, after Eylau, he commanded the right wing, and was created Duke of Rivoli. In the campaign of 1809 against Austria he covered himself with glory and earned the title of Prince of Essling. In 1810 he compelled **Wellington** to fall back upon his impregnable lines at Torres Vedras, was forced after five months, by total lack of supplies, to make a masterly retreat, but was recalled with ignominy by his imperious master. At the Restoration he adhered to the Bourbons and on Napoleon's return from Elba Masséna refused to follow him.

MASSENET, Jules (1842–1912) French composer, born near St Étienne. He studied at the Paris Conservatoire, where he was professor (1878–96). He made his fame by the comic opera *Don César de Bazan* in 1872. Other operas are *Hérodiade* (1884), *Manon* (1885), *Le Cid* (1885), *Werther* (1892) and *Thaïs* (1894); among his other works are oratorios, orchestral suites, music for piano and songs. He wrote *Mes Souvenirs* (1912, trans 1919).

MASSEY, Gerald (1828–1907) English mystic and poet, born near Tring. He became a Christian Socialist, edited a journal, lectured, and between 1851 and 1869 published several volumes of poetry, including *Babe Christabel and other Poems* and *Craigcrook Castle*. He also wrote mystical and speculative theological or cosmogonic works, and claimed to have discovered a 'Secret Drama' in **Shakespeare**'s sonnets.

MASSEY, (Charles) Vincent (1887–1967) Canadian statesman and diplomat, brother of **Raymond Massey**, born in Toronto, joined the Canadian cabinet after World War I, became Canadian minister in Washington (1926–30), high commissioner in London (1935–46), and governor-general of Canada (1952–59).

MASSEY, Raymond (1896–1983), Canadian actor, brother of **Vincent Massey**. He made his stage début in 1922 in *In the Zone*, and played **Lincoln** in *Abe Lincoln* (1938–39). On film he played leading parts in *Things to come*, *49th Parallel*, etc, and on television 'Dr Gillespie' in the long-running *Dr Kildare* series during the 1960s. See his autobiography (1976).

MASSEY, William Ferguson (1856–1925) New Zealand statesman, born in Ireland, went to New

Zealand and became a farmer. Elected to the House of Representatives he became opposition leader and in 1912 prime minister, which office he held until his death.

MASSILLON, Jean Baptiste (1663–1742) French prelate, born in Hyéres in Provence. Trained for the church in the oratory, he preached before **Louis XIV**, became bishop of Clermont, and the next year preached before **Louis XV** his celebrated *Petit Carême*—a series of ten short Lenten sermons. In 1723 he preached the funeral oration of the Duchess of **Orléans**, his last public discourse in Paris.

MASSINE, Léonide (1896–1979) Russian dancer and choreographer, born in Moscow. Having trained with the Imperial ballet school at St Petersburg, he became principal dancer in the early days of **Diaghilev** and the Ballet Russe, going on to develop his interests in choreography with ballets like *La Boutique fantasque* (1919) and *Parade* (1917), with music by **Erik Satie** and design by **Picasso**. Though he worked periodically in America, Massine settled in Europe working freelance for companies like Sadler's Wells and Ballets des Champs Elysées. He appeared in the ballet films *The Red Shoes* (1948) and *The Tales of Hoffmann* (1950).

MASSINGER, Philip (1583–1640) English dramatist, the son of a retainer of the Earl of Pembroke. After leaving Oxford without a degree he became a playwright and was associated with **Henslowe**, who died in 1616. In later years he wrote many plays on his own, but much of his work is mixed up with that of other men, particularly **Fletcher**. He and Fletcher are buried in the same grave. Probably the earliest of Massinger's extant plays is *The Unnatural Combat*, a dreadful tragedy, printed in 1639. The first in order of publication is *The Virgin Martyr* (1622), partly written by **Dekker**. In 1623 was published *The Duke of Milan*, a fine tragedy, but too rhetorical. Other plays include *The Bondman*, *The Roman Actor* (1626), *The Great Duke of Florence* (1627), and *The Emperor of the East* (1631). **Nathaniel Field** joined Massinger in writing the fine tragedy *The Fatal Dowry*, printed in 1632. *The City Madam*, licensed in 1632, and *A New Way to Pay Old Debts*, printed in 1633, are Massinger's most masterly comedies—brilliant satirical studies, though without warmth or geniality. It is difficult to say how much Massinger was involved in the plays under the names of **Beaumont** and **Fletcher**.

MASSON, David (1822–1907) Scottish historian and literary critic, born in Aberdeen, the son of a stonemason, and best known for his epic biography of **John Milton**. Educated at Aberdeen Grammar School and Marischal College, he studied divinity at Edinburgh, but moved to London in 1847 for a career in writing. He was appointed professor of English at University College, London (1853–65), and was editor of *Macmillan's Magazine* (1859–68). He returned to Scotland as professor of rhetoric at Edinburgh (1865–95). His six-volume biography of Milton was published between 1859 and 1880; his many other works include editions of **Goldsmith** (1869) and **De Quincey** (1889–90), and critical studies of **Drummond of Hawthornden** (1873) and **Carlyle** (1885). He also wrote *Modern Essays, Biographical and Critical* (1856), and two lively autobiographical works, *Memories of London in the Forties* (1908) and *Memories of Two Cities* (1911).

MASSYS See **MATSYS**

MASTERS, Edgar Lee (1869–1950) American author, born in Garnett, Kansas. A successful lawyer in Chicago, he wrote poetry, and became famous with the satirical *Spoon River Anthology* (1915), a book of epitaphs in free verse about lives of people in Illinois. He published several more collections and some novels, and returned to his first success with *The New Spoon River* (1924), attacking the new style of urban life.

MASTERS, William Howell (1915–) American gynaecologist and sexologist, born in Cleveland, Ohio. He received his MD from Rochester University in 1943. He joined the faculty of the Washington University School of Medicine (St Louis) in 1947, where his studies in the psychology and physiology of sexual intercourse were carried out using volunteer subjects under laboratory conditions. Much of his research has been done in collaboration with **Virginia Johnson**, whom he married in 1971, and with whom he published *Human Sexual Response* in 1966, which became an international best-seller. They also wrote *On Sex and Human Loving* (1986).

MASTROIANNI, Marcello (1924–) Italian actor, born in Fontana Liri, near Frosinone, the son of a carpenter. Trained as a draughtsman, and a survivor of a wartime Nazi labour camp, he became a cashier in post-war Rome, pursuing amateur dramatics as a hobby. He made his film début in *I Miserabli* (1947) and, from 1948, was employed by **Luchino Visconti**'s theatrical troupe in productions of *A Streetcar Named Desire* and *Death of a Salesman*. *Peccato che sia una Canaglia* (1955) began an enduring partnership with **Sophia Loren**, while his performances in Visconti's *Le Notte Bianchi* (1957) and **Federico Fellini**'s *La Dolce Vita* (1960) established him as an international star. Stereotypically perceived as a 'latin lover', his prolific career has encompassed a wide diversity of characterizations and work with some of the most distinguished European film directors. He has received Academy Award nominations for *Divorzio all'Italiano* (1962), *Una Giornata Speciale* (1977) and *Oci Ciornie* (1987).

MATA HARI, stage name of **Margarete Gertrude Zelle** (1876–1917) Dutch spy, born in Leeuwarden. She became a dancer in France (1905), had many lovers, several in high military and governmental positions (on both sides) and, found guilty of espionage for the Germans, was shot in Paris.

MATEJKO, Jan Alois (1838–93) Polish painter, born in Cracow. He is noted for his paintings of scenes from Polish history.

MATHER, Cotton (1663–1728) American clergyman, born in Boston, son of **Increase Mather**. After graduating at Harvard he became a colleague to his father at the Second Church, Boston, and succeeded him in 1683. He published 382 books, and his *Memorable Providences relating to Witchcraft and Possessions* (1685) did much to fan the cruel fury of the New Englanders. During the Salem witchcraft mania (1692–93) he wrote his *Wonders of the Invisible World* (1692), but with hindsight disapproved. He supported smallpox inoculation and other progressive ideas. His *Magnalia Christi Americana* (1702) contains a mass of material for the church history of New England. Other major works include *Curiosa Americana* (1712–24) and *Christian Philosopher* (1721).

MATHER, Increase (1639–1723) American theologian, born in Dorchester, Massachusetts, the eldest son of an English Nonconformist minister who emigrated in 1635. He graduated at Harvard in 1656, and again at Trinity College, Dublin, in 1658. His first charge was Great Torrington in Devon; but in 1661, finding it impossible to conform, he returned to America, and from 1664 till his death was pastor of the Second Church, Boston, and from 1681 also president of Harvard. He published no fewer than 136 separate works, including *Remarkable Providences* (1684) and a *History of the War with the Indians* (1676). Sent to

England in 1689 to lay colonial grievances before the king, he obtained a new charter from **William III**. He was less of an alarmist about witchcraft than his son, **Cotton Mather**, and his *Cases of Conscience Concerning Witchcraft* (1693) helped to cool the heated imaginations of the colonists.

MATHEW, Theobald, known as **Father Mathew** (1790–1856) Irish temperance reformer, born in Thomastown, Tipperary. He took priest's orders in the Capuchin order in 1814, and became provincial of the Capuchins at Cork (1822–51). In 1838 he became an ardent advocate of total abstinence. He carried out crusades in Ireland, England, and Scotland, and later in America (1849–51).

MATHEWS, Charles (1776–1835) English comedian, father of **Charles James Mathews**. He made his début as an actor at Richmond in 1793, but left the legitimate stage in 1818 and achieved great success as an entertainer, visiting America twice.

MATHEWS, Charles James (1803–78) English comedian, son of **Charles**. He was a delightful light comedian of charming grace and delicacy. In 1838 he married **Lucia Vestris**.

MATHEWSON, Christy (Christopher) (1880–1925) American baseball player, born in Factoryville, Pennsylvania. An outstanding right-handed pitcher, he played 17 seasons (1900–16) for the New York Giants (now the San Francisco Giants), and holds the record (with **Grover Cleveland Alexander**) of 373 wins. In the 1905 World Series he pitched three shut-outs against the Philadelphia Athletics. He won more than 30 games in three successive seasons, and struck out 2499 batters in his career. He was one of the first five players to be elected to the National Hall of Baseball Fame in 1936.

MATHIAS CORVINUS See **MATTHIAS I CORVINUS**

MATHIEU, Georges (1921–) French painter, born in Boulogne. He took a degree in literature, but began to paint in 1942; he settled in Paris in 1947, and exhibited there and in New York. With Bryen and others, he has perfected a form of lyric, nongeometrical abstraction, in close sympathy with the American neo-Expressionists.

MATHIS See **GRÜNEWALD, Matthias**

MATILDA, called **'the Empress Maud'** (1102–67) English princess, the only daughter of **Henri I**. In 1114 she married the emperor **Henry V**, but returned to England as 'Empress Maud' after his death in 1125 and was acknowledged as the heir to the English throne. In 1128 she married Geoffrey Plantagenet of Anjou, by whom she had a son, 'Henry FitzEmpress', the future **Henry II** of England. When Henri I died in 1135, his nephew Stephen of Blois seized the throne in a swift *coup d'état*; in 1139 Matilda invaded England from Anjou with her half-brother, Robert, Earl of **Gloucester**. After capturing Stephen, she declared herself 'Lady of the English', but was never crowned. Stephen and his queen gradually regained control, and in 1148 Matilda left England and returned to her son in Normandy.

MATILDA OF TUSCANY (c.1046–1115) known as the 'Great Countess' of Tuscany. Daughter of the Margrave Boniface II of Canossa, as an infant she inherited vast tracts of land in northern Italy. Intelligent, well-educated and determined, she married first Godfrey the Hunchback, Duke of Lorraine (d.1076), and later, at the age of 43, the 17-year-old Guelf of Bavaria. She was a devoted supporter of the papacy and, in particular, Pope **Gregory VII (Hildebrand)**, even taking the field at the head of her troops to aid him in his struggle against the Holy Roman Empire. In 1077 it was at her stronghold of Canossa that the emperor **Henry IV** did barefoot penance to the pope. After Gregory's death in 1085 her lands were ravaged by Henry's allies, but she refused to make peace or recognize the anti-pope Clement III; instead she steadfastly supported Pope **Urban II** until his death in 1099. She died at the Benedictine monastery of Polirone, near Mantua.

MATISSE, Henri (1869–1954) French painter, born in Le Cateau. He first studied law in Paris and then worked as a lawyer's clerk in St Quentin. In 1892 he began studying seriously in Paris, first under **Bouguereau** at the Académie Julian and then under **Moreau** at the École des Beaux Arts, where he met **Rouault**. Between 1899 and 1900 he was working at the Académie Carrière where he met **Derain**. In the 1890s he came under the influence of Impressionism and Neo-Impressionism and, in particular, of the Divisionism developed by **Seurat** and **Signac**, but this was eclipsed for a time by his admiration for **Cézanne**. Although poverty-stricken he managed to buy Cézanne's small *Bathers* from the dealer Ambroise Vollard (1865–1939). In 1904 he returned to his Divisionist technique while working in the brilliant light of St Tropez and started using high-pitched colour, as in his celebrated *Woman with the Hat* (1905). From this departure grew the movement irreverently dubbed the Fauves (Wild Beasts) by critics. Matisse was the leader of this group which also included Derain, **Vlaminck**, **Dufy** and Rouault. His most characteristic paintings display a bold use of luminous areas of primary colour, organized within a rhythmic two-dimensional design. The purity of his line drawing is seen in his many sketch books and book illustrations. Resident in Nice from 1914, he designed some ballet sets for **Diaghilev**. The art of Matisse owes a great deal to oriental influences and his sensuous art has been as influential in the 20th century as more cerebral movements such as Cubism. In his later years he began working with large paper cut-outs, creating abstract designs. He also designed the stained glass for the Dominican Chapelle du Rosaire at Vence, Alpes-Maritimes.

MATSYS, or **Massys, Jan** (1509–75) Flemish painter, son of **Quentin Matsys**. An imitator of his father, he worked in Antwerp. His brother, Cornelius (1513–79), was also a painter.

MATSYS, or **Massys, Quentin** (c.1466–c.1531) Flemish painter, born in Louvain. According to legend, he was a blacksmith. In 1491 he joined the painters' guild of St Luke in Antwerp. His paintings are mostly religious and genre pictures, treated with a reverent spirit, but with decided touches of realism (as in *The Banker and His Wife*), and exquisite finish. He also ranks high as a portrait painter, notably his portrait of **Erasmus**.

MATTEOTTI, Giacomo (1885–1924) Italian politician. A member of the Italian Chamber of Deputies, in 1921 he began to organize the United Socialist party on a constitutional basis in opposition to **Mussolini**'s Fascists. Matteotti's protests against Fascist outrages led to his murder in 1924, which caused a crisis and nearly brought the Fascist régime to an end.

MATTHAY, Tobias (1858–1945) English pianist and teacher, of German descent, born in London. He was professor of pianoforte at the Royal Academy of Music from 1880 to 1925, when he resigned to devote himself to his own school, which he had founded in 1900. His method of piano playing was enunciated in *The Act of Touch* (1903) and subsequent publications.

MATTHESON, Johann (1681–1764) German composer, born in Hamburg. He was a singer and orchestral player before beginning to compose operas and many choral and instrumental pieces, and was also the author of manuals on continuo playing.

MATTHEW, St (1st century) one of the Twelve Apostles in the New Testament. He was a tax gatherer before becoming a disciple of **Jesus**, and is identified with Levi in Mark (ii, 14) and Luke (v, 27). According to tradition he was the author of the first gospel, was a missionary to the Hebrews in Judaea, Ethiopia and Persia, and suffered martyrdom, but nothing is known with certainty about his life. His feast day is 21 September.

MATTHEW PARIS See **PARIS, Matthew**

MATTHEWS, Alfred Edward (1869–1960) English actor, born in Bridlington. He began his career in 1887, and played innumerable comedy roles from *Charley's Aunt* to *Quiet Weekend* and was still a popular favourite at 90. He published his autobiography in 1952.

MATTHEWS, Sir Stanley (1915–) English footballer, known as the 'Wizard of Dribble'. Born in Hanley, he was the son of a notable featherweight boxer, Jack Matthews, 'the fighting barber of Hanley'. He started his sporting career as a sprinter, but soon switched to football, and joined Stoke City as a winger in 1931. First picked for England at the age of 20, he won 54 international caps, spread over 22 years. He played for Blackpool from 1947 to 1961, winning an FA Cup Winner's medal in 1953 at the age of 38. He retired in 1955, a fitness fanatic and consummate professional to the last.

MATTHIAS (1557–1619) Holy Roman Emperor, the third son of emperor **Maximilian II**. A tolerant man in religious matters, he favoured a policy of moderation towards German Protestants although, as governor of Austria, he was responsible for suppressing risings of Protestant peasants (1594–97). Elected emperor on his brother **Rudolf II**'s death in 1612, he continued to pursue a conciliatory policy which aroused the antagonism of other Catholic princes, including his nephew and heir, Ferdinand (later **Ferdinand II**), whose more rigid policy was instrumental in provoking the Thirty Years' War in 1618.

MATTHIAS, Bernard Teo (1918–) German-born American physicist, born in Frankfurt. He studied at Rome University and the Federal Institute of Technology, Zürich, before moving to the USA in 1947, where he was naturalized in 1951. After a period with Bell Telephones he was appointed professor of physics at the University of California, San Diego. In his search for new superconducting materials, he discovered that alloys of metals with five or seven valence electrons were the most effective. His work was a useful advance in the period before ceramic superconductors were found, in the late 1980s.

MATTHIAS I CORVINUS (c.1443–1490) king of Hungary, the second son of **Janos Hunyady**. He was elected in 1458, but it cost him six years' hard struggle against Turks, Bohemians, the emperor **Frederick III** and disaffected magnates before he could have himself crowned. He drove the Turks back across the frontiers; made himself master of Bosnia (1462) and of Moldavia and Wallachia (1467); and in 1478 concluded peace with Ladislaus of Bohemia, obtaining Moravia, Silesia, and Lusatia. Out of this war grew another with Frederick III, in which Matthias besieged and captured Vienna (1485), and took possession of a large part of Austria proper. His conquests were facilitated by the creation of a standing army and reform of the fiscal system, although his heavy taxation was unpopular. He codified the laws, patronized the arts, and founded a magnificent library, the *Bibliotheca Corvina*.

MATTHIESSEN, Peter (1927–) American novelist, travel writer, naturalist and explorer, born in New York City. He has made anthropological and natural history expeditions to Alaska, the Canadian Northwest Territories, Peru, New Guinea, Africa, Nicaragua and Nepal. The author of five novels and a number of eloquent ecological and natural history studies, he won the National Book award with the best-selling *The Snow Leopard* (1978), one man's inner story of a mystical trek across the Tibetan plateau to the Crystal Mountain to catch a glimpse of the rarest and most beautiful of the great cats.

MATURIN, Basil William (1847–1915) Irish preacher and writer, born in Dublin, the son of an Anglican clergyman. He was a curate in England before he went to the USA as rector of St Clements in Philadelphia in 1881. He was recalled in 1888 after doubts were expressed about his Anglicanism. He became one of the Cowley brotherhood, and a well-known pulpit orator, but in 1897 he was converted to Roman Catholicism. He was chaplain to Oxford University in 1914, but on his way home from a preaching tour in the USA he lost his life on the torpedoed *Lusitania*.

MATURIN, Charles Robert (1782–1824) Irish dramatist and novelist, born in Dublin. Educated at Trinity College, Dublin, he became a curate in Loughrea and Dublin. He made his name with a series of extravagant novels in macabre vein that rivalled those of **Anne Radcliffe**. These included *The Fatal Revenge*, *Melmoth the Wanderer* (1820), which influenced **Balzac**, and *The Albigenses*. His tragedy, *Bertram*, had a success at Drury Lane in 1816; its successors, *Manuel* and *Fredolpho*, were failures.

MAUCHLY, John William (1907–80) American physicist and inventor, born in Cincinnati. He graduated in physics at Johns Hopkins University and after a few years in teaching joined **John P Eckert** in 1943 at the University of Pennsylvania in the development of ENIAC, one of the first modern computers. They continued to collaborate in the design of electronic computers, founding in 1948 the Eckert-Mauchly Computer Corporation (which they had to sell in 1950). Following ENIAC they built EDVAC, an Electronic Discrete Variable Automatic Computer, and finally UNIVAC, a Universal Automatic Computer first used in 1951 by the US Census Bureau. The success of these machines played a large part in launching the computer revolution in the second half of the 20th century.

MAUD See **MATILDA**

MAUDE, Cyril (1862–1951) English actor-manager. He made his name in *The Second Mrs Tanqueray* and *The Little Minister* and became associate-manager of the Haymarket Theatre (1896–1905) In 1907–15 he directed his own company at the Playhouse. He was famous as Andrew Bullivant in *Grumpy* (1915). His son, John Cyril (1901–), an eminent judge and QC, was MP for Exeter (1945–51).

MAUDE, Sir Frederick Stanley (1864–1917) British soldier, born in Gibraltar. He served in the Sudan and in the 2nd Boer War (1899–1902). In World War I he took part in the Dardanelles evacuation (1915). In command in Mesopotamia in 1916 he reversed the tide against the Turks and captured Baghdad in 1917, but died of cholera.

MAUDLING, Reginald (1917–79) British Conservative politician, born in London, was educated at Merchant Taylors' and Merton College, Oxford, was called to the bar, served in the air force during World War II and in 1945 became one of **Butler**'s 'back-room boys' in the Conservative central office. He entered parliament in 1950 and after two junior ministerial posts, became minister of supply (1953–57), paymaster-general (1957–59), president of the board of trade (1959–61), colonial secretary (1961), Chancellor of the Exchequer (1962–64), and deputy leader of the opposition in 1964. In 1970 he became home secretary in the Heath government but resigned in 1972. He published his Memoirs in 1978.

MAUDSLAY, Henry (1771–1831) English engineer, and inventor of the metal lathe. He learned his job as apprentice to **Joseph Bramah**, set up on his own in 1797 and invented various types of machinery, including a screw-cutting lathe. He also invented the slide rule, and a method of desalinating sea water. With Joshua Field (1757–1863) he began producing marine engines and started the firm of Maudslay, Sons and Field (1810).

MAUDSLEY, Henry (1835–1918) English psychiatrist, born near Giggleswick. He was physician to the Manchester Asylum, and professor of medical jurisprudence at University College, 1869–79. The Maudsley Hospital, Denmark Hill, London, is named after him.

MAUGHAM, William Somerset (1874–1965) British writer, a modern master of the short story, born in Paris, of Irish origin. He was educated at King's School, Canterbury, read philosophy and literature at Heidelberg and qualified as a surgeon at St Thomas's Hospital, London. Afflicted by a bad stammer, he turned to writing in his student days and a year's medical practice in the London slums gave him the material for his first novel, the lurid *Liza of Lambeth* (1897), and the magnificent autobiographical novel, *Of Human Bondage*, eventually published in 1915. Attempts to have his plays accepted having failed, he settled in Paris and with **Laurence Housman** revived a 19th-century annual, *The Venture* (1903–04). With the success of *Lady Frederick* (1907), four of his plays ran in London in 1908. In 1914 he served first with a Red Cross unit in France, then as a secret agent in Geneva and finally in Petrograd, attempting to prevent the outbreak of the Russian Revolution. *Ashenden* (1928) is based on these experiences. He travelled in the South Seas, visiting Tahiti, which inspired *The Moon and Sixpence* (1919), in which an Englishman, Strickland, leaves his wife and stockbroking to end his life in a leper's hut. Maugham spent two years in a Scottish tuberculosis sanatorium and this again finds expression in several short stories. He then visited the Far East, writing such plays as *East of Suez* (1922) and *Our Betters* (1923). In 1928 he settled in the South of France, where he wrote his astringent, satirical masterpiece, *Cakes and Ale* (1930). A British agent again in World War II, he fled from France in 1940 with only a suitcase, and lived until 1946 in the USA where he ventured into mysticism with *The Razor's Edge* (1945). But he is best known for his short stories, several of which were filmed under the titles *Quartet* (1949), *Trio* (1950) and *Encore* (1951). The best of them, 'Rain', was originally published in the collection, *The Trembling of a Leaf* (1921). His sparse, careful prose has sometimes unjustly been mistaken for superficiality. He refused to do more than tell a story; all else is propaganda, which seriously impairs a work of art. Other works include *Catalina* (1948), *The Complete Short Stories* (3 vols, 1951), *A Writer's Notebook* (1949) and essays on **Goethe**, **Chekhov**, **James** and **Mansfield** in *Points of View* (1958).

MAUNDEVILLE, or **-VYLLE** See **MANDEVILLE, Jehan de,** or **Sir John**

MAUPASSANT, Guy de (1850–93) French novelist, born in the Norman château of Miromesnil. He was educated at Rouen and spent his life in Normandy. After a short spell as a soldier in the Franco-German war he became a government clerk, but encouraged by **Flaubert**, a friend of his mother's, he took to writing and mingled with **Zola** and other disciples of Naturalism. His stories range from the short tale of one or two pages to the full-length novel. Free from sentimentality or idealism, they lay bare with minute and merciless observation the pretentiousness and vulgarity of the middle class of the period and the animal cunning and traditional meanness of the Norman peasant. His first success, *Boule de suif* (1880), exposes the hypocrisy, prudery and ingratitude of the bourgeois in the face of a heroic gesture by a woman of the streets, while *La Maison Tellier* (1881) tells with penetrating satire and humour the tale of an outing for the inmates of a provincial house of ill-repute. At the other end of the scale *Le Horla* and *La Peur* describe madness and fear with a horrifying accuracy which foreshadows the insanity which beset de Maupassant in 1892 and finally caused his death. His short stories number nearly 300, and he wrote several full-length novels, including *Une Vie* (1883) and *Bel Ami* (1885)

MAUPERTUIS, Pierre Louis Moreau de (1698–1759) French mathematician, born in St Malo. In 1736–37 he was at the head of the French Academicians sent to Lapland to measure a degree of the meridian. **Frederick, II the Great**, made him president of the Berlin Academy in 1746. He formulated the principle of least action in mechanics, and formed a theory of heredity which was a century ahead of its time, but his temper provoked general dislike and the special enmity of **Voltaire**, who satirized him in *Micromégas*, driving him to Basel, where he died.

MAUREPAS, Jean Frédéric Phélippeaux, Comte de (1701–81) French statesman, and later minister of marine. He rendered services to his department by promoting the French expedition to the North Pole and the Equator in 1736–37, but he displeased the all-powerful **Pompadour**, and was banished from court in 1749. Recalled and made first minister in 1774, he sought to humiliate England by recognizing the USA.

MAURIAC, François (1885–1970) French novelist, born in Bordeaux of Roman Catholic parentage, and regarded as the leading novelist of that faith. He started as a poet, publishing his first volume of verse in 1909. In his novels, his treatment of the themes of temptation, sin and redemption, set in the brooding Bordeaux countryside, showed his art as cathartic, exploring the universal problems of sinful, yet aspiring, man. His principal novels, all translated into English, are *Le Baiser au Lépreux* (1922); *Génitrix* (1923); the *Thérèse* novels; and *Noeud de Vipères* (1932). Also important is his play *Asmodée* (1938). He was awarded the 1952 Nobel prize for literature.

MAURICE (1521–53) Duke and Elector of Saxony, son of Duke Henry of Albertine Saxony. Although a Catholic, he was married, by his father's wishes, to the daughter of the prominent Lutheran prince, Landgrave Philip of Hesse. Maurice continued his father's policy of friendship with the Protestants but refused to join the Schmalkaldic League. Following the Protestants' defeat at Mühlberg in 1547, Maurice became Elector of Ernestine Saxony in place of **John Frederick** who had been stripped of his title and lands. As ruler of a unified Saxony, he pursued a more strongly Protestant policy, protecting the theologian, **Philip Melanchthon**, and re-establishing the Lutheran University of Wittenberg.

MAURICE (1567–1625) Count of Nassau, Prince of Orange, second son of **William the Silent**. He was appointed stadthouder of Holland by the states-general of the United Provinces at the age of 17 upon his father's murder in 1584 and took command of the fledgling republic's army in its continuing struggle for independence from Spain. With English aid, he was able to inflict a series of humiliating defeats on the Spanish in the 1590s, leading to the recognition of the republic at the Hague in 1608 and the Twelve Years' Truce of 1609. He became Prince of Orange on the death of his elder brother in 1618 and, after the execution of his rival, the veteran statesman Oldenbarnevelt, was able to establish a virtually monarchical authority over the state, but left the constitution unchanged on his death. He died childless and was succeeded by his brother, Frederick Henry, grandfather of **William III** (William of Orange).

MAURICE, Prince See **RUPERT**

MAURICE, Sir John Frederick (1841–1912) English soldier and military historian, son of **Frederick Denison Maurice**. He was professor (1885–92) of military history at the Staff College, and the author of *Life of Frederick Denison Maurice* (1884), a *System of Field Manœuvres* (1872), *The Ashantee War* (1874), *War* (1891), and other works.

MAURICE, (John) Frederick Denison (1805–72) English theologian and writer, born in Normanston near Lowestoft, the son of a Unitarian minister. He studied at Trinity College and Trinity Hall, Cambridge, but as a Dissenter, left in 1827 without a degree, and began a literary career in London. He wrote a novel, *Eustace Conway*, and for a time edited the *Athenaeum*. Influenced by **Coleridge**, he took orders in the Church of England, became chaplain to Guy's Hospital (1837) and to Lincoln's Inn (1841–60); in 1840 he became professor of literature at King's College, London, where he was professor of theology 1846–53, and from 1866 professor of moral philosophy at Cambridge. The publication in 1853 of his *Theological Essays*, dealing with atonement and eternal life, lost him his professorship of theology. His books include *Moral and Metaphysical Philosophy*, *The Conscience*, and *Social Morality*. Maurice strenuously controverted **Mansel**'s views on our knowledge of God, and denounced as false any political economy founded on selfishness and not on the universe. With **Thomas Hughes** and **Charles Kingsley** he founded the Christian socialism movement. He also was the founder and first principal of the Working Man's College (1854) and of the Queen's College for Women.

MAURIER See **DU MAURIER**

MAUROIS, André, pseud of **Emile Herzog** (1885–1967) French novelist and biographer, born in Elbeuf. He was one of a family of Jewish industrialists from Alsace who settled in Normandy after 1870. During World War I he was a liaison officer with the British army, and began his literary career with two books of shrewd and affectionate observation of British character, *Les Silences du Colonel Bramble* (1918) and *Les Discours du Docteur O'Grady* (1920). His large output includes such distinguished biographies as his *Ariel*, a life of **Shelley** (1923), *Disraeli* (1927), *Voltaire* (1935), *A la recherche de Marcel Proust* (1949), and *The Life of Sir Alexander Fleming* (trans 1959).

MAUROY, Pierre (1928–) French politician, prime minister from 1981 to 1984. He was a teacher before becoming involved with trade unionism and socialist politics. He was prominent in the creation of a new French Socialist party in 1971 and in the subsequent unification of the left. He became mayor of Lille in 1973, the same year that he was first elected to the National Assembly, and held the post until President **Mitterrand** made him prime minister in 1981. He oversaw the introduction of a radical, but unsuccessful, reflationary programme and was replaced as prime minister by **Laurent Fabius** in July 1984 as a major switch in policy course became essential. A representative of the 'traditional left' faction, he became first secretary of the Socialist party in May 1988.

MAURRAS, Charles (1868–1952) French journalist and critic, born in Martigues (Bouches-du-Rhône). A student of philosophy at Paris, he was influenced by the ideas of **Auguste Comte**, and this influence, combined with discipleship to the *Félibrige* movement, fostered in him a spirit critical of the contemporary scene, but by 1894 he had outgrown the association and was established as an avant-garde journalist. A trip to Greece made him a pronounced admirer of Greek culture, and influenced by the **Dreyfus** case, he moved away from republicanism to a belief in the efficacy of monarchy. *Trois idées politiques...* (1898) and *Enquête sur la monarchie* (1901) state his views with clarity and vigour. From 1908, in *Action française*, his articles wielded a powerful influence on the youth of the country and this was reinforced by such studies as *Les Conditions de la victoire* (1916–18). *Action française* was finally discredited and in 1936 Maurras was imprisoned for violent attacks on the government of the day, the culmination of his bitter campaign in *Figaro*, *Gazette de France*, and other newspapers, against democratic ideals. At the fall of France in 1940 he supported the Vichy government. When the country was liberated in 1945, he was brought to trial and sentenced to life imprisonment. He was released, on medical grounds, in 1952, just before he died.

MAURY, Jean Siffrein (1746–1817) French prelate, born in Valréas (Vaucluse). Ordained a priest in 1770, he wrote a series of eloquent *éloges* on the dauphin, which gained him admission to the Academy in 1784. In 1789 he was sent to the States General, where as an orator he rivalled **Mirabeau** and was one of the chief supporters of the crown. At the dissolution of the Constituent Assembly in 1791 he withdrew to Rome, and was made an archbishop *in partibus*, and cardinal (1794). In 1804 he returned to France and made his submission to **Napoleon**, who in 1810 appointed him archbishop of Paris.

MAURY, Matthew Fontaine (1806–73) American hydrographer, born in Spotsylvania, Virginia. He entered the US navy in 1825, and during a voyage round the world (1826–30) commenced his well-known *Navigation* (1834). Lamed for life in 1839, he was appointed superintendent in 1842 of the hydrographical office at Washington, and in 1844 of the observatory. There he wrote his *Physical Geography of the Sea* (1856), and his works on the Gulf Stream, ocean currents, and Great Circle sailing. He became an officer of the Confederate navy, and later professor of physics at Lexington.

MAUSER, Peter Paul von (1838–1914) German firearm inventor, born in Oberndorf, Neckar. With his brother Wilhelm (1834–82) he was responsible for the improved needle-gun (adopted by the German army in 1871) and for the improved breech-loading cannon. He produced the Mauser magazine-rifle in 1897.

MAUSOLUS See **ARTEMISIA, Queen of Caria**

MAUSS, Marcel (1872–1950) French sociologist and anthropologist, born in Épinal, Lorraine, the nephew of **Émile Durkheim**. He studied philosophy under his uncle at Bordeaux, and the history of religion at Paris. In 1901 he became professor in the philosophy and religion of 'non-civilized' peoples, and in 1925 was co-founder of the Institute of Ethnology at Paris University. From 1931 to 1939 he was at the Collège de France. During the period up to World War I, he collaborated closely with Durkheim and other members of the *Année sociologique* school which had grown up around him. Though he never carried out any fieldwork, his knowledge of classic and ethnographic sources was prodigious. From this period date his studies of sacrifice, magic, collective representations and social morphology. After World War I, he devoted himself to editing the work of the *Année* school and to writing his masterpiece, *Essai sur le don* (1925), in which he demonstrated the importance of gift exchange in primitive social organization. His last significant work, a lecture on the concept of the person, appeared in 1938. The renewed outbreak of war in 1939 dealt a blow to his sanity from which he never recovered.

MAUVE, Anton (1838–88) Dutch painter, born in Zaandam. One of the greatest landscapists of his time, he was influenced by **Corot** and **Millet** and painted country scenes. From 1878 he lived in Laren, gathering other painters round him in a kind of Dutch Barbizon school.

MAVOR, O H See **BRIDIE, James**

MAWLAY AHMAD-AL-MANSUR (1578–1603) sultan of Maghrib (Morocco), brought peace and prosperity to the country, instituted administrative reforms and developed trade, especially in sugar and saltpetre.

MAWLAY ISMA'IL (1672–1727) sultan of Maghrib (Morocco). He consolidated the authority of the state and took firm control of piracy which he turned into a state enterprise. He also established an élite corps of black slaves (*abid al-Bukhari*), who owed personal devotion to the sultan.

MAWLAY SIDI MUHAMMAD (1757–90) sultan of Maghrib (Morocco). He restored peace and prosperity after a period of political chaos. He developed Mogador as the principal port for trade with Europe, strengthened central authority and limited the intervention of Europeans in Moroccan affairs.

MAWSON, Sir Douglas (1882–1958) English-born Australian explorer and geologist, born in Bradford, Yorkshire. He was educated at Sydney University. In 1907 he was appointed to the scientific staff of **Ernest Shackleton**'s Antarctic expedition and discovered the South Magnetic Pole. From 1911 to 1914 he was leader of the Australasian Antarctic expedition, which charted 2000 miles of coast; he was knighted on his return. He also led the joint British-Australian-New Zealand expedition to the Antarctic from 1929 to 1931.

MAX, Adolphe (1869–1939) Belgian politician and patriot, born in Brussels. First a journalist, then an accountant, he became burgomaster of Brussels in 1909. When the German troops approached Brussels in August 1914, he boldly drove to meet them and opened negotiations. He defended the rights of the Belgian population against the invaders, and in September was imprisoned by the Germans, later refusing an offer of freedom on condition that he went to Switzerland and desisted from anti-German agitation. In November 1918 he returned to Belgium, was elected to the House of Representatives, and became a minister of state.

MAX-MÜLLER See **MÜLLER, Friedrich Max**

MAXIM, Sir Hiram Stevens (1840–1916) American-born British inventor and engineer, born in Sangersville, Maine. He became a coachbuilder in an engineering works in Fitchburg, Massachusetts (1865), and from 1867 he took out patents for gas apparatus, electric lamps, etc. He emigrated to England in 1881, where he perfected his Maxim machine-gun in 1883. He also invented a pneumatic gun, a smokeless powder, a mousetrap, carbon filaments for light bulbs, and a flying machine (1894).

MAXIMILIAN, Ferdinand-Joseph (1832–67) emperor of Mexico, the younger brother of **Francis Joseph I**. He became an Austrian admiral. In 1863, the French called together a Mexican assembly, which offered the crown of Mexico to Maximilian; he accepted it, and in June 1864 entered Mexico. But **Juarez** again raised the standard of independence, and **Napoleon III** had to withdraw his troops. In vain the empress Charlotte (1840–1927), a daughter of **Leopold I** of Belgium, went to Europe to enlist support; her reason gave way under grief and excitement. Maximilian felt bound to remain and share the fate of his followers. With 8000 men he made a brave defence of Querétaro, but in May 1867 was betrayed, and on June 19 shot. He has been called a 'marionette emperor'. Seven volumes of his sketches of travel, essays, etc (*Aus meinem Leben*) were published in 1867.

MAXIMILIAN I (1459–1519) German emperor, the son of **Frederick III**. By his marriage with Mary, heiress of **Charles the Bold**, he acquired Burgundy and Flanders; but this involved him in war with **Louis XI** of France, and in 1482 he was forced to give Artois and Burgundy to Louis. In 1486 he was elected king of the Romans. In 1490 he drove out the Hungarians who, under **Matthias I Corvinus**, had seized (1487) much of the Austrian territories. At Villach in 1492 he routed the Turks, and in 1493 he became emperor. Having next married a daughter of the Duke of Milan, he turned his ambition towards Italy. But after years of war he was compelled (1515) to give up Milan to France and Verona to the Venetians; and in 1499 the Swiss completely separated themselves from the German Empire. The hereditary dominions of his house, however, were increased by the peaceful acquisition of Tirol; the marriage of his son Philip with the Infanta Joanna united the Houses of Spain and Habsburg, Philip becoming **Philip I** of Spain; while the marriage in 1521 of his grandson Ferdinand with the daughter of Ladislaus of Hungary and Bohemia brought both these kingdoms to Austria. He also improved the administration of justice, greatly encouraged the arts and learning, and caused to be written *Theuerdank* in verse and *Weisskunig* in prose, of both of which he himself is the hero, and probably part-author. He was succeeded by his grandson **Charles V**.

MAXIMILIAN I (1573–1651) Duke and Elector of Bavaria. Educated at the Jesuit college at Ingolstadt, he succeeded to the dukedom in 1598 and instituted energetic reforms of the country's inefficient bureaucracy and disordered finances. He placed himself at the head of the Catholic League in 1609 and pledged his support to the emperor **Ferdinand II** in the Thirty Years' War, obtaining as a reward the confiscated lands of **Frederick V** of the Palatinate. By the Peace of Westphalia (1648), the Palatinate was returned to Frederick's heir, Charles Louis, but Maximilian retained the electoral title. The foremost Catholic prince in Germany after the emperor, Maximilian was a keen defender of German liberties and resisted imperial attempts to turn the empire into a centralized Habsburg monarchy.

MAXIMILIAN II (1527–76) Holy Roman Emperor, eldest son of the emperor **Ferdinand I** and Anna of Bohemia and Hungary. He became king of Bohemia in 1548 and emperor in 1564. An intelligent, tolerant and cultivated man who considered himself 'neither Catholic nor Protestant but a Christian', he embarrassed his family by his Protestant leanings and was obliged in 1562 to swear to live and die within the Catholic church. As emperor he secured considerable religious freedom for Austrian Lutherans and deplored the intolerance of the Catholic reaction in Spain and France. A patron of the arts and sciences, he set out to make Vienna a centre of European intellectual life.

MAXTON, James (1885–1946) Scottish politician, born in Glasgow. He was educated at the university there and became a teacher. A supporter of the

Independent Labour party, he became its chairman in 1926 and he sat as MP for Bridgeton in Glasgow from 1922 until his death. A man of strong convictions, he was a staunch pacificist, and suffered imprisonment for attempting to foment a strike of shipyard workers during World War I, in which he was a conscientious objector. His extreme views claimed few supporters, but his sincerity won the respect of all.

MAXWELL, James Clerk (1831–79) Scottish physicist, born in Edinburgh, the son of a lawyer. One of the greatest theoretical physicists the world has known, he was nicknamed 'Dafty' at school (The Edinburgh Academy) because of his gangling appearance; but at the age of 15 he devised a method for drawing certain oval curves, which was published by the Royal Society of Edinburgh. He studied mathematics, physics and moral philosophy at Edinburgh University, where he published another paper, on rolling curves, and later graduated from Cambridge University as second wrangler. He was appointed professor of natural philosophy at Marischal College, Aberdeen (1856) and King's College, London (1860), but resigned in 1865 to pursue his researches at home in Scotland. In 1871 he was appointed the first Cavendish professor of experimental physics at Cambridge, where he organized the Cavendish laboratory. In his brilliant career he published papers on the kinetic theory of gases; established theoretically the nature of Saturn's rings (1857), later to be confirmed by **James Edward Keeler**; investigated colour perception and demonstrated colour photography with a picture of tartan ribbon (1861). But his most important work was on the theory of electromagnetic radiation, with the publication of his great *Treatise on Electricity and Magnetism* in 1873, which treated mathematically **Michael Faraday**'s theory of electrical and magnetic forces considered as action in a medium rather than action at a distance. He suggested that electromagnetic waves could be generated in a laboratory—as **Heinrich Hertz** was to demonstrate in 1887. His work is considered to have paved the way for **Albert Einstein** and **Max Planck**.

MAXWELL, (Ian) Robert (1923–) British publisher and politician, born in Czechoslovakia. Self-educated, he served in the war (1940–45) before founding the Pergamon Press, a publishing company specializing in scientific journals and one of the first to use computerization. A former Labour MP (1964–70), Maxwell, who has many business interests including film production, rescued the large British Printing Corporation from financial collapse in 1980 and rapidly transformed it into the successful British Printing and Communications Corporation.

MAXWELL, Sir William Stirling See **STIRLING-MAXWELL**

MAXWELL DAVIES, Sir Peter (1934–) English composer, born in Manchester. He studied at the Royal Manchester College of Music, at Manchester University and in Rome. After three years as director of music at Cirencester Grammar School he went to Princeton University in 1962 for further study. He has lectured in Europe, Australia and New Zealand, and was composer in residence at the University of Adelaide in 1966. Most of his music is written for chamber ensembles, often including a large percussion section. The Fires of London, a group founded by him, is particularly associated with his work. He has a keen interest in early English music, in particular the 16th-century composer **John Taverner**, the subject of his opera *Taverner* (1962–70), and has always experimented with different orchestral combinations; in later works he introduced stereo tape and electronic sounds. The scoring of one of the parts in *Vesalii Icones* (1970) for a dancer-pianist exemplifies his idea of 'music theatre', with no artificial division between the forms of expression. His works include *Prolation* (1959), *Revelation and Fall* (1965), two *Fantasies on an In Nomine of John Taverner* (1962, 1964), *Eight Songs for a Mad King* (1969), *Le Jongleur de Notre Dame* (1978), four symphonies, and an opera, *The Lighthouse*, 1979. Since 1970 Maxwell Davies has done most of his work in Orkney, frequently using Orcadian or Scottish subject matter or music. He directed the St Magnus Festival (1977–86).

MAY, Peter Barker Howard (1929–) English cricketer and administrator, born in Reading. Educated at Charterhouse and Pembroke College, Cambridge, he was an outstanding schoolboy batsman and earned a double Blue at Cambridge for cricket and football. One of the last great amateur cricketers, he was first capped for Surrey in 1950. He played in 66 Tests for England (41 as captain), scoring 4537 runs at an average of 46.77 and making a century on his Test début against South Africa at Leeds in 1951. With **Colin Cowdrey** of Kent he set up the record fourth-wicket Test partnership of 411, against West Indies at Edgbaston in 1957. He retired from first-class cricket in his early thirties to concentrate on his work as a Lloyd's insurance broker. He was chairman of the England Cricket Selection Committee from 1982 to 1988.

MAY, Phil (Philip William) (1864–1903) English caricaturist, born in Wortley near Leeds. Orphaned at the age of nine, he endured years of poverty before he became poster artist and cartoonist of the *St Stephen's Review*. He went to Australia and on his return in 1890 established himself by his *Annual* and contributions to *Punch* and other periodicals. He excelled in depicting East London types and brought a new simplicity of line to popular cartooning.

MAY, Thomas (1594–1650) English dramatist and historian, born in Sussex. He was educated at Sidney Sussex College, Cambridge, and became a member of Gray's Inn and a courtier. He wrote dramas, comedies, poems and translations of **Lucan**'s *Pharsalia* (1627), **Virgil**'s *Georgics* (1628), and **Martial** (1629). A Puritan, he was secretary and official historian to the Long Parliament, and produced a *History of the Parliament 1640–1643* (1647), and a *Breviary* (1650).

MAY, Sir Thomas Erskine, 1st Baron Farnborough (1815–86) English constitutional jurist. Educated at Bedford School, he became assistant librarian of the House of Commons in 1831, clerk-assistant in 1856, and clerk of the House in 1871. He was created a baron in 1881 on his retirement. His *Treatise on the Law, Privileges, Proceedings, and Usage of Parliament* (1844) has been translated into various languages and remains a standard work. He also wrote *Constitutional History of England 1760–1860* (1861–63).

MAYAKOVSKY, Vladimir Vladimirovich (1894–1930) Russian poet and playwright, born in Bagdadi (now Mayakovsky), Georgia. The son of an impoverished Russian nobleman, he was involved in the Social-Democratic movement during his youth, but when he was imprisoned for eleven months he renounced politics for art. Writing was his first love, however, and in 1912 he wrote a poem that was published in the miscellany, *Poshchochina obshchestvennomu vkusu* (A Slap in the Face of Public Taste). An enthusiastic supporter of the Revolution in 1917, both his play *Misteriya-Buff* (Mystery-Bouffe 1918) and the long poem *150,000,000* (1919–20) are masterpieces of the period. But when the Civil War ended and the National Economy Policy was introduced in 1921, he found himself at odds with the new, conservative leaders. In response he wrote *Pro eto* (1923), poems pre-Revolution in sentiment, and satirical plays like *Klop* (The Bedbug, 1929) and *Banya* (The Bath-House, 1930), concerned with the betrayal of the Revolution by its self-appointed officials. His fame in the Soviet Union is dependent on three works: *Vladimir Illich Lenin* (1924), *Khorosho!* (Good!, 1927) and the unfinished *Vo ves golos* (At the Top of My Voice, 1929–30). Towards the end of his life he was severely castigated by more orthodox Soviet writers and critics for his outspoken criticism of the bureaucracy and his unconventional opinions on art, and was even forced to abandon the Left Front for the Arts for the reactionary Russian Association of Proletarian Writers. But he was always regarded as an outsider, and this, together with an unstable personal life, undoubtedly contributed towards his suicide.

MAYBACH, Wilhelm (1846–1929) German inventor and car manufacturer, born in Heilbronn. He joined **Gottlieb Daimler** in 1869 as a draughtsman, and became his partner in 1882 when he established a factory at Cannstatt near Stuttgart. He was responsible for one innovation that was crucial to the development of high-speed petrol engines suitable for motor cars, the float-feed carburettor (1893), as well as improvements in timing, gearing and steering, all of which played their part in the success of a Daimler car which won the first international road race in 1894. He left the Daimler firm in 1907 and set up his own works at Friedrichshafen (1909), where he made engines for **Zeppelin** airships, and (1922–39) luxury Maybach cars.

MAYER, Julius Robert von (1814–78) German physician and physicist, born in Heilbronn. In 1842 he announced, from physiological considerations, the equivalence of heat and work and the law of the conservation of energy, independently of **James Prescott Joule**, and his mental health suffered on account of the dispute over priority.

MAYER, Louis Burt (1885–1957) Russian-born American film mogul, born in Minsk. Brought to St John, New Brunswick, at the age of three, he was working in the junk and scrap metal business at the age of eight and later expanded his activities to ship salvaging. In 1907 he purchased a house in Haverhill, Massachusetts, refurbished it as a nickelodeon and opened one of the earliest custom-designed cinemas. He subsequently acquired a chain of theatres in New England and displayed a shrewd knowledge of commercial and artistic achievement by buying the regional rights to such popular attractions as *Birth of a Nation* (1915). He later moved into film production with the formation of Metro Films (1915) and Louis B Mayer Productions (1917) which later joined with **Sam Goldwyn** to form Metro-Goldwyn-Mayer (M-G-M) in 1924. The first vice-president in charge of production, he was instrumental in the creation of Hollywood as a dream factory and the establishment of the star system. A canny entrepreneur and showman with an eye for talent and a sense of popular taste, he oversaw such enduring successes as *Ben Hur* (1926), *Grand Hotel* (1932), the Andy Hardy series, *Ninotchka* (1939) and countless others prior to his enforced retirement in 1951. He received an honorary Academy Award in 1950.

MAYHEW, Henry (1812–87) English author, born in London, and first joint editor of *Punch* with **Mark Lemon**. He ran away from Westminster School and collaborated with his brother Augustus (1826–75) in writing numerous successful novels such as *The Good Genius that turns everything to Gold* (1847) and *Whom to Marry* (1848). He also wrote on many subjects, his best-known work being the classic social survey, *London Labour and the London Poor* (1851–62). Another brother, Horace (1816–72), also collaborated with Henry and was a contributor to *Punch*.

MAYO, Charles Horace (1865–1939) American surgeon, born in Rochester, Minnesota. He made a special study of goitre, and helped his brother **William James Mayo** to organize the Mayo Clinic in 1905 within what is now St Mary's Hospital, Rochester, which their father had founded (1899).

MAYO, Katherine (1868–1940) American journalist, born in Ridgeway, Pennsylvania. She is remembered for her books exposing social evils, especially *Isles of Fear* (1925), condemning American administration of the Philippines, and *Mother India* (1927), a forthright indictment of child marriage and other customs.

MAYO, Richard Southwell Bourke, Earl of (1822–72) Irish politician and administrator, born in Dublin. He was educated at Trinity College, Dublin. He entered the House of Commons as a Conservative in 1847, and was appointed chief-secretary of Ireland by Lord **Derby** in 1852, 1858, and 1866. Sent out in 1868 to succeed Lord **Lawrence**, he was eminently successful as viceroy of India, but was fatally stabbed by a convict while inspecting the settlement at Port Blair on the Andaman Islands.

MAYO, William James (1861–1939) American surgeon, born in Le Sueur, Minnesota. A specialist in stomach surgery, he established the Mayo Clinic with his brother **Charles Horace Mayo** at St Mary's Hospital, Rochester, Minnesota, and set up the Mayo Foundation for Medical Education and Research (1915).

MAYOW, John (1640–79) English chemist. A fellow of All Souls, Oxford, he preceded **Joseph Priestley** and **Antoine Lavoisier** by a century with his discoveries relating to respiration and the chemistry of combustion.

MAYR, Ernst Walter (1904–) German-born American zoologist, born in Kempten, West Germany. He studied at Berlin and emigrated to the USA in 1932. He was professor of zoology at Harvard from 1953 to 1975. His early work was on the ornithology of the Pacific, leading three scientific expeditions to New Guinea and the Solomon Islands (1928–30), but in his later career he was best known for his neo-Darwinian views on evolution, as developed in his books such as *Animal Species and Evolution* (1963) and *Evolution and the Diversity of Life* (1976).

MAYS, Willie Howard Jr (1931–) American baseball player, known as the 'Say Hey Kid', born in Fairfield, Alabama. He played for the San Francisco Giants (1951–72) and the New York Mets (1973). A magnificent fielder, batter and base runner, only he and **Hank Aaron** have performed the baseball double of more than 3000 hits and 600 home runs. He was twice voted the Most Valuable Player (1954, 1965), and was voted the Baseball Player of the Decade (1960–69). He was elected to the National Baseball Hall of fame in 1979.

MAZARIN, Jules, originally **Giulio Mazarini** (1602–61) Italian-born French prelate and statesman, born in Pescina in the Abruzzi, studied under the Jesuits at Rome and at Alcalá in Spain. He accompanied a papal legate to the court of France, was papal nuncio there (1634–36), entered the service of **Louis XIII** as a naturalized Frenchman (1639), and two years later became cardinal through the influence of **Richelieu**, who before his death in 1642 recommended Mazarin to the king as his successor as minister of France. Louis died in 1643, but Mazarin knew how to retain his power under the queen-regent, **Anne of Austria**; she certainly loved him, even if it cannot be proved that there was a private marriage between them (the cardinal had never taken more than the minor orders). He ruled more efficiently than Richelieu, and was almost as powerful. The parliament resisted the registration of edicts of taxation; but Mazarin caused the leaders of the opposition to be arrested (August 1648), upon which the disturbances of the Fronde began. The court retired to St Germain, but at length triumphed by the aid of **Condé**. The hatred against Mazarin, however, blazed out anew in the provinces, when at his instigation the queen-regent arrested Condé, Conti and Longueville in January 1650. Mazarin triumphed at Réthel, but soon had to succumb and retire to Brühl. Meantime the press teemed with pamphlets and satires against him— the *Mazarinades*. The cardinal used all his influence to form a new royal party, won the support of **Turenne**, and in February 1653 returned to Paris, regaining all his power and popularity. He acquired the alliance of **Cromwell** at the price of Dunkirk; and by the marriage of **Louis XIV** with the Infanta **Maria Theresa** (1659), brought the succession to the throne of Spain nearer. Mazarin died leaving an immense fortune. His magnificent library was bequeathed to the Collége Mazarin, and his name lives in the rare 'Mazarin Bible'.

MAZEPPA, Ivan Stepanovich (c.1644–1709) Russian nobleman, and hetman of the Cossacks. Having become a page at the court of Poland, he was surprised in an intrigue with a nobleman's wife, and was sent home bound naked upon his horse. Mazeppa now joined the Cossacks, and in 1687 was elected hetman of the Ukraine. He won the confidence of **Peter the Great**, who made him Prince of the Ukraine; but when Peter curtailed the freedom of the Cossacks, Mazeppa entered into negotiations with **Karl XII** of Sweden. His hopes of an independent crown of the Ukraine perished in the disaster of Pultowa (1709), and he fled with Karl to Bender, where he died. His story is the theme of poems (notably that by **Byron**), plays, novels, opera, and paintings.

MAZZINI, Giuseppe (1805–72) Italian patriot, and a leader of the Risorgimento, born in Genoa. He studied at the university there, and at 19 was practising as an advocate. He wrote in favour of romanticism, became an ardent champion of liberalism, and joining the Carbonari in 1829, was betrayed (1830) to the Sardinian police, and imprisoned in Savona. Released and exiled next year, he organized in Marseilles the Young Italy Association, which sought to create a free and united republic of Italy. In 1831 he addressed an appeal to **Charles Albert** of Piedmont, urging him to put himself at the head of the struggle for Italian independence; the answer, under **Metternich**'s influence, was a sentence of perpetual banishment, and in 1832 the French authorities expelled him from France. Henceforward he was the most untiring political agitator in Europe. He wrote incessantly with fervid eloquence and intense conviction. In 1834 he organized an abortive invasion of Savoy. The next years Mazzini spent in Switzerland scattering, by means of his underground journal *Young Italy*, the seeds of republican revolt throughout Europe. Banished from Switzerland, he found a refuge in London in 1837; and, struggling with poverty, contrived to teach and civilize many of his poorer countrymen, the organ-boys of London. In 1844 he proved his charge against the British government of opening his letters and communicating their contents to the rulers in Italy—a charge which raised a storm of indignation throughout the country. He threw himself into the thick of the Lombard revolt in 1848. After Milan capitulated he tried with **Garibaldi** to keep the war alive in the valleys of the Alps. Leghorn received him with wild enthusiasm in February 1849, just before the republic was proclaimed at Rome, where he was elected one of a triumvirate with dictatorial powers. In April the French arrived; after a struggle the republic fell; and the triumvirs indignantly resigned (June). From London Mazzini planned the attempted risings at Mantua (1852), Milan (1853), Genoa (1857), and Leghorn (1857). Here also he founded, along with **Kossuth** and **Ledru-Rollin**, the republican European Association, and organized the Society of the Friends of Italy. In 1859 Mazzini condemned the alliance between Piedmont and **Napoleon III**. He supported Garibaldi in his expedition against Sicily and Naples; and when Piedmont defeated and took him prisoner at Aspromonte (1862), Mazzini broke finally with the monarchical party. From 1866 to 1867 Messina in protest elected him its deputy to the Italian parliament four times in succession. Again expelled from Switzerland, he was (1870) arrested at sea and imprisoned for two months at Gaeta; he then settled at Lugano, and died in Pisa. It was Mazzini who prepared the ground for Italian unity, Garibaldi who did most of the harvesting, and **Cavour** who entered into their labours. Mazzini's writings are mostly political. *On the Duties of Man* contains an outline of ethical theory; *Thoughts upon Democracy in Europe* is a discussion of economics and Socialism.

MBITI, John Samuel (1931–) African theologian, born in Kenya. Teaching theology and comparative religion at Makere University College, Uganda, before becoming director of the World Council of Churches Ecumenical Institute, Bossey, Switzerland (1972–80), he now teaches Christianity and African religions at Berne University and is a pastor in Burgdorf, Switzerland. His books, which include *African Religions and Philosophy* (1969), *Concepts of God in Africa* (1970), *New Testament Eschatology in an African Background* (1970), *The Prayers of African Religion* (1975), and *Bible and Theology in African Christianity* (1987), maintain that the African is naturally religious and that the Christian message should be seen as a fulfilment of traditional African beliefs rather than a rejection of them.

MBOYA, Tom (1930–69) African nationalist leader, born on a sisal estate in the white highlands of Kenya. Educated at Holy Ghost College, Mangu, he became a sanitary inspector (1951) but soon came under the influence of **Kenyatta** and joined his Kenya African Union, of which he was PRO and later (1953) treasurer. On the suppression of the party, he turned to trade union activity, becoming secretary of the Kenya Federation of Labour. The unsatisfactory new Constitution of 1954 drove him to passive resistance and campaigning for independence. At the round-table conference in London (1960), he obtained important constitutional concessions for Africans, especially on land reform. After the resurgence of Kenyatta's party as the Kenya African National Union in 1960 he became its general secretary; he was Kenyan minister of labour (1962–63), minister of justice (1963–64), and minister of economic development and planning from 1964. He was assassinated in Nairobi in 1969.

MEAD, George Herbert (1863–1931) American social psychologist, born in South Hadley, Massachusetts. He studied at Oberlin College, Harvard University and the universities of Leipzig and Berlin. He taught at Michigan from 1891 to 1894, then moved to the philosophy department at Chicago (1894–1931). His main interest lay in the theory of the mind, and he was particularly concerned with the notion of the self, and how this is developed through communication with others. His work gave rise to symbolic interactionism, a social science tradition which is concerned with the meanings that people give to the world, and how these are worked out through interpersonal interaction. His books include *The Philosophy of the Present* (1932) and *Mind, Self and Society* (1934, based on his lecture courses).

MEAD, Margaret (1901–78) American anthropologist, born in Philadelphia. She was appointed assistant curator of ethnology at the American Museum of Natural History in 1926, associate curator from 1942, and curator from 1964. After expeditions to Samoa and New Guinea she wrote *Coming of Age in Samoa* (1928) and *Growing up in New Guinea* (1930). Later publications included *Male and Female* (1949) and *Growth and Culture* (1951). In these works she argued that personality characteristics, especially as they differ between men and women, are shaped by cultural conditioning rather than heredity. Her writings have proved very popular, and have made anthropology accessible to a wide public.

MEAD, Richard (1673–1754) fashionable London physician. He succeeded **John Radcliffe** as leader of his profession and published on poisons and infections. Physician to Queen **Anne**, he was consulted by the consumptive French painter **Jean Antoine Watteau**, who visited London specially for the purpose.

MEADE, George Gordon (1815–72) American soldier, born in Cadiz in Spain. He graduated at West Point in 1835, and served against the Seminoles and in the Mexican War. In the American Civil War (1861–65) he distinguished himself at Antietam and Fredericksburg (1601), and in 1863 he commanded the Army of the Potomac and defeated **Lee** at Gettysburg.

MEADE, James Edward (1907–) English economist, born in Swanage, Dorset. After working for the League of Nations in the 1930s, he was a member (latterly director) of the economic section of the Cabinet Office (1940–46), then professor of economics at London School of Economics (1947–57) and of political economics at Cambridge (1957–74). A prolific writer, his principal contributions have been in the area of international trade, including *The Theory of International Economic Policy* (2 vols, 1951–55), *Principles of Political Economy* (4 vols, 1965–76) and *The Intelligent Radical's Guide to Economic Policy* (1975). He shared the 1977 Nobel prize for economics with **Bertil Ohlin**.

MEADS, Colin Earl (1935–) New Zealand rugby player, born in Cambridge. A lock forward, he was the first New Zealand player to win more than 100 international caps. A dour, uncompromising player, he was sent off against Scotland at Murrayfield in 1967, but continued to be selected for another four years. He was a prodigious worker and immensely strong, but for many followers of Rugby Union he communicated a new and disturbing image of the game.

MEAGHER, Thomas Francis (1822–67) Irish nationalist and American politician, born in Waterford. He became a prominent member of the Young Ireland party and a founder-member (1847) of the Irish Federation, and in 1848 was transported for life to Van Diemen's Land (Tasmania) after an abortive rising. He made his escape in 1852, and made his way to the United States, where he studied law and became a journalist. At the outbreak of the Civil War in 1861 he organized the 'Irish brigade' for the Federals, and distinguished himself at Richmond and elsewhere. While secretary of Montana territory, and keeping the Indians in check, he was drowned in the Missouri.

MEALE, Richard Graham (1932–) Australian composer, conductor and teacher, born in Sydney. He studied at the New South Wales State Conservatorium for Music, and later at the University of California where he researched the music of Japan, Java and Bali. Returning to Australia he made an immediate impact with his compositions *Los Alboradas* (1963) and *Homage to Garcia Lorca* (1964). The influence of Japanese music on him is apparent in *Images: Nagauta* (1966) and *Clouds Now and Then* (1969). Later works, such as *Viridian* (1979) and his second string quartet reflect **Debussy**. His first opera *Voss* (1982, with a libretto by **David Malouf** based on the novel by **Patrick White**) demonstrates the strength of his orchestral and vocal writing. From 1969 he was reader in music at Adelaide University.

MECHNIKOV, Ilya Ilich (1845–1916) Russian biologist, born in Ivanovka near Kharkov. Educated in Russia and Germany, he became professor of zoology and comparative anatomy at Odessa (1870–82). He conducted research into the transparent larvae of starfish at Medina in Italy (1882–86), where he discovered the phagocytes, cells which devour infective organisms.

MEDAWAR, Sir Peter Brian (1915–87) British zoologist and one of the world's leading immunologists, born in Rio de Janeiro of an English mother and a Lebanese father. He went to school at Marlborough and studied zoology at Magdalen College, Oxford, and during World War II began to study skin-grafts for burn victims. He was appointed professor of zoology at Birmingham University (1947–51) and Jodrell professor of comparative anatomy at University College, London (1951–62), where he pioneered experiments in the prevention of rejection in transplant operations. He was director of the National Institute for Medical Research from 1962. In 1960 he shared the Nobel prize with the Australian Sir **Macfarlane Burnet** for researches on immunological tolerance in relation to skin and organ grafting. He gave the brilliant Reith Lectures on *The Future of Man* in 1959. His writings included *The Uniqueness of the Individual* (1957), *The Future of Man* (1959), *The Art of the Soluble* (1967), *The Hope of Progress* (1972) and *Pluto's Republic* (1982).

MEDICI a Florentine family which amassed great wealth from banking during the 14th and 15th centuries, starting with Giovanni di Bicci de Medici (1360–1429), who used his fortune to establish himself as a public benefactor and patron of the arts. Although the Medici remained rulers of Tuscany until its cession to Austria by the Peace of Vienna in 1736, the later Grand Dukes, following **Cosimo I, 'the Great'**, were undistinguished. Francis I (1541–87) began work on what is today the Uffizi gallery. Ferdinand I (1549–1609) developed the port of Livorno (Leghorn), amassed a striking collection of Greek and Roman sculputre, and had the fine family mausoleum built at San Lorenzo. His daughter **Marie de'Medici** married **Henri IV** of France, while his son and successor Cosimo II (1590–1620) was the patron of **Galilei**. Both he and his sons, Ferdinand and Leopold, maintained Florence's reputation throughout the first half of the 17th century as a centre for art and learning.

MEDICI, Cosimo (1389–1464) Florentine financier, statesman and philanthropist, known posthumously as 'Pater Patriae', the son of **Giovanni de Bicci Medici**. He began the glorious epoch of the family. As ruler of Florence he procured for Florence (nominally still republican) security abroad and peace from civil dissensions. He employed his wealth in encouraging art and literature, building the Medici library, the first public library in Europe, as well as many other magnificent buildings, and made the city the centre of the new learning.

MEDICI, Cosimo I, 'the Great' (1519–74) Florentine magnate, Duke of Florence from 1537, and Grand Duke of Tuscany from 1569. He possessed the astuteness of character of his greater predecessors, but was cruel and relentless in his enmities, though one of the ablest rulers of his century. A skilled soldier, he annexed the republic of Sienna in 1555 and doubled the territory of Tuscany during his rule. He devoted his considerable energies to developing the trade, agriculture and economic infrastructure of Tuscany, and to building up its armed forces. At the same time, he was a notable patron of artists and a great collector of Etruscan antiquities.

MEDICI, Giovanni (1475–1521), Florentine prelate, pope in 1513 as **Leo X**. He was the brother of **Pietro II Medici, 'the Unfortunate'**. With his election as pope, the rule of Florence passed first to his younger brother, Giuliano, and then to his nephew, Lorenzo, Duke of Urbino. The real power of the family, however, remained with the pope and his cousin, Guilio, grandson of **Cosimo Medici**, who succeeded to the papacy in 1523 as **Clement VII**.

MEDICI, Lorenzo, 'the magnificent' (1449–92) Florentine ruler, son of **Pietro I Medici** and grandson of **Cosimo Medici**. He succeeded as head of the family upon the death of his father, Pietro, in 1469, and was an able, if autocratic, ruler who made Florence the leading state in Italy. In 1478 he showed courage and judgment in thwarting an attempt by malcontents, with the encouragement of Pope **Sixtus IV**, to overthrow the Medici, although the rising led to the assassination of Lorenzo's brother, Giuliano (1453–78). Lorenzo was a distinguished lyric poet as well as being, in the words of **Macchiavelli** 'the greatest patron of literature and art that any prince has ever been'.

MEDICI, Pietro, 'the Unfortunate' (1471–1503), Florentine ruler, eldest son of **Lorenzo Medici**. He succeeded his father in 1492, but his disregard of republican forms made him unpopular. With the invasion of Italy by **Charles VIII** of France in 1494, Pietro was obliged to surrender key Florentine forces to the aggressor, a step strongly resented by the civic authorities, who banished the Medici from the state in November, placed a price on Pietro's head and permitted the plundering of the Medici palace. Pietro died fighting against the French. The Medici did not return to Florence until 1512, when the head of the family was Pietro's brother, **Giovanni Medici**.

MEDINA-SIDONIA, Alonzo Perez de Gusman el Bueno, 7th Duke of (1550–1619) Spanish naval commander, captain general of Andalusia and one of the wealthiest and most influential men in Spain. He was a distinguished administrator with a good record in conquest of Portugal. Appointed to command the Great Armada in the Enterprise of England on the death of the Marquis of Santa Cruz (1588), he led the Armada successfully up the English Channel to rendezvous with Parma off the Dutch coast, but was thwarted by the latter's failure to break out, action by the English fleet and adverse weather. He returned to Spain north-about round Britain, and continued in royal service.

MEDLICOTT, William Norton (1900–87) English diplomatic historian, born in Wandsworth, London. He was known especially for his studies of the **Bismarck** period in international relations, and British diplomacy in the 20th century. Educated at Aske's School, Hatcham, and University College, London, he was lecturer at University College, Swansea (1926–39), and professor (later principal) of history at Exeter University (1939–53), and Stevenson professor of international history at the London School of Economics (1953–67). Amongst his many publications were *The Congress of Berlin and After* (1938), *British Foreign Policy since Versailles* (1940), and *Bismarck, Gladstone and the Concert of Europe* (1956), as well as a history of British economic warfare against Germany, *The Economic Blockade* (2 vols, 1952–59). He also edited eleven volumes of the multi-volume *Documents on British Foreign Policy, 1919–1939*. The Norton Medlicott Medal, awarded by The Historical Association, was instituted in his honour (1984).

MEDTNER, Nikolai (1880–1951) Russian composer and pianist of German descent, born in Moscow. He went to live in western Europe in 1922. His classical-romantic compositions included three piano concertos, songs and much piano music. He died in London, his home since 1935.

MEDWALL, Henry (1462–c.1505) English dramatist. He wrote *Fulgens and Lucres*, the earliest extant English secular play written before 1500.

MEE, Arthur (1875–1943) English journalist, editor and writer, born in Stapleford, Nottingham. He is most widely known for his *Children's Encyclopaedia* (1908) and for his *Children's Newspaper*. He also produced a *Self-Educator* (1906), a *History of the World* (1907), both with Sir John Hammerton, a *Popular Science* (1912), a *Children's Shakespeare* (1926), and *The King's England* (1936–53), a series of topographical books describing the English counties.

MEE, Margaret Ursula (1909–88) English botanical artist and traveller. Trained at the Camberwell School of Art, she first visited the Amazon forests when she was 47. Ten years later, having settled in Brazil, she began her outstanding career as a botanical artist, travelling extensively in the Brazilian Amazonia and collecting new species and painting many others, some of which have since become extinct. She was well-known for her outspoken anger at the destruction of the Amazonia, which she called 'a valley of death'; the Margaret Mee Amazon trust was set up in 1988 to draw attention to the area's ecological crisis.

MEEGEREN, Van See **VAN MEEGEREN**

MEEHAN, Patrick Connolly (1927–) convicted Scottish thief who was also found guilty of murder, but later received a royal pardon. Born in the Gorbals, Glasgow, he spent most of his teenage life in approved schools and in Borstal for theft. In December 1947 he was arrested and charged with blowing up a safe. He was convicted and sentenced to three years' imprisonment in 1948. Other prison sentences followed. On 14 July, 1969, after a routine interview with police on 12 July in which Meehan admitted that he had passed through Ayr on 6 July, two men, who called each other 'Jim' and 'Pat' broke into the Ayr home of Abraham and Rachel Ross. They assaulted the Rosses, and Rachel Ross died of her injuries shortly after. Ross identified Meehan's voice and Meehan was charged. Meanwhile, Griffiths, who had been on the run, was killed in a shoot-out with the police, during which he killed one person and wounded others. Suspicions arose about some of the police's evidence, but Meehan was nonetheless found guilty on 24 October. The next seven years were filled with appeals which failed, new evidence and confessions from the real killer. In May 1976, after the publication of **Ludovic Kennedy**'s book *A Presumption of Innocence* (1976), Meehan was pardoned.

MEGASTHENES (fl.300 BC) Greek historian. He was ambassador (306–298 BC) at the Indian court of Sandrakottos or **Chandragupta**, where he gathered materials for his *Indica*, from which **Arrian**, **Strabo**, and others borrowed.

MÈGE MOURIÉS, Hippolyte (1817–80) French chemist and inventor, born in Draguignan. He patented margarine in its original form in 1869 after several years of research into the food value of various animal fats. The French government had offered a prize for a satisfactory and economic substitute for butter, which had become very difficult to supply in adequate quantities to the rapidly increasing urban populations and armed forces. Mège Mouriés' margarine was manufactured from tallow, and although he was awarded the prize it was not until F Boudet patented a process for emulsifying it with skimmed milk and water in 1872 that it could be made sufficiently palatable to be a commercial success.

MEGERLE, Ulrich See **ABRAHAM-A-SANTA-CLARA**

MEHEMET 'ALI (c.1769–1849) better known as Mohammed 'Ali, viceroy of Egypt. An Albanian officer of militia, he was sent to Egypt with a Turkish-Albanian force on the French invasion in 1798. After the departure of the French, at the head of his Albanians, he supported the Egyptian rulers in their struggles with the Mamluks. Having become the chief power in Egypt, he had himself proclaimed viceroy by his Albanians (1805), and was confirmed in this post by the sultan. He secured for Egypt a boost in prosperity by the massacre of the Mamelukes in the citadel of Cairo (1811), the formation of a regular army, the improvement of irrigation, and the introduction of the elements of European civilization. In 1816 he reduced part of Arabia by the generalship of his adopted son **Ibrahim Pasha**; in 1820 he annexed Nubia and part of the Sudan; and from 1821 to 1828 his troops, under Ibrahim, occupied various points in the Morea and Crete, to aid the Turks in their war with the insurgent Greeks. The Egyptian fleet was annihilated at Navarino, and Ibrahim remained in the Morea till forced to evacuate by the French in 1828. In 1831 Ibrahim began the conquest of Syria, and in 1832 totally routed the Ottoman army at Koniya, after which the Porte ceded Syria to Mehemet 'Ali on condition of tribute. The victory at Nezib in 1839 might have elevated him to the throne of Constantinople; but the quadruple alliance in 1840, the fall of Acre to the British, and the consequent evacuation of Syria compelled him to limit his ambition to Egypt. In 1848 he became insane and was succeeded by Ibrahim.

MEHMET I (c.1387–1421) sultan of Turkey from 1413. He led recovery from conquests of **Tamerlane**.

MEHMET III (1566–1603) sultan of Turkey from 1595, Ottoman emperor, son of Murad III. On his succession he invoked the law of fratricide by which the sultan could have his brothers put to death. All 19, of whom the eldest was only 11, were executed by strangulation.

MEHMET IV (1642–93) sultan of Turkey from 1648–1687. He succeeded his deposed father, Ibrahim I, as a child, in the middle of a long war with Venice (1645–64). Anarchy in the country was quelled by the appointment of able viziers, Mohammed Kiuprili (1656) and his son Ahmed (1661). In 1664 the Turks were defeated by the Austrians under **Montecucculi** at the battle of St Gotthard; in a war with Poland (1672–76) the Turks were twice defeated by King **John III Sobieski**, but gained Polish Ukraine, which they lost to Russia in 1681. In 1683 the Turks, under a new grand vizier, Kara Mustafa, laid siege to Vienna, which was relieved by John Sobieski. After defeat at the second battle of Mohacs (1687), Mehmet was deposed, and replaced by **Süleyman II**.

MEHMET VI (1861–1926) sultan of Turkey 1918–1922, brother of Mehmet V, unsuccessful in suppressing the nationalists led by **Mustafa Kemal**; he died in exile.

MEHRING, Franz (1846–1919) German left-wing writer and historian, born in Schlawe, Pomerania. He was a founder of the German Communist party and author of historical studies of the workers' movement, including *Geschichte der deutsche Sozialdemocratie* (1898) and a life of **Karl Marx** (1919).

MEHTA, Ved Parkash (1934–) Indian writer, born in Lahore. He was one of seven children of a Hindu doctor who was an officer in the Health Services of the Indian government. Blind from the age of eight, he went to the USA for his education when he was 15 and attended the Arkansas School for the Blind at Little Rock and Pomona College, before going to Oxford and Harvard universities. While at Pomona he published his first book, the autobiography *Face to Face* (1957). He has had a distinguished career as a journalist, contributing chiefly to the *New Yorker*. Employing amanuenses he has written biographies (*Mahatma Gandhi and His Apostles*, 1977), stories, essays and portraits of India. His enduring achievement, however, is 'Continents of Exile', an acclaimed series of autobiographical books: *Daddyji* (1972), *Mamaji* (1979), *Vedi* (1982), *The Ledge Between the Streams* (1984), *Sound-Shadows of the New World* (1986), and *The Stolen Light* (1989).

MÉHUL, Étienne Nicolas (1763–1817) French operatic composer, born in Givet. In 1795 he became professor of the Paris Conservatoire. Of his numerous operas, *Joseph* (1807) is his masterpiece.

MEI LANFANG (1894–1961) Chinese opera singer and actor, born in Yanchow, Kiangsu. The son of an actor, he is best-known for his female roles in opera and was the doyen of theatre in the first half of the 20th century. He made his stage début in Peking at the age of ten, and went on to study at the Hsi-lien-ch'eng Dramatic Training School before forming a professional troupe, and establishing his reputation in 1913 in Shanghai as a gifted performer of the 'tan' (female) role. He was the first Chinese actor to perform outside his own country when he appeared to great acclaim in Tokyo (1919), and following this travelled widely abroad. He made his first colour film *Sheng-ssu-ken* (The Wedding is a Dream) in 1947, and after the revolution (1949) held various prestigious cultural posts. A well-loved performer, he played a major role in preserving the essential heritage of Chinese dramatic art.

MEI SHENG (d.140 BC) Chinese poet. He is often credited with the introduction of the five-character line. For this reason he is sometimes called the father of modern Chinese poetry.

MEIDNER, Ludwig (1884–1966) German painter and lithographer, born in Bernstadt, Silesia. He moved to Berlin in 1905, and in 1906 visited Paris, where he first saw the work of **Van Gogh**, which impressed him deeply. Although he did not belong to any of the major artistic movements, most of his work has strong links with Expressionism in style and subject-matter. Shortly before the outbreak of World War I he produced a series of apocalyptic visions—scenes of disaster and chaos which were remarkable prefigurations of the horrors to come.

MEIGHEN, Arthur (1874–1960) Canadian politician, born in Anderson, Ontario. He became a lawyer and sat in the Canadian House of Commons as a liberal Conservative, (1908–26). He was solicitor-general (1913), and secretary of state (1917) and of the interior (1917). He succeeded Sir **Robert Borden** as leader of the Conservatives in 1920. A brilliant parliamentary debater, his skill helped to carry the controversial Military Service Bill in 1917. He was briefly prime minister in 1920 and 1921 and again in 1926. From 1932 to 1941 he was a senator, and minister without portfolio from 1932 to 1935.

MEIKLE, Andrew (1719–1811) Scottish millwright and inventor, born at Houston Mill near Dunbar. He was the son of James Meikle (c.1690–1717), who invented fanners for winnowing grain in 1710 and a barley mill. Andrew inherited his father's mill and showed a keen interest and considerable talent in devising improvements to the machinery of the mill. He also turned his attention to the design of windmills, and in 1750 invented the fantail which kept the sails rotating at right angles to the direction of the wind; in 1768 he patented a machine for dressing grain; in 1772 he invented the 'spring' sail which counteracted the effect of sudden gusts of wind. His most significant invention was a drum threshing machine which could be worked by wind, water, horse or (some years later) steam power; he obtained a patent in 1788 and built a factory to produce them, but as with all his other inventions he derived very little financial return, and in his old age the sum of £1500 was raised by his friends to alleviate his distress.

MEILHAC, Henri (1831–97) French playwright, born in Paris. From 1855 he produced a long series of light comedies—some in conjunction with **Ludovic Halévy**, and, some, including *La Belle Hélène*, well known through **Offenbach**'s music. His *chief-d'œuvre* is *Frou-Frou* (1869). He also collaborated with Halévy and Gille respectively in the libretti of the operas *Carmen* and *Manon*.

MEILLET, Antoine (1866–1936) French philologist, born in Moulins. A great authority on Indo-European languages, he was professor at the École des Hautes Études (1891–1906) and at the Collège de France from 1906. He wrote standard works on Old Slavonic, Greek, Armenian, Old Persian, etc, on comparative Indo-European grammar, and on linguistic theory.

MEINHOF, Ulrike Marie (1934–76) West German terrorist, born in Oldenburg, the daughter of a museum director. While studying at Marburg University, she campaigned for the creation of a neutral, nuclear-free 'Greater Germany' and subsequently became a respected left-wing journalist. In 1961 she married the communist activist, Klaus Rainer Röhl (divorced 1968), by whom she had twin daughters. After an interview with the imprisoned arsonist, **Andreas Baader**, she became committed to the use of violence to secure radical social change. In May 1970, she helped free Baader and they both then headed an underground urban guerrilla organization, the Red Army Faction, which conducted brutal terrorist attacks against the post-war West German 'materialist order'. As the Faction's chief ideologist, she was arrested in 1972, and in 1974 was sentenced to eight years' imprisonment. She committed suicide in Stammheim high-security prison.

MEINHOLD, Johann Wilhelm (1797–1815) German pastor and poet, born on the island of Usedom. He was the Lutheran pastor there and at Krummin and Rehwinkel. He published poems and dramas, but is best known for his *Amber Witch* (trans 1894).

MEINONG, Alexius von (1853–1920) Austrian philosopher and psychologist, born in Lemberg. A disciple of **Franz Brentano** in Vienna, he became professor at Graz in 1882 and founded there in 1894 Austria's first institute of experimental psychology. His main work was *Untersuchungen zur Gegenstandstheorie und Psychologie* (1904), in which he distinguishes sharply between the content and the objects of thoughts and makes further distinctions between different kinds of objects, to the point of paradox if not absurdity—as **Bertrand Russell** devastatingly demonstrated, wielding '**Ockham**'s razor'.

MEIR, Golda, née **Mabovich** (1898–1978) Israeli politician, born in Kiev. Her family emigrating to Milwaukee, USA, when she was eight years old. She married in 1917 and settled in Palestine in 1921, where she took up social work and became a leading figure in the Labour movement. She was Israeli ambassador to the Soviet Union (1948–49), minister of labour (1949–56), and foreign minister (1956–66). She was elected prime minister in 1969 and resigned in 1974.

MEISSONIER, Jean Louis Ernest (1813–91) French painter born in Lyon. He specialized in small genre and military scenes.

MEITNER, Lise (1878–1968) Austrian physicist, born in Vienna. Professor in Berlin (1926–38) and member (1907–38) of the Kaiser Wilhelm Institute for Chemistry, in 1917 she shared with **Otto Hahn** the discovery of the radioactive element protactinium. She is known for her work on nuclear physics. In 1938 she fled Nazi Germany and went to Sweden, to the Nobel Physical Institute, and in 1947 to the Royal Swedish Academy of Engineering Sciences, Stockholm, retiring to England in 1960.

MELA, Pomponius (fl.40) Latin geographer, born in Tingentera, in southern Spain. He lived under the Emperor **Claudius**. He was the author of an unsystematic compendium entitled *De Situ Orbis*, in three volumes.

MELACOMBE, Lord See **DODINGTON, George Bubb**

MELANCHTHON, (Greek for original surname, **Schwarzerd,** 'black earth'**), Philip** (1497–1560) German Protestant reformer, born in Bretten in the Palatinate. He was appointed professor of Greek at Wittenberg in 1516 and became **Luther**'s fellow-worker. His *Loci Communes* (1521) is the first great Protestant work on dogmatic theology. The Augsberg Confession (1530) was composed by him. After Luther's death he succeeded to the leadership of the German Reformation movement but lost the confidence of some Protestants by concessions to the Catholics; while the zealous Lutherans were displeased at his approximation to the doctrine of **Calvin** on the Lord's Supper. His conditional consent to the introduction of the stringent Augsburg Interim (1549) in Saxony led to painful controversies.

MELBA, Dame Nellie, née **Mitchell** (1861–1931) Australian prima donna, born in Melbourne from which she took her professional name. She appeared at Covent Garden in 1888, and the wonderful purity of her soprano voice won her worldwide fame. She was created DBE in 1927. She published her autobiographical *Melodies and Memories* in 1925.

MELBOURNE, William Lamb, 2nd Viscount (1779–1848) English statesman, born in London. Educated at Eton, Trinity College, Cambridge and Glasgow, he became Whig MP for Leominster in 1805, but accepted in 1827 the chief-secretaryship of Ireland in **Canning**'s government, and retained it under Goderich (the Earl of **Ripon**) and **Wellington**. Succeeding as second viscount (1828), he returned to the Whigs, became home secretary in 1830, for a few months of 1834 was premier, and, premier again in 1835, was still in office at the accession of Queen **Victoria** (1837), when he showed remarkable tact in introducing her to her duties. In 1841 he passed the seals of office to **Peel**, and after that took little part in public affairs. His wife (1785–1828), a daughter of the

Earl of Bessborough, wrote novels as Lady **Caroline Lamb**, and was notorious for her nine month's devotion (1812–13) to Lord **Byron**. The charge brought against Melbourne in 1836 of seducing the Hon Mrs **Caroline Norton** was thrown out at once.

MELCHETT, 1st Baron See **MOND, Alfred Moritz**

MELCHIOR, Lauritz Lebrecht Hommel (1890–1973) Danish-born American tenor, born in Copenhagen. His career began as a baritone (in *Pagliacci*, 1913). From 1918 he appeared as a tenor, making his Covent Garden début in 1924. One of the foremost Wagnerian singers of the century, he sang at Bayreuth (1924–31) and regularly at the New York Metropolitan (1926–50). He became a US citizen in 1947 and retired to California.

MELEAGER (fl.80 BC) Greek poet and epigrammatist, from Gadara, in Syria. He was the author of 128 exquisite short elegiac poems, and many epigrams, collected in his anthology *Stephanos* (Garland).

MELÉNDEZ VALDÉS, Juan (1754–1817) Spanish poet, born near Badajoz. He became a professor of classics at the University of Salamanca and fought for **Napoleon** in the War of Independence. Considered the greatest lyric poet of his time, he is known for his odes, ballads and romantic verses.

MELISSUS (5th century BC) Greek philosopher and statesman. He commanded the Samian fleet which defeated the Athenians under **Pericles** in a battle in 441 BC. He was probably a pupil of **Parmenides of Elea** and wrote a book entitled *On Nature* which elaborated Parmenides' views on the properties of reality and which most influenced the atomists, **Democritus** and **Leucippus**, in their response to Eleatic doctrines.

MELLANBY, Kenneth (1908–) Scottish entomologist and environmentalist, born in Barrhead, Renfrewshire. Educated at King's College, Cambridge, and London University, his early career was in medical entomology at the London School of Hygiene and Tropical Medicine. In 1955 he was appointed head of the entomology department at Rothamsted Experimental Station, and in 1961 founded and directed the Nature Conservancy's experimental station at Monks Wood, Huntingdon. Here he led research into the deleterious affects of pesticides on the environment and advocated the advantages of biological control of insect pests. He wrote several books on entomology, ecology and pollution, notably *Pesticides and Pollution* (1967), and founded the leading journal, *Environmental Pollution*, in 1970.

MELLON, Andrew William (1855–1937) American financier, philanthropist and statesman, born in Pittsburgh, Pennsylvania. Trained as a lawyer, he entered his father's banking house in 1874 and took over in 1882, soon establishing himself as a banker and industrial magnate. Entering politics, he was secretary of the Treasury from 1921 to 1932 under presidents **Harding**, **Coolidge** and **Hoover** and made controversial fiscal reforms, drastically reducing taxation of the wealthy. He was ambassador to the UK from 1932 to 1933. He endowed the National Gallery of Art at Washington DC.

MELLON, Harriot (c.1777–1837) English actress, born in London. She appeared at Drury Lane in 1795. In 1815 she married her elderly protector, **Thomas Coutts**, who left her all his money when he died in 1822. In 1827 she married the Duke of St Albans.

MELLONI, Macedonio (1798–1854) Italian physicist, born in Parma. As professor of physics at Parma (1824–31), he had to flee to France on account of political activities. Returning to Naples in 1839, he directed the Vesuvius Observatory till 1848. He is specially noted for his work on radiant heat. He introduced the term 'diathermancy' to denote the capacity of transmitting infrared radiation.

MELO, Francisco Manuel de (1608–66) Portuguese writer, born in Lisbon. He had an arduous and hazardous life as soldier, political prisoner, and exile in Brazil, whence he returned in 1657. He wrote in both Spanish and Portuguese, and is better remembered for his critical works and his history of the Catalan wars than for his voluminous poetry.

MELVILL, Thomas (1726–53) Scottish scientist. Educated at Glasgow University for the church, he was the first (1752) to study the spectra of luminous gases. His early death in Geneva obscured the importance of his experiments.

MELVILLE, Andrew (1545–c.1622) Scottish Presbyterian religious reformer, born in Baldowie, Angus, and educated at St Andrews and Paris. In 1568 he became professor at Geneva. On his return to Scotland he was principal of Glasgow University (1574–80), and did much to reorganize university education; he also had an important share in drawing up the *Second Book of Discipline*. Chosen principal of St Mary's College, St Andrews in 1580, he taught Hebrew, Chaldee and Syriac besides lecturing on theology. In 1582 he preached boldly against absolute authority before the General Assembly and advocated a presbyterial system of church government; in 1584, to escape imprisonment, he went to London. He was repeatedly moderator of the General Assembly of the Church of Scotland. In 1596 he headed a deputation to 'remonstrate' with King **James VI**; and in 1606, with seven other ministers, was called to England to confer with him. Having ridiculed the service in the Chapel Royal in a Latin epigram, he was summoned before the English privy council, and sent to the Tower. In 1611 he was released through the intercession of the Duke of Bouillon, who wanted his services as a professor of theology in his university at Sedan.

MELVILLE, George John Whyte See **WHYTE-MELVILLE**

MELVILLE, Henry Dundas, 1st Viscount See **DUNDAS, Henry**

MELVILLE, Herman (1819–91) American novelist, born in New York. He became a bank clerk but, in search of adventure, joined a whaling ship bound for the South Seas. He deserted at the Marquesas and spent some weeks with a savage tribe in the Typee valley, an episode which inspired his first book, *Typee* (1846). Having been taken off by an Australian whaler, he was jailed in Tahiti as a member of a mutinous crew, but escaped and spent some time on the island. This adventure was the basis of his second book, *Omoo* (1847). *Mardi* (1849) also dealt with the South Seas, but entered the realm of satire not too successfully, so that Melville returned to adventure fiction with *Redburn* (1849) and *White Jacket* (1850), in which he drew on his experiences as a seaman on the man-of-war which brought him home from Tahiti. In 1847 he had married, and after three years in New York he took a farm near Pittsfield, Massachusetts, where **Nathaniel Hawthorne** was his neighbour and friend. It was during this period that he wrote his masterpiece, *Moby Dick* (1851), a novel of the whaling industry, whose extraordinary vigour and colour and whose philosophical and allegorical undertones reflecting on the nature of evil have given it a place among the classic sea stories. Later novels included *Pierre* (1852), in a symbolic vein which was not appreciated by his readers, the satirical *Confidence Man* (1857), and *Billy Budd*, published posthumously in 1924 and used as the subject of an opera by **Benjamin Britten** in 1950. Now regarded as one of America's greatest novelists, he was not so successful during his life, even *Moby Dick* being unappreciated. After 1857, disillusioned and by then a New York customs official, he wrote only some poetry. Recognition did not come until some 30 years after his death.

MELVILLE, Sir James, of Halhill (1535–1617) Scottish soldier and diplomat. He went to France in 1550 as page to the young **Mary, Queen of Scots**, and subsequently undertook missions to the courts of England and the Palatinate. He wrote *Memoirs of his Own Time* (Bannatyne Club, 1827).

MELVILLE, James (1556–1614) Scottish Reformer and diarist, born near Montrose, nephew of **Andrew Melville**. He was professor of Oriental languages at St Andrews and minister in 1586 of Kilrenny, Fife. He took a leading part with his uncle in ecclesiastical politics and went to London in 1606. He was moderator of the general assembly in 1589. He is best known for his *Diary* (1556–1601), written in racy, vigorous and idiomatic Scots.

MEMLINC, or **Memling, Hans** (c.1440–1494) Flemish religious painter, born in Seligenstadt (Germany) of Dutch parents. He lived mostly in Bruges. A pupil of **Roger van der Weyden**, he repeated the types of his master. The triptych of the *Madonna Enthroned* at Chatsworth (1468), the *Marriage of St Catherine* (1479) and the *Shrine of St Ursula* (1489), both at Bruges, are among his best works. He was also an original and creative portrait painter.

MEMMI, Simone See **MARTINI**

MENAECHMUS (4th century BC) Greek mathematician. One of the tutors of **Alexander the Great**, he was the first to investigate conics as sections of a cone.

MÉNAGE, Giles (1613–92) French lexicographer, born in Angers. He gave up the bar for the church, but chiefly spent his time in literary pursuits. He founded, in opposition to the Academy, a salon, the 'Mercuriales', which gained him European fame and **Molière**'s ridicule as Vadius in *Femmes savantes*. His chief work is his *Dictionnaire étymologique* (1650).

MENANDER (c.343–291 BC) Greek poet, and the greatest writer of Attic comedy, born in Athens. His comedies were more successful with cultured than with popular audiences; but **Quintilian** praised him, and **Terence** imitated him closely. He wrote more than 100 comedies, but only a few fragments of his work were known until 1906, when **Lefebvre** discovered in Egypt a papyrus containing 1328 lines from four different plays. In 1957, however, the complete text of the comedy *Dyskolos* ('The Bad-Tempered Man') was brought to light in Geneva.

MENCHIKOV See **MENSHIKOV, Alexander Danilovich**

MENCIUS, properly **Meng-tzu** (c.371–c.289 BC) Chinese philosopher and sage, born in Shantung. He helped to develop and popularize Confucian ideas and founded a school to promote their study. From the age of 40 he travelled China for some 20 years searching for a princely ruler to espouse and implement Confucian moral and political ideals. The search was unsuccessful but his conversations with rulers, disciples and others are recorded in a book of sayings which his pupils compiled after his death (*Book of Meng-tzu*). His ethical system was based on the belief that human beings were innately and instinctively good but required the proper conditions and support for moral growth; like **Confucius** he emphasized the cardinal virtues of magnanimity (*jen*), sense of duty (*i*), politeness (*li*) and wisdom (*chih*), and he made many proposals for social and political reform, down to the level of very practical recommendations about taxes, road maintenance and poor law.

MENCKEN, Henry Louis (1880–1956) American journalist and linguist, born in Baltimore. A reporter on the *Baltimore Herald*, he became city editor, then editor. He joined the *Sunpapers* in 1906 for whom he worked continuously. In 1908 he was literary editor of *Smart Set* and was co-editor from 1914 to 1923. In 1924 he and George Jean Nathan founded the *American Mercury*. Throughout the early decades of the 20th century he was a literary Vesuvius, iconoclastically attacking what he called the 'booboisie', particularly in the Bible belt. Unstinting in his criticism of many public figures, he flouted religion, rapped newpapers over the knuckles, denounced traditionally-minded authors, eulogized radical writers and tongue-whipped politicians. During the Scopes trial he contributed a series of masterly articles, heaped scorn on prohibitionists and wrote a po-faced account of the invention of the bath-tub in America from which President **Truman** quoted as if it were the Gospel. His many books illustrate his eclecticism: *Ventures into Verse* (1903), *The Artist* (1912), a play, *A book of Prefaces* (1917), *Damn: A Book of Calumny* (1918), *Menckeniana: A Schimpflexicon* (1927), a collection of fugitive pieces, and *The American Language* (1921), a remarkable study motivated by his dislike of England. *The Vintage Mencken*, edited by **Alistair Cooke**, appeared in 1955.

MENDEL, Gregor Johann (1822–84) Austrian biologist and botanist, born near Udrau in Austrian Silesia, the son of a peasant farmer. Entering an Augustinian cloister in Brünn in 1843, he was ordained a priest in 1847. After studying science at Vienna (1851–53) he returned to Brünn, and in 1868 became abbot there. Meanwhile he had been pursuing remarkable researches on the inheritance characters in plants, especially the edible peas in the monastery garden. His experiments in hybridity in plants led to the formulation of Mendel's Law of Segregation and his Law of Independent Assortment. His principle of factorial inheritance and the quantitative investigation of single characters have become the basis of modern genetics.

MENDEL, Lafayette Benedict (1872–1935) American chemist, born in Delhi, New York. Professor at Yale (1897–1935), he did much original work on nutrition, discovering Vitamin A (1913) and the function of Vitamin C.

MENDELEYEV, Dmitri Ivanovich (1834–1907) Russian chemist, born in Tobolsk. Professor of chemistry at St Petersburg from 1866, he formulated the periodic law by which he predicted the existence of several elements which were subsequently discovered. Element No 101 is named mendelevium after him.

MENDELSOHN, Erich (1887–1953) German-born American architect, born in Allenstein (now Olszlyn, in Poland). A leading exponent of functionalism, he designed the Einstein Tower in Potsdam (1919–21) and various factories and department stores. In 1933 he fled to England, and designed hospitals. He designed the Hebrew University at Jerusalem. He emigrated to the USA in 1941, where he designed synagogues and hospitals.

MENDELSSOHN, Felix, properly **Mendelssohn-Bartholdy** (1809–47) German composer, born in Hamburg, the grandson of **Moses Mendelssohn**. He was born the son of a Hamburg banker who added the name Bartholdy. He was carefully educated, especially in music, and at ten made his first public appearance as pianist. Within the next few years he formed the acquaintance of **Goethe**, **Carl Weber** and **Ignaz Moscheles**, and composed his Symphony in C minor and the B minor Quartet. In 1825 he completed his opera, *Camacho's Wedding*. With the *Midsummer Night's Dream* overture (1826) he attained musical maturity. A tour of Scotland in the summer of 1829 inspired him with the *Hebrides* overture and the *Scotch Symphony*. He conducted the Lower Rhine festival at Düsseldorf in 1833 and 1834 and in 1835 the Gewandhaus concerts at Leipzig. He settled in Berlin in 1841 when the king of Prussia asked his assistance in the founding of an Academy of Arts. In 1843 the new music school at Leipzig was opened for him with **Schumann** and the violinist Ferdinand David among his associates. He produced his *Elijah* in Birmingham in 1846. He had scarcely returned from his tenth and last visit to England, in 1847, when the news of his sister Fanny's death reached him. Periods of illness and depression followed rapidly; and he died soon after. Although eminent as pianist and organist, his music suffers from lack of emotional range, often deteriorating into fairylike prestos and sugary sentimental andantes. His violin concerto (1844) characterizes this criticism, yet its charm almost defies it.

MENDELSSOHN, Moses (1729–86) German Jewish philosopher and biblical scholar, born in Dessau, grandfather of **Felix Mendelssohn**. He studied in Berlin and went on to become the partner to a silk manufacturer. He is an important figure in the history of Jewish philosophy and in the Enlightenment, and his main works reflect his commitment both to Judaism and rationalism: *Phädon* (1767) is an argument for the immortality of the soul, based on **Plato**'s *Phaedo*; *Jerusalem* (1783) advocates Judaism as the religion of reason; *Morgenstunden* (1785) argues for the rationality of belief in the existence of God. He was a friend of **Lessing** and the prototype of his *Nathan*.

MENDERES, Adnan (1899–1961) Turkish statesman, born near Aydin. Though educated for the law, he became a farmer, entered politics in 1932, at first in opposition, then with the party in power under **Mustafa Kemal Ataturk**. In 1945 he became one of the leaders of the new Democratic party and was made prime minister when it came to power in 1950. Re-elected in 1954 and 1957, in May 1960 he was deposed and superseded by General Cemal Gursel after an army *coup*. He appeared as defendant with over 500 officials of his former Democratic party administration at the Yassiada trials (1960–61), was sentenced to death and hanged in Imrali.

MENDÈS, Catulle (1841–1909) French writer, born in Bordeaux of Jewish parentage. A Parnassian, he founded the *Revue Fantaisiste* (1859), but switched to Romanticism and wrote poems, novels, dramas and libretti as well as journalistic articles and criticisms.

MENDÈS-FRANCE, Pierre (1907–82) French statesman. He entered parliament in 1932 as a Radical. In 1941 he made a daring escape from imprisonment in Vichy France and went to England to join the Free French forces. After a short time as minister for national economy under **de Gaulle** in 1945, he became prominent on the opposition side, and in June 1954 succeeded M Laniel as prime minister. At a troubled period he handled France's foreign affairs with firmness and decision, but his government was defeated on its North African policy, and he resigned in 1955. A firm critic of de Gaulle, he lost his seat in the 1958 election. He returned to the Assembly in 1967, but retired due to ill-health in 1973, later giving much attention to Israeli affairs.

MENDOZA, Diego Hurtado de (1503–75) Spanish politician of Basque origin, great-grandson of **Inigo Lopez de Mendoza**. He was entrusted by **Charles V** with the conduct of his Italian policy and the representation of his views at the Council of Trent. He inherited his ancestor's gifts as a statesman and man of letters. His *War of Granada* is a masterpiece of prose.

MENDOZA, Inigo Lopez de (fl.1450) Spanish statesman and poet, father of **Pedro Gonzalez de Mendoza** and great-grandfather of **Diego Hurtado de Mendoza**. He was created Marquis of Santillana by John II of Castile in 1445 for his services on the field. He was a wise statesman, a sturdy patriot, and an admired poet of Petrachan sonnets, lyrics, allegories and didactic poems. He left an excellent account of the Provençal, Catalan and Valencian poets, and was an early folklorist and collector of popular proverbs.

MENDOZA, Pedro Gonzalez de (1428–95) Spanish prelate and statesman, son of **Inigo Lopez de Mendoza**. He was created a cardinal in 1473, and chancellor of Castile. As archbishop of Castile in 1474 he helped **Isabella of Castile** gain the throne. He became the archbishop of Toledo and primate of Spain in 1482, and was a trusted minister of **Ferdinand** and Isabella.

MENELAUS according to Greek legend, king of Sparta, younger brother of **Agamemnon** and husband of Helen of Troy. It was the abduction of Helen by Paris, son of **Priam**, that caused the combined expedition of the Greeks against Troy, episodes of which form the subject matter of **Homer**'s *Iliad*. Menelaus took part in the Trojan War, recovered his wife Helen, and Homer's *Odyssey* shows him once more back in Sparta with Helen after an adventurous return from Troy.

MENEM, Carlos Saul (1935–) Argentinian politician, born in Anillaco, in La Rioja province. While training for the legal profession he became politically active in the Peronist (Justice party) movement, founding the Youth Group in 1955. In 1963 he was elected president of the party in La Rioja and in the same year unsuccessfully contested the governorship of the province, eventually being elected in 1983 and re-elected in 1987. In 1989 he defeated the Radical Union party (UCR) candidate and became president of Argentina. Despite inflammatory speeches during the election campaign, soon after assuming office he declared a wish to resume normal diplomatic relations with the United Kingdom and to discuss the future of the Falkland Islands rationally in a spirit of compromise.

MENÉNDEZ PIDAL, Ramon (1869–1968) Spanish philologist and critic, born in Coruña. A pupil of **Menéndez Y Pelayo**, he became professor at the University of Madrid in 1899, founded the Madrid Centre of Historical Studies, and carried on the tradition of exact scholarship. His *La España del Cid* (1929) is the finest Spanish modern historical study. He published critical works on Spanish ballads and chronicles and important historical grammars of Spanish.

MENÉNDEZ Y PELAYO, Marcelino (1856–1912) Spanish scholar, critic and poet. He is regarded as the founder of modern Spanish literary history. He was professor at Madrid (1878–98) and director of the Biblioteca National from 1898. His writings, all exemplifying his traditionalism and Catholicism, include the *History of Aesthetic Ideas in Spain* (1844–91) and *History of Spanish heterodoxies* (1880–81). His verse includes *Odes* (1883) and anthologies.

MENG-TZU See **MENCIUS**

MENGER, Karl von (1840–1921) Austrian economist. A native of Silesia, and a founder of the 'Austrian school' of economics, he was professor in Vienna from 1879 to 1901.

MENGISTU, Mariam Haile (1937–) Ethiopian soldier and politician. Educated at Holetu military academy, he joined the Ethiopian army, rising to the rank of colonel. He took part in the 1974 coup which removed Emperor **Haile Selassie** and then, in 1977, he himself led another coup which ousted the military régime. He was confronted with secessionist guerrilla activities in the north and drought, eventually surviving with aid, initially from the Soviet Union and then from the West. In 1987 civilian rule was formally reintroduced, with the Marxist-Leninist Workers' party of Ethiopia (WPE) as the only legally permitted political group. Mariam became the country's first president.

MENGS, Anton Raphael (1728–79) German painter, born in Aussig in Bohemia, the son of a Danish artist. Having eventually settled at Rome, he turned Catholic, married, and directed a school of painting. A close friend of **Winckelmann**, he became the most famous of the early Neoclassical painters. In Madrid (1761–70 and 1773–76) he decorated the dome of the grand salon in the royal palace with the *Apotheosis of the Emperor Trajan*.

MENKEN, Adah Isaacs, née **Adah Bertha Theodore** (?1835–1868) American actress, born near New Orleans. She appeared on stage in New York in 1859, and later appeared in *Mazeppa* with immense success in London (1864) and elsewhere. She had many husbands, including **Charles Dickens**, and many literary friends. No reports of her acting ability are extant and her reputation rests, apparently, on her audacity which reached its apotheosis when she appeared in a state of virtual nudity after she was bound to the back of a wild horse.

MENNIN, Peter (1923–) American composer, born in Erie, Pennsylvania. He studied at the Eastman College of Music and rapidly established himself as a composer of large-scale works. He has composed eight symphonies, including *The Cycle*, a choral work to his own text, concertos, choral and chamber music.

MENNO SIMONS (1496–1561) Dutch Anabaptist leader, and founder of the Mennonite sect. Ordained a Roman Catholic priest in 1524, he withdrew from the church under the influence of Lutheran thought in 1536. He was made an elder at Groningen in 1537, and organized Anabaptist groups in northern Europe that were persecuted by Catholics and Protestants alike. The evangelical Mennonite sect, named after him, practises adult baptism, excommunication, close adherence to Scriptural authority, restriction of marriage to members of the group, and aloofness from the State.

MENON See **KRISHNA MENON**

MENOTTI, Gian-Carlo (1911–) Italian-born American composer, born in Milan. He settled in America at the age of 17. Instinctively imbued with the Italian operatic tradition, he achieved international fame with a series of operas that began with *Amelia goes to the Ball*, produced in 1937 at Philadelphia, where he was a student. He writes his own libretti, and his later works, *The Medium* (1946), *The Consul* (1950; Pulitzer prize), *Amahl and the Night Visitors* (1951) composed for television performance, *The Saint of Bleecker Street* (1954; Pulitizer prize), *Maria Golovin* (1958), *The Most Important Man* (1971), and others, have great theatrical effectiveness although their musical style is derived from a wide variety of models. In 1958 he founded the Festival of Two Worlds in Spoleto.

MENSHIKOV, Alexander Danilovich (c.1660–1729) Russian field-marshal and statesman, born of poor parents in Moscow. Entering the army, he distinguished himself at the siege of Azov, and afterwards accompanied **Peter I the Great** in his travels to Holland and England. During the war with Sweden (1702–13) he played an important part at Pultowa—Peter made him a field marshal there—Riga, Stettin and elsewhere. At the capture of Marienburg the girl who became **Catherine I** fell into Menshikov's hands, and was through him introduced to the tsar. Towards the end of Peter's reign Menshikov lost favour owing to extortions and suspected duplicities. But when Peter died he secured the succession of Catherine, and during her reign and that of her young successor, **Peter II**, he governed Russia with almost absolute authority. He was about to marry his daughter to the young tsar when the jealousy of the old nobility led to his banishment to Siberia and the confiscation of his estates.

MENSHIKOV, Alexander Sergeievich (1789–1869) Russian soldier, great-grandson of **Alexander Danilovich Menshikov**. He rose to the rank of general in the Napoleonic campaigns of 1812–15, was severely wounded at Varna in the Turkish campaign of 1828, and was made head of the Russian navy. His overbearing behaviour as ambassador at Constantinople brought about the Crimean War. He commanded at Alma and Inkerman, and defended Sebastopol, but in 1855 was recalled because of illness.

MENTEITH, Sir John de (13th–14th century) Scottish knight. He was captured by the English in 1296 but released in 1297 and made governor of Dumbarton. In 1305 he captured the Scottish patriot **William Wallace** in Glasgow and delivered him to his fate in London. Created Earl of Lennox he joined **Robert I, the Bruce** in 1307, and was one of the signatories to the Declaration of Arbroath in 1320.

MENUHIN, Sir Yehudi (1916–) American-born British violinist, born in New York. At the age of seven he appeared as soloist with the San Francisco Symphony Orchestra. This was followed by appearances all over the world as a prodigy, and after 18 months' retirement for study, he continued his career as a virtuoso, winning international renown. In 1962 he started a school for musically talented children. He was awarded an honorary KBE in 1965 and OM in 1987, two years after taking British citizenship. His sister Hephzibah (1920–81) was a gifted pianist. He published his autobiography in 1977.

MENZEL, Adolf (1815–1905) German painter, illustrator and engraver, born in Breslau. He is known for his drawings illustrating the times of **Frederick II, the Great** and **Wilhelm I**.

MENZEL, Donald Howard (1901–76) American astrophysicist, born in Florence, Colorado. Educated at the universities of Denver and Princeton, he joined the staff of the Lick Observatory in California, and was appointed director of the Harvard College Observatory (1954–66). He did valuable work on planetary atmospheres and on the composition of the Sun.

MENZEL, Wolfgang (1798–1873) German critic and historian, born in Waldenburg in Silesia. He studied at Jena and Bonn, but from 1825 lived mainly in Stuttgart. He edited magazines, and wrote poems, novels, histories of German literature and poetry, a history of the world, literary criticism and polemics.

MENZIES, Sir Robert Gordon (1894–1978) Australian statesman, born in Jeparit, Victoria. He practised as a barrister before entering politics, becoming member of the Victoria parliament in 1928. Six years later, in 1934, he went to the Federal House of Representatives, sitting as the member for Kooyang. He was Commonwealth attorney-general for the years 1935 to 1939, prime minister from 1939 to 1941, and leader of the opposition from 1943 to 1949, when he again took office as premier of the coalition government. He had been appointed a privy councillor in 1937; and his qualities of high purpose and warm humanity were displayed during the war and the succeeding years. In 1956 he headed the Five Nations

Committee which sought to come to a settlement with **Nasser** on the question of Suez.

MERBECKE, John See **MARBECK**

MERCATOR, Gerardus (the Latinized form of **Gerhard Kremer)** (1512–94) Flemish geographer and map-maker, born in Rupelmonde. He graduated at Louvain in philosophy and theology. He studied mathematics, astronomy and engraving, and produced a terrestrial globe (1536) and a map of the Holy Land (1537). In 1544 he was imprisoned for heresy, but released for lack of evidence. In 1552 he settled at Duisburg in Germany, becoming cosmographer to the Duke of Cleves, and produced maps of many parts of Europe, including Britain. To aid navigators, in 1569 he introduced the map projection that bears his name, in which the path of a ship steering on a constant bearing is represented by a straight line on the map; it has been used for nautical charts ever since. In 1585 he published the first part of an 'Atlas' of Europe, said to be the first time that this word was used to describe a book of maps; it was completed by his son in 1595. On the cover was a drawing of Atlas holding a globe on his shoulders, hence the word 'atlas' became applied to any book of maps.

MERCATOR, (German **Kaufmann), Nicolaus** (c.1620–1687) German mathematician and astronomer. As an engineer he planned the fountains at Versailles, as a mathematician he was one of the discoverers of the series for log $(1 + x)$. From 1660 he lived in England.

MERCER, Cecil William See **YATES, Dornford**

MERCER, David (1928–80) English dramatist, born in Wakefield. After studying painting at King's College, Newcastle, he moved to Europe and began to write. His first television play, *Where the Difference Begins* (1961) signalled his interest in fusing the personal and the political in work that challenged the conventions of television drama. Further plays, like *A Climate of Fear* (1962), *A Suitable Case for Treatment* (1962) and *In Two Minds* (1967), explored his fascination with mental health, psychiatry and his struggle to reconcile a belief in socialism with the repression revealed during his stays in Eastern Europe. Winner of the 1965 *Evening Standard* Award for most promising playwright, his stage work includes *Ride A Cock Horse* (1965), *Flint* (1970) and *Cousin Vladimir* (1978). His film scripts include *Morgan* (1965) and *Providence* (1977). He continued to address issues of personal alienation and the class system in later television plays like *Huggy Bear* (1976), *The Ragazza* (1978) and *Rod of Iron* (1980).

MERCER, Joe (1914–) English footballer and manager, born in Cheshire. Frail and spindly-legged, he belied appearances by playing professional football for more than 20 years. Already an established player with Everton when war broke out in 1939, he began a new career with Arsenal in 1946, with whom he gained two more championship medals and an F A Cup winners' medal. He was chosen Player of the Year in 1950 when 35 years old. With Aston Villa and Manchester City he was a highly successful manager, and he had a spell later as caretaker of the England side.

MERCER, John (1791–1866) English dye chemist, born near Blackburn, Lancashire. He is chiefly known for his invention of mercerization—a process by which cotton is given a silky lustre resembling silk. Almost entirely self-educated, he made many important discoveries connected with dyeing and calico printing.

MERCKX, Eddy (1945–) Belgian racing cyclist, born in Brussels. As a cyclist he had no discernible weaknesses, and in the 1969 Tour de France he won the major prizes in all three sections: overall, points classification and King of the Mountains. He won the Tour de France five times (1969–72, and 1974), and came out on top in the Tours of Spain and Italy also.

MEREDITH, George (1828–1909) English novelist, born in Portsmouth, the grandson of a famous naval outfitter (the 'great Mel' of *Evan Harrington*). He was educated privately in Germany and was thus able to view the English class system with detachment. In London, after being articled to a solicitor, he turned to journalism and letters, his first venture appearing in *Chambers's Journal* in 1849, the year in which he married Mary Ellen Nicolls, a widowed daughter of **Thomas Love Peacock**. This disastrous marriage gave him an insight into relations between the sexes, which appear as largely in his work as his other great interest, natural selection as Nature's way of perfecting man. His works did not bring him much financial reward and he had to rely on his articles in *The Fortnightly* and his work as a reader in the publishing house of Chapman and Hall. His prose works started with a burlesque Oriental fantasy, *The Shaving of Shagpat* (1855), followed in 1859 by *The Ordeal of Richard Feverel*, which is based on parental tyranny and a false system of private education. He did not achieve general popularity as a novelist until the delightful *Diana of the Crossways* appeared in 1885. In the meantime he wrote less successful works, such as his two novels on the Italian revolt of 1848, *Sandra Belloni* (1864) and *Vittoria* (1866). Other popular works are *Evan Harrington* (1860), which throws light on Meredith's origins; *Harry Richmond* (1871); and best of all, *Beauchamp's Career* (1875), which poses the question of class and party and is well constructed and clearly written. This cannot be said of Meredith's later major novels, *The Egoist* (1879), a study of refined selfishness, and *The Amazing Marriage* (1895). These two powerful works are marred by the artificiality and forced wit which occurs in so much of his poetry. His first volume of verse (1851) is quite unremarkable, but *Poems and Lyrics of the Joy of Earth* (1883) displays his new cryptic manner and discusses the two master themes—the 'reading of earth' and the sex duel. His masterpiece on the latter theme had appeared in 1862 when he was influenced by the pre-Raphaelite poets and painters. This is *Modern Love*, a novelette in pseudo-sonnet sequence form in which the novelist in him plays powerfully on incompatibility of temper. His 'reading of earth' is expressed cryptically in the magnificent *Woods of Westermain*, intelligibly in *The Thrush in February* and thrillingly in *The Lark Ascending*. The volume called *A Reading of Life* (1901) adds little to the record. The modern revaluation of the Victorians has enhanced the fame of this very cerebral poet.

MEREDITH, Owen See **LYTTON, Edward Robert Bulwer**

MEREZHKOVSKI, Dmitri Sergeyevich (1865–1941) Russian novelist, critic and poet, born in St Petersburg. He wrote a historical trilogy, *Christ and Antichrist* (*The Death of the Gods*, *The Forerunner*, *Peter and Alexis*), and books on **Tolstoy**, **Ibsen**, and **Gogol**. He opposed the Revolution in 1917 and fled to Paris in 1919. His wife, Zinaida Nikolayevna Hippius (1870–1945), was also a poet, novelist and critic.

MERGENTHALER, Ottmar (1854–99) German-born American inventor, born in Hachtel in Germany. He went to the USA in 1872 and became an American citizen in 1878. He invented the Linotype typesetting machine (patented in 1884).

MERIKANTO, Aarre (1893–1958) Finnish composer, born in Helsinki, the son of the notable song-composer Oskar Merikanto (1868–1924). He studied in

Helsinki, with **Reger** in Leipzig, and in Moscow (where **Scriabin**'s music influenced him). His compositions of the 1920s display remarkable individuality, but they were largely unrecognized in his lifetime. His masterpiece, the opera *Juha* (1922), was premiered only in 1963. From 1936 till his death he was an influential teacher at the Sibelius Academy.

MÉRIMÉE, Prosper (1803–70) French novelist, born in Paris, the son of a painter. He studied law, visited Spain in 1830, and held posts under the ministries of the navy, commerce and the interior. He was appointed inspector-general of historical remains in France in 1833, and became a senator in 1853. His last years were clouded by ill-health and melancholy, and the downfall of the empire hastened his death. He wrote novels and short stories, archaeological and historical dissertations, and travel stories, all of which display exact learning, keen observation, real humour, and an exquisite style. Among his novels are *Colomba*, *Mateo Falcone*, *Carmen*, *La Vénus d'Ille*, *Lokis*, *Arsène Guillot*, *La Chambre bleue* and *L'Abbé Aubain*. His letters include the famous *Lettres á une inconnue* (1873), the *Lettres á une autre inconnue* (1875) and the letters to **Panizzi** (1881). He also wrote some plays.

MERLEAU-PONTY, Maurice (1908–61) French philosopher, born in Rochefort-sur-mer, Charente-Maritime. He studied in Paris, taught in various lycées, served as an army officer in World War II, and then held professorships at Lyon University (1948) and in Paris (from 1949). He helped **Sartre** and **de Beauvoir** found the journal *Les Temps Modernes* in 1945, and was a fellow-traveller with Sartre in the Communist party in the early post-war years, becoming disillusioned and more detached after the Korean War. His two main philosophical works are *La Structure du comportement* (1942) and *Phénoménologie de la perception* (1945), which investigate the nature of consciousness, and reject the extremes of both behaviouristic psychology and subjectivist accounts; the world is neither wholly 'given' nor wholly 'constructed' for the perceiving subject, but is essentially ambiguous and enigmatic.

MEROVECH, or **Merovius** (5th century) Frankish ruler and grandfather of **Clovis**. He gave his name to the Merovingian dynasty.

MERRIAM, Clinton Hart (1855–1942) American naturalist and zoologist, and early conservationist, born in New York. A physician by training, he became head of the US Bureau of Biological Survey (1885–1910). He wrote on grizzly bears, brown bears and the birds of Connecticut, but his most important work was his *Life Zones and Crop Zones of the United States* (1898).

MERRIFIELD, (Robert) Bruce (1921–) American organic chemist, born in Fort Worth, Texas. He studied at the University of California at Los Angeles and from 1949 worked at the Rockefeller Institute for Medical Research in New York City. There he devised (1959–62) the important and now much-used 'solid phase' method for synthesizing peptides and proteins from amino acids, for which he received the Nobel prize for chemistry in 1984.

MERRILL, Stuart Fitzrandolph (1863–1915) American symbolist poet, born in Hempstead, Long Island, New York. He was educated in Paris, where he lived from 1889. His French poems *Les Gammes* (1895), *Les Quatre Saisons* (1900), and others developed the musical conception of poetry, and made full use of alliteration.

MERRIMAN, Brian (1747–1805) Irish-Gaelic poet, born in Ennistymon, County Clare, the son of a stonemason. He became a schoolteacher and small farmer in Feakle, later (1790) marrying and settling as a mathematics teacher in Limerick. His reputation depends on a stupendous mock-heroic epic, traditional in its use of dream-vision, but satirical and feminist in content: *Cúirt an Mheáin Oidhche* ('The Midnight Court', c.1786). Imagining its author's presence at a ferocious fairy inquisiton against bachelors, it lampoons sexual mores, celibacy, the clergy and male chauvinism, and all in vigorously earthy and erotic language. The poem was banned in all English translations (by **Frank O'Connor** and others) after Irish independence, but the Irish language itself was deemed incapable of corrupting influence. Liberal (and ribald) Irish intellectuals have established an annual Merriman Summer School, convening in August in Clare.

MERRIMAN, John Xavier (1841–1926) English-born South African statesman, born in Street, Somerset. He went early to South Africa, where his father was Bishop of Grahamstown. He was a member of various Cape ministries from 1875, and premier (South African party) 1908–10.

MERSENNE, Marin (1588–1648) French mathematician and scientist, born in Oize. He became a Minim Friar in 1611, and lived in Paris. Devoting himself to science, he corresponded with all the leading scientists of his day including **Descartes**, **Fermat**, **Pascal** and **Hobbes**, acting as a clearing house for scientific information. He experimented with the pendulum and found the law relating its length and period of oscillation, studied the acoustics of vibrating strings and organ pipes and measured the speed of sound. He also wrote on music, mathematics, optics and philosophy.

MERTENS, Eva See **KEITH, James**

MERTON, Robert King (1910–) American sociologist, born in Philadelphia. He was educated at Temple and Harvard Universities, going on to teach at Harvard (1934–39) and Tulane University (1939–41), before moving in 1941 to the department of sociology at Columbia University, where he remained until his retirement in 1979. He was also associate director of the Bureau of Applied Social Research, collaborating with **Paul Lazarsfeld**. His interests were very diverse, including theory, methods, and a wide range of empirical issues. His work is particularly noted for its emphasis on the connections between theory and empirical evidence. He is also regarded as the founder of the sociology of science in its modern form. His works include *Social Theory and Social Structure* (1949), *On Theoretical Sociology* (1967), *Science, Technology and Society in Seventeenth-Century England* (1938, 1970) and *The Sociology of Science* (1973).

MERTON, Thomas (1915–68) American Cistercian monk, born in Prades, France, of New Zealand and American parentage. He studied and taught English at Columbia, but in 1938 he became a convert to Roman Catholicism and in 1941 joined the Trappist order at Our Lady of Gethsemane Abbey, Kentucky. His best-selling autobiography, *The Seven Storey Mountain* (1946), prompted many to become monks, but Merton himself was to discover intense tensions between his hermitic inclinations and community living. However, ways were found for him to follow his vocation free *for* the world rather than free *from* it (cf, *Contemplation in a World of Action*, 1971), keeping up a voluminous correspondence and writing many books, ranging from personal journals and poetry to social criticism. His growing interest in Eastern spirituality led him to attend a conference in Bangkok, where he was accidentally electrocuted by a faulty fan.

MERTON, Walter de (d.1277) English prelate, born probably in Surrey. In 1264 he founded Merton

College, Oxford, the prototype of the collegiate system in English universities. He was Bishop of Rochester from 1274.

MERYON, Charles (1821–68) French etcher, the illegitimate son of an English doctor and Paris opera dancer. He entered naval college in 1837 and travelled until 1842, when he returned to Paris and decided to become an artist. Throughout his life he was a victim to mental disorder which brought his career to a premature end. His total output comprised some 100 etchings and although many were in the syle of others, a sizeable number are generally regarded as masterpieces of 19th-century etching. Particularly, acclaimed is his 1850 series *Eaux-Fortes sur Paris* (1850–54).

MESDAG, Hendrik Willem (1831–1915) Dutch marine painter, born in Groningen. He settled at The Hague, where his personal collection is housed in the Mesdag Museum.

MESELSON, Matthew Stanley (1930–) American molecular biologist, born in Denver, Colorado. He studied chemistry at the California Institute of Technology and was professor of biology at Harvard from 1964. With F W Stahl in 1957 he carried out some notably ingenious experiments which both verified **James Dewey Watson** and **Francis Crick**'s ideas on the way the double helix of the DNA molecule carries genetic information, and gave new information on the details.

MESMER, Friedrich Anton or **Franz** (1734–1815) Austrian physician and founder of mesmerism. Born near Constance, he studied and practised medicine at Vienna, and about 1772 took up the idea that there exists a power which he called 'animal magnetism'. In 1778 he went to Paris, where he created a sensation curing diseases at séances. He refused 20000 livres for his secret; but in 1785, when a learned commission denounced him as an imposter, he retired into obscurity in Switzerland.

MESSAGER, André Charles Prosper (1853–1929) French composer, mostly of operattas, born in Montlugon. *La Basoche* (1890), a comic opera, was his best. His works also include several ballets and piano pieces. He was artistic director of Covent Garden Theatre, London (1901–07) and director of Opéra Comique, Paris, (1898–1903, 1919–20).

MESSALINA, Valeria (c.25–c.48) Roman matron, the third wife of the emperor **Claudius**, whom she married at the age of 14. She bore him two children, Octavia (wife of **Nero**) and **Britannicus**. Her name has became a byword for avarice, lust and cruelty. In the emperor's absence she publicly married one of her favourites, the consul-designate Silius, and the emperor at last had her executed.

MESSERER, Asaf (1903–) Russian dancer, teacher and choreographer, born in Viln, into a ballet family. He studied with **Mikhail Mordkin** and Gorsky at the Bolshoi Ballet School, graduating in 1921 to join the company. A versatile principal, he retired from dancing in 1954 to concentrate on teaching, the element of his work for which he is best known. His choreography includes *Football Player* (1924) and *Ballet School* (1962).

MESSERSCHMITT, Willy (Wilhelm) (1898–1978) German aviation designer and production chief. He studied at the Munich Institute of Technology, and in 1923 established the Messerschmitt aircraft manufacturing works. His ME-109 set a world speed record in 1939, and during World War II he supplied the Luftwaffe with its foremost types of combat aircraft. In 1944 he produced the ME-262 fighter, the first jet-plane flown in combat. From 1955 he continued his activities with the revived Lufthansa and later also entered the automobile industry.

MESSIAEN, Olivier Eugène Prosper Charles (1908–) French composer and organist, son of the poet Cécile Sauvage, born in Avignon. He studied under Duprès and **Paul Dukas**, and was appointed professor at the Schola Cantorum. In 1941 he became professor of harmony at the Paris Conservatoire. He composed extensively for organ, orchestra, voice and piano, and made frequent use of new instruments such as the 'Ondes Martenot'. His music, which has evolved intricate mathematical rhythmic systems, is motivated by religious mysticism, and is best known outside France by the two-and-a-half-hour piano work, *Vingt regards sur l'enfant Jésus*, and the mammoth *Turangalila* Symphony, which makes use of Indian themes and rhythms. His great interest in birdsong has proved the stimulus for several works including the *Catalogue d'oiseaux* for piano (1956–58). Other works include an oratorio *La Transfiguration de Notre Seigneur Jésus-Christ* (1965–69) and an opera *St François d'Assisi* (1975–83) and *Technique de mon language musicale* (2 vols, 1944, trans 1957).

MESSIER, Charles (1730–1817) French astronomer, born in Badonviller. He mapped the faint unmoving objects in the sky which he could discard in comet-searching, and so produced the first nebula catalogue in 1784. The prefix 'M' is still applied to these objects, which are either nebulae or star clusters.

MESSMER, Otto (1894–1985) American animator, born in New Jersey, the creative force behind *Felix the Cat*. He contributed joke cartoons to *Life* magazine (1914) and entered animation in 1916, scripting and animating many films including the *Charlie Chaplin* cartoons (1917). In 1920 he created *Feline Follies*, the first Felix the Cat cartoon, and Felix was the first cartoon film star to win international favour; one of the many spin-offs was a comic strip for newspaper syndication (1923) which he drew in his spare time. Felix failed to make the transition to sound, but Messmer continued the strip until 1954.

MESTROVIC, Ivan (1883–1962) Yugoslav-born American sculptor, born in Vrpolje in Dalmatia. A shepherd boy, he was taught stone-cutting and woodcarving by his father, eventually studying in Vienna and Paris, where he became a friend of **Rodin**. He designed the national temple at Kossovo (1907–12), and the colossal *Monument to the Unknown Soldier* in Belgrade (1934). He lived in England during World War II and executed many portrait busts, including that of Sir **Thomas Beecham**. After the war he emigrated to the USA. His work is naturalistic, emotionally intense and is characterized by an impressive simplicity.

METASTASIO, Pietro, originally **Trapassi** (1698–1782) Italian poet, born in Rome. A gift for versifying gained him a patron in Gravina, a lawyer, who educated him, and left him his fortune (1718). He gained his reputation by his masque. *The Garden of Hesperides* (1722), wrote the libretti for 27 operas, including **Mozart**'s *Clemenza di Tito*, and became court poet at Vienna in 1729.

METAXAS, Yanni (1870–1941) Greek politician, born in Ithaka. He graduated from the Military College in 1890, fought in the Thessalian campaign against the Turks in 1897, and later studied military science in Germany. He took a leading part in reorganizing the Greek army before the 1912–13 Balkan Wars and in 1913 became chief of the general staff. A Royalist rival of the Republican **Venizelos**, he opposed Greek intervention in World War I. On King **Constantine I**'s fall he fled to Italy, but returned with him in 1921. In 1923 he founded the Party of Free Opinion. In 1935 he became deputy prime minister after the failure of the Venizelist coup, and in April 1936 became prime minister, in August establishing an authoritarian government with a cabinet of specialist and retired service officers. His work of reorganizing Greece economically and militarily bore fruit in the tenacious Greek resistance to the Italian invasion of 1940–41.

METCALF, John (1717–1810) English engineer, known as 'Blind Jack of Knaresborough'. He lost his sight at six, but became an outstanding athlete and horseman. During the 1745 Jacobite rising he fought at Falkirk and Culloden (1746), set up a stagecoach between York and Knaresborough, and from 1765 constucted 185 miles of road and numerous bridges in Lancashire and Yorkshire.

METCHNIKOFF See **MECHNIKOV, Ilya**

METELLUS a Roman plebeian family which rose to front rank in the nobility. One member of it twice defeated **Jugurtha** (109 BC); another conquered Crete (97 BC).

METFORD, William Ellis (1824–99) English engineer and inventor, born in Taunton. He invented an explosive rifle bullet which was outlawed by the St Petersburg Convention of 1869. He turned to the design of a breech-loading rifle (1871); it was adapted by the American **James Paris Lee** as the Lee-Metford rifle, adopted by the British War Office in 1888.

METHODIUS See **CYRIL**

METHUEN, Sir Algernon Methuen Marshall, originally **Stedman** (1856–1924) English publisher, born in London. He was a teacher of classics and French (1880–95), and began publishing as a sideline with Methuen & Co in 1889 to market his own textbooks. His first publishing success was **Kipling**'s *Barrack-Room Ballads* (1892), and, amongst others, he published works of **Belloc**, **Chesterton**, **Conrad**, **Masefield**, **R L Stevenson** and **Oscar Wilde**.

METSU, Gabriel (1630–67) Dutch painter, born in Leiden. He settled in Amsterdam in 1650, and is known for his religious and domestic genre works.

METTERNICH, Prince Clemens Lothar Wenzel (1773–1859) Austrian statesman, born in Coblenz, the son of an Austrian diplomat. He studied at Strasburg and Mainz, was attached to the Austrian embassy at The Hague, and at 28 was Austrian minister at Dresden, two years later at Berlin, and in 1805 (after Austerlitz) at Paris. In 1807 he concluded the treaty of Fontainebleau; in 1809 was appointed Austrian foreign minister, and as such negotiated the marriage between **Napoleon** and **Marie Louise**. In 1812–13 he maintained at first a temporizing policy, but at last declared war against France; the Grand Alliance was signed at Teplitz; and Metternich was made a prince of the empire. He took a very prominent part in the congress of Vienna, rearranging a German confederation (while disfavouring German unity under Prussian influence), and guarding Austria's interests in Italy. From 1815 he was the most active representative of reaction all over Europe, persistently striving to repress all popular and constitutional aspirations. As the main supporter of autocracy and police despotism at home and abroad he is largely responsible for the tension that led to the upheaval of 1848. The French Revolution of that year, which overturned for a time half the thrones of Europe, was felt in Vienna, and the government fell. Metternich fled to England, and in 1851 retired to his castle of Johannesberg on the Rhine. A brilliant diplomat, a man of iron nerve and will, though personally kind, he had few deep convictions, no warm sympathies, and no deep insight into the lessons of history.

METTRIE See **LA METTRIE**

MEULEN, Adam François van der (1632–90) Flemish painter and tapestry designer, born in Brussels. From 1666 he was battle painter to **Louis XIV**.

MEUNG, Jean de, or **Jean Clopinel** (c.1250–1305) French poet and satirist. He flourished in Paris under **Philip IV, 'the Fair'**. He translated many books into French, and left a witty *Testament*. His great work is his lengthy continuation (18000 lines) of the *Roman de la Rose* by **Guillaume de Lorris**, which substituted for tender allegorizing his own satirical pictures of actual life and an encyclopaedic discussion of every aspect of contemporary learning, which inspired many later authors to write in support of or in opposition to his views.

MEURSIUS, Latin form of **De Meurs, Johannes** or **Jan** (1579–1639) Dutch classical scholar, born in Loozduinen near The Hague. In 1610 he became professor of history, and in 1611 of Greek, at Leiden, historiographer to the States-General, and in 1625 professor of history at Sorö in Denmark. He edited **Cato**'s *De Re Rustica*, **Plato**'s *Timaeus*, **Theophrastus**'s *Characters*, and a long series of the later Greek writers; he also wrote on Greek antiquities and Dutch and Danish history.

MEYER, Adolf (1866–1950) Swiss-born American psychiatrist, born in Niederweingen. After medical and psychiatric training in Zürich and elsewhere, he emigrated to the USA in 1892, where he held posts in a number of universities and psychiatric hospitals, especially Johns Hopkins Medical School (1910–41). He was an eclectic at a time when psychoanalytical concepts dominated American psychiatry. Through his notion of 'psychobiology' he sought to integrate psychiatry and medicine, seeing mental disorder as the consequence of unsuccessful adjustment patterns. He also tried to improve the standards of patient record-keeping and long-term follow-up care in psychiatry, and lent his considerable prestige to the mental hygiene movement of Clifford Beers. His *Collected Papers* were published after his death.

MEYER, Conrad Ferdinand (1825–98) Swiss poet and novelist, born in Zürich. After a period during which he concentrated mainly on ballads and verse romances, he composed the epic poem *Huttens Letzte Tage* (1871) and a number of historical novels such as *Jürg Jenatsch* (1876) and *Der Heilige* (1880), in which he excels in subtle and intricate psychological situations and complex characters.

MEYER, Joseph (1796–1856) German publisher, born in Gotha. He issued many important serial works, editions of German classics, the encyclopaedia known as *Konversations-lexikon*, historical libraries, and other works. His business, the 'Bibliographical Institute', was transferred from Gotha to Hildburghause in 1828, and in 1874 (by his son) to Leipzig.

MEYER, Julius Lothar von (1830–95) German chemist, born in Varel, Oldenburg. He became the first professor of chemistry at Tübingen in 1876. He discovered the periodic law independently of **Dmitri Mendeleyev** in 1869 and showed that atomic volumes were functions of atomic weights.

MEYER, Viktor (1848–97) German chemist. He studied under **Robert Wilhelm Bunsen** in Heidelberg, became professor at Zürich, Göttingen, and finally at Heidelberg (1889). He discovered and investigated thiophene and the oximes. The nature of his work undermined his health and he died by his own hand.

MEYER-LÜBKE, Wilhelm (1861–1936) Swiss-born German linguist, born in Dübendorf, near Zürich.

Professor successively in the universities of Jena, Vienna, and Bonn, his studies of the Romance languages and Vulgar Latin revolutionized Romance linguistics. Among his most important works are *Grammatik der romanischen Sprachen* (1890–1902), *Einführung in das Studium der romanischen Sprachwissenschaft* (1901), and the *Romanisches etymologisches Wörterbuch* (1911–20).

MEYERBEER, Giacomo, originally **Jakob Beer** (1791–1864) German operatic composer, born in Berlin, the son of a Jewish banker. He adopted the name Meyer from a benefactor, and reconstructed and Italianized the whole. At seven he played in public **Mozart**'s D-minor piano concerto, and at 15 was received into the house of Abt Vogler at Darmstadt, where **Weber** was his fellow-pupil. His earlier works were unsuccessful, but in Vienna he attracted attention as a pianist. After three years' study in Italy he produced operas in the new (**Rossini**'s) style, which were immediately well received. From 1824 to 1831 he lived mostly in Berlin. He next applied himself to a minute study of French opera. The result of this was seen in the production at Paris in 1831 of *Robert le Diable* (libretto by **Augustin Scribe**), whose dramatically new style brought unparalleled success across Europe. It was followed in 1836 by the even more successful *Huguenots*. Appointed kapellmeister at Berlin, he wrote the opera *Ein Feldlager in Schlesien*. His first comic opera, *L'Étoile du nord* (1854), was a success, as was *L'Africaine*, produced after his death at Paris. Praised extravagantly by **François Fétis** and others, he was severely concondemned by **Schumann** and **Wagner** on the ground that he made everything subsidiary to theatrical effect. His successive adoption of widely different styles bears this out. But even opponents concede the power and beauty of some of his pieces.

MEYERHOF, Otto Fritz (1884–1951) German physiologist, professor at Kiel (1918–24), director of the physiology department at the Kaiser Wilhelm Institute for Biology (1924–29), and professor at Heidelberg (1930–38). His work on the metabolism of muscles won him the 1922 Nobel prize for physiology or medicine (with **Archibald Vivian Hill**). Forced to leave Germany in 1938, he continued his work in France, and in 1940 escaped to America, where he was professor at Pennsylvania University.

MEYERHOLD, Vsevolod Emillevich (1874–c.1940) Russian actor and director. He joined the Moscow Art Theatre when it opened in 1898, but soon rejected the naturalism of **Stanislavsky** and from 1902 to 1905 he toured Russia with his own company, the Society of New Drama, both acting and directing. Later he founded his own studio in Moscow, where he developed his theories of a director's theatre, with the actor subservient to the director's vision. He became an ardent Bolshevik, and directed the first Soviet play, **Mayakovsky**'s *Mystery-Bouffe*, in 1918. In 1920 he was provided with the former Sohn Theatre in Moscow in which to work, (it was officially known as the Meyerhold Theatre from 1926). He directed several new and revolutionary works, including two more Mayakovsky plays, *The Red Bug* (1929) and *The Bath House* (1930). During the 1930s, when socialist Realism was decreed the official art form, he fell from the favour of the cultural authorities. His theatre was closed in 1938 and he was arrested, and disappeared in prison.

MEYNELL, Alice Christiana Gertrude, née **Thompson** (1847–1922) English essayist and poet, born in Barnes, London, the daughter of a scholar and a concert pianist, and sister of the battle-painter **Elizabeth Butler**. She spent her childhood on the Continent, and became a convert to Catholicism. Her volumes of essays include *The Rhythm of Life* (1893), *The Colour of Life* (1896) and *Hearts of Controversy* (1917). She published several collections of her own poems, starting in 1875 with *Preludes*, and anthologies of **Patmore**, of lyric poetry, and of poems for children. In 1877 she married Wilfrid Meynell (1852–1948), author and journalist, with whom she edited several periodicals.

MEYRINK, Gustav (1868–1932) German writer, born in Vienna. He translated **Dickens** and wrote satirical novels with a strong element of the fantastic and grotesque. Among the best known are *Der Golem* (1915), *Das grüne Gesicht* (1916) and *Walpurgisnacht* (1917).

MIALL, Edward (1809–81) English clergyman, born in Portsmouth. An Independent minister at Ware and Leicester,he was a lifelong advocate of disestablishment of the Church of England. In 1841 he founded the weekly *Nonconformist* newspaper, and tried to amalgamate with the Chartists (1842). He was MP for Rochdale (1852–57) and Bradford (1869–74).

MIASKOVSKY, Nikolai Yakovlevich (1881–1950) Russian composer, born in Novogeorgievsk, near Warsaw. Originally a military engineer, he turned to music in 1907. His teachers included **Liadov** and **Rimsky-Korsakov**. After army service (1914–21) he became an influential professor of composition at Moscow Conservatory. He composed 27 symphonies and other orchestral works, concertos for violin and cello, 13 string quartets and other chamber music, songs, nine piano sonatas and other works.

MICAH (735–665 BC) Old Testament minor prophet, a native of Moresheth Gath in SW Judah. He prophesied during the reigns of Jotham, Ahaz and Hezekiah, being a younger contemporary of **Isaiah**, Hosea and **Amos**.

MICHAEL (1921–) king of Rumania from 1927 to 1930, 1940 to 1947, son of **Carol II**. He first succeeded to the throne on the death of his grandfather Ferdinand I, his father having renounced his own claims in 1925. In 1930 he was supplanted by Carol, but was again made king in 1940 when the Germans gained control of Rumania. In 1944 he played a considerable part in the overthrow of the dictatorship of **Antonescu**. He announced the acceptance of the Allied peace terms, and declared war on Germany. His attempts after the war to establish a broader system of government were foiled by the progressive Communization of Rumania. In 1947 he was forced to abdicate and has since lived in exile.

MICHAEL ROMANOV (1596–1676) tsar of Russia from 1613, great-nephew of **Ivan IV 'the Terrible'**. He was the founder of the Romanov dynasty that would rule Russia until the revolution of 1917. He was elected by the boyars after a successful revolt against the Poles, when Russian was threatened with invasion from Sweden, and brought an end to the Time of Troubles that had plagued Russia since the death of **Boris Godunov** in 1605. He concluded peace with Sweden (1617) and Poland (1618). He left the business of government largely in the hands of his father, the patriarch Filaret (Fedor Nikitch Romanov), who reorganized the army and industry with the help of experts from abroad, and consolidated the system of serfdom.

MICHAEL VIII PALAEOLOGUS (c.1224–1282) Byzantine emperor from 1261. He was born into the Greek nobility and rose to be a successful general in the Empire of Nicaea. In 1258 he became a regent for, and soon co-ruler with, the eight-year-old emperor, John IV Lascaris, whom he later had blinded and imprisoned. In 1261 an opportunistic attack brought him control of Constantinople, thereby extinguishing the feeble empire of **Baldwin II**, and Michael was crowned sole emperor on August 15. This triumph, however, brought him the enmity of the Papacy and **Charles of Anjou** who aimed to re-establish the Latin Empire; Byzantium survived precariously, preserved only by Michael's diplomatic skill. The forced re-union of the Orthodox Church with Rome aroused great discontent among his subjects but warded off attacks until 1281; the hostile Pope **Martin IV** proclaimed a crusade against him, but Michael fomented discontent in Sicily, which was invaded by his allies the Aragonese, thereby ending the Angevin threat.

MICHAELIS, Johann David (1717–91) German Protestant theologian, born in Halle. Professor of philosophy (1746) and oriental languages (1750) at Göttingen, he pioneered historical criticism in biblical interpretation. He wrote an *Introduction to the New Testament* (1750), and *Autobiography* (1793).

MICHAELIS, Leonor (1875–1949) German-born American biochemist, born in Berlin. He was professor at Berlin (1908–22) and the Nagoya Medical School in Japan (1922–26), then went to the USA to Johns Hopkins (1926–29) and the Rockefeller Institute (1929–40). He made early deductions on enzyme action, and is especially known for the Michaelis-Menten equation on enzyme-catalyzed reactions.

MICHEL, Claude, pseud **Clodion** (1738–1814) French sculptor. Perhaps the greatest sculptor of the Napoleonic era, he is famous for his small terracotta figures of classical subjects such as fauns, satyrs and nymphs.

MICHEL, Francisque (1809–87) French antiquary, born in Lyon. Professor at Bordeaux from 1839, he earned a reputation by researches in Norman history, French *chansons*, argot and the Basques. He wrote *Les Écossais en France et les français en Écosse* (1862) and *A Critical Inquiry into the Scottish Language* (1882).

MICHEL, Louise (1830–1905) French anarchist, born in Vroncourt. A teacher in Paris, she spent many years preaching revolution, and suffered much imprisonment. She lived for ten years in London (1886–96), and returned to Paris to spread anarchist propaganda. She wrote *Mémoires* (1886) and various other works.

MICHELANGELI, Arturo Benedetti (1920–) Italian pianist, born in Brescia. He studied in Brescia and Milan, and won the International Music Competition in Geneva in 1939. After war service in the Italian air force, he acquired a legendary reputation as a virtuoso in the post-war years, enhanced by the rarity of his public performances. He is a noted teacher.

MICHELANGELO, properly **Michelagniolo di Lodovico Buonarroti** (1475–1564) Italian sculptor, painter and poet, born in Caprese in Tuscany, where Lodovico his father was mayor. Brought up in Florence, he was placed in the care of a stonemason and his wife at Settignano where Lodovico owned a small farm and marble quarry. At school he devoted his energies more to drawing than to his studies. Despite his father's opposition, in 1488 Michelangelo was bound to **Domenico Ghirlandaio** for three years. By this master he was recommended to **Lorenzo de' Medici** and entered the school for which the 'Magnifico' had gathered together a priceless collection of antiques (1490–92). To this period belong two interesting reliefs. In the *Battle of the Centaurs* the classical influence of Lorenzo's garden is strikingly apparent, though the straining muscles and contorted limbs, which mark the artist's mature work, are already visible. A marvellous contrast to the *Centaurs* is the *Madonna of the Steps*, conceived and executed in the spirit of **Donatello**. After Lorenzo's death in 1492, **Pietro II Medici**, his son and successor, is said to have treated the artist with scant courtesy; and Michelangelo fled to Bologna for a time, but in 1495 he returned to Florence. During this sojourn to his native city he fashioned the marble *Cupid*. An acquaintance persuaded him to bury the work to give it an antique look and then send it to Rome to be sold. The *Cupid* was bought by Cardinal San Giorgio who discovered the fraud but recognized the talent of the sculptor and summoned him to Rome in 1496. The influence of Rome and the antique is easily discernible in the *Bacchus*, now in the National Museum in Florence. The *Pieta* (1497), now in St Peter's, shows a realism wholly at variance with the antique ideal. For four years the sculptor remained in Rome and then, returning to Florence, fashioned his *David* out of a colossal block of marble. *David* is the Gothic treatment of a classical theme; in pose and composition there is a stately grandeur, a dignified solemnity. During the same period he painted the *Holy Family of the Tribune* and the *Madonna* in the National Gallery in London, proving that he had not wholly neglected the art of painting. His genius, however, was essentially plastic; he had far more interest in form than in colour. In 1503 **Julius II**, succeeding to the pontificate, summoned the painter-sculptor back to Rome. Michelangelo could as little brook opposition as the pope, and their dealings were continually interrupted by bitter quarrels and recriminations. The pope commissioned the sculptor to design his tomb, and for forty years Michelangelo clung to the hope that he would yet complete the great monument; but other demands were continually made upon his energy, and the sublime statue of **Moses** is the best fragment that is left to us of the tomb of Julius. Instead of being allowed to devote himself to the monument, he was ordered to decorate the ceiling of the Sistine Chapel with paintings. In vain he protested that sculpture was his profession, in vain he urged **Raphael**'s higher qualifications for the task; the pope was obdurate, and from 1508 to 1512 Michelangelo achieved a masterpiece of decorative design. Almost superhuman invention, miraculous variety of attitude and gesture, place this marvellous work among the greatest achievements of human energy. No sooner had he finished his work in the Sistine Chapel than he returned with eagerness to the tomb. But in 1513 Pope Julius II died, and the cardinals, his executors, demanded a more modest design. Then Pope **Leo X**, of the Medici family, commissioned Michelangelo to rebuild the façade of the church of San Lorenzo in Florence and enrich it with sculptured figures. The master reluctantly complied, and set out for Carrara to quarry marble; from 1514 to 1522 his artistic record is a blank, as the elaborate scheme was ultimately given up, though the sculptor remained in Florence. But in 1528 danger to his native city forced him to the science of fortification, and when in 1529 Florence was besieged Michelangelo was foremost in its defence. After the surrender he completed the monuments to Giuliano and Lorenzo de' Medici, which are among the greatest of his works. In 1533 yet another compact was entered into concerning Pope Julius's ill-fated sepulchre; whereupon he was once again commissioned to adorn the Sistine Chapel with frescoes. After some years he began in 1537 to paint *The Last Judgement*. In 1547 he was appointed architect of St Peter's, and devoted himself to the work with loyalty until his death. Michelangelo is by far the most brilliant representative of the Italian Renaissance. He was not only supreme in the arts of sculpture and painting—in which grandeur and sublimity rather than beauty was his aim—but was versed in all the learning of his age, and wrote copious poetry.

MICHELET, Jules (1798–1874) French historian, born in Paris. He lectured on history at the École Normale, assisted **Guizot** at the Sorbonne, worked at the Record Office, and was appointed professor of history at the Collège de France (1838–51). The greatest of his many historical works are his monumental *Histoire de France* (24 vols, 1833–67) and his *Histoire de la Révolution* (7 vols, 1847–53). By refusing to swear allegiance to **Louis Napoleon** he lost his appointments, and henceforth worked mostly in Brittany and the Riviera. His second wife, Adèle Mialaret, collaborated with him in several nature books, including *L'Oiseau* (1856), *L'Insecte* (1857) and *La Mer* (1861). In his last years he set himself to complete his great *Histoire*, but lived to finish only three volumes (1872–75).

MICHELL, John (1724–93) English geologist, born in Nottinghamshire. A fellow of Queen's College, Cambridge, and professor of geology (1762–64), he described a method of magnetization, founded the science of seismology, and is credited with the invention of the torsion balance. In 1767 he became rector of Thornhill, Yorkshire.

MICHELOZZI, Michelozzo di Bartolommeo (1396–1472) Italian architect and sculptor, born in Florence. He was associated with **Ghiberti** on his famous bronze doors for the baptistery there, and collaborated with **Donatello** in several major sculpture groups, including monuments to (the anti-pope) Pope **John XXIII** and Cardinal Brancacci (1427). He was court architect to **Cosimo de' Medici**, with whom he was in exile at Venice, where he designed a number of buildings. One of his finest works is the Ricardi Palace in Florence.

MICHELSON, Albert Abraham (1852–1931) German-born American physicist, born in Strelno (now Strzelno, Poland). Professor of physics at Chicago from 1892, he became in 1907 the first American scientist to win a Nobel prize. He invented an interferometer and an echelon grating, and did important work on the spectrum, but is chiefly remembered for the Michelson-**Morley** experiment to determine ether drift, the negative result of which set **Albert Einstein** on the road to the theory of relativity.

MICHIE, Donald (1923–) British specialist in artificial intelligence, born in Rangoon, Burma. Educated at Rugby School and Balliol College, Oxford, he served in World War II with the foreign office at Bletchley Park (1942–45), where work on the Colossus code-breaking project acquainted him with computer pioneers, such as **Alan Turing**, M H A Newman and T H Flowers. After a biological career in experimental genetics he developed the study of machine intelligence at Edinburgh University as director of experimental programming (1963–66) and professor of machine intelligence (1967–84). He is editor-in-chief of the *Machine Intelligence* series, of which the first 12 volumes span the period 1967–90. Since 1986 he has been chief scientist at the Turing Institute which he founded in Glasgow in 1984. In publications such as *The Creative Computer* (1984) and *On Machine Intelligence* he has argued that computer systems are able to generate new knowledge. His research contributions have primarily been to the study of machine learning.

MICHURIN, Ivan Vladimirovich (1855–1935) Russian horticulturist, born in Koslov (later Michurinsk). At his private orchard at Koslov, which became a state institution, he developed many new varieties of fruit and berries. His theory of cross-breeding ('Michurinism'), which postulated the idea that acquired characteristics were heritable, became State doctrine and influenced the pernicious anti-Mendelian doctrines of **Lysenko**.

MICKIEWICZ, Adam (1798–1855) Polish poet, born near Novogrodek in Lithuania (Minsk). He published his first poems in 1822, and as founder of a students' secret society was banished to Russia (1824–29); there he produced three epic poems, glowing with patriotism. After a journey through Germany, France and Italy his masterpiece, the epic *Pan Tadeusz*, appeared in 1834 ('Thaddeus', trans 1886)—a brilliant delineation of Lithuanian scenery, manners and beliefs. After teaching at Lausanne, he was appointed Slavonic professor at Paris in 1840, but was deprived of the post in 1843 for political utterances. He went to Italy to organize the Polish legion, but in 1852 **Louis Napoleon** appointed him a librarian in the Paris Arsenal. He died in Constantinople, where the emperor had sent him to raise a Polish legion for service against Russia. His body, first buried at Montmorency in France, was in 1890 laid beside **Kosciuzko**'s in Cracow Cathedral. Mickiewicz is the national poet of the Poles, and one of the greatest of all Slav poets.

MICKLE, William Julius (1735–88) Scottish poet, born in Langholm manse. Educated at Edinburgh High School, he failed as a brewer, and turned author in London. In 1765 he published a poem, *The Concubine* (or *Syr Martyn*), and in 1771–75 his version rather than translation of the *Lusiad* of **Camoens**. In 1779 he went to Lisbon as secretary to Commodore Johnstone, but his last years were spent in London. His ballad of *Cumnor Hall* (which suggested *Kenilworth* to Sir **Walter Scott**) is poor poetry, but 'There's nae luck aboot the hoose' assures his immortality.

MIDAS (8th century BC) king of Phrygia. He is mentioned in Assyrian records, and was the first non-Greek ruler to have made a dedication to the Oracle of Apollo at Delphi, thus anticipating **Gyges** of Lydia. Many stories were told about him (or about a namesake), notably that the god Dionysus gave him the power to turn to gold anything he touched, in gratitude for his hospitality to the satyr Silenus.

MIDDLETON, Conyers (1683–1750) English controversialist and clergyman, born in Richmond in Yorkshire. A fellow of Trinity College, Cambridge, he became librarian to Cambridge University (1719), and rector of Hascombe in Surrey. He fiercely attacked Roman Catholic ritual in his *Letter from Rome, showing an exact Conformity between Popery and Paganism* (1729). He next assailed the orthodox **Daniel Waterland**, giving up literal inspiration and the historical truth of the Old Testament. In 1747–48 he published his *Introductory Discourse* and the *Free Inquiry* into the miraculous powers claimed for the post-Apostolic church. He also published a *Life of Cicero* (1741), which was was largely borrowed from William Bellenden.

MIDDLETON, Thomas (c.1570–1627) English dramatist. He is first mentioned in **Henslowe**'s *Diary* in 1602, when he was engaged with **Munday**, **Drayton** and **Webster** on a lost play, *Cæsar's Fall*. First on the list of his printed plays is *Blurt, Master Constable* (1602), a light, fanciful comedy. Two interesting tracts, *Father Hubbard's Tale* and *The Black Book*, exposing London rogues, were published in 1604, to which year belongs the first part of *The Honest Whore* (mainly written by **Dekker**, partly by Middleton). *The Phœnix* and *Michaelmas Term* (1607) are lively comedies; even more diverting is *A Trick to Catch the Old One* (1608); and *A Mad World, My Masters*, from which **Aphra Behn** pilfered freely in *The City Heiress*, is singularly adroit. *The Roaring Girl* (1611; written with Dekker) idealizes the character of a noted cutpurse and virago.

Middleton was repeatedly employed to write the Lord Mayor's pageant. *A Chaste Maid in Cheapside* was probably produced in 1613, as was *No Wit, No Help like a Woman's*. *A Fair Quarrel* (1617) and *The World Lost at Tennis* (1620) were written in conjunction with **William Rowley**, as were probably *More Dissemblers Besides Women* (?1622) and *The Mayor of Quinborough*. In 1620 Middleton was appointed city chronologer, and a MS Chronicle by him was extant in the 18th century. The delightful comedy, *The Old Law*, first published in 1656, is mainly the work of Rowley, with something by Middleton, all revised by **Massinger**. In the three posthumously-published plays, *The Changeling*, *The Spanish Gypsy* and *Women Beware Women*, Middleton's genius is seen at its highest. Rowley had a share in the first two and probably in the third. A very curious and skilful play is *A Game at Chess*, acted in 1624. *The Widow*, published in 1652, was mainly by Middleton. *Anything for a Quiet Life* (*c*. 1619) may have been revised by **Shirley**. Middleton was concerned in the authorship of some of the plays included in the works of **Beaumont** and **Fletcher**.

MIDGLEY, Thomas, Jr (1889–1944) American engineer and inventor, born in Beaver Falls, Pennsylvania. He studied engineering at Cornell. During World War I, on the staff of Dayton (Ohio) Engineering Laboratories (1916–23), he worked on the problem of 'knocking' in petrol engines, and by 1921 found tetra-ethyl lead to be effective as an additive to petrol, used with 1,2-dibromoethane to reduce lead oxide deposits in the engine. Since 1980 there has been rising concern that the emitted lead produces a health hazard. As president of Ethyl Corporation from 1923, he also introduced Freon 12 as a non-toxic non-inflammable agent for domestic refrigerators. Again there is concern that chlorofluorocarbons (CFCs), such as Freon, cause destruction of the ozone layer of the upper atmosphere with damaging climatic and other effects as a result of the increased passage of ultraviolet radiation. He also devised the octane number method of rating petrol quality. He died by accidental strangulation through the failure of a harness he used to help him rise in the morning, needed because he was a polio victim.

MIDLER, Bette (1945–) American comedienne and actress, born in Honolulu, Hawaii. After studying drama at the University of Hawaii she was hired as an extra in the film *Hawaii* (1966). Moving to New York, she made her stage début in *Miss Nefertiti Regrets* (1966). She then developed a popular nightclub act as a chanteuse and purveyor of outrageously bawdy comic routines. Her album *The Divine Miss M* (1974) won her a Grammy Award as Best New Artist, and the same year she received a Tony Award for her record-breaking Broadway show. Her dramatic performance in the film *The Rose* (1979) earned her an Academy Award nomination and she has continued to excel in all media, writing a modest memoir *A View from A Broad* (1980) and enjoying considerable commercial success in a string of film farces including *Outrageous Fortune* (1987) and *Big Business* (1988).

MIERIS, Frans van (1635–81) Dutch painter, born in Leiden. He excelled in small-scale, exquisitely finished genre paintings in the style of Dou and Ter Borch. His sons Jan (1660–90) and Willem (1662–1747) followed his example. Willem's son Frans (1689–1773) was less successful as a painter, but made his name as a writer of antiquarian works.

MIES VAN DER ROHE, Ludwig (1886–1969) German-born American architect, born in Aachen. A pioneer of glass skyscrapers, in pre-war Berlin he designed high-rise flats for the Weissenhof Exhibition in 1927, and the German Pavilion for the Barcelona International Exposition (1929). He also designed tubular-steel furniture, particularly the 'Barcelona chair'. He was director of the Bauhaus in Dessau (1930–33), and emigrated to the USA in 1937, where he became professor of architecture at the Illinois Institute of Technology in Chicago. There he designed two glass apartment towers on Lake Shore Drive, and the Seagram Building in New York (1956–58). He also designed the Public Library in Washington, DC (1967), and two art galleries in Berlin (1968).

MIFSUD BONNICI, Carmelo (1933–) Maltese politician. A graduate of Malta University, he lectured in law at University College London and then in Malta. In 1969 he became legal consultant to the General Workers' Union and then moved more openly into politics, becoming deputy leader of the Malta Labour party (MLP) in 1980, under **Dom Mintoff**, and then leader, and prime minister, on Mintoff's retirement in 1984. In the 1987 general election the MLP won 34 seats to the Nationalist party's 31, but because they had won a larger share of the vote the Nationalists were, under the terms of the constitution, awarded four more seats, and Mifsud Bonnici went out of office.

MIGNARD, Pierre (1612–95) French painter, born in Troyes. After studying under **Simon Vouet** he worked in Rome from 1636 to 1657, where he developed a classicizing style much influenced by **Poussin**. He was summoned to Paris by **Louis XIV** and became a successful court portraitist and favourite of the king. Upon the death of his great rival **Charles Le Brun**, the king appointed him *premier peintre* as well as director and chancellor of the Académie. His brother, Nicolas (1608–68) was also a painter.

MIGNAULT, Pierre-Basile (1854–1945) Canadian text-writer and judge. He taught civil law at McGill University, Montreal, before serving as a judge (1918–29) of the Supreme Court of Canada. He wrote extensively, and his *Le droit civil canadien* (9 vols, 1895–1916), is still an important work. By his writings and judgments he stoutly defended the integrity and distinction of Quebec civil law in the Canadian Supreme Court.

MIGNE, Jacques Paul (1800–75) French churchman and writer, born in St Flour. He was ordained in 1824. A disagreement with his bishop drove him to Paris in 1833, where he started the Catholic *L'Univers*. In 1838 he sold the paper, and soon after set up a great publishing house at Petit Montrouge near Paris, which gave to the world *Scripturae Sacrae Cursus* and *Theologiae Cursus* (each 28 vols, 1840–45), *Collection des orateurs sacrés* (100 vols, 1846–48), *Patrologiae Cursus* (383 vols, 1844 *et seq*), and *Encyclopédie théologique* (171 vols, 1844–66). The archbishop of Paris, thinking that the undertaking had become a commercial speculation, forbade it to be continued, and when Migne resisted, suspended him. A great fire put an end to the work in 1868.

MIGNET, François Auguste Marie (1796–1884) French historian, born in Aix en Provence. He studied law there with **Thiers**. In 1821 he went to Paris, wrote for the *Courrier français*, and lectured on modern history. His *Histoire de la révolution française* (1824) was the first, a sane and luminous summary. With Thiers he signed the famous protest of the journalists in 1830, and after the Revolution became keeper of the archives at the foreign office (till 1848). In 1833 he explored the Simancas Archives. Elected to the Academy of Moral Sciences at its foundation in 1832, he succeeded **Auguste Comte** as its permanent secretary in 1837, and was elected to fill **Raynouard**'s chair among the Forty in 1836. His works include *La Succession* *d'Espagne sous Louis XIV* (1836–42), *Antonio Perez et Philippe II* (1845), *Franklin* (1848), *Marie Stuart* (1851), *Charles-Quint* (1854), *Éloges historiques* (1843–64–77), and *François I et Charles V* (1875).

MIGUEL, properly **Miguel, Maria Evaristo de Brangança** (1802–66) king of Portugal, born in Lisbon, the third son of King John VI. He plotted (1824) to overthrow the constitutional form of government granted by his father; but was banished with his mother, his chief abettor. On John's death in 1826 the throne devolved upon Miguel's elder brother, **Pedro I**, emperor of Brazil; he, however, resigned it in favour of his daughter, Maria de Gloria, making Miguel regent; but Miguel summoned a *Cortés*, which proclaimed him king in 1828. In 1832 Pedro captured Oporto and Lisbon, and **Charles Napier** destroyed Miguel's fleet off Cape St Vincent (1833). Next year Maria was restored, and Miguel withdrew to Italy.

MIHAILOVICH, Draza (1893–1946) Serbian soldier. He distinguished himself in World War I, after which he rose to the rank of colonel in the Yugoslav army. In 1941 when Germany occupied Yugoslavia, he remained in the mountains and organized resistance, forming groups called Chetniks to wage guerrilla warfare. He became minister of war for the Yugoslavian goverment in exile (1943). When **Tito**'s Communist Partisans' resistance developed, Mihailovich allied himself with the Germans and then with the Italians in order to fight the Communists. After the war he was captured and executed by the Tito government for collaboration with the occupying powers.

MIKAN, George Lawrence (1924–) American professional basketball player, born in Joliet, Illinois. He set the stage for the big men who now dominate the sport. Six foot ten inches tall, he graduated from Chicago University in 1946. He played with Minneapolis in the National Basketball Association from 1948 to 1956, winning the championship five times. He led the NBA in points-scoring three times. A trend-setter, he helped launch basketball into a new era.

MIKLOSIC, Franz Xavier von (1813–91) Slavonic scholar, born in Luttenberg. He studied at Graz, worked in the Imperial library at Vienna, and was professor of Slavonic at the University of Vienna (1850–85). His numerous works include *Lexicon Linguae Palaeoslovenicae* (1850), *Vergleichende slawische Grammatik* (1852–74), works on the Gypsies (1872–80) and the great *Etymologica Slav Dictionary* (1886).

MIKOLAJCIK, Stanislaw (1901–67) Polish politician, born, a miner's son, in Westphalia. He became leader of the Peasant party in Poland in 1937. From 1940 to 1943 he held office in the exiled Polish government in London, and in 1943–44 was prime minister. After the German defeat he became deputy premier in the new coalition government in Warsaw, but fled to the USA when the Communists seized power in 1947.

MIKOYAN, Anastas Ivanovich (1895–1978) Soviet politician, brother of **Artem Ivanovich Mikoyan**, born in Armenia, of poor parents, studied theology and became a fanatical revolutionary. Taken prisoner in the fighting at Baku, he escaped and made his way to Moscow, where he met **Lenin** and **Stalin**. A member of the Central Committee in 1922, he helped Stalin against **Trotsky**, and in 1926 became minister of trade, in which capacity he did much to improve Soviet standards of living. He showed himself willing to learn from the West, eg, in the manufacture of canned goods and throughout the food industry generally. While other politicians came and went, Mikoyan's genius for survival enabled him to become a first vice-chairman of the council of ministers (1955–64), and president of the presidium of the Supreme Soviet from 1964.

MIKOYAN, Artem Ivanovich (1905–70) Soviet aircraft designer, born in Sanain, Armenia, brother of **Anastas Ivanovich Mikoyan**. He worked as a metal-worker in Rostov-on-Don and Moscow and served in the Red Army before graduating from the NE Zhukovsky Air Force Academy (1936). His career began as an engineer at the N N Polikarpov Design Bureau where he worked on refinements to the I-16 monoplane and the development of the I-153 ('Seagull') fighter. He was best known for the fighter aircraft produced by the design bureau he headed with **Mikhail Iosifovich Gurevich**, the MiG (M̄ikoyan 'ī' (= 'and') Ḡurevich) series. The most notable of this series were: the MiG-1 (1940), a single-engine fighter and its refinement, the MiG-3 (1941), both used in World War II; the MiG-9 (1946), one of the Soviet Union's first jet fighters; the MiG-15 (1947), single-turbojet fighter, and the MiG-17, which were deployed in the Korean War; the MiG-19 (1955) supersonic twin-turbojet all-weather fighter-interceptor; the MiG-21 (1967) single-turbojet Mach 2 fighter-interceptor, on which design the world's first supersonic passenger aircraft, the Tu-144, was based; and the MiG-25 (1971) single-turbojet reconnaissance fighter.

MIKULIC, Branko (1928–) Yugoslav politician, born in Gornji Vakuf, in Bosnia and Herzegovina. He participated in the national liberation struggle from 1943 and joined the League of Communists in 1945. After World War II he held party posts in his home republic and became party boss in 1965, premier in 1967 and federal prime minister in 1986. In the light of mounting economic difficulties and republic rivalries he introduced a package of radical 'market socialist' reforms to encourage private enterprise and foreign inward investment, but an attempt to freeze wages provoked a wave of industrial unrest and an unprecedented parliamentary 'no-confidence' challenge. He stepped down as prime minister in 1988.

MILES, Bernard, Baron (1907–) English actor, stage director and founder of the Mermaid Theatre, London, born in Uxbridge. He made his London début as an actor in 1930, and worked in several repertory theatres as a designer, scene-painter, carpenter, property-manager and character actor before touring with the Old Vic company as Iago in *Othello* in 1941. He rejoined the company in 1947–48. In 1950, he went on to the music-hall stage, including the London Palladium. In 1951 he founded the Mermaid Theatre as a small private theatre in the grounds of his home at St John's Wood, London. In 1953, the Mermaid was re-erected in the City of London, and in 1959 a permanent, professional Mermaid Theatre, financed by public subscription, was built at Puddle Dock, Blackfriars.

MILGRAM, Stanley (1933–84) American psychologist, born in New York City. He was educated at Harvard, spending 1959–60 at the Institute for Advanced Study at Princeton. He was professor at Yale (1960–63) and later became professor of psychology at the City University of New York (1967–84). Like many other postwar social psychologists, he became concerned to understand how apparently ordinary people in Nazi Germany had committed the atrocities of the Holocaust against the Jews and other minority groups. In his most famous research programme, published in *Obedience to Authority: An Experimental View* (1974), he set out to examine what factors would influence the tendency of ordinary people to 'obey orders' in an artificial situation where they were given to believe (wrongly) that they were administering electric shocks to other experimental subjects. The most striking result of this controversial study was that the vast majority of people were apparently prepared to give huge shocks in the cause of 'science' when requested to do so by an authority figure (an apparently respectable academic scientist).

MILHAUD, Darius (1892–1974) French composer, born in Aix-en-Provence. He studied under **Widor** and **D'Indy**, and from 1917 to 1918 was attached to the French Embassy at Rio de Janeiro. There he met the playwright **Paul Claudel**, with whom he frequently collaborated, as on the opera *Christopher Columbus*. For a time he was a member of *Les Six*. In 1940 he went to the USA, where he was professor of music at Mills College, California (1940–47), and afterwards lived both in France and America. He was one of the most prolific of modern composers, his work including several operas, much incidental music for plays, ballets (including the jazz ballet *La Création du monde*), symphonies and orchestral, choral and chamber works. He wrote an autobiography, *Notes without Music* (trans 1952).

MILL, James (1773–1836) Scottish philosopher, historian and economist, father of **John Stuart Mill**, born a shoemaker's son in Logiepert, near Montrose. He studied for the ministry at Edinburgh and was ordained in 1798, but moved in 1802 to London and supported himself through journalism and editorial work for periodicals such as the *Edinburgh Review* and *St James's Chronicle*. He became a disciple and friend of **Jeremy Bentham**, an enthusiastic proponent of utilitarianism, and a prominent member of the circle of 'Philosophical Radicals' which included **George Grote**, **David Ricardo**, **John Austin** and in due course his son John Stuart Mill. The group was active in social and educational causes and James Mill took a leading part in the founding of University College London, in 1825. His first major publication was the *History of British India* (1817–18) on which he had worked for 11 years and which secured him a permanent position with the East India Co., where he rose to become head of the Examiner's Office in 1830. He continued writing utilitarian essays for publications like the *Westminster Review* and the *Encyclopaedia Britannica*, and published three further important books: *Elements of Political Economy* (1821), which derived from **Ricardo** and was an important influence on **Marx**; *Analysis of the Phenomenon of the Human Mind* (1829), his main philosophical work, which provides a psychological basis for utilitarianism; and *A Fragment on MacKintosh* (1835), which argues that morality is based on utility.

MILL, John (1645–1707) English New Testament critic, born in Shap in Westmorland. He entered Queen's College, Oxford, as servitor in 1661 and became fellow and tutor there, rector of Blechingdon, Oxfordshire (1681), principal of St Edmund's Hall (1685), and prebendary of Canterbury (1704). His *Novum Testamentum Graecum*, the labour of 30 years, sponsored by Dr **John Fell**, appeared a fortnight before his death.

MILL, John Stuart (1806–73) English philosopher and social reformer, one of the major intellectual figures of the 19th century and a leading exponent of the British empiricist and utilitarian traditions. Born in London, son of the Scottish philosopher **James Mill**, his father was wholly responsible for his remarkable and rigorous education. He was taught Greek at the age of 3, Latin and arithmetic at 8, logic at 12, and political economy at 13. He was shielded from association with other boys of his age and his only recreation was a daily walk with his father, who meanwhile conducted oral examinations. After a visit to France in 1820 he broadened his studies into history, law and philosophy and in 1823 began a career under his father at the India Office, where he advanced to become head of his department and retired in 1858 on the dissolution of the East India Co. This forced education gave him an advantage, as he put it, of a quarter of a century over his contemporaries, and he began enthusiastically to fulfil the ambitions his father had designed for him of becoming leader and prophet of the Benthamite utilitarian movement. He began publishing in the newspaper *The Traveller* in 1822; he helped form the Utilitarian Society, which met for reading and discussion in **Jeremy Bentham**'s house (1823–26); he was a major contributor to the *Westminster Review* and a regular performer in the London Debating Society; he corresponded with **Carlyle** and met **Maurice** and **Sterling**; he espoused Malthusian doctrines and was arrested in 1824 for distributing birth control literature to the poor in London. But in 1826 he underwent a mental crisis which he describes in his famous *Autobiography* (1873) and which was the unsurprising consequence of his precocious but emotionally restricted development. For a while he was in 'a dull state of nerves', but the depression passed and he recovered, with his sympathies broadened and his intellectual position importantly modified, as his reviews of **Tennyson** (1835), **Carlyle** (1837), **Bentham** (1838) and **Coleridge** (1840) indicate. He effectively 'humanized' utilitarianism by recognizing differences in the quality as well as the quantity of pleasures and by thus restoring the importance of cultural and idealistic values. He published his major work, *A System of Logic*, in 1843; it ran through many editions, established his philosophical reputation, and greatly influenced **Venn**, **John Neville Keynes**, **Frege** and **Bertrand Russell**, particularly in its treatment of induction. In 1830 he had met Harriet Taylor, bluestocking wife of a wealthy London merchant, and after a long, intense but apparently chaste romance he married her in 1851, two years after her husband's death. She took an active interest in his writing and though he undoubtedly exaggerated her role in the *Autobiography*, she helped him draft the brilliant essay *On Liberty* (1859), the most popular of all his works, which eloquently defines and defends the freedoms of the individual against social and political control. Harriet died in 1858, but her views on the marriage contract and the status of women helped inspire *The Subjection of Women* (1869), which provoked great antagonism. His other main works include *Principles of Political Economy* (1848), *Considerations on Representative Government* (1861), *Utilitarianism* (1863), *Examination of Sir William Hamilton's Philosophy* (1865), *Auguste Comte and Positivism* (1873) and *Three Essays on Religion* (1874). He remained politically active in later life and was elected to Parliament in 1865, campaigning for women's suffrage and generally supporting the Advanced Liberals. In 1872 he became godfather, 'in a secular sense', to Lord Amberley's second son, **Bertrand Russell**. His last years were spent in France and he died in Avignon.

MILLAIS, Sir John Everett (1829–96) English painter, born in Southampton. He became the youngest ever student at the Royal Academy in 1840, and in 1846 exhibited his *Pizarro Seizing the Inca of Peru*. Along with **Dante Gabriel Rossetti** and **Holman Hunt** he was a founder member of the Pre-Raphaelite Brotherhood, and was markedly influenced by them and by **Ruskin**. His first Pre-Raphaelite picture, the banquet scene from the *Isabella* of **Keats**, figured in the Academy in 1849, where it was followed in 1850 by *Christ in the House of His Parents*, which met the full force of the anti-Pre-Raphaelite reaction. The exquisite

Gambler's Wife (1869) and *The Boyhood of Raleigh* (1870) mark the transition of his art into its final phase, displaying brilliant and effective colouring, effortless power of brushwork, and delicacy of flesh-painting. The interest and value of his later works, largely portraits, lie mainly in their splendid technical qualities. A late painting, *Bubbles* (1886), achieved huge popularity. Millais executed a few etchings, and his illustrations in *Good Words*, *Once a Week*, *The Cornhill*, etc (1857–64) place him in the very first rank of woodcut designers. He was buried in St Paul's Cathedral.

MILLAR, John (1735–1801) Scottish jurist, born in Shotts, Lanarkshire. Educated at Hamilton Grammar School and Glasgow University, he was professor of law at Glasgow. A friend of **Adam Smith** and Lord **Kames**, he had a great reputation as a law teacher and a leading liberal. His main works are the *Origin of the Distinction of Ranks* (1771), a pioneer work on sociology; and *An Historical View of the English Government* (1787), the first constitutional history of Britain or England, and a pioneering work with many new and original insights. Both books were widely influential. An ardent Whig, he was regarded at the time as a radical, even a near-revolutionary.

MILLAY, Edna St Vincent (1892–1950) American poet, born in Rockland, Maine. Her first poem was published when she was a student at Vassar College. Moving into Greenwich Village, then at its height as a meeting place for artists and writers, she published *A Few Figs from Thistles* (1920). In 1923 came *The Harp Weaver and Other Poems*, for which she was awarded a Pulitzer prize. During her lifetime she was a feminist and though latterly dismissed as arrogant, egotisic and whimsical, the admiration of writers like **Maya Angelou** has caused her to be re-evaluated and there has been renewed interest in her sonorous verse.

MILLE, De See **DE MILLE**

MILLER, Arthur (1915–) American playwright, born in New York City. His *Death of a Salesman* (1949) won the Pulitzer prize and brought him international recognition, though *All My Sons* (1947) had already placed him in the front rank of American dramatists. *The Crucible* (1953) is probably, to date, his most lasting work, since its theme, the persecution of the Salem witches equated with contemporary political persecution, stands out of time. Other works include *A View from the Bridge* (1955), the film script of *The Misfits* (1960), *After the Fall* (1963), *Incident at Vichy* (1964), *The Creation of the World and Other Business* (1972), and *Playing for Time* (1981). His marriage to **Marilyn Monroe**, from whom he was divorced in 1961, and his brush with the authorities over early Communist sympathies, brought him considerable publicity. Recent plays include *Danger: Memory!* (1987). During the 1980s, almost all of Miller's plays have been given major British revivals, including a definitive account of *A View From The Bridge*, starring **Michael Gambon** and directed by **Alan Ayckbourn** at the National Theatre in 1987. Without doubt, Miller is now more revived, and consequently more popular, in Britain than in America, where the apparent spurning of serious work by Broadway has made it difficult even for the voice of Miller to be heard in his native land. In 1989, an Arthur Miller Centre for American Studies opened at the University of East Anglia.

MILLER, (Alton) Glenn (1904–44) American trombonist and bandleader, born in Clarinda, Iowa, and educated at University of Colorado. Before completing his studies, he joined the Ben Pollack Band in 1924, moving to New York in 1928 and working as a freelance musician and arranger. From 1937, he led a succession of popular dance orchestras and joined the US Army Air Force in 1942, forming another orchestra—the Glenn Miller Army Air Force Band—to entertain the troops. While they were stationed in Europe, Miller was a passenger in a small aircraft lost without trace over the English Channel. His music has continued to be performed since his death by orchestras rehearsed in his distinctive style.

MILLER, Henry Valentine (1891–1980) American writer, born in New York. His parents were German-Americans and he was brought up in Brooklyn. He rebelled against a conventional upbringing and a traditional career pattern, and after two months at the City College in 1909 took a job with a cement company. With money from his father which was intended to finance him through Cornell, he travelled in the south west and Alaska. When he returned home he went to work in his father's tailor shop but left after trying to unionize the workforce. In 1920 he became employment manager for the Western Union Telegraph Co; in 1927 he ran a speakeasy in Greenwich Village. But in 1930 he moved to France for nine years during which time he published *Tropic of Cancer* (1934) and *Tropic of Capricorn* (1938), as well as *Black Spring* (1936). He returned to the USA in 1940 but travelled extensively both at home and abroad before settling in Big Sur, California. He has been described as a folk hero, an ardent Bohemian whose life was his work. Though much of his fiction is autobiographical and explicitly sexual, he regarded his childhood as seminal: 'From five to ten were the most important years of my life; I lived in the street and acquired the typical American gangster spirit'. This undoubtedly helped him overcome many impecunious years and rebuffs from state censors. (American editions of the *Tropics* were not published until 1961 and 1962 respectively.) In his time, however, he became one of the most read American authors, solipsistic, surrealistic and blackly comic, empathizing with the outcast; prostitutes, hobos and artists. Important books are *The Colossus of Maroussi* (1941), *The Air-Conditioned Nightmare* (1945), and *The Rosy Crucifixion* trilogy: *Sexus* (1949), *Plexus* (1953) and *Nexus* (1960). A guru of the sexually liberated 1960s, he fell foul of feminist critics in the 1970s.

MILLER, Hugh (1802–56) Scottish geologist and man of letters, born in Cromarty. Having lost his father at sea at the age of 5, he had a rebellious school career in various schools, and was apprenticed as a stonemason at 16. Working with stone for the next 17 years, he developed an interest in fossils, and he devoted the winter months to reading, writing and natural history; in 1829 he published *Poems written in the Leisure Hours of a Journeyman Mason*, followed by *Scenes and Legends of the North of Scotland* (1835). He contributed to **John Mackay Wilson**'s *Tales of the Borders* (1834–40), and to *Chambers's Journal*. He married the daughter of an Inverness businessman and became a bank acountant for a time (1834–39), but becoming involved in the controversy over church appointments that led to the Disruption of the Church of Scotland (1843) with a ferocious open *Letter to Lord Brougham* (1839), he was invited to Edinburgh to start *The Witness*, the newspaper of the anti-patronage 'Evangelicals' within the Church of Scotland, and became the outstanding journalist of the Disruption. At the same time he wrote a series of geological articles in *The Witness*, later collected as *The Old Red Sandstone* (1841). In 1845 he visited England for the first time and wrote *First Impressions of England* (1847); his *My Schools and Schoolmasters* (1854), is the story of his youth. A pioneer of popular science books, he combated the Darwinian evolution theory with

Footprints of the Creator (1850), *The Testimony of the Rocks* (1857), and *Sketchbook of Popular Geology* (published posthumously, 1859). Worn out by illness and overwork, he shot himself. The old thatched cottage at Cromarty in which he was born is now a museum run by the National Trust for Scotland.

MILLER, Joaquin, pen-name of **Cincinnatus Heine Miller** (1839–1913) American poet, born in Liberty, Indiana. He became a miner in California, and fought in the Indian wars. After practising law in Oregon, he edited a paper suppressed for showing Confederate sympathies. In 1866–70 he was a county judge in Oregon, after a spell as a Washington journalist, in 1877 he settled in California as a fruitgrower. His poems include *Songs of the Sierras* (1871); his prose works, *The Danites in the Sierras* (1881). He also wrote a successful play, *The Danites*. He wrote his autobiography in *My Life among the Modocs* (1873) and *My Own Story* (new ed 1891).

MILLER, Jonathan Wolfe (1934–) English stage director and author, born in London. He qualified as a doctor at Cambridge University, and co-authored and performed in the revue, *Beyond the Fringe*, at the 1960 Edinburgh Festival. In 1962, he made his directorial début with *Under Plain Cover*, a play by **John Osborne**, at the Royal Court Theatre. From 1964 to 1965 he was editor and presenter of the BBC Television arts programme, *Monitor*. He has been responsible for many memorable productions, and from 1974 has also specialized in opera productions for the English National Opera and other major companies. He has written and presented two BBC television series related to the world of medicine, *The Body in Question* (1977) and *States of Mind* (1982). In 1985, he became Research Fellow in Neuropsychology at Sussex University. One of the most original of directors, he has written several books, including *Subsequent Performances* (1986), an illuminating and invigorating discussion of his views on the theatre and directing plays and operas.

MILLER, Keith Ross (1919–) Australian cricketer, born in Melbourne. In the great **Don Bradman** Test side of 1948, he established himself as the world's leading all-rounder of the time. He scored 2598 runs in 55 Test matches including seven centuries, and took 170 wickets. He could generate astonishing pace off a short run-up and his batting was as cavalier as that of **Denis Compton**.

MILLER, Patrick (1731–1815) Scottish inventor, and pioneer of early experimental steamboats. In 1788 he launched a steamboat, with an engine by **William Symington**, on the loch at his estate at Dalswinton, near Dumfries.

MILLER, Stanley Lloyd (1930–) American chemist, born in Oakland, California. He studied at California University and taught there from 1960. His most familiar work was done in Chicago in 1953, and concerns the possible origin of life on earth. He passed electric discharges (similar to miniature thunderstorms) through a mixture of those gases which probably formed the early planetary atmosphere. After some days, analysis showed the presence of some typical organic substances, including amino acids and urea. This result is certainly suggestive, although the probable path from these chemicals to a living system is still very unclear.

MILLER, William (1781–1849) American religious leader, born in Pittsfield, Massachusetts. A New York farmer, he believed that the Second Coming of Christ was imminent, and founded the religious sect of Second Adventists or Millerites. When the event did not materialize in 1843 or 1844 his followers organized the Seventh Day Adventist church in 1863.

MILLER, William (1810–72) Scottish poet, born in Glasgow. He was a woodturner by profession, having relinquished a medical career through ill-health. He is now remembered only as the author of *Wee Willie Winkie*, one of his numerous dialect poems about children and childhood.

MILLERAND, Alexandre (1859–1943) French statesman, born in Paris. He edited socialist papers, entered parliament 1885, was minister of commerce 1899–1902, of works 1909–10, of war 1912–13, when he resigned over a personal incident but was reinstated until 1915, when he resigned on complaints of deficiency of supplies. His chief critic, **Clemenceau**, later appointed him commissaire général in Alsace-Lorraine 1919. As prime minister (1920), he formed a coalition (Bloc National) and gave support to the Poles during the Russian invasion of 1920. He became president in 1920 and resigned in 1924 in face of opposition from *cartel des gauches* under **Herriot**. He later entered the senate and organized the opposition to the *cartel*.

MILLES, Carl Vilhelm Emil (1875–1955) Swedish-born American sculptor, born near Uppsala. He executed numerous monumental works, such as the **Sten Sture** monument near Uppsala and the **Gustav I Vasa** statue, and was especially renowned as a designer of fountains. Much of his work is in Sweden and the USA, where he settled in 1931, noteworthy examples being *Wedding of the Rivers* (1940) in St Louis, and *St Martin of Tours* (1955) in Kansas City, his last work.

MILLET, Jean François (1814–75) French painter, born in Grouchy near Gréville. He worked on the farm with his father, a peasant, but, showing a talent for art, he was placed under a painter at Cherbourg in 1832. In 1837 he went to Paris and worked under **Delaroche** achieving recognition in 1844 at the Salon. The 1848 Revolution and poverty drove him from Paris, and he settled with his wife and children at Barbizon, near the forest of Fontainebleau, living much like the peasants around him, and painting the rustic life of France with sympathetic power. His famous *Sower* was completed in 1850. His *Peasants Grafting* (1855) was followed by *The Gleaners* (1857), *The Angelus* (1859) and other masterpieces. He also produced many charcoal drawings of high quality, and etched a few plates. He received little public notice, and was never well off, but after the Great Exhibition of 1867 at Paris, in which nine of his best works were on show, his merit came to be recognized, and he was awarded the *Légion d'honneur*.

MILLIGAN, Spike (Terence Alan) (1918–) English humorist, born in Ahmadnagar, India. A singer and trumpeter before doing war service, he made his radio début in *Opportunity Knocks* (1949) and, along with **Peter Sellers**, **Harry Secombe** and **Michael Bentine**, co-wrote and performed in *The Goon Show* (1951–59). His unique perspective on the world, allied to an irrepressible sense of the ridiculous and the surreal, has been expressed in all the artistic media and has left an indelible influence on British humour. On stage, he has appeared in *Treasure Island* (1961,1973,1974,1975) and *The Bed-Sitting Room* (1963,1967) which he also co-wrote. Aside from numerous television series and small roles in feature films, he has published a variety of children's books, poetry, autobiography and comic novels including *Puckoon* (1963), *Adolf Hitler, My Part in His Downfall* (1971), *Where Have All the Bullets Gone?* (1985) and *The Looney: An Irish Fantasy* (1987).

MILLIKAN, Robert Andrews (1868–1953) American physicist, born in Illinois. He studied at Columbia University, Oberlin College, Berlin, and Göttingen, and taught physics at Chicago University from 1896 (as professor from 1910) till 1921 when he became head of Pasadena Institute of Technology. He determined the charge on the electron, for which he was awarded the Nobel prize for physics in 1923, and did important work on cosmic rays (1925), which he explained as due to atom-building.

MILLS, Charles Wright (1916–62) American sociologist, born in Waco, Texas. Educated at Texas A and M, and the universities of Texas and Wisconsin, he taught at Wisconsin and Maryland, and was professor at Columbia from 1946 to 1962. One of the most controversial figures in American social science, he was strongly critical of mainstream American sociology, which he felt did not fulfil the social responsibility that he saw as being the duty of social science, and he was something of an outcast from academic life. But his writings attracted a large popular audience, and he had an important influence on the American New Left. His books include *White Collar* (1951), *The Power Elite* (1956), *The Sociological Imagination* (1959), *Images of Man* (1960) and *The Marxists* (1962).

MILLS, Sir John Lewis Ernest Watts (1908–) English actor, born in Felixstowe, Suffolk. An early interest in amateur dramatics led to his London stage début as a chorus boy in *The Five O'Clock Revue* (1927). More prestigious theatre work followed in *Cavalcade* (1931) and *Words and Music* (1932) before his film début in *The Midshipmaid* (1932). Of slight build, he established himself as one of the hardest-working mainstays of the British film industry, portraying dependable servicemen and stiff upper-lip heroes in such films as *In Which We Serve* (1942), *Scott of the Antarctic* (1948) and *The Colditz Story* (1954). As a character actor his many credits include *Great Expectations* (1946), *Tunes of Glory* (1960) and *Ryan's Daughter* (1970), for which he received an Academy Award. Active in the theatre and on television, he also directed the film *Sky West and Crooked* (1965). Knighted in 1977, he published his autobiography, *Up in the Clouds, Gentlemen Please*, in 1980. Married to the playwright Mary Hayley Bell since 1941, both his daughters Juliet (1941–) and Hayley (1946–) are actresses.

MILMAN, Henry Hart (1791–1868) English poet and church historian, born in London, son of Sir Francis Milman (1746–1821), physician to **George III**. He was educated at Eton and Oxford, where he won the Newdigate prize (1812). In 1816 he became vicar at Reading from 1821 to 1831 professor of poetry at Oxford and in 1849 dean of St Paul's. His *Poems and dramatic works* (3 vols, 1839) are almost forgotten, except for a few hymns.

MILN, James (1819–81) Scottish antiquary. A former naval officer and merchant in China and India, he made excavations on a Roman site at Carnac, Brittany, and published the results in *Excavations at Carnac* (1877 and 1881). Miln Museum, Carnac, contains his collection.

MILN, Walter See **MYLNE**

MILNE, A A (Alan Alexander) (1882–1956) English author, born in St John's Wood, London. He was educated at Westminster and Trinity College, Cambridge, where he edited the undergraduate magazine *Granta*. He joined the staff of *Punch* as assistant editor, and became well known for his light essays and his comedies, notably *Wurzel-Flummery* (1917), *Mr Pim Passes By* (1919) and *The Dover Road* (1922). In 1924 he achieved world fame with his book of children's verse, *When We were Very Young*, written for his own son, Christopher Robin. Further children's classics include *Winnie-the-Pooh* (1926), *Now We are Six* (1927) and *The House at Pooh Corner* (1928). He wrote an autobiography, *It's Too Late Now* (1939).

MILNE, Edward Arthur (1896–1950) English astrophysicist, born in Hull. Assistant director of the Cambridge Solar Physics Observatory (1920–24), professor of mathematics at Manchester (1924–8) and Oxford (from 1928), he made notable contributions to the study of cosmic dynamics. He estimated the age of the universe to be c.2000000000 years.

MILNE, John (1859–1913) English seismologist, born in Liverpool. He worked in Newfoundland as a mining engineer, then became professor of geology in Tokyo (1875–94). He took a Japanese wife, became a supreme authority on earthquakes, travelled widely, and finally established a private seismological observatory at Newport, Isle of Wight. He published important works on earthquakes, seismology and crystallography.

MILNE-EDWARDS, Henri (1800–85) French naturalist and zoologist, born in Bruges, of an English father. He studied medicine at Paris, became professor at the Jardin des Plantes, and wrote a famous *Cours élémentaire de zoologie* (1834; rewritten 1851), works on the crustacea, the corals, physiology and anatomy, researches on the natural history of the French coasts (1832–45) and the coasts of Sicily, and on the natural history of the mammalia (1871).

MILNER, Alfred, 1st Viscount Milner (1854–1925) English statesman, born in Bonn, son of the university lecturer in English at Tübingen. He had a brilliant career at Oxford, winning a New College fellowship. For a time he was assistant editor of the *Pall Mall Gazette*, and then private secretary to **Goschen**, who recommended him (1889) for the under-secretaryship of finance in Egypt, where he wrote *England in Egypt* (1892). From 1892 to 1897 he was chairman of the board of inland revenue, from 1897 to 1901 governor of the Cape Colony, governor of the Transvaal and Orange River Colony (1901–05), and high commissioner for South Africa (1897–1905), receiving a barony (1901) and a viscountcy (1902) for his services before and during the Boer War. In December 1916 he entered the War Cabinet; in 1918–19 he was secretary for war; from 1919 to 1921 colonial secretary. He recommended virtual independence for Egypt.

MILNER, Brenda Atkinson, née **Langford** (1918–) English-born Canadian psychologist, one of the most significant figures in the growth of neuropsychology. She studied at Cambridge and at McGill University, Montreal. She worked at the ministry of supply (1941–44), at which point she emigrated to Canada. She taught at the Université de Montreal from 1944 to 1952, leaving to join McGill University and then becoming head of the Neuropsychology Research Unit at the Montreal Neurological Institute (1953). She won the Distinguished Scientific Contribution Award of the American Psychological Association (1973), and the Ralph W Gerard Prize of the Society for Neuroscience (1987). Her contributions to the field have been mainly empirical, the best-known being a series of investigations of a man rendered profoundly amnesic following a radical brain operation for the relief of epilepsy. This work has formed the basis for a large body of subsequent research, in which the brain structures implicated in laying down a new memory, and their mode of function, are now becoming better understood. Other important research has concerned the asymmetrical activities of the two sides of the brain, particularly in relation to the temporal lobes (at the side of the brain), but also in relation to the frontal lobes. As well as contributing to our knowledge of how the brain works, much of her research has also had application to the clinic, particularly in relation to the surgical treatment of temporal-lobe epilepsy.

MILNER, John (1752–1826) English clergyman, born in London, called by Newman 'the English **Athanasius**'. Ordained in 1777, he was a Catholic priest at Winchester from 1779, and in 1803 he was made a bishop *in partibus* and vicar-apostolic of the Midlands. He wrote a great history of Winchester (1798–1801) and much polemical theology.

MILNER, Joseph (1744–97) English church historian, born in Leeds. Educated at Cambridge, he was headmaster of Hull grammar school, and in 1797 vicar of Holy Trinity, Hull. His principal work, *History of the Church of Christ* (1794-1908), was completed by his brother Isaac (1750–1820), a noted mathematician and theologian.

MILNER-GIBSON See **GIBSON, Richard**

MILNES, Richard Monckton, 1st Baron Houghton (1809–85) English politician and man of letters, born in London. His father, 'single-speech Milnes' (1784–1858), declined the Chancellorship of the Exchequer and a peerage; his mother was a daughter of the fourth Lord Galway. At Cambridge he was a member of the Apostles Club with many future leading literary figures like **Tennyson** and **Thackeray**. He was MP for Pontefract from 1837 until he entered the House of Lords in 1863. A patron of young writers, he befriended **David Gray**, and was one of the first to recognize **Swinburne**'s genius, and secured the poet laureateship for **Tennyson** (1850). He was the 'Mr Vavasour' of **Disraeli**'s novel *Tancred*. A traveller, a philanthropist, and an unrivalled after-dinner speaker, he went up in a balloon and down in a diving-bell; he was the first publishing Englishman who gained access to the harems of the East; he championed oppressed nationalities, liberty of conscience, fugitive slaves, the rights of women; and carried a bill for establishing reformatories (1846). As well as his poetry and essays, he published *Life, Letters and Remains of Keats* (1848). His son, Robert Offley Ashburton Crewe Milnes (1858–1945), was viceroy of Ireland from 1892 to 1895, and was made Earl of Crewe (1895) and Marquis (1911). He married Lord **Rosebery**'s daughter and wrote his Life (1931). He held cabinet rank (1905–16), 1931, and was British ambassador in Paris 1922 to 1928.

MILO OF CROTON (6th century BC) legendary Greek wrestler from the Greek colony of Croton in southern Italy. The best-known Greek athlete of all time, he won the wrestling contest at five successive Olympic Games and swept the board at all other festivals. A man of huge stature, he boasted that no one had ever brought him to his knees. It is said that he carried a live ox upon his shoulders through the stadium at Olympia and then ate it all in a single day. He played a leading part in the military defeat of Sybaris in 511 BC. Tradition has it that in his old age he tried to split a tree which closed upon his hands and held him fast until he was devoured by wolves.

MILSTEIN, Cesar (1927–) Argentinian-born British molecular biologist and immunologist, and joint winner of the 1984 Nobel prize for physiology or medicine. Educated at Buenos Aires University and at Cambridge, he joined the Medical Research Council Laboratory of Molecular Biology there in 1963. He worked there on antibody research, and in 1975 developed monoclonal antibodies (MCAs), with **Georges Köhler**, which revolutionized biological research, and for which they shared the Nobel prize with **Niels Jerne**.

MILSTEIN, Nathan Mironovich (1904–) Russian-born American violinist, born in Odessa. He began his concert career there in 1919, soon playing with **Horowitz** and **Piatigorsky**. He left Russia in 1925, was encouraged by Ysaÿe in Brussels, and gave recitals in Paris. He made his American début under **Stokowski** (1929) and became a US citizen in 1942.

MILTIADES, the Younger (c.550–489 BC) Greek soldier. He became a vassal of **Darius I** of Persia and accompanied him on his Scythian expedition (c.514). He returned to Athens in 493, and masterminded the Greek victory against the Persians at Marathon (490). In the following year he attacked the island of Paros to gratify a private enmity, but, failing in the attempt, was impeached and condemned to pay a fine of fifty talents, but died in prison of a wound received in Paros before paying it.

MILTON, John (1608–74) English poet, born in Bread Street, Cheapside, the son of a composer of some distinction. From St Paul's School he went up to Christ's College, Cambridge, where he spent seven not altogether blameless years, followed by six years of studious leisure at Horton which he regarded as preparation for his life's work as a poet. His apprentice work at Cambridge—apart from some poems of elegant Latin written there or at Horton—includes the splendid 'Nativity Ode', the brilliant epitaph on **Shakespeare** and 'At a Solemn Music'. The poems he wrote at Horton—*L'Allegro* and *Il Penseroso*, *Comus* and *Lycidas*—he also regarded as preparatory for the great poem or drama which was to be 'doctrinal and exemplary for a nation'. *Lycidas* (1637) is an excellent pastoral elegy, though it was censured for its outburst against the Laudian clergy by critics who were ignorant of the Renaissance pastoral convention. On this ominous note Milton concluded his formal education with a visit to Italy (1638–39). The fame of his Latin poems had preceded him and he was received in the academies with distinction. His Italian tour was interrupted by news of the imminent outbreak of Civil War in England. This event, into which he threw himself with revolutionary ardour, silenced his poetic outpourings for 20 years except for occasional sonnets, most of which were published in a volume of *Poems* in 1645. They range from civilities to friends to trumpet-blasts against his and the Commonwealth's detractors. Two stand out—the noble 'On His Blindness' and 'On the Late Massacre in Piedmont'. On his return to London in 1639 Milton undertook the education of his two nephews, but in 1641 he emerged as the polemical champion of the revolution in a series of pamphlets against episcopacy, including an *Apology for Smectymnuus* (1642). *Smectymnuus* was an attack on episcopacy by five Presbyterians. He was now launched on his second series of controversial pamphlets—the divorce pamphlets which were occasioned by the refusal of his 17-year-old bride, Mary Powell, daughter of a Royalist, whom he married in 1642, to return to him after a visit to her home. The first of these, *The Doctrine and Discipline of Divorce* (1643), involved him in three supplementary pamphlets against the opponents of his views on divorce, and these occasioned a threat of prosecution by a parliamentary committee dominated by the Presbyterians who were now to be reckoned his chief enemies after the episcopacy pamphlets. *Areopagitica, A Speech for the Liberty of Unlicensed Printing* (1644) was the famous vindication which is still quoted when the press is in danger. The contemporary *Tractate on Education*, a brilliant exposition of the Renaissance ideals of education, has much less appeal today. Meanwhile his wife returned to him in 1645 accompanied by her whole family as refugees after Naseby, and two years later, his father having left him enough to live on comfortably, he was able to give up schoolmastering. The execution of King **Charles I** launched him on his third public controversy, now addressed however to the conscience of Europe. As Latin secretary to the new council of state to which he was appointed immediately after his defence of the regicides (*The Tenure of Kings and Magistrates*, 1649), he became official apologist for the Commonwealth. As such he wrote *Eikonoklastes* and two *Defensiones*, the first, *Pro Populo Anglicano Defensio* (1650), addressed to the celebrated humanist **Salmasius**. The second, also in Latin, *Defensio Secunda* (1654), contains autobiographical matter and so supplements the personal matter in the *Apology for Smectymnuus*. Meanwhile, his wife having died in 1652, leaving three daughters, he married Catherine Woodcock, whose death two years later is the theme of his beautiful sonnet 'Methought I saw my late espoused Saint'. Although blind from 1652 onwards, he retained his Latin secretaryship until the Restoration (1660), which he roused himself to resist in a last despairing effort as pamphleteer. But the fire had gone out of him, and *The Readie and Easie Way*, which pointed to dictatorship, became the target of the Royalist wits. After the Restoration Milton went into hiding for a short period, and then after the Act of Oblivion (August 1660) he devoted himself wholly to poetry with the exception of his prose *De Doctrina Christiana* (which did not appear until 1823). He married his third wife, Elizabeth Minshull, in 1662 and spent his last days in what is now Bunhill Row. His wife survived him. The theme of *Paradise Lost* (completed 1665, published 1667) had been in Milton's mind since 1641. It was to be a sacred drama then; but when in 1658 his official duties were lightened so as to allow him to write, he chose the epic form. The first three books reflect the triumph of the godly—so soon to be reversed; the last books, written in 1663, are tinged with despair. God's kingdom is not of this world. Man's intractable nature frustrates the planning of the wise. The heterodox theology of the poem which is made clear in his late *De Doctrina Christiana* did not trouble Protestant readers till modern critics examined it with hostile intent; at the same time they made him responsible for that 'dissociation of sensibility' in the language of poetry which had fatal effects on his 18th-century imitators. *Paradise Regained* (1671) ought to have appeased these critics, for its manner is quiet and grave, though not without grand rhetorical passages. The theme here is the triumph of reason over passion; Christ is more the elevated stoic than the redeemer. Resignation is the note of *Paradise Regained*, but *Samson Agonistes*, published along with it in 1671, shows the reviving spirit of rebellion, due no doubt to the rise of Whig opposition about 1670. The parallel of his own fortunes, both in the private and the public sphere, with those of Samson made Milton pour out his great spirit into this Greek play, which also became the libretto of **Handel**'s oratorio. His last years were spent in sociable comfort in Cripplegate; he was buried next to his father in St Giles' Churchyard, Cripplegate.

MINDSZENTY, Jozsef, Cardinal (1892–1975) Hungarian Roman Catholic prelate, born in Mindszent, Vas. Primate of Hungary (1945) and created cardinal (1946), he became internationally known in 1948 when he was arrested and charged with treason by the Communist government in Budapest. He was sentenced to life imprisonment in 1949. Temporarily released in the wake of the 1956 uprising, he was granted asylum in the American legation at Budapest where he remained as a voluntary prisoner until 1971 when he went to Rome, where he criticized the Vatican's policy towards Hungary, and was asked by Pope **Paul VI** to resign his primacy. He settled in Vienna, where he spent his last years in a Hungarian religious community. His memoirs were published in 1974.

MING the name, meaning 'bright', given to the dynasty of Chinese rulers founded by Chu Yüan-Chang, a rebel leader who captured the capital, Nanking, in 1356 and unified China, ruling as the Hung-wu emperor. Under his successor, Jung-lo (reigned 1403–24), the capital was moved to Peking and the process of reconstruction begun in earnest. The reigns of Chia-ching (1521–67) and Wan-li (1572–1620) were periods of great economic growth. Wan-li's reign was also one of cultural brilliance although, in his later years, he withdrew from affairs of state and became increasingly dependent upon the palace eunuchs. Pressure from the Mongols on the northern borders and the increasing burden of taxation seriously weakened Ming government and the last 20 years of the dynasty were also marred by the growth of eunuch power and by corruption and factionalsim at court. A rising against the government in the 1630s led eventually to the Manchu invasion of 1644 and the end of the Ming dynasty.

MINGHETTI, Marco (1818–86) Italian statesman, **Cavour**'s successor, born in Bologna. He studied there, and travelled in Europe and Britain. Pope **Pius IX** in 1846 made him, now a journalist, minister of public works. The pope's reforming zeal was short-lived, and Minghetti entered the Sardinian army, and at Custozza earned a knighthood. After Novara he settled at Turin, an ardent student of economics, a free-trader and a devoted friend of Cavour. Premier in 1863, he concluded with **Napoleon** the 'September Convention' in 1864. At Rome from 1873 to 1876 he was prime minister for the second time. He wrote on Raphael and Dante, *Economia publica* (1859), and *La Chiesa e lo Stato* (1878).

MINGUS, Charles (1922–79) American jazz bassist, composer and bandleader, born in Nogales, Arizona, and brought up in Los Angeles. While at Jordan High School, he was taught to play the cello, eventually performing with Los Angeles Junior Philharmonic Orchestra, but contact with jazz musicians led him to take up the double-bass. His first professional work as a bassist was with traditional-style bands but as a child, he had sung gospel music at the Holiness Church, and his later work as a leader and composer brought elements of this background together with modern and avant garde ideas. During the 1940s, Mingus worked with big bands led by **Louis Armstrong** and **Lionel Hampton**. In the following decade, he moved to New York, generally working with smaller groups under Red Norvo, **Art Tatum** and others, before becoming involved in the experimental Jazz Composers Workshop. His experience there shaped the later works where he attempted to overcome lack of spontaneity in arranged jazz by teaching each musician his arranged part by ear, often shouting instructions to improvising soloists during the performance. An emotional campaigner for black rights, Mingus was crippled by sclerosis in 1978.

MINIÉ, Claude Étienne (1804–79) French army officer, born in Paris. Rising from private to colonel, in 1849 he invented the conical pointed expanding bullet for the Minié rifle.

MINKOWSKI, Hermann (1864–1909) Russian-born German mathematician, born near Kovno. He was professor at Königsberg (1895), Zürich (1896), where he taught **Einstein**, and at Göttingen (1902). He discovered a new branch of number theory, the geometry of numbers, and gave a precise mathematical description of space-time as it appears in Einstein's relativity theory.

MINNELLI, Liza May (1946–) American singer and actress, born in Los Angeles, daughter of director Vincente Minnelli (1910–86) and **Judy Garland**. She first appeared on screen in her mother's film *In The Good Old Summertime* (1949) and acted in a school production of *The Diary of Anne Frank* (1960). She made her off-Broadway début in *Best Foot Forward* (1963) and became the youngest actress to win a Tony Award for *Flora, the Red Menace* (1965). Seen on television and in cabaret, her vibrant vocal talents and emotional rendition of plaintive songs earned comparisons with her mother. Dramatic roles in films like *Charlie Bubbles* (1967), *The Sterile Cuckoo* (1969) and *Tell Me That You Love Me, Junie Moon* (1970) revealed her as a skilled portrayer of social outcasts: the fragile, insecure and gauche. She won an Academy Award for *Cabaret* (1972), and a television special, *Liza with a Z* (1972), confirmed her many talents. Subsequent dramatic appearances include *New York, New York* (1977) and the television film *A Time to Live* (1985). Her private life has often appeared to emulate the volatility of her mother's but she remains a potent attraction as a recording artist and concert performer.

MINOS in Greek legend, king of Crete, the son of Zeus and Minerva. It is from him that the modern designation 'Minoan' has been derived, to refer to the brilliant civilization of Bronze Age Crete that archaeology has revealed. Whether Minos was himself a historical figure is another matter. According to legend, Minos' wife Pasiphae had been caused by the god Poseidon to fall in love with a bull, whom Minos had refused to sacrifice to him, thus breaking a promise. From this union, Pasiphae gave birth to a monster, half-human, half-bull, the Minotaur, who was shut up in a maze, the Labyrinth, constructed by the craftsman Daedalus. As a result of a war against the Athenians, Minos extracted from them a yearly tribute of youths and maidens, who were offered to the Minotaur. Eventually **Theseus** of Athens slew the Minotaur with the help of Minos' daughter Ariadne and of Daedalus. Minos later met his death in Sicily while pursuing Daedalus, who had escaped from Crete to avoid the anger of Minos.

MINOT, George Richards (1885–1950) American physician, professor of medicine at Harvard (1928–48). He first suggested, with **William Murphy**, the importance of a liver diet in the treatment of pernicious anaemia. In 1934 they shared the Nobel prize for physiology or medicine with **George Whipple**.

MINSHEU, John (fl.1617) English lexicographer who taught languages in London. His dictionary, *Guide into Tongues* (1617), providing equivalents of eleven languages, is of great value for the study of Elizabethan English.

MINTER, Alan (1951–) English boxer, born in Crawley. He held the European middleweight title in 1977 and from 1978 to 1979, and the British crown 1975–77 and 1977–78. He became world champion in 1980, and of 49 bouts he won 39.

MINTOFF, Dom (Dominic) (1916–) Maltese Labour politician. He was educated at Malta and Oxford universities, afterwards becoming a civil engineer. In 1947 he joined the Malta Labour party and in the first Malta Labour government that year he became minister of works and deputy prime minister. He became prime minister in 1955 and in 1956–57 undertook negotiations with Britain to integrate Malta more closely with the former. These broke down in 1958, when his demands for independence and political agitation over the transfer of the naval dockyard to a commercial concern led directly to the suspension of Malta's constitution in January 1959. Having resigned in 1958 to lead the Malta Liberation Movement, he became opposition leader in 1962, and was prime minister from 1971 to 1984, during which period he followed a policy of moving away from British influence.

MINTON, (Francis) John (1917–57) English artist, born in Cambridge. He studied in London and Paris, and from 1943 to 1956 taught at various London art schools. He was noted for his book illustrations and his brilliant watercolours, and also as a designer of textiles and wallpaper.

MINTON, Thomas (1765–1836) English pottery and china manufacturer, born in Shrewsbury, founder of the firm which bears his name. Originally trained as a transfer-print engraver, he worked for **Josiah Spode** for a time, but in 1789 he set up his own business in Stoke-on-Trent, producing copperplates for transfer-printing in blue underglaze. He is reputed to have invented the willow pattern (for which an original copperplate engraved by him is in the British Museum). In 1793 he built a pottery works at Stoke, where he very soon produced a fine bone china (approximating to hard paste) for which the best period is 1798–1810. Much of it was tableware, decorated with finely painted flowers and fruit. His son, Herbert (his partner from 1817 to 1836), took over the firm at his death.

MINTON, Yvonne Fay (1938–) Australian operatic and concert mezzo-soprano, born in Earlwood, Sydney. She attended the New South Wales Conservatorium of Music, and after winning a scholarship and the Shell aria contest, studied in London where in 1961 she won the **Kathleen Ferrier** prize. She made her operatic début in 1964 at the Royal Opera House, Covent Garden, where she has since been resident artist. Minton has also been a guest member of the Cologne Opera since 1969, and guest artist with the New York Metropolitan, the Chicago, Paris and Australian opera companies. She is noted for her Octavian in **Strauss**'s *Rosenkavalier* and for Wagnerian roles to which her voice is well suited.

MINUCIUS FELIX (c. 2nd century) early Christian apologist, possibly born in Africa. A lawyer in Rome, he was converted to Christianity and was the author of *Octavius*, a dialogue between a pagan and a Christian.

MIRABEAU, André Boniface Riqueti, Vicomte de (1754–92) French soldier and politician, son of **Victor Riqueti Mirabeau** and brother of **Honoré Mirabeau**. In the American War of Independence (1775–83) he served in the American army (1780–1785) and at the outbreak of the French Revolution was returned to the Estates-General. He raised a legion of *emigrés* against the republic but was accidentally killed at Freiburg-im-Breisgau. Notorious for his thirst and his corpulence, he was nicknamed *tonneau*—ie, barrel.

MIRABEAU, Honoré Gabriel Riqueti, Comte de (1749–91) French revolutionary politican and orator, born in Bignon, in Loiret, the son of **Victor Riqueti Mirabeau** and brother of **André Boniface Riqueti Mirabeau**. At 17 he entered a cavalry regiment (1767), but lived so recklessly and profligately that he was imprisoned on several occasions for his disorderly behaviour. In hiding in Amsterdam, having eloped with a young married woman, he wrote *Essai sur le despotisme*, which made a sensation by its audacity. Meantime the *parlement* of Besançon sentenced him to death; and in May 1777 he was handed over by the States-General and flung into the castle of Vincennes, where, in close imprisonment for three and a half years, he wrote *Erotica biblion*, *Ma conversion*, and his famous *Essai sur les lettres de cachet* (2 vols, 1782). In 1780 he was released, and in 1782 he had his sentence annulled. In England in 1784 he was able to study English politics, which taught him the good of moderation, compromise and opportunism. In 1786 he was sent on a secret mission to Berlin, and there obtained the materials for his work, *Sur la monarchie prussienne sous Frédéric le Grand* (4 vols, 1787). In 1789 he was elected to the States General as deputy for the Third Estate for both Marseilles and Aix. When the Third Estate constituted itself the National Assembly, Mirabeau's political sagacity made him a great force, while his audacity and volcanic eloquence endeared him to the mob. He advocated a constitutional monarchy on the English model but was distrusted both by the court and the extremists. Nonetheless he was elected president of the Assembly in January 1791, but died soon afterwards.

MIRABEAU, Victor Riqueti, Marquis de (1715–89) French soldier and economist. An associate of **Quesnay**, he expounded physiocratic political philosophy in *Ami des hommes* (1756) and *La Philosophie rurale* (1763).

MIRANDOLA See **PICO DELLA MIRANDOLA**

MIRBEAU, Octave (1850–1917) French dramatist, novelist, journalist, born in Trevières (Calvados). A radical, he attracted attention by the violence of his writings. His *Les Affaires sont les affaires* (1903) was adapted by Sidney Grundy (1905).

MIRÓ, Joán (1893–1983) Spanish artist, born in Montroig. He studied in Paris and Barcelona and exhibited with the Surrealists in 1925. In his early years he had great admiration for primitive Catalan art and the Art Nouveau forms of **Gaudi**'s architecture. Before World War I he painted in Cézannesque and Fauve styles but in 1920 he settled in Paris and came into contact with **Picasso** and **Juan Gris**. Seduced by Surrealism he invented a manner of painting using curvilinear, fantastical forms which suggest all kinds of of dreamlike situations. Eventually, these pictures became almost entirely abstract and had a great influence on American Abstract Expressionist artists such as **Gorky** in the late 1940s and 50s.

MISES, Richard von (1883–1953) Austrian-born American mathematician and philosopher. He was professor at Dresden (1919), Berlin (1920–33), Istanbul, and from 1939 at Harvard. An authority in aerodynamics and hydrodynamics, he set out in *Wahrscheinlichkeit, Statistik und Wahrheit*, ('Probability, Statistics and Truth' 1928) a frequency theory of probability which has had a wide influence, even though not generally accepted.

MISHIMA, Yukio, pen-name of **Hiraoka Kimitake** (1925–70) Japanese writer, born in Tokyo. He published his first story in 1944 at the age of 19. He attended Tokyo University before becoming a civil servant and embarking on a prolific writing career which, as well as 40 novels, produced poetry, essays and modern Kabuki and Noh drama. His first major work was *Confessions of a Mask* (1949, trans 1958) which dealt with his discovery of his own homosexuality and the ways in which he attempted to conceal it. After many other works, notably the novels *The Temple of the Golden Pavilion* (1956, trans 1959) and *After the Banquet* (1960, trans 1963), he wrote his great tetralogy, *Sea of Fertility* (1965–70), which, with a central theme of reincarnation, spanned Japanese life and events in the twentieth century. Passionately interested in the chivalrous traditions of Imperial Japan, he believed implicitly in the ideal of a heroic destiny, the pursuit of an absolute ideal of beauty, and the concept of a glorious and honourable death in battle. He became an expert in the martial arts of *karate* and *kendo*, and in 1968 founded the Shield Society, a group of a hundred youths dedicated to a revival of *Bushido*, the Samurai knightly code of honour. The most extreme expression of his elitist right-wing views was in an essay *Sun and Steel* (1970), and in the same year he committed suicide by performing hara-kiri after a carefully-staged token attempt to rouse the nation to a return to pre-war nationalist ideals. Among his other novels are *Thirst for Love* (1950, trans 1969), *The Sound of Waves* (1954, trans 1956), and *The Sailor Who Fell From Grace with the Sea* (1963, trans 1966); his plays include *Madame de Sade* (1965, trans 1968) and *My Friend Hitler* (1968).

MISSONI, Tai Otavio (1921–) Italian knitwear designer, born in Yugoslavia, the son of an Italian father and a Serbian mother. He founded the Missoni company in Milan with his wife, Rosita, in 1953. At first manufacturing knitwear to be sold under other labels, they later created, under their own label, innovative knitwear notable for its sophistication and distinctive colours and patterns.

MISTINGUETT, stage name of **Jeanne Marie Bourgeois** (1874–1956) French dancer, singer and actress, born in Pointe de Raquet. Making her début in 1895, she became the most popular French music hall artiste of the first three decades of the century, reaching the height of success with **Maurice Chevalier** at the Folies Bergère. She also distinguished herself as a straight actress in *Madame Sans-Gène* and *Les Misérables*, etc.

MISTRAL, Frédéric (1830–1914) Provençal poet, born in Maillane near Avignon. After studying law at Avignon, he went home to work on the land and write poetry. He helped to found the Provençal renaissance movement (Félibrige school). In 1859 his epic *Miréio* (trans 1890) gained him the poet's prize of the French academy and the *Légion d'honneur*. He was awarded a Nobel prize for literature in 1904. Other works are an epic, *Calendau* (1861), poems *Lis Isclo d'or* (1876), a tragedy *La Reino Jano* (1890), and a Provençal-French dictionary (1878–86).

MISTRAL, Gabriela, pseud of **Lucila Godoy de Alcayaga** (1889–1957) Chilean poet, diplomat and teacher, born in Vicuña. As a teacher she won a poetry prize with her *Sonetos de la muerte* at Santiago in 1915. She taught at Columbia University, Vassar and in Puerto Rico, and was formerly consul at Madrid and elsewhere. The cost of publication of her first book, *Desolación* (1922), was defrayed by the teachers of New York. Her work is inspired by her vocation as a teacher, by religious sentiments and a romantic preoccupation with sorrow and death, infused with an intense lyricism. She was awarded the Nobel prize for literature in 1945.

MITCHEL, John (1815–75) Irish patriot, born, a Presbyterian minister's son, near Dungiven, County Derry. He studied at Trinity College, Dublin, practised as an attorney, and became assistant editor of the *Nation*. Starting the *United Irishman* (1848), he was tried for his articles on a charge of 'treason-felony' and sentenced to 14 years' transportation; but in 1853 he escaped from Van Diemen's Land (Tasmania) to the USA, and published his *Jail Journal* (1854). Returning in 1874 to Ireland, he was next year elected to parliament for Tipperary, declared ineligible and re-elected, but died the same month. He published a *Life of Hugh O'Neill* (1845) and a *History of Ireland from the Treaty of Limerick* (1868).

MITCHELL, Arthur (1934–) American dancer, choreographer and director, born in New York. After studying with the High School for the Performing Arts, he trained with the School of American Ballet. In 1956 he joined New York City Ballet and created roles in **Balanchine**'s *Agon* (1957) and *A Midsummer Night's Dream* (1962). The first black principal dancer to join that company, his dream, following the assassination of **Martin Luther King** in 1968, was to found his own group in order to develop opportunities for fellow black dancers. In 1968 he began laying the foundations of this dream, and Dance Theatre of Harlem made its début in New York in 1971 with resounding success. Quickly growing from a school in a garage to a company of international standing, Dance Theatre of Harlem enjoys world-wide attention.

MITCHELL, James Fitzallen (1931–) St Vincent and the Grenadines politician. He trained and worked as an agronomist (1958–65) and then bought and managed an hotel in Bequia, St Vincent. He entered politics through the St Vincent Labour party (SVLP) and in the pre-independence period served as minister of trade (1967–72). He was then premier (1972–74), heading the People's Political party (PPP). In 1975 he founded the New Democratic party (NDP) and, as its leader, became prime minister in 1984.

MITCHELL, James Leslie See **GIBBON, Lewis Grassic**

MITCHELL, Joni (1943–) Canadian singer and songwriter, born in McLeod, Alberta. Her compositions, highly original and personal in their lyrical imagery, first attracted attention among folk-music audiences in Toronto while she was still in her teens. She moved to the USA in the mid 1960s and in 1968 recorded her first album, *Joni Mitchell*. Other highly successful albums that followed include *Clouds*, *Ladies of the Canyon* and *Blue*. Many of her songs, notably 'Both Sides Now', have been recorded by other singers.

MITCHELL, Margaret (1900–49) American novelist, born in Atlanta, Georgia. She studied for a medical career, but turned to journalism. After her marriage to J R Marsh in 1925, she began the ten-year task of writing her only novel, *Gone with the Wind* (1936), which won the Pulitzer prize, sold over 25 million copies, was translated into 30 languages and was the subject of a celebrated film in 1939.

MITCHELL, Sir Peter Chalmers (1864–1945) Scottish zoologist and journalist, born in Dunfermline. He started his career as a lecturer at Oxford and London, and in 1903 was elected secretary of the Zoological Society. He inaugurated a period of prosperity at the London Zoo and was responsible for the Mappin terraces, Whipsnade, the Aquarium and other improvements. He wrote a number of books on zoological subjects including *The Nature of Man* (1904) and *Materialism and Vitalism in Biology* (1930).

MITCHELL, Peter Dennis (1920–) English biochemist born in Mitcham, Surrey. He graduated from Cambridge and taught there (1943–55) and at Edinburgh (1955–63) before creating his own research institute, the Glynn Research Laboratories, at Bodmin, Cornwall, in 1964. In the 1960s he proposed an entirely novel theory of the way energy is generated at the molecular level in biochemical cells. Although at first greeted with scepticism, by his views became widely accepted, and his position was formally established by his award of the unshared Nobel prize for chemistry in 1978.

MITCHELL, Reginald Joseph (1895–1937) English aircraft designer. Trained as an engineer, he was led by his interest in aircraft to join the Vickers Armstrong Supermarine Co in 1916, where he soon became chief designer. He designed world-beating sea-planes for the Schneider trophy races (1922–31) and later the famous Spitfire, the triumph of which he did not live to see.

MITCHELL, Silas Weir (1829–1914) American physician and author, born in Philadelphia. A surgeon in the Union army in the American Civil War, he specialized in nervous diseases and pioneered in the application of psychology to medicine. As well as a host of historical novels and poems he wrote medical texts, including *Injuries of Nerves* (1872) and *Fat and Blood* (1877).

MITCHELL, Sir Thomas Livingstone (1792–1855) Scottish explorer, born in Craigend, Stirlingshire. After service in the Peninsular War, from 1828 he was surveyor-general of New South Wales. In four expeditions (1831, 1835, 1836, 1845–47) he did much to explore Eastern Australia ('Australia Felix') and Tropical Australia, especially the Murray, Glenelg and Barcoo rivers.

MITCHELL, Warren (1926–) English actor, born in London. After studying at Oxford and RADA he made his first appearance at the Finsbury Park Open Air Theatre in 1950. He won great acclaim for his interpretation of Willy Loman in **Arthur Miller**'s *Death of a Salesman* at the National Theatre in 1979. He is most widely known for playing the character of Alf Garnett, a garrulous, foul-mouthed, right-wing Cockney in the television series *Till Death Us Do Part*, which ran from 1966 to 1978. A stage show, *The Thoughts of Chairman Alf*, starring Mitchell opened at the Theatre Royal, Stratford East, in 1976, and the character returned in further television series, *In Sickness and In Health* (1985–).

MITCHELL, William (1879–1936) American aviation pioneer. Beginning his army career in the signal service, he became an early enthusiast for flying and commanded the American air forces in World War I. He foresaw the development and importance of air power in warfare, but his outspoken criticism of those who did not share his convictions resulted in a court martial which suspended him from duty. His resignation followed and he spent the rest of his life lecturing and writing in support of his ideas. His vindication came with World War II and he was posthumously promoted and decorated.

MITCHISON, Naomi Margaret, née **Haldane** (1897–) British writer, born in Edinburgh, the daughter of **J S Haldane**. Educated at the Dragon School, Oxford, she won instant attention with her brilliant and personal evocations of Greece and Sparta in a series of novels such as *The Conquered* (1923), *When the Bough Breaks* (1924), *Cloud Cuckoo Land* (1925) and *Black Sparta* (1928). In 1931 came the erudite *Corn King and Spring Queen*, which brought to life the civilizations of ancient Egypt, Scythia and the Middle East. She has travelled widely, and in 1963 was made Tribal Adviser and Mother to the Bakgatla of Botswana. She has written more than 70 books, including her memoirs in *Small Talk* (1973), *All Change Here* (1975) and *You May Well Ask* (1979), among many other writings. She married Gilbert Richard Mitchison (1890–1970, created life peer in 1964) in 1916. He was a Labour MP (1945–64), and joint parliamentary secretary, ministry of land (1964–66). Since 1937 she has lived in Carradale in the Mull of Kintyre, Scotland.

MITCHUM, Robert (1917–) American film actor, born in Bridgeport, Connecticut. A peripatetic youth spent as a labourer, vagrant and professional boxer brought him to Hollywood where he found employment in the film industry, initially as an extra but later as a prolific leading man particularly associated with the post-war film noir thriller. His laconic, heavy-lidded manner is deceptively casual, disguising a potent screen presence and thorough professionalism that have enlivened many routine assignments. His talents are seen to advantage in more stimulating material such as *Out of the Past* (1947), *The Night of the Hunter*

(1955) and *Farewell My Lovely* (1975, as Philip Marlowe).

MITFORD, Diana See **MOSLEY, Sir Oswald**

MITFORD, Jessica (1917–) English writer, daughter of the 2nd Baron Redesdale, and sister of Diana Mitford, **Nancy Mitford** and **Unity Mitford**. She wrote *Hons and Rebels* (1960), her autobiography and story of the unconventional Mitford childhood. She went to the USA in 1939 and became a communist. Her other books include *The American Way of Death* (1963), *The Trial of Dr Spock* (1970) and *The Making of a Muckraker* (1979).

MITFORD, John (1781–1859) English clergyman and man of letters, born in Richmond, Surrey. Much of his time was devoted to literary pursuits, collecting and gardening. He edited the *Gentleman's Magazine* from 1834 to 1850, and also volumes for the *Aldine Poets* including **Gray**, **Cowper** and **Milton**. He published his own *Miscellaneous Poems* in 1858.

MITFORD, Mary Russell (1787–1855) English novelist and dramatist, daughter of a spendthrift physician. At the age of ten she won £20000 in a lottery and went to school in Chelsea. As the family became more and more impoverished she had to write to earn money. Several plays were produced successfully but failed to keep the stage. Her gift was for charming sketches of country manners, scenery and character, which after appearing in magazines were collected as *Our Village* (5 vols, 1824–32). She received a civil list pension in 1837 which was increased on her father's death from subscriptions raised to pay his debts. In 1852 she published *Recollections of a Literary Life*.

MITFORD, Nancy Freeman (1904–73) English writer, daughter of the 2nd Baron Redesdale and sister of Diana Mitford, **Jessica Mitford** and **Unity Mitford**. She established a reputation with her witty novels such as *Pursuit of Love* (1945) and *Love in a Cold Climate* (1949), followed by *The Blessing* (1951) and *Don't Tell Alfred* (1960). After the war she settled in France and wrote her major biographies *Madame de Pompadour* (1953), *Voltaire in Love* (1957), *The Sun King* (1966), and *Frederick the Great* (1970). As one of the essayists in *Noblesse Oblige*, edited by herself (1956), she helped to originate the famous 'U', or upper-class, and 'non-U' classification of linguistic usage and behaviour.

MITFORD, Unity Valkyrie (1914–48) English socialite, daughter of the 2nd Baron Redesdale and sister of Diana Mitford, **Jessica Mitford** and **Nancy Mitford**. She was notorious for her associations with leading Nazis in Germany but returned to Britain during World War II in January 1940, suffering from a gunshot wound.

MITFORD, William (1744–1827) English historian, born in London. He studied at Queen's College, Oxford, in 1761 succeeded to the family estate of Exbury, and in 1769 became a captain in the South Hampshire Militia, of which **Edward Gibbon** was major. On Gibbon's advice he undertook his pugnacious anti-democratic *History of Greece* (5 vols, 1784–1818), which, by virtue of careful research, held the highest place in the opinion of scholars until the appearance of **Thirlwall** and **Grote**. He sat in parliament from 1785 to 1818.

MITHRADATES VI (d.63 BC) surnamed **Eupator**, called the Great, king of Pontus. He succeeded to the throne about 120 BC as a boy, but soon subdued the tribes who bordered on the Euxine as far as the Crimea, and made an incursion into Cappadocia and Bithynia, at that time Roman. In the First Mithradatic War, commenced by the Romans (88), Mithradates' generals repeatedly defeated the Asiatic levies of the Romans, and he himself occupied the Roman possessions in Asia Minor and invaded Greece. Defeated by Roman generals, he was compelled to make peace with **Sulla** (85), relinquishing all his conquests in Asia, giving up 70 war galleys, and paying 2000 talents. The aggressions of the Roman legate gave rise to the Second Mithradatic War (83–81), in which Mithradates was wholly successful. In the Third Mithradatic War (74) he obtained the services of Roman officers of the Marian faction, and at first prospered; but **Lucullus** compelled him to take refuge with **Tigranes I** of Armenia (72), and defeated both of them at Artaxata (68). In 66 **Pompey** defeated Mithradates on the Euphrates, and compelled him to flee to his territories on the Cimmerian Bosporus. Here his new schemes of vengeance were frustrated by his son's rebellion, and he killed himself. He had received a Greek education, spoke 22 languages, and made a great collection of pictures and statues.

MITSCHERLICH, Eilhard (1794–1863) German chemist, born in Neuende near Jeve. Professor of chemistry at Berlin from 1822, he studied Persian at Heidelberg and Paris, medicine at Göttingen, and geology, mineralogy, chemistry and physics at Berlin and Stockholm. His name is identified with the discovery of the laws of isomorphism and dimorphism, and with artificial minerals, benzene and ether.

MITTERRAND, François Maurice Marie (1916–) French statesman and author, president of France (1981–). Born in Jarnac in South West France, the fifth child of a stationmaster, he attended the University of Paris during the mid 1930s, studying law and politics and immersing himself in French literature. During World War II he served with the French forces (1939–40), was wounded and captured, but escaped (on the third attempt) in December 1941 from a prison camp in Germany and became a network commander in the French resistance. He has been awarded the Legion d'Honneur, the Croix de Guerre and the Rosette de la Resistance. He was a deputy in the French national assembly almost continuously from 1946, representing the constituency of Nievre (near Dijon), and held ministerial posts in 11 centrist governments between 1947 and 1958. A firm believer in the democratic traditions of Republican France, which he now saw to be under threat, he opposed **de Gaulle**'s creation of the Fifth Republic in May 1953 and, as a result, lost his Assembly seat in the November 1958 election. He became radicalized, leaving the Catholic church during the early 1960s, and began to set about building up a strong new, left-of-centre anti-Gaullist alliance, the 'Federation of the Left'. After returning to the national assembly in 1962, he performed creditably as the Federation's candidate in the 1965 presidential election against de Gaulle and in 1971 became leader of the new Socialist party (PS). He proceeded to embark on a successful strategy of electoral union with the (then important) Communist party which brought major gains for the Socialists, establishing them as the single most popular party in France by 1978 and in May 1981 was elected president, defeating **Giscard d'Estaing**. As president, Mitterrand initially introduced a series of radical economic and political reforms, including programmes of nationalization and decentralization. However, deteriorating economic conditions after 1983 forced a policy U-turn and in the March 1986 election the Socialists lost their National Assembly majority. This compelled him to work with a prime minister, **Jacques Chirac**, drawn from the opposition 'right coalition'. However, despite being forced to concede considerable executive authority to Chirac in this unique 'co-habitation' experiment, the wily Mitterrand, nicknamed 'the fox', outmanouevred his younger rival, comfortably defeating Chirac in the presidential election of May 1988. Following fresh national assembly elections in which the conservative parties lost their majority, the moderate socialist, **Michel Rocard**, was appointed prime minister in a new left-of-centre administration.

MIVART, St George Jackson (1827–1900) English biologist. Educated for the bar, he devoted himself to the biological sciences, and before his death was excommunicated for his liberalism. In 1874–84 he was professor of zoology and biology at the Roman Catholic University College in Kensington, and in 1890 accepted a chair of the philosophy of natural history at Louvain. An evolutionist save as regards the origin of mind, he was an opponent of the 'Natural Selection' theory. Among his works are *The Genesis of Species* (1871), *Nature and Thought* (1883), and *The Origin of Human Reason* (1889).

MIYAKE, Issey (1938–) Japanese fashion designer, born in Hiroshima. After studying at Tama Art University in Toyko, he spent six years in Paris and New York fashion houses. Although he showed his first collection in Tokyo in 1963, he founded his studio there only in 1971. His first subsequent show was in New York the same year, followed by a show in Paris in 1973. His distinctive style combines eastern and western influences in garments which have an almost theatrical quality. Loose fitting but with dramatic often asymmetric outline, his clothes achieve richness by varied textures, weaves and patterns rather than by colour which is frequently subdued.

MNOUCHKINE, Arianne (1938–) French stage director, dramatist and founder of the Théâtre du Soleil. In 1959 she founded the Association Théâtrale des Étudiants de Paris with fellow students of the Sorbonne, putting on plays, organizing workshops and lectures. In 1962 she travelled to Cambodia and Japan and on her return in 1963 founded the Théâtre du Soleil as a theatre co-operative. The early productions were influenced by the teachings of **Stanislavsky**, and their first major success came with a production of **Arnold Wesker**'s *The Kitchen* in 1967. After the student uprising of May 1968, the company performed a series of collective improvizations based on techniques of collage, circus and continuous and discontinuous narrative, *1789*, first produced in 1970, is one of the company's best-known works.

MOBERG, (Carl Artur) Vilhelm (1898–1973) Swedish author, born in Algutsboda in Småland. He came from a family of crofters and enlisted soldiers and remained loyal to his background. His best-known work is the series of novels that deal with documentary accuracy with the 19th-century mass migration of Swedes to the USA: *Utvandrarna* (The Emigrants, 1949), *Invandrarna* (The Immigrants, 1952), *Nybyggarna* (The Settlers, 1956) and *Sista brevet till Sverige* (Last Letter to Sweden, 1959). His unfinished *Min svenska historia 1–2* (My Swedish History, 1970–71) looks at history from the viewpoint of the common people. He was a popular dramatist and several of his novels, notably *The Emigrants*, have been filmed.

MÖBIUS, August Ferdinand (1790–1868) German mathematician. As professor at Leipzig he worked on analytical geometry, topology and theoretical astronomy but is chiefly known for the discovery of the Möbius strip (a one-sided surface formed by giving a rectangular strip a half-twist and then joining the ends together) and the Möbius net, important in projective geometry. He also introduced barycentric coordinates into geometry.

MOBUTU, Sese Seko Kuku Ngbendu Wa Za Banga, formerly **Joseph Désiré Mobutu** (1930–) Zairean soldier and politician. After army training and a period of study in Brussels, he rose quickly to become commander in the Belgian army at the age of 30 with the rank of colonel. In 1958 he joined **Lumumba**'s Congolese National Movement party (MNC). In 1960, immediately after independence, the government in Leopoldville was so indecisive in its dealings with dissidents in Katanga province that Mobutu stepped in and took over. Five months later he handed power back to the civilian government. After the civil war of 1963–65 he again took over but this time retained power. As president, with a new constitution and a new name for his country, he adopted a new name for himself and the rank of marshal. Although his régime has been harsh and highly personalized, he has, at least, brought stability to what at one time seemed to be an ungovernable country.

MODERSOHN-BECKER, Paula, née **Becker** (1876–1907) German painter, born in Dresden. After art school in London and academic training in Berlin from 1896 to 1898, she joined an artists' colony at the village of Worpswede, and married a fellow-artist, Otto Modersohn. She made several trips to Paris between 1900 and 1906 where she came under the influence of *avant-garde* painters such as **Gauguin** and **Cézanne**. Her subsequent paintings, in which personal response in the form of simple forms and strong colour takes precedence over realistic portrayal, place her at the beginning of the German Expressionist movement.

MODIGLIANI, Amedeo (1884–1920) Italian painter and sculptor of the modern school of Paris, born in Leghorn. His early work was influenced by the painters of the Italian Renaissance, particularly the primitives, and in 1906 he went to Paris, where he was further influenced by **Toulouse-Lautrec** and 'les Fauves'. In 1909, influenced by the Rumanian sculptor **Brancusi**, he took to sculpture and produced a number of elongated stone heads in African style, a style he continued to use when he later resumed painting, with a series of richly-coloured, elongated portraits—a feature characterizing all his later work. In 1918 in Paris he held virtually his first one-man show, which included some very frank nudes; the exhibition was closed for indecency on the first day. It was only after his death from tuberculosis that he obtained recognition and the prices of his paintings soared.

MODIGLIANI, Franco (1918–) Italian-born American economist, born in Rome. Having taken a law degree in Rome in 1939, he emigrated to the USA and held professorships at a number of smaller institutions (1942–48), then at Illinois (1949–52), Carnegie-Mellon (1952–60) and Northwestern (1960–62) universities and at Massachusetts Institute of Technology (1962–). He was awarded the 1985 Nobel prize for economics for his work on two fundamental theories: personal saving and corporate finance.

MODJESKA, Helena (1844–1909) Polish actress, born in Cracow. She began to act in 1861, and made a great name in Cracow in 1865. From 1868 to 1876 she was the first actress of Warsaw. After learning English, however, she achieved her greatest triumphs in the USA and in Great Britain, in such roles as Juliet, Rosalind, and Beatrice, and in *La Dame aux camélias*. She wrote *Memories and Impressions* (1910).

MOE, Jørgen Engebretsen (1813–82) Norwegian folklorist and poet, bishop of Christiansand (1875–81). With **Peter Christian Asbjørnsen** he collected and edited *Norwegian Folk Stories* (1841–44). He also published a book of Romantic verse (1850), and a children's classic, *I brønden og i kjærnet* (1851).

MOERAN, Edward James (1894–1950) English composer, born in Middlesex. He was a pupil at the Royal College of Music and, after service in World War I, studied under **John Ireland**. He first emerged as a composer in 1923, but left London to live in Herefordshire, where he worked prolifically in all forms. As well as a large number of songs, he composed a symphony and concertos for violin, piano and cello.

MOFFAT, Robert (1795–1883) Scottish missionary, born in Ormiston, East Lothian. He turned from gardening to the mission field in 1815, and began his work in Great Namaqualand (1818). He finally settled at Kuruman in Bechuanaland (1826–70), which soon became, through his efforts, a centre of Christianity and civilization. He printed both New (1840) and Old (1857) Testaments in Sechwana and published *Labours and Scenes in South Africa* (1842). **David Livingstone** married his daughter, Mary.

MOFFATT, James (1870–1944) Scots-born American theologian, born in Glasgow. Ordained a minister of the Free Church of Scotland in 1896, he was professor at Mansfield College, Oxford (1911–14), and at the United Free Church College, Glasgow, (1914–27). In 1927 he went to the USA and became professor of church history at Union Theological Seminary, New York (1927–39). His most famous work is the translation of the Bible into modern English; his New Testament was published in 1913 and his Old Testament in 1924. He also wrote theological works, including *Presbyterianism* (1928).

MOHAMMED, sultans of Turkey See **MEHMET**

MOHAMMED, or **MEHMET II, 'the Conqueror'** (1432–81) sultan of Turkey from 1451 and founder of the Ottoman empire, born in Adrianople. He succeeded his father, Murad II, in 1451, and took Constantinople in 1453 renaming it Istanbul, thus extinguishing the Byzantine Empire and giving the Turks their commanding position on the Bosphorus. Checked by **Janos Hunyady** at Belgrade in 1456, he nevertheless annexed most of Serbia, all Greece, and most of the Aegean Islands, threatened Venetian territory, was repelled from Rhodes by the Knights of St John (1479), took Otranto in 1480 and died in a campaign against Persia.

MOHAMMED or **MAHOMET** See **MUHAMMAD**

MOHAMMED AHMED (1848–85) known as the Mahdi (or Muslim Messiah), born in Dongola. He was for a time in the Egyptian Civil Service, then a slave trader, and finally a relentless and successful rebel against Egyptian rule in the Eastern Sudan. He made El Obeid his capital in 1883, and on November 5 annihilated an Egyptian army under **William Hicks** (Pasha). On January 26 1885, Khartum was taken, and General **Gordon** killed.

MOHAMMED 'ALI See **MEHEMET 'ALI**

MOHAMMED BEN YOUSSEF See SIDI MOHAMMED BEN YOUSSEF

MOHAMMED NADIR SHAH (c.1880–1933) king of Afghanistan from 1929 to 1933. The brother of Dost Mohammed, as commander-in-chief to **Amanullah Khan** (ruler and later king of Afghanistan from 1926) he played a prominent role in the 1919 Afghan War against Britain which secured the country's full independence in 1922. He subsequently fell into disfavour and was forced to live in exile in France. In 1929, with British diplomatic support, he returned to Kabul and seized the throne, immediately embarking on a programme of economic and social modernization. These reforms, however, alienated the Muslim clergy and in 1933 he was assassinated. He was succeeded by his son, Mohammed Zahir Shah.

MOHL, Hugo von (1805–72) German botanist. He was professor of botany at Tübingen (1835–72), and carried out researches on the anatomy and physiology of vegetable cells. In 1846 he discovered and named protoplasm.

MOHL, Julius von (1800–76) German orientalist, born in Stuttgart. He became professor of Persian at the Collège de France in 1847. His great edition of the *Sháh Námeh* was published in 1838–78. The salon of his accomplished wife, Mary Clarke (1793–1883), was a popular centre for Parisian intellectuals.

MÖHLER, Johann Adam (1796–1838) German theologian, born in Igersheim. Professor of Roman Catholic theology at Tübingen and Munich, he wrote *Symbolik* (1832), on the doctrinal differences of Catholics and Protestants.

MOHN, Henrik (1835–1916) Norwegian meteorologist, born in Bergen. He studied at Oslo, and became director of the university meteorological institute (1866–1913). He wrote on meteorology, on the climate of Norway, on the Arctic ocean, and first worked out the theory of Arctic drift and currents that **Fridtjof Nansen** utilized.

MOHOLY-NAGY, László (1895–1946) Hungarian-born American artist and photographer, born in Bucsborsod. He studied law in Budapest and painted with Dada and Constructionist groups in Vienna and Berlin (1919–23). He produced his first 'photograms' (non-representational photographic images made directly without a camera) in 1923 and joined the Bauhaus under **Walter Gropius** in 1925. Here he began to use a camera and was quickly recognized as a leading avant-garde artist in the New Photographers movement in Europe (1925–35), his work including film-making and typography integrated with photographic illustration. He left Germany in 1935 and after working as a designer in Amsterdam and London was invited to the USA in 1937 to head the New Bauhaus school in Chicago, later the Institute of Design. Here he taught photography, becoming a US citizen shortly before his death.

MOHOROVICIC, Andrija (1857–1936) Yugoslavian geophysicist, born in Volosko. He discovered the boundary between the Earth's crust and the mantle. Mohorovicic was educated at Prague University, he became professor initially at the Zagreb Technical School in 1891, and later at Zagreb University. In 1909, while observing the Croatian earthquake in the Kulpa Valley at a distance, he discovered that some seismic waves from a distant earthquake travelling through deep higher-velocity rocks arrived before waves travelling through the Earth's crust. He deduced that the Earth's crust must overlay a denser mantle and calculated the depth to this transition (the Mohorovicic discontinuity or Moho) to be about 30 km. The depth of the Moho has now been extensively mapped using reflection seismic techniques.

MOHS, Friedrich (1773–1839) German mineralogist, born in Gernrode. He became successively professor at Graz, Freiburg and Vienna. The Mohs scale of hardness he introduced is still in use. He wrote *The Natural History System of Mineralogy* (1821), and *Treatise on Mineralogy* (3 vols, 1825).

MOHUN, Charles, 4th Baron Mohun (c.1675–1712) notorious English nobleman and rake. He was involved in frequent duels and brawls. He was twice tried by the House of Lords for murder and acquitted. In 1701 he was involved in lawsuit with James Douglas, 4th Duke of **Hamilton**, which ended in a duel in which both were killed. This duel figures in **Thackeray**'s *Henry Esmond*.

MOI, Daniel Arap (1924–) Kenyan politician, born in Rift Valley Province, the son of a poor farmer. A young teacher without a university education, he was chosen by **Jomo Kenyatta** to be his successor. When

Kenyatta died, in 1978, few people expected him to be capable of surviving under that enormous shadow, but, adopting the motto 'nyayo' (footsteps to freedom), he gradually asserted his authority. He purged the army, launched an impressive development plan, and in 1982 made the Kenyan African National Union (KANU) the only legally permitted party. Despite his increasingly firm style of government, he was re-elected in 1983 and 1988.

MOINAUX See **COURTELINE, Georges**

MOIR, David Macbeth (1798–1851) Scottish physician and writer, born in Musselburgh, where he practised as a physician from 1817 till his death. Under his pen-name of *Delta* (δ) he contributed verses to *Blackwood's Magazine* (coll. 1852), and is remembered for his humorous *The Life of Mansie Wauch, Tailor in Dalkeith* (1828).

MOISEIWITSCH, Benno (1890–1963) Russian-born British pianist, born in Odessa. He studied at the Imperial Academy of Music, Odessa, where he won the **Rubinstein** prize at the age of 9, and subsequently worked in Vienna under Leschetitzky. Rapidly winning recognition as an exponent of the music of the romantic composers, he first appeared in Britain in 1908, and took British nationality in 1937.

MOISEYEV, Igor Alexandrovich (1906–) Soviet dancer, choreographer and ballet director, born in Kiev. He studied privately and at the Bolshoi Ballet School, graduating in 1924 into the main company where he remained, as character soloist and choreographer, until 1939. Always interested in folk dance, he accepted an appointment as director of the new dance department of the Moscow Theatre for Folk Art in 1936. From this he formed a professional folk dance company the following year, developing simple steps and primitve patterns into full theatrical expression. This ensemble has since toured both the world and all 15 republics of the USSR, meanwhile amassing a vast repertoire of dances from other nations. As a choreographer, he is best at creating scenes from daily life and genre pieces. In 1967 he founded the State Ensemble of Classical Ballet.

MOISSAN, Henri (1852–1907) French chemist, born in Paris. A noted experimenter and teacher, he was professor of toxicology at the School of Pharmacy in Paris (1886) and of inorganic chemistry at the Sorbonne (1900). He was awarded the Nobel prize for chemistry (1906). He is chiefly known for his work on fluorine and the electric furnace, which he developed to further his researches into the carbides, silicides and borides. He discovered carborundum and was able to produce tiny artificial diamonds in his laboratory.

MOIVRE, Abraham de See **DE MOIVRE**

MOKANNA, al (Arabic **'The Veiled')**, properly **Hakim ben Atta** (d.778) Arab prophet, the founder of a sect in the Persian province of Khorasan. Ostensibly to protect onlookers from the dazzling rays from his divine countenance, but actually to conceal the loss of an eye, he wore a veil. Setting himself up as a reincarnation of God he gathered enough followers to seize several fortified places, but the caliph Almahdi, son of **Almansur**, after a long siege, took his stronghold of Kash (778), when, with the remnant of his army, Mokanna took poison. His story is the subject of one of **Thomas Moore**'s poems in *Lalla Rookh*.

MOLÉ, Louis Matthieu, Comte (1781–1855) French politician and writer. His father was guillotined during the Terror. In his *Essai de morale et de politique* (1806) he vindicated **Napoleon**'s government on the ground of necessity, and was made a count. **Louis XVIII** made him a peer and minister for the navy; and **Louis-Philippe** made him foreign minister and, in 1836, prime minister, but his régime was unpopular. He left politics after the *coup d'état* of 1851.

MOLESWORTH, Mary Louisa, née **Stewart** (1839–1921) Scottish novelist and writer of children's stories, born in Rotterdam, of Scottish parentage. She spent her childhood in Manchester, Scotland and Switzerland. She began writing as a novelist under the pseudonym 'Ennis Graham', but she is best known as a writer of stories for children, such as *The Carved Lion* and *Cuckoo Clock*.

MOLESWORTH, Sir William (1810–55) English radical politician, born in London. He studied at Offenbach, near Frankfurt, Edinburgh and Cambridge, but was expelled for challenging his tutor to a duel. He was MP for East Cornwall (1832–37), Leeds (1837–41) and Southwark (1845–55). In 1835 he founded the *London Review*, which he merged with the *Westminster Review* in 1836, transferring the ownership to **John Stuart Mill**. He edited the works of **Hobbes** (16 vols, 1839–45), denounced penal transportation, and was a champion of colonial self-government.

MOLESWORTH, William Nassau (1816–90) English historian, born in Milbrook. Educated at Canterbury and Cambridge, he held a living near Rochdale (1844–89). A friend of **John Bright** and **Cobden**, he was an early supporter of the co-operative movement, with which he became acquainted through the Rochdale Pioneers. His works include *History of the Reform Bill of 1832* (1864), *History of England from 1830* (1871–73), and *History of the Church of England from 1660* (1882).

MOLIÈRE, stage name of **Jean Baptiste Poquelin** (1622–73) French playwright, born in Paris, the son of a well-to-do upholsterer. He studied with the Jesuits at the Collège de Clermont, under **Pierre Gassendi**. He may have been called to the bar. His mother, who had some property, died when he was ten years old, and thus when he came of age he received his share of her fortune. He declined to follow his father's business, hired a tennis-court, and embarked on a theatrical venture (1643) with the Béjart family and others, under the title of L'Illustre Théâtre, which lasted for over three years in Paris. The company then proceeded to the provinces from Lyon to Rouen, and had sufficient success to keep going from 1646 to 1658. Prince **François de Conti** took it under his protection for a time; and when he took to Catholic Methodism, Molière obtained the patronage of the king's brother, **Philippe d'Orléans**, so that his troupe became the servants of Monsieur. He played before the king on 24 October 1658, and organized a regular theatre, first in the Petit Bourbon, then, on its demolition, in the Palais Royal. In the provinces Molière had acquired experience as a comic writer, mostly in the style of the old farces. But he had also written *L'Étourdi* and *Le Dépit amoureux*. As a theatre manager he had to perform tragedy as well as comedy. **Corneille**'s *Nicomède*, with which he opened, was not a success; and though the other great tragedian of the day, **Racine**, was a personal friend of Molière's, their connection as manager and author was brief and unfortunate. But Molière soon realized his own immense resources as a comic writer. *Les Précieuses ridicules* was published in November 1659, and every year until his death he produced at least one of his comic masterpieces. In the spring of 1662 he married Armande Béjart, an actress in his own company, probably about 19, and the youngest member of the Béjart family, of which two other sisters, Madeleine and Geneviève, and one brother, Joseph, had been members of L'Illustre Théâtre. It has been suggested that Madeleine Béjart and Molière were lovers, that Armande was Madeleine's daughter, even that Molière was the father of his own wife! It is also said that Armande was unfaithful to her husband. In August 1665 the king adopted Molière's troupe as his own servants. In 1667 symptoms of lung disease showed themselves. He died in his home in the rue de Richelieu the night after having acted as the *Malade* in the seventh representation of his last play. He was generous and amiable; and there are insufficient grounds for the accusations of irreligion brought against him. The dates and titles of his plays are: *L'Étourdi, Le Dépit amoureux* (1658; in the provinces 1656); *Les Précieuses ridicules* (1659); *Sganarelle* (1660); *Don Garcie de Navarre* (1661); *L'Ecole des maris, Les Fâcheux, L'Ecole des femmes* (1662); *La Critique de l'école des femmes, Impromptu de Versailles* (1663); *Le Mariage forcé, La Princesse d'Élide, Tartuffe* (partially, 1664); *Le Festin de Pierre [Don Juan], L'Amour médecin* (1665); *Le Misanthrope, Le médecin malgré lui, Mélicerte, Le Sicilien* (1666); *Tartuffe* (1667); *Amphitryon, George Dandin, L'Avare* (1668); *Monsieur de Pourceaugnac* (1669); *Les Amants magnifiques, Le Bourgeois gentilhomme* (1671); *Les Fourberies de Scapin* (1671); *La Comtesse d'Escarbagnas, Les Femmes savantes* (1672); *Le Malade imaginaire* (1673). To this must be added part of *Psyché* (1671), in collaboration with **Quinault** and **Corneille**, two farces, a few court masques, and some miscellaneous poems. Of all French writers he is the one whose reputation stands highest among his own countrymen and foreigners.

MOLINA, Luis de (1535–1600) Spanish Jesuit theologian, born in Cuenca. He studied at Coimbra, was professor of theology at Evora for 20 years, and died in Madrid. His principal writings are a commentary on the *Summa* of **Aquinas** (1593); a treatise, *De Justitia et Jure* (1592); and the celebrated treatise on grace and free will, *Concordia Liberi Arbitrii cum Gratiae Donis* (1588). Molina asserts that predestination to eternal happiness or punishment is consequent on God's foreknowledge of the free determination of man's will. This view was assailed as a revival of Pelagianism, and hence arose the dispute between Molinists and Thomists. A papal decree in 1607 permitted both opinions; and Molinism has been taught by the Jesuits.

MOLINOS, Miguel de (1640–97) Spanish priest and mystic, born of noble parentage near Saragossa. Ordained in 1652, in 1675 he published *Guida spirtuale*, which embodied an exaggerated form of Quietism, and was arrested for heresy. After a public retraction, he was condemned by the Inquisition to life imprisonment.

MÖLLER, Poul Martin (1794–1838) Danish literary figure, born in Uldum. He graduated in theology at Copenhagen and later became a professor of philosophy, first in Oslo, and then in Copenhagen. His chief work, *A Danish Student's Tale*, which he finished in 1824, but which was published posthumously, is a charming, light-hearted account of student life in Copenhagen. During a journey to China he wrote in verse nostalgically of his homeland. *Leaves from Death's Diary* is a representative work, showing how he avoids the abstract and metaphysical, for his credo was 'all poetry that does not come from life is a lie'. He made the first Danish translation of *The Odyssey*, wrote philosophical essays and coined brilliant aphorisms.

MOLLET, Guy Alcide (1905–75) French socialist politician, born in Flers, Normandy, of working-class parentage. He joined the Socialist party in 1923 and shortly afterwards became English master at the Arras Grammar School, a post which he occupied till World War II, from which he emerged as a captain in the secret resistance army. In 1946 he became mayor of Arras, and MP, secretary-general of the Socialist party and a cabinet minister in the **Léon Blum** government. A keen supporter of a Western European Federation, he became in 1949 a delegate to the Consultative Assembly of the Council of Europe and was its president in 1955. He became prime minister in February 1956. He survived the international crisis over the Anglo-French intervention in Suez in November, but fell from office in May 1957 after staying in power longer than any French premier since the war. In 1959 he was elected a senator of the French Community.

MOLLISON, James Allan (1905–59) Scottish aviator, born in Glasgow. A consultant engineer by profession, he was commissioned into the RAF in 1923, and won fame for his record fight, Australia–England in 1931 in 8 days 19 hours and 28 minutes. In 1932 he married **Amy Johnson**. He made the first solo east-west crossing of the north Atlantic in 1932, and in February 1933 the first England–South America flight. With his wife, he made the first flight across the Atlantic to the USA in 1933, and to India in 1934. He was awarded the Britannia Trophy (1933). The marriage was dissolved in 1938.

MOLNÁR, Ferenc (1878–1952) Hungarian novelist and dramatist, born in Budapest. He is best known for his novel *The Paul Street Boys* (1907), and his plays *The Devil* (1907), *Liliom* (1909) and *The Good Fairy* (1930), all of which have achieved success in English translation.

MOLOTOV, originally **Skriabin, Vyacheslav Mikhailovich** (1890–1986) Russian politician, born in Kukaida, Vyatka. He was educated at Kazan High School and Polytechnic. In the 1905 revolution he joined the Bolshevik section of **Lenin**'s Social Democratic Workers' party and in 1912 became the staunch disciple of **Stalin** when *Pravda* was launched. During the March 1917 revolution he headed the Russian bureau of the central committee of the Bolshevik party and in October was a member of the military revolutionary committee which directed the coup against **Kerensky**. In 1921 he became secretary of the central committee of the Russian Communist party and the youngest candidate-member of the Politburo. In 1928 his appointment to the key position of secretary of the Moscow committee of the all-Union party marked the launching of the first Five-Year Plan. Molotov, who was chairman of the council of people's commissars from 1930 to 1941, became an international figure in May 1939 when he took on the extra post of commissar for foreign affairs, shaping the policy which led to the nonaggression pact with Nazi Germany. In 1942 he signed in London the 20 years' Treaty of Alliance with Britain. He was Marshal Stalin's chief adviser at Teheran and Yalta and represented the Soviet Union at the 1945 founding conference of the United Nations at San Francisco and at the Potsdam Conference. After the war Molotov, who negotiated the pacts binding the satellite states to the Soviet Union, emerged as the uncompromising champion of world Sovietism. His 'no' at meetings of the United Nations and in the councils of foreign ministers became a byword. His attitude led to the prolongation of the 'Cold War' and the division of Germany into two conflicting states. In 1949 he was released from his duties as foreign minister but retained his post as deputy prime minister. He was re-appointed foreign minister in the 1953 **Malenkov** government and switched to the 'peace offensive'. He resigned in 1956 and was appointed minister of state control. In 1957 **Khrushchev** called him a 'saboteur of peace', accused him of policy failures and appointed him ambassador to Outer Mongolia until 1960.

MOLTKE, Helmuth, Count von (1800–91) Prussian soldier. In 1819 he became lieutenant in a Danish regiment, but in 1822 entered the Prussian service. In 1832 he was appointed to the staff, and in 1835 obtained leave to travel. Asked by the sultan to remodel the Turkish army, he did not return to Berlin till 1839. From 1858 to 1888 he was chief of the general staff in Berlin, and reorganized the Prussian army. His strategical skill was displayed in the successful wars with Denmark in 1863–64, with Austria in 1866, and with France in 1870–71. He married in 1841 his stepsister's daughter by an English father, Marie von Burt (1825–1868). Known as 'The Silent', he was a man of great modesty and simplicity of character.

MOLTKE, Helmuth (1848–1916) German soldier nephew of Count **Helmuth von Moltke**. Like his uncle, he rose to be chief of the general staff (in 1906), but in World War I, after losing at the battle of the Marne in September 1914, was superseded by **Falkenhayn**.

MOLTMANN, Jürgen (1926–) German Reformed theologian, born in Hamburg. A professor at Wuppertal (1958–63), Bonn (1963–67), and Tübingen (1967–), he is best known for his influential trilogies, *Theology of Hope* (1967), *The Crucified God* (1974), and *The Church in the Power of the Spirit* (1977), *The Trinity and the Kingdom of God* (1981), and the Gifford Lectures *God in Creation* (1985), and *The Way of Jesus Christ* (1990). Probably the most significant Protestant theologian of the 20th-century since **Karl Barth**, Moltmann's espousal of a theology of hope marked a reacton against the individualistic existential approach of **Rudolf Bultmann**, and a revival in Protestant theology of concern for the social nature of Christian faith in the modern world. His other books include *Hope and Planning* (1971), *On Human Dignity* (1984), and *Creating a Just Future* (1989).

MOLYNEUX, Edward Henry (1891–1974) English fashion designer, born in London. After studying art, he worked for Lucile in London and abroad. After service as a captain in the British Army in World War I, in which he lost an eye, he opened his own couture house in Paris in 1919 with branches in London, Monte Carlo, Cannes and Biarritz, and became famous for the elegant simplicity of his tailored suits with pleated skirts and his evening wear. He closed his salons in 1950 and retired to Jamaica. He reopened in 1965 but soon retired again.

MOMMSEN, Theodor (1817–1903) German historian, born in Garding in Schleswig, the son of a pastor. He studied at Kiel for three years, examined Roman inscriptions in France and Italy for the Berlin Academy (1844–47), and in 1848 was appointed to a chair of law at Leipzig, of which he was deprived two years later for the part he took in politics. In 1852 he became professor of Roman law at Zürich, and in 1854 at Breslau, in 1858 professor of ancient history at Berlin. He edited the monumental *Corpus Inscriptionum Latinarum*, helped to edit the *Monumenta Germaniae Historica*, and from 1873–95 was permanent secretary of the Academy. In 1882 he was tried and acquitted on a charge of slandering **Bismarck** in an election speech. His greatest works remain his *History of Rome* (3 vols, 1854–55) and *The Roman Provinces* (1885). He was awarded the Nobel prize for literature in 1902. Amongst his 920 separate publications were works on the Italic dialects (1845, 1850), Neapolitian inscriptions (1857), Roman coins (1850), Roman constitutional law (1871), and an edition of the Pandects (1866–70).

MOMOH, Joseph Saidu (1937–) Sierra Leone soldier and politician. Born in Binkolo, in the Northern Province, he was trained at military schools in Ghana, Britain and Nigeria before being commissioned in the Sierra Leone army in 1963. Twenty years later he was army commander, with the rank of major-general. In 1985, when the president, **Siaka Stevens**, announced his retirement at the age of 80, Momoh was endorsed by Sierra Leone's only political party, the All-People's Congress (APC), as the sole presidential candidate. Since taking office he has disassociated himself from the policies of his predecessor, pledging to fight corruption and improve the economy.

MOMPESSON, William (1639–1709) English clergyman. He was rector of Eyam, Derbyshire, when in 1665–66 the plague (brought from London in a box of infected cloths) carried off 267 of his 350 parishioners. He persuaded his people to confine themselves entirely to the parish, and the disease was not spread. In 1669 he became rector of Eakring, Nottinghamshire, and in 1676 was made a prebendary of Southwell.

MONASH, Sir John (1865–1931) Australian soldier, born in Melbourne of German parentage. Educated at Scotch College and Melbourne University, he practised as a civil engineer and also held a commission in the Australian Citizen Force (1887). He commanded the 4th Australian Brigade at Gallipoli (1914–15), the 3rd Australian Division in France (1916), and the Australian Corps as lieutenant-general (1918). Recognized as one of the outstanding generals of World War I, he was noted for the meticulous preparation and planning of his operations. He retired in 1930 with the rank of general.

MONBODDO, James Burnett, Lord (1714–99) Scottish judge and pioneer anthropologist, born at Monboddo House, Kincardineshire. Educated at Aberdeen, Edinburgh and Gröningen, he was called to the Scottish bar, and in 1767 was raised to the bench as Lord Monboddo. His *Origin and Progress of Language* (6 vols, 1773–92) is a learned but eccentric production, but his theory of human affinity with monkeys anticipated **Charles Darwin** and the modern science of anthropology. He also published, anonymously, *Ancient Metaphysics* (6 vols, 1779–99).

MONCK See **MONK, George**

MONCKTON, Lionel (1861–1924) English composer, born in London. Prominent as an amateur actor while at Oxford, he turned to composition and contributed songs to many of the shows of **George Edwardes**, at the Gaiety Theatre and elsewhere in London. He was composer of several musical comedies, of which *The Quaker Girl* and *The Country Girl* were popular.

MONCKTON, Walter Turner, 1st Viscount Monckton of Brenchley (1891–1965) English lawyer and statesman, born in Plaxtol, Kent. Educated at Harrow and Balliol College, Oxford, he was called to the bar in 1919, and became attorney-general to the Prince of Wales in 1932, in which capacity he was adviser to him (as **Edward VIII**) in the abdication crisis of 1936. He held many legal offices, and in World War II was director-general of the ministry of information; in the 1945 caretaker government he was solicitor-general. MP for Bristol West from 1951 until his elevation to the peerage in 1957, he was minister of labour (1951–55), of defence (1955–56) and paymaster-general (1956–57).

MONCRIEFF, Colonel Sir Alexander, (1829–1906) Scottish soldier and engineer, born in Edinburgh. He invented the Moncrieff Pits and disappearing carriages for siege and fortress guns.

MOND, Alfred Moritz, 1st Baron Melchett (1868–1930) British industrialist and politician, son of

Ludwig Mond. After some years in industry and chairman of the Mond Nickel Co, he was a Liberal MP from 1906 to 1928, was the first commissioner of works (1916–21) and was minister of health (1922). In 1926 he helped to form ICI (Imperial Chemical Industries Ltd), of which he became chairman. A powerful advocate of industrial co-operation, in 1927 he instituted the Mond-Turner conference with the TUC which suggested the formation of a national industrial council.

MOND, Ludwig (1839–1909) German-born British chemist and industrialist, born in Cassel. Settling in England in 1864, he perfected at Widnes his sulphur recovery process. He founded in 1873, with John Tomlinson Brunner, great alkali-works at Winnington, Cheshire, and made discoveries in nickel manufacture. In 1896 he gave to the Royal Institution for the nation a physico-chemical laboratory costing £100000.

MONDALE, Walter Frederick (Fritz) (1928–) American politician born in the small town of Ceylon, Minnesota, the son of a Methodist preacher of Norwegian stock. After graduating from the University of Minnesota Law School, he made his reputation as a local Democrat 'machine politician' in his home state, before serving in the US senate between 1964 and 1976. He was selected as **Jimmy Carter**'s running-mate in the 1976 presidential election and served as an active vice-president between 1977 and 1980. In November 1984 he was the Democratic presidential nominee, but was crushingly defeated by the Republican, **Ronald Reagan**. Following this reverse, Mondale retired from national politics to resume his law practice.

MONDRIAN, Piet, properly **Pieter Cornelis Mondriaan** (1872–1944) Dutch artist, born in Amersfoort. He was associated with **van Doesburg** in founding the De Stijl movement in architecture and painting. He began by painting landscape in a traditional sombre Dutch manner but after moving to Paris in 1909 he came under the influence of **Matisse** and Cubism. He then began painting still lifes which are analysed in terms of the relationship between the outlines and the planes. In the hands of Mondrian these became increasingly abstract so that eventually the patterns made become more important than the subject itself. During World War I he discarded the subject altogether and concentrated on constructing grids of simple black lines filled in with primary colours. These rectilinear compositions depend for their beauty on the simple relationships between the coloured areas. He was a great theoretician and in 1920 published a pamphlet called Neo-Plasticism which inspired the Dutch philosopher Schoenmaekers. He went to London in 1938, and from 1940 he lived in New York. Mondrian's work has been a major influence on all purely abstract painters.

MONET, Claude (1840–1926) French Impressionist painter, born in Paris. He spent his youth in Le Havre, where he met **Boudin**, who encouraged him to work in the open air. Moving to Paris, he associated with **Renoir**, **Pissarro** and **Sisley**, and exhibited with them at the first Impressionist Exhibition in 1874; one of his works at this exhibition, *Impression: soleil levant*, gave name to the movement. Later he worked much at Argenteuil. With Pissarro, Monet is recognized as being one of the creators of Impressionism, and he was one of its most consistent exponents. He visited England, Holland and Venice, and he spent his life expressing his instinctive way of seeing the most subtle nuances of colour, atmosphere and light in landscape. Apart from many sea and river scenes, he also executed several series of paintings of subjects under different aspects of light—eg, *Haystacks* (1890–91), *Rouen Cathedral* (1892–95) and the almost abstract *Waterlilies* (at the Orangerie, Paris). The last years of his life were spent as a recluse at Giverny.

MONGE, Gaspard (1746–1818) French mathematician and physicist, born in Beaune. The founder of descriptive geometry, he became professor of mathematics at Mézières in 1768, and in 1780 professor of hydraulics at the Lycée in Paris. In 1783, independently of **James Watt** or **Henry Cavendish**, he discovered that water resulted from an electrical explosion of oxygen and hydrogen. During the Revolution he was minister for the navy, but soon took charge of the national manufacture of arms and gunpowder. He helped to found (1794) the École Polytechnique, and became professor of mathematics there. The following year there appeared his *Leçons de géométrie descriptive*, in which he stated his principles regarding the general application of geometry to the arts of construction (descriptive geometry). He was sent by the Directory to Italy, from where he followed Napoleon to Egypt. In 1805 he was made a senator and Count of Pelusium, but lost both dignities on the restoration of the Bourbons.

MONICA See **AUGUSTINE, St**

MONIER-WILLIAMS See **WILLIAMS, Sir Monier Monier-**

MONIZ, Antonio Egas See **EGAS MONIZ, Antonio**

MONK or **MONCK, George, 1st Duke of Albemarle** (1608–70) English soldier, the second son of a Devonshire baronet of loyalist sympathies. He was a volunteer in the *Île de Rhé* expedition of 1628. He campaigned for 10 years in the Low Countries (1629–38). In the Civil War (1642–51) he was at first a Royalist, fought in Ireland (1642–43) but was captured at the battle of Nantwich, (1644). After two years' imprisonment in the Tower he was persuaded to support the Commonwealth cause. His successful activities in Ireland brought him to the notice of **Cromwell**. He defeated the Scots at Dunbar in 1650, and was successful in pacifying Scotland. In the 1st Dutch War he speedily adapted his talents to sea fighting, and played a major part in the 1653 victory over **Tromp** off the Gabbard. Returning to his command in Scotland, with the Lord Protector's death Monk's intensely practical nature revolted at the turmoil and confusion that characterized **Richard Cromwell**'s faction-torn régime. Convinced that the catalyst required to heal the nation's health was a revival of monarchical rule, he was instrumental in bringing about the restoration of **Charles II**. He was rewarded with the Dukedom of Albermarle, and the appointment of lieutenant-general of the forces. In the 2nd Dutch War he played a conspicuous and useful part, defeating the Dutch at St James's Fight in July, 1666. Throughout the Great Plague (1665) he exercised a wise and enheartening rule over stricken London. In 1667, with **De Ruyter** raiding the Medway virtually unopppsed, Monk hastened to Gillingham to take command of the defences. Thereafter canny, taciturn 'Old George' retired more and more into private life. He was buried in Westminster Abbey.

MONK, Maria (c.1817–1850) Canadian impostor, born in St John's, Quebec. She pretended in 1835 to have escaped from cruel treatment in a nunnery at Montreal, and published *Awful Disclosures by Maria Monk* (1836) and *Further Disclosures* (1837) before being exposed as a fake.

MONK, Meredith (1943–) American dancer, choreographer and musician, born in Lima, Peru. The daughter of a professional singer, she took dance classes as a child and began composing music as a teenager. She was briefly associated with the experimental Judson Dance Theatre in mid 1960s, but broke away to develop multimedia music/theatre/dance events of her own. These are either solos or inventive group performances featuring her own company, The House (formed in 1968). They frequently occur in unconventional venues (churches, museums, car parks) and utilize film, props, sound, gestures and other movement, public history and personal myth.

MONK, Thelonious Sphere (1917–82) American jazz pianist and composer, born in Rocky Mount, North Carolina, and brought up in New York. After piano lessons at eleven, he began to perform at 'rent parties' in Harlem and to play in church. While in his twenties, he worked as a freelance musician and studied briefly at the Juilliard School of Music. Between 1939 and 1945 he worked under a succession of leaders in New York, including Kenny Clarke, Lucky Millinder, Cootie Williams and Kermit Scott. Monk first recorded while with the Coleman Hawkins Sextet in 1944. During this period the bebop style was causing a ferment among young jazz musicians in New York, and Monk was a key figure in these experiments at Minton's Playhouse. He joined **Dizzy Gillespie**'s first big band in 1946, formed specifically to perform bebop-style arrangements. Monk formed his own small group in 1947, and from that time his performing and recording was done largely with small groups, latterly with a quartet using such tenor saxophone players as **John Coltrane**, Johnny Griffin and (for eleven years) Charlie Rouse. World tours from the 1960s brought wide recognition for Monk's percussive and harmonically iconoclastic style. He played little after the mid 1970s but many of his compositions, such as 'Round Midnight' and 'Straight No Chaser' are frequently performed.

MONMOUTH, James, Duke of (1649–85) English claimant to the throne, born in Amsterdam, the illegitimate son of **Charles II** and **Lucy Walter**. Charles committed the boy to the care of Lord Crofts; and in 1662 'Mr James Crofts' came to England with the queen-dowager. In 1663 he was created Duke of Monmouth, wedded to a rich heiress, Anne, Countess of Buccleuch (1651–1732), and also made Duke of Buccleuch; in 1670 he succeeded **George Monk** as captain-general. A weak, pretty, affable libertine, he became the idol of the populace, thanks to his humanity towards the Scottish Covenanters at Bothwell Brig (1679), to the Popish Plot and the Exclusion bill, and to his two semi-royal progresses (1680–82). The first Earl of **Shaftesbury** pitted the 'Protestant Duke' against the popish heir-presumptive (later **James II**), and enmeshed him in the Rye House Plot (1683), on whose discovery Monmouth fled to the Low Countries. At Charles' death, in concert with the Scottish expedition by the 9th Duke of **Argyll**, he landed at Lyme Regis with 82 followers in June 1685, branded James as a popish usurper, and asserted his own legitimacy and right to the crown. At Taunton he was proclaimed King James II; and on 6 July he attempted with 2600 foot and 600 horse (peasants mostly and miners) to surprise the king's forces, 2700 strong, encamped on Sedgemoor near Bridgwater. His men were mown down by the artillery. Monmouth fled, but was captured in a ditch near Ringwood. Brought before James, he wept and even offered to turn Catholic; but on 15 July he was beheaded on Tower Hill. His followers were persecuted in the 'Bloody Assize' of Judge **Jeffreys**.

MONNET, Jean (1888–1979) French statesman, born in Cognac. He was educated locally, and in 1914 entered the ministry of commerce. A distinguished economist and expert in financial affairs, he became in 1947 commissioner-general of the 'Plan de modernisation et d'équipement de la France' (Monnet plan). He was awarded the Prix Wateler de la Paix (1951), and he was president of the European Coal and Steel High Authority (1952–55). In 1956 he became president of the Action Committee for the United States of Europe.

MONOD, Adolphe (1802–56) French protestant pastor, born of Swiss parentage in Copenhagen, brother of **Frédéric Monod**. He worked as a preacher in Naples and Lyon. In 1833 he founded a Free Evangelical Church. He became professor at Montauban and minister at the Oratoire in Paris. He was the author of *Sermons* (1844).

MONOD, André Théodore (1902–) French naturalist and explorer, born in Rouen. Educated at the Sorbonne, he made extensive botanical and geological studies of remote regions of the Sahara. His most memorable trans-Saharan crossing of 560 miles was by camel from Wadan, Mauritania to Arawan, Mali, made by laying down advance depots of food and water. He subsequently became director of the Institut Français d'Afrique Noire (1938–64), and dean of the faculty of sciences of Dakar University, Senegal.

MONOD, Frédéric (1794–1863) French Protestant pastor, brother of **Adolphe Monod**. He was for 30 years a prominent pastor in Paris, and in 1849 helped to found the Free Reformed Church of France.

MONOD, Jacques (1910–76) French biochemist, and joint winner of the 1965 Nobel prize for physiology or medicine. A graduate of Paris, he served in the French Resistance during World War II before joining the Pasteur Institute in Paris. He became head of the cellular biochemistry department in 1954, and director in 1971, as well as being professor of molecular biology at the Collège de France from 1967. With **François Jacob** he discovered genes that regulate other genes which they named as operons (groups of genes clustered round a chromosome). Their discovery may have great significance for cancer research. They shared the Nobel prize with **André Lwoff**.

MONRO, Alexander (1697–1767) 'Monro Primus', Scottish anatomist, born in London. He studied at London, Paris, and in Leiden under **Hermann Boerhaave**. From 1719 he lectured at Edinburgh on anatomy and surgery (professor 1725–59). He helped to found the Edinburgh Royal Infirmary, and made Edinburgh a major centre for medical training. He wrote *Osteology* (1726), *Essay on Comparative Anatomy* (1744), *Observations Anatomical and Physiological* (1758), and *Account of the Success of Inoculation of Smallpox in Scotland*.

MONRO, Alexander (1733–1817) 'Monro Secundus', Scottish anatomist, son of **Alexander Monro** 'Monro Primus'. He succeeded his father's chair in anatomy at Edinburgh University. He wrote on the nervous system (1783), the physiology of fishes (1785), and the brain, eye and ear (1797).

MONROE, Harriet (1860–1936) American poet and critic, born in Chicago. In 1912 she founded the magazine *Poetry*, which was influential in publicizing the work of **Lindsay**, **Eliot**, **Pound** and **Frost**, among others. She wrote the 'Columbian Ode' for the Chicago World's Columbian Exposition (1892), celebrating the 400th anniversary of the west's 'discovery' of America.

MONROE, James (1758–1831) fifth president of the USA, born in Westmoreland County, Virginia. After serving in the War of Independence he was elected to the assembly of Virginia and in 1783 to congress, where he sat for three years. He was chairman of the committee (1785) that prepared the way for framing the constitution, of which, however, as a States' Rights man, he disapproved. As a member of the United

States senate (1790–94), he opposed **Washington** and the Federalists; the government recalled him in 1796 from the post of minister to France. He was governor of Virginia 1799–1802, and in 1803 he helped to negotiate the Louisiana purchase. The next four years were spent in less successful diplomacy at London and Madrid. In 1811 he was again governor of Virginia, from 1811 to 1817 secretary of state, and in 1814–15 also secretary of war. In 1816 he was elected president of the USA, and in 1820 re-elected almost unanimously. His most popular acts were the recognition of the Spanish American republics, and the promulgation in a message to congress (1823) of the 'Monroe Doctrine', embodying the principle 'that the American continents ... are henceforth not to be considered as subjects for future colonization by any European power', though existing colonies were not to be interfered with. In 1825 Monroe retired to his seat at Oak Hill, Virginia, till, deep in debt, he found refuge with relatives in New York.

MONROE, Marilyn, originally **Norma Jean Mortenson** or **Baker** (1926–62) American film star, born in Los Angeles. After a disturbed childhood spent largely in foster homes because of her mother's mental illness, she became a photographer's model in 1946. Following several small film parts and a high-powered studio publicity campaign, she became the star of many successful films as a beautiful, sexy 'dumb blonde' in, for instance, *How to Marry a Millionaire* and *Gentlemen Prefer Blondes* (both 1953). She developed her flair for light comedy in *The Seven Year Itch* (1955) and *Some Like It Hot* (1959). Wanting more serious roles, she had studied at **Lee Strasberg**'s Actors' Studio and went on to win acclaim in *Bus Stop* (1956) and *The Misfits* (1961), written for her by her third husband, **Arthur Miller**. She came to London to make *The Prince and the Showgirl* (1957) with Sir **Laurence Olivier**, returning after two years to Hollywood. Divorced from Arthur Miller in 1961, she died in 1962 of an overdose of sleeping pills, and has become something of a symbol of Hollywood's ruthless exploitation of beauty and youth.

MONSARRAT, Nicholas John Turney (1910–79) English novelist, born in Liverpool. He was educated at Winchester and at Trinity College, Cambridge, abandoned law for literature and wrote three quite successful novels, and a play, *The Visitors*, which reached the London stage. During the war he served in the navy, and out of his experiences emerged his bestselling novel *The Cruel Sea* (1951), which was filmed. *The Story of Esther Costello* (1953) repeated that success, followed by *The Tribe That Lost Its Head* (1956) and *The Pillow Fight* (1965). He settled in Ottawa, Canada, as director of the UK Information Office (1953–56) after holding a similar post in South Africa (1946–52).

MONSON, Sir William (1569–1643) English naval commander, born in South Carlton, Lincolnshire. He served at sea against the Spaniards (1585–1602), was taken prisoner and sentenced to the galleys (1591) but returned to active service with **Essex**. He distinguished himself in the Cadiz expedition of 1596. He was imprisoned briefly on charges of treason and corruption, but was released and became admiral of the narrow seas (1604–16). He wrote *Naval Tracts* which are partly autobiographical (5 vols, 1902–14, ed M Oppenheim).

MONSTRELET, Enguerrand de (c.1390–1453) French chronicler, born near Boulogne. Provost of Cambrai, he wrote a *Chronicle, 1400–44*, from the Burgundian standpoint.

MONTAGNA, Bartolomeo (c.1450–1523) Italian painter, a native of Brescia. He probably studied at Venice under **Giovanni Bellini** and **Carpaccio**. He founded a school of painting at Vicenza and also worked in Verona and other places.

MONTAGU See **HALIFAX, Charles, MANCHESTER, Edward** and **SANDWICH, Edward**

MONTAGU, Ashley, originally **Montague Francis Ashley Montague** (1905–) English-born American anthropologist, born in London. He was educated in London and studied at London, Florence and Columbia universities. Throughout his work on human biosocial evolution he has argued strongly against the view that cultural phenomena are genetically determined. His many influential publications, both scholarly and popular, include *Coming Into Being among the Australian Aborigines* (1937), *The Natural Superiority of Women* (1953), *Man's Most Dangerous Myth: the Fallacy of Race* (1964), *The Elephant Man* (1971), *The Nature of Human Aggression* (1976) and *Growing Young* (1981). He has held posts at the Wellcome History Museum, London, New York University, Hahnemann Medical College, Philadelphia, and was head of anthropology at Rutgers University, New Jersey, from 1949 to 1955.

MONTAGU, Eizabeth, née **Robinson** (1720–1800) English writer and society leader. In 1742 she married Edward Montagu, grandson of the **1st Earl of Sandwich** and cousin of Edward Wortley Montagu (husband of Lady **Mary Wortley Montagu**). The first of the 'bluestockings', with £10 000 a year, she established a salon in Mayfair which became the heart of London social and literary life, for people like **Lyttelton, Garrick, Reynolds** and many others. She wrote an essay on **Shakespeare** (1768).

MONTAGU, George (1753–1815) English naturalist and soldier, born at Lackham House in Wiltshire. A failed career in the army and a disastrous marriage that led to the loss of his estates turned his attention to ornithology. He moved to Devon, where he produced his notable *Ornithological Dictionary; or Alphabetical Synopsis of British Birds* (2 vols, 1802). Montagu's Harrier is named after him.

MONTAGU, Lady Mary Wortley (1689–1762) English writer, eldest daughter of the Earl (later Duke) of Kingston. A well-known society hostess, she had a celebrated quarrel with **Alexander Pope**. She was instrumental in introducing vaccination against smallpox into Britain.

MONTAGU, Richard (1577–1641) English prelate. He was appointed chaplain to **James VI and I** in 1617, and as an opponent of Puritanism was the centre of much controversy, but with **Laud**'s influence he became successively bishop of Chichester (1628) and Norwich (1638). He published several theological books.

MONTAGUE, Charles Edward (1867–1928) English novelist and essayist, of Irish parentage. He was on the staff of *The Manchester Guardian* from 1890 to 1925. His numerous writings include the novels *A Hind Let Loose*, and *Rough Justice* (1926), and a collection of essays, *Disenchantment* (1922).

MONTAIGNE, Michel Eyquem de (1533–92) French essayist, third son of the Seigneur de Montaigne, born at the Château de Montaigne in Périgord. As an experiment in humanist upbringing, he spoke no language but Latin until he was six, and at the Collège de Guienne in Bordeaux he remained for seven years, boarding in the rooms of his famous teachers, **George Buchanan** and **Marc Muret**. He subsequently studied law; but from the age of 13 to 24 little is known of him, though it is certain that he was frequently in Paris, knew something of court life, and took his full share of its pleasures. He obtained a post in connection with the *parlement* of Bordeaux, and for 13 years was a city counsellor. He formed a close friendship with Étienne de la Boëtie (1530–63). He married (1565) Françoise de la Chassaigne, daughter of a fellow counsellor. A translation (1569) of the *Natural History* of a 15th-century professor at Toulouse was his first attempt at literature, and supplied the text for his *Apologie de Raymon Sebond*, in which he exhibited the full scope of his own sceptical philosophy. In 1571, as his two elder brothers had died, he succeeded to the family estate at Château de Montaigne, and there lived the life of a country gentleman, varied only by visits to Paris and a tour in Germany, Switzerland and Italy. There he began those *Essais* (1572–80, and 1588) which were to give him a place among the first names in literary history. The record of his journey (1580–81), in French and Italian, was first published in 1774. Unanimously elected mayor of Bordeaux (against his wish), he performed his duties to the satisfaction of the citizens, and was re-elected. Despite the free expression of scepticism in his writings, he devoutly received the last offices of the church. From the very first, men like **Pascal**, differing completely from him in all the fundamental problems of life (as in his inconclusive philosophy, his easy moral opinions, his imperfect sense of duty), have acknowledged their debt to his fearless and all-questioning criticism, expressed mainly in haphazard remarks, seemingly inspired by the mere caprice of the moment, but showing the highest originality, the very broadest sympathies, and a nature capable of embracing and realizing the largest experience of life.

MONTALE, Eugenio (1896–1981) Italian poet, born in Genoa. He was the leading poet of the modern Italian 'Hermetic' school, and his primary concern was with language and meaning. His works include *Ossi di Seppia* (1925), *Le occasioni* (1939), *La bufera* (1956), *Satura* (1962) and *Xenia* (1966). He was awarded the Nobel prize for literature in 1975.

MONTALEMBERT, Charles René Forbes de (1810–70) French historian and politician, born in London, the eldest son of a noble French *émigré* and his English wife. Educated at Fulham and the Collège Ste Barbe, in 1830 he eagerly joined the Abbé **Lamennais** and **Lacordaire** in the *Avenir*, a High Church liberal newspaper. In 1831 Montalembert and Lacordaire opened a free school in Paris, which was immediately closed by the police. Montalembert, who had succeeded to his father's peerage, pleaded with great eloquence the cause of religious liberty, and when the *Avenir*, being condemned by the pope (1831), was given up, Montalembert lived for a time in Germany, where he wrote the *Historie de Ste Élizabeth*. In 1835 again in Paris, he spoke in the Chamber in defence of the liberty of the press, and a famous protest against tyranny was his great speech in January 1848 upon Switzerland. After the revolution he was elected a member of the National Assembly; and he supported Louis Napoleon (**Napoleon III**) until the confiscation of the Orléans property, when he became a determined opponent of the imperial régime. He visited England in 1855, and wrote *De l'Avenir politique de l'Angleterre*. In 1858 an article in the *Correspondant* made such exasperating allusions to the imperial government that he was sentenced to six months' imprisonment and a fine of 3000 francs—a sentence remitted by the emperor. Besides his great work, *Les Moines d'occident* (7 vols, 1860–77), he wrote *Une Nation en deuil: la Pologne* (1861), *L'Église libre dans l'état libre* (1863), *Le Pape et la Pologne* (1864) and other works.

MONTAND, Yves, originally **Ivo Livi** (1921–) Italian-born French actor-singer, born in Monsummano in Tuscany. He worked at a variety of jobs before performing as a singer and impressionist in Marseilles and Paris. A protégé of **Edith Piaf**, he made his film début with her in *Etoile sans lumière* (1946). A star attraction with his one-man show, his film career temporarily blossomed with *Le Salaire de la Peur* (*The Wages of Fear*, 1953). An international cabaret star, he appeared on stage in *The Crucible* (1954) and ventured abroad for films like *Let's Make Love* (1960). His acting reputation was enhanced by an association with the director Costa-Gavras and films like *Z* (1968) and *L'Aveu* (The Confession, 1970), which also reflected his sympathy for a variety of left-wing causes. Married to actress **Simone Signoret** from 1951 until her death in 1985, he became a distinguished elder statesman of the French film industry, in productions like *Jean De Florette* (1986) and *Manon Des Sources* (1986).

MONTANO See **ARIAS, Benito**

MONTCALM, Louis Joseph, Marquis de Montcalm Gezan de Saint Véran (1712–59) French soldier, born near Nîmes. A soldier at 15, in 1746 he was severely wounded and made prisoner at the battle of Piacenza. In the Seven Years' War (1756–63) he assumed command of the French troops in North America in 1756, and captured the British post of Oswego, and also Fort William Henry, where the prisoners (men, women and children) were massacred by the Indian allies. In 1758 with a small force he successfully defended Ticonderoga, and after the loss to the French of Louisburg and Fort Duquesne, moved to Quebec, and with 16000 troops prepared to defend it against a British attack. In 1759 General **Wolfe** ascended the St Lawrence with about 8000 troops. After repeated attempts to scale the heights of Montmorency, he gained the plateau with 5000 men, and in a battle on the plains of Abraham drove the French in disorder on the city. Montcalm tried in vain to rally his force, was borne back by the rush, and, mortally wounded, died next morning.

MONTECUCCULI, Raimondo, Count (1608–81) Italian-born Austrian soldier, born near Modena. He entered the Austrian service in 1625, and distinguished himself during the Thirty Years' War, against the Turks (1664), and against the French on the Rhine (1672–75). He was made a Prince and Duke of Melfi.

MONTEFIORE, Sir Moses Haim (1784–1885) Italian-born British philanthropist, born in Leghorn, Italy. He retired with a fortune from stockbroking in 1824, and from 1829 was prominent in the struggle for removing Jewish disabilities. After long exclusion and repeated re-election, he was admitted sheriff of London in 1837. Between 1827 and 1875 he made seven journeys to Palestine in the interests of his oppressed co-religionists in Poland, Russia, Rumania and Damascus. He endowed a hospital in Jerusalem in 1855 and a Jewish college in Ramsgate in 1865.

MONTELIUS, Oscar (1843–1921) Swedish archaeologist, born in Stockholm. He became director of archaeology there, wrote on early Swedish culture and developed the typological method.

MONTEMAYOR, Jorge de (c.1515–1561) Spanish novelist and poet, born in Portugal. He wrote the unfinished pastoral romance *Diana* (1559) in Castilian, which influenced Sir **Philip Sidney** and **Shakespeare**.

MONTESI, Wilma (1932–53) Italian model, the daughter of a Roman middle-class carpenter. The finding of her body on the beach near Ostia in April 1953 led to prolonged investigations involving sensational allegations of drug and sex orgies in Roman society. After four years of debate, scandal, arrests, re-arrests and libel suits, the Venice trial in 1957 of the son of a former Italian foreign minister, a self-styled marquis and a former Rome police chief for complicity in her death, ended in their acquittal after many conflicts of evidence. The trial left the mystery unsolved, but exposed corruption in high public places and helped to bring about the downfall of the Scelba Government in 1955.

MONTESPAN, Françoise Athénais, Marquise de (1641–1707) French courtier, and favourite of **Louis XIV**. The daughter of the Duc de Mortemart, in 1663 she married the Marquis de Montespan, and became attached to the household of the queen. Her beauty and wit captivated Louis XIV, and about 1668 she became his mistress. The marquis was flung into the Bastille, and in 1676 his marriage was annulled. The marquise de Montespan reigned supreme till 1682, and bore the king seven children, who were legitimized, but was then supplanted by Madame **de Maintenon**, the governess of her children. In 1691 she left the court, and retired to a convent.

MONTESQUIEU, Charles de Secondat, Baron de la Brède et de (1689–1755) French philosopher and jurist, born at the Château La Brède near Bordeaux. He became counsellor of the *parlement* of Bordeaux in 1714, and its president in 1716. He discharged the duties of his office faithfully, but, till defective eyesight hindered him, by preference devoted himself to scientific researches. His first great literary success was the *Lettres persanes* (1721), containing a satirical description, put in the mouths of two Persian visitors to Paris, of French society. Weary of routine work, he sold his office in 1726 and settled in Paris. He travelled for three years to study political and social institutions, visiting, among other places, England, where he remained for two years (1729–31), mixing with its best society, frequenting the Houses of Parliament, studying the political writings of **Locke**, and analysing the English constitution. *Causes de la grandeur des Romains et de leur décadence* (1734) is perhaps the ablest of his works. His monumental *De l'esprit des lois* (1748) was published anonymously and put on the Index, but passed through twenty-two editions in less than two years. By the spirit of laws he means their *raision d'être*, and the conditions determining their origin, development and forms; the discussion of the influence of climate was novel. The work, which held up the free English constitution to the admiration of Europe, had an immense influence. In 1750 he published a *Défense de l'esprit des lois*, followed afterwards by *Lysimaque* (1748), a dialogue on despotism, *Arsace et Isménie*, a romance, and an essay on taste in the *Encyclopédie*. A member of the French Academy since 1728, he died totally blind.

MONTESSORI, Maria (1870–1952) Italian physician and educationist, born in Rome. The first woman in Italy to receive a medical degree (1894), she founded a school for feeble-minded children (1899–1901), and developed a system of education for children of three to six based on spontaneity of expression and freedom from restraint. The system was later worked out for older children, and applied in Montessori schools throughout the world. She opened the first Montessori school for children in the slums of Rome in 1907.

MONTEUX, Pierre (1875–1964) French-born American conductor, born in Paris. He trained at the Paris Conservatoire, where he began his career as a viola player. From 1911 to 1914, and in 1917, he conducted **Diaghilev**'s Ballets Russes in Paris, leading the world premières of **Stravinsky**'s *Petrushka* (1911) and *The Rite of Spring* (1913) and **Ravel**'s *Daphnis and Chloë* (1912), and in 1914 he organized the 'Concerts Monteux' whose programmes gave prominence to new French and Russian music. After serving in the army in World War I he went to America where he conducted in New York and Boston before returning to Europe in 1924 to the Amsterdam Concertgebouw Orkest. Founding and directing the Orchestre Symphonique de Paris, in 1936 he took over the newly organized San Francisco Symphony Orchestra, and in 1941 established a summer school for student conductors at Hanover, New Hampshire. From 1960 until his death he was principal conductor of the London Symphony Orchestra, and was one of the 20th century's leading conductors, his interpretations equally admired in ballet, opera and symphonic music.

MONTEVERDI, Claudio (1567–1643) Italian composer, born in Cremona, the eldest son of a doctor. As a pupil of Ingegneri at Cremona Cathedral between 1580–90 he became a proficient violist and learnt the art of composition, publishing a set of three-part choral pieces, *Cantiunculae Sacrae*, at the age of 15. About 1590 he was appointed court musician to the Duke of Mantua, with whose retinue he travelled in Switzerland and the Netherlands, and whose *maestro di capella* he became in 1602. In 1612 the duke died and his successor dismissed Monteverdi, who returned to Cremona in straitened circumstances with arrears of salary unpaid. Luckily the post of *maestro di capella* at St Mark's, Venice, fell vacant in 1613 and he was appointed, remaining there until his death. By his efforts the musical reputation of that church, sadly declined since the great days of the **Gabrielis**, was restored to its former high position. Monteverdi left no purely instrumental compositions. His eight books of madrigals, which appeared at regular intervals between 1587 and 1638, embody in the later examples some audaciously experimental harmonies which brought much criticism from academic quarters but underlined the composer's originality and pioneering spirit, while his first opera, *Orfeo* (1607), with its programmatic use of orchestral sonorities, its dramatic continuity and the obbligato character of the accompaniment, marked a considerable advance in the evolution of the genre. The two surviving operas of his later period, *Il Ritorno d'Ulisse* (1641) and *L'Incoronazione di Poppea* (1642), both written when he was well past seventy, show further development towards the Baroque style and foreshadow the use of the *leitmotif*. His greatest contribution to church music is the magnificient *Mass* and *Vespers* of the Virgin (1610), the excellence of which was a deciding factor in his appointment to St Mark's, and which contained tone colours and harmonies well in advance of its time. Other new features which he introduced were the orchestral ritornello, and the use of tremolo and pizzicato. He has been called the 'last madrigalist and first opera composer', an inaccurate designation which, even if it were entirely true, would not be the reason for the immense importance of his role, which is that of a great innovator at one of the most formative periods in the history of musical style.

MONTEZ, Lola, originally **Maria Délores Gilbert** (1818–61) Irish-born American dancer, born in Limerick. After an unsuccessful marriage she turned dancer at Her Majesty's Theatre in London, and while touring Europe, went to Munich (1846), where she soon won over the eccentric artist-king, **Louis I** of Bavaria, with whom she had a scandalous affair, a great boost to her career as a dancer. After a tour of the USA she decided to settle in California. She died in New York.

MONTEZUMA I (c.1390–1464) Aztec emperor of Mexico, ascended the throne about 1437, annexed Chalco, and crushed the Tlascalans.

MONTEZUMA II (1466–1520) last Aztec emperor, succeeded to the title in 1502. A distinguished warrior and legislator, he died during the Spanish conquest of **Hernando Cortés**. One of his descendants was viceroy of Mexico (1697–1701). The last, banished from Spain for liberalism, died at New Orleans in 1836.

MONTFAUCON, Bernard de (1655–1741) French scholar and monk, the founder of the science of palaeography. A Benedictine monk at Saint-Maur, he went to Paris to edit the Latin works of the Greek fathers of the church, and published *Palaeographia graeca* (1708), the first work to be based on a study of manuscript handwriting. He also published editions of **Athanasius** and St **John Chrysostom**.

MONTFORT, Simon IV de, Earl of Leicester (c.1160–1218) Norman crusader. He took part in the 4th Crusade (1202–04), and also undertook in 1208 a crusade against the Albingenses and fell at the siege of Toulouse.

MONTFORT, Simon de, Earl of Leicester (c.1208–1265) English statesman and soldier, son of **Simon IV de Montfort**. Young Simon was well received by **Henry III** of England in 1230, was confirmed in his title and estates in 1232, and in 1238 married the king's youngest sister, Eleanor. In 1239 he quarrelled with the king and crossed to France, but, soon nominally reconciled, he was again in England by 1242. In 1248, sent as king's deputy to Gascony, Simon put down disaffection with a heavy hand. But his jealous master listened eagerly to complaints against his rule, and arraigned him. De Montfort, acquitted, resigned his post in 1253, and returned to England. Bad harvests, famine, fresh exactions of Rome and the rapacity of foreign favourites had exhausted the endurance of the country, and in 1258, at Oxford, the parliament drew up the Provisions of Oxford, which the king swore solemnly to observe. Prince Edward (the future **Edward I**) intrigued with the subtenants, and the barons quarrelled among themselves; and in 1261 the king announced that the pope had declared the Provisions null and void. All men now looked to de Montfort as leader of the barons and the whole nation, and he at once took up arms. After some varying success, both sides sought an arbitrator in **Louis IX** of France, who decided in the *Mise* of Amiens for surrender to the royal authority. London and the Cinque Ports repudiated the agreement, and de Montfort, collecting his forces, surprised the king's army at Lewes, and captured Prince Edward (1264). The *Mise* of Lewes arranged that there were to be three electors: de Montfort, the Earl of **Gloucester**, and the bishop of Hereford, who were to appoint nine councillors to nominate the ministers of state. To aid these councillors in their task a parliament was called, in which, together with the barons, bishops and abbots, there sat four chosen knights from each shire, and for the first time two representatives from certain towns. This, the Model Parliament, held the germ of modern parliaments. But the great earl's constitution was premature; the barons soon grew dissatisfied with the rule of 'Simon the Righteous'; and his sons' arrogance injured his influence. Prince Edward, escaping, combined with Gloucester, and defeated Simon at Evesham.

MONTGOLFIER, Joseph Michel (1740–1810) and **Jacques Étienne** (1745–99), French aeronautical inventors, sons of a paper manufacturer of Annonay. In 1782 they constructed a balloon whose bag was lifted by lighting a cauldron of paper beneath it, thus heating and rarifying the air it contained. A flight of $7\frac{1}{2}$ miles, at 3000 feet, carrying Pilatre de Rozier and the Marquis d'Arlandes, was achieved in 1783: the world's first manned flight. Further experiments were frustrated by the outbreak of the French Revolution, Étienne being proscribed, and his brother returning to his paper factory. Joseph was subsequently elected to the Académie des Sciences and created a *Chevalier de la légion d'honneur* by **Napoleon**.

MONTGOMERIE See **EGLINTON AND WINTON, 13th Earl of**

MONTGOMERIE, Alexander (c.1545–c.1611) Scottish poet, born probably at Hessilhead Castle near Beith. He was 'maister poet' to **James VI**. He was detained in a continental prison, and embittered by the failure of a lawsuit involving loss of a pension. Implicated in Barclay of Ladyland's Catholic plot, he was denounced as a traitor in 1597, and went into exile. His fame rests on the *Cherrie and the Slae*, published twice in 1597, and his love lyrics, especially 'To his Mistress'.

MONTGOMERY, Bernard Law, 1st Viscount Montgomery of Alamein (1887–1976) English soldier, the son of the Bishop Montgomery. Educated at St Paul's School and the Royal Military College, Sandhurst, he served with the Royal Warwickshire Regiment in World War I. In World War II he commanded the 3rd Division, with which he shared the retreat to Dunkirk. In North Africa in 1941 the 8th Army had only partially recovered from its rough handling by the Axis forces when Montgomery was appointed to its command. He quickly restored bruised confidence and the will to win. Conforming to General Sir **Harold Alexander**'s strategic plans, he launched the successful battle of Alamein (October 1942). This was followed up by a series of hard-fought engagements that eventually drove the Axis forces back to Tunis. Montgomery's subsequent activities in Sicily and Italy were solid if somewhat pedestrian. Appointed commander for the ground forces for the Normandy invasion in 1944, his strategy was characterized by wariness and unflagging tenacity. By deliberately attracting the main weight of the German counter-offensive to the British flank, he freed the American armoured formations to inaugurate the joint drive across France and Belgium. His attempt to roll up the German right flank by way of Arnhem (September 1944) lacked co-ordination and the deployment of the proper means to ensure success and ended in disaster, but his timely intervention helped materially to frustrate **Rundstedt**'s surprise offensive of December 1944. He accepted the German capitulation on Lüneburg Heath, and was commander of the British occupied zone in Germany (1945–46) and chief of the imperial general staff (CIGS) in 1946–48. He was deputy commander of NATO forces (1951–58). His publications include *Normandy to the Baltic* (1947), his controversial *Memoirs* (1958), *The Path to Leadership* (1961) and *History of Warfare* (1968).

MONTGOMERY, Gabriel, Comte de (c.1530–1574) French soldier. As an officer in the French king's Scottish Guard, at a tournament in 1559 he mortally wounded **Henri II** in a joust. He retired to Normandy and England, turned Protestant, and returned to France to become a leader of the Huguenot cause, narrowly escaping to Jersey and England from the massacre of St Bartholomew's Day (1572). He later landed in Normandy, but was compelled to surrender, taken to Paris, and beheaded.

MONTGOMERY, James (1771–1854) Scottish poet, born in Irvine. The son of a Moravian pastor, he settled down, after various occupations, as a journalist in Sheffield, where in 1794 he started the *Sheffield Iris*, which he edited till 1825. In 1795 he was fined £20, and spent three months in York Castle for printing a 'seditious' ballad; in 1796 it was £30 and six months for describing a riot. Yet by 1832 he had become a moderate Conservative, and in 1835 accepted from **Peel** a pension of £150. He died in Sheffield, his poems (4 vols, 1849) are 'bland and deeply religious'.

MONTGOMERY, Lucy Maud (1874–1942) Canadian novelist, born in Clifton, Prince Edward Island. She qualified as a schoolteacher from Prince of Wales College, Charlottetown, and after studying at Dalhousie College, Halifax, Nova Scotia, she returned to Cavendish to care for her grandmother for 13 years. She published as her first book the phenomenally successful *Anne of Green Gables* (1908), the story of an orphan girl adopted in error for a boy by an elderly brother and sister. She followed it with several sequels, of which *Rilla of Ingleside* (1921) is an invaluable description of the impact of World War I on the island community. She married the Rev Ewan MacDonald in 1911, and moved to his manse at Leaskdale, Ontario. Her works are sometimes highly satirical; at her best she captures memorably the mysteries and terrors of early childhood, as in *Magic for Marigold* (1929), while her later works show qualities which recall **Maupassant**.

MONTGOMERY, Robert (1807–55) English preacher and poet, born in Bath, the illegitimate son of a clown. He studied at Lincoln College, Oxford; and from 1843, after some years in Glasgow, became minister of Percy Chapel, London. *The Omnipresence of the Deity* (1828) and *Satan* (1830) are remembered by **Macaulay**'s onslaught in the *Edinburgh Review* (April 1830).

MONTHERLANT, Henri Millon de (1896–1972) French novelist and playwright, born in Neuilly-sur-Seine. He was severely wounded in World War I, after which he travelled in Spain, Africa and Italy. A man of athletic interests, in his novels, as in his plays, he advocates the overcoming of the conflicts of life by vigorous action, disdaining the consolation of bourgeois sentiment. His novels, all showing his mastery of style, include the largely autobiographical *La Relève du matin* (1920), *Le Songe* (1922), *Les Bestiaires* (trans 1927, as *The Bullfighters*), *Les Jeunes filles* (1935–39) and *L'Histoire d'amour de la rose de sable* (1954). His plays include *La Reine morte* (1942), *Malatesta* (1946), *Don Juan* (1958) and *Le Cardinal d'Espagne* (1960).

MONTHOLON, Charles Tristan, Marquis de (1783–1853) French soldier and diplomat, born in Paris. He joined the army in 1798, served in the navy and cavalry, was wounded at Wagram (1809), and in 1809 was made **Napoleon**'s chamberlain. He was promoted general in 1811, and was Napoleon's aide-de-camp at Waterloo (1815). He accompanied him to St Helena, and published *Mémoires pour servir à l'histoire de France sous Napoléon, écrits sous sa dictée* (8 vols, 1822–25). Condemned in 1840 to 20 years' imprisonment for helping Louis Napoleon's (**Napoleon III**) attempted seizure of power, he was liberated in 1848, having published in 1846 *Récits de la captivité de Napoléon á Ste Hélène*.

MONTI, Vincenzo (1754–1828) Italian poet, born in Afonsine. He was professor at Pavia and official historian to **Napoleon**. He wrote epics and tragedies and translated **Homer**.

MONTICELLI, Adolphe Joseph Thomas (1824–86) French painter, born in Marseilles. He studied in Paris, where he lived mainly till 1870, then returned to Marseilles, and died there in poverty. His most characteristic paintings are notable for masses of warm and luxurious colour, and vague, almost invisible, figures, in Impressionistic style, though he is placed with the Barbizon group.

MONTLUC, Blaise de (1502–77) French soldier. He fought in Italy, and as governor of Guienne treated the Huguenots with great severity. His *Mémoires* were called 'la bible du soldat' by **Henri IV**.

MONTMORENCY, Anne, 1st Duc de (1493–1567) Marshal and Constable of France. He distinguished himself under his childhood friend, **Francis I**, at Marignano (1515), Mézières and Bicocca, was taken prisoner along with Francis at Pavia (1525), defeated **Charles V** at Susa (1536) and became constable (1538). Suspected by the king of siding with the Dauphin, he was banished from court in 1541. He was restored to his dignities by **Henri II** (1547), commanded at the disaster of St Quentin (1557), and was taken prisoner by the Spaniards. He opposed the influence of **Catherine de' Medici**, commanded against the Huguenots at Dreux (1562), and was taken prisoner a third time. In 1563 he drove the English out of Le Havre. He again engaged **Condé** at St Denis (1567), but received his death-wound.

MONTMORENCY, Henri, Duc de (1595–1632) French marshal, grandson of **Anne, Duc de Montmorency**. He commanded the Catholics of the south in the religious wars (1621–30), took Ré and Oléron (1625), and penetrated into Piedmont (1630). But provoked into rebellion against **Richelieu**, he was defeated at Castelnaudary and beheaded at Toulouse.

MONTPENSIER, Anne Marie Louise d'Orléans, Duchesse de (1627–93) French noblewoman, known as 'La Grande Mademoiselle'. A niece of **Louis XIII**, she supported her father and **Condé** in the revolt of the Fronde (1651–52), where she commanded an army that occupied Orléans and later the Bastille. After a period in disgrace she returned to the court and wished to marry M de Lauzun, but the king refused his consent for many years. Her marriage in the end was not successful and her last years were spent in religious duties.

MONTROSE, James Graham, Marquis of (1612–50) Scottish soldier and royalist. He was educated at St Andrews and travelled in Italy, France and the Low Countries. He returned in the very year (1637) of the 'Service-book tumults' in Edinburgh (see **Jenny Geddes**), and he was one of the four noblemen who drew up the National Covenant. In 1638 he was dispatched to Aberdeen, which he occupied for the Covenanters. When **Charles I** invited several Covenanting nobles to meet him in Berwick, Montrose was one of those who went; and the Presbyterians dated his 'apostasy' from that interview. In the General Assembly of 1639 he expressed misgivings about the Covenant. In the second Bishops' War, Montrose was the first of the Scottish army to ford the Tweed (20 August 1640); but that very month he had entered into a secret engagement against Archibald, 8th Earl of **Argyll**. It leaked out that he had been communicating with the king; he was cited before a committee of the Scottish parliament, and next year was confined for five months in Edinburgh Castle. In 1644 he quitted his forced inaction at Oxford, and, disguised, made his way into Perthshire as lieutenant-general and Marquis of Montrose. At Blair Atholl he met 1200 Scoto-Irish auxiliaries under Alastair MacDonald of Colonsay (d.1647), and the clans quickly rallied round him. He routed the Covenanters under Lord Elcho at Tippermuir near Perth. He next gained a victory at Aberdeen and took the city, which was this time abandoned for four days to the horrors of war. The approach of Argyll with 4000 men compelled Montrose to retreat; but he suddenly appeared in Angus, where he laid waste the estates of the Covenanting nobles. Later, receiving large accessions from the clans, he marched into the Campbell country, devastated it, drove Argyll himself from his castle at Inveraray, and then wheeled north towards Inverness. The 'Estates' placed a fresh army under William Baillie of Letham, who was to take Montrose in front, while Argyll should fall on his rear; but Montrose instead surprised and utterly routed Argyll at Inverlochy (1645). He then passed with fire and sword through Moray and Aberdeenshire, eluded Baillie at Brechin, captured and pillaged Dundee and escaped into the Grampians. He defeated Baillie's lieutenant at Auldearn near Nairn, routed Baillie himself at Alford; and in July 1645 he marched southward with over 5000 men. Baillie, following, was defeated with a loss of 6000 at Kilsyth; this, the most notable of Montrose's six victories, seemed to lay Scotland at his feet, but the clansmen slipped away home to secure their booty. Still, with 500 horse and 1000 infantry, he had entered the Border country, when, on 13 September he was surprised and routed by 6000 troopers under **David Leslie** at Philiphaugh near Selkirk. Escaping to Athole, he endeavoured, vainly, to raise the Highlands; on 3 September 1646, he sailed for Norway, and so passed to Paris, Germany and the Low Countries. When news of Charles' execution reached him, he swore to avenge the death of the martyr, and, undertaking a fresh invasion of Scotland, lost most of his little army by shipwreck in the passage from Orkney to Caithness, but pushed on to the borders of Ross-shire, where, at Invercharron, his dispirited remnant was cut to pieces on 27 April 1650. He was nearly starved to death in the wilds of Sutherland, when he fell into the hands of Macleod of Assynt, who delivered him to Leslie, and taken to Edinburgh as quickly as possible, he was hanged in the High Street, 21 May 1650. Eleven years afterwards his mangled remains were collected and buried in St Giles', where a stately monument was reared to him in 1888. Montrose's few passionately loyal poems are little known, save the one stanza beginning, 'He either fears his fate too much'; even its ascription to Montrose (first made in 1711) is doubtful.

MONTUCLA, Jean Étienne (1725–99) French mathematician, born in Lyon. In 1758 he wrote the first history of mathematics worthy of the name, *Histoire des Mathématiques*.

MONTYON, Jean Baptiste Auget, Baron de (1733–1820) French lawyer and philanthropist. He is best known for the prizes he established for scientific and literary achievements, and for good deeds. He also wrote on economics from a philanthropic point of view.

MOODY, Dwight Lyman (1837–99) American evangelist, born in Northfield, Massachusetts. He was a shoe salesman in Boston and in 1856 went to Chicago, where he gave up his job to engage in missionary work, and organized the North Market Sabbath School. In 1870 he was joined by Ira David Sankey (1840–1908), who was born in Edinburgh, Pennsylvania. In 1873 and 1883 they visited Great Britain as evangelists, Moody preaching and Sankey singing; afterwards they worked together in America. They published the *Sankey and Moody Hymn Book* (1873) and *Gospel Hymns* (1875). In 1899 he founded the Moody Bible Institute in Chicago.

MOON, William (1818–94) English inventor, born in Kent. Partially blind from the age of four, he became totally blind in 1840 and began to teach blind children. Dissatisfied with existing systems of embossed type, he invented (in 1845) a system based on Roman capitals, and he later invented a stereotype plate for use with his type. Although requiring more space, his type is easier to learn than **Braille** and is still widely used.

MOORCROFT, William (1872–1945) English potter, from Staffordshire. In 1913 he set up his own firm in Burslem, producing a range of white-bodied ceramics decorated with stylized flowers and leaves, titled 'Florian Ware'. More colourful were his 'Hazledene' (landscape and trees) and 'Claremont' (toadstools). His main interest, however, was the flambé glazes and he won many prizes for his work in Paris, Brussels and America. In 1928 he was appointed potter to the crown.

MOORE, Albert Joseph (1841–93) English painter, son of **William Moore**, and brother of the painter **Henry Moore**. He is best known for his Hellenic decorative paintings.

MOORE, Archie (Archibald Lee Wright) (1913–) American boxer, born in Benoit, Wisconsin. He became a professional boxer in 1936, and eventually, in 1952, won the world light-heavyweight title by defeating Joey Maxim. He held the title for 10 years (1952–62), when he retired at the age of 49. He also challenged for the heavyweight title, despite a lack of weight and height, and in 1955 gave **Rocky Marciano** a hard fight before being knocked out. He also fought Floyd Patterson for the title in 1956. Of his 229 fights he won more than half inside the distance, and ranks high in any list of the world's greatest-ever fighters.

MOORE, Bernard (1850–1935) English potter, born in Staffordshire. He succeeded his father in the firm of Moore Brothers, where he traded with his brother until the sale of the business in 1905. During the same year he set up his own business where he was joined by his son in 1906. As a chemist he was particularly interested in glazes and his experiments led him to produce a series of superb rouge flambés, turquoise, sang-de-bœuf, crystalline and aventurine glazes as well as fine lustres. He worked as a consultant with many British, European and American companies, assisting them with problems relating to technical production. He was greatly concerned with health risks to pottery workers and delivered an influential paper to the Ceramic Society in 1932 suggesting changes in production to minimalize lung disease. His firm closed in 1915.

MOORE, Bobby (Robert) (1941–) English footballer, born in London. In a long career with West Ham United (1958–74) and later Fulham (1974–77), he played 1000 matches at senior level, winning an FA Cup-winner's medal in 1964 and a European Cup-winner's medal in 1965. A tall and shrewd central defender, he was an automatic choice for his country and was capped a record 108 times (107 in succession), 90 of them as captain. He played in the World Cup finals in Chile in 1962, captained the victorious England side in the 1966 World Cup, and led the team with some success in Mexico in 1970 despite being the victim of a trumped-up charge of theft in Bogota in the run-up to the finals.

MOORE, Brian (1921–) Northern Irish-born Canadian novelist, born in Belfast. He served with the British Ministry of War Transport during the latter stages of World War II. After the war he worked for the United Nations in Europe before emigrating to Canada in 1948, where he became a journalist and adopted Canadian citizenship. He spent time in New York before moving to California. Though he has written thrillers under the pseudonym Michael Bryan, he is best known for novels like *The Feast of Lupercal* (1957), *The Luck of Ginger Coffey* (1960), *Catholics* (1972) and *The Temptation of Eileen Hughes* (1981). Particularly admired for his portrayal of women, he won the Author's Club First Novel award with *The Lonely Passion of Judith Hearne* (1955), though it was not, strictly speaking, his first novel. *The Great Victorian Collection* (1975) was awarded the James Tait Black Memorial prize, and both *The Doctor's*

Wife (1976) and *Black Robe* (1985) were short-listed for the Booker prize.

MOORE, Edward (1712–57) English dramatist, born in Abingdon, Berkshire, the son of a dissenting minister. He was a draper in London who, to avoid going bankrupt, took to writing plays. The comedy *Giil Blas* (1751), based on *Le Sage*, and the tragedy *The Gamester* (1753), are his best-known productions. He also edited the weekly journal *The World* (1753–57).

MOORE, Francis (1657–1715) English astrologer, born in Bridgnorth. He practised physic in London, and in 1700 started 'Old Moore's' astrological almanac.

MOORE, George Augustus (1852–1933) Irish writer, born in Ballyglass, County Mayo. He was the son of a landed gentleman in southwest Ireland who was an MP and bred horses for racing. His youth was spent partly there and partly in London. He was educated at Oscott College, Birmingham, and intended for the army, but soon became an agnostic, abandoned a military career and lived a bohemian life in London until his father's death in 1870 left him free to become a dilettante artist and writer in Paris. After ten years of this life, **Zola**'s example revealed to him his true métier as a novelist of the realist school. His importance as a writer is that in the years of relative poverty in London, from 1880 to 1892, he introduced this type of fiction into England, with *A Modern Lover* (1883), *A Mummer's Wife* (1885) and others. *Esther Waters* (1894), the last of his novels in this vein, was regarded as rather offensive, but these novels of low life, drawn from Moore's own experience of racing touts and shabby lodgings, introduced the public to a wider world than the fashionable novel of the day. During the Boer War Moore sought exile in Ireland—such was his hatred of England's wars—and this had the double effect of arousing his interest, as in *Evelyn Innes* (1898), and *Sister Teresa* (1901), in love, theology and the arts, and encouraging his preoccupation with the texture of his prose which increasingly engaged his attention. The Irish scene also helped to turn his attention away from sordid realism as in *A Drama in Muslin* (1886), and the stories in *An Untilled Field* (1903). Moore returned to England early in the century and eventually occupied a flat in Ebury Street where he wrote dialogues, conversations (*Conversations in Ebury Street*) and confessions—a sure sign that he had exhausted his experience for novel writing. He had already written *Confessions of a Young Man* (1888), but then came *Memoirs of My Dead Life* (1906) and the belated and inferior *In Single Strictness* (1926). The most famous of his works of this sort is *Hail and Farewell* in three parts, *Ave* (1911), *Salve* (1912) and *Vale* (1914). The malicious element in this trilogy, in which he wrote about his friends and his associates in setting up the Abbey Theatre in Dublin, particularly **W B Yeats**, does not detract from his claim to be one of the great memoirists. With this prose style now perfected, Moore turned in his last phase to romanticize history, beginning with the masterpiece *The Brook Kerith* (1916), which relates an apocryphal story of **Paul** and **Christ** among the Essenes. *Héloïse and Abelard* (1921) tells the famous love story with distinction and compassion. He also wrote the mythical *Aphrodite in Aulis* (1930).

MOORE, George Edward (1873–1958) English philosopher, born in London. He was educated at Dulwich College and Trinity College, Cambridge, where a fellow student, **Bertrand Russell**, helped persuade him to switch from classics to philosophy. After some years of private study in Edinburgh and London he returned to Cambridge to teach philosophy in 1911 and was professor of mental philosophy and logic (1925–39). After a brief, early infatuation with the prevailing Hegelian idealism of **John McTaggart** and others, in 1903 he published an article 'The Refutation of Idealism' (in the journal *Mind*), and a book, the celebrated *Principia Ethica*. These marked an important change of direction and the effective revival, in a new form, of a British empiricist philosophical tradition, emphasizing in particular the intellectual virtues of clarity, precision and honesty and identifying as a principal task of philosophy the analysis of ordinary concepts and arguments. Moore and Russell, and later their student **Wittgenstein**, were in fact the dominant figures in this tradition in the inter-war years. *Principia Ethica* was a philosophical analysis of the fundamental moral concept of goodness which went on to commend the particular value of friendship and aesthetic experience, and it was taken up as a text by the so-called 'Bloomsbury circle' which included **Leonard Woolf**, **Lowes Dickenson**, **John Maynard Keynes** and **E M Forster**. His other works include *Ethics* (1916), an elaboration and restatement of these views, and three important collections of his influential articles and papers: *Philosophical Studies* (1922), *Some Main Problems of Philosophy* (1953) and *Philosophical Papers* (1959). He also edited the journal *Mind* (1921–47) and made it the major English-language journal in the field.

MOORE, Gerald (1899–1987) English pianoforte accompanist, born in Watford. He studied music at Toronto and established himself as an outstanding accompanist of the world's leading singers and instrumentalists, a constant performer at international music festivals and a notable lecturer and television broadcaster on music. He wrote an engaging and instructive account of his art and experiences in *The Unashamed Accompanist* (1943; new ed 1959).

MOORE, Henry (1831–95) English painter, son of **William Moore**, and brother of **Albert Joseph Moore**. Starting as a landscape painter, he later achieved great success as a sea painter.

MOORE, Henry Spencer (1898–1986) English sculptor, born in Castleford, Yorkshire, the son of a coal miner. He studied at Leeds and at the Royal College of Art, London, where he taught sculpture from 1924–31; from 1931–39 he taught at the Chelsea School of Art. He travelled in France, Italy, Spain, USA and Greece, and was an official war artist from 1940–42. During this time he produced a famous series of drawings of air-raid shelter scenes. In 1948 he won the International Sculpture prize at the Venice biennale. He is recognized as one of the most original and powerful modern sculptors, producing mainly figures and groups in a semi-abstract style based on the organic forms and undulating rhythms found in landscape and natural rocks, and influenced by primitive African and Mexican art. His interest lay in the spatial, three-dimensional quality of sculpture, an effect he achieved by the piercing of his figures. His principal commissions included the well-known *Madonna and Child* in St Matthew's Church, Northampton (1943–44), the decorative frieze (1952) on the Time-Life building, London, and the massive reclining figures for the UNESCO building in Paris (1958) and the Lincoln Center in New York (1965).

MOORE, Sir (John) Jeremy (1928–) English soldier. From Cheltenham College he joined the Royal Marines at the age of 19 as a probationary second-lieutenant. He saw service in Britain, Brunei and Australia in a variety of roles, including that of commandant of the RM School of Music. By 1979 he had reached the rank of major-general in the commando forces and in 1982, when the decision was taken to recapture the Falkland Islands from Argentina, he was made commander of land forces. His success in the brief campaign brought him unexpected fame as well as a knighthood. He retired from the forces in 1983.

MOORE, John (1729–1802) Scottish physician and writer, father of Sir **John Moore**. After studying medicine and practising in Glasgow, he travelled with the young Duke of **Hamilton** (1772–78), and then settled in London. His *View of Society in France, Switzerland, Germany and Italy* (1779–81) was well received but it is for the novel *Zeluco* (1789), which suggested **Byron**'s *Childe Harold*, that he is best remembered today.

MOORE, Sir John (1761–1809) Scottish soldier, born in Glasgow, son of the physician **John Moore**. He served in the American War of Independence from 1779–83, and during the Revolutionary War in France distinguished himself in the attack on Corsica (1794) and served in the West Indies (1796), in Ireland (1798), and in Holland (1799). He was in Egypt in 1801, and in 1802 served in Sicily and Sweden. In 1808 he was sent with a corps of 10 000 men to strengthen the English army in the Peninsula, and in August assumed the chief command. In October he received instructions to co-operate with the Spanish forces in the expulsion of the French, and moved his army from Lisbon towards Vallodolid. But Spanish apathy, French successes elsewhere, and the intrigues of his own countrymen soon placed him in a critical position. When the news reached him that Madrid had fallen, and that **Napoleon** was marching to crush him with 70000 men, Moore, with only 25 000, was forced to retreat. In December he began a disastrous march from Astorga to Coruña, nearly 250 miles, through a mountainous country, made almost impassable by snow and rain, and harassed by the enemy. They reached Corrunna (La Coruña) in a lamentable state, and **Soult** was waiting to attack as soon as the embarkation should begin. In a desperate battle on 19 January 1809, the French were defeated with the loss of 2 000 men. Moore himself was mortally wounded by grape-shot in the moment of victory, and was buried early next morning (as in **Wolfe**'s poem).

MOORE, John Bassett (1860–1947) American lawyer, born in Smyrna, Delaware. Educated at the University of Virginia, he served in the Department of State and became professor of international law at Columbia (1891–1924). He wrote a massive *History and Digest of International Arbitrations* (6 vols, 1898), a *Digest of International Law* (8 vols, 1906), *International Adjudications* (7 vols, 1929–36) and other works on international law. From 1921 to 1928 he served as a judge of the Permanent Court of International Justice.

MOORE, Marianne Craig (1887–1972) American poet, born in Kirkwood, Missouri, and educated at the Metzger Institute, Carlisle, Pennsylvania, Bryn Mawr College, and Carlisle Commercial College. She taught commercial studies there, tutored privately, and was a branch librarian in New York (1921–25). She contributed to the Imagist magazine, *The Egoist*, from 1915, and edited *The Dial* from 1926 until its demise in 1929. America's most popular female poet of the 20th century, she was acquainted with seminal modernists like **Pound** and **T S Eliot**, but New York was her milieu not Paris, and she associated with the Greenwich Village group including **William Carlos Williams** and **Wallace Stevens**. She was much liked and admired by contemporaries, even those—like Eliot—at odds with her artistic beliefs. Idiosyncratic, a consummate stylist and unmistakably modern, her first publication was *Poems* (1921). *Selected Poems* appeared in 1935 and *The Complete Poems* in 1968. She published *Predilections*, a collection of essays, in 1955.

MOORE, Mary Tyler (1936–) American actress, born in Brooklyn, New York City. Trained as a dancer, her first professional job in 1955 was as the Happy Hotpoint Pixie in a series of television commercials. Small acting roles followed and she was seen in the series *Richard Diamond, Private Eye* (1957–59) and made her film début in *X-15* (1961). The series *The Dick Van Dyke Show* (1961–66) highlighted her talent for domestic comedy and won her Emmys in 1964 and 1965. Her small screen popularity was used to launch a multi-media career on Broadway with *Breakfast at Tiffanys* (1966) and in the cinema, but she returned to television with *The Mary Tyler Moore Show* (1970–77) where her charm and self-reliance were seen to embody the average single working girl. Among numerous awards the series won her Emmys in 1973, 1974 and 1976. She subsequently won an Emmy for *First, You Cry* (1978), a Tony for *Whose Life Is It Anyway?* (1980) and an Oscar nomination for *Ordinary People* (1980). Unable to repeat the success of earlier series she has appeared in television films like *Finnegan, Begin Again* (1984), *Heartsounds* (1984) and *Lincoln* (1988). MTM Enterprises, formed with her second husband Grant Tinker in 1970, has been responsible for such television series as *Lou Grant* and *Hill Street Blues*.

MOORE, Roger George (1927–) English actor, born in London. An art school student of painting, he made his film début as an extra in *Perfect Strangers* (1945) and appeared in small roles on stage and in films prior to National Service in the army. Subsequently performing in America, he appeared on Broadway in *A Pin to See the Peepshow* (1953) and in the Hollywood film *The Last Time I Saw Paris* (1954). On television his boyish good looks, smooth manner and athletic prowess won him stardom as the action-man hero of such series as *Ivanhoe* (1957), *The Alaskans* (1959–60), *The Persuaders* (1971–72) but most especially, *The Saint* (1962–68). His own wittiest critic, he brought a lightweight insouciance to the role of James Bond in seven films between *Live and Let Die* (1973) and *A View to a Kill* (1985).

MOORE, Stanford (1913–82) American biochemist, born in Chicago. He studied chemistry at Vanderbilt University and Wisconsin, and spent his career at the Rockefeller Institute (1939–82). There in the 1950s, with **William Stein**, he devised a general method for finding the identity of the number of amino acids in protein molecules; by 1958 they had developed an ingenious automated analyzer to carry out all the steps of the analysis of the structure of RNA on a small sample. Moore, Stein and **Christian Anfinsen** shared the Nobel prize for chemistry in 1972. Moore and Stein later devised a method of analyzing DNA as well.

MOORE, Thomas (1779–1852) Irish poet, born in Dublin, the son of a Catholic grocer. He was educated at Whyte's School, Trinity College, Dublin, and the Middle Temple. His translation of **Anacreon** (1800) proved a great success, followed by *Poems* (1801) and, with his musical talent as a singer, procured him admission to the best society. In 1803, after being appointed registrar of the Admiralty Court in Bermuda, he arranged for a deputy and returned after a tour of the USA and Canada. In 1811 he married an actress, Bessy Dyke, and later settled in Wiltshire. Meanwhile he had published the earlier of the *Irish Melodies* (1807–34) and *The Twopenny Post-bag* (1812). In 1817 the long-expected *Lalla Rookh* appeared, for which Longmans paid him 3000 guineas; the *Irish Melodies* brought in £500 a year. Moore had 'a generous contempt for money', his Bermuda deputy embezzled £6000, and in 1819, to avoid arrest, he went to Italy and then to Paris. He returned in 1822 to

Wiltshire, where he spent his last 30 years, during which he published *The Loves of the Angels* (1823), and a novel (*The Epicurean*, 1827), and wrote lives of **Sheridan** and **Byron** and other works. In 1835 he received a pension of £300, but his last days were clouded by the loss of his two sons. In his lifetime he was as popular as his friend, Byron. His poetry was light, airy, graceful, but soulless. He is best in his lyrics.

MOORE, Thomas Sturge (1870–1944) English poet, critic and wood-engraver, born in Hastings in Sussex, brother of the philosopher **George Edward Moore**. He is known as the author of polished verse of classical style, works on **Dürer** and other artists and as a distinguished designer of book-plates.

MOORE, William (1790–1851) English painter. A well-known portrait painter in York, he was the father of thirteen sons, several of whom also became well-known artists.

MOR, More, or **Moro, Anthonis** (1519–75) Dutch portrait-painter, born in Utrecht. In 1547 he entered the Antwerp guild of St Luke; in 1550–51 he visited Italy, in 1552 Spain, and in 1553 England, where he was knighted (Sir Anthony More), and painted Queen **Mary I** for her bridegroom, **Philip II** of Spain. From about 1568 he lived in Antwerp.

MORAND, Paul (1889–1975) French diplomat and writer, born in Paris. In the French diplomatic service from 1912 to 1944, his early posts included the secretaryship of the French embassies in London (where he was also minister plenipotentiary in 1940), Rome and Madrid. In 1939 he was head of the French mission of economic warfare in England, in 1943 minister at Bucharest and in 1944 ambassador at Berne. He turned to writing in 1920, beginning with poetry, then publishing short stories and novels, with a background of cosmopolitan life in post war Europe. These include *Ouvert la nuit* (1922), *Fermé la nuit* (1923) and *Lewis et Irène* (1924). He also wrote travel books, studies of cities, and political and biographical works. Among his later works were *Vie de Maupassant* (1942), *Journal d'un attaché d'ambassade* (1948), *Fouquet* (1961) and *Tais-toi* (1965).

MORANDI, Giorgio (1890–1964) Italian painter, born in Bologna. He studied at the Academy of Fine Arts, Bologna, where he later taught (1930–56). Although influenced c.1918–19 by the Italian Metaphysical painters, he otherwise eschewed the changing fashions of the modern movement, concentrating on landscapes, portraits and above all still life. His arrangements of everyday objects on a tabletop were painted in subdued tones and with a monumental simplicity of form reminiscent of **Cézanne**. He won the Grand Prix for Painting at the Venice Biennale, 1948, and other honours followed.

MORANT, Harry Harbord (1865–1902) English-born Australian adventurer and minor poet, born probably in Bridgewater, Somerset, under the name Edwin Henry Murrant. Under this name he arrived in northern Queensland in 1883 and the following year married Daisy May O'Dwyer, later **Daisy Bates**. About this time he changed his name and ranged about Queensland and New South Wales earning a living by his undoubted skills as a rider and horse-breaker. Under the pseudonym 'Breaker' he contributed ballads and bush verse to the Sydney magazine *The Bulletin* from 1891, writing some 60 poems. In 1899 Morant, then in Adelaide, enlisted in the Australian contingent sailing for the Boer wars. In South Africa, after the murder and mutilation by the Boers of a close friend, Morant and others of his patrol shot a number of Boers who were coming to surrender. Morant was also implicated in the murder of a British missionary who was witness to these events. After a lengthy and confused court-martial, Morant and a companion were found guilty, and executed by firing squad.

MORANT, Philip (1700–70) British antiquary and historian, born in Jersey. Curate of Great Waltham in Essex, he wrote *The History and Antiquities of Colchester* (1748) and *The History and Antiquities of the County of Essex* (2 vols, 1760–68), other historical and theological works, and also edited the records of parliament, 1278–1413.

MORANT, Sir Robert (1863–1920) English educationist and civil servant, born in Hampstead, London. Educated at Winchester and New College, Oxford, he became tutor to the crown prince of Siam and laid the foundation of public education there (1886–94). He joined the education department in England in 1895, and became permanent secretary to the board of education in 1902, and first secretary at the ministry of health (1919). He remodelled the English educational machinery and constructed the ministry of health. He devised the Balfour Education Act of 1902 which made county and county borough councils the local education authorities in place of the school boards, and brought voluntary schools under the new authorities. The act led to the development of the county grammar schools, but caused fierce political disputation for several years. His *Regulations for Secondary Schools* (1904), by ignoring the practical and quasi-vocational curricula developed in the Higher Grade Schools of the School Board era, are now thought to have inhibited the development of vocational education in secondary schools.

MORATA, Olympia (1526–55) Italian Humanist scholar and poet, daughter of the poet and scholar Pellegrino Morato. She gave public lectures when 15; but, having in 1548 married the German physician Andreas Grundler, she followed him to Germany, became a Protestant, and died penniless, leaving numerous Latin and Greek poems, a treatise on **Cicero**, dialogues and letters.

MORATIN, Leandro de (1760–1828) Spanish dramatist and poet, born in Madrid. He wrote a number of successful comedies influenced by French ideas and especially by **Molière**. His acceptance of the post of librarian to **Joseph Bonaparte** resulted in his exile to Paris in 1814.

MORAVIA, Alberto, pseud of **Alberto Pincherle** (1907–) Italian novelist and short-story writer, born in Rome of middle-class parents. He spent some years in a sanatorium as a result of a tubercular infection. Before the outbreak of World War II he travelled extensively and lived for a time in the USA when out of favour with the Fascist government. His first novel, *Gli indifferenti* (The Time of Indifference, 1929), which achieved popular success, contains many of the ingredients of his later novels and short stories. He analyses without compassion but without explicit moral judgment the members of decadent bourgeois society in Rome, portraying in a fatalistic way their preoccupation with sex and money, their apathy, their lack of communication, the total incapability of action of even the intellectuals who acknowledge the corruption but cannot break away from it. In *La Romana* (Woman of Rome, 1947) many of these themes remain but his canvas has broadened to include the corruption and socio-economic problems of the working-class. In *Raconti romani* (Roman Tales, 1954), he turns his critical eye to the corruption of the lower-middle class. His works include *Agostino* (1957), *L'Amore conjugale* (Conjugal Love, 1949), *La ciociara* (Two Women, 1957), *L'Attenzione* (The Lie, 1965) and *La Vita Interiore* (Time of Desecration, 1978).

MORAY, James Stewart, Earl of (1531–70) regent of Scotland, the second eldest of the many illegitimate sons of **James V** of Scotland, by a daughter of Lord Erskine. In 1538 he was made prior *in commendam* of St Andrews. He emerged as one of the leaders of the Protestant Lords of the Congregation whose revolt produced the Scottish Reformation of 1560. In 1561 he visited his half-sister, **Mary, Queen of Scots**, in France and after her return his robust defence of her right to attend mass in her private chapel resulted in his disaffection from **John Knox**. He was granted the earldoms of Mar and Moray in 1562, which resulted in the revolt and death of the Earl of **Huntly**, the greatest Catholic magnate in Scotland. He remained the queen's chief adviser until her marriage to Darnley in 1565, which triggered an abortive coup by him and the **Hamiltons** and his flight to England. He returned to Edinburgh on the day after **Rizzio**'s murder in 1566 and was rehabilitated. His fore-knowledge of the plot to murder Darnley in 1567 induced another diplomatic absence, and he was also in France when Mary was overthrown and imprisoned at Lochleven. He returned in August to accept the regency during the minority of Mary's infant son, **James VI**. His regency was chequered: it saw for the first time a Prostestant government, but little was done by it to advance the fortunes of the reformed church; the civil war continued, despite attempts made to blacken the queen's reputation, and the majority of the major nobles ranged against him. He was assassinated at Linlithgow by James Hamilton of Bothwellhaugh. One of the few Protestant nobles who acted consistently for religious motives, it was he as much as any of the ministers, including Knox, who helped give a Calvinist tone to the Scottish Reformation. His reputation has ironically been obscured by the brilliance of the case put in his defence in the writings of **George Buchanan**.

MORDAUNT See **PETERBOROUGH, Charles, 3rd Earl of**

MORDKIN, Mikhail (1880–1944) Russian-born American dancer, teacher and director, born in Moscow. After graduating from the Bolshoi Ballet School in 1899, he became first soloist with and then ballet master of the company. His career in the West was launched with his appearance in **Diaghilev**'s 1909 Paris season, from which he went on to tour with **Anna Pavlova**. After touring the USA with his own group, he returned to the Bolshoi in 1912, becoming director in 1917. The October Revolution sent him back to the USA, where he settled and became a pioneer of American ballet. He twice attempted to establish his own company, but these efforts were short-lived. Latterly he was best known for his teaching, counting stars like **Judy Garland** and **Katharine Hepburn** among his pupils.

MORE, Anthonis or Sir **Anthony** See **MOR**

MORE, Hannah (1745–1833) English playwright and religious writer, born in Fishponds, near Bristol, daughter of a schoolteacher. She was educated at the boarding school in Bristol run by her elder sisters, where she wrote verses at an early age. She was engaged in 1767 to a Mr Turner, who failed to marry her for six years and eventually settled £200 a year on her and left her. In 1773 she published *The Search after Happiness*, a pastoral drama for schools, and then went to London in 1774, where she joined the 'Blue Stocking' coterie of **Elizabeth Montagu** and her friends. She wrote two tragedies for **David Garrick**: *Percy* (1777), and *The Fatal Secret* (1779). Led by her religious views to withdraw from society, she retired to Cowslip Green near Bristol, where she did much to improve the condition of the poor. She published *Sacred Dramas* (1782) and a collection of religious poems in *Bas Bleu* (1786), and an essay *Estimate on the Religion of the Fashionable World* (1790). Her moral tracts for the poor, *Village Politics by Will Chip* (1793) and *Cheap Repository Tracts* (1795–98), led to the founding of the Religous Tracts Society. She also wrote a didactic, novel, *Coelebs in Search of a Wife* (1809).

MORE, Henry (1614–87) English philosopher and theologian, a leading figure in the circle of 'Cambridge Platonists' which included **Whichcote** and **Cudworth**. Born in Grantham, Lincolnshire, his father being 'a gentleman of fair estate and fortune', he was educated at Eton and Christ's College, Cambridge, where he remained all his life. He devoted himself entirely to study, despite the turbulent political times in which he lived, and developed a particular affinity for **Plato**, **Plotinus** and **Descartes**, with the last of whom he corresponded enthusiastically at first, though his admiration for him later waned as his interest in occultism and mysticism grew. He was, however, generally concerned in his philosophy to demonstrate the compatibility of reason and faith. He wrote in both prose and verse and his main works were: *Philosophical Poems* (1647), *An Antidote against Atheism* (1653), *The Immortality of the Soul* (1659), *Enchiridion Ethicum* (1666) and *Divine Dialogues* (1668).

MORE, Sir Thomas, St (1478–1535) English statesman and scholar, born in London, the son of a judge. Educated at Oxford under **Colet** and **Linacre**, he completed his legal studies at New Inn and Lincoln's Inn, and was for three years reader in Furnival's Inn, and spent the next four years in the Charterhouse in 'devotion and prayer'. During the last years of **Henry VII** he became under-sheriff of London and member of parliament. Introduced to **Henry VIII** through **Wolsey**, he became master of requests (1514), treasurer of the exchequer (1521), and chancellor of the Duchy of Lancaster (1525). He was speaker of the House of Commons, and was sent on missions to France to **Francis I** and **Charles V**. On the fall of Wolsey in 1529, More, against his own strongest wish, was appointed Lord Chancellor. In the discharge of his office he displayed a primitive virtue and simplicity. The one stain on his character as judge is the harshness of his sentences for religious opinions. He sympathized with Colet and **Erasmus** in their desire for a more rational theology and for radical reform in the manners of the clergy, but like them also he had no promptings to break with the historic church. He saw with displeasure the successive steps which led Henry to the final schism from Rome. In 1532 he resigned the chancellorship. In 1534 Henry was declared head of the English Church; and More's steadfast refusal to recognize any other head of the church than the pope led to his sentence for high treason after a harsh imprisonment of over a year. Still refusing to recant, he was beheaded. More was twice married; his daughter Margaret, the wife of his biographer William Roper, was distinguished for her high character, her accomplishments, and her pious devotion to her father. By his Latin *Utopia* (1516; English trans 1556), More takes his place with the most eminent humanists of the Renaissance. His *History of King Richard III* (1513) 'begins modern English historical writing of distinction'. From Erasmus we realize the virtues and attractions of a winning rather than an imposing figure. He was canonized in 1935.

MORÉAS, Jean, originally **Yannis Papadiamantopoulos** (1856–1910) Greek-born French poet, born in Athens. He wrote first in Greek, then settled in Paris (1879) and became a leader of the Symbolist school, to which he gave its name, though his later work shows a return to classical and traditional forms. His works include *Les Syrtes* (1884), *Cantilènes* (1886), *Le Pèlerin passioné* (1891) and *Les Stances* (1905), the masterpiece of his classical period.

MOREAU, Gustave (1826–98) French painter and teacher, born in Paris. He studied at the École des Beaux-Arts, Paris. An eccentric Symbolist, he painted colourful but usually rather sinister scenes from ancient mythology and the Bible (eg *Salome*, 1876, which inspired **Huysmans** to write an enthusiastic description). A good teacher, in 1892 he was appointed professor of painting at the École des Beaux-Arts; his pupils included **Rouault** and **Matisse**.

MOREAU, Jean Victor (1761–1813) French soldier, born in Morlaix, the son of an advocate. He studied law, but at the Revolution in 1789 commanded the volunteers from Rennes, served under **Dumouriez** in 1793, and in 1794 was made a general of division. He took part, under **Pichegru**, in reducing Belgium and Holland. In command on the Rhine and Moselle, he drove the Austrians back to the Danube, but was forced to retreat and later deprived of his command (1797). In 1798 he took command in Italy and skilfully conducted the defeated troops to France. The party of **Sieyès**, which overthrew the Directory, offered him the dictatorship; he declined it, but lent his assistance to **Napoleon** in the *coup d'état* of 18th Brumaire. In command of the army of the Rhine, he gained victory after victory over the Austrians in 1800, drove them back behind the Inn, and at last won the decisive battle of Hohenlinden. Napoleon, grown very jealous of Moreau, accused him of sharing in the plot of **Cadoudal** and sentenced him to two years' imprisonment (1804). The sentence was commuted to banishment, and Moreau settled in New Jersey. In 1813 he joined the Russian service and accompanied the Russian attack on Dresden, where a French cannon-ball broke both his legs. Amputation was performed, but he died in Laun in Bohemia. He was buried in St Petersburg.

MOREAU, Jeanne (1928–) French actress and director, born in Paris. A pupil at the Conservatoire National D'Art Dramatique, she made her stage début with the Comédie Française in *A Month in the Country* (1948) and her film début in *Dernier Amour* (1948). An association with the directors of the French New Wave brought her recognition as an intense, hypnotic film actress, capable of immersing her own personality in a succession of generally world-weary, sensual characterizations. Her most famous films include *Les Amants* (1958), *La Notte* (1961), *Jules et Jim* (1961), *Diary of a Chambermaid* (1964) and *Viva Maria* (1965). Occasional English-language ventures met with little acclaim but she proved herself a formidable director with *La Lumière* (1976) and *L'Adolescente* (1978).

MORECAMBE, Eric originally **Eric Bartholomew** (1926–84) English comedian, born in Morecambe. Having appeared in working men's clubs since the age of eleven, he teamed up in 1943 with fellow entertainer, Ernie Wise (Wiseman) (1925–). They made their West End début in the revue *Strike a New Note* in 1943. In 1947 they teamed up again and, as Morecambe and Wise, subsequently became the finest British comedy double-act for many years, working in music-hall, summer-shows, pantomimes, radio, films, and television. In 1968, Morecambe had a heart attack; they reduced their work-load, concentrating on their television shows, programmes of sketches interspersed with the double-act routine. Their films, *The Intelligence Men* (1964), *That Riviera Touch* (1966), and *The Magnificent Two* (1967), were not successful; the small screen and the stage were their media, and quick-fire repartee their true forte.

MORELLI, Giovanni (1816–91) Italian art critic, born in Verona. After studying natural philosophy and medicine at Munich University, he returned to Italy in 1846 and became active in the Italian liberation movement against Austrian rule. In 1861 he became a deputy for Bergamo in the first free Italian parliament and later, in 1873, a senator. From that year he began writing art criticism and, in 1880, published *Die Werke Italienischen Meister in den Galerien von München, Dresden und Berlin* (trans *Italian Masters in German Galleries*). This was followed, from 1890 to 1893, by *Kunstkritische Studien über italienischer Maleri* (trans as *Critical Studies of Italian Painters*). His criticism concentrated on attribution, which he claimed to have reduced to scientific principles by the close analysis of the artist's depiction of details such as eyes, hands and ears—the so-called 'Morellian method'. He was also instrumental in the passing of an act, later named after him, which gave state protection to important works of art.

MORERI, Louis (1643–80) French scholar, born in Provence. He took orders, and was a noted preacher at Lyon, where he pubished a *Grand dictionnaire historique ou Mélange curieux de l'histoire sacrée et profane* (1674). In 1675 he went to Paris, and laboured at the dictionary's expansion till his death.

MORESBY, John (1830–1922) English naval commander and explorer, born in Allerton, Somerset. He conducted exploration and survey work in New Guinea, where he discovered the fine natural harbour now fronted by Port Moresby, which was named after him.

MORETTO DA BRESCIA, properly **Alessandro Bonvicino** (1498–1554) Italian painter, born in Brescia. He painted for several churches there and also became a fine portrait painter.

MOREY, Samuel (1762–1843) American inventor, born in Hebron, Connecticut. He showed early mechanical aptitude and built up a successful business in timber and sawmills; he also acted as local consulting engineer for the construction of locks on the Bellows Falls Canal. After 1790 he and his older brother became interested in steam navigation and built a series of paddle-wheel steamboats, but in spite of encouragement and financial support from Robert R **Livingston** none of them was commercially successful. He took out more than 20 patents in all, some of them many years ahead of their time, such as his American Water Burner (1817–18) which was ridiculed when it appeared but was a precursor of the water-gas process widely used half a century later; his triple pipe steam boiler of 1818 and a gasoline-powered internal combustion engine patented in 1826 were both pointers to the way technology would develop in the future.

MORGAGNI, Giovanni Battista (1682–1771) Italian physician, born in Forli. He became professor of medicine at Padua in 1711 and is considered the founder of the science of pathological anatomy.

MORGAN, Augustus de See **DE MORGAN**

MORGAN, Charles Langbridge (1894–1958) English author, born in Kent, the son of a civil engineer. He served in Atlantic and China waters as a midshipman (1911–13), but finding it uncongenial, resigned. He rejoined the navy in 1914 and was later interned in Holland until 1917. On repatriation he went to Oxford University, where he published *The Gunroom* (1919) on his early experiences, and became a well-known personality. In 1921, on leaving Oxford, he joined the editorial staff of *The Times*, and was their principal drama critic from 1926 to 1939. Under the pen-name of 'Menander' he also wrote for *The Times Literary Supplement* critical essays called *Reflections in a Mirror*, which were later (1944–45) collected in two series. His novels and plays show high professional competence, but lack vividness and urgency. *Portrait in a Mirror* (1929), which won the Femina Vie Heureuse prize in 1930, is his most satisfying novel. Later works show too much preoccupation with values of the heart to the detriment of narrative sweep, and his earnestness seems unduly solemn, pompous and vaguely sentimental. None the less, *The Fountain* (1932) won the Hawthornden prize and *The Voyage* (1940) won the James Tait Black Memorial prize. His plays are *The Flashing Stream* (1938), *The River Line* (1952) and *The Burning Glass* (1953).

MORGAN, Sir Henry (c.1635–1688) Welsh buccaneer, born in Glamorganshire of good family. He appears to have been kidnapped in Bristol and shipped to Barbados. Joining the buccaneers, he conducted triumphant, unbridled expeditions against Spanish possessions (Porto Bello, Maracaibo, Panama). He died lieutenant-governor of Jamaica.

MORGAN, John Pierpont (1837–1913) American banker, financier and art collector, born in Harford, Connecticut, the son of the financier John Spencer Morgan (1813–90). He built his father's firm into the most powerful private banking house in the USA. His house financed the Federal Reserve system in the depression of 1895, developed the railroad system, and formed the US Steel Corporation (1901). He compiled one of the greatest private art collections of his day, which he bequeathed to the Metropolitan Museum of Art in New York. He was also noted for his extensive philanthropic benefactions. His son, John Pierpont Morgan Jr (1867–1943), inherited his father's firm and fortune, and raised loans for Britain during World War I.

MORGAN, Lewis Henry (1818–81) American ethnologist, born in Aurora, New York. He became a lawyer in Rochester, and served in the state assembly (1861) and senate (1868). He undertook extensive investigations of the cultures of native North American Indians, publishing *The League of the Iroquois* (1851), and *Houses and House-Life of the American Aborigines* (1881). His *Systems of Consanguinity and Affinity* (1869) laid the foundations for the modern social anthropological study of kinship, but his best-known work is *Ancient Society* (1877). A treatise on the origins and evolution of the institutions of government and property, it was hailed by **Marx** and **Engels** as furnishing independent confirmation for their materialist theory of history. Morgan is also remembered as the author of an authoritative study on *The American Beaver and his Works* (1868), in which he argued that animals as well as humans possess powers of rational thought.

MORGAN, Lady Sydney, née **Owenson** (1783–1859) Irish novelist, born in Dublin. Her father, a theatrical manager, got into financial difficulties and she supported the family, first as governess, next as author of sentimental poems and novels. In 1812 she married a surgeon, Thomas Charles Morgan (1783–1843), who was later knighted. Her works—lively novels, verse and travels—include *St Clair* (1804), *The Wild Irish Girl* (1806), *O'Donnel* (1814), *The O'Briens and the O'Flahertys* (1827) and *Memoirs* (1862).

MORGAN, Thomas Hunt (1866–1945) American geneticist and biologist, born in Lexington, Kentucky. He studied zoology at Kentucky State College and Johns Hopkins University, and became professor of experimental zoology at Columbia (1904–28) and the California Institute of Technology (1928–45). He carried out experiments with the *Drosophila* fruit fly, from which he established a chromosome theory of heredity involving genes for specific tasks aligned on chromosomes. This major breakthrough in genetics earned him the 1933 Nobel prize for physiology or medicine. His many books included *Evolution and Adaptation* (1911), *Mechanism of Mendelian Heredity* (1915), *The Theory of the Gene* (1926) and *Embryology and Genetics* (1933).

MORGAN, William De See **DE MORGAN**

MORGANWG, Iolo See **WILLIAMS, Edward**

MORGHEN, Raphael (1758–1833) Italian engraver, born in Naples. He is known for his plates after **Raphael**, **Leonardo da Vinci** (notably *The Last Supper*) and others, under the patronage of the Grand Duke of Tuscany.

MORIER, James Justinian (1780–1849) English novelist, son of the consul at Smyrna. He turned to literature after a diplomatic career. His great work is that inimitable picture of Persian life, *The Adventures of Hajji Baba of Ispahan* (1824), with the less brilliant *Hajji Baba in England* (1828).

MÖRIKE, Eduard (1804–75) German poet and novelist, born in Ludwigsburg. He entered the theological seminary at Tübuingen in 1822 and became vicar of Kleversulzback in 1834, retiring in 1843. He was weak, hypochondriacal, unhappily married and lazy, yet he produced a minor masterpiece in *Mozart auf der Reise nach Prag* (1856) and many poems of delicacy and beauty with something of the deceptive simplicity of **Heine**. These were collectively published in 1838.

MORIN, or **Morinus, Jean** (1591–1659) French theologian. He was a founder of biblical criticism, and wrote on ecclesiastical antiquities.

MORISON, James (1816–93) Scottish clergyman, born in Bathgate. Minister of Kilmarnock in 1840, he was suspended by the United Secession church in 1841 for preaching universal atonement, and in 1843, with three other ministers, founded the Evangelical Union of Congregational churches, its system a modified Independency.

MORISON, Robert (1620–83) Scottish botanist, born in Aberdeen. A Royalist, he escaped to France, took his MD at Angers (1648), and had charge of the garden of the Duke of Orléans. **Charles II** made him one of his physicians, 'botanist royal', and the first professor of botany at Oxford. His chief work is *Plantarum Historia Universalis Oxoniensis* (1680–99).

MORISON, Stanley (1889–1967) English typographer. He was typographical adviser to Cambridge University Press (1923–44 and 1947–59) and to the Monotype Corporation from 1923. On the staff of the London *Times* from 1929 he designed the Times New Roman type, introduced in 1932. He edited *The Times Literary Supplement* (1945–47) and was the author of many works on typography and calligraphy. He also edited the history of *The Times* (1935–52). In 1961 he was appointed to the editorial board of the *Encylopaedia Britannica*.

MORISOT, Berthe Marie Pauline (1841–95) French painter, grand-daughter of **Fragonard**. She painted especially women and children, and was the leading female exponent of Impressionism. Her early work shows the influence of **Corot**, who was her friend and mentor, but her later style owes more to **Renoir**. She herself exercised an influence on **Manet**, whose brother Eugène she married.

MORITA, Akio (1921–) Japanese manufacturer, born in Nagoya. With Masaru Ibuka he founded, after World War II, the electronics firm which since 1958 has been known as Sony. Like many Japanese companies, Sony has been at the forefront of technological developments and has had a strong design policy. Among its most important products have been early tape recorders for the domestic market (c.1950), advanced television equipment and (one of the best examples of miniaturization) the 'Walkman' range of radios and cassette players, first produced in 1980.

MORITZ, Karl Philipp (1756–93) German writer, born in Hameln. He was in turn hat-maker's apprentice, actor, teacher and professor. Self-educated, he travelled in England and Italy and wrote *Reisen eines Deutschen in England* (1783), and *Reisen eines Deutschen in Italien* (1792–93). His autobiographical novel, *Anton Reise* (1785–90), influenced **Goethe**. He was a precursor of the German Romantic movement, delved into the past, and wrote *Versuch einer deutschen Prosodie* (1786), which he dedicated to **Frederick II, the Great**.

MORLAND, George (1763–1804) English painter, born in London, the eldest son of the painter Henry Morland (1712–97), who brought him up with extreme rigour. He exhibited sketches at the Royal Academy when only ten years old, but from the time he was his own master, his life was a downward course of drunkenness and debt. Yet in the last eight years of his life he turned out nearly 900 paintings and over 1000 drawings, many of them hastily completed to bring in money and inferior in quality. His strength lay in country subjects (pigs, gipsies, and stable interiors). His best known work is *The Interior of a Stable* (1791). He died in destitution.

MORLEY, Christopher Darlington (1890–1957) American novelist and essayist, born in Haverford, Pennsylvania. He was a Rhodes scholar at Oxford, and joined the editorial staff of Doubleday's from 1913 to 1917 and later contributed to numerous periodicals such as *Ladies' Home Journal*, the New York *Evening Post* and the *Saturday Review of Literature*. His chief works, whimsical and urbane, included *Parnassus on Wheels* (1917), *Thunder on the Left* (1925), *Swiss Family Manhattan* (1932), *Human Being* (1932), *Streamlines* (1937), *Kitty Foyle* (1939), *The Ironing Board* (1949) and a book of poems, *The Middle Kingdom* (1944).

MORLEY, Edward Williams (1838–1923) American chemist and physicist, born in Newark, New Jersey, the son of a Congregational minister. He was taught at home, and studied at Williams College. He became a Congregational minister, like his father, but from 1869 to 1906 taught science at the college which became Western Reserve University in Ohio. His work in science is marked by his precise and accurate measurements. His early research was on the oxygen content of air, and he also studied the relative atomic mass of oxygen (measured to within 1 in 10000). He worked with **Albert Abraham Michelson** in their famous experiments to detect the 'ether-drift' (1887).

MORLEY, Henry (1822–94) English writer and editor, born in London. He studied medicine at King's College, London, but after practising for a while he turned to journalism, and eventually became a lecturer (1857–65) and professor of English (1865–89) at London University. He was assistant editor for **Dickens'** *Household Words* and *All the Year Round* (1850–65), and edited *The Examiner* (1859–65). A champion of adult education he wrote biographical and critical works, and edited 'Morley's Universal Library' of English classics (63 vols, 1883–88), *Cassell's Library of English literature* (1875–81) and *Cassell's National Library* (214 vols, 1886–90). He also wrote the first 11 volumes of an ambitious history of English literature, *English Writers* (1864–95).

MORLEY, John, 1st Viscount Morley (1838–1923) English journalist, biographer, philosophical critic, Radical politician and statesman, born in Blackburn, Lancashire, the son of a doctor. Educated at Cheltenham and Lincoln Colleges, Oxford, he was called to the bar, but chose literature as a profession. His works (collected 1921 *et seq*) include *Edmund Burke* (1867), *Critical Miscellanies* (1871–77), *Voltaire* (1872), *On Compromise* (1874), *Rousseau* (1876), *Diderot and the Encyclopaedists* (1878), *Richard Cobden* (1881) and *Studies in Literature* (1891). From 1867–82 he edited the *Fortnightly Review* and he was editor of the 'English Men of Letters' series, writing the volume on **Burke**, while for the 'English Statesmen' series he wrote *Walpole* (1889). From 1880–83 he edited the *Pall Mall Gazette*. His articles and speeches in favour of Home Rule made him **Gladstone**'s most conspicuous supporter. In 1886 he was a successful Irish Secretary, and again from 1892 to 1895. He sat for Newcastle from 1883 to 1895, and for Montrose Burghs from 1896 until his elevation to the peerage in 1908. He was secretary for India from 1905 to 1910 (repressing sedition and making the government more representative), and lord president of the council from 1910 until the outbreak of World War I in August 1914. He wrote a great life of Gladstone (4 vols, 1903), and *Recollections* (1917).

MORLEY, Samuel (1809–86) English woollen manufacturer, politician and philanthropist, born in Homerton, the son of a hosier. By 1860 he had greatly extended his father's business with mills in Nottingham, Leicester and Derbyshire. Deeply religious, he was a conscientious employer, a supporter of the temperance movement and was a Liberal MP (1865–85). His son, Arnold (1849–1916), was chief Liberal whip and postmaster general (1892–95).

MORLEY, Thomas (1557–1603) English composer. A pupil of **William Byrd**, he became organist at St Paul's Cathedral, and from 1592 was a Gentleman of the Chapel Royal. He is best known for his *A Plaine and Easie Introduction to Practicall Musicke* (1597), written in entertaining dialogue with the purpose of encouraging part-singing for pleasure; also for his volumes of madrigals and canzonets, which include such evergreen favourites as 'Now is the month of maying', 'My bonny lass she smileth' and 'It was a lover and his lass'. He was compiler of the collection, in honour of Queen **Elizabeth**, called *The Triumphes of Oriana* (1603).

MORNAY, Philippe de, Seigneur de Plessis-Marly (1549–1623) French statesman. He was converted to Protestantism in 1560, and nicknamed the 'Pope of the Huguenots'. His treatise on Christianity was translated into English in 1589 at the request of his dead friend, Sir **Philip Sidney**.

MORNY, Charles Auguste Louis Joseph, Duc de (1811–65) French nobleman, believed to be the son of Queen Hortense and the Comte de **Flahaut**, and so half-brother of **Napoleon**. Born in Paris, and adopted by the Comte de Morny, he served in Algeria; but soon he left the army, and in 1838 became a manufacturer of beet sugar. From that time he was mixed up in all sorts of speculations. Chosen a deputy in 1842, he quickly became prominent in financial questions. After 1848 he supported Napoleon, took a leading part in the *coup d'état*, and became minister of the interior. From 1854 to 1865 he was president of the *corps législatif*, and was ambassador to Russia in 1856–57. He is the 'Duc de Mora' in **Daudet**'s *Nabab*.

MORO See **MOR, Anthonis**

MORONI, Giovanni Battista (1525–78) Italian portrait and religious painter, born in Bondo near Albino. He painted altarpieces, but is best known for his portraits, especially *The Tailor* in the National Gallery, London.

MORPHY, Paul Charles (1837–84) American chess player, born in New Orleans. He had a meteoric chess career from 1857 to 1859, because he graduated early in law and could not practise until reaching the age of 21. During this short period he won the American championship and beat the strongest masters in Europe, establishing him as unofficial world champion (the championship not being instituted until 1886). Foreshadowing the career of fellow American chess genius **Bobby Fischer**, he retired from competitive chess and returned to his native New Orleans to make abortive attempts to commence his legal career, failures which contributed to the bouts of delusion and paranoia he suffered before his death from a stroke while taking a bath. His brilliantly conducted games, particularly his approach to attack, continued to exert a strong influence upon generations of chess players long after his death.

MORRIS, Arthur Robert (1922–) Australian cricketer, born in Sydney. An invaluable left-handed opening batsman for Australia, he was capped 46 times, and his 3533 Test runs at an average of 46.48 included twelve centuries. Twice he made two centuries in the same Test match.

MORRIS, Desmond John (1928–) English zoologist. Educated at Birmingham University and Magdalen College, Oxford, he studied animal behaviour under **Nikolaas Tinbergen**. His later career as head of Granada TV (1956–59) and curator of mammals at the Zoological Society of London (1959–67) developed his interest in the explanation and demonstration of animal behaviour to the public. In addition to many television programmes on animal and social behaviour, he has written several books, including *The Naked Ape* (1967), *The Human Zoo* (1969) and *Manwatching* (1977), which analyze human behaviour when viewed as an animal. His books and films have popularized sociology and zoology.

MORRIS, George Pope (1802–64) American journalist and poet, born in Philadelphia. In 1823 he founded the *New York Mirror* (editor 1824–42), and later edited the *Evening Mirror* and the *Home Journal* (1846–64). He published many poems, including the celebrated *Woodman, Spare that Tree*.

MORRIS, Gouverneur (1752–1816) American statesman, born in Morrisania, New York. He was admitted to the bar in 1771. In 1780 he lost a leg by an accident. Assistant in the finance department (1781–84), in 1787 he took his seat in the convention that framed the US constitution, and in 1788 sailed for Paris. The greater part of 1791 he spent in England as **Washington**'s agent, and then till 1794 was US minister to France. Returning to America in 1798, he sat in the senate from 1800 to 1803.

MORRIS, Sir Lewis (1833–1907) Welsh poet and barrister, born in Carmarthen, and educated at the town's Queen Elizabeth Grammar School, Sherborne, and Jesus College, Oxford. His main literary works were *Songs of Two Worlds* (3 vols, 1872–75), followed in 1876 by *The Epic of Hades* and more verse and drama, largely drawing on incidents in Welsh history and mythology. In the later stages of his career he campaigned for the fostering of higher education in Wales and the establishment of a National University. In 1895 he was made knight-bachelor and therafter entertained fruitless hopes of becoming poet laureate.

MORRIS, Mark (1956–) American dancer and choreographer, born in Seattle, Washington. His training included ballet, flamenco and Balkan folk dance. He danced for several important modern choreographers (**Eliot Feld**, **Laura Dean**, and **Twyla Tharp**) before making an informal New York début with his company in 1980. Within a few years he became the most talked-about and, in some quarters, revered choreographer of his generation. He has devised dances for his own and other companies, and for opera. In 1988 the Mark Morris Dance Group began a permanent residency at Theatre de le Monnaie in Brussels.

MORRIS, Robert (1734–1806) English-born American financier and statesman, born in Liverpool, known as the 'Financier of the American Revolution'. In 1747 he went from Lancashire to Philadelphia, and working in the shipping business. A member of the Continental Congress, he was a signatory of the Declaration of Independence. He organized the finance for **Washington**'s military supplies, and in 1782 founded the Bank of North America. He died bankrupt.

MORRIS, Thomas ('Old Tom') (1821–1908) Scottish golfer, born in St Andrews, and known as the 'Nestor of Golf'. After serving an apprenticeship as a golfball-maker in St Andrews he went to Prestwick as a greenkeeper in 1851, returning to St Andrews as a professional in 1861. He won the British championship belt four times, (1861, 1862, 1864 and 1866). His son, **'Young Tom' Morris**, became champion after him.

MORRIS, Thomas ('Young Tom') (1851–75) Scottish golfer, the son of **'Old Tom' Morris**. Precociously brilliant, he won the British championship three times in succession (1868, 1869, 1870), thereby winning the championship belt outright; there was no contest in 1871, but he won it again in 1872. His early death was said to have been caused by grief at the loss of his young wife.

MORRIS, William (1834–96) English craftsman, poet and socialist, born in Walthamstow, near London, of middle-class parents. Educated at Marlborough School and Exeter College, Oxford, he studied for holy orders, but his friendship with members of the Pre-Raphaelite Brotherhood, particularly the painter **Edward Burne-Jones**, aroused a deep love of Gothic architecture, and they both renounced the church. He turned to the study of architecture under **George Edmund Street**, but on the advice of **Dante Gabriel Rossetti** became a professional painter (1857–62). In 1859 he married a model, Jane Burden, and moved into the Red House at Bexley Heath, which he designed and furnished with the architect **Philip Webb**; from the ideas expressed there he founded in 1861, with the help of his pre-Raphaelite associates, the firm of Morris, Marshall, Faulkner and Company, which would revolutionize the art of house decoration and furniture in England. His literary career began with a volume of poetry, *The Defence of Guinevere, and other Poems*, in 1858, followed by *The Life and Death of Jason* (1867), a long narrative poem in rhyming couplets and the three-volumed *The Earthly Paradise* (1868–70), a collection of 24 classical and medieval tales in a Chaucerian mould. He developed a passionate interest in the heroic literature of Iceland, and worked with **Eiríkur Magnússon** on a series of saga translations. He visited Iceland twice, in 1871 and 1873, and was inspired to write *Three Northern Love Songs* (1875) and a four-volumed epic, *The Story of Sigurd the Volsung and the Fall of the Nibelungs* (1876), regarded as his greatest work. Also at this time he published a verse morality, *Love is Enough, or The Freeing of Pharamond* (1972), a translation of **Virgil**'s *Aeneid* (1875), and a translation of **Homer**'s *Odyssey* (1887). He founded a Society for the Protection of Ancient Buildings in 1877. His experience as a master-craftsman, and his devotion to the Gothic, persuaded him that the excellence of medieval arts and crafts sprang from the joy of free craftsmen, which was destroyed by Victorian mass-production and capitalism. He joined the Social Democratic Federation in 1883; his Utopian ideals did much to develop the philosophy of socialism, and when the Social Democratic Federation suffered disruption in 1884 he led the seceders into a Socialist League. His socialist zeal inspired two prose romances, *The Dream of John Ball* (1888) and *News from Nowhere* (1891). Further prose romances concentrated more on story-telling: *The House of the Wolfings* (1889), *The Roots of the Mountains* (1889), and *The Story of the Glittering Plain* (1891), all set in the far north. His last books were a book of verse (*Poems by the Way*, 1891), and further prose romances: *The Wood beyond the World* (1895), *The Well at the World's End* (1896), *The Water of the Wondrous Isles* and *The Story of the Sundering Flood* (published posthumously in 1897). In 1890, in a further rejection of Victorian values, he founded a publishing house, the Kelmscott Press at Hammersmith, for which he designed clear typefaces and wide ornamental borders; it produced a stream of his own works and reprints of English classics.

MORRISON, Arthur (1863–1945) English novelist, born in Poplar, Kent, the son of an engine fitter. He became clerk to the People's Palace in Mile End Road, then a journalist on the *National Observer*, for which he wrote a series of stories published as *Tales of Mean Streets* (1894). His reputation rests on his powerfully realistic novels of London life such as *A Child of the Jago* (1896) and *The Hole in the Wall* (1902). He also wrote detective stories featuring a private investigator, Martin Hewett.

MORRISON, Herbert Stanley, Baron Morrison of Lambeth (1888–1965) English politician, born in Lambeth, London. He was educated at an elementary school and by intensive private reading. After being an errand-boy and a shop-assistant, he helped to found the London Labour party and became its secretary in 1915. Mayor of Hackney from 1920 to 1921, he entered the London County Council in 1922, becoming its leader in 1934; he grouped together London's passenger transport system, and much of the credit for the 'Green Belt' was due to him. He was MP for South Hackney three times between 1923 and 1945, when he was elected for East Lewisham. In **Winston Churchill**'s Cabinet he was home secretary and minister of home security. He was a powerful figure in the postwar social revolution, uniting the positions of deputy prime-minister, lord president of the Council, and leader of a Commons which enacted the most formidable body of legislation ever entrusted to it. For seven months in 1951 he was, less felicitously, foreign secretary. In 1951 he became deputy leader of the opposition and a Companion of Honour, and in 1955 was defeated by **Hugh Gaitskell** in the contest for the leadership of the Labour party. He was created a life peer in 1959. He wrote *How London is Governed* (1949) and *Government and Parliament* (1954). He wrote his *Autobiography* (1960).

MORRISON, Richard James See **ZADKIEL**

MORRISON, Robert (1782–1834) Scottish scholar and missionary, born near Jedburgh. After studying theology in his spare time, in 1807 he was sent to Canton by the London Missionary Society as the first Protestant missionary to China. In 1809–14 he translated and printed the New Testament (1819); with some help, the Old Testament into Chinese; and in 1823 he completed his great *Chinese Dictionary*. In 1818 he established an Anglo-Chinese College at Malacca.

MORRISON, Toni Chloe Anthony, née **Wofford** (1931–) American novelist, born in Lorain, Ohio. She was educated at Howard University and Cornell University, and taught at Howard before moving to New York in 1965. She worked in publishing as senior editor at Random House before turning to fiction. Labelled as a black **Joyce** or **Faulkner**, she explores in rich vocabulary and cold-blooded detail the story of rural black Americans. *The Bluest Eye* (1970) focuses on the incestuous rape of an eleven-year-old girl; *Sula* (1974) again confronts a generation gap, but between a grandmother and the eponymous scapegoat; *Song of Solomon* (1977) is a merciless study of genteel blacks. Her two most recent novels, *Tar Baby* (1981) and *Beloved* (1987), formidable in their mastery of technique and courageous in their subject matter, confirmed her as one of the most important novelists of her generation. She won a Pulitzer prize in 1988.

MORSE, Samuel Finley Breese (1791–1872) American artist and inventor, born in Charlestown, Massachusetts, the eldest son of Rev Dr Jedidiah Morse (1761–1826), a noted geographer. He graduated at Yale in 1810, went to England to study painting, and was a founder and first president of the National Academy of Design at New York (1826) and a professor at New York University (from 1832). He studied chemistry and electricity, and in 1832 conceived the idea of a magnetic telegraph, which he exhibited to congress in 1837, and attempted in vain to patent in Europe. He struggled on against scanty means until 1843, when congress voted him $30000 for an experimental telegraph line between Washington and Baltimore, built by **Ezra Cornell**, over which he sent the historic message, 'What hath God wrought?' on 24 May 1844. His system, widely adopted, at last brought him honours and rewards. The Morse code (originally called the Morse alphabet) was evolved by him for use with his telegraph.

MORSHEAD, Sir Leslie James (1889–1959) Australian soldier, born in Ballarat, Victoria. He enlisted in the Australian Imperial Forces in 1914 and commanded a company at Gallipoli, and later a batallion on the Western Front, where he won the DSO and the Legion d'Honneur. In World War II he commanded the 18th Brigade in the Middle East and led the 9th Division at Tobruk during the siege of 1941, and in 1941 at the battles of El Alamein. He returned to Australia to lead the New Guinea Force and to become general officer commanding of the First Australian Corps, ending the war in 1945 as commander of the Australian and USA Task Force in Borneo.

MORT, Thomas Sutcliffe (1816–78) English-born Australian businessman and pioneer of refrigeration, born in Bolton, Lancashire. He went to Sydney in 1838 as agent for an English firm and later established his own wool-broking business, for some years the largest in Australia. In 1854 he constructed a dry dock at Balmain, Sydney, a venture in which half of the company shares were held by his employees. Shipbuilding began there in 1855 and the first Australian railway locomotive was built there in 1870. He established a scientific farm at Bodalla on the south coast of New South Wales, building a model community for his workers. His experience there in the wastage of perishable foods led to an interest in refrigeration and to a large freezing plant being built at Darling Harbour, Sydney, in 1875.

MORTARA, Edgar (1852–1940) Italian religious, born into a Jewish family, and the unwitting principal in the celebrated 'Mortara' case. In 1858 he was carried off from his parents by the archbishop of Bologna, on the ground that he had been secretly baptized when a gravely ill infant, by a Catholic maid servant. The refusal of the authorities to give him up to his parents excited great indignation in Britain. Eventually he was discovered in Rome in 1870, but preferred to retain his Christian faith, and became an Augustinian monk.

MORTENSEN, Erik (1926–) Danish fashion designer. Since 1948 he has been attached to the Balmain fashion house in Paris, becoming the artistic director in 1960. He took over the management of the fashion house after the death of **Pierre Balmain** in 1982. He was awarded the Golden Thimble of the French Haute Couture in 1983 and 1987.

MORTIER, Édouard Adolphe Casimir Joseph, Duke of Treviso (1768–1835) French soldier. In the Napoleonic war he became a marshal of France in 1804, and campaigned brilliantly in Germany, Russia and Spain. He rejoined Napoleon in the Hundred Days (1816), and was deprived of his peerage. Later he held high office under **Louis-Philippe**, as ambassador to Russia, and prime minister (1834–35). He was mortally wounded at the king's side by the bomb thrown by **Joseph Fieschi**.

MORTIMER, Earls of March See **EDWARD II** and **III**

MORTIMER, John Clifford (1923–) English dramatist, novelist and barrister, born in London. He was called to the bar in 1948, participating in several celebrated civil cases, and is a constant defender of liberal values. His series of novels featuring Horace Rumpole, an amiable, late-middle-aged defence barrister and frequenter of Pomeroy's bar, have been adapted for television as *Rumpole of the Bailey*. His other novels, including *Paradise Postponed* (1985), and *Summer's Lease* (1988), are highly popular, evoking, often savagely, what Mortimer perceives as the moral decline of the English middle-class. His plays include *The Dock Brief* (1958), *The Wrong Side of the Park* (1960), *Two Stars for Comfort* (1962) and an autobiographical play, *A Voyage round My Father* (1971) which was filmed for television in 1982 with **Laurence Olivier** as the father. He has made notable translations, especially of **Feydeau**, and several TV screenplays including *I, Claudius* (1976), *Brideshead Revisited* (1981), and *Paradise Postponed* (1986).

MORTON, Alan Lauder (1893–1971) Scottish footballer, born in Glasgow. Possibly the best left-winger ever produced by Scotland, he won 31 international caps in a period when such matches occurred infrequently. Known as the 'Wee Blue Devil', he was a member of the famous 'Wembley Wizards' side which defeated England 5–1 in 1928. On his retirement from playing in 1934 he became a director of Glasgow Rangers, the club with which he had spent his entire playing career.

MORTON, H V (Henry Vollam) (1892–1979) English author and journalist. He began his career on the staff of the *Birmingham Gazette* in 1910 and became assistant editor in 1912. He was the author of many informative and informal travel books, including *The Heart of London* (1925), *In the Steps of the Master* (1934), *Middle East* (1941), *In Search of London* (1951), others in the *In Search of*... series, and *A Wanderer in Rome* (1957).

MORTON, James Douglas, 4th Earl (c.1516–1581) regent of Scotland, the younger son of Sir George Douglas of Pittendriech near Edinburgh. He became Earl of Morton in right of his wife in 1550, and in 1563 was made chancellor. Conspicuous in **Rizzio**'s assassination (1566), he fled to England, but obtained his pardon from the queen. He was privy to the plan for Darnley's murder, though absent from Edinburgh (1567); he joined the confederate nobles who defeated **Bothwell** and **Mary, Queen of Scots** at Carberry Hill: 'discovered' the 'Casket Letters'; led the van at Langside (1568); and, after the brief regencies of **Moray**, Lennox, and Mar, in November 1572 was himself elected regent. After the end of the civil war in 1573 he bound Scotland more tightly to the 'amity' with England, but his attempts to control ecclesiastical appointments and to bring the church into episcopal conformity with England brought him into sharp conflict with the radical ministers, led by **Andrew Melville**, whose 'overseas dreams' of a Genevan polity Morton derided. His regency brought a welcome restoration of law and order, especially to the Borders, but it was achieved at the cost of an unwonted **Douglas** monopoly of many offices, which caused intense resentment. He fell briefly from power in 1578, but the arrival of the young king's cousin, Esme Stuart, in 1579 recast political expectations. His fall was engineered by Captain James Stewart, nominally for his part in Darnley's murder and he was beheaded by means of the 'Maiden', which he had himself introduced to Scotland, in Edinburgh's Grassmarket. His regency, though brief, was in many respects a turning-point, not least in the beginning of the restoration of royal power which was to be continued in **James VI**'s personal reign.

MORTON, Jelly Roll (Ferdinand Joseph La Menthe) (1890–1941) American jazz pianist, composer and bandleader, born into a Creole family in New Orleans. He worked as a gambler and pimp as well as a piano entertainer in 'sporting houses'. After playing under such leaders as Fate Marable and W C Handy, he formed the recording band of six to eight players, called the 'Red Hot Peppers' in 1926, probably the first in jazz to combine arranged ensemble passages with collective improvisation and improvised solos. In 1938, Morton made a series of recordings, including spoken recollections on his early years, for the American Library of Congress.

MORTON, John (c.1420–1500) English prelate and statesman, born at Milborne St Andrew in Dorset. He practised as an advocate in the Court of Arches. He adhered with great fidelity to **Henry VI**, but after the battle of Tewkesbury (1417) he made his peace with **Edward IV** and was made master of the rolls and bishop of Ely. **Richard III** imprisoned him, but he escaped, and joining **Henry VII**, was made archbishop of Canterbury and chancellor (1486). In 1493 he became a cardinal.

MORTON, John Cameron Andrieu Bingham Michael (1893–1979) English author and journalist. After serving in World War I he took up writing and published many books of humour, fantasy and satire, as well as a number of historical works including several on the French Revolution. From 1924 to 1975 he contributed a regular humorous column, 'By the Way' to the *Daily Express* under the name of 'Beachcomber'.

MORTON, John Maddison (1811–91) English dramatist, son of **Thomas Morton**, born in Pangbourne. He became a prolific writer of farces (mostly from the French), but is best remembered as the author of *Cox and Box* (1847). The rise of burlesque was his ruin and he became a 'poor brother' of the Charterhouse.

MORTON, Levi Parsons (1824–1920) American banker and politician, born in Shoreham, Vermont. He began as a country storekeeper's assistant, and in 1863 founded banking-houses in New York and London. In 1878–80 he was returned to congress as a Republican and in 1881–85 was minister to France. He was vice-president of the USA to President **Benjamin Harrison** (1889–93), and governor of New York state (1895–97).

MORTON, Thomas (1764–1838) English dramatist, father of **John Maddison Morton**, born in Durham. He abandoned Lincoln's Inn for play writing, and produced *Speed the Plough* (1798, with its invisible 'Mrs Grundy'), *The Blind Girl* (1801), *Town and Country* (1807), *School for Grown Children* (1826), and other popular plays.

MORTON, Thomas (1781–1832) Scottish shipbuilder. In 1819 he invented the patent slip for docking vessels, which provides a cheap substitute for a dry dock.

MORTON, William Thomas Green (1819–68) American dentist who claimed the patent for the use of sulphuric ether ('letheon') as an anaesthetic. Born in Charlton, Massachusetts, he practised in Boston from 1842. Having learned of experiments with ether as an anaesthetic, he tried it out on a patient in 1846, and patented the process, which was hotly disputed by **Crawford Long** and other medical men.

MORYSON, Fynes (1566–1630) English traveller, born in Cadeby, Lincolnshire. After becoming a fellow of Peterhouse, Cambridge, he travelled through Europe and the East, and published his *Itinerary* (1617; complete ed 4 vols, 1907–08).

MOSCHELES, Ignaz (1794–1870) Bohemian pianist and composer, born in Prague of Jewish parents. By 1808 he was the favourite musician and music-master of Vienna. He taught in London from 1825, and from 1844 in Leipzig. He edited, in English, Anton Felix Schindler's *Life of Beethoven* (1841).

MOSCICKI, Igancy (1867–1946) Polish chemist, and later president of Poland, born in Mierzanow. An ardent patriot, he spent many years in Switzerland, where he became a chemist. He later returned to Poland, where he was a professor of chemistry at Lwow (1912–26). In 1926, his friend **Józef Pilsudski** made him president of Poland. In 1939 he fled to Rumania and then retired to Switzerland where he died.

MOSELEY, Harry (Henry Gwyn Jeffreys) (1887–1915) English physicist. A brilliant graduate of Oxford University, he worked under **Ernest Rutherford** at Manchester University (1910–14). By his researches into radioactivity he determined by means of X-ray spectra the atomic numbers of the elements (Moseley's Law), the basis of 20th-century atomic and nuclear physics. He also predicted the unknown element hafnium. He was killed in action at Gallipoli.

MOSER, George Michael (1704–83) Swiss gold chaser and enameller. Moving early to London, he became the head of his profession. A founder member of the Royal Academy, he was elected the first keeper.

MOSER, Mary (?1744–1819) English flower painter, daughter of **George Michael Moser**. She was one of the founder members of the Royal Academy, and an intimate friend of the royal family.

MOSES BEN MAIMON See **MAIMONIDES**

MOSES, Anna Mary, known as **Grandma Moses** (1860–1961) American primitive artist, born in Washington County, New York. She was a farmer's wife in Staunton, Virginia, and in New York State, and did embroideries of country scenes. She began to paint at about the age of 75, mainly country scenes remembered from her childhood—'old, timey things ... all from memory'. From her first show in New York in 1940, she had great popular success in the United States.

MOSES, Sir Charles Joseph Alfred (1900–88) English-born Australian broadcaster and administrator, born in Little Hulton, Bolton, Lancashire. Trained as a soldier at the Royal Military College, Sandhurst, he emigrated to Australia in 1922 and, after a number of ventures, became an announcer with the then Australian Broadcasting Company in 1930. On the formation of the Australian Broadcasting Commission in 1934 he was appointed controller of talks and school broadcasts. The following year he became general manager of the ABC, a position he was to hold for the next 30 years, the formative years of Australian broadcasting. During this period he pioneered broadcasting to schools and to rural areas, introduced the ABC's own independent news service and national television, and established ABC symphony orchestras in each state. He joined the Australian Imperial Forces in 1940, and escaped after the fall of Singapore in 1942 to serve in New Guinea. On his retirement from the ABC in 1965 he became secretary-general of the Asian Broadcasting Union until 1976.

MOSES, Ed (Edwin Corley) (1955–) American athlete, born in Dayton, Ohio, the greatest 400-metre hurdler ever. He was unbeaten in any race in this gruelling event from August 1977 to June 1987. Olympic champion in 1976 and 1984 and four times world record holder, he dominated this discipline for over a decade. He would have been favourite for the gold medal in the 1980 Moscow Olympics as well, but missed them because of the American boycott. A popular athlete with both the spectators and his fellow competitors, he is an ardent critic of drug-taking in sport. His third place in the 1988 Olympic final marked the end of a unique era.

MOSES, Hebrew *Môsheh* (15th–13th century BC) Old Testament Hebrew prophet and lawgiver. According to the Pentateuch he led the people of Israel out of Egypt by way of Sinai, Kadesh and Moab (where he died) towards the Promised Land. On Mount Sinai he was given the Ten Commandments by Yahweh (Jehovah). As a child in Egypt he was saved from the slaughter of all male Jewish children by being hidden in bulrushes in the Nile, where he was found and brought up by one of Pharaoh's daughters.

MOSES, Robert (1888–1981) American public official, born in New Haven, Connecticut, the son of a department-store owner. He was educated at Yale, Oxford, and Columbia universities. In 1919 he became chief of staff of the New York state reconstruction committee, and in 1924 was appointed president of the New York state council of parks and chairman of Long Island State park commission, thus giving him almost total supervision of the state park system. In 1934 he was appointed commissioner of the city parks, and became an eminent and committed spokesman for parks and limited-access roads. Widely known for his part in the constitution of the Triborough Bridge (which gave New Yorkers access to parkland), he has the Jones Beach development and many other projects, such as slum clearance and housing estates, to his credit. He is considered to be responsible for much of the modern appearance of New York City.

MOSHOESHOE II, Constantine Bereng Seeiso (1938–) king of Lesotho. Educated at Oxford, he was installed as Paramount Chief of the Basotho people in 1960 and proclaimed king when Lesotho became independent six years later. His desire for political involvement led to his being twice placed under house arrest, and in 1970 an eight-month exile in Holland ended when Moshoeshoe agreed to take no further part in the country's politics.

MOSLEY, Sir Oswald Ernald, 6th Baronet (1896–1980) English politician, successively Conservative, Independent and Labour MP, was a member of the 1929 Labour government. He later resigned and became leader of the British Union of Fascists. Detained under the Defence Regulations during World War II, he founded a new 'Union' Movement in 1948. His vision of a politically and economically united Europe is embodied in his *Europe: Faith and Plan*

(1958). He married Cynthia, 2nd daughter of Earl **Curzon** of Kedleston in 1920, and, three years after her death, the Honourable Diana Mitford in 1936.

MOSSADEQ, Mohammed (1881–1967) Iranian statesman, born in Tehran. He held office in Iran in the 1920s, returned to politics in 1944, and directed his attack on the Anglo-Iranian Oil Co, which, by his Oil Nationalization Act of 1951 (in which year he became prime minister), he claimed to have expropriated. His government was overthrown by a royalist uprising in 1953, and he was imprisoned. He was released in 1956.

MÖSSBAUER, Rudolph (1929–) German-born American physicist, born in Munich. He discovered the 'Mössbauer effect' concerning gamma radiation in crystals, and shared the 1961 Nobel prize with **Robert Hofstadter** for research into atomic structure. He has been professor of experimental physics at the Technische Hochschule, Munich, and visiting professor of physics at the Californian Institute of Technology since 1964.

MOSZKOWSKI, Moritz (1854–1925) Polish composer and pianist, born in Breslau. He taught at the Kullak Academy, Berlin, and later lived in Paris. A prolific composer for piano and orchestra, he is now remembered almost solely for his lively *Spanish Dances*.

MOTHERWELL, Robert Burns (1915–) American painter, born in Aberdeen, Washington. He briefly attended the California School of Fine Arts in San Francisco and studied philosophy at Stanford, Harvard, Grenoble and later at Columbia. He has written a good deal on the theory of modern art and helped found the Abstract Expressionist group in New York in the 1940s. His images often resemble semi-automatic doodles of a kind that the Surrealists had explored, but enlarged to fill huge canvases. He married the artist **Helen Frankenthaler** in 1955.

MOTHERWELL, William (1797–1835) Scottish collector of ballads, born in Glasgow. From 1819 to 1829 he was sheriff-clerk depute of Renfrewshire. He published *Minstrelsy, Ancient and Modern* (1819) and other verse collections, including *Poetical Remains* (1848).

MOTLEY, John Lothrop (1814–77) American historian and diplomat, born in Dorchester, Massachusetts. He studied at Harvard and several German universities, and began a diplomatic career. He soon turned to literature, however, and ten years were spent on his *Rise of the Dutch Republic* (1856), which established his fame. This was continued in the *History of the United Netherlands* which appeared in 1860–69. In 1861–67 he was minister to Austria, in 1869–70 to Great Britain. His last work was *The Life and Death of John Barneveld*, a biography which is virtually a part of his main theme.

MOTT, John Raleigh (1865–1955) American religious leader and social worker, born in Livingston Manor, New York. A Methodist layman, he became known the world over by his work for the Young Men's Christian Association (1915–31), the Student Volunteer Movement (1888–1920) and the World Missionary Council (1941–42). He shared the 1946 Nobel peace prize with **Emily Balch**.

MOTT, Lucretia, née **Coffin** (1793–1880) American feminist and reformer, born in Nantucket, Massachusetts. She married James Mott (d.1868) in 1811, bearing him six children. She rose to prominence as a speaker at Quaker meetings, beginning in 1817, and became an active campaigner for temperance, peace, women's rights and anti-slavery. She attended the Anti-Slavery Convention of 1833 and was organizer and president of the Philadelphia women's branch but was denied membership in the World Anti-Slavery Convention in London, for which **Daniel O'Connell** savagely denounced it. She was strongly supported by her husband in this, and under her influence he left his commission business because of its connection with slave-produced cotton, in which he had dealt throughout the 1820s. James Mott published *Three Months in Great Britain* in 1841, describing their ill-fated mission of the previous year. Lucretia Mott and **Elizabeth Cady Stanton** organized the first Woman's Rights Convention in 1848. She remained prominent and active in the feminist movement until her death.

MOTT, Sir Nevill Francis (1905–) English physicist, born in Leeds. He studied mathematics at Cambridge and became a lecturer and fellow there working with **Ernest Rutherford**. He later became professor of theoretical physics at Bristol, and in 1954 Cavendish professor of physics at Cambridge, decisively shaping the Cavendish Laboratory's research activities. In 1965 he 'retired' and returned to full-time research to work on the new area of noncrystalline semiconductors. He shared the 1977 Nobel prize for physics (with **Philip Anderson** and **John van Vleck**) for his work on the electronic properties of disordered materials. Mott is one of the major theoretical physicists of this century, opening new and difficult areas of solid-state physics and materials science. He influenced a generation in showing how to model the complexity of physical problems such as fracture of metals and electronic processes in disordered semiconductors.

MOTTELSON, Benjamin Roy (1926–) American-born Danish physicist, born in Chicago, Illinois, and educated at Purdue University and Harvard. From Harvard he moved to the Institute of Theoretical Physics in Copenhagen (now the Neils Bohr Institute) on a travelling fellowship, where he worked with **Aage Bohr** on the problem of combining the two models of the atomic nuclei. They secured experimental evidence in support of **Leo James Rainwater**'s collective model of the atomic nuclei and Bohr, Mottelson and Rainwater shared the 1975 Nobel prize for physics. From 1953 to 1957 Mottelson held a research position in CERN (the European Centre for Nuclear Research) before returning to Copenhagen where he became professor at Nordita (Nordic Institute for Theoretical Atomic Physics). He took Danish nationality in 1973.

MOTTEUX, Peter Anthony (1660–1718) British author, born in Rouen. He left France for London after the revocation of the Edict of Nantes (1685) and after a time took up journalism. He edited the *Gentleman's Journal* (1691–94), but is best known for his translations of **Rabelais** (1693–1708) and *Don Quixote* (1703).

MOTTRAM, Ralph Hale (1883–1971) English novelist, born in Norwich. He began his working life as a banker. **Galsworthy** is the main influence in his work, as is clearly seen in his first book, *Spanish Farm* (1924), and its sequels, *Sixty-Four, Ninety-Four* (1925), and *The Crime at Vanderlynden* (1926).

MOULE, Charles Francis Digby (1908–) English biblical scholar, born in Hanchow, China. He graduated at Cambridge and was ordained into the Anglican church in 1933. After several curacies and theological appointments he returned to Cambridge as lecturer before becoming professor of divinity (1951–76). One of the most versatile scholars of his time, he has made substantial contributions to the *Encyclopaedia Britannica* and has written many books including *An Idiom Book of New Testament Greek* (1953), *The Origin of Christology* (1977), *The Holy Spirit* (1978), *The Birth of the New Testament* (1981), and *Essays in New Testament Interpretation* (1982).

MOULINS, Master of (c.1460–c.1529) the name given to an unknown French artist whose principal work was the triptych in Moulins Cathedral of the *Virgin and Child.* He is regarded as the most accomplished French artist of the time. The influence of **Hugo van der Goes** can be seen in his vividly coloured and realistic paintings, and some authorities identify him with Jean Perreal or Jean de Paris, court painter to **Charles VIII**.

MOUNTBATTEN, Edwina Cynthia Annette, née **Ashley, Countess of** (1901–60) wife of **Louis, Earl Mountbatten of Burma**, whom she married in 1922. She rendered distinguished service during the London 'blitz' (1940–42) to the Red Cross and St John Ambulance Brigade, of which she became superintendent-in-chief in 1942. As vice-reine of India (1947), her work in social welfare brought her the friendship of **Gandhi** and Pandit **Nehru**. She died suddenly on an official tour of Borneo for the St John Ambulance Brigade.

MOUNTBATTEN, originally **Battenburg, Prince Louis Alexander, 1st Marquess of Milford Haven** (1854–1921) British naval commander, born in Austria, the son of Prince Alexander of Hesse. He became a naturalized British subject and entered the Royal Navy in 1868. He served with distinction as a commodore in the Mediterranean fleet, as director of naval intelligence and senior sea commands. He was first sea lord at the outbreak of World War I, but was forced to resign by anti-German prejudice. By royal command he gave up his German titles in 1917 and changed the family name from Battenberg to Mountbatten, and was created Marquess of Milford Haven. He was promoted admiral in 1919.

MOUNTBATTEN, Louis Francis Victor Albert Nicholas, 1st Earl Mountbatten of Burma (1900–79) British naval commander and statesman, born near Windsor. The younger son of Prince **Louis Mountbatten** and great-grandson of Queen **Victoria**, he was known as Prince Louis Francis of Battenberg until 1917. Educated at Royal Naval Colleges Osborne and Dartmouth (1913–16), he served at sea in World War I in HMS *Lion* and HMS *Elizabeth.* In World War II he commanded the 5th destroyer flotilla (1939–41), and became chief of combined operations (1941–43). He was supreme allied commander south-east Asia from 1943 to 1945, and was then appointed the last viceroy of India (1947) to oversee the rapid transfer of power. He returned to service afloat as 4th sea lord and commander of the Mediterranean fleet (1952–55), and was appointed first sea lord (1955–59) and chief of defence staff (1959–65). He was murdered by an IRA bomb while sailing near his holiday home in County Sligo, Ireland.

MOUNTBATTEN, Prince Philip See **EDINBURGH, Duke of**

MOUNTCASTLE, Vernon Benjamin (1918–) American neurophysiologist, born in Shelbyville, Kentucky. He received his undergraduate education at Roanoke College and his medical training at the Johns Hopkins University School of Medicine. He joined the faculty at Johns Hopkins in 1946. His research has been concerned with neural mechanisms in sensation and perception, and his book (with G M Edelman), *The Mindful Brain* (1978) has been very influential.

MOUNTEVANS, Edward Ratcliffe Garth Russell Evans, 1st Baron (1881–1957) English naval commander. Educated at Merchant Taylors' School, he entered the Royal Navy in 1897. From 1910 to 1913 he was second-in-command to **Scott**'s Antarctic expedition. In Word War I he fought at Jutland, and in command of HMS *Broke* he scored an outstanding victory over four German destroyers. In 1929 he was appointed rear admiral commanding the Royal Australian Navy. He later was commander-in-chief of the Africa station and deputy high commissioner of the British Protectorates, where his actions against the paramount chief Tshkedi Kama of Bechuanaland were criticized. Recalled in 1939, he served in World War II as London regional commissioner. He wrote *Keeping the Seas* (1920) and *South with Scott* (1921).

MOUNTFORD, Charles Pearcy (1890–1976) Australian ethnologist, author and film director, born in Hallett, South Australia. During his early years as a mechanic for the post office he was brought into contact with the aborigines and became an expert on their way of life, although he had no formal training. In 1937 he led an expedition in search of the lost explorer **Ludwig Leichhardt**, and between 1938 and 1960 he led ten expeditions into central Australia. In 1948 he was leader of expeditions into Arnhem Land and to Melville Island, for the National Geographic Society of the USA. Beginning with *Brown Men and Red Sand* (1948), Mountford wrote a series of books, illustrated with his own photographs, about the aborigines and their culture. He received awards for his photography and went on to direct feature films on aboriginal life from 1950.

MOUNTJOY, Charles Blount, Lord see **BLOUNT**

MOUSSORGSKY or **MUSORGSKY, Modest Petrovich** (1835–81) Russian composer, born in Karevo (Pskov). He was educated for the army but resigned his commission in 1858 after the onset of a nervous disorder and began the serious study of music under **Balakirev**. A member of the **Glinka**-inspired nationalist group in St Petersburg, which included **Dargomizhsky** and **Rimsky-Korsakov**, he first made a name with his songs, among them the well-known setting of **Goethe**'s satirical 'Song of the Flea' (1879); but his masterpiece is the opera *Boris Godunov*, first performed at St Petersburg in 1874; his piano suite *Pictures from an Exhibition* (1874) has also kept a firm place in the concert repertoire. Other operas and large-scale works remained uncompleted as the composer sank into the chronic alcoholism which hastened his early death. His friend Rimsky-Korsakov undertook the task of musical executor, arranged or completed many of his unfinished works and rearranged some of the finished ones, sometimes to the detriment of their robust individuality.

MOYNIHAN, Berkeley George Andrew, 1st Baron Moynihan of Leeds (1865–1936) English surgeon, born in Malta. He held various posts at the Leeds General Infirmary, specializing in the techniques of abdominal, gastric and pancreatic operations, and became professor at Leeds in 1909. The driving impulse of his life was the promotion of scientific surgery, and he set out his doctrine in his *Abdominal Operations* (1905). He formed the Moynihan Chirurgical Club, was active in starting the Association of Surgeons of Great Britain and Ireland, and was also a leader of the movement to found the *British Journal of Surgery*.

MOYNIHAN, Rodrigo (1910–) English painter. He studied at the Slade school, and joined the London Group in 1933. From 1943–44 he was an official war artist, and was professor of painting at the Royal College of Art 1948–57. Most of his works are of an Impressionist nature, with soft tones (eg, his portrait of Queen **Elizabeth** as *Princess Elizabeth*), but he later changed to non-figurative painting—of equal sensitivity.

MOZART, (Johann Chrysostom) Wolfgang Amadeus (1756–91) Austrian composer, born in Salzburg, the son of a violinist, composer and theorist, Leopold

Mozart (1719–87). He displayed his musical gifts early, playing the keyboard confidently when aged four, composing his first pieces for it, at the age of five, and soon mastering the violin. Leopold was keen to exhibit his son's extraordinary talents along with those of his pianist-daughter, Maria-Anna or 'Nannerl' (1751–1829), and he undertook a series of tours with them. In 1762 they played before the Elector of Bavaria in Munich and before Empress **Maria Theresa** in Vienna. In 1763 they gave concerts in Munich, Augsburg, Mainz and Frankfurt, en route for Paris where they stayed five months, and then to London for fifteen months, where a friendship was formed with **J C Bach**. During the next six months in the Netherlands, both children took seriously ill. In 1766 they began the homeward journey, stopping in Paris for two months, and making many appearances throughout Switzerland and Germany. Accounts of this tour mention Mozart's precocity, spirited playing and talent for improvization. In September 1767 the family went for five months to Vienna, where he wrote an opera buffa, *La finta semplice*, and a Singspiel, *Bastien und Bastienne*, the latter commissoned by Dr **Franz Anton Mesmer**. On returning to Salzburg Mozart was appointed honorary konzsertmeister to the court. There followed three extended visits by father and son to Italy (1770–72). His musical experiences on these tours helped mould his style, especially in dramatic music, although he was prolific also in writing sacred vocal pieces and instrumental works: by 1772 he had written about 25 symphonies (some are lost) and his first quartets. Further quartets and symphonies followed during and after a Vienna visit in 1772, on which Mozart came into contact with **Haydn**'s music. 1775–76 saw two stage works, *La finta giardiniera* and *Il rè pastore*, five violin concertos, the *Haffner* Serenade, and Masses for the Salzburg Court Chapel. Unhappy with the austere and unmusical Archbishop Colloredo of Salzburg, Mozart left his service in 1777 and, travelling with his mother, sought employment elsewhere. They stayed at Mannheim, but no post was offered. Instead he composed some piano concertos and flute quartets, and fell in love with a singer, Aloysia Weber. Then, in Paris, where his mother died, he composed the *Paris* Symphony. Leopold persuaded him to return to Salzburg, and Mozart reluctantly accepted the post of court organist. At this time he composed the Symphonies (**Köchel** Nos 318–19), the *Coronation* Mass, and the Sinfonia Concertante for violin and viola. 1780 saw an important commission from Munich, the opera seria *Idomeneo*. In 1781 Colloredo summoned Mozart to Vienna for the coronation of Emperor **Joseph II**. Again, he soon left the Archbishop's service, after a stormy scene, but remained in Vienna, which became home for the rest of his short, crowded life. Here his reputation as composer and pianist was to reach its peak within a few years. Aloysia Weber had married a court actor, and Mozart turned his attentions to her sister Constanze, whom he married in 1782, the year of his Singspiel *The Abduction from the Seraglio*. Married life was happy, but insecure financially (they had six children, of whom two survived); Mozart eked out his income by teaching. He became a freemason in 1784, and produced six piano concertos; in 1785 a further three; in 1786 three more. This was the rich flowering of his maturity, along with the six quartets dedicated to Haydn, the *Linz* and *Prague* Symphonies and the three Italian comic masterpieces composed to libretti by **Giacomo da Ponte**: *The Marriage of Figaro* (after **Beaumarchais**, 1786), *Don Giovanni* (first performed in Prague, 1787), and *Cosi fan tutte* (1790). The String Quintets in C major and G minor (1787), the last three symphonies (1788) the quartets for the king of Prussia (K575,589,590) and the Clarinet Quintet mark the peak of his instrumental powers. The letters to fellow masons in his last three years make sad reading, reflecting countless anxieties about finance or health. He hoped for new commissions or a court post on the accession of Emperor **Leopold II**, but none was forthcoming. In 1791 he applied unsuccessfully for the kapellmeistership of St Stephen's Cathedral. His last works were the Masonic Singspiel *Die Zauberflöte*, and an opera seria, *La Clemenze di Tito* (also of 1791) and for Leopold's coronation in Prague a clarinet concerto and a requiem. The last was unfinished when he died on 5 December. In many ways Mozart remained a child, and his irresponsible way of life may have contributed to the troubles of his last years. But he was not a wicked man: his most grievous vice was probably billiards. Nor was he an intellectual. Instead he was quite simply a universal genius of music; his facility, grace and polish, the swiftness and fecundity of his thought, his innate sense for phrasing and gift of melodic beauty, his mastery of form and the richness of his harmony, all contributing to his excelling in every *genre* of the music of his day, which he raised to a sublime pitch of perfection.

MU'AWIYAH (c.602–680) first Umayyad caliph, from 661. He opposed the prophet **Muḥammad** until the conquest of Mecca in 630, then became his secretary. Under the 2nd caliph, **Omar**, he took part in the conquest of Syria and was made governor in 640. He rebelled against the 4th caliph, **Ali**, for the murder of his kinsman, the caliph **Uthman**, and fought him at the indecisive battle of Siffin (657). With the help of **Amr ibn al-'As** he gained control of Egypt, and after the assassination of Ali in 661 took over the caliphate, thus founding the Omayyad dynasty, and moved the capital to Damascus. He centralized control of the caliphate and extended it through conquests in North Africa and Afghanistan. He was succeeded by his son, Yazid (d.683).

MUBARAK, Hosni (?1928–) Egyptian politician, president of Egypt since 1981. A former pilot and flying instructor who rose to become commander of the Egyptian Air Force, Mubarak was vice-president under **Anwar Sadat** from 1975 until the latter's assassination in 1981. The only candidate for the presidency, Mubarak pledged to continue Sadat's domestic and international policies, including firm treatment of Muslim extremists, and the peace process with Israel.

MUCHA, Alphonse, originally **Alfons Maria** (1860–1939) Czech graphic artist and designer, born in Ivancise. He studied in Munich, in Vienna, and at the Académie Julian and the Académie Colarossi, Paris. He designed jewellery, wallpaper and furniture, but his best-known works are his posters for **Sarah Bernhardt**, in the rich curvilinear Art Nouveau style of the 1890s. He designed a shop for a jeweller in Paris in 1901, before devoting himself mainly to painting from c.1903.

MUDIE, Charles Edward (1816–90) English bibliophile, born in Chelsea. After some experience as a bookseller, he established in 1842 his library, which became a well-known institution.

MUELLER, Baron Sir Ferdinand Jakob Heinrich von (1825–96) German-born Australian explorer and botanist, born in Rostock, Schleswig-Holstein. After emigrating to Australia in 1847, he was appointed government botanist for the state of Victoria in 1853, and in the next few years travelled extensively, building up a valuable collection of native flora. He also explored Western Australia and Tasmania, promoted expeditions into New Guinea and was a member of the first Australian Antarctic Exploration committee. Mueller sponsored a fund organized by Melbourne ladies for an expedition in search of the lost explorer **Ludwig Leichhardt**, and he organized the 1875 trip into the central desert by **Ernest Giles**. He published a large number of scientific works on the plants of Australia.

MUELLER, Erwin Wilhelm (1911–77) German-born American physicist, born in Berlin. He studied engineering in Berlin and worked for industrial laboratories there and at the Fritz Haber Institute until 1952, when he joined the Pennsylvania State University. He became a naturalized American in 1962. In 1936 he invented the field-emission microscope, and in 1951 the field-ion microscope, which gave the first photographs affording a direct view of atoms and some heat-stable molecules.

MUGABE, Robert Gabriel (1924–) African nationalist and Zimbabwean politician, Zimbabwe's first prime minister. Largely self-educated (by means of correspondence courses) Mugabe became a teacher in 1942, and while working in Ghana was influenced by **Nkrumah**'s radical policies. After short periods in the (subsequently banned) National Democratic Party and Zimbabwe African People's Union (ZAPU) he was briefly detained but escaped to co-found, with **Ndabaningi Sithole**, the Zimbabwe African National Union (ZANU). After a ten-year detention in Rhodesia (1964–74) he spent five years in Mozambique gathering support in preparation for Zimbabwe's independence in 1980. In 1987 Mugabe persuaded parliament to agree to combine the roles of head of state and head of government, and he became the country's first executive president. In 1988 ZANU and ZAPU merged to make Zimbabwe effectively a one-party state, under Mugabe's leadership.

MUGGERIDGE, Malcolm (1903–) English journalist and sage, born in London. A lecturer at the Egyptian University in Cairo (1927–30), he joined the *Manchester Guardian* (1930–33), serving as their Moscow correspondent, was assistant editor of the *Calcutta Statesman* (1934–35) and joined the editorial staff of the *Evening Standard.* Serving with the Intelligence Corps during World War II, he received the Legion of Honour and the Croix de Guerre with Palm. Resuming his journalistic career, he worked with *The Daily Telegraph* (1946–52) and was editor of *Punch* (1953–57). Later a television reporter and interviewer, he contributed regularly to *Panorama* (1953–60) and had his own series *Appointment With* ... (1960–61) and *Let Me Speak* (1964–65), in which he quizzed the great figures of the day and challenged minorities to defend their beliefs. A controversial rector of Edinburgh University (1967–68), he resigned over student liberalism and promiscuity. Once an iconoclastic gadfly and self-confessed rake, he has characterized his life as a spiritual journey towards a greater understanding of faith and, in 1982, became a Roman Catholic. More recent television appearances include the autobiographical *Muggeridge Ancient and Modern* (1981). His many books include *The Earnest Atheist* (1936), *Tread Softly for You Tread on My Jokes* (1966) and *Chronicle of Wasted Time* (1982).

MUGGLETON, Lodowick (1609–98) English Sectarian, a London Puritan tailor. With his cousin, John Reeve (1608–58), he presented himself as the messenger of a new divine dispensation in 1652, and founded the sect of Muggletonians. They held that the Devil became incarnate in Eve, and denied the Holy Trinity. He was imprisoned, and later fined for blasphemy, and published a *Spiritual Transcendental Treatise* (1652).

MUHAMMAD, or **Mohammed** (c.570–c.632) Arab prophet, and founder of Islam, born in Mecca. He was the son of Abdallâh, a poor merchant of the powerful tribe of Quaraysh, hereditary guardians of the shrine in Mecca. Orphaned at six, he was brought up by his grandfather and uncle, Abu Tâlib, who trained him to be a merchant. At the age of 24 he entered the service of a rich widow, Khadija (c.595–619), whom he eventually married. They had six children, including their daughters **Fatima** and Umm Kulthum, who married **Uthman**, the 3rd caliph. While continuing as a trader, Muhammad became increasingly drawn to religious contemplation. Soon after 600 (the traditional date is c.610) he began to receive revelations of the word of Allah, the one and only God. This Qur'an (Koran), or 'reading', commanded that the numerous idols of the shrine should be destroyed and that the rich should give to the poor. This simple message attracted some support but provoked a great deal of hostility from those who felt their interests threatened. When his wife and uncle died, Muhammad was reduced to poverty, but began making a few converts amongst pilgrims to Mecca from the town of Yathrib, an agricultural community to the north. By 622 the position of Muhammad and his small band of devoted followers had become untenable, but they were saved by an invitation from the people of Yathrib, who wanted Muhammad to come and arbitrate in the feuds that racked their community. He migrated there, and this migration, the Hegira, marks the beginning of the Muslim era. The name of the town was changed to Medina, 'the city of the prophet'. The most important act in the first year of the Hegira was Muhammad's permission to go to war with the enemies of Islam—especially the Meccans—in the name of God. In December 623 his Muslims defeated a Meccan force, but he was severely wounded at a battle at Ohod (January 625). In 627 he repelled a Meccan siege of Medina. By 629 he was able to take control of Mecca, which recognized him as chief and prophet. By 630 he had control over all Arabia. In March 632 he undertook his last pilgrimage to Mecca, and there on Mount Arafat fixed for all time the ceremonies of the pilgrimage. He fell ill soon after his return and died on 8 June in the home of the favourite of his nine wives, **Aishah**, daughter of one of his first followers, **Abu Bakr**. His tomb in the mosque at Medina is venerated throughout Islam.

MUIR, Edwin (1887–1959) Scottish poet, born in Deerness on the Mainland of Orkney. The son of a crofter, he left the Orkneys at 14 when his family migrated to Glasgow, where he suffered the period of drab existence described in his *The Story and the Fable* (1940), revised as *An Autobiography* in 1954. He moved from job to job, but spent much time reading **Nietzsche**, **Shaw**, **Ibsen**, **Heine** and **Blatchford**, and he became interested in left-wing politics. In 1919 he married the novelist Willa Anderson (1890–1970), with whom he settled in London, and travelled on the Continent from 1921 to 1924, where the couple collaborated in translations of **Kafka** and **Feuchtwanger**. Back in Scotland in 1925 he published his first volume of verse (*First Poems*), then returned to France where he wrote novels, notably *The Marionette* (1927). He spent most of the 1930s in Sussex and St Andrews. On the outbreak of World War II he joined the staff of the British Council in 1942, and in 1945 returned to Prague as first director of the British Institute there, which was closed after the Communist coup of 1948. He then took over the British Institute in Rome until 1950, when he was appointed warden of the adult education college at Newbattle Abbey, Midlothian. After a year as Eliot Norton professor of poetry at Harvard (1955–56), he retired to Swaffham Prior near Cambridge. His verses appeared in eight slim volumes—*First Poems* (1925), *Chorus of the Newly Dead* (1926, omitted from *Collected Poems*), *Variations on a Time Theme* (1934), *Journeys and Places* (1937), *The Narrow Place* (1943), *The Voyage* (1946), *The Labyrinth* (1949), *New Poems* (1949–51) and finally *Collected Poems* (1952). Other poems appeared in *The Listener* and other periodicals later. Muir's critical work includes a controversial study of **John Knox**, *Scott and Scotland* (1936), *Essays on Literature and Society* (1949) and *Structure of the Novel* (1928).

MUIR, Jean Elizabeth (1933–) English fashion designer, born in London. Educated at Dame Harper School, Bedford, she started as a salesgirl with Liberty's in London in 1950, then moved to Jaeger in 1956. In 1961 she started on her own as Jane & Jane. In 1966 she established her own company, Jean Muir. Her clothes are noted for their classic shapes and their softness and fluidity.

MUIR, John (1810–82) Scottish Sanskrit scholar, born in Glasgow, brother of Sir **William Muir**. After spending 25 years in the East India Company's Civil Service in Bengal, he settled in Edinburgh, where he founded a chair of Sanskrit. His great work was his *Original Sanskrit Texts* (5 vols, 1858–70). Another of his books is *Metrical Translations from Sanskrit Writers* (1878).

MUIR, John (1838–1914) Scots-born American naturalist, born in Dunbar, East Lothian, and considered the father of the modern environment movement. He emigrated with his family to the USA in 1849, and after a difficult childhood, with a harsh father, studied at Wisconsin University. He was an ingenious inventor and constructor of devices until he lost an eye in 1867 in an industrial accident, and thereafter concentrated his interest on natural history, exploring the American west and especially the Yosemite area. After marriage to Louie Wanda Strentzel, the daughter of an Austrian who established the Californian fruit and wine industry in 1880, he farmed very successfully in California, and also campaigned with his friend Robert U Johnson (1853–1937), editor of *Century Magazine*, for a national park there. In 1890 came apparent success; congress approved a bill creating the Yosemite National Park. However, active opposition to the Park's ideals did not cease, and it needed a decade of Muir's vigorous oratory and article-writing, and President **Roosevelt**'s support, before the idea of wildlife conservation became widely accepted. Muir wrote a number of books, covering his own life and explorations, including *The Mountains of California* (1894), *Our National Parks* (1901), *My First Summer in the Sierra* (1911) and *The Yosemite* (1912). The John Muir Trust to acquire wild land in Britain was established in 1984.

MUIR, Thomas (1765–99) Scottish advocate, born in Glasgow. He advocated parliamentary reform, was transported for sedition to Botany Bay, escaped in 1796, but died in France of a wound received (1796) on a Spanish frigate in a fight with British vessels.

MUIR, Sir William (1819–1905) Anglo-Indian administrator and scholar, born in Glasgow, brother of the Sanskrit scholar **John Muir**. He joined the Bengal Civil Service, and became foreign secretary to the Indian government in 1865. He held other high offices in India and from 1885 to 1902 was principal of Edinburgh University. His works include a *Life of Mahomet* (4 vols, 1858–61), *The Caliphate* (new ed. 1915), and *The Corân* (1878).

MUIRHEAD, (Litellus) Russell (1896–1976) English editor and traveller. Educated at University College School and Christ's College, Cambridge, in 1930 he became editor of the 'Blue Guides' to Europe, his other editorial work including scientific journals and the Penguin guides to England and Wales (1938–49). He was also author of numerous travel books and articles.

MUJIBUR RAHMAN, known as **Sheikh Mujib** (1920–75) Bangladesh politician. Born in Tungipana, into a landowning family, he was educated in Calcutta and Dacca University, from which he was expelled for political activities. In 1949 he co-founded the Awami (People's) League, campaigning for autonomy for East Pakistan (Bangladesh), became its leader in 1953, and led it to electoral victory in 1970. In 1972, after the civil war between East and West Pakistan, he became prime minister of newly independent Bangladesh. He introduced a socialist economic programme but became increasingly intolerant of opposition, establishing a one-party state. In August 1975 he and his wife were assassinated in a military coup.

MULCASTER, Richard (c.1530–1611) English educationist, a native of Cumberland. A brilliant Greek and Oriental scholar, he was head of Merchant Taylors School, London, and one of the great Elizabethan schoolmasters, his ideas on education being well in advance of his time. In 1582 he published in *Elementaire* a list of 7000 words in his proposed reformed spellings ('guest' to be spelled 'gest' and 'guide' to be spelled 'gide'; an accent 'u' to show the short 'a' in, eg 'babble': 'băbble' etc).

MULDOON, Robert David (1921–) New Zealand politician, born in Auckland. He served as an infantryman in World War II before becoming an accountant. He was first elected to parliament (as a National party MP) in 1960, and after five years as minister of finance became deputy prime minister. Though the government was defeated in elections later that year, Muldoon (having become party leader and leader of the opposition in 1974) led the National party to victory in the 1975 elections. He was prime minister from 1974 to 1984, when he gave up leadership of the National party. Since 1986 he has been shadow foreign affairs spokesman.

MÜLLER, Sir Ferdinand (1825–96) German-born Australian botanist, born in Rostock. He emigrated to Australia in 1847, and was director of Melbourne Botanic Gardens (1857–73). He introduced the blue gum tree into America, Europe and Africa, but is chiefly important for his many publications describing new species of Australian plants.

MÜLLER, Franz Joseph, Baron von Reichenstein (1740–1825) Austrian chemist and mineralogist. In 1783 he discovered a new metal which **Heinrich Klaproth** named tellurium.

MÜLLER, Georg (1805–98) German-born British preacher and philanthropist, born in Kroppenstedt. He studied at Halle, and came to London in 1829. Called to a Nonconformist chapel in Teignmouth, he abolished church-plate collections and depended entirely on voluntary gifts. In 1836 he founded an Orphan House at Ashleydown, Bristol. He wrote an *Autobiography* (1905), and *The Lord's Dealings with George Müller* (1837–56).

MÜLLER, Hermann Joseph (1890–1967) American geneticist, born in New York. He held academic appointments in Moscow (1933–37), Edinburgh (1938–40) and Indiana (from 1945), and was awarded the 1946 Nobel prize for physiology or medicine for his discovery of the use of X-rays to induce genetic mutations.

MÜLLER, Johann See **REGIOMONTANUS**

MÜLLER, Johannes Peter (1801–58) German physiologist, born in Coblenz. In 1826 he became professor of physiology and anatomy at Bonn, and from 1833 at

Berlin. He studied the nervous system and comparative antomy, and his *Handbuch der Physiologie des Menschen* (1833–40); trans 1840–49) was extremely influential.

MÜLLER, Johannes von (1752–1809) Swiss historian, born in Schaffhausen. He studied at Göttingen, taught in Geneva (1774–80), wrote his *Allgemeine Geschichte* (3 vols, 1810), and commenced his *Gerschichte der schweizerischen Eidgenossenschaft* (5 vols, 1786–1808; new ed 1826). He held posts at Cassel, Mainz and Vienna. In Berlin in 1804 he was installed as royal historiographer; and **Napoleon** appointed him (1807) secretary of state for Westphalia.

MÜLLER, Julius (1801–78) German theologian, brother of Karl Otfried Müller. He was professor of theology at Halle from 1839 and wrote *Der christliche Lehre von der Sünde* (1839).

MÜLLER, (Friedrich) Max (1823–1900) German-born British philologist and orientalist, born in Dessau, where his father, the poet Wilhelm Müller (1794–1827), was ducal librarian. He studied at Dessau, Leipzig and Berlin, and took up the then novel subject of Sanskrit and its kindred sciences of philology and religion. In Paris, under **Eugène Burnouf**, he began to prepare an edition of the *Rig-Veda*, the sacred hymns of the Hindus; he came to England in 1846 to examine the MSS, and the East India Company commissioned him (1847) to edit and publish it at their expense (1849–74). He was appointed Taylorian professor of modern languages at Oxford (1854) and professor of comparative philology (1868 onwards), a study he did more than anyone else to promote in Britain. Among his most popular works were *Lectures on the Science of Language* (1861–64), *Auld Lang Syne* (1898), and *My Indian Friends* (1898), and he edited the *Sacred Books of the East* (51 vols, 1879–1910).

MÜLLER, Otto Frederick (1730–84) Danish biologist, born in Copenhagen. He was the first to describe diatoms and bring to notice the animal kingdom of *Infusoria*. He was the inventor of the naturalist's dredge.

MÜLLER, Paul Hermann (1899–1965) Swiss chemist. As research chemist for the J R Geigy company, in 1939 he synthesized DDT (Dichlorodiphenyltrichloroethane) and demonstrated its insecticidal properties. He gained the Nobel prize for physiology or medicine in 1948. The use of DDT has now been discontinued in many countries.

MÜLLER, William James (1812–45) English painter, born in Bristol. His early landscapes dealt mainly with Gloucestershire and Wales. He later travelled abroad and produced many masterly sketches.

MULLIKEN, Robert Sanderson (1896–1986) American chemist and physicist, born in Newburyport, Massachusetts. Professor at Chicago University, he won the Nobel prize for chemistry in 1966 for work on chemical bonds and the electronic structure of molecules.

MULOCK, Miss See **CRAIK, Dinah Maria**

MULREADY, William (1786–1863) Irish painter, born in Ennis, Country Clare, the son of a leather-breeches maker. His family moved to London when he was a boy, and he studied at the Royal Academy, painting such subjects as *A Roadside Inn*, *Barber's Shop*, and *Boys Fishing* (1813). He also worked at portrait painting and book illustration, and designed the first penny postage envelope.

MULRONEY, (Martin) Brian (1939–) Canadian politician, born in Baie Comeau, Quebec province, the son of an Irish immigrant. He attended St Francis Xavier University in Nova Scotia and studied law at Laval University, Quebec City, and then practised as a labour lawyer in Montreal, while becoming increasingly active in the Progressive Conservative party. In 1976 he failed to wrest the party leadership from **Joe Clark** and returned to business as president of a US-owned iron ore company. In 1983 he replaced Clark and in 1984 became prime minister, with a landslide victory over the Liberals. He initiated a number of radical measures, including the 'Meech Lake Accord', settling disputes between the provinces and the centre, and a free trade agreement with the United States, and in 1988 was decisively re-elected.

MULTATULI See **DEKKER, Eduard Douwes**

MUMFORD, Lewis (1895–1990) American author, editor and critic, a lecturer on social problems, born in Flushing, Long Island. He wrote *The Story of Utopias* (1922), *The Brown Decades* (1931), *Faith for Living* (1940), *The Human Prospect* (1955), *The Myth of the Machine* (1967), *The Pentagon of Power* (1971) and other works. He also wrote his autobiography as *My Works and Days: A Personal Chronicle* (1979).

MUNCH, Edvard (1863–1944) Norwegian painter, born in Löten. He studied in Oslo, travelled in Europe and finally settled in his homeland in 1908. His earliest work is influenced by his friend Christian Krogh, but in Paris he came under the influence of **Gauguin**. He began working in a distinctly Expressionist style around the turn of the century and his work was widely disseminated in periodicals. His use of primary colours and tortuously curved designs were a great influence on German Expressionists in particular. Becoming obsessed by subjects such such as death and love, his mature paintings are really non-representative but evocative of these themes. His most characteristic work is a picture entitled *The Scream*, in which an anonymous figure on a bridge clasps his hands to his ears and screams out, swirling lines of colour contributing to the mood of desperation. Munch's work is represented in most major collections, and there is a Munch museum in Oslo.

MÜNCHHAUSEN, Karl Friedrich Hieronymus, Baron von (1720–97) German soldier, born in Bodenwerder, a member of an ancient Hanoverian house. He was the narrator of ridiculously exaggerated exploits, and served in Russian campaigns against the Turks. A collection of marvellous stories attributed to him was first published in English as *Baron Munchausen's Narrative of his Marvellous Travels and Campaigns in Russia* (1785) by **Rudolf Erich Raspe**. *Munchausen* is based partly on 16th-century German jokes, partly as a satire on **James Bruce** and other travellers.

MUNDAY, Anthony (1553–1633) English poet and playwright, born in London. A stationer and actor, he wrote many poems and pamphlets and plays, mostly in collaboration. He reported on the activities of English Catholics in France and Italy and was pageant writer for London.

MUNGO, St See **KENTIGERN, St**

MUNK, Kaj, born **Kaj Harald Leininger Petersen** (1898–1944) Danish playwright, priest and patriot, born in Maribo, Laaland. He studied theology at Copenhagen University, and as priest of a small parish in Jutland wrote heroic and religious plays that led the Danish dramatic revival in the 1930s. His first play was *En Idealist* (1928), followed by *Cant* (1931), *Henrik VIII* (1931), *Ordet* (The Word, 1932), and *Han sidder ved smeltedigien* (He Sits by the Melting-Pot, 1938). During World War II he was one of the spiritual leaders of the Danish Resistance. In 1943 he wrote a patriotic drama, *Niels Ebbeson*; early in 1944 he was taken from his home by the Gestapo one night and was found murdered in a ditch near Silkeborg next morning.

MUNKÁCSY, or **Lieb, Michael** (1846–1900) Hungarian painter, born in Munkács. He went as apprentice to Vienna, studied painting, and in 1872 settled in Paris. His best known pictures include *Christ before Pilate* (1881) and *Death of Mozart* (1884).

MUNNINGS, Sir Alfred (1878–1959) English painter, born in Suffolk. A specialist in the painting of horses and sporting pictures, he became president of the Royal Academy (1944–49). His work is in many public galleries and he was well known for forthright criticism of modern art.

MUNRO, Alice (1931–) Canadian short story writer and novelist, born in Wingham, Ontario, where she was brought up before attending the University of Western Ontario. She wrote short stories from an early age, waiting until she was 'ready' to write the great novel. Her only novel to date, *Lives of Girls and Women* (1971), accomplished though it is, cannot claim to be that. Her stories, however, published for many years without being collected, are recognized as among the finest of the day. Invariably set in rural and semi-rural Ontario, the landscape of her childhood, she has had seven collections from *Dance of the Happy Shades* (1968)—winner of the Governor-General's Award for Fiction—to *The Progress of Love* (1987).

MUNRO, Hector Hugh, pseud **Saki** (1870–1916) British novelist and short-story writer, born in Burma, the son of a police inspector. Educated in England at Bedford Grammar School, he returned to Burma and joined the police force in 1893, but went to London in 1896 and took up writing for *The Westminster Gazette*, and from 1902 as the Balkans correspondent for *The Morning Post*. He settled in London again in 1908. He is best known for his short stories, humorous and macabre, which are highly individual, full of eccentric wit and unconventional situations. Collections of his stories are *Reginald* (1904), *The Chronicles of Clovis* (1911) and *Beasts and Superbeasts* (1914). His novels *The Unbearable Bassington* (1912) and *When William Came* (1913) show his gifts as a social satirist of his contemporary upper-class Edwardian world. He was killed on the Western front during World War I.

MUNRO, Neil (1864–1930) Scottish novelist and journalist, born in Inveraray, the son of a farmer. He worked in a law office before taking up journalism in Glasgow, where he became editor of the *Glasgow Evening News* (1918–27). He wrote romantic Celtic tales in *The Lost Pibroch* (1896) and *Gilian the Dreamer* (1899), and historical Highland novels in *John Splendid* (1898), *Doom Castle* (1901) and *The New Road* (1914). But he is best known for his humorous tales about a Clyde puffer, published as *The Vital Spark* (1906) and collected as *Para Handy and Other Tales* (1931). He published his autobiography, *Brave Days*, in 1931.

MUNRO, Robert (1835–1920) Scottish archaeologist. After practising as a doctor, he retired and founded (1911) at Edinburgh a lectureship in anthropology and prehistoric archaeology. He wrote *Lake-Dwellings of Scotland* (1882), *Lake-Dwellings of Europe* (1890), *Bosnia* (1896), *Prehistoric Problems* (1897), *Prehistoric Britain* (1914). He also wrote *Autobiographic Sketch* (1921).

MÜNSTER, Sebastian (1489–1552) German theologian and cosmographer, born in Ingelheim. He became a Franciscan monk, but after the Reformation taught Hebrew and theology at Heidelberg, and from 1536 mathematics at Basel. He brought out a Hebrew bible (1534–35), Hebrew and Chaldee grammars, and wrote a famous *Cosmographia* (1544).

MUNTHE, Axel (1857–1949) Swedish physician and writer, born in Oskarshamn. He practised as a physician and psychiatrist in Paris and Rome, was Swedish court physician and retired to Capri, where he wrote his best-selling autobiography, *The Story of San Michele* (1929).

MÜNZER, Thomas (c.1489–1525) German religious reformer and Anabaptist, born in Stolberg. He studied theology, and in 1520 began to preach at Zwickau. His socialism and mystical doctrines soon brought him into collision with the authorities. After preaching widely, in 1525 he was elected pastor of the Anabaptists of Mülhausen, where his communistic ideas soon aroused the whole country. He joined the Peasants' Revolt of 1524–25, but was defeated at Frankenhausen, and executed a few days later.

MUQADDASI (945–88) Arab geographer, and pioneer of fieldwork, born in Jerusalem. He travelled widely and described Moslem lands in a geographical compendium published in 985.

MURAD IV (1609–40) Ottoman emperor, succeeded on the deposition of his father, Mustafa I, in 1623 when the state was in political and financial anarchy. A savage disciplinarian, he successfully put down a serious revolt among the Janissaries in the 1630s, and eliminated corruption in administration and justice. In 1638 he led an expedition against Persia, recapturing Baghdad, which had been taken by **Abbas the Great** in 1624.

MURASAKI, Shikibu (978–c.1031) Japanese author. A member of a noble family, she wrote the world's earliest surviving long novel, *Genji Monagatari* or *The Tale of Genji*, translated by Arthur Waley in 1925–33.

MURAT, Joachim (1767–1815) French soldier and king of Naples, father of **Napoléon Lucien Murat** and Charles Murat, born, an innkeeper's son, in La Bastide-Fortunière near Cahors. At the Revolution he entered the army, and soon rose to be colonel. He served under **Napolean** in Italy and in Egypt, rose to be general of division (1799), returned with Napoleon to France, and on 18th Brumaire dispersed the Council of Five Hundred at St Cloud. Napoleon gave him his sister, Caroline, in marriage. In command of the cavalry at Marengo he covered himself with glory, and in 1801 was nominated governor of the Cisalpine Republic. He contributed to the victories of Austerlitz (1805), Jena and Eylau; in 1806 the grand-duchy of Berg was bestowed on him, and in 1808 he was proclaimed king of the Two Sicilies as Joachim Napoleon. He took possession of Naples, though the Bourbons, supported by Britain, retained Sicily, and won the hearts of his subjects. In the Russian expedition he commanded the cavalry, and indeed the army after Napoleon left it. He crushed the Austrians at Dresden (1813), fought at Leipzig, and concluded a treaty with Austria and a truce with the British admiral; but, on Napoleons's escape from Elba, he commenced war against Austria and was twice defeated. With a few horsemen he fled to Naples, and thence to France. After Napoleon's final overthrow, he proceeded with a few followers to the coast of Calabria, and proclaimed himself king; but was taken, court-martialled and shot.

MURAT, Napoléon Lucien Charles (1803–78) French senator, son of **Joachim Murat**. He suffered reverses in fortune, but, returning to France after 1848, attached himself to Louis Napoleon (**Napoleon III**), who in 1849 sent him as ambassador to Turin, and in 1852 made him a senator.

MURATORI, Lodovico Antonio (1672–1750) Italian historian, born near Modena. In 1695 he was appointed Ambrosian librarian at Milan, and ducal librarian and archivist at Modena in 1700. He published *Rerum Italicarum Scriptores* (29 vols fol, 1723–51), *Annali* *d'Italia* (12 vols, 1744–49), and *Antiquitates Italica* (6 vols, 1738–42), containing the 'Muratorian Fragment', a canon of the New Testament books, apparently written by a contemporary of **Irenaeus**. In later years he was attacked by the Jesuits for teaching heresies, but found a protector in Pope **Benedict XIV**.

MURCHISON, Sir Roderick Impey (1792–1871) Scottish geologist, born in Tarradale. After leaving the army in 1816, he devoted himself to geology. He established the Silurian system (1835) and, with **Adam Sedgwick**, the Devonian system. From 1840 to 1845, with others, he carried out a geological survey of the Russian empire. Struck with the resemblance between the Ural mountains and Australian chains, he foreshadowed the discovery of gold in Australia (1844). Murchison Falls (Uganda) and Murchison River (Western Australia) are named after him. In 1855 he was made director-general of the geological survey and director of the Royal School of Mines. His principal works were *The Silurian System* (1839) and *The Geology of Russia in Europe and the Urals* (1845).

MURDOCH, Dame (Jean) Iris (1919–) Irish novelist and philosopher, born in Dublin of Anglo-Irish parents, she was educated at Badminton School, Bristol, and Oxford, where she was fellow and tutor in philosophy at St Anne's College from 1948 to 1963. She published a study of **Sartre** (like her, both a novelist and a philosopher) in 1953 and two important but unfashionable philosophical works, much influenced by **Plato**, *The Fire and the Sun* (1977) and *The Sovereignty of the Good* (1970). These deal with the relationships between art and philosophy, and between love, freedom, knowledge and morality. She began writing novels as a hobby. *Under the Net* appeared in 1954, to be followed by more than 20 titles in the next 25 years, including such well-known works as *The Sandcastle* (1957), *The Bell* (1958), *A Severed Head* (1961), *An Unofficial Rose* (1962), *The Red and the Green* (1965), *The Nice and the Good* (1968), *The Black Prince* (1972), *The Sea, The Sea* (1978, winner of the Booker Prize), *Nuns and Soldiers* (1980), *The Good Apprentice* (1985), *The Book and the Brotherhood* (1987) and *The Message to the Planet* (1989). The popularity of the fiction derives largely from her narrative skill in controlling tangled and shifting patterns of relationships, the ironic or even startling circumstances in which the characters find themselves, and the pervasive blend of realism and symbolism. She has also written several plays, including *A Severed Head* (adapted with **J B Priestley** in 1963), *Servants and the Snow* (1970), *The Two Arrows* (1972) and *Art and Eros* (1980).

MURDOCH, (Keith) Rupert (1931–) Australian-born American newspaper publisher, born in Melbourne. His grandfather was a prominent Presbyterian minister in Scotland, his father a celebrated World War I correspondent who later became chief executive of the Melbourne Herald newspaper group. He was educated at Geelong Grammar School and Oxford University where he was active in Labour politics. When his father died in 1952 he inherited the Adelaide *News* and, employing shrewdly the experience gained at the *Daily Express* in London, he soon made it a success. By judicious buying, innovation and unflagging energy, he became in the space of a decade Australia's second largest publisher and began to set his sights on expansion abroad. First he acquired the *News of the World* in London in 1969, which at the height of the **Profumo** scandal had a circulation of 6000000. Then, at the end of the same year, he bought the *Sun*, whose introduction of a daily 'Page 3' girl earned him the sobriquet 'Thanks-for-the Mammary' Murdoch. Denounced for its puerile taste, the *Sun* defied its critics and maintained its lead in the circulation war. In 1981 he struck at the heart of the English Establishment when his company, News International, acquired *The Times* and *The Sunday Times* after a bitter struggle. He moved into the American market in 1976 with the purchase of the New York *Post*, and then acquired The New York Magazine Company, whose titles include *The New York Magazine*, *New West* and *Village Voice*. He became an American citizen in 1985. Thought by some to be a latter-day Citizen Kane, and frequently compared to Lord **Beaverbrook**, his communications empire is ever dynamic. In 1989 he bought Collins the publishers and inaugurated Sky Television, a satellite television network.

MURDOCK, George Peter (1897–1985) American cultural anthropologist, born in Meriden, Connecticut. He studied at Yale, and taught there (1928–60) and at Pittsburgh (1960–71). He initiated the cross-cultural survey, later known as the 'human relations area files', as an instrument of sociological and anthropological generalization. His best-known work is *Social Structure* (1949), in which he focused on family and kinship organization, seeking sets of functionally interrelated traits in a wide range of societies.

MURDOCK, William (1754–1839) Scottish engineer, and pioneer of coal gas for lighting, born near Auchinleck. He worked with his father, a millwright, and then with **Boulton** and **James Watt** of Birmingham, by whom he was sent to Cornwall to erect mining engines. At Redruth he constructed in 1784 the model of a high-pressure engine to run on wheels, introduced labour-saving machinery, a new method of wheel rotation, an oscillating engine (1785), and a steam-gun; and he also improved Watt's engine. His distillation of coal gas began at Redruth in 1792, when he illuminated his own home with it; successful experiments were made at Neath Abbey in 1796; but it was not until 1803 that Boulton's engineering works at Soho were lighted with gas.

MURE, Sir William (1594–1657) Scottish poet, born in Rowallan in Ayrshire. A staunch Protestant and Royalist, he was wounded at Marston Moor (1644). He wrote a long religious poem, *The True Crucifixe for True Catholikes* (1629), a fine version of the Psalms (1639), and some love and courtly poems. He also translated parts of **Virgil**'s *Aeneid*.

MURET, Marc Antoine (1526–85) French humanist and poet, born in Muret near Limoges. He lectured on civil law and classics in France, but later fled on a charge of heresy to Italy, where he edited Latin authors and wrote orations, poems and commentaries.

MURFREE, Mary See **CRADDOCK**

MURGER, Henri (1822–61) French writer, born in Paris. He began life as a notary's clerk, and, devoting his time to literature, led the life of privation and adventure described in his first and best novel, *Scènes de la vie de Bohème* (1845), the basis of **Puccini**'s opera. During his later years he led a dissipated life and wrote slowly and fitfully. *Le Manchon de Francine* is one of the saddest short stories ever written. Other prose works are *La Vie de jeunesse* (1861) and *Le Pays Latin* (1861). His poems, *Les Nuits d'hiver*, are graceful and often deeply pathetic; several were translated by **Andrew Lang** in his *Lays of old France*.

MURILLO, Bartolomé Esteban (1618–82) Spanish painter, born in Seville, where he spent most of his life. In 1645 he painted eleven remarkable pictures for the convent of San Francisco, which made his name. In 1660 he founded the Academy of Seville, of which he became first president. He frequently chose the Immaculate Conception or the Assumption of the Virgin as a subject, and treated them much alike. In 1681 he fell from a scaffold when painting an altarpiece at Cadiz, and died in Seville. His pictures naturally fall into two groups—scenes from low life, such as gipsies and beggar children (mostly executed early in his life), and religious works.

MURNAU, F W, originally **Friedrich Wilhelm Plumpe** (1888–1931) German film director, born in Bielefeld. He studied philology in Berlin, and art history and literature at Heidelberg, and was briefly an actor with **Max Reinhardt**'s theatre troupe before World War I. A combat pilot, he crash-landed in Switzerland during 1917. Returning to Germany two years later, he founded the Murnau Veidt Filmgesellschaft and made his directorial début with *Der Knabe in Blau* (1919). Experimenting with the mobility of the camera, his expressive use of light and shade heightened the menace in such macabre works as *Der Januskopf* (1920, a version of *Dr Jekyll and Mr Hyde*), and *Nosferatu* (1922, a chilling and faithful rendition of the Dracula story). After a successful trio of films with actor **Emil Jannings**, including *Der Letzte Mann* (The Last Laugh, 1924), he moved to America and made *Sunrise* (1927), a lyrical tale of a young rural couple whose love is threatened by the sophistication of the big city. This won three of the first-ever Academy Awards. He had just completed the much-praised South Seas documentary *Tabu* (1931) before his death in a car crash.

MURPHY, Arthur (1727–1805) Irish actor and playwright, born in Clomquin, Roscommon. He was educated at St Omer. He worked as a clerk in Cork and then London from 1747–51. From 1752 to 1774 he published the weekly *Gray's Inn Journal*, and so got to know Dr **Johnson**. By going on the stage he paid his debts, and entered Lincoln's Inn in 1757. In 1758 he produced *The Upholsterer*, a successful farce; in 1762 he was called to the bar, but continued to write farces and adaptations for the stage. His translation of **Tacitus** (1793) is excellent, unlike his *Essay on Johnson* and *Life of Garrick*.

MURPHY, Eddie (Edward Regan) (1961–) American comic performer, born in the Bushwick section of Brooklyn, New York. A popular prankster and mimic at school, he hosted a talent show at the Roosevelt Youth Center in 1976 and subsequently decided to pursue a career in showbusiness. A stand-up comic in Long Island night spots, he first came to national prominence on the television show *Saturday Night Live* (1980–84). A charismatic, self-confident humorist whose act relies on scatalogical observation, sharp satire, impersonation and profanity, his dynamic, scene-stealing début in the film *48 Hrs* (1982) was followed by an unbroken string of box-office hits including *Trading Places* (1983), *Beverly Hills Cop* (1984) and *Coming to America* (1988). His bestselling albums include *Eddie Murphy Comedian* (1982) and *How Could it Be?* (1984). Currently one of the film world's most potent attractions, he made his directorial début with *Harlem Nights* (1989).

MURPHY, Graeme (1951–) Australian dancer, choreographer and ballet director, born in Melbourne. He trained at the Australian Ballet School, the youngest boy ever to enter, and subsequently joined the company. Dance studies in New York were succeeded by six months as a member of Sadler's Wells Royal Ballet in England. He worked as a freelance choreographer in 1975 before rejoining Australian Ballet as dancer and resident choreographer. Appointed director of Sydney Dance Company in 1976, he has brought international stardom to this young contemporary ensemble by creating dances which feature a sexy, eclectic range of subjects and styles, all rooted in the classical idiom. Several of his pieces are in the repertory of the Australian Ballet. In 1988 he created *Vast*, an Australian bicentennial performance featuring Australian Dance Theatre, Queensland Ballet, West Australian Ballet and his own troupe.

MURPHY, William Parry (1892–) American physician, born in Stoughton, Wisconsin. He taught for some years at Harvard and then in 1923 took up private practice in Boston. He made a special study of anaemia and with **George Minot** first suggested the liver diet. They shared the 1934 Nobel prize for physiology or medicine with **George Whipple**.

MURRANT See **MORANT, Harry Harbord**

MURRAY, Alexander (1775–1813) Scottish philologist, born in Minnigaff parish, Kirkcudbright, the son of a shepherd. While he was a shepherd himself, he acquired a mastery of the classics, the chief European tongues and Hebrew, and after 1794 studied at Edinburgh. In 1806 he became minister in the parish of Urr, and in 1812 professor of oriental languages at Edinburgh. He left a *History of the European Languages* (published in 1823).

MURRAY, Andrew (1828–1917) South African religious leader and writer, born in Graaf-Reinet. Educated in Aberdeen and Utrecht, he was ordained a minister in the Scottish Dutch Reformed Church and posted to a vast frontier parish. Later, prompted by a national religious revival that started in his Worcester, Cape Colony, pastorate in 1860, he became an evangelistic preacher, holding meetings throughout South Africa, Europe, and America, from 1879. His emphasis on prayer and personal holiness was expounded in *With Christ in the School of Prayer* (1885), *The Spirit of Christ* (1888), *The Full Blessing of Pentecost* (1907), and numerous other books and pamphlets. Murray also took a keen interest in the welfare of Africans, opposed both to Afrikaner nationalism and British colonialism.

MURRAY, Charles (1864–1941) Scottish poet, born in Alford, Aberdeenshire. He trained as an engineer and had a successful career in South Africa, where in 1917 he became director of defence. His poems were written in the Aberdeenshire dialect and admirably portrayed country life and character at the turn of the century. His first major collection, *Hamewith* (1900), was his best and most characteristic.

MURRAY, Lord George (c.1700–1760) Scottish Jacobite soldier, son of the Duke of Atholl. He took part in the Jacobite risings of 1715 and 1719, fled to France but was pardoned in 1726. In 1745 he joined the Young Pretender (Prince **Charles Stewart**), and was one of his generals. He won a victory at Prestonpans (September 1745), and conducted a masterly retreat from Derby. He had a victory at Falkirk (January, 1746). He opposed the decision to fight at Culloden, but commanded the right wing. He resigned the next day, escaped abroad, and died in Holland.

MURRAY, George Gilbert Aimé (1866–1957) Australian classical scholar and writer, born in Sydney, New South Wales. Arriving in England at the age of eleven, he went to the Merchant Taylors's School and Oxford. He was appointed professor of Greek at Glasgow (1889) and regius professor of Greek at Oxford (1908). His work as a classical historian and translator of Greek dramatists brought him acclaim as 'the foremost Greek scholar of our time'. His celebrated verse translations of Greek plays, including *The Trojan Women*, *Bacchae*, *Medea* and *Electra*, were performed at London's Court Theatre from 1902. His many works on classics include *History of Ancient Greek Literature* (1897), *The Rise of the Greek Epic* (1907),

Five Stages of Greek Religion (1913). As a lifelong Liberal, he stood for parliament, unsuccessfully, six times. President of the League of Nations Union (1923–38), he was first president of the United Nations Association General Council.

MURRAY, Sir James Augustus Henry (1837–1915) Scottish philologist and lexicographer, born in Denholm. He was for many years a schoolmaster at Mill Hill school. His *Dialects of the Southern Counties of Scotland* (1873) established his reputation. The great work of his life, the editing of the Philological Society's *New English Dictionary* (later called the *Oxford English Dictionary*), was begun at Mill Hill (1879), and completed (1928) at Oxford. Murray himself edited about half the work, but he created the organization and the inspiration for completing it.

MURRAY, John (1741–1815) English-born American theologian, born in Alton. Coverted to Universalism in 1759, he went to the USA in 1770, where he preached the doctrine of universal salvation and became known as the 'Father of American Universalism'. In 1779 he became the first pastor of the new Independent Church of Christ in Gloucester, Massachusetts.

MURRAY, John, originally **McMurray** (1745–93) Scottish publisher, born in Edinburgh. He became an officer in the Royal Marines in 1762, but in 1768 bought Sandy's book-selling business in London, and published the *English Review*, **Disraeli**'s *Curiosities of Literature*, and other works. His son, John (1778–1843), who carried the business from Fleet Street to Albemarle Street, launched the *Quarterly Review* of which the first issue appeared in 1809. **Byron** received £20000 for his works, **Crabbe**, **Moore** and **Campbell** also being treated generously. His 'Family Library' was begun in 1829, and he issued the travels of **Mungo Park**, **Belzoni**, **Parry**, **Franklin**, and others. His son, John Murray the third (1808–92), issued the works of **Livingstone**, **Borrow**, **Darwin**, **Smiles**, **Smith**'s dictionaries, and *Handbooks for Travellers* (begun 1836). His son and successor, Sir John Murray (1851–1928), absorbed Smith, Elder & Co. in 1917, edited **Gibbon**'s *Autobiography* and Byron's letters, and began publication of the *Letters of Queen Victoria*. Sir John (1884–1967), his son, completed their publication.

MURRAY, Sir John (1841–1914) Scots-Canadian marine zoologist, born in Cobourg, Ontario, of parents who had left Scotland in 1834. He studied in Canada and at Edinburgh University, and after a voyage on a whaler, was appointed one of the naturalists to the Challenger Expedition (1872–76). He was successively assistant editor and editor-in-chief (1882) of the *Reports* of the scientific results. He wrote a *Narrative* of the expedition and a report on deep-sea deposits, and published many papers on oceanography and biology, and fresh-water lakes.

MURRAY, Sir John of Broughton (1715–77) Scottish Jacobite soldier, born in Peeblesshire. Educated at Edinburgh and Leyden, he visited Rome and made contact with the Jacobite court. He was Prince **Charles Edward Stewart**'s secretary during the 1745 Rising, but, captured after Culloden, saved his life by betraying his fellow Jacobites. He succeeded as baronet in 1770.

MURRAY, Keith Bay Pearce (1892–) New Zealand architect and designer, born in Auckland. He went to England in 1906, and after service in the air force, began designing glass in the 1930s, moving to silver and then to ceramics, principally for Josiah Wedgwood & Sons, where he designed a number of successful shapes. His hallmark was the simple, functional, clean shapes relying a great deal on turned grooves and stepped surfaces. These were executed in black basalt or earthenware with matt glaze effects in cream, green or straw colours. He exhibited widely, including a one-man show at the Medici Gallery in 1935 and the 5th Triennial in Milan in 1933. He designed the new Wedgwood factory at Barlaston (1946).

MURRAY, Len (Lionel), Baron Murray of Epping Forest (1922–) English trade union leader, born in Shropshire. His studies at London University were interrupted by World War II and completed at New College, Oxford, in 1947 when he joined the staff of the Trades Union Congress (TUC). He progressed from the economic department to become assistant general secretary (1969–73) and then general secretary (1973–84). He played a major role in the 'social contract' partnership between the TUC and the Labour governments of **Harold Wilson** and **James Callaghan** (1974–78), but, from 1979, had an unhappy relationship with the new Conservative administration of **Margaret Thatcher**. He was made a life peer in 1985.

MURRAY, Les (1938–) Australian poet, born in Nabiac, New South Wales. His childhood and adolescence were spent on a dairy farm. He attended Sydney University but left in 1960 without taking a degree. He has worked as a translator but has long been a freelance writer, frequently contributing literary journalism to newspapers and magazines. His poetry, which has made him one of Australia's leading literary figures, is revered for its perceptive and pungent evocation of rural life. Significant collections include *The Ilex Tree* (1965), *The Weatherboard Cathedral* (1969), *Selected Poems: The Vernacular Republic* (1982) and *The People's Otherworld* (1983).

MURRAY, Lindley (1745–1826) American grammarian, born in Swatara Creek, Pennsylvania. He practised law, made a fortune in New York during the War of Independence and then, for health reasons, retired to England in 1784 and bought an estate near York. His *English Grammar* (1795) was for long the standard text, and was followed by *English Exercises*, the *English Reader*, and various religious works.

MURRAY, Matthew (1765–1826) English inventor and mechanical engineer, born near Newcastle-upon-Tyne. Apprenticed to a blacksmith at the age of 14, in 1788 he moved to Leeds as a qualified mechanic. He devised and patented several improvements in flax spinning machinery before establishing his own engineering works in 1795, where he manufactured textile machinery and also steam engines of his own design. When **Watt**'s master patent expired in 1800, Murray was one of the first to make significant improvements to the steam engine, his designs being smaller, lighter, more efficient and easier to assemble. His success and the rapid expansion of his firm led to an intense rivalry with the firm of Boulton & Watt, and there is no doubt that he was a more versatile engineer than Watt himself, making use of the new powers of steam in locomotives and ships as well as stationary engines.

MURRAY, William Staite (1881–1962) English potter. He started work on a bulb plantation in Holland and spent ten years there, but returned to England in 1908. He learnt his craft as a potter at Camberwell School of Art and began working as an individual potter at Yeoman's Row in South Kensington in 1919. He worked at Brockley in Kent and Bray in Berkshire, and then started teaching at the Royal College, where he became head of the Pottery School in 1926. He taught pottery as a fine art medium, placing on it as much importance as that of painting and sculpture. He lived in Rhodesia from 1939.

MURROW, Edward (Edgar) Roscoe (1908–65) American journalist and broadcaster, born near Pole Cat Creek in North Carolina. He first visited Europe as assistant director of the Institute of International Education (1932–35). Joining CBS in 1935, he returned to Europe in 1937, ostensibly to report on cultural items, but he extended his brief to political matters and became an incisive and compassionate conveyor of the wartime spirit in Britain. In postwar America he became a producer and presenter of such hard-hitting, current affairs programmes as *See It Now* (1951–58) and *Person to Person* (1953–60). Passionately committed to the pursuit of truth and excellence, his intelligent and courageous questioning of Senator **McCarthy** in 1954 contributed to the latter's fall from grace and he received five Emmy Awards between 1953 and 1958. Worried by the ease with which the power of television could be subverted by genial personalities and pyrotechnical glibness, he retired from the medium to head the United States Information Agency (1961–64). The recipient of numerous international distinctions, he was awarded an honorary KBE in 1964.

MURRY, John Middleton (1889–1957) British writer and critic, born in Peckham. He wrote some poetry and many volumes of essays and criticism which had a strong influence on the young intellectuals of the 1920s. In 1911 he met **Katherine Mansfield**, whom he married in 1918, and introduced her work in *The Adelphi*, of which he was founder and editor from 1923 to 1948. He also produced posthumous selections from her letters and diaries, and a biography in 1932. He edited the *Athenaeum* (1919–21). He became a pacifist and was editor of *Peace News* from 1940 to 1946. Towards the end of his life he became interested in agriculture, and started a community farm in Norfolk. His major works include critical studies on *Keats and Shakespeare* (1925), his friend *D H Lawrence* (1931), *William Blake* (1933) and *Swift* (1954). He also wrote religious works, including *To The Unknown God* (1924) and *The Life of Jesus* (1926). He published his autobiography, *Between Two Worlds*, in 1935).

MUSA IBN NOSAIR (640–717) Arab soldier. He conquered northern Africa from 699 to 709 and Spain in 712, fell under the displeasure of the caliph of Damascus, and died in poverty in the Hejaz.

MUSAEUS (5th–6th century) Greek poet, wrote a beautiful Greek poem, *Hero and Leander*, which has been translated into many languages.

MUSÄUS, Johann Karl August (1735–87) German writer, born in Jena. He studied theology there, and in 1770 became professor at the Weimar gymnasium. His first book (1760) was a parody of **Richardson**'s *Sir Charles Grandison*; in 1798 he satirized **Lavater** in *Physiognomische Reisen*. But his fame rests on his German popular tales, which claimed, falsely, to be a collection taken down from the lips of old people. (*Volksmärchen der Deutsche*, 1782–86). Their chief note is artificial naïveté, but they are a blend of satirical humour, quaint fancy and graceful writing.

MUSEVENI, Yoweri Kaguta (1945–) Ugandan soldier and politician. After graduating at Dar-es-Salaam University he worked for President **Milton Obote** until his overthrow, in 1971, by **Idi Amin**. From exile in Tanzania he formed the Front for National Salvation and, fighting with the Tanzanian army, took part in the defeat and expulsion of Amin in 1979. He became minister of defence in the governments of Yusof Lule and Godfrey Binaisa (1979–80) but was in disagreement with Obote, who returned to the presidency in 1980 but only retained power with the help of Tanzanian troops. When they withdrew in 1982, a virtual civil war ensued and reasonable normalcy did not return until 1986 when Museveni became president, pledging himself to follow a policy of national reconciliation.

MUSGRAVE, Thea (1928–) Scottish composer, born in Edinburgh. She studied at Edinburgh University, the Paris Conservatoire, and with **Nadia Boulanger**. Her early work was largely Scottish in inspiration: her *Suite o' Bairnsangs* (1953) and the ballet *A Tale for Thieves* (1953), were followed by *Cantata for a Summer's Day* (1954) a chamber opera, *The Abbot of Drimock* (1955), and her *Scottish Dance Suite* (1959). In the late 1950s her work became more abstract, and she has used serial and aleatory devices. Her music includes two choral and orchestral works, *The Phoenix and the Turtle* (1962), and *The Five Ages of Man* (1963), an opera *The Decision* (1964–65), a full-length ballet, *Beauty and the Beast* (1968), works for instruments and prerecorded tapes, the chamber opera *The Voice of Ariadne* (commissioned for the Aldeburgh Festival of 1974), the operas *Mary, Queen of Scots* (1977), and *A Christmas Carol* (1979), and a radio opera, *An Occurrence at Owl Creek Bridge* (1981).

MUSHET, David (1772–1847) Scottish iron-master, born in Dalkeith. Like many of his contemporaries he was continually experimenting with new materials and processes in the search for better and cheaper iron and steel. He discovered black band ironstone at Calder Ironworks near Glasgow in 1801 and maintained against strong opposition that it was suitable for smelting; after the invention of the hot blast process by **James Beaumont Neilson** in 1828 it became widely used in the Scottish iron industry. He showed that non-phosphoric oxides of iron could be used to make better quality wrought iron, patented a process for making cast steel from wrought iron, and discovered the beneficial effects of adding manganese to iron and steel. He moved from Scotland in 1805 to Derbyshire and later to the Forest of Dean.

MUSHET, Robert Forester (1811–91) English metallurgist, born in Coleford, Gloucestershire, the son of **David Mushet**. He assisted with and continued his father's researches into the manufacture of iron and steel. In 1856 **Henry Bessemer** patented his new steel-making process, but it was soon found that it could not be applied to the majority of iron ores, and only through Mushet's discovery, also patented in 1856, of the beneficial effects of adding ferro-manganese to the blown steel, did the Bessemer process become a profitable commercial success. Ironically, Mushet's patent was allowed to lapse and his vital discovery became common property from which he derived little or no benefit. He was much more successful with his invention of 'R Mushet's Special' steel in 1868, a self-hardening tungsten alloy steel which was the forerunner of a whole family of tool steels.

MUSIAL, Stanley Frank (1920–) American baseball player, born in Domona, known as 'Stan the Man'. An outstanding left-handed hitter, he played a record number of major-league games (3026) with the St Louis Cardinals (1941–63). He scored a record number of hits (3360), and won the batting championship seven times. He was voted the Most Valuable Player (MVP) three times, and elected to the National Hall of Baseball Fame in 1969. There is a lifesize statue of him in the Busch Stadium, St Louis.

MUSIL, Robert (1880–1942) Austrian novelist, born in Klagenfurt. He was trained as a scientist (he invented a chromatometer) and as a philosopher. During World War I he was an officer and drew on his experience for *Die Verwirrungen des Zöglings Törless* (1906, trans *Young Törless*, 1963), a terrifying, sadistic story of life inside a military academy. Memorable though it is, it is eclipsed by *Der Mann ohne Eigenschaften* (1930–43;

trans *The Man Without Qualities*, 1953–60), his unfinished *tour de force*. Portraying a society on the brink of the abyss through the eyes of Ulrich, the man who has dispensed with conventional qualities, its narrative covers just one year, 1913–14. Plotless but dealing in inter-related facts, it is multi-storeyed. It is widely acknowledged as one of the great novels of the century despite the confusionof final drafts which the author did not have time to tidy up before his sudden death in Geneva.

MUSORGSKI See **MOUSSORGSKY, Modest Petrovich**

MUSPRATT, James (1793–1886) British chemist, born in Dublin of English parents. He took part in the Peninsular War and then returned to his trade of druggist. He began manufacturing acids, etc, and greatly improved the methods of so doing. With Josias Gamble he was the founder of the chemical industry in St Helens.

MUSSARGSKY See **MOUSSORGSKY, Modest Petrovich**

MUSSCHENBROEK, Pieter van (1692–1761) Dutch physicist, born in Leiden. Professor of physics at Duisburg, Utrecht, and Leiden (1740–61), he invented the pyrometer and in 1746 discovered the principle of the Leiden jar.

MUSSET, Alfred de (1810–57) French poet and dramatist, born in Paris. After tentative study first of the law, then of medicine, he found he had a talent for writing and at 18 published a translation of **De Quincey**'s 'Confessions of an Opium Eater'. His first collection of poems, *Contes d'Espagne et d'Italie* (1830), won the approval of **Victor Hugo** who accepted him into his *Cénacle*, the inner shrine of militant Romanticism. But Musset had no real desire to commit himself to any particular cult; indeed he had already begun to poke gentle fun at the Movement, and had indicated that he wished to 'se déhugotiser'. His first excursion into drama, *La Nuit vénitienne*, failed at the Odéon in 1830, and from then on he conceived an 'armchair theatre' with plays intended for reading only. The first of these, *La Coupe et les lèvres* and *À quoi rêvent les jeunes filles*, together with the narrative poem *Namouna*, were published as *Spectacle dans un fauteuil* in 1832, and next year the tragi-comedies *André del Sarto* and *Les Caprices de Marianne* appeared in the *Revue des deux mondes*. Also among his *Comédies et proverbes*, as these pieces were called, are *Lorenzaccio* (1834), *On ne badine pas avec l'amour* (1836) and *Il ne faut jurer de rien* (1836). *Un Caprice*, published in 1837, and several of his other 'armchair' plays were staged successfully more than ten years later, and thus reassured he wrote *On ne saurait penser de tout* (1849), *Carmosine* (1850) and *Bettine* (1851) for actual performance. In 1833 Musset had met **George Sand**, and there began the stormy love affair which coloured much of his work after that date. The pair set out to spend the winter together at Venice, but Musset became ill, George became capricious, and in April the poet returned alone, broken in health and sunk in depression. His *Nuits*, from *Nuit de mai* (1835) through *Nuit de décembre* (1835) and *Nuit d'août* (1836) to *Nuit d'octobre* (1837), trace the emotional upheaval of his love for George Sand from despair to final resignation. His autobiographical poem *Confessions d'un enfant du siècle* (1835) is a study of the prevalent attitude of mind—the *mal du siècle*—resulting from the aftermath of revolution and the unrest of the early years of the century. *L'Espoir en Dieu*, an expression of the soul's longing for certainty, is perhaps not altogether convincing. In 1838 he was appointed Home Office librarian. He died of heart failure.

MUSSOLINI, Benito (1883–1945) Italian dictator, born a blacksmith's son, at Predappio, near Forli, Romagna. He edited the socialist *Avanti*, but after serving in World War I founded the *Popolo d'Italia*, and organized the Fascisti as militant nationalists to defeat socialism. In October 1922 his blackshirts marched on Rome; and 'Il Duce' established himself as dictator by melodramatic means, including murder. He ruled forcefully and intolerantly, not without efficiency. Greece was bullied, the League of Nations flouted. The Vatican State was set up by the Lateran Treaty (1929). The Axis with Germany was formed. **Franco** was aided in Spain. With the annexation of Abyssinia (1936) and Albania (1939) to the Italian crown, Mussolini's dream of a new Roman empire seemed to be coming true. At the most favourable moment (1940) he entered World War II, but met with disaster everywhere. In 1943 his followers fell away and he resigned (25 July), was arrested, and rescued by German parachutists. He sought to regain what he had lost. On 28 April 1945, he and other Fascists were caught by Italians at Dongo on the Lake of Como, and, after some form of trial, shot, their bodies being exposed to insult in Como and in Milan, the old headquarters of Fascism.

MUSTAFA KEMAL ATATÜRK (1881–1938) Turkish general and statesman, born in Salonika. He led the Turkish nationalist movement from 1909 and was a general in World War I. Elected president (1923–38), he was responsible for many reforms and for the modernization of Turkey.

MUTHESIUS, Hermann (1861–1927) German architect, writer and propagandist, born in Gross-Neuhausen, Thuringia. After study in Berlin and practice in Toyko, he worked from 1893 as a Prussian government architect and editor of the official architectural journal. Attached to the German embassy in London from 1896 to 1903, he studied the remarkable developments taking place in British architecture and design, and knew most of the practitioners. The reports and articles he wrote during that period were followed, on his return, by the three-volume study *Das Englische Haus* (1904–05), which was very influential in Germany and remains an invaluable document on the period. With **Van de Velde** he was one of the main initiators in 1907 of the Deutsche Werkbund, whose aim was to accomplish a much-needed improvement in German design. It was an integral part of a movement, to which the Bauhaus and its successors contributed, and which led to the very high design standards of contemporary German industry.

MUTSUHITO (1852–1912) emperor of Japan, born in Kyoto, son of the titular emperor, Komei, whom he succeeded in 1867. Within a year he had recovered the full powers of the emperors when, after a brief civil war, he overthrew the last of the shoguns, who had exercised dictatorial authority in Japan for 700 years. His long reign saw the rapid political and military westernization of Japan, under the initiative of the emperor himself. The feudal system was abolished in 1871; most restrictions on foreign trade were removed; a constitution providing for an advisory cabinet and an Imperial Diet was promulgated in 1889; a navy was created on the British model and an army on the German. Military success against China in 1894 and 1895 was followed by Japan's victories in the Russo-Japanese War (1904–05) and by the economic penetration of Korea and Manchuria. When Mutsuhito died he was succeeded by his only son, Crown Prince **Yoshihito**. Assigned a posthumous title, in accordance with Japanese custom, Mutsuhito was styled Meiji Tenno.

MUYBRIDGE, Eadweard, originally **Edward James Muggeridge** (1830–1904) English-born American photographer and inventor, born in Kingston-on-Thames. He emigrated to California in 1852, and about 1866 became a professional photographer; eventually he became chief photographer to the US government. To settle an argument about the gait of horses he was commissioned by ex-Governor Leland Stanford of California to take a series of action photographs, but had to wait until 1877 when faster photo plates became available and he was able to prove that a trotting horse has all its feet off the ground at times. In 1880 he devised the zoopraxiscope to show his picture sequences, achieving a rudimentary kind of cinematography in his Zoopraxographical Hall in Chicago (1893), which has been hailed as the world's first motion picture theatre. In 1884–85 he carried out for the University of Pennsylvania an extensive survey of the movements of animals and humans, publishing the results as *Animal Locomotion* (1887).

MUZOREWA, Abel Tendekayi (1925–) Zimbabwean clergyman and politician. Ordained in 1953, he was consecrated the first black bishop of the United Methodist Church, in 1968. In 1971 he became president of the African National Council (ANC), a non-violent organization intended to pave the way for an internal settlement of the political situation in Rhodesia. In 1975 the ANC split into two factions, the gradualists, led by Muzorewa, working for a transition to majority rule, and the more extreme elements, led by **Joshua Nkomo**. Muzorewa was prime minister of 'Zimbabwe Rhodesia' for six months in 1979, but after independence his movement was defeated by the parties of **Robert Mugabe** and **Joshua Nkomo**.

MWATA YAMVO (1600–mid 19th century) the dynastic title of the paramount chiefs of the Lunda empire of central Africa. The empire expanded steadily from its inception c.1600 so that by the mid-19th century as many as 36 great chiefs of the region were reputed to pay tribute to the *mwata yamvo*.

MWENE MUTAPA the dynastic title of the kings of northern Zimbabwe with whom Portuguese traders established close relations in the 16th century. Gatsi Rusere (d.1622) appealed to the Portuguese for aid in suppressing a rebellion, ceding in return the mineral wealth of the kingdom to his 'brother-in-arms', the king of Portugal. Towards the end of his reign relations with the Europeans deteriorated although the king received Christian baptism on his death-bed. His son, Nyambo Kapararidze broke openly with the Portuguese and placed himself at the head of an uprising in 1631. He was defeated in battle in 1633 and replaced by the puppet-king Mavura (d.1652), after which the dynasty survived only in subordination to the Portuguese.

MWINYI, Ndugu Ali Hassan (1925–) Tanzanian politician, born in Zanzibar. He trained as a teacher on the island and in Britain before returning to hold progressively important posts in teaching. He then joined the ministry of education and, after working in a parastatal trading corporation on the mainland, entered the government of **Julius Nyerere**. He held a variety of ministerial and ambassadorial posts until, in 1985, he succeeded Nyrere as president of the United Republic of Tanzania.

MYDDELTON, or **Middleton, Sir Hugh** (c.1560–1631) Welsh goldsmith, banker and clothier, born in Galch Hill near Denbigh. He is best known for improving London's water-supply. In 1609–13 he constructed the New River, a 38-mile canal bringing water from springs in Hertfordshire to the New River Head reservoir at Clerkenwell. He represented Denbigh in Parliament from 1603 to 1628.

MYERS, Ernest James (1844–1921) English poet and translator, the son of a clergyman, brother of **Frederic William Henry Myers**. He published several volumes of verse, translated **Pindar**, and collaborated in a translation of the *Iliad*.

MYERS, Frederic William Henry (1843–1901) English poet and essayist, brother of **Ernest James Myers**, the son of a clergyman. A classical scholar, and a school inspector from 1872 to 1900, he wrote poems (collected 1921), essays, a book on *Wordsworth* (1881), and *Human Personality and its Survival of Bodily Death* (1903). He was one of the founders of the Society for Psychical Research in 1882.

MYLNE, Robert (1734–1811) Scottish architect, born in Edinburgh of a notable family of stonemasons, architects and engineers. He studied on the Continent and designed Blackfriars' Bridge (erected in 1769 and pulled down in 1868) and planned the Gloucester and Berkeley Ship Canal and the Eau Brink Cut for fen drainage at King's Lynn. His buildings, for example St Cecilia's Hall, Edinburgh (1763–65), show an elegance typical of the best late 18th-century work. His brother, William, designed the North Bridge in Edinburgh.

MYLNE, or **Miln, Walter** (d.1558) Scottish Protestant martyr. While on a visit to Germany he became imbued with the doctrines of the Reformation, and later as priest of Lunan in Angus was denounced for heresy. Condemned by Cardinal **Beaton** to be burnt wherever he might be found, he fled the country, but after the cardinal's death he mistakenly thought it safe to return. Taken prisoner at Dysart, he was tried at St Andrews and although by this time over 80 years old was condemned to the stake, the last Scottish Protestant martyr.

MYLONAS, Professor George (1898–1988) Greek archaeologist, born in Smyrna on the Anatolian coast. He taught for many years in the USA and became president of the Archaeological Society of America; he was also secretary-general of the Greek Historical Society. His main excavation was at the Outer Grave Circle at Mycenae, and before that the Neolithic material at Olyathus, and the small Bronze Age site at Ayios Kosmas, near Athens Airport. He was also responsible for the building of a new museum at Mycenae.

MYRDAL, Alva, née **Reimer** (1902–86) Swedish sociologist, politician and peace reformer, born in Uppsala. She was educated at the universities of Uppsala, Stockholm, and Geneva, and in 1924 married **Gunnar Myrdal**. A proponent of child welfare and equal rights for women, she was director of the United Nations department of social sciences (1950–56). Appointed Swedish ambassador to India, Burma and Ceylon from 1955 to 1961, she was elected to the Swedish parliament in 1962, acting as Swedish representative on the UN Disarmament Committee from 1962 to 1973. As minister for disarmament and church affairs (1966–73) she played a prominent part in the international peace movement; her works include *The Game of Disarmament: How the United States and Russia Run the Arms Race* (1977). She was awarded the 1980 Albert Einstein Peace Prize, and in 1982 received the Nobel prize for peace, jointly with **Alfonso García Robles**.

MYRDAL, (Karl) Gunnar (1898–1987) Swedish economist, politician and international civil servant. He studied law, and then economics, at Stockholm, and taught economics at Stockholm from 1927 to 1950 and from 1960 to 1967. He wrote a classic study of race relations in the USA (*An American Dilemma*, 1944), then was minister of trade and commerce in Sweden (1945–47), and was executive secretary of the

UN Economic Commission for Europe (1947–57). His later works include *Beyond the Welfare State* (1960) and *The Challenge of Affluence* (1963). He was awarded the Nobel prize in economics in 1974 (jointly with **Friedrich A Hayek**), principally for his work on the critical application of economic theory of Third World countries. His wife, the sociologist, **Alva Myrdal**, won the Nobel peace prize for her work on disarmament.

MYRON (5th century BC) Greek sculptor. A contemporary of **Phidias**, he worked in bronze and is best known for the celebrated *Discobolos* and *Maryas*.

MYTENS, Daniel (c.1590–1642) Flemish portrait-painter, born in The Hague. He worked for **James I** and **Charles I**, who made him 'King's painter'. He painted portraits of many notable persons of the time.

N

NABOKOV, Vladimir (1899–1977) Russian-born American novelist, born in St Petersburg (now Leningrad). His family was wealthy and aristocratic and he was a precocious child. He attended St Petersburg's relatively progressive Tenishev School, where he was accused of 'not conforming' to his surroundings. In 1919, following the Bolshevik Revolution, his family became émigrés, and he and his brother went to Cambridge on a scholarship, where he studied Russian and French literature. When he graduated in 1922 he rejoined his family in Berlin, where his father was the victim of a senseless murder. He lived for more than 15 years in Berlin but admitted to never having mastered the language, though his first literary success was a translation of some of **Heine**'s songs. From 1937 to 1940 he was in Paris, where he met **James Joyce**, and then emigrated to the USA where he took out citizenship in 1945. He published his first novels in Berlin: *Mashenka* (1926), *King, Queen, Knave* (1928), *The Defense* (1936) and *Despair* (1936). In Paris he wrote *The Eye* (1938) and *Invitation to a Beheading* (1938). All were written in Russian, under the pseudonym V Sirin, the author himself later collaborating on English translations. In the USA he taught at Wellesley College and Cornell University, and earned distinction as a lepidopterist. Writing now in English he published many short stories and novels including *The Real Life of Sebastian Knight* (1941), *Bend Sinister* (1947), *Pale Fire* (1962) and *Ada* (1969). *Lolita* (1959) was a *succès de scandale* and brought his name before the general public, and allowed him to abandon teaching and devote himself full time to writing. From 1959 he lived in Montreux in Switzerland. Among 20th-century novelists he is regarded for his linguistic ingenuity and dazzling intellect. **H G Wells** was his first love but his debt to **Jane Austen**, **Charles Dickens**, **R L Stevenson** and others is acknowledged in *Lectures on Literature* (1980). He also translated **Pushkin**'s *Eugene Onegin* (1963).

NACHTIGAL, Gustav (1834–85) German traveller, born in Eichstedt. He studied medicine, served as army surgeon, and in 1863 went to North Africa. He travelled across the Sahara from Tripoli to Cairo (1869–74) via Tiberti and Lake Chad, which resulted in the first detailed description of the south-eastern Sahara. As German consul in Tunis, in 1884 he went to annex Togo and Cameroon for Germany, and died on the return journey off Cape Palmas.

NADAR, pseud of **Gaspard-Felix Tournachon** (1820–1910) French journalist, artist and photographer, born in Paris where he worked as a left-wing journalist from 1840. In 1852 he published a series of caricatures, some of which were based on his photographs, and soon afterwards opened a studio which became a favourite haunt of the intelligentsia. For many years he produced lively portraits of distinguished literary and artistic contemporaries, successfully capturing individual personalities in intimate and natural studies. In 1886 he produced the first 'photo-interview', a series of 21 photographs of the scientist **Eugène Chevreul**, each captioned with the sitter's replies to Nadar's questions. Among other innovations he proposed the use of aerial photographs for map-making and in 1858 he took the first photographs from a balloon, of the city of Paris. In his later years he was active as a writer and journalist.

NADEL, Siegfried Frederick (1903–56) Austrian-born British social anthropologist. His early interests were in music, but he studied psychology and philosophy at Vienna University. In 1932 he moved to England to study anthropology under **Bronislaw Malinowski** at the London School of Economics. He was reader at Durham (1948–50), and professor at Canberra University, Australia (1950–56). He carried out fieldwork among the Nupe in northern Nigeria (1934–36) and the Nuba of the Sudan (1938–40), which resulted in three major monographs: *A Black Byzantium* (1942), *The Nuba* (1947) and *Nupe Religion* (1954). However, Nadel's major contribution to anthropology lay not in ethnography but in theory, in his *The Foundations of Social Anthropology* (1951) and *The Theory of Social Structure* (1957).

NADELMAN, Elie (1882–1946) Polish-born American sculptor, born in Warsaw. He studied at Warsaw Art Academy, left Poland in 1904 and settled in Paris. His drawings and sculptures after 1906 reveal a simplification of forms and stylization close to Cubism but also show an affinity with antique sculpture. In 1914 he moved to the USA, taking a studio in New York. There he produced a number of unusual painted figure sculptures in wood. He became an American citizen in 1927 and from the 1930s worked extensively in ceramics.

NADER, Ralph (1934–) American lawyer and consumer activist, born in Winsted, Connecticut. Educated at Princeton and Harvard Law School, he was admitted to the Connecticut bar in 1959. Since then he has ceaselessly campaigned for improved consumer rights and protection, encouraging the establishment of powerful 'civic interest lobbies' of which the US congress, state legislatures and corporate executives have had to take note. His best-seller about the automobile industry, *Unsafe at Any Speed* (1965), led to the passage of improved car safety regulations in 1966. He became head of the Public Citizen Foundation in 1980. His other books include *The Menace of Atomic Energy* (1977) and *Who's Poisoning America?* (1981).

NADIR SHAH, (Nadir Quli) (1688–1747) king of Persia from 1736, born in Khorasan of Turkish origin. A military commander under his brother-in-law, Shah Tahmasp II, he fought the Afghans and the Turks, and subjugated Azarbaijan, Georgia and most of Armenia. In 1732 he deposed Tahmasp and put on the throne as his puppet Tahmasp's infant son as Abbas III—the last of the **Safavid** dynasty. The boy-king died in 1736, and Nadir took the throne himself. He campaigned successfully in Central Asia, conquered Afghanistan and invaded India, where he took and sacked Delhi (1740), and carried off the Koh-i-noor diamond and the Peacock Throne. He tried to impose the Sunnite form of Islam, the state religion, on Shi'ite Persia, but failed. He resumed the war with the Turks (1742–47), but was assassinated by one of his own tribesmen.

NAEVIUS, Gnaeus (c.264–194 BC) Roman poet and dramatist, born probably in Campania. He served in the first Punic war (264–241 BC), and started producing his own plays in 235. A plebeian, for 30 years he satirized the Roman nobles in his plays, and was compelled to leave Rome, ultimately retiring to Utica in Africa. Fragments of an epic, *De Bello Punico*, are extant.

NAGANO, Osami (1880–1947) Japanese naval officer. Educated at the Naval Academy, Etajima, he studied law at Harvard and served as naval attaché in Washington (1920–23). Promoted rear admiral in 1928, he was superintendent of the Naval Academy (1928–29). As head of the Japanese delegation to the 2nd London Naval Conference (1935–36), he advocated the expansion of Japanese naval power. He was navy minister (1936–37), commander-in-chief Combined Fleet (1937), and chief of naval general staff (1941–44). He planned and ordered the Japanese attack on Pearl Harbor in December 1941. He died while on trial for war crimes.

NAGEL, Ernest (1901–85) Czech-born American philosopher of science, born in Nové Město, Bohemia (now Czechoslovakia). He went to the USA in 1911 and became a naturalized American citizen in 1919. He taught philosophy at Columbia University from 1931 to 1970 and published widely on the philosophy of science. His best-known works are *An Introduction to Logic and Scientific Method* (1934, with M R Cohen), *Logic without Metaphysics* (1957) and *The Structure of Science* (1961).

NÄGELI, Karl Wilhelm von (1817–91) Swiss botanist and physicist. Professor at Munich (from 1858), he was one of the early writers on evolution. He investigated the growth of cells and originated the micellar theory relating to the structure of starch grains, cell walls, etc.

NAGLE, Kelvin (1920–) Australian golfer, born in north Sydney. With **Peter Thomson** he was the first of the Australian golfers to make a considerable mark abroad. After winning the Australian Open in 1959, he won the British Open in 1960 and came second in the same event two years later. He was also moderately successful in the USA at a time when comparatively few foreign golfers competed there, coming second in the US Open of 1965. An amiable man with a relaxed swing, he represented Australia in their World Cup side on nine occasions between 1954 and 1966, taking part in two trophy-winning sides. He set up a record low aggregate of 260 (64-65-66-65) when winning the Irish Hospitals event in 1961 and continued to be a formidable golfer even in his 50s, taking the World Senior title in 1971.

NAGY, Imre (1895–1958) Hungarian politician, born in Kaposvar, Hungary. He was captured in the Austrian army in World War I, and sent to Siberia. At the revolution he escaped, joined the Bolshevik forces and became a Soviet citizen in 1918. Back in Hungary in 1919, he had a minor post in the **Béla Kun** revolutionary government, but later fled to Russia where he remained throughout World War II. Returning with the Red Army, he became minister of agriculture in the provisional government, enforcing communist land reforms. In 1947 he became speaker of the Hungarian parliament, and in 1953 prime minister, introducing a 'new course' of milder political and economic control. In February 1955 the régime of Matyas Rakosi (1892–1971) removed him from office as a 'right deviationist'. He returned to the premiership in 1956 on Rakosi's downfall. When the revolution broke out in October 1956 he promised free elections and a Russian military withdrawal. When, in November, Soviet forces began to put down the revolution he appealed to the world for help, but was displaced by the Soviet puppet **Janos Kadar** and later executed. He has recently been rehabilitated, having been declared, by the Hungarian Supreme Court, innocent of all alleged past crimes. In 1989 he was given a hero's reburial in Budapest.

NAHAYAN, Sheikh Zayed bin Sultan al- (1918–) Emir of Abu Dhabi. He was governor of the eastern province of Abu Dhabi, one of seven Trucial States on the southern shores of the Persian Gulf and the Gulf of Oman, which were under British protection, until in 1969 he deposed his brother, Sheikh Shakhbut, and became Emir. When the States decided to federate as the United Arab Emirates in 1971 he became president of its supreme council. He was unanimously re-elected in 1986.

NAHUM (7th century BC) Old Testament minor prophet. He seems to have been an Israelite or Judaean who had been a captive in Nineveh, and prohesied the destruction of Nineveh by the Medes in 612 BC.

NAIDU, Sarojini, née **Chattopadhyay** (1879–1949) Indian feminist and poet, born in Hyderabad and educated at Madras, London and Cambridge. Known as the 'nightingale of India', she published three volumes of lyric verse: *The Golden Threshold* (1905), *The Bird of Time* (1912) and *The Broken Wing* (1915). She organized flood-relief in Hyderabad (1908), and lectured and campaigned on feminism, particularly the abolition of purdah. Associated with **Mahatma Gandhi**, she was the first Indian woman to be president of the Indian National Congress, in 1925. She was imprisoned several times for civil disobedience incidents, and took part in the negotiations leading to independence. In 1947 she was appointed govenor of United Provinces (now Uttar Pradesh).

NAIPAUL, Vidiadhar Surajprasad (1932–) Trinidadian novelist, born in Trinidad. His brother, Shiva Naipaul (1945–85), was also a writer. Educated at Queen's Royal College, Port of Spain, he left the Caribbean for Oxford in 1950, where he took his degree. The editor of 'Caribbean Voices' for the BBC, he dabbled in journalism before his first novel, *The Mystic Masseur* (1957), was published. His first book, however, was *Miguel Street* (1959), a series of sketches depicting lower-class life in Trinidad through the eyes of a growing boy. The book which made his name was *A House for Mr Biswas* (1961), a spicy satire spanning three Trinidadian generations but focusing on its eponymous six-fingered sign-writer. Thereafter the Caribbean figured less prominently in his work, which grew steadily darker and more complex. *A Bend in the River* (1979), a masterly re-creation of what it is like to live under an African dictatorship, won the Booker prize. As well as novels he has written several trenchant 'travel' books including *An Area of Darkness: An Experience of India* (1964) and *Among the Believers: An Islamic Journey* (1981). *Finding the Centre* (1984) is autobiographical.

NAIRNE, Carolina, née **Oliphant, Lady** (1766–1845) Scottish song writer, born in Gask in Perthshire, the daughter of a Jacobite laird. In 1806 she married her second cousin, Major Nairne (1757–1830), who became Lord Nairne in 1824. She lived in Edinburgh, but travelled widely in Ireland and Europe after her husband's death. She collected traditional airs and wrote songs to them under the pseudonym 'Mrs Bogan of Bogan', which were published in *The Scottish Minstrel* (1821–24), and posthumously as *Lays from Strathearn*. They include the lament for Prince **Charles Edward Stewart**, *Will ye no' come back again*, *The Land o' the Leal*, *Caller Herrin'*, *The Laird o' Cockpen*, *The Rowan Tree*, and *The Auld Hoose*, as well as the martial setting for *The Hundred Pipers*.

NAISMITH, James (1861–1939) Canadian educationist, born in Almonte, Ontario. He is regarded as the originator of basketball in 1891 at the YMCA college in Springfield, Massachusetts, using peach baskets on a gym wall. The game was originally designed merely to bridge the gap between the baseball and American football season, but it soon became popular in its own right. He taught at the YMCA, Denver, Colorado (1895–98), and the University of Kansas (1898–1937). He attended the Berlin Olympics of 1936, at which basketball was elevated to the status of an Olympic sport.

NAKASONE, Yasuhiro (1917–) Japanese politician, born in Takasaki and educated at Tokyo Imperial University. After service in World War II he entered politics as a member of the conservative Liberal Democratic party (LDP), and held a number of ministerial posts from 1967 to 1982. He established his own faction within the LDP and was elected secretary-general (1974–76), chairman (1977–80) and, in October 1982, LDP president, and thus prime minister. He introduced an innovative programme which combined greater economic liberalism at home with a more assertive posture abroad, and became Japan's most forceful and popular political leader for decades. He was the first LDP president to be re-elected for a second term since the 1960s, stepping down as prime minister in 1987.

NAMATH, Joe Willie (Joseph William) (1943–) American football player, born in Beaver Halls, Pennsylvania, known as 'Broadway Joe' for his high living off the field. An outstanding quarterback in Alabama University's unbeaten team of 1964, he turned professional in the American Football League with the New York Jets in 1965. In a phenomenally successful career, he played for a total of 23 seasons, he passed for a total of 27663 yards and 173 touchdowns; in 1967 he passed for a record 4007 yards, and in 1969 inspired the Jets to an upset victory over the Baltimore Colts in the Superbowl.

NAMIER, Sir Lewis Bernstein, originally surnamed **Bernstein** (1888–1960) British historian, born in Poland of Russian origin. Educated at Balliol College, Oxford he became a naturalized citizen in 1913 and had a long and distinguished career in diplomacy and journalism, crowned with the professorship of modern history at the University of Manchester from 1931 to 1952. His influence created a Namier school of history, in which the emphasis was on microscopic analysis of events and institutions, particularly parliament, so as to reveal the entire motivation of the individuals involved in them. He compelled a 're-thinking' of history through his *Structure of Politics at the Accession of George III* (1929) and *England in the Age of the American Revolution*, (vol i, 1930).

NANA SAHIB, properly **Brahmin Dundhu Panth** (c.1820–c.1859) Indian rebel, adopted son of the ex-peshwa of the Mahrattas. At the outbreak of the Indian Mutiny (1857) he became the leader of the Sepoys in Cawnpore and organized the massacre of the British residents. After the collapse of the rebellion he escaped into Nepal, and died in the hills, probably after 1859.

NANAK, known as **Guru Nanak** (1469–1539) Indian religious leader, and founder of Sikhism, born near Lahore. A Hindu by birth and belief, he travelled widely to Hindu and Muslim centres in search of spiritual truth. He settled in Kartarpur, in the Punjab, where he attracted many followers. His doctrine, set out later in the *Adi-Granth*, sought a fusion of Brahmanism and Islam on the grounds that both were monotheistic, although his own ideas leaned rather towards pantheism.

NANNI, di Banco (c.1384–1421) Florentine sculptor, one of the most important artists of the early Renaissance. He was recorded as a member of the Stonemasons' Guild in 1405, and was working with his father shortly thereafter on the Porta della Mandorla of Florence cathedral. In his early years he shared two cathedral commissions, for pairs of free-standing figures, with his contemporary **Donatello**. Later he contributed statues to three of the niches on the guild hall Orsanmichele; his best work here was the group of *Four Crowned Saints*, which shows strong classical influence. However, in his most important later commission, the relief of the *Assumption of the Virgin* above the Porta della Mandorla (1414–21), he returned to a more Gothic manner.

NANSEN, Fridtjof (1861–1930) Norwegian explorer, born near Oslo. He studied at Oslo university and later at Naples. In 1882 he made a voyage into the Arctic regions in the sealer *Viking*, and on his return was made keeper of the natural history department of the museum at Bergen. In the summer of 1888 he made an adventurous journey across Greenland from east to west. But his great achievement was the partial accomplishment of his scheme for reaching the North Pole by letting his ship get frozen into the ice north of Siberia and drift with a current setting towards Greenland. He started in the *Fram*, built for the purpose, in August 1893, reached the New Siberian islands in September, made fast to an ice floe, and drifted north to 84° 4′ on 3 March 1895. There he left the *Fram* and pushed across the ice, reaching the highest latitude till then attained, 86° 14′ N, on 7 April and over-wintering in Franz Josef Land. Professor of zoology (1897) and of oceanography (1908) at Oslo, he furthered the cause of Norwegian independence from Sweden, and was the first Norwegian ambassador in London (1906–08). In 1922 he was awarded the Nobel peace prize for Russian relief work, and he did much for the League of Nations.

NAOROJI, Dadhabai (1825–1917) Indian politician, born in Bombay. He became professor of mathematics in Elphinstone College there, and a member of the Legislative Council; and from 1892 to 1895 represented Finsbury in the House of Commons—the first Indian MP—and was also president of the Indian National Congress.

NAPIER, Sir Charles (1786–1860) Scottish naval commander, born at Merchiston Hall near Falkirk, a cousin of Sir **Charles James Napier**. He went to sea at 13, received his first command in 1808, and later served as a volunteer in the Peninsular army. Commanding the *Thames* in 1811, he inflicted great damage on the French in the Mediterranean. In the American War of 1812–14 he led the way in the ascent of the Potomac, and took part in the operations against Baltimore. From 1831 to 1833, in command of the loyalist Portuguese fleet, he defeated the fleet of the pretender, **Maria Evaristo Miguel**, and restored Queen Maria II to the throne. Returning to the British navy in 1839, in the war between the Porte and **Mehemet Ali**, he stormed Sidon, defeated **Ibrahim Pasha** in Lebanon, attacked Acre, blockaded Alexandria, and concluded a convention with Ali. He commanded the Baltic fleet in the Crimean War (1854–55); but the capture of Bomarsund failed to realize expectations, and he was superseded. He twice sat in parliament, and until his death he worked to reform the naval administration.

NAPIER, Sir Charles James (1782–1853) Scottish soldier, the conqueror of Sind, born in London, the brother of Sir **William Napier**. He was a descendant of

John Napier of Merchiston, the mathematician. He served in Ireland during the rebellion, in Portugal (1810), against the United States (1813), and in the storming of Cambrai (1815). In 1841 he was ordered to India to command in the war with Sind, and at the battle of Meeanee (1843) broke the power of the amirs. As governor of Sind, he was soon engaged in an acrimonious war of dispatches with the home authorities, and allegedly sent the classically punny telegram 'Peccavi' ('I have sinned'). In 1847 he returned to England, but was back in India before the close of the Sikh War. As commander-in-chief of the army in India, he quarrelled with Lord **Dalhousie** about military reform, and bade a final adieu to the East in 1851.

NAPIER, John (1550–1617) Scottish mathematician, the inventor of logarithms, born at Merchiston Castle, Edinburgh. He matriculated at St Andrews University in 1563, travelled on the Continent, and settled down to a life of literary and scientific study. In 1593 he published his *Plaine Discouery of the whole Reuelation of Saint John*. He made a contract with Logan of Restalrig for the discovery of treasure in Fast Castle (1594), devised warlike machines (including primitive tanks) for defence against **Philip II** of Spain, and recommended salt as a fertilizer. A strict presbyterian, he was also a believer in astrology and divination. He described his famous invention of logarithms in *Mirifici Logarithmorum Canonis Descriptio* (1614), and the calculating apparatus called 'Napier's Bones' in *Rabdologiae* (1617).

NAPIER, Macvey (1776–1847) Scottish lawyer and editor, born in Glasgow. In 1799 he became a Writer to the Signet in Edinburgh, in 1805 Signet librarian (until 1837), and in 1824 first professor of conveyancing at Edinburgh. He edited the supplement to the fifth edition of the *Encyclopaedia Britannica* (1816–24), the seventh edition (1830–42) and from 1829 the *Edinburgh Review*.

NAPIER, Robert (1791–1876) Scottish shipbuilder and engineer, born in Dumbarton. He built the engines for the first four Cunard steamships, and also built some of the earliest ironclad warships, including the *Black Prince* in 1860, and helped to make the Clyde a great shipbuilding centre.

NAPIER, Robert Cornelis, 1st Baron Napier of Magdala (1810–90) British soldier, born in Colombo, Ceylon. Educated at Addiscombe, he entered the Bengal Engineers in 1826. He served in campaigns in India, and during the Indian Mutiny (1857) he distinguished himself at the siege of Lucknow. He received the thanks of parliament for his services in the Chinese war of 1860 and for his brilliant conduct of the expedition in Abyssinia in 1868. In 1870 he became commander-in-chief in India and a member of the Indian Council, and was subsequently governor of Gibraltar, field marshal, and constable of the Tower.

NAPIER, Sir William Francis Patrick (1785–1860) English soldier and military historian, brother of Sir **Charles James Napier**. He served through the Peninsular campaign and retired from the army in 1819. He began writing and published his *History of the War in the Peninsula* (1828–40), *The Conquest of Scinde* (1845) and a Life of his brother (1857).

NAPOLEON I, or **Napoleon Bonaparte** (1769–1821) emperor of France, second son of **Charles Bonaparte**, born in Ajaccio, Corsica. Granted free military education in France, he studied French at Autun before entering the military schools at Brienne (1779) and Paris (1784). In 1785 he was commissioned second-lieutenant of artillery in the regiment of la Fère, garrisoned at Valence. At Auxonne he saw the beginnings of the French Revolution, but, more concerned with Corsica than France, he went home on leave to organize a revolution and was temporarily struck off the army list for returning to his regiment late (1792). He was given command of the artillery at the siege of Toulon (1793) and was promoted general of brigade. On the fall of **Robespierre** Napoleon was arrested on a charge of conspiracy because of his friendship with the younger Robespierre, but the charges were not proven and he was released. In 1795 he helped to defeat supporters of the counter-revolution in Paris with the celebrated 'whiff of grapeshot' against the mob at the Tuileries, and was then appointed commander of the army of Italy (1796), in which role he was able to demonstrate his great military genius. Two days before his departure for Italy he married **Joséphine**, widow of General Vicomte de **Beauharnais**, who had been executed during the Reign of Terror. On arrival in Nice he was appalled by the poverty and indiscipline of the French army. Since his army was outnumbered by the combined Piedmontese-Austrian forces he determined to separate them. He finally routed the Piedmontese at Mondovi, after which Sardinia sued for peace, and the Austrians at Lodei, after which he entered Milan. He next broke through the Austrian centre and occupied the line of the Adige, taking Verona and Legnago from the neutral republic of Venice. Austria made attempts to recover Lombardy, but she was defeated at Arcola and Rivoli. When Napoleon's position in Italy was secured he advanced on Vienna, and reached Leoben in April 1797. Negotiations for a peace settlement with Austria began, but progressed slowly as Austria hoped to benefit from the political crisis in France, where the moderates and royalists were gaining power on the legislative councils. Napoleon, however, despatched General **Augereau** to assist the Directory in disposing of their opponents by force. In October 1797 Austria signed the Treaty of Campo Formio, by which France obtained Belgium, the Ionian Islands and Lombardy, while Austria got Istria, Dalmatia and Venetia and engaged to try to get the left bank of the Rhine for France. The Directory, fearing Napoleon's power and ambition, hoped to keep him away from Paris by giving him command of the army of England. But, realizing the folly of invading England while her fleet was supreme, he set out on an expedition to Egypt in the hope of damaging Britain's trade with India. He set sail in May 1798, captured Malta and, escaping the British fleet, arrived at Alexandria on 30 June. He then twice defeated the Mamluks and entered Cairo on 24 July, but his position was endangered by the destruction of the French fleet on 1 August by **Nelson** at the battle of the Nile. He defeated the Turks at Mount Tabour but failed to capture St Jean d'Acre, defended by the British squadron under Sir **Sidney Smith**, and was obliged to return to Egypt. He defeated a Turkish army which had landed at Aboukir, but learning of French reverses in Italy and on the Rhine, he secretly embarked for France on 22 August 1799. **Sieyès**, one of the Directors, realizing the unpopularity and weakness of the government, was considering a *coup d'état* when Napoleon arrived. They coalesced, despite their distrust of each other, and the revolution of 18th Brumaire followed (9 November 1799), when Sieyès, Roger Ducos and Napoleon drew up a new constitution. Under it the executive was vested in three consuls, Napoleon, Cambacérès and Lebrun, of whom Napoleon was nominated first consul for ten years. Before embarking on military campaigns Napoleon had to improve the perilous state of the French Treasury. He made plans to found the Bank of France, stabilize the franc and regulate the collection of taxes by employing paid officials; he also tried to improve the system of local government and the judicial system which had become very lax. Offers of peace negotiations were made to England and Austria but he was not surprised when these were rejected. While **Masséna** occupied the attention of the Austrian general Mélas in Piedmont, Napoleon secretly collected an army, reached the plains of Italy, and occupied Milan. In June 1800 the Austrians were routed at Marengo. Napoleon returned to Paris to disprove the rumours about his defeat and death. **Moreau**'s victory at Hohenlinden (1800) led to the signing of the Treaty of Luneville (February 1801) by which the French gains of the Campo Formio treaty were reaffirmed and increased. France's power in Europe was further consolidated by the Concordat with Rome by which Pope **Pius VII** recognized the French Republic and by the peace of Amiens with war-weary England (1802). By this treaty England was allowed to retain Ceylon and Trinidad but relinquished Egypt, Malta and the Cape of Good Hope; France agreed to evacuate Naples; the independence of Portugal and the Ionian Islands was recognized. Napoleon then continued his domestic reforms: he restored the church, realizing that many people, especially the peasants, felt the need of religion; he made an effort to improve secondary education; and he instituted the Légion d'Honneur. He was elected first consul for life. Peace between England and France did not last long because Napoleon annexed Piedmont, occupied Parma and interfered in Swiss internal affairs, and because Britain refused to give up Malta. Napoleon made vast preparations for the invasion of England, at the same time seizing Hanover. England sent help to the royalist conspirators led by **Cadoudal**, who were plotting against Napoleon's life, but Napoleon arrested the conspirators and rid himself of Moreau, his most dangerous rival, by accusing him of conspiring with the royalists. He also executed the Duc **d'Enghien**, a young **Bourbon** prince, although his connection with the conspirators was not proved. He assumed the hereditary title of emperor (18 May 1804) because France did not want to be left without a rightful leader in the event of his death. In 1805 he found himself at war with Russia and Austria, as well as with England. Forced by England's naval supremacy to abandon the notion of invasion, he suddenly, in August 1805, led his armies from Boulogne to the Danube, leaving **Villeneuve** to face the English fleet. He succeeded in surprising the Austrians under **Mack** at Ulm and they surrendered (19 October), leaving him free to enter Vienna on 13 November. On 2 December he inflicted a disastrous defeat on the Russians and Austrians at Austerlitz. The Holy Roman Empire came to an end, the Confederation of the Rhine was formed under French protection, and Napoleon then entered into negotiations for peace with Russia and England. Prussia, afraid that an Anglo-French alliance would mean the loss of Hanover to England, mobilized her army in August 1806; but Napoleon crushed her at Jena and Auerstadt on 14 October. Russia, who had intervened, was defeated at Friedland (14 June 1807). By the peace of Tilsit Prussia lost half her territory and Napoleon was now the arbiter of Europe. Knowing England's reliance on her trade he tried to cripple her by the Continental System, by which he ordered the European states under his control to boycott British goods. He sent an army under **Junot** to Portugal, which refused to adhere to the Continental System, another under **Murat** to Spain because he was uncertain of her loyalty. When he placed his brother **Joseph Napoleon** on the throne many of the nobles and clergy rebelled against the French, while a British army, under Wellesley (**Wellington**), landed in Portugal, defeated Junot at Vimeiro (1808) and forced him to evacuate Portugal under the terms of the Convention of Cintra. So began the Peninsular War which was to occupy a large part of the French army until 1813 when Wellington routed the French and forced them out of Spain. Meanwhile the Prussian reformer **Heinrich Stein** was trying to rouse the Prussians to rebel against the French domination but Napoleon forced the government to dismiss him (1808). In 1809 Austria took advantage of the French troubles in Spain to declare war on France. Napoleon drove the Austrians out of Ratisbon, and entered Vienna (13 May) and won the battle of Wagram on 5 and 6 July. Although resistance was kept up for a time in Tirol by the patriot **Andreas Hofer**, by the treaty of Schönbrunn (20 October 1809) France obtained from Austria the Illyrian provinces, and a heavy money indemnity. In December Napoleon, desirous of an heir, divorced Joséphine, who was childless, and married the archduchess **Marie Louise** of Austria. A son (the future **Napoleon II**) was born on 20 March 1811. Still bent on the humiliation of England, he soon increased the stringency of the Continental System, and annexed Holland and Westphalia. Russia opened its ports to neutral shipping, and this convinced Napoleon that the tsar was contemplating alliance with England. He decided to invade Russia and teach her a lesson. He narrowly defeated the Russians at Borodino (6 September) leaving him free to enter Moscow, which he found deserted and which was destroyed by the fires which broke out the next night. He was then forced to retreat from Moscow, his army hungry, encumbered by the sick and wounded and suffering from the effects of the Russian winter which he had underestimated. Only a mere fraction of the Grand Army that had set out for Russia reached Vilna. Napoleon hurried to Paris to raise new levies, stem the rising panic and belie rumours of his death. Meanwhile the Prussian and Austrian contingents withdrew from the Grand Army. Prussia and Saxony allied with Russia, but Austria and the middle states doubted the ability of the allies to defeat Napoleon and disliked the idea of an alliance with Russia. Napoleon left Paris on 15 April 1813, moved on Leipzig, and won the battle of Lützen on 2 May. He then followed the allies, beat them at Bautzen, 20 and 21 May, and forced them to retire into Silesia. Austria then asked for concessions of territory; but he merely offered to concede Illyria to them, and Austria joined the allies. Napoleon inflicted a crushing defeat on the Austrians near Dresden but part of the French army under **Vandamme** was forced to surrender at Kulm. In October he was defeated at Leipzig and led back the remnant of his army across the Rhine. The invasion of France followed the rejection of peace terms which deprived France of much of her territorial conquests. Napoleon won four battles in four days at Champaubert, Montmirail, Vauchamps and Montereau but benefited little from the battles of Craonne and Laon which followed. On 30 March 1814 the allies attacked Paris, and **Marmont** signed the capitulation of Paris. Napoleon fell back to Fontainebleau; but his position was desperate and Wellington had now led his army across the Pyrenees into France. The French marshals forced him to abdicate, first in favour of his son, then unconditionally (11 April). By the treaty of Fontainbleau he was given the sovereignty of Elba, allowed to retain the title of emperor, and awarded a revenue from the French government. The Bourbons in the person of **Louis XVIII** were restored to the throne of France, but their return was unpopular. The army was disgusted at their treatment by the king and also at the appointment to commands of *émigrés* who had fought against France, and alarm was caused by proposals to return national lands to the *émigrés* and the church. The coalition, too, broke up because of quarrels over territorial settlement, especially over Prussia. Napoleon hoped to take advantage of the situation and landed on the French coast on 1 March 1815. On the 20th he entered Paris at the start of the 'Hundred Days', having been joined by the army. Europe had declared war against him but only a mixed force under Wellington in Belgium and a Prussian army under **Blücher** in the Rhine provinces were in the field. Napoleon's aim being to strike suddenly and then defeat each force separately, he occupied Charleroi and on 16 June defeated Blücher at Ligny. But not until the next day did he send **Grouchy** to follow the retreating Prussians, thus enabling Blücher to move on to Wavre to join Wellington who had retired to Mont St Jean, while Grouchy was engaged with the Prussian rear-guard only. After his defeat by Wellington and Blücher at Waterloo, Napoleon fled to Paris, abdicated on 22 June, decided to throw himself on the mercy of England, and surrendered to Captain Maitland of the *Bellerophon* at Rochefort on 15 July 1815. He was banished by the British government to St Helena, where he died on 5 May 1821, of either liver disease or cancer of the stomach.

NAPOLEON II, properly **François Charles Joseph Bonaparte** (1811–32) Son of **Napoleon I** by **Marie Louise**, born in Paris. He was styled king of Rome upon his birth at the Tuileries in 1811. From 1814 until his death (from tuberculosis) he lived at the Austrian court and was created Duke of Reichstadt (1818) by his grandfather, **Francis I**. Loyal Bonapartists proclaimed him Napoleon II in Paris on 28 June 1815, but he was formally deposed five days later. He spent the rest of his life in Vienna.

NAPOLEON III, Charles Louis Napoléon Bonaparte (1808–73) emperor of France, born in Paris, the third son of **Louis Bonaparte**, king of Holland, and nephew of **Napoleon I**. He was brought up in Geneva, Augsburg, and his mother's residence, the Swiss castle of Arenenberg on the Lake of Constance. He hastened with his elder brother Louis into Italy in 1831 to assist the Romagna in its revolt against pontifical rule, an expedition in which Louis perished of fever. On the death of the Duke of Reichstadt, only son of **Napoleon I**, in 1832, he became the head of the Napoleonic dynasty. He published in 1832–36 his *Rêveries politiques*, *Projet de constitution*, and *Considérations politiques et militaires sur la Suisse*. In 1836 he put his chances to a premature test by appearing among the military at Strasbourg, was easily overpowered, and conveyed to America. He was recalled to Europe by his mother's last illness (1837); and when the French government demanded of Switzerland his expulsion he settled in London. In 1838 he published his *Idées napoléoniennes*. In 1840 he made at Boulogne a second and equally abortive attempt on the throne of France, and was condemned to perpetual imprisonment in the fortress of Ham. Here he continued his Bonapartist propaganda by writing *Aux mânes de l'empereur*, etc, and actually helped to edit the *Dictionnaire de la conversation*. After an imprisonment of more than five years he made his escape (25 May 1846), and returned to England. The revolution of February 1848 was a victory of the workers, to whom some of his political theories were especially addressed; he hurried back to France as a virtual nominee of the Fourth Estate, or working-classes. Elected deputy for Paris and three other departments, he took his seat in the Constituent Assembly on 13 June 1848. On the 15th he resigned and left France. His quintuple election recalled him in September, and he commenced his candidature of the presidency; 5 562 834 votes were recorded for him, only 1 469 166 for General **Cavaignac**, his genuinely Republican competitor. On 20 December he took the oath of allegiance to the Republic. For a few days concord seemed established between the different political parties in the Assembly; but the beginning of 1849 witnessed the commencement of a struggle between the president and the majority of the Assembly. Then he committed the command of the army to those devoted to him, and established his supporters in posts of influence. He paraded as a protector of popular rights and of national prosperity; but, hampered by the National Assembly in his efforts to make his power perpetual, he threw off the mask of a constitutional president. On 2 December 1851, with the help of the military, he dissolved the Constitution. Imprisonment, deportation, and the bloody repression of popular rebellion, marked this black day's work. France appeared to acquiesce; for when the vote was taken on it in December, he was re-elected for ten years by 7 000 000 votes. The imperial title was assumed a year after the *coup d'état*, in accordance with another plebiscite. Political parties were either demoralized or broken. Napoleon III gagged the press, awed the *bourgeoisie*, and courted the clergy to win the peasantry. On 29 January 1853 he married Eugénie de Montijo (1826–1920), a Spanish countess, born in Granada. The emperor now proclaimed the right of peoples to choose their own masters, availing himself of it in the annexation (1860) of Savoy and Nice to France, in his Mexican intervention through **Maximilian** of Austria, and in his handling of the Italian question. At home the price of bread was regulated, public works enriched the working-men, while others were undertaken to enhance in value the property of the peasantry. The complete remodelling of Paris under the direction of Baron **Haussmann** raised the value of house property. International exhibitions and treaties of commerce were a further inducement to internal peace. A brilliant foreign policy seemed to dawn on the Crimean War (1854–56); the campaign in Lombardy against Austria (1859), to which Napoleon was somewhat paradoxically encouraged by the murderous attack of **Orsini** on his person; and the expeditions to China (1857–60). In all these undertakings Napoleon had the support if not the co-operation of Great Britain. With Prussia his relations were very different. At the death of **Morny** in 1865 the controlling power of Napoleon's measures was almost spent. His *Vie de César*, written to extol his own methods of government, met with loud protests. Forewarned, Napoleon reorganized his army, set himself up more proudly as an arbiter in Europe, and took a more conciliatory attitude to liberalism. In 1869 his prime minister **Rouher**, an advocate of absolutism, was dismissed, and new men were called into power to liberalize the constitution. By another plebiscite the new parliamentary scheme was sanctioned by 7 million votes (8 May 1870). But 50 000 dissentient votes given by the army revealed an unsuspected source of danger. Anxious to rekindle its ardour, and ignorant of the corruption that existed in his ministry of war, he availed himself of a pretext—the scheme to place Leopold of Hohenzollern on the Spanish throne—to declare war against Prussia (15 July 1870). By 30 July, Prussia had 500 000 men in the field, while the French had with great exertion collected 270 000 by the beginning of August. The emperor assumed the command, but never got across the Rhine, and had to fight at a disadvantage within Alsace and Lorraine.

The campaign opened with a small success at Saarbrücken (2 August), followed by the defeats of Weissenburg (4 August), Wörth and Spicheren (6 August). Napoleon had retired to Metz, and abandoned the chief command to Marshal **Bazaine**, whose escape from Metz was prevented by the defeats of Mars-la-Tour (16 August) and Gravelotte (18 August), Metz surrendered on 27 October. Meanwhile a hastily organized force of 120000 men under Marshal **Macmahon** was moved to the assistance of Bazaine. On reaching Sedan Macmahon found himself surrounded by the Prussians, and on 1 September suffered a crushing defeat. Next day the emperor surrendered with 83000 men. On 4 September the Second Empire was ended. Until the conclusion of peace he was confined at Wilhelmshöle. In March 1871 he joined the ex-empress at Chislehurst, Kent, and resided there in exile until his death. His son, Eugène Louis Jean Joseph (1856–79), Prince Imperial, was in the field with his father in 1870, but escaped to England, where he entered Woolwich Academy. He was killed in the Zulu campaign of 1879.

NARAYAN, Rasipuram Kirshnaswamy (1906–) Indian novelist, born in Madras, south India. He was educated there and at Maharaja's College in Mysore. His first novel, *Swami and Friends* (1935), and its successor *The Bachelor of Arts* (1937), are set in the enchanting fictional territory of 'Malgudi'. Other Malgudi novels are *The Dark Room* (1938), *The English Teacher* (1945)—a thinly veiled account of his own marriage and the event that most matured and shaped his character, the early death of his beloved wife—*Mr Sampath* (1949), *The Financial Expert* (1952), *The Man-Eater of Malgudi* (1961), *The Painter of Signs* (1977) and *The Tiger for Malgudi* (1983). His novel *The Guide* (1958) won him the National prize of the Indian Literary Academy. He has also published stories, travel books, books for children and essays, as well as *My Days: A Memoir* (1974). The best Indian novelist of his generation, his publication in Britain was brought about by **Graham Greene**.

NARES, Sir George Strong (1831–1915) Scottish naval commander and explorer, born in Aberdeen. Educated at the Royal Naval College, New Cross, he entered the navy in 1846. He served as mate on the *Resolute* during its Arctic expedition of 1852, in the Crimea, and as commander of the cadet sail-training ship *Britannia*, and worked on surveys of north-east Australia and the Mediterranean (1872–74). He commanded the *Challenger* (1872–74) on its oceanographic voyage around the world which resulted in a 50-volume report for its sponsors, the Admiralty and the Royal Society. In 1875 he was transferred to command the *Alert* and *Discovery* in the Arctic, and later, on the *Alert*, surveyed the Magellan Straits.

NARSES (c.478–573) Byzantine statesman and Persian general, born in Armenia. He rose in the imperial household in Constantinople to be keeper of the privy purse to **Justinian I**. In 538 he was sent to Italy, but recalled the next year. In 552 **Belisarius** was recalled from Italy and Narses succeeded him, defeated the Ostrogoths, took possession of Rome, and completely extinguished the Gothic power in Italy. Justinian appointed him prefect of Italy in 554, and he administered its affairs with vigour and ability. But he was charged with avarice; and on Justinian's death the Romans complained to **Justin II**, who deprived him in 567 of his office.

NARVÁEZ, Ramón Maria (1800–68) Spanish soldier and statesman, born in Loja. A supporter of **Isabella II** he defeated the Carlists in 1836, and then took part in an unsuccessful insurrection against **Espartero** in 1840 and fled to France, where he was joined by **Maria Christina**. In 1843 he led a republican insurrection in Madrid that drove Espartero from power, and became virtual dictator. He lost power temporarily in 1851, and was briefly exiled as special ambassador to France, but from 1856 he was premier again several times.

NASH, John (1752–1835) English architect, born in London or Cardigan. He trained as an architect, but after coming into a legacy retired to Wales. Having lost heavily by speculations in 1792, he resumed practice in London and gained a reputation by his country house designs. He came to the notice of the Prince of Wales, later the Prince Regent (the future **George IV**), and was engaged (1811–25) to plan the layout of the new Regent's Park and its environs of curved terraces. He laid out Regent Street (1825) to link the Park with Westminster. He built Carlton House Terrace, and laid out Trafalgar Square and St James's Park. He recreated Buckingham Palace from old Buckingham House, designed the Marble Arch which originally stood in front of it (moved to its present site in 1851), and rebuilt Brighton Pavilion in oriental style. On the strength of a patent (1797) for improvements to the arches and piers of bridges, he claimed much of the credit for introducing steel girders. The skilful use of terrain and landscape featured in his layouts marks him as one of the greatest town planners.

NASH, (Frederic) Ogden (1902–71) American light versifier, born in Rye, New York. Educated at Harvard, he tried various occupations—teaching, editing, selling bonds, copy writing—before devoting himself to verse. Taking outrageous liberties with the English language ('I would live all my life in nonchalance and insouciance/Were it not for making a living, which is rather a nouciance'), he soon became the most popular modern versifier, frequently to be seen in the *New Yorker*, whose sophisticated tone he helped establish. No subject, however odd, inconsequential or mundane was safe from his wit. Puns, parody and pastiche—as well as alliteration—were his stock in trade, which he used to amuse as well as shock. He published many collections including *Free Wheeling* (1931), *Hard Lines* (1931), *Parents Keep Out: Elderly Poems for Youngerly Readers* (1951), *The Private Dining Room and Other New Verses* (1953), and *Boy is a Boy* (1960). *I Wouldn't Have Missed It: Selected Poems of Ogden Nash* was published in 1983.

NASH, Paul (1899–1946) English painter, born in London. Educated at St Paul's and the Slade School, he became an official war artist in 1917 (remembered particularly for his poignant *Menin Road*, 1919). Developing a style which reduced form to bare essentials without losing the identity of the subject, he won renown as a landscape painter and also practised scene painting, commercial design, and book illustration. For a while he taught at the Royal College of Art. Experiments in a near abstract manner were followed by a phase of Surrealism until, in 1939, he again filled the role of war artist, this time for the Air Ministry and the Ministry of Information, producing such pictures as *Battle of Britain* and *Totes Meer*. Shortly before his death he turned to a very individual style of flower painting. His autobiography, *Outline*, was published in 1949.

NASH, Richard, known as **'Beau Nash'** (1674–1762) Welsh dandy, born in Swansea. Educated at Carmarthen and Oxford, he held a commission in the army, and in 1693 entered the Middle Temple. He then made a shifty living by gambling, but in 1704 became Master of Ceremonies at Bath, where he conducted the public balls with a splendour never before witnessed. His reforms in manners, his influence in improving the streets and buildings and his leadership in fashion helped to transform Bath into a fashionable holiday centre.

NASH, Sir Walter (1882–1968) English-born New Zealand politician, born in Kidderminster. From 1919 to 1960 he served on the national executive of the New Zealand Labour party, encouraging the adoption of a moderate reform programme in the Christian Socialist tradition. A member of parliament from 1929, he held numerous ministerial appointments from 1936 onwards and in World War II was deputy prime minister to **Peter Fraser**, although from 1942 to 1944 he headed a special mission to the USA. He was prime minister from 1957 to 1960, but as his government possessed a majority of only one there were few political innovations.

NASHE, Thomas (1567–1601) English dramatist and satirist, born in Lowestoft. He studied for seven years at St John's College, Cambridge, travelled in France and Italy, and then went to London to earn a precarious living by his pen. His first work was the *Anatomie of Absurditie* (1589), perhaps written at Cambridge. He plunged into the Martin Marprelate controversy, showing a talent for vituperation which he expressed in his works. *Pierce Penilesse, his Supplication to the Divell* (1592) began the series of attacks on the Harveys (Richard Harvey had criticized Nashe's preface to **Greene**'s *Menaphon*) which culminated in *Have with you to Saffron Walden* (1596), against **Gabriel Harvey**, who had by then assailed Greene's memory in *Foure Letters*. In 1599 the controversy was suppressed by the archbishop of Canterbury. Nashe's satirical masque *Summer's Last Will and Testament* (1592) contains the song 'Spring the sweet Spring is the year's pleasant king'. *The Unfortunate Traveller* (1594) is a picaresque tale, one of the earliest of its kind. After **Marlowe**'s death, Nashe prepared his unfinished tragedy *Dido* (1596) for the stage. His own play *The Isle of Dogs* (1597), now lost, drew such attention to abuses in the state that it was suppressed, the theatre closed, and the writer himself thrown into the Fleet prison. His last work was *Lenten Stuffe* (1599), a panegyric on the red herring trade at Yarmouth.

NASMYTH, Alexander (1758–1840) Scottish painter, born in Edinburgh. He was a pupil of **Allan Ramsay** and became a well-known portrait painter in Edinburgh. His portrait of **Burns** in the Scottish National Gallery is particularly famous. He later confined himself to landscape painting.

NASMYTH, James (1808–90) Scottish engineer, son of **Alexander Nasmyth**, born in Edinburgh. From boyhood he evinced a bent for mechanics; in 1834 he started in business at Manchester, and in 1836 established at Patricroft the Bridgewater Foundry. His steam hammer was devised in 1839 for forging an enormous wrought-iron paddle-shaft, and in 1842 he found an identical steam hammer at work at Le Creusot in France; it had been adapted from his own scheme-book. Nasmyth patented his invention, and it was adopted by the Admiralty in 1843. Among others of his inventions was a steam pile-driver, a planing machine and a hydraulic punching machine. He published *Remarks on Tools and Machinery* (1858) and *The Moon* (1874).

NASMYTH, Patrick (1787–1831) Scottish landscape painter, born in Edinburgh, son of **Alexander Nasmyth**. He settled in England, painted many English scenes and became known as the 'English **Hobbema**'.

NASO See **OVID**

NASR-ED-DIN, (1829–96) shah of Persia from 1848. He visited England in 1873 and 1889, introduced European ideas into Persia, granted trade concessions to Britain and Russia, and was shot near Teheran by an assassin. He was succeeded by his second son Muzzaffar-ed-Din.

NASSER, Gamal Abdel (1918–70) Egyptian political leader, president of the United Arab Republic, born in Alexandria. As an army officer with bitter experience of the mismanaged Palestine campaign of 1948, he became dissatisfied with the inefficiency and corruption of the **Farouk** régime, and founded the military Junta which encompassed its downfall. Chief power behind the *coup* of 1952, he was mainly responsible for the rise to power of General **Neguib**, but tension between the two, as a result of Neguib's suspected dictatorial ambitions, culminated in Nasser's assumption of the premiership in April 1954 and of presidential powers in November 1954, when Neguib was deposed. Nasser was officially elected president in June 1956, and his almost immediate action in expropriating the Suez Canal led to a state of tension in the Middle East which culminated in Israel's invasion of the Sinai peninsula. When Anglo-French forces intervened, widespread differences of opinion in Britain and elsewhere, coupled with veiled Russian threats, enabled Nasser to turn an abject military débâcle into a political victory. His aim was clearly now to build an Arab empire stretching across North Africa, the first step being the creation, by federation with Syria, of the United Arab Republic in February 1958. In March 1958 the Yemen and the UAR formed the United Arab States. This was followed by a sustained effort to break up the Baghdad Pact and liquidate the remaining sovereign states in the Middle East, a policy which succeeded in Iraq, but was thwarted in Jordan and the Lebanon by the deployment of American and British forces. His plans for unity among the Arab states received a setback when Syria withdrew from the UAR and when the union with the Yemen was dissolved (1961). In 1964, however, the UAR formed joint presidency councils with Iraq and the Yemen. After the six-day Arab-Israeli war in June 1967, heavy losses on the Arab side led to Nasser's resignation, but he was persuaded to withdraw it almost immediately.

NATHAN, Isaac (1790–1864) English-born Australian composer and music teacher, born in Canterbury, Kent. Musical librarian to King **George IV**, he was a friend of the poet **Byron** whose *Hebrew Melodies* (1815) Nathan set to music inspired by Jewish chants. He moved with his family to Australia in 1841 where he quickly became involved in the musical scene as choirmaster of St Mary's Cathedral, Sydney. He published *Australia the Wide and Free* in 1842, and the first opera to be composed and performed in Australia, *Don John of Austria* in 1847. He also composed a dramatic scena, *Leichhardt's Grave*, and in 1849 published *The Southern Euphrosyne*, which included the first harmonisations of aboriginal music.

NATHANS, Daniel (1928–) American microbiologist, and joint winner of the 1978 Nobel prize for physiology or medicine. Professor at Johns Hopkins University from 1962, he pioneered the use of restriction enzymes to fragment DNA molecules, and shared the Nobel prize with **Hamilton Smith** and **Werner Arber**.

NATION, Carry Amelia, née **Moore** (1846–1911) American temperance agitator, born in Garrard County, Kentucky. A large, powerful woman of volcanic emotions, she went on saloon-smashing expeditions with a hatchet in many American cities, attacking what she considered illegal drinking places, and was frequently imprisoned for breach of the peace.

NATORP, Paul Gerhard (1854–1924) German philosopher, born in Düsseldorf. He became professor at Marburg from 1885 and a leading member of the neo-Kantian 'Marburg school', which sought to apply Kantian methods to the philosophy of science, and which also included **Hermann Cohen**, **Ernst Cassirer** and Rudolf Stammuler. Among his publications are *Sozialpädagogik* (1899), *Philosophie und Pädagogik* (1909), *Die logischen Grundlagen der exakten Wissenschaft* (1910) and *Sozialidealismus* (1920).

NATTA, Giulio (1903–79) Italian chemist. Professor at Pavia, Rome and Turin, from 1939 he held the chair of industrial chemistry at Milan Institute of Technology. With **Karl Ziegler**, he was awarded the Nobel prize for chemistry in 1963 for his researches on polymers which led to important developments in plastics and other industrial chemicals.

NATTIER, Jean Marc (1685–1766) French artist, born in Paris. He executed historical pictures and portraits, including those of **Peter the Great** and the empress **Catherine II, the Great** of Russia, but after losing his money in the **John Law** financial crisis he took up the fashionable stereotyped style of court portraiture now labelled 'le portrait Nattier' for the court of **Louis XV**.

NAUDIN, Charles (1815–99) French botanist, born in Autun. He studied in Paris and taught botany at the Natural History Museum there until total deafness forced him to abandon teaching for research. In the 1850s he experimented on plant hybridization, and his 'theory of disjunction' correctly recognized that inheritance is particulate and not a blending process. However, his experiments on hybridization were inferior to those of his contemporary, **Mendel**, so that he did not discover any statistical regularities in inheritance; and he failed to recognize the importance of natural selection.

NAUMAN, Bruce (1941–) American sculptor, born in Fort Wayne, Indiana. He studied mathematics and art at Wisconsin University. In the 1960s he became a leading exponent of Conceptual Art, using neon lights and holograms in addition to producing minimalist sculptures from more conventional materials. Since 1970 he has worked chiefly with fibreglass and wood, exploring the relationship between sculpture and the gallery space.

NAUNDORF, Karl Wilhelm See **LOUIS XVII**

NAUNTON, Sir Robert (1563–1635) English statesman and writer, born in Alderton, Suffolk. He became public orator at Cambridge in 1594, travelled, entered parliament, and was secretary of state (1618–23). He wrote *Fragmenta Regalia* (1641), a sketch of **Elizabeth**'s courtiers.

NAVIER, Claude Louis Marie Henri (1785–1836) French civil engineer, born in Dijon. Educated at the École Polytechnique and the École des Ponts et Chaussées, for much of his life he taught at one or the other of these schools, being principally occupied in developing the theoretical basis of structural mechanics and the strength of materials, as well as the work done by machines. Recognizing the importance of being able to predict the limits of elastic behaviour in structural materials, his formulae represented one of the greatest single advances in structural analysis ever made.

NAVILLE, Henri Edouard (1844–1926) Swiss Egyptologist, born in Geneva. He became professor of Egyptology there, excavated in Egypt for many years, edited the *Book of the Dead*, and wrote a number of books on Egypt.

NAVRATILOVA, Martina (1956–) Czechoslovakian-born American tennis player, born in Prague. For three years she played for Czechoslovakia in the Federation Cup, but in 1975 she defected to the USA and immediately turned professional. Her rivalry with **Chris Evert** was one of the great features of the game from 1975. She won Wimbledon seven times and the US Open three times and recorded more than 100 tournament successes. In 1985 she wrote *Being Myself*.

NAYLER, James (c.1617–1660) English Quaker preacher, born in Ardsley near Wakefield. He served in the parliamentary army. Later he became a Quaker, and gathered a band of disciples and rode into Bristol (1656) as the reincarnation of Christ. He was flogged, branded and imprisoned for blasphemy.

NAZIANZEN See **GREGORY OF NAZIANZUS**

NAZIMOVA, Alla, originally **Alla Leventon** (1879–1945) Russian-born American actress, born in the Crimea. She studied in Moscow under **Stanislavsky** and made her début in St Petersburg in 1904, and in 1905 appeared in New York as Hedda Gabler. In 1910 she took the 39th Street Theatre, rechristening it 'The Nazimova', and became a highly popular emotional actress. She had a successful period in films, which included *The Brat*, *Camille*, *A Doll's House*, *The Red Lantern* and her own *Salomé*, based on the **Beardsley** illustrations to **Wilde**'s play. She specialized in the plays of **Ibsen**, **Turgenev**, **Chekhov** and **O'Neill**.

NAZOR, Vladimir (1876–1949) Croatian poet, born in Postire on the island of Brač. He wrote lyrics and ballads as well as epic poems and dramatic works in a style similar to the Symbolists. His works include *Slav Legends* (1900), *Lirika* (1910), *Carmen Vitae*, an anthology (1922), and a diary of his experiences with the Yugoslav partisans in World War II.

NAZRUL ISLAM, Kazi See **ISLAM, Kazi Nazrul**

NE WIN, (Maung Shu Maung) (1911–) Burmese politician, whose name means 'Brilliant Sun'. Educated at Rangoon University, he was an active anti-British nationalist in the 1930s. In World War II he became chief of staff in the collaborationist army after the Japanese invasion of Burma, but joined the Allied forces later in the war, and held senior military and cabinet posts after Burma's independence (1948), before becoming caretaker prime minister (1958–60). In 1962, following a military coup, he ruled the country as chairman of the revolutionary council and became state president in 1974. After leaving this office in 1981, he continued to dominate political affairs as chairman of the ruling Burma Socialist Programme party (BSPP), following an isolationist foreign policy and a unique domestic 'Burmese Way to Socialism' programme, a blend of Marxism, Buddhism and Burmese nationalism. In 1988, with economic conditions rapidly deteriorating, and riots in Rangoon, he was forced to step down as BSPP leader.

NEAGLE, Dame Anna, originally **Marjorie Robertson** (1904–86) English actress, born in London. She studied dance as a child and was an instructor before becoming a chorus girl in *Charlot's Revue of 1925*. She graduated to leading roles in *Stand Up and Sing* (1931), making her film début in *Should A Doctor Tell?* (1930). Under the tutelage of director Herbert Wilcox, who became her husband in 1943, she emerged as a major star of historical film dramas, offering genteel portraits of inspiring heroines in *Victoria, the Great* (1937), *Nurse Edith Cavell* (1939), *Odette* (1950) and *The Lady With the Lamp* (1951). A series of escapist musicals opposite Michael Wilding made her Britain's number one box-office attraction but later attempts to tackle contemporary subjects were ill-judged and she retired from the screen after *The Lady is a Square* (1958). She retained the affection of British audiences with appearances in such theatrical candyfloss as *Charlie Girl* (1965–71), *No, No, Nanette* (1973) and *My Fair Lady*

(1978–79). Created DBE in 1969 she wrote two autobiographies, *It's Been Fun* (1949) and *There's Always Tomorrow* (1974).

NEAL, Daniel (1678–1743) English clergyman and historian, born in London. In 1706 he became an Independent minister there. He wrote a *History of New England* (1720) and the laborious and accurate *History of the Puritans* (1732–38).

NEAL, John (1793–1876) American writer, born of Quaker parentage in Falmouth (now Portland, Maine). He failed in business in 1816, and turned to law, supporting himself in the meantime by his writings. He was one of the first Americans to write in the larger English magazines, and lived in England from 1823 to 1827. After his return he practised law, edited newspapers and lectured. He wrote an autobiographical *Wandering Recollections of a Somewhat Busy Life* (1869).

NEALE, Edward Vansittart (1810–92) English social reformer, born in Bath. A graduate of Oxford, he became a barrister, and from 1851 he was a pioneer Christian Socialist and an advocate of co-operation, founding the first co-operative shop in London. He became general secretary of the Central Co-operative Board (1875–91).

NEALE, John Mason (1818–66) English hymnologist, born in London. He was a scholar of Trinity College, Cambridge, and from 1846 warden of Sackville College, East Grinstead. An advanced High Churchman, he was inhibited by his bishop. He wrote many books on church history, but is remembered chiefly for his hymns, and many of his translations are cherished worldwide. Among his best-known pieces are 'Jerusalem the golden' and 'O happy band of pilgrims'. His *Collected Hymns* was published in 1914.

NEANDER, Johann August Wilhelm, originally **David Mendel** (1789–1850) German church historian, born in Göttingen of Jewish parentage. In 1806 he renounced Judaism and changed his name. In 1813 he became professor of church history at Berlin. Profoundly devotional, sympathetic, glad-hearted and profusely benevolent, he inspired universal reverence, and attracted students from all countries. He probably contributed more than any other to overthrowing anti-historical rationalism and dead Lutheran formalism. He wrote many books on church history, of which the best known is his *General History of the Christian Religion and Church* (Eng trans 9 vols, 1847–55).

NEARCHUS (4th century BC.) Macedonian general, from Crete. He settled in Amphipolis during the reign of **Philip II** of Macedon, and became the companion of the young **Alexander the Great**. In 330 BC he was governor of Lycia; in 329 he joined Alexander in Bacria with a body of Greek mercenaries, and took part in the Indian campaigns. Having built a fleet on the Hydaspes (Jhelum), Alexander gave Nearchus the command. He left the Indus in November 325, and, skirting the coast, reached Susa in February 324. His narrative is preserved in the *Indica* of **Arrian**.

NEBUCHADREZZAR, or **NEBUCHADNEZZAR II** (d.562 BC) king of Babylon. He succeeded his father Nabopolassar in 605 BC. During his 43-year reign he recovered the long-lost provinces of the kingdom, and once more made Babylon a supreme nation. He not only restored the empire and rebuilt Babylon, but almost every temple throughout the land underwent restoration at his hands. Not a mound has been opened by explorers which has not contained bricks, cylinders or tablets inscribed with his name. In 597 he captured Jerusalem; and in 586 he destroyed the city, and removed most of the inhabitants to Chaldea.

NECKAM, or **Nequam, Alexander** (1157–1217) English scholar, born in St Albans on the same night as **Richard I**. He was nursed by his mother along with the future king. Educated at St Albans and Paris (where he lectured), he returned to England to be schoolmaster at Dunstable. In 1213 he became Abbot of Cirencester. In his *De naturis rerum* and *De utensilibus* he was the first in Europe to describe the use of a magnetic needle by sailors.

NECKER, Jacques (1732–1804) French statesman and financier, born in Geneva. At 15 he went to Paris as a banker's clerk, and in 1762 established the London and Paris bank of Thellusson and Necker. In 1776 he was made director of the treasury, and next year director-general of finance. Some of his remedial measures were a boon to suffering France, but his most ambitious scheme—the establishment of provincial assemblies, one of whose functions should be the apportionment of taxes—proved a disastrous failure. His retrenchments were hateful to the queen, and his famous *Compte rendu* (1781) occasioned his dismissal. He retired to Geneva, but in 1787 returned to Paris; and when **Charles de Calonne** cast doubt on the *Compte rendu*, he published a justification which drew upon him his banishment from Paris. Recalled to office in September 1788, he quickly made himself the popular hero by recommending the summoning of the States-General. But the successful banker proved himself unfit to steer the ship of state amid the storms of revolution. On 11 July he received the royal command to leave France at once, but the fall of the Bastille three days later frightened the king into recalling him amid the wildest popular enthusiasm. But after spurning the help of **Lafayette** and **Mirabeau**, and leading the king to surrender his suspensive veto, he finally resigned (September 1790). He retired to his estate near Geneva where he died.

NEDREAAS, Torborg (1906–) Norwegian novelist, born in Bergen. She turned to writing late in life, after World War II. A left-wing feminist, her books highlight social life and class struggle in Norwegian urban society. Especially powerful are *Music from a Blue Well* (1960) and *At the Next New Moon* (1971), about a girl called Herdis growing up in Bergen between the wars.

NEEDHAM, Joseph (1900–) English biochemist and historian of Chinese science, born in London, the son of a Harley Street doctor. Educated at Oundle and Gonville and Caius College, Cambridge, he was university demonstrator in biochemistry (1928–33), working mainly to discover the process underlying the development of the fertilized egg into a differentiated and complex organism, which he published in *Chemical Embryology* (1931). He was reader from 1933 to 1966, and master of Gonville and Caius College, Cambridge, from 1966 to 1976. His publications at first reflected philosophical problems in science, such as *Man a Machine* (1927) and *The Sceptical Biologist* (1929), but these began to give way to historical preoccupations shown in *A History of Embryology* (1934), and *History is on Our Side* (1945). During World War II he became head of the British Scientific Mission in China and Scientific Counsellor at the British Embassy, Chungking, and adviser to the Chinese National Resources Commission, Chinese Army Medical Administration and Chinese Air Force Research Bureau, following this from 1946 to 1948 as director of the department of natural sciences, UNESCO. He published *Chinese Science* in 1946, and 1954 saw the appearance of the first instalment of *Science and Civilisation in China* (12 vols, 1954–84), a work of the foremost significance in the development of the history of science and in the exposition to a western audience of the Chinese historical achievement. He has also published studies in the history of acupuncture (*Celestial Lancets*, 1980), of Korean astronomy and clocks, and of the development of Chinese technology in iron and steel, as well as a vast body of other work.

NÉEL, Louis Eugène Félix (1904–) French physicist, born in Lyon. A graduate of the École Normale Supérieure, he was later professor of physics at Strasbourg University (1937–40). In 1940 he moved to Grenoble and became the driving force in making it one of the most important scientific centres in France, becoming director of the Centre for Nuclear Studies there in 1956. His research has been concerned with magnetism in solids, which led to the development of the 'memories' in computers. He predicted in 1936 that a special type of magnetic ordering called 'antiferromagnetism' should exist, and this was experimentally confirmed in 1938, with full neutron diffraction confirmation in 1949. He shared the Nobel prize for physics in 1970 with **Hannes Alfvén**. He has also studied the past history of the Earth's magnetic field.

NEER, Aert van der (1603/4–1677) Dutch painter, born in Amsterdam. He specialized in moonlit canal and river scenes and, although these paintings are now regarded as major works of the Dutch school, he received little recognition in his own time. In 1658 he gave up painting in order to open a wineshop. He was no more successful in this venture and returned to painting in 1662 after being declared bankrupt. Two of his sons became artists: Eglon (1634–1703) and Jan (1638–65).

NEFERTITI (14th century BC) Egyptian queen, the consort of **Akhenaton**, by whom she had six children. She is immortalized in the beautiful sculptured head found at Amarna in 1912, now in the Berlin museum.

NEGRI, Ada (1870–1945) Italian poet, born in Milan. She became a teacher, wrote socialistic verse and short stories.

NEGUIB, Mohammed (1901–) Egyptian leader. As general of an army division in 1952 he carried out a *coup d'état* in Cairo which banished King **Farouk I** and initiated the 'Egyptian Revolution'. Taking first the offices of commander-in-chief and prime minister, he abolished the monarchy in 1953 and became president of the republic. He was deposed in 1954 and succeeded by Colonel **Gamal Abdel Nasser**.

NEGUS, Arthur George (1903–85) English broadcaster and antiques expert, born in Reading. The son of a cabinet maker, he took over the family shop in 1920 and spent the next 20 years as an antique dealer. The shop was bombed during World War II, and in 1946 he joined the Gloucester firm of fine art auctioneers, Bruton, Knowles & Co, becoming a partner in 1972. Asked to expound on the merits and value of antiques for television, he became a regular panel member on the series *Going for a Song* (1966–76). His avuncular manner, wry humour and expertise made him a popular broadcaster in such series as *Arthur Negus Enjoys* (1982) and *The Antiques Roadshow* (1982–83). His books include *Going for a Song*: *English furniture* (1969) and *A Life Among Antiques* (1982).

NEHEMIAH (5th century BC) Old Testament prophet. He was cupbearer to **Artaxerxes Longimanus**, who in 444 BC gave him full powers to act as governor-extraordinary of Judaea. He had the walls of Jerusalem rebuilt, and repopulated the city by drafts from the surrounding districts. In 432 he revisited Jerusalem, and either initiated or renewed and completed certain reforms which henceforth were among the most characteristic features of post-exilic Judaism. The canonical book of Nehemiah originally formed the closing chapters of the undivided work, Chronicles-Ezra-Nehemiah.

NEHRU, Jawaharlal (1889–1964) Indian statesman, son of **Motilal Nehru**, born in Allahabad. After an undistinguished career at Harrow School and Trinity College, Cambridge, where he took the natural sciences tripos, he read for the bar (Inner Temple 1912), returned home and served in the high court of Allahabad. A persistent vision of himself as an Indian **Garibaldi** made him become a member of the Indian Congress Committee in 1918 and brought him, if with scientific reservations, under the spell of **Mahatma Gandhi**. He was imprisoned in 1921 and spent 18 of the next 25 years in jail. In 1928 he was elected president of the Indian National Congress, an office he often held afterwards, and was the leader of the movement's socialist wing. Although sympathetic to the Allied Cause in World War II, he, in common with other Congress party leaders, did not co-operate and turned down the **Cripps** offer of dominion status for India made in 1942. But in 1947, when India achieved independence, Nehru became her first prime minister and minister of external affairs. As democratic leader of the first republic within the Commonwealth, he followed a policy of neutralism and peace-making during the Cold War, often acting as a go-between between the Great Powers, and originated the theory of non-aligment. He committed India to a policy of industrialization, to a reorganization of its states on a linguistic basis and, although championing his people's claim to Kashmir, acted with restraint to bring this outstanding dispute with Pakistan to a peaceful solution. His many works include *Soviet Russia* (1929), *India and the World* (1936), *Independence and After* (1950) and an *Autobiography* (1936). His daughter **Indira Gandhi** also served later as prime minister.

NEHRU, Motilal (1861–1931) Indian nationalist leader, lawyer and journalist, father of **Jawaharlal Nehru**. He became a follower of **Mahatma Gandhi** in 1919, founded the *Independent* of Allahabad and became the first president of the reconstructed Indian National Congress.

NEILL, Alexander Sutherland (1883–1973) Scottish educationist and author, born in Kingsmuir, the son of a village schoolmaster. He became a pupil-teacher at Kingsmuir (1899–1903), and then assistant master at Kingskettle School, Fife (1903–06) and Newport Public School, Fife (1906–08), before studying English at Edinburgh University. After a spell in publishing he became headmaster of Gretna Public School (1914–17). After World War I he taught at King Alfred School, Hampstead (1918–20). He was editor of *New Era* (1920–21). He started a community school at Hellerau, near Salzburg, which eventually settled at Leiston, Suffolk, in 1927 as Summerhill School, a co-educational progressive school which 'began as an experiment and became a demonstration'. It was an attempt to provide an education free even of the authoritarian overtones of other progressive schools. He held with **Freud** that 'emotions are more important than intellect'. Like many progressive schools, Summerhill became a school for children, especially American children, from higher income groups. Many pupils were 'difficult' and Neill spent a lot of time in psychotherapy, at first called 'Private Lessons'. He was the most extreme and radical of British progressive schoolmasters and a great publicist, publishing over 20 books from *A Dominie's Log* (1916) to *Neill! Neill! Orange Peel!* (1973). Summerhill's importance is greater as an idea than as an institution. He believed in love and was generally loved, despite a cantankerous character. He ran an independent school, but his philosophy influenced many teachers in the maintained sector and he was revered abroad as well as in Britain.

NEILL, Stephen Charles (1900–84) Scottish missionary and theologian of mission, born in Edinburgh. From 1924 he worked in south India as an evangelist, theological teacher, and latterly as Anglican bishop of Tinnevelly (Tirunelveli). He became deeply concerned with producing Tamil Christian literature and promoting church union. Returning to Europe in 1944 he maintained his ecumenical interests through working with the World Council of Churches and lecturing in Hamburg, Nairobi, and elsewhere. Author of many books, his *Anglicanism* (1958), *Interpretation of the New Testament* (1962), and *History of Christian Missions* (1964) remain classics in their fields, as does the *History of the Ecumenical Movement* (1954, edited with Ruth Rouse).

NEILSON, Donald, originally **Donald Nappey** (1936–) convicted English murderer and kidnapper, born near Bradford. He was convicted of four murders, three of which occurred in 1974 when the victims interrupted him as he was robbing their houses. Because of the black hood he wore as a disguise, he became known as 'the Black Panther'. Three murders were followed by a kidnapping. Seventeen-year-old Lesley Whittle was taken from her home on 13 January 1974, and a ransom demand of £50000 was accompanied by a death-threat. Lesley's naked body was found at the bottom of a ventilation shaft two months later. Neilson evaded the police until late 1975, when a security guard he had shot and wounded was able to provide a description. He was disarmed by police on 11 December 1975. He received life-sentences for the murders and 21 years for kidnapping.

NEILSON, James Beaumont (1792–1865) Scottish engineer, born in Shettleston, Glasgow. He invented the hot-blast which revolutionized iron manufacture in 1828, and was chief engineer and manager of Glasgow Gasworks from 1817 to 1847.

NEILSON, Julia (1868–1957) English actress, born in London. After a brilliant career at the Royal Academy of Music, she made her début at the Lyceum in 1888; her greatest success was as Rosalind in the record-breaking run of *As You like It* (1896–98). She married **Ellen Terry**'s brother Fred (1863–1933), who often appeared with her and who partnered her in management from 1900. Their children Dennis (1895–1932) and Phyllis (1892–1977) Neilson-Terry also became famous for their acting, the latter especially in the title role of *Trilby*, and for their productions.

NEISSER, Ulric Richard Gustav (1928–) German-born American psychologist, born in Kiel. He emigrated with his family to the USA in 1933, gained his PhD at Harvard University in 1956, and subsequently taught at Brandeis University (1957–66), Cornell University (1967–80), and Emory University from 1980. The modern growth of cognitive psychology received a major boost from the publication in 1967 of the first (and most influential) of his books, *Cognitive Psychology*. It synthesized a large body of experimental data on memory, attention, thought and perception in a timely theoretical package, setting the agenda and serving as a framework for much research in the area. However in his later writings he has become critical of the methodology of much cognitive psychology, faulting it for being 'ecologically invalid'.

NEKRASOV, Nikolai Alexeievich (1821–78) Russian lyrical poet of the Realistic school, born near Vinitza, Podolia. He worked as a journalist and critic, and made his name with poems depicting the social wrongs of the peasantry. His unfinished narrative epic, *Who can be Happy and Free in Russia*? (1879), was translated in 1917.

NELSON, (John) Byron Jr (1912–) American golfer, born in Fort Worth, Texas. One of America's outstanding players, he won the US Open in 1939, the US Masters twice (1937, 1942), and the PGA title twice (1940, 1945); in 1945 he won a remarkable eleven consecutive US Tour events—an all-time record. He played in two Ryder Cup matches, and retired in 1955 to become a broadcaster and coach.

NELSON, George (1907–86) American designer, architect and writer, born in Hartford, Connecticut. After graduating in architecture he travelled in Europe during the early 1930s, familiarizing himself with the work of the 'Modern Movement'. Its influence is evident in his design work, the best known being his range of wall storage furniture (1946) for the manufacturer Herman Miller, whose design policy he directed. It was he who commissioned **Charles Eames** to collaborate with the firm. He was editor of *Architectural Forum* from 1935 to 1944, and wrote widely on design and architectural subjects.

NELSON, Horatio, Viscount Nelson (1758–1805) English naval commander, born in Burnham Thorpe rectory, Norfolk. He entered the navy in 1770, made a voyage to the West Indies, served in the arctic expedition of 1773, and afterwards in the East Indies, whence he returned invalided in September 1776. As lieutenant of the *Lowestoft* frigate (1777) he went to Jamaica, and in 1779 was posted to the *Hinchingbrook* frigate. In January 1780 he commanded the naval force in the expedition against San Juan; in 1781 he commissioned the *Albemarle*, and joined the squadron under Lord **Hood** in America. In 1784 he was appointed to the frigate *Boreas* for service in the West Indies, where he enforced the Navigation Act against the Americans. Here he married Mrs Frances Nisbet (1761–1831), the widow of Dr Nisbet of Nevis and in 1787 retired with his wife to Burnham Thorpe for five years. At the outbreak of the French revolutionary wars (1792–1802) he was given command of the *Agamemnon* and accompanied Lord Hood to the Mediterranean. When Toulon was given up to the Allies Nelson was ordered to Naples, where he first met **Emma Hamilton**, the wife of the British ambassador. In 1794 he commanded the naval brigade at the reduction of Bastia and of Calvi, where a blow from a bit of gravel, scattered by a shot, destroyed his right eye. In 1796 he inflicted a signal defeat with Sir **John Jervis** on the Spanish fleet off Cape St Vincent. Promoted rear admiral, he was sent with an inadequate squadron to seize a richly-laden Spanish ship at Santa Cruz, where he lost his right arm. In 1798, commanding the *Vanguard*, he inflicted a massive defeat on the French fleet by his victory at the battle of the Nile, off Aboukir Bay. He returned in triumph to Naples, to a hero's welcome from Emma Hamilton. Nelson was raised to the peerage as Baron Nelson of the Nile, parliament voted him a pension of £2000 a year, the East India Company awarded him £10000 and the king of Naples conferred on him the title of Duke of Bronte, in Sicily. He resigned his command and returned to England with the Hamiltons, where Emma gave birth to a daughter, Horatia and Nelson separated from his wife. In 1801 he was promoted to vice admiral, and appointed second in command of the expedition to the Baltic, under Sir **Hyde Parker**. In the face of Parker's irresolution, Nelson disregarded orders and engaged in the battle of Copenhagen, which he won decisively. In 1803, on the resumption of the war, he was made commander in the Mediterranean. He blockaded Toulon for 18 months, but in March 1805 the French fleet slipped out to sea, and were eventually caught by Nelson off Cape Trafalgar in October 1805. Nelson directed the engagement from the *Victory*, but was mortally wounded by a sniper's bullet in the hour of victory. His body was brought home and buried in St Paul's Cathedral.

NELSON, Robert (1656–1714) English nonjuror born in London, son of a rich Turkish merchant. From the first a (passive) Jacobite, in 1691 he joined the nonjurors, and would not pray for Queen **Anne**. One of the earliest members of the Society for Promoting Christian Knowledge and the Society for the Propagation of the Gospel Nelson was the author of five devotional works, of which *Festivals and Fasts* (1703) sold 10000 copies in four and a half years.

NELSON, Thomas (1780–1861) Scottish publisher, born in Edinburgh. The company of the same name was established in 1798. His son William (1816–87) entered the business in 1835, and did much to improve the city of Edinburgh, including the restoration of Parliament House. Another son, Thomas (1822–92), is credited with the invention of a rotary press (1850), and established an office in London (1844). Specializing in tracts, educational books and affordable reprints, the company's authors included **John Buchan**.

NENNI, Pietro (1891–1980) Italian socialist politician, born in Faenza, Romagna. An agitator at 17, as editor of *Avanti* he was exiled by the Fascists in 1926. In the Spanish War he was political commissar of the Garibaldi Brigade. He became secretary-general of the Italian Socialist party in 1944, vice-premier in the **De Gasperi** coalition cabinet (1945–46), and foreign minister (1946–47). His pro-Soviet party did not break finally with the communists till 1956. In 1963 Nenni became deputy prime minister in the new centre-left four-party coalition government, including social democrats and socialists. In 1966 he succeeded in his longstanding aim of uniting the two groups as the United Socialist party. In the 1968 elections the coalition had overall gains, but the socialists lost ground, mainly to the Communist party, and against Nenni's advice, withdrew from the coalition in June 1968. He was foreign minister in a new coalition in government from December 1968, but resigned in July 1969.

NENNIUS (fl.769) Welsh writer, reputedly author of the early Latin compilation known as the *Historia Britonum*, which purports to give an account of British history from the time of **Julius Caesar** to towards the end of the 7th century. The book gives a mythical account of the origins of the Britons, and recounts the Roman occupation, the settlement of the Saxons and King **Arthur**'s twelve victories. Although it contains fanciful material of doubtful historical significance, its real value lies in its preservation of material needed for the study of early Celtic literature in general, and the Arthurian Legend in particular.

NEOT, St (d.877) According to legend, a monk of Glastonbury who became a hermit in Cornwall. His relics were brought to Crowland about 1003.

NEPOMUK, St John of See **JOHN OF NEPOMUK, St**

NEPOS, Cornelius (c.99–25 BC) Roman historian, a native of Pavia or Hostilia. He was the contemporary of **Cicero**, **Atticus** and **Catullus**. He wrote a lost universal history in three books (*Chronica*), and a series of *Lives of Famous Men* (*De Viris Illustribus*), of which only 25 (mainly Greek warriors and statesmen) survive—untrustworthy, but written in a clear and elegant style. He also wrote love poems and a book of anecdotes (*Exempla*), and lives of the elder **Cato** and **Atticus**.

NEQUAM, Alexander See **NECKAM**

NERI, St Philip (1515–95) Italian mystic, born in Venice and founder of the Oratory. He went to Rome at the age of 18, and for many years spent most of his time in works of charity and instruction, and in solitary prayer. In 1551 he became a priest, and gathered around him a following of disciples which in 1564 became the Congregation of the Oratory and later received the approbation of the pope. The community was finally established at Vallicella, where Philip built a new church (Chiesa Nuova) on the site of Sta Maria. He was canonized with **Ignatius Loyola** and others in 1622.

NERNST, Walter Hermann (1864–1941) German physical chemist, born in Briesen in west Prussia. He became professor of chemistry in Göttingen (1891) and in Berlin (1905), and in 1925 director of the Berlin Physical Institute. In 1906 he proposed the heat theorem (third law of thermodynamics). He also investigated the specific heat of solids at low temperature in connection with quantum theory, and proposed the atom chain-reaction theory in photochemistry. He won the Nobel prize for chemistry in 1920.

NERO (37–68) Roman emperor from 54 to 68, born in Antium, son of Cnaeus Domitius Ahenobarbus and of **Agrippina** the younger daughter of **Germanicus**. His mother became the wife of the emperor **Claudius**, who adopted him (50). After the death of Claudius (54) the Praetorian Guards declared him emperor. His reign began with much promise, but owing to the influence of his mother and his own moral weakness and sensuality, he soon plunged headlong into debauchery, extravagance and tyranny. He caused **Britannicus**, the son of Claudius, to be poisoned, and afterwards murdered his mother and his wife Octavia. In July 64 two-thirds of Rome was destroyed by fire. Nero is stated to have been the incendiary. We are told that he admired the spectacle from a distance, reciting verses about the burning of Troy, but he found a scapegoat in the Christians, many of whom were cruelly put to death. He rebuilt the city with great magnificence, and built a splendid palace on the Palatine hill; but in order to provide for his expenditure Italy and the provinces were plundered. A conspiracy against Nero in 65 failed, and **Seneca** and the poet **Lucan** fell victims to his vengeance. In a fit of passion he murdered his wife Poppaea, by kicking her when she was pregnant. He then offered his hand to Antonia, daughter of Claudius, but was refused; whereupon he had her executed, and married Statilia Messallina, after murdering her husband. He also executed or banished many eminent persons. His vanity led him to seek distinction as poet, philosopher, actor, musician and charioteer. In 68 the Gallic and Spanish legions, and after them the Praetorian Guards, rose against him to make **Galba** emperor. Nero fled to the house of a freedman, four miles from Rome, and saved himself from execution by suicide.

NERUDA, Jan (1834–91) Czech writer, born in Prague. He was a disciple of Romanticism but developed into the foremost classical poet in modern Czech literature. He is also known for some excellent prose and drama.

NERUDA, Madame See **HALLÉ**

NERUDA, Pablo Neftali Reyes (1904–73) Chilean poet, born in Parral, in southern Chile. He was educated at Santiago. He made his name with *Veinte poemas de amor y una canción desesperada* (Twenty Love Poems and a song of Despair, 1924). From 1927 he held diplomatic posts in various East Asian and European countries (in Spain during the Civil War) and in Mexico from 1940. It was on his way back to Chile from Mexico in 1943 that he visited the Inca city of Macchu Picchu, which was the inspiration of one of his greatest poems. Once settled in Chile again he joined the Communist party and was elected to the senate in 1945. When the party was outlawed in 1948 he left to travel in Russia and China, returning in 1952. He was awarded the Stalin prize in 1953. He was the Chilean ambassador in Paris (1970–72). His works include *Residencia en la Tierra* (I, II and III, 1933, 1935, 1947), *Alturas de Macchu Picchu* (1945), which later became part of *Canto General* (published in Mexico, 1950), and *Odas elementales* (1954). In 1971 he was awarded the Nobel prize for literature.

NERVA, Marcus Cocceius (c.32–98) Roman emperor, was elected in 96 by the Senate after the assassination of **Domitianus**. He introduced liberal reforms but lacked military support, and had to adopt **Trajan** as his successor.

NERVAL, Gérard de, properly **Gérard Labrunie** (1808–55) French writer, born in Paris. He published at the age of 20 a translation of *Faust*. Desultory work, a love affair, fits of restless travel, dissipation, gloom and insanity, and death by his own hand, sum up the story of his life. Nerval wrote admirably both in prose and verse. But his travels, criticism, plays and poems are less interesting than his fantastic short tales, the *Contes et facéties* (1852), the semi-autobiographic series of *Filles du feu* (1856) and *La Bohéme galante*.

NERVI, Pier Luigi (1891–1979) Italian architect and engineer. After graduating as an engineer he set up as a building contractor. His many works include the Berta Stadium in Florence (1930–32) and a complex of exhibition halls in Turin (1948–50). He achieved an international reputation by his designs for the two Olympic stadia in Rome (1960), in which bold and imaginative use is made of concrete for roofing in the large areas. He also designed San Francisco cathedral (1970). He was professor at Rome from 1947 to 1961.

NESBIT, Edith (1858–1924) English writer, born in London, the daughter of an agricultural chemist who died when she was three. She was educated at a French convent, and began her literary career by writing poetry, having met the **Rossettis** and their friends. In 1880 she married the Fabian journalist Hubert Bland. To help with the family finances she turned to popular fiction and children's stories about the Bastaple family, including *The Story of the Treasure Seekers* (1899), *The Would-be-Goods* (1901), *Five Children and It* (1902), *The New Treasure Seekers* (1904), *The Railway Children* (1906), and *The Enchanted Castle* (1907). She also wrote other novels, and ghost stories. After her husband's death in 1914 she married an engineer, Terry Tucker, in 1917. Her last novel was *The Lark* (1922).

NESSELRODE, Karl Robert, Count (1780–1862) Russian diplomatist, born in Lisbon, son of the Russian ambassador. He gained the confidence of the Emperor **Alexander I**, took a principal part in the negotiations which ended in the Peace of Paris, and in the Congress of Vienna, and was one of the most active diplomatists of the Holy Alliance. He dealt a deadly blow to the revolutionary cause in Hungary in 1849. He exerted himself to preserve peace with the Western Powers, and in 1854 strove for the re-establishment of peace.

NESTORIUS (d.451) Syrian ecclesiastic, a native of Germanicia in northern Syria. As a priest he became so eminent for his zeal, ascetic life, and eloquence that he was selected as patriarch of Constantinople (428). The presbyter Anastasius having denied that the Virgin **Mary** could be truly called the Mother of God, Nestorius warmly defended him; and so emphasized the distinction of the divine and human natures that antagonists accused him—falsely—of holding that there were two persons in Christ. A controversy ensued, and at a general council in Ephesus in 431 Nestorius was deposed. He was confined in a monastery near Constantinople, was banished to Petra in Arabia, and died after confinement in the Greater Oasis in Upper Egypt and elsewhere. There are still a few Nestorians in Kurdistan and Iraq, and a small body of Christians in India are nominally Nestorian.

NESTROY, Johann (1801–62) Austrian dramatist, born in Vienna. He began life as an operatic singer, turned playwright and was director of the Vienna Carl-Theater (1854–60). His sixty-odd plays, which include *Der böse Geist lumpazivagabundus* (1833), *Einen Jux will er sich machen* (1842), *Der Undbedeu tende* (1846), and *Judith und Holofernes* (1849), are mostly elaborate jibes at theatrical sentimentality characterized by a deft play on words, thoughts and afterthoughts. They revolutionized the Viennese theatre and influenced **Wittgenstein**.

NETTLESHIP, Henry (1839–93) English classical scholar, born in Kettering. Educated at Lancing, Durham, Charterhouse and Corpus Christi College, Oxford, he was elected a fellow of Lincoln, was a master at Harrow (1868–73), and from 1878 was Corpus professor of Latin at Oxford. He completed **Conington**'s *Virgil*, and published *Contributions to Latin Lexicography* (1889).

NEUMANN, (Johann) Balthasar (1687–1753) German architect, born in Eger. He was at first a military engineer in the service of the archbishop of Würzburg, but soon found his true *métier*, and after visiting Paris and absorbing new ideas, he became professor of architecture at Würzburg. Many outstanding examples of the Baroque style were designed by him, the finest being probably Würzburg palace and Schloss Bruchsal.

NEUMANN, John (Johann) von (1903–57) Hungarian-born American mathematician, born in Budapest. He taught at Berlin (1927–29), Hamburg (1929–30) and Princeton (1930–33). In 1933 he became a member of the newly-founded Institute for Advanced Study at Princeton. In 1943 he became a consultant to the Los Alamos project on the construction of the first atomic bomb and in 1954 a member of the Atomic Energy Commission. His best-known mathematical work was on the theory of linear operators, but he also gave a new axiomatization of set theory, later used by **Kurt Gödel**; formulated a precise mathematical description of the recently developed quantum theory (1932); and worked on **Lie** groups. His work during the war led him to study the art of numerical computation and to design some of the earliest computers, and his theoretical description of a programmable computer has governed computer architecture until quite recently. In *The theory of games and economic behavior* (1944), written with G Morgenstern, he created a theory applicable both to games of chance and to games of pure skill, such as chess. These ideas have since become important in mathematical economics and operational research.

NEUMEIER, John (1942–) American dancer, choreographer and artistic director, born in Milwaukee, Wisconsin. A choreographer with a large European following and a strong attachment to Germany, he danced with Stuttgart Ballet (1963–69) before assuming leadership of Frankfurt Ballet (1969–73) and Hamburg Ballet (since 1973). He creates acrobatically expressive contemporary ballets to match the grand themes and important composers he favours in his work.

NEURATH, Baron Konstantin von (1873–1956) German administrator, and Nazi 'Protector of Bohemia and Moravia', born in Klein-Glattbach, Württemberg. After consular service, he joined the German Embassy in Istanbul and in 1921 became ambassador to Italy and in 1930 to Britain. He was foreign minister from 1932 to 1938. From 1939 to 1943 he was the Reich protector of the Czech territories. At the Nuremberg trial he was sentenced to 15 years' imprisonment for war crimes, but released in 1954.

NEURATH, Otto (1882–1945) Austrian philosopher and social theorist, born in Vienna. He was a member of the influential 'Vienna Circle' which also included **Schlick**, **Gödel** and **Carnap**. The group were logical positivists, generally hostile to metaphysics and theology and respectful of empirical science. Neurath is particularly associated with the radical version of positivism called 'physicalism', which aimed to establish an entirely materialist foundation of knowledge. His best philosophical work was published in the group's journal *Erkenntnis*, but he also wrote books on sociology, education and social policy, including *International Picture Language* (1936) and *Modern Man in the Making* (1939), and was active in public affairs as an independent Marxist. He was an energetic organizer, and at different stages in his life was involved with bodies as diverse as the Carnegie Endowment for International Peace (1911–13), the Central Planning Office, Munich (1919), the Museum for House and Town Planning (1919–24), the Social and Economic Museum, Vienna (1924–34), the International Foundation for Visual Education (1933–40), and the International Unity of Science movement (1934–40). He was founding editor of the uncompleted *International Encyclopaedia of Unified Science*.

NEUVILLE, Alphonse Marie de (1836–85) French painter. He is best known for his pictures of French military exploits in the Crimea, Italy and Mexico, and against Germany. He excelled as an illustrator of books.

NEVELSON, Louise, née **Berliawsky** (1899–) Russian-born sculptor and printmaker, born in Kiev. Her family settled in Portland, Maine, in 1905. After marriage in 1920, she studied at the Art Students' League in New York (1929–33) and (after separating from her husband) with the influential theorist **Hans Hofmann** in Munich. In 1932 she worked as an assistant to the Mexican mural-painter **Diego Rivera**. She is best known for her 'environmental' sculptures, abstract, wooden box-like shapes stacked up to form walls and painted white or gold. In 1966 she began to use plexiglas and aluminium.

NEVILLE, Richard See **WARWICK**

NEVINSON, Christopher Richard Wynne (1889–1946) English artist, born in Hampstead, London, the son of **Henry Wood Nevinson**. He studied at the Slade School and for a brief period went into journalism before venturing back to painting and etching in Paris. He became a leader of the pre-1914 avant garde, joining **Emilio Marinetti** as co-signatory of the Futurist Manifesto, published in England in 1914. He volunteered for the Red Cross and was discharged in 1916, but returned the following year as an artist attached to the Bureau of Information. Many of his most famous works reflect his experiences at the front. After the war he moved away from Futurism to paint, in a poetic manner, New York, Paris and the English landscape. In his etchings he particularly maintained an assured realist vein. In 1937 he published the autobiographical *Paint and Prejudice*.

NEVINSON, Henry Woodd (1856–1941) English war correspondent and journalist, born in Leicester. He was correspondent for various papers in, among many other campaigns, the Boer War, the Balkans and the Dardanelles. In 1904 he exposed the Portuguese slave trade in Angola. His publications include *Lines of Life* (verse, 1920), *Essays in Freedom and Rebellion* (1921) and a study of **Goethe** (1931). He also wrote an autobiographical series, *Changes and Chances* (1925–28).

NEWBERY, John (1713–67) English publisher and bookseller, born in Berkshire, a farmer's son. He settled about 1744 in London as a seller of books and patent medicines. He was the first to publish little books for children, and he was himself— perhaps with **Goldsmith**—part author of some of the best of them, notably *Goody Two-Shoes*. In 1758 he started the *Universal Chronicle*, or *Weekly Gazette*, in which the *Idler* appeared. In the *Public Ledger* (1760) appeared Goldsmith's *Citizen of the World*. Since 1922 the Newbery medal has been awarded annually for the best American children's book.

NEWBIGIN, James Edward Lesslie (1909–) English missionary and theologian of mission, born in Northumberland. He went to Madras as a Church of Scotland missionary in 1936 and spent most of the next 38 years in south India, being appointed bishop of Madurai and Ramnad (1947–59) and bishop in Madras (1956–74), in the Church of South India. In his retirement he lectured at the Selly Oak Colleges, was appointed moderator of the United Reformed Church (1978–79), and became a parish minister in Birmingham. His many writings on the uniqueness of Christianity and on Christian responses to secularism in modern Western culture are put in context by his autobiography, *Unfinished Agenda* (1985).

NEWBOLT, Sir Henry John (1862–1939) English poet, born in Bilston, Staffordshire. He studied at Clifton School and Oxford, became a barrister, and published a novel *Taken from the Enemy* (1892), followed by *Mordred: A Tragedy* (1895). He is best known, however, for his sea songs—*Admirals All* (1897), which contained 'Drake's Drum', *The Island Race* (1898), *Songs of the Sea*, and others. In World War I he was controller of telecommunications and an official war historian, and published *The Naval History of the Great War* in 1920.

NEWBY, Eric (1919–) English travel writer, born in London. He worked briefly in advertising before joining a Finnish four-masted bark in 1938, an adventure described in *The Last Grain Race* (1956). In 1942 he was captured off Sicily while trying to rejoin the submarine from which he had landed to attack a German airfield. For some years he worked in the rag trade, which he eagerly left to take *A Short Walk in the Hindu Kush* (1958). In 1963, after some years as a fashion buyer to a chain of department stores, he made a 1200-mile descent of the Ganges, described with typical aplomb and wit in *Slowly Down the Ganges* (1966). Later he became travel editor of *The Observer*. Other significant books are *The Big Red Train Ride* (1978), the story of a journey from Moscow to the Pacific on the Trans-Siberian Railway, *Love and War in the Apennines* (1971), his autobiography, *A Traveller's Life* (1982), and *Round Ireland in Low Gear* (1987), about a wet journey on mountain bikes.

NEWCASTLE See **CAVENDISH** and **PELHAM**

NEWCOMB, Simon (1835–1909) Canadian-born American astronomer, born in Wallace, Nova Scotia. A graduate of Harvard, from 1861 to 1897 he was professor of mathematics in the US navy, had charge of the naval observatory at Washington, and edited the American *Nautical Almanac*. From 1884 to 1894 and 1898 to 1900 he was professor in the Johns Hopkins University. He made many astronomical discoveries, and wrote a long series of works, including *Elements of*

Astronomy, *The Stars*, and his own *Reminiscences of an Astronomer* (1903).

NEWCOMEN, Thomas (1663–1729) English inventor, born in Dartmouth. A blacksmith to trade, in 1698 he teamed up with **Thomas Savery**, who had just patented an atmospheric steam engine for pumping water from mines, and by 1712 had constructed a practical working engine that was widely used in collieries.

NEWDIGATE, Sir Roger (1719–1806) English antiquary, born in Arbury, Warwickshire. He was MP for 36 years for Middlesex (1741–47) and Oxford University (1750–80). He built up a famous collection of antiquities and endowed the Newdigate prize for English verse at Oxford, winners of which have included **Haber**, **Ruskin**, **Matthew Arnold**, **Laurence Binyon** and **John Buchan**.

NEWLANDS, John Alexander Reina (1837–98) English chemist. He worked in a sugar refinery at the Victoria Docks, London. He was the first to arrange the elements in order of atomic number and to see the connection between every eighth. This 'Law of Octaves' brought him ridicule at the time (1864), but it was the first idea of a periodic law and in 1887 the Royal Society awarded him its Davy medal in recognition of his work.

NEWMAN, Barnet (1905–70) American painter, born in New York City. He studied at the Art Students' League in the early 1920s and from 1929 to 1930. Until c.1948 his art was Biomorphic in style, and he was always interested in the primitive, and in the psychiatrist **C G Jung**'s primordial archetypes. In 1948, with **Baziotes**, **Motherwell** and **Rothko**, he founded the 'Subject of the Artist' school, and produced *Onement I*, the first of his stripe paintings, which consist of vertical bands of colour and look forward to the Minimalist art of the 1960s, such as *Vir Heroicus Sublimis* (1950–51) and *Station of the Cross* (1966).

NEWMAN, Ernest (1868–1959) English music critic, born in Liverpool. He was successively music critic of the *Manchester Guardian*, the *Birmingham Post* and the *Sunday Times* (from 1920). His writings are noted for their wit and elegance, and for their strict factual accuracy. His works include studies of **Gluck** and **Hugo Wolf**, and of opera (eg *Opera Nights* and *Wagner Nights*); but it is for his far-reaching studies and deep understanding of **Wagner** that he is best known—his four-volume biography of Wagner (1933–37) is the most complete and authoritative account of the composer in existence. In *A Musical Critic's Holiday* he vindicates music criticism as a valuable study.

NEWMAN, Francis William (1805–97) English scholar, born in London, and brother of **John Henry Newman**. In 1826 he obtained a double first at Worcester College, Oxford, and was elected to a fellowship at Balliol College. After losing sympathy with Anglicanism, he withdrew from the university in 1830, declining subscription to the Thirty-nine Articles. He went as an unsectarian missionary to Baghdad (1830–33), then returned to England and became classical tutor at Bristol College in 1834, professor at Manchester New College (1840) and, from 1846 to 1869, professor of Latin at University College, London. In religion he took a position directly opposite to his brother's, being eager for a religion including whatever is best in all the historical religions. *Phases of Faith* (1853), the best known of his works, was preceded by *The Soul* (1849). His other works include a *History of the Hebrew Monarchy* (1847), and a small book on his brother (1891).

NEWMAN, Sir George (1870–1948) English medical officer and pioneer in public health, born in Leominster. A Quaker, he was educated at Bootham School, King's College London, and Edinburgh University. After qualifying as a doctor, he became medical officer for Bedfordshire (1897–1900) and Finsbury (1900–1907), and chief medical officer for the board of education (1907–19), and worked at the ministry of health from 1919 to 1935. He was responsible for drafting the 1907 Act which empowered local education authorities to provide medical treatment, and he pioneered school medical inspection, probably as influential in raising educational standards as any other factor between the wars. He advocated open-air schools for the delicate, and new techniques in physical education. By 1935, Britain's school medical service was more complex and universal than any other country's. He was also influential in the establishment of the London School of Hygiene and Tropical Medicine. His brillant annual reports, 15 to the minister of health, 26 to the minister of education, have had a lasting effect on the development of public health and education.

NEWMAN, John Henry, (1801–90) English prelate and theologian, born in London, brother of **Francis William Newman**. His father was a banker; his mother, a moderate calvinist, deeply influenced his early religious views. He went up to Trinity College, Oxford, in 1817, and in 1822, in spite of taking a second class degree, he was elected a fellow of Oriel College, and here he formed his close intimacy with **Pusey** and **Richard Hurrell Froude**. In 1824 he was ordained, in 1828 became vicar of St Mary's, Oxford and in 1830 broke definitely with Evangelicalism. His first book, *The Arians of the Fourth Century* (1833), argued that Arianism was a Judaizing heresy which sprang up in Antioch. In 1832–33 Newman accompanied Hurrell Froude and his father on a Mediterranean tour, when many of the poems in *Lyra Apostolica* (1834) were written and also 'Lead, kindly Light'. He was present at **Keble**'s Oxford assize sermon on National Apostasy (July 1833), which he regarded as the beginning of the Tractarian movement ('Oxford Movement'). Into the *Tracts for the Times* Newman threw himself with energy, and he himself composed a number of them. Tract 90 (1841) was the most famous of the tracts. Newman contended that the intention of the Thirty-nine Articles was Catholic in spirit, and that they were aimed at the supremacy of the pope and the popular abuses of Catholic practice, and not at Catholic doctrine. But Tract 90 provoked an explosion which was the end of the Tractarian movement, and brought on the conversion to Rome of those of the Tractarians who were most logical as well as most earnest. Newman struggled for two years longer to think his position tenable, but in 1843 resigned the vicarage of St Mary's, which he had held since 1828, and retired to Littlemore. The magnificent sermon on 'Development in Christian Doctrine' was the last which he preached in the university pulpit. In October 1845 he invited the Passionist Father Dominic to his house at Littlemore in order that he might be received into the Roman Catholic Church. He went to Rome for a year and a half, where he joined the Oratorians and became a priest, and on his return in 1847 he established an Oratorian branch in England at Edgbaston, Birmingham; here he did a great deal of hard work, devoting himself to the sufferers from cholera in 1849 with the utmost zeal. The lectures on *Anglican Difficulties* (1850) drew public attention to Newman's great power of irony and the delicacy of his literary style, and were followed by his lectures on *Catholicism in England* (1851) and *The Idea of a University* (1852) while he was rector of Dublin Catholic University

(1851–58). His long series of Oxford sermons contains some of the finest ever preached from an Anglican pulpit, and his Roman Catholic volumes—*Sermons Addressed to Mixed Congregations* (1849) and *Sermons on Various Occasions* (1857)— though less remarkable for their pathos, are even fuller of fine rhetoric. In 1864 a casual remark by **Charles Kingsley** in *Macmillan's Magazine* on the indifference of the Roman Church to the virtue of truthfulness, an indifference which he asserted that Dr Newman approved, led to a correspondence which resulted in the publication of the remarkable *Apologia pro Vita Sua*. In 1865 he wrote a poem of singular beauty, 'The Dream of Gerontius', republished in *Verses on Various Occasions* (1874). In 1870 he published his *Grammar of Assent*, on the philosophy of faith. In the controversies which led to the Vatican Council, Newman sided with the Inopportunists. He was at this time in vehement opposition to the Ultramontanes under **Manning** and William George Ward, and the bitterness between the two parties ran very high. **Leo XIII**, anxious to show his sympathy with the moderates, in 1879 summoned Newman to Rome to receive the cardinal's hat. He died in Edgbaston.

NEWMAN, Paul (1925–) American film actor and director, born in Cleveland, Ohio. He turned to acting after a knee injury ended a promising sports career. Studying at the Yale School of Drama and the Actor's Studio in New York, he made a disastrous film début in *The Silver Chalice* (1954) but recovered to become one of the key stars of his generation, combining blue-eyed masculinity with a rebellious streak in films like *The Hustler* (1961), *Hud* (1963) and *Cool Hand Luke* (1967). Frustrated by the limitations imposed by his image, he later chose to pursue interests in motor racing, politics and food production, but returned as a powerful character actor and director of such sensitive works as *The Glass Menagerie* (1987). Married to the actress Joanne Woodward since 1958, he has been nominated seven times for the Academy Award, finally winning for *The Color of Money* (1986).

NEWNES, Sir George (1851–1910) English publisher, the son of a Matlock Congregational minister. He was educated at Shireland Hall, Warwickshire, and the City of London School. He founded *Tit-Bits* (1881), *The Strand Magazine* (1891), *The Westminster Gazette* (1873), *Country Life* (1897), *The Wide World Magazine* (1898) and others. He was MP for the Newmarket division (1885–95).

NEWTON, Alfred (1829–1907) English zoologist, born in Geneva. In 1866 he was appointed the first professor of zoology and comparative anatomy at Cambridge, and wrote valuable works on ornithology, the most important being *A Dictionary of Birds* (1893–96).

NEWTON, Sir Charles Thomas (1816–94) English archaeologist, born in Bredwardine. From 1840 to 1852 he held a post at the British Museum. As vice-consul at Mitylene he made important finds (*Discoveries in the Levant*, 1865), and he became keeper of antiquities at the British Museum (1861–1885).

NEWTON, Sir Isaac (1642–1727) English scientist and mathematician, born in Woolsthorpe, Lincolnshire. Educated at Grantham Grammar School and Trinity College, Cambridge, in 1665 he committed to writing his first discovery on fluxions (an early form of differential calculus); and in 1665 or 1666 the fall of an apple in his garden suggested the train of thought that led to the law of gravitation. He turned to study the nature of light and the construction of telescopes. By a variety of experiments upon sunlight refracted through a prism, he concluded that rays of light which differ in colour differ also in refrangibility—a discovery which suggested that the indistinctness of the image formed by the object-glass of telescopes was due to the different coloured rays of light being brought to a focus at different distances. He concluded (rightly for an object-glass consisting of a single lens) that it was impossible to produce a distinct image, and was led to the construction of reflecting telescopes; and the form devised by him is that which reached such perfection in the hands of **William Herschel** and the **Earl of Rosse**. Newton became a fellow of Trinity College, Cambridge in 1667, and Lucasian professor of mathematics in 1669. By 1684 he had demonstrated the whole gravitation theory, which he expounded first in *De Motu Corporum* (1684), and more completely in *Philosophiae Naturalis Principia Mathematica* (1687); this great work was edited and financed by **Edmond Halley**. He also wrote *Opticks* (1703). The part he took in defending the rights of the university against the illegal encroachments of **James II** procured him a seat in the Convention parliament (1689–90). In 1696 he was appointed warden of the Mint, and was master of the Mint from 1699. He again sat in parliament in 1701 for his university. He solved two celebrated problems proposed in June 1696 by **Jean Bernoulli**, as a challenge to the mathematicians of Europe; and performed a similar feat in 1716, by solving a problem proposed by **Gottfried Leibniz**. He superintended the publication of **Flamsteed**'s *Greenwich Observations*, which he required for the working out of his lunar theory—not without much disputing between himself and Flamsteed. In the controversy between Newton and Leibniz as to priority of discovery of the differential calculus of the method of fluxions, Newton acted secretly through his friends. The verdict of science is that the methods were invented independently, and that although Newton was the first inventor, a greater debt is owing to Leibniz for the superior facility and completeness of his method. In 1705 he was knighted by Queen **Anne**; he lies buried in Westminster Abbey. Newton was also a student of alchemy; and he left a remarkable MS on the prophecies of Daniel and on the Apocalypse, a history of creation, and some tracts.

NEWTON, John (1725–1807) English clergyman and writer, born in London, the son of a shipmaster. He sailed with his father for six years, and for ten years engaged in the African slave trade. In 1748 he was converted to Christianity, but still went on slave trading; in 1755 he became tide surveyor at Liverpool; and in 1764 he was offered the curacy of Olney in Buckinghamshire and took orders. **Cowper** went there four years later, and an extraordinary friendship sprang up. In 1779 Newton became rector of St Mary Woolnoth, London. His prose works are little read, apart from the *Remarkable Particulars in his own Life*. But some of his *Olney Hymns* (1779) are still sung, including 'Approach, my soul, the mercy-seat', 'How sweet the name of Jesus sounds' and 'One there is above all others'.

NEXÖ, Martin Andersen (1869–1954) Danish novelist, born in a poor quarter of Copenhagen. He spent his boyhood in Bornholm near Nexö (from where he took his name). From shoemaking and bricklaying he turned to books and teaching, and in 1906 won European fame with *Pelle the Conqueror* (trans 1915–17; 4 parts), describing poor life from within and the growth of the Labour movement.

NEY, Michel (1769–1815) French soldier, born in Saarlouis, a cooper's son. He rose to be adjutant-general (1794) and general of brigade (1796). For the capture of Mannheim he was made general of division in 1799. Under the empire he was made marshal. In

1805 he stormed the entrenchments of Elchingen, and was created Duke of Elchingen. He distinguished himself at Jena and Eylau, and his conduct at Friedland earned him the grand eagle of the Légion d'honneur. Serving in Spain, he quarrelled with **Masséna** and returned to France. In command of the 3rd Corps (1813) he covered himself with glory at Smolensk and Borodino, received the title of Prince of the Moskwa, and led the rear-guard in the disastrous retreat. In 1813 he was present at Lützen and Bautzen, but was defeated by **Bülow** at Dennewitz. He fought heroically at Leipzig, but submitted to **Louis XVIII**, who loaded him with favours. On **Napoleon**'s return from Elba, Ney, sent against him, went over to his old master's side. He opposed and killed Frederick William Brunswick (1771–1815) at Quatrebras, and led the centre at Waterloo. After the capitulation of Paris he was condemned for high treason, and shot.

NGUYEN VAN LINH (1914–) Vietnamese politician, born in what is now northern Vietnam. He joined the anti-colonial Thanh Nien, a forerunner of the current Communist party of Vietnam (CPV), in Haiphong in 1929, and spent much of his subsequent party career in the south, gaining a reputation as a pragmatic reformer. A member of CPV's politburo and secretariat (1976–81), his career suffered a temporary setback during the early 1980s when party conservatives gained the ascendancy. He re-entered the politburo in 1985, becoming CPV leader in December 1986. Under Nguyen's stewardship, there has been notable economic liberalization, and he has undertaken a phased withdrawal of Vietnamese troops from Kampuchea and Laos.

NI TSAN, or **Ni Zan** (1301–74) Chinese landscape painter, calligrapher and poet, born in Wu-hsi (Kiangsu Province). Of the Four Great Masters of the Yuan period, he may not be the greatest, but he certainly is the purest. A passionate lover of culture and aesthetics, he nevertheless spent the last 20 years of his life travelling the lakes of the lower Yangtze river with no possessions. His solitary temperament, search for purity and an absolute spiritual certainty and technical discipline permeate his work. Instead of showing the typical development from early to mature, his work consists of a rational, austere and disembodied assemblage of expressive forms, almost reduced to signs, which constituted a radical departure from all previous traditions.

NIARCHOS, Stavros Spyros (1909–) Greek shipowner, born in Athens. Controller of one of the largest independent fleets in the world, he served during World War II in the Royal Hellenic navy, then pioneered the construction of super-tankers, in competition with his brother-in-law **Aristotle Onassis**. He is also a major art collector.

NICCOLA PISANO See **PISANO, Nicola**

NICHOLAS, St (300–99) Christian prelate, and patron saint of Greece and Russia. He is said to have been the bishop of Myra in Lycia (now Turkey), imprisoned under **Diocletian** and released under **Constantine I**, and his supposed relics were conveyed to Bari in 1087. He is also the patron of children, scholars, merchants, sailors, travellers and thieves. In legend he gave gifts of gold to three poor girls for their dowries, which gave rise to the custom of giving gifts on his feast day (6 December), still followed in the Netherlands and Germany; elsewhere this has transferred to 25 December, Christmas Day, through his identification with 'Santa Claus', an American corruption of his name.

NICHOLAS I, 'the Great', St (c.820–867) pope from 858 to 867. He asserted the supremacy of the church against secular rulers such as Lothair, king of Lorraine (whose divorce he forbade) and church leaders like **Hincmar**, archbishop of Reims. He had problems with the Eastern church, however, particularly with **Photius**, whom he tried to depose as patriarch of Constantinople, leading to the Photian schism. His feast day is 13 November.

NICHOLAS II, originally Gerard of Burgundy (c.980–1061) pope from 1058 to 1061. He enacted regulations for papal elections.

NICHOLAS V, originally Pietro Rainalducci (d.1033) antipope from 1328 to 1330. He set up in opposition to **John XXII**.

NICHOLAS V, originally **Tommaso Parentucelli** (1397–1455) pope from 1447. He prevailed on the antipope, Felix V (**Amadeus VIII**) to abdicate in 1449, and thus restored the peace of the Church. A liberal patron of scholars, he rebuilt the Vatican, restored St Peter's, and the Vatican Library. He vainly endeavoured to arouse Europe to the duty of succouring the Greek empire.

NICHOLAS I (1796–1855) emperor of Russia, third son of **Paul**. In 1817 he married the daughter of **Frederick-William III** of Prussia. As Grand Duke Constantine had resigned his right to the throne in 1822, Nicholas became tsar on the death of the elder brother **Alexander I** (1825), and suppressed a military conspiracy with vigour and cruelty. After a brief outburst of reforming zeal, he reverted to the ancient policy of the tsars—absolute despotism, supported by military power. Wars with Persia and Turkey increased Russia's territories. The movement of 1830 in the west of Europe was followed by a Polish rising, which was suppressed after a severe contest of nine months; and Nicholas, converting Poland into a Russian province, strove to extinguish the Polish nationality. In Russia intellectual activity was kept under official guidance. The tsar's Panslavism also prompted him to Russianize all the inhabitants of the empire, and to convert Roman Catholics and Protestants to the Russian Greek church. During the political storm of 1848–49 he assisted the emperor of Austria in quelling the Hungarian insurrection, and tightened the alliance with Prussia. The re-establishment of the French empire confirmed these alliances, and Nicholas thought that the time had come for absorbing Turkey; but the opposition of Britain and France brought on the Crimean War, during which he died.

NICHOLAS II (1868–1918) emperor of Russia. The eldest son of **Alexander III**, he succeeded his father in 1894. He married a princess of Hesse (née **Alexandra Feodorovna**), and initiated (1898) The Hague Peace Conference. His reign was marked by the alliance with France, *entente* with Britain, disastrous war with Japan (1904–05), and the establishment of the Duma (1906). He took command of the Russian armies against the Central Powers in 1915. Forced to abdicate (17 March 1917) at the revolution, he was shot with his entire family at Yekaterinburg by the Red Guards (July 1918).

NICHOLAS, Grand-Duke (1856–1929) Russian soldier, nephew of **Alexander II**. In World War I he was Russian commander-in-chief against Germany and Austria, and commander-in-chief in the Caucasus (1915–17). After 1919 he lived quietly in France.

NICHOLAS OF CUSA (1401–64) German philosopher, scientist and churchman, born in Cues, Trier. He studied at Heidelberg (1416) and Padua (1417–23), received a doctorate in canon law, and was ordained about 1430. He was active at the Council of Basel in 1432, supporting in his *De concordantia catholica* (1433) the 'conciliarists' who advocated the supremacy of Church councils against the pope; but he later switched allegiance to the papal party, undertook various papal missions as a diplomat, and was created cardinal in 1448. His main philosophical work is *De docta ignorantia* (1440), which emphasizes the limitations of human knowledge but at the same time argues that faith, science, theology and philosophy all pursue convergent though different paths towards the ultimately unattainable goal of absolute reality. He also wrote on mathematics and cosmology and anticipated **Copernicus** in his non-geocentric theories.

NICHOLLS, Sir Douglas Ralph (1906–88) Australian clergyman, activist and administrator, born in southern New South Wales, near Echuca, Victoria. Reared and educated on a mission station, he worked on the land until his Australian-rules football skills took him to Melbourne where, in 1935, he became the first aboriginal to represent his state in football. As pastor, he established an aborigines' mission at Fitzroy in 1943 and worked actively for aboriginal advancement. Having received the MBE in 1957, in 1972 he became the first aboriginal to be knighted. In December 1976 he was appointed governor of South Australia, but was forced to relinquish the position through ill-health four months later.

NICHOLS, John (1745–1826) English printer and writer. He was apprenticed to **William Bowyer** in 1757 and became his successor in 1777. He was editor of the *Gentleman's Magazine* (1778–1826). He edited and published literary and historical works, including *Bibliotheca Topographica* (1780–90), *The History and Antiquities of Leicestershire* (1795–1815) and *Literary Anecdotes of the Eighteenth Century* (1812–15). He also published the works of **Swift** in 19 volumes (1801) and *Illustrations of Literary History of the Eighteenth Century* (1817–31).

NICHOLS, John Bowyer (1779–1863) English printer, son of **John Nichols**. He succeeded his father as editor of the *Gentleman's Magazine* for a time and published many important county histories.

NICHOLS, John Gough (1806–73) son of **John Bowyer Nichols**. He, too, edited the *Gentleman's Magazine* and also made valuable contributions to English history and genealogy.

NICHOLS, Mike, originally **Michael Igor Peschkowsky** (1931–) German-born American film and theatre director, born in Berlin. A US citizen from 1944, he studied acting with **Lee Strasberg** before joining the improvisational theatre group Compass Players in Chicago (1955–57). From 1957 to 1961 he gained great popularity on radio, records and stage with Elaine May dissecting the American psyche through offbeat, satirical duologues. The partnership culminated in a year-long Broadway engagement after which he turned to direction, revealing a flair for comedy, a liking for literate scripts and a talent to elicit polished performances from his casts. He has received seven Tony Awards for his theatre work which includes *Barefoot in the Park* (1963), *The Odd Couple* (1965), *The Prisoner of Second Avenue* (1971) and *The Real Thing* (1984). He also produced the hit musical *Annie* (1977). He directed his first film, *Who's Afraid of Virginia Woolf?*, in 1966 and received an Academy Award for *The Graduate* (1967). His films offer sardonic portraits of American life, social mores and sexual politics, and include *Catch* 22 (1970), *Carnal Knowledge* (1971) and *Working Girl* (1988).

NICHOLSON, Ben (1894–1982) English artist, born in Denham, London, son of Sir **William Newzam Prior Nicholson**. He exhibited with the Paris Abstraction-Création group in 1933–34 and at the Venice Biennale in 1954, designed a mural panel for the Festival of Britain (1951) and in 1952 executed another for the Time-Life building in London. As one of the leading abstract artists, he gained an international reputation and won the first Guggenheim award in 1957. Although he produced a number of purely geometrical paintings and reliefs, in general he used conventional still-life objects as a starting point for his finely drawn and subtly balanced and coloured variations. Three times married, his second wife was **Barbara Hepworth**.

NICHOLSON, Jack (1937–) American film actor, born in Neptune, New Jersey. An office boy at M-G-M, he studied acting with Jeff Corey and worked with the Players Ring Theater before making his film début in *Cry Baby Killer* (1958). He spent the next decade in a succession of low budget exploitation films before a supporting role in *Easy Rider* (1969) brought him belated critical recognition. He then established himself as one of the best portrayers of explosive nonconformists in *Five Easy Pieces* (1970) and *The Last Detail* (1973). His intense charisma and acute sense of humour have illuminated a wide range of characters in such diverse films as *Chinatown* (1974), *The Shining* (1980), *Prizzi's Honor* (1985) and *Ironweed* (1987). He has also written scripts and occasionally directs. Nominated nine times for the Academy Award, he won Oscars for *One Flew Over the Cuckoo's Nest* (1975) and *Terms of Endearment* (1983).

NICHOLSON, John (1822–57) Irish soldier and administrator, born in Lisburn (or possibly Dublin). In 1839 he joined the East India Company's service, and in 1842 was captured at Ghazni in Afghanistan. During the Sikh rebellion of 1848 he saved the fortress of Attock, and at Chillianwalla and Gujrat earned the special approval of Lord **Gough**. He was appointed deputy-commissioner (1851) of the Punjab, and during the Indian Mutiny of 1857 he did more than any other man to hold the province. As brigadier-general, he led the storming party at the siege of Delhi, and was mortally wounded.

NICHOLSON, Joseph Shield (1850–1927) English economist, born in Wrawby near Brigg. From 1880 to 1925 he was professor of political economy at Edinburgh. He wrote on *Money* (1888), *Principles of Political Economy* (3 vols, 1893–1901), and other works on economics advocating the ideas of **Adam Smith**.

NICHOLSON, Seth Barnes (1891–1963) American astronomer, born in Springfield, Illinois. On the staff of the Mount Wilson Observatory (1915–57), he discovered the 9th, 10th, and 11th satellites of Jupiter.

NICHOLSON, William (1753–1815) English physicist. A waterworks engineer for Portsmouth and Gosport, he invented the hydrometer named after him, and also a machine for printing on linen. He constructed the first voltaic pile in England, and in so doing discovered that water could be dissociated by electricity (1800).

NICHOLSON, William (1816–64) Scots-born Australian statesman, born near Whitehaven. He emigrated as a grocer to Melbourne in 1841, became mayor 1850, and premier of Victoria 1859. He had the ballot adopted in 1855.

NICHOLSON, Sir William Newzam Prior (1872–1949) English artist, born in Newark. He studied in Paris and was influenced by **Whistler** and **Manet**. He became a fashionable portrait painter, but is principally remembered for the posters produced (with his brother-in-law, James Pryde) under the name of J and W Beggarstaff, for his woodcut book illustrations, and for his glowing still-life paintings (eg, the *Mushrooms* in the Tate Gallery).

NICIAS (d.413 BC) Athenian statesman and soldier. A member of the aristocratic party, he opposed **Cleon** and **Alcibiades**. In 427–426 BC he defeated the Spartans and the Corinthians. In 424 he ravaged Laconia, but in 421 made a short-lived peace between Sparta and Athens (the Peace of Nicias). In the naval expedition against Sicily (418) he was one of the commanders, albeit reluctantly. He laid siege to Syracuse (415), and was at first successful, but subsequently experienced a series of disasters; his troops were forced to surrender, and he was put to death.

NICKLAUS, Jack (1940–) American golfer, born in Columbus, Ohio, known as the 'Golden Bear'. As a student at Ohio State University he won two US Amateur Championships and played in the Walker Cup twice before turning professional in 1962. He immediately won the US Open (1962), and since then has won more major tournaments than any other player in the world: four US Opens, three British Opens, five PGA championships, and six US Masters—the last from semi-retirement in 1986. He is the first golfer to have earned more than $84 million from the game, and is now in great demand as a golf course architect.

NICOL, Erskine (1825–1904) Scottish painter, born in Leith. He studied art in Edinburgh and taught in Dublin before moving to London in 1862. He painted homely incidents in Irish and Scottish life, such as *Donnybrook Fair.*

NICOL, William (c.1744–1797) Scottish schoolmaster, a classics master in the High School of Edinburgh. He was a convivial intimate of **Robert Burns** who immortalized him in the poem 'Willie Brewed a Peck O' Maut'.

NICOL, William (1768–1851) Scotish geologist and physicist, born in Edinburgh, where he lectured in natural philosophy at the university. In 1828 he invented the Nicol prism which utilizes the doubly refracting property of Iceland Spar, and which proved invaluable in the investigation of polarized light. He also devised a new method of preparing thin sections of rocks for the microscope, by cementing the specimen to the glass slide and then grinding until it was possible to view by transmitted light, thus revealing the mineral's internal structure. His reluctance to publish delayed the use of thin sections for some 40 years, until **H C Sorby** and others introduced them into petrology.

NICOLAI, Christoph Friedrich (1733–1811) German author, bookseller and publisher, born in Berlin. A champion of the German Enlightenment, he soon distinguished himself by a series of critical letters (1756), contributed to many literary journals, and for many years edited the *Allgemeine deutsche Bibliothek* (106 vols, 1765–92). He wrote topographical works, satires, anecdotes of **Frederick II, the Great**, and an autobiography, recording strange apparitions and hallucinations.

NICOLAI, Otto (1810–49) German composer, born in Königsberg. In 1847 he became kapellmeister at Berlin, where his opera *The Merry Wives of Windsor* was produced just before he died.

NICOLAS, Sir Nicholas Harris (1799–1848) English antiquary, born in Dartmouth. He served in the navy (1808–16), and was called to the bar in 1825. He devoted himself chiefly to genealogical and historical studies; his works included *History of British Orders of Knighthood* (1841–42), and *Synopsis of the Peerage* (1825).

NICOLE, Pierre (1625–95) French Jansenist theologian, born in Chartres. He was one of the most distinguished of the Port Royalists, the friend of **Antoine Arnauld** and **Pascal**, and author of *The Logic of Port Royal* (1662) and *Essais de morale* (1671 *et seq*).

NICOLINI See **PATTI, Adelina**

NICOLL, Sir William Robertson (1851–1923) Scottish churchman and man of letters (pseudonym Claudius Clear), born in Lumsden, Aberdeenshire. Educated at Aberdeen, he was Free Church minister at Dufftown (1874–77) and Kelso (1877–85). He moved to London for health reasons and turned to literary work, and became editor of *The Expositor* and *The British Weekly*. In 1891 he founded *The Bookman*, and in 1893 *The Woman at Home*, whose main contributor was **Annie S Swan**. He wrote books on theology, and edited *The Bookman's Illustrated History of English Literature* (1897) and the complete works of **Emily Brontë** (1910). His collected articles were published as *The Daybook of Claudius Clear* (1905) and *A Bookman's Letters* (1915).

NICOLLE, Charles Jules Henri (1866–1936) French physician and bacteriologist, a pupil of **Louis Pasteur**. He was director of the Pasteur Institute at Tunis (1903), and professor at the Collège de France (1932). He discovered that the body louse is a transmitter of typhus fever, and in 1928 was awarded the Nobel prize for physiology or medicine.

NICOLSON, Adela Florence See **HOPE, Sir John**

NICOLSON, Alexander (1827–93) Scottish Gaelic scholar, born in Usabost in Skye. Educated for the Free Church at Edinburgh, he became assistant to the philosopher Sir **William Hamilton**, and became an advocate. A prolific writer in both English and Gaelic, he was a member of the Napier Commission that reported on crofting conditions in the Highlands and Islands (1884) and established the Crofters' Commission. He helped to revise the Gaelic Bible, and published *A Collection of Gaelic Proverbs and Familiar Phrases* (1881).

NICOLSON, Sir Harold George (1886–1968) English diplomat, author and critic, born in Teheran, where his father (later 1st Baron Carnock) was British chargé d'affaires. Educated at Wellington College and Balliol College, Oxford, he had a distinguished career as a diplomat, entering the service in 1909, and holding posts in Madrid, Constantinople, Teheran and Berlin until his resignation in 1929, when he turned to journalism. From 1935 to 1945 he was National Liberal MP for West Leicester. He wrote several biographies, including those of **Tennyson**, **Swinburne** and the official one of **George V**, as well as books on history, politics and, in *Good Behaviour* (1955), manners. He was highly regarded as a literary critic. In 1913 he married **Victoria Sackville-West**.

NICOLSON, William (1655–1727) English prelate and antiquary, born in Plumbland. He became successively bishop of Carlisle (1702) and Derry (1718). His main interest was the collection and preservation of official papers, which he published as the *Historical Library* (English, Scottish and Irish), and other important works and colllections.

NICOT, Jean (1530–1600) French diplomat and scholar, born in Nîmes. He became French ambassador in Lisbon (1559–61), and in 1561 introduced into France from Portugal the tobacco plant, called after him *Nicotiana*. The word 'nicotine' derives from his name. He compiled one of the first French dictionaries (1606).

NIEBUHR, Barthold Georg (1776–1831) German historian, born in Copenhagen, son of **Carsten Niebuhr**. He studied at Kiel, London and Edinburgh (1798–99). In 1800 he entered the Danish state service, and in 1806 the Prussian civil service. The opening of Berlin University in 1810 introduced a new era in his life. He gave (1810–12) a course of lectures on Roman history, which established his position as one of the most original and philosophical of modern historians. In 1816 he was appointed Prussian ambassador at the papal court, and on his return in 1823 he took up his residence at Bonn, where his lectures gave a powerful impetus to historical learning. He possessed great intuitive sagacity in sifting true from false historic evidence; and though his scepticism as to the credibility of early history goes too far, the bulk of his contribution to history still stands substantially unshaken. His *Römische Geschichte* and other important works were translated into English.

NIEBUHR, Carsten (1733–1815) German traveller, born in Lauenburg. From 1761 to 1767 he was on a Danish expedition to explore Yemen, of which he was the only survivor. His five companions died during the journey, but in his reports he gave them full credit, and provided important and accurate scientific accounts of Arabia.

NIEBUHR, Helmut Richard (1894–1962) American theologian, born in Wright City, Missouri, brother of **Reinhold Niebuhr.** He taught at Yale University from 1931, becoming professor of theology and Christian ethics and director of graduate studies. Like his brother, he had enormous influence on generations of students. His classic study *The Meaning of Revelation* (1941) was followed by *Christ and Culture* (1951), *Radical Monotheism and Western Culture* (1960), and *The Responsible Self* (1963): a series of books advocating critical reflection on the relation between faith and moral action and a quest for a Christian transformation of society. Niebuhr's concern that ministers be adequately trained for this task was reflected in his direction of a survey of American Protestant theological education (1954–56).

NIEBUHR, Reinhold (1892–1971) American theologian, born in Wright City, Missouri, brother of **Helmut Richard Niebuhr**. Educated at Elmhurst (Illinois) College, Eden Theological Seminary and Yale Divinity School, he became an evangelical pastor in working-class Detroit (1915–28) and professor of Christian ethics in the Union Theological Seminary, New York, from 1928 to 1960. An advocate of Christian Realism, he wrote *Moral Man and Immoral Society* (1932), *The Nature and Destiny of Man* (2 vols, 1941–43), *Faith and History* (1949), *The Irony of American History* (1952), *Structure of Nations and Empires* (1959) and many other books.

NIEL, Adolphe (1802–69) French soldier, born in Muret (Upper Garonne). He entered the army as an engineer officer, and took part in the storming of Constantine in Algeria (1836), the siege of Rome (1849), the bombardment of Bomarsund (1854), the fall of Sebastopol (1856), and the battles of Magenta and Solferino (1859); and became minister of war in 1867.

NIELSEN, Carl August (1865–1931) Danish composer, born in Nörre-Lyndelse, near Odense, Fünen, the son of a house-painter who was also a village fiddler. He became a bandsman at Odense, and in 1883 entered Copenhagen Conservatory. His compositions from this period—including the G minor quartet and oboe fantasias—are not revolutionary, being rather in the tradition of **Gade**, but with his first symphony (1894) his progressive tonality and rhythmic audacity become apparent, though still within a classical structure. His second symphony ('The Four Temperaments', 1901–02) shows the first use in Danish music of polytonality, along with the contrapuntal style which was to become characteristic of him. His other works include four further symphonies (1912, 1916, 1922 and 1925), the tragic opera *Saul and David* (1902), the comic opera *Masquerade* (1906), chamber music, concertos for flute, clarinet and violin, and a huge organ work, *Commotio* (1931). In 1915 he was appointed director of Copenhagen Conservatory. Denmark's greatest 20th-century composer, striving through new harmonies, rhythms and melodic ideas of truly Nordic character to divest Danish music of its prevalent romanticism, Nielsen was also a conductor of note, and exerted a tremendous influence on the musical development of Denmark.

NIEMBSCH See **LENAU, Nikolaus**

NIEMEYER, Oscar (1907–) Brazilian architect, born in Rio de Janeiro. He studied at the National School of Fine Arts in Brazil and began work in the office of **Lúcio Costa,** (1935). From 1936 to 1943 he joined Costa and others to design the ministry of education and public health, Rio (1937–42, with **Le Corbusier** as consultant architect). With Costa he designed the Brazilian Pavilion at the New York World Fair (1939). He became architectural adviser to Nova Cap, serving as its chief architect (1957–59), co-ordinating the development of Brasilia. His Expressionist powers are well displayed in a group at Pampúlha, including the Church of São Francisco (1942–44), where parabolic sections indicate the organic, anti-rationalist principles underlying his works. Further major works are the Exhibition Hall, São Paolo (1953), and the President's Palace, Law Courts and Cathedrals, Brasilia.

NIEMÖLLER, Martin (1892–1984) German Lutheran pastor and outspoken opponent of **Hitler**, born in Lippstadt, Westphalia. He rose from midshipman to become one of Germany's ace submarine commanders in World War I, studied theology, was ordained in 1924 and became pastor at Berlin-Dahlem in 1931. Summoned with other Protestant church leaders to meet Hitler, who wished to get their co-operation for the Nazi régime, Niemöller declared that he, like Hitler, also had a responsibility for the German people, given by God, which he could not permit Hitler to take away from him. His house was ransacked by the Gestapo and, continuing openly to preach against the Führer, he was arrested and confined from 1937 to 1945 in Sachsenhausen and Dachau concentration camps. Acclaimed by the Allies as one of the few 'good Germans' at the end of the war, he caused great astonishment when it was discovered that he had in 1941 volunteered in vain to serve again in the German navy, despite his opposition to Hitler. His explanation was that he had a duty to 'give unto Caesar what is Caesar's'. In 1945 he was responsible for the 'Declaration of Guilt' by the German churches for not opposing Hitler more strenuously. On the other hand he loudly condemned the abuses of the de-Nazification courts. He vigorously opposed German rearmament and the nuclear arms race. Federal Germany he described as 'begotten in Rome and born in Washington'. From 1947 to 1964 he was church president of the Evangelical church in Hesse and Nassau. In 1961 he became president of the World Council of Churches. He wrote *Vom U-Boot zur Kanzel*, 'From U-Boat to the Pulpit' (1934), and collections of his sermons were published in 1935, 1939, 1946, and 1956, particularly *Six Dachau Sermons* (1946, trans 1959).

NIEPCE, Joseph Nicéphore (1765–1833) French chemist, born in Chalon-sur-Saône. One of the inventors of photography, he served in the army, and in 1795 became administrator of Nice. At Chalon in 1801 he devoted himself to chemistry, and at length succeeded in producing a photograph on metal (1826), said to be the world's first. From 1829 he co-operated with **Louis Daguerre** in further research.

NIETZSCHE, Friedrich Wilhelm (1844–1900) German philosopher, scholar and writer, though really unclassifiable by conventional labels. He was born in

Röcken, Saxony, son of a Lutheran pastor (who died in 1849), and proved himself a brilliant classical student at the school at Schulpforta and at the universities of Bonn and Leipzig. He was appointed professor of classical philology at the University of Basel at the age of 24 and became a Swiss citizen, serving briefly as a medical orderly in 1870 in the Franco-Prussian war but returning to the university in poor health. His first book *Die Geburt der Tragödie* (1872, The Birth of Tragedy), with its celebrated comparison between 'Dionysian' and 'Apollonian' values, was dedicated to **Richard Wagner**, who had become a friend and whose operas he regarded as the true successors to Greek tragedy. But he broke violently with Wagner in 1876, nominally at least because he thought the Christian convictions expressed in *Parsifal* 'mere playacting' and political expediency. In 1878 he was forced to resign his university position after worsening bouts of his psychosomatic illnesses and he spent most of the next ten years at various resorts in France, Italy and Switzerland writing and trying to recover his 'shattered health'. But in 1889 he had a complete mental and physical breakdown, a collapse that was probably syphilitic in origin, and he was nursed for the next twelve years first by his mother at Naumberg then by his sister Elizabeth at Weimar. He never recovered his sanity. In the 16 years from 1872 he had produced a stream of brilliant, unconventional works, often aphoristic or poetical in form, which have secured him an enormous, if sometimes cultish, influence in modern intellectual history. The best known writings are: *Unzeitgemässe Betrachtungen* (1873–76, Untimely Meditations), *Die Fröliche Wissenschaft* (1882, The Joyous Science), *Also Sprach Zarathustra* (1883–92, Thus Spake Zarathustra), *Jenseits von Gut und Böse* (1886, Beyond Good and Evil), *Zur genealogie der Moral* (1887, On the Genealogy of Morals), and *Ecce Homo* (his autobiography, completed in 1888 but withheld by his sister and not published till 1908). One cannot derive systematic 'theories' from these often highly-wrought literary works but the characteristic themes are: the vehement repudiation of Christian and liberal ethics, the detestation of democratic ideals, the celebration of the *Übermensch* (superman) who can create and impose his own law, the death of God, and the life-affirming 'will to power'. His reputation suffered when his views were taken up in a simple-minded and perverted form by the German Nazis, but he is now regarded as a major, though very individual, influence on many strands of 20th century thought, including existentialism and psychoanalysis, and on figures as various as **Jaspers**, **Heidegger**, **Mann**, **Yeats**, **Mannheim** and **Foucault**.

NIEUWLAND, Julius Arthur (1878–1936) Belgian-born American chemist. In 1903 he took holy orders, and later became professor of organic chemistry at Notre Dame university (1918). His researches led to the production of the first commercially successful synthetic rubber, **Du Pont**'s 'neoprene', in 1932.

NIGHTINGALE, Florence (1820–1910) English nurse and hospital reformer, born in Florence, daughter of William Edward Nightingale of Embly Park, Hampshire. She trained as a nurse at Kaiserswerth (1851) and Paris and in 1853 became superintendent of a hospital for invalid women in London. In the Crimean War she volunteered for duty and took 38 nurses to Scutari in 1854. She organized the barracks hospital after the battle of Inkerman (5 November) and by discipline and sanitation reduced the hospital mortality rate drastically. She returned to England in 1856 and a fund of £50 000 was subscribed to enable her to form an institution for the training of nurses at St Thomas's and at King's College Hospital. She devoted many years to the question of army sanitary reform, to the improvement of nursing and to public health in India. Her main work, *Notes on Nursing* (1859), went through many editions.

NIJINSKA, Bronislava (1891–1972) Russian ballet dancer and choreographer, born in Minsk, sister of **Vaslav Nijinsky**. Her parents were professional dancers, and she, like her brother, studied at the Imperial Ballet School in St Petersburg, graduating in 1908 and going on to become a soloist with the Maryinsky company. She danced with **Diaghilev's** Ballet Russe in Paris and London before returning to Russia during World War I, when she started a school in Kiev, but went back to Diaghilev in 1921, following **Léonide Massine** as principal choreographer. Among the ballets she created for the company were her masterpieces *Les Noces* (1923) and *Les Biches* (1924). After working in Buenos Aires and for Ida Rubinstein's company in Paris she briefly formed her own company in 1932. From 1935 she choreographed for many companies in Europe and the USA, but lived mainly in the USA and started a ballet school in Los Angeles (1938). She was persuaded to stage a notable revival of *Les Noces* and *Les Biches* at Covent Garden in 1964.

NIJINSKY, Vaslav (1890–1950) Russian dancer, born in Kiev. Considered to be the greatest male dancer of the 20th century, he was, like his sister **Bronislava Nijinska**, trained at the Imperial Ballet School in St Petersburg, and first appeared in ballet at the Maryinski Theatre. As the leading dancer in **Diaghilev**'s Ballet Russe, taken to Paris in 1909, he became enormously popular, and in 1911 he appeared as Petrouchka in the first perfomance of **Stravinsky**'s ballet. His choreographic portfolio is slim but has two exceptional high points, *L'Après-midi d'un Faune* (1912) and *Sacre du Printemps* (1913). He married in 1913 and was interned in Hungary during the early part of World War I. He rejoined Diaghilev for a world tour, but was diagnosed a paranoid schizophrenic in 1917. Even before his death Nijinsky had become a legendary figure.

NIKISCH, Arthur (1855–1922) Hungarian conductor and composer. He was conductor of the Boston Symphony Orchestra (1889–93), the Gewandhaus Orchestra of Leipzig from 1895, and the Berlin Philharmonic Orchestra from 1897. His compositions include a string quartet and a symphony.

NIKODIM, Boris Georgyevich Rotov (1929–78) Russian prelate, and metropolitan of Leningrad, born in Frolovo. He entered the Orthodox monastery at Ryazan, and assumed the name of Nikodim when made deacon in 1947. His rise was meteoric, He combined parochial work with studies at Leningrad, and was archimandrite in charge of the Russian Orthodox Mission in Jerusalem before consecration in 1960 as bishop of Podolsk and head of foreign relations of the Russian church, which led into the World Council of Churches amid geat acclaim in 1961. Two years later, still only 34, he was appointed metropolitan, and became known at ecumenical meetings all over the world. He collapsed and died during an audience with Pope **John Paul I** in the Vatican.

NIKOLAIS, Alwin (1910–) American dancer, choreographer, teacher and director, born in Southington, Connecticut. A pianist for silent films and former puppeteer, he turned to dance and studied with **Hanya Holm**, after seeing **Mary Wigman** perform in 1933. Moving to New York City in 1948, he produced children's theatre at the Henry Street Playhouse, out of which he founded his own dance company, Nikolais Dance Theatre. His style was idiosyncratic and uninhibited by conventional artistic boundaries. He designed his own sets with painted slides and tin cans punctured with holes to fantastic effect, and composed scores out of chopped tape. Always an innovator, he became, in 1963, the first artist to use the Moog Synthesizer. His work includes *Noumenon* (1953), *Kaleidescope* (1956), *Imago* (1963), *Sanctum* (1964), *Gallery* (1978) and, more recently for the Paris Opéra Ballet, *Schema* (1980) and *Arc-en-Ciel* (1987).

NILAND, D'Arcy Francis (1919–67) Australian author, born in Glen Innes, New South Wales. After his early years working in the bush, he went to Sydney and in 1942 married the New Zealand writer **Ruth Park**, after which he settled down to writing. Between 1949 and 1952 he won many prizes for short stories and novels, and in 1955 achieved international fame with his novel *The Shiralee*. This was followed by *Call Me When the Cross Turns Over* (1957) and four more novels. Niland also wrote radio and television plays, and hundreds of short stories, some of which were published in four books between 1961 and 1966.

NILES, Daniel Thambyrajah (1908–70) Tamil Methodist and ecumenical leader and evangelist, born near Jaffna. A fourth-generation Tamil Christian he became increasingly involved in the developing ecumenical movement. The youngest delegate at the 1938 International Missionary Council Tambaram Conference, he was appointed a president of the World Council of Churches after Uppsala (1968), and at the time of his death was chairman of the East Asian Christian Conference and president of the Methodist church in Ceylon. He wrote 45 hymns for the *EACC Hymnal* (1963), and these, along with the posthumous *A Testament of Faith* (1972), convey the spirit of his many books.

NILSSON, (Märta) Birgit (1922–) Swedish operatic soprano, born near Karup, Kristianstadslaen. She was educated at the Stockholm Royal Academy of Music, where her teachers included **Joseph Hislop**. Following her début in 1946, she sang with the Stockholm Royal Opera (1947–51), and at Bayreuth Festivals from 1953 to 1970. She was the leading Wagnerian soprano of that period, having a voice of exceptional power, stamina and intense personality. She sang at most of the great houses and festivals of the world, and her repertoire included **Verdi**, **Puccini** and **Strauss**. She retired from the stage in 1982.

NILSSON, Christine (1843–1921) Swedish operatic singer, born in Wexiö. She made her début at Paris in 1864, and became a leading prima donna in Europe and the USA. She retired in 1888.

NILSSON, Lennart (1922–) Swedish photographer. He worked as a freelance press photographer and gained respect for several portraits such as *Sweden in Profiles* (1954) but went on to pioneer microfilm showing the anatomy of plants and animals. He has since become best known for his microbiological and medical photography. Working in close contact with medical teams he has successfully combined the techniques of photography and endoscopy. He perfected special lenses to film inside the human body, which enabled him to produce pictures of the human foetus in the womb from conception to birth. His pictorial record entitled *Ett barn blir till* (1965, The Everyday Miracle: A Child is Born), which won him the American National Press Association Picture of the Year Award, was syndicated and gained international fame.

NIMERI, (Nemery) Gaafar Mohamed al- (1930–) Sudanese soldier and politician, born in Omdurman. Educated at Sudan Military College in Khartoum, he joined the army, and continued his training in Egypt, where he became a disciple of **Gamal Abdel Nasser**. In 1969, with the rank of colonel, he led the military coup which removed the civilian government and established a Revolutionary Command Council (RCC). In 1971, under a new constitution, he became president. Although twice re-elected, by the 1980s his regional policies and his attempts to impose strict Islamic law had made his régime unpopular and in 1985, while visiting the USA, he himself was deposed by an army colleague, General Swar al-Dahab.

NIMITZ, Chester William (1885–1966) American naval commander, born in Fredericksburg, Texas. He graduated from the US Naval Academy in 1905, served mainly in submarines, and by 1938 had risen to the rank of rear admiral. Chief of the bureau of navigation during 1939–41, from 1941 to 1945 he commanded the US Pacific fleet and Pacific Ocean areas, contributing largely to the defeat of Japan. He was made a fleet admiral in 1944, and signed the Japanese surrender documents for the USA on board the USS *Missouri* in Tokyo Bay (1945). He became chief of naval operations from 1945 to 1947 and special assistant to the secretary of the Navy (1947–49), and led the UN mediation commission in the Kashmir dispute in 1949.

NIN, Anaïs (1903–77) American writer, born in Paris to parents of mixed Spanish-Cuban descent. She spent her childhood in Europe until, at the age of eleven, she left France to live in the USA. Ten years later, after her marriage to Hugh Guiler, a banker, she returned to Paris, where she studied psychoanalysis under Otto Rank, became acquainted with many well-known writers and artists and began to write herself. Her first novel, *House of Incest*, was published in 1936 and was followed by volumes of criticism, among them *The Novel of the Future* (1968), and a series of novels including *Winter of Artifice* (1939), *A Spy in the House of Love* (1954) and *Collages* (1964). She also published an early collection of short stories, *Under a Glass Bell* (1944). Ultimately, however, her reputation as an artist and seminal figure in the new feminism of the 1970s rests on her seven *Journals* (1966–83). Spanning the years 1931–74 they are an engrossing record of an era and some of its most intriguing and avant garde players, as well as a passionate, explicit and candid account of one woman's voyage of self-discovery.

NINAGAWA, Yukio (1935–) Japanese stage director. After completing his studies at the Seihari Theatre Company, he emerged as a leading light in Japanese avant-garde theatre with his work at Toyko's Small Basement Theatre. In 1974, he staged *Romeo and Juliet* as his first production for the Toho Company, followed by a series of classical works and numerous Japanese plays. In 1985 he created a sensation at the Edinburgh Festival with a vibrant, colourful, violent, Samurai-influenced production of *Macbeth*, followed by an open-air production in a Georgian courtyard of **Euripides**' *Medea* in 1986. Both productions were subsequently seen at the National Theatre in London, for which Ninagawa won the 1987 Olivier award for director of the year.

NINIAN, St, also known as **Nynia** or **Ringan** (fl.390) bishop and missionary associated with Whithorn in Wigtownshire, and the earliest-known Christian leader in Scotland. According to **Bede**, writing about 730, he was a bishop of the Old Welsh British, and was instructed in Rome; he built a stone church for his see, called Candida Casa. According to his 12th-century biographer, Ailred of Reivaulx, he was the son of a Christian king and born near the Solway Firth. He was consecrated bishop by the pope (394) and sent as an apostle to the western parts of **Britain**. On his way home from Rome he visited St **Martin** of Tours, who supplied him with masons and to whom he later dedicated his church. He selected Wigtownshire for the site of a monastery and church, which was built around 400. Successful in converting the southern Picts, he died at Whithorn and was buried there, although other sources suggest he may have withdrawn to Ireland.

NIPKOW, Paul (1860–1940) German engineer, born in Lauenburg. One of the pioneers of television, he invented in 1884 the Nipkow disc, a mechanical scanning device consisting of a revolving disc with a spiral pattern of apertures. In use until 1932, it was superseded by electronic scanning.

NIRENBERG, Marshall Warren (1927–) American biochemist, born in New York. He studied at Florida and Michigan and worked from 1957 at the National Institutes of Health, Bethesda, Maryland. Others had proposed that there are different combinations of three nucleotide bases (triplets or 'codons') in nucleic acid chains in DNA and RNA, each coded for a different amino acid in the biological synthesis of proteins, and that this was the fundamental process in the chemical transfer of inherited characteristics. There are 64 possible combinations of bases, and only 20 amino acids to be coded. Nirenberg attacked the problem of the 'code dictionary' by synthesizing a nucleic acid with a known base sequence, and then finding which amino acid it converted to protein. With his success, **Har Gobind Khorana** and others soon completed the task of deciphering the full code. Nirenberg, Khorana and **Robert Holley** shared the Nobel prize for physiology or medicine in 1968 for this work.

NITHARDT, Mathis See **GRÜNEWALD, Matthias**

NITHSDALE, William Maxwell, 5th Earl of (1676–1744) Scottish Jacobite. He succeeded his father at the age of seven, in 1699 married Lady Winifred Herbert (1679–1749), youngest daughter of the Marquis of Powis, and lived at his Kirkcudbrightshire seat, Terregles. A Catholic, he joined the English Jacobites in the 1715 Rising and was taken prisoner at Preston. He was tried for high treason in London, and sentenced to death; but on the night before the day fixed for his execution he escaped from the Tower in woman's apparel, through the heroism of his countess who had changed clothes with him. They settled in Rome, where the earl died.

NITSCH, Hermann (1938–) Austrian performance artist, born in Vienna. He lives and works in Prinzendorf. After reading **Schopenhauer** and **Nietzsche**, he decided that 'art was something similar to religion, and the performance of art corresponded to a ritual'. His work consists of 'installations' in which, for example, slaughtered cattle are hung up before naked men who lie on stretchers, spattered with blood, while music is played.

NITZSCH, Karl Immanuel (1787–1868) German Lutheran theologian. He became professor at Bonn in 1822, and in 1847 at Berlin. Subordinating dogma to ethics, he was one of the leaders of the broad evangelical school. His chief books are *System der christlichen lehre* (1829), *Praktische Theologie* (1847–67), *Christliche Glaubenslehre* (1858), and several volumes of sermons and essays.

NITZSCH, Karl Wilhelm (1818–80) German historian, nephew of **Karl Immanuel Nitzsch**. A pupil of **Niebuhr**, he was professor at Kiel, Königsberg and Berlin. His writings embrace historical studies on **Polybius** (1842) and the **Gracchi** (1847), *Die römische Annalistik* (1873), *Deutsche Studien* (1879), German history to the peace of Augsburg (1883–85), and a history of the Roman republic (1884–85).

NIVELLE, Robert (1857–1924) French soldier, born in Tulle. He was an artillery colonel in August 1914, and made his name when in command of the army of Verdun by recapturing Douaumont and other forts (October–December 1916). He was commander-in-chief, December 1916 to May 1917, when his Aisne offensive failed and he was superseded by **Pétain**.

NIVEN, David, originally **James David Graham Nevins** (1910–83) English actor, born in London. A graduate of the Royal Military College at Sandhurst, he had a variety of jobs before he arrived in Hollywood, where he joined the social set led by **Errol Flynn** and **Clark Gable**, and worked as an extra in *Mutiny on the Bounty* (1935). Signed by **Samuel Goldwyn** he developed into a polished light-comedian and gallant hero in films like *The Charge of the Light Brigade* (1936), *The Dawn Patrol* (1938) and *Bachelor Mother* (1939). After service as an army officer in World War II he spent 30 years as an urbane leading man, perfectly cast as the gentlemanly voyager Phineas Fogg in *Around the World in 80 Days* (1956), and winning an Academy Award for *Separate Tables* (1958). An inimitable raconteur, he published two volumes of lighthearted autobiography: *The Moon's A Balloon* (1972) and *Bring on the Empty Horses* (1975).

NIVEN, Frederick John (1878–1944) Scottish novelist, born in Chile of Scots parentage. Educated at Hutcheson's Grammar School, Glasgow, and Glasgow School of Art, he travelled widely in South America and worked as a journalist (1898–1914). After World War I he emigrated to Canada. He wrote more than 30 novels, mostly set in Glasgow or Canada, including *The Lost Cabin Mine* (1908), *The Justice of the Peace* (1914) and *The Staff at Simsons* (1937). His major work was a trilogy on Canadian settlement, comprising *The Flying Years*, *Mine Inheritance*, and *The Transplanted* (1935–44). He also published his autobiography, *Coloured Spectacles* (1938).

NIXON, Richard Milhous (1913–) 37th president of the USA, born in Yorba Linda, California, into a lower-middle class Quaker family of Irish descent which had migrated from the Midwest. After five years practice as a lawyer, he served in the US navy (1942–46), prior to his election to the House of Representatives in 1946. He became senator in 1950, and vice-president in 1952. His swift climb in political circles was a result of fearless outspokenness and brilliant political tactics, and he was particularly prominent as a member of the Committee on Un-American Activities, working on the **Alger Hiss** case. In May 1958 he and his wife were subjected to violent anti-American demonstrations in Peru and Venezuela, during a goodwill tour of Latin America, and in 1959 on a visit to Moscow he achieved notoriety by his outspoken exchanges with **Nikita Khrushchev**. As the Republican candidate, he lost the presidential election (1960) to **John F Kennedy** by a tiny margin. Standing for the governorship of California in 1962, he was again defeated. He won the presidential election in 1968 by a small margin, and was re-elected in 1972 by a large majority. During an official investigation into a break-in attempt in June 1972 at the Democratic National Committee's headquarters in the Watergate Hotel, Washington, Nixon lost credibility with the American people by at first claiming executive privilege for senior White House officials to prevent them being questioned, and by refusing to hand over tapes of relevant conversations. He resigned in August 1974 under the threat of impeachment after several leading members of his government had been found guilty of being involved in the Watergate scandal. In September 1974 he was given a full pardon by President **Gerald Ford**. He wrote his autobiography, *Six Crises* (1962) and his Memoirs (1978).

NKOMO, Joshua Mqabuko Nyongolo (1917–) African Nationalist and Zimbabwean politician, born in Matabeleland. During periods away from his native country he strove to bring the Rhodesian problem to the attention of the world. He was a member of the African National Congress from 1952 until the organization was banned in 1959, and two years later became President of the Zimbabwe African People's Union (ZAPU). There followed a long period during which he was placed under Government restrictions, but Nkomo re-emerged in 1975 to sign (with Rhodesian Prime Minister **Ian Smith**) an agreement to hold a constitutional conference. The following year he formed the ZAPU-ZANU Popular Front with **Robert Mugabe** in order to press for black majority rule in an independent Zimbabwe, and he was given a Cabinet post in the Mugabe government in 1980. However, tension between ZAPU and ZANU and their respective leaders led to Nkomo's dismissal from the goverment in 1982. Nkomo later fled the country after alleged attempts to assassinate him, returning after several months. Gradually relations between the two men improved and Mugabe reinstated Nkomo in his Cabinet. In 1988 ZAPU and ZANU merged to become ZANU-PF, under Mugabe's leadership, and Nkomo became, in effect, an elder statesman.

NKRUMAH, Kwame (1909–72) Ghanaian politician, born in Ankroful. He was educated at Achimota College, Lincoln University, Pennsylvania and the London School of Economics. He returned to Africa and in 1949 formed the nationalist Convention People's party with the slogan 'self-government now'. In 1950 he was imprisoned for his part in calling strikes and was elected to parliament while still in jail. A year later he was released, and became virtual prime minister with the title of Leader of Business in the Assembly. He was confirmed in power at the 1956 election and in 1957 became the first prime minister of the independent Commonwealth State of Ghana. Called the 'Gandhi of Africa' he was a significant leader first of the movement against white domination and then of Pan-African feeling. Ghana became a republic in 1960. Nkrumah was the moving spirit behind the Charter of African States (1961). Economic reforms sparked off political opposition, and several attempts on his life. Legal imprisonment of political opponents for five years and more without trial, and interference with the judiciary in the treason trial (1963, when he dismissed the chief justice), heralded the successful referendum for a one-party state in 1964, in which the secrecy of the ballot was called in question. In 1966 his régime was overthrown by a military *coup* during his absence in China. He returned to Ghana where he was appointed head of state. His publications included *Towards Colonial Freedom* (1946), an autobiography (1957), and *Consciencism* (1964).

NOAILLES, Adrien Maurice, 3rd Duke of (1678–1766) French nobleman and soldier, son of **Anne Jules, 2nd Duke of Noailles**. He won his marshal's baton in **Louis XV**'s wars.

NOAILLES, Anna-Elisabeth, Comtesse de (1876–1933) French poet and novelist. She wrote many poems and novels and was acclaimed 'Princesse des lettres'.

NOAILLES, Anne Jules, 2nd Duke of (1650–1708) French nobleman and soldier. He commanded against the Huguenots and in Spain, and became marshal.

NOAILLES, Emanuel Henri Victurnien de (1830–1909) French diplomat, son of Paul, 6th Duke of Noailles. He was ambassador in Italy, Constantinople and Berlin, and wrote on Poland.

NOAILLES, Emanuel Marie Louis de (1743–1822) French diplomat, brother of Paul Francois, 5th Duke of Noailles. He was ambassador at Amsterdam, London and Vienna.

NOAILLES, Louis Antoine de (1651–1729) French ecclesiastic, brother of **Anne Jules Noailles**, and archbishop of Paris (1695). He became cardinal in 1700 and was a reformer of clerical practice.

NOAILLES, Louis Marie de (1756–1804) French soldier, grandson of **Adrien Maurice, 3rd Duke of Noailles**. He served in America under **Lafayette**, supported the French Revolution for a time, then returned to America in 1792 and defended San Domingo against the English (1802–04).

NOBEL, Alfred (1833–96) Swedish chemist and manufacturer, the inventor of dynamite and the founder of the Nobel prizes, born in Stockholm. The son of an engineer, he moved in his childhood to Russia, where his father was working on an underwater mine he had devised. He studied chemistry in Paris, worked in the USA with the Swedish-born **John Ericsson**, and settled in Sweden in 1859. An explosives expert like his father, in 1866 he invented a safe and manageable form of nitroglycerin he called 'dynamite', and, later, smokeless gunpowder. In 1875 he invented gelignite. With them he created an industrial empire manufacturing many of his other inventions, from artificial gutta-percha to mild steel for armour-plating. He amassed a huge fortune, much of which he left to endow annual Nobel prizes (first awarded in 1901) for physics, chemistry, physiology or medicine, literature and peace (a sixth prize, for economics, was instituted in his honour in 1969). The synthetic transuranic element nobelium was named after him.

NOBILE, Umberto (1885–1978) Italian aviator, born in Lauro. He became an aeronautical engineer and built the airships *Norge* and *Italia*. He flew across the North Pole in the *Norge* with **Amundsen** and **Ellsworth** in 1926, but in 1928 he was wrecked in the airship *Italia* when returning from the North Pole, and was adjudged (1929) responsible for the disaster. In the USA from 1936 to 1942, he later returned to Italy and was reinstated in the Italian air service.

NOBILI, Leopoldo (1784–1835) Italian physicist. Professor of physics at Florence, he invented the thermopile used in measuring radiant heat, and the astatic galvanometer.

NOBLE, Adrian (1950–) English stage director. He studied at Bristol University and the Drama Centre in London, and worked for two years in community and young people's theatre in Birmingham. He became an associate director of the Bristol Old Vic (1976–79), and joined the Royal Shakespeare Company in 1980 as a resident director, becoming an associate director in 1982.

NOCARD, Edmond Isidore Étienne (1850–1903) French biologist. He made important discoveries in veterinary science, and showed that meat and milk from tubercular cattle could transmit the disease to man.

NODDACK, Ida Eva (1896–) and **Walter Karl Friedrich** (1893–1960), German chemists, husband and wife. In 1925 they discovered the elements masurium and rhenium.

NODIER, Charles (1780–1844) French writer. He had a profound influence on the Romanticists of 1830, but only his short stories and fairy tales are remembered, such as *Les Vampires* (1820) and *Le Chien de Brisquet* (1844).

NOEL-BAKER, Baron Philip (1889–1982) English Labour politician. After a brilliant athletic and academic career at Cambridge, he captained the British Olympic team (1912), and in World War I commanded a Friends' ambulance unit. He served on the secretariat of the peace conference (1919) and of the League of Nations (1919–22), was MP for Coventry (1929–31) and for Derby from 1936. He was Cassel professor of international relations at London (1924–29) and Dodge lecturer at Yale (1934), where he was awarded the Howland prize. He wrote a number of books on international problems, including *Disarmament* (1926), and a standard work, *The Arms Race* (1958). During and after World War II he held several junior ministerial posts and was Labour secretary of state for air (1946–47), of commonwealth relations (1947–50) and minister of fuel and power (1950–51). He was awarded the Nobel peace prize in 1959 and created a life peer in 1977. His son, Francis Edward Noel-Baker (1920–), was a Labour MP from 1945 to 1950 and from 1955 to 1968. He resigned from the Labour party in 1969, joined the SDP (1981–83), and the Conservative party in 1984.

NOETHER, (Amalie) Emmy (1882–1935) German mathematician, born in Erlangen. The daughter of the mathematician Max Noether, she studied at Erlangen and Göttingen. Though invited to Göttingen in 1915 by **David Hilbert**, as a woman she could not hold a full academic post at that time, but worked there in a semi-honorary capacity until she emigrated to the USA in 1933 to Bryn Mawr and Princeton. She was one of the leading figures in the development of abstract algebra, working in ring theory and the theory of ideals; the theory of Noetherian rings has been an important subject of later research.

NOGUCHI, Hideyo (1876–1928) Japanese-born American bacteriologist, born in Inawashiro. He graduated from the Tokyo Medical College and worked in the USA from 1900, and made important discoveries in the cause and treatment of syphilis and also of yellow fever, from which he died.

NOGUCHI, Isamu (1904–88) American sculptor, born in Los Angeles. His father was a Japanese writer, his mother an American writer, and from 1906 to 1917 he was brought up in Japan. He studied medicine at Columbia University, then moved to New York where he attended sculpture classes. A Guggenheim fellowship permitted him to study with **Brancusi** in Paris from 1927 to 1929. He returned to New York and made stylized sculptures which owed much to his teacher. From 1940 his work moved closer to Surrealism, incorporating bone-like elements. From the mid 1940s he became one of the best-known American sculptors, gaining worldwide commissions for large-scale public sculptures.

NOKE, Charles John (1858–1941) English ceramic specialist, modeller and designer, born in Worcester. Apprenticed to the Worcester Porcelain Factory at 15, he joined Doulton & Co in 1889 as head modeller, where he produced large vases, table services and ornamental centrepieces. He was later responsible for many parian ware figures, including the Diana and Columbus vases and the ivory glazed **Henry Irving** and **Ellen Terry** figures in theatrical costume in 1894. He was instrumental in introducing the Holbein and Rembrandt wares. In 1914 he succeeded John Slater as art director in Doulton's art department in Burslem, where he experimented with reproducing red rouge flambé and sang-de-bœuf glazes from the Sung, Ming and early Ching dynasties.

NOLAN, Sir Sidney Robert (1917–) Australian painter, born in Melbourne. He took up full-time painting in 1938 and held his first exhibition in 1940. He made his name with a series of '**Ned Kelly**' paintings begun in 1946, and followed this with an 'explorer' series based on the travels of **Burke** and **Wills**. He first came to Europe in 1950, and although he has worked in Italy, Greece and Africa, he remains best-known for his Australian paintings. He is also a theatrical designer, and has designed the Covent Garden productions *The Rite of Spring* (1962) and *Samson and Delilah* (1981), and has illustrated books by **Robert Lowell** and **Benjamin Britten**. He published a volume of poems, drawings and paintings, *Paradise Garden* (1972).

NOLAND, Kenneth (1924–) American painter, born in Asheville, North Carolina. He studied under Ilya Bolotowsky and **Josef Albers** at Black Mountain College (1946–48). He met **Ossip Zadkine** while studying in Paris, (1948–49). Influenced initially by **Klee** and **Matisse** and by the New York Action Painters, he developed his own kind of hard-edge minimalist abstract painting by c.1957. He likes to restrict his shapes to circles, ovals or chevrons or—after c.1966—horizontal stripes. His 'plaid' paintings date from c.1971.

NOLDE, Emil, pseud of **Emil Hansen** (1867–1956) German painter and printmaker, born in Nolde. One of the most important Expressionist painters, he was briefly a member of the Expressionist *Die Brücke* (1906–07), but produced his own powerful style of distorted forms in his violent religious pictures such as *The Life of Christ* (1911–12). He also produced a large number of etchings, lithographs and woodcuts.

NOLLEKENS, Joseph (1737–1823) English sculptor, born in London. A pupil of **Scheemakers**, he executed likenesses of most of his famous contemporaries, including **Garrick**, **Sterne**, **Goldsmith**, **Johnson**, **Fox**, **Pitt**, and **George III**.

NOLLET, Jean Antoine (1700–70) French abbé and physicist. First professor of physics at the Collège de Navarre, in Paris, in 1748, he discovered osmosis (1748), invented an electroscope, and improved the Leiden jar invented by **Pieter van Musschenbroek**.

NONIUS MARCELLUS (?4th century) Latin grammarian who lived sometime between the 2nd and 5th centuries and was perhaps born in Numidia. He wrote *De compendiosa doctrina*, a sort of lexicon in 20 chapters, of no great merit in itself but valuable to scholars in that it preserves forgotten senses of many words and passages from ancient Latin authors now lost.

NONO, Luigi (1924–90) Italian composer, born in Venice, He attended the Venice Conservatoire in 1943–45 and again from 1946 (after having graduated in law from Padua University), studying under **Malipiero** and later **Bruno Maderna**, with whom he and **Luciano Berio** helped to establish Italy in the forefront of contemporary music. Unlike Maderna and Berio, however, he was a strongly politically-committed artist, his music as much deriving from and gaining its purpose through a deep concern with human and social injustice as from the purely abstract creation of formal musical relationships. He worked for a time at the electronic studio in Darmstadt, and though radically avant-garde in technique, his concern for artist-to-audience communication, and the readily-understandable inspiration of pieces such as *La Victoire de Guernica* (1954), prevented his work from degenerating into obscurity. *Il Canto Sospero* in 1956, based on the letters of victims of wartime oppression, brought him to international notice. His opera *Intolleranza* (1961), an attack on the restrictions of freedom, aroused violent hostility at its first performance in Venice. This was followed the next year by *Canti di vita e d'amore* (*Sul ponte di Hiroshima*). Among his other compositions are *Variazioni canoniche* (1950), *Polyfonica-Monodia-Ritmica* (1951), *Canto per il Vietnam* (1973); the operas *Al gran sole carico* *d'amore* (1972–75) and *Prometeo* (1981–85);*...sofferte o de serene...* (1976) for piano and tape, and a *String Quartet* (1980). In 1955 he married **Schoenburg**'s daughter Nuria.

NOODT, Gerhardus (1647–1725) Dutch jurist, educated at Nijmegen school and university, Leiden and Utrecht. Professor at several universities, chiefly Leiden, he was a scholar of European reputation and regarded as an authority on Roman law. A leading member of the Elegant School, which concentrated on pure Roman law, he was a follower of the French or Humanistic approach. His works include a *Commentarius* on the first 27 books of **Justinian**'s *Digest* (1713), and *Ad Legem Aquiliam* (1690), *De pactis et transactionibus* (1713) and *De Usufructu* (1713).

NORDAL, Sigurður (Jóhanneson) (1886–1974) Icelandic scholar, the leading authority on classical Icelandic literature, born in Vatnsdalur. He studied philology at Copenhagen, and psychology and philosophy in Germany and at Oxford. He was professor of Old Icelandic literature at the new University of Iceland (1918–45), and Charles Eliot Norton professor of poetry at Harvard (1931–32). He was appointed Icelandic ambassador to Denmark (1951–57) at the time when the return of the **Árni Magnússon** manuscript collection to Iceland was being negotiated. His seminal publications, on *Ólafs saga helga* (1914), *Snorri Sturluson* (1920), *Völuspá* (1923), *Hrafnkatla* (1940) and particularly *Íslenzk menning I* (Icelandic Culture I, 1942), had a profound impact. He founded the *Íslenzk Fornrit* series of literary editions of the sagas, to which he contributed *Egils saga* (1933) and *Borgfiroðingar sögur* (1938). He also published some poetry, a play, and a collection of short stories (*Fornar ástir*, 1919).

NORDAU, Max Simon, originally **Südfeld** (1849–1923) Hungarian author and physician, born of Jewish descent in Budapest. He studied medicine and established himself as physician, first in Budapest (1878), and then in Paris (1886). He wrote several books of travel, but became known as the author of works on moral and social questions, including *Conventional Lies of Society* (1883; trans 1895) and *Degeneration* (1895), and as a novelist. He was also an active Zionist leader in Europe.

NORDENSKJÖLD, Nils Adolf Erik, Baron (1832–1901) Finnish-born Swedish arctic navigator, born in Helsingfors (now Helsinki). A naturalized Swede, he made several expeditions to Spitsbergen, mapping the south of the island. After two preliminary trips proving the navigability of the Kara Sea, in 1878–79 he accomplished the navigation of the Northeast Passage (on the *Vega*) from the Atlantic to the Pacific along the north coast of Asia. He later made two expeditions to Greenland.

NORDENSKJÖLD, (Nils) Otto (1869–1928) Swedish explorer and geologist, nephew of Baron **Nils Nordensjöld**. He accompanied a Swedish scientific expedition to Patagonia and in 1898 travelled through Klondike and Alaska. In 1900 he was a member of Georg Karl Amdrup's Danish expedition to Greenland and in 1901 he led a Swedish party on *Antarctica* to the South Pole. They reached the Weddell Sea and spent two winters on Snow Hill Island. *Antarctica* was crusted by ice, but they were rescued by the *Uruguay*, an Argentinian gunboat. In 1920–21 he explored the Andes. He was appointed professor of geography at Gothenburg University in 1905, and principal of Gothenburg University Business School in 1923.

NØRGÅRD, Per (1932–) Danish composer. Educated at the Royal Danish Academy of Music, he continued his studies in Paris. His compositions include operas, symphonies, ballet and chamber music. He wrote the music for the Oscar-winning Danish film *Babette's Feast* (*Babettes Gæstebud*), directed by **Gabriel Axel** in 1987.

NORIEGA, General Manuel Antonio Morena (1940–) Panamanian soldier and politician. Born in Panama City and educated at the university there and a military school in Peru, he was commissioned in Panama's National Guard in 1962 and rose to become head of intelligence (1970) and chief of staff (1982). As head of the National Guard, he wielded considerable power, eventually becoming 'de facto' ruler of the country, in which there was growing evidence of undemocratic practices. Despite this, his pivotal role was recognized by the USA which sought his help in CIA activities, but his indictment in February 1988 by a US grand jury on charges of drug trafficking made that association embarrassing. An attempted coup against him, in October 1989, failed and US president **George Bush** was criticized for not supporting it. However, in December 1989, with relations rapidly deteriorating, he sent troops into Panama to arrest him. Noriega initially took refuge in the Vatican embassy but eventually surrendered and was taken for trial in the USA.

NORMAN, Jessye (1945–) American soprano, born in Augusta, Georgia. She made her operatic début at the Deutsche Oper, Berlin (1969), and at both La Scala and Covent Garden in 1972. Her US début was at the Hollywood Bowl (1972). She is widely admired in opera and concert music for her beauty of tone, breadth of register and mastery of dynamic range.

NORMAN, Montagu, 1st Baron (1871–1950) English banker. After serving in the South African war he entered banking and became associated with the Bank of England. He was elected governor of the Bank in 1920 and held this post until 1944. During this time he wielded great infuence on national and international monetary affairs.

NORRIS, Frank Benjamin Franklin (1870–1902) American novelist, born in Chicago. He first studied art but later turned to journalism, and while a reporter for the San Francisco *Chronicle* (1895–96) was involved in the **Jameson** raid in South Africa. He was influenced by **Zola** and was one of the first American naturalist writers, his major novel being *McTeague* (1899), a story of lower-class life in San Francisco. He also wrote the first two volumes of an unfinished 'epic of the wheat' trilogy, *The Octopus* (1901) and *The Pit* (1903).

NORRIS, George William (1861–1944) American politician, born in Sandusky, Ohio. He obtained a law degree in what is now Valparaiso University, moving to Beaver City, Nebraska, in 1885. He became county prosecuting attorney, and served as district judge from 1895 to 1902. He was elected as a Republican to the House of Representatives (1902–12), was identified with the growing progressive movement for national reform, and under his leadership the House was democratized to the extent of breaking the virtually monarchical rule of the speaker. He was senator for Nebraska from 1912 to 1942, voted against entry into World War I and was irreconcilably opposed to the Versailles Treaty. He maintained the progressive struggle in the cynical capitalist 1920s, sponsored the Norris-**La Guardia** anti-injunction Act (1932), and broke with his party on the issue of public ownership of water power. His hopes were realized under the New Deal, and the Tennessee Valley Authority's first dam was named in his honour. His memoirs, written after defeat, were posthumously published as *Fighting Liberal*.

NORRIS, John (1657–1711) English philosopher and Anglican priest, born in Collingbourne-Kingston,

Wiltshire. He became a fellow of All Souls College, Oxford, in 1680, and was then vicar of Newton St Loe in Somerset (1689–92) and vicar at Bemerton, Wiltshire from 1692 until his death. He was a prolific writer and his books include a political tract *A Murnival of Knaves, or Whiggism Planely Displayed and Laughed out of Countenance* (1683), various moral and mystical writings, heavily influenced by the Cambridge Platonists **Cudworth** and **More**, such as *An Idea of Happiness* (1683), and an exposition of the views of **Malebranche** against those of **Locke** in *An Essay Towards the Theory of the Ideal or Intelligible World* (1701–04).

NORRIS, Kathleen, née **Thompson** (1880–1966) American novelist, born in San Francisco. She began writing stories and published her first novel, *Mother*, in 1911. After that she wrote many popular novels and short stories, including *Certain People of Importance* (1922) and *Over at the Crowleys* (1946).

NORRISH, Ronald George Wreyford (1897–1978) English chemist, born in Cambridge. Educated at Cambridge, he was professor of physical chemistry there from 1937 to 1965. His research was in the field of photochemistry and chemical kinetics. He collaborated with **George Porter** to develop flash photolysis and kinetic spectroscopy for the investigation of very fast reactions. They shared the 1967 Nobel prize for chemistry with **Manfred Eigen**.

NORTH, Christopher See **WILSON, John**

NORTH, Sir Dudley (1641–91) English economist and entrepreneur, brother of **Francis** and **Roger North**. A merchant in Turkey, he lived for a time in Constantinople and amassed a fortune. He became a sheriff of London and a commissioner of customs. He was a keen-eyed observer, and had great mechanical genius, and his *Discourses upon Trade* (1691) anticipated **Adam Smith**.

NORTH, Sir Edward, 1st Baron (1496–1564) English lawyer, father of Sir **Thomas North**. A privy councillor, he held important posts during the reigns of **Henry VIII, Edward VI, Mary I** and **Elizabeth**.

NORTH, Francis, 1st Baron Guilford (1637–85) English lawyer, brother of Sir **Dudley North**, and **Roger North**. Educated at Cambridge, he was called to the bar in 1655, and was successively solicitor-general, attorney-general, chief-justice of the court of common pleas (1675), privy councillor, Lord Chancellor (1682), and Baron Guilford (1683). He was a learned lawyer and reformer of abuses.

NORTH, Frederick, 8th Lord North and 2nd Earl of Guilford (1732–92) English statesman. He entered parliament at the age of 22, became a lord of the treasury, Chancellor of the Exchequer and in 1770 prime minister. He was largely responsible for the measures that brought about the loss of America, being too ready to surrender his judgment to the king's. In 1782 he resigned and later entered into a coalition with **Fox**, hitherto his opponent, and served with him under the 3rd Duke of Portland (**William Bentinck**) in 1783.

NORTH, John Dudley (1893–1968) English applied mathematician, aircraft engineer and designer, born in London. He went to Bedford school, took a brief marine apprenticeship and at 20 became **Claude Grahame-White**'s chief engineer at his flying school at Hendon. Thereafter he created a succession of highly original aircraft, both for his first company and then in 1917 for Boulton Paul Aircraft Ltd, of which he eventually became chairman and managing director. His aircraft included the Grahame-White Popular, Type XIII, and Charabanc, and for Boulton Paul the Bobolink, Bourges, Bugle, Phoenix, Sidestrand, Overstrand and Defiant. His company specialized in hydraulic gun turrets and, later, power controls. Renowned also for his advanced mathematical ideas on cybernetics, operational research and ergonomics, he contributed significant papers on these subjects to the Royal Aeronautical Society.

NORTH, Marianne (1830–90) English flower painter, a descendant of **Roger North**. At the age of 40, after the death of her father, she set off to paint colourful and exotic flowers in many countries and with the encouragement of Sir **Joseph Dalton Hooker** gave her valuable collection to Kew Gardens where they can be seen in a gallery, opened in 1882, which bears her name.

NORTH, Oliver (1943–) American soldier, born into a San Antonio military family. A graduate of the US Naval College, Annapolis, during the Vietnam War he led a counter-insurgency marines platoon, winning a Silver Star and Purple Heart, before returning home wounded. After working as an instructor and security officer, he was appointed a deputy-director of the National Security Council by President **Reagan** in 1981. Here he played a key role in a series of controversial military and security actions. In November 1986, when the 'Iran-Contragate' affair became public, he resigned. In May 1989, despite appeals to patriotism, a Washington Court found him guilty on three of twelve charges arising from the affair. He was given a three-year suspended jail sentence, fined $150000 and sentenced to perform 1200 hours of community service. He subsequently appealed against this conviction.

NORTH, Robert (1945–) American-born British dancer and choreographer, born in Charleston, South Carolina. He has spent all his working life in Britain. In 1965 he joined the Royal Ballet School and later took classes with London Contemporary Dance School, going on to become one of the founding members of London Contemporary Dance Theatre. He spent twelve years with that company as dancer and choreographer. A classical training spiced with jazz has given him popular appeal. Early work includes *Still Life* (1975), *Scriabin Preludes and Studies* (1978) and *Troy Game* (1974), arguably his best work. In 1981 he was made artistic director of Ballet Rambert, but was dismissed five years later. He now works as a freelance choreographer. He is married to the dancer Janet Smith.

NORTH, Roger (1653–1734) English lawyer and writer, brother of Sir **Dudley North** and **Francis North**. Educated at Jesus College, Cambridge, he entered the Middle Temple and rose to a lucrative practice at the bar. A nonjuror, he retired after the Revolution. His three hypereulogistic biographies of his brothers (*Lives of the Norths*, 1742–44), his autobiography and his *Examen* (1740, on the history of England) are noteworthy.

NORTH, Sir Thomas (?1535–?1601) English translator, son of Sir **Edward North, 1st Baron**. He is known for his translation of **Plutarch** (1579), from which **Shakespeare** drew his knowledge of ancient history.

NORTHBROOK See **BARING, Sir Francis Thornhill**

NORTHCLIFFE, Lord See **HARMSWORTH, Alfred Charles William**

NORTHCOTE, James (1746–1831) English painter, the son of a Plymouth watchmaker. A pupil and assistant of **Reynolds**, he painted portraits and historical pictures, among them the well-known *Princes in the Tower* and *Prince Arthur and Hubert*. He is also remembered by **Hazlitt**'s *Conversations with Northcote*.

NORTHCOTE, Sir Stafford See **IDDESLEIGH**

NORTHROP, John Howard (1891–1987) American biochemist, born in New York. Educated at Columbia University, he became professor of bacteriology at California in 1949. He discovered the fermentation process for the manufacuture of acetone, worked on enzymes and published *Crystalline Enzymes* (1939). He shared the 1946 Nobel prize for chemistry with **Wendell Meredith Stanley** and **James Batcheller Sumner** for their study of ways of producing purified enzymes and virus products.

NORTHROP, John Knudsen (1895–1981) American aircraft manufacturer, born in Newark, New Jersey. He began as a project engineer for the Loughead Aircraft Co in 1916, continued with Douglas Aircraft Co and was a co-founder and chief engineer of the Lockheed Aircraft Co of Burbank California, (1927–28). He was vice-president and chief engineer of The Northrop Corporation, a subsidiary of Douglas Aircraft (1933–37), and became president and director of engineering of Northrop Aircraft Inc, (1939–52). He was an engineering consultant from 1953. His company built many famous aircraft, including two very large all-wing types; the first was propeller driven and a later version was jet-propelled.

NORTHUMBERLAND, Dukes of See **PERCY** family

NORTON, Caroline Elizabeth Sarah, née **Sheridan** (1808–77) Irish writer and reformer, born in London, granddaughter of **Richard Brinsley Sheridan**. In 1827 she married a dissolute barrister, the Hon George Chapple Norton (1800–75), and bore him three sons. She took up writing to support the family, and published a successful book of verse, *The Sorrows of Rosalie* (1829). In 1836 she separated from her husband, who brought an action of 'criminal conversation' (adultery) against Lord **Melbourne**, obtained custody of the children and tried to obtain the profit from her books. Her spirited pamphlets led to improvements in the legal status of women in relation to infant custody (1839) and marriage and divorce (1857). She married Sir **William Stirling-Maxwell** in 1877, but died soon afterwards. Her other books of verse included an attack on child labour in *Voice from the Factories* (1836), *The Dream* (1840) and *The Lady of Garaye* (1862), and she also published three novels. She was the model for **George Meredith**'s central character in his novel *Diana of the Crossways* (1885).

NORTON, Charles Eliot (1827–1908) American writer and scholar, born in Cambridge, Massachusetts, the son of a Unitarian theologian. With **James Russell Lowell** he was joint editor of the *North American Review* (1964–68), and was a co-founder of *The Nation* (1865). He was professor of art at Harvard (1873–97), where he instituted a course in the history of fine arts as related to society and general culture. A personal friend of **Carlyle**, **Ruskin**, **Longfellow**, **Emerson** and many other leading literary figures, he wrote on medieval church-building, translated **Dante**'s *Commedia Divina* (1891–92), edited the poems of **John Donne** (1895) and **Anne Bradstreet** (1897), and the letters of Carlyle (1883–91).

NORTON, Mary (1903–) English children's novelist, born in Leighton Buzzard. Aiming to become an actress she joined the Old Vic Theatre Company in the 1920s, but marriage took her to Portugal, where she first began to write, and later to America. Returning to Britain in 1943, she published her first book two years later. But it was *The Borrowers* (1952), an enchanting story about tiny people living beneath the floorboards of a big house, which established her as one of the foremost children's writers of her generation, and which won the Carnegie Medal. There have been four sequels, the latest being *The Borrowers Avenged* (1982).

NORTON, Thomas (1532–84) English lawyer, MP, and poet, born in London. He was a successful lawyer and a zealous Protestant, married to a daughter of **Thomas Cranmer**. He translated **Calvin**'s *Christianae Religionis Institutio* (1561). With **Sackville** he was joint author of the tragedy *Gorboduc*, which was performed before Queen **Elizabeth** in 1562.

NORWAY, Nevil Shute See **SHUTE**

NORWICH, 1st Viscount See **COOPER, Sir Alfred Duff**

NORWOOD, Sir Cyril (1875–1956) English educationist, born in Whalley, Lancashire, the son of a headmaster. Educated at Merchant Taylors' School and St John's College, Oxford, he taught at Leeds Grammar School (1901–06) and became headmaster of Bristol Grammar School (1906–16), master at Marlborough College (1916–26), headmaster of Harrow (1926–34) and president of St John's College, Oxford (1934–46). He was chairman of the Committee on Curriculum and Examinations in Secondary Schools from 1941 which reported in 1943. The report contained a plan for the main features of a new secondary education for all children which incorporated a tripartite system of grammar schools and modern schools as proposed in the Hadow Report of 1926 and of technical schools as proposed in the Spens Report of 1938. It affected many of the development plans presented by local education authorities after the Education Act of 1944.

NOSSAL, Sir Gustav Joseph Victor (1931–) Austrian-born Australian immunologist, born in Bad Ischl. He arrived in Australia in 1939 and was educated at the universities of Sydney and Melbourne. He was appointed research fellow at the Walter and Eliza Hall Institute of Medical Research in 1957, deputy director (immunology) in 1961, director of the Institute in 1965, and also professor of medical biology at Melbourne University. In 1978 he gave the ABC's Boyer Lecture entitled 'Nature's Defences'. His discovery of the 'one cell-one antibody' rule is crucial to modern work in immunology.

NOSTRADAMUS, or **Michel de Notredame** (1503–66) French physician and astrologer, born in St Rémy in Provence. He became doctor of medicine in 1529, and practised in Agen, Lyon, and other places. He set himself up as a prophet about 1547. His *Centuries* of predictions in rhymed quatrains (two collections, 1555–58), expressed generally in obscure and enigmatical terms, brought their author a great reputation. **Charles IX** on his accession appointed him physician-in-ordinary.

NOTKE, Bernt (c.1440–1509) German painter and sculptor, born in Lübeck. A surviving reference in 1467 to his exemption from guild rules suggests that he enjoyed an unusually high social status amongst German artists. In 1477 he carved and painted the great cross for Lübeck cathedral. He executed major works outside Germany, such as the high altar of Aarhas cathedral in Denmark, and, during a period of several years spent in Sweden, produced a huge monument for the church of St Nicholas in Stockholm depicting St George killing the dragon.

NOTT, Sir John William Frederick (1932–) English Conservative politician and merchant banker, born in Bideford, Devon. He was commissioned in the 2nd Gurkha Rifles and served in Malaysia (1952–56). He left the army to study law and economics at Trinity College, Cambridge (1957–59), and was called to the bar in 1959. In the same year he married Miloska Sekol, in Maribor, Yugoslavia. He entered the House of Commmons in 1960 as Conservative member for St Ives, Cornwall, and was a junior Treasury minister in the government of **Edward Heath** (1972–74). In **Margaret Thatcher**'s administration he was trade secretary (1979–81), and then defence secretary during the Falklands War. He left the House of Commons, with a knighthood, in 1983 and moved into the City of London, becoming chairman and chief executive of Lazard Brothers, the merchant bankers, in 1985.

NOTTINGHAM, Heneage Finch See **FINCH, Heneage**

NOVÁK, Vitezslav (1870–1949) Czech composer, born in Kamenitz. A pupil of Dvořák, he studied at Prague Conservatory, later becoming professor there (1909–20). His many compositions, which include operas and ballets, show the influence of his native folk melody.

NOVALIS, pen-name of **Friedrich von Hardenberg** (1772–1801) German Romantic poet and novelist called the 'Prophet of Romanticism'. At Weissenfels (1795) he fell in love with a beautiful girl, whose early death left a lasting impression upon him, and in whose memory he wrote the prose lyrics of *Hymnen an die Nicht* (1800). He also published *Geisliche Leider* (1799, Sacred Songs). He left two philosophical romances, both incomplete, *Heinrich von Ofterdingen* and *Die Lehrlinge zu Sais*. He died of consumption.

NOVATIAN (fl.3rd century) Roman Stoic. He was converted to Christianity and ordained a priest. In 251, soon after the Decian persecution under the emperor **Decius**, a controversy arose about those who fell away during persecution. Pope Cornelius (251–53) defended indulgence towards the lapsed; Novatian was chosen by a small party and ordained bishop in opposition to Cornelius. The Novations denied the lawfulness of readmitting the lapsed to communion. The sect, in spite of persecution, survived into the 6th century.

NOVELLO, Ivor, in full **Ivor Novello Davies** (1893–1951) Welsh actor, composer, songwriter and dramatist, born in Cardiff. He was the son of the singer Dame Clara Novello Davies and was educated at Magdalen College School, Oxford, where he was a chorister. His song 'Keep the Home Fires Burning' was one of the most successful of World War I. He first appeared on the regular stage in London in 1921 and enjoyed great popularity, his most successful and characteristic works being his 'Ruritanian' musical plays such as *Glamorous Night* (1935), *The Dancing Years* (1939) and *King's Rhapsody* (1949).

NOVELLO, Vincent (1781–1861) English organist, composer and music publisher, born in London of an Italian father and English mother. In 1811 he arranged the publication of two volumes of sacred music, which was the start of the publishing house of Novello & Co. He was a founder-member of the Philharmonic Society (1813), and subsequently its pianist and conductor. His compositions improved church music, and he was a painstaking editor of unpublished works. His son, Joseph Vincent (1810–96), was also an organist and music publisher, and from 1857 lived in Nice and in Genoa with his sister, Mary Victoria (Mrs **Cowden Clarke**). His daughter Clara Anastasia Novello (1818–1908), won triumphs all over Europe as a concert and operatic singer; in 1843 she married Count Gigliucci, but returned to the stage from 1850 to 1860.

NOVERRE, Jean-Georges (1727–1810) French dancer, choreographer and ballet master, born in Paris and renowned in posterity as a ballet reformer and theorist. He claimed invention of the notion of the ballet d'action, in which truthful movement expression was integrated with plot, music and décor; it is commonly identified as one of the greatest influences on ballet as it is known and practised today. Although he studied dance with Louis Dupré of the Paris Opéra, he eventually opted for a career as a prolific choreographer instead. He was ballet master at the Paris Opéra Comique (1754), the royal court theatre of Württemberg (now the Stuttgart Ballet, 1760–66) and the Paris Opéra (under the patronage of Queen **Marie Antoinette**, 1776–79). He also worked extensively in Lyon, Vienna and Milan. In 1760 he published his enormously significant *Lettres sur la danse*. During the French Revolution he formed a company at the King's Theatre, London, where he staged his last of approximately 150 ballets, none of which has survived.

NOVOTNÝ, Antonin (1904–75) Czech politician, born the son of a bricklayer in Letnany, near Prague. Becoming a communist at the age of seventeen, he survived four years in a Nazi concentration camp. After his release (1945) he rose rapidly in the Czechoslovak Communist party, and played a leading part in the Soviet take-over of the Czech government. He was first secretary of the party, and virtual dictator from 1953 to 1968. From 1957 to 1968 he was president of the republic. He remained a dedicated Stalinist, basing his state planning so much on the needs of heavy industry that by 1961 there was an economic recession. His unpopularity forced him to make token concessions from 1962 onwards, especially in the hope of placating the Slovaks, but these gestures of liberalization failed to satisfy his critics. He was succeeded as first secretary by the reformist Slovak, **Alexander Dubček**, in 1968, and resigned the presidency two months later.

NOYES, Alfred (1880–1958) English poet, born in Staffordshire. He began writing verse as an undergraduate at Oxford, and on the strength of getting a volume published in his final year he left without taking a degree. This book, *The Loom of Years* (1902), which was praised by **George Meredith**, was followed by *The Flower of Old Japan* (1903) and *The Forest of Wild Thyme* (1905), both of which attracted some notice. Noyes now turned to the subject of some of his most successful work—the sea, and in particular the Elizabethan tradition. *Forty Singing Seamen* (1908) and the epic *Drake* (1908) were in this vein. Having married an American, he travelled in the USA and became visiting professor of poetry at Princeton (1914–23). Between 1922 and 1930 appeared his trilogy *The Torchbearers*, praising men of science. He published literary essays in *Some Aspects of Modern Poetry* (1924), a defence of traditionalism. He also wrote plays, and studies of **William Morris** and **Voltaire**.

NOYES, Eliot (1910–77) American designer and architect, born in Boston, Massachusetts. As a student of architecture he came under the influence of **Gropius, Breuer** and **Le Corbusier**, and it is not surprising that he was the most 'European' of the prominent American designers working from the 1930s to the 1970s. In 1940 he set up and directed the department of industrial design at the Museum of Modern Art, New York. After working for the American stage designer and architect Norman Bel Geddes (1893–1958), he established his own practice in 1947. He set high ethical standards, working only for clients who shared his approach to design, and who allowed sufficient time and money for the proper execution of the project. This did not prevent his working for major companies such as Westinghouse, Mobil and, most notably, IBM, for which he became consultant design director. At his death it was said that 'objects the world over were his monument'.

NOYES, John Humphrey (1811–86) American social reformer, born in Brattleboro, Vermont. As a theological student he decided that the prevailing theology was wrong, and that sinlessness was attainable. He founded a 'Perfectionist' church at Putney, Vermont, and he and his converts put their property into a common stock. In 1846 he was arrested for his views on free love. In 1848 the communists removed to New York State, where they established a community at Oneida. It flourished and became an incorporated company in 1881, manufacturing silverware. He himself fled to Canada to escape prosecution for adultery. He published several books on his views.

NU U, (Thakin Nu) (1907–) Burmese politician. Educated at Rangoon University, he began his career as a teacher and in the 1930s joined the Dobhama Asiayone (Our Burma) nationalist organization. He was imprisoned by the British authorities at the outbreak of World War II, during the Japanese occupation, and in 1942 was released to serve in a nationalist puppet government. However, in 1945 he formed the Anti-Fascist People's Freedom League (AFPFL), which collaborated with the British against the Japanese, and on independence, in 1948, he became Burma's first prime minister. He held this post until 1962, apart from short breaks (1956–57 and 1958–60). In 1962, with regionalist discontent mounting, his parliamentary régime was overthrown by General **Ne Win**, and he was imprisoned until 1966 when he lived abroad, in Thailand and India, organizing exiled opposition forces. He returned to Burma in 1980, and in 1988 helped found the National League for Democracy political movement.

NUFFIELD, William Richard Morris, 1st Viscount (1877–1963) English motor magnate and philanthropist. He started in the bicycle repair business and by 1910 was manufacturing prototypes of Morris Oxford cars at Cowley, in Oxford. He was the first British manufacturer to develop the mass production of cheap cars. He received a baronetcy in 1929 and was raised to the peerage in 1934. He used part of his vast fortune to benefit hospitals, charities and Oxford University. In 1987 he endowed Nuffield College, Oxford, and in 1943 he established the Nuffield Foundation for medical, scientific and social research.

NUJOMA, Sam Daniel (1929–) Namibian politician. Born in Ongandjern and educated at a Finnish missionary school in Windhoek, he entered active politics as a co-founder of the South West Africa People's Organisation of Namibia (SWAPO) in 1958. After being exiled in 1960 he set up a provisional headquarters for SWAPO in Dar es Salaam, and on his return to Namibia in 1966 was again arrested and expelled. Feeling that peaceful opposition to South Africa's exploitation of his country was unproductive, he established a military wing, the People's Liberation Army of Namibia (PLAN), in the mid 1960s, and his long struggle for Namibia's independence eventually bore fruit in 1989. He was elected president of the new republic in February 1990, and formally instated the following month.

NUMA POMPILIUS (8th–7th century BC) the second of Rome's early kings. According to tradition he ruled from 715 to 673 BC. He is described as a peaceful ruler, and was credited with organizing the religious life of the community.

NUNCOMAR See **HASTINGS, Warren**

NÚÑEZ DE ARCE, Gaspar (1834–1903) Spanish poet, dramatist and statesman, born in Valladolid. He held office in the government in 1883 and 1888, and in 1894 received a national ovation at Toledo. As a lyric poet he may be styled the 'Spanish **Tennyson**', and among his poems are *Gritos del Combate* (1875), *Última Lamentación de Lord Byron* (1879), *El Vértigo* (1879), *La Pesca* (1884) and *La Maruja* (1886). His plays include *La Cuenta del Zapatero* (1859) and *El Haz de Leña* (1872).

NUNN, Sir (Thomas) Percy (1870–1944) English education administrator and teacher trainer, born in Bristol. Educated at his father's school (Weston-super-Mare) and Bristol University College, he taught in Halifax and London grammar schools, becoming vice-principal of London Day Training College in 1905. Director from 1922 to 1936, he transformed it into the Institute of Education of University of London (1932). His principal claim to fame is his book, *Education: its Data and First Principles* (1920), which derived its child-centred philosophy from **John Dewey**, the American educationist, and which dominated English teacher training for more than 25 years. He was on the drafting committee of the **Hadow** Committee (1926) and on the curriculum sub-committee of the **Spens** Committee (1938). Both reports incorporated his views on the validity and liberality of vocational education.

NUNN, Trevor (1940–) English stage director, born in Ipswich. A graduate of Cambridge University, he joined the Belgrade Theatre, Coventry, as a trainee director before joining the Royal Shakespeare Company in 1965. In 1968 he succeeded **Peter Hall** as the company's artistic director, being joined as co-artistic director by **Terry Hands** ten years later. He has directed many outstanding productions for the RSC, and during his directorship (1968–87) the RSC took many strides forward, including the opening of two new theatres in Stratford: The Other Place (1974) and The Swan (1986). He directed **Andrew Lloyd Webber**'s musical *Cats*, followed by *Starlight Express* (1984), *Chess* (1986) and *Aspects of Love* (1989).

NŪR AL-DĪN, also known as **al-Malik al-Ādil ('the Just Ruler')** (1118–74) sultan of Egypt and Syria. He was the son of the Turkish atabeg Zangī, whom he succeeded as ruler of Aleppo in 1146. He devoted himself to the jihād, the holy war against the Christian Franks of the crusader states, defeating and killing Prince Raymond of Antioch (1149) and completely extinguishing the most exposed Frankish state, the county of Edessa (1146–51). He saw the unification of the Muslim Middle East as the key to his aim, and worked to bring about the conquest of Damascus (1154) and Mosul (1170), while through his generals Shīrkūh and **Saladin** he took control of Egypt and abolished the Fatimid caliphate. Nūr al-Dīn's empire began to fall apart soon after his death, and it was left to **Saladin**, who by this time had made himself independent, to carry on his mission.

NUREYEV, Rudolf (1939–) Russian ballet-dancer, born in Siberia. He trained first as a folk dancer and then at the Leningrad Choreographic School, obtained political asylum in Paris in 1961 and became a member of Le Grand Ballet du Marquis de Cuevas. Since then he has had many different roles, often appearing with **Margot Fonteyn**, with whom he made his Covent Garden début in 1962. As a guest performer, he has danced with most of the prominent companies of the world. He has also had a successful career as a producer of full length ballets. Films in which he has appeared include *Swan Lake* (1966), *Don Quixote* (1974) and *Valentino* (1977).

NURI ES-SA'ID See **ES-SA'ID**

NURMI, Paavo Johannes (1897–1973) Finnish athlete, born in Turku. Known as 'the Flying Finn', he dominated long-distance running in the 1920s, during which decade he won nine gold medals at three Olympic games (1920, 1924 and 1928). From 1922 to 1926 he set four world records at 3000 metres, bringing the time down to 8:20.4 seconds. He also established world records at six miles (1921, 29:7.1), one mile (1923, 4:10.4) and two miles (1931, 8:59.5). Disqualified in 1932 for alleged professionalism, he nevertheless remained a Finnish national hero. His statue stands outside the stadium in Helsinki where, in 1952, he was given the honour of lighting the Olympic flame.

NUTTALL, Thomas (1786–1859) English-born American naturalist, born in Settle, Yorkshire. In 1808 he emigrated to Philadelphia, Pennsylvania, where he took up botany, accompanied several scientific expeditions, and discovered many new American plants. He wrote *Genera of North American Plants* (1818), and became curator of the Botanical Garden at Harvard (1822–32). Here he turned his attention to ornithology, and published *A Manual of the Ornithology of the United States and Canada* (1832).

NYERERE, Julius Kambarage (?1922–) Tanzanian politician, born in Butiama village, Lake Victoria. He qualified as teacher at Makerere College and, after a spell of teaching, took a degree in history and economics at Edinburgh. On his return, he reorganized the nationalists into the Tanganyika African National Union (1954) of which he became president, entered the Legislative Council (1958) and in 1960 became chief minister. In 1961, Tanganyika was granted internal self-government and Nyerere became premier. During 1962 he retired for a while to reorganize his party, but was elected president in December when Tanganyika became a republic. In 1964 he negotiated the union of Tanganyika and Zanzibar (which became Tanzania in October of the same year). He had genuine hopes of bringing a unique form of African socialism, based on rural values, to his country but his efforts were largely frustrated by economic difficulties, particularly following the debilitating war against the Ugandan dictator, **Idi Amin** in 1978–79. He gave up the presidency in 1985 but retained leadership of his party (CCM). Nyerere, known affectionately as Mwalimu, or teacher, has been one of Africa's most respected political figures.

NYS, Ernest (1851–1920) Belgian jurist. Professor of international law at Brussels, he was a member of the Permanent Court of Arbitration at The Hague, and wrote *La Guerre maritime* (1881), *Le droit de la guerre et les precurseurs de Grotius* (1882), *Les Origines du droit internationel* (1894) and *Le droit internationel et les principes, les théories, les faits* (1904).

NZINGA (d.1663) queen of Matamba. A royal princess of the Ndongo (a small kingdom adjoining the Portuguese colony of Angola), she fought to establish a kingdom independent of the Portuguese, free from war and the depredations of the slave-trade. In 1623 she went personally to Angola to negotiate with the governor and was baptized a Christian as Dona Aña de Souza. Driven out of Ndongo by Portuguese troops the following year, she created the new kingdom of Matamba. Here she trained up military élites to resist the Portuguese and allied herself with the Dutch following their capture of Luanda, the Angolan capital, in 1641. Although she had abandoned Christianity, she re-converted towards the end of her life, by which time Matamba had become a thriving commercial kingdom (largely through acting as a broker in the Portuguese slave-trade).

O

OAKESHOTT, Michael Joseph (1901–) English philosopher and political theorist, born in Harpenden, Hertfordshire. He was educated at Cambridge where he taught from 1929 to 1949, and in 1950 became professor of political science at the London School of Economics, retiring in 1969. His first and main philosophical work was *Experience and its Modes* (1933), written broadly from within the English idealist tradition. This view of human experience and conduct is developed in the political theory, which tends to be conservative, pragmatic and sceptical of systematization and ideology, as represented in *Rationalism in Politics* (1962), *On Human Conduct* (1975), and *On History, and other Essays* (1983).

OAKLEY, Annie, stage name of **Phoebe Anne Oakley Moses** (1860–1926) American rodeo star and sharp-shooter, born into an Ohio Quaker family. She learned to shoot at an early age, helping to provide food for her family after her father's death, and married Frank E Butler in 1880 after beating him in a shooting match. They formed a trick-shooting act, and from 1885 toured widely with the Buffalo Bill Wild West Show. A tiny woman just under five feet tall, she shot cigarettes from her husband's lips, and could shoot through the pips of a playing card tossed in the air (hence an 'Annie Oakley' for a punched free ticket). She retired in 1922. Her story was fictionalized in the **Irving Berlin** musical comedy *Annie Get Your Gun* (1946), starring Ethel Merman.

OAKSEY See **LAWRENCE, Geoffrey**

OASTLER, Richard (1789–1861) English factory reformer, known as the factory king, born in Leeds. Steward of the Fixby estates near Huddersfield from 1820, he campaigned against slavery, and agitated against the employment of children in factories. He advocated a ten-hour working factory day, which led to the Ten-Hours Act of 1847. He resisted the new poor law and was dismissed by his employer and imprisoned in the Fleet prison for debt (1840–44). From prison he published the *Fleet Papers* (1841–43).

OATES, Joyce Carol (1938–) American writer, born in Millersport, New York. She was educated at Syracuse University and the University of Wisconsin. Married to Raymond Smith in 1961, she taught English at the University of Detroit (1961–67), then she was appointed professor of English at the University of Windsor in Ontario. A prolific novelist, story writer and essayist, her first novel was *With Shuddering Fall* (1964). Splintered with violence and impressive in its social scope, her fiction challenges received ideas about the nature of human experience. *Them* (1969), her fourth novel, won a National Book award. Later novels include *Marya: A Life* (1986) and *You Must Remember This* (1989). Her interest in pugilism emerged in *On Boxing* (1987), first published in the *Ontario Review*, with which she has long had a connection.

OATES, Lawrence Edward Grace (1880–1912) English explorer, born in Putney. Educated at Eton College, he left school to serve in the South African War with the Inniskilling Dragoons. In 1910 he set out with Captain **Robert Scott**'s antarctic expedition, and was one of the party of five to reach the South Pole (17 January 1912). On the return journey the explorers suffered dangerous delay and became weatherbound. Lamed by severe frostbite, Oates, convinced that his crippled condition would fatally handicap his companions' prospect of winning through, walked out into the blizzard, deliberately sacrificing his life to enhance his comrades' chances of survival.

OATES, Titus (1649–1705) English conspirator and perjurer, born in Oakham, the son of an Anabaptist preacher. He attended Cambridge University, took orders, and held curacies and a naval chaplaincy, from all of which he was expelled for infamous practices. With the Rev Dr Tonge he resolved to concoct the 'narrative of a horrid plot', and, feigning conversion to Catholicism, was admitted to the Jesuit seminaries of Valladolid and St Omer. He was expelled from both for misconduct, but, returning to London in 1678, he told the authorities his pretended plot, the main features of which were a rising of the Catholics, a general massacre of Protestants, the burning of London, the assassination of the king (**Charles II**), and his brother James (**James II**) being placed on the throne. He swore to the truth of it before a magistrate, Sir Edmund Berry Godfrey, who was found dead in a ditch—murdered possibly by Titus and his confederates. All London immediately went wild with fear and rage, and Oates became the hero of the day. Several others came forward to back or emulate his charges; the queen herself was assailed; and many Catholics were cast into prison. He was directly or indirectly the cause of 35 judicial murders; but after two years a reaction set in. In 1683 Oates was fined £100000 for calling the Duke of York (the future James II) a traitor, and being unable to pay, was imprisoned; in May 1685 he was found guilty of perjury, and sentenced to be stripped of his canonicals, pilloried, flogged and imprisoned for life. He was set free in the Revolution of 1688 when he was even granted a pension.

OATLEY, Sir Charles (1904–) English electronic engineer and inventor, born in Frome, Somerset. He graduated in physics from St John's College, Cambridge in 1925 and shortly afterwards joined the staff of King's College, London. During World War II he was a member of the Radar Research and Development Establishment, and in 1945 he returned to Cambridge where in 1960 he became professor of electrical engineering. From 1948 his research was concentrated on the development of the scanning electron microscope, capable of producing three-dimensional images at magnifications of 100000 or more.

OBA (15th century–end 18th century) the dynastic title of the rulers of Benin, a city-state in western Africa which reached its imperial apogee in the 15th century under Ewuare the Great, who ruled c.1440–1473. In the 16th and 17th centuries the *oba* welcomed Portuguese traders and Benin became one of the most prosperous towns in Africa, but its economy was fatally reliant on supplying subject peoples as slaves to the Portuguese and, as the peoples of the surrounding territories became increasingly able to resist, Benin declined, losing most of its affluence by the end of the 18th century.

OBEL, Matthias de l' See **L'OBEL**

OBERLIN, Johann Friedrich (1740–1826) Alsatian clergyman, born in Strasbourg. In 1767 he became Protestant pastor of Waldbach, in the Ban de la Roche, which had suffered in the Thirty Years' War. Oberlin introduced better methods of cultivation and manufacture, made roads and bridges, founded a library and schools.

OBERTH, Hermann Julius (1894–1990) Hungarian-born German astrophysicist, born in Transylvania at Sibiu (Hermannstadt), called the father of German rocketry. Abandoning a medical career for mathematics and astronomy he published his first book *By Rocket to Interplanetary Space* in 1923. In 1928 he was elected president of the German Society for Space Travel (Verein für Raumschiffahrt). He designed a manned rocket and space cabin for **Fritz Lang**'s film *Woman in the Moon* in 1929. In World War II he worked at the experimental rocket centre at Peenemünde, and later, from 1955 to 1961, he assisted **Werner von Braun** in developing space rockets in the USA.

OBOLENSKY, Alexander, Prince (1916–40) Russian-born British rugby player, born in St Petersburg (Leningrad). Brought to England as an infant when the Russian Revolution broke out, he became a brilliant rugby union winger and played for Oxford University. Capped against the All-Blacks when they visited England in 1936 he scored two tries, the second being regarded as one of the classic tries of all time. He was killed in a flying accident while training with the RAF.

OBOTE, (Apollo) Milton (1924–) Ugandan politician. Educated at Makerere College, Kampala, in his mid-twenties he went to Kenya and worked as a labourer, clerk and salesman (1950–55). He returned to Uganda and was elected to the legislative council in 1957, and founded the Uganda People's Congress (UPC) in 1960. At independence in 1962 he became the new nation's first prime minister, under King Mutesa II of Buganda (1924–69) as head of state. Obote wanted to create a one-party state and, when this was opposed by the king, in 1966 he mounted a *coup*, declared a republic and made himself executive president. In 1971 he was, in turn, deposed by **Idi Amin** and took refuge in Tanzania. After Amin's removal in 1979, Obote returned and was re-elected president in 1980. His government was soon under pressure from opposition groups outside and inside Uganda and in 1985 he was ousted by Brigadier Basilio Okello. Obote fled to Kenya and was then granted political asylum in Zambia.

O'BRIEN, (Donal) Conor (Dermod David Donat) Cruise (1917–) Irish historian, critic and politician, born into a strongly nationalist Dublin family, described in his *States of Ireland* (1973). He had one of the most brilliant student careers in the history of Trinity College, Dublin. His doctoral dissertation, later published as *Parnell and his Party* (1957), was an outstanding historical mingling of political analysis and literary insight. Already his *Maria Cross* (1953), on imaginative patterns among certain Catholic writers, had established him as an outstanding critic. His finest work is *To Katanga and Back* (1962), an autobiographical narrative of the Congo crisis of 1961 which he had seen as UN secretary-general **Dag Hammarskjöld**'s representative in Kataga; the earlier tragedy of **Patrice Lumumba** formed the theme of his play *Murderous Angels* (1968). Following academic office in Ghana and New York, he was elected Irish Labour TD (MP) for Dublin Clontarf (1969), became minister for posts and telegraphs in 1973, and was defeated in 1977 because of his ruthless opposition to IRA violence in Northern Ireland and the self-indulgent romanticism in the Republic which fuelled it. He was subsequently editor-in-chief of *The Observer*, and a mordant political columnist, as well as the author of studies of **Albert Camus** and **Edmund Burke**.

O'BRIEN, Edna (1932–) Irish novelist, short story writer and playwright born in Tuamgraney, County Clare. Educated at the Convent of Mercy, Loughrea, and at the Pharmaceutical College of Dublin, she practised pharmacy briefly before becoming a writer. Her dominant themes are loneliness, guilt and loss, articulated in musical prose. 'My aim', she has written, 'is to write books that in some way celebrate life and do justice to my emotions'. Among her celebrated books are *The Country Girls* (1960), *The Lonely Girl* (1962), *Girls in Their Married Bliss* (1964), *August is a Wicked Month* (1965) and *A Pagan Place* (1970). *The Collected Edna O'Brien*, containing nine novels, was published in 1978.

O'BRIEN, Flann, pseud of **Brian O'Nolan** (1911–66) Irish writer, born in Strabane, County Tyrone, the third child in a family of twelve. His father working in the Customs and Excise, his early life was peripatetic but the family settled for a spell in a large house near Tullamore where Irish was the common tongue. Later they moved to Dublin and it was here that his formal education began at the Christian Brothers' school, renowned for its rigidly basic and brutally applied methods of education. In 1927, the family moved to the seaside suburb of Blackrock, where he wrote his earliest and finest books. He attended Blackrock College and University College, Dublin, studying German, Irish and English, although much of his time was frittered away at billiards or in pubs. From 1933 to 1934 he was in Germany where there is speculaton (but no proof) that he married a girl called Clara who died of consumption a month later. He returned to Dublin, finished his thesis, had it rejected (it was finally accepted in 1935) and founded *Blather*, whose six editions he wrote mainly himself. On Irish radio he gave talks on literature, completed his eccentric but brilliant novel *At-Swim-Two-Birds* (published four years later in 1939) and joined the Irish Civil Service which occupied him until his premature retirement in 1953. The death of his father and the need to supplement his salary to support his kin led him reluctantly to submit *At-Swim-Two-Birds* to publishers. Its acceptance by Collins owed much to **Graham Greene**'s enthusiasm and led to the birth of the Flann O'Brien pseudonym. A year later, in 1940, came the début of 'Myles na Gopaleen', the pseudonym under which he contributed a column to the *Irish Times* for some 20 years, and which he regarded as not so much a *nom de plume* as a *nom de guerre*. His second novel *An Béal Bocht* was published in Irish in 1941 (trans *The Poor Mouth*, 1973); *The Third Policeman*, written and rejected in 1940, was published posthumously in 1967. Best known as an idiosyncratic newspaper columnist, various anthologies appeared after his death—*The Best of Myles* (1968), *The Various Lives of Keats and Chapman and the Brother* (1976) and *Myles From Dublin* (1985).

O'BRIEN, James 'Bronterre' (1805–64) Irish journalist and Chartist, born in County Longford. Educated at Edgeworthstown school and Trinity College, Dublin, he went to London and was admitted to Gray's Inn where he came to know **Henry ('Orator') Hunt** and **William Cobbett**. He wrote extensively in the *Poor Man's Guardian* and the *Poor Man's Conservative* from 1831, signing himself 'Bronterre'. He studied and wrote on the French Revolution, with particular admiring attention to **Babeuf** and **Robespierre**, conducting ill-fated ideological journals in a revolutionary socialist spirit: *Bronterre's National Reformer*' (1837) and *The Operative* (1838–39). He was prominent in London Chartism from its beginnings in 1838, and established links with Manchester and secretly advocated physical force. He wrote violent articles for **Feargus O'Connor**'s *Morning Star* (1839), but opposed the idea of a general strike. He was indicted unsuccessfully for conspiracy at Newcastle but was sentenced to 18 months' imprisonment at Liverpool for seditious speaking (1840). He became editor of the *British Statesman* (1842) and denounced alliance with the Anti-Corn-Law League whose success he believed would strengthen agrarian and commercial capitalism. As editor of the *National Reformer* (1845), he advocated credit banks and 'symbolic' money. He opposed physical force in 1848 and left the Chartist revival of that year. He edited *Reynold's Newspaper* briefly, lectured extensively, and wrote at great length but instructively and influentially. He died in poverty, and the posthumous edition of his writings resulted in a book of major value, *The Rise, Progress, and Phases of Human Slavery* (1885).

O'BRIEN, Kate (1897–1974) Irish playwright and novelist, born in Limerick. She was educated at Laurel Hill Convent, Limerick, and University College, Dublin. At 30 she began a career in London as playwright and in 1931 she published her prizewinning *Without My Cloak*, followed by *Mary Lavelle* (1936), *Pray for the Wanderer* (1938), *The Land of Spices* (1941), *The Last of Summer* (1943), *That Lady* (1946) and *As Music and Splendour* (1958). A remarkable observer of life, she was injured by a deeply unhappy marriage to the Dutch historian **Gustaaf Johannes Renier**, and her novels are best understood by appreciation of her consciousness of a lesbian sexual identity. Her work reflected deep knowledge of Ireland and Spain as may be seen from her *Farewell Spain* (1937) and *My Ireland* (1962).

O'BRIEN, Richard Barry (1847–1918) Irish nationalist historian and biographer, born in Kilrush, County Clare. He studied at **Newman**'s ill-fated Catholic University of Dublin, after which he was called to the Irish (1874) and English (1875) bars without practising much. He was drawn into skilful and detailed historical writing in the cause of Irish home rule, producing many detailed works whose nationalist apologetics did not greatly weaken their considerable historical value. His masterpiece, *The Life of Charles Stewart Parnell* (1898), is one of the great political biographies of all time. He was founder, chairman and (from 1906) president of the Irish Literary Society in London from 1892 to 1911.

O'BRIEN, (Michael) Vincent (1917–) Irish horse trainer from Tipperary. He made an immediate impact on the post-war English National Hunt scene when he trained Cottage Rake, which won the Cheltenham Gold Cup in three consecutive years from 1948. Later he turned his attention to the Flat and on several occasions led the list of winning trainers. Two notably successful seasons were those of 1966, when he trained the winners of the Oaks, the 1000 Guineas, the Eclipse Stakes and the Champion Stakes; and 1977, when one of his horses, The Minstrel, won the Derby, the Irish Derby, the King George VI and Queen Elizabeth Stakes. On the Flat, he was closely associated with **Lester Piggott**, especially from 1968 to 1980.

O'BRIEN, William (1852–1928) Irish journalist and nationalist, born in Mallow, County Cork. A Catholic by birth, he was educated at the Protestant Cloyne Diocesan College and Queen's College, Cork. He became a journalist, founded the Land League journal, *United Ireland* (1881), sat in parliament as a Nationalist for Mallow (1883–95), founded the agrarian United Irish League (1898) and was nine times prosecuted and imprisoned for two years. He retired from parliament in 1895 owing to dissensions in the party. He headed the Independent Nationalists, but returned to parliament (1900–18) for Cork. He withdrew from politics in 1918 when the Sinn Fein party swept the polls. He wrote *Recollections* (1905), *Evening Memories* (1920), *An Olive Branch* (on 'All-for-Ireland', 1910) and *The Irish Revolution* (1923).

O'BRIEN, William Smith (1803–64) Irish nationalist, son of Sir Lucas O'Brien, born in County Clare. Educated at Harrow School and Cambridge, he was Conservative MP for Ennis (1825) and County Limerick (1835) and though a Protestant, supported the Catholic claims as a Whig. In October 1843 he joined **O'Connell**'s Repeal Association. Disillusioned by O'Connell's aversion to physical force he joined the Young Ireland party. After many disputes O'Brien in 1846 withdrew from the Association, and the Young Irelanders founded the Irish Confederation (1847). In March 1848 he urged the formation of a National Guard and a national rebellion. The sentence of **John Mitchel** for 'treason-felony' in 1848 hastened the projected rising, which ended ludicrously in an almost bloodless battle in the widow McCormack's cabbage-garden at Ballingarry in County Tipperary. O'Brien was arrested, tried and sentenced to death; but the sentence was commuted to transportation for life. He served five years in Tasmania, and in 1854 he was released on condition of not returning to Ireland. In 1856 he received an unconditional pardon. He returned to Ireland but took no further part in politics.

Ó BRUADAIR, Dáibhidh (David) (?1625–1698) Irish-Gaelic poet, recording the destruction of his culture, born in Cork into a family of some substance. He was impressively educated, but the wars and proscriptions drove his FitzGerald patrons in Kerry into danger and exile, and the poet's later verses dramatically and lyrically convey his fall from places of patronage and honour to the status of farm labourer. His work, complex and resourceful, innovative as well as traditional, offers a bridge from the earlier, assured world of the Gaelic bards to the dark dispossession of the next century. The Irish Texts Society published a bilingual edition of his surviving poems, *Duanaire Dháibhidh Uí Bhruadair* (1913–17).

O'BRYAN, William (1778–1868) English Nonconformist clergyman, son of a Cornish yeoman. He quarrelled with the Methodists and in 1815 founded a new methodist communion, the (Arminian) Bible Christians or Bryanites. In 1831 he went to the USA as an itinerant preacher.

Ó CADHAIN, Máirtín (ie **Martin Kane**) (1906–70) Irish Gaelic novelist, born in Galway. He became a schoolteacher, a post he lost having joined the Irish Republican Army in the 1930s. Working as a labourer and freelance teacher, he was IRA recruiting officer, his converts including **Brendan Behan**. Interned during World War II in the Curragh Camp, Kildare, he taught Irish to his fellow-prisoners and published Irish short stories, followed in 1949 by his masterpiece, *Cré na Cille*, a ruthless social analysis of rural community ill-feeling revealed by conversations and monologues of the corpses in the local graveyard. He was an official translator of Irish parliamentary debates from 1949, and was made lecturer in modern Irish in Trinity College, Dublin in 1956 (professor in 1969). He translated **Saunders Lewis**'s account of the Welsh language into Irish, and was fluent also in Scots Gaelic, Breton, German, Russian, Italian and French.

UNESCO translated his novel into several major European languages.

O'CASEY, Sean (1884–1964) Irish playwright, born in a poor part of Dublin. He picked up whatever education he could and worked as a labourer and for nationalist organizations before beginning his career as a dramatist. His early plays, dealing with low life in Dublin—*Shadow of a Gunman* (1923) and *Juno and the Paycock* (1924)—were written for the Abbey Theatre. Later he became more experimental and impressionistic. Other works include *The Plough and the Stars* (1926), *The Silver Tassie* (1929), *Cockadoodle Dandy* (1949) and *The Bishop's Bonfire* (1955). He also wrote essays, such as *The Flying Wasp* (1936). He was awarded the Hawthornden prize in 1926. His autobiography, begun in 1939 with *I Knock at the Door*, continued through several volumes to *Sunset and Evening Star* (1954).

OCCAM, William See **OCKHAM**

OCCLEVE, Thomas See **HOCCLEVE**

OCHINO, Bernardino (1487–1564) Italian Protestant reformer, born in Siena. He joined the Franciscans, but in 1534 changed to the Capuchins, becoming vicar-general of the order after four years. In 1542 he was summoned to Rome to answer for evangelical tendencies, but fled to **Calvin** in Geneva. In 1545 he became preacher to the Italians in Augsburg. **Cranmer** invited him to England, where he was pastor to the Italian exiles and a prebend in Canterbury. At **Mary I**'s accession (1553) he fled to Switzerland, and ministered to the Italian exiles in Zürich for ten years. The publication of *Thirty Dialogues*, one of which the calvinists said contained a defence of polygamy, led to his being banished. Ochino fled to Poland, but was not permitted to stay there and died at Slavkow in Moravia.

OCHOA, Severo (1905–) Spanish-born American biochemist, and joint winner of the 1959 Nobel prize for physiology or medicine. He studied medicine in Madrid and did research work at Heidelberg and Oxford. He emigrated to the USA in 1941 and joined the staff of the New York University Medicine School. He did research on the biological synthesis of nucleic activities, and shared the Nobel prize with **Arthur Kornberg**.

OCKHAM, William of (c.1285–c.1349) English philosopher, theologian and political writer, born in Ockham, Surrey. He entered the Franciscan order young, studied theology at Oxford as an 'inceptor' (beginner), but never obtained a higher degree or a teaching chair because of his controversial views, and left technically still an 'undergraduate'—hence his nickname 'the Venerable Inceptor'. He was summoned to Avignon by Pope **John XXII** to answer charges of heresy, and became centrally involved in the dispute about Franciscan poverty which the Pope had denounced on doctrinal grounds. He was forced to flee to Bavaria in 1328, was excommunicated, and stayed under the protection of Emperor Louis of Bavaria until 1347. He died in Munich, probably of the Black Death. He published many works on logic while at Oxford and Avignon, particularly the *Summa Logicae*, *Quodlibeta Septem* and commentaries on the *Sentences* of **Peter Lombard** and on **Aristotle**; and also several important political treatises in the period 1333–47, generally directed against the papal claims to civil authority and including the *Dialogus de potestate Papae et Imperatoris* and the *Opus nonaginta dierum*. His best-known philosophical contributions are his successful defence of nominalism against realism, and his deployment in theology of 'Ockham's razor', a rule of ontological economy to the effect that 'entities are not to be multiplied beyond necessity'. He was perhaps the most influential of later medieval philosophers.

O'CLERY, Michael, originally **Tadhg,** ie **Thaddeus Ó Cléirigh** (1575–?1643) Irish annalist, born in Kilbarron, County Donegal. He studied in Louvain as a Franciscan lay brother, and was sent back to Ireland in 1627 to gather manuscript material for the *Acta Sanctorum Hiberniae*. He also compiled materials for factual history, ultimately translated and edited by **John O'Donovan** as *The Annals of the Four Masters* (6 vols, 1848–57); and *Réim Rioghraidhe* (1630), an Irish royal genealogical listing; *Leabhar Gabhála*, a record of invasions of Ireland, mythological and historical; and an Irish lexicon, *Sanasán* or *Foclóir* (printed in Louvain in 1643), chiefly glossing difficult Irish words. His own original research task was enshrined in *Martyrologium Sanctorum Hiberniae*.

OCONAIRE, Pádraic (ie **Patrick Conroy**) (1883–1928) Irish Gaelic writer, born in Galway and educated in Gaelic-speaking Rosmuc. He went to sea, and spent many years in the London civil service, which he left in 1913 having won prizes in 1904 and 1909 for stories in Gaelic. He won fame as a novelist, essayist, travel-writer and short-story writer of deceptive simplicity and fine construction, sometimes working in children's fiction, sometimes taking up themes of psychological complexity which worried the more puritanical elements in the Gaelic revival. His later years were spent in writing and teaching Irish, chiefly in Galway.

O'CONNELL, Daniel (1775–1847) Irish political leader, called 'the liberator', born near Cahirciveen, County Kerry. Called to the Irish bar in 1798, he built up a highly successful practice. Leader of the agitation for the rights of Catholics, he formed in 1823 the Catholic Association which successfully fought elections against the landlords. Elected MP for Clare in 1828, he was prevented as a Catholic from taking his seat, but was re-elected in 1830, the Catholic Emancipation Bill having been passed in the meantime. He formed a new society for repeal of the Union, revived as often as suppressed by others under new names. He denounced the ministry of **Wellington** and **Peel**, but in the face of a threatened prosecution (1831) he temporized, saved himself, and was made king's counsel. In 1830 the potato crop had been very poor, and under O'Connell's advice the people declined to pay tithes, and that winter disorder was rampant everywhere. He had sat last for Kerry, when at the general election of 1832 he was returned for Dublin. At this time he nominated about half of the candidates returned, while three of his sons and two of his sons-in-law composed his 'household brigade'. Of the 105 Irish members, 45—his famous 'tail'—were declared Repealers. He fought fiercely against the Coercion Act of 1833. By **Feargus O'Connor**, the *Freeman's Journal*, and his more ardent followers he was forced to bring the Repeal movement prematurely into parliament; a motion for inquiry was defeated by 523 to 38. For the next five years (1835–40) he gave the Whigs a steady support. The Earl of Mulgrave and **Thomas Drummond** governed Ireland so mildly that O'Connell was prepared to abandon the Repeal agitation. In 1836 he was unseated on petition for Dublin, and he was returned for Kilkenny. In 1837 the mastership of the rolls was offered to him but declined. In August he founded his 'Precursor Society', and in April 1840 his famous Repeal Association. Yet the agitation languished until the appearance of the *Nation* in 1842 brought him the aid of **Dillon**, **Duffy**, **Davis**, **Mangan** and Daunt. In 1841 O'Connell lost his seat at Dublin, but found another at Cork, and in November he was elected lord mayor of Dublin. In 1843 he brought up Repeal in the Dublin corporation, and carried it by 41 to 15. The agitation now leaped into prominence, but the Young Ireland party began to grow impatient of the old chief's tactics, and O'Connell allowed himself to outrun his better judgment. **Wellington** poured 35000 men into Ireland. A great meeting was fixed at Clontarf for Sunday 8 October 1843, but it was proclaimed the day before, and O'Connell issued a counter-proclamation abandoning the meeting. Early in 1844, with his son and five of his chief supporters, he was imprisoned and fined for a conspiracy to raise sedition. The House of Lords set aside the verdict on 4 September; but for 14 weeks O'Connell lay in prison. He opposed Peel's provincial 'godless colleges', and it soon came to an open split between him and Young Ireland (1846). Next followed the potato famine. A broken man, he left Ireland for the last time in January 1847, and died in Genoa on his way to Rome.

O'CONNOR, Feargus Edward (1794–1855) Irish Chartist, born in Connorville, County Cork. He studied at Trinity College, Dublin, was called to the Irish bar, and entered parliament for Cork County in 1832. Estranged from **O'Connell**, he devoted himself to the cause of the working classes in England. His eloquence and enthusiasm gave him vast popularity, and his Leeds *Northern Star* (1837) did much to advance Chartism. Elected for Nottingham in 1847, he presented the monster Chartist petition in London in April 1848. In 1852 he became hopelessly insane.

O'CONNOR, (Mary) Flannery (1925–64) American novelist, born in Savannah, Georgia, whose environs she rarely left during her short life. She was educated at Peabody High School, Midgeville, Georgia, graduating in 1942. Thereafter she attended Georgia State College for Women and the University of Iowa. Brought up a Catholic and in the 'Christ-haunted' bible-belt of the Deep South, she homed in on the Protestant fundamentalists who dominated the region. The characters in her work seem superficially similar to those photographed by **Diane Arbus**: grotesque, deformed, freakish. This to her, however, was reality, and her heightened depicton of it is unforgettable. *Wise Blood* (1952), the first of her two novels, is a bizarre tragicomedy, and its theme of vocation is taken up again in her second, *The Violent Bear It Away* (1960). Regarded as one of the finest short-story writers of her generation, her work in that form can be found in *A Good Man Is Hard To Find and other stories* (1955) ('nine stories about original sin'), and *Everything That Rises Must Converge* (1965), affected by the pain she was suffering in the closing stages of chronic disseminated lupus. *The Habit of Being*: *Letters of Flannery O'Connor* was published in 1979.

O'CONNOR, Frank, pseud of **Michael O'Donovan** (1903–66) Irish writer, born in Cork. He was a member of the Irish Republican Army in his teens (1921–22), fought in the War of Independence and was imprisoned. He then worked as a railway clerk in Cork, and later a librarian in Wicklow, Cork and Dublin. Although he wrote plays and some excellent literary criticism—*Art of the Theatre* (1947), *The Modern Novel* (1956), *The Mirror in the Roadway* (1957)—his best medium was almost exclusively the short story. **Yeats** said of him that he was 'doing for Ireland what **Chekhov** did for Russia'. Representative titles are *Guests of the Nation* (1931), *Bones of Contention* (1936), *Crab Apple Jelly* (1944), *Travellers' Samples* (1956), and collections of short stories (1946, 1953, 1954 and 1956). He also wrote a memoir, *An Only Child* (1961), and critical studies, *The Lonely Voice* (1963) and *Shakespeare's Progress* (1960), and a biography of **Michael Collins**, *The Big Fellow* (1937).

O'CONNOR, Sandra Day (1930–) American judge, born in El Paso, Texas. She studied law and was admitted to the bar in California but then took up practice in Arizona, where she became assistant attorney-general (1965–69) and then a state senator. She was then a superior court judge of Maricopa County (1974–79) and a judge of the Arizona Court of Appeals (1979–81) before being named an associate justice of the Supreme Court of the US, the first woman to attain that office. As a justice she has taken full share in the work of the court and shown an independent spirit.

O'CONNOR, Thomas Power (1848–1929) Irish journalist and politician, born in Athlone. He was educated at Queen's College, Galway, and became a journalist for the *Saunders' Newsletter* in Dublin and the *Daily Telegraph* in London. Elected a Parnellite MP for Galway in 1880, he sat for Liverpool (Scotland division) in 1885, and was a conspicuous Irish Nationalist. He founded various Radical newspapers, including *TP's Weekly* (1902). He wrote *The Parnell Movement* (1886) and *Memoirs of an Old Parliamentarian* (1928). He became a privy councillor in 1924, and was 'Father of the House' of Commons for many years.

OCTAVIA (d.11 BC) Roman matron, sister of the emperor **Augustus**, distinguished for beauty and 'womanly' virtues. On the death of her first husband, Marcellus, in 40 BC she consented to marry **Marcus Antonius** (Mark Antony), to reconcile him and her brother; but in 32 BC Antony divorced and forsook her for **Cleopatra**.

OCTAVIAN See **AUGUSTUS**

O'CURRY, Eugene See **O'DONOVAN, John**

ODESCALCHI See **INNOCENT XI**

ODETS, Clifford (1903–63) American playwright and actor, born in Philadelphia. In 1931 he joined the Group Theatre, New York, under whose auspices his early plays were produced. The most important American playwright of the 1930s, his works are marked by a strong social conscience and grow largely from the conditions of the great depression of that time. They include *Waiting for Lefty*, *Awake and Sing* and *Till the Day I Die*, all produced in 1935, and *Golden Boy* (1937). He was responsible for a number of film scenarios, including *The General Died at Dawn*, *None but the Lonely Heart* (which he directed), *Deadline at Dawn*, and *The Big Knife*.

ODLING, William (1829–1921) English chemist, born in London. Waynflete professor of chemistry at Oxford, he classified the silicates and advanced suggestions with regard to atomic weights which made O = 16 instead of 8.

ODO (c.1036–1097) Anglo-Norman prelate, bishop of Bayeux, and half-brother of **William I, 'the Conqueror'.** He fought at the battle of Hastings (1066) and was created Earl of Kent. He played a conspicuous part under William in English history, and was regent during his absences in Normandy, but left England after rebelling against **William II Rufus**. He rebuilt Bayeux Cathedral, and may have commissioned the Bayeux tapestry.

ODOACER, or **Odovacar** (d.493) Germanic warrior, and first barbarian king of Italy from 467, the son of a tribal captain in the service of the western Roman empire. A leader of the Heruli, he was the German commander of the imperial guard in Rome. He took part in the revolution (476) which drove Julius Nepos from the throne after a 12-month reign and conferred on Orestes's son Romulus the title of Augustus, scoffingly turned to **Augustulus**. With the Herulians and other Germanic mercenaries he marched against Pavia, and stormed the city (476). Romulus abdicated in favour of Odoacer and thus perished the western Roman empire. Odoacer was a politic ruler; but his increasing power excited the alarm of the Byzantine Emperor **Zeno**, who encouraged **Theodoric the Great**, King of the Ostrogoths, to undertake an expedition against Italy (489). Odoacer, defeated in three great battles, shut himself up in Ravenna, which he defended for three years. Compelled by famine, he capitulated (493); a fortnight later he was assassinated by Theodoric himself.

O'DONNELL, Hugh Roe (?1571–1602) Irish rebel, known as Red Hugh, Lord of Tyrconnel. He fought against the English in Ireland with **Hugh O'Neill** , and went to Spain to seek military aid in 1602, leaving his power to his brother, Rory (1575–1608), who kissed the king's hand and was made Earl of Tyrconnel (1603); but having plotted to seize Dublin Castle (1607) Rory fled, and died in Rome.

O'DONNELL, Leopoldo (1809–67) Spanish soldier and politician, born in Tenerife, descended from an Irish family. He supported the infant Queen **Isabella II** against her uncle **Don Carlos** and later supported her mother, the regent **Maria Christina**, but was forced into exile with her in 1840. In 1843 his intrigues against Espartero were successful; and as governor-general of Cuba he amassed a fortune. He returned to Spain in 1846; was made war minister by **Espartero** in 1854, but in 1856 supplanted him as prime minister by a *coup d'état*. He was in three months' time succeeded by **Narváez**, but in 1858 he returned to power; in 1859 he led a successful campaign against the Moors in Morocco and was made Duke of Tetuan. He was prime minister again in 1863 and 1865, but in 1866 his government was upset by Narváez.

O'DONNELL, Peadar (Peter) (1893–1986) Irish revolutionary and writer, born in Meenmore, County Donegal, the son of a small farmer. He reflected the vigorous agrarian traditions of his native Donegal and added to them a lifelong republicanism and socialism. First a teacher, then labour organizer, then guerrilla republican leader, he opposed the 1921 Anglo-Irish Treaty, was captured in Civil War fighting, and escaped after a 41-day hunger-strike. A vigorous publicist and editor of *An Phoblacht*, the official IRA newspaper, he gave (and then withdrew) qualified support for **Eamon de Valera** in 1932, left the IRA in 1934, fought for the Spanish Republic in 1936–37 and wrote extensively on his experiences: the novel *Storm* (1925) on the Anglo-Irish war, *The Gates Flew Open* (1934) on his imprisonment, *Salud!* (1937) on the Spanish Civil War, and *There Will Be Another Day* (1963) on his campaign against land annuities which led to the Anglo-Irish Economic War of the 1930s. His editorship of the literary monthly, *The Bell* (1946–54), was invaluable in furthering Irish writing. His finest work is *Islanders* (1927), but his last novel, *The Big Windows* (1955), is also evocative of his power in social depiction.

O'DONOVAN, John (1809–61) Irish Gaelic scholar, born in Kilkenny. Educated in Dublin, he worked in the Irish Record Office and, with his brother-in-law Eugene O'Curry (1796–1862), on the Ordnance Survey, for which he visited every Irish parish to obtain accurate Irish place-names, his authoritative *Letters* on these and allied questions proving an invaluable historical source when published (50 vols, 1924–32). He worked from 1836 on Irish MSS in Trinity College, Dublin, from which came his analytical catalogue, generally regarded as the first step in scientific Gaelic scholarship. Together with O'Curry he founded the Archaeology Society and prepared a seminal Irish grammar. Editor of many Irish texts, his masterpieces are his editions of **Michael O'Clery**. He became professor of Celtic studies at Queen's College, Belfast in 1850, and collaborated in the translation of the *Senchus Mór*, corpus of ancient Irish laws.

O'DONOVAN, Michael See **O'CONNOR, Frank**

ODOVACAR See **ODOACER**

O'DUFFY, Eimar Ultan (1893–1935) Irish satirical playwright and novelist, born in Dublin. Educated at Stonyhurst (Jesuit) College in Lancashire, at first he followed his father in studying dentistry at University College, Dublin, but embraced the new Irish revolutionary cultural nationalism under the influence of **Thomas MacDonagh** and Joseph Plunkett, who published and produced his first play, *The Walls of Athens*, and whose Irish Theatre also staged his *The Phoenix on the Roof* (1915). He broke with them on the Easter Rising of 1916 where, as an Irish volunteer loyal to **John MacNeill**, he was one of the couriers who tried to transmit the order countermanding it. His best play, *Bricriu's Feast* (1919), satirized neo-Gaelicism, and his first novel, *The Wasted Island* (1919, revised 1929), is a valuable source on the origins of the Rising. He was responsive to **James Joyce**'s *Ulysses*, and wrote many novels of which the Butlerian fantasies *King Goshalk and the Birds*, *The Spacious Adventures of the Man in the Street*, and *Asses in Clover* are the most noteworthy. Emigrating to England in 1925, he ultimately espoused the Social Credit philosophy of Major C H Douglas, his *Life and Money* (1932) winning some success. He was married to Cathleen Cruise O'Brien, aunt of **Conor Cruise O'Brien**.

OECOLAMPADIUS, Joannes, Latinized Greek for **Hüssgen,** or **Hausschein** (1482–1531) German clergyman and scholar, born in Weinsberg in Swabia. He studied at Heidelberg, became tutor to the sons of the Elector Palatine, and subsequently preacher at Weinsberg (1510) and Basel (1515), where **Erasmus** employed him on his Greek New Testament. In 1520 he entered a monastery at Attomünster, but under **Luther**'s influence became a reformer at Basel in 1522 as preacher and professor of theology. On the Lord's Supper he gradually adopted the views of **Zwingli**, disputed with Luther at Marburg in 1529, and wrote treatises.

OEDIPUS Greek legendary figure, who killed his father Laius and married his mother Jocasta, as told notably in **Sophocles**' tragedy *Oedipus Rex*. An oracle had warned Laius, king of Thebes, that he would be killed by his son. Laius therefore exposed the infant Oedipus to die on the mountains, after piercing his feet with a spike (hence the name Oedipus, which in Greek means 'with swollen feet'). The young Oedipus was rescued and adopted by Polybus, king of Corinth, and grew up in the belief that the rulers of Corinth were his parents. When told by an oracle that he was fated to kill his father and marry his mother, he left Corinth in an attempt to avoid fulfilling the prophecy. On his way through Boeotia, he was involved in a quarrel with his (to him unknown) father Laius, and killed him. He freed Thebes from the scourge of the Sphinx by solving her riddles, and in return married the now-widowed Jocasta, his mother, and became king of Thebes. At length, the terrible truth about his origins and parenthood was revealed to him. Jocasta took her life, and Oedipus blinded himself. He was succeeded by Jocasta's brother, **Creon**.

OEHLENSCHLÄGER, Adam Gottlob (1779–1850) Danish poet and playwright, born in Copenhagen. The founder of Danish Romanticism, and the greatest Danish poet of his day, he was much influenced by

Goethe and the **Schlegel** brothers. He published his symbolic poem, *Goldhornene* (The Golden Horns) in 1802 and a verse fantasy, *Aladdin*, in 1805. He wrote some 24 blank-verse historical tragedies, starting with *Hakon Jarl* (Earl Hakon, 1807), followed by *Baldur hin Gode* (Baldur the Good) in 1808, *Palnetoke* (1809), *Correggio* (1909, written in German), and *Axel og Valborg* (1910). He later wrote a cycle of verse romances, *Helge* (1814), and *Nordens Guder* (Gods of the North), an epic ballad cycle based on the Norse mythology of the *Edda*. He was appointed professor of aesthetics at Copenhagen in 1910. In 1829 he was crowned 'king of the Scandinavian singers' by **Tegnér** at Lund, and in 1849 was publicly proclaimed as the national poet of Denmark.

OERSTED, Hans Christian (1777–1851) Danish physicist. Professor at the university of Copenhagen, he discovered in 1820 the magnetic effect produced by an electric current, made an extremely accurate measurement of the compressibility of water, and succeeded in isolating aluminuium for the first time in 1825.

OERTER, Al (Alfred) (1936–) American athlete and discus-thrower, born in Astoria, New York State. An outstanding Olympic competitor, he won four consecutive gold medals for the discus, at Melbourne (1956), Rome (1960), Tokyo (1964) and Mexico (1968), breaking the Olympic record each time. No other athlete has dominated his event so overwhelmingly for so long.

OETINGER, Christoph Friedrich (1702–82) German theosophic theologian. He was the leader of the Pietists and a disciple of **Swedenborg** and **Böhme**.

O'FAOLAIN, Sean (1900–) Irish writer, born in Dublin. He was educated at the National University of Ireland, and took his MA at Harvard. He lectured for a period (1929) at Boston College, then took a post as a teacher in Strawberry Hill, Middlesex and in 1933 returned to Ireland to teach. His first writing was in Gaelic, and he produced an edition of translations from Gaelic—*The Silver Branch*—in 1938. Before this, however, he had attracted attention with a novel, *A Nest of Simple Folk* (1933). He never quite repeated its success with later novels, and from then on wrote many biographies, including *Daniel O'Connell* (1938), *De Valera* (1939), and *The Great O'Neill* (1942), this last being a life of the 2nd Earl of Tyrone. He edited the autobiography of **Wolfe Tone** (1937). His *Stories of Sean O'Faolain* (1958) cover thirty years of writing and progress from the lilting 'Irishry' of his youth to the deeper and wider artistry of his maturity.

OFFA (d.796) king of Mercia from 757, and overlord of all England south of the Humber. He extended his dominion over Kent, Sussex, Wessex and East Anglia, and styled himself *rex Anglorum* in his charters. To protect his frontiers to the west after constant wars with the Welsh, he built the great earthwork known as Offa's Dyke, stretching for 70 miles along the Welsh border. He was probably the most powerful English monarch before the 10th century, and considered himself on an equal footing with **Charlemagne** in diplomatic correspondence. He founded a new archbishopric of Lichfield in 788 with the sanction of Pope Hadrian I. To secure the royal succession for his own line, he had his son Ecgfrith annointed as king of Mercia in 787; but Ecgfrith only survived him by a few months in 796.

OFFENBACH, Jacques (1819–80) German composer of *opéra bouffe*, born in Cologne. He came to Paris in 1833, becoming *chef d'orchestre* in the Théâtre-Français in 1848, and manager of the *Bouffes parisiens* in 1855. He composed a vast number of light, lively operettas, such as *Le Mariage aux lanternes*, but is best known as inventor of modern *opéra bouffe*, represented by *Orphée aux enfers* (1858), *La Belle Hélène*, *La Barbe bleu*, *La Grande Duchesse*, *Geneviève de Branant*, *Roi Carotte*, *La Vie Parisienne* and *Madame Favart*. The well-known *Contes d'Hoffmann* was not produced till after his death.

O'FLAHERTY, Liam (1897–1984) Irish writer, born on Inishmore in the Aran Islands. Educated at Rockwell College, Tipperary and University College, Dublin, he fought in the British army during World War I and later wandered in North America and Latin America. He returned to Ireland in 1921 and fought on the Republican side in the Irish Civil War. He went to London in 1922 to become a writer, and published his first novels, *Thy Neighbour's Wife* (1923) and *The Black Soul* (1924). *The Informer* (1926) won the James Tait Black prize and was a popular success. Other books, reflecting the intensity of his feeling and style, include *Spring Sowing* (1926), *The Assassin* (1928), *The Puritan* (1932), *Famine* (1937) and *Land* (1946). He also wrote three volumes of autobiography, *Two Years* (1930), *I went to Russia* (1931) and *Shame the Devil* (1934).

OFTERDINGEN, Heinrich von (12th–13th century) one of the famous *minnesinger* or lyric poets of Germany, who flourished between the years 1170 and 1250.

OGDEN, Charles Kay (1889–1957) English linguistic reformer, educated at Rossall School. He studied classics at Cambridge, where he was founder-editor of the *Cambridge Magazine* (1912–22) and founder in 1917 of the Orthological Institute. In the 1920s he conceived the idea of 'Basic English', a simplified system of English as an international language with a restricted vocabulary of 850 words, which he developed, with the help of **I A Richards**. With Richards he wrote *The Foundations of Aesthetics* (1921) and *The Meaning of Meaning* (1923).

OGDON, John Andrew Howard (1937–89) English pianist and composer, born in Mansfield Woodhouse, Nottinghamshire; he studied at the Royal Manchester College of Music. In 1962 he was joint winner (with **Ashkenazy**) of the Moscow Tchaikovsky Competition. He excelled in the repertoire of the virtuoso pianist-composer tradition, notably **Liszt**, **Busoni**, **Stevenson** and **Sorabji**; and his own works, both large and small, are very much part of that distinguished line. His career was sadly interrupted by the onset of mental illness, from which he was recovering before his death.

OGILBY, John (1600–76) Scottish topographer, printer and map-maker, born in Edinburgh. He became a dancing teacher in London and a tutor in the household of the Earl of **Strafford**, lost everything in the Civil War, but after the Restoration obtained court recognition and became a London publisher. The great fire of 1666 destroyed his stock but got him the job of surveying the gutted sites in the city. With the proceeds he established a thriving printing house and was appointed 'king's cosmographer and geographic printer'. His early productions include his own translations of **Virgil** and **Homer** (sneered at by **Alexander Pope** in the *Dunciad*), but his most important publications were the maps and atlases engraved in the last decade of his life, including Africa (1670), America (1671) and Asia (1673), and a road atlas of Britain (1675) unfinished at his death.

OGILVIE, St John (1579/80–1615) Scottish Jesuit priest and martyr, born in Banff. He worked in Edinburgh, Glasgow and Renfrew, and was hanged at Glasgow Cross for his defence of the spiritual supremacy of the pope. Beatified in 1927 and finally canonized in 1976, he is the only officially recognized martyr in post-Reformation Scotland.

OGILVY See **ALEXANDRA, Princess**

OGLETHORPE, James Edward (1696–1785) English general, born in London, the son of Sir Theophilus Oglethorpe. He served with Prince **Eugène** of Savoy, and from 1722 to 1754 sat in parliament. He projected a colony in America for debtors from English jails and persecuted Austrian Protestants. Parliament contributed £10000; **George II** gave a grant of land, after him called Georgia; and in 1732 Oglethorpe went out with 120 persons and founded Savannah. In 1735 he took out 300 more, including **Charles** and **John Wesley**; and in 1738 he was back again with 600 men. War with Spain was declared in 1739; in 1740 Oglethorpe invaded Florida, and in 1742 repulsed a Spanish invasion of Georgia. In 1743 he left the colony to repel malicious charges. He was tried and acquitted after the 1745 Jacobite Rising for failing as major-general to overtake Prince **Charles Edward Stewart**'s army.

O'GORMAN, Juan (1905–82) Mexican architect, born and trained in Mexico City. He was apprenticed to Carlos Santacilia in 1927, subsequently studying painting under **Diego Rivera**. Thereafter he worked as a draughtsman and as director of the Town Planning Administration, beginning independent practice in 1934. He began as a Functionalist, eschewing the ideas of **Le Corbusier**, apparent in early works such as the studio for Diego Rivera. He later rejected the purist simplicity of Functionalism and, inspired by **Frank Lloyd Wright**, turned in the 1950s to the artistry of traditional Mexican architecture. His masterpieces include the Library of the National University of Mexico in Mexico City (1952, in collaboration), and his own house, San Angelo, Avenida San Jeronimo (1953–56). He also created many striking murals and frescoes for his buildings. In later years, disillusioned, he turned to painting. He died by his own hand.

O'HARA, John (1905–70) American novelist and short story writer, born in Pottsville, Pennsylvania. In his fiction Pottsville becomes 'Gibbsville', the setting for *Appointment in Samarra* (1934). Its naturalistic, fatalistic account of the last three days in the life of Julian English made him almost overnight a success. 'Brash as a young man', wrote **John Updike**, 'he became with success a slightly desperate braggart'. Notoriously irascible and hypersensitive, his best known works—*Butterfield 8* (1935) and *Pal Joey* (1940)—became film and stage successes. His short stories are obsessed with class, social privilege and feminist issues.

O'HIGGINS, Bernardo (1778–1842) Chilean revolutionary, born in Chillán, the illegitimate son of Ambrosio O'Higgins (c.1720–1801), the Irish-born viceroy of Chile (1789) and of Peru (1795). He played a great part in the Chilean revolt of 1810–17, and became known as the 'Liberator of Chile'. In 1817–23 he was the new republic's first president, but was deposed after a revolution and retired to Peru.

O'HIGGINS, Kevin Christopher (1892–1927) Irish politician, born in Stradbally, County Laois. He joined the newly emerging Sinn Féin party after the Rising of 1916, became MP as abstentionist candidate in his family constituency (1918), and his formidable legal powers consolidated his ascendancy in Dáil Éireann. After the Dáil split on the Treaty issue in 1922, his cruel skill in debate and defence of hard policies of repression made him the most hated opponent of his former comrades now in arms against the Irish Free State. As minister for justice, he was assassinated by unknown gunmen.

OHLIN, Bertil Gotthard (1899–1979) Swedish economist and politician, born in Klippan. Educated in Sweden and at Harvard, he was professor at Copenhagen (1925–30) and at Stockholm (1930–65). He was a member of the Swedish parliament from 1938 to 1970 and leader of the Liberal party from 1944 to 1967. He was awarded the 1977 Nobel prize for economics, jointly with **James Meade**.

OHM, Georg Simon (1789–1854) German physicist. He became professor at Nuremburg (1833–49) and Munich (1849–54), after a long struggle to get due recognition for the importance of his work. Ohm's Law had been published in 1827 as a result of his researches in electricity, and the measure of resistance is called the Ohm.

OHNET, George (1848–1918) French novelist, born in Paris. Under the general title of *Les Batailles de la vie*, he published a series of novels, some of which went beyond 100 editions.

OHTHERE, Norse **Óttar** (9th century), wealthy Norwegian merchant and mariner from Halogalond in the far north of Norway. In the 880s he visited the court of King **Alfred** of Wessex with gifts and a cargo of exotic furs, skins and walrus-ivory. He gave Alfred valuable geographical information about northern Scandinavia, which the king incorporated in his translation of Orosius' *History of the World*.

OISTRAKH, David Feodorovitch (1908–74) Russian violinist, born in Odessa. He studied at Odessa Conservatory, graduating in 1926. In 1928 he went to Moscow and began to teach at the Conservatory there in 1934, being appointed professor in 1939. He made concert tours in Europe and America, and was awarded the Stalin prize in 1945 and the Lenin prize in 1960. His son Igor Davidovitch (1931–), born in Odessa, is also a noted violinist.

O'KEEFE, Georgia (1887–1986) American painter, born on a farm at Sun Prairie, Wisconsin. Educated at a convent in Madison, she studied at the Art Institute of Chicago, 1905–06, and at the Art Students' League in New York, 1907–08, where she met **Alfred Stieglitz**, whom she married in 1924. As early as 1915 she pioneered abstract art in America (eg *Blue and Green Music*, 1919) but later moved towards a more figurative style, painting flowers and architectural subjects, frequently with a Surrealist flavour. After her husband's death in 1946 she lived in New Mexico from 1949, but travelled extensively in Europe, Asia and the Middle East in the 1950s and 1960s.

OKEGHEM or **OCKEGHEM, Johannes** (c.1430–1497) Flemish composer, born probably in Termonde. By 1452 he had become a court musician to **Charles VII** of France, and was in 1459 treasurer of the abbey of St Martin at Tours. He was also kapellmeister to **Louis XI**. He played an important part in the stylistic development of church music in the 15th century and was renowned as a teacher; **Josquin** was probably among his pupils.

O'KELLY, James (1845–1916) Irish war correspondent and politician, born in Dublin. He seems to have done some studying at Trinity College, Dublin, and at the Sorbonne, before joining the French Foreign Legion in which he served against **Maximilian** in Mexico and remained as Captain until the fall of Paris in 1870. He covered the Cuban revolt for the *New York Herald*, was captured by Spanish troops, sentenced to be shot, and respited in Spain partly through intervention by **Isaac Butt**. He remained a top war reporter for the *Herald*, covering the Brazilian imperial tour of the USA and **Sitting Bull**'s war of 1876–77, but was drawn into Fenian negotiations with the young **Charles Stewart Parnell**. As Clan-na-Gael emissary he was converted to Parnell's cause, apparently becoming his closest political friend, and became MP for Roscommon (1880–1916, being ousted in 1892–95 as Parnellite after the divorce scandal). He kept up international journalism for a time, covering the revolt of the Mahdi (**Muhammad Ahmed**) in the Sudan for the *Daily News*. In his *Herald* years he was surpassed by **H M Stanley** alone.

O'KELLY, Sean Thomas, properly **Ó Ceallaigh, Seán Thomas** (1882–1966) Irish statesman, born in Dublin. A pioneer in the Sinn Fein movement and the Gaelic league, he fought in the Easter Rising (1916) and was imprisoned. Elected to the first Dáil in 1918, he became speaker (1919–21), minister for local government (1932–39) and for finance and education (1939–45). He was president of the Irish Republic from 1945 to 1952, and again from 1952 to 1959.

OKEN, Lorenz, originally **Ockenfuss** (1779–1851) German naturalist and nature philosopher. He became professor of medicine at Jena in 1807. In 1816 he issued a journal called *Isis*, which led to government interference and his resignation. In 1828 he obtained a professorship at Munich, and in 1832 at Zürich. His theory that the skull is a modified vertebra was later discredited.

OLAF I TRYGGVASON (c.965–1000) king of Norway from 995. The great-grandson of **Harald I Halfdanarson ('Fine Hair')**, he became the most spectacular Viking of his time and the subject of much legend. He was brought up in Novgorod at the court of Prince **Vladimir I** of Russia and became a Viking mercenary in the Baltic at the age of 18. In the early 990s he took part in Viking expeditions to Britain, and was the leader of the Viking army that defeated a gallant Anglo-Saxon force at the celebrated battle of Maldon in Essex in 991. He returned to harry England in 994 in a huge expedition led by the king of Denmark, **Svein I Haraldsson** ('Fork-Beard'). While in England he was converted to Christianity; in the following year he returned to Norway, where he seized the throne for himself and attempted to convert Norway to Christianity by force, but with only limited success. After a lurid five-year reign he was overwhelmed by a combined Danish and Swedish fleet at the battle of Svold in 1000; when defeat became inevitable he leapt overboard and was never seen again.

OLAF II HARALDSSON, (St Olaf) (c.995–1030) king of Norway from 1014, the half-brother of King **Harald III 'Hardraade'**. He became a Viking mercenary in the Baltic at the age of twelve, graduating to attacks on England, Frisia and Spain. In England in 1010 he took part in a celebrated attack on London when London Bridge was torn down by grappling irons ('London Bridge is falling down'). He was converted to Christianity in Normandy in 1013, and returned to Norway in 1014, where he seized the throne and worked hard to complete the conversion of Norway begun by **Olaf I Tryggvason** and establish the church. In 1028, faced by rebellion abetted from Denmark, he was forced to flee to Russia for safety; in 1030 he came back in an attempt to regain his crown, but was defeated and killed at the battle of Stiklestad. Within twelve months he was regarded as a national hero and the patron saint of Norway.

OLAF III HARALDSSON, 'the Peaceful' (d.1093) king of Norway from 1067, the son of **Harald III Hardraade**. He was at the battle of Stamford Bridge in Yorkshire in 1066 when his father was defeated and killed by King **Harold II Godwinsson** of England, but was allowed to return to Norway with the survivors of the Norwegian invasion force, and assumed the throne of Norway the following year. His long reign was marked by unbroken peace and prosperity in Norway. He was succeeded by his illegitimate son, **Magnus III 'Barelegs'**.

ÓLAFSSON, Eggert (1726–68) Icelandic antiquarian and poet, born in Snæfellsnes. Educated at Copenhagen University, he was a pioneer in the preservation of Iceland's language and culture. From 1752 to 1757 he conducted (with the physician and naturalist Bjarni Pálsson) the first comprehensive survey of Iceland's geography, natural resources and people, which was published in Danish as *Reise igiennem Island* (2 vols, 1772) and soon translated into many languages. Before its publication, however, he was drowned at sea.

OLAUS See **MAGNUS** and **PETRI, Olaus**

OLAV V (1903–) king of Norway from 1957, son and successor of **Haakon VII** and Maud, daughter of **Edward VII** of Britain. Born in England, he was educated in Norway and at Balliol College, Oxford. An outstanding sportsman and Olympic yachtsman in his youth, he stayed in Norway when it was invaded by Germany in 1940, and was appointed head of the Norwegian armed forces. Later he escaped with his father to England, returning in 1945. In 1929 he married Princess Martha of Sweden (1901–54), and has two daughters and a son, Harald, the heir to the throne.

OLBERS, Heinrich Wilhelm Matthäus (1758–1840) German physician and astronomer. While practising medicine at Bremen, he calculated the orbit of the comet of 1779; discovered the minor planets Pallas (1802) and Vesta (1807); discovered five comets (all but one already observed at Paris); and invented a method for calculating the velocity of falling stars.

OLBRICH, Joseph Maria (1867–1908) German architect and designer, born in Troppau in Silesia. He was a contemporary of **Josef Hoffmann** at Vienna Academy of Fine Arts, where he won the Rome Prize. He, too, was a prominent member of the Vienna Secession and in 1897–98 built its exhibition building. In 1899 he joined the Darmstadt Artists' Colony where **Peter Behrens** was also working. In Darmstadt he designed a number of buildings, including the outstanding Wedding Tower (1907), as well as furniture, lighting, cutlery and graphics.

OLCOTT, Henry Steel (1832–1907) American theosophist, born in Orange, New Jersey. A lawyer by training, he studied theosophy under **Madame Blavatsky** and was founder president of the Theosophical Society in 1875. He travelled to India and Ceylon as her partner (1879–84), but fell out with her in 1885. He opened schools for untouchables in India, and became an associate of **Annie Besant**.

OLD MORTALITY See **PATERSON, Robert**

OLDCASTLE, Sir John (c.1378–1417) English Lollard leader and rebel, known as the 'good Lord Cobham'. He served under **Henry IV** on the Welsh marches. He acquired the title of Lord Cobham by marrying the heiress in 1409, and presented a remonstrance to the Commons on the corruptions of the church. He had **Wycliffe**'s works transcribed and distributed, and paid preachers to propagate his views. In 1411 he commanded an English army in France, and forced the Duke of Orléans to raise the siege of Paris; but in 1413, after the accession of **Henry V**, he was examined, and condemned as a heretic. He escaped from the Tower into Wales; a Lollard conspiracy in his favour was stamped out; and after four years' hiding he was captured, brought to London, and was 'hanged and burnt hanging'. **Halliwell-Phillipps** first proved in 1841 that **Shakespeare**'s Sir John Falstaff was based on a popular tradition of dislike for the heretic Oldcastle. Though he stood high in the favour of 'Prince Hal', there is no historical ground for representing him as his 'boon companion'.

OLDENBARNEVELDT See **BARNEVELDT, Jan van Olden**

OLDENBURG, Claes Thure (1929–) Swedish-born American sculptor, born in Stockholm. He lived in America from 1936 and became a US citizen in 1953. he studied at Yale and the Art Institute of Chicago before moving to New York in 1956. There he came into contact with leading artists of the avant-garde, and from c.1958 became part of the milieu from which 'happenings' and Pop Art developed. In the early 1960s he worked on 'total environment' exhibitions inspired by New York street life, and in 1962 began to make giant versions of foodstuffs such as hamburgers. The following year he introduced soft sculptures of normally hard objects like light switches, made of vinyl or canvas stuffed with kapok. His projects for colossal monuments in public places (eg giant lipsticks in Piccadilly Circus) have occasionally been realized, as in the *Giant Clothespin* (1975) in Philadelphia.

OLDFIELD, Anne (1683–1730) English actress, born in London. She made her début in 1700, and by 1705 had become one of the most popular actresses of her time. She continued to act until the last year of her life.

OLDFIELD, Barney (Berna Eli) (1878–1946) American motor-racing driver, born in Wauseon, Ohio, who specialized in short 'match' races on dirt-tracks at the turn of the century. He was chief driver from 1902 of **Henry Ford**'s '999' racer. In 1903 he became the first American to race a mile in a minute (at Indianapolis), then in 1910 he set records at one mile, two miles and one kilometre. An extrovert showman, he preferred the one-off challenges to organized races like the Indianapolis 500, but competed in them too with some success. He retired in 1918. His success in motor-sport earned him a fortune, but he was reported to have lost $1 million in the Wall Street crash.

OLDFIELD, Bruce (1950–) English fashion designer, born in London. He taught art then studied fashion in Kent (1968–71) and in London (1972–73), after which he became a freelance designer. He designed for Bendel's store in New York and sold sketches to **Yves Saint Laurent**. He showed his first collection in 1975 in London. His designs include evening dresses for royalty and screen stars, and ready-to-wear clothes.

OLDHAM, Richard Dixon (1858–1936) British geologist and seismologist born in Dublin, discoverer of the Earth's core. Educated at the Royal School of Mines, he was a member of the Geological Survey of India (1878–1903) and director of the Indian Museum in Calcutta (from 1903). His report on the Assam earthquake of June 1897 distinguished for the first time between primary and secondary seismic waves. In 1906 he established from seismographic records the existence of the Earth's core.

OLDMIXON, John (1673–1742) English author. He wrote dull, partisan histories of England, Scotland, Ireland and America, and works on logic and rhetoric. He was satirized by **Pope** in *The Dunciad*.

OLDYS, William (1696–1761) English antiquary and bibliographer, illegitimate son of Dr Oldys, chancellor of Lincoln. He was librarian to the Earl of Oxford (1738–41), whose valuable collections of books and MSS he arranged and catalogued. He was appointed Norroy king-of-arms (1755–61). His chief works are a *Life of Sir Walter Raleigh*, prefixed to **Raleigh**'s *History of the World* (1736), and *The British Librarian* (1737). He worked with **Samuel Johnson** on a catalogue of the Harleian Library, and issued with him *The Harleian Miscellany* (1753).

OLE-LUK-OIE See **SWINTON, Sir Ernest Dunlop**

OLGA, St (d.968) Russian saint, wife of prince Igor of Kiev. She ruled Kiev during the minority of her son (945–64). She was baptized at Constantinople (c.657) and, returning to Russia, laboured for the new creed. Her grandson was **St Vladimir I**.

OLIPHANT, Carolina See **Nairne, Lady**

OLIPHANT, Laurence (1829–88) English travel writer and mystic, born in Capetown, son of the attorney-general there. His first work, *A Journey to Khatmandu* (1852), was followed by *The Russian Shores of the Black Sea* (1853). As secretary to James Bruce, 8th Earl of **Elgin**, he travelled to China in 1857–58, thus finding material for further books. In 1861, while acting as *chargé d'affaires* in Japan, he was severely wounded by assassins. From 1865 to 1868 he sat for the Stirling burghs. His satirical novel, *Piccadilly* (1870), was a book of exceptional promise, full of wit and delicate irony. He joined the religious community of **Thomas Lake Harris** in the USA, and later settled in Haifa in Palestine. His mystical views he published in 1886 in *Sympneumata* (written with his wife and advocating purity in one's sex life) and *Scientific Religion* (1888).

OLIPHANT, Margaret, née **Wilson** (1828–97) Scottish novelist, born in Wallyford, near Edinburgh. When she was ten years old her family moved to England. She took her name from her mother; little is known of her father, Francis Wilson, except that he once 'took affadavits' in a Liverpool customs house. Precocious, she wrote a novel when she was 16 but her first published work was *Passages in the Life of Mrs Margaret Maitland* (1849), and two years later she began her lifelong connection with the Edinburgh publishers Blackwood and *Blackwood's Magazine*, culminating in a history of the firm, published posthumously (1897). In 1852 she married her cousin, Frances Oliphant, an artist, but she was widowed in 1859 and found herself £1000 in debt with an extended family to support and educate. Her output was astonishing and uneven, hardly surprising in an author who wrote almost 100 novels. The best known are in the group known as *The Chronicles of Carlingford*, consisting of *The Rector and the Doctor's Family* (1863), *Salem Chapel* (1863), *The Perpetual Curate*, (1864), *Miss Majoribanks* (1866), and *Pheobe Junior* (1876), which have earned her the sobriquet, a 'feminist **Trollope**'. She wrote novels of Scottish life, including *The Minster's Wife* (1869), *Effie Ogilvie* (1886), and *Kirsteen* (1890). Other notable works include *Hester* (1883), *Lady Car* (1889), *The Railway Man and his Children* (1891) and *Sir Robert's Fortune* (1895). She was awarded a Civil List pension in 1868 but her industry was unabated and she produced a spate of biographies, literary histories, translations, travel books and tales of the supernatural.

OLIPHANT, Sir Mark (Marcus Laurence Elwin) (1901–) Australian nuclear physicist, born in Adelaide. He studied there and at Trinity College and Cavendish Laboratory, Cambridge, where he did valuable work on the nuclear disintegration of lithium. Professor at Birmingham (1937), he designed and built a 60-inch cyclotron, completed after World War II. He worked on the atomic bomb project at Los Alamos (1943–45), but at the end of hostilities strongly argued against the American monopoly of atomic secrets. In 1946 he became Australian representative of the UN Atomic Energy Commission, designed a proton-synchrotron for the Australian Government and from 1950 to 1963 was research professor at Canberra.

OLIVARES, Gaspar de Guzmán, Count of (1587–1645) Spanish nobleman and politician, Duke of San Lücar. He was born in Rome where his father was ambassador. He was the favourite of **Philip IV** of Spain, and his prime minister for 22 years. He wrung money from the country to carry on foreign wars. His attempts to rob the people of their privileges provoked insurrections and roused the Portuguese to shake off the Spanish yoke in 1640, and the king was obliged to dismiss him in 1643.

OLIVE, 'Princess', assumed title of **Mrs Olivia Serres,** née **Wilmot** (1772–1834) English impostor, born in Warwick, the daughter of a house painter, Robert Wilmot. In 1817 she claimed to be an illegitimate daughter of the Duke of **Cumberland**, brother of **George III**, then in 1821 had herself rechristened as Princess Olive, legitimate daughter of the Duke and his first wife, Olive. The same year, arrested for debt, she produced an alleged will of George III, leaving £15000 to her as his brother's daughter, but in 1823 her claims were found to be baseless, and she died within the rules of the King's Bench. Her elder daughter, Mrs Lavinia Ryves (1797–1871), took up her mother's claim of legitimacy, which a jury finally repudiated in 1866.

OLIVER, Isaac (c.1560–1617) English miniature painter, of French Huguenot origin. He was the pupil and later the rival of **Nicholas Hilliard**, and executed portraits of Sir **Philip Sidney**, **Anne of Denmark**, and others.His son and pupil, Peter (1594–1648), continued his work, and was employed by **Charles I** to copy old master paintings in miniature.

OLIVER, King (Joe) (1885–1938) American cornettist, composer and bandleader, born in Abend, Louisiana, and raised in New Orleans. His first instrument was the trombone, and as a youth he played in various parade bands as well as in early jazz groups. He moved to Chicago where in 1922 he formed his Creole Jazz Band; featuring his cornet partnership with **Louis Armstrong**, the band made some of the finest recordings of the period. Although Oliver worked as a musician until 1937, he made no recordings after 1931. Some of his compositions, such as 'Dippermouth Blues' and 'Dr Jazz', are part of the standard traditional repertoire.

OLIVETTI, Adriano (1901–60) Italian manufacturer, born in Ivrea. After a period in the USA assimilating the methods of mass-production, he returned to transform the manufacturing methods of the typewriter firm founded by his father Camillo Olivetti (1868–1943). As well as vastly increasing production, he established a strong design policy which embraced products, graphics and the architecture of the company's buildings. Many notable designers such as Marcello Nizzoli, Marco Zanuso and **Ettore Sottsass Jnr** are associated with Olivetti. His strong social concerns, for which he was widely noted, led him to provide housing and facilities of a high standard for his employees. He made the company the exemplary manufacturer of the 'Modern Movement'. The firm survived a period of stagnation in the 1970s to regain its primacy by exploiting modern technological advances in office equipment.

OLIVIER, Laurence Kerr, Baron (1907–89) English actor, producer and director, born in Dorking. His first professional appearance was as the Suliot officer in *Byron* in 1924, after which he played all the great Shakespearean roles, including a memorable Titus, while his versatility was underlined by a virtuoso display in *The Entertainer* (1957) as a broken-down low comedian. After war service he became in 1944 co-director of the Old Vic Company. He produced, directed and played in films of *Henry V*, *Hamlet* and, notably, *Richard III*. He was knighted in 1947. He was divorced from his first wife, Jill Esmond, in 1940 and in the same year married **Vivien Leigh**. They were divorced in 1960. In 1961 Olivier married **Joan Plowright** (b.1929), the English stage actress. In 1962 he succeeded brilliantly as director of a new venture, the Chichester Theatre Festival, and later the same year was appointed director of the National Theatre, where among many successes he directed and acted a controversial but outstanding *Othello* (1964). He was director of the National Theatre until 1973, and then Associate Director for a year. After 1974 he appeared chiefly in films and on television. He was made a life peer in 1970 and awarded the OM in 1981.

OLLIVIER, Émile (1825–1913) French politician, born in Marseilles. He established a reputation at the Parisian bar, and after 1864 acquired influence as a member of the Legislative Assembly. In 1865 the viceroy of Egypt appointed him to a judicial office. In January 1870 **Napoleon III** charged him to form a constitutional ministry, but 'with a light heart' he rushed his country into war with Germany. He was overthrown on 9 August and withdrew to Italy for a time. He was the author of numerous works, including *L'Empire libéral*, a defence of his policy (16 vols, 1894–1912).

OLMSTED, Frederick Law (1822–1903) American landscape architect, born in Hartford, Connecticut. He was co-designer of Central Park, New York, and of other famous parks, and planned the layout of the Chicago World's Fair of 1893.

OLNEY, Richard (1835–1917) American Democratic statesman, born in Oxford, Massachusetts. He was educated at Harvard, and called to the bar. In 1893 he became attorney-general under **Cleveland**, in June 1895 secretary of state, and within six months caused a crisis by his interference, in virtue of the Monroe Doctrine, in the boundary question between British Guiana and Venezuela. In 1897 he returned to the bar at Boston. In 1913 he declined the ambassadorship to London.

OLSON, Harry Ferdinand (1901–82) American radio engineer and inventor, born in Mount Pleasant, Iowa. He graduated from the University of Iowa and joined the RCA laboratories in 1928, his first invention being a directional microphone, later developed into a true unidirectional microphone of the type still in use today. In the late 1940s he carried out a series of tests which established the standards for high-fidelity sound reproduction, then he developed the first electronic music synthesizer (1955) with which Charles Wuorinen (1938–) produced his composition *Time's Encomium* which was awarded the Pulitzer prize for music in 1971. Olson held more than 100 US patents for acoustic devices and systems.

OLYMPIAS (d.316 BC) Macedonian queen, wife of **Philip II** of Macedon, and mother of **Alexander the Great**. She was the daughter of king Neoptolemus of Epirus. When Philip divorced her and married Cleopatra, niece of Attalus, she left Macedon and ruled Epirus by herself, and is said to have brought about the murder of Cleopatra. After Alexander's death in 323 she returned to Macedon, where she secured the death of his half-brother and successor, and made Alexander's posthumous son, Alexander IV, king. Eventually **Cassander** besieged her in Pydna, and on its surrender put her to death.

OLYMPIODORUS, of Alexandria, called 'the Elder' (5th century) Greek author and Peripatetic philosopher at Alexandria. He was the teacher of **Proclus**.

OLYMPIODORUS, of Alexandria, called 'the Younger' (6th century) Greek Neoplatonist philosopher. He left a *Life of Plato*, with commentaries on several of his dialogues.

OLYMPIODORUS (5th century) Greek historian from Thebes. He wrote in Greek a history of the western Roman empire.

O'MAHONY, John (1816–77) Irish Fenian leader and American politician, born in Kilbeheny, County Limerick. He studied at Trinity College, Dublin, and in 1848 joined in **William Smith O'Brien**'s rebellion. He fled to France, and from there to the USA (1852), where he joined **John Mitchel** in New York. In 1858 he helped **James Stephens** found the Irish Republican Brotherhood, popularly known as the Fenians.

OMAN, Sir Charles William Chadwick (1860–1946) English historian, born in Muzaffarpur in India. Educated at Winchester and New College, Oxford, he was made a fellow of All Souls College in 1883, establishing his reputation with brilliant studies on **Warwick** the Kingmaker (1891), Byzantine history (1892), and the art of war in the middle ages (1898). The appearance in 1902 of the first part of his great 7-volume history of the Peninsular War, which took him 28 years to complete, gave an indication of the immense scholarship and meticulous research which became the hallmark of his many authoritative works on medieval and modern history. In 1905 he was elected Chichele professor of modern history at Oxford, and from 1919 to 1935 sat in parliament for the university. He also wrote *Things I have Seen* (1933), *On the Writing of History* (1939) and *Memories of Victorian Oxford* (1941).

OMAR, or **'Umar** (c.581–644) the second caliph. He was father of one of **Muhammad**'s wives, and succeeded **Abu-bakr** in 634. By his generals he built up an empire comprising Persia, Syria and all North Africa. He was assassinated in Medina by a Persian slave.

OMAR KHAYYÁM, or **'Umar Khayyám** (c.1048–c.1122) Persian poet, mathematician and astronomer, born in Níshápūr. His father was a tentmaker, hence his surname. He was well educated, particularly in the sciences and philosophy, in his home town and in Balkh. Later he went to Samarkand where he completed a seminal work on algebra. Consequently he was invited by Seljuq sultan Malik-Sháh to make the necessary astronomical observations for the reform of the calendar, and collaborated on an observatory in Isfahan. When his patron died in 1092 he made a pilgrimage to Mecca, on his return from which he served at the court as an astrologer. In his own country and time he was known for his scientific achievements but in the English-speaking world he is indelibly associated with the collection of robáīyát, or quatrains, attributed to him. As a poet he had attracted little attention until **Edward Fitzgerald** translated and arranged the fugitive pieces into *The Rubáiyát of Omar Khayyám*, first published anonymously in 1859. Replete with memorable sayings, they have been translated into all the world's major languages and have influenced Western ideas about Persian poetry. Though some questioned their authorship, it has been established that at least 250 robáīyát were the work of Omar.

OMAR PASHA, properly **Michael Latas** (1806–71) Croatian-barn Ottoman general, born in Plasky. He served in the Austrian army but in 1828 he deserted, fled to Bosnia, and became a Muslim. He was appointed writing-master to **Abdul-Medjid**, on whose accession to the Ottoman throne in 1839 Omar Pasha was made colonel, and in 1842 governor of Lebanon. From 1843 to 1847 he suppressed insurrections in Albania, Bosnia and Kurdistan. On the invasion of the Danubian Principalities by the Russians in 1853 he defeated the Russians in two battles. In the Crimean War he repulsed the Russians at Eupatoria in February 1855. He was sent too late to relieve Kars. He was governor of Baghdad from 1857 to 1859. In 1861 he again pacified Bosnia and Herzegovina, and overran Montenegro in 1862.

O'MEARA, Barry Edward (1786–1836) Irish physician. He served as surgeon in the army, but was dismissed in 1808 for taking part in a duel. He was on the *Bellerophon* when **Napoleon** came on board, and accompanied him as private physician to St Helena, took part in his squabbles with Sir **Hudson Lowe**, and was compelled to resign in 1818. Asserting in a letter to the Admiralty that Sir Hudson Lowe had dark designs against his captive's life, he was dismissed from the service. His *Napoleon in Exile* (1822) made a great sensation.

OMNIUM, Jacob See **HIGGINS, Matthew James**

ONASSIS, Aristotle Socrates (1906–75) Greek-born Argentinian ship-owner, born in Smyrna, Turkey, son of a Greek tobacco importer. At 16 he left Smyrna for Greece as a refugee, and from there went to Buenos Aires where he made a fortune in tobacco and was Greek consul for a time. Buying his first ships in 1932–33, he built up one of the world's largest independent fleets, and was a pioneer in the construction of super-tankers. His first marriage, to Athina, daughter of Stavros Livanos, a Greek shipowner, ended in divorce (1960), and after a long relationship with **Maria Callas**, in 1968 he married Jacqueline Kennedy, widow of US president **John F Kennedy**.

O'NEILL, Eugene Gladstone (1888–1953) American playwright, born in New York, the son of the actor James O'Neill (1847–1920). After a fragmentary education and a year at Princeton, he took various clerical and journalistic jobs and signed on as a sailor on voyages to Australia, South Africa and elsewhere. Then he contracted tuberculosis and spent six months in a sanatorium where he felt the urge to write plays, the first being *The Web*. He joined the Provincetown Players in 1915, for whom *Beyond the Horizon* (1920; Pulitzer prize) was written. This was followed, during the next two years, by *Exorcism*, *Diff'rent*, *The Emperor Jones* (1921), *Anna Christie* (1922; Pulitzer prize) and *The Hairy Ape* (1922). *Desire Under the Elms*, his most mature play to date, appeared in 1924. He then began experimenting in new dramatic techniques, in *The Great God Brown* (1926) he used masks to emphasize the differing relationships between a man, his family and his soul. *Marco Millions* (1931) is a satire on tycoonery. *Strange Interlude* (1928; Pulitzer prize), a marathon nine-acter, lasting five hours, uses asides, soliloquies and 'streams of consciousness'. In the same year he wrote *Lazarus Laughed*, a humanistic affirmation of his belief in the conquest of death. *Mourning Becomes Electra* (1931) is a re-statement of the Orestean tragedy in terms of biological and psychological cause and effect. *Ah, Wilderness*, a nostalgic comedy, appeared in 1933 and *Days Without End* in 1934. Then, for twelve years he released no more plays but worked on *The Iceman Cometh* (New York 1946, London 1958) and *A Moon for the Misbegotten* (1947). The former is a gargantuan, broken-backed, repetitive parable about the dangers of shattering illusions. It is impressive by its sheer weight and redeemed by O'Neill's never-failing sense of the theatre. *Long Day's Journey into Night* (1957; Pulitzer prize), probably his masterpeice, whose tragic Tyrone family is closely based on O'Neill's early life, *Hughie* and *A*

Touch of the Poet were published posthumously. He was awarded the Nobel prize for literature in 1936, the first American dramatist to be thus honoured.

O'NEILL, Hugh, 2nd Earl of Tyrone (c.1540–1616) Irish rebel, born in Dungannon, son of an illegitimate son of Con O'Neill (?1484–?1559), a warlike Irish chieftain who was made Earl of Tyrone on his submission to **Henry VIII** in 1542. Hugh O'Neill was invested with the title and estates in 1587, but soon plunged into intrigues with the Irish rebels and the Spaniards against **Elizabeth**. As 'the O'Neill' he spread insurrection in 1597 all over Ulster, Connaught and Leinster. In spite of Spanish support he was defeated by **Mountjoy** at Kinsale and badly wounded. He made submission, but intrigued with Spain against **James VI and I**, and in 1607 fled. He died in Rome. His nephew, Owen Roe (?1590–1649), won a distinguished place in the Spanish military service, came to Ireland in 1642, fought for a time with great success against Scots and English for an independent Ireland, but died suddenly when about to measure himself against **Cromwell**. A kinsman, Sir Phelim, was the leader of the insurrection, not so much against the English government as against the English and Scots settlers in Ulster, in which occurred the massacre of 1641.

O'NEILL, Jonjo (John Joseph) (1952–) Irish National Hunt jockey, born in Castletownroche, County Cork. He started as an apprentice jockey at The Curragh in Kildare, followed by a short spell at the stable of Sir **Gordon Richards**. When this proved unsuccessful, he decided to become freelance, and concentrated on the National Hunt. Establishing a reputation for utter fearlessness and an astonishing ability to endure pain, he suffered innumerable broken bones, but fought on to become champion jockey twice, in 1977–78 and 1979–80. He set the remarkable record of 148 winners in a season and won the Champion Hurdle on Sea Pigeon in 1980 and the Gold Cup on Dawn Run in 1986.

O'NEILL, Peggy See **EATON, Margaret**

ONIONS, Charles Talbut (1873–1965) English scholar and lexicographer, born in Edgbaston, Birmingham. He was recruited to the staff of the *Oxford English Dictionary* by Sir **J A H Murray** in 1895. After the completion of that dictionary, he was commissioned to revise and complete the unfinished *Shorter Oxford English Dictionary*, which was published in 1933 and which he continued to revise and enlarge until 1959. He was reader in English philology at Oxford University between 1927 and 1949, and editor of the journal *Medium Aevum* from 1932 to 1956. His last great work was the *Oxford Dictionary of English Etymology* (1966) produced with the collaboration of **R W Burchfield** and G W S Friedrichsen.

ONKELOS Palestinian Jewish scholar, the reputed author of an Aramaic Targum of the Pentateuch, produced by the scholars of R Akiba between 150 and 200 in Palestine. 'Onkelos' is a corruption of Akylas (Greek for Aquila), the name of the actual translator of the Old Testament into Greek, c.130.

ONNES, Heike Kamerlingh (1853–1926) Dutch physicist, born in Groningen. Professor of physics at Leiden (1882–1923), he obtained liquid helium, and discovered that the electrical resistance of metals cooled to near absolute zero all but disappears ('superconductivity'). In 1913 he was awarded the Nobel prize for physics.

O'NOLAN Brian See **O'BRIAN Flann**

ONSAGER, Lars (1903–76) Norwegian-born American physical chemist, born in Christiania (now Oslo). He studied at the Norwegian Institute of Technology and under **Debye** at Zürich. In 1928 he went to Yale, where he studied and then taught for the rest of his career (1934–72). He became a naturalized citizen in 1945. His researches in solution chemistry and in chemical thermodynamics led to his award of the Nobel prize for chemistry in 1968.

OORT, Jan Hendrik (1900–) Dutch astronomer, born in Franeker. He worked mainly in Leiden Observatory from 1924 (director from 1945 to 1970). He proved (1927) by observation that our galaxy is rotating, and calculated the distance of the Sun from the centre of the galaxy and the period of its orbit. In 1950 he suggested the existence of a sphere of incipient cometary material surrounding the solar system. He proposed that comets detached themselves from this 'Oort cloud' and went into orbits about the Sun. With his co-workers in Leiden he also carried out notable work in radioastronomy from 1940 onwards.

OPECHANCANOUGH (d.1644) American Indian chief of the **Powhatan** confederacy. He succeeded Powhatan, the father of **Pocohontas** in 1618. Less peaceable than his predecessor, he attacked the white settlers of Virginia in 1622. Years of reprisals and crop-stealing by the whites had effectively all but destroyed the livelihood of the Indians when Opechancanough led a renewed attack on the settlements in 1644. The chief, then in his nineties, was captured and killed, and the confederacy ceased to exist.

OPIE, John (1761–1807) English portrait and historical painter, born near St Agnes, Cornwall, a carpenter's son. His attempts at portrait painting interested John Wolcot (**Peter Pindar**), by whom he was taken to London in 1789 to become the 'Cornish Wonder'. In 1798 he married the writer Amelia Opie (1769–1853). He became renowned as a portraitist of contemporary figures, and also painted historical pictures like the well-known *Murder of Rizzio*, *Jephtha's Vow* and *Juliet in the Garden*. He wrote a Life of **Reynolds**, and published his *Lectures on Painting* (1809) at the Royal Institution.

OPIE, Peter Mason and **Iona** (1918–82 and 1923–) British children's literature specialists. They married in 1943 and the birth of their first child prompted them to study the folklore of childhood. This culminated in *The Oxford Book of Nursery Rhymes* (1951), acknowleged widely for its scholarship as well as its sense of humour. Through their work on this they amassed a peerless collection of children's books which is now housed in the Bodleian Library.

OPITZ, Martin (1597–1639) German poet, born in Bunzlau in Silesia. The founder of the Silesian school of poets, he championed the purity of the German language in *Aristarchus* (617, written in Latin) and other works. In 1620 he fled to Holland to escape war and the plague, but still fell victim to that terrible disease. His didactic poems are cold and formal and lacking in feeling. His works include translations from classical authors (**Sophocles** and **Seneca**), the Dutchmen **Daniel Heinsius** and **Grotius**, and from the Bible. He also wrote a prose idyll, *Daphne*, which formed the basis of the first German opera in 1627.

OPPENHEIM, Edward Phillips (1866–1946) English novelist, born in London. He had his first book published in 1887 and went on to become a pioneer of the novel of espionage and diplomatic intrigue. Among his best are *Mr Grex of Monte Carlo* (1915), *Kingdom of the Blind* (1917), *The Great Impersonation* (1920) and *Envoy Extraordinary* (1937).

OPPENHEIM, Lassa Francis Lawrence (1858–1919) German international lawyer, born near Frankfurt-am-Main. Educated at Frankfurt Gymnasium and Göttingen, Berlin, Heidelberg and Leipzig universities, he taught law in Germany, Switzerland and England, where he settled in 1895, holding a chair at Cambridge from 1908. His major work, *International Law: a Treatise* (1905–06 and later editions) is a standard British text. He stressed positive international law, based on the usages of and agreements between states rather than on theoretical principles, and the supremacy of national sovereignty and national laws over international law. He nevertheless accepted the necessity for—and indeed advocated—the League of Nations after World War I.

OPPENHEIMER, Sir Ernest (1880–1957) German-born South African mining magnate, politician and philanthropist, born in Freidberg, the son of a Jewish cigar merchant. At the age of 17 he worked for a London firm of diamond merchants and, sent out to Kimberley as their representative in 1902, soon became one of the leaders of the diamond industry. In 1917, with **John Pierpoint Morgan**, he formed the Anglo-American Corporation of South Africa and at the time of his death his interests extended over 95 per cent of the world's supply of diamonds. He was mayor of Kimberley (1912–15), raised the Kimberley Regiment and, a friend of **Smuts**, was MP for Kimberley (1924–38). He endowed university chairs and slum clearance schemes in Johannesburg.

OPPENHEIMER, Harry Frederick (1908–) South African industrialist, born in Kimberley, son of Sir **Ernest Oppenheimer**. Educated at Oxford, he succeeded his father as chairman of Anglo-American from 1957 to 1983. As an MP (1947–88) he was a critic of the South African government's policy of apartheid. His son, Nicholas Frederick (1945–), born in Johannesburg and educated at Oxford, was chairman of de Beers (1984–85).

OPPENHEIMER, Julius Robert (1904–67) American nuclear physicist, born in New York. He studied at Harvard, Cambridge (England), Göttingen, Leiden and Zürich, became assistant professor of physics at the California Institute of Technology (1929), studied electron-positron pairs, cosmic ray theory and worked on deuteron reactions. In 1942 he joined the atom bomb project and in 1943 became director of the Los Alamos laboratory, resigning in 1945. He argued for joint control with the Soviet Union of atomic energy. He was chairman of the advisory committee to the US Atomic Energy Commission (1946–52) and in 1947 became director and professor of physics at the Institute for Advanced Study, Princeton. In 1953 he was suspended from secret nuclear research by a security review board for his left-wing associations, although many people disagreed with the charges brought against him. He delivered the BBC Reith Lectures (1953), and received the Enrico Fermi award in 1963.

OPPERMAN, Sir Hubert Ferdinand (1904–) Australian cyclist and politician, born in Rochester, Victoria. After leaving school he started work as a telegraph boy and it was this which developed his phenomenal cycling speed. Between 1924 and 1937 he held at various times every long-distance, track and road record in Australia, and also competed with success in France, where in 1931 he was voted sportsman of the year. His paced record for 24 hours and for 1000 miles, set in 1932, still stands. Opperman served with the Royal Australian Air Force in World War II, and was involved in federal politics from 1949 to 1967, during which time he held two ministerial posts and was government whip. In 1967 he became Australian high commissioner to Malta until 1972.

ORANGE, Princes of See **WILLIAM III, WILLIAM THE SILENT**

Ó RATHAILLE, Aodhagán (Little Hugh O'Rahilly) (1670–?1730) Classical Irish-Gaelic poet, born in Kerry on lands formerly ruled by the MacCarthy earls of Clancarty, whose memory he idolized as a descendant of their hereditary bards. His poetry embodies the great Jacobite lament for the overthrow of Catholic Gaelic Ireland, much of it realized in rich lyrical and elegant development of the *Aisling* (patriotic dream-vision). Although essentially oral, his Gaelic poems survived in part and were edited for the Irish Texts Society bilingually (1900, revised edition 1911). His death-date is unknown, usual estimates being based on a poem avowedly written on his death-bed which shows not the slightest sign of diminution of powers of proficiency, intricacy, beauty or invective.

ORBISON, Roy (1936–88) American country-pop singer and songwriter, born in Vernon, Texas. He began playing in public at the age of eight on local radio stations and was discovered in his early teens by the record producer Norman Petty. Moving to the Sun record label he had his first minor success with 'Ooby Dooby' (1956) but subsequently spent four years writing for other artists. He re-emerged with the hit single 'Only The Lonely' (1960). The death of his wife Claudette in 1966, and two of his sons in 1968, coincided with a low period in his career and he spent ten years in relative obscurity. In the late 1970s and early 1980s a series of successful cover versions of his songs by other artists, and the patronage of a younger generation of musicians, helped to reverse his fortunes. In 1988 he helped to form the ageing 'super-group', The Travelling Wilburys, but he died of heart failure later that year.

ORCAGNA, properly **Andrea de Cione** (c.1308–1368) Florentine sculptor, painter, architect and poet, the son of a silversmith. His tabernacle in Or San Michele at Florence is a triumph of sculpture. His greatest paintings are frescoes, an altarpiece in S Maria Novella, and *Coronation of the Virgin* in the National Gallery. His brothers Nardo (active 1343/6–1365/6) and Jacopo (active 1365–98) were both painters who worked in his style.

ORCHARDSON, Sir William Quiller (1832–1910) Scottish painter, born in Edinburgh. He studied at the Trustees' Academy with **John Pettie** and went to London in 1862. He painted portraits, but is best known for historical and social subject paintings; his most famous is the scene of **Napoleon** on board the *Bellerophon* (1880) in the Tate Gallery; among other well-known subjects are *Queen of the Swords* (1877), *Mariage de convenance* (1884) and *Her Mother's Voice* (1888).

ORCZY, Baroness Emmuska (1865–1947) Hungarian-born British novelist and playwright, born in Tarnaörs, the daughter of a musician. *The Scarlet Pimpernel* (1905) was the first success in the Baroness's long writing career. It was followed by many popular adventure romances, including *The Elusive Pimpernel* (1908) and *Mam'zelle Guillotine* (1940), which never quite attained the success of her early work.

ORDERICUS VITALIS (1075–1143) Anglo-Norman historian, born in Atcham near Shrewsbury, the son of a French priest and an English woman. Educated in the Norman abbey of St Évroul, he spent most of his life there, but he visited England to collect materials for his *Historia Ecclesiastica* (1123–41), a history mainly of Normandy and England from 1082 to 1141.

O'REILLY, John Boyle (1844–90) Irish-born American journalist and Fenian agitator, born in Dowth Castle, near Drogheda, the son of a schoolmaster. He was apprenticed as a printer, and became a reporter on the *Manchester Guardian* in Preston, Lancashire. He joined the Fenians and returned to Dublin, where he enlisted in the 10th Hussars in 1863. In 1866 he was sentenced to 20 years' penal servitude and transportation for spreading Fenianism in the army. He escaped in 1869 from Western Australia to the USA, and settled as a journalist in Boston, where he became known as an author of songs and novels.

O'REILLY, Tony (Anthony John Francis) (1936–) Irish industrialist and rugby internationalist, born in Dublin. Educated at Belvedere College and University College, Dublin, and Bradford University (PhD), he was an outstanding and buccaneering wing-threequarter. He won 23 caps for Ireland, spanning 15 years (his last cap against England came after an interval of seven years). He was particularly in his element with the British Lions teams, for whom he scored a record number of tries touring in South Africa and New Zealand. After a busy and productive business career, he became chief executive and chairman of the Heinz International Corporation.

O'REILLY, William (1905–) Australian cricketer, born in White Cliffs, New South Wales. One of the world's great spin bowlers, he was a mainstay of Australian Test sides in the 1920s and 1930s. He played 27 Test matches at a time when they occurred comparatively infrequently, and of 144 Test wickets no fewer than 102 were taken against England. He could also bat in a crisis, putting on 78 with **Don Bradman** for the 9th wicket against South Africa in Adelaide in 1931–32. In later life he became a trenchant newspaper reporter on the game.

O'RELL, Max See **BLOUET**

ORELLANA, Francisco de (c.1500–1549) Spanish explorer, born in Trujillo. He went to Peru with **Francisco Pizarro**. After crossing the Andes in 1541, he descended the Amazon river to its mouth. The river's original name was Rio Santa Maria de la Mar Dulce; but Orellana is said to have renamed it after an attack by a tribe in which he believed women were fighting alongside men.

ORESME, Nicole (c.1320–1382) French cleric, philosopher and mathematician, born in Normandy. He probably studied at the University of Paris, became tutor to the Dauphin, dean of Rouen (1364), and bishop of Lisieux (1377). An early student of mechanics within the framework of the scholastic philosophy of his time, he translated **Aristotle** from Latin into French, and was an opponent of astrology.

ORFF, Carl (1895–1982) German composer, born in Munich. He studied under Kaminski and in 1925 helped to found the Günter school in Munich, where he subsequently taught; his aim, to which his didactic composition *Schulwerk* (1930–54) testifies, was to educate in the creative aspects of music. The influence of **Stravinsky** is apparent in his compositions, which include three realizations of **Monteverdi**'s *Orfeo* (1925, 1931, 1941), an operatic setting of a 13th-century poem entitled *Carmina Burana* (1936), *Die Kluge*, 'The Prudent Woman' (1943), an operatic version of **Johann Hölderlin**'s translation of *Antigone* (Salzburg Festival, 1949) and *Astutuli* (1953). Later works include *Oedipus* (1958), and *Prometheus* (1968).

ORFILA, Mathieu Joseph Bonaventure (1787–1853) French chemist, founder of toxicology, born in Mahón in Minorca. He studied at Valencia, Barcelona and Paris. In 1811 he lectured on chemistry, botany and anatomy. In 1813 appeared his celebrated *Traité de toxicologie générale*. In 1819 he became professor of medical jurisprudence, and in 1823 of chemistry.

ORFORD, Earl of See **WALPOLE, Sir Robert**

ORHAN or **ORKHAN** (1288–1359) sultan of Turkey from 1324, son of Osman. He took Brusa in his father's time, and afterwards reduced Nicaea and Mysia. He organized the state and established the Ottoman bridgehead in Europe.

ORIGEN (c.185–c.254) Christian scholar and teacher, the most learned and original of the early church fathers, born probably in Alexandria, the son of a Christian martyr. He studied in the catechetical school in Alexandria, where he made a thorough study of **Plato**, the later Platonists and Pythagoreans, and the Stoics, under the Neoplatonist **Ammonius**. He was head of the school in Alexandria for 20 years (c.211–232), and composed there the chief of his dogmatic treatises, and began his great works of textual and exegetical criticism. During a visit to Palestine in 216 the bishops of Jerusalem and Caesarea employed him to lecture in the churches, and in 230 they consecrated him presbyter without referring to his own bishop. An Alexandrian synod deprived him of the office of presbyter. The churches of Palestine, Phoenicia, Arabia and Achaea declined to concur in this sentence; and Origen, settling in Caesarea in Palestine, founded a school of literature, philosophy and theology. In the last 20 years of his life he travelled widely. In the persecution under **Decius** in Tyre he was cruelly tortured and there he died. His exegetical writings extended over nearly the whole of the old and new Testaments, and included *Scholia*, *Homilies* and *Commentaries*. Of the homilies only a small part has been preserved in the original, although much has been saved in the Latin translations by **Rufinus** and **Jerome**; but, unfortunately, the translators tampered with them. Of the Commentaries a number of books on **Matthew** and **John** are extant in Greek. His gigantic *Hexapla*, the foundation of the textual criticism of the Scriptures, is mostly lost. His *Eight Books against Celsus*, preserved entire in Greek, constitute the greatest of early Christian apologies. The speculative theology of the *Peri Archon* is extant mostly in the garbled translation of Rufinus. Two books on *The Resurrection* and ten books of *Stromata* are lost. The eclectic philosophy of Origen bears a Neoplatonist and Stoical stamp in which the idea of the proceeding of all spirits from God, their fall, redemption and return to God, is the key to the development of the world; at the centre of this is the incarnation of the logos. All scripture admits of a threefold interpretation—literal, psychical or ethical, and pneumatic or allegorical.

ORLANDO, Vittorio Emmanuele (1860–1952) Italian politician. Born in Palermo, where he inherited a fiery Sicilian temperament, he began his career teaching law, and gradually moved into the political arena, becoming minister of justice in 1916. In 1917 the Italian army suffered a humiliating defeat by Austro-German forces at the battle of Caporetto and, in the depths of this humiliation, Orlando became prime minister. He eventually succeeded in restoring some Italian pride by the victory at Vittorio Veneto, towards the end of the war, but his failure to extract suitable territorial concessions from the other world leaders at the Paris Peace Conference in 1919 resulted in his eclipse, resignation and subsequent retirement from politics after **Mussolini** came to power, in 1925. After World War II he served as the first president of the Constituent Assembly from 1946 to 1947, and ran unsuccessfully for the presidency in 1948.

ORLÉANS, (Eng Orleans) a ducal title thrice conferred by French kings on their brothers—in 1392 by **Charles VI** on Louis (1372–1407); in 1626 by **Louis XIII** on John Baptiste Gaston, Duc **d'Orléans**, and in 1660 by **Louis XIV** on Philippe (1640–1701). His son was the regent, **Philippe, Duc d'Orléans** (1674–1723), and his great-grandson was Louis Philippe Joseph,

Duc **d'Orléans**, Égalité. Égalité's son was King **Louis Philippe**. His eldest son (1810–42) took the title, but it was not borne by that duke's son, the **Comte de Paris**, who settled in England in 1883, became head of the **Bourbon** house, and died in 1894.

ORLÉANS, Charles, Duc d' (1391–1465) French nobleman and soldier. He married in 1406 his cousin Isabella, widow of **Richard II** of England. In alliance with Bernard d'Armagnac, he did his best to avenge on the Duke of Burgundy his father's murder. He commanded at Agincourt (October 1415), and was taken prisoner and carried to England, where he spent over a quarter of a century composing ballades, rondels, etc, in French and English, conventional, musical and graceful. He was ransomed in 1440, and during the last third of his life he maintained a kind of literary court at Blois. His son became **Louis XII**.

ORLÉANS, Jean Baptiste Gaston, Duc d' (1608–60) French nobleman and soldier, third son of **Henri IV** of France. He troubled his country with bloody but fruitless intrigues against **Richelieu**. He was lieutenant-general of the kingdom during the minority of **Louis XIV**, was at the head of the Fronde, but soon made terms with **Mazarin**.

ORLÉANS, Louis Philippe Joseph, Duc d' (1747–93) known as **Égalité**. He succeeded to the title on his father's death in 1785. He early fell into debauchery, and was looked upon coldly at court, especially after the accession of **Louis XVI** (1774). He visited London frequently, became an intimate friend of the Prince of Wales, afterwards **George IV**, infected young France with Anglomania in the form of horse-racing and hard drinking, and made himself popular by profuse charity. In 1787 he showed his liberalism boldly against the king, and was sent by a *Lettre-de-cachet* to his château of Villers-Cotterets. As the States-General drew near he lavished his wealth in disseminating throughout France books and papers by **Sieyès** and other liberals. In 1788 he promulgated his *Délibérations*, written by **Laclos**, to the effect that the *tiers état* was the nation, and in June 1789 he led the 47 nobles who seceded from their own order to join it. He dreamed of becoming constitutional king of France, or at least regent. He gradually lost influence, felt hopeless of the Revolution, and thought of going to America. In 1792, all hereditary titles being swept away, he adopted the name of Philippe Égalité, became 20th deputy for Paris to the Convention, and voted for the death of the king. His eldest son, afterwards King **Louis-Philippe**, rode with **Dumouriez**, his commander, into the Austrian camp. Égalité was at once arrested, with all the Bourbons still in France, and, after six months' durance, was found guilty of conspiracy and guillotined.

ORLÉANS, Philippe, Duc d' (1674–1723) regent of France during the minority of **Louis XV**, son of the first duke Philippe, and grandson of **Louis XIII**. He possessed excellent talents, but was early demoralized. He showed courage at Steenkirk and Neerwinden, and commanded with success in Italy and Spain. For some years he lived in exile from the court, spending his time by turns in profligacy, the fine arts and chemistry. **Louis XIV** at his death (1715) appointed the Duc d'Orléans sole regent. (Orléans had married Mlle de Blois, daughter of Louis XIV and Mme de **Montespan**.) He was popular, but his adoption of **John Law**'s financial schemes led to disaster. His alliance with England and Holland (1717) was joined by the emperor, and overthrew Alberoni. He expelled **James Francis Stewart** from France, debarred the parliament of Paris from meddling with political affairs, and to appease the Jesuits sacrificed the Jansenists.

ORLEY, Bernard, or **Barend van** (c.1491–1542) Flemish painter, born in Brussels. He became court painter to the regent, **Margaret of Austria**, and was one of the first Flemish painters to adopt the Italian Renaissance style. He executed a number of altarpieces and triptychs of biblical subjects, and in his later years he designed tapestries and stained glass.

ORLOV a Russian family that rose to eminence when one of its members, Gregory (1734–1783), succeeded **King Stanislaus Augustus Poniatowski** of Poland as the favourite of **Catherine II, the Great**. It was he who planned the murder of **Peter III**, and his brother Alexis (1737–1808) who committed the deed (1762). The legitimate line of Orlov became extinct; but Feodor, a brother of Gregory and Alexis, left four illegitimate sons, one of whom, Alexis (1787–1862), distinguished himself in the French wars and in Turkey. He represented Russia at the London conference of 1832, in 1844 was at the head of the secret police, stood high in favour with the emperor **Nicholas**, in 1856 was Russian representative at the congress of Paris, and was made president of the grand council of the empire.

ORM, or **Ormin** (fl.c.1200) English monk and spelling reformer, born probably in Lincolnshire. He invented an orthography based on phonetic principles, in which he wrote the *Ormulum*, a series of homilies in verse on the gospel history.

ORMIN See **ORM**

ORMOND, John (1923–90) Welsh poet and film-maker, born in Dunvant, near Swansea, and educated at University College, Swansea. After training as a journalist he joined BBC Wales in 1957 as a director and producer of documentary films, including studies of Welsh painters and writers such as Ceri Richards, **Dylan Thomas**, **Alun Lewis** and **R S Thomas**. He himself established a reputation as a fine Anglo-Welsh poet.

ORMONDE, James Butler, 1st Duke of (1610–88) Anglo-Irish nobleman, born in London. A member of the ancient family of Butler, in 1632 he succeeded to the earldom and estates of Ormonde. During the **Strafford** administration he greatly distinguished himself, and in the Civil War of 1640 was appointed to the chief command of the army; but when, in 1643, he concluded an armistice, his policy was condemned by both great parties. In the last crisis of King **Charles I**'s fortunes he retired to France, returned again to Ireland with the all but desperate design of restoring the royal authority, but after a gallant struggle was compelled (1650) to return to France. At the Restoration he was rewarded by the ducal title of Ormonde. He twice again returned to the government of Ireland. In 1679 an attempt was made on his life by the notorious Colonel **Blood**, supposed to have been instigated by the Duke of **Buckingham**. He escaped uninjured.

ORMONDE, James Butler, 2nd Duke of (1665–1746) grandson of James Butler, 1st Duke of **Ormonde**, was born in Dublin. As Earl of Ossory he served in the army against **Monmouth**. After his accession to the dukedom in 1688, he took his share in the revolution conflict. He headed **William III**'s lifeguards at the battle of the Boyne. In 1702 he commanded the troops in **Rooke**'s expedition against Cadíz; in 1703 he was appointed lord-lieutenant of Ireland, and in 1711 commander-in-chief against France and Spain. Under **George I** he fell into disgrace, and was impeached in 1715 of high treason, his estates being attainted; he retired to France, spent years in the intrigues of the Pretender **James Francis Stewart**, and died abroad.

ORNSTEIN, Leo (1895–) Russian-born American composer, born in Kremenchug. He had appeared as a child prodigy at the piano in Russia before his parents settled in the USA in 1906, and he made his American début at 16. In the years following 1915, he composed much music that placed him among the avant-garde and has had considerable influence upon younger American composers; but his later works, which include a symphony and various pieces of piano music, are more traditional in style.

OROSIUS, Paulus (5th century) Spanish priest and historian. He visited **Augustine** in 415, and went to study under **Jerome** at Bethlehem. He was the author of a seven-volume universal history, *Historiarum adversus Paganos*, from the Creation to 417, a favourite textbook during the middle ages which was translated into Anglo-Saxon by King **Alfred**.

O'ROURKE, Sir Brian-na-Murtha (d.1591) Irish chieftain in Galway, Sligo, and the west of Ulster. He was in frequent collision with the English authorities, sheltered the Spaniards of the Armada wrecked on Irish coasts, and in 1591 went to Scotland to seek support from **James VI and I**, who handed him over to the English. He was tried and executed at Tyburn in 1591.

OROZCO, José Clemente (1883–1949) Mexican painter, born in Zapotlán, Jalisco. He studied engineering and architectural drawing in Mexico City and from 1908 to 1914 studied art at the Academia San Carlos. His first exhibition was in Paris, 1925; a major retrospective was held in Mexico City, 1947. One of the greatest mural painters of the 20th century, he decorated many public buildings in Mexico and the USA. His powerful realistic style, verging on caricature, was a vehicle for revolutionary socialist ideas—his murals in the Rockefeller Center, New York, were later destroyed.

ORPEN, Sir William (1878–1931) Irish painter, born in Stillorgan, County Dublin. He studied at the Metropolitan School of Art at Dublin and at the Slade School. He did many sketches and paintings at the front in World War I, and was present at the Paris peace conference as official painter. The results may be seen at the Imperial War Museum. He is also known for Irish genre subjects, but is most famous for his portraits, whose vitality and feeling for character place them among the finest of the century.

ORR, Bobby (Robert Gordon) (1948–) Canadian-born North American hockey player, born in Parry Sound, Ontario. The highest goal-scorer ever in North American National League hockey, he was fast, courageous, elusive and a deadly finisher. He played mainly with Boston Bruins and became that city's greatest-ever sporting hero, but by the time he moved to Chicago Black Hawks in the 1976–77 season (for a contract reputed to be worth 3 million dollars), his career was already almost over. Six major leg operations had left him unable to stand the stress of major-league hockey and he played only a handful of games for Chicago before being compelled to retire.

ORR, Boyd See **BOYD ORR**

ORR, James (1844–1913) Scottish theologian, born in Glasgow. As a long-time parish minister, professor of church history at the United Presbyterian Divinity Hall from 1891, and professor of apologetics and theology at the new Trinity College, Glasgow (1900–13), he defended and promoted conservative evangelical views against contemporary challenges. His books, including *The Christian View of God and the World* (1893), *The Ritschlian Theology and the Evangelical Faith* (1897), *The Virgin Birth of Christ* (1907), and *Revelation and Inspiration* (1910), gave him considerable influence in North America as well as Britain. His standing as a major representative of evangelical orthodoxy in the early 20th century was consolidated by his editorship of the *International Standard Bible Encyclopaedia* (1915).

ORRERY See **BOYLE**

ORSINI, Felice (1819–58) Italian revolutionary, born in Meldola, of an ancient and distinguished family. The son of a conspirator, he was early initiated into secret societies, and in 1844 was sentenced at Rome to the galleys, amnestied, and again imprisoned for political plots. In 1848 he was elected to the Roman Constituent Assembly. He took part in the defence of Rome and Venice, agitated in Genoa and Modena, and in 1853 was shipped by the Sardinian government to England, where he joined the Young Italy movement and formed close relations with **Mazzini**. Next year he was in Parma, Milan, Trieste, Vienna, until arrested and confined in Mantua. In 1856 he escaped to England, where he supported himself by public lecturing, and wrote *Austrian Dungeons in Italy* (1856). In 1857 he went to Paris to assassinate **Napoleon III** as an obstacle to revolution in Italy. Orsini and three others threw three bombs under Napoleon's carriage (14 January 1858); 10 persons were killed, 156 wounded, but Napoleon and the empress remained unhurt. Orsini and another were guillotined.

ØRSTED, Niels-Henning (1946–) Danish jazz musician. He has played with **Oscar Peterson**, Dexter Gordon, **Sonny Rollins**, **Dizzy Gillespie**, Kenny Drew, **Count Basie**, **Ella Fitzgerald** and others, and has performed on several hundred recordings, including *Jaywalkin*, *Trio I* and *Trio II*. In 1977 he was voted the 'World's Best Bass Player' by *Melody Maker* magazine.

ORTEGA SAAVEDRA, Daniel (1945–) Nicaraguan politician, born in La Libertad, Chontales, into a middle-class family. Educated at the University of Central America, Managua, he became active in his teens in the resistance movement against the Somoza régime, and in 1963 joined the Sandinista National Liberation Front (FSLN), which had been founded in 1960. He became national director of the FSLN in 1966, was imprisoned for seven years for urban guerrilla bank raids, and then, in 1979, played a major part in the overthrow of Anastasio Somoza. A junta led by Ortega established a provisional government, and in 1985 he became president, but counter-revolutionary forces, the 'Contras', with US support threatened his government's stability. By 1989, however, there were encouraging signs of peace being achieved. He surprisingly lost the 1990 General Election to Violeta Chamorro, and supervised the peaceful handover of power.

ORTEGA Y GASSET, José (1883–1955) Spanish writer and philosopher, born in Madrid. He was professor there from 1911. His introduction of such writers as **Proust** and **Joyce** to Spain, and his critical writings, made him the most influential author of his time. *Meditaciones del Quijote* (1914) outlines national symbols in Spanish literature and compares them with those of others. In *Tema de nuestro tiempo* (1923) he argues that great philosophies demarcate the cultural horizons of their epochs. *La Rebelión de Las Masas* (1930) foreshadowed the Civil War. He lived in South America and Portugal (1931–46). *Man of Crisis* (1959) is a collection of lectures, posthumously translated, also *On Love* (trans 1959).

ORTELIUS, Abraham Ortel (1527–98) Flemish geographer, born of German parents in Antwerp. His *Theatrum Orbis Terrarum* (1570) was the first great atlas.

ORTON, Arthur, alias **Thomas Castro,** known as the **'Tichborne Claimant'** (1834–98) English butcher and impostor, born in Wapping, London. He emigrated to Australia in 1852, where he met Sir Alfred Joseph

Tichborne, 11th baronet (1839-66). On the death of the 11th baronet, he persuaded the widow of the 10th baronet (Sir James Francis Doughty Tichborne) that he was actually her eldest son, Roger Charles Tichborne (b.1829), who was presumed to have been lost at sea off America in 1854. Invited to England in 1866, he brought an action as the 'Tichborne Claimant' against the 12th baronet, but his action collapsed after 102 days in court. Orton was charged with perjury and found guilty after a trial of 188 days, and sentenced to 14 years' hard labour. Released in 1884, he confessed the imposture.

ORTON, Joe, originally **John Kingsley** (1933–67) English dramatist, born in Leicester. After training as an actor, he turned to writing vivid, outrageous farces, beginning with *The Ruffian on the Stair* (1963) and *Entertaining Mr Sloan* (1964). Subsequent plays include *Loot* (1966), *The Erpingham Camp* (1966), and *What the Butler Saw* (1969). He was murdered by his lover, failed artist Kenneth Halliwell, who subsequently killed himself.

ORWELL, George, pseud of **Eric Arthur Blair** (1903–50) English novelist and essayist, born in Motihari in Bengal. He was educated at Eton, served in Burma in the Indian Imperial Police from 1922 to 1927 (later recalled in 1935 in the novel *Burmese Days*, and then was literally *Down and Out in Paris and London* (1933), making an occasional living as tutor or bookshop assistant. In 1935 he became a small country shopkeeper, and published two novels, *A Clergyman's Daughter* (1935) and *Keep the Aspidistra Flying* (1936). *Coming Up for Air* (1939) is a plea for the small man against big business. He fought and was wounded in the Spanish Civil War and he developed his own brand of socialism in *The Road to Wigan Pier* (1937), *Homage to Catalonia* (1938) and *The Lion and the Unicorn* (1941). During World War II, he was war correspondent for the BBC and *The Observer*, and wrote for *Tribune*. His intellectual honesty motivated his biting satire of Communist ideology in *Animal Farm* (1945) which was made into a cartoon film; and the terrifying prophecy for mankind in *Nineteen Eighty-Four* (1949), the triumph of the scientifically-perfected servile state, the extermination of political freedom by thought-control and an ideologically delimited basic language of *newspeak* in which 'thought crime is death'. Other penetrating collections of essays include *Inside the Whale* (1940) and *Shooting an Elephant* (1950).

OSBORN, Henry Fairfield (1857–1935) American zoologist and palaeontologist, born in Fairfield, Connecticut. He studied at Princeton, and became professor of zoology at Columbia University (1891–1910), and was thereafter research professor. His work especially on fossil vertebrates is important, but he is best known for his work at the American Museum of Natural History in New York (curator of vertebrate palaeontology, 1891–1910, and president 1908–33). He revolutionized museum display with innovative instructional techniques and popularized palaeontology and dinosaurs. His books included *The Age of Mammals* (1910), *Man of the Old Stone Age* (1915), and *The Origin and Evolution of Life* (1917).

OSBORN, Sherard (1822–75) English naval officer, born in Madras. He entered the navy in 1837, took part in the Chinese War of 1841–42, commanded vessels in two expeditions (1849 and 1852–55) in search of Sir **John Franklin**, was head of the British squadron in the Sea of Azov during the Crimean War, and took a leading share in the Chinese War of 1857–59. As a director of the Telegraph Construction and Maintenance Company he was involved in laying a cable between Great Britain and Australia; hence Osborn Deep in the Indian Ocean bears his name. Promoted rear admiral in 1873, he helped to fit out the Arctic expedition of **Nares** and **Markham** (1875). He published *Arctic Journal* (1851), *Journals of McClure* (1956) and *Fate of Sir John Franklin* (1860).

OSBORNE, Dorothy See **TEMPLE, Sir William**

OSBORNE, John James (1929–) Welsh playwright and actor, son of a commercial artist. He left Belmont College, Devon, at 16 and became a copywriter for trade journals. Hating it, he turned actor (1948) and by 1955 was playing leading roles in new plays at the Royal Court Theatre. There his fourth play, *Look Back in Anger* (1956; filmed 1958), and *The Entertainer* (1957; filmed 1960), with Sir **Laurence Olivier** playing Archie Rice, established Osborne as the leading young exponent of British social drama. The 'hero' of the first, Jimmy Porter, the prototype 'Angry Young Man', as well as the pathetic, mediocre music hall joker Archie Rice, both echo the author's uncompromising hatred of outworn social and political institutions and attitudes. An earlier play, *Epitaph for George Dillon*, written in collaboration with A Creighton and exploring the moral problems of the would-be literary genius, was also staged in 1957. Among other works are *Luther* (1960), *Inadmissible Evidence* (1965), *Time Present* and *The Hotel in Amsterdam* (1968), and the filmscript of *Tom Jones*. He wrote his credo in *Declarations* (1957), and his autobiography, *A Better Class of Person* (1981).

OSBORNE, Thomas See **LEEDS**

OSBOURNE, Lloyd (1868–1947) American writer, born in San Francisco. He was the son of Fanny Osbourne (née Vandegrift, 1840–1914) and stepson of **Robert Louis Stevenson**. He collaborated with Stevenson on several books, including *The Wrong Box* (1889), *The Wrecker* (1892), and *The Ebb Tide* (1894). He became American vice-consul in Samoa, and published several books of his own including *An Intimate Portrait of RLS* (1925).

O'SHAUGHNESSY, Arthur William Edgar (1844–81) English poet, born in London. In 1861 he began work in the British Museum moving to the natural history department in 1863. An associate of the Pre-Raphaelites, he published *An Epic of Women* (1870), *Lays of France* (1872), *Music and Moonlight* (1874) and *Songs of a Worker* (1881). His best-known poem is 'The Music-Makers'.

OSIANDER, Andreas (1498–1552) German Lutheran reformer, born in Gunzenhausen. A preacher at Nürnberg (1522), he persuaded the city to declare for **Luther**. Deprived for refusing to agree to the Augsburg Interim (1548), he was made professor of theology at Königsberg, but soon became entangled in bitter theological strife, disputing the imputation of **Jesus Christ**'s righteousness in favour of an infusion doctrine.

OSKAR I (1799–1859) king of Sweden and Norway from 1844, only son and successor of **Karl XIV Johan**. A liberal by temperament, he sought to conciliate nationalist feelings in Norway, encouraged social and economic reforms, developed schools, railways, banks and industry, and pursued a policy of Scandinavian unity and Swedish neutrality. He married Josephine of Leuchtenberg, the daughter of the empress **Joséphine**'s son, Eugène de Beauharnais, Duke of Leuchtenberg, and his wife Augusta Amalia of Bavaria. He was succeeded by his eldest son, **Karl XV**.

OSKAR II (1829–1907) king of Sweden from 1872 and of Norway 1872–1905. He was the younger son of **Oskar I** and brother of **Karl XV**, whom he succeeded. A vigorous, intelligent man of literary bent, his foreign policy was marked by admiration of the new German Empire of **Otto von Bismarck**. He served as mediator in international disputes, but found it impossible to keep the union of Norway and Sweden intact, and in 1905 surrendered the crown of Norway to Prince Carl of Denmark, elected King of Norway as **Haakon VII**. He wrote a number of poems and historical works (including a *Life of Karl XII*), and translated German literature including **Goethe**'s *Faust*. Married to Sofia of Nassau (1836–1913), sister of Adolf, Grand Duke of Luxemburg, he was succeeded as king of Sweden by his son, **Gustav V**.

OSLER, Sir William (1849–1919) Canadian physician, born in Bond Head, Ontario. He became professor of medicine at McGill (1875–84), Pennsylvania (1884–88), Johns Hopkins (1889–1905), and finally Oxford (1905–19). He wrote widely on many aspects of clinical medicine and medical history and amassed a superb library, now at McGill University. His *Principles and Practice of Medicine* (1892) became a standard work.

OSMAN See **UTHMAN**

OSMAN I (1259–1326) founder of the Ottoman (Turkish) empire, born in Bithynia. The son of a border chief, he founded a small Turkish state in Asia Minor called Osmanli (Ottoman). On the overthrow of the Seljuk sultanate of Iconium in 1299 by the Mongols, he gradually subdued a great part of Asia Minor.

OSMAN DIGNA, originally **George Nisbet** (1836–1926) French slave dealer, born in Rouen. From 1881 he was a Mahdist leader on the Red Sea coast and the Abyssinian frontier. He was defeated and taken at Tolar (1900).

OSMAN NURI PASHA (1837–1900) Turkish general, born in Amasia or in Tikat. He fought in the Crimean War (1853–56) and numerous other campaigns, and became a national hero for his defence of Plevna against the Russians, in 1877.

OSMUND, St (d.1099) Norman prelate, nephew and chaplain to **William I, the Conqueror**. He became chancellor of England (1072) and helped to compile the *Domesday Book*. From 1078 he was bishop of Salisbury, where he established the so-called 'Use of Sarum' (a version of the Latin liturgy of worship). His feast day is 4 December.

OSSIAN, or **Oisín Mac Fhinn Mhic Cumhail Mhic Tréanmóir Uí Baoisne** legendary Gaelic bard and warrior, the son of Finn (Fingal). After many years' service in the *Fianna*, or sworn band of heroes, he departed for *Tír na n-Óg*, the land of perpetual youth with its queen, Niamh Chinn Óir, from whom he returned after 300 years to age catastrophically and, after extended acrimony, to be converted to Christianity by St **Patrick**. Oral ballads, lyrics and prose ascribed to him, and a disputation supposedly recorded between Patrick and himself, were circulated in Ireland and Scotland, but the texts are probably from the 2nd century. The *Ossian* of **James Macpherson** supposes a coherence and royal status lacking in the original, since after Ossian's departure his father Fionn and his followers were finally defeated by the actual king of Ireland (or Tara), Cairbre Lifeachar, son of the Fianna's former suzerain, Cormac Mac Airt. The Fionn of Ossianic folklore had the intellectual's moral ambiguity also found in contrasting Odysseus myths: Macpherson's Fingal was of impeachable but interesting probity.

OSSIETZKY, Carl von (1888–1938) German pacifist and writer. He was a reluctant conscript in the German army in World War I. He was co-founder of *Nie Wieder Krieg* (No More War) in 1922, and his success as a journalist culminated in his being appointed editor of the weekly *Weltbühne*, in which his articles denounced German military leaders' secret rearmament activities. He was convicted of treason in 1931 but his 18-month imprisonment sentence was commuted so that he was once more editor when **Hitler** became chancellor, after which he was sent to Papenburg concentration camp. While he was in prison hospital he was awarded the 1935 Nobel peace prize, to Hitler's fury. He died of tuberculosis while under prison conditions in a private hospital.

OSSOLI, Margaret Fuller See **FULLER**

OSTADE, Adriaan van (1610–85) Dutch painter and engraver, born probably in Haarlem. He was a pupil of **Frans Hals**, and his use of chiaroscuro shows the influence of **Rembrandt**. His subjects are taken mostly from everyday life—tavern scenes, farmyards, markets, village greens, etc. His *Alchemist* is in the National Gallery. His brother Isaac (1621–49) treated similar subjects, but excelled at winter scenes and landscapes.

ÖSTBERG, Raynor (1866–1945) Swedish architect, leader of the quest for a modern national style and a giant of early 20th-century Swedish architecture. His principal and most influential building was Stockholm City Hall, (1911–23) in which many Swedish influences combine to create not only a city hall but a national monument commanding a magnificent waterfront site. His other important work is the classical Swedish Patent and Registration Office (1921). Although his popularity declined with the rise of functionalism, he is now acknowledged as a modern master.

OSTROVSKY, Alexander (1823–85) Russian dramatist, born in Moscow. His best-known play is *The Storm* (1860; trans in 1899).

OSTWALD, Friedrich Wilhelm (1853–1932) German chemist, born in Riga. He was professor at Leipzig (1887–1906), and was awarded the Nobel prize for physics (1909). He discovered the dilution law which bears his name, and invented a process for making nitric acid by the oxidation of ammonia. He also developed a new theory of colour.

Ó SÚILLEABHÁIN, Eoghan Ruadh (Red Owen O'Sullivan) (1748–84) Irish-Gaelic poet, born in County Kerry. He symbolizes the last phase of native Irish vernacular poetry. He was variously a teacher in proscribed Catholic ('hedge') schools, an itinerant labourer, a sailor serving with **Rodney** in the West Indies, a British soldier, and at all times an insatiable lover. His work followed Irish patriotic poetic traditions, his obvious parallels exist with his contemporary **Robert Burns**, and **Yeats**'s 'Red Hanrahan' was based on him, as is 'Owen MacCarthy' in Thomas Flanagan's *The Year of the French* (1979).

OSWALD, St (c.605–642) king of Northumbria. The second son of King Æthelfrith of Bernicia, he fled to Iona for safety when his father was overwhelmed by King **Edwin** (St Edwin) of Deira in 616. After Edwin's death at the hands of the Welsh king **Cadwallon** and **Penda** of Mercia in 633, Oswald returned from Iona and fought his way to the throne of Northumbria (Deira and Bernicia) with a victory over the pagan Cadwallon near Hexham in 634. He re-established Christianity in Northumbria with the help of the Celtic monk St **Aidan** whom he summoned from Iona to set up a bishopric on Lindisfarne, the Holy Isle, but was later killed by Penda of Mercia at the battle of Maserfelth (Old Oswestry).

OSWALD, Lee Harvey (1939–63) American alleged assassin of President **John Kennedy**, born in New Orleans. He was alleged to have shot Kennedy, who was passing through Dealey Plaza in Dallas in a motor cavalcade, from the sixth floor of the Texas School Book Depository where he worked. Oswald, who had lived for some time in the USSR and was deemed to have Cuban sympathies, was arrested some hours after the assassination on 22 November 1963, on a charge of murdering a police officer in another incident. On 23 November he was also charged with the murder of President Kennedy. He repeatedly denied both killings, saying that he had been set up as a scapegoat. Before he could come to trial, he was shot at close range by Jack Ruby (1911–64), who claimed to be avenging Jacqueline Kennedy. Ruby was reputedly a small-town gangster with Mafia links. Subsequent studies of events, of the direction of the bullets and of witnesses' evidence showed several inconsistencies. Claims were made that Oswald had links with the US secret service and with the Mafia. In 1976, the US senate ordered a fresh inquiry. This confirmed that shots had indeed been fired from a grassy knoll to the side of the president's car and that more than one gunman had been involved. In 1979, the House Assassination's Committee decided that Kennedy 'was probably assassinated as a result of a conspiracy'.

OTAKE, Eiko and Koma (1952– and 1948–) Japanese dance-theatre artists, now resident in New York City. They met in 1971 as law and political science students who joined butoh master **Tatsumi Hijikata**'s company in Toyko. What began as an experiment developed into an exclusive partnership in which they perform and choreograph only their own work. They made their début in 1972, and began studying with Kazuo Uhno, the other central figure of Japan's mid 20th-century avant-garde. That same year their interest in the roots of German modern dance took them to Hanover, where they studied with a disciple of **Mary Wigman**. They made their American début in 1976, since when they have regularly toured North America and Europe with both short and full-length pieces.

OTHO, Marcus Salvius (32–69) Roman emperor. He was a close friend of the emperor **Nero** and husband of Sabina Poppeia, who became Nero's second wife, and was murdered by him. He was governor of Lusitalia, and joined **Galba** in his revolt against Nero (68). When he was not proclaimed Galba's successor, he rose against the new emperor, who was slain. Otho was recognized as emperor everywhere except in Germany, whence **Aulus Vitellius** marched on Italy, and completely defeated Otho's forces. Next day Otho, who had worn the purple only three months, stabbed himself.

OTIS, Elisha Graves (1811–61) American inventor, born in Halifax, Vermont. He was a master mechanic in a firm making bedsteads when he was put in charge of the construction of their new factory at Yonkers. The factory had several floors connected by a hoist, and Otis, knowing of the many serious accidents caused by runaway lifting platforms, designed a spring-operated safety device which would hold the platform securely if there was any failure of tension in the rope (1853). He patented his 'elevator' and exhibited it at an Exposition in New York in 1854, after which orders came in rapidly for passenger as well as goods lifts; he patented a new type of steam-powered lift in 1861 just before he died, and his two sons afterwards continued the successful expansion of the business.

OTIS, James (1725–83) American statesman, born in West Barnstable, Massachusetts. He became a leader of the Boston bar. He was advocate-general in 1760, when the revenue officers demanded his assistance in obtaining from the superior court general search warrants allowing them to enter any man's house in quest of smuggled goods. Otis refused, resigned, and appeared in defence of popular rights. In 1761, elected to the Massachusetts assembly, he was prominent in resistance to the revenue acts. In 1769 he was savagely beaten by revenue officers and others, and lost his reason. He was killed by lightning. His fame chiefly rests on *The Rights of the Colonies Asserted* (1764).

O'TOOLE, Peter Seamus (1932–) Irish actor, born in Connemara. A journalist and member of the submarine service, he attended RADA before joining the Bristol Old Vic where he made his professional début in *The Matchmaker* (1955). He made his film début in *Kidnapped* (1959). West End success in *The Long and The Short and The Tall* (1959) and a season with the RSC established his stage reputation, while his performance in *Lawrence of Arabia* (1962) made him an international film star. Adept at drama, comedy or musicals, he has tackled many of the great classical roles and is frequently cast as mercurial or eccentric characters. Stage work includes *Hamlet* (1963, London), *Waiting for Godot* (1971, Dublin), *Uncle Vanya* (1978, Toronto) and a critically roasted *Macbeth* (1980, London). Nominated seven times for the Academy Award, his films include *The Lion in Winter* (1968), *Goodbye Mr. Chips* (1969), *The Ruling Class* (1972), *My Favourite Year* (1982) and *The Last Emperor* (1987).

OTT, Mel (Thomas Melvin) (1909–58) American baseball player, born in Gretna, Louisiana. He was a player and later manager with the New York Giants in the National League for 22 years, from 1926 to 1948. In that time he played 2732 games and hit 511 home runs. After arriving at the club as a baby-faced 17-year-old, he went on to play in three World Series (1933, 1936, 1937) and twice scored six runs in a single game (1934 and 1944). He became manager of New York in 1942, and was elected to the Baseball Hall of Fame in 1951.

OTTO I, 'the Great' (912–73) Holy Roman Emperor. The son of **Henry I** the Fowler, he was crowned king of the Germany in 936 and emperor in 962. He brought the great tribal duchies under the control of the monarchy, and made the church the main instrument of royal government. He was married in 930 to Edith, daughter of **Edward the Elder** and sister of **Athelstan** of England; and later, in 951, to **St Adelaide**. He preserved Germany from the Hungarian invasions by his great victory on the Lechfeld near Augsburg (955), and re-established imperial rule in Italy in a revival of the Carolingian tradition.

OTTO II (955–83) Holy Roman Emperor, son of **Otto I**. He became emperor in 973, successfully fought the Danes and Bohemians, and subdued insurgent Bavaria which he reduced in size by splitting it up. In 972 he married Theophano, daughter of the Byzantine emperor Romanus II. He invaded France, but overreached himself in attempts on the Eastern Empire.

OTTO III (980–1002) Holy Roman Emperor, son of **Otto II**. He came to the throne at the age of three. His mother, the empress Theophano, ruled as regent until her death in 991; thereafter his grandmother **Adelaide**, widow of **Otto I**, ruled as regent until his accession in 996. In his brief reign he managed to engineer into the papacy first his cousin (Gregory V) and then his tutor (Sylvester II). He lived most of his short life in Rome and tried to make it the capital of the empire, but was driven out by the hostility of the people in 1002 and died in Paterno.

OTTO IV (c.1174–1218) Holy Roman Emperor, son of **Henry the Lion**. He grew up at the court of his uncle **Richard I** of England, who created him Count of Poitou. He was elected king in 1198 in opposition to Philip of Swabia, against whom he struggled for surpremacy for ten years. Philip's murder in 1208 left the way free for his coronation as Emperor (1209), but his subsequent invasion of Sicily lost him the support of Pope **Innocent III** who raised up Philip's nephew **Frederick II** as a rival, and Otto's cause finally collapsed after his defeat by **Philip II** of France at Bouvines in 1214.

OTTO, Nikolaus August (1832–91) German engineer, born near Schlangenbad. He invented in 1876 the four-stroke internal combustion engine, the sequence of operation of which is named the Otto cycle after him.

OTTO, Rudolf (1869–1937) German Protestant theologian and philosopher, born in Peine, Hanover. A professor at Göttingen and Breslau before settling at Marburg in 1917, he was prompted by **Kant**, **Schleiermacher**, and several journeys he made to the east to study non-Christian religions, to define religion in a new way. In *Das Heilige* (1971, trans *The Idea of the Holy*, 1923) he describes religious experience as a non-rational but objective sense of the 'numinous', a *mysterium tremendum et fascinans* inspiring both awe and a promise of exaltation and bliss. His other books include *India's Religion of Grace and Christianity* (1930), *The Philosophy of Religion* and *Religious Essays* (1931), and *Mysticism East and West* (1932).

OTWAY, Thomas (1652–85) English dramatist, born in Trotton in Sussex. From Winchester he passed in 1669 to Christ Church College, Oxford. He left the university without a degree in 1672, failed utterly as an actor, but made a fair hit with his tragedy *Alcibiades* (1675). In it the actress **Elizabeth Barry** made her first appearance, and with her Otway is said to have fallen in love. In 1676 **Betterton** accepted his *Don Carlos*, a good tragedy in rhyme. In 1677 Otway translated **Racine**'s *Bérénice*, as well as **Molière**'s *Cheats of Scapin*. In 1678–79 he was in Flanders as a soldier; in the May of the former year appeared his coarse but diverting comedy, *Friendship in Fashion*. The year 1680 yielded two tragedies, *The Orphan* and *Caius Marius*, and his one important poem, *The Poet's Complaint of his Muse*; to 1681 belongs *The Soldier's Fortune*. His greatest work, *Venice Preserved, or a Plot Discovered* (1682), is a masterpiece of tragic passion. For a time he sinks out of sight, to reappear again in 1684 with *The Atheist*, a feeble comedy, and in February 1685 with *Windsor Castle*, a poem addressed to the new king, **James VII and II**. He died in poverty. In 1719 a badly edited tragedy, *Heroick Friendship* was published as his.

OUD, Jacobus Johann Pieter (1890–1963) Dutch architect, born in Purmerend. He collaborated with **Mondrian** and others in launching the review *de Stijl* and became a pioneer of the modern architectural style based on simplified forms and pure planes. Appointed city architect at Rotterdam in 1918, he designed a number of striking buildings, including municipal housing blocks.

OUDINOT, Nicolas Charles (1767–1847) French soldier, born in Bar-le Duc. He served in the revolutionary wars. In 1805 he obtained the command of ten reserve battalions, the 'grenadiers Oudinot'. He fought at Austerlitz and Jena, won the battle of Ostrolenka (1807), and helped at Friedland. Conspicuous in the Austrian campaign of 1809, he was created marshal of France and Duke of Reggio. In 1810 he was charged with the occupation of Holland, and took part in the Russian campaign and in the battles in 1813 with the Russians and Austrians. He was one of the last to abandon **Napoleon**. At the second restoration (1815) he became a minister of state and commander-in-chief of the royal and national guards. In 1823 he commanded in Spain.

OUDINOT, Nicolas Charles Victor, Duke of Reggio (1791–1863) French soldier, son of **Nicolas Oudinot** (1767–1847). He fought in Algeria, and commanded the expedition to Rome in 1849.

OUGHTRED, William (1575–1660) English mathematician, born in Eton College. Educated there and at Cambridge, he wrote extensively on mathematics, notably *Clavis Mathematica* (1631), a textbook on arithmetic and algebra in which he introduced many new symbols including multiplication and proportion signs. He also invented the slide rule and is said to have died of joy at hearing of the restoration of **Charles II**.

OUIDA, pseud of **Marie Louise de la Ramée** (1839–1908) English popular novelist, born in Bury St Edmunds. Her mother was English, her father a French teacher. 'Ouida' was a childish mispronunciation of 'Louise'. Educated in Paris, she settled in London in 1857. Starting her career by contributing stories to magazines, in particular to *Bentley's Miscellany* (1859–60), her first success was *Held in Bondage* (1863). This was followed by *Strathmore* (1865), another three-decker aimed at the circulating libraries. She was soon established as a writer of hot-house romances, often ridiculed for her opulent settings, preposterous heroes and improbable plots, as well as for her ignorance of male sports and occupations. But her narratives were powerful and readers responded to her emotional energy and until her popularity waned in the 1890s she was a bestseller. From 1860 she spent much time in Italy and in 1874 settled in Florence where she lived lavishly in a style recognizable from her novels. She wrote almost 50 books, mainly novels, such as *Under Two Flags* (1867), *Folle-Farine* (1871) which was praised by **Bulwer-Lytton**, *Two Little Wooden Shoes* (1874), *A Village Commune* (1881) and *In Maremma* (1882)—but also animal stories, essays and tales for children. Latterly her royalties dried up. She fell into debt, moved to Lucca in 1894, and her last years in Viareggio were spent in destitution.

OUIMET, Francis (1893–1967) American golfer, born in Brookline, Massachusetts. He recorded the first major success in American golfing history when he defeated **Harry Vardon** and Ted Ray in a play-off for the US Open of 1913 and broke the British stranglehold on top-level events. He was a member of every Walker Cup team from 1922 to 1949, either as player or non-playing captain, and in 1951 he became the first foreigner ever to be made captain of the R & A at St Andrews.

OUSELEY, Sir Frederick Arthur Gore, 2nd Bart. (1825–89) English musician, born in London. He graduated at Oxford, where he became professor of music in 1855. He was founder and benefactor of St Michael's College, Tenbury, to which he bequeathed his music library.

OUTRAM, Sir James (1803–63) English soldier and colonial administrator, the 'Bayard of India', born in Butterley Hall, Derbyshire, the residence of his father, Benjamin Outram (1764–1805), engineer. Educated in Aberdeen, in 1819 he joined the Bombay native infantry, organized a corps of wild Bhils (1825–35), and was political agent in Gujrat (1835–38). He made his name in the 1st Afghan War (1839–42), particularly with his eight days' ride of 355 miles from Kelat through the Bolan Pass. Political agent in Sind (1840), he defended the residency at Hyderabad against 8000 Beluchis (1843), and opposed Sir **Charles Napier**'s aggressive policy towards the amir. He was afterwards resident at Satara and Baroda, and in 1854, on the eve of the annexation of Oudh, was made resident at Lucknow. In 1857 he commanded the brief and brilliant Persian expedition, and returned to India when the Mutiny (1857–59) was raging. Lord **Canning** offered him the command of the forces advancing to the relief of Lucknow, but he waived the honour in favour of his old lieutenant, **Havelock**, and accompanied him as a volunteer and as chief-commissioner of Oudh. Lucknow was relieved, and Outram took command, only to be in turn himself besieged. He held out against overwhelming odds, until Sir **Colin Campbell** relieved him; and his skilful movement up the Gumti led to a complete victory. He took his seat as a member of the Supreme Council at Calcutta, but in 1860 had to return to England. He spent a winter in Egypt, died in Pau, and was buried in Westminster Abbey.

OVERBECK, Johann Friedrich (1789–1869) German painter, born in Lübeck. He studied art in Vienna (1806–10), and settled in Rome, where he allied himself with the like minded **Cornelius**, **Schadow**, **Schnorr** and **Veit**, who, from the stress they laid on religion and moral significance, were nicknamed the Nazarenes. In 1813 he became a Roman Catholic. He painted in fresco as well as oil, mainly religious and historical subjects.

OVERBURY, Sir Thomas (1581–1613) English courtier and poet, born in Compton-Scorpion, Warwickshire. He studied at Oxford and at the Middle Temple. In 1611 **James VI and I** made him Viscount Rochester. He became a close friend of **Robert Carr** (later Earl of Somerset), and a member of the king's court. Within this circle he became involved in numerous intrigues and scandals, one of which resulted in his death in the Tower at the instigation of Carr's mistress, Lady Essex. Four years later four of the conspirators were hanged, but Carr and his ex-mistress, now wife, received a royal pardon. Overbury's works, published posthumously, include *The Wife* (1614) and *Crumm's fal'n from King James's Table* (1715, but of doubtful authorship).

ØVERLAND, Arnulf (1889–1968) Norwegian poet, born in Kristiansund. He wrote radical poetry in volumes such as *Brød og vin* (Bread and Wine, 1919) and *Berget det Blå* (The Blue Rock, 1937). A committed anti-Fascist, he wrote *Den røde front* (1937) and circulated Resistance poetry during the German occupation of Norway, for which he was imprisoned in a concentration camp.

OVERSTONE, Samuel Jones Loyd, Baron (1796–1883) English economist, born in London. He entered his father's banking house, later merged in the London and Westminster Bank, and established himself as a leading authority on banking and currency by his famous series of tracts (1837–57). He was Whig MP for Hythe (1819–26).

OVETT, Steve (1955–) English runner, born in Brighton. With **Sebastian Coe**, he launched a new era of British dominance in middle distance athletics. Gold medallist in the 800 metres at the 1980 Olympics, he also won a bronze in the 1500 metres. He broke the world record at 1500 metres (three times), at one mile (twice) and at two miles. An outspoken and sometimes controversial figure, he occasionally upset the press but remained generally popular with his fellow athletes and the spectators. As his competitive career faded he began a new role as a television commentator.

OVID, (Publius Ovidius Naso) (43 BC–17 AD) Roman poet, born in Sulmo (Solmona), in the Abruzzi, son of a well-to-do *eques*. He was trained for the law in Rome, but in spite of extraordinary aptitude for the legal profession he gave his whole energies to poetry. His first literary success was his tragedy *Medea*. Then came his *Epistolae* or *Heroides*, imaginary love letters from ladies of the heroic days to their lords, and his *Amores*, short poems about his mistress, Corinna. His *Medicamina Faciei* (a practical poem on artificial aids to personal beauty) seems to have been preliminary to his true masterpiece, the *Ars Amandi*, or *Ars Amatoria*, in three books, which appeared about 1 BC, followed by a subsidiary book entitled *Remedia Amoris*. His second period of poetic activity opens with the *Metamorphoses*, in 15 books, and with the *Fasti*, designed to be in twelve, of which six only were completed. Midway in composition he was banished by **Augustus** (8 AD), for some reason unknown, to Tomi on the Black Sea, where he died. On his way from Rome he began his third period with the elegies which he published in five books, the *Tristia*. Similar in tone and theme are the four books of the *Epistolae ex Ponto*. His *Ibis*, written in imitation of **Callimachus**, and his *Halieutica*, a poem extant only in fragments, complete the list of his remains. A master of metrical form, Ovid is the most voluminous of Latin poets.

OVIEDO Y VALDÉS, Gonzalo Hernández de (1478–1557) Spanish historian, born in Madrid. He was sent to San Domingo in 1514 as inspector-general of goldmines, and, as historiographer of the Indies, wrote after his return a *Historia general y natural de las Indias occidentales* (1535).

OWEN, David Anthony Llewellyn (1938–) English politician. He trained as a doctor before becoming Labour MP for Plymouth in 1966. He was minister of state at the Department of Health and Social Security (1974–76), then at the foreign and commonwealth office (1976–77) before becoming the youngest foreign secretary for over 40 years (1977–79). Owen was one of the so-called 'Gang of Four' who broke away from the Labour party to found the Social Democratic party in 1981. He succeeded **Roy Jenkins** as SDP leader after the party's rather poor election perfomance in 1983. When the Liberal leader, Sir **David Steel**, called for a merger of his party with the SDP, immediately after the 1987 general election, Owen resigned the leadership and persuaded a minority of members to join him in a breakaway, reconstituted, SDP, but the party was dissolved in 1990.

OWEN, John (c.1560–1622) Welsh epigrammatist, born in Llanarmon, Pwllheli. Educated at Winchester, he became a jurist fellow at New College, Oxford, in 1584. He was later employed as a schoolmaster at Trelleck, Gwent, and in 1595 became headmaster of Warwick school. He published ten books of *Epigrammata*, written in Latin, between 1606 and 1613. His epigrams were bestsellers in their day, and particularly popular on the Continent.

OWEN, John (1616–83) English Puritan clergyman, born in Stadhampton vicarage, Oxfordshire. He graduated in 1632 from Queen's College, Oxford, and in 1637 was driven from Oxford by dislike of **Laud**'s statutes. He spent some years as a private chaplain; then in 1642 he moved to London, and published *The Display of Arminianism* (1643), for which he was rewarded with the living of Fordham in Essex. In 1646 he moved to Coggeshall, and showed his preference for Independency over presbyterianism. **Cromwell** took him in 1649 as his chaplain to Ireland, where he regulated the affairs of Trinity College, Dublin. Next year (1650) he went with Cromwell to Scotland. In 1651–52 he became dean of Christ Church College and vice-chancellor of Oxford University. Here he wrote a number of theological works. He was one of the Triers appointed to purge the church of scandalous ministers. He opposed giving the crown to the Protector, and the year after Cromwell's death he was ejected from his deanery. He bought an estate at Stadhampton, and formed a congregation. In 1673 he became pastor in

Leadenhall Street. To the end he preached and wrote incessantly.

OWEN, Sir Richard (1804–92) English zoologist, born in Lancaster. He studied medicine at Edinburgh and at St Bartholomew's and became curator in the museum of the Royal College of Surgeons, where he produced a fine series of descriptive catalogues. In 1856 he became superintendent of the natural history departments of the British Museum, but continued to teach at the Royal Institution and elsewhere. His essay on *Parthenogenesis* was a pioneer work. A pre-Darwinian, he maintained a hostile attitude to detailed evolutionist theories.

OWEN, Robert (1771–1858) Welsh social and educational reformer, born in Newtown, Montgomeryshire, a saddler's son. At the age of ten he was put into a draper's shop at Stamford, and by 19 had risen to be manager of a cotton mill. In 1799 he married Anne Caroline, eldest daughter of **David Dale**, and bought from him his cotton-mills and manufacturing village at New Lanark in Scotland. Here he established a model community with improved housing and working conditions, and built an Institute for the Formation of Character, a school (including the world's first day-nursery and playground, and also evening classes) and a village store, the cradle of the co-operative movement. In 1813 he formed New Lanark into a new compnay with **Jeremy Bentham** and others. In *A New View of Society* (1813) he contended that character was formed by the social environment, and went on to found several co-operative 'Owenite' communities, including one at New Harmony in Indiana (1825–28), but all were unsuccessful. In 1825 he ceased to be manager at New Lanark after disagreements with his partners, and in 1828 sold all his shares. He organized the Grand National Consolidated Trades Union in 1833, and spent the rest of his life campaigning for various causes, including (later) spiritualism. He also wrote *Revolution in Mind and Practice* (1849). He died in his home town of Newtown. Vigorous conservation and restoration work at New Lanark Village since the 1970s has made it a living community again; it was awarded a Europa Nostra Medal of Honour in 1988.

OWEN, Robert Dale (1801–77) Scots-born American social reformer, born in Glasgow, son of **Robert Owen**. In 1825 he accompanied his father to America to help set up the New Harmony colony in Indiana. He taught in the School there and edited the *New Harmony Gazette*. In 1829 he moved to New York, where he edited the *Free Inquirer*. He returned to Indiana in 1832 and became a member of the Indiana legislature, and entered congress in 1843. He was US ambassador to India (1855–58). An advocate of emancipation of slaves, he became a spiritualist. He wrote *The Policy of Emancipation* (1863) and *The Wrong Slavery* (1864), and an autobiography, *Threading My Way* (1874).

OWEN, Wilfred (1893–1918) English poet, born in Plas Wilmot, near Oswestry, Shropshire, where his father worked on the railway. Educated at the Birkenhead Institute and at Shrewsbury Technical School, he worked as a pupil-teacher at Wyle Cop School while preparing for the matriculation exam for the University of London. But money was too short for him to be able to take up courses there. In 1913 he left England to teach English in Bordeaux at the Berlitz School of Languages. He was tutoring a private pupil in the Pyrenees when war was declared. He enlisted in 1915 and in 1917 suffered concussion and trench fever on the Somme. In the summer of that year he was sent to recuperate at Craiglockart War Hospital, near Edinburgh, where he introduced himself to **Siegfried Sassoon**, who suggested improvements to his poems and encouraged him. However, he was posted back to France near the end of the war where he won the MC, but was killed on the bank of the Oise-Sambre Canal, near Ors, just a week before the Armistice was signed. Only five of his poems were published while he was alive, most of them being published between the summer he arrived at Craiglockhart and the time of his death. His work was first collected in 1920 by Sassoon and reappeared in 1931 with a memoir by **Edmund Blunden**. *The Collected Poems* were published in 1963. His poetry is distinguished by its directness, realism and vivid imagery, and individual poems like 'Dulce et Decorum Est' and 'Anthem for doomed Youth' have shaped the attitude of many towards war.

OWEN AP GRUFFYDD (d.1169) prince of Gwynedd, North Wales. He fiercely resisted **Henry II**, but ultimately submitted.

OWEN GLENDOWER See **GLENDOWER**

OWENS, Jesse James Cleveland (1913–80) American athlete, born in Danville, Alabama, the greatest sprinter of his generation. While competing for the Ohio State University team on 25 May 1935, he set three world records and equalled another (all within the space of an hour), including the long jump (26 feet $8\frac{1}{4}$ inches), which lasted for 25 years. At the 1936 Olympics in Berlin he won four gold medals (100 metres, 200 metres, long jump, and 4×100 metres relay); it caused a sensation when the German Nazi leader, **Adolf Hitler**, left the stadium, apparently to avoid having to congratulate a black non-Aryan athlete. Back in the USA, Owens gained no recognition for his feat and was reduced to running 'freak' races against horses and dogs. Later he held an executive position with the Illinois Athletic Commission, and attended the 1956 Olympics as President **Eisenhower**'s personal representative; and in 1976 he was awarded the Presidential Medal of Freedom.

OWENS, John (1790–1846) English philanthropist from Manchester. A cotton merchant, he left a fortune for the foundation of a nonsectarian college there (Owens College, opened in 1851).

OXENSTIERNA, Count Axel Gustafsson (1583–1654) Swedish statesman, born in Uppland into one of Sweden's great families. Trained abroad for the church, he entered the royal service in 1605, and was instrumental in achieving the smooth accession of **Gustav II Adolf** in 1611. From then on he was Gustav's chancellor, a man of outstanding administrative and diplomatic ability; he negotiated the favourable peace treaties with Denmark (1613), Sweden (1617), and Poland (1629). During the Thirty Years' War (1618–48) he governed Sweden during the king's absence on military expeditions; after the king's death in 1632, he kept the Swedish armies together and became director of the Protestant League (1633). He was regent for Queen **Kristina** (1632–44), and continued to exercise considerable authority in policy-making after she came of age.

OXFORD, Earl of See **ASQUITH, HARLEY, VERE**

OYAMA, Iwao, Prince (1842–1916) Japanese soldier born in Satsuma. In the Sino-Japanese War of 1894–95 he took Port Arthur and Wei-hei-Wei from China, and in the Russo-Japanese War of 1904–05 defeated **Kuropatkin** in several encounters.

OZ, Amos (1939–) Israeli Hebrew-language writer, born in Jersualem. At the age of 14 he went to live in a kibbutz, where he taught in the school and became a writer of international stature. His works, which deal with historical and contemporary themes of guilt and persecution, include *Elsewhere, Perhaps* (1966), *The*

Hill of Evil Counsel (1976), *In the Land of Israel* (1983) and *A Perfect Peace* (1984). His work has been widely translated and he has won many awards. *My Michael* (1972), described by the *New York Times* as 'a modern Israeli *Madame Bovary*', is the book by which he is best known. *Black Box* appeared in 1988.

ÖZAL, Turgut (1927–) Turkish politician, born in Malatya. Educated at Istanbul Technical University, he entered government service and in 1967 became under-secretary for state planning. From 1971 he worked for the World Bank and in 1979 joined the office of prime minister **Bülent Ecevit**, and in 1980 was deputy to prime minister Bülent Ulusu, within the military régime of Kenan Evren. When political pluralism returned in 1983, Ozal founded the Islamic, right-of-centre Motherland party (ANAP) and led it to a narrow, but clear victory in the elections of that year. In the 1987 general election he retained his majority, and in 1984 became Turkey's first civilian president for 30 years.

OZANAM, Antoine Frédéric (1813–53) French literary historian, born in Milan. He was a Neo-Catholic of the school of **Lacordaire**, and one of the founders of the Society of St Vincent de Paul. In 1841 he became professor of foreign literature at the Sorbonne. He wrote *Dante et la philosophie catholique* (1839), *Histoire de la civilisation au Vesiècle* (1845), and *Études germaniques* (1847–49).

OZENFANT, Amédée (1886–1966) French artist, born in St Quentin. He was the leader of the Purist movement in Paris and published a manifesto of Purism with **Le Corbusier** in 1919. From 1921 to 1925 they published an avant-garde magazine, *Espirit nouveau*. They also collaborated in writing *Après le Cubisme* (1918) and *La Peinture moderne* (1925). His still-lifes based on this theory reduce vases and jugs to a static counterpoint of two-dimensional shapes. He founded art schools in London (1935) and New York (1938); his publications include *Art* (1928) and his diaries for the years 1931–34.

OZICK, Cynthia (1928–) American novelist and short-story writer, born in New York City. Educated at New York University and Ohio State University, she has said she began her first novel—*Trust* (1966)—an American writer and ended it six and a half years later a Jewish one. Powerfully and originally expressing the Jewish ethos, her slight but significant oeuvre includes *The Pagan Rabbit and Other Stories* (1971), *Bloodshed* (1976), *Levitation* (1982), *The Cannibal Galaxy* (1983) and *The Messiah of Stockholm* (1987).

OZU, Yasujiro (1903–63) Japanese film director, born in Tokyo. An inveterate cinema-goer as a youngster, he joined the industry as an assistant cameraman, became an assistant director and made his fully-fledged directorial début with *Out of College* (*Gakuso O Idete*, 1925). Adept at many popular genres, from comedies to thrillers, he began to specialize from the 1930s in 'home drama'. A precise and rigorous cinematic stylist, his films offered gentle, compassionate portraits of everyday family life laced with humour and, latterly, underlying tragedy. A prolific filmmaker, his most widely-seen work was made in the 1950s and includes *The Flavour of Green Tea Over Rice* (*Ochazuke No Aji*, 1952), *Tokyo Story* (*Tokyo Monogatari*, 1953) and *Good Morning!* (*Ohayo*, 1959).

P

PAASIKIVI, Juo Kusti (1870–1956) Finnish statesman, born in Tampere. He became Conservative prime minister after the civil war in 1918. He recognized the need for friendly relations with Russia, and took part in all Finnish–Soviet negotiations. He sought to avoid war in September 1939, conducted the armistice negotiations and became prime minister again in 1944. He succeeded **Mannerheim** as president (1946–56).

PACHECO, Francisco (1571–1654) Spanish painter, born in Seville. Influenced by **Raphael**, he painted portraits and historical subjects, and he opened a school of art at Seville, where **Velazquez** was his pupil and became his son-in-law. He wrote a notable technical treatise, *Arte de la pintura* (1639).

PACHELBEL, Johann (c.1653–1706) German composer and organist, born in Nuremberg. He held a variety of organist's posts before, in 1695, he returned to Nuremberg as organist of St Sebalds' Church. His works, which include six suites for two violins, and organ fugues, profoundly influenced **J S Bach**.

PACHER, Michael (c.1435–1498) Austrian painter and wood-carver, born in the Tyrol, one of the earliest artists to import Italian Renaissance ideas into northern Europe. He may have travelled to Italy but, in any case, his paintings show the influence of Italian artists, especially the Paduan painter **Mantegna**, in their convincing foreshortening and perspective. Most of his work remains in the parish churches for which it was commissioned, including his masterpiece of 1481, the high altar for the church of St Wolfgang on the Abersee, depicting the life of the Virgin **Mary** and the legend of St Wolfgang.

PACHMANN, Vladimir de (1848–1933) Russian pianist, born in Odessa. He studied at Vienna, and won fame as an interpreter of **Chopin** although he was rather eccentric, sometimes talking to the audience during his performance.

PACHOMIUS, St (4th century) Egyptian hermit. He superseded the system of solitary reclusive life by founding (c.318 AD), the first monastery on the island of Tabenna on the Nile, with its properly regulated communal life and rule. He founded ten other monasteries, including two convents for women.

PACKER, Kerry Francis Bullmore (1937–) Australian media proprietor, born in Sydney. He inherited the Australian Consolidated Press (ACP) group from his father, Sir **Frank Packer**. In the 1977–78 season Packer created 'World Series Cricket', contracting the leading Test cricketers for a knock-out series of one-day matches and 'Super-Tests', played in colourful costume and often under floodlights, sole television rights for which were held by ACP's Channel Nine. This led to disputes with the Australian Cricket Board and other national cricket bodies, and provoked many legal battles, before a *modus operandi* was established.

PACKER, Sir (Douglas) Frank Hewson (1906–74) Australian newspaper proprietor, born in Sydney. The son of Robert Clyde Packer (1879–1934), founder of *Smith's Weekly*, he became a cadet reporter on his father's *Daily Guardian* in 1923. He established the magazine *Australian Women's Weekly* in 1933, the success of which led to the formation of the Australian Consolidated Press group, publishers of the (Sydney) *Daily Telegraph* (sold to **Rupert Murdoch** in 1972), *The Bulletin* magazine, and television and radio interests. In 1962 and 1970 his racing yachts *Gretel I* and *Gretel II* unsuccessfully contested the America's Cup.

PADEREWSKI, Ignace Jan (1860–1941) Polish pianist, composer and patriot, born in Kurylowka in Podolia. Beginning to play as a child of three, he studied at Warsaw, becoming professor at the Conservatory there in 1878. In 1884 he taught at the Strasbourg Conservatory, but thereafter became a virtuoso, appearing with prodigious success in Europe and America. He became director of Warsaw Conservatory in 1909. In 1919 he was one of the first premiers of Poland, for whose freedom he had striven. Very soon, however, he retired from politics and went to live in Switzerland. He resumed concert work for some years, but when Poland's provisional parliament was established in Paris in 1940, he was elected president. He died in Switzerland.

PADILLA, Juan de (1490–1521) Spanish rebel and popular hero. He was commandant of Saragossa under **Charles V**, headed an insurrection against the intolerable taxation, and after some success was defeated and beheaded. His wife Maria (d.1531) held Toledo against the royal forces from 1521 to 1522, and then fled to Portugal.

PAGANINI, Niccolo (1782–1840) Italian violin virtuoso, born, a porter's son, in Genoa. He gave his first concert in 1793 (when his father reduced his age by two years in advertisements); beginning his professional tours in Italy in 1805, in 1828–31 he created a sensation in Austria and Germany, Paris and London. His dexterity and technical brilliance acquired an almost legendary reputation and it was said that he was in league with the devil. He revolutionized violin technique, among his innovations being the use of stopped harmonics. He published several concertos and, in 1820, the celebrated 24 *Capricci*.

PAGE, Sir Earle Christian Grafton (1880–1961) Australian politician, born in Grafton, New South Wales. He practised medicine and sat in the federal parliament from 1919 until his death. He wrote a persuasive study of a hydro-electric scheme for the Clarence River Gorge, near his home town, but achieved wider recognition as the first permanent leader of the Australian Country party (1921–39), and was made a privy councillor in 1929. He served as deputy prime minister (1934–39) and was briefly prime minister in April 1939. In 1941 and 1942 he travelled to London as special Australian envoy to the war cabinet. His memoirs, *Truant Surgeon*, were published in Sydney two years after his death.

PAGE, Sir Frederick Handley (1885–1962) English aircraft designer. In 1909 he founded the first British aircraft manufacturing firm, Handley-Page Ltd. His twin-engined 0/400 (1915) was the first twin-engined bomber, and saw service in World War I, and his Hampden and Halifax bombers were used in World War II. His civil aircraft include the Hannibal, Hermes and Herald transports.

PAGE, Thomas Nelson (1853–1922) American novelist and diplomat, born in Hanover County, Virginia. He practised law in Richmond, wrote many stories, some in Negro dialect, and became American ambassador to Italy from 1913 to 1919.

PAGE, Violet See **LEE, Vernon**

PAGE, Walter Hines (1855–1918) American journalist and diplomat, born in Cary, North Carolina. He edited the *Forum* (1890–95) and *Atlantic Monthly* (1896–99), and became a partner in Doubleday's in 1900. He was founder editor of *World's Work* (1900–13), and was American ambassador in London (1913–18).

PAGÈS See **GARNIER-PAGÈS**

PAGET, Sir James (1814–99) English physician and pathologist, born in Yarmouth. One of the founders of modern pathology, he studied at St Bartholomew's Hospital, London, where he became full surgeon in 1861. He discovered the cause of trichinosis, and described Paget's disease. He published his *Lectures on Surgical Pathology* and *Clinical Lectures* in 1853.

PAHLAVI, Mohammad Reza (1919–80) shah of Persia. He succeeded on the abdication of his father, Reza Shah, in 1941. His first two marriages, to Princess Fawzia, sister of **Farouk I**, and to Soraya Esfandiari, ended in divorce after the failure of either to produce a male heir. By his third wife Farah Diba, daughter of an army officer, he had two sons, Crown Prince Reza (1960), Ali Reza (1966), and two daughters, Princess Farahnaz (1963) and Princess Leila (1970). He had a daughter, Princess Shahnaz (1940–) from his first marriage. His reign was for many years marked by social reforms and a movement away from the old-fashioned despotic concept of the monarchy, but during the later 1970s the economic situation deteriorated, social inequalities worsened, and protest at western-style 'decadence' grew among the religious fundamentalists. After several attempts at parliamentary reform the shah, having lost control of the situation, left the country, and a revolutionary government was formed under Ayatollah **Khomeini**. The ex-shah having been admitted to the USA for medical treatment, the Irani government seized the US embassy in Teheran and held many of its staff hostage for over a year, demanding his return to Iran. He made his final residence in Egypt at the invitation of President **Sadat** and died there.

PAIGE, Elaine (1951–) English actress and singer, born in Barnet. She joined the west end cast of *Hair*, in 1969, but it was her performances in *Jesus Christ Superstar* (1972) and *Billy* (1974) that established her as a musicals actress. She appeared at Chichester Festival Theatre and at Stratford East before she became a star as *Evita* in 1978. In 1981 she played in *Cats*, followed by *Chess* (1986) and *Anything Goes* (1989–).

PAIGE, Satchel (Leroy Robert) (1906–82) American baseball player, born in Mobile, Alabama, and one of the first blacks to make a breakthrough into the major leagues. As pitcher, he enjoyed success in the 'negro' leagues (1925–47) before moving into the majors with the Cleveland Indians, whom he helped to win the 1948 World Series. In his forties he played for St Louis and Kansas City and went on briefly to coach the Atlanta Braves. He was elected to the Baseball Hall of Fame in 1971. He published his autobiography *Maybe I'll Pitch Forever* in 1962.

PAINE, Thomas (1737–1809) English-born American revolutionary philosopher and writer, born in Thetford, Norfolk, the son of a Quaker smallholder and corset-maker. He worked as a corset-maker from the age of 13, then became a sailor and a schoolmaster. In 1771 he became an exciseman, but was dismissed as an agitator after fighting for an increase in excisemen's pay. In London he met **Benjamin Franklin**, who in 1774 helped him to emigrate to America, where he settled in Philadelphia as a radical journalist. After the outbreak of the American Revolutionary War (1775–83) he published a pamphlet, *Common Sense* (January 1776), which outlined the history of the transactions that led to the war and urged an immediate declaration of independence. He served in the continental army, and issued a series of pamphlets, *The American Crisis* (1776–83), urging the colonial cause, and became secretary to the congress committee on foreign affairs (1777–79). He went on a mission to France in 1781, and published *Dissertations on Government* in 1786. He returned to England in 1787, where he published *The Rights of Man* (1791–92), a reply to **Edmund Burke**'s *Reflections on the Revolution in France*; in it he supported the French Revolution and appealed for an overthrow of the British monarchy. He was indicted for treason, but slipped away to Paris, where he was made a citizen of France and became a member of the National Convention as deputy for Pas-de-Calais (1792–93). A supporter of the Girondins, he opposed the execution of the king, thus falling foul of **Robespierre**, who had his French citizenship rescinded and arrested him as an enemy Englishman (1794). After the Terror was over, he was released on the plea that he was an American citizen (1795). Just before his arrest he published Part I of his powerful attack on accepted religion, *The Age of Reason* (1794; Part II, written in prison, was published in 1796). The book alienated most of his old friends, including **Washington**. After his release he stayed on in Paris, writing and studying, but in 1802 he returned to America, where he was ostracized as an atheist and a free-thinker. He died, alone and in poverty, on the farm at New Rochelle which a grateful state of New York had once given him.

PAINLEVÉ, Paul (1863–1933) French mathematician and statesman, born in Paris. He was professor at Lille, the Sorbonne, and the École polytechnique, repeatedly minister for war, twice air minister, and twice (1917, 1925) premier.

PAINTER, William (?1540–1594) English translator. He studied at Cambridge, was master of Sevenoaks school, but in 1561 became clerk of ordnance in the Tower of London. His *Palace of Pleasure* (1566–67), largely composed of stories from **Boccaccio**, **Bandello**, and **Margaret of Navarre**, became popular, and was a major source for many dramatists, including **Shakespeare**

PAISH, Frank Walter (1898–1988) English economist, educated at Winchester and Trinity College, Cambridge. Appointed lecturer at the London School of Economics in 1932, and reader in 1938, he was professor of economics (with special reference to business finance) from 1949 until his retirement in 1965. In the 1960s he advocated an inbuilt level of 'therapeutic' unemployment (around $2\frac{1}{2}$ per cent) as a government policy to keep inflation in check, and attacked the validity of incomes policy as an instrument of economic control. He published several books on his economic principles, in particular *Studies in an Inflationary Economy* (1962) and *The Rise and Fall of Incomes Policy* (1969).

PAISIELLO, Giovanni (1740–1816) Italian composer, born in Taranto. He studied at Naples, wrote at first only church music, but turned successfully to opera, and from 1776 to 1784 was court musician to the empress **Catherine** at St Petersburg. In 1799 he was appointed director of national music by the republican government of France and later enjoyed the patronage of **Napoleon**. He returned to Naples in 1804. The most successful Neapolitan opera composer of his time, his

Barbiere di Seviglia was so popular that **Rossini**'s use of the same libretto met with considerable hostility, but his ninety-odd pieces are seldom if ever staged today, possibly because of their comparative superficiality, though they contain a wealth of delightful tunes, one of which, *Nel cor più non mi sento*, was used by both **Beethoven** and **Paganini** as a theme for variations.

PAISLEY, Ian Richard Kyle (1926–) Northern Ireland clergyman and politician, and founder of the Free Presbyterian Church of Ulster, born in Northern Ireland. Ordained by his Baptist minister father in 1946, he began his own denomination in 1951, and by 1985 his Free Presbyterian Church had some 10750 members, with Paisley himself as minister of its largest congregation, in Belfast. He became increasingly involved in politics, and (with one brief self-imposed break) has been a Westminster MP since 1970, and leads his own Democratic Unionist party. He is also a member of the European parliament, in which he staged a well-publicized one-man protest against the pope as guest speaker in 1988. Strongly pro-British and strenously opposed to the unification of Ireland, he is a rousing orator who inspires both fanatical devotion and deep distrust. Roman Catholic constituents nonetheless have given credit to his impartiality in carrying out routine constituency tasks on their behalf.

PALACH, Jan (1948–69) Czech philosophy student. As a protest against the August 1968 invasion of Czechoslovakia by the Russians, he set fire to himself in Wenceslas Square, Prague, on 16 January 1969. After his death five days later he became a hero and symbol of hope, and was mourned by thousands.

PALACIO VALDÉS See **VALDÉS, Armando Palacio**

PALACKÝ, Františêk (1798–1876) Czech historian and politician in Prague, and the founder of historiography in Bohemia. He served in the first Austrian Reichstag, and campaigned for the formation of a separate Czech nation. His chief work was *Geschichte von Böhmen* (1836–67).

PALADE, George Emil (1912–) Romanian-born American cell biologist, born in Iasi. He trained as a doctor in Bucharest, and became professor of anatomy there until he moved to the USA in 1946; he worked at the Rockefeller Institute (1946–72), and from 1972 he headed cell biology at Yale Medical School. His work on the fine structure of cells as revealed by electron microscopy led him in 1956 to discover the small organelles within cells, called ribosomes, in which RNA synthesizes protein. He shared the 1974 Nobel prize for physiology or medicine with Albert Claude and **Christian de Duve**.

PALAFOX Y MELZI, José de (1780–1847) Spanish patriot. Nominally head of the heroic defence of Saragossa (July 1808 to February 1809), he was carried prisoner to France, and not released until 1813. He was made Duke of Saragossa (1836) and grandee of Spain (1837).

PALESTRINA, Giovanni Pierluigi da (c.1525–1594) Italian composer, born in Palestrina. He was sent at the age of ten to the choir school of S Maria Maggiore in Rome, where he learnt composition and organ playing. In 1544 he became organist and *maestro di canto* at the cathedral of St Agapit in his native town, and at the age of 22 married the heiress of a well-to-do citizen. The new pope, **Julius III**, had been bishop of Palestrina and, aware of the talent possessed by his late organist, appointed him master of the Julian choir at St Peter's, for which he composed many fine masses. In 1555 Julius engineered him into the exclusive and highly privileged Pontifical Choir without an entrance examination or the customary election by existing members, but **Paul IV**, coming to the papal throne in the same year, tightened up the regulations and Palestrina was compulsorily retired. He then became choirmaster at the Lateran, but walked out without notice in 1560, probably owing to his disagreement with economy cuts imposed by the impoverished canons. In 1561 he returned to S Maria Maggiore as choirmaster, remaining until 1567, though only on a part-time basis after 1565, when he was appointed music master at the new Roman Seminary set up by the Council of Trent. The years between 1572 and 1580 were tragic ones for Palestrina, who during that time lost his wife and three sons in the terrible epidemics which intermittently ravaged Rome. Eight months after his wife's death he was married again, this time to a wealthy widow who had come into a furrier's business, which he took over, apparently with success. A great task entrusted to him at this time was the revision of the Gradual, ordained in 1577 by the Council of Trent, a monumental labour which was abandoned after a few years. He continued to live in Rome, composing and working at St Peter's, refusing an offer from the Duke of Mantua, an old friend of his, to become his musical director. He was buried in St Peter's. His place as the most distinguished composer of the Renaissance remains unchallenged, as does his status as one of the greatest figures in musical history, to whom generations of later composers, including **Bach**, **Mozart**, **Wagner**, **Liszt** and **Debussy**, have acknowledged their debt. His works include over 90 masses and a large number of motets, hymns and other liturgical pieces as well as some excellent madrigals. Apart from a few organ *ricercari* of doubtful authenticity, no instrumental music has been ascribed to him. His compositions, free from sentimentality yet with an extraordinary depth of feeling, are characterized by an uncanny skill in the handling of contrapuntal texture, but also contain examples of homophony and subtle dissonances which are immensely effective chorally. Having in its original form no division into bars, his music is free-flowing and unhampered by rhythmic conventions.

PALEY, William (1743–1805) English theologian, born in Peterborough. He was fellow and tutor of Christ's College, Cambridge (1768–76), and became archdeacon of Carlisle (1782) and subdean of Lincoln (1795). He published *Principles of Moral and Political Philosophy* (1785), expounding a form of utilitarianism. In 1790 he published his most original work, *Horae Paulinae*, the aim of which is to prove the improbability of the hypothesis that the New Testament is a cunningly devised fable. It was followed in 1794 by his famous *Evidences of Christianity*. In 1802 he published perhaps the most widely popular of all his works, *Natural Theology, or Evidences of the Existence and Attributes of the Deity*.

PALGRAVE, Sir Francis (1788–1861) English historian, born in London, the son of Meyer Cohen, a stockbroker. On his marriage (1823) he assumed his mother-in-law's maiden name. He was called to the bar in 1827; in 1838 he was appointed deputy-keeper of records. Among his works are *The English Commonwealth* (1832), *The Merchant and the Friar*, and a *History of Normandy and of England* (1851–64, incomplete). He also edited *Parliamentary Writs* (1830–34), *Rotuli Curiae Regis* (1835), *Ancient Kalendars of the Treasury of the Exchequer* (1836), and *Documents illustrating the History of Scotland* (1837).

PALGRAVE, Francis Turner (1824–97) English poet and critic, born in London, eldest son of Sir **Francis Palgrave**. He became a scholar of Balliol College, Oxford, and fellow of Exeter College, was successively vice-principal of a training college, private secretary to

George Leveson-Gower (Earl Granville), an official in the education department, and professor of poetry at Oxford (1886–95). His works include *Idylls and Songs* (1854), *Essays on Art* (1866), *Hymns* (1867), *Lyrical Poems* (1871), *Visions of England* (1881), and *Landscape in Poetry* (1897). He is best known as the editor of the *Golden Treasury of Lyrical Poetry* (1875); *Sonnets and Songs of Shakespeare* (1877); selections from **Herrick** (1877) and **Keats** (1885); and *Treasury of Sacred Song* (1889).

PALGRAVE, William Gifford (1826–88) English diplomat and traveller, second son of Sir **Francis Palgrave**. He graduated from Oxford in 1846. He joined the Bombay Native Infantry, but becoming a Jesuit, studied at Rome, and was sent as a missionary to Syria. For **Napoleon III** he went disguised as a physician on a daring expedition through Arabia (1862–63), described in his *Narrative of a Year's Journey through Central and Eastern Arabia* (1865). Leaving the Jesuits in 1864, he joined the diplomatic service. He became consul at Trebizond, St Thomas and Manila; consul-general in Bulgaria (1878) and Siam (1880); and British minister to Uruguay (1884). There he married, was reconciled to the church, and died.

PALISSY, Bernard (c.1509–1589) French potter, born in Agen. A glass-painter by trade, he settled in Saintes and devoted 16 years to experimentation on how to make enamels. From 1557 his ware, bearing in high relief plants and animals coloured to represent nature, made him famous. He was imprisoned as a Huguenot in 1562, but in 1564 was taken into royal favour and he established his workshop at the Tuileries, and was specially exempted from the St Bartholomew's Day massacre (1572). From 1575 to 1584 he lectured on natural history, physics and agriculture. In 1588 he was again arrested as a Huguenot and was thrown into the Bastille of Bucy, where he died.

PALLADIO, Andrea (1508–80) Italian architect, born in Vicenza. Trained as a stonemason, he developed a modern Italian architectural style based on classical Roman principles, as against the ornamentation of the Renaissance. This Palladian style was widely imitated all over Europe, especially by **Inigo Jones** and **Christopher Wren**. Palladio started by remodelling the basilica in Vicenza, and extended his style to villas and palaces and churches, especially in Venice (San Giorgio Maggiore). His *Quattro Libri dell' Architetura* (1570) greatly influenced his successors.

PALLADIUS, Rutilius Taurus Aemilianus (4th century) Roman author. He wrote *De Re Rustica* (On Agriculture), in 14 books.

PALLAS, Peter Simon (1741–1811) German naturalist, born in Berlin. The son of a professor of surgery, he studied medicine at Halle, Göttingen and Leiden but his interests always tended towards natural history. He published *Miscellania Zoologica* in 1766 and *Spicilegia Zoologica* (1767 onwards), and was invited to St Petersburg by the empress **Catherine the Great** as professor at the Academy of Sciences in order to survey her domains. He spent six years (1768–74) exploring the Urals, the Kirghiz Steppes, the Altai Range, part of Siberia and the steppes of the Volga, returning with an extraordinary treasure of specimens. He wrote a series of works on the geography, ethnography, flora and fauna of the regions he had visited (*Reise durch verschiedene Provinzen des Russischen Reichs*, 1771–76). He made another expedition in 1793–94, and stayed on in Russia, and wrote *Zoographica Russo-Asiatica* (3 vols, 1811–31). Several birds, including Pallas's Sandgrouse, are named after him.

PALLAVICINO, Sforza (1607–67) Italian prelate and historian. In 1638 he became a Jesuit, and a cardinal in 1659. His best-known work is *Istoria del Concilio di Trento* (1656–57), a reply to the work of **Pietro Sarpi**.

PALLES, Christopher (1831–1920) Irish judge, born in Dublin. Educated at Clongaves Wood College and Trinity College, Dublin, he was successively solicitor-general and attorney-general for Ireland (1872–74), and chief baron of the Irish Court of Exchequer (1874–1916). He had an encyclopaedic knowledge of law and many of his judgments are classics, though he showed reluctance to develop principles beyond cases for which there was precedent. In his day he was highly esteemed, even revered. He also played a major part in education in Ireland, especially the establishment of University College, Dublin.

PALMA, Jacopo, called **Palma Vecchio ('Old Palma')** (c.1480–1528) Italian painter of the Venetian School. He is particularly remembered for the ample blonde women who appear in many of his works. His pictures are sacred subjects or portrait groups; his brother's grandson, Jacopo (1544–1628), called Il Giovane ('the Younger'), was a prolific painter of poorish religious pictures in a style influenced by **Tintoretto** and late **Titian**.

PALME, (Sven) Olof (1927–86) Swedish politician, born in Stockholm. He was educated in the USA at Kenyon College, and studied law at Stockholm University. He joined the Social Democratic Labour party (SAP) in 1949 and became leader of its youth movement in 1955. After election to the Riksdag in 1956, he entered the government in 1963 and held several ministerial posts before assuming the leadership of the party, and becoming prime minister, in 1969. Although losing his parliamentary majority in 1971, he successfully carried out major constitutional reforms but was eventually defeated in 1976 over taxation proposals to fund the welfare system. He was returned to power, heading a minority government, in 1982, and was re-elected in 1985, but was shot and killed in the centre of Stockholm while walking home with his wife after a visit to a cinema.

PALMER, Arnold (1929–) American golfer, born in Latrobe, Pennsylvania. One of the post-war golfing greats, he turned professional in 1955 after a brilliant amateur career, and between 1958 and 1964 he won the US Masters four times, the British Open twice, and the US Open once. He attracted a huge following on both sides of the Atlantic, known as 'Arnie's Army', whom he delighted with his characteristic 'charges' in the later stages of a tournament. He was twice captain of the American Ryder Cup team. An accomplished businessman, his career earnings topped $80 million.

PALMER, Daniel David (1845–1913) American osteopath and founder of chiropractic, born in Toronto. In 1895 he settled at Davenport, Iowa, where he first practised spinal adjustment and founded the Palmer School of Chiropractic in 1898. Later he established a college of chiropractic in Portland, Oregon.

PALMER, Edward Henry (1840–82) English orientalist, born in Cambridge. He made oriental studies his speciality at Cambridge, and in 1871 was appointed professor of Arabic there. In 1874 he was called to the bar. In 1881 he turned journalist, writing principally for the *Standard*. In 1882, on the eve of **Ahmed Arabi**'s Egyptian rebellion, he was sent by the government to win over the Sinai tribes, but was murdered by robbers in an ambush. Among his works are the *Desert of the Exodus* (1871) and a translation of the *Koran* (1880).

PALMER, Geoffrey Winston Russell (1942–) New Zealand politician. After graduating from Victoria University, Wellington, he taught law in the USA and

New Zealand before entering politics, entering the House of Representatives as Labour party member for Christchurch in 1979. By 1984 he had become attorney-general and deputy prime minister and in 1989, when Prime Minister **David Lange** resigned, he succeeded him.

PALMER, Roundell and **William** See **SELBORNE**

PALMER, Samuel (1805–81) English landscape painter and etcher, born in London. He produced chiefly watercolours in a mystical and imaginative style derived from his friend **William Blake** as in *Repose of the Holy Family* (1824). From 1826 to 1835 he lived in Shoreham, Kent, where he was surrounded by friends like John Linnell and George Richmond, who formed a group which called itself *The Ancients*. Palmer later visited Italy and began producing more academic, conventional work in a completely different style. He was then forgotten until a group now called the Neo-Romantics—**Sutherland**, **Minton**, and **Nash**—rediscovered him during World War II, seeing in his work something essentially English but with overtones of Surrealism.

PALMERSTON, Henry John Temple, 3rd Viscount (1784–1865) English politician, born in Westminster, of the Irish branch of the ancient English family of Temple. In 1800 he went to Edinburgh University, in 1802 succeeded his father as viscount, and was at Cambridge University (1803–06). As Tory candidate for the university he was rejected in 1806, but was elected in 1807 for Newport (Wight); but from 1811 he represented his *alma mater* for 20 years, and only lost his seat when he supported the Reform Bill. Afterwards he was returned for South Hampshire, lost his seat in 1835, but found a seat for Tiverton. He was junior lord of the Admiralty and secretary at war under **Perceval**, the Earl of **Liverpool**, **Canning**, **Ripon** and the Duke of **Wellington** (1809–28). His official connection with the Tory party ceased in 1828. Wellington's government was swept away in 1830, and Earl **Grey** offered the seals of the foreign office to Palmerston. For the first time on record England and France acted in concert. Palmerston took a leading part in securing the independence of Belgium, in establishing the thrones of **Isabella II** of Spain and Maria of Portugal, and in endeavouring, in alliance with Austria and Turkey, to check Russian influence in the East. In 1841 Palmerston went out of office with the Whigs on the question of free trade in corn, and under Lord **John Russell** in 1846 again became foreign minister. His second term was embarrassed by the Spanish marriages (see **Guizot**), the revolutions in 1848, the rupture between Spain and Great Britain, the affair of Don Pacifico (a Gibraltar Jew living in Athens, who claimed the privileges of a British subject), and the consequent quarrel with Greece. His self-assertive character, his brusque speech, and his interferences in foreign affairs, were little calculated to conciliate opponents at home, and secured for 'Firebrand Palmerston' many enemies abroad. A vote of censure on the foreign policy was carried in the House of Lords in 1850, but defeated in the Lower House. In December 1851 Palmerston expressed to the French ambassador his approbation of the *coup d'état* of Louis Napoleon (**Napoleon III**), without consulting either the premier or the queen, and Lord John Russell advised his resignation. Next February he shattered the Russell administration on a militia bill. He refused office under the Earl of **Derby**, but was home secretary in **Aberdeen**'s coalition (1852), whose fall (1855) brought Palmerston the premiership. He vigorously prosecuted the Russian war. Defeated in 1857 on **Cobden**'s motion condemning the Chinese war, he appealed to the country, and met the House of Commons with a greatly increased majority, but fell in February 1858 over the Conspiracy Bill. In June 1859 he again became prime minister, remaining in office till his death; the chief events of his premiership were the American Civil War, Napoleon III's war with Austria, and the Austro-Prussian war with Denmark. It was his ambition to be the minister of a nation rather than of a political party, and his opponents admitted that he held office with more general acceptance than any minister since **Chatham**.

PALMIERI, Luigi (1807–96) Italian meteorologist. In 1847 he became professor at Naples, and in 1854 director of the Vesuvius observatory. He invented a rain gauge and other meteorological instruments.

PALTOCK, Robert (1697–1767) English lawyer and writer, born in London. He took up law and practised as an attorney at Clement's Inn. He wrote the fantasy novel, *The Life and Adventures of Peter Wilkins* (1751); its authorship remained a mystery till 1835.

PALUDAN-MÜLLER, Frederick (1809–76) Danish poet. He wrote poems, dramas and romances, but his fame rests on *Adam Homo* (1841–49), a humorous, satiric, didactic epic.

PANAETIUS (c.185–c.110 BC) Greek Stoic philosopher, from Rhodes. He taught in Athens and Rome and became head of the Stoa in Athens in 129 BC. His writings are now lost but he was an important figure in the popularization of stoicism in Rome. He was a friend of the younger **Scipio**, and his ethical and political works were an important source for **Cicero**'s influential treatise *De Officiis*.

PANCRAS, St (d.304) Christian martyr, the son of a heathen noble of Phrygia. He was baptized in Rome, but immediately afterwards was slain in the **Diocletian** persecutions while only a young boy. One of the patron saints of children, his feast day is 12 May.

PANDER, Christian Heinrich (1794–1865) Russian-born German anatomist, born in Riga, and regarded as the father of embryology. At Würzburg with **Karl Ernst von Baer** he did valuable research on chick development in the egg, with particular regard to the embryonic layers now called by his name. Having published his findings in 1817, in 1820 he accompanied as a naturalist a Russian mission to Bokhara, and was elected a member of the St Petersburg Academy of Sciences in 1826.

PANDULF, Cardinal (d.1226) Italian prelate. He was the commissioner sent by **Innocent III** to King **John** of England after his excommunication to receive his submission (1213). He returned to England as legate (1218–21), in 1218 was made bishop of Norwich, and exercised great authority during the minority of **Henry III** (1299–1321).

PANETH, Friedrich Adolf (1887–1958) Austrian chemist, born in Vienna. He studied at Munich, Glasgow and Vienna, and taught at Hamburg, Berlin and Königsberg, before moving to England in 1933. He worked at Imperial College, London, and Durham University, where he was appointed professor of chemistry (1939). In 1953 he returned to Germany and the directorship of the Max Planck Institute. With **George de Hevesy** he developed the concept of radioactive tracers (1912–13), and from the 1920s he used them to establish the age of rocks and meteorites by their helium content, and to detect novel metal hydrides and short-lived free radicals.

PANHARD, René (1841–1908) French engineer and inventor, born in Paris, a pioneer of the motor industry. With Émile Levassor, his partner from 1886, he was the first to mount an internal combustion engine on a chassis (1891). He founded the Panhard Company.

PĀṆINI (5th–7th century BC) Indian grammarian. He was the author of the *Aṣṭādhyāyī* (Eight Lectures), a grammar of Sanskrit comprising 4000 aphoristic statements which provide the rules of word-formation and, to a lesser extent, sentence structure. Pāṇini's work has been reckoned by many to be the finest grammar ever written, but it is composed in a very condensed style and has required extensive commentary. It forms the basis of all later Sanskrit grammars.

PANIZZI, Sir Anthony (1797–1879) Italian bibliographer, born in Brescello in Modena. An advocate by training, he fled to Liverpool after the 1821 revolution, and in 1828 became Italian professor at University College London. In 1831 he was appointed assistant librarian, and later chief librarian (1856–66), of the British Museum, where he showed great administrative ability, undertook a new catalogue, and designed the famous Reading Room.

PANKHURST, Emmeline, née **Goulden** (1857–1928) English suffragette, born in Manchester. In 1879 she married Richard Marsden Pankhurst (d.1898), a radical Manchester barrister who had been the author of the first women's suffrage bill in Britain and of the Married Women's Property Acts of 1870 and 1882. In 1889 Mrs Pankhurst founded the Women's Franchise League, and in 1903, with her daughter Christabel Harriette (1880–1958), the Women's Social and Political Union, which fought for women's suffrage with extreme militancy. She was frequently imprisoned and underwent hunger strikes and forcible feeding. She later joined the Conservative party. She wrote her autobiography in *My Own Story* (1914). Her daughter, Estelle Sylvia Pankhurst (1882–1960), was also a suffragette.

PANNENBERG, Wolfhart (1928–) German Lutheran theologian, born in Stettin (now Poland). Professor of systematic theology at Wuppertal, Mainz, and Munich (1968–), his best-known work is *Jesus — God and Man* (1964, trans 1968), which opposes **Bultmann**'s programme of demythologization with the claim that revelation and history *are* significant theological categories and that the resurrection of **Jesus** is the pivot on which everything turns. His other works, including *Basic Questions in Theology, I-III (1970–73), Theology and the Philosophy of Science* (1976), and *Anthropology in Theological Perspective* (1985), defend the place of reason in theology. He has also written on ethics, spirituality, the church and secularization.

PANOFSKY, Erwin (1892–1968) German-born American art historian, born in Hanover. Classically educated in Berlin and at the universities of Munich, Berlin and Freiburg (Baden), where he took his doctorate in 1914, he taught at Hamburg (1926–33) and, from 1935, was professor at the Institute for Advanced Study at Princeton. He set new standards for the study of the meaning of works of art (iconology); his many books include seminal studies of **Dürer**, **Titian** and early Netherlandish painting, as well as his classic *Studies in Iconology* (1939) and *Meaning in the Visual Arts* (1955).

PANOV, Valeri (1938–) Russian dancer, born in Vitebsk. Trained in Leningrad, he made his début with the Maly Theatre Ballet in 1957 and then moved to the Kirov (1964–72). There his reputation as a virtuoso performer grew as he created sparkling roles in both classical works and new ballets like *Gorianka* (1968) by Vinogradov, *Hamlet* (1970) by Sergeyev and *Land of Miracles* (1967) by Iacobson. He became known internationally when he was refused emigration papers by the Soviet authorities, who eventually allowed him to resettle in Israel in 1974. From that time he made guest appearances with companies around the world. His choreography includes *Sacré du printemps* (1978), *The Idiot* (1979, for Berlin Opera Ballet) and *Cinderella* (1977).

PAOLI, Pasquale de (1725–1807) Corsican patriot, born in Stretta, the son of a patriot driven into exile to Naples in 1739. In 1755 Pasquale returned to Corsica to take part in the patriotic struggle against the Genoese, and was appointed to the chief command. The Genoese sold the island (1768) to France. For a year he held out against a French army, but was overpowered, and escaped to England, where he was welcomed. **Boswell**, who had visited him in Corsica, introduced him to Dr **Johnson**. On the French Revolution he became governor of Corsica in 1790, but he organized a fresh insurrection against the Convention, favouring union with England. He returned to England in 1796.

PAOLO, Fra See **SARPI, Pietro**

PAOLOZZI, Eduardo Luigi (1924–) Scottish sculptor and printmaker, born in Leith, Edinburgh. He studied at Edinburgh College of Art and at the Slade School in London. He has held many teaching posts (eg London, Hamburg, California). His first one-man show was at the Mayor Gallery in 1947, and he has held many since, also at the Museum of Modern Art, New York (1964) and the Tate Gallery, London (1971). His early collages were inspired by Surrealism, and his use of magazine cuttings made him a pioneer of Pop Art. In the 1960s he made large, brightly-painted metal sculptures.

PAPADOPOULOS, Georgios (1919–) Greek soldier and politician, born in Eleochorion, Achaia. He underwent army training in the Middle East and fought in Albania against the Italians before the German occupation of Greece in World War II. He was a member of the resistance during the occupation and then rejoined the army, reaching the rank of colonel. In 1967 he led a coup against the government of King **Constantine II** and established a virtual military dictatorship. In 1973, following the abolition of the monarchy, he became president under a new republican constitution, but before the year was out he was himself ousted in another military coup. In 1974 he was arrested, tried for high treason and convicted, but his death sentence was commuted.

PAPAGOS, Field Marshal Alexander (1883–1956) Greek statesman, a distinguished soldier who, after a brilliant military career, became in 1952 prime minister of Greece at the head of an exclusively Greek Rally government.

PAPANDREOU, Andreas George (1919–) Greek politician. The son of **George Papandreou**, a former prime minister, he was educated at Athens University Law School and Harvard. Before entering active politics he had an impressive academic career, holding professorial posts at universities in the USA and Canada, and became a US citizen in 1944. He returned to Greece as director of the Centre for Economic Research in Athens (1961–64) and economic adviser to the Bank of Greece, and resumed his Greek citizenship. His political activities led to imprisonment and exile after the military coup led by **Papadopoulos** in 1967. He returned to Greece in 1974 and threw himself wholeheartedly into national politics, and founded the Pan-Hellenic Liberation Movement, which later became the Pan-Hellenic Socialist Movement (PASOK). He was leader of the opposition from 1977 and in 1981 became Greece's first socialist prime minister. He was re-elected in 1985. In 1988 a heart operation and news of his impending divorce, following his association with a young former air stewardess, created speculation about his future. The 1989 general election produced no clear result and, after unsuccessful attempts to form a new government, he resigned and was succeeded by Tzannis Tzannetakis.

PAPANDREOU, George (1888–1968) Greek politician, born in Salonika. A lawyer by training, he moved into politics in the early 1920s. The monarchy had been temporarily removed in 1923 and reinstated by the army in 1925 but Papandreou, a left-of-centre republican, held office in several administrations including the brief period when the monarchy was temporarily removed (1923–25) and in the following decade. In 1942 he escaped from Greece during the German occupation and returned in 1944 to head a coalition government, but, suspected by the army because of his socialist credentials, remained in office for only a few weeks. He remained an important political figure, founding the Centre Union party in 1961, and returning as prime minister (1963 and 1964–65). A disagreement with the young king **Constantine II** in 1965 led to his resignation, and in 1967, when a coup established a military régime, he was placed under house arrest. His son, **Andreas Papandreou**, was to carry forward his political beliefs.

PAPANEK, Victor (1925–) Viennese-born American designer, teacher and writer. He has worked in many parts of the world including developing countries, where he has specialized in design appropriate to local materials and to the local level of technology, and on programmes to further such countries' interests. In the western context he has demonstrated particular concern for the handicapped. These preoccupations are reflected in the book for which he is best known, *Design for the Real World* (1971), in which he questioned the role of the designer, and encouraged a sense of his responsibility towards mankind as a whole, and to ecological considerations, rather than simply to the interests of western commercial economies.

PAPANICOLAOU, George Nicholas (1883–1962) Greek-born American physiologist and microscopist who developed the 'pap smear', born in Kimi, where his father was a physician. He received his MD from Athens University (1904) and a PhD from Munich University (1910). He went to the USA in 1913, where for most of his career he was associated with the Cornell Medical College in New York City. His research on reproductive physiology led him to discover that the cells lining the wall of the guinea pig vagina changed with the oestrus cycle. Similar changes take place in women, but, more importantly, Papanicolaou noticed that he could identify cancer cells from scrapings from the cervixes of women with cervical cancer. He subsequently pioneered the techniques, now familiar as the 'pap smear', of routine microscopical examination of exfoliated cells for the early detection of cervical and other forms of cancer.

PAPEN, Franz von (1879–1969) German politician, born in Werl, Westphalia. He was military attaché in Mexico and Washington, chief of staff with a Turkish army, and took to centre party politics. As **Hindenburg**'s chancellor (1932) he suppressed the Prussian socialist government, as **Hitler**'s vice-chancellor (1933–34) he signed a concordat with Rome. He was ambassador to Austria (1936–38) and Turkey (1939–44) and was taken prisoner in 1945. He stood trial at Nuremberg in 1946 but was acquitted.

PAPIAS (2nd century) Greek prelate and writer. Bishop at Hierapolis in Phrygia, he was a companion of **Polycarp**. **Irenaeus** and **Eusebius** preserve fragments of his lost 'Exposition of the Sayings of the Lord'.

PAPIN, Denis (1647–?1712) French physicist, born in Blois. He helped **Christiaan Huygens** and thereafter **Robert Boyle** in their experiments. He invented in 1679 the steam digester, forerunner of the domestic pressure cooker, and in about 1690 made a working model of an atmospheric condensing steam engine on principles later developed by **Thomas Newcomen** and **James Watt**.

PAPINEAU, Louis Joseph (1789–1871) French-Canadian politician, born in Montreal. He was speaker of the House of Assembly for Lower Canada (1815–37). He opposed the union with Upper Canada, and agitated against the imperial government. At the rebellion of 1837 a warrant was issued against him for high treason. He escaped to Paris; but returned to Canada, amnestied, in 1847.

PAPINI, Giovanni (1881–1956) Italian author and philosopher, born in Florence. He was educated there, and founded the literary periodicals *Leonardo* (1903–07) and *Lacerba* (1913–15). He became a Catholic in 1920. His works included *Un Uomo finito* (1913), *Storia di Cristo* (1921) and *Sant' Agostino* (1929). He also wrote a history of Italian literature (1937).

PAPINIANUS, Aemilius (c.140–212) One of the greatest of the classical Roman jurists. He held offices at Rome under **Septimius Severus**, but was put to death by **Caracalla**. Nearly 600 excerpts from his legal works were incorporated in **Justinian**'s *Pandects*.

PAPP, Joseph originally **Papirofsky** (1922–) American stage director and producer, born in Brooklyn, New York City. Following acting and backstage experience, he formed a Shakespeare Workshop at the Emanuel Presbyterian Church on the Lower East Side, New York, in 1952. In 1954 the Workshop started performing free shows during the summer in Central Park, and in 1960 the Shakespeare Workshop officially became the New York Shakespeare Festival. A permanent open-air theatre, the Delacorte, was built in the Park for the company in 1962. In 1967 he founded the off-Broadway Public Theater dedicated to new work by American writers, opening with the original production of the rock musical, *Hair*. He was director of the theatres at the Lincoln Center (1973–78).

PAPPENHEIM, Gottfried Heinrich Graf zu (1594–1632) German imperial soldier in the Thirty Years' War, born in Pappenheim in Franconia, of an ancient Swabian family. At 20 he went over to the Roman Catholic Church, served the king of Poland, joined the army of the Catholic League, and decided the battle of Prague (1620). In 1625 he became general of the Spanish horse in Lombardy; but in 1626 he re-entered the Austrian service, and after suppressing a peasant revolt, co-operated with **Tilly** against Danes, Swedes and Saxons. On his head rests in great measure the guilt of the ferocious massacres at Magdeburg. He involved Tilly in the disastrous battle of Breitenfeld, but made heroic efforts to protect the retreat. After Tilly's death he served under **Wallenstein**. He arrived at Lützen when Wallenstein's army was on the point of being routed by **Gustav II Adolf**, and charged the Swedes' left wing with such fury as to throw it into confusion. He was mortally wounded in the last charge, and died the following day.

PAPPUS OF ALEXANDRIA (4th century) Greek mathematician. He wrote a mathematical *Collection* covering a wide range of geometrical problems, some of which inspired **Descartes** and contributed to the development of projective geometry in modern times.

PARACELSUS, a name coined for himself by **Theophrastus Bombastus von Hohenheim** (1493–1541) German alchemist and physician, born in Einsieden, Switzerland: the name meant 'beyond Celsus' (the

Roman physician **Aulus Cornelius Celsus**). He studied alchemy and chemistry at Basel University, and then learned about metals and minerals and mining diseases at the mines in the Tirol. He wandered through Europe, Russia and the Middle East (1510–24), amassing a vast store of erudition, and learning the practice of medicine. In 1526 he became town physician in Basel and lectured at the university (in German, not Latin), but was driven out in 1528 and finally settled in Salzburg in 1541. Despite his obsession with alchemy, he nonetheless made new chemical compounds, and coined the word 'alkahest', apparently from Arabic, for the hypothetical universal solvent sought by alchemists. He encouraged research, observation and experiment, and revolutionized medical methods. He was the first to describe silicosis, and to connect goitre with minerals found in drinking water. He improved pharmacy and therapeutics, and established the role of chemistry in medicine.

PARDEE, Arthur Beck (1921–) American biochemist, born in Chicago. He studied in California and became professor of pharmacology at Harvard in 1975. His work concentrated especially on the way in which cells control their own synthetic processes; in the 1950s and 1960s he and his co-workers elucidated the details of some cell processes which are inhibited by their own metabolic end-product, so that its production is self-limiting.

PARDESSUS, Jean Marie (1772–1853) French jurist and judge. He was the author of *Cours de droit commercial* (1813), *Collection des lois maritimes antérieures au XVIIme siècle* (1828), *Us et coûtumes de la mer* (1847) and other works, mainly on maritime law.

PARDO BAZÁN, Emilia, Condesa de (1851–1921) Spanish novelist, born near La Coruña, Galicia, into an ancient Spanish family. She married at 16 and moved to Madrid. Her first novel was *Pascual Lopez* (1879), about the life of a medical student. She turned from Romanticism to Naturalism. Her greatest works are *La Cuestión palpante* (1883), *Los Pazos de Ulloa* (The Son of a Bondswoman, 1886), *La Madre naturaleza* (1887), *La Piedra Angular* (1891) and *Dulce Dueño* (1911). She also wrote plays, and was an ardent feminist. She was professor of romantic literature at Madrid from 1916.

PARÉ, Ambroise (c.1510–1590) French surgeon, 'the father of modern surgery', born near Laval. In 1537 he joined the army as a surgeon, and became surgeon to **Henri II**, **Charles IX** and **Henri III**. He improved the treatment of gunshot wounds, and substituted ligature of the arteries for cauterization with a red-hot iron after amputation. His *Cinq Livres de chirurgie* (1562) and other writings exercised a great influence on surgery.

PARER, Damien (1912–44) Australian news photographer, born in Malvern, Victoria. Trained for the priesthood, he instead developed an interest in cinematography and worked with the pioneer film director Charles Chauvel on *Heritage* (1933) and the epic *Forty Thousand Horsemen* (1940). In 1940 he became an official cameraman with the 2nd Australian Imperial Forces and went with the first troops to the Middle East, filming the action at the siege of Tobruk, later working in Greece and Syria, and in New Guinea. He shot a number of documentary films in the heat of battle, and his *Kokoda Front* (1942) was the first Australian film to win an Oscar. In 1943 he joined the American troops for the liberation of the Pacific and was killed while filming their landing at Peleliu, Caroline Islands.

PARES, Sir Bernard (1867–1949) English historian. He was educated at Harrow and Cambridge, and was professor of Russian history, language and literature at Liverpool University (1908–17) and at London University (1919–36). Among his many authoritative books on Russian subjects are *A History of Russia* (1926), *Fall of the Russian Monarchy* (1939) and *Russia and the Peace* (1944). He also contributed the chapters on Russia in the *Cambridge Modern History*.

PARETO, Vilfredo (1848–1923) Italian economist and sociologist, born in Paris. He was professor of political economy at Lausanne from 1893, writing well-known textbooks on the subject in which he demonstrated a mathematical approach. In sociology his *Trattato di sociologica generale* (1916; trans *The Mind and Society*) anticipated some of the principles of Fascism.

PARINI, Giuseppe (1729–99) Italian poet, born near Milan. He became a priest in 1754, and was professor at Palatine and Brera schools (1769–99). He made his name as a poet by the sequence of poems called collectively *Il Giorno* (1763–1803).

PARIS, (Bruno Paulin) Gaston (1839–1903) French philologist and medievalist, born in Paris. In 1872 he became professor of Old French at the Collège de France in succession to his father, Alexis Paulin Paris (1800–81). He edited medieval poems, wrote a long series of valuable works on medieval French literature, and founded *Romani* (1872), a review of Romance philology.

PARIS, Louis Philippe, Comte de (1834–94) French nobleman, grandson of King **Louis-Phillippe** ('Égalité'), and pretender to the French throne. He served as a captain of volunteers on the staff of General **George McClellan** in the American Civil War (1861–62), and wrote *Histoire de la guerre civile en Amérique* (1874–89). He returned to France in 1871 and renounced his claim to the throne, and on the death of the Comte de **Chambord** in 1883 became head of the **Bourbon** house.

PARIS, Matthew (c.1200–1259) English chronicler. He entered the monastery of St Albans as a Benedictine monk in 1217, where he succeeded **Roger of Wendover** as the abbey chronicler in 1236. He also made two journeys to France, and was sent on a mission to Norway on behalf of Pope Innocent IV. His *Chronica Majora* is a revision of the earlier work of Roger of Wendover, with an additional 23 years of his own first-hand work, which establishes him as the finest chronicler of the 13th century. He also produced an abridged form for the years 1200–50, known as the *Historia Anglorum sive Historia Minor*. He also wrote Lives of abbots, and a book of *Additamenta*.

PARK, Maud May, née **Wood** (1871–1955) American suffrage leader, born in Boston, Massachusetts. Educated at Radcliffe College, where she had a glittering career, with Inez Haynes Gillmore (Irwin) she joined the Massachusetts Woman Suffrage Association, and in 1897, while still at college, married an architect, Charles Edward Park (d.1904). Becoming deeply involved in woman suffrage issues, she became co-founder and leader of Boston Equal Suffrage Association for Good Government and with Inez Gillmore founded the College Equal Suffrage League (from 1901), aiming to involve young women in the fight for equality. In 1908 she made a secret marriage with a theatrical agent, Robert Hunter (d.1928). An efficient, strong-minded campaigner, she helped to bring about the 19th Amendment (1920), thus securing the vote for women. She became first president of the League of Women Voters (1920–24), and shortly afterwards head of the Women's Joint Congressional Committee. Following her retirement from the LWV she continued to lecture and advise.

PARK, Mungo (1771–1806) Scottish explorer of Africa, born in Foulshiels on the Yarrow. He studied medicine at Edinburgh (1789–91), and through Sir **Joseph Banks** was named assistant surgeon on the *Worcester* bound for Sumatra (1792); and in 1795 his services were accepted by the African Association. He learnt Mandingo at an English factory on the Gambia, started inland in December, was imprisoned by a chief, but escaped and reached the Niger at Sego in July 1796. He pursued his way westward along its banks to Bammaku, but fell ill while crossing mountainous country, and was eventually brought back to the factory by a slave trader after an absence of 19 months. He told his adventures in *Travels in the Interior of Africa* (1799), which at last determined the direction of flow of the Niger. Marrying in 1799 he settled as a surgeon in Peebles, but, unhappy in this, in 1805 undertook another journey to Africa at government expense. Again he started from Pisania on the Gambia, with a company of 45; but by the time he reached the Niger he had only seven followers. From Sansanding he sent back his journals and letters in November 1805 and embarked in a canoe with four European companions. Battling against great dangers and difficulties they reached Boussa, where they were attacked by the natives, and drowned in the fight.

PARK, Robert Ezra (1864–1944) American sociologist, born in Luzerne County, Pennsylvania. Educated at the universities of Minnesota and Michigan, from 1887 to 1898 he worked as a newspaper reporter, before returning to study at Harvard, Strasbourg and Heidelberg universities. From 1905 he worked as publicity officer for the black leader, **Booker T Washington**. In 1913 he was invited to teach at Chicago University, where he remained for 20 years. He spent the last nine years of his life at Fisk University. He played a formative part in the founding of urban sociology, as well as making important contributions to the study of race relations (*Race and Culture*, 1950). He created the Chicago school of sociology, which flourished in the 1920s and 1930s, and which was characterized by the use of the participant observation methods that he pioneered.

PARK, Ruth (?1923–) New Zealand-born Australian writer, born in Auckland, and educated at the university there. She went to Australia in 1942 and married the author **D'Arcy Niland**. Her first success was in 1947 with the novel *The Harp in the South*, which won a major newspaper competition. This story of slum life in the Surry Hills district of Sydney has been translated into ten languages and forms a trilogy with *Poor Man's Orange* (1949) and *Missus* (1986). She has written six other novels, as well as short stories, and many scripts for film, television and radio. She created the popular *Muddle-Headed Wombat* series of children's books, and has written novels for adolescent readers including the haunting *Playing Beatie Bow*, filmed in 1987.

PARK CHUNG-HEE (1917–79) South Korean soldier and politician, born in Sangmo-ri, in Kyongsang province, the son of a Buddhist farmer. He was educated at a Japanese military academy and fought with the Japanese forces during World War II. He joined the South Korean army in 1946, becoming a major general by 1961, when he ousted the civilian government of Chang Myon in a bloodless coup. He formed the Democratic Republican party (DRP) and was elected state president in December 1963. He embarked on an ambitious, and remarkably successful, programme of export-led industrial development, based on strategic government planning and financial support, which attained 'miracle' annual growth rates of 10–20% during the 1960s and 1970s. However, he ruled in an austere and authoritarian manner, imposing martial law in October 1972 and introducing restrictive 'emergency measures' in May 1975. In October 1979, during a brief economic downturn, he was assassinated by the head of the Korean central intelligence service.

PARKER, Bonnie (1911–34) notorious American thief, partner of **Clyde Barrow**. Despite the popular romantic image of the duo as glamorous robbers, they and their gang were also responsible for a number of murders. The pair met in 1932 when Parker was working as a waitress. Shortly after, when Barrow was convicted of theft and was sentenced to two years in jail, Parker smuggled a gun to him and he escaped. Parker herself spent a short time in jail on suspicion of car theft. With their gang, which included Barrow's brother and wife, Parker and Barrow continued to rob and murder until they were shot dead in their car by police at a road-block in Louisiana on 23 May 1934. Their demise was predicted by Parker in a poem, variously called *The Story of Bonnie and Clyde* and *The Story of Suicide Sal*.

PARKER, Charlie or **Bird (Charles Christopher)** (1920–55) American alto (and tenor) saxophonist, bandleader and composer, born in Kansas City, and the most influential performer in post-1940s modern jazz. Learning to play baritone horn and alto sax while at school, he frequented the clubs and halls where jazz was played, leaving school at 14 to practise and find casual work. In 1939 he went to New York, living by menial jobs but working out rhythmic and harmonic ideas which would form the basis of the bebop style. He worked from 1940 to 1942 with the Jay McShann Band, then joined the Earl Hines Band where he began an important musical association with trumpeter **Dizzy Gillespie**, another of the young adherents to the new jazz idiom. Both joined Billy Eckstine's orchestra in 1944, but the following year Parker led the first of his influential bebop quintets, with Gillespie on trumpet. Despite addiction to heroin and alcohol and recurring mental illness, Parker continued to lead and record with the style-setting small groups of modern jazz, using trumpeters such as **Miles Davis** and Red Rodney, and pianists like Al Haig and Duke Jordan. He made two European tours (1949, 1950), which strengthened the development of modern jazz on the continent and in Britain. Although he died young, his influence on the development of jazz cannot be overestimated. Many of his compositions, such as 'Now's The Time' and 'Ornithology', have become standard jazz works.

PARKER, Dorothy, née **Rothschild** (1893–1967) American wit, short-story writer and journalist, born in West End, New Jersey, daughter of a clothes salesman. Her mother died when she was five and her father remarried; Dorothy could barely contain her antipathy to her stepmother and refused to address her. She attended Blessed Sacrament Academy in New York, a private parochial school run by the Sisters of Charity, and Miss Dana's School in Morristown, New Jersey, where the typical girl was 'equipped with a restfully uninquiring mind'. She lasted only a few months and her formal education ended in 1908 at the age of 14. But she was a voracious reader and, having read **Thackeray** when she was eleven, decided to make literature her life. In 1916 she sold some of her poetry to the editor of *Vogue*, and was subsequently given an editorial position on the magazine, writing captions for fashion photographs and drawings. She then became drama critic of *Vanity Fair* (1971–20), where she met **Robert Benchley** and **Robert Sherwood** and formed with them the nucleus of the legendary Algonquin Hotel Round Table luncheon group in the 1920s. Famed for her spontaneous wit and acerbic criticism, she has had attributed to her many cruel wisecracks and backhanded compliments. She was at her most trenchant in book reviews and stories in the early issues (1927–33) of the *The New Yorker*, a magazine whose character she did much to form. Her work continued to appear in the magazine at irregular intervals until 1955. Her reviews were collected in *A Month of Saturdays* (1971). She also wrote for *Esquire* and published poems and sketches. Her poems are included in *Not So Deep as a Well* (1930) and *Enough Rope* (1926), which became a bestseller. Her short stories were collected in *Here Lies* (1936). She also collaborated on several film scripts, including *The Little Foxes* and *A Star Is Born*. Her own last play was *Ladies of the Corridor* (1953). Twice married (1917 and 1933), she took her surname from her first husband. As is often the case, her public persona was not mirrored in her personal life. Both marriages foundered, there was a string of one-night stands and lacerating love affairs, abortive suicide attempts, abortions, debts and drinking bouts, and she died alone in a Manhattan apartment with Troy, her poodle, at her side.

PARKER, Sir Hyde (1739–1807) English naval commander, son of vice admiral Sir Hyde Parker (1714–82). In 1801 he was appointed to command the fleet sent to the Baltic to act against the armed coalition of Russia, Sweden and Denmark. He had no share in the battle of Copenhagen, which was directed by **Nelson** in defiance of his order.

PARKER, Joseph (1830–1902) English Congregationalist preacher and author, born in Hexham, the son of a stonecutter. He studied at Moorfields Tabernacle and University College London (1852), and became pastor of Congregational chapels at Banbury, Manchester, and, in 1869, of what became in 1874 the City Temple in London. He was noted as a pulpit orator, and as the author of many religious works.

PARKER, Matthew (1504–75) English prelate, and the second Anglican archbishop of Canterbury, born in Norwich. He became chaplain to Queen **Anne Boleyn** (1535), dean of a college at Stoke in Suffolk, a royal chaplain, canon of Ely, master of Corpus Christi College, Cambridge (1544), vice-chancellor (1545) and dean of Lincoln. He married, and was deprived of his preferments by Queen **Mary I**. Under **Elizabeth** he was consecrated archbishop of Canterbury (1559). The ritual was not the Roman one; but the scandalous fable that he was informally consecrated in an inn called the Nag's Head originated in Catholic circles 40 years later. The new primate strove to bring about more general conformity. The Thirty-nine Articles of Anglican doctrine, as revised by him, were passed by convocation in 1562; and his 'Advertisements' for the regulation of service, and measures of repression perhaps forced upon him by the queen, provoked great opposition in the growing Puritan party. Parker originated the revised translation of the scriptures known as the Bishops' Bible (1572). He edited works by **Aelfric**, **Gildas**, **Asser**, **Matthew Paris**, **Walsingham** and **Giraldus Cambrensis**, was an indefatigable collector of books, and maintained printers, transcribers and engravers. His *De Antiquitate Britannicae Ecclesiae* (1572) is said to be the first privately printed English book.

PARKER, Richard (c.1767–1797) English seaman, born in Exeter. He volunteered into the navy in 1797, and from May 10 till June 13 of that year was ringleader of the mutiny at the Nore, having for a time 13 ships of the line, besides frigates, under his orders. He was hanged on June 30.

PARKER, Theodore (1810–60) American Unitarian clergyman, born in Lexington, Massachusetts. He graduated at Harvard in 1836, and settled as Unitarian minister in West Roxbury (now in Boston). The rationalistic views which separated him from conservative Unitarians were expounded in *A Discourse of Matters Pertaining to Religion* (1841), followed by *Sermons for the Times*. In 1845 he resigned his ministry and became pastor of a new free church, the 28th Congregational Society in Boston. From then on he wrote incessantly. He lectured throughout the States, and plunged into social causes like antislavery agitation. His health broke down, and he died in Florence.

PARKES, Alexander (1813–90) English chemist and inventor, born in Birmingham. He was noted for his inventions in connection with electroplating, in the course of which he even electroplated a spider's web. He invented xylonite (a form of celluloid), first patented in 1855.

PARKES, Sir Harry Smith (1828–85) English diplomat, born near Walsall. He went to China in 1841, served as consul at Canton, Amoy and Foochow, figured prominently in the *Arrow* episode, and in 1858 was appointed a commissioner after the capture of Canton. His treacherous seizure by the Chinese while acting as Lord **Elgin**'s envoy in 1860 led to the burning of the Summer Palace in Peking. He was British minister in China from 1883.

PARKES, Sir Henry (1815–96) English-born Australian statesman, born, the son of a yeoman, in Stoneleigh, Warwickshire. He emigrated to New South Wales in 1839, and in Sydney became eminent as a journalist. A member of the colonial parliament in 1854, he held various offices, from 1872 was repeatedly prime minister, and was identified with free trade.

PARKINSON, Cecil Edward (1932–) English Conservative politician, born in Carnforth, Lancashire. Educated at the Royal Lancaster Grammar School and Emmanuel College, Cambridge, where he read English, he joined the Metal Box Company as a management trainee and then qualified as an accountant. His wife introduced him to local Conservative party politics and in 1970 he entered the House of Commons as MP for Enfield West; he was elected MP for Herts South (1974–83), and Hertsmere in 1983. On the advice of his father-in-law, a builder, he had bought a bankrupt northern building firm and, from that base, established a successful business career and a comfortable personal fortune. In 1979 he was made a junior minister at the department of trade by **Margaret Thatcher** and, two years later, surprisingly, chairman of the Conservative party. He became prominent as a close confidant of the prime minister and a member of her inner cabinet during the Falklands War. After his successful direction of the 1983 general election campaign his political future seemed secure until the news of an affair with his former secretary, Sara Keays, resulting in her pregnancy, forced his resignation. After a period on the back benches he returned to the cabinet as secretary of state for energy in 1987, and became secretary of state for transport in 1989.

PARKINSON, Cyril Northcote (1909–) English political scientist. He graduated from Emmanuel College, Cambridge, of which he became a fellow in 1935. Professor of history at the University of Malaya (1950–58), and visiting professor at Harvard and Illinois, he has written many works on historical, political and economic subjects, but achieved wider renown by his seriocomic tilt at bureaucratic malpractices *Parkinson's Law, the Pursuit of Progress* (1958). 'Parkinson's Law'—that work expands to fill the time available for its completion, and subordinates multiply at a fixed rate, regardless of the amount of work produced—has passed into the language.

PARKINSON, James (1755–1824) English physician and amateur paleontologist. In 1817 he gave the first description of paralysis agitans, or Parkinson's disease. He had already (1812) described appendicitis and perforation, and was the first to recognize the latter condition as a cause of death.

PARKINSON, John (1567–1650) London herbalist, a native probably of Nottinghamshire. He was apothecary to **James VI and I** and author of *Paradisus Terrestris* (1629) and *Theatrum Botanicum* (1640), for a long time the most comprehensive English book of medicinal plants.

PARKINSON, Norman, originally **Ronald William Parkinson Smith** (1913–90) English photographer, born in London and educated at Westminster School. Apprenticed as a photographer, he opened his own studio in 1934 and became one of Britain's favourite portrait and fashion artists. His work was widely used in quality magazines. His style was essentially elegant and romantic but some of his later portraits of the famous achieved a dramatic insight into the sitter's personality. In the 1950s his advertising work took him to exotic locations all over the world and he settled in Tobago in 1963, regularly returning to Britain and the United States for exhibitions and awards.

PARKMAN, Francis (1823–93) American historian, born in Boston. He graduated at Harvard in 1844, studied law, and became the authoritative writer on the rise and fall of the French dominion in America. His works included *The California and Oregon Trail* (1849), *The Pioneers of France in the New World* (1865), *La Salle and the Great West* (1869), *Frontenac and New France* (1877), *A Half-Century of Conflict* (1893), and *Montcalm and Wolfe* (1884).

PARLEY, Peter See **GOODRICH, Samuel Griswold**

PARMENIDES OF ELEA (fl.5th century BC) Greek philosopher from Southern Italy, founder of the Eleatic school (which included his pupils **Zeno** and **Melissus**). Little is known of his life but he produced a remarkable philosophical treatise, *On Nature*, written in hexameter verse, of which substantial fragments survive and which represents a radical departure from the cosmologies of his Ionian predecessors like **Thales** and **Anaximander**. The first part is a sustained deductive argument about the nature of being, which argues for the impossibility of motion, plurality and change. He contrasts this 'way of truth' with the 'way of seeming' in the second part of the poem, which is very obscure but apparently presents a more traditional cosmology. This highly original work set an agenda of problems for the subsequent pre-Socratic philosophers, and in some ways foreshadows the dualism of **Plato**'s metaphysics.

PARMIGIANO, or **Parmigianino,** properly **Girolamo Francesco Maria Mazzola** (1503–40) Italian painter of the Lombard school, born in Parma. He first worked as a painter in Parma, especially on the frescoes in S Giovanni Evangelista, but after 1523 worked in Rome, whence he fled to Bologna when the city was sacked in 1527. At Bologna he painted his famous Madonna altarpiece for the nuns of St Margaret before returning to Parma in 1531. He shows the influence of **Correggio** and **Raphael**. His *Vision of St Jerome* and *Self-Portrait in a convex mirror* are particularly celebrated.

PARNELL, Charles Stewart (1846–91) Irish politician, born in Avondale, County Wicklow. His father belonged to an old Cheshire family which purchased an estate in Ireland under **Charles II**. His great-grandfather, Sir John Parnell (1744–1801), was Chancellor of the Irish Exchequer. **Thomas Parnell**, the poet, belonged to the same family. Charles, whose mother was the daughter of an American admiral, studied for four years at Magdalen College, Cambridge, but took no degree. In 1874 he became high sheriff of County Wicklow; that same year he contested County Dublin without success, but in April 1875 was returned as a Home Ruler for County Meath. In 1877–78 he gained great popularity in Ireland by his audacity in the use of deliberate obstruction in parliamentary tactics. In 1878 he threw himself into agrarian agitation, and was elected president of the Irish National Land League. From the United States he brought home £70000 for the cause. In 1880 he was returned for Meath and Mayo and for the city of Cork, sat for the last, and was chairman of the Irish parliamentary party. In 1880 too he formulated the method of 'boycotting'. **Gladstone**'s government put Parnell and other leading members of the Land League on trial, but the jury failed to agree. In opposing the government's Coercion Bill, Parnell was ejected from the House, with 34 of his followers (3 February 1881). He refused to accept Gladstone's Land Bill as a final settlement. In October Gladstone sent him to Kilmainham jail; he was released on 2 May 1882. Parnell in the House of Commons expressed his detestation of the tragedy of Phoenix Park. The Crimes Act was then hurried through parliament in spite of the Irish party. The Land League, proclaimed illegal after the issue of the 'No Rent' manifesto, was revived in 1884 as the National League, Parnell being president; the previous year the sum of £35000, mostly raised in America, had been presented to him by his admirers. After an unsuccessful attempt to make terms with the Conservatives, Parnell flung his vote—now 86 strong— into the Liberal scale, and brought about the fall of the short-lived first **Salisbury** government. Gladstone's Home Rule Bill was defeated owing to the defection of Liberal members. The consequent appeal to the country (July 1886) gave Lord Salisbury a Unionist majority of over 100, and threw Parnell into a close alliance with Gladstone. Now it was that *The Times* published 'Parnellism and Crime'—with letters as by Parnell, expressing approval of the murder of **Thomas Henry Burke**. A Special Commission sat 128 days, and, after the flight and suicide in Madrid of **Richard Pigott**, who had imposed upon *The Times* with forgeries, cleared Parnell (November 1889) of the charge of having been personally guilty of organizing outrages; but his party were declared guilty of incitements to intimidation, out of which had grown crimes which they had failed to denounce. Parnell now raised an action against *The Times*, settled by a payment of £5000. The 'uncrowned king' of Ireland was presented with the freedom of Edinburgh in July 1889. His frequent mysterious absences from his parliamentary duties were explained by his appearance as co-respondent in a divorce case brought by Captain William Henry O'Shea (1840–1905) against his wife Katherine, and decree was granted with costs against Parnell (17 November 1890). The Gladstonian party now demanded his retirement from leadership; and though the Irish members had reappointed him chairman, they met to reconsider the position a week later, and, after five days of wrangling, the majority elected **Justin McCarthy** chairman. Parnell, with the remnants of his party, carried the warfare into Ireland; but his condemnation by the church and the emphatic defeat of his nominees at by-elections fore-tokened the collapse of his party at the general election of 1892, when 72 anti-Parnellites were returned against 9 of his supporters. Before this, Parnell had died suddenly in Brighton, 5 months after his marriage to Katherine O'Shea; he is buried in Glasnevin cemetery, Dublin.

PARNELL, Thomas (1679–1718) Irish poet and clergyman, born in Dublin. He was educated at Trinity College, took holy orders in 1700, and received the archdeaconry of Clogher (1706), and the vicarage of Finglass (1716). He also owned property in Cheshire, and he lived much in London, where his wit brought him the friendship of **Harley**, **Swift** and **Pope**. After his wife's death in 1711 he took to drink, and died while on his way to Ireland. The following year Pope published a selection of his poems, the best-known of which are 'The Hermit', 'The Nightpiece on Death' and 'Hymn to Contentment'.

PARR, Catherine (1512–48) English queen, the sixth wife of **Henry VIII**, daughter of Sir Thomas Parr of Kendal. She first married Edward Borough, and next Lord Latimer, and in 1543, became queen of England by marrying Henry VIII. She was distinguished for her learning and knowledge of religious subjects, her discussion of which with the king almost brought her to the block. She persuaded Henry to restore the succession to his daughters Mary (**Mary I**) and **Elizabeth**. Very soon after Henry's death (1547) she married a former lover, Lord **Thomas Seymour** of Sudeley, and died in childbirth the following year at Sudeley Castle near Cheltenham.

PARR, Thomas, known as **Old Parr** (?1483–1635) English centenarian, born, according to the tradition, in 1483. He was a Shropshire farm-servant, and when 120 years old married his second wife, and till his 130th year performed all his usual work. In his 152nd year his fame had reached London, and he was induced to journey thither to see **Charles I**, where he was treated at court so royally that he died. **John Taylor**, the 'Water-poet', wrote his Life.

PARRHASIUS (4th century BC) Greek painter, working in Athens. According to tradition he was the greatest painter of ancient Greece, and reputedly the first to use shading.

PARRINGTON, Vernon Louis (1871–1929) American literary historian, born in Aurora, Illinois, the son of a schoolteacher. A graduate of Harvard (1893), he taught at Emporia, then at Oklahoma University (1897–1908), then at the University of Washington in Seattle for the rest of his life. He published little until his masterpiece, *Main Currents in American Thought* (1927), which charted American literature from colonial times, seeking evidence of growing liberal values and democratic idealism. He also published *The Connecticut Wits* (1926) and a study of **Sinclair Lewis** (1927).

PARRY, Sir Charles Hubert Hastings (1848–1918) English composer, born in Bournemouth, the son of Thomas Gambier Parry, inventor of the spirit-fresco process. Educated at Eton and Oxford, in 1883 he became professor at the Royal College of Music, and in 1895 its director. He composed the oratorios *Judith*, *Job* and *King Saul*; an opera on *Lancelot and Guinevere*; symphonies, quartets and cantatas, and wrote *Evolution of the Art of Music* (1896), a Life of **Bach**, and *The Oxford History of Music*, vol iii (1907).

PARRY, Sir William Edward (1790–1855) Arctic navigator, born in Bath, son of Caleb Hillier Parry (1755–1822), an eminent physician. Entering the navy as midshipman, he served against the Danes in 1808, and in 1810 was sent to the Arctic regions to protect the whale fisheries. He took command in five expeditions to the Arctic regions—in 1818 (under Sir **John Ross**), 1819, 1821–23, 1824–25, and 1827—the last an unsuccessful attempt to reach the Pole on sledges from Spitsbergen but which reached further north than anyone had done before. In 1829 he was knighted, and in 1837 was made controller of a department of the navy. He was subsequently superintendent of Haslar (1846), rear-admiral (1852), and governor of Greenwich Hospital (1853).

PARSONS, Sir Charles Algernon (1854–1931) Irish engineer, born in London, 4th son of the 3rd Earl of **Rosse**. Educated at Dublin and Cambridge, he became an engineering apprentice, and in 1884 developed the high-speed steam turbine. He also built the first turbine-driven steamship, the *Turbinia*, in 1897.

PARSONS, Robert (1546–1610) English Jesuit, born in Nether Stowey, Somerset. He became a fellow and tutor of Balliol College. His enemies secured his forced retirement from Oxford in 1574. He then turned Catholic, and in Rome entered the Society of Jesus (1575), becoming a priest in 1578. With **Thomas Campion** he landed in disguise at Dover in 1580, amazed Catholics and Protestants by his activity and success, and for twelve months baffled all the attempts of government to catch him. In 1581 he escaped to the Continent. In 1582 he was in Paris conferring with the Provincial of the French Jesuits, the archbishop of Glasgow, the papal nuncio, and the agent of the king of Spain, concerning his own project for the invasion of England; and this plan he himself carried to King **Philip II** in Madrid. Thus began his influence with the Spanish king, and the series of political enterprises which culminated in the Armada of 1588. At Rouen in 1582 he had finished his *Christian Directory* (1585); in 1588 he was rector of the college at Rome, and he founded a number of Jesuit seminaries. In *The Conference on the next Succession to the Crown* he insisted on the right of the people to set aside, on religious grounds, the natural heir to the throne.

PARSONS, Talcott (1902–79) American sociologist, born in Colorado Springs, Colorado. Educated at Amherst College, the London School of Economics and Heidelberg, from 1926 to 1927 he taught in the department of economics at Amherst, before moving in 1927 to teach economics at Harvard. In 1931 he joined the newly-created sociology department there. In 1946 he set up the interdisciplinary department of social relations. He retired in 1973. He was a leading proponent of functionalism, which attempts to explain social practices in terms of the function they have in maintaining society. The functionalist school dominated American sociology from the 1940s to the 1960s. He also undertook a number of empirical studies, of which the most influential have been those in the sociology of medicine. His books include *The Structure of Social Action* (1937), *The Social System* (1952), *Sociological Theory and Modern Society* (1968) and *Politics and Social Structure* (1969).

PÄRT, Arvo (1935–) Estonian composer, born in Paide. He emigrated in 1980, and settled in West Berlin in 1982. His many compositions (orchestral, choral, piano and chamber works) evince an eclectic range of musical techniques: neo-Baroque, strict serialism, aleatory methods, minimalism, impressionism, polytonality, etc. In his religious works especially, he evokes old polyphonic forms, medieval harmonies and plainsong.

PARTRIDGE, Sir Bernard (1861–1945) English artist and caricaturist, born in London. He began as a stained-glass designer, but made his name as staff cartoonist for *Punch* (from 1891).

PARTRIDGE, Eric Honeywood (1894–1979) New Zealand-born British lexicographer, born near Gisborne. Educated at Queensland and Oxford universities, he was elected Queensland travelling fellow at

Oxford after World War I. He was a lecturer at Manchester and London Universities from 1925 to 1927 and wrote on French and English literature, but later made a specialized study of slang and colloquial language. His works in this field include the standard *Dictionary of Slang and Unconventional English* (1937), *Usage and Abusage* (1947), *Dictionary of Forces Slang* (1948), and *A Dictionary of the Underworld, British and American* (1950).

PARTRIDGE, John (1644–1715) English astrologer and almanac-maker. A shoe-maker in East Sheen, he contrived to learn Latin, Greek, Hebrew, medicine and astrology, and published a number of astrological books. The manifold quackery of his prophetic almanac, *Merlinus Liberatus*, led **Swift** (under the name of Bickerstaff) to ridicule and expose him.

PASCAL, Blaise (1623–62) French mathematician, physicist, theologian and man-of-letters, born in Clermont-Ferrand, the son of the local president of the court of exchequer. The mother having died, the family moved to Paris (1630), where the father, a considerable mathematician, personally undertook his children's education. Blaise was not allowed to begin a subject until his father thought he could easily master it. Consequently it was discovered that the eleven-year-old boy had worked out for himself in secret the first 23 propositions of **Euclid**, calling straight lines 'bars' and circles 'rounds'. Inspired by the work of **Girard Desargues**, at 16 he published an essay on conics which **Descartes** refused to believe was the handiwork of a youth. It contains his famous theorem on a hexagram inscribed in a conic. Father and son collaborated in experiments to confirm **Torricelli**'s theory, unpalatable to the schoolmen, that nature does not, after all, abhor a vacuum. These experiments consisted in carrying up the Puy de Dôme two glass tubes containing mercury, inverted in a bath of mercury, and noting the fall of the mercury columns with increased altitude. This led on to the invention of the barometer, the hydraulic press and syringe. In 1647, he patented a calculating machine, later simplified by **Gottfried Leibniz**, which Blaise had built to assist his father in his accounts. In 1651 Pascal's father died, and his sister, Jacqueline, entered the Jansenist convent at Port-Royal. Blaise divided his time between mathematics and the social round in Paris. His correspondence with **Pierre de Fermat** in 1654 laid the foundations of probability theory. Then, just before midnight on 23 November 1654, he had the first of two revelations, according to a note found sewn into his clothes, and he came to see that his religious attitude had been too intellectual and remote. He joined his sister in her retreat at Port-Royal, gave up mathematics and the social life almost completely and joined battle for the Jansenists against the Jesuits of the Sorbonne who had publicly denounced **Antoine Arnauld**, the Jansenist theologian and mathematician, as a heretic. In 18 brilliant anonymous pamphlets, the *Lettres provinciales* (1656–57), Pascal attacked the Jesuits' meaningless jargon, casuistry and moral laxity. This early prose masterpiece in the French language, the model for **Voltaire**, failed to save Arnauld, but undermined for ever Jesuit authority and prestige, while Pascal's papers on the area of the cycloid (1669) heralded the invention of the integral calculus. Notes for a case book of Christian truths were discovered after his death, and published as the *Pensées* in 1669. The groundwork for Pascal's intended Christian apology, they contain profound insights into religious truths coupled, however, with scepticism of rationalist thought and theology. Their style owes much to **Montaigne** and **Pierre Charron**.

PASCOLI, Giovanni (1855–1912) Italian poet and writer, born in San Mauro di Romagna. He was professor of Latin at Bologna from 1907. Much of his poetry, set in the background of his native Romagna, is of a tragic nature; his volumes of verse include *Myricae* (1891), *In Or San Michele* (1903) and *Canti di Castelvecchio* (1903). *Sotto il Velame* (1900) and *La Mirabile Visione* (1902) are critical studies of **Dante**'s *Commedia Divina*.

PASHUKANIS, Evgeny Bronislavitch (1894–?1937) Russian legal philosopher. He was the author of *General Theory of Law and Marxism* (1924), which led to his appointment as People's Commissar for Justice in 1936. He contended that law was a feature of societies which practised commodity exchange through markets. He argued that law embodied a concept of the individual which corresponded to the individual involved as buyer or seller in market exchange. This approach made him unpopular with **Stalin** and he disappeared in 1937. His work has been more influential outside Russia than that of any other Marxist legal philosopher.

PAŠIĆ, Nicola (c.1846–1926) Serbian statesman, born in Zaječar. He was condemned to death in 1883 for his part in the 'Revolution of Zaječar', a plot against King Milan, but escaped to Austria, and on the accession of King **Peter I** became prime minister of Serbia (1891–92, 1904–05, 1906, and from 1908 almost continuously until 1918). He was instrumental in the creation of Yugoslavia, and was prime minister from 1921 to 1924 and 1924 to 1926.

PASKEVICH, Ivan Feodorovich (1782–1856) Russian soldier, born in Poltava. He served against the French in 1805, and against the Turks, and took a prominent part in the campaign of 1812. In 1826, conquering Persian Armenia and taking Yerevan, he was made Count of Yerevan; in 1828–29 he made two campaigns against the Turks in Asia, taking Kars and Erzerûm. In 1831 he suppressed the rising in Poland, and was made prince of Warsaw. Under his governership Poland was incorporated with Russia (1832). In 1848, sent to the support of Austria, he defeated the insurgent Hungarians. In 1854 he commanded the Russian army on the Danube, was wounded at Silistria and retired to Warsaw, where later he died.

PASMORE, (Edwin John) Victor (1908–) English artist, born in Chelsham. Largely self-taught, he was one of the founders of the London 'Euston Road School' (1937). He became an art teacher and after World War II began to paint in a highly abstract style, in which colour is often primarily used to suggest relief. His works include *Rectangular Motif* (1949), *Inland Sea* (1950, Tate, London) and *Relief Construction in White, Black, Red and Maroon* (1957).

PASOLINI, Pier Paolo (1922–75) Italian critic, poet, novelist, film director and screen-writer, born and educated in Bologna. Most of his childhood was spent in Casara della Delizia, in his mother's birthplace of Friuli. Unheard of until the 1940s, he became notorious in the 1950s, due principally to the publication of the first two parts of a projected trilogy, *Ragazzi di vita* (1955, trans *The Ragazzi*, 1968) and *Una vita violenta* (1959, trans *A Violent Life*, 1968). Superficially works of protest, they exhibit a strong thematic continuity with his early youthful poetry, portraying the timeless innocence of Friuli. His later writings did not match those of his youth and during the 1960s and 1970s he devoted himself to directing films, many based on literary sources: *The Gospel According to Saint Matthew* (1964), *The Decameron* (1971) and *Salò or the 120 Days of Sodom* (1975). He was murdered, probably as the result of a homosexual encounter, though some believe he was killed for political reasons.

PASQUIER, Étienne Denis, Duc de (1767–1862) French statesman under **Napoleon**, the **Bourbons** and **Louis-Philippe**. He was chancellor of France from 1837 to 1848.

PASSAGLIA, Carlo (1812–87) Italian theologian, born in Lucca. In 1827 he entered the Society of Jesus, and in 1844 became professor at the Collegium Romanum. From 1849 to 1851 he taught in England. In 1855 he wrote on the Immaculate Conception; he then left the Jesuits and wrote against the temporal power of the pope, *Pro Causo Italica* (1859). He withdrew to Turin, where he was professor of moral philosophy (1861).

PASSFIELD, Baron See **WEBB, Sidney James**

PASSMORE, John (1914–) Australian philosopher, born in Manly, New South Wales. He studied at Sydney University under **John Anderson**, and from 1935 to 1949 he held academic posts in philosophy there, before becoming professor of philosophy at Otago University, New Zealand. In 1955 he returned as reader in philosophy at the Australian National University's Institute of Advanced Studies, Canberra. He later held the chair for 20 years from 1959, and was president of the Australian Academy of the Humanities from 1975 to 1977. He is regarded as a principal exponent of the 'Andersonian' school of philosophy, and has published much, particularly his classic *A Hundred Years of Philosophy* (1957) and the ABC's Boyer Lecture for 1981, *The Limits of Government*.

PASSOW, Franz (1786–1833) German scholar, born in Ludwigslust in Mechlenburg. In 1815 he became professor of Greek at Weimar gymnasium and of ancient literature at Breslau. His *Handwörterbuch der griechischen Sprache* (1819–24) formed the basis of **Liddell** and **Scott**'s *Greek Lexicon*.

PASSY, Frédéric (1822–1912) French economist and author, born in Paris. He became a member (1881–89) of the Chamber of Deputies, was a founder member of the International Peace League in 1867, and a member of the International Peace Bureau in Bern in 1892. In 1901 he shared the Nobel prize for peace with **Jean Dunant**. His writings include *Mélanges économiques* (1857), *L'Histoire du travail* (1873) and *Vérités et paradoxes* (1894).

PASSY, Paul Édouard (1859–1940) French philologist and phonetician, son of **Frédéric Passy**, born in Versailles. An advocate of phonetic spelling, he was one of the founders of the Phonetic Teachers' Association (later the International Phonetic Association) in 1886, and was assistant professor of phonetics at the Sorbonne. His publications include *Le Français parlé* (1886) and *Études sur les changements phonétiques* (1890).

PASTERNAK, Boris Leonidovich (1890–1960) Russian lyric poet, novelist and translator of **Shakespeare**, born in Moscow. He was the son of Leonid Pasternak, (1862–1945), painter and illustrator of **Tolstoy**'s works. He studied law at the university, then musical composition under **Scriabin**, abandoning both for philosophy at Marburg. A factory worker in the Urals during World War I, he was employed in the library of the education ministry in Moscow after the Revolution. His early collections of verse, written between 1912 and 1916, were published under the title *Above the Barriers* (1931), followed by *My Sister, Life* (1922) and *Themes and Variations* (1923). Under the influence of his friend **Mayakovsky** he wrote the political poems *The Year 1905* (1927), on the Bolshevik uprising, and *Lieutenant Schmidt* (1927), on the *Potemkin* mutiny. *Spectorsky* and *Second Birth* (both 1932) are autobiographical. Among his outstanding short stories are the collection *Aerial Ways* (1933) and particularly *The Childhood of Lyuvers* (1924), a delicate presentation of a girl's first impressions of womanhood, and *A Tale* (1934) translated as 'The Last Summer' (1959), in which Pasternak's imagery is at its freshest and most unexpected. The long years under **Stalin** turned Pasternak into the official translator into Russian of **Shakespeare**, **Verlaine**, **Goethe** and **Kleist**, but he did compose incidental verse such as *In Early Trains* (1936–41) and *The Sapper's Death* (1943). With **Khrushchev**'s misleading political 'thaw' Pasternak caused a political earthquake with his first novel, *Dr Zhivago* (trans 1958), banned in the Soviet Union. A fragmentary, poet's novel, it describes with intense feeling the Russian revolution as it impinged upon one individual, both doctor and poet. Its strictures on the post-revolutionary events are those not of an anti-Marxist but of a communist who is disappointed that history has not conformed to his vision. Expelled by the Soviet Writers' Union, he had to take the unprecedented step of refusing the 1958 Nobel prize for literature, and in a thoroughly self-critical letter to Khrushchev, echoed **Ovid** by his plea that exile would for him be the equivalent of death.

PASTEUR, Louis (1822–95) French chemist, the father of modern bacteriology, born in Dôle. He studied at Besançon and Paris, and held academic posts at Strasbourg, Lille and Paris, where in 1867 he became professor of chemistry at the Sorbonne. His work was at first chemical, as on tartrate crystals and 'left-handed' tartrates. He discovered a living ferment, a micro-organism comparable in its powers to the yeast plant, which would, in a solution of paratartrate of ammonia, select for food the 'right-handed' tartrates alone, leaving the 'left-handed'. He next showed that other fermentations—lactic, butyric, acetic—are essentially due to organisms, not spontaneous generation. He greatly extended **Theodor Schwann**'s researches on putrefaction, and gave valuable rules for making vinegar and preventing wine disease. After 1865 he tackled silkworm disease, injurious growths in beer, splenic fever, and fowl cholera. He showed that it was possible to attenuate the virulence of injurious micro-organisms by exposure to air, by variety of culture, or by transmission through various animals. He thus demonstrated by a memorable experiment that sheep and cows 'vaccinated' with the attenuated bacilli of anthrax were protected from the evil results of subsequent inoculation with virulent virus; and, by the culture of antitoxic reagents, prophylactic treatment of diphtheria, tubercular disease, cholera, yellow fever and plague has been found effective. His treatment of hydrophobia depends on similar proofs, and in 1888 the Institut Pasteur, of which he became first director, was founded for the treatment by inoculation of this disease.

PASTON a Norfolk family, named after the village of Paston. Their letters and papers, published in 1787, 1789 and 1823 as the *Paston Letters*, shed a vivid light on domestic life in the 15th century. **James Gairdner** edited them with more fullness between 1872 and 1875, and again completely in 1904, after the recovery of two long lost volumes. The chief members of the family were William Paston (1378–1444), justice of common pleas; his son John (1421–66); Clement (c.1515–1597), a sailor; and Sir Robert (1631–83), Earl of Yarmouth.

PASTOR, Ludwig, Freiherr von Campersfelden (1854–1928) German historian of the papacy, born in Aachen. From 1881 to his death he taught and studied either in Austria or in the Austrian service in Rome. He influenced Pope **Leo XIII** to open the Vatican archives to scholars in 1881 on the principle that the Roman Catholic Church had nothing to fear from the truth, and he himself also laid other major archives heavily under siege. In 1886 he published the beginning of his great work, the 16-volume *Geschichte der Päpste seit dem Ausgang des Mittelalters*, translated as *History of the Popes from the Close of the Middle Ages*. His approach was biographical, although firmly placing the individual popes within the widest historical context of their times; but his work also included challenging essays asserting pagan and Christian Renaissances whereby he linked Catholicism firmly to ideals of intellectual and cultural advancement. He was made lecturer at Innsbruck University in 1881, professor of modern history there in 1886, director of the Austrian Historical Institute at Rome in 1901, and Austrian ambassador to the Vatican in 1920.

PATAÑJALI Indian founder of the *Yoga* system of Hindu philosophy. The four books of his *Yoga Sūtra*, extant versions dating from the 3rd century AD but drawing on earlier traditions, expound the moral and physical disciplines necessary for attaining absolute freedom of the self. He is not to be confused, according to modern scholarship, with Patañjali the Grammarian (c.140 BC), who wrote a substantial commentary on *Astādhyāyī* (4th century BC), the Sanskrit grammar of **Pānini**.

PATAUDI, Iftikhar Ali, Nawab of (1910–52) Indian cricketer, born in Bhopal. Educated at Oxford University, where he gained his blue, he played cricket in England with Worcestershire, and was first capped by England on the controversial 'Bodyline' tour of Australia under **D R Jardine** in 1932–33, where he made a century on his first Test appearance. After World War II he captained India on their visit to England in 1946 but his health was never robust and he retired from the game. He made seven Test centuries in all. His son, **Mansur Ali Pataudi**, also captained India shortly afterwards.

PATAUDI, Mansur Ali, Nawab of (1941–) Indian cricketer and captain, born in Bhopal, the son of **Iftikhar Ali Pataudi**. Despite the loss of an eye in a car crash, he captained the Indian Test team; in all he made 2793 runs, scoring six centuries, and his brisk energetic captaincy gave India the self-confidence which took her to a leading place among the world's cricketing nations.

PATENIER, (Patinier, Patinir) Joachim (c.1485–1524) Flemish painter, probably born in Bouvignes, Belgium. Nothing is known of his early life, although it has been suggested that he studied under **Hieronymus Bosch**. In 1515 he is recorded as a member of the Antwerp painters' guild. He was arguably the first Western artist to paint scenes in which the natural world, whilst not the whole subject of the painting, clearly dominates the religious narrative. A drawing of him was made by **Dürer** in 1521 who described him as a 'good landscape painter'.

PATER, Jean Baptiste Joseph (1695–1736) French genre painter, born in Valenciennes. A talented pupil and follower of **Watteau**, he is known for paintings such as *La Balançoire* and *Conversation Galante*.

PATER, Walter Horatio (1839–94) English critic and essayist, born in London, the son of a doctor. He was educated at King's School, Canterbury, and Queen's College, Oxford, became a fellow of Brasenose College and from then on lived the life of a scholar. His *Studies in the History of the Renaissance* (1873) shows the influence of the pre-Raphaelites with whom he associated. His philosophic romance, *Marius the Epicurean* (1885) appealed to a wider audience. His *Imaginary Portraits* (1887) and *Appreciations* (1889), followed by *Plato and Platonism* (1893), established his position as a critic, but already people were beginning to talk of his influence as being unhealthy, in the sense that he advocated a cultivated hedonism. That his neo-Cyrenaism, as it might be called, involved strenuous self-discipline hardly occurred to his critics, who found in his style alone an enervating quality. His influence on Oxford, however, was profound. He died having left unfinished another romance, *Gaston de Latour* (1896).

PATERSON, Andrew Barton, nicknamed **'Banjo'** (1864–1941) Australian journalist and poet. He was a World War I correspondent and the author of several books of light verse including *The Animals Noah Forgot* (1933). He is best known as the author of 'Waltzing Matilda', adapted from a traditional ditty, which became Australia's national song.

PATERSON, Helen See **ALLINGHAM, William**

PATERSON, Robert (1715–1801) Scottish stone-cutter, the original 'Old Mortality', born, a farmer's son, near Hawick. In 1758 he deserted his wife and five children, and for over 40 years devoted himself to the task of repairing or erecting headstones to Covenanting martyrs. He was buried at Caerlaverock.

PATERSON, William (1658–1719) Scottish financier and founder of the Bank of England, born at Skipnayre farm in Tinwald parish, Dumfriesshire. He spent some years trading in the West Indies. Returning to Europe, he consolidated his fortune in London, and in 1691 proposed the establishment of the Bank of England. When it was founded in 1694 he became a director, but resigned in 1695. Instead he went to Edinburgh, where he promoted a scheme for establishing a new colony at Darien, on the Panama Isthmus. The Scottish parliament created the Company of Scotland to finance the enterprise, and the whole nation backed it. He sailed with the first expedition in a private capacity, shared all its troubles, and returned with its survivors a broken man in December 1699. But his energy remained unabated. He had a considerable share in promoting the Union of the parliaments of Scotland and England in 1707, and was elected to the first united parliament by the Dumfries burghs. He prepared the scheme for **Walpole**'s Sinking Fund, and the conversion and consolidation of the National Debt (1717). In 1715 he was awarded £18000 as indemnity for his Darien losses.

PATHÉ, Charles (1863–1957) French film pioneer, the inaugurator of the newsreel in France in 1909 and in America in 1910. In 1896, with his brother Émile (1860–1937), he founded the company of Pathé Frères which gave Britain her first newsreel and the screen magazine Pathé Pictorial. He produced the cliff-hanger series, *The Perils of Pauline*, with **Pearl White** (1914). In 1949 the Company became Associated British Pathé Ltd.

PATMORE, Coventry Kersey Dighton (1823–96) English poet, born in Woodford, Essex. An assistant librarian at the British Museum, he was associated with the Pre-Raphaelite brotherhood whose members were much taken with his verse. The epitome of Victorian values, a father to six children and a husband to three wives, his best work is *The Angel in the House* (4 vols, 1854), a poetic treatment of married love which delighted a generation devoid of cynicism. A rabid Tory who put England's decline down to 'the disenfranchisement (in 1867) of the upper and middle classes by the false English nobles and their Jew', his conversion to Roman Catholicism after the death of his first wife may well have been responsible for the plummet in his popularity.

PATON, Alan (1903–88) South African writer and educator, born in Pietermaritzburg. Educated at the University of Natal, he spent ten years as a schoolteacher, first at a native school and later at Pietermaritzburg College. From 1935 to 1948 he was principal of the Diepkloof Reformatory for young offenders, where he became known for the success of his enlightened methods. From his deep concern with the racial problem in South Africa sprang the novel *Cry the Beloved Country* (1948). His other novels were *Too Late the Phalarope* (1953), and *Ah, But Your Land is Beautiful* (1981). He also wrote *Hope for South Africa* (1958), a political study written from the Liberal standpoint, *Debbie Go Home* (1961, short stories), *Instrument of Thy Peace* (1968), *Apartheid and the Archbishop* (1973), and his autobiography, *Towards the Mountain* (1981). He was national president of the South African Liberal party from 1953 to 1960.

PATON, John (d.1684) Scottish Covenanter, the son of a farmer at Fenwick in Ayrshire. He became a captain in the army of **Gustav II Adolf** of Sweden, fought at Rullion Green and Bothwell Brig (1679), and, apprehended in 1684, was hanged.

PATON, John Gibson (1824–1907) Scottish missionary, the son of a stocking-maker, born in Kirkmahoe, Dumfriesshire. In 1858 he went as a missionary of the Reformed Presbyterian Church to the cannibals of the New Hebrides. His brother published and edited his missionary narratives (1889).

PATON, Sir Joseph Noel (1821–1901) Scottish painter, born in Dunfermline. He studied at the Royal Academy, London, and became a painter of historical, fairy, allegorical and religious subjects, in a style close to that of the Pre-Raphaelites. He was appointed Queen's Limner for Scotland from 1865. He also published two volumes of poems.

PATON, William (1886–1943) Scottish missionary statesman and writer, born in England of Scottish parents. He was educated at Oxford and Cambridge, and served the Student Christian Movement (1911–21). Though a pacifist, he worked as an evangelist among British troops in India, and returned there to minister under ecumenical auspices (1922–27). He organized the international conferences in Jerusalem (1928) and Madras (1938), and edited the prestigious *International Review of Missions*. Among his numerous writings are *Jesus Christ and the World's Religions* (1916), *The Church and the New Order* (1941), and *The Ecumenical Church and World Order* (1942).

PATOU, Jean (1880–1936) French fashion designer, born in Normandy, the son of a prosperous tanner. In 1907 he joined an uncle who dealt in furs. In 1912 he opened Maison Parry in Paris, and in 1913 sold his collection outright to an American buyer. After war service he successfully opened again as couturier in 1919. He was noted for his designs for sports stars, actresses and society ladies, and for his perfume 'Joy'.

PATRICK, St (5th century) the Apostle and patron saint of Ireland, born perhaps in South Wales, less probably at Boulogne-sur-Mer, or Kilpatrick near Dumbarton. His father was a Romano-British deacon named Calpurnius. His own Celtic name or nickname was Succat. According to legend he was seized by pirates in his 16th year, carried off to Ireland and sold to an Antrim chief called Milchu. After six years he escaped, and, probably after a second captivity, went to France, where he became a monk, first at Tours and afterwards at Lérins. He was consecrated a bishop at 45, and in 432 it is thought he was sent by Pope **Celestine I** as a missionary to Ireland. He landed at Wicklow; thence he sailed north to convert his old master Milchu. In Down he converted another chief, Dichu. At Tara in Meath he preached to the king of Tara, Laoghaire. Thence he proceeded to Croagh-Patrick in Mayo, to Ulster, and as far as Cashel in the south. He addressed himself first to the chiefs, and made use of the spirit of clanship. After 20 years spent in missionary labours, he fixed his see at Armagh (454). He died at Saul (Saul-Patrick; *Sabhal*, 'barn'), the spot which Dichu had given him on his arrival, and was very probably buried at Armagh. The only certainly authentic literary remains of the Saint (both in very rude Latin) are his spiritual autobiography 'Confession', and a letter addressed to Coroticus, a British chieftain who had carried off some Irish Christians as slaves. His feast day is 17 March.

PATTEN, Chris (Christopher Francis) (1944–) English politician. After Balliol College, Oxford, he joined the Conservative party's research department and then, under **Edward Heath**, worked in the cabinet and home offices and became personal assistant to the party chairman (1972–74). In opposition he was director of the research department (1974–79) and when the Conservatives returned to power in 1979, under **Margaret Thatcher**, held a number of non-cabinet posts, culminating in that of minister for overseas development, in 1986. With Mrs Thatcher's sudden interest in ecological issues, Patten's 'green credentials' and valuable presentational skills made him the obvious choice to replace **Nicholas Ridley** as secretary of state for the environment in 1989.

PATTERSON-BONAPARTE See **BONAPARTE, Jerome**

PATTESON, John Coleridge (1827–71) English martyr-bishop, born in London, the son of Sir John Patteson, judge in the King's Bench, and of a niece of **Coleridge**. He passed through Eton and Balliol, and was a fellow of Merton, and curate of Alfington in Devonshire. From 1855 he spent 16 years in missionary work in the New Hebrides, Banks, Solomon and Loyalty Islands; and in 1861 he was consecrated bishop of Melanesia. He was killed by natives of the Santa Cruz group.

PATTI, Adelina (1843–1919) Italian-born British singer, born in Madrid, the daughter of a Sicilian tenor. At seven she sang in New York, and there made her début as 'Lucia' in 1859. She appeared in London in 1861. Her voice was an unusually high, rich, ringing soprano. In 1866 she married the Marquis de Caux, and, on her divorce in 1886, the Breton tenor Ernesto Nicolini (1834–98), followed in 1899 by the Swedish Baron Cederström. Her home was Craig-y-nos Castle near Swansea. In 1898 she was naturalized. Her sister Carlotta (1840–89) was also a fine soprano.

PATTISON, Dorothy Wyndlow (1832–78) English philanthropist, known as 'Sister Dora', and sister of **Mark Pattison**, born in Hauxwell. In 1861 she became schoolmistress at Little Woolston near Bletchley, and in 1864 joined the Sisterhood of the Good Samaritan at Coatham near Redcar. As 'Sister Dora' she became a nurse at Walsall, and in 1877 became head of the municipal epidemic hospital at Walsall (mainly for smallpox). She was indefatigable in all good works.

PATTISON, Mark (1813–84) English scholar and critic, brother of **Dorothy Pattison**, born in Hornby, Yorkshire. He graduated from Oriel College, Oxford, in 1837, and was elected fellow of Lincoln College, Oxford (1839). Under **John Newman**'s influence he forsook Evangelicalism and almost followed his master into Catholicism, but then reacted towards liberalism, and soon became a tutor of exceptional influence. An attempt to deprive him of his fellowship failed; but for ten years he took little share in Oxford life. He published an article on education in the *Oxford Essays*, went with a commission on education to Germany, and served for three months in 1858 as *The Times* correspondent in Berlin. In 1861 he was elected rector of Lincoln College, and in 1862 he married Emilia Frances Strong (afterwards Lady **Dilke**). He wrote the *Life of Isaac Casaubon* (1875) and a *Life of Milton* (1879), but the greatest project of his life—the study of **Scaliger**—remains a fragment.

PATTON, George Smith, known as **'Old Blood and Guts'** (1885–1945) American soldier, born in San Gabriel, California. He graduated from West Point in 1909. In World War I he commanded an armoured brigade on the western front, using tanks. In 1941 he commanded the 1st Armoured Corps and later led the first US troops to fight in North Africa. In 1943 he commanded the US 7th Army in the Sicilian campaign. At the head of the 3rd Army he swept across France and Germany in 1944–45 and reached the Czech frontier. He wrote his memoirs, *War As I Knew it* (1947).

PAUL (1st century) the Apostle of the Gentiles, born of Jewish parents at Tarsus in Cilicia (now in Turkey). At the age of about 14, he trained as a rabbi under **Gamaliel** at Jerusalem, also acquiring the trade of tent-maker. A strenuous Pharisee, he assisted in persecuting the Christians, including St **Stephen**. He was on his way to Damascus on this mission when a vision of **Jesus Christ** converted him into a fervent adherent of the new faith. After three years spent mainly in Damascus, but partly in Arabia, he visited Jerusalem again, and after the apostles had been persuaded by Barnabas of his conversion, he began to preach: but opposition to him was strong and for ten years he lived in retirement in Tarsus. Brought to Antioch by Barnabas, he was there for a year before undertaking with him and **Mark** his first mission-tour in Cyprus, Pisidia, Pamphylia and Lycaonia. Returning to Antioch, he found the controversy raised as to the condition under which Gentiles and Jews respectively were to be admitted to the Christian Church, a controversy which led to the first apostolic council in Jerusalem c.49 or 50. Paul opposed **Peter** during the debate and when the question was finally settled by a compromise, he addressed himself thereafter mainly to the Gentiles. His second mission-journey led him, with Silas, again to Asia Minor and through Galatia and Phrygia to Macedonia and Achaia, where in Corinth he was especially successful. A year and a half later he was again in Jerusalem and Antioch, and then undertook a third mission-tour—to Galatia and Phrygia. Driven from Ephesus, he visited Achaia and Macedonia again, and by way of Miletus returned by sea to Jerusalem. There the fanaticism of the Jews against him led to disturbances, whereupon he was brought to Caesarea to be tried before **Felix** the procurator, and after two years' imprisonment, before Felix's successor **M Porcius Festus**. Then, using his right as a Roman citizen, Paul 'appealed to Caesar', and in the spring of 62 arrived in Rome, where he spent two years a prisoner, but in his own hired house. He was executed under **Nero**—probably at the end of the two years' captivity, though tradition makes him visit Spain and other countries. The ancient church recognized 13 of the New Testament *Epistles* as Paul's, but did not unanimously regard *Hebrews* as his. All but the most destructive modern critics accept unhesitatingly as Paul's the Epistles to the Galatians, Romans and Corinthians (1st and 2nd), but a considerable body of scholars dispute the Pauline authorship of the Pastoral Epistles, 2nd Thessalonians and Ephesians, and some also Colossians and Philippians. The order of the Epistles is certainly not chronological, though it is difficult to fix the succession.

PAUL III, named **Alessandro Farnese** (1468–1549) pope from 1534. A Tuscan, created cardinal-deacon in 1493, one of his first acts was to give cardinals' hats to two of his young grandsons, and throughout his reign he laboured to advance his bastard sons. Yet he surrounded his throne with good cardinals like **Contarini**, **Pole** and **Sadoleto**. He convoked a general council in 1542, but it did not actually assemble (in Trent) until 1545. In 1538 he issued the bull of excommunication and deposition against **Henry VIII** of England, and also the bull instituting the order of the Jesuits in 1540.

PAUL IV, named **Giovanni Pietro Caraffa** (1476–1559) pope from 1555, born in Naples. As bishop of Chieti he laboured for the reformation of abuses and for the revival of religion and morality. A rigorous enemy of heresy, under his influence **Paul III** organized the Inquisition in Rome. As pope he enforced upon the clergy the observance of all the clerical duties, and enacted laws for the maintenance of public morality. He established a censorship, issued a full *Index librorum prohibitorum*, completed the organization of the Roman Inquisition, and helped the poor. He was embroiled with the emperor **Ferdinand the Catholic**, with **Philip II** of Spain, and with Cosmo, Grand Duke of Tuscany.

PAUL V, named **Camillo Borghese** (1552–1621) pope from 1605, born in Rome. He became nuncio in Spain, and cardinal, and was elected pope in succession to Leo XI. In his time took place the great conflict with the republic of Venice as to the immunity of the clergy from the jurisdiction of civil tribunals, and other questions. Paul issued a decree denouncing excommunication against the doge and senate, placing the republic under an interdict. By the intervention of **Henri IV** of France the dispute was settled in 1607, after the pope had abandoned his claims. Paul promoted charities and useful public works.

PAUL VI, named **Giovanni Battista Montini** (1897–1978) pope from 1963, born in Concesio, son of the editor of a Catholic daily paper. He graduated at the Gregorian University of Rome, was ordained in 1920, and entered the Vatican diplomatic service, where he remained until 1944. He was then appointed archbishop of Milan, in which important diocese he became known for his liberal views and support of social reform. Made a cardinal in 1958, he was elected pope on the death of **John XXIII**, many of whose opinions he shared. He travelled more widely than any previous pope, and initiated important advances in the move towards Christian unity.

PAUL I (1901–64) king of Greece from 1947, son of **Constantine I**, brother and successor of **George II**. Born in Athens and educated at the naval academy there, he was in exile with his father during his first deposition (1917–20). In 1922 he served with the Greek navy in the campaign against the Turks, but went into exile again in 1923 when his brother George was deposed and a republic was proclaimed. In 1935 he returned to Greece with his brother, as crown prince. At the start of World War II he served with the Greek general staff in the Albanian campaign, and was a member of the Greek government in exile in London for the rest of the war; he succeeded to the throne on the death of his brother in 1947. He married, in 1938, Princess Frederika, daughter of the Duke of Brunswick, whose political views aroused controversy, but his reign was seen as a symbol of Greek post-war recovery. He was succeeded by his son **Constantine II**.

PAUL (1754–1801) emperor of Russia. Second son of **Peter III** and **Catherine II, 'the Great'**, he succeeded his mother in 1796. His father's murder and his mother's neglect had exerted a baneful influence on his character. His earliest measures were the exile of the murderers and the pardon of Polish prisoners, including **Kosciuszko**, but he soon revealed his violent temper and lack of capacity, and irritated his subjects by vexatious regulations. He suddenly declared for the allies against France, and sent an army of 56 000 men under **Suvorov** into Italy; he sent a second army to co-operate with the Austrians, retired from the alliance, quarrelled with England, and entered into close alliance with **Napoleon**. After his convention with Sweden and Denmark, England sent a fleet into the Baltic under **Nelson** to dissolve the coalition (1801). His own officers conspired to compel Paul to abdicate, and in a scuffle he was strangled.

PAUL, Alice (1885–1977) American feminist and social reformer, born into a Quaker family in Moorestown, New Jersey. Educated at Swarthmore College and Pennsylvania University, where she gained a PhD in 1912, she spent some years in England, becoming involved in the militant branch of the suffrage movement, and was several times arrested and imprisoned. Back in the USA (from 1912) she formed the Congressional Union for Woman Suffrage (later the National Woman's party), her magnetic, forceful personality attracting wide support and equally wide mistrust. She devoted her whole career to fighting for equal rights for women, in particular for the 19th Amendment, and in 1928 founded the World Party for Equal Rights for Women.

PAUL, Charles Kegan (1828–1902) English author and publisher, born in White Laekington in Somerset. He was a graduate of Oxford and entered the church, becoming in 1852 a chaplain at Eton and in 1862 vicar at Sturminster Hall. During this time he wrote religious works and edited the *New Quarterly Magazine*. In 1874 he left the Church to settle in London, where he wrote *William Godwin, his Friends and Contemporaries* (1876). In 1877 he took over a publishing firm which became C Kegan Paul & Co. Among his first publications were the monthly *Nineteenth Century*, and the works of **G W Cox**, **Tennyson**, **Meredith** and **Stevenson**. Paul became a Roman Catholic and among his many works were *Biographical Sketches* (1883), *Maria Drummond* (1891), works on religion and translations from **Goethe** and **Pascal.**

PAUL, Jean See **RICHTER, Johann Paul Friedrich**

PAUL, Lewis (d.1759) English inventor, of French descent. He invented a roller-spinning machine and opened two mills, one in Birmingham and one in Northampton. This machine was a failure commercially, although the idea was later utilized by **Arkwright**. In 1738 he invented a carding machine which was used in Lancashire after his death, and in 1758 patented another type of spinning machine.

PAUL, Vincent de See **VINCENT DE PAUL**

PAULA, St Francesco di See **FRANCIS, St, of Paola**

PAULDING, James Kirke (1778–1860) American writer, born in Putnam County, New York. He was a friend and associate of **Washington Irving** in *Salmagundi* (1807–08), and during the 1812 war published the *Diverting History of John Bull and Brother Jonathan*. In 1814 a more serious work, *The United States and England*, gained him an appointment on the Board of Naval Commissioners. He also wrote *The Dutchman's Fireside* (1831), *Westward Ho!* (1832), a *Life of Washington* (1835), and a defence of *Slavery in the United States* (1836). From 1838 to 1841 he was secretary of the navy.

PAULET, or **Poulet, Sir Amyas** (c.1536–1588) English courtier. He succeeded his father as governor of Jersey, was ambassador to France (1576–79), and was keeper of **Mary, Queen of Scots** from 1585 till her death (1587).

PAULI, Wolfgang (1900–58) Austrian-born American theoretical physicist, born in Vienna, the son of a professor of chemistry. He studied under **Arnold Sommerfeld** in Munich and **Niels Bohr** in Copenhagen. He formulated the 'exclusion principle' (1924), that no two electrons can be in the same energy state, of great importance in the application of the quantum theory to the periodic table of chemical elements, and postulated (1931) the existence of an electrically neutral particle in sub-atomic physics, later confirmed by **Enrico Fermi**. In 1957 he carried out experiments confirming the nonparity theory of **Chen Ning Yang** and **Tsung-dao Lee** in nuclear interactions. He was visiting professor at Princeton in 1935 and, at **Albert Einstein**'s invitation, again from 1939 to 1946. He won the Nobel prize for physics in 1945, and became a naturalized American citizen in 1946.

PAULING, Linus Carl (1901–), American chemist, born in Portland, Oregon. He was professor of chemistry at the California Institute of Technology (1961–63) and at the University of California at San Diego from 1967. He was awarded the Nobel prize for chemistry in 1954 for his work on chemical bonding and on molecular structure, was elected a foreign member of the Royal Society, and in 1962 won the Nobel peace prize, so becoming the first to win two unshared Nobel prizes. For a period after 1955 his criticism of nuclear deterrence policy made him a controversial figure, as has his belief in the value of vitamin C in combatting a wide range of non-nutritional diseases. His scientific work is of remarkable range and importance, covering chemical bonding, crystal structures, inorganic complexes, protein structure, antibodies, and the molecular basis of some genetic diseases.

PAULINUS, St, of Nola **(Pontius Meropius Anicius Paulinus)** (353–431) French prelate, born in Bordeaux. He accepted Christian baptism (c.389) and settled in Nola in Italy, where he became known for his charity and his rigid asceticism. He was consecrated bishop of Nola (c.409). He is remembered for his *Carmina* and for his epistles to **Augustine**, **Jerome**, **Sulpicius Severus**, and Ausonius.

PAULINUS (d.644) first archbishop of York. A Roman Christian missionary to England with St **Augustine** in 601, he was consecratated bishop in 625 and went north with princess Æthelburh of Kent on her marriage to the pagan King **Edwin** of Northumbria. He baptized Edwin and all his court in York at Easter, 627, and was made bishop of York, later archbishop (633). Edwin's death at the hands of the pagan **Penda** of Mercia and **Cadwallon** of Wales in 633 drove him back to Kent, where he was appointed bishop of Rochester.

PAUL OF SAMOSATA (3rd century) Christian churchman, born in Samosata on the Euphrates. In 260 he became bishop or patriarch of Antioch, and so was practically the viceregent of Queen **Zenobia** of Palmyra; but in 272 he was deposed for monarchianism—the doctrine that the Son is rather an attribute of the Father than a person.

PAULUS See **AEMILIUS PAULUS** and **SCIPIO AFRICANUS**

PAULUS, Friedrich (1890–1957) German soldier and tank specialist. As commander of the 6th Army he capitulated to the Russians with the remnants of his army at the siege of Stalingrad in February 1943. Released from captivity in 1953, he became a lecturer on military affairs under the East German communist government.

PAULUS, Heinrich Eberhard Gottlob (1761–1851) German pioneer of rationalism, born in Leonberg near

Stuttgart. He studied at Tübingen and, as professor at Jena (1789–1803), produced a New Testament commentary (1800–04), one on the Psalms (1791), and one on Isaiah (1793). He was afterwards professor at Würzburg and at Heidelberg. In his theological works he asserted the impossibility of the supernatural, and explained the miracles as due to mistaken opinions and errors.

PAULUS, Julius (c.190–c.225) Roman jurist, legal councillor of the praetorian prefect **Papinianus** and the emperor **Severus**. He was a voluminous writer and many passages from his works are included in **Justinian**'s *Digesta*. His *Decrees*, reports of cases heard by Severus, are the only law reports surviving from ancient times.

PAULUS AEGINETA (7th century) Greek physician. He wrote a compendium of all medical knowledge of his time, *Epitomae medicae libri septem*, which went through many editions and had a great influence on Arab physicians in particular.

PAULUS DIACONUS, known as **'Paul the Deacon'** (8th century) Lombard historian, born in Friuli. He probably resided at the court of the Duke of Beneventum. He became a monk about 774, but spent some years at the court of **Charlemagne**, and retired to Monte Cassino in 787. His *Historia Romana* is based on **Eutropius**. The *Historia Langobardorum* comes down to 744. Other works are a *Life of Gregory the Great*; *Gesta Episcoporum Mettensium*; a *Book of Homilies*, selected from **Augustine**, **St John Chrysostom**, and others; and poems and letters.

PAUL VERONESE See **VERONESE**

PAUSANIAS (5th century BC) Spartan soldier and regent, nephew of **Leonidas**. He commanded the Greek forces at Plataea (479 BC), where the Persians were routed. He then compelled the Thebans to give up the chiefs of the Persian party, and haughtily treated the Athenians and other Greeks. Capturing the Cyprian cities and Byzantium, he negotiated with **Xerxes** in the hope of becoming ruler under him of all Greece, and was twice recalled for treachery. He tried to stir up the helots, was betrayed, and fled to a temple of Athena on the Spartan acropolis, where he was walled up and only taken out when dying of hunger (c. 470 BC).

PAUSANIAS (2nd century AD) Greek geographer and historian, born probably in Lydia. He travelled through almost all Greece, Macedonia and Italy, and also through part of Asia and Africa, and composed from his observations and researches an *Itinerary* of Greece, describing the different parts of that country and the monuments of art. Intended as a guide-book, it is an invaluable source of information.

PAVAROTTI, Luciano (1935–) Italian tenor, born in Modena, the son of an amateur tenor. He abandoned a career in school teaching to become a singer, and won the international competition at the Teatro Reggio Emilia in 1961, making his operatic début there in *La Bohème* the same year. He performed with the La Scala tour of Europe 1963–64 and in 1965 toured Australia with **Joan Sutherland** in *Lucia di Lammermoor*. He made his American début in 1968. His voice and performance are very much in the powerful style of the traditional Italian tenor, and he is also internationally known as a concert performer. He has made many recordings, and appeared in the film *Yes, Giorgio* (1981). He wrote his autobiography (with W Wright) in 1981.

PAVESE, Cesare (1908–50) Italian novelist, poet, critic and translator, born in Piedmont. He was brought up in Turin where he worked for Einaudi, the publisher. Among his translations, *Moby Dick* is regarded as a classic. A leader of the Italian post-war Neorealist school he was politically disillusioned and sexually neurotic and he committed suicide. His poetry is slight; his finest works are novels like *La casa in collina* (1949, trans *The House on the Hill*) and *La luna e i falò* (1950, trans *The Moon and the Bonfire*) which express precisely and definitely his abhorrence of war and Fascism.

PAVIE, Auguste Jean Marie (1847–1925) French explorer and diplomat. He served in the French Marines before joining the Telegraph Department in Cochin China (southern Vietnam) and being posted to Kampot in Cambodia where he learnt the language and explored locally. In 1880 he supervised the laying of the telegraph line between Phnom Penh and Bangkok, before being granted permission to explore French Indochina. The series of expeditions which he organized (1881–95), known as the Pavie Mission, surveyed 260000 square miles, collected much important scientific data, which was published in eleven volumes with accompanying maps (*Mission Pavie*, 1898–1919), and led to French political domination over the Laotian states. He was vice-consul in Luang Prabang (1886–91) and consul-general in Bangkok (1891–93).

PAVLOV, Ivan Petrovich (1849–1936) Russian physiologist, born near Ryazan. A village priest's son, he studied medicine at St Petersburg, conducted research in Breslau and Leipzig, and returned to St Petersburg, where he became professor (1890) and director of the Institute of Experimental Medicine (1913). He worked on the physiology of circulation and digestion, but is most famous for his study of 'conditioned ' or acquired reflexes, each associated with some part of the brain cortex—the brain's only function being in his view the coupling of neurones to produce reflexes. He was awarded the Nobel prize for physiology or medicine in 1904.

PAVLOVA, Anna (1885–1931) Russian ballerina, born in St Petersburg. She trained there at the Imperial Ballet School, and became world famous, creating roles in work by **Fokine**, in particular *The Dying Swan* (1907). After a period with **Diaghilev**'s Ballet Russe, in 1909 she began touring Europe with her own company. She choreographed over a dozen works of which the best known are *Snowflakes* (1915) and *Autumn Leaves* (1919). She did much to create the stereotyped image of the ballerina which persists today.

PAXTON, Sir Joseph (1801–65) English gardener and architect, born in Milton-Bryant near Woburn. As superintendent of gardens to the Duke of Devonshire at Chiswick and Chatsworth (from 1826), he remodelled the gardens and designed a glass and iron conservatory at Chatsworth (1836–40) which became the model for his design of the building for the Great Exhibition of 1851 (it was later re-erected as the Crystal Palace in Sydenham, and destroyed by fire in 1936). He was Liberal MP for Coventry from 1854.

PAXTON, Steve (1939–) American experimental dancer and choreographer, born in Tucson, Arizona. As a schoolboy gymnast, he was drawn to dance, which with a move to New York in 1958 became his primary concern. His training included three years with **Merce Cunningham** and a year with **José Limón**. An experimental composition course with musician Robert Dunn led to his involvement with the Judson Dance Theatre, with whom he performed works by **Yvonne Rainer**, **Trisha Brown** and others. He was also a founding member of the experimental Grand Union. In 1972 he invented the dance form known as contact improvisation which has now been absorbed into the choreography of dancers the world over. Contact relies only on the performer's own weight to determine the shape of the dance, without any reliance on set steps.

Though one of the most important dancers of his generation, he is one of the most invisible and reclusive, now choosing to live in the Vermont countryside and performing rarely and usually alone.

PAYN, James (1830–98) English novelist, born in Cheltenham. He was educated at Eton, Woolwich Academy, and Trinity College, Cambridge. In 1853 he published a volume of *Poems*, from 1859 to 1874 was editor of *Chambers's Journal*, and from 1882 to 1896 edited the *Cornhill*. He wrote a hundred novels, such as *Lost Sir Massingberd* (1864), *By Proxy* (1878) and *The Luck of the Darrells* (1885).

PAYNE, John Howard (1791–1852) American actor and playwright, born in New York. He made his début there in February 1809, and in 1813 appeared in London. For 30 years he had a successful career as an actor and author of plays, chiefly adaptations. His play *Clari* contains the song 'Home, Sweet Home', the music being by Sir **Henry Bishop**. Payne was appointed American consul in Tunis in 1841.

PAYNE, Peter (c.1380–1455) English Wycliffite, born near Grantham. He studied at Oxford, and in 1410 became principal of St Edmund Hall. Charged with heresy, he fled about 1416 to Bohemia, where, till his death, he played a conspicuous part as a controversialist amongst the Hussites, taking the Taborite view.

PAYNE-SMITH, Robert (1819–95) English theologian and Orientalist, born in Chipping Camden. He studied at Pembroke College, Oxford, and, as sub-librarian of the Bodleian (1857–65), began his great Syrian dictionary, *Thesaurus Syriacus* (1870–93). Sermons on *Isaiah* (1862) led to his appointment as Regius professor of theology at Oxford (1865–70); he moved to the deanery of Canterbury in 1870. He was a member of the Old Testament Revision Committee (1870–75).

PAYTON, Walter (1954–) American footballer, born in Columbia, Missouri. He played college football for Jackson State before joining the Chicago Bears as a running back in 1975. Between then and his retiral in 1987 he established a National Football League rushing record of 16726 yards. In a sport often characterized by naked aggression and rampant egomania, Payton's cheerfulness and humility earned him the nickname 'Sweetness'. He remained loyal to Chicago throughout his career. Regarded as one of the greatest ever American footballers, his loyalty was rewarded when, in 1986, the Bears defeated the New England Patriots 46-10 to win the Super Bowl.

PAZ, Octavio (1914–) Mexican poet, born in Mexico City. He attended the National University of Mexico, and fought on the Republican side in the Spanish Civil War. Diplomat (he was ambassador to India in the 1960s), essayist and editor, with strong metaphysical leanings, he is best known for his poetry. His long poem, *Sun Stone* (*Piedra de sol*, 1957), is one of the most remarkable of ten volumes that have appeared. There is also a perceptive study of Mexican character and culture, *The Labyrinth of Solitude*, originally published in 1950. *Postdata* (1970), written after the student massacre and other events in 1968, revises views he had held earlier. Thereafter he emigrated to Britain.

PAZ ESTENSSORO, Victor (1907–) Bolivian politician and economist. Educated at the University Mayor de San Andres, he held a number of financial posts before entering politics in the 1930s. In 1942 he founded the National Revolutionary Movement (MNR), a centre-right grouping, but in 1946 went into exile in Argentina during one of Bolivia's many periods of military rule. He returned to fight for the presidency in 1951 and, although he did not win an outright victory, eventually became president in 1952. He immediately embarked on a programme of political reform, retaining the presidency until 1956 and being re-elected (1960–64) and again in 1985, returning from near-retirement at the age of 77. During a long career he was Bolivian ambassador in London (1956–59) and a professor at London University (1966).

PEABODY, George (1795–1869) American merchant, financier and philanthropist, born in South Danvers, Massachusetts, now called Peabody. He became a partner in a Baltimore dry-goods store in 1815. He established himself in London in 1837 as a merchant and banker, raising loans for American causes. In his lifetime he gave away a fortune for philanthropic purposes. He fitted out **Kane**'s Arctic expedition to search for **Franklin**, and founded and endowed the Peabody Institutes in Baltimore and Peabody, and the Peabody Museums at Yale and Harvard. He also set up the Peabody Education Fund for the promotion of education in the American south, and built working men's tenements in London. He died in London but was buried in Peabody.

PEACE, Charles (1832–79) English criminal and murderer, born in Sheffield. First imprisoned for robbery at the age of 18, he subsequently divided his time between picture-frame making by day and burglary by night. In August 1876 he shot a policeman in Whalley Range, Manchester, and after escaping attended the trial of William and John Habron for his crime. John was found not guilty, and William was, on account of his youth, sentenced to life imprisonment for the crime. In November 1876 in Sheffield Peace murdered Arthur Dyson, whose wife he had been annoying, but again escaped. He made his way to London, where he lived a life of seeming respectability, and was, two years later, arrested for attempted murder, having fired upon a policeman while attempting a burglary in Blackheath. In the following January, while serving sentence for the latter crime, he was accused of the murder of Dyson and found guilty. Shortly before his execution, he confessed to the Whalley Range murder.

PEACOCK, Andrew Sharp (1939–) Australian politician. A former foreign minister (1975–80) and minister for industrial relations (1980–81), he resigned from the government in 1981 over differences between himself and prime minister **Malcolm Fraser** The following year, he unsuccessfully challenged Fraser for the leadership of the Liberal party before being appointed minister for industry and commerce. Peacock suceeded Fraser as Liberal leader after the party lost the 1983 general election.

PEACOCK, Thomas Love (1785–1866) English novelist and poet, born in Weymouth, the son of a London merchant. He was a friend of **Shelley**. He entered the service of the East India Company in 1819 after producing three satirical romances, *Headlong Hall* (1816), *Melincourt* (1817) and *Nightmare Abbey* (1818). *Crochet Castle* (1831) concluded this series of satires, and in 1860 *Gryll Grange* appeared. He also published two romances, *Maid Marian* (1822) and *The Misfortunes of Elphin* (1829). The framework of his satirical fictions is always the same—a company of humorists meet in a country house and display the sort of crotchets or prejudices which Peacock, the reasonable man, most disliked: morbid romance, the mechanical sort of political economy, the 'march of science' and transcendental philosophy. The poets of the Romantic school, **Wordsworth**, **Coleridge**, **Shelley**, **Byron** and **Southey**, are caricatured along with the

Edinburgh Reviewers, who offer the extra target of being Scots.

PEAKE, Mervyn Laurence (1911–68) English author and artist, born in south China, where his father was a missionary. He was educated at Tientsin Grammar School, Eltham College and the Royal Academy Schools. While living on Sark (1933–35) and thereafter teaching at the Westminster School of Art, his reputation as an artist grew. His first book was a children's story, *Captain Slaughterboard Drops Anchor* (1939), with his own illustrations. *The Craft of the Lead Pencil* (1946), a book on drawing, was published in the same year as his first novel, *Titus Groan*, the first part of a Gothic fantasy trilogy completed in *Gormenghast* (1950) and *Titus Alone* (1959). Another novel, *Mr Pye*, appeared in 1953, and his only play, *The Wit to Woo*, in 1957. He published two volumes of verse, *Shapes and Sounds* (1941) and *The Glassblowers* (1950), and illustrated several classics, notably *The Hunting of the Snark* and *The Ancient Mariner*.

PEALE, Charles Willson (1741–1827) American painter, born in Maryland, the eldest member of a family of painters. He began his career as a saddler and silversmith but in 1767 travelled to London where he studied painting for two years under **Benjamin West**. He became best known for his many portraits of the leading figures of the American Revolution, painted in a neo-classical style after the manner of **J-L David**. He is said to have caused a stir when, as a staunch Democrat, he refused to remove his hat in the presence of **George III**. In 1775 he settled in Philadelphia and from 1779 to 1780 was a Democratic member of the Pennsylvania Assembly. He established the first art gallery in America when he opened his Portrait Gallery of the Heroes of the Revolution in 1782. In 1786 he founded the Peale Museum of natural history and technology. Seemingly prolific in all his ventures, he had 17 children, all of whom he named after great artists of the past. Amongst them, Raphaelle (1774–1825) was a painter of still lifes, and Rembrandt (1778–1860) a portrait painter and early lithographer. Rubens (1784–1865) and Titian (1799–1881) were also painters.

PEALE, Norman Vincent (1898–) American Christian Reformed pastor and writer, born in Bowersville, Ohio, the son of a physician and pastor. Educated at Ohio Wesleyan University and Boston University, he was ordained as a Methodist Episcopal minister in 1922, and held three pastorates before beginning his long ministry at Marble Collegiate Reformed Church, New York City (1932–84). He established a psychiatric clinic, the American Foundation of Religion and Psychiatry, next door to his church. He wrote the bestseller, *The Power of Positiive Thinking* (1952), and was much in demand as a lecturer on public affairs. His other works include *The Tough-Minded Optimist* (1962), *Jesus of Nazareth* (1966), and *Power of the Positive Factor* (1987).

PEANO, Giuseppe (1858–1932) Italian mathematician, born in Cuneo. He taught at the University of Turin, and was known for his work on mathematical logic. The symbolism he invented was the basis of that used by **Bertrand Russell** and **Alfred Whitehead** in *Principia Mathematica*. He also promoted Interlingua, a universal language based on uninflected Latin.

PEARLSTEIN, Philip (1924–) American painter, born in Pittsburgh. Following army service from 1943 to 1946, he worked as a graphic designer and in 1949 moved to New York. In the 1950s he produced landscapes in a bold painterly style, but from 1960 turned to making detailed studies of the male and female nude. His work emphasizes the impersonal aspect of the subject, often omitting the head of his model to concentrate on an unidealized representation of the naked body.

PEARS, Sir Peter (1910–86) English tenor, born in Farnham. After being organ scholar of Hertford College, Oxford, he studied singing (1933–34) at the Royal College of Music. He toured the USA and Europe with **Benjamin Britten**, and in 1943 joined Sadler's Wells. After the success of *Peter Grimes* (1945) he joined Britten in the English Opera Group, and was co-founder with him, in 1948, of the Aldeburgh Festival. He was noted for his sympathy with and understanding of modern works.

PEARSE, Patrick (or **Padraic) Henry** (1879–1916) Irish writer, educationist and nationalist, born in Dublin, the son of an English monumental sculptor and an Irish mother. A leader of the Gaelic revival, he joined the Gaelic League in 1895, became editor of its journal, and lectured in Irish at University College. In 1908 he founded a bilingual school, St Enda's, at Ranelagh, later moved to Rath Farnham. In 1915 he joined the Irish Republican Brotherhood. In the 1916 Easter Rising he was commander-in-chief of the insurgents, and was proclaimed president of the provisional government. After the revolt had been quelled he was arrested, court-martialled and shot. He wrote poems, short stories and plays in English and Irish.

PEARSON, Sir Cyril Arthur (1866–1921) English newspaper and periodical proprietor, born in Wookey, Somerset. Educated at Winchester, he became a journalist, founded *Pearson's Weekly* in 1890 and various other periodicals. In 1900 he became associated with newspapers, founding the *Daily Express*, and amalgamating the *St James Gazette* with the *Evening Standard*. Turning blind, he founded St Dunstan's home for blinded soldiers and was president of the National Institution for the Blind.

PEARSON, Hesketh (1887–1964) English biographer, born in Hawford in Worcestershire. He worked in a shipping office before beginning a successful stage career in 1911. In 1931 he emerged as a writer of popular and racy biographies. Among these are *Gilbert and Sullivan* (1935), *Shaw* (1942), *Conan Doyle* (1943), *Oscar Wilde* (1946), whose *Works* and *Essays* he edited, *Dizzy* (**Disraeli**, 1951), *Sir Walter Scott* (1955), *Johnson and Boswell* (1958) and *Charles II* (1960).

PEARSON, John (1613–86) English prelate and theologian, born in Great Snoring, Norfolk, son of the archdeacon of Suffolk. He was educated at Eton and at Queen's and King's Colleges, Cambridge. In 1640 he was appointed chaplain to the lord-keeper Finch, and later became rector of Thorington in Suffolk. In 1659 he published his learned *Exposition of the Creed*, and edited the works of **John Hales** of Eton. In 1660 he was made rector of St Christopher's in London, and then prebendary of Ely, archdeacon of Surrey, and master of Jesus College, Cambridge. In 1661 he was the principal antagonist of **Richard Baxter** in the Savoy Conference, and became Lady Margaret professor of divinity; in 1662 he was made master of Trinity College, Cambridge, and in 1673 bishop of Chester. He defended the genuineness of the Epistles of **Ignatius** (1672), and in 1684 published his *Annales Cyprianici*.

PEARSON, Karl (1857–1936) English mathematician and scientist, born in London. He turned from the law to mathematics, becoming professor of applied mathematics at University College, London, and Galton professor of eugenics. He published *The Grammar of Science* (1892), and works on eugenics, mathematics, and biometrics. He was a founder of modern statistical theory and his work established statistics as a subject in its own right. He was motivated by the study of evolution and heredity. In his *Life of Galton* (1914–30) the head of the Eugenics Laboratory applied the methods of his science to the study of its founder. He founded and edited the journal *Biometrika* (1901–36).

PEARSON, Lester Bowles (1897–1972) Canadian politician, born in Newtonbrook, Ontario, and educated at Toronto and Oxford Universities. He became successively first secretary at the London office of the Canadian high commissioner (1935–39), assistant under-secretary of state for external affairs (1941), and ambassador in Washington (1945–46). He was a senior adviser at the Charter Conference of the UN in 1945 and was later leader of Canadian UN delegations. In 1952–53 he was president of the UN General Assembly, and in 1957 was awarded the Nobel peace prize. Secretary of state for external affairs (1948–57), and leader of the opposition party from 1958, he became prime minister in 1963, retaining power with a minority government in 1965. He resigned as party leader and as prime minister in 1968.

PEARY, Robert Edwin (1856–1920) American naval commander and explorer, born in Cresson Springs, Pennsylvania. He made eight Arctic voyages by the Greenland coast, arriving on the east coast by crossing the ice in 1891–92. In 1906 he reached 87° 6′ N lat, and on 6 April 1909 attained the North Pole. His claim to be first to reach the North Pole was substantiated when Dr **Frederick Cook**'s own claim was discredited.

PEASE, Edward (1767–1858) English industrialist, born in Darlington. He carried on until 1817 his father's woollen mill there. He later promoted railways, and was **George Stephenson**'s supporter in his famous Stockton to Darlington project of 1825. The family were Quakers and worked for the Peace and Anti-slavery Societies.

PEASE, Francis Gladheim (1881–1938) American astronomer and designer of optical instruments, born in Cambridge, Massachusetts. He was observer and optician at Yerkes Observatory, Wisconsin (1901–04), and instrument-maker (1908–13) at the Mount Wilson Observatory, Pasadena, where he designed the 100-inch telescope, and the 50-foot interferometer telescope by means of which he gained direct measurements of star diameters. He was also associated in the design of the 200-inch Palomar telescope.

PECHSTEIN, Max (1881–1955) German painter and print-maker, born in Zwickau. He studied in Dresden, where he joined the avant-garde Die Brücke group in 1906. Going to Berlin in 1908 he helped found the rival Neue Sezession. He developed a colourful style indebted to **Matisse** and to the Fauvists; he visited the Pacific just before World War I, and at Palau he painted figures in tropical settings reminiscent of **Gauguin**. He taught at the Berlin Academy from 1923 until he was dismissed by the Nazis in 1933; he was reinstated in 1945.

PECK, (Eldred) Gregory (1916–) American film actor, born in La Jolla, California. After two years with the Neighbourhood Playhouse in New York, his Broadway début in *Morning Star* (1942) led to a flood of film offers and his cinema debut as a Russian guerrilla in *Days of Glory* (1944). One of the first major independent post-war film stars, his good looks and soft-spoken manner were employed to illuminate many men of action and everyday citizens distinguished by their sense of decency. Nominated five times for the Academy Award, he won it as a liberal Southern lawyer in *To Kill A Mockingbird* (1962). He also produced films, including *The Trial of the Catonsville Nine* (1972), an anti-Vietnam war drama reflecting his own off-screen involvement with liberal causes and support of the Democratic party.

PECOCK, Reginald (c.1395–c.1460) Welsh theologian and writer, born in Laugharne, Dyfed. A fellow of Oriel, Oxford, he was ordained a priest in 1421. He was rector of St Michael Royal and master of Whittington College, London, (1431–44), bishop of St Asaph (1444–50), and bishop of Chichester (1450–58). He was involved in several theological controversies of the day, and compiled many treatises in English including a tract against the Lollards, *The Repressor of Overmuch Wijting* [*Blaming*] *of the Clergy* (1457), *The Book of Faith* (1456), *The Poor Men's Mirror*, and *The Reule of Cristen Religioun*. His philosophic breadth and independence of judgment brought upon him the suspicions of the church. In 1457 he was denounced for having written in English, and for making reason paramount to the authority of the old doctors. Condemned as a heretic, he was given the alternative of retracting or being burned. He chose to recant. Deprived of office, he was sent to Thorney Abbey, Cambridgeshire, where he died.

PECQUET, Jean (1622–74) French anatomist, born in Dieppe. He worked at Montpellier, where in 1647 he was the first to see clearly the thoracic duct. He described his findings in *Experimenta nova anatomica* (1651).

PEDEN, Alexander (c.1626–1686) Scottish Covenanter, born in Ayrshire. He studied at Glasgow, became a schoolmaster in Tarbolton, and minister at New Luce, Galloway (1660). In 1662 he was ejected from his charge, and subsequently wandered about preaching at conventicles and hiding in caves. Declared a rebel in 1665, he went to Ireland, but returned in 1673 and from 1673 to 1678 was imprisoned on the Bass Rock. Many of his utterances were regarded as prophecies.

PEDERSEN, Christiern (1480–1554) Danish theologian and historian, born probably in Elsinore. In 1523 he accompanied King Kristian II of Denmark into exile in the Low Countries, and was converted to Protestantism. He made the first translation into Danish of the New Testament (1529). He returned to Denmark as a leader of the Reformation, and worked on the famous **'Kristian III'** version of the Bible, which appeared in 1550. He also compiled a Danish-Latin dictionary.

PEDRELL, Felipe (1841–1922) Spanish composer, born in Tortosa, leader of the Spanish nationalist music movement. Self-taught, he wrote operas, choral works, songs, and other works. He became professor at Madrid, and lived later in Barcelona. He was the author of critical and historical works on music and edited important anthologies of classical composers (**Cabezón**, **Victoria** and others) and a three-volume collection of Spanish folk songs.

PEDRO I (1798–1834) emperor of Brazil, second son of John VI of Portugal. He fled to Brazil with his parents on **Napoleon**'s invasion, and became prince-regent of Brazil on his father's return to Portugal (1821). A liberal in outlook, he declared for Brazilian independence in 1822, and was crowned as Pedro I in 1826. The new empire did not start smoothly, and in 1831 Pedro abdicated and withdrew to Portugal. He was Pedro IV of Portugal on the death of his father, but abdicated in favour of his daughter, Donna Maria da Glória (1831).

PEDRO II (1825–91) emperor of Brazil, son of **Pedro I**. He succeeded on his father's abdication, and, distinguished by his love of learning and scholarly tastes, reigned in peace until the 1889 revolution drove him to Europe. He died in Paris.

PEDRO, 'the Cruel' (1334–69) king of Castile and León. He succeeded his father, Alfonso XI, in 1349. Both their attempts to assert strong monarchic government aroused resentment among the nobility, who found a leader in Pedro's illegitimate brother Henry of Trestamara. A revolt in 1354 was suppressed and Henry fled to France, but returned in 1366 with French and Aragonese support. With the help of **Edward the Black Prince** Pedro defeated his rival at Najera (1367) but after Edward's departure from Spain Pedro was finally routed and killed by Henry at Montiel (1369).

PEEL, Sir Robert (1788–1850) English statesman, born near Bury in Lancashire. His father, Sir Robert Peel (1750–1830), MP from 1790, created baronet in 1800, was a wealthy cotton manufacturer and calico printer, and from him he inherited a great fortune. He had three years at Harrow, took a double first from Christ Church College, Oxford, in 1808, and entered parliament in 1809 as Tory member for Cashel. In 1811 he was appointed under-secretary for the colonies, and from 1812 to 1818 was secretary for Ireland. In this capacity 'Orange Peel' displayed a strong anti-Catholic spirit, and was so fiercely attacked by **O'Connell** that he challenged him to a duel. From 1818 till 1822 Peel remained out of office, but was MP for the University of Oxford. In 1819 he was chairman of the Bank Committee, and moved the resolutions which led to the resumption of cash payments. In 1822 he re-entered the ministry as home secretary, and he and **Canning** as foreign secretary worked together pretty well, Peel devoting himself to the currency. But on Roman Catholic emancipation Canning was in advance of Peel, and when Canning formed a Whig-Tory ministry, Peel, along with the Duke of **Wellington** and others, withdrew from office (1827). Yet, when the death of Canning led to the Wellington-Peel government, its great measure was that for the relief of the Roman Catholics (1829). As home secretary he reorganized the London police force ('Peelers' or 'Bobbies'). Peel opposed parliamentary reform, and in 1830 the Wellington-Peel ministry was succeeded by a Whig ministry under Earl **Grey**, which, in 1832, carried the Reform Bill. Peel shrank from factious obstruction of the measure, but as leader of the Conservative opposition, sought by vigilant criticism of Whig measures to retard the too rapid strides of Liberalism. Rejected by Oxford in 1829, but returned for Westbury, Peel represented Tamworth from 1833 till his death. In November 1834 he accepted office as prime minister but gave place to Lord **Melbourne** in April 1835. The general election of 1841 was virtually a contest between Free Trade and Protection, and Protection won. The Conservative party, headed by Peel, then came into office. The Whigs were bent upon a fixed but moderate duty on foreign corn; the Anti-Corn-Law League would hear of nothing short of repeal; while Sir Robert carried (1842) a modification of the sliding-scale. The deficit in the revenue led him to impose (1842) an income tax of 7d in the pound, to be levied for three years. To alleviate the new burden Peel revised the general tariff, and either abolished or lowered the duties on several very important articles of commerce. He resolutely repressed the malcontents of Ireland, and O'Connell's influence was broken. In 1845 the allowance to Maynooth was changed into a permanent endowment, and the Irish unsectarian colleges were founded. But the potato rot in Ireland, followed by a terrible famine, rendered cheap corn a necessity. **Cobden** and the League redoubled their exertions. Peel again yielded, telling his colleagues that the corn-laws were doomed. Lord Stanley (afterwards Earl of **Derby**) seceded, and, with Lord **George Bentinck**, **Disraeli** and others, formed a 'no-surrender' Tory party; but the Duke of Wellington, **Graham**, **Aberdeen**, **Gladstone** and other eminent Conservatives stood by him, and repeal was carried. Defeated on an Irish Protection of Life Bill, he retired in June 1846, giving place to a Whig administration under Lord **John Russell** to which he gave independent but general support. In the critical times of 1847–48 he was one of the most important props of the government, whose free trade principles he had now accepted. He had a keen interest in sport, and a cultivated taste in matters literary and artistic. On 29 June 1850, he was thrown from his horse, and was so badly injured that he died. Peel's eldest son, Sir Robert (1822–95), and the second, Sir Frederick (1823–1906), held office as ministers; Arthur Wellesley, the fifth and youngest (1829–1912), was speaker of the House of Commons (1884–95), and then was created Viscount Peel.

PEELE, George (c.1558–1598) English Elizabethan dramatist, born in London. He went up to Oxford in 1571, where he took his bachelor's degree in 1577 and his master's in 1579. By 1581 he had moved to London, where for 17 years he lived a roistering Bohemian life as actor, poet and playwright. He was one of those warned to repentance by **Henry Greene** in his *Groatsworth of Wit* (1592). *The Arraignment of Paris* (1584) is a dramatic pastoral containing ingenious flatteries of Queen **Elizabeth**. Other works include his *Farewell* to Sir John Norris on his expedition to Portugal (1589, eked out by *A Tale of Troy*), *Eclogue Gratulatory* (1589) to the Earl of Essex, *Polyhymnia* (1590), *Speeches* for the reception of Queen Elizabeth (1591), and *Honour of the Garter* (1593). The historical play of *Edward I* (1593) is marred by its slanders against Queen **Eleanor**. His play, *The Old Wives' Tale* (1595), probably gave **Milton** the subject for his *Comus*. *David and Bethsabe* was published in 1599.

PÉGUY, Charles Pierre (1873–1914) French nationalist, publisher, and neo-Catholic poet, born of peasant stock in Orléans. He was educated at the École Normale and the Sorbonne, after which he opened a bookshop. In 1900 he founded the *Cahiers de la quinzaine* in which were first published his own works as well as those of such writers as **Romain Rolland**. Deeply patriotic, he combined sincere Catholicism with socialism and his writings reflect his intense desire for justice and truth. His most important works include *Le Mystère de la charité de Jeanne d'Arc* (1910), *Victor Marie, Comte Hugo* (1910), *L'Argent* (1912) and *La Tapisserie de Notre Dame* (1913). He was killed in World War I.

PEI, Ieoh Meng (1917–) Chinese-born American architect, born in Canton. He emigrated to the USA in 1935, where he studied at the Massachusetts Institute of Technology. He became a naturalized citizen in 1954 and in 1955 founded his own firm. His principal projects include Mile High Center, Denver, the 60-storey John Hancock Tower, Boston, and the glass pyramids at the Louvre, Paris. A controversial, adventurous designer, he won the 1983 Pritzker prize for architecture.

PEIERLS, Sir Rudolf Ernest (1907–) German-born British theoretical physicist, born in Berlin. Educated in Berlin, he then studied under **Sommerfeld** in Munich, **Heisenberg** in Leipzig and as **Pauli**'s assistant in Zürich. Research in Rome, Cambridge and Manchester followed, and in 1937 he was appointed professor at Birmingham. In 1963 he moved to Oxford and from 1974 to 1977 was at the University of Washington, Seattle. He contributed to solid-state physics, quantum mechanics and nuclear physics. He studied the theory of solids and analyzed how electrons move in them; he developed the theory of diamagnetism in metals, and in nuclear physics he worked on the problem of how protons and neutrons interact. During World War II Peierls and **Otto Robert Frisch** studied uranium fission and the neutron emission that accompanies it with a release of energy. In a report in 1940 they showed that a chain reaction could be generated in quite a small mass of enriched uranium, giving an atomic bomb. The British government took this up and Peierls led a group developing ways of separating uranium isotopes and calculating the efficiency of the chain reaction. The work was moved to the USA as part of the combined Manhattan Project (1943), which yielded the first atomic bombs (1945) and brought the war with Japan to an end.

PEIRCE, Benjamin (1809–80) American mathematician, born in Salem, Massachusetts. In 1833 he became professor at Harvard, in 1849 astronomer to the American Nautical Almanac, and from 1867 to 1874 was superintendent of the Coast Survey. His papers on the discovery of Neptune (1848) and on Saturn's rings (1851–55) and his *Treatise on Analytic Mechanics* (1857) attracted great attention. He also did important work in algebra.

PEIRCE, Charles Sanders (1839–1914) American philosopher, logician and mathematician, born in Cambridge, Massachusetts, the son of **Benjamin Peirce**. He graduated from Harvard in 1859 and began his career as a scientist, working for the US Coast and Geodetic Survey from 1861. In 1879 he became a lecturer in logic at Johns Hopkins University but left in 1894 to devote the rest of his life in seclusion to the private study of logic and philosophy. His enormous output of papers was collected and published posthumously in eight volumes (1931–58). He was a pioneer in the development of modern, formal logic and the logic of relations, but is best known as the founder of pragmatism, which he later named 'pragmaticism' to distinguish it from the work of **William James**. His theory of meaning helped establish the new field of semiotics, which has become central in linguistics as well as philosophy.

PEISISTRATOS See **PISISTRATUS**

PELAGIUS (c.360–c.420) British monk and heretic, of either British or Irish origin, his name being a Greek translation of the Celtic *Morgan* ('sea-born'). He never took orders, and settled in Rome about 400. There he wrote *On the Trinity*, *On Testimonies* and *On the Pauline Epistles*, and attached Celestius, an Irish Scot, to his views. About 409 the two withdrew to Africa, and Pelagius made a pilgrimage to Jerusalem. Celestius having sought ordination in Carthage, his doctrines were examined and condemned; and in 415 Pelagius too was accused of heresy before the synod of Jerusalem. The Pelagian heresy rejected the doctrine of original sin and predestination, insisting on free will and man's innate capacity to do good. The impeachment failed, but a new synod of Carthage in 416 condemned Pelagius and Celestius; ultimately Pope **Zosimus** adopted the canons of the African Council, and Pelagius was banished from Rome in 418. The Pelagian sect was soon extinguished, but Pelagianism and Semi-Pelagianism often troubled the church.

PELAYO, or **Pelagius** (8th century) Christian Visigothic nobleman. He led an uprising against the Moors after their conquest of Spain, and laid the foundations of the kingdom of Asturias.

PELÉ, pseud of **Edson Arantes do Nascimento** (1940–) Brazilian footballer, born in Três Corações, Minas Gerais, one of the finest inside-forwards in the history of the game. He made his international début at the age of 16, and in 1958 won his first World Cup medal, scoring twice in Brazil's win in the final over Sweden. He won another World Cup medal in 1970, and in the intervening two tournaments played in the early matches. For most of his senior career he played for Santos, and in November 1969 he achieved the staggering mark of 1000 goals in first-class football. In 1975 he signed a multi-million dollar contract for New York Cosmos, and led the team to the 1977 North American Soccer League Championship, as well as giving football a temporary burst of popularity in the USA.

PELHAM, Henry Pelham (c.1695–1754) English statesman, younger brother of **Thomas Pelham**. He took an active part in suppressing the Jacobite Rising of 1715, became secretary for war in 1724, and was a zealous supporter of **Walpole**. In 1743 he took office as prime minister. Events during his ministry (reconstructed in 1744 as the 'Broad-bottom administration') were the Austrian Succession war, the Jacobite Rising of 1745, the Financial Bill of 1750, the reform of the calendar, and Hardwicke's Marriage Act.

PELHAM, Henry Pelham-Clinton (1811–64) English statesman, 5th Duke of Newcastle and 12th Earl of Lincoln. He represented South Nottinghamshire from 1832 to 1846, when he was ousted for supporting **Peel**'s Free Trade measures. He was a lord of the Treasury in 1834–35, first commissioner of woods and forests (1841–46), and then Irish secretary. He succeeded to the dukedom in 1851, and returned to office in 1852, being colonial secretary in the **Aberdeen** government. At the Crimean war he was made secretary of state for war—the first to hold that office. But the sufferings of the British army in the winter of 1854 raised a storm, and he resigned. He was colonial secretary under **Palmerston** (1859–64).

PELHAM, Thomas Pelham Holles (1693–1768) English statesman, son and successor of Sir Thomas Pelham (d.1712). He succeeded in 1711 to the estates of his maternal uncle, John Holles, Duke of Newcastle. **George I** created him Earl of Clare (1714) and Duke of Newcastle (1715). A Whig and a supporter of **Walpole**, in 1724 he became secretary of state, and held the office for 30 years. In 1754 he succeeded his brother, **Henry Pelham**, as premier, but retired in 1756. In July 1757 he was again premier, and was compelled to take the first **William Pitt** into his ministry and to give him the lead in the House of Commons and the supreme direction of the war and of foreign affairs. On the accession of **George III**, **Bute** superseded Pelham (1762). In the **Rockingham** ministry (1765), he was for a few months Lord Privy Seal.

PÉLISSIER, Aimable Jean Jacques, Duc de Malakoff (1794–1864) French soldier, born near Rouen. He served in Spain in 1823, in the Morea in 1828, and in Algeria in 1830 and 1839. In 1845 he acquired notoriety by suffocating 500 fugitive Arabs in caves in the Dahna. In the Crimean War (1854) he commanded the first corps, and succeeded **Canrobert** in the chief command before Sebastopol. For storming the Malakoff he was made marshal and Duc de Malakoff. In 1858–59 he was French ambassador in London and thereafter governor of Algeria.

PELL, John (1610–85) English mathematician and clergyman, born in Southwick, Sussex. A brilliant student at Cambridge, he was appointed professor of mathematics at Amsterdam in 1643 and lecturer at the New College, Breda, in 1646. Employed by **Oliver Cromwell**, first as a mathematician and later in 1654 as his agent, he went to Switzerland in an attempt to persuade Swiss Protestants to join a Continental Protestant league led by England. In 1661 he became rector at Fobbing in Essex and in 1663 vicar of

Laindon. He is remembered chiefly for the equation named after him and for introducing the division sign ÷ into England.

PELLEGRINI, Carlo (1839–89) Italian caricaturist, born in Capua. He went to London in 1864, and from 1869 till his death was the cartoonist, 'Ape', of *Vanity Fair*.

PELLETIER, Pierre Joseph (1788–1842) French chemist, born in Paris. Professor and later director at the School of Pharmacy in Paris, with **Joseph Bienaimé Caventou** he discovered strychnine, quinine, brucine and other alkaloids. He was responsible for the naming of chlorophyll.

PELLICO, Silvio (1788–1854) Italian writer and patriot, born in Saluzzo in Piedmont. He spent four years in Lyon, and in Milan (1810) was French tutor at the military school. His tragedies of *Laodamia* and *Francesca da Rimini* (1815) made his name, and he translated **Byron**'s *Manfred*. In 1820 he was arrested and imprisoned for two years in Venice. He was then, on a charge of Carbonarism, condemned to death, but had his sentence commuted to 15 years' imprisonment in the Spielberg near Brünn, and was liberated in 1830. During this time he wrote two other dramas. He published an account of his imprisonment, *Le mie Prigioni* (1833), and subsequently numerous tragedies, poems and a catechism on the duties of man.

PELOPIDAS (d.364 BC) Theban soldier. In 382 BC he was driven from Thebes by the oligarchic party, who were supported by the Spartans, and sought refuge in Athens; he returned with a few associates in 379, and recovered possession of the citadel. His 'sacred band' of Theban youth largely contributed to **Epaminondas**' victory at Leuctra (371), which drove the Spartans out of central Greece. In the expedition against Alexander of Pherae (368) he was treacherously taken prisoner, but rescued by Epaminondas the following year. He was then ambassador to the Persian court. In 364, in command of a third expedition against Alexander of Pherae, he marched into Thessaly, and won the battle of Cynoscephalae, but was himself slain.

PELTIER, Jean Charles Athanase (1785–1845) French physicist, born in Hain, Somme. Originally a watchmaker, he discovered the thermoelectric reduction of temperature known as the Peltier effect and later used by **Heinrich Lenz** as a method of freezing water.

PELTON, Lester Allen (1829–1918) American inventor and engineer, born in Vermillion, Ohio. He was a carpenter when he joined the gold-rush to California in 1849. He failed to strike it rich but became interested in the water-wheels used to drive mining machinery, and devised an improved type of undershot wheel powered by a jet of water striking pairs of hemispherical cups. He tested a prototype at the University of California and was granted a patent in 1880, later selling the rights to the Pelton Water Wheel Company of San Francisco. Pelton wheels are now in use all over the world for high-head hydro power generation, at efficiencies approaching 90 per cent.

PEMBERTON, Sir Max (1863–1950) English writer, born in Birmingham. Educated at Merchant Taylors' School and Gonville and Caius College, Cambridge, he was editor of *Chums* (1892–93) and of *Cassell's Magazine* from 1984 to 1906. He produced a succession of historical romances including *Impregnable City* (1895), *Queen of the Jesters* (1897), *The Show Girl* (1909), *Captain Black* (1911) and *The Mad King Dies* (1928). He also wrote revues and plays. He founded the London School of Journalism, and in 1920 became a director of Northcliffe newspapers, two years later publishing a biography of Lord Northcliffe (**Alfred Harmsworth**).

PEMBROKE See **HERBERT, Earls of; MARSHALL, William, 1st Earl of; STRONGBOW**

PENCK, Albrecht (1858–1945) German geographer and geologist, born in Leipzig. Educated at Leipzig, he was appointed to a professorship of physical geography at Vienna (1885–1906), and at Berlin (1906–26). He examined the sequence of past Ice Ages, providing a basis for later work on the European Pleistocene. In 1894 he produced his classic *Morphology of the Earth's Surface*; he identified six topographic forms and is believed to have introduced the term geomorphology.

PENDA (c.577–655) king of Mercia, champion of paganism and hammer of Christian Northumbria. He came to power in 633 with his defeat (in alliance with the Welsh king **Cadwallon**) of **Edwin** (St Edwin) of Northumbria at Hatfield Chase. He attacked Northumbria again in 642, defeating and killing King **Oswald** at Maserfelth (Old Oswestry). An Anglo-Saxon war-leader in the old heroic mould, he made inroads on Wessex and East Anglia, but in another onslaught on Northumbria in 655 he was defeated and killed by King Oswiu at the battle of Winwaed in Yorkshire.

PENDERECKI, Krzysztof (1933–) Polish composer, born in Debica. He studied at Cracow Conservatory and later taught there and in Essen. He achieved worldwide recognition for two strikingly adventurous scores of the late 1960s: *Threnody to the Victims of Hiroshima* for 52 strings (1960) and *The Passion according to St Luke* (1965). Several oratorios followed, as well as operas (including *Die schwarze Maske*, 1986) and other large-scale pieces (*Paradise Lost*, 1976–78; *Polish Requiem*, 1983–84), two symphonies, concertos and many others.

PENFIELD, Wilder Graves (1891–1976) American-born Canadian neurosurgeon, born in Spokane, Washington. He went to Oxford University as a Rhodes Scholar in 1914, but the outbreak of war interrupted his studies. Wounded in the war, he returned to the USA, where he finished his medical education at Johns Hopkins University. Further scientific study in Oxford and Spain prepared him for his experimental neurosurgical work, which he carried out above all at the Montreal Neurological Institute, of which he was the first director (1934–60). An outstanding practical neurosurgeon, he was even more famous for his experimental work on the exposed brains of living human beings. These helped in understanding the higher functions of the brain and the causes of symptoms of brain disease such as epilepsy. He became a naturalized Canadian citizen in 1934. Following his retirement in 1960, he began a second career as a novelist and biographer and was the grand old man of Canadian medicine for many years.

PENG TEH-HUAI (1899–) Chinese communist general, born in Hunan. He fought in the Sino-Japanese War (1937–45), became second-in-command to **Zhu De**, and led the Chinese 'volunteer' forces in the Korean war.

PENIAKOFF, Vladimir, nicknamed **Popski** (1897–1951) Belgian soldier and author, born in Belgium of Russian parentage and educated in England. He joined the British army and from 1940 to 1942 served with the Long Range Desert Group and the Libyan Arab Force. In October 1942, with the sanction of the army, he formed his own force, Popski's Private Army, which carried out spectacular raids behind the German lines. He rose to the rank of lieutenant-colonel and was decorated for bravery by Britain, France and

Belgium. His book *Private Army* was published in 1950.

PENN, William (1644–1718) English Quaker reformer and colonialist, founder of Pennsylvania, born in London, the son of Admiral Sir William Penn (1621–70). He was sent down from Christ Church College, Oxford, for refusing to conform to the restored Anglican church, and his father sent him to the Continent, in the hope that the gaiety of French life would alter the bent of his mind. He returned a polished man of the world, having seen brief naval service in the Dutch war. He studied law at Lincoln's Inn for a year, and in 1666 his father dispatched him to look after his estates in Cork. There he attended Quaker meetings, and was imprisoned. He returned to England a convinced Quaker. In 1668 he was thrown into the Tower for writing *Sandy Foundation Shaken*, in which he attacked the ordinary doctrines of the Trinity. While in prison he wrote the most popular of his books, *No Cross, No Crown*, and *Innocency with her Open Face*, a vindication of himself that contributed to his liberation, obtained through the intervention of his father's friend, the Duke of York (the future **James VII and II**). In September 1670 he was again imprisoned for preaching; and in 1671 he was sent to Newgate for six months. He took advantage of the Indulgence for making preaching tours, championing religious tolerance, and visited Holland and Germany for the advancement of Quakerism. Meanwhile, as one of the Quaker trustees of the American province of West Jersey, he had drawn up the settlers' celebrated 'Concessions and Agreements' charter. In 1681 he obtained from the crown, in lieu of his father's claim upon it, a grant of territory in North America, called 'Pensilvania' in honour of the old admiral, with the intention of establishing a home for his co-religionists. Penn with his emigrants sailed for the Delaware in 1682, and in November held his famous interview with the Indians on the site of Philadelphia. He planned the city of Philadelphia, and for two years governed the colony wisely, with full tolerance for all that was not regarded as wicked by Puritanism (card-playing and play-going, however, being strictly forbidden as 'evil sports and games'). He returned to England (1684–99) to exert himself in favour of his persecuted brethren at home. His influence with James VII and II and his belief in his good intentions were curiously strong. Through his exertions, in 1686 all persons imprisoned on account of their religious opinions (including 1200 Quakers) were released. After the accession of **William III**, Penn was repeatedly accused of treasonable adherence to the deposed king, but was finally acquitted in 1693. In 1699 he paid a second visit to Pennsylvania, where his constitution had proved unworkable, and had to be much altered. He did something to mitigate the evils of slavery, but held black slaves himself. He departed for England in 1701. His last years were embittered by disputes about boundaries, etc; he was even thrown into the Fleet Street debtors' prison for nine months in 1708. He was twice married, and wrote over 40 works and pamphlets.

PENNANT, Thomas (1726–98) Welsh naturalist and writer, born in Downing near Holywell, Flintshire. In 1744 he went to Oxford, but left without a degree. His many tours included visits to Ireland (1754), the Continent (1765), Scotland (1769 and 1772), and the Isle of Man (1774), besides rambles through England and Wales. His principal work on zoology (*British Zoology*) appeared between 1761 and 1777 in four volumes. His most ambitious literary undertaking was *Outlines of the Globe* in 22 manuscript volumes, only four of which were ever published. He is remembered for his well illustrated *Tours in Wales* (2 vols, 1778 and 1781) and *Tours in Scotland* (1771–75). Most of the information that is known of his life is derived from his *Literary Life of the Late Thomas Pennant Esq. by Himself* (1793).

PENNELL, Joseph (1857–1926) American etcher and book illustrator, born in Philadelphia. He did illustrations for **George Cable** and **William Dean Howells**, and in 1885 with his wife Elizabeth Robins (1855-1936) made his base in London. Together they produced illustrated tours of the Thames, Provence, Hungary and elsewhere, Elizabeth writing the text, Joseph providing the illustrations.

PENNEY, Baron William George (1909–) British physicist, born in Gibraltar. Professor of mathematics at the Imperial College of Science, London, he became well known for his research work on nuclear weapons and was an observer when the atomic bomb was dropped on Nagasaki. He became director of the Atomic Weapons Research Establishment at Aldermaston (1953–59), and was chairman (1964–67) of the UK Atomic Energy Authority.

PENNINGTON, Michael (1943–) English actor. He has appeared at the Royal Court Theatre, London, the Cambridge Theatre and in the West End, but is one of Britain's leading Shakespearian actors, and spent seven years with the Royal Shakespeare Company (1975–81). He joined the National Theatre in 1984, and in 1986 co-founded and became co-artistic director, with the stage director **Michael Bogdanov**, of the English Shakespeare Company.

PENNY, Thomas (d.1589) English clergyman and botanist. Educated at Cambridge, he was a prebendary of St Paul's. His interest in botany and entomology was such that he assisted **Conrad Gessner** in his work. After his death his insect drawings passed into the possession of Thomas Moffet, who made use of them in his *Insectorum Theatrum* (1634).

PENROSE, Sir Roland Algernon (1900–84) English painter, connoisseur and art collector, born in London. He graduated from Queen's College, Cambridge, in 1922, and lived in Paris from 1922 to 1935, when he began to collect Cubist and Surrealist art. In 1936 he organized the International Surrealist Exhibition in London. He founded the Institute of Contemporary Arts, London, in 1947. His friendship with **Picasso** led to his writing the standard biography (1958) and organizing a major exhibition of his work (Tate Gallery, 1960).

PENTREATH, Dolly (1685–1777) English fishwife, born in Mousehole on Mounti Bay, Cornwall. She is reputed to have been the last person to speak native Cornish. An itinerant fishwife and fortune-teller, she married a man called Jeffery.

PENZIAS, Arno Allan (1933–) German-born American astrophysicist, born in Munich. A refugee with his family from Nazi Germany, he was educated at Colombia University, New York, and joined the Bell Telephone Laboratories in 1961. In 1964 Penzias and his colleague **Robert Wilson**, exploring the Milky Way with a radio telescope, discovered the cosmic microwave background radiation. Their discovery has provided some of the strongest evidence for the 'big bang' theory for the origin of the universe, and is arguably the most important discovery, bearing on cosmology, made this century. Penzias and Wilson were awarded the Nobel prize for physics in 1978, along with **Peter Kapitza**.

PÉPIN (777–810) king of Italy, second son of **Charlemagne**. He was crowned king of Italy in 781, and fought against the Avars, Slavs, Saxons and Saracens.

PÉPIN, of Héristal (d.714) Frankish ruler, was mayor of the Palace in Austrasia, to which he added after 687 the similar vice-royalties of Neustria and Burgundy, and called himself 'Duke and Prince of the Franks'. He was their real ruler during several Merovingian reigns. He was the father of **Charles Martel**.

PEPIN, 'the Short' (c.715–768) king of the Franks, illegitimate son of **Charles Martel** and father of **Charlemagne**, founder of the Frankish dynasty of the Carolingians. Pépin was chosen king in place of Childeric III, the last of the Merovingians, in 751. When Pope **Stephen III** was hard pressed by the Longobards, Pépin led an army into Italy (754), compelled the Longobard Aistulf to become his vassal, and laid the foundation of the temporal sovereignty of the popes (756). The rest of his life was spent in wars against Saxons and Saracens.

PEPLOE, Samuel John (1871–1935) Scottish artist, born in Edinburgh. As a mature and established painter, he went to Paris in 1911 and returned to Edinburgh to remodel his style in accordance with Fauve colouring and Cézannesque analysis of form. His later still-life paintings brought him fame as a colourist.

PEPUSCH, Johann Christoph (1667–1752) German composer and musical theorist, born in Berlin. He was appointed to the Prussian court at the age of 14, subsequently emigrating to Holland and settling in London in his early thirties. Best known as the arranger of the music for **John Gay**'s *The Beggar's Opera* from popular and traditional sources, Pepusch was a prolific composer of music for the theatre and church as well as of instrumental works.

PEPYS, Samuel (1633–1703) English diarist and Admiralty official, son of a London tailor. He was educated at St Paul's School and Trinity Hall and Magdalene College, Cambridge. After the Civil War he lived poorly with his young wife, Elizabeth St Michel, whom he married in 1655, but after the Restoration, through the patronage of the Earl of **Sandwich**, his father's cousin, he rose rapidly in the naval service and became secretary to the Admiralty in 1672. He lost his office and was imprisoned on account of his alleged complicity in the Popish Plot (1679), but was re-appointed in 1684 and in that same year became president of the Royal Society. At the Revolution (1688) he was again removed from office. The celebrated Diary, which ran from 1 January 1660 to 31 May 1669, the year his wife died and his eyesight failed him, is of extraordinary interest, both as the personal record (and confessions) of a man of abounding love of life, and for the vivid picture it gives of contemporary life, including naval administration and Court intrigue. The highlights are probably the accounts of the three disasters of the decade—the great plague (1665–66), the great fire of London (1666) and the sailing up the Thames by the Dutch fleet (1665–67). The veracity of the Diary has been accepted. It was apparently written in cipher (a kind of shorthand), in which form it remained at Magdalene College till 1825, when it was deciphered and edited.

PERCEVAL, John de Burgh (1923–) Australian ceramic artist and painter, born in Bruce Rock, Western Australia. A self-taught artist, he developed his precocious talent for surrealist paintings while confined to bed with poliomyelitis at the age of twelve. In 1939 he joined the Australian Army Survey Corps, where he met artists such as **Sydney Nolan**, Albert Tucker, and **Arthur** and **Guy Boyd**. After being exhibited in Melbourne, some of Perceval's paintings were reproduced in the avant-garde periodical *Angry Penguins*. In 1944 he joined Arthur Boyd, (whose sister Mary he was to marry), at the Murrumbeena pottery. After travelling to Europe he returned in 1965 to take up the first creative arts fellowship at the Australian National University, Canberra.

PERCEVAL, Spencer (1762–1812) English statesman, second son of the second Earl of Egmont, was educated at Harrow and Trinity, Cambridge, and called to the bar in 1786. He soon obtained a reputation as a diligent lawyer, in 1796 entered parliament for Northampton, and became a strong supporter of **William Pitt**. In the Addington (Lord **Sidmouth**) administration he became solicitor-general in 1801 and attorney-general in 1802, and in the second Portland administration, of 1807, Chancellor of the Exchequer, and was even then the real head of government, being trusted by **George III** for his opposition to Catholic claims. At Portland's death in 1809 Perceval became premier also, and retained office till his tragic death, when he was shot while entering the lobby of the House of Commons by a bankrupt Liverpool broker, John Bellingham, who was later hanged for the murder.

PERCIER, Charles (1764–1838) French architect, born in Paris. With his friend and partner, Pierre Fontaine (1762–1853), he was among the first to create buildings in the Empire style. For **Napoleon** they remodelled the Malmaison, worked on the Rue de Rivoli, the palace of St Cloud, the Louvre and the Tuileries, and in the gardens of the latter erected the Arc du Carrousel in 1807.

PERCIVAL, James Gates (1795–1856) American poet, born in Berlin, Connecticut. He graduated from Yale in 1815, studied botany and medicine, and became professor of chemistry at West Point in 1824 and of geology at Wisconsin in 1854. His poems *Prometheus* and *Clio* appeared between 1822 and 1827; and *The Dream of a Day* in 1843.

PERCY a noble north of England family, whose founder, William de Percy (c.1030–1096), came with **William I, the Conqueror**, and received lands in Yorkshire, Lincolnshire, Hampshire and Essex. Richard (c.1170–1244) was one of the barons who extorted Magna Carta. Henry (c.1272–1315) aided **Edward I** in subduing Scotland and was governor of Galloway. Driven out of Turnberry Castle by **Robert Bruce**, he received from **Edward II** a grant of Bruce's forfeited earldom of Carrick and the wardenship of Bamburgh and Scarborough Castles. In 1309 he purchased from Bishop Antony Bek the barony of Alnwick, the chief seat of the family ever since. His son defeated and captured **David II** of Scotland at Neville's Cross (1346); his grandson fought at Crécy; his great-grandson, Henry (1342–1408), fourth Lord Percy of Alnwick, in 1377 was made marshal of England and Earl of Northumberland. The fourth lord's son, Henry (1364–1403), was the famous Harry Hotspur whom James, 2nd Earl of **Douglas** defeated at Otterburn (1388), and who himself fell fighting against **Henry IV** at Shrewsbury, where his uncle, Sir Thomas, Earl of Worcester, was captured and soon after executed. The father, who had helped Henry to the throne, was dissatisfied with the king's gratitude, and with his sons plotted the insurrection. Later he joined Archbishop **Scrope**'s plot, and fell at Bramham Moor (1408), when his honours were forfeited, but restored (1414) to his grandson, who became High Constable of England, and fell in the first battle of St Albans (1455). His son, the third earl, fell at Towton (1461). The title and estates were then given to a brother of **Warwick**, the kingmaker, but in 1469 Henry, son of the third earl, was restored by **Edward IV**. The sixth earl, who had in youth been the lover of **Anne Boleyn**, died childless in 1537, and as his brother, Sir Thomas Percy, had been attainted and executed for his share in the Pilgrimage of Grace, the title of Duke of Northumberland was conferred by **Edward VI** upon John Dudley, Earl of Warwick, who in turn was attainted and executed under **Mary I** in 1553. In 1557 Mary granted the earldom to Thomas Percy (1528–72), son of the attainted Sir Thomas. A devoted Catholic, he took part in the Rising of the North, and was beheaded at York. His brother Henry, eighth earl, became involved in **Francis Throckmorton's** conspiracy in favour of **Mary, Queen of Scots**, and was committed to the Tower, where he was found dead in bed (1585). His son, ninth earl, was imprisoned for 15 years in the Tower, and fined £30000 on a baseless suspicion of being privy to the Gunpowder Plot. His son, tenth earl, fought for parliament in the Civil War; on the death of his son (1670), eleventh earl, the male line of the family became extinct. **Charles II** created his third bastard by the Duchess of Cleveland Earl, and afterwards Duke, of Northumberland, but he died childless in 1716. The eleventh earl's daughter, Baroness Percy, married **Charles Seymour**, 6th Duke of Somerset; their son was created in 1749 Baron Warkworth and Earl of Northumberland, with remainder to his son-in-law, Sir Hugh Smithson (1715-86), who assumed the name of Percy, and in 1766 was created Duke of Northumberland.

PERCY, Eustace, 1st Baron of Newcastle (1887–1958) English statesman, seventh son of the Duke of Northumberland. He entered the diplomatic service and was for several years in Washington. Member of parliament for Hastings from 1921 to 1937, he became president of the board of education (1924–29) and minister without portfolio (1935–36). His books include *The Responsibilities of the League* (1920), *Education at the Crossroads* (1930), *Democracy on Trial* (1931) and *The Heresy of Democracy* (1954). *Some Memories* was published in the year of his death.

PERCY, Thomas (1729–1811) English antiquary, poet and churchman, author of *Percy's Reliques*, born in Bridgenorth, the son of a grocer. Educated at Bridgenorth Grammar School and Christ Church College, Oxford, he became vicar of Easton Maudit in Northamptonshire (1753) and also rector of Wilby (1756). Later he was appointed chaplain to the Duke of Northumberland and **George III**, dean of Carlisle (1778) and bishop of Dromore (1782). As a man of letters his fame rests on his *Reliques of Ancient English Poetry* (1765), largely compiled from a 17th-century manuscript of medieval ballads and other material found in a house in Shifnal, Shropshire, and much 'restored' by him. Earlier he had published the first English version of a Chinese novel, *Hau Kiou Choaun* (1761, translated from the Portuguese), and *Miscellaneous Pieces translated from the Chinese* (1762). Prompted by the success of **James Macpherson**'s spurious Ossianic translations, he also published, anonymously, *Runic Poetry translated from the Icelandic language* (1763), a group of five poems actually translated from Latin versions. He later wrote a ballad of his own, *The Hermit of Warkworth* (1771).

PERCY, Walker (1916–90) American novelist, born in Birmingham, Alabama. He studied medicine, intending to make this his career, but had to abandon it when he contracted tuberculosis. His first novel, *The Moviegoer* (1961), won a National Book award. A philosophical writer, his novels are firmly grounded in social observation seen from the standpoint of a Catholic Southerner. He is the author of several novels, including *The Last Gentleman* (1966), *The Second Coming* (1980) and *The Thanatos Syndrome* (1987). He also wrote *Novel-Writing in an Apocalyptic Time* (1984).

PERDICCAS (d.321 BC) Macedonian soldier, second-in-command to **Alexander the Great**. He became virtually regent of the empire after Alexander's death, but was soon murdered by mutineers from his own army.

PEREDA, José Maria de (1833–1906) Spanish novelist, born in Polanco near Santander. His novels give a realistic picture of the people and scenery of the region where he was born and where much of his life was spent, an outstanding example being *Sotileza* (1885). Other novels are *Del Tal palo tal astilla* (1880), *Pedro Sanchez* (1883), and perhaps his finest, *Peñas arriba* (1895). He was called 'the modern **Cervantes**'.

PEREGRINUS, Petrus (Peter the Pilgrim, Peter de Maricourt) (13th century) French scientist and soldier. A native of Picardy, and a Crusader, he was the first to mark the ends of a round natural magnet and call them poles. He also invented a compass with a graduated scale.

PEREIRA, Aristedes Maria (1923–) Cape Verde politician. Born on Boa Vista island, he began his career as a radio telegraphist and progressed to head of the telecommunications service of Guinea-Bissau. He became politically active and co-founded the African party for the Independence of Portuguese Guinea and Cape Verde (PAIGC) in 1956. When Cape Verde won its independence in 1975 he became its first president and was re-elected in 1981 and 1986. His careful leadership earned him and his country wide respect.

PEREIRE, originally **Pereira, Giacobbo Rodriguez** (1715–80) Spanish-born inventor of a sign language for deaf-mutes. He gave up business in Bordeaux to devote himself to his humanitarian work with such success that in 1749 he presented a pupil before the Paris Academy of Sciences.

PERELMAN, S J (Sydney Joseph) (1904–79) American humorous writer, born in Brooklyn, New York City. Graduating from Brown University in 1925 he contributed to magazines until the publication of *Dawn Ginsbergh's Revenge* (1929), which had the nation in stitches and secured the author's fame. He went to Hollywood and wrote scripts for, among others, the **Marx** Brothers. Latterly his work found its way to the *New Yorker* (from 1931) before coming to rest between hard covers. His writing is remarkable for its linguistic dexterity and ingenuity; he took pot shots at modern sitting ducks and most sunk under a side-splitting fusillade, though somehow the entertainment and advertising industries survived. He is at his best in *Crazy Like a Fox* (1944), *Westward Ha! or, Around the World in 80 Clichés* (1948), *The Swiss Family Perelman* (1950) and *The Road to Miltown, or, Under the Spreading Atrophy* (1957). *The Most of S J Perelman* was published in 1958.

PERES, Shimon (1923–) Polish-born Israeli politician. He emigrated with his family from Poland to Palestine as a child in 1934, and was raised on a kibbutz, but received most of his education in the USA, studying at New York and Harvard universities. In 1948 he became head of naval services in the new state of Israel, and later director-general of the defence ministry (1953–59). In 1959 he was elected to the Knesset. He was minister of defence (1974–77), and in 1977 became chairman of the Labour party and leader of the opposition until 1984, when he entered into a unique power-sharing agreement with the leader of the Consolidation party (Likud), **Yitzhak Shamir**. Under this agreement, Peres was prime minister from 1984 to 1986, when Shamir took over. After the inconclusive 1988 general election Peres eventually rejoined Shamir in a new coalition.

PÉREZ DE AYALA, Ramón (1881–1962) Spanish novelist, poet and critic, born in Oviedo. He first attracted attention with his poetry when *La Paz del sendero* was published in 1904. A sequel volume appeared in 1916 under the title *El Sendero innumerable*. As a novelist he combines realism with beauty, best shown in the philosophical *Belarmino y Apolonio* (1921). Other novels include the humorous and satirical *Troteras y Danzaderas* (1913), the anti-Jesuit *A.M.D.G.* (1910), and perhaps his best, *Tigre Juan* (1924), which with *El Curandero de ru honra* appeared in English as *Tiger Juan* (1933). Among his works of criticism are *Máscaras* and *Política y Toros*. He was ambassador to London from 1931 to 1936.

PÉREZ DE CUELLAR, Javier (1920–) Peruvian diplomat. The son of a businessman who died when Javier was only four, he graduated at Lima University and embarked on a career in the Peruvian diplomatic service, representing his country at the first United Nations assembly in 1946. He succeeded the openly ambitious **Kurt Waldheim** as UN secretary-general in 1982, his quiet, modest approach contrasting sharply with that of his predecessor. His patient diplomacy secured notable achievements, particularly in his second term, including a ceasefire in the Iran-Iraq War and the achievement of independence for Namibia. His work has enhanced not only his own reputation but that of the UN as well.

PÉREZ DE HITA, Ginés (1544–1619) Spanish writer and soldier. He fought in the Moorish war in 1569–70 and wrote a semi-romantic history entitled *Historia de los bandos de los Zegríes y Abencérajes* in two parts (1595 and 1604). Known as *Las Guerras civiles de Granada*, it was republished in Madrid (1913–15).

PÉREZ GALDÓS, Benito (1843–1920) Spanish novelist and dramatist, born in the Canary Islands, and brought up in Madrid. Regarded as Spain's greatest novelist after **Cervantes**, he was deeply interested in his own country and its history. His short *Episodios nacionales*, of which there are 46, gives a vivid picture of 19th-century Spain from the viewpoint of the people. The longer novels included in the *Novelas españolas contemporáneas* number 31, and in these the conflicts and ideas of the Europe of his day are recorded forcefully but often with humour. Some of these, including *Trafalgar*, *Gloria*, *Doña Perfecta* and *León Roch*, have been translated. His plays, many of them based on his novels, also achieved success.

PERGOLESI, Giovanni Battista (1710–36) Italian musician, born in Jesi near Ancona. His first great works were the oratorio *San Guglielmo* (1731) and the comic operetta *La Serva Padrona* (1732). His last works were the cantata *Orfeo* and his great *Stabat Mater*, described by **Bellini** as 'a divine poem of grief'. He also composed operas and oratorios. He died of consumption.

PERI, Jacopo (1561–1633) Italian composer, born in Rome. As a student he became attached to the **Medici** family in Florence, and became the leading composer in a group of artists whose aim was to restore what they believed to be the true principles of Greek tragic declamation. Experimenting in an instrumentally-accompanied declamatory style, Peri wrote *Dafne* (1597–89) and *Euridice* (1600), with libretti by the poet **Ottavio Rinuccini**, which have been historically accepted as the first genuine operas.

PERIANDER (c.625–585 BC) tyrant of Corinth, successor to his father **Cypselus**. Under him Corinth's power and position in the Greek world developed further and Periander cultivated extensive links with foreign rulers. Later tradition remembered him as an example of a repressive tyrant, yet he was also included in the canon of the Seven Wise Men of Greece. The tyranny came to an end soon after his death.

PERICLES (c.490–429 BC) Athenian statesman, born of distinguished parents. He was carefully educated, and rapidly rose to the highest power as leader of the dominant democracy. About 463 he struck a great blow at the oligarchy by depriving the Areopagus of its most important political powers. His successful expeditions to the Thracian Chersonese and to Sinope, together with his numerous colonies, increased the naval supremacy of Athens. His greatest project was to form a grand Hellenic confederation to put an end to mutually destructive wars; but the Spartan aristocrats brought the scheme to nothing. Athens and Sparta were already in the mood which rendered the Peloponnesian war inevitable; but the first troubles were allayed by a 30 years' peace with Sparta (445). **Cimon** was now dead, and the next leaders of the aristocratic party sought in vain (in 444 BC) to overthrow the supremacy of Pericles by attacking him in the popular assembly for squandering public money on buildings and in festivals and amusements. Thereafter Pericles reigned undisputed master in the city of **Aeschylus**, **Sophocles**, **Euripides**, **Anaxagoras**, **Zeno**, **Protagoras**, **Socrates**, **Myron** and **Phidias**. In the Samian war (439) Pericles gained high renown as a naval commander. His enemies, who dared not attack himself, struck at him in the persons of his friends—**Aspasia**, Phidias and Anaxagoras. Greek architecture and sculpture under the patronage of Pericles reached perfection. To him Athens owed the Parthenon, the Erechtheum, the Propylaea, the Odeum and numerous other public and sacred edifices; he liberally encouraged music and the drama; and during his rule industry and commerce flourished. At length in 431 the inevitable Peloponnesian war broke out between Athens and Sparta. The plague ravaged the city in 430, and in the autumn of 429 Pericles himself died after a lingering fever.

PÉRIER, Casimir (1777–1832) French statesman, born in Grenoble. He founded a Paris bank with his brother Antoine Scipion (1776–1821). He secured a seat in the Chamber of Deputies in 1817, was minister of finance in 1828, president of the council in 1830, and premier in 1831.

PERKIN, Sir William Henry (1838–1907) English chemist, born in London. He worked as an assistant to **August Hofmann**, and in 1856 made the discovery of mauve, which led to the foundation of the aniline dye industry. His son William Henry (1860–1929) became professor of chemistry at Manchester (1892) and Oxford (1912).

PERKINS, Francis (1882–1965) American social reformer and politician, the first US female Cabinet member. Born in Boston, Massachusetts, into a well-off middle-class family, she was educated at Mount Holyoak College, Massachusetts, where a speech by **Florence Kelley** first sparked her interest in feminism. Later, while a teacher, she visited various Chicago settlement houses, in particular Hull House, and grew convinced that the workers' conditions would be improved by practical deeds not political doctrines. Moving to New York, she became secretary of the New York Consumers' League (1910–12), during which time she campaigned with enormous energy on many fronts. She achieved several legislative successes as secretary of the Committee on Safety of the City of New York. In 1918 she became the first woman member of the New York State Industrial Commission (chairman 1926, commissioner 1929). She joined the Democratic party and for 30 years played a significant role in introducing women's issues into party policy.

She was appointed US secretary of labor (1933–45), and in this post made perhaps her greatest contribution to women's rights in her supervision of the New Deal labour regulations, which included the Social Security Act (1935) and the Wages and Hours Act (1938). A controversial figure, she resigned in 1945, but served on the Civil Service Commission until 1952.

PERKINS, Jacob (1766–1849) American mechanical engineer and inventor, born in Newburyport, Massachusetts. He was apprenticed at the age of 13 to a goldsmith, and after making dies for the state coinage he invented (c.1790) an improved nail-making machine, which was not commercially successful. He next developed steel plates that could be used in place of copper in the engraving process, enabling much more complicated patterns to be used for bank-notes and making counterfeiting more difficult. He and his partner moved to England in 1818 and established an engraving factory which in 1840 printed the first penny postage stamps. While in England he became interested in high-pressure steam boilers and experimented with pressures of more than 1000 lb per square inch when most engineers considered it dangerous to exceed about 25 lb per square inch. In 1831 he invented an early form of water tube boiler, but engineers in general were not then ready for such advances and his experiments had to be abandoned.

PERKINS, Maxwell Evarts (1884–1947) American editor, publisher and journalist, born in New York city. He studied economics at Harvard, worked as a reporter on *The New York Times* (1907–10), then joined Scribner's the publishers, eventually becoming vice-president and editor-in-chief. Associated with writers of the stature of **Ernest Hemingway** and **F Scott Fitzgerald**, he was a sympathetic and tireless editor whose greatest achievement was to convert **Thomas Wolfe**'s manuscript of *Look Homeward, Angel* from an indigestible mass into an American classic. Wolfe made him the prototype for his character Foxhall Edwards in his *You Can't Go Home Again* (1941).

PERLMAN, Itzhak (1945–) Israeli violinist, born in Tel Aviv, the son of Polish immigrants. A victim of polio from the age of four, he plays seated, and made débuts on American radio aged ten, at Carnegie Hall (1963) and in London (1968). He is a noted chamber music player.

PERMEKE, Constant (1886–1951) Belgian painter and sculptor, born in Antwerp. He studied at Bruges and Ghent, and later settled in Laethem-Saint-Martin, where he became the leader of the modern Belgian Expressionist school. After 1936, he concentrated on sculpture.

PERÓN, Isabelita, popular name of **Maria Estela Martínez de Perón** (1931–), second wife of **Juan Domingo Perón**. A dancer, born in La Rioja Province, Argentina, she married Juan Perón in 1961, living with him in Spain until his return to Argentina as president in 1973, when she was made vice-president. She took over the presidency at his death in 1974, but her inadequacy in office led to a military take-over in 1976. She was imprisoned for five years on a charge of abuse of public property and on her release in 1981 settled in Madrid.

PERÓN, Juan Domingo (1895–1974) Argentine soldier, and president, born in Lobos, southern Buenos Aires province. He joined the army in 1913, and took a leading part in the army revolt of 1943 which toppled the pro-Axis president, Ramón Castillo. Well-read, a hypnotic public speaker and a close student of **Benito Mussolini**, he developed a broad base of popular support, augmenting his rule with force. He used his position as secretary of labour to gain union support, while using his other position as under-secretary of war to cultivate junior officers. He organized the *descamisados*, a civilian paramilitary organization which, like **Hitler**'s Brownshirts and Mussolini's Blackshirts, was drawn from the lower classes. Their affections were secured by his politically astute wife, **Eva Duarte Perón**, whose death in 1952 they greatly mourned. In 1945, senior army and navy officers, alarmed at Perón's mobilization of the masses, imprisoned Perón, but released him after thousands gathered in the public squares demanding his return. In 1946 after a populist campaign laced with strong nationalist and anti-American rhetoric, 'El Líder' was elected president and set about building a corporatist state. He reduced the legislature and the judiciary to rubber-stamps, tried to crush all opposition by any means including torture, and sought to modernize and industrialize the economy through large-scale government intervention and by nationalizing foreign-owned enterprises (eg railways). In 1955, with the economy in a shambles and having alienated the church, the military, the middle-class and some of the labour movement, he was deposed by the army and fled to Spain. But his movement remained. Failing to crush the Perónists, the military returned the government to civilian rule until 1966 when it again took over to prevent a Perónist party electoral victory. It again failed to destroy the Perónists by force, and again allowed elections, which were won by the Perónist candidate who resigned in favour of 'El Líder'. Perón died a year after his triumphal return in 1973, leaving his office to the vice-president, his second wife, **Isabelita Perón**.

PERÓN, (Maria) Eva Duarte De, known as **Evita** (1919–52) first wife of **Juan Perón**, born in Los Toldos, Buenos Aires. An actress before her marriage in 1945, she became a powerful political influence, agitating for women's suffrage, and acquiring control of newspapers and business companies. Revered by the populace, she founded the Eva Perón Foundation for the promotion of social welfare. Her life story was the theme of the **Andrew Lloyd-Webber** and **Tim Rice** musical *Evita* (1978).

PEROSI, Lorenzo (1872–1956) Italian priest and composer, born in Tortona, Piedmont, the son of a musician. He was ordained priest, and was the author of *The Resurrection of Lazarus*, *The Passion of Christ* and other oratorios. He was organist at Monte Cassino and St Mark's, Venice, before becoming chapelmaster at the Sistine Chapel, Rome.

PEROT, (Henry) Ross (1930–) American computer software executive, born in Texarkana, Texas. After a spell as a salesman with IBM, he founded the Electronic Data Systems Corporation Inc, Dallas, in 1962, which now has over 50000 employees. He was its chairman and chief executive (1982–86) until a buy out by General Motors.

PÉROUSE See **LA PÉROUSE, Jean François de Galaup**

PEROWNE, John James Stewart (1823–1904) English prelate, the son of a missionary in Bengal. Educated at Corpus Christi College, Cambridge, he held office at King's College (London), Lampeter, and Trinity College, Cambridge, and became dean of Peterborough in 1878. From 1875 he had been also Hulsean professor of divinity at Cambridge. From 1891 to 1901 he was bishop of Worcester. Perowne sat on the committee for the revision of the Old Testament. His works include a commentary on the Psalms (1864–68), the Hulsean Lectures on *Immortality* (1869) and *Remains* of **Thirlwall** (1878).

PERRAULT, Charles (1628–1703) French writer, born in Paris. He studied law, and from 1654 to 1664 had an easy life working for his brother, the receiver-general of Paris. In 1663 he became a secretary or assistant to **Colbert**. His poem, *Le Siècle de Louis XIV*, and **Boileau**'s outspoken criticisms of it, opened up the dispute about the relative merits of the ancients and moderns. To the modern cause Perrault contributed his poor *Parallèle des anciens et des modernes* (1688–96), and his *Hommes illustres du siècle de Louis XIV* (1696–1700). His *Mémoires* appeared in 1769. All his writings would have been forgotten but for his eight inimitable fairy tales, the *Histoires ou Contes du temps passé* (1697), including 'The Sleeping Beauty', 'Red Riding Hood' and 'Bluebeard'.

PERRET, Auguste (1874–1954) French architect, born in Brussels. He spent most of his life in Paris, where he pioneered the use of reinforced concrete in a number of buildings, mainly in the Neoclassical style, including the Théâtre des Champs Élysées and the Musée des travaux publics. He also designed churches at le Raincy and Montmagny.

PERRIN, Jean Baptiste (1870–1942) French physicist, born in Lille. From 1910 he was professor of physical chemistry at the University of Paris. For important researches in molecular physics and radioactivity, and for his discovery of the equilibrium of sedimentation, he was awarded the Nobel prize for physics in 1926.

PERRONET, Jean Rodolphe (1708–94) French civil engineer, born in Suresnes. After training as an architect and working as a civil engineer in French government service, he was appointed in 1747 the first director of the newly-created École des Ponts et Chaussées. He built a number of outstanding masonry arch bridges, including the Pont de Neuilly and the Pont de la Concorde in Paris, setting new standards of aesthetic and engineering design, for example by his realisation that if all the spans were built simultaneously the thickness of the interior piers could be greatly reduced.

PERRONNEAU, Jean Baptiste (c.1715–1783) French pastellist painter, best known for his *Girl with a Kitten* painted in 1745. He travelled widely in Europe and died in Amsterdam.

PERROT, Georges (1832–1914) French archaeologist. He travelled in Greece and Asia Minor, in 1877 became professor of archaeology at Paris University and in 1833 director of the École normale. He wrote on Crete (1866) and archaeology, most notably, with Charles Chipiez, a *History of Art in Antiquity* (in Egypt, Chaldaea, primitive Greece, etc; 1882 *et seq*).

PERROT, Sir John (c.1527–1592) English courtier, commonly reputed to be a son of **Henry VIII**. He was lord deputy of Ireland during the troublous time there of Queen **Elizabeth**, and died in the Tower, under trial for treason with Spain.

PERROT, Jules Joseph (1810–94) French dancer, choreographer and ballet master, born in Lyon. The most prolific choreographer and greatest male dancer of the Romantic movement, he started his theatrical career as a child acrobat and pantomimist before studying ballet with master teacher **Auguste Vestris**. He danced at the Paris Opéra Ballet (1830–34), partnering **Maria Taglioni**. He met **Carlotta Grisi** while touring Europe in 1836, becoming her lover, partner and mentor; though uncredited, he fashioned the steps for her solos in *Giselle* (1841). He switched his base to London (1842–48) and choreographed nearly two dozen ballets, the most famous being *Pas de Quatre* (1845). From 1850 he was ballet master and principal dancer in St Petersburg. Afterwards he retired to Brittany with his wife, the Russian ballerina Capitoline Samovskaya.

PERRY, (Mary) Antoinette (1888–1946) American actress and director, born in Denver. She had a long career on the stage from 1905 and as a director from 1928. In 1941 she founded the American Theatre Wing. The annual 'Tony' Awards of the New York theatre are named after her.

PERRY, Fred (Frederick John) (1909–) English-born American tennis player, born in Stockport, Cheshire, the son of a Labour MP. His first sport was table-tennis, at which he was world singles champion in 1929. He only took up lawn tennis when he was 19, and between 1933 and the end of 1936, when he turned professional, he won every major amateur title, including the Wimbledon singles three times, the US singles three times, and the Australian and French championships, and helped to keep the Davis cup in Britain for four years. He made his professional début at Madison Square Garden, New York, and went on to a career in coaching, writing and broadcasting.

PERRY, Matthew Galbraith (1794–1858) American naval officer, brother of **Oliver Hazard Perry**, born in Newport, Rhode Island. In 1837 he was appointed commander of the *Fulton*, one of the first naval steamships. He was active in suppression of the slave trade on the African coast in 1843. In the Mexican War of 1846–48 he captured several towns and took part in the siege of Veracruz. From 1852 to 1854 he led the naval expedition to Japan that forced it to open diplomatic negotiations with the USA and grant the first trading rights.

PERRY, Oliver Hazard (1785–1819) American naval officer, born in South Kingston, Rhode Island, brother of **Matthew Galbraith Perry**. In the War of 1812 he defeated a British squadron on Lake Erie in 1813. He died of yellow fever on a mission to Venezuela.

PERSEUS (c.213–c.165 BC) the last king of Macedon in the Antigonid dynasty. He succeeded his father **Philip V** in 179. He pursued Philip's policy of consolidating his kingdom after the defeat by Rome, but his success provoked the jealousy of Rome and her supporters in the Greek world, who accused him of hostile designs. This brought about the Third Macedonian War (171–168), in which Perseus was defeated at the battle of Pydna (168) and taken to Italy, where he died in captivity. The monarchy of Macedon was then abolished.

PERSHING, John Joseph, known as **'Black Jack'** (1860–1948) American soldier, born in Linn County, Missouri. He was first a schoolteacher, went to West Point, and became military instructor there and at Nebraska University. He served on frontier duty against the Sioux and Apache Indians (1886–98), in the Cuban War in 1898, during the Moro insurgencies in the Philippines (1903), in the Japanese army during the Russo-Japanese War (1904–05), and in Mexico in 1916. In 1917 he was appointed commander-in-chief of the American Expeditionary Force in Europe and was chief of staff, US Army, 1921–24. He wrote *My Experience in the World War* (1931).

PERSIGNY, Jean Gilbert Victor Fialin, Duc de (1808–72) French politician, born in Saint-Germain Lespinasse. He was expelled from the army in 1831, secured the favour of Louis Napoleon (**Napoleon III**), and had the chief hand in the affairs of Strasbourg (1836) and Boulogne (1840), where he was captured, and condemned to 20 years' imprisonment. Released in 1848, he strongly supported his patron then and in 1851, from 1852 to 1855 and 1860 to 1863 was minister of the interior, from 1855 to 1860 ambassador to England, and a senator until the fall of the empire.

PERSIUS, (Aulus Persius Flaccus) (34–62) Roman satirist, born of a distinguished equestrian family in

Volaterrae in Etruria. He was educated in Rome, where he came under Stoic influence. He wrote fastidiously and sparingly, leaving at his death only six admirable satires, the whole not exceeding 650 hexameter lines. These were published by his friend Caesius Bassus after his death. **Dryden** and others have translated them into verse.

PERTHES, Friedrich Christoph (1772–1843) German publisher, nephew of **Johann Georg Justus Perthes**. He started business in Hamburg in 1796, and soon was in the front rank of publishers. An ardent patriot, in 1810 he started the National Museum in Hamburg and resisted the establishment of French authority in Germany. After the peace, he moved in 1821 to Gotha.

PERTHES, Johann Georg Justus (1749–1816) German publisher. He established a publishing-house in Gotha in 1785, which acquired, in the hands of his sons, a great reputation as a geographical institute. It issued *Petermann's Mitteilungen*, Stieler's *Atlas*, books of travel and geography, and the *Almanach de Gotha*.

PERTINAX, Publius Helvius (126–93 AD) Roman emperor, born in Alba-Pompeia in Liguria. When the assassins of **Commodus** forced him to accept the purple, his accession was hailed with delight by the Senate; but he was slain by rebellious praetorians three months after.

PERUGINO, properly **Pietro di Cristoforo Vannucci** (c.1450–1523) Italian painter, born in Città della Pieve in Umbria. He established himself in Perugia (hence the nickname). He executed works, no longer extant, at Florence, Perugia (1475) and Cerqueto (1478). In Rome, where he went about 1483, **Sixtus IV** employed him in the Sistine Chapel; his fresco of *Christ giving the Keys to Peter* is the best of those still visible, others being destroyed to make way for **Michelangelo**'s *Last Judgment*. In Florence (1486–99) he had **Raphael** for his pupil. In Perugia (1499–1504) he adorned the Hall of the Cambio; after 1500 his art visibly declined. In his second Roman sojourn (1507–12) he also, along with other painters, decorated the Stanze of the Vatican; and one of his works there, the Stanza del Incendio, was the only fresco spared when Raphael was commissioned to repaint the walls and ceilings. He died of the plague near Perugia.

PERUTZ, Max Ferdinand (1914–) Austrian-born British biochemist. After graduating at Vienna, he came to Cambridge in 1936 to carry on research at the Cavendish Laboratory, where he began work on the structure of haemoglobin and became director of the Medical Research Council's unit for molecular biology (1962–79). He was awarded the 1962 Nobel prize for chemistry, jointly with **John Kendrew**.

PERUZZI, Baldassare Tommaso (1481–1536) Italian architect, born in Ancajano near Volterra. In 1503 he went to Rome, where he designed the Villa Farnesina and the Ossoli Palace, and painted frescoes in the Church of S Maria della Pace in 1516. After a short period as city architect in Siena, he returned to Rome in 1535 and designed the Palazzo Massimo. He was influenced by **Bramante** and ancient Italian architecture; drawings and designs by him are in the Uffizi Gallery, Florence.

PESTALOZZI, Johann Heinrich (1746–1827) Swiss educationist, born in Zürich, who devoted his life to the children of the very poor. Believing, like **Rousseau**, in the moralizing virtue of agricultural occupations and rural environment, he set up a residential farm school for his collected waifs and strays on his estate at Neuhof in 1774; but owing to faulty domestic organization it had to be abandoned after a five-year struggle (1780). He then for a time withdrew to think out the educational problem, and wrote his *Evening Hours of a Hermit* (1780). In 1798 he opened his orphan school at Stanz, but at the end of eight months it was broken up. He was appointed to the people's school at Berthoud (Burgdorf) in 1799, but was ejected by the jealous senior master. In partnership with others, and under the patronage of the Swiss government, he opened a school of his own at Berthoud. While there he published *How Gertrude Educates her Children* (1801), the recognized exposition of the Pestalozzian method. In 1805 he moved his school to Yverdon, and applied his method in a large secondary school, but his incapacity in practical affairs resulted in the school's closure in 1825. He addressed to mankind the *Song of the Swan*, a last educational prayer, and withdrew to Brugg, where he died.

PÉTAIN, Henri Philippe Omer (1856–1951) French soldier and statesman, born in Cauchy-à-la-Tour of peasant parents. He passed through St Cyr to a commission in the *chasseurs alpins*. As a junior officer his confidential report was marked, 'If this officer rises above the rank of major it will be a disaster for France'; but seniority brought him the military governorship of Paris and appointments on the instructional staff. A temporary brigadier in 1914, by 1916 he was in command of an army corps. His defence of Verdun ('They shall not pass') made him a national hero. Succeeding as commander-in-chief in 1917, his measures of appeasement, while 'puttying-up' the widespread mutinies that had followed on General **Nivelle**'s disastrous offensive, ended by virtually removing the French army as a fighting force from the war. He was promoted marshall of France in 1918. Minister for war in 1934, his eager sponsorship of the useless Maginot Line defence system only too faithfully reflected the defeatist spirit of contemporary France. With the French collapse in early 1940, he succeeded **Paul Reynaud** as the head of the government at the age of 84 and immediately sought terms from the Germans. Convinced that France could 'only be regenerated through suffering', his administration at Vichy was the tool of such outright collaborationists as **Laval** and **Déat**. With the liberation of France Pétain was brought to trial, his death sentence for treason being commuted to life imprisonment on the Île de Yeu. He died in captivity in 1951.

PETAVIUS, Dionysius, or **Denys Petau** (1583–1652) French theologian, born in Orléans. In 1621 he became professor of theology in Paris. In 1646 he retired and devoted himself to the completion of about 50 works on philology, history and theology. An ardent Jesuit, among his learned writings are *Rationarium Temporum* (1634) and *De Theologicis Dogmatibus* (1644–50).

PETER, St (1st century) One of the Twelve Apostles, named originally **Symeon** or **Simon**. He came from Bethsaida, but during the public ministry of **Jesus** had his house at Capernaum. Originally a fisherman, and brother of **Andrew**, he soon became leader amongst the twelve apostles, regarded by Jesus with particular favour and affection. Despite his frailty at the time of the Crucifixion, when he denied Jesus three times, he was named as the rock on which the Church was to be built, and was entrusted with the 'keys of the Kingdom of Heaven'. He was the spokesman for the others on the day of Pentecost, he was the first to baptize a Gentile convert, and he took a prominent part in the council at Jerusalem. In Antioch he for a time worked in harmony with **Paul**, but ultimately the famous dispute arose (Gal ii. 11–21) which, with other causes, led to the termination of Paul's ministry in that city. Peter's missionary activity seems to have extended to Pontus, Cappadocia, Galatia, Asia and Bithynia. That he suffered martyrdom is clear from John xxi. 18, 19, and is confirmed by ecclesiastical tradition: **Eusebius of Caesarea** says he was impaled or crucified with his head downward; as to the place, tradition from the end of the 2nd century mentions Rome. But the comparatively late tradition which assigns him a continuous bishopric of 25 years in Rome from 42 to 67 is unhistorical. The first Epistle of Peter is usually accepted as genuine, but not the second. His feast day is 29 June.

PETER I, the Great (1672–1725) tsar of Russia from 1682, fourth son of the tsar **Alexei I Mihailovitch** by his second wife. He was made co-tsar jointly with his half-brother Ivan V (1666–96) on the death of their elder brother, Fedor III, under the regency of their sister, the grand-duchess Sophia. In his teens, Peter became notorious for his limitless energy, his capacity for drink, his absorption in military affairs and his coarse contempt for political and religious ceremonial. In 1689 he had his sister arrested and immured in a convent (she died in 1704), and ruled on his own with his weak-minded brother as a figurehead. In 1689 he married Eudoxia (1669–1731), the pious daughter of a boyar, by whom he had a son in 1690, the tsarevitch Alexis (father of the future **Peter II**). In 1695, after six years of preparation, his army moved against the Turks, the tsar himself serving as a humble bombardier, and in 1696 captured the vital sea-port of Azov. In 1697 he set off on a tour of Europe, travelling incognito in a 'Grand Embassy' whose main official purpose was to secure allies against the Turks. He spent 16 months travelling through Germany, Holland, England, and Austria, and worked as a shipwright in Holland and at Deptford in England. In the course of the journey he amassed knowledge of western technology and hired thousands of craftsmen and military personnel to take back to Russia. He returned hurriedly to Russia in the summer of 1698 to deal with a revolt of the *streltsy* (regiments of musketeers), which was savagely repressed in the weeks that followed with the help of the Scottish general **Patrick Gordon**. The tsarina Eudoxia, accused of conspiracy, was divorced and sent to a convent. Peter proceeded to offend many sensibilities by his vigorous espousal of western customs, insisting that beards be shaven at court and that 'German' dress be adopted. Houses were to be built in western style; his son Alexis was put in the charge of a German tutor. In 1700, in alliance with Denmark and **Augustus II the Strong**, king of Poland and Elector of Saxony, he launched the Great Northern War against Sweden (1700–21), but **Karl XII** of Sweden force-marched his troops in a pre-emptive strike and routed the Russian forces at Narva in Estonia (1700). Undaunted, Peter ordered the church bells in Moscow to be melted down to make new cannon, and by refusing to permit the election of a new patriarch was able to divert ecclesiastical revenues to the war effort. In 1703 Peter set about the construction of the new city and port of St Petersburg (now Leningrad), which was designated as the capital of the empire. In 1709, at the battle of Poltava in the Ukraine, Narva was finally avenged and the Swedish army decisively defeated. By the eventual Peace of Bystadt in 1721, Sweden ceded to Russian parts of Finland and the provinces of Ingria, Estonia and Latvia. In 1712 he married as his second wife his Lithuanian mistress, Catherine (the future **Catherine I**). In 1718 his son Alexis, who had wanted to renounce the succession, was imprisoned for suspected treason and died after torture. In 1722 the Act of Succession gave the ruling sovereign liberty to choose his or her successor, and in the following year Peter had Catherine crowned empress. The move was unpopular, but at his death she succeeded him without opposition. Peter had achieved during his reign a kind of cultural revolution that made Russia part of the general European state system for the first time in its history, and established it as a major power.

PETER II (1715–30) tsar of Russia from 1727, grandson of **Peter I, the Great**. The son of the tsarevitch Alexis (1690–1718), he succeeded to the throne on the death of his step-grandmother, **Catherine I**. He died of smallpox on the day designated for his wedding. He was succeeded by the empress **Anna Ivanova**, daughter of Peter the Great's half-brother and co-tsar, Ivan V.

PETER III (1728–62) tsar of Russia from 1762, grandson of **Peter I, the Great**. The son of Peter's youngest daughter, Anna, and Charles Frederick, Duke of Holstein Gottorp, he was born in Kiel. In 1742 he was declared heir-presumptive to his aunt, the empress **Elizabeth Petrovna** (daughter of Peter the Great and **Catherine I**), and in 1745 he married Sophia-Augusta von Anhalt-Zerbst (the future empress **Catherine II the Great**). A weak and unstable man, and a great admirer of **Frederick II, the Great**, he withdrew Russia's forces from the Seven Years' War as soon as he succeeded to the throne in January 1762, and restored East Prussia to Frederick. This enraged the army and aristocracy, and in June of that year Peter was deposed by a group of nobles inspired by his wife Catherine and led by her lover, Count **Orlov**. He was strangled in captivity a few days later, and Catherine was proclaimed empress.

PETER I (1844–1921) king of Serbia, son of Prince Alexander **Karadjordjević**, born in Belgrade. He fought in the French army in the Franco-Prussian war (1870–71), and was elected king of Serbia by the Serbian parliament in 1903. In World War I he accompanied his army into exile in Greece in 1916. He returned to Belgrade in 1918 and was proclaimed titular king of the Serbs, Croats and Slovenes until his death, although his second son, Alexander (later **Alexander I**), was regent.

PETER II (1923–70) king of Yugoslavia (1934–45), born in Belgrade, the son of **Alexander I**. He was at school in England when his father was assassinated in 1934. His uncle, Prince Paul Karadjordjević (1873–1976), a nephew of **Peter I**, was regent until 1941 when he was ousted by pro-Allied army officers, who declared King Peter of age and he assumed sovereignty. The subsequent German attack on Yugoslavia forced the king to go into exile within three weeks. He set up a government in exile in London, but lost his throne when Yugoslavia became a republic in 1945. From then on the ex-king lived mainly in California.

PETER LOMBARD See **LOMBARD**

PETER MARTYR (c.1205–1252) Italian preacher, and patron saint of the Inquisition. A Dominican of Verona, he was slain at Como by the populace, for the severity with which he exercised his inquisitorial functions. He was canonized in 1253.

PETER MARTYR, Italian **Pietro Martire Vermigli** (1500–62) Florentine reformer. He became an Augustinian canon and abbot at Spoleto and Naples. As visitor-general of his order in 1541 his rigour made him very unpopular with the dissolute monks, and he was sent to Lucca as prior. There he came under the influence of the Spanish reformer **Juan de Valdès** and soon fell under the suspicions of the Inquisition, and fled to Zürich (1542). At Strasbourg he was made Old Testament professor. In 1547 he went to England at the invitation of **Cranmer** and was professor of divinity at Oxford (1541–53). **Mary I**'s accession drove him back to Strasbourg, and in 1555 to Zürich. His *Loci Communes* was printed at London in 1575.

PETER MARTYR ANGLERIUS (1459–1525) Italian historian, born in Arona on Lake Maggiore. From 1487 he rose to high ecclesiastical preferment in Spain, and was named bishop of Jamaica. He wrote *De Orbe Novo* (1516), giving the first account of the discovery of America, *De Legatione Babylonica* (1516), and *Opus Epistolarum* (1530).

PETER THE CRUEL, See **PEDRO, 'the Cruel'**

PETER THE HERMIT, or **Peter of Amiens** (c.1050–c.1115) French monk, a preacher of the First Crusade, born in Amiens. He served some time as a soldier, became a monk, and is said to have made a pilgrimage to Palestine before 1095. When **Urban II** launched the First Crusade at a council in Clermont (France) in 1096, Peter traversed Europe, preaching and producing extraordinary enthusiasm by impassioned descriptions of the cruelties of the Turks towards pilgrims, and their desecration of the holy places. He rallied an army of 20 000 peasants, and led one section of the Crusading army to Asia Minor, where it was utterly defeated by the Turks at Nicaea. Peter then joined the 'army of the princes' in 1097. During the siege of Antioch, which lasted seven months, the besiegers' ranks were fearfully thinned by famine and disease. Many lost heart, and among the deserters was Peter, who was several miles on his way home when he was brought back to undergo a public reprimand. He later founded the monastery of Neufmoutier at Liée, Belgium.

PETER THE WILD BOY (d.1785) German freak found in July 1725 in a wood near Hameln in Hanover; 'he was walking on his hands and feet, climbing up trees like a squirrel, and feeding upon grass and moss trees'. Brought to England in 1726 by **George I**, he could never be taught to articulate more than a few syllables, and was apparently an idiot. From 1737 till his death he lived on a Hertfordshire farm near Berkhampstead.

PETERBOROUGH, Charles Mordaunt, 3rd Earl of (c.1658–1735) English commander and statesman. Between 1674 and 1680 he took part in naval expeditions to the Barbary coast. He began to take an active part in politics, identifying himself with the extreme Whig party, and was an early intriguer in the overthrow of **James II**. After the revolution he rose high in the eyes of the new king who made him Earl of Monmouth, but later he opposed **William III** and his policies and in 1697 was committed to the Tower for three months. In 1705, during the War of the Spanish Succession, now as the Earl of Peterborough, he was put in change of an army of 4000 Dutch and English soldiers which he took to Spain. A series of victories led them to Valencia early in 1706 and Peterborough then went on to defeat a French army, under the Duke of Anjou, which was blockading Barcelona. However, disagreements with his colleagues, and outbreaks of his violent temper, led to his recall to England in March 1707 and the virtual end of his military career.

PETERMANN, August See **PERTHES, Johann Georg Justus**

PETERS, Hugh (1598–1660) English Independent divine, born in Cornwall. He emigrated to Holland, then to New England, but returned in 1641 and became army chaplain, and was active in parliamentarian politics. He published numerous pamphlets, and was executed for assumed complicity in the death of **Charles I**.

PETERS, Karl (1856–1918) German traveller and administrator, born in Neuhaus in Hanover. In 1884 he helped to establish German East Africa as a colony by his negotiations with native chiefs. In the same year he had formed the Gesellschaft für deutsche Kolonisation (German Colonization Society). Without the sanction of **Bismarck**, he claimed Uganda for Germany and was made commissioner of Kilimanjaro (1891–93), but his harsh treatment of the natives caused his recall. He returned to Africa in 1906 when gold was discovered in the Zambesi district.

PETERS, Mary Elizabeth (1939–) Irish athlete, born in Halewood, Lancashire. She started competing in the pentathlon, a gruelling discipline covering five events over two days, at the age of seventeen. She won the gold medal at her third Olympics in 1972, at the age of 33, setting a new world record (4801 points). She was also the Commonwealth champion twice, winning the shot as well in the 1970 Games. Perennially cheerful and good-natured, she campaigned for more sports facilities in Northern Ireland, and an athletics stadium in Belfast is now named after her.

PETERSEN, Nis (1897–1943) Danish poet and novelist, cousin of **Kaj Munk**, born in South Jutland. He rebelled against a strict upbringing and became a journalist, casual labourer and vagabond until he became famous for his novel of Rome in the time of **Marcus Aurelius**, *Sandalmagernes Gade* (trans 1932 as *The Street of the Sandal-makers*). His later poetry is highly considered.

PETERSON, Oscar Emmanuel (1925–) Canadian jazz pianist and composer, born in Montreal, the son of immigrants from the West Indies. He studied piano from childhood and developed a phenomenal technique and driving style, comparable with that of **Art Tatum** of whom he was an admirer and friend. From 1949 Peterson's work with the touring 'Jazz at the Philharmonic' groups brought him international recognition. A prolific recording artist, some of his finest work has been as leader of a trio, but he has also worked extensively as a soloist.

PETERSON-BERGER, Wilhelm (1867–1942) Swedish composer, writer and music critic. After studying at the Stockholm conservatory (1886–89) and later at Dresden (1889–90), he settled in Stockholm and was music critic for *Dagens Nyheter* from 1896 to 1930, after which he withdrew to his beloved Frösö, Jämtland. He won early acclaim for his lyric pieces *Frösöblomster* (1896–1914) and three series of *Svensk lyrik* (1896–1926), settings of poems by **Karlfeldt**, **Heidenstam** and others. They show clearly the influence of Scandinavian folk music and of **Grieg**, and were a major contribution to the Swedish national dramas for which he provided his own text, achieving a Swedish *Gesamtkunstwerk*. Most popular of these is *Arnljot* (1909), about a warrior found in **Snorri Sturluson**'s *St Olaf's saga*, performed annually from 1936 at Frösö. Of his prolific but uneven output, his Symphony No 3 (1913–15, known as the Lappland because of its use of the Lapp *jojka*, and infused with nature mysticism), the *Cantata Norrbötten* (1922), *Opera Cantata* (1923) and his violin concerto (1928), are among the best known. His idealistic music criticism, which could be ruthless and personal, attacking old established composers and radical young ones, antagonized many and hampered his career, but his atmospheric, colourful music greatly influenced Swedish cultural life early in this century.

PÉTION DE VILLENEUVE, Jérôme (c.1756–1794) French revolutionary, born in Chartres. In 1789 he was elected deputy to the *tiers-état*. He was a prominent member of the Jacobin Club, and became a great ally of **Robespierre**. He was one of those who brought back the royal family from Varennes (1789) and advocated the deposition of the king. He was elected mayor of Paris and was the first president of the Convention. On the triumph of the Terrorists, he cast in his lot with the Girondists. He voted at the king's trial for death, but headed the unsuccessful attack on Robespierre. Proscribed on 2 June 1793, he escaped to Caen, and thence, on the failure of the attempt to make armed opposition against the Convention, to the Gironde, where his and Buzot's bodies were later found in a cornfield, partly devoured by wolves. His *Oeuvres* fill three volumes (1792).

PETIPA, Marius (1818–1910) French ballet-master and choreographer, credited with the development of Russian classical ballet. After touring France, Spain and the USA as a dancer, he went to St Petersburg in 1847 to dance with the Imperial Theatre where his father Jean had been a teacher. In 1858 he became the company's second ballet master, and four years later staged his first ballet, *Pharaoh's Daughter*, setting the style of *ballet à grand spectacle* which was to dominate Russian ballet for the rest of the century. In 1869 he became ballet-master, and in the 34 years until his retirement in 1903 he created 50 original ballets and restagings, the most famous being **Tchaikovsky**'s *The Sleeping Beauty*, the supreme example of 19th-century classical ballet.

PETIT, Alexis Thérèse (1791–1820) French physicist, born in Vesoul. Professor at the Lycée Bonaparte, he enunciated with **Pierre Louis Dulong** the 'law of Dulong and Petit' that for all elements the product of the specific heat and the atomic weight is the same.

PETIT, Jean Louis (1674–1750) French surgeon. He gained experience with the army and then lectured in Paris on anatomy and surgery. The inventor of the screw tourniquet, he was the first to operate with success for mastoiditis.

PETIT, Roland (1924–) French choreographer and dancer, born in Paris. At the age of nine he began his studies at the Paris Opéra under **Serge Lifar** to become the company's principal dancer (1943–44). Following a short period with the Ballets des Champs-Elysées, he founded his own troupe in 1948, Les Ballets de Paris de Roland Petit. In 1972 he became artistic director of the Ballet de Marseilles. He created many new ballets including *Le Rossignol et la Rose* (1944), a story by **Oscar Wilde** set to **Schumann**'s music; *Les Forains* (1945) with **Cocteau**; *Le Jeune Homme et la Mort* (1946), which Cocteau had rehearsed strictly to jazz until the opening night when **Bach** was substituted; **Anouilh**'s *Les Desmoiselles de la Nuit* (1948); *Pink Floyd Ballet* (1972); *Nana* (1976) and *Marcel Proust Remembered* (1980). During the 1950s he was very active in the film industry, creating the ballet sequences in the film *Hans Christian Andersen* (1952), danced by his wife, Zizi Jeanmaire, and *Daddy Long Legs* (1954).

PETIT DE JULLEVILLE, Louis (1841–1900) French critic, born in Paris. He became professor at the École normale supérieure and the Sorbonne. He wrote the *Histoire du théâtre en France* and edited a monumental *Histoire de la langue et de la littérature française*.

PETITOT, Jean (1607–91) Swiss painter in enamel, born in Geneva. After some years in Italy he went to England and obtained the patronage of **Charles I**. After the king's execution he moved to Paris, where **Louis XIV** gave him lodgings in the Louvre and a share in his patronage. As a Protestant, he fled back to Geneva after the revocation of the Edict of Nantes (1685).

PETO, Sir Samuel Morton (1809–89) English civil engineer and contractor, born in Woking, Surrey. He attained great wealth as a contractor, laying railways in England, Russia, Norway, Algiers and Australia. He was a Liberal MP from 1847 to 1868.

PETÖFI, Sandor (1823–49) Hungarian poet, born in Kiskörös. He was successively actor, soldier and literary hack, but by 1844 had made his name as a poet. In 1848 he threw himself into the revolutionary cause, writing numerous war songs. He fell in battle at Segesvár. His poetry broke completely with the old pedantic style, and, full of national feeling, began a new epoch in Hungarian literature. He also wrote a novel, *The Hangman's Rope*, and translated **Shakespeare**'s *Coriolanus*.

PÉTOMANE, Le See **PUJOL, Joseph**

PETRARCH, Francesco Petrarca (1304–74) Italian poet and scholar. One of the earliest and greatest of modern lyric poets, he was the son of a Florentine notary, who, exiled (1302) along with **Dante**, settled in Arezzo, where Francesco was born. In 1312 his father went to Avignon, then the seat of the papal court; and there and in Bologna the boy devoted himself with enthusiasm to the study of the classics. After his father's death Petrarch returned to Avignon (1326). Being without means, he became a churchman, though perhaps never a priest, and lived on the small benefices conferred by his many patrons. It was at this period (1327) that he first saw Laura (possibly Laure de Noves, married in 1325 to Hugo de Sade; she died, the mother of eleven children, in 1348). She inspired him with a passion which has become proverbial for its constancy and purity. Now began also his friendship with the powerful Roman family of the **Colonnas**. As the fame of Petrarch's learning and genius grew, his position became one of unprecedented influence. His presence at their courts was competed for by the most powerful sovereigns of the day. He travelled repeatedly in France, Germany and Flanders, searching for MSS. In Liège he found two new orations of **Cicero**, in Verona a collection of his letters, in Florence an unknown portion of **Quintilian**. Invited by the senate of Rome on Easter Sunday, 1341, he ascended the capitol clad in the robes of his friend and admirer, King Robert of Naples, and there, after delivering an oration, he was crowned poet laureate. In 1353, after the death of Laura and his friend Cardinal Colonna, he left Avignon and his country house at Vaucluse for ever, disgusted with the corruption of the papal court. His remaining years were passed in various towns of northern Italy. Petrarch may be considered as the earliest of the great humanists of the Renaissance. He himself chiefly founded his claim to fame on his epic poem *Africa*, the hero of which is **Scipio Africanus**, and his historical work in prose, *De Viris Illustribus*, a series of biographies of classical celebrities. Other Latin works are the eclogues and epistles in verse; and in prose the dialogues, *De Contemptu Mundi* (or *Secretum*), the treatises *De Otio Religiosorum* and *De Vita Solitaria*, and his letters—he was in constant correspondence with **Boccaccio**. It is as a poet that his fame has lasted for over five centuries. His title deeds to fame are in his *Canzoniere*, in the Italian sonnets, madrigals, and songs, almost all inspired by his unrequited passion for Laura. The *Opera Omnia* appeared at Basel in 1554. His Italian lyrics were published in 1470, and have since gone through innumerable editions.

PETRAZHITSKY, Leo Josifovitch (1867–1931) Russian pre-revolution jurist. Professor at St Petersburg, he was author of *Introduction to Legal Policy* (1900), *Introduction to the Study of Law and Morals* (1905) and *Theory of Law and the State in connection with a Theory of Morals*. In 1921 he moved to Warsaw and contributed to the project of unifying the civil code of the revived Polish state.

PETRE, Edward (1631–99) English religious, born in London of an old Catholic house. He studied at St Omer, but was not admitted a Jesuit until 1671. His influence as confessor of **James II** made him extremely unpopular. In 1693 he became rector of St Omer.

PETRI, Laurentius (1499–1573) Swedish reformer. He studied under **Luther** at Wittenberg, was made professor at Uppsala, and in 1531 the first Protestant archbishop of Uppsala. He and his brother **Olaus** did most to convert Sweden to the Reformed doctrines, and superintended the translation of the New Testament into Swedish (1541).

PETRI, Olaus (1493–1552) Swedish reformer and statesman, brother of **Laurentius Petri**. After his return (1519) from Wittenberg, he gained the ear of **Gustav I Vasa**, who made him (1531) chancellor of the kingdom—a post he resigned in 1539 to spend the rest of his life as first pastor of Stockholm. His works include memoirs, a mystery-play, hymns and controversial tracts.

PETRIE, Sir (William Matthew) Flinders (1853–1942) English archaeologist and Egyptologist, born in Charlton, Kent. He surveyed Stonehenge (1874–77), but turned from 1881 entirely to Egyptology, beginning by surveying the pyramids and temples of Giza and excavating the mounds of Tanis and Naucratis. The author of more than 100 books, renowned for his energy and spartan tastes, he became the first Edwards professor of archaeology at London (1892–1933), continuing excavations in Egypt and Palestine until well into his 80s.

PETRIE, George (1789–1866) Irish archaeologist, born in Dublin. Although trained to be a landscape-painter, he was early attracted by the old buildings of Ireland. From 1833 to 1846 he was attached to the Ordnance Survey of Ireland, and from 1832 he contributed to the *Dublin Penny Journal*, and his famous *Essay on Round Towers* proved that they were Christian ecclesiastical buildings.

PETRONIO, Stephen (1956–) American dancer and choreographer, born in Nutley, New Jersey. He was studying medicine at college when a chance visit to a dance class changed the course of his life. He trained in contact improvisation with **Steve Paxton** and also with such leading modern dance experimentalists as **Yvonne Rainer** and **Trisha Brown**. He began choreographing while still a member of Brown's company (1979–86). He now heads his own troupe, and is establishing a reputation as one of America's most exciting young choreographers.

PETRONIUS ARBITER (1st century) Latin satirical writer, and author of the *Satyricon* (Tales of Satyrs). He is usually supposed to be the voluptuary Gaius Petronius, whom **Tacitus** calls 'arbiter elegantiae' at the court of **Nero**. He was governor of Bithynia for a time. The *Satyricon* is a long satirical romance in prose and verse, of which only parts of the 14th, 15th and 16th books, in a fragmentary state, are still extant. The work depicts with wit, humour and realism the licentious life in southern Italy of the upper or moneyed class. The favour Petronius enjoyed as aider and abettor of Nero and his entourage in every form of sensual indulgence aroused the jealousy of another confidant, Tigellinus, who procured his disgrace and banishment. Ordered to commit suicide, he opened his veins.

PETROSIAN, Tigran Vartanovich (1929–84) Russian chess player, born in Tbilisi, and world champion (1963–69). He won the title from **Mikhail Botvinnik** in 1963 and made one successful defence, before losing it to **Boris Spassky** in 1969. His awkward, prophylactic style of chess earned him the sobriquet, 'Iron Tigran'.

PETROV-VODKIN, Kuzma Sergeevich (1878–1939) Russian painter, born in Khvalynsk (now Saratov region). Initially trained as an icon painter, he later studied painting in St Petersburg and Moscow, after which he travelled in Africa. Although he was a member of the World of Art and The Four Arts Societies, and was associated with the Blue Rose Group (whose exhibition in 1907 marked the beginning of the Russian avant-garde), he ultimately did not become identified with any particular school. After the 1917 Revolution, the titles of his paintings reflect new concerns, eg *The Year 1918 in Petrograd* (1920), and *Workers* (1926). Later he developed and wrote about a new theory concerning the depiction of space. His importance rests mainly on his influence as a teacher of the first generation of Soviet painters at the Leningrad Art Academy.

PETROVITCH See **ALEXEI**

PETRUS DE ALLIACO See **AILLY, Pierre d'**

PETT, Peter (fl.1560) English shipwright, of Deptford. He was master shipwright there under **Edward VI** and responsible for the building of most of the English fleet at that time, including the *Elizabeth Jonas*, one of the largest vessels to engage the Spanish Armada. His son Phineas (1570–1647) studied at Emmanuel College, Cambridge, was appointed to the same post in succession to his half-brother Joseph in 1605, and later became naval commissioner at Chatham. He built both warships, such as the 1200-ton *Royal Prince* and the even larger *Sovereign of the Seas*, and merchant vessels such as the East India Company's *Increase* and *Peppercorn*. His son Peter (1610–70) succeeded him in 1648 at Chatham, but was dismissed after the Dutch fleet inflicted severe damage on the laid-up English fleet in the Medway.

PETTENKOFER, Max von (1818–1901) German chemist, born near Neuburg. Professor of chemistry at Munich (1847–94), he made valuable contributions to science on gold refining, gas-making, ventilation, clothing, epidemics and hygiene. Of his works, the best known is his *Handbuch der Hygiene* (1882 *et seq*).

PETTIE, John (1839–93) Scottish painter, born in Edinburgh. He trained at the Trustee's Academy under **Robert Scott Lauder**, and joined **Orchardson** in London in 1862. His works, apart from his portraits, were mainly of historical and literary subjects and had considerable popularity. Examples of these are *Juliet and Friar Lawrence* (1874) and *The Vigil* (1884).

PETTIT, Bob (1932–) American professional basketball player, born in Baton Rouge, Louisiana. After graduating from university in Louisiana he joined the Milwaukee (later the St Louis) Hawks in the National Basketball Association in 1954, and stayed with the franchise right through to 1965. Unusually he led the NBA in both scoring (twice) and rebounding, helping the Hawks to one championship. Throughout his career he averaged 26.4 points per game and was twice voted the NBA's Most Valuable Player.

PETTY, Sir William (1623–87) English economist, born in Romsey, Hampshire, the son of a clothier. He went to sea, and then studied at a Jesuit college in Caen, in Utrecht, Amsterdam, Leiden, Paris and Oxford. He taught anatomy at Oxford, and music at Gresham College, London. Appointed physician to the army in Ireland (1652), he executed a fresh survey of the Irish lands forfeited in 1641 and started ironworks, lead-mines, sea-fisheries and other industries on estates he bought in southwest Ireland. He was made surveyor-general of Ireland by **Charles II**. Inventor of a copying machine (1647), and a double-keeled sea-boat (1663), he was one of the first members of the Royal Society. In political economy he was a precursor of **Adam Smith**, and wrote a *Treatise on Taxes* (1662) and *Political Arithmetic* (1691), the latter a discussion of the value of comparative statistics. He married Baroness **Shelburne**, and his sons were successively Lord Shelburne.

PÉTURSSON, Hallgrímur (1614–74) Icelandic poet, pastor and hymn-writer, the greatest devotional poet in Icelandic literature, who struggled with poverty all his life and died afflicted with leprosy. Born in the north of Iceland, he ran away to Denmark to become a blacksmith's apprentice, but was put to school in Copenhagen by an Icelandic patron, the future bishop **Brynjólfur Sveinsson**, who recognized his unusual abilities. He was entrusted with the task of rehabilitating the Icelandic survivors of a Moorish pirate raid on Iceland by 'Turks' (1627), whose captives had been sold as slaves and were now in Copenhagen after being ransomed. He fell in love with one of them, a 38-year-old Icelandic woman known as Turkish-Gydda. They married in Iceland, where Hallgrímur worked as a labourer before becoming pastor of the church at Saurbær in the west of Iceland (1651). Here he wrote his masterpiece, *Passion Hymns* (1666), a cycle of 50 meditations on the Crucifixion. One of the hymns, *Allt eins og blómstrið eina* (Just as the one true flower) is still sung at every funeral in Iceland. The new cathedral in Reykjavík, Hallgrímskirkja, is named after him.

PEUERBACH See **PURBACH, Georg von**

PEUTINGER, Conrad (1465–1547) German scholar and antiquary. A keeper of the archives of Augsburg, he published a series of Roman inscriptions. His *Tabula Teutingeriana*, now in Vienna, is a copy, made in 1264, of an itinerary or a Roman map of the military roads of the 4th century AD.

PEVSNER, Antoine (1886–1962) Russian-born French Constructivist sculptor and painter, born in Orël, brother of **Naum Gabo**. In Moscow he helped to form the Suprematist Group with **Malevitch**, **Tatlin** and his brother. In 1920 he broke away from the Suprematists and issued the *Realist Manifesto* with his brother: this ultimately caused their exile from Russia, and he migrated to Paris. Several of his completely nonfigurative constructions (mainly in copper and bronze) are in the Museum of Modern Art, New York.

PEVSNER, Sir Nikolaus Bernhard (1902–83) German-born British art historian, born in Leipzig. He was lecturer in art at Göttingen University until the Nazis came to power in 1933, when he fled to Britain and became an authority on English architecture. From 1934 he investigated British industrial design, and wrote *An Enquiry into Industrial Art in England* (1937). He also wrote *Pioneers of the Modern Movement* (1936), and an enormously popular Pelican paperback, *An Outline of European Architecture* (1942), and became art editor of Penguin Books (1949). He was Slade professor of fine art at Cambridge (1949–55). He also produced a monumental series for Penguin Books, *The Buildings of England* (50 vols, 1951–74).

PFEFFER, Wilhelm Friedrich Philipp (1845–1920) German botanist, born near Cassel. Trained as a pharmacist, he became a specialist in plant physiology, professor successively at Bonn, Basel, Tübingen and Leipzig, and was noted particularly for his researches on osmotic pressure. His *Handbuch der Pflanzenphysiologie* (1881) was a standard work.

PFEIFFER, Ida, née **Reyer** (1797–1858) Austrian traveller, born in Vienna. After making two journeys round the world (1846–48, 1851–54), in 1856 she went on an expedition to Madagascar, endured terrible hardships, and came home to die. She wrote accounts of all her journeys.

PFEIFFER, Richard Friedrich Johannes (1858–?1945) German bacteriologist, born near Posen (now Poznań, Poland). He studied under **Robert Koch**, and became professor at Berlin (1894), Königsberg (1899) and Breslau (1901). He worked on the immunization of man against typhoid, on the influenza bacillus, discovered a serum against cholera, and published books on hygiene and microbiology. He was presumed dead in 1945.

PFITZNER, Hans Erich (1869–1949) German musician and composer, born in Moscow. He taught in various German conservatoria, and conducted in Berlin, Munich and Strasbourg. He composed *Palestrina* (1917) and other operas, choral and orchestral music (*Von deutscher Seele*, 1921) and chamber music. A romantic, he went his own way, refusing to follow passing fashions.

PFLEIDERER, Otto (1839–1908) German Protestant theologian, born in Stetten in Württemberg. He studied at Tübingen (1857–61), became pastor at Heilbronn in 1868, in 1870 professor of theology at Jena, and in 1875 at Berlin. In New Testament criticism Pfleiderer belonged to the critical school which grew out of the impulse given by **Baur**, and was an independent thinker, suggestive and profoundly learned. His works include *Primitive Christianity* (14 vols, trans 1906–11), *The Influence of the Apostle Paul on Christianity* (Hibbert Lectures, 1885) and *The Philosophy of Religion* (Gifford Lectures, 1894).

PFLÜGER, Eduard Friedrich Wilhelm (1829–1910) German physiologist, born in Hanau. Professor at Bonn (1859), he did important work on the sensory function of the spinal cord and on the digestive and metabolic systems. He also helped in the construction of the mercurial blood pump.

PHAEDRUS, Gaius Julius (1st century) Thracian slave, and translator of **Aesop**'s fables into Latin verse. He was taken to Rome at an early age and became the freedman of **Augustus** or **Tiberius**. Under Tiberius he published the first two books of his fables, but his biting though veiled allusions to the tyranny of the emperor and his minister Sejanus caused him to be accused and condemned—his punishment is unknown. On the death of Sejanus he published his third book. The fourth and fifth books belong to his last years. He died probably at an advanced age. He was more than a reproducer of Aesop; he invented fables of his own, and it seems certain that the five books contain many fables that are not his own work.

PHALARIS (6th century BC) Greek tyrant of Agrigentum in Sicily. He greatly embellished the city, and extended his sway over large districts in Sicily. After holding power for 16 years he was overthrown, and allegedly roasted alive in his own invention, the brazen bull. The 148 letters bearing his name were proved by **Richard Bentley** in 1697–99 to be spurious.

PHEIDIPPIDES (5th century BC) Greek long-distance runner who was sent to Sparta to ask for aid against the Persians before the battle of Marathon in 490 BC. To do this, he is reputed to have covered 150 miles in two days. Legend has confused him with the man who ran from the battlefield of Marathon to bring news of the victory to Athens. The Marathon race in the modern Olympics, although at 26 miles 385 yards not precisely the same distance, commemorates this event.

PHELPS, Samuel (1804–78) English actor-manager, born in Devonport. His first career was as a reader on the *Globe* and *Sun* newspapers, but by 1826 his interest in acting led him to the stage. By 1837 he was a success, especially with his performance as Shylock, but he did not fully exercise his talent until he became manager of Sadler's Wells. For 18 years with an excellent company of actors he produced legitimate plays, appearing himself equally successfully in comic and tragic roles.

PHIDIAS, Greek Pheidias (5th century BC) Greek sculptor, born in Athens c.500 BC. Considered the greatest sculptor in ancient Greece, he received from **Pericles** a magnificent commission to execute the chief statues with which he proposed to adorn the city, and was superintendent of all public works. He had under him architects, statuaries, bronze-workers, stone-cutters, etc. He constructed the Propylaea and the Parthenon, designed the sculpture on the walls; and is thought to have made the gold and ivory Athena there, and the Zeus at Olympia, himself. Charged with appropriating gold from the statue and carving his own head on an ornament, he was accused of impiety, and disappeared from Athens.

PHILARET (1782–1867) Russian prelate, the greatest preacher and the most influential Russian churchman of his day. In 1817 he became bishop of Reval, in 1819 archbishop of Tver, and in 1821 of metropolitan Moscow.

PHILBY, Harry St John Bridger (1885–1960) English Arabist and explorer, born in Ceylon (Sri Lanka). Educated at Westminster and Trinity College, Cambridge, he joined the Indian Civil Service in 1907 and served in the Punjab, learning several local languages. He served as political officer in Mesopotamia in 1915, and while in charge of the British Political Mission to Central Arabia (1917–18), crossed Arabia by camel from Uqayr to Jedda, exploring a large area of south-central Arabia and becoming the first European to visit the Nejd. For this he was awarded the Founder's Medal of the Royal Geographical Society in 1920 and later wrote *The Heart of Arabia* (1922). He returned to Mesopotamia and Trans-Jordan but retired from the Indian Civil Service in 1925 after quarrelling with British government policy in Arabia. He set up business in Jedda in 1926, advised King **Ibn Saud**, and became a Muslim in 1930. In 1931 he made an epic crossing of the Empty Quarter from north to south, shortly after Bertram Thomas made his crossing. From 1932 to 1937 he mapped the Yemen highlands, and in 1937 made a return journey from the Empty Quarter of Saudi Arabia to the Hadhramaut, described in *Sheba's Daughters* (1939). He lived in Arabia until his death.

PHILBY, 'Kim' (Harold Adrian Russell), (1911–88) British double agent, born in Ambala, India, son of **Harry St John Philby**. He was educated at Westminster and Trinity College, Cambridge, where, like **Guy Burgess**, **Donald Maclean** and **Anthony Blunt**, he became a communist. Already recruited as a Soviet agent, he was employed by the British Secret Intelligence Service (MI6), from 1944 to 1946, as head of the anti-communist counter-espionage. He was first secretary of the British embassy in Washington, working in liaison with the CIA, from 1949 to 1951, when he was asked to resign because of his earlier communist sympathies. From 1956 he worked in Beirut as foreign correspondent for the *Observer* and the *Economist*, obtaining the posts with the help of the British foreign office, until 1963, when he admitted the truth and disappeared to Russia, where he was granted citizenship. In 1968 he published *My Silent War* (1968). His third wife, Eleanor, joined him in Russia (1963) but returned to the West (1965). She wrote *Kim Philby: The Spy I Loved* (1968).

PHILIDOR, François André Danican (1726–95) French composer of operas, and chess master. Born in Dreux, into a family of Scots origin who had served for several generations as court musicians at Versailles, he was destined to a career as composer and arranger. His 1765 adaptation of **Fielding**'s *Tom Jones* was the most popular of the 21 operas he wrote; but he had sustained a dual career in chess, which brought him greater financial rewards. Unchallenged as the strongest player of his day, he established himself as a phenomenon and a scientific curiosity by giving public exhibitions in Paris, Holland, Germany and England of his ability to defeat two opponents simultaneously while blindfolded. His *L'Analyze du jeu des Échecs* (1749) was the first book to lay down the theoretical and strategical principles of chess, appearing in over a hundred editions in ten languages. He died in London, where he had become exiled following the French Revolution.

PHILIP, Prince See **EDINBURGH, Duke of**

PHILIP, 'the Bold' ('le Hardi') (1342–1404) Duke of Burgundy, founder of the second and last ducal House of Burgundy. He was the fourth son of **John II 'the Good'**, king of France. As a boy at the battle of Poitiers (1356) he displayed heroic courage, shared his father's captivity in England, and was made Duke of Burgundy in 1363. He married Margaret, daughter of the count of Flanders, in 1369. In 1372 he commanded with success against the English, and in 1380 helped to suppress the sedition of the Flemish towns against his father-in-law; but the rebels, especially the burghers of Ghent, were finally subdued only after the defeat of Rosbeck (1382). He inherited Flanders by the death of the count in 1384, and his wise government won the esteem of his new subjects. He encouraged arts, manufactures and commerce, and his territory was one of the best governed in Europe. For his imbecile nephew, **Charles VI** of France, he was obliged to take the helm of affairs.

PHILIP, 'the Good' (1396–1467) Duke of Burgundy, son of Duke John the Fearless and grandson of **Philip the Bold**. Bent on avenging his father's murder by the dauphin, in 1419 he entered into an alliance with **Henry V** of England, recognizing him as heir to the French crown. This agreement was sanctioned by the French king and States-General (1420), but the dauphin (**Charles VII** after 1422) took to arms, and was twice defeated. Disputes with the English prompted Philip to conclude a treaty with Charles in 1429. But by ceding to him Champagne and paying a large sum, the English regained his alliance. At this time, by falling heir to Brabant, Holland and Zeeland, he was at the head of the most powerful realm in Europe. Smarting under fresh insults of the English viceroy, he made final peace (1435) with Charles. When the English committed great havoc on Flemish ships, Philip declared war against them and, with the king of France, gradually expelled them from their French possessions. The imposition of taxes excited a rebellion, headed by Ghent; but the duke inflicted a terrible defeat (July 1454) upon the rebels, of whom 20000 fell. The later part of his reign was troubled by the quarrels between Charles VII and his son (afterwards **Louis XI**) who sought shelter with Philip. Under him Burgundy was the most wealthy, prosperous and tranquil state in Europe. He was founder of the order of the Golden Fleece in 1492.

PHILIP I, 'the Handsome' (1478–1506) king of Castile, the son of the emperor **Maximilian I** and Mary of Burgundy. As Archduke of Austria and Duke of Burgundy he married, in 1496, the Infanta of Spain, Joanna, daughter of **Ferdinand the Catholic** of Aragon and **Isabella of Castile**. Isabella's death in 1504 made Joanna the legal heiress to Castile, but Ferdinand promptly declared himself her regent. In 1506 Philip went to claim the throne, but died in the same year, and Joanna lost her reason and was put into confinement. Their children were the emperors **Charles V** and his successor, **Ferdinand I**.

PHILIP I (1052–1108) king of France, son of **Henri I**. He ruled from 1067. His reign marked a low point in the prestige of the Capetian monarchy, largely due to his elopement with Bertrada, wife of Fulk of Anjou, a scandal which led to his excommunication.

PHILIP II, known as **Philip-Augustus** (1165–1223) the first great Capetian king of France. The son of **Louis VII**, he was crowned joint king in 1179, succeeded his father in 1180, and married Isabella of Hainault, the last direct descendant of the Carolingians. His first war, against the Count of Flanders, gave him Amiens. He supported the sons of **Henry II** of England against their father. **Richard I** and he set out on the Third Crusade (1190–91), but they quarrelled in Sicily. After three months in Syria he returned to France, having sworn not to molest Richard's dominions; but no sooner had he returned than he made a bargain with **John** for the partition of Richard's French territories. Richard's sudden return occasioned an exhausting war till 1199. On Richard's death Philip supported Prince **Arthur** against his uncle John in the French domains of the English crown, but was for a while fully occupied by his quarrel with the pope. He had put away his second wife Ingeborg of Denmark, in order to marry Agnes of Meran, but the anger of the Vatican forced him to replace Ingeborg upon her throne. The murder of Arthur in 1203 again gave him excuse to win back English possessions in France. The fortress of Château Gaillard surrendered to him in 1204, and that same year he added to his dominions Normandy, Maine, Anjou and Touraine, with part of Poitou, as well as the overlordship of Brittany. The victory of Bouvines in 1214 over the Flemish, the English, and the Emperor **Otto IV** established his throne securely, and the rest of his reign he devoted to reforms of justice and to the building and fortifying of Paris—Notre Dame remaining a lasting monument of this great king. He died in Nantes.

PHILIP III, 'the Bold' ('le Hardi') (1245–85) king of France from 1270. He was with his father **Louis IX** (St Louis) at his death in Tunis (1270), and fought several unlucky campaigns in Spain, the last of which, the attack on Aragon, caused his death.

PHILIP IV, 'the Fair' ('le Bel') (1268–1314) king of France. He succeeded his father, **Philip III**, in 1285. By his marriage with Queen Joanna of Navarre he acquired Navarre, Champagne and Brie. He overran Flanders, but was defeated by the Flemings at Courtrai (1302). His struggle with Pope **Boniface VIII** arose from his attempts to tax the French clergy. In 1296 the Pope forbade this in the bull *Clericis laicos*, to which Philip replied by prohibiting the export of money or valuables. A temporary reconciliation was ended by a fresh quarrel in 1301, precipitated by Philip's arrest and trial of Bernard Saisset, bishop of Pamiers. The king's reply to the bull *Unam Sanctam* was to send his minister William de Nogaret to seize Boniface, who escaped but died soon afterwards (1303). After the short pontificate of Benedict XI, Philip procured the elevation of the pliant Frenchman, **Clement V** (1305), who came to reside at Avignon, thus beginning the 70 years' 'Babylonish captivity' of the papacy. Coveting the wealth of the Templars, Philip forced the pope to condemn and dissolve the order, whose property he appropriated (1314).

PHILIP V, 'the Tall' ('le Long') (1293–1322) king of France, second son of **Philip IV**. He succeeded his brother, Louis X, in 1316. He ended the war with Flanders (1320), and tried to unify the coinage.

PHILIP VI, of Valois (1293–1350) first French king of the house of Valois. The son of Charles of Valois, younger brother of **Philip IV**, he succeeded to the throne of France on the death of **Charles IV** in 1328. His right was denied by **Edward III** of England, son of the daughter of **Philip IV**, who declared that females, though excluded by the Salic law, could transmit their rights to their children. Marching into Flanders in 1328 to support the Count of Flanders against his rebellious subjects, he vanquished them at Cassel. He gave up Navarre, but retained Champagne and Brie. The Hundred Years' War with England began in 1337. The French fleet was destroyed off Sluys (1340). In 1346 Edward III landed in Normandy, ravaged to the environs of Paris, and defeated Philip at Crécy. A truce was concluded just as destruction threatened France in the 'Black Death'.

PHILIP II (382–336 BC) king of Macedon, father of **Alexander the Great**, and the founder of Macedonian greatness. He was born in Pella, the youngest son of Amyntas. The assassination of his eldest brother (367), and the death in battle of his second (359), left him guardian to his infant nephew Amyntas, but in a few months he made himself king. He rapidly secured his position internally and externally, built up the army, developed the resources of Macedon, and pursued a policy of expansion and opportunism. He captured Amphipolis (357), Pydna and Potidaea (356), and in the same year refounded Crenides as Philippi. He advanced into Thessaly but retreated when he found Thermopylae strongly guarded by the Athenians (352). He turned against the Thracians and captured all the towns of Chalcidice, including Olynthus (348). Requested by the Thebans to interfere in the 'Sacred War' raging between them and the Phocians, he marched into Phocis, destroyed its cities, and sent many of the inhabitants as colonists to Thrace (346). In the same year he made peace with the Athenians, but was back at war with them in 340 when he besieged Byzantium and Perinthus. In 339 the Amphicytyonic Council, of which Philip had been a member since 346, declared war against the Locrians of Amphissa, and in 338 appointed Philip to be their commander-in-chief. The Athenians, alarmed, formed a league with the Thebans against him, but their forces were decisively defeated at the battle of Chaeronea (338), and Philip was now in a position to organize the Greek states in a federal league with himself as their general (the 'League of Corinth'). Preparations for an invasion of Persia were started, but Philip was assassinated before he could begin the war himself (336). His son Alexander the Great was able to take over where Philip had left off and carry out the conquest of the Persian empire.

PHILIP V (238–179 BC) king of Macedon in the Antigonid dynasty, adopted by Antigonus Doson whom he succeeded in 221. Ambitious and active, he inherited a strong kingdom from his predecessor, but it was his misfortune to come into conflict with the growing power of Rome. He made an alliance with **Hannibal** in 215 BC during the Second Punic War, which resulted in a first (indecisive) conflict with Rome (214–05). Conflict broke out again with Rome, in the Second Macedonian War of 200–196. Decisively defeated at Cynoscephalae in 197, he had to give up all control of Greece and follow Rome's dictates. He was succeeded by his son **Perseus**.

PHILIP II (1527–98) king of Spain from 1556, the only son of the emperor **Charles V**, born in Valladolid. In 1543 he married the Infanta Mary of Portugal, who died in 1546 giving birth to their ill-fated son, **Don Carlos**. In 1554 he married **Mary I** (Mary Tudor) of England, but spent only 14 months in that country, where the marriage was not popular. Although he had little personal interest in England nor in its queen, England was a potentially useful ally for Spain upon the Continent, while the marriage opened the prospect of a union between England and the Spanish Netherlands. In 1555–56 Charles abdicated the sovereignty of Spain, the Netherlands, and all Spanish dominions in Italy and the New World to Philip, who nevertheless remained in Flanders until after his father's death in 1558. The Spain to which he returned in autumn 1559 was in the grip of a serious financial crisis and in a state of panic at the apparent spread of religious heresy. In championing religious orthodoxy, Philip increasingly indentified himself with the Spanish Inquisition, which he saw as a useful instrument both for combating heresy and for extending his control over his own dominions. Despite the bankrupt exchequer he had inherited from his father, he was involved in war against France and the papacy (1557–59) and, in 1560, against the Turks in the Mediterranean. These wars necessitated a sharp increase in domestic taxation which served only to increase unrest within his dominions. Mary Tudor died in 1558 and, when Philip failed to secure the hand of her sister and successor, **Elizabeth**, he married Isabella of France (daughter of **Henri II**) in 1559, and in 1570 married as his fourth wife, his cousin Anna, daughter of the emperor **Maximilian II**, by whom he had a son, the future **Philip III**. At home, Philip's government had to meet threats from the Moriscos (converted Muslims) of Granada, who rebelled between 1568 and 1570 and, more seriously, from the Netherlands, in open revolt from 1573. Abroad, Spain contributed to the Holy League against the Turks, which, under the command of Philip's half-brother, Don **John of Austria**, defeated the Ottoman fleet at Lepanto in 1571. In 1575, for the second time in Philip's reign, the Spanish crown was obliged to declare itself bankrupt and in November 1576 the discontented and unpaid Spanish troops in the Netherlands ran wild and sacked the city of Antwerp. Don John of Austria was sent to take command in the Low Countries, but he was unable to prevent the seven United Provinces from gaining their independence in 1579, although this was not formally accepted by Spain until the truce of 1609. In 1580 Philip succeeded to the Portuguese throne. The increase in trade-revenue from the New World in the 1580s resulted in a new prosperity and a more confident expansionist policy. Portugal was annexed to Spain in 1580, and attempts to re-conquer the northern Netherlands came close to success. In 1588, the year after **Drake**'s sack of Cadiz, the great Armada was launched against England, which had lent aid to the United Provinces, but failed in its objective when storms wrecked a substantial proportion of the fleet. By contrast the 1590s were dark years, with a further revolt in Aragon (1591–92), and renewed financial crisis leading to a third bankruptcy in 1596. Philip died two years later, leaving his empire divided, demoralized and economically depressed. The violence of his campaign against Protestants had destroyed all harmony within his dominions, while continual wars continued to deplete the financial resources of Spain.

PHILIP III (1578–1621) king of Spain from 1598, the son and successor of **Philip II** by his fourth and last marriage. An introspective and deeply religious man, he left government to corrupt ministers and devoted himself to the interests of the church. During his reign, agriculture and industry declined, and foreign wars drained the treasury. In 1606 the Moriscos (Muslim converts to Christianity) were expelled from Spain. He was succeeded by his son, **Philip IV**.

PHILIP IV (1605–65) king of Spain from 1621, son and successor of **Philip III**. A discerning patron of the arts (particularly of **Velazquez**), he had no interest in politics and left the administration of government to his favourite minister, the able and patriotic count of **Olivares**. His reign continued the rapid decline of Spain as a dominant European power. In 1640 Portugal regained its independence after a revolt. In 1648 Holland was lost by the Treaty of Westphalia; and in 1659 the Treaty of the Pyrenees cost Spain her frontier fortresses in Flanders. His daughter, Maria Theresa (1638–83), was the first wife of **Louis XIV** of France. He was succeeded by his four-year-old son, **Charles II**, the last of the Habsburgs.

PHILIP V (1683–1746) Duke of Anjou and first Bourbon king of Spain from 1700, grandson of **Louis XIV** of France. He succeeded to the Spanish throne under the will of **Charles II**. The prospect of a French prince ruling Spain caused widespread alarm throughout Europe and precipitated the War of the Spanish Succession (1701–13). The war resulted in the loss of all Spanish territories outside Spain itself and spelt the end of Spanish power in Europe. Spain lost Gibraltar and Minorca to the British, the Spanish Netherlands and Naples to Austria, and Sicily to the House of Savoy. Within Spain, the Catalans had been in open revolt since 1705 and Barcelona was not recaptured until 1714. Philip was a weak king and the government was dominated by his second wife, Isabella Farnese of Parma and her Italian favourite, **Guilio Alberoni**. In 1724 he abdicated, for some unknown reason, in favour of his son, Louis I, but resumed the throne when Louis died in the same year. In 1732 Oran was reconquered from the Moors and war with Austria (1733–36) regained Naples and Sicily. At Philip's death, Spain was embroiled in the War of Austrian Succession (1741–48).

PHILIP NERI, St See **NERI**

PHILIP THE ARAB (3rd century) Roman emperor from 244 to 249. He came to power by causing the death of **Gordian III**. He celebrated the 1000th anniversary of the founding of Rome with a mammoth secular games in 248, the last time they were celebrated in Roman history. He also founded the city of Philipopolis. His reign was plagued by usurpations, and he was killed in battle by **Decius**, who succeeded him.

PHILIP, 'the Magnanimous' (1504–67) Landgrave of Hesse. He was converted to Lutheranism in 1524 and was a major driving force in the Protestant Schmalkaldic League of 1531. He established Hesse as a sovereign state where the Protestant church was prominent in the provision of state schools and hospitals. Despite pressure from radical Anabaptists, Hesse maintained a tolerant religious régime that accommodated pastors of different Protestant persuasions and where no one was executed for religious reasons. In 1539 Philip developed syphilis and in 1540 contracted a bigamous marriage with Margaret van der Saale. This moral ambiguity, and his long imprisonment after the Schmalkaldic War (1547–52), lessened his influence in European affairs.

PHILIP (d.1676) American-Indian chief (Indian name, Metacomet), the son of Massoit, chief of the Wampanoag Indians of Massachusetts (d.1661). He led a confederation of tribes against the European settlers in an attempt to stem the erosion of his ancestral domain. King Philip's War (1675–76) was characterized by atrocities on both sides. Philip himself was shot on the battlefield by one of his own braves and his wife and nine-year-old son, along with hundreds of his people, were sold into slavery by the victorious colonists.

PHILIPPA OF HAINAULT (c.1314–1369) queen of England, married her second cousin **Edward III** at York in 1327. She brought Flemish weavers to England and encouraged coal-mining, and made the French poet and historian **Jean Froissart** her secretary. She is said to have roused the English troops before the defeat of the Scots at the battle of Neville's Cross in 1346, and to have interceded with Edward for mercy for the burgesses of Calais after the long seige in 1347. The Queen's College, Oxford, founded by Philippa's chaplain in 1341, was named after her.

PHILIPS, Ambrose (?1674–1749) English poet, born in Shrewsbury. He was educated at St John's College, Cambridge, and became a fellow there. A friend of **Addison** and **Steele**, he did hack work for **Tonson**, and gained a reputation by the *Winter-piece* in the *Tatler* and six Pastorals in Tonson's *Miscellany* (1709). These were praised in the *Guardian* at **Pope**'s expense, and Pope's jealousy started a bitter feud. He was dubbed 'Namby Pamby' by either **Carey** or **Swift** for the oversentimentality of some of his poetry. Of his plays only *The Distrest Mother* (1712), based on **Racine**'s *Andromaque*, found favour with his contemporaries. He was MP for Armagh, secretary to the archbishop of Armagh, purse-bearer to the Irish Lord Chancellor, and registrar of the Prerogative Court.

PHILIPS, John (1676–1709) English poet, born in Bampton, Oxfordshire. He was the son of the archdeacon of Shropshire, and was educated at Winchester and Christ Church College, Oxford. He wrote three very popular poems: *The Splendid Shilling* (1701), a Miltonic burlesque; *Blenheim* (1705), a Tory celebration of **Marlborough**'s great victory; and *Cyder* (1708), an imitation of Virgil's *Georgics*. He has a monument in Westminster Abbey.

PHILIPS, Katherine, née **Fowler,** pseud **'Orinda'** (1631–64) English poetess, born in London, the daughter of a merchant. Called 'the matchless Orinda', at 16 she married James Philips of Cardigan Priory. She is the first English woman poet to have her work published (it included an address to the Welsh poet **Henry Vaughan**). She received a dedication from **Jeremy Taylor** (*Discourse on the Nature, Offices and Measures of Friendship*, 1659). She ran a literary salon, described in the *Letter of Orinda to Poliarchus* (1705). She translated **Corneille**'s *Pompée*, which was performed in Dublin in 1663, and the greater part of his *Horace*. Her poems, surreptitiously printed in 1663, were issued in 1667. She died of smallpox on a visit to London.

PHILIPSON, Sir Robin (Robert James) (1916–) Scottish painter, born in Broughton-in-Furness. He studied at Edinburgh College of Art from 1936 to 1940, where he was head of drawing and painting (1960–82). During World War II he served in India and Burma. His first one-man show was at the Scottish Gallery, Edinburgh, 1954. He was president of the Royal Scottish Academy from 1973 to 1983. Like many Scottish artists of his generation, he handles paint freely and colours boldly, but has always retained a precise figurative element in his work.

PHILLIMORE, Sir Robert Joseph (1810–85) English judge, son of the Regius professor of civil law at Oxford. Educated at Westminster and Christ Church College, Oxford, he served on the board of control and later had a brilliant career at the bar. He sat in parliament as a Whig (1853–57), and became advocate-general (1862), judge advocate-general (1871), judge of the Arches Court (1867–75), and of the High Court of Admiralty (1867–83). He wrote *Commentaries upon International Law* (1854–61) and *Ecclesiastical Law* (1873–76). His son Walter (1845–1929) became a lord justice of appeal and edited his father's works.

PHILLIP, Arthur (1738–1814) English naval commander, born in London, founder and first governor of New South Wales. He trained at Greenwich and joined the navy in 1755. He saw service in the Mediterranean with **Byng**, and was at the taking of Havana. In 1787 he was appointed commander of the 'First Fleet' carrying convicts to Australia. He landed on 26 January 1788 (subsequently celebrated as Australia Day). Finding the site unsuitable, he founded his penal colony settlement at Sydney. He explored the Hawkesbury River, piloted his colony through difficulties and predicted its future importance. He left in 1792, being made vice admiral in 1810.

PHILLIP, John (1817–67) Scottish painter, born in Aberdeen, an old soldier's son. Apprenticed to a decorator and glazier, he was sent to London for art studies. Most of his early subjects were Scottish, but after a visit to Spain (1851) for health reasons, his main triumphs were in Spanish themes, and earned him the nickname of Phillip of Spain.

PHILLIPPS See **HALLIWELL-PHILLIPPS**

PHILLIPS, David Graham (1867–1911) American feminist novelist and journalist, born in Madison, Indiana. He played a part in the 'muckraker' movement of reform-minded journalism in the early 20th century. He also wrote powerfully in several novels in favour of the emancipation of women, notably in *The Plum Tree* (1905) and *Susan Lennox: Her Fall and Rise* (1917), and was ultimately assassinated by a lunatic who regarded his efforts in this direction as contributory to female moral depravity. Despite the identification of his name with his attacks on political servitude to capitalist interests, it is for his devoted service to the cause of women's rights that he deserves best to be remembered.

PHILLIPS, Edward (1630–c.1696) English writer, son of **John Milton**'s sister, Ann. He was brought up and educated by his uncle. He went to Oxford in 1650, but left next year without taking a degree. In 1633 he was tutor to the son of **John Evelyn**, and is mentioned in Evelyn's *Diary* as 'not at all infected by Milton's principles', yet he not only extolled his uncle in his *Theatrum Poetarum*, but wrote a short life of the poet. Among his numerous works are a complete edition (the first) of the poems of **William Drummond** of Hawthornden (1656); *New World of English Words* (1658), a philological dictionary; the *Continuation* of Sir **Richard Baker**'s *Chronicle of the Kings of England* (1665); and *Theatrum Poetarum, or a Complete Collection of the Poets* (1675).

PHILLIPS, John (1631–1706) English writer, brother of **Edward Phillips**, nephew of **John Milton**. He was educated by his uncle, and replied to **Salmasius**'s attack on him, and acted as his secretary. His *Satyr against Hypocrites* (1655) was a bitter attack on Puritanism, and *Speculum Crape Gownorum* (1682) on the High Churchmen.

PHILLIPS, John Bertram (1906–82) English bible translator, writer and broadcaster, born in Barnes. He was made famous by *Letters to Young Churches* (1947), translations of Paul's epistles begun in 1941 to encourage his church youth club, and in due course by the complete *New Testament in Modern English* (1958). He wrote a dozen best-sellers, including *Your God is Too Small* (1952), *A Man Called Jesus* (1959), and *Ring of Truth: A Translator's Testimony* (1967). Few were aware, until the posthumous publication of his autobiography, *The Price of Success* (1984), and letters to others in similar situations (*The Wounded Healer*, 1984), of his continuous battle against depression from 1961.

PHILLIPS, Captain Mark Antony Peter (1948–) husband of Princess **Anne**, and a noted horseman. Educated at Marlborough College and Sandhurst, he joined the Queen's Dragoon Guards in 1969. In 1973 he married Princess Anne (now the Princess Royal), but separated from her in 1989. He was a regular member of the British equestrian team, 1970–76, and won many team events, including the gold medal at the Olympic Games in Munich in 1972.

PHILLIPS, Ulrich Bonnell (1877–1934) American historian, born in La Grange, Georgia. A graduate of Georgia University and Columbia, a pupil of **W A Dunning**, he studied the ante-bellum South rather than its post-war Reconstruction, and won fame for his *American Negro Slavery* (1918), which defended slavery as preferable for black slaves as well as white owners. His *Life and Labour in the Old South* (1929) was an impressive contribution to environmentalist determinism, with particular stress on climate. He also wrote *Georgia and States Rights* (1902), *History of Transportation in the Eastern Cotton Belt* (1908) and *The Life of Robert Toombs* (1913).

PHILLIPS, Wendell (1811–84) American abolitionist, born in Boston, Massachusetts. He graduated at Harvard in 1831, and was called to the bar in 1834. By 1837 he was the chief orator of the anti-slavery party, closely associated with **William Lloyd Garrison**. He also championed the causes of temperance and women, and advocated the rights of Indians.

PHILLPOTTS, Dame Bertha Surtees (1877–1932) English Scandinavian scholar and educationist, born in Bedford. She studied medieval and modern languages at Girton College, Cambridge (1898–1902), and was a research student in Iceland and Denmark from 1903 to 1906. In 1913 she was appointed the first Lady Carlisle fellow at Somerville College, Oxford, and became principal of Westfield College, London, in 1920. She was mistress of Girton (1922–25), and director of Scandinavian Studies at Cambridge from 1926 to 1932. She wrote *The Elder Edda and Ancient Scandinavian Drama* (1920) and *Edda and Saga* (1931). In 1931 she married the astronomer Hugh Frank Newall (1857–1944).

PHILLPOTTS, Eden (1862–1960) English novelist, dramatist and poet, born in Mount Aboo, India. He studied for the stage in London, but turned to literature instead (1893), and made his name by realistic novels chiefly dealing with Devonshire, such as *Lying Prophets* (1896) and *Children of the Mist* (1898). Of his plays, *The Farmer's Wife* (1917: staged 1924) and *Yellow Sands* (1926), which he wrote with his daughter Adelaide, were perhaps the most successful. He wrote more than 250 books.

PHILLPOTTS, Henry (1778–1869) English prelate, born in Bridgwater. He was elected fellow of Magdalen College, Oxford in 1795, and became dean of Chester in 1828, and bishop of Exeter in 1831. A zealous Tory, a High Churchman and a keen controversialist, he opposed the Reform Bill in the House of Lords.

PHILO (2nd century) Byzantine scientist. He wrote a treatise on military engineering of which some fragments remain. He was probably the first to record the contraction of air in a globe over water when a candle is burnt in it.

PHILO JUDAEUS (1st century) Hellenistic Jewish philosopher, born in Alexandria, where he was a leading member of the Jewish community. A prolific author, he sought to effect a synthesis between Greek philosophy and Jewish scripture, and greatly influenced subsequent Greek Christian theologians like **Clement** and **Origen**. In c.40 AD he headed a deputation to the mad Emperor **Caligula** to plead with him on behalf of Jews who refused to worship him, as he records in the *De Legatione*. Most of his other works consist in allegorical interpretations of the Pentateuch, many of which survive in the original Greek.

PHILO OF BYBLIUS (fl.1st–2nd century AD) Greek grammarian from Byblus in Phoenicia. He wrote a distorted and misleading account of the religion and history of the Phoenicians, much of it professedly translated from Sanchoniathon.

PHILOPOEMEN (c.252–183 BC) Greek soldier, born in Megalopolis in Arcadia. As commander in chief of the Achaean League he crushed the Spartans at Mantinea (208), and sought to unite Greece against the Romans. In his old age he took part in an expedition against Messene, but was captured and poisoned by the Messenians.

PHILOSTRATUS, Flavius (c.170–245) Greek sophist. He studied at Athens, and established himself in Rome, where he wrote an idealized Life of **Apollonius of Tyana**, the bright *Lives of the Sophists*, and the amatory *Epistles*. The *Heroicon* and the *Imagines*, a description of 34 paintings on mythological themes supposedly in a villa near Naples, are now ascribed to his son-in-law, Philostratus the Lemnian; and further *Imagines* to a third and related Philostratus, probably a grandson.

PHIPPS, Sir William (1651–95) American colonial governor, born in Pemmaquid (Bristol), Maine. He was successively shepherd, carpenter and trader, and in 1687 recovered £300000 from a wrecked Spanish ship off the Bahamas. This gained him a knighthood and the appointment of provost-marshal of New England. In 1690 he captured Port Royal (now Annapolis) in Nova Scotia, but failed in 1691 in a naval attack upon Quebec. In 1692 he became governor of Massachusetts. He died in London.

PHIZ See **BROWNE, Hablot Knight**

PHOCAS (547–610) Byzantine emperor who overthrew his predecessor, Maurice, in 602. Through his monstrous vices, tyranny and incapacity the empire sank into utter anarchy, and he was overthrown in 610 by **Heraclius**.

PHOCION (c.402–318 BC) Athenian soldier. He commanded a division of the Athenian fleet at Naxos in 376, and helped to conquer Cyprus in 351 for **Artaxerxes III**. In 341 he crushed the Macedonian party in Euboea, and in 340 forced **Philip II** to evacuate the Chersonesus, but advised Athens to make friends with him. The advice was not taken; but the disastrous battle of Chaeronea (338) proved its soundness. After the murder of Philip (336) he struggled at Athens to repress the reckless desire for war; on the death of **Alexander** in 323 BC he vainly endeavoured to prevent the Athenians from going to war with **Antipater**, regent in Macedon. During a brief return to democracy in Athens, he was put to death on a charge of treason.

PHOMVIHANE, Kaysone (1920–) Laotian politician. Born in Savannakhet province and educated at Hanoi University, he fought with the anti-French forces in Vietnam after World War II and joined the exiled Free Lao Front (Neo Lao Issara) nationalist movement in Bangkok in 1945. He later joined the communist Pathet Lao, becoming, with North Vietnamese backing, its leader in 1955. Phomvihane successfully directed guerrilla resistance to the incumbent rightist régime and in 1975 became prime minister of the newly formed People's Democratic Republic of Laos and general-secretary of the Lao People's Revolutionary party. Initially he attempted to follow a radical socialist programme of industrial nationalization and rural collectivization, but later began a policy of economic and political 'liberalization'. Phomvihane is now viewed as a mellowing radical.

PHOTIUS (c.820–891) Byzantine prelate, and patriarch of Constantinople. On the deposition of **Ignatius** from the patriarchate of Constantinople for correcting the vices of the emperor Michael, Photius, a soldier and courtier, was hurried through all the stages of holy orders, and installed in his stead. In 862, however, Pope **Nicholas I** called a council at Rome which declared Photius's election invalid, excommunicated him, and reinstated Ignatius. Supported by the emperor, Photius assembled a council at Constantinople in 867, which condemned many points of doctrine and discipline of the western church as heretical, excommunicated Nicholas, and withdrew from the communion of Rome. Under the emperor Basilius, in 867 Photius was banished to Cyprus and Ignatius reinstated. In 869 the eighth general council, at which Pope Adrian II's legates presided, assembled at Constantinople; Photius was again excommunicated, and the intercommunion of the churches restored. Yet, on the death of Ignatius, Photius was reappointed. In 879 he assembled a new council at Constantinople, renewed the charges against the western church, and erased the *filioque* from the creed. Photius was finally deprived, and exiled to Armenia by Leo, son of Basilius, in 886. His main surviving works are *Myriobiblon* or *Bibliotheca*, a summary review of 280 works which Photius had read, and many of which are lost; a *Lexicon*; the *Nomocanon*, a collection of the acts and decrees of the councils and ecclesiastical laws of the emperors; and a collection of letters.

PHRYNE (4th century BC) Greek courtesan, born in Thespiae in Boeotia. She became enormously rich through her many lovers. Accused of profaning the Eleusinian mysteries, she was defended by the orator **Hyperides**, who threw off her robe in court, showing her loveliness, and so gained the verdict.

PIAF, Edith, originally **Edith Giovanna Gassion** (1915–63) French singer, born in Paris, the daughter of the famous acrobat Jean Gassion. She started her career by singing in the streets, and she soon graduated to music hall and cabaret, becoming known as Piaf, from the Parisian argot for 'little sparrow', which perfectly suited her waif-like appearance and the 'life at street-level' subject-matter of her songs. She appeared in stage-plays—**Jean Cocteau** wrote *Le Bel Indifferent* for her—and in films, including Renoir's *French-Cancan*; but it was for her songs with their undercurrent of sadness and nostalgia, written by herself and songwriters such as Jacques Prévert, that she became legendary, travelling widely in Europe and America. After a severe illness she made a greatly successful but brief return to the stage in 1961, before recurring ill-health led to her death two years later. Among her best-remembered songs are *Le Voyage du pauvre nègre*, *Mon Légionnaire*, *Un Monsieur m'a suivi dans la rue*, *La vie en rose*, and *Non, je ne regrette rien*.

PIAGET, Jean (1896–1980) Swiss psychologist and pioneer in the study of child intelligence, born in Neuchâtel. After studying zoology he turned to psychology and became professor of psychology at Geneva university (1929–54), director of the Centre d'Epistémologie génétique and a director of the Institut des Sciences de l'Education. He is best-known for his research on the development of cognitive functions (perception, intelligence, logic), for his intensive case study methods of research (using his own children), and for postulating 'stages' of cognitive development. His books include *The Child's Conception of the World* (1926), *The Origin of Intelligence in Children* (1936), and *The Early Growth of Logic in the Child* (1958).

PIAST (fl.c.870) legendary Polish ploughman and progenitor of a line of princes to which his name was attached 800 years later. His son Siemowit was first of the new line of princes of Gniezno (or Gnesen), commencing the loose consolidation of Great Poland to culminate in Piast's great-great-grandson Boleslaw I (the Brave) being crowned king shortly before his death in 1025. Boleslaw's great-grandson, Boleslaw II (the Generous) briefly won back the title of king after it had fallen into abeyance but after his death in 1079 his successors lost it once more, Boleslaw III (the Wry-Mouthed) restoring lost lands to include the territories of Pomerania, Silesia and Little Poland (first held under Miezko I, Christianizer of Poland and father of Boleslaw I). Boleslaw III divided the lands among his descendants, resulting in constant struggles among the cousins and attempts at unification. Boleslaw III's great-great-grandson, Przemysl II of Great Poland, was crowned king in 1295, but died in 1296. But the kingship then passed to his Bohemian son-in-law Wenceslas or Waclaw II (1300–05). It then passed to the Mazovian Piast line from Wladyslaw I (the Short) who became king in 1320, and consolidated his situation by marriage alliances with Hungary and Lithuania. His son Casimir III, the Great, (1310–70) reigned from Wladyslaw's death in 1333 until his own in 1370, during which time he finally relinquished Silesia and Pomerania but annexed Galicia, modernized its state and army administration, strengthened its economy and founded the university at Krakow (1364), also codifying the Polish laws. His death marked the end of the Piast dynasty as he was succeeded by his nephew, Louis I of Hungary from whom descended the Jagiellon dynasty.

PIATIGORSKY, Gregor (1903–76) Russian-born American cellist, born in Ekaterinoslav. He gave concerts throughout Russia at the age of nine, and studied at the Moscow Conservatory. He was prinicipal cellist of the Moscow Imperial Opera from 1919 to 1921. He emigrated in 1921 and was first cellist with the Warsaw (1921–23) and Berlin (1924–28) Philharmonic orchestras, before embarking on a solo career. He toured internationally and made his US début in 1929. Recital partners included **Horowitz**, **Schnabel**, **Heifetz**, and **Rachmaninov**, and many works were composed for him. An American citizen from 1942, he was a distinguished teacher at the Curtis Institute, Philadelphia, and subsequently at several universities.

PIAZZI, Giuseppe (1746–1826) Italian astronomer and monk. Professor of mathematics in Palermo, he set up an observatory there (1789) and published a catalogue of the stars (1803, 1814).

PICABIA, Francis (1879–1953) French Dadaist painter, born in Paris. Originally an Impressionist, he took part in every modern movement—Neo-Impressionism, Cubism, Futurism, and finally, with **Marcel Duchamp**, Dadaism, which they introduced to New York in 1915. His anti-art productions, often portraying senseless machinery, include *Parade Amoureuse* (1917), *Infant Carburettor*, and many of the cover designs for the American anti-art magazine *291*, which he edited.

PICARD, Charles Émile (1856–1941) French mathematician. Professor at the Sorbonne (1886–97) and president of the French Academy of Science (1910), he was specially noted for his work in complex analysis and integral and differential equations.

PICARD, Jean (1620–82) French astronomer, born in La Flèche, Anjou. In 1645 he became professor in the Collège de France and helped to found the Paris observatory. He made the first accurate measurement of a degree of a meridian and thus arrived at an estimate of the radius of the earth. He visited **Tycho Brahe**'s observatory on the island of Hven, and determined its latitude and longitude.

PICASSO, Pablo (1881–1973) Spanish painter, born in Malaga, Andalusia, the dominating figure of early 20th-century French art and, with **Braque**, a pioneer of Cubism. At the age of 14 he entered the academy at

Barcelona and painted *Barefoot Girl* (1895) and two years later transferred to Madrid for advanced training. In 1898 he won a gold medal for *Customs of Aragon*, which was exhibited in his native town. In 1901 he set up in a studio at 13 Rue de Ravignon (now Place Émile-Goudeau), Montmatre. By now a master of the traditional forms of art, to which such works as his *Gypsy Girl on the Beach* (1898) abundantly testify, Picasso quickly absorbed the Neo-Impressionist influences of the Paris school of **Toulouse-Lautrec**, **Degas** and **Vuillard**, exemplified by such works as *Longchamp* (1901) and *The Blue Room* (1901), but soon began to develop his own idiom. The blue period (1902–04), a series of striking studies of the poor in haunting attitudes of despair and gloom, gave way to the bright, life-affirming pink period (1904–06), in which Picasso achieved for harlequins, acrobats and the incidents of circus life what Degas had previously done for the ballet. Pink turned to brown in *La Coiffure* (1905–06) and the remarkable portrait of **Gertrude Stein** (1906). His first dabblings in sculpture and his new enthusiasm for black art are fully reflected in the transitional *Two Nudes* (1906), which heralded his epoch-making break with tradition in *Les Demoiselles d'Avignon* (1906–07), the first full-blown exemplar of analytical Cubism, an attempt to render the three-dimensional on the flat picture surface without resorting to perspective. Nature was no longer to be copied, decorated or idealized, but exploited for creative ends. Its exclusive emphasis on formal, geometrical criteria contrasted sharply with the cult of colour of the Fauvists, to whom Braque for a time belonged, before joining forces with Picasso in 1909 for their exploration of Cubism through its various phases; analytic, synthetic, hermetic and rococo, in which collage, pieces of wood, wire, newspaper and string became media side by side with paint. The *Ma Jolie* series of pictures, after the music-hall song score which appears in them (1911–14), are examples of the last phase. Braque broke with Picasso in 1914. From 1917 Picasso, through **Jean Cocteau**, became associated with **Diaghilev**'s Russian Ballet, designing costumes and sets for *Parade* (1917), *Le Tricorne* (1919), *Pulcinella* (1920), *Le Train bleu* (1924), in both Cubist and Neo-Classical styles, and thus made the former acceptable to a wider public. The grotesque facial and bodily distortions of the *Three Dancers* (1925) foreshadows the immense canvas of *Guernica* (1937), which expressed in synthetic Cubism Picasso's horror of the bombing of this Basque town during the Civil War, of war in general and compassion and hope for its victims. The canvas was exhibited in the Spanish Pavilion in the Paris World Fair (1937) and Picasso became director of the Prado Gallery, Madrid (1936–39). During World War II he was mostly in Paris, and after the liberation joined the communists. Neither *Guernica* nor his portrait of **Stalin** (1953) commended him to the party. Only the 'Picasso Peace Dove' has some propagandist value. He designed stage sets for Cocteau and **Petit**, illustrated translations of classical texts, experimented in sculpture, ceramics and lithography, allowed his canvas to be filmed while at work and wrote a play. He was above all the great innovator.

PICCARD, Auguste Antoine (1884–1962) Swiss physicist, born in Basel, twin brother of **Jean Felix Piccard**. He became professor at Brussels in 1922 and held posts at Lausanne, Chicago and Minnesota universities. He ascended 16–17 km by balloon (1931–32) into the stratosphere. In 1948 he explored the ocean depths off west Africa in a bathyscaphe constructed from his own design. His son Jacques, together with an American naval officer, Donald Walsh, established a world record by diving more than seven miles in the US bathyscaphe *Trieste* into the Marianas Trench of the Pacific Ocean in January 1960.

PICCARD, Jean Felix (1884–1963) Swiss-born American chemist, born in Basel, twin brother of **Auguste Piccard**. He took a chemical engineering degree at the Swiss Institute of Technology in 1907, subsequently held a chair at New York, and became professor emeritus of aeronautical engineering at Minnesota University. His chief interest was in exploration of the stratosphere and he designed and ascended (with his wife) in a balloon from Dearborn, Detroit, in 1934, to a height of 57 579 ft, collecting valuable data concerning cosmic rays.

PICCAVER, Alfred (1884–1958) English tenor, born in Long Sutton. He studied in New York, made his début in Prague (1907) and was the leading tenor at Vienna (1910–37), singing **Beethoven**, **Wagner**, **Verdi** and **Puccini** roles. He taught in Vienna from 1955.

PICCINNI, Niccola (1728–1800) Italian composer, born in Bari. He wrote over a hundred operas as well as oratorios and church music. In 1766 he was summoned to Paris, and became the representative of the party opposed to **Gluck**.

PICCOLOMINI an old Italian family, who obtained possession of the duchy of Amalfi. It produced numerous *littérateurs* and warriors, one pope, Eneo Silvio or Aeneas Silvius (**Pius II**), and several cardinals. Ottavio, Duke of Amalfi (1599–1656), entered the Spanish service and, sent to aid the emperor **Ferdinand II**, fought against the Bohemians (1620), in the Netherlands, and against **Wallenstein**'s army at Lützen (1632), and contributed to the fall of Wallenstein. He won great distinction at Nördingen (1634), and next year was sent to aid the Spaniards in the Netherlands to drive out the French. In 1640 he stopped the advance of the Swedes for a time, but he was worsted by them in Silesia. In 1643 he commanded the Spanish armies in the Netherlands, and after the peace of Westphalia (1648) was created field marshal. His son Max, who figures in **Schiller**'s *Wallenstein*, is a poetical fiction.

PICHEGRU, Charles (1761–1804) French soldier, born in Arbois, a labourer's son. He enlisted in 1783, and by 1793 was a general of division. With **Hoche**, he drove back the Austrians and overran the Palatinate; then defeating the Austrians at Fleurus in 1794, he continued the struggle into the winter, and entered Amsterdam in 1795. Recalled by the Thermiodorians, he crushed an insurrection in Paris, and next took Mannheim. But at the height of his fame he sold himself to the **Bourbons** and, by deliberately remaining inactive, allowed **Jourdan** to be defeated. The Directory superseded him with **Moreau**. In 1797 he became president of the council of Five Hundred, and continued his Bourbon intrigues, but was arrested and deported to Cayenne. Escaping next year, he made his way to London, and thereafter lived in Germany and England until the Bourbon conspiracy of **Cadoudal** for the assassination of **Napoleon III**. The pair reached Paris but were betrayed, and Pichegru was lodged in the Temple prison, where he was later found strangled in bed.

PICHON, Stéphen Jean Marie (1857–1933) French statesman and journalist, born in Arnay-le-Duc in Burgundy. He served on **Clemenceau**'s paper *La Justice* before entering the Chamber of Deputies in 1885. Sent in turn as minister to Port-au-Prince, San Domingo, Rio de Janeiro, Peking and Tunis, he represented the powers in negotiations with China during the Boxer Rebellion. He became minister of foreign affairs twice, in 1906 and again from 1917 to 1920, when he joined *Le Petit Journal* as its political editor.

PICK, Frank (1878–1941) English administrator and design patron, born in Spalding. A solicitor by training, he joined the London Underground Electric Railways in 1906 as assistant to the general manager, and was promoted rapidly, becoming vice-chairman of the London passenger transport board from 1933 to 1940. It was his vision which transformed London Transport into the model, unified, modern system that it became. A founder-member of the Design and Industries Association, he employed some of the best artistic and design talents available; among them the architect Charles Holden, the sculptors **Eric Gill** and **Jacob Epstein**, and graphic artists such as **E McKnight Kauffer**.

PICKEN, Ebenezer (1769–1816) Scottish poet, born in Paisley. A teacher in Edinburgh, he published several volumes of Scots poems and a *Pocket Dictionary of the Scottish Dialect* (1818).

PICKERING, Edward Charles (1846–1919) American astronomer, born in Boston, brother of **William Henry Pickering**. Educated at Harvard, he became professor of physics at the Massachusetts Institute of Technology. In 1876 he was appointed professor of astronomy and director of the observatory at Harvard, where his work was concerned with stellar photometry and classification of spectra of the stars. He invented the meridian photometer.

PICKERING, Sir George (1904–80) English clinician who pioneered the study of blood pressure. Born in Whalton, Northumberland, he came to medicine through a natural sciences degree in Cambridge. He pursued clinical training at St Thomas's Hospital and spent eight years with Sir **Thomas Lewis** at University College Hospital in London. Lewis infused in him a love of clinical research which Pickering put into practice, first at St Mary's Hospital and, from 1956, as Regius professor of medicine at Oxford. He did important experimental work on the mechanism of pain in peptic ulcer, and on the physiological causes and epidemiology of high blood pressure in human populations. He was a key figure in medical education in Britain from the 1950s, and wrote widely on historical and cultural issues.

PICKERING, William (1796–1854) English publisher. He set up his own business in London in 1820, and became known by his 'Diamond Classics' (1821–31) and his 'Aldine' edition of the English poets.

PICKERING, William Henry (1858–1938) American astronomer, born in Boston, brother of **Edward Charles Pickering**. In 1919 he discovered Phoebe, the 9th satellite of Saturn. He was in charge of an observation station at Arequipa, Peru and from 1900 was director of a station at Mandeville, Jamaica.

PICKFORD, Mary, née **Gladys Mary Smith** (1893–1979) Canadian-born American actress, born in Toronto. She first appeared on the stage at the age of five, and in 1909 made her first film, *The Violin Maker of Cremona*, directed by **D W Griffith**. Her beauty and ingenuous charm soon won her the title of 'The World's Sweetheart' and her many successful films include *Rebecca of Sunnybrook Farm* (1917), *Poor Little Rich Girl* (1917) and *The Taming of the Shrew* (1929). She made her first talkie, *Coquette*, in 1929 and retired from the screen in 1933. She founded United Artists Film Corporation in 1919. Her second husband was **Douglas Fairbanks Jr** (1920–35).

PICO DELLA MIRANDOLA, Giovanni, Comte (1463–94) Italian philosopher and humanist, born in Mirandola, Ferrara. He studied in Italy and France, and settled later in Florence, where he came under the influence of **Ficino**. In 1486 in Rome he wrote his *Conclusiones*, offering to dispute his 900 theses on logic, ethics, theology, mathematics and the *Kabbala* against all-comers, but the debate was forbidden by the pope (Innocent VIII) on the grounds that many of the theses were heretical, and he suffered persecution until Pope **Alexander VI** finally absolved him in 1493. He wrote various Latin epistles and elegies, a series of florid Italian sonnets, *Heptaplus* (1490, a mystical interpretation of the Genesis creation myth), and some important philosophical works including *De ente et uno* (1492, an attempt to reconcile Platonic and Aristotelian ontological doctrines) and *De hominis dignitate oratio* (1486, on freewill).

PICTET, Marcus Auguste (1752–1825) Swiss physicist. He published results of researches on heat (1790).

PICTET, Raoul (1846–1929) Swiss chemist and physicist, professor at Geneva and Berlin. He is known for his liquefaction of oxygen, hydrogen and carbon dioxide.

PICTON, Sir Thomas (1758–1815) English soldier, born in Poyston, Pembrokeshire. He entered the army in 1771. In 1794 he went out to the West Indies, took part in the conquest of several of the islands and was appointed (1797) governor of Trinidad, in 1801 becoming general. In 1803 he was superseded, but immediately after appointed commandant of Tobago. He returned, however, to England to face trial for having permitted, under the old Spanish laws, a female prisoner to be tortured. He was found technically guilty (1806), but on appeal was acquitted. He saw active service again in the Walcheren expedition (1809), and was made governor of Flushing. In 1810 he went to Spain, and in command of the 'Fighting Division' rendered brilliant service at Busaco, Fuentes de Oñoro, Ciudad Rodrigo, Badajoz, Vittoria, the battles of the Pyrenees, Orthez and Toulouse. He was seriously wounded at Quatre Bras, and fell leading his men to the charge at Waterloo.

PIECK, Wilhelm (1876–1960) East German politician. Born near Berlin, the son of a labourer, he initially worked as a carpenter and was active from an early age in socialist politics. In 1915 he helped found the Spartacus League and in 1918 the German Communist party (KPD), leading the unsuccessful 'Spartacus uprising' in Berlin in 1919. During the Weimar Republic, Pieck was elected as a communist to the Reichstag in 1928, but was forced into exile in 1933 when **Hitler** came to power. He fled to Moscow where he became, in 1935, secretary of the Comintern. In 1945 he returned to Berlin in the wake of the Red Army and founded, in 1946, the dominant Socialist Unity party (SED). From 1949 he served as president of the German Democratic Republic, the post being abolished on his death.

PIERCE, Franklin (1804–69) 14th president of the USA, born in Hillsborough, New Hampshire. He studied law, and was admitted to the bar in 1827. From 1829 to 1833 he was a member of the state legislature, and for two years speaker; he was then elected to congress as a Jacksonian Democrat, and in 1837 to the US senate. As a leader of his party, he advocated the annexation of Texas with or without slavery, and—after his opponents, the Whigs and Freesoilers, had been victorious in 1846—volunteered for the Mexican War and was made brigadier-general. In 1852 Pierce was nominated as a compromise candidate for the presidency against Scott Winfield, the Whig nominee, and elected. He defended slavery and the fugitive slave law. The events of his administration were the treaty for reciprocity of trade with the British American colonies, the treaty with Japan, the filibustering expeditions of

Walker to Nicaragua and of others to Cuba, and, especially, the repeal of the Missouri Compromise and the passing of the Kansas-Nebraska Act, which kindled a flame that ultimately led to the Civil War. The unpopularity of this act led to his enforced retirement from politics in 1857.

PIERCE, John Robinson (1910–) American electrical engineer, born in Des Moines, Iowa. He graduated at the California Institute of Technology and worked in the Bell Telephone Laboratories from 1936 to 1971, when he returned to CIT as professor of engineering. A man of wide scientific interests, he made important discoveries in the fields of microwaves, radar and pulse-code modulation. In the 1950s he was one of the first to see the possibilities of satellite communication, taking a leading part in the development work that resulted in the launch of *Echo* in 1960 and *Telstar* in 1962. He has published many books and technical papers as well as works of science fiction.

PIERO DELLA FRANCESCA (c.1420–1492) Italian painter, born in the provincial town of Borgo San Sepolcro. He also worked in Urbino, Ferrara, Florence and Rome, but by 1442 he was a town councillor at Borgo. A number of influences can be seen in his work, notably **Domenico Veneziano**, his teacher, but also **Masaccio**, **Alberti** and **Uccello**. As a scientist and mathematician he developed a very precise and geometric attitude towards composition, which he wrote about in his treatise *On Perspective in Painting*. Complementing this is a subtle use of pale colour and a concern for proportion and scale. **Perugino** and **Signorelli** were both pupils of his and through them his influence extends to the entire Italian school. In his own lifetime Piero was overshadowed by his more fashionable contemporaries but during this century his work has become the favourite from this period. His major work is a series of frescoes illustrating *The Legend of the True Cross* in the choir of San Francesco at Arezzo, painted 1452–66. An unfinished *Nativity* in the London National Gallery shows some Flemish influence.

PIERO DI COSIMO, properly **Piero di Lorenzo** (1462–1521) Florentine painter. He was a pupil of Cosimo Rosselli, whose name he adopted. His later style was influenced by **Signorelli** and **Leonardo da Vinci**, and among his best-known works are *Perseus and Andromeda* and *The Death of Procris*.

PIERRE, Abbé, properly **Grouès, Henri Antoine** (1912–) French priest, born in Lyon. He served with distinction during World War II and became a member of the Resistance movement in 1942. Elected deputy in the constituent assembly after the war, he resigned in 1951 to concentrate on helping the homeless of Paris. Forming his band of Companions of Emmaus, he provided, with little monetary assistance, at least a minimum of shelter for hundreds of families and finally secured the aid of the French government in dealing with this problem.

PIETRO See **PETER**

PIGALLE, Jean Baptiste (1714–85) French sculptor, born in Paris. Extremely popular in his day, he was patronized by **Louis XV** and **Madame de Pompadour**. His works include a statue of Voltaire and the tomb of Marshal Maurice de Saxe in Strasbourg. His *Vénus, l'Amour et l'Amitié* is in the Louvre.

PIGGOTT, Lester Keith (1935–) English jockey, the most brilliant and controversial since World War II, born in Wantage into a family steeped in racing tradition. Appearing aloof and severe, partly due to imperfect hearing and a speech impediment, champion jockey in England on eleven occasions, he rode his first winner in 1948, and within two years was eleventh on the list of top British jockeys. A bold rider, he frequently came into conflict with the stewards of the Jockey Club, and received various suspensions and fines. From 1955 to 1966 he had an extremely successful partnership with Noel Murless. He became officially freelance in 1967. At five feet nine inches, Piggott was known as the 'the Long Fellow', and had to waste rigorously to make the weight. In all he rode 29 Classic winners, including nine Derbies. Many of his greatest successes came on horses trained by **Vincent O'Brien**. Retiring from riding he became a trainer, but he was tried for tax irregularities (1987) and sentenced to three years' imprisonment. He was released on parole after one year, and resumed his career as a trainer.

PIGNON, Edouard (1905–) French painter, born in Marles-les-Mines. He was much influenced by the Cubists and by **Villon**. Many of his pictures are studies of miners—eg, the *Mineur mort* (1952)—and of harvest scenes and peasants.

PIGOTT, Richard (c.1828–1889) Irish journalist and forger, born in County Meath. He became editor and proprietor of *The Irishman* (1865) and two other papers of Fenian or extreme nationalist type, which he disposed of in 1881 to **Parnell** and others. Already suspected by his party, in 1886 he sold to the Irish Loyal and Patriotic Union (an anti-Home Rule organization) papers accusing Parnell of complicity in the Phoenix Park tragedy, on which were based *The Times* articles 'Parnellism and Crime' (1887). Under cross examination in court, he confessed that he had forged the more important papers, fled, and shot himself in Madrid.

PIJPER, Willem (1894–1947) Dutch composer, born in Zeist, one of the foremost of modern composers of the Netherlands. He taught at Amsterdam Conservatory, and wrote symphonies and other orchestral pieces and an opera, *Halewijn*.

PIKE, Kenneth Lee (1912–) American linguist, born in Woodstock, Connecticut. After graduating in theology in 1933, he became involved in linguistic studies through the Summer Institute of Linguistics whose purpose is to study previously unwritten languages with the aim of producing translations of the Bible in them. Between 1948 and 1979, he was first associate professor, then professor, of linguistics at the University of Michigan at Ann Arbor. He developed the system of linguistic analysis known as tagmemics. Among his many books are *Phonetics* (1943), *Phonemics* (1947), *Tone Languages* (1948), and *Language in Relation to a Unified Theory of the Structure of Human Behavior* (1954–60).

PILATE, Pontius (d.c.36) Roman procurator of Judaea and Samaria, from 26 to 36 AD. In his time **Jesus** suffered. Under his rule there were many uprisings, and at length **Vitellius** sent him to Rome to answer to the emperor **Tiberius** (36 AD) on charges of rapacity and cruelty. **Eusebius** says that Pilate committed suicide; others say he was banished to Vienna Allobrogum (*Vienne*), or beheaded under **Nero**. Tradition makes him (or his wife) accept Christianity, and associates him with Pilatus in Switzerland. The so-called *Acts of Pilate* are utterly unauthentic.

PILBEAM, David Roger (1940–) English physical anthropologist, born in Brighton. He trained at Cambridge and Yale, and became professor at Harvard. A leading student of human and primate evolution, his many publications include *Evolution of Man* (1970) and *The Ascent of Man* (1972).

PILE, Sir Frederick Alfred (1884–1976) English soldier. In World War I he won the DSO and the MC, and throughout World War II commanded Britain's anti-aircraft defences. In 1945 he was appointed director-general of the ministry of works.

PILKINGTON, Sir Lionel Alexander Bethune (Sir Alastair) (1920–) English inventor. Educated at Trinity College, Cambridge, he joined the family firm of glass-makers and in 1952 conceived the idea of float glass as a method of manufacturing plate glass without having to grind it to achieve a satisfactory finish. He led the team which, after seven years' work, successfully introduced the new technique of pouring glass straight from the furnace on to the surface of a bath of molten tin; it floats while cooling, the mirror-perfect surface of the tin giving to the glass a similarly perfect finish allied to an extremely uniform thickness and an absence of defects.

PILNYAK, Boris, real name **Boris Andreyevich Vogau** (1894–?1938) Russian author. He wrote novels and short stories including *The Naked Year* (1922) and *The Volga Flows Down to the Caspian Sea* (1930; trans 1932). His main theme was the effect of the Revolution on the middle classes in Russia. He was arrested in 1938 and is thought to have died shortly after.

PILON, Germain (1537–90) French sculptor, born in Paris. Among his works are the statues of **Henry II** and **Catherine de' Medici** at St Denis, the 'Virgin' in St Paul de Louis in Paris and the bronze Cardinal René de Biraque in the Louvre. In these, in contrast with his earlier more conventional work, such as 'The Three Graces', his keen feeling for and observation of nature have produced figures which are both more realistic and more emotional. He also produced skilful medals, especially of the French royal family.

PILOTY, Karl von (1836–86) German painter, born in Munich. He became head of a new Munich school of painters, in 1856 professor of painting at the Munich Academy, and in 1874 director. A pronounced realist, his finest pictures belong to the class of historical genre. Most have melancholy subjects.

PILPAY See **BIDPAI**

PIŁSUDSKI, Józef (1867–1935) Polish soldier and statesman, born in Zulöw (Wilno). He suffered frequent imprisonment in the cause of Polish independence. In 1887 he was sent to Siberia for five years, on his return becoming leader of the Polish Socialist party and from 1894 editor of the unauthorized *Workman*. After further terms of imprisonment in Warsaw and St Petersburg he escaped to Cracow and began to form a band of troops which at the beginning of World War I fought on the side of Austria. In 1917, realizing that Poland's situation was not to be bettered by a change from Russian to Austro-German domination, he disbanded his fighting force and was imprisoned in Magdeburg by the Germans. In 1918 a republic was set up in Poland with Piłsudski as its provisional president. In 1919, now a marshal, he led an army in a struggle to establish Poland's frontiers, but was driven back in 1920 by the Bolshevik army. In 1921 he went into retirement owing to disagreement with the government which he returned to overthrow in 1926, becoming minister of war and later premier. His reforms in the constitution produced in Poland a dictatorship which prevailed until his death. Although he had resigned the premiership in 1928, he remained the real ruler of the country in his capacity of minister of war.

PINAY, Antoine (1891–) French politician, born in the Rhône department. Primarily an industrialist and very successful mayor of the town of St Chamond, he entered politics in 1936 as deputy, becoming senator in 1938. He was minister of transport and public works and of tourism; in 1952 became prime minister from March to December; and was minister of foreign affairs (1955–56), and of finance and economic affairs (1958–60).

PINCHBECK, Christopher (c.1670–1732) London clockmaker and toymaker. He invented the gold coloured alloy of copper and zinc, called after him, for making imitation gold watches.

PINCHBECK, Christopher (c.1710–1783) English inventor, son of **Christopher Pinchbeck**(c.1670–1732). He invented astronomical clocks, automatic pneumatic brakes, patent candle snuffers, etc.

PINCKNEY, Charles Cotesworth (1746–1825) American statesman, born in Charleston, South Carolina. He was sent to England and educated at Oxford, read law, and studied at Caen Military Academy. He afterwards settled as a barrister in Charleston. He was **Washington**'s aide-de-camp at Brandywine and Germantown, but was taken prisoner at the surrender of Charleston (1780). A member of the convention that framed the US constitution (1787), he introduced the clause forbidding religious tests. In 1796 the Directory refused to receive him as minister to France. From 1804 to 1808 he was twice Federalist candidate for the presidency.

PINCUS, Gregory Goodwin (1903–67) American physiologist, born in Woodbine, New Jersey, the man who introduced the oral contraceptive pill. Educated at Cornell, Harvard, Cambridge and Berlin, he then founded his own consultancy in experimental biology at Shrewsbury, Massachusetts. In 1951 he was influenced by the birth control campaigner **Margaret Sanger** to concentrate on reproductive biology. With John Rock and M C Chang he studied the antifertility effect of those steroid hormones which inhibit ovulation in mammals; in this way re-fertilization is prevented during pregnancy. Synthetic hormones became available in the 1950s and Pincus organized field trials of their antifertility effects in Haiti and Puerto Rico in 1954. The results were successful, and oral contraceptives (the 'pill') have since been widely used, despite concern over some side effects. Their success is a pharmaceutical rarity; synthetic chemical agents do not usually show near-100% effectiveness in a specific physiological action, or have such remarkable social effects.

PINDAR, Greek **Pindaros** (c.522–c.440 BC) Greek lyric poet, born of an old and illustrious family in Cynoscephalae near Thebes, the capital of Boeotia. He began his career as a composer of choral odes at 20 with a song of victory still extant (*Pyth.* X, written in 502 BC). He soon reached the highest rank in his profession, and composed odes for a wide range of people—for the tyrants of Syracuse and Macedon, as well as for the free cities of Greece. In his poems he gives advice and reproof as well as praise to his patrons. He wrote hymns to the gods, paeans, dithyrambs, odes for processions, mimic dancing songs, convivial songs, dirges, and odes in praise of princes. Of all these poems only fragments are extant, but his *Epinikia* or Triumphal Odes can be read in their entirety. They are divided into four books, celebrating the victories won in the Olympian, Pythian, Nemean and Isthmian games. They show the intense admiration of the Greeks for bodily prowess and beauty; such gifts come from the gods and are sacred. The groundwork of Pindar's poems consists of those legends which form the Greek religious literature, and his protest against myths dishonouring to the gods shows his pious nature.

PINDAR, Peter See **WOLCOT, John**

PINDLING, Sir Lynden Oscar (1930–) Bahamanian politician. Educated in the Bahamas and at London University, he practised as a lawycr before becoming centrally involved in politics, eventually as leader of the Progressive Liberal party (PLP). He became prime minister in 1969 and led his country to full independence, within the Commonwealth, in 1973. The PLP, under Pindling, was re-elected in 1977, 1982 and 1987.

PINEL, Philippe (1745–1826) French physician and pioneer in psychiatry, born in Languedoc. He graduated at Toulouse, worked in Montpellier and in 1793 became head of the Bicêtre, later working at the Salpêtrière. His humanitarian methods, emphasizing the psychological approach, reformed the old barbarous treatment of the insane and are contained in his great *Traité médico-philosophique sur l'aliénation mentale* (1801).

PINERO, Sir Arthur Wing (1855–1934) English playwright, born in London. He studied law, but in 1874 made his début on the stage in Edinburgh, and in 1875 joined the Lyceum company. His first play, *£200 a Year*, appeared in 1877, followed by a series of comedies. In 1893, with *The Second Mrs Tanqueray*, generally reckoned his best, he began a period of realistic tragedies which were received with enthusiastic acclamation and made him the most successful playwright of his day. He was the author of some 50 plays which included *The Squire* (1881), *The Magistrate* (1885), *Dandy Dick* (1887) and *The Profligate* (1889) from his earlier works, and from his later *The Gay Lord Quex* (1899), *His House in Order* (1906), and *Mid-Channel* (1909).

PINKERTON, Allan (1819–84) Scottish-born American detective, born in Glasgow. A cooper by trade and a Chartist, he emigrated to the USA in 1842 and settled in West Dundee, Illinois. He became a detective and deputy-sheriff in Chicago (1850). In 1852 he formed a detective agency which solved a series of train robberies. In 1861 he guarded **Abraham Lincoln** on his way to his inauguration in Washington and foiled a plot to assassinate him when his train stopped at Baltimore. He became head of the American secret service during the Civil War (1861–62). His Chicago detective agency, the first in the USA, was carried on after his death by his sons Robert and William.

PINOCHET UGARTE, Augusto (1915–) Chilean soldier and politician. He began his army career in 1933 at the age of 18 and rose to the rank of full general by 1973. He was an instructor at Chile's senior military school, the Academy of War, from 1954 to 1964, when he became deputy director. He was made commander in chief of the armed forces in 1973 and in the same year led a coup which ousted, and resulted in the death of, the Marxist president, **Salvador Allende**. Pinochet took over the presidency and ruled firmly, crushing all opposition. A man of contrasts, vain, with a passion for physical fitness, he was, despite his outward display of sternness, very much in the sway of his wife, Lucia. In 1980 he promised a return to democratic government by 1989 but in 1986, despite widespread opposition to his harsh régime, and an assassination attempt, he announced that he was considering remaining in office for another eight years, by which time he would have reached the age of 79. However a plebiscite in 1988, asking for support for his continuing in office, produced a decisive 'No'. His presidency ended in March 1990 but he retained his military command.

PINTER, Harold (1930–) English dramatist, the son of a London East End tailor of Portuguese-Jewish ancestry (da Pinta). He became a repertory actor and wrote poetry and later plays. His first London production was trounced by the critics unused to his highly personal dramatic idiom. A superb verbal acrobat, he exposes and utilizes the illogical and inconsequential in everyday talk, not to illustrate some general idea (as does **Ionesco**), but to induce an atmosphere of menace in *The Birthday Party* (1957), or of claustrophobic isolation in *The Caretaker* (1958; filmed 1963). His TV play *The Lover* (1963) won the Italia prize. Other plays include *The Collection* (TV 1961; stage 1962), *The Dwarfs* (radio 1960; stage 1963), and *The Homecoming* (1965). Filmscripts include *The Servant* (1963) and *The Pumpkin Eaters* (1964). Later plays include *No Man's Land* (1975), and *Betrayal* (1978), the story of an adulterous relationship told in reverse chronological order, since when he has not produced a full-length play. Three short pieces, under the title *Other Voices*, were shown at the National Theatre in 1982. The subsequent plays, *One for the Road* (1984), and *Mountain Language* (1988), both about 25 minutes in length, show that while he has lost none of his ability to create quickly an atmosphere of threat, his subject matter is now explicity political, *Mountain Language* being a play set in a prison camp in which the guards brutalize the inmates and their visiting relatives. More recent filmscripts include *The French Lieutenant's Woman* (1981), from the novel by **John Fowles**. He was married first (1956–80) to the actress Vivien Merchant (1929–83); in 1980 he married the writer and biographer Lady Antonia Fraser.

PINTO, Fernão Mendez (c.1510–1583) Portuguese adventurer and writer, born near Coimbra. At the age of 27 he made his way to India, and remained for 21 years in south-east Asia, leading a life of adventure, fighting pirates, trading and going on special missions to Japan or elsewhere. He returned in 1558, and wrote an extravagant account of his adventures, *Peregrinaçao* (1614; trans 1663).

PINTURICCHIO, properly **Bernardino di Betto Vagio** (1454–1513) Italian painter, born in Perugia. As assistant to **Perugino**, he helped him with the frescoes in the Sistine Chapel at Rome, and he himself painted frescoes in several Roman churches and in the Vatican Library, also in Orvieto, Siena and elsewhere. His delight in brilliant colour and ornamental detail is evident in these lavish decorative schemes.

PINZÓN, Vicente Yáñez (c.1460–c.1524) Spanish discoverer of Brazil, from a wealthy Andalusian family. He commanded the *Nina* in the first expedition of **Columbus** (1492), and his brother, Martin, commanded the *Pinta*. In 1499 he sailed on his own account, and in 1500 landed near Pernambuco on the Brazil coast, which he followed north to the Orinoco. He was made governor of Brazil by **Ferdinand V** and **Isabella of Castile**.

PIOMBO, Sebastian del, properly **Luciani** (1485–1547) Italian painter, called Del Piombo ('of the Seal') from his becoming in 1523 sealer of briefs to Pope **Clement VII**. He studied under **Giovanni Bellini** and **Giorgione**, and went to Rome about 1510, where he worked in conjunction with **Michelangelo**. In 1519 he painted his masterpiece, the *Raising of Lazarus* (now in the National Gallery, London); he was also an excellent portrait painter.

PIOZZI, or **THRALE, Mrs Hester Lynch**, née **Salusbury** (1741–1821) Welsh writer, born in Bodvel in Caernarvonshire. In 1763 she married Henry Thrale, a prosperous Southwark brewer. Dr **Samuel Johnson** in 1765 conceived an extraordinary affection for her, was domesticated in her house at Streatham Place for over 16 years, and for her sake learned to soften many of his eccentricities. Thrale also esteemed Johnson, took him to Brighton, to Wales in 1774, and to France in 1775, and made him one of his four executors. Thrale died in April 1781, after his wife had borne him twelve children, and in 1784 the brewery was sold for £135 000.

Dr Johnson began to feel himself slighted as the widow became attached to the Italian musician Gabriel Piozzi, whom she married in 1784. After extensive travels in Europe, the couple returned to England in 1787, to Streatham in 1790; soon afterwards Mrs Piozzi built Brynbella on the Clwyd, where Piozzi died in 1809. She wrote poems and published *Anecdotes of Dr Johnson* (1786) and *Letters to and from Dr Johnson* (1788).

PIPER, John (1903–) English artist, born in Epsom. In 1933 he met **Braque**, and experiments in many media, including collage, led to a representational style which grew naturally from his abstract discipline. He designed sets for the theatre and painted a series of topographical pictures, eg, the watercolours of *Windsor Castle* commissioned by the Queen from 1941 to 1942, and dramatic pictures of war damage. He designed the stained glass for Coventry Cathedral. His publications include *Brighton Aquatints* (1939) and *Buildings and Prospects* (1949).

PIPER, Otto (1891–) German theologian, born in Lichte. A student in Jena, Marburg, Paris and Göttingen, and a theological teacher at Göttingen and Münster, he fled from the Nazis in 1933 to Britain. He taught briefly in Bangor and Swansea, then moved to Princeton in 1937, where he was professor of New Testament from 1941. He advocated a 'biblical realism' which neither took Scripture literally nor ignored its teaching, but sought to be true to the writer's intentions. His books include *God in History* (1936); *The Christian Interpretation of Sex* (1941), rewritten as *The Biblical View of Sex and Marriage* (1960); and *Christian Ethics* (1970).

PIPPI See **GIULIO ROMANO**

PIPPIN See **PÉPIN**

PIRANDELLO, Luigi (1867–1936) Italian dramatist, novelist and short-story writer, born in Girgenti (Agrigento), Sicily. He studied philology at Rome and Bonn, becoming a lecturer in literature at Rome (1897–1922). After writing powerful and realistic novels and short stories, including *Il Fu Mattia Pascal* (1903) and *Si Gira* (1916), he turned to the theatre and became a leading exponent of the 'grotesque' school of contemporary drama. Among his plays are *Six Characters in Search of an Author* (1920), *Enrico IV* (1922) and *Come Tu Mi Vuoi* (1930). In 1925 he established a theatre of his own in Rome, the Teatro d'Arte, and his company took his plays all over Europe. Many of his later plays have been filmed. In 1934 he was awarded the Nobel prize for literature.

PIRANESI, Giambattista (1720–78) Italian architect and copper-engraver of Roman antiquities, born in Venice. He worked in Rome, producing innumerable etchings of the city both in ancient times and in his own day.

PIRE, (Dominiques) Georges (1910–69) Belgian Dominican priest, born in Dinant. He lectured in moral philosophy at Louvain (1937–47) and was awarded the Croix de Guerre for resistance work as priest and intelligence officer in World War II. After the war he devoted himself to helping refugees and displaced persons, and was awarded the 1958 Nobel prize for peace for his scheme of 'European villages', including the 'Anne Frank village' in Germany for elderly refugees and destitute children.

PIRENNE, Henri (1862–1935) Belgian historian of Belgium and medieval Europe. He studied medieval history at the universities of Liège, Leipzig and Berlin and also in Paris, and was professor of medieval and Belgian history at Ghent (1886–1930). He quickly developed expertise in the history of the medieval town, beginning with that of the medieval constitution of Dinant (1889), a theme culminating in *Medieval Cities* (1925). His *Economic and Social History of Medieval Europe* (1936) summarizes his life's work in this connection. His seven-volume *Histoire de Belgique* (1900–32) is his classic exposition of his country's history. During World War I he was imprisoned by the Germans (1916–18) for refusing to teach during their occupation of Belgium; while imprisoned he wrote from memory a great *History of Europe* (posthumously published, and unfinished). His other major posthumous work, *Mahomet et Charlemagne* (1937), is a challenging assertion of Arab imperialism and not Roman decline or Germanic invasion as the great break which closed medieval civilization in on itself, envisaging economic forces as the great determinant. He is at once the father of Belgian history and of medieval economic history.

PIRIE, (Douglas Alastair) Gordon (1931–) English athlete, born in Leeds. A fine middle-distance runner who at various times held the world records for 3000 metres and 5000 metres, he never produced his top form during the Olympics, and his best performance was a silver medal in the 5000 metres in Melbourne in 1956.

PIRON, Alexis (1689–1773) French poet, playwright and wit, born in Dijon. His works include the comic opera *Endriaque* (1723) and a variety of plays. Piron described himself as 'nothing, not even an Academician'.

PISANELLO, Antonio, real name **Antonio Pisano** (1395–1455) Italian court painter, born in San Visilio. The foremost draughtsman of his day, his drawings are marked by an accurate observation of reality and a naturalism which contrasts with the stylized manner of his great contemporary, **Gentile da Fabriano**. These drawings became models for later Renaissance artists. Pisanello was also the greatest medallist of his day. Unfortunately, his frescoes have all been lost except for two in Verona. His most famous picture is the *Vision of Saint Eustace*.

PISANO, Andrea (c.1270–1349) Italian sculptor, born in Pontedera. He became famous as a worker in bronze and a sculptor in marble, settling in Florence. In 1337 he succeeded **Giotto** as chief artist in the cathedral at Florence, and in 1347 became chief artist in the cathedral at Orvieto, working on reliefs and statues.

PISANO, Giovanni (c.1250–c.1320) Italian sculptor and architect, son of **Nicola Pisano**. He worked with his father on the pulpit in Siena and on the fountain in Perugia and then between 1284 and 1286 on the façade of Siena Cathedral on which were positioned a number of life-size statues which are particularly expressive. He also sculpted figures for the entrance to the Baptistery at Pisa (now in the Museo Nazionale). He made a number of free-standing Madonnas, the most famous of which is in the Arena Chapel, Padua. His style is intensely dramatic and expressive, more dynamic than that of his father. Undoubtedly the greatest sculptor of his day in the Italian Gothic tradition, his innovation pointed the way to Renaissance sculptural ideals.

PISANO, Nicola (c.1225–c.1284) Italian sculptor, architect and engineer, father of **Giovanni Pisano**. His first great work was the sculpted panels for the pulpit in the Baptistery in Pisa, finished in 1260, whose powerful dramatic composition carved in high relief makes all earlier pulpit decoration look feeble and old-fashioned. On a second pulpit, this time for the cathedral at Siena, and on the Fontana Maggiore in Perugia, he collaborated with his son. Although working in a traditional Gothic style, Nicola studied classical sculpture—in particular the Roman sarcophagi he found in the Campo Santo at Pisa—and incorporated their forms into his own work.

PISCATOR, Erwin (1893–1966) German stage director. He was the first to use the term 'epic theatre' to describe a theatre composed of short, episodic plays with political ambitions, and pioneered staging techniques using films and mechanical devices. He joined the German Communist party in 1918, and opened his own theatre in Berlin in 1926. Among his notable productions was *The Adventures of the Good Soldier Schweik*, adapted by **Brecht** from the novel by **Hašek** (1927). He was in the Soviet Union from 1933 to 1936, and went to New York in 1938, where he became head of the Dramatic Department of the New School for Social Research, and mounted several productions. In 1951 he decided to settle in West Germany, becoming director of the West Berlin new Volksbühne Theatre in 1962, where he produced a number of German plays, including **Hochhuth**'s *The Representative* (1963), and **Weiss**'s *The Investigation* (1965).

PISISTRATUS, Greek **Peisistratos** (600–527 BC) tyrant of Athens. He rose to power during the aristocratic factional struggles that followed the reforms of **Solon**. His first two bids for power (c.561 and c.556) failed against the opposition of rival aristocrats, but at length he established himself with help from supporters in other Greek states which enabled him to defeat his opponents (c.546). He curbed aristocratic factioning, enforced a period of internal peace and stability, favoured the peasantry of Attica, and was remembered as a popular ruler. At his death he transmitted his power to his sons Hippias and Hipparchus.

PISSARRO, Camille (1830–1903) French Impressionist artist, born in St Thomas, West Indies. He went in 1855 to Paris, where he was much influenced by **Corot**'s landscapes. In 1870 he lived in England for a short time, this being the first of several visits. Most of his works were painted in the countryside round Paris, and he lived in Pontoise from 1872 to 1884. In the next year he met **Signac** and **Seurat** and for the next five years adopted their Divisionist style. Pissarro was the leader of the original Impressionists, and the only one to exhibit at all eight of the Group exhibitions in Paris from 1874 to 1886. He had considerable influence on **Cézanne** and **Gauguin** at the beginning of their artistic careers. His famous painting of the *Boulevard Montmartre* by night (1897) is in the National Gallery, London.

PISSARRO, Lucien (1863–1944) French painter, designer, wood-engraver and printer, son of **Camille Pissarro**. He went to England in 1890, where he founded (1894) the Eragny press, designed types, and painted landscapes showing the Divisionist touch.

PISTON, Walter (1894–1976) American composer of Italian descent, born in Rockland, Maine. He trained as an artist, and first took a serious interest in music as a student at Harvard. He later studied in Paris under **Nadia Boulanger** and returned to Harvard as professor of music. He produced books on harmony, counterpoint and orchestration. His compositions are in a modern, neoclassical style that includes elements from jazz and popular music.

PITCAIRN, Robert (c.1745–1770) English sailor, son of a British Royal Marine officer killed at Bunker Hill in the American War of Independence. He was a midshipman on board the *Swallow* in July 1767, when he was the first to sight the island later called Pitcairn Island, which was to become the refuge of the *Bounty* mutineers (see **Fletcher Christian**).

PITCAIRN, Robert (1793–1855) Scottish writer and antiquary, born in Edinburgh. He was the editor of *Criminal Trials in Scotland, 1484–1624* (1830–33). He held a post in the Register House at Edinburgh.

PITCAIRNE, Archibald (1652–1713) Scottish physician and satirist, born in Edinburgh. He practised medicine there before being appointed professor at Leiden (1692). Returning to Edinburgh in 1693, he was notorious as a Jacobite, an Episcopalian and satirist of Presbyterianism. He founded the medical faculty at Edinburgh and his medical writings appeared in 1701 under the title *Dissertationes medicae*.

PITMAN, Benjamin (1822–1910) English educationist and pioneer of shorthand in the USA, brother of Sir **Isaac Pitman**. In 1852 he was sent to the USA by his brother to teach his shorthand system there, and established the Phonographic Institute in Cincinnati (1853). He invented an electrochemical process of relief engraving (1855), and taught at Cincinnati Art School from 1873.

PITMAN, Sir Isaac (1813–97) English educationist and inventor of a shorthand system, born in Trowbridge, Wiltshire, brother of **Benjamin Pitman**. First a clerk, he became a schoolmaster at Barton-on-Humber (1832–36) and at Wotton-under-Edge, where he issued his *Stenographic Sound Hand* (1837). Dismissed from Wotton because he had joined the New (Swedenborgian) church, he established a Phonetic Institute for teaching shorthand in Bath (1839–43). In 1842 he brought out the *Phonetic Journal*, and in 1845 opened premises in London.

PITOT, Henri (1695–1771) French hydraulic and civil engineer, born in Aramon in the Languedoc. He had little formal education but was fortunate in making the acquaintance of the great physicist **Réaumur** whose laboratory assistant he became in 1723. He developed a particular interest in hydraulic engineering, was appointed superintendent of the Canal du Midi and constructed an aqueduct for the water supply of Montpellier. In 1730 he invented the device now known as the Pitot tube, by means of which the relative velocity of a fluid past the orifice of the tube may be measured.

PITSCOTTIE, Lindsay Robert of (c.1532–1580) Scottish historian, born in Pitscottie near Cupar. He was the author of *The Historie and Cronicles of Scotland*, extending from 1436–1575. His style is quaint and graphic, but his facts trustworthy, except where he deals in marvels.

PITT, Thomas (1653–1726) English merchant, son of the rector of Blandford. He became a wealthy East India merchant, governor of Madras, and purchaser for £20 400 of the Pitt Diamond, which he sold in 1717 to the French regent to become one of the state jewels of France. In 1791 it was valued at £480 000. His eldest son, Robert, was father of the Earl of **Chatham**; his second, Thomas (c.1688–1729), was first Earl of Londonderry.

PITT, William 'the Younger' (1759–1806) English statesman, second son of the Earl of **Chatham**, born in Hayes near Bromley. Because of early ill health, he did not attend school and was educated at home, being able to translate Latin and Greek at the age of 11. When he reached 14 his condition had improved sufficiently for him to go to Pembroke Hall, Cambridge, where he graduated at the age of 17. He was called to the bar in 1780 but clearly saw his career in the political field. He failed to win a seat at Cambridge on his first attempt but was elected for Appleby in 1781. He joined the opposition to Lord **North** and soon made his mark as an orator. At the age of 22 he declined a junior post under **Rockingham**, reserving himself for greater things, and a year later became Chancellor of the Exchequer and leader of the Commons in **Shelburne**'s ministry, usurping **Charles James Fox**, who then became his bitter rival. When Shelburne resigned in 1783 the king offered Pitt the premiership but he declined, leaving it to the Duke of Portland (**William Cavendish Bentinck**). However, when Portland's government collapsed in December of the same year, Pitt decided to accept the challenge and, at the age of 24, became Britain's youngest prime minister. The youthful leader and his newly-formed administration were derided by more experienced politicians, and particularly by Fox, who said that it would not last for more than a few weeks. In the event, it continued for 17 years. Pitt had clear ideas of what he wished to achieve. He wanted good relations with America, union with Ireland, a reduction in the national debt, reform of parliament, and reorganization of the East India Company. He did not achieve all his aims but, despite his inexperience and fierce opposition from Fox, made considerable progress. He established a sinking fund to reduce the national debt, passed the India Act of 1784 to establish dual control of the East India Company, effected a division between the French and English through the Canada Act of 1791, and achieved union with Ireland in 1800. In 1801 the king refused to approve his Bill to emancipate the Catholics and Pitt resigned in protest, but within three years, with **Napoleon** planning to invade England, he was persuaded to return, despite failing health. He formed a coalition with Russia, Austria and Sweden, and the French were defeated at Trafalgar (1805). Pitt was hailed as the saviour of Europe. His words of reply became immortal: 'England has saved herself by her exertions, and will, I trust, save Europe by her example.' He was dismayed when the coalition he had formed broke up and Napoleon triumphed against the Russians and Austrians at Austerlitz in 1805. He died nearly ten years before Napoleon's final defeat at Waterloo. Although Pitt was a popular national figure his private life was comparatively sad and lonely. He had no close friends and did not marry. He died so heavily in debt that the House of Commons raised £40000 to pay off his creditors.

PITT, William, 'the Elder' See **CHATHAM**

PITT-RIVERS, Augustus Henry Lane-Fox (1827–1900) English soldier and archaeologist, born in Yorkshire. Educated at Sandhurst, he worked to improve army small arms training and was a promoter of the Hythe school of musketry, ultimately becoming a lieutenant-general (1882). Having in 1880 inherited Wiltshire estates, rich in Romano-British and Saxon remains, from his great-uncle, Lord Rivers, he devoted himself to archaeology, evolving a new scientific approach to excavation which became a model for later workers. His collections were presented to Oxford museum. He became the first inspector of ancient monuments in 1882.

PITTACUS OF MITYLENE (650–570 BC) Greek ruler, one of the Seven Wise Men of Greece. His experience, according to the ancients, was embodied in 'Know thine opportunity' and other aphorisms.

PITTER, Ruth (1897–) English poet, born in Ilford, Essex, the daughter of a schoolmaster. She wrote verse from a very early age and later was encouraged by **Hilaire Belloc**. Her writing belongs to no particular school and for inspiration she has drawn mainly upon the beauty of natural things. In 1955 she was awarded the Queen's Gold Medal for Poetry, having already won the Hawthornden Prize in 1936 with *A Trophy of Arms*. Other volumes include *First and Second Poems* (1927), *A Mad Lady's Garland* (1934), *Urania* (1951), *The Ermine* (1953), *Still by Choice* (1966) and *End of Drought* (1975).

PIUS II, named **Enea Silvio de Piccolomini** (1405–64) pope from 1458. As a youngster he wrote poems, letters and a novel. At 26 he was secretary to the bishop of Fermo at the Council of Basel, and from 1432 to 1435 was employed on missions to Scotland, England and Germany. He took office as secretary and court poet under the emperor **Frederick III**, regulated his life, took orders, was made bishop of Trieste and, after returning to Italy (1456), a cardinal. On the death of **Callixtus III** in 1458 he was elected pope, and took the name of Pius II. His reign is memorable for his vain efforts to organize an armed confederation of Christian princes to resist the Turkish army. Aeneas Sylvius was one of the most eminent scholars of his age. His works are chiefly historical; his letters throw a vivid light upon their age.

PIUS IV, named **Giovanni Angelo Medici** (1499–1565) pope from 1559, born in Milan. He became archbishop of Requsa in 1547 and cardinal in 1549, before being elected pope. He brought to a close the deliberations of the Council of Trent, and issued (1564) the Creed of Pius IV, or Tridentine Creed. He reformed the sacred college of cardinals, instituted the Index of Forbidden Books, and encouraged St **Teresa of Avila**. A notable patron of the arts, he built many public buildings and patronized **Michelangelo**.

PIUS V, St, named **Michele Ghislieri** (1504–72) pope from 1566, a Dominican friar noted for his asceticism, born near Alessandria. He became a bishop in 1556, and a cardinal in 1557. As inquisitor-general for Lombardy he rigorously repressed the Reformed doctrines. As pope he laboured to restore discipline and morality, and reduce the expenditure of his court. The bull *In Coena Domini* (1568) applied to the 16th century the principles and the legislation of **Gregory VII**. He excommunicated Queen **Elizabeth** of England in 1570, and issued a bull releasing her subjects from their allegiance, but to little effect. The most momentous event of his pontificate was the expedition which he organized, with Spain and Venice, against the Turks, resulting in the naval engagement of Lepanto (1571). He was canonized in 1712. His feast day is 6 May.

PIUS VI, named **Giovanni Angelo Braschi** (1717–99) pope from 1775, born in Cesena. He became cardinal in 1773. To him Rome owes the drainage of the Pontine Marsh, the improvement of the port of Ancona, the completion of St Peter's, the foundation of the New Museum of the Vatican, and the embellishment of the city. In the American War of Independence he released the American Catholic clergy from the jurisdiction of the vicar apostolic in England. In the 1780s he went to Vienna, but failed to restrain the reforming Emperor **Joseph** from further curtailing papal privileges. Soon after came the French Revolution and the confiscation of church property in France. The pope launched his thunders in vain, and then the murder of the French agent in Rome (1793) gave the Directory an excuse for the attack. **Napoleon** took possession of the Legations, and afterwards of the March of Ancona, and extorted (1797) the surrender of these provinces from Pius. The murder of a member of the French embassy in December was avenged by **Berthier**'s taking possession of Rome. Pius was called on to renounce his temporal sovereignty, and on his refusal was seized, carried to Siena, the Certosa, Grenoble and finally Valence, where he died.

PIUS VII, named **Luigi Barnaba Chiaramonti** (1742–1823) pope from 1800, born in Cesena. He became bishop of Tivoli, and, already a cardinal, succeeded **Pius VI**. Rome was now restored to the papal authority and next year the French troops were withdrawn from most of the papal territory. Pius restored order in his states, and in 1801 concluded a concordat with **Napoleon**, which the latter altered by autocratic *Articles organiques*. In 1804 Napoleon compelled Pius to come to Paris to consecrate him as emperor. He failed to get any modification of the articles, and soon after his return to Rome the French seized Ancona and entered Rome. This was followed by the annexation (May 1809) of the papal states to the French empire. The pope in June retaliated by excommunicating the robbers of the Holy See. Next he was removed to Grenoble, and finally to Fontainebleau, where he was forced to sign a new concordat and sanction the annexation. The fall of Napoleon (1814) allowed him to return to Rome, and the Congress of Vienna restored to him his territory. Brigandage was suppressed, as well as secret societies; while the Jesuits were restored.

PIUS IX, named **Giovanni Maria Mastai Ferretti** (1792–1878) pope from 1846, born in Sinigaglia. He took deacon's orders in 1818, in 1827 was made archbishop of Spoleto, and in 1832 bishop of Imola. In 1840 he became a cardinal, and was elected pope on the death of **Gregory XVI**. He entered at once on a course of reforms. He granted an amnesty to all political prisoners and exiles, removed most of the disabilities of the Jews, authorized railways, projected a council of state, and in March 1848 published his *Statuto Fondamentale*, a scheme for the temporal government of the papal states by two chambers, one nominated by the pope, the other (with the power of taxation) elected by the people. At first the new pope was the idol of the populace. But the revolutionary fever of 1848 spread too fast for a reforming pope, and his refusal to make war upon the Austrians finally forfeited the affections of the Romans. In 1848 his first minister, Count **Pelegrino Rossi**, was murdered, and two days later a mob assembled in the square of the Quirinal. The pope escaped to Gaeta, and a republic was proclaimed in Rome. In April 1849 a French expedition was sent to Civita Vecchia; in July General **Oudinot** took Rome after a siege of 30 days; and henceforward the papal government was re-established. Pius IX proved an unyielding conservative and Ultramontane, closely allied with the Jesuits. The war of the French and Sardinians against Austria in 1859 and the popular vote of 1860 incorporated a great part of papal territory with the Sardinian (Italian) kingdom; but Pius always refused to recognize the fact. He re-established the hierarchy in England, sanctioned a Catholic University in Ireland, and condemned the Queen's Colleges. He concluded a reactionary concordat with Austria. By the bull *Ineffabilis Deus* (1854) he decreed the Immaculate Conception; his famous encyclical *Quanta Cura* and the *Syllabus of Errors*, appeared in 1864. The Vatican Council (1869–79) proclaimed the infallibility of the pope. For the last ten years the pope's temporal power had only been maintained by the French garrison; on its withdrawal in 1870 the soldiers of **Victor Emmanuel II** entered Rome. For the rest of his days the pope lived a voluntary 'prisoner' within the Vatican.

PIUS X, named **Giuseppe Sarto** (1835–1914) born in Riese near Venice. Ordained in 1858, he became bishop of Mantua in 1884, in 1893 cardinal and patriarch of Venice and in 1903 was elected pope. He condemned theological modernism in 1907 in his encyclical *Pascendi*, and revolutionary movements, but was a champion of social reforms (especially in the Catholic Action movement). He reformed the liturgy, re-codified canon law, and was canonized in 1954.

PIUS XI, named **Achille Ratti** (1857–1939) pope from 1922, born in Desio near Milan. He was ordained in 1879. Holder of three doctorates, he was papal nuncio to Poland, archbishop of Lepanto, and cardinal archbishop of Milan in 1921. He consolidated the church's role in post-World War I years, gained independence for the Vatican State through the Lateran Treaty with **Mussolini** (1929), but later condemned Fascism (1931) as well as Nazism (1937) and Communism (1937). He broke new ground by appointing six Chinese bishops, improved the Vatican's strained relations with France, and clarified the basis for Catholic school education.

PIUS XII, named **Eugenio Pacelli** (1876–1958) pope from 1939, born in Rome. He distinguished himself in the papal diplomatic service and as secretary of state to the Holy See before succeeding **Pius XI**. During World War II under his leadership the Vatican did much humanitarian work, notably for prisoners of war and refugees. There has been continuing controversy, however, over his attitude to the treatment of the Jews in Nazi Germany critics arguing that he could have used his influence with Catholic Germany to prevent the massacres, others that any attempt to do so would have proved futile and might possibly have worsened the situation. In the post-war years the plight of the persecuted churchmen in the communist countries, and the fate of Catholicism there, became the Pope's personal concern. Pius XII was widely respected both in the Catholic and non-Catholic world as a distinguished scholar and as a man of immense moral authority.

PIZARRO, Francisco (c.1478–1541) Spanish conqueror of Peru, born in Trujillo. He served under Gonsalvo di Cordova in Italy, in 1509 he was in Darien, and he served under **Balboa** when he discovered the Pacific. In 1526 Pizarro and **Diego de Almagro** sailed for Peru and, after many misadventures and delays, they reached its port of Tumbes, where they collected full information about the empire of the Incas. Pizarro returned to Spain for authority to undertake the conquest, which he received in 1529, being made captain-general and Almagro marshal. He sailed again from Panamá in 1531, with 183 men and 37 horses; Almagro was to follow with reinforcements. Landing at Tumbes, the Spaniards began the march inland in May 1532, and in November entered Cajamarca. Near this, Pizarro captured the Inca **Atahualpa** by treachery, and after extorting an enormous ransom, amounting to £3 500 000, put him to death (1533). Pizarro then marched to Cuzco, set up the young Inca Manco as nominal sovereign, and was himself created a marquis by the Emperor **Charles V**. Almagro undertook the conquest of Chile, Pizarro was busy founding Lima and other cities on the coast, and his brothers were at Cuzco, when an Indian insurrection broke out. Both Cuzco and Lima were besieged, and Juan Pizarro was killed, but in the spring of 1537 Almagro returned from Chile, raised the siege of Cuzco, and took possession of the city. Pizarro had no intention of allowing his rival to retain Cuzco. Too old to take the field himself, he entrusted the command of his forces to his brothers, who defeated Almagro soon afterwards. One of Almagro's followers, named Juan de Rada, matured a conspiracy for the assassination of Pizarro. The conspirators attacked his house in Lima, and murdered him. His brother, Hernando Pizarro, for having beheaded Almagro at Cuzco, was imprisoned until 1560 on his return to Spain.

PIZARRO, Gonzalo (c.1506–1548) Spanish conquistador, half-brother of **Francisco Pizarro**. He accompanied him in the conquest of Peru, and did good service when the Indians besieged Cuzco (1535–36), and in the conquest of Charcas. In 1539 he undertook an expedition to the east of Quito, and endured fearful hardships. One of his lieutenants, **Francisco de Orellana**, sent in advance for supplies, deserted his starving comrades, discovered the whole course of the Amazon, and returned to Spain. Only 90 out of 350 Spaniards returned with Gonzalo in June 1542. On his brother's assassination (1541) Gonzalo retired to Charcas. In 1544 the new viceroy, Vela, arrived in Peru to enforce the 'New Laws'. The Spaniards, dismayed, entreated Gonzalo to protect their interests. He mustered 400 men, entered Lima in October 1544, and was declared governor of Peru; the viceroy Vela was defeated and killed in battle (1546). When news of this revolt reached Spain, Pedro de la Gasca, an able ecclesiastic, was sent to Peru as president to restore order, and landed at Tumbes in June 1547. Gonzalo Pizarro defeated a force sent against him, and met Gasca near Cuzco in April 1548. But his forces deserted him, and he gave himself up and was beheaded.

PIZZETTI, Ildebrando (1880–1968) Italian composer, born in Parma. The son of a piano teacher, he studied at Parma Conservatory, and in 1908 became professor of harmony and counterpoint at the Instituto Musicale, Florence. He was director there from 1917 to 1924, when he became director of the Guiseppe Verdi Conservatory, Milan. He won a high reputation as an opera composer with *Fedra* (1912) and *Debora e Jaele* (1923), and in 1936 he succeeded **Ottorino Respighi** as professor of composition at the Accademia di Sancta Cecilia, Rome. He composed extensively in all forms.

PLACE, Francis (1771–1854) English radical and reformer, born in London. A self-educated tailor, he was a champion of radicalism and the right of forming trade unions, and contrived the repeal of the anti-union Combination Acts in 1824. He was a leading figure in the agitation which brought about the passing of the Reform Bill in 1832. Drafter of the People's Charter, and a pioneer of birth-control study, he wrote *The Principle of Population* (1822).

PLANCHÉ, James Robinson (1796–1880) English playwright, antiquary and herald, born in London of Huguenot ancestry. He was a prolific writer of burlesque and extravaganzas, such as *Amoroso, King of Little Britain* (1818), *Success; or, a Hit if you like it* (1825) and *High, Low, Jack and the Game* (1833). He wrote the libretto for **Weber**'s *Oberon*. As a heraldic scholar he wrote *History of British Costumes* (1834) and other works. He was appointed Somerset Herald in 1866.

PLANCK, Max Karl Ernst (1858–1947) German theoretical physicist, born in Kiel, the formulator of the quantum theory which revolutionized physics. He studied at Munich and under **Gustav Kirchhoff** and **Hermann von Helmholtz** at Berlin, where he succeeded the former in the professorship (1889–1926). His work on the law of thermodynamics and black body radiation led him to abandon classical dynamical principles and formulate the quantum theory (1900), which assumed energy changes to take place in violently abrupt instalments or quanta. This successfully accounted for and predicted certain phenomena inexplicable in the Newtonian theory. **Albert Einstein**'s application of the quantum theory to light (1905) led to the theories of relativity and in 1913 **Niels Bohr** successfully applied it to the problems of subatomic physics. He was awarded the Nobel prize for physics (1918). One of his sons, Erwin, was executed in 1944 for plotting against **Hitler**.

PLANQUETTE, Robert (1850–1903) French composer, born in Paris. Educated at the Paris Conservatoire, he composed *Paul Jones* (1889) and other highly successful light operas.

PLANTAGENET a surname applied to the Angevin family which in 1154 succeeded to the throne of England in the person of **Henry II**. *Plante-geneste* was the nickname of Geoffrey, Count of Anjou, husband of **Matilda**, daughter of **Henry I**—possibly from the sprig of broom (*planta genista*) which he wore in his cap, possibly because he used a broom-switch in penance, possibly from the village of Le Genest in Maine. The first to use *Plantaginet* (*sic*) as his family name was Richard, Duke of **York**, in 1460, in laying claim to the crown. But the sovereigns called Plantagenet kings are **Henry II**, **Richard I**, **John**, **Henry III**, **Edward I–III**, **Richard II**, **Henry IV–VI**, **Edward IV-V** and **Richard III**.

PLANTÉ, Gaston (1834–89) French physicist, born in Orthy. Professor in Paris from 1860, he followed up **Johann Ritter**'s discovery of the secondary cell and constructed the first practical storage battery (1860).

PLANTIN, Christophe (1514–89) French printer, born in St Avertin near Tours. He settled as a bookbinder in Antwerp in 1549 and six years later he began to print. His *Biblia Polyglotta* (1569–73), his Latin, Hebrew and Dutch Bibles, and his editions of the classics are all famous. His printing-houses in Antwerp, Leiden and Paris were carried on by his sons-in-law. His office in Antwerp, bought by the city in 1876, is now the 'Musée Plantin'.

PLANTINGA, Alvin (1932–) American philosopher of religion, born in Ann Arbor, Michigan. A professor at Calvin College, Grand Rapids (1963–82) and the University of Notre Dame, Indiana (1982–), he is concerned with philosophical questions about God, as in *Does God have a Nature*? (1980). In other books he argues that God's existence is no less probable than our own (*God and Other Minds*, 1967): it can be supported by the ontological argument (*The Nature of Necessity*, 1974), and belief in His goodness is tenable despite the fact of evil (*God, Freedom and Evil*, 1974).

PLANUDES, Maximus (c.1260–1310) Greek Orthodox monk of Constantinople. He established a lay school there that became famous for its scholarship. He published theological works, and translations of classical authors.

PLASKETT, John Stanley (1865–1941) Canadian astronomer, born in Woodstock, Ontario. At the Dominion Observatory, Ottawa, his work included research in spectroscopy and improvements in the design of the spectrograph. In 1918 the Dominion astrophysical observatory was built at Victoria to accommodate a huge telescope with a 72-inch reflector which he had designed. He was director there until he retired in 1935. During these years important investigations were carried out into motion and matter in interstellar space, and results included the discovery of the largest known star, which was named Plaskett's star.

PLATEAU, Joseph Antoine Ferdinand (1801–83) Belgian physicist, born in Brussels, professor of physics at Ghent from 1835. In his study of optics he damaged his own eyesight by looking into the sun for twenty seconds in order to find out the effect on the eye. By 1840 he was blind, but continued his scientific work with the help of others. He was the discoverer of the tiny second drop, named after him, which always follows the main drop of a liquid falling from a surface.

PLATER, Alan Frederick (1935–) English dramatist, born in Jarrow-on-Tyne. Trained as an architect, his writing was first published in *Punch* (1958) and, since 1960, he has built up an enormous body of work, both originals and adaptations, reflecting his working-class origins, political beliefs and interest in jazz. A regular writer for *Z Cars* (1963–65), his many television plays include *Ted's Cathedral* (1964), *Close the Coalhouse Door* (1968) and *The Land of Green Ginger* (1974). He is also responsible for such literate and skilled screen translations as *The Good Companions* (1980), *Fortunes of War* (1987) and *A Very British Coup* (1988). Equally prolific in other media, he has contributed to *The Guardian*, and written film scripts like *The Virgin and the Gypsy* (1969) and *Priest of Love* (1980), as well as such novels as *Misterioso* (1987) and *The Beiderbecke Affair* (1985) from his television series of the same title.

PLATH, Sylvia (1932–63) American poet, born in Boston, Massachusetts, the daughter of a German-born professor of biology and a school-teacher. Educated at Bradford High School and Smith College, where she suffered from deep depression and attempted suicide, she won a Fulbright Fellowship to Newnham College, Cambridge, in 1956, where she studied English and met and married **Ted Hughes** (1930–). After a spell of teaching in the USA they settled in England, first in London and then in Devon, but separated in 1962; a year later Sylvia committed suicide. She wrote poetry from early childhood; her first volume, *A Winter Ship* (1960), was published anonymously, but she put her name to her second volume, *The Collossus* (1960). After the birth of her second child she wrote a radio play, *Three Women* (1962), set in a maternity home. Often termed a 'confessional' poet because of the inclusion in her work of personal details about her own life and the influence of poets such as **Robert Lowell**, her earlier, highly controlled poetry gave way to an almost visionary expression and intensity, reaching its culmination in the last few days before her death. This late poetry was published posthumously in *Ariel* (1965), *Crossing the Water* (1971) and *Winter Trees* (1972). Her only novel, *The Bell Jar* (1963), about her student collapse, was published just before her death, under the pseudonym Victoria Lucas. Her *Collected Poems*, edited by Ted Hughes, were published in 1982.

PLATO (c.428–c.348 BC) Greek philosopher, indisputably one of the most important philosophers of all time and so enormously influential that **Whitehead** was able to characterize the subsequent history of Western philosophy as a series of 'footnotes to Plato'. He was the pupil (or at least the associate) of **Socrates** and the teacher of **Aristotle**, and this trio were the great figures in ancient philosophy. Plato was probably born in Athens, of a distinguished aristocratic family, but little is known of his early life. Any youthful political ambitions must have withered when his friend and mentor, Socrates, was condemned to death in 399 BC by the restored democracy in Athens. Plato immortalized the story of Socrates' trial and last days in three of his dialogues: the *Apology*, the *Crito* and the *Phaedo*, where his profound affection and respect for Socrates come through vividly. After the execution he and other disciples of Socrates took temporary refuge at Megara with the philosopher **Euclides**, and he then travelled widely in Greece, Egypt, the Greek cities in southern Italy (where he no doubt encountered Pythagoreans) and Sicily (where he made friends with **Dion**, brother-in-law of **Dionysius I**, the ruler of Syracuse). He returned to Athens in c.387 BC to found the Academy, which became a famous centre for philosophical, mathematical and scientific research, and over which he presided for the rest of his life. He visited Sicily again in 367 BC, at Dion's request, to try and train **Dionysius II** to become a philosopher-statesman, but despite a second visit in 361–60, which placed him in some personal danger, the attempt failed completely. His corpus of writings consists of some 30 philosophical dialogues and a series of *Letters*, of which the Seventh is the most important (biographically and philosophically) and only the Seventh and Eighth are likely to be genuine. The dialogues are conventionally divided into three groups—early, middle and late—though the exact relative chronology of individual dialogues is a vexed and probably insoluble problem of scholarship. The early, 'Socratic' dialogues have Socrates as the principal character, usually portrayed interrogating his unfortunate interlocutors about the definition of different moral virtues (piety in the *Euthyphro*, courage in the *Laches*, and so on); their initially confident assertions are shown to be confused and contradictory and all parties end up sharing Socrates' professed perplexity. The middle dialogues show the character 'Socrates' expressing more positive, systematic views, which are taken to be Plato's own. This group includes the most dramatic and literary of the dialogues, the *Symposium*, *Gorgias*, *Phaedo*, and *Republic*, and presents such famous Platonic doctrines as the theory of knowledge as recollection, the immortality of the soul, the tripartite division of the soul, and above all the theory of forms (or 'ideas') which contrasts the transient, material world of 'particulars' (objects merely of perception, opinion and belief) with the timeless, unchanging world of universals or forms (the true objects of knowledge). The *Republic* also describes Plato's celebrated political utopia, ruled by philosopher-kings who have mastered the discipline of 'dialectic' and studied the hierarchy of the forms, including its apex, the form of the Good. The details of this visionary state—the rigid class structure of workers, soldiers and rulers, the education of the rulers (both men and women), their communism of property and family, their totalitarian powers—have been variously idealized, attacked, misinterpreted and imitated in subsequent political theory and literature, but the *Republic* remains one of the most compelling and influential works in the history of philosophy. The third group of 'late' dialogues is generally less literary in form and represents a series of sustained and highly sophisticated criticisms of the metaphysical and logical assumptions of Plato's doctrines of the middle period. The *Parmenides*, *Theaetetus* and *Sophist* in particular have attracted the interest of contemporary analytical philosophers and contain some of Plato's most demanding and original work. Taken as a whole, his philosophy has had a pervasive and incalculable influence on almost every period and tradition, rivalled only by that of his greatest pupil Aristotle, which was its principal competitor for much of the Hellenistic period, the middle ages and the Renaissance.

PLATOV, Matvei Ivanovich, Count (1757–1818) Russian soldier, born in Azov. He served in the Turkish campaign of 1770–71, and in 1801 was named by **Alexander I** 'Hetman of the Cossacks of the Don'. He took part in the campaigns against the French (1805–07), and hung on their retreat from Moscow with pitiless pertinacity (1813), defeating **Lefebvre** at Altenburg, gaining a victory at Laon, and making his name memorable by the devastations of his hordes of semi-savages.

PLAUTUS, Titus Maccius, or **Maccus** (c.250–184 BC) Roman writer of comedies, born in Sarsina in Umbria. It is probable that he went to Rome while still young, and there learned his mastery of the most idiomatic Latin. In Rome he found employment in connection with the stage, and saved enough money to enable him to leave Rome and start in business on his own account in foreign trade. His plays show close familiarity with seafaring life and adventure, and an intimate knowledge of all the details of buying and selling and book-keeping. He failed, however, in business, and returned to Rome in such poverty that he had to earn his livelihood in the service of a baker by turning a handmill. While thus employed he wrote three plays which he sold to the managers of the public games. The money for these enabled him to leave the mill, and he spent the rest of his life in Rome. Probably he began to write about 224 BC, and, until his death, he continued to produce comedies. His plays appear to have been left in the hands of the actors, who probably interpolated and omitted passages to suit them for the stage. Almost all the prologues were written after his death. About 130 plays were attributed to him in the time of **Gellius**, who held most of them to be the work of earlier dramatists revised and improved by Plautus. Roman critics considered most of them spurious. **Varro** limited the genuine comedies to 21; and these so-called 'Varronian comedies' are those which are now extant, the *Vidularia* being fragmentary. Plautus borrowed his plots to a large extent from the New Attic Comedy, which dealt with social life to the exclusion of politics.

PLAYER, Gary (1936–) South African golfer, born in Johannesburg. Small and slightly built, he nonetheless won three British Opens (1959, 1968, 1974), the US Masters twice (1961, 1974), the US Open once (1965), and the US PGA title twice (1962, 1972). He also won the South African Open eight times, and the Australian Open six times. His fitness and skill have remained undiminished: in 1988 he won both the British and the American Seniors' Championship.

PLAYFAIR, John (1748–1819) Scottish mathematician, physicist and geologist, born in Benvie near Dundee. He studied at St Andrews University and in 1785 became joint professor of mathematics at Edinburgh, but in 1805 he exchanged his chair for that of natural philosophy. He was a strenuous supporter of the Huttonian theory in geology, and travelled widely to make geological observations. His *Illustrations of the Huttonian Theory* (1802) was a landmark in British geological writing.

PLAYFAIR, Lyon, 1st Baron Playfair (1819–98) Scottish scientist, born in India at Meerut. He studied at St Andrews, Glasgow, London and Giessen, was manager of textile-printing works at Clitheroe (1840–43), professor of chemistry at Edinburgh (1858–68), and Liberal MP from 1868. He wrote on chemistry and political economy and education.

PLAYFAIR, Sir Nigel Ross (1874–1934) English actor-manager and producer, born in London. After a career as a barrister, he went on the stage and from 1902 to 1918 was a successful character actor. In 1919 he became manager of the Lyric Theatre, Hammersmith, and was responsible for a long series of successful productions, many of which were drawn from 18th-century comedy. One of the most outstanding of these was *The Beggar's Opera*, and others included *The Duenna* and *The Rivals*. He wrote *The Story of the Lyric Theatre, Hammersmith* (1925) and *Hammersmith Hoy* (1930).

PLAYFAIR, William Henry (1789–1857) Scottish architect, born in London, nephew of **John Playfair**. He was brought up in Edinburgh and designed many of Edinburgh's most prominent buildings including the National Gallery of Scotland, the Royal Scottish Academy, the National Monument on Calton Hill, Surgeon's Hall and Donaldson's Hospital.

PLAYFORD, Sir Thomas (1896–1981) Australian politician, born in Norton Summit, South Australia. He served with the Australian Imperial Forces during World War I at Gallipoli and in France. In 1933 he was elected to the South Australian House of Assembly, entering the ministry in March 1938 and becoming premier of South Australia in November the same year, a position which he was to hold until March 1965. His grandfather, Thomas Playford (1837–1915), was premier of South Australia between 1887 and 1892, and was a senator in the first federal government between 1901 and 1906.

PLEASANCE, Donald (1919–) English stage and film actor, born in Worksop. He made his first appearance in Jersey in 1939, served in the RAF during the war and returned to the stage in 1946. He worked at various repertory theatres, including Birmingham and the Bristol Old Vic, but scored a huge success as the malevolent tramp, Davies, in **Harold Pinter**'s *The Caretaker* in 1960. Since the 1960s, his London stage appearances have been rare, but he is in constant demand for film work, usually as a villain, as in *Dr Crippen* (1962) and *Cul-de-Sac* (1966).

PLEKHANOV, Georgi Valentinovich (1857–1918) Russian revolutionary and Marxist philosopher, born in Tambov province. He joined the Narodnist Populist movement as a student and in 1876 led the first popular demonstration in St Petersburg. In 1883 he helped to found the League for the Emancipation of Labour (which became the Russian Social Democratic Workers' party in 1898) and spent the years 1883–1917 in exile in Geneva. From 1889 to 1904 he was Russian delegate to the Second International. With **Lenin**, whose revolutionary mentor he was, he edited the journal *Spark* (1900). He argued that Russia would have to go through industrialization and capitalism before arriving at socialism, and after the Bolshevik-Menshevik break he supported the latter faction against Lenin. He returned to Russia in 1917, where he edited a paper. After the Bolshevik victory he lived in Finland. His commentaries on Marxist theory fill 26 volumes.

PLESSNER, Helmuth (1892–) German philosopher and social theorist, born in Wiesbaden. He studied zoology, medicine and philosophy at the universities of Freiburg, Heidelberg and Berlin. He was professor at Cologne from 1926 to 1934, then moved to Groningen in Holland to escape the Nazis and became professor of sociology there from 1934 to 1942, was expelled during the Nazi occupation, then became professor of philosophy there again from 1946 to 1951, before returning finally to Göttingen in 1951. He helped found, with **Max Scheler**, the new discipline of 'philosophical anthropology': humans are distinguished from animals by the 'eccentric position' by which they can distance themselves from their own bodies through self-consciousness and can thus have access to experiences, expressions, language and institutions of a quite different order of significance. This philosophy is explained in such works as *Die Einheit der Sinne* ('The Unity of the Senses' 1923), *Die Stufen des Organischen und der Mensch* ('Man and the Stages of the Organic', 1928), and *Lachen und Weinen* ('Laughter and Weeping', 1941). He also wrote on social philosophy and the origins of Fascism in *Das Schicksal deutschen Geistes im Ausgang seiner bürgerlichen Epoche* ('The Destiny of the German Spirit at the End of the Bourgeois Epoch', 1935) and *Grenzen der Gemeinschaft: Eine Kritik des sozialen Radikalismus* ('Limits of Society: a Critique of Social Radicalism', 1972).

PLETHON, Georgios Gemistos (c.1355–1450) Greek scholar, probably a native of Constantinople. He was counsellor in the Peloponnesus to **Manuel II, Palaeologus**, and was sent to the Council of Florence in 1439. Here he did much to spread a taste for **Plato**, and founded the Platonic Academy of Florence.

PLEYDELL-BOUVERIE, Katherine (1895–1985) English potter. She studied at the Central School of Arts and Crafts in London and with **Bernard Leach** at St Ives, Cornwall, in 1924. She established a pottery in Wiltshire, producing domestic wares in stoneware, experimenting with wood and vegetable ash glazes. In 1946 she established an oil-fired kiln in Kilmington Manor near Warminster where her output consisted of a series of unique small works often decorated with vertical ribbing.

PLEYEL, Ignaz Joseph (1757–1831) Austrian composer, born near Vienna. In 1783 he became kapellmeister of Strasbourg Cathedral. In 1791 he visited London, in 1795 opened a music shop in Paris and in 1807 added a pianoforte manufactory. His compositions included quartets, concertos and sonatas.

PLIMSOLL, Samuel (1824–98) English social reformer, known as 'the sailors' friend', born in Bristol. In 1854 he started business in the coal trade in London and soon began to interest himself in the dangers affecting the mercantile marine. He entered parliament for Derby in 1868; but it was not until he had published *Our Seamen* (1873) and had made a public appeal that the Merchant Shipping Act (1876) was passed, by which, *inter alia*, every owner was ordered to mark upon his ship a circular disc (the 'Plimsoll Mark'), with a horizontal line drawn through its centre, down to which the vessel might be loaded. He retired from parliamentary life in 1880. In 1890 he published *Cattle-ships*, exposing the cruelties and dangers of cattle-shipping.

PLINY, Gaius Plinius Secundus, known as **'the Elder'** (23–79) Roman writer on natural history. He came of a wealthy north Italian family owning estates at Novum Comum (Como), where he was born. He was educated in Rome, and when about 23 entered the army and served in Germany. He became colonel of a cavalry regiment, and a comrade of the future emperor **Titus**, and wrote a treatise on the throwing of missiles from horseback and compiled a history of the Germanic wars. He also made a series of scientific tours in the region between the Ems, Elbe and Weser, and the sources of the Danube. Returning to Rome in 52, he studied for the bar, but withdrew to Como and devoted himself to reading and authorship. Apparently for the guidance of his nephew, he wrote his *Studiosus*, a treatise defining the culture necessary for the orator, and the grammatical work, *Dubius Sermo*. By **Nero** he was appointed procurator in Spain, and through his brother-in-law's death (71) became guardian of his sister's son, **Pliny the Younger**, whom he adopted. **Vespasian**, whose son Titus he had known in Germany, was now emperor, and became a close friend; but court favour did not wean him from study, and he brought down to his own time the history of Rome by Aufidius Bassus. A model student, amid metropolitan distraction he worked assiduously, and by lifelong application filled the 160 volumes of manuscript which, after using them for his universal encyclopaedia in 37 volumes, *Historia Naturalis* (77), he bequeathed to his nephew. In 79 he was in command of the Roman fleet stationed off Misenum when the great eruption of Vesuvius was at its height. Eager to witness the phenomenon as closely as possible, he landed at Stabiae (*Castellamare*), but had not gone far before he succumbed to the stifling vapours rolling down the hill. His *Historia Naturalis* alone of his many writings survives. Under that title the ancients classified everything of natural or non-artificial origin. Pliny adds digressions on human inventions and institutions, devoting two books to a history of fine art, and dedicates the whole to Titus. His observations, made at second-hand, show no discrimination between the true and the false, between the probable and the marvellous, and his style is inartistic, sometimes obscure. But he supplies information on an immense variety of subjects about which, but for him, we should have remained in the dark.

PLINY, Gaius Plinius Caecilius Secundus, known as **'the Younger'** (62–113) Roman writer and orator, born in Novum Comum, the nephew and adopted son of **Pliny** 'the Elder'. He wrote a Greek tragedy in his 14th year, and made such progress under **Quintilian** that he became noted as one of the most accomplished men of his time. His proficiency as an orator enabled him at 18 to plead in the Forum, and brought him much practice. He served as military tribune in Syria, and was *quaestor Caesaris*, then praetor, and afterwards consul in 100 AD, in which year he wrote his laboured panegyric of **Trajan**. From 103 to 105 he was propraetor of the Provincia Pontica and, among other offices, held that of curator of the Tiber, chiefly for the prevention of floods. He married twice; his second wife, Calpurnia, is fondly referred to in one of his most charming letters for the many gifts and accomplishments with which she sweetened his rather invalid life. It is to his ten volumes of letters that Pliny owes his assured place in literature, giving an intimate picture of the upper class in the 1st century; above all, it is from his correspondence with Trajan that we get our clearest knowledge of how even the most enlightened Romans regarded the then obscure sect of the Christians and their 'depraved and extravagant superstition'.

PLISETSKYA, Maya (1925–) Russian dancer, born in Moscow into a family with dance in its blood (she was the niece of Asaf and Sulamith **Messerer**). Trained at the Bolshoi school, success came early and she was made a principal immediately on joining the company in 1943. Celebrated for her dazzling, fast technique, she shone in classical roles like Odile/Odette in *Swan Lake* and came to represent the epitome of the Bolshoi style. A performer of great charisma both on and off stage, she was able to travel at a time when this was difficult for most Soviet artists. Best known for the role created for her in *Carmen Suite* (1967) by Alberto Alonso, she also danced in **Roland Petit**'s company in *La Rose malade* (1973) and in **Maurice Béjart**'s company in 1979. Film roles, both dancing (*Vernal Floods*, 1975) and acting (*Anna Karenina*, 1972), punctuated the career of one of the most exciting dancers of the century.

PLOMER, William Charles Franklin (1903–76) British writer, born in Pietersburg, Transvaal. He was educated at Rugby, was a farmer and trader in South Africa before becoming an author, and also lived for a while in Greece and Japan. With **Roy Campbell** he ran a South African literary review, and in World War II he served at the Admiralty. His works include the novels *Turbott Wolfe* (1926), *Sado* (1931) and *Ali the Lion* (1936); collections of short stories *I Speak of Africa* (1928) and *Paper Houses* (1929); and *Collected Poems* (1960). He edited the diaries of **Francis Kilvert**. He also wrote the autobiographical *Double Lives* (1943).

PLOTINUS (c.205–270) Neoplatonist philosopher, probably born in Egypt of Roman parentage, though his education and intellectual background was Greek. He studied in Alexandria (under **Ammonius Saccas**), and in Persia, and in 244 settled in Rome where he became a popular lecturer, advocating asceticism and the contemplative life, though he seemed to live in some style himself. At the age of 60 he tried to found in Campania a 'Platonopolis' modelled on **Plato**'s utopian *Republic*, but the Emperor **Gallienus** in the end put a stop to it. His prolific writings, produced between 253 and 270, were posthumously edited and arranged by his pupil **Porphyry** into six 'groups of nine books' (or *Enneads*). They established the foundations of neoplatonism as a philosophical system, combining Platonic with Pythagorean, Aristotelian and Stoic doctrines. He greatly influenced early Christian theology, and neoplatonism was the dominant philosophy in Europe for a millenium, establishing a link between ancient and medieval thought.

PLOWDEN, Bridget Hortia Lady, née **Richmond** (1907–) English educationist, educated at Downe House. She was the first woman to chair the Central Advisory Council for Education (1963–66), and subsequently became chairman of the Independent Broadcasting Authority (1975–80). Her report, *Children and their Primary Schools* (1967), concentrated public attention on the relationship between the primary school and the home and social background of children. It argued that education must be concerned with the whole family and that increased resources were needed for nursery education and for areas starved of new investment—'educational priority areas'. It took child-centred approaches to their logical limits, insisting on the principle of complete individualization of the teaching/learning process and holding it impossible 'to describe a standard of attainment that should be reached by all or most children'. The *Plowden Report* marks a watershed in the development of English primary education.

PLOWDEN, Edmund (1518–85) English Catholic lawyer, born in Shropshire. Educated at Cambridge, he sat in parliament in the reign of Queen **Mary I**, retiring with 39 other members over the question of heresy laws. One of the ablest lawyers of his day, from 1561 to 1571 he was treasurer of the Middle Temple. His excellent *Commentaries*, notably accurate reports, which brought out the decisive issues in cases, were first published in 1571. A monument was erected to him in Temple church.

PLOWRIGHT, Joan (1929–) English actress and stage director, born in Brigg, Lincolnshire. Trained at the Old Vic Theatre School, she became a member of the English Stage Company at the Royal Court Theatre, London, in 1956. There she played opposite **Laurence Olivier**, whom she married in 1961. In 1957 she played Jean Rice in **Osborne**'s *The Entertainer*, and Beattie in **Arnold Wesker**'s *Roots* in 1959. In 1963 she joined the National Theatre in its first season. A formidably talented classical actress, she is also an accomplished stage director.

PLÜCKER, Julius (1801–68) German mathematician and physicist, born in Eberfeld. Professor of mathematics at Bonn (1836) and of physics (1847), he investigated diamagnetism, originated the idea of spectrum analysis, and in 1859 discovered cathode rays, produced by electrical discharges in gases at low pressures. His mathematical work was concerned with line geometry and algebraic curves.

PLUME, Thomas (1630–1704) English theologian, born in Maldon. Educated at Chelmsford and Christ's College, Cambridge, he was vicar of Greenwich from 1658 and archdeacon of Rochester from 1679. He endowed an observatory and the Plumian chair of astronomy and experimental philosophy at Cambridge, and bequeathed his extensive library to the town of Maldon, where it still exists intact.

PLUMER, Herbert Charles Onslow (1857–1932) English soldier and colonial administrator. He served in Sudan (1884) and led the Rhodesian relief force to Mafeking (1900). In World War I he distinguished himself as commander of the 2nd army of the British Expeditionary Force (1915–18), notably at the great attack on Messines, and GOC Italian Expeditionary Force (1917–18). He was made a field marshal in 1919, was governor of Malta (1919–24), and high commissioner for Palestine (1925–28).

PLUNKET, William Conyngham, 1st Baron Plunket (1764–1854) Irish lawyer, born in Enniskillen. He opposed the Union (1798), prosecuted **Robert Emmet** (1803), and rose to be Lord Chancellor of Ireland (1830–41).

PLUNKETT, Sir Horace Curzon (1854–1932) Irish agricultural reformer, third son of Lord Dunsany. Educated at Eton and Oxford, he spent ten years on a cattle ranch in Wyoming (1879–89), from 1889 promoted agricultural co-operation in Ireland, and in 1894 founded the Irish Agricultural Organization Society. He was MP for Dublin Co (S) (1892–1900), vice-president of the Irish department of agriculture (1899–1907), and chairman of the Irish Convention (1917–18). He was a senator of the Irish Free State (1922–23).

PLUTARCH, Roman **Ploutarchos** (c.46–c.120) Greek historian, biographer and philosopher, born in Chaeroneia in Boeotia. His higher education was begun at Athens in 66. He paid more than one visit to Rome—once as *chargé d'affaires* of his native town —and there gave public lectures in philosophy. He spent all his mature life at his native place. His extant writings comprise his historical works, and those which are grouped under the general head of *Opera Moralia*. To the former belong his *Parallel Lives*—the work by which he is best known. These contain a gallery of 46 portraits of the great characters of the ages preceding his own. They were published in successive books, each pair forming one book, and a Greek and Roman, with some resemblance between their respective careers, being chosen for the subject of each. The sequels which come after most of the Lives, giving a detailed comparison of each warrior, statesman, legislator or hero, are regarded as spurious by some critics. Plutarch's *Biographies* are monuments of great literary value for the precious materials which they contain, based as they are on lost records. The author adheres throughout to his professed purpose—portraiture of character; he either omits or briefly touches upon the most famous actions or events which distinguish the career of each subject of his biography, holding that these do not show a man's virtues or failings so well as some trifling incident, word or jest. The others and less known half of his writings—the *Morals*—are a collection of short treatises, 60 or more (although certainly not all from Plutarch's hand), upon various subjects—*Ethics*, *Politics*, *History*, *Health*, *Facetiae*, *Love-stories*, *Philosophy* and *Isis and Osiris*. Some of the essays breathe quite a Christian spirit, although the writer probably never heard of Christianity. The nine books of his *Symposiaca* or Table-talk exhibit him as the most amiable and genial of boon companions; while his dialogue *Gryllus* reveals a remarkable sense of humour. Though not a profound thinker, Plutarch was a man of rare gifts, and occupies a unique place in literature as the encyclopaedist of antiquity. The translation by Sir **Thomas North** (1579) was the major source for **Shakespeare**'s Roman plays.

POBEDONOSTSEV, Constantin Petrovich (1827–1907) Russian jurist, son of a Moscow professor. Tutor to **Alexander III** and **Nicholas II**, he became professor of civil law at Moscow in 1858 and favoured liberal reforms in the law. Later he reacted against this, becoming strongly opposed to any westernization of Russia, and was the most uncompromising champion of the autocracy and of the supremacy of the Russian orthodox church.

POCAHONTAS, Indian name **Matoaka** (1595–1617) American Indian princess, daughter of an Indian chief, **Powhatan**. According to the English adventurer **John Smith**, she saved his life on two occasions when he was at the mercy of her tribe. Cajoled to Jamestown, Virginia in 1612, she embraced Christianity, was baptized Rebecca, in 1613 married an Englishman, John Rolfe (1585–1622), and came to England with him in 1616, where she was received by royalty. Having embarked for Virginia the following year, she died of smallpox off Gravesend. She left one son, and several Virginia families claim descent from her.

PO-CHÜ-I (772–846) Chinese poet under the T'ang dynasty, born in Honan, of which he became governor in 831. He was so esteemed as a lyric poet that his poems were collected by imperial order and engraved on stone tablets.

POCOCKE, Edward (1604–91) English orientalist, born in Oxford. Elected a fellow of Corpus Christi College, Oxford in 1628, he sailed for Aleppo in 1630 as chaplain to the English factory, but in 1636 became Oxford professor of Arabic, and in 1643 rector of Childrey. He was appointed to the chair of Hebrew in 1648. His main writings were *Specimen Historiae Arabum* (1649) and an edition of **Abulfaraj's** History (1663).

PODIEBRAD, George of (1420–71) king of Bohemia from 1458. Born into the Czech nobility in Podiebrad or Poděbrady, he became an adherent of the moderate Hussite Protestant followers of **Jan Huss**. When the Catholic barons (1438) carried the election of the Emperor Albert II to the Bohemian crown, Podiebrad allied himself with the Utraquist faction of Hussites in Tabor, who offered it to Casimir, king of Poland. After forcing Albert to raise the siege of Tabor and retire to Prague, Podiebrad became leader of the Utraquists, seized Prague (1448), and had himself made regent (1453–57) for the young King Ladislaus Posthumus. On Ladislaus's death, Podiebrad was crowned his successor in 1458. He succeeded for a while in allaying the bitternesses of religious zeal. In 1462 he refused to abolish the terms of the *compactata* of Prague (1433) which legitimized the Ultraquists; this angered Pope **Pius II**, but the emperor restrained him from excommunicating Podiebrad. The next pope (**Paul II**), however, excommunicated him in 1466. King **Matthias Corvinus** of Hungary took the field to enforce the ban; but Podiebrad forced him into a truce at Wilamow (1469). Nevertheless Matthias was crowned King of Bohemia by the Catholic barons. Podiebrad left the succession to Bohemia to a Polish prince.

POE, Edgar Allan (1809–49) American poet and story writer, born in Boston, Massachusetts. After being orphaned in his third year, he was adopted by John Allan (1780–1834), a wealthy and childless merchant in Richmond, Virginia. From 1815 to 1820 the family lived in England, and the boy went to school in Stoke Newington. The year 1826 was spent at the University of Virginia; but, offended by his dissipation and gambling debts, his patron moved him to the counting-room, from where he ran away to Boston. He published *Tamerlane and other Poems* (1827), enlisted in the US army that same year, and rose to be sergeant-major in 1829. He then procured his discharge and after a year's delay his admission to West Point Military Academy (1830), but the following March he was dismissed for deliberate neglect of duty. Now he was thrown on his own resources. A third edition of his *Poems* (1831) contained 'Israfel', his earliest poem of value, and 'To Helen'. In Baltimore he won a prize in 1833 for his story 'A MS. found in a Bottle'. From then on he lived with his aunt, Mrs Clemm, and wrote for the *Saturday Visitor*. His connection with the *Southern Literary Messenger* began with his tale *Berenice* in 1835 and he went to Richmond as its assistant editor (1835–37). In 1836 he married his cousin Virginia. He left Richmond in 1837, and after a year or less in New York, of which the chief result was *The Narrative of Arthur Gordon Pym*, in 1838 he established himself in Philadelphia. Here he published *Tales of the Grotesque* and *Arabesque* (1840), was connected with Burton's *Gentleman's Magazine* (1839), and for a year (1842–43) edited *Graham's Magazine*. He won another short story competition in 1843 with 'The Gold Bug'. In 1844 he moved to New York, and in *The Evening Mirror* (1845) published 'The Raven', which won immediate fame. In 1847 his wife died. 'The Bells', 'The Domain of Arnheim', the wild 'prose poem' *Eureka* (1848) and a few minor pieces belong to the brief remainder of his life. He attempted suicide in November 1848, and had an attack of *delirium tremens* in June 1849. Recovering, he spent over two months in Richmond, lecturing there and at Norfolk. He became engaged to a lady of means, and in September went to wind up his affairs in the north. In October he was found in a wretched condition in Baltimore, and died in the hospital. Weird, wild, fantastic, dwelling by choice on the horrible, Poe's genius was yet great and genuine. His short stories show great originality, and from some of them, such as 'The Murders in the Rue Morgue', Poe emerges as a pioneer of the modern detective story. The chief charm of his poems is exquisite melody.

POELZIG, Hans (1869–1936) German Expressionist architect, born in Berlin. He joined the Prussian ministry of works in 1899, becoming professor of architecture at the Academy of Arts in Breslau in 1900 (subsequently director). Between 1916 and 1920 he served as city architect of Dresden. The early inventive projects such as the Luban Chemical Works, Posen, Silesia (1911–12), and the monumental Water Tower and Exhibition Hall, Posen (1910–11), disseminated his uncompromising Expressionist ideals. Later works include the remodelling of Grosses Shauspielhaus, Berlin (1919), Salzburg Festival Theatre (1920–22), and the imposing and conservative design of the I G Farben Headquarters, Frankfurt (1928–31).

POERIO, Carlo (1803–67) Italian lawyer and patriot, born in Naples. In 1848 he became director of police, minister of public instruction and deputy for Naples. In July 1849 **Ferdinand II** had him arrested, and sentenced to 24 years in irons; but in 1858 shipped him with other prisoners to America. They persuaded the captain to land them at Cork, and Poerio returned to Turin, where he became a member of parliament, and in 1861 its vice-president. His brother, Alessandro (1802–48), was a patriotic poet; his lyrics included *Il Risorgimento*. He fell in battle for the liberation of Venice.

POGGENDORFF, Johann Christian (1796–1877) German physicist and chemist. He was professor of chemistry at Berlin from 1834. He made discoveries in connection with electricity and galvanism, and invented a multiplying galvanometer. He was the founder and editor of the journal *Annalen der Physik und Chemie* (1824–74).

POGGIO, Gian Francesco Bracciolini (1380–1459) Italian humanist, born in Florence. In 1403 he became a secretary to the Roman curia. At the Council of Constance (1414–18) he explored the Swiss and Swabian convents for MSS. He recovered MSS of **Quintilian**, **Ammianus Marcellinus**, **Lucretius**, **Silius**

Italicus, **Vitruvius** and others. In 1453 he retired to Florence, and became chancellor and official historian to the republic. His writings include letters, moral essays, a rhetorical Latin *History of Florence*, a series of invectives against his contemporaries, and—his most famous book—the *Liber Facetiarum*, a collection of humorous stories, mainly against monks and secular clergy.

POHL, Frederik (1919–) American science fiction writer, born in Brooklyn, New York City. In 1938 he became a founder-member of a group of left-wing science fiction writers known as the Futurists, which included **Isaac Asimov** and others. He served in the air force in World War II, worked as a literay agent, and edited various science fiction magazines (1953–69). He describes his own multifarious books as 'cautionary literature', seeing science fiction as a kind of alarm signal. Of his vast output of novels, stories and anthologies, *The Space Merchants* (1953) and *Gladiator-at-Law* (1955), both written with C M Kornbluth, exemplify his social concern and strength as a storyteller.

POINCARÉ, Jules Henri (1854–1912) French mathematician, born in Nancy. He studied at the École Polytechnique and, as an engineer at the École des Mines, became professor of mathematics in Paris in 1881. Following the work of Immanuel Fuchs and **Felix Klein**, he created the theory of automorphic functions, and showed the importance of topological considerations in differential geometry. Many of the basic ideas in modern topology—such as triangulation, homology, the **Euler-Poincaré** formula and the fundamental group—are due to him. In a paper on the three-body problem in 1889 he opened up new directions in celestial mechanics and began the study of dynamical systems in the modern sense. In his last years he published several books on the philosophy of science and scientific method, such as '*Science et méthode*' (1909).

POINCARÉ, Raymond Nicolas Landry (1860–1934) French statesman, cousin of **Jules Poincaré**, born in Bar-le-Duc. He studied law, became a deputy in 1887, senator 1903, minister of public instruction (1893, 1895), of finance (1894, 1906), and premier (1911–13, 1922–24 and 1926–29). He was elected president of the Republic in 1913, remaining in office until 1920. He occupied the Ruhr (1923), and his National Union ministry averted ruin in 1926. Member of the Académie Française (1909), he wrote on literature and politics, *Memoirs* (trans 1925), and *How France is Governed* (1913).

POINDEXTER, Rear-Admiral John Marlan (1936–) United States naval officer and statesman. Born in Washington, Indiana, the son of a bank manager, he was educated at the US Naval Academy and California Institute of Technology, where he secured a doctorate in nuclear physics. He became chief of naval operations during the 1970s and was deputy head of naval educational training (1978–81). In 1981 he joined President **Reagan**'s National Security Council (NSC), becoming National Security Adviser (NSA) in 1985. He resigned, together with his assistant, Lieutenant-Colonel **Oliver North**, in November 1986 in the aftermath of the 'Irangate Scandal'. Poindexter retired from the navy in December 1987, and in 1990 was convicted by a Federal court on charges of conspiracy, of obstructing congressional inquiries, and of lying to congress.

POIRET, Paul (1879–1944) French fashion designer, born in Paris. He worked for Jacques Doucet and **Worth** before opening his own fashion house in 1904. Influenced by the exotic oriental costumes of the Ballets Russes, which was first in Paris in 1908, his designs of the period featured such garments as turbans and harem pants. A brochure of 1911, illustrated by Georges Lepape under the title *Les Choses de Paul Poiret*, showed a rich and varied collection of an early leader of fashion rather than a designer for the individual client. After World War I he was never able to adapt sufficiently to changed circumstances to re-establish his prominence, and he died in poverty.

POISSON, Siméon Denis (1781–1840) French mathematical physicist, born in Pithiviers. He became the first professor of mechanics at the Sorbonne and achieved a leading position in the French scientific establishment. He published extensively on mathematical physics but his work was criticized for lack of originality by many of his contemporaries.

POITIER, Sidney (1924–) American actor and director, born in Miami, Florida. A student at the American Negro Theater in New York, he appeared on stage in *Lysistrata* (1946) and *Anna Lucasta* (1946–48) before making his film début in the documentary *From Whence Cometh My Help* (1949). His Hollywood début followed in *No Way Out* (1950). Cast mainly in supporting roles he made an impression in *Cry, the Beloved Country* (1952), *The Blackboard Jungle* (1955) and *The Defiant Ones* (1958). He won an Academy Award for *Lilies of the Field* (1963) which consolidated his position as the cinema's first black superstar. Handsome and unassuming, he brought dignity to the portrayal of noble and intelligent characters in films like *In the Heat of the Night* (1967) and *Guess Who's Coming to Dinner* (1967). Latterly a director of lowbrow comedies, including *Stir Crazy* (1980), he returned to acting after a ten-year absence in *Little Nikita* (1988) and *Shoot to Kill* (1988). His autobiography, *This Life*, was published in 1980.

POITIERS See **DIANE DE POITIERS**

POLANSKI, Roman (1933–) Polish filmmaker, born in Paris. An actor on radio and in the theatre, he attended the State Film School in Todz (1954–59), making a number of short films beginning with the uncompleted *Rower* (The Bicycle, 1955). His feature-length début *Nóż w Wodzie* (Knife in the Water, 1962) brought him international recognition and he has subsequently worked in London, Paris and Los Angeles on such films as *Repulsion* (1965), *Cul de Sac* (1966), *Rosemary's Baby* (1968), *Chinatown* (1974) and *Tess* (1979). A traumatic life that includes his internment in a German concentration camp, the early death of his mother and the horrifying murder of his second wife, actress Sharon Tate, has been reflected in his artistic concern with alienation, individual isolation and the understanding of evil. On stage, he has directed *Lulu* (1974) and *Rigoletto* (1976) and acted in *Amadeus* (1981) and *Metamorphosis* (1988). His candid autobiography, *Roman*, was published in 1984.

POLANYI, Michael (1891–1976) Hungarian-born British physical chemist and social philosopher, born in Budapest. He studied there and at Karlsruhe, lectured at Berlin, but emigrated to Britain after **Hitler**'s rise to power and was professor of physical chemistry (1933–1948) and of social studies (1948–58) at Manchester. He did notable work on reaction kinetics and crystal structure, published *Atomic Reactions* (1932) and wrote much on the freedom of scientific thought, philosophy of science and latterly social science, including *Personal Knowledge* (1958), *The Study of Man* (1959), and *Beyond Nihilism* (1960).

POLDING, John Bede (1794–1877) English-born Australian clergyman, born in Liverpool. Ordained in 1819, in 1834 when the Catholic mission to Australia was removed from the control of the vicariate in

Mauritius, he was appointed first vicar apostolic of New Holland and Van Diemen's Land. He arrived in Sydney in 1835 and consecrated St Mary's as his cathedral in the following year. In 1842 he was made archbishop of Sydney and metropolitan of Australia, positions which he was to hold until his retirement in 1875. During this period he saw the Catholic church in Australia grow from a priesthood of eight into twelve dioceses, with 135 priests, under a strong central administration with its own schools, a hospital, and its own college, St John's, within Sydney University.

POLE, de la a family descended from a Hull merchant, whose son Michael (c.1330–1389) in 1383 became chancellor, in 1385 was made Earl of Suffolk, and died an exile in France. His grandson, William (1396–1450), was in 1449 raised to be Duke of Suffolk, having since 1445 been virtually prime minister. His administration was disastrous; and he was on his way to a five years' banishment in Flanders when he was intercepted off Dover and beheaded. John de la Pole, 2nd Duke (1442–91), married Elizabeth, sister to **Edward IV** and **Richard III** and from this marriage sprang John, Earl of Lincoln (c.1464–1487), Edmund, Earl of Suffolk (c.1472–1513, executed by **Henry VIII**), two churchmen, four daughters, and Richard, on whose death at the battle of Pavia (1525) the line became extinct.

POLE, Reginald (1500–58) English prelate, and archbishop of Canterbury, born in Stourton Castle near Stourbridge. He was the son of Sir Richard Pole and Margaret, Countess of Salisbury (1473–1541), daughter of the Duke of **Clarence** and niece of **Edward IV**. At 19 he went to Italy to finish his studies. He returned in 1527 to become dean of Exeter, and was then high in **Henry VIII**'s favour. When the question of the divorce was raised, Pole seemed at first disposed to take the king's side; but later expressed disapproval, refused the archbishopric of York and, going to Italy in 1532, formed intimate friendships with many eminent men eager for an internal reformation of the church. In 1535 he entered into a political correspondence with the emperor **Charles V**, and was now compelled by Henry to declare himself, which he did in a violent letter to the king, afterwards expanded into the treatise *Pro Unitatis Ecclesiasticae Defensione*. The king withdrew Pole's pension and preferments. **Paul III** made him a cardinal (1536), and sent him as legate to the Low Countries to confer with the English malcontents. Henry retaliated by setting a price on his head and beheading his mother and other relatives. Pole's several attempts to procure the invasion of England were not successful. From 1541 to 1542 he was governor of the 'Patrimony of St Peter', and at the Council of Trent (1545) he was one of the presidents. In 1549 he was on the point of being elected pope; after the election of **Julius III** he lived in retirement until the death of **Edward VI**, when he was commissioned to Queen **Mary I** as legate *a latere*. Pole was still only in deacon's orders, and cherished the idea of marrying the queen; but Charles V carried the match with his son, **Philip II** of Spain. Pole arrived in London in November 1554, with powers to allow the owners of confiscated church property to retain their possessions. He absolved parliament and country from their schism, and reconciled the Church of England to Rome. As long as **Cranmer** lived, Pole would not accept the archbishopric of Canterbury, but Pole was ordained priest (March 1556), and consecrated archbishop after Cranmer was burnt. Pope **Paul IV**, indignant at the concessions made by authority of his predecessor to the holders of church property, revived the accusations of heresy formerly brought against Pole. Paul IV was, moreover, now at war with Spain, and could not tolerate Pole as his ambassador at the court of Mary. So his legation was cancelled and he was summoned before the Inquisition. Mary angrily protested, and the pope relented, but would not reinstate Pole. When the queen died in 1558, Pole was dangerously ill; he died on the same day. It has been disputed how far he was responsible for Mary's persecution of Protestants; certainly when Pole became the queen's supreme adviser the persecution increased in violence.

POLE, William (1814–1900) English engineer and musician, born in Birmingham. He became professor of engineering at Bombay (1844–47), at University College, London (1859–67), and from 1871 to 1883 was consulting engineer in London for the imperial railways in Japan. He was also an authority on music and whist.

POLIAKOFF, Stephen (1952–) English dramatist. He achieved recognition with the plays *Hitting Town* and *City Sugar* (1975), both looking at the plight of urban young in a Britain of concrete shoppng arcades and consumerism. Several plays followed on the same theme, but *Breaking the Silence* (1984), set in the aftermath of the Russian Revolution, is his finest work to date. *Coming Into Land* (1987) follows the fortunes of a Polish refugee as she tries to enter Britain. Other stage plays include *Strawberry Fields* (1977) and *Shout Across the River* (1978). His television plays include *Caught on a Train* (1980).

POLIGNAC an ancient French family to which belonged Cardinal Melchior de Polignac (1661–1742), plenipotentiary of **Louis XIV** at Utrecht (1712) and French minister at Rome. A Duchesse de Polignac (1749–93) who died at Vienna, and her husband (died at St Petersburg, 1817), grand-nephew of the cardinal, were among the worst, but unhappily most favoured, advisers of **Marie Antoinette**, and were largely responsible for the shameful extravagance of the court. Their son, Auguste Jules Armand Marie, Prince de Polignac (1780–1847), born at Versailles, at the Restoration returned to France and became intimate with the Comte d'Artois, afterwards **Charles X**. In 1820 he was made a prince by the pope, appointed ambassador at the English court in 1823, and in 1829 became head of the last **Bourbon** ministry, which promulgated the fatal ordinances that cost Charles X his throne. He was condemned to imprisonment for life in the castle of Ham, but was set at liberty by the amnesty of 1836. He took up residence in England, but died in Paris.

POLITIAN, properly **Angelo Ambrogini** (1454–94) Italian humanist, scholar and poet, born in Montepulciano in Tuscany, and called *Poliziano* (Politian) from the Italian name of his birthplace. At the age of 10 he was sent to Florence, and made incredible progress in the ancient languages. By his sixteenth year he had written brilliant Latin and Greek epigrams; at 17 he began the translation of the *Iliad* into Latin hexameters, and having secured the friendship of the all-powerful **Lorenzo de' Medici** (whose sons he taught) he was soon recognized as the prince of Italian scholars. He was appointed canon of Florence in 1480, and became professor of Greek and Latin at Florence (1482–86). Lorenzo's death in 1492 was a serious blow, and he mourned his death in a remarkable Latin elegy. Among his other works were Latin translations of a long series of Greek authors, and an excellent edition of the *Pandects* of **Justinian**. His original works in Latin fill a thick quarto, half of which is made up of letters; the rest with miscellanies in prose and verse. His *Orfeo* (1480) was the first secular drama in Italian.

POLK, James Knox (1795–1849) 11th president of the USA, born in Mecklenburg County, North

Carolina. He later moved to Tennessee and was admitted to the bar in 1820 and elected to congress as a Democrat in 1825, becoming house speaker in 1835. He served as governor of Tennessee between 1839 and 1841 and in 1844 was elected president, defeating the Whig candidate **Henry Clay**, mainly because of his 'firm' attitude with regard to the annexation of Texas. In December 1845 Texas was admitted to the Union, and jurisdiction was extended to the disputed territory. The president next forced hostilities by advancing the American army to the Rio Grande; the capital was taken in September and by the terms of peace the USA acquired California and New Mexico. The Oregon boundary was settled by a compromise with England. Polk condemned the antislavery agitation, and he was devoted to the Democratic principles of **Thomas Jefferson** and **Andrew Jackson**—state rights, a revenue tariff, independent treasury, and strict construction of the constitution.

POLK, Leonidas (1806–64) American soldier, born in Raleigh, North Carolina, a cousin of **James K Polk**. Graduating at West Point in 1827, he held a commission in the artillery, but resigned to study divinity and in 1831 received holy orders in the Episcopal church. In 1838 he was consecrated a missionary bishop of Arkansas, and from 1841 till his death was bishop of Louisiana, even when at the head of an army corps. In the Civil War (1861–65) he was made major-general by **Jefferson Davis**. At Belmont, in November 1861, he was driven from his camp by **Grant**, but finally forced him to retire. At Shiloh and Corinth he commanded the first corps; promoted lieutenant-general, he conducted the retreat from Kentucky. After Chickamauga, where he commanded the right wing, he was relieved of his command; reappointed in December 1863, he opposed **Sherman**'s march. He was killed reconnoitring on Pine Mountain.

POLLAIUOLO, Antonio (1429–98) Florentine goldsmith, medallist, metal-caster and painter. He cast sepulchral monuments in St Peter's in Rome for Popes **Sixtus IV** and Innocent VIII. His pictures are distinguished for life and vigour. He was one of the first painters to study anatomy and apply it to his art, and was skilled in suggesting movement. His brother Piero (1443–96) was associated with him in his work.

POLLARD, Albert Frederick (1869–1948) English historian, born in Ryde. After graduating at Oxford, he became assistant editor of *The Dictionary of National Biography*, and later professor of Constitutional History at London University from 1903 to 1931, founding in 1920 its Institute of Historical Research. From 1908 to 1936 he was a fellow of All Souls College, Oxford. Among his many historical works are lives of *Henry VIII* (1902), *Thomas Cranmer* (1904) and *Wolsey* (1929), *A Short History of the Great War* (1920) and *Factors in American History* (1925). The Historical Association was founded by him in 1906 and he was editor of *History* from 1916 to 1922.

POLLARD, Alfred William (1859–1944) English scholar and bibliographer, born in London. A graduate of Oxford, he was an assistant in the department of printed books at the British Museum (from 1883), and keeper from 1919 to 1924. He was appointed reader in bibliography at Cambridge (1915) and professor of English bibliography at King's College, London (1919–1932). An authority on **Chaucer** and **Shakespeare**, his contributions to Shakespearean criticism included his *Shakespeare Folios and Quartos* (1909) and *Shakespeare's Fight with the Pirates* (1917). Important earlier work on Chaucer had produced *A Chaucer Primer* (1893) and his edition of the Globe *Chaucer* (1898). In 1926 was completed the *Short Title Catalogue of Books Printed in England, Scotland and Ireland, 1475–1640*, for which he was largely responsible.

POLLIO, Gaius Asinius (76 BC–4 AD) Roman orator, poet and soldier. In the Civil War against **Pompey** he sided with **Caesar**; in 39 BC he commanded in Spain, and, appointed by **Marcus Antonius** (Mark Antony) to settle the veterans on the lands assigned them, saved **Virgil**'s property from confiscation. He founded the first public library in Rome, and was the patron of Virgil and **Horace**. His orations, tragedies and history of the civil wars have perished save for a few fragments.

POLLITT, Harry (1890–1960) English communist politician, born in Droylesden, Lancashire. He entered a cotton mill at twelve and joined the Independent Labour party at 16. Later he became a boilermaker and was a shop steward by the age of 21. He was secretary of the National Minority Movement from 1924 to 1929, when he became secretary of the Communist party of Great Britain. A stormy demagogue, he frequently clashed with authority, being imprisoned for seditious libel in 1925 and being deported from Belfast in 1933. During the Spanish Civil War he helped to found the British battalion of the International Brigade. In 1956 he resigned the secretaryship of the party and became its chairman. He wrote an autobiography *Serving My Time* (1940).

POLLOCK, Sir Charles Edward (1823–97) English jurist, fourth son of Sir Jonathan Frederick Pollock and brother of Sir **William Frederick Pollock**. He was a baron of Exchequer (1873) and from 1875 justice of the High Court.

POLLOCK, Sir David (1780–1847) English jurist, eldest son of David Pollock, saddler to **George III**. He became chief-justice of Bombay.

POLLOCK, Sir Frederick (1845–1937) English jurist, born in London, eldest son of Sir **William Frederick Pollock** and brother of Sir **Charles Edward** and **Walter Herries Pollock**. Educated at Eton College and Trinity College, Cambridge, in 1868 he obtained a fellowship. He was called to the bar in 1871, became professor of jurisprudence at University College, London (1882), Corpus professor of jurisprudence at Oxford (1883), professor of common law in the Inns of Court (1884–90), editor of the Law Reports (1895) and the Law Quarterly Review (1885–1919), judge of Admiralty Court of Cinque Ports (1914). Besides his *Spinoza* (1880), he published *Principles of Contract* (1875), *Digest of the Law of Partnership* (1877), *Law of Torts* (1887), all of which went through many editions, *Oxford Lectures* (1891), *History of English Law before Edward I* (with **Frederic William Maitland**, 1895), *The Etchingham Letters* (with Mrs Fuller-Maitland, 1899) and other books. Over many years he corresponded with **Oliver Wendell Holmes**.

POLLOCK, Sir George (1786–1872) English soldier, third son of David Pollock (saddler to **George III**) and brother of Sir **David Pollock**. He entered the East India Company's army in 1803. He was engaged at the siege of Bhartpur (1805) and in other operations, saw service in the Nepal (Gurkha) campaigns of 1814–16, and in the first Burmese war (1824–26) won his colonelcy. In 1838 he became major-general. After the massacre of General **Elphinstone** in Afghanistan, the Indian government sent him to the relief of Sir Robert Sale in Jelalabad. In April 1842 he forced the Khyber Pass and reached Sale, pushed on to Kabul, defeated the Moghul emperor **Akbar**, and recovered 135 British prisoners. Then he conducted the united armies back to India, and was rewarded with a political appointment at Lucknow. He returned to England in 1846, was director of the East India Company (1854–56), was created a field marshal in 1870, and in 1871 was appointed constable of the Tower.

POLLOCK, (Paul) Jackson (1912–56) American artist, born in Cody, Wyoming. Educated at the Art Students' League in New York, he became the first exponent of tachism or action painting in America. His art developed from Surrealism to abstract art and the first drip paintings of 1947. This technique he continued with increasing violence and often on huge canvases as in *One* which is 17 feet long. Other striking works include *No. 32*, and the black and white *Echo and Blue Poles*. He was killed in a motor accident.

POLLOCK, Robert Graeme (1944–) South African cricketer, born in Durban. One of the great batsmen of the 1960s, he was the last South African cricketer to make an impact at international level before that country's exclusion from Test cricket. In 23 Tests he averaged more than 60.9. Against Australia at Durban in 1969-70 he made 274, and he shares three record partnerships.

POLLOCK, Walter Herries (1850–1926) younger son of Sir **William Frederick Pollock**. He was called to the bar in 1874, edited the *Saturday Review* (1884-94), and published *Lectures on French Poets*, *Verses of Two Tongues*, *A Nine Men's Morrice*, *King Zub*, etc.

POLLOCK, Sir William Frederick (1815–88) English jurist, eldest son of Sir Jonathan Frederick Pollock and brother of Sir **Charles Edward Pollock**. Educated at St Paul's and Trinity College, Cambridge, he was called to the bar in 1838. He was appointed a master of the Court of Exchequer (1846) and Queen's Remembrancer (1874). In 1876 he became senior master of the Supreme Court of Judicature and resigned his offices in 1886. He published a blank verse translation of **Dante** (1854) and *Personal Remembrances* (1887).

POLO, Marco (1254–1324) Venetian traveller, born of a noble family in Venice, while his father and uncle (both merchants), were away on an expedition to Bokhara and Cathay (China). Well-received there by the great **Kublai Khan**, they were commisioned by the mongol prince as envoys to the pope, to ask him to send 100 Europeans learned in the sciences and arts—a commission they unsuccessfully tried to carry out (1269). The Polos started again in 1271, taking with them young Marco, and arrived at the court of Kublai Khan in 1275, after travelling by Mosul, Baghdad, Khorassan, the Pamir, Kashgar, Yarkand and Khoton, Lob Nor, and across the desert of Gobi, to Tangut and Shangtu. The khan took special notice of Marco, and soon sent him as envoy to Yunnan, northern Burma, Karakorum, Cochin-China and Southern India. For three years he served as governor of Yang Chow, and helped to subdue the city of Saianfu. The khan at first refused to think of the Polos leaving his court; but eventually they sailed to Persia, finally reaching Venice in 1295, and bringing with them the great wealth they had accumulated. In 1298 Marco was in command of a galley at the battle of Curzola, where the Venetians were defeated by the Genoese, and he was taken prisoner for a year at Genoa. It was once thought that he dictated to another captive, one Rusticiano of Pisa, vivid account of his travels, but it is now believed that he had his notes (which he had written for Kublai) sent to him from Venice and that Rusticiano helped to make a record from them, entitled *Divisament dou Monde*. After his liberation he returned to Venice, where he died.

POL POT, also known as **Saloth Sar** (1926–) Kampuchean (Cambodian) politician. After working on a rubber plantation in his early teens, he joined the anti-French resistance movement under **Ho Chi-Minh** during the early 1940s, becoming a member of the Indo-Chinese Communist party and Cambodian Communist party in 1946. During the 1960s and early 1970s he led the pro-Chinese communist Khmer Rouge in guerrilla activity against the Kampuchean governments of Prince Sihanouk and Lieutenant General Lon Nol, and in 1976, after the overthrow of Lon Nol, became prime minister. He proceeded brutally to introduce an extreme communist régime which resulted in the loss of more than 2 500 000 lives. The régime was overthrown by Vietnamese troops in January 1979 and Pol Pot took to the resistance struggle once more. Despite announcing his 'official' retirement as the Khmer's military leader in August 1985, he remains an influential and feared figure within the movement.

POLYBIUS (c.205–c.123 BC) Greek historian, born in Megalopolis in Arcadia. He was one of the 1000 noble Achaeans who, after the conquest of Macedonia in 168, were sent to Rome and detained as political hostages in honourable captivity. Polybius was the guest of **Aemilius Paulus** himself, and became the close friend of his son, **Scipio Aemilianus**, who helped him to collect materials for his great historical work. In 151 the exiles were permitted to return to Greece; Polybius, however, soon rejoined Scipio, followed him in his African campaign, and was present at the destruction of Carthage in 146. The war between the Achaeans and Romans called him back to Greece, and, after the taking of Corinth by Rome (146), he used all his influence to procure favourable terms for the vanquished. In furtherance of his historical labours he undertook journeys to Asia Minor, Egypt, upper Italy, southern France and even Spain. His *History*, the design of which was to show how and why it was that all the civilized countries of the world fell under the dominion of Rome, covers the period 221–146 BC. The greater part has perished; of 40 books only the first five are preserved complete, but the plan of the whole is fully known. The merits of Polybius are the care with which he collected his materials, his love of truth, his breadth of view, and his sound judgment; but his tone is didactic and monotonous.

POLYCARP (c.69–c.155) Greek Christian martyr, and one of the 'Apostolic Fathers'. He was bishop of Smyrna during the earlier half of the 2nd century. He bridges the little-known period between the age of his master, the Apostle **John**, and that of his own disciple **Irenaeus**. His parentage was probably Christian. Ephesus had become the new home of the faith, and there Polycarp was 'taught by apostles', John above all, and 'lived in familiar intercourse with many who had seen Christ'. He was intimate with Papias and **Ignatius**. At the close of his life Polycarp visited Rome to discuss the vexed question of the time for keeping the Easter festival; and he returned to Smyrna, only to win the martyr's crown in a persecution which broke out during a great pagan festival. The fire, it was said, arched itself about the martyr, and he had to be dispatched with a dagger. The graphic *Letter of the Smyrnaeans* tells the story of the martyrdom. The only writing of Polycarp extant is the *Epistle to the Philippians*, incomplete in the original Greek, but complete in a Latin translation. Somewhat commonplace in itself, it is of great value for questions of the canon, the origin of the Roman Church, and the Ignatian epistles.

POLYCLITUS (5th century BC) Greek sculptor from Samos, specializing in athletes, contemporary with **Phidias**. He was highly thought of by **Pliny**, especially for his bronze *Doryphorus*, which he deemed perfect sculpture.

POLYCRATES (c.536–522 BC) tyrant of Samos. He conquered several nearby islands and towns on the

Asiatic mainland and was one of the most conspicuous and powerful Greek tyrants of his time. He made an alliance with Amasis II, king of Egypt, but later broke it by giving support to the Persian king **Cambyses** in his invasion of Egypt. He successfully resisted an attack from Spartans, Corinthians and disaffected Samians, but was later lured to the mainland by a Persian satrap, seized, and crucified.

POLYDORE VERGIL See **VERGIL, Polydore**

POLYGNOTUS (5th century BC) Greek painter, born on the isle of Thasos. He was the first to give life and character to painting. His principal works were in Athens, Delphi and Plataea.

POMBAL, Sebastião José de Carvalho e Mello, Marquês de (1699–1782) Portuguese statesman, born near Coimbra. In 1739 he was sent as ambassador to London and to Vienna. Appointed secretary for foreign affairs (1750), he reattached many crown domains unjustly alienated; at the great Lisbon earthquake (1755) he showed much calmness and resource, and next year was made prime minister. He sought to subvert the tyranny of the church, opposed the intrigues of nobles and Jesuits, and in 1759 banished the Jesuits. He established elementary schools, reorganized the army, introduced fresh colonists into the Portuguese settlements and established West India and Brazil companies. The tyranny of the Inquisition was broken. Agriculture, commerce and finance were improved. In 1758 he was made Count of Oeyras, and in 1770 Marquis of Pombal. On the accession of Maria I (1777), who was under clerical influence, the 'Great Marquis' lost his offices.

POMPADOUR, Jeanne Antoinette Poisson, Marquise de (1721–64) mistress of **Louis XV**, born in Paris, supposedly the child of Le Normant de Tournehem, a wealthy *fermier-général*. In 1741 she was married to Le Normant's nephew, Le Normant d'Étoiles, became a queen of fashion, and attracted the eye of the king at a ball; she was installed at Versailles, and ennobled as Marquise de Pompadour. She assumed control of public affairs, for twenty years swayed the policy of the state, and lavished its treasures on her own ambitions. She reversed the traditional policy of France because **Frederick II, the Great** lampooned her, filled all public offices with her nominees, and made her own favourites ministers of France. Her policy was disastrous, her wars unfortunate—the ministry of Choiseul was the only fairly creditable portion of the reign. She founded the École Militaire and the royal factory at Sèvres. A lavish patron of the arts, she heaped her bounty upon poets and painters. She held her difficult position to the end, and retained the king's favour by relieving him of all business, by diverting him with private theatricals, and at last by countenancing his debaucheries. The *Mémoires* (1766) are not genuine.

POMPEY, Gnaeus Pompeius Magnus (106–48 BC) Roman soldier and statesman. At 17 he fought in the Social War against **Marius** and **Cinna**. He supported **Sulla**, and destroyed the remains of the Marian faction in Africa and Sicily. He next drove the followers of **Lepidus** out of Italy, extinguished the Marian party in Spain under **Sertorius** (76–71), and annihiliated the remnants of the army of **Spartacus**. He was now the idol of the people, and was elected consul for the year 70. Hitherto Pompey had belonged to the aristocratic party, but latterly he had been looked upon with suspicion, and he now espoused the people's cause and carried a law restoring the tribunician power to the people. He cleared the Mediterranean of pirates; defeated **Mithridates VI** of Pontus, **Tigranes** of Armenia, and **Antiochus** of Syria, subdued the Jews and captured Jerusalem, and entered Rome in triumph for the third time in 61. But now his star began to wane. Henceforward he was distrusted by the aristocracy, and second to **Caesar** in popular favour. When the senate declined to accede to his wish that his acts in Asia should be ratified he formed a close intimacy with Caesar, and the pair, with the plutocrat **Crassus**, formed the all-powerful 'First Triumvirate'. Pompey's acts in Asia were ratified; Caesar's designs were gained; and Caesar's daughter, Julia, was given in marriage to Pompey. Next year Caesar repaired to Gaul, and for nine years carried on a career of conquest, while Pompey was wasting his time in Rome. Jealousies arose between the two, and Julia died in 54. Pompey now returned to the aristocratic party. Caesar was ordered to lay down his office, which he consented to do if Pompey would do the same. The senate insisted on unconditional resignation, otherwise he would be declared a public enemy. But crossing the Rubicon, Caesar defied the senate and its armies. After his final defeat at Pharsalia in 48, Pompey fled to Egypt, where he was murdered. His younger son, Sextus, secured a fleet manned largely by slaves and exiles, and, occupying Sicily, ravaged the coasts of Italy. But in 36 he was defeated at sea by **Agrippa**, and in 37 slain at Mitylene.

POMPIDOU, Georges Jean Raymond (1911–74) French statesman, born in Montboudif in the Auvergne, and trained as an administrator. In 1944 he joined **de Gaulle**'s staff, their continued association being based on a similarity of opinion, though he had more moderate views. He held various government posts from 1946, culminating in his appointment as prime minister in 1962 (he was elected to the National Assembly in 1967). During the 'May Events' of 1968 Pompidou played a key role in defusing and resolving the political crisis, but was dismissed by his increasingly jealous patron, de Gaulle, soon after the parliamentary election held in June. However, in June 1969, following de Gaulle's resignation, he was comfortably elected president and proceeded to pursue a somewhat more liberal and internationalist policy programme, as reflected in his own more open and gregarious personality.

PONCE DE LEÓN, Juan (1460–1521) Spanish explorer, born in San Servas. A court page, he served against the Moors and became governor, first of part of Hispaniola, then (1510–12) of Puerto Rico. On a quest for the fountain of perpetual youth, he discovered Florida in March 1512, and was made governor. Failing to conquer his new subjects, he retired to Cuba, and died there from a wound inflicted by a poisoned arrow.

PONCE DE LEÓN, Luis (1527–91) Spanish monk, scholar and poet, born in Granada. In 1544 he entered the Augustinian order, and became professor of theology at Salamanca in 1561. From 1572 to 1576 he was imprisoned by the Inquisition for his translation and interpretation of the *Song of Solomon*; but shortly before his death he became general of his order. His poetical remains, published in 1631, comprise translations from **Virgil**, **Horace** and the *Psalms*; his few original poems are lyrical masterpieces.

PONCELET, Jean Victor (1788–1867) French engineer and geometrician, born in Metz. A military engineer, he became professor of mechanics at Metz (1825–35) and Paris (1838–48). His *Traité des propriétés projectives des figures* (1822) gives him an important place in the development of projective geometry.

PONCHIELLI, Amilcare (1834–86) Italian composer, born in Paderno Fasolare near Cremona. He studied for eleven years at Milan Conservatory, and became musical director at Bergamo Cathedral

(1881–86). He wrote several operas, including *La Gioconda* (1876), and a successful ballet, *Le due Gemelle* (1873).

POND, John (1767–1836) English astronomer. Astronomer-royal from 1811, he improved methods and instruments of observation at Greenwich. His work was notable for its extreme accuracy.

PONIATOWSKI, Joseph Antony (1762–1813) Polish prince and soldier, born in Warsaw, nephew of **Stanislaw Augustus Poniatowski**. He trained in the Austrian army. In 1789 the Polish Assembly appointed him commander of the army of the south, with which he gained brilliant victories over the Russians (1792); and he commanded under **Kosciuszko** (1794). When the duchy of Warsaw was constituted (1807), he was appointed minister of war and commander-in-chief. In 1809, during the war between Austria and France, he invaded Galicia. Three years later with a large body of Poles he joined **Napoleon** in his invasion of Russia, and distinguished himself at Smolensk at Borodino, and at Leipzig, where, in covering the French retreat, he was drowned in the Elster.

PONIATOWSKI, Stanislas (1677–1762) father of **Stanislas Augustus Poniatowski**, last king of Poland. He joined **Charles XII** of Sweden in supporting **Stanislaus Leszczynski** and later under Augustus II and III was appointed to several administrative posts in Lithuania and Poland.

PONIATOWSKI, Stanislas Augustus (1732–98) last king of Poland, son of **Stanislas Poniatowski**. In St Petersburg in 1755, while in the suite of the British ambassador, he became much favoured by the Empress **Catherine II, the Great**. Largely through her influence he was elected king in 1764, though not fitted to rule the country at a time of such crisis. **Frederick II, the Great**, who had gained the consent of Austria to a partition of Poland, made a similar proposal to Russia, and the first partition was effected in 1772. The diet tried, too late, to introduce reforms. The intrigues of discontented nobles led again to Russian and Prussian intervention, and a second fruitless resistance was followed in 1793 by a second partition. The Poles now became desperate; a general rising took place (1794), the Prussians were driven out, and the Russians were several times routed. But Austria now appeared on the scene, **Kosciuszko** was defeated, Warsaw was taken, and the Polish monarchy was at an end. Stanislaw resigned his crown (1795), and died in St Petersburg.

PONS, Lily (Alice Joséphine) (1898–1976) French-born American soprano, born in Draguignan. A fine dramatic coloratura, she excelled in opera, achieving immense success in Paris, London, South America and, especially at the New York Metropolitan. She also sang in films, and during World War II toured North Africa and the Far East.

PONSELLE, (Ponzillo) Rosa (1897–1981) American soprano, born in Meridan, Connecticut. Her career began in vaudeville. At **Caruso**'s suggestion she appeared as Leonora in *La forza del destino* at the New York Metropolitan (1918), where she sang in leading French and Italian grand opera roles until 1937, also appearing at Covent Garden in 1929–31. She later taught and directed opera in Baltimore.

PONSONBY, Sarah See **BUTLER, Lady Eleanor**

PONT, Timothy (c.1560–1630) Scottish cartographer. He graduated at St Andrews in 1584, became minister of Dunnet (1601), and in 1609 subscribed for 2000 acres of forfeited land in Ulster. He first projected a Scottish atlas, and surveyed all the counties and isles of the kingdom. His collections were rescued from destruction by Sir John Scot of Scotstarvet, and his maps, revised by Robert Gordon of Straloch, appeared in Blaeu's *Theatrum Orbis Terrarum* (1654).

PONTECORVO, Guido (1907–) Italian-born British geneticist, born in Pisa, where he studied agricultural science. Thereafter he supervised cattle breeding in Tuscany. After moving in 1938 to the Institute of Animal Genetics in Edinburgh, he became interested in pure genetics, especially using fungi. In 1950, with J Roper, he discovered the parasexual cycle in fungi, which allows genetic analysis of asexual fungi. Soon afterwards he proposed that the gene is the unit of function in genetics, an idea proved by **Seymour Benzer** and others in 1955.

PONTIAC (c.?1720–1769) chief of the Ottawa Indians. In 1763 he organized a rising against the English garrisons, and for five months besieged Detroit. He was murdered by an Illinois Indian.

PONTOPPIDAN, Erik (1698–1764) Danish theologian, born in Aarhus. He was professor of theology at Copenhagen (1738), bishop of Bergen (1747), and wrote *Annales Ecclesiae Danicae Diplomaticae*, a Danish topography, a Norwegian glossary, and *Norges Naturlige Historie* (trans 1755), describing the Kraken (sea-serpent) amongst others.

PONTOPPIDAN, Henrik (1857–1944) Danish novelist, born in Fredericia, the son of a pastor. He trained as an engineer but turned to writing. Among his novels were *Land of Promise* (1891–95), *Lykke-Per* (1898–1904) and *The Realm of the Dead* (1912–16). He shared the Nobel prize for literature in 1917 with his fellow Danish novelist, Karl Gjellerup (1857–1919).

PONTORMO, Jacopo da (1494–1552) Florentine painter, whose family name was Carucci. He was influenced by **Leonardo da Vinci** and **Piero di Cosimo** and worked under **Andrea del Sarto**. His works included frescoes, notably of the Passion (1522–25), in the Certosa near Florence. The *Deposition* (c.1525), which forms the altarpiece in a chapel in Sta Felicità, Florence, is probably his masterpiece, and is a prime example of the early Mannerist style. He also painted portraits and the **Medici** villa at Poggio a Caiano was partly decorated by him. His later work shows the influence of **Michelangelo**.

PONTRYAGIN, Lev Semyonovich (1908–88) Russian mathematician, born in Moscow. The loss of his sight in an accident at the age of 14 did not prevent him from graduating from Moscow University where he became professor in 1935. One of the leading Russian topologists, he worked on topological groups and their character theory, on duality in algebraic topology, and on differential equations with applications to optimal control. His book *Topological groups* (trans 1939) is still a standard work.

POOLE, Reginald Stuart (1832–95) English archaeologist, born in London. He lived in Cairo from 1842 to 1849, subsequently becoming an eminent Egyptologist. He was keeper of coins and medals at the British Museum (1870–93) and, from 1889 until his death, professor of classical archaeology at University College, London. One of the founding members of the Egypt Exploration Fund (later Society), he served as secretary (1882–87), and vice-president (1887–95).

POOLE, William Frederick (1821–94) American librarian, born in Salem, Massachusetts. He graduated at Yale, where in 1848 he published an *Index of Periodical Literature*, to which supplements were later added. From 1856 to 1869 he was librarian of the Boston Athenaeum, and from 1888 of the Newberry Library at Chicago.

POPE, Alexander (1688–1744) English poet, born in London. His father was a linen merchant who retired soon after his son was born, and the family moved to

Binfield in Windsor Forest when Alexander was an infant. He was educated erratically at Catholic schools but was largely self-taught, which left gaps in his knowledge of literature. At the age of three he suffered his first serious illness and at twelve he was crippled by a tubercular infection of the spine which accounted for his stunted growth (4 ft 6 in). He began writing at an early age; 'Ode to Solitude' was completed in the same year as his illness. Reading and writing feverishly, he got to know members of the literati—William Walsh, Henry Cromwell, and Sir William Trumball—who acted as mentors, critics and encouragers. He wrote *The Pastorals* while a teenager and they were eventually published by **Jacob Tonson** in 1709. Metrically adept, they are remembered for his mastery of technique rather than their poetry. But already he had moved on and was working on the seminal work *An Essay on Criticism* (1711), whose couplets caused a stir. *The Rape of the Lock* followed in 1712 and confirmed him as a poetic force. A mock epic, this exquisite work can be enjoyed throughout as a true epic diminished to contemporary proportions. With *Windsor Forest* (1713) his popularity was further enhanced and he became a favourite in London where he was now living. **Addison** and **Swift** were among his acquaintances and he became a member of the Scriblerus Club. His persistent ambition was to translate **Homer**, and the first instalment of the *Iliad* appeared in 1715; when completed in 1720 its genius was immediately acknowledged though it bore flimsy resemblance to the original. During this time he also issued his *Works* (1717), a pot-pourri of odes, epistles, elegies and a translation of **Chaucer**'s *The House of Fame*. He also met and befriended Lady **Mary Wortley Montagu**, a friendship which foundered after they quarrelled in 1723. Pope contemptuously dismissed her in a few lines in his *Imitations of Homer*. With the success of the *Iliad*, Pope was financially secure and was regarded as the senior figure of English letters, much sought after and revered. He bought a villa in Twickenham and lived there until his death. In 1726 he completed the *Odyssey*, following the failure of his edition of **Shakespeare** (1725) which **Lewis Theobald** criticized for its slip-shoddiness and poor scholarship. Pope got his revenge in *The Dunciad* (1728), a mock-heroic satire, published anonymously, whose butt is 'Dulness' in general and, in particular, all the authors whom he wanted to hold up to ridicule. It is not, however, confined to personal animus, and literary vices are likewise exposed and scorned. With **Swift**, **Gay**, Lord **Oxford**, **Arbuthnot** and **Bolingbroke** he arranged the publication of a *Miscellany* of which three volumes appeared between 1727 and 1728. Pope's contributions included *An Epistle to Dr Arbuthnot* (published separately in 1735) and *Martinus Scriblerus peri Bathous: or The Art of Sinking in Poetry*, a satirical invective that insulted various poetasters. That and *The Dunciad* prompted a tiresome literary feud which dragged on interminably. In 1733–34 he published his *Essay on Man* and wrote *Moral Essays* (1731–35). His last years were engaged in organizing his correspondence for publication but while this marked a new development in English literature he tinkered too much with the originals and their value as social documents was impaired. Since his death his reputation has waxed, waned and waxed again. His technical brilliance has never been in doubt, but he lacked the surface warmth that endears lesser poets to the reading public. Nor was he an attractive figure, either in manner or physique. Much of this may have been due to inconsistent health, but without his abrasive side English satire would be the poorer, for he was the sharpest and most innovative of its practitioners.

POPE, John (1822–92) American soldier, born in Louisville, Kentucky. He graduated at West Point in 1842, and served with the engineers in Florida (1842–44) and in the Mexican war. He was exploring and surveying in the west until the Civil War (1861–65), when as brigadier-general in 1861 he drove the guerrillas out of Missouri. As major-general he commanded the army of the Mississippi (1862) and then that of Virginia, but was defeated at the second battle of Bull Run (1862). He was transferred to Minnesota, where he kept the Indians in check, and held commands until 1886, when he retired.

POPE, Sir William Jackson (1870–1939) English chemist, born in London. He studied chemistry at Finsbury Technical College and the Central Institution, London (later to become Imperial College). He became head of chemistry at Goldsmith's College, London; then professor of chemistry at Manchester, and in 1908 at Cambridge. He demonstrated that in an optically active compound the asymmetric centres could be due to elements other than carbon. He also showed that compounds containing no asymmetric atoms could still be optically active.

POPE-HENNESSY, Sir John (1913–) English art historian, born in London and educated at Balliol College, Oxford. He joined the staff of the Victoria and Albert Museum in 1938, and has subsequently held many academic and curatorial posts, including Slade professor of fine art at Oxford (1956–57), and at Cambridge (1964–65); he was director of the V & A (1967–73), and director of the British Museum, (1974–76), before going to New York, where he has been consultative chairman, department of European paintings, at the Metropolitan Museum since 1977. A leading authority on Italian renaissance art, his many books include studies of Sienese painting, **Uccello**, **Fra Angelico** and a series of definitive volumes on Italian sculpture.

POPHAM, Sir John (c.1531–1607) English lawyer, born in Huntworth near Bridgwater. He became speaker in the House of Commons in 1580 and lord chief justice in 1592. He presided at the trial of **Guy Fawkes**.

POPIELUSKO, Jerzy, originally **Alfons Popielusko** (1947–84) Polish priest, born in Okopy, near Svchowola, Podlasie. Serving in several Warsaw parishes after ordination, and inspired by the faith of his compatriot St Maximilian Kolbe (1894–1941), he became an outspoken supporter of the Solidarity trade union, especially when it was banned in 1981. His sermons at 'Masses for the Country' regularly held in St Stanislaw Kostka church were widely acclaimed. He ignored harassment and resisted official moves to have him silenced, but was kidnapped and murdered by the secret police in October 1984.

POPOV, Aleksandr Stepanovich (1859–1905) Russian physicist. Independently of **Guglielmo Marconi**, he is acclaimed in Russia as the inventor of wireless telegraphy (1895). He was the first to use a suspended wire as an aerial.

POPOVA, Liubov Sergeevna, née **Eding** (1889–1924) Russian painter and stage designer, born near Moscow. After studying in Paris (1912–13) she returned to Russia where she met **Tatlin**, the founder of Soviet Constructivism. In the year before her death she designed textiles for the First State Textile Print Factory, Moscow, where she was given a memorial exhibition in 1924. Her work was especially important for its exploration of abstract colour values.

POPPER, Sir Karl Raimund (1902–) Austrian-born British philosopher, born in Vienna. He studied at the university there and associated with the 'Vienna Circle' of philosophers, though he sharply criticized their logical positivism and their views, for example, on meaning and verification. He published in 1934 a major work in scientific methodology, *Die Logik der Forschung* (trans as *The Logic of Scientific Discovery*, 1959). This stressed the importance of 'falsifiability' as a defining factor of true scientific theories, and he contrasted these with 'pseudosciences', like Marxism and psychoanalysis, that would never specify in advance the conditions under which they could be tested and refuted. He extended the critique of Marxism in *The Open Society and its Enemies* (1945), a brilliant polemic directed against all philosophical systems with totalitarian political implications from **Plato** to **Marx**; and both here and in *The Poverty of Historicism* (1957) he attacks more generally the idea that historians and social scientists can discover large-scale laws of historical development with predictive potential. He left Vienna in 1937 under the threat of German occupation, and taught philosophy at Canterbury University College, New Zealand (1937–45), and then was reader (1945–48) and later professor (1949–69) at the London School of Economics. His later works include *Conjectures and Refutations* (1963), *Objective Knowledge* (1972), and *The Self and Its Brain* (1977, with Sir **John Eccles**).

POPSKI See **PENIAKOFF, Vladimir**

PORDAGE, John See **BÖHME, Jakob**

PORDENONE, Il, properly **Giovanni Antonio Licinio de Sacchis** (1483–1539) Italian religious painter, born in Corticelli near Pordenone. In 1535 he settled in Venice, and in 1538 was summoned by the duke to Ferrara. He painted frescoes in the cathedral at Cremona and in Sta Maria da Campagna at Piacenza.

PORPHYRY (c.232–c.305) Neoplatonist philosopher, born of Syrian parents, probably in Tyre, where he spent his boyhood. He studied at Athens and gained a reputation as a polymathic scholar, 'a living library and a walking museum'. In 263 he went to Rome where he became a devoted pupil of **Plotinus**, and later his biographer and editor. He is probably most important as a popularizer of Plotinus's thought, but his own works include a celebrated treatise *Against the Christians* (now lost), influential commentaries on **Plato**, Plotinus, and **Aristotle** (especially his *Introduction* to the *Categories*, which **Boethius** translated into Latin), *De Abstinentia* (a vegetarian tract), and a moral address to his wife, Marcella.

PORPORA, Niccola Antonio (1686–1766) Italian composer and teacher of singing, born in Naples. He established a school for singing, which fostered many famous singers. During the period 1725–55 he was in Dresden, Venice, London (1734–36) and Vienna (where he taught **Haydn**), composing operas and teaching. He figures in **George Sand**'s *Consuelo*.

PORSCHE, Ferdinand (1875–1951) German car designer, born in Hafersfdorf, Bohemia. He designed cars for Daimler and Auto Union, but set up his own independent studio in 1931, and in 1934 produced the plans for a revolutionary cheap car with rear engine, to which the Nazis gave the name *Volkswagen* ('People's car') and which they promised to mass-produce for the German workers. After World War II the 'Beetle' became a record-breaking German export. He also designed the distinctive sports car that bears his name.

PORSENNA (LARS PORSENNA) (6th century BC) according to Roman patriotic tradition the Etruscan ruler of Clusium, who laid siege to Rome after the overthrow in 510 BC of **Tarquinius Superbus**, but was prevented from capturing the city by the heroism of Horatius Cocles defending the bridge across the Tiber. However, this tradition may conceal a temporary occupation of Rome by Porsenna.

PORSON, Richard (1759–1808) English classical scholar, born in East Rushton, Norfolk, the son of the parish clerk. Prodigiously precocious as a child, he was educated by benefactors at Eton and Trinity College, Cambridge, and was appointed Regius professor of Greek at Cambridge in 1792. He made his name as a defender of **Erasmus Darwin** in his brilliant *Letters to Archdeacon Travis* (1788–89) in the *Gentleman's Magazine* on the authenticity of the text of a passage in the First Epistle of St John (v 7). He edited four plays by **Euripides** (1797–1801), and contributed hugely to Greek scholarship through his elucidation of idiom and usage and prosody.

PORTA, Baccio della See **BARTOLOMMEO**

PORTA, Carlo (1776–1821) Italian poet, born in Milan. Writing in the dialect of Milan, he showed his insight into human character in narrative poems which are satirical and grimly realistic. These include *La Nomina del Capellan*, *La Guerra di Pret* and *I Disgrazzi di Giovannin Bongee*.

PORTA, Giacomo della (1541–1604) Italian architect. A pupil of **Vignola**, he is best known for the cupola of St Peter's and his work on the Palazzo Farnese, left unfinished by **Michelangelo**. He was also responsible for some of the fountains of Rome.

PORTA, Giovanni Battista della (1543–1615) Italian physicist and philosopher. He wrote on physiognomy, natural magic, the steam pump, the properties of lenses, and gardening, besides several comedies.

PORTA, Guglielmo della (c.1510–1577) Italian sculptor. His main work was the tomb of Pope **Paul III** in the choir of **St Peter**'s.

PORTAL, Charles Frederick Algernon, 1st Viscount Portal of Hungerford (1893–1971) English air force officer, born in Hungerford, Berkshire, of an old Huguenot family. Educated at Winchester and Christ Church College, Oxford, he joined the Royal Engineers as a motor-cyclist in August 1914. He was commissioned in the Royal Engineers, but served in the Royal Flying Corps (1915–18). Promoted air vice marshal in 1937, he was director of organization at the air ministry (1937–38). In 1940 he was commander in chief of Bomber Command (April–October), before becoming chief of air staff (1940–46). He was controller of the Atomic Energy Authority (1946–51), and was appointed chairman of the British Aircraft Corporation in 1960.

PORTALIS, Jean Étienne Marie (1745–1807) French jurist and statesman. He practised law in Paris, was imprisoned during the Revolution, but under **Napoleon** was a principal draftsman of the *Code Civil*.

PORTEOUS, John (d.1736) Scottish soldier, born in the Canongate, Edinburgh, the son of a tailor. Trained as a tailor, his father disowned him because of his violent temper. He enlisted in the army and served in Holland, and soon after 1715 he returned home and was appointed drill-master of the Edinburgh town guard, which was being trained as a civil militia against the 1715 Jacobite Rising. He became captain of the guard in 1726. On 14 April 1736 he was in charge at the execution of Andrew Wilson, a smuggler who had robbed the Pittenweem custom-house. There was some stone-throwing; whereupon the guard fired on the mob, wounding 12 persons and killing three (the so-called 'Porteous Riot'). Porteous was tried and condemned to death (20 July), but reprieved by Queen **Caroline**. But on the night of 7 September an organized mob burst open the Tolbooth, dragged Porteous to the

Grassmarket, and hanged him from a dyer's pole. The story is told in **Walter Scott**'s *The Heart of Midlothian*.

PORTER, Anna Maria (1780–1832) English novelist, born in Durham, younger sister of **Jane Porter** and **Robert Ker Porter**. Her novel *The Hungarian Brothers* (1807), about the French Revolution, was highly successful and achieved numerous editions.

PORTER, Cole (1891–1964) American composer, born in Peru, Indiana. He studied law at Harvard before deciding upon a musical career and entering the Schola Cantorum in Paris. Attracted to musical comedy, he composed lyrics and music for many stage successes. In 1937 he was severely hurt in a riding accident, leaving him in permanent pain, but he continued to compose, reaching the height of his success with, in 1948, *Kiss me Kate* and, in 1953, *Can-Can*. His highly personal style and dramatic sense is illustrated by such popular songs as 'Night and Day' and 'Begin the Beguine'.

PORTER, David (1780–1843) American naval officer, born in Boston, Massachusetts, the son of a naval officer. He entered the navy in 1798, became captain in 1812, and captured the first British warship taken in the war. In 1813 he nearly destroyed the English whale fishery in the Pacific, and took possession of the Marquesas Islands; but in 1814 his frigate was captured by the British off Valparaíso. He afterwards commanded an expedition against pirates in the West Indies (1823–25). He resigned in 1826, and for a time commanded the Mexican navy. In 1829 the United States appointed him consul-general to the Barbary States, and then minister at Constantinople, where he died.

PORTER, David Dixon (1813–91) American naval officer, born in Chester, Pennsylvania, son of **David Porter**. He accompanied his father against the pirates in the West Indies, and in the Mexican navy. In the Civil War, as commander of the federal mortar flotilla, he bombarded the New Orleans forts in April 1862. In September, with the Mississippi squadron, he passed the batteries of Vicksburg, and bombarded the city; in December 1864 he silenced Fort Fisher, taken the following month. Superintendent till 1869 of Annapolis naval academy, he was made admiral of the navy in 1870. As well as three romances, he wrote *Incidents of the Civil War* (1885), and *History of the Navy During the War of the Rebellion* (1887).

PORTER, Eleanor, née **Hodgman** (1868–1920) American novelist, born in Littleton, New Hampshire. She studied music at the New England Conservatory. She married in 1892. Her first novels included *Cross Currents* (1907) and *Miss Billy* (1911). In 1913 *Pollyanna* appeared; this was an immediate success and has retained its popularity ever since. A sequel, *Pollyanna Grows Up*, was published in 1915, and two volumes of short stories, *The Tangled Threads* and *Across the Years*, appeared posthumously in 1924.

PORTER, Endymion (1587–1649) English royalist, servant to **James VI and I**, was groom of the bedchamber to **Charles I**, and fought for him in the Civil War. He wrote verses and was painted by Van Dyck.

PORTER, Eric (1928–) English actor, born in London. He made his first appearance in 1945 at the Arts Theatre, Cambridge, and his London début in 1946. He was in the RAF from 1946 to 1947 and subsequently toured with **Donald Wolfit**'s company. From 1952 to 1953, he was with **John Gielgud**'s company at the Lyric Theatre, Hammersmith. He has built up a formidable reputation as an actor in both classical and modern roles at the Old Vic, the Royal Shakespeare Company, and the National Theatre, where he gave a magnificent performance as Big Daddy in **Tennessee Williams**'s *Cat on a Hot Tin Roof* in 1988 and, the following year, as King Lear in **Jonathan Miller**'s dark and brooding revival at the Old Vic. He has made several film and television appearances, notably in the BBC television series, *The Forsyte Saga*.

PORTER, Gene, née **Stratton** (1868–1924) American novelist, born on a farm in Wabash County, Indiana. She married Charles D Porter in 1886, and as Gene Stratton Porter attained great popularity with *A Girl of the Limberlost* (1909) and other stories full of sentiment and nature study.

PORTER, Sir George (1920–) English physical chemist, born in Stainforth. Educated at Thorne Grammar School, he studied radio physics at Leeds. As a naval officer in World War II he worked with radar. In Cambridge from 1945 with **Ronald Norrish** he studied the detection and identification of the short-lived radical intermediates involved in photochemical gas reactions. Later, he was able to trap radicals in supercooled liquid, and he was an early user of lasers in photochemistry. He became director of the Royal Institution in 1966 and shared the Nobel prize for chemistry in 1967 with Norrish and **Manfred Eigen**.

PORTER, Jane (1776–1850) English writer, born in Durham, sister of **Anna Maria Porter** and **Robert Ker Porter**, and daughter of an army surgeon. She made a great reputation in 1803 by her high-flown romance, *Thaddeus of Warsaw*, and had even more success in 1810 with *The Scottish Chiefs*. Other books were *The Pastors' Fireside* (1815), *Duke Christian of Lüneburg* (1824), *Tales Round a Winter's Hearth* (with her sister Anna Maria, 1824), and *The Field of Forty Footsteps* (1828). *Sir Edward Seaward's Shipwreck* (1831), a clever fiction, edited by her, was almost certainly written by her eldest brother, Dr William Ogilvie Porter (1774–1850).

PORTER, Katherine Anne Maria Veronica Callista Russell (1890–1980) American writer, born in Indian Creek, Texas. Brought up by a grandmother near Kyle, Texas, she ran away and got married at 16, but divorced at 19. She worked as a reporter and actress, moved to Greenwich Village, and went to Mexico (1920–22) and took up Mexican causes. She had started writing at a very early age, but allowed nothing to be published until 1928, with her first collection of stories, *Flowering Judas*. Later, in Paris, she married a consular official (divorced 1938), and wrote her first novel, *Hacienda* (1934). Back in the USA she married for a third time, a professor of English, but divorced four years later. Three short novels, published as *Pale Horse, Pale Rider* (1939), were a success. *Ship of Fools* (1962), an immense allegorical novel analyzing the German state of mind in the 1930s, aroused great controversy. A volume of essays, *The Days before*, appeared in 1952. Her *Collected Short Stories* (1965) won a Pulitzer prize.

PORTER, Michael (c.1947–) American management theorist, born in Ann Arbor, Michigan. Trained as an economist at Princeton and Harvard Business School, he became a lecturer at Harvard (1973) and subsequently professor (1982). In 1983 he founded Monitor Co Inc, a strategic consulting organization. He was in great demand throughout the 1980s as a lecturer and consultant to many leading US and UK organizations. His book *Competitive Analysis* (1980) has been translated into 13 languages and has had over 30 printings. In 1989 he published *The Competitive Advantage of Nations and their Firms*.

PORTER, Noah (1811–92) American clergyman, born in Farmington, Connecticut. He studied at Yale, was a Congregational pastor (1836–46), then became professor of moral philosophy at Yale, and from 1871 to 1886 was president of the college. He was editor in chief of *Webster's American Dictionary of the English Language* (1864) and *Webster's International Dictionary of the English Language* (1890). Among his other works are *The Human Intellect* (1868), *Books and Reading* (1870), and *Moral Science* (1885).

PORTER, Peter (1929–) Australian poet and critic, born in Brisbane. He lived in England from 1951 to 1974 and London has been his base since, though he frequently visits Australia. He has worked as a bookseller, journalist, clerk and advertising copywriter. A difficult, clever and allusive poet, his several collections include *Words Without Music* (1968), *A Porter Portfolio* (1969), *The Last of England* (1970) and *The Cost of Seriousness* (1978). His *Collected Poems* (1983) confirmed him as a gifted aphorist.

PORTER, Robert Ker (1775–1842) English battle painter, brother of **Anna Maria Porter** and **Jane Porter**. He visited Russia in 1804, where he was historical painter to the tsar. He accompanied Sir **John Moore**'s expedition in 1808. He was afterwards British consul in Venezuela, and published books of travel in Russia, Sweden, Spain, Portugal, Georgia, Persia and Armenia.

PORTER, Rodney Robert (1917–85) English biochemist, born in Liverpool. He studied there and in Cambridge with **Frederick Sanger** (1946–49), and worked at the National Institute for Medical Research (1949–60) and St Mary's Hospital Medical School in London (1960–67), and became professor of biochemistry at Oxford in 1967. He had worked in London on antibodies from 1949, and, using his own results, together with studies by **Gerald Edelman** and others, he was able to propose an overall molecular structure for antibodies which later results have confirmed and refined. These ideas of the 1960s linked the biochemistry of antibodies with immunology in a fruitful way; and led to Porter and Edelman sharing the Nobel prize for physiology or medicine in 1972.

PORTER, William S See **HENRY, O**

PORTO-RICHE, Georges de (1849–1930) French dramatist, born in Bordeaux. He wrote several successful psychological plays, including *L'Amoureuse* (1891), *Le Vieil homme* (1911) and *Le Marchand d'Estampes* (1917). .

PORTSMOUTH, Louise de Kéroualle, Duchess of (1649–1734) French courtesan, mistress of **Charles II** of Britain, born in Brittany. She went to England in 1670 in the train of **Henrietta-Anne, Duchess of Orléans**, Charles II's cherished sister, ostensibly as a lady-in-waiting, but secretly charged to influence the king in favour of the French alliance. Charles made her his mistress and ennobled her (1673) and her son, who became Duke of Richmond. Rapacious and haughty, 'Madame Carwell' was universally detested.

PORUS See **ALEXANDER THE GREAT**

POSIDONIUS (c.135–c.51 BC) Greek Stoic philosopher, scientist and polymath, born in Apamea in Syria, and nicknamed 'the Athlete'. He studied at Athens as a pupil of **Panatius**, spent many years on travel and scientific research in Europe and Africa, then settled in Rhodes and became an active citizen there. In 86 BC he was sent as an envoy to Rome, where he settled and became a friend of **Cicero** and other leading figures of the day. He wrote on an enormous range of subjects, including geometry, geography, astronomy, meteorology, history and philosophy (though only fragments of all these survive), and made important contributions to the development of Stoic doctrines.

POST, Wiley (1900–35) American pioneer aviator, born in Grand Saline, Texas. In the early 1920s he went barnstorming as a mechanic, stunt parachutist and wingwalker, learning to fly in 1924. On 23 June 1931 he left Roosevelt Field, New York City, in a Lockheed Vega monoplane with the Australian Harold Gatty (1903–57) as navigator to fly around the world in eight days, 15 hours and 51 minutes. He gained instant fame, since the previous record had been made by the Graf Zeppelin in 21 days. In 1933 he made the first solo flight round the world, in seven days, 18 hours and 49 minutes. He was killed in an air crash in Alaska.

POTEMKIN, Grigori Aleksandrovich (1739–91) Russian solder and statesman, born near Smolensk, of a noble but impoverished Polish family. He entered the Russian Horse Guards in 1755, and attracted the notice of **Catherine II, the Great** by his handsome face and figure. He distinguished himself in Catherine's 1st Turkish War (1768–74), and in 1774 became her recognized paramour, and directed Russian policy. There is reason to believe they were secretly married. In charge of the new lands in the south acquired by conquest, he made an able administrator, and constructed a fleet in the Black Sea. In the 2nd Turkish War (1787–92) he was placed at the head of the army, and reaped the credit of **Suvorov**'s victories (1791). He died in the same year. Licentious, astute and unscrupulous, in spite of his lavish extravagance he heaped up an immense fortune. He gained for Russia the Crimea and the north coast of the Black Sea, and he founded Sebastopol, Nikolaev and Ekaterinoslav (Dnepropetrovsk).

POTHIER, Robert Joseph (1699–1772) French jurist and judge, who worked in Orléans for 50 years. He closely studied **Justinian**'s *Corpus Juris Civilis* with its confused order of texts, and between 1748 and 1752 published the texts rearranged within the titles in logical order, with a learned preface about the sources of Roman law and the characteristics of the jurists from whose works excerpts appear in the *Digest*. In 1749 he became professor of law at Orléans and revived that law school. In 1761 he produced a work on the customary law of Orléans, comparing it with other regional customs. This was followed by a series of texts on the specific topics of the law, such as sale, hiring, ownership, possession etc; the most influential of these has been the *Treatise on Obligations*. Large parts of his works were incorporated almost verbatim in the French Civil Code of 1808.

POTT, August Friedrich (1802–87) German philologist, born in Nettelrede in Hanover. In 1833 he became professor of the science of language at Halle. The foundation of Pott's reputation was laid by his *Etymologische Forschungen* (1833–36); among his other notable works are the articles he contributed to **Ersch** and Gruber's *Encyklopädie*.

POTT, Percival (1714–88) English surgeon, born in London. He became assistant and then senior surgeon at St Bartholomew's Hospital, where he introduced many improvements to make surgery more humane. He wrote *Fractures and Dislocations* (1765), in which he described a compound leg fracture suffered by himself, still called 'Pott's fracture', and gave a clinical account of a disease of the spine called 'Pott's disease'.

POTTER, (Helen) Beatrix (1866–1943) English author and illustrator of books for children, born in Kensington, London, into a wealthy family. The atmosphere at home was oppressively quiet and Beatrix, supervised by nurses and educated by governesses, grew up a lonely town child longing for the country. She taught herself to draw and paint, and while still quite young did serious natural history studies of fungi with the intention of making a book of watercolours. She turned to sketching pet animals dressed as human beings to amuse younger children. The original version of *The Tale of Peter Rabbit* was enclosed with a letter to her ex-governess's child in 1893 and later published at her own expense, with fuller illustrations, in 1900, as was *The Tailor of Gloucester* (1902). When Frederick Warne took over publication in 1903 she had her first popular success with *The Tale of Squirrel Nutkin* (1903). In an appreciative, if gently satirical, review **Graham Greene** considered *The Roly-Poly Pudding* (1908) (later changed to *The Tale of Samuel Whiskers*), to be her masterpiece. Miss Potter was not amused. In 1913, eight years after she had moved to a farm at Sawrey, near Lake Windermere (where six of her books are set), she married William Heelis, a Lake District solicitor. Thereafter she devoted herself almost entirely to farming and the new National Trust. *Johnny Town-Mouse* (1918) was her last book in the familiar style. She devised an elaborate cryptic diary whose code was broken by Leslie Linder and published as *The Journal of Beatrix Potter 1881–1897* (1966). She was the outstanding writer and artist of picture-story books of her time, and Peter the Rabbit, Jemima Puddle-Duck, Mrs Tiggy-Winkle, Benjamin Bunny and the rest have become classics of children's literature.

POTTER, Dennis (1935–) English dramatist. Although he has written for the stage (*Sufficient Carbohydrate*, 1984), he is primarily a television dramatist. Since *Vote, Vote, Vote for Nigel Barton* (1965), he has written over 25 television plays and series. *Son of Man* (1969) was the first television screenplay that depicted Christ as a man who struggled as much with his own doubts as with those opposed to his teaching. Other controversial plays include *Brimstone and Treacle* and *The Singing Detective*. He is also technically innovative: *Pennies from Heaven* (1978) required the actors to mime to popular songs of the 1920s and 30s that intercut the action; *Blue Remembered Hills* (1979), a memory play, required the adult actors to impersonate children.

POTTER, John (c.1674–1747) English scholar and prelate, born in Wakefield. He became Regius professor of divinity at Oxford in 1707, bishop of Oxford in 1715, and in 1737 archbishop of Canterbury. He published *Archaeologia Graeca, or Antiquities of Greece* (1696–99), among other works.

POTTER, Paul (1625–54) Dutch painter and etcher, born in Enkhuizen, the son of a painter. His best pictures are small pastoral scenes with animal figures. He also painted large pictures, the life size *Young Bull* (1647) being especially celebrated.

POTTER, Philip (1921–) West Indian ecumenical leader, born in Roseau, Dominica. After studying law and pastoring a Methodist church in Haiti, he became secretary of the youth department of the World Council of Churches in 1954. Appointed Methodist Missionary Society (London) field secretary for Africa and the West Indies (1960–67) and chairman of the World Student Christian Federation (1960–67), he was promoted director of World Mission and Evangelism (1967–72) and then general secretary (1972–84) of the World Council of Churches. His aim has been described as one of keeping the ecumenical movement theologically faithful and socially credible, as in *Life in All its Fullness* (1981).

POTTER, Stephen (1900–69) English writer and radio producer. He joined the BBC in 1938, and was co-author with **Joyce Grenfell** of the *How* series. He wrote a novel, *The Young Man* (1929), and an educational study, *The Muse in Chains* (1937), but made his name with a series of comic books on the art of establishing personal supremacy by demoralizing the opposition, with *Gamesmanship* (1947), *Lifemanship* (1950), *One-Upmanship* (1952), *Potter on America* (1956) and *Supermanship* (1958).

POUJADE, Pierre (1920–) French political leader, born in Saint Cére. After serving in World War II, he became a publisher and bookseller. In 1951 he was elected a member of the Saint Cére municipal council, and in 1954 he organized his Poujadist movement (union for the defence of tradesmen and artisans) as a protest against the French tax system. His party had successes in the 1956 elections to the National Assembly. He published his manifesto, *J'ai choisi le combat*, in 1956.

POULENC, Francis (1899–1963) French composer, born in Paris. He fought in World War I, studied composition under Koechlin, came under the influence of **Satie**, and as a member of 'Les Six' was prominent in the reaction against Debussyesque impressionism. He wrote a good deal of chamber music in a cool, limpid style, often for unusual combinations of instruments, and is also known for some excellent stage works, especially the ballet *Les Biches* and the operas *Les Mamelles de Tirésias* and *Dialogues des Carmélites*. His cantata *Figure humaine* (1945) has as its theme the occupation of France. Perhaps his major contribution to music is his considerable output of songs, more romantic in outlook than his other compositions; they include *Poèmes de Ronsard* (1924), and *Fêtes Galantes* (1943).

POULSEN, Valdemar (1869–1942) Danish electrical engineer, born in Copenhagen. Working for the Copenhagen Telephone Company, he invented the telegraphone, a wire recording device, forerunner of magnetic tape recorders (1898). In 1903 he invented an arc generator for use in wireless telegraphy.

POUND, (Alfred) Dudley Pickman Rogers (1877–1943) English naval commander. He became captain in 1914, commanded with distinction the battleship *Colossus* at the battle of Jutland (1916), and for the remaining two years of World War I directed operations at the Admiralty. Promoted to the rank of rear admiral, he was commander-in-chief, Mediterranean fleet (1936–39), becoming in 1939 Admiral of the Fleet. In the same year he was appointed First Sea Lord, and this post he held through the most difficult years of the war.

POUND, Ezra Loomis (1885–1972) American poet and critic, born in Hailey, Idaho. Brought up in Wyncote, near Philadelphia, he graduated at Pennsylvania University in 1906, became an instructor in Wabash College in Crawfordsville, Indiana, but after four months left for Europe, travelling widely in Spain, Italy and Provence. He published his first collection of poems, *A Lume Spento* (With Tapers Quenched, 1908), in Venice. In London later that year he met **Ford Madox Ford**, **James Joyce** and **Wyndham Lewis**, and published *Personae* and *Exultations* in 1909, followed by a book of critical essays, *The Spirit of Romance*, in 1910. He was co-editor of *Blast* (1914–15), the magazine of the short-lived 'Vorticist' movement, and London editor of the Chicago *Little Review* (1917–19), and in 1920 became Paris correspondent for *The Dial*. From 1924 he made his home in Italy. He became involved with Fascist ideas and stirred up much resentment by antidemocracy broadcasts in the early stages of the war. In 1945 he was escorted back to the USA and indicted for treason. The trial did not proceed, however, as he was adjudged insane, and placed in an asylum. In 1958 he was certified sane and released, and returned to Italy. In addition to his poetry he wrote books on literature, music, art and economics, and translated much from Italian, French, Chinese and Japanese. As a poet, of the Imagist school at the outset of his career, he was a thorough-going experimenter, deploying much curious and often spurious learning in his illustrative imagery and in the development of his themes. **T S Eliot** regarded him as the motivating force behind 'modern' poetry, the poet who created a climate in which English and American poets could understand and appreciate each other. *Homage to Sextus Propertius* (1919) and *Hugh Selwyn Mauberley* (1920) are among his most important early poems. His *Cantos*, a loosely-knit series of poems, appeared first in 1917, continuing in many instalments, via the *Pisan Cantos* (1948) to *Thrones: Cantos 96–109* (1959). His work in the classics and Chinese poetry are discernible in their form. Apart from his life work in poetry, significant collections are *Translations of Ezra Pound* (1933) and *Literary Essays* (1954).

POUND, Roscoe (1870–1964) American jurist and botanist, born in Lincoln, Nebraska. He was educated at Nebraska University and Harvard Law School. Among his appointments were those as commissioner of appeals of the Supreme Court of Nebraska (1901–03), assistant professor of law at Nebraska University (1899–1903), and successively professor of law at Northwestern University (1907), Chicago University (1909) and Harvard Law School (1910–37). An able and influential teacher, especially of jurisprudence, his theories, with their emphasis on the importance of social interests in connection with the law, have had a universal effect. His many legal writings include *Readings on the History and System of the Common Law* (1904), *Introduction to the Philosophy of Law* (1922), *Law and Morals* (1924), *Criminal Justice in America* (1930) and *Jurisprudence* (5 vols, 1959). An authority also on botany, he was largely responsible for the botanical survey of Nebraska, and on this subject, in collaboration with Dr F E Clements, wrote *Phyto-geography of Nebraska* (1898). A rare lichen is named after him.

POUNDS, John (1766–1839) English cripple shoemaker, born in Portsmouth. He became unpaid teacher of poor children, and is regarded as the founder of ragged schools.

POUSSIN, Gaspard, properly **Gaspond Dughet** (1613–75) French painter, the brother-in-law and pupil of **Nicolas Poussin**. He worked in Rome and became well known as a landscapist. His popularity in the 18th century was high, though many paintings attributed to him may not have been his work.

POUSSIN, Nicolas (1594–1665) French painter, born in Les Andelys, Normandy, the greatest French painter of the 17th century. After struggling in Paris he earned enough money to visit Rome in 1624, where he recived commissions from Cardinal **Barberini** and soon became rich and famous. Among the masterpieces dating from this period is *The Adoration of the Golden Calf*, now in the London National Gallery. In 1640 he was ordered by King **Louis XIII** and Cardinal **Richelieu** to return to France, where he was appointed painter in ordinary to the king. However, the types of work he was expected to carry out—altarpieces and mural decorations for example—were unsuited to his genius and in 1643 he returned to Rome. He constructed his historical pictures with great deliberation and after much experimentation, even going so far as to make small clay models of his scenes to get the lighting right. From this relentless search for perfection he evolved the prototype for the History Picture. Considered academically as the highest form of art, painters strove to emulate Poussin's achievements for the next two centuries. His œvre also includes mythological works, biblical subjects and, in his later years, landscape.

POWDERLY, Terence Vincent (1849–1924) American labor leader, born into an Irish immigrant family in Carbondale, Pennsylvania. He began working on the railroad at the age of 13. After four years' apprenticeship he became a machinist in 1869, joined its union in 1871, became president in 1872, and worked as Pennsylvania organizer for the Industrial Brotherhood. He joined the secret oath-bound Knights of Labor in 1874, and became its grand master workman in 1879 and general master workman from 1883 to 1893. He worked to make the Knights a union for all forms of labor, brought it into touch with developing new ideas of labor organization and philosophy such as that of **Henry George**, politicized it, and sought to further labor causes wherever possible. He was critical of the use of strikes, although strongly interested in the development of the boycott from its use in Ireland in the Land War of 1879–82. He sought to encourage constructive relations between labor and management. He saw the Knights mushroom to a million members in 1886, but his ideas and charisma were not matched by administrative skills; the bubble soon burst, and the Knights had declined badly by the time Powderly took up a second career in law. He was commissioner-general of immigration (1897–1902), and head of the division of information in the Immigration Bureau (1907–21). He wrote *Thirty Years of Labor* (1889) and a posthumously published autobiography, *The Path I Trod* (1940).

POWELL, Anthony Dymoke (1905–) English novelist, born in London, the son of an army officer. He was educated at Eton and Balliol College, Oxford, where he met several other young writers, including **Evelyn Waugh** and **Graham Greene**. He worked in publishing and journalism before World War II, and by 1936 had published four satirical novels, among them *Afternoon Men* (1931), *Venusberg* (1932) and *What's Become of Waring?* (1939). After the war he returned to book-reviewing, wrote a biography of **John Aubrey** (1948), and began the series of novels he called *A Dance to the Music of Time*—twelve volumes, beginning with *A Question of Upbringing* (1951), covering fifty years of British upper middle-class life and attitudes. The light, witty, satirical tone of the prewar novels developed, in *The Music of Time*, into an intricate and disciplined interweaving of personal relationships, ironic, humorous, and with extraordinary scope and depth of vision. He has won the James Tait Black prize and W H Smith Literary award. Since the completion of the cycle with *Hearing Secret Harmonies* (1975), he has published a four-volume autobiography, *To Keep the Ball Rolling* (1976–82), and two novels, *O, How the Wheel Becomes It!* (1983) and *The Fisher King* (1986).

POWELL, Baden See **BADEN-POWELL**

POWELL, Bud (Earl) (1924–66) American jazz pianist, born in New York, the most influential of bebop stylists. Playing from the age of six, he became interested in jazz as a teenager, involving himself with the modern jazz movement in the 1940s with encouragement from **Thelonious Monk**. A head injury sustained in an attack heralded a series of visits to mental hospitals; nevertheless, he was the first choice to work and record with top New York players until he moved to Paris from 1959 to 1964, where he led a trio featuring American expatriate drummer Kenny Clarke. Powell, a great jazz virtuoso, died shortly after returning to New York.

POWELL, Cecil Frank (1903–69) English physicist, born in Tonbridge, Kent. Professor of physics at

Bristol (1948–63), director of the Wills Physics Laboratory, Bristol, from 1964, he is known for his work on the photography of nuclear processes. He was awarded the Nobel prize for physics in 1950, and was one of the leaders of the movement to increase the social responsibility of scientists.

POWELL, (John) Enoch (1912–) English Conservative politician and scholar, born in Stechford, Birmingham. He was educated at King Edward's School, Birmingham, and Trinity College, Cambridge, becoming professor of Greek at Sydney University (1937–39). He enlisted in World War II as a private in 1939, was commissioned in 1940 and rose to the rank of brigadier. In 1946 he joined the Conservative party, in 1950 entering parliament as MP for Wolverhampton, and held office as parliamentary secretary, ministry of housing (1955–57), as financial secretary to the treasury from 1957, resigning with **Thorneycroft** in 1958, and as minister of health from 1960, again resigning over the appointment of Sir **Alec Douglas-Home** as prime minister in 1963. His austere brand of intellectualism, his adherence to the principles of high Toryism in economic planning, and his radical views on defence and foreign commitments made him a significant figure within his party. He created more general controversy by his outspoken attitude to black immigration and racial integration. Because of his opposition to the common market, he did not stand for election in February 1974, but returned to parliament as an Ulster Unionist from October 1974 until he was defeated in the 1987 general election.

POWELL, Frederick York (1850–1904) English historian and Old Icelandic scholar, born in London. Educated at Rugby and Christ Church, Oxford, he taught Old English and Old German at Oxford. In 1894 with **Guðbrandhur Vigfússon** he worked on the records and ancient poetry of Scandinavia and compiled with him *Icelandic Prose Reader* (1879), *Corpus Poeticum Boreale* (2 vols, 1883) and *Origines Islandicae* (2 vols, 1905). In 1894 he was appointed Regius professor of modern history at Oxford. He translated the Icelandic *Faereyinga Saga* (1896), and helped to found the *English Historical Review* (1885).

POWELL, John Wesley (1834–1902) American geologist, born in Mount Morris, New York. He lost his right arm in the Civil War, and became a professor of geology, surveyor (1868–72) of the Colorado River and its tributaries, and director of the bureau of ethnology and of the US geological survey. He wrote on the arid region, the Uinta Mountains, the Colorado River and its canyons, and on Indian languages.

POWELL, Mary See **MILTON, John**

POWELL, Michael (1905–90) English filmmaker, born in Bekesbourne near Canterbury. Frustrated by the mundane routine of his job in a bank, he took work at the studios of director Rex Ingram and learnt every technical aspect of the filmmaking process. *Two Crowded Hours* (1931), his directorial début, was one of two dozen 'quota quickies' he made over six years. More prestigious assignments followed, including *The Edge of the World* (1937), and *The Spy in Black* (1939) began a partnership with writer Emeric Pressburger that lasted until 1957. Known as 'the Archers', they collaborated on films like *The Life and Death of Colonel Blimp* (1943), *Black Narcissus* (1947) and *Red Shoes* (1948), creating a body of work unique in its flamboyant use of colour, expressionism and sensuality. Later Powell made the controversial *Peeping Tom* (1959), which was attacked for its 'bad taste' and 'sadism' but later reclaimed as a masterly commentary on the voyeurism of film. Often considered ahead of his time, he lived to see 'the Archers' hailed as one of the most daring and distinctive forces in the history of British cinema. The first volume of his autobiography, *A Life in Movies*, was published in 1986.

POWERS, Hiram (1805–73) American sculptor, born in Woodstock, Vermont, the son of a farmer. He worked as an artist for a waxworks museum in Cincinnati, and in 1835 went to Washington, where he executed busts, and in 1837 to Florence in Italy, where he resided till his death. There he produced his *Eve*, and in 1843 the still more popular *Greek Slave*. Among his other works were busts of **Washington**, **Calhoun** and **Daniel Webster**.

POWHATAN (d.1618) American Indian chief of confederacy of Tidewater tribes of New England. Despite considerable provocation he managed to maintain an uneasy peace with white settlers in Virginia. His favourite daughter, **Pocahontas**, was carried off by settlers in 1609, but married a white colonist with her father's consent. Powhatan was succeeded by his more warlike brother, **Opechancanough**.

POWYS, John Cowper (1872–1963) English novelist, poet and essayist, born in Shirley, Derbyshire, where his father was vicar; his mother was descended from **John Donne** and **William Cowper**. He was brought up in the Dorset-Somerset countryside and though he spent much of his later life in America, his formative years greatly influenced his work. Educated at Sherborne and Corpus Christi College, Cambridge, he taught and lectured before becoming a prolific author. Of some 50 books, his best known are his novels, particularly *Wolf Solent* (1929), *A Glastonbury Romance* (1932), gargantuan in scale, in which the myths surrounding the ancient abbey have a supernatural effect on the citizens of the town, *Weymouth Sands* (1934) and *Maiden Castle* (1936).

POWYS, Llewelyn (1884–1939) English essayist and novelist, brother of **John Powys** and **Theodore Francis Powys**, born in Dorchester. He suffered from recurrent tuberculosis which caused him to spend some years in Switzerland and in Kenya, and from which he died. From 1920 to 1925 he was a journalist in New York. Works include *Ebony and Ivory* (1922), *Apples be Ripe* (1930) and the biographical *Confessions of Two Brothers* (with his brother John, 1916), *Skin for Skin* (1925) and *The Verdict of Bridlegoose* (1926).

POWYS, Theodore Francis (1875–1953) English novelist and short-story writer, brother of **John** and **Llewelyn Powys**, born in Shirley. He lived in seclusion and wrote original and eccentric novels of which the best known is *Mr Weston's Good Wine* (1927). He also wrote *Mr Tasker's Gods* (1925), *Captain Patch* (1935) and *Goat Green* (1937).

POYNINGS, Sir Edward (1459–1521) English soldier and diplomat. He took part in a rebellion against **Richard III**, escaped to the Continent and joined the Earl of Richmond (**Henry VII**), with whom he later returned to England. In 1493 he was governor of Calais, and in 1494 went to Ireland as deputy-governor for Prince Henry (**Henry VIII**). His aim was to anglicize the government of Ireland. This he accomplished by means of the Statutes of Drogheda, known as Poynings' Law, to the effect that all Irish legislature had to be confirmed by the English privy council. This was not repealed until 1782. He was often abroad on diplomatic missions. In 1520 he was present at the Field of the Cloth of Gold, which he had taken an active part in arranging.

POYNTER, Sir Edward John (1836–1919) English painter, born of Huguenot ancestry in Paris, the son of the architect Ambrose Poynter (1796–1886). Educated at Westminster and Ipswich, he studied

(1853–54) at Rome and from 1856 to 1860 in Paris and elsewhere. He made designs for stained glass, and drawings on wood for *Once a Week* and other periodicals, and for **Dalziel**'s projected illustrated Bible. This led to studies in Egyptian art, which resulted in his *Israel in Egypt* (1867). His watercolours are numerous. In 1871 he became Slade professor at University College London, director for art at South Kensington 1876–81, director of the National Gallery 1894–1905, and in 1896 was made president of the Royal Academy. Among his works are *The Ides of March* (1883), *The Visit of the Queen of Sheba to Solomon* (1891), the portrait of **Lillie Langtry** bequeathed in her will to the Jersey Museum, and *Nausicaa and her Maidens*, painted (1872–79) for the Earl of Wharncliffe at Wortley Hall. In 1869–70 he designed the cartoons for a mosaic of St **George** in the Houses of Parliament.

POYNTING, John Henry (1852–1914) English physicist, born in Monton, Lancashire. Educated at Manchester and Cambridge, he became professor of physics at Birmingham (1880). He wrote on electrical phenomena and on radiation, and determined the constant of gravitation by a torsion experiment. He wrote *On the Mean Density of the Earth* (1893) and *The Earth* (1913). With **Joseph John Thomson** he wrote a *Textbook of Physics* (1899–1914).

POZZO, Andrea (1642–1709) Italian artist, born in the north of Italy. In 1665 he became a Jesuit lay brother. In Rome from 1681, his main work was the decoration of the church of S Ignazio, the ceiling of which he painted in the perspective style known as *sotto in sù*. In Vienna from 1702, his work in the Liechtenstein palace is all that survives. His treatise *Perspectiva pictorum...* (1693–98) had considerable influence on 18th-century artists.

POZZO DI BORGO, Carlo Andrea, Count (1764–1842) Corsican-born Russian diplomatist, born in Alala. He practised as an advocate in Ajaccio, in 1790 joined the party of **Paoli**, who made him president of the Corsican council and secretary of state, but in 1796 was obliged to seek safety from the Bonapartes in London. In 1798 he went to Vienna and effected an alliance of Austria and Russia against France. In 1803 he entered the Russian diplomatic service. He laboured strenuously to unite **Napoleon**'s enemies against him, seduced **Bernadotte** from the Napoleonic cause, and urged the allies to march on Paris. He represented Russia at Paris, the Congress of Vienna, and the Congress of Verona, and was ambassador to London from 1834 to 1839, when he settled in Paris, where he died.

PRAAGH, Peggy van (1910–90) English dancer, teacher and ballet director, born in London. She danced as a soloist with Ballet Rambert (1933–38) and Antony Tudor's London Ballet (1938) before becoming a principal dancer with Sadler's Wells Ballet (1941). Having studied ballet, modern dance and mime, in 1946 she was appointed ballet mistress of Sadler's Wells Theatre Ballet, and between 1951 and 1956 served as assistant director, during which time she nurtured important young talents such as **John Cranko** and **Kenneth MacMillan**. Freelance producing and teaching followed, until she was invited to become artistic director of the Borovansky Ballet's final season in Australia (1962). The following year she converted the troupe into the Australian Ballet, a company firmly based on the Royal Ballet. She remained in charge until 1974.

PRANDTL, Ludwig (1875–1953) German pioneer of the science of aerodynamics, born in Freising, Bavaria. He studied mechanical engineering in Munich and gained a PhD in 1900. Although apparently destined for a career in elasticity, while working for the company MAN his interest was redirected to aerodynamics. In this field he made outstanding contributions to boundary layer theory, airship profiles, supersonic flow, wing theory and meteorology. He was director of technical physics at the University of Göttingen (1904–53), and director of the Kaiser Wilhelm Institute for fluid mechanics from 1925.

PRASAD, Rajendra (1884–1963) Indian statesman. He left legal practice to become a follower of **Mahatma Gandhi**. A member of the Working Committee of the All-India Congress in 1922, he was president of the Congress several times between 1934 and 1948. In 1946 he was appointed minister for food and agriculture in the government of India, and president of the Indian Constituent Assembly. He was the first president of the Republic of India from 1950 to 1962. He wrote several books, including *India Divided At the Feet of Mahatma Gandhi* and an autobiography, *Atma Katha* (1958).

PRATI, Giovanni (1815–84) Italian lyric and narrative poet, born near Trento. Court poet to the House of Savoy, he became a deputy to the Italian parliament (1862) and a senator (1876). His lyrics, which fill several volumes, include *Canti lirici*, and *Canti del popolo*.

PRATT, John Henry (1809–71) English clergyman and geophysicist. A missionary in India from the 1830s, he was archdeacon of Calcutta from 1850 to 1871. A keen amateur scientist, he postulated the isostasy principle to account for gravity anomalies resulting from nearby mountains, such as those observed by Sir **George** Everest in his classic survey of India. The same idea was offered very soon afterwards, also in 1854, by Sir **George Airy**.

PRAXITELES (5th century BC) Greek sculptor from Athens, considered one of the greatest of Greek sculptors. His works have almost all perished, though his *Hermes carrying the boy Dionysus* was found at Olympia in 1877.

PREECE, Sir William Henry (1834–1913) Welsh electrical engineer, born in Caernarfon. He was instructed in electrical engineering by **Michael Faraday** at the Royal Institution. After service with several telegraph companies, in 1870 he was attached to the Post Office, of which he became engineer-in-chief and finally consulting engineer. A pioneer of wireless telegraphy and telephony, he also improved the system of railway signalling and introduced the first telephones to Great Britain. He wrote several books, including *Telegraphy* (1876) with J Sivewright and *A Manual of Telephony* (1893) with A J Stubbs.

PREGL, Fritz (1869–1930) Austrian chemist, born in Laibach (now Ljubljana in Yugoslavia). He became professor of applied medical chemistry at Innsbruck and later at Graz. He was specially noted for the microchemical methods of analysis, which gained him the Nobel prize for physics in 1923.

PRELOG, Vladimir (1906–) Swiss organic chemist, born in Sarajevo (now in Yugoslavia). He was educated at the Prague Institute of Technology and then worked as an industrial chemist, before moving to Zagreb University. In 1941, when the Germans invaded Yugoslavia, he taught at the Federal Institute of Technology in Zürich, and became professor of chemistry (1950–76). Following his notable work in organic chemistry, and especially in stereochemistry, he shared the Nobel prize for chemistry in 1975 with Sir **John Warcup Cornforth**.

PREMADASA, Ranasinghe (1924–) Sri Lankan politician. Born in a North Colombo slum, a member of the lowly dhobi (laundrymen's) caste, he was educated at St Joseph's College, Colombo. He began his political career attached to the Ceylon Labour party, forming a temperance group dedicated to moral uplift, then joined the United National party (UNP) in 1950 and became deputy mayor of the Colombo municipal council in 1955. Elected to Sri Lanka's parliament in 1960, he served, successively, as UNP chief whip (1965–68 and 1970–77), the minister of local government (1968–70) and leader of the house (1977–78), before becoming prime minister, under President **Jayawardene**, in 1978. During ten years as prime minister, Premadasa implemented a popular housebuilding and poverty alleviation programme, which provided the basis for his election as president in December 1988. As president, he faced mounting civil unrest, both in the Tamil north and Sinhala south, and deteriorating relations with India.

PREMINGER, Otto (1906–86) Austrian-born American film and stage director, born in Vienna. He studied law at Vienna University, then acting with **Max Reinhardt**, joining the Theater in der Josefstadt in 1928 and becoming its director in 1933. He directed his first film, *Die Grosse Liebe*, in 1931. Moving to the USA in 1935 he directed several Broadway productions including *Libel!* (1935) and *Outward Bound* (1938) before journeying to Hollywood, first as an actor then as a director under contract to Twentieth Century Fox, where he specialized in costume dramas and film noir thrillers like *Laura* (1944) and *Where the Sidewalk Ends* (1950). An independent filmmaker from 1952, he boldly tackled controversial themes such as drug addiction in *The Man with the Golden Arm* (1955), rape in *Anatomy of a Murder* (1959), Jewish repatriation in *Exodus* (1960), homosexuality in *Advise and Consent* (1962) and racism in *Hurry Sundown* (1966). To the public he maintained the stereotype of the old-style film director: autocratic, bullying and a strict disciplinarian; but he was also a showman, a craftsman, a talent-spotter and a man who took the fight against antiquated notions of censorship to the Supreme Court. An American citizen from 1943, his other theatrical work includes *The Trial* (1953) and *Full Circle* (1973). He also acted in the film *Stalag 17* (1953) and the television series *Batman* (1966), and published an autobiography, *Preminger*, in 1977. His last film, *The Human Factor*, was released in 1979.

PREMPEH (d.1931) last king (1888–96) of Ashanti. He was deposed by the British, imprisoned at Elmina, and exiled to the Seychelles. He was allowed to return in 1924, with chief's rank from 1926.

PREM TINSULANONDA, General (1920–) Thai soldier. Educated at the Chulachomklao Royal Military Academy, Bangkok, he began as a sub-lieutenant in 1941 and rose to become commander-general of the 2nd Army Area in 1974 and assistant commander-in-chief of the Royal Thai Army in 1977. During the military administration of General Kriangsak Chomanam (1977–80) he served as deputy minister of the interior and, from 1979, as defence minister, before being appointed prime minister in March 1980. Prem formally relinquished his army office and established a series of civilian coalition governments. He withstood coup attempts in April 1981 and September 1985 and ruled in a cautious, apolitical manner, retaining the confidence of key business and military leaders. Under his stewardship, 'newly industrializing' Thailand achieved rapid annual economic growth rates in excess of 9%. He retired on 'personal grounds', in July 1988.

PRESCOTT, John Leslie (1938–) English politician, After leaving Ellesmere Port Secondary Modern School he began work as a trainee chef and then served in the merchant navy (1955–63). He continued his education through part-time classes, correspondence tuition and then full-time study at Ruskin College, Oxford and Hull University. He became a full-time officer of the National Union of Seamen (NUS) in 1968 and two years later entered the House of Commons, sponsored by the NUS, as Labour member for Hull East. Although opposed to Britain's membership of the European Community, in 1975 he was elected to the European parliament and was leader of the Labour Group (1976–79). Never afraid to voice his feelings publicly, he has sometimes been openly critical of his party's leadership and in 1988 unsuccessfully opposed **Roy Hattersley** for the deputy leader's post. In the Labour party's shadow cabinet he has been spokesman for employment, energy and transport.

PRESCOTT, William Hickling (1796–1859) American historian, born in Salem, Massachusetts, the son of a lawyer. He studied at Harvard (where a piece of bread playfully thrown blinded his left eye, and greatly weakened his right one), travelled in England, France and Italy, married in 1820, and, abandoning law for literature, devoted himself to severe study, and, in spite of his disabilities, formed splendid literary projects. His first studies were in Italian literature, but by 1826 he had found his life's work in Spanish history. His *History of Ferdinand and Isabella* (1838) quickly carried his name to the Old World, and was translated into French, Spanish and German. The *History of the Conquest of Mexico* (1843), followed by the *Conquest of Peru* (1847), confirmed his reputation; he was chosen a corresponding member of the French Institute. In 1855–58 he published three volumes of his *History of Philip II*, but died in New York before completing it. Prescott's scholarly but vivid style alone would have assured him popularity.

PRESLEY, Elvis Aaron (1935–77) American popular singer, born in Tupelo, Mississippi. From a religious family, he began singing in his local church choir and taught himself the rudiments of the guitar. He was discovered in 1953 by Sam Phillips, president of Sun Records, in Memphis, Tennessee, who heard a record Presley had made privately for his mother. By 1956 the singer was the most popular performer in the USA and, shortly after, the world. His unparalleled contribution to popular music sprang from his ability to combine white country and western with black rhythm and blues. This, together with his overtly sexual style, made him controversial: moralists accused him of obscenity; racists attacked him for performing black music. Two years of national service with the US army in West Germany saw a falling off in creativity, but did little to dim his popularity. During the 1960s his appearances were largely restricted to a succession of mediocre films made at the behest of his domineering manager, Colonel Tom Parker. In the 1970s Presley re-emerged as a night-club performer in Las Vegas with a grandiose stage act based on lachrymose ballads and inferior versions of his early hits. Suffering in his last years from ill-health caused by obesity and narcotics, he died suddenly in 1977. His most popular records include 'Heartbreak Hotel', 'Blue Suede Shoes', 'Hound Dog', 'Love Me Tender', 'All Shook Up', 'It's Now or Never', 'King Creole', 'Crying in the Chapel', 'Suspicious Minds' and 'In the Ghetto'. His films include *Loving You* (1957), *G I Blues* (1960) and *That's the Way It Is* (1971).

PRESSENSÉ, Edmond Dehaut de (1824–91) French Protestant theologian and politician. He studied at Paris, Lausanne, Berlin and Halle, and in 1847 became a pastor in Paris. He was deputy to the National Assembly for the Seine (1871–76), and elected a life senator in 1883. A vigorous writer as well as eloquent preacher, he took a leading part in the great theological and ecclesiastical controversies of the day. Among his works are *L'Église et la Révolution* (1864) and *Les Origines* (1882).

PRESSENSÉ, Francis de (1853–1914) born in Paris, son of **Edmond Pressensé**. He was a notable socialist and journalist, and a defender of **Dreyfus**.

PRESTON, Margaret Rose (1875–1963) Australian artist and teacher, born in Port Adelaide, South Australia. Educated in Sydney and Melbourne, in 1904 she went to Germany where she attended the Government Art School for Women in Munich. She travelled widely in Europe before returning to Sydney in 1919. An enthusiastic traveller, she visited various south Pacific islands, south-east Asia and China in the 1920s, and Africa and India in the late 1950s. She was an active champion of aboriginal painting, and its influence is clearly seen in her still-lifes of Australian flowers and her wood and linocut engravings with their strong design and use of colour.

PRESTWICH, Sir Joseph (1812–96) English geologist, born in Pensbury, Clapham. He was a wine merchant until the age of 60, but in 1874 became Oxford professor of geology. His work on the water-bearing strata round London (1851) was a standard authority.

PRETORIUS, Andries Wilhelminus Jacobus (1799–1853) Boer leader, in whose honour the town of Pretoria was named. Born in the Cape Colony and a prosperous farmer, he was one of the leaders of the Great Trek of 1837 into Natal. After Zulu atrocities, he defeated Dengaan's force of 10000 at Blood River in December 1838. He accepted British rule, but later led another trek across the river Vaal and made war against the British. Eventually in 1852 the British recognized the Transvaal Republic (later the South African Republic), whose capital, Pretoria, was founded in 1855.

PRETORIUS, Marthinus Wessels (1819–1901) South African soldier, son of **Andries Pretorius**, whom he succeeded as commandant-general in 1853. In 1854 he led a punitive expedition against the natives. He was elected president of the South African Republic in 1857, and of the Orange Free State in 1859. Failing in his ambition to unite the two republics, he resigned the presidency of the Orange Free State in 1863. The discovery of gold in Bechuanaland and diamonds in the Vaal led to difficulties with the *Volksraad*, and he resigned the presidency of the South African Republic in 1871. He fought against the British again in 1877, until the independence of the Republic was recognized. He lived to see it extinguished in 1901.

PRÉVERT, Jacques (1900–77) French poet and screenwriter. Associated with the Surrealist movement in the 1920s, he made his name with humorous, anarchic 'song poems' about street life in Paris, collected in *Paroles* (1946), *Spectacle* (1951) and *Imaginaires* (1970). He also wrote several distinguished screenplays, all for **Marcel Carné**, including the celebrated *Les Enfants du Paradis* (1944).

PREVIN, André (George) (1929–) German-born American conductor and composer, born in Berlin. He went to the USA in 1938 and was naturalized in 1943. He studied music mainly in California and Paris. He was musical director of the Houston Symphony Orchestra (1967–69), of the London Symphony Orchestra (1968–79), of the Pittsburgh Symphony Orchestra (1976–86), of the Royal Philharmonic Orchestra from 1985, and of the Los Angeles Philharmonic Orchestra from 1986. He has composed musicals, film scores and orchestral works, including a cello concerto (1967) and a guitar concerto (1971). He has achieved great popular success through his work, on television and in the concert hall, bringing classical music to the attention of a wider public. He wrote *Music Face to Face* (1971).

PRÉVOST, Abbé (Antoine François Prévost d'Exiles) (1697–1763) French novelist, born in Artois. Educated by the Jesuits, at 16 he enlisted in the army, but soon returned to the Jesuits, and had almost joined the order when he was again tempted to the soldier's life. In 1720, following an unhappy love affair, he joined the Benedictines of St Maur, and spent the next seven years in religious duties and in study. But about 1727 he fled for six years, first to London, where he started to write *Histoire de Cleveland*, and then to Holland (1729–31). He issued volumes i–iv of *Mémoires d'un homme de qualité* in 1728 and volumes v–vii in 1731, *Manon Lescaut* forming volume vii. He employed himself in additional novels—*Cleveland* and *Le Doyen de Killerine*—and in translations. In London again after another affair he started *Le Pour et contre* (1733–40), a periodical review of life and letters, modelled on the *Spectator*. In France by 1735, he was appointed honorary chaplain to the Prince de Conti, and compiled over a hundred volumes more. He died suddenly at Chantilly. Prévost's reputation stands securely on *Manon Lescaut*. It remains fresh, charming and perennial, from its perfect simplicity, the stamp of reality and truth throughout, and a style so flowing and natural that the reader forgets it altogether in the interest of the story.

PRÉVOST, Eugène Marcel (1862–1941) French novelist, born in Paris. A civil engineer, he worked in a tobacco factory until 1891. From the age of 25 he wrote in his leisure hours. Of his clever novels and plays many have been translated, including *Cousin Laura*, *Frédérique* and *Léa*.

PRÉVOST, Pierre (1751–1839) Swiss physicist, classicist and philosopher, born in Geneva. He occupied chairs of philosophy and physics at Berlin and Geneva. He formulated the theory of exchanges in connection with the laws of radiation. His writings and translations covered many subjects.

PRÉVOST-PARADOL, Lucien Anatole (1829–70) French journalist and diplomat, born in Paris. After a year at Aix as professor of French literature he became a journalist in Paris in 1856, and from time to time published collections of essays, the best being his *Essais sur les moralistes français* (1864). In 1868 he visited England. Opposed as a moderate liberal to the empire, he accepted the post of envoy to the USA under **Ollivier** in January 1870. His mind unhinged by republican attacks and the struggle with Germany, he committed suicide in Washington just after the outbreak of the Franco-Prussian War.

PREY, Hermann (1929–) German baritone, born in Berlin. Equally distinguished as an interpreter of lieder and in stage roles, he sang at the Hamburg Opera (1953–60) and (as Wolfram in *Tannhäuser*) made his début at Bayreuth (1956) and the New York Metropolitan (1960). He excels in the **Mozart** repertoire and is accomplished in 20th-century German from **Berg** to **Henze**.

PRIAM according to Greek legend, son of Laomedon and king of Troy. His son Paris fell in love with Helen, wife of **Menelaus**, king of Sparta, and abducted her. This was the origin of the Trojan War, when a coalition of Greek forces led by **Agamemnon** came to lay siege to the city of Priam. **Homer**'s *Iliad* portrays him as an elderly and mild ruler. He was killed during the sack of Troy by Neoptolemus, son of Achilles, despite having taken refuge at the altar of Zeus.

PRICE, George (1919–) Belize politician. Educated in Belize City and the USA, he was elected to the Belize

City council in 1947 and in 1950 founded the People's United party (PUP), a left-of-centre grouping which grew out of a smaller group calling for the independence of Belize, the People's Committee. Partial self-government was achieved in 1954 and Price became prime minister, continuing to lead his country until it achieved full independence in 1981. In 1984 PUP's 30 years of uninterrupted rule ended when the general election was won by the United Democratic party (UDP), led by Manuel Esquivel, but Price unexpectedly returned to power in 1989.

PRICE, Henry Habberley (1899–1985) Welsh philosopher, born in Neath, Glamorgan. He was educated at Oxford, where he was professor of logic from 1935 to 1959. His first and major work was *Perception* (1932), in which he presented a theory of our knowledge of the external world, arguing that what we know directly are sense-data, though material objects do not just consist in sense-data but have other causal powers. He also wrote sympathetically on religion, parapsychology and psychic phenomena, and published *Thinking and Experience* (1953), *Belief* (1969) and *Essays in the Philosophy of Religion* (1972).

PRICE, (Mary Violet) Leontyne (1927–) American soprano, born in Laurel, Mississippi. She studied at the Juillard Music School in New York City. She was a notable Bess (1952–54) in **Gershwin**'s *Porgy and Bess*, an outstanding **Verdi** singer, and was much associated with **Barber**'s music.

PRICE, Richard (1723–91) Welsh moral philosopher and unitarian minister, born in Tynton, Glamorgan. He attended a Dissenting Academy in London and became a preacher at Newington Green and Hackney. He first established his reputation with the *Review of the Principal Questions in Morals* (1758), which was directed principally against **Hume** in arguing that 'morality is a branch of necessary truth'. But his interests were quite diverse: he was admitted to the Royal Society in 1765 for his work on probability; his *Obervations on Reversionary Payments* (1771) helped to establish a scientific system for life-insurance and pensions; and he published *An Appeal to the Public on the subject of the National Debt* (1772), which influenced **William Pitt**, 'the Younger'. He also wrote books on the American Revolution (*Observations on the nature of Civil Liberty, the Principles of Government, and the Justice and Policy of the War with America*, 1776) and the French Revolution (*A Discourse on the Love of our Country*, 1789) which brought him into political prominence, the latter also provoking **Burke**'s *Reflections on the Revolution in France*.

PRICHARD, James Cowles (1786–1848) English physician and ethnologist, born in Herefordshire, the son of a Quaker merchant. He studied medicine and from 1810 practised in Bristol. In 1813 appeared his *Researches into the Physical History of Mankind*, in which he argued for a single human species. In *The Eastern Origin of the Celtic Nations* (1831) he established Celtic as an Indo-European language with close affinity with the Sanskrit, Greek, Latin and Teutonic languages. Besides several medical works, he published an *Analysis of Egyptian Mythology* (1819) and *The Natural History of Man* (1843).

PRICHARD, Katharine Susannah (1883–1969) Australian writer, born in Levuka, on Ovalau, where her father was editor of the *Fiji Times*. She started work on a Melbourne newspaper, for which she made a trip to London in 1908. Four years later she again travelled to London to further her career as a novelist, and in 1915 her first novel, *The Pioneers*, won the colonial section of a publisher's competition. In 1916 she returned to Australia, and in the next 50 years produced twelve novels, many poems, plays and short stories, and an autobiography. In 1920 she had become a founding member of the Australian Communist party, and her socialist convictions coloured much of her subsequent work, especially her powerful trilogy set in the West Australian goldfields, *The Roaring Nineties* (1946), *Golden Miles* (1948) and *Winged Seeds* (1950). She married Captain Hugo Vivian Hope Throssell (1884–1933); their son, Ric Prichard Throssell (1922–), diplomat and playwright, wrote *For Valour* (1960, published 1976), and a life of his mother *Wild Weeds and Wind Flowers* (1975).

PRIDE, Thomas (d.1658) English parliamentarian, born perhaps near Glastonbury. He had been a London drayman or brewer when, at the beginning of the Civil War, he became parliamentary captain, and quickly rose to be colonel. He commanded a brigade in Scotland, and when the House of Commons betrayed a disposition to effect a settlement with the king, was appointed to expel its Presbyterian royalist members. By 'Pride's Purge' over 100 were excluded, and the House, reduced to about 80 members, proceeded to bring **Charles I** to justice. Pride sat among his judges, and signed the death warrant. He was present at the battles of Dunbar (1650) and Worcester (1651); opposed to **Cromwell** becoming 'king', he played little additional part in protectorate politics.

PRIDEAUX, Humphrey (1648–1724) English Orientalist, born in Padstow. Educated at Westminster School and Christ Church College, Oxford, his *Marmora Oxoniensia* (1676), an account of the Arundel Marbles, procured for him the friendship of **Heneage Finch**, and ecclesiastical appointments. His chief work, *The Old and New Testament connected in the History of the Jews* (1715–17), ran to many editions.

PRIESTLEY, J B (John Boynton) (1894–1984) English novelist, playwright and critic, born in Bradford. He was educated there and at Trinity Hall, Cambridge. He had already made a reputation by critical writings such as *The English Comic Characters* (1925), *The English Novel* (1927), *English Humour* (1928), and books on **Meredith** (1926) and **Peacock** (1927) in 'The English Men of Letters' series when the geniality of his novel *The Good Companions* (1929) gained him a wide popularity. It was followed by other humorous novels, though not all of equal merit, including *Angel Pavement* (1930), *Let the People Sing* (1939), *Jenny Villiers* (1947) and *The Magicians* (1954). His reputation as a dramatist was established by *Dangerous Corner* (1932), *Time and the Conways* (1937), and other plays on space-time themes, as well as popular comedies such as *Laburnum Grove* (1933). Best known as a writer of novels, Priestley was also master of the essay form. He was an astute, original and controversial commentator on contemporary society—*Journey Down the Rainbow* (1955), written with his wife Jacquetta Hawkes the archaeologist, was a jovial indictment of American life; in serious vein, his collected essays, *Thoughts in the Wilderness* (1957), deal with both present and future social problems.

PRIESTLEY, Joseph (1733–1804) English Presbyterian minister and chemist, born, a cloth-dresser's son, in Fieldhead in Birstall Parish, Leeds. After four years at a Dissenting academy in Daventry, in 1755 he became minister at Needham Market, and wrote *The Scripture Doctrine of Remission*. In 1758 he went to Nantwich, and in 1761 became a tutor at Warrington Academy. In visits to London he met **Benjamin Franklin**, who supplied him with books for his *History of Electricity* (1767). In 1767 he became minister of a chapel at Mill Hill, Leeds, where he took up the study of chemistry. In 1774, as literary companion, he accompanied Lord **Shelburne** on a continental tour and published *Letters to a Philosophical Unbeliever*. But at home he was branded as an atheist in spite of his *Disquisition relating to Matter and Spirit* (1777), affirming from revelation our hope of resurrection. He was elected to the French Academy of Sciences in 1772 and to the St Petersburg Academy in 1780. He became in that year minister of a chapel in Birmingham. His *History of Early Opinions concerning Jesus Christ* (1786) occasioned renewed controversy. His reply to Burke's *Reflections on the French Revolution* led a Birmingham mob to break into his house and destroy its contents (1791). He then settled in Hackney, and in 1794 moved to America, where he was well received; he died in Northumberland, Pennyslvania, believing himself to hold the doctrines of the primitive Christians, and looking for the second coming of **Jesus Christ**. Priestley was a pioneer in the chemistry of gases, and one of the discoverers of oxygen (see **Scheele**).

PRIGOGINE, Ilya (1917–) Russian-born Belgian theoretical chemist, born in Moscow. Living in Belgium from the age of twelve, he was educated in Brussels and has been a professor there from 1951; he was also founder-director in 1967 of the Center for Statistical Mechanics and Thermodynamics at Texas. He developed irreversible thermodynamics as opposed to classical thermodynamics, which is concerned with reversible processes. He developed mathematical models of these non -equilibrium systems, and was able to show in general terms how such dissipative structures are created and sustained. His ideas have applications in studies on the origin of life and its evolution, and on ecosystems in general. He was awarded the Nobel prize for chemistry in 1977. His books include *Order out of Chaos* (1979) and *From Being to Becoming* (1980).

PRIM (Y PRATS), Juan (1814–70) Spanish soldier, born in Reus. As a progressist he opposed the dictatorship of **Espartero**, and was exiled (1839), but came back and defeated him in 1843. He was captain general of Puerto Rico from 1847 to 1848, and deputy in the Cortes (1850–56). Failing in an insurrectionary attempt in 1866, he fled to England and Brussels, and from there guided the revolution that in 1868 overthrew **Isabella II**. He was war minister under **Serrano**, but soon became a virtual dictator. Prim secured the election of **Amadeus** as king in 1870, but was later shot by an assassin.

PRIMATICCIO, Francesco (c.1504–1570) Italian painter, born in Bologna. He went to France in 1531 at the invitation of **Francis I**, to help in the decoration of the palace of Fontainebleau. A collection of his drawings is in the Louvre.

PRIMO DE RIVERA, Miguel, Marqués de Estella (1870–1930) Spanish soldier, born in Jerez de la Frontera. During the Spanish-American war (1898) he served in Cuba and the Philippines, and from 1909 to 1913 he was in Morocco, in 1915 becoming military governor of Cadiz and in 1922 of Barcelona. He effected a military *coup d'état* in 1923, and ruled Spain as dictator until he was forced to resign in 1930.

PRIMUS, Pearl (1919–) American dancer, choreographer and teacher, born in Trinidad. A star athlete in school, she studied medicine and anthropology at Columbia University before making an accidental dance début in 1941 as a last-minute replacement. Her first solo recital followed two years later, and in 1944 the first appearance of her own group. She continued to present concerts and choreographed on Broadway, but her real direction lay in dance and anthropological research in Africa. She made her first extended study trip there in 1948. On subsequent trips she was assisted in the preservation of primitive dance forms by her husband, dancer Percival Borde. She took a PhD in educational anthropology at New York University in 1978.

PRINCE, in full **Prince Roger Nelson** (1958–) American pop-singer and composer, born in Minneapolis, Minnesota. Raised in a musical family (he was named after the Prince Roger Trio, a jazz band in which his father was a pianist), he was signed to Warner Brother Records while still in his teens, releasing his first album *For You* in 1978. Subsequent albums included *Prince* (1979), *Dirty Mind* (1980) and *Controversy* (1981) which attracted increasing controversy with their tendency to mix religious and overtly sexual themes. International success followed the release of *1999* (1982), and the film and album *Purple Rain* (1984) confirmed him as one of America's most commercially successful artists, comparable only to **Bruce Springsteen** in the 1980s. Other albums have included *Sign 'O' The Times* (1987) and *Lovesexy* (1988).

PRINCE, Hal (Harold Smith) (1928–) American stage director and producer, born in New York City. He took part in student productions at the University of Pennsylvania, became a stage manager on Broadway, and is now one of the most successful producers and directors of stage musicals in the world. His first production was *The Pajama Game* (1954), followed by *Damn Yankees* (1955), *West Side Story* (1957), **Sondheim**'s *A Funny Thing Happened on the Way to the Forum* (1963), *Fiddler on the Roof* (1964) and *Cabaret* (1968). He has maintained a long association with Stephen Sondheim, producing and directing many of the composer's shows, including *Company* (1970), *Follies* (1971), *A Little Night Music* (1973), *Pacific Overtures* (1976), *Sweeney Todd* (1979), and *Merrily We Roll Along* (1981). He also directed *Evita* (1978) and *The Phantom of the Opera* (1986).

PRINCE, Henry James (1811–99) English clergyman and eccentric, founder of the notorious 'Agapemone' in Somerset. Born in Bath, he studied medicine but took Anglican orders, and in 1849 at Spaxton near Bridgewater he founded what he called the Agapemone ('Abode of Love'), a community of religious visionaries who shared all their property and, it was believed, their womenfolk.

PRINCIP, Gavrilo (1895–1918), Serbian nationalist and revolutionary, born in Bosnia. He was a member of a secret Serbian terrorist organization known as the 'Black Hand', dedicated to the achievement of independence for the South Slav peoples from the Austro-Hungarian empire. On 28 June 1914, he and a group of young zealots assasinated the archduke Francis Ferdinand of Austria and his wife Sophie on a visit to Sarajevo. The murder precipitated World War 1, after Austria declared war on Serbia on 28 July. Princip died in an Austrian prison.

PRINGLE, Mia Lilly Kellmer (1920–83) Austrian educational psychologist, born in Vienna. Educated at Vienna Grammar School, King's College and Birkbeck College, London, she taught in primary schools from 1942 to 1945. She was appointed psychologist in the Hertfordshire School Psychology and Child Guidance Service (1945–50), deputy head of the Child Study Centre (1954–63) and lecturer (senior lecturer from 1960) in educational psychology at Birmingham University (1950–63). She was director of the National Children's Bureau from 1963 to 1981. Her many publicatons, such as *Early Child Care and Education* (1974) and *Psychological Approaches to Child Abuse* (1980), have greatly influenced parent-child relationships.

PRINGLE, Sir John (1707–82) Scottish physician and reformer, born in Roxburgh. He studied philosophy and classics at St Andrews University and medicine at Leiden. After a stint of teaching philosophy in Edinburgh, he moved to London where he rose to become head of the Army Medical Service and physician to various members of the Royal Family, including King **George III**. His *Observations on Diseases of the Army* (1752) is a classic of humane common sense, emphasizing cleanliness and hygiene in the prevention and treatment of many camp diseases. He participated fully in 18th-century intellectual life, corresponded with many European savants, and was president of the Royal Society from 1772 to 1778.

PRINGLE, Thomas (1789–1834) Scottish writer, born in Blakelaw, Roxburghshire, the son of a farmer. He was educated at Kelso Grammar School and Edinburgh University, and in 1811 became an archivist in the Register Office. In 1817 he started the *Edinburgh Monthly Magazine*, later *Blackwood's Magazine*. In 1820 he emigrated to Cape Colony, and for three years was government librarian at Cape Town. He started a Whig paper, but it was suppressed by the governor. Returning to London in 1826 he became secretary of the Anti-Slavery Society. He wrote *African Sketches* (1834), and published two collections of poems and lyrics, *The Autumnal Collection* (1817), and *Ephemerides* (1828).

PRINGSHEIM, Ernst (1859–1917) German physicist. Professor at Berlin and Breslau, he is noted for his work with Otto Lummer on black-body radiation. His results influenced **Max Planck** in his development of the quantum theory.

PRINGSHEIM, Nathanael (1823–94) German botanist, born in Wziesko in Silesia. Noted for his research on the fertilization of cryptogamic plants, he was professor at Jena for a short time, but for the most part worked privately in Berlin, having inherited wealth from his industrialist father. He was the first scientist to observe and demonstrate sexual reproduction in algae.

PRINTEMPS, Yvonne (1894–) French actress, born in Ermont, Seine-et-Oise. She made her first appearance at the Théâtre Cigale, Paris, in 1908, and appeared regularly in revue and musical comedy until 1916, when she began to work with **Sacha Guitry**, whom she subsequently married. She appeared in London and New York, but did not undertake English parts until 1934, when she played in **Noël Coward**'s *Conversation Piece*. In 1937 she returned to Paris as manager of the Théâtre de la Michodière.

PRIOR, Matthew (1664–1721) English poet and diplomat, born in Wimborne, Dorset, the son of a joiner. Under the patronage of Lord Dorset he was sent to Westminster School, and from there with a scholarship from the Duchess of Somerset to St John's College, Cambridge. He was first employed as secretary to the ambassador to The Hague. In Queen **Anne**'s time he turned Tory, and was instrumental in bringing about the treaty of Utrecht (1713), for which dubious service he was imprisoned for two years (1715–17) after the queen's death. His Tory friends recouped his fortunes by subscribing handsomely to a folio edition of his works (1719). He also received a gift of £4000 from Lord Harley to purchase Down Hall in Essex. Prior was a master of neat, colloquial and epigrammatic verse. His first work, a collaboration with Charles Montagu (Lord **Halifax**), was *The Hind and the Panther Transvers' to the story of the Country and the City Mouse* (1687), a witty satire on **Dryden**'s *Hind and the Panther*. His long poem, *Alma or The Progress of the Mind* (1718), was composed in prison. The long soliloquy in couplet form, *Solomon on the Vanity of the World*, is definitely tedious. His political verse, with the exception of his brilliant burlesque of **Boileau**'s *Epître au roi* (*An English Ballad on the Taking of Namur*), is now of historical interest only. He is best known as the poet of light occasional verse—mock-lyrics such as *A Better Answer* (*to Chloe Jealous*), or charming addresses to noble children (*A Letter to the Lady Margaret Cavendish when a Child*), and, in serious vein, *Lines Written in the Beginning of Mézeray's History of France*, a favourite with Sir **Walter Scott**. His wittiest trifle is *The Secretary*, but *Jinny the Just* is also popular. He was buried in Poets' Corner in Westminster Abbey.

PRISCIAN, (Priscianus Caesariensis) (fl.500) Latin grammarian of Caesarea. At the beginning of the 6th century he taught Latin at Constantinople. As well as his 18-volume *Institutiones Grammaticae*, which was highly thought of in the Middle Ages, he wrote six smaller grammatical treatises and two hexameter poems.

PRISCILLIAN (c.340–385) bishop of Ávila. He was excommunicated by a synod at Saragossa in 380, then tolerated, but ultimately executed—the first case of capital punishment for heresy in the history of the Church. His doctrine, said to have been brought to Spain from Egypt, contained Gnostic and Manichaean elements, and was based on dualism. The Priscillianists were ascetics, eschewed marriage and animal food, and were said to hold strict truth obligatory only between themselves.

PRITCHARD, Charles (1808–93) English astronomer and clergyman. From 1870 he was Savilian professor at Oxford, where he established an observatory. He wrote on stellar photometry in *Uranometria Nova Oxoniensis* (1885).

PRITCHARD, Ernest William (1825–65) English doctor and murderer, son of a naval captain. He grew up in Hampshire, was apprenticed to Portsmouth surgeons, and served as ship's doctor from 1846 to 1851. Having married an Edinburgh silk-merchant's daughter, Mary Jane Taylor, he practised medicine in Yorkshire for six years, graduated MD (Edinburgh) in 1857, and set up his practice in Glasgow in 1860. In 1863 he may or may not have been responsible for the death of one of his maidservants; she perished in a fire in his home, possibly having been drugged when it started. On 25 February 1865 his mother-in-law died in his house, on 18 March his wife died there, and on 3–7 July he was tried for their murder in Edinburgh. A remarkable feature was the evidence of Dr Paterson, who testified that on attending the ladies, at the prisoner's request, he concluded that Dr Pritchard was poisoning them, but that it was contrary to medical ethics for him to interfere. Pritchard was found guilty and was hanged on 28 July on Glasgow Green, the last public execution in Scotland.

PRITCHETT, Sir Victor Sawdon (1900–) English writer and critic, born in Ipswich. He was educated at Alleyn's School, Dulwich, and Dulwich College. After working in the leather trade he became a newspaper correspondent in France, Morocco and Spain, and in 1929 published his first novel, *Claire Drummer*. His style is witty and idiosyncratic, his themes satirical, and he is particularly interested in the 'puritan' character with its fanaticism and guilt, which he portrays with increasing humour in his novels *Nothing Like Leather* (1935), *Dead Man Leading* (1937) and *Mr Beluncle* (1951). A highly-regarded literary critic, he travelled and lectured widely, especially in the USA. Among his critical works are *The Living Novel* (1946), *Books in General* (1953), and a biography of **Balzac** (1973), and he is the author of many volumes of short stories, and two autobiographical books, *A Cab at the Door* (1968) and *Midnight Oil* (1973).

PROBUS, Marcus Aurelius (232–82) Roman emperor, born in Sirmium in Pannonia. He came to power through a military career, though the details are little-known. He became sole emperor in 276, and fought campaigns in Gaul, Germany and Illyricum. A strict disciplinarian, he was murdered by discontented troops near Sirmium.

PROBUS, Marcus Valerius (1st century) Latin grammarian and critic, from Berytus (Beirut). He wrote a biography of **Persius**, and prepared annotated editions of classical authors, including Persius, **Horace**, **Terence** and **Lucretius**. The *Institutia Artium*, a grammatical treatise on the parts of speech attributed to Probus, cannot have been written before the 4th century. The *Appendix Probi*, a list of misspelt words coupled with the correct spelling which dates from the end of the 3rd century, was found appended to a manuscript of the *Instituta*; it is useful in that it indicates the pronunciation of the colloquial Latin of the time.

PROCLUS (c.410–485) Greek neoplatonist philosopher, born in Constantinople of patrician parents from Lycia in Asia Minor. He was educated in Lycia, Alexandria and then Athens, where he was a pupil of Syrianus whom he succeeded as head of Plato's Academy. He never married, and his only recorded defects were a jealous nature and a short temper. He was a champion of paganism above Christianity and theurgy above philosophy. His metaphysics were an elaborate synthesis of elements from **Pythagoras**, the Orphics and **Plato**, and from Roman, Syrian and Alexandrian schools of Greek philosophy. He was quite influential on medieval and Renaissance thought.

PROCOP, Andrew, also known as **Procopius the Great** (c.1380–1434) Bohemian Hussite leader. Originally a monk, he became a member of the conservative Ultraquist Hussite movement and later the commander of the peasant Taborites. Under him the fearful raids into Silesia, Saxony and Franconia were carried out, and he repeatedly defeated German armies. He headed the internal conflict of the Taborites with the more moderate Calixtines and fell at Lipan near Böhmischbrod.

PROCOPIUS (c.499–565) Byzantine historian, born in Caesarea in Palestine. He studied law, and accompanied **Belisarius** against the Persians (526), the Vandals in Africa (533), and the Ostrogoths in Italy (536). He was highly honoured by **Justinian**, and seems to have been appointed prefect of Constantinople in 562. His principal works are his *Historiae* (on the Persian, Vandal and Gothic wars), *De Aedifiis*, and *Anecdota* or *Historia Arcana*, an attack on the court of Justinian and the empress **Theodora**.

PROCTER, Adelaide Ann, pseud **Mary Berwick** (1825–64) English poet, born in London, daughter of **Bryan Waller Procter**. In 1851 she turned Roman Catholic. By her *Legends and Lyrics* (1858–60), some of which were written for *Household Words*, she won poetical renown. Her poems included *The Lost Chord*, which was set to music by Sir **Arthur Sullivan**.

PROCTER, Bryan Waller, pseud **Barry Cornwall** (1787–1874) English poet, born in Leeds. After studying at Harrow with **Byron** and **Peel** he became a solicitor, went to London and in 1815 began to contribute poetry to the *Literary Gazette*. In 1823 he married Anne Benson Skepper (1799–1888). He had meanwhile published poems and produced a tragedy at Covent Garden, *Mirandola*, whose success was largely due to the acting of **Macready** and **Kemble**. He was called to the bar in 1831, and from 1832 to 1861 was a metropolitan commissioner of lunacy. His works comprise *Dramatic Scenes* (1819), *Marcian Colonna* (1820), *The Flood of Thessaly* (1823), and *English Songs* (1832), besides memoirs of **Kean** (1835) and **Charles Lamb** (1866).

PROCTER, Michael John (1946–) South African all-round cricketer, born in Durban. Confined to a mere seven Tests, he was, with **Barry Richards**, the most prominent South African lost to Test cricket. In all first-class cricket he scored 48 centuries, six of them in succession, and performed the hat-trick on four occasions. Highly individual in style, he was for many years the mainstay of Gloucestershire cricket.

PROCTOR, Richard Anthony (1837–88) English astronomer, born in Chelsea. A graduate of St John's College, Cambridge, he devoted himself from 1863 to astronomy. His name is associated with the determination of the rotation of Mars, the theory of the solar corona, and stellar distribution. He charted the 324 198 stars contained in **Argelander**'s great catalogue. He founded a popular scientific magazine, *Knowledge* (1881).

PRODICUS (5th century) Greek Sophist and teacher, born in the Ionian city of Iulis on Ceos. He seems often to have visited Athens on official missions, and became one of the professional, freelance educators who were dubbed 'Sophists' and were caricatured in **Plato**'s dialogues. He is supposed to have written works *On Nature*, *On the Nature of Man*, and *Horai*, and to have composed the celebrated story 'The Choice of Herakles'. He was evidently a humanist, with a rationalistic view of religion; and he had special linguistic interests in 'the correctness of names'—there was a standing joke about the difference between his one-drachma lecture and his 50-drachma course on semantics.

PROFUMO, John Dennis (1915–) English politician. Educated at Harrow and Oxford, he first became a Conservative MP in 1940 and was awarded the OBE in 1944. He held several government posts before becoming secretary of state for war in 1960. He resigned three years later during the scandal following his admission that he had earlier been guilty of a grave misdemeanour in deceiving the House of Commons about the nature of his relationship with **Christine Keeler**, who was at the time also involved with a Russian diplomat. He was awarded the CBE in 1975 for charitable services. *Scandal*, a film based on an account of his affair with Miss Keeler, appeared in 1989.

PROKHOROV, Alexander Mikhailovich (1916–) Russian physicist, born in Australia of Russian emigré parents. His family returned to the Soviet Union after the Revolution, and he became professor at Lebedev Physics Institute, Moscow. He won the Nobel prize for physics in 1964 with **Nikolai Basov** and **Charles Townes** for work on the development of laser beams.

PROKOFIEV, Sergei Sergeyevich (1891–1953) Russian composer, born in Sontsovka in the Ukraine. He wrote his first piano piece at the age of five, and by the time Glièe became his teacher (1902) had already composed two operas. He entered the St Petersburg Conservatory in 1904, and remained for ten years, studying for part of that time with **Rimsky-Korsakov**, forming a lifelong friendship with **Miaskovsky**, and proving in personality, pianism and composition, a radical, indeed rebellious student. His compositions of this period, including his first two piano concertos and two piano sonatas, caused a furore among teachers and critics. In 1914 he visited London, heard **Stravinsky**'s music and met **Diaghilev**. He returned to St Petersburg and avoided war service by again enrolling at the conservatory. There he completed his opera *The Gambler*, the 3rd and 4th piano sonatas, the *Classical* symphony and the Violin Concerto No 1. In May 1918 he left Russia, intending to return when political stability might ensure a hearing for new music. Instead, he remained in exile for 18 years. In the USA he had success as a pianist, and saw his *The Love for Three Oranges* mounted by **Mary Garden** at the Chicago Opera. In Paris he completed other operas, *The Fiery Angel* (1927) and *The Gambler* (Brussels, 1929), a 5th piano sonata, a cantata, *We are Seven*, the symphonies 2–4, piano concertos 4–5, and a ballet, *The Prodigal Son*. Throughout this time he remained in contact with musical life in the Soviet Union where he had several premières, touring there often from 1927, and finally settling in Moscow in 1936. In heart and artistic soul he felt drawn to his homeland rather than to the West. The ballets *Romeo and Juliet* and *Cinderella*, the operas *Semyon Kotko*, *Betrothal in a Monastery* and (his greatest opera) *War and Peace*, the symphonies 5–7, the piano sonatas 6–9, his last piano concerto and film scores for **Sergi Eisenstein** (including *Alexander Nevsky*, first written for Hollywood and later recast as a dramatic cantata) were his most notable works of the Soviet period, as well as his 'children's piece', *Peter and the Wolf* (1936). 1936 saw the beginning of Russia's artistic isolation from the West; Prokofiev made his last visit to western Europe and the USA in 1938; in 1939 he wrote a cantata *Hail to Stalin*, and at the entry to the war (1941) his health declined progressively owing to a heart condition. From 1941 he became estranged from his first wife (who was sent to labour camps from 1948) and lived with Mira Mendel'son who wrote the texts for several late works. In 1948 Prokofiev was named, among others, by the party central committee as the composer of music 'marked with formalist perversions ... alien to the Soviet people'. His last opera, *The Story of a Real Man*, was deemed unfavourable by the Union of Composers, and performed only after **Stalin** died (coincidentally on the same day as Prokofiev, 5 March 1953).

PROKOP See **PROCOP, Andrew**

PROKOPOVICH, Feofan (1681–1736) Russian prelate and statesman. He was educated at Kiev Orthodox Academy (where in 1711 he was appointed rector), and Rome. In St Petersburg in 1716 his sermons and theories for church reforms brought him to the notice of **Peter II, the Great**, who made him his adviser, bishop of Pskov and in 1724 archbishop of Novgorod. He was responsible for setting up a Holy Synod instead of the existing patriarchate, whereby the respective powers of church and state were established.

PRONY, Gaspard François Clair Marie Riche, Baron de (1755–1839) French civil engineer, born in Chamelet. He studied at the École des Ponts et Chaussées from 1776 to 1780, and three years later became assistant to **Perronet** in Paris, for whom he undertook some analyses of masonry arch bridges. After the Revolution he occupied several teaching posts until in 1805 he was appointed inspector general of roads and bridges. He is most noted for the equations he developed dealing with the flow of water, and for the Prony brake (1821) which measures the power of an engine under test.

PROPERTIUS, Sextus (c.48–c.15 BC) Roman elegiac poet, born probably in Asisium (Assisi) in Umbria. He had a portion of his patrimony confiscated after Philippi by the Triumvirs (41 BC), to reward their veterans, but he retained sufficient funds to proceed to Rome for education, and became a poet. He won the favour of **Maecenas**, to whom he dedicated a book of his poems, and even ingratiated himself with **Augustus**, whose achievements he duly celebrated. But the central figure of his inspiration was his mistress Cynthia. Propertius left Rome apparently only once, on a visit to Athens. Of his poems only the first book, devoted to Cynthia, was published during his lifetime.

PROSPER OF AQUITAINE, St (c.390–c.463) French theologian, born in Aquitaine, the champion of Augustinian doctrine against the Semi-Pelagians. He was prominent in southern Gaul from 428 to 434, and then settled in Rome. Besides letters, *Responsiones* and pamphlets on grace and free will, he wrote a chronicle coming down to 455, a hexameter poem against the Pelagians, and *Epigrammata ex sententiis Sancti Augustini*, compiled from St **Augustine**.

PROST, Alain (1955–) French racing driver, born in St Chamond. He had the talent to become a professional footballer, but opted instead for racing driving, and won his first Grand Prix in 1981. The runner-up in the world championships of 1983–84, he became world champion in 1985–86. In 1987 he surpassed **Jackie Stewart**'s record of 27 Grand Prix wins, thus becoming the most successful driver in the history of the sport.

PROTAGORAS (c.490–c.420 BC) Greek Sophist and teacher, born in Abdera in north-east Greece. He was a regular visitor to Athens, and was the first and most famous of the 'Sophists' who, for a fee, offered a professional training in public life and in other skills. He became a friend of **Pericles** and was invited by him to draft a legal code for the new pan-Hellenic colony of Thurii. His many works are lost, except for an agnostic first sentence from *On the Gods*, and much of our information about him comes from **Plato**'s dialogues, one of which was named after him and portrays him memorably (and respectfully). His most famous maxim was 'Man is the measure of all things', which is usually taken to imply a sceptical or relativistic view of human knowledge.

PROTOGENES (5th century BC) Greek painter, born in Caunus in Caria. He lived in Rhodes, where he worked steadily on through the siege of 305–304 BC.

PROUDHON, Pierre Joseph (1809–65) French journalist and socialist, born in Besançon. He tried as a compositor to complete and extend his education. He became partner (1837) in the development of a new typographical process, contributed to an edition of the Bible notes on the Hebrew language, and in 1838 published an *Essai de grammaire générale*. He subsequently contributed to an *Encyclopédie catholique*. In 1840 he issued *Qu'est-ce que la propriété?*, affirming the bold paradox 'Property is Theft', as appropriating the labour of others in the form of rent. In 1842 he was tried for his revolutionary opinions, but acquitted. In 1846 he published his greatest work, the *Système des contradictions économiques*. During the Revolution of 1848 he was elected for the Seine department, and published several newspapers advocating the most advanced theories. He attempted also to establish a bank which should pave the way for a socialist transformation by giving interest-free credit, but this failed completely. The violence of his utterances at last resulted in a sentence of three years' imprisonment, and in March 1849 he fled to Geneva, but returned to Paris in June and gave himself up. While in prison he published *Confessions d'un révolutionnaire* (1849), *Actes de la Révolution* (1849), *Gratuité du crédit* (1850) and *La Révolution sociale démonstrée par le coup d'état* (1852). In June 1852 he was released, but in 1858 was again condemned to three years' imprisonment, and went to Belgium, receiving an amnesty in 1860. A forerunner of **Marx**, his theories emphasized liberty, equality and justice, and one of his main themes was that as man becomes morally mature the artificial restrictions of law and government can be dispensed with.

PROUST, Joseph Louis (1754–1826) French chemist, born in Angers. He was director of the royal laboratory in Madrid (1789–1808), but he returned to France after the fall of **Charles IV**, his patron, and the destruction of the laboratory by the French. He stated the law of constant proportion, known as Proust's Law, was in a controversy with **Claude Berthollet** lasting eight years, and was the first to isolate and identify grape sugar.

PROUST, Marcel (1871–1922) French novelist, born in Auteuil, Paris. A semi-invalid all his life, he was cosseted by his mother, and her death in 1905, when he was 34 years old, robbed him of any desire to continue his 'social butterfly' existence. Instead he withdrew from society, immured himself in a sound-proof flat and gave himself over entirely to introspection. Delving into the self below the levels of superficial consciousness, he set himself the task of transforming into art the realities of experience as known to the inner emotional life. Despite the seemingly dilettante approach to life prior to his start on his novel, *À la recherche du temps perdu* (13 volumes), it is evident from the various volumes which make up this title that no detail ever escaped his amazingly observant eye, and he subjected experience to searching analysis to divine in it beauties and complexities that escape the superficial response of ordinary intelligence. Thinking about the philosophy of **Henri Bergson** on the subconscious, his distinctions between the various aspects of time, and insistence on the truths perceived by involuntary memory, Proust evolved a mode of communication by image, evocation and analogy for displaying his characters—not as a realist would see them, superficially, from the outside, but in terms of their concealed emotional life, evolving on a plane that has nothing to do with temporal limitations. *À la recherche* started off with *Du côté de chez Swann* (1913), and, after a delay caused by the war, *À l'ombre des jeunes filles en fleur*, which won the Prix Goncourt in 1919. *Le Côté de Guermantes* (1920–21, 2 vols) and *Sodome et Gomorrhe* (1922, 3 vols) followed. These achieved an international reputation for Proust and an eager public awaited the posthumously-published titles, *La Prisonnière*, *Albertine disparue*, and *Le Temps retrouvé*, each of two volumes. Apart from his masterpieces, there was also posthumous publication of an early novel, *Jean Santeuil* (1957) and a book of critical credo—*Contre Sainte-Beuve* (trans 1958).

PROUT, Ebenezer (1835–1909) English composer and writer on musical theory, born in Oundle, Northamptonshire. He edited **Handel**'s Messiah, for which he provided additional accompaniments. In 1894 he became professor of music at Dublin.

PROUT, Father See **MAHONY, Francis**

PROUT, Samuel (1783–1852) English watercolourist, born in Plymouth. In 1815 he was elected to the Watercolour Society, and in 1818 went to Rouen. His numerous elementary drawing-books influenced many. He was famed for his picturesque views of buildings and streets, and he was admired by **Ruskin**.

PROUT, William (1785–1850) English chemist and physiologist, born in Horton near Chipping Sodbury. A graduate of Edinburgh, he practised in London from 1812. He is noteworthy for his discovery of the presence of hydrochloric acid in the stomach and for his 'Hypothesis' (1815), which, rejected at first, is now looked upon as a modification of the Atomic Theory.

PRUDENTIUS, Marcus Aurelius Clemens (348–c.410) Latin Christian poet, born in the north of Spain. He practised as a pleader, acted as civil and criminal judge, and afterwards received high office at the imperial court. A Christian all his life, he devoted himself in his later years to the composition of religious poetry. Of his poems the chief are *Cathemerinon Liber*, a series of twelve hymns (trans 1845); *Peristephanon*, 14 lyrical poems in honour of martyrs; *Apotheosis*, a defence of the Trinity; *Hamartigeneia*, on the origin of evil; *Psychomachia*, on the Christian Graces; and *Contra Symmachum*, against the heathen gods; and *Diptychon*, on scriptural incidents. He is the best of the early Christian verse-makers.

PRUD'HON, Pierre Paul (1758–1823) French painter, born in Cluny. He studied in Dijon, trained with engravers in Paris and, having won the Rome prize, went to Italy. He did little work there, returning to Paris to draw and paint in a refined style not in accord with revolutionary Paris. Patronized, however, by the empresses of **Napoleon**, he was made court painter, and among his best work is a portait of the empress **Josephine**. Many of his paintings had mythological and allegorical subjects and were commissioned for public buildings, such as his celebrated *Crime Pursued by Justice and Vengeance* (1808). He also designed furniture and interiors on classical lines.

PRUS, Boleslaw, pseud of **Aleksander Glowacki** (1847–1912) Polish novelist, born in Hrubieszów. He belonged to the period of realism in literature which followed the unsuccessful revolt against Russian domination in 1863–64. His novels and short stories are written as social novels, mainly about common people, and include *The Blunder*, *The Outpost* (1884), *The Doll* (1887), considered to be his masterpiece, a vivid and sympathetic picture of Warsaw, and *Emancipated Women* (1893).

PRYDE, James See **NICHOLSON, Sir William Newzam Prior**

PRYNNE, William (1600–69) English pamphleteer, born in Swanswick near Bath. He graduated from Oriel College, Oxford, in 1621, and was called to the bar, but was soon drawn into controversy, and between 1627 and 1630 published *The Unloveliness of Love-lockes*, *Healthes Sicknesse* (against drinking of healths), and three other Puritan diatribes. In 1633 appeared his *Histrio-Mastix: the Players Scourge*, for which, on account of a supposed reflection on the virtue of Queen **Henrietta Maria**, he was in 1634 sentenced to have his book burnt by the hangman, pay a fine of £5000, be expelled from Oxford and Lincoln's Inn, lose both ears in the pillory, and suffer life imprisonment. Three years later, for attacking **Laud** and the hierarchy in two more pamphlets, a fresh fine of £5000 was imposed; he was again pilloried, and was branded on both cheeks with *S L* ('seditious libeller'; rather than 'stigmata Laudis' as Prynne interpreted it). He remained a prisoner until he was released by a warrant of the House of Commons (1640). He acted as Laud's bitter prosecutor (1644), and in 1647 became recorder of Bath, and in 1648 member for Newport in Cornwall. But, opposing the Independents and **Charles I**'s execution, he was one of those of whom the House was 'purged', and was even imprisoned (1650–52). On **Cromwell**'s death he returned to parliament as a royalist; and, after the Restoration, **Charles II** made him keeper of the Tower records. A great compiler of constitutional history, his best works were the *Calendar of Parliamentary Writs* and his *Records*.

PRYS-JONES, Arthur Glyn (1888–1987) Welsh poet, born in Denbigh and educated at Llandovery College and Jesus College, Oxford. A teacher by profession, he edited the first anthology of Anglo-Welsh poetry, *Welsh Poets* (1917), and published six volumes of his own, including *Poems of Wales* (1923), *Green Places* (1948), *High Heritage* (1969) and *Valedictory Verses* (1978). The doyen of Anglo-Welsh writers, he was president of the Welsh Academy from 1970 until his death.

PRZHEVALSKI, Nikolai Mikhailovich (1839–88) Russian traveller, born near Smolensk. From 1867 to his death at Karakol (Przhevalsk) he made important journeys in Mongolia, Turkestan and Tibet, reaching to within 160 miles of Lhasa. He explored the upper Hwang-ho, reaching as far as Kiachta. During his travels he amassed a valuable collection of plants and animals, including a wild camel and a wild horse which now bears his name.

PRZYBYSZEWSKI, Stanislaw (1868–1927) Polish novelist, dramatist and critic. He was educated in Germany, and lived from 1898 in Cracow, where he became editor of *Life* and a leader of the new literary 'Young Poland' movement. His work, reflecting his 'naturalist' ideas, included *Homo Sapiens* (1901), *Matka* (1903) and the drama *Śnieg* (*Snow*), which was translated into English in 1920.

PSALMANAZAR, George, known as **'the Formosan'** (c.1679–1763) French literary imposter, born probably in Languedoc. Educated by monks and Jesuits, he turned vagabond at the age of 16, and wandered through France, Germany and the Low Countries, by turns an 'Irish pilgrim', a 'Japanese convert', a waiter, a 'heathen Formosan' and a soldier. At Sluys in 1703 he found an accomplice in one Innes, chaplain to a Scottish regiment, who baptized him 'George Lauder' and brought him to London. For Bishop Compton he translated the Church Catechism into the 'Formosan' language; and to him he dedicated his *Historical and Geographical Description of Formosa* (1704), which found many believers in spite of its patent absurdities. Later he was the alleged importer of a white 'Formosan' enamel, a tutor, a regimental clerk (1715–17), a fan-painter and, lastly, for years a diligent hack-writer. The *Universal History* was largely of his compiling; and his, too, a popular *Essay on Miracles*. But in all his strange life there is nothing stranger than the esteem expressed for him by **Samuel Johnson** as 'the best man he ever knew'.

PSELLUS, Michael (11th century) Byzantine politician and teacher of philosophy. He wrote *Synopsis in Aristotelis logicam* and *Chronographia*, valuable both historically and autobiographically. He had considerable influence during the reigns of Constantine Monomachus (who appointed him head of the new faculty of philosophy at the university of Constantinople), **Isaac Comnenus** and Constantine Ducas, whose son was his pupil.

PTOLEMY, or **Claudius Ptolemaeus** (c.90–168) Egyptian astronomer and geographer, who flourished in Alexandria. His 'great compendium of astronomy' seems to have been denominated by the Greeks *megistē*, 'the greatest', whence was derived the Arab name *Almagest*, by which it is generally known. With his *Tetrabiblos Syntaxis* is combined another work called *Karpos* or *Centiloquium*, because it contains a hundred aphorisms—both treat of astrological subjects, so have been held by some to be of doubtful genuineness. Then there is a treatise on the fixed stars or a species of almanac, the *Geographia*, and other works dealing with map making, the musical scale and chronology. Ptolemy, as astronomer and geographer, held supreme sway over the minds of scientific men down to the 16th–17th century; but he seems to have been not so much an independent investigator as a corrector and improver of the work of his predecessors. In astronomy he depended almost entirely on **Hipparchus**. But, as his works form the only remaining authority on ancient astronomy, the system they expound is called the *Ptolemaic System*, which, the system of **Plato** and **Aristotle**, was an attempt to reduce to scientific form the common notions of the motions of the heavenly bodies. The Ptolemaic astronomy, handed on by Byzantines and Arabs, assumed that the Earth is the centre of the universe, and that the heavenly bodies revolve round it. Beyond and in the ether surrounding the earth's atmosphere were eight concentric spherical shells, to seven of which one heavenly body was attached, the fixed stars occupying the eighth. The apparent irregularity of their motions was explained by a complicated theory of epicycles. As a geographer Ptolemy is the corrector of a predecessor, Marinus of Tyre. His *Geography* contains a catalogue of places, with latitude and longitude; general descriptions; and details regarding his mode of noting the position of places—by latitude and longitude, with the calculation of the size of the earth. He constructed a map of the world and other maps.

PTOLEMY I, Soter (d.283 BC) a son of Lagos. He was one of the greatest of the generals of **Alexander the Great**, upon whose death he obtained Egypt (323). Nominally subject to the Macedonian kings, Ptolemy occupied the first half of his reign in repelling outside attacks and consolidating his government. In 306 he was defeated by **Demetrius Poliorcetes** in a sea-fight off Salamis in Cyprus. He was nevertheless able to assume the royal title (305), and defended his territories against **Antigonus** and **Cyclops** and Demetrius. In 305 he defended the Rhodians against Demetrius, and received from them his title Soter (Saviour). Alexandria, his capital, became the centre of commerce and Greek culture.

PTOLEMY II, Philadelphus (308–246 BC) king of Egypt from 283, son and successor of **Ptolemy I, Soter**. Under him the power of Egypt attained its greatest height. He was generally successful in his external wars, founded the Museum and Library, purchased many valuable manuscripts of Greek literature, and attracted leading Greek intellectuals to his court. The Egyptian history of **Manetho** was dedicated to him, but the story that he commissioned the Greek translation of the Hebrew scriptures (the Septuagint) is open to doubt.

PTOLEMY III, Eurgetes (d.222 BC) king of Egypt from 246, son and successor of **Ptolemy II, Philadelphus**. He extended the limits of the empire in the Aegean and to the south.

PTOLEMY IV, Philopator (d.204 BC) king of Egypt from 222, son and successor of **Ptolemy III, Eurgetes**. He began his reign by murdering his mother, Berenice. A hostile tradition portrays him as indolent and ascribes to him the decline of Ptolemaic power at home and abroad.

PTOLEMY V, Epiphanes (c.210–180 BC) king of Egypt from 203, son and successor of **Ptolemy IV, Philopater**. Egypt's decline dates rather from his reign, and from the internal conflicts that plagued the dynasty for most of the rest of Ptolemaic history. The belated attempt of **Cleopatra** to revive Ptolemaic power with Roman help ended in failure, and after her, Egypt became a Roman province.

PUAPUA, Dr Tomasi (1938–) Tuvaluan politician. After training at the Fiji School of Medicine and Otago University, New Zealand, he worked as a doctor and gradually moved into the political arena. In September 1981 he was elected prime minister of Tuvalu, replacing Toaripi Lauti, who had been implicated in an investment scandal. He was re-elected in 1985, but defeated in the general election of 1989 and replaced as premier by Bikenibeu Paeniu. During his period as prime minister he was outspoken in his opposition to France's testing of nuclear weapons on Mururoa Atoll, in French Polynesia.

PUCCI, Emilio, Marchese di Barsento (1914–) Italian fashion designer, born in Naples. He studied social sciences in Italy and the USA, and was a member of Italy's Olympic ski team (1933–34). He served in the Italian air force in World War II and became a member of the Italian Parliament (1963–72). He started designing ski clothes in 1947, and in 1950 opened his own couture house, creating casual, elegant, print dresses for women. He became renowned for his use of bold patterns and brilliant colour.

PUCCINI, Giacomo (Antonio Domenico Michele Secondo Maria) (1858–1924) Italian composer, born in Lucca. At 19, he was an organist and choirmaster in Lucca, his first extant compositions being written for use in the church. Poverty prevented his undertaking regular studies until a grant from the queen in 1880 enabled him to attend the Milan Conservatory. His first opera, *Le Villi*, failed to secure a prize in the competition for which it was composed, but impressed Ricordi, the publisher, sufficiently to induce him to commission a second work, *Edgar*, which failed at its first performance in 1889. *Manon Lescaut* (1893) was his first great success, but it was eclipsed by *La Bohème* (1896). *Tosca* and *Madame Butterfly* (both 1900) have also remained popular favourites. His last opera, *Turandot*, was left unfinished at his death, and was completed by his friend Alfano. He was, perhaps, the last great representative of the Italian operatic tradition, which absorbed almost all his energies throughout his mature working life.

PUFFENDORF, or **Pufendorf, Samuel, Freiherr von** (1632–94) German writer on jurisprudence, born near Chemnitz. After studies at Leipzig and at Jena, he was tutor to the sons of the Swedish ambassador at Copenhagen when war broke out between Denmark and Sweden, and he was imprisoned. There he thought out his *Elementa Jurisprudentiae Universalis*, dedicated to the Elector Palatine, who made him professor of the law of nations at Heidelberg (1661). As 'Severinus de Monzambano' he exposed absurdities of the constitution of the Germanic empire in *De Statu Imperii Germanici* (1667). In 1670 he became professor at Lund, and wrote his great *De Jure Naturae et Gentium* (1672), based upon **Grotius** with features from **Hobbes**. Appointed Swedish historiographer to King **Karl XI**, he published a history of Sweden from the wars of **Gustav II Adolf** to the death of Queen **Kristina**. In 1688 the Elector of Brandenburg invited him to Berlin to write the history of **Frederick-William**, the Great Elector.

PUGACHEV, Yemelyan Ivanovich (c.1744–1775) Russian Cossack soldier and pretender. He fought in the Seven Years' War (1756–63) and in the war against Turkey (1769–74) before retiring to a lawless life in the south of Russia. In 1773 he proclaimed himself to be **Peter III**, the assassinated husband of **Catherine II, the Great**, and began a reign of organized rebellion in the south, gathering to him the discontented masses out of which he created a military force. Promising his followers freedom and possessions, he besieged fortresses and towns and his power by 1774 had spread alarmingly. Catherine made half-hearted attempts to curb Pugachev with a weak and badly-led force, but finally sent a proper army against him, and in a battle near Tsaritsyn he was defeated, captured and conveyed in an iron cage to Moscow, where he was executed.

PUGET, Pierre (1622–94) French sculptor, painter and architect, born in Marseilles, where later he did most of his architectural work. He worked on the ceilings of the Berberini Palace in Rome and the Pitti Palace in Florence. Examples of his sculpture may be seen in the Louvre (Hercules, **Milo of Crotona**, **Alexander** and **Diogenes**, etc).

PUGH, Clifton Ernest (1924–) Australian artist, born in Richmond, Victoria. He studied under Sir William Dargie at the Art School of the National Gallery of Victoria, Melbourne, after war service. He had his first major exhibition in 1957 and made his mark with exhibitions at the Whitechapel and Tate Galleries, London, in the early 1960s. His paintings divide into two genres: his love of native Australian wildlife is reflected in his 'bush' paintings, and his perceptive portraits of academics and politicians won him the Archibald prize in 1965, 1971 and 1972. He has also designed stage sets and illustrated a number of popular books on conservation.

PUGIN, August Welby Northmore (1812–52) English architect, born in London, son of a French architectural draughtsman, Auguste Pugin (1762–1832). Educated at Christ's Hospital School, he trained in his father's office in London by making drawings for his father's books on Gothic buildings. He was employed by Sir **Charles Barry** to make detailed drawings for the Houses of Parliament (1836–37), for which he designed and modelled a large part of the decorations and sculpture. A convert to Roman Catholicism, he designed several Roman Catholic churches, including the cathedral in Birmingham and St Oswald's in Liverpool. He did much to revive Gothic architecture in England, and his aesthetic theories were influential on people as diverse as **John Ruskin** and Sir **Henry Cole**, and provided much of the foundation for the Arts and Crafts Movement. He wrote *Contrasts between the Architecture of the 15th and 19th Centuries* (1836), *Chancel Screens* (1851), and *True Principles of Christian Architecture* (1841).

PUJOL, Joseph, known as **'Le Pétomane'** (1857–1945) French entertainer, born in Marseilles, the son of an artisan stone mason and sculptor. A baker by trade, he became a music hall entertainer as a result of his phenomenal capacity for farting, by drawing in air through his rectum and expelling it. He appeared in public in Marseilles in 1887, and in 1892 moved to Paris, where his extraordinary act topped the bill at the Moulin Rouge. In 1895 he opened his own theatre, the Pompadour. Three years later he sued the Moulin Rouge for presenting a female 'Pétomane', but before the case came to court she was exposed as a fraud, having concealed various whistles and bellows in her skirts. He retired from the stage in 1914 when the outbreak of World War I made his speciality act of mock artillery barrages seen less than funny.

PUŁASKI, Kazimierz (1748–79) Polish nobleman and soldier. He fought against Russia, and was outlawed at the partition of Poland (1772). In 1777 he went to America, and for his conduct at Brandywine was given a brigade of cavalry. In 1778 he organized 'Pułaski's legion', in May 1779 entered Charleston, and held it until it was relieved. He was mortally wounded at the siege of Savannah.

PULCI, Luigi (1432–84) Italian poet. A protégé of **Cosimo de' Medici**, he wrote *Il Morgante Maggiore* ('Morgante the Giant', 1481), a burlesque epic with **Roland** for hero, one of the most valuable specimens of the early Tuscan dialect. He also produced a comic novel and several humorous sonnets.

PULITZER, Joseph (1847–1911) Hungarian-born American newspaper proprietor, born in Makó of Magyar–Jewish and Austro-German parentage. In 1864 he emigrated to join the US army. Discharged the following year, he came penniless to St Louis. There he became a reporter, was elected to the State legislature, and began to acquire and revitalize old newspapers. The New York *World* (1883) sealed his success. He endowed the Columbia University School of Journalism, and in his will established annual Pulitzer prizes for literature, drama, music and journalism.

PULLMAN, George Mortimer (1831–97) American inventor and businessman, born in Brocton, New York state. A cabinet-maker to trade, he became a contractor in Chicago and a storekeeper in Colorado, before designing a Pullman railroad sleeping-car (patented in 1864 and 1865). The Pullman Palace Car Company was formed in 1867. He also introduced dining-cars in 1868. In 1880 he founded 'Pullman City' for his workers, since absorbed by Chicago.

PULSZKY, Francis Aurelius (1814–97) Hungarian politician and author, born in Eperies. He studied law, travelled, and published (1837) a successful book on England. In 1848 he became **Esterházy**'s factotum, but, having joined the revolution, fled to London, where he became a journalist. When **Kossuth** came to England Pulszky became his companion, and went with him to America. His wife, Theresa (1815–66), wrote *Memoirs of a Hungarian Lady* (1850) and *Tales and Traditions of Hungary* (1851). Pulszky was condemned to death in 1852, but after living in Italy 1852–66, and being imprisoned in Naples as a Garibaldian, was pardoned in 1867. He returned to Hungary, sat in parliament, and was director of museums.

PULTENEY, William, Earl of Bath (1684–1764) English politician, the son of a London knight. He was educated at Westminster and Christ Church College, Oxford. He became Whig member for Heydon in 1705, and was an eloquent speaker. Disgusted with **Walpole**'s indifference to his claims, in 1728 he headed a group of malcontent 'patriots', and was thenceforth Walpole's bitterest opponent. He was **Bolingbroke**'s chief assistant in the *Craftsman*, which involved him in many political controversies, and called forth some of his finest pamphlets. On Walpole's resignation Pulteney was sworn into the privy council, and in 1742 created Earl of Bath. **Horace Walpole** places him amongst his *Royal and Noble Authors*.

PUPIN, Michael Idvorsky (1858–1935) Hungarian-born American physicist and inventor, born in Idvor, Austria-Hungary (now in Yugoslavia). He arrived in the USA in 1874 as a penniless immigrant, graduated at Columbia University in 1883, and subsequently studied under **Helmholtz** and **Kirchhoff** in Germany, returning to become professor of electromechanics at Columbia (1901–31). His many inventions included a system of multiplex telegraphy using electrical tuning; the fluoroscope, by which X-rays can be observed and photographed on a fluorescent screen; and the Pupin inductance coil, which made long-distance telephony practical by amplifying the signal at intervals along the line without distortion. His autobiography, *From Immigrant to Inventor* (1923), won the Pulitzer prize.

PURBACH, or **Peuerbach, Georg von** (1423–61) Austrian astronomer and mathematician, considered to be the first great modern astronomer, and teacher of **Regiomontanus**. Court astrologer to **Frederick III** and professor at Vienna, he is thought to have been the first to introduce sines into trigonometry, and compiled a sines table.

PURCELL, Edward Mills (1912–) American physicist, born in Taylorville, Illinois. He taught at Massachusetts Institute of Technology and Harvard University, where he was appointed professor of physics in 1949 and Gerhard Gade professor in 1960. He was awarded the Nobel prize for physics in 1952 (with **Ernest Bloch**) for his work on the magnetic moments of atomic particles.

PURCELL, Henry (1659–95) English composer, born probably in Westminster, the son of Thomas Purcell, a court musician and Chapel Royal chorister. He was himself one of the 'children of the chapel' from about 1669 to 1673, when, his voice having broken, he was apprenticed to the keeper of the king's keyboard and wind instruments, whom he ultimately succeeded in 1683. In the meantime he had followed **Matthew Locke** as 'composer for the king's violins' (1677), and had been appointed organist of Westminster Abbey (1679) and of the Chapel Royal (1682). It is known that he began to compose when very young, though some early pieces ascribed to him are probably the work of his uncle Henry, also a professional musician. In about 1680 he began writing incidental music for the Duke of York's Theatre, and from this time until his early death his output was prolific. Though his harpsichord pieces and his well-known set of trio-sonatas for violins and continuo have retained their popularity, his greatest masterpieces are among his vocal and choral works. In his official capacity he produced a number of fine 'odes' in celebration of royal birthdays, St Cecilia's Day, and other occasions, also many anthems and services, but had he never written these, his incidental songs such as 'Nymphs and Shepherds' (**Thomas Shadwell**'s *The Libertine*), 'I Attempt from Love's Sickness' (*The Indian Queen*), and 'Arise, ye Subterranean Winds' (*The Tempest*) would ensure his immortality. He is credited with six operas, but of these only the first, *Dido and Aeneas*, written to a libretto by **Nathum Tate** in 1689, is opera in the true sense. The others—*Dioclesian* (1690; adapted from **Beaumont** and **Fletcher**), *King Arthur* (1691; **Dryden**), *The Fairy Queen* (1692; adapted from *A Midsummer Night's Dream*), *The Tempest* (1695; Shadwell's adaptation) and *The Indian Queen* (1695; Dryden and Sir **Robert Howard**)—consist essentially of spoken dialogue between the main characters interspersed with masques and other musical items supplied by nymphs, shepherds, allegorical figures and the like. Purcell was writing at a time when the new Italian influence was first beginning to be felt in England, and his music includes superb examples in both this and the traditional English style, as well as in the French style exemplified by **Giovanni Lully**. **John Blow**'s fine ode on his untimely end, and tributes by other contemporary musicians, show that he was recognized in his own time, as now, as the greatest English composer of the age. His brother Daniel (c.1663–1718) was also a distinguished composer and was for some time organist of Magdalen College, Oxford.

PURCHAS, Samuel (1577–1626) English compiler of travel books, born in Thaxted in Essex. He studied at St John's College, Cambridge, and became vicar of Eastwood in 1604, and in 1614 rector of St Martin's, Ludgate. He assisted **Hakluyt** in his later years. His own great works were *Purchas his Pilgrimage, or Relations of the World in all Ages* (1613) and *Hakluytus Posthumus, or Purchas his Pilgrimes* (1625), based on the papers of Hakluyt and archives of the East India company. Another work is *Purchas his Pilgrim: Microcosmus, or the History of Man* (1619).

PURKINJE, Jan Evangelista (also **Purkyne**) (1787–1869) Czech physiologist, born in Libochowitz. He was professor at Breslau (1823) and Prague (1850). He did research on the eye, the brain, muscles, embryology, digestion and sweat glands. 'Purkinje's figure' is an effect by which one can see in one's own eye the shadows of the retinal blood vessels. 'Purkinje's cells' are situated in the middle layer of the cerebellar cortex.

PUSEY, Edward Bouverie (1800–82) English theologian, and leader of the 'Oxford Movement', born in Pusey, in Berkshire. His father, the youngest son of the first Viscount Folkestone, had assumed the name Pusey when he inherited the Pusey estates. He was educated at Eton and Christ Church, Oxford, in 1823 was elected a fellow of Oriel College, Oxford, and from 1825 to 1827 in Germany acquainted himself with German theological teaching. In 1828 he was ordained deacon and priest and appointed Regius professor of Hebrew at Oxford, a position which he retained until his death. His first work was an essay on the causes of rationalism in recent German theology, which was criticized as being itself rationalistic. The aim of his life was to prevent the spread of Rationalism in England. Hence, when in 1833 **Newman** began the issue of the *Tracts for the Times*, Pusey very soon joined him; and they, with **Keble**, were the leaders of the movement. They endeavoured to make the church live again before the eyes and minds of men as it had lived in times past. With this aim Pusey wrote his contributions to the *Tracts*, especially those on Baptism and the Holy Eucharist, and commenced in 1836 the *Oxford Library of the Fathers*, to which his chief contributions were translations of **Augustine**'s Confessions and works of **Tertullian**. In 1843 Pusey was suspended for two years from preaching in Oxford for a university sermon on the Holy Eucharist; at the first opportunity he reiterated his teaching, and this time was left alone. But before his suspension was over Newman, with several of his leading disciples, had joined the Roman communion. With Keble, Pusey at once set himself to reassure those who were distressed by this development. But soon another band of distinguished men, including Archdeacon (Cardinal) **Manning** and Archdeacon **Wilberforce**, departed to the Roman Church. Still Pusey loyally laboured on. His numerous writings during this period, include a letter on the practice of confession (1850) and *A Letter to the Bishop of London* (1851), a general defence of his position. *The Doctrine of the Real Presence* (1856–57), and the series of three *Eirenicons* (1865–69), clear the way for reunion between the Church of England and that of Rome. The reform of Oxford University, which destroyed the intimate bond between the university and the church, greatly occupied Pusey's mind. His evidence before the commission, his remarkable pamphlet on *Collegiate and Professorial Teaching*, and his assiduous work on the Hebdomadal Council are proofs of the interest he took in the university. By 1860 the tide had turned. The teaching for which the Tractarians had laboured was beginning to be recognized. But the fruits of the intolerance and persecution of which Oxford had been the scene were also ripening into religious indifference and rationalism. Against such teaching Pusey contended for the rest of his life. In private life Pusey was an ascetic, deeply religious man of warm affection, widely known for his gentleness, sincerity and humility, and was constantly sought as a spiritual guide by persons of every station. He spent large sums in helping to provide churches in East London and Leeds, and in founding sisterhoods. He married in 1828 and his only son, Philip Edward (1830–80), predeceased him.

PUSHKIN, Alexander Sergevich (1799–1837) Russian poet, born in Moscow. His lineage was illustrious, and he attended the Lyceum at Tsarkoe Selo, in the environs of St Petersburg, where his talent for poetry first emerged. In 1817 he entered government service, but because of his liberalism was exiled in 1820 to the south. In 1824 he was dismissed and confined to his estate near Pskov, and did not return to Moscow until after the accession of **Nicholas I**. He married Natalia Goncharova in 1832, whose beauty attracted Baron Georges D'Anthès, a French royalist in the Russian service. Pushkin challenged him to a duel and was killed. Regarded as Russia's greatest poet, his first success was the romantic poem *Ruslan and Lyudmilla* (1820), followed by *The Prisoner of the Caucasus* (1822), *Fountain of Bakhchisarai* (1826), *Tzigani* (1827), and his masterpiece, *Eugene Onegin* (1828), a sophisticated novel in verse that was much imitated but never rivalled. Prolific for one whose life was so short, he also wrote lyric poems, essays, the blank verse historical drama *Boris Godunov* (1825), and, in 1830, the four 'Little Tragedies': 'Mozart and Salieri', 'The Covetous Knight', 'The Stone Guest', and 'The Feast during the Plague'. He is to Russian literature what **Shakespeare** is to English.

PUSKAS, Ferenc (1927–) Hungarian footballer, born in Budapest. A member of the great Hungarian side of the early 1950s, he was severely criticized for playing in the final of the 1954 World Cup tournament when his fitness was in doubt, and was blamed for the defeat by West Germany. His career looked likely to end with the invasion of Hungary by the Russians in 1956, but, touring in South America at the time, he decided to sign for Real Madrid. He became a Spanish national and formed a devastating partnership with **Di Stefano**. He has the unique distinction of having scored four goals and three goals in two separate European Cup finals. Puskas did not look athletic and was often overweight, but his left foot was deadly. He played until he was almost 40 years old, when he turned to coaching and took the Greek side Panathinaikos to the European Cup final.

PUTNAM, Frederic Ward (1839–1915) American archaeologist and ethnographer, born in Salem, Massachusetts, the founding father of archaeology in the USA. He trained as a zoologist, turning to archaeology on being appointed curator of the Peabody Museum at Harvard (1875–1909); he was also professor of American archaeology and ethnology at Harvard from 1887, and curator of anthropology at the American Museum of Natural History in New York City from 1894. The author of more than 400 articles, he was also an energetic excavator, one of the first to study archaeological remains of the native Americans. He directed pioneer field expeditions to the Ohio river valley, and to New Jersey, the American southwest, Mexico, and South America. Organizer of the anthropological exhibit at the 1893 Chicago Exposition, he helped found the Field Museum of Natural History in Chicago and the department of anthropology at the University of California at Berkeley (1903). For 25 years he also served as secretary of the American Association for the Advancement of Science.

PUTNAM, George Palmer (1814–72) American publisher, born in Brunswick, Maine, grand-nephew of **Israel Putnam**. He went to London in 1840 and opened a branch bookshop selling American books. In 1848 he returned to the USA and founded a book-publishing business, established in 1866 as the firm of G P Putnam & Sons (now G P Putnam's Sons). In 1853 he founded *Putnam's Monthly Magazine*.

PUTNAM, Hilary (1926–) American philosopher, born in Chicago. He held teaching positions at Northwestern University and Princeton, and was professor of the philosophy of science at the Massachusetts Institute of Technology from 1961 to 1965. Since 1965 he has been professor of philosophy at Harvard. Much of his early work was on problems arising out of physics, mathematics and logic, but he has gone on to work creatively in virtually all the main areas of philosophy, and has argued strongly for a conception of philosophy that makes it essential to a responsible view of the real world and our place in it. His main publications are *Philosophical Papers* (3 vols, 1975, 1975, 1979), *Meaning and the Moral Sciences* (1978), and *Reason, Truth and History* (1982).

PUTNAM, Israel (1718–90) American revolutionary soldier, born in Danvers, Massachusetts, a cousin of **Rufus Putnam**. He became a farmer, but in the French and Indian War of 1755–63 he helped as a captain to repel a French invasion of New York, and was present at the battle of Lake George (1755). In 1758 he was captured by Indians, tortured, and about to be burnt when a French officer rescued him. In 1759 he was given command of a regiment, in 1762 went on the West India campaign, and in 1764 helped to relieve Detroit, then besieged by **Pontiac**. In 1775, after Concord, he was given command of the forces of Connecticut, was at Bunker Hill, and held the command at New York and in August 1776 at Brooklyn Heights, where he was defeated by **Howe**. In 1777 he was appointed to the defence of the Highlands of the Hudson.

PUTNAM, Rufus (1738–1824) American revolutionary soldier, born in Sutton, Massachusetts, a cousin of **Israel Putnam**. He served against the French from 1757 to 1760, and then settled as a farmer and millwright. In the American War of Independence he rendered good service as an engineer, commanded a regiment, and in 1783 became brigadier-general. In 1788 he founded Marietta, Ohio; in 1789 he was appointed a judge of the Supreme Court of the Northwest Territory; and from 1793 to 1803 was surveyor-general of the United States.

PUTTNAM, David Terence (1941–) English film-maker, born in Southgate, London. A very successful background in advertising and photography led him to produce his first feature film *S.W.A.L.K* (1969). Subsequently he helped encourage new directorial talents with stylish, low-budget features such as *Bugsy Malone* (1976) and *The Duellists* (1977). *Chariots of Fire* (1981), which won four Academy Awards, epitomized the type of intelligent, humanist drama he wanted to make, and its international commercial appeal allowed him to progress to larger scale explorations of human and moral dilemmas in films such as *Local Hero* (1983), *The Killing Fields* (1984) and *The Mission* (1986). A tireless spokesman and figurehead of the British film industry in the early 1980s, he was appointed chairman and chief executive of Columbia Pictures in 1986, but his anti-establishment stance led him to return to independent production with *Memphis Belle* (1990).

PUVIS DE CHAVANNES, Pierre (1824–98) French decorative, symbolic painter, born in Lyon. Murals by him of the life of St **Geneviève** may be seen in the Panthéon, Paris, and large allegorical works such as 'Work' and 'Peace' on the staircase of the Musée de Picardie, Amiens.

PU-YI, personal name of **Hsuan T'ung** (1906–67) last emperor of China (1908–12) and the first of Manchukuo (from 1934 until it ceased to exist in 1945). After the revolution of 1912 the young emperor was given a pension and a summer palace near Beijing. He became known as Henry Pu-yi, but in 1932 he was called from private life to be provincial dictator of Manchukuo and from 1934 to 1945 he was emperor under the name of **Kang Teh**. From 1945 to 1950 he was imprisoned by the Russians and subsequently by the Chinese communists, who undertook his political re-education. After then he lived as a private citizen in Beijing until his death. He wrote *From Emperor to Citizen* (1964).

PUZO, Mario (1920–) American novelist, born in New York City. Educated at Columbia University, he served in the US air force during World War II and worked for 20 years as an administrative assistant in government offices at home and overseas. His first novel was *The Dark Arena* (1955), but his breakthrough came with his novel about the Mafia, *The Godfather* (1969), the epic story of Don Corleone and his extended 'family' of Sicilian immigrants who impose their will by brutal force and terror. It became a bestseller, and was filmed by **Frances Coppola** in 1972 with **Marlon Brando** playing Corleone.

PYAT, Félix (1810–89) French journalist and communist. He was admitted to the bar in 1831, but chiefly wrote articles, feuilletons and plays. He signed **Ledru-Rollin**'s appeal to the masses to arm in 1849, escaped to Switzerland, Brussels and London, and was a member of the 'European revolutionary committee'. Returning to Paris on amnesty in 1870, he was a leader of the communards, and again escaped to London. He was condemned to death, in absence, in 1873, but pardoned in 1880.

PYE, Henry James (1745–1813) English poet, born in London. He studied at Magdalen College, Oxford. He held a commission in the Berkshire militia, in 1784 became MP for that county, and in 1790 succeeded **Thomas Warton** as poet laureate. In 1792 he was appointed a London police magistrate. The works of 'poetical Pye' number nearly 20, and include *Alfred: an Epic* (1801), with numerous birthday and New-Year odes, all extremely loyal and extremely dull.

PYE, John David (1932–) English zoologist, born in Mansfield, Nottingham. Educated at University College of Wales, Aberystwyth and Bedford College, London, he taught at King's College, London, and from 1977 to 1982 was appointed head of the department of zoology, Queen Mary College, London (professor since 1973). His principal research has been into the use of ultrasound by animals. Ultrasound (which is inaudible to humans) is used by a wide range of animals as a means of communication and navigation. Much of his work has concerned the echo-location used by bats to obtain food and avoid obstacles while flying, but the applications of his work have raised the possibility of controlling the social behaviour of insects, in particular those which are pests.

PYM, Francis Leslie, Baron Pym (1922–) English politician. Educated at Eton and Cambridge, he served in World War II and was awarded the Military Cross. A Conservative MP since 1961, Pym's political advancement came through the whips' office (assistant whip 1962, deputy chief whip 1967, Government chief whip 1970) before he was appointed secretary of state for Northern Ireland (1973–74). He spent two years as defence secretary (1979–81), and was appointed foreign secretary during the 'Falklands Crisis' of 1982. However, his comparatively gloomy assessments of economic prospects did not endear him to the prime minister, **Margaret Thatcher**, and he was dropped from the government following the Conservatives' 1983 landslide election victory. It seemed for a time that he might lead an anti-Thatcher faction within the Conservative party, but support for his 'Centre Forward' group failed to coalesce and he accepted a life peerage in 1987.

PYM, John (1584–1643) English politician, born in Brymore near Bridgwater. He entered Broadgates Hall (now Pembroke College), Oxford, in 1599, as a gentleman-commoner, but left in 1602 without taking a degree, and then became a student of the Middle Temple. In 1614 he was returned to parliament for Calne, exchanging that seat in 1625 for Tavistock. He attached himself to the Country party, and made war against monopolies, papistry, the Spanish match and absolutism with a vigour that brought him three months' imprisonment. In 1626 he took a prominent part in the impeachment of **Buckingham**. In the parliament of 1628 he stood second only to Sir **John Eliot** in supporting the Petition of Right, but he opposed him on tonnage and poundage. In the Short Parliament (1640) he 'brake the ice by a two hours' discourse, in which he summed up shortly and sharply all that most reflected upon the prudence and justice of the government, that they might see how much work they had to do to satisfy their country'. And in the Long Parliament, having meanwhile joined with the Scots, and ridden with **Hampden** through England, urging the voters to their duty, Pym on 11 November named **Strafford**, twelve years earlier his friend and ally, as the 'principal author and promotor of all those counsels which had exposed the kingdom to so much ruin'. In the impeachment of Strafford which followed, resulting in his execution, Pym took the leading part. In the proceedings against **Laud**, Pym was also conspicuous, as in the carrying of the Grand Remonstrance and in every other crisis up to the time when war became inevitable; he was the one of the 'Five Members' whom **Charles I** singled out by name. On the breaking out of hostilities he remained in London, and there in the executive rendered services to the cause no less essential than those of a general in the field. He died a month after being appointed Lieutenant of the Ordnance.

PYNCHON, Thomas (1937–) American novelist, born in Glen Cove, New York, and educated at Cornell University. Seen by some as wilfully obscure, by others as a swashbuckling experimentalist, his sprawling, loquacious novels are ingenious, fabulous structures in which the normal conventions of the novel have been largely abandoned. Studiously avoiding public forums, he is more studied than read. *V*, generally regarded as his best book, was published in 1963. Subsequent publications include *The Crying of Lot 49* (1966) and *Gravity's Rainbow* (1973), concerning Tyrone Slothrop, lost in a surreal labyrinth but imbued with the wherewithal—in his reproductive organ—to predict exactly the sites of V-2 explosions in London.

PYNSON, Richard (d.1530) French printer of Norman birth. He studied at the University of Paris, learned printing in Normandy, and practised his trade in England. In 1497 appeared his edition of **Terence**, the first classic to be printed in London. He became printer to King **Henry VIII** (1508), and introduced roman type in England (1509).

PYRRHO (c.365–270 BC) Greek philosopher, born in Elis. He travelled in Persia and India with **Alexander the Great**, and returned to Elis where he effectively established the philosophical tradition later called Scepticism. Like **Socrates**, he wrote nothing himself but had a great effect on his pupils and contemporaries. His views were reported by his disciple Timon the Sillographer. He seems to have held a strong form of scepticism and recommended 'suspending judgement' as an appropriate response which would bring with it 'an imperturbable peace of mind'.

PYRRHUS (c.318–322 BC) king of Epirus, one of the greatest generals of the age after **Alexander the Great**, best-known for his wars against the Romans in Italy. His early years were insecure, as he had to struggle to maintain his throne and emancipate Epirus from Macedonian control. In this he was at length successful, but his opportunity came in 281 when the Tarentines, a Greek colony in the south of Italy, appealed to him for support against the growing power of Rome. In 280 he sailed for Tarentum with 25000 men and a number of elephants—the first time elephants had been seen in Italy. The first battle, on the River Siris, was long and bloody, and though Pyrrhus won, the casualties on both sides were heavy—hence the phrase a 'Pyrrhic victory'. Many Italians now joined Pyrrhus, and he marched north, but finding Rome too well-prepared and the Romans unwilling to negotiate, was forced to withdraw to Tarentum for the winter. In 279 the Romans were again defeated (at Asculum), but once more Pyrrhus' losses were heavy. He then crossed over to Sicily to assist the Sicilian Greeks against the Carthaginians in 278. Initially successful, he suffered a setback at Lilybaeum, and relations with his Greek allies broke down. In 275 he left the island to resume his war against the Romans, but was defeated by the consul Curius Dentatus near Beneventum. He was then forced to abandon Italy and return to Epirus, where he engaged in war with **Antigonus Gonatas**, king of Macedonia, then invaded the Peloponnese, where he failed to capture Sparta and was killed in a street fight in Argos.

PYTHAGORAS (6th century BC) Greek philosopher, sage and mathematician, born in Samos. About 530 he settled in Crotona, a Greek colony in southern Italy, where he established a religious community of some kind. He may later have moved to Megapontum, after persecution. He wrote nothing, and his whole life is shrouded in myth and legend. Pythagoreanism was first a way of life rather than a philosophy, emphasizing moral asceticism and purification, and associated with doctrines of the transmigration of souls, the kinship of all living things and various ritual rules of abstinence (most famously, 'do not eat beans'). He is also associated with mathematical discoveries involving the chief musical intervals, the relations of numbers, the theorem which bears his name, and with more fundamental beliefs about the understanding and representation of the world of nature through numbers. The equilateral triangle of ten dots, the tetracys of the decad, itself became an object of religious veneration, referred to in the Pythagoran oath 'Nay, by him that gave us the *tetracys* which contains the fount and root of ever-flowing nature'. It is impossible to disentangle Pythagoras' own views from the later accretions of mysticism and neoplatonism, but he had a profound influence on **Plato** and later philosophers, astronomers and mathematicians.

PYTHEAS, of Marseilles (4th century BC) Greek navigator and geographer. About 330 BC he was commissioned to reconnoitre a new trade-route to the tin and amber markets of northern Europe. He sailed past Spain, Gaul and the east coast of Britain, and reached 'Thule', six days' sail to the north, formerly identified as Iceland but more probably northern Norway. His report on his voyage survives only in fragmentary references in later writers.

PYTHIAS See **DAMON**

Q

QABOOS, bin Said (1940–) Sultan of Oman, born in Salalah, the son of Said bin Taimar, and the 14th descendant of the ruling dynasty of the Albusaid family. He was educated in England and trained at Sandhurst military academy. He disagreed with the conservative views of his father and in 1970 overthrew him in a bloodless coup and assumed the sultanship. He proceeded to pursue more liberal and expansionist policies, while maintaining an international position of strict non-alignment.

QUANT, Mary (1934–) English fashion designer, born in London. She studied at Goldsmith's College of Art and began fashion design when she opened a small boutique in Chelsea in 1955. Two years later she married one of her partners, Alexander Plunkett Greene. Her clothes became extremely fashionable in the 1960s when the geometric simplicity of her designs, especially the mini-skirt, and the originality of her colours, became an essential feature of the 'swinging Britain' era. In the 1970s she extended into cosmetics and textile design.

QUANTZ, Johann Joachim (1697–1773) German flautist and composer, born near Göttingen. He spent many years in the service of the king of Saxony, toured extensively in Italy, France and England, and became teacher of **Frederick II, the Great** and later his court composer. Author of a treatise on flute-playing, he composed some 300 concertos for one or two flutes as well as a vast quantity of other music for this instrument.

QUARLES, Francis (1592–1644) English poet, born in the manor house of Stewards near Romford, Essex, the son of the surveyor-general of victualling for the navy. He studied at Christ's College, Cambridge, and at Lincoln's Inn, and was successively cup-bearer to the princess **Elizabeth** (queen of Bohemia) when she went to marry Elector **Frederick V** in Germany (1613), secretary to Archbishop Ussher (c.1629), and chronologer to the City of London (1639). He married in 1618 a wife who bore him 18 children and prefixed a touching memoir to his *Solomon's Recantation* (1645). Quarles was a royalist and churchman who suffered in the cause by having his books and manuscripts destroyed. He wrote abundantly in prose and verse. His *Emblems* (1635), in spite of many imperfections, occasionally shows a flash of poetic fire. Other poetical works include *A Feast of Wormes* (1620), *Argalus and Parthenia* (1629), *Divine Poems* (1630), *The Historie of Samson* (1631) and *Divine Fancies* (1632). The prose includes a book of aphorisms (*Enchyridion*, 1640) and *The Profest Royalist* (1645).

QUARTON, sometimes **Charonton** or **Charrenton, Enguerrand** (15th century) French painter, active in Avignon and the best known late-medieval French artist. Documents relating to six of his important paintings survive, one of which, for a Coronation of the Virgin, is one of the most complete and interesting documents of early French art as it includes the views both of the patron and artist. His style united French and Italian influences and some have attributed to him, on stylistic grounds, the most famous of 15th-century French paintings, the Pietà of Villeneuve-lès-Avignon.

QUASIMODO, Salvatore (1901–68) Italian poet, born in Syracuse, Sicily. A student of engineering, he became a travelling inspector for the Italian state power board before taking up a career in literature and music. A professor of literature at the Conservatory of Music in Milan, he wrote several volumes of spirited poetry. These reflect above all his deep interest in the fate of Italy, and his language is made particularly striking by the use simultaneously of both Christian and mythological allusions. He won the Nobel prize for literature in 1959. His works include *Ed è Subito Sera* (And suddenly it is Evening, 1942), *La Vita non è sogno* (Life is not a Dream, 1949) and *La Terra impareggiabile* (The Matchless Earth, 1958).

QUATREFAGES DE BRÉAU, Jean Louis Armand de (1810–92) French naturalist and ethnologist, born in Berthezème (Gard). Professor in the Lycée Napoléon and at the Natural History Museum (1855), his chief works are *Souvenirs d'un naturaliste* (1854), *L'Espèce humaine* (1877), *Crania Ethnica* (1875–82), *Les Pygmées* (1887) and *Darwin et ses précurseurs français* (1892).

QUAYLE, Sir Anthony (1913–89) English actor and director, born in Ainsdale. He made his first stage appearance in 1931, and was with the Old Vic Company from 1932 to 1939. After six years' army service in World War II he joined the Shakespeare Memorial Theatre company at Stratford-upon-Avon as actor and theatre director (1948–56). During his years at Stratford he played 20 leading roles, directed 12 plays, and transformed a provincial repertory company into a theatre of international standing. This provided much of the foundation work for the successful creation of the Royal Shakespeare Company in 1960. He returned to work in London, and during the next decade appeared in several contemporary plays now established as classics. In 1982 he founded the Compass Theatre Company, dedicated to touring classical plays to the regions of Britain. He has also appeared in films, including *The Guns of Navarone*, and *Lawrence of Arabia*.

QUAYLE, Dan (J Danforth) (1947–) American politician, born in Indianapolis, Indiana, into a rich and influential newspaper-owning family. After taking a political science degree, he underwent legal training and was admitted to the Indiana bar in 1974. He was elected to the House of Representatives as a Republican in 1977 and to the senate, representing Indiana, in 1981. Admired by the right wing of the party for his conservative views on defence, fiscal and moral matters, he was chosen as the running-mate of **George Bush** in 1988. His selection was strongly criticized, but he became vice-president in January 1989.

QUEEN, Ellery, pseud of **Frederick Dannay** (1905–82) and his cousin **Manfred B Lee** (1905–71), American writers of crime fiction, both born in Brooklyn, New York City. As businessmen they entered for a detective-story competition, and won with *The Roman Hat Mystery* (1929). From then on they concentrated on detective fiction, using Ellery Queen both as pseudonym and as the name of their detective. Others of their very popular stories are *The French Powder Mystery* (1930), *The Greek Coffin Mystery* (1932), *The Tragedy of X* (1940), *Double, Double* (1950) and *The Glass Village* (1954). They also wrote under the pseudonym Barnaby Ross, featuring the detective Drury Lane. In 1941 they founded *Ellery Queen's Mystery Magazine*.

QUEENSBERRY, Sir John Sholto Douglas, 8th Marquis of (1844–1900) Scottish representative peer, and patron of boxing. In 1867 he supervised the formulation by **John Graham Chambers** of new rules to govern the sport, since known as the 'Queensberry rules'. In 1895 he was unsuccessfully sued for criminal libel by **Oscar Wilde**, of whose friendship with his son, Lord **Alfred Douglas**, he disapproved; it was his allegations of homosexuality that led in turn to Wilde's trial and imprisonment.

QUEENSBERRY, William Douglas, Duke of (1724–1810) English nobleman, known as **'Old Q'**. He succeeded his father as Earl of March, his mother as Earl of Ruglen, and his cousin in 1778 as 4th Duke of Queensberry. From 1760 to 1789 he was lord of the bedchamber to **George III**. He was famous as a patron of the turf, and infamous for his shameless debaucheries. He died unmarried, worth over a million pounds.

QUEIPO DE LLANO, Gonzalo, Marquis of Queipo de Llano y Sevilla (1875–1951) Spanish soldier, born in Valladolid. After military service in Cuba and Morocco, he was promoted to the rank of major-general in the Republican army, but went over to the rebel side at the beginning of the Spanish Civil War. In July 1936 he led the forces which captured Seville, and became commander-in-chief of the Southern army. In one of his many propaganda broadcasts from Seville he originated the phrase 'fifth column', using it to describe the rebel supporters inside Madrid, who were expected to add their strength to that of the four columns attacking from outside. In April 1950 he was given the title of marquis.

QUENNELL, Peter Courtney (1905–) English biographer, born in London, the son of the illustrator Marjorie Quennell (1884–1972). He was educated at Berkhamsted and Balliol College, Oxford. He became professor of English at Tokyo in 1930, and wrote *A Superficial Journey through Tokio and Pekin* (1932). Author of several books of verse and a novel, and editor of *The Cornhill Magazine* (1944–51), he is best known for his biographical studies of **Byron** (1935; 1941), Queen **Caroline** (1939), **John Ruskin** (1949), **Shakespeare** (1963), **Pope** (1968) and **Samuel Johnson** (1972), as well as those of **Boswell**, **Gibbon**, **Sterne** and **Wilkes** in *Four Portraits* (1945), and *Hogarth's Progress* (1955). He has edited many volumes of literary studies, and written two autobiographical books, *The Marble Foot* (1976) and *The Wanton Chase* (1980).

QUENTAL, Anthero de (1842–91) Portuguese poet, born in Ponta Delgada in the Azores. He studied at Lisbon and Coimbra, publishing his first collection of sonnets in 1861 and his *Odes Modernas* in 1865. He followed the latter with a pamphlet, *Good Sense and Good Taste*, which exposed the view that poetry depends upon richness and vitality of ideas rather than upon technical skill with words. He lived in Paris and America from 1866 to 1871, and on his return to Portugal became a leading socialist until, after a severe nervous illness, he committed suicide.

QUERCIA, Jacopa Della (c.1367–1438) Italian sculptor, born in Quercia Grossa, Siena. He went to Lucca, where one fine example of his work is the beautiful tomb of Ilaria del Carretto in the cathedral. In direct contrast are the strongly dramatic reliefs for the doorway of the church of San Petronio in Bologna which he left unfinished at his death.

QUEROUAILLE, or **Kéroualle** See **PORTSMOUTH, Louise de**

QUESADA, Gonzalo Jiménez de (c.1497–1579) Spanish conquistador, born in Córdoba or Granada. Appointed magistrate at Santa Marta in what is now Colombia, in 1536 he headed an expedition and after many hardships and loss of men conquered the rich territory of the Chibchas in the east. This he called New Granada, and its chief town Santa Fé de Bogotá. In 1569, during a later expedition in search of El Dorado, he reached the river Guaviare not far from the point where it meets the Orinoco. His history, *Los tres ratos de Suesca*, has been lost.

QUESNAY, François (1694–1774) French physician and economist, born in Mérey, near Paris. He studied medicine at Paris, and rose to become first physician to **Louis XV**. But the fame of the 'European **Confucius'** depends on his essays in political economy. Around him and his friend, M de Gournay, the famous group of the *Économistes* gathered, also called the Physiocratic School. Quesnay's views were set forth in *Tableaux économiques*. Only a few copies were printed (1758), and these are lost; yet Quesnay's principles are well known from his contributions to the *Encyclopédie* and from his *Maximes du gouvernement économique* and *Le Droit naturel*.

QUESNEL, Pasquier (1634–1719) French Jansenist theologian, born in Paris. He studied at the Sorbonne, became in 1662 director of the Paris Oratory, and here wrote *Réflexions morales sur le Nouveau Testament*. In 1675 he published the works of **Leo the Great**, which, for Gallicanism in the notes, was placed on the *Index*. Having refused to condemn Jansenism in 1684, he fled to Brussels, where his *Réflexions* were published (1687–94). The Jesuits were unceasing in their hostility, and Quesnel was flung into prison (1703), but escaped to Amsterdam. His book was condemned in the bull *Unigenitus* (1713).

QUESNOY, François (Il Flammingo) (1594–1646) Flemish sculptor, born in Brussels. He worked in Rome from 1618 to 1643. His style was more Classical and restrained than the prevailing Baroque typified by **Bernini**.

QUÉTELET, Lambert Adolphe Jacques (1796–1874) Belgian statistician and astronomer, born in Ghent. He became professor of mathematics at the Brussels Athenaeum (1819) and professor of astronomy at the Military School (1836). In his greatest book, *Sur l'homme* (1835), as in *L'Anthropométrie* (1871), he showed the use that may be made of the theory of probabilities, as applied to the 'average man'.

QUEVEDO Y VILLEGAS, Francisco Gómez de (1580–1645) Spanish writer, born in Madrid. His father was secretary to the queen, and his mother a lady-in-waiting. He left the University of Alcalá with a reputation for varied scholarship. The fatal issue of a duel drove him in 1611 to the court of the Duke of Ossuna, viceroy of Sicily, who made him his right-hand man, and, when promoted to the viceroyalty of Naples, chose him for minister of finance. Quevedo was involved in Ossuna's fall in 1619, and put in prison, but allowed to retire to the Sierra Morena. He returned to Madrid in 1623 and was one of the favourites at the court of **Philip IV**. In his *Politica de Dios* (1626) he appealed to the king to be a king, not in name only, but in fact; in 1628 he followed up this attack on government by favourites with an apologue, *Hell Reformed*. He remained, however, on friendly terms with **Olivares** and accepted the honorary title of royal secretary. In 1639 a memorial in verse to the king, imploring him to look to the miserable condition of his kingdom, was one day placed in Philip's napkin. Quevedo was denounced as the author, arrested and imprisoned in a convent at Leon, where he was struck down by an illness, from which he never recovered. In 1643 Olivares fell from power, and Quevedo was free to return to Madrid. He died two years later. Quevedo was one of the most prolific Spanish poets, but his verses were all written for his friends or for himself, and, except those in the *Flores* of Espinosa (1605), the few pieces published in his lifetime were printed without his consent. His poetry is therefore largely of an occasional character. About a dozen of his short pieces are extant, but of his comedies almost nothing is known. His prose is even more varied than his verse. His first book (1620) was a Life of St Thomas de Villanueva, and his last one of St **Paul** (1644), and most of his prose is devotional. Of his political works the *Política de Dios* is the main one. His brilliant picaresque novel, the *Vida del Buscón Pablos* (1626), or, as it was called after his death, the *Gran Tacaño*, at once took its place beside *Guzmán de Alfarache*. His five *Visions* were printed in 1627; to obtain a licence they were barbarously mutilated.

QUEZON, Manuel Luis (1878–1944) first Philippine president, born in Baler, Luzon. He studied at Manila, served with **Aguinaldo** during the insurrection of 1898 and in 1905 became governor of Tayabas. In 1909 he went to Washington as one of the resident Philippine commissioners and began to work for his country's independence. President of the Philippine senate (1916–35), he was elected first president of the Philippine commonwealth (1935). He established a highly centralized government verging on 'one-man' rule and displayed great courage during the Japanese onslaught on General **MacArthur**'s defences in December 1941, refusing to evacuate to the USA until appealed to by President **Roosevelt**. He died in Saranac, USA. The new capital of the Philippines on the island of Luzon is named after him.

QUICK, Robert Hebert (1831–91) English educationist, born in London. Educated at Harrow and Trinity College, Cambridge, he was a curate in Whitechapel and Marlebone, a schoolmaster, and vicar of Sedbergh (1883–87). Deeply interested in education, he brought considerable wisdom and learning to debates over educational theories. His main work was *Essays on Educational Reformers* (1868). In 1875 he published his *Account of Celebrated Methods*, a review of language teaching through the ages from Asekam (1570) to **Jacotot** (1826).

QUILLER-COUCH See **COUCH, Sir Arthur Quiller-**

QUILTER, Roger (1877–1953) English composer, born in Brighton. He studied in Germany and lived entirely by composition, holding no official posts and making few public appearances. His works include an opera, *Julia*, a radio opera *The Blue Boar*, and the *Children's Overture*, based on nursery tunes; but he is best known for his songs.

QUIN, James (1693–1766) Irish actor, born in London. He made his début at Dublin in 1714 but it was at Drury Lane that he found success, when in 1716 the sudden illness of a leading actor led to Quin's being called on to play Bajazet in *Tamerlane*. At Lincoln's Inn Fields (1718–32) and at Drury Lane (1734–41) he was by universal consent the first actor in England; then **Garrick** largely eclipsed him. He retired in 1751.

QUIN, Wyndham- See **DUNRAVEN, Earl of**

QUINCEY See **DE QUINCEY, Thomas**

QUINCY, Josiah (1772–1864) American statesman, born in Boston, Massachusetts, the son of the lawyer Josiah Quincy (1744–75). He graduated at Harvard, was called to the bar in 1793, was a leading member of the Federal party, and elected in 1804 to congress, distinguished himself as an orator. He denounced slavery, and in one most remarkable speech declared that the admission of Louisiana would be a sufficient cause for the dissolution of the union. Disgusted with the triumph of the Democrats and the war of 1812, he declined re-election to congress, and devoted his attention to agriculture; but he was a member of the Massachusetts legislature, served as mayor of Boston 1823–28, and from 1829 to 1845 was president of Harvard. Among his works are Memoirs of his father (1825) and **John Quincy Adams** (1858), histories of Harvard (1840), the Boston Athenaeum (1851), and Boston (1852). His *Speeches* were edited (1874) by his son, Edmund Quincy (1808–77), who was secretary of the American Anti-Slavery Society.

QUINE, William Van Orman (1908–) American philosopher and logician, born in Akron, Ohio. He was trained, initially in mathematics, at Oberlin College in Ohio, then at Prague, Oxford and at Harvard under **Whitehead**, and was professor of philosophy at Harvard from 1948 to 1978. He was much influenced by **Carnap**, the Vienna Circle and the empiricist tradition generally, but went on to make his own distinctive and original contributions to philosophy and became most influential. He made many important technical contributions to mathematical logic, but is best known through such philosophical works as *Two Dogmas of Empiricism* (1951), *From a Logical Point of View* (1953), *Word and Object* (1960) and *The Roots of Reference* (1973). In these he challenges the standard, sharp distinctions between analysis and synthetic truths and between science and metaphysics, and presents a systematic philosophy of language of his own which successfully challenged the hitherto dominant linguistic philosophy of **Wittgenstein** and **J Langsham Austin**.

QUINET, Edgar (1803–75) French writer and politician, born in Bourg. He studied at Strasbourg, Geneva, Paris and Heidelberg. The remarkable introduction to his translation of **Herder**'s *Philosophy of History* (1825) won him the friendship of **Cousin** and **Michelet**; a government mission to Greece produced *La Grèce moderne* (1830). *Ahasvérus* (1833), a kind of spiritual imitation of the ancient mysteries, was followed by the less successful poems, 'Napoléon' (1836) and 'Prométhée' (1838); in his *Examen de la vie de Jésus* (1838) he showed that **Strauss** was too analytic, and that religion is the very substance of humanity. Appointed professor of foreign literature at Lyon in 1839, he began the lectures which formed his brilliant *Du génie des religions* (1842); then once recalled to the Collège de France in Paris, he joined Michelet in attacking the Jesuits. His lectures caused so much excitement that the government suppressed them in 1846. At the revolution Quinet took his place on the barricades, and in the National Assembly voted with the extreme left. After the *coup d'état* he was exiled to Brussels, from where in 1857 he emigrated to Switzerland. At Brussels he produced *Les Esclaves* (1853), and in Switzerland *Merlin l'Enchanteur* (1860). Other works were *La Révolution religieuse au XIXe siècle* (1857), *Histoire de mesidées* (1858), *Histoire de la campagne de* 1815 (1862), and *La Révolution* (1865). After the downfall of **Napoleon III** he returned to Paris, and during the siege strove to keep patriotism alive. He sat in the National Assemblies at Bordeaux and Versailles, and aroused great enthusiasm by his speeches. His last books were *La Création* (1870), *La République* (1872), *L'Esprit nouveau* (1874), and *Le Livre de l'exilé* (1875).

QUINTANA, Manuel José (1772–1857) Spanish poet and advocate, born in Madrid, where his house became a resort of advanced liberals. Besides his classic *Vidas de los Españoles célèbres* (1807–34), he published tragedies and poetry written in a classical style, the best of which are his odes, ardently patriotic yet restrained. On the restoration of **Ferdinand VII** he was imprisoned (1814–20); but he recanted, and by 1833 had become tutor to Queen **Isabella**. He was crowned national poet in 1855.

QUINTERO, Serafín Álvarez (1871–1938) and **Joaquín Álvarez** (1873–1944), brothers, born at Utrera, Seville. They wrote many plays in collaboration, usually depicting Andalusian life. These include comedies and shorter pieces such as *El Pario*, *Las de Caín* and *Malvaloca*, all written with delightful insight into Spanish life and character.

QUINTILIAN, Marcus Fabius Quintilianus (c.35–c.100) Roman rhetorician, born in Calagurris (Calahorra) in Spain. He studied oratory at Rome, and returned there in 68 in the train of **Galba**, and became eminent as a pleader and still more as a state teacher of the oratorical art. His pupils included **Pliny the Younger** and the two grand-nephews of **Domitianus**. The emperor named him consul and gave him a pension. His reputation rests securely on his great work, *Institutio Oratoria* (Education of an Orator), a complete system of rhetoric in twelve books, remarkable for its sound critical judgments, purity of taste, admirable form and the perfect familiarity it exhibits with the literature of oratory. Quintilian's own style is excellent, though not free from the florid ornament and poetic metaphor characteristic of his age.

QUINTUS CURTIUS See **CURTIUS, Rufus Quintus**

QUISLING, Vidkun (1887–1945) Norwegian diplomat and Fascist leader, born in Fyresdal. He was an army major, a League of Nations official, had the care of British interests in Russia 1927–29, was defence minister in Norway 1931–33, and in 1933 founded the *Nasjonal Samlung* (National party) in imitation of the German National Socialist party. As puppet prime minister in occupied Norway he gave his name to all who play a similarly traitorous part. He gave himself up in May 1945, was tried and executed.

R

RAAB, Julius (1891–1964) Austrian statesman, born in St Pölten. He became an engineer and was a Christian Socialist member of the Austrian Diet (1927–34), and federal minister of trade and transport (1938). He retired from politics during the Nazi régime, and in 1945 was one of the founders of the People's party, chairman of the party (1951–60) minister of economic reconstruction, and in 1953 was elected chancellor of Austria.

RAABE, Wilhelm, pseud **Jakob Corvinus** (1831–1910) German novelist, born in Eschershausen in Brunswick. Reacting against 19th-century progress, he wrote novels which were often grim, tragic and pessimistic. They include *Der Hungerpastor* (1864), *Des Reiches Krone* (1870) and *Meister Autor* (1871).

RABELAIS, François (?1494–?1553) French satirist, said to have been born at a farmhouse near Chinon, or possibly in the town of Chinon, where his father was an advocate. At nine he was sent to the Benedictine abbey of Seuilly, and from there to the Franciscan house of La Baumette near Angers. He became a novice of the Franciscan order, and entered the monastery of Fontenay le Comte, where he had access to a large library, learned Greek, Hebrew and Arabic, and studied all the Latin and old French authors within his reach, as well as medicine, astronomy, botany and mathematics. In Fontenay he found a friend, Andrés Tiraqueau, a lawyer and scholar; his patron, the bishop of Maillezais, lived close by and he corresponded with **Budaeus**. But Franciscan jealousy of the old learning was transformed into jealousy of the new. His books were taken from him and he conceived a loathing for the convent, and fled to a Benedictine house near Orléans. Perhaps through his friend the bishop, he obtained the pope's permission (1524) to pass from the Franciscan to the Benedictine order. He stayed with the bishop for at least three years. After studying medicine at Montpellier he left in 1532 and became a physician in the hospital. Lyon was then a great intellectual centre. There he began the famous series of books by which he will for ever be remembered. In 1532 there appeared at Lyon fair a popular book, *The Great and Inestimable Chronicles of the Grand and Enormous Giant Gargantua*. It was almost certainly not by Rabelais, but to this book he wrote, in the same year, a sequel, *Pantagruel*, in which serious ideas are set forth side by side with overwhelming nonsense. In 1534 he supplied a first book of his own, a new *Gargantua*, fuller of sense and wisdom than *Pantagruel*. Both books (published under the name of Alcofri bas Nasier, an anagram of François Rabelais) had a prodigious success. Meanwhile he had begun his almanacs or *Pantagrueline Prognostications*, which he continued for a number of years; few of them survive. In 1533 he accompanied Jean du Bellay, bishop of Paris, to Rome; in 1536 he was in Italy again with du Bellay, the latter then a cardinal. There he amused himself with collecting plants and curiosities—to him France owes the melon, artichoke and carnation. He also received permission to go into any Benedictine house which would receive him, and was enabled to hold ecclesiastical offices and to practise medicine. From 1537 (when he took his doctorate) to 1538 he taught at Montpellier. From 1540 to 1543 he was in the service of the cardinal's brother, Guillaume du Bellay, sometimes in Turin (where Guillaume was governor), sometimes in France. Guillaume died in 1543, in which year Rabelais was appointed one of the *maîtres des requêtes*. In 1546 he published his third book, this time under his own name. The Sorbonne condemned it—as it had done its predecessors—and Rabelais fled to Metz, where he practised medicine. In 1547 **Francis I** died; **Henri II** sent the French cardinals to Rome; and thither du Bellay summoned Rabelais as his physician (1548). In Rome until 1549, he thereafter stayed near Paris; he received two livings from the cardinal in 1551–52, and resigned them two years later. A 'partial edition' of a fourth book had appeared in 1548, the complete book in January 1552–53 (to be banned by the theologians); and a professed fifth book, *L'Isle sonante*, perhaps founded on scraps and notes by Rabelais, in 1562. The riotous licence of his mirth has made Rabelais as many enemies as his wisdom has made him friends, yet his works remain the most astonishing treasury of wit, wisdom, commonsense and satire that the world has ever seen.

RABI, Isidor Isaac (1898–1988) Austrian-born American physicist, born in Rymanow, which he left in childhood. He was a graduate of Cornell and Columbia Universities, where he became professor of physics in 1937. An authority on nuclear physics and quantum mechanics, in 1944 he was awarded the Nobel prize for physics for his precision work on neutrons.

RABIN, Itzhak (1922–) Israeli soldier and politician, born in Jerusalem. After studies at an agriculture school he embarked on an army career, completing his training in Britain. He fought in the 'War of Independence' (1948–49) and represented the Israeli Defence Forces (IDF) at the armistice in Rhodes. In the IDF he rose to become chief-of-staff in 1964, heading the armed forces during the successful 'Six-Day War' of 1967. After serving as ambassador to the USA (1968–73) he moved decisively into the political arena, becoming Labour party leader and prime minister (1974–77) and defence minister from 1984.

RABINOWITZ, Solomon J See **ALEICHEM**

RABUKA, Sitiveni (1948–) Fijian soldier and politician, born in the village of Drekeniwai, north of Sura. After leaving the Queen Victoria School he joined the Fijian army and was trained in England, at Sandhurst. After serving with the UN peacekeeping force in Lebanon, he returned to Fiji with the rank of colonel. After the 1987 elections which resulted in an Indian-dominated coalition government, he staged a coup which removed prime minister Kamisese Mara, and set up his own provisional government. The country was declared a republic and in December prime minister Mara was reinstated, but Rabuka retained control of the security forces and internal affairs.

RABUTIN See **BUSSY-RABUTIN**

RACHEL, Élisa, properly **Élisa Félix** (1821–58) French actress, born in Mumpf in Aargau, the daughter of Alsatian-Jewish pedlars. Brought to Paris about 1830, she received singing and elocution lessons, and made her début in *La Vendéenne* in 1837 with moderate success, but in June 1838 appeared as Camille in *Horace* at the Théâtre Français. From then on she was unrivalled in classical roles, scoring her greatest triumph as Phèdre. In *Adrienne Lecouvreur*, written for her by **Legouvé** and **Scribe**, she had immense success. She visited London (and was witnessed by **Charlotte Brontë**), Brussels, Berlin and St Petersburg, everywhere meeting with enthusiastic applause. In 1855, in America, her health gave way. She died of consumption.

RACHMAN, Peter (1919–62) Polish-born British property developer and notorious landlord whose name gave rise to the term 'Rachmanism', the exploitation of poor tenants by unscrupulous landlords. A Polish Jew by birth, Rachman survived persecution by the Nazis and a Stalinist labour camp. When **Hitler** invaded Russia in 1941, he was sent to fight alongside the British in the Middle East. In 1946 he came to Britain and was settled at various refugee camps. After some years spent working in a factory and as a tailor's assistant, he turned his attention to property. In 1950 he started renting and sub-letting flats to prostitutes for an inflated sum, to be paid in cash. By 1953 he was acquiring properties all over London. Three years later he was able to indulge his taste for a lavish and expensive lifestyle. He let rooms and flats to poor West Indian tenants, whom no-one else would house, for exorbitant rents, counting on the fact that his tenants would not know that they could go to a rent tribunal. By 1959, many of his tenants did take him to the tribunal and he was obliged to sell off his properties. He became involved with **Christine Keeler** and **Mandy Rice-Davies**. Obese, with assorted phobias and a huge appetite for prostitutes, gambling and high society, Rachman only really achieved notoriety after his death. Neither his creditors nor his family could believe that he had no money, and the supposedly 'missing million' was hunted voraciously by all.

RACHMANINOV, or **Rakhmaninov, Sergey Vasilyevich** (1873–1943) Russian composer and pianist, born in Nizhni-Novgorod. He studied at St Petersburg Conservatory and later in Moscow, where he won the gold medal for composition. A brilliant performer, he travelled all over Europe on concert tours, visiting London in 1899. Having fled from the Russian revolution, he settled in the USA in 1918. An accomplished composer, he wrote operas, orchestral works and songs, but is best known for his piano music, which includes four concertos, the first three of which achieved enormous popularity, and the inveterate *Prelude in C Sharp Minor*, the demand for which at his own concerts nauseated even the composer himself. His style, devoid of national characteristics, epitomizes the lush romanticism of the later 19th century, which is still apparent in his last major composition, *Rhapsody on a Theme of Paganini* (1934) for piano and orchestra, a work of great craftsmanship which has remained a concert favourite.

RACINE, Jean (1639–99) French dramatist and poet, born in La Ferté-Milan (Aisne department), the son of a solicitor. He was sent to the college of Beauvais, from where he went to Port Royal in 1655. He studied hard, and discovered a faculty for verse-making and a liking for romance that perturbed his teachers. At 19, when he went to study philosophy at the Collège d'Harcourt, he appears to some extent to have exchanged the severity of his Jansenist upbringing for libertinism and the life of letters. He wrote an ode, *La Nymphe de la Seine*, on the marriage of **Louis XIV**, finished one piece and began another for the theatre, made the acquaintance of **La Fontaine**, **Chapelain** and other men of letters, and assisted a cousin who was a secretary to the Duc de Luynes. In 1661 he went to Uzès in Languedoc, hoping in vain to get a benefice from his uncle, the vicar-general of the diocese. Having returned to Paris, he obtained in 1664 a gift from the king for a congratulatory ode. Another ode, *La Renommée aux muses*, gained him the lifelong friendship of **Boileau**; and now began the famous friendship of 'the four'—Boileau, La Fontaine, **Molière** and Racine. His earliest play, *La Thébaïde ou Les Frères ennemis*, was acted by Molière's company at the Palais Royal (1664). His second, *Alexandre le grand* (1665), was after its sixth performance played by the rival actors at the Hotel de Bourgogne, which led to a rupture with Molière. Racine showed himself as hostile to **Corneille**. Stung by one of **Nicole**'s *Lettres visionnaires* (1666) condemning in accordance with Port Royal ethics the romancer or dramatist as an *empoisonneur public*, he published a clever letter to the author, full of indecent personal remarks. During the following ten years Racine produced his greatest works—*Andromaque* (1667); *Les Plaideurs* (1668), satirizing lawyers; *Britannicus* (1669); *Bérénice* (1679); *Bajazet* (1672); *Mithridate* (1673), produced almost at the moment of his admission to the Academy; *Iphigénie* (1675), a masterpiece of pathos; and *Phèdre* (1677), a marvellous representation of human agony. Then the *troupe du roi* introduced a rival *Phèdre*, by Jacques Pradon, which was supported by a powerful party. Whether from mortification or from alleged conversion, Racine retired from dramatic work, made his peace with Port Royal, married in June 1677, and settled down to 20 years of domestic happiness. His wife brought him money (as well as two sons and five daughters); and he had found ample profit in the drama, besides enjoying an annual *gratification* that grew to 2000 livres, at least one benefice, and, from 1677, jointly with Boileau, the office of royal historian. In 1689 he wrote *Esther* for Madame **de Maintenon**'s schoolgirls at Saint-Cyr; *Athalie* followed in 1691. Four *cantiques spirituelles* and an admirable *Histoire abrégée de Port Royal* make up Racine's literary work. In his later years he somehow lost the favour of the king. In France Racine is regarded as the greatest of all masters of tragic pathos; this estimate is not inflated. He took the conventional French tragedy from the stronger hands of Corneille, and added to it all the grace of which it was capable, perfecting exquisitely its versification, and harmoniously subordinating the whole action to the central idea of the one dominant passion.

RACKHAM, Arthur (1867–1939) English artist and book illustrator. He studied at Lambeth School of Art. He excelled in illustrating fairy tales and the like, such as *Peter Pan* (1906) and *Hans Andersen* (1932), in Art Nouveau style.

RACOCZY See **RÁKÓCZI**

RADCLIFFE, Ann, née **Ward** (1764–1823) English romantic novelist, born in London. At 23 she married William Radcliffe, a graduate of Oxford and student of law, who became proprietor and editor of the weekly *English Chronicle*. In 1789 she published the first of her Gothic romances, *The Castles of Athlin and Dunbayne*, followed by *A Sicilian Romance* (1790), *The Romance of the Forest* (1791), *The Mysteries of Udolpho* (1794), and *The Italian* (1797). She travelled much, and her journal shows how keen an eye she had for natural scenery and ruins. A sixth romance, *Gaston de Blondeville*, with a metrical tale, 'St Alban's Abbey', and a short Life, was published in 1826. Her reputation among her contemporaries was considerable. She was praised by Sir **Walter Scott**, and influenced writers such as **Byron**, **Shelley** and **Charlotte Brontë**. Her particular brand of writing found many imitators, most of them unfortunately inferior to herself, and prompted **Jane Austen**'s satire *Northanger Abbey*.

RADCLIFFE, Cyril John, Viscount (1899–1978) English lawyer. Educated at Haileybury and New College, Oxford, from 1941 to 1945 he was director-general of the ministry of information. In 1949 he was appointed a lord of appeal in ordinary and a life peer, and in 1962 he was created viscount. He was chairman of many commissions and committees, notably those on taxation of profits and income, and on the frontier between India and Pakistan. In 1956, as constitutional commissioner, Cyprus, he drew up a constitution for the future of the island.

RADCLIFFE, John (1650–1714) English physician, born in Wakefield. He studied at University College, Oxford, became a fellow of Lincoln, took his MB in 1675 and his MD in 1682. In 1684 he moved to London, where he soon became the most popular physician of his time. Despite being a Jacobite, he attended **William III** and Queen **Mary**; in 1713 he was elected MP for Buckingham. He bequeathed the bulk of his large property to the Radcliffe Library, Infirmary and Observatory, and University College in Oxford, and St Bartholomew's Hospital, London.

RADCLIFFE-BROWN, Alfred Reginald (1881–1955) English social anthropologist, born in Birmingham. After studying at Cambridge, he carried out field research in the Andaman islands (1906–08) and Australia (1910–11), which served as a basis for his later works on *The Andaman Islanders* (1922) and *The Social Organization of Australian Tribes* (1930–31). After moving to South Africa in 1920 he became professor of anthropology at Cape Town, but in 1926 returned to Australia to take up the chair in anthropology at Sydney. He was subsequently professor at Chicago and Oxford. Along with **Bronislaw Malinowski**, Radcliffe-Brown was the principal architect of modern social anthropology, but despite his early fieldwork his major contribution was more theoretical than ethnographic. Greatly influenced by the sociology of **Émile Durkheim**, he regarded social anthropology as the comparative study of 'primitive' societies, whose aim was to establish generalizations about the forms and functioning of social structures. According to his structural-functional theory, institutions serve to maintain the total social order of which they are parts, as organs of the body maintain the whole body. His concern throughout was to emulate the methods of natural science, and he attacked the 'pseudo-historical' conjectures of many of his predecessors. He also distinguished social anthropology sharply from ethnology, which he saw as a descriptive rather than a theoretical enterprise. His *Structure and Function in Primitive Society* (1952) contains all the essentials of his theoretical programme.

RADCLYFFE, James See **DERWENTWATER**

RADDE, Gustav Ferdinand Richard (1831–1903) German naturalist, ornithologist and explorer, born in Danzig. Trained as an apothecary, he abandoned his career for a study of natural history. He travelled widely in the Caucusus and surrounding regions, and became director of a museum he established in Tiflis (Tbilisi). He wrote *Ornis Caucasica* (1884) and many other works. Radde's Warbler and Radde's Accentor are named after him.

RADEK, Karl, originally **Solbelsohm** (1885–?1939) Russian politician, born of Jewish parentage in Lwów. He studied at Cracow and Bern. A member of the Polish Social Democratic party, he was imprisoned for taking part in the Russian revolution of 1905, and later wrote for Polish and German newspapers. During World War I he published propaganda literature from Switzerland. He crossed Germany with **Lenin** after the outbreak of the Russian revolution (1917), and took part in the Brest-Litovsk peace negotiations. He organized the German communists during their revolution (1918) and was imprisoned (1919). Returning to the Soviet Union, he became a leading member of the Communist International, but lost standing with his growing distrust of extremist tactics. Nevertheless he became editor of *Pravda* and rector of the Sun Yat-Sen Chinese university in Moscow. He was charged as a **Trotsky** supporter and expelled from the party (1927–30) but readmitted, only to fall victim to one of **Stalin**'s 'trials' for treason in 1937, when he was sentenced to ten years' imprisonment, but died in a labour camp a few years later. In June 1988 the Soviet Supreme Court annulled the 1937 conviction, posthumously rehabilitating Radek.

RADETZKY, Johann Joseph, Count (1766–1858) Austrian soldier, born in Trebnitz near Tabor in Bohemia. He fought against the Turks in 1788–89 and in nearly all the wars between the Austrians and the French. He was appointed commander-in-chief in Lombardy from 1831, and promoted field marshal in 1836. In 1848 he was driven out of Milan by the insurgents, but held Verona and Mantua for the Habsburgs. Defeated at Goito, he won a victory at Custozza (1848), and re-entered Milan. In March 1849 he almost destroyed the Sardinian army at Novara, forced Venice to surrender, and till 1857 again ruled the Lombardo-Venetian territories with an iron hand. He died in Milan.

RADHAKRISHNAN, Sir Sarvepalli (1888–1975) Indian philosopher and statesman, born in Tiruttani, Madras. He was educated at Madras Christian College. He was professor at the universities of Mysore, Calcutta and Oxford, where he gave the Upton lectures at Manchester College in 1926 and 1929, and in 1936 he became Spalding professor of eastern religions and ethics at Oxford. He also lectured abroad, in America in 1926 and 1944 and in China in 1944. From 1931 to 1939 he attended the League of Nations at Geneva as a member of the Committee of Intellectual Co-operation. In 1946 he was chief Indian delegate to Unesco, becoming chairman of Unesco in 1949. A member of the Indian Assembly in 1947, he was appointed first Indian ambassador to Russia in 1949, vice-president of India from 1952 to 1962, and president from 1962 to 1967. He was awarded the OM in 1963. He wrote many scholarly philosophic works including *Indian Philosophy* (1927), his Hibbert lectures of 1929 published as *An Idealist View of Life* (1932), which is often thought to be his greatest work, and *Eastern Religion and Western Thought* (2nd ed 1939).

RADIGUET, Raymond (1903–23) French novelist and poet, born in Saint-Maur. He is best known for two stories, *Le Diable au Corps* (1923) and *Le Bal du Comte d'Orgel* (1924). Acclaimed as the '**Rimbaud** of the novel', his writing is as austerely controlled as his personal behaviour was erratic and unpredictable. The nature of love is his dominant theme, comparable in his fiction to the high moral conception of love in the tragedies of **Racine**.

RADOWITZ, Joseph von (1797–1853) Prussian soldier, born in Blankenburg in the Harz. In 1813 he entered the Westphalian army, in 1823 the Prussian, and in 1830 became chief of the artillery staff. Connected by marriage with the Prussian aristocracy, he headed the anti-revolutionary party, and was **Frederick-William IV**'s adviser. After 1848 the Prussian scheme of a German constitution by means of the alliance of the three kings was largely his work. He wrote political treatises.

RADZINOWICZ, Sir Leon (1906–) Polish-born English criminologist. He taught law in Poland before coming to England, where he directed the department of criminal science at Cambridge (1946–59) and taught as Wolfson professor of criminology (1959–). He wrote a major *History of English Criminal Law* (5 vols, 1948–) and edited many works on criminal science.

RAE, John (1813–93) Scottish Arctic traveller, born near Stromness in Orkney. After studying medicine at Edinburgh, in 1833 he became doctor to the Hudson Bay Company. In 1846–47 he made two exploring expeditions, and in 1848 he accompanied **Sir John Richardson** on a **Franklin** search voyage. In 1853–54 he commanded an expedition to King William's Land, and it was on this journey that he met the Eskimos who gave him definite news of Franklin's expedition and its probable fate. In 1860 he surveyed a telegraph line to America via the Faroes and Iceland, visited Greenland, and in 1864 made a telegraph survey from Winnipeg over the Rockies.

RAEBURN, Sir Henry (1756–1823) Scottish portrait painter, born in Edinburgh. Apprenticed to a goldsmith, he took to art, producing first watercolour miniatures and then oils. At 22 he married the widow of Count Leslie, a lady of means, studied two years in Rome (1785–87), then settled in Edinburgh, and soon attained pre-eminence among Scottish artists. He was knighted by **George IV** in 1822, and appointed king's limner for Scotland a few days before his death. His style was to some extent founded on that of **Reynolds**, to which a positiveness was added by his bold brushwork and use of contrasting colours. Among his sitters were Sir **Walter Scott**, **Hume**, **Boswell**, **John Wilson** ('Christopher North'), Lord Melville (**Henry Dundas**), Sir **David Baird**, **Henry Mackenzie**, Principal **Robertson**, Lord **Jeffrey** and Lord **Cockburn**.

RAEDER, Erich (1876–1960) German naval commander. He entered the navy in 1894 and during World War I was chief of staff to Admiral von **Hipper**. In 1928 he was promoted admiral and became commander-in-chief of the navy, and rebuilt the fleet, especially submarines and fast cruisers. In 1939 **Hitler** made him a grand admiral. In 1943 he was dismissed from command for strategic disagreements with Hitler. At the Nuremberg Trials in 1946 he was sentenced to life imprisonment for having helped to prepare a war of aggression. He was released in September 1955.

RAEMAEKERS, Louis (1869–1956) Dutch political cartoonist and artist, born in Roermond. He attained worldwide fame in 1915 by his striking anti-German war cartoons.

RAFF, Joachim (1822–82) Swiss composer, born in Lachen on the Lake of Zürich. In 1850–56 he lived near **Liszt** in Weimar, taught music at Wiesbaden until 1877, and then was director of the conservatory at Frankfurt-am-Main. Among his compositions are the symphonies *Lenore* and *Im Walde*, and violin and piano works. In support of **Wagner** he wrote *Die Wagner-Frage* (1854).

RAFFAELLO See **RAPHAEL**

RAFFLES, Sir Thomas Stamford (1781–1826) English colonial administrator and oriental scholar, born off Port Morant in Jamaica, the son of a sea-cook. In 1795 he was appointed to a clerkship in the East India House, and in 1805 secretary to an establishment at Penang. In 1811 he accompanied an expedition against Java, and on its capture, as lieutenant-governor, completely reformed the internal administration. In 1816 ill-health brought him home to England, where he wrote his *History of Java* (1817). Lieutenant-governor of Bengkulu in West Sumatra (1818–23), he formed, without authority, a settlement at Singapore to counter Dutch influence in the area, but in 1824 had again to return to England. His ship took fire off Sumatra, and his natural history collections, East Indian vocabularies, etc, were lost. He founded the London Zoo and was its first president.

RAFN, Carl Christian (1795–1864) Danish philologist. He became sub-librarian of Copenhagen University in 1821, and a professor in 1826. In 1825 he founded the Society for Northern Antiquities, which published many editions of the Icelandic sagas. His own works include a Danish translation of Norse sagas (1821–26) and *Antiquitates Americanae* (1837), on the Norse discovery of America in the 10th century.

RAFSANJANI, Hojatoleslam Ali Akbar Hashemi (1934–) Iranian cleric and politician, born near Rafsanjan, in south-eastern Iran, into an affluent pistachio-farming family. He trained as a mullah under Ayatollah **Ruholla Khomeini** at the holy city of Qom, from 1950. His friendship with Khomeini led him into opposition against Shah **Mohammed Reza Pahlavi** and brief imprisonment in 1963. During the 1970s he became wealthy through the construction business in Tehran, but continued to keep in close touch with the exiled Khomeini. Following the 'Islamic Revolution' of 1979–80 he became speaker of the Iranian parliament (Majlis), emerging as an influential and pragmatic power-broker between fundamentalist and technocrat factions within the ruling Islamic Republican party, playing a key role in securing an end to the Gulf War (1980–88). In August 1989, soon after the death of Ayatollah Khomeini, Rafsanjani became state president and 'de facto' national leader.

RAGAZ, Leonhard (1862–1945) Swiss Reformed pastor and social activist, born in Canton-Graubuenden. Educated at Basel, Jena and Berlin, and ordained in 1890, he encountered opposition through his profound social concern. In World War I he denouonced violence as an evil solution; he later rejected Fascism, Nazism and Communism. Visiting the USA he found the status of black people 'utterly offensive'. In 1921 he resigned his theological chair at Zürich 'to represent Christ in poverty', and established an educational centre for working people. He saw social change and religious reform as interdependent.

RAGLAN, Fitzroy James Henry Somerset, 1st Baron (1788–1855) English soldier, youngest son of the 5th Duke of Beaufort. He entered the army in 1804, graduating from regimental duty to service on **Wellington**'s staff in the Peninsular War (1808–12). He fought at Waterloo (1815), losing his sword arm. Thereafter he sat in parliament as MP for Truro, and spent many years at the war office, being appointed master-general of the ordnance and elevated to the peerage in 1852. In 1854 he was promoted field marshal and nominated to head a grossly ill-prepared expeditionary force against the Russians, in the Crimea, in alliance with the French. He won the battle of Alma, but lack of cohesion amongst the Allies prevented an effective follow-up. At Balaclava he gave the order that led to the heroic but disastrous charge of the Light Brigade. He won the battle of Inkerman and was promoted field marshal, but was blamed for the failure of the Commisariat during the terrible winter of 1854–55. He died shortly before the storming of Sebastopol. The raglan overcoat, with sleeves extending to the neck without a shoulder seam, is named after him.

RAHBEK, Knud Lyne (1760–1830) Danish poet, critic and editor, born in Copenhagen. He became professor of aesthetics at Copenhagen University, edited several literary journals, notably *Den Danske Tilskuer* (the Danish *Spectator*). As well as poetry, he wrote many plays, songs and works on drama.

RAHERE (d.1144) English churchman of Frankish descent, the founder of St Bartholomew's Hospital in London. On a pilgrimage to Rome he suffered an attack of malarial fever. During his convalescence he made a vow to build a hospital, and on his return to London he was granted the site at Smithfield by **Henry I**. In 1123 the building of St Bartholomew's Hospital and St Bartholomew's Church was begun. In charge of the hospital until 1137, he retired in that year to the priory.

RAHNER, Karl (1904–84) German Roman Catholic theologian, born in Freiburg. He joined the Society of Jesus in 1922 and was ordained a priest in 1932. Much influenced by transcendental Thomism, he began his teaching career in Innsbruck in 1937. Here, and later at Munich and Münster, his lectures and writings maintained a dialogue between traditional dogma and contemporary existential questions, based on the principle that grace is already present in human nature. As a prolific writer, editor, and adviser to Vatican Council II, he has probably been the most influential Catholic theologian of the 20th century. The substance of his magisterial *Theological Investigations* (1961–81) is laid out in *Foundations of Christian Faith* (1978) and *The Practice of Faith* (1985). A man of prayer and deep love for God, his mystical beliefs may be glimpsed in his *Prayers for a Lifetime* (1984) and the autobiographical interviews *I Remember* (1985).

RAIBOLINI, Francesco See **FRANCIA**

RAIKES, Robert (1735–1811) English publisher and philanthropist, born in Gloucester. In 1757 he succeeded his father as proprietor of the *Gloucester Journal*. In 1780 he started a Sunday school for children, which became the forerunner of the present system.

RAIMONDI See **MARCANTONIO**

RAIMU, originally **Jules Auguste César Muraire** (1883–1946) French actor, born in Toulon. An amateur performer as a child, he was professionally engaged for the first time at the Casino de Toulon (1899–1900). He worked in mime and as a croupier before moving to Paris, making his film début in *L'Homme Nu* (1912) and his legitimate stage début in *Monsieur Chasse* (1916). He appeared throughout the 1920s in revues, operettas and comedies before creating the character of César in *Marius* (1929), which he repeated on film in 1931. Able to combine pathos and humour in his truculent portrayals of the dignified French working man, his films include *Fanny* (1932), *Gribouille* (1937), *Un Carnet de Bal* (1937) and *Les Inconnus dans la Maison* (1942). From 1944 to 1945 he played with the Comédie Française, and died following a car accident.

RAINER, Yvonne (1934–) American experimental dancer, choreographer and filmmaker, born in San Francisco, California. One of the greatest influences on post-modern dance, she moved to New York in 1956, took classes at the **Martha Graham** School, and returned in 1969 to California where she joined Anna Halprin's experimental summer course, which had a profound effect on her future work. Back in New York she studied with **Merce Cunningham**, and enrolled in Robert Dunn's pioneering composition class along with **Trisha Brown**, **Steve Paxton**, **David Gordon** and **Lucinda Childs**. The radical Judson Dance Theatre, for which she was the most prolific choreographer, was born out of these alternative sessions. *Trio A* (part of the larger work *The Mind is a Muscle*), her signature piece, was made to be performed by anyone of any age whether trained or not. *Continuous Project—Altered Daily* was started in 1970 and *Grand Union Dreams* was made in 1971. In 1973, she gave up her involvement in dance and took up filmmaking.

RAINIER III (1923–), properly **Rainier Louis Henri Maxence Bertrand de Grimaldi, prince of Monaco**. Born in Monaco, he succeeded his grandfather, Louis II, in 1950, as 26th ruling prince of the House of Grimaldi, which dates from 1297. In 1956 he married the American film actress **Grace Kelly** by whom he has a son, Prince Albert (b.1958, heir presumptive to the throne of the principality), and two daughters, Princess Caroline (b.1957) and Princess Stephanie (b.1965).

RAINWATER, (Leo) James (1917–) American physicist, born in Council, Idaho. He unified two theoretical models of the atomic nucleus. He was educated at the California Institute of Technology and Columbia University. During World War II he contributed to the Manhattan (atomic bomb) project. He became professor of physics at Columbia University in 1952 and was director of the Nevis Cyclotron Laboratory there from 1951 to 1953 and 1956 to 1961. There were two theories to describe the atomic nucleus in 1950; in one the nuclear particles were arranged in concentric shells, in the other, the nucleus was described as analogous to a liquid drop. Rainwater produced a collective model combining the two ideas. Together with **Aage Bohr** and **Ben Roy Mottelson**, he developed this theory and obtained experimental evidence in its support. The three shared the Nobel prize for physics in 1975 for this work.

RAINY, Robert (1826–1906) Scottish theologian, born in Glasgow. He studied at Glasgow and at New College in Edinburgh, and, after being minister of the Free Church in Huntly (1851) and the Free High Church in Edinburgh (1854), was from 1862 to 1900 professor of church history in the New (Free Church) College in Edinburgh, becoming its principal in 1874. He organized the union in 1900 of the Free and United Presbyterian Churches as the United Free Church of Scotland, of whose general assembly he became the first moderator.

RÁJÁ RÁM MOHÁN RÁI See **RAMMOHUN ROY**

RAJASINHA II (d.1687) king of Kandy (Ceylon). He succeeded his father, **Senerat**, in 1635, and continued the struggle for independence against the Portuguese. When the latter invaded Kandy in 1638, they were heavily defeated by Rajasinha at the battle of Gannoruwa. In alliance with the Dutch, the king was able to capture all the island's important towns from the Portuguese, but a breach between the allies allowed the Portuguese to recover for a time until war again broke out in 1652. In 1655 Colombo fell, after a six-month siege, to a combined force of Dutch and Sinhalese. Rajasinha's government was, according to an English observer, 'tyrannical and arbitrary in the highest degree', but he maintained the independence of his people from both the Portuguese and the Dutch until his death.

RAKHMANINOV, Sergey Vassilyevich See **RACHMANINOV**

RÁKÓCZI a princely family of Hungary and Transylvania that became extinct in 1780. The most important member was the popular Francis (Ferenc) II (1676–1735), who in 1703 led a Hungarian revolt against Austria. He had little success but was hailed by his countrymen as a patriot and a hero. His later years were spent as a Carmelite monk first in France and then in Turkey, where he died.

RALEIGH, Sir Walter (1552–1618) English courtier, navigator and poet, born in Hayes Barton, near

Sidmouth in Devon, half-brother of Sir **Humphrey Gilbert**. He went to Oriel College, Oxford, but left in order to volunteer in the Huguenot cause in France, and fought at Jarnac and Moncontour. In 1578 he joined a piratical expedition against the Spaniards organized by his half-brother; in 1580 he went to Ireland, where he suppressed the rising of the **Desmonds** in Ulster with ruthless savagery. He became a favourite of Queen **Elizabeth**, who heaped favours upon him—estates, the 'farm of wines', and a licence to export woollen broadcloths. In 1585 he was appointed lord warden of the Stannaries and vice-admiral of Devon and Cornwall; that same year he entered parliament for Devon. From 1584 to 1589 he sent an expedition to America to take unknown lands in the queen's name, and despatched an abortive settlement to Roanoke Island, North Carolina (1585–86). He later made unsuccessful attempts to colonize Virginia, but at least brought about the introduction of tobacco and potatoes. Eclipsed as court favourite in 1587 by the young earl of **Essex**, he went to Ireland and planted his estates in Munster with settlers, and became a close friend of the poet **Spenser**. In 1592 he was committed to the Tower for a secret affair with Bessy Throckmorton, one of the queen's maids of honour, and for more than four years after this was excluded from the queen's presence; he and Bessy later married. In 1595, with five ships, he explored the coasts of Trinidad, and sailed up the Orinoco, which he described in *The Discovery of Guiana*, and in 1596 took part with **Howard** and **Essex** in the sack of Cadiz. In 1600 he became governor of Jersey, and in three years did much to foster its trade. In the dark intrigues at the close of Elizabeth's reign he took little part, but he was arrested on 17 July 1603, and in his first despair tried to kill himself. His defence on his trial at Winchester was splendid; yet he was condemned to death, and only on the scaffold was his sentence commuted to perpetual imprisonment. Within the Tower Raleigh employed himself with study and chemical experiments and with writing his *History of the World* (1614), whose first and only volume comes down to the second Roman war with Macedonia. Other writings of Raleigh's captivity were *The Prerogative of Parliaments* (1628), *The Cabinet Council* (1658), and *A Discourse of War*. In 1616, he was released to make an expedition to the Orinoco in search of a goldmine. But the mission was a failure; Raleigh lost his fleet, and his son, and broke his terms by razing a Spanish town. On his return in 1618 the Spanish minister in London invoked the suspended death-sentence, and he was beheaded at Whitehall. Only fragments of his poetry survive.

RALEIGH, Sir Walter Alexander (1861–1922) English scholar, critic and essayist, born in London. He was professor of English literature at Liverpool (1899), Glasgow (1900) and at Oxford from 1904. Among his writings are *The English Novel* (1894), *Milton* (1900), *Wordsworth* (1903) and *Shakespeare* (1907). Chosen to compile the official history of the war in the air (1914–18), he died while collecting material for it.

RALSTON, William Ralston, originally **Shedden** (1828–89) English scholar and folklorist, born in London. He trained for the bar, but worked in the British Museum library (1853–75). He wrote on Russian folksongs and tales, besides a translation of **Turgenev**'s *Liza* (1869), and *Kriloff and his Fables* (1869).

RAMADHIN, Sonny (1930–) West Indian cricketer, born in Trinidad. With **Alfred Valentine** he formed a devastating spin attack in the West Indies Test sides of the 1950s. In 43 Tests he took 188 wickets, on one occasion taking ten wickets in a match. He was extremely difficult to 'read', but **Peter May** and **Colin Cowdrey** destroyed him at Birmingham in 1957 by padding up to almost every delivery, which the laws at that time permitted them to do. In this match Ramadhin bowled more balls (774) than any other bowler in the history of Test cricket. In later years he played county cricket with Lancashire. A peculiarity of his was that he invariably bowled in a cap.

RAMAKRISHNA PARAMAHASA, originally **Gadadhar Chatterjee** (1836–86) Indian mystic, born in the Hooghly district of Bengal. A priest at Dakshineswar Kali temple, near Calcutta, he took instruction from several *gurus* of different schools in his spiritual search, finally coming to believe in self-realization and God-realization, and that all religions were different paths to the same goal. His simple but effective re-telling of traditional stories, and personal charisma, attracted the interest of Calcutta intellectuals, including **Swami Vivekananda**, who became Ramakrishna's spiritual heir.

RAMAN, Sir Chandrasekhara Venkata (1888–1970) Indian physicist, born in Trichinopoly. Educated at Madras University, he became professor of physics at Calcutta (1917–33) and then director of the Indian Institute of Science at Bangalore. In 1930 he was awarded the Nobel prize for physics for important discoveries in connection with the diffusion of light (the Raman effect). He also worked on the theory of musical instruments.

RAMANA MAHARISHI (1879–1950) South Indian sage, born in Tirukuli, Madurai district. Attracted to the holy mountain Arunachala (at Tiruvannamalai, about 100 miles south-west of Madras) in 1896 at the age of 17, following a religious experience, he remained there until his death. Much of the time he lived in caves on the mountain and avoided publicity, but he later allowed devotees to establish an *ashram* at Villupuram, at the foot of the mountain. His philosophy of seeking self-knowlege through integration of the personality in the 'cave of the heart' became known to Westerners through the books of Paul Brunton as well as his own *Collected Works* (1969), *Forty Verses on Reality* (1978) and other anthologies.

RĀMĀNUJA (11th–12th century) Tamil Brahmin philosopher, born near Madras, South India. Dateable biographical information within a century of his death is not available, but his position in Indian thought is unassailable. Rejecting **Śankara**'s *a/madvaita* or non-dualistic Vedanta for *Viśishtādvaita* (which held that the soul was united with a personal god rather than absorbed into the Absolute) he prepared the way for the *bhakti* or devotional strain of Hinduism that was taken up by **Madhva**, Nimbarka, Vallabha and **Caitanya**.

RAMANUJAN, Srinivasa (1887–1920) Indian mathematician, born in Eroda, Madras, one of the most remarkable self-taught prodigies in the history of mathematics. The child of poor parents, he taught himself mathematics from an elementary English textbook. Although he attended college, he did not graduate. While working as a clerk, he was persuaded to send over 100 remarkable theorems that he had discovered to **Godfrey Hardy** at Cambridge, including results on elliptic integrals, partitions, and analytic number theory. Hardy was so impressed that he arranged for him to come to Cambridge in 1914. There Ramanujan published many papers, some jointly with Hardy. Having no formal training in mathematics, he arrived at his results by an almost miraculous intuition, often having no idea of how they could be proved or even what an orthodox proof might be like. He was elected FRS and a fellow of Trinity in 1918, but soon returned to India suffering from poor health, and died shortly after.

RAMAZZINI, Bernardini (1633–1714) Italian physician and pioneer of occupational health, born in Capri. He studied both philosophy and medicine at Parma University. He practised medicine for a while near Rome, and then settled in Modena where he eventually became professor of medicine at the university. He moved to Padua in 1700. His major work *De morbis artificum* (1700, trans 1705), was the first systematic treatise on occupational diseases, and includes many shrewd observations about environmental hazards (for instance, exposure to lead by potters and painters). He also made important observations on epidemics in human beings and animals, especially cattle plague.

RAMBAUD, Alfred Nicolas (1842–1905) French historian, born in Besançon. From 1896 to 1898 he was minister of public instruction. From 1870 he wrote on Russia, French civilization, colonial France, etc, and edited the *Histoire générale, du IV siècle à nos jours* (12 vols, 1892–99).

RAMBERT, Dame Marie, stage name of **Cyvia Rambam** (1888–1982) Polish-born British ballet dancer and teacher, born in Warsaw. She was sent to Paris to study medicine, but became involved in artistic circles and began to study eurhythmics. In 1913 she worked on **Stravinsky**'s *Rite of Spring* with **Diaghilev**'s Ballet Russe. She moved to London and began to dance and teach, marrying playwright Ashley Dukes in 1918. In 1931, eleven years after opening her own dance studio, she formed the Ballet Club, a permanent producing and performing organization which featured dancer **Alicia Markova** and choreographer **Frederick Ashton**. Particularly interested in promoting new ballets, she always encouraged her pupils to produce works, and this inevitably led to periodical financial shortages. Her company (which had become Ballet Rambert in 1935) had been expanding since the 1940s, but by 1966 was reduced to a small group which concentrated on new works and began to embrace modern dance techniques. In the mid 1970s the company performed work by Glen Tetley, John Chesworth and Christopher Bruce, and has grown to become one of Britain's major touring contemporary dance companies. She was made a DBE in 1962.

RAMBOUILLET, Catherine de Vivonne, Marquise de (1588–1665) French noblewoman, born in Rome, the daughter of Jean de Vivonne, Marquis of Pisani. At the age of twelve she was married to the son of the Marquis de Rambouillet, who succeeded to the title in 1611. From the beginning she disliked both the morals and manners of the French court. Virtuous and spiritual, she gathered together in the famous Hôtel Rambouillet for 50 years the talent and wit of France culled from both the nobility and the literary world.

RAMEAU, Jean Philippe (1683–1764) French composer and musical theorist, born in Dijon. He had been an organist, when he settled in Paris (1721) and wrote his *Traité de l'harmonie* (1722), a work of fundamental importance in the history of musical style. In 1732 he produced his first opera, *Hippolyte et Aricie*, which created a great sensation; his best was *Castor et Pollux* (1737). He composed over 30 operas and ballets, besides harpsichord pieces, and was ennobled by **Louis XV**. His nephew, who gave the title to a singular work by **Diderot**, was Louis Sébastien Mercier (1740–1814), author of the *Tableau de Paris*.

RAMÉE, De la See **RAMUS** and **OUIDA**

RAMELLI, Agostino (c.1531–c.1610) Italian military engineer, born in Ponte Tresa. He trained in the arts of war in the service of the Marquis of Marignano, and about 1570 was summoned to France by the Duke of Anjou (later King **Henri III**), and took part in the siege of La Rochelle in 1572. He achieved a high reputation as a military engineer in his lifetime, and lasting fame through the publication in 1588 of his one work, *The Various and Ingenious Machines of Agostino Ramelli*, in which he described and illustrated in great detail almost 200 devices such as water pumps, cranes, grain mills, military bridges and ballistic engines. There is no evidence that he had actually constructed any of the machines, but such collections played a valuable part in the dissemination of ideas.

RAMENSKI, Johnny, also known as **Johnny Ramsay** (c.1905–1972) convicted Scottish safe-breaker and jail-breaker of Polish extraction. He spent much of his life in Scotland compulsively breaking into banks and safes or breaking out of prisons. He escaped five times from Peterhead Prison and several times from Barlinnie. Police dubbed him 'Gentle Johnny' because he was never violent. Indeed, his genial nature endeared him to many. One of his last coups, after which he planned to retire, was a bank break-in at Rutherglen. He eventually died in Perth Prison.

RAMESES II (1304–1237 BC) usually called **the Great**, Egyptian ruler, third king of the 19th dynasty. He defeated the Hittites at Kadesh, then formed a peace with them, and married a Hittite princess. During his long reign (c.1292–c.1225 BC) he built magnificent monuments, temples, etc, completing the mortuary temple of Seti I at Luxor and the colonnaded hall of the Karnak temple, and building the rock temple of Abu Simbel. Tradition identifies him with the Pharaoh of the oppression, and Merenptah or Rameses III with the Pharaoh of the Exodus; the identification is doubtful. The mummy of Rameses II was found at Deir-el-Bahari in 1881.

RAMESES III (1198–1167 BC) Egyptian ruler, second king of the 20th dynasty. He warred with the Philistines and the invading 'Sea Peoples' and repeated the conquest of Ethiopia. The mummy of Rameses III was found at Bulak in 1886.

RAMMOHUN ROY, or **Rájá Rám Mohán Rái** (1774–1833) Indian religious reformer, born in Burdwan in Bengal of high Brahman ancestry. He came early to question his ancestral faith, and studied Buddhism in Tibet. Revenue collector for some years in Rangpur, in 1811 he succeeded to affluence on his brother's death. He published various works in Persian, Arabic and Sanskrit, with the aim of uprooting idolatry; and he helped in the abolition of suttee. He issued an English abridgment of the *Vedanta*, giving a digest of the Veda. In 1820 he published *The Precepts of Jesus*, accepting the morality preached by **Christ**, but rejecting His deity and miracles; and he wrote other pamphlets hostile both to Hinduism and to Christian Trinitarianism. In 1828 he began the Brahma Samaj association, and in 1830 the emperor of Delhi bestowed on him the title of raja. In 1831 he visited England, where he gave invaluable evidence before the board of control on the condition of India.

RAMÓN Y CAJAL, Santiago (1852–1934) Spanish physician and histologist, born in Petilla de Aragon. He graduated at Saragossa University, and became professor of anatomy at Valencia (1881–86), of histology at Barcelona (1886–92) and at Madrid (1892–1922). He was specially noted for his work on the brain and nerves; he isolated the neuron and discovered how nerve impulses are transmitted to brain cells. In 1906 he shared (with **Camillo Golgi**) the Nobel prize for physiology or medicine.

RAMPHAL, Sir Shridath Surrendranath ('Sonny'), (1928–) Guyanan and Commonwealth lawyer and diplomat. After studying law at King's College, London, he was called to the bar in 1951. He returned to the West Indies, and from 1952 held increasingly responsible posts in Guyana and the West Indies before becoming Guyana's foreign minister and attorney general in 1972, and justice minister in 1973. During much of this time he sat in the Guyanan National Assembly. From 1975 to 1989 he was secretary-general of the Commonwealth.

RAMS, Dieter (1932–) German product designer, born in Wiesbaden. Although he trained and worked as an architect, he is best known as the chief designer, since 1955, for the Frankfurt electrical appliance manufacturer, Braun AG. In association initially with Hans Gugelot, of the Hochschule für Gestaltung ('High School for Design') in Ulm, he transformed the company's product range. His food mixers, record players and radios, shavers, hair driers and clocks are all examples of rational, unadorned and beautiful modern design. He was made an honorary royal designer for industry in 1968.

RAMSAY, Sir Alexander (d.1342) Scottish patriot of Dalhousie, famed for his deeds of bravery. He relieved Dunbar Castle (1338), and captured Roxburgh Castle from English occupation (1342). He was captured and starved to death at Hermitage Castle in 1342 by William Douglas of Liddesdale.

RAMSAY, Allan (c.1685–1758) Scottish poet, born in Leadhills, Lanarkshire. His father was manager of Lord Hopetoun's mines there, and his mother, Alice Bower, was the daughter of a Derbyshire mining expert. In 1704 he was apprenticed for five years to a wigmaker in Edinburgh. By 1718 he had become known as a poet, having issued several short humorous satires printed as broadsides. He had also written (1716–18) two additional cantos to the old Scots poem of *Christ's Kirk on the Green*, cheerful pictures of rustic life and broad humour. Ramsay then commenced business as book-seller, later adding a circulating library (1725), apparently the first in Britain. 'Honest Allan's' career was eminently prosperous, though the theatre he built in Edinburgh at his own expense (1736) was soon closed down by the magistrates. In 1740 he built himself a quaint house (the 'goose-pie') on the Castle Hill, where he spent his last years in retirement. He was buried in Greyfriars' Churchyard. Among his works are: *Tartana, or the Plaid* (1718); *Poems* (collected edition published by subscription in 1721, by which it is said he realised 400 guineas—other editions, 1720, 1727, 1728); *Fables and Tales* (1722); *Fair Assembly* (1723); *Health, a Poem* (1724); *The Monk and the Miller's Wife* (1724), *The Tea-table Miscellany*, a collection of songs (4 vols, 1724–37); *The Evergreen* (1724); *The Gentle Shepherd, a Pastoral Comedy* (1725), his best and most popular work; and *Thirty Fables* (1730).

RAMSAY, Allan (1713–84) Scottish portrait painter, eldest son of the poet **Allan Ramsay**. He was a distinguished portrait painter, who trained in Italy, worked first in Edinburgh, but in 1762 settled in London, and in 1767 was appointed portrait painter to **George III**. In his best works his painting is simple and delicate and he excels in portraits of women, notably that of his wife. He delighted in conversation and was acquainted with many of the writers of his day, including **Samuel Johnson**; he also corresponded with such men as **Rousseau** and **Voltaire**.

RAMSAY, Andrew Michael, originally **André Michel** (1686–1743) the 'Chevalier de Ramsay', French writer, of Scottish parentage, born in Ayr, the son of a baker. He served in the Low Countries, in 1710 was converted by **Fénelon** to Catholicism, and lived with him for five years. In 1724–25 he was tutor to Prince **Charles Edward Stewart** in Rome, and in 1730 he visited England. He wrote *Vie de Fénelon* (1723), *Les Voyages de Cyrus* (1727), and other works.

RAMSAY, Sir Bertram Home (1883–1945) English naval officer, born in London, the son of a brigadier-general. He entered the Royal Navy as a cadet in 1898, and served as a destroyer commander in the Dover Patrol in World War I. He resigned from the navy after a disagreement in 1938, but was recalled to service on the outbreak of World War II and served as flag officer, Dover (1939–42). He directed the Dunkirk evacuation of 338 000 Allied troops in May–June 1940. He was deputy to Admiral **Andrew Cunningham** for the North African landings in 1942, and commanded the British naval forces for the Allied invasion of Sicily (1943). Reinstated on the active list as an admiral in 1944, he was Allied Naval commander-in-chief for the Normandy landings in 1944. He was killed in an aircraft accident near Paris.

RAMSAY, Edward Bannerman Burnett (1793–1872) Scottish theologian, born in Aberdeen, the son of Alexander Burnett, sheriff of Kincardineshire. In 1806 his father succeeded to his uncle Sir Alexander Ramsay's estates, took the surname Ramsay, and was created a baronet. Young Ramsay was educated at Durham and St John's College, Cambridge, held two Somerset curacies (1816–24), and then moved to Edinburgh. In 1830 he became incumbent of St John's, and in 1846 also dean of the diocese. He wrote various religious works, and the delightful *Reminiscences of Scottish Life and Character* (1857).

RAMSAY, James Andrew Brown See **DALHOUSIE, Marquis of**

RAMSAY, Johnny See **RAMENSKI, Johnny**

RAMSAY, Sir William (1852–1916) Scottish chemist, born in Glasgow. Professor of chemistry at Bristol (1880–87) and at University College, London (1887–1912), in conjunction with Lord **John Rayleigh** he discovered argon in 1894. Later he obtained helium, neon, krypton and xenon, and won the Nobel prize for chemistry in 1904. His writings include *The Gases of the Atmosphere* and *Elements and Electrons*.

RAMSAY, Sir William Mitchell (1851–1939) Scottish archaeologist, born in Glasgow. He was professor of humanities at Aberdeen (1886–1911). An authority on Asia Minor, he wrote a *Historical Geography of Asia Minor* (1890), and on the history of early Christian times he published several works, the best known being *The Church in the Roman Empire before AD 170* (1893).

RAMSDEN, Jesse (1735–1800) English instrument-maker, born near Halifax. He opened a business in London in 1762, improved optical and survey instruments and devised the mural circle.

RAMSEY, Sir Alf (Alfred) (1922–) English footballer and team manager, born in Dagenham. A thoughtful tactical player with Southampton and Tottenham Hotspur, he made his lasting mark as a manager at club and international level. He took Ipswich Town to the 2nd and 1st Division championships in successive years (1961, 1962), and became England manager a year later (1963–74). Criticized for being over-defensive and for not using wingers sufficiently, he won the World Cup for England in 1966 in England.

RAMSEY, Arthur Michael, Baron (1904–88) English prelate, 100th archbishop of Canterbury from 1961 to 1974, the son of a Cambridge don. He was educated at Repton School (where the headmaster was the man he would succeed as archbishop, Dr **Geoffrey Fisher**), and Magadelene College, Cambridge, where he was president of the Union (1926). His advance was rapid. After his first book (*The Gospel and Catholic Church*, 1936) he was appointed vicar at St Benet's, Cambridge, in 1938, professor of divinity at Durham and a canon of the cathedral in 1940, Regius professor of divinity at Cambridge in 1950, bishop of Durham in 1952 and bishop of York in 1956. As archbishop of Canterbury he worked tirelessly for Church unity, making a historic visit to Pope **Paul VI** in the Vatican in 1966, but was disappointed in his attempts to forge a reconciliation with the Methodist Church. An eminent scholar, he published many theological works, notably *The Resurrection of Christ* (1945) and *The Glory of God and the Transfiguration of Christ* (1949). His last book was *Be Still and Know* (1982).

RAMSEY, Frank Plumpton (1903–30) English philosopher and mathematician, born in Cambridge. He read mathematics at Trinity College, Cambridge, and went on to be elected fellow of King's College when he was only 21. In his tragically short life (he died after an operation) he made outstanding contributions to philosophy, logic, mathematics and economics, to an extent which was only properly recognized years after his death. He was much stimulated by his Cambridge contemporaries **Bertrand Russell**, whose programme of reducing mathematics to logic he ingeniously defended and developed, and **Ludwig Wittgenstein**, whose *Tractatus* he was among the first both to appreciate and to criticize, rejecting the idea of ineffable metaphysical truths beyond the limits of language with the famous remark, 'What we can't say we can't say, and we can't whistle it either'. The best of his work is collected in *Philosophical Papers* (ed D H Mellor, 1990).

RAMSEY, Ian Thomas (1915–72) English prelate, theologian and philosopher of religion, born in Kearsley, near Bolton. Having taught at Cambridge from 1941 and become a professor at Oxford in 1951, he was appointed bishop of Durham in 1966. He was respected both as a diocesan bishop and for his intellectual contribution to the Church of England's Board for Social Responsibility, Doctrine Commission, and the committee on religious education that produced *The Fourth R* (1970). His enthusiasm for new causes left him relatively little time to develop his philosophical work on language about God and the understanding of religious experiences as 'disclosure' situations, as in *Models and Mystery* (1964) and *Models for Divine Activity* (1973).

RAMUS, Petrus, or **Pierre de la Ramée** (1515–72) French humanist, born at Cuth near Soissons. He became servant to a rich scholar at the Collège de Navarre, and by studying at night made rapid progress in learning. The dominant philosophy dissatisfied him, and he put higher value on 'reason' than on 'authority'. Graduating at 23, he had great success as lecturer on the Greek and Latin authors, and undertook to reform the science of logic. His attempts excited much hostility among the Aristotelians, and his *Dialectic* (1543) was fiercely assailed by the doctors of the Sorbonne, who had it suppressed. But cardinals de Bourbon and Lorraine (**Charles Guise**) in 1545 had him appointed principal of the Collège de Presles; and Lorraine in 1551 instituted a chair for him at the Collège Royal. He mingled largely in the literary and scholastic disputes of the time, and ultimately turned Protestant. He had to flee from Paris, and travelled in Germany and Switzerland; but, returning to France in 1571, he perished in the massacre of St Bartholomew. He wrote treatises on arithmetic, geometry and algebra, and was an early adherent of the Copernican system. His theories had no small influence after his death, and all over Europe the Ramist system of logic was adopted and taught.

RAMUZ, Charles Ferdinand (1878–1947) Swiss writer, born in Cully near Lausanne. He wrote in French, mainly about life in his native canton of Vaud. His first book, *Le Petit Village*, appeared in 1903, and from then on he wrote prolifically. His pure prose style and fine descriptive power won him wide admiration and repute, his European popularity being somewhat tempered in Britain, though he has been translated into English—*Beauté sur la terre* (1927; trans *Beauty on Earth*) and *Présence de la mort* (1922; trans *The Triumph of Death*). Other writings include *Jean Luc persécuté* (1909), *La Guérison de maladies* (1917), *Adam et Ève* (1932) and *Besoin de grandeur* (1937).

RANCÉ, Armand Jean le Bouthillier de (1626–1700) French monk, founder of the Trappists. An accomplished but worldly priest, he became abbot of the Cistercian abbey of La Trappe in 1662. Affected by the tragic deaths of two of his friends, he underwent a conversion, undertook a reform of his monastery, and finally established what was practically a new religious order, its principles perpetual prayer and austere self-denial. Intellectual work was forbidden; only manual labour was allowed to the monks. He wrote of his order in *Traité de la sainteté et des devoirs de la vie monastique* (1683), which caused much controversy on the place of study in monastic life.

RANDALL, James Ryder (1839–1908) American poet, born in Baltimore. He was first a teacher, then a journalist. His lyrics, which in the Civil War gave powerful aid to the Southern cause, include 'Maryland, my Maryland' (1861), 'Stonewall Jackson' and 'There's life in the old land yet'.

RANDALL, Samuel Jackson (1828–90) American Democratic statesman, born in Philadelphia. He was a member of the House of Representatives (1863–90). As speaker (1876–81), he codified the rules of the House and considerably strengthened the speaker's power.

RANDOLPH, Asa Philip (1889–1979) American black labor leader and civil rights activist, born in Crescent City, Florida, the son of a clergyman. Educated locally, he studied economics, philosophy and science at City College of New York. He worked in various jobs, in which he tried to organize the workers, and founded a black labor monthly, the *Messenger*, in 1917. After World War I he sought to unionize blacks in laundries, clothes factories and cinemas, and from 1925 began to concentrate on sleeping-car porters staffing the long-distance passenger trains. He broke an anti-union protection racket in Pullman Cars, using public opinion and government regulation apparatus, and was president of the Brotherhood of Sleeping-Car Porters (1925–68). He obtained amendment to the Railroad Labor Act, 1934, ensuring benefits for black workers under its provisions, and won wage increases from Pullman in 1937. In 1941 he called a march on Washington of 50000 blacks protesting against unfair government and war industry employment practices, to avert which he was granted the Fair Employment Practices Commission. He influenced President **Truman** to desegregate the armed forces in 1948. Made vice-president of AFL-CIO in 1957, he formed the Negro American Labor Council within it in 1960. He directed the great march on Washington in 1963, when 200000 protested against continuing discrimination against blacks in the largest civil rights demonstration in American history, with **Martin Luther King** as the chief speaker ('I have a dream').

RANDOLPH, Edmund Jennings (1753–1813) American statesman, born in Williamsburg, Virginia. He studied at William and Mary College, and in 1786–88 was governor of Virginia, in 1787 a member of the convention which framed the US constitution. He was working on a codification of the state laws of Virginia when **Washington** appointed him attorney-general (1789). In 1794 he was made secretary of state, but, falsely charged with bribery, resigned (1795), and was practically ruined. He resumed law practice at Richmond, Virginia, and was chief counsel for **Aaron Burr** at his treason trial.

RANDOLPH, John (1773–1833) 'of Roanoke', American statesman, born in Cawsons, Virginia, a second cousin of **Edmund Randolph**. In 1799 he entered congress, where he became distinguished for his eloquence, wit, sarcasm and eccentricity. He was the Democratic leader of the House of Representatives, but quarrelled with **Jefferson** and opposed the war of 1812; he also opposed the Missouri Compromise and Nullification. From 1825 to 1827 he sat in the senate, and in 1830 was appointed minister to Russia. By his will he emancipated his slaves.

RANDOLPH, Sir Thomas (d.1332) Scottish soldier and statesman, nephew of **Robert I the Bruce**, who created him Earl of Moray. He recaptured Edinburgh Castle from the English (1314), commanded a division at Bannockburn, took Berwick (1318), won the victory of Mitton (1319), reinvaded England (1320, 1327), and was Guardian of the kingdom from Bruce's death (1329) until his own death at Musselburgh.

RANDOLPH, Sir Thomas (1523–90) English political agent and ambassador. A zealous Protestant, he lived abroad during **Mary I**'s reign, and by **Elizabeth** was employed on diplomatic missions in Germany, Russia, France and especially Scotland, where off and on between 1559 and 1586 he played his mistress's cards. He was twice shot at there, and in 1581 had to flee for his life. From 1585 he was Chancellor of the Exchequer in England.

RANDOLPH, Thomas (1605–35) English poet and dramatist, born in Newnham near Daventry. He studied at Westminster School and Trinity College, Cambridge, where he was elected a fellow, and soon began to write, gaining the friendship of **Ben Jonson** and leading a boisterous life. He left a number of bright, fanciful poems, and six plays: *Aristippus, or the Jovial Philosopher* (1631); *The Conceited Peddler* (1631); *The Jealous Lovers* (1632); *The Muses' Looking-glass* (1632); *Amyntas, or the Impossible Dowry* (1635); and *Hey for Honesty* (1651).

RANJIT SINGH (1780–1839) known as the 'Lion of the Punjab'. At the age of twelve he succeeded his father, a Sikh chief, as ruler of Lahore, and directed all his energies to founding a kingdom which would unite all the Sikh provinces. With the help of an army trained by western soldiers, including generals Ventura and Allard, he became the most powerful ruler in India. He was a firm ally of the British, the boundary between their territories having been amicably fixed at the river Sutlej. In 1813 he procured from an Afghan prince, as the price of assistance in war, the Koh-i-noor diamond.

RANJITSINHJI, Prince (1872–1933) Indian nobleman and England cricketer, known as the 'Black Prince of Cricketers'. After studying at Cambridge University, he became a star batsman (with **C B Fry**) for Sussex and England. He succeeded as Jam Sahib of Nawanagar in 1906 (maharaja in 1918), and did much to modernize and improve conditions in his home state. His nephew, Duleepsinhji, also played cricket for England in 1930.

RANK, Joseph Arthur, 1st Baron Rank (1888–1972) English film magnate, born in Hull. Starting in his father's flour-milling business, he developed an interest in films as a means of propagating the Gospel. He became chairman of many film companies, including Gaumont-British and Cinema-Television, and did much to promote the British film industry at a time when Hollywood and the American companies seemed to have the monopoly. A staunch and active supporter of the Methodist church, he was keenly interested in social problems. He was raised to the peerage in 1957.

RANKE, Leopold von (1795–1886) German historian, born in Wiehe in Thuringia. He studied at Halle and Berlin, and in 1818 became a schoolmaster at Frankfurt-an-der-Oder, but his heart was set on the study of history. A work on the Romance and Teutonic peoples in the Reformation period, and another criticizing contemporary historians, procured his call to Berlin as professor of history (1825–72). In 1827–31 he was sent to examine the archives of Vienna, Venice, Rome and Florence. The fruits of his labours were a work on south Europe in the 16th and 17th centuries (1827), books on Serbia and Venice, and *History of the Popes in the 16th and 17th Centuries* (1834–37; trans 1846), perhaps his greatest achievement. Then he turned his attention to central and northern Europe, and wrote on German Reformation history, Prussian history (1847–48), French history in the 16th and 17th centuries (1852–61), and English history in the 17th century (1859–67; trans 1875). Other books were on the origin of the Seven Years' War (1871), the German Powers and the Confederation (1871), the Revolutionary Wars of 1791–92 (1875), Venetian history (1878), a universal history (1881–88), and the history of Germany and France in the 19th century (1887), besides monographs on **Wallenstein** (1869), **Hardenberg** (1877–78), and **Frederick II, the Great** and **Frederick-William IV** (1878).

RANKIN, Dame Annabelle Jane Mary (1908–86) Australian politician, born in Brisbane, Queensland. Daughter of a former minister of the Queensland parliament, she became the first Queensland woman to enter federal politics, as a senator for the state in 1946. She became the first woman whip in the British Commonwealth, serving as opposition whip (1947–49) and government whip (1951–66). She was also the first Australian woman of ministerial rank, holding the housing portfolio (1966–71). In 1971 she was Australia's first woman head of a diplomatic mission on being appointed high commissioner to New Zealand, from which position she retired in 1974. She was appointed DBE in 1957.

RANKIN, Jeannette (1880–1973) American feminist and pacifist, the first female member of congress, born near Missoula, Montana. Educated at Montana University and the New York School of Philanthropy, she went on to work as a social worker in Seattle (1909), where she became involved in the fight for women's rights. In 1914 she was appointed legislative secretary of the National American Woman Suffrage Association, and in 1916 entered the House of Representatives as a Republican, the first woman to do so. During her two terms there (1917–19; 1941–43) she consistently voted against American participation in both world wars, promoted women's welfare and rights, and was instrumental in the adoption of the first bill granting married women independent citizenship. Continuing to campaign for women's issues throughout her career, she worked for the National Council for the Prevention of War from 1928 to 1939, and led the Jeannette Rankin March (1968) in which 5000 women gathered on Capitol Hill, Washington, to protest against the Vietnam War.

RANKINE, William John Macquorn (1820–72) Scottish engineer and scientist, born in Edinburgh. In 1855 he was appointed to the chair of engineering at Glasgow. Elected a fellow of the Royal Society in 1853, his works on the steam engine, machinery, shipbuilding and applied mechanics became standard textbooks; and he also did much for the new science of thermodynamics and the theories of elasticity and of waves. He wrote humorous and patriotic *Songs and Fables* (1874).

RANSOM, John Crowe (1888–1974) American poet and critic, born in Tennessee. His family were Methodists and he was educated locally and at Oxford. He had a long association with Kenyon College (1937–58) and was formative in the founding of the *Kenyon Review*, which beat a drum for the New Criticism. His poetry came early in his career. *Poems About God* (1919), *Chills and Fever* (1924), and *Two Gentlemen in Bonds* (1927) illustrate his aptitude as a balladist and elegist. Critical books include *God Without Thunder* (1930) and *The New Criticism* (1941).

RANSOME, Arthur Mitchell (1884–1967) English journalist and writer of children's books, born in Leeds. His father was a history professor, and he was educated at Rugby where he was a poor scholar and—by virtue of bad eyesight—inept at games. He worked as an office boy in a publishing house before graduating to ghost-writing, reviewing and writing short stories, meanwhile living a bohemian existence. He became a reporter on the *Daily News* and, in 1919, for the *Manchester Guardian*. He was widely travelled and, having learned Russian in 1913, was sent to cover the Revolution, a welcome relief from his stormy relationship with his first wife. They divorced in 1924 and he married **Trotsky**'s secretary, Evgenia Shelepin, with whom he fled from Russia, staying for a while in Estonia before settling in the Lake District. He had been a published author for a quarter of a century before the appearance of *Swallows and Amazons* (1930), the first of twelve perennially popular novels featuring two families of adventurous but responsible children, the Blacketts and the Walkers, who spend their school holidays revelling in the open air, free from the cramping attention of adults. Of his numerous other books, *Old Peter's Russian Tales* (1916) is worthy of note. *The Autobiography of Arthur Ransome* (1976) is interesting but unrevealing.

RANSOME, Robert (1753–1830) English agricultural implement maker, born in Wells in Norfolk. In 1789 he founded at Ipswich the great Orwell Works for agricultural implements.

RANTZEN, Esther Louise (1940–) English television presenter and producer, born in Berkhamsted. Educated at Somerville College, Oxford, she joined the BBC in 1963, making sound effects for radio drama. Shifting into research for *Man Alive* (1965–67), she joined *Braden's Week* (1968–72) as a reporter. Since 1973 she has produced, written and presented *That's Life*, a populist consumer programme combining investigative journalism with a potpourri of comical items. She also produced the talent show *The Big Time* (1976) and *Esther Interviews . . .* (1988), and has used her position of influence to campaign on issues of child abuse and drug problems in a variety of documentaries such as *Childwatch* (1987). In 1977 she married broadcaster Desmond Wilcox (1931–); their joint publications include *Kill the Chocolate Biscuit* (1981) and *Baby Love* (1985). In 1988 she received the Richard Dimbleby Award for her contributions to factual television.

RAOULT, François Marie (1830–1901) French chemist, born in Fournes (Nord). Educated at Paris, in 1870 he became professor of chemistry at Grenoble. He discovered the law (named after him) which relates the vapour pressure of a solution to the number of molecules of solute dissolved in it.

RAPHAEL, properly **Raffaello Santi** or **Sanzio** (1483–1520) Italian painter, born in Urbino, the son of the poet-painter, Giovanni Santi (d. 1494). He studied from about 1500 at Perugia under **Perugino**. Among his early paintings were the *Mond Crucifixion* (1502–03), and *Assumption of the Virgin* (1504), which clearly show Peruginesque influence. In 1505 he went to Siena, where he assisted **Pinturicchio**, and then moved to Florence; but before starting he probably took commissions, which produced the *Madonna Ansidei*, the *Madonna of Sant' Antonio* and the *Madonna of Terranuova*. Raphael, who now had painting-rooms in Florence and in Perugia, resolved to acquire and assimilate some of the boldness of **Michelangelo** and the sweetness of **Leonardo da Vinci**. In portraiture more than elsewhere da Vinci's influence is visible, and the likeness of *Maddalena Doni* (Florence) is inspired by the *Mona Lisa*. Of special interest is the *St George*, sent by the Duke of Urbino to **Henry VII** of England; while attractive in other ways are the painter's own likeness and the *Madonnas* of Orléans, of the Palm, of St Petersburg and of Canigiani in which **Raphael** finally appears as a pure Tuscan. The Borghese *Entombment* (1507) is an embodiment of all the new principles which Raphael acquired in Florence and of colour such as only he could give. He became attracted by the style of **Fra Bartolommeo**; and, under that influence, finished the *Madonna del Baldacchino* in Florence. Some of the best work of his Florentine period was now produced —the small *Holy Family*, the *St Catherine*, the *Bridgewater* and *Colonna Madonnas*, the *Virgin and Sleeping Infant*, the large *Cowper Madonna*, the *Belle Jardinière*, and the *Esterhazy Madonna*. In 1508 he went to Rome at the instigation of his relative **Bramante**, then in high favour with pope **Julius II**, who had laid the foundation of the new cathedral of St Peter, and who caused the papal chambers to be decorated afresh because he disliked the frescoes of the older masters. The date of Raphael's engagement to paint the *Camere* of the Vatican is now fixed as 1509. Raphael divided his time between the labours of the Vatican and easel pictures. The portraits of Julius II and the Virgin of the Popolo were now executed, drawings were furnished to the copperplate-engraver Marcantonio for the Massacre of the Innocents, and Madonnas and Holy Families were composed. The constant employment of disciples also enabled Raphael in the three years 1511–14 to finish the *Madonna di Foligno*, the *Isaiah of St Agostino*, the *Galatea of the Farnesina*, the *Sibyls of the Pace*, and the mosaics of the Popolo ordered by Agostino Chigi. He also painted the *Madonna of the Fish* (Madrid) and *Madonna della Sedia* (Florence), while in portraits such as *Altoviti* (Munich) and *Inghirami* (Florence) he rises to the perfect rendering of features and expression which finds its greatest triumph in the *Leo X* (Florence). **Leo X** selected Raphael to succeed **Bramante** as architect of St Peter's in 1514, and secured from him for the Vatican chambers the frescoes of the Camera dell' Incendio, which all illustrate scenes from the lives of Leonine Popes. But much of Raphael's attention was taken up with the cartoons executed, with help from assistants, for the tapestries of the Sistine Chapel. When Leo X succumbed to **Francis I**, Raphael followed the pontiff to Florence and Bologna, and found there new patrons for whom he executed the *Sistine Madonna*, the *St Cecilia* of Bologna, and the *Ezechiel* of the Pitti, Florence. The labours subsequently completed were immense, including the *Spasimo*, the *Holy Family* and *St Michael*, which the pope sent to the king of France in 1518, the likeness of the vice-queen of Aragon, and the *Violin-player*. In wall-painting he produced, with help, the cycle of the Psyche legend at the Farnesina, the gospel scenes of the Loggie of the Vatican, and the Frescoes of the Hall of Constantine. His last work, the *Transfiguration*, was left unfinished when he died.

RAPIN, Paul de (1661–1725) French historian, born in Castres in Languedoc, the son of the seigneur de Thoyras. He studied at the Protestant college of Saumur, and passed as advocate in 1679. After the revocation of the Edict of Nantes (1685) he went to Holland, enlisted in a Huguenot volunteer corps, followed the Prince of Orange (**William III**) to England in 1688, was made ensign in 1689, and distinguished himself at the Boyne and at Limerick. For some years he travelled as tutor with the Earl of Portland's son, then settled at Wesel where he devoted his remaining years to the composition of his great *Histoire d'Angleterre* (1724), undoubtedly the best work on English history that had until then appeared.

RAPP, George (1770–1847) German-born American religious leader, founder of the Harmony Society, born in Württemberg. A linen-weaver by trade, he became leader of a group of separatists. In 1803, to escape persecution, he and some of his followers emigrated to Western Pennsylvania where they established a settlement named Harmony. After migrating to New Harmony in Indiana (1815), they returned in 1824 to Pennsylvania and built Economy on the Ohio, 15 miles north-west of Pittsburgh. Looking for the speedy second coming of Christ, the community of Harmonites (or Rappites) sought to amass wealth for the Lord's use, practised rigid economy, self-denial and celibacy, all things being held in common, and, diminished in number, owned farms, dairies and vineyards, and railway and bank shares worth millions of dollars. The community came to an end in 1906.

RAPP, Jean, Comte de (1772–1821) French soldier, born in Colmar. He entered the French army in 1788, distinguished himself in Germany and Egypt, and became aide-de-camp to **Napoleon**. For his brilliant charge at Austerlitz he was made general of division (1805); in 1809 he became a count of the Empire. He accompanied the emperor on the Russian expedition, defended Danzig for nearly a year, on its surrender was sent as a prisoner to Russia, and did not return until 1814. During the Hundred Days (1816) he supported Napoleon, but after the Restoration he was made a peer.

RASHDALL, Hastings (1858–1924) English moral philosopher and theologian, born in London. Educated at Harrow and Oxford, he was elected a fellow of Hertford College, Oxford, in 1888, divinity tutor and chaplain at Balliol, and from 1895 to 1917 was tutor in philosophy at New College. Given a canonry at Hereford in 1909, in 1917 he became dean of Carlisle. Among his writings are the scholarly *Universities of Europe in the Middle Ages* (3 vols, new ed 1936), and *Theory of Good and Evil* (2 vols, 1917), containing his nonhedonistic 'ideal utilitarian' system of ethics in which right and wrong are judged by the ideal and which may, but not of necessity, be pleasurable. *Idea of Atonement in Christian Theology* (1919) includes his Bampton lectures given in 1915.

RASK, Rasmus Christian (1787–1832) Danish philologist, born on the island of Fyn. He mastered some 25 languages and dialects, and is said to have studied twice as many. Along with the works of **Bopp** and **Grimm**, his *Essay on the Origin of the Ancient Scandinavian or Icelandic Tongue* (1818), in which he demonstrated the affinity of Icelandic to other European languages, opened up the science of comparative philology. He was one of the first to recognize that the Celtic languages are Indo-European, and, developing the work of the Swedish philologist **Johan Ihre**, he anticipated Grimm in formulating the Germanic consonant shift described in what has become known as Grimm's Law. Between 1819 and 1823 he travelled to India and Ceylon, returning to Copenhagen with many manuscripts. He became professor of literary history in 1825, of oriental languages in 1828, and of Icelandic in 1831.

RASMUSSEN, Knud Johan Victor (1879–1933) Danish explorer and ethnologist, born in Jacobshavn, Greenland, the son of a Danish Eskimo mother. From 1902 onwards he directed several expeditions to Greenland in support of the theory that the Eskimos and the North American Indians were both descended from migratory tribes from Asia. In 1910 he established Thule base on Cape York, and in 1921–24 crossed from Greenland to the Bering Strait by dog sledge to visit all the Eskimo groups along the route.

RASP, Charles (1846–1907) German-born Australian prospector, born in Stuttgart. Illness forced him to emigrate to Australia in 1869, and after trying his luck on the Victorian goldfields he became a boundary rider in the south-west of New South Wales, at a time when considerable discoveries of tin were being made. Although not a geologist, he pegged the very first claim on 'the Broken Hill' in 1883, later being joined in a syndicate by six others, but met with disappointing assay results. Two years later further tests indicated not tin but rich silver ore. The Broken Hill Proprietory Company was formed, and Rasp became a rich man. Now known as BHP Ltd, the company is the largest industrial company in Australia, with wealth founded on lead, coal, iron ore and silver.

RASPAIL, François Vincent (1794–1878) French chemist, doctor, deputy, and advocate of universal suffrage. As a revolutionist he was banished from France in 1848, but allowed to return in 1859. His camphor system (1845) was a forerunner of antiseptic surgery.

RASPE, Rudolf Erich (1737–94) See **MÜNCHHAUSEN**

RASPUTIN, Grigoriy Efimovich (?1871–1916) Russian peasant and mystic, self-styled 'strannik', or holy man, born in Pokrovskoye in Tobolsk province. In 1904 he left his village and devoted himself to religion. In St Petersburg from 1905, his apparent ability to ease the bleeding of the haemophiliac crown prince gave him a magnetic influence over the empress **Alexandra** and her husband, **Nicholas II**. He extended his malign influence over the court and government, until he was assassinated at the Yusupov Palace by a party of noblemen led by the Grand Duke Dimitry Pavlovich and Prince Yusupov.

RASSAM, Hormuzd (1826–1910) Turkish Assyriologist, born in Mosul, the son of Chaldaean Christians. An English national, he assisted **Layard** at Nineveh in 1845–47 and 1849–51, and succeeded him, until 1854, as British agent for Assyrian excavations, finding the palace of Ashur-bani-pal (**Sardanapalus**). After holding political offices at Aden and Muscat, he was sent (1864) to Abyssinia, where King **Theodore** cast him into prison till 1868, when he was released by Sir **Robert Napier**. In 1876–82 he made explorations in Mesopotamia for the British Museum, conducting notable excavations at Tell Balawat and Abu Habbah (ancient Sippar). He wrote on his Abyssinian experiences (1869), and did much work for the British Academy.

RASTELL, John (1475–1536) English printer, lawyer and dramatist, born in Coventry. He was called to the bar and in 1510 set up his own printing press. Married to the sister of Sir **Thomas More**, he printed More's *Life of Pico*, a grammar by **Linacre**, the only copy of **Medwall**'s play *Fulgens and Lucres*, and many law books. Himself a dramatist, his plays, printed on his own press, include *Nature of the Four Elements* (1519), *Of Gentylness and Nobylyte...* (c.1527) and *Calisto and Meleboea* (c.1527). An ingenious deviser of pageants, he presented several of them at court. His expedition to found a settlement in the 'New Found Lands' in 1517 came to nothing through mutiny on his ship.

RASTELL, William (1508–65) English printer and lawyer, son of **John Rastell** and nephew of Sir **Thomas More**. He worked until 1529 with his father, then set up his own printing press and during the next five years printed many of More's works, **Robert Fabyan**'s *Chronicle*, **Henry Medwall**'s *Nature*, plays by his brother-in-law, **John Heywood**, as well as many law books, notably *A Collection of All the Statutes* (1557) and *A Collection of Entrees* (1566). Abandoning printing for law when More fell from favour with the king, he was by 1549 treasurer of Lincoln's Inn. His kinship with More and his relationship through marriage with a daughter of More's protégé, John Clement, drove him into exile with the Clements at Louvain. With him went letters and other works written by More in the Tower. These, which he edited and printed, appeared in More's *English Works* (1557). Exiled again during the reign of **Elizabeth**, he died abroad.

RASTRICK, John Urpeth (1780–1856) English civil and mechanical engineer, born in Morpeth. Articled to his father, an engineer and machinist, at the age of 15, from about 1801 he gained experience with several firms of iron-founders, and from 1815 to 1816 he designed and built the cast-iron bridge over the Wye at Chepstow. In 1822 he was engineer of the Stratford & Moreton horse-drawn railway, and in 1826, with **George Stephenson**, supported the use of steam locomotives on the Liverpool & Manchester railway. He was one of the judges at the Rainhill trials in 1829, and in the same year built a colliery railway in Staffordshire which he worked with the locomotive *Agenoria*; a similar engine, the *Stourbridge Lion*, was the first to run in North America. His greatest achievement was the London & Brighton railway, opened in 1841, which included the 37-span Ouse viaduct and three major tunnels.

RATHBONE, Eleanor Florence (1872–1946) English feminist and social reformer, born in Liverpool into a philanthropic merchant family of Quaker antecedents. After reading classics at Somerville College, Oxford, she made an extensive study of the position of widows under the poor law, and became the leading British advocate for family allowances in *The Disinherited Family* (1924) and *The Case for Family Allowances* (1940). She was a leader in the constitutional movement for female suffrage, and as independent member of Liverpool city council from 1909 she worked vigorously in the housing campaign between the wars. Elected as independent MP for the Combined English Universities, she fought to gain the franchise for Indian women, denounced child marriage in India (*Child Marriage: The Indian Minotaur*, 1934), and attacked appeasement of **Hitler** in *War Can Be Averted* (1937), non-intervention in the Spanish Civil War, and Italian aggression in Ethiopia. She was a vigorous worker in the service of refugees, as a result of which she became an enthusiastic proponent of Zionism.

RATHBONE, Harold Stewart (1858–1929) English painter, designer and poet. He founded the Della Robbia Pottery with the sculptor, Conrad Dressler, in 1893 in Birkenhead, Liverpool, producing architectural earthenware, relief plaques, vases and bottles, plates, dishes and clock cases. They were decorated with sgraffito and elaborate modelled relief decoration inspired by Italian maiolica. The Italian sculptor, Carlo Manzoni, joined in 1895, and among the many designers were **Ford Maddox Ford**, **Robert Anning Bell** and **Christopher Dresser**. The pottery merged with a firm of ecclesiastical sculptors in 1900 and went into liquidation in 1906.

RATHENAU, Walther (1867–1922) German electro-technician and industrialist, born in Berlin of Jewish parents. He organized the Allgemeine Elektrizitäts Gesellschaft, founded by his father, and German war industries during World War I. In 1921 as minister of reconstruction he dealt with reparations. His works include *Von kommenden Dingen* and other works. Soon after becoming foreign minister he was murdered.

RATHKE, Martin Heinrich (1793–1860) German biologist, born in Danzig. He was professor of physiology at Dorpat (1829) and Königsberg (1835). In 1829 he discovered gill-slits and gill-arches in embryo birds and mammals. 'Rathke's pocket' is the name given to the small pit on the dorsal side of the oral cavity of developing vertebrates.

RATICH, or Ratke, Wolfgang (1571–1635) German educationist, born in Holstein. He based a new system of education on **Francis Bacon**'s *The Advancement of Learning*, which he tried unsuccessfully to practice at Köthen in 1618. A second trial at Magdeburg in 1620 also ended in failure, and after some years of ineffectual wanderings he died in Erfurt. Though his ideas on education and methods of teaching were unsuccessful and unpopular in his lifetime, they had some influence on later reformers, especially **Comenius**.

RATSIRAKA, Didier (1936–) Malagasy sailor and politician, born in Vatomandry. Educated and trained for naval service in Madagascar and France, he served in the navy (1963–70) and was military attaché in Paris, with the rank of lieutenant-commander (1970–72). Since independence in 1960 there had been frequent clashes between the country's two main ethnic groups, the highland Merina and the coastal Cotiers. From independence in 1960 until 1972 the government had favoured the Cotiers but in 1972 the army, representing the Merina, took control. A deteriorating economy and Cotier unrest resulted in the imposition of martial law in 1975, but this was lifted and, under a new constitution, Ratsiraka, a Cotier, was elected president. In 1976 he formed the Advance Guard of the Malagasy Revolution (AREMA) which became the nucleus of a one-party state, based on the National Front for the Defence of the Malagasy Socialist Revolution (FNDR). Although AREMA won overwhelming support in the Assembly elections of 1983 and 1989, discontent, particularly among the Merina, remained.

RATTAZZI, Urbano (1808–73) Italian statesman, born in Alessandria. He practised as advocate at Casale, and in 1848 entered the Second Chamber at Turin, becoming minister of the interior and later of justice until after Novara. In 1853 he took the justice portfolio under **Cavour**; but, accused of weakness in suppressing the Mazzinian movement, retired in 1858. In 1859 he was minister of the interior, but retired because of the cession of Savoy and Nice (1860). Twice prime minister for a few months (1862, 1867), he twice had to resign because of his opposition to **Garibaldi**.

RATTENBURY, Alma (d.1935) alleged murderer of unknown extraction. In Canada in 1928 she met and married a successful British architect, Francis Rattenbury (1867–1935), who was reputedly 30 years her senior. Upon Rattenbury's retirement, the couple settled in Britain. In 1934, Alma advertised for a chauffeur/handyman. The employee, 18-year-old George Stoner, soon became her lover. On 24 March 1935 Alma found her husband with blood streaming from his head at their home, Villa Madeira, in Bournemouth. He later died. The murder weapon was found to be a mallet. Alma and Stoner confessed independently. At the trial Stoner was found guilty and sentenced to death, but Alma was acquitted. She then committed suicide. Following a petition with over 300000 signatures, Stoner was reprieved shortly after.

RATTIGAN, Terence Mervyn (1911–77) English playwright, born in London. Educated at Harrow and Oxford, he scored a considerable success with his comedy *French Without Tears* (1936). After that, most of his works, with the possible exception of *Adventure Story* (1949), a play about **Alexander the Great**, were internationally acclaimed; they reveal not only a wide range of imagination but a deepening psychological knowledge. Best known are *The Winslow Boy* (1946), based on the Archer Shee case, *The Browning Version* (1948), *The Deep Blue Sea* (1952), *Separate Tables* (1954) and *Ross* (1960), a fictional treatment of **T E Lawrence**. He was responsible for several successful films made from his own and other works.

RATTLE, Simon (1955–) English conductor, born in Liverpool. He won the Bournemouth International Conducting Competition at the age of 17, and made his London début at both the Royal Albert and Festival Halls in 1976, and was assistant conductor of the BBC Scottish Symphony Orchestra (1977–80), and since 1980 has been principal conductor of the City of Birmingham Symphony Orchestra, and principal guest conductor of the Los Angeles Philharmonic since 1981. He is married to the American soprano Elise Ross.

RAU, Johannes (1931–) West German politician, born in Wuppertal, in North-Rhine-Westphalia, the son of a Protestant pastor. He began his career as a salesman for a church publishing company before being attracted to politics as a follower of **Gustav Heinemann**. He joined the Social Democratic party (SPD) and was elected to the Diet of his home *Land* (state), the country's most populous, in 1958. He served as chairman of the SPD's parliamentary group (1967–70), and as minister of science and research in the *Land* (1970–78) before becoming its minister-president in 1978. His successful record as *Land* leader, his moderate policy outlook, and his optimistic and youthful personality persuaded the SPD to elect him federal party deputy chairman in 1982 and chancellor-candidate for the 1987 Bundestag election. However, the party was heavily defeated, and since this setback he has concentrated on his work as *Land* premier.

RAUCH, Christian Daniel (1777–1857) German sculptor, born in Arolsen. He practised sculpture while still valet to **Frederick-William III** of Prussia, and in 1804 went to Rome. From 1811 to 1815 he carved the recumbent effigy for the tomb of Queen **Louisa** at Charlottenburg. His works included statues of **Blücher**, **Dürer**, **Goethe**, **Schiller** and **Schleiermacher**; his masterpiece was that of **Frederick the Great** (1851) in Berlin.

RAUMER, Friedrich Ludwig Georg von (1781–1873) German historian, born in Wörlitz near Dessau. He entered the Prussian state service in 1801; in 1811 became professor of history at Breslau; in 1819–53 filled the chair of political science at Berlin; and was secretary of the Berlin Academy. In 1848 he went to Paris as German ambassador. His chief works are a history of the Hohenstaufen emperors (1823–25) and a history of Europe from the 16th century (1832–50).

RAUSCHENBERG, Robert (1925–) American avant-garde artist, born in Port Arthur, Texas, of German and Indian descent. He studied art at the Kansas City Art Institute and in Paris, and at Black Mountain College, North Carolina, under **Josef Albers** (1948–49). His collages and 'combines' incorporate a variety of rubbish (rusty metal, old tyres, stuffed birds, fragments of clothing, etc) splashed with paint. Sometimes categorized as a Pop artist, his work has strong affinities with Dadaism and with the 'ready-mades' of **Marcel Duchamp**.

RAVAILLAC, François (1578–1610) French schoolmaster and assassin. After long imprisonment for bankruptcy and a brief service in the Order of Feuillants, he was moved by Catholic fanaticism to stab **Henry IV** of France. For this he was torn to pieces by horses.

RAVEL, Maurice (1875–1937) French composer, born in Ciboure in the Basque country. He entered the Paris Conservatoire as a piano student in 1889. Eschewing the formal type of study and practice, he was something of a rebel; his early compositions met with considerable disapproval from the authorities, but after joining **Gabriel Fauré**'s composition class in 1898 he developed considerably, though his first orchestral piece, the overture to *Schéhérazade*, an opera which was never performed, had a hostile reception on its first performance in 1899. In the same year, however, he won recognition with the *Pavane pour une infante défunte*, strongly redolent of his Basque background. In 1901 he was runner-up for the Prix de Rome with his cantata *Myrrha*, and his *Jeux d'eau* for piano won a popular success. He made two more fruitless attempts at the Prix de Rome and was intending to try a fourth time, but was barred from entering. He himself was indifferent, but the case was seized upon by the press as an example of personal prejudice in high quarters. Significantly, all Ravel's successful rivals were consigned to oblivion by posterity within a half-century. Now at the height of his powers, he wrote his *Sonatina* (1905), *Miroirs* (1905), *Ma Mère l'Oye* (1908) and *Gaspard de la nuit* (1908) for piano; and in 1909 he began the music for the **Diaghilev** ballet *Daphnis et Chloë*, which was first performed in 1912. His comic opera *L'Heure espagnole* was completed in 1907 and produced in 1911. When World War I broke out he was 40, but he joined the army and saw active service; his *Tombeau de Couperin* (1917), a piano suite on the 18th-century pattern, which he later orchestrated, was dedicated to friends killed in action. The opera *L'Enfant et les sortilèges*, written to a libretto by **Colette**, was performed with great success in 1925, and the 'choreographic poem' *La Valse*, epitomizing the spirit of Vienna, had been staged in 1920. These two works, both begun in 1917, were Ravel's last major contributions. The *Boléro* (1928), despite its popularity in Promenade concerts and elsewhere, is of smaller stature and was intended as a miniature ballet. He visited England in 1928 and received an honorary doctorate at Oxford. In 1933 his mental faculties began to fail, and it was found that he had a tumour on the brain. He composed no more but remained fairly active physically, and was able to tour Spain before he died. His music is scintillating and dynamic; he defied the established rules of harmony with his unresolved sevenths and ninths and other devices, his syncopation and strange sonorities, and he made the piano sound as it had never sounded before. His orchestrations are brilliant, especially in their masterly use of wind instruments and unusual percussion effects, often characteristically French, sometimes with a Spanish flavour. It is interesting that his only work written purely for orchestra is *Rapsodie espagnole* (1907);

everything else orchestral is either opera, ballet, or orchestrated piano pieces.

RAVENSCROFT, Thomas (1592–1640) English composer and author. He wrote *Pammelia* (1609), *Melismata* (1611) and *The Whole Book of Psalms* (1621). *Pammelia*, a collection of rounds and catches, was the first book of its kind in England. He wrote some well-known tunes, such as St Davids and Bangor.

RAVILIOUS, Eric William (1903–42) English artist, designer and illustrator. He studied at Eastbourne School of Art (1919–22) and at the Design School of the Royal College of Art (1922–25), where he was taught by **Paul Nash**. He designed printed patterns for J Wedgwood & Sons, including many famous designs such as the travel series, coronation mugs and Christmas tableware. Wood engraving, however, was the centre of his activity, and he was commissioned to illustrate many books including *Twelfth Night* (Golden Cockerel Press, 1932) and *Elm Angel* (1930). During the late 1930s he turned increasingly to watercolour painting and colour lithography. He was appointed official war artist in 1940 and was lost on air patrol off the coast of Iceland.

RAVI SHANKAR (1920–) Indian musician. He is widely regarded as India's most important musician, not only because of his virtuosic playing of the sitar, but also as a teacher and composer. His own early training as a dancer was followed by years of intensive musical study. He set up schools of Indian music, founded the National Orchestra of India, and by the mid 1950s his reputation had spread so widely that he became the first Indian instrumentalist to undertake an international tour. He found himself in demand in the West as a performer and teacher in all areas of music—from the Edinburgh International Festival to the jazz and rock worlds. George Harrison of the **Beatles** was one of his pupils. He has written several film scores, the most notable being for **Satyajit Ray**'s trilogy, *Apu*. His autobiography, *My Music, My Life*, was published in 1968.

RAWLINGS, Flight-Lieutenant Jerry John (1947–) Ghanaian leader. He was at the centre of a peaceful coup in 1979, the intentions of which were to root out widespread corruption and promote 'moral reform'. Rawlings and his supporters returned power to a civilian government four months later, but he threatened to take over again if the politicians put their own interests before those of the nation. Despite being forcibly retired from the Armed Forces and discredited by the civilian government, his popularity remained high among the lower ranks of the army and the general public, and he returned with his Armed Forces Revolutionary Council to seize power again at the end of 1981. Since then the country has remained under military rule.

RAWLINSON, Sir Henry Creswicke (1810–95) English diplomat and Assyriologist, born in Chadlington. He entered military service with the East India Company in 1827. In 1833–39 he helped to reorganize the Persian army, at the same time studying the cuneiform inscriptions, and translating **Darius**'s Behistun inscription. He was political agent at Kandahar 1840–42, at Baghdad from 1843, later consul also, and made excavations and collections. A director of the East India Company in 1856, in 1859–60 he was British minister in Persia, MP (1858, 1865–68), and in 1858–59, 1868–95 a member of the Council of India. He wrote books on cuneiform inscriptions, the Russian question, and a *History of Assyria* (1852).

RAWLINSON, Henry Seymour, 1st Baron Rawlinson (1864–1925) English soldier, eldest son of Sir **Henry Creswicke Rawlinson**. He served in Burma, Sudan and South Africa. In World War I he commanded the 4th Army at the Somme (1916). In 1918 he broke the Hindenburg line near Amiens. He was commander-in-chief in India (1920).

RAWLS, John (1921–) American philosopher, born in Baltimore, Maryland. He studied at Princeton, and taught at Princeton and Cornell, before going to Harvard as professor in 1962. In 1971 he published *A Theory of Justice*, which has probably been the most discussed text in social and political philosophy since World War II and which gave this field a new direction and energy. In it he presents a fully elaborated description first of the theoretical principles of his theory of justice, second of its implications in detail for social institutions, and third of its grounding and support in moral psychology.

RAWSTHORNE, Alan (1905–71) English composer, born in Haslingden, Lancashire. He first studied dentistry, but turned to music at the age of 20 and studied at the Royal Manchester College of Music. From 1932 to 1934 he taught at Dartington Hall, but settled in London in 1935. His works, forthright and polished, include symphonies, *Symphonic Studies* for orchestra, concertos for piano and for violin, and various pieces of choral and chamber music.

RAY, James Earl See **KING, Martin Luther**

RAY, John (1627–1705) English naturalist, born in Black Notley, near Braintree, Essex, the son of a blacksmith. Educated at Cambridge, he became a fellow of Trinity College in 1649, but lost his post in 1662 when he refused to take the oath of Act of Uniformity after the Restoration. Accompanied and subsidized by a wealthy former pupil and fellow naturalist, **Francis Willoughby**, he toured extensively in Europe (1662-66), studying botany and zoology. He originated the basic principles of plant classification into cryptograms, monocotyledons and diocotyledons in his pioneering *Catalogus Plantarum Angliae* (1670) and *Methodus Plantarum Nova* (1682). His major work was *Historia Generalis Plantarum* (3 vols, 1686–1704), but he also wrote books on birds, fishes and insects. His *Wisdom of God Manifested in the Works of the Creation* (1691) was immensely influential in its time. The Ray Society was founded in his memory in 1844.

RAY, Man (Emanuel Rabinovich) (1890–1976) American painter, photographer and filmmaker, born in Philadelphia, Pennsylvania. He studied art in New York, and became a major figure in the development of Modernism, founding (with **Marcel Duchamp** and **Francis Picabia**), the New York Dadaist movement. He experimented with new techniques in painting and photography, moved to Paris, where he became interested in filming, and, after working with **René Clair**, made Surrealist films such as *Anemic Cinema* with Marcel Duchamp in 1924 and *L'Étoile de Mer* (Star of the Sea, 1928). During the 1930s he published and exhibited many photographs and 'rayographs' (photographic images made without a camera), and returned to America in 1940, teaching photography in Los Angeles. In 1961 he was awarded the gold medal at the Biennale of Photography in Venice. He published his autobiography, *Self Portrait*, in 1963.

RAY, Satyajit (1921–) Indian film director, born in Calcutta. A graduate of Santiniketan University, he worked as a commercial artist in an advertising agency while writing screenplays and looking for finances to make his first film. With government support he eventually completed *Pather Panchali* (1955), which together with *Aparajito* (1956) and *Apu Sansar* (1959), formed the Apu trilogy: an understated, affectionate portrait of social change in rural life. Later, he made documentaries and filmed tales from Indian folklore, such as *Devi* (1960), before revealing a strong interest in the complex political issues facing his country, tackling famine in *Distant Thunder* (*Ashanti Sanket*, 1973) and business ethics in *The Middle Man* (*Jana-Arnaya*, 1975). He has frequently composed the music for his films, and worked in Hindi for the first time with *The Chess Players* (*Shatranj Ke Khilari*, 1977). Poor health temporarily interrupted his career, but he returned to direction with *Ganashatru* (1989).

RAYLEIGH, John William Strutt, 3rd Baron (1842–1919) English physicist, born near Maldon in Essex. In 1865 he graduated from Trinity College, Cambridge, as senior wrangler and Smith's prizeman, and was elected a fellow (1866). He succeeded his father as third baron in 1873; was Cambridge professor of experimental physics (1879–84), and of natural philosophy at the Royal Institution (1888–1905); and president of the Royal Society (1905–08). He became chancellor of Cambridge University in 1908. He won the Nobel prize for physics in 1904. His work included valuable studies and research on vibratory motion, the theory of sound, and the wave theory of light. With Sir **William Ramsay** he was the discoverer of argon (1894). Interested in psychical problems, he was a member, and president in 1901, of the Society for Psychical Research. His writings include *The Theory of Sound* (1877–78; 2nd ed. 1894–96) and *Scientific Papers* (1899–1900).

RAYLEIGH, Robert John Strutt, 4th Baron (1875–1947) English physicist, son of **John Rayleigh**, born at Terling Place, Essex. He became professor of physics at the Imperial College of Science from 1908 to 1919. Notable for his work on rock radioactivity, he became a fellow of the Royal Society in 1905 and a Rumford medallist. His writings include two excellent biographies, one of his father, the other of Sir **Joseph John Thomson**.

RAYMOND, Alex (Alexander Gillespie) (1909–56) American strip cartoonist, born in New Rochelle, New York. After studying at the Grand Central School of Art, he was asked by King Features Syndicate to create three new strips, all of which started in January 1933: *Jungle Jim* and the science-fiction adventurer, *Flash Gordon*, every Sunday, and *Secret Agent X9* (scripted by **Dashiell Hammett**) every day. In 1946 he created a new daily strip, *Rip Kirby*, whose realism was far removed from Flash's fantasy.

RAYNOUARD, François Juste Marie (1761–1836) French poet and philologist, born in Brignoles in Provence. A prosperous Paris advocate, in 1791 he entered the legislative assembly. Later he joined the Girondins, and was imprisoned. His poems and tragedies were successful, and in 1807 he was elected to the Academy, of which he became permanent secretary in 1817. He was elected to the imperial legislative body in 1806 and 1811. After 1816 he wrote on the Provençal language and literature, notably his *Lexique Roman* (1838–44).

RĀZI See **RHAZES**

READ, Sir Herbert (1893–1968) English art historian, critic and poet, born near Kirby Moorside, Yorkshire. Educated in Halifax and at Leeds University, he became assistant keeper at the Victoria and Albert Museum in London (1922–31) and professor of fine art at Edinburgh University (1931–33); he was editor of the *Burlington Magazine* (1933–39), and held academic posts at Cambridge, Liverpool, London, and Harvard universities. As an art critic he revived interest in the 19th-century Romantic movement, and championed modern art movements in Britain. His broad interests extended to industrial design, and his *Art and Industry* (1936) was seminal in the development of this new discipline. He was director of the first major British design consultancy, the Design Research Unit. As a poet he wrote *Naked Warriors* (1919, based on his war experiences), and published his *Collected Poems* in 1946. His other publications include *English Prose Style* (1928), *The Meaning of Art* (1931), *Form in Modern Poetry* (1932), *Art Now* (1933), *Art and Society* (1936), *The Philosophy of Modern Art* (1952), and the autobiographical *Annals of Age and Experiences* (1940).

READE, Charles (1814–84) English novelist and playwright, born in Ipsden House, Oxfordshire, the youngest of eleven. After five harrowing years at Iffley, and six under two milder private tutors, in 1831 he gained a scholarship at Magdalen College, Oxford, and in 1835, having taken third-class honours, was duly elected to a lay fellowship. Next year he entered Lincoln's Inn, and in 1843 was called to the bar, but never practised. In 1850 he first tried to write for the stage, producing about thirteen dramas. Through one of these dramas he formed a platonic friendship with Mrs Seymour, a warmhearted actress, who from 1854 until her death (1879) kept house for him. His life after 1852 is a succession of plays by which he lost money, and novels that won profit and fame. These novels illustrate social injustice and cruelty in one form or another, and his writing is realistic and vivid. They include *Peg Woffington* (1852), *Hard Cash* (1863), *Foul Play* (1869, with **Dion Boucicault**), *A Terrible Temptation* (1871), and *A Woman-hater* (1877). His masterpiece was his long, historical novel of the 15th century, *The Cloister and the Hearth* (1861).

READING, Rufus Daniel Isaacs, 1st Marquess of (1860–1935) English lawyer and statesman, born in London. Educated in London, Brussels and Hanover, he entered parliament as Liberal member for Reading in 1904, and began to gain a reputation as an advocate. In 1910 he was appointed solicitor-general and later attorney-general, and as such in 1912 was the first Jew to become a member of the cabinet. Lord chief justice in 1913, during World War I he was special envoy to the USA in negotiating financial plans. He was British ambassador in Washington (1918–21), and thereafter viceroy of India until 1926. Created marquess on his return, he took charge of many business concerns, including the chairmanship of United Newspapers Ltd and the presidency of Imperial Chemical Industries. In 1931 he was for a short time foreign secretary in the National government.

REAGAN, Ronald Wilson (1911–) 40th president of the USA, and former film and television actor. Born in Tampico, Illinois, the son of an Irish-immigrant shoe salesman who was bankrupted during the Great Depression, Reagan graduated in economics from Eureka College, Illinois, and worked as a sportscaster in Des Moines, Iowa, before being signed as a film actor by Warner Brothers in 1937. He moved to Hollywood and, after making his début in *Love is in the Air* (1937), starred in 50 films, including *Bedtime for Bonzo* (1951) and *The Killers* (1964). He married the actress Jane Wyman (1914–) in 1940, but they divorced in 1948. During this period Reagan was a liberal Democrat and admirer of **Franklin Roosevelt**. He became interested in politics when serving as president of the Screen Actors' Guild between 1947 and 1952, and moved increasingly towards Republicanism, particularly following his marriage in 1952 to the affluent actress Nancy Davis (1923–), a devout Presbyterian. During the later 1950s he became a committed free-enterprise conservative and began promotional work for the General Electric Corporation, before officially joining the Republicans in 1962 and delivering a rousing television appeal for the party's 1964 presidential election candidate, Barry Goldwater. In 1966 Reagan was elected governor of California, having been persuaded to stand by businessmen friends, and remained in the post for eight years. He unsuccessfully contested the Republican presidential nomination in 1968 and 1976, being defeated by **Nixon** and **Ford** respectively. In 1980, however, after eventually capturing the party's nomination, he proceeded convincingly to defeat the incumbent **Jimmy Carter**. His campaign stressed the need to reduce taxes, deregulate the economy and build up and modernize America's defences to enable the country to negotiate abroad 'from a position of strength'. He survived an attempted assassination in 1981 and, despite initial serious economic problems between 1981 and 1983, secured re-election by a record margin in 1984. The successful anti-Marxist invasion of Grenada (October 1983), which served to generate a revival in national self-confidence, and his domestic programme of tax cuts and deficit financing, which brought about a rapid economic upturn between 1983 and 1986, were crucial factors behind this victory. During his second term, Reagan, the one-time arch 'hawk', despite advocating a new Strategic Defence ('Star Wars') Initiative of space-based military defence, became a convert to detente, holding four summit meetings with Soviet leader **Mikhail Gorbachev** between 1985 and 1988, and signing a treaty for the scrapping of intermediate nuclear forces. During 1986–87, however, the president's position was temporarily imperilled by the 'Iran-Contragate Scandal' concerning illegal arms-for-hostages deals with Iran by senior members of his administration and the 'laundering' of profits intended, equally illegally, to supply the anti-Marxist Contra guerrillas fighting in Nicaragua. As a result of the scandal, White House chief-of-staff **Donald Regan** and his National Security Adviser Rear-Admiral **John Poindexter** were forced to resign, but Reagan escaped surprisingly unscathed. Described as the 'great communicator' for his accomplished use of modern media, Reagan had a unique, populist rapport with 'mainstream America' and left office an immensely popular figure. His courage in bravely coping with a series of operations to remove cancerous polyps added to this appeal. However, his policies in Central America and with respect to domestic social programmes were less widely supported, and he left for his successor, **George Bush**, the serious problem of record budget and trade deficits.

RÉAMUR, René Antoine Ferchault de (1683–1757) French physicist, born in La Rochelle. In 1708 he became a member of the Academy of Sciences, and superintended an official *Description des arts et métiers*. He made researches in natural history, and in metallurgy and glassmaking. His thermometer (with spirit instead of mercury) has 80 degrees between the freezing- and boiling-points.

REBER, Grote (1911–) American radio engineer, born in Wheaton, Illinois. He was already an enthusiastic radio 'ham' when he began his studies at the Illinois Institute of Technology. Hearing of **Jansky**'s discovery of weak radio noise originating outside the solar system, he built the first radio telescope, 31 feet in diameter, in his own back yard, and for several years after its completion in 1938 he was the only radio astronomer in the world. He found that the radio map of the sky is quite different to that produced by conventional telescopes.

RÉCAMIER, Jeanne Françoise Julie Adélaïde, née **Bernard** (1777–1849) French beauty, born in Lyon. In 1792 she married a rich banker, Jacques Récamier, thrice her own age. Her salon was soon filled with the brightest wits of the day, but her temperament prevented any hint of scandal. When her husband was financially ruined she visited Madame de **Staël** at Coppet (1806), who featured her in her novel *Corinne* (1807). Here she met Prince August of Prussia. A marriage was arranged, provided M Récamier would consent to a divorce. He did, but Madame could not desert him in adversity. The most distinguished friend of her later years was **Chateaubriand**.

RECLUS, Jean Jacques Élisée (1830–1905) French geographer, born in Ste-Fois-la-Grande (Gironde). Educated at Montauban and Berlin, he left France after the *coup d'état* of 1851, and spent seven years in England, Ireland and America. He returned in 1858, and published *Voyage à la Sierra Nevada de Ste Marthe* (1861). For his share in the Paris Commune (1871) he was banished. In Switzerland he began his masterpiece, *Nouvelle Géographie universelle* (19 vols 1876–94). He also wrote a physical geography, *La Terre* (1867–68), and *Histoire d'une montagne* (1880).

RECORDE, Robert (c.1510–1558) English mathematician, born in Tenby. He studied at Oxford, and in 1545 took his MD at Cambridge. He practised medicine in London, and was in charge of mines in Ireland, but died in prison after losing a lawsuit brought against him by the Duke of Pembroke. He wrote the first English textbooks on elementary arithmetic and algebra, which became the standard works in Elizabethan England, including *The Ground of Artes* (1543) and *The Whetstone of Witte* (1557).

REDDING, Otis (1941–67) American soul singer, born in Dawson, Georgia. Although he never achieved a major American pop hit until after his death, he was one of the most influential soul singers of the late 1960s. As a high school student in Macon, Georgia, he was so impressed by the success of the local luminary **Little Richard** that he decided to become a full-time performer. His early work, including 'Shout Bamalama' (1960), was heavily influenced by Richard's frantic jump-blues style. Despite several minor hits he did not gain the widespread acceptance of American rock fans until an appearance at the Monterey pop festival in 1967, and he died in a plane crash in December of that year. The posthumously-released ballad 'Dock Of The Bay' became his first number one American hit early in 1968. Several of his songs, including 'I've Been Loving You Too Long' (1965), 'Try A Little Tenderness', and 'Mr Pitiful' (1965), are now regarded as classics of their style.

REDFIELD, Robert (1897–1958) American cultural anthropologist, born in Chicago. Educated at Chicago, he studied biology at Harvard but returned to Chicago to study law. Discontented with law practice and influenced by a trip to Mexico, he was encouraged by his father-in-law, the sociologist **Robert Ezra Park**, to take up anthropology. He went on to conduct field research in an Aztec community near Mexico City, on which he based his monograph *Tepoztlán, a Mexican Village* (1930). During the ensuing years, he continued to carry out field research in Central America, publishing *The Folk Culture of the Yucatán* in 1941. He became a leading theorist in the study of peasant societies, introducing the concept of the 'folk-urban continuum', and examining the process of urbanization in terms of an interplay between 'great and little traditions'. His major works include *The Primitive World and Its Transformations* (1953), *The Little Community* (1955) and *Peasant Society and Culture* (1956). He was professor of anthropology at Chicago from 1934 to 1958.

REDFORD, (Charles) Robert (1937–) American film actor and director, born in Santa Monica, California. After studying at the AADA, he landed small roles in television and on stage before making his film début in *War Hunt* (1962). The long-running Broadway comedy *Barefoot in the Park* (1963) established his leading-man potential, and cinema stardom was guaranteed by the 1967 film version of the play. Tall, blond and athletic, his good looks and image of integrity made him a popular sex symbol in films like *Butch Cassidy and the Sundance Kid* (1969, with **Paul Newman**), *The Candidate* (1972), *The Way We Were* (1973), *The Sting* (1973) and *Out of Africa* (1985). Later projects have reflected his interests in the American West, ecology and politics. In 1976 he produced and starred in *All The President's Men*. He has directed two films, the first of which, *Ordinary People* (1980) earned him an Academy Award.

REDGRAVE, Sir Michael Scudamore (1908–85) English stage and film actor, born in Bristol, the son of actor parents and grandfather. Educated at Clifton College, Bristol, and Magdalene College, Cambridge, he was first a modern-language teacher at Cranleigh school, then began his acting career with Liverpool Repertory Company (1934–36). His sensitive, intellectual approach to acting was most successful in classical roles, such as the title parts of *Hamlet* (Old Vic and Elsinore, 1949–50) and *Uncle Vanya* (Chichester and National Theatre, 1963–64). Modern plays in which he appeared include *Tiger at the Gates* (1955) and his own adaptation of *The Aspern Papers* (1959). He also acted in many films after his début in *The Lady Vanishes* (1938), including *The Way to the Stars* (1945) and the outstanding *The Browning Version* (1951). Knighted in 1959, he became director of the Yvonne Arnaud Theatre at Guildford in 1962. He married the actress Rachel Kempson (1910–) in 1935, and their three children are all in acting professions, **Vanessa** (1937–), Corin (1939–), and Lynn (1944–).

REDGRAVE, Richard (1804–88) English subject painter. Inspector-general of art schools from 1857, he was much involved with the Sir **Henry Cole** circle, and edited the *Journal of Design and Manufactures*. With his brother Samuel (1802–76) he wrote *A Century of English Painters* (1866), and *Dictionary of Artists of the English School* (1874).

REDGRAVE, Vanessa (1937–) English actress, born in London, the eldest daughter of Sir **Michael Redgrave** and actress Rachel Kempson. A student at the Central School of Speech and Drama (1954–57), she made her professional début at the Frinton Summer Theatre (1957) and her London stage début opposite her father in *A Touch of the Sun* (1958). A classical actress with the Royal Shakespeare Company, she made her film début in *Behind the Mask* (1958) and achieved stardom with her performance in *Morgan!* (1965) and *Blow-Up* (1966). Active in all media, she has proved herself one of the most distinguished performers of her generation. Her luminous grace, conviction and integrity have served a vast emotional spread of characterizations. On stage her work includes *The Prime of Miss Jean Brodie* (1966), *The Lady from the Sea* (1976–77) and *Orpheus Descending* (1988–89). She has received Academy Award nominations for *Morgan!*, *Isadora* (1968), *Mary, Queen of Scots* (1971) and *The Bostonians* (1984), winning an Oscar for *Julia* (1977). On television she won an Emmy for *Playing for Time* (1980). She is also noted for her espousal of various left-wing and humanitarian causes.

REDI, Francesco (1626–97) Italian physician and poet, born in Arezzo. He studied at Florence and Pisa, and became physician to the dukes of Tuscany. He wrote a book on animal parasites and proved by a series of experiments that maggots cannot form on meat which has been covered. He also wrote the dithyrambic *Bacco In Toscana* (1685).

REDMAN, Don (Donald Matthew) (1900–64) American saxophonist, arranger and bandleader, born in Piedmont, West Virginia, to a musical family. He was able to play a wide range of wind instruments while still at school, and after studies at music schools, including Boston Conservatory, he began to work professionally as a clarinettist, alto saxophonist and arranger. His first achievement was the creation in the mid 1920s of a distinctive style for the **Fletcher Henderson** Orchestra. Redman's principles of swing-style orchestration, heard in recordings by McKinney's Cotton Pickers and Redman's own band from 1931 to 1940, influenced nearly every important jazz composer of the era and are still respected in big band music.

REDMOND, John Edward (1856–1918) Irish politician, born in Dublin, the son of a Wexford MP. He was called to the bar at Gray's Inn in 1886, and entered parliament in 1881. A champion of Home Rule, he became chairman of the Nationalist party in 1900. He declined a seat in **Asquith**'s coalition ministry (1915), but supported the war, deplored the Irish rebellion, and opposed Sinn Fein.

REDON, Odilon (1840–1916) French painter and lithographer, born in Bordeaux, usually regarded as a forerunner of Surrealism because of his use of dream images in his work. He made many charcoal drawings and lithographs of extraordinary imaginative power, but after 1900 he painted, especially in pastel, pictures of flowers and portraits in intense colour. He was also a brilliant writer; his diaries (1867–1915) were published as *À soi-même* in 1922, and his *Letters* in 1923.

REDOUTÉ, Pierre Joseph (1759–1840) Belgian-born French botanical painter, born in St Hubert. Patronized by successive French courts from **Louis XV** to **Louis-Philippe**, and specializing in roses, he made countless prints for china, table mats, wall-pictures, etc. He published *Les Liliacées* (1802–15), a collection of lilies in 500 plates, and *Choix des plus belles fleurs* (1827–37), but his finest achievement is generally considered to be *Les Roses* (1817–21).

REDPATH, Anne (1895–1965) Scottish painter, born in Galashiels. She studied at Edinburgh Art College, and lived in France from 1919 to 1934. One of the most important modern Scottish artists, her paintings in oil and watercolour show great richness of colour and vigorous technique.

REDPATH, James (1833–91) Scottish-born American reformer and journalist, born in Berwick-on-Tweed. His family emigrated to Michigan in 1850. A vehement abolitionist reporter for **Horace Greeley**'s New York *Tribune*, he covered the Kansas conflict (1854–58), reported on his tour of Southern slavery in *The Roving Editor* (1858), defended **John Brown**'s Harper's Ferry Raid in his adulatory and inaccurate *The Public Life of Captain John Brown* (1860), published incendiary *Southern Notes for National Circulation* (1860), supported ex-slave migration to Haiti, encouraged **Walt Whitman** and **Louisa May Alcott**, covered General **W T Sherman**'s punitive march through Georgia and South Carolina, and was made superintendent of schools in captured Charleston, South Carolina, in 1865. He organized the Redpath Lecture Lyceum Bureau, covered Ku Klux Klan atrocities in Louisiana (1875), the disputed Hayes-Tilden election (1876–77) and the Irish Land War (1880–82), godfathering the term 'Boycott' which he publicized with influence on the American labor movement. He was assistant editor of the *North*

American Review in the 1880s, supported **Henry George** for mayor of New York City (1886) and helped **Jefferson Davis** prepare his memoirs. His *Talks About Ireland* (1881) convey something of his Land League work; although non-violent, his partisanship led *The Times* counsel at the **Parnell** Special Commission to label him 'advocate of crime'.

REDPATH, Jean (1937–) Scottish singer, born in Edinburgh. She became involved in folk music while studying at Edinburgh University. In 1961 she emigrated to the USA, where her outstanding ability, particularly as an interpreter of traditional Scots ballads and the songs of **Robert Burns**, was quickly recognized. She made her mark at academic level, too, and for several years lectured in music at Wesleyan University. In the mid 1970s she returned to live and perform in Scotland, but she continued to pay frequent visits to the USA, where she had already embarked on a project to record all of the songs of Robert Burns—numbering more than 300—to musical arrangements written by the American composer, Serge Hovey.

REED, Sir Carol (1906–76) English film director, born in Putney. Educated at King's School, Canterbury, he took to the stage (1924) and acted and produced for **Edgar Wallace** until 1930. He produced or directed such memorable films as *Kipps* (1941), *The Young Mr Pitt* (1942), *The Way Ahead* (1944), the Allied War Documentary *The True Glory* (1945), and *The Fallen Idol* (1948), but is best remembered for his Cannes Film Festival prizewinning version of **Graham Greene**'s novel, *The Third Man* (1949), depicting the sinister underworld of postwar, partitioned Vienna. *Outcasts of the Islands* (1952), based on a **Conrad** novel, was another triumph of location work in the East, and *Our Man in Havana* (1959) marked a return to his post-war brilliance. He won an Academy Award for *Oliver!* (1968).

REED, Isaac (1742–1807) English editor, born in London. A conveyancer by profession, he developed a considerable interest in archaeology and literature. A meticulous commentator and editor, he is best known for his revisions of Dr **Johnson**'s and **George Stevens**'s 'variorum' edition of **Shakespeare**.

REED, Lou, real name **Louis Firbank** (1944–) American rock singer, guitarist and songwriter, born in Long Island, New York. He initially gained fame as a member of The Velvet Underground, a band which was closely associated with **Andy Warhol** and his organization, The Factory, and whose importance and influence was not fully realized until after it had split up in 1970. The Velvet Underground's albums include *The Velvet Underground & Nico* (1967), *White Light, White Heat* (1968) and *The Velvet Underground* (1969). After the group split up he moved to England to record *Lou Reed* (1972). His 1973 album, *Transformer*, included 'Walk On The Wild Side', a paean to transsexuality which somehow bypassed radio censorship to become the first 'top ten' hit of his career. Subsequent albums have included *Rock 'n' Roll Animal* (1974), *Street Hassle* (1978) and *New Sensations* (1984).

REED, Talbot Baines (1852–93) English author of books for boys, born in London, the son of Sir Charles Reed (1819–81), chairman of the London School Board. He became head of his father's firm of typefounders, and wrote books on the history of printing (such as *History of the Old English Letter-foundries* (1887). His robust, moral, but entertaining school stories first appeared in the *Boy's Own Paper*. They include *The Fifth Form at St Dominic's* (1881), *The Master of the Shell* (1887), and *Cockhouse at Fellsgarth* (1891).

REED, Walter (1851–1902) American army surgeon, born in Belroi, Virginia. He entered the medical corps in 1875, and was appointed professor of bacteriology in the Army Medical College, Washington, in 1893. Investigations carried out by him in 1900 proved that transmission of yellow fever was by mosquitoes, and his researches led to the eventual eradication of this disease from Cuba.

REES, Lloyd Frederick (1895–1988) Australian artist, born in Yeronga, Queensland. Influenced by the pen drawings of **Joseph Pennell**, he worked in **Sydney Ure Smith**'s studio in Sydney from 1917 and then travelled in Europe for two years. His early drawings, meticulous in draughtsmanship and romantic in style, were etched or lithographed, and in 1931 Rees held his first exhibition, in Sydney. He turned to oils, mainly landscapes of the south coast of New South Wales, and in 1942 the Art Gallery of New South Wales held a retrospective exhibition of his work, with another in 1969. Rees made four more journeys to Europe between 1952 and 1973, and the influence of the Italian landscape lightened the tone of his oils. His later works were more lightly covered, almost abstract, landscapes, capturing the pearly light of Sydney and of Tasmania where he spent his last years.

REES-MOGG, William, Baron (1928–) English journalist, born in Bristol. Educated at Charterhouse and Balliol College, Oxford, he joined *The Financial Times* in 1952, becoming chief leader writer and assistant editor. In 1960 he moved to *The Sunday Times*, as city editor, and became deputy editor in 1964. In 1967 he assumed the editorship of *The Times*, which he held for 14 years. By this time he had become an accepted establishment figure, on the boards of several companies, and, having been vice-chairman of the BBC and chairman of the Arts Council, in 1988 he was appointed to head the new, controversial, Broadcasting Standards Council.

REEVE, Clara (1729–1807) English novelist of the 'Gothic' school, born in Ipswich, the daughter of the rector of Freston. She translated **John Barclay**'s *Argenis* (1772), and wrote *The Champion of Virtue, a Gothic Story* (1777), renamed *The Old English Baron*, which was avowedly an imitation of **Walpole**'s *The Castle of Otranto*. She wrote four other novels and *The Progress of Romance* (1785).

REGAN, Donald Thomas (1918–) American politician, born in Cambridge, Massachusetts, the son of a Roman Catholic Irish-immigrant railway security guard. He studied English and economics at Harvard, where he was a classmate of **John F Kennedy**. He switched allegiance from the Democrats to the Republicans in 1940, and during World War II distinguished himself by becoming the youngest ever US Marine line-major. After the war he joined Merrill Lynch as a sales trainee and rose to become its president in 1968, building the company into America's largest securities brokerage corporation. Attracted by his strong belief in supply-side free-market economics, President **Reagan** appointed him Treasury secretary in 1981. He proceeded to push through radical tax-cutting legislation, but left a growing budget deficit. He became White House chief-of-staff in January 1985, but was forced to resign two years later as a result of criticisms of his role in the 1985–86 'Irangate Affair'.

REGENER, Erich (1881–1955) German physicist, professor of physics at Berlin and Stuttgart. He was dismissed for political reasons in 1937, but reinstated in 1946. He is known for his pioneering work on cosmic rays, and for his researches on the stratosphere.

REGER, Max (1873–1916) German composer, born in Brand, Bavaria. He taught music at Wiesbaden and Munich, became director of music at Leipzig University (1907), and professor (1908). He composed organ music, piano concertos, choral works and songs.

REGIOMONTANUS (1436–76) the name given to **Johannes Müller**, German mathematician and astronomer, from his Franconian birthplace, Königsberg (*Mons Regius*). He studied at Vienna, and in 1461 accompanied Cardinal **Bessarion** to Italy to learn Greek. In 1471 he settled in Nuremberg, where the patrician Bernhard Walther subsidized him. The two laboured at the *Alphonsine Tables*, and published *Ephemerides 1475–1506* (1473), which **Christopher Columbus** made good use of. He established the study of algebra and trigonometry in Germany, and wrote on waterworks, burning-glasses, weights and measures, the quadrature of the circle, etc. He was summoned to Rome in 1474 by Pope **Sixtus IV** to help to reform the calendar, and died there.

REGNARD, Jean François (1655–1709) French comic dramatist, born in Paris, the son of a rich shopkeeper. He found himself at the age of 20 the master of a considerable fortune, and set out on his travels. In his autobiographical romance, *La Provençale*, he tells of his and his Provençal mistress's capture and sale as slaves by Algerian corsairs, their bondage in Constantinople, and their ransom. After wanderings as far as Lapland, he found his vocation in the success of *Le Divorce* at the Théâtre-Italien in 1688. *Le Joueur* (1696), a hit at the Théâtre-Français, was followed by *Le Distrait* (1697), *Le Retour imprévu* (1700), *Les Folies amoureuses* (1704), and his masterpiece, *Le Légataire universel* (1708).

REGNAULT, Alexandre Georges Henri (1843–71) French painter of mythological, Spanish and Moorish subjects, born in Paris, son of **Henri Victor Regnault**. He won the Prix de Rome in 1866. In 1869 he painted his equestrian portrait of **Prim**, and in 1870 his *Salome* and *Moorish Execution*. He was killed in the Franco-Prussian war .

REGNAULT, Henri Victor (1810–78) French chemist and physicist, born in Aix-la-Chapelle. A shop assistant in Paris and a professor at Lyon, in 1840 he was recalled to Paris as a member of the Academy of Sciences. Having filled chairs in the École Polytechnique and the Collège de France, he became in 1854 director of the Sèvres porcelain factory where he investigated gases, latent heat, steam-engines, and published a *Cours élémentaire de chimie* (14th ed 1871).

RÉGNIER, Henri François Joseph de (1864–1936) French Symbolist poet, novelist and critic, born in Honfleur. He studied law in Paris, and then turned to letters. His *Poèmes anciens et romanesques* (1890) revealed him as a Symbolist, though later he returned to more traditional versification. In both poetry and prose his style and mood were admirably suited to evocation of the past, and expressive of a melancholy disillusionment induced by the passage of time. Poetical works include *La Sandale ailée* (1906), *Vestigia flammae* (1921) and *Flamma tenax* (1928). His novels were mainly concerned with France and Italy in the 17th and 18th centuries. Two of these are *La Double Maîtresse* (1900) and *Le Bon Plaisir* (1902).

RÉGNIER, Mathurin (1573–1613) French satirist, born in Chartres. After taking orders he grew up dissipated and idle, obtained a canonry at Chartres, and enjoyed the favour of **Henri IV**. His whole work hardly exceeds 7000 lines—16 satires, three epistles, five elegies, and some odes, songs and epigrams, yet it places him high among French poets. He is best at satires, admirably polished, but vigorous and original and giving a lively picture of the Paris of the day.

REGULUS, or **Rule, St** (4th century) according to legend a monk of Constantinople or bishop of Patras, who in 347 came to Muckross or Kilrimont (afterwards St Andrews), bringing relics of St **Andrew** from the East. **William Skene** suggested his possible identification with an Irish St Riagail of the 6th century.

REGULUS, Marcus Atilius (d.c.250 BC) Roman statesman, obtained a triumph as Roman consul in 267 BC. Consul again (256), he defeated the Carthaginian fleet, then landed in Africa, and, although at first victorious, suffered a total defeat and was taken prisoner (255). He remained five years in captivity, until, reverses inducing the Carthaginians to sue for peace, he was released on parole and sent to Rome with the Punic envoys. He successfully dissuaded the senate from agreeing to their proposals, then, according to legend, returned to Carthage, and was put to death with horrible tortures.

REHNQUIST, William (1924–) American jurist, born in Milwaukee, Wisconsin. He studied political science at Stanford and Harvard and law at the Stanford Law School. After securing his LLB in 1952 he practised law in Phoenix, Arizona, and became active in the Republican party. In 1969 he was appointed head of the Office of Legal Counsel in the justice department by President **Nixon**, and in this post supported such controversial measures as pre-trial detention and wiretapping. Impressed with this approach, Nixon appointed him associate justice of the Supreme Court in 1972. He duly emerged as the Court's most conservative member and in 1986 was appointed chief justice. Initially, the new 'Rehnquist Court' differed little from its predecessor, but by 1989 a 'new right' majority had been established by President **Reagan** and a series of conservative rulings on abortion, affirmative action and capital punishment was framed.

REICH, Ferdinand (1799–1882) German physicist. Professor at the Freiberg School of Mines, he was the co-discoverer with **Hieronymous Richter** of the element indium (1863).

REICH, Steve (1936–) American composer, born in New York. Strongly influenced by his training in drumming, his love of early **Stravinsky**, the pulse of jazz and the rhythms of African and Balinese music, he has evolved a style of vigorous tonality, hypnotic contrapuntal patterns, and percussive virtuosity. He writes for a kaleidoscopic variety of vocal and instrumental forces and timbres, including taped and electronic effects.

REICH, Wilhelm (1897–1957) Austrian psychoanalyst. He became a practising psychoanalyst while still a medical student in Vienna, and apparently had become preoccupied with sex at a very early age. He became convinced of the necessity of regular orgasms for the mental health of both men and women, and much of his writing reflects this conviction (*The Function of the Orgasm*, 1927, trans 1942). One of his most notorious eccentricities was the invention of the 'orgone accumulator', which purported to collect massless particles and transmit them to the user, to the alleged benefit of his or her sex life and emotional health. He attempted a synthesis of psychoanalysis with Marxism, arguing that abolition of the bourgeois family would eliminate the oedipal complex and also allow fuller sexual satisfaction in adults. He was expelled from the German Communist party in 1933 and the International Psychoanalytical Association in 1934, left Germany for Scandinavia in 1933 and emigrated to the USA in 1939. He established an Orgone Institute, but died in gaol after being prosecuted for promoting a fraudulent treatment. During the sexual revolution of the 1960s, he became something of a cult figure in the USA. His other works included *Character Analysis* (1933, trans 1945) and *The Sexual Revolution* (1936-45).

REICHA, Antonín (1770–1836) Czech composer, teacher, and music theorist, born in Prague. From 1785 he played flute with the Electoral orchestra at Bonn in which **Beethoven** played; from 1794 to 1799 he taught piano in Hamburg; then proceeded to Paris hoping for operatic success. He failed to achieve this, but had two symphonies performed. From 1801 to 1808 he lived in Vienna, seeing much of his friends Beethoven and **Haydn**, and taking lessons from **Salieri**. Subsequently he lived in Paris, where his pupils included **Liszt**, **Berlioz**, **Franck** and **Gounod**. His use of counterpoint and instrumental sonority was highly original as seen in his 36 *Fugues* (dedicated to Haydn) and in his use of timpani chords. His 24 quintets for woodwind have remained popular.

REICHENBACH, Georg Friedrich von (1772–1826) German engineer, instrument-maker and inventor, born in Durlach near Karlsruhe. He graduated from the School of Army Engineers in Mannheim, and, on the initiative of Benjamin Thompson, Count **Rumford**, spent the next two years in England studying the latest advances in engineering and scientific instrument-making with such eminent men as **Watt** and **Ramsden**. Returning to Germany, he designed improved muskets and a rifled cannon for the Bavarian army, and in 1804 established a firm in Munich for the manufacture of precision instruments which became famous among astronomers and surveyors for their high quality. In his later years he turned to hydraulic engineering and built a pipeline 67 miles long, in the course of which he used eleven hydraulic rams to pump salt water to a height of 1200 feet.

REICHENBACH, Hans (1891–1953) German philosopher of science, born in Hamburg. He became professor of philosophy at Berlin (1926–33), Istanbul (1933–38) and Los Angeles (from 1938). He was an early associate of the Vienna School of logical positivists, and with **Rudolph Carnap** founded the journal *Erkenntnis* in 1930 (which lasted till 1938, then reappeared in 1975 in the USA, in English). He made an important technical contribution to probability theory in which two truth tables are replaced by the multivalued concept 'weight', and wrote widely on logic and the philosophical bases of science in such works as *Philosophie der Raum-Zeit-Lehre* (1927–28), *Elements of Symbolic Logic* (1947) and *The Rise of Scientific Philosophy* (1951).

REICHENBACH, Karl, Baron von (1788–1869) German natural philosopher and industrialist, born in Stuttgart. He discovered paraffin (1830) and creosote (1833) and, after studying animal magnetism, discovered, as he thought, a new force, which he called Od, intermediate between electricity, magnetism, heat and light, and recognizable only by the nerves of sensitive persons. He wrote on the geology of Moravia, on magnetism, and several works on 'odic force' (1852–58).

REICHSTADT, Duke of See **NAPOLEON II**

REICHSTEIN, Tadeusz (1897–) Polish-born Swiss chemist. He has done outstanding work on the adrenal hormones and received (with **Edward Kendall** and **Philip Hench**) the Nobel prize for physiology or medicine in 1950.

REID, Beryl (1920–) English comedienne and actress, born in Hereford. She made her first stage appearance in a concert party at the Floral Hall, Bridlington, in 1936. In the ensuing years she built a reputation as a variety entertainer and soubrette-cum-impressionist. The radio series *Educating Archie* (1952–56) established the comic character of schoolgirl Monica, and her other creations include Midlands Teddy girl Marlene. A veteran of numerous revues and pantomimes, she made her film début in *Spare a Copper* (1940), and her extensive list of television roles includes such series as *The Most Likely Girl* (1957), *Man o' Brass* (1964) and *The Secret Diary of Adrian Mole* (1985). *The Killing of Sister George* (1965) established her as a serious actress and she won a Tony award for its Broadway production (1966), repeating her role on film (1968). In demand for eccentric character roles and malaprops, her films include *Star!* (1968) and *Entertaining Mr. Sloane* (1969). Her stage work encompasses *Blithe Spirit* (1970), *Spring Awakening* (1974), *Born in the Gardens* (1979–80) and *Gigi* (1985). On television she received a BAFTA for *Smiley's People* (1982). Her autobiography, *So Much Love*, written with Eric Braun, appeared in 1984.

REID, Sir George Houstoun (1845–1918) Scottish-born Australian politician and statesman, born in Johnstone, Renfrew. He arrived in Melbourne with his parents in 1852, and in 1858 moved to Sydney, where he obtained a post with the colonial treasury. He studied law, and in 1878 became secretary to the attorney-general of New South Wales. In 1880 he was elected to the Legislative Assembly of NSW, and in 1891 succeeded Sir **Henry Parkes** as Leader of the New South Wales opposition, becoming premier of the state from 1894 to 1899. He moved to the first federal parliament in 1901, still representing his old constituency, and became leader of the opposition in the House of Representatives. He became prime minister of Australia for a short time in 1904, but was defeated in 1905 and retired from politics in 1908. In 1909 he was appointed Australia's first high commissioner to London, a post which he held with distinction until the end of his term in 1916. He then took up the seat for Hanover Square in the British House of Commons, which he held until his death.

REID, James Scott Cumberland, Lord, of Drem (1890–1975) Scottish judge, born in Drem, East Lothian. Educated at The Edinburgh Academy, Jesus College, Cambridge, and Edinburgh University, he served in World War I, and practised at the Scottish bar. He became dean of the Faculty of Advocates (1945–48). An MP from 1931 to 1935 and 1937 to 1948, he was solicitor-general for Scotland (1936–41) and Lord Advocate (1941–48). He then sat as a lord of appeal in ordinary (1948–75), and won a high reputation for accurate thought, precise reasoning and careful application of principle.

REID, or **Robertson, John** (1721–1807) Scottish soldier and musician, of Perthshire stock. He entered the army in 1745 and rose to be general. A flute-player and composer, he left £50000 to found a chair of music at Edinburgh University.

REID, John Richard (1928–) New Zealand cricketer, born in Auckland. He assumed the mantle of **Bert Sutcliffe** and for almost 15 years was the batting lynchpin in a weak New Zealand Test side. Six of his 39 first-class centuries were made in Tests, for which he was selected 58 times. He took part in four record Test stands for New Zealand, including the highest-ever partnership for the third wicket: 222 unbroken with Bert Sutcliffe against India at Delhi in 1955–56.

REID, Robert Paul (1934–) Scottish industrial executive. He joined Shell when he left St Andrews University in 1956, and worked in overseas subsidiaries until 1983, when he returned to the UK. He was appointed chairman and chief executive of Shell UK in 1985. In 1988, as chairman of the British Institute of Management, he took a leading role in the reshaping of management education in the UK. In 1990 he was appointed chairman of British Rail.

REID, Sir Robert Threshie See **LOREBURN**

REID, Thomas (1710–96) Scottish philosopher, born in Strachan, Kincardineshire. Educated at Aberdeen, he became librarian of Marischal College there in 1733, and in 1737 minister of New Machar in Aberdeenshire. He became professor of philosophy at Aberdeen in 1751, and succeeded **Adam Smith** in the chair of moral philosophy at Glasgow from 1764 to 1780. He was leader of the group known as the 'commonsense' or later the 'Scottish' school, which rejected **Hume**'s scepticism with its assumption that the immediate objects of knowledge are ideas in the mind and its conclusion that we cannot prove the existence of anything outside the mind or even the existence of mind itself. Reid reasserted the real existence of external objects and mind by denying that simple 'ideas' are our primary data; it is rather a natural and original part of experience to make a complex judgment which apprehends these ideas in the context of mind and an objective order. His main publications are *Inquiry into the Human Mind on the Principles of Common Sense* (1764), *Essays on the Intellectual Powers of Man* (1785) and *Essays on the Active Powers of Man* (1788).

REID, Thomas Mayne (1818–83) Irish writer of boys' stories, born in Ballyroney, County Down. In 1840 he emigrated to New Orleans, settled as a journalist in Philadelphia (1843), and served in the US army during the Mexican war (1847), where he was severely wounded. Returning to Britain in 1849, he settled down to a literary life in London. His vigorous style and hairbreadth escapes delighted his readers. Among his books, many of which were popular in translation in Poland and Russia, were *The Rifle Rangers* (1850), *Scalp Hunters* (1851), *Boy Hunters* (1853), *War Trail* (1857), *Boy Tar* (1859), and *Headless Horseman* (1866). He went back to New York in 1867 and founded the *Onward Magazine*, but returned to England in 1870.

REID, Sir Thomas Wemyss (1842–1905) Scottish journalist and biographer, born in Newcastle. He edited the *Leeds Mercury* (1870–87), then was manager at Messrs Cassell, and from 1890 to 1899 editor of the *Speaker*. He wrote lives of **Charlotte Brontë** and Lord **Houghton**, a book about Tunis, and several novels.

REID, Sir William (1791–1858) Scottish meteorologist, soldier and administrator, a writer on winds and storms, born in Kinglassie, Fife. He served with high distinction in the Peninsular War, and was governor of Bermuda, the Windward Islands and Malta.

REIMARUS, Hermann Samuel (1694–1768) German theologian and philosopher, born in Hamburg, where he became a teacher of oriental languages from 1727. His first book was published quite late in life, at the age of 60, and was a moderate defence of natural religion entitled *Abhandlungen von den vornehmsten Wahrheiten der natürlichen Religion* (1754). But he went on to write a far more radical attack on revelation, a series of rationalistic essays rejecting altogether the accounts of miracles in the Gospels and the supernatural origins of Christianity. These were published posthumously, and only in part, by **Gotthold Lessing**, who claimed they were fragments from an anonymous manuscript found in the Wolfenbüttel Library, Brunswick, where Lessing was librarian. The work was described as *Wolfenbüttler Fragmente eines Ungenannten* (1774–77); it caused something of a sensation on publication, and was very influential in later German theology.

REINHARDT, Ad (Adolf Frederick) (1913–67) American painter and critic, born in Buffalo, New York. He studied at the National Academy of Design, New York (1936), and the following year joined the American Abstract Artists, an avant-garde association which promoted hard-edge abstraction. Between 1946 and 1950 he was influenced by oriental art. His final style was typified by five-foot square canvases divided into nine equal squares, each painted black.

REINHARDT, Django (Jean Baptiste) (1910–53) Belgian guitarist, born in Liverchies to a family of gipsy entertainers, who became one of the first European jazz virtuosi. Despite losing the use of two fingers of his left hand in a caravan fire, he developed an outstanding technique. After working as a cabaret player in Paris cafés, he joined violinist **Stephane Grappelli** in 1934 to form the Quintette du Hot Club de France, which established a distinctive French jazz style. In 1946, he joined the **Duke Ellington** Orchestra for an American tour, changing from acoustic to electric guitar; but although this project was not a success, he became a powerful influence among swing-style guitarists.

REINHARDT, Max (1873–1943) Austrian theatre manager, born in Baden near Vienna. He did much to reorganize the art and technique of production. His most notable success was *The Miracle* in London in 1911. Other productions were *Everyman* and *Faust* for the Salzburg festivals of 1920 and subsequent years. He left Germany for the USA in 1933.

REISNER, George Andrew (1867–1942) American Egyptologist, born in Indianapolis. A Harvard law graduate, he studied Egyptology in Berlin, returning to Harvard, first as assistant professor (1905–14), and later (1914–42) as professor, of Egyptology. His reputation for meticulous excavation was established early when he assumed leadership of California University's expedition to explore the burial grounds of Koptos (1899–1905). Subsequently he directed for the Egyptian government the important campaign to survey Nubian monuments threatened by the raising of the first Aswan dam (1907–09), returning (1916–23) to explore the pyramids of Meroe and Napata. In Egypt itself, he excavated the valley temple and pyramid of Mycerinus at Giza and many private or mastaba tombs. Outstanding was the discovery in 1925 of the tomb of Queen Hetepheres, mother of **Cheops**, the only major find of jewellery and furniture surviving from the Old Kingdom.

REITH, John Charles Walsham, 1st Baron Reith of Stonehaven (1889–1971) Scottish engineer and pioneer of broadcasting, born in Stonehaven. Educated at Glasgow Academy and Gresham's School, Holt, he served an engineering apprenticeship in Glasgow. Later entering the field of radio communication, he became the first general manager of the British Broadcasting Corporation in 1922 and its director-general from 1927 to 1938. He was MP for Southampton in 1940, and minister of works and buildings from 1940 to 1942. He was chairman of the Commonwealth Telecommunications Board from 1946 to 1950. He wrote the autobiographical *Into the Wind* (1949) and *Wearing Spurs* (1966). The BBC Reith Lectures on radio were instituted in 1948 in honour of his influence on broadcasting.

REITZ, Dana (1948–) American dancer and choreographer, born in New York. She spent part of her teenage years in Japan, prior to studying dance theatre at the University of Michigan, Ann Arbor. Graduating in 1970, she moved to New York to study classical ballet and t'ai chi chuan, and to study with **Merce Cunningham**. Briefly a member of **Twyla Tharp** and **Laura**

Dean's companies, she began choreographing in 1973. Her work is noted for its quiet energy and gestural detail. Although she is best known as a soloist, she has collaborated with other dancers, musicians and lighting designers. She made a significant contribution to **Robert Wilson** and **Philip Glass**'s opera *Einstein on the Beach* (1976).

REIZENSTEIN, Franz (1911–68) German composer and pianist. He studied under **Paul Hindemith** and in 1934 moved to England, where he was a pupil of **Vaughan Williams**. Among his compositions are cello, piano and violin concertos, the cantata *Voices by Night*, two radio operas, and chamber and piano music.

RÉJANE, Gabrielle (1856–1920) French actress, born in Paris. She was noted for her playing of such parts as Zaza and Madame Sans-Gêne. Equally gifted in both tragic and comic roles, she was regarded in France almost as highly as **Sarah Bernhardt**, and was also popular in England and the USA.

REMAK, Robert (1815–65) German physician and pioneer in electrotherapy, born in Posen. He studied pathology and embryology, and discovered the 'fibres of Remak' (1830), and the nerve cells in the heart called Remak's ganglia (1844).

REMARQUE, Erich Maria (1898–1970) German novelist, born in Osnabrück. He served in World War I, and published his famous war novel, *All Quiet on the Western Front*, in 1929. He lived in Switzerland from 1929 to 1939, and published *The Road Back* (1931). In 1939 he emigrated to the USA, and became a naturalized citizen. There he wrote *Flotsam* (1941), *Arch of Triumph* (1946), *The Black Obelisk* (1957) and *The Night in Lisbon* (1962).

REMBRANDT, properly **Rembrandt Harmensz van Rijn** (1606–69) Dutch painter, born in Leiden, the son of a prosperous miller. The greatest northern European painter of his age, he is commonly regarded as one of the greatest artists of all time. After early training he moved to Amsterdam, where he worked under Pieter Lastman before returning to his home town and setting up independently. He quickly achieved a high reputation as a portrait painter, and excelled at group portraits of professional burghers after his return to Amsterdam in 1631. Married to Saskia van Ulenburgh, Rembrandt prospered until her death in 1642. In that year he produced his masterpiece, *The Night Watch*, a dramatically lit, dynamically composed group portrait of a local militia band. In spite of a second marriage and increasing fame, Rembrandt's personal financial situation declined over the next 25 years, and he died a pauper. Apart from group portraits, his greatest achievements were his portraits and superb series of self-portraits, and his etchings—mostly of biblical subjects and ink-and-wash drawings. Rembrandt virtually re-invented all these media, bringing to them an original technical mastery, a sense of drama created by a subtle use of chiaroscuro and his own overwhelming sense of humanity. Although working to satisfy the demands of patrons in prosperous 17th-century Holland, Rembrandt used the various genres as vehicles by which to express his own personality. This qualifies him as the first truly 'modern' artist. His self-portraits are the first psychological studies in the history of art. In spite of the eclipse his reputation suffered after his death, his genius was rediscovered in the 19th century and his work influenced Realists like **Courbet**. Even **Van Gogh** copied his works. He has been much forged. Recently, many works previously attributed to him have been labelled as copies or works of pupils.

REMÉNYI See **BRAHMS, Johannes**

REMIGIUS, St See **REMY**

REMINGTON, Philo (1816–89) American inventor, born in Litchfield, New York, the son of the inventor, Eliphalet Remington (1793–1863). He entered his father's small-arms factory, and for 25 years superintended the mechanical department. As president of the company from 1860, he perfected the Remington breech-loading rifle.

REMIZOV, Alexei Mikhailovich (1877–1957) Russian writer, born in Moscow. He lived in St Petersburg, but left Russia at the Revolution, going first to Berlin and finally settling in Paris. His writing is full of national pride and a deep love of old Russian traditions and folklore; it contains realism, fantasy and humour. His main works are the novels, *The Pond*, *The Clock*, *Fifth Pestilence* and *Sisters of the Cross*, legends, plays and short stories.

RÉMUSAT, Charles François Marie, Comte de (1797–1875) French aristocrat, born in Paris, son of the Comte de Rémusat (1762–1823) who was chamberlain to **Napoleon**. He early developed liberal ideas, and took to journalism. He signed the journalists' protest which brought about the July Revolution (1830), was elected deputy for Toulouse, in 1836 became under-secretary of state for the interior and in 1840 minister of the interior. Exiled after the *coup d'état* of 1848, he devoted himself to literary and philosophical studies, until, in 1871, **Thiers** called him to the portfolio of foreign affairs, which he retained until 1873. Among his writings are *Essais de philosophie* (1842); *Abélard* (1845); *L'Angleterre au XVIII*ᵉ siècle (1856); studies on *St Anselm* (1853), *Bacon* (1857), *Channing* (1857), *John Wesley* (1870) and *Lord Herbert of Cherbury* (1874); *Histoire de la philosophie en Angleterre de Bacon à Locke* (1875); and two philosophical dramas, *Abélard* (1877) and *Le Saint Barthélemy* (1878).

RÉMUSAT, Jean Pierre Abel (1788–1832) French physician and Sinologist, born in Paris. He took his diploma in medicine in 1813, but in 1811 had published an essay on Chinese literature. In 1814 he was made professor of Chinese in the Collège de France. Among his numerous works are one on the Tartar tongues (1820) and his great *Grammaire chinoise* (1822). He wrote also on Chinese writing (1827), medicine, topography and history, and *Mélanges* (1843). In 1822 he founded the Société Asiatique, and in 1824 became curator of the oriental department in the Bibliothèque Royale.

REMY, St (c.438–533) Frankish prelate, and bishop of Reims. According to **Gregory of Tours** he baptized **Clovis**, king of the Franks, in the Christian faith. He was known as the Apostle of the Franks.

RENAN, (Joseph) Ernest (1823–92) French philologist and historian, born in Tréguier in Brittany. Trained for the church, he abandoned traditional faith after studying Hebrew and Greek Biblical criticism. In 1850 he started work at the Bibliothèque Nationale, and published *Averroès et l'Averroïsme* (1852), *Histoire générale des langues sémitiques* (1854), and *Études d'histoire religieuse* (1856). His appointment as professor of Hebrew at the Collège de France in 1861 was not confirmed (until 1870) by the clerical party, especially after the appearance of his controversial *La Vie de Jésus* (1863), which undermined the supernatural aspects of **Christ**'s life and his teachings. It was the first of a monumental series on the history of the origins of Christianity, which also included books on the Apostles (1866), St **Paul** (1869) and **Marcus Aurelius** (1882). Among his other works were books on Job (1858) and Ecclesiastes (1882), and an *Histoire du peuple d'Israël* (1887–94).

RENAUDOT, Théophraste (1586–1653) French physician and journalist, founder of the first French newspaper. Born in Loudoun, he settled in Paris in 1624 and was physician to the king. Appointed commissary general for the poor, he started an information agency for them, which in 1631 became a regular journal, *Gazette de France*. He opened a free medical clinic in 1635, with free dispensaries, and also opened the first pawnshop, in 1637.

RENDEL, Stuart, 1st Baron (1834–1913) English politician and industrialist, born in Plymouth. He trained as a barrister, but became an engineer with an interest in armaments. Elected Liberal MP for Montgomeryshire (1880–94) he promoted the reform of Welsh education and the disestablishment of the Welsh church. He was a generous supporter of the University College of Wales, Aberystwyth, and helped to found the National Library of Wales.

RENÉ, France-Albert (1935–) Seychelles politician. Educated in the Seychelles, Switzerland and Britain, at King's College, London, he was called to the bar in 1957. He returned to the Seychelles and threw himself into politics, establishing the Seychelles People's United party (SPUP), a socialist grouping, in 1964. In 1970 he pressed for full independence for the Seychelles, while his contemporary, James Mancham of the Seychelles Democratic party (SDP), favoured integration with the United Kingdom. Despite their differences the two men agreed to form a coalition and, when independence was achieved in 1976, Mancham became president and René prime minister. In 1977, however, while Mancham was abroad, René staged a *coup*, made himself president and created a one-party state. Since then he has followed a non-nuclear policy of non-alignment and resisted several attempts to remove him.

RENE I, 'the Good' (1409–80) Duke of Anjou, Count of Provence and Piedmont, known as the 'Last of the Troubadours'. Having failed in his efforts (1438-42) to make good his claim to the crown of Naples, he married his daughter Margaret to **Henry VI** of England (1445), and ultimately devoted himself to Provençal poetry and agriculture at Aix.

RENFREW, (Andrew) Colin (1937–) English archaeologist, born in Stockton-on-Tees, County Durham. He was educated at St Albans School and St John's College, Cambridge. Inspired by the writings of **Gordon Childe**, his work has ranged widely, but exhibits a central preoccupation with the nature of cultural change in prehistory. The origin, development, and interaction of such fundamental features of European civilization as language, agriculture, urbanism, metallurgy, trade, and social hierarchy are constant themes, pursued in such books as *Before Civilization* (1973) and *Archaeology and Language* (1987). He has excavated in Greece (1964–76) and on Orkney (1972–74), notably at the chambered tomb of Quanterness. Since 1981 he has been professor of archaeology at Cambridge, and master of Jesus College, Cambridge, since 1986. His other major publications include *The Emergence of Civilization* (1972), *The Archaeology of Cult* (1985) and *Approaches to Social Archaeology* (1986). He has also contributed to several pioneering archaeological programmes on BBC television, notably in the *Chronicle* series.

RENI, GUIDO (1575–1642) Italian painter, born near Bologna. He studied under **Calvaert** and **Ludovico Carracci**, and went to Rome in 1599 and again in 1605. *Aurora and the Hours* there is usually regarded as his masterpiece. Because of a quarrel with Cardinal Spinola regarding an altarpiece for St Peter's he left Rome and settled in Bologna, where he died. He was a prolific painter, and his works are in all the chief European galleries. He also produced some vigorous etchings.

RENIER, Gustaaf Johannes (1892–1962) Dutch historian, born in Flushing. After study in Louvain, and the universities of Ghent and London, he became London correspondent of Dutch newspapers from 1914 to 1927, and then concentrated on writing and translation, mixing high scholarship (*Great Britain and the Establishment of the Kingdom of the Netherlands 1813–15*) with popular lives of **William III** of Orange and **Oscar Wilde** (partly because of his common homosexual identity with them both), and a sardonic and stimulating enquiry *The English: are they human?* (1931). He joined the staff of University College London as lecturer in English history in 1934, and was professor of Dutch history and institutions there from 1945 to 1957. His other books include *The Dutch Nation* (1944) and *History, its Purpose and Method* (1950). He was married for a time to the novelist **Kate O'Brien**.

RENNEL, James (1742–1830) English geographer. He served in the navy, became a major in the East India Company's army, and surveyor-general of Bengal. His *Bengal Atlas* was published in 1779, and in 1781 he was elected a fellow of the Royal Society. Interested in hydrography, ancient geography and oceanography, he was the author of a *Treatise on the Comparative Geography of Western Asia* (published posthumously in 1831).

RENNENKAMPF, Pavel Karlovich von (1853–1918) Russian cavalry officer, of Baltic German origins. He commanded a force in the Russo-Japanese War (1904–05). In World War I, in command of the 1st Army, he defeated the German 8th Army at Insterburg and Gumbinnen (August 1914), but was decisively defeated by **Hindenberg** at Tannenberg a few days later. He was appointed governor of St Petersburg (Leningrad) in 1915, and commander-in-chief of the northern front in 1916. After the October Revolution he was shot by the Bolsheviks.

RENNER, Karl (1870–1950) Austrian statesman who became first chancellor of the Austrian republic (1918–20). He was imprisoned as a Socialist leader in 1934, and was chancellor again (1945). He wrote political works, and a national song. From 1946 until his death he was president of Austria.

RENNIE, George (1791–1866) Scottish engineer, eldest son of Sir **John Rennie**, born in London. He was superintendent of the machinery of the Mint, and aided his father. With his brother Sir **John Rennie** he carried on an immense business—shipbuilding, railways, bridges, harbours, docks, machinery and marine engines. He built the first screw vessel for the Royal Navy, the *Dwarf*.

RENNIE, John (1761–1821) Scottish civil engineer, born at Phantassie farm, East Linton. After working as a millwright with Andrew Meikle (1719–1811), he studied at Edinburgh University (1780–83). In 1784 he entered the employment of Messrs **Boulton & Watt**, and in 1791 he set up in London as an engineer and soon became famous as a bridge-builder—building Kelso, Leeds, Musselburgh, Newton-Stewart, Boston, New Galloway, and the old Southwark and Waterloo Bridges, and planning London Bridge. He made many important canals; drained fens; designed the London Docks, and others at Blackwall, Hull, Liverpool, Dublin, Greenock and Leith; and improved harbours and dockyards at Portsmouth, Chatham, Sheerness and Plymouth, where he constructed the celebrated breakwater (1811–41).

RENNIE, Sir John (1794–1874) Scottish engineer, second son of Sir **John Rennie**, born in London. He completed London Bridge to his father's design (1831). He was engineer to the Admiralty and wrote on harbours.

RENOIR, Jean (1894–1979) French-born American film director, born in Paris, son of **Pierre Auguste Renoir**. He won the Croix de Guerre in World War I, and from script-writing turned to filmmaking. His version of **Zola**'s *Nana* (1926), *La Grande Illusion* (1937), *La Bête humaine* (1939), *The Golden Coach* (1953) and *Le Déjeuner sur l'herbe* (1959) are among the masterpieces of the cinema. He left France in 1941 during the German invasion and became a naturalized American. His later films include *Le Caporal épinglé* (1962) and *Le Petit théâtre de Jean Renoir* (1969).

RENOIR, Pierre Auguste (1841–1919) French Impressionist artist, born in Limoges. He began as a painter on porcelain; in this trade, and then as a painter of fans, he made his first acquaintance with the work of **Watteau** and **Boucher** which was to influence his choice of subject matter as deeply as Impressionism was to influence his style. He entered the studio of **Charles Gleyre** in 1862 and began to paint in the open air about 1864. From 1870 onwards he obtained a number of commissions for portraits. In 1874–79 and in 1882 he exhibited with the Impressionists, his important, controversial picture of sunlight filtering through leaves, the *Moulin de la Galette* (in the Louvre), dating from 1876. He visited Italy in 1880 and during the next few years painted a series of *Bathers* in a more cold and classical style influenced by **Ingres** and **Raphael**. He then returned to hot reds, orange, and gold to portray nudes in sunlight, a style which he continued to develop to the end, although his hands were crippled by arthritis in later years.

RENOUF, Sir Peter Le Page (1822–97) British Egyptologist, born in Guernsey. He studied at Oxford and turned Catholic in 1842. He was professor of ancient history and oriental languages in Dublin (1855–64), a school inspector (1864–85), and keeper of Egyptian and Assyrian antiquities at the British Museum (1885–91). He wrote on ancient Egypt, notably a translation of *The Book of the Dead*, and gave the Hibbert Lectures on Egyptian religion in 1879.

RENOUVIER, Charles Bernard (1815–1903) French philosopher, born in Montpellier and educated in Paris. He developed a modified Kantian philosophy called 'neocriticism', emphasizing individual freedom and personal experience. His works include *Essai de critique générale* (4 vols, 1859–64), *La Science de la Morale* (1869), *Psychologie rationelle* (3 vols, 1875) and *Le Personnalisme* (1903).

RENWICK, James (1662–88) Scottish Covenanter, born in Moniaive. He studied at Edinburgh University, joined the 'Cameronians' as a field preacher, proclaimed the Lanark Declaration (1682), and was sent to complete his studies in Holland. In 1683 he preached his first sermon at Darmead Moss near Cambusnethan; in 1684 he was outlawed for his *Apologetic Declaration*. On the accession of **James VII and II** he published at Sanquhar a declaration rejecting him. A reward was offered for his capture; and at last he was taken in Edinburgh, and executed.

RENWICK, James (1790–1863) English physicist, born in Liverpool of Scottish-American parents. Professor at Columbia College, New York, he wrote books on mechanics. His son James (1818–95) designed Grace Church and St Patrick's Cathedral, New York, the Smithsonian Institution and the Bank of the State of New York.

REPIN, Ilya Efimovich (1844–1930) Russian painter, born in Chuguyev. Initially trained as an icon painter and then at the St Petersburg Academy, he lived in France from 1873 to 1876. He and his family then joined the Abramtsevo colony, a community of the most progressive personalities of the time, gathered by Savva Mamontov, the Russian railway tycoon, at his estate near Moskov, and today considered the cradle of the modern movement in Russian art. Repin is possibly the most famous of the Realist group 'The Wanderers' which had founded a new artistic code aimed at 'bringing art to the people'. The major representative of naturalism in Russian during the second half of the 19th century, he gained popularity with paintings such as *The Reply of the Cossacks of Zaporoguus to Sultan Mahmoud IV*, which his contemporaries saw as a symbol of the Russian people throwing off their chains; but he also painted portraits of famous contemporaries such as **Mussorgsky** (1881) and **Tolstoy** (1887). Although he prepared the development of Russian painting towards colourism, he did not support the new movements, such as World of Art and the Blue Rose, and his own painting eventually exhausted itself in a stale naturalism. A professor of painting at the St Petersburg Academy (1893–1907), he retired to his estate in Finland after the Revolution of 1917.

REPSOLD, Johann Georg (1770–1830) German instrument-maker. He designed a special pendulum, named after him, for the accurate determination of 'g'. Chief of the Hamburg fire brigade, he was killed when a wall collapsed during a fire.

REPTON, Humphrey (1752–1818) English landscape designer, born in Bury St Edmunds, the successor to **Lancelot 'Capability' Brown**. He completed the change from formal gardens of the early 18th century to the 'picturesque'. He designed for Uppark in Sussex and Sheringham Hall in Norfolk, and wrote *Observations on the Theory and Practice of Landscape Gardening* (1803).

RESNAIS, Alain (1922–) French film director, born in Vannes, Brittany. After studying at l'Institut des Hautes Études Cinématographiques in Paris, he made a series of outstanding and prizewinning short documentaries, such as *Van Gogh* (1948, Academy Award), *Guernica* (1950) and *Nuit et Bruillard* (1955), a haunting evocation of the horror of Nazi concentration camps. His first feature film, *Hiroshima mon amour* (1959), intermingles the nightmare war memories of its heroine with her unhappy love for a Japanese against the tragic background of contemporary Hiroshima. His next film, *L'Année dernière à Marienbad* (1961), illustrates his interest in the merging of past, present and future to the point of ambiguity, being hailed as a Surrealistic and dreamlike masterpiece by some, as a confused and tedious failure by others. Works as diverse as *Je t'aime, Je t'aime* (1967), *Mon Oncle D'Amérique* (1980) and *Héo* (1985) had similarly mixed receptions.

RESPIGHI, Ottorino (1879–1936) Italian composer, born in Bologna. A pupil of **Max Bruch** and of **Rimsky-Korsakov**, his works include nine operas, the symphonic poems, *Fontane di Roma* and *Pini di Roma*, and the ballet *La Boutique fantasque*. A vivid, melodic composer, he was the leading Italian composer of orchestral music of his day.

RESTIF, (Rétif) de la Bretonne, Nicolas Edme (1734–1806) French writer, born in Sacy, Yonne. His many voluminous and licentious novels, such as *Le Pied de Fanchette*, *Le Paysan perverti* and *Mémoires d'un homme de qualité*, give a vividly truthful picture of 18th-century French life, and entitle him to be considered as a forerunner of Realism. His own not unsullied life he described in the 16-volume *Monsieur Nicolas* (1794–97). He also wrote on social reform.

RESZKE, Edouard de (1856–1917) Polish operatic bass, born in Warsaw. He was successful throughout Europe in a wide range of parts, and often appeared with his brother **Jean de Reszke**.

RESZKE, Jean de (1850–1925) Polish operatic tenor, born in Warsaw. He began his career as a baritone, and, after his début as a tenor in 1879, succeeded in most of the leading French and Italian operatic roles, adding Wagnerian parts after 1885.

RESZKE, Joséphine de (1855–91) Polish operatic soprano, born in Warsaw, sister of **Edouard** and **Jean de Reszke**. She sang at the Paris Opéra but withdrew from the stage on her marriage with Baron von Kronenburg.

RETHEL, Alfred (1816–59) German historical painter and graphic artist, born in Diepenbend near Aachen. He decorated the imperial hall of the Römer, Frankfurt-am-Main, the Council House of Aachen with frescoes of the *Life of Charlemagne*, and executed a series of fantastic designs (1842–44; Dresden) on the theme of **Hannibal**'s crossing of the Alps.

RETZ, Rais, or **Raiz, Gilles de Laval, Baron de** (1404–40) French murderer, a Breton of high rank who fought by the side of **Joan of Arc**. He became marshal of France at 25, but soon retired to his estates, where for over ten years he is alleged to have indulged in the most infamous orgies, kidnapping 150 children, who were sacrificed to his lusts or sorceries. He was hanged and burned at Nantes, after a trial closed by his own confession.

RETZ, Jean Paul de Gondi, Cardinal de (1614–79) French prelate, born in Montmirail. He was bred for the church in spite of love affairs, duels and political intrigues. He became in 1643 coadjutor to his uncle, the archbishop of Paris, plotted against **Mazarin**, and instigated the outbreak of the Fronde in 1648. He became a cardinal, but in 1652 was flung into prison. After two years he made his escape, wandered in Spain and England, appeared in Rome, and in 1662 made his peace with **Louis XIV** by resigning his claim to the archbishopric in exchange for the abbacy of St Denis and restoration to his other benefices. His debts (four million francs!) he provided for in 1675 by making over to his creditors his entire income save 2000 livres. Retz figures pleasingly in the letters of **Madame de Sévigné**. His own masterly *Memoirs* (1655) throw much light on the Fronde.

RETZSCH, Friedrich August Moritz (1779–1897) German painter and engraver, born in Dresden. He became a professor there in 1824. He acquired great celebrity by his etchings in outline of **Schiller**, **Goethe**, **Fouqué** and **Shakespeare**.

REUCHLIN, Johann (1455–1522) German humanist and Hebraist, born in Pforzheim. He studied Greek at Paris, and wrote a Latin dictionary at Basel (1476). In 1481 he set up as lecturer at Tübingen, and in 1496 went to Heidelberg, where he became the main promoter of Greek studies in Germany; in 1500 he received a judicial appointment at Stuttgart. In 1506 he published the first Hebrew grammar, *Rudimenta Linguae Hebraicae*. From 1510 to 1516 he was involved in controversy with the Dominicans of Cologne over the burning of Jewish books, but in 1519 the Duke of Bavaria appointed him professor at Ingolstadt. He edited various Greek texts, published a Greek grammar, a whole series of polemical pamphlets, and a satirical drama (against the Obscurantists), and in *De Verbo Mirifico* and *De Arte Cabbalistica* showed a theosophico-cabbalistic tendency.

REUTER, Fritz (1810–74) German humorist, born in Stavenhagen in Mecklenburg-Schwerin. He studied law at Rostock and Jena. In 1833 he was condemned to death, as with other Jena students he had indulged in wild talk about the fatherland, but his sentence was commuted to 30 years' imprisonment. Released in 1840, with his career spoilt and his health ruined, he tried to resume his legal studies, learned farming, and taught pupils. His rough Plattdeutsch (Low German) verse setting of the jokes and merry tales of the countryside, *Läuschen un Rimels* (1853), became at once a great favourite, and another humorous poem, *Reis' nah Belligen* (1855), was equally successful, followed by a second volume of *Läuschen un Rimels* (1858) and the tragic poem *Kein Hüsung* (1858). The rest of his best works, except the poem *Hanne Nüte* (1860), were all written in Low German prose. *Ut de Franzosentid* (1860, trans *The Year '13*, 1873), *Ut mine Festungstid* (1862), and *Ut mine Stromtid* (1862–64) made him famous throughout Germany. He lived in Eisenach from 1863 until his death.

REUTER, Paul Julius, Freiherr von, originally **Israel Josaphat** (1816–99) German journalist born in Cassel. He changed his name to Reuter in 1844. In 1849 he formed in Aachen an organization for transmitting commercial news by telegraph and pigeon post. In 1851 he fixed his headquarters in London; and gradually his system spread to the remotest regions.

REUTHER, Walter Philip (1907–70) American trade-union leader. President of the American Auto Workers' Union, in 1935 he began to organize the automobile workers into what later became the largest union in the world, and fought against communist influence in trade unionism.

REVANS, Reginald William (1907–) English management consultant and promoter of action learning, born in London. Educated at University College, London, and at Cambridge, he was an Olympic athlete in 1928. As deputy chief officer of Essex (1935–45) and as director of education in the coal industry (1945–50), he pioneered 'action learning'. This approach to management development holds that the skills of managing are better learnt by managers reviewing their own experience with their peers and asking appropriate questions of each other, than by studying the programmed information of experts. He was professor of industrial administration at Manchester University (1955–65), and has subsequently worked as an action learning consultant in many overseas countries.

REVELLE, Roger (1909–) American oceanographer and sociologist, born in Seattle, Washington. He worked mainly at the Scripps Institution of Oceanography at La Jolla (1931–64). As a result of his geophysical studies of the Pacific Ocean, he contributed to the theory of sea-floor spreading. Between 1964 and 1976 he was professor of population policy at Harvard.

REVERE, Paul (1735–1818) American patriot, born in Boston, Massachusetts. A silversmith and copperplate printer to trade, he served as a lieutenant of artillery (1756). He was one of the party that destroyed the tea in Boston harbour (1773), and he was at the head of a secret society formed to watch the British. On 18 April 1775, the night before Lexington and Concord, he rode from Boston to Lexington and Lincoln, warning the people of Massachusetts that the British were on the move. His ride was celebrated in **Longfellow**'s *The Midnight Ride of Raul Revere*. In the war he became a lieutenant-colonel of artillery. He designed and printed the first issue of Continental money. In 1801 he founded the Revere Copper Company at Canton, Massachusetts, for rolling sheet copper.

REVIE, Don (1927–89) English footballer and manager, born near Middlesbrough. Always a thoughtful player, he was one of the first to introduce the deep-lying centre-forward method to British soccer, which the Hungarians had used with such success in the mid 1950s. Footballer of the Year in 1955, he won an FA Cup medal the following year with Manchester City. In 1961 he was appointed player-manager of Leeds United, and over the next 13 years transformed the struggling club into a powerful force in British football, taking all three major honours. He succeeded Sir **Alf Ramsey** as England team manager in 1974, but abruptly abandoned the job in 1977 to take up a coaching post in the Middle East. He died of motor neurone disease.

RÉVILLE, Albert (1826–1906) French Protestant theologian of the advanced school, born in Dieppe. He was pastor of the Walloon Church in Rotterdam (1851–72), lectured at Leiden, and in 1880 became professor of the history of religions in the Collège de France. His works include a comparative history of philosophy and religion (1859).

REYBAUD, Louis (1799–1879) French journalist and politician, born in Marseille. He travelled in the Levant and India and, returning to Paris in 1829, wrote for the Radical papers and edited a history of the French expedition to Egypt (1830–36). His *Réformateurs ou Socialistes modernes* (1840–43) popularized the word 'socialism'. He also wrote satirical novels, ridiculing the manners and institutions of his time.

REYMONT, Wladyslaw Stanislaw (1867–1925) Polish novelist, born in Kobiele Wielke. He was the author of the tetralogy, *The Peasants* (1904–09), and was awarded the Nobel prize for literature in 1924. Other books are *The Comédienne* (1896; trans 1920) and *The Year 1794* (1913–18).

REYNAUD, Paul (1878–1966) French statesman, born in Barcelonnette. Originally a barrister, he held many French government posts, being premier during the fall of France in 1940. He was imprisoned by the Germans during World War II. Afterwards he re-entered politics, until losing his seat in 1962, and was a delegate to the Council of Europe (1949). Among several works are *La France a sauvé l'Europe* (1947), *Au Coeur de la mêlée 1930–45* (trans 1955), and his *Mémoires* (1960, 1963).

REYNOLDS, George William MacArthur (1814–79) English journalist, Chartist, and blood-and-thunder novelist, born in Sandwich. In 1850 he started *Reynolds's Weekly*.

REYNOLDS, Sir Joshua (1723–92) English portrait painter, born in Plympton Earls near Plymouth, the seventh son of a clergyman and schoolmaster. Sent in 1740 to London to study art, in 1747 he settled in Plymouth Dock, now Davenport. In Rome (1749–52) he studied **Raphael** and **Michelangelo**, and in the Vatican caught a chill which permanently affected his hearing. He then established himself in London, and by 1760 was at the height of his fame. In 1764 he founded the Literary Club of which Dr **Johnson**, **Garrick**, **Burke**, **Goldsmith**, **Boswell** and **Sheridan** were members. He was one of the earliest members of the Incorporated Society of Artists, and on the establishment of the Royal Academy (1768) was elected its first president; in 1769 he was knighted. In that year he delivered the first of his Discourses to the students of the Academy, which, along with his papers on art in the *Idler*, his annotations to Du Fresnoy's *Art of Painting*, and his *Notes on the Art of the Low Countries* (the result of a visit in 1781), show a cultivated literary style. In 1784 he became painter to the king, and finished his **Sarah Siddons** as the *Tragic Muse*, a work existing in several versions. In 1789 his sight became affected, and he ceased to paint. He was buried in St Paul's. It is by virtue of his portraits that Reynolds ranks as the head of the English school. They are notable for the power and expressiveness of their handling, and the beauty of their colouring. His pictures of children have an especial tenderness and beauty, as in *The Strawberry Girl*, *Simplicity*, and many others.

REYNOLDS, Osborne (1842–1912) English engineer, born in Belfast of a Suffolk family. He became the first professor of engineering at Manchester (1868) and a Royal Society gold medallist (1888). He greatly improved centrifugal pumps. The 'Reynolds number', a dimensionless ratio characterizing the dynamic state of a fluid, takes its name from him.

REYNOLDS, Samuel William (1773–1835) English engraver, born in London. He was an accomplished mezzotinter, and produced many engravings after portraits by Sir **Joshua Reynolds**, **Turner**, **Lawrence** and **Opie**.

REYNOLDS, Walter (d.1327) English prelate, the son of a Windsor baker. He was made treasurer by **Edward II** (1307), and bishop of Worcester (1308), chancellor (1310), and archbishop of Canterbury (1314), despite the opposition of the monks. He later declared for **Edward III**, whom he crowned in 1327.

RHAZES, or **Räzi** (9th century) Persian physician and alchemist of Baghdad, considered the greatest physician of the Arab world. He wrote many medical works, some of which were translated into Latin and had considerable influence on medical science in the middle ages. He distinguished smallpox from measles.

RHEE, Syngman (1875–1965) Korean statesman, born near Kaesong. Imprisoned from 1897 to 1904 for campaigning for reform and a constitutional monarchy, he went soon after his release to America, where he was influenced by **Wilson**, the apostle of self-determination. In 1910 he returned to Japanese-annexed Korea, and after the unsuccessful rising of 1919 he became president of the exiled Korean Provisional Government. On Japan's surrender in 1945 he returned to Korea, and in 1948 was elected president of the Republic of South Korea. He opposed the Korean truce of 1953, calling Korea's continued partition 'appeasement of the Communists'. Re-elected for a fourth term as president in March 1960, he was obliged to resign in April after large-scale riots and the resignation of his cabinet. A man of inflexible and often bellicose patriotism, his immense personal authority was derived from a lifetime of resistance and exile. His publications include *Japan Inside Out* (1941).

RHEINBERGER, Joseph (1839–1901) German composer, born in Vaduz in Liechtenstein. At the age of twelve he entered Munich Conservatory, where he remained for seven years, later becoming a teacher there. He became royal professor and kapellmeister. His works include two operas and 18 organ sonatas.

RHETICUS, real name **Georg Joachim von Lauchen** (1514–74) Austrian-born German astronomer and mathematician, born in Feldkirch. He became professor of mathematics at Wittenberg (1537). He is noted for his trigonometrical tables, some of which went to 15 decimal places. For a time he worked with **Copernicus**, whose *De Revolutionibus Orbium Coelestium* he was instrumental in publishing. His own *Narratio Prima de Libris Revolutionum Copernici* (1540) was the first account of the Copernican theory.

RHIGAS, Konstantinos (1760–98) Greek poet. He organized the anti-Turkish revolutionary movement in Vienna, but was betrayed and shot.

RHIND, Alexander Henry (1833–63) Scottish antiquary, born in Wick. He studied at Edinburgh

University, but was forced to travel for the sake of his health, and published a book on Egyptian antiquities, *Thebes, its Tombs and their Tenants* (1862). The Rhind Lectures in archaeology, delivered at Edinburgh, were founded in his memory.

RHINE, Joseph Banks (1895–1980) American psychologist, pioneer of parapsychology, born in Waterloo, Pennsylvania. He studied botany at Chicago, switched to psychology under **William McDougall** at Duke University, and in 1937 became professor of psychology there. He co-founded the Parapsychology Laboratory there (1930), and the Institute of Parapsychology in Durham, New Carolina (1964). His laboratory-devised experiments involving packs of specially designed cards established the phenomenon of extrasensory perception and of telepathy on a statistical basis, since some guessers achieved considerably better results than the average chance successes. He wrote *New Frontiers of the Mind* (1937), *Extrasensory Perception* (1940), and *The Reach of the Mind* (1948).

RHODES, Cecil John (1853–1902) South African statesman, born in Bishop's Stortford, where his father was vicar. He was sent for his health to Natal, and subsequently made a fortune at the Kimberley diamond diggings, and succeeded in amalgamating the several diamond companies to form the De Beers Consolidated Mines Company in 1888. (In that year he sent £10000 to **Parnell** to forward the cause of Irish Home Rule.) He came back to England, entered Oriel College, Oxford, and although his residence was cut short by ill-health, he ultimately took his degree. He entered the Cape House of Assembly as member for Barkly. In 1884 General **Gordon** asked him to go with him to Khartoum as secretary; but Rhodes declined, having just taken office in the Cape ministry. In 1890 he became prime minister of Cape Colony; but even before this he had become a ruling spirit in the extension of British territory in securing first Bechuanaland as a protectorate (1884) and later (1889) the charter for the British South Africa Company of which until 1896 he was managing director, and whose territory was later to be known as Rhodesia. His policy was the ultimate establishment of a federal South African dominion under the British flag. In 1895 he was made a member of the privy council. In 1896 he resigned the Cape premiership in consequence of complications arising from the 'unauthorized' raid into the Transvaal of Dr **Jameson**, the Chartered Company's administrator, in aid of the Uitlanders' claims. His action was condemned by the South Africa Commission and by the British government. In the same year he succeeded in quelling the Matabele rebellion by personal negotiations with the chiefs. In 1899 he was capped DCL at Oxford. He was a conspicuous figure during the war of 1899–1902, when he organized the defences of Kimberley during the siege. He left a remarkable will which, besides making great benefactions to Cape Colony, founded scholarships at Oxford for Americans, Germans and colonials.

RHODES, Zandra (1940–) English fashion designer, born in Chatham, Kent. She studied textile printing and lithography at Medway College of Art, then won a scholarship to the Royal College of Art. She designed and printed textiles, and, with others, opened The Fulham Road Clothes Shop, afterwards setting up on her own. She showed her first dress collection in 1969, and is noted for her distinctive, exotic designs in floating chiffons and silks.

RHONDDA, David Alfred Thomas, 1st Viscount (1856–1918) Welsh coal owner, financier and politician, born in Ysgyborwen, near Aberdare, Glamorganshire. Educated at Caius College, Cambridge, he was Liberal MP for Merthyr Tydfil from 1888 to 1910. During World War I, he was sent to the USA by **Lloyd George** to negotiate the supply of munitions to Britain. His success led to a peerage, and was followed by an equally successful period as minister of food (1917–18), with the introduction of war-time food rationing. On his death in 1918 his peerage passed, by special remainder, to his daughter, Viscountess Rhondda (**Margaret Haig Thomas**).

RHONDDA, Viscountess. See **THOMAS, Margaret Haig**

RHYS, Ernest Percival (1859–1946) Anglo-Welsh editor and writer, born in London. He spent much of his youth in Carmarthen and became a mining engineer. Abandoning this for a writing career in 1886 he was first a freelance, then on the staff of **Walter Scott**'s publishing house, Constable's, for whom he edited the Camelot Classics series. He is best known as editor of the Everyman Library of classics. He wrote two novels and some volumes of verse.

RHYS, Jean, pseud of **Gwen Williams** (1894–1979) British novelist, born in the West Indies. Her father was a Welsh doctor, her mother a Creole. Educated at a convent in Roseau, Dominica, she came to England in 1910 to train at the Royal Academy of Dramatic Art, but her father's death after only one term obliged her to join a touring theatre company. At the end of World War I she married a Dutch poet, Max Hamer, and went to live on the Continent, spending many years in Paris where she met writers and artists, including **Hemingway**, **Joyce** and **Ford Madox Ford** (the last-named in particular encouraged her writing). In 1927 she published *The Left Bank and Other Stories*, set mostly in Paris or in the West Indies of her childhood. Four novels followed, *Quartet* (originally published as *Postures*, 1928), *After Leaving Mr Mackenzie* (1930), *Voyage in the Dark* (1934), and *Good Morning Midnight* (1939); her heroines were women attempting to live without regular financial support, adrift in European cities between the worlds of wealth and poverty. After nearly 30 years she published in 1966 what was to become her best-known novel, *Wide Sargasso Sea*, based on the character of Rochester's mad wife in **Charlotte Brontë**'s *Jane Eyre*. Further short stories followed in 1968 and 1976, and an autobiography, *Smile Please*, was published posthumously in 1979.

RHYS, Sir John (1840–1915) Welsh philologist, born in Cardiganshire. He taught in Anglesea until 1865, when he entered Jesus College, Oxford, and continued his studies in France and Germany. From 1871 an inspector of schools in Wales, in 1877 he became the first professor of Celtic at Oxford, in 1881 a fellow of Jesus College, Oxford, and in 1895 its principal. He was a distinguished authority on Celtic philology, and author of numerous works, including *Celtic Britain* (1882) and *Celtic Heathendom* (1888).

RHYS-DAVIDS See **DAVIDS, Thomas William Rhys**

RIBALTA, Francisco de (1550–1628) Spanish painter, born in Castellón de la Plana. He studied in Rome, and settled in Valencia. Noted as a painter of historical subjects and for his use of chiaroscuro, his works include *The Last Supper* and his *Christ* in Madrid. His sons, José (1588–1656) and Juan (1597–1628), were also Valencian painters.

RIBBENTROP, Joachim von (1893–1946) German politician. He was a wine merchant who became a member of the National Socialist party in 1932. Finally **Hitler**'s adviser in foreign affairs, he was responsible in

1935 for the Anglo-German naval pact, becoming the following year ambassador to Britain, and, foreign minister (1938–45). He was taken by the British in 1945 and condemned to death and executed at Nuremberg.

RIBERA, Jusepe de (1588–1656) called **Lo Spagnoletto** ('The Little Spaniard'), Spanish painter and etcher, born in Játiva. He settled in Naples, and became court painter there. He delighted in the horrible, often choosing such subjects as the martyrdom of the saints and painting them with a bold, unsympathetic power. Later works were calmer and more subtle, and include *The Immaculate Conception* and paintings of the Passion.

RIBOT, Alexandre (1842–1923) French statesman, born in St Omer. He was premier in 1892, 1895 and 1917, foreign minister (1890–93), and finance minister (1914–17). An academician in 1906, he wrote *Letters to a Friend*, which were translated in 1925.

RIBOT, Théodule Armand (1839–1916) French psychologist, born in Guingamp. He became professor at the Sorbonne (1885) and the Collège de France (1888). A pioneer in experimental psychology, he wrote many works, including *English Psychology* (1873), *Heredity* (1875) and *Diseases of the Will* (1884).

RICARDO, David (1772–1823) English political economist, born in London. He was brought up by his father, a Jewish stockbroker, to the same business. In 1793 he married Priscilla Ann Wilkinson, a Quaker, and turned Christian; then, starting for himself, he made a large fortune by 1814. In 1799 his interest in political economy was awakened by **Adam Smith**'s *Wealth of Nations*. His pamphlet, *The High Price of Bullion, a Proof of the Depreciation of Banknotes* (1809), was an argument in favour of a metallic basis. In 1817 appeared the work on which his reputation chiefly rests, *Principles of Political Economy and Taxation*, a discussion of value, wages, rent, etc. In 1819 he became Radical MP for Portarlington. He died at his Gloucestershire seat, Gatcombe Park.

RICARDO, Sir Harry Ralph (1885–1974) English mechanical engineer, born in London. He studied at Trinity College, Cambridge (1903–07), where he designed and built several small petrol engines and began to work on the problems of ignition, combustion and detonation. He soon recognised the importance of the type of fuel in avoiding detonation or 'knocking', and this led to the use of octane numbers to measure the anti-knock properties of petrols. His improved design of the combustion chamber in side-valve engines has been universally adopted, and he has many other important inventions to his credit.

RICASOLI, Bettino, Baron (1809–80) Italian statesman, born in Florence. He was a leading agriculturist, and for ten years worked successfully at draining the Tuscan Maremma. In 1859 he opposed the Grand Duke, on whose flight he was made dictator of Tuscany. A strong advocate of the unification of Italy, he supported **Cavour** in the struggle to join Piedmont with Tuscany. He was head of the ministry in 1861–62 and 1866–67.

RICCI, Marco (1676–1730) Italian painter, born in Belluno. He was a pupil of his uncle **Sebastiano Ricci**, and, although based in Venice like him, he travelled extensively. He was brought to England by the Earl of Manchester in 1708, and seems to have worked mostly on the design of stage scenery for the opera. In 1710 he returned to Venice to bring his uncle to England, where they worked together from 1712 to 1716. Little is known of his later career; he appears to have worked for Sebastiano painting landscape backgrounds for large religious pictures.

RICCI, Matteo (1552–1610) Italian missionary, founder of the Jesuit missions in China, born in Macerata. He studied at Rome, and lived in Nanking and in Peking. He so mastered Chinese as to write dialogues, etc, which received much commendation from the Chinese literati, and he met with extraordinary success as a missionary, although his methods aroused much controversy.

RICCI, Sebastiano (1659–1734) Italian painter, born in Belluno. He was trained in Venice, where he fully assimilated the work of **Veronese** and developed a decorative style which was to influence **Tiepolo**. After extensive travel in Italy he worked for two years (1701–03) in Vienna. In 1712 he travelled to England, via the Netherlands, with his nephew **Marco Ricci**. The only complete work to survive from this time is a *Resurrection* in the apse of Chelsea Hospital chapel. He left England for Venice in 1716 when he failed to gain the commission to decorate the dome of St Paul's (which went to **Thornhill**).

RICCIO See **RIZZIO, David**

RICE, Edmund Ignatius (1762–1844) Irish philanthropist, born near Callan, County Kilkenny. A wealthy provision merchant in Waterford, he retired from business on the death of his wife in 1789 and devoted himself to good works. He founded a school for poor boys at Waterford in 1803, and many others elsewhere. In 1808 he took religious vows, and in 1802 he founded the Irish Christian Brothers for the education of the poor (sanctioned by the Pope in 1820). He was superior-general of the order as Brother Ignatius till 1838.

RICE, Elmer, originally **Elmer Reizenstein** (1892–1967) American dramatist, born Elmer Reizenstein in New York. He studied law and turned to writing plays. His prolific output includes *The Adding Machine* (1923), *Street Scene* (1929), which won a Pulitzer prize, *The Left Bank* (1931), *Two on an Island* (1940), *Cue for Passion* (1958), etc.

RICE, James (1843–82) English novelist, born in Northampton. He studied at Queen's College, Cambridge, drifted from law into literature, and was proprietor and editor of *Once a Week* (1868–72). From 1872 he was involved in writing novels with Sir **Walter Besant**.

RICE, Tim (1944–) English lyricist, born in Buckinghamshire. He studied to be a lawyer, but left a lawyer's firm to join the record company EMI. His musical début was writing the lyrics to music by **Andrew Lloyd Webber** for *Joseph and the Amazing Technicolour Dreamcoat* (1968), followed by *Jesus Christ Superstar* (1971), *Evita* (1978) and *Chess* (1986).

RICE-DAVIES, Mandy (Marilyn) (1944–) Welsh model and show girl. Born in Wales, the daughter of a police officer, she grew up in the West Midlands where, after leaving school, she worked in a department store. Her striking looks and figure won her a contract as a model in the promotion of the new Mini motor car and, with her appetite for show business whetted, she moved to London where, at an early age, she became a show girl at Murray's Cabaret Club. Here she met and became close to **Christine Keeler** and, through the osteopath, Stephen Ward, was introduced to influential London society, receiving several marriage offers. As a witness at Ward's trial, in reply to a suggestion that Lord **Astor** denied knowing her, she gave the celebrated retort: 'He would, wouldn't he?' After the trial she moved to Israel, where she established two night clubs, called Mandy. She married twice and published her autobiography, eventually returning to live in London.

RICH, Barnabe (c.1540–1620) English soldier and romance writer, born in Essex. Under the patronage of Sir **Christopher Hatton** he served as a soldier in France, the Low Countries and Ireland. He was the author of exaggerated tales in *The Strange and Wonderful Adventures of Don Simonides* (1581) and *The Adventures of Brusanus, Prince of Hungaria* (1592). His *Apolonius and Silla* (contained in *Riche, his Farewell to the Military Profession*, 1581) was used by **Shakespeare** as a source for the plot of *Twelfth Night*. He was also a prolific pamphleteer on military matters, and on Ireland.

RICH, Edmund See **EDMUND, St**

RICH, Penelope See **SIDNEY, Sir Philip**

RICHARD I, Coeur de Lion (1157–99) king of England from 1189, third son of **Henry II**, born in Oxford. While still a child, he was invested with the duchy of Aquitaine, his mother **Eleanor of Aquitaine**'s patrimony. Richard did not spend in all his life a full year in England; it may reasonably be doubted whether he could speak English. He was induced by his mother to join his brothers Henry and Geoffrey in their rebellion (1173) against their father Henry II; and in 1189 he was again in arms against his father and in league with **Philip II Augustus** of France. Richard became king of England, Duke of Normandy and Count of Anjou on 5 July 1189. But he had already taken the crusader's vow; and in 1190 he and Philip set out for Palestine. Both spent the winter in Sicily, whose throne had just been seized by the Norman **Tancred**. The latter made his peace by giving up to Richard his sister Johanna, the widowed queen, and her possessions, and by betrothing his daughter to **Arthur**, Richard's nephew and heir. In 1191 part of Richard's fleet was wrecked on Cyprus, and the crews were most inhospitably treated by the sovereign, **Isaac I Comnenus**. Richard sailed back from Rhodes, routed Isaac, deposed him, and give his crown to **Guy of Lusignan**. In Cyprus he married Berengaria of Navarre, and on 8 June landed near Acre, which surrendered. Richard's exploits—his march to Joppa, his two advances on Jerusalem (the city he never beheld), his capture of the fortresses in the south of Palestine, and his relief of Joppa—excited the admiration of Christendom. In September he concluded a three years' peace with **Saladin**, and started off home alone. He was shipwrecked in the Adriatic, and in disguise made his way through the dominions of his bitter enemy, **Leopold**, Duke of Austria, but was recognized, seized and handed over to the emperor **Henry VI** (1193), who demanded a heavy ransom. Richard's loyal subjects raised the money, and he returned home (March 1194) having established useful political alliances with the empire. Although his brother **John** used his utmost endeavours to prevent his return, Richard generously forgave him; and, proceeding to France, spent the rest of his life warring against Philip, mainly on the Norman-French border which he held for the Angevins. He was killed while besieging the castle of Chalus, and was buried at Fontevrault.

RICHARD II (1367–1400) king of England from 1377 to 1399, son of **Edward the Black Prince**, born in Bordeaux. He succeeded his grandfather, **Edward III**, in 1377. The government was entrusted to a council of twelve, but **John of Gaunt** gained control of it. The war with France and the extravagance of the court cost money; and more was wasted by the government, for which John of Gaunt was held to be mainly responsible. The poll tax of 1380 provoked popular risings; the men of Essex and Kent, 100000 strong, marched upon London. The Essex men consented to return home when Richard (14 June 1381) assured them at Mile End that he would liberate the villeins and commute their service into money rent. The men of Kent, after destroying the Savoy (Gaunt's palace), burning Temple Bar, opening the prisons, breaking into the Tower, and slaying the archbishop of Canterbury, met the king at Smithfield (15 June) where, during the negotiations, William Walworth, mayor of London, struck down **Wat Tyler**, their leader. The king at once rode amongst them, exclaiming he would be their leader, and granted them the concessions demanded. From this time John of Gaunt kept much in the background, until in 1386 he retired to the Continent. In 1385 Richard invaded Scotland and burned Edinburgh. About the same time another coalition of the baronial party, headed by the Duke of Gloucester, began to oppose the king. They impeached several of his friends in 1388, and secured convictions and executions. But on 3 May 1389, Richard suddenly declared himself of age; for eight years he ruled as a moderate constitutional monarch, and the country was fairly prosperous. But in 1394 Richard's first wife, **Anne of Bohemia**, died, and in 1396 he married Isabella (1389–1409), daughter of **Charles VI** of France, and seems to have adopted French tastes, manners, and ideas, and to have adopted a more despotic view of the monarchy. He had Gloucester, Arundel and Warwick arrested for conspiracy. Arundel was beheaded; Gloucester was sent a prisoner to Calais, and died in prison, probably murdered; Warwick was banished, and so was the archbishop of Canterbury. In 1398 the Duke of Norfolk and the Duke of Hereford (Henry, later **Henry III**, John of Gaunt's son)) were accused of treason; Norfolk was banished for life and Hereford for ten years. In 1399 John of Gaunt died, and Hereford succeeded him as Duke of Lancaster. Richard went over to Ireland in May, and Henry of Lancaster landed on 4 July. Richard hurried back, submitted to his cousin at Flint (19 August), and was put in the Tower. On 29 September he resigned the crown, and next day was deposed by parliament, which chose Henry as his successor. Richard seems to have been murdered at Pontefract Castle early in 1400. It was the fear that he inspired in men of property that, in the end, made Richard's downfall inevitable.

RICHARD III (1452–85) king of England from 1483, youngest brother of **Edward IV**, born in Fotheringay Castle. After the defeat and death of his father, Richard, 3rd Duke of **York**, in 1460, he was sent to Utrecht for safety, but returned to England after Edward had won the crown (1461), and was created Duke of Gloucester. In the final struggle between York and Lancaster he took an active part, and is believed to have had a hand in the murder of Prince Edward, **Henry VI**'s son, after Tewkesbury, and of Henry himself. In 1472 he married Anne, younger daughter of Warwick. This alliance was resented by his brother, the Duke of Clarence, who had married the elder sister, and wished to keep Warwick's vast possessions to himself. Clarence was impeached and put to death in the Tower in 1478. Of this judicial murder Richard is likewise accused; but the evidence is slight. In 1482 Richard commanded the army that invaded Scotland and captured Berwick. In 1483, while still in Yorkshire, he heard of King Edward's death, and learned that he himself was guardian of his son and heir, **Edward V**, then aged 13. On his way south the Protector arrested Earl **Rivers** and Lord Richard Grey, the uncle and stepbrother of the young king, and rallied to himself the old nobility. He accused Lord Hastings, a leading member of the council, of treason, and had him beheaded. The queen-dowager was induced to give up her other son, the little Duke of York, and he was put into the Tower to keep his brother, the king, company. The parliament desired Richard to become king and on 6 July 1483 he was crowned, Rivers and Grey having been executed on 25 June. Richard's principal supporter all through had always been Henry Stafford, 2nd Duke of Buckingham; but soon after Richard's coronation he entered into a plot with the friends of Henry Tudor, Earl of Richmond (afterwards **Henry VII**), the chief representative of the House of Lancaster, to effect Richard's overthrow and proclaim Henry king. The attempted rising collapsed, and Buckingham was executed on 2 November. It seems to have been shortly before this that Richard is believed to have had his nephews murdered in the Tower. The deed was done so secretly that the nation did not know of it until some time after, and Richard has never been proved guilty. Henry landed at Milford Haven on 7 August 1485; Richard met him at Bosworth on 22 August, and there lost his kingdom and his life. Had Richard succeeded to the throne peacefully, he would probably have been a great king, for he was a very capable ruler.

RICHARD, Cliff, real name **Harry Roger Webb** (1940–) English pop-singer, born in Lucknow, India. He moved to England at the age of eight. He began his professional career playing with the Dick Teague Group, and formed his own band in 1958. Originally called The Drifters, the group changed its name to The Shadows to avoid confusion with an American vocal group of that name. Following the success of 'Living Doll' (1959), The Shadows were hailed as Britain's answer to American rock. He made a series of family musical films during the 1960s, including *Expresso Bongo* (1960), *The Young Ones* (1961) and *Summer Holiday* (1962). Following his conversion to Christianity, his clean-cut image damaged his reputation with rock fans, but he has nevertheless become a British entertainment institution. His many recorded albums have included *21 Today* (1961), *Rock and Roll Juvenile* (1979) and *Love Songs* (1981).

RICHARD, Henry (1812–88) Welsh politician, born in Tregaron, Cardiganshire. A Nonconformist minister devoted to the cause of pacifism, he was secretary of the Peace Society. Elected Liberal MP for Merthyr Tydfil (1868–88), he spoke for Wales in parliament and was a strong advocate of international arbitration in lieu of war. In his homeland he was known as the apostle of peace, 'Apostol Heddwch'.

RICHARD, of Bury See **AUNGERVILLE**

RICHARDS, Alun (1929–) Welsh novelist, short-story writer and playwright, born in Pontypridd, Glamorgan. He was educated at the Monmouthshire Training College, Caerleon, and at University College, Swansea. He has published six novels, including *The Elephant You Gave Me* (1963), *A Woman of Experience* (1969), and *Barque Whisper* (1979), and two collections of short stories (*Dai Country*, 1973, and *The Former Miss Merthyr Tydfil*, 1976), often drawing on his varied experiences working as a probation officer, a sailor and a teacher. Besides editing several short-story anthologies, he has written a book about Welsh rugby, and many plays and adaptations for television, notably *The Onedin Line*.

RICHARDS, Barry Anderson (1945–) South African cricketer, born in Durban. Restricted to only four Test matches at the very end of South Africa's international career, he scored two centuries. He spent most of his time playing Sheffield Shield cricket with Western Australia, Currie Cup cricket with Natal, and county cricket with Hampshire. His first-class aggregate of 28 358 and average of 54.74 gives some indication of what he might have contributed to the wider arena of Test cricket.

RICHARDS, Ceri (1903–71) Welsh artist, born in Dunvant, near Swansea. He studied at Swansea School of Art (1920–24) and at the Royal College of Art (1924–27), holding his first one-man show at the Glynn Vivian Art Gallery, Swansea, in 1930. In 1932 he began making collages and constructions which showed the clear influence of **Max Ernst** and the Surrealists generally. He joined the London Group in 1937, taught at Chelsea School of Art (1945–55), at the Slade School (1956–61), and at the Royal College (1961–62). In addition to his paintings, he designed opera sets, stained-glass windows and vestments. He won the Einaudi prize at the Venice Biennale in 1962.

RICHARDS, Dickinson Woodruff (1895–1973) American physician, born in Orange, New Jersey. Educated at Yale, he specialized in cardiology, which he taught at Columbia University (1928–61), becoming professor of medicine there from 1947 to 1961. He was awarded jointly with **André Cournand** and **Werner Forssmann** the 1956 Nobel prize for physiology or medicine for developing cardiac catheterization.

RICHARDS, Frank, properly **Charles Hamilton** (1875–1961) English children's writer, author of the 'Tom Merry', 'Billy Bunter' of Greyfriars School and other school-story series. He wrote for boys' papers, and particularly for *The Gem* (1906–39) and *The Magnet* (1908–40). After World War II he published school stories in book and play form, and his *Autobiography* (1952).

RICHARDS, Sir Gordon (1904–86) English jockey, born in Oakengates, Shropshire, the son of a coalminer. In 34 seasons (1921–54) he was champion jockey 26 times, and rode 4870 winners. Towards the end of his career he eventually rode his first Derby winner, Pinza, in 1953, the year in which he was knighted.

RICHARDS, Henry Brinley (1819–85) Welsh pianist and composer, born in Carmarthen and educated at the Royal Academy of Music, London. His father was an organist and also kept a music shop. Regarded as the finest piano player in the country, he was also a prolific composer of songs, piano pieces and choruses. During a study trip to Paris he befriended **Chopin**. His best remembered piece is 'God Bless the Prince of Wales'.

RICHARDS, Ivor Armstrong (1893–1979) English scholar and literary critic, and initiator of the so-called 'New Criticism' movement. Professor at Cambridge (1922–29), with **Charles Key Ogden** he developed the idea of Basic English, and in 1924 published the influential *Principles of Literary Criticism*, followed by *Science and Poetry* (1825) and *Practical Criticism* (1929). In 1939 he left Cambridge for Harvard, where he was professor (1939–63). There he taught **William Empson**, became a friend of **Robert Lowell**, and began himself to write poetry, publishing, among other collections, *Goodbye Earth and other poems* (1958), *The Screens* (1960), and *New and Selected Poems* (1978).

RICHARDS, Theodore William (1868–1928) American chemist, born in Germantown, Pennsylvania. He became professor at Harvard in 1901 and won the Nobel prize for chemistry in 1914. Best known for his work on atomic weights, he also carried out important investigations in thermochemistry and thermodynamics.

RICHARDSON, Alan (1905–75) English Anglican theologian, born in Highfield, Wigan. Professor of theology at Nottingham (1953–64), and dean of York (1964–75), he communicated on many levels. His *Creeds in the Making* (1935) heralded a series of student texts, culminating in *An Introduction to the Theology of the New Testament* (1958), the Bampton lectures *History, Sacred and Profane* (1964), and major contributions to *A Dictionary of Christian Theology* (1969), which he also edited. Masterly surveys of current issues appeared in more popular books, including *The Bible in an Age of Science* (1961), *Religion in Contemporary Debate* (1966), and *The Political Christ* (1973).

RICHARDSON, Charles (1775–1865) English lexicographer, born in Tulse Hill, Norwood. He studied law, kept school till 1827 at Clapham, and published *Illustrations of English Philology* (1815), but is remembered for his *New Dictionary of the English Language* (2 vols, 1835–37), with etymologies. A later work was *On the Study of Language* (1854).

RICHARDSON, Dorothy M (Miller) (1873–1957) English novelist, born in Abingdon, Berkshire. After her mother's suicide in 1895 she moved to London and worked as a teacher, a clerk, and a dentist's assistant. She became a Fabian, and had an affair with **H G Wells** which led to a miscarriage and a near-collapse in 1907. Later (1917) she married a painter, Alan Odle. She started her writing career with works on the Quakers and **George Fox** (1914). Her first novel, *Painted Roofs* (1915), was the first of a twelve-volume sequence entitled *Pilgrimage*, culminating with *Clear Horizon* (1935) and *Dimple Hill* (1938). She was the first exponent of the 'stream of consciousness' style later made famous by **Virginia Woolf**.

RICHARDSON, Henry Handel, pen-name of **Ethel Florence Lindesay** (1870–1946) Australian novelist, born in Melbourne, the daughter of an Irish immigrant doctor. Educated at the Presbyterian Ladies' College, Melbourne, she travelled and studied music at Leipzig. In 1895 she married a fellow music student from Dublin, John George Robertson, and they lived in Strasbourg. In 1904 they settled in England, when her husband became a professor of German language and literature at the University of London. Her first novel was *Maurice Guest* (1908), based on her musical experience. She made her name with a trilogy set in Australia, *The Fortunes of Richard Mahony*, comprising *Australia Felix* (1917), *The Way Home* (1925), and *Ultima Thule* (1929). She also wrote an autobiography, *Myself When Young* (1948).

RICHARDSON, Henry Hobson (1838–86) American architect, born in Priestley Plantation, Louisiana. Educated at Harvard, he studied architecture in Paris, and initiated the Romanesque revival in the USA, leading to a distinctively American style of architecture. He designed a number of churches, especially Trinity Church, Boston (1872), the Allegheny Co Buildings in Pittsburgh, and halls of residence at Harvard; but his range covered private houses as well as railway stations and wholesale stores.

RICHARDSON, Sir John (1787–1865) Scottish naturalist and explorer, born in Dumfries. He was a surgeon in the Royal Navy (1807–55), and served in the Arctic expeditions of **Parry** and **Franklin** (1819–22, 1825–27), and the Franklin search expedition of 1848–49. He wrote *Fauna Boreali-Americana* (1829–37), and *Ichthyology of the Voyage of HMS Erebus and Terror* (1844–48), and made great contributions to the knowledge of ichthyology of the Indo-Pacific region especially.

RICHARDSON, Sir Owen Willans (1879–1959) English physicist, born in Dewsbury, Yorkshire. He was educated at Cambridge, where at the Cavendish Laboratory he began his famous work on *thermionics*, a term he coined to describe the phenomenon of the emission of electricity from hot bodies; for this work he was awarded the Nobel prize for physics in 1928. He was appointed professor of physics at King's College, London, in 1914, and from 1924 to 1944 was Yarrow research professor of the Royal Society.

RICHARDSON, Sir Ralph (1902–83) English actor, born in Cheltenham. He made his London début in 1926 at the Haymarket, and played leading parts with the Old Vic Company, including the title roles of **Maugham**'s *Sheppey* and **Priestley**'s *Johnson over Jordan* (1930–32 and 1938). After war service he became co-director of the Old Vic, playing with the Stratford-on-Avon company in 1952, and toured Australia and New Zealand in 1955. His many stage appearances included *Home at Seven*, *The White Carnation*, *A Day at the Sea* and, later, *West of Suez* (1971), *The Cherry Orchard* (1978) and *The Understanding* (1982). His films include *The Shape of Things to Come*, *Anna Karenina*, *The Heiress*, *Oh, What a Lovely War*, *A Doll's House* and *Invitation to the Wedding*.

RICHARDSON, Samuel (1689–1761) English novelist, born in Derbyshire, where his father, a London joiner, had apparently taken refuge after the **Monmouth** rebellion. He may have gone to Merchant Taylor's School. He was apprenticed to a printer, married his master's daughter, and set up in business for himself in Salisbury Court, where in the heyday of his fame (and in much enlarged premises) he received Dr **Johnson, Edward Young** and the blue stockings. He was represented as the model parent and champion of women, but his three daughters seem to have had a repressed upbringing. In a letter he says that as a boy he wrote love letters for a group of young women, and this may have been the origin of his epistolary novels. In 1741 he published *Letters Written to and for Particular Friends*, generally referred to as *Familiar Letters*, which gave advice on 'how to think and act justly and prudently in the common concerns of human life'. *Pamela* (1749), his first novel, is also 'a series of familiar letters now first published in order to cultivate the Principles of Virtue and Religion', and this was the aim of all his works; but the virtue taught was of the prudential sort and the manners mean and bourgeois. After holding out for conditions against her brutal employer, Pamela, in the sequel, plays the Lady Bountiful and mingles easily in genteel life. In his second novel, *Clarissa, Or the History of a Young Lady*, Richardson depicts the high life, of which he confessed he knew little. Clarissa Harlowe in the toils of Lovelace is the main theme, but parental repression is also to be corrected. With all her charm Clarissa is too much the victim of her pride for her tragedy to be truly moving, and Lovelace is too ambiguous a character to be credible. Nevertheless, the seven volumes issued in 1748 made Richardson famous, and he was flattered by society as he took the cure at Tunbridge Wells or was visited at his fine new house, Northend. He corresponded with several society women. Fine ladies and gentlemen such as Lady **Mary Wortley Montagu, Horace Walpole** and Lord **Chesterfield** might 'hesitate dislike', but the middle classes were enthusiastic. Richardson's third novel, *Sir Charles Grandison* (1754), designed to portray the perfect gentleman, turns on the question of divided love. Not only English bluestockings but Continental writers raved about Richardson's novels. **Diderot**'s eulogy in *Le Journal étranger*, though extravagant, is sincere—his *La Religieuse* is modelled on Richardson—and **Rousseau**'s *La Nouvelle Héloïse* confesses his discipleship. Apart from its technical advantages and disadvantages, the epistolary method was a means to suggest authenticity at a time when mere fiction was frowned upon. Thus Richardson called himself the editor, not author, of his works. He was also a redoubtable correspondent.

RICHELIEU, Armand Jean Duplessis, Cardinal, Duc de (1585–1642) French prelate and statesman, born into a noble but impoverished family, of Richelieu near Chinon, and baptized in Paris. He abandoned the military profession for the clerical in order to keep in the family the bishopric of Luçon, to which he was consecrated at 22. In 1614 he became adviser to **Marie de' Medici**, regent for her son **Louis XIII**; and in 1616 he rose to be secretary at war and for foreign affairs, but next was sent back to his diocese. In 1622 he was named cardinal, in 1624 minister of state to Louis XIII. His first important measure was the blow to Spain of an alliance with Britain, cemented by the marriage (1625) of the king's sister **Henrietta Maria** with **Charles I**. His next great task was to destroy the political power of the Huguenots. La Rochelle was starved into submission (1628); and he destroyed Montauban, the last refuge of Huguenot independence. From 1629 he was chief minister and actual ruler of France. In 1630 he entered Italy with a splendid army, and reduced Savoy. Meanwhile he plunged into tortuous intrigues with the Italian princes, the pope, and the Protestants of the North against the House of Austria. He promised a large subsidy to **Gustav II Adolf**, and succeeded in persuading **Ferdinand II** to dismiss **Wallenstein**. The first treaty of Cherasco (April 1631) ended the Italian war; the second gave France the strategic position of Pinerolo. Just before this final triumph Richelieu successfully surmounted a great combination formed for his downfall by the queen-mother, the House of Guise and others. He was then made duke, and governor of Brittany. Further intrigues and attempted rebellions were crushed with merciless severity. In July 1632 Richelieu seized the duchy of Lorraine. He continued his intrigues with the Protestants against Ferdinand, subsidizing them with his gold, but until 1635 took no open part in the Thirty Years' War. In that year, after completing his preparations and concluding an alliance with Victor Amadeus of Savoy, Bernard of Saxe-Weimar and the Dutch, he declared war on Spain. His first efforts were unsuccessful; Piccolomini entered Picardy and threatened Paris. But Richelieu rose to the height of his genius; with 30000 foot and 12000 horse he swept the enemy out of Picardy while Bernard drove them across the Rhine, and in 1638 destroyed the imperial army at Rheinfelden. His policy soon led to the disorganization of the power of Spain, the victories of Wolfenbüttel and Kempten over the Imperialist forces in Germany, and at length in 1641 in Savoy, as well as the ascendancy of the French party. But the hatred of the great French nobles continued, and his safety lay in the king's helplessness without him. The last conspiracy against him was that of Henri Cinq-Mars, whose intrigues with the Duke of Bouillon and the Spanish court were soon revealed to the cardinal, the centre of a network of espionage which covered the whole of France. Cinq-Mars and De Thou were arrested and executed. While overwhelming the citizens with taxation, he had built up the power of the French crown, achieved for France a preponderance in Europe, destroyed the local liberties of France, and crushed every element of constitutional government. He never sacrificed to personal ambition what he thought the interests of his country, but he often forgot in his methods the laws of morality and humanity. The weakest point in Richelieu's character was his literary ambition. His plays sleep in safe oblivion, but his *Mémoires* are still read with interest. Other works include *Instruction du chrétien* (1619) and *Traité de la perfection du chrétien* (1646). He founded the French Academy in 1634.

RICHEPIN, Jean (1849–1926) French poet, playwright and novelist, born in Medeah, Algeria. Before the appearance of his first romance in 1872 he had been *franc-tireur*, sailor and actor. His revolutionary book of poems, *La Chanson des Gueux* (1876), led to a fine and his imprisonment.

RICHER, Jean (1630–96) French astronomer. He went to Cayenne, French Guiana, in 1671 to observe meridian transits of the Sun and measure the apparent distance of Mars from nearby stars; at the same time **Giovanni Cassini** would make the same observations from Paris, thus providing a base line from which the Earth-Sun distance could be calculated. To his surprise Richer found that his pendulum was running slow, which could be explained if Cayenne was further from the centre of the Earth than Paris, ie the Earth bulged at the equator. This gave **Newton** valuable information for his work on the size and shape of the Earth.

RICHET, Charles Robert (1850–1935) French physiologist, born and educated in Paris. He was professor there from 1887 to 1927. For his work on the phenomenon of anaphylaxis he was awarded the 1913 Nobel prize for physiology or medicine. He also did research on serum therapy.

RICHLER, Mordecai (1931–) Canadian novelist, born in Montreal. He grew up in a Jewish working-class neighbourhood and attended Baron Byng high school and Sir George Williams College. He travelled in Europe, but returned to Canada in 1952, working for the Canadian Broadcasting Corporation before moving to England in 1959, since when he has been a professional writer. His first novel, *The Acrobats* (1954), was derivative of **Hemingway** and subsequently disowned. In 1955 he published *Son of a Smaller Hero*, about a young man endeavouring to escape the Jewish ghetto and North American society in general. It was the first of several books for which he was accused of anti-semitism. It was followed by *A Choice of Enemies* (1957), but his break-through came with *The Apprenticeship of Duddy Kravitz* (1959), about an endearing shyster. Subsequent novels—*St Urbain's Horseman* (1971), *The Incomparable Auk* (1963) and *Cocksure* (1968)—have enhanced his reputation as one of Canada's richest novelists, a bawdy humorist and vitriolic satirist.

RICHMOND, Legh (1772–1827) English clergyman, born in Liverpool. He wrote the *Dairyman's Daughter*, *Negro Servant*, and *Young Cottager*, three famous evangelical tracts, collected as *Annals of the Poor* (1814).

RICHTER, Burton (1931–) American particle physicist, born in New York City. He studied at the Massachusetts Institute of Technology, and then joined the high-energy physics laboratory at Stanford University, where he became a professor in 1967. He was largely responsible for the Stanford Positron-Electron Accelerating Ring (SPEAR), a machine designed to collide positrons and electrons at high energies, and to study the resulting elementary particles. In 1974 a team led by him discovered the J/psi hadron, a new heavy elementary particle whose unusual properties supported **Sheldon Glashow**'s hypothesis of charm quarks. Many related particles were subsequently discovered, and stimulated a new look at the theoretical basis of particle physics. He shared the 1976 Nobel prize for physics with **Samuel Ting**, who had discovered the J/psi almost simultaneously. Richter became a strong proponent of the modern trend in particle physics towards building ever-larger particle accelerator rings.

RICHTER, Charles Francis (1900–85) American seismologist, born near Hamilton, Ohio. Educated at the University of Southern California and the California Institute of Technology, he worked at the Carnegie Institute before returning in 1936 to the California Institute of Technology, where he became professor of seismology in 1952. With **Beno Gutenburg**

he devised the scale of earthquake strength which bears his name (1927–35). It is an absolute scale based on the logarithm of the maximum amplitude of the earthquake waves observed on a seismograph, adjusted for the distance from the epicentre of the earthquake. Earthquakes of magnitude 5.5 or greater cause significant damage.

RICHTER, Hans (1843–1916) Hungarian conductor, born in Raab. After conducting in Munich, Budapest and Vienna, he began the Orchestral Concerts in London in 1879. In 1893 he became first court kapellmeister at Vienna, from 1900 to 1911 was conductor of the Hallé orchestra. He was an authority on the music of **Wagner**, with whom he was closely associated in the Bayreuth festival.

RICHTER, Hieronymus Theodor (1824–98) German chemist, born in Dresden. At the age of 19, with **Ferdinand Reich**, he discovered by spectroscopic analysis the element indium in zinc-blende.

RICHTER, Jeremias Benjamin (1762–1807) German chemist, born in Silesia. He studied under **Kant** at Königsberg, and discovered the law of equivalent proportions.

RICHTER, Johann Paul Friedrich, pseud **Jean Paul** (1763–1825) German novelist and humorist, born in Wunsiedel in north Bavaria. In 1781 he was sent to Leipzig to study theology, but turned to literature. He got into debt, and in 1784 fled from Leipzig, to hide in the poverty-stricken home of his widowed mother at Hof. His first literary efforts were satires which no-one would publish, until in 1783 **Voss** of Berlin gave him 40 louis d'or for *The Greenland Law-suits*. The book was a failure, and for three years Jean Paul struggled on at home. In 1787 he began to teach, and during his nine years of tutorship produced the satirical *Extracts from the Devil's Papers* (1789); the beautiful idylls *Dominie Wuz* (1793), *Quintus Fixlein* (1796; trans by **Carlyle**, 1827), and the *Parson's Jubilee* (1797); grand romances, such as *The Invisible Lodge* (1793), *Campanerthal* (1797) on the immortality of the soul; and the prose idyll, *My Prospective Autobiography* (1799). *The Invisible Lodge* was his first literary success; but *Hesperus* (1795) made him famous. For a few years he was the object of extravagant idolatry on the part of the women of Germany. In 1801 he married and three years later settled at Bayreuth, living there until his death. The principal works of his married life were the romances *Titan* (1800–03), which he himself considered his masterpiece and *Wild Oats* (1804–05), *Schmeltzle's Journey to Flätz* (1809; trans by Carlyle, 1827) and *Dr. Katzenberger's Trip to the Spa* (1809), the best of his satirico-humorous writings; the idyll *Fibel's Life* (1812); the fragment of another grand romance, *Nicholas Markgraf, or The Comet* (1820–22); reflections on literature (*Vorschule der Aesthetik*; improved ed 1812); another series on education (*Levana*, 1807), a book that ranks with **Rousseau**'s *Émile*; various patriotic writings (1808–12); and an unfinished *Autobiography* (1826). Jean Paul stands alone in German literature. All his great qualities of imagination and intellect were made subservient to his humour, which has the widest range, moving from the petty follies of individual men and the absurdities of social custom up to the paradoxes rooted in the universe. (1859).

RICHTER, Sviatoslav (Teofilovitch) (1914–) Russian pianist, born in Zhitomir. He studied at the Moscow Conservatory in 1942–47. He had made extensive concert tours, with a repertoire ranging from **Bach** to 20th-century composers, and was awarded the Stalin prize in 1949 and the Order of Lenin in 1965.

RICHTHOFEN, Ferdinand Baron von (1833–1905) German geographer and traveller, born in Karlsruhe in Silesia. In 1860 he accompanied a Prussian expedition to eastern Asia, then during the next twelve years travelled in Java, Siam, Burma, California, the Sierra Nevada, and China and Japan (1868–72). After his return (1872) he became president of the Berlin Geographical Society (1873–78), professor of geology at Bonn (1875), and of geography at Leipzig (1883), and at Berlin (1886). His reputation rests upon his great work on *China* (1877–1912), *Aufgaben der Geographie* (1833), etc.

RICHTHOFEN, Manfred, Baron von (1882–1918) German airman, born in Schweidnitz. At first in the cavalry, he later joined the German air force, and during World War I, as commander of the 11th Chasing Squadron ('Richthofen's Flying Circus'), was noted for his high number (80) of aerial victories. He was shot down behind the British lines.

RICKENBACKER, Edward Vernon (1890–1973) American aviator and World War I ace, born in Columbus, Ohio. His pre-war skill as a leading racing-car driver earned him the position of chauffeur to General **Pershing** in World War I, but he applied for aviation duties. In four months of combat flying he scored 26 victories and received a hero's welcome in the USA and the Congressional Medal of Honor. He returned to motor racing and formed the Rickenbacker Motor Company (1921). He became vice president and sales director of the Fokker Aircraft Company, and joined Eastern Air Lines in 1934 as pilot, becoming president and general manager in 1938 (chairman, 1959). During World War II he undertook a variety of assignments in military aviation; in November 1942 his plane ditched in the Pacific and he spent 23 days adrift on a raft before being rescued.

RICKERT, Heinrich (1863–1936) German philosopher, born in Danzig (now Gdansk, Poland). He became professor at Freiburg (1894) and Heidelberg (1916). He was a pupil of **Windelband**, and with him a founder of the Baden school of neo-Kantianism, which developed a distinctive theory of historical knowledge and the foundations of the social sciences. Rickert argued for a *Kulturwissenschaft* (science of culture) which could be an objective science of those universal concepts like religion, art and law that emerge from the multiplicity of individual cultures and societies. His views were strongly contrasted to those of **Dilthey** and were a great influence on, among others, **Max Weber**. His main works are *Die Grenzen der naturwissenschaftlichen Begriffsbildung* (1896–1902), and *Kulturwissenschaft und Naturwissenschaft* (1899).

RICKEY, Wesley Branch (1881–1965) American baseball manager and administrator, born in Stockdale, Ohio. Nicknamed 'The Mahatma', he had a profound influence on top-class baseball. In 1919, as manager of the St Louis Cardinals, he introduced the 'farm system' whereby major league clubs linked themselves to lower-grade clubs to develop their own young players; this brought his team four world championships and made them the most profitable in baseball. While manager of the Brooklyn Dodgers (1942–50) he broke the colour barrier in major league baseball by signing the first black player, **Jackie Robinson**. In 1967 he was posthumously elected to the National Baseball Hall of Fame.

RICKLIS, Meshulam (1923–) Turkish-born American financier. Born in Istanbul and educated in Israel, he went to the USA at 24 as a teacher of Hebrew, but soon became involved in business and in 1955 became an American citizen.

RICKMAN, Thomas (1776–1841) English architect, born in Maidenhead. He was in succession chemist, grocer, doctor, cornfactor and insurance agent in Liverpool, before becoming in 1820 an architect in Birmingham. He designed a number of churches in the revived Gothic style; also the New Court at St John's College, Cambridge. He wrote *Styles of Architecture in England* (1817).

RICKOVER, Hyman George (1900–86) Russian-born American naval engineering officer, born in Makov (now Poland). Taken to the USA as a child, he graduated from the US Naval Academy in 1922, and in 1929 received a master's degree in electrical engineering from Columbia University. His greatest achievement was leadership of the team that successfully adapted nuclear reactors as a means of ship propulsion, the first vessel so equipped being the USS *Nautilus*, the world's first nuclear submarine, launched in 1954.

RICOEUR, Paul (1913–) French philosopher, born in Valence, Drôme. Educated at the Lycée de Rennes and at the University of Paris, he became professor successively at Strasbourg (1948–56), Paris-Nanterre (1956–70) and Chicago (1970). He was a pupil of **Marcel**, and as a prisoner in World War II read deeply in **Jaspers, Heidegger** and **Husserl**. Their influences are all evident in his work, and he published commentaries on Husserl—in particular *Husserl: an analysis of his Phenomenology* (1967), and a dialogue with Marcel (*Entretiens Paul Ricoeur-Gabriel Marcel*, 1973). He has been an influential if rather unclassifiable figure in both French and Anglo-American philosophy, engaging critically with various contemporary methodologies—structuralism, phenomenology, psychoanalysis and hermeneutics—across a whole range of problems about the nature of language, interpretation, human action and will, freedom and evil. His other publications include a major work on the will, *Philosophie de la Volonté* (3 vols, 1950–60), *Histoire et Verité* (1955), *De l'interprétation: Essai sur Freud* (1965), *Le Conflit des interprétations: Essais d'herméneutique* (1969) and *La Métaphore vive* (1975).

RIDDELL, George Allardice Riddell, 1st Baron (1865–1934) Scottish lawyer and newspaper proprietor, born in Duns, Berwickshire. Educated in London, he rose from boy clerk to solicitor, and through one of his clients, the Cardiff *Western Mail*, became further involved in the newspaper world, at first as legal adviser to the *News of the World*, later as its chairman; he also became chairman of George Newnes, Ltd. Knighted in 1909, he represented the British press at the Paris peace conference in 1919, and the following year was raised to the peerage.

RIDDELL, William Renwick (1852–1945) Canadian judge and legal historian. Educated at Cobourg Collegiate Institute, Victoria University and Syracuse University, he was judge of the High Court of Ontario from 1906 and of the Supreme Court of Canada from 1917. A prolific writer, he made notable contributions to Canadian history, particularly legal history, such as *The Legal Profession of Upper Canada in its Early Years* (1916), and *The Bar and the Courts of the Province of Upper Canada or Ontario* (1928), and wrote biographies of early Canadian public men and judges, as well as a vast number of papers in legal and historical journals.

RIDE, Sally Kristen (1951–) American astronaut, born in Los Angeles, the first American woman in space. Educated at Westlake High School, Los Angeles, and Stanford University, she studied in physics and English, taking a doctoral degree in physics in 1978. While a student she achieved national ranking as a tennis player, but chose not to follow this as a career. In 1978 she was selected as an astronaut candidate by NASA, and became a mission specialist on future Space Shuttle flight crews. She was selected to serve on a planned six-day flight of the orbiter Challenger (June 1983). In August 1987 she published a report to the Administrator of Nasa on 'Leadership—and America's Future in Space'.

RIDEAL, Sir Eric Keightley (1890–1974) English chemist. He worked at Cambridge (1930–46), the Royal Institution, London (1946–49), and London University (1950–55). He studied colloids and catalysis, and devised the Rideal-Walker test for the germicidal power of a disinfectant.

RIDGE, William Pett (1857–1930) English writer, born in Chatham, Kent. He is best known as an exponent of cockney humour, in works like *A Clever Wife* and *Mord Em'ly*.

RIDGEWAY, John (1938–) English trans-Atlantic oarsman and explorer. Educated at the Nautical College, Pangbourne, he served in the Merchant Navy, before doing his national service with the Royal Engineers. After two years at the Royal Military Academy, Sandhurst, he was commissioned into the Parachute Regiment and served in Canada, Norway, Greece, the Arabian Gulf, Kenya and Malaysia. In 1966 he rowed the Atlantic in 92 days from the USA to Eire with Chay Blyth. He then sailed the Atlantic single-handed to South America, led an expedition that followed the River Amazon from source to sea, and another which crossed the Chilean ice-cap. He participated in the 1977–78 Round the World Race with a team from the School of Adventure run from his home at Ardmore in Scotland.

RIDGWAY, Mathew Bunker (1895–) American soldier, born in Virginia. Educated at US Military Academy, West Point, he commanded the 82nd Airborne Division in Sicily (1943), and Normandy (1944). He commanded the 18th Airborne Corps in the North West Europe campaign (1944–45) and the US 8th Army in United Nations operations in Korea (1950). He succeeded **Douglas Macarthur** in command of US and UN forces (1951), and was supreme allied commander Europe in succession to **Eisenhower** (1952–53), and chief of US Army Staff (1953).

RIDGWAY, Robert (1850–1929) American ornithologist, born in Mount Carmel, Illinois. Curator of birds at the US National Museum, he devised the Ridgway colour system for bird identification. His books included *A History of North American Birds* (1874–84) and *The Birds of Middle and North America* (8 vols, 1901–19).

RIDING, Laura, original surname **Reichenthal** (1901–) American poet, critic, novelist and polemicist, born in New York, the daughter of an Austrian immigrant. Educated at Cornell, she married a history lecturer, Louis Gottschalt (divorced in 1925). She went to Europe in 1925 and remained there until the outbreak of World War II. She published her first collection of verse, *The Close Chaplet*, in 1926, and took the name Riding. She was long associated with **Robert Graves**, with whom she lived in various Mediterranean locations and with whom she collaborated on several projects including *A Survey of Modernist Poetry* (1927). In 1941 she married Schulyer B Jackson, editor of *Time*, and signed herself 'Laura (Riding) Jackson'. Although overshadowed by Graves, her poetry is much anthologized. The *Collected Poems* appeared in 1938, a year after *The Trojan Ending*, a poor historical novel. Other titles are *Contemporaries and Snobs* (1918), *Anarchism is not Enough* (1928), and *Experts are Puzzled* (1930).

RIDLEY, Nicholas (c.1500–1555) English Protestant martyr, born in Unthank Hall near Haltwhistle. He was elected in 1524 a fellow of Pembroke College, Cambridge, studied at Paris and Louvain (1527–30), and became proctor at Cambridge in 1534, domestic chaplain to **Cranmer** and **Henry VIII**, master of Pembroke in 1540, canon, first of Canterbury, then of Westminster, rector of Soham, and in 1547 bishop of Rochester. An ardent and outspoken reformer, he was in 1550, on the deprivation of **Edmund Bonner**, bishop of London, made his successor. In this high position he distinguished himself by his moderation, learning and munificence, and assisted Cranmer in the preparation of the Thirty-Nine Articles. On the death of **Edward VI** he denounced **Mary I** and **Elizabeth** as illegitimate, and espoused the cause of Lady **Jane Grey**; on Mary's accession he was stripped of his dignities and sent to the Tower. In 1554 he was tried at Oxford, with **Latimer** and Cranmer, by a committee of Convocation; all three were adjudged obstinate heretics and condemned. Ridley lay in jail for 18 months, and after a second trial was burnt, along with Latimer, in front of Balliol College, Oxford.

RIDLEY, Nicholas (1929–) English politician, born in Newcastle-upon-Tyne, the son of the 3rd Viscount Ridley. After Eton and Oxford he embarked on an industrial career then moved into politics, winning the safe Conservative seat of Cirencester and Tewkesbury in 1959. He held junior ministerial posts under **Harold Macmillan**, Sir **Alec Douglas-Home** and **Edward Heath** (1962–70), and in 1979 joined the **Margaret Thatcher** government, entering the cabinet in 1983. Regarded in ideological terms as one of Mrs Thatcher's closest allies, he has also been singled out for an apparent insensitivity in his relations with the media and the public. This led to his being moved, in 1989, from the department of environment, where he had had responsibility for the controversial 'poll tax', to the department of trade and industry.

RIDOLFO, Robert di (1531–1612) Florentine conspirator, operating in England against Queen **Elizabeth**. A businessman in London, in 1570 he organized a Roman Catholic plot, supported by Spain, to marry **Mary, Queen of Scots** to **Thomas Howard**, 4th Duke of Norfolk, and overthrow Elizabeth. The plot was discovered when an emissary was seized.

RIDPATH, George (c.1717–1772) Scottish historian, born in Ladykirk manse in Berwickshire. Minister from 1742 of Stitchell, he wrote a *Border History* (1776).

RIE, Lucie (1902–) Austrian potter, born in Vienna. Trained at the Kunstwerbeschule, in 1938 she moved to England where she shared a workshop with **Hans Coper**, producing ceramic jewellery and buttons while continuing her individual work. She has produced stoneware, tin glazed earthenware and porcelain pots throughout her working life with a precision and technical control that has influenced many of today's leading contemporary potters.

RIEFENSTAHL, Leni (1902–) German filmmaker, born in Berlin. She studied fine art and ballet, but turned to film acting. After appearing in several films she formed her own production company and directed and starred in *The Blue Light* (1932). Her *Triumph of the Will* (1936)—a compelling record of a Nazi rally at Nuremberg—vividly illustrated **Hitler**'s charismatic appeal, but tainted Riefenstahl's career, having prompted criticism that she had glorified and sympathized with the event. *Olympia* (1938), her epic documentary of the 1936 Berlin Olympic Games, was given a gala premiere on Hitler's 49th birthday. After the war, she was blacklisted by the Allies until 1952, when she completed a film based on **Eugene D'Albert**'s opera *Tiefland*. A 1956 film, *Schwarze Fracht*, was never completed, and a 1977 documentary, *Nuba*, was never released.

RIEGGER, Wallingford (1885–1961) American composer, born in Albany, Georgia. He studied at Cornell University, the Institute of Musical Art, New York, and in Berlin, and went on to hold posts at Drake University and Ithaca Conservatory, New York. His works, which show the influence of **Schoenberg**'s 'twelve-note' system and his German training, received little attention until the performance of his third symphony in 1948, since when he has been increasingly recognized. He wrote extensively for orchestra and for chamber music combinations.

RIEL, Louis (1844–85) Canadian insurgent, born in St Boniface, Manitoba. He succeeded his father as a leader of the Métis (French half-breeds) opposed to the incorporation of the North-West Territories into the dominion of Canada, and headed the Red River rebellion in 1869–70, setting up a provisional government with himself as president. He fled in 1870. In 1885 he again established a rebel government, and in November, the rising having been quelled, he was executed.

RIEMANN, Georg Friedrich Bernhard (1826–66) German mathematician, born in Breselenz. He studied in Göttingen under **Carl Friedrich Gauss** and in Berlin, and succeeded **Gustav Dirichlet** as professor of mathematics at Göttingen in 1859. He was forced to retire by illness in 1862 and died of tuberculosis in Italy. His first publication (1851) was on the foundations of the theory of functions of a complex variable including the result now known as the Riemann mapping theorem. In this and a later paper (1857) on abelian functions he introduced the concept of 'Riemann surface' to deal with 'multi-valued' algebraic functions; this was to become a key idea in the development of analysis. His famous lecture in 1854, 'On the hypotheses that underlie geometry', given in the presence of the aged Gauss, first introduced the concept of a 'manifold', an *n*-dimensional curved space, greatly extending the non-Euclidean geometry of **János Bolyai** and **Nikolai Lobachevski**. These ideas were essential in the formulation of **Einstein**'s theory of general relativity, and have led to the modern theory of differentiable manifolds which plays a vital part in current attempts to unify relativity and quantum theory. Riemann's name is also associated with the zeta-function which is central to the study of the distribution of prime numbers; the 'Riemann hypothesis' is a famous unsolved problem concerning this function.

RIEMANN, Hugo (1849–1919) German musicologist, born in Sondershausen. Author of many works on the history and theory of music, he wrote exercises and studies for piano, as well as composing chamber music and a variety of songs. He was professor at Leipzig from 1901.

RIEMENSCHNEIDER, Tilman (1460–1531) German sculptor, born in Osterode. He spent his life after 1483 in Würzburg, where he rose to become burgomaster, but was imprisoned for participating in the Peasants' Revolt of 1525. The greatest carver of his period, he executed many fine sepulchral monuments and church decorations. His best work was in wood, but he also worked in stone.

RIEMERSCHMID, Richard (1868–1957) German architect and designer, born in Munich. In 1897, after varied experience, he founded werkstätten (craft workshops) in Munich, for which he designed furniture. His early furniture possessed some of the linear freedom of Art Nouveau without the naturalistic decoration. However, his designs of 1905 for the Deutsche Werkstätten in Dresden were functional, of simple construction and suitable for mass-production as befitted a future founder-member of the Deutsche Werkbund (1907). His enormous output over almost 50 years included architecture, furniture and interiors, glass and ceramics, cutlery, light-fittings and graphics. He was a major figure and influence in the development of 20th-century German design and industry.

RIENZO, or **Rienzi, Cola di** (c.1313–1354) Italian patriot, born in Rome of humble parentage. In 1343 he was spokesman of a deputation sent in vain to Avignon to beseech Pope **Clement VI** to return to Rome. In May 1347 he incited the citizens to rise against the rule of the nobles. The senators were driven out, and Rienzo was invested with practically dictatorial power. At his request the Italian states sent deputies to Rome to devise measures for unification and common good, and Rienzo was crowned tribune. But the nobles were still bitterly hostile. The papal authority was turned against him; and, his seven months' reign over, he fled to Naples. After two years of religious meditation Rienzo resumed his life as political reformer, but was taken prisoner by the emperor and sent to Clement VI at Avignon. A new pope, Innocent VI, sent him to Rome to crush the power of the nobles, but after accomplishing this Rienzo aimed at re-establishing himself in supreme authority. In August 1354, having raised a small body of soldiers, he made a sort of triumphal entry into Rome, but his conduct then was such that the Romans murdered him. **Wagner**'s opera on his story was produced in 1842.

RIESENER, Jean Paul (1734–1806) French cabinet-maker, born in München-Gladbach, Prussia. He worked in Paris from 1754, and was a master of marquetry and ebony work, favoured by **Louis XVI**'s court.

RIESZ, Frigyes (Frédéric) (1880–1956) Hungarian mathematician, born in Györ. He studied at Zürich, Budapest and Göttingen, then lectured at the University of Szeged. He worked in functional analysis, integral equations and subharmonic functions, and developed a new approach to the **Lebesgue** integral. His textbook on functional analysis, written in 1952 with Bela Szökefalvi-Nagy (1887–1953), has been translated into English.

RIETSCHEL, Ernst (1804–61) German sculptor, of the Dresden school. He executed the **Goethe** and **Schiller** monument at Weimar, the **Luther** memorial at Worms, and many other monuments and portrait busts.

RIETVELD, Gerrit Thomas (1888–1964) Dutch architect and furniture designer, born in Utrecht. He started his career as a woodworker, opening his own cabinet-making workshop in Utrecht in 1911. At evening school he studied architecture, and started to make furniture designed by his teacher P J Klaarhamer. Sparked off by these remarkable pieces, Rietveld began to design his own furniture leading to the famous 'red-blue' chair of 1918, which is an experiment concerning form in space as much as a piece of furniture. Space, its exploitation and how objects impinge upon it, was at the core of all Rietveld's work. The architectural equivalent of the chair was the Schröder House in Utrecht (1924); both also exhibit the rectilinear quality and use of colour associated with the De Stijl movement. He designed many buildings and pieces of furniture, but the culmination of his work is the Van Gogh Museum, Amsterdam, completed posthumously in 1973.

RIEU, Emile Victor (1887–1972) English editor and translator, born in London. A classical scholar, he formed the habit of translating aloud to his wife, and it was her interest in *The Odyssey* that encouraged him to start on his own version. It was offered to Allen Lane, the founder of Penguin, the paperback publisher, and published in 1946. It became the cornerstone of the new Penguin Classics of which Rieu became editor. By his retirement in 1964 *The Odyssey* had sold over two million copies.

RIGAUD, Hyacinthe (1659–1743) French portrait painter, born in Perpignan. He settled in Paris in 1681 as a portrait painter to the French Court. His portrait of **Louis XIV** in full robes (1701) is in the Louvre.

RIISAGER, Knudäge (1897–1975) Danish composer, born in Port Kunda, Russia, by 1900 he had returned with his parents to Denmark. He took a political economy degree at Copenhagen, then went to Paris, where he studied under Paul le Flem and **Albert Roussel**, and was influenced by other French composers. On his return to Denmark he shocked conventional musical circles by his revolutionary compositions and writings. Polytonality, polyrhythm and unique syncopations abound in his works, which include the overtures *Erasmus Montanus* and *Klods Hans*, symphonies, ballets, including the well-known *Quarrtsiluni*, and a piano sonata (1931).

RILEY, Bridget Louise (1931–) English painter, born in London. Educated at Cheltenham Ladies' College, she studied at Goldsmith's College of Art (1949–52) and at the Royal College of Art (1952–55), holding her first one-woman show in London at Gallery One in 1962; this was followed by others worldwide. She is a leading Op artist, manipulating overall flat patterns, originally in black and white but later in colour, using repeated shapes or undulating lines which dazzle the beholder, often creating an illusion of movement, eg *Fall*, 1963. She was the first English painter to win the major painting prize at the Venice Biennale (1968).

RILEY, James Whitcomb (1849–1916) American poet, known as the 'Hoosier poet', born in Greenfield, Indiana. He made his name contributing homely dialect poems to the *Indianapolis Journal* (1877–85). He published several volumes, and is also known for his poems about children, including 'Little Orfant Annie'.

RILKE, Rainer Maria (1875–1926) Austrian lyric poet, born in Prague. He deserted a military academy to study art history in Prague, Munich and Berlin. The spiritual melancholy of his early verse turns into a mystical quest for the deity in such works as *Geschichten vom lieben Gott* (1900) and *Das Stundenbuch* (1905), written after two journeys to Russia (1899–1900), where he met **Tolstoy** and was deeply influenced by Russian pietism. In 1901 he married Klara Westhoff, a pupil of **Rodin**, whose secretary Rilke became in Paris, publishing *Das Rodin-Buch* (1907). Mysticism was abandoned for the aesthetic ideal in *Gedichte* (1907, 1908). *Die Aufzeichnungen des Malte Laurids Brigg* (1910) portrays the anxious loneliness of an imaginary poet. In 1923 he wrote two masterpieces, *Die Sonnette an Orpheus* and *Duineser Elegien*, in which he exalts the poet as the mediator between crude nature and pure form. His work greatly extended the range of expression and subtlety of the German language.

RIMBAUD, (Jean Nicolas) Arthur (1854–91) French poet, born in Charleville, Ardennes, the son of an army captain and his stern, disciplinarian wife. After a brilliant academic career at the Collège de Charleville, he published in 1870 his first book of poems, and the same year ran away to Paris, the first stage in his life of wandering. He soon returned to Charleville, where he wrote, while leading a life of leisure, drinking and bawdy conversation, *Le Bateau ivre*, which, with its verbal eccentricities, daring imagery and evocative language, is perhaps his most popular work. Soon after its publication in August 1871, **Verlaine** invited Rimbaud to Paris, where they began a homosexual affair. In Brussels in July 1873 he threatened to terminate the friendship, and was shot at and wounded by Verlaine, who was imprisoned for attempted murder. The relationship had, however, given Rimbaud some measure of stability, and from its height, the summer of 1872, date many of *Les Illuminations*, the work which most clearly states his poetic doctrine. These prose and verse poems show Rimbaud as a precursor of symbolism, with his use of childhood, dream and mystical images to express dissatisfaction with the material world and a longing for the spiritual. In 1873 he published the prose volume *Un Saison en enfer*, which symbolized his struggle to break with his past—his 'enfer' (hell); he was bitterly disappointed at its cold reception by the literary critics, burned all his manuscripts, and at the age of 19 turned his back on literature. Then began years of varied and colourful wandering in Europe and the East—in Germany, Sweden, Aden, Cyprus and Harar, as soldier, trader, explorer and gun-runner. During these years, in 1866, Verlaine published *Les Illuminations* as by the 'late Arthur Rimbaud', but the author ignored, rather than was ignorant of, the sensation they caused and the reputation they were making for him. In April 1891, troubled by a leg infection, he left Harar and sailed to Marseilles, where his leg was amputated, and where he died.

RIMINI See **FRANCESCA DA RIMINI**

RIMSKY-KORSAKOV, Nikolai Andreievich (1844–1908) Russian composer, born in Tikhvin, Novgorod. His early musical education was perfunctory until 1859, when he took some piano lessons and developed a taste for composition, making arrangements of the operatic tunes of **Glinka**, whom he greatly admired. In 1861 he was introduced to **Balakirev**, who became his friend and mentor, and to **Mussorgsky**. Encouraged by his new companions, he started a symphony, completed during his years of duty as a naval officer. His knowledge of the tools of the composer's trade was still extremely limited when, in 1867, he wrote his first version of the fairy-tale fantasy *Sadko*, and began his opera *The Maid of Pskov* in 1868. In 1871 he was offered a professorship at the St Petersburg Conservatory which, conscious of his technical shortcomings, he hesitated to accept, but eventually he took the plunge and by assiduous study caught up on his academic deficiences. He was greatly helped at this time by Nadezhda Purgold, a musician and a composer in her own right, whom he married in 1872. In 1877 he published a collection of Russian folk songs, and he spent a good deal of time studying instrumentation with his friend **Borodin**, after whose death he and **Glazunov** completed the unfinished *Prince Igor*. He also arranged and reorchestrated much of Mussorgsky's output. In 1887–88 he produced his three great orchestral masterpieces—*Capriccio Espagnol*, *Easter Festival* and *Scheherazade*—but thereafter turned to opera, which occupied his attention, apart from revisions of earlier works, for the rest of his life. Among his best in this genre are *The Snow Maiden* (1882), *The Tsar Saltan* (1900), *The Invisible City of Kitesh* (1906) and *The Golden Cockerel*, his last work, begun in 1906, based on a satire against autocracy by **Pushkin** and banned at first from the Russian stage. A revised version of *Sadko* appeared in 1898, and *The Maid of Pskov* reappeared, staged by **Diaghilev** as *Ivan the Terrible*, in 1908. Since 1892 Rimsky-Korsakov had suffered with cerebro-spinal neurasthenia, and his life was saddened by the loss of two children in 1891 and 1893. His music is notable, however, for its brilliance and native vitality, and for the colour engendered by his great flair for orchestration. Constantly aware of his earlier technical shortcomings, he rewrote almost all his early work. **Stravinsky** was his pupil. His *My Musical Life* was translated by Joffe in 1942.

RINGAN, St See **NINIAN**

RINUCCINI, Ottavio (1562–1621) Italian poet. He wrote *Dafne* (1594), the first Italian melodrama, based on the earlier Greek work.

RIPLEY, George (1802–80) American social reformer and literary critic, born in Greenfield, Massachusetts. A graduate of Harvard, he was a Unitarian pastor in Boston until 1841. He joined in the Transcendental movement with **Amos Bronson Alcott**, founded *The Dial* in 1840, and helped **Sarah Margaret Fuller** to edit it. In 1841 he organized and led the idealistic communal experiment at Brook Farm, near Boston, based on the socialist theories of **François Fourier**, but this went bankrupt in 1847. He edited *The Harbinger* (1845–49), and became literary critic for the *New York Tribune* (1849–80). In 1850 he founded *Harper's New Monthly Magazine*, and was joint-editor with **Charles Anderson Dana** of the *New American Cyclopaedia* (1858–63).

RIPON, Frederick John Robinson, Earl of (1782–1859) English statesman, second son of the second Lord Grantham. He was educated at Harrow and St John's College, Cambridge. In 1806 he entered parliament as a moderate Tory, and had successively been under-secretary for the colonies, vice-president of the board of trade, and Chancellor of the Exchequer, when, as Viscount Goderich, in 1827 he became head of a brief administration. He was later colonial secretary, lord privy seal, and president of the board of trade, and in 1833 was created Earl of Ripon.

RIPON, George Frederick Samuel Robinson, Marquis of (1827–1909) English statesman, son of Frederick, Earl of **Ripon**. He succeeded his father as Earl of Ripon and his uncle as Earl de Grey. From 1852 he sat in parliament as a Liberal, and he became successively under-secretary for war (1859), under-secretary for India (1861), secretary for war (1863–66), secretary for India (1866), lord president of the Council (1868–73), grand master of the Freemasons (1870), which office he resigned in 1874 on his conversion to Catholicism, Marquis of Ripon (1871), and viceroy of India (1880–84). He was First Lord of the Admiralty in 1886, colonial secretary in 1892–95, and lord privy seal in 1905–08.

RIPPERDA, Johann Wilhelm, Baron de (1680–1737) Dutch political adventurer, born in Groningen. He was Dutch ambassador to Spain, then turned Catholic and joined the Spanish diplomatic service (1718), became prime minister (1725) but was imprisoned, escaped to Holland and became a Protestant again, then turned Muslim in the service of the sultan of Morocco and commanded an army against Spain. He died in Tetuan.

RIPPON, Geoffrey, Baron Rippon of Hexham (1924–) English politician. Educated at King's College, Taunton, and Brasenose College, Oxford, he qualified as a barrister in his mid-twenties, entering private practice and, at the same time, becoming increasingly active in local politics for the Conservative party. He entered the House of Commons in 1955 and served in the governments of **Harold Macmillan**, **Alec Douglas-Home** and **Edward Heath**. A committed European, he led the UK delegation to the Council of Europe and the Western European Union (WEU) (1967–70). He left the House of Commons in 1987 to concentrate on business interests, and was made a life peer.

RIQUET DE BONREPAS, Baron Pierre Paul (1604–80) French land owner, administrator and promoter of the Languedoc or Canal du Midi, born in Béziers. Through his intimate knowledge of the region he became convinced that a canal linking the Atlantic with the Mediterranean by way of the rivers Garonne and Aude would be a practical proposition. Eventually, through **Colbert**, he obtained the support of **Louis XIV**, and work began in 1666. With a labour force of more than 8000 he supervised the construction of the canal from Toulouse to Sète, a distance of 260 km involving over 100 locks, several aqueducts and a short tunnel. He died a few months before the completion of the canal in 1681.

RISTORI, Adelaide (1822–1906) Italian tragédienne, born in Cividale in Friuli. She rapidly became the leading Italian actress of her day. In 1847 her marriage with the Marquis del Grillo temporarily interrupted her dramatic career. She won a complete triumph before a French audience in 1855, when **Elisa Rachel** was at the height of her fame; and gained fresh laurels in nearly every country of Europe, in the USA (1866, 1875, 1884–85), and in South America. She wrote *Memoirs and Artistic Studies* (trans 1907).

RITCHIE, Anne Isabella, Lady (1837–1919) English writer, daughter of **William Makepeace Thackeray**, born in London. A close companion of her father, and well acquainted with his friends of literary and artistic note, she contributed valuable personal reminiscences to an 1898–99 edition of his works, and also wrote memoirs of their contemporaries, such as **Tennyson** and **Ruskin**. Her novels include *The Village on the Cliff* (1867) and *Old Kensington* (1873).

RITS, Jacob August (1849–1914) Danish-born American journalist and social critic, born in Ribe. He emigrated to the USA in 1870 and became a police reporter on the New York *Tribune* (1877–88) and the New York *Sun* (1888–99). He published a horrifying description of immigrant poverty in New York in 1890 entitled *How the Other Half Lives*: it was the first use of photographic evidence in reportage of social content. He followed this up with several more books, enthusiastically championed the reforms of **Theodore Roosevelt** and wrote a study of him, and a useful autobiography, *The Making of an American* (1901). He was active in the movement for small parks and playgrounds, and in tenement housing and school reform.

RITSCHL, Albrecht (1822–89) German Protestant theologian, born in Berlin, cousin of **Friedrich Wilhelm Ritschl**. He became professor of theology at Bonn (1851), and Göttingen (1864). His principal work is on the doctrine of justification and reconciliation (1870–74). Other works were on Christian perfection (1874), conscience (1876), pietism (1880–86), theology and metaphysics (1881). The distinguishing feature of the Ritschlian theology is the prominence it gives to the practical, ethical, social side of Christianity.

RITSCHL, Friedrich Wilhelm (1806–76) German classical scholar, born near Erfurt, cousin of **Albrecht Ritschl**. He received classical chairs at Breslau (1834), Bonn (1839) and Leipzig (1865). His great edition of **Plautus** (1848–54) was preceded by *Parerga Plautina et Terentiana* (1845). His *Priscae Latinitatis Monumenta Epigraphica* (1864) was the forerunner of the *Corpus Inscriptionum*.

RITSON, Joseph (1752–1803) English antiquary, born in Stockton-on-Tees. He went to London in 1775 and practised as a conveyancer, but was enabled to give most of his time to antiquarian studies. He was as notorious for his vegetarianism, whimsical spelling and irreverence as for his attacks on literary reputations. His first important work was an onslaught on **Thomas Warton**'s *History of English Poetry* (1782). He assailed (1783) **Johnson** and **Steevens** for their text of **Shakespeare**, and **Thomas Percy** for his *Reliques*, in *Select Collection of English Songs* (1783). In 1792 appeared his *Cursory Criticisms* on **Malone**'s Shakespeare. He also exposed **John Pinkerton's** forgeries, in *Select Scottish Ballads* (1784), and the Shakespeare forgeries of Samuel Ireland.

RITTER, Johann Wilhelm (1776–1810) German physicist, born in Silesia. While working in Jena he discovered (1802) the ultraviolet rays in the spectrum (see **W H Wollaston**). He also worked on electricity.

RITTER, Karl (1779–1859) German geographer, born in Quedlinburg. He became professor of geography at Berlin (1829), and director of studies of the Military School. He laid the foundations of modern scientific geography, his most important work, *Die Erkunde...* (1817), stressing the relation between man and his natural environment. He also wrote a comparative geography (English ed 1865).

RIVAROL, Antoine (1753–1801) French writer, born in Bagnols in Languedoc. He went to Paris in 1780, and in 1788 set the whole city laughing at the sarcasms in his *Petit Almanach de nos grands hommes*. Emigrating in 1792, and supported by royalist pensions, he wrote pamphlets in Brussels, London, Hamburg and Berlin.

RIVAS, Angel de Saavedra, Duque de (1791–1865) Spanish politician and writer, born in Córdoba, educated in Madrid. He served in the Civil War, lived in exile (1823–34), became minister of the interior in 1835, and was soon exiled again. In 1837 he returned, became prime minister, and later was ambassador in Naples, Paris (1856) and Florence (1860). Alongside his political life, Rivas led his literary one, as an early exponent of Spanish romanticism. His works include the epics *Florinda* (1826) and *El Moro expósito* (1834), the dramatic poems *Romances históricos* (1841), and several dramas, including *Don Alvaro* or *La Fuerza del Sino* (1835), on which **Verdi** based his opera *La Forza del Destino*.

RIVERA, Diego (1886–1957) Mexican painter, born in Guanajuato. In 1921 he began a series of murals in public buildings depicting the life and history (particularly the popular uprisings) of the Mexican people. From 1930 to 1934 he executed a number of frescoes in the USA, mainly of industrial life. His art is a curious blend of the rhetorical realism of folk art and revolutionary propaganda, with overtones of Byzantine and Aztec symbolism. His *Man at the Crossroads* mural for the Rockefeller Center in New York (1933) was removed and put up in Mexico City because it contained an apparent portrait of **Lenin**. He was married to **Frida Kahlo**.

RIVERA Y ORBANEJA, Miguel Primo de, Marquis of Estella (1878–1930) Spanish soldier and statesmen, born in Jerez de la Frontera, the nephew of General **Primo de Rivera**, Marquis of Estella. Educated at the Military Academy, Madrid, he distinguished himself from an early age on active service in Morocco, in the Philippines and Cuba. He was governor of Cadiz (1915) and captain general of Madrid (1919) and of Catalonia (1922). He led the *pronunciamiento* and established the Directory to govern Spain under King **Alfonso** (1923). He personally commanded the combined Franco-Spanish operations against an uprising by Riffs in Morocco (1925), but was dismissed by the king for breach of the constitution in 1930.

RIVERS, Anthony Woodville, 2nd Earl (?1442–1483) English nobleman, son of **Richard Woodville** 1st Earl, and brother of **Elizabeth Woodville** (who married

Edward IV in 1464). He had given his allegiance in 1461 to Edward, who made him captain-general of the forces. He followed him into exile in 1470, becoming lieutenant of Calais, and helped him make his triumphant return in 1471. He was tutor to the Prince of Wales (the future **Edward V**), translated from French the *Dictes or Sayings of the Philosophers* which **Caxton** published (1477). After King Edward's death in 1483, he was put to death by **Richard III**.

RIVERS, Augustus Pitt- See **PITT-RIVERS**

RIVERS, Joan, originally **Joan Alexandra Molinsky** (1933–) American comedienne and writer, born in Larchmont, New York. A starstruck child, keen on amateur dramatics, she appeared as an extra in the film *Mr. Universe* (1951). After graduating from college, she became a fashion co-ordinator for Bond stores whilst still harbouring notions of a showbusiness career. Concentrating on these aspirations from 1958, she appeared in *Seawood* (1959) and other minor plays before working with the Chicago improvisational troupe Second City (1961–62) and developing her prowess as an acid-tongued, stand-up comedienne dealing in personal intimacies and vituperative assaults on public figures. Success came with an appearance on *The Tonight Show* in 1965. She made her Las Vegas début in 1969, wrote a regular column in *The Chicago Tribune* (1973–76), directed the film *Rabbit Test* (1978), recorded an album *What Becomes A Semi-Legend Most* (1983), and was the regular guest host of *The Tonight Show* (1983–86). She has also hosted *The Late Show* (1986–87) and *Hollywood Squares* (1987–). Her books include *Having A Baby Can Be A Scream* (1974) and an autobiography, *Enter Talking* (1986).

RIVERS, Richard Woodville, 1st Earl (d.1469) English soldier. He was esquire to **Henry V**, and during his son's reign was made governor of the Tower (1424) and knighted (1425). He fought in France, and for the Lancastrians in the Wars of the Roses. He married Jacquetta of Luxembourg, widow of the Duke of Bedford, and it was their daughter Elizabeth whom **Edward IV** married. This led him to go over to the Yorkists, and Edward made him constable of England, Baron Rivers (1448) and Earl Rivers (1466). But the favour shown to the Rivers family offended the old nobility, and their avarice aroused popular enmity, and in 1469 Earl Rivers was beheaded at Northampton.

RIVERS, William Halse Rivers (1864–1922) English anthropologist and psychologist, born in Luton, near Chatham, Kent. He trained in medicine, but lectured at Cambridge in neurophysiology and psychology. His anthropological interests were kindled through participation in the Cambridge University expedition to the Torres Straits in 1898–99, and he subsequently worked among the Todas of India and in Melanesia. He was the first to develop and apply the genealogical method for the systematic study of kinship materials. Later in his career, influenced by Elliot Smith, he came to believe that cultural uniformities could be explained by migrations of peoples in the distant past from a common point of origin. He never lost his original interest in psychoanalysis, and in *Instinct and the Unconscious* (1920) he sought to construct a theory of the unconscious based on the conflict of instinct, censorship and reason.

RIVIÈRE, Jacques (1886–1925) French writer and critic, born in Bordeaux. In 1919 he became the first editor of the *Nouvelle revue française*, as such playing a prominent part in the cultural life of post-war France. His writings include novels, essays and a justification of the Christian conception of God, *Á la trace de Dieu* (1925).

RIVINGTON, Charles (1688–1742) English publisher, born in Chesterfield, Derbyshire. He went to London, where he founded in 1711 the Rivington publishing firm which remained under family direction until absorbed by Longmans in 1890.

RIX, Sir Brian (1924–) English actor and manager, born in Cottingham, renowned for the Whitehall farces which he both appeared in and managed at the Whitehall Theatre during the 1950s and 1960s. He made his professional début in **Shakespeare** in 1942, and appeared with the **Donald Wolfit** Company in 1943. In 1943–44 he appeared with the White Rose Players, Harrogate, and served in the RAF from 1944 to 1947. He founded his own company, Rix Theatrical Productions, at Ilkley, Yorkshire, in 1948, forming a second company at the Hippodrome, Margate, in 1949. He had a great success with the farce *Reluctant Heroes* in 1950 which ran at the Whitehall Theatre for four years. In 1967 he moved to the Garrick Theatre. He has also produced and appeared in several films. In 1980 he left the theatre to work for Mencap, a charity for the mentally handicapped, but returned to the Lyric to star in a revival of *Dry Rot* in 1988.

RIZAL, José (1861–96) Filipino patriot and writer, born in Calamba, Luzon. He studied medicine at Madrid, and on his return to the Philippines published a political novel, *Noli me tangere* (1886), whose anti-Spanish tone led to his exile. He practised in Hong Kong, where he wrote *El Filibusterismo* (1891), a continuation of his first novel. Returning to the Philippines, he arrived just when an anti-Spanish revolt was erupting; he was accused of instigating it, and was shot.

RIZZIO, or **Riccio, David** (?1533–1566) Italian courtier and musician. He entered the service of **Mary, Queen of Scots** in 1561, and rapidly becoming her favourite, was appointed private foreign secretary in 1564. He negotiated Mary's marriage (1565) with Darnley, with whom he was at first on friendliest terms, but the queen's husband soon became jealous of his influence over Mary and of his strong political power, and entered with other nobles into a plot to kill him. Rizzio was dragged from the queen's presence and brutally murdered at the palace of Holyrood.

ROACH, Hal (Harriett Eugene) (1892–) American filmmaker, born in Elmira, New York. After an adventurous life as a muleskinner and gold prospector in Alaska, he entered the film industry as a stuntman and extra in 1911. Three years later, he began producing short comedy films featuring **Harold Lloyd** as the character Willie Work and later as Lonesome Luke. He became an expert in the mechanics of screen humour and slapstick, helping to foster the careers of Charlie Chase, **Will Rogers** and, most successfully, the partnership of **Laurel** and **Hardy**. He also devised the series of Our Gang films and won Academy Awards for *The Music Box* (1932) and *Bored of Education* (1936). His range of full-length productions includes *Bonnie Scotland* (1935), *Way Out West* (1937), *Of Mice and Men* (1939) and *One Million B.C.* (1940) which he co-directed. During World War II he made a number of propaganda and training films and subsequently diversified into television production. His final film was the compilation feature *The Crazy World of Laurel and Hardy* (1967). In 1984, he received a special Academy Award.

ROBARDS, Jason (1922–) American actor, born in Chicago. He made his New York début as the back end of the cow in *Jack and the Beanstalk* at the Children's World Theater in 1947, going on to become an understudy and stage-manager. In 1956, he won critical acclaim for his performances in two **O'Neill** plays. He joined the Stratford Festival Company, Ontario, in

1958. A powerful classical actor, he also made a reputation as one of the greatest interpreters of O'Neill's work. He has appeared in several films and television dramas, but is primarily recognized as a stage actor of great stature.

ROBBE-GRILLET, Alain (1922–) French novelist, born in Brest. Educated in Paris, he worked for some time as an agronomist and then in a publishing house. His first novel, *Les Gommes* (The Erasers, 1953), aroused much controversy and with the appearance of his later ones (*Dans le labyrinthe*, 1959, etc) he emerged as a leader of the *nouveau roman* group. He uses an unorthodox narrative structure and concentrates on external reality, believing this to be the only one. He has also written film scenarios, eg, *L'Année dernière à Marienbad*, and essays, *Pour un nouveau roman* (1963). Other publications include *Projet pour une révolution à New York* (1970), *La Belle Captive* (1976) and *Djinn* (1981).

ROBBIA, DELLA, Luca (c.1400–1482) Italian sculptor in Florence. Between 1431 and 1440 he executed ten unequalled panels of angels and dancing boys for the cathedral there, for whose sacristy he also made (1448–67) a bronze door with ten panels of figures in relief. In marble he sculptured, in 1457–58, the tomb of the bishop of Fiesole. He is amost equally famous for his figures in terracotta, including medallions and reliefs, white or coloured. He established a business producing glazed terracottas which was carried on by his nephew Andrea (1435–1525) and Andrea's son Giovanni (1469–c.1529).

ROBBINS, Frederick Chapman (1916–) American physiologist and pediatrician. After war service as an army medical researcher into epidemic diseases, he joined **John Enders** and **Thomas Weller** in devising techniques for cultivating the poliomyelitis virus, thus making a polio vaccine possible. For this they were awarded the 1954 Nobel prize for physiology or medicine. He was professor of pediatrics at Case Western Reserve University, Cleveland (1952–80).

ROBBINS, Harold (1916–) American bestseller novelist, born of unknown parentage in the Hell's Kitchen area of Manhattan, New York City. At 15 he dropped out of George Washington high school, left his foster parents and eventually became an inventory clerk in a grocery store. During the Depression he showed entrepreneurial flair by buying up crops and selling options to canning companies and the canning contracts to wholesale grocers. He was a millionaire by the time he was 20, but speculation in sugar before the outbreak of World War II relieved him of his fortune. He became interested in writing in 1949. Drawing on his knowledge of street life, high finance and Hollywood, he produced a string of earthy bestsellers: *Never Love a Stranger* (1948), *The Dream Merchants* (1949), *A Stone for Danny Fisher* (1952), *79 Park Avenue* (1955) and *The Carpetbaggers* (1961), which sold six million copies throughout the 1960s.

ROBBINS, Jerome (1918–) American dancer and choreographer, born in New York City. He danced with American Ballet Theatre for four years and in Broadway musicals, before making choreography his main interest with *Fancy Free* (1944), his first piece. He joined New York City Ballet in 1949, dancing principal roles in **Balanchine** ballets and choreographing a total of nine ballets in ten years. During that time he also worked on Broadway in *The King and I* (1951), *Peter Pan* (1954) and *West Side Story* (1957), a unique achievement which perfectly combined the commercial theatre with artistic excellence. In order to free himself to experiment, he formed the small company Ballet:USA, out of which came *Moves*, a ballet without music. Further Broadway successes included *Gypsy* (1959) and *Fiddler on the Roof* (1964). He returned to New York City Ballet in 1969 when he made *Dances at a Gathering*. He has remained with the company and, after the death of Balanchine in 1983, was made joint ballet master with **Peter Martins**. Blending classical ballet with more earthy folk styles, he is one of America's greatest choreographers. Other works include *The Goldberg Variations* (1971), *Watermill* (1972), *Piano Concerto in G* (1975), *Opus 19/The Dreamer* (1979) and *Glass Pieces* (1983). He won two Oscars for the 1961 Hollywood version of *West Side Story*.

ROBBINS, Lionel Charles, Baron Robbins of Clare Market (1898–1984) English economist, born in Middlesex. Professor of economics at the London School of Economics from 1929 to 1961, he was also director of the economic section of the war cabinet. He resigned from the LSE to become chairman of the *Financial Times* (1961–70). From 1961 to 1964 he chaired the 'Robbins Committee' on the expansion of higher education. His best-known work is *An Essay on the Nature and Significance of Economic Science* (1932). He also wrote *The Economic Problem in Peace and War* (1947), *Classical Political Economy* (1952) and *The Evolution of Modern Economic Theory* (1970).

ROBENS, Alfred, Lord Robens of Woldingham (1910–) English trade unionist and industrialist, born in Manchester. He became a full-time trade union officer of the Union of Distributive and Allied Workers. In 1945 he was elected to parliament and, for six months in 1951, was a member of the cabinet as minister of labour and national service. From 1961 to 1971 he was chairman of the National Coal Board.

ROBERT I See **BRUCE, Robert**

ROBERT II (1316–90) king of Scotland from 1371, the son of **Walter Stewart** and of Marjory, only daughter of **Robert I, Bruce**. He twice acted as guardian during the imprisonment in England of **David II**. On David's death (1371) he obtained the crown, founding the **Stewart** dynasty. His reign, though usually characterized as that of a king lacking in prestige and unsuited to rule, did not see serious factional disputes over either the succession or Anglo-Scottish politics, despite English invasions in 1384 and 1385. It saw, vitally, the extension of Stewart lands and patronage by grants made to his many legitimate sons and the beginnings of a transformation of the greater nobility. His complicated matrimonial history, however, was to bring problems for later Stewart kings. His first marriage, to Elizabeth, daughter of Sir Adam Mure of Rowallan, was within the prohibited degrees; his second, in 1355, was to Euphemia, Countess of Moray, daughter of Hugh, Earl of Ross. A papal dispensation for the children of the first marriage was obtained in 1347, and they were further recognized by an Act of Succession passed by parliament in 1373.

ROBERT III (c.1340–1406) king of Scotland from 1390, the eldest son of **Robert II** by his first marriage. He was originally called John. He was created Earl of Carrick in 1368 and took the name Robert on his accession in 1390. The issue of guardianship dominated politics since he was a permanent invalid, the result of a kick from a horse. The main contenders were his brother, Robert, Duke of **Albany** (?1340–1420), and his elder son, David, Duke of Rothesay (?1378–1402), who was appointed lieutenant of the kingdom by a general council in 1398. Rothesay's fall in 1402, imprisonment and subsequent death at Falkland, brought Albany to an unrivalled position of power, made more secure by the imprisonment in England of many magnates captured at the battle of Homildon Hill (1402). Robert, anxious for the safety of his younger son, James (the future **James I**), sent him to France; he died shortly after news arrived of James's capture by the English. Perhaps the least impressive of Scotland's medieval kings, his reign was dominated by a family quarrel rather than by civil war.

ROBERT, Duke of Normandy See **HENRY I, of England**

ROBERT OF ANJOU, 'the Wise' (1278–1343) king of Naples, grandson of **Charles of Anjou**. He succeeded his father (Charles II) to the throne in 1309. A leader of the **Guelf** papal party, he nonetheless broke with Pope **John XXII** in 1330. A notable patron of learning and the arts, he was a friend of **Boccaccio** and **Petrarch**.

ROBERT OF BRUNNE, See **MANNYNG, Robert**

ROBERT OF CURTHOSE (c.1054–1134) Duke of Normandy, the eldest son of **William I, the Conqueror** and Mathilda of Flanders. Although designated as his father's successor, his exclusion from government led to his unsuccessful revolt, followed by exile in France. On William's death (1087) Robert succeeded only to Normandy, while England passed to the second son, **William II, Rufus**. A protracted struggle between the two brothers was interrupted by Robert's participation in the First Crusade (1096–1101), which did much for his prestige, but in his absence the throne of England was seized by his younger brother **Henry I** on the death of Rufus. In 1106 Henry invaded Normandy and Robert was captured at the battle of Tinchebray. He spent the rest of his life a prisoner at Devizes, Bristol and Cardiff, where he died. His only legitimate offspring, William Clito, was killed in battle in 1128.

ROBERT OF GLOUCESTER (fl.1260–1300) English chronicler. He was the reputed author of a metrical English chronicle to 1135.

ROBERT OF JUMIÈGES (fl.1037–52) Norman prelate, and archbishop of Canterbury. Abbot of Jumiéges from 1037, he came to England in 1043 with **Edward the Confessor**, who made him bishop of London (1044) and archbishop of Canterbury in 1050. He was the head of the anti-English party which in 1051 banished Earl **Godwin** and his sons. Their return next year drove him to Normandy. The Witan stripped him of his archbishopric, and he died at Jumiéges.

ROBERT OF MELUN (d.1167) English theologian. He taught in Paris and Melun, and was elected bishop of Hereford in 1163. He acted as a mediator between **Becket** and **Henry II**, latterly, however, giving his support to Becket.

ROBERTI, Ercole de' (c.1455–1496) Italian painter, born in Ferrara. His *Madonna* in the Brera Gallery, Milan, and *Pietà*, in the Walker Art Gallery, Liverpool, are characteristic of his work, which is less austere than that of **Cossa** and **Tura**, his contemporaries of the Ferrarese school.

ROBERTS, Sir Charles George Douglas (1860–1943) Canadian writer and naturalist, born in Douglas, New Brunswick. A graduate of Fredericton, he was professor in King's College, Nova Scotia (1885–95), and settled in New York as an editor, joining the Canadian army at the outbreak of World War I. An outstanding lyric poet, he wrote *Orion and Other Poems* (1880), *In Divers Tones* (1887), and other verse, a history of Canada, *Canada in Flanders* (1918), and nature studies, in which he particularly excelled, including *The Feet of the Furtive* (1912) and *Eyes of the Wilderness* (1933).

ROBERTS, David (1796–1864) Scottish painter, born in Edinburgh. A scene-painter at Drury Lane he attracted attention with pictures of Rouen and Amiens cathedrals while he exhibited at the Royal Academy. Among his pictures, inspired by his wide travels, were *Departure of the Israelites from Egypt* (1829), *Jerusalem* (1845), *Rome* (1855) and *Grand Canal at Venice* (1856).

ROBERTS, Frederick Sleigh Roberts, Earl, of Kandahar, Pretoria, and Waterford (1832–1914) English soldier, born in Cawnpore, India. Educated at Clifton, Eton, Sandhurst and Addiscombe, he entered the Bengal Artillery in 1851. During the Indian Mutiny (1857–58) he was at the siege of Delhi and took an active part in the subsequent operations down to the relief of Lucknow, and won the VC at Khudagani in 1858. He was assistant quartermaster general in the Abyssinian (1868) and Lushai (1871–72) expeditions. In the 2nd Afghan War of 1878–79, now major-general, he forced the Afghan position on Peiwar Kotul, defeated the Afghans at Charásia, took possession of Kabul, and assumed the government. In August 1880, he set out with 10000 men on a memorable march through Afghanistan to the relief of Kandahar; three weeks later he reached it, and routed Ayub Khan. In 1881 he was appointed commander-in-chief of the Madras army, and from 1885 to 1893 he was commander-in-chief in India. Created Lord Roberts of Kandahar and Waterford in 1892, he became field marshal, and commander-in-chief in Ireland in 1895. He published *The Rise of Wellington* (1895) and *Forty-One years in India* (1895). After the first checks of the 2nd Boer War he was sent out in 1899 to assume the chief command, relieved Kimberley and made the great advance to Pretoria, and came home in 1901 to be commander-in-chief. Created earl in 1901, he retired in 1904, and died while visiting troops in the field in France.

ROBERTS, Sir Gilbert (1899–1978) English civil engineer. Educated at the City and Guilds of London Institute, he assisted **Ralph Freeman** on the design of the Sydney Harbour bridge, then joined Sir William Arrol & Company in Glasgow where he became director and chief engineer, extending the uses of welding and high-tensile steels in bridges and other structures. In 1949 he joined Freeman, Fox & Partners for whom after the death of Sir **Ralph Freeman** he was in charge of the design of the Forth, Severn, Auckland Harbour, Bosphorus (Turkey) and Humber bridges as well as radio telescopes, goliath cranes and many other steel structures.

ROBERTS, Kate (1891–1985) Welsh novelist and short-story writer, born in Rhosgadfan, near Caernarfon, Gwynedd. She was educated at the University College of North Wales, Bangor. Sometimes described as 'the Welsh **Chekhov**', she is generally regarded as the most distinguished prose writer in Welsh this century. She was a teacher of Welsh at Ystalyfera (1915–17) and Aberdare (1917–28), and later (with her husband Morris T Williams) bought Gwasg Gee, the publishers of the newspaper *Baner ac Amserau Cymru* (later *Y Faner*), and settled in Denbigh.

ROBERTS, (Granville) Oral (1918–) American evangelist and faith healer, born in Ada, Oklahoma, the son of a Pentecostal preacher and a half-Creole mother. He was ordained at 18 in the Pentecostal Holiness Church. Flamboyant and enterprising, he gained a reputation for faith healing, and when he founded Oral Roberts University in Tulsa in 1967 the state governor attended and Roman Catholics and Jews were among its backers. By 1978 it had 3800 students and assets of about $150 million. Roberts has a weekly national TV programme, a radio station, and a mass circulation monthly magazine. His writings include *If You Need Healing, Do These Things* (1947), *The Miracle Book* (1972), and *Don't Give Up* (1980).

ROBERTS, Richard (1789–1864) Welsh mechanical engineer and inventor, born in Carreghofa. He had only an elementary education and worked for a while as a labourer in a quarry before moving to England, where he worked for **John Wilkinson** and **Henry Maudslay**. In 1816 he established his own machine-tool business in Manchester, where he devised a number of improvements to Maudslay's screw-cutting lathe and built one of the first metal-planing machines. His power loom, introduced in 1822, was a successful development of Horrocks' earlier model, and from 1825 to 1830 he developed the self-acting spinning mule, an improvement on **Crompton**'s original design of 1779. He was offered a partnership by Thomas Sharp in 1828, and the firm of Sharp, Roberts and Company manufactured his spinning mule as well as railway locomotives, beginning with the *Experiment* for the Liverpool & Manchester Railway in 1833, until Sharp's death in 1842. Although Roberts continued to invent useful machines and other devices, his fortunes thereafter went into decline and he died impoverished.

ROBERTS, Sir Stephen Henry (1901–71) Australian historian and political writer, born in Maldon, Victoria. Educated at Melbourne University, and at London and Paris, he then joined the history department of Melbourne University and wrote his first book, *History of Australian land settlement* (1923). In 1929 he became Challis professor of history at Sydney University. His *History of Modern Europe* (1933), *The Problems of Modern France* (1937) and *The House that Hitler Built* (1937) brought him wider attention, and, with war approaching, Roberts became a radio and newspaper commentator. In 1947 he resigned his chair to become vice-chancellor of Sydney University, and was also principal from 1955.

ROBERTS, Tom (Thomas William) (1856–1931) English-born Australian landscape and portrait painter, born in Dorchester, Dorset. He arrived in Melbourne in 1869, where he studied at the National Gallery of Victoria's Art School, and in 1881 he returned to London to study at the Royal Academy. On his return to Australia he formed, in 1886, with **Frederick McCubbin** and friends, the first artists' camp at Box Hill, Victoria. In 1888 he joined **Arthur Streeton** and **Charles Conder** in Heidelberg, Victoria, to form the first indigenous Australian school of painting. Sixty-two of his paintings were exhibited in 1889 in the famous '9 x 5 Impression' exhibition, so styled because most of the paintings were done on old cigar-box lids. With Streeton, he camped at Sirius Cove on Sydney harbour from 1891 to 1896, producing a sparkling series of harbour and beach scenes which beautifully captured the prevailing light. He was commissioned to paint the official opening of the first Australian federal parliament, in Melbourne in 1903, a subject which required over 250 individual portraits.

ROBERTS, William Patrick (1895–1980) English artist, born in London. He was associated with **Roger Fry**, **Wyndham Lewis** (as a Vorticist), and the London group, and in both World Wars was an official war artist. His art was then devoted to the portrayal of Cockney characters in a very formal Cubist, or rather cylindrical, style, with a certain satirical emphasis.

ROBERTS-AUSTEN, Sir William Chandler (1843–1902) English metallurgist, born in Kennington, London. In 1880 he was appointed professor at the Royal School of Mines, two years later becoming chemist and assayer at the Mint. A pioneer of alloy research, he demonstrated the possibility of diffusion occurring between a sheet of gold and a block of lead.

ROBERTSON, Frederick William (1816–53) English clergyman, born in London. He was educated for the army at Tours and Edinburgh, but, devoting himself to the church, studied at Oxford (1837–40), and in 1847 became incumbent of Trinity Chapel, Brighton, where his earnestness, originality and sympathies for revolutionary ideals arrested attention, but provoked suspicion. He resigned in 1853 because his vicar had refused to confirm his nomination of a curate. He published only one sermon; the five series of *Sermons* (1855–80), so well known over the English-speaking world, are really recollections, sometimes dictated and sometimes written out.

ROBERTSON, George Croom (1842–92) Scottish philosopher, born in Aberdeen. He studied philosophy at Aberdeen University under **Alexander Bain**, who had a formative influence on his thought. In 1866 he became professor of mental philosophy and logic at University College London. He published a monograph on **Hobbes** (1886), and there were two posthumous volumes of lectures, *Elements of General Philosophy* and *Elements of Psychology* (1896), but he is best remembered as the founding editor of *Mind* (from 1876), the first journal in English devoted to psychology and philosophy. Volume 1 contained contributions from **Helmholtz**, **Sidgwick**, **Herbert Spencer**, **Henry Venn** and **Wundt**, and Robertson remarked in his opening editorial, 'Long as English inquiry has been turned on the things of the mind, it has, until quite lately, been distinguished from the philosophical thought of other countries by what may be called its unprofessional character. Even now the notion of a journal being founded to be wholly taken up with metaphysical subjects ... will little commend itself either to those who are in the habit of declaring with great confidence that there can be no science in such matters, or to those who would only play with them now and again.'

ROBERTSON, James Logie See **HALIBURTON, Hugh**

ROBERTSON, Jeannie (1908–75) Scottish folk singer, born in Aberdeen, described by the American folklorist, Alan Lomax, as 'a monumental figure of world folk-song'. She was virtually unknown beyond the north-east of Scotland until 'discovered' in 1953 by **Hamish Henderson**. Her huge repertoire of classic traditional ballads and other songs, together with her powerful and magnetic singing style, exerted a profound influence on the folk-music revival. Although she lived most of her life in Aberdeen, she belonged to the 'travelling folk', whose music was passed down orally from generation to generation, and she represented an important link with this ancient culture.

ROBERTSON, Joseph (1810–66) Scottish antiquary and historian, born in Aberdeen. Educated at Aberdeen Grammar School and Marischal College, he turned from law to literature. He was editor of the Edinburgh *Evening Courant* (1848 –53), and in 1853 became historical curator at the Edinburgh Register House. He was a founder-member of the Aberdeen Spalding Club (1839–70), which published works of Scottish historical interest, and contributed much to Chambers' *Encyclopaedia*. Among his works are *The Book of Bon-Accord* (1839) and *Concilia Scotiae: Ecclesiae Scoticanae Statuta 1225–1559* (1866).

ROBERTSON, Madge See **KENDAL**

ROBERTSON, Oscar (1938–) American professional basketball player and commentator, born in Charlotte, Tennessee. Known as 'The Big O', he graduated from Cincinnati University in 1960, having been voted three times the college player of the year. He was also the leading scorer in college games for three seasons, and helped the USA win the gold medal in the 1960 Olympics. After graduating he joined the Cincinnati Royals and played with them from 1961 to 1970, moving on to the Milwaukee Bucks for the last four years of his playing career. He won only one NBA championship (1971), but throughout his career averaged 25.7 points per game. He went on to commentate on the sport for television.

ROBERTSON, Thomas William (1829–71) English dramatist, brother of **Madge Kendal**, born in Newark-on-Trent, of an old acting family. Going to London in 1848, he was an actor, prompter and stage manager, wrote unsuccessful plays, contributed to newspapers and magazines, and translated French plays. His first notable success as a dramatist was with *David Garrick* (1864) and *Society* (1865), and his next comedy, *Ours* (1866), established his fame. *Caste* (1867), *Play* (1868), *School* (1869), *M.P.* (1870)—all performed by the **Bancrofts** at the Prince of Wales Theatre—and *Home* (1869) and *Dreams* (1869) were all equally successful.

ROBERTSON, William (1721–93) Scottish historian, born in the manse of Borthwick in Midlothian. He studied at Edinburgh, and at 22 was ordained minister of Gladsmuir, and of Lady Yester's in Edinburgh (1756). He volunteered for the defence of Edinburgh against the Jacobite rebels in 1745, from 1751 took a prominent part in the General Assembly, and soon became leader of the 'Moderates'. From 1761 he was joint minister of Greyfriars, Edinburgh. In 1761 he became a royal chaplain, in 1762 principal of Edinburgh University, and in 1764 king's historiographer. His *History of Scotland 1542–1603* (1759) was a splendid success. Next followed the *History of Charles V* (1769), his most valuable work, highly praised by **Voltaire** and **Gibbon**. The *History of America* appeared in 1777, and a disquisition on *The Knowledge which the Ancients had of India* in 1791.

ROBERTSON, Sir William Robert (1860–1933) English soldier. He enlisted as a private in 1877 and rose to be field marshal in 1920. In World War I he was quarter-master general (later chief of general staff) of the British Expeditionary Force, and became chief of the Imperial General Staff from 1915 to 1918. He wrote his autobiography, *From Private to Field-Marshal* (1921).

ROBESON, Paul Le Roy (1898–1976) Black American singer and actor, born in Princeton, New Jersey. He was admitted to the American bar before embarking on a stage career in New York in 1921, appearing in Britain in 1922. Success as an actor was matched by popularity as a singer, and he appeared in works ranging from *Show Boat* to plays by **O'Neill** and **Shakespeare**. He was known particularly for his Othello, a part which he first played in London in 1930 and in which he scored a triumphant American success ten years later. He gave song recitals, notably of black spirituals, throughout the world, and appeared in numerous films. From the end of World War II his racial and political sympathies somewhat embittered his relationship with the USA, and from 1958 to 1963, when he retired and returned to the USA, he lived in England. He published his autobiography *Here I Stand* in 1958.

ROBESPIERRE, Maximilien Marie Isidore de (1758–94) French revolutionary, born, of Irish origin, in Arras. He was admitted *avocat* in 1781, and was elected to the states general in 1789. He attached himself to the extreme left, and soon commanded attention. His influence grew daily, and the mob frantically admired his earnest cant and his boasted incorruptibility. In 1791 he carred the motion that no member of the present Assembly should be eligible for the next, and was appointed public accuser. Next followed the flight of **Louis XVI** and the royal family to Varennes (June 21), **Lafayette**'s last effort to control the right of insurrection on the Champ-de-Mars (July 17), the abject terror of Robespierre, his hysterical appeal to the Club, the theatrical oath taken by every member to defend his life, and his conduct home in triumph by the mob at the close of the Constituent Assembly (30 September). The Girondist leaders in the new Legislative Assembly were eager for war. Robespierre offered strenuous opposition in the Jacobin Club. In April 1792 he resigned the post of public accuser. In August he presented to the Legislative Assembly a petition for a revolutionary tribunal and a new Convention. It does not appear that he was responsible for the September massacres. He was elected first deputy for Paris to the National Convention, where the bitter attacks upon him by the Girondists threw him into closer union with **Danton**. Robespierre vigorously opposed the Girondist idea of a special appeal to the people on the king's death, and Louis XVI's execution (21 January 1793) opened up the final stage of the struggle, which ended in a complete triumph for the Jacobins on 2 June. The first Committee of Public Safety was decreed in April 1793, and Robespierre, elected in July, was now one of the actual rulers of France; but it is doubtful whether henceforth he was not merely the stalking-horse for the more resolute party within the Twelve. Next came the dark intrigues and desperate struggles that sent **Hébert** and his friends to the scaffold in March 1794, and Danton and **Camille Desmoulins** in April. For the next three months Robespierre reigned supreme. He nominated all the members of the government committees, placed his supporters in all places of influence in the commune of Paris, and assumed complete control of the revolutionary tribunal. But as his power increased his popularity waned. On 7 May 1794 Robespierre, who had previously condemned the cult of Reason, advocated a new state religion and recommended the Convention to acknowledge the existence of God; on June 8 the inaugural festival of the Supreme Being took place. Meantime the pace of the guillotine grew faster; public finance and government generally drifted to ruin, and **Saint-Just** demanded the creation of a dictatorship in the person of Robespierre. On 26 July Robespierre delivered a long harangue complaining that he was being accused of crimes unjustly. The Convention, after at first obediently passing his decrees, next rescinded them and referred his proposals to the committees. That night at the Jacobin Club his party again triumphed. Next day at the Convention Saint-Just could not obtain a hearing, and Robespierre was vehemently attacked. A deputy proposed his arrest; at the fatal word Robespierre's power crumbled to ruin. He flew to the Common Hall, whereupon the Convention declared him an outlaw. The National Guard under **Barras** turned out to protect the Convention, and Robespierre had his lower jaw broken by a shot fired by a gendarme. Next day (28 July; 10th Thermidor 1794) he was sent to the guillotine with Saint-Just, **Couthon**, and 19 others.

ROBEY, Sir George, originally **George Edward Wade** (1869–1954) English comedian, born in Herne Hill. He first appeared on the stage in 1891 and changed his name from Wade to Robey. He made a name for himself in musical shows such as *The Bing Boys* (1916) and later emerged as a Shakespearean actor in the part of Falstaff. Dubbed the 'Prime Minister of Mirth', he was famous for his robust, often Rabelaisian humour, his bowler hat, long black collarless frockcoat, hooked stick and thickly painted eyebrows. He was knighted in 1954.

ROBIN HOOD (c.1250–c.1350) legendary English outlaw, hero of a group of old English ballads, the gallant and generous outlaw of Sherwood Forest, where he spent his time gaily under the greeenwood tree with Little John, Scarlet, Friar Tuck, and his merry men. Unrivalled with bow and quarter-staff, he waged war on proud abbots and rich knights, helping himself to riches but giving generously to the poor and needy. The 'rymes of Robyn Hood' are named in *Piers Plowman* (c.1377) and the plays of Robin Hood in the *Paston Letters* (1473). Tradition made the outlaw into a political personage, a dispossessed Earl of Huntingdon and other characters, and in Sir Walter **Scott**'s *Ivanhoe* he is a Saxon holding out against the Normans; but there is no evidence that he was anything but the creation of popular imagination, a yeoman counterpart to the knightly King **Arthur**.

ROBINS, Benjamin (1707–51) English mathematician and father of the art of gunnery, born, of Quaker family, in Bath. He set up as teacher of mathematics in London, published several treatises, commenced his experiments on the resisting force of the air to projectiles, studied fortification, and invented the ballistic pendulum. In 1735 he demolished, in a treatise on *Newton's Methods of Fluxions*, **Berkeley**'s objections. His *New Principles of Gunnery* appeared in 1742. Engineer to the East India Company (1749), he died in Madras. His works were collected in 1761.

ROBINSON, Anastasia See **PETERBOROUGH, Charles Mordaunt**

ROBINSON, Arthur Howard (1915–) American geographer, born in Montreal and educated at the universities of Miami and Wisconsin. He taught at Wisconsin (1936–38) and Ohio State (1938–41) universities, followed by a period as chief of the map division at the Office of Strategic Services (1941–46). Thereafter he was appointed professor of geography at Wisconsin (1945–80), also becoming Lawrence Martin professor of cartography in 1967. He has held various senior government posts and received numerous awards. He is known internationally through his major cartographic textbooks, notably *Elements of Cartography*, now in its fifth edition.

ROBINSON, Arthur Napoleon (Ray) (1926–) Trinidad and Tobago politician. He was educated in Trinidad and the United Kingdom, where he studied at Oxford and then qualified as a barrister. Returning to the West Indies he became politically active, and in 1967, on independence, was deputy leader of the moderate-centrist People's Nationalist Movement (PNM). In 1984, with other colleagues, he broke away to form a left-of-centre coalition which became the National Alliance for Reconstruction (NAR), which in the 1986 general election swept the PNM from power, making Robinson prime minister.

ROBINSON, Brooks (1937–) American baseball player, born in Little Rock, Arkansas. A highly proficient batter who hit more than 250 home runs and over 1300 runs batted in, he was outstanding for the quality of his work in the field, and is universally recognized as the greatest third baseman of all time. He won the Golden Glove in that position for 15 consecutive years from 1960 and was named as the American League's Most Valuable Player in 1960 and the Outstanding Player of the 1970 World Series.

ROBINSON, Edward (1794–1863) American scholar, born in Southington, Connecticut, considered the 'father of Biblical geography'. He studied in Germany, and became professor of theology at Andover (1830–37) and at the Union Theological Seminary, New York (1937–63). In 1838 he explored Palestine and Syria, and wrote *Biblical Researches in Palestine and Adjacent Countries* (1841). He was the founder-editor of *American Biblical Repository* (1831–35), and compiled a *Hebrew and English Lexicon of the Old Testament* and a *Greek and English Lexicon of the New Testament* (both 1836).

ROBINSON, Edward G, originally **Emanuel Goldenberg** (1893–1973) Romanian-born American actor, born in Bucharest. He emigrated to the USA with his parents and studied at the American Academy of Dramatic Arts in New York before making his stage début in *Paid in Full* (1913). He made his Broadway début in *Under Fire* (1915) and served in the US navy during World War I. A prolific stage performer, his work includes *Banco* (1922), *Androcles and the Lion* (1925) and *The Racket* (1927). He made his film début in *The Bright Shawl* (1923), but it was his vivid portrayal of a snarling, vicious gangster in *Little Caesar* (1930) that brought him stardom. A short, squat figure with thick features and a wide mouth, he brought magnetism and a refreshing humanity to a rogues' gallery of larcenous hoodlums in films like *The Whole Town's Talking* (1935), *The Last Gangster* (1937) and *Key Largo* (1948). A cultured man and art connoisseur in real life, his screen versatility was displayed as the paranoid captain in *The Sea Wolf* (1941), a dogged insurance investigator in *Double Indemnity* (1944), a hen-pecked husband in *Scarlet Street* (1945) and the patriarch in *All My Sons* (1948). The hysteria of the **McCarthy** witchhunts harmed his career, but he reasserted his reputation as a powerful character star on stage in *Middle of the Night* (1956–58) and in films like *The Cincinnati Kid* (1965) and *Soylent Green* (1973). His autobiography, *All My Yesterdays*, was published in 1973, and he received a posthumous Academy Award.

ROBINSON, Edwin Arlington (1869–1935) American poet, born in Head Tide, Maine. He was brought up in the town of Gardiner, Maine, which provided the background for 'Tilbury Town', the fictional New England village setting of his best poetry. He was educated at Harvard, and went to New York to find work. He made a name with an early collection of poetry *The Children of the Night* (1897), followed by *Captain Craig* (1902), *The Town down the River* (1910), *The Man against the Sky*, which confirmed his reputation, and *King Jasper* (1935). He was three times a Pulitzer prizewinner, for his *Collected Poems* (1922), *The Man Who Died Twice* (1925) and *Tristram* (1928), one of his several modern renditions of Arthurian legends.

ROBINSON, Frederick John See **RIPON, Earl of**

ROBINSON, George Augustus (1788–1866) English-born Australian social worker, born probably in London. Trained as a builder and engineer, he showed an interest in community and religious affairs. He emigrated to Australia, arriving in Hobart, Tasmania, in 1824, and set up in business. This prospered, and in 1829 he was appointed 'Protector of Aboriginals' by the lieutenant-governor of Van Diemen's Land (Tasmania), Sir **George Arthur**, ostensibly to act as conciliator, but actually to put into practice Arthur's policy of relocating the aboriginal tribes. Robinson spent nearly five years travelling round Tasmania, persuading the natives to leave their traditional areas, but earlier armed clashes between them and the settlers had effectively solved the problem: of the estimated aboriginal population of 4000 at the white settlement of Tasmania in 1803, less than 100 remained to be transferred to their new home, on Flinders Island in Bass Strait. Arthur thought the same policies could be effective on the mainland and in 1839 he left for the settlement of Port Phillip. There he was less successful; the aboriginals could not so easily be confined as on the island. In 1849 the Port Phillip protectorate was abolished, and Robinson, now a wealthy man, left for Europe, travelling on the Continent and later settling in Bath.

ROBINSON, George Frederick Samuel See **RIPON, Marquis of**

ROBINSON, (William) Heath (1872–1944) English artist, cartoonist and book-illustrator, born in Hornsey Rise, London. He attended the Islington School of Art and the Royal Academy Schools, and in 1897 appeared an edition of *Don Quixote*, the first of many works to be illustrated by him; others include editions of *Arabian Nights* (1899), *Twelfth Night* (1908) and *Water Babies* (1915). But his fame rests mainly on his humorous drawings—in his ability to poke fun at the machine age with magnificent drawings of countless 'Heath Robinson contraptions' of absurd and fantastic design to perform simple and practical operations, such as the raising of one's hat, the shuffling and dealing of cards, or the recovering of a collar-stud which has slipped down the back.

ROBINSON, Henry Crabb (1775–1867) English journalist and diarist. He was articled to a Colchester attorney (1790–95), then travelled in Germany where he met **Goethe** and **Schiller**, and studied at Jena University. He joined *The Times* in 1807 as a foreign correspondent, and covered the Peninsular War as a war correspondent (1808-09)—the first of his kind. He worked as a barrister from 1813 to 1828. He knew and corresponded with many of the major literary figures of the day (**Coleridge**, **Wordsworth**, **Lamb**, **Blake**, etc), who all figure in his voluminous diaries, correspondence and reminiscences. He was one of the founders of London University (1828) and the Athenaeum Club in London.

ROBINSON, Henry Peach (1830–1901) English photographer, born in Ludlow. He opened a studio at Leamington Spa in 1857, but tired of formal portraiture and moved to 'high art photography', creating literary and narrative genre scenes in the mid-Victorian style, often by composites of several separate images of costumed models and painted settings. Although criticized for artificiality, he exercised considerable influence until the end of the century and was a founder member of The Linked Ring (1892), an association of photographers seeking artistic creation rather than technical pictorialism, which developed into the international Photo-Secession under **Stieglitz** and others. He wrote *Pictorial Effect in Photography* (1869).

ROBINSON, Sir Hercules George Robert, Lord Rosmead (1824–97) English colonial administrator, second son of Admiral Hercules Robinson (1789–1864). After being administrator in Ireland during the Potato Famine (1848), he became governor of Hong Kong (1859), Ceylon (1865), New South Wales (1872), New Zealand (1878), and Cape Colony, perhaps the scene of his ablest administration (1880 and again in 1895). In 1896 he was created 1st Baron Rosmead.

ROBINSON, Jackie (Jack Roosevelt) (1919–72) American baseball player, born in Cairo, Georgia, the first black player to play major league baseball. Having done well in sports at the University of California at Los Angeles before World War II, he became a star infielder and outfielder for the Brooklyn Dodgers (1947–56). He led the Dodgers to six National League pennants and one World Series, in 1955. He was Rookie of the Year in 1947, and in 1949 he was league batting champion and was named Most Valuable Player (MVP). He retired in 1956, and in 1962 was elected to the National Baseball Hall of Fame. Largely responsible for the acceptance of black athletes in professional sports, he wrote of the pressures on him in his autobiography *I Never Had It Made* (1972).

ROBINSON, James Harvey (1863–1936) American historian, born in Bloomington, Illinois. He taught European history at Pennsylvania (1891–95), and at Columbia (1895–1919). He began as a successful textbook writer, collaborating with **Charles Beard** in *The Development of Modern Europe* (1907), and published *The New History* (1911), an exciting demand for history to reflect the totality of human experience, scientific, environmental, intellectual, cultural and social. His masterpiece was an optimistic study of the development of human understanding in what he saw as its enlargement, *The Mind in the Making* (1921). He lost some of his optimism in his later, less popular, *The Ordeal of Civilization* (1926).

ROBINSON, Joan Violet, née **Maurice** (1903–83) English economist, born in Camberley, Surrey. Educated at Girton College, Cambridge, she married an economist, Austin Robinson, in 1926, and after a brief period in India taught economics at Cambridge from 1931 to 1971 (in 1965 she succeeded her husband as professor). She was one of the most influential economic theorists of her time and a leader of the Cambridge school, which developed macroeconomic theories of growth and distribution, based on the work of **J M Keynes**. Her books include *The Economics of Imperfect Competition* (1933), *Introduction of the Theory of Employment* (1937), *Essay of Marxian Economics* (1942), *The Accumulation of Capital* (1956), *Essays in the Theory of Economic Growth* (1962) and *Economic Heresies* (1971).

ROBINSON, John (c.1576–1625) English clergyman, pastor of the Pilgrim Fathers, born in Lincolnshire. He studied at Cambridge, held a curacy at Norwich, became a Puritan and in 1608 escaped to Leiden, where he established a church in 1609. In 1620, after a memorable sermon, he saw part of his congregation set sail in the *Speedwell* for Plymouth, where they joined the *Mayflower*.

ROBINSON, John Arthur Thomas (1919–83) English Anglican prelate and theologian, born in Canterbury. He was educated at Cambridge where he lectured before appointment as bishop of Woolwich (1959–69). In 1963 he published *Honest to God*, which he described as an attempt to explain the Christian faith to modern man. It scandalized the conservatives, became a bestseller, and blocked his chances of further ecclesiastical advancement. He also made weighty—and more orthodox—contributions to biblical studies in other volumes, including *Jesus and His Coming* (1957), *The Human Face of God* (1973), and *Redating the New Testament* (1976).

ROBINSON, (Esmé Stuart) Lennox (1886–1958) Irish dramatist, born in Douglas, County Cork. His first play, *The Clancy Game*, was produced in 1908 at the Abbey Theatre, Dublin, where he was appointed manager in 1910 and then director from 1923 to 1956. Other plays include *The Cross Roads* (1909), *The Dreamers* (1915) and *The White-Headed Boy* (1920). He also compiled volumes of Irish verse, including the Irish *Golden Treasury* (1925), and edited Lady **Gregory**'s *Journals* (1946). His autobiographical works were *Three Homes* (1938) and *Curtain Up* (1941).

ROBINSON, Mary, known as **'Perdita'** (1758–1800) English actress, born in Bristol. She played Perdita and other Shakespearian parts at Drury Lane (1776–80), and became mistress in 1779 to the future **George IV**, who gave her a bond for £20000 which he never paid. She wrote poems, plays and novels; in 1783 she received a pension of £500, but died poor and ill.

ROBINSON, Sir Robert (1886–1975) English chemist, born in Chesterfield. Educated at Manchester University, he held chairs at Sydney, Liverpool, St Andrews, Manchester, London and Oxford, where he was Waynflete professor from 1930 to 1955. He is particularly noted for his work on plant pigments, alkaloids and other natural products, and in the development of penicillin. From 1945 to 1950 he was president of the Royal Society, and won the Nobel prize for chemistry in 1947.

ROBINSON, Sugar Ray, originally **Walker Smith** (1920–89) American professional boxer, born in Detroit. He held world titles at welterweight and middleweight, holding the latter crown on five separate occasions. His skill and speed brought him close to winning the world light-heavyweight championship in 1952 despite conceding enormous advantages in weight and height to Joey Maxim. He lost the middleweight title to **Randolph Turpin** in 1951, but soon regained it. He was a professional boxer for 20 years but bore few, if any, visible signs of his calling. Very popular in Europe, he travelled in considerable style with a large entourage.

ROBINSON, William (1838–1935) Irish gardener and horticultural writer, born in County Down. He began as a garden-boy at Ballykilcaven, County Laois, and in 1861 went to the Royal Botanic Society's gardens at Regent's Park, London. He published 18 books, including *Gleanings from French Gardens* (1868), *Alpine Flowers for English Gardens* (1870), and *The English Flower Garden* (1883), and founded and edited three horticultural journals: *The Garden* (1872), *Gardening Illustrated* (1879), and *Flora and Sylva* (1903).

ROBINSON, Sir William Cleaver Francis (1834–97) English colonial administrator, brother of Sir **Hercules Robinson**. From 1874 he was three times governor of Western Australia.

ROB ROY, (Gaelic for '**Red Robert**'), properly **Robert Macgregor** (1671–1734) Scottish freebooter, the second son of Lieut-Col Donald Macgregor of Glengyle. Until 1661 the 'wicked clan Gregor' had for a century been pursued with fire and sword; the very name was proscribed. But from that year until the 'Glorious Revolution' of 1688 the severe laws against them were somewhat relaxed, and Rob Roy lived quietly enough as a grazier at Balquhidder. His herds were so often plundered by the outlaws from the north, however, that he had to maintain a band of armed followers to defend both himself and such of his neighbours as paid him protection money. And so with those followers espousing in 1691 the Jacobite cause, he did a little plundering for himself, and, two or three years after having purchased from his nephew the lands of Craigroyston and Inversnaid, laid claim to be chief of the clan. Suffering losses (1712) in cattle speculations, for which he had borrowed money from the Duke of Montrose, his lands were seized, his houses plundered, and his wife turned adrift with her children in midwinter. Rob Roy now gathered his clansmen and made open war on the duke. This was in 1716, the year after the Jacobite rebellion, in which, at Sheriffmuir, Rob Roy had stood watch for the booty. Marvellous stories were current round Loch Katrine and Loch Lomond of his hairbreadth escapes, of his evasions when captured, and of his generosity to the poor, whose wants he supplied at the expense of the rich. They in return warned him of the designs of his arch-foes, the Dukes of Montrose and Atholl, and of the redcoats; besides, he enjoyed the protection of John, 2nd Duke of **Argyll**, having assumed his mother's name—Campbell. In 1727 he was arrested and sentenced to transportation, but pardoned. His life was romanticized in Sir **Walter Scott**'s *Rob Roy* (1818). He left five sons, two of whom died in 1754—James, the notorious outlaw James Mohr, in Paris; and Robin, the youngest, on the gallows in Edinburgh for abduction.

ROBSART, Amy See **LEICESTER, Earl of**

ROBSON, Dame Flora (1902–) English actress, born in South Shields. She first appeared in 1921 and gained fame mainly in historical roles in plays and films, such as Queen **Elizabeth** in *Fire over England* (1931), and Thérèse Raquin in *Guilty* (1944). She consolidated her reputation with memorable stage performances in **G B Shaw**'s *Captain Brassbound's Conversion* (1948) and **Ibsen**'s *Ghosts* (1958). She was made DBE in 1960.

ROCARD, Michel (1930–) French politician, born in the Paris suburb of Courbevoie, the son of a nuclear physicist who worked on France's atomic bomb. He trained at the École National d'Administration, where he was a classmate of **Jacques Chirac**. He began his career in 1958 as an inspector of finances, and in 1967 became leader of the radical Unified Socialist party (PSU), standing as its presidential candidate in 1969 and being elected to the National Assembly in the same year. He joined the Socialist party (PS) in 1973, emerging as leader of its moderate social democratic wing, and unsuccessfully challenged **François Mitterrand** for the party's presidential nomination in 1981. After serving as minister of planning and regional development (1981–83) and agriculture (1983–85) in the ensuing Mitterrand administration, he resigned in April 1985 in opposition to the government's expedient introduction of proportional representation. In May 1988, however, as part of a strategy termed the 'opening to the centre', he was appointed prime minister by President Mitterrand.

ROCHAMBEAU, Jean Baptiste Donatien de Vimeur, Comte de (1725–1807) French soldier, born in Vendôme. He entered the French army in 1742, was at the siege of Maestricht, and distinguished himself at Minorca in 1756. In 1780 he was sent out with 6000 men to support the Americans, and in 1781 rendered effective help at Yorktown. Back in France (1783) he served with the Napoleonic army, and was made a marshal in 1803.

ROCHEFORT, Victor Henri, Marquis de Rochefort-Luçay (1832–1913) French journalist and politician, born in Paris. He became a clerk in the hôtel-de-ville, but was dismissed in 1859 for neglecting his duties. He took to journalism, in 1868 starting *La Lanterne*, which was quickly suppressed. He fled to Brussels, but returning in 1869 on his election to the Chamber of Deputies, started the *Marseillaise*, in which he renewed his attacks on the imperial régime. On the cowardly murder of his contributor, Victor Noir, by Prince Pierre Bonaparte, the paper was suppressed and its editor imprisoned. The fall of the empire opened up a role for him. In 1871 he was elected to the National Assembly, and soon sided with the communards in *Le Mot d'ordre*. He escaped from Paris, but the Prussians caught him and sent him to Versailles; sentenced to life imprisonment, he escaped from New Caledonia in 1874, and returned to France after the amnesty of 1880. His *L'Intransigeant* showed him intractable as ever. He sat in the National Assembly (1885–86), buried his influence in Boulangism, fled in 1889 to London, returned to Paris in 1895, and was an active anti-Dreyfusard. He wrote *Adventure of my Life* (trans 1896).

ROCHEFOUCAULD See **LA ROCHEFOUCAULD, François**

ROCHEJACQUELEIN See **LA ROCHEJACQUELEIN**

ROCHESTER, John Wilmot, Earl of (1647–80) English courtier and poet, born in Ditchley, Oxfordshire. He was educated at Burford school and Wadham College, Oxford. He travelled in France and Italy, and then returned to court, where his good looks and lively wit made him a prominent figure. In 1665 he showed conspicuous courage against the Dutch. He is said to have been a patron of the actress **Elizabeth Barry**, and of several poets. In 1667 he married a wealthy heiress, Elizabeth Malet, and plunged into a life of debauchery, yet wrote excellent letters, satires (particularly 'A Satyr against Mankind', 1675), and bacchanalian and amatory songs and verses. Finally he was moved to repentance by Bishop **Burnet**. Among the best of his poems are imitations of **Horace** and **Boileau**, *Verses to Lord Mulgrave*, and *Verses upon Nothing*.

ROCHESTER, Viscount See **OVERBURY, Sir Thomas**

ROCKEFELLER, John Davison (1839–1937) American oil magnate and philanthropist, born in Richford, New York. In 1857 he was clerk in a commission house and then in a small oil refinery at Cleveland, Ohio. In 1870 he founded the Standard Oil Co. with his brother William (1841–1922), and through it secured control of the oil trade of America. He gave over 500 million dollars in aid of medical research, universities, and Baptist churches, and in 1913 established the Rockefeller Foundation 'to promote the well-being of mankind'. His son John Davison, II (1874–1960), was chairman of the Rockefeller Institute of Medical Research, and built the Rockefeller Center in New York (1939). He also restored colonial Williamsburg in Virginia. Of his sons, John Davison, III, (1906–78), became chairman of the Rockefeller Foundation in 1952; Nelson Aldrich (1908–79), elected Republican governor of New York state in 1958, was re-elected in 1962, again in 1966, and was vice-president of the USA from 1974 to 1977; and Winthrop (1912–73), a racial moderate, became Republican governor of Arkansas in 1966.

ROCKINGHAM, Charles Watson Wentworth, Marquis of (1730–82) English statesman. In 1750 he was created Earl of Malton and succeeded his father as second Marquis. In 1751 he was made KG; but, opposing the policy of **Bute**, was dismissed from his appointments in 1762. As leader of the Whig Opposition, he was in 1765 called on to form his first ministry and became premier. He repealed the Stamp Act, and would have done more for progress but for court intrigues and the defection of the Duke of **Grafton**. He resigned in 1766, and opposed Lord **North** and his ruinous American policy. He again became premier in March 1782, but died four months later.

ROCKNE, Knute Kenneth (1888–1931) Norwegian-born American football coach, born in Voss. Taken to the USA as a child, he graduated from Notre Dame in 1914 and became head football coach there shortly after the end of World War I. He dominated American college football, having markedly changed the emphasis from sheer physical brawn to pace, elusiveness and ball handling. He died in an air crash.

ROD, Edouard (1857–1910) Swiss writer, born in Nyon in Vaud. He studied at Lausanne, Bonn and Berlin, was professor at Geneva, and settled in Paris. Among his 30 works are *La Chute de Miss Topsy* (1882), *La Course à la mort* (1885), *Le Sens de la vie* (1889), *Le Dernier Refuge* (1896) and *Les Unis* (1909).

RODBERTUS, Johann Karl (1805–75) German economist and politician, the founder of scientific socialism. He held law appointments under the Prussian government, but in 1836 settled down on his estate. In 1848 he entered the Prussian National Assembly, and for a fortnight was minister of education; in 1849 he carried the Frankfurt constitution. He held that the socialistic ideal would come to pass gradually according to the natural laws of change and progress. The state would then own all land and capital, and superintend the distribution of all products of labour.

RODCHENKO, Alexander Mikhailovich (1891–1956) Russian painter, designer and photographer, born in St Petersburg (Leningrad). He trained at the Kazan Art School (1910–14) and soon met **Tatlin** and the young Russian avant-garde. After the revolution he worked for the People's Commissariat of Enlightenment and taught at the Moscow Proletkult School from 1918 to 1926. His most original works were his abstract spatial constructions and his documentary photographs of the new communist society.

RODDICK, Anita Lucia (1943–) English retail entrepreneur, born in Brighton. In 1976 she founded with her husband, Thomas Gordon, the Body Shop International plc to sell cosmetics 'stripped of the hype' and made from natural materials. The company has over 100 stores in the United Kingdom (many of them franchised) and twice this number overseas.

RODERIC (d.711) last Visigothic king of Spain. He was elected on the death of Witiza (710), and died on the Guadalete in battle against the invading Moors, who proceeded to conquer most of Spain.

RODGERS, John (1771–1838) American naval officer, born in Maryland. He entered the US navy in 1798, and in 1805 he extorted treaties from Tripoli and Tunis, and in the war with Britain took 23 prizes. He became secretary of the navy in 1823.

RODGERS, John (1812–82) American naval officer, son of **John Rodgers** (1771–1838). In 1863 he captured the Confederate ironclad *Atlanta*, and became rear admiral and (1877) superintendent of the US naval observatory.

RODGERS, Richard (1902–79) American composer, born in New York City. He collaborated with the lyricist **Lorenz Hart** in a number of musicals such as *The Garrick Gaieties* (1925), *Babes in Arms* (1937, whose songs included 'The Lady is a Tramp'), *The Boys from Syracuse* (1938, including 'Falling in Love with Love') and *Pal Joey* (1940, which included 'Bewitched, Bothered and Bewildered'). After Hart's death (1943) he collaborated in a spectacular series of hit musicals with **Oscar Hammerstein II**, especially *Oklahoma!* (1943, which won the Pulitzer prize), *Carousel* (1945), *South Pacific* (1949, Pulitzer prize), *The King and I* (1951), *The Flower Drum Song* (1958), and *The Sound of Music* (1959).

RODGERS, William Thomas (1928–) English politician, born in Liverpool. Educated at Oxford, he served as general-secretary of the Fabian Society between 1953 and 1960 before being elected a Labour MP for Stockton-on-Tees in 1962. He held a succession of posts in the Labour governments of the 1960s and 1970s, culminating in that of transport secretary between 1976 and 1979. A fervent supporter of membership of the European Community, and concerned at the party's leftward lurch, Rodgers left Labour to form, along with **Roy Jenkins**, **David Owen** and **Shirley Williams** (the 'Gang of Four'), the Social Democratic party (SDP) in 1981. Although defeated in Stockton in the 1983 election, he proceeded to play an influential organizational role as SDP vice-president between 1982 and 1987, directing the party's alliance with the Liberals. Despite expressing support for the SDP–Liberal merger of 1987–88, he formally withdrew from party politics in December 1987 to become director-general of the Royal Institute of British Architects.

RODIN, (François) Auguste (René) (1840–1917) French sculptor, born in Paris, the son of a clerk. He made three unsuccessful attempts to enter the École des Beaux-Arts, and from 1864 (the year in which he produced his first great work, *L'Homme au nez cassé*) until 1875 he worked in Paris and Brussels under the sculptors **Barye**, **Carrier-Belleuse** and Van Rasbourg, collaborating with the latter in some of the decorations for the Brussels Bourse. In 1875 he travelled in Italy, studying the work of **Donatello**, **Michelangelo** and others, and in 1877 made a tour of the French cathedrals (he published *Les Cathédrales de la France* much later, in 1914). The Italian masters and the Gothic cathedrals both influenced Rodin's work considerably, as did his interest in the ancient Greeks, but the greatest influence on him was the current trend of Romanticism. In 1877 he exhibited anonymously at the Paris Salon *L'Âge d'airain* (The Age of Bronze), which aroused controversy because of its realism—the sculptor was accused of taking the cast from a living man! In 1879 he exhibited the more highly developed *Saint Jean Baptiste*. In 1880 he was commissioned by the government to produce the *Porte de l'enfer* (The Gate of Hell), inspired by **Dante**'s *Inferno*, for the Musée des Arts Décoratifs, and during the next 30 years he was primarily engaged on the 186 figures for these bronze doors. It was never completed, but many of his best-known works were originally conceived as part of the design of the doors, among them *Le Baiser* (1898) and *Le Penseur* (1904). From 1886 to 1895 he worked on *Les Bourgeois de Calais*. His statues include those of a nude **Victor Hugo** (1897) and **Balzac** in a dressing gown (1898), the latter being refused recognition by the Societé des Gens de Lettres who had commissioned it; and among his portrait busts are those of Madame Rodin, **Bastien-Lepage**, **Puvis de Chavannes**, Victor Hugo and **Bernard Shaw**. His works are represented in the Musée Rodin, Paris, in the Rodin Museum, Philadelphia, and in the Victoria and Albert Museum, London, where there is a collection of his bronzes which he presented to the British nation in 1914.

RODNEY, George Brydges Rodney, 1st Baron (1719–92) English naval commander, born in London of an old Somerset family. He entered the navy in 1732, was made lieutenant in 1739, in 1742 post-captain, and in 1747 had a brilliant share in **Hawke**'s victory against the French off Cape Finisterre. He was governor of Newfoundland 1748–52. In 1759 as rear admiral he commanded the squadron which bombarded Le Havre and destroyed the flotilla for the invasion of England. In 1761 he was appointed commander-in-chief on the Leeward Islands station, where in 1762 he captured Martinique, St Lucia and Grenada. In 1765 he was appointed governor of Greenwich Hospital, but was recalled to active service and sent out as commander-in-chief in Jamaica (1771–74). In 1779–82, commander-in-chief in the Leeward Islands again, he captured a Spanish convoy off Cape Finisterre and defeated another squadron off Cape St Vincent (1780). In 1781 he captured Dutch islands in the West Indies on which American contraband trade depended before sailing for England. In 1782 he gained a brilliant victory over the French off Dominica.

RODÓ, José Enrique (1872–1917) Uruguayan writer and critic, born in Montevideo. He was professor at Montevideo from 1898. He wrote in Spanish a collection of essays, *Ariel* (1900), in which he stresses the importance of spiritual as compared with materialistic values, and other philosophical essays, such as *Motivos de Proteo* (1908) and *El Mirador del Prospero* (1913).

ROE, Edward Rayson (1838–88) American clergyman and novelist, born in New Windsor, New York. He became chaplain in the volunteer service (1862–65), and afterwards pastor of a Presbyterian church in Highland Falls. The Chicago fire of 1871 furnished him with the subject of his first novel, *Barriers Burned Away* (1872), whose success led him to resign his pastorate in 1874. His other moralistic best sellers included *A Knight of the Nineteenth Century* (1877).

ROE, Sir Edwin Alliot Verdon (1877–1958) English aircraft manufacturer, born in Patricroft, near Manchester. When only 15 he went to Canada to assist in making drawings for a flying machine. After apprenticeship in locomotive engineering and a study of naval engineering at King's College, London, he went to sea as a marine engineer from 1899 to 1902. He won the highest award for a competition for model aeroplanes in 1907 and built his first biplane in 1907 at Brooklands, being the first Englishman to design, build and fly his own aircraft. With his brother Humphrey Verdon Roe (1878–1949, husband of Dr **Marie Stopes**) he formed A V Roe & Co in 1910, producing the famous AVRO 504 bomber/trainer type that set a standard for design for many years. He sold out to Armstrong Siddeley in 1928 and formed Saunders–Roe (SARO) to build flying boats at Cowes. AVRO is known for its Lancaster and Vulcan Bombers and SARO for the first jet-propelled flying boat, the SR-A1 and the Princess.

ROE, Sir Thomas (c.1580–1644) English diplomat, born in Low Leyton, near Wanstead. He studied at Magdalen College, Oxford, and, after holding court appointments, was knighted in 1605, and sent as a political agent to the West Indies, Guiana and Brazil. MP for Tamworth (1614), from 1615 to 1619 he was ambassador to the great mogul Jahangir at Agra, to the Porte in 1621–28, and afterwards to Germany.

ROEBLING, John Augustus (1806–69) German-born American civil engineer, born in Mühlhausen. Educated in the Royal Polytechnic Institute in Berlin, he emigrated to the USA in 1831 and began farming with his brother near Pittsburgh. He soon took up work as a canal engineer, where his observation of hemp ropes on inclines led him to develop machinery for the fabrication of much superior wire ropes, the first to be made in America. At the same time he worked on the design of suspension bridges, completing the first to use his wire ropes in 1846. He went on to build the pioneer railway suspension bridge at Niagara Falls (1851–55, replaced 1897), and had completed the design for the Brooklyn bridge in New York when an injury to his foot resulted in tetanus from which he died. His son Washington Augustus (1837–1926), after graduating at Rensselaer Polytechnic Institute, became his assistant and succeeded him as chief engineer of the Brooklyn bridge project, which he saw through to its completion in 1883.

ROEBUCK, John (1718–94) English inventor, born in Sheffield. He studied at Edinburgh, and graduated MD at Leiden. He gave up his practice in Birmingham to return to chemistry research, which led to improvements in methods of refining precious metals and in the production of chemicals. In 1759 he founded the Carron ironworks in Stirlingshire, and later was a friend and patron of **James Watt**.

ROEMER, Olaus (1644–1710) Danish astronomer, born in Aarhus, Jutland. He became professor of astronomy at Copenhagen, and discovered the finite velocity of light, which he measured by observing the time variations in the eclipse of Jupiter's satellites. He erected the earliest practical transit instrument.

ROETHKE, Theodore (1908–63) American poet, born in Saginaw, Michigan. He was educated at Michigan University and Harvard and was professor of English at Washington University from 1948. It was not until the publication of *The Waking* (1953), his fourth volume, that he became widely known. He had a history of mental illness and while some of his work borders on hysteria he convinced enough admirers of his sincerity. **Lowell** and others of the 'Confessional' poets were influenced by him. *Words for the Wind* (1958) is a selection from his first four books; the *Collected Poems* appeared posthumously in 1968.

ROGER I (1031–1101) Norman ruler in Sicily, brother of **Robert Guiscard**. He joined Robert in South Italy, and helped him to conquer Calabria. In 1060 he was invited to Sicily to fight against the Saracens, and took Messina. Everywhere the Normans were welcomed as deliverers from the Muslim yoke; in 1071 the Saracen capital, Palermo, was captured, and Robert made Roger Count of Sicily. After Robert's death (1085) Roger succeeded to his Italian possessions, and became the head of the Norman power in southern Europe.

ROGER II (1095–1154) first Norman king of Sicily. The second son of **Roger I**, he succeeded his older brother Simon as Count of Sicily in 1105, his mother Adelaide at first acting as regent. On the death (1127) of the Duke of Apulia, grandson of **Robert Guiscard**, his duchy passed to Roger, who thereupon welded Sicily and South Italy into a strong Norman kingdom, of which he was crowned king by Anacletus the antipope in 1130. He next added to his dominions Capua (1136), Naples and the Abruzzi (1140). In 1139 he took prisoner Pope Innocent II, with whom he concluded a bargain, Innocent recognizing him as king of Sicily, while Roger acknowledged Innocent and held his kingdom as a fief of the Holy See. The Byzantine emperor **Manuel I Comnemus** having insulted his ambassador, Roger's admiral, George of Antioch, ravaged the coasts of Dalmatia and Epirus, took Corfu, and plundered Corinth and Athens (1146). He carried off silk-workers, and introduced that industry into Sicily. Finally (1147), Roger won Tripoli, Tunis and Algeria. His court at Palermo was one of the most magnificent in Europe, a meeting point for Christian and Arab scholars, and his government was firm and enlightened.

ROGER OF HOVEDON (12th century) English chronicler, probably born in Howden in Yorkshire. He was a civil servant of **Henry II** and accompanied **Richard I** on his Crusade to the Holy Land. He wrote a Latin *Chronicle* covering the main events of Henry II's reign.

ROGER OF TAIZÉ, Brother, originally **Roger Louis Schutz-Marsache** (1915–) Swiss founder of the Taizé Community, born in Provence, the son of a Protestant pastor. In 1940 he went to Taizé, a French hamlet between Cluny and Citeaux, to establish a community devoted to reconciliation and peace in church and society. Since Easter 1949, when the first seven brothers took their vows, this vision has attracted thousands of pilgrims, especially young people drawn by the distinctive worship in the Church of Reconciliation which was built in 1962. His publications include *The Dynamic of the Provisional* (1965), *Violent for Peace* (1968), and several volumes of extracts from his journal.

ROGER OF WENDOVER (d.1236) English chronicler. A Benedictine monk at the monastery of St Albans, he revised and extended the abbey chronicle from the Creation to the year 1235, under the title *Flores Historiarum* (Flowers of History). The section from 1188 to 1235 is believed to be Roger's first-hand account. The chronicle was later extended by **Matthew Paris**.

ROGERS, Carl Ransom (1902–87) American psychotherapist, born in Oak Park, Illinois, the originator of client-centred therapy, sometimes known as non-directive therapy. He first studied theology but abandoned this for psychology, in which he took his doctorate at Columbia University Teachers College (1931). His first book, *Clinical Treatment of Problem Children* (1939), arose from his work as director of the child guidance centre in Rochester, New York. Later he taught at Chicago University (1945–57), where his research on the one-to-one relationship in therapy produced the book *Client-Centred Therapy* (1951). This form of psychotherapy attempts to elicit and resolve a neurotic person's problems by verbal means, but explicitly renounces attempts to talk the patient ('client') into accepting any particular doctrinaire interpretation of his symptoms, the procedure practised by **Freud** and his followers. It led to the proliferation of open therapy sessions and encounter groups in which patients talk out their problems under the supervision of a passive therapist. He was also a notable pioneer in carrying out systematic evaluations of the efficacy of psychotherapy. He was resident fellow at the Western Behavioral Science Institute (1964–68) and the Centre for Studies of the Person at La Jolla, California (1968–87). His other books included *Psychotherapy and Personality Change* (1954) and *On Becoming a Person* (1961).

ROGERS, Claude (1907–79) English artist, born in London. He studied and lectured at the Slade School, was professor of fine art at Reading University (1963–72), and president of the London Group from 1952–65. With **Victor Pasmore** and **William Coldstream** he founded the Euston Road School in 1937.

ROGERS, James Edwin Thorold (1823–90) English economist, born in West Meon, Hampshire. He became professor of political economy at Oxford (1862–67), but made so many enemies by his outspoken zeal for reforms that he was not re-elected till 1888. An advanced Liberal, he was MP for Southwark (1880–85), and Bermondsey (1885–86). He wrote many works on economics.

ROGERS, John (c.1500–1555) English Protestant reformer, born near Birmingham. He was a London rector from 1532 to 1534, and at Antwerp and Wittenberg embraced the Reformed doctrines. He helped to prepare a revised translation of the bible pseudonymously called 'Thomas Matthew's Bible' in 1537, and, having married and returned to England in 1548, preached at St Paul's Cross in 1553, just after **Mary**'s accession, against Romanism, and was burned as a heretic.

ROGERS, Randolph (1825–92) American sculptor, born in Waterloo, New York. He studied in Florence and Rome, and lived in Rome from 1885. His statues include *Ruth* (Metropolitan Museum) and *Lincoln* (Philadelphia), and he is best known for his *Columbus Doors* of the Capitol in Washington DC, and the heroic figure of *Michigan* on the Detroit monument.

ROGERS, Richard (1933–) English architect, born in Florence. He studied at the Architectural Association in London, and was a founder member with **Norman Foster** and their wives of Team 4. Like Foster, he was concerned with advanced technology in architecture and pushed the limits of design through exhaustive research. Two important works have caused widespread praise and controversy: the Beaubourg or Pompidou Centre, Paris (1971–79) with Renzo Piano, a large open interior space clothed in highly-coloured services; and Lloyds of London (1979–85), a masterful and dramatic exercise in steel and glass which exemplifies his architectural optimism.

ROGERS, Samuel (1763–1855) English poet, born in Stoke-Newington. He entered his father's bank, in 1784 was taken into partnership, and in 1793 became head of the firm. In 1781 he contributed essays to the *Gentleman's Magazine*, next year wrote a comic opera, and in 1786 published *An Ode to Superstition*. In 1792 appeared *The Pleasures of Memory*, on which his poetical fame was chiefly based. There followed *An Epistle to a Friend* (Richard Sharp, 1798), the fragmentary *Voyage of Columbus* (1812), *Jacqueline* (1814, bound up with **Byron**'s *Lara*), and the inimitable *Italy* (1822–28). The last, in blank verse, proved a monetary failure; but the loss was recouped by the splendid edition of it and his earlier poems, brought out at a cost of £15000 (1830–34), with 114 illustrations by **Turner** and **Stothard**. In 1803, with £5000 a year, he retired from the bank as a sleeping partner, and settled down to bachelor life and an art collection which sold at his death for £50000. He was quietly generous to **Thomas Moore**, as well as to some unknown writers. But with the kindest heart he had so unkind a tongue that 'melodious Rogers' is better remembered today by a few ill-natured sayings than by his poetry.

ROGERS, Will (William Penn Adair) (1879–1935) American humorist-philosopher, born in Oolagah, Indian Territory (now Oklahoma), the son of a rancher. A colourful early life included foreign travels in Buenos Aires and Johannesburg and spells as a ranch hand and cow-puncher, where he gained a proficiency in riding and lariat-throwing that gained him employment from 1902 as 'The Cherokee Kid' in a variety of Wild West shows. He appeared at the St Louis World's Fair of 1904 and featured in the musical *The Girl Rangers* (1907). He made his legitimate Broadway début in *The Wall Street Girl* (1912) and later became a regular attraction at the *Ziegfeld Follies* (1917–18). By now his act had grown to include homespun philosophy, cracker-barrel wit and rustic ruminations. He made his film début in *Laughing Bill Hyde* (1918) and appeared, with moderate success, in such silent features as *Jubilo* (1919) and *Doubling for Romeo* (1921). The first of many books, *The Cowboy Philosopher at the Peace Conference*, was published in 1919. He began a newspaper column, wrote for the *Saturday Evening Post*, made frequent radio broadcasts, and came to personify the common man offering simple sagacity to the great and powerful. He returned to Broadway in *Three Cheers* (1928) and made his sound début in *They Had to See Paris* (1929). Films like *State Fair* (1933), *Judge Priest* (1934) and *Steamboat Round the Bend* (1935) catapulted him to the top of cinema popularity polls. At the time of his death in a plane crash, with his friend, the aviator **Wiley Post**, he was widely regarded as an irreplaceable American folk hero.

ROGERS, William Pierce (1913–) US Republican politician, born in Norfolk, New York. He was educated at the University of Colgate and Cornell University law school. He was assistant district attorney in New York under **Dewey**. In 1957 he became attorney general in the **Eisenhower** government. In this capacity he played a leading role in drafting the Civil Rights Act of 1957. In 1967 he was a delegate to the United Nations. He was secretary of state in the **Nixon** administration from 1969 until 1973.

ROGERS, Woodes (d.1732) English navigator. He led a privateering expedition against the Spanish (1708–11) which took off **Alexander Selkirk** from Juan Fernández island, and on his successful return wrote *Voyage Round the World* (1712). As governor of the Bahamas (1718–21, 1729–32) he suppressed piracy, founded a house of assembly and resisted Spanish attacks.

ROGET, Peter Mark (1779–1869) English physician and scholar, creator of 'Roget's Thesaurus'. The son of a Huguenot minister, he became physician to the Manchester Infirmary in 1804; physician to the Northern Dispensary, London, in 1808; secretary of the Royal Society, 1827–49; Fullerian professor of physiology at the Royal Institution 1833–36; and an original member of senate of London University. He wrote *On Animal and Vegetable Physiology* (Bridgewater Treatise, 1834). He is best known for his *Thesaurus of English Words and Phrases* (1852).

ROGIER VAN DER WEYDEN See **WEYDEN**

ROHAN-GIÉ, Henri, Duc de (1579–1638) French Duke of Léon, born in the Château of Blain in Brittany. He was a favourite of **Henri IV**, and in 1605 married the daughter of **Sully**. After the king's murder (1610) he became a Huguenot leader. On the surrender of La Rochelle (1628) a price was set on his head, and he made his way to Venice, but soon after was summoned by **Richelieu** to serve his king in the Valtelline, out of which he drove Imperialists and Spaniards. He next served under Bernard of Saxe-Weimar, but died in 1638 of a wound received at Rheinfelden.

ROHAN-GUÉMÉNÉE, Louis René Édouard, Prince de (1734–1803) French prelate. He embraced the clerical life in spite of dissolute morals, and became coadjutor to his uncle the bishop of Strasbourg. In 1772 he was sent as minister to Vienna, but injured himself at the French court by slanderous gossip about **Marie Antoinette**, and was recalled in 1774. In 1778 he became a cardinal, and in 1779 became bishop of Strasbourg. His eagerness to recover his footing at court made him an easy prey to **Cagliostro** and the **Comtesse de La Motte**, who tricked him into believing that the queen, who knew nothing of the affair, wished him to stand security for her purchase by instalments of a priceless diamond necklace. The adventurers collected the necklace from the jewellers supposedly to give it to the queen, but left Paris in order to sell the diamonds for their own gain. When the plot was discovered Rohan Guéménée was sent to the Bastille, but was acquitted by the *parlement* of Paris (1786). He was elected to the states-general in 1789, but refused to take the oath to the constitution in 1791, retiring to the German part of his diocese.

ROHDE, Ruth, née **Bryan** (1885–1954) American diplomat and feminist, born in Jacksonville, Illinois. The daughter of **William Jennings Bryan**, she gained political insight from a young age. In 1899 she went to Monticello Female Academy, and later entered Nebraska University, but left soon after to marry (1903). Divorcing in 1909 with two children, in 1910 she married Reginald Owen, an English army major, by whom she also had two children. Her husband was badly injured in service, and was left a chronic invalid. Ruth, to support her family, took to public speaking and in 1926 entered politics as a Democrat in Florida. In 1927 Major Owen died, and in 1928 she successfully ran for congress, becoming the first congresswoman from the deep south. Defending herself against accusations of ineligibility for congress because of dubious citizenship (the result of marrying an alien) she won a brilliant victory on feminist grounds, resulting in an amendment to the Cable Act, and as a member of congress continued to campaign for women's rights. In 1933 she was appointed US minister to Denmark, the first American diplomatic post ever held by a woman. In 1936 she married Börge Rohde, a Danish soldier, and was obliged to resign her ministerial post. Returning to the USA, she continued to lecture and write, helped to draft the United States Charter, and received the OM from King **Frederik IX** of Denmark.

ROHLFS, Gerhard (1831–96) German explorer, born in Vegesack near Bremen. He studied medicine, and joined (1855) the Foreign Legion in Algeria. While travelling through Morocco (1861–62), he was plundered and left for dead in the Sahara. From 1864 he travelled widely in North Africa, the Sahara and Nigeria, and, commissioned by the German emperor, undertook expeditions to Wadai (1878) and Abyssinia (1885) before becoming German consul in Zanzibar.

RÖHM, Ernst (1887–1934) German soldier, politician and Nazi leader. In 1921 he organized a private force of Brown Shirts. Early a supporter of **Hitler**, he was organizer and commander of the stormtroopers (Brown Shirts and Black Shirts, 1931). He became state commissar of Bavaria, but in 1934 he was charged with conspiracy to overthrow Hitler, and was executed without trial.

ROHMER, Sax, pseud of **Arthur Sarsfield Ward** (1886–1959) English author of mystery stories, born in Birmingham. Interested in things Egyptian, he found literary fame with his sinister, sardonic, oriental criminal genius villain, Fu Manchu, whose doings were told in many spine-chilling tales, including *Dr Fu Manchu* (1913), *The Yellow Claw* (1915), *Moon of Madness* (1927) and *Re-enter Fu Manchu* (1957).

ROH TAE WOO (1932–) South Korean politician, born in the farming hamlet of Sinyong, in the south-eastern region of Kyongsang. He was educated at the Korean Military Academy (1951–55), where he was a classmate of a future president, **Chun Doo-Hwan**. He fought briefly in the Korean War and was a battalion commander during the Vietnam War. He became commanding general of the Capital Security Command in 1979, from which position he helped General Chun seize power in the coup of 1979–80. He retired from the army in 1981 and successively served, under President Chun, as minister for national security and foreign affairs (1981–82) and for home affairs (from 1982). He was elected chairman of the ruling Democratic Justice party in 1985 and in 1987, following serious popular disturbances, drew up a political reform package which restored democracy to the country. He was elected president in 1987.

ROKITANSKY, Karl, Baron von (1804–78) Austrian pathologist, born in Königgrätz. Professor of pathological anatomy at Vienna (1834–75), he was one of the founders of modern pathological anatomy, and wrote the great *Handbuch der pathologischen Anatomie* (1842–46).

ROKOSSOVSKY, Konstantin (1896–1968) Russian soldier, born in Warsaw of Polish descent. He served in World War I in the tsarist army, and joined the Red Guards in 1917. In World War II he was one of the defenders of Moscow, played a leading part in the battle of Stalingrad (1943), recaptured Orel and Warsaw, and led the Russian race for Berlin. In 1944 he was promoted marshal of the Soviet Union. In 1949 he was appointed Polish minister of defence, a post he was made to resign when **Gomulka** became premier in November 1956. He then became a deputy-minister of defence of the Soviet Union, and in 1957 he was appointed to a military command in Transcaucasia.

ROLAND (acc. to tradition d.778) semi-legendary French knight, hero of the *Chanson de Roland* (11th century). The most celebrated of the Paladins of **Charlemagne**, he is said to have been the nephew of Charlemagne, and the ideal of a Christian knight. The only evidence for his historical existence is a passage in **Einhard**'s *Life of Charlemagne*, which refers to Roland as having fallen at Roncesvalle. **Boiardo**'s *Orlando Inamorato* and **Ariosto**'s *Orlando Furioso* depart widely from the old traditions.

ROLAND DE LA PLATIÈRE, Jean Mari (1734–93) French statesman, born near Villefranche-sur-Saône. He had risen to be inspector of manufactures at Amiens, when in 1775 he made the acquaintance of Marie Jeanne Phlipon (1754–93), the daughter of an engraver, whom he married in 1780. In 1791 Roland was sent to Paris by Lyon to watch the interests of the municipality; and there Madame Roland became the queen of a coterie of young and eloquent enthusiasts that included all the leaders of the Gironde, such as **Brissot**, **Pétion** and François Buzot (1760–94). In March 1792 Roland became minister of the interior, but was dismissed three months later for a remonstrance to the king. He was recalled after the king's removal to the Temple, made himself hateful to the Jacobins by his protests against the September massacres, and took part in the last struggle of the Girondists. It was then that the friendship between Madame Roland and Buzot grew into love, but she sacrificed passion to duty. On 31 May 1793, the 22 were proscribed, Roland had been arrested, but escaped and fled to Rouen; Buzot and others fled to Caen to organize insurrection, but in vain; next day Madame Roland was carried to the Abbaye. Set at liberty two days later, she was arrested anew and taken to Sainte-Pélagie. During her five months in prison she wrote her unfinished Memoirs, in which we have a serene and delightful revelation of her youth, though she is best and most natural in her letters. On 8 November 1793 she was guillotined. Two days later her husband committed suicide by his sword near Rouen.

ROLFE, Frederick William, styled **Baron Corvo** (1860–1913) English novelist and essayist. A convert to Roman Catholicism, his life was shattered by his rejection from the novitiate for the Roman priesthood at the Scots College in Rome; but it prompted his most famous work, *Hadrian VII* (1904), in which a comparable and obviously self-modelled 'spoiled priest' is unexpectedly chosen for the papacy, institutes various reforms and is ultimately martyred. He contributed to the *Yellow Book* in the 1890s *Stories Toto Told Me* (afterwards republished in book form, 1895) and is also remembered for *Chronicles of the House of Borgia* and the posthumous *The Desire and Pursuit of the Whole*, published in 1934.

ROLLAND, Romain (1866–1944) French musicologist and author, born in Clamecy, Nièvre. He studied in Paris and at the French School in Rome, and in 1895 gained his doctorate of letters with a thesis on early opera, *L'Histoire de l'opéra en Europe avant Lulli et Scarlatti*. A number of dramatic works written at this time won comparatively little success. In 1910 he became professor of the history of music at the Sorbonne, and in the same year published *Beethoven*, the first of many biographical works including lives of **Michelangelo** (1906), **Handel** (1910), **Tolstoy** (1911) and **Gandhi** (1924). His ten-volume novel cycle *Jean-Christophe*, the hero of which is a musician, was written between 1904 and 1912, and in 1915 he was awarded the Nobel prize for literature. During World War I he aroused unpopularity by his writings, out of Switzerland, showing a pacifist attitude; these were published in 1915 as *Au dessus de la mêlée*. He lived in Switzerland until 1938, completing another novel cycle, *L'Âme enchantée* (1922–33), a series of plays upon the French Revolution, and a further study of **Beethoven**, as well as numerous pieces of music criticism. On his return to France he became a mouthpiece of the opposition to Fascism and the Nazis, and his later works contain much political and social writing.

ROLLE OF HAMPOLE, Richard (c.1290–1349) English hermit, mystic and poet, born in Thornton in Yorkshire. He studied at Oxford, but at 19 turned into a hermit, first at Dalton and then at Hampole, near Doncaster. He wrote lyrics, meditations and religious works in Latin and English, and translated and expounded the Psalms in prose.

ROLLIN, Charles (1661–1741) French historian, born in Paris. He was the author of *Traité des études* (1726–31), *Histoire ancienne* (1730–38) and *Histoire romaine* (1738–48). He lost the rectorship of Paris University (1720) and other academic posts because of his Jansenist sympathies.

ROLLIN, Ledru See **LEDRU-ROLLIN**

ROLLING STONES, The British rock group, formed in 1961. Members: **Mick (Michael Phillip) Jagger** (1943–), **Keith Richard** (1943–), **Bill Wyman** (1936–), **Charlie Watts** (1941–), and former member **Brian Jones** (1944–69). One of the longest-running, most successful and controversial pop groups, they first performed together in London in 1962 and released their first single, a version of **Chuck Berry**'s 'Come On' in 1963. At first they were very much in the shadow of the **Beatles** but their carefully cultivated rebellious image and greater reliance on black blues and rhythm and blues soon won them their own, large following. Although their uninhibited lifestyles often hit the headlines—with Jones dying as a result of drug abuse and Jagger and Richard both convicted of drugs possession—it was the excellence of their compositions and the popularity of their stage act which ensured their continuing success. Controversy continued to surround them, with a murder taking place at one of their US performances and Richard being convicted in Canada in 1977 for heroin possession. They will be remembered, however, for their quintessential rock and roll, and such singles as 'The Last Time' (1965), 'Jumpin' Jack Flash' (1968), 'Honky Tonk Women' (1969), and albums such as *Beggar's Banquet* (1968), *Let it Bleed* (1969), *Sticky Fingers* (1971), *Exile on Main Street* (1972), *Some Girls* (1978) and *Tattoo You* (1981).

ROLLINS, Sonny (Theodore Walter) (1930–) American jazz saxophonist and composer, born in New York, who learned to play piano, alto and tenor saxophone while at school. Before reaching 25, he worked and recorded with major bebop figures such as **Charlie Parker**, **Bud Powell** and **Miles Davis**. But it was from the mid 1950s that he emergeed as an important if highly individual voice in the 'hard bop' movement. Rollins, whose use of calypso themes reflects his mother's roots in the Virgin Islands, is one of the most powerful improvisers (on tenor and soprano saxophones) to emerge in the post-Parker period, creating a thematic style distinct from that of the **Coltrane** school.

ROLLO (HROLF) (c.860–c.932) Viking founder of the duchy of Normandy. The son of a Norse earl of Orkney (Rognvald of Möre), he was the leader of a band of mercenary Vikings foraging in France in 911. He laid siege unsuccessfully to Chartres, but in peace talks with King **Charles III 'the Simple'** he was offered a large tract of land on the lower Seine in return for becoming Charles' vassal. This territory was the nucleus of the future duchy of Normandy ('Northmandy'). One of his descendants was **William I, the Conqueror**. Rollo (Hrolf) was such a huge man that no horse could carry him, hence his nickname of Hrolf 'the Ganger' (walker).

ROLLS, Charles Stewart (1877–1910) English motor car manufacturer and aviator, born in London, the third son of the 1st Baron Llangattock. Educated at Eton and Cambridge, from 1895 he experimented with the earliest motor cars and founded C S Rolls & Co in 1902. In 1906 he went into partnership with **Henry Royce**. The same year he crossed the English Channel by balloon, and in 1910 made the first non-stop double crossing by aeroplane. He lost his life in a plane crash soon afterwards.

RÖLVAAG, Ole Edvart (1876–1931) Norwegian-born American novelist, born on Dönna Island. He emigrated to the USA in 1896 and became professor of Norwegian at St Olaf College (1906–31). A naturalized citizen since 1908, but writing in Norwegian, he published *Letters from America* (1912). His best-known novel, also written in Norwegian, was translated as *Giants in the Earth* (1927), dealing with the life of Norwegian settlers in South Dakota in the 1870s; it was followed by *Peder Victorious* (1929) and *Their Fathers' God* (1931).

ROMAINS, Jules, pseud of **Louis Farigoule** (1885–1972) French writer, born in Saint-Julien Chapteuil. After graduating in both science and literature at the École Normale Supérieure, he taught in various lycées. In 1908 his poems, *La Vie unanime*, established his name and, along with his *Manuel de déification* (1910), the Unanimist school. He remained prominent in French literature, and from 1936 to 1941 was president of the International PEN Club. His works include the books of poems *Odes et prières* (1913), *Chants des dix années 1914–1924* (1928) and *L'Homme blanc* (1937), the dramas *L'Armée dans la ville* (1911) and *Knock, ou le triomphe de la médecine* (1923), his most successful play, the novels *Mort de quelqu'un* (1910) and *Les Copains* (1913), and the great cycle *Les Hommes de bonne volonté* in 27 volumes (1932–46), covering the early 20th-century era of French life. He published his autobiographical *Souvenirs et confidences d'un écrivain* in 1958.

ROMAN, Johan Helmich (1694–1758) Swedish composer. He twice visited England, where he met **Handel**, Geminiani and other leading figures in contemporary music. He travelled in France and Italy, and in 1745 was appointed *intendent* of music to the Swedish court. His compositions include symphonies, concerti grossi, trio sonatas, a Swedish Mass, settings in the vernacular of the Psalms, and occasional music, all showing the influence of the Italian style and, less markedly, of Handel and the French and North German schools.

ROMANES, George John (1848–94) Canadian-born English naturalist, born in Kingston, Canada, but brought to England as an infant. While at Cambridge University he became a close friend of **Charles Darwin**, whose arguments he supported in his various works, including *Animal Intelligence* (1881) and *Scientific Evidences of Organic Evolution* (1881). He also wrote *Mental Evolution in Man* (1888).

ROMANO, Giulio See **GIULIO ROMANO**

ROMANOV a family that originally emigrated from (Slavonic) Prussia to the principality of Moscow. Its head, **Michael Romonov**, was elected tsar by the other Russian boyars in 1613, and the tsardom became hereditary in his house till in 1762, on the death of the Tsaritsa Elizabeth, the Duke of Holstein-Gottorp, son of **Peter I, the Great**'s daughter, succeeded as **Peter III**. Later tsars (till the 1917 revolution) were descended from him and his wife, **Catherine II**.

ROMBERG, Sigmund (1887–1951) Hungarian-born American composer of operettas, born in Nagy Kaniza; he settled in the USA in 1909. Of more than 70 works, his most famous were *Blossom Time* (1921), *The*

Student Prince (1924), *The Desert Song* (1926) and *The New Moon* (1928).

ROMER, Alfred Sherwood (1894–1973) American palaeontologist, born in White Plains, New York, an authority on the evolutionary history of vertebrates. He studied at Columbia and became professor of biology at Chicago (1923–34) and Harvard (1934–65). Especially interested in the evolution of the lower vertebrates, he used his own and other collections of fossils to trace the evolution of fishes to terrestrial vertebrates, as recorded in his book *The Vertebrate Story* (1959).

ROMERO Y GALDAMES, Oscar Arnulfo (1917–80) Salvadorean Roman Catholic prelate, born in Ciudad Barrios. Ordained in 1942, and generally conservative in outlook, he was made bishop in 1970 and (to the dismay of progressives) archbishop in 1977. Acts of political violence and repression of the poor made his public utterances and actions more outspoken. After thousands had died in a brutal persecution the archbishop himself was murdered while preaching, one year after he was nominated for the Nobel peace prize by a large number of American and British parliamentarians. Some of his 'Thoughts' appeared in translation (by James Brockman) as *The Church Is All of You* (1984).

ROMILLY, Sir Samuel (1757–1818) English lawyer and law reformer, born in London, the son of a watchmaker of Huguenot descent. At 21 he entered Gray's Inn, and found his chief employment in Chancery practice. In 1790 he published an able pamphlet on the French Revolution. Appointed solicitor-general in 1806, he entered parliament and obstinately set himself to mitigate the severity of the criminal law. He shared in the anti-slavery agitation, and opposed the suspension of the Habeas Corpus Act and the spy system. He committed suicide three days after his wife's death. He wrote *Observations on the Criminal Law of England* (1810), *Speeches* (1820), and *Memoirs* (1840). His second son, John, Baron Romilly (1802–74), was solicitor-general in 1848, attorney-general in 1850, master of the rolls in 1851 and a baron in 1866.

ROMMEL, Erwin (1891–1944) German soldier, born in Heidenheim. Educated at Tübingen, he distinguished himself in World War I. An instructor at the Dresden Military Academy, he was an early Nazi sympathizer. He commanded **Hitler**'s headquarters guard during the Austrian, Sudetenland and Czech occupations and throughout the Polish campaign. Leading a panzer division during the 1940 invasion of France, he displayed such drive and initiative that he was promoted to command the Afrika Korps, where his spectacular successes against the attenuated 8th Army earned him the sobriquet of the 'Desert Fox' and the admiration of his opponents. He captured Tobruk (1942) and drove the British right back to El-Alamein, but in November 1942 was defeated there by **Montgomery** and retreated to Tunis. In March 1943 he was withdrawn—a sick man—from North Africa at **Mussolini**'s insistence. Hitler subsequently appointed him commander of the Channel defences in France. Returning home wounded in 1944, his condoning of the plot against Hitler brought him the choice between the firing squad and suicide. He chose to die by self-administered poison, thus preserving his estate for his family.

ROMNEY, George (1734–1802) English painter, born in Dalton-in-Furness, Lancashire. For ten years he worked at his father's trade of cabinetmaker, and in 1755 was articled to a 'Count' Steel in Kendal to be taught how to paint. From 1757 he specialized in portraiture, and was greatly influenced by **Reynolds** and, to a lesser extent, **Gainsborough**. Leaving his wife and two children behind he went to London in 1762. Most of the leading aristocratic and cultural figures of his day sat for him, including Emma, Lady **Hamilton**. His technique was ostentatiously fluent and, at times, slick. In 1798 he returned to Kendal and his wife in poor health, and died there.

ROMULUS legendary founder and first king of Rome. According to tradition the son of Mars and Rhea Silvia, the daughter of King Numitor of Alba Longa. With his twin brother Remus he was exposed by a usurping uncle, but suckled by a she-wolf. In 753 BC he founded his city on the Tiber, and in 716 was said to have been carried up to heaven in a chariot of fire.

ROMULUS AUGUSTUS See **AUGUSTULUS**

RONALD, originally **Russell, Sir Landon** (1873–1938) English conductor, composer and pianist, born in London, son of Henry Russell, the songwriter. He toured with **Nellie Melba**, conducted the New Symphony Orchestra, notably in **Elgar**, **Strauss** and **Tchaikovsky**, and was principal of the Guildhall School of Music (1910–37). He wrote many songs, including 'Down in the Forest Something Stirred', and was knighted in 1922. He wrote the autobiographical *Variation on a Personal Theme* (1922) and *Myself and Others* (1931).

RONALDS, Sir Francis (1788–1873) English inventor, born in London, the son of a merchant. After studying practical electricity, in 1816 he fitted up in his garden at Hammersmith an electric telegraph. His offer of the invention to the Admiralty was refused; he published a description of it in 1823. He also invented (1845) a system of automatic photographic registration for meteorological instruments. He was made superintendent of the Meteorological Observatory at Kew in 1843.

RONSARD, Pierre de (1524–85) French poet, born in the Château de la Possonnière in Vendôme. He served the dauphin and the Duc d'**Orléans** as page, and accompanied **James V** with his bride, Mary of Lorraine (**Guise**), to Scotland, where he stayed three years. Becoming partially deaf, he abandoned arms for letters, and studied under the great humanist **Jean Daurat**, at first with his future fellow member of the Pléiade, **Jean Antoine de Baïf**, at the house of his father the scholar and diplomat Lazare de Baïf, and later at the Collège de Coqueret, where **du Bellay** and **Belleau** joined them. His seven years of study resulted first in the *Odes* (1550), which excited violent opposition from the older national school. In 1552 appeared his *Amours*, a collection of Petrarchan sonnets, followed by his *Bocage* (1554), his *Hymnes* (1555), the conclusion of his *Amours* (1556), and the first collected edition of his poetry(1560). He subsequently wrote two bitter reflections on the political and economic state of the country, *Discours des misères de ce temps* (1560–69) and *Remonstrance au peuple de France* (1563), and in 1572, following the massacre of St Bartholomew, *La Françiade*, an unfinished epic. **Charles IX**, like his predecessors, heaped favours on the poet, who, despite recurrent illness, spent his later years in comfort at the abbey of Croix-Val in Vendôme. The most important poet of 16th-century France, Ronsard was the chief exemplar of the doctrines of the Pléiade, which aimed at raising the status of French as a literary language and ousting the formal classicism inherited from the middle ages. Despite the great success of Ronsard's poems in his lifetime, the classicists regained the upper hand after his death, and his fame suffered an eclipse until the 19th century, when the Romantic movement brought recognition of his true worth.

RÖNTGEN, Wilhelm Konrad von (1845–1923) German physicist, born in Lennep in Prussia. He studied at Zürich, and was professor at Strasbourg, Giessen, Würzburg, and (1899–1919) Munich. At Würzburg in 1895 he discovered the electromagnetic rays which he called X-rays (known also as Röntgen rays), and for his work on them he was awarded in 1896, jointly with **Lenard**, the Rumford medal, and in 1901 the Nobel prize for physics. He also did important work on the heat conductivity of crystals, the specific heat of gases, and the electromagnetic rotation of polarized light.

ROOKE, Sir George (1650–1709) English admiral, born near Canterbury. He became at 30 post-captain, and in 1689 rear-admiral. In 1692 he did splendid service at Cape La Hogue, and was knighted. In 1702 he commanded the expedition against Cadiz, and destroyed the plate-fleet at Vigo. With Sir **Cloudesley Shovel** he captured Gibraltar (1704), and then engaged off Malaga a much heavier French fleet.

ROOSEVELT, (Anna) Eleanor (1882–1962) American humanitarian, born in New York City, niece of **Theodore Roosevelt** and wife of **Franklin D Roosevelt**, whom she married in 1905. She took up extensive political work during her husband's illness from polio and proved herself an invaluable social adviser to him when he became president. In 1941 she became assistant director of the office of civilian defence; after her husband's death in 1945 she extended the scope of her activities, and was a delegate to the UN Assembly in 1946, chairman of the UN Human Rights Commission (1947–51) and US representative at the General Assembly (1946–52). She was also chairman of the American UN Association. Her publications include *This Is My Story* (1937), *The Lady of the White House* (1938), *The Moral Basis of Democracy* (1940), *India and the Awakening East* (1953), *On My Own* (1958), and her Autobiography (1962).

ROOSEVELT, Franklin Delano (1882–1945) 32nd president of the USA, a distant cousin of **Theodore Roosevelt**, born in Hyde Park, New York, into a wealthy family. Educated in Europe and at Harvard and Columbia Law Schools, he was admitted to the New York bar in 1907 and successively served as a state senator (1910–13) and as assistant secretary of the navy (1913–20), before becoming Democratic candidate for the vice-presidency in 1920. Stricken by paralysis (1921–23), he was governor of New York (1928–32). In the presidential election of 1932 he defeated **Hoover**, the repeal of prohibition being made a vital party issue, and at once in 1933 was faced by a serious economic crisis, the 'Great Depression', which he successfully met by launching an innovative 'New Deal' programme, involving abandonment of the gold standard, devaluation of the dollar, state intervention in the credit market, agricultural price support, and the passage of a Social Security Act (1935) which provided for unemployment and old age insurance. With this programme beginning to work, Roosevelt was elected by a landslide in 1936 and secured a third term (unique in American history) in 1940 and a fourth in 1944. In the process, Roosevelt, who inculcated a new spirit of hope through his skilful and optimistic radio 'fireside chats', constructed a new rural-urban 'majority coalition' for the Democratic party. He also served significantly to extend the reach of the 'presidential sector'. During the late 1930s he strove in vain to ward off war, but when World War II began he modified America's neutrality to favour the allies (as by the Lend-Lease plan), before the country was brought into the conflict by Japan's attack on Pearl Harbour (December 1941). A conference with **Churchill** at sea produced the 'Atlantic Charter', a statement of peace aims; and there were other notable meetings with Churchill and **Stalin** at Tehran (1943) and Yalta (1945). He died three weeks before the Nazi surrender.

ROOSEVELT, Theodore (1858–1919) 26th president of the USA, born, of Dutch and Scottish descent, in New York. He studied at Harvard, was leader of the New York legislature in 1884, and president of the New York police board from 1895 to 1897. He was assistant secretary of the navy when in 1898 he raised and commanded 'Roosevelt's Roughriders' in the Cuban War, returning to be governor of New York State (1898–1900). Appointed (Republican) vice-president (1901), he became president on the death (by assassination) of **McKinley** (1901), and was re-elected in 1905. An 'expansionist', he insisted on a strong navy, the purification of the civil service, and the regulation of trusts and monopolies. He returned from a great hunting tour in Central Africa in time to take an active part in the elections of 1910, and helped to split the Republican party, those with whom he acted forming the 'progressive' section. As Progressive candidate for the presidency in 1912 he was defeated by **Woodrow Wilson**. After exploring the Rio Duvida, of Teodoro, in Brazil (1914), he worked vigorously during World War I pressing for America's intervention. He wrote on American ideals, ranching, hunting, and zoology.

ROOT, Elihu (1845–1937) American jurist and statesman, born in Clinton, New York. He was US secretary of war 1899–1904, of state 1905–09, and was awarded the Nobel prize for peace in 1912 for his promotion of international arbitration. He participated in founding the League of Nations.

ROOZEBOOM, Hendrick Willem Bakhuis (1854–1907) Dutch physical chemist, born in Alkmaar. He became professor of chemistry at Amsterdam, where he demonstrated the practical application of **Josiah Gibbs**'s phase rule.

ROPER, Margaret See **MORE, Sir Thomas**

ROPS, Félicien (1833–98) Belgian artist, born in Namur. He was known for his lithographs and etchings, which often had satirical or social significance, and for his illustrations of the works of **Baudelaire**.

ROREM, Ned (1923–) American composer and writer, born in Richmond, Indiana. After studies at the Juilliard School in New York he spent the greater part of the 1950s in Paris and was much influenced by contemporary French culture. As well as a rich corpus of songs, he has composed three symphonies and much other orchestral music, six operas, numerous concertos, ballets and other music for the theatre, choral and chamber music. His published essays, diaries and literary criticism are products of a candid and elegant stylist.

RORSCHACH, Hermann (1884–1922) Swiss psychiatrist and neurologist, born in Zürich. He devised a diagnostic procedure for mental disorders based upon the patient's interpretation of a series of standardized ink blots (the Rorschach test).

RORTY, Richard McKay (1931–) American philosopher, born in New York City. He studied at Chicago and Yale, and taught at Yale (1955–57), Wellesley College (1958–61) and Princeton (1961–82), before becoming professor of humanities at Virginia University (from 1982). In 1979 he published *Philosophy and the Mirror of Nature*, which mounted a forceful and dramatic attack on the foundationalist, metaphysical aspirations of traditional philosophy. It was hailed by sympathizers as the first major text in 'post-analytical philosophy' and denounced by opponents as unscholarly special pleading. He has subsequently attracted a wider, though no less polarized, readership among those interested in literary criticism, social theory and intellectual history generally, with works such as *Contingency, Irony and Solidarity* (1988).

ROSA, originally **Rose, Carl August Nicolas** (1842–89) German impresario and violinist, born in Hamburg. He became konzertmeister there in 1863, appeared in London as a soloist in 1866, and in 1873 founded the Carl Rosa Opera Company, giving a great impulse to opera sung in English, and also to operas by English composers.

ROSA, Salvator (1615–73) Italian painter and poet, born near Naples. At Rome his rebellious talents as a painter brought him fame, but he made powerful enemies by his satires, and withdrew to Florence for nine years. After that he returned to Rome, where he died. He owes his reputation mainly to his landscapes of wild and savage scenes. He executed numerous etchings. His *Satires* were published in 1719.

ROSAMOND See **ALBOIN; CLIFFORD** family

ROSAS, Juan Manuel de (1793–1877) Argentine dictator, born in Buenos Aires. He became commander-in-chief in 1826, and was governor of the province from 1829 to 1832. Disappointed of re-election, he headed a revolt, and from 1835 to 1852 governed as dictator. His rule was one of terror and bloodshed. In 1849 Rosas secured for Buenos Aires the entire navigation of the Plate, the Uruguay and the Paraná. This roused the other river provinces, and Urquiza, governor of Entre Rios, supported by Brazil, routed him at Monte Caseros near Buenos Aires in February 1852. Rosas escaped to England, where he lived until his death.

ROSCELLINUS, Johannes (c.1050–after 1120) French scholar, born probably in Compiègne. He studied at Soissons, and defended Nominalism, of which he is considered the founder, against attacks by his pupil **Abelard**. In 1092 the council of Soissons condemned his teaching as implicitly involving the negation of the doctrine of the Trinity.

ROSCIUS, Quintus (c.134–62 BC) Roman actor, a slave by birth. He became the greatest comic actor in Rome. His patrons included the dictator **Sulla** and **Cicero** and he gave the latter lessons in elocution. He wrote a treatise on eloquence and acting. On his being sued at law for 50000 sesterces, Cicero defended him in his extant oration, *Pro Q. Roscio Comoedo*.

ROSCOE, Sir Henry Enfield (1833–1915) English chemist, grandson of **William Roscoe**, born in London. He was educated at Liverpool High School, University College, London, and Heidelberg, where with **Robert Bunsen** he did research on quantitative photochemistry. From 1857 to 1886 he was professor of chemistry at Manchester, and worked on the preparation and properties of pure vanadium. He was Liberal MP for South Manchester (1885–95), and vice-chancellor of London University (1896–1902). His works include *Spectrum Analysis* (1868), the great *Treatise on Chemistry* (with Schorlemmer; 6 vols, 1878–89), a book on **John Dalton**, and his own *Life and Experiences* (1906).

ROSCOE, William (1753–1831) English historian, born in Liverpool. In 1769 he was articled to an attorney, and began to practise in 1774. In 1777 he published a poem, *Mount Pleasant*, and in 1787 *The Wrongs of Africa*, a protest against the slave trade. But it was his *Life of Lorenzo de' Medici* (1796) that established his literary reputation. His second great book, *Life of Leo X* (1805), like the former, was translated into German, French and Italian. He had retired from business in 1796, but in 1799 became partner in a Liverpool bank, which involved him in pecuniary embarrassment (1816–20). He also wrote poems, of which the best known is the children's classic, *The Butterfly's Ball and the Grasshopper's feast* (1807); an edition of **Pope**; and a monograph on Monandrian plants.

ROSE-INNES, Sir James (1855–1942) South African judge, born in Uitenkage. Educated at the University of the Cape of Good Hope, he became attorney-general (1890–93 and 1900–02), and then judge president (later chief justice) of the Supreme Court of the Transvaal (1902–10), judge of appeal (1910–14), and chief justice of the Union of South Africa (1914–27). He advocated a liberal policy towards the Bantu and, as head of a strong bench, was probably the greatest of all South African judges. His opinions are notable for their clarity and their willingness to rely on both the English and Roman-Dutch traditions in South African law. He was also one of the early translators of the works of **Johannes Voet**.

ROSE, Hugh See **STRATHNAIRN**

ROSE, Sir John (1820–88) Scots-born Canadian diplomat, born in Turriff, Aberdeenshire. Educated at Udny Academy and King's College, Aberdeen, he emigrated with his parents to Huntingdon, Lower Canada, in 1836, and was called to the Montreal bar in 1842. He was identified with Hudson's Bay Company operations, acquired numerous directorates, and became a close friend and political associate of **John A Macdonald**. He was drawn into Anglo-American arbitration initially in deciding Oregon-related questions directly arising from his Hudson's Bay brief (1863–69), while at the same time entering into partnership in London with the American financier and future vice-president, **Levi P Morton**. He played a critical part in adjusting British-American hostilities after the Civil War. He later settled in England, but died in Scotland during a stag shoot.

ROSE, Lionel Edmund (1948–) Australian bantamweight boxer, born in Warragul, Victoria, the first Aborigine to hold a world title. Brought up in an Aboriginal camp, he was inspired by the success of **Jimmy Carruthers**, and determined to emulate him; he did this by winning the bantamweight championship of the world in Tokyo against Fighting Harada of Japan (1968) just four years after turning professional. He followed this up by defeating Alan Rudkin of Great Britain on points over 15 rounds in a bout at Melbourne in which the Commonwealth title was also at stake, but in March 1969 lost his title to Ruben Olivares. He is currently an adviser on Youth, Sport and Recreation to the minister for Aboriginal Affairs.

ROSE, Murray (1939–) Australian swimmer. At the 1956 Melbourne Olympics he became the youngest-ever triple gold medallist in swimming, with wins in the 400 and 1500 metres freestyle and the relay team. In Rome in 1960 he became the first swimmer to defend successfully the 400 metres title. He received the Helms Foundation World Trophy in 1962 and for three or four years had no serious rivals.

ROSE, Pete (Peter Edward) (1941–) American professional baseball player and manager, born in Cincinnati, Ohio. He played with the Cincinnati Reds from 1963 to 1978, then went on to Philadelphia and Montreal before returning to the Reds as player/manager in 1984. In September 1985 he broke **Ty Cobb**'s 57-year-old record of career base hits (4191). By the time he retired from playing in 1986 he had hit 4256 base hits. In 1989 he accepted a life ban from the sport.

ROSE, William Cumming (1887–1984) American biochemist, born in Greenville, South Carolina. He studied at Yale and spent his career at Illinois. From the 1930s he studied mammalian nutrition; in one series of experiments he replaced all protein by amino acids, and so found that not all 20 of them are essential for a given species; in the rat, ten are essential (including threonine, discovered by Rose in 1936). In the adult human diet, only eight are essential, as he showed by experiments using student volunteers.

ROSEBERY, Archibald Philip Primrose, 5th Earl of (1847–1929) Scottish statesman, born in London. Educated at Eton and Christ Church College, Oxford, he succeeded his grandfather in 1868. In 1874 he was president of the Social Science Congress, in 1878 lord rector of Aberdeen University, in 1880 of Edinburgh, in 1899 of Glasgow, from 1881 to 1883 under-secretary for the home department, and in 1884 became first commissioner of works. In July 1886, and again from 1892 to 1894, he was secretary for foreign affairs in the **Gladstone** administration. In 1889–90 and 1892 he was chairman of the London County Council. On the retirement of Gladstone he became Liberal premier (March 1894); and after his government had been defeated at the general election (1895), he remained leader of the Liberal opposition till 1896, when he resigned the leadership. A spokesman for imperial federation, he was an imperialist during the Boer war, and as head of the Liberal League from 1902 represented a policy, first set forth in a famous speech at Chesterfield, but not accepted by official Liberals. His attitude in 1909–10 was Independent or Conservative. In 1911 he was created Earl of Midlothian. Lord Rosebery published books on **Pitt** (1891), **Peel** (1899), the 'last phase' of **Napoleon**'s career (1900), **Chatham** (1910), and *Miscellanies* (2 vols, 1921). In 1878 he married Hannah (1851–90), the only daughter of Baron Meyer de Rothschild. A devoted race-goer, he won the Derby thrice (1894, 1895, 1905).

ROSECRANS, William Starke (1819–98) American soldier, born in Kingston, Ohio. At the outbreak of the Civil War (1861–65) he became aide to **McClellan**, whom he succeeded, and kept **Lee** out of Western Virginia. In 1862 he commanded a division at the siege of Corinth, and after its capture commanded the army of the Mississippi; in September he defeated **Price** at Iuka, and in October defended Corinth against Price and Van Dorn. In the battles at Stone River (December 1862 and January 1863), against **Bragg**, he converted what had nearly been a defeat into a victory; but at Chickamauga (September 1863), he was defeated by Bragg, although he held Chattanooga. He was superseded by **Grant**, but in 1864 repelled Price's invasion of Missouri. In 1868–69 he was minister to Mexico, from 1881 to 1885 a member for California of the US House of Representatives, and then registrar of the US treasury (1885–93).

ROSEGGER, Peter, known until 1894 as **P K (Petri Kettenfeier)** (1843–1918) Austrian poet and novelist, born of peasant parents near Krieglach, Styria. In 1870 he published *Zither und Hackbrett*, a volume of poems in his native dialect, and followed this with autobiographical works such as *Waldheimat* (1897) and *Mein Himmelreich* (1901), and novels, including *Die Schriften des Waldschulmeisters* (1875), *Der Gottsucher* (1883) and *Jakob der Letzte* (1888), vividly portraying his native district and its people.

ROSENBERG, Alfred (1893–1946) German politician, born in Estonia. An avid supporter of national socialism, he joined the party in 1920, edited Nazi journals, for a time (1933) directed the party's foreign policy, and in 1934 was given control of its cultural and political education policy. In his *The Myth of the 20th Century* (1930) he expounded the extreme Nazi doctrines which he later put into practice in eastern Europe, for which crime he was hanged at Nuremberg in 1946.

ROSENBERG, Isaac (1890–1918) English poet and artist, born in Bristol, the son of Jewish émigrés from Russia. Educated at council schools in the east end of London, he was apprenticed as an engraver before studying art at Slade School. He kept poor health and went to South Africa in 1914 but returned to England the following year, enlisted in the army and was killed in action in France. He published his first collection, *Night and Day*, in 1912, and *Youth* in 1915 before the posthumous appearance of *Poems* in 1922, a selection edited by **Gordon Bottomley** and introduced by **Laurence Binyon**. Though revered by the cognoscenti, his reputation languished until the appearance in 1937 of his *Collected Works* (newly edited in 1979). His comparatively poor upbringing, highly charged vocabulary and bluntly realistic attitude to the war mark him out from other war poets.

ROSENBERG, Julius (1917–53) and his wife **Ethel** (1916–1953), American communists, part of a transatlantic spy ring uncovered after the trial of **Klaus Fuchs** in Britain. Julius was employed by the American army, and Ethel's brother, David Greenglass, at the nuclear research station at Los Alamos. They were convicted of passing on atomic secrets through an intermediary to the Soviet vice-consul. Greenglass turned witness for the prosecution and saved his life. The Rosenbergs were sentenced to death in 1951 and, despite numerous appeals from many West European countries and three stays of execution, were executed at Sing Sing prison, New York.

ROSENFELD See **KAMENEV**

ROSENKRANZ, Karl (1805–79) German philosopher, born at Magdeburg. In 1833 he became professor of philosophy at Königsberg. His works include an encyclopaedia of theology, criticisms of **Schleiermacher** and **David Strauss**, and books on poetry, education, **Diderot** and **Goethe**; but he is best known by his works on the Hegelian system (1840–56) and his life of **Hegel** (1844). He wrote an unfinished autobiography (1873).

ROSENQUIST, James Albert (1933–) American painter, born in Grand Falls, North Dakota. He studied at the Minneapolis School of Art (1948), at Minnesota University (1952–54), and at the Art Students' League in 1955. He began as an abstract painter but c.1960 took to Pop Art and painted enlarged bits and pieces of unrelated everyday objects. He held an exhibition at the Whitney Museum of American Art in 1972.

ROSENTHAL, Jack Morris (1931–) English dramatist, born in Manchester. Educated at Sheffield University, he joined the promotions department of Granada television in 1956 and made his professional writing début with over 150 episodes of *Coronation Street* (1961–69). He created the series *The Lovers!* (1970), followed by individual plays like *Another Sunday and Sweet F.A.* (1972), *The Evacuees* (1975) and *Barmitzvah Boy* (1976). His film scripts include *Lucky Star* (1980) and *Yentl* (1983) in collaboration with **Barbra Streisand**, whilst stage work includes *Smash!* (1981) and *Our Gracie* (1983). Among his more recent television plays are *The Knowledge* (1979) and *London's Burning* (1986). In 1973 he married the actress Maureen Lipman.

ROSENZWEIG, Franz (1886–1929) German theologian, born in Kassel into a Jewish family. He first studied medicine, then switched to modern history and philosophy and did his doctoral dissertation on **Hegel**'s political philosophy. But he came to react against Hegel and German Idealism in favour of an existential approach that emphasized the experience and interests of the individual. He was on the point of converting from Judaism to Christianity, but a critical religious experience in 1913 caused him to reaffirm his Jewishness and devote the rest of his life to the study and practice of Judaism. His major work was *Der Stern der Erlösung* (The Star of Redemption), begun while on active service in World War I and published in 1921. From 1922 he suffered progressive paralysis, but still collaborated with **Martin Buber** from 1925 on a new German translation of the Hebrew Bible, and after his death exercised a profound influence on Jewish religious thought.

ROSEWALL, Ken (Kenneth Ronald) (1934–) Australian tennis player, born in Sydney. Small and wiry, and an impeccable stylist, he is regarded as the best player never to have won the Wimbledon singles title, although playing in three finals. In the course of a brilliant career, however, he won every other major title, including the US title twice, and with **Lew Hoad** he won the British, American, French and Australian doubles titles in 1956, the year in which he turned professional. He won the professional world championship in 1971 and 1972.

ROSMINI-SERBATI, Antonio (1797–1855) Italian theologian and philosopher, born in Rovereto in the Italian Tirol. He was ordained in 1821 and after some years of planning founded in 1828 a new institution for the training of teachers and priests called the 'Institute of the Fathers of Charity', which eventually gained papal approval but hostility from the Jesuits. In 1830 he published *Nuovo saggio sull'origine delle ide* (New Essay on the Origin of Ideas). His next important work was *Il rinnovamento della filosofia in Italia* (The Renewal of Philosophy in Italy, 1936). He developed an interest in political affairs, became an adviser to Pope **Pius IX**, and worked for a federation of the Italian states under the pope as permanent president, embodied in his *La constituzione secondo la giustizia sociale* (Constitution according to Social Justice, 1848). But he fell into disfavour and several of his works, including *Delle cinque piaghe della santa Chiesa* (The Five Wounds of the Holy Church, 1848), were prohibited in 1849 by the Congregation of the Index. He retired to Stresa to immerse himself in philosophy and in devotion.

ROSNY joint pseudonym of the brothers **Joseph Henri** (1856–1940) and **Séraphin Justin François** (1859–1948) **Boëx**, French novelists, born in Brussels. Their vast output of social novels, naturalistic in character, includes *L'Immolation* (1887) and *L'Impérieuse Bonté* (1905), signed jointly, and after 1908, when they separated, the older Rosny's *L'Appel au bonheur* (1919) and *La Vie amoureuse de Balzac* (1930), and *La Courtesane passionée* (1925) and *La Pantine* (1929) by the younger Rosny.

ROSS, Harold Wallace (1892–1951) American editor, born in Aspen, Colorado. He attended high school in Salt Lake City but did not attend college. At the age of 13 he was a reporter for *The Salt Lake City Tribune* and in 1910 he was with the *Marysville Appeal* in California. He worked for a variety of newspapers until 1917, when he enlisted in the Railway Engineer Corps of the US army, becoming editor of *Stars and Stripes*, the army newspaper, where his flair for discovering humorous writing first emerged. After the war he resumed his career and when the *New Yorker* began in February 1925 he was its first editor. After a stuttering start the new magazine caught on and became legendary for its attention to detail, urbane and sophisticated writing, and the quality of its cartoons. A quixotic, instinctive and obsessive editor, he was frequently eccentric and irascible, but loyal to his contributors. Under his wing for a quarter of a century, the *New Yorker* published and nurtured many notable writers including **Thurber**, **E B White**, **Edmund Wilson**, **Truman Capote**, **John Cheever** and **John O'Hara**.

ROSS, Sir James Clark (1800–62) Scottish polar explorer and naval officer, born in London, son of a rich merchant and nephew of Sir **John Ross**. He first went to sea with his uncle at the age of twelve, conducting surveys of the White Sea and the Arctic, and accompanied **Parry** on four Arctic expeditions (1819–27). From 1829 to 1833 he was joint leader with his uncle of a private Arctic expedition financed by the distiller, Sir **Felix Booth**, and in 1831 he located the magnetic north pole. After conducting a magnetic survey of the British Isles, he led an expedition to the Antarctic (1839–43) on the *Erebus* and the *Terror*, during which he discovered Victoria Land and the volcano Mt Erebus, and wrote an account of it in *Voyage of Discovery* (1847). He made a last expedition in 1848–49, searching for the ill-fated **Franklin** expedition in Baffin Bay. Ross Island, the Ross Sea and Ross's Gull are named after him.

ROSS, Sir John (1777–1856) Scottish Arctic explorer and naval officer, born at Inch manse in Wigtownshire. He joined the navy at the age of nine and served with distinction in the Napoleonic wars. From 1812 he conducted surveys in the White Sea and the Arctic; in 1818 he led an expedition, including his nephew Sir **James Clark Ross** and Sir **Edward Sabine**, in search of the northwest passage. He led another such expedition with his nephew, financed by the distilling magnate Sir **Felix Booth**, in 1829–33, during which he discovered and named Boothia Peninsula, King William Land and the Gulf of Boothia. In 1850 he made an unsuccessful attempt to discover the fate of Sir **John Franklin**.

ROSS, Martin See **MARTIN, Violet Florence**

ROSS, Robert Baldwin (1869–1918) Canadian authority on art, and **Oscar Wilde**'s literary executor, the son of the attorney-general of Upper Canada. On his father's death he was taken to Europe at the age of two. He became a literary journalist and art critic, associated with Wilde (whom he is believed to have drawn into homosexual life) and the decadents, later writing a study of **Beardsley**, but also associated with their critics such as **W E Henley**. He left England briefly after Wilde's fall, returned, acted as Wilde's main psychological support in his imprisonment and subsequent life, and after Wilde's death in 1900 worked to pay off the bankruptcy on the Wilde Estate, reclaim its properties, and produce a comprehensive edition of Wilde's works (1908). His action in pubishing part of Wilde's long prison letter as *De Profundis* (1905) ultimately led to violent persecution from Lord **Alfred Douglas**, who by repeated libels and entrapments sought to ruin him; but Ross was well regarded among a wide circle of literary figures who gave him a public testimonial.

ROSS, Sir Ronald (1857–1932) British physician, born in Almara in India, discoverer of the malaria parasite and of its life history. He studied medicine at St Bartholomew's. From 1881 to 1899 he was in the Indian Medical Service; later he became professor of tropical medicine at Liverpool and directed the Rose Institute for tropical diseases from 1926. He won the 1902 Nobel prize for physiology or medicine. He also wrote poems, romances and his Memoirs (1923).

ROSS, William, Lord Ross of Marnock (1911–88) Scottish Labour politician, the longest-serving secretary of state for Scotland (1964–70, 1974–76). Born in Ayr, the son of a train driver, he was educated at Ayr Academy and Glasgow University and became a school-teacher before World War II. He entered parliament as MP for Kilmarnock in a by-election in 1946, and represented that constituency until 1979, when he was created a life peer. As secretary of state for Scotland, he was responsible for the creation of the Highlands and Islands Development Board and the Scottish Development Agency.

ROSSBY, Carl-Gustaf Arvid (1898–1957) Swedish-born American meteorologist, born in Stockholm. Educated in Stockholm, he joined the Bergen Geophysical Institute in 1919. He emigrated to America in 1926, and was professor at the Massachusetts Institute of Technology (1931–39), Chicago University (1941–1950), and Stockholm University (1950–57). In 1940 he showed that large-scale undulatory disturbances exist in the flow of the westerly winds in the upper atmosphere. There are usually three to five such *Rossby waves* in each hemisphere. He also showed that the strength of the westerly winds has an important influence on global weather, and is credited with the discovery of the jet stream, the broad ribbon of upper westerly winds travelling at about 45 m s^{-1} in the mid-latitudes. His ideas, together with computers and weather satellites introduced after his death, did much to create modern weather-prediction methods.

ROSSE, William Parsons, 3rd Earl of (1800–67) Irish astronomer, born in York. He graduated from Magdalen College, Oxford, with a first in mathematics (1822). During his father's lifetime he sat in parliament for King's County as Lord Oxmantown from 1821 to 1834; in 1841 he succeeded as third earl. He experimented in fluid lenses, and made great improvements in casting specula for the reflecting telescope. From 1842 to 1845 he constructed his great reflecting telescope, 58 feet long, in the park at Birr Castle, his Irish home, at a cost of £30000; from 1848 to 1854 he was president of the Royal Society. Sir Charles Parsons (1854–1931), the inventor and engineer, was his son.

ROSSELLINI, Roberto (1906–77) Italian film director, born in Rome. He began in the film industry as a sound technician and editor before graduating, via short films, to his feature-length directorial début with *La Nave Bianca* (1940). Immediately after the war, his trilogy of *Rome, Open City* (*Città Apperta*, 1945), *Paisan* (*Paisà*, 1946) and *Germany, Year Zero* (*Germania, anno Zero*, 1947) helped establish the neo-realist movement; raw, naturalistic depictions of everyday life which combined drama with factual accuracy. An adulterous liaison with **Ingrid Bergman** (whom he later married, 1949–57) provoked world-wide condemnation, and the films they made together, such as *Stromboli* (1950) and *Voyage to Italy* (*Viaggio in Italia*, 1953), were critically undervalued and sometimes banned. This damaged his international stature, but he enjoyed a popular success with *Il Generale della Rovere* (1959) and spent his later years creating television documentaries on historical figures, including *Socrates* (1970) and *The Messiah* (1977). His daughter by Ingrid Bergman, Isabella Rossellini (1952–) has become an actress.

ROSSELLINO, Antonio (1427–c.1479) Italian sculptor, born in Florence, youngest brother and pupil of **Bernardo Rossellino**. He is best known for sculptural reliefs of the Madonna and Child and portrait busts, most notably that of the Florentine Matteo Palmieri (1468). His style is less austere than his brother's and his preference for suggesting movement is well demonstrated in his most important monument, the tomb of the cardinal of Portugal (1466) in San Miniato al Monte, Florence.

ROSSELLINO, Bernardo (1409–64) Italian architect and sculptor, born in Florence, brother and teacher of **Antonio Rossellino**. As an architect he worked under **Leon Battista Alberti** executing his designs for the church of Sta Maria Novella, Florence. His most complete architectural work is the palace and cathedral of Pienza. In 1451 he was appointed architect to Pope **Nicholas V** and designed, though never built, a new façade for St Peter's in Rome. His sculptural masterpiece is the tomb of the chancellor **Leonardo Bruni** (1450) in S Croce, Florence, which in its austere classical style is the very epitome of Italian Renaissance art.

ROSSETER, Philip (1568–1623) English lutenist and composer. He was a musician at the court of **James VI and I** when he published his *Ayres* (1601). His *Lessons for Consort* appeared in 1609, and from that time he was active in court theatricals.

ROSSETTI, Christina Georgina (1830–94) English poet, born in London, daughter of **Gabriele Rossetti** and sister of **Dante Gabriel Rossetti**. Educated at home, she was to have been a governess but she retired through ill-health which may originally have been feigned or psychosomatic. She was precocious poetically; her grandfather printed a pamphlet by her before she was in her teens. She was engaged to James Collinson, the painter, but this was broken off when he returned to the Catholic faith, Christina being a devout High Anglican. Her first lyrics, including 'An End' and 'Dream Lane', were published in the first issue of *The Germ* (1850) under the pseudonym Ellen Alleyne. *Goblin Market*, her first and best-known collection, was published in 1862, and in 1866 came *The Prince's Progress*. *Sing Song*: *A Nursery Rhyme Book*, illustrated by **Arthur Hughes**, appeared in 1872. By the 1880s recurrent bouts of illness had made her an invalid, but she still continued to write, later works including *A Pageant and Other Poems* (1881), *Time Flies*: *A Reading Diary* (1895), and *The Face of the Deep*: *A Devotional Commentary on the Apocalypse* (1892). Technically a virtuoso, she ranged far emotionally and imaginatively.

ROSSETTI, Dante Gabriel, in full **Gabriel Charles Dante Rossetti** (1828–82) English poet, painter and translator, son of **Gabriele Rossetti** and brother of **Christina** and **William Rossetti**, born in London. His father was Gabriele Pasquale Giuseppe Rossetti, a Neapolitan political refugee; his mother was Frances Mary Lavinia Polidori Rossetti, daughter of Gaetano Polidori and sister of Lord **Byron**'s physician, Dr John Polidori. The household was artistic and more Italian than English. He was educated at King's College School and attended Cary's Art Academy, having shown early his inclination towards poetry and art. There was a short spell at the Antique School of the Royal Academy before he persuaded **Ford Madox Brown** to tutor him, but this was short-lived. With **Holman Hunt** and **Millais** he formed the Pre-Raphaelite Brotherhood. Throughout the 1840s his poetry and painting prospered, completing on canvas 'The Girlhood of Mary Virgin', 'How They Met Themselves' and 'Ecce Ancilla Domini', symbolic, historical, overpowering. Like Christina, several of his poems—'The Blessed Damozel' and 'My Sister's Sleep'—had appeared in *The Germ* in 1850, the year he met Elizabeth Siddal (or Siddall) whom he married in 1860 after a fraught and prolonged courtship. Already an invalid, she died in 1862 from a surfeit of laudanum. He met **Ruskin** in 1854 and two years later **William Morris**, whom he manifestly influenced. His wife's death, however, affected him deeply and his work took on the taint of morbidity. (He exhumed her body to place manuscript poems by her side.) *The Early Italian Poets* was published in 1861, translations from 60 poets such as **Dante** and **Cavalcanti**. *Poems* appeared in 1870, drawing on those he had interred with his wife, but though he replied robustly to **Robert Buchanan**'s attack on him in 'The Fleshly School of Poetry' with 'The Stealthy School of Criticism', he fell into a depression and attempted suicide in 1872. Nevertheless, *Ballads and Sonnets* with the sonnet sequence 'The House of Life' and 'The King's Tragedy' appeared in 1881. At odds with Victorian morality, his work is lush, erotic and medieval, romantic in spirit, and of abiding interest and fascination.

ROSSETTI, Gabriele (1783–1854) Italian poet and writer, father of **Christina Rossetti**, **Dante Gabriel Rossetti** and **William Michael Rossetti**, and sometime curator of ancient bronzes in the Museum of Bronzes at Naples. He was a member of the provisional government set up by **Murat** in Rome (1813). After the restoration of **Ferdinand I** to Naples, he joined the Carbonari secret society and greeted the constitution demanded by the patriots in 1820 in a famous ode. On the overthrow of the constitution he went to London (1824), where he became professor of Italian at the new University of London. Besides writing poetry he was a close student of **Dante**, whose *Inferno* he maintained was chiefly political and anti-papal.

ROSSETTI, William Michael (1829–1919) English critic, son of **Gabriele Rossetti** and brother of **Christina** and **Dante Gabriel Rossetti**. He was an inland revenue official as well as a man of letters and one of the seven pre-Raphaelite 'brothers', and editor of their manifesto *The Germ* (1850). He was art critic of *The Spectator* from 1850, wrote biographies of **Shelley** and **Keats**, and published editions of **Coleridge**, **Milton**, **Blake** and **Whitman**. Like all his family he was devoted to the study of **Dante**, whose *Inferno* he translated. He was equally devoted to his family, as his memoirs of his brother (1895) and his sister (1904) witness.

ROSSI, Bruno (1905–) Italian-American physicist, born in Venice. In 1940 he became professor of physics at Cornell University. His work includes the identification of photons, and study of cosmic rays.

ROSSI, Giovanni Battista de (1822–94) Italian archaeologist, born in Rome. He is known for his researches on the Christian catacombs of St Callistus in Rome, and has been called the founder of Christian archaeology.

ROSSI, Pellegrino, Count (1787–1848) Italian statesman and economist, born in Carrara. He became professor of law at Bologna at 25. Exiled after the fall of **Murat**, he obtained a chair at Geneva, and there wrote his *Traité de droit pénal*. In 1833 **Louis-Philippe** made him professor of political economy at the Collège de France. He was sent to Rome as French ambassador in 1845. Called to the ministry by **Pius IX**, Rossi, opposing the Savoy party and striving for an Italian confederation with the pope as president, roused the hatred of the Romans and was assassinated.

ROSSINI, Gioacchino Antonio (1792–1868) Italian composer, born in Pesaro, the son of a strolling horn player and a baker's daughter turned singer. He was taught to sing and play at an early age in order to help the family, and in 1806 began to study composition at the Liceo in Bologna, where in 1808 he won the prize for counterpoint with a cantata. Tiring of the stern academic routine he wrote several slender comic operas, among them *La Scala di seta* (1812), whose lively overture has remained popular although the opera itself was a failure. At Milan in the same year *La Pietra del Paragone* made a great impression; in 1813 at Venice *Tancredi* and *L'Italiana in Algeri* were a success, though *Sigismondo* (1815) failed, possibly because it was an *opera seria* and Rossini's talents were more scintillating in the lighter vein; *Elisabetta*, a version of the **Amy Robsart** story, succeeded at Naples in the same year but gained little favour elsewhere. The title role in the latter was taken by the beautiful Spanish singer, Isabella Colbran, whom he married in 1821. In 1816 his masterpiece, *Il Barbiere de Seviglia*, was received in Rome with enthusiasm despite a disastrous opening night. *Otello* (1816) marked an advance, but the libretto was weakened by pandering to the whims of the audience and has been eclipsed by **Verdi**'s masterpiece. *La Cenerentola* was favourably received in Rome, *La Gazza Ladra* (*The Thieving Magpie*) at Milan in 1817, and these were followed at Naples by *Armide* and *Mosè in Egitto* (1818), *La Donna del Lago* (1819) and *Maometto Secondo* (1820). *Semiramide* (1823), the most advanced of his works, had only a lukewarm reception from the Venetians. Meantime Rossini and his wife had won fresh laurels in Vienna and in London, and he was invited to become director of the Italian Theatre in Paris, where he adapted several of his works to French taste: *Maometto* (as *Le Siège de Corinth*), *Moïse* and *Le Comte Ory*. In 1829 his greatest work, *Guillaume Tell* was first performed. Conceived and written in a much nobler style than his Italian operas, its success was immense but not lasting. In 1837 he separated from Colbran, whose extravagance and selfishness had become insupportable, and in 1847 he married Olympe Pelissier, who had been nurse to his children. After 1829 he produced little but the *Stabat Mater* (1841), the *Petite messe solennelle* (1863) and a number of vocal and piano pieces. In 1836 he retired to Bologna and took charge of the Liceo, which he raised from an almost moribund state to a high position. The revolutionary disturbances in 1847 drove him to Florence in deep depression, but he recovered and returned to Paris in 1855. He has been criticized for immoderate use of long crescendos and other devices in his overtures, but he was a superb craftsman, using the tools of his trade quite legitimately to create an atmosphere of excitement and expectancy in his audience, and the sheer sparkle and vivacity of his music, enlivened as it is by flashes of the puckish sense of humour for which he was renowned, are sufficient to ensure its immortality.

ROSSITER, Leonard (1926–84) English actor, born in Liverpool. Originally an insurance clerk, he first appeared on stage in *The Gay Dog* (1954) at Preston and made his London début in *Free As Air* (1957–58). His hawk-like features, predatory mouth and lizard-like tongue, combined with expert timing and energetic attack, could portray the furtively sinister or the manically comic. He made his film début in *A Kind of Loving* (1962) and subsequently appeared in *Billy Liar* (1963), *King Rat* (1965) and *Barry Lyndon* (1975). Following his Broadway début in *Semi-Detached* (1963) his notable theatre work included *The Resistible Rise of Arturo Ui* (1968–69), *Richard III* (1971) and *Banana Box* (1973). The latter was transformed into the television series *Rising Damp* (1974–78) where his leering landlord won great acclaim. His comic talents were further employed on television in *The Fall and Rise of Reginald Perrin* (1976–80), and in a variety of stage appearances including *Tartuffe* (1976), *Rules of the Game* (1982) and *Loot* (1984).

ROSSO, Fiorentino, real name **Giovanni Battista de Jacopo di Gasparre** (1494–1540) Florentine painter and leading exponent of Mannerism. Trained under **Andrea del Sarto**, his angular, tortured style owes more to **Michelangelo**. Along with other Italian painters of his generation he was invited to France by **Francis I** in 1530. There he was responsible for what, in many ways, was the fullest flowering of the Mannerist style—the Fontainebleau School. His most famous work is an extraordinary, almost 'expressionist', *Descent From the Cross* at Volterra.

ROSTAND, Edmond (1868–1918) French poet and dramatist, born in Marseilles. He published *Les Musardises*, a volume of verse, in 1890 but rose to fame with *Cyrano de Bergerac* (1897), *L'Aiglon* (1900), *Chantecler* (1910), and other plays in verse.

ROSTOPCHINE, Feodor Vassilievich, Count (1763–1826) Russian soldier and writer. He won great influence over the Emperor **Paul I**, and in 1812 became, under **Alexander I**, governor of Moscow. It was he who planned, or at least had a share in, the burning of Moscow against **Napoleon** (1812). He wrote historical memoirs and two comedies and other plays, in Russian and French.

ROSTOW, Walt Whitman (1916–) American economist, born in New York. A graduate of Yale, he was a Rhodes Scholar at Oxford (1936–38). After serving with the US army as a major (1942–45), he was assistant chief of the German-Austrian Economic Division of the State Department until becoming Harmsworth professor of history at Oxford and then professor of American history at Cambridge until 1950. He worked at the Massachusetts Institute of Technology Center for International Studies (1950–60), and became special adviser to presidents **Kennedy** (1961–63) and **Johnson** (1966–69). Since 1969 he has been professor of economics and history at Texas University. He has published many books, particularly relating to questions of economic growth, and is best known for his theory that societies pass through five stages of economic growth. His publications include *The Stages of Economic Growth: A Non-Communist Manifesto* (1960), *Politics and the Stages of Growth* (1971), and *The World Economy: History and Prospect* (1978).

ROSTROPOVICH, Mstislav Leopoldovitch (1927–) Russian cellist and composer, born in Baku. He studied at the Moscow Conservartory (1937–48), where he was professor (1960–74). He was awarded the Lenin prize in 1964. In 1974 he left Russia with his wife, the soprano Galina Vishnevskaya (1926–), and in 1978 they were both deprived of Soviet citizenship. Since 1977 he has been an artistic director of the Aldeburgh Festival and musical director and conductor of the National Symphony Orchestra, Washington.

ROSWITHA See **HROSWITHA**

ROTH, Joseph (1894–1939) Austrian novelist, short-story writer and critic, brought up on the eastern frontiers of the Austro-Hungarian Empire. His father was Austrian, his mother a Russian Jew. He had a miserable life. His father left his mother before he was born, the war disrupted his education, his wife went mad, and he survived by doing menial jobs and journalism until the 1930s when, exiled in Paris, he became an alcoholic and died destitute. A prolific writer, his major themes were not dissimilar to those of **Robert Musil**. His concern for those brought up in the Austro-Hungarian Empire, however, was linked with that of the Jewish diaspora. Narratively conventional, he was a versatile and readable writer, still underrated though more of his work has been translated in recent years. Key works are *Job: The Story of a Simple Man* (1930), *The Emperor's Tomb*, *The Radetzky March* (1932), *Confessions of a Murderer*, *Hotel Savoy* and *Tarabas* (1935).

ROTH, Philip Milton (1933–) American novelist, born in Newark, New Jersey. He attended Bucknell University as an undergraduate and received a master's degree from Chicago University where he taught (1956–58). His upbringing was Jewish, conventional and lower-middle-class; he did not begin to fight the 'taboos that had filtered down to me' until he was in his late teens, An uncompromising, tough-minded writer, his portraits of Jews adept at scheming and compromise have frequently irritated rabbis and Jewish organizations. Daring to talk about abortion, masturbation and other sexual matters has led him into conflict with conservatives who have sought to restrict access to his books. His first book was *Goodbye Columbus* (1959), a collection of short stories, each obsessed with confrontations between Jews of radically different persuasions and temperaments. Two accomplished novels succeeded these—*Letting Go* (1962) and *When She Was Good* (1967)—before publication of his 'masturbation' masterpiece, *Portnoy's Complaint* (1969), made him notorious. The success of the monotone confession of Alexander Portnoy to his psychiatrist lies in the fascination of the narrator's 'voice'. His prolific career has taken many turns; much more than a one-joke writer, he is constantly exploring the relationship 'between the written and the unwritten world', a distinction he finds more useful than that between imagination and reality, or art and life. Nathaniel Zuckerman, a writer, is the central presence in the trilogy of novels—*The Ghost Writer* (1979), *Zuckerman Unbound* (1981) and *The Anatomy Lesson* (1983)—and its epilogue, *The Prague Orgy* (1985), collected in *Zuckerman Bound* (1985). He is married to the actress Claire Bloom.

ROTHACKER, Erich (1888–1965) German philosopher, born in Pforzheim, Baden-Württemberg. He was a leading exponent of 'philosophical anthropology', which aims to construct a coherent picture of human beings in their biological, cultural and social aspects. Rothacker proposed an empirical examination of all human cultures and historical periods on their own terms and in all their authentic particularity and diversity. The human sciences therefore have an essential involvement with the *Weltanschauungen* (worldviews) of their objects. His main works were *Logik und Systematik der Geisteswissenschaften* (1920), *Probleme der Kulturanthropologie* (1948) and *Philosophische Anthropologie* (1966).

ROTHENSTEIN, Sir John (Knewstub Maurice) (1901–) English art historian, born in London, the son of Sir **William Rothenstein**. He studied at Worcester College, Oxford, and University College, London. From 1927 to 1929 he taught in the United States, and was director of Leeds and Sheffield city art galleries between 1932 and 1938, when he was appointed director and keeper of the Tate Gallery, retiring in 1964. His many works on art include *Modern English Painters* (1952–73) and his Autobiography (3 vols, 1965, 1966, 1970).

ROTHENSTEIN, Sir William (1872–1945) English artist, born in Bradford. He studied at the Slade School and in Paris, won fame as a portrait painter, and was principal of the Royal College of Art. He was an official war artist in both world wars.

ROTHERMERE, Viscount See **HARMSWORTH, Harold Sydney**

ROTHESAY, David See **ROBERT III**

ROTHKO, Mark, originally **Marcus Rothkovitch** (1903–70) Latvian-born American painter, born in Dvinsk, Latvia. His family emigrated when he was a child to the USA where he studied at Yale (1921–23). Largely self-taught as an artist, he had his first one-man show in New York in 1933. During the 1940s he was influenced by Surrealism but by the early 1950s he had evolved his own very peaceful and meditative form of Abstract Expressionism, staining huge canvases with rectangular blocks of pure colour.

ROTHSCHILD, Meyer Amschel (1743–1812) German financier, born in Frankfurt, named from the 'Red Shield' signboard of his father's house. Trained as a rabbi, he founded a business as a moneylender and became the financial adviser to the landgrave of Hesse. The house received a heavy commission for transmitting money from the English government to **Wellington** in Spain, paid the British subsidies to Continental princes, and negotiated loans for Denmark between 1804 and 1812. At his death, the founder left five sons, all of whom were made barons of the Austrian empire in 1822. Anselm Meyer (1773–1855), eldest son, succeeded as head of the firm in Frankfurt; Solomon (1774–1855) established a branch in Vienna; Nathan Meyer (1777–1836), one in 1798 in London; Charles (1788–1855), one in Naples (discontinued about 1861); and James (1792–1868), one in Paris. They negotiated many of the great government loans of the 19th century, and Nathan raised the house to be first amongst the banking houses of the world. He staked his fortunes on the success of Britain in her duel with **Napoleon**, and, receiving the first news of Waterloo, sold and bought stock which brought him over £1 000 000 profit. His son Lionel (1808–79) did much for the civil and political emancipation of the Jews in Great Britain. Lionel's son, Nathan (1840–1915), succeeded (1876) to his uncle Anthony's baronetcy (1846), and was made Baron Rothschild in 1885. His son, Lionel (1868–1937), second Baron, set up a valuable zoological museum at Tring.

ROTHSCHILD, Nathaniel Mayer Victor, 3rd Baron (1910–90) English administrator, born in London. He served in military intelligence from 1939 to 1945, then spent two years with BOAC. From 1948 to 1958 he was chairman of the Agricultural Research Council, from 1950 to 1970 assistant director of the department of zoology at Cambridge and research director/co-ordinator of Shell UK. From 1971 to 1974 he was in government service as director-general of the central policy review staff.

ROTHWELL, Evelyn See **BARBIROLLI, Sir John**

ROTROU, Jean de (1609–50) French playwright, born in Dreux. He went to Paris, qualified as a lawyer, and turned to writing plays, as well as becoming one of the five poets who worked into dramatic form the ideas of **Richelieu**. His first pieces were in the Spanish romantic style. Next followed a classical period, culminating in three masterpieces, *Saint-Genest*, a tragedy of Christian martyrdom, *Don Bertrand* and *Venceslas*. He died of the plague. Thirty-five of his plays are still extant.

ROUAULT, Georges (Henri) (1871–1958) French painter and engraver, born in Paris. He was apprenticed to a stained-glass designer in 1885, and in all his work he retained the characteristic glowing colours, outlined with black, to achieve a concise statement of his feelings about the clowns, prostitutes and biblical characters he chose as his subjects. He studied under **Gustave Moreau**, and in 1898 was made curator of the Moreau Museum. About 1904 he joined the Fauves (**Matisse**, **Derain** and others), and in 1910 held his first one-man show. Many of his works were acquired by the art dealer Ambroise Vollard (1865–1939), who commissioned the series of large religious engravings published after Vollard's death as *Miserere* and *Guerre*.

ROUBILLAC, or **Roubiliac, Louis François** (1702/1705–1762) French sculptor, born in Lyon. He studied at Paris, and in the 1730s settled in London. His statue of **Handel** for Vauxhall Gardens in 1738 first made him popular. His other most famous statues are those of **Newton** (1755) at Cambridge, of **Shakespeare** (1758), now in the British Museum, and another of Handel in Westminster Abbey.

ROUGET DE LISLE, Claude Joseph (1760–1836) French soldier, born in Lons-le-Saunier. He wrote and composed the *Marseillaise* (originally *Chant de guerre pour l'armée du Rhin*) when stationed in 1792 as captain of engineers at Strasbourg. Wounded at Quiberon (1795), he left the army, and published in 1796 a volume of *Essais en vers et en prose*. The *Marseillaise*, was made known in Paris by troops from Marseilles.

ROUGHEAD, William (1870–1952) Scottish criminologist, son of a wealthy Edinburgh family of drapers. He was led to a life-long fascination with murder when as legal apprentice in 1889 he covered the trial of the baby-farmer Jessie King, and then that of John Watson Laurie for murder on Arran. Admitted Writer to the Signet in 1893, he married Janey More, daughter of an Edinburgh accountant, in 1900. In 1906, with the *Trial of Dr Pritchard*, he commenced his great partnership with the publisher Harry Hodge, to result in 10 volumes in the Hodge 83-volume 'Notable British Trials' series. In addition to **Pritchard**, Roughead handled Deacon **William Brodie**, Captain **Porteous**, **Burke** and **Hare**, **Oscar Slater**, and many others. Harshly moralistic towards the guilty, he proved a formidable critic where he believed justice had erred, and his edition of the Slater trial (1909) was of major value in obtaining Slater's ultimate if horribly delayed pardon (1928), duly chronicled by Roughead in his next edition. He also published 119 essays on criminal cases in 14 individual books. He was an industrious pioneer, and was probably unrivalled in his influence on popular criminology.

ROUHER, Eugène (1814–84) French statesman, born in Riom. In 1848 he was returned to the Constituent Assembly, and until 1869 held various offices in the government. He negotiated the treaty of commerce with England in 1860 and with Italy in 1863. In 1870 he was appointed president of the Senate. A staunch Napoleonist, after the fall of the empire he fled abroad. Later he represented Corsica in the National Assembly.

ROUMANILLE, Joseph (1818–91) French writer, born in Saint-Rémy, Bouches-du-Rhône. He taught at Avignon, his pupils including **Frédéric Mistral**. In 1847 he published *Li Margarideto*, a book of his own poems, in 1852 a volume of Provençal poems, and later many volumes of verse and prose in Provençal dialect. With Mistral and others he founded the 'Soci dou Félibrige' for the revival of Provençal literature.

ROUS, Francis (1579–1659) English hymnist, born in Dittisham, Devon. Educated at Oxford, he was a member of the Long Parliament, sat in the Westminster Assembly of Divines, and in 1644 was made provost of Eton. His writings were collected in 1657. His metrical version of the psalms (1643) was recommended by the House of Commons to the Westminster Assembly, and is still substantially the presbyterian psalter.

ROUS, Francis Peyton (1879–1970) American pathologist, born in Baltimore. Educated at Johns Hopkins University and Medical School, he became assistant (1909–10), associate (1910–12), associate member (1912–20) and member (1920–45) of the Rockefeller Institute for Medical Research. In 1910 he discovered a virus to induce malignant tumours in hens, the outstanding importance of which has become apparent over the years. In 1962 he received the UN prize for cancer research, and in 1966 shared the Nobel prize for physiology or medicine with **Charles Huggins**.

ROUSSEAU, Henri Julien Félix, known as **Le Douanier** (1844–1910) French primitive painter, born in Laval. He joined the army at about 18, but spent most of his life as a minor tax collector in the Paris toll office, hence his nickname. He retired in 1885 and spent his time painting and copying at the Louvre. From 1886 to 1898 he exhibited at the Salon des Indépendants and again from 1901 to 1910. He met **Gauguin**, **Pissarro** and later **Picasso**, but his painting remained unaffected. Despite its denial of conventional perspective and colour, it has a fierce reality more Surrealist than primitive. He produced painstaking portraits, and painted dreams, such as the *Sleeping Gipsy* (1897), and exotic, imaginary landscapes with trees and plants which he had seen in the Jardin des Plantes.

ROUSSEAU, Jean Baptiste (1671–1741) French poet, born in Paris, the son of a shoemaker. He wrote for the theatre, and lampoons on the literary frequenters of the Café Laurent which started feuds leading to recriminations, lawsuits and a sentence of banishment (1712). Thereafter he lived abroad, in Switzerland, Vienna (with Prince **Eugene**) and Brussels. His sacred odes and *cantates* are splendidly elaborate, frigid and artificial; his epigrams are bright, vigorous and unerring in their aim.

ROUSSEAU, Jean Jacques (1712–78) French political philosopher, educationist and author, born in Geneva. His mother died at his birth, and he had little early family life and no formal education. In 1728 he ran away to Italy and Savoy, where he lived with Baronne Louise de Warens (1700–62) and was baptized a Catholic, and after an itinerant existence for a few years eventually became her lover and general factotum (1733–41). In 1741 he was supplanted, and moved to Paris where he began to thrive, making a living from secretarial work and music copying. There he began a lifelong association with an illiterate maidservant at his inn, Thérèse le Vasseur; by her he had five children, all of whom he consigned to foundling hospitals, despite his later proclamations about the innocence of childhood. He composed an operetta, *Les Muses Galantes* (1745), which led to correspondence with **Voltaire** and acquaintance with **Diderot**, and through that came to contribute articles on music and political economy to the *Encyclopédie*. In 1750 he made his name with a prize essay, *Discours sur les arts et sciences*, which argued that civilization had corrupted our natural goodness and decreased our freedom; and in 1752 he triumphed with a second operetta, *Le Devin du village*. He was now a celebrity, and in 1754 wrote *Discours sur l'origine et les fondements de l'inégalité permi les hommes*, in which he attacked private property and argued that man's perfect nature was corrupted by society. He travelled restlessly first to Geneva, where he was much influenced by Calvinism, back to Paris and then to Luxembourg in 1757, and in 1758 published his *Lettre á d'Alembert sur les spectacles*, in which he argued against the establishment of a theatre in Geneva on Puritan grounds. In 1762 he published his masterpiece, *Du contrat social* (The Social Contract), which begins with the ringing paradox, 'Man is born free; and everywhere he is in chains'. It postulated a social contract in which every individual surrenders his rights totally to the collective 'general will', which is the sole source of legitimate sovereignty and by definition represents the common good; the aberrant can then, in the sinister phrase, 'be forced to be free' in their own interests. His text, with its slogan 'Liberty, Equality, Fraternity', became the bible of the French Revolution and of progressive movements generally, though clearly the main thesis was vulnerable to totalitarian perversions. Also in 1762 he published in novel form *Émile, ou Traité de l'éducation*, a simple romance of a child reared apart from other children as an experiment; it greatly influenced educationists like **Pestalozzi** and **Froebel**, but so outraged the political and religious establishment that he had to flee to Switzerland. He moved to England in 1766 at the invitation of **David Hume** and went to live at Wootton Hall near Ashbourne in Derbyshire (1766–67), where he began writing his *Confessions*, a remarkably frank if somewhat narcissistic volume of self-revelations. He became seriously unstable at about this time, quarrelled with his English friends (particularly Hume), and fled back to France in 1767 with a full-blown persecution complex. In Paris from 1770 to 1778 he completed his *Confessions* (published 1782–89), wrote a justification of his past actions (*Rousseau, juge de Jean Jacques*, 1782) and *Rêveries du promeneur solitaire* (1782), and eked out a living as a music copyist again. He declined further, became seriously insane, and died in Ermenonville. In 1794 his remains were placed alongside Voltaire's in the Panthéon in Paris. By the time of his death he had became very much a spokesman for Romanticism in Britain and Europe.

ROUSSEAU, (Pierre Étienne) Théodore (1812–67) French landscape painter, born in Paris. He began painting directly from nature in the Forest of Fontainbleau in the 1830s and first exhibited in the Salon of 1831; and in 1834 his *Forest of Compiègne* was bought by the Duc d'Orléans. Some twelve years of discouragement followed. He moved to Barbizon and became leader of the Barbizon school. In 1849 he resumed exhibiting, and was thenceforward prominent. He was an exceedingly prolific, if a somewhat unequal, painter.

ROUSSEL, Albert (1869–1937) French composer, born in Tourcoing. Educated for the navy, at the age of 25 he resigned his commission to study music in Paris with Gigout, in 1896 joining the Schola Cantorum under **Vincent d'Indy**. His works, after his period of study, are adventurous in harmony and texture, reconciling modern experimental styles with the conservative tradition of his teachers. A journey to India and the Far East gave him an interest in Oriental music which inspired the choral *Évocations* (1912) and the opera *Padmâvati*, begun in 1914 and completed after World War I. Service in the war ruined his health, and after his demobilization he largely retired into seclusion, devoting his time entirely to composition. His works include ballets (the best-known of which are *Bacchus and Ariane* and *Le Festin de l'araignée*), four symphonies and numerous choral and orchestral works.

ROUSSEL, Ker Xavier (1867–1944) French artist, born in Lorry-les-Metz. He was a member of the Nabis, and associated with **Bonnard**, **Vuillard** and **Denis**. He is best known for his classical subjects portrayed in typical French landscapes, using the Impressionist palette.

ROUTH, Martin Joseph (1755–1854) English patristic scholar, born in South Elmham, Suffolk. Educated at Queen's College, Oxford, he became president of Magdalen College in 1791. In 1810 he became rector of Tylehurst near Reading. He died at Magdalen in his hundredth year. He was a great patristic scholar when patristic scholars were few, a Caroline churchman, a liberal Tory, a lover of animals, fond of jokes, and an inveterate book-buyer—his 16000 volumes he bequeathed to Durham University. Throughout 70 years he published only six works, including his *Reliquiae Sacrae* (1814–48), a collection of fragments of early Christian writings.

ROUTLEDGE, George (1812–88) English publisher, born in Brampton, Cumberland. He went to London in 1833, starting up as a bookseller in 1836, and as a publisher in 1843. In 1848, the year in which he founded his 'Railway Library' of cheap reprints, and 1851 respectively, he took his two brothers-in-law, W H and Frederick Warne, into partnership. In 1947 the firm acquired the undertaking of Kegan Paul, Trench, Trubner and Co. Ltd.

ROUX, Pierre Émile (1853–1933) French bacteriologist, born in Confolens (Charente). He studied at Clermont-Ferrand, became assistant to **Pasteur**, and from 1905 to 1918 was his successor. With **Yersin** he discovered (1894) the antitoxic method of treating diphtheria, and he also worked on cholera and tuberculosis.

ROUX, Wilhelm (1850–1924) German anatomist and physiologist, born in Jena. He became professor at Breslau in 1886, Innsbruck in 1889, and Halle in 1895. He did extensive practical and theoretical work on experimental embryology (his *Entwicklungsmechanik*, or developmental mechanics).

ROW, John (c.1525–1580) Scottish Reformer and ecclesiastical lawyer, born near Stirling. Educated at Stirling and St Andrews, in 1550 he was sent by the archbishop to Rome as Scottish agent. In 1558 he returned to Scotland, and next year turned Protestant. He helped in compiling the *Confession of Faith* (1560) and *First Book of Discipline* (1561), became minister of Perth, and sat in the first General Assembly. He was four times moderator and took a share in preparing the *Second Book of Discipline*.

ROW, John (1568–1646) Scottish clergyman, son of **John Row** (c.1525–1580). He was minister from 1592 of Carnock near Dunfermline, and wrote a prolix but reliable *History of the Kirk of Scotland from 1558 to 1637*. He was strongly opposed to the introduction of episcopacy into Scotland.

ROWAN, Archibald Hamilton (1751–1834) Irish nationalist, born in London, the son of Gawin Hamilton; on his maternal grandfather's death he took the name of Rowan. Educated at Westminster School and Queen's College, Cambridge, he settled in Ireland in 1784. In 1791 he joined the United Irishmen, and three years later was imprisoned for sedition. He escaped to France, went to America in 1795, obtained a pardon in 1903 and returned to Ireland, where he supported the cause of Catholic emancipation.

ROWBOTHAM, Sheila (1943–) English social historian and feminist, born in Leeds. Educated at Oxford, she became involved in the women's movement in the late 1960s. An active socialist, she wrote for several socialist papers, and provoked controversy with *Beyond the Fragments: Feminism and the Making of Socialism* (1979, with Segal and Wainwright). Among her most important historical works are *Women, Resistance and Revolution* (1972) and *Hidden from History* (1973).

ROWE, Nicholas (1674–1718) English poet and dramatist, born in Little Barford, Bedfordshire. He was educated at Westminster, was called to the bar, but from 1692 devoted himself to literature. Between 1700 and 1715 he produced eight plays of which three were popular—*Tamerlane* (1702), *The Fair Penitent* (1703) and *The Tragedy of Jane Shore* (1714), followed by *The Tragedy of Lady Jane Grey* (1715). Lothario in *The Fair Penitent* was the prototype of Lovelace in **Richardson**'s *Clarissa* and the name is still the synonym for a fashionable rake. Rowe translated **Lucan**'s *Pharsalia* and his edition of **Shakespeare** (1709–10) at least contributed to the popularity of his author. Rowe was under-secretary to the Duke of Queensberry from 1709 to 1711; in 1715 he was appointed poet laureate and a surveyor of customs to the port of London; the Prince of Wales made him clerk of his council, and Lord Chancellor Parker appointed him clerk of presentations in chancery.

ROWLAND, Henry Augustus (1848–1901) American physicist, born in Honesdale, Pennsylvania. From 1875 to1901 he was first professor of physics at Johns Hopkins University. He invented the concave diffraction grating used in spectroscopy, discovered the magnetic effect of electric convection, and improved on **James Joule**'s work on the mechanical equivalent of heat.

ROWLAND, 'Tiny' (Rowland W), originally **Rowland W Furhop** (1917–) British financier, born in India. He joined Lonrho (London and Rhodesian Mining and Land Company) in 1961 and became chief executive and managing director. In 1983 he became chairman of *The Observer* newspaper.

ROWLANDSON, Thomas (1756–1827) English caricaturist, born in London. From the age of 15 he studied art in Paris, where he acquired a taste for high living on the strength of a £7000 legacy from a French aunt, which he dissipated on gambling and tavern life. In 1777 he returned to London to work as a portrait painter, but soon turned to vigorous watercolour caricatures, and book-illustrations for authors like **Smollett**, **Sterne**, and **Goldsmith**. He also engraved a popular series, *Tour of Dr Syntax in Search of the Picturesque* (1812, with sequels in 1820 and 1821), also *The English Dance of Life* (1815) and *The Dance of Death* (1816).

ROWLEY, Thomas See **CHATTERTON, Thomas**

ROWLEY, William (c.1585–c.1642) English actor and playwright. Little is known about him, except that he collaborated with **Dekker**, **Middleton**, **Heywood**, **Webster**, **Massinger** and **Ford**. Four plays published with his name are extant: *A New Wonder, a Woman Never Vext* (1632); *All's Lost by Lust*, a tragedy (1633); *A Match at Midnight* (1633); and *A Shoomaker a Gentleman* (1638).

ROWLING, Sir Wallace Edward (1927–) New Zealand politician, born in Motueka, South Island. After graduating at Canterbury University he joined the New Zealand army and served in the education corps before becoming active in the Labour party. He entered parliament in 1962 and was finance minister in the administration of **Norman Kirk**. When Kirk died in 1974 he succeeded him as prime minister until the National party, under **Robert Muldoon**, returned to power in 1985. Rowling was then appointed ambassador to the USA.

ROWNTREE, Joseph (1836–1925) English Quaker industrialist and reformer, born in York, the son of Joseph Rowntree, a Quaker grocer. With his brother, Henry Isaac (d.1883), he became a partner in a cocoa manufactury in York in 1869, and built up welfare organizations for his employees.

ROWNTREE, (Benjamin) Seebohm (1871–1954) English manufacturer and philanthropist, born in York, son of **Joseph Rowntree**. He was chairman of the family chocolate firm (1925–41), and introduced enlightened schemes of worker-participation. He devoted his life to the study of social problems and welfare and wrote many books, including *Poverty: a Study of Town Life* (1901), *Poverty and Progress* (1941), and *Poverty and the Welfare State* (1951).

ROWSE, Alfred Leslie (1903–) English historian, born in St Austell. Educated at Oxford, he became a fellow of All Souls College and wrote many works on English history including *Tudor Cornwall* (1941), *The Use of History* (1946) and *The England of Elizabeth* (1950). He also wrote some poetry, much of it on Cornwall, and many literary works, including several on aspects of **Shakespeare**, a Life of **Marlowe** (1964), and his own autobiography, *A Cornishman at Oxford* (1965).

ROWTON, Montagu William Lowry-Corry, 1st Baron (1838–1903) English politician and philanthropist, born in London. Called to the bar in 1863, he became private secretary to **Disraeli** (1866–68, 1874–80). He was created baron in 1880. Later he devoted his time and money to the provision of good cheap accommodation for working men, and six Rowton hostels were built in London, with total accommodation for 5000. Although Rowton's motives were entirely philanthropic his houses in fact made a profit.

ROXBURGHE, Duke of See **KERR** family

ROY See **RAMMOHUN ROY**

ROY, William (1726–90) Scottish military surveyor, born in Miltonhead, Carluke, Lanarkshire. In 1747 he was engaged on the survey of Scotland, in 1755 held an army commission, was elected FRS in 1767, and rose to be major-general in 1781. In 1784, in connection with the triangulation of the southeastern counties, he measured with great accuracy a base line of $5\frac{1}{5}$ miles of Hounslow heath, for which he received the Royal Society's Copley medal. In 1764 he studied the Roman remains in Scotland, and his *Military Antiquities of the Romans in Britain* was published in 1793 by the Society of Antiquaries.

ROYCE, Sir (Frederick) Henry (1863–1933) English engineer, born near Peterborough. He was apprenticed to the Great Northern Railway but, becoming interested in electricity and motor engineering, he founded (1884) in Manchester the firm of Royce, Ltd, mechanical and electrical engineers. He made his first car in 1904, and his meeting with **Rolls** in that year led to the formation (1906) of Rolls-Royce, Ltd, motor-car and aero-engine builders, of Derby and London. He later designed the aero-engines that became the Merlin engines for Spitfires and Hurricanes in World War II.

ROYCE, Josiah (1855–1916) American philosopher, born in Grass Valley, California. Trained as an engineer he switched to philosophy, studied in Germany and at Johns Hopkins, Baltimore (under **Charles Sanders Peirce**) and taught philosophy at Harvard from 1882. He was much influenced by **Hegel** and developed a philosophy of idealism emphasizing the importance of the individual in *Religious Aspects of Philosophy* (1885) and *The World and the Individual* (1900–01). He also wrote on mathematical logic, social ethics, psychology and religion.

ROYDEN, Agnes Maud (1876–1956) English social worker and preacher, born in Liverpool. Educated at Lady Margaret Hall, Oxford, she was prominent in the women's suffrage movement. From 1917 to 1920 she was assistant at the City Temple, and published, amongst others, *Woman and the Sovereign State*, *The Church and Woman*, and *Modern Sex Ideals*.

ROYER-COLLARD, Pierre Paul (1763–1845) French philosopher and politician, born in Sompuis in Champagne. He began as an advocate, and on the outbreak of the revolution was elected member of the municipality of Paris. In 1792 he fled from the Jacobins to his birthplace, and in 1797 served for a few months on the Council of Five Hundred. Professor of philosophy in Paris from 1810, he exercised an immense influence on French philosophy, rejecting the purely sensuous system of **Condillac**, and giving special prominence to the principles of the Scottish School of **Thomas Reid** and **Dugald Stewart**. Strongly 'spiritualist' as opposed to materialist, he originated the 'Doctrinaire' school of **Jouffroy** and **Victor Cousin**. From 1815 to 1820 he was president of the Commission of Public Instruction, in 1815 was returned as deputy for Marne, and in 1827 entered the French Academy. He became president in 1828 of the Chamber of Representatives, and presented the address of March 1830, which the king refused to hear read.

ROZANOV, Vasili Vasilievich (1856–1919) Russian writer, thinker and critic, born in Vetluga, Kostroma. He became a teacher in provincial schools. His literary studies include that of **Dostoyevsky**'s *Grand Inquisitor*, which, published in 1894, first brought him into prominence. Though a Christian, in his prolific writings he criticized from a Nietzschean standpoint the contemporary standards in morals, religion, education, and particularly the too-strict attitude towards sex, which was for him the very soul of man. Much of his work is highly introspective, and his literary reputation is firmly based on the two books of fragments and essays, *Solitaria* (1912; trans 1927) and *Fallen Leaves* (1913, 1915; trans 1929).

RÓZSA, Miklós, (Nicholas) (1907–) Hungarian composer, born in Budapest. A composer of orchestral works from an early age, he graduated from the University of Leipzig in 1931. In Paris and then London, he composed symphonies and ballet music before being commissioned to write his first film score for *Knight Without Armour* (1937). In Hollywood from 1940, his use of jolting chords and pounding rhythms heightened the emotional impact of psychological melodramas and film noirs like *Double Indemnity* (1944), *The Lost Weekend* (1945) and *The Killers* (1946). Later, he concentrated on lush accompaniments to historical epics, including *Quo Vadis* (1951) and *El Cid* (1961). His work outside the film industry is equally renowned and includes a Violin Concerto (1953) for **Jascha Heifetz** and a Cello Concerto (1968) for Janos Starker. He received Academy Awards for *Spellbound* (1945), *A Double Life* (1947) and *Ben Hur* (1959). His autobiography, *A Double Life*, was published in 1982.

RUBBIA, Carlo (1934–) Italian-born American physicist, born in Gorizia. Educated at Pisa, Rome and Columbia universities, from 1960 he headed the team at CERN (the European Organisation for Nuclear Research) in Geneva using the proton-antiproton collider. In 1971 he became professor of physics at Harvard, and in 1989 director-general of the European Organisation for Nuclear Research. He shared the Nobel prize for physics in 1984 with **Simon van der Meer** for their work on the CERN project which led to the discovery of the field particles W and Z, which transfer the weak nuclear interaction.

RUBBRA, Edmund (1901–86) English composer and music critic, born in Northampton. While working as a railway clerk, he had piano lessons from **Cyril Scott**, and in 1919 won a composition scholarship to Reading University. There he studied under Howard Jones and **Holst**, and won a scholarship to the Royal College of Music, where he was a pupil of **Vaughan Williams** and, most influentially, of Reginald Owen Morris. An interest in the polyphonic music of the 16th and 17th centuries is reflected in his characteristic contrapuntal style of composition, which he uses not only in works such as his Spenser sonnets (1935), his madrigals and his Masses (1945 and 1949), but also in his larger symphonic canvases. In these he has progressed from a relentless prosecution of polyphonic principles in the first two to a more flexible interpretation of them in his later symphonies. As well as his eleven symphonies he wrote chamber, choral and orchestral music, songs and works for various solo instruments. He was senior lecturer in music at Oxford 1947–68, was made a fellow of Worcester College in 1963, and professor of composition at the Guildhall School of Music 1961–74.

RUBENS, Peter Paul (1577–1640) Flemish painter, born in Siegen in Westphalia. He studied from 1587 in Antwerp, and in 1600 went to Italy; in Venice he studied the works of **Titian** and **Veronese**. He next entered the service of Vincenzo Gonzago, Duke of Mantua; and in 1605 was dispatched on a mission to **Philip III** of Spain, thus beginning his career as a diplomat. While in Madrid he executed many portraits, as well as several historical subjects. On his return from Spain he travelled in Italy, copying celebrated works for the Duke of Mantua. His paintings of this Italian period are much influenced by the Italian Renaissance, and already show the Rubens characteristics of vigorous composition and brilliant colouring. In 1608 he returned home, and, settling in Antwerp, was appointed in 1609 court painter to the archduke Albert, and soon afterward married his first wife, Isabella Brant, whom he often portrayed. Rubens was then approaching his artistic maturity, and his triptych *Descent from the Cross* (1611–14) in Antwerp Cathedral is usually regarded as his masterpiece. By this time he was famous, and pupils and commissions came in a steady stream to the master's studio, from which issued vast numbers of works, witnesses to his extraordinary energy and ability. In 1620 he was invited to France by **Marie de' Medici**, who was then engaged in decorating the palace of the Luxembourg; and he undertook for her 21 large subjects on her life and regency. In 1628 he was dispatched on a diplomatic mission to **Philip IV** of Spain. In Madrid he made the acquaintance of **Velazquez**, and executed some 40 works, including five portraits of the Spanish monarch. In 1629 he was appointed envoy to **Charles I** of Britain, to treat for peace; and, while he conducted a delicate negotiation with tact and success, he painted the *Peace and War* (National Gallery) and also made sketches for the *Apotheosis* of **James VI and I** for the banqueting hall at Whitehall, completing the pictures on his return to Antwerp. His first wife having died in 1626, in 1630 he married Helena Fourment, and retired to his estate at Steen. In 1635 he designed the decorations which celebrated the entry of the cardinal Infant Ferdinand into Antwerp as governor of the Netherlands; and, having completed *The Crucifixion of St Peter* for the church of that saint in Cologne, he died in Antwerp. A successful diplomat, a distinguished humanist, a man of wide erudition and culture, Rubens was outstanding for versatility even in his time, and the main characteristics of his production —their power, spirit and vivacity, their sense of energy, of exuberant life—may be largely attributed to the comprehensive qualities of the man himself.

RUBIK, Ernö (1944–) Hungarian architectural designer, inventor and puzzle-maker, born in Budapest, creator of the Rubik cube. He studied architecture and industrial design at the Technical University in Budapest, and teaches at the School of Industrial Design there. In 1974 he conceived the idea of his puzzle cube and patented it in 1975; by 1981 it had become a world craze and millions had been sold, many of which were pirated. The remarkable mechanical ingenuity of the apparently impossible way in which its faces can be turned and the 43 252 003 274 489 856 000 different possible patterns of its colours, have fascinated both children and mathematicians, who have studied its theory in considerable detail. Other puzzles followed, but have not caught the public imagination.

RUBINSTEIN, Anton (1829–94) Russian pianist and composer, born in Moldavia. He studied in Berlin and Vienna, and in 1848 settled in St Petersburg, where he taught music and took a part in founding the conservatory, of which he was for a time director. He made concert tours in Europe and, in 1872–73, the USA, gaining widespread acclaim and lasting distinction for his mastery of technique and musical sensitivity. His compositions, which include operas, oratorios and piano concertos, have not stood the test of time, apart from some songs and melodious piano pieces. His brother Nikolai (1835–81) founded Moscow Conservatory. He wrote an Autobiography (trans 1891).

RUBINSTEIN, Artur (1888–1982) Polish-born American pianist, born in Łódź, Poland. At the age of 12 he appeared successfully in Berlin, and after further study with **Paderewski**, began his career as a virtuoso, appearing in Paris and London in 1905 and visiting the USA in 1906. After World War II he lived in America, making frequent extensive concert tours. He was made an honorary KBE in 1977. He published his autobiographical *My Young Years* (1973) and *My Many Years* (1980).

RUBLEV, Andrei (fl.1400) Russian painter. Although little is known about his life or works, he is generally regarded as the greatest of Russian icon painters. It is known that he became a monk, probably quite late in life, in the monastery of Troitsky-Sergieva and was an assistant of the Greek painter from Constantinople **Theothanes**, with whom he worked in Moscow from 1405. In 1422 he returned to Troitsky-Sergieva and, tradition has it, executed his most famous work, the icon of the Old Testament Trinity in which the subject is represented by three graceful angels.

RUBRUCK, William of (fl.13th century) French traveller, born probably in Rubrouck near St Omer. He entered the Franciscan order, and was sent on a religious mission in 1253 by **Louis IX** to visit the son of the Mongol prince, Batú Khan, a supposed Christian. Friar William travelled across the Black Sea and the Crimea to the Volga. At Sartak his father sent him to the Mongol emperor, Mangú Khan, whom he found about ten days' journey south of Karakorum in Mongolia. He stayed there until 1254, then returned to the Volga, by way of the Caucasus, Armenia, Persia and Asia Minor, arriving at Tripoli in 1255. He was still living in 1293, when **Marco Polo** was returning from the East.

RUCCELLAI, Giovanni (1475–1525) Italian poet, a nephew of **Lorenzo de' Medici**. He lived in Rome and took orders. His works include the blank verse *Le Api*, an instructive poem based on book four of **Virgil**'s *Georgics*. He also wrote early Italian tragedies, such as *Rosamunda* (1515) and *Oreste* (1525).

RÜCKERT, Friedrich (1788–1866) German poet and scholar, born in Schweinfurt. He studied law, philology and philosophy at Würzburg, and during the Napoleonic wars stirred up German patriotism with his *Deutsche Gedichte* (1814). After the wars he studied oriental languages, of which he became professor at Erlangen (1826–41) and Berlin (1841–48), and recast in German verse many famous books of countries of the orient. His original work includes the lyrical *Liebesfrühling* (1923), the reflective poems *Die Weisheit des Brahmanen* (1836–39), and the personal *Kindertotenlieder*, posthumously published in 1872 and set to music by **Mahler** in 1902.

RUDBECK, Olof (1630–1702) Swedish anatomist, botanist and architect, the discoverer of the lymphatic system (simultaneously with **Thomas Bartholin** in Copenhagen). Educated at Uppsala and Leiden, he was appointed professor of medicine at Uppsala in 1660. He planned a vast illustrated work on all known plants but his manuscripts and the 3200 wood blocks were destroyed in the great Uppsala fire of 1702. His son Olof Rudbeck, the younger (1660–1740), professor of medicine at Uppsala, visited Lapland and was the patron of young **Carl Linnaeus**. The botanical genus *Rudbeckia* is named after him. He also wrote *Atlantikan* (1675–98) on Sweden as the cradle of civilization.

RUDDIMAN, Thomas (1674–1757) Scottish classical grammarian and philologist, born in the parish of Boyndie, Banffshire. He studied classics at Aberdeen, and in 1700 obtained a post in the Advocates' Library in Edinburgh, being appointed assistant keeper in 1702 and principal keeper in 1730, in the meantime also setting up business as a book auctioneer (1707) and printer (1715). He edited Latin works of **Arthur Johnston**, and published in 1715 his great edition of the works of **George Buchanan**, with its controversial introduction in which he is severely critical of Buchanan's character and political views (Ruddiman was an ardent Jacobite). He also produced his own *Rudiments of the Latin Tongue* (1714), and the *Grammaticae Latinae Institutiones* (1725–32), on which his philological reputation mainly rests.

RUDE, François (1784–1855) French sculptor, originally a smith, born in Dion. He worked in Brussels and Paris, and is known for his public monuments in Paris. His most famous work is the relief group *Le Départ* (1836) on the Arc de Triomphe in Paris.

RUDOLF I (d.912) king of Transjuranic Burgundy from 888.

RUDOLF II (d.937) king of Burgundy, son of **Rudolf I**, whom he succeeded in 912, and father of the empress **St Adelaide**. Became king of Italy in 922, but resigned the throne in 926 in return for Provence.

RUDOLF III (d.1032) last king of Burgundy, grandson of **Rudolf II**, ruled from 993 to 1032.

RUDOLF I (1218–91) uncrowned Holy Roman Emperor, founder of the Habsburg dynasty, was the most powerful prince in Swabia when he was elected king of Germany in 1273, although he was never crowned Emperor. He attempted to restore the power of the monarchy by the resumption of lands and rights usurped by the princes since 1245. His victory at Durnkrüt on the Marchfeld (1278) over Ottokar II of Bohemia, who had occupied Austria and Styria, brought him control of these two duchies, which passed to his son **Albert I** and became the seat of Habsburg power.

RUDOLF II (1552–1612) Austrian emperor, elected Holy Roman Emperor on the death of his father, **Maximilian II**, in 1576. Residing for most of his reign in Prague, he made the city a centre for writers, artists and humanist scholars, including the astronomers **Tycho Brahe** and **Johan Kepler** and mystics such as **Giordano Bruno** and **John Dee**. He waged an indecisive and underfinanced war against the Turks (1591–1606). His catholicizing policies provoked opposition amongst Bohemian protestants, who looked to his younger brother, Matthias, for support. Remaining unmarried, he became increasingly tactiturn and withdrawn in his later years. In 1611 he was obliged to recognize Matthias as king of Bohemia.

RUDOLF, Prince See **FRANZ-JOSEPH**

RUDOLPH, Wilma (1940–) American sprinter, born in Clarksville, Tennessee, the 20th of 22 children. Overcoming childhood polio she came to prominence as a teenager as part of an athletics team known as the 'Tennessee Belles'. As a 16-year-old she won a sprint relay bronze medal at Melbourne in the 1956 Olympic Games, and took first place in the 100 metres, 200 metres and sprint relay events at Rome in 1960. She retired in 1964.

RUE See **DE LA RUE, Warren**

RUEDA, Lope de (c.1510–1565) Spanish dramatist, born in Seville. He became manager of a group of strolling players. A pioneer of Spanish drama, he wrote comedies in the Italian style, short humorous pastoral dialogues, and ten burlesques.

RUETHER, Rosemary Radford (1936–) American theologian, born in Minneapolis. Professor of applied theology at Garrett-Evangelical theological seminary, Evanston, she has written extensively on women and theological issues. Her books, analyzing the effects of male bias in official Church theology and seeking to affirm the feminine dimension of religion and the importance of women's experience, include *New Woman/New Earth* (1975), *Mary: The Feminine Face of the Church* (1979), *Sexism and God-Talk* (1983), and *Women-Church* (1985).

RUFF, William (1801–56) London sporting reporter. In 1842 he started his annual *Ruff's Guide to the Turf.*

RUFFINI, Giovanni Domenico (1807–81) Italian writer, born in Genoa. In 1833 he joined Young Italy, and in 1836 had to flee to England. From 1875 he lived in Taggia in the Riviera. He wrote *Lorenzo Benoni: Passages in the Life of an Italian* (1853), *Dr Antonio* (1855), *Vincenzo* (1863), and other novels in English, and the libretto for **Donizetti**'s *Don Pasquale* (1843).

RUFINUS (c.345–410) Italian theologian. He was the friend and later the opponent of St **Jerome**, the orthodoxy of **Origen** being their subject of dispute.

RUGE, Arnold (1802–80) German writer and political thinker, born in Bergen in Rügen. In 1837 he helped to found the *Hallesche* (later *Deutsche*) *Jahrbücher*, the organ of Young Germany. Its liberal tendencies were condemned, and Ruge went to Paris and Switzerland. He published in 1848 the democratic *Reform*, entered the Frankfurt parliament for Breslau, and took part in the disturbances at Leipzig in 1849. In 1850 he fled to England, where with **Mazzini** and **Ledru-Rollin** he organized the Democratic Committee. He settled in Brighton, and lived by teaching, writing and translating.

RUGGLES, Carl (1876–1971) American composer, born in Marion, Massachusetts. He was the founder of the Winona Symphony Orchestra, Massachusetts (1912), and taught composition at Miami University (1938–43). His radical modernity and remarkable individuality were met largely with incomprehension, and in later years he concentrated on painting. He published only eight works, the longest of which is the 17-minute orchestral *Sun-treader* (1926–31).

RUGGLES-BRISE, Sir Evelyn John (1857–1935) English penal reformer, born in Finchingfield, Essex. A civil servant, he was appointed chairman of the Prison Commission (1895–1921). He introduced many reforms to humanize penal treatment, including the borstal system, brought in under the Children Act, 1908.

RUHMKORFF, Heinrich Daniel (1803–77) German instrument-maker, born in Hanover. In 1839 he settled in Paris, where in 1855 he invented his induction coil.

RUÏSDAEL, or **Ruysdael, Jacob van** (c.1628–1682) Dutch landscape painter, born in Haarlem. Perhaps a pupil of his uncle Salomon van Ruïsdael (c.1600–1670), a Haarlem landscape painter, he became a member of the Haarlem painters' guild in 1648, and about 1655 moved to Amsterdam, thereafter travelling in Holland and Germany. He died in an almshouse in Haarlem. One of the greatest landscape painters of the Dutch school, his best works are country landscapes, and he also excelled in cloud effects, particularly in his seascapes. He was not highly regarded by his contemporaries, but modern appreciation of him has prevailed. He is represented in the National Gallery, London (*Holland's Deep* and *Landscape with Ruins*),

Glasgow Art Gallery (*View of Katwijk*), the Louvre (*Le Coup de Soleil*), and elsewhere.

RULE, St See **REGULUS, St**

RUMFORD, Benjamin Thompson, Count (1753–1814) Anglo-American administrator and scientist, born in Woburn, Massachusetts. He was assistant in a store and a school teacher, but in 1771 married a wealthy Mrs Rolfe (1739–92). He was made major in a New Hampshire regiment, but left wife and baby daughter, and fled to England (1776), possibly because he was politically suspect. He gave valuable information to the government as to the state of America, and received an appointment in the Colonial Office. In England he experimented largely with gun-powder, and was elected FRS (1779). In 1782 he was back in America, with a lieutenant-colonel's commission. After the peace he was knighted, and in 1784 entered the service of Bavaria. In this new sphere he reformed the army, drained the marshes round Mannheim, established a common foundry and military academy, planned a poor-law system, spread the cultivation of the potato, disseminated a knowledge of nutrition and domestic economy, improved the breeds of horses and cattle, and laid out the English Garden in Munich. For these services he was made head of the Bavarian war department and count of the Holy Roman Empire. During a visit to England (1795–96) he endowed the two Rumford medals of the Royal Society, and also two of the American Academy, for researches in light and heat. Back in Munich, he found it threatened by both French and Austrians. The Elector fled, leaving Count Rumford president of the Council of Regency and generalissimo. Out of his supervision of the arsenal at Munich, where he was impressed by the amount of heat generated in cannon boring, arose his experiments proving the motion, as opposed to the caloric, theory of heat. In 1799 he left the Bavarian service, returned to London, and founded the Royal Institution; in 1802 he moved to Paris, and, marrying **Lavoisier**'s widow in 1804, lived in her villa at Auteuil, where he died. He also invented the Rumford shadow photometer.

RUMSEY, James (1743–92) American engineer and inventor, born in Cecil County, Maryland. His steamboat, propelled by the ejection of water from the stern and exhibited on the Potomac in 1787, was one of the earliest constructed. He died in London while preparing a second version for exhibition on the Thames.

RUNCIE, Robert Alexander Kennedy (1921–) English prelate, and archbishop of Canterbury. He served in the Scots Guards during World War II, and earned an MC, was ordained a priest in 1951, and was bishop of St Albans for ten years before being consecrated archbishop of Canterbury in 1980. Many significant events marked his career, among them a papal visit to Canterbury, the war with Argentina when he stressed reconciliation rather than triumphalism in victory, the ongoing controversies over homosexuality and women in the church, and his highly acclaimed chairmanship of the Lambeth conference. He retired from the post in 1990.

RUNCIMAN, Lord Walter, 1st Viscount (1870–1949) English politician. He entered the House of Commons as a Liberal in 1899 and held a number of ministerial posts in Liberal and coalition administrations from 1908 to 1939. He is remembered for his mission to Czechoslovakia in 1938 to persuade the government to make concessions to Nazi Germany as part of Britain's 'appeasement strategy'.

RUNDSTEDT, Karl Rudolf Gerd von (1875–1953) German soldier, born in the Old Mark of Brandenburg. He served in World War I, rising to chief of staff of the 1st Army Corps. In the early 1930s he was military commander of Berlin and in 1938 commanded occupation troops in the Sudetenland, but was 'purged' for his outspokenness about **Hitler**. Recalled in 1939, he directed the *Blitzkrieg* in Poland and France. Checked in the Ukraine in 1941, he was relieved of his command, but in 1942 was appointed to the command of the Western Front stretching from Holland to the Italian frontier. On the success of the Allied invasion of France in 1944 he was again relieved of his command, but returned as commander-in-chief in September, his last great action being the Ardennes offensive the 'Battle of the Bulge' (1944). Once more he lost his command and in May 1945 was captured by the Americans in Munich. War crimes proceedings against him were dropped on the grounds of his ill-health, and he was a prisoner in Britain from 1946.

RUNEBERG, Johan Ludvig (1804–77) Finnish poet, born in Pietarsaari. Writing in Swedish, his style was much influenced by his studies of Finnish folk-poetry, and he is considered the greatest poet of the national-Romantic school. He taught at Helsinki (1830–37), and at Porvoo (1837–57). He wrote several volumes of lyric verse, but his major works were *Elgskyttaråe* (The Elk Shooters, 1832), a Norse epic, *Kung Fjalar* (King Fjalar, 1844), and his collection of patriotic ballads, *FänrikStåls Sägner* (Tales of Ensign Stål, 2 vols, 1848–60), about Finland's war of independence 1808–09. It begins with 'Vårt land' (Our land), which has become the Finnish national anthem. He also wrote some plays, and edited for the Lutheran Church of Finland a Psalm Book which contained some 60 pieces of his own.

RUNGE, Friedlieb Ferdinand (1795–1867) German chemist, born in Hamburg, discovered carbolic acid and aniline in coal tar (1834).

RUNGE, Philipp Otto (1777–1810) German Romantic painter, born in Wolgast in what was then Swedish Pomerania. After studies in Copenhagen (1799–1801), in Dresden he met the great Romantic landscape painter **Caspar David Friedrich**, and visited **Goethe** in Weimar. His art, intensely mystical, was described by Goethe as 'enough to drive one mad, beautiful and at the same time nonsensical'. His allegorical figures were influenced, not least in their linearity, by **Blake** and **Flaxman**.

RUNYON, (Alfred) Damon (1884–1946) American author and journalist, born in Manhattan, Kansas. After service in the Spanish-American war (1898) he turned to journalism and sports reporting for the *New York American* from 1911, and then feature writing with syndicated columns *Both Barrels* (1918–36) and *The Brighter Side*, from 1937. His first books were volumes of verse, *Tents of Trouble* (1911) and *Rhymes of the Firing Line* (1912), but it was his short stories, written in a characteristic racy style, using the present tense, with liberal use of American slang and jargon, and depicting life in underworld New York and on Broadway, which won for him his great popularity. One collection, *Guys and Dolls* (1932), was adopted for a musical revue (1950). Other books include *Blue Plate Special* (1934) and *Take it Easy* (1939), and the play, with Howard Lindsay, *A Slight Case of Murder* (1935). From 1941 he worked as a film producer.

RUPERT, Prince (1619–82) English cavalry officer, third son of the Elector Palatine **Frederick V** and Elizabeth, daughter of **James VI and I**, of Scotland and England, and nephew of **Charles I**, born in Prague. In the Thirty Years' War (1818–48) he fought against the Imperialists, until at Lemgo he was taken prisoner, and confined for nearly three years at Linz. In 1642 he returned to England and was appointed Commander of Horse, and for the next three years the 'Mad Cavalier' was the life and soul of the royalist cause, winning many a battle by his resistless charges, to lose as many by a too headlong pursuit. He fought at Worcester, Edgehill, Brentford, Chalgrove, Newbury, Bolton, Marston Moor, Newbury again, and Naseby; in August 1645 his surrender of Bristol so irritated Charles (who in 1644 had created him Duke of Cumberland and generalissimo), that he dismissed him. A court martial, however, cleared him, and he resumed his duties, only to surrender at Oxford to **Fairfax** in June 1646. He now took service with France, but accepting in 1648 the command of that portion of the English fleet which had espoused the king's cause, acquitted himself with all his old daring and somewhat more caution. But in 1650 Admiral **Robert Blake** attacked his squadron, and burned or sank most of his vessels. With the remnant the prince escaped to the West Indies, where with his brother, Prince Maurice (1620–52), he maintained himself by seizing English and other merchantmen. In 1653 he was back in France, where he chiefly lived until the Restoration. Thereafter he served under the Duke of York (**James VII and II**), and in naval operations against the Dutch. He took part in founding the Hudson's Bay Company, which was granted its charter in 1670. His last years were spent in chemical, physical and mechanical researches. Though he was not the inventor of mezzotint, he improved the processes of the art, which he described to the Royal Society in 1662; and he invented an improved gunpowder and an alloy called 'Prince's metal'.

RÜPPELL, Wilhelm Peter Eduard Simon (1794–1884) German zoologist and explorer, born in Frankfurt-am-Main, the son of a wealthy banker. He studied natural history at Pavia and Genoa, and made his first major expedition to the Sudan from 1821 to 1827, and to Ethiopia (1830–34). He published extensive maps and scientific accounts of his travels, including the monumental *Reise in Abyssynien* (1838–40). Rüppell's Warbler is named after him.

RUSH, Benjamin (1745–1813) American physician and politician, born in Byberry, Pennsylvania. He studied medicine at Edinburgh and Paris, and in 1769 became professor of chemistry at Philadelphia and at Pennsylvania in 1791. Elected a member of the Continental Congress, he signed the Declaration of Independence (1776). In 1777 he was appointed surgeon-general, and later physician-general, of the Continental army. In 1778 he resigned his post because he could not prevent frauds upon soldiers in the hospital stores, and resumed his professorship. In 1799 he became treasurer of the US Mint. He wrote *Medical Inquiries and Observations* (1789–93), and *Diseases of the Mind* (1821).

RUSH, Ian (1961–) Welsh footballer, born in St Asaph. After playing one season with Chester, he moved to Liverpool in 1981 and immediately began to score heavily (110 goals in 182 league matches). He won all the major honours in British football and, in addition, a European Cup medal in 1984. In 1986 he joined Juventus, the side which had defeated Liverpool in the European Cup final of 1985, but returned to Liverpool in 1988. He has been a regular member of the Welsh international team since 1980.

RUSHDIE, (Ahmed) Salman (1947–) British novelist, born in Bombay. His family moved to Pakistan when he was 17. He was educated at the Cathedral School, Bombay, then at Rugby in England where he experienced 'minor persecutions and racist attacks which felt major at the time'. He emigrated to Britain in 1965 and graduated from King's College, Cambridge, in 1968. He worked as an actor and an advertising copywriter before becoming a full-time writer. Writing in the traditon of **James Joyce**, **Gunter Grass** and the South American 'magic realists', he published his first novel, *Grimus*, in 1975, a muddled fable which sold poorly. With *Midnight's Children* (1981), a *tour de force* poised at the moment when India achieves independence, he emerged as a major international writer, inventive, imaginative and an intoxicating storyteller. It was awarded the Booker prize. *Shame* (1983), a trenchant satire and a revisionist history of Pakistan and its leaders, was similarly conceived on a grand scale and was acclaimed another virtuoso performance. In *The Satanic Verses* (1988) he turned his attention towards Islam, in his familiar hyperbolic mode. The book was banned in India in 1988, and in 1989 Iran's Ayatollah **Khomeini** declared it blasphemous and issued a death threat. Demonstrations followed and copies of the book were burned in Bradford along with effigies of the author, who was forced into hiding under police protection.

RUSHWORTH, John (c.1612–1690) English historian, born in Ackington Park, Warkworth. He studied at Oxford, and settled in London as a barrister. When the Long Parliament met in 1640 he was appointed clerk-assistant to the House of Commons; he represented Berwick 1657–60, 1679, and 1681; he was secretary to **Fairfax** (1645–50), and in 1677 to the lord keeper. In 1684 he was flung into the King's Bench for debt, and there he died. His *Historical Collections of Private Passages of State* (8 vols, 1659–1701) cover the period 1618–48, and are valuable on the Civil War.

RUSK, Dean (1909–) American politician, born in Cherokee County, Georgia. He was educated at Davidson College, North Carolina, and at Oxford, and in 1934 was appointed associate professor of government and dean of faculty at Mills College. After service in the army in World War II, he held various governmental posts, including that of special assistant to the secretary of war (1946–47), assistant secretary of state for UN affairs, deputy under-secretary of state and assistant secretary for Far Eastern affairs (1950–51). In 1952 he was appointed president of the Rockefeller Foundation and from 1961 was secretary of state, in which capacity he played a major role in handling the Cuban crisis of 1962. He retained the post under the **Johnson** administration, retiring in 1969.

RUSKIN, John (1819–1900) English author and art critic, the son of a prosperous wine merchant in London. Private tutoring took the place of schooling so that when he went up to Christ Church, Oxford, in 1836, he was lacking in experience of the world. At Oxford he won the Newdigate prize for poetry, and fancied himself as a poet until shortly after graduating, when he met **Turner** and discovered that his immediate task was to rescue the great painter from obscurity and neglect. *Modern Painters* (1843) was the result of this championship, which may well have embarrassed the painter. This work developed through another four volumes (1846–60) into a spiritual history of Europe with comments on every phase of morals and taste. For his task he had the advantage of frequent visits to the Continent with his parents. His marriage in 1848 to Euphemia (Effie) Chalmers Gray, who afterwards became **Millais**' wife, was legally annulled about the time he began his crusade on behalf of a new set of obscure or vilified painters, the pre-Raphaelite brotherhood, with which Millais was associated. *Modern Painters* and the offshoots of that great work, *The Seven Lamps of Architecture* (1848) and *The Stones of Venice* (1851–53), with its great chapter three 'On the nature of the Gothic', made him the critic of the day and something more than that, for the moral and social criticism in those works raised him into a moral guide or prophet, even though he had rejected the religious upbringing of his childhood. Following on the publication of the completed *Modern Painters* in 1860 he transferred his interest in art to the social question which had been implicit in much pre-Raphaelite painting. **Carlyle**'s attacks on utilitarianism no doubt helped, but Ruskin's resentment of the social injustice and squalor resulting from unbridled capitalism led him to a sort of Christian communism, for which he was denigrated. *Unto This Last* (1862), a protest against the law of supply and demand, was discontinued after four essays in *Cornhill Magazine* by **Thackeray** (1860). The contemptuous rejection of his social economics in this work, and in *Munera Pulveris* (1872), which was stopped after six essays in *Fraser's Magazine* (1862–63), was almost mortal to Ruskin. In *Sesame and Lilies* (1864–69), addressed to privileged young ladies and admonishing them on their duties, he likened his temper to that of Dean **Swift**. In 1869 Oxford made him its first Slade professor of fine art. He settled at Coniston, in the Lake District, and his incomparable vitality showed in the publication of various Slade lectures, but more memorably in *Fors Clavigera*, a series of papers addressed 'To the Workmen and Labourers of Great Britain' (1871–84), in which his social philosophy is fully discussed. Meanwhile he began to spend his fortune on such individual enterprises as the St George's Guild, a non-profit-making shop in Paddington Street, in which members gave a tithe of their fortunes, the John Ruskin school at Camberwell, and the Whitelands College at Chelsea. His last regret was that he had not, like St **Francis**, denuded himself of all wealth. In 1878, in failing health, he resigned the Slade professorship, but returned to it briefly in 1883–84. In his last work, his unfinished autobiography *Praeterita*, also published in numbers (1886–88), he reminisced quietly, all passion spent save for a final jab at the railways which disturbed rural beauty. His last years were spent at Brantwood, Coniston, his solitude being consoled by the affection of his cousin Mrs Arthur Severn and her family. His influence was profound and enduring.

RUSSEL, Alexander (1814–76) Scottish journalist, editor of *The Scotsman* from 1848, born in Edinburgh. A Liberal and an opponent of the corn-laws, he was a caustic wit and a great angler.

RUSSELL a great Whig house whose origin goes back to Henry Russell, an MP from Weymouth, and a merchant in the Bordeaux wine trade, who lived at the beginning of the 15th century.

RUSSELL, Bertrand Arthur William, 3rd Earl Russell (1872–1970) Welsh philosopher, mathematician, prolific author and controversial public figure throughout his long and extraordinarily active life. He was born in Trelleck, Gwent; his parents died when he was very young and he was brought up by his grandmother, the widow of Lord **John Russell**, the Liberal prime minister and 1st Earl. He was educated privately and at Trinity College, Cambridge, where he took first-class honours in mathematics and philosophy. He graduated in 1894, was briefly British Embassy attaché in Paris, and became a fellow of Trinity in 1895, shortly after his marriage to Alys Pearsall Smith. A visit to Berlin led to his first book, *German Social Democracy* (1896), and he was thus launched on an amazingly long, wide-ranging and fertile intellectual career. His most original contributions to mathematical logic and philosophy are generally agreed to belong to the period before World War I, as expounded for example in *The Principles of Mathematics* (1903), which argues that the whole of mathematics could be derived from logic, and the monumental *Principia Mathematica* (with **Alfred North Whitehead**, 1910–13), which worked out this programme in a fully developed formal system and stands as a landmark in the history of logic and mathematics. Russell's famous 'theory of types' and his 'theory of descriptions' belong to this same period. **Wittgenstein** came to Cambridge to be his student from 1912 to 1913 and began the work that led to the *Tractatus Logico-philosophicus* (1922), for the English version of which Russell wrote an introduction. He wrote his first genuinely popular work in 1912, *The Problems of Philosophy*, which can still be read as a brilliantly stimulating introduction to the subject. Politics became his dominant concern during World War I and his active pacifism caused the loss of his Trinity fellowship in 1916 and his imprisonment in 1918, during the course of which he wrote his *Introduction to Mathematical Philosophy* (1919). He had now to make a living by lecturing and journalism, and became a celebrated controversialist. He visited the Soviet Union, where he met **Lenin**, **Trotsky** and **Gorky**, which sobered his early enthusiasm for communism and led to the critical *Theory and Practice of Bolshevism* (1919). He also taught in Peking from 1920 to 1921. In 1921 he married his second wife, Dora Black, and with her founded (in 1927) and ran a progressive school near Petersfield; he set out his educational views in *On Education* (1926) and *Education and the Social Order* (1932). In 1931 he succeeded his elder brother, John, 2nd Earl **Russell**, as 3rd Earl Russell. His second divorce (1934) and marriage to Patricia Spence (1936) helped to make controversial his book *Marriage and Morals* (1932); and his lectureship at City College, New York, was terminated in 1940 after complaints that he was an 'enemy of religion and morality', though he later won substantial damages for wrongful dismissal. The rise of Fascism led him to renounce his pacifism in 1939; his fellowship at Trinity was restored in 1944, and he returned to England after the war to be honoured with an OM, and to give the first BBC Reith Lectures in 1949. He was awarded the Nobel prize for literature in 1950. He had meanwhile continued publishing important philosophical work, mainly on epistemology, in such books as *The Analysis of Mind* (1921), *An Enquiry into Meaning and Truth* (1940) and *Human Knowledge: Its Scope and Limits* (1948), and in 1945 published the best-selling *History of Western Philosophy*. He also published a stream of popular and provocative works on social, moral and religious questions, some of the more celebrated essays later being collected in *Why I am not a Christian* (1957). After 1949 he became increasingly preoccupied with the cause of nuclear disarmament, taking a leading role in CND and later the Committee of 100, and engaging in a remarkable correspondence with various world leaders. In 1961 he was again imprisoned, with his fourth and final wife, Edith Finch, for his part in a sit-down demonstration in Whitehall. His last years were spent in North Wales, and he retained to the end his lucidity, independence of mind and humour. The last major publications were his three volumes of *Autobiography* (1967–69).

RUSSELL, Edward, Earl of Orford (1683–1727) nephew of William Russell, 1st Duke of Bedford (1613–1700), English naval commander, a supporter of **William III (of Orange)**, and is remembered as the commander of a combined British and Dutch fleet in the victory over the French at La Hogue (1692). He was created an earl in the same year.

RUSSELL, Francis, 2nd Earl of Bedford (1527–85) English courtier, son of **John Russell**, 1st Earl of Bedford. He was involved in the Lady **Jane Grey** affair and fled the country until **Elizabeth**'s accession, when he returned and held several offices, among them that of lord president of Wales.

RUSSELL, Francis, 4th Earl of Bedford (1593–1641) English nobleman, son of Sir **William, Baron Russell**. With the help of **Inigo Jones** he developed Covent Garden and built the mansion of Woburn; he also continued the fen drainage scheme intitiated by his father and known as the Bedford Level.

RUSSELL, Francis, 5th Duke of Bedford (1765–1802) English nobleman, a friend of the Prince of Wales. He built Russell and Tavistock Squares in London and employed **Henry Holland** to make additions to Woburn.

RUSSELL, Herbrand, 11th Duke of Bedford (1858–1940) English nobleman. He declined political office, preferring to preside autocratically over his landed estates. He established the collections of rare animals at Woburn, including the Prjevalsky wild horses and the Père David deer. His duchess, Mary du Caurroy (1865–1937), from 1898 kept a model hospital at Woburn, in which she later worked as a radiographer; she took up flying at the age of sixty and participated in record-breaking flights to India and Africa before being lost off the east coast of England while flying solo in 1937.

RUSSELL, John, 1st Earl of Bedford (c.1486–1555) English courtier. He became a gentleman usher to king **Henry VIII**; was entrusted with several diplomatic missions and later held many court appointments, including those of comptroller of the household and lord privy seal. Among the rich possessions which he amassed were the abbeys of Woburn and Tavistock, and the London properties of Covent Garden and Long Acre. Created earl in 1550, he led the mission to Spain in 1554 which escorted back **Philip** to marry **Mary I, Tudor**.

RUSSELL, John, 1st Earl Russell (1792–1878) English statesman, born in London, the third son of the sixth Duke of Bedford. He studied at the University of Edinburgh, and in 1813 was returned for Tavistock. His strenuous efforts in favour of reform won many seats for the Liberals at the 1830 election; **Wellington** was driven from office; and in **Earl Grey**'s ministry Lord John became paymaster of the forces. He was one of the four members of the government entrusted with the task of framing the first Reform Bill (1832), and on him devolved the honour of proposing it. In November 1834 Lord John left office with **Melbourne**; but with the downfall of **Peel** in 1835 he became home, and later colonial, secretary and leader of the Lower House. In the general election of 1841 he was returned for the City, which he represented until his elevation to the Upper House. Immediately after the repeal of the corn-laws in 1846 Peel was defeated and Lord John became prime minister, at the head of a Whig administration (1846–52). In Lord **Aberdeen**'s coalition of 1852 he was foreign secretary and leader of the Commons again but his inopportune Reform bill (1854), the mismanagement of the Crimean campaign and his bungling of the Vienna conference all combined to make him unpopular, and for four years he was out of office. In June 1859, however, he returned as foreign secretary, under **Palmerston**, and in 1861 was created Earl Russell. On Palmerston's death in 1865 he again became prime minister but was defeated in June on his Reform Bill and resigned. Although he remained out of office, he continued to speak and to write on issues of the day until his death.

RUSSELL, John, 4th Duke (1710–71) English statesman, a member of the anti-**Walpole** group. He was First Lord of the Admiralty under **Pelham**; lord-lieutenant of Ireland (1755–61) and ambassador to France (1762–63).

RUSSELL, John Francis Stanley, 2nd Earl Russell (1865–1931) English politician, grandson of Lord **John Russell** (1st Earl); and brother of **Bertrand Russell, 3rd Earl**. He held secretaryships in the second Labour administration. An American divorce and marriage led to three months' imprisonment for bigamy (1901).

RUSSELL, John Robert, 13th Duke of Bedford (1917–) English nobleman. He was estranged from his family at an early age and lived for a while on a slender pittance in a Bloomsbury boarding house until, having been invalided out of the Coldstream Guards in 1940, he became in turn house agent, journalist and South African farmer. After succeeding to the title he became famous for his energetic and successful efforts to keep Woburn Abbey for the family by running it commercially as a show place with popular amenities and amusements.

RUSSELL, Sir William, Baron Russell (cr. 1603) **of Thornhaugh** (c.1558–1613) English statesman, son of **Francis Russell**, 2nd Earl of Bedford. He was governor of Flushing (1587–88) and lord deputy of Ireland (1594–97). His experience of lowland drainage methods while in the former post led him to initiate reclamation work in the Cambridgeshire fens.

RUSSELL, William, Lord Russell (1639–83) English Whig statesman, third son of **William Russell**, 5th Earl and 1st Duke of Bedford. He studied at Cambridge, made the Grand Tour, and at the Restoration was elected MP for Tavistock. He was 'drawn by the court into some disorders' (debts and duelling), from which he was rescued by his marriage (1669) with Lady Rachel Wriothesley (1636–1723), second daughter and co-heiress of the Earl of Southampton and widow of Lord Vaughan. In 1674 he spoke against the actions of the Cabal, and thenceforth was an active adherent of the Country party. He dallied unwisely with France, but took no bribe; he shared honestly in the delusion of the Popish Plot; he presented the Duke of York (**James II**) as a recusant; and he carried the Exclusion Bill up to the House of Lords. He was arrested with Essex and **Sidney** for participation in the Rye House Plot, was arraigned for high treason, and, infamous witnesses easily satisfying a packed jury, was found guilty, and beheaded. The pity of his judicial murder, the pathos of **Gilbert Burnet**'s story of his end, and the exquisite letters of his noble wife, who at his trial appeared in court as his secretary, have secured him a place in history.

RUSSELL, William, 5th Earl and 1st Duke of Bedford (1613–1700) English nobleman. He was created Marquess of Tavistock and 1st Duke in 1694. He fought with **Cromwell** at Edgehill (1642), turned royalist the following year, but after the battle of Newbury changed his coat yet again for parliament. He completed the Bedford Level.

RUSSELL, William, 12th Duke of Bedford (1888–1953) English nobleman, son of **Herbrand Russell**, 11th Duke of Bedford. He acquired a reputation for his collection of parrots and homing budgerigars and for his adherence to pacifism, Buchmanism and near-Fascism which nearly landed him in difficulties during World War II. He was killed in a shooting accident.

RUSSELL, Anna, stage name of **Claudia Anna Russell-Brown** (1911–) English singer and musical satirist, born in London. She studied singing, and began an orthodox operatic career before realizing the possibilities of satire offered by opera and concert singing. She first appeared as a concert debunker of musical fads in New York in 1948, since when she has achieved universal fame in this medium.

RUSSELL, Bill (William Felton) (1934–) American professional basketball player, coach and commentator, born in Monroe, Louisiana. He played with the Boston Celtics from 1956 to 1969, and is considered one of the greatest 'big men' in the sport. A member of eleven National Basketball Association championship teams, he went on to coach in Boston, Seattle and Sacramento. Between playing and coaching he worked as a commentator for American network television. His book, *Second Wind, Memoirs of an Opinionated Man*, was published in 1979.

RUSSELL, Charles Taze, known as **'Pastor Russell'** (1852–1916) American religious leader, and founder of the Jehovah's Witnesses movement, born in Pittsburgh. A congregationalist, he became a travelling preacher. In Pittsburgh in 1872 he founded the international Bible Students' Association (Jehovah's Witnesses), a sect with peculiar views on prophecy and eschatology. He founded the journal *The Watchtower* in 1879.

RUSSELL, Sir Edward John (1872–1965) English agriculturist, born in Frampton-on-Severn, Gloucestershire. He studied chemistry at Owens College (later Manchester University) and then decided to study the improvement of agriculture with a view to founding rural settlements for the unemployed. The latter ideal failed, but his interest in agricultural science increased and in 1912 he became director of the Rothamsted Experimental Station and also published his classic *Soil Conditions and Plant Growth* (1912). His own researches on soil were valuable, and his contributions to the rising status of Rothamsted and of agricultural science were substantial. In his long working life he published some 20 books.

RUSSELL, Frederick Stratten (1897–1984) English marine biologist, born in Dorset. Educated at Oundle School and Gonville and Caius Colleges, Cambridge, he served with distinction in the Royal Naval Air Service during World War I, then joined the staff of the Plymouth Laboratory, of which he eventually became director. He main work was concerned with plankton and medusae; his *The Medusae of the British Isles* (2 vols, 1953 and 1970), and *Eggs and Planktonic Stages of British Marine Fishes* (1976) are classic reference works. His work with plankton was instrumental in elucidating the movement of water masses in the ocean (distinguished by their characteristic plankton) and allowing the prediction of annual variation in fishes of commercial importance.

RUSSELL, George (1857–1951) English horticulturist, born in Stillington, Yorkshire. After 25 years of research and experiment he succeeded in producing lupins of greatly improved strains and of over 60 different colours.

RUSSELL, George William, pseud Æ (1867–1935) Irish poet, painter, writer and economist, born in Lurgan, County Armagh. In 1877 the family went to Dublin, where at the Metropolitan School of Art Russell met **Yeats**, and, already something of a mystic, through him became interested in theosophy. This led him to give up painting, except as a hobby. Having worked first in a brewery, then as a draper's clerk, he published his first book in 1894, *Homeward: Songs by the Way*, and from then on became a recognized figure in the Irish literary renaissance. He was editor of the *Irish Homestead* from 1906 to 1923, when it amalgamated with the *Irish Statesman*, and as editor of the latter from 1923 to 1930 he aimed at expressing balanced Irish opinion of the 1920s, although he held nationalistic sympathies. His writings include books on economics, *The Candle of Vision* (1918), which is an expression of his religious philosophy, books of essays, many volumes of verse, all expressing his mysticism, among then *The Divine Vision* (1903) and *Midsummer Eve* (1928), and a play, *Deirdre* (1907).

RUSSELL, Sir (Sydney) Gordon (1892–1980) English designer, manufacturer and administrator, born in Cricklewood, London. In 1923 he started a furniture-making business in Broadway, Worcestershire, with designs very much in the Cotswold Arts and Crafts tradition. However, under the influence of his architect younger brother R D (Dick) Russell (1903–81), who later became professor in charge of furniture at the Royal College of Art, London (1948–64), Gordon Russell Limited produced some of the finest furniture of the 1930s in a logical modern idiom. In World War II he was chairman of the panel responsible for 'Utility' furniture (1943–47), and from 1947 to 1959 was director of the Council of Industrial Design (now the Design Council) during its crucial formative years. He was elected a royal designer for industry in 1940.

RUSSELL, Henry Norris (1877–1957) American astronomer, born in Oyster Bay, New York. Educated at Princeton and Cambridge, he became professor of astronomy at Princeton in 1911. He developed a theory of stellar evolution, from dwarf to giant stars, which has now been superseded.

RUSSELL, Jack (John) (1795–1883) English 'sporting parson', born in Dartmouth and educated at Oxford. He was perpetual curate of Swymbridge near Barnstaple (1832–80), and master of foxhounds. He developed the West Country smooth-haired, short-legged terrier named 'Jack Russell' after him.

RUSSELL, John (1745–1806) English portrait painter and Methodist enthusiast, born in Guildford. He was painter to **George III**, and produced vividly coloured chalk portraits.

RUSSELL, John Scott (1808–82) Scottish engineer born near Glasgow. He invented the 'wave-line system' of shipbuilding, and took a large part part in the design and building of **Brunel**'s *Great Eastern* steamship (1858).

RUSSELL, Ken (Henry Kenneth Alfred) (1927–) English film director, born in Southampton. After service in the merchant navy and Royal Air Force, he pursued a variety of careers as a ballet dancer, actor and photographer before his amateur film efforts secured him employment at the BBC. His numerous television documentaries include *Portrait of a Goon* (1959), *Lotte Lenya Sings Kurt Weill* (1962) and *Isadora Duncan, The Biggest Dancer in the World* (1966). He made his feature film début with *French Dressing* (1963) and enjoyed an international success with *Women in Love* (1969). A controversial figure, his flamboyant style and unorthodox biographies of musical notables have divided viewers into outraged observers or staunch followers. His more eye-catching films include *The Music Lovers* (1970), *The Devils* (1971) and *Crimes of Passion* (1984). He has also staged operas and directed pop videos.

RUSSELL, Morgan (1886–1953) American painter, born in New York City. He moved to Paris in 1906 and studied briefly with **Matisse**. In 1912 he and the American painter Stanton McDonald-Wright (1890–1973) developed the theory of Synchromist colour, in which colour was given precedence over descriptive form. One of his best-known works in this genre is *Synchromy in Orange: To form* (1913–14). From 1920 he reverted to figurative painting. He returned to the USA in 1946.

RUSSELL, Sir William Howard (1821–1907) Irish war correspondent, born near Tallaght, County

Dublin. Educated at Trinity College, Dublin, he joined *The Times* in 1843, and after entering the Middle Temple was called to the bar in 1850, but never practised. From the Crimea (1854–55) he wrote the famous despatches (published in book form in 1856) which opened the eyes of the British to the sufferings of the soldiers during the winter of 1854–55. He next witnessed the events of the Indian mutiny (1858). He established the *Army and Navy Gazette* in 1860; and in 1861 the Civil War took him to America, where his candid account of the Federal defeat at the first battle of Bull Run made him unpopular. He accompanied the Austrians during the war with Prussia (1866), and the Prussians during the war with France (1870–71). He visited Egypt and the East (1874) and India (1877) as private secretary to the Prince of Wales (**George V**), and went with Viscount **Wolseley** to South Africa in 1879. Among his books are a novel, *The Adventures of Dr Brady* (1868), *Hesperothen* (1882) and *A Visit to Chile* (1890).

RUSSELL OF KILLOWEN, Charles Russell, 1st Baron (1832–1900) Irish lawyer, born in Newry, Ireland. He studied at Trinity College, Dublin, and was called to the English bar in 1859. He became a QC (1872), a Liberal MP (1880), attorney-general (1886, 1892–94), lord chief justice (1894), and a life peer. A supporter of Irish home rule, he was leading counsel for **Charles Parnell** in the tribunal of 1888–89. His son Frank (1867–1946) became a lord of appeal (1929–46) and the latter's son Charles (1908–) a lord of appeal (1975–82).

RUST, Mathias (1968–) West German aviator. He achieved worldwide fame in May 1987 when he piloted a light Cessna 172 turboprop plane from Finland to the heart of Moscow, landing in Red Square, on the doorstep of the Kremlin. His exploit, which was carefully timed to take place on the Soviet Union's 'national border guards' day', highlighted serious deficiencies in the Soviet air defence system and led to the immediate dismissal of defence minister, Marshal Sergei Sokolov. Despite pleading that his actions had been designed to promote world peace, he was found guilty of 'malicious hooliganism' by the Soviet authorities and sentenced to four years' imprisonment. After serving 14 months in a KGB prison in Lefortovo he was released in August 1988 and flown home to West Germany as a goodwill humanitarian gesture by the **Gorbachev** administration.

RUTEBEUF (c.1230–1286) French trouvère, Champenois in origin but Parisian by adoption. He was the author of the semi-liturgical drama *Miracle de Théophile* (c.1260, a prototype of the Faust story), the *Dit de L'Herberie*, a monologue by a quack doctor, full of comic charlatanesque rhetoric, and also several typical stories.

RUTH, Babe (George Herman) (1895–1946) American baseball player, born in Baltimore, the greatest all-rounder in the history of the game. Starting his career as a left-handed pitcher with the Boston Red Sox (1914–19), he became legendary for his power hitting with the New York Yankees (1920–34). In 1920 he scored a then-record of 54 home runs; in 1927 he hit 60 home runs. In all he played in ten World Series, and hit 714 home runs, a record that stood for 30 years until it was surpassed by **Hank Aaron** in 1974. In 1935 he moved to the Boston Braves, and ended his career as coach for the Brooklyn Dodgers (1938). In 1936 he was elected to the National Baseball Hall of Fame.

RUTHERFORD, Alison See **COCKBURN, Alison**

RUTHERFORD, Daniel (1749–1819) Scottish physician and botanist, born in Edinburgh, where he became professor of botany in 1786. In 1772 he published his discovery of the distinction between 'noxious air' (nitrogen) and carbon dioxide.

RUTHERFORD, Ernest Rutherford, 1st Baron Rutherford of Nelson (1871–1937) New Zealand-born British physicist, one of the greatest pioneers of subatomic physics, born in Spring Grove (later Brightwater) near Nelson, the fourth of twelve children of a wheelwright and flaxmiller. Winning scholarships to Nelson College and Canterbury College, Christchurch, his first research projects were on magnetization of iron by high-frequency discharges (1894) and magnetic viscosity (1896). In 1895 he was admitted to the Cavendish Laboratory and Trinity College, Cambridge, on a scholarship. There he made the first successful wireless transmissions over two miles. Under the brilliant direction of **Joseph John Thomson**, Rutherford discovered the three types of uranium radiations. In 1898 he became professor of physics at McGill University, Canada, where, with **Frederick Soddy**, he formulated the theory of atomic disintegration to account for the tremendous heat energy radiated by uranium. In 1907 he became professor at Manchester and there established that alpha particles were doubly ionized helium ions by counting the number given off with a **Geiger** counter. This led to a revolutionary conception of the atom as a miniature universe in which the mass is concentrated in the nucleus surrounded by planetary electrons. His assistant, **Niels Bohr**, applied to this the quantum theory (1913) and the concept of the 'Rutherford-Bohr atom' of nuclear physics was born. During World War I, Rutherford did research on submarine detection for the admiralty. In 1919, in a series of experiments, he discovered that alpha-ray bombardments induced atomic transformation in atmospheric nitrogen, liberating hydrogen nuclei. The same year he succeeded J J Thomson to the Cavendish professorship at Cambridge and reorganized the laboratory, the world centre for the study of *The Newer Alchemy* (1937). In 1920 he predicted the existence of the neutron, later discovered by his colleague, **James Chadwick**. He was awarded the Nobel prize for chemistry in 1908. He published nearly 150 original papers, and his books include *Radioactivity* (1904), *Radioactive Transformations* (1906) and *Radioactive Substances* (1930).

RUTHERFORD, Dame Margaret (1892–1972) English stage and film actress, born in London. She made her first stage appearance in 1925 at the Old Vic theatre, and her film début in 1936. She gradually gained fame as a character actress and comedienne, her gallery of eccentrics including such notable roles as Miss Prism in *The Importance of Being Earnest* (stage 1939, film 1952), Madame Arcati in *Blithe Spirit* (stage 1941, film 1945), and Miss Whitchurch in *The Happiest Days of Your Life* (stage 1948, film 1950). She also scored a success as **Agatha Christie**'s Miss Marple in a series of films from 1962, appearing with her husband, the actor Stringer Davis (1896–1973), whom she married in 1945. She was created DBE in 1967, and won an Oscar as Best Supporting Actress for her part in *The V.I.P's* (1963).

RUTHERFORD, Mark See **WHITE, William Hale**

RUTHERFORD, Samuel (c.1600–1661) Scottish theologian and preacher, born in Nisbet near Jedburgh. He graduated from Edinburgh in 1621. In 1623 he was appointed professor of humanity there, but was dismissed in 1626, having 'fallen in fornication'. In 1627 he was settled as minister of Anwoth. Here he began that correspondence with his godly friends which formed 'the most seraphic book in our literature': *Exercitationes pro divina Gratio* (1636) was against the Arminians, and brought him both an invitation to a divinity chair in Holland and a summons before the High Commission Court in July 1636, when he was forbidden to preach, and banished to Aberdeen (until 1638). He became professor of divinity at St Andrews in 1639, and in 1648 principal of St Mary's College, St Andrews. In 1643 he was sent to the Westminster assembly, his *Due Right of Presbyteries* (1644) belonging to this period. At the Restoration he was deposed, having written *Lex Rex* (1661), a work of biblical and scholarly erudition which refuted the divine right of kings and argued for the limited powers of the ruler subject to the role of law and popular sovereignty. It was burned by the hangman in Edinburgh in 1661, and its author deposed and summoned for high treason; but he received the citation when on his deathbed.

RUTHVEN, John, 3rd Earl of Gowrie (c.1578–1600) Scottish nobleman, second son of **William Ruthven**, 1st Earl of Gowrie. He succeeded a brother as 3rd Earl in 1588, and travelled in Italy, Switzerland and France. Soon after his arrival back in Scotland he was killed with another brother in his house in Perth in the 'Gowrie Conspiracy'—an alleged attempt to murder or kidnap **James VI**.

RUTHVEN, William, 1st Earl of Gowrie (c.1541–1584) Scottish nobleman, created Earl of Gowrie in 1581. He was involved in the murder of **David Rizzio** (1566), and later was the custodian of **Mary, Queen of Scots** during her captivity at Loch Leven (1567–68). In 1582 he kidnapped the boy king, **James VI**, to Castle Ruthven near Perth, for which he was first pardoned and then ordered to leave the country, but was beheaded at Stirling for his part in a conspiracy to take Stirling Castle.

RUTLAND, John James Robert Manners, 7th Duke of Belvoir (1818–1906) English politician, born in Belvoir Castle. He entered parliament in 1841, succeeded to the dukedom in 1888, and held office in the various Conservative ministries between 1852 and 1892. A member of the Young England party (1842–45), he wrote poems, descriptions of tours and a yachting cruise, ballads, etc.

RUYSBROEK, Johannes (1293–1381) Flemish mystic, born in Ruysbroek near Brussels. He was vicar of St Gudule's in Brussels, but in 1353 founded the Augustinian monastery of Groenendael near Waterloo, of which he became prior. His mysticism is expressed in his *Book of Supreme Truth* and other works.

RUYSDAEL, Jacob van See **RUÏSDAEL**

RUYTER, Michiel Adrianszoon de (1607–76) Dutch naval commander, born in Flushing. He went to sea as a cabin boy, but by 1635 had become a captain in the Dutch navy. In the Dutch War with England (1652–54) he served with distinction under **Tromp** against **Blake** and **Monk**, until the death of Tromp at the battle off the Texel (1653). In the second Anglo-Dutch War (1665–67) he defeated Monk in the 'Four Days' battle off Dunkirk (1666). In 1667 he sailed up the Medway to Rochester, burned some of the English ships, and next sailed up the Thames to Gravesend, besides attacking Harwich. In the third Dutch War (1672–78) he attacked the English and French fleets in Solebay (28 May 1672); he defeated Prince **Rupert** and **d'Estrées** in June 1673, and again in August, thus preventing an English invasion. In 1675 he sailed for the Mediterranean to help the Spaniards against the French, but was mortally wounded in a battle in the Bay of Catania, off Sicily.

RUŽIČKA, Leopold (1887–1976) Yugoslavian chemist, born in Vukovar. He became professor of chemistry at Utrecht in 1926 and at Zürich in 1929. He made the earliest synthesis of musk, worked on higher terpenes and steroids, and was the first to synthesize sex hormones, for which he was awarded, with **Adolf Butenandt**, the 1939 Nobel prize for chemistry.

RUZZANTE, real name **Angelo Beolco** (1502–42) Italian dramatist and actor, born in Padua. He wrote mainly comedies of rural life.

RYAN, Desmond (1893–1964) Irish socialist and historian, born in London, son of **William Patrick Ryan**. He grew up in the Dublin of the Irish Renaissance, as brilliantly described in his autobiography of youth, *Remembering Sion* (1934). Educated at **Patrick Pearse**'s school, St Enda's, he became Pearse's secretary, fought in the General Post Office in the Easter Rising (1916), and edited Pearse's account of the school on release from internment, after which he wrote slight studies of Pearse and **James Connolly**. He supported the Anglo-Irish treaty but left Ireland in disgust at the Civil War, and in London wrote novels (*Invisible Army*, (1932), an emotive account of **Michael Collins**, and the hypnotically picaresque *St Eustace and the Albatross*, 1934), and penetrating analyses of **de Valera**, **Devoy**, and of the Irish language (*The Sword of Light*, 1938). He returned to Dublin in the 1940s and produced in *The Rising* (1946) the definitive narrative of the Easter Rising, and became an invaluable editor of *Devoy's Post Bag* (1948,1953—Fenian correspondence) as well as biographer of James Stephens (*The Fenian Chief*, posthumously published in 1957).

RYAN, Nolan (1947–) American baseball player, born in Refugio, Texas. In 1974 he was measured as the fastest baseball pitcher of all time, his fast ball in that year being recorded at 100.8 miles per hour. He played for the New York Mets (1966–71), and with the California Angels (1972–79) he threw three no-hitters, a record exceeded only by Sandy Koufax. In 1973 he set up a record number of strike-outs (383). He later played for the Houston Astros.

RYAN, William Patrick also writing by his name in Irish, **Liam P O Riain,** and as **W P O'Ryan** (1867–1942) Irish journalist and historian, born in Templemore, County Tipperary. He worked in London as a journalist, but returned to Ireland to edit the *Irish Peasant* and other journals (1906–11), only to find his expectations of cultural emancipation blighted by clerical intervention. He expressed his anger in *The Plough and the Cross* (1918) and *The Pope's Green Island* (1912), both of social value, while his contemporary histories *The Irish Literary Revival* (1894) and *The Irish Labour Movement* (1919) are admirable starting-points on their subjects. He returned to London to become assistant editor of the *Daily Herald*, and in later life published his own creative writing in Irish, *Seanchas Filídheachta* (1940), and a study of European contributions to Gaelic scholarship, *Gaelachas i Gléin* (1933).

RYDBERG, Abraham Viktor (1828–95) Swedish writer and scholar, born in Jönköping. After a hard childhood and early struggles to gain an education he worked as a journalist on the liberal newspaper *Götebergs Handels- och Sjöfartstidning* (1855–76), and was professor at Stockholm (1884–95). He wrote historical novels, including *Fribytaren på Östersjön* (Freebooter in the Baltic, 1857), *Singoalla* (1857), *Den siste atenaren* (The Last Athenian, 1859) and *Vapensmeden* (The Armourer, 1891), and several volumes of Biblical criticism. The leading cultural figure of his day, he also wrote works on philosophy, philology and aesthetics, translated **Goethe**'s *Faust*, and published a mythological study, *Undersökningar i germanisk mytologi* (1886–89).

RYDBERG, Johannes Robert (1854–1919) Swedish physicist, born in Halmstad. Professor at Lund from

1901 to 1919, he developed a formula for spectral lines, incorporating the constant known by his name.

RYDER, Albert Pinkham (1847–1917) American painter, born in New Bedford, Massachusetts. He excelled in figures and landscapes, executed in a romantic style.

RYDER, Samuel (1859–1936) English businessman, born in Cheshire, the son of a nurseryman. He built up a prosperous business in St Albans, mainly through selling penny packets of seeds. In 1927 he donated the Ryder Cup, competed for between teams of British (now European) and American professional golfers.

RYDER, Sue, Baroness Ryder of Warsaw and Cavendish (1923–) English philanthropist, born in Leeds, and promoter of residential care for the sick and disabled. Educated at Benenden School in Kent, she joined the First Aid Nursing Yeomanry in World War II and worked with the Polish section of the Special Operations Executive in occupied Europe. As a result of her experiences she determined to establish a 'living memorial' to the dead and those, like refugees, who continued to suffer. The Sue Ryder Foundation, begun at Cavendish, near Sudbury, Suffolk, in 1953, now links 80 centres worldwide. In some countries projects function under the auspices of the Ryder-Cheshire Foundation, which links her work with that of **Leonard Cheshire**, whom she married in 1959. She has written *And the Morrow Is Theirs* (1975), and an autobiography, *Child of My Love* (1986).

RYLANDS, John (1801–88) English textile manufacturer and merchant, born in St Helens. In 1899 his widow established the John Rylands Library in Manchester.

RYLE, Gilbert (1900–76) English philosopher, born in Brighton, Sussex. He studied at Queen's College, Oxford, and became professor of philosophy at Oxford (1945–68) after war service. He was one of the most influential exponents of 'linguistic' or 'ordinary language' philosophy, holding that 'philosophy is the detection of the sources in linguistic idioms of recurrent misconstructions and absurd theories'. He was editor of *Mind* from 1947 to 1971 and helped make Oxford the centre of philosophy in the English-speaking world in the post-war years. His first and best-known work is *The Concept of Mind* (1949), which aimed to exorcize 'the ghost in the machine' in a behaviourist analysis directed against the traditional Cartesian theory that mind and matter were two distinct and problematically-related things. His other works include *Dilemmas* (1954) and *Plato's Progress* (1966).

RYLE, Sir Martin (1918–84) English radio-astronomer, educated at Bradfield and Christ Church College, Oxford. He worked at the Cavendish laboratory, Cambridge (1945–48), and subsequently became a fellow of Trinity College, Cambridge, lecturer in physics (1948–59), and professor of radio-astronomy (1959–82). Using the Cambridge radio-telescope to plot the intensity-distribution curve of stars up to 3000 million and more light years distant, he obtained controversial data which led him in 1961 to throw doubt on the generally accepted 'steady state' theory of the universe. He was appointed astronomer royal in 1972, and awarded the Nobel Prize for physics in 1974, jointly with **Antony Hewish**.

RYMER, Thomas (1641–1713) English critic and historian, born in Yafforth Hall, Northallerton, Yorkshire, the son of a Roundhead gentleman who was hanged at York in 1664. He studied at Sidney Sussex College, Cambridge, and entered Gray's Inn in 1666. He published translations, critical discussions on poetry, dramas and works on history, and in 1692 was appointed historiographer royal (1692). His principal critical works are *The Tragedies of the Last Age Consider'd* (1678) and *A Short View of Tragedy* (1693), which later earned him scorn for its attacks on **Shakespeare**. But he is chiefly remembered as the compiler of the collection of historical materials known as the *Foedera* (20 vols, 1704–35).

RYMOUR See **THOMAS THE RHYMER**

RYSBRACK, (John) Michael (c.1693–1770) Flemish sculptor, born perhaps in Antwerp. He settled in London in 1720. Among his works are the monument to Sir **Isaac Newton** in Westminster Abbey (1731), statues of **William III**, Queen **Anne**, and **George II**, and busts of **Gay**, **Rowe**, **Pope**, Sir **Robert Walpole** and others.

RYUN, Jim (James) (1947–) American athlete, born in Wichita, Kansas. In 1966, while still in his teens, he set a world record time of 3:51.3 for the mile. The following year he established a world record in the 1500 metres, clocking 3:33.1. Never as successful in top class competition as he was against the clock, at the Olympic Games of 1964, 1968 and 1972 he failed to take the gold medal. He turned professional shortly after the 1972 Games.

RYVES, Mrs See **OLIVE, Princess**

RYZHKOV, Nikolai Ivanovich (1929–) Soviet politician, born in the Urals industrial region. He began his working life as a miner before studying engineering at the Urals Polytechnic in Sverdlovsk. He then worked his way up from welding foreman in a local heavy machine building plant to head of the giant Uralmash engineering conglomerate, the largest industrial enterprise in the Soviet Union, at the age of 41. A member of the Communist party of the Soviet Union (CPSU) since 1956, he was was brought to Moscow in 1975 to work as first deputy minister for heavy transport and machine building. Four years later, he became first deputy chairman of Gosplan, and in 1982 was inducted into the CPSU Secretariat by **Yuri Andropov**, as head of economic affairs. He was brought into the Politburo by **Mikhail Gorbachev** in April 1985 and made prime minister in September 1985, with the task of restructuring the Soviet planning process on the quasi-autonomous Uralmash model. A low-profile technocrat, he is viewed as a more cautious and centralist reformer than Gorbachev.

S

SA'ADI, See **SÁDI**

SAARINEN, Eero (1910–61) Finnish-born American architect and furniture designer, born in Kirkknonummi. At the age of 13 he moved with his father, **Eliel Saarinen**, to the USA; after studying sculpture in Paris and architecture at Yale University he went into partnership with his father in 1937. He designed many public buildings in the USA and Europe, including the Jefferson Memorial Arch in St Louis, the General Motors Technical Centre in Warren, Michigan, the Columbia Broadcasting System HQ in New York City, the American embassies in London and Oslo, the TWA terminal at New York's John F Kennedy Airport and Washington's Dulles International Airport.

SAARINEN, (Gottlieb) Eliel (1873–1950) Finnish-born American architect, born in Rantasalmi. The leading architect in his native country, he designed the Helsinki railway station (1904–14) before emigrating to the USA in 1923, where he designed the buildings for the Cranbrook Academy of Art in Michigan, of which he became president (1932–48). An eloquent opponent of skyscrapers, he formed a partnership with his son, **Eero Saarinen**, and designed many churches such as the Tabernacle Church of Christ in Columbus, Independence, and the Christ Lutheran Church in Minneapolis. His writings include *The City, Its Growth, Its Decay, Its Future* (1943) and *Search for Form* (1948).

SABATIER, Louis Auguste (1839–1901) French protestant theologian, born in Vallon (Ardèche). Professor at Strasbourg (1868–73) and Paris (1877-1901), he applied strict historical critism to Biblical interpretation, and wrote the influential *Esquisse d'une philosophie de la religion* (1897), amongst other works. His brother, Paul (1858-1928), a theologian, was also professor at Strasbourg in 1919, and wrote on St **Francis** of Assissi.

SABATIER, Paul (1854–1941) French chemist, born in Carcassonne. In 1882 he became professor at Toulouse. He did notable work in catalysis, discovering with **Senderens** a process for the catalytic hydrogenation of oils, and shared with **Grignard** the 1912 Nobel prize for chemistry.

SABATINI, Rafael (1875–1950) Italian-born novelist, born of Italian and British parentage in Jesi. Writing in English, he first made his name as an author of historical romances with *The Tavern Knight* (1904), which he followed after he settled in England in 1905 with many other such tales, including *The Sea Hawk* (1915), *Scaramouche* (1921) and *Captain Blood* (1922), historical biographies, and a study of *Torquemada* (1913).

SABBATAI Z'VI (1626–75) Jewish mystic, born in Smyrna. In 1648 he declared himself the Messiah and gained a great following, with which he travelled in the Middle East. In Constantinople he was arrested (1666), and promptly embraced Islam to save his life.

SABIN, Albert Bruce (1906–) Polish-American microbiologist. After working on developing vaccines against dengue fever and Japanese B encephalitis, he became interested in polio vaccine and attempted to develop a live attenuated vaccine (as opposed to **Salk**'s killed vaccine). He succeeded in persuading the Russians to help with the testing of his live virus, and in 1959 he was able to produce the results of 4.5 million vaccinations. His vaccine was found to be completely safe, possessing a number of advantages over that of Salk: it gave a stronger, longer-lasting immunity and could be administered orally, consequently there was a widespread international adoption of the Sabin vaccine in the early 1960s. Some years later, he reported a major advance in cancer research, claiming to have evidence in support of the viral origin of human cancer. Later, however, he rejected his own experimental results.

SABINE, Sir Edward (1788–1883) Irish soldier, physicist, astronomer and explorer, born in Dublin. Educated at Marlow and the Royal Military Academy at Woolwich, he was commissioned in the artillery and served in Gibraltar and Canada. He accompanied his lifelong friend Sir **James Clark Ross** as astronomer on **John Ross**'s expedition to find the North-west Passage in 1818 and on **Parry**'s Arctic expedition of 1819–20. He conducted valuable pendulum experiments to determine the shape of the earth at Spitzbergen and in tropical Africa (1821–23), and devoted the rest of his life to work on terrestrial magnetism. He retired from the army in 1877 as a general. Sabine's Gull is named after him. His brother, Joseph Sabine (1770–1837), inspector-general of taxes, was a noted botanist.

SABINE, Wallace Clement Ware (1868–1919) American physicist, born in Richwood, Ohio, regarded as the founder of architectural acoustics. He studied physics at Harvard and became an instructor there in 1890; apart from service during World War I (he was in effect the first chief scientist for the US air force, 1917–18), he never left Harvard. A major new lecture theatre there was found to be useless, due to poor acoustics. Sabine saw the problem in terms of the size, shape and materials of a room affecting the reverberation time. Making tests at night, after two years of experimentation he prescribed 22 hair-felt blankets and rendered the theatre useable. Working further on acoustics, by 1898 he devised the Sabine formula and with its aid advised on the projected new Boston Symphony Hall (1898–1900). From 1904 he was much in demand to advise on architectural acoustics.

SACCHETTI, Franco (c.1330–1400) Italian novelist, born in Florence. He held several diplomatic offices. He wrote *Trecento Novelle* in the style of **Boccaccio**, first printed in 1724, of which ten are translated in **Roscoe**'s *Italian Novelists* (1825). He also published poetry and burlesques.

SACCHI, Andrea (c.1599–1661) Italian painter, born in Netturo near Rome. A pupil of **Francesco Albani**, he upheld the classical tradition in Roman painting, and is represented by the *Vision of St Romuald* and *Miracle of Saint Gregory*, painted for Pope **Urban VIII**, and by religious works in many Roman churches.

SACCO, Nicola (1891–1927) and **Bartolomeo Vanzetti** (1888–1927), Italian-born American political radicals, chief figures in an American *cause célèbre* which had world-wide reverberations. Accused of a payroll murder and robbery in 1920, they were found guilty, and seven years later were executed in spite of conflicting and circumstantial evidence, and the confession of another man to the crime. Both had been anarchists, and the suspicion that this had provoked deliberate injustice aroused an outcry in all parts of the world.

SACHARISSA See **WALLER, Edmund**

SACHER-MASOCH, Leopold von (1836–95) Austrian lawyer and writer, born in Lemberg. He wrote many short stories and novels, including *Der Don Juan von Kolomea* (1866), depicting the life of small-town Polish Jews. The term 'masochism' has been coined to describe the form of eroticism detailed in his later works.

SACHEVERELL, Henry (c.1674–1724) English political preacher, born in Marlborough, the son of a High Church rector. In 1689 he went to Magdalen College, Oxford, where he shared rooms with **Addison**, who dedicated to his 'dearest Henry' *An Account of the Greatest English Poets* (1694). Gaining his doctorate in 1708, he had held the Staffordshire vicarage of Cannock, when in 1709 he delivered the two sermons—one at Derby assizes, the other at St Paul's—attacking the Whig government with such rancour that he was impeached (1710) before the House of Lords. Ardent crowds, shouting 'High Church and Sacheverell!' and now and then wrecking a meeting house, attended him to Westminster. He was found guilty, and suspended from preaching for three years. The **Godolphin** ministry fell that same summer, and in 1713 Sacheverell was selected by the House of Commons to preach the Restoration sermon. He was presented to the rich rectory of St Andrew's Holborn, after which little is heard of him save that he squabbled with his parishioners, and was suspected of complicity in a Jacobite plot.

SACHEVERELL, William (1638–91) English politician, sometimes called the 'First Whig'. He studied law, entered the House of Commons as member for Derbyshire in 1670, and rapidly became one of the leaders of the anti-Court party, instrumental in framing the Test Act, which overthrew **Charles II**'s 'cabal' ministry. He was prominent amongst those later demanding the resignation of **Thomas Leeds**, Lord Danby, and was a keen supporter of the Exclusion Bill. Fined by Judge **Jeffreys** in 1682 for opposing the king's remodelled charter for Nottingham, and defeated in the 1685 election, he sat in the Convention parliament of 1689 which offered the throne to **William III**. Throughout his career of opposition Sacheverell was distinguished for his powers of parliamentary oratory.

SACHS, Hans (1494–1576) German poet and dramatist, born in Nuremberg, the son of a tailor. He was bred a shoemaker, and early learnt verse-making from a weaver. On finishing his apprenticeship in 1511 he travelled through Germany, practising his craft in various cities, and frequenting the schools of the *Meistersinger*. On his return to Nuremberg in 1516 he commenced business as a shoemaker, becoming a master of his guild in the following year. Sachs' literary career, which resulted in the tremendous output of more than 6300 pieces, falls into two periods. In the first he celebrated the Reformation and sang **Luther**'s praises in an allegorical tale entitled *Die Wittenbergisch Nachtigall* 1523, while his poetical fly-sheets, numbering about 200, furthered in no small measure the Protestant cause. In his second period his poetry deals more with common life and manners, and is distinguished by its vigorous language, good sense, homely morality and fresh humour. His best works are *Schwänke*, or Merry Tales; serious tales; allegorical and spiritual songs; and Lenten dramas. He was the central character in **Wagner**'s opera *Die Meistersinger von Nürnberg* (1886).

SACHS, Julius von (1832–97) German botanist, born in Breslau (Wroclaw), one of nine children of a poor engraver. He was befriended by Porkyne and enabled to study at the University of Prague, then became botany lecturer at an agricultural college near Bonn, and from 1698 professor of botany at Wuřzburg. There he carried on important experiments, especially on the influence of light and heat upon plants, and the organic activities of vegetable growth. He exerted widespread influence through his *Lehrbuch der Botanik* (1868) and its English translation, *Textbook of Botany* (1875).

SACHS, Nelly Leonie (1891–1970) German-born Swedish poet and playwright, born in Berlin of a wealthy Jewish family. Between the wars she published a book of stories, *Tales and Legends* (1921), and several volumes of lyrical poetry. With the rise of Nazi power she studied Jewish religious and mystical literature, and in 1940 escaped to Sweden through the intercession of the Swedish royal family and **Selma Lagerlöf**. After World War II she wrote plays and poetry about the anguish of the Jewish people. She was awarded the 1966 Nobel prize for literature, jointly with the Israeli novelist **Shmuel Yosef Agnon**.

SACKVILLE, Charles, 6th Earl of Dorset (1638–1706) English courtier and poet. He succeeded to the earldom in 1677, having two years before been made Earl of Middlesex. He was returned by East Grinstead to the first parliament of **Charles II**, and became an especial favourite of the king, and notorious for his boisterous and indecorous frolics. He served under the Duke of York (**James II**) at sea, but could not endure his tyranny as king and ardently supported the cause of **William III**. His later years were honoured by his generous patronage of **Prior**, **Wycherley** and **Dryden**. He died at Bath, 19 January 1706. He wrote lyrics (such as 'To all you Ladies now at Land') and satirical pieces.

SACKVILLE, George Sackville Germain, 1st Viscount (1716–85) English nobleman, youngest son of the first Duke of Dorset, was wounded at Fontenoy (1745), and dismissed from the service for not charging at Minden (1759). Colonial secretary 1775–82, in 1770 he took the surname Germain, and in 1782 was created Viscount Sackville.

SACKVILLE, Thomas, 1st Earl of Dorset (1536–1608) English poet and statesman, born in Buckhurst in Sussex, the only son of Sir Richard Sackville, Chancellor of the Exchequer. He studied law at Hart Hall, Oxford, and St John's College, Cambridge, and entered the Inner Temple and became a barrister. In 1555 he married, and in 1558 was in parliament. With **Thomas Norton** he produced the blank-verse tragedy of *Ferrex and Porrex* (later called *Gorboduc*) which in 1560–61 was acted before Queen **Elizabeth**, Sackville's second cousin. This work, after the style of **Seneca**, is claimed to be the earliest tragedy in English. He also wrote the verses *Induction* and *Buckingham's Complaint* for *A Mirror for Magistrates* (1563). His prodigality brought Sackville into disgrace, and he travelled in France and Italy (c.1563–66), was imprisoned in Rome as a suspected spy, received Knole as a gift from the queen (1566), and in 1567 was knighted and created Lord Buckhurst. He was then employed as a diplomat in France and the Low Countries and in 1586 it was he who announced her death sentence to **Mary, Queen of Scots**. In 1599 he was made lord high treasurer, and in 1604 Earl of Dorset.

SACKVILLE-WEST, Vita Victoria Mary (1892–1962) English poet and novelist, born in Knole House, Kent, daughter of the 3rd Baron Sackville. Educated privately, she started writing novels and plays as a child. In 1913 she married the diplomat

Harold Nicolson, and their marriage survived despite Nicolson's homosexuality and her own lesbian affair with Violet Trefusis. Her first published works were a collection of poems, *Poems of West and East* (1917), and a novel, *Heritage* (1919). In her *Orchard and Vineyard* (1921) and her long poem *The Land*, which won the 1927 Hawthornden prize, her close sympathy with the life of the soil of her native county is expressed. Her prose works include the novels *The Edwardians* (1930), *All Passion Spent* (1931), and *No Signposts in the Sea* (1961), an account of her family in *Knole and the Sackvilles* (1947), and studies of **Andrew Marvell** and **Joan of Arc**. *Passenger to Teheran* (1926) records her years in Persia with her husband. A passionate gardener at Sissinghurst, Kent, her married home, she wrote a weekly gardening column for *The Observer* for many years. She was the model for **Virginia Woolf**'s *Orlando*.

SACROBOSCO, Johannes de, or **John Holywood,** or **Halifax** (fl. mid 13th century) English mathematician, probably born in Halifax. He is said to have studied at Oxford, and taught at Paris, where he died in 1244 or 1256. He was one of the first to use the astronomical writings of the Arabians. His treatise, *De Sphaera Mundi*, based on **Ptolemy**'s *Almagest* and Arab writings, became the basic astronomy text of the middle ages, and more than 60 editions were printed between 1472 and 1547.

SADAT, Mohamed Anwar El- (1918–81) Egyptian army officer and political leader, president of the United Arab Republic, born in the Tala district of an Egyptian-Sudanese family, joined the army and was commissioned in 1938. Imprisoned in 1942 for contacts with the Germans in World War II, he continued to work for the overthrow of the British-dominated monarchy, and in 1952 was one of the group of officers who carried out the coup deposing King **Farouk**. He held various posts under **Gamal Abdel Nasser**, being one of the four vice-presidents from 1964 to 1967, and sole vice-president in 1969–70 when the office was revived. An ardent Egyptian nationalist and Muslim, he was editor of *Al-Jumhuriya* and *Al-Tahrir* in 1955–56, and held strong anti-Communist views. He became president in 1970 after the death of Nasser at a time when Egypt's main preoccupation was the confrontation with Israel. In March 1973 he temporarily assumed the post of prime minister, also proclaiming himself military governor-general, the fourth Arab-Israeli war taking place in November of that year. In September 1974 he relinquished the premiership to Dr Hagazy, and from then sought diplomatic settlement of the conflict, meeting the prime minister of Israel in Jerusalem in December 1977 and at Camp David at President **Carter**'s invitation in September 1978, in which year he and **Begin** were jointly awarded the Nobel peace prize. The only Arab leader to sign a peace treaty with Israel, he was criticized by other Arab statesmen and hard-line Muslims. He failed to match his undoubted international success with an improvement in Egypt's own struggling economy and he was suspected of harsh treatment of his political opponents. He was assassinated by Muslim extremists while reviewing troops.

SADE, Donatien Alphonse François, Comte de, (known as **Marquis)** (1740–1814) French writer, born in Paris. An army officer in the Seven Years' War (1756–63), in 1772 he was condemned to death at Aix for his cruelty and unnatural sexual practices. He made his escape, but was afterwards imprisoned at Vincennes and in the Bastille, where he wrote works of sexual fantasy and perversion, including *Les 120 Journées de Sodome* (1784), *Justine* (1791), *La Philosophie dans le boudoir* (1793), *Juliette* (1798) and *Les Crimes de l'amour* (1800). He died in a mental asylum at Charenton. The word 'sadism', derived from his name, is used to describe the type of sexual activities which he practised.

SÁDI, Saadi, or **Sa'adi,** the assumed name of **Sheikh Muslih Addin** (c.1184–?1292) Persian poet highly regarded in his native land. He was a descendant of **'Alī, Muhammad**'s son-in-law. He studied at Baghdad, travelled much, and near Jerusalem was taken prisoner by the Crusaders, but was ransomed by a merchant of Aleppo, who gave him his daughter in marriage. The catalogue of his works comprises 22 different kinds of writings in prose and verse, in Arabic and Persian, of which odes and dirges form the predominant part. The most celebrated of his works, however, is the *Gulistan*, or rose garden, a kind of moral work in prose and verse, intermixed with stories, maxims, philosophical sentences, puns and the like. Next comes the *Bostan*, or orchard garden, written in verse, and more religious than the *Gulistan*. Third comes the *Pend-Nameh*, or Book of Instructions.

SADLEIR, Michael (1888–1957) English author and publisher, born in Oxford, a son of Sir **Michael Ernest Sadler**, and great-grand-nephew of **Michael Thomas Sadler**; he took an older form of the name to avoid confusion. Educated at Rugby and Oxford, he joined the publishing firm of Constable, becoming a director in 1920. As well as numerous bibliographical works—he was Sandars reader in bibliography at Cambridge in 1937—he published novels, including *Hyssop* (1915), *These Foolish Things* (1937) and *Fanny by Gaslight* (1940), and biographies, of which *Michael Ernest Sadler: a memoir by his son* (1949) and *Anthony Trollope* (1927) are noteworthy.

SADLER, Sir Michael Ernest (1861–1943) English educational pioneer, born in Barnsley and educated at Rugby and Trinity College, Oxford. Secretary of the extension lectures sub-committee of the Oxford University examinations delegacy (1885), he oversaw an enormous expansion in its work but realized much of the value was lost because of the early age at which most students had left school. He was a member of the Bryce Commission on secondary education which reported in 1895, and he became director of the office of special inquiries and reports in the department of education that year. He made his office a powerful research bureau and virtually founded the study of comparative education in the process. Resigning in 1903, he became (part-time) professor of education at Manchester University and advised extensively on the organization of secondary education. Vice-chancellor of Leeds from 1911, he transformed the university from a little-known college to a major institution. President of a commission on Calcutta University (1917), he produced a notable report which had widespread and long-lasting effects. Master of University College, Oxford (1923–34), he raised funds for the Bodleian Library. He was one of the greatest promoters of education.

SADLER, Michael Thomas (1780–1835) English social reformer, born in Snelston, Derbyshire. An importer of Irish linen in Leeds, he sat as a Tory MP (1829–32) and wrote copiously on Irish social questions. He was a leader of the factory reform movement, and promoted the Factory Act of 1833 which reduced the working-hours in textile mills.

SADLER, Sir Ralph (1507–87) English diplomat, born in Hackney. From 1537 he was employed in diplomacy with Scotland. He was left one of the twelve councillors of **Edward VI**'s minority, fought at Pinkie, sat in the commission on **Mary, Queen of Scots** at

York, was her jailer at Tutbury, and was perhaps sent with the news of her execution to her son. His Papers, valuable for Border and Scottish history, were edited by Arthur Clifford, with historical notes by Sir **Walter Scott** (1809).

SADOLETO, Jacopo (1477–1547) Italian prelate, born in Modena. He went to Rome in 1502, and took orders. **Leo X** made him apostolical secretary, an appointment he retained under **Clement VII** and **Paul III**. By Leo he was made bishop of Carpentras in 1517, and by Paul in 1536 a cardinal. In 1544 he was legate to **Francis I**. Sadoleto ranks as one of the great churchmen of his age. He corresponded with many Protestant leaders, and sought to find a basis for reunion.

SAENREDAM, Pieter Jansz (1597–1665) Dutch painter, born in Assendelft. He was the son of an engraver, and trained in Haarlem. He was acquainted with the architect **Jacob van Campen**, and may have been inspired by his architectural drawings to specialize in paintings of church interiors, a subject of which he is the acknowledged master. His paintings not only effectively convey—in a distinctive high tonality—the subtle effects of light and atmosphere, but also, and unlike previous architectural paintings, are precisely drawn images of known and identifiable churches.

ŠAFAŘIK, Pavel Josef (1795–1861) Czech author and scholar. He was director of the Serbian Orthodox school at Novi Sad (1819–33) and professor at Prague University from 1848, and produced important works on Slavonic literature and antiquities.

SAFAVIDS a dynasty of possibly Kurdish origin, shahs of Persia from 1501 to 1722. Its eponymous ancestor Safī al-Dīn, a Shaykh from Azerbaijan, married the daughter of Shaykh Ẕāhid-i Gīlānī, leader of a Muslim mystic order (*Sūfī*). After he succeeded as its head in 1301, the order gradually developed into a revolutionary religious movement, the *Safaviyya*, under the hereditary leadership of his descendants, and was based at Ardabil near the Caspian Sea. Its military strengh was provided by many of the Turkmen tribesmen of Azerbaijan and eastern Anatolia, who came to be known as Qizilbash ('redheads') from their uniform headgear. By the end of the 15th century the *Safaviyya* had grown strong enough to challenge for political power in Persia, and at Sharur in 1501 Ismā'īl I (1487–1524) defeated the leading Turkmen confederation, the Ak-Koyunlu ('White Sheep'), and proclaimed himself shah. He proceeded to impose a variety of Islam called Twelver Shī'ism which has remained the predominant religion of Iran up to the present. Although Ismā'īl took over a Persian bureaucracy, military power remained with the Qizilbash leaders whose internecine struggles led to civil war in the reign of his son Tahmāsp I (1514–76). Their supremacy was not ended until the reign of **'Abbās I, the Great** (1588–1629) whose military and administrative reforms constituted a lasting achievement which enabled the Safavid state to survive a series of mediocre successors and pressure from Ottomans and Uzbeks until its overthrow by the Afghans in 1722.

SAGAN, Carl Edward (1934–) American astronomer, born in New York. After studying at Chicago and Berkeley, he worked at Harvard then moved to Cornell, becoming professor of astronomy and space science in 1970. Interested in most aspects of the solar system, Sagan has done work on the physics and chemistry of planetary atmospheres and surfaces. He has also investigated the origin of life on earth and the possibility of extraterrestrial life. Through books and a television programme, *Cosmos*, Sagan has done much to interest the general public in this aspect of science. His *Cosmic Connection* (1973) dealt with advances in planetary science; *The Dragons of Eden* (1977) and *Broca's Brain* (1979) helped to popularize recent advances in evolutionary theory and neurophysiology.

SAGAN, Françoise, pen-name of **Françoise Quoirez** (1935–) French novelist, born in Cajare in the Lot region, and educated at a convent in Paris and private schools. At the age of 18 she wrote, in only four weeks, the best-selling *Bonjour tristesse* (1954; filmed 1958), followed by *Un Certain Sourire* (1956; filmed 1958), both remarkably direct testaments of wealthy adolescence, written with the economy of a remarkable literary style. Irony creeps into her third, *Dans un mois, dans un an* (1957), but moral consciousness takes over in her later novels, such as *Aimez-vous Brahms ...* (1959; filmed 1961 as *Goodbye Again*) and *La Chamade* (1966). A ballet to which she gave the central idea, *Le Rendez-vous manqué*, enjoyed a temporary *succès de scandale* in Paris and London in 1958. Her later works, including several plays, such as *Château en Suède* (1960), *Les Violins, parfois...* (1961), *Un Piano dans l'herbe* (1970), and *Zaphorie*, and novels such as *L'Echarde* (1966), *Le lit défait* (1977), *La Femme Fardé* (1981), and *Un orage immobile* (1983) have had a mixed critical reception.

SAGASTA, Práxedes Mateo (1827–1903) Spanish Liberal leader, born in Torrecilla. A member of the Cortes from 1855, he took part in insurrections in 1856 and 1866, and had twice to flee to France. Several times premier, he introduced universal male suffrage and trial by jury.

SAHA, Meghnad (1894–1956) Indian astrophysicist, born in Dacca (now in Bangladesh), the son of a small shopkeeper. He was educated at Presidency College, Calcutta, and afterwards visited Europe on a travelling scholarship. He taught at Allahabad University, and in 1938 was appointed professor of physics at Calcutta. He worked on the thermal ionization that occurs in the extremely hot atmosphere of stars, and in 1920 demonstrated that elements in stars are ionized in proportion to their temperature ('Saha's equation'). He later moved to nuclear physics, and became interested in the creation in India of an institute for its study, which was named after him.

SAHLINS, Marshall David (1930–) American cultural anthropologist, born in Chicago. Educated at Michigan and Columbia, he became professor of anthropology at Michigan in 1964, and later professor at Chicago University. He has made major contributions in the field of Oceanic ethnography, cultural evolution, economic anthropology and the analysis of symbolism. In his early work, as in *Evolution and Culture* (1960), he presented a materialist and progressivist view of cultural evolution heavily influenced by the theory of **Leslie White**. In *Culture and Practical Reason* (1976), however, he inverts this perspective, insisting on the autonomy of cultural systems. In economic anthropology, he has been a strong advocate of the substantivism of **Michael Polanyi**, as in *Stone Age Economics* (1972).

SA'ID PASHA (1822–63) Ottoman viceroy of Egypt from 1854. He granted the concession for making the Suez Canal.

SAINSBURY, Alan John, Baron Sainsbury of Drury Lane (1902–) English retailer, born in Hornsey, Middlesex. Educated at Haileybury, he joined the family grocery business (founded by his grandparents) in 1921. He was chairman from 1956 to 1967, and since 1967 has been joint president of J Sainsbury plc with his younger brother, Sir Robert (1906–). His elder son, Sir John Davan (1927–), has been chairman of the company since 1969. Sir Robert's son, David John (1940–) became deputy chairman in 1988.

SAINT AMANT, Antoine Girard de (1594–1661) French poet, born in Rouen. An early exponent of French burlesque poetry, as in *Rome ridicule* (1649), he also wrote the mock heroic *Albion* (1643), the biblical epic, *Moyse sauvé* (1653), and an ode, *À la solitude*.

SAINT ARNAUD, Jacques Leroy de (1796–1854) French soldier, born in Bordeaux. He fought for the Greeks (1822–26), but made his reputation in Algeria, and in 1851 carried on bloody but successful warfare with the Kabyles. Louis Napoleon (**Napoleon III**) recalled him in 1851, and as war minister (1851–54) he took an active part in the *coup d'état* of 2 December that gave Napoleon the crown. He was rewarded with the marshal's baton. In the Crimean war he commanded the French forces, and co-operated with Lord **Raglan** at Alma, but nine days later died on his way home to France.

SAINT DENIS, Ruth, originally **Ruth Dennis** (1879–1968) American dancer, director, choreographer and teacher, born in Somerville, New Jersey, the daughter of a farmer and inventor. The other half of the Denishawn partnership with **Ted Shawn** (1891–1972), she began performing in vaudeville at an early age and became known, first in Europe, for the exotic, colourful, eastern dances which were to characterize her work (*Cobras*, *The Incense* and *Radha* were all made in 1906). She married Shawn in 1914 on her return to the USA, and founded a school and company with him in Los Angeles in 1915 (later in New York), which was frequented by many Hollywood stars. In 1916 she choreographed the Babylonian dances for **D W Griffith**'s film *Intolerance*. Fusing all manner of dance forms together, from ballet to Indian, the company toured the USA until it folded in 1931, when the couple separated. She danced into her eighties. She wrote an autobiography, *An Unfinished Life*, in 1939.

SAINTE-BEUVE, Charles Augustin (1804–69) French writer, the greatest literary critic of his time, born in Boulogne-sur-Mer. His father was a commissioner of taxes who died three months before the birth of his son, leaving his wife in straitened circumstances. He attended school in Boulogne, then went to the Collège Charlemagne in Paris, and next (1824–27) took a course of medical study. One of his teachers at the Collège Charlemagne founded a literary and political paper called the *Globe*, and to it, along with **Jouffroy**, **Rémusat**, **Ampère** and **Mérimée**, Sainte-Beuve became a contributor. For three years he wrote the short articles collected as *Premiers Lundis*. In 1827 a review praising the *Odes et Ballades* of **Victor Hugo** led to the closest relations between the poet and his critic, which lasted until broken in 1834 by Sainte-Beuve's affair with Madame Hugo. For a time he was a zealous advocate of the Romantic movement. In 1828 he published *Tableau de la poésie française au seizième siècle*, and in 1829 and 1830 *Vie et Poésies de Joseph Delorme* and *Les Consolations*, poems full of morbid feeling. In 1829 in the *Revue de Paris* he began the *Causeries* or longer critical articles on French literature. After the Revolution of July 1830 he again wrote for the *Globe*, now in the hands of the Saint-Simoniens, but he soon fell out with his new colleagues and for the next three years he was on the staff of the *National*, the organ of extreme republicanism. From 1830 to 1836 he became a sympathetic listener of **Lamennais**, but with the ultra-democratic opinions of Lamennais after his breach with Rome he had no sympathy. His single novel, *Volupté* (1835), belongs to this period. In 1837 he lectured on the history of Port Royal at Lausanne, and in book form these lectures contain some of his finest work. In Lausanne he produced his last volume of poetry, *Pensées d'août*. A journey to Italy closes the first period of his life. In 1840 he was appointed keeper of the Mazarin Library. During the next eight years he wrote mainly for the *Revue des deux mondes*. The political confusions of 1848 led him to become professor of French literature at Liège, where he lectured on *Chateaubriand et son groupe*. In 1849 he returned to Paris, and began to write for the *Constitutionnel*, producing an article on some literary subject, to appear on the Monday of every week. In 1861 these *Causeries du lundi* were transferred to the *Moniteur*, in 1867 back to the *Constitutionnel*, and finally in 1869 to the *Temps*. In 1854, on his appointment by the emperor as professor of Latin poetry at the Collège de France, the students refused to listen to his lectures, and he was forced to resign the office. The undelivered lectures contained his critical estimate of **Virgil**. Nominated a senator in 1865, he regained popularity by his spirited speeches in favour of that liberty of thought which the government was doing its utmost to suppress. It was his special instruction that he should be buried without religious ceremony. It is by the amount and variety of his work, and the ranges of qualities it displays, that Saint-Beuve holds such a place among literary critics. He published many other literary works, including *Critiques et portraits littéraires* (1836–39), *Portraits de femmes* (1844), and, posthumously, *M. de Talleyrand* and *Souvenirs et indiscrétions*.

SAINTE-CLAIRE DEVILLE, Henri Étienne (1818–81) West Indian-born French chemist, born in St Thomas. In 1851 he became professor of chemistry at the École Normale at Paris, and shortly afterwards at the Sorbonne. It was he who first produced aluminium (1855) and platinum in commercial quantities, and demonstrated the general theory of te dissociation of chemical compounds at a high temperature. He also examined the forms of boron and silicon, and produced artificially sapphire, aluminium, etc. Besides many papers, he published *De l'aluminium* (1859) *and Métallurgie du platine* (1863).

SAINT-ÉVREMOND, Charles Marguetel de Saint Denis, Seigneur de (1610–1703) French writer and wit, born in St Denis le Guast near Coutances. He fought at Rocroi, Freiburg and Nördlingen, was steadily loyal throughout the Fronde, but in 1661 fled by way of Holland to England on the discovery of his witty and sarcastic letter to Créqui on the Peace of the Pyrenees. He was warmly received by **Charles II**, and in London he spent almost all the rest of his days, delighting the world with his wit. His satire, *La Comédie des académistes* (1644), is masterly, and his letters to and from **Ninon de Lenclos** charming.

SAINT-EXUPÉRY, Antoine de (1900–44) French novelist and airman, born in Lyon. He became a commercial airline pilot and wartime reconnaissance pilot. His philosophy of 'heroic action' based on the framework of his experiences as a pilot is expressed in his sensitive and imaginative *Courier sud* (1929), *Vol de nuit* (1931), *Terre des Hommes* (1939) and *Pilote de guerre* (1942); but his most popular work is *Le Petit Prince* (1943), a touching allegorical story of a little boy from another planet who befriends a pilot stranded in the desert. He was declared missing after a flight in World War II.

SAINT-GAUDENS, Augustus (1848–1907) Irish-born American sculptor, born in Dublin, a French shoemaker's son. Taken to the USA as a baby, he was trained as a cameo-cutter, then studied sculpture in Paris and in Rome, where he was influenced by the

Italian Renaissance. He returned to the USA in 1873, and became the foremost sculptor of his time. His major works include *Lincoln* in Lincoln Park, Chicago, *The Puritan* (Deacon Chapin) in Springfield, Massachusetts, and the **Henry Adams** Memorial in Rock Creek Cemetery in Washington, DC.

SAINT GERMAIN, Christopher (c.1460–1540) English legal writer, born in Shilton, Warwickshire and educated at Oxford. He is remembered for the treatise known as *Doctor and Student* (1523), a dialogue between a doctor of divinity and a student of the common law of England, urging that principles of law must sometimes be applied with discretion and reason to temper the otherwise excessive rigidity of the common law. The first significant critical discussion of the common law to be published, it provoked a *Replication of a Serjeant at the Laws of England*, to which he answered with *A Little Treatise Concerning Writs of Subpoena*. He also wrote a *Treatise concerning the Division between the Spirituality and the Temporality* (1532) which argued for the power of parliament to reform the church.

SAINT-HILAIRE See **BARTHÉLEMY SAINT-HILAIRE** and **GEOFFROY SAINT-HILAIRE**

SAINT JOHN, Henry See **BOLINGBROKE, 1st Viscount**

SAINT-JOHN PERSE, pen-name of **Marie René Auguste Alexis Saint-Léger Léger** (1887–1975) French poet and diplomat, born in St Léger des Feuilles, an island near Guadeloupe. He studied at Bordeaux, and after many adventures in New Guinea and a voyage in a skiff along the China coast he entered the French foreign ministry in 1904. He became secretary-general in 1933, was dismissed in 1940 and fled to the USA, where he became an adviser to **Roosevelt** on French affairs. The Vichy government burnt his writings and deprived him of French citizenship, but it was restored in 1945. His blank verse utilizes an exotic vocabulary of little-used words. The best known of his earlier works, which include *Images à Crusoë* (1909), *Éloges* (1910), and *Amitié du prince* (1924), is the long poem *Anabase* (1924; translated by **T S Eliot**, 1930). Later works include *Exil* (1942), *Pluies* (1944), *Amers* (1957) and *Chroniques* (1960). He was awarded the Nobel prize for literature in 1960.

SAINT JOSEPH, John Kenneth Sinclair (1912–) English aerial photographer and archaeologist, born in Worcestershire. Educated at Selwyn College, Cambridge, he was successively curator, director, and professor of aerial photographic studies at Cambridge (1948–80). Trained as a geologist, he came to recognize the value of aerial survey in the 1930s through meeting and working with **O G S Crawford**. After wartime service in Operational Research at RAF Bomber Command, in 1948 he was involved in the development of a unique university department with its own aircraft, pilot, and servicing facilities, establishing a photographic archive which grew in size and value with every season. The emphasis from the first was on systematic reconnaissance designed to reveal new sites, and on low level oblique photography of natural landscapes and of archaeological monuments in their landscape setting. The often spectacular results were published in *The Journal of Roman Studies* (1951–77), the journal *Antiquity* (1964–80), and in a sequence of books, including *Monastic Sites from the Air* (with David Knowles, 1952) *Medieval England: An Aerial Survey* (with Maurice Beresford, 1958, 1979), and *Roman Britain from the Air* (with Sheppard Frere, 1983).

SAINT-JUST, Louis Antoine Léon Florelle de (1767–94) French Revolutionary, born in Decize near Nevers. Educated by the Oratorians at Soissons, he studied law at Reims, but early gave himself to letters. At 19 he set off for Paris, with some of his mother's valuables, and was, at her request, imprisoned for selling them. He published (1789) a poor poem, *L'Organt*, and in 1791 a revolutionary essay, *L'Esprit de la Révolution et de la Constitution de France*. Returned for Aisne to the Convention (1792), he attracted notice by his fierce tirades against the king; and as a devoted follower of **Robespierre** was sent on missions to the armies of the Rhine and the Moselle. He made bombastic speeches before the Convention, and began the attacks on **Hébert** which sent him and **Danton** to the guillotine. In 1794 he led the attack on the Austrians at Fleurus. In that year, too, he laid before the Convention a comprehensive report on the police, and soon after proposed, along with other fanciful schemes of like Spartan character, Robespierre's scheme for institutions in which boys were to be taken from their parents at seven and brought up by the state. He fell with Robespierre by the guillotine.

SAINT LAURENT, Louis Stephen (1882–1973) Canadian politician, born in Compton, Quebec. He trained as a lawyer in Quebec, and entered the Dominion parliament in 1941 as a Liberal. He was minister of justice and attorney-general (1941–46) and minister of external affairs (1946–48), and in 1948 became leader of the Liberal party and prime minister of Canada. He resigned the latter office on the defeat of his party in the 1957 election, and in 1958 was succeeded as leader of the party by **Lester Pearson**.

SAINT LAURENT, Yves, originally **Henri Donat Mathieu** (1936–) French designer, born in Oran, Algeria. He studied in Paris, graduating in modern languages, and was employed by **Christian Dior** in 1955 after winning an International Wool Secretariat design competition. On Dior's death in 1957, he took over the house. In 1962 he opened his own house, and launched the first of his 160 Rive Gauche boutiques in 1966, selling ready-to-wear clothes, a trend which many other designers were to follow.

SAINT-LÉGER, Alexis See **SAINT-JOHN PERSE**

SAINT LEGER, Sir Anthony (c.1496–1559) English statesman. In 1540 he was appointed lord deputy of Ireland, where he was at first highly successful in his treatment of the fractious clans, who, however, later rebelled. Accused of fraud, he died during the investigation.

SAINT LEGER, Barry (1737–89) British army officer and racing enthusiast, founder of the St Leger. As a colonel during the American Revolution, he was with General **Wolfe** at Quebec. In 1776 he founded the classic St Leger Stakes at Doncaster.

SAINT-LÉON, (Charles Victor) Arthur (1821–71) French dancer, choreographer, ballet master and dance notator, born in Paris. He studied with his father, a ballet master in Stuttgart, before making his teenage début dancing and playing the violin in Munich. He later danced and staged ballets all over Europe (1845–51), often with and for his wife, the ballerina Fanny Cerrito; they created leading roles in **Jules Perrot**'s *Ondine* (1843) and *La Esmeralda* (1844). He was ballet master with the St Petersburg Imperial Theatre (1859–69) and Paris Opéra (1863–70). The classic *Coppelia*, his last and only surviving ballet, dates from 1870. In this and other works, he was one of the first choreographers to incorporate national and ethnic dances into classical ballet.

SAINT LEONARDS, Edward Burtenshaw Sugden, Lord, of Slaugham (1781–1875) English legal writer and judge. He early achieved professional renown with his *Practical Treatise of the Law of Vendors and Purchasers of Estates* (1805) and his *Practical Treatise* *on Powers* (1808). He became MP in 1828 and solicitor-general in 1829, then Lord Chancellor of Ireland (1834 and 1841–46) and Lord Chancellor of Great Britain (1852). A very learned and industrious judge, his main fame rests on his legal texts which were standard works during most of the nineteenth century.

SAINT-MARC GIRARDIN See **GIRARDIN, François Saint-Marc**

SAINT-MARTIN, Louis Claude de (1743–1803) French mystical philosopher, born in Amboise. He was influenced successively by the mystics Martinez Pasqualis, **Jacob Böhme** and **Emmanuel Swedenborg**, and was a vigorous opponent of the prevailing rationalism and materialism of the 18th century. His best-known works are *Des Erreurs et de la Vérité* (1775), *L'Homme de Désir* (1790) and *L'Esprit des choses* (1800). He signed his works 'le philosophe inconnu'.

SAINT-PIERRE, Charles Irénée Castel, Abbé de (1658–1743) French writer and reformer. He was abbot of Tiron from 1695. He published an optimistic *Projet de la paix perpétuelle* (1713), and was expelled from the Academy in 1718 for his *Discours sur la polysynodie*. He also wrote on political economy and philosophy, in which his principles were those of the physiocratic school.

SAINT PIERRE, Jacques Henri Bernardin de (1737–1814) French author, born in Le Havre. After a voyage to Martinique he served for some time in the army engineers, but quarrelled with his chiefs and was dismissed, and next year was sent to Malta, with the same result. He was greatly influenced by the writings of **Rousseau**, and he made public employment impossible by the innumerable utopian criticisms with which he deluged the ministers. With dreams of a new state to be founded on the shores of the Aral Sea, he travelled to Russia, and returned in dejection to Warsaw. He abandoned a government expedition to Madagascar at the Île de France (Mauritius), to spend there almost three years of melancholy and observation. His *Voyage à l'Île de France* (1778) gave a distinctly new element to literature in its close portrayal of nature. His *Études de la nature* (3 vols, 1784) showed the strong influence of Rousseau. A fourth volume (1788) contained the popular *Paul et Virginie*, the story of the love between two young people, untainted by civilization, in the natural surroundings of Mauritius. His next works were *Voeux d'un solitaire* (1789) and the novel, *La Chaumière indienne* (1791). His *Harmonies de la nature* (1796) was a pale repetition of the *Études*. **Napoleon** heaped favours upon him, and he lived comfortably for the rest of his days.

SAINT-RÉAL, César Vichard, Abbé de (1631–92) French historian, born in Chambéry. He visited London, and in 1679 returned to his birthplace as historiographer to the duke of Savoy. He wrote *Dom Carlos* (1672) and *La Conjuration que les Espagnols formèrent en 1618 contre Venise* (1674), early examples of the serious French historical novel.

SAINT-SAËNS, (Charles) Camille (1835–1921) French composer and music critic, born in Paris. He entered the Paris Conservatoire in 1848, was a pupil of Benoist and **Framental Elias Halévy**, and at the age of 16 had begun his long and prolific career of composition with his prizewinning *Ode à Sainte Cécile* (1852), followed shortly afterwards by his first symphony (performed 1853, published 1855). He was a distinguished pianist, and from 1858 to 1877 won considerable renown as organist of the Madeleine in Paris, also giving recitals in London, Russia and Austria. Although conservative as a composer, he was a founder in 1871 of the Société Nationale de Musique, and as such was influential in encouraging the performance of works by young contemporary French composers, for whom his style was also an impeccable model of directness, clarity and technical skill. He wrote four further symphonies, 13 operas, including his best-known, *Samson et Dalila* (1877), four symphonic poems, *Le Rouet d'Omphale* (1871), *Phaëton* (1873), *Danse macabre* (1874) and *La Jeunesse d'Hercule* (1877), five piano, three violin and two cello concertos, *Carnival des animaux* (1886) for two pianos and orchestra, church music, including his *Messe solennelle* (1856), and chamber music and songs. He was a sound music critic, although latterly somewhat prejudiced, because of his own temporarily declining reputation, against his younger contemporaries; his writings include *Harmonie et mélodie* (1885), *Portraits et souvenirs* (1899) and *Au courant de la vie* (1914).

SAINT-SIMON, Claude Henri de Rouvroy, Comte de (1760–1825) French social reformer, and founder of French socialism, born in Paris. He served in the American War of Independence; during the French Revolution he was imprisoned as an aristocrat, but made a small fortune by speculating in confiscated lands. His marriage (1801) was terminated by a divorce; and his lavish expenditure reduced him to utter poverty. Beginning to be in straits, he published his *Lettres d'un habitant de Genève à ses contemporains* (1803); but the first enunciations of socialism occurred in *L'Industrie* (1817), followed by *L'Organisateur* (1819), *Du système industriel* (1821), *Catéchisme des industriels* (1823), and his last and most important work, *Nouveau christianisme* (1825). But for the kindness of friends and a small pension allowed him by his family in 1812 he would have died of starvation. In 1823 he tried to shoot himself, and lost an eye in the attempt; he later died in Paris. Saint-Simon's works are wanting in judgment and system; but notwithstanding all his vagaries, the man who originated Comtism and French socialism must be regarded as a seminal thinker of high rank. In opposition to the destructive spirit of the Revolution, he sought a positive reorganization of society. He desired that the feudal and military system should be superseded by an industrial order controlled by industrial chiefs, and that the spiritual direction of society should pass from the church to the men of science.

SAINT-SIMON, Louis de Rouvroy, Duc de (1675–1755) French courtier and author, born in Paris, son of a page and favourite of **Louis XII** who had become duke in 1636 but later fallen from favour. He served in the army from 1691 to 1702, and went to Versailles. After the death of **Louis XIV** in 1715 he was sent to Spain in 1721 to demand the hand of the Infanta for the young king, **Louis XV**. In 1723 he retired to his château of La Ferté Vidame near Chartres. He died bankrupt. He is best known for his Memoirs (1752), with his impressions and detailed descriptions of court life between 1695 and 1723.

SAINT VINCENT, Gregorius de (1584–1667) Flemish mathematician and astronomer, born in Bruges. He was received into the Jesuit Order in Rome in 1607. His major work, the *Opus geometricum* of 1647, contains a method of finding areas which anticipates the work of **Newton** and **Leibniz** in integral calculus later in the century.

SAINT VINCENT, John Jervis, Earl (1735–1823) English naval commander, born in Meaford Hall, Stone, Staffordshire. He entered the navy in 1749, became a lieutenant in 1755, and so distinguished himself in the Quebec expedition of 1759 that he was made commander. In 1778 he fought in the action of Brest, and in 1782 captured the *Pégase* of 74 guns. In 1793 he commanded a successful expedition against the

French in the West Indies. In 1795, now admiral, he commanded the Mediterranean fleet. In 1797, during preparations for the invasion of England by French, Dutch and Spanish fleets, he intercepted them off Cape St Vincent and completely defeated them. Created Earl St Vincent, he was forced by ill-health to give up command and returned home (1799), but not before his dispositions led to **Nelson**'s victory at the battle of the Nile. As commander of the Channel fleet he subdued the spirit of sedition, and as First Lord of the Admiralty from 1801 to 1804 reformed innumerable abuses. He resumed Channel command in 1806–07.

SAINTINE, or **Boniface, Joseph Xavier** (1798–1865) French writer. He was the author of many plays, poems and tales, the best known being the sentimental *Picciola, the Story of a Prison Flower* (1836).

SAINTSBURY, George Edward Bateman (1845–1933) English literary critic and scholar, born in Southampton. He was educated at King's College School, London, and Merton College, Oxford. From 1868 to 1876 he was a schoolmaster in Manchester, Guernsey and Elgin, but soon afterwards established himself as one of the most active critics of the day, and from 1895 to 1915 he was professor of English literature at Edinburgh. He contributed to the major magazines (he edited *Macmillan's*) and to encyclopaedias. Among his books are histories of literature, both French and English; books on **Dryden**, **Marlborough**, Sir **Walter Scott**, **Matthew Arnold**, **Thackeray**, the early Renaissance, and minor Caroline poets; histories of criticism (3 vols, 1900–04), English prosody (1906–10), and prose rhythm (1912); and a novel (1912). After his retirement came *The Peace of the Augustans* (1916), *A History of the French Novel* (1917–19), *Notes on a Cellar-book* (1920) and *Scrapbooks* (1922–24).

SAKHAROV, Andrei Dimitrievich (1921–89) Soviet physicist and dissident, born in Moscow, the son of a scientist. He graduated in physics from Moscow State University in 1942 and won his doctorate for work on cosmic rays. He was mainly responsible for the development of the Soviet hydrogen bomb and in 1953 became the youngest-ever entrant to the Soviet Academy of Sciences. During the early 1960s he became increasingly estranged from the Soviet authorities because of his campaigning for a nuclear test-ban treaty, peaceful international co-existence and improved civil rights within the USSR. In 1975 he was awarded the Nobel peace prize, but in 1980, during a 'cold war' crackdown against dissidents, he was sent into internal exile in the 'closed city' of Gorky. Here he undertook a series of hunger strikes in an effort to secure permission for his wife, **Yelena Bonner**, to receive medical treatment overseas. Under the personal orders of **Mikhail Gorbachev**, he was eventually released in December 1986. He continued to campaign for improved civil rights and in 1989 was elected to the Congress of the USSR People's Deputies. His non-scientific writing includes *Progress, Co-existence and Intellectual Freedom* (1968) and *Alarm and Hope* (1978).

SAKI See **MUNRO, Hector Hugh**

SALA, George Augustus Henry (1828–95) English journalist and novelist, born in London of Italian ancestry. He studied art and drew book illustrations, but in 1851 became a contributor to *Household Words*, and later contributed to the *Welcome Guest*, *Temple Bar* (which he founded and edited 1860–66), the *Illustrated London News* and *Cornhill*. As a special correspondent of the *Daily Telegraph* he was in the USA during the Civil War, in Italy with **Garibaldi**, in France in 1870–71, in Russia in 1876, and in Australia in 1885. *Twice Round the Clock* (1859) is a social satire, and he also wrote novels such as *The Strange Adventures of Captain Dangerous* (1863) and *Quite Alone* (1864), many books of travel, and the autobiographical *Life and Adventures* (1895).

SALADIN, properly **Salāh al-Dīn al-Ayyūbī** (1137–93) sultan of Egypt and Syria and founder of a dynasty, born in Takrit, on the Tigris, of which his father Ayyūb, a Kurd, was governor under the Seljuks. He entered the service of **Nūr al-Dīn**, emir of Syria, held command in the expeditions to Egypt (1167–68), and was made grand vizier of the Fatimid caliph, whom in 1171 he overthrew, constituting himself sovereign of Egypt. On Nūr al-Dīn's death (1174) he further proclaimed himself sultan of Egypt and Syria, reduced Mesopotamia, and received the homage of the Seljuk princes of Asia Minor. His remaining years were occupied in wars with the Christians and in the consolidation of his extensive dominions. In 1187 he defeated King Guy of Jerusalem and a united Christian army at Hattin near Tiberias, and then captured Jerusalem and almost every fortified place on the Syrian coast. A great army of crusaders, headed by the kings of France and England, captured Acre in 1191, **Richard Cœur-de-Lion** defeated Saladin, took Caesarea and Jaffa, and obtained a three years' treaty. Saladin died in Damascus. His wise administration left traces for centuries in citadels, roads and canals. His opponents recognized his chivalry, good faith, piety, justice and greatness of soul.

SALAM, Abdus (1926–) Pakistani theoretical physicist, born in Jhang. Educated at Punjab University and Cambridge, he became professor of mathematics at the Government College of Lahore and at Punjab University (1951–54). He lectured at Cambridge (1954–56) and in 1957 became professor of theoretical physics at Imperial College of Science and Technology, London. His concern for his subject in developing countries led to his setting up the International Centre of Theoretical Physics in Trieste in 1964. In 1979 he was awarded the Nobel prize for physics, with **Steven Weinberg** and **Sheldon Glashow**. Independently each had produced a theory explaining both the 'weak' nuclear force and 'electromagnetic' interactions between elementary particles, whose predictions were confirmed experimentally in the 1970s and 1980s.

SALANDRA, Antonio (1853–1931) Italian statesman, professor of administrative science at Rome, was premier (1914–16) when Italy entered World War I. Though at first an opponent of Fascism, he became a senator under **Mussolini** in 1928.

SALAZAR, António de Oliviera (1889–1970) Portuguese dictator, born near Coimbra, studied and became professor of economics there. In 1928 he was made minister of finance by **Carmona**, with extensive powers to deal with the widespread economic chaos. Having been elected prime minister in 1932, he gradually converted Portugal into a corporate state by virtue of his considerable financial skill. His tenure of the ministries of war (1936–44) and of foreign affairs (1936–47) included the delicate period of the Spanish Civil War. He further curtailed political opposition, which in any case was only permitted during the brief election periods, after his opponent polled relatively well in 1959. He retired in 1968.

SALDANHA, João Carlos, Duke of (1790–1876) Portuguese statesman and soldier, born in Arinhaga. He fought at Busaco (1810), helped Brazil against Montevideo (1817–22), sided with Dom **Pedro** against Dom **Miguel** as a moderate constitutionalist, and from 1846 to 1856 was alternately head of the government and in armed opposition. Created a duke in 1846, he was twice ambassador at Rome, prime minister in 1870, and ambassador at London from 1871.

SALEH, Ali Abdullah (1942–) North Yemeni soldier and politician. A colonel in the army of the Yemen Arab Republic, he took part in the 1974 coup when Colonel Ibrahim al-Hamadi seized power, with rumours that the monarchy was to be restored. Hamadi was assassinated in 1977 and Colonel Hussein al-Ghashmi took over, only to be killed by a South Yemen terrorist bomb in 1978. Against this background of death and violence Saleh became president. Under his leadership, the war with South Yemen was ended and the two countries agreed to eventual reunion. He was re-elected in 1983 and 1988.

SALES, Francis of See **FRANCIS of Sales**

SALIERI, Antonio (1750–1825) Italian composer, born in Verona. He worked in Vienna for 50 years. A teacher of **Beethoven** and **Schubert**, he was bitterly antipathetic towards **Mozart**, although, contrary to popular myth, he did not poison him. He wrote over 40 operas, an oratorio and masses.

SALINGER, J D (Jerome David) (1919–) American novelist and short story writer, born in New York. His father was a Jewish cheese importer, his mother Scots. Brought up 'an affluent big-city boy', he attended schools in Manhattan, but instead of going to high school in 1932 he transferred to MacBurney's, a private institution which he left after a year. Two years later his father enrolled him at Valley Forge Military Academy, 'Pencey Prep' of *The Catcher in the Rye* (1951). He left school at 17, provided a dancing-partner for wealthy spinsters on a cruise liner, dabbled in writing, and went to Austria to retrace his father's footsteps. At 19 he enrolled at Ursinus College, Collegeville, Pennsylvania, where he lasted a semester before going to Columbia University where his performance was 'below average'. His constant ambition was to become a writer and after service as an infantryman in World War II he graduated from popular magazines to *The New Yorker*. *The Catcher in the Rye*, his first and enduringly popular novel (which sells 250000 copies annually), made him the guru of disaffected youth. Its hero, Holden Caulfield, plays hooky from his Pennsylvania boarding-school and goes to New York, where he tries in vain to lose his virginity. Written in a slick and slangy first-person narrative, disrespectful to adults and authority, it provoked a hostile response from some critics who objected to the forthright language, iconoclasm and élitism. This did not prevent it becoming a college set text. It was succeeded by three 'skimpy' books of short stories about the Glass family of hypersensitive geniuses—*Nine Stores* (1953), published in Britain as *For Esmé—With Love and Squalor, and Other Stories*, *Franny and Zooey* (1961), and two long short stories, *Raise High the Roof Beam, Carpenters* and *Seymour: an Introduction* (1963). Twice married and divorced, Salinger is one of the best-known men in America, and lives in rural reclusion apparently still writing and cultivating Zen philosophy.

SALISBURY, Earls and **Marquises of** See **CECIL**

SALISBURY, Sir Edward James (1886–1978) English botanist, born in Harpenden, Hertfordshire. He studied botany at University College London, where he became reader in plant ecology (1924) and professor of botany (1929–45). He was director of the Royal Botanic Gardens, Kew (1943–56), and wrote *The Reproductive Capacity of Plants* (1942), *Weeds and Aliens* (1966) and *The Living Garden* (1935).

SALISBURY, John of See **JOHN OF SALISBURY**

SALISBURY, originally **Markham, Richard Anthony** (1781–1829) English botanist and horticulturist, born in Leeds, the son of a cloth manufacturer. Educated at Edinburgh University, he assumed his surname to fulfill the conditions of a bequest. He wrote *Prodromus Stirpium* (1796) and *Paradisus Londinesis* (1805–08), but earned opprobrium for unethical professional behaviour and the unwarranted changing of botanical names. His *Genera Plantarum* was edited and published posthumously (1866).

SALISBURY, William (c.1520–c.1600) Welsh lexicographer. He published a Welsh and English Dictionary (1547), and translated the New Testament into Welsh (1567).

SALK, Jonas Edward (1914–) American virologist, born in New York City, the son of a garment worker. Educated in medicine at the New York University College of Medicine, he taught there and at several other schools of medicine or public health until, in 1963, he became director of the Salk Institute in San Diego, California. Some of his early research had been on the influenza virus, but by the time he moved to California, he was known world-wide for his work on the 'Salk vaccine' against poliomyelitis. This used killed polio virus, as opposed to the **Sabin** vaccine, which used a live attenuated strain and could be given orally instead of by injection, which Salk's vaccine required.

SALLÉ, Marie (1707–56) French dancer, born in Paris. A child performer and daughter of an acrobat, she appeared in London in pantomime, making her Paris début in 1718. She studied with **François Prévost** there and in 1727 first performed with the Paris Opéra in the Lavals' *Les Amours des dieux*. Rival to **Marie Camargo**, the other illustrious dancer of the time, she knew a large number of great talents, including **Handel** and **Voltaire**, who were inspired by her. She is known to have excelled in the Lavals' *Castor et Pollux* (1737), Ramean's *Les indes gallantes*, and in the comedy ballets of **Molière** and **Lully**. She created some roles of her own, most notably a sensational *Pygmalion* (1733), and Terpsichore, in the prologue to *Pastor fido* (1734) by Handel. Having worked all her career between London and Paris, she resigned in 1739. She is known today as one of the pioneers of the ballet d'actions.

SALLINEN, Aulis (1935–) Finnish composer, born in Salmi. He studied at the **Sibelius** Academy (1955–60) with **Merikanto** and Joonas Kokkonen, and taught there himself from 1963 to 1976. His works include four operas, *The Horseman* (Savonlinna, 1975), *The Red Line* (Helsinki, 1978), *The King Goes Forth to France* (Savonlinna, 1984) and *Kullervo* (for the new Helsinki opera house), orchestral works including six symphonies, chamber music including five string quartets, concertos, songs and choral music, all in an eclectic, adventurous but mainly tonal idiom.

SALLINEN, Tyko Konstantin (1879–1955) Finnish painter, born in Narmes. After studying art in Helsinki he went to Paris in 1909 and was deeply affected by the works of Kees van Dongen (1877–1968) and the Fauvists. His favourite subjects were landscapes and Finnish peasants, painted in a colourful style.

SALLUST, Latin Gaius Sallustius Crispus (86–34 BC) Roman historian and politician, born of plebeian family in Amiternum in the Sabine country. He had risen to be tribune in 52 when he helped to avenge the murder of **Clodius** upon Milo and his party. Such was the scandal of his licentious life that he was expelled in 50 from the senate—though his attachment to **Caesar**'s party doubtless strengthened the reasons for his expulsion. In 47 he was made praetor and restored to senatorial rank. He served in the African campaign, and was left as governor of Numidia. His administration was sullied by oppression and extortion, but the charges brought against him failed before the partial tribunal of Caesar. With the fruit of his extortion he laid out famous gardens on the Quirinal and the splendid mansion which became an imperial residence of **Nerva**, **Vespasian** and **Aurelian**. In his retirement he wrote his famous histories, the *Bellum Catalinae*, the *Bellum Iugurthinum* and the *Historiarum Libri Quinque* (78–67 BC), of which latter but a few fragments survive. He was one of the first Roman writers to look directly for a model to Greek literature.

SALMASIUS, Claudius, or **Claude de Saumaise** (1588–1653) French scholar, born in Semur in Burgundy. He studied philosophy at Paris and law at Heidelberg (1606–09), where he professed Protestantism. In 1629 appeared his chief work, *Plinianae Exercitationes in Solinum* (1629), after the publication of which he mastered Hebrew, Arabic and Coptic. In 1631 he was called to Leiden to occupy **Joseph Scaliger**'s chair. He is best known for his *Defensio Regio pro Carolo I*, published in 1649 at the request of **Charles II**, which was answered by **Milton** in 1651 with his *Pro Populo Anglicano Defensio*.

SALMOND, Sir John William (1862–1924) New Zealand jurist and judge. He served as professor of law at Adelaide (1897–1906) and Wellington (1906–07), and then in government legal service till 1921 when he was appointed a judge of the Supreme Court of New Zealand. While at Adelaide he published *Jurisprudence* (1902) and *Torts* (1907), the latter still a staple work which has been extensively relied on by the Bench as an authoritative text.

SALOME (1st century AD) Judaean princess, granddaughter of **Herod the Great** and daughter of Herodias by her first husband, Herod Philip, the brother of her second husband, **Herod Antipas**. She is identified (by the historian **Josephus**) as the unnamed girl who danced before Herod Antipas and, at her mother's instigation, demanded the head of **John the Baptist**, who had inveighed against the marriage.

SALOTE (1900–65) queen of Tonga. Educated in New Zealand, she succeeded her father, King George Tupou II, in 1918. Her prosperous and happy reign saw the reunion, for which she was mainly responsible, of the Tongan Free Church majority with the Wesleyan Church (1924). Queen Salote is remembered in Britain for her colourful and engaging presence during her visit in 1953 for the coronation of Queen **Elizabeth**.

SALT, Sir Titus (1803–76) English manufacturer and benefactor, born in Morley near Leeds. He was a wool stapler at Bradford, started wool-spinning in 1834, and was the first to manufacture alpaca fabrics in England. Round his factories in a pleasant valley, three miles from Bradford, on the Aire, rose the model village of Saltaire (1853). Mayor of Bradford in 1848, and its Liberal MP from 1859 to 1861, he was created a baronet in 1869.

SALTEN, Felix, pen name of **Siegmund Salzmann** (1869–1945) Hungarian-born Austrian novelist and essayist, born in Budapest. He is known especially for his animal stories, particularly *Bambi* (1929) which, in translation and filmed by **Walt Disney**, achieved great popularity in America and Britain. He also wrote *Florian, the Emperor's Stallion* (1934) and *Bambi's Children* (1940).

SALTYKOV, Michail Evgrafovich, pseud **N Shchedrin** (1826–89) Russian writer and satirist, born in Tver. He was exiled (1848–56) because of his satirical story *Contradictions* (1847), but later became a provincial vice-governor of Ryazen (1858–60) and Tver (1860–64). He edited with **Nekrasov** the radical *Notes of the Fatherland*, and of his many books, *The Golovlyov Family* (1876) and the *Fables* are among those translated.

SALVATOR ROSA See **ROSA**

SALVIATI, Antonio (1816–90) Italian mosaicist born in Vicenza. He revived in 1860 the glass factories of Murano and the art of mosaic.

SALVIATI, Cecchino, originally **Francesco de' Rossi** (1510–63) Italian painter, born in Florence. He was a pupil of **Andrea del Sarto** and a close friend of **Vasari**. In c.1530 he travelled to Rome and entered the service of Cardinal Giovanni Salviati, whose name he adopted. He travelled extensively in Italy and executed decorative schemes, painted portraits and designed tapestries in Rome, Venice and Florence. In 1554 he was called to the French court but, unable to settle, returned to Rome the following year. He is regarded as one of the major Italian Mannerist painters whose work is characterized by strong colour, complex figure arrangements and spatial ambiguity.

SALVINI, Tommaso (1830–1915) Italian actor, born in Milan. He first became well known as a member of **Ristori**'s company. In Paris he played in **Racine** and in London he enjoyed immense popularity in Shakespearean roles, especially as Othello and Hamlet. He played also in comedies such as those of **Goldoni**, but won fame mainly as a tragedian. The part which he played in fighting in the revolutionary war of 1848 added to his popularity. In 1884 he retired.

SALVIUS JULIANUS (c.100–c.169) Roman jurist. About 130 he was commissioned by the emperor **Hadrian** to revise and rearrange the praetorian edict, which was thereafter fixed and settled. He later held high offices and was a member of the emperor's *consilium*. He wrote a *Digesta* in 90 books, much quoted in later works and in **Justinian**'s *Digest*, commentaries and *Responsa*. He was a masterly jurist, and in him Roman legal science reached its peak.

SAMAIN, Albert Victor (1858–1900) French poet, born in Lille. He was a clerk in the Prefecture of the Seine. His symbolist poetry, though not original in subject, is delicate, fresh and musical, and was well received in his lifetime. Among his collections of verse are *Au jardin de l'infante* (1893), *Aux flancs de la vase* (1898) and *Le Chariot d'or*, published posthumously.

SAMBOURNE, Edward Linley (1844–1910) English cartoonist and illustrator, born in London. At the age of 16 he was apprenticed to marine engineering works at Greenwich, but later joined the staff of *Punch* as a cartoonist (1867–1910). He illustrated **Kingsley**'s *Water Babies*, **Andersen**'s *Fairy Tales*, and other books.

SAMSON, St (c.485–c.565) Welsh bishop, born in south Wales, the son of Amwn of Dyfed and Anna of Gwent. He was educated and ordained by St Illtud in Glamorgan, became an abbot and was later consecrated bishop. He is said to have evangelized in Cornwall and the Channel Islands, and later went to Brittany, where he established a monastery at Dol which became an episcopal see.

SAMSON Old Testament ruler, and the last of the twelve judges in the Book of Judges. His life as recounted in the bible, however, represents him not as a leader but as an individual whose deeds on behalf of Israel made him a popular hero. After a number of encounters with the Philistines he was lured into a trap by Delilah, who cut off his hair to reduce his strength. Blinded by the Philistines, he took his revenge by pulling down the temple at Gaza.

SAMSON OF TOTTINGTON (1135–1211) English ecclesiastic. In 1182 he became abbot of Bury St Edmunds. He built up the abbey, and is featured in **Jocelin de Brakelond**'s *Chronica*.

SAMSONOV, Alexander (1859–1914) Russian soldier. He commanded a force in the Russo-Japanese War (1904–05). In World War I he commanded the army which invaded East Prussia in August 1914, but was decisively defeated by **Hindenberg** at the Battle of Tannenburg on 26–31 August, and committed suicide.

SAMUEL, (Hebrew *Shemû'el*, probably 'name of God') (11th century BC) Old Testament ruler, and first of the Hebrew prophets. Next to **Moses** he was the greatest personality in the early history of Israel. An Ephraimite, he was a native of Ramathaim or Ramah in Mount Ephraim. As a child he was dedicated to the priesthood. The story of 1 Sam vii-xvi combines two widely different accounts of his career. According to one of these, Israel lay under the Philistine yoke for 20 years when a national convention was summoned to Mizpah by Samuel. The Philistines came upon them, only to sustain a decisive repulse. The prophet thenceforward ruled peacefully and prosperously as judge over Israel till age compelled him to associate his sons with him in the government. Dissatisfaction with their ways gave the elders a pretext for asking for a king such as every other nation had. Although seeing the folly of this, equivalent to a rejection of Yahweh (Jehovah), after some remonstrance he granted their prayer, and at Mizpah **Saul** was chosen. The older account makes him a 'man of God', a man 'held in honour', and a seer whose every work 'cometh surely to pass', but occupying a position hardly so prominent as that of judge of Israel. Saul was divinely made known to him as God's instrument to deliver Israel, and the seer secretly anointed him. A month later Saul's relief of Jabesh-Gilead resulted in his being chosen king. The accounts of Samuel's conduct during Saul's reign are also inconsistent.

SAMUEL, Herbert Louis, 1st Viscount Samuel (1870–1963) English Liberal statesman and philosophical writer, born into a banking family. He was educated at University College School and Balliol College, Oxford. Entering parliament in 1902, he held various offices, including that of chancellor of the Duchy of Lancaster (1909), postmaster-general (1910 and 1915), and home secretary (1916, 1931–32) and was high commissioner for Palestine (1920–25). His philosophical works include *Practical Ethics* (1935), *Belief and Action* (1937) and *In Search of Reality* (1957).

SAMUELSON, Paul Anthony (1915–) American economist and journalist, born in Gary, Indiana. Educated at Chicago and Harvard, he was a professor at the Massachusetts Institute of Technology (1940–85). He was the author of *Foundations of Economic Analysis* (1947), and a classic textbook on *Economics* (1948). He was awarded the Nobel prize for economics in 1970 for raising the level of scientific analysis in economic theory.

SANCHEZ, Francisco (1550/51–1623) Portuguese or Spanish physician and philosopher, probably from Braga in Portugal. He became professor of philosophy (1585) and then medicine (1612) at Toulouse. His main work is a study of philosophical scepticism, *Quod Nihil Scitur* (written in 1576, published in 1581, 'That Nothing is Known'), which is a radical critique of **Aristotle** and argues that true knowledge is impossible; we must settle for the limited information available from careful experiment and observation.

SANCHEZ, Thomas (1550–1610) Jesuit moral theologian and casuist. He became master of novices at Granada. His *Disputationes de Sancto Matrimonii Sacramento* (1592) deals with the legal, moral and religious questions that arise out of marriage.

SANCROFT, William (1617–93) English prelate, and archbishop of Canterbury, born in Fressingfield, Suffolk. He was elected fellow of Emmanuel College, Cambridge, in 1642, but in 1651 was expelled from his fellowship for refusing to take the 'Engagement', and in 1657 crossed over to Holland. After the Restoration his advancement was rapid—king's chaplain and rector of Houghton-le-Spring (1661), prebendary of Durham and master of Emmanuel (1662), dean first of York and next of St Paul's (as such having a principal hand in the rebuilding of the cathedral), archdeacon of Canterbury (1668), and archbishop (1678). A Tory and High Churchman, he crowned **James VII and II** in 1685 but refused to sit in his Ecclesiastical Commission (1686), and in 1688 was sent to the Tower as one of the seven bishops charged with seditious libel. But after the Revolution, having taken the oath of allegiance to James, he would not take it to **William III** and **Mary**, so was suspended (1689), and retired to his native village. The *Fur Praedestinatus* (1651), an attack on Calvinism by an unknown author, has been ascribed to him.

SANCTORIUS, (Santorio Santorio) (1561–1636) Italian physician and friend of **Galileo**, born in Capodistria. He studied at Padua and in 1611 became professor of theoretical medicine there. He invented the clinical thermometer, a pulsimeter, a hygrometer and other instruments, but he is best known for his investigations into the fluctuations in the body's weight under different conditions due to 'insensible perspiration'. His experiments were conducted on a balance made by himself.

SAND, George, pseud of **Amandine Aurore Lucie Dupin, Baronne Dudevant** (1804–76) French novelist, born in Paris, the illegitimate daughter of Marshal de Saxe. Her father died when she was very young, and she lived principally at Nohant in Berri with her grandmother, Madame Dupin, on whose death she inherited the property. At the age of 18 she married Casimir, Baron Dudevant, and had two children, but after nine years left him and went to Paris with her children to make her living by literature in the Bohemian society of the period (1831). For the best part of 20 years her life was spent in the company and partly under the influence of various distinguished men. She scandalized bourgeois society with her unconventional ways and her love affairs. Her first lover was **Jules Sandeau**, from whose surname she took her pseudonym, and with whom she wrote a novel, *Rose et Blanche* (1831). She was always interested in poets and artists, including **Prosper Merimée**, Alfred de Musset, with whom she travelled in Italy, and **Chopin**, who was her lover for ten years. In the second decade her attention shifted to philosophers and politicians, such as **Lamennais**, the socialist **Pierre Leroux**, and the republican Michel de Bourges. After 1848 she settled down as the quiet 'châtelaine of Nohant', where she spent the rest of her life in outstanding literary activity, varied by travel. Her work can be divided into four periods. When she first went to Paris, her candidly erotic novels—*Indiana* (1832), *Valentine* (1832), *Lélia* (1833) and *Jacques* (1834)—shared in the Romantic extravagance of the time, and declared themselves against marriage. In the next period her philosophical and political teachers inspired the socialistic rhapsodies of *Spiridion* (1838), *Consuelo* (1842–44), *Comtesse de Rudolstadt* (1843–45) and *Le Meunier d'Angibault* (1845). Between the two periods came the fine novel *Mauprat* (1837). Then she began to turn towards the studies of rustic life—*La Mare au diable* (1846), *François le Champi*, (1847–48) and *La Petite Fadette* (1849—which are, by modern standards, her best works. The fourth period comprises the miscellaneous works of her last 20 years—some of them, such as *Les Beaux Messieurs de Bois Doré*, *Le Marquis de Villemer*, and *Mlle la Quintinie*, of high merit. Her complete works (over 100 vols), besides novels and plays, include the autobiographical *Histoire de ma vie* (1855), *Elle et lui* (on her relations with de Musset, 1859), and delightful letters, published after her death.

SANDAGE, Allan Rex (1926–) American astronomer, born in Iowa City. He studied at Illinois University and California Institute of Technology before joining the Hale Observatories, initially as an assistant to **Hubble**. In 1960 he made the first optical identification of a quasar. With Thomas Matthews, a junior colleague, he found a faint optical object at the same location as the quasar 3C 48 and showed that it had a very unusual spectrum (soon shown by **Maarten Schmidt** to be the result of a massive red shift). Sandage went on to identify many more quasars via this peculiarity of their spectra, and showed that most quasars are not radio emitters.

SANDBURG, Carl (1878–1967) American poet, born in Galesburg, Illinois, of Swedish stock. After trying various jobs, fighting in the Spanish-American war and studying at Lombard College, he became a journalist in Chicago and started to write for *Poetry*. His verse, realistic and robust but often also delicately sensitive, reflects industrial America. Among his volumes of poetry are *Chicago Poems* (1915), *Corn Huskers* (1918), *Smoke and Steel* (1920), *Slabs of the Sunburnt West* (1922) and *Good Morning, America* (1928). His *Complete Poems* gained him the Pulitzer prize in 1950. Interested in American folksongs and ballads, he published a collection in *The American Songbag* (1927). He also wrote a vast *Life of Abraham Lincoln* (1926–39).

SANDBY, Paul (1725–1809) English painter, born in Nottingham, brother of **Thomas Sandby**. He has been called the father of the watercolour school. His career began as a draughtsman, but later, living at Windsor with his brother, he made seventy-six drawings of Windsor and Eton. His watercolours, outlined with the pen, and only finished with colour, take, however, the purely monochrome drawing of this school one step forward. He was an original member of the Royal Academy.

SANDBY, Thomas (1721–98) English artist and architect, brother of **Paul Sandby**. He ran an academy at Nottingham with his brother, and became private secretary and draughtsman to William Augustus, Duke of **Cumberland**. He was deputy ranger of Windsor Park from 1746, and became the first professor of architecture to the Royal Academy (1770). He built Lincoln's Inn Fields (1776) and was joint architect of His Majesty's works with **James Adam** (1777).

SANDEAU, Jules Léonard Sylvian Julien (1811–83) French author, born in Aubusson. He went to Paris to study law, but soon devoted himself to letters. He co-wrote *Rose et Blanche* (1831) with **George Sand**. His first independent novel was *Madame de Sommerville* (1834) and his first success was *Marianna* (1840). His books give an accurate picture of the social conflicts of the France of his day, and he was master of the *roman de moeurs*. He became keeper of the Mazarin Library in 1853, and librarian at St Cloud in 1859.

SANDEMAN, Robert See **GLAS, John**

SANDER, August (1876–1964) German photographer. Born in Herdorf, he studied painting in Dresden and opened a studio in Linz in 1902 and also in Cologne. For many years he planned and worked towards a massive photographic documentary study, *Men in the 20th Century*. He published the first part, entitled *Faces of Our Times*, in 1929, but his social realism was discouraged by the Nazi Ministry of Culture after 1934 and he published little thereafter. Much of his enormous collection of negatives was destroyed in the bombing of Cologne and in a fire at his studio in 1946, but surviving material has provided penetrating portraits of all levels of German life in the early part of the century.

SANDERS, or **Saunder, Nicholas** (c.1530–1581) English Catholic historian and controversialist, born near Reigate. Educated at Winchester and New College, Oxford, he was elected a fellow in 1548, lectured on canon law in 1558, and in 1559 he went abroad. At Rome he was created DD and ordained priest, and in 1561 accompanied Cardinal Hosius to the Council of Trent. He was theological professor at Louvain for 13 years, and twice visited Spain (1573–77), where he tried to incite an invasion of England. As a papal agent in 1579 he was sent to Ireland to stir up rebellion and later died there after the defeat of his supporters. His best known works are *De Visibili Monarchia Ecclesiae* (1571) and *De Origine ac Progressu Schismatis Anglicani* (completed by Rishton, 1585).

SANDERSON, Robert (1587–1663) English theologian and casuist, born in Yorkshire. He graduated at Lincoln College, Oxford, of which he became a fellow (1606–19), reader of logic (1608) and thrice subrector (1613–16). Regius professor of divinity (1642–48), he was deprived of his professorship during the Civil War but was reinstated and became bishop of Lincoln in 1660. To him are due the second preface to the Prayer Book and perhaps the General Thanksgiving, as well as works on casuistry.

SANDOW, Eugene (1867–1925) German-born American strong-man, born in Königsberg of Russian parents. He made his name as a strong-man at the Chicago World's Fair in 1893, then became an artist's model and exponent of physical culture, and opened an Institute of Health in London's St James's Street.

SANDRAKOTTOS See **CHANDRAGUPTA**

SANDS, Bobby (Robert) (1954–81) Irish revolutionary, born in Belfast. He joined the IRA in 1972, and was sentenced to five years' imprisonment in 1973 for possession of guns. In 1977 he was sentenced to 14 years after the bombing of a furniture factory. On 1 March 1981, while at Long Kesh prison, Northern Ireland, he went on hunger-strike in protest against the authorities' refusal to treat himself and his fellow-IRA prisoners as 'political'. On 9 April he was elected Westminster MP for Fermanagh-South Tyrone in a by-election. He remained on hunger-strike for 66 days, dying on 5 May, the first of ten to die throughout that summer.

SANDWICH, Edward Montagu, 1st Earl of (1625–72) English naval commander. In the Civil War he fought on the parliamentary side as a soldier at Marston Moor (1644), sat in parliament 1645–48 and shared the command of the fleet with **Blake** from 1653 and fought in the first Dutch War. For services in the restoration of the monarchy (1660), he was appointed admiral of the narrow seas. Ambassador to Spain (1666–69), he helped to negotiate King **Charles II**'s marriage, and escorted **Catherine of Braganza** to England. In the third Dutch war (1672–78) he fought in the battle of Southwold Bay, and was blown up with his flagship, the *Royal James*.

SANDWICH, John Montagu, 4th Earl of (1718–92) English politician, and inventor of the 'sandwich'. He succeeded his grandfather in 1729 and became First Lord of the Admiralty (1748–51). He held the same post from 1771 to 1782, where his ineptness contributed to British failures in the American War of Independence.

Notoriously corrupt, he was a member of **Francis Dashwood**'s 'Mad monks of Medmenham Abbey', and was involved in the persecution of his former friend, **John Wilkes**. The Sandwich (now Hawaiian) Islands were named after him by Captain **Cook**. The 'sandwich' is reputed to have been invented by him as a snack for eating at the gaming-table.

SANDYS, Duncan See **DUNCAN-SANDYS**

SANDYS, George (1578–1644) English colonist and traveller, born in Bishopthorpe, Yorkshire, the son of the archbishop of York. Educated at St Mary Hall, Oxford, he travelled in Europe and the Middle East and wrote *Relation of a Journey Begun An. Dom 1610* (4 vols, 1615). In America (1621–31) he acted as treasurer of the colony of Virginia and made a verse translation of **Ovid**'s *Metamorphoses* (1626). He also wrote poetic versions of the *Psalms* (1636) and the *Song of Solomon* (1641) and translated a tragedy from the Latin of Hugo Grotius, *Christ's Passion* (1640).

SANGALLO, Antonio Giamberti da, known as **the Younger** (1485–1546) Italian architect and engineer, born in Florence. He was the most notable of a family of architects, nephew of Giuliano (c.1445–1535) and Antonio the Elder (1455–1535), with whom he trained before departing for Rome c.1503. He began as draughtsman to **Donato Bramante** and **Baldassare Peruzzi**, and from 1516 served as assistant to **Raphael** at St Peter's, becoming chief architect there in 1539. He was the leading architect of the High Renaissance in Rome, designing in a confident manner disliked by **Michelangelo**. His works include the Palazzo Palma-Baldassini, Rome (c.1520), and his great masterpiece, the Palazzo Farnese, Rome (1534–46, completed by Michelangelo). Also a military engineer, he designed the fortifications around Rome.

SANGER, Frederick (1918–) English biochemist, born in Rendcombe. A double Nobel prize winner, he pioneered chemical studies on the structure of proteins and nucleic acids. The son of a physician, he was educated at Bryanston, and St John's College, Cambridge. He has researched there ever since, and has been on the staff of the Medical Research Council laboratories since 1951. In the 1940s he devised methods to deduce the sequence of amino acids in the chains of the protein hormone, insulin; by the 1950s he had worked out the sequence of the 51 amino acids in its two-chain molecule, and found the small differences in this sequence in insulins from pig, sheep, horse and whale. For this he was awarded the Nobel prize for chemistry in 1958. He moved to the structure of nucleic acids, working on RNA and DNA. Using a highly ingenious combination of radioactive labelling, gel electrophoresis, and selective enzymes, he and his group were able, by 1977, to deduce the full sequence of bases in the DNA of the virus Phi X 174, with over 5400 bases, and mitochondrial DNA with 17000 bases. Such methods led, by 1984, to the full base sequence in Epstein-Barr virus. For his nucleic acid work Sanger shared (with **Walter Gilbert** and **Paul Berg**) the 1980 Nobel prize for chemistry, thus becoming the first to win two Nobel prizes for chemistry. His inspiring work has given new, surprising and detailed knowledge of both proteins and genes.

SANGER, John (1816–89) and his brother **George** (1825–1911), English showmen. They both called themselves 'Lord', and became famous with their travelling circuses first in the provinces and then in London.

SANGER, Margaret Louise, née **Higgins** (1883–1966) American social reformer and founder of the birth control movement, born in Corning, New York. Educated at Claverack College, she became a trained nurse, and married William Sanger in 1902. Appalled by the tragedies she encountered as a nurse, she published a radical feminist magazine, *The Woman Rebel*, with advice on contraception, in 1914, and in 1916 founded the first American birth-control clinic, in Brooklyn, New York, for which she was imprisoned. After a world tour, she founded the American Birth Control League in 1921. Divorced in 1920, she married J Noah H Slee in 1922. Her many books include *What Every Mother Should Know* (1917), *Motherhood in Bondage* (1928) and *My Fight for Birth Control* (1931).

SANGUINETTI, Julio Maria (1936–) Uruguayan politician. A member of the long-established, progressive Colorado party (PC), which had its origins in the civil war of 1836, he was elected to the assembly in 1962, and then headed the ministries of labour and industry, and education and culture (1969–73). The oppressive régime of Juan Maria Bordaberry (1972–76) was forcibly removed, and military rule imposed before democratic government was restored in 1985. The 1966 constitution was, with some modifications, restored, and Sanguinetti was elected president. He took office in 1986, leading a government of National Accord.

ŚANKARA, (Śamkara or Śankarāchārya) (?700–?750) South Indian philosopher, born in Kalati, Kerala. The author of commentaries on the Hindu scriptures, and founder of monastic centres in different parts of India, he taught *ādvaita* or non-dualistic *Vedanta*: Brahma alone has true existence and the goal of the self is to become one with the Divine, to be absorbed in the ocean of being. This view, familiar to modern westerners through the teaching of Ramakrishna Mission, was strongly opposed by **Rāmānuja** and his successors in the *bhakti* tradition.

SANKEY, Ira David See **MOODY, Dwight Lyman**

SANKEY, John, Viscount (1866–1948) English judge, born in Moreton-in-Marsh, educated at Lancing and Jesus College, Oxford. As a judge of the King's Bench (1914–28) he was chairman of the Coal Commission which in 1919 recommended nationalization of the mines. He went to the Court of Appeal in 1928 and was Lord Chancellor in the Labour and National Governments of 1929–35. As such he secured the appointment in 1929 of the (Donoughmore) Committee on Ministers' Powers and the permanent Law Revision Committee in 1934.

SAN MARTIN, José de (1778–1850) Argentine soldier and statesman, the national hero of Argentina, born in Yapeyu. He played a great part in winning independence for his native land, Chile and Peru. He was an officer in the Spanish army (1789–1812), but helped Buenos Aires in its struggle for independence (1812–14). He raised an army in Argentina (1814–16), which in January 1817 he led across the Andes into Chile, and with **Bernardo O'Higgins** defeated the Spanish at Chacabuco (1817) and Maipo (1818), thus achieving independence for Chile. In 1821, after creating a Chilean navy with **Cochrane**, he entered Lima and declared the independence of Peru. He became Protector of Peru but resigned in 1822 after differences with **Bolivar**, and died an exile in Boulogne.

SANMICHELE, Michele (c.1484–1559) Italian architect and military engineer, responsible with **Jacopo Sansovino** for introducing the Roman High Renaissance to the Veneto. Regarded as the true successor of **Bramante**, and a friend of **Vasari**, he gained direct contact with classical antiquities through designing forts across the Venetian Empire. Capella Pellegrini, in Verona (1527–57), was his first church, in which a simply detailed domed cylinder rises severely from a more elaborate centralized plan. Palazzo Grimani,

Venice (1551–59), is the quintessential Renaissance palace where the skeletal structure of columns dissolves the wall plane. Through numerous influences he produced a cohesive architecture which, amongst others, influenced **Palladio**.

SANNAZARO, Jacopo (c.1458–1530) Italian poet, born in Naples. He sought favour at the court there. His *Arcadia* (1485), a pastoral medley of prose and verse, is full of beauty. He also wrote Latin elegies, and religious works.

SANSON a family of Paris executioners. 'M de Paris', Charles Henri Sanson, executed **Louis XVI**.

SANSOVINO, properly **Andrea Contucci** (1460–1529) Italian religious sculptor, born in Monte Sansovino, from which he took his name. He worked in Florence, Portugal at the court of John II, and in Rome. Some of his work survives, including, at S Maria del Popolo in Rome, the tomb of Cardinal Ascanio Sforza.

SANSOVINO, Jacopo, originally **Tatti** (1486–1570) Italian sculptor and architect, born in Florence. He was a pupil of **Andrea Contucci Sansovino**, and took his name. From 1529 he was state architect in Venice, where he did his best work. As an architect his most noteworthy works are the Libreria Vecchia, the Palazzo della Zecca and the Palazzo Corner, and as a sculptor, the two giants on the steps of the ducal palace.

SANTA ANNA, Antonio López de (1797–1876) Mexican president, born in Jalapa, in 1821 joined **Itúrbide**, but in 1822 overthrew him, and in 1833 became president of Mexico. His reactionary policy in 1836 cost the country Texas. He invaded the revolted province, but was routed by **Houston**, and imprisoned for eight months. In 1838 he lost a leg in the gallant defence of Vera Cruz against the French. From 1841 to 1844 he was either president or the president's master, and was recalled from exile in 1846 to be president during the unlucky war with the United States, in which he was twice defeated in the field. He was recalled from Jamaica by a revolution in 1853, and appointed president for life, but in 1855 he was driven from the country. Under **Maximilian** he intrigued industriously, and ultimately had to flee. In 1867, after the emperor's death, he tried to effect a landing, was captured, and sentenced to death, but allowed to retire to New York. He returned at the amnesty in 1872.

SANTAMARIA, Bartholomew Augustine (1915–) Australian social and political writer, born in West Brunswick, Victoria. After graduating in law from Melbourne University he became involved with the Catholic Rural Movement and other organizations, becoming president of the Catholic Social Movement in 1943, director of Catholic Action in 1947, and president of the National Civic Council in 1957. He was a leading force against Communist influence in Australia, and in the establishment of the Democratic Labour party, though its power, however, waned after 1972. Santamaria has written a number of right-wing texts, including *The Price of Freedom* (1964) and *The Defence of Australia* (1970), and in 1978 a biography of his patron, Archbishop **Daniel Mannix**.

SANTAYANA, George (1863–1952) Spanish philosopher, poet and novelist, born in Madrid, and educated from 1872 in the USA. He taught at Harvard from 1889 and was professor there from 1907 to 1912, but always retained his Spanish citizenship and returned to Europe in 1912. He spent much time in England but settled in Rome in 1924 and passed his last years as the guest of a convent of nuns there. Santayana is always regarded as a very literary philosopher, and a fine stylist. He was a poet (*Sonnets and Other Verses*, 1894), a successful novelist (*The Last Puritan*, 1935) and a cultivated literary critic, aesthetician and essayist. Philosophy, however, became his main interest, though never in a narrow or technical sense. He had quite broad and somewhat paradoxically combined sympathies. His general outlook was naturalistic and materialistic, and he was very critical of the transcendental claims of religion and of German idealism. He was also a sceptic: our knowledge of the external world depends on an act of 'animal faith'. But he was at the same time a Platonist in temperament and attitude, and was devoted to the institutions if not the doctrines of the Catholic Church. His main philosophical works are: *The Sense of Beauty* (1896), *The Life of Reason* (1905–06), *Scepticism and Animal Faith* (1923), which is itself an introduction to the comprehensive four-volume work *Realms of Being* (1927–40), and *Platonism and the Spiritual Life* (1927). He also wrote a three-volume autobiography, *Persons and Places* (1944–53).

SANTERRE, Antoine Joseph (1752–1809) French Revolutionary and soldier. A wealthy brewer, he received a command in the National Guard in 1789, took part in the storming of the Bastille and was in charge at king **Louis XVI**'s execution. Appointed general of division (1793), he marched against the Vendéan royalists, but, miserably beaten, was recalled and imprisoned.

SANTILLANA, Iñigo López de Mendoza, Marqués de (1398–1458) Spanish scholar, soldier and poet. He led expeditions against the Moors in Spain, but is best known as a patron of the arts. Influenced by the poetry of **Dante** and **Petrarch**, he introduced their style and methods into Spanish literature. His shorter poems, especially his *serranillas* (pastoral songs), are among his best work, and he was the first Spanish poet to write sonnets. His principal prose work, *Carta Proemio*, is a discourse on European literature of his day.

SANTLEY, Sir Charles (1834–1922) English baritone, born in Liverpool. He trained partly in Milan (1855–57), made his début in **Haydn**'s *Creation* in 1857, and from 1862 devoted himself to Italian opera. Latterly he became better known at concerts and in oratorio. He was knighted in 1907, and published his *Reminiscences* in 1909.

SANTOS-DUMONT, Alberto (1873–1932) Brazilian aeronaut, born in São Paolo. In 1898 he built and flew a cylindrical balloon with a gasoline engine. In 1901 he did the same with an airship in which he made the first flight from St Cloud round the Eiffel Tower and back. Two years later he built the first airship station, at Neuilly. He then experimented with heavier-than-air machines, and eventually flew 715 feet in a plane constructed on the principle of the box-kite. In 1909 he succeeded in building a light monoplane, a forerunner of modern light aircraft.

SAN YU, U (1919–) Burmese politician and soldier, born in Prome. Educated at Rangoon University, he gained military experience during World War II, fighting under **Ne Win**. Following independence, he held a succession of senior army posts and was a member of the Revolutionary Council which seized power in the March 1962 coup. From the late 1960s he was, successively, minister of finance, minister of defence, army chief-of-staff and, between 1973 and 1981, secretary-general of the ruling Burmese Socialist Programme party (BSPP). Popular within the BSPP and viewed as more pragmatic than Ne Win, San Yu succeeded him as state president in November 1981. With other senior BSPP figures he was forced to resign in July 1988, after popular anti-government demonstrations in Rangoon.

SAPIR, Edward (1884–1939) German-born American linguist and anthropologist, born in Lauenburg, Pomerania (now Poland). He went to the USA with his family in 1889, and studied ethnology and American Indian languages at Columbia. One of the founders of ethnolinguistics, he is best known for his work on the languages of the North American Indians, particularly his studies of the relationship between language and culture. His insights into the effect that the grammatical structure and vocabulary of a language may have on the way its speakers perceive the world were developed by his pupil **Benjamin Lee Whorf**, and came to be known as the Sapir-Whorf hypothesis. After serving as head of anthropology at the Canadian National Museum (1910–25) and as professor of anthropology and linguistics at Chicago University (1925–31), he became Sterling professor of anthropology and linguistics at Yale (1931–39). His best-known book is *Language* (1921).

SAPPHO (b.c.650 BC) Greek lyric poet, born in Erebos on the island of Lesbos. She went into exile about 596 BC from Mitylene to Sicily, but after some years returned to Mitylene. She married Cercylas, and had a daughter, Cleis. She seems to have been the centre of a circle of women and girls, probably her pupils. Tradition represents her as exceptionally immoral, because of the passion she apparently expresses in a love poem to a girl. The greatest woman poet of antiquity, she wrote lyrics unsurpassed for depth of feeling, passion and grace. Only two of her odes are extant in full, but many fragments have been found in Egypt.

SARASATE, Martin Meliton (1844–1908) Spanish violinist and composer, born of Basque parentage in Pamplona. He studied at the Paris Conservatoire, where he was a star pupil, and in 1857 began to give concerts. A skilled performer in concertos, he was perhaps best at playing the Spanish dance music he composed himself. One of the greatest violinists of his day, various works were specially composed for him, including **Max Bruch**'s second violin concerto and his 'Scottish fantasy'.

SARDANAPALUS, the Greek form of **Ashurbanipal** (669–640 BC) king of Assyria, eldest son of **Esarhaddon** and grandson of **Sennacherib**, with all the ambition but without the genius of his father. He was a generous patron of art and letters, and his reign marks the zenith of Assyrian splendour. He extended his sway from Elam to Egypt, but the revolt of Babylon shook the empire.

SARDOU, Victorien (1831–1908) French dramatist, born in Paris. His first efforts were failures, but through his marriage to the actress Brécourt, who nursed him when sick, he became acquainted with **Déjazet**, for whom he wrote successfully *Monsieur Garat* and *Les Prés Saint-Gervais* (1860). Soon he had amassed a fortune and had become the most successful European playwright of his day, and his popularity was immense in the USA. Pieces like *Les Pattes de monde* (1860), *Nos intimes* (1861), *La Famille Benoîton* (1865), *Divorçons* (1880), *Odette* (1882), and *Marquise* (1889) are fair samples of his work. For **Sarah Bernhardt** he wrote *Fédora* (1883), *La Tosca* (1887), etc, and with Moreau *Madame Sans-Gene*; for **Irving** *Robespierre* (1899) and *Dante* (1903). He attempted the higher historical play in *La Patrie* (1869). Today his plays appear over-technical and over-theatrical, and the plot and characters shallow and rather obvious.

SARGENT, John Singer (1856–1925) American painter, born in Florence, the son of an American physician. He studied painting there and in Paris, where he first gained attention at the Salon with *Madame X* (1884). Most of his work was, however, done in England from 1885, where he became the most fashionable and elegant portrait painter of his age. His early painting shows the influence of France, but Spain had a more lasting effect and *Carmencita* is perhaps the best example of this. He made constant visits to the USA where as well as portraits he worked on series of decorative paintings for public buildings. He also, especially in later life, painted landscapes, often in watercolour. He was an official war artist in World War I.

SARGENT, Sir (Harold) Malcolm Watts (1895–1967) English conductor, born in Stamford. Originally trained as an organist, he first appeared as a conductor when his *Rhapsody on a Windy Day* was performed at a Promenade Concert in 1921. He was conductor of the Royal Choral Society from 1928, was in charge of the Liverpool Philharmonic Orchestra (1942–48), and of the BBC Symphony Orchestra (1950–57). His outstanding skill in choral music, his sense of occasion and unfailing panache won him enormous popularity at home and abroad.

SARGESON, Frank (1903–82) New Zealand short story writer and novelist, born in Hamilton. He qualified as a lawyer but did not practise. In 1926 he went to Europe but returned to New Zealand two years later. He worked briefly as a market gardener, milkman, pantryman and freelance journalist, but his main energy was devoted to writing novels and short stories. He made his name with collections of short stories like *Conversations with My Uncle* (1936), *A Man and His Wife* (1940), and *That Summer and Other Stories* (1946), satirizing the provincial attitudes of his surroundings. His novels include *I Saw in My Dream* (1949), *The Hangover* (i967) and *Man of England Now* (1972).

SARGON, of Akkad (fl.c.2370 BC) Mesopotamian ruler. He extended his power over the Sumerian cities in Mesopotamia, and established the first large empire of the ancient Near East. He was long remembered as a conquering ruler and a model for later Near–Eastern empire builders.

SARGON II (d.705 BC) king of Assyria from 721 to 705 BC. He was probably a son of Tiglath-Pileser III, named partly after **Sargon** of Akkad. One of the most powerful of Assyrian kings, he consolidated the empire he had inherited in a long series of campaigns to the north, east, and west of Assyria. He was succeeded by his son **Sennacherib**.

SARICH, Ralph (c.1939–) Australian inventor, born in Perth, Western Australia, of a Yugoslav immigrant family. His early interest in machinery and engines led to an apprenticeship as fitter and turner, and to engineering studies which he pursued through correspondence courses and at night school. In 1972 he developed a working model of an orbital two-stroke reciprocating piston engine. This won him the Australian Broadcasting Corporation's 'Inventor of the Year' award. The following year, with support from Broken Hill Propriety (BHP Ltd), he founded a company to market the engine, which is now being developed under licence by Ford and General Motors in the USA, and by Mercury for marine applications.

SARMIENTO See **DARÍO, Felix Rubén**

SARNEY COSTA, Jose (1930–) Brazilian soldier and politician, born in Maranhao state. He became assistant to the governor at the age of 20, and 6 years later was elected to the state assembly. In 1965 he became governor of Maranhao and in 1970 a senator and president of the government-controlled party, the National Renewal Alliance (ARENA), which was reconstructed in 1980 as the Social Democratic party

(PDS). In 1985, when restrictions on opposition party activity were lifted, Tancredo Neves became the first civilian president for 21 years, with Sarney as his deputy. The new president died within months and Sarney took over, despite some public disquiet about his former military associations.

SAROYAN, William (1908–81) American playwright and novelist, born in Fresno, California. His first work, *The Daring Young Man on the Flying Trapeze* (1934), a volume of short stories, was a tremendous success, and was followed by a number of highly original novels and plays. *The Time of Your Life* (1939), a play, was awarded the Pulitzer prize. Among later works are the autobiographical *My Name is Aram* (1940), *The Bicycle Rider in Beverley Hills* (1952), *The Human Comedy* (1943, a novel) *Days of Life and Death* and *Escape to the Moon* (1971), *Places Where I've Done Time* (1973), and the autobiographical *Obituaries* (1979).

SARPI, Pietro, or **Fra Paolo** (1552–1623) Italian historian, scientist, theologian and patriot, born in Venice. He entered the Servite Order there in 1565, and became vicar-general in 1599. He studied a wide range of subjects, including oriental languages, mathematics, astronomy, physiology and medicine, and is credited with various later anatomical discoveries to do with the venous valves and the circulation of blood. He became the champion of Venice in the dispute with Pope **Paul V** over the immunity of clergy from the jurisdiction of civil tribunals, resisting the intrusion of Rome in the internal affairs of the Republic and opposing the interdict that sought to debar all priests from their functions; he was himself excommunicated and was seriously wounded by assassins. His main preoccupation then became the great *Istoria del Concilio Tridentino*, which was published in London in 1619 under the pseudonym Pietro Soave Polano.

SARRAIL, Maurice Paul Emmanuel (1856–1929) French soldier, born in Carcassonne. In World War I he led the 3rd army at the battle of the Marne (1914), commanded the Allied forces in the East (Salonica) from 1915 to 1917, where he deposed **Constantine I** of Greece. He was high commissioner in Syria (1924–25), but was recalled after the bombardment of Damascus during a rising.

SARRAUTE, Nathalie, née **Tcherniak** (1920–) Russian-born French writer, born in Ivanovno-Voznesenk. Her parents settled in France when she was a child. She was educated at the Lycée Fénelon and the Sorbonne, graduating in arts and law. She spent a year at Oxford (1922–23) doing graduate studies, and then studied sociology in Berlin, before establishing a law practice in Paris (1922–39). Her first book was a collection of sketches on bourgeois life, *Tropismes* (1939, trans 1964), in which she rejected traditional plot development and characterization to describe a world between the real and the imaginary. She developed her theories further in her later novels: *Portrait d'un Inconnu* (1948, trans 1958), *Martereau* (1953, trans 1959), *Le Planétarium* (1959, trans 1960), *Les Fruits d'or* (1963, trans 1964), *Entre la vie et la mort* (1968) and *Vous les entendez?* (1972, trans 1973). She has also written plays, *Le Silence*, *Le Mensonge* (1967), *Isma* (1970) and *Elle est là* (1978).

SARSFIELD, Patrick, Earl of Lucan (?1645–1693) Irish soldier, born in Lucan, County Dublin. He joined the English Life Guards, and in 1685 fought against **Monmouth** at Sedgemoor. In 1688 he was defeated at Wincanton, and crossed over to Ireland. Created Earl of Lucan by **James VII and II**, he drove the English out of Sligo, was present at the Boyne (1690) and Aghrim (1691), defended Limerick, and on its capitulation (1691) left Ireland under amnesty and entered the French service in the Irish Brigade. He fought at Steenkirk (1692), and was mortally wounded at Neerwinden.

SARTI, Giuseppe (1729–1802) Italian composer, born in Faenza. He held posts at Copenhagen, Venice, Milan and St Petersburg, and composed a dozen operas, masses and sonatas. **Cherubini** was one of his pupils.

SARTO, Andrea Del properly **d'Agnolo** (1486–1531) Florentine painter of the Renaissance. He got his name, 'del Sarto', from his father's trade of tailor. From 1509 to 1514 he was engaged by the Servites in Florence to paint for their church of the Annunciation a series of frescoes, and a second series was next painted for the Recollets. In 1518, on the invitation of **Francis I**, he went to Paris, returned next year to Italy, with a commission to purchase works of art, but squandered the money and dared not return to France. He died of the plague in Florence. Many of Andrea's most celebrated pictures, such as *Madonna of the Harpies* (1517), are in Florence. He was a rapid worker and accurate draughtsman, displaying a refined feeling for harmonies of colour. His pupils included **Pontormo**, **Rosso** and **Vasari**.

SARTON, George Alfred Leon (1884–1956) Belgian-born American historian of science, born in Ghent. He studied at the university there, and emigrated to the USA in 1915. From his youth he moved steadily to become the dominant figure in the history of science, founding its principal journal, *Isis*, in 1912, and *Osiris* in 1936; his magisterial *Introduction to the History of Science* (3 vols, 1927–48) reaches only to AD 1400. His many other books and articles largely shaped the subject as a separate dicipline; his career was devoted to this, sustained financially by the Carnegie Institution and based at Harvard.

SARTRE, Jean-Paul (1905–80) French philosopher, dramatist and novelist, born in Paris. He studied at the Sorbonne with **Simone de Beauvoir** and taught philosophy at Le Havre, Paris and Berlin (1934–35). He joined the French army in 1939, was a prisoner of war in Germany (1941), and after his release became an active member of the Resistance in Paris. In 1945 he emerged as the leading light of the left-wing, left-bank intellectual life of Paris, but he eventually broke with the communists. In 1946, with Simone de Beauvoir, he founded and edited the avant-garde monthly *Les Temps modernes*. A disciple of **Heidegger**, he developed his own characteristic existentialist doctrines, derived from an early anarchistic tendency, which found full expression in his autobiographical novel *La Nausée* (1938) and in *Le Mur* (1938), a collection of short stories. The Nazi occupation provided the grim background to such plays as *Les Mouches*, a modern version of the Orestes theme, and *Huis clos* (both 1943). *Les Mains sales* (1952), filmed as *Crime Passionel*, movingly portrayed the tragic consequences of a choice to join an extremist party. He became the most prominent exponent of atheistic existentialism. His doctrines are outlined in *L'Existentialisme est un humanisme* (1946; trans 1948) and fully worked out in *L'Être et le néant* (1943, trans as 'Being and Nothingness', 1957). Other notable works include the novels which comprise *Les Chemins de la liberté* (1945–49), the play *Les Séquestrés d'Altona* (1959), and a study of **Flaubert**, *L'Idiot de la famille* (1971). In 1964 he was awarded, but declined to accept, the Nobel prize for literature. In the late 1960s he became closely involved in opposition to American policies in Vietnam, and expressed support for student rebellion in 1968.

SASSAU-NGUESSO, Denis (1943–) Congolese soldier and politician. A member of the left-wing Congolese Labour party (PCT), he became president of the Congo in 1979, two years after the former president, Marien Ngouabi, had been assassinated in a coup led by Colonel Yhombi-Opango. He, in turn, fearing another coup, handed over power to the central committee of the PCT, resulting in Sassau-Nguesso's accession. Since assuming office he has loosened his country's ties with the Soviet Union and strengthened them with France and the USA. He has also consolidated his own power and was re-elected in 1984.

SASSETTA, originally **Stefano do Giovanni** (c.1392–1450) Italian painter, born in Siena. Though trained in the rather backward-looking late 14th-century Sienese manner, he was receptive to the diverse contemporary developments of both the courtly International Gothic style and the Florentine Early Renaissance. These influences he blended into a unique, highly inventive style, full of narrative interest though never truly concerned with naturalism. His finest work was the altarpiece of St Francis (1437–44), painted for San Francesco, Borgo San Sepolcro, but now dispersed; some of the finest predella panels are in the National Gallery in London.

SASSOON, Siegfried Lorraine (1886–1967) English poet and novelist, born in Kent. His experiences in World War I formed in him a hatred of war, fiercely expressed in his *Counterattack* (1918) and *Satirical Poems* (1926). A semi-fictitious autobiography, *The Complete Memoirs of George Sherston* (1937),started with *Memoirs of a Fox-Hunting Man* (1928; Hawthornden prize 1929), and continued in *Memoirs of an Infantry Officer* (1930) and *Sherston's Progress* (1936). Truly autobiographical are *The Old Century* (1938), *The Weald of Youth* (1942) and *Siegfried's Journey 1916–20* (1945). He became a Roman Catholic in 1957.

SATIE, Erik Alfred Leslie (1866–1925) French composer, born in Honfleur of French-Scottish parents. After working as a café composer, he studied under **Vincent D'Indy** and **Albert Roussel**. In his own work (ballets, lyric dramas, whimsical pieces) he was in violent revolt against Wagnerism and orthodoxy in general, and had some influence on **Debussy**, **Ravel** and others.

SAUD IBN See **IBN SAUD**

SAUER, Carl Ortwin (1889–1975) American geographer, born in Warrenton, Missouri. Educated at Northwestern University and at Chicago, he became professor of the department of geology and geography at Michigan (1915–22) and made vital and practical contributions to the improved use of land in Michigan State. He was professor of geography at the University of California, Berkeley (1923–54), researching the historical geography of Latin America and the relationships between human societies and plants. He had a major impact on the growth of geography in the USA. He held various government posts from 1910, and was president of the Association of American Geographers in 1940.

SAUL (11th century BC) Old Testament ruler, a Benjamite, the son of Kish, the first king elected by the Israelites. He conquered the Philistines, Ammonites and Amalekites, but became madly jealous of **David**, his son-in-law, and was ultimately at feud with the priestly class. At length **Samuel** secretly anointed David king. Saul fell in battle with the Philistines at Mount Gilboa.

SAUMAISE See **SALMASIUS**

SAUMAREZ, James, 1st Baron de (1757–1836) British naval commander, born in Guernsey. He served in the navy during the American war (1774–82), and distinguished himself in the 3rd Dutch War. He fought at L'Orient (1795) and Cape St Vincent (1797), and was second in command at the battle of the Nile (1798). In 1801, as vice-admiral, he fought his greatest action, off Cadiz, defeating fourteen French-Spanish ships with six. He commanded the British Baltic fleet sent to assist the Swedes from 1809 to 1813. He was promoted admiral in 1814, and subsequently commanded at Plymouth (1824–27).

SAUNDER, Nicholas See **SANDERS**

SAUNDERS, Dame Cicely Mary Strode (1918–) English founder of the modern hospice movement, born in Barnet, Greater London. She was educated at Roedean School and St Anne's College, Oxford, and trained at St Thomas's Hospital Medical School and the Nightingale School of Nursing. Founder (1967), medical director (1967–85) and chairman (1985–) of St Christopher's Hospice, Sydenham, she promotes the principles of dying with dignity, maintaining that death is not a medical failure but a natural part of living and that its quality can be enhanced by sensitive nursing and effective pain-control. She has received many awards for her pioneering work, including the Templeton prize (1981) and the BMA gold medal (1987). She has written and edited a number of books, including *Care of the Dying* (1960), *The Management of Terminal Disease* (1978), *Hospice: The Living Idea* (1981), *Living With Dying* (1983) and *St Christopher's in Celebration* (1988).

SAUNDERS, Howard (1835–1907) English ornithologist, born in London. He became a merchant banker and travelled widely, to Brazil and Chile (1855–62), Spain (1883–84), Switzerland (1891) and France (1893). He became a world-renowned authority on gulls and terns, and compiled a popular *Illustrated Manual of British Birds* (1889).

SAUSSURE, Ferdinand de (1857–1913) Swiss linguist, born in Geneva, often described as the founder of modern linguistics. In 1878 he published his *Mémoire sur le système primitif des voyelles dans les langues indo-europées*. He was appointed professor of Indo-European linguistics and Sanskrit at the University of Geneva in 1901, and also professor of general linguistics in 1907. His lectures on general linguistics showed his dissatisfaction with the theoretical foundations of linguistics as then practised, and constituted the first serious attempt to determine the nature of the object of which linguistics is the study. His *Course in General Linguistics* (1916; 5th ed 1955; English translation by Baskin, 1959) was compiled by two of his students after his death, mainly from lecture notes. Saussure regarded language as a social phenomenon, and favoured the type of investigation which looks for an underlying system; as well as introducing the important dichotomy of *langue* (the system of language, language as a structured system of signs) and *parole* (actual speech, the speech acts that are made possible by the *langue*), he pointed out that language can be viewed descriptively (synchronically) or historically (diachronically). His methodology inspired a great deal of the later work done by semiologists and structuralists.

SAUSSURE, Horace Benédict de (1740–99) Swiss physicist and geologist, born at Conches near Geneva. Professor of physics and philosophy at Geneva (1762–88), he travelled in Germany, Italy and England, and crossed the Alps by several routes. He was the first traveller (not a guide) to ascend Mont Blanc (1787). A pioneer in the study of mineralogy, botany, geology and meteorology, his invaluable observations are recorded in his *Voyages dans les Alpes* (1779–96). He devised the hair hygrometer and other instruments and published an *Essai sur l'hygrométrie* (1783). The mineral saussurite is named after him and it was he who introduced the word *geology* into scientific nomenclature.

SAUSSURE, Nicolas Théodore (1767–1845) Swiss botanist, son of **Horace Saussure**. He wrote *Recherches chimiques sur la végétation* (1804), which contains valuable discoveries about the growth of plants.

SAVAGE, Michael Joseph (1872–1940) New Zealand politician, born in Australia. In 1907 he emigrated to the South Island of New Zealand, where he became a moderate trade unionist. He later moved into politics, and helped to found the Labour party in 1916. He was elected to parliament in 1919 and in 1933 became leader of the New Zealand Labour party. By cultivating the support of rural interests he secured a win for his party in the November 1935 general election, thus becoming the country's first Labour prime minister. His popularity grew and he was re-elected in 1938 but died in office two years later, to be succeeded by **Peter Fraser**.

SAVAGE, Richard (?1697–1743) English poet, claimed to be the illegitimate child of Richard Savage, fourth and last Earl Rivers, and the countess of Macclesfield. In the dedication to his comedy *Love in a Veil* (1718) he asserted the parentage, but in Curll's *Poetical Register* (1719) the story is for the first time fully given. **Aaron Hill** befriended him, and in 1724 published in *The Plain Dealer* an outline of his story which brought subscribers for his *Miscellanies* (1726). In 1727 he killed a gentleman in a tavern brawl, and narrowly escaped the gallows. His attacks upon his alleged mother (now Mrs Brett) became louder and more bitter in his poem *The Bastard* (1728). *The Wanderer* (1729) was dedicated to Lord Tyrconnel, nephew of Mrs Brett, who had befriended him. Savage led a dissipated life and the queen's pension (1732) of £50 for a birthday ode was squandered in a week's debauchery. On Queen **Caroline**'s death (1737) **Pope** tried to help him, but after about a year he went to Bristol, was jailed for debt, and died there. He wrote a comedy, *Love in a Veil* (1718), and *The Tragedy of Sir Thomas Overbury* (1723), and at least one notable poem, *The Wanderer* (1729). He owes his reputation mainly to **Samuel Johnson**, who wrote what is perhaps the most perfect Life in English literature, though it was later discredited.

SAVARIN See **BRILLAT-SAVARIN**

SAVART, Félix (1791–1841) French physician and physicist, born in Mézières in the Ardennes. He taught physics in Paris, and invented *Savart's wheel* for measuring tonal vibrations, and the *Savart quartz plate* for studying the polarization of light. With **Jean Baptiste Biot** he discovered the law (named after them) governing the force in a magnetic field round a long straight current.

SAVARY, Anne Jean Marie René, Duc de Rovigo (1774–1833) French soldier, born in Marcq in Ardennes. In 1800 he became aide-de-camp to **Napoleon**, who employed him in diplomatic affairs as chief of his secret police. In 1804 he presided at the execution of the Duc **d'Enghien**, and in the wars of 1806–08 distinguished himself at Jena and Ostroteka. Now Duke of Rovigo (1808), he was sent to Spain, and negotiated the kidnapping of the Spanish king and his son. From 1810 to 1814 he was minister of police. After Napoleon's fall he wished to accompany him to St Helena, but was confined at Malta. He escaped and in 1819 was reinstated in his honours. From 1831 to 1833 he was commander-in-chief in Algeria.

SAVERY, Thomas (c.1650–1715) English inventor and military engineer. In 1696 he patented an invention for rowing vessels by means of paddle-wheels, and in 1698 he patented the first practical high-pressure steam engine for pumping water from mines; it was superseded in 1712 by the much improved version designed in partnership with **Thomas Newcomen**.

SAVI, Paolo (1798–1871) Italian naturalist and zoologist, born in Pisa. He studied physics and natural science at Pisa, and soon became professor of natural history (zoology from 1840) at Pisa University, and also director of the Pisa Museum. He extended the museum considerably, and became a senator in 1862. His great work, *Ornitologia Italiana*, was published posthumously (1873–76). Savi's Warbler is named after him.

SAVIGNY, Friedrich Karl von (1779–1861) German jurist, born in Frankfurt of an Alsatian family. In 1803 he became a law professor at Marburg, and published a treatise on the Roman law of possession that won him European fame. In 1808 he was called to Landshut and in 1810 to Berlin, where he was (1810–42) a member of the commission for revising the code of Prussia. He resigned office in 1848. He attacked the call for a German Civil Code and was leader of the historical school of jurists, contending that law evolved from the spirit of a people and was not made for them. His greatest books were his *Roman Law in the Middle Ages* (1815–31), and *System of Roman Law* (1840–49), with its continuation in *Obligations* (1851–53). All are still of great value.

SAVILE, George See **HALIFAX, 1st Marquis of**

SAVILE, Sir Henry (1549–1622) English scholar and courtier, born in Bradley, near Halifax. Educated at Brasenose College, Oxford, he became a fellow of Merton College, Oxford, and was later appointed warden of Merton (1585) and also provost of Eton (1596). In 1578 he visited the centres of European learning to meet students of astronomy and mathematics. On his return to England he became Latin secretary and tutor in Greek to Queen **Elizabeth**, and later he was one of the scholars appointed by King **James VI and I** to prepare the Authorized Version of the Bible. He translated part of the histories of **Tacitus** (1591) and the *Cyropaedia* of **Xenophon**. He also published the first edition of **St John Chrysostom** (1610–13). He helped Sir **Thomas Bodley** in the founding of the Bodleian library, and in 1619 he founded the Savilian chairs of mathematics and astronomy at Oxford.

SAVILE, Jimmy (James Wilson Vincent) (1926–) English broadcaster and charity worker, born in Leeds. A miner and ballroom manager with Mecca, he became a radio disc-jockey and television personality, with regular appearances on *Top of the Pops* (1963–). An ebullient figure with a shock of platinum blonde hair and an ostentatious lifestyle, he has used his celebrity status to work tirelessly for worthwhile causes, raising £10 million to construct a National Spinal Injuries Centre at Stoke Mandeville Hospital, acting as a voluntary helper at Leeds Infirmary and Broadmoor Hospital and running countless fund-raising marathons. On television he has campaigned for car safety and, since 1975, hosted *Jim'll Fix It*, helping to realise the dreams of ordinary people. He has written several books, including *As It Happens* (1975) and *Love Is An Uphill Struggle* (1976).

SAVIMBI, Jonas (1934–) Angolan soldier and revolutionary. Educated at Lausanne University, he moved to Lusaka and was active in the struggle for independence from Portugal which developed, in 1961, into a civil war. The People's Movement for the Liberation of Angola (MPLA), led by Agostinho Neto, and supported by socialist and communist states, including Cuba, eventually triumphed, and in 1975 Neto became the new country's first president. Meanwhile, in 1966, Savimbi had formed the National Union for the Total Independence of Angola (UNITA) which, even after independence had been won, continued its fight against MPLA, with the assistance of South Africa. By 1988 South Africa was clearly seeking an end to the hostilities and in 1989 a ceasefire between UNITA and MPLA was agreed.

SAVONAROLA, Girolamo (1452–98) Italian religious and political reformer, born of a noble family in Ferrara. In 1474 he entered the Dominican order at Bologna. He seems to have preached in 1482 in Florence; but his first trial was a failure. In a convent at Brescia his zeal won attention, and in 1489 he was recalled to Florence. His second appearance in the pulpit of San Marco—on the sinfulness and apostasy of the time—was a great popular triumph; and by some he was hailed as an inspired prophet. Under **Lorenzo de' Medici, the Magnificent** art and literature had felt the humanist revival of the 15th century, whose spirit was utterly at variance with Savonarola's conception of spirituality and Christian morality. To the adherents of the Medici therefore, Savonarola early became an object of suspicion, but until the death of Lorenzo (1492) his relations with the church were at least not antagonistic; and when, in 1493, a reform of the Dominican order in Tuscany was proposed under his auspices, it was approved by the pope, and Savonarola was named the first vicar-general. But now his preaching began to point plainly to a political revolution as the divinely-ordained means for the regeneration of religion and morality, and he predicted the advent of the French under **Charles VIII**, whom he soon afterwards welcomed to Florence. Soon, however, the French were compelled to leave Florence, and a republic was established, of which Savonarola became the guiding spirit, his party ('the Weepers') being completely in the ascendant. Now the puritan of Catholicism displayed to the full his extraordinary genius and the extravagance of his theories. The republic of Florence was to be a Christian commonwealth, of which God was the sole sovereign, and His Gospel the law; the most stringent enactments were made for the repression of vice and frivolity; gambling was prohibited; the vanities of dress were restrained by sumptuary laws. Even the vainest flocked to the public square to fling down their costliest ornaments, and Savonarola's followers made a huge 'bonfire of vanities'. Meanwhile his rigorism and his claim to the gift of prophecy led to his being cited in 1495 to answer a charge of heresy in Rome, and on his failing to appear he was forbidden to preach. Savonarola disregarded the order, but his difficulties at home increased. The new system proved impracticable and although the conspiracy for the recall of the Medici failed, and five of the conspirators were executed, this very rigour hastened the reaction. In 1497 came a sentence of excommunication from Rome; and thus precluded from administering the sacred offices, Savonarola zealously tended the sick monks during the plague. A second 'bonfire of vanities' in 1498 led to riots; and at the new elections the Medici party came into power. Savonarola was again ordered to desist from preaching, and was fiercely denounced by a Franciscan preacher, Francesco da Puglia. Dominicans and Franciscans appealed to the interposition of divine providence by the ordeal of fire. But when the trial was to have come off (April 1498) difficulties and debates arose, destroying Savonarola's prestige and producing a complete revulsion of public feeling. He was brought to trial for falsely claiming to have seen visions and uttered prophecies, for religious error, and for sedition. Under torture he made avowals which he afterwards withdrew. He was declared guilty and the sentence was confirmed by Rome. On 23 May 1498, this extraordinary man and two Dominican disciples were hanged and burned, still professing their adherence to the Catholic Church. In morals and religion, not in theology, Savonarola may be regarded as a forerunner of the Reformation. His works are mainly sermons, theological treatises, the chief *The Triumph of the Cross*, an apology of orthodox Catholicism, some poems, and a discourse on the government of Florence.

SAVUNDRA, Emil, originally **Michael Marion Emil Anecletus Savundranayagam,** (1923–76) Singalese convicted swindler and fraudster, born in Ceylon (now Sri Lanka). Although from a highly respected family, Savundra, who gave himself the title of 'Doctor', was an inveterate conman. Before coming to Britain he perpetrated huge financial swindles in Costa Rica, Goa and Ghana. He also initiated a bogus oil deal in which he sold non-existent oil to the government of Communist China. He was a devout Catholic and in tense moments he would send a cable to a nunnery asking to be remembered in prayers. He donated vast sums of money to the Catholic Church. When he was arrested in Britain on charges of forgery in 1954, he had the first of many convenient, but generally considered genuine, heart-attacks. He was extradited to Belgium and tried in January 1956, and was found guilty. An appeal in July confirmed his sentence of five years' imprisonment. However, a Catholic cardinal interceded for him, and he was released on grounds of ill-health. He is best known in Britain for his lavish and flamboyant lifestyle and for the crash of his Fire, Auto and Marine Insurance company which left 400 000 British motorists without insurance cover in 1966. He disappeared but was traced by the Fraud Squad. In an attempt to defend his actions he made a famous television appearance on 'The Frost Programme' which was later described as 'trial by television'. He was arrested in February 1967, was found guilty in March 1968 and sentenced to eight years' imprisonment. He was freed in October 1974.

SAX, Antoine Joseph, known as **Adolphe** (1814–94), Belgian musician and inventor, born in Dinant, the son of a Brussels musical instrument maker. With his father he invented (patented 1845) a valved brass wind-instrument he called the sax-horn, also the saxophone, the saxtromba and the sax-tuba. He moved to Paris to promote his inventions, and was an instructor at the Paris Conservatoire, but failed to make his expected fortune despite the encouragement of **Berlioz** and other musicians.

SAXE, Maurice, Comte de (1696–1750) usually called **Marshal de Saxe**, French soldier, born in Goslar, the illegitimate son of **Augustus II**, Elector of Saxony and king of Poland, and Countess Aurora von Königsmark. At 12 he ran off to join the army of **Marlborough** under **Eugene of Savoy** in Flanders, and next the Russo-Polish army before Stralsund (1711). He fought against the Turks in Hungary under Prince Eugene, and studied the art of war in France. In 1726, elected Duke of Courland, he maintained himself against Russians and Poles, but was compelled to retire in 1729. In the War of the Polish Succession (1733–38) he opposed his half-brother Augustus III, and took a brilliant part in the siege of Philippsburg (1734). In the War of the Austrian Succession (1740–48) he invaded Bohemia and took Prague by storm (1741). In 1744, now marshal of France, he commanded the French army in Flanders, showed splendid tactical skill, and took several fortresses. In 1745 he defeated the Duke of

Cumberland at Fontenoy. In 1746 he gained the victory at Raucoux, and was made marshal-general. For the third time, at Laffeld (July 1747), he defeated Cumberland and captured Bergen-op-Zoom. He then retired to his estate of Chambord. His treatise on the art of war, *Mes Rêveries*, was published in 1751.

SAXE-COBURG-GOTHA, Alfred Ernes Albert, Prince of (1844–1900) British prince, second son of Queen **Victoria**, born in Windsor Castle. He studied at Bonn and Edinburgh before entering the royal navy in 1858. He was elected king of Greece in 1862, but declined the dignity. In 1866 he was created Duke of Edinburgh and in 1874 married the Russian Grand Duchess Marie Alexandrovna (1853–1920). In 1893 he succeeded his uncle as reigning Duke of Saxe-Coburg-Gotha.

SAXO GRAMMATICUS, 'the Scholar' (c.1150–c.1220) Danish chronicler, born on Zealand. Secretary or clerk to Bishop **Absalon** of Roskilde, he compiled a monumental *Gesta Danorum*, a Latin history of legendary and historical kings of Denmark down to 1186, in 16 volumes (probably written 1185–1216). Acclaimed as the first national historian of Denmark, his work has great scope and imaginative power as an interpretation of ancient legendary lore.

SAXTON, Christopher (1542 or 1544–c.1611) English surveyor and cartographer, probably born in Sowood, Yorkshire. He was possibly educated at Cambridge University and, in cartography, by John Rudd, Vicar of Dewsbury. He was commissioned by Queen **Elizabeth** to carry out the first survey of all the counties of England and Wales and worked under the patronage of Thomas Seckford, Master of the Queen's Requests. His atlas (1579) was the first national atlas of any country. He also published a wall map of England and Wales (1583). This record and legacy has led modern writers to name him 'the father of English cartography'.

SAY, Jean Baptiste (1767–1832) French political economist, born in Lyon. He passed part of his youth in England. On the outbreak of the Revolution he was secretary to the minister of finance. From 1794 to 1800 he edited *La Décade*, and in it expounded the views of **Adam Smith**. A member of the tribunate in 1799, he resigned in 1804 in protest against the arbitrary tendencies of the consular government. In 1803 he issued his *Traité d'économie politique*. He operated a cotton mill from 1807 to 1813, and in 1814 the government sent him to England to study its economics. From 1817 he lectured on political economy at the Conservatoire des Arts et Métiers, and in 1831 became professor at the Collège de France. As a disciple of Adam Smith and through his own writings his influence on French economics of the first half of the 19th century was of the greatest importance.

SAY, Thomas (1787–1834) American naturalist and entomologist, born in Philadelphia. He made expeditions to the Rocky Mountains, Minnesota, Florida, Georgia and Mexico (1818–29), and was the author of *American Entomology* (1824–28). Curator of the American Philosophical Society (1821–27) and professor at Pennsylvania (1822–28), he eloped with a young girl to **Robert Owen**'s Utopian settlement at New Harmony, Indiana, in 1824; she made the illustrations for his *American Conchology* (1830–34).

SAYCE, Archibald Henry (1845–1933) English philologist, born in Shirehampton near Bristol. Educated at Grosvenor College, Bath, and Queen's College, Oxford (where he read classics), he became professor of Assyriology at Oxford (1891–1919). A member of the Old Testament Revision Company, he wrote on biblical criticism and Assyriology, including an *Assyrian Grammar* (1872), *Principles of Comparative Philology* (1874–75), *The Monuments of the Hittites* (1881), and *The Early History of the Hebrews* (1897).

SAYERS, Dorothy L (Leigh) (1893–1957) English detective-story writer, born in Oxford. Educated at the Godolphin School, Salisbury, and Somerville College, Oxford (a first in modern languages), she taught for a year and then worked in an advertising agency until 1931. In 1924 she had an illegitimate son, and in 1926 married Captain Oswald Fleming. Her novels are distinguished by taste and style. Beginning with *Whose Body?* (1923) and *Clouds of Witness* (1926), she told the adventures of her hero Lord Peter Wimsey in various accurately observed milieux—such as advertising in *Murder Must Advertise* (1933) or campanology in *The Nine Tailors* (1934). Her other stories included *Strong Poison* (1930), *Gaudy Night* (1935), *Busman's Honeymoon* (1937) and *In the Teeth of the Evidence* (1939). She earned a reputation as a leading Christian apologist with two successful plays, *The Zeal of Thy House* (1937) and *The Devil to Pay* (1939), a series for broadcasting (*The Man Born to be King*, 1943) and a closely reasoned essay (*The Mind of the Maker*, 1941). A translation of **Dante**'s *Inferno* appeared in 1949 and of *Purgatorio* in 1955. The *Paradiso* was left unfinished at her death.

SAYERS, Gale (1943–) American football player and star running back with the Chicago Bears from 1965 to 1972, born in Wichita, Kansas. The holder of numerous records, he was elected to the sport's Hall of Fame in 1977. He once scored 6 touchdowns in a single game (12 December 1965). After retiring from the sport, he coached and also went into business as a computer company executive.

SAYERS, James (1912–) English physicist, a member of the British team associated with the atomic bomb project. He became professor of electron physics at Birmingham (1946) and in 1949 was given a government award for his work on the cavity magnetron valve, which was of great importance in the development of radar.

SAYERS, Peig (1873–1958) Irish Gaelic story-teller, born in Dunquin, County Kerry, among purely Irish-speaking neighbours. She lived most of her life on the Great Blasket Island. The disappearance of the Irish language from most of Ireland made her powers of recollection and her hold on traditional narratives deeply respected by scholars. Her prose, as recorded in *Peig* (edited by Máire Ní Chinnéide, 1936) and *Machtnamh Sean-Mná* (1939, translated as *An Old Woman's Reflections*, 1962), is straightforward and clear, with decided authority and a touch of complacency.

SAYERS, Tom (1826–65) English pugilist, known as the 'Napoleon of the Prize Ring'. Born in Pimlico, he became a bricklayer before taking up boxing in 1849. He became English heavyweight champion in 1857 despite weighing only 11 stone, which would be normal for a middleweight. Throughout his career he lost only one fight. His last and most famous contest was with the American champion John Heenan, the 'Benicia Boy', for the first world championship title; the fight lasted 2 hours and 6 minutes, and was declared a draw after 42 rounds.

SA'ADIA, Ben Joseph (882–942) Jewish philosopher, polemicist and scholar, born in Dilaz in al-Fayyum, Egypt. He left Egypt in about 905 and after a period in Palestine settled eventually in Babylonia, where he became *gaon* (head) of the rabbinic Academy of Sura in two periods of tenure (928–35, 937–42) separated by a brief spell in which he was excommunicated after various personal and political struggles by the head of

Babylonian Jewry, David ben Zakkai. He was one of the most important medieval Jewish thinkers and produced a Hebrew-Arabic dictionary, translated much of the Old Testament into Arabic, and wrote treatises on Talmudic law, religious poetry and a major philosophical work, the *Book of Beliefs and Opinions* (935), a rationalistic study in theology which became a basic Jewish text.

SCALA, Della See **SCALIGER, Julius Caesar**

SCALIGER, Joseph Justus (1540–1609) French scholar, son of **Julius Caesar Scaliger**, born in Agen. After studying at Bordeaux, with his father, and in Paris, he acquired a surpassing mastery of the classics and eventually boasted that he spoke 13 languages, ancient and modern. While in Paris he became a Calvinist (1562) and later visited Italy, England and Scotland, only the last of which seems to have appealed to him, especially through the beauty of its ballads. In 1570 he settled at Valence and for two years studied under the jurist **Cujacius**. From 1572 to 1574 he was professor at Calvin's College at Geneva. He then spent 20 years in France and there produced works which placed him at the head of European scholars. Among them are his editions of **Catullus**, **Tibullus**, **Propertius** and **Eusebius**. By his edition of Manilius and his *Opus De Emendatione Temporum* (1583) he founded modern chronology. From 1593 he held a chair at Leiden and to his inspiration Holland owes her long line of scholars. His last years were embittered by controversy, especially with the Jesuits, who charged him with atheism and profligacy. By his combined knowledge, sagacity and actual achievement he holds the first place among the scholars of his time.

SCALIGER, Julius Caesar, originally probably **Benedetto Bordone** (1484–1558) Italian-born French scholar and physicist, the son of a sign-painter. He claimed descent from the princely della Scala family of Verona, and that he was brought up a soldier under his kinsman the Emperor **Maximilian**, gaining distinction in the French armies attempting the conquest of Italy. He changed his name to Scaliger, and graduated in medicine at Padua. He became a French citizen in 1528 and settled at Agen, where he produced learned works on Latin grammar, on **Theophrastus**, **Aristotle** and **Hippocrates**. His poems of invective, as in his attack on **Erasmus**, were considerable.

SCANDERBEG See **SKANDERBEG**

SCARFE, Gerald (1936–) English cartoonist, caricaturist and animator, born in London. His first cartoon, drawn as a schoolboy, was published in *Eagle* comic (1952). He studied art at St Martin's School, London and freelanced cartoons to the *Daily Sketch* and *Punch*. As a cruel ugliness began to appear in his work, he found a home in the satirical *Private Eye*, where the first of several bannings occurred when newsagents refused to display his *Annual* cover of **Harold Macmillan**. *The Sunday Times* refused to publish his commissioned caricature of **Winston Churchill**. His work met with more approval in the American magazines *Life* and *Esquire*, but America so disgusted him he animated a savage computerized cartoon for television. He designed the animated sequences for the film, *Pink Floyd: The Wall* (1982).

SCARGILL, Arthur (1938–) English trade union leader. Educated at primary and secondary schools in Yorkshire, he entered the mining industry at the age of 18 and was soon involved in politics, joining the Young Communist League (1955–62), the Co-operative party in 1963, and the Labour party in 1966. He was also active in the National Union of Mineworkers (NUM), becoming a Yorkshire branch committee member in 1960 and area president in 1973. He steadily established himself as a striking orator and in 1981 became national president. Warning his members of the threat of massive pit closures, in 1984 he led them into a national strike. Its collapse ten months later raised doubts about his leadership tactics, but his predictions of pit closures and job losses proved to be correct.

SCARLATTI, Alessandro (1659–1725) Italian composer, born in Palermo, Sicily. His musical career began in Rome, where in 1680 he produced his first opera. This gained him the patronage of Queen **Kristina** of Sweden, whose *maestro di cappella* he became. A few years later he went to Naples, where he was musical director at the court (1693–1703) and conducted the conservatory there. He was the founder of the Neapolitan school of opera. He wrote nearly 120 operas; about 70 of these survive, the most famous being *Tigrane* (1715). He also wrote 200 masses, 10 oratorios, 500 cantatas and many motets and madrigals.

SCARLATTI, (Giuseppe) Domenico (1685–1757) Italian composer, founder of the modern piano technique, son of **Alessandro Scarlatti**, born in Naples. In Rome (1709) he was official composer to the queen of Poland, for whom he composed several operas. In Lisbon (1720) he served the king, taught the Infanta Barbara, and in 1729 went to the Spanish court in Madrid. He was also (1714–19) choirmaster of St Peter's, Rome, and wrote much church music. He was a skilled performer on the harpsichord, beating **Handel** in a competition on the instrument, and it is as a writer of brilliant harpsichord sonatas that he is best remembered. He wrote over 600, and his work had an important effect on the development of the sonata form.

SCARLETT, James, Baron Abinger (1769–1844) English lawyer and statesman, born in Jamaica. He studied at Trinity College, Cambridge, took silk in 1816, and in 1819 became Whig MP for Peterborough. He was made attorney-general by **Cannning**, and in 1834, by then lord chief baron of the Exchequer, was created Baron Abinger.

SCARLETT, Sir James Yorke (1799–1871) English soldier, second son of **James Scarlett**, Baron Abinger. Educated at Eton and Trinity College, Cambridge, he commanded the 5th Dragoon Guards (1840–53), and in October 1854, led the heavy cavalry in the charge at Balaclava after the disastrous charge of the Light Brigade. He subsequently commanded all the cavalry in the Crimea, and from 1865 to 1870 commanded at Aldershot.

SCARRON, Paul (1610–60) French writer, born in Paris, the son of a lawyer. He became an *abbé*, and gave himself up to pleasure. About 1634 he paid a long visit to Italy, and in 1638 began to suffer from a malady which ultimately left him paralysed. He obtained a prebend in Mans (1643), tried physicians in vain, and, giving up all hope of remedy, returned to Paris in 1646 to depend upon letters for a living. From this time he began to pour forth endless sonnets, madrigals, songs, epistles and satires. In 1644 he published *Typhon, ou la giganto-machie*; and made a still greater hit with his metrical comedy, *Jodelet, ou le maître valet* (1645), followed by *Les Trois Dorothées* and *Les Boutades du Capitan Matamore* (the plots taken from the Spanish). In 1648 appeared his *Virgile travesti* (part one) and the popular comedy, *L'Héritier ridicule*. One of the bitterest satires against **Mazarin** which he wrote for the *Fronde* probably lost him his pensions. The burlesque predominates in most of his writing, but it is as the creator of the realistic novel that he will always be remembered. *Le Roman comique* (1651–57) was a reaction against the euphuistic and interminable novels of **Madeleine de Scudéry** and **Honoré d'Urfé**. The work of **Le Sage**, **Defoe**, **Fielding** and **Smollett** owes much to him. In 1652 he married Françoise d'Aubigné, afterwards Madame **de Maintenon**, who brought an unknown decorum into his household and writings.

SCARRY, Richard McClure (1919–) American illustrator and writer of children's books, born in Boston. He was educated at Boston Museum School of Fine Arts and served in the US army in the Mediterranean and North Africa. Didactic, detailed and scatty, his output is prolific and he is hugely popular with children tolerant of his formulaic approach. Indicative titles are *What Do People Do All Day?* (1968) and *Hop Aboard, Here We Go!* (1972).

SCÈVE, Maurice (1510–64) French renaissance poet, born in Lyons. He was a leader of the *école lyonnaise*, which paved the way for the *Pléiade* (see **Ronsard**).

SCHACHT, Hjalmar Horace Greely (1877–1970) German financier, born of Danish descent in Tinglev, North Schleswig. He was brought up in New York, where his father was a merchant. In 1923 he became president of the Reichsbank, and founded a new currency which ended the inflation of the mark. He resigned in 1929, was called back by the Nazis in 1933, and the following year, as minister of economics, he restored the German trade balance by unorthodox methods and by undertaking an expansionist credit policy. He resigned his post in 1937, and in 1939 was dismissed from his office as president of the Reichsbank because of his disagreement with **Hitler** over the latter's rearmament expenditure. Charged with high treason and interned by the Nazis, in 1945 he was acquitted by the Allies at Nuremberg of crimes against humanity, and was finally cleared by the German de-Nazification courts in 1948. In 1952 he advised Dr **Mossadegh** on Persia's economic problems, and in 1953 set up his own bank in Düsseldorf.

SCHADOW, Friedrich Wilhelm von (1788–1862) German artist, born in Berlin, younger son of **Johann Gottfried Schadow**. A painter of the Overbeck school, from 1819 he was professor at Berlin, and from 1826 to 1859 head of the Düsseldorf Academy. He changed his name to Schadow-Godenhaus.

SCHADOW, Johann Gottfried (1764–1850) Prussian sculptor, born in Berlin. He became court sculptor in 1788 and director of the Academy of Arts in Berlin from 1816. He executed many public monuments, including the *Quadriga of Victory* for the Brandenburg Gate (1793).

SCHADOW, Rudolf (1786–1822) Prussian sculptor, born in Berlin, son of **Johann Gottfried Schadow**. He executed *Spinning Girl* and the *Daughters of Leucippos* at Chatsworth.

SCHAEFER, Vincent Joseph (1906–) American physicist, born in Schenectady, New York. He graduated from the Davey Institute of Tree Surgery in 1928, and went as assistant to **Irving Langmuir** at the research laboratories of the General Electric Company. He became director of research at the Munitalp Foundation in 1954, and professor of physics at the State University of New York, Albany, in 1959. During World War II he worked on the problem of icing on aeroplane wings, which led him in 1946 to demonstrate for the first time the possibility of inducing rainfall by seeding clouds with dry ice (solid CO_2).

SCHAFER, Sir Edward Sharpey- See **SHARPEY-SCHAFER**

SCHAFF, Philip (1819–93) Swiss-born American Presbyterian theologian, born in Coire. He was *privatdozent* in Berlin, when in 1844 he was called to a chair at the German Reformed seminary at Mercersburg, Pennsylvania. In 1870 he became professor at the Union Seminary, New York. A founder of the American branch of the Evangelical Alliance, he was president of the American Old Testament Revision Committee. Among his works are a *History of the Christian Church* (1883–93) and *The Creeds of Christendom* (1877).

SCHALL, Johann Adam von (1591–1669) German Jesuit missionary and astronomer, born in Cologne. He was sent out to China as a missionary in 1622, and at Peking was entrusted with the reformation of the Chinese calendar and the direction of the mathematical school. By favour of the Manchu emperor the Jesuits obtained liberty to build churches (1644), and in 14 years they are said to have made 100 000 converts. But in the next reign Schall was accused of plotting against the emperor (1664) and thrown into prison, where he died. A large MS collection of his Chinese writings is preserved in the Vatican. He wrote a Latin history of the China Mission (1655).

SCHALLY, Andrew Victor (1926–) Polish-born American biochemist, joint winner of the 1977 Nobel prize for physiology or medicine. He fled from Poland at the German invasion of 1939 and studied at the National Institute for Medical Research in London and McGill University in Montreal. He worked at the Baylor Medical School (1957–62) and Tulane University (from 1962). He discovered and synthesized the hormones produced by the hypothalamus that control the pituitary gland, and shared the Nobel prize with **Roger Guillemin** and **Rosalyn Yalow**.

SCHAMYL or **SHAMYL** See **SHAMIL**

SCHARNHORST, Gerhard Johann David von (1755–1813) German soldier, the son of a Hanoverian farmer. He fought in Flanders against the French (1793–95), and directed the training-school for Prussian officers (1801). Wounded at Auerstädt and taken prisoner at Lübeck, he was present at Eylau; from 1807 he reorganized the Prussian army, introduced the short-service system and restored morale, so making it possible to defeat **Napoleon** at Leipzig (1813). But before that he died at Prague of a wound received at Grossgörschen.

SCHARWENKA, Xaver (1850–1924) German-Polish pianist and composer, born in Samter near Posen. In 1881 he started a music school in Berlin, and spent the years 1891–98 in New York directing the Scharwenka Music School. He composed symphonies, piano concertos and Polish dances.

SCHAUDINN, Fritz Richard (1871–1906) German zoologist and microbiologist, born in Röseningken, in East Prussia. He studied philology at Berlin, but turned to zoology, and after research work in Berlin he became director of the department of protozoological research, Institute for Tropical Diseases, Hamburg (1904). He demonstrated the amoebic nature of tropical dysentery, and with Erich Hoffmann discovered the *spirochaeta pallida* which causes syphilis (1905).

SCHAUFUSS, Peter (1949–) Danish dancer and director, born in Copenhagen. With a ballet background (his mother and father were both principals with the Royal Danish Ballet) he began his training at the age of seven and made his professional début the same year. In 1964 he moved to Canada to become soloist with the National Ballet of Canada, with whom he danced leading roles in *Don Quixote* and *The Nutcracker*. But he returned home less than two years later and contributed to the first workshop performance at the Royal Danish Ballet. Independent of spirit, he spent the next ten years moving from company to company, eventually becoming a principal with London Festival Ballet in 1970 and spending several seasons (1974–77) with New York City Ballet. In 1984 he was appointed artistic director of London Festival Ballet, where he has fostered a strong commitment to contemporary ballet as well as the classics. The company was renamed English National Ballet in 1989.

SCHAUKAL, Richard (1874–1942) Austrian symbolist poet, born in Brünn. He was in the Austrian civil service, and like **Hofmannsthal** turned away from the decadence of the declining Austrian empire to seek perfection in lyrical expression of poetic dreams in *Verse* (1896), *Tage und Träume* (1899), *Sehnsucht* (1900), and *Spätlese* (1943).

SCHAWLOW, Arthur Leonard (1921–) American physicist, and co-inventor of the laser, born in Mount Vernon, New York. He studied at Toronto and Columbia (1949–51), where he worked with **Charles Townes** and married his sister. He moved to Bell Telephones (1951–61) and became professor of physics at Stanford University in 1961. Townes and Schawlow collaborated to extend the maser principle to light by devising the laser and showed its feasibility and discussed its properties and oscillation theoretically, but **Theodore Maiman** constructed the first working laser in 1960. From the early 1970s Schawlow used laser methods to simplify atomic spectra and to give improved values for basic physical quantities such as the **Rydberg** constant. For his work on laser spectroscopy Schawlo shared the Nobel prize for physics in 1981 with **Nicolas Bloembergen** and Kai Siebahn.

SCHEEL, Walter (1919–) West German statesman, born and educated in Solingen. After serving in the Luftwaffe in World War II he went into business, joined the Free Democratic party (FDP), and was elected to the city council of Solingen in 1948, and to the Bundestag in 1953. In 1958 he became vice-chairman of the Free Democrats and guided their policies closer to the SPD, thus preparing the ground for the coalition of 1969. In 1970 he negotiated treaties with Russia and Poland, regarded as major advances in east-west relations. From 1969 to 1674 he was vice-chancellor and foreign minister, and became president (for five years) of the Federal Republic of Germany in 1974 on the resignation of **Gustav Heinemann**.

SCHEELE, Carl Wilhelm (1742–86) Swedish chemist, born in Stralsund (then Swedish). He was apprenticed to a chemist at Gothenburg, and was afterwards chemist at Malmö, Stockholm, Uppsala and Köping. He discovered hydrofluoric, tartaric, benzoic, arsenious, molybdic, lactic, citric, malic, oxalic, gallic, and other acids, and separated chlorine (1774), baryta, oxygen, glycerine (1783), and sulphuretted hydrogen. He first described the pigment called Scheele's green, or arsenite of copper, and scheelite or tungsten. Independently of **Joseph Priestley**, he showed in 1777 that the atmosphere consists chiefly of two gases, one supporting combustion, the other preventing it. In 1783 he described prussic acid. His papers were translated by Dobbin (1931).

SCHEEMAKERS, Pieter (1691–1770) Belgian sculptor, born in Antwerp. The teacher of **Joseph Nollekens**, he lived in London (1735–69), and executed several monuments and portrait busts, including those of **Shakespeare**, **Mead** and **Dryden** in Westminster Abbey.

SCHEER, Reinhard (1863–1928) German naval commander, born in Hesse-Nassau. He went to sea as a naval cadet in torpedo craft. As vice admiral he commanded the 2nd Battle Squadron of the German High Seas fleet at the outset of World War I. He succeeded as commander in chief in 1916 and was in command at the indecisive battle of Jutland (1916).

SCHEFFEL, Joseph Viktor von (1826–86) German poet and novelist, born in Karlsruhe. He studied law at Heidelberg, Munich and Berlin, but in 1852 went to Italy to write. His best book is *Der Trompeter von Säckingen* (1854), a romantic and humorous tale in verse.

SCHEFFER, Ary (1795–1858) French painter, born in Dordecht, Holland, of a German father. He studied under **Guérin**, and became known for his subject pictures and portraits in the romantic style. **Puvis de Chavannes** was his pupil.

SCHEIDEMANN, Philipp (1865–1939) German socialist political leader. He was minister of finance and colonies in the provisional government of 1918, and first chancellor of the republic in 1919.

SCHELER, Max (1874–1928) German philosopher and social theorist, born in Munich. He taught at the universities of Jena (1900–06), Munich (1907–10), Cologne (1919–27) and Frankfurt (1928). He was much influenced by **Husserl**'s phenomenology, but he developed a distinctive version of it which emphasized the importance of emotions as well as reason in apprehending and ranking values. This is set out in two major works in ethics, *Der Formalismus in der Ethik und die materiale Wertethik* (1913, translated as *Formalism in Ethics and Non-Formal Ethics of Values*, 1973), and *Die Sinngesetze des emotionalen Lebens: Wesen und Formen der Sympathie* (1923, translated as *The Nature of Sympathy*, 1954). He also did influential work in the sociology of knowledge, for example in *Die Wissensformen und die Gesellschaft* (1926, translated as *Problems of a Sociology of Knowledge*, 1979), where he shows how social and economic conditions ('real factors') influence the way in which ideas are historically realized. His *Die Stellung des Menschen im Kosmos* (1928, translated as *Man's Place in Nature*, 1961) is a work of philosophical anthropology with a pantheistic view of how God is realized in history and in the world.

SCHELLING, Friedrich Wilhelm Joseph von (1775–1854) German idealist philosopher, born in Leonberg in Württemberg. He studied at Tübingen and Leipzig, and taught at Jena (1798–1803, as **Fichte**'s successor), Würzburg (1803–08), Munich (until 1820, as secretary of the Royal Academy of Arts), Erlangen (1820–27), Munich again (1827–40), then finally Berlin (1841–46). His early work, influenced by **Kant** and Fichte, culminated in the *Ideen zur einer Philosophie der Natur* (1797), and the *System des transzendentalen Idealismus* (1800), which examined the relation of the self to the objective world and argued that consciousness itself is the only immediate object of knowledge and that only in art can the mind become fully aware of itself. He thus became an important influence on romanticism, associated with the view that art is the condition to which true philosophical reflection should aspire. His later works include *Philosophische Untersuchungen über das Wesen der menschlichen Freiheit* (1809) and *Die Weltalter* (1811).

SCHENKEL, Daniel (1813–85) German Protestant theologian, born in Dägerlen in Zürich. He was professor of theology at Heidelberg from 1851. His *Charakterbild Jesu* (1864) was an attempt to construct the human character of Jesus and entirely eliminate the supernatural.

SCHEPISI, Fred (1939–) Australian film director, born in Melbourne. Originally intending to join the Catholic church, he spent 18 months in a monastery. As a teenager he joined an advertising agency and, by 1966, had bought the company and was making documentaries and commercials. Acquiring a comprehensive knowledge of filmmaking technique, he made a short fictional film *The Party* (1970) and one segment of the multi-part *Libido* (1972). His first major feature, *The Devil's Playground* (1976), reflecting his early experiences with Catholicism, won the Australian Film Institute Award for Best Film, and established him as one of the indigenous industry's most promising talents. After *The Chant of Jimmie Blacksmith* (1978), a true story of racism, he moved to the USA where his fascination for myth and superstition was seen in *Barbarosa* (1982) and *The Iceman* (1984). He enjoyed an international success with the comedy *Roxanne* (1987), whilst *Plenty* (1985) and *A Cry in the Dark* (1988) reveal his continuing concern with issues of class and social injustice.

SCHEUTZ, Edvard Georg Raphael (1821–81) Swedish engineer, born in Stockholm, the son of **Pehr Georg Scheutz**, educated at the Royal Technological Institute, Stockholm. In 1843 he completed the world's first complete Difference Engine (started by his father), and built a second version in 1853. The device mechanized the production of numerical tables, but the limited demand for such machines meant that the Scheutzes were unable to market it successfully

SCHEUTZ, Pehr Georg (1785–1873) Swedish lawyer, publisher, and inventor of a calculating machine. Born in Jönköping, he was educated in law at Lund. In the 1830s he read about **Charles Babbage**'s Difference Engine and then designed his own machine, later completed by his son, **Edvard Scheutz**.

SCHIAPARELLI, Elsa (1890–1973) Italian-born French fashion designer, born in Rome, the daughter of a professor of oriental languages. She studied philosophy and lived in the USA for a time, working as a film script writer. Her husband left her and in 1920 she took her daughter and moved to Paris, where she designed and wore a black sweater knitted with a white bow that gave a *trompe d'œil* effect, as a result of which she received orders from an American store, which started her in business in 1929. Her designs were inventive and sensational, and she was noted for her use of colour, including 'shocking pink', and her original use of traditional fabrics. She featured zippers and buttons, and made outrageous hats. She opened a salon in New York in 1949, and retired in 1954.

SCHIAPARELLI, Giovanni Virginio (1835–1910) Italian astronomer, born in Savigliano, Piedmont. He worked under **FGW Struve** at Pulkova, was head of Brera observatory, Milan, studied meteors and double stars, and discovered the 'canals' of Mars (1877) and the asteroid Hesperia (1861).

SCHICKARD, Wilhelm (1592–1635) German polymath, born in Herrenberg. Educated at the University of Tübingen, he was a pioneer in the construction of calculating machines. His Calculating Clock was designed and built in about 1623, but lay forgotten until the discovery of Schickard's papers allowed its reconstruction in 1960.

SCHICKELE, René (1883–1940) German Alsatian writer, born in Oberehnheim. A journalist by profession, he wrote poems, plays and novels, including the trilogy *Das Erbe am Rhein* (1925–31).

SCHIEFNER, Franz Anton von (1817–79) Russian philologist, born in Reval (now Tallinn), Estonia. He contributed to the study of Tibetan language and literature, of Finnic philology, mythology and ethnology, of the Caucasian languages, and of Samoyedic and Ossetic. He was also responsible for a revision of the New Testament in Mongolian.

SCHIELE, Egon (1890–1918) Austrian painter, born in Tulln. He studied at the Vienna Academy of Art from 1906 to 1909. Much influenced by **Gustav Klimt**, he joined the Wiener Werkstätte, a craft studio which promoted the fashionable Art Nouveau style. He developed a personal form of Expressionism in which figures, often naked and emaciated and drawn with hard outlines, fill the canvas with awkward, anguished gestures. In 1912 he was arrested and some of his work was destroyed by the police. He also painted intense, psychologically disturbing portraits. He died in the influenza epidemic of 1918.

SCHILLEBEECKX, Edward Cornelis Florentius Alfons (1914–) Belgian Dominican theologian, born in Antwerp. Professor of dogmatics and the history of theology at Nijmegen in the Netherlands from 1958 to 1983, his publications have ranged widely across the whole field of theology, from sacraments (*Christ the Sacrament*, 1963), to the presentation of the gospel in contemporary society (*Jesus in our Western Culture*, 1987). Like **Hans Küng**, he has attracted Vatican investigations for questioning received interpretations of doctrine and church order, as in *The Church with a Human Face* (1985), replacing *Ministry* (1981); and *Jesus* (1979) and *Christ* (1980), the first two volumes of a promised trilogy on Christology. He has also published sermons (*God Among Us*, 1983, and *For the Sake of the Gospel*, 1989), and autobiographical interviews, *God is New Each Moment* (1983).

SCHILLER, Ferdinand Canning Scott (1864–1937) English philosopher. He taught at Oxford (1903–26) and the University of Southern California (from 1929). He was a pragmatist, much influenced by his friend **William James**, and a humanist, in the spirit of the Greek philosopher **Protagoras**, as Schiller explained in his major publications *Humanism: Philosophical Essays* (1903) and *Studies in Humanism* (1907).

SCHILLER, Johann Christoph Friedrich von (1759–1805) German dramatist, poet and historian, born in Marbach on the Neckar. His father was an army surgeon in the service of the Duke of Württemberg. He was educated at the grammar school in Ludwigsburg, and was intended for the church, but at the age of 13, at the personal request of the duke, was obliged to attend the latter's military academy, studying the law instead of theology, but finally qualified as a surgeon (1780) and was posted to a regiment in Stuttgart. Although outwardly conforming well, he found an outlet for his true feelings in the reading and eventually writing of *Sturm und Drang* verse and plays. His first play, *Die Räuber* (1781), published at his own expense, was, on account of its seemingly anarchical and revolutionary appeal, an instant success when it reached the stage at Mannheim the following year. Schiller played truant from his regiment to attend the performance, was arrested but, forbidden to write anything but medical works in the future, fled and, in hiding at Bauerbach, finished the plays, *Fiesko* and *Kabale und Liebe* (1783). For a few months he was dramatist to the Mannheim theatre. He next issued a theatrical journal, *Die rheinische Thalia*, begun in 1784, in which were first printed most of his *Don Carlos*, many of his best poems, and the stories *Verbrecher aus verlorener Ehre* and *Der Geisterseher*. In 1785 he went by invitation to Leipzig and in Dresden, where **Karl Theodor Körner** was living, he found rest from emotional excitement and financial worries. Here he finished *Don Carlos* (1787), written in blank verse, not prose, his first mature play, though it suffers artistically from excessive length and lack of unity. Amongst the finest fruits of his discussions with Körner and his circle are the poems *An die Freude*, later magnificently set to music by **Beethoven** in his choral symphony, and *Die Künstler*. After two years in Dresden and an unhappy love affair he went to Weimar, where he studied **Kant**, met his future wife,

Charlotte von Lengefeld, and began his history of the revolt of the Netherlands. In 1788 he was appointed honorary professor of history at Jena, and married, but his health broke down due to overwork from writing a history of the Thirty Years' War, the letters on aesthetic education (1795) and the famous *Über naive und sentimentalische Dichtung* (1795–96), in which he distinguishes ancient from modern poetry by their different approaches to nature. His short-lived literary magazine, *Die Horen* (1795–97), was followed by the celebrated *Xenien* (1797), a collection of satirical epigrams against philistinism and mediocrity in the arts, in which the newly-found friendship between **Goethe** and Schiller found mutual expression. This inspired the great ballads (1797–98), *Der Taucher*, *Der Ring des Polykrates*, *Die Kranische des Ibykus*, the famous *Lied von der Glocke* (Song of the Bell, completed in 1799) and, under the influence of **Shakespeare**, the dramatic trilogy, *Wallenstein* (1796–99), comprising *Wallensteins Lager*, *Die Piccolomini*, and *Wallensteins Tod*, the greatest historical drama in the German language. This was followed by *Maria Stuart* (1800; trans **Stephen Spender** 1957), a remarkable psychological study of the two queens, **Elizabeth** and **Mary, Queen of Scots**, in which the latter by her death gains a moral victory. Schiller the historian is here at odds with Schiller the dramatist. Again, in *Die Jungfrau von Orleans* (1801), **Joan of Arc** dies on the battlefield and is resurrected. *Die Braut von Messina* (1803) portrays the relentless feud between two hostile brothers and the half-legend of *Wilhelm Tell* (1804) is made by Schiller a dramatic manifesto for political freedom. There is a fragment of *Demetrius*, his unfinished work. He was ennobled (1802), fell ill (1804) and died.

SCHIMPER, Andreas Franz Wilhelm (1856–1901) German botanist, son of **Wilhelm Philipp Schimper**. Professor at Basel (1898–1901), he was noted as a plant geographer, and divided the continents into floral regions. He also proved, in 1880, that starch is a source of stored energy for plants.

SCHIMPER, Carl Friedrich (1803–67) German naturalist and poet, a pioneer in modern plant morphology. He was notable for his work on phyllotaxis, and in geology for his theory of prehistoric alternating hot and cold periods. Despite his talents, he failed to secure any academic post. Many of his scientific ideas were published as poems; several hundred are known.

SCHIMPER, Wilhelm Philipp (1808–80) German botanist, cousin of **Carl Friedrich Schimper** and father of **Andreas Schimper**. Director of the Natural History Museum in Strasbourg, he was an authority on mosses and with P Bruch wrote *Bryologia Europaea* (1836–55).

SCHINKEL, Karl Friedrich (1781–1841) German architect and painter, born in Neuruppin in Brandenburg. State architect of Prussia from 1815 and professor at the Berlin Royal Academy from 1820, he designed numerous military buildings, museums and churches in romantic-classical style and designed boulevards and squares in Berlin. He also attained distinction as a painter and illustrator.

SCHIRACH, Baldur von (1907–74) German Nazi politician, born in Berlin. He became a party member in 1925, a member of the Reichstag in 1932, and in 1933 founded and organized the **Hitler** Youth, of which he was leader until his appointment as *gauleiter* of Vienna in 1940. Captured in Austria in 1945 and tried before the Nuremberg Tribunal, he was found guilty of participating in the mass deportation of Jews, and was sentenced to 20 years' imprisonment. He was released from Spandau prison in 1966.

SCHLAF, Johannes (1862–1941) German novelist and dramatist, born in Querfurt. He studied at Berlin and with **Arno Holz** wrote *Papa Hamlet* (1889), a volume of short stories, *Die Familie Selicke* (1890), a social drama, *Peter Boies Freite* (1902), and others.

SCHLAGINTWEIT, Adolf von (1829–57) German geographer, born in Munich, one of five brothers who were all travellers and writers on geography. With his elder brother Hermann (1826–82) he published two books on the physical geography of the Alps (1850, 1854). **Wilhelm von Humboldt** then had them recommended to the British East India Company, which sent them, with a younger brother, Robert (1833–85), to India to make observations on terrestrial magnetism, altitudes in the Deccan, the Himalayas, Tibet and Assam. They published their *Results of a Scientific Mission to India and High Asia* (1860–69). Hermann was the first European to cross the Kunlun mountains. Adolf was put to death by the emir of East Turkestan. Robert became professor of geography at Giessen in 1863, travelled to the United States and wrote on the Pacific railway (1870), California (1871) and the Mormons (1874).

SCHLAGINTWEIT, Eduard von (1831–66) German traveller and writer, brother of **Adolf von Schlagintweit**. He took part in the Spanish invasion of Morocco (1859–60), wrote an account of it and fell at Kissingen fighting for Bavaria against the Prussians.

SCHLAGINTWEIT, Emil von (1835–1904) German traveller, brother of **Adolf von Schlagintweit**. He, the fifth brother, became a lawyer, but wrote *Buddhism in Tibet* (London 1860), *Die Könige von Tibet* (1865), *Indien in Wort und Bild* (1880–81) and other works.

SCHLAGINTWEIT, Hermann von See **SCHLAGINTWEIT, Adolf von**

SCHLAGINTWEIT, Robert von See **SCHLAGINTWEIT, Adolf von**

SCHLEGEL, August Wilhelm von (1767–1845) German man of letters and pioneer of the German Romantic movement, brother of **Friedrich von Schlegel**, born in Hanover. He studied theology at Göttingen, but soon turned to literature. In 1795 he settled in Jena, and in 1796 married a widow, Caroline Böhmer (1763–1809), who separated from him in 1803 and married **Friedrich Schelling**. In 1798 he became professor of literature and fine art at Jena, and founded with his brother the literary journal *Das Athenäum*. In 1801–04 he lectured at Berlin. Most of the next 14 years he spent in the house of Madame **de Staël** at Coppet, though he lectured on *Dramatic Art and Literature* (English translation 1815) at Vienna in 1808, and was secretary to the crown prince of Sweden (1813–14). From 1818 till his death he was professor of literature at Bonn. He translated 17 plays of **Shakespeare**, and also translated works by **Dante**, **Calderón**, **Cervantes** and **Camoens**, and edited the *Bhagavad-Gita* and the *Ramayana*.

SCHLEGEL, (Karl Wilhelm) Friedrich von (1772–1829) German man of letters and critic, and pioneer of the German Romantic movement, brother of **August von Schlegel**, born in Hanover. Educated at Göttingen and Leipzig, in 1798 he eloped with Dorothea (1763–1839), daughter of **Moses Mendelssohn** and wife of a Jewish merchant, Simon Veit, and mother of **Philipp Veit** the religious painter, and next year utilized his experiences in a notorious romance, *Lucinde*. He then joined his brother at Jena, and with him wrote and edited the journal *Das Athenäum*, in the interests of Romanticism. The *Charakteristiken und Kritiken* (1801) contain some of both brothers' best writing. He studied oriental languages at Paris (1802–04), and in 1808 he published a pioneering work on Sanskrit and Indo-Germanic linguistics, *Über die Sprache und Weisheit der Indier*. In 1808 he became a Roman Catholic, and joined the Austrian foreign service; it was he who penned the Austrian proclamations against **Napoleon** in 1809. His best-known books are lectures on the *Philosophy of History* (English translation 1835) and *History of Literature* (translation 1859). There are also English versions of his *Philosophy of Life* (1847) and *Lectures on Modern History* (1849).

SCHLEICHER, August (1821–68) German philologist. He became professor of Slavonic languages at Prague (1850), and honorary professor at Jena (1857). He compiled the *Comparative Grammar of the Indo-Germanic Languages* (1861–62).

SCHLEICHER, Kurt von (1882–1934) German soldier and politician, born in Brandenburg. He was on the general staff during World War I. Minister of war in von **Papen**'s government of 1932, he succeeded him as chancellor, but his failure to obtain dictatorial control provided **Hitler** with his opportunity to seize power in 1933. Schleicher and his wife were executed by the Nazis on a trumped-up charge of treason.

SCHLEIDEN, Matthias Jakob (1804–81) German botanist, born in Hamburg. He studied law in Heidelberg and started a practice in Hamburg, but switched to botany and became professor at Jena (1839–62), and in 1863 at Dorpat. He did much to establish the cell theory.

SCHLEIERMACHER, Friedrich Ernst Daniel (1768–1834) German theologian and philosopher, born in Breslau in Lower Silesia. He was brought up in the Moravian faith but became intellectually disillusioned with its dogmatism and studied philosophy and theology at the University of Halle. In 1796 he became a clergyman at the Charité, a Berlin hospital, and joined the literary and intellectual circles associated with figures like the **Schlegels** and **von Humboldt**. He became Professor at Halle (1804–06) and Berlin (1810), and had a significant role in the union of the Lutheran and Reformed Churches in Prussia in 1817. His works include *Reden über die Religion* (1799), *Monologen* (1800), a translation of **Plato** (started in collaboration with Schlegel, 1804–10), his major treatise *Der Christliche Glaube* (1821–22), and an influential, posthumous life of Jesus. He was much involved in German romanticism and the critique of traditional and Kantian religious and moral philosophy. He defends a view of religious liberalism and an understanding of Christianity rooted in historical tradition, and is now regarded by many as the founder of modern Protestant theology.

SCHLEMMER, Oskar (1888–1943) German painter, sculptor, designer, dancer and theorist, born in Stuttgart. He was on the faculty of the Bauhaus from 1919 to 1933, where he developed his notions of theatre as a mix of colour, light, form, space and motion. Using puppet-like human figures as the centrepiece, he called his experimental productions 'architectonic dances'. All were created between 1926 and 1929 except for the best-known *Triadic Ballet* (three versions: 1911, 1916, and 1922). He exerted a considerable, if indirect, impact on the creation and perception of dance in the 20th-century.

SCHLESINGER, Arthur Meier (1888–1965) American historian, born in Xenia, Ohio. He was educated at Columbia University, New York, and taught at Ohio State University (1912–19), the University of Iowa (1919–24) and Harvard (from 1924). His most important work is *New Viewpoints in American History* (1922), in which he emphasized social and cultural history. This concern, together with his interest in the history of urban growth (*The Rise of the City 1878–98* (1933)), was a new departure in American historiography. His *History of American Life* (13 vols, 1928–43) was an attempt to describe all aspects of human life in America. While at Harvard he established the Schlesinger Library on the History of Women.

SCHLESINGER, Arthur Meier Jr (1917–), American historian, son of **Arthur Meier Schlesinger**, born in Columbus, Ohio, and educated at Harvard (graduated 1938) and Cambridge. He was professor of history at Harvard (1954–61) before becoming special assistant to President **Kennedy** (1961–63). His publications include *The Age of Jackson* (1945, Pulitzer prize 1946), *The Politics of Freedom* (1950), *The Age of Roosevelt* (3 vols, 1957–60), *The Politics of Hope* (1963), *A Thousand Days: John F Kennedy in the White House* (1965, Pulitzer Prize 1966) and *The Imperial Presidency* (1973). He has been professor of humanities at the City University of New York since 1966, and president of the American Institute of Arts and Letters since 1981.

SCHLESINGER, John Richard (1926–) English film director, born in London. As a student at Oxford University from 1945 to 1950 he was a member of the dramatic society and directed his first short film, *Black Legend*, in 1948. Thereafter he worked as a small-part actor, making his film acting début in *Singlehanded* (1952). At the BBC (1956–61), he directed documentaries for the *Tonight* and *Monitor* series. He made his feature film directing début with *A Kind of Loving* (1962), followed by *Billy Liar* (1963) and *Darling* (1965). Interested in illuminating complex human relationships and noted for his sensitive handling of actors, he won an Academy Award for his first American film *Midnight Cowboy* (1969). His enduring trans-Atlantic career encompasses *Sunday, Bloody Sunday* (1971), *Marathon Man* (1976) and *Madame Sousatzka* (1988). He has also staged opera, including *The Tales of Hoffman* (1980, London), and occasionally directs for television, notably *An Englishman Abroad* (1982).

SCHLICK, Moritz (1882–1936) German philosopher, born in Berlin. He was first trained in physics, and studied at the universities of Heidelberg, Lausanne and Berlin. He taught at Rostock and Kiel, and from 1922 to 1936 was professor of inductive sciences at Vienna, where he became a leader of the 'Vienna Circle' of logical positivists. He elaborated their central verificationist theory of meaning and applied it also in the field of ethics, which he argued was a factual science of the causes of human actions. His main publications were *Allgemeine Erkenntnislehre* (General Theory of Knowledge, 1918) and *Fragen der Ethik* (Problems of Ethics, 1930). He was murdered by a deranged student on the steps of the university library.

SCHLIEFFEN, Alfred, Count von (1833–1913) Prussian soldier, born in Berlin. Chief of general staff (1891–1905), he devised the 'Schlieffen Plan' in 1895 on which German strategy was unsuccessfully based in World War I. In the event of a German war on two fronts, he envisaged a German breakthrough in Belgium and the defeat of France within six weeks by a colossal right-wheel flanking movement through Holland and then southwards, cutting off Paris from the sea, meanwhile holding off any Russian intervention with a smaller army in the east.

SCHLIEMANN, Heinrich (1822–90) German archaeologist, the excavator of the sites of Mycenae and Troy, and the creator of Greek prehistoric archaeology. Born in Neubuckow, he went into business at home, in Amsterdam (1842–46) and in St Petersburg (1846–63), acquiring a considerable fortune and a knowledge of the principal modern and ancient European languages. At the age of 46 he retired to realize his childhood ambition, set out in *Ithaka, der Peloponnes und Troja* (1869), of finding the site of the Homeric poems by excavating the mound of Hisarlik in Asia Minor, the traditional site of Troy. Excavations were begun 1871–73, and continued in 1879, 1882–83, and 1889–90. Assisted by the professional **Wilhelm Dörpfeld**, he discovered nine superimposed city sites, one of which contained a considerable treasure, overhastily identified as Priam's though in fact belonging to an earlier, pre-Homeric site. The Trojan finds he presented to the German nation in violation of his agreement with the Turkish government, and after compensation was paid, they were housed in the Ethnological Museum in Berlin (1882). He also excavated the site of Mycenae (1876), in Ithaca (1869 and 1878), at Orchomenos (1874–76, 1880) and at Tiryns (1884). An amateur who consistently kept his own counsel in the face of expert opinion, he was responsible for some of the most spectacular archaeological discoveries of recent times. Verging at times on monomania, his obsessional enthusiasm is well conveyed in his autobiography (1891).

SCHLUTER, Poul Holmskov (1929–) Danish politician. After studying at Aarhus and Copenhagen universities he qualified as a barrister and Supreme Court attorney but was politically active at an early age, becoming leader of the Conservative Youth movement (KU) in 1944. He became its national leader in 1951 and in 1952 a member of the executive committee of the Conservative People's party (KF). He was elected to parliament (Folketing) in 1964 and ten years later became chairman of the KF, and in 1982 prime minister, heading a centre-right coalition which survived the 1987 election but was reconstituted, with Liberal support, in 1988.

SCHMELZER, Johann Heinrich (1623–80) Austrian composer, son of a soldier. He was trained as a musician in the emperor's service and won fame throughout Europe as a violinist. In 1679 he became kapellmeister to **Leopold I**, but the following year died of the plague in Prague, where the court had fled from the great epidemic in Vienna. The first to adapt the tunes of the Viennese street musicians and Tyrolean peasants to the more sophisticated instrumental styles of the court, he is often regarded as the true father of the Viennese waltz.

SCHMIDT, Bernhard (1879–1935) German astronomer of Swedish-German origin, born in Nargen, Estonia. He studied optics in Sweden and made a precarious living grinding reflectors at Jena with his left hand, as his right had been lost in early youth. In 1926 he became associated with the Bergedorf observatory near Hamburg. In 1932 he devised a method to overcome aberration of the image in spherical mirrors and lenses by the introduction of a correcting plate at the centre of curvature. This was utilized in the Palomar Schmidt telescope.

SCHMIDT, Franz (1874–1939) Austrian composer, born in Pressburg. His teachers included **Anton Bruckner** for composition and Leschetizsky for piano. He played cello in the Vienna Philharmonic Orchestra (1896–1911) and from 1901 to 1937 was a distinguished teacher at various Viennese institutions. He continued the style of Austro-German lavish late-Romanticism in his four symphonies, an oratorio *Das Buch mit sieben Siegeln* (Vienna, 1938), the operas *Notre Dame* (Vienna, 1914) and *Fredigundis* (Berlin, 1922), two piano concertos for the left-hand alone, chamber and organ music.

SCHMIDT, Helmut (Heinrich Waldemar) (1918–) West German chancellor and international statesman, born in a working-class district of Hamburg. He was a group leader in the **Hitler** Youth organization, and won the Iron Cross for his service in the Wehrmacht in World War II. After the war he studied economics at Hamburg University and in 1947 became the first national chairman of the Socialist Student Leagues. He had joined the Social Democratic party (SPD) in 1946, and after graduating became manager of transport administration of the state of Hamburg. In the centre-right of his party, he was a member of the Bundestag for the first time in 1953, and while senator for domestic affairs in Hamburg in 1962 he won acclaim for his efficient handling of the Elba flood-disaster. From 1967 to 1969 he was SPD 'floor leader' in the Bundestag and from 1969 to 1972 minister of defence, but it was as minister of finance from 1972 to 1974 that his policy of the achievement of monetary stability, created a firm basis for economic growth, consolidated the Wirtschaffswunder (economic miracle), giving Germany the most stable currency and economic position in the world. In 1974 he succeeded **Willy Brandt** as chancellor, and has described his aim as the 'political unification of Europe in partnership with the United States'. He established himself as an energetic international statesman, pressing for European co-operation and international economic co-ordination, and, with his close friend **Valery Giscard d'Estaing**, helped introduce the concept of annual world economic summits and European 'mini-summits'. In 1977 he emerged as the 'hero of Mogadishu' after taking a firm stand against domestic and international terrorism. He gained re-election as chancellor in 1980, but was defeated in parliament in 1982 following the switch of allegiance by the SPD's coalition allies, the Free Democratic party. He retired from federal politics at the general election of 1983, having encountered growing opposition from the SPD's left wing, who opposed his moderate stance on defence and economic issues.

SCHMIDT, Johannes (1877–1933) Danish biologist, born in Jägerspris. He solved the problem of the European eel's life history by his discovery of the breeding-ground on the ocean bed near Bermuda in 1904.

SCHMIDT, Maarten (1929–) Dutch-born American astronomer, born in Groningen. He was educated there and at Leiden, moving to the California Institute of Technology in 1959. He became director of the Hale Observatories in 1978. He studied the spectrum of an optically identified quasar and discovered that the peculiarities of its spectrum were caused by a massive red shift; it appeared to be receding at nearly 16 per cent of the speed of light. Such high velocities are now interpreted as implying that quasars are very distant objects. He also found that the number of quasars increases with distance from Earth, providing evidence for the 'big bang' theory for the origin of the universe.

SCHMIDT, Wilhelm (1868–1954) German priest and ethnologist, born in Hörde, Westphalia. He joined the Society of the Divine Word Missionary order (SVD) in 1883 and was ordained a priest in 1892. After studying oriental languages at Berlin University (1893–95), he became professor in the St Gabriel Mission Seminary at Mödling, where he remained until 1938. He also taught at Vienna and Fribourg. His interest in ethnology stemmed from the observations of the SVD missionaries, and from the influence of **Fritz Graebner**. He sought to develop and refine Graebner's system of 'Kulturkreise' or trait clusters, proposing a theory of devolution to counter that of cultural evolution. In 1906 he founded the journal *Anthropos*.

SCHMIDT-ROTTLUFF, Karl (1884–1976) German painter and print-maker, born in Rottluff. He began as an architectural student in Dresden but in 1905 was one of the founder members of the avant-garde group of painters known as *Die Brücke*. He developed a harsh, angular style which is well exemplified in his powerful woodcuts. In Berlin from 1911, he shared the current interest in African sculpture. Appointed to the Prussian Academy in 1931 he was dismissed from it by the Nazis in 1933, and in 1941 was forbidden to paint; he was reinstated after World War II, and taught at the Berlin Academy of Fine Arts.

SCHNABEL, Artur (1882–1951) Austrian pianist and composer, born in Lipnik. He studied under Leschetizsky and made his début at the age of eight. He taught in Berlin, making frequent concert appearances throughout Europe and America, and, with the advent of the Nazi government, settled first in Switzerland, then in the USA from 1939. He was an authoritative player of a small range of German classics—notably **Beethoven**, **Mozart** and **Schubert**; his compositions include a piano concerto, chamber music and piano works.

SCHNITTKE, Alfred (1934–) Russian composer, born in Engels, near Saratov. His musical studies began in 1946 in Vienna where his father worked for a Soviet German-language paper. In 1948 he moved to Moscow, trained as a choirmaster, and studied composition at Moscow Conservatory (1953–58), teaching there himself from 1962 to 1972. His prolific output has attracted more Western attention than any Soviet composer's since **Shostakovich**; it is characterized by bold eclectic flair, frequent reference to music of the past and to popular styles such as jazz. Yet, underlying his originality and experimental tendencies, he retains formal, melodic and harmonic characteristics that anchor him in the mainstream of Russian music. His works include four symphonies, many other orchestral works, numerous concertos, choral-orchestral works, ballets, film scores, chamber, vocal and piano works.

SCHNITZER, Eduard See **EMIN PASHA**

SCHNITZLER, Arthur (1862–1931) Austrian dramatist and novelist of Jewish origin, born in Vienna. He practised as a physician in Vienna from 1885 before he turned playwright. His highly psychological, often strongly erotic short plays and novels, executed with great technical skill, frequently underline some social problem, mostly against the familiar easy-going Viennese background. *Anatol* (1893) and *Reigen* (1900) are cycles of one-act plays linked with one another by the overlapping of one of the characters until the chain is completed by a character of the last meeting one from the first. Other notable works include *Der grüne Kakadu* (1899), *Liebelei* (1895), *Der Weg ins Freie* (1908), *Professor Bernhardi* (1912), on anti-Semitism, and *Flucht in die Finsternis* (1931).

SCHNORR VON CAROLSFELD, Baron Julius (1794–1872) German historical and landscape painter, born in Leipzig. In Rome from 1818 to 1825 he became associated with the school of **Cornelius** and **Overbeck** (Nazarenes), and helped decorate with frescoes the Villa Massimo. He went to Munich in 1825, and became professor of historical painting, painting frescoes of the *Nibelungenlied*, **Charlemagne, Barbarossa**, etc. In 1846 he became professor at Dresden and director of the gallery. He painted many frescoes, and in addition designed stained-glass windows among others for Glasgow Cathedral and St Paul's, London.

SCHOENBERG, Arnold Franz Walter (1874–1951) Austro-Hungarian Jewish composer, conductor and teacher, born in Vienna. He learned the violin as a boy but, apart from encouragement and advice from his friend **Alexander von Zemlinsky** (whose sister he married, 1901), he was entirely self-taught. In his twenties he earned his living by orchestrating operettas and from 1901 to 1903 he was in Berlin as conductor of a cabaret orchestra. The works of his first period were in the most lush vein of late German Romanticism and include the string sextet *Verklärte Nacht* (1899), a symphonic poem *Pelleas und Melisande* (1903) and the mammoth choral-orchestral *Gurrelieder* (1900–01; orchestrated by 1911). He was a notable teacher from his Berlin days until his last years, and his two most famous pupils, **Webern** and **Berg**, joined him in Vienna in 1904. His search for a new and personal musical style began to show in such works as the first *Chamber Symphony* (1907) and the second *String Quartet* (1908) which caused an uproar at their first Vienna performances through their free use of dissonance. His works up till World War I, including *Erwartung* (1909) and *Pierrot Lunaire* (1912), may be described as expressionist: extremely chromatic in harmony, with tonality almost obscured, they met with incomprehension and hostility. During periods of compositional crisis Schoenberg turned to painting, and he exhibited with **Kandinsky**'s group, Der Blaue Reiter. During the war he was twice called up and discharged as physically unfit. From 1915 to 1922 he worked on the text and music for an oratorio, *Die Jacobsleiter*, which remained unfinished. Gradually Schoenberg saw the need to harness his totally free chromatic style, and he logically evolved the discipline known as the 'twelve-note method', dodecaphony, or serialism; its first use was in the Piano Suite Op 25 (1921–23). Although he never 'taught' this method or publicized his theory, it was adopted by Webern and a whole succession of others. Schoenberg himself used thematic serialism both strictly and freely, and in some later works departed from it entirely, even returning to tonality. In the 1920s he made many tours, conducting his own works, and in 1925 succeeded **Busoni** as director of the composition masterclass at Berlin Academy of the Arts. There he wrote his third *String Quartet*, *Variations for Orchestra*, a one-act opera, *Von Heute auf Morgen*, a cello concerto and two acts of his greatest stage work, *Moses und Aaron* (unfinished). When the Nazis came to power he left Berlin for Paris, where he formally rejoined the Jewish faith, and set sail for the USA (October 1933), never to return to Europe. In America, Schoenberg suffered from bouts of ill health, money troubles, and general misunderstanding and neglect of his work. Yet he created much fine music after settling in Los Angeles (1934), became a popular teacher at the University of California there, also taught privately, and wrote a number of valuable textbooks on composition. The Violin Concerto (1935–36) and fourth *String Quartet* are complex twelve-note works, while the Suite for Strings (1934) and a Hebrew setting *Kol Nidre* (1938) are more traditionally tonal. His isolation in an alien cultural atmosphere and his spiritual agony over the atrocities committed against his race in Europe are felt in such powerful works as the Piano Concerto (1942), *Ode to Napoleon* (1942) and *A Survivor from Warsaw* (1947). Sickness, financial cares and fear of neglect dogged Schoenberg's last years, but interest in his works was already increasing among a younger generation; a few years after his death his stature as a composer and teacher of immense influence was realized, even if he never attained the popular audience with whom he strove to communicate.

SCHOENHEIMER, Rudolf (1898–1941) German-born American biochemist, born in Berlin. He studied there and taught in Germany for ten years before moving to the USA in 1933. There, working at Columbia with the chemist **Harold Clayton Urey**, he used two new isotopes discovered by Urey (deuterium and heavy nitrogen) to trace biochemical pathways. His work soon showed that many materials of the human body which had been regarded as rather static, have in reality a steady turnover (eg, depot fats, proteins and even bone); and the methods he pioneered have since been used with a variety of isotopic tracers for a range of biochemical studies. He comitted suicide during World War II.

SCHÖFFER, Peter (c.1425–1502) German printer in Mainz. With his father-in-law **Johann Fust** he took over and ran the printing works of **Gutenberg**. They completed the Gutenberg Bible (1456), and in 1457 they issued the *Mainz Psalter*, the first work on which the name of the printer and date of publication appears. After the death of Gutenberg and Fust, Schöffer claimed to be the inventor of printing.

SCHOFIELD, John McAllister (1831–1906) American soldier, born in Gerry, New York. In the Civil War (1861–65) he distinguished himself at Franklin (1864) and Wilmington (1865). He became secretary of war (1868–69), and was commander-in-chief 1888–95.

SCHOLES, Percy Alfred (1877–1958) English musicologist, born in Leeds. He graduated at Oxford in 1908, and as university extension lecturer there, at Manchester, London and Cambridge, as music critic to the *Observer* (1920–25), as the first music adviser to the BBC, and as the editor of *The Oxford Companion to Music* (1938), widely fostered musical appreciation and knowledge. But it is as the author of *The Puritans and Music* (1934) and *The Life of Dr Burney* (1948) that his reputation as musicologist rests.

SCHOMBERG, Frederick Hermann, 1st Duke of (1615–90) German-born French and later British soldier of fortune, born in Heidelberg of a German father and English mother. He fought against the Imperialists in the Thirty Years' War (1618–48) for the Dutch and the Swedish. He was captain in the Scottish Guards in the French army (1652–54) and fought at the battle of the Dunes (1658). He was in Portuguese service from 1660 to 1668, but became a French citizen in 1668 and, though a Protestant, obtained a marshal's baton in 1675. After the revocation of the Edict of Nantes (1685), he retired to Portugal and afterwards took service under the Elector of Brandenburg. He commanded under William of Orange (**William III**) in the English expedition (1688), became a naturalized British citizen and was created Duke of Schomberg (1689), and was commander-in-chief in Ireland. He conducted the Ulster campaign, but was killed at the Boyne.

SCHOMBURGK, Sir Robert Hermann (1804–65) Prussian-born British traveller and official. He surveyed (1831) in the Virgin Islands, where he was a merchant, and was sent by the Royal Geographical Society to explore British Guiana (1831–35). In ascending the Berbice River he discovered the magnificent Victoria Regia lily. In 1841–43 he was employed by the government in Guiana to draw the controversial 'Schomburgk-line' as a provisional boundary with Venezuela and Brazil. In 1848–57 he was British consul in San Domingo, in 1857–64 in Siam.

SCHÖNBEIN, Christian Friedrich (1799–1868) German chemist, born in Metzingen, Württemberg. From 1828 he was professor at Basel. He discovered ozone, gun-cotton and collodion, and experimented on oxygen.

SCHONGAUER, or **Schön, Martin** (1450–91) German painter and engraver, born in Colmar. His famous *Madonna of the Rose Garden* altarpiece at Colmar, one of the most exquisite of early representations of the Virgin, shows Flemish influence, probably that of **Rogier van der Weyden**. Other religious paintings attributed to Schongauer have not been authenticated, but well over 100 of his engraved plates have survived, including *The Passion*, *The Wise and Foolish Virgins*, *Adoration of the Magi*, and other religious subjects, executed with a delicacy of line and a feeling for modelling and composition unequalled among 15th-century German engravers.

SCHOOLCRAFT, Henry Rowe (1793–1864) American ethnologist, born in Albany county, New York. In 1820 he went with **Lewis Cass** to Lake Superior as geologist. In 1822 he became Indian agent for the tribes round the lakes, and in 1823 married a wife of Indian blood. In 1832 he commanded an expedition which discovered the sources of the Mississippi (*Narrative*, 1834). While superintendent for the Indians, he negotiated treaties by which the government acquired 16 000 000 acres. In 1845 he collected the statistics of the Six Nations (*Notes on the Iroquois*, 1848). For the government he prepared his *Information respecting the Indian Tribes of the US* (6 vols, 1851–57).

SCHOPENHAUER, Artur (1788–1860) German philosopher, born in Danzig, where his father was a banker and his mother a novelist. The family moved to Hamburg in 1793 and he was reluctantly prepared for a business career. But after his father's sudden death in 1805 he embarked on an academic education at Gotha, Weimar, Göttingen (where he first studied medicine and natural science), and finally Berlin and Jena (where he completed his dissertation in philosophy in 1813). Throughout his unhappy life his disposition remained dark, distrustful, misogynistic and truculent. He reacted strongly (indeed indignantly) against the post-Kantian idealist tradition represented by **Hegel**, **Fichte** and **Schelling** and found his inspiration in the work of **Plato**, **Kant** himself, the ancient Indian philosophy of the *Vedas*, and **Goethe** (with whom he collaborated on the poet's 'theory of colours'). His major work was *Die Welt als Wille und Vorstellung* (The World as Will and Idea, 1819), which included reflections on the theory of knowledge and the implications for the philosophy of nature, aesthetics and ethics. He emphasized the active role of Will, as the creative but covert and irrational force in human nature, in a way that was greatly to influence **Nietzsche** and **Freud**; and he argued that art represented the sole kind of knowledge that was not subservient to the Will. His work is often characterized as a systematic philosophical pessimism. He took a teaching position in Berlin in 1820 and combatively staged his lectures at exactly the same time as **Hegel**, but he failed to attract students, his book was virtually ignored, and he retired to live a bitter, reclusive life in Frankfurt-am-Main, accompanied for the most part only by his poodle. He continued to work on, defiantly elaborating and defending the same basic ideas in such publications as *Über den Willen in der Natur* (On the Will in Nature, 1889), *Die Beiden Grundprobleme der Ethik* (The Two Main Problems of Ethics, 1841) and a second edition of the major work (1844). But he did finally begin to attract attention with a collection of diverse essays and aphoristic writings published under the title *Parerga und Paralipomena* (1851), and subsequently influenced not only philosophical movements like existentialism but a wide range of figures including **Wagner**, **Tolstoy**, **Proust** and **Mann**.

SCHOPPE See **SCIOPPIUS, Kaspar**

SCHOUTEN, Willem Corneliszoon (c.1580–1625) Dutch mariner, the first man to round Cape Horn. In the service of the East India Company, he was the first to traverse Drake Passage in 1615, and discovered Cape Horn in 1616, which he named after Hoorn, his birthplace in Holland.

SCHOUVALOFF See **SHUVALOV**

SCHREIBER, née **Bertie, Lady Charlotte Elizabeth** (1812–95) Welsh scholar diarist, born in Uffington, Lincolnshire, a daughter of the earl of Lindsey. She became interested in the literature and traditions of Wales after her marriage in 1833 to Sir **Josiah John Guest**, the iron-master of Dowlais, Merthyr Tydfil. Widowed in 1852, in 1855 she married Charles Schreiber, former MP for Cheltenham and Poole. She is best known for her part in translating and editing *The Mabinogion* (1838–1849), being helped by Thomas Price, John Jones and others. A lifelong collector, she became an authority on fans and playing cards, and bequeathed her collections of these to the British Museum. Her famous collection of china was presented to the Victoria and Albert Museum.

SCHREINER, Olive (1855–1920) South African author and feminist, born in Wittebergen Mission Station, Cape of Good Hope, the daughter of a German Methodist missionary and an English mother. She grew up largely self-educated and at the age of 15 became a governess to a Boer family near the Karoo desert. She lived in England (1881–89), where her novel, *The Story of an African Farm* (1883), the first sustained, imaginative work to come from Africa, was published under the pseudonym Ralph Iron. She had a fiery, rebellious temperament and a lifelong hatred of her mother; in her later works the creative artist gave way to the passionate propagandist for women's rights, pro-Boer loyalty and pacificism. These include the allegorical *Dreams* (1891) and *Dream Life and Real Life* (1893), the polemical *Trooper Peter Halket* (1897), a sociological study, *Woman and Labour* (1911), and her last novel *From Man to Man* (1926). In 1894 she married S P Cronwright, who took her name, wrote a Life of her (1924) and edited her letters (1926).

SCHRIEFFER, John Robert (1931–) American physicist, born in Oak Park, Illinois. He studied electrical engineering and physics at the Massachusetts Institute of Technology and Illinois University. Working for his PhD under **John Bardeen** on superconductivity, collaboration with Bardeen and **Leon Cooper** led to the BCS (Bardeen-Cooper-Schrieffer) theory of superconductivity, for which all three shared the 1972 Nobel prize for physics. Schrieffer's particular contribution to the theory was the generalization from the properties of a single Cooper electron pair to that of a solid containing many pairs. He became professor at Pennsylvania University in 1962.

SCHRÖDINGER, Erwin (1887–1961) Austrian physicist, born and educated in Vienna. He became professor at Stuttgart, Breslau, Zürich, Berlin, fellow of Magdalen College, Oxford (1933–38), professor at the Dublin Institute for Advanced Studies (1940) and returned to Vienna as professor in 1956. He originated the study of wave mechanics as part of the quantum theory with his celebrated wave equation, for which he shared with **Paul Dirac** the Nobel prize for physics in 1933, and also made contributions to the field theory. He wrote *What is Life?* (1946) and *Science and Man* (1958).

SCHUBART, Christian Friedrich Daniel (1739–91) German poet, born in Obersontheim in Swabia. He wrote satirical and religious poems. He was imprisoned at Hohenasperg (1777–87) by the Duke of Württemberg, whom he had offended by an epigram. He is largely remembered for his influence on **Schiller**.

SCHUBERT, Franz Peter (1797–1828) Austrian composer, born in Vienna, the son of a schoolmaster. He received early instruction in the violin and piano, and at eleven entered the Stadtkonvikt, a choristers' school attached to the court chapel. During the five austere years he spent there, he tried his hand at almost every kind of musical composition, including a symphony in D (1813). In 1814 he became assistant master at his father's school, composed an opera, the Mass in F and that masterpiece of song, *Gretchen am Spinnrade*, from **Goethe**'s *Faust*. Another, equally famous, the *Erlkönig*, followed in 1815, but was not performed until 1819. From 1817 he lived fairly precariously on his wits, earning a living by giving lessons. His friends at this time included amateur artists and poets and the operatic baritone, Vogl, with whom he was to found the new Viennese entertainment, the 'Schubertiads', private and public accompanied recitals of his songs, which made them known throughout Vienna. In 1818, and again in 1824, he stayed at Zseliz as the tutor of Count Esterházy's three daughters. The famous 'Trout' piano quintet in A major was written after a walking tour with Vogl in 1819. Schubert's veneration of **Beethoven** made him visit the same coffee house, but he was too awestruck ever to approach the great man, except when the latter was sick, when he sent him his compositions; in 1822 a set of variations for a piano duet dedicated to Beethoven, and in 1827 a collection of his songs, which the dying Beethoven greatly admired. In 1822 he composed the Unfinished Symphony (No 8), and the 'Wanderer' fantasia for piano; in the same year he discovered he had contracted syphilis. The song cycle, *Die schöne Müllerin*, which includes the well-known refrain, *Das Wandern*, and the incidental music to *Rosamunde* followed in 1823, the string Quartets in A and D minor in 1824. In 1825 he sent Goethe a number of settings of his poems, but the latter returned them ungraciously without acknowledgment. In 1826 he applied unsuccessfully for the post of assistant musical director to the court, wrote the *Winterreise* song cycle, the string quartets in G major and D minor and the songs *Who is Sylvia?* and *Hark, Hark the Lark*, which, contrary to popular belief, he did not hurriedly scribble on the back of a menu or bill. Before he died of typhus, he had written the great C major symphony (No 9), the fantasy in F minor for four hands and the posthumously published songs, the *Schwanengesang*, or 'Swan-song'. He was buried as near as possible to Beethoven's grave under Grillparzer's well-meant but unjust epitaph: 'Music has here entombed a rich treasure, but still fairer hopes'. Schubert's works are sufficient to preserve his place among the great masters, not least for his infectiously lyrical spontaneity, his lavish musical inventiveness and as the originator and greatest exponent of the art of the German Lieder.Other works include six masses, the dramatic oratoria *Lazarus*, the opera *Alfonso und Estrella*, and the incidental music to *Rosamunde*.

SCHUCHARDT, Hugo (1842–1927) German philologist, born in Gotha. He was professor of philology at Halle and Gotha, chiefly known for his studies in Romance philology which concentrated on linguistic rather than social or historical phenomena, and which include *Der Vokalismus des Vulgärlateins* (1866–68). He also made studies of Basque and the languages of the Caucasus.

SCHULENBURG, Countess Ehrengard Melusina von der (1667–1743) German noblewoman and mistress of **George I** of Britain, nicknamed 'the Maypole' because of her lean figure. She was created Duchess of Kendal in 1719.

SCHULTZ, Theodore William (1902–) American economist, born in Arlington. He held professorships at Iowa State College (1930–43) and the University of

Chicago (1943–72), and wrote *Transforming Traditional Agriculture* (1964). He was awarded the Nobel prize in economics in 1979 (with Sir **Arthur Lewis**) for his work, which stressed the importance of the human factor in agriculture.

SCHULTZE, Max Johann Sigismund (1825–74) German zoologist, born in Frieburg. He studied at Greifswald and Berlin and taught zoology at Bonn. Although he studied the anatomy of a variety of animals, his best-known work was on unicellular organisms: in 1861 he argued that cells in general contain a nucleus and protoplasm as 'the basis of life' and that a boundary membrane is not always present. His duplicity theory of vision of 1866, based on his study of the retina of birds, ascribed separate functions to the retinal rods and cones and was a step towards later theories of vision.

SCHULZ, Charles Monroe (1922–) American strip cartoonist, born in Minneapolis, the creator of Charlie Brown and Snoopy. Learning cartooning from a correspondence course, he became letterer for a religious magazine freelancing cartoons to the *Saturday Evening Post* (1947). He submitted a sample strip about children entitled *Li'l Folks* to many newspapers before United Features accepted it, retitling it *Peanuts* (1950). The strip features the loser, Charlie Brown (based on Schulz himself), the thinking dog, Snoopy, Linus and his security blanket, and became the world's most successful strip.

SCHULZE-DELITZSCH, Hermann (1808–83) German co-operative politician and economist, born in Delitzsch in Prussian Saxony. He advocated constitutional and social reform on the basis of self-help in the National Assembly in Berlin. He started the first 'people's bank' at Delitzsch, on a co-operative basis. Other branches were founded and joined in 1864 under one organization which eventually spread over middle Europe. He wrote on banks and co-operation.

SCHUMACHER, Kurt Ernst Karl (1895–1952) German statesman, born in Kulm, Prussia. He studied law and political science at the universities of Leipzig and Berlin, and from 1930 to 1933 was a member of the Reichstag and of the executive of the Social Democratic parliamentary group. An outspoken opponent of National Socialism, he spent ten years from 1933 in Nazi concentration camps, where he showed outstanding courage. He became in 1946 chairman of the Social Democratic party and of the parliamentary group of the Bundestag, Bonn. He strongly opposed the German government's policy of armed integration with Western Europe.

SCHUMAN, Robert (1886–1963) French statesman, born in Luxemburg. A member of the Resistance during World War II, prime minister in 1947 and 1948, propounded (1950) the 'Schuman plan' for pooling the coal and steel resources of Western Europe, was elected president of the Strasbourg European Assembly in 1958 and awarded the Charlemagne prize. He survived **de Gaulle**'s electoral reforms, being re-elected to the National Assembly in November 1958.

SCHUMAN, William Howard (1910–) American composer, born in New York. He studied under **Roy Harris** and at Salzburg, winning in 1943 the first Pulitzer prize to be awarded to a composer. In 1945 he became president of the Juilliard School of Music in New York. His work ranges from the lighthearted (eg, his opera, *The Mighty Casey*) to the austere and grim. He composed ten symphonies, concertos for piano and violin and several ballets as well as choral and orchestral works.

SCHUMANN, Clara Josephine, née **Wieck** (1819–96) German pianist and composer, born in Leipzig, wife of **Robert Schumann** and daughter of a Leipzig pianoforte teacher, Friedrich Wieck, who turned her into one of the most brilliant concert pianists of her day. She gave her first *Gewandhaus* concert when only eleven and the following year four of her Polonaises were published. After their marriage in 1840, the Schumanns made concert tours to Hamburg and she alone to Copenhagen (1842) and to Russia. From 1856 she very often played for the Philharmonic Society in London, fostering her husband's work wherever she went. Her own compositions include piano music and songs. From 1878 she was principal pianoforte teacher in the Frankfurt-am-Main Conservatory.

SCHUMANN, Elisabeth (1889–1952) German-born American operatic soprano and lieder singer, born in Merseburg. In 1919 she was engaged by **Richard Strauss** for the Vienna State Opera and sang in his and **Mozart**'s operas all over the world, making her London début in 1924. Latterly she concentrated more on Lieder by such composers as **Schubert**, **Hugo Wolf** and Richard Strauss. She left Austria in 1936 and in 1938 became a US citizen.

SCHUMANN, Robert Alexander (1810–56) German composer, born in Zwickau. He spent his boyhood browsing in his father's bookshop, and began at 21 a desultory course of legal studies at Leipzig and Heidelberg. After hearing **Rossini**'s operas performed in Italy and **Paganini** playing at Frankfurt-am-Main, he persuaded his parents to allow him to change over to the pianoforte, under the formidable teacher Friedrich Wieck of Leipzig. The latter, however, was mostly away on his daughter's concert tours and Schumann, left to his own devices, studied **Bach**'s *Well-tempered Clavier*, wrote a prophetic newspaper article on the talents of the young **Chopin**, and broke a finger of his right hand on a finger-strengthening contraption (1832), thus ruining for good his prospects as a performer. The deaths of a brother and a sister-in-law and an obsessive fear of insanity drove him to attempt suicide. Fortunately, his first compositions, the Toccata, Paganini studies, and Intermezzi, were published in 1833 and in 1834 he founded and edited (for ten years) the biweekly *Neue Leipzige Zeitschrift für Musik*, his best contributions to which were collected and translated under the title, *Music and Musicians* (1877–80). In these, he championed romanticism, and in 1853 contributed another prescient essay, this time on the young **Brahms**. In 1835 he met Chopin, **Moscheles** and **Mendelssohn,** who had become director of the Leipzig *Gewandhaus*. The F sharp minor sonata was begun and another in C major, written post-haste for the **Beethoven** commemorations, but not published until 1839. His attachment to Clara Wieck (the future **Clara Schumann**) did not escape her disapproving father, who whisked her away on concert tours as much as possible. He did not know that they were secretly engaged, however. Clara dutifully repudiated Schumann, who retaliated by a brief encounter with the Scottish pianist, Robina Laidlaw, to whom he dedicated his *Fantasiestücke*. In 1839 the lovers were reconciled and after a long legal wrangle to obtain permission to marry without her father's consent, they married in 1840, after Schumann had written his first songs, the Fool's Song in *Twelfth Night*, and aptly, the Chamisso songs *Frauenliebe und Leben*, or 'Woman's Love and Life'. Clara immediately brought pressure on him to attempt some major orchestral composition, and her efforts were rewarded by the first symphony in B flat major, which was performed under Mendelssohn's direction at the *Gewandhaus*. This was followed by the A Minor piano concerto the Piano

Quintet, the choral *Paradise and the Peril*, and his best work in that medium, the scenes from *Faust*, completed in 1848, the 'Spring' Symphony in B flat, etc. In 1843 he was appointed professor of the new Leipzig Conservatory. The Schumanns' Russian concert tour, during which Clara played before **Nicholas I** (1844), inspired him to write five poems on the Kremlin. Recurring symptoms of mental illness prompted the move from Leipzig to Dresden. The Symphony in C major was completed in 1847 and the death of his great friend prompted him to write *Reminiscences of Mendelssohn-Bartholdy*, first published in 1947. Revolution broke out in Dresden in 1849 when Prussian troops confronted republican revolutionaries, among them **Wagner**. The Schumanns fled, but Robert wrote some stirring marches. His mental state allowed him one final productive phase in which he composed pianoforte pieces, many songs and the incidental music to **Byron**'s *Manfred*. His appointment as musical director at Düsseldorf in 1850 saw a happy interlude and the composition of the *Rhenish* Symphony, but his condition remained unstable and in 1854 he threw himself into the Rhine, only to be rescued by fishermen. He died in an asylum two years later. Schumann was primarily a composer for the pianoforte. His early works show a tremendous fertility of musical and extra-musical ideas, to which the names of many of them, '*Abegg*' variations (after a dancing partner), *Carnaval*, *Kreisleriana*, *Papillons*, etc, testify.

SCHUR, Issai (1875–1941) Russian-German mathematician, born in Mogilev. He taught in Berlin from 1916 to 1935, when as a Jew he was forced to retire, in 1939 escaping to Israel. A pupil of **Ferdinand Georg Frobenius**, he worked on representation theory and group characters.

SCHURZ, Carl (1829–1906) German-born American statesman and journalist, born near Cologne. He joined the revolutionary movement of 1849. In America from 1852 he was politician, lecturer, major-general in the Civil War, journalist, senator (1869–75), secretary of the interior (1877–1881). He wrote Lives of **Henry Clay** and **Lincoln**, and *Reminiscences* (1909).

SCHUSCHNIGG, Kurt von (1897–1977) Austrian statesman, born in Riva, South Tirol. He served and was decorated in World War I and then practised law. He was elected a Christian Socialist deputy in 1927, became minister of justice (1932) and education (1933). After the murder of **Dollfuss** in 1934, he succeeded as chancellor until March 1938, when **Hitler** occupied Austria. Imprisoned by the Nazis, he was liberated by American troops in 1945. He was professor of political science at St Louis in the USA (1948–67).

SCHUSTER, Sir Arthur (1851–1934) British physicist, born in Frankfurt of Jewish parents. He studied at Heidelberg and Cambridge and became professor of applied mathematics (1881) and physics (1888–1907) at Manchester. He carried out important pioneer work in spectroscopy and terrestrial magnetism. The Schuster-Smith magnetometer is the standard instrument for measuring the earth's magnetic force. He led the eclipse expedition to Siam in 1875.

SCHUTZ, Alfred (1899–1959) Austrian-born American social philosopher, born in Vienna. A banker by profession, he emigrated to the USA and continued his banking career in New York from 1939, and became professor in the New School of Social Research there in 1952. He reacted against the positivism and behaviourism of the Vienna Circle and developed a phenomenological, descriptive sociology which assumes that the sociologist is himself a factor in whatever he investigates. He was an influence on the ethnomethodologists and on the critical theory of **Habermas**. His main work is *Die sinnhafte Aufbau der sozialen Welt* (1932, translated as *The Phenomenology of the Social World*, 1967).

SCHÜTZ, Heinrich, also known by the Latin form **Sagittarius** (1585–1672) German composer, born in Köstritz near Gera. In 1608 he went to Marburg to study law. The following year he went to Venice to study music, becoming a pupil of **Gabrieli**, and published in 1611 a book of five-part madrigals, showing the Italian influence. He returned to Germany in 1613, continued his law studies at Leipzig, and in 1617 was appointed *Hofkapellmeister* in Dresden, where he introduced Italian-type music and styles of performance—madrigals, the use of continuo, and instrumentally-accompanied choral compositions, for example his *Psalms of David* (1619); he may thus be regarded as the founder of the Baroque school of German music. A visit to Italy in 1628 acquainted him with the more recent developments effected by **Monteverdi** in Italian music, and from 1633 until his return to Dresden in 1641 he travelled between various courts, including those at Copenhagen and Hanover, preaching his gospel of Italianism. Creatively he lies between the polyphony of **Palestrina** and the more elaborate orchestration of such composers as **Bach** and **Handel**, his compositions including much church music—psalms, motets, passions ('The Seven Words on the Cross' and 'The Resurrection'), a German requiem, and the first German opera, *Dafne*, produced in Torgau in 1627.

SCHUYLER, Philip John (1733–1804) American politician born in Albany, New York, raised a company and fought at Lake George in 1755. He was a member of the colonial assembly from 1768, and delegate to the Continental congress of 1775, which appointed him one of the first four major-generals. **Washington** gave him the northern department of New York, and he was preparing to invade Canada when ill -health compelled him to tender his resignation. He still retained a general direction of affairs from Albany, but jealousies rendered his work both hard and disagreeable, and in 1779 he finally resigned. Besides acting as commissioner for Indian affairs and making treaties with the Six Nations, he sat in congress 1777–81, and was state senator for 13 years between 1780 and 1797, US senator 1789–91 and 1797–98, and surveyor-general of the state from 1782. With **Hamilton** and **John Jay** he shared the leadership of the Federal party in New York; and he aided in preparing the state's code of laws.

SCHWABE, Heinrich Samuel (1789–1875) German amateur astronomer, born in Dessau. In 1843 he discovered a ten-year sunspot cycle (later found to be rather more than eleven years) which was brought to recognition by **von Humboldt**.

SCHWANN, Theodor (1810–82) German physiologist, born in Neuss. In 1838 he became professor at Louvain, in 1848 at Liège. He discovered the enzyme pepsin, investigated muscle contraction, demonstrated the role of micro-organisms in putrefaction and brilliantly extended the cell theory, previously applied to plants, to animal tissues.

SCHWARTZ, Delmore (1913–66) American poet, story writer and critic, born in Brooklyn, New York City. He was educated at New York University and made a startling début as a poet while still a student. Writing lyrics, fiction, drama and criticism, he was associated with the *Partizan Review* group of writers as editor (1943–55), and editor of *The New Republic* (1955–57). In 1960 he became one of the youngest winners of the Bollingen prize. A profound ironist, his collections of verse include *In Dreams Begin Re-*

sponsibilities (1938), *Shenandoah* (1941), *Vaudeville for a Princess* (1950) and *Summer Knowledge* (1959). His stories are collected in *The World is a Wedding* (1948) and *Successful Love* (1961). **Saul Bellow** portrayed him eponymously in *Humbolt's Gift* (1975).

SCHWARZ, Berthold (fl.1320) semi-legendary German Franciscan monk of Freiburg (or Dortmund), whose real name was Konstantin Anklitzen, Schwarz ('black') being a nickname due to his chemical experiments. About 1320 he is said to have brought gunpowder (or guns) into practical use.

SCHWARZ, Harvey Fisher (1905–88) American electrical engineer, born in Edwardsville, Illinois. He was the co-inventor (with William J O'Brien) of the Decca radio-navigation system for ships and aircraft. He studied electrical engineering at Washington University, St Louis. Working for the General Electric Company in Schenectady, New York, he helped to develop 'Radiola 44', the first domestic radio receiver to use the newly invented screen-grid valve. As chief engineer of Brunswick Radio Corporation, he was sent to Britain in 1932 to design radios and radiograms for manufacture in the UK, and made his home there for the rest of his life although remaining a US citizen. During World War II, working for Decca, he and O'Brien developed a prototype radio-navigation system that was put into operation for the first time during the D-Day landings in the seaborne invasion of Normandy in 1944.

SCHWARZENBERG, Felix Ludwig Johann Friedrich (1800–52) Austrian statesman, nephew of **Karl Philipp Schwarzenberg**. He was sent on a mission to London in 1826, became involved in the **Ellenborough** divorce suit, was Austrian ambassador at Naples (1846–48), then distinguished himself in the Italian campaign. As prime minister he called in the aid of the Russians against Hungary, and pursued a bold absolutist policy.

SCHWARZENBERG, Karl Philipp, Prince of (1771–1820) Austrian soldier and diplomat. He entered the army in 1787 and took part in the War of the Second Coalition (1792–1802) where he distinguished himself at Hohenlinden (1800). He was ambassador to Russia in 1808, and when Austria declared war on France in 1809 he took part in the defeat at Wagram. After the peace treaty, he conducted the negotiations for the marriage between **Napoleon** and the archduchess Maria Louisa of Austria (1810), and as ambassador at Paris gained the esteem of Napoleon, who demanded him as general of the Austrian contingent in the invasion of Russia in 1812. When Austria turned on Napoleon, he became generalissimo of the allied armies which won the battles of Dresden and Leipzig in 1813. In 1814 he helped to occupy Paris.

SCHWARZKOPF, Elisabeth (1915–) German soprano, born in Janotschin. She studied at the Berlin High School for Music and sang in the Vienna State Opera (1944–48) and Royal Opera, Covent Garden (1949–52), at first specializing in coloratura roles and only later appearing as a lyric soprano. A singer of great dramatic range and versatility, she later concentrated on recitals of German songs.

SCHWARZSCHILD, Karl (1873–1916) German astronomer, born in Frankfurt-am-Main; he was the first to predict the existence of 'black holes'. He became interested in astronomy as a schoolboy and published papers on binary orbits at 16. Educated at the universities of Strasbourg and Munich, he was appointed director of the Göttingen observatory in 1901 and the Astrophysical Observatory in Potsdam in 1909. His lasting contributions are theoretical and were largely made during the last year of his life. In 1916, while serving on the Russian front, he wrote two papers on **Einstein**'s general theory of relativity, giving the first solution to the complex partial differential equations of the theory. He also introduced the idea that when a star contracts under gravity, there will come a point at which the gravitational field is so intense that nothing, not even light, can escape The radius to which a star of given mass must contract to reach this stage is known as the *Schwarzschild radius*. Stars that have contracted below this limit are now known as black holes.

SCHWATKA, Frederick (1849–92) American Arctic explorer, born in Galena, Illinois. He was lieutenant of cavalry on the frontier till 1877, meanwhile being admitted to the Nebraska bar and taking a medical degree in New York. From 1878 to 1880 he commanded an expedition which discovered the skeletons of several of Sir **John Franklin**'s party, and filled up all gaps in the narratives of Sir **John Rae** and Admiral **McClintock**, besides performing a sledge-journey of 3251 miles. In 1883 he explored the course of the Yukon, in 1886 led the *New York Times* Alaskan expedition, and in Alaska, in 1891, opened up 700 miles of new country.

SCHWEIGGER, Johann Salomo Christoph (1779–1857) German physicist, born in Erlangen. He invented the string galvanometer.

SCHWEINFURTH, Georg August (1836–1925) German explorer, botanist and anthropologist, born in Riga. He studied botany and palaeontology at Heidelberg, Munich and Berlin universities. From 1864 to 1866 he botanized along the Red Sea and inland along the Nile to Khartoum and as a result was commissioned to return in 1869, travelling from Khartoum up the White Nile and through the country of the Dinka, Bongo and Niam-Niam tribes, confirming the existence of dwarf people, the Pygmy Akka. He discovered the Welle River and wrongly thought it to be part of the Niger drainage system (it was later confirmed to be part of the Congo). Although his collections were destroyed by fire, his *Heart of Africa* (2 vols, 1873) contains much important detail. From 1873 to 1874 he travelled with Gerhard Rholfs in the Libyan desert and then settled in Cairo, becoming curator of museums and establishing a geographical society, whilst still travelling in the Nile region. In 1889 he moved to Berlin but continued his explorations in Eritrea.

SCHWEITZER, Albert (1875–1965) Alsatian medical missionary, theologian, musician and philosopher, born in Kaysersberg in Alsace, and in terms of intellectual achievement and practical morality probably the noblest figure of the 20th century. He was brought up in Günsbach in the Münster valley, where he attended the local *realgymnasium*, learnt the organ eventually under **Widor** in Paris, studied theology and philosophy at Strasbourg, Paris and Berlin, and in 1896 made his famous decision that he would live for science and art until he was 30 and then devote his life to serving humanity. In 1899 he obtained his doctorate on **Kant**'s philosophy of religion, became curate at St Nicholas Church, Strasbourg, in 1902 *privat-dozent* at the university, and in 1903 principal of the theological college. In 1905 he published his authoritative study, *J S Bach, le musicien-poète* (1905), translated by **Ernest Newman** (1911), followed in 1906 by a notable essay on organ-design. Schweitzer was all for the preservation of old organs, many of which he considered had a better tone than modern factory-built ones. The same year appeared the enlargement of his theological thesis (1901), *Von Reimarus zu Wrede*, re-issued in 1913 as *Geschichte der Leben-Jesu Forschung*, (The Quest of the

Historical Jesus, trans 1910), a thoroughgoing demolition of Liberal theology which had emphasized the role of **Jesus Christ** as ethical teacher, in favour of an eschatological interpretation; ie, Christ as the herald of God's kingdom at hand, in which the ethical teaching which would only serve a short interim period is correspondingly devalued. It marked a revolution in New Testament criticism. His Pauline studies *Geschichte der Paulinischen Forschung* (1911; trans 1912) and *Die Mystik des Apostels Paulus* (1930; trans 1931) were intended as companion volumes to these. True to his vow, despite his international reputation as musicologist, theologian and organist, he began to study medicine (1905), resigned as principal of the theological college (1906) and, duly qualified (1913), went off with his newly-married wife to set up a hospital to fight leprosy and sleeping sickness at Lambaréné, a deserted mission station on the Ogowe river in the heart of French Equatorial Africa. Except for his internment by the French (1917–18) as a German and periodic visits to Europe to raise funds for his mission by organ recitals, he made his self-built hospital the centre of his paternalistic service to Africans, in a spirit 'not of benevolence but of atonement'. His newly discovered ethical principle 'reverence for life' was fully worked out in relation to the defects of European civilization in *Verfall und Wiederaufbau der Kultur* (1923), (The Decay and Restoration of Civilization, trans 1923) and philosophically in *Kultur und Ethik* (1923; trans 1923). He was Hibbert lecturer at Oxford and London (1934) and Gifford lecturer at Edinburgh (1934–35). He was awarded the Nobel prize for peace (1952). His other works include *On the Edge of the Primeval Forest* (trans 1922), *More from the Primeval Forest* (trans 1931), *Out of My Life and Thought* (1931; postscript 1949), and *From My African Notebook* (1938).

SCHWENKFELD, Kaspar von (c.1490–1561) German reformer and mystic, born in Ossig near Liegnitz, founder of a Protestant sect named after him. He served at various German courts, and about 1525 turned Protestant, though he differed widely from **Luther**. His doctrines resembled those of the Quakers, and brought him banishment and persecution; but he gained disciples everywhere. Most of his 90 works were burned by both Protestants and Catholics. Some of his persecuted followers (most numerous in Silesia and Swabia) emigrated to Holland. In 1734, 40 families emigrated to England, and from there to Pennsylvania, where, as Schwenkfeldians, they maintained a distinct existence, numbering some 300 members.

SCHWIMMER, Rosika (1877–1948) Hungarian feminist and pacifist, born in Budapest. As a journalist she was active in the Hungarian women's movement, and was a co-founder of a feminist-pacifist group. She became vice-president of the Women's International League for Peace and Freedom, and from 1918 to 1919 was Hungarian minister to Switzerland. In 1920, fleeing from the country's anti-semitic leadership, she emigrated to the USA, but was refused citizenship since, as a pacifist, she could not promise to fight should war break out. For the rest of her life she continued to campaign for pacifism and before the outbreak of World War II was outspoken in her criticism of growing European Fascism.

SCHWINGER, Julian (1918–) American physicist, one of the founders of quantum electrodynamics. One of Harvard's youngest professors, he shared the 1963 Nobel prize for physics with **Richard Feynman** and **Sin-Itiro Tomonaga**.

SCHWITTERS, Kurt (1887–1948) German artist, born in Hanover. He studied at the Dresden Academy and painted abstract pictures before joining the Dadaists. His best-known contribution to the anarchic movement was *Merz*, his name for a sort of collage made from everyday detritus: broken glass, tram tickets, scraps of paper picked up in the street. From 1920 he slowly built a three-dimensional construction (his '*Merzbau*') which filled his house until it was destroyed in an air raid in 1943. In 1937 he fled to Norway from the Nazi régime, and thence in 1940 to England, where he built but did not complete, another *Merzbau* (1947–48).

SCIASCIA, Leonardo (1921–89) Sicilian novelist, born in Racalmuto. Taking Sicily for the focus of his work, his themes embrace its society past and present which he saw as exemplifying the political, social and spiritual tensions to be found on the wider stage of Europe. A teacher and politician, he first published *Favole della dittatura* (1950). *Le parrocchie di Regalpetra* (1956, trans *Salt in the Wound*, 1969) pointed the way ahead for his fiction and subsequent works developed his early themes. *Candido* (1977) was published in English in 1977 and in the 1980s his novels, several of which were re-translated, reached a wider English-speaking audience. These include *Il Consiglio d'Egitto* (1963, trans *The Council of Egypt*, 1988) and *A ciascuno il suo* (1968, trans *To Each His Own*, 1989).

SCIOPPIUS, or **Schoppe, Kaspar** (1576–1649) German classical scholar and controversialist, born in Neumarkt, at Prague. In 1598 he abjured Protestantism and attacked his former coreligionists, together with **Joseph Justus Scaliger** and King **James VI and I**. He devoted himself at Milan to philological studies and theological warfare (1617–30), and died in Padua. A great scholar, his works included *Grammatica Philosophica* (1628); *Verisimilium Libri Quatuor* (1596), and *Suspectae Lectiones* (1597).

SCIPIO, Publius Cornelius, Africanus Major (237–183 BC) Roman soldier. He fought against the Carthaginians at the Trebia and at Cannae. In 210 he was sent as a general extraordinary to Spain. By a sudden march he captured (209) Nova Carthago, stronghold of the Carthaginians, checked **Hasdrubal**, and soon held the whole of Spain. He was consul in 205, and in 204 sailed with 30000 men to carry on the war in Africa. His successes compelled the Carthaginians to recall **Hannibal** from Italy, and the great struggle between Rome and Carthage was terminated by the Roman victory at Zama in 202. Peace was concluded in 201. The surname of Africanus was conferred on Scipio, and popular gratitude proposed to make him consul and dictator for life—honours Scipio refused. In 190 he served as legate under his brother Lucius in the war with **Antiochus III, the Great**, king of Syria, whose power they crushed in the victory of Magnesia. But on their return the brothers were charged with having been bribed by Antiochus, the excuse being the too lenient terms granted. Popular enthusiasm supported Scipio against the ill-will of the senatorial oligarchy; but he soon retired to his country-seat at Liternum in Campania. His daughter was Cornelia, mother of the **Gracchi**. He is regarded as the greatest Roman general before **Julius Caesar**.

SCIPIO ÆMILIANUS, Publius Cornelius, Africanus Minor (185–129 BC) Roman statesman and general. He was a younger son of Lucius Aemilius Paulus who conquered Macedon, but was adopted by his kinsman Publius Scipio, son of the great **Scipio Africanus**. He accompanied his father against Macedon, and fought at Pydna (168). In 151 he went to Spain under **Lucius Lucullus**, and in 149 the third and last Punic war began. The incapacity of the consuls, Manilius and Calpurnius Piso (149–148), and the brilliant manner in which their subordinate rectified their blunders, drew all eyes to him. In 147 he was elected consul and invested with supreme command. The story of the siege of Carthage, the despairing heroism of its inhabitants, the determined resolution of Scipio, belongs to history. The city was finally taken in the spring of 146, and by orders of the senate levelled to the ground. Scipio was now sent to Egypt and Asia on a special embassy; but affairs meanwhile were going badly in Spain, where the Roman armies had suffered the most shameful defeats. At last in 134 Scipio, re-elected consul, went to Spain, and after an eight months' siege forced the Numantines to surrender, and utterly destroyed their city. He then returned to Rome, where he took part in political affairs as one of the leaders of the aristocratic party, and although a brother-in-law of **Tiberius Gracchus**, disclaimed any sympathy with his aims. The Latins, whose lands were being seized under the Sempronian law, appealed to Scipio, and he succeeded (129) in getting the execution suspended. But his action caused the most furious indignation, and shortly after Scipio was found dead in his bed, doubtless murdered by an adherent of the Gracchi.

SCOFIELD, (David) Paul (1922–) English actor, born in Hurstpierpoint, Sussex. Interested in amateur dramatics as a child, he joined the Croydon Repertory School and studied at the London Mask Theatre before making his professional début in *Desire Under the Elms* (1940). He appeared with various repertory companies before settling in London where his early successes included *The Seagull* (1949), *Ring Round the Moon* (1950) and *Time Remembered* (1954–55). An imposing, ageless figure capable of both intensity and eloquent stillness, his versatility and daring vigour earned comparisons with **Laurence Olivier**. His range was constantly broadened in plays as diverse as *The Power and the Glory* (1956), *Expresso Bongo* (1958) and as Sir **Thomas More** in *A Man for All Seasons* (1960) which he repeated on Broadway in 1962, winning a Tony Award. He made his film début in *That Lady* (1955) but has made only rare forays into that medium despite winning an Academy Award for the screen version of *A Man for All Seasons* (1966). Associate director of the National Theatre from 1970 to 1972, his recent stage work has included *Amadeus* (1979), *Othello* (1980) and *I'm Not Rappaport* (1986).

SCOGAN, John (fl.1480–1500) English jester at the court of **Edward IV** whose *Jests* are said to have been compiled by **Andrew Boorde**.

SCOPAS (4th century BC) Greek sculptor from Paros. He was the founder, with **Praxiteles**, of the later Attic school, and settled in Athens.

SCOPOLI, Giovanni Antonio (1723–88) Italian physician and naturalist, born in the Tyrol. A graduate of Innsbruck, he became physician at the quicksilver mines of Idria at Carniola in 1754, professor of mineralogy at Schemitz, Hungary (1764–66), and professor of chemistry and botany at Pavia (1775–88). A naturalist of worldwide reputation, he wrote *Annus I Historico-Naturalis* (1769).

SCOREL, Jan van (1495–1562) Netherlandish painter, born in Schoorel. He was trained in Amsterdam and, by 1517, was working in Utrecht. In 1519 he travelled to Germany in order to visit **Dürer** at his home in Nuremberg but found him too preoccupied with the activities of **Luther** to be of any use as a teacher. He continued on to Venice where he was very much influenced by the work of **Giorgione**. After a pilgrimage to Jerusalem, he returned to Italy in 1521 and was fortunate to arrive in Rome during the pontificate of the Utrecht pope **Adrian VI**, who appointed him inspector of the Belvedere, canon of Utrecht and sat for a portrait. During this stay he studied the work of **Michelangelo** and **Raphael**. On the death of Adrian he returned to Utrecht where, except for a journey to France in 1540, he was to remain. Much of his work was destroyed by the iconoclasts of the Reformation but his surviving work demonstrates how much he was affected by the art of the south and developed a style that had considerable influence on subsequent Netherlandish painters.

SCORESBY, William (1789–1857) English Arctic explorer, born near Whitby. As a boy he went with his father, a whaling captain, to the Greenland seas, and himself made several voyages to the whaling grounds. He attended Edinburgh University, and published *The Arctic Regions* (1820), the first scientific accounts of the Arctic seas and lands. In 1822 he surveyed 400 miles of the east coast of Greenland. Having studied at Cambridge, and been ordained (1825), he held various charges at Exeter and Bradford but continued his scientific investigations, going to Australia in 1856 to study terrestrial magnetism.

SCORSESE, Martin (1942–) American film director, born in Queens, New York. As a student at New York University he made a number of short films, beginning with *What's A Nice Girl Like You Doing in a Place Like This?* (1963). He then worked towards his first feature, *Who's That Knocking at My Door?* (1969) and subsequently lectured, made commercials and served as an editor before returning to direction with *Boxcar Bertha* (1972). Considered one of the foremost directors of his generation, his work has sought to illuminate masculine aggression and sexual inequality and he has frequently questioned traditional American values. His many films include *Alice Doesn't Live Here Anymore* (1974), *Taxi Driver* (1976) and *Raging Bull* (1980). In 1988 he achieved a long-held ambition to film **Kazantzakis**' controversial novel *The Last Temptation of Christ*. He has also directed pop videos, documentaries and Broadway shows and has acted in his own and other films, including *Round Midnight* (1986).

SCOT, Michael See **SCOTT**

SCOT, or **Scott, Reginald** (c.1538–1599) English author, a younger son of Sir John Scot of Smeeth in Kent. He studied at Hart Hall, Oxford, was a collector of subsidies for the lathe of Shepway in 1586–87 and was MP (1588–89). He is credited with the introduction of hop-growing into England, and his *Perfect Platform of a Hop-garden* (1574) was the first manual on hop culture in the country. His famous *Discoverie of Witchcraft* (1584), is an admirable exposure of the childish absurdities which formed the basis of the witchcraft craze, and excited the antipathy of King **James VI**, who wrote his *Daemonologie* (1597), and had Scot's book burnt by the hangman.

SCOTT name of a great Scottish Border family originating in Peeblesshire, possessors of Buccleuch in Selkirkshire in 1415, and of Branxholm near Hawick, from 1420 onwards. Sir Walter Scott fought for **James II** at Arkinholm against the Douglases (1455), and received a large share of the forfeited Douglas estates; his descendants acquired Liddesdale, Eskdale, Dalkeith, etc, with the titles Lord Scott of Buccleuch (1606) and Earl of Buccleuch (1619). Among them were two Sir Walters, one of whom (c.1490–1552) fought at Flodden (1513), Melrose (1526), Ancrum (1544) and Pinkie (1547), and in 1552 was slain in a street fray in Edinburgh by Kerr of Cessford; while the other Sir Walter, 1st Baron Scott of Buccleuch (1565–1611), was the rescuer of **William Armstrong** ('Kinmont Willie') from Carlisle Castle (1596). Francis, 2nd Earl (1626–51), left two daughters—Mary

(1647–61), who married the future Earl of Tarras, and Anna (1651–1732), who married James, Duke of **Monmouth**, who took the surname Scott and was created Duke of Buccleuch. After his execution (1685) his duchess, who had borne him four sons and two daughters, retained her title and estates, and in 1688 married Lord Cornwallis. Her grandson Francis succeeded her as 2nd Duke, and through his marriage in 1720 with a daughter of the Duke of Queensberry that title and estates in Dumfriesshire devolved in 1810 on Henry, 3rd Duke of Buccleuch (1746–1812), a great agriculturist. Walter Francis, 5th Duke (1806–84), was the builder of the pier and breakwater at Granton. The Harden branch (represented by Lord Polwarth) separated from the main stem in 1346; and from this sprang the Scotts of Raeburn, ancestors of the novelist Sir **Walter Scott**.

SCOTT, Alexander (c.1525–1584) Scottish lyrical poet of the school of **Dunbar**. Little is known of his early life, except that he became musician and organist at the Augustinian priory of Inchmatome, in the Firth of Forth, in 1548. He had associations with the court of **Mary, Queen of Scots**, and in 1565 was a canon of Inchaffray in Perthshire. He bought an estate in Fife in 1567 and became a wealthy landowner. He wrote 36 short poems, either courtly love lyrics or poems offering moral advice and rectitude. He is considered the last of the Scottish 'Makars'.

SCOTT, C P (Charles Prestwich) (1846–1932) English newspaper editor, born in Bath. Educated at Corpus Christi College, Oxford, at the age of 26 he became editor of the *Manchester Guardian*, which he raised into a serious Liberal rival of *The Times* by highly independent and often controversial editorial policies, such as opposition to the Boer War, and by his high literary standards. He was a Liberal MP (1895–1906).

SCOTT, Cyril Meir (1879–1970) English composer, born in Oxton, Cheshire. As a child he studied the piano in Frankfurt-am-Main, later returning there to study composition. His works won a hearing in London at the turn of the century, and in 1913 he was able to introduce his music to Vienna; his opera, *The Alchemist*, had its first performance in Essen in 1925. He composed three symphonies, piano, violin and cello concertos, and numerous choral and orchestral works, but is best known for his piano pieces and songs. He also wrote poems, studies of music, homoeopathy and occultism.

SCOTT, David (1806–49) Scottish historical painter, brother of **William Bell Scott**, born in Edinburgh. Apprenticed to his father as a line-engraver, he studied at the Trustee's Academy and in 1831 he designed his 25 'Illustrations to the *Ancient Mariner*' (1837). From 1823 to 1833 he visited Italy, and painted *The Vintager*, now in the National Gallery; many imaginative and historical paintings followed, such as *The Traitor's Gate* and *Ariel and Caliban*.

SCOTT, Dred (?1795–1858) American slave, born in Southampton County, Virginia. He made legal and constitutional history as the nominal plaintiff in a test case that sought to obtain his freedom on the ground that he lived in the free state of Illinois—the celebrated Dred Scott Case (1848–57). The Supreme Court ruled against him, but he was soon emancipated, and became a hotel porter in St Louis, Missouri.

SCOTT, Dukinfield Henry (1854–1934) English botanist, son of Sir **George Gilbert Scott**. He studied at Oxford and Würzburg, and became assistant professor at the Royal College of Science and in 1892 keeper of Jodrell Laboratory, Kew, devoting himself to plant anatomy and later to palaeobotany. He collaborated with **William Crawford Williamson** in a number of brilliant studies of fossil plants, and established in 1904 the class Pteridospermeae. He published important textbooks, *Structural Botany* (1896) and *Studies in Fossil Botany* (1900).

SCOTT, Francis George (1880–1958) Scottish composer, born in Hawick. He studied at the universities of Edinburgh and Durham, and in Paris under Roger-Ducasse. From 1925 to 1946 he was lecturer in music at Jordanhill Training College for Teachers, Glasgow. His *Scottish Lyrics* (five volumes, 1921–39) comprise original settings of songs by **Dunbar**, **Burns** and other poets, most notably of **Hugh MacDiarmid**, and exemplify Scott's aim of embodying in music the true spirit of Scotland. Primarily a song composer, Scott also wrote the orchestral suite *The Seven Deadly Sins* (after Dunbar's poem) and other orchestral works.

SCOTT, Sir George Gilbert (1811–78) English architect, born in Gawcott, Buckinghamshire. Aroused by the Cambridge Camden Society and an article of **Pugin** (1840–41), he became the leading practical architect in the Gothic revival, and, as such, the building or restoration of most of the public buildings, ecclesiastical or civil, was in his hands. The Martyrs Memorial at Oxford (1841), St Nicholas at Hamburg (1844), St George's at Doncaster, the new India office (exceptionally, owing to pressure by Lord **Palmerston**, in the style of the Italian Renaissance), the Home and Colonial Offices (from 1858), the Albert Memorial (1862–63), St Pancras station and hotel in London (1865), Glasgow University (1865), the chapels of Exeter and St John's Colleges, Oxford, and the Episcopal Cathedral in Edinburgh are examples of his work. He was professor of architecture at the Royal Academy (1868). The establishment of the Society for Protection of Ancient Buildings (1877) was due to his inspiration. He was buried in Westminster Abbey. He wrote works on English medieval church architecture.

SCOTT, Sir Giles Gilbert (1880–1960) English architect, grandson of Sir **George Gilbert Scott**. Educated at Beaumont College, Old Windsor, he won a competition in 1903 for the design of the Anglican cathedral in Liverpool (consecrated 1924), and also designed, among many other public buildings, the new nave at Downside Abbey, the new buildings at Clare College, the new Bodleian Library at Oxford (1936–46) and the new Cambridge University Library (1931–34). He planned the new Waterloo Bridge (1939–45) and was responsible for the rebuilding of the House of Commons after World War II.

SCOTT, Hew (1791–1872) Scottish theologian, born in Haddington and educated in Aberdeen. From 1839, he was minister of Wester Anstruther, and compiled *Fasti Ecclesiae Scoticanae* (1866–71), still regularly revised as a record of Church of Scotland ministers.

SCOTT, James Brown (1866–1943) Canadian-born American international lawyer, born in Kincardine, Ontario. Educated at Philadelphia and Harvard, he taught law in several universities and was solicitor to the US department of state (1906–10), delegate to the Second Hague Peace Conference (1907) and an arbitrator in international disputes. He wrote *The Hague Peace Conferences of 1899 and 1907* (1909) and *Law, the State and the International Community* (1939); he edited the *American Journal of International Law* (1907–24) and was president of the American Institute of International Law (1915–40).

SCOTT, John See **ELDON**

SCOTT, Lady John See **SPOTTISWOODE, Alicia, Ann**

SCOTT, John (1794–1871) English horse-trainer, born in Chippenham and brought up in West Australia.

He trained six Derby winners, including West Australian, which won the three great racing events in 1853, the Two Thousand Guineas, the Derby and the St Leger.

SCOTT, Mackay Hugh Baillie (1865–1945) English architect and designer, born in Kent. He designed the decoration for the palace of the Grand Duke of Hesse at Darmstadt which was carried out by the Guild of Handicraft in consultation with **Ashbee** in 1898. In 1901 he gave up his practice in Douglas and moved to Bedford. His furniture is simple, solid, bold and generally decorated with a degree of Art Nouveau ornamentation. He went on to design numerous houses in Britain and Europe before retiring in 1939.

SCOTT, Michael (c.1175–c.1230) Scottish scholar and astrologer, the 'wondrous wizard', born probably in Durham, of Border ancestry. He studied at Oxford, Paris and Padua, was tutor and astrologer at Palermo to **Frederick II, the Great**, settled at Toledo 1209–20 and translated Arabic versions of **Aristotle**'s works and **Averroës**' commentaries. Returning to the Imperial court at Palermo, he refused the proffered archbishopric of Cashel (1223). He wrote a learned work on astrology, *Quaestio curiosa de natura solis et lunae* (1622), and his translations of Aristotle were seemingly used by **Albertus Magnus**, and was one of the two familiar to **Dante**. Dante alludes to him in the *Inferno* in a way which proves that his fame as a magician had already spread over Europe; and he is also referred to by **Albertus Magnus** and Vincent de Beauvais. In Border folklore he is credited with having, in the words of Sir **Walter Scott** 'cleft the Eildon Hills in three and bridled the Tweed with a curb of stone'; and his alleged grave is shown in Melrose Abbey.

SCOTT, Michael (1789–1835) Scottish author, born in Cowlairs, Glasgow, the son of a merchant. Educated at Glasgow High School and at Glasgow University (1801–05), he went to seek his fortune in Jamaica. He spent a few years in the West Indies, but in 1822 settled in Glasgow. His vivid, amusing stories, *Tom Cringle's Log* (1829–33) and *The Cruise of the Midge* (1834–35), first appeared serially in *Blackwood's Magazine*.

SCOTT, Michael (1907–83) English Anglican missionary and social and political activist. He was educated at King's College, Taunton, and St Paul's College, Grahamstown, and served in a London east end parish and as chaplain in India (1935–39), where he collaborated with the communists. Invalided out of the RAF in 1941, he served (1943–50) in various missions in South Africa. No longer associating with communists, he exposed the atrocities in the Bethal farming area and in the Transvaal, defended the Basutos against wrongful arrest, and brought the case of the dispossessed Herero tribe before the United Nations. He became *persona non grata* in the Union and in the Central African Federation. He founded the London Africa Bureau in 1952. In 1958 he suffered a short imprisonment for his part in nuclear disarmament demonstrations. He was expelled from Nagaland in 1966. He wrote an autobiography, *A Time to Speak* (1958), and *A Search for Peace and Justice* (1980).

SCOTT, Paul Mark (1920–78) English novelist, born in London. He served in the British army (1940–43), and in the Indian army, in India and Malaya (1943–46). His great achievement is *The Raj Quartet* (*The Jewel in the Crown*, 1966; *The Day of the Scorpion*, 1968; *The Towers of Silence*, 1971; *A Division of Spoils*, 1975). Set in the years 1939–47, the overlapping novels give a vivid portrait of India at the demise of the Raj. Critical acclaim came late for the author, encouraged by a popular television adaptation of the books. *Staying On* (1977), which can be seen as a coda to the *Quartet*, was awarded the Booker prize.

SCOTT, Sir Percy Moreton, 1st bartonet. (1853–1924) English naval commander and gunnery expert, born in London. He entered the navy in 1866 and saw active service in Ashanti (Gold Coast), Egypt, South Africa and China. Retiring in 1909, he returned to active service as gunnery adviser to the fleet. His methods and inventions transformed naval gunnery but he had influential opponents. He commanded the anti-aircraft defences of London (1915–18), and foresaw the importance of air power at sea. He wrote *Fifty Years in the Royal Navy* (1919).

SCOTT, Sir Peter Markham (1909–89) English artist and ornithologist, born in London, son of **Robert Falcon Scott**. Educated at Oundle and Cambridge, he became an enthusiastic wildfowler, making paintings of his quarry. He went on to the State Academy School at Munich and the Royal Academy of Art Schools in London to study painting, and became a professional artist, with his first exhibition in 1933. He represented Britain (single-handed dinghy sailing) at the 1936 Olympic Games, served with distinction with the Royal Navy in World War II, founded the Severn Wild Fowl Trust in 1948, explored in the Canadian Arctic in 1949, and was leader of several ornithological expeditions (Iceland, 1951 and 1953; Australasia and the Pacific, 1956–57). Through television he helped to popularize natural history, and his writings include *Morning Flight* (1935), *Wild Chorus* (1938), *The Battle of the Narrow Seas* (1945) and *Wild Geese and Eskimos* (1951). He also published an autobiography, *The Eye of the Wind* (1961).

SCOTT, Reginald See **SCOT**

SCOTT, Robert See **LIDDELL, Henry George**

SCOTT, Robert Falcon (1868–1912) English Antarctic explorer, father of Sir **Peter Markham Scott**, born near Devonport. He entered the navy in 1881 and in the *Discovery* commanded the National Antarctic Expedition (1900–04) which explored the Ross Sea area, and discovered King Edward VII Land. Scott was promoted captain in 1906; in 1910 he embarked upon his second expedition in the *Terra Nova* and with a sledge party which consisted of **Edward Wilson**, **Laurence Oates**, Bowers, Evans and himself reached the South Pole on 17 January 1912, only to discover that the Norwegian expedition under **Roald Amundsen** had beaten them by a month. Delayed by blizzards and the sickness of Evans, who died, and Oates, who gallantly left the tent in a blizzard, the remainder eventually perished in the tantalizing vicinity of One Ton Depot at the end of March, where their bodies and diaries were found by a search party eight months later. Scott was posthumously knighted and the statue of him by his wife, Kathleen, Lady Scott, the sculptor, stands in Waterloo Place, London. The Scott Polar Research Institute at Cambridge was founded in his memory.

SCOTT, Sheila, originally **Sheila Christine Hopkins** (1927–88) English aviator, born in Worcester. Leaving school at 16 she joined the Royal Naval Section of the VAD, and after the war spent a year acting with a repertory company under the stage name of Sheila Scott. Following an unhappy marriage (1945–50), she worked as a model and actress until, in 1959, she took her pilot's licence and came fifth in the first race she competed in, from London to Cardiff. Supported financially by several sponsors, she took part in many races and gained wide flying experience and a commercial pilot's licence. In 1966, in 33 days and 189 flying hours, she flew 31 000 miles, the longest solo flight in a single-engined aircraft. She followed this with further light-aircraft records, including in 1971 a solo flight from equator to equator, over the North Pole. She wrote three books describing her career: *I Must Fly* (1968), *On Top of the World* (1973) and *Bare Feet in the Sky* (1974).

SCOTT, Walter of Satchells (c.1614–c.1694) Scottish soldier and genealogist. He served in Holland and at home 1629–86, and wrote a metrical *History of the Scotts* (1688).

SCOTT, Sir Walter (1771–1832) Scottish novelist and poet, born in Edinburgh, son of a Writer to the Signet and of Anne Rutherford, a daughter of the professor of medicine at the university. When young he contracted polio in his right leg and was sent to his grandfather's farm at Sandyknowe to recuperate, and thus came to know the Border country which figures often in his work. Neither at the High School, Edinburgh, nor at the university did he show much promise. His real education came from people and from books—**Fielding** and **Smollett**, **Walpole**'s *Castle of Otranto*, **Spenser** and **Ariosto** and, above all, **Percy**'s *Reliques* and German ballad poetry. He did better in his father's office as a law clerk and became an advocate in 1792. His first publication was rhymed versions of ballads by Bürger in 1796. The following year he was an ardent volunteer in the yeomanry and on one of his 'raids' he met at Gilsland spa Charlotte Charpentier, daughter of a French émigré, whom he married in Carlisle on Christmas Eve, 1797. Two years later he was appointed sheriff-depute of Selkirkshire. The ballad meanwhile absorbed all his literary interest. *Glenfinlas* and *The Eve of St John* were followed by a translation of **Goethe**'s *Göetz von Berlichingen*. His skill as a writer of ballads led to the publication by **James Ballantyne**, a printer in Kelso, of Scott's first major work, *The Border Minstrelsy* (vols 1 and 2, 1802, vol 3, 1803). The *Lay of the Last Minstrel* (1805) made him the most popular author of the day. The other romances which followed, *Marmion* (1808), and *The Lady of the Lake* (1810), enhanced his fame, but the lukewarm reception of *Rokeby* (1811), of *Lord of the Isles* (1815) and *Harold the Dauntless* (1817) warned him that he should turn his attention away from the ballad form and concentrate on writing novels. In 1811 he built his country seat, Abbotsford, near Galashiels, in the Borders. The business troubles which darkened his later career began with the setting up with James Ballantyne and his brother John as publishers in the Canongate. All went well at first, but with expanding business came expanding ambitions, and when **Archibald Constable** with his London connections entered the scene, Scott lost all control over the financial side of the vast programme of publication, much of it hack publication, on which he now embarked; hence the bankruptcy in the middle of his great career as a novelist (1826). The Waverley novels fall into three groups—first from *Waverley* (1814) to *The Bride of Lammermoor* (1819) and *A Legend of Montrose* (1819); next from *Ivanhoe* (1820) to *The Talisman* (1825), the year before his bankruptcy; *Woodstock* (1826) opens the last period, which closes with *Castle Dangerous* and *Count Robert of Paris* (1832), in the year of his death. The first period established the historical novel based, in Scott's case, on religious dissension and the clash of races English and Scottish, Highland and Lowland, his aim being to illustrate manners but also to soften animosities. In *Guy Mannering* (1815) his great humorous characters first appear and are found in *The Heart of Midlothian* (1818) and *Old Mortality* (1816). *The Bride of Lammermoor* has the stark outlines of the ballad. His Scottish vein exhausted, he turned to England in the middle ages in *Ivanhoe*. With *The Monastery* and *The Abbot* (1820) he moved to Reformation times, where he showed a respect for what was venerable in the ancient church which might have been predicted from his harshness to the Covenanters in *Old Mortality*. This group is distinguished by its portrait gallery of queens and princes. The highlights in the last period are *Woodstock* (1826), not quite successful, and *The Fair Maid of Perth* (1828), where again the ballad motif appears. He worked best on a traditional or ballad theme, as in *Proud Maisie*, but Highland themes, as in *The Pibroch* and *The Coronach*, equally proved his lyric powers. He was also writing other works for the publishers, much of which was simply hack work—the editions of **Dryden** (1808), of **Swift** (1814), and the *Life of Napoleon* (9 vols, 1827). The *Tales of a Grandfather* (1828–30), however, keeps its charm, and his three letters 'from Malachi Malagrowther' (1826), are remembered for their patriotic assertion of Scottish interests. A national figure, he helped to supervise the celebration for **George IV**'s visit to Edinburgh in 1822. His last years were plagued by illness, and in 1831–32 he toured the Mediterranean in a government frigate. He died at Abbotsford soon after his return, and was buried in the ruins of Dryburgh Abbey.

SCOTT, William See **STOWELL**

SCOTT, William (1913–) Scottish-Irish painter, born in Greenock. He studied at Belfast College of Art (1928–31) and at the Royal Academy Schools (1931–35). After World War II he taught at Bath Academy of Art, Corsham (1946–56). He visited Canada and New York in 1953, meeting **Jackson Pollock, de Kooning**, and other leading Abstract Expressionists. His preferred subject is still-life, painted in a simplified, nearly-abstract way. He won first prize in the John Moores Liverpool Exhibition in 1959.

SCOTT, William Bell (1811–90) Scottish painter and poet, brother of **David Scott** and son of an engraver, born in Edinburgh. While training as an engraver, he also began to write poetry and had verses published for the first time in 1831. He exhibited paintings at the Royal Scottish Academy from 1834. He moved to London in 1837 and, in the following year his first volume of poetry was published. He married in 1839. He began exhibiting at the Royal Academy from 1842 and, in 1843, became master of the Government School of Design in Newcastle. His major paintings were of scenes of Northumberland history which were exhibited in London and Newcastle prior to their installation (1861) at Wallington Hall, Northumberland. He moved back to London in 1864 and, in 1875, published *Poems* dedicated to his friends **D G Rossetti**, **William Morris** and **A C Swinburne**. His *Autobiographical Notes* were published posthumously in 1892.

SCOTT, Winfield (1786–1866) American soldier, born near Petersburg, Virginia. He was admitted to the bar in 1807, but obtained a commission as artillery captain in 1808. As major-general, he framed the 'General Regulations' and introduced French tactics and helped (1839) to settle the disputed boundary line of Maine and New Brunswick. He succeeded to the chief command of the army in 1841. He took Vera Cruz (26 March 1847), put **Santa Anna** to flight, and entered the Mexican capital in triumph (14 September). Unsuccessful Whig candidate for the presidency (1852), he retained nominal command of the army until October 1861.

SCOTT-MONCRIEFF, Charles Kenneth Michael (1889–1930) Scottish man of letters, celebrated as the translator into English of **Proust**, **Stendhal**, **Pirandello**, *Beowulf* and the *Song of Roland*. He was educated at

Winchester and Edinburgh University, and was on the staff of *The Times* (1921–23).

SCOTUS See **DUNS SCOTUS, ERIGENA, MARIANUS SCOTUS**

SCRIABIN, Alexander (1872–1915) Russian composer and pianist, born in Moscow. He studied at the conservatory with **Rachmaninov** and **Nikolai Medtner** and became professor of the pianoforte (1898–1904). His compositions include a piano concerto, three symphonies, two tone poems, ten sonatas, studies and preludes. His piano music is technically and harmonically highly original, and he increasingly relied on extramusical factors and applied religion, occultism and even coloured light (eg in *Prometheus*).

SCRIBE, Augustin Eugène (1791–1861) French dramatist, born in Paris. After 1816 his productions became so popular that he established a type of theatre workshop in which numerous *collaborateurs* worked under his supervision turning out plays by 'mass-production' methods. The best known are *Le Verre d'eau* (1840), *Adrienne Lecouvreur* (1848) and *Bataille des dames* (1851). Scribe also wrote novels and composed the libretti for 60 operas, including *Masaniello, Fra Diavolo, Robert le Diable, Les Huguenots*, and *Le Prophète*.

SCRIBLERUS See **ARBUTHNOT, John**

SCRIBNER, Charles, original surname **Scrivener** (1821–71) American publisher, born in New York. He graduated from Princeton in 1840, and in 1846 founded with Isaac Baker the New York publishing firm which became Charles Scribner's Sons in 1878. He founded *Scribner's Monthly* (1870–81), which became *Scribner's Magazine* from 1887 to 1939. His three sons continued the business.

SCRIPPS a family of American newspaper publishers: James Edmund (1835–1906), born in London, was the founder of the *Detroit Evening News* and was associated with his half-brother, Edward Wyllis (1854–1926), in the foundation of many newspapers, notably in St Louis and Cleveland. His sister, Ellen Browning (1836–1932), born in London, served on many of the family newspapers. The family interest passed to Robert Paine (1895–1938), Edward's son. The Scripps were first in the field of syndicated material with the Newspaper Enterprises Association (1902).

SCROGGS, Sir William (1623–83) English judge, born in Deddington, Oxfordshire. Chief justice of the King's Bench from 1678, he was notorious for cruelty and partiality during the 'Popish Plot' trials (see **Titus Oates**). In 1680 he was impeached, but removed from office by the king on a pension.

SCROPE a north of England family that produced Richard le Scrope, chancellor in 1378 and 1381–82; Richard le Scrope (c.1350–1405), archbishop of York, beheaded for conspiracy against **Henry IV**; and Henry Lord Scrope, warden of the West Marches under Queen **Elizabeth**.

SCRUTTON, Sir Thomas Edward (1856–1934) English legal text-writer and judge, born in London. Educated at Mill Hill and London University, after an outstanding academic career he developed a busy practice in commercial cases and wrote *The Contract of Affreightment as Expressed in Charter-parties and Bills of Lading* (1886). A century later this is still the standard text, while several other of his legal works remain useful. A judge of the King's Bench Division (1910–16) and of the Court of Appeal (1916–34), he was an extremely powerful judge, especially in commercial cases.

SCUDDER, Samuel Hubbard (1837–1911) American entomologist, born in Boston. An authority on fossil insects, he also wrote on the Orthoptera and Lepidoptera, and wrote *Butterflies of the Eastern United States and Canada* (1888–89).

SCUDÉRY, Georges de (1601–67) French writer, born in Le Havre, brother of **Madeleine de Scudéry**. After a brief military career he wrote a number of plays which achieved some success. In 1637 his *Observations sur le Cid* led to a controversy with **Pierre Corneille**. He later wrote novels and had a small share in his sister's works, which first appeared under his name.

SCUDÉRY, Madeleine de (1608–1701) French novelist, born in Le Havre, sister of **Georges de Scudéry**. Left an orphan at six, she went to Paris in 1639 and with her brother was accepted into the literary society of Mme **de Rambouillet**'s salon. From 1644 to 1647 she was in Marseilles with her brother. She had begun her literary career with the romance *Ibrahim ou l'illustre Bassa* (1641), but her most famous work was the ten-volume *Artamène, ou le Grand Cyrus* (1649–59), written with her brother, followed by *Clélie* (10 vols, 1654–60). These highly artificial, ill-constructed pieces, full of pointless dialogue, were popular at the court because of their sketches of and skits on public personages.Her last novel was *Mathilde d'Anguilon* (1667). She was satirized by **Molière** in *Les précieuses ridicules* (1659).

SCULTHORPE, Peter Joshua (1929–) Australian composer, born in Launceston, Tasmania. He studied at the Conservatorium of Melbourne University, and later in Oxford with **Egon Wellesz** and **Edmund Rubbra**. A leading figure in bringing about the recognition of Australian compositions overseas, his work, though never prolific, is much influenced by the vast spaces of the Australian landscape. Small-scale works, chamber music and the *Irkanda* series, were followed by his four *Sun Music* pieces. In 1974 the Australian Opera performed his opera *Rites of Passage* and in 1982 the Australian Broadcasting Corporation commissioned an opera for television, *Quiros*, to mark its 50th anniversary. *Sun Song* (1989), specially written for the Australian group Synergy, employs aboriginal themes originally noted down by the French explorer Nicolas Baudin in the early 19th century. Other major works include the cello requiem (1979) and a piano concerto (1983).

SEABORG, Glenn Theodore (1912–) American nuclear chemist. After taking his PhD at the University of California at Berkeley, he became professor of chemistry there in 1945, and was part of the team which discovered the transuranic elements plutonium (1940), americium and curium (1944). By bombarding the last two with alpha rays he produced the elements berkelium and californium in 1950. He was awarded the Nobel prize for chemistry in 1951 with **Edwin McMillan**, and from 1961 to 1971 was chairman of the US Atomic Energy Commission.

SEABURY, Samuel (1729–96) American clergyman, born in Groton, Connecticut. He graduated at Yale in 1748, studied medicine at Edinburgh, and received orders in the Church of England in 1753. Three years a missionary, in 1757 he became rector of Jamaica, Long Island, and in 1767 of Westchester, New York. Despite imprisonment for his loyalty to Britain which he maintained through the War of American Independence as a royalist army chaplain, he was elected first Episcopal bishop of Connecticut in 1783. The Church of England refusing to consecrate him because he could not take the Oath of Allegiance, three bishops of the Scottish Episcopal Church performed the ceremony at Aberdeen (1784).

SEAGA, Edward Philip George (1930–) American-born Jamaican politician. He went to school in Kingston, Jamaica, and then returned to study at Harvard University. He was on the staff of the

University of West Indies before moving into politics, joining the Jamaica Labour party (JLP) and becoming its leader in 1974. He entered the House of Representatives in 1962 and served in the administration of Hugh Shearer (1967–72) before becoming leader of the opposition. In 1980 he and the JLP had a resounding, and surprising, win over **Michael Manley**'s People's National party (PNP), and Seaga became prime minister. He called a snap election in 1983 and won all the assembly seats, but in 1989 Manley and the PNP returned to power with a landslide victory.

SEAMAN, Sir Owen (1861–1936) English writer. He was educated at Shrewsbury and Clare College, Cambridge, became professor of literature at Newcastle (1890), and was editor of *Punch* (1906–32). His parodies and verses on society which include *Paulopostprandials* (1833), *In Cap and Bells* (1889) and *From the Home Front* (1918) were very popular.

SEARLE, Humphrey (1915–82) English composer, born in Oxford. He studied at the Royal College of Music and in Vienna with **Webern**. He became musical adviser to Sadler's Wells Ballet, 1951–57. He wrote *Twentieth Century Counterpoint*, and a study of the music of **Liszt**. An exponent of the 'twelve note system', he composed five symphonies, two piano concertos and a trilogy of works for speaker, chorus and orchestra to words by **Edith Sitwell** and **James Joyce**, many other choral-orchestral works and three operas, the last of them *Hamlet* (1968).

SEARLE, John (1932–) American philosopher, born in Denver, Colorado. He taught at Oxford from 1956 to 1959 and since 1959 has been professor of philosophy at the University of California at Berkeley. In such works as *Speech Acts* (1969) and *Expression and Meaning* (1979) he expounded a distinctive approach to the study of language and its relation to mind, which has greatly influenced linguists and cognitive scientists as well as philosophers. He also wrote a famous account of the student riots in California, *The Campus War* (1971), and delivered the Reith lectures on *Minds, Brains, and Science* in 1984.

SEARLE, Ronald William Fordham (1920–) English cartoonist, painter, author and creator of the girls of St Trinian's, born in Cambridge. He studied at Cambridge School of Art while working as a solicitor's clerk and drew his first cartoon for The *Cambridge Daily News* in 1935, contributing 200 before moving to magazines, including *Lilliput*, *London Opinion*, and *Punch*. Serving in the Royal Engineers painting camouflage (1939), he was a prisoner of war for three and a half years, later publishing a book of his sketches made in Changi Camp. In 1956 he became staff theatrical caricaturist for *Punch* and in 1961 moved to Paris, becoming the first foreign artist to exhibit at the *Bibliothèque Nationale* (1973). He designed animated films like *Dick Deadeye* (1975), the animated sequences for *Those Magnificent Men in Their Flying Machines* (1965) and titles for features based on his St Trinian's schoolgirls.

SEBASTIAN, St (d.c.288) Christian martyr, a native of Narbonne and a victim of the **Diocletian** persecution. He is said to have been a captain of the praetorian guard, and secretly a Christian. Diocletian, according to tradition, hearing that he favoured Christians, ordered him to be slain. But the archers did not quite kill him: a woman named Irene nursed him back to life. When he upbraided the tyrant for his cruelty, Diocletian had him beaten to death with rods. His feast day is 20 January.

SEBASTIAN (1554–78) king of Portugal, a grandson of the emperor **Charles V** and nephew of **Philip II** of Spain. He succeeded his grandfather John III in 1557. Following the regencies of his grandmother, Catalina (1557–62) and great-uncle, Cardinal Henry (1562–68), he took control of the government at the age of 14. Lost in dreams of conquest and crusading zeal, he launched a futile and costly war against the Moors of North Africa, and fell in the battle of Alcazar-Qivir in Algeria. His death without an heir opened the way for the union of Portugal with Spain under his uncle, but continuing rumours that he was still alive fuelled Portuguese nationalism and gave rise to a series of impostors. The popular belief that he would come again revived as late as 1807–08 when Portugal was occupied by the French.

SÉBASTIANI, François Horace Bastien, Count (1772–1851) French soldier and diplomat, born near Bastia in Corsica. He became one of **Napoleon**'s most devoted partisans. He fought at Marengo (1800), was wounded at Austerlitz (1805), twice undertook missions to Turkey (1802–06), commanded an army corps in Spain, and distinguished himself in the Russian campaign (1812) and at Leipzig (1813). He joined Napoleon on his return from Elba, but after 1830 was twice in the ministry, and was ambassador at Naples and London. He was made marshal of France in 1840.

SEBASTIANO DEL PIOMBO See **PIOMBO**

SÉBILLOT, Paul (1843–1918) French folklorist, born in Matignon, Côtes-du-Nord. He abandoned law for painting, and from 1870 to 1883 exhibited in the Salon. He then held a post in the ministry of public works, and devoting himself to the study of Breton folk tales, published the standard work *Le Folklore de France* (1907).

SECCHI, Angelo (1818–78) Italian astronomer, born in Reggio. Trained as a Jesuit, he became professor of physics at Washington, USA, and in 1849 director of the observatory at the Collegio Romano. He originated classification of stars by spectrum analysis.

SECKENDORFF, Veit Ludwig von (1626–92) German statesman and historian. He served the princes of Saxony and Brandenburg, was chancellor of the University of Halle, and wrote a Latin compendium of church history (1664) and a work *De Lutheranismo* (1688).

SECOMBE, Sir Harry (1921–) Welsh entertainer, born in Swansea. A choir boy and office worker, he served in the army during World War II, making his stage début in *Revuedeville* (1946) before becoming a regular on the radio show *Variety Bandbox* (1947). An exuberant, roly-poly comic with an irrepressible laugh, he joined with **Peter Sellers**, **Spike Milligan** and **Michael Bentine** in *The Goons* (1951–59), a much-loved radio show whose iconoclasm and lunacy had a wide-reaching influence. Besides countless variety shows, his stage appearances include *Humpty Dumpty* (1959), *Pickwick* (1963), *The Four Musketeers* (1967) and *The Plumber's Progress* (1975). A popular singer with dozens of albums to his credit, his films include *Oliver!* (1968) and *Song of Norway* (1970). As a writer he has contributed regularly to *Punch*, and his fiction includes *Twice Brightly* (1974) and *Katy and the Nurgla* (1978). Recently he has acted as singer and host of the religious television series *Highway* (1983–). He was knighted in 1981.

SEDGMAN, Frank (1927–) Australian tennis player, born in Mont Albert, Victoria. In 1951 he defeated **Jaroslav Drobny** in the Wimbledon singles final, thus becoming the first Australian to win there since World War II. Under the shrewd captaincy of Harry Hopman, the Australian team of Sedgman, Bromwich and McGregor (with whom he accomplished the Grand Slam in Doubles in 1951) regained the Davis Cup from the USA in 1950 and only lost it on Sedgman's turning professional in 1953. His game was based on the modern style of heavy and early vollying and he was influential on the careers of such younger players as **Lew Hoad**.

SEDGWICK, Adam (1785–1873) English geologist, born in Dent, Cumbria. Graduating in mathematics from Trinity College, Cambridge (1808), he became Woodwardian professor of geology in 1818. In 1835 he calculated the stratigraphic succession of fossil -bearing rocks in North Wales, naming the oldest of them the Cambrian period. His best work was on *British Palaeozoic Fossils* (1854); with Sir **Roderick Murchison** he studied the Alps and the Lake District, and identified the Devonian system in south-west England. He strongly opposed Darwin's *Origin of Species*.

SEDLEY, Sir Charles (1639–1701) English courtier and poet, born probably in London. He was notorious at court for debauchery and wit. He became an MP in 1668. He is remembered less for his plays—*The Mulberry Garden*, *Antony and Cleopatra*, *Bellamira*—than for a few songs and *vers de société*.

SEEBECK, Thomas Johann (1770–1831) Estonian-born German physicist, born in Tallin (now in the USSR). A member of a wealthy merchant family, he went to Germany to study medicine, qualifying in 1802, but spending his time thereafter in research in physics. In 1822 he showed that if a circuit is made of a loop of two metals with two junctions, then when the junctions are at different temperatures a current flows; he had thus discovered the thermoelectric effect, now much used in thermocouples for temperature measurement.

SEEBOHM, Frederic (1833–1912) English economic historian, born in Yorkshire, brother of **Henry Seebohm**. Called to the bar in 1856, he became a partner in a bank at Hitchin. A revisionist of Anglo-Saxon history, he wrote *The Oxford Reformers of 1498* (1867), *The English Village Community* (1883), *The Tribal System in Wales* (1895) and *Tribal Custom in Anglo-Saxon Law* (1902).

SEEBOHM, Henry (1832–95) English industrialist and ornithologist, born in Yorkshire, brother of **Frederic Seebohm**. Of Swedish and German descent, he set up a steel works in Sheffield, where he prospered. He travelled in Greece, Asia Minor, Russia and Japan in pursuit of his hobby, and wrote *A History of British Birds* (1883–85). His *Coloured Figures of Eggs of British Birds* (1896) and *The Birds of Siberia* (1901) were published posthumously.

SEEFRIED, Irmgard (1919–88) Austrian soprano, born in Köngetried, Germany. She is famous for her performances with Vienna State Opera, especially in the operas of **Mozart** and **Richard Strauss**.

SEEGER, Pete (1919–) American folk-singer and songwriter, born in New York. The father figure of the American folk-music revival, he studied sociology at Harvard University before becoming a professional musician in the late 1930s. In 1940, along with **Woody Guthrie**, he formed the Almanac Singers, whose repertoire of radical songs marked the start of the 'protest' movement in contemporary folk-music. A later Seeger group, the Weavers, carried on this tradition. Seeger's unpretentious singing style and homely banjo playing made him a popular solo artist, but his uncompromising political stance caused him to fall foul of the Un-American Activities Committee in the 1950s, and for many years he was shunned by the American media. His best-known songs include 'Where Have All the Flowers Gone?' and 'Little Boxes', although his name will always be associated with 'We Shall Overcome', which he adapted from a traditional song.

SEELEY, Sir John Robert (1834–95) English historian, son of the publisher Robert Benton Seeley (1798–1866). Educated at City of London School and Christ's College, Cambridge, he became professor of Latin at University College, London (1863), and of modern history at Cambridge (1869). His *Ecce Homo* (1865), a popular Life of Christ, caused much controversy in religious circles. Other works include *Natural Religion* (1882), the authoritative *Life and Times of Stein* (1874) and *The Expansion of England* (1883).

SEFERIADES, George, pseud **Seferis** (1900–71) Greek poet and diplomat, born in Smyrna. He was educated at Athens and the Sorbonne. Ambassador to the Lebanon (1953–57) and the UK (1957–62), he wrote lyrical poetry, collected in *The Turning Point* (1931), *Mythistorema* (1935) and others. He translated **T S Eliot**'s *The Waste Land* into Greek. In 1963 he was awarded the Nobel prize for literature.

SEFSTRÖM, Nils Gabriel (1787–1854) Swedish physician and chemist. In 1831 he discovered the element vanadium in a specimen of soft iron.

SEGAL, George (1924–) American sculptor, born in New York. He studied at Cooper Union (1941) and Pratt Institute of Design (1947), finally graduating from New York University in 1950 and Rutgers in 1963. Beginning as a painter, he turned to sculpture and is best-known for his life-size plaster figures, cast from life and usually unpainted, which exist as ghostly presences within the realistic environments he creates for them, using real objects, eg *Girl in a Doorway*, 1969.

SEGAR, Elzie Crisler (1894–1938) American strip cartoonist, born in Chester, Illinois, the creator of *Popeye the Sailor*. Son of a house-painter, he took a correspondence course in cartooning and went to Chicago for the daily strip, *Charlie Chaplin's Comic Capers* (1916). His first creation was *Barry the Boob* (1917) for the *Chicago Herald*. In New York he started *Thimble Theater* (1919) for King Features, originally a burlesque on stage melodramas. The cast included heroine Olive Oyl, whose brother Castor encountered a one-eyed sailor named Popeye in January 1929. Popeye moved into **Max Fleischer** animated cartoons from 1933, and had his statue erected in Crystal City (the home of spinach). He also popularized the hamburger, and added 'jeep', 'goon' and 'wimp' (from the character Wimpy) to the language.

SEGHERS, Hercules Pietersz (1589/90–c.1635) Dutch landscape painter and etcher, probably born in Haarlem. He was a pupil of **G van Coninxloo** and, from 1614, was working in Amsterdam. His landscapes are unprecedented in their dramatic nature and, as they seem to be taken from nature, it has been argued that he must have travelled, most likely to Italy via the Alps. His paintings and etchings were highly regarded in his own day and were very influential: **Rembrandt** is known to have owned eight of his paintings. A virtuoso etcher, he would often use tinted paper to modify lighting effects. Despite his reputation, little is known of his personal life. In 1678 a biography was published by the Dutch painter Samuel van Hoogstraten, in which the artist is pictured as a destitute drunkard who ended his life by falling downstairs in a state of intoxication. While there is some evidence that Seghers had financial problems towards the end of his life, much of the account seems to be the result of a fanciful equation of the wild and romantic character of the work with the artist.

SEGONZAC, André Dunoyer de (1884–1974) French painter and engraver, born in Boussy-Saint-Antoine. He was influenced by **Courbet** and **Corot**, and produced many delicate watercolour landscapes, etchings and illustrations. His series of engravings of *Beaches* was published in 1935.

SEGOVIA, Andres (1894–1987) Spanish guitarist, born in Linares. Influenced by the Spanish nationalist composers, he evolved a revolutionary guitar technique permitting the performance of a wide range of music, and many composers wrote works for him. In 1981 he was created Marquis of Salobrēna by royal decree.

SEGRAVE, Sir Henry O'Neal de Hane (1896–1930) American-born British racing driver, born of Irish parentage in Baltimore. Educated at Eton and Sandhurst, he served in the Royal Flying Corps in World War I. Wounded in 1916, he became technical secretary to the air minister. A leading postwar racing driver, he helped to design the Sunbeam car, in which he broke the land speed record with a speed of 203.9 mph, raising this to 231 mph in 1929. He was killed in his boat *Miss England* on Lake Windermere, on a trial run, during which he had surpassed the world water speed record.

SEGRÈ, Emilio (1905–89) Italian-born American physicist who discovered the antiproton. A pupil of **Fermi**, he fled from the **Mussolini** régime to the USA. He took American nationality in 1944, having already been on the staff of the University of California for several years and having helped to develop the atomic bomb at Los Alamos. He shared the 1959 Nobel prize for physics with **Owen Chamberlain** for researches on the antiproton.

SEGUIER, William (1771–1843) English artist, born in London of Huguenot descent. He studied under **George Morland**, but abandoned painting for the art of the restorer and connoisseur, and helped **George IV** to gather together the Royal Collection. When the National Gallery was inaugurated, he became its first keeper. As superintendent of the British Institution, he was succeeded at his death by his brother John (1785–1856), also a painter and his partner in the picture-restoring business.

SÉGUIN, Marc (1786–1875) French mechanical and civil engineer, born in Annonay. He was taught science informally by his uncle **Joseph Montgolfier**, and maintained an interest throughout his life in problems such as the mechanical equivalent of heat. His principal achievements were in engineering, notably his association with the development of wire-rope suspension bridges from 1825 onwards, and his invention of the multi-tubular (fire-tube) boiler which he patented in 1827. He used this successfully in 1829, on the railway he had built between Lyon and St-Étienne, in a locomotive which employed forced draught from a fan driven by the wheels of the tender. It was also used by **George Stephenson** in his *Rocket* locomotive.

SEGUNDO, Juan Luis (1925–) Uruguayan Jesuit liberation theologian, born in Montevideo. After studying in Argentina and Europe he became director of the Pedro Fabbro Institute of socio-religious research in Montevideo. Though critical of the methodology of some liberation theologians in *The Liberation of Theology* (1976), he defended them against Vatican criticisms in *Theology and the Church* (1986). He advocates employing a 'hermeneutical circle', in which questioning of prevailing ideological and theological assumptions that govern the received way of interpreting scripture leads to new understanding. His own multi-volume exposition of liberation theology is entitled *Jesus of Nazareth Yesterday and Today* (5 vols, 1984–88).

SÉGUR, Louis Philippe, Comte de Ségur d'Aguesseau (1753–1820) French soldier and man of letters. As French ambassador in St Petersburg he was a great favourite of the empress **Catherine II, the Great**. Later he served in the American War of Independence, and hailed the French Revolution. Among his writings (33 vols) was *La Politique de tous les cabinets de l'Europe* (1793).

SÉGUR, Philippe Paul (1780–1873) French soldier, son of **Louis Philippe Ségur**. A general in the first empire under **Napoleon**, he wrote a history (1824) of the Russian campaign of 1812, and *Histoire de Russie et de Pierre le Grand* (1829).

SÉGUR, Sophie Rostopchine, Comtesse de Ségur (1799–1874) Russian-born French author, daughter of a Russian soldier and statesman, Count Fyodor Rostopchin. She married Comte Eugéne de Ségur and lived in France, writing children's books based on a central character called 'Sophie', such as *Les malheurs de Sophie* (1859) and *Mémoires d'un Âne*.

SEIBER, Mátyás (1905–60) Hungarian-born British composer, born in Budapest. He studied there under **Kodály**, and later became a private music teacher (1925) and professor of jazz (1928–33) at Hoch's Conservatory at Frankfurt-am-Main. He settled in Britain in 1935 and in 1942 became a tutor at Morley College, London. He gained only belated recognition as a composer, with strong musical affinities to **Bartok** and **Schoenberg**. His compositions include three string quartets, of which the second (1935) is the best known, other chamber works, piano music and songs and the *Ulysses* cantata (1946–47) based on **James Joyce**'s novel. He was killed in a motor accident in South Africa.

SEIDLER, Harry (1923–) Austrian-born Australian architect, born in Vienna. He studied at the Vasa Institute in Vienna, and later at Harvard where he studied under **Gropius**. He worked in New York, and later with **Oscar Niemeyer** in Brazil, before setting up practice in Sydney in 1948. His first design, for a private house, won the coveted Sulman medal three years later, since which time Seidler has won many awards for public and private buildings. He has worked in Mexico and Hong Kong, and designed the Australian embassy in Paris. His application of modern building techniques were well demonstrated in his MLC Centre and the award- winning Australia Square tower, in central Sydney.

SEIFERT, Jaroslav (1901–) Czech poet, brought up in a poor family in a working-class suburb of Prague. His first collection was *Město v slzáck* (1921, City of Tears) in which he looked back in anger at the human waste of World War I, urging a working-class revolution. In 1923 he moved to and fell under the spell of Paris and translated **Apollinaire**. His second collection was *Samá láska* (1923, All Love) in which his private experience is to the fore. He was expelled from the Communist party in 1929 and joined the Social Democrats. After Munich (1938) and the Nazi occupation his patriotism emerged in *Přílba Llíny* (1945, A Helmet of Earth), in which he identifies himself with the people's grief. Most memorable are the poems which evoke the four days in May 1945 when the citizens of Prague rose against the tatters of the Nazi forces. He edited *Práce*, a trade union paper, but he was too much his own man to enjoy the trust of the Communist party. New work was shunned and *Morový sloup* (1977, trans *The Prague Column*, 1979) had to be published abroad. He was awarded the Nobel prize for literature in 1984.

SEJANUS See **TIBERIUS**

SELBORNE, Roundell Palmer, 1st earl of (1812–95) English jurist and hymnologist, born in Mixbury, Oxfordshire. He was solicitor-general (1861) and attorney-general (1863–66), but his opposition to

Gladstone's Irish Church policy delayed his promotion to lord chancellor (1872–74, 1880–85). He was an outstanding judge, promoted much legislation, and reformed the English court system, merging all the old courts into the Supreme Court of Judicature (1875). He also wrote hymnological and liturgical studies.

SELBORNE, William Waldegrave Palmer, 2nd Earl of (1859–1942) English politician. He was under-secretary for the colonies (1895–1900), First Lord of the Admiralty (1900–05), high commissioner for South Africa (1905–10), president of the board of agriculture (1915–16) and warden of Winchester (1920–25).

SELBY, Prideaux John (1788–1857) English naturalist, born in Alnwick, Northumberland. A fellow of University College, Oxford, he was appointed high sheriff of Northumberland in 1823. He produced *Illustrations of British Ornithology* (19 vols, 1821–34), the first book of British birds to be shown life-size, and *Illustrations of Ornithology* (1825–43). With Sir **William Jardine** he founded and edited the *Magazine of Zoology and Botany* (1837), and also wrote *A History of British Forest Trees* (1842).

SELCRAIG See **SELKIRK, Alexander**

SELDEN, John (1584–1654) English jurist, historian and antiquary, born near Worthing. He studied at Oxford and London, where he acquired wealth, yet found time for profound and wide study. His *Duello*, or *Single Combat*, was published in 1610, while his *Titles of Honour* (1614) is still an authority. *Analecton Anglo-Britannicon* (1615) dealt with the civil government of Britain previous to the Norman Conquest. In 1617 he published his erudite work on the Syrian gods, *De Diis Syriis*. His *History of Tithes* (1618), demolishing their divine right, earned him the fulminations of the clergy, and was suppressed by the privy council. In 1621 he was imprisoned for advising parliament to repudiate King **James**'s doctrine that their privileges were originally royal grants. In 1623 he was elected member for Lancaster and in 1628 he helped to draw up the Petition of Right; the year after he was committed to the Tower with **Eliot**, **Holles** and others. In 1635 he dedicated to the king his *Mare Clausum* (an answer to the *Mare Liberum* of **Grotius**). In 1640 he entered the Long Parliament for Oxford University, and opposed the policy that led to the expulsion of the bishops from the House of Lords and finally to the abolition of Episcopacy. He took no direct part in the impeachment of **Strafford**, voted against the Attainder Bill, and had no share in **Laud**'s prosecution. He sat as a lay member in the Westminster Assembly (1643), and was appointed keeper of the records in the Tower and (1644) an Admiralty commissioner. In 1646 he subscribed the Covenant. In 1647 he was appointed a university visitor, and sought to moderate the fanaticism of his colleagues. After the execution of **Charles I**, of which he disapproved, he took little share in public matters. He was buried in the Temple Church. He had also written in Latin books on the Arundel Marbles (1624) and on Hebrew law (1634–50), besides posthumous tracts and treatises, of which the most valuable is his *Table Talk* (1689).

SELEUCUS the name of six kings of the Seleucidae, the dynasty to whom fell that portion of **Alexander I the Great**'s Asiatic conquests which included Syria, part of Asia Minor, Persia and Bactria. See **Antiochus**.

SELEUCUS I, surnamed **Nicator** (c.358–280 BC) Macedonian general under **Alexander the Great**, obtained Babylonia, to which he added Susiana, Media and Asia Minor. He founded Greek and Macedonian colonies, and also built Antioch, Seleucia on the Tigris, etc, but was assassinated.

SELEUCUS II, surnamed **Callinicus** (d.c.226 BC) son of **Antiochus II**. His reign (246–26 BC) was beset by conflict. He suffered invasion from **Ptolemy III Euergetes** of Egypt, his half-brother, lost control of his eastern territories to the rising power of the Parthians and the Greek rulers of Bactria, and lost Asia Minor to his younger brother Antiochus Hierax.

SELFRIDGE, Harry Gordon (1858–1947) American-born British merchant, born in Ripon, Wisconsin. Educated privately, he joined a trading firm in Chicago and brought new ideas and great organizing ability into the business. In 1892 he was made a junior partner. While visiting London in 1906 he bought a site in Oxford Street, and built upon it the large store, which bears his name (opened 1909). He took British nationality in 1937.

SELIGMAN, Charles Gabriel (1873–1940) English anthropologist, born in London. He trained as a physician in London, then joined the Cambridge Anthropological Expedition to the Torres Straits (1898–99), and carried out subsequent field research in New Guinea, Ceylon and the Sudan. His principal works, based on this research, include *The Melanesians of British New Guinea* (1910), *The Veddas* (*Ceylon*) (1911) and *Pagan Tribes of the Nilotic Sudan* (1932), the latter two volumes co-authored with his wife, Brenda, who collaborated in all his later research. Throughout the earlier part of his career, he continued with his studies in pathology, until his appointment in 1913 to the first chair of ethnology at London University turned his interests decisively towards anthropology. He pioneered the application of a psychoanalytic approach and had a strong influence on the later work of both **Bronislaw Malinowski** and Sir **Edward Evans-Pritchard**.

SELIM I (1467–1520) Ottoman sultan of Turkey. In 1512 he dethroned his father, **Bayezit II**, and caused him, his own brothers, and nephews to be put to death. In 1514 he declared war against Persia, and took Diyarbakir and Kurdistan. He conquered in 1517 Egypt, Syria and the Hejaz, with Medina and Mecca; won from the **Abbasid** calif at Cairo the headship of the Muslim world; chastized the insolence of the Janissaries; sought to improve the condition of the peoples he had conquered; and cultivated the poetic art. He was succeeded by his son, **Süleyman II, the Magnificent**.

SELIM II (1524–74) Ottoman emperor of Turkey from 1566, son of **Süleyman the Magnificent**. He proved to be an indolent drunkard. During his reign Cyprus was sacked by Turkish troops and 30000 inhabitants of Nicosia were massacred. A naval force under Don **John of Austria** succeeded in defeating the Turkish fleet at the battle of Lepanto in 1571, but the victors did not follow up their success, and Selim recaptured Tunisia in 1574.

SELIM III (1761–1807) Ottoman sultan of Turkey. Succeeding his brother in 1780, he prosecuted the war with Russia; but the Austrians joined the Russians, and Belgrade surrendered to them, while the Russians took Bucharest, Bender, Akerman and Ismail. Selim's attempts to reform the administration cost him his throne and life.

SELJUKS a Turkish dynasty belonging to a group of tribes known as the Oghuz, whose ancestor, Seljük, converted to Sunni Islam in Transoxania in the late 10th century. In the 1040s his grandsons, Tüghrül-Beg (c. 990–1063) and Chagri-Beg (c.990–1060) conquered most of Persia, dividing up their conquests between them. In 1055 Tüghrül-Beg and his troops entered Baghdad, freeing the 'Abbasid caliph from the tutelage of the Shī'ite Buyids and receiving from him the title of 'sultan' which legitimized his position as the real ruler over most of the caliphate. He was succeeded by

Chagri-Beg's son **Alp-Arslan**, who united the family domains; under him and his son Malik-Shāh (1055–92), sultan from 1072, the Great Seljuk empire attained its greatest extent, incorporating Persia, Iraq, Syria, and Anatolia. The basis of Seljuk power was their regular army of Turkish mamluk slaves, frequently augmented by nomadic Turkmen tribesmen, and the Persian administrative system which they took over. However, in accordance with the Seljuk tradition of joint rule, Malik-Shāh divided up the empire among his family, a development which coincided with the arrival of the First Crusade. The loss of Syria to the Franks at the beginning of the 12th century was accompanied by the factual independence of many of the Turkmen leaders and even of the *atabegs*, provincial governors who were in theory regents for infant Seljuks. The most enduring of the various Seljuk successor states was the sultanate of Rūm in Anatolia, established by Alp-Arslan's cousin Süleyman (d. 1084) and his son Kilij-Arslan I (d. 1107) on territory won from the Byzantine ('Roman') empire. Thereafter the sultanate, based on Iconium (Konya), fell under the domination of the Danishmends, a rival Turkmem emirate in northern Anatolia, a situation reversed in the 1140s by Mas'ūd (d. 1155), whose son Kilij-Arslan II (d. 1192) won a decisive victory over the Byzantine emperor **Manuel Comnenus** at Myrioke phalon (1176). After the reign of Kay-Qubād (d.1237), who ruled from 1220, the sultanate gradually crumbled under Mongol pressure, to be finally destroyed in 1308.

SELKIRK, Alexander or **Alexander Selcraig** (1676–1721) Scottish sailor, born in Largo, Fife, the original of **Defoe**'s Robinson Crusoe. He ran away to sea in 1695, and in 1704 joined the South Sea buccaneers. In 1704 he quarrelled with his captain, **William Dampler**, and at his own request was put ashore on the uninhabited island of Juan Fernández. Having lived alone there for four years and four months, he was at last taken off by **Thomas Dover**. He returned to Largo in 1712, and at his death was a lieutenant on a man-of-war.

SELKIRK, Thomas Douglas, 5th Earl of (1771–1820) Scottish colonizer. He settled 800 emigrants from the Scottish Highlands in Prince Edward Island (1803) and in the Red River Valley, Manitoba, although twice evicted by soldiers from the Fort William post of the Northwest Fur Company (1815–16).

SELLAR, Patrick (1780–1851) Scottish lawyer and estate factor, born in Moray. He became notorious during the Highland Clearances as factor to the 1st Duke of Sutherland for the brutality with which he evicted the crofting tenant families of Strathnaver in 1814 to make room for sheep. He was brought to trial by Robert MacKid, the sheriff-substitute of Sutherland, but was acquitted, and later became a sheep farmer in Morvern.

SELLAR, William Young (1825–90) Scottish scholar, born near Golspie, son of the notorious **Patrick Sellar**. Educated at The Edinburgh Academy, he studied classics at Glasgow University and Balliol College, Oxford. He was professor of Greek at St Andrews (1859–63), and thereafter professor of Latin at Edinburgh. He made his name by his brilliant *Roman Poets of the Republic* (1863), which was followed by *The Roman Poets of the Augustan Age—Virgil* (1877) and *Horace and the Elegiac Poets* (1892), the latter edited by his nephew, **Andrew Lang**.

SELLARS, Peter (1958–) American stage director, born in Pittsburgh, Pennsylvania. He directed several plays while still a student at Harvard, where he took an array of courses in music, film and art history. From 1983 to 1984 he was director of the Boston Shakespeare Company, and from 1984 to 1986 director of the American National Theater at the Kennedy Center in Washington, where his radical staging of **Sophocles**' *Ajax* divided audiences and critics. He is internationally recognized as a daringly innovative director of opera, setting his productions in the cultural landscape of 20th-century America.

SELLERS, Peter (1925–80) English actor and comedian, born in Southsea. After a spell as a stand-up comic and impressionist first with the Entertainments National Services Association, then at the Windmill Theatre, he moved into radio. His meeting with comedian **Spike Milligan** heralded *The Goon Show*, one of the funniest radio shows of all time, which ran for seven years (1951–59). He made his film début with *Penny Points to Paradise* (1951) and became one of the stalwarts of British film comedy in the 1950s and '60s. His range of characterizations included the spiv member of *The Ladykillers* (1955), a pompous union leader in *I'm Alright Jack* (1959) and a Welsh librarian in *Only Two Can Play* (1962). Two films with **Stanley Kubrick** established his international reputation: *Lolita* (1962) and *Dr Strangelove* (1963), in which he played three roles. His popularity was sustained as the incompetent French detective Inspector Clouseau in a series of films that began with *The Pink Panther* (1963) and extended beyond his death to *The Trail of the Pink Panther* (1982). He received an Academy Award nomination for *Being There* (1979).

SELLON, Priscilla Lydia (1821–76) English religious reformer. In 1849, at Plymouth, she founded the second Anglican sisterhood. Its spiritual director was **Edward Pusey**.

SELOUS, Frederick Courtenay (1851–1917) English explorer and big-game hunter, born in London. He first visited South Africa in 1871, fought in Matabeleland (1893, 1895), and in 1916 won the DSO and fell in action in West Africa. The Selous National Park, Tanzania is named after him.

SELWYN, George Augustus (1809–78) English prelate, born in Hampstead. He was educated at Eton and St John's College, Cambridge, where he rowed in the first university boat race (1829), and graduated in 1831. In 1841 he was consecrated the first (and only) bishop of New Zealand and Melanesia, of whose church he played a large part in settling the constitution. In 1867 he was appointed bishop of Lichfield, where upon his initiative the first Diocesan Conference in which the laity were duly represented met in 1868. Selwyn College, Cambridge, was founded (1882) in his memory. His son, John Richardson (1844–98), was bishop of Melanesia 1877, and master of Selwyn College, Cambridge.

SELWYN-LLOYD, Baron (John) Selwyn Brooke (1904–78) originally **LLoyd**, English politician, born in Liverpool of Anglo-Welsh parentage. Educated at Fettes and Cambridge, he studied law and became a barrister in 1930 with a practice in Liverpool. He stood unsuccessfully as Liberal candidate for Macclesfield and in 1931 transferred his allegiance to the Conservative party. Meantime he entered local government, becoming in 1936 chairman of the Hoylake Urban District Council. During World War II he was a staff officer rising to the rank of colonel general staff, Second Army. In parliament in 1945 as Conservative member for Wirral, he continued to practise law, becoming a KC in 1947. In 1951 he was appointed minister of state, and in 1954 became successively minister of supply and minister of defence. As foreign secretary in 1955, he defended **Eden**'s policy on Suez, and was retained in this post until 1960 when he became Chancellor of the Exchequer, resigning in **Harold Macmillan**'s 'purge' in 1962. Refusing a peerage, he was given the task of investigating the Conservative party organization. He was lord privy seal and leader of the House (1963–64) and speaker of the House of Commons (1971–76). He was created a life peer in 1976.

SELYE, Hans Hugo Bruno (1907–82) Austrian-born Canadian physician, born in Vienna, the son of a surgeon. He studied medicine in Prague, Paris and Rome before emigrating to North America in the 1930s. After a decade at McGill University in Montreal (1933–45), he became in 1945 director of the Institute for Experimental Medicine and Surgery at the French-language University of Montreal. He was best known for his 'Stress-General Adaptation Syndrome', an attempt to link stress and anxiety and their biochemical and physiological consequences to many of the disorders of modern man.

SELZNICK, David O (Oliver) (1902–65) American cinema mogul, born in Pittsburgh, Ohio. He worked for his father Lewis J Selznick (1870–1933) in film distribution and promotion before turning producer on the short film *Will He Conquer Dempsey?* (1923). Employment as a story editor and associate producer at M-G-M and Paramount led to his appointment as vice president in charge of production at RKO when the studio created such films as *A Bill of Divorcement* (1932) and *King Kong* (1933). A stickler for detail, he was renowned for masterminding every aspect of a production and for despatching voluminous memos to those who worked with him. In 1936 he formed his own production company and produced *A Star Is Born* (1937) and his greatest achievement, the enduring screen adaptation of *Gone With the Wind* (1939), for which he received an Academy Award. Other successes included *Rebecca* (1940), *Duel in the Sun* (1946), and *A Farewell to Arms* (1957), which starred his second wife, the actress Jennifer Jones (1919–).

SEMENOV, Nikolai Nikolaevich (1896–1986) Russian physicist, and co-winner of the Nobel prize for chemistry in 1956 with Sir **Cyril Hinshelwood**. He was born at Saratov and graduated from the University of St Petersburg (now Leningrad). After a spell as assistant director at the Leningrad Physical Technical Institute (1920–31), he was appointed director of the newly-created Institute of Chemical Physics of the Academy of Sciences in Moscow, where he remained until shortly before his death. An expert in molecular physics, he carried out important research on the kinetics of gas reactions, for which he shared the Nobel prize in 1956—the first Soviet citizen ever to win a Nobel prize, and the first Russian resident in Russia since Ivan Pavlov in 1904.

SEMIRAMIS (9th century BC) semi-legendary queen of Assyria, the wife of Ninus, with whom she is supposed to have founded Babylon. The historical germ of the story seems to be the three years' regency of Sammu-ramat (811–808 BC), widow of Shamshi-Adad V, but the details are legendary, derived from **Ctesias** and the Greek historians, with elements of the Astarte myth.

SEMLER, Johann Salomo (1725–91) German theologian, born in Saalfeld. In 1753 he became professor of theology at Halle. He exercised a profound influence as a pioneer of the historical methods in biblical criticism. He was distinctively a rationalist, but he sincerely believed in revelation. In insisting on the distinction of the Jewish and Pauline types of Christianity he anticipated the Tübingen school.

SEMMELWEISS, Ignaz Philipp (1818–65) Hungarian obstetrician, born in Budapest. He studied there and at Vienna. Appalled by the heavy death rate in the Vienna maternity hospital where he worked, he introduced antiseptics. The death rate fell from 12% to $1\frac{1}{4}$%, but his superiors would not accept his conclusion and he was compelled to leave Vienna and return to Budapest. He contracted septicaemia in a finger and died in a mental hospital near Vienna from the disease he had spent his life combating.

SEMMES, Raphael (1809–77) American naval officer, born in Charles County, Maryland. He joined the US navy in 1826, but also studied law during periods of leave. He saw active service during the Mexican war, and in 1858 was made secretary to the Lighthouse Board. On the outbreak of the Civil War he first commanded the confederate raider *Sumter*, and then the *Alabama*, with which he proceeded to capture 65 vessels, nearly all of which were sunk or burned, and to destroy property estimated at $6000000. In 1864, the *Alabama* was sunk in action off Cherbourg by the US cruiser *Kearsarge*, but Semmes escaped. Later he edited a paper, was a professor, and practised law in Mobile. He wrote several books on service afloat.

SEMPER, Gottfried (1803–73) German architect, born in Hamburg. He deserted law for architecture and travelled in France, Italy and Greece. In 1834 he was appointed professor at Dresden, but his part in the revolution of 1848 compelled him to flee to England, where he designed the Victoria and Albert Museum. He eventually settled in Vienna, where the Burgtheater, the imperial palace and two museums, as well as the art gallery and railway station at Dresden testify to his adaptation of the Italian renaissance style.

SEMPILL, Robert (?1530–1595) Scottish author of witty ballads full of coarse vigour, such as *The Legend of a Lymaris Life* and *Sege of the Castel of Edinburgh*. He was an enemy of **Mary, Queen of Scots** and wrote satirical Reformation pieces, such as the *Life of the Tulchene Bishop of St Andrews*.

SEMPILL, Robert (?1595–?1665) Scottish poet, of Beltrees. He revived the methods of the Scottish *makaris* and started a trend for poetry in the vernacular, and invented a 'Standard Habbie' six-line stanza. He wrote *Habbie Simson*, *The Blythesome Bridal* and, possibly, *Maggie Lauder*.

SEN, Amartya Kumar (1933–) Indian economist. Educated in India and Cambridge, he was a fellow of Trinity College, Cambridge from 1957 to 1963, when he became professor of economics at New Delhi University, until 1971. He was professor of economics at the London School of Economics from 1971 to 1977, and then moved to Oxford where he became Drummond professor of political economy until 1988, when he took up a professorship at Harvard. He is noted for his work on the nature of poverty and famine.

SEN, Keshub Chunder (1838–84) Indian religious reformer, a native of Bengal. In about 1858 he was attracted by the Brahjma Samâj (see **Rammohun Roy**), and in 1866 founded the more liberal 'Brahma Samâj of India'. He visited England in 1870. In 1878 a schism broke out in his church, caused largely by his autocratic temper; and his last years brought disappointment.

SÉNANCOUR, Étienne Pivert de (1770–1846) French author, born in Paris. After nine years in Switzerland he returned to Paris about 1798. His fame rests on three books; *Rêveries sur la nature primitive de l'homme* (1799), *Obermann* (1804) and *Libres Méditations d'un solitaire inconnu*. The influence of **Goethe**'s *Werther* is persistent in his work. Sénancour, neglected in his day, was appreciated by **George Sand**, **Saint-Beuve** and **Matthew Arnold**.

SENDAK, Maurice Bernard (1928–) American illustrator and writer of children's books, born in

Brooklyn, New York City. His family were indigent Jewish immigrants from Poland. Like many American children brought up in the 1930s, he thrived on a stew of comics, **Walt Disney**, King Kong and **Charlie Chaplin**, supplemented with tales told to him by his father from the Old Testament and Jewish folklore. Sickly (he was often quarantined) and bookish, he attended Lafayette High School, but formal education did not appeal to him. Working as a window-dresser, he encountered classic illustrators in a toy store and was subsequently introduced to and commissioned by a publisher to illustrate *The Wonderful Farm* (1951) by Marcel Aymé. For *A Hole Is To Dig* (1952), he produced humorous, unsentimental drawings and in 1956 came *Kenny's Window*, the first book he both illustrated and wrote. But it was *Where the Wild Things Are* (1963) that made him internationally famous. Exploring the fantasy world of mischievous Max in whose room grows a forest inhabited by scary monsters, it fascinated children and perturbed parents. It won the Carnegie Medal and sold hugely. After this acknowledged classic he produced another, *In The Night Kitchen* (1970), in which Mickey falls out of bed into bread-dough being mixed by Ollie Hardy (from **Laurel** and **Hardy**) lookalikes. Latterly he has collaborated on operas as well as continuing to produce the distinctive, disturbing and daring books—*Outside Over There* (1981), *Nutcracker* (1981) and *Dear Mili* (1988)—that have made him the premier practitioner of his métier.

SENDERENS, Jean Baptiste (1856–1936) French chemist, born in Barbachen, Hautes-Pyrénées. With **Paul Sabatier** he discovered the hydrogenation of oils by catalysis in 1899.

SENEBIER, Jean (1742–1809) Swiss botanist and pastor, and city librarian of Geneva from 1773. In 1782 he first demonstrated the basic principle of photosynthesis.

SENECA, Marcus Annaeus, called **'the Elder'** (c.55 BC–c.40 AD) Roman rhetorician, born in Córdoba, Spain. Besides a history of Rome, now lost, he wrote for his sons a collection of imaginary court cases, *Oratorum et Rhetorum Sententiae*, *Divisiones*, *Colores Controversiae* (partly lost), and *Suasoriae*, a collection of earlier, rhetorical styles. He was the father of **Seneca the Younger** and grandfather of **Lucan**.

SENECA, Lucius Annaeus, called **'the Younger'** (c.4 BC–c.65 AD) Roman Stoic philosopher, statesman and tragedian, born in Cordova, Spain, the son of **Seneca the Elder**. He was educated in rhetoric and philosophy for a career in politics and law, which he began in Rome in 31. But in 41 he was banished to Corsica by the Emperor **Claudius** on a charge of adultery with the emperor's niece Julia, sister of **Caligula**; he spent eight years there in study and wrote the three treatises called *Consolationes*. He was recalled to Rome in 49 through the influence of **Agrippina the younger**, 3rd wife of Claudius and sister of Julia and became tutor to her son, the future Emperor **Nero**. He enjoyed considerable political influence for a while and was made consul by Nero in 57. But his moral influence waned, and though he tried to withdraw progressively from public life to devote himself to philosophy he lost favour with Nero, was denounced as a party to the conspiracy of Piso, and was ordered to commit suicide, which he did with composure and dignity. He was an eclectic Stoic, a moralist rather than a theorist, and a stylist much imitated by later essayists. His writings include: *De Ira*, *De Clementia*, *De Beneficiis*, *Epistolae morales ad Lucilium* and the *Apocolocyntosis divi Claudii* (literally, 'The Pumpkinification of the Divine Claudius', a scathing satire); he also wrote a number of verse tragedies which were influential in Elizabethan drama in England.

SENEFELDER, Aloys (1771–1834) Bavarian printer and inventor, born in Prague. Having been successfully an actor and playwright, about 1796 he invented lithography after accidentally discovering the possibilities of drawing with greasy chalk on wet stone. After various trials in 1806 he opened an establishment of his own in Munich. He became director of the Royal Printing Office in Munich, and established a training school at Offenbach.

SENERAT (d.1635) king of Kandy (Ceylon). He succeeded to the throne in 1604, having served as commander-in-chief of the army in his predecessor's wars with the Portuguese, who controlled the remainder of the island. The early part of his reign was a period of peace and prosperity with increased trade with the Portuguese. Portuguese aggression led to the renewal of hostilities in 1629 but Senerat was able completely to destroy the Portuguese army at the battle of Radenwiela in 1630. He was unable to capture the Portuguese capital of Colombo and in 1634 a peace settlement was agreed.

SENGHOR, Léopold Sédar (1906–) Senegalese politician and poet. Educated in Dakar and at the Sorbonne in Paris, he taught classics in France from 1935, where he became involved with literary figures and wrote poetry advocating the concept of 'negritude' to glorify African civilization and values. After World War II he sat in the French National Assembly (1946–58) and was a leader of the Senegalese independence movement. After independence in 1960, as leader of the Senegalese Progressive Union (UPS), he became the new nation's first president. In 1976 he reconstituted the UPS as the Senegalese Socialist party (PS) and gradually the one-party political system which he had created became more pluralist, although the PS remained the dominant force. Senghor was consistently re-elected until his retirement in 1980, his successor being **Abdou Diouf**.

SENIOR, Nassau William (1790–1864) English economist and 'prince of interviewers', born in Compton Beauchamp, Berkshire. Educated at Eton and Magdalen College, Oxford, in 1819 he was called to the bar; from 1825 to 1830, and again from 1847 to 1862, he was professor of political economy at Oxford; in 1832 he was appointed a poor-law commissioner; and in 1836–53 he was a master in chancery. He stressed the importance of the last hour's work in the cotton factories and opposed the trade unions. His publications include *On the Cost of Obtaining Money* (1830), *An Outline of the Science of Political Economy* (1836), and *Value of Money* (1840).

SENNACHERIB, (d.681 BC) king of Assyria. He succeeded his father, **Sargon II**, in 705 BC. He sacked Babylon in 689 BC. He invaded Judaea and besieged Hezekiah in Jerusalem. His great achievement was the rebuilding of Nineveh, but was instrumental in various other projects such as the making of the embankment of the Tigris, canals, water-courses. He was slain by one of his sons, and was succeeded by **Esarhaddon**.

SENNETT, Mack, originally **Michael Sinnott** (1880–1960) Canadian filmmaking pioneer, known as the King of Comedy, born in Danville, Quebec. A child singing prodigy, he hoped to pursue a career in opera and appeared in minor roles on Broadway and in burlesque between 1902 and 1908. He joined Biograph Studios in 1908, making his film début that year in *Baked in the Altar*. Under the tutelage of **D W Griffith**, he became a leading man and turned to direction with *The Lucky Toothache* (1910). By 1912 he had formed his own company, Keystone Co in Los Angeles, and set about altering and defining the conventions of American screen comedy. An ability to spot comic talent led to his discovery of **Charles Chaplin**, Fatty Arbuckle and numerous others, whilst scores of short comedies illustrated his skill for staging breathless chases, custard pie fights and the pricking of pomposity. He also established the popular Keystone Kops and the Sennett Bathing Beauties. His feature-length films include *Tillie's Punctured Romance* (1914), *The Goodbye Kiss* (1928) and *Way Up Thar* (1935). Semi-retired from 1935, he received a special Academy Award in 1937. *Mack Sennett: King of Comedy*, an as-told-to autobiography, was published in 1954.

SENUSRIT See **SESOSTRIS**

SEPÜLVEDA, Juan Ginés de (1490–1574) Spanish historian and churchman, born near Cordoba. He become historiographer to **Charles V**, preceptor to the future **Philip II**, and a canon of Salamanca. He was a champion of humanism. His Latin works include histories of Charles V and Philip II, a Life of **Albornoz**, and a History of Spain in the New World.

SÉQUARD See **BROWN-SÉQUARD, Édouard**

SEQUOYAH, or George Guess (c.1770–1843) American half-Cherokee scholar. In 1826 he invented a Cherokee syllabary of eighty-five characters. His name was given to a genus of giant coniferous trees (*Sequoia*) and to a national park.

SERAO, Matilde (1856–1927) Italian novelist and journalist, born in Patras in Greece, the daughter of a Greek father and a Neapolitan political refugee. She graduated as a teacher in Naples, worked in a telegraph office, and started writing articles for newspapers (1876–78) Her first novel of Neapolitan life was *Cuore Infermo* (1881), after which she joined the Rome newspaper *Capitan Fracassa*. She had a huge success with her next romantic novel, *Fantasia* (1882), followed by *Conquista di Roma* (1886), *Riccardo Joanna* (1887), *All' Erta Sentinella* (1889) and *Il Paese di Cuccagna* (1891).

SERF, St Scottish saint who founded the church of Culross between 697 and 706, but who yet figures in the legend of St **Kentigern** as his teacher. He is associated with an island on Loch Leven.

SERGEYEV-TSENSKY, Sergey (1875–1958) Russian novelist, born in Tambov province. From a Dostoevskian passion for morbid characterization, as in *The Tundra* (1902), he developed greater simplicity of style and social sense in the massive ten-volume novel sequence, *Transfiguration* (1914–40), which won him the Stalin prize in 1942.

SERKIN, Rudolf (1903–) Austrian-born American pianist, born in Eger, Bohemia. He studied composition with Joseph Marx and **Schoenberg** in Vienna and made his début there in 1915. He was closely associated with **Adolf Busch** (whose son-in-law he became) in chamber music. He settled in the USA in 1939 and directed the Curtis Institute, Philadelphia from 1968 to 1976. He founded the Marlboro School of Music (1949) and the Marlboro Music Festival (1950).

SERLING, Rod (1924–75) American television playwright, born in Syracuse, New York. A combat paratrooper during World War II, he attended Antioch College and began writing radio scripts before securing a radio staff job in Cincinnati. He first wrote for television in 1951 and won the first of six Emmy Awards for *Patterns* (1955). His other plays include *Requiem for a Heavyweight* (1956) and *The Comedian* (1957). He created, wrote and hosted the popular anthology series *The Twilight Zone* (1959–64) which often reflected his interest in the individual's struggle against social and political pressures, while also showing his mastery of the surprise, twist-in-the-tail ending. He created, hosted and occasionally wrote the similar series *Night Gallery* (1970–73) and frequently narrated documentaries on scientific and nature subjects. The author of over 200 television plays, his few film scripts include *Seven Days in May* (1964).

SERLIO, Sebastiano (1475–1554) Italian architect and painter, born in Bologna. After training there, he moved to Rome in 1514, to continue with **Baldassare Peruzzi**. He moved to Venice in 1527, and in 1540 was called to France by **Francis I**. More influential than his architecture was his treatise on Italian architecture, *Regole generali di architettura* (1537–51, and posthumously 1575), including plans bequeathed by **Peruzzi**: the treatise was widely consulted, and later received English, German and Dutch editions. As master of works at Fontainebleau, his most important work was the Grand Ferrare (1541–48, demolished), where the pioneering use of an enclosed U-plan set the precedent for French town-houses in subsequent years. The quadrangular chateau at Ancy-le-Franc, Tonnerre (from 1546), was similarly exemplary.

SERRA, Richard (1939–) American sculptor, born in San Francisco. He studied art at Berkley and Yale. From 1964 to 1966 he studied in Paris and Florence before settling in New York. In the late 1960s he produced a series of films and began manufacturing austere minimalist works from sheet steel, iron and lead, barely altering the original form of the metal. Many of his works are of huge dimensions: notable are the long arcs of sheet metal which can span city squares and the cubic structures composed of massive metal plates balanced vertically against one another. Public commissions for such works have made him a controversial but highly influential artist.

SERRANO, Francisco, Duke de la Torre (1810–85) Spanish statesman, fought against the Carlists and, nominally a liberal, favoured by **Isabella II**, played a conspicuous part in various ministries. Banished in 1866, in 1868 he drove out the queen and was regent until the accession of **Amadeus I of Savoy** (1870). He waged successful war against the Carlists in 1872 and 1874; and again regent (1874), resigned the power into the hands of **Alfonso XIII**.

SERRE, Jean-Pierre (1926–) French mathematician, born in Bages. He studied at the École Normale Supérieure before working at the Centre National de la Recherche Scientifique and the University of Nancy, becoming professor at the Collège de France in 1956. He has worked in homotopy theory, algebraic geometry, class field theory, group theory and number theory. In 1954 he was awarded the Fields Medal (the mathematical equivalent of the Nobel prize).

SERRES, Olivia See **OLIVE, Princess**

SERTORIUS, Quintus (123–72 BC) Roman soldier, born in Nursia in the Sabine country. He fought with **Marius** in Gaul (102 BC) and supported him against **Sulla**. In 83, as praetor, he was given Spain as his province: in 80 he headed a successful rising of natives and Roman exiles against Rome, holding out against Sulla's commanders (including **Pompey**) for eight years until he was assassinated by his chief lieutenant.

SERTÜRNER, Friedrich Wilhelm Adam (1783–1841) German chemist, born in Neuhaus near Paderborn. In 1805 he isolated morphine from opium and proved that organic bases contained nitrogen.

SERVETUS, Michael (1511–53) Spanish theologian and physician, born in Tudela. He worked largely in France and Switzerland. In *De Trinitatis Erroribus* (1531) and *Christianismi Restitutio* (1553) he denied the Trinity and the divinity of **Jesus**; he escaped the

Inquisition but was burnt by **Calvin** in Geneva for heresy. He lectured on geography and astronomy, practised medicine at Charlien and Vienna (1538–53), and discovered the pulmonary circulation of the blood.

SERVICE, Robert William (1874–1958) English-born Canadian poet, born in Preston. He went to Canada, travelled as a reporter for the *Toronto Star*, served as ambulance driver in World War I and wrote popular ballads, such as *Rhymes of a Rolling Stone* (1912) and *The Shooting of Dangerous Dan McGrew*. He also wrote novels, of which *Ploughman of the Moon* (1945) and *Harper of Heaven* (1948) are autobiographical.

SERVIUS TULLIUS (578–535 BC) 6th semi-legendary king of Rome. He allegedly distributed all freeholders (for military purposes primarily) into tribes, classes and centuries, making property, not birth, the standard of citizenship.

SESOSTRIS, or **Senusrit** according to Greek legend an Egyptian monarch who invaded Libya, Arabia, Thrace and Scythia, subdued Ethiopia, placed a fleet on the Red Sea, and extended his dominion to India; but he was possibly Sesostris I (c.1980 BC–1935), II (c.1906 BC–1887) and III (c.1887 BC–1849) compounded into one heroic figure.

SESSHU, Toyo (1420–1506) Japanese painter and priest, born in Bitchu Province. He was educated as a Zen monk and painter at the Shokokuji in Kyoto, where the teaching of Tensho Shubun (d.c.1445) became the determining factor of his career. From 1467 to 1469 he travelled in **Ming** China, and his mature style, determined by a clear and solid composition, shows the influence of Chinese painting. Eventually he returned to his original monastery. His knowledge of Zen Buddhism and his intimate communion with nature allowed him to renew the traditional lyricism of Japanese landscapes, at the same time retaining a unique expression which distinguishes him from his contemporaries. His genius still exerts its influence: his technique of 'pom' shows certain similarities to **Jackson Pollock**'s 'dripping' and related techniques of lyrical abstraction of the 20th century.

SESSIONS, Roger (1896–1985) American composer, born in Brooklyn, New York. He studied under **Ernest Bloch** and from 1925 to 1933 was in Europe. He later taught in the USA, becoming professor of music at California University in 1945 and professor at Princeton University (1953–65). He has taught at the Juilliard School of Music since 1965. His compositions include five symphonies, a violin concerto, piano and chamber music, a one-act opera of **Brecht**'s *The Trial of Lucellus*, a three-act opera (1947), *Montezuma* (1959–63), and a *Rhapsody for Orchestra* (1970).

SETON, St Elizabeth Ann, née **Bayley** (1774–1821) American religious, and the first native-born saint of the USA. Born into New York upper-class society, she married at 19 into a wealthy trading family, and in 1797 founded the Society for the Relief of Poor Widows with Small Children. In 1803 she herself was left a widowed mother of five. She was converted to Catholicism from Episcopalianism, took vows, founded a Catholic elementary school in Baltimore, and in 1809 founded the USA's first religious order, the Sisters of Charity. She was beatified by Pope **John XXIII** in 1963, and canonized in 1975.

SETTLE, Elkanah (1648–1724) English dramatist, born in Dunstable. He went from Oxford to London to make a living by his pen. In 1671 he had a success with his bombastic tragedy of *Cambyses*. To annoy **Dryden**, the Earl of **Rochester** arranged for Settle's *Empress of Morocco* to be played at Whitehall by the court lords and ladies. In *Absalom and Achitophel* Dryden scourged 'Doeg' with his scorn, and Settle speedily relapsed into obscurity.

SEURAT, Georges Pierre (1859–91) French artist, born in Paris. He studied at the École des Beaux-Arts in Paris. A founder of Neo-Impressionism, he developed the system known as Pointillism in which the whole picture is composed of tiny rectangles of pure colour which merge together when viewed from a distance. The system was founded on the colour theories of **Delacroix** and the 'chroma' theory of the chemist **Michel Eugène Chevreul**, and the compositions were constructed architecturally according to scientific principles. He only completed seven canvasses in this immensely demanding discipline, including *Une Baignade* (1883), *Un Dimanche d'été à la Grande-Jatte* (1885-86), *Les Poseuses* (1887-88) and *Le Cirque* (1891). His colour theories influenced **Signac**, **Pissarro**, **Degas** and **Renoir**, but his principal achievement was the marrying of an Impressionistic palette to classical composition.

SEUSE, Heinrich See **SUSO**

SEUSS, Dr, pseud of **Theodor Seuss Giesel** (1904–) American author and illustrator of a profusion of children's books, born in Springfield, Massachusetts. Though his animals have been described as 'boneless wonders', there is no denying his ingenuity, particularly in early books like *And to Think that I Saw it on Mulberry Street* (1937) and *The 500 Hats of Bartholemew Cubbins* (1938). He wrote the screenplay for the animated cartoon *Gerald McBoing Boing* (1950), which won several awards. In 1957 he began to write and draw a series of 'Beginner Books', intended to help teach reading, for Random House, starting with *The Cat in the Hat* (1958) and *Yertle the Turtle* (1958). By 1970, 30 million copies had been sold in America and Seuss had become synonymous with learning to read. He also wrote a best-selling book for adults, *You're Only Old Once!* (1986).

SEVERIN, (Giles) Timothy (1940–) English historian, traveller and author. He was educated at Tonbridge School and Keble College, Oxford, where he took a research degree in medieval Asian exploration. He has recreated many voyages following the routes of early explorers and navigators, using vessels reconstructed to the original specifications, including those of St **Brendan**, the legendary Irish monk, Sinbad whose seven long voyages in an Arab dhow took him from Arabia to China, and the early Greek quests of Jason and Ulysses in a bronze age galleon.

SEVERINI, Gino (1883–1966) Italian artist, born in Cortona. He studied in Rome under **Balla** from 1900–1906, then moved to Paris, where he worked as a Pointillist. In 1910 he signed the first Futurist manifesto in 1910, associating with **Balla** and **Boccioni**, with whom he exhibited in Paris and London especially *Dynamic Hieroglyphic of the Bal Tabarin* (1912). After 1914 he evolved a personal brand of Cubism and Futurism in which he painted many striking nightclub scenes. In 1921 he reverted to a more representational Neoclassical style, which he used in fresco and mosaic work, particularly in private houses and a number of Swiss and Italian churches. From 1940 onwards he adopted a decorative Cubist manner. His many publications include *Du Cubisme au classicisme* (1921).

SEVERN, Joseph (1793–1879) English portrait and subject painter, born in Hoxton. In 1816 he befriended **Keats**, whom he painted and accompanied on his last journey to Rome in 1820. He was British consul in Rome (1861–1872).

SEVERUS, Lucius Septimius (146–211) Roman emperor and founder of the Severan dynasty, born near Leptis Magna in Africa. He rose to be consul in 190 and commander of the army in Pannonia and Illyria. After the murder of **Pertinax** (193) he was proclaimed emperor, marched upon Rome, defeated his two rivals in 195 and 197, and between these dates made a campaign in the East, and took Byzantium. Between 197 and 199 he waged successfully his campaigns against the Parthians. At Rome in 202 he gave shows of unparalleled magnificence, and distributed extravagant largesse. In 208 he marched, it is said, to the extreme north of Britain to quell a rebellion. To shield south Britain from the Meatae and Caledonians, he repaired Hadrian's wall and died soon after at Eboracum (York). See also **Alexander Severus**.

SEVERUS, Sulpicius See **SULPICIUS SEVERUS**

SÉVIGNÉ, Madame de, née **Marie de Rabutin-Chantal** (1626–96) French letter writer, born in Paris. She was orphaned at an early age and was carefully brought up by an uncle, the Abbé de Coulanges, at the Abbaye de Livry in Brittany. She married the dissolute Marquis Henri de Sévigné in 1644, but he was killed in a duel in 1651. From then on, in the most brilliant court in the world, her thoughts were centred on her children, Françoise Marguerite (b.1646) and Charles (b.1648). On the marriage of the former to the Comte de Grignan in 1669, she began the series of letters to her daughter which grew sadder as friend after friend passed away. She died of smallpox, after nursing her daughter through a long illness. Madame de Sévigné's 25 years of letters reveal the inner history of the time of **Louis XIV** in wonderful detail, but the most interesting thing in the whole 1600 (one-third letters to her from others) remains herself.

SEWARD, Sir Albert Charles (1863–1941) English palaeobotanist, born in Lancaster. He studied at Cambridge and Manchester, and was professor of botany at Cambridge (1906–36). He is best known for his work on *English Wealden Flora* (1894–95) and *Jurassic Flora* (1900–03) and a panoramic survey, *Plant Life Through the Ages* (1931).

SEWARD, Anna (1747–1809) English poet, known as the 'Swan of Lichfield', born in Eyam Reactory, Derbyshire. She lived from the age of ten at Lichfield, where her father, himself a poet, became a canon. He died in 1790, but she continued to live on in the bishop's palace, and wrote romantic poetry. Her 'Elegy on Captain Cook' (1780) was commended by Dr **Johnson**. She bequeathed all her poems to Sir **Walter Scott**, who published them in 1810 (*Poetical Works*).

SEWARD, William Henry (1801–72) American statesman, born in Florida, New York. He graduated at Union College in 1820, and was admitted to the bar at Utica in 1822. In 1830 he was elected to the state senate, where he led the Whig opposition to the dominant democratic party. In 1838 and 1840 he was governor of New York State; in 1849 he was elected to the US senate, and re-elected in 1855. In 1850, while urging the admission of California to the Union, he declared that the national domain was devoted to liberty by 'a higher law than the constitution'. He opposed the Compromise Bill of 1850, separated himself from those Whigs who followed President **Fillmore** in his proslavery policy, and on the formation of the republican party became one of its leaders. In 1860 he was a candidate for the presidential nomination, but, failing, became **Lincoln**'s secretary of state (1861–69). In 1867 he negotiated the purchase of the territory of Alaska from Russia for $7200000. The Civil War rendered the foreign relations of the United States unusually delicate, especially in view of the attitude of France and Britain. In the 'Trent affair' during the Civil War he advised that the Confederate envoys should be given up to England. He protested against the fitting out of the *Alabama* and similar vessels in British ports, and declared that the United States would claim indemnities. He supported President **Andrew Johnson**'s reconstruction policy, thereby incurring much censure from his own party. In 1870–71 he made a tour round the world.

SEWELL, Anna (1820–78) English novelist, born in Yarmouth. She was an invalid for most of her life. *Black Beauty, The Autobiography of a Horse* (1877), written as a plea for the more humane treatment of animals, is perhaps the most famous fictional work about horses.

SEXTON, Ann, née **Harvey** (1928–74) American poet, born in Newton, Massachusetts. A confessional poet in the mould of her teacher, **Robert Lowell**, and her friend, **Sylvia Plath**, with whom she is often bracketed, her main subjects are herself, her depression and mental illness, and her various roles as a woman. In 1948 she married Alfred Sexton and had two daughters. She taught at Boston University (1969–71) and Colgate (1971–72). *To Bedlam and Part Way Back* (1962) was her first collection of poetry; others are *All My Pretty Ones* (1962), *Live or Die* (1966), *Love Poems* (1969), *Transformations* (1971), *The Book of Folly* (1972), *The Death Notebooks* (1974), *The Awful Rowing Towards God* (1975), and the posthumously published *45 Mercy Street* (1976). The *Complete Poems* were published in 1981, seven years after she committed suicide.

SEXTON, Thomas (1848–1932) Irish nationalist politician, born in Ballygannon, County Waterford. He worked as a railway clerk before becoming leader-writer on the *Nation*. He was elected MP for Sligo as Home Rule supporter of **Parnell** in 1880, capturing West Belfast for Parnell in 1886; he was defeated there in 1892 after the Parnell split, and subsequently being MP for Kerry North from 1892 to 1896. He was lord mayor of Dublin in 1888–89. He controlled the leading Home Rule daily newspaper, the *Freeman's Journal*, from 1892 to 1912. Sexton is generally hailed as a parliamentary orator second only to **Gladstone**.

SEXTUS EMPIRICUS (2nd century) Greek philosopher and physician, active at Alexandria and Athens, who is the main source of information for the Sceptical school of philosophy. Little is known of his life, but his extant writings (*Outlines of Pyrrhonism* and *Against the Dogmatists*) had an emormous influence when they were rediscovered and published in Latin translations in the 1560s.

SEYDLITZ, Friedrich Wilhelm, Baron von (1721–73) Prussian cavalry officer, born in Kalkar Cleve. He served in the Silesian wars and so distinguished himself at Kolin (1757) and at Rossbach (1757) that **Frederick II, the Great** promoted him over the heads of two generals to take charge of the cavalry, which under his brilliant charges won the battle practically without infantry. Seydlitz was wounded but won another victory at Zorndorf (1758) and covered the Prussian retreat at Hochkirch. Severely wounded at the defeat of Kunersdorf (1758), he did not return to the front until 1761, when in command of both cavalry and infantry groups, he won the battle of Freyburg (1762).

SEYMOUR an historic family, originally from St Maur in Normandy (hence the name), who obtained lands in Monmouthshire in the 13th century, and in the 14th at Hatch Beauchamp, Somerset, by marriage with an heiress of the Beauchamps.

SEYMOUR, Charles, 6th Duke of Somerset (1662–1748) English nobleman, known as the 'proud Duke of Somerset'. He held high posts under **Charles II**, **William III** and Queen **Anne**. He married Elizabeth, daughter of the last Earl of Northumberland and the heiress of the Percies.

SEYMOUR, Edward, 1st Duke of Somerset (c.1506–1552) English soldier and statesman, known as the 'Protector Somerset', eldest son of Sir **John Seymour** and brother of **Jane Seymour**. Successively created Viscount Beauchamp and 1st Earl of Hertford, he enjoyed high office under his brother-in-law, **Henry VIII**. As warden of the Scottish marches, he led the invading English army that devastated southern Scotland and Edinburgh in the 'Rough Wooing' of 1543-44, after the Scots turned down a proposed marriage between Prince Edward (the future **Edward VI**) and the infant **Mary, Queen of Scots**. At Henry's death in 1547 he was named Protector of England during the minority of Edward VI and was king in all but name. He defeated a Scottish army at Pinkie (1547), and furthered the Reformation with the first Book of Common Prayer (1549). In 1549 his younger brother, **Thomas Seymour**, was executed for attempting to marry Princess Elizabeth (the future Queen **Elizabeth**), and soon he himself was indicted for 'over-ambition' and deposed by John Dudley, Earl of **Warwick** (1549) and eventually executed.

SEYMOUR, Edward, Earl of Hertford (1539–1621) son of **Edward Seymour**, 1st Duke of Somerset, by his second wife. Created Earl of Hertford by Queen **Elizabeth** in 1559, in 1560 he secretly married Lady Catherine Grey, sister of Lady **Jane Grey**, for which he was imprisoned for nine years (1561–71) and fined £15000. He later achieved high office under Queen **Anne**.

SEYMOUR, Jane (c.1509–1537) queen of England, the third wife of **Henry VIII**. The daughter of Sir **John Seymour**, she was lady in waiting to both of Henry's former wives, **Catherine of Aragon** and **Anne Boleyn**. She married Henry eleven days after Anne Boleyn's execution in 1536, and gave birth to a son, Edward (the future **Edward VI**), but died twelve days later. Her portrait was painted by **Holbein**.

SEYMOUR, Sir John (c.1476–1536) English soldier, father of **Jane Seymour**, **Edward Seymour** (Duke of Somerset), and **Thomas Seymour**. He helped to suppress a Cornish insurrection in 1497, and accompanied **Henry VIII** to France.

SEYMOUR, Thomas (c.1508–1549) created Lord Seymour of Sudeley: English soldier and statesman, son of Sir **John Seymour** and younger brother of **Edward Seymour**, Duke of Somerset, and brother-in-law to **Henry VIII** through the marriage to **Jane Seymour**. He became high admiral of England in 1547, and in the same year married the dowager queen **Catherine Parr**, widow of Henry VIII. He schemed against his brother to marry **Edward VI** to Lady **Jane Grey**. After Catherine Parr's death in 1548 he tried to marry princess **Elizabeth** of England, but was executed by his brother for treason.

SEYMOUR, William (1588–1660) 2nd Earl of Hertford and 3rd Duke of Somerset, grandson of **Edward Seymour**, Earl of Hertford. He fell into disfavour in 1610 by secretly marrying Lady Arabella Stuart (1575–1615), first cousin to King **James VI and I**. He fled to Paris, but later played a conspicuous part in the Royalist cause during the Civil War (1642–43), capturing Hereford, Cirencester and Bristol, and defeating Sir **William Waller** at Lansdown. At the Restoration he took his seat in the House of Lords as the 3rd Duke of Somerset.

SEYMOUR, Lynn (1939–) Canadian-born British dancer, born in Wainwright, Alberta. Trained in Vancouver, she spent two years at the Royal Ballet School, making her début in 1956 with the Sadler's Wells branch of the company. She is best known for her passionate interpretations of the choreography of **Kenneth MacMillan** and **Frederick Ashton**. The former cast her first in *The Burrow* (1958). Following that she was frequently teamed with **Christopher Gable**. Her dancing career was a volatile one and disappointments such as being shifted out of MacMillan's premiere of *Romeo and Juliet* in favour of **Margot Fonteyn** took their toll, though the roles in Ashton's *Five Brahms Waltzes in the Manner of Isadora Duncan* and *A Month in the Country* (both 1976) were outstandingly performed. In 1978 she spent an unsuccessful season as director of the Bavarian Opera in Munich, but in recent years she has returned as a mature ballerina as Tatiana in *Onegin* and the mother in Gable's *A Simple Man* (both 1988). While best known as a dancer, she has choreographed several pieces, *Rashomon* (1976) and *Wolfi* (1987) being perhaps the best known. Her book *Lynn* (1984) describes the trials and triumphs of her life as a ballerina at the top.

SEYSS-INQUART, Artur von (1892–1946) Austrian 'Quisling', born in the Sudetenland. He practised as a lawyer in Vienna and saw much of **Schuschnigg**. When the latter became chancellor in 1938, he took office under him, informing **Hitler** of every detail in Schuschnigg's life, in the hope of becoming Nazi chancellor of Austria after the 'Anschluss'. Instead, he was appointed commissioner for the Netherlands in 1940, where he ruthlessly recruited slave labour. In 1945, he was captured by the Canadians, tried at Nuremberg and executed for war crimes.

SFORZA name of a celebrated Italian family founded by a peasant of the Romaga called Muzio Attendolo (1369–1424), who became a great *contottiere* or soldier of fortune, and received the name of Sforza ('Stormer'—ie, of cities).

SFORZA, Carlo, Count (1873–1952) Italian statesman, born in Lucca. He became minister of foreign affairs (1920–1921) and negotiated the Rapallo treaty. A senator (1919–1926) he became leader of the anti-fascist opposition and from 1922 lived in Belgium and the USA (1940).

SFORZA, Francesco (1401–66) Duke of Milan from 1450. The illegitimate son of Muzio Attendolo Sforza, he was the father of **Galeazzo Maria** and **Ludovico Sforza**. He sold his sword to the highest bidder, fighting for or against the pope, Milan, Venice and Florence. From the Duke of Milan he obtained his daughter's hand and the succession to the duchy; and before his death had extended his power over Ancona, Pesaro, all Lombardy and Genoa.

SFORZA, Galeazzo Maria (1444–76) Italian nobleman, son of **Francesco Sforza** and Duke of Milan from 1466. A competent ruler, he was nonetheless notorious for debauchery and prodigality, and was assassinated.

SFORZA, Ludovico, 'the Moor' (1451–1508) ruler of Naples and patron of **Leonardo da Vinci**. The son of **Francesco Sforza**, he acted as regent for his nephew Gian Galeazzo (1469–94) from 1476, but expelled him in 1481 and usurped the Dukedom for himself. He made alliance with **Lorenzo de' Medici** of Florence; under his rule, Milan became the most glittering court in Europe. He helped to defeat the attempts of **Charles VIII (the 'Affable')** of France to secure Naples, but in 1499 was expelled by **Louis XII** and imprisoned in France, where he died.

SGAMBATI, Giovanni (1841–1914) Italian composer and pianist, born in Rome. A friend of **Liszt**, his compositions include two symphonies, a requiem and chamber and piano music.

SHACKLETON, Sir Ernest Henry (1874–1922) Irish explorer, born in Kilkee. He was apprenticed in the Merchant Navy, and became a junior officer under Captain **Robert Scott**, on the *Discovery*, in the National Antarctic Expedition (1901–03). In 1908–09, in command of another expedition, he reached a point 97 miles from the South Pole—at that time a record. While on another expedition, in 1914–16, his ship *Endeavour* was crushed in the ice. By sledges and boats he and his men reached Elephant Island, from where he and five others made a perilous voyage of 800 miles to South Georgia and organized relief for those remaining on Elephant Island. He died in South Georgia while on a fourth Antarctic Expedition, begun in 1920.

SHADWELL, Thomas (c.1642–1692) English dramatist, born at Broomhill House, Brandon. He made a hit with the first of his 13 comedies, *The Sullen Lovers* (1668). He also wrote three tragedies. **Dryden**, grossly assailed by him in the *Medal of John Bayes*, heaped deathless ridicule upon him in *MacFlecknoe* ('Shadwell never deviates into sense'), and as 'Og' in the second part of *Absalom and Achitopel*. His works exhibit talent and comic force. He succeeded Dryden as Laureate in 1689.

SHAFFER, Peter (1926–) English dramatist, born in Liverpool. His plays are variations on the themes of genius and mediocrity, faith and reason, and the question of whether God, if he exists, is benevolent or not. These ideas form the intellectual core of *The Royal Hunt of the Sun* (1964); *Equus* (1973), and *Amadeus* (1979). His first play was *Five Finger Exercise* (1958), followed by the comedies *The Private Ear* and *The Public Eye* (1962). *Yonadab* (1985), a story of incest and envy set in the Jerusalem of 1000 BC, was not well-received, but *Lettice and Lovage* (1987), a comedy, proved a great success. Other plays include *Black Comedy* (1965), *White Lies* (1967), and *The Battle of Shrivings* (1970). His twin brother, Anthony, also writes plays, his works including the successful thriller *Sleuth* (1970).

SHAFTESBURY, Anthony Ashley Cooper, 1st Earl of (1621–83) English statesman, born in Wimborne St Giles, Dorset. In the Civil War, after ten months' service with the royalists he joined the parliamentarians and was a member of **Cromwell**'s Council of State. He was always suspected of royalist sympathies, however, and in 1659 was tried and imprisoned. He was one of twelve commissioners sent to France to invite **Charles II** home and at the Restoration came under royal favour. In 1661 he was created Baron Ashley and from then until his elevation as the Earl of Shaftesbury, in 1672, was Chancellor of the Exchequer. He was subsequently made lord chancellor but dismissed by Charles a year later. He was a leading member of the movement to exclude the Roman Catholic Duke of York (**James II**) from the throne, exploiting the fictitious 'Popish plot' allegedly uncovered by **Titus Oates**, for his own purposes. In the subsequent reaction to the plot's clear falsity, Shaftesbury was tried for treason but acquitted. He sought refuge in Amsterdam, where he died. He was satirized as 'Achitobel' in **Dryden**'s *Absolom and Achitobel* (1651). Although a man of great deviousness, he had basic liberal instincts, as revealed by his association with **John Locke** in securing the amendment of the Habeas Corpus Act in 1679.

SHAFTESBURY, Anthony Ashley Cooper, 3rd Earl of (1671–1713) English moral philosopher, politician and essayist, grandson of Anthony Ashley Cooper, 1st Earl of **Shaftesbury**, born in London. **John Locke** supervised his early education and he then attended Winchester College. He entered parliament in 1695 and sat as a Whig for Poole until 1698, succeeding as 3rd Earl in 1699 and regularly attending the House of Lords until ill-health forced him to abandon an active political life in 1702. He moved to Naples in 1711 and died there. He wrote stylish (if to a modern taste, overwrought) essays on a wide range of philosophical and cultural topics, and these are collected in three volumes under the title *Characteristicks of Men, Manners, Opinions, Times* (1711). He is usually regarded as one of the principal English deists, and he argued (both against orthodox Christianity and against **Hobbes**) that we possess a natural 'moral sense' and natural affections directed to the good of the species and in harmony with the larger cosmic order. He gained more favourable attention abroad, perhaps, than at home, and **Leibniz**, **Voltaire**, **Diderot** and **Lessing** were among those attracted by his work.

SHAFTESBURY, Anthony Ashley Cooper, 7th Earl of (1801–85) English factory reformer and philanthropist, born in London. Educated at Harrow and Christ Church College, Oxford, he entered parliament in 1826. As Lord Ashley, he undertook the leadership of the factory reform movement from **Michael Sadler** in 1832. He also piloted successive factory acts (1847, 1850 and 1859) through the House, achieving the ten-hour day and the provision of lodging-houses for the poor (1851). His Lunacy Act (1845) achieved considerable reforms, as a result of the Lunacy Commission he chaired from 1834. His Coal Mines Act (1842) prohibited underground employment of women and of children under 13. He was chairman of the Ragged Schools Union for 40 years, assisted **Florence Nightingale** in her schemes for army welfare and took an interest in missionary work. Strongly evangelical, he opposed radicalism although he worked with the trade unions for factory reforms.

SHAGALL, Marc See **CHAGALL**

SHAH JAHAN (1592–1666) Mogul emperor (1627–58), the ablest and most ambitious of the sons of **Jahangir**. He was in open revolt against his father from 1624 until the latter's death in 1627 when he succeeded him as emperor. Disputes with the Sikhs of the Punjab led to defeats of the Mogul troops in both 1628 and 1631, and Kandahar was lost in 1653 to the Persians, but the emperor was able to consolidate his power in the Deccan, subjugating Ahmadnagar, Bijapur and Golconda (1636). In 1658 he fell ill and his sons seized the opportunity to rebel. The eventual victor was the emperor's third son, **Aurangzeb**, who became effective ruler of the empire. Shah Jahan was an able administrator and a great patron of architecture and engineering work. His reign saw the construction of the dazzling Peacock Throne, the Taj Mahal (tomb of the empress Mimtaz Mahal), the Pearl Mosque, the Ali Masjid and the fort at Shahjahanabad, and also witnessed the construction of the great gardens at Delhi, Lahore and Kashmir and the 98-mile Ravi Canal.

SHAHN, Ben (Benjamin) (1898–1969) Lithuanian-born American painter, born in Kaunas. He emigrated with his parents to New York in 1906, and studied painting in night school. In 1922 he visited the European art centres and came under the influence of **Rouault**. His didactic pictorial commentaries on contemporary events such as his 23 satirical gouache paintings on the trial of the Italian anarchists **Nicola Sacco** and Bartolomeo Vanzetti (1932), and the 15 paintings on Tom Mooney, the Labour leader (1933), earned him the title of 'American **Hogarth**'. He was the first painter to deliver the Charles Eliot Norton Lectures at Harvard, published as the *The Shape of Content* (1958).

SHAKA (c.1787–1828) Zulu leader, and founder of the Zulu nation. An illegitimate son, he seized power from his half-brother to become clan chief in 1816. He organized a permanent army and conquered the Nguni peoples of modern Natal, exterminating many smaller clans, and built up a centralized, militaristic Zulu kingdom covering most of southern Africa. Increasingly autocratic, to the point of insanity, he was murdered by his half-brothers, and was succeeded by one of them, **Dingaan**.

SHAKESPEARE, John (c.1530–1601) glover and wool dealer of Stratford-upon-Avon, father of **William Shakespeare**, born in Snitterfield, near Stratford, the son of a tenant farmer. After apprenticeship to a whittawer ('white leather' maker) and glover, he set up his own business in Stratford. It prospered and he was soon securely established in his house and workshop in Henley Street. In 1557 he married Mary, daughter of Robert Arden, a gentleman farmer and landowner in the nearby parish of Wilmcote, who inherited good farm land when her father died. In 1559 he was elected burgess, and six years later became an alderman. In 1568 he was made bailiff (mayor) of Stratford and a justice of the peace. In 1576–77 his wool business failed. He managed to retain possession of his house in Henley Street, but his wife's inheritance had to be mortgaged. At times he dared not leave the house for fear of being arrested for debt. In 1592 he was rescued by his son William, whose earnings in the London theatre were by then enough to restore the family's position. John Shakespeare never again played an active part in Stratford's civic life, but he got his coat of arms in 1596, and died a gentleman. He was buried in Stratford churchyard in 1601. Mary, his widow, died in 1608 and was buried by his side. They had eight children. Of their four daughters, only Joan survived childhood. She married William Hart, outlived him by 30 years, and died in 1646, aged 77. Direct descendants of William and Joan Hart are now living in England and in Australia. Of John and Mary Shakespeare's four sons, William, the eldest, lived to be 52. Gilbert died at the age of 46, Richard at 39 and Edmund at 27.

SHAKESPEARE, William (1564–1616) English playwright, poet, actor, joint-manager of a London acting company and part-owner of one of its theatres, born in Stratford-upon-Avon in Warwickshire, the eldest son of **John Shakespeare**, glover and wool dealer. By long-established tradition, his birthday is celebrated on 23 April, St George's Day. The register of Holy Trinity Church, Stratford, records that he was christened there on 26 April 1564. He lived for 52 years, partly in Stratford and partly in London, and died at his home in Stratford on 23 April 1616. Two days later, he was buried in the church in which he had been christened. His life turned on its Stratford-London axis: Stratford, where he grew up, where his parents, his wife and his children lived; London, where he made the theatre career that brought him fame and fortune, and from which he withdrew while still pre-eminent. His life can be divided into three consecutive periods. The first period, spent wholly in Stratford, included boyhood and education, early marriage and the birth of his three children. The second period began when, still a very young man, he left Stratford to work in London as an actor and playwright. It lasted for 25 years, in the course of which he became a permanent and leading member of a great acting company. For that company he then wrote plays that gave it a commanding place in the London theatre. With his principal colleagues, he was responsible for the day-to-day business management and artistic direction of the company, receiving a share of its profits in return and becoming part-owner of one of the two theatres in which it was based. On top of all that, he acted for many years, performing in his own plays and in those of other dramatists whose work was in his company's repertory. Throughout this period he had lodgings in London and he used most of his very considerable income to increase the security and status of his family in their Stratford home, spending time with them between theatre seasons. The beginning of the third period of his life was marked by his carefully-planned and gradual withdrawal from his heavy commitments in the theatre. Then, when he was in his late forties and possessed of ample means, he left London to live full time in Stratford, where he spent the remainder of his days. There is no documentary proof that he was educated at Stratford Grammar School, but the numerous classical allusions in his plays and poems were drawn from the Latin and Greek poets, dramatists, philosophers and historians closely studied by Elizabethan grammar school pupils; and John Shakespeare's civic status entitled him to send his son to Stratford's excellent school free of charge. In the winter of 1582–83, at the age of 18, he married Anne Hathaway, a farmer's daughter who lived in Shottery, near Stratford. She was 26, and pregnant by him. Having no income of their own, they lived with the elder Shakespeares. Less than six months after their wedding, their first child, Susanna, was baptized in Stratford church. Early in 1585, Anne gave birth to twins: Hamnet, their only (and short-lived) son, and Judith, their second daughter. With a wife and three children to maintain, and still dependent on his father, Shakespeare decided to try his luck in the London theatre. Stratford was a regular touring venue for the London acting companies, and three troupes were playing there from 1583 to 1588. He must have begun to work in the theatre soon after the twins were born. There is evidence that he had written several very successful plays in 1592. The theatre impresario **Philip Henslowe** recorded in his diary that 'Harey the vj' played to packed houses at the Rose Theatre between March and June 1592. Clearly, he was referring to *Henry VI*; but whether to one part of that play or to all three is not plain. In the September of that year, **Robert Greene** wrote a pamphlet, *Greene's Groatsworth of Wit, Bought with a Million of Repentance*, which included a ranting and envious attack on 'an upstart crow', a 'Shake-scene'. The pun on Shakespeare's name was obvious, but Greene identified his target even more precisely by parodying a line from *Henry VI* Part 3. The three parts of *Henry VI* were not the only successes of these first seven years. He wrote two other histories (*King John* and *Richard III*); three comedies (*The Comedy of Errors*, *The Taming of the Shrew*, *The Two Gentlemen of Verona*); and a revenge-tragedy (*Titus Andronicus*). By 1592 he had tried out each of the then most popular forms of drama and made his own distinctive contributions to them. Theatre-going London was well aware that a new star had risen, its light shining as brightly as any then burning—even **Marlowe**'s. In June 1592 the theatres were closed by an outbreak of the plague and they were not allowed to reopen until the summer of 1594. While the London stages were silent, Shakespeare wrote two long narrative poems: *Venus and Adonis* (published 18 April 1593) and *The Rape of Lucrece* (published 9 May 1594). Both were dedicated to the 3rd Earl of **Southampton**; but no reliable information about his connection with that young patron of the arts has been discovered. In the literary and courtly circles in which they were read, the poems were highly praised for their eloquent treatment of classical subjects. The sonnets were probably in private circulation by 1598. Though not published until 1609, it is generally held that they were written between 1592 and 1598. The order in which he composed these 154 poems is not known; and nobody has succeeded in arranging them to tell a coherent 'story'. The temptation to read them as autobiography has been—and still is—strong, and many attempts have been made to identify the mysterious people—'young man', 'dark lady', 'rival poet'—who appear in them. Sonnet sequences were in vogue, and Shakespeare's own added greatly to his contemporary reputation. Later generations have ranked many of the individual sonnets in the collection among the world's finest poems. The language in which they treat recurrent themes—love's ecstasy and despair, implacable time, lust and its shames, separation, betrayal, fame and death—echoes that of the plays. When the theatres re-opened, Shakespeare joined the newly-formed Lord Chamberlain's Men as a 'sharer'. It was the turning point in his career. In the first years as an actor he had been a 'hired man', working for a wage. From now on, he was entitled to a share of the company's profits. Previously, too, he had been a freelance playwright and, though his work had found a ready market, he had little security. The founder of the Chamberlain's Men, James Burbage, and the other sharers, knew what they were about when they brought him into their company. They already had some of the best actors. For example, **Richard Burbage**, James's son, was considered to be as good a tragic and heroic actor as the great **Edward Alleyn** of the Admiral's Men; and **Will Kempe** was a very popular comic. It was with those two fellow sharers that Shakespeare, on behalf of the Chamberlain's Men, received the queen's payment for the company's performances at court during the Christmas festivities of 1594–95. By securing the exclusive services of the best playwright in London, the Chamberlain's Men were justifiably confident that they would outdo all their rivals. It is clear that Shakespeare wrote the following plays for his company between 1594 and 1598: *The Merchant of Venice*, *A Midsummer Night's Dream*, *The Merry Wives of Windsor*, *Much Ado About Nothing*, *As You Like It*; *Richard II*, *Henry IV* Parts 1 and 2 and *Romeo and Juliet*. The prodigious output of five comedies, three histories and one tragedy took the London theatre world by storm. The language and the characters of the plays captured people's imagination and entered their daily conversation: 'dull as a Justice Shallow' was a term used by a letterwriter of the day; and a comptemporary dramatist noted rather sourly that playgoers were talking 'pure Juliet and Romeo'. The material rewards of these triumphs enabled Shakespeare to meet the heavy expenses incurred when his father was awarded a grant of arms in October 1596. Henceforth, John Shakespeare was entitled to the style of 'Gentleman', an honour that would descend in due course to his eldest son. That style, and the heraldic display that went with it, was prized in an age of rigid social distinction, For the Shakespeares it was also a tangible sign that the family had regained—surpassed, indeed—its former status in Stratford. Ironically, the award of honour was received little more than two months after Shakespeare's only son, Hamnet, died, aged eleven. Given the dynastic ambition common in that age and evident in Shakespeare's conduct of his worldly affairs, it was a heavy blow. Of his personal grief we have no record. The welfare of his wife and his daughters was now his main family preoccupation. In 1597 he bought New Place, a large and imposing mansion in Stratford, close by the Guild Chapel and the grammar school and a few minutes' walk from his parents' house. He spent freely on improvements to the house and garden before Anne, Susanna and Judith moved into their new home. At about this time, trouble with the owner of the site on which Burbage's playhouse (called the Theatre) stood, forced the Chamberlain's Men to move. They dismantled the Theatre and used much of its material to build a new playhouse—the Globe—on Bankside, south of the Thames. It was a bold and successful venture. Sited in the heart of London's pleasure-land—dicing-houses, bear-gardens, brothels and theatres—the Globe was the finest playhouse of them all, bigger and better equipped than any of its rivals. Its huge stage, with 'cellarage' below and balcony above, provided the space and permitted the rapidity and continuity of action which the dramas of the day demanded and which Shakespeare most notably exploited in the plays he wrote for performance there. He followed the brilliant success of *Henry V* (the Globe's opener) with *Julius Caesar*, *Twelfth Night*, *Hamlet* and *Othello*. In all, he had now written fourteen plays which were the exclusive property of the Chamberlain's Men, and nine before he joined them. Nor did his current successes lead to the neglect of his earlier plays. Unwilling to allow popular plays to 'fust unused', the company rang the changes on its play stock and often revived former works. Takings at the Globe far exceeded those at the Theatre. The accession of King **James VI and I** in 1603 brought the company new and very great benefits. He immediately conferred his own royal patronage on Shakespeare and his fellow sharers. They became the King's Men—'His Majesty's Servants'—and were granted a patent. James thought it good to see them often. Court performances had always been a prestigious and lucrative addition to their ordinary programme. They had played for Queen **Elizabeth** on average three times a year. Between 1603 and 1614, the King's Men averaged 13 royal command shows a year and got for each twice as much as Queen Elizabeth had paid. The darker tone of the plays that Shakespeare wrote in the early years of James I's reign has led to speculation that it reflected some kind of personal and spiritual crisis. But nothing that is known about him amounts to a feasible 'explanation' of why he wrote a succession of 'problem plays' (or 'dark comedies') and tragedies between 1603 and 1608–09: *All's Well*, *Measure for Measure*, *King Lear*, *Macbeth*, *Antony and Cleopatra*, *Timon of Athens*, *Coriolanus* and *Troilus and Cressida*. Great popular successes at the Globe, these plays were also received with acclaim at court and when performed for wealthy and socially exclusive audiences in private halls and in the lawyers' Inns of Court. It was audiences of this kind who were now flocking to the so-called 'private theatres'. The term is misleading. Like the 'public playhouses', they were commercial enterprises. They charged much more for admission and attracted fashionable patrons willing to pay to sit in comfort, protected from the elements. Because they were roofed over, these theatres were artificially lit. Stage illusion of a kind not possible in the public theatres was an integral part of their more sophisticated entertainments. In 1608 Shakespeare's company decided to beat the opposition by joining it. The King's Men took over the most successful of the private theatres—the Blackfriars—using it for their winter seasons and performing at the Globe in the summer. They now got the best of both worlds and prospered exceedingly. Shakespeare, who had bought a share in the Blackfriars Theatre, immediately began to write plays that could be performed with equal success on two very different stages. He solved the technical problems with increasing sureness: *Pericles*, *Cymbeline*, *The Winter's Tale*, and *The Tempest*. Those plays were enthusiastically received at the Blackfriars, at the Globe and at Court; and they have all held the stage to this day. Collectively known now as the 'Last Plays', they were the results of Shakespeare's characteristic urge to experiment with and make a distinctive contribution to developments in the art and craft of drama. Tragi-comedy was then all the rage and he wanted to find his own way of writing it. Meanwhile, there were signs that he was preparing to return to Stratford, where there was much to demand his attention. His parents were now dead and he was the head of the family, a position he took seriously. He had long been investing in land and tithes in and around the town. In 1607, Susanna had married a respected physician, Dr John Hall. Their daughter Elizabeth, Shakespeare's first grandchild, was born in 1608. Soon after writing *The Tempest*, he freed himself of his major commitment to his company by bringing forward **John Fletcher** to take over as the King's Men's chief dramatist. Shakespeare—whose own still very popular plays were company property, to be staged whenever the sharers wished—could now spend more time in Stratford. By 1612 he had completed his withdrawal, leaving management in the safe hands of his 'fellows'. In a legal document that he signed while visiting London in that year, he identified himself in these terms: 'William Shakespeare of Stratford-on-Avon in the County of Warwick, gentleman of the age of 48 years'. Even so he did not quite abandon his writing. In 1613, with John Fletcher's collaboration, he wrote *Henry VIII*. In the same year, he helped Fletcher by contributing several scenes and most of one act to *The Two Noble Kinsmen*. Shakespeare died on 23 April 1616. The nature of his fatal illness is not known, but the male Shakespeares of his generation were not long-lived. Of John Shakespeare's four sons, he was the last to go. He had made provision in his will to keep the bulk of his estate intact, entailed for the benefit of his descendants. His intentions were soon thwarted. His direct line of descent ended when his granddaughter died childless in 1670. In 1623, his monument was erected in Holy Trinity Church. A few months later, John Hemminge and Henry Condell—two of his friends and principal colleagues in the King's Men—published his collected plays in the First Folio. But for them much of his work would have been lost; and all subsequent editions of his plays have been based on the text they so diligently and lovingly established.

SHALIAPIN, Fedor Ivanovich See **CHALIAPIN**

SHĀMIL, ie Samuel (c.1797–1871) Caucasian chief, who led the tribes in the Caucasus in their 30 years' struggle against Russia. He became a Sufi mullah or priest, and strove to end the tribal feuds. He was one of the foremost in the defence of Gimry against the Russians in 1831, in 1834 was chosen head of the Lesghians, and by abandoning open warfare for guerilla tactics, secured numerous successes for the mountaineers. In 1839, and again in 1849, he escaped from the stronghold of Ahulgo after the Russians had made themselves masters of it, to continue preaching a holy war against the infidels. The Russians were completely baffled, their armies sometimes disastrously beaten, though Shāmil began to lose ground. During the Crimean War (1853–56) the Allies supplied him with money and arms, but after peace was signed the Russians compelled the submission of the Caucasus. In 1859, Shāmil's chief stronghold, Vedeno, was taken. For several months he was hunted till surprised, and after a desperate resistance captured. He was exiled to Kaluga, to south of Moscow.

SHAMIR, Yitzhak, originally **Yitzhak Jazernicki** (1915–) Polish-born Israeli politician. He studied law at Warsaw University and, after emigrating to Palestine, at the Hebrew University of Jerusalem, and in his twenties became a founder member of the Stern Gang ('Fighters for the Freedom of Israel'), a Zionist terrorist group which carried out anti-British attacks on individuals and strategic targets in Palestine. He was arrested by the British in 1941 and exiled to Eritrea in 1946, but given asylum in France. He returned to the new state of Israel in 1948 but spent the next 20 years on the fringe of politics, immersing himself in business interests. He entered the Knesset in 1973, becoming speaker from 1977 to 1980. He was foreign minister (1980–83), before taking over the leadership of the right-wing Consolidation party (Likud) from **Menachem Begin**, and becoming prime minister in 1983. Since 1984 he has shared power in an uneasy coalition with the Israel Labour party and its leader **Shimon Peres**. Renowned for his forthright views, Shamir has consistently refused to enter into discussions with the Palestine Liberation Organisation (PLO).

SHANKLY, Bill (William) (1913–81) Scottish footballer and manager. With **Jock Stein** and Sir **Matt Busby** he was one of the greatest football managers in recent times. A tireless, biting wing-half, he won an FA Cup medal with Preston North End and five Scotland caps. As a post-war manager he found success with Liverpool after unremarkable spells with Carlisle, Grimsby, Workington and Huddersfield. He created a team which was not only highly successful in Britain and Europe but one which encouraged individual expression and communicated great exhilaration to the spectators. Although he was fanatically committed to the game, there was nothing grim in the football which his team produced.

SHANNON, Claude Elwood (1916–) American applied mathematician and pioneer of communication theory, born in Gaylord, Michigan. He was educated at Michigan University and at the Massachusetts Institute of Technology (MIT), where he gained a PhD in mathematics. A student of **Vannevar Bush**, in 1938 he published a seminal paper ('A Symbolic Analysis of Relay and Switching Circuits') on the application of symbolic logic to relay circuits, which helped transform circuit design from an art into a science. After graduating from MIT, he worked at the Bell Telephone Laboratories (1941–72) in the esoteric discipline of information theory. He wrote *The Mathematical Theory of Communications* (1949, with Warren Weaver).

SHAPLEY, Harlow (1885–1972) American astrophysicist, born in Nashville, Missouri. The son of a farmer, he first worked as a newspaper crime reporter before going to the University of Missouri, where he quickly switched from journalism to astronomy. From 1914 he worked at the Mount Wilson Observatory and was director of Harvard University Observatory (1921–52). He demonstrated that the Milky Way is much larger than had been supposed, and that the Solar System is located on the Galaxy's edge, not at its centre. He did notable work on photometry and spectroscopy and his writings included *Star Clusters* (1930), *Galaxies* (1943), *Climatic Changes* (1954) and *The View from a Distant Star* (1963).

SHARP, Cecil James (1859–1924) English collector of folk songs (of which he published numerous collections) and folk dances, born in London. He practised law in Australia, then turned to music and worked as an organist. Returning to England (1892) he was principal of the Hampstead Conservatory from 1896 to 1905. His work is commemorated by Cecil Sharp House in London, the headquarters of the

English Folk Dance (founded by him in 1911) and song societies.

SHARP, Granville (1735–1813) English abolitionist, born in Durham. Apprenticed to a London linen-draper, in 1758 he got a post in the ordnance department, but resigned in 1776 through sympathy with America. He was active in the anti-slavery movement and, defending a black immigrant, James Sommersett (or Somerset), won a legal decision that as soon as any slave sets foot in England he or she becomes free. He worked with **Thomas Clarkson** for the abolition of negro slavery, and his idea for a home for freed slaves in Sierra Leone was adopted. He also wrote many philological, legal, political and theological pamphlets, and was active in various religious associations.

SHARP, James (1613–79) Scottish prelate, born in Banff. He studied for the church at King's College, Aberdeen (1633–37). He signed the National Covenant against **Charles I** in 1638, and became minister at Crail in 1647. In 1651–52 he was taken prisoner to London with some other ministers; and in 1657 he was chosen by the more moderate party in the church to plead their cause before **Cromwell**. Sent by **Monk** to Breda, he had several interviews with **Charles II** in exile there (1660). His correspondence for some months after his return from Holland is full of apprehensions of Prelacy; but its perfidy stands revealed in a letter to the Earl of Middleton, which proves that he was then in hearty co-operation with **Clarendon** and the English bishops for the re-establishment of Episcopacy in Scotland. The bribe was a great one, for in December he was consecrated archbishop of St Andrews. The wily tool of **Lauderdale**, an oppressor of those he had betrayed, he soon became an object of popular detestation and of contempt to his employers. On 3 May 1679, twelve Covenanters, led by **John Balfour** of Kinloch and David Hackston dragged him from his coach on Magus Muir and murdered him.

SHARP, Sir Percival (1867–1953) pioneer English educationist. Educated at the Endowed School, Bishop Auckland, and Homerton College, Cambridge, he was head of Bowerham School, Lancashire (1898–1902). He became secretary for education at St Helen's (1905–14) and director of education at Newcastle-upon-Tyne (1914–19) and Sheffield (1919–32). He was a member of the Burnham committee (1919–49). As secretary of the Association of Education Committees (1933–44) his work was formative in relations between local authorities and teachers' associations, and he played a prominent part in the development of English education in the first half of this century.

SHARP, William (1749–1824) English engraver, born in London, a businessman in the city. He was an eminent engraver of portraits and of historical, religious and decorative subjects in the style of his contemporaries and old master painters, including **Benjamin West**, and **Joshua Reynolds**. He was a friend of **Thomas Paine** and **Horne Tooke**.

SHARP, William (1855–1905) Scottish writer, born in Paisley. He settled in London (1879), and published *Earth's Voices* (1884). He wrote books on contemporary English, French and German poets, but is chiefly remembered as the author of the remarkable series of Celtic—or neo-Celtic—tales and romances by 'Fiona Macleod'—a pseudonym he systematically refused to acknowledge. They include *Pharais* (1894), *The Mountain Lovers* and *The Sin-Eater* (1895) and *The Immortal Hour* (1900).

SHARPE, Charles Kirkpatrick (1781–1851) Scottish antiquary, born in Hoddam Castle, Dumfries. Educated in Edinburgh and at Christ Church College, Oxford, he was a lifelong friend of Sir **Walter Scott** and contributed two original ballads to Scott's *Minstrelsy of the Scottish Border*. He edited editions for the Bannatyne Club and the Abbotsford Club, but is chiefly remembered for his lively correspondence (2 vols, 1888).

SHARPE, Richard Bowdler (1847–1909) English ornithologist. Librarian of the Zoological Society from 1867, and on the staff of the British Museum from 1872, he wrote half of the British Museum's *Catalogue of Birds* (27 vols, 1874–98). He was a founder of the British Ornithologists' Club.

SHARPEY-SCHAFER, Sir Edward (1850–1935) English physiologist, born in Hornsey. Educated at University College, London, he became professor there (1883–99) and at Edinburgh (1899–1933). Known especially for his researches on endocrinology and muscular contraction, he devised the prone-pressure method of artificial respiration.

SHASTRI, Lal Bahadour (1904–66) Indian politician, born in Benares, the son of a clerk in **Nehru**'s father's law office. He joined **Mahatma Gandhi**'s independence movement at 16 and was seven times imprisoned by the British. He excelled as a congress party official and politician in the United Provinces and joined Nehru's cabinet in 1952 as minister for the railways, becoming minister of transport (1957) and of commerce (1958) and home secretary (1960). Under the Kamaraj plan to invigorate the Congress party at 'grass-roots' level he resigned with other cabinet ministers in 1963 but was recalled by Nehru in 1964, after the latter's stroke, as minister without portfolio, and succeeded him as prime minister in 1964. He died suddenly of a heart attack while in Tashkent, USSR, for discussions on the India-Pakistan dispute.

SHAW, Anna Howard (1847–1919) English-born American suffragist, one of the most influential leaders of the suffrage movement, born in Newcastle-upon-Tyne. Emigrating with her family to the USA as a young child (1851), in 1880 she became the first woman ordained as a Methodist Protestant preacher.In 1886 she graduated from Boston University as a doctor, but decided to work for the cause of women's suffrage and devoted herself entirely to this. An eloquent, powerful lecturer, she campaigned widely. From 1904 to 1915 she was president of the National American Woman Suffrage Association. She was head of the Women's Committee of the Council of National Defense during World War I. She published her autobiography, *The Story of a Pioneer*, in 1915.

SHAW, George Bernard (1856–1950) Irish dramatist, essayist, critic, vegetarian and pamphleteer, born of Irish Protestant parents in Dublin. His mother was a singing-teacher in Dublin and later in London, and from her he inherited strength of character and the great love and knowledge of music so influential in his life and work. After short and unhappy periods at various schools, in 1871 he entered a firm of land-agents, disliked office routine, and left Ireland for good to follow his mother and sister Lucy, a musical-comedy actress, to London. His literary life had already begun in 1875 with a letter to the press (one of his favourite means of expression), shrewdly analysing the effect on individuals of sudden conversion by the American evangelists, **Moody** and Sankey. In London his early years were a long period of struggle and impoverishment, and of the five novels he wrote between 1879 and 1883, the best of which are probably *Love Among the Artists* and *Cashel Byron's Profession*, all were rejected by the more reputable publishers. An encounter (1882) with **Henry George** and the reading of **Karl Marx** turned his thoughts towards socialism, and while any direct propagation of it is absent from his plays, his faith in it and a 'kindly dislike' (if not dread) of capitalist society form the backbone of all his work. Political and economic understanding stood him in good stead as a local government councillor in St Pancras (1897–1903) and also on the executive committee of the small but influential Fabian Society, to which he devoted himself selflessly for many years (1884–1911) and for which he edited *Fabian Essays* (1889) and wrote many well-known socialist tracts. Journalism provided another lively platform for him, and it was as 'Corno di Bassetto', music critic for the new *Star* newspaper (1888–90), that he made his first indelible impact on the intellectual and social consciousness of his time. In this and in his later music criticism for *The World* (1890–94) and, above all, in his dramatic criticism for **Frank Harris**'s *Saturday Review* (1895–98), he was making his name. To this period also belong *The Quintessence of Ibsenism* (1891) and *The Perfect Wagnerite* (1898), tributes to fellow 'artist-philosophers' who, together with **Bunyan**, **Dickens**, **Samuel Butler** and **Mozart**, he acknowledged had influence on his work. The rest of Shaw's life, especially after his marriage (1898) to the Irish heiress Charlotte Payne-Townshend, is mainly the history of his plays. His first, *Widowers' Houses*, was begun in 1885 in collaboration with his friend William Archer, but was finished independently in 1892 as the result of the challenge he felt to produce the newer drama of ideas he had been advocating. Into the earliest plays, which also include *Mrs Warren's Profession* (1898), *Arms and the Man* (pub 1898) and *Candida* (1897) (one of the first in a long series of remarkable female portrayals), comes already the favourite Shavian theme of conversion—from dead system and outworn morality towards a more creatively vital approach to life—and this is further developed in *Three Plays for Puritans*: *The Devil's Disciple* (pub 1897), *Caesar and Cleopatra* (1901), and *Captain Brassbound's Conversion* (1900). His long correspondence with the famous Lyceum actress, **Ellen Terry**, was also at its peak during these years. At last Shaw was becoming more widely known, first of all in the USA and on the Continent, and then, with the important advent of the playwright-producer-actor, **Harley Granville-Barker**, in England itself, especially after the epoch-making Vedrenne-Barker Court Theatre season of 1904–07. This had been preceded by one of Shaw's greatest philosophical comedies, *Man and Superman* (1902), in which, in quest of a purer religious approach to life, Shaw advocated through his Don Juan the importance of man's unceasing creative evolutionary urge for world-improvement. Other notable plays from the early part of the century are *John Bull's Other Island* (1904), *Major Barbara* (1905), *The Doctor's Dilemma* (1906), and two uniquely Shavian discussion plays, *Getting Married* (1908) and *Misalliance* (1910). They further display Shaw's increasing control of his medium and the wide range of his subject matter (from politics and statecraft to family life, prostitution and vaccination). Before the Joint Committee on Stage Censorship of 1909 he proudly proclaimed himself as 'immoralist and heretic', and insisted on the civilized necessity for toleration and complete freedom of thought. Just before World War I came two of his most delightful plays; *Androcles and the Lion* (1912), a 'religious pantomime', and *Pygmalion* (1913), an 'anti-romantic' comedy of phonetics (adapted as a highly successful musical play, *My Fair Lady* in 1956, filmed in 1964). During the war, though he later toured the front at official invitation, he created controversy and recrimination with his fearless and provocative *Common Sense About the War* (1914). After the war followed three of his greatest dramas in near succession: *Heartbreak House* (1919), an attempt to analyse in an English Chekhovian social environment the causes of present moral and political discontents; *Back to Methuselah* (1921), five plays in one, in which Shaw conducted a not altogether successful dramatic excursion from the Garden of Eden to 'As Far as Thought Can Reach'; and *Saint Joan* (1923), in which Shaw's essentially religious nature, his genius for characterization (above all of saintly yet very human women), and his powers of dramatic argument are most abundantly revealed. In 1925 Shaw was awarded the Nobel prize for literature, but donated the money to inaugurate the Anglo-Swedish Literary Foundation. In 1931 he visited Russia, and during the 1930s made other long tours, including a world one with his wife in 1932, during which he gave a memorable address on political economy in the Metropolitan Opera House, New York. Greater perhaps than any of the plays written during the last years of his life are the two prose works: *The Intelligent Woman's Guide to Socialism and Capitalism* (1928), one of the most lucid introductions to its subjects, and *The Black Girl in Search of God* (1932), a modern *Pilgrim's Progress*. The later plays, except for *The Apple Cart* (1929), have scarcely received adequate public stage presentation but they continue to preach the stern yet invigorating Shavian morality of individual responsibility, self-discipline, heroic effort without thought of reward or 'atonement', and the utmost integrity. Plays such as *Too True to Be Good* (1932) and *The Simpleton of the Unexpected Isles* (1934) also show signs of sounding a newer and even more experimental dramatic note altogether.

SHAW, Henry Wheeler See **BILLINGS, Josh**

SHAW, Jack (1780–1815) English pugilist of prodigious strength. Serving in the Life Guards, he fell at Waterloo (1815), first killing ten curassiers.

SHAW, Martin Fallus (1876–1958) English composer, born in London. He studied under **Charles Stanford** at the Royal College of Music, composed the ballad opera, *Mr Pepys* (1926), with Clifford Bax, and set **T S Eliot**'s poems to music. He is best known, however, for his songs and as co-editor with his brother, Geoffrey Turton Shaw (1879–1943), a church musician, of national songbooks, and with **Vaughan Williams** of *Songs of Praise* and the *Oxford Carol Book*.

SHAW, (Richard) Norman (1831–1912) English architect, born in Edinburgh. He worked with his partner William Eden Nesfield (1835–88) in many styles ranging from Gothic Revival to neo-Baroque, but became an acknowledged leader in the trend away from the Victorian style back to traditional Georgian design, leading to the English Domestic Revival. His major buildings include the Old Swan House, Chelsea (1876), New Scotland Yard (1888), the Gaiety Theatre, Aldwych (1902, now demolished), and the Piccadilly Hotel (1905). He also designed the garden suburb at Bedford Park, London.

SHAW, Sir William Napier (1854–1945) English meteorologist, born in Birmingham. In 1877 he became assistant director of the Cavendish Laboratory; he was director of the Meteorological Office, London (1907–20), and from 1918 scientific adviser to the government. He became professor of the Royal College of Science in 1920. In his *Life History of Surface Air Currents* (1906) he established with Lempfert the 'polar front' theory of cyclones propounded by **Bjerknes**. His *Manual of Meteorology* (1919–31) became a standard work.

SHAWCROSS, Sir Hartley William, Baron Shawcross (1902–) English jurist, born in Giessen,

Germany. Educated at Dulwich College, he was called to the bar at Gray's Inn in 1925 and was senior lecturer in law at Liverpool (1927–34). After service in World War II, he was attorney-general (1945–51) and president of the board of trade (1951) in the Labour government. He established an international legal reputation for himself as chief British prosecutor at the Nuremberg Trials (1945–46), led the investigations of the Lynskey Tribunal (1948) and prosecuted in the **Fuchs** atom spy case (1950). Finding the narrow opposition tactics of the Labour party irksome, he resigned his parliamentary seat in 1958. He was created a life peer in 1959.

SHAW-LEFEVRE, George John, Baron Eversley (1832–1928) English Liberal politician, born in London. He served in Liberal ministries (1881–84, 1892–95), and formed with **Grote**, **Stephen** and **John Stuart Mill** in 1866 the Commons Preservation Society to protect common lands from the encroaching builder. As postmaster-general (1883–84) he introduced sixpenny telegrams, and as commissioner of works (1880–83, 1892–94) threw open Hampton Court park and Kew Palace. He served on the London County Council from 1897 and in 1906 was created baron.

SHAWN, Ted (Edwin Myers) (1891–1972) American dancer and director, born in Kansas City, Missouri. He studied theology and began dancing in order to strengthen his legs after suffering diphtheria. In 1914 he met **Ruth St Denis** in New York, and from 1914 to 1931 they were married—a relationship which was to have a major effect on the dance world. In 1915 they founded Denishawn, a dance school which was favoured by the Hollywood studios and branched out right across America with a uniquely wide-ranging curriculum of classes from ballet to oriental dance. When the couple separated in 1931, Denishawn broke up and Ted Shawn moved to a farm in Lee, Massachusetts, where he founded his own group, Ted Shawn and His Men Dancers, who toured with dance inspired by native American and aboriginal work, until 1941. The farm then became the setting for Jacob's Pillow, an annual summer school/festival. His books include *The American Ballet* (1925), *Dance We Must* (1940) and *One Thousand And One Night Stands* (1960).

SHAWN, William (1901–) American journalist and editor, born in Chicago. Educated at Michigan University, he was the second editor of the *New Yorker* (1952–87), in succession to **Harold Wallace Ross**.

SHAYS, Daniel (1747–1825) American soldier and insurgent leader of the rebellion in western Massachusetts (1786–87) which bears his name, born probably in Hopkinton, Massachusetts. During the American War of Independence (1775–83) he served against the British at Bunker's Hill, Ticonderoga, etc, and was commissioned. In 1786 he led the insurrection by the farmers against the US government, which was imposing heavy taxation and mortgages. After raiding the arsenal at Springfield, Massachusetts, the insurrectionists were routed at Petersham (1787) and Shays was condemned to death, but pardoned (1788).

SHCHARANSKY, Natan, originally **Anatoly Borisovich** (1948–) Soviet dissident, born in Donetsk, in the Ukraine, the son of a Jewish filmwriter and journalist. A brilliant mathematician who was disillusioned with Soviet society, in 1973 he applied for a visa to emigrate to Israel. This was repeatedly refused, prompting him to become increasingly active in the Soviet dissident movement. In 1976 he joined Yuri Orlov's Helsinki Watch Group, a body formed to monitor Soviet human rights violations, and in 1977 was sentenced to 13 years in a labour colony for allegedly spying on behalf of the CIA. He was freed from confinement in February 1986 as part of an east-west 'spy' exchange and joined his wife Avital in Israel, where he assumed the name Natan. In 1989 he was nominated as Israeli ambassador to the UN.

SHEEHY-SKEFFINGTON, Francis Joseph Christopher (1878–1916) Irish pacifist and feminist, born in Cavan, the son of a school inspector. Educated at University College, Dublin, he was the first lay registrar (1902–04) and married Hanna Sheehy, daughter of David Sheehy, the Irish Nationalist MP. They added one another's names to their own, becoming active socialists and secularists and campaigning for female suffrage and women's rights. He became increasingly drawn to pacifism, edited the *Irish Citizen* from 1912, contributed to the *Manchester Guardian*, *L'Humanité* and the *Call* (US). On the outbreak of World War I he was sentenced to six months' imprisonment for campaigning against recruiting, being released after six days' hunger-strike, after which he went, still campaigning, to the USA. Opposing the Easter Rising of 1916 he sought to organize an attempt to stop the looting but was arrested and shot in Portobello Barracks.

SHEELER, Charles (1883–1965) American painter and photographer, born in Philadelphia, where he studied art. As a painter much influenced by the Cubist movement, he contributed to the Armory Show in New York (1913). From 1912 he worked as an industrial photographer, moving towards creative industrial records, especially the skyscrapers of Manhattan, publishing *Mannahatta* with **Paul Strand** (1920). In 1927 he was commissioned to record the building of the Ford Motor installation at River Rouge, Michigan (1927). Widely acclaimed for this, he was staff photographer at the New York Museum of Modern Art 1942–45 but came to regard photography as a basis for his abstract-realistic paintings and graphic work.

SHEEN, Fulton John (1895–1979) American Roman Catholic prelate and broadcaster, born in El Paso, Illinois, the son of a farmer. He graduated from the Catholic University of America, then took a PhD at Louvain, Belgium. Ordained in 1919, he returned to the Catholic University to teach philosophy (1926–59) before becoming national director of the Society for the Propagation of the Faith. Meanwhile he had gained a reputation as a broadcaster on the 'Catholic Hour' which was heard worldwide (1930–52), and he gained an even larger hearing with the TV programme Life is Worth Living (1952–65). He was auxiliary bishop of New York (1951–65) and bishop of Rochester (1966–69), then retired as titular archbishop. His many writings include *Peace of Soul* (1949), *Those Mysterious Priests* (1974) and *The Electronic Christian* (1979).

SHEEPSHANKS, John (1787–1863) English art-collector, born in Leeds. In 1857 he presented his collection (233 oil paintings and 103 drawings) to the nation.

SHEFFIELD, John, 1st Duke of Buckingham and Normanby (1648–1721) English political leader and poet. He succeeded his father as third Earl of Mulgrave in 1658, served in both navy and army, and was lord chamberlain to **James II** and a cabinet councillor under **William III**, who in 1694 made him Marquis of Normanby. Queen **Anne** made him Duke of (the county of) Buckingham (1703); but for his opposition to **Godolphin** and **Marlborough** he was deprived of the Seal (1705). After 1710, under the Tories, he was lord steward and lord president till the death of Anne, when he lost all power, and intrigued for the restoration of the Stuarts. Patron of **Dryden** and friend of **Pope**, he wrote two tragedies, a metrical *Essay on Satire*, an *Essay on Poetry*, and other works.

SHEIL, Richard Lalor (1791–1851) Irish dramatist and politician, born in Drumdowney, Kilkenny. He wrote a series of plays, aided **O'Connell** in forming the new Catholic Association (1825), and supported the cause by impassioned speeches. He was MP and in 1839 under **Melbourne** became vice-president of the board of trade, and a privy councillor—the first Catholic to gain that honour. In 1846 he was promoted master of the Mint.

SHELBURNE, William Petty, 2nd Earl of (1737–1805) English statesman, great-grandson of Sir **William Petty**, born in Dublin. He studied at Christ Church College, Oxford, served in the army, entered parliament, succeeded his father to the earldom in 1761, and in 1763 was appointed president of the board of trade and in **Chatham**'s second administration (1766) secretary of state. Upon the fall of Lord **North**'s ministry in 1782 Shelburne declined to form a government, but became secretary of state under **Rockingham**. Upon the latter's death the same year, the king offered Shelburne the Treasury. **Fox** resigned, and Shelburne introduced **William Pitt** into office as his Chancellor of the Exchequer. This ministry resigned when outvoted by the coalition between Fox and North (February 1783). Shelburne was in 1784 made Marquis of Lansdowne, and at Lansdowne House and Bowood, Wiltshire, he collected a splendid gallery of pictures and a fine library.

SHELDON, Gilbert (1598–1677) English prelate. Chaplain to **Charles I**, he was warden of All Souls, Oxford (1626–48), but was ejected by the parliamentarians. At the Restoration in 1660 he was appointed bishop of London, and in 1663 archbishop of Canterbury. He built the Sheldonian Theatre at Oxford (1669).

SHELLEY, Mary Wollstonecraft, née **Godwin** (1797–1851) English writer, the daughter of **William Godwin** and **Mary Wollstonecraft Godwin**. In 1814 she eloped with **Percy Bysshe Shelley**, and married him as his second wife in 1816. They lived abroad throughout their married life. Her first and most impressive novel was *Frankenstein* (1818), her second *Valperga* (1823). After her husband's death in 1822 she returned from Italy to England with their son in 1823. Her husband's father, in granting her an allowance, insisted on the suppression of the volume of Shelley's *Posthumous Poems* edited by her. *The Last Man* (1826), a romance of the ruin of human society by pestilence, fails to attain sublimity. In *Lodore* (1835) the story is told of Shelley's alienation from his first wife. Her last novel, *Falkner* appeared in 1837. Of her occasional pieces of verse the most remarkable is 'The Choice'. Her *Journal of a Six Weeks' Tour* (partly by Shelley) tells of the excursion to Switzerland in 1814; *Rambles in Germany and Italy* (1844) describes tours of 1840–43; her *Tales* were published in 1890. Two unpublished mythological dramas, *Proserpine* and *Midas*, were edited and published in 1922.

SHELLEY, Percy Bysshe (1792–1822) English poet, born in Field Place, near Horsham in Sussex. He was educated at Syon House Academy and Eton, where he acquired the sobriquet 'Mad Shelley' for his independent spirit and was later dubbed 'Eton Atheist'. While at Eton he published *Zastrozzi* (1810), a Gothic novel. That year, with his sister Elizabeth, he produced *Original Poetry by Victor and Cazire*, and the following year another Gothic romance, *St Irvine, or, The Rosicrucian*. He attended University College, Oxford, where he read radical authors like **William Godwin** and **Paine**, and dressed and behaved in an eccentric and provocative manner. In 1811, he produced a pamphlet, co-authored with Thomas Jefferson Hogg, called *The Necessity of Atheism*, a formative declaration. Both authors were expelled. That and Shelley's elopement to Scotland with 16-year-old Harriet Westbrook caused a rift between him and his family that was never repaired. Shelley would not recant, and relinquished his right to his inheritance. He lived itinerantly for the next three years; in York, in the Lake District where only **Southey** was at home, in Dublin where he advocated the repeal of the Union and Catholic emancipation, and at Lynmouth in Devon where he set up a commune of 'like spirits'. *Queen Mab* (1813) was the poetic fruit of this time but it made little impact. In London he met, befriended, subsidized and fell out with Godwin, and was close to **Thomas Love Peacock**. Despite having two children, his marriage to Harriet failed and he fell in love with Mary, the 16-year-old daughter of Godwin and **Mary Wollstonecraft**. Predictably they eloped, making up a *ménage à trois* with Mary's half-sister, Jane 'Claire' Clairmont. The three travelled on the continent where Shelley wrote an unfinished novella, *The Assassins* (1814), collaborated on a journal, and published *The History of a Six Weeks' Tour* (1817). Shelley returned to London, to face financial problems, and Mary gave birth to a daughter who died prematurely. The couple took a house near Windsor Great Park and he wrote *Alastor* (1816), its publication coinciding with the birth of his beloved son, William. 1816 was a traumatic year. He spent time with **Byron** at Lake Geneva, Harriet Westbrook drowned herself, and Shelley immediately married Mary. His reputation was growing. He met **Keats** and **Hazlitt** and, having moved to Marlow in 1817, he wrote *An Address to the People on the Death of Princess Charlotte*, a fine political pamphlet. He published *The Revolt of Islam* in 1818, the year he finally left England for Italy where he was to spend the rest of his life. In Este he wrote *Julian and Maddalo* (1818), which explores his relationship with Byron, and in 1819 came the major part of *Prometheus Unbound*, his masterpiece. William's death in Rome devastated him and he moved to Tuscany, finally settling in Pisa. From the middle of 1819 to summer 1820 came an extraordinary burst of creative energy resulting in the completion of the fourth part of *Prometheus*, *The Masque of Anarchy* (1819, inspired by the Peterloo massacre), 'The Ode to the West Wind', 'To Liberty' and 'To Naples', the *Letter to Maria Gisborne* (1820) and *The Witch of Atlas*. His son Percy was born in November 1819. Still to come was *A Philosophical View of Reform* (1820), *Essay on the Devil* (1821), poems, *The Defence of Poetry* (1821) and *Swellfoot the Tyrant* (1820), a burlesque. *Adonais* (1821), an elegy and meditation on death, was prompted by the death of Keats. *Epipsychidion* (1821) was the fruit of a platonic affair with a beautiful Italian heiress locked away in a convent. Byron came to Pisa in 1821, where a bohemian group gathered. Roused by the Greek war of independence, Shelley wrote *Hellas* (1822), a verse drama. It was to be his last work. The *ménage* moved to Lerici. Mary had a miscarriage and Claire was distraught at the death of her daughter, Allegra, whom she had had by Byron. Returning from a visit to Byron and **Leigh Hunt** at Livorno in August 1822 in the schooner 'Ariel', Shelley, Edward Williams and an English boatboy were drowned when they were surprised by a sudden squall. Shelley's body was cremated at Viareggio. As much a political activist as a poet, Shelley's adventurous life and unconventional behaviour have tended to overshadow his poetry. He was revolutionary in both spheres of life, turning away from **Coleridge**'s German Romanticism and reaffirming Mediterranean values: an inspirational polemicist and a poet of genius. His Letters in two volumes appeared in 1964.

SHEN KUA (1030–93) Chinese administrator, engineer and scientist, born in Hangchow. He made significant contributions to such diverse fields as astronomy, cartography, medicine, hydraulics and fortification. As director of the astronomical bureau from 1072 he improved methods of computation and the design of several observational devices; in 1075 he constructed a series of relief maps of China's northern frontier area, and designed fortifications as defences against nomadic invaders. He surveyed and improved the Grand Canal over a distance of some 150 miles, using stone-filled gabions, wooden piles and long bundles of reeds to strengthen the banks and close gaps. In 1082 he was forced by intrigue to resign from his government posts, and occupied his last years in the writing of *Brush Talks from Dream Brook*, a remarkable compilation of about 600 observations which has become one of the most important sources of information on early science and technology.

SHENSTONE, William (1714–63) English poet, born near Halesowen, Worcestershire. He studied at Solihull Grammar School and Pembroke College, Oxford. In 1735 he inherited the estate of the Leasowes, and spent most of his income on 'landship gardening' to turn it into a show garden. In 1737 he published his best-known poem, 'The Schoolmistress', which, written in imitation of **Spenser**, foreshadowed **Gray**'s *Elegy*. He published *The Judgement of Hercules* in 1741. His *Pastoral Ballad* (1755) was commended by Gray and **Samuel Johnson**.

SHEPARD, Alan Bartlett (1923–) American astronaut, the first American in space, born in East Derry, New Hampshire. He graduated from the US Naval Academy in 1945 and served in the Pacific. He won his wings in 1947 and subsequently flew jet aircraft on test and training missions. One of the original seven NASA astronauts, on 5 May 1961, 23 days after **Yuri Gagarin**'s historic orbit of the earth, he was launched in 'Freedom 7' by a Redstone rocket vehicle, on a ballistic sub-orbital trajectory to a height of 116 miles, landing 302 miles downrange, controlling the whole 15-minute flight manually. He was director of astronaut training at NASA (1965–74), and commanded the Apollo 14 lunar mission in 1971.

SHEPARD, Ernest Howard (1879–1976), English artist and cartoonist. He worked for *Punch*, but made his name with his illustrations for children's books such as **A A Milne**'s *Winnie the Pooh* (1926) and **Kenneth Grahame**'s *The Wind in the Willows* (1931).

SHEPARD, Sam, originally **Samuel Shepard Rogers** (1943–) American dramatist and actor, born in Illinois. He moved to New York City and worked in the avant-garde theatre of the 1960s with one-acters. His first plays, *Cowboy*, and *The Rock Garden*, were written in 1964 and produced by Theater Genesis in New York, followed by *Dog* and *Rocking Chair* (1965) at La Mama. *The Tooth of Crime*, a rock drama, was staged at the Royal Court Theatre, London, in 1974, followed by *The Curse of the Starving Class*, at the New York Shakespeare Festival, in 1976. He won the Pulitzer prize with his 1978 play, *Buried Child*. He was resident playwright at the Magic Theater, San Francisco, for several years, and two of his plays were first staged there, *True West* (1979), and *Fool For Love* (1983). *A Lie of the Mind* (1985) was very successful in America. Few living American playwrights have such sensitivity for landscape and time as Shepard, and few can produce such economic theatrical intensity. He also appeared in films, and has written screenplays, including *Paris, Texas* (1984), a tale of drifting and homecoming.

SHEPILOV, Dmitri Trofimovitch (1905–) Soviet politician, born in Ashkhabad and educated at Moscow University. From 1926 to 1931 he was a public prosecutor in Siberia and later became a lecturer in political economy. In 1952 he became chief editor of *Pravda*; in 1954 a member of the Supreme Soviet; and in 1956 foreign minister. He was 'purged' by the party leadership in 1957 and banished to a distant teaching post.

SHEPPARD, David Stuart (1929–) English Anglican prelate, and former Test cricketer, born in Reigate, Surrey. He graduated at Cambridge and worked in London's East End as Warden of the Mayflower Family Centre, Canning Town (1957–69). He was bishop of Woolwich before becoming bishop of Liverpool in 1975. There his profound social concern, the remarkable rapport in which he and his Roman Catholic counterpart work together, and perhaps also his past record as former England and Sussex cricket captain, have made a lasting impact on the city. He has written *Parson's Pitch* (1964), *Built as a City* (1974), and *Bias to the Poor* (1983).

SHEPPARD, Dick (Hugh Richard Lawrie) (1880–1937) Anglican clergyman and pacifist, born in Windsor. A popular preacher with distinctly modern views on the Christian life and a pioneer of religious broadcasting, he was vicar of London's St Martin-in-the-Fields (1914–27), published *The Human Parson* (1927) and *The Impatience of a Parson* (1927), and became dean of Canterbury (1929–31) and canon of St Paul's Cathedral (1934–37). He was an ardent pacifist and founded the Peace Pledge Union in 1936.

SHEPPARD, Jack (1702–24) English robber, born in Stepney, London. He committed the first of many robberies in 1720, and in 1724 was five times caught, and four times escaped. He was hanged at Tyburn in the presence of 200 000 spectators. He was the subject of many plays and ballads, tracts by **Daniel Defoe** and a novel by **William Ainsworth**.

SHER, Antony (1949–) South African-born British actor and writer. He came to England in 1968 and studied at the Webber-Douglas Academy of Dramatic Art. He appeared in plays at the Royal Court Theatre, including **David Hare**'s *Teeth 'n' Smiles* in 1975, and joined the Royal Shakespeare Company in 1982. In 1984 he gave a performance of macabre brilliance in the title role of **Bill Alexander**'s production of *Richard III*, a performance given theatrical virtuosity by his use of crutches. An immensely powerful stage presence, he has appeared occasionally in television drama, notably in *The History Man* (1981). His book, *The Year of the King* (1985), describes his work on *Richard III*. His first novel, *Middlepost*, was published in 1988. He illustrated both himself.

SHERARD, Robert Harborough, originally surnamed **Kennedy** (1861–1943) English biographer and defender of **Oscar Wilde**, the son of a clergyman and great-grandson of **William Wordsworth**. He lived most of his life in France and Corsica, wrote lives of **Zola**, **Daudet** and **Maupassant**, all of whom he had known, as well as interesting memoirs of French life, *Twenty Years of Paris*, *Modern Paris*, *My Friends the French*, and an important exposé *The White Slaves of England*. He was not homosexual, and befriended Oscar Wilde in 1883 several years before his homosexual career. Although deeply shocked by the Wilde scandal, he stood by him, sometimes hysterically, and wrote several books and pamphlets on him, by far the best being that courageously (if initially anonymously) issued two years after Wilde's death: *Oscar Wilde: the Story of an Unhappy Friendship* (1902).

SHERATON, Thomas (1751–1806) English furniture designer, born in Stockton-on-Tees. He settled in London around 1790, but never had a workshop of his own. Although there is no extant furniture attributable to him, he achieved great renown for his elegant Neoclassical designs, influenced by **Thomas Chippendale** and **George Hepplewhite**. His major work, *The Cabinet-Maker and Upholsterer's Drawing Book*, was published in parts between 1791 and 1794. His later publications were less successful: *The Cabinet Dictionary* (1803) and *The Cabinet-Maker, Upholsterer and General Artists' Encyclopaedia* (1805). He was ordained in 1800.

SHERBROOKE, Robert Lowe, 1st Viscount (1811–92) English politician, born in Bingham, Nottinghamshire. From Winchester he went in 1829 to University College, Oxford. Called to the bar in 1842, he emigrated the same year to Australia, soon attained a lucrative practice, and also took a leading part in politics. Home again in 1850, and returned to parliament (1852), he took office under **Aberdeen** and **Palmerston**. From 1859 to 1864 he was vice-president of the education board, and introduced the Revised Code of 1862 with its 'payment by results'. In 1868 his feud with the Liberals was forgotten in his strenuous aid towards disestablishing the Irish Church, and **Gladstone** made him Chancellor of the Exchequer. In 1873 he became home secretary; in 1880 he went to the Upper House as Viscount Sherbrooke. He opposed the exclusive study of the classics.

SHERE ALI (1825–79) amir of Afghanistan, a younger son of **Dost Mohammed**, succeeded as amir in 1863. Disagreements with his half-brothers soon arose, which kept Afghanistan in anarchy; Shere Ali fled to Kandahar; but in 1868 regained possession of Kabul, with assistance from the viceroy of India, Sir **John Lawrence**. In 1879 his eldest son, Yakub Khan, rebelled but was captured and imprisoned. Shere Ali's refusal to receive a British mission (1878) led to war; and, after severe fighting, he fled to Turkestan, where he died. He was succeeded by Yakub Khan.

SHERIDAN, Philip Henry (1831–88) American calvary officer, born in Albany, New York, of Irish parentage. In 1848 he entered West Point, and graduated in 1853. At the outbreak of the Civil War in 1861 he was an infantry captain in the Federal army, but in 1862 was given a cavalry regiment, and rose rapidly to command a division. He distinguished himself at Perryville and at Stones River, fought at Chickamauga (1863), and was engaged in all the subsequent operations of the Civil War, gaining credit for the gallantry with which his division drove the enemy over Missionary Ridge. In 1864 he was given command of the cavalry of the Army of the Potomac, took part in the battle of the Wilderness, made a notable raid on Confederate communications with **Richmond**, and led the advance to Cold Harbor. In August **Grant** placed him in command of the Army of the Shenandoah with instructions to make the valley 'a barren waste'. In September he attacked the enemy under **Early**, drove him beyond Winchester, again dislodged him from Fisher's Hill, and pursued him through Harrisonburg and Staunton; but Early, reinforced by **Lee**, again appeared in the Shenandoah Valley, and on 19 October surprised the Northern army at Cedar Creek and drove it back in confusion. Sheridan, who was at Winchester, 20 miles away, galloped to the field and turned defeat into victory. He was promoted major-general and received the thanks of congress. Defeating the enemy at Five Forks on 1 April, he had an active share in the final battles which led to Lee's surrender at Appomattox Courthouse on 9 April 1865. A lieutenant-general in 1870, he was with **Moltke** at Gravelotte and other battles. In 1883 he succeeded **Sherman** as general-in-chief. He died at Nonquitt, Massachusetts. Sheridan never lost a battle. Among the northern generals he ranks next to Grant and Sherman. He wrote *The Personal Memoirs of P H Sheridan* (1888).

SHERIDAN, Richard Brinsley (1751–1816) Irish dramatist, born in Dublin. He was grandson of **Swift**'s friend, Thomas Sheridan, (1687–1738), and son of Thomas Sheridan (1719–88), a teacher of elocution, actor and author of a *Life of Swift*. His mother, Frances Sheridan, née Chamberlaine (1724–66), was the author of a novel called *Sidney Biddulph* and of one or two plays. Richard Sheridan was educated at Harrow, and after leaving school, with a school-friend named Halhed wrote a three-act farce called *Jupiter* and tried a verse translation of the *Epistles of Aristoenetus*. After a romantic courtship, Richard married Elizabeth Linley in 1773. The young couple settled in London to a life much beyond their means. Sheridan now made more serious efforts at dramatic composition. On 17 January 1775 *The Rivals* was produced at Covent Garden, and after a slight alteration in the cast met with universal approval. In the same year appeared a poor farce called *St Patrick's Day* and also *The Duenna*. In 1776 Sheridan, with the aid of **Linley** and another friend, bought half the patent of Drury Lane Theatre for £35000 from **Garrick**, and in 1778 the remaining share for £45000. His first production was a purified edition of **Vanbrugh**'s *Relapse*, under the title of *A Trip to Scarborough*. *The Critic* (1779), teeming with sparkling wit, was Sheridan's last dramatic effort, with the exception of a poor tragedy, *Pizarro*. On the dissolution of parliament in 1780 Sheridan was elected for Stafford, and in 1782 became under-secretary for foreign affairs under **Rockingham**, afterwards secretary to the Treasury in the coalition ministry (1783). His parliamentary reputation dated from some great speeches in the impeachment of **Warren Hastings**. In 1794 he again electrified the House by a magnificent oration in reply to Lord Mornington's denunciation of the French Revolution. He remained the devoted friend and adherent of **Fox** till Fox's death, and was also the defender and mouthpiece of the prince regent. In 1806 he was appointed receiver of the Duchy of Cornwall, and in 1806 treasurer to the navy. In 1812 he was defeated at Westminster, and his parliamentary career came to an end. In 1792 his first wife died, and three years later he married Esther Ogle, the silly and extravagant daughter of the dean of Winchester, who survived him. The affairs of the theatre had gone badly. The old building had to be closed as unfit to hold large audiences, and a new one, opened in 1794, was burned in 1809. This last calamity put the finishing touch to Sheridan's pecuniary difficulties, which had long been serious. He died in great poverty, but was given a magnificent funeral in Westminster Abbey.

SHERIFF, Lawrence (d.1567) London grocer, born in Rugby. He was the founder of Rugby School in 1567 by his bequest and endowment.

SHERLOCK, William (1641–1707) English prelate, born in Southwark. He became master of the Temple in 1685 and dean of St Paul's in 1691. He was a nonjuror, but took the oaths in 1690. The most controversial of his 60 works were *Vindication of the Doctrines of the Trinity and of the Incarnation* (1690), which made **South** charge him with Tritheism, and *Case of Allegiance* (1691).

SHERMAN, Henry Clapp (1875–1955) American biochemist. Educated at Maryland and Columbia, he became professor of organic chemistry (1907), of nutritional chemistry (1911) and of chemistry (1924) at Columbia. He did important quantitative work on vitamins.

SHERMAN, John (1823–1900) American statesman, born in Lancaster, Ohio, brother of General **William Sherman**. He was in turn chairman of financial committees in both houses of congress. He was largely author of the bills for the reconstruction of the seceded states and for the resumption of specie payment in 1879. He was appointed in 1877 secretary of the Treasury, and in 1878 had prepared a redemption fund in gold that raised the legal tender notes to par value. In 1881 and 1887 he was again returned to the senate, was its president, and afterwards chairman of the foreign relations committee. In 1897 he was made secretary of state, but retired on the war with Spain in 1898. The Sherman Act (1890; repealed 1893) sanctioned large purchases of silver by the Treasury.

SHERMAN, Roger (1721–93) American statesman and patriot, born in Newton, Massachusetts. He lived in Connecticut from 1743. First elected to the state assembly in 1755, he became a judge of the superior court (1766–89) and mayor of New Haven (1784–93). A signatory of the Declaration of Independence, as a delegate to the Convention of 1787 he took a prominent part in the debates on the constitution.

SHERMAN, William Tecumseh (1820–91) American soldier, born in Lancaster, Ohio, brother of **John Sherman**. He graduated at West Point in 1849. After serving in Florida and California, he became a banker in San Francisco. At the outbreak of the Civil War he was commissioned colonel of the 13th Infantry in the Federal army in May 1861; at Bull Run he won his promotion to Brigadier-general of volunteers. In August he was sent to Kentucky, at first under **Anderson**, but when he asked for 200000 men to put an end to the war there, he was deprived of his command. Soon in command of a division, he took a distinguished part in the battle of Shiloh (April 1862) and was made major-general. In July 1863, promoted brigadier, he drove General **Johnston** out of Jackson, Missisippi. In November he joined **Grant** at Chattanooga, and rendered excellent service in the victory of the 25th; soon after, he relieved **Burnside**, besieged at Knoxville. In March 1864 he was appointed by Grant to the command of the southwest. In April he began his campaign against Atlanta. He first encountered Johnston at Dalton on 14 May, and drove him beyond the Eaowah, and finally to Atlanta, which was evacuated on 1 September. After giving his army a rest, Sherman set out on his famous march to the sea, with 65000 men. Meeting with little serious opposition, he reached Savannah on 10 December. The works were soon carried, and on the 29th the city was evacuated. In February 1865 he left Savannah for the north, and by the 17th, compelling the evacuation of Charleston, had reached Columbia. Thence he moved on Goldsboro', fighting two battles on the way. On 9 April **Lee** surrendered, and Johnston made terms with Sherman (disapproved as too lenient by Secretary **Stanton**). For four years he commanded the Mississippi division; when Grant became president he was made head of the army. In 1874, at his own request, to make room for **Philip Sheridan**, he was retired on full pay. He died in New York.

SHERRIFF, R C (Robert Cedric) (1896–1975) English playwright, novelist and scriptwriter, born in Kingston-upon-Thames. He achieved an international reputation with his first play, *Journey's End* (1929), based on his experiences in the trenches during World War I. He became a scriptwriter in Hollywood, and wrote the scripts for films like *The Invisible Man* (1933), *Goodbye Mr Chips* (1936), *The Four Feathers* (1938), *Lady Hamilton* (1941) and *The Dambusters* (1955).

SHERRINGTON, Sir Charles Scott (1857–1952) English physiologist, born in London. After studying at Caius College, Cambridge, he became professor of physiology at Liverpool (1895–1913) and Oxford (1913–35). His researches on reflex action and especially on *The Integrative Action of the Nervous System* (1906) consititute a landmark in modern physiology. He was awarded the 1932 Nobel prize for physiology or medicine with Lord **Adrian**.

SHER SHAH (SHER KHAN) (d.1545) ruler of the Afghans. He was able to contest the supremacy of the Mughals, defeating the emperor **Hamayun** at Chausa on the Ganges in 1539 and forcing him into exile. A formidable warrior and able administrator, he also built a new city at Delhi and a fine mausoleum at Sahasram in Bihar. Only his death in battle and the inefficiency of his successors allowed the Mughals to emerge triumphant.

SHERWOOD, Mary Martha, née **Butt** (1775–1851) English writer of children's books, daughter of a chaplain to **George II**, born in Stanford, Worcestershire. In 1803 she married Henry Sherwood and went to India with him (1805–66). Her 77 works include *Little Henry and his Bearer* (1815), and the long-popular *History of the Fairchild Family* (1818–47).

SHERWOOD, Robert Emmet (1896–1955) American playwright and author, born in New Rochelle, New York. He wrote his first play, *Barnum Was Right*, while at Harvard, and after service in World War I he became editor of *Life* (1924–28), and a member of **Dorothy Parker**'s celebrated Algonquin Round Table. He won four Pulitzer prizes, the first three for drama—*Idiot's Delight*, (1936), *Abe Lincoln in Illinois* (1939) and *There Shall be No Night* (1941) and the last (1949) for his biographical *Roosevelt and Hopkins* (1949).

SHEVARDNADZE, Eduard Ambrosievich (1928–) Soviet politician, born in the Georgian village of Mamati, the son of a teacher. He studied history at the Kutaisi Institute of Education, joined the Communist party of the Soviet Union (CPSU) in 1948 and worked in the Komsomol youth league during the 1950s and the Georgian interior ministry during the 1960s, where he gained a reputation as a stern opponent of corruption. He became Georgian party chief in 1972 and introduced imaginative agricultural experiments. In 1978 he was inducted into the CPSU politburo as a candidate member and, having enjoyed longstanding connections with the new Soviet leader **Mikhail Gorbachev**, was promoted to full politburo status and appointed foreign minister in 1985, contrasting starkly with his dour predecessor, **Andrei Gromyko**. He rapidly overhauled the Soviet foreign policy machine to equip it for a new era of détente.

SHEVCHENKO, Taras (1814–61) Ukrainian poet and prose writer, born a serf in Kirilovka (Kiev). He was freed and became professor at Kiev (1845), and founded an organization for radical social reforms. He was exiled to Siberia for ten years, and published collections of poems in the Ukrainian language.

SHIELD, William (1748–1829) English viola player and composer, born in Swalwell in Durham. He was apprenticed to a boatbuilder, and, encourged by Giardini, studied music, composed anthems that were sung in Durham Cathedral, and conducted at Scarborough. He published a comic opera, *The Flitch of*

Bacon, in 1778, and, as composer to Covent Garden (1778–97), produced others. Some of his songs are still known. From 1817 he was master of the King's Musicians.

SHIH HUANG TI (259–210 BC) Chinese emperor from 246, and 4th monarch of the Chin dynasty. Assuming the title of 'the first emperor', he greatly extended the empire and built the Great Wall, completed in 294, to keep out barbarians. He had all historical documents burnt in 212 to maintain himself and his successors in power.

SHILLABER, Benjamin Penhallow (1814–90) American humorist. He was the author of *The Life and Sayings of Mrs Partington* (1854).

SHILLIBEER, George (1797–1866) English pioneer of London omnibuses, born in London. He established a coach-building business in Paris in 1825, and from 1829 ran the first London omnibus coach service from the City to Paddington.

SHILTON, Peter (1949–) English footballer, born in Leicester. He made his international début for England in 1970 and became a fixture in the England international side for the next 18 years, at the same time becoming the first England goalkeeper to gain 100 caps, and has won all the major honours in the game, including League championship and European Cup medals. Starting his career with Leicester City at the age of 16 he moved on to Stoke City, then to Nottingham Forest where he achieved his greatest successes. He then left the Midlands for Southampton before returning to Derby County. For the first four clubs he established an extraordinary record by making over 100 league appearances for each of them. In 1989 he set a new record by winning his 109th cap against Denmark, thus toppling the record established by **Bobby Charlton**.

SHINWELL, Emmanuel, Baron (1884–1986) English Labour politician, born in Spitalfields, London. He began work as an errand boy in Glasgow at the age of twelve. An early student of public library and street-corner socialism, he was elected to Glasgow Trades Council in 1911 and, one of the 'wild men of Clydeside', served a five months' prison sentence for incitement to riot in 1921. MP in 1931 and secretary to the department of mines (1924, 1930–31), in 1935 he defeated **Ramsay MacDonald** at Seaham Harbour, Durham, in one of the most bitterly contested election battles of modern times. From 1942 he was chairman of the Labour party committee which drafted the manifesto 'Let us face the future' on which Labour won the 1945 election. As minister of fuel and power he nationalized the mines (1946), and the following year, when he was said to be a scapegoat for the February fuel crisis, he became secretary of state for war. From 1950 to 1951 he was minister of defence. In these last two offices, Manny's considerable administrative ability outshone his prickly party political belligerence and earned him the respect of such discerning critics in defence matters as **Churchill** and **Montgomery**. In his later years he mellowed into a back-bench 'elder statesman'. He was parliamentary Labour party chairman 1964–67, was created CH in 1965 and awarded a life peerage in 1970. See his autobiographical works, including *Conflict without Malice* (1955), *I've Lived through it All* (1973), and *Lead with the Left* (1981).

SHIPTON, Eric Earle (1907–77) English mountaineer. He gained his early mountaineering experience during five expeditions to the mountains of East and Central Africa, climbing Kamet (25 447 ft) in 1931. He obtained much of his knowledge of the east during his terms as consul-general in Kashgar (1940–42 and 1946–48) and in Kunming (1949–51). Between 1933 and 1951 he either led or was member of five expeditions to Mount Everest. He probably did more than anyone else to pave the way for the successful **Hunt-Hillary** expedition of 1953.

SHIPTON, Mother (1488–c.1560) English witch, born near Knaresborough, and baptized as Ursula Southiel. At the age of 24 she married Tony Shipton, a builder, and died at over 70 years of age—according to S Baker, who edited her 'prophecies' (1797). A book (1684) by Richard Head tells how she was carried off by the devil, bore him an imp, etc. A small British moth, with wing-markings resembling a witch's face, is named after her.

SHIRER, William Lawrence (1904–) American journalist, broadcaster and author. After working as a newspaper correspondent in Europe he joined CBS in 1937 and broadcast on the momentous events in Europe from both sides until 1940. He wrote a column for the New York *Herald Tribune* (1942–48). His monumental history of *The Rise and Fall of the Third Reich* (1960) won the National Book Award. His other books include *Berlin Diary: The Journal of a Foreign Correspondent, 1934–41* (1941), *The Collapse of the Third Republic* (1969), and *Ghandhi: A Memoir* (1979).

SHIRLEY or **Sherley, Sir Anthony** (1565–c.1635) English adventurer. After following the Earl of **Essex** from 1597, he was knighted by the king of France without the assent of Queen **Elizabeth**, who had him imprisoned until he renounced the title, which is therefore nominal only. His voyage to America and Jamaica (1595) is recorded by **Richard Hakluyt**. In 1599 he went to Persia on a trade mission, and returned as the shah's envoy in an unsuccessful attempt to form an alliance against the Turks. His account of this adventure was published in 1613. Proscribed from entering Britain, he wandered in Europe and died in Madrid.

SHIRLEY, James (1596–1666) English late-Elizabethan dramatist, born in London. From Merchant Taylors' he passed in 1612 to St John's, Oxford, but migrated to Catharine Hall, Cambridge. He took orders, and held a living at St Albans. Turning Catholic, he taught (1623–24) in the grammar school there, but soon went to London and became a playwright. The suppression of stage plays in 1642 ended his livelihood, and he took to teaching again. The Restoration revived his plays, but brought him no better fortunes. His death was a result of the Great Fire of London. **Beaumont** and **Fletcher** and **Ben Jonson** were his models, but he has little of the grand Elizabethan manner. Most of his plays are tragicomedies. His chief works are *Eccho* (1618), a poem on the Narcissus subject; comedies, *The Witty Fair One* (1628); *The Wedding* (1628); *The Grateful Servant* (1629); *The Example* (1634); *The Opportunity* (1634); *The Lady of Pleasure*, the most brilliant of his comedies (1635); tragedies, *The Cardinal*, to the author himself 'the best of his flock' (1641); *The Traytor* (1631), a great drama. As a masque writer he is second only to Jonson; among his best masques are *The Triumph of Peace* (1633) and *The Contention of Ajax and Ulysses* (1659, including 'the glories of our blood and state').

SHIRLEY, John (?1366–1456) English traveller and transcriber of **Chaucer** and **Lydgate**.

SHIRLEY, Lawrence See **FERRERS**

SHIRLEY, Robert (?1581–1628) brother of Sir **Anthony Shirley**. He accompanied him to Persia and remained there. He made two journeys to European courts as envoy of the shah of Persia (1608, 1615), being accepted by **James I** of Britain for three years (1624–27), when he returned to Persia and died out of favour.

SHIRREFF, Emily Anne Eliza (1814–97) English pioneer of women's education. With her sister, Maria Georgina Gray, she wrote *Thoughts on Self-Culture, Addressed to Women* (1850) and founded the National Union for the Higher Education of Women (1872). She was mistress of Girton College, Cambridge (1870–97), and also published works on kindergartens and the Froebel system.

SHIRREFF, Patrick (1791–1876) Scottish farmer, born near Haddington. He was the pioneer of cereal hybridizing, and produced many varieties of wheat and oats.

SHIVAJI (1627–80) ruler of the Maratha empire, the son of Shahaji Bhosle, a Maratha nobleman who had defied the power of the Mughals in Bijapur. He was able to gather a considerable following among the Mawali hill-dwellers of the region, and, when the Bijapur authorities sent a large army against him in 1659, he succeeded in killing their general and ambushing the leaderless army. During the 1660s Maratha power continued to increase and he had himself crowned as raja in 1674. He profited from the conflict between the Mughal emperor **Aurangzeb** and the Afghans to make extensive conquests in the South before his death. Although his empire remained essentially a 'robber-state', exacting 'protection-money' from areas under its control, he was also intensely devoted to the cause of Hinduism, and the Maratha empire that he created maintained its independence until 1818.

SHOCKLEY, William Bradford (1910–89) American physicist, born in London, the son of two American mining engineers. Brought up in California, he was educated at the California Institute of Technology and Massachusetts Institute of Technology before starting work at the Bell Telephone Laboratories in 1936. During World War II he directed anti-submarine warfare research and became consultant to the secretary for war 1945. Returning to Bell Telephones he collaborated with **John Bardeen** and **Walter Brattain** in trying to produce semiconductor devices to replace thermionic valves. Using a germanium rectifier with metal contacts including a needle touching the crystal, they invented the point-contact transistor (1947). A month later Shockley developed the junction transistor (for *transfer* of current across a *resistor*). These devices led to the miniaturization of circuits in radio, TV and computer equipment. Shockley, Bardeen, and Brattain shared the Nobel prize for physics in 1956. From 1963 to 1974 Shockley was professor of engineering at Stanford.

SHOEMAKER, William Lee (1931–) American jockey, born in Fabens, Texas, one of the most successful jockeys in the history of racing. In 1953 he rode a record 485 winners. In a season in the USA his major successes included four Kentucky Derbies, five Belmont Stakes, and two wins in the famous Preakness event at Baltimore. The first jockey to saddle more than 8000 winners, he moved to Europe late in his career, proving equally successful there.

SHOLOKHOV, Mikhail Alexandrovich (1905–84) Russian novelist, born in Kruzhilin. He was educated at schools in Moscow, Boguchar and Veshenskaya. From 1920 to 1922 he served in the army, after which he had multifarious occupations: teacher, clerk, tax inspector, labourer, playwright, actor and journalist. During World War II he was a war correspondent. His literary career began with some 30 short stories written between 1923 and 1927. Most focus on the merciless socio-political struggle within Don Cossack families and villages during the civil war and early years of Soviet rule. Uneven in quality, they nevertheless demonstrate a rapid development from a sedulous ape into an original craftsman. His masterpiece is *And Quiet Flows the Don* (trans 1934–40, 4 vols). Set in the years 1912–22, it is a monument to the Don Cossacks, offering a panoramic view of their life in time of peace and during the turbulent years of war and revolution. The characterization is splendid and the dialogue earthy. Since 1928 his authorship of the novel has been questioned on the grounds that he was too young and had previously shown no form to indicate he could write such an epic work, but the evidence to support these allegations is thin. *Virgin Soil Upturned* (trans 1935–60, 2 vols) is much inferior, attributable to his toeing of the official line, alcoholism and decline of his creative powers. He received the Stalin prize in 1941 and the 1965 Nobel prize for literature.

SHORE, Jane (d.c.1527) English courtesan, born in London. She early married William Shore, a goldsmith. In 1470 she captivated **Edward IV** with her wit and beauty and became his mistress. Her husband abandoned her, but she lived till Edward's death in 1483 in luxury. Thereafter she became the mistress of Thomas, Lord Hastings and on his death, it is said, of the Marquis of Dorset. **Richard III**, to make his brother's life odious, caused the bishop of London to make her walk in open penance, taper in hand, dressed only in her kirtle. She forms the subject of a tragedy by **Rowe** (1714).

SHORE, John, 1st Baron Teignmouth (1751–1834) English governor-general of India (1793–98). He originated the Bengal *zamindari* system and many of Lord **Cornwallis**' reforms. He supported **Warren Hastings** during his impeachment (1788–95) and settled the Oude succession. He was first president of the British and Foreign Bible Society and was created an Irish peer (1798).

SHORE, Peter David (1924–) English politician. Educated at Cambridge, he joined the Labour party in 1948 and headed its research department for five years before becoming an MP in 1964. A former parliamentary private secretary to **Harold Wilson**, Shore held several government posts, notably those of secretary of state for economic affairs (1967–69), for trade (1974–76) and for the environment (1976–79). A member of the Fabian society, he was unsuccessful candidate in the Labour party leadership elections of 1983. He was shadow leader of the commons (1983–87).

SHORT, Sir Frank (1857–1945) English artist, born in Stourbridge. Educated in London, he became a great teacher and authority, and was a master of all the engraving processes. Head of the Engraving School at the Royal College of Art, he spent a great deal of time interpreting other masters, in particualr **Turner**'s 'Liber Studiorum'. He was president of the Royal Society of Painter Etchers (1910–39).

SHORTER, Frank C (1947–) American marathon runner, born in Munich. He won the 1972 Olympic title and silver at the 1976 Games. His first Olympic gold came in only his sixth marathon. A track runner before stepping up to marathon distance, his victory in the 1972 Munich Games is best remembered because he was 'led' into the stadium for the finish by a student hoaxer. His success helped inspire the running and jogging boom in the USA. He went on to a career as a television sports commentator.

SHORTER, Wayne (1933–) American jazz saxophonist, leader and composer, born in Newark, New Jersey. He studied music at New York University, and after a period of freelancing, his first long association was with the **Art Blakey** Jazz Messengers (1959–63); six subsequent years with **Miles Davis**, covering the trumpeter's first experiments in electric jazz-rock fusion, set Shorter on his future direction. He co-founded the quintet Weather Report which performed from 1971 until the mid 1980s. Since then, Shorter has continued in the electric jazz style, playing tenor and soprano saxophones, at the head of small combos.

SHORTHOUSE, Joseph Henry (1834–1903) English novelist, born in Birmingham. He became a chemical manufacturer. In 1881 his romance, *John Inglesant*, revealed a subtle and sympathetic insight into old-world phases of the spiritual mind. It was followed by *The Little Schoolmaster Mark* (1883–84), *Sir Percival* (1886), *A Teacher of the Violin* (1888), *The Countess Eve* (1888), and *Blanche, Lady Falaise* (1891).

SHOSTAKOVICH, Dmitri (1906–75) Russian composer, born in St Petersburg (now Leningrad). He entered St Petersburg Conservatory in 1919, and his First Symphony, composed in 1925, the year his studies ended, attracted considerable attention. His music, in which he attempted to support Soviet principles, was at first highly successful, but the development of a more conservative attitude on the part of the Soviet government, coinciding with his own development of a more experimental outlook, led to official criticism of his opera *The Nose*, and his Second ('October') Symphony; and a second opera, *A Lady Macbeth of Mtensk*, had to be withdrawn after violent press attacks on its decadence and its failure to observe the principles of 'Soviet realism'. He was reinstated by his Fifth Symphony (1938). He composed prolifically in all forms, and his Seventh ('Leningrad'), and Tenth Symphonies won considerable popularity outside Russia. His Eleventh Symphony, for which he was awarded a Lenin prize in 1958, is based upon the events of the October Revolution of 1905, his Twelfth celebrates the 1917 Revolution, No 13 includes male-voice settings of **Yevtushenko**, No 14 consists of eleven vocal movements; his Fifteenth and last Symphony (1974) is purely instrumental. He composed two violin, two cello and two piano concertos, many vocal works, 15 string quartets and much other chamber music. His son Maxim (1938–) is a pianist and conductor.

SHOVEL, Sir Cloudesley (1650–1707) English naval commander. He served against the Dutch and in the Mediterranean, burned four corsair galleys at Tripoli (1676), and commanded a ship at the battle in Bantry Bay (1689). In 1690 he took part in the battle off Beachy Head; in 1692 he supported **Russell** at La Hogue, and burned 20 of the enemy's ships. He served under **Rooke** in the Mediterranean, and with him took Gibraltar in 1704. In 1705 he was made rear admiral of England. That year he took part with **Peterborough** in the capture of Barcelona, but failed in his attack on Toulon in 1707. On the voyage home his ship (and others) struck a rock off the Scilly Isles on the foggy night of 22 October 1707, and went down. His body was washed up, and buried in Westminster Abbey.

SHRAPNEL, Henry (1761–1842) English artillery officer. He saw service in many parts of the world, and invented the shrapnel shell. He was made inspector of artillery in 1804.

SHREWSBURY See **TALBOT** family

SHULTZ, George Pratt (1920–) American politician, born in New York City into an affluent financial family. Educated at Princeton, he was an artillery officer during World War II. After the war he taught as a labour economist at Massachusetts Institute of Technology (1946–57) and at Chicago University (1957–68), before serving as labour secretary (1969–70), budget director (1970–72) and Treasury secretary (1972–74) in the **Nixon** administration. He was subsequently vice-chairman of the giant Bechtel industrial corporation and economic adviser to President **Reagan** in 1980, before replacing **Alexander Haig** as state department secretary in June 1982. He retained this post for the remainder of the Reagan administration (1981–89). A moderate and pragmatic Atlanticist and supporter of arms control, he acted as a counterweight to the 'hawkish' defence secretary **Caspar Weinberger** and helped to shift US-Soviet relations away from 'cold war' to, following the accession of **Mikhail Gorbachev**, renewed 'détente'. His crowning achievement was the December 1987 Intermediate Nuclear Forces (INF) treaty. As secretary of state, he also directed a campaign against international terrorism, backing America's bombing of Tripoli in 1986. In 1989 he became professor of political economy at Stanford University.

SHUMWAY, Norman Edward (1923–) American cardiac surgeon, born in Kalamazoo, Michigan. He received his MD from Vanderbilt University and his PhD in surgery from Minnesota University. He joined the faculty at the Stanford University School of Medicine in 1958 where he and his team have been active in many aspects of cardiovascular surgery, including cardiac transplantation. Shumway did much of the early experimental work in the field, before heart transplants were attempted in human beings.

SHUSTER, Joseph (1914–) Canadian-born American strip cartoonist, born in Toronto, artist and co-creator with **Jerry Siegel** of the world's most popular comic book hero, *Superman*.

SHUTE, John See **BARRINGTON, 1st Viscount**

SHUTE, Nevil, pseud of **Nevil Shute Norway** (1899–1960) English novelist, born in Ealing. He served in World War I and immediately afterwards began an aeronautical career. He was chief calculator of the Airship Guarantee Company during the construction of the airship R100, and he flew the Atlantic twice in her. He founded Airspeed Ltd, aircraft constructors, and became its managing director. He emigrated to Australia after World War II. His novels include *The Pied Piper* (1942), *Most Secret* (1945), *The Chequer board* (1947), *No Highway* (1948), *A Town Like Alice* (1949), *Round the Bend* (1951), *Requiem for a Wren* (1955), *Beyond the Black Stump* (1956) and *On The Beach* (1957), about an atomic war catastrophe. His success was largely due to his brisk style and his ability to make technical language and procedure understandable to a lay public. He published his autobiography, *Slide Rule*, in 1954.

SHUVALOV, Count Petr Andreyevich (1827–89) Russian diplomatist. He became head of the secret police in 1866. In 1873, sent on a secret mission to London, he arranged the marriage between the Duke of **Edinburgh** and the only daughter of **Alexander II**. In 1878 he was one of the Russian representatives at the Congress of Berlin.

SIBBALD, Sir Robert (1641–1722) Scottish naturalist and physician, born in Edinburgh. He became a physician there, but gave much time to botany and zoology. He helped to establish a botanic garden, and was virtual founder of the Royal College of Physicians of Edinburgh. He was appointed professor of medicine and Scottish geographer royal. He wrote *History of Fife* (1710), and pamphlets on medical subjects, natural history and antiquities.

SIBELIUS, Jean (1865–1957) Finnish composer, born in Hämeenlinna. The son of a surgeon, he studied the piano as a child, but was sent to Helsinki University to study law. He abandoned a legal career for full-time musical study in 1885, leaving Helsinki Conservatory in 1889 with a state grant which enabled him to continue his studies in Berlin and Vienna. A passionate nationalist, on his return to Finland he began the series of symphonic poems (including the well-known *Swan of Tuonela*) based on episodes in the Finnish epic *Kalevala*, and his first great success came with *En Saga* (1892). From 1897 until his death a state grant enabled him to devote himself entirely to composition, and his symphonies, symphonic poems—notably *Finlandia* (1899)—and violin concerto won great popularity, in Britain and America as well as in Finland, for their originality of form and idiom. After his Seventh Symphony (1924–25) and *Tapiola* (1926), he released no more music for performance or publication.

SIBLEY, Antoinette (1939–) English dancer, born in Bromley, Kent. She trained with the Royal Ballet, and appeared as a soloist for the first time in 1956 when, due to illness, she stepped from the ranks into the main role of *Swan Lake*. It was an unprecedented casting move which hit the headlines and set her at the top overnight. Her partnership with **Anthony Dowell** was one of enchanting compatibility, leading them to be dubbed 'The Golden Pair'. A dancer of great sensuality and beauty, her roles in **Frederick Ashton**'s *The Dream* and **Kenneth MacMillan**'s *Manon* are among her most celebrated. A knee injury forced an early retirement in 1976, but she was persuaded by Ashton to dance again five years later to great acclaim.

SIBLEY, Henry Hastings (1811–91) American statesman, born in Detroit. First governor and 'Father of Minnesota', he put down the Sioux outbreak of 1862.

SICKERT, Walter Richard (1860–1942) German-born British artist, born in Munich of mixed Dutch and Danish parentage. After three years on the English stage (an interest reflected in many pictures of music halls) he studied at the Slade School, and under **Whistler**. While working in Paris, he was much influenced by **Degas**. He had many studios in London, paying regular visits to France, and he used Degas' technique to illustrate London low life. Sickert was a member of the New English Art Club, and about 1910 the Camden Town Group (later the London Group) was formed under his leadership. His famous interior *Ennui* (Tate Gallery) belongs to this period. Both his painting and his writings on art have had great influence on later English painters. His autobiography *A Free House!* was published in 1947.

SICKINGEN, Franz von (1481–1523) German knight, born in Ebernburg near Kreuznach. He fought in 1508 against the Venetians for the Emperor **Maximilian I**, but in peace led the life of a soldier of fortune, and in 1519 supported the election of **Charles V** as emperor. **Ulrich von Hutten** the German humanist was his constant guest from 1520, and won him over to the cause of the Reformation. In 1521 he assisted the emperor in his French campaign; in 1522 he opened a Protestant war against the Archbishop of Trier. That war miscarried; and, put to the ban of the empire and besieged in his castle of Landstuhl, he was killed.

SIDDAL, Elizabeth Eleanor See **ROSSETTI, Dante Gabriel**

SIDDONS, Sarah (1755–1831) English actress, born in Brecon, the eldest child of **Roger Kemble**, manager of a small travelling theatrical company, of which Sarah was a member from her earliest childhood. In 1773 she married at Coventry her fellow actor, William Siddons. Her first appearance at Drury Lane in December 1775 as Portia was unremarkable. But her reputation grew so fast in the provinces that in 1782 she returned to Drury Lane, and made her appearance in October as Isabella in **Garrick**'s adaptation of **Southerne**'s *Fatal Marriage*. Her success was immediate, and from then on she was the unquestioned queen of the stage. In 1803 she followed her brother, **John Philip Kemble**, to Covent Garden, where she continued until her formal farewell to the stage as Lady Macbeth, on 29 June 1812. Thereafter she appeared occasionally, and sometimes gave public readings. Endowed with a gloriously expressive and beautiful face, a queenly figure, and a voice of richest power and flexibility, she worked assiduously to cultivate her gifts until as a tragic actress she reached a height of perfection. In comedy, however, she was less successful.

SIDGWICK, Henry (1838–1900) English philosopher, born in Skipton, Yorkshire. He was educated at Rugby and Cambridge, where he became a fellow of Trinity College in 1859 and Knightbridge professor of moral philosophy in 1883. His best known work, *Methods of Ethics* (1874), contains a sophisticated and distinctive development of the utilitarian theories of **John Stuart Mill**, combining them with views drawn from **Kant**. He was a founder and the first president of the Society for Pyschical Research in 1882. He was also active in promoting higher education for women and was involved in founding in 1871 a house for women students which became Newnham College, Cambridge in 1880; his wife, Eleanor Balfour (sister of **A J Balfour**) was its principal from 1892 to 1910.

SIDGWICK, Nevil Vincent (1873–1952) English theoretical chemist. After taking a first in science at Oxford he then took a first in classics. In 1901 he became professor at Oxford. He is known for his work on molecular structure and his formulation of a theory of valency. He was awarded the Royal Society's Royal Medal in 1937.

SIDI MOHAMMED BEN YOUSSEF (1911–61) sultan of Morocco from 1927, was born in Meknès, a scion of the Alouite dynasty. Exercising both spiritual and temporal power, he privily supported the nationalist Istaqlal party and constantly obstructed French hegemony. Tribal hostility to him gave the French the chance to depose him in 1953, but he was restored in 1955, and when Morocco attained independence in 1957 he became King Mohammed V. He died suddenly after a minor operation and was succeeded by his eldest son, Prince Moulay Hassan, who had already emerged as the spokesman of chauvinistic Moroccan youth. His eldest daughter, Princess Lalla Ayesha, repudiated the *yasmak* and became a leader of the women's emancipation movement.

SIDMOUTH, Henry Addington, 1st Viscount (1757–1844) English statesman and briefly Tory prime minister (1801–04), educated at Winchester and Brasenose College, Oxford. He entered Parliament as MP for Devizes in 1783, and was speaker of the House of Commons 1789–1801. When **William Pitt** (the Younger) resigned in 1801, Addington formed an administration that turned out to be weak and vacillating. He was created Viscount Sidmouth in 1805 and held several Cabinet posts. As home secretary (1812–21) he took severe measures against Luddite rioters and suspended the Habeas Corpus Act; it was in his period of office that the 'Peterloo Massacre' took place in Manchester in 1819, during an open-air meeting in support of parliamentary reform.

SIDNEY, Algernon (?1622–1683) English politician, grandnephew of Sir **Philip Sidney**, and second son of the second Earl of Leicester, born probably in Penshurst, Kent. During the Civil War he was wounded at Marston Moor (1644), fighting on the parliamentary side, although later resenting **Cromwell**'s usurpation of power. After the Restoration he lived on the Continent until 1677, when he returned to England. He was always thought to be dangerous and unreliable and in 1683 was alleged to be implicated in the Rye House Plot of the Whigs to kill **Charles II**. He was tried and found guilty, on slender evidence, and, with the Duke of **Monmouth** and Lord **Russell**, beheaded in the same year.

SIDNEY, Dorothea See **WALLER, Edmund**

SIDNEY, Sir Henry (1529–86) English administrator. As lord deputy of Ireland (1565–71; 1575–78), he crushed Shane O'Neill in Ulster (1566–67), failed to establish English settlers, but organized a system of presidency councils. He served also as president of the council of Wales (1559–86).

SIDNEY, Sir Philip (1554–86) English poet and patron, born in Penshurst Place, Kent. The eldest son of Sir **Henry Sidney** (lord deputy of Ireland), he was educated at Shrewsbury School and Christ Church College, Oxford. He may also have been enrolled at Cambridge. From 1572 to 1575 he travelled in France, Germany, Austria and Italy, where he spent a year studying history and ethics, and was painted by **Veronese**. Returning to England he did not rise politically as anticipated and waited until 1585 for his appointment as governor of Flushing, having been knighted in 1582. Much of his life was reposeful and conducive to composition. None of his work was published in his lifetime. The revised *Arcadia* was published in 1590 in three books, and again in an augmented edition in 1593. *Astrophel and Stella* appeared first, in 1591, with a corrupt text in a pirated edition, then in the authorized version. *A Defence of Poetry* was published in 1595. The *Arcadia* was probably written while he was lodging with his sister, Mary, Countess of Pembroke. It is probable that Penelope Devereux, whose father approved of Sidney and wished him to marry his daughter, is the 'Stella' of the sonnets. However, she married another, and Sidney, in 1583, married Frances, daughter of Sir **Francis Walsingham**. Throughout this time he bestowed patronage on a number of poets as dedications in various works testify, the most notable being that in **Spenser**'s *The Shepheardes Calendar* in 1579. He spent his last years in the Netherlands, where he successfully plotted an attack on the town of Axel. In September of the same year he led an attack on a Spanish convoy transporting arms to Zutphen, was shot in the thigh and died from the infection. He was buried in St Paul's Cathedral, much loved by contemporary poets and alluded to with affection and respect by **Yeats**, **Ruskin** and others.

SIDONIUS APOLLINARIS, Gaius Sollius (c.430–c.483) Gallo-Roman poet and prelate, born in Lugdunum (Lyon) of a prominent Chistian family. He held high civil offices in Rome, and in 472 became Bishop of Clermont-Ferrand in the Auvergne. His letters are modelled on **Pliny**'s; his poems comprise panegyrics on three emperors, and two poems celebrating a marriage. He was canonized as St Sidonius Apollinaris.

SIEBOLD, Karl Theodor Ernst (1804–65) German zoologist, brother of **Philipp Franz von Siebold**. He became professor at Munich. He worked on invertebrate research, and studied parthenogenesis, salamanders, and the freshwater fish of central Europe.

SIEBOLD, Philipp Franz von (1796–1866) German physician and botanist, born in Wüburg of a distinguished medical family, and brother of **Karl Siebold**. He became medical officer to the Dutch in Batavia (now Djakarta), Java, and as such was stationed at a Dutch outpost in Nagasaki from 1823 to 1829, when he was expelled for obtaining too much information about Japan. He was largely responsible for the introduction of Western medicine into Japan and many Japanese plants into European gardens, and in collaboration with German and Dutch scientists published important works on the flora and fauna of Japan.

SIEFF, Israel Moses, Baron Sieff of Brimpton (1889–1972) English commercial executive, born in Manchester. There he was a schoolfellow of **Simon Marks**, and each married the other's sister. Together they developed Marks and Spencer. He was joint managing director of the company from 1926 to 1967 and succeeded Lord Marks as chairman (1964–1967). His younger son, Marcus Joseph (1913–), who took a life peerage in 1980 as Lord Sieff of Brimpton, was chairman of Marks and Spencer from 1972 to 1984, when he became president of the company.

SIEGBAHN, Kai (1918–) Swedish physicist, born in Lund, the son of **Karl Manne Georg Siegbahn**. Educated at Stockholm, he was professor of physics at the Royal Institute of Technology, Stockholm until 1954 and thereafter at Uppsala University. He devised ESCA (electron spectroscopy for chemical analysis), and also worked on the related technique of ultraviolet photoelectron spectroscopy developed by D W Turner. He shared the Nobel prize for physics in 1981 with **Nicolas Bloembergen** and **Arthur Schawlow**.

SIEGBAHN, Karl Manne Georg (1886–1978) Swedish physicist, born in Örebro. Professor at Lund (1920), at Uppsala (1923) and professor of the Royal Academy of Sciences and director of the Nobel Institute for Physics at Stockholm from 1937, he discovered the M series in X-ray spectroscopy, for which he was awarded the Nobel prize for physics in 1924. He also constructed a vacuum spectrograph.

SIEGEL, Jerry (1914–) American strip cartoonist, born in Cleveland, Ohio, writer and co-creator with **Joseph Shuster** of the *Superman* series. He met Shuster at high school where they published their own science fiction magazine. After a series of strips for various comic books, they created *Superman* for *Action Comics* in 1938. It became an instant success, leading to huge spin-offs in films and television. The partners had no copyright on the characters in the strip and failed to benefit until the owners (Warner Communications) agreed, after protracted lawsuits, to pay them a comfortable pension in 1975.

SIEGEN, Ludwig von (1609–c.1675) German engraver, a German military officer of Dutch origin, thought to have been influenced by **Rembrandt**. In 1642 he invented the mezzotint process, sending a portrait of Landgravine Amelia Elizabeth of Bohemia to the Landgrave with a letter stating that the invention was his. He also disclosed his invention to Prince Rupert at Brussels in 1654. Only a handful of his prints are in existence.

SIEGFRIED, André (1875–1959) French economist, historian and Academician. He was specially noted for his studies of Canada, the States and Latin America. His works included *Les États-unis d'aujourd'hui* (1927, trans *America comes of Age*), *Le Canada, Puissance internationale* (1937), *Suez and Panama* (trans 1940) and *America in Mid-century* (1955).

SIEGMUND See **SIGISMUND**

SIELMANN, Heinz (1917–) German naturalist and photographer specializing in nature films, born in Königsberg. Interested in animal photography from boyhood, he started making films in 1938 and won the German Oscar for documentary films three years running (1953–55). He evolved techniques enabling him to take films of happenings inside the lairs of animals and inaccessible types of birds' nests (eg, the woodpecker), which have revolutionized the study of animal behaviour.

SIEMENS, Sir Charles William (Karl Wilhelm) (1823–83) German-born British electrical engineer, brother of **Ernst Werner von Siemens**, born in Lenthe, Hanover. In 1843 he visited England to introduce a process for electro-gilding invented by Ernst Werner and himself. In 1844 he patented his differential governor, and was naturalized in 1859. As manager in England of the firm of Siemens Brothers, he was actively engaged in the construction of telegraphs, designed the steamship *Faraday* for cable-laying, promoted electric lighting, and constructed the Portrush Electric Tramway in Ireland (1883). In 1861 he designed an open-hearth regenerative steel furnace which became the most widely used in the world. Other inventions were a water-meter, pyrometer and bathometer. He was assisted in England by another brother, Friedrich (1826–1904), who invented a regenerative smelting oven (1856) extensively used in glassmaking.

SIEMENS, Ernst Werner von (1816–92) German electrical engineer, brother of Sir **Charles William Siemens**, born in Lenthe, Hanover. In 1834 he entered the Prussian artillery, and in 1844 took charge of the artillery workshops at Berlin. He developed the telegraphic system in Prussia, discovered the insulating property of gutta-percha, and devoted himself to making telegraphic and electrical apparatus. In 1847 he established factories for making telegraphy equipment in Berlin and elsewhere (in 1867 the business became known as Siemens Brothers). Besides devising numerous forms of galvanometer and other electrical instruments, he was one of the discoverers of the self-acting dynamo. He determined the electrical resistance of different substances, the SI Unit being named after him. In 1886 he endowed a technological institute. One of his sons, Wilhelm (1855–1919) was one of the pioneers of the incandescent lamp.

SIENKIEWICZ, Henryk (1846–1916) Polish novelist, born near Luków. He lived in the USA from 1876 to 1878, and after a hunting expedition in East Africa (1892) wrote the children's story *Desert and Wilderness*. Most of his works, however, are strongly realistic; many have been translated, among them *With Fire and Sword* (1884), *The Deluge* (1886), *Pan Michael* (1887–88), *Children of the Soil* (1893) and *Quo Vadis* (1896). He was awarded the Nobel prize for literature in 1905.

SIERPIŃSKI, Wactaw (1882–1969) Polish mathematician, born in Warsaw. He studied there, and was professor from 1919 to 1960. The leader of the Polish school of set theorists and topologists, he was a prolific author, publishing more than 700 research papers on set theory, topology, number theory and logic, and several books. In 1919 he founded the still-important journal *Fundamenta Mathematicae* to publish work in these areas.

SIERRA See **MARTINEZ SIERRA, Gregorio**

SIEYÈS, Emmanuel Joseph Comte (1748–1836) French prelate and Revolutionary leader, generally called the Abbé Sieyès, born in Fréjus. He studied theology and became canon at Tréguier (1775), then chancellor and vicar-general of Chartres (1788), and as such was sent to the assembly of the clergy of France. His three pamphlets carried his name over France: *Vues sur les moyens d'exécution* (1788), *Essai sur les privilèges* (1788), and, the most famous of all, *Qu'est-ce que le tiers-état?* (1789). He was elected deputy for Paris, and had much to do with the formation of the National Assembly. He gained great influence, and the division of France into departments was mainly his work. He took part in the declaration of the Rights of Man (26 August 1789), and opposed the royal veto. He was elected to the Legislative Assembly, sat in the centre, and also voted for the king's death; but as the Revolution grew, he lapsed into 'philosophic silence'. He opposed the new constitution of Year III (1795), and declined a seat on the Directory named by the new *corps législatif*, but had a share in the *coup d'état* of 3 September 1797. In 1798 he went on a mission to Berlin, in 1799 was elected to the Directory. **Napoleon** returned from Egypt in October, and together they plotted the Revolution of 18 Brumaire (9 November 1799), the result of which was the institution of the Consulate of Sieyès, Napoleon and Pierre Roger Ducos. Sieyès drew up a constitution, a masterpiece of complexity, its aim to break the force of democracy by dividing it. Finding himself deceived by Napoleon, he threw up his consulship, but received the title of count, 600000 francs, and the estate of Crosne. Exiled at the Restoration, he lived in Belgium for 15 years, but returned in 1830.

SIGFÚSSON, Sæmundur, 'the Learned' (1056–1133) Icelandic scholar and historian, born in Oddi. Educated at Paris or in Franconia, he succeeded his father as priest and chieftain in Oddi. He was the first Icelandic historian, writing a Latin *History of the Kings of Norway* (now lost). His formidable reputation for erudition led later scholars to assume, erroneously, his authorship of the *Elder* or *Poetic Edda*, and many folk-tales about his intellectual duels with the devil accrued around his name.

SIGISMUND (1368–1437) Holy Roman Emperor from 1433, younger son of the emperor **Charles IV**. He became king of Hungary in 1387 as husband of Mary, daughter of Louis I the Great, after defeating his Angevin rival Charles of Durazzo, king of Naples; however his dominions were continually eaten away by Venetians, Angevins and the Turks, who defeated him and his crusading allies at Nicopolis (1396). As emperor he presided over the Council of Constance, which ended the Great Schism and condemned **John Huss** to death (1414–18). Despite launching repeated invasions he was unable to conquer Bohemia where the Hussites had seized control on the death of his elder brother, **Wenceslas IV** (1419). Only a year before his death did he negotiate a compromise settlement which allowed his return as king in exchange for recognition of the Hussite principles embodied in the *Four Articles of Prague*.

SIGISMUND I, the Old (1466–1548) king of Poland. Grand Prince of Lithuania, he was elected in 1506 at the age of 40, and spent most of his reign attempting to stem the tide of Muscovite expansion in the east and the ambitions of the Teutonic Order in the west. Smolensk was lost to Russia in 1514, but in 1525, Albrecht, Master of the Teutonic Order and first Duke of Prussia was obliged to recognize publicly the sovereignty of the king of Poland at Cracow. He was succeeded by his son, **Sigismund II Augustus**.

SIGISMUND II AUGUSTUS (1520–72) king of Poland, son of **Sigismund I, the Old**. He was crowned co-ruler with his father in 1530, and succeeded on his death in 1548. His reign saw the wide spread of Protestantism, the union of Poland and Lithuania, and the conquest of Livonia. Despite initial problems with the gentry he was able to achieve a measure of constitutional reform.

SIGISMUND III, VASA (1561–1632) king of Poland (1587–1632) and of Sweden (1592–99). The Catholic son of King **Johan III** of Sweden and nephew of **Sigismund II Augustus** of Poland, he was elected to the Polish throne in 1587. For most of his reign the government and army were dominated by the chancellor, John Zamoyski, who in 1588–89 defeated an attempt by the Archduke Maximilian to invade Poland and obliged the emperor to relinquish all Habsburg claims there. In 1592 he succeeded his father as king of

Sweden. Before he arrived in Sweden for his coronation in 1594, however, his uncle, the future **Karl IX**, had promoted a convention which renounced Catholicism in Sweden; after Sigismund's return to Poland, Karl ruled as regent. In 1598, when he tried to return to Sweden, he was defeated at the battle of Stångebro by Karl, who effectively deposed him the following year. For several years he waged intermittent war with Sweden in a futile attempt to regain his crown. In 1609 he invaded Russia in pursuit of his claim to the Russian crown, and captured Moscow and Smolensk, causing his son Ladislaus to be elected tsar (although he never occupied the throne). He fought in Moldavia against Ottoman forces (1617–21), and lost Livonia in a long war with **Gustav II Adolf** of Sweden (1621–29). He was succeeded in Poland by his son, Ladislaus IV Vasa.

SIGNAC, Paul (1863–1935) French artist, born in Paris. He exhibited in 1884 with the Impressionists and was later associated with Henri Edmond Cross (1856–1910) and **Seurat** in the Neo-Impressionist movement. Signac, however, used mosaic-like patches of pure colour (as compared with Seurat's Pointillist dots). He published *D'Eugène Delacroix au Néo-impressionisme*, in which he sought to establish a scientific basis for his 'divisionist' theories (1899).

SIGNORELLI, Luca (c.1441–1523) Italian painter, born in Cortona. He worked, especially in frescoes, in Loreto, Rome, Florence, Siena, Cortona and Orvieto. Orvieto Cathedral contains his greatest works, the frescoes of *The Preaching of Anti-Christ* and *Last Judgment* (1499–1504), which display his great technical skill in the drawing of male nudes. He was one of the painters summoned by Pope **Julius II** in 1508 to adorn the Vatican, and dismissed to make way for **Raphael**.

SIGNORET, Simone, originally **Simon-Henriette Charlotte Kaminker** (1921–85) French actress, born in Wiesbaden, Germany. She left her job as a typist to become a film extra in *Le Prince Charmant* (1942) and soon graduated to leading roles. Frequently cast as a prostitute or courtesan, her warmth and sensuality found international favour in such films as *La Ronde* (1950), *Casque d'Or* (1952) and *Les Diaboliques* (1954). A rare participant in English language productions, she won an Academy Award for *Room at the Top* (1959) and gained further distinction for *Ship of Fools* (1965). Unafraid to show her age, she matured into one of France's most distinguished character actresses, in films like *Le Chat* (1971) and *Madame Rosa* (1977). Married to actor **Yves Montand** from 1951, she later turned to writing, completing an autobiography, *Nostalgia Isn't What It Used To Be* (1976), and a novel, *Adieu Volodia* (1985).

SIGURD I MAGNUSSON, 'the Crusader' (c.1090–1130) king of Norway from 1103. The youngest of the three sons of **Magnus III Olafsson** ('Barelegs'), he ruled jointly with his brothers until their deaths (1015 and 1022). Between 1107 and 1111 he made an expedition with 60 ships to the Holy Land, the first Scandinavian king to take part in the Crusades (hence his nickname, *Jorsalafari*, 'Jerusalem-farer'). At home he did much to strengthen the church, building cathedrals and imposing tithes for the first time.

SIGURÐSSON, Jón (1811–79) Icelandic scholar and statesman, known as the 'father of Iceland's independence'. He was born in Hrafnseyri in the Westfjords of Iceland, and educated at the University of Copenhagen, where he lived for the rest of his life. As archivist of the Royal Norse Archaeological Society (1847–65), he published several editions of Icelandic saga classics as well as authoritative works on the history and laws of Iceland. As a statesman, he became the revered leader of the movement to secure from Denmark political autonomy and freedom of trade. He persuaded King **Kristian IX** to restore the ancient Althing (parliament) as a consultative assembly, and sat as MP for the Westfjords from 1845. His independence campaign culminated in 1874 with the granting by Denmark of a constitution allowing limited self-government in domestic affairs. His statue stands in the Old Town Square in Reykjavík, facing Parliament House; and when full independence was finally achieved in 1944, 17 June—his birthday—was chosen as Iceland's National Day.

SIGURJÓNSSON, Jóhann (1880–1919) Icelandic dramatist and poet, pioneer of Icelandic theatre and the first Icelandic writer in modern times to achieve international recognition. Born in Laxamýri in the north of Iceland, he studied veterinary science in Copenhagen but turned to literature instead. He wrote simultaneously in Danish and Icelandic in order to gain a wider audience, and used Icelandic folk-tale motifs for his most successful plays: *Fjalla-Eyvindur* in 1911 (trans *Eyvind of the Mountains*), which was made into a film as *Berg Eyvind och hans hustru* (1917) by the Swedish director **Victor Sjöström**, and *Galdra-Loftur* in 1914 (Danish *Önsket*, trans *The Wish*). His other plays were *Dr Rung* (1908), *Bonden á Hrauni* (The Farmer at Hraun, 1908), and *Løgneren* (The Liar, 1917), based on a theme from *Njál's Saga*. He also wrote lyric poetry of touching sensitivity.

SIHANOUK, Prince Norodom (1922–) Cambodian (Kampuchean) politician. Educated in Vietnam and Paris, he was elected king of Cambodia in 1941. He negotiated the country's independence from France (1949–53), before abdicating in 1955 in favour of his father so as to become an elected leader under the new constitution. As prime minister and then, from 1960 after his father's death, as head of state also, he steered a neutralist course during the Vietnam War. In 1970 he was deposed in a right-wing military coup led by the US-backed Lt-General Lon Nol. Fleeing to Peking (Beijing), he formed a joint resistance front with **Pol Pot** which successfully overthrew Lon Nol in April 1975. Prince Sihanouk was re-appointed head of state but a year later was ousted by the communist Khmer Rouge leadership. In 1982, while living in North Korea, he was elected head of a new broad-based Democratic Kampuchea (Cambodia) government-in-exile, which aimed to overthrow the Vietnamese-installed puppet régime in Cambodia. Following the Vietnamese troop withdrawal in 1989, he has been involved in attempting to negotiate a settlement to the country's civil war, and appears set to return as head of state.

SIKORSKI, Wladyslaw (1881–1943) Polish statesman and soldier, born in Galicia, studied engineering at Cracow and Łwów universities, joined the underground movement for Polish freedom from tsarist rule, served under General **Piłsudski** as head of the war department, but after the treaty of Brest-Litovsk was imprisoned by the Austrians. In 1919 he commanded a Polish Infantry Division at Vilna during the Russian-Polish war and in 1920 defended Warsaw. In 1921 he became commander-in-chief and in 1922 was elected premier. After Piłsudski's *coup d'état* (1926) he retired and wrote military history in Paris. He returned to Poland in 1938, advocated a strong alliance with Britain and France, but was treated with suspicion and refused a command when Poland was invaded. He fled, fought in France, became commander-in-chief of the Free Polish forces and premier of the Polish government in exile from June 1940 in London. He signed a treaty with the Soviet Union in 1941 which annulled the Russo-German partition of Poland in 1939. But the discovery of Polish officers' graves at Katyn (1943) led to the breaking off of diplomatic relations between the two countries. He was killed in an air-crash over Gibraltar, 4 July 1943.

SIKORSKY, Igor Ivan (1889–1972) Russian-born American aeronautical engineer, born in Kiev. He began experimenting with building helicopters in 1909, but turned to aircraft, and built and flew the first four-engined aeroplane in 1913. He emigrated to Paris in 1918 and to the USA (1919) and founded the Sikorsky Aero Engineering Corporation (1923), which later was merged into the United Aircraft Corporation. He built several flying-boats, including the *American Clipper*; and in 1939 he finally built the first successful helicopter, the VS-300.

SILHOUETTE, Étienne de (1709–67) French politician. As the extremely parsimonious minister of finance in 1759, his name was applied to cheap blacked-in shadow outlines.

SILIUS ITALICUS, Tiberius Catius Asconius (25–101) Latin poet and politician. He became a prominent orator in the Roman courts, was consul in 68, and then proconsul in Asia (77). He lived thereafter in retirement on his rich estates near Naples, and became a patron of literature and the arts. Having contracted an incurable disease, he starved himself to death. He was the author of the longest surviving Latin poem, *Punica*, an epic in 17 books on the 2nd Punic War.

SILLANPÄÄ, Frans Eemil (1888–1964) Finnish novelist, born in Hämeenkyrö. The foremost Finnish writer of his time, his major works were *Hurskas kurjuus* (Meek Heritage, 1919), a novel about the Finnish civil war, and *Nuorena nukkunut* (Fallen Asleep When Young, trans as *The Maid Silja*, 1931), about the collapse of traditional values in Finland, and *Ihmiset suviyössä* (People in the Summer Night, 1934). He was awarded the 1939 Nobel prize for literature.

SILLIMAN, Benjamin (1779–1864) American chemist, born in Trumbull, Connecticut. He was admitted to the bar in 1802, but became professor of chemistry at Yale and studied this subject at Philadelphia, Edinburgh and London, specializing in electrolysis. He was founder (1818) and editor of the *American Journal of Science*.

SILLIMAN, Benjamin (1816–85) American chemist, son of **Benjamin Silliman** (1779–1864), born in New York. He became professor at Yale, assisted his father in his editorial work and showed that petroleum was a mixture of hydrocarbons, different in character from vegetable oils, and could be separated by fractional distillation.

SILLS, Beverley, originally **Belle Miriam Silverman** (1929–) American soprano, born in Brooklyn, New York, of Russian Jewish descent. After a varied and remarkable career as a child star, she made her operatic début in 1947, subsequently appearing with various American companies, and in Vienna and Buenos Aires (1967), La Scala in Milan (1969), Covent Garden and the Deutsche Oper Berlin (1970). A most musical, intelligent and dramatically gifted coloratura, she retired from the stage aged 50, to become general director of New York City Opera.

SILVA, Antonio José da (1705–39) Portuguese playwright and Offenbachian librettist, born in Rio de Janeiro. He studied law at Coimbra, and was burnt with wife and mother by the Inquisition at Lisbon as a relapsed Jew.

SILVERS, Phil, originally **Philip Silver** (1912–85) American comic actor, born in Brownsville, Brooklyn. An archetypal stage-struck youngster, he made his professional bow as part of the *Gus Edwards Revue* (1925) in Philadelphia. He worked in vaudeville and with the *Minsky Burlesque Troupe* (1934–39) before his Broadway début in *Yokel Boy* (1939). Signed to a contract with M-G-M, he appeared as bald, bespectacled hapless suitors and friends of the leading man in films like *Tom, Dick and Harry* (1941) and *Cover Girl* (1944). After World War II, he enjoyed notable Broadway hits with *High Button Shoes* (1947) and *Top Banana* (1951), for which he received a Tony Award. The television series *The Phil Silvers Show* (1955–59) earned him three Emmy Awards and established him irrevocably as Sergeant Bilko, 'a Machiavellian clown in uniform', forever pursuing get-rich-quick schemes with fast-talking bravado. He achieved further Broadway success in *Do Re Me* (1960) and *A Funny Thing Happened on the Way to the Forum* (1972, Tony Award). Latterly in poor health, he continued to make guest appearances on television and in increasingly inferior films. His autobiography, *The Laugh Is On Me*, was published in 1973.

SILVESTER See **SYLVESTER**

SILVIA (1943–) queen of Sweden since 1976, married to King **Carl XVI Gustaf**. She was born in Heidelberg as Silvia Renate Sommerlath, the daughter of a West German businessman, Walther Sommerlath and his Brazilian wife, Alice (née Soares de Toledo). She lived for many years in São Paulo in Brazil, where her father represented a Swedish company. Back in the Federal Republic of Germany, she attended the Interpreters' School in Munich and graduated in 1969 as an interpreter in Spanish. In 1971 she was appointed Chief Hostess in the Organization Committee for the Olympic Games in Munich in 1972, where she met Carl Gustaf, then heir to the Swedish throne. They were married in Stockholm Cathedral in 1976 and have three children, Crown Princess Victoria (1977–), Prince Carl Philip (1979–), and Princess Madeleine (1982–).

SIM, Alastair (1900–76) Scottish actor, born in Edinburgh. Destined to follow in the family tailoring business, his theatrical interests pulled in a different direction. He was a lecturer in elocution at Edinburgh University from 1925 to 1930 and made his professional stage début in a London production of *Othello* (1930). Further stage work, including a season with the Old Vic, led to his film début in *Riverside Murder* (1935). His lugubrious manner, distinctive physiognomy and inimitable vocal range made him a cherished comic performer, equally adept at mirthful or menacing characterizations. His numerous films include *Green for Danger* (1946), *The Happiest Days of Your Life* (1950), *Scrooge* (1951), *Laughter in Paradise* (1951) and *The Belles of St. Trinians* (1954). On stage he enjoyed a long association with playwright **James Bridie** and also appeared in *The Tempest* (1962), *Too True To Be Good* (1965), *The Magistrate* (1969) and *Dandy Dick* (1973) among many others.

SIMAK, Clifford Donald (1904–88) American science fiction writer, born in Milville, Wisconsin, of an immigrant Czech father and an American mother. During the Depression he entered journalism in Michigan and then joined the Minneapolis *Star*, to which he contributed a weekly science column for the rest of his life. He started publishing science fiction stories in 1931; his major work was the story sequence *The City* (1952), a chronicle in which dogs and robots take over a world abandoned by men.

SI-MA QIA (c.145–87 BC) Chinese historian, born in Lungmen. He succeeded his father Ssuma T'an in 110 BC as grand astrologer, but incurred the emperor's wrath for taking the part of a friend who, in command of a military expedition, had surrendered to the enemy. Ssu-ma Ch'ien was imprisoned for three years and castrated, but was gradually restored to favour. He is chiefly remembered for the *Shih Chi*, the first history of China compiled as dynastic histories in which annals of the principal events are supplemented by princely and other biographies and notes on economic and institutional history. It had been begun by his father.

SIMENON, Georges Joseph Christian (1903–89) Belgian-born French novelist, born in Liège. At 16 he began work as a journalist on the *Gazette de Liège*. He moved to Paris in 1922 and became a prolific writer of popular fiction, writing under a plethora of pseudonyms. He also wrote serious psychological novels, much-admired but neglected in favour of almost 100 short, economical novels featuring Jules Maigret, the pipe-smoking, persistent detective. His prototype is popularly supposed to have been the French detective Marcel Guillaume, though Simenon said he could not remember where the inspiration for him came from. A 'Commissaire Maigret' appeared in three of the *romans populaires* that Simenon produced but he bears little resemblance to the character now known the world over, partly through films and television adaptations. The first two in the series were published in 1931: *M. Gallet déceçé* and *Le Pendu de Saint-Pholien*. Like **Conan Doyle** with Sherlock Holmes, Simenon often tried to shake off his sleuth but he reappeared at least once a year until the 1970s, when he finally put the cover on his typewriter. In *Les Mémoires de Maigret* (1960), in which Maigret is ostensibly the author, he describes his childhood and career, and with laboured humour displays slight resentment at the liberties taken by his creator. Simenon published more than 500 novels and innumerable short stories but told The *New Yorker*, 'I have no imagination; I take everything from life'. Autobiographical writings include *When I Was Old* (trans 1971) and *Intimate Memoirs* (trans 1984).

SIMEON, Charles (1759–1836) English evangelical clergyman, born in Reading. A fellow of King's College, Cambridge, he was appointed perpetual curate (1783–1836). A renowned preacher, he led the evangelical revival in the Church of England, and helped form the Church Missionary Society (1793).

SIMEON OF DURHAM English chronicler. He became a Benedictine monk at Jarrow (c.1081), and wrote *Historia Ecclesiae Dunelmensis* (a history of the church at Durham), and *Historia Regum Anglorum et Dacorum*.

SIMEON STYLITES, St (387–459) Syrian ascetic, and the earliest of the Christian 'Pillar-saints' (Stylite = 'pillar-dweller'). After living nine years in his Syrian monastery without leaving his cell, at Telanessa near Antioch he established himself on the top of a pillar 72 feet high. There he spent 30 years, preaching to crowds.

SIMMEL, Georg (1858–1918) German sociologist and philosopher, born in Berlin. He studied at Berlin University, where he became a lecturer in 1885, teaching philosophy and ethics. He gradually began setting up courses in the new discipline of sociology, and was appointed professor of sociology in 1900. In 1914 he moved to a chair in philosophy at Strasbourg. He was the principal representative of German sociological formalism, an approach which emphasizes the form of a phenomenon, rather than its nature or content. He was particularly concerned to encourage the growth of an independent sociology, with a concrete object of its own, and to define its boundaries with other disciplines. A man of wide interests, he also wrote extensively on philosophy. His books include *Philosophy of Money* (1900, trans 1978), and a collection of essays published as *Georg Simmel: On Women, Sexuality and Love* (1984).

SIMMONDS, Kennedy Alphonse (1936–) St Christopher-Nevis politician and physician. He studied medicine at the University of the West Indies, worked in hospitals in Jamaica, the Bahamas and the USA, and returned to his native country in 1964 to establish his own practice. He entered politics and in 1965 founded the People's Action Movement (PAM) as a centre-right alternative to the Labour party. After a series of unsuccessful elections, in 1980 Simmonds and PAM won enough seats in the Assembly to form a coalition government with the Nevis Reformation party (NRP) and he became prime minister. Full independence was achieved in 1983 and Simmonds' coalition was re-elected in 1984.

SIMMS, William Gilmore (1806–70) American novelist, born in Charleston. He edited the *City Gazette* in Charleston and published *Lyrical and other Poems* (1827), *The Vision of Cortes* (1829), *The Tricolour* (1830), *Atalantis* (1832), *The Yemassee* (1835), *The Partisan* (1835), *Charlemont* (1856), and many other works. He was an apologist for slavery and the South.

SIMNEL, Lambert (c.1477–c.1534) English imposter, a baker's son. After careful coaching in 1487 by an Oxford priest, Roger Simon, he was set up in Ireland as, first, a son of **Edward IV**, and then as the Duke of **Clarence**'s son, Edward, Earl of Warwick (1475–99). Backed by Margaret of Burgundy, his suppositious aunt, Simnel had some success in Ireland and was crowned at Dublin as Edward VI, but, landing in Lancashire with 2000 German mercenaries, he was defeated at Stoke Field, Nottinghamshire, and subsequently became a royal scullion and falconer.

SIMON MAGUS, ('Simon the Magician') (1st century) Samaritan sorcerer. According to the bible (Acts, 8), he became a commanding personality in Samaria through his sorceries. He was converted by the preaching of Philip the evangelist, and tried to buy the power of the Holy Spirit from **Peter** and **John** (hence the term 'Simony'). Later Christian authors bring him to Rome and make him the author of heresies.

SIMON, Claude Eugène Henri (1913–) French novelist, born in Tananarive, Madagascar. Educated at Collège Stanislas, Paris, and briefly at Oxford and Cambridge universities, he studied painting before serving in the French cavalry. In World War II he joined the Resistance in Perpignan. Some align him with practitioners of the *nouveau roman* but he owes more to **Proust**, **Conrad**, **Joyce**, and **Faulkner** than his contemporary, **Camus**. The absence of story, time and punctuation is his hallmark, his style rich, sensuous and complex. *Le Vent* (1957, trans *The Wind*, 1959) and *La Route de Flandres* (1960, trans *The Road to Flanders*, 1962) are his most important novels, both eloquently expressing his innate pessimism. In 1985 he was awarded the Nobel prize for literature.

SIMON, Sir Francis Eugen (1893–1956) German physicist, born in Berlin. He was educated at the universities of Munich, Göttingen, and Berlin, and served in World War I. Nazism forced him to leave his chair at Breslau and he came to Oxford to the Clarendon Laboratory at the invitation of Frederick Lindemann (Lord **Cherwell**); he became reader in thermodynamics in 1935 and succeeded Lindemann as professor in 1956. He verified experimentally the third law of thermodynamics. Under Simon's influence Oxford became one of the leading low-temperature physics centres in the world. Probably uniquely, he held the Iron Cross of Imperial Germany, and a knighthood of the British Empire.

SIMON, Herbert Alexander (1916–) American economist, born in Milwaukee. A man of wide talents, who has written on psychology and computers, as well as on economics and political science, he was awarded the Nobel prize for economics in 1978 for his 'pioneering research into the decision-making process in economic organization'. A university administrator and a professor, he has held chairs at Illinois Institute of Technology (1946–49) and Carnegie-Mellon university (1949–). His books include *Administrative Behavior* (1947), *Models of Man* (1957), *Human Problem Solving* (1972), and *Reason in Human Affairs* (1983).

SIMON, Sir John (1816–1904) English pathologist. He was surgeon at St Thomas's Hospital, London, and in 1848 became the first medical officer of health for London. He later became chief medical officer to the Privy Council, and was responsible for many sanitary reforms.

SIMON, John Allsebrook Simon, 1st Viscount (1873–1954) English jurist and statesman, born in Bath. Educated at Fettes College, Edinburgh, and Wadham College, Oxford, he was junior counsel for the British government in the Alaska boundary arbitration. He became Liberal MP in 1906, took silk in 1908 and was knighted in 1910 when he became solicitor-general. He was attorney-general (1913–15) and home secretary (1915–16), resigned from the Cabinet for his opposition to conscription, served at the front in World War I (1917–18) and returned to become one of the wealthiest members of the legal profession. As chairman of the Indian statutory commission (1927–30) he proved in advance of Conservative opinion of the time. Deserting the Liberals, he fully supported **Ramsay MacDonald**'s coalition governments and became foreign secretary (1931) and leader of the National Liberals. He attempted a middle-of-the-road policy in European affairs but without much success, proposing the 'Eastern Locarno' pact. He was home secretary again (1935–1937), Chancellor of the Exchequer (1937–40) and Lord Chancellor in **Churchill**'s wartime coalition government (1940-45). His second wife, Kathleen Harvey, was a well-known anti-slavery crusader. He was created viscount in 1940.

SIMON, Jules François (1814–96) French statesman and philosopher. A philosophy lecturer at the Sorbonne in 1839, he became a deputy in 1848 and, refusing the oath of allegiance, established himself as a leader of the left-wing republicans in 1873, when he resigned as minister of public instruction because his educational reforms were severely attacked. He directed the *Siècle* newspaper from 1874, became prime minister in 1876, but resigned following a dispute with President **Macmahon**. He edited the French rationalists **Descartes**, **Malebranche** and **Arnauld**, and wrote a number of works on political philosophy and biographical studies.

SIMON, (Marvin) Neil (1927–) American dramatist, born in New York, the only living American playwright to have had a Broadway theatre named after him. He began by writing gags for radio and television personalities, and had a New York hit with his first comedy, *Come Blow Your Horn* (1961). His plays include the musical farce, *Little Me* (1962); *Barefoot in the Park* (1963); *The Odd Couple* (1965); the musical, *Sweet Charity*, and *The Star-Spangled Girl* (1966); *Plaza Suite*; and the musical *Promises, Promises* (1968). *The Gingerbread Lady*, a play about alcoholism, was not as enthusiastically received, but he persevered with more serious themes, as in *The Prisoner of Second Avenue* (1972) and *The Sunshine Boys* (1972). Moving from New York to California he made another hit with *California Suite* (1976). *Chapter Two* opened in 1977, and in 1979, his fourth musical, *They're Playing Our Song*, gave him yet another hit. Later he produced a semi-autobiographical trilogy: *Brighton Beach Memoirs* (1983), *Biloxi Blues* (1984), and *Broadway Bound* (1986).

SIMON, Paul (1941–) American singer, songwriter and guitarist, born in Newark, New Jersey. One of America's finest pop lyricists, he had the most successful album of the early 1970s as one half of the duo Simon and Garfunkel, with *Bridge Over Troubled Water* (1970). Simon originally worked with Art Garfunkel at the age of 15 when they were known as Tom and Gerry, but he also pursued a solo career, under various pseudonyms, before 'The Sound Of Silence' (1965) brought Simon and Garfunkel their first major success as a duo. In 1968 the film *The Graduate* became one of the first major films to use rock music in its soundtrack, using songs written by Simon. After splitting from Garfunkel, Simon returned to a solo career taking songwriting classes in New York prior to releasing his album *Paul Simon* in 1972. *Graceland* (1986)—which featured the work of several African musicians—was one of the most successful albums of the 1980s.

SIMON, Richard (1638–1712) French theologian and biblical critic, born in Dieppe. He entered the Oratory in 1659, lectured on philosophy, and catalogued the oriental manuscripts in the library of the order at Paris. His criticisms of **Arnauld** caused great displeasure among the Port-Royalists, and the scandal caused by the liberalism of his *Histoire critique du Vieux Testament* (1678), in which he denied that **Moses** was the author of the Pentateuch, led to his expulsion from the order and retirement to Belleville as *curé*. In 1682 he resigned his parish, and lived thereafter in literary retirement. Few writers of his age played a more prominent part in polemics. His *Histoire critique* (trans 1682), suppressed through **Bossuet**'s and the Jansenists' influence, often anticipates the later German rationalists, and is the first work which treats the Bible as a literary product.

SIMONIDES OF CEOS (556–468 BC) Greek lyric poet, born on the island of Ceos. He travelled extensively, and lived many years in Athens. When Persia invaded Greece he devoted his powers to celebrating the heroes and the battles of that struggle in elegies, epigrams, odes and dirges. He won poetical contests 56 times, and beat **Aeschylus** in a contest with an elegy on the heroes who fell at Marathon in 490 BC.

SIMONOV, Konstantin Mikhailovich (1915–79) Russian writer. He achieved a considerable reputation by his historical poem about **Alexander Nevski**, his poems of World War II, *Days and Nights*, a novel about the defence of Stalingrad, and the play *The Russians*. He was awarded the Stalin prize three times.

SIMPSON, Sir George (1792–1860) Canadian explorer, born in Scotland. He was administrator (1821–56) of the Hudson's Bay Company's territory. In 1828 he made an overland journey round the world. Simpson's Falls and Cape George Simpson are named after him.

SIMPSON, Sir George Clarke (1878–1965) English meteorologist, born in Derby. He became a lecturer at Manchester University (1905). He was Captain **Scott**'s meteorologist on the Antarctic expedition (1910), investigated the causes of lightning, and was elected president of the Royal Meteorological Society (1940–42).

SIMPSON, George Gaylord (1902–84) American palaeontologist, born in Chicago. Educated at the universities of Colorado and Yale, he joined the staff of the American Museum of Natural History in New York City in 1927, and from 1959 to 1970 taught at Harvard. Now widely regarded as this century's leading palaeontologist, he travelled extensively for his studies on fossil mammals. He was a central figure in the fusion of modern genetics and palaeontology to form modern Darwinism, which owes much to his influential books *Tempo and Mode in Evolution* (1944) and *The Major Features of Evolution* (1949), with a popular account in *The Meaning of Evolution* (1949).

SIMPSON, Sir James Young (1811–70) Scottish obstetrician, born in Bathgate. He studied medicine at Edinburgh, where he became professor of midwifery in 1840. He originated the use of ether as anaesthetic in childbirth (January 1847), and experimenting on himself in the search for a better anaesthetic, discovered the required properties in chloroform (November 1847), and championed its use against medical and religious opposition until its employment by Queen **Victoria** at the birth of Prince **Leopold** (1853) signalled general acceptance. He founded gynaecology by his sound tests, championed hospital reform, and in 1847 became physician to the Queen in Scotland.

SIMPSON, Orenthal James (1947–) American football player, born in San Francisco, California. Known as 'O.J.', he starred in the running back position for the University of Southern California in 1967 and 1968, being adjudged the outstanding player in the major conferences in the latter year. He combined blistering pace with an astute strategical appreciation of the game, and in 1973, playing with the Buffalo Bills, he established an all-time record of 2003 yards gained in rushing.

SIMPSON, Robert Baddeley (1936–) Australian cricketer, born in Sydney. After a slow start in Test cricket, he became a mainstay of Australian batting in the 1960s. He scored 4869 Test runs and made ten of his 60 centuries in Test matches. A brilliant fielder, he took 110 catches in his 62 appearances for Australia. His first Test century was a triple one, 311 against England at Old Trafford in 1964. Against Pakistan at Karachi in 1964–65 he scored two centuries in the same Test. When over 40, he unselfishly came out of semi-retirement to captain an Australian side greatly weakened by defections to the **Kerry Packer** organization.

SIMPSON, Robert Wilfred Levick (1921–) English composer and writer on music, born in Leamington, Warwickshire. He studied with **Herbert Howells** and was for almost 30 years a BBC music producer in London, until 1980. His works include ten symphonies, twelve string quartets, much other chamber music and concertos for violin and piano. He is a symphonic thinker of unswerving logic and integrity, a traditionalist who is never dully conventional and an orchestrator sure of colour and effect. He has written important studies of **Nielsen** and **Bruckner**.

SIMPSON, Tom (1938–67) English cyclist, born in Easington, County Durham. In 1962 he became the first Briton ever to wear the leader's yellow jersey in the Tour de France. Known as 'Major Tom' to the French, he led the race for just one day. During the 1967 Tour de France he died from heart failure while riding the thirteenth stage, the climb of Mont Ventoux. A post-mortem revealed traces of amphetamines in his blood. A memorial stone was built near the spot where he died.

SIMROCK, Karl Joseph (1802–76) German scholar and mythologist, born in Bonn. A member of the Prussian state service (1823–30), he translated the *Nibelungenlied* (1827), edited German medieval poets and legends, and wrote on **Shakespeare**'s sources (1831). He was professor of Old German at Bonn from 1850.

SIMS, William Sowden (1858–1936) American naval officer, born in Port Hope, Ontario, of American parents. Educated at the US Naval Academy, Annapolis, he became a gunnery specialist. He served in China during international action against the Boxer rebellion (1900). He served as a naval attaché in Paris and St Petersburg (Leningrad), wrote a classic textbook on navigation, and did much to improve US naval gunnery. In World War I he was president of the US Naval War College (1914–17). On government instructions he travelled to England in secrecy with false identity before the US declaration of war on Germany in April 1917. He made a distinguished contribution to Anglo-American action against the U-boat campaign as Commander of US Naval Forces in Europe, devising a convoy system to protect merchant shipping.

SIMSON, Robert (1687–1768) Scottish mathematician, professor of mathematics at Glasgow from 1711. His life-work was the editing and restoration of the work of the ancient Greek geometers; his edition of Euclid's *Elements* (1758) was the basis of nearly all editions for over a century.

SINATRA, Frank (Francis Albert) (1915–) American singer and film actor, born in Hoboken, New Jersey. He started his long and highly successful career as recording artist singing with the bands of Harry James and **Tommy Dorsey** on radio, becoming one of the most adulated teenage idols. He made his film début in musicals in 1941, leading to films like *Anchors Aweigh* (1945) and *On The Town* (1949), but later successfully switched to dramatic roles, most notably *From Here to Eternity* (1953, Academy Award as Best Supporting Actor), *The Man With the Golden Gun* (1955), *Pal Joey* (1957), *The Manchurian Candidate* (1962) and *The Detective* (1968). His impeccable musical phrasing and choice of material made him one of the bestselling recording artists of the 1950s and 60s as well as a top concert performer and television star into the 1980s. His highly publicized private life includes four marriages to, among others, **Ava Gardner** and Mia Farrow.

SINCLAIR, or **St Clair** the name of the Earls of Orkney and afterwards of Caithness. They were hereditary grandmaster masons of Scotland 1455–1736. Roslin Castle near Edinburgh was the seat of the St Clairs.

SINCLAIR, Sir Archibald Henry MacDonald, 1st Viscount Thurso (1890–1970) Scottish Liberal politician, descendant of Sir **John Sinclair**. Educated at Eton and Sandhurst, he served in the army (1910–21), entered parliament in 1922, became chief whip (1930–31) and leader of the Liberals (1935–45), and was secretary of state for air in the **Churchill** administration (1940–45).

SINCLAIR, Sir Clive (Marles) (1940–) English electronic engineer and inventor. He worked for three years as a publisher's editor before launching his own electronics research and manufacturing company which developed and successfully marketed a wide range of calculators, miniature television sets and personal computers. He later embarked on the manufacture of a small three-wheeled 'personal transport' vehicle powered by a washing-machine motor and rechargeable batteries; it was widely condemned as unsafe and impractical, and its failure led to a period of retrenchment in Sinclair's business activities.

SINCLAIR, Sir John, 1st Baronet (1754–1835) Scottish politician and agricultural improver, born in Thurso Castle. He studied at Edinburgh, Glasgow and Oxford, was admitted to both the Scottish and English bars (1775–82), and sat in parliament (1780–1811). In 1784 he published a *History of the Revenue of the British Empire*; and in 1786 was created a baronet. He established the board of agriculture in 1793 and supervised the compilation of the first *Statistical Account of Scotland* (1791–99), comprising a description of every parish in Scotland, mainly with the help of the parish ministers. He developed the town of Thurso, in Caithness, and gave it its present lay-out; his statue (by Sir **Francis Chantrey**) stands in the main square. His daughter, Catherine (1800–64), wrote children's books, including *Holiday House* (1839).

SINCLAIR, May (?1865–1946) English novelist, born in Rock Ferry, Cheshire. She was educated at Cheltenham College, and wrote *The Divine Fire* (1904), *The Creators* (1910), *The Dark Night* (1924), *Anne Severn*, and other novels. She also wrote books on philosophical idealism.

SINCLAIR, Upton Beall (1878–1968) American novelist and social reformer, born in Baltimore, Maryland. He horrified the world with his exposure of meat-packing conditions in Chicago in his novel *The Jungle* (1906). Later novels such as *Metropolis* (1908), *King Coal* (1917), *Oil!* (1927) and *Boston* (1928) were increasingly moulded by his socialist beliefs. He was for many years prominent in Californian politics and attempted to found a communistic colony in Englewood, New Jersey (1907). He also wrote a monumental eleven-volume series about 'Lanny Budd', starting with *World's End* (1940) and including *Dragon's Teeth* (1942) which won the Pulitzer prize. He wrote autobiographical works (1932, 1962) and *A World to Win* (1946).

SINDEN, Donald (1923–) English actor, born in Plymouth. He made his first appearance in the Mobile Entertainments Southern Area in 1941, and remained with the company for four years, touring comedies to the armed forces. In 1946 he joined the Shakespeare Memorial Theatre company at Stratford-upon-Avon, and the Old Vic company in 1948. From 1952 he spent five years in films. For many years he alternated between lightweight comedy in the West End and classical roles with the RSC, increasingly in recent years in farce. For several seasons he played an English butler in the television comedy series, *Two's Company*.

SINDIA the title of the Mahratta princes of Gwalior. Their founder was Ranaji Sindia, who rose to high rank in the bodyguard of the Peshwa, and had a grant of half the province of Mala. His most noteworthy successors were:

SINDIA, Baji Rao (d.1886) Muhrato prince of Gwalior. During the Indian Mutiny he took the field against the rebels; but most of his troops deserted him, and he fled to Agra. He was reinstated, and was succeeded by his adopted son.

SINDIA, Daulat Rao Sindia (1779–1827) Mahrato prince of Gwalior, grandnephew of Ranaji Sindia. He ravaged Indore and Poona, but was routed by Holkar (1802), and next year brought upon himself the vengeance of the East India Company. The Mahrattas were routed at Assaye and Argaum by Sir Arthur Wellesley (**Wellington**), and were scattered at Laswari by Lord **Lake**. Thereupon Sindia ceded all his possessions in the Doab and along the right bank of the Jumna to the British. Gwalior was restored in 1805.

SINDIA, Mádhava Ráo Sindia (d.1794) illegitimate son of Ranaji Sindia, joined the Mahratta confederation, and was crippled for life at Panipat (1761). In 1770, along with the Peshwa and Holkar, he aided the Mughal to expel the Sikhs and became virtually supreme in Hindustan. He came into collision with the British in 1779, and was thoroughly beaten by **Hastings**, but by the treaty of Salbai (1783) was confirmed in all his possessions. In 1784 he captured Gwalior, in 1785 marched on Delhi, and subsequently seized Agra, Alighur and nearly the whole of the Doab. He raised and drilled an army in European fashion, neglecting the cavalry, and won Akbar and crushed Jodhpur, Udaipur and Jaipur, three Rajput states, while Holkar remained his ally. He died, or was murdered, at Poona.

SINDING, Christian (1856–1941) Norwegian composer, born in Königsberg. He studied in Germany, wrote two violin and a piano concerto, and three symphonies, as well as chamber music and songs. His brother, Otto (1842–1909), was a painter. Another, Stephan (1846–1922), was a sculptor.

SINGER, Esther (Mrs Kreitman) (1892–) Polish Yiddish novelist, born in Radzymin, sister of **Isaac Bashevis** and **Israel Joshua Singer**. Her *Der sheydim tants* was published in Warsaw in 1936 and translated ten years later as *Deborah*.

SINGER, Isaac Bashevis (1904–) Polish-born American Yiddish writer, born in Radzymin, the son of a rabbi, brother of **Esther** and **Israel Joshua Singer**. He was educated at the Tachkemoni Rabbinical Seminary in Warsaw 1920–22, and worked for ten years as a proof-reader and translator. He emigrated to the USA in 1935, where he joined his brother, as a journalist for the *Jewish Daily Forward*. A firm believer in story-telling rather than commentary by the author, he set his novels and short stories among the Jews of Poland, Germany and America, combining a deep psychological insight with dramatic and visual impact. Considered by many the last and greatest Yiddish writer, he was awarded the Nobel prize in 1978. His novels include *The Family Moskat* (1950), *Satan in Goray* (1955), *The Magician of Lublin* (1960), *The Manor* (1967), *The Estate* (1970) and *Enemies: A Love Story* (1972). Among his short stories are *Gimpel the Fool and Other Stories* (1957), *The Spinoza of Market Street* (1961), *The Séance* (1968), *A Friend of Kafka* (1970) and *A Crown of Feathers* (1973). He also wrote a play, *Schlemiel the First* (1974) and many stories for children. He wrote his autobiography, *In My Father's Court*, in 1966.

SINGER, Isaac Merritt (1811–75) American inventor and manufacturer, born in Pittstown, New York. He patented a rock drill in 1839, a carving machine in 1849 and at Boston in 1852 an improved single-thread, chain-stitch sewing machine. He was sued by Elias Howe (1819–67) for infringement of patent for the Howe needle, but despite having to pay compensation the success of his Singer Manufacturing Company was assured.

SINGER, Israel Joshua (1893–1944) Polish-born American Yiddish writer, born in Bilgorai, the son of a rabbi, brother of **Esther** and **Isaac Bashevis Singer**. He studied at the Rabbinical Yeshivah School in Warsaw, and after World War I became a journalist in Kiev. He became foreign correspondent in Warsaw for the New York *Jewish Daily Forward*, for whom he continued to write after emigrating to the USA in 1933. His novels have been widely translated, and include *The Sinner* (*Yoshe Kalt*, 1933), *The Brothers Ashkenazi* (1936), *The River Breaks Up* (1938) and *East of Eden* (1939).

SINGH, Vishwanath Pratap ('VP') (1931–) Indian politician, born in Allahabad, Uttar Pradesh, the son of an influential local Raja. He was educated at Poona and Allahabad universities and in 1971 was elected to the Lok Sabha (federal parliament) as a representative of the Congress (I) party. During the administrations of **Indira Gandhi** and **Rajiv Gandhi**, he served as minister of commerce (1976–77 and 1983), chief minister of Uttar Pradesh (1980–82), minister of finance (1984–86) and minister of defence (1986–87), instigating a zealous anti-corruption drive in the finance and defence posts. In 1987 he was ousted from the government and Congress (I) when he unearthed the 'Bofors scandal', which involved the payment of alleged arms deal 'kickbacks' to senior officials closely connected to Rajiv Gandhi. Respected for his probity and sense of principle, as head of the broad-based Janata Dal coalition he emerged as the most popular opposition politician in India. He was elected prime minister in 1990.

SIQUEIROS, David Alfaro (1896–1974) Mexican mural painter, born in Chihuahua. He was a revolutionary from youth, and fought in **Madero**'s revolution of 1910–11 that overthrew **Diaz**. With **Rivera** and **Orozco**, he launched the review *El Machete* in Mexico City in 1922, and painted the frescoes for the National Preparatory School there. An active trade unionist, he was frequently imprisoned for revolutionary activities. He was expelled from the USA in 1932 after founding the Experimental Workshop in New York City, and during the 1930s he worked in South America. In 1944 he founded the Centre of Realist Art in Mexico City. One of the principal figures in 20th-century Mexican mural painting, and notable for his experiments in the use of modern synthetic materials, his most celebrated works include *From Porfirio's Dictatorship in the Revolution* (National History Museum), and *March of Humanity* (Hotel de Mexico).

SIRHAN, Sirhan (c.1943–) Palestinian-born convicted American assassin of Senator **Robert Kennedy**, he was a refugee whose family settled in Pasadena, California, in 1956, having fled from Israeli bombings in Beirut. Sirhan was committed to the Arab cause. When Robert Kennedy, who was running for the presidential nomination in 1968, took an overtly pro-Israeli stance in order to gain Jewish votes, Sirhan became enraged. He had reputedly idolized Kennedy until this point. On the night of 4 June 1968 Sirhan took a revolver and shot Kennedy in the head as Kennedy passed through the kitchen of the Ambassador Hotel in Los Angeles on his way to a victory press conference. Sirhan, who was 24, was charged on 5 June. At his trial, it emerged that Sirhan had written in his diary on 18 May, 'Robert Kennedy must be assassinated before 5 June 1968'. He said that Kennedy's repeated statements that he would send 20 bomber planes to Israel 'burned' him up. When Sirhan was reputedly asked, under hypnosis, to relive the assassination, he could only say: 'You can't send the bombers!' He was found guilty of pre-meditated murder of the first degree and the death penalty was recommended. Senator **Edward Kennedy**'s plea for leniency led to this sentence being commuted to life imprisonment. A petition for parole in 1983 failed. Since the assassination, suspicion that Sirhan was involved in a Mafia conspiracy has been voiced but never proven.

SISLEY, Alfred (1839–99) French Impressionist painter and etcher, born in Paris, of English ancestry. He joined **Monet** and **Renoir** in the studio of Charles Gleyre (1808–74) and was also influenced by **Corot**. He painted landscapes almost exclusively, particularly in the valleys of the Seine, the Loire and the Thames, and was noted for his subtle treatment of skies.

SISMONDI, Jean Charles Léonard Simond de (1773–1842) Swiss historian and economist of Italian descent, born in Geneva. The French Revolution drove his family into exile, but in 1800 Sismondi himself went back to Geneva, and obtained a municipal office. His *Histoire des républiques italiennes du moyen âge* (1807–18), a pioneer work, contributed greatly to the Italian liberal tradition. In 1813 appeared his *Littérature du midi de l'Europe* (English trans by Roscoe), and in 1819 he began his *Histoire des Françaises*. His *Richesse commerciale* (1803) is written from the standpoint of the *Wealth of Nations*; but his *Nouveaux Principes d'économie politique* (1819) inclines to socialism.

SITHOLE, Reverend Ndabaningi (1920–) Zimbabwean clergyman and politician. He was a prominent member of the National Democratic party and the Zimbabwe African People's Union (ZAPU) before becoming president of the Zimbabwean African National Union (ZANU) in 1963. With **Abel Muzorewa**, he was regarded as one of the more moderate advocates of independence based on majority rule and in 1978 was party to an agreement with prime minister **Ian Smith** for an internal constitutional settlement. This was, however, rejected as insufficient by the two nationalist leaders, **Robert Mugabe** and **Joshua Nkomo**, and by the United Nations. When an internationally accepted settlement was achieved in 1979, Sithole's power and influence waned.

SITSKY, Larry (1934–) Chinese-born Australian composer, pianist and teacher, born in Tientsin, northern China, where he made his piano début at the age of eleven. He emigrated to Australia aged 17, with his parents, and attended the New South Wales Conservatorium of Music until 1955, studying composition with **Raymond Hanson**. He also studied at Oxford University and at the San Francisco Conservatorium, California. Returning to Australia, he held various teaching positions before joining the Canberra School of Music in 1966 as head of keyboard studies. He has been head of composition and electronic music there since 1978. A prolific writer in many genres, his compositions include *Fall of the House of Usher* (1965), *Fiery Tales* (1975), and the opera *Lenz* (1970). Orchestral and instrumental works include *Sinfonia for Ten Players* (1964), a Concerto for Wind Quintet and Orchestra (1971) and a Concerto for Violin, Orchestra and Female Voices (1971).

SITTER, Willem de (1872–1934) Dutch astronomer. He became director and professor of astronomy at Leiden (1908). He computed the size of the universe as two thousand million light years in radius, containing about 80 000 million galaxies. As opposed to **Einstein**'s static concept ('matter with no motion'), he characterized the universe as an expanding curved space-time continuum of 'motion with no matter'.

SITTING BULL, Indian name **Tatanka Iyotake** (1834–90) American Indian warrior, chief of the Dakota Sioux, born near Grand River, South Dakota. He was a leader in the Sioux War of 1876–77, and led the massacre of **Custer** and his men at the Little Big Horn (1876). He escaped to Canada but surrendered in 1881, and was put into the reservation at Standing Rock. He was featured in Buffalo Bill **Cody**'s Wild West Show (1885), but was still rebellious and was killed attempting to evade the police in the 'ghost dance' uprising of 1890.

SITWELL, Dame Edith (1887–1964) English poet, born in Scarborough, Yorkshire, daughter of an eccentric, Sir George Sitwell, and sister of **Osbert** and **Sacheverell Sitwell**. She had an unhappy, lonely and frustrated childhood in the family home in Renishaw Hall, Derbyshire, until her governess introduced her to music and literature, especially the poetry of **Swinburne** and the Symbolists. She first attracted notice by her editorship of an anthology of new poetry entitled *Wheels* (1916–21). This was a new type of poetry which repudiated the flaccid quietism of Georgian verse, but her shock tactics were not fully displayed till *Façade* appeared in 1923, with **William Walton**'s music, and was given a stormy public reading in London. It was followed by *Bucolic Comedies* (1923), which is for the most part in the same fantastic vein, but the elegiac romantic style begins to appear and this vein is fully exploited in *The Sleeping Beauty* (1924), and finally worked out in the amazing *Elegy for Dead Fashion* (1926). The short poems of this romantic period, 'Colonel Fantock', 'Daphne', 'The Strawberry' and above all 'The Little Ghost who died for Love' are probably the most beautiful things she ever wrote. At the close of this period she suddenly flamed into indignation over the evil in society—in *Gold Coast Customs* (1929) expressing the horror underlying civilization. In the 1930s she turned to prose work. During World War II she denounced with great vehemence the cruelty of man in the prophetic utterance of *Street Songs* (1942), *Green Song* (1944), and *The Song of the Cold* (1945). She set out to refresh the exhausted rhythms of traditional poetry by introducing the rhythms of jazz and other dance music, and also by free association in expression and the transference of the bodily senses with the result that sense was sacrificed to the evocation of states of feeling. She abandoned this style in her later verse but there is a certain lack of control in her poems on the age of the atom bomb—*Dirge for the New Sunrise*, *The Shadow of Cain* and *The Canticle of the Rose* (1949). Other works include *The English Eccentrics* (1933), *Victoria of England* (1936), *Fanfare of Elizabeth* (1946), *The Outcasts* (verse; 1962), and *The Queens and the Hive* (1962). Her autobiography, *Taken Care Of*, was published posthumously in 1965.

SITWELL, Sir Osbert (1892–1969) English author, born in London, brother of **Edith** and **Sacheverell Sitwell**. He was educated at Eton, and his youth was spent mainly at the family home at Renishaw Hall, Derbyshire with occasional visits to Scarborough, which figures a good deal in his own satiric work, as a symbol of Victorian decrepitude. He served in the Brigade of Guards in World War I, and in 1916 was invalided home. This provided him with the leisure to set up as a satirist of war and the types which ingloriously prosper at home. Many of his satirical poems were published in the *Nation* and collected in *Argonaut and Juggernaut* (1919) and *Out of the Flame* (1923). After the war he narrowed his literary acquaintance to his sister and brother, **Ezra Pound**, **T S Eliot** and **Wyndham Lewis**. The object of the group was the regeneration of arts and letters, and in this pursuit the Sitwells acquired notoriety, Sir Osbert not least by his novel *Before the Bombardment* (1927), which anatomized the grandees of Scarborough and by implication the social orders in general. Neither this nor his other novel, *Miracle on Sinai* (1933), was successful, and his forte was always the short story, especially those, like the collection *Dumb Animal* (1930), where his delicacy of observation and natural compassion are more in evidence than his satire. The paternalism of the aristocracy is expressed in *England Reclaimed, a Book of Eclogues* (1927). His collected works show the contrast between his mordant satire and human kindliness—the satiric sharpness of *Triple Fugue* (1924) with the humanity of the stories in *Dumb Animal* parallels the resentment of the early verse with the acceptance of rural manners in the *Eclogues*. His aristocratic disposition took the form of travel in the grand manner in the 1930s. He had published *Discursions on Travel, Art and Life* in 1925, but then *Winters of Content* (1932) displayed mature descriptive powers. *Brighton* (1935, in collaboration with Margaret Barton) anticipated the vogue of 18th- and early 19th-century architecture. At the close of the 1930s *Escape with Me*, describing a journey to China, proved his most charming book of travel. All these elements contributed to the great autobiography he was planning. The first volume of *Left Hand: Right Hand* appeared in 1944, to be followed by *The Scarlet Tree* (1946), *Great Morning* (1947) and *Laughter in the Next Room* (1948). *Noble Essences* (1950) completed this work. Other collections of essays and stories include *Penny Foolish* (1935), *Sing High, Sing Low* (1944), *Alive-Alive Oh* (1947) and *Pound Wise* (1963).

SITWELL, Sacheverell (1897–1988) English writer and art critic, younger brother of **Edith** and Sir **Osbert**. Educated at Eton, he became an officer in a Guards regiment and enjoyed unlimited travel abroad. After World War I the brothers toured Spain and Italy. Italy became their second country, resulting in Sacheverell's *Southern Baroque Art* (1924), followed by *The Gothic North* (1929). His *German Baroque Art* (1927) completed his study of European art. The popularity of the Baroque today owes much to his persistent praise of this mode. A prolific writer, he published many books on travel and music and other art subjects, and poetry (especially *The People's Palace*, 1918). His works include *The Dance of the Quick and the Dead* (1986) and *Cupid and the Jacaranda* (1962).

SIVERTSEN, Cort See **ADELAER**

SIXTUS the name of five popes. The first was beheaded c. AD 125; the second was martyred in 258; the third was pope (432–440) when St **Patrick** began his mission in Ireland

SIXTUS IV, Francesco della Rovere (1414–84) pope from 1471, a famous Franciscan preacher. His nepotism led to many abuses, and he is said to have connived at the Pazzi conspiracy against the **Medici** at Florence; it was certainly engineered by his nephew, the future **Julius II**. He fostered learning, built the Sistine chapel and the Sistine bridge, and enriched painters; but he lowered the moral authority of the papacy. In 1482 he entered into an alliance with the Venetians which led to a general Italian war. His private life seems to have been blameless.

SIXTUS V, Felice Peretti (1521–90) pope from 1585. A great Franciscan preacher and a professor of theology, he was created a cardinal (Montalto) in 1570. His assumed feebleness procured him election to the papacy in succession to **Gregory XIII** in 1585. But his rule was marked by vigorous measures of improvement. He repressed licence and disorder, reformed the administration of the law and the disposal of patronage, carried on many public enterprises, and having found an empty treasury, secured a surplus of five million crowns. To the Jews he extended liberty. The great aim of his foreign policy was to combat Protestantism and uphold the balance of the Catholic powers. He fixed the number of cardinals at 70. Under his authority were published new editions of the Septuagint and Vulgate—the latter very inaccurate. He instigated the building of the Vatican Library at the Lateran Palace.

SJÖSTRÖM, Victor (1879–1960) Swedish actor and film director. Together with **Mauritz Stiller** he created the first golden age of Sweden's cinema. In 1912 he joined the expanding film company Svenska Bio where he worked as both actor (often under Stiller's direction) and director. His notable successes as actor/director included *Ingeborg Holm* (1913), a social drama, *Terje Vigen* (1918, based on **Ibsen**'s poem) and above all *Körkarlen* (1920, The Phantom Carriage), where his psychological portrayal of David Holm and use of double exposure were landmarks in cinematic acting and philosophy. His ability to adapt classic Swedish writers, above all **Selma Lagerlöf**, to the screen gave Swedish cinema popular appeal. He was in Hollywood from 1923 to 1930 (using the name Seastrom) and made a **Lon Chaney** film, *He who gets slapped* (1924) and two masterpieces, *The Scarlet Letter* (1926) and *The Wind* (1928), with **Lillian Gish**. As a director he did not adapt well to sound cinema and directed only two films after returning home. As an actor however he created several memorable parts, as Knut Borg in Molander's *The Word* (1943) and above all Professor Borg in *Wild Strawberries* (1957), an egocentric academically successful old doctor forced to admit his failure in human relationships. It crowned his career and was said to be a tribute from one great artist, **Ingmar Bergman**, to another.

SKALKOTTAS, Niko(lau)s (1904–49) Greek composer, born in Chalkis. A pupil of **Weill** and **Schoenberg** in Berlin, he returned to Greece (1933) and was an outstanding but individual exponent of the 12-note method. The works of his last decade also exploited Greek and Balkan folk elements. Most of his music was ignored in his lifetime.

SKALLAGRÍMSSON, Egill (c.910–990) Icelandic poet and warrior, born on the farm of Borg in Iceland. His father had emigrated to Iceland after falling foul of King **Harald Fine-Hair** of Norway, and Egill became a professional Viking and court-poet. He fought in the service of King **Athelstan** of England at the battle of Brunanburh (937), fell out with King **Erik Blood-Axe Haraldsson** of Norway, but visited him when he was king in the city of York in 948; there he only escaped execution by composing a eulogy in Erik's honour, the *Höfuðlausn* (Head Ransom). In 960 he lost two young sons, and composed the greatest lament in Old Icelandic poetry, *Sonatorrek* (On the Loss of Sons). His other major verse-sequence was *Arinbjarnarkviða* (The Lay of Arinbjörn), a eulogy to his friend and protector, Arinbjörn. Egill is the eponymous hero of the Icelandic *Egils saga*, probably written by his descendant, **Snorri Sturluson**, which also contains more than 40 occasional verses ascribed to him.

SKANDERBEG, Muslim **Iskander Bey,** properly **George Kastrioti** (1403–68) Albanian national hero, born of Serb descent, the son of a prince of Emathia. Carried away as a hostage by Turks when seven and brought up a Muslim, he was a favourite commander of Sultan Murat II. In 1444 he changed sides, renounced Islam, and drove the Turks from Albania, where he valiantly defeated every force sent against him. For 20 years he maintained the independence of Albania with only occasional support from Naples, Venice and the pope. After his death Albanian opposition to the Turks collapsed.

SKEAT, Walter William (1835–1912) English philologist, born in London. Educated at King's College School and Christ's College, Cambridge, he became a fellow in 1860 and in 1878 professor of Anglo-Saxon. He was founder and first director of the Dialect Society (1873), and he contributed more than any scholar of his time to a sound knowledge of Middle English and English philology generally. He edited important texts like *Piers Plowman* (1867–85). Other works are *A Moeso-Gothic Glossary* (1868), his admirable *Etymological English Dictionary* (1879–82); *Principles of English Etymology* (1887–91); his great *Chaucer* (6 vols, 1894–95); the *Student's Chaucer* (1895); *A Student's Pastime* (1896); *Chaucerian and other Pieces* (1897); *The Chaucer Canon* (1900); *Glossary of Tudor and Stuart Words* (1914); and papers on place names.

SKELTON, John (c.1460–1529) English satirical poet, born in Norfolk. He studied at both Oxford and Cambridge, and was created 'poet laureate' by both. Later he was tutor to Prince Henry (the future **Henry VIII**), took holy orders in 1498, and became rector of Diss in 1502, but seems to have been suspended in 1511 for having a concubine or wife. He had produced some translations and elegies in 1489, but began to write satirical vernacular poetry, overflowing with grotesque words and images and unrestrained joviality, as in *The Bowge of Courte*, *Colyn Cloute* and *Why come ye nat to Courte*. Of these, the first is an allegorical poem; the second an unsparing attack on the corruptions of the church; and the last a sustained invective against **Wolsey**, for which Skelton had to take sanctuary at Westminster.

SKENE, Sir John, Lord Curriehill (c.1543–1617) Scottish advocate, regent of St Mary's College, St Andrews. He lived in Scandinavia, was ambassador, lord advocate, lord clerk-register and lord of session. He published the first collection of the old Scots Acts (1597), compiled a Scottish legal dictionary, *De Verborum Significatione* (1597) and edited and translated a collection of old Scots laws, *Regiam Majestatem* (1609). He was the first Scottish legal antiquary.

SKENE, William Forbes (1809–92) Scottish historian, born in Inverie, Knoydart. Educated at the Royal High School, Edinburgh, Frankfurt, and Aberdeen, he was also privately tutored in Gaelic. He graduated in law and practised as a lawyer in Edinburgh. He wrote *The Highlanders of Scotland* (1837), but his chief work was *Celtic Scotland; a History of Ancient Alba* (3 vols, 1876–80), based on research into original documents. In 1881 he succeeded **John Hill Burton** as historiographer royal for Scotland.

SKINNER, Burrhus Frederic (1904–) American psychologist, born in Susquehanna. Pennsylvania. He was educated first at Hamilton College and then at Harvard where he taught for many years (1931–36 and 1947–74). He also taught at Minnesota University (1936–45). He has been the most consistent and radical proponent of Behaviorism. He took the ideas of **John Broadus Watson**, who advocated the study of behaviour as the only possible road for a scientific psychology to travel, developing and refining them during the 1930s and throughout the post-war years. He invented the 'Skinner Box', a simple device for training animals (usually rats or pigeons), and discovered a range of behavioural phenomena which have provided gainful employment for numerous academic psychologists and laboratory animals for over half a century. A prolific writer, his influence has extended widely. In education, his ideas led to the development and proliferation of 'programmed learning', a technique which seeks to tailor teaching to the needs of each individual and to reinforce learning by regular and immediate feedback. In clinical psychology his ideas have proved useful for the behavioural training and care of the severely mentally handicapped. His writings extend beyond psychology and 'radical behaviorism' into fiction, autobiography (four volumes), and philosophy. He has been emeritus professor at Harvard since his retiral. His honours include both the Distinguished Scientific Contribution Award (1958) and the Gold Medal (1971) of the American Psychological Association and also the National Medal of Science (1968).

SKINNER, James (1778–1841) celebrated soldier of Eurasian origin in the Indian army. He joined at 15, was promoted to lieutenant for gallantry, but dismissed by General **Perron** in 1803 because of his mixed origin. Under General Lord **Lake**, he formed Skinner's Horse, one of the most famous regiments in India. His rank of lieutenant-colonel was not recognized in London until 1827. With the fabulous wealth of 30 years' looting, and several wives, he settled down to the life of a rich Moghul in his town house at Delhi and his country seat nearby. Always inclined to scholarship and philanthropy, he then wrote books in flawless Persian, with decorations and numerous paintings by local' artists, on the princes, castes and tribes of Hindustan; and built a mosque, a temple and the Church of St James in Delhi. Of his burial there it has been said that 'None of the Emperors of Hindustan was ever brought into Delhi in such a state as Sikander Sahib'—the name associates his military genius with Alexander (Sikander) the Great.

SKINNER, James Scott (1843–1927) Scottish fiddler and composer, known as the 'Strathspey King', born in Banchory. As a child he learned the rudiments of Scots music but also received classical tuition. At the age of 19 he was able to outplay many leading Scots fiddlers in a national competition, moving the judge to say: 'Gentlemen, we have never before heard the like of this from a beardless boy'. His virtuoso playing continued to dazzle audiences during his long career as a concert performer both in Britain and the USA. Several recordings, made when he was probably past his peak, are available. Of his many compositions—over 600—some of the most popular are 'The Bonnie Lass o' Bon-Accord', 'The Laird o' Drumblair' and 'The Miller o' Hirn'.

SKINNER, John (1721–1807) Scottish historian and songwriter, born in Birse, Aberdeenshire. After working as a schoolmaster and tutor, he became an Episcopalian minister at Longside near Peterhead (1742). Although no Jacobite, his house was pillaged and his chapel burnt in 1746. He wrote *The Ecclesiastical History of Scotland* (1788) and *A Preservative against Presbytery*, and several songs, of which 'The Ewie wi' the crookit horn' and 'Tullochgorum' are the best known. His son, John (1744–1816), was a bishop of Aberdeen.

SKOBELEFF, Mikhail Dmitrievich (1843–82) Russian soldier. He fought against the Polish insurgents (1863), and from 1871 to 1875 was at the conquest of Khiva and Khokland. In the Russo-Turkish war of 1877–78 he played a conspicuous part at Plevna, in the Shipka pass, and at Adrianople; in 1881 he stormed the Turkoman stronghold of Göktepe. He was an ardent Panslavist.

SKOBTSOVA, Maria (1891–1945) Russian Orthodox nun, born in Riga. She early identified herself with the Social Revolutionaries when a student in St Petersburg, where she was the first woman to enrol at the Ecclesiastical Academy. Bolshevik excesses having disillusioned her, she was among those who escaped to France. She began work with the Russian Orthodox Student Christian Movement which adminstered also to refugees, and in 1932, despite having had two divorces, became a nun. Unconventional and radical, she worked among society's cast-offs whom she fed and housed. Nazi measures against the Jews in wartime Paris provided a new challenge. She was arrested and sent to Ravensbrück concentration camp in 1943, where she brought Christian light and hope despite appalling conditions. She was gassed on the eve of Easter, 1945, reportedly going voluntarily 'in order to help her companions to die'.

SKODA, Joseph (1805–81) Austrian physician, born in Pilser, Bohemia. He studied first theology and then natural sciences and medicine, receiving his MD from Vienna University in 1831. He worked at the General Hospital in Vienna for almost all of his career, where he was particularly concerned with using the stethoscope, invented by **Laennec**, in understanding diseases of the heart and lungs. He worked closely with the pathologist **Rokitansky**, and between them they made the medical school in Vienna one of international standing. Skoda was extremely sceptical of the value of most of the remedies routinely used by doctors of his day.

SKORZENY, Otto (1908–75) Austrian soldier, born in Vienna. He was the officer personally chosen by **Hitler** to kidnap **Mussolini** from internment in a mountain hotel on the Gran Sasso range. In September 1943 he succeeded in landing with a detachment of men in gliders on the short inclined slope in front of the hotel and after a short engagement whisking the dictator off in a small aeroplane, and so to Hitler's headquarters in East Prussia. In September 1944 he daringly infiltrated into the Citadel of Budapest and forcibly prevented **Horthy** from making a separate peace with **Stalin**, thus endangering German troops. During the Ardennes offensive in December 1944 he carried out widespread sabotage behind Allied lines, for which he was tried as a war criminal but acquitted.

SKRAM, Bertha Amalie, née **Alver** (1847–1905) Norwegian feminist novelist, born in Bergen. After divorcing her first husband in 1878, she worked as a critic and short-story writer. In 1884 she married Erik Skram, a Danish writer, and following this wrote a collection of novels in which she explored women's issues, and sex in particular. Her best-known works include *Constance Ring* (1885), the tetralogy *Hellemyrstolket* (1887–98) and *Foraadt* (1892). She was divorced from Skram in 1900, and thereafter never recovered her mental health.

SKRIABIN, Alexander See **SCRIABIN**

SKUM, Nils Nilsson (1872–1951) distinguished Lappish artist of the Sami people. Born into a nomadic family of reindeer hunters, he was the first of his people to draw pictures, but using the traditional inspiration of Sami craftwork. His paintings form one of the first comprehensive studies of traditional Sami life.

SLADE, Felix (1790–1868) English antiquary and art collector, born in Halsteads, Yorkshire. He bequeathed to the British Museum his engravings and Venetian glass, and founded art professorships at Oxford and Cambridge, and the Slade School of Art in London.

SLATER, Oscar (1873–1948) German Jew resident in Glasgow, Scotland, wrongly convicted of the murder of Marion Gilchrist in 1909. Three witnesses identified him as the man seen leaving the scene of the crime, although their descriptions varied considerably and at least one of them was thought to have seen Slater's photograph before identifying him. After the trial, at which he was not called to give evidence, he was sentenced to death but this was commuted to life imprisonment. Because of protests of injustice by **Conan Doyle** and others, he was released after 19 years and received £6000 in compensation.

SLATER, Samuel (1768–1835) English-born American mechanical engineer, born in Belper, Derbyshire. Apprenticed to Jedediah Strutt, he gained a detailed knowledge of the most advanced textile machinery and its operation. At the time the textile industry in the USA was offering bounties to skilled mechanics from Europe, but Britain had made both the export of machinery or data, and the emigration of textile workers, illegal. Nevertheless, Slater sailed from England in 1789 in disguise and under an assumed name. Blessed with a photographic memory, he was able within a year to build up-to-date spinning machines for a struggling cotton mill in Rhode Island, becoming a partner in the firm of Almy, Brown & Slater, whose prosperity laid the foundation for the success of the American cotton industry.

SLATIN, Baron Rudolf Carl von (1857–1932) Austrian soldier in the British service, born near Vienna. In 1878 he took service under General **Gordon** in the Sudan. Governor of Darfur (1881), on the defeat of **William Hicks** he surrendered (1883) to the Mahdi **Mohammad Ahmed**, escaped in 1895, and wrote a vivid description of his experiences, *Fire and Sword in the Soudan* (1896). As colonel he served in the Dongola and Omdurman expeditions (1896–98). He was inspector-general of the Sudan from 1900 to 1914; and in World War II president of the Austrian Red Cross.

SLEEP, Wayne (1948–) English dancer and choreographer, born in Plymouth. As a child he studied tap and ballet, joining the Royal Ballet School at the age of twelve and graduating into the company itself in 1966. Promoted to principal dancer in 1973, his small stature, extrovert personality and technical prowess landed him choice roles in such ballets as **Frederick Ashton**'s *A Month in the Country* (1976) and **Kenneth MacMillan**'s *Manon* (1974), among others. His talents extend to the musical stage, cinema and television. He appeared as Squirrel Nutkin and one of the Bad Mice in the 1971 film *Tales of Beatrix Potter* (choreography by **Ashton**) and in the original production of *Cats* (1981). In 1980 he formed his own touring group, Dash, and later adapted his series *The Hot Shoe Show* (1983–84) into a fast-paced, eclectic live revue.

SLEIDANUS, properly **Philippi, Johannes** (1506–56) German historian, born in Schleiden. In 1537 he entered the service of **Francis I** of France; but turning Protestant, was dismissed (1541), and served as ambassador of the Protestant princes of Germany. He wrote a Latin history of **Charles V** (1555).

SLESSOR, Sir John Cotesworth (1897–1979) British air-marshal, born in Rhanikhet, India. Educated at Haileybury, he served in the Royal Flying Corps in World War I and was awarded the MC. He was instructor at the RAF Staff College (1924–25) and at Camberley (1931–34). His part in the Waziristan operations (1936–37) earned him the DSO. During World War II he was commander-in-chief of Coastal Command (1943) and of the Mediterranean theatre (1944–45). Promoted marshal in 1940, he was chief of the Air Staff (1950–52). His often original, penetrating and unorthodox views on nuclear strategy are expressed in *Strategy for the West* (1954) and *The Great Deterrent* (1957).

SLESSOR, Kenneth Adolf (1901–71) Australian poet and journalist, born in Orange, New South Wales. He worked as reporter and columnist on various Sydney and Melbourne newspapers until he joined *Smith's Weekly* in 1927, later becoming editor-in-chief until 1939. He was appointed an official war correspondent and covered the Battle of Britain and then followed the Australian Imperial Forces through the Near East and North Africa, and on to New Guinea. Slessor contributed many poems to various periodicals, and, beginning with *Thief of the Moon* (1924), he published six books of verse, with two collections in 1944 and 1957. He also edited the 1945 collection in the series 'Australian Poetry' and co-edited *The Penguin Book of Australian Verse* (1958). Although essentially a poet of the town, his feeling for the romanticized past is shown in his poem entitled 'Five Visions of Captain Cook' (1931).

SLESSOR, Mary (1848–1915) Scottish missionary, born in Aberdeen. She worked as a mill girl in Dundee from childhood but, conceiving a burning ambition to become a missionary, got herself accepted by the United Presbyterian Church for teaching in Calabar, Nigeria (1876), where she spent many years of devoted work among the natives. She was known among the natives as 'Great Mother'.

SLEVOGT, Max (1868–1932) German Impressionist painter and engraver, born in Landshut. He studied in Munich and Berlin (where he later taught at the Academy), and worked with the Impressionist **Louis Corinth**. His works comprise murals of historical scenes and swiftly executed landscapes and portraits.

SLEZER, John (d.1714) Dutch engraver, employed by **Charles II** and the Duke of York to make engravings of Scottish buildings. His *Theatrum Scotiae* (1693) was reprinted, with a memoir, in 1874.

SLIM, William Joseph, 1st Viscount (1891–1970) English soldier, educated at King Edward's School, Birmingham. During World War I he served in Gallipoli, France and Mesopotamia. Transferring to the Gurkha Rifles, a succession of command and staff appointments brought him to high command in World War II. In 1943 he became commander of the 14th 'forgotten' army in Burma, which he led to victory over the Japanese. In 1945–46 he was supreme Allied commander in south-east India. He was chief of the Imperial General Staff (1948–52), and governor-general of Australia (1953–60). He wrote *Defeat into Victory* (1956) and his memoirs, *Unofficial History* (1959).

SLIPHER, Vesto Melvin (1875–1969) American astronomer, born in Mulberry, Indiana. He studied at Indiana University, before working for over 50 years at the Lowell Observatory, Arizona, becoming its director in 1926. He used spectroscopic techniques to measure the **Doppler** shift in light reflected from the edges of planetary discs, thereby determining the periods of rotation of Uranus, Jupiter, Saturn, Venus and Mars in 1912. Extending his methods to spiral galaxies, he discovered the general recession of galaxies (outside the Local Group) from our own galaxy, a result later seen to be in accord with the idea of an expanding universe.

SLOAN, Alfred Pritchard, Jr (1875–1966) American industrialist, born in New Haven, Connecticut. From 1920 to 1924 he worked with **Pierre Du Pont** to reorganize and restructure General Motors. He became president in 1924 and chairman of the board from 1937 to 1956. Under his guidance the company became one of the largest industrial corporations in the world. A noted philanthropist, he founded the Alfred P Sloan Foundation in 1937 and the Sloan-Kettering Institute for Cancer Research in 1945. His autobiography, *My Years with General Motors* (1964) is a classic in management literature.

SLOAN, John (1871–1951) American artist, born in Lock Haven, Pennsylvania. He worked initially as a commercial artist and newspaper art reporter after studying at Philadelphia Spring Garden Institute and Pennsylvania Academy of Fine Arts. Influenced by **Robert Henri**, he produced a series of intimate warm-hearted etchings based on New York City life. Throughout his career he continued to depict his individual visual documentation of life in the metropolis, placing him in the forefront of the American Realist tradition.

SLOANE, Sir Hans (1660–1753) British physician and naturalist, born in Killyleagh, County Down, the son of an Ulster Scot. He studied in London and in France, and settled in London as a physician. From 1685 to 1686 he was physician to the governor of Jamaica, and collected a herbarium of 800 species. He was secretary to the Royal Society (1693–1713), and was physician-general to the army (1716) and first physician to **George II**. He founded the Chelsea Physic

Garden in 1721. He bequeathed his museum and library of 50 000 volumes and 3560 MSS to the British Museum. His great work was the *Natural History of Jamaica* (1707–25).

SLOCUM, Joshua (1844–c.1910) American mariner, born in Wilmot Township, Nova Scotia. Going early to sea as a ship's cook, in 1869 he captained a trading vessel off the Californian coast. In 1886 he set off with his second wife and two sons on a converted bark, *Aquidneck*, for South America, was wrecked on a Brazilian sandbar, but from the wreckage built a canoe which took them all back to New York. In 1895 he set out from Boston without capital on the sloop *Spray* for the first solo cruise around the world, arriving back at Newport in 1898, having supported himself by lecturing on the way. In November 1909 he set out once more, but was not heard of again.

SŁOWACKI, Juljusz (1809–49) Polish poet, born in Krzemieniec. He settled in Paris in 1831. He belonged to the Romantic school, the influence of **Byron**, among others, being perceptible in his work, which includes the historical drama *Marie Stuart* (1830), the dramatized legend *Balladyna* (1834), *Lilla Weneda* (1840), perhaps the most famous Polish tragedy, and *Mazeppa* (1839).

SLUTER, Claus (c.1350–1405) Flemish sculptor born probably in Haarlem. He went to Dijon under the patronage of **Philip the Bold of Burgundy**, and died there. His chief works are the porch sculptures of the Carthusian house of Champmol near Dijon, and the tomb of Philip the Bold.

SMART, Christopher (1722–71) English poet, born in Shipbourne near Tonbridge. He studied at Pembroke College, Cambridge, and was elected a fellow in 1745. Improvidence, wit and a secret marriage upset his academic career and he settled to a precarious living in London. He died insane. **Samuel Johnson** assisted him in his monthly *Universal Visitor*. Smart's works include sacred poems, epigrams, birthday odes and occasional poems; the *Hilliad* (1753), a satire on a quack doctor; and several translations from the Bible and the classics. His most celebrated work is *A Song to David* (1763).

SMEATON, Bruce James (1938–) Australian composer for film and television, born in Brighton, Victoria. His work for major feature films, such as *Picnic at Hanging Rock* (1975), *The Cars that Ate Paris* (1974), *The Chant of Jimmie Blacksmith* (1978) and, for television, *Seven Little Australians* (1973), *A Town Like Alice* (1981) and *Naked under Capricorn* (1988), is internationally recognized and has won many awards. His other works include a cello concerto, music for brass, and chamber music, including a setting for woodwind quintet of **Shostakovich**'s *Twenty-Four Preludes* (1988). *Mithe, a ballet in fourteen movements* (1988) was written for the Twyla Tharp Dance Foundation of New York.

SMEATON, John (1724–94) English civil engineer, born in Austhorp near Leeds. He gave up law and about 1750 moved to London as a mathematical-instrument maker. Elected FRS in 1753, he won the Copley Medal for his researches into the mechanics of waterwheels and windmills and established his reputation with his novel design for the third Eddystone lighthouse (1756–59), which remained in use till 1877, and was re-erected on Plymouth Hoe as a memorial. Through systematic study and experiment he improved the atmospheric steam engine of **Thomas Newcomen**. His other chief engineering works include Ramsgate Harbour (1774), the Forth and Clyde Canal, and bridges at Coldstream and Perth.

SMECTYMNUUS a composite pseudonym used by Stephen Marshal, Edward Calamy, Thomas Young, Matthew Newcomen, and William Spurstow, who published in 1641 a pamphlet attacking Episcopacy which was answered by **Joseph Hall** and defended by **Milton**.

SMELLIE, William (1740–95) Scottish editor, printer and antiquary, born in Edinburgh. Educated at the High School, he was apprenticed to a printer in 1752 but he gained permission to attend classes in botany at the university. In 1765 he set up his own printing business and, with Andrew Bell and Colin MacFarquhar, produced the first edition of the *Encyclopaedia Britannica* (1768–71), much of which was later ascribed to him. A founder member of the Society of Antiquities in 1780, he helped prepare the first statistical account of Scotland. **Robert Burns** found his company congenial and described him as 'that old Veteran in Genius, Wit and B[awd]ry'. Smellie printed the first edition of Burns' poems for **William Creech**, the publisher.

SMETANA, Bedřich (1824–84) Czech composer, born in Litomyšl. He studied in Prague, and in 1848 opened a music school with the financial support of **Liszt**, who recommended his music to the German publisher Kistner. From 1856 to 1859 and again in 1860 he was conductor of the Philharmonic Orchestra in Göteborg, Sweden, but after his return to Prague he opened a new music school, and in 1866 became conductor of the new National Theatre, for which his operas were composed. Overwork destroyed his health, and in 1874 he became totally deaf, though he continued to compose until his mental breakdown in 1883. His compositions, intensely national in character, include nine operas (one unfinished), of which the best known are *The Bartered Bride*, *Dalibor* and *The Kiss*; his many orchestral and chamber works include the series of symphonic poems entitled *Má Vlast* (My Country) and the string quartet *Aus meinem Leben* (From My Life), both composed when he was deaf.

SMILES, Samuel (1812–1904) Scottish writer and social reformer, born in Haddington. He studied medicine at Edinburgh, and published *Physical Education* (1838). He practised in Haddington, and then settled as a surgeon in Leeds, but became editor of the *Leeds Times*, secretary of the Leeds and Thirsk Railway in 1845, and in 1854 secretary of the Southeastern Railway, retiring in 1866. While at Leeds he met **George Stephenson**, and undertook a Life of him (1857). His most celebrated work was *Self-Help* (1859), with its short Lives of great men and the admonition 'Do thou likewise', which made the ideal Victorian school-prize. He wrote many other improving works, including *Character* (1871), *Thrift* (1875), and *Duty* (1880), and also 'Lives of the Engineers' (1861–62).

SMILLIE, Robert (1857–1940) Scottish Labour politician, born of Scottish parents in Belfast. He was president of the Scottish Miners' Federation 1894–1918, and again from 1921; and from 1912 to 1921 president of the Miners' Federation of Great Britain. He was Labour MP for Morpeth (1923–29).

SMIRKE, Sir Robert (1781–1867) English architect, son of Robert Smirke (1752–1845), painter and book-illustrator. Architect to the board of works, his public buildings are usually classical, his domestic architecture Gothic. Covent Garden Theatre (1809) was his first great undertaking; the British Museum (1823–47), his best known. He also designed the General Post Office (1824–29) and the College of Physicians (1825). His brother, Sydney (1799–1877), completed the west wing of the museum and the reading room (1854), and rebuilt the Carlton Club (1857).

SMITH, Adam (1723–90) Scottish economist and philosopher, born in Kirkcaldy; his *Wealth of Nations* is the first masterpiece in political economy. The posthumous son of the comptroller of customs, he studied at Glasgow and Oxford. From 1748 he became one of the brilliant circle in Edinburgh which included **David Hume**, **John Home**, **Hugh Blair**, Lord **Hailes** and **William Robertson**. In 1751 he became professor of logic at Glasgow, later exchanging for the chair of moral philosophy (1755–64). In 1759 he published his *Theory of Moral Sentiments*, based on Hume's doctrines. The essence of moral sentiments, Smith argued, was sympathy—but a specialized, conscience-stricken sympathy, like that of an impartial and well-informed spectator. While travelling as tutor to Henry, 3rd Duke of **Buccleuch**, he met in Paris **Quesnay**, **Turgot**, **Necker** and others. He watched the illness and death of his friend Hume and edited his non-controversial papers. A moving account of Hume's end, written to a Mr Strahan of London, attracted controversy; many resented the idea that an atheist could die with such dignity. In 1776 Smith went to London. He became a member of the club to which **Joshua Reynolds**, **David Garrick** and Dr **Johnson** belonged. That same year he published a volume of five chapters, which he originally intended to be only the first part of a complete theory of society in the tradition of Scottish moral philosophy, which would cover natural theology, ethics, politics and law. This single volume, *Inquiry into the Nature and Causes of the Wealth of Nations*, examined the consequences of economic freedom, such as the division of labour, the function of markets and mediums of exchange and the international implications. He attacked medieval mercantile monopolies and the theories of the French physiocrats, who saw land as the economic basis of wealth. His doctrine did not, however, support full 'laissez faire', for he sought to implement, through economics, his earlier work on moral influence. At a public dinner, **Pitt** invited Smith to be seated first, as 'we are all your scholars'. Appointment as commissioner of customs took Smith back to Edinburgh in 1778; there he died and was buried in the Canongate churchyard. He was elected FRS in 1767 and lord rector of Glasgow University in 1787. His works (edited by **Dugald Stewart** in 1811–12) include essays on the formation of languages; the history of astronomy; classical physics and logic; and the arts. His Glasgow *Lectures on Justice, Police, Revenue, Arms* (1896), were edited from notes by a student.

SMITH, Alexander (1830–67) Scottish poet and essayist, born in Kilmarnock, Ayrshire, the son of a pattern designer. He himself became a pattern designer in Glasgow, sending occasional poems to the *Glasgow Citizen*. His *Life Drama* (1851) was highly successful at first but was satirized by **Aytoun** in *Firmilian, a Spasmodic Tragedy*, and the adjective 'spasmodic' has stuck to Smith's poetry ever since. In 1854 he was appointed secretary to Edinburgh University, and next year produced *Sonnets on the War* with **Sydney Dobell**, his brother poet of the 'Spasmodic' school. *City Poems* (1857) and *Edwin of Deira* (1861) were followed by essays, collected under the title *Dreamthorp* (1863), novels, and *A Summer in Skye* (1865), an enthusiastic and vivid evocation of the island.

SMITH, Alfred Emanuel (1873–1944) American Democrat politician, born in New York City. He rose from newsboy to be governor of New York State (1919–20, 1923–28). 'Al' Smith was beaten as Democratic candidate for the US presidency in 1928.

SMITH, Annie See **SWAN, Annie Shepherd**

SMITH, Augustus John (1804–72) English lessee or 'king' from 1834 of the Scilly Islands. He was MP for Truro from 1857.

SMITH, Benjamin Eli (1857–1912) American lexicographer, born in Urumiah, Syria, the son of **Eli Smith**. He became managing editor (1882) and later editor-in-chief (1894) of the *Century Dictionary and Cyclopaedia* and associated enterprizes, such as the *Century Atlas*.

SMITH, Bernard, originally **Bernhardt Schmidt** (c.1630–1708) German-born British organ-builder, known as 'Father Smith', born in Halle. He moved to London in 1666, and was organist at St Margaret's, Westminster, from 1675. He built organs for Westminster Abbey, and for the Sheldonian Theatre in Oxford. He also built the organs for Durham Cathedral, St Paul's in London (1697), and Trinity College, Cambridge. His chief rival as an organ-builder was **Renatus Harris**, whom he defeated in a contest in 1684.

SMITH, Bessie (Elizabeth) (1894–1937) American blues singer, born in Chattanooga, Tennessee. Later to be advertized as 'The Empress of the Blues', she began her career in the modest circuit of vaudeville tents and small theatres, but her magnificent voice, blues-based repertoire and vivacious stage presence soon gained her recognition as one of the outstanding black artistes of her day. She made a series of recordings throughout the 1920s, accompanied by leading jazz musicians, including **Louis Armstrong**, and these are regarded as classic blues statements. In 1929 she had the leading role in a film, *St Louis Blues* the title of one of her favourite songs. She died following a car crash.

SMITH, David Roland (1906–65) American sculptor, born in Decatur, Indiana. In 1925 he worked in the Studebaker car factory at South Bend and learnt how to cut and shape metal. From 1926 he studied under the Czech abstract artist Jan Matulka at the Art Students' League in New York. His first welded-steel pieces, inspired by magazine photographs of similar work by **Picasso**, date from 1932. During the 1930s he assimilated avant-garde European styles, including Cubism, Surrealism and Constructivism; his personal idiom developed from c.1940.

SMITH, Dodie, pseud (until 1935) **C L Anthony** (1896–) English playwright, novelist, and theatre producer. She started as an actress but took up a business career. Her first play, *Autumn Crocus* (1930) was an instant success and enabled her to devote all her time to writing. Other plays include *Dear Octopus* (1938), *Letter from Paris* (adapted from *The Reverberator* by **Henry James**, 1952) and *I Capture the Castle* (adapted from her own novel, 1952). Other works include the children's book *The Hundred and One Dalmations* (1956). She also published the autobiographical works *Look Back With Love* (1974), *Look Back With Mixed Feelings* (1978) and *Look Back With Astonishment* (1979).

SMITH, Eli (1801–57) American churchman and missionary, born in Northford, Connecticut. A Congregationalist, he went to Syria in 1926 as a missionary, and founded the American Mission at Urumiah. He translated the Bible into Arabic.

SMITH, Florence Margaret see **SMITH, Stevie**

SMITH, Sir Francis Pettit (1808–74) English inventor, born in Hythe, inventor of the screw propellor. In 1836 he took out a patent for the screw propellor, just ahead of the Swedish inventor **John Ericsson**. In 1839 he built the first successful screw-propelled steamer, the *Archimedes*, which eventually convinced the Admiralty of their superiority, and in 1841–43 he built the first screw warship for the Royal Navy, the *Rattler*. In 1860 he was appointed curator of the Patent Office Museum in London.

SMITH, Frederick Edwin See **BIRKENHEAD**

SMITH, George (1824–1901) English publisher. He joined his father's firm of Smith & Elder in 1838, and becoming head in 1846. He founded the *Cornhill Magazine* in 1860 with **Thackeray** as editor, and the *Pall Mall Gazette* in 1865. He published the works of **George Eliot**, the **Brownings**, Mrs **Gaskell**, **Trollope**, and others. He also published the *Dictionary of National Biography* (63 vols, 1885–1900).

SMITH, George (1840–76) English Assyriologist, born in London. He was a banknote engraver who studied cuneiform inscriptions in the British Museum, and in 1867 became an assistant there. He helped Sir **Henry Rawlinson** with his *Cuneiform Inscriptions* (1870), furnished (1871) the key to the Cypriote character, and deciphered from **Layard**'s tablets in 1872 the *Epic of Gilgamesh*, a pre-Biblical account of a Deluge. In 1873 he found the missing fragments of the tablet in Nineveh. He made two further expeditions on behalf of the British Museum, and died at Aleppo. He wrote *Assyrian Discoveries* (1875) and the popular *Chaldean Account of Genesis* (1876).

SMITH, Sir George Adam (1856–1942) Scottish Biblical scholar, born in Calcutta. He was a minister in Aberdeen (1882–92), professor of Hebrew at the Free Church College, Glasgow (1892–1909) and wrote studies on **Isaiah** and the minor prophets. From 1909 to 1935 he was principal of Aberdeen University. His books include *Modern Criticism and the Preaching of the Old Testament* (1901), *Jerusalem* (1907–08), and *The Early Poetry of Israel* (1913).

SMITH, George Joseph (1872–1915) English murderer, born in London. He drowned his three 'brides in the bath', Beatrice Williams, Alice Burnham and Margaret Lofty, for the total gain of £3500, the first and last in London (1912, 1914), the second in Blackpool (1913).

SMITH, Gerrit (1797–1874) American reformer and philanthropist, born in Utica, New York. He was active in movements such as Sunday observance, total abstinence, vegetarianism, reform, dress, prison reform, and women's suffrage. He became a prominent abolitionist in 1835, and aided **John Brown** (1800–59).

SMITH, Sir Grafton Elliot (1871–1937) Australian anatomist and ethnologist, authority on brain anatomy and human evolution, born in Grafton, NSW, was professor in Cairo School of Medicine, Manchester and London. He built his reputation on studies of cranial morphology and the Egyptian practice of mummification. His books, *Migrations of Early Culture* (1915), *The Evolution of the Dragon* (1919), *The Diffusion of Culture* (1933), etc, explain similarities in culture all over the world by diffusion from pharaonic Egypt.

SMITH, Hamilton Othanel (1931–) American molecular biologist, born in New York City. He graduated from Johns Hopkins Medical School, and did genetic research there from 1967. He became professor of microbiology at Johns Hopkins in 1973. In the 1970s he obtained enzymes from bacteria which would split genes to give genetically active fragments; these 'restriction enzymes' therefore allowed the possibility of genetic engineering of a new kind, as well as providing a tool for DNA sequencing. He shared the Nobel prize for physiology or medicine in 1978 with **Werner Arber** and **Daniel Nathams**, who had worked in the same field.

SMITH, (Robert) Harvey (1938–) English show-jumper, born in Yorkshire. He won the British championships, and the British Grand Prix, on several occasions, and represented Britain in the 1968 Mexico City Olympics and at Munich in 1972. Horses most closely associated with him include Salvador, O'Malley, Mattie Brown, Farmer's Boy and Harvester. With the increasing prominence and popularity of show-jumping, Smith became a well-liked figure, though parodying the blunt, bluff, Yorkshireman. He wrote two books, *Show Jumping with Harvey Smith* (1979) and *Bedside Jumping* (1985).

SMITH, Henry John Stephen (1826–83) Irish mathematician, born in Dublin. He was educated at Rugby School and Balliol College, Oxford, of which he was elected a fellow. In 1860 he became Savilian professor of geometry. He was the greatest authority of his day on the theory of numbers, and also wrote on elliptic functions and modern geometry.

SMITH, Horace or **Horatio** See **SMITH, James** (1775–1839)

SMITH, Ian Douglas (1919–) Zimbabwean politician, born in Selukwe. He was educated in Rhodesia, and at Rhodes University, South Africa. He was a fighter pilot in World War II and became an MP in 1948. From 1953 he was a member of the United Federal party, resigning in 1961 to become a founder of the Rhodesian Front, dedicated to immediate independence for Rhodesia without African majority rule. He was minister of the treasury (1962–64), and prime minister from April 1964, and of external affairs (to August 1964), of defence (to May 1965). With an overwhelming majority, despite lengthy talks and strenuous attempts to avert it, he unilaterally declared independence in November 1965. Britain declared his government rebels and, supported by many other countries, applied increasingly severe economic sanctions. His meetings (1966 and 1968) with **Harold Wilson**, the British prime minister, aboard HMS *Tiger* and HMS *Fearless* off Gibraltar, failed to resolve the situation, but in 1979 majority rule was granted. Bishop **Abel Muzorewa**'s caretaker government made him minister without portfolio and a member of the Transitional Executive Council of 1978–79 to prepare for the transfer of power. He was then elected a member of parliament in the government of **Robert Mugabe**. He was suspended from parliament in April 1987 because of his suspicious connections with South Africa, and in May of that year he resigned the leadership of the white opposition party.

SMITH, James (1775–1839) and **Horace** (1779–1849), English authors of *The Rejected Addresses*. They were educated at Chigwell, Essex. James succeeded his father as solicitor to the Board of Ordnance; Horace made a fortune as a stockbroker. Both wrote for magazines. When a prize was advertised for an address to be spoken at the opening of the new Drury Lane Theatre in 1812, the brothers produced a series of supposed 'Rejected Addresses', James furnishing imitations of **Wordsworth**, **Southey** and **Coleridge**; Horace those of Sir **Walter Scott**, **Byron**, 'Monk' **Lewis** and **Moore**. James also wrote for **Charles Mathews** and Horace wrote the *Tin Trumpet* (1836) and more than a score of novels. Of Horace's *Poems* (1846) the best known is the 'Ode to an Egyptian Mummy'.

SMITH, James (1789–1850) Scottish agricultural engineer and philanthropist, of Deanston, Perthshire. Manager of the cotton mills there from 1807, he was the inventor of 'thorough drainage' by means of a subsoil plough.

SMITH, Sir James Edward (1759–1828) English botanist, born in Norwich,. He studied medicine in Edinburgh, but his chief interest was in botany. At the age of 24 he bought the entire natural history collection of **Linnaeus** from his widow and brought it to London. He was one of the founders and first president (1788), of the Linnaean Society. He wrote *Flora Britannica* (1804) and *English Botany* (36 vols, 1790–1814) and 76 other publications.

SMITH, Jedediah Strong (1799–1831) American fur trader and explorer, born in Jericho, New York. He went to St Louis to trade furs, and undertook two major explorations in the Far Southwest of North America between 1823 and 1830, covering more than 16000 miles, first in the Central Rockies and Columbia River areas, trapping and providing intelligence on the activities of the Hudson's Bay Company; later he became the first white man to reach California overland across the Sierra Nevada mountains and Great Basin to the Pacific. He was killed by Comanche Indians while leading a wagon train to Santa Fe, thus preventing the publication of his extensive discoveries.

SMITH, John (1580–1631) English adventurer and colonist, born in Willoughby, Lincolnshire. Apprenticed to a Lynn merchant, he left to seek fame and fortune in France, and saw some soldiering under **Henri IV**. Next he served with distinction against the Turks in Hungary, but was captured and sold as a slave. He escaped and returned to England, and in 1606 he joined an expedition to colonize Virginia, landing at Jamestown. On one of his hunting expeditions he was taken prisoner by the Indians and only saved from death by Princess **Pocahontas**. His energy and tact in dealing with the Indians were useful to the colonists and he was elected president of the colony in 1608, but returned to England in 1609. In 1614 he was sent to New England and explored the coast. His works include *A True Relation of Virginia Since the First Planting of that Colony* (1612), *A Description of New England* (1616) and *The Generall Historie of Virginia, New England, and the Summer Isles* (1624). He also wrote *The True Travels, Adventures, and Observations of Captaine John Smith* (1630).

SMITH, John (1790–1824) English missionary in Demerara, who was sentenced to death by the governor for refusing to help in suppressing a Negro uprising. Public protests at home, led by **Wilberforce**, caused the government to override the governor, but instructions arrived after Smith had perished in an insanitary jail. His fate hastened the passing of the Emancipation Act (1833).

SMITH, John (1825–1910) Scottish dentist, and founder of Edinburgh Dental Hospital and School, the son of an Edinburgh dentist, whose practice he inherited in 1851. He published a *Handbook of Dental Anatomy and Surgery* in 1864. He was appointed surgeon dentist to the Royal Public Dispensary in 1857–59, and founded the Edinburgh Dental Dispensary in 1860. Largely as a result of his efforts, the Edinburgh Dental Hospital and School was established in 1879, the Dispensary being merged with it. Smith left the running of the school to others, but remained a significant influence on its development. His practice was later shared and ultimately inherited by his son-in-law **William Guy**. He was also a theatre enthusiast, wrote the scripts of several Edinburgh Lyceum pantomimes and successfully adapted Sir **Walter Scott**'s *Waverley* for the stage.

SMITH, John (1938–) Scottish politician. Educated at Dunoon Grammar School and Glasgow University, where he studied law, he was called to the Scottish bar in 1967 and made a QC in 1983. He distinguished himself as a public speaker at an early age, winning the 'Observer Mace' debating competition in 1962. He entered the House of Commons, representing Lanarkshire North, in 1970 and from 1983 Monklands East. He served in the administrations of **Harold Wilson** and **James Callaghan**, becoming trade secretary in 1978. Since 1979, in opposition, he has been front bench spokesman on trade, energy, employment and economic affairs. His political career seemed threatened by a heart attack in 1988, but he made a complete recovery and returned in 1989 as one of Labour's most respected politicians.

SMITH, John Raphael (1750–1812) English miniaturist, portrait painter and especially mezzotinter, son of Thomas Smith (c.1709–1767), Derby landscapist. Many of his plates are from the works of **Reynolds**, **Romney** and others.

SMITH, John Stafford (1750–1836) English composer and musical scholar. He wrote vocal music and the tune of *The Star-spangled Banner*.

SMITH, Joseph (1805–44) American religious leader, regarded as the founder of the Mormons, born in Sharon, Vermont. He received his first 'call' as a prophet at Manchester, New York, in 1820. In 1823 an angel told him of a hidden gospel on golden plates, with two stones which should help to translate it from the 'Reformed Egyptian'; and on the night of 22 September 1827, the sacred records were delivered into his hands. The *Book of Mormon* (1830) contains a postulated history of America from its colonization at the time of the confusion of tongues to the 5th century of the Christian era, and said to have been written by a prophet named Mormon. In 1830, the new 'Church of the Latter-day Saints' was founded in Fayette, New York, and despite ridicule and hostility, and sometimes open violence, it rapidly gained converts. In 1831 it established its headquarters at Kirtland, Ohio, and built Zion in Missouri. Things culminated in 1838 in a general uprising in Missouri against the Mormons; and Smith was often arrested. In 1840 they moved to Illinois, near Commerce, where they founded the community of Nanvoo, and within three years, the Mormons in Illinois numbered 20000. Smith meanwhile started having 'spiritual wives'. He was imprisoned, with his brother Hyrum, but on 27 June 1844, 150 masked men broke into Carthage jail and shot them dead. Thereafter the Mormons continued their westward migration, to Utah, under **Brigham Young**.

SMITH, Logan Pearsall (1865–1946) American-born British writer, born in Millville, New Jersey, a member of a Philadelphia Quaker family. Educated at Harvard and Oxford, he settled in England and took British nationality in 1913. He produced critical editions of various authors, and *Milton and His Modern Critics* (1941), but is best remembered for his delightful essays, collected in *All Trivia* (1933) and *Reperusals and Re-collections* (1936), his short stories, and his love of adverbs.

SMITH, Madeleine Hamilton (1835–1928) Scottish gentlewoman, born in Glasgow, the daughter of a Glasgow architect. She is notorious as the defendant in a sensational murder trial. In 1857 she stood trial at the High Court in Edinburgh for the alleged murder by arsenic poisoning of her former lover Pierre Émile L'Angelier, a clerk and native of Jersey (Channel Islands) whom she had met in Glasgow in 1855. Her uninhibited love letters to him, published during the trial, stirred up considerable resentment against her. But although she had sufficient motive for ridding herself of L'Angelier, after her engagement to a more wealthy suitor, William Kinnock, and although she had purchased arsenic on three occasions, evidence was lacking of any meeting between them on the last days or nights prior to his last violent illness. She was brilliantly defended by **John Inglis**, dean of the faculty of advocates, and the verdict was 'not proven'. Spurned by her family, she moved to London, where she became a popular social figure. In 1861 she married an artist-publisher George Wardle, an associate of **William Morris**, and after a normal family life in Bloomsbury, separated from her husband and eventually emigrated to the USA, where she married again, and refused all Hollywood offers to play herself in a silent film of her life.

SMITH, Maggie (1934–) English actress, born in Ilford, Essex. A student at the Oxford Playhouse School, she made her stage début with the Oxford University Dramatic Society in a production of *Twelfth Night* (1952) and, after revue experience, appeared in New York as one of the *New Faces of '56*. Her inimitable vocal range, mastery of stagecraft and precise timing have enabled her to portray vulnerability to both dramatic and comic effect. Gaining increasing critical esteem for her performances in *The Rehearsal* (1961) and *Mary, Mary* (1963), she joined the National Theatre to play in *Othello* (1963), *Hay Fever* (1966) and *The Three Sisters* (1970) among others. Her film début in *Nowhere to Go* (1958) was followed by scene-stealing turns in such films as *The VIPs* (1963) and *The Pumpkin Eater* (1964) but her tour de force was in *The Prime of Miss Jean Brodie* (1969), gaining her an Academy Award. Recent stage work includes *Virginia* (1980) and *Lettice and Lovage* (1988), while her selection of film roles shows a penchant for eccentric comedy and acid spinsters, and includes award-winning performances in *California Suite* (1978), *A Private Function* (1984, BAFTA Award for Best Actress), *A Room With a View* (1985) and *The Lonely Passion of Judith Hearne* (1987).

SMITH, Maria Ann (c.1801–1870) Australian orchardist. In the 1860s she was growing various seedlings on her orchard in Eastwood, near Sydney, and experimented with a hardy French crab-apple from the cooler climate of Tasmania. From this was developed the late-ripening 'Granny Smith' apple which, because of its excellent keeping qualities, formed for many years the bulk of Australia's apple exports.

SMITH, Sir Matthew Arnold Bracy (1879–1959) English artist, born in Halifax. He studied at the Slade School, and first went to Paris in 1910, when he met **Matisse** and the Fauves. In 1915 he exhibited with the London Group and he later painted much in Provence.

SMITH, Rodney (1860–1947) English evangelist, known as 'Gipsy Smith', born of nomadic gipsy parents near Epping Forest. He was converted at a Primitive Methodist meeting in 1876. Soon afterwards he joined **William Booth** and became one of the first officers in the newly formed Salvation Army, which he left in 1882 to carry on his evangelism under the auspices of the Free Church, preaching forcefully in America, Australia and elsewhere as well as in Britain.

SMITH, Sir Ross Macpherson (1892–1922) Australian aviator, born in Semaphore, South Australia. He joined the Australian Imperial Forces and fought with the 3rd Light Horse at Gallipoli. He transferred to the Australian Flying Corps in 1916 and became its most decorated pilot. He flew over Jerusalem, the first pilot to do so, taking **T E Lawrence** to meet Sharif Nazir. After the war he flew a Handley-Page bomber from Cairo to Calcutta, a distance of nearly 2400 miles and a record for the day, to survey an air route from England to Australia. In 1919 the Australian Government offered £10000 for the first Australian-crewed plane to fly there from England within 30 days. Ross joined his elder brother Keith (1890–1955) in London and in a Vickers Vimy bi-plane, with two Australian engineers, they set out, arriving in Darwin 28 days later, a feat for which both brothers were knighted. In 1922 Ross was killed in a trial flight of a Vickers Viking amphibian plane, while preparing for a round-the-world flight with his brother.

SMITH, Sophia (1796–1870) American philanthropist, born in Hartfield, Massachusetts. Inheriting her brother's fortune, on her pastor's advice she willed this money to be used to found a women's college. Smith College, Northampton, in Massachusetts, was opened in 1875.

SMITH, Stevie, pen-name of **Florence Margaret Smith** (1902–71) English poet and novelist, born in Hull. At the age of three she moved with her family to the house in the London suburb of Palmer's Green where she was to live with her aunt for most of her life. She attended the local High School and the North London Collegiate School for Girls before working for the Newnes publishing company. In 1935 she took a collection of her poems to a publisher, who rejected them and advised her to try a novel. This she did, and the result was *Novel on Yellow Paper*, published in 1936, a largely autobiographical monologue in an amusing conversational style, which proved a success and was followed in 1938 by *Over the Frontier*, in similar style. *The Holiday* (1949) was again to a great extent autobiographical but had a more conventional structure and told the story of a doomed love affair. Meanwhile her reputation as a poet was becoming established. *A Good Time Was Had By All* was published in 1937, the poetry light and childlike in tone, with chatty amusing language and short verses. She developed a more serious tone, with stronger themes, moving towards the concepts and language of Christianity. Loneliness is often her theme, as in *Not Waving but Drowning* (1957) and she is considered to be a comic writer, but as one who talks of serious matters in an amusing tone. Her work also includes *Mother, What is Man?* (1942), *Harold's Leap* (1950), *Selected Poems* (1962), *The Frog Prince* (1966) and *Scorpion* (1972). She wrote many reviews and critical articles, and produced a volume of the line-drawings that often accompanied her poems, entitled *Some Are More Human Than Others* (1958).

SMITH, Sydney (1771–1845) English clergyman, essayist and wit, born in Woodford, Essex. He was educated at Winchester and New College, Oxford, of which he became a fellow. He was ordained (1794) and served at Netheravon near Amesbury, and Edinburgh. In 1802, with **Francis Jeffrey**, **Francis Horner** and **Lord Brougham**, he started the *Edinburgh Review*. He next lived six years in London, and soon made his mark as a preacher, a lecturer at the Royal Institution on moral philosophy (1804–06), and a brilliant talker; but in 1809 was 'transferred' to the living of Foston in Yorkshire. In 1828 Lord Lyndhurst presented him to a prebend of Bristol, and next year enabled him to exchange Foston for Combe-Florey rectory, Somerset. In 1831 **Charles Grey, 2nd Earl Grey** appointed him a canon of St Paul's. His writings include 65 articles, collected in 1839 from the *Edinburgh Review*; *Peter Plymley's Letters* (1807–08) in favour of Catholic emancipation; *Three Letters on the Ecclesiastical Commission* (1837–39); and other letters and pamphlets on the ballot, American repudiation, the game laws, prison abuses, etc. Their author is chiefly remembered as the creator of 'Mrs Partington', a kindly, sensible humourist who stands immeasurably above **Theodore Hook**, if a good way below **Charles Lamb**.

SMITH, Sir Sydney Alfred (1883–1969) New Zealand forensic medical expert, born in Roxburgh. Educated at Victoria College, Wellington, and Edinburgh University, he was medical officer of health for New Zealand, professor of forensic medicine at Cairo and from 1917 principal medico-legal expert for the Egyptian government. He was Regius professor of forensic medicine at Edinburgh (1928–53) and dean of the medical faculty from 1931, playing a foremost part in the medical and ballistic aspects of crime detection, not least in the Merrett (1926) and Ruxton (1936) murder cases, often effectively opposing his brilliant English colleague, Sir **Bernard Spilsbury**. He wrote a *Text-Book of Forensic Medicine* (1925) and edited Taylor's *Principles and Practices of medical Jurisprudence*, and wrote an autobiography, *Mostly Murder* (1959).

SMITH, Sydney Goodsir (1915–75) New Zealand-born Scottish poet, born in Wellington, son of Sir **Sydney Alfred Smith**. He moved to Edinburgh in 1928 when his father was appointed a professor there. He studied at Edinburgh University and Oriel College, Oxford, and with such works as *Skail Wind* (1941), *The Devil's Waltz* (1946), *Under the Eildon Tree* (1948, a great modern love poem), *Orpheus and Eurydice* (1955), *So Late into the Night* (1952), *Figs and Thistles* (1959), established a reputation as the best modern Lallans poet after **MacDiarmid**. He published a loving description of Edinburgh in *Kynd Kittock's Land* in 1965. His first play, *The Wallace*, was commissioned for the Edinburgh Festival of 1960. He also wrote a comic novel, *Carotid Cornucopius* (1947).

SMITH, Theobald (1859–1934) American microbiologist and immunologist, born in Albany, New York, the greatest American bacteriologist of his generation. He received his medical degree from the Albany Medical College, and was subsequently associated with several American institutions, including Harvard University (professor, 1896–1915) and the Rockefeller Institute for Medical Research (1915–29). He studied both animal and human diseases, and first implicated an insect vector in the spread of disease when he showed that Texas cattle fever is spread by ticks. He worked on human and bovine tuberculosis, laid the scientific foundations for a cholera vaccine, improved the production of smallpox vaccine and diphtheria and tetanus antitoxins, and established precise techniques for the bacteriological examination of water, milk and sewage.

SMITH, Thomas See **SMITH, John Raphael**

SMITH, Sir Thomas (1514–77) English classical scholar, author of *De Republica Anglorum*, born in Saffron Walden. He became a fellow of Queen's College, Cambridge, and was knighted in 1548. He served as secretary of state and negotiated the peace of Troyes (1564).

SMITH, Thomas Southwood (1788–1861) English physician and sanitary reformer, born in Martock, Somerset. He took charge of a Unitarian chapel in Edinburgh in 1812 and at the same time studied medicine. In 1824 he became physician at the London Fever Hospital, publishing in 1830 his *Treatise on Fever*. **Jeremy Bentham** left him his body for dissection and Smith kept the skeleton fully clothed until it was transferred to University College, London.

SMITH, Tommie (1944–) American athlete, born in Ackworth, Texas. An outstanding sprinter, he set world records for both the 220 yards and the 200 metres in 1966 and was a member of the United States team which broke the world record for the 4 x 400 metres relay. In the 1968 Olympics at Mexico City he won the gold medal in the 200 metres in a world record time of 19.8 seconds, but caused considerable controversy by giving the Black Power salute while standing on the victor's rostrum.

SMITH, William (1769–1839) English civil engineer, known as the father of English geology, born in Churchill, Oxfordshire. In 1794 he was appointed engineer to the Somerset Coal Canal and began his study of the strata of England, introducing the law of strata identified by fossils. His epoch-making Geological Map of England (1815) was followed by 21 geologically-coloured maps of English counties (1819–24), in which he was assisted by his nephew, John Phillips (1800–74). He was awarded the first Wollaston medal (1831) and was an expert on irrigation.

SMITH, Sir William (1813–93) English lexicographer, born in London and educated at University College, London. His great work was as editor and part-author of the *Dictionary of Greek and Roman Antiquities* (1840–42), followed by the *Dictionary of Greek and Roman Biography and Mythology* (1843–49) and the *Dictionary of Greek and Roman Geography* (1853–57). He edited **Gibbon**'s *Decline and Fall* (1854), and also produced a *Dictionary of the Bible* (1860–63), a *Dictionary of Christian Antiquities* (1875–80), and a *Dictionary of Christian Biography and Doctrines* (1877–87). He was editor of *The Quarterly Review* from 1867 to his death.

SMITH, Sir William (1854–1914) Scottish businessman, and founder of the Boys' Brigade, born near Thurso, Caithness. An active worker in the Free College Church, Glasgow, and a member of the Lanarkshire Volunteers from 1874, he was well embarked on a successful career in commerce when he began his movement for 'the advancement of Christ's Kingdom among Boys' in 1883. Intended to meet a need at a vital stage in their lives, the organization instilled habits of discipline, provided recreation through camps and other pursuits, and was firmly based on Christian principles. By the year of Queen **Victoria**'s Jubilee (1897) (in which a B B captain was Lord Mayor of London), the movement had spread to every continent.

SMITH, William Henry (1792–1865) English newsagent. He entered the newsagent's business of his father in the Strand, London, in 1812 and aided by his brother, Henry Edward, expanded it into the largest in Britain by making extensive use of railways and fast carts for country deliveries.

SMITH, William Henry (1825–91) English newsagent, bookseller and statesman, born in London, son of **William Henry Smith** (1792–1865). He became his father's partner in 1846 and later assumed full control. The business steadily expanded, and in 1849 secured the privilege of selling books and newspapers at railway stations. Smith entered parliament in 1868, was financial secretary of the Treasury (1874–77), First Lord of the Admiralty (1877–80), and secretary for war (1885). In the second **Salisbury** ministry he was First Lord of the Treasury and leader of the Commons until his death.

SMITH, William Robertson (1846–94) Scottish theologian and orientalist, born in Keig, Aberdeenshire. He studied at Aberdeen, Edinburgh, Bonn and Göttingen, and in 1870 became professor of Hebrew and Old Testament Exegesis in the Free Church College, Aberdeen. His *Encyclopaedia Britannica* article 'Bible' (1875) was strongly attacked for heterodoxy, but he was acquitted of heresy (1880). He was deprived of his professorship (1881) for another article on 'Hebrew Language and Literature'. In 1883 he became Lord Almoner's professor of Arabic at Cambridge, in 1886 university librarian and Adams professor of Arabic (1889). He became co-editor and chief editor (1887) of the *Encyclopaedia Britannica*. His chief works were *The Old Testament in the Jewish Church* (1881), *The Prophets of Israel* (1882), and *The Religion of the Semites* (1889).

SMITH, Sir William Sidney (1764–1840) English naval commander, born in Westminster. He entered the navy in 1777, and in 1780 was promoted lieutenant for his bravery at Cape St Vincent. He became captain in 1782, and from 1790 to 1792 acted as adviser to the king of Sweden, and was decorated—hence his nickname 'the Swedish Knight'. In 1793 he aided **Hood** in burning the shops and arsenal at Toulon. In 1798 he was sent as plenipotentiary to Constantinople, and in 1799 raised Napoleon's siege of Acre. He aided **Abercromby** in Egypt, destroyed the Turkish fleet off Abydos (1807), blockaded the Tagus, and became vice admiral of the blue in 1810.

SMITHERS, Leonard Charles (1861–1907) English publisher of **Wilde**, **Beardsley** and other 1890s writers, born in Sheffield. At first he practised as a solicitor, being drawn into publishing through editing Sir **Richard Burton**'s verse translation of **Catullus**, adding his own prose translation of the remainder with scholarly skill (1894). It showed high aesthetic standards in production which he sought to maintain as he brought out Wilde's *The Ballad of Reading Gaol* (1898) and the hitherto unpublished and no longer performed *Importance of Being Earnest* and *An Ideal Husband* (1899), as well as the *Savoy* (which replaced the *Yellow Book*). He also published most of Beardsley's later work, the poems of **Ernest Dowson** and **Arthur Symons**, and the first collection of **Max Beerbohm**'s drawings. He was adjudged bankrupt in 1900, and, after trafficking in piracy and pornography, ended in utter destitution, supposedly exacerbated by women, drink and drugs.

SMITHSON, James Louis Macie (1765–1829) English chemist, born in Paris, the founder of the Smithsonian Institution. An illegitimate son of Sir Hugh Smithson Percy, 1st Duke of Northumberland, he devoted himself to chemistry and mineralogy. In a fit of pique at the Royal Society's rejection of a paper by him in 1826, he bequeathed the reversion of £105 000 to found an institution in Washington 'for the increase and diffusion of knowledge among men'. The Institution was established by an act of congress in 1846.

SMITHSON, Robert (1938–73) American 'Land artist', born in Passaic, New Jersey. He studied at the Art Students' League (1955–56) and at the Brooklyn Museum School. He took up Minimal Art in the 1960s, but from c.1966 he began to exhibit his 'Non-Sites'—maps of sites he had visited, together with samples of rocks and soil. He is best known for such earth works as the *Spiral jetty on the Great Salt Lake, Utah* (1970). He was killed in a plane crash while taking photographs of one of his earth works in Texas.

SMOLLETT, Tobias George (1721–71) Scottish novelist, born on the farm of Dalquharn in the Vale of Leven, Dunbartonshire, grandson of Sir James Smollett. He was educated at Dumbarton Grammar School and Glasgow University, where he took a degree in medicine. He moved to London in 1740 to find a producer for his tragedy, *The Regicide*, but, disappointed in his quest, sailed as surgeon's mate in the expedition to Carthagena against the Spanish in 1741. Three years later he settled in London, practising as a surgeon, but literature in the form of novel writing was his real interest. His first efforts were successes—*Roderick Random* (1748) and *Peregrine Pickle* (1751). The former is modelled on **Le Sage**'s *Gil Blas*, and as well as describing episodes in the life of the unprincipled hero it made use of Smollett's experiences in the Carthagena expedition. *Peregrine Pickle* pursues the hero's adventures in love and war throughout Europe. *Ferdinand, Count Fathom* (1753) is the story of another heartless villain, whom an easy repentance saves from the gallows. **Cervantes** was now his model—he translated *Don Quixote* in 1755—but his imitation of the master, *Sir Launcelote Greaves*, is crude work. In 1753 he settled in Chelsea editing the new *Critical Review*—which led to his imprisonment for libel in 1760—and writing his *History of England* (3 vols, 1757–58). Ordered abroad for his health, he visited France and Italy and saw little to please him. His caustic record, *Travels in France and Italy* (1766), earned for him **Sterne**'s nickname of 'Smelfungus'. His next publication was a coarse satire on public affairs, *The Adventures of an Atom* (1769). He wrote *Humphrey Clinker* (1771), which is much more kindly in tone and is still a favourite, in the form of a series of letters from and to members of a party touring round England and 'North Britain'. He spent the last years of his life abroad, and died in Livorno, Italy.

SMUTS, Jan Christian (1870–1950) South African statesman, born in Malmesbury, Cape Colony, and educated at Christ's College, Cambridge. In the Boer War he took the field with de la Rey; he entered the House of Assembly in 1907 and held several cabinet offices, subsequently succeeding **Louis Botha** as the premier of the Union of South Africa (1919). Entrusted during World War I with operations in German East Africa, he was made a member of the Imperial War Cabinet. As minister of justice under **Hertzog**, his coalition with the Nationalists in 1934 produced the United party, and he became prime minister in 1939; during World War II his counsel was sought by the War Cabinet.

SMYSLOV, Vasily Vasiliyevich (1921–) Russian chess player, born in Moscow, and world champion (1957–58). He made chess his career after narrowly failing an audition for the Bolshoi Opera in 1950. After drawing a world championship match against **Mikhail Botvinnik** in 1954, which allowed the holder to retain his title, he beat the same player in 1957, only to relinquish the championship in the 1958 re-match.

SMYTH, Dame Ethel Mary (1858–1944) English composer and suffragette, born in London. After studying at Leipzig she composed a Mass in D Minor, symphonies, choral works, and operas like *Der Wald* (1901), *The Wreckers* (1906), and *The Boatswain's Mate* (1916). As a crusader for women's suffrage she composed the battle-song of the Women's Social and Political Union ('The March of the Women', 1911), and was imprisoned for three months. Created DBE in 1922, she wrote the autobiographical *Female Pipings for Eden* (1933) and *What Happened Next* (1940).

SMYTHE, Francis Sydney (1900–49) English mountaineer, born in Maidstone. He was member of three Everest expeditions (1933, 1936 and 1938), and he shared the world's altitude climbing record. In 1930 he was a member of the Swiss Kanchenjunga expedition and was the first to climb the Himalayan peak Kamet in 1931. During World War II he commanded the Commando Mountain Warfare School. His many books, beautifully illustrated by his fine mountain photography, include *Kamet Conquered* (1932), *Camp Six* (1937), *Adventures of a Mountaineer* (1940), and *Over Welsh Hills* (1941).

SMYTHE, George Augustus See **STRANGFORD**

SMYTHE, Reg (Reginald Smith) (1917–) English strip cartoonist, born in Hartlepool, the creator of *Andy Capp*, the most popular British strip of all time. He started as a butcher's errand boy (1931), then became a regular soldier. After World War II he joined the Post Office and freelanced joke cartoons to the *Daily Mirror*, who invited him to contribute a regular joke for their new Northern edition in 1958. This became *Andy Capp*, the adventures of a feisty little layabout fonder of beer than of his wife, Florrie. He eventually became the first British strip to be syndicated worldwide. The strip was adapted as a stage musical and television series starring James Bolam (1987).

SMYTHSON, Robert (c.1535–1614) English architect. Trained as a mason, his first recorded work was at Longleat (1568), but his first major work was Wollaton Hall, Nottingham (1580–88), a lavish palace richly modelled and detailed. He developed a new vertical plan with the great hall set transversely, which revolutionized the spatial possibilities of contemporary buildings. Hardwick Hall, Derbyshire (1591–97) provides the quintessential Elizabethan house of state, combining a magnificent suite of state rooms, a grand processional route and the distinctive large costly windows. Other buildings attributed to Smythson include Worksop Manor, Balborough and Bolsover Little Castle.

SNEAD, Sam (Samuel Jackson) (1912–) American golfer, born in Hot Springs, Virginia. The leading postwar American professional golfer, he won the British Open in 1946, had three PGA championship wins and three Masters, and only the US Open eluded him. Known as 'Slamming Sam', his uncomplicated rhythmic style endeared him to spectators, while his relaxed, drawling delivery made him much in demand as a TV commentator. He holds the record number of US Tour victories (84), and did much to popularize his sport in the United States.

SNELL, George Davis (1903–) American immunologist, and joint winner of the 1980 Nobel prize for physiology or medicine. At the Jackson Laboratory, Bar Harbour, in Maine (1935–73), he conducted experiments in immunology that did much to make future organ transplants possible. He shared the Nobel prize with **Jean Dausset** and **Baruj Benacerraf**.

SNELL, John (1629–79) Scottish philanthropist, born in Colmonell, Ayrshire. Educated at Glasgow University, he fought for the royalists at Worcester (1651). He founded the Snell exhibitions at Balliol College, Oxford.

SNELL, Peter (1938–) New Zealand athlete, born in Opunake, Taranaki. He was a surprise winner of the Olympic 800 metres in 1960, but then went on to win gold in both the 800 and 1500 metres in the 1964 Olympics. He also achieved the Commonwealth Games 'double' in 1962 and set world records at 800 metres and one mile (twice). In 1962 he broke the world mile record at Wanganui, New Zealand, on an outdated all-grass track, to become his country's first sub-four-minute miler.

SNELL, Willebrod van Roijen, Latin **Snellius** (1580–1626) Dutch mathematician. He was professor of mathematics at Leiden (1613) and discovered the law of refraction known as Snell's law. He extensively developed the use of triangulation in surveying.

SNOW, C P (Charles Percy), 1st Baron (1905–80) English novelist and physicist, born in Leicester. He was educated at Alderman Newton's School, and then studied science at Leicester University College, and Christ's College, Cambridge, and became a fellow of Christ's College (1930–50) and a tutor there (1935–45). During World War II he was chief of scientific personnel for the ministry of labour, and was a Civil Service commissioner from 1945 to 1960. As a writer he started with a detective story, *Death Under Sail* (1932), followed by *The Search* (1934), set in the corridors of science and power. This heralded his major sequence of novels, under the general title *Strangers and Brothers*, starting with a novel of that name in 1940. The continuity is maintained by means of the character Lewis Eliot, through whose eyes the dilemmas of the age are focused. It was followed after the war by *The Light and the Dark* (1947) and *Time of Hope* (1949). *The Masters* (1951) stages the conflict aroused by the election of a new master in a Cambridge college. *The New Men* (1954) poses the dilemma of the scientists in the face of the potentials of nuclear fission. Other volumes are *Home-comings* (1956), *The Conscience of the Rich* (1958), *The Affair* (1960), *Corridors of Power* (1964), and *The Sleep of Reason* (1968). Several have been adapted for theatre and television. Though the chief characters of his cycle are rather supine, being manipulated to exhibit the expressed problems, mostly of power and prestige in all their facets, his work shows a keen appreciation of moral issues in a science-dominated epoch. His controversial *Two Cultures* (Rede lecture, 1959) discussed the dichotomy between science and literature and his belief in closer contact between them. Created a life peer in 1964, he was appointed parliamentary secretary at the ministry of technology (1964–66), and lord rector of St Andrews University (1961–64). In 1950 he married the novelist, **Pamela Hansford Johnson**.

SNOW, John (1813–58) English anaesthetist and epidemiologist, born in York. He was a young general practitioner when cholera first struck Britain in 1831–32, and his experience then convinced him that the disease was spread through contaminated water. After 1836 he practised in London, where, during the cholera outbreaks of 1848 and 1854, he carried out some brilliant epidemiological investigations, tracing one local outbreak to a well in Broad (now Broadwick) Street, Soho, into which raw sewage seeped. He had the pump handle removed. His additional work implicated the Thames, into which many of London's sewers drained and from which much of London's domestic water was obtained. Snow was also a pioneer anaesthetist. He did fundamental experimental work on ether and chloroform, devised apparatus to administer anaesthetics, and gave chloroform to Queen **Victoria** in 1853, during the birth of Prince **Leopold**.

SNOWDEN, Philip Snowden, 1st Viscount (1864–1937) English Labour statesman, born near Keighley. He was crippled in a cycling accident and forced to leave the civil service. He was chairman of the ILP (1930–36), socialist MP from 1906, opposed conscription (1915) and as Chancellor of the Exchequer in the Labour governments of 1924 and 1929 maintained orthodox policies and aggravated the financial crises. As a free trader he resigned from the national government in 1932, having been created viscount in 1931. He wrote an *Autobiography* (1934).

SNOWDON, Antony Armstrong-Jones, 1st Earl of (1930–) English photographer. Born in London and educated at Eton and Cambridge, he married HRH Princess **Margaret** in 1960 (divorced 1978). Starting as an assistant in the studios of Baron (Nahum), he became a free-lance photographer from 1951 and an artistic adviser to many publications, designing the Aviary of the London Zoo in 1965. A versatile photo-journalist, his informal portraits of the famous have often captured unusual facets of the subjects' personalities, especially those taken during stage performances. Within recent years he has brought great sympathy to photographic stories, recording the plight of the handicapped and disabled, both old and young, and has produced telling documentaries for television on similar themes.

SNYDER, Gary (1930–) American poet, born in San Francisco. He was educated at the University of California and is associated with the 'Beat' poets. From the outset he identified with the natural world and the values of simple living and hard physical work. His writing is informed with his interest in Asian religious practices and literary traditions. *Turtle Island* (1975) was awarded a Pulitzer prize.

SNYDERS, Frans (1579–1657) Flemish painter, born in Antwerp. A pupil of **Pieter Brueghel** the Younger, he specialized in still life and animals, often assisting **Rubens** and other painters in hunting scenes. He was court painter to the governor of the Low Countries.

SOAMES, Arthur Christopher John Soames, Baron Soames (1920–87) English Conservative politician. Educated at Eton and Sandhurst, he was commissioned in the Coldstream Guards and during World War II served in the Middle East, Italy and France. In 1947 he married Mary, daughter of Sir **Winston Churchill**, and embarked on a political career, entering the House of Commons in 1950. He held junior ministerial posts under Churchill and Sir **Anthony Eden** before becoming war secretary in 1958 in **Harold Macmillan**'s administration and then agriculture minister (1960–64). He was ambassador to France (1968–72) and a member of the European Commission (1973–77). He was made a life peer in 1978 and, with the return of the Conservatives under **Margaret Thatcher** in 1979, was made lord president and leader of the House of Lords. He will be best remembered for his successful governorship of Rhodesia (1979–80), overseeing its transition to the independent state of Zimbabwe.

SOANE, Sir John (1753–1837) English architect, born near Reading, the son of a mason. He trained under **George Dance** (the Younger) and was assistant to **Henry Holland**, then won the travelling scholarship of the Royal Academy and spent 1777–80 in Italy, developing a restrained Neo-Classical style of his own. He designed the Bank of England (1788–1833, now destroyed), Dulwich College Art Gallery (1811–14), and his own house in Lincoln's Inn Fields, London, which he bequeathed to the nation as the Sir John Soane Museum. He was professor at the Royal Academy from 1806.

SOARES, Mario Alberto Nobre Lopez (1924–) Portuguese politician. Educated at Lisbon University and in the Faculty of Law at the Sorbonne, Paris, he was politically active in the democratic socialist movement from his early twenties and was imprisoned for his activities on twelve occasions. In 1968 he was deported by **Salazar** to Sao Tome, returning to Europe in 1970 and living in exile in Paris until 1974 when he returned to co-found the Social Democratic party (PSD). In the same year he was elected to the Assembly and was soon brought into the government. He was prime minister (1976–78 and 1983–85), and then in 1986 was elected Portugal's first civilian president for 60 years.

SOBERS, Gary (Sir Garfield St Auburn) (1936–) West Indian cricketer, born in Bridgetown, Barbados, and arguably the greatest all-rounder in cricket history. In 93 Test matches for West Indies (captain 1953–74), he scored more than 8000 Test runs (including 26 centuries), and took 235 wickets and 110 catches. A cricketing phenomenon, he could deliver three kinds of bowling (fast, medium and slow spin) and bat with tireless brilliance and power. He holds the world record for the highest Test innings (365 not out, made at Kingston, Jamaica, in 1958). In county cricket he played for Nottinghamshire (captain 1968–74), and achieved the remarkable feat of scoring a maximum of 36 runs (six sixes) off one over against Glamorgan at Swansea in 1968. He was knighted on his retirement from cricket in 1975.

SOBIESKI See **JOHN III** of Poland; and for the 'Sobieski-Stuarts', see **ALBANIE**

SOBxRERO, Ascanio (1812–88) Italian chemist. He was the discoverer of nitroglycerine (1847).

SOCINUS, Faustus, or **Fausto Paulo Sozini** (1539–1604) Italian Protestant reformer, nephew of **Lælius Socinus**, born in Siena. A co-founder with his uncle of Socinianism, he studied theology at Basel, where he developed his uncle's anti-Trinitarian doctrines, arguing that **Luther** and **Calvin** had not gone far enough, and that human reason alone was the only solid basis of Protestantism. Later he became secretary to Duke Orsini in Florence (1563–75). In 1578, on the publication of his *De Jesu Christo Servatore*, he narrowly escaped assassination, and moved to Poland, where he became leader of an anti-Trinitarian branch of the Reformed church in Cracow. At the synod of Bresz in 1588 he argued against all the chief Christian dogmas—the divinity of **Christ**, propitiatory sacrifice, original sin, human depravity, the doctrine of necessity, and justification by faith. Denounced by the Inquisition in 1590, his possessions were confiscated. Destitute, he sought refuge in the village of Luclawice, where he died.

SOCINUS, Lælius, or **Lelio Francesco Maria Sozini** (1525–62) Italian Protestant reformer, and co-founder of the doctrine of Socinianism, born in Siena. A lawyer by training, he turned to Biblical research and settled in Zürich in 1548. He travelled widely, meeting leading Protestant reformers like **Calvin** and **Melanchthon**, and developed an anti-Trinitarian doctrine that tried to reconcile Christianity with humanism, which profoundly influenced his nephew, **Faustus Socinus**.

SOCRATES (469–399 BC) Greek philosopher, born in Athens, where he spent his whole life and died. He wrote nothing, founded no school and had no sect of disciples, but along with **Plato** and **Aristotle** is one of the three great figures in ancient philosophy. His pivotal influence was such that all earlier Greek philosophy is classified as 'preSocratic', and he was responsible for the decisive shift of philosophical interest from speculations about the natural world and cosmology to ethics and conceptual analysis. What little we know of his life and personality has to be gleaned, and interpreted, from three very different and each rather biased sources. **Aristophanes** the comic playwright caricatured him in his play *The Clouds* as a professional sophist of the kind he actually seems to have opposed and exposed. **Xenophon** was an admirer, but a soldier not a philosopher, and presents him as the sort of practical commonplace figure he was himself. Plato was by far his most brilliant associate and pupil and is the best and main source. He gives an unforgettable, dramatized portrait in such dialogues as the *Apology*, *Crito* and *Phaedo*, which describe Socrates' trial, last days and death; in later dialogues he makes Socrates the mouthpiece for what were undoubtedly Plato's own opinions. Socrates was apparently ugly, snub-nosed, with a paunch, and with a shrewish wife, Xanthippe. He took part as a good citizen in three military campaigns at Potidaea (432–29), Delium (424) and Amphipolis (422), and distinguished himself by his bravery, remarkable physical endurance and indifference to fatigue, climate and alcohol. He otherwise held aloof from politics, guided by his 'voice' which impelled him to philosophy and to the examination of conventional moral attitudes and assumptions with his fellow citizens and with the notable politicians, poets and gurus of the day. He represented himself as just the midwife for the opinions of others, and gave that as the reason for the Delphic Oracle's pronouncement that he was the wisest man alive. The 'Socratic method' was to ask for definitions of familiar concepts like justice, courage and piety, to elicit contradictions in the responses of his unfortunate interlocutors, and thus to demonstrate their ignorance, which he claimed ironically to share, and the need for a deeper and more honest analysis. This unpopular activity no doubt contributed to the demands for his conviction for 'impiety' and 'corrupting the youth', and he was tried at the age of 70; he rejected the option of merely paying a fine, declined a later opportunity to escape from prison, and was sentenced to die by drinking hemlock.

SODDY, Frederick (1877–1956) English radio chemist, born in Eastbourne. He studied at the University College of Wales and Merton College, Oxford, and became professor of chemistry at Glasgow, Aberdeen and Oxford. He collaborated with **Ernest Rutherford**, and in 1904 with **William Ramsay** discovered the transformation of radium emanation into helium. In 1913 he gave the name *isotope* to forms of the same element having identical chemical qualities but different atomic weights; and his discovery of this phenomenon earned him the Nobel prize for chemistry in 1921 and in 1955 the Albert medal.

SÖDERBERG, Hjalmar (1869–1941), Swedish novelist and playwright, known as 'the **Anatole France** of Sweden'. He wrote several collections of witty short stories, such as *Historietter* (1898), and novels of upper-middle-class life in Stockholm like *Förvillelser* (Aberrations, 1895), *Martin Bircks ungdom* (The Youth of Martin Birck), and *Doktor Glas* (1905). His plays included *Gertrud* (1905).

SÖDERBLOM, Nathan (1866–1931) Swedish churchman, born in Trönö near Söderhamm. Educated at Uppsala, he was ordained in 1893 and was Lutheran minister of the Swedish church in Paris, and later professor of history of religion at Uppsala (1901) and Leipzig (1912). In 1914 he was appointed archbishop of Uppsala and primate of the Swedish Lutheran Church. A leader in the ecumenical movement, he wrote several works on comparative religion and was the principal promoter of the Life and Work movement. He was awarded the 1930 Nobel prize for peace.

SÖDERGRAN, Edith (Irene) (1892–1923) Finnish Expressionist poet writing in Swedish, born in St Petersburg, Russia. Regarded as the originator of the Swedish-Finnish Modernist movement with her first collection of poems, *Dikter* (1916), she lived in total isolation in a house in the Karelian Isthmus (now in Soviet territory). Her best-known work is *Landet som icke är* (The Non-Existent Country), published posthumously in 1925.

SÖDERSTRÖM, Elisabeth Anna (1927–) Swedish soprano opera singer. After studying at the Stockholm Opera School she was engaged by the Royal Opera, Stockholm, in 1950. She made her début at Glyndebourne in 1957, the Metropolitan Opera Company in 1959 and Covent Garden in 1960 and has subsequently sung in all the leading international opera houses and toured extensively in Europe, the USA and the USSR. Her roles range from Nero in **Monteverdi**'s *Poppea*, through **Mozart**, **Tchaikovsky**'s Tatyana, **Strauss**, **Débussy**'s Mélisande to **Janácék**'s Jenúfa and Elena Makropoulos and Daisy Doody in **Blomdahl**'s *Aniara*. In the 1959 season she sang all three leading female roles in *Der Rosenkavelier*. She has published two autobiographical works, *I min tonart* (1978) and *Sjung ut, Elisabeth* (1986).

SODOMA, Il, sobriquet of **Giovanni Antonio Bazzi** (1477–1549) Italian religious and historical painter, born in Vercelli. A Lombard, he painted frescoes in Monte Oliveto Maggiore near Siena, before being called to the Vatican in 1508, where he was painting the fresco of *The Marriage of Alexander and Roxane* in the Villa Farnesian, but was later superseded by **Raphael**. His masterpieces date from his second Siena period and include *Christ at the Column*, *St Sebastian* and *Ecstasy of St Catherine*.

SOEHARTO See **SUHARTO**

SOEKARNO, Achmad See **SUKARNO**

SOFFICI, Ardengo (1878–1964) Italian artist and author, born in Rignano. He lived in Paris from 1900–1908, where his early experiments in Futurism were followed by a return to a more representational style founded on a study of the techniques of early Italian masters. Among his writings are *Giornale di bordo* (1915), *Estetica futurista* (1920) and *Diario di Borghi* (1933).

SOKOLOW, Anna (1912–) American dancer, choreographer and teacher, born in Hartford, Connecticut. She studied at the School of American Ballet and Metropolitan Opera Ballet School, leaving home as a teenager to become one of **Martha Graham**'s original dancers (1930–39). She began choreographing in 1934, founded her own troupe and, in 1939, the first modern dance company in Mexico, called La Paloma Azul. She retired from the stage in 1954, but continued to teach and make dances for her own and other companies, stage, television and film. As a choreographer, she is an uncompromising social critic. She has also conducted pioneering collaborations with experimental jazz composers.

SOLARIO, Antonio (c.1382–1455) Neapolitan painter, born in Civita in the Abruzzi, and nicknamed 'Lo Zingaro' (the Gipsy). Originally a blacksmith, he painted frescoes in the Benedictine monastery at Naples.

SOLIMAN See **SÜLEYMAN**

SOLIS Y RIBADENEYRA, Antonio de (1610–86) Spanish author. He was private secretary to **Philip IV** and historiographer of the Indies. He wrote poems and dramas, and *Historia de la Conquista de Mexico* (1684).

SOLOGUB, Fedor, pseud of **Fedor Kuzmich Teternikov** (1863–1927) Russian novelist. He wrote *The Little Demon* (trans 1916), and many short stories, fables, fairy tales and poems.

SOLOMON (c.1015–977 BC) king of Israel, the second son of **David** and Bathsheba. His reign was outwardly splendid. The kingdom attained its widest limit; the temple and royal palaces were built on an unprecedented scale of magnificence. But the taxation entailed by the luxury of the court bred the discontent that led in the next reign to the disruption of the kingdom; and the king's alliance with heathen courts and his idolatrous queens and concubines provoked the discontent of the prophetic party. Solomon was credited with transcendent wisdom; in later Jewish and Muslim literature he was believed to control the spirits of the invisible world. There is no reason to suppose that he had anything to do with any of the works to which his name has been attached—Proverbs, Ecclesiastes, Song of Solomon, and, in the Apocrypha, the Wisdom of Solomon.

SOLOMON, professional name of **Solomon Cutner** (1902–88) English pianist, born in London. After appearing with enormous success as a child prodigy, he retired for some years' further study, and won a high reputation as a performer of the works of **Beethoven**, **Brahms** and some modern composers. In 1955 he suffered a stroke which cut short his career.

SOLOMON, Solomon Joseph (1860–1927) English portrait and mural painter, born in London. He served in World War I and initiated the use of camouflage in the British army.

SOLON (640 or 638–559 BC) Athenian lawgiver, a merchant and a poet. Archon in 594 (or 591), in a time of economic distress, he was appointed to reform the constitution. He set free all people who had been enslaved for debt (Seisachtheia), reformed the currency, and admitted a fourth class (Thetes) to the Ecclesia, so that they elected the magistrates, and to the Heliaea, so that they judged them. Thus he laid the foundations for the Athenian democracy; but he was a moderate and kept many privileges of the wealthy. After ten years' voluntary exile, he returned (580), and, in a poem, stirred up the Athenians to capture 'lovely Salamis' (c. 569). He died soon after the usurpation of **Pisistratus**, the story of his connection with Croesus being legendary.

SOLOVIEV, Vladimir (1853–1900) Russian philosopher, theologian and poet, born in Moscow, son of the historian Sergei Mikhailovitch Soloviev. He proposed a universal Christianity which would unite the Catholic and Orthodox churches, and attempted a synthesis of religious philosophy with science. His main works were *The Crisis of Western Philosophy* (1875), *The Philosophical Principles of Integral Knowledge* (1877), *Russia and the Universal Church* (1889) and *The Justificaion of the Good* (1898).

SOLOW, Robert Merton (1924–) American economist, born in Brooklyn. Educated at Harvard, he has been a professor at the Massachusetts Institute of Technology since 1958. He was awarded the 1987 Nobel prize for economics for his 'study of the factors which permit production growth and increased welfare'.

SOLTI, Sir Georg (1912–) Hungarian-born British conductor, born in Budapest. He appeared as a pianist, aged twelve, and entered the Franz Liszt Academy of Music, studying with **Bartók**, **Dohnányi**, and **Kodály**. He assisted **Bruno Walter** and **Toscanini** at Salzburg (1935–37) and made a notable conducting début at the Budapest Opera with *Le nozze di Figaro* (1938). Anti-semitic pressure led him to leave for Switzerland in 1939, where he had success as pianist and conductor. Post-war appointments included musical directorships of the Bavarian State Opera (1946–52) and at Covent Garden (1961–71). Between these he established an outstanding reputation in the USA, and also conducted the Chicago Symphony Orchestra (from 1969), with which he toured extensively. He made a pioneering recording of **Wagner**'s *Ring* cycle for the Decca company, and conducted it at Salzburg and Bayreuth (1983). He took British nationality in 1972.

SOLVAY, Ernest (1838–1922) Belgian industrial chemist, born in Rebecq. He solved the practical problems of the ammonia–soda process for the production of sodium carbonate (1863) which eventually replaced the earlier Leblanc process.

SOLZHENITSYN, Aleksandr Isayevich (1918–) Russian writer, born in Kislovodsk. He was brought up in Rostov where he graduated in mathematics and physics in 1941. After distinguished service with the Red Army in World War II, he was imprisoned (1945–53) for unfavourable comment on **Stalin**'s conduct of the war. Rehabilitated in 1956, his first novel, *One Day in the Life of Ivan Denisovich* (1962, trans 1963), set in a prison camp, was acclaimed both in **Khrushchev**'s Russia and the West, but his denunciation in 1967 of the strict censorship in Russia led to the banning of his later novels, *The Cancer Ward* (2 vols, trans 1968, 1969) and *The First Circle* (trans 1968). They are semi-autobiographical, as he himself has suffered from cancer, and expose corruption in Russian society while defending socialism. He was expelled from the Soviet Writers' Union in 1969, and was awarded the Nobel prize for literature in 1970. After some trouble with the authorities, he accepted it. His novel, *August, 1914*, the first part of a projected trilogy on the theme of the emergence of modern Russia, was published in the West in 1971 (trans 1972), and *The Gulag Archipelago 1918–56* (3 vols), a factual account of the Stalinist terror, between 1973 and 1975. In 1974 he was deported to West Germany and later settled in the USA. His memoirs, *The Oak and the Calf* (1975), were published in translation in 1980.

SOMARE, Michael Thomas (1936–) Papua New Guinea politician. Educated at Sogeri Secondary School, he worked initially as a teacher (1956–62) and then a journalist (1966–68) before founding the pro-independence Pangu Pati (PP: Papua New Guinea party) in 1967. He was elected to the House of Assembly a year later and in 1972 became chief minister. After independence in 1975 he was prime minister, heading a coalition government. He was forced to resign in 1980 in the wake of a government corruption scandal, but returned as prime minister (1982–85). In 1988 he stepped down as PP leader and became foreign minister in the government of Rabbie Namaliu.

SOMERS, Sir George (1554–1610) English colonist. A founder of the South Virginia company, in 1610 he was commander of a fleet of settlers which was shipwrecked on the Bermudas (originally known as the Somers Islands), and claimed the islands for the British crown.

SOMERS, John, 1st Baron (1651–1716) English Whig statesman, born in Worcester, an attorney's son. He studied at Trinity College, Oxford, and was called to the bar in 1676. Associated with the 'country party', he was one of the counsel for the Seven Bishops (1688) and presided over the drafting of the Declaration of Rights; and after the Revolution was successively solicitor-general, attorney-general, and lord keeper of the Great Seal, until in 1697 he became Lord Chancellor and Baron Somers of Evesham. Highly regarded as a judge, he was **William III**'s most trusted minister, and was the object of frequent attacks. One of these resulted in his being deprived of the seal (1700), and another the following year in an impeachment by the Commons, rejected by the Lords. The *Somers Tracts* (1748), state papers from his library, were re-edited by Sir **Walter Scott** (1809–15).

SOMERSET, Dukes of See **SEYMOUR**

SOMERSET, Edward See **WORCESTER, Marquis of**

SOMERSET, Henry See **BEAUFORT, Duke of**

SOMERSET, James See **SHARP, Granville**

SOMERVELL, Sir Arthur (1863–1937) English composer, born in Windermere. He is known for the cantata *The Forsaken Merman*, *Thalassa*, a symphony, children's operettas and for his collection of English folksongs.

SOMERVILLE, Edith (Anna Oenone) (1858–1949) Irish novelist, born in Corfu, the daughter of an army officer and cousin of **Violet Martin** ('Martin Ross'). As a baby she returned to the family home of Drishane in Skibbereen, County Cork. Educated at Alexandra College, Dublin, she studied painting in London, Düsseldorf and Paris, and became a magazine illustrator. She met her cousin, Violet Martin in 1886, with whom she began a lasting literary partnership as 'Somerville and Ross'. Starting with *An Irish Cousin* (1889), they completed 14 works together, including *The Real Charlotte* (1894), *Some Experiences of an Irish RM* (1899) and *In Mr Knox's Country* (1915). After Violet's death in 1915, Edith continued to write as 'Somerville and Ross', producing *Irish Memoirs* (1917) and *The Big House at Inver* (1925). A forceful character, she became the first woman Master of Foxhounds in 1903, and was Master of the West Carberry pack from

1912 to 1919. She was also a founder-member of the Irish Academy of Letters (1933).

SOMERVILLE, Sir James Fownes (1882–1949) English naval commander. As a radio communications specialist he served in the Dardanelles (1915), and in the Grand Fleet (1915–18). In the West Indies (1938–39), he was invalided home with suspected tuberculosis but volunteered at the time of Dunkirk and was recalled to the active list in 1940. As vice admiral in the Mediterranean, he sank the French ships at Oran (1940), shelled Genoa (1941), helped in the sinking of the *Bismarck* (1941), took part in the Malta convoy battle (1941), and after the entry of the Japanese into the war, became commander-in-chief of the British fleet in the Indian ocean. In 1945 he was promoted admiral of the fleet.

SOMERVILLE, Mary née **Fairfax** (1780–1872) Scottish scientific writer, born in Jedburgh. The daughter of Admiral Sir William Fairfax, she lived in London from 1816, where she moved in intellectual and scientific circles, and corresponded with foreign scientists. In 1831 she published *The mechanism of the heavens*, an account for the general reader of **Pierre Simon Laplace**'s *Mécanique Céleste*. This had great success and she wrote several further expository works on science. She supported the emancipation and education of women, and Somerville College (1879) at Oxford is named after her.

SOMERVILLE, William (1675–1742) English poet, born in Wolseley in Staffordshire. Educated at Winchester School and New College, Oxford (where he became a fellow), he was the squire of Edstone, Warwickshire. He wrote *The Chase* (1735) a long poem in praise of hunting. He also wrote *Field Sports* (1742), and on hawking, and *Hobbinol* (1740), a burlesque on rural May Day games.

SOMMERFELD, Arnold (1868–1951) German physicist, born in Königsberg. Professor of mathematics at Clausthal (1897), of physics at Aachen (1900) and at Munich (1906), with Felix Klein he developed the theory of the gyroscope. He researched into wave spreading in wireless telegraphy, applied the quantum theory to spectral lines, developed the **Bohr** atomic model, and evolved a theory of the electron in the metallic state.

SON OF SAM See **BERKOWITZ, David**

SONDHEIM, Stephen Joshua (1930–) American composer and lyricist. As a young man, he studied lyric-writing with **Oscar Hammerstein II**, and wrote incidental music for *Girls of Summer* (1956), before writing the lyrics for **Bernstein**'s *West Side Story* (1957). The first shows for which he wrote both the music *and* the lyrics—still rather unusual in musicals—were *A Funny Thing Happened on the Way to the Forum* (1962) and *Anyone Can Whistle* (1964). *Company* (1970), about married life in New York, was followed by *Follies* (1971) and *A Little Night Music* (1973), *Pacific Overtures* (1976), *Sweeney Todd, The Demon Barber of Fleet Street* (1979), *Merrily We Roll Along* (1981), *Sunday in the Park with George* (1984), and *Into the Woods* (1986).

SONNINO, Baron Sidney (1847–1922) Italian statesman, born in Pisa of an English mother. He entered parliament in 1880, was finance minister 1893–96, premier 1906 and 1909–10, and as foreign minister (1914–20) denounced the Triple Alliance and brought Italy into the European War (May 1915).

SONTAG, Susan (1933–) American critic, born in New York City. Though she has written novels and stories, she is best known for her innovative essays for which she has been dubbed a 'new intellectual'. Her influential books include *The Style of Radical Will* (1969), *On Photography* (1976) and *Illness as Metaphor* (1978).

SOONG, Charles Jones (d.1927) Chinese merchant and Methodist missionary, father of **Ching Ling, Mayling** and **Tse-ven Soong**, born on Hainan Island. He went to the USA in 1880, was converted to Christianity and educated at Vanderbilt University. He returned to Shanghai, founded the first YMCA there and set up as Bible publisher and salesman.

SOONG, Mayling See **CHIANG KAI-SHIEK**

SOONG, Tse-ven, abbreviated **T V** (1894–1971) Chinese financier, born in Shanghai, son of **Charles Jones Soong**. He studied at Harvard and Columbia, and became finance minister of the Nationalist Government at Canton (1925–27) and at Nanking (1928–33). He westernized Chinese finances and standardized the Chinese currency, and founded the Bank of China in 1936. He was foreign minister from 1942 to 1945. In 1949 he went to the USA.

SOPER, Baron Donald Oliver (1903–) English Methodist minister, born in Wandsworth, London. Widely known for his open-air speaking on London's Tower Hill, he was superintendent of the West London Mission (1936-78), and has written many books on Christianity and social questions, and particularly on international issues from the pacifist angle. He was president of the Methodist Conference in 1953, and was created a life peer in 1965.

SOPHIA (1630–1714) Electress of Hanover, youngest daughter of **Elizabeth**, queen of Bohemia. In 1658 he married Ernest Augustus, Duke of Brunswick-Lüneburg, afterwards Elector of Hanover. She was the mother of **George I**.

SOPHIA (1657–1704) regent of Russia from 1682 to 1689, half-sister of **Peter the Great**. On the death of her father, Fedor, in 1676, she became regent for her mentally handicapped brother, Ivan, and for her half-brother, Peter, who was still a minor. During her regency a treaty of 'permanent peace' was signed with Poland and treaties were also signed with Sweden and Denmark (1684) and with China (1689). Unsuccessful campaigns against the Turks in the Crimea (1687,1689) did much to discredit the regent and in 1689 Peter assumed power, confining Sophia to a convent, where, following a rising in her favour in 1698, she was obliged to take the veil under the name of Susanna.

SOPHIA CHARLOTTE (1668–1705) queen of Prussia as wife of **Frederick I**, and sister of **George I** of Britain. She was the daughter of Ernest Augustus, the first Elector of Hanover, and **Sophia**, daughter of **Elizabeth**, queen of Bohemia. In 1684 she married Prince Frederick, and greatly encouraged his patronage of learning and the arts. The district of Charlottenburg in West Berlin was named after her.

SOPHOCLES (c.496–405 BC) Athenian tragedian, one of the great figures of Greek drama, born in Colonus Hippius, an Athenian suburb. He had to forgo his ambitions for the stage on account of a weak voice. He wrote well over a hundred items, most of them conventional satirical plays of which only the *Ichneutae* survives, as well as seven major plays, still extant, all written after his victory over **Aeschylus** in a dramatic contest in 468. He won first prize at the Great Dionysia 18 times. The problem of burial is prominent in both the *Ajax* and *Antigone* (possibly c.441), in the first an Olympian directive that hatred should not pursue a noble adversary beyond the grave, in the second as a clash between sisterly compassion for a dead traitor brother and the stately proprieties of King Creon. Aeschylus, **Euripides** and Sophocles each wrote versions of *Electra*, the gruesome matricide by Orestes in revenge for his father's death at the hands of his mother's paramour. The great Sophoclean masterpiece, however, is *Oedipus Tyrannus*, on which Aristotle based his aesthetic theory of drama in the *Poetica* and from which **Freud** derived the name and function of the 'Oedipus complex'. King Oedipus proclaims sentence on the unknown murderer of his father Laius, whose presence is thought to be the cause of a plague at Thebes. By a gradual unfolding of incidents, he learns that he was the assassin and that Jocasta his wife is also his mother. He blinds himself, goes into exile and Jocasta commits suicide. The dramatic characteristics are the gradual reversal in fortune of an estimable, conventionally 'good' person, through some untoward discovery in personal relationships, but also linked to some seemingly minor defect in character, in Oedipus' case, pride. This combination of a minor defect with the external cruel machinations of *até*, or personal destiny abetted by the gods, constitutes, according to Aristotle, the famous 'tragic flaw' which arouses the tragic emotions of pity and fear in the spectator and allows their purgation in a harmless manner. This is in sharp contrast to Aeschylean tragedy, which is essentially static. There is no development in the plot; the hero is doomed from the beginning. The *Trachiniae* explores the ruinous love of Heracles and Deianira. The *Philoctetes* (produced in 409) and *Oedipus Coloneus* would hardly be called tragic, except for the grave circumstances which attend the achievement of glory.

SOPHONISBA (d.c.204 BC) Carthaginian noblewoman, daughter of a Carthaginian general. She was betrothed to the Numidian prince Masinissa but for reasons of state during the 2nd Punic War (218–202 BC) married his rival Syphax. In 203 Syphax was defeated by a Roman army led by Masinissa, who took Sophonisba captive and married her. The Romans objected to this marriage and Masinissa gave her up, but sent her poison to prevent her being sent as a captive to Rome. **Corneille**, **Voltaire** and **Alfieri** have written tragedies around this theme.

SOPWITH, Sir Thomas Octave Murdoch (1888–1989) British aircraft designer and sportsman. He won the Baron de Forest prize in 1910 for flying across the English Channel. In 1912 he founded the Sopwith Aviation Company at Kingston-on-Thames, where he designed and built many of the aircraft used in World War I. Chairman of the Hawker Siddeley Group from 1935, he was president from 1963, and chairman of the Society of British Aircraft Constructors (1925–27). A keen yachtsman, he competed for the America's Cup in 1934.

SORABJI, (Leon Dudley) Kaikhosru Shapurji (1892–1988) British composer, pianist, and polemical essayist of Parsi and Spanish-Sicilian descent, born in Chingford, Essex. Largely self-taught, his compositional style combines extraordinary technical complexity with contrapuntal ingenuity, lavishness of texture and epic form. These qualities are exemplified in his *Opus Clavicembalisticum* (premiered by him in Glasgow, 1930): a work of four hours, in three parts with twelve subdivisions, written on three or four staves throughout, including one theme with 49 variations, a passacaglia with 81 variations, and four colossal fugues. Not every work is on this scale, but some actually exceed it. In 1936 Sorabji forebade performance of his music, a ban lifted only in 1975. In addition to piano music he wrote concertos, organ works, choral music and songs. His pungent, witty and outspoken critical writings were collected in *Around Music* (1932) and *Mi Contra Fa* (1947).

SORAYA, properly **Princess Soraya Esfandiari Bakhtiari** (1932–) ex-queen of Persia, born in Isfahan of Persian and German parents. She was educated at Isfahan, and later in England and Switzerland, and became queen of Persia on her marriage to his majesty **Muhammad Reza Shah Pahlavi** (1951). The marriage was dissolved in 1958.

SORBON, Robert de (1201–74) French churchman, and **Louis IX**'s confessor. He founded the college of the Sorbonne in c.1257.

SORBY, Henry Clifton (1826–1908) English geologist and metallurgist, born in Woodbourne, Sheffield. He was the first to study rocks in thin sections under the microscope, and he adapted the technique to metals by treating polished surfaces with etching materials. He also wrote on biology, architecture and Egyptian hieroglyphics, and was elected FRS in 1857.

SOREL, Agnes (c.1422–1450) French lady, born in Fromenteau, Touraine. She was the mistress from 1444 of **Charles VII** of France. She exerted considerable influence over him, and was given an estate at Beauté-sur-Marne. She may have died of poison.

SOREL, Albert (1842–1906) French historian, born in Honfleur. He wrote *L'Europe et la révolution française* (8 vols, 1885–1904).

SOREL, Georges (1847–1922) French social philosopher, born in Cherbourg, Manche. He was trained as an engineer and worked in the government department of bridges and roads from 1870; but he resigned in 1892 to devote himself to the study of philosophy and social theory, his particular mentors being **Nietzsche**, **Marx** and **Bergson**. In his political commitments he seemed to veer rapidly and often from one extreme position to another—Marxism, anarchism, royalism—but he consistently affirmed the moral importance of self-expression and self-realization through the free and creative exercise of the Will. His best-known work is *Réflexions sur la violence* (1908) which enlarged the usual definition of 'violence' to include the violence implicit in conventional moral and religious principles and in laws and institutions. He argued that serious political opposition must also resort to violence and that socialism would only be achieved by confrontation and revolution. He advocated the use of 'social myths' like the idea of a general strike, to inspire and focus the necessary collective action. His work was read by political leaders as different as **Lenin** and **Mussolini**, and some of his ideas were enthusiastically invoked in the student unrest of the 1960s.

SÖRENSEN, Sören Peter Lauritz (1868–1939) Danish biochemist. He studied chemistry at Copenhagen, and was director of chemistry at the Carlsberg Laboratory from 1901, did pioneer work on hydrogen-ion concentration, and in 1909 invented the pH scale for measuring acidity.

SORLEY, Charles Hamilton (1895–1915) Scottish poet, born in Aberdeen where his father was professor of moral philosophy. Educated at King's College Choir School, in 1908 he won a scholarship to Marlborough College where, impressed by the rolling Wiltshire countryside, he started to write poetry. Just before the outbreak of World War I, and prior to taking his place at University College, Cambridge, he visited Germany, which coloured ambivalently his attitude to the events that followed. One of the first to enlist, he believed in the war as a necessary evil, as his poems show. In 1915, he went with his battalion to France, where he was killed by a sniper at the battle of Loos. *Marlborough and Other Poems* was published in 1916, thanks to his family, and his best and probably unfinished work is unsentimental, direct and free from cant. *The Collected Poems of Charles Hamilton Sorley* were edited in 1985.

SOROKIN, Pitirim Alexandrovich (1889–1968) Russian-born American sociologist, born in Turia. He lived in the United States after 1923. After a varied career as factory hand, journalist, tutor, cabinet minister (1917), he became professor of sociology at Leningrad (1919–22), specializing in the study of the social structure of rural communities. Banished by the Soviet government in 1922, he became professor at Minnesota and then (1931–64) at Harvard. His works include *Sociology of Revolution* (1925), *Principles of Rural-Urban Sociology* (1929), *Crisis of our Age* (1941), *Russia and the United States* (1944), *Altruistic Love* (1950), and *Fads and Foibles of Modern Sociology* (1956).

SOROLLA Y BASTIDA, Joaquin (1863–1923) Spanish painter, born in Valencia. He became one of the leading Spanish Impressionists, known especially for his sunlight effects, as in *Swimmers* and *Beaching the Boat* (Metropolitan, New York).

SORSA, (Taisto) Kalevi (1930–) Finnish politician, born in Keuruu. Educated at what is now the University of Tampere, he worked in publishing, with the United Nations and in the ministry of education, before moving directly into politics, becoming secretary-general of the Social Democratic party (SDP) in 1969 and its president in 1975. He entered parliament (Eduskunta) in 1970, soon becoming a central figure, foreign minister (1972 and 1975–76), prime minister (1972–75, 1977–79, 1982–87) and deputy prime minister from 1987, when the SDP entered into a coalition with their main rivals, the conservative National Coalition party (KOK).

SOSIGENES (fl.50 BC) Greek astronomer, probably of Alexandria. He assisted **Julius Caesar** with his reform of the calendar (c.46 BC). The resulting Julian calendar is based on a $365\frac{1}{4}$-day year (having a 'leap year' with an extra day every four years) and conforms with the Sun and seasons. The modern (Gregorian) calendar is closely similar. Sosigenes's writings have been almost entirely lost.

SOTHEBY, John (1740–1807) English auctioneer and antiquarian. He was the nephew of Samuel Baker (d.1778) who founded at York Street, Covent Garden, London, in 1744 the first sale room in Britain exclusively for books, manuscripts and prints. He became a director of the firm (1780–1800) which became known as Leigh and Sotheby. In 1803 it was transferred to the Strand. His nephew, Samuel (1771–1842), and grand-nephew, Samuel Leigh (1806–61), an authority on cataloguing and early printing, continued the business.

SOTHERN, Edward Askew (1826–81) English comic actor, born in Liverpool. In 1849 he joined a company of players in Jersey, and soon afterwards the stock company in Birmingham. From 1852 he appeared in the USA, with small success, until in 1858 he made his name as Lord Dundreary in **Tom Taylor's** *Our American Cousin*.

SOTO, Fernando de (c.1496–1542) Spanish explorer, born in Jerez de los Caballeros. In 1518–20 he accompanied Pedro Arias de Ávila to Darien, served in Nicaragua in 1527, and assisted **Pizarro** in the conquest of Peru, returning to Spain with 180000 ducats. **Charles V** gave him permission to conquer Florida, and appointed him governor of Cuba; in May 1539 with 600 men he anchored in Tampa Bay, and the long search for gold was begun. For three years, harassed by hostile Indians, the ever-decreasing company continued their toilsome march. In 1541 the Mississippi was crossed, and the third winter was spent on Washita River. Returning to the Mississippi in the spring, Soto died of a fever on its banks; and to conceal his death from the Indians, his body was lowered at midnight into the great river he had discovered. Barely half of his followers finally reached Mexico.

SOTTSASS, Ettore Jnr (1917–) Italian architect and designer, born in Innsbruck. He trained as an architect in Turin, graduating in 1939. After serving in World War II and a short period in an architectural practice, he moved to Milan and set up his own design office in 1946, becoming involved in the reconstruction of northern Italian towns. As an industrial designer he is closely associated with the firm of Olivetti for which, after 1958, he designed several typewriters and other office equipment including furniture systems. His departure from 'mainstream' design in the 1970s, culminating in his leading role in the 'Memphis' group (formed 1981), caused much bewilderment and to him, perhaps, a good deal of amusement. The Memphis style, characterized by bizarre, often asymmetric designs, bright colours and patterned plastic laminates, has had its influence and, probably, its day, but it has not prevented Sottsass from continuing his serious design work.

SOUBISE, Charles de Rohan, Prince de (1715–87) French soldier. In the Seven Years' War (1756–63) he was defeated by **Frederick II, the Great** at Rossbach (1757), but next year gained victories at Sondershausen and Lützelburg.

SOUFFLOT, Jacques Germain (1709–80) French architect, born in Irancy. He trained in Italy (1731–38) and became the leading French exponent of Neo-Classicism. He designed the Panthéon and the École de Droit in Paris, the Hôtel Dien in Lyon, and the cathedral in Rennes.

SOULAGES, Pierre (1919–) French artist, born in Rodez. One of the most original of the established non-figurative painters, he designed décors for the theatre and ballet.

SOULT, Nicolas Jean de Dieu (1769–1851) French soldier, born in Saint-Amans-la-Bastide, Tarn. He enlisted in 1785, and in 1794 became general of brigade. **Masséna** made him general of division (April 1799), and owed to him much of the glory of his Swiss and Italian campaigns. In 1804 Soult was appointed a marshal of France by **Napoleon**. He led the right wing in the campaign that closed at Austerlitz, did good service in the Prussian and Russian campaigns (1806-07), and after the peace of Tilsit was created Duke of Dalmatia. In Spain he pursued the retreating British, and, though repulsed at La Coruña, forced them to evacuate the country. He then conquered Portugal, and governed it till the arrival of Wellesley (**Wellington**) at Coimbra made him retreat to Galicia. In 1809–10, as commander-in-chief in Spain, he gained a brilliant victory at Ocaña and overran Andalusia. In attempting to succour Badajos he was defeated by **Beresford** at Albuera (1811). After Salamanca and the advance of the British on Madrid, Soult, vexed at the obstinacy of **Joseph Bonaparte** and the rejection of his plans, demanded his recall; but Napoleon, after Vitoria, sent him back to Spain. By brilliant tactics he neutralized the strategy of Wellington, but was defeated at Orthez and Toulouse. He turned a royalist after Napoleon's abdication, but joined him again on his return from Elba and was made chief of staff. After Waterloo he rallied the wreck of the army at Laon, but agreed with **Carnot** as to the uselessness of further resistance. He was banished and not recalled till 1819, but was gradually restored to all his honours and was minister of war (1830–34).

SOUPHANOUVONG, Prince (1902–) Laotian politician and half-brother of Prince Souvanna Phouma. Prime minister of Laos for much of the period between 1951 and 1975, and head of the moderate Lao Issara, he was educated in Paris, where he studied engineering. On returning to Laos in 1938 he became active in the nationalist movement. In 1950 he founded the Chinese-backed, communist Lao Independence Front, which later became known as the Pathet Lao (Land of the Lao), to fight, first, against French rule and then, from 1954, against the ruling Lao Issara and rightist forces. In 1975, following the declaration of a socialist republic, he became state president, retaining this largely ceremonial position until he retired in 1986. He was a moderating influence within the ruling Lao People's Revolutionary party.

SOUSA, John Philip (1854–1932) American composer and bandmaster, born in Washington, DC. His early training as a conductor was gained with theatre orchestras, and in 1880 he became conductor of the United States Marine Band. His own band, formed twelve years later, won an international reputation. As well as more than a hundred popular marches, he composed ten comic operas, the most successful of which was *El Capitán*.

SOUTAR, William (1898–1943) Scottish poet, born in Perth, the son of a joiner. Educated at Perth Academy, he was conscripted into the Royal Navy (1916–19), where he contracted a form of spondylitis (ossification of the vertebrae), which was to confine him to bed for the last 13 years of his life. After demobilization he studied first medicine and then English at Edinburgh, returning to Perth in 1923. As an undergraduate he published his first volume of verse, anonymously, in *Gleanings by an Undergraduate* (1923), followed by *Conflict* (1931). In 1933 he published his first volume of verse in Scots, *Seeds in the Wind*, for children. This was followed by his *Poems in Scots* (1935) and *Riddles in Scots* (1937), which gave him a permanent place in the Scottish literary revival. The best examples of his work in English are *In the Time of Tyrants* (1939) and the collection *The Expectant Silence* (1944). His remarkable *Diaries of a Dying Man*, published in 1954, mark him out as an outstanding diarist.

SOUTH, Robert (1634–1716) English High Church theologian and preacher, born in Hackney. From Westminster he passed as a student to Christ Church College, Oxford, in 1651. He was for a time in sympathy with Presbyterianism, but in 1658 he received orders secretly and in 1660 was appointed public orator of Oxford. His vigorous sermons, full of mockery of the Puritans, delighted the restored royalists. He became domestic chaplain to **Clarendon**, prebendary of Westminster in 1663, canon of Christ Church in 1670, and rector of Islip in 1678, but his outspokenness prevented any further preferment. He 'aquiesced in' the Glorious Revolution of 1688, but strongly opposed the scheme of Comprehension. He published *Sermons on Several Occasions* (new ed 1878).

SOUTHAMPTON, Henry Wriothesley, 2nd Earl (1545–81) English courtier, son of Sir **Thomas Wriothesley**, 1st Earl. He turned Catholic and became involved in intrigues for the advancement of **Mary, Queen of Scots**, for which activity he was imprisoned in the Tower.

SOUTHAMPTON, Henry Wriothesley, 3rd Earl (1573–1624) English soldier, son of **Henry Wriothesley, the 2nd Earl**. He was a patron of poets, particularly of **Shakespeare**, who dedicated to him his *Venus and Adonis* (1593) and *The Rape of Lucrece* (1594). He graduated from Cambridge in 1589, accompanied **Essex** to the Azores (1597), incurred Queen **Elizabeth**'s displeasure by marrying Essex's cousin and took part in Essex's rebellion. He revived *Richard II* in order to arouse antimonarchic feeling, and was sentenced to death (afterwards commuted to life imprisonment) but was released by **James VI and I**. He helped the expedition to Virginia (1605), was imprisoned in 1621 on charges of intrigue, and died of fever at Bergen-op-Zoom while in charge of the English volunteer contingent helping the Dutch against Spain.

SOUTHAMPTON, Sir Thomas Wriothesley, 1st Earl (1505–50) English statesman, son of William Wriothesley the York Herald. He held various state offices under **Thomas Cromwell**, with whom he actively participated in the iconoclastic measures associated with the Dissolution, and in 1538 as ambassador to the Netherlands. Having avoided sharing Cromwell's fate only by turning evidence against him and through his own erstwhile opposition to **Anne of Cleves** as a wife for **Henry VIII**, he again came into favour, and as the author of the defensive treaty with Spain was created a baron. Lord Chancellor from 1544 to 1547, he won an unenviable reputation for brutality, especially towards reformers; he is said to have personally racked **Anne Askew**. He was created an earl on the accession of **Edward VI**, but soon after was deprived of the Great Seal for dereliction of duty.

SOUTHAMPTON, Thomas Wriothesley, 4th Earl (1607–67) English statesman, son of **Henry Wriothesley**, 2nd Earl. Educated at Eton and Magdalen College, Oxford, he sided with the Commons on certain aspects of royal privilege, but became one of **Charles I**'s foremost advisers. Owing perhaps to his moderate views, he was leniently treated by **Cromwell**, and at the Restoration was made lord high treasurer.

SOUTHCOTT, Joanna (c.1750–1814) English religious fanatic, a farmer's daughter in Devon. About 1792 she declared herself to be the woman of Rev xii. She came to London on the invitation of **William Sharp** the engraver (1749–1824), and published *A Warning* (1803), and *The Book of Wonders* (1813–14). At length she announced that she was to give birth on 19 October 1814, to a second Prince of Peace. Her followers received this announcement with devout reverence. But she fell into a coma and died of a brain tumour in December 1814. Her followers, who believed that she would rise again, still numbered over 200 in 1851, and were not yet extinct at the beginning of the 20th century.

SOUTHERNE, Thomas (1660–1746) Irish dramatist, born in Oxmantown, County Dublin. From Trinity College, Dublin, he passed to the Middle Temple, London, and in 1682 began his career with a compliment to the Duke of York in *The Loyal Brother*. **Dryden** wrote the prologue and epilogue, and Southerne finished Dryden's *Cleomenes* (1692). He served a short time under the Duke of Berwick and, at his request, wrote the *Spartan Dame*. His best plays were *The Fatal Marriage* (1694) and *Oroonoko* (before 1696), based on **Aphra Behn**.

SOUTHEY, Robert (1774–1843) English poet and writer, born in Bristol, the son of a linen draper. After his father's death an uncle sent him to Westminster School, but he was expelled in 1792 for his Jacobin sympathies and for denouncing whipping in the school magazine. He went on to Balliol College, Oxford. He met **Coleridge** in Bristol in 1794 and they planned to form a 'pantisocracy' or communist society but this fell through. They wrote a topical drama together, *The Fall of Robespierre* (1794), and Southey published an early volume of *Poems* (1795) and an epic poem, *Joan of Arc* (1795). Also in 1795 he married Edith Fricker, whose elder sister Sara married Coleridge. He made two trips to Lisbon (1795 and 1800), and then, after studying law, settled at Great Hall, Keswick (where Coleridge and his wife and sister-in-law were already); and there he remained. He had only £160 a year from his school friend Charles Wynn on which to live, until the government gave him a similar amount in 1807. By this time his political views had mellowed and Southey had become something of a Tory. He became poet laureate in 1813, and **Peel** raised his pension by £300 in 1835. He had joined the *Quarterly Review* in 1809 and remained a contributor under **William Gifford** and **Lockhart**. Essentially a family man, he sustained a great shock when his wife died insane in 1838; and, though he married Caroline Anne Bowles, the poet, in 1839, she became little more than a nurse for his last years of life. His literary output was prodigious, and many of his short poems are familiar, such as 'Holly Tree', 'After Blenheim', 'The Scholar', 'Inchcape Rock', 'Old Woman of Berkeley' and 'God's judgement on a wicked Bishop'. His other works include *The Curse of Kehama* (1810), *Roderick* (1814); Lives of *Nelson* (1813), *Wesley* (1820) and *Bunyan* (1830), *A Vision of Judgment* (1821), *Book of the Church* (1824), *Colloquies on Society* (1829), *Naval History* (1833–40), and *The Doctor* (1834–47), a miscellany, in which appears the nursery classic, *The Three Bears*. He also published a *Journal of a Tour of Scotland in 1819* (1929).

SOUTHWELL, Robert (?1561–1595) English poet and Jesuit martyr, born in Horsham, Norwich. He was educated at Douai and Rome, and entered into the Society of Jesus in 1578. He was appointed prefect of the English College, was ordained priest in 1584, and two years later, arriving in England with **Henry Garnet**, was first sheltered by Lord Vaux, and next became chaplain to the Countess of Arundel, when he wrote his *Consolation for Catholics* and most of his poems. In 1592 he was betrayed, tortured and thrown into the Tower, and finally he was hanged and quartered at Tyburn for high treason. He was beatified in 1929. His longest poem is *Saint Peter's Complaint*; his most famous, *The Burning Babe*.

SOUTINE, Chaim (1893–1943) Lithuanian-born French artist, born in Smilovich. He studied at Vilna and went to Paris in 1913. He is best known for his paintings of carcases, his series of *Choirboys* (1927) and the magnificent psychological study, *The Old Actress* (1924; Moltzau collection, Norway). After his death his vivid colours and passionate handling of paint gained him recognition as one of the foremost Expressionist painters.

SOUZA, Madame de, née **Adelaïde Marie Emilie Filleul** (1761–1836) French novelist, born in the Norman château of Longpré. She married the Comte de Flahaut (1727–93). At the outbreak of the French Revolution (1789) she found refuge with her only son in Germany and England, and there learned of her husband's execution at Arras. She turned to writing, and her first book was the delightful *Adèle de Sénange* (1794). In 1802 she married the Marquis de Souza-Botelho (1758–1825), Portuguese minister in Paris. Later novels include *Émilie et Alphonse* (1799) and *Charles et Marie* (1801).

SOWERBY, James (1757–1822) English artist and illustrator, born in Lambeth, London. He started as a portraitist and miniaturist, but is remembered by his illustrated *English Botany* (1792–1807) and *British Mineralogy* (1804–19).

SOWERBY, Leo (1895–1968) American composer and organist, born in Grand Rapids, Michigan. He studied in Chicago and Rome and became a teacher at the American Conservatory of Music in Chicago. His music, which includes a wide range of symphonies, concertos and choral works, employs a traditional European style in works often evocative of American scenes, such as *Prairie*, an orchestral tone poem, and the suite *From the Northland*.

SOYER, Alexis (1809–58) French chef, born in Meaux. Destined for the church, he became the most famous cook of his time. He fled to London in 1830, and was chef in the Reform Club, 1837–50. He went to Ireland during the famine (1847), and in 1855 tried to reform the food system in the Crimea, by introducing the 'Soyer Stove'. He wrote, amongst other works, *Culinary Campaign in the Crimea* (1857).

SOYINKA, Wole, pen-name of **Akinwande Oluwole Soyinka** (1934–) Nigerian dramatist, poet and novelist. Born in Western Nigeria, he was educated in Abeokuta and Ibadan before coming to England to do research at Leeds University and study the contemporary theatre. He was for a while attached to the Royal Court Theatre as a play-reader, and it was there that his first play, *The Inventor*, was given a performance in 1957, his verse-tragedy, *The Swamp Dwellers*, being produced by students in London the following year. He returned to Ibadan in 1959, and productions of *The Swamp Dwellers*, and a contrasting joyously ribald comedy *The Lion and the Jewel*, immediately established him in the forefront of Nigerian literature. In 1960 he founded the Masks amateur theatre company, and four years later, the professional Orisun Repertory. These companies played an essential part in Soyinka's building up of a new Nigerian drama, in English but using the words, music, dance and pantomime of the traditional festivals. His plays, like all his writing, are deeply concerned with the tension between the old and the new in modern Africa; history opposes tradition, and while there is value in many of the old ways, he condemns an uncritical clinging to the past. The richness of his language ranges from high-flown biblical English to the slang of the Lagos slums. His first poems were published while he was still an Ibadan undergraduate, but his first major collection, *Idanre and Other Poems* (1967) turned from his earlier humorous verse to more sombre themes; *A Shuttle in the Crypt* (1972) appeared after his release in 1969 from two years' political detention, and was as powerfully expressive of his ordeal as his play of 1970, *Madmen and Specialists*. His first novel, *The Interpreters* (1970) has been called the first really modern African novel. His other works include the plays *The Trials of Brother Jero* (1961) and *Kongi's Harvest* (1964), the novel *Season of Anomy* (1973), and the mostly prose 'prison notes', *The Man Died* (1973). He is presently professor of comparative literature and head of the department of dramatic arts at Ife University. Little of Soyinka's later work has been seen in Britain. He was awarded the Nobel prize for literature in 1986.

SPAAK, Paul Henri (1899–1972) Belgian statesman, born in Brussels, where he began to practise law in 1922. A socialist deputy for Brussels in 1932, he rose to become, in 1938, the first socialist premier of Belgium, but resigned the following year. He was foreign minister with the government-in-exile in London during World War II, and in 1946 was elected president of the first General Assembly of the United Nations. Prime minister again in 1946 and from 1947 to 1949, as president of the consultative assembly of the Council of Europe (1949–51) he was in the forefront of the movement for European unity. He was again foreign minister (1954–57), secretary-general of NATO (1957–61), and foreign minister from 1961 until his resignation from parliament in 1966.

SPAGNOLETTO See **RIBERA, Jusepe de**

SPAHN, Warren (1921–) American baseball player, born in Buffalo, New York. He holds the record for games won by a left-handed pitcher (363). He played for Boston in the National League from 1942 to 1952, then moved on to Milwaukee (1953–64). He was elected to the Baseball Hall of Fame in 1973.

SPALDING, John (c.1609–1670) Scottish historian and antiquary. He was an ecclesiastical lawyer attached to the church of St Machar in Aberdeen. He wrote a valuable *History of the Troubles and Memorable Transactions of Scotland, 1624–45* (posthumously published in 1792), an account of the events of King **Charles I**'s reign in Scotland. The Spalding Club was founded in Aberdeen in 1839 in his memory to edit and print works of Scottish historical interest.

SPALLANZANI, Lazaro (1729–99) Italian biologist and naturalist, born in Scandiano in Modena. He studied law at Bologna, but switched to physics and became a priest. He was professor of natural history at Reggio, Modena and Pavia, and disposed of the doctrine of spontaneous generation. In 1780 he demonstrated the true nature of digestion, and the functions of spermatozoa and ova. He also discovered artificial insemination.

SPARK, Muriel Sarah, née **Camberg** (1918–) Scottish novelist, short story writer, biographer and poet, born in Edinburgh the daughter of a Jewish engineer and a suffragette mother. She was educated in Edinburgh at James Gillespie's School for Girls (the model for Marcia Blaine School in *The Prime of Miss Jean Brodie*) where she was 'the school's Poet and Dreamer', and Heriot Watt College (now University). After her marriage in 1938, she spent a few years in Central Africa, a period rarely reflected in her work. She came back to England in 1944 when her marriage broke down, and worked in Intelligence in the Foreign Office, and stayed on in London after the war to become general secretary of the Poetry Society and editor of *Poetry Review* (1947–49). Since then she has devoted herself to writing, from the early 1960s living mainly in New York and Rome. She became a Catholic in 1954, an event of central importance to her life and work. Her early books were biographical studies of **Wordsworth** (1950), **Mary Shelley** (1951), **Emily Brontë** (1953) and **John Masefield** (1953), but she also published a collection of poems, *The Fanfarlo and Other Poems* (1952). Nevertheless, she is pre-eminently a novelist and short-story writer. *The Comforters* (1957) was hailed by **Evelyn Waugh** as 'brilliantly original and fascinating' and her reputation grew steadily among the cognoscenti. She continued with *Memento Mori* (1959), *The Ballad of Peckham Rye* (1960), and *The Batchelors* (1961), but it was only with the publication of her sixth novel, *The Prime of Miss Jean Brodie* (1961), an eerie portrait of a school-teacher with advanced ideas and her influence over her 'crème de la crème' pupils, that she achieved popular success. She has written 18 novels in all, invariably slim, elegant and imbued with bizarre elements. They include *The Girls of Slender Means* (1963), set in a Kensington hostel, *The Abbess of Crewe* (1974), an allegorical fantasy set in an abbey but with parallels to the Watergate scandal, *Loitering with Intent* (1981), *The Only Problem* (1984), echoing the Book of Job, and *A Far Cry From Kensington* (1988), an evocative, comic but sinister portrayal of London in the 1950s. Her stories were collected in 1985.

SPARKS, Jared (1789–1866) American historian and biographer, born in Willington, Connecticut. He was a tutor at Harvard and, for a time, a Unitarian minister at Baltimore, and chaplain to congress (1821). He edited the *North American Review* (1823–29) and in 1832 began his *Library of American Biography*. At Harvard, he was McLean professor of history (1839–49) and president (1849–53). He wrote, among other works, Lives of John Ledyard (1828) and **Gouverneur Morris** (1832), and edited works of **Washington** (1834–37) and **Franklin** (1836–40).

SPARTACUS (d.71 BC) Roman gladiator and rebel, born in Thrace. A shepherd who became a robber, he was captured and sold to a trainer of gladiators at Capua. In 73 BC he escaped, with about 70 others, to Vesuvius, where he was joined by many runaway slaves. He repulsed C Claudius Pulcher, defeated several Roman armies and laid waste much of Italy. He was defeated by **Marcus Licinius Crassus** near the river Silarus in 71, and executed with his followers by crucifixion.

SPASSKY, Boris Vasilyevich (1937–) Russian chess player, born in Leningrad, and world champion (1969–72). He gained the title against **Tigran Petrosian** in 1969, and carried Soviet hopes in his first defence, against **Bobby Fischer** in Reykjavík, Iceland, in 1972. His defeat before the full glare of international attention gave him the unfortunate legacy of the most famous loser in sporting history. In 1975, following a third marriage, he took up residence in Paris.

SPEAIGHT, Robert William (1904–76) English actor and author, son of Frederick William (1869–1942) the architect. He played most of the major Shakespearean roles for the Old Vic from 1930, and played Becket in **Eliot**'s *Murder in the Cathedral* at the Canterbury Festival (1935). He wrote many biographies including *Hilaire Belloc* (1956), edited the latter's correspondence (1958) and published works on drama.

SPECKBACHER, Joseph (1767–1820) Tirolese patriot, known as 'Der Mann vom Rinn'. Like **Hofer**, he fought with distinction in 1809 against the French.

SPEDDING, Frank Harold (1902–84) American inorganic chemist, born in Hamilton, Ontario. He spent his working career at Iowa State University. He devised a method for purifying uranium metal in quantity in World War II, and 'Spedding's eggs' formed the core of **Fermi**'s first atomic pile, set up in Chicago in 1942. Thereafter he worked on the problem of separating the closely similar lanthanides ('rare earth metals') and devised an ion-exchange chromatographic method for this purpose, which was also suitable for the separation of the actinides (trans-uranium elements).

SPEDDING, James (1808–81) English scholar, born in Mirehouse near Bassenthwaite. He entered the colonial service, and served as secretary to **Alexander Baring**'s mission to the USA (1842) and to the newly founded civil service commission (1855). He was a fellow of Trinity College, Cambridge, and the editor and vindicator of **Francis Bacon**. He published Bacon's *Life and Letters* (1861–74) and *Evenings with a Reviewer* (1848), a refutation of **Macaulay**'s *Essay* on Bacon.

SPEE, Count Maximilian von (1861–1914) German naval commander, born in Copenhagen. He entered the Imperial German navy in 1878. In 1908 he became chief of staff of the North Sea Command. At the outbreak of World War I in 1914 he was in command of a commerce-raiding force in the Pacific. Off Coronel (Chile) he encountered an inferior British squadron, which he punished severely, sinking HMS *Good Hope* and *Monmouth*. He attempted an attack on British coaling and wireless stations in the Falklands, but was surprised by the appearance of two battlecruisers in a reinforced British squadron under **Sturdee**. Six German ships were sunk and Von Spee and two of his sons went down with his flagship.

SPEED, John (1542–1629) English antiquary and cartographer, born in Cheshire. He worked for most of his life in London as a tailor, but his extraordinary historical learning gained him the acquaintance of Sir **Fulke Greville** and Sir **Henry Spelman**, and opened up the door for the publication of his 54 *Maps of England and Wales* (1608–10), incorporated into *The Theatre of Great Britain*, and *History of Great Britain* (both 1611).

SPEER, Albert (1905–81) German architect and Nazi government official. He joined the National Socialist party in 1931 and undertook architectural commissions for the party, becoming **Hitler**'s chief architect in 1934. From 1941 to 1945 he was a member of the Reichstag, representing Berlin, and in 1942 was made minister of armaments; his talent for organization resulted in greatly improved industrial performance. Always more concerned with technology and administration than Nazi ideology, he openly opposed Hitler in the final months of the war, and was the only Nazi leader at the Nuremberg trials to admit responsibility for the régime's actions. He was sentenced to 20 years' imprisonment in Spandau fortress, and after his release in 1966 published *Inside the Third Reich* (1970) and *Spandau: The Secret Diaries* (1976).

SPEIDEL, Hans (1897–) German soldier, born in Metzingen, Württemberg. He served in World War I and in 1939 was senior staff officer. From 1940 to 1942 he was chief of staff to the German commander in occupied France. In July 1944, when he was chief of staff to **Rommel** during the allied invasion of Europe, he was imprisoned after the anti-**Hitler** bomb plot. In 1951 he became military adviser to the West German government. His NATO appointment as commander-in-chief land forces, Central Europe (1957–63), aroused wide controversy. He became president of the Institution of Science and Politics in 1964. He wrote *Invasion 1944*, and *The Destiny of Rommel and the Reich* (1949).

SPEIGHT, Johnny (1920–) English comic writer, born in London. A milkman, insurance salesman and member of a jazz band, he began writing after World War II for such comic stars as **Frankie Howerd**, Arthur Haynes and **Morecambe** and Wise. He made his mark on television with the play *The Compartment* (1962), and the creation of the loud-mouthed, working-class bigot Alf Garnett in the controversial assault on sacred cows like religion and royalty, *Till Death Do Us Part* (1964–74). The series earned him Screenwriters' Guild Awards in 1966, 1967 and 1968, and the character was revived for *In Sickness and In Health* (1985–). His other television series include *Spooner's Patch* (1979–82) and *The Nineteenth Hole* (1989–). His publications include *It Stands to Reason* (1973) and *The Thoughts of Chairman Alf* (1973).

SPEKE, John Hanning (1827–64) English explorer, born in Jordans, Ilminster. In the Indian army he saw service in the Punjab. In 1854 he joined **Richard Francis Burton** in a hazardous expedition to Somaliland and in 1857 the Royal Geographical Society sent them out to search for the equatorial lakes of Africa. Speke, while travelling alone, discovered the Victoria Nyanza, and saw in it the headwaters of the Nile. In 1860 he returned with Captain **James Grant**, explored the lake, and tracked the Nile flowing out of it. He was about to defend the identification against Burton's doubts at the British Association meeting at Bath, when he accidentally shot himself while partridge-shooting.

SPELMAN, Sir Henry (1562–1641) English antiquary, born in Congham, Lynn. From Trinity College, Cambridge, he passed to Lincoln's Inn. He was high sheriff of Norfolk in 1604, was employed in public affairs at home and in Ireland, and was knighted. In 1612 he settled in London to pursue his studies. His ponderous *Glossarium Archaiologicum* (1626–64) was completed by his son and Sir **William Dugdale**; he also left his *Concilia Ecclesiastica Orbis Britannici* (1639–64) incomplete. *Reliquiae Spelmannianae* was edited, with a Life, by **Edmund Gibson** (1698). His son, Sir John (1594–1643), is remembered for his Life of King **Alfred**.

SPEMANN, Hans (1869–1941) German zoologist. Educated in Stuttgart and Heidelberg, he was professor at Rostock (1908–14), director of the Kaiser Wilhelm Institute of Biology in Berlin (1914–19), and professor at Freiburg (1919–35). He worked on embryonic development, discovering the 'organizer function' of certain tissues, and won the 1935 Nobel prize for physiology or medicine.

SPENCE, Sir Basil Urwin (1907–76) Scottish architect, born in India of Scots parents. Educated at George Watson's College, Edinburgh, and London and Edinburgh Schools of Architecture, he assisted **Lutyens** with the drawings of the Viceregal Buildings in Delhi. He was twice mentioned in dispatches during World War II, and gradually emerged as the leading post-war British architect with his fresh approach to new university buildings and conversions at Queen's College, Cambridge, Southampton, Sussex, and other universities; his pavilions for the Festival of Britain (1951); the British Embassy in Rome; and his prize-winning designs for housing estates at Sunbury-on-Thames (1951). His best-known work is his prize design for the new Coventry Cathedral (1951) which boldly merged new and traditional structural methods. He was professor of architecture at Leeds (1955–56) and at the Royal Academy from 1961.

SPENCE, Catherine Helen (1825–1910) Scottish-born Australian writer and feminist, born near Melrose. She arrived in Adelaide in 1839 with her parents, with the ambition to be 'a teacher first and a great writer afterwards'. While a governess she worked on the first novel of Australian life written by a woman, published in London in 1854 as *Clare Morrison*. She wrote five more novels, the last one not published until after her death. Her early preoccupation with social problems, especially of the destitute and the young, led her more into the public arena, and she made lecture tours in Britain and the USA. She advocated a modification of Hare's system of proportional representation and formed an Effective Voting League in South Australia. She stood as a candidate in the elections for the federal convention in 1897, to become Australia's first woman political candidate.

SPENCE, Joseph (1699–1768) English anecdotist. He was educated at Winchester and New College, Oxford, where he became professor of poetry (1727). He is remembered for his *Essay on Pope's Odyssey* (1727) and his anecdotes of **Pope** and other celebrities.

SPENCE, (James) Lewis Thomas Chalmers (1874–1955) Scottish poet and anthropologist, born in Broughty Ferry, Dundee. He studied dentistry at Edinburgh, but turned to writing and in 1899 became a sub-editor on *The Scotsman* newspaper, and subsequently *The British Weekly* (1906–09). He became an authority on the folklore and mythology of central and South America, and elsewhere, with numerous books including *Mythologies of Mexico and Peru* (1907), *Dictionary of Mythology* (1913), *Encyclopaedia of Occultism* (1920), and *The Magic Arts in Celtic Britain* (1945). As a poet he was a pioneer of the use of archaic Scots language, in such collections as *The Phoenix* (1924) and *Weirds and Vanities* (1927). An ardent nationalist, he was one of the founder members of the National Party of Scotland in 1928, and the first nationalist to contest a parliamentary seat.

SPENCE, Peter (1806–83) Scottish industrial chemist, born in Brechin. He worked in a grocery and a gasworks and then in 1845 patented and operated a novel process for making potash alum, then much used as a mordant in dyeing textiles. His works at Manchester used shale and sulphuric acid and produced much of the world's alum, and also such noxious fumes that he was forced to move from Manchester in 1857.

SPENCER, Earls a family founded by the Honourable John Spencer, younger son of the 3rd Earl of Sunderland by Anne, daughter of the great Duke of Marlborough (his brother became 3rd duke). His only son, John (1734–83), was created Earl Spencer in 1765.

SPENCER, Lady Diana Frances See **CHARLES, Prince of Wales**

SPENCER, George John Spencer, 2nd Earl (1758–1834) English statesman, son of the 1st Earl. As **Pitt**'s First Lord of the Admiralty (1794–1801), he improved naval administration. During his tenure of office, mutinies were suppressed at the Nore and Spithead, and the British fleet achieved notable successes, including St Vincent, Camperdown, and the Nile. He resigned on the fall of government, but became home secretary in 1806–07. He was a famous collector of books and was founder-president of the Roxburgh Club.

SPENCER, John Charles Spencer, 3rd Earl, Lord Althorp (1782–1845) English politician, educated at Harrow and Trinity College, Cambridge. Known under his courtesy title of Lord Althorp, he became Whig Chancellor of the Exchequer and leader of the House of Commons, and was mainly responsible for carrying through the Reform Bill of 1832, and the bill for reforming the Irish Church. He resigned on account of the Irish Coercion Bill, but resumed office in the **Melbourne** administration. On succeeding as earl in 1834 he passed to the House of Lords.

SPENCER, John Poyntz Spencer, 5th Earl (1835–1910) English statesman. He was lord-lieutenant of Ireland (1868–74 and 1882–85). In 1880 he became lord president of the Council, and again in 1886, having embraced **Gladstone**'s Home Rule policy. He was First Lord of the Admiralty (1892–95).

SPENCER, Sir (Walter) Baldwin (1860–1929) English-born Australian anthropologist and biologist, born in Stretford, Lancashire. Graduating from Exeter College, Oxford, he obtained a fellowship at Lincoln College and in 1887 became foundation professor of biology at Melbourne University. In 1894 he joined Horn's expedition to central Australia, the reports of which he edited, and where he met Francis James Gillen. They began a collaborative study of the local aboriginal tribes which was to last until Gillen's death, resulting in a number of invaluable published works. In 1912 Spencer was appointed chief protector of the Aborigines, becoming the first white man to make contact with some previously isolated tribes. He became ill while on a trip to the world's most southerly settlement, on Tierra del Fuego, and died there.

SPENCER, Herbert (1820–1903) English philosopher, born in Derby. He had a varied career as a railway engineer, teacher, journalist and sub-editor at *The Economist* (1848–53) before devoting himself entirely to writing and study. His particular interest was in evolutionary theory which he expounded in *Principles of Psychology* in 1855, four years before **Darwin**'s *The Origin of Species*, which Spencer regarded as welcome scientific evidence for his own *a priori* speculations and a special application of them. He also applied his evolutionary theories to ethics and sociology and became an advocate of 'social Darwinism', the view that societies naturally evolve in competition for resources and that the 'survival of the fittest' is therefore morally justified. He announced in 1860 a *System of Synthetic Philosophy*, a series of volumes which were to comprehend metaphysics, ethics, biology, psychology, and sociology, and nine of these appeared between 1862 and 1893. He viewed philosophy itself as the science of the sciences, distinguished by its generality and unifying function. His other works include *Social Statics* (1851), *Education* (1861), *The Man Versus the State* (1884) and *Autobiography* (1904).

SPENCER, Sir Stanley (1891–1959) English painter, born in Cookham, Berkshire. He studied at the Slade School of Art, London, where he learnt the linear drawing style which informs most of his work. Never part of any of the main movements in 20th-century British art, Spencer remained an eccentric figure, tackling unfashionable religious subjects in his precise, distinctive style. These he transposed into his own local context at Cookham, especially *The Resurrection* (1922–27). He was an official war artist in World War II when he painted a series of panels depicting *Shipbuilding on the Clyde*. His best-known work is his decorative scheme of murals of army life for the Sandham Memorial Chapel, Burghclere (1926–32). His brother Gilbert (1892–1976) was also an artist.

SPENCER-CHURCHILL, Baroness See **CHURCHILL, Sir Winston**

SPENDER, Edward Harold (1864–1926) English journalist, biographer and novelist, son of **Lilian Spender**. He wrote *One Man Returns* (1914), and biographies of **Asquith**, **Botha** and **Lloyd George**.

SPENDER, John Alfred (1862–1942) English journalist and biographer, son of **Lilian Spender**, born in Bath. He became editor of the Liberal *Westminster Gazette* (1896–1922) and one of the leading journalists of the day. A member of Lord **Milner**'s special mission to Egypt (1919–20), he wrote a number of political books and biographies of **Campbell-Bannerman**, **Asquith**, and others.

SPENDER, Lilian (1835–95) English novelist. She married John Kent Spender in 1858 and became mother of **Edward Harold** and **John Alfred Spender**. Her novels include *Lady Hazleton's Confession* (1890).

SPENDER, Sir Stephen (1909–) English poet and critic, son of **Edward Harold Spender**, born in London. Educated at University College, Oxford, in the 1930s he was one of the 'modern poets', left-wing in outlook, who set themselves the task of recharging the impulses of poetry both in style and subject matter. In his thought he is essentially a liberal, despite his earlier flirtings with communism. He translated **Schiller**, **Toller**, **Rilke** and **Lorca**, among others, besides writing much penetrating literary criticism. From his beginnings in 1930 with *Twenty Poems* to *Engaged in Writing* (a novella) (1957), he relived his experiences in his work. *Poems from Spain* (1939) links up with his service in the Spanish Civil War. In World War II he served as a fireman in the London blitz, and volumes of poems, *Runes and Visions* (1941), *Poems of Dedication* (1941) and *The Edge of Darkness* (1949), continue his self-analysis. Alongside these are critical evaluations such as *The Destructive Element* (1936), *Life and the Poet* (1942), *The Creative Element* (1944), and his first autobiography, *World within World* (1951). From 1939 to 1941 he was co-editor, with **Cyril Connolly**, of the brilliant monthly, *Horizon*, and from 1953 to 1967 was co-editor of *Encounter*. He was professor of English at University College, London (1970–77). His later work includes *The Struggle of the Modern* (1963), *The Year of the Young Rebels* (1969), *The Thirties and After* (1978) and *Chinese Journal* (with **David Hockney**, 1982).

SPENER, Philipp Jakob (1635–1705) German philosopher of history, 'the Father of Lutheran Pietism', born in Alsace. At Strasbourg and Frankfurt he tried to reawaken the dormant Christianity of the day. His *Pia Desideria* (1675) spread the movement far beyond the range of his personal influence, but not without enmity.

SPENGLER, Oswald (1880–1936) German historicist writer, born in Blankenburg, Harz. He studied at Halle, Munich and Berlin and taught mathematics (1908) in Hamburg before devoting himself entirely to the compilation of the morbidly prophetic *Untergang des Abendlandes* (1918 and 1922, trans as *Decline of the West* 1926–29), in which he argues by analogy, in the historicist manner of **Hegel** and **Marx**, that all civilizations or cultures are subject to the same cycle of growth and decay in accordance with predetermined 'historical destiny'. The soul of Western civilization is dead. The age of soulless expansionist Caesarism is upon us. It is better for Western man, therefore, to be engineer rather than poet, soldier rather than artist, politician rather than philosopher. Unlike **Toynbee**, whom he influenced, he was concerned with the present and future rather than with the origins of civilizations. His verdict, achieved by his specious method, greatly encouraged the Nazis although he never became one himself. Another work attempted the identification of Prussianism with socialism (1920).

SPENS, Sir William (Will) (1882–1962) Scottish educational administrator, born in Glasgow. Educated at Rugby School and King's College, Cambridge, where he studied both science and theology, he was master of Corpus Christi College, Oxford, from 1927 to 1952. He was chairman of the Consultative Committee on Education from 1934 and produced the report on *Secondary Education* (*Grammar Schools and Technical High Schools*) in 1938 which recommended the raising of the school-leaving age to 15 and a widening of the provision of secondary education. It embodied the best thinking of the inter-war period and paved the way for the *Norwood Report* (1943) and the Education Act of 1944.

SPENSER, Edmund (c.1552–1599) English poet, born in London, the son of a gentleman tradesman who was connected with the Spencers of Althorp. He was educated at Merchant Taylors' School and Pembroke Hall, Cambridge. His early writings, partly written at Cambridge, include translations of the *Visions* of **Petrarch** and some sonnets of **Du Bellay**. Shortly after leaving Cambridge (1576) he obtained a place in the Earl of **Leicester**'s household and this led to a friendship with Sir **Philip Sidney** and the Areopagus, a society of wits. His first original work, *The Shepheard's Calender* (1579), dedicated to Sydney, heralded the age of Elizabethan poetry and no doubt assisted in his career as a courtier. In 1580 he was appointed secretary to Lord Grey de Wilton, lord deputy in Ireland, whose assignment was to crush Irish rebellion, and Spenser was involved in this. His reward for his work as one of the 'undertakers' for the settlement of Munster was Kilcolman Castle in the county of Cork, where he settled in 1586 and where he hoped to have leisure to write his *Faerie Queene* and other courtly works, written with an eye to the court no less than as a brilliant presentation of the art and thought of the Renaissance. In 1589 he visited London in company with Sir **Walter Raleigh**, who had seen the first three books of *The Faerie Queene* at Kilcolman and now carried him off to lay them at Queen **Elizabeth**'s feet. Published in 1590, they were an immediate success, but a previous misdemeanour, the attack in *Mother Hubberd's Tale* on the proposed match between Elizabeth and the Duc d'Alençon, was not forgotten and the poet returned to Ireland in 1591 a disappointed man; he later published his wry reflections on his visit in *Colin Clout's Come Home Again* (1595). *Complaints*, published in 1591, contains, beside his early work, the brilliantly coloured but enigmatic *Muiopotmos*; *Mother Hubberd's Tale*, to which was now added a bitter satire on Court favour; *The Early Tears of the Muses*, which lamented the lack of patronage; and his pastoral elegy for Sir Philip Sydney which is so frigid as to make us question their friendship. In 1594 he married again, celebrating his wooing of Elizabeth Boyle in the sonnet sequence *Amoretti* and his wedding in the supreme marriage poem *Epithalamion*. He revisited London in 1596, with three more books of *The Faerie Queene*, which were published along with the *Four Hymns*. This was a year of uncommon activity. Under the roof of Lord **Essex** he wrote *Prothalamion*, and his prose *View of the Present State of Ireland*, which, taken with the fifth book of *The Faerie Queene*, is probably the first explicit statement of the imperialism which is now discredited. In 1598 the Irish rose in rebellion and Kilcolman Castle was burned, but the Spensers escaped to Cork and from there to safety in London. He died the following year and was buried in Westminster Abbey.

SPERANSKI, Mikhail, Count (1722–1839) Russian statesman and reformer. He became Tsar **Alexander I**'s adviser and in 1809 produced a plan for the reorganization of the Russian structure of government on the Napoleonic model, but was dismissed when **Napoleon** invaded Russia (1812). Under **Nicholas I** he was restored to power and was responsible for the trial and conviction of the Decembrist conspirators of 1825. He also prepared major works on Russian law.

SPERRY, Elmer Ambrose (1860–1930) American inventor and electrical engineer, born in Cortland, New York. He invented dozens of new devices, including a new-type dynamo, arc-light and searchlight. His chief invention was the gyroscopic compass (1911) and stabilizers for ships and aeroplanes. He also devised an electrolytic process for obtaining pure caustic soda from salt, and a high intensity arc searchlight (1918). He founded several companies for the manufacture of these inventions.

SPERRY, Roger Wolcott (1913–) American neuroscientist, born in Hartford, Connecticut. Educated at Oberlin College, he studied zoology at Chicago University (PhD 1941), then worked as a research fellow at Harvard and at the Yerkes Laboratory of Primate Biology (1941–46). He taught at Chicago University (1946–52), and was Hixon professor of psychobiology at the California Institute of Technology from 1954 to 1984. He first made his name in the field of developmental neurobiology, his experiments helping to establish the means by which nerve cells come to be 'wired up' in particular ways in the central nervous system. In the 1950s and 1960s he pioneered the behavioural investigation of 'split-brain' animals and humans, arguing that two separate realms of consciousness could coexist under one skull. His experiments led him into philosophy and the 'mind/brain problem'. His view is that mind is an 'emergent property' arising from the very complexity of the physical system that constitutes the brain. He shared the Nobel prize for physiology or medicine in 1981 with **David Hubel** and **Torsten Wiesel**.

SPEUSIPPUS (c.407–339 BC) Greek philosopher, who lived in Athens. He was **Plato**'s nephew and his successor as head of the Academy in 348. He produced a large corpus of writings, but only one fragment of this work, on Pythagorean numbers, survives.

SPIELBERG, Steven (1947–) American filmmaker, born in Cincinnati, Ohio. An amateur filmmaker as a child, he became one of the youngest television directors at Universal on such projects as *Night Gallery* (1969). A highly praised television film, *Duel* (1971), brought him the opportunity to direct for the cinema, and a string of hits have made him the most commercially successful director of all time. His films have explored primeval fears, as in *Jaws* (1975), or expressed childlike wonder at the marvels of this world and beyond, as in *Close Encounters of the Third Kind* (1977) and *E.T.* (1982). More recently he has concentrated on grand literary adaptations such as *The Color Purple* (1985) and *Empire of the Sun* (1987) and on the continuing adventures of his dare-devil hero Indiana Jones. His company, Amblin', has been instrumental in the production of many other films including *Poltergeist* (1982), *Back to the Future* (1985) and *Who Framed Roger Rabbit* (1988).

SPIELHAGEN, Friedrich (1829–1911) German novelist, born in Magdeburg. As well as poems, plays, books of travel, his works include *Durch Nacht zum Licht* (1861), *Die von Hohenstein* (1863), *In Reih und Glied* (1866) and *Susi* (1895). He also worked as an actor.

SPIES-KJÆR, Janni (1962–) Danish businesswoman, owner of Scandinavia's largest group of tour operators, the *Spies Concern* and the *Tjæreborg Concern*. In 1983 she married Simon Spies, the charismatic and unconventional founder of *Spies Travel* (who died in 1984) and she became one of Scandinavia's richest women. She married again in 1988.

SPILSBURY, Sir Bernard Henry (1877–1947) British pathologist, born in Leamington. He studied physiology at Magdalen College, Oxford, then entered the medical school of St Mary's Hospital, Paddington, and specialized in what was then the new science of forensic pathology. He made his name at the trial of **Hawley Harvey Crippen** (1910), and was appointed pathologist to the Home Office. As expert witness for the Crown, he was involved in many notable murder trials, such as those of Mahon (1924), Thorne (1925) and Rouse (1931). His last important case was the murder of de Antiquis (1947).

SPINELLO ARETINO (c.1330–1410) Italian painter, born in Arezzo. He spent nearly all his life between there and Florence. His principal frescoes were done for San Miniato, in Florence, for the *campo santo* of Pisa, and for the municipal buildings of Siena.

SPINK, Ian (1947–) Australian dancer, choreographer and director, born in Melbourne. Trained in classical ballet, he joined the Australian Ballet in 1969. He made his first works there, but left the world of ballet in 1974 to perform with the Dance Company of New South Wales (now Sydney Dance Company). Moving to England in 1977 he formed the Ian Spink Group. But it was in partnership with **Siobhan Davies** and **Richard Alston** in Second Stride (founded 1982) that he first found success there. He became sole artistic director in 1987. Up-beat and theatrical, his work is both innovative and popular, and includes *Further and Further . . .*, *Bosendorfer Waltzes*, *Weighing the Heart* (1987), and *Dancing and Shouting* (1988).

SPINKA, Matthew (1890–1972) Czech-born American church historian, born in Stitary. He graduated from the University of Chicago and the Faculty of Protestant Theology, Prague, and taught church history at Central Theological Seminary, Dayton, Ohio and Chicago University before appointment as professor at Hartford Theological Seminary in 1943, a post he held till his retirement. A brilliant scholar who specialized in Central and Eastern European subjects, he edited the prestigious *Church History* journal (1932–49). His numerous books include *The Church and the Russian Revolution* (1927), *Christianity Confronts Communism* (1936), *John Amos Comenius* (1943), *Nicholas Berdyaev* (1950), and *John Hus* (1968).

SPINOLA, Ambrogio, Marquis of Los Balbases (1539–1630) Italian soldier in Spanish service, born in Genoa. In 1602 he raised and maintained at his own cost 9000 troops and served against **Maurice of Nassau** (1567–1625) in the Spanish Netherlands. In 1603 he succeeded to the marquisate on the death of his brother Frederigo in a naval battle against the Dutch. Spinola was meanwhile besieging Ostend, which fell in 1604 after a three years' siege. He was one of the plenipotentiaries at the Hague Conference which made the twelve-year truce in 1609. Early in the Thirty Years' War (1618–48) he was in Germany, subduing the Lower Palatinate. But he was recalled to the Netherlands to fight once more against Maurice of Nassau, who, however, died of fever while attempting to relieve Breda, which fell to Spinola in 1625. Shortly afterwards, ill-health forced him to resign. In 1629 he was in Italy, acting as governor of Milan; and in the same year, while besieging Casale, he died.

SPINOZA, Baruch, or **Benedictus, de** (1632–77) Dutch philosopher, born in Amsterdam into a Jewish emigré family that had fled from Portugal to escape Catholic persecution. His deep interests in optics and the new astronomy and his radical ideas in theology and philosophy led to his expulsion from the Jewish community for heresy in 1656. He became the leader of a small philosophical circle and made a living grinding and polishing lenses, moving in 1660 to Rijnsburg near Leiden, where he wrote his 'Short Treatise on God, Man and His Well-Being' (about 1662), the *Tractatus de Intellectus Emendatione* ('Treatise on the Correction of the Understanding', 1662) and most of his geometrical version of **Descartes**' *Principia Philosophiae*, which was published in 1663 (the only book published in his lifetime with his name on the title page), and which marks the point at which Spinoza moved decisively beyond Descartes' influence. He moved in 1663 to Voorburg near The Hague and in 1670 to The Hague itself. The *Tractatus Theologico-Politicus* was published anonymously in 1670 and aroused great interest but was banned in 1674 for its controversial views on the Bible and Christian theology. He advocated a strictly historical approach to the interpretation of biblical sources and argued that complete freedom of philosophical and scientific speculation was consistent with what was really important in the Bible—the moral and practical doctrines, not the factual beliefs assumed or expressed. He had sent **Leibniz** his tract on optics in 1671, and Leibniz came to The Hague to visit him in 1676. But Spinoza was by then in an advanced stage of consumption, aggravated by the glass-dust in his lungs, and he died the next year in Amsterdam, leaving no heir and few possessions. His major work was the *Ethics*, which was published posthumously in 1677. As the Latin title suggests (*Ethica Ordine Geometrico Demonstrata*), this was a complete, deductive metaphysical system, intended to be a proof of what is good for human beings derived with mathematical certainty from axioms, theorems and definitions. He rejects the Cartesian dualism of mind and matter in favour of a God who is identified with the ultimate substance of the world—infinite, logically necessary and absolute— which has mind and matter as two of his attributes. Spinoza's God is thus not a personal creator, but more a pantheistic nature, the ultimate explanation of why everything must exist and happen exactly as it does. His work was first condemned as atheistical and subversive, but his reputation was restored by literary critics like **Lessing**, **Goethe** and **Coleridge** and later by professional philosophers, and he is now regarded, along with Descartes and Leibniz, as one of the great Rationalist thinkers of the 18th century.

SPITTELER, Karl Friedrich Georg (1845–1924) Swiss poet and novelist, born in Liestal (Basel). He studied law and theology at Basel, Zürich and Heidelberg, was a tutor in Russia, teacher and journalist in Switzerland, and retired to Lucerne in 1892. *Der Olympische Frühling* (1900–03) is a great mythological epic, but perhaps his most mature work is *Prometheus der Dulder* (1924). As well as poetry he wrote tales (*Konrad der Leutnant*, and others), essays (*Lachende Wahrheiten*) and reminiscences. He was awarded the Nobel prize for literature in 1919.

SPITZER, Lyman Jr (1914–) American astrophysicist, born in Toledo, Ohio. He was educated at Yale and Princeton, where he was professor of astronomy from 1947 to 1979. His interest in energy generation in stars led to his early attempt to achieve controlled thermonuclear fusion, for which he devised a method of 'containing' a plasma in a magnetic field; the principle continues to form part of experimentation in this area.

SPOCK, Dr Benjamin McLane (1903–) American paediatrician who transformed the attitudes of the postwar generation to their babies with his seminal book *The Common Sense Book of Baby and Child Care* (1946), which has sold more than 30 million copies. He was born in New Haven, Connecticut, and studied at both Yale (where he became a star oarsman and rowed in the 1924 Olympics) and Columbia. He qualified as a doctor, having trained in both paediatrics and psychiatry, and started a practice in Manhattan in 1933. In the 1960s he was a vocal opponent of the Vietnam War, and was in turn accused of having been responsible for raising a permissive, spineless generation of pacifists. In 1968 he was sentenced to jail on a charge of helping young men to evade the draft, but appealed successfully against the conviction and published *Dr Spock on Vietnam*. He continued his political interest with *Decent and Indecent: Our Personal Political Behaviour* (1970), and helped to form the People's party, running for the US presidency in 1972 and the vice-presidency in 1976.

SPODE, Josiah (1754–1827) English potter, born in Stoke-on-Trent. He learnt his trade in his father's workshops, and in 1800 began to use bone as well as feldspar in the paste, which resulted in porcelain of a special transparency and beauty. He did much to popularize the willow pattern and he became the foremost china manufacturer of his time. He was appointed potter to **George III** in 1806.

SPOERLI, Heinz (1941–) Swiss dancer, choreographer and ballet director, born in Basel. He studied locally and at the School of American Ballet and the London Dance Centre before joining Basel Ballet (1960–63), Cologne Ballet (1963–66), Royal Winnipeg Ballet (1966–67), Les Grands Ballets Canadiens (1967–71) and Geneva Ballet (1971–73). He assumed directorship of Basel Ballet in 1973, gradually turning what was strictly a provincial ballet company attached to the state opera into one of the best of Europe's smaller dance ensembles. He is a prolific dancemaker for companies throughout the Continent, both creating new, contemporary ballets and staging his versions of the classics.

SPOFFORTH, Frederick Robert (1853–1926) Australian cricketer, known as 'the demon', the greatest bowler in the history of the game, born in Balmain, Sydney. On 26 May 1878, he took 11 wickets for 20 runs against the MCC, and during 1884 he took 218 wickets in first-class cricket with a bowling average of 12.53.

SPOHR, Ludwig (1784–1859) German composer, violinist and conductor, born in Brunswick. He was kapellmeister at the court of Hesse-Kassel from 1822 to 1857. Remembered chiefly as a composer for the violin, for which he wrote 17 concertos, he also composed operas, oratorios and symphonies.

SPONTINI, Gasparo Luigi Pacifico (1774–1851) Italian composer, born near Ancona into a peasant family. He was intended for the priesthood, like his brothers, but insisted on following a musical career. He studied at Naples, where he began to compose. In 1803 he settled in Paris, and his operas *La Vestale* (1807) and *Ferdinand Cortez* (1809) were greeted with enthusiasm. In Berlin from 1820 to 1842 only court influence supported him against the public and the press. *Agnes von Hohenstaufen* (1829, revised 1837) is his greatest work.

SPOONER, William Archibald (1844–1930) English clergyman and educationist, dean (1876–89) and warden (1903–24) of New College, Oxford. As an albino he suffered all his life from weak eyesight, but heroically surmounted his disabilities and earned a reputation for kindness and hospitality. His name is associated with his own nervous tendency to transpose initial letters or half-syllables (metathesis), which has given it the name 'spoonerism'—for instance, 'a half-warmed fish' for 'a half-formed wish'.

SPOTTISWOODE, Alicia Ann, Lady John Scott (1810–1900) Scottish poet and song-writer, born in Westruther, Berwickshire. A friend of **Charles Kirkpatrick Sharpe**, she was a busy collector of traditional songs and wrote 69 of her own, often reworking original material, as with her most famous compositions, *Annie Laurie* and *Durrisdeer*. In 1836 she married Lord John Scott, a brother of the 5th Duke of Buccleuch.

SPOTTISWOODE, John (1565–1639) Scottish prelate, son of a minister. Educated at Glasgow University, he was at first a Presbyterian, but later became Episcopalian. He became an assistant at Calder, and accompanied **James VI** to London on his accession as James I in 1603. He was archbishop of Glasgow (1610) and of St Andrews (1615). He promoted Episcopal government, and forced the Perth Assemby (1618) to sanction the 'Five Articles of Perth'. He officiated at the coronation of **Charles I** at Holyrood in 1633, and in 1635 was appointed chancellor of Scotland. He reluctantly entered into the king's code of canons and prayer book, and so made himself hateful to the Covenanters. The king compelled him to resign the chancellorship in 1638, and he was deposed and excommunicated by the Glasgow General Assembly. His chief work is the *History of the Church of Scotland* (1655).

SPOTTISWOODE, William (1825–83) English mathematician, physicist and publisher, born in London. He was educated at Harrow and Balliol, where he lectured in mathematics. In 1846, he succeeded his father as head of the printing house of Eyre and Spottiswoode and did original work in polarization of light and electrical discharge in rarefied gases, and wrote a mathematical treatise on determinants.

SPRAGUE, Frank Julian (1857–1934) American electrical engineer and inventor, born in Milford, Connecticut. He graduated from the US Naval Academy in 1878 and served in the US navy until 1883, when he worked for a year with **Edison** before setting up the Sprague Electric Railway and Motor Company. He developed a new type of motor for street railways (trams) which was first used in 1887 in Richmond, Virginia, and by 1890 had become so successful that his company was absorbed by the Edison General Electric Company. He turned to the manufacture of electric lifts and as a result of his experience with them he perfected in 1895 a system of control for multiple-unit trains, which he later developed into an automatic train control system. He has been called 'the father of electric railway traction'.

SPRENGEL, Christian Konrad (1750–1816) German botanist, born in Brandenburg. He became rector of Spandau, but neglected his duties to make discoveries about the part played in the pollination of plants by nectaries and insects, which aroused **Darwin**'s interest. His nephew, Kurt (1766–1833), wrote histories of medicine (1803) and botany (1818).

SPRENGEL, Hermann Johann Philipp (1834–1906) German-born British chemist, born near Hanover. He came from Göttingen and Heidelberg for research in Oxford and London and remained in Britain. He invented a new type of vacuum pump (1865) and devised the U-tube method for comparing liquid densities.

SPRENGER, Aloys (1813–93) Austrian orientalist, born in Nassereut in Tyrol. He studied at Vienna, came to London, sailed to Calcutta in 1843 and worked as interpreter, librarian, and translator. In 1857 he became Oriental professor at Bern. In 1881 he settled in Heidelberg. He wrote a great *Leben und Lehre des Mohammed* (1861–65) and books on the ancient geography of Arabia and Babylonia.

SPRENGER, Jacob (15th century) German theologian. A Dominican, and professor of theology in Cologne, with Henricus Institor (Latinized form of Krämer) he compiled the famous *Malleus Maleficarum* (1489), which first formulated the doctrine of witchcraft, and formed a textbook of procedure for witch trials. They were appointed inquisitors by **Innocent VIII** in 1484.

SPRING, Howard (1889–1965) Welsh novelist, born in Cardiff. From errand boy he became a newspaper reporter and literary critic and established himself as a writer with his best-selling *Oh Absalom* (1938), renamed *My Son, My Son*. Other novels include *Fame is the Spur* (1940), *Dunkerleys* (1946), *These Lovers Fled Away* (1955) and *Time and the Hour* (1957), as well as three autobiographical works (1939, 1942 and 1946).

SPRINGSTEEN, Bruce (1949–) American rock singer and guitarist, born in Freehold, New Jersey. From the release of his first album, *Greetings From Asbury Park, NJ* (1973), he was hailed by critics as the new **Bob Dylan**, but although he quickly developed a strong cult following it was not until the release of *Born To Run* (1975) that he met with major commercial success. Subsequently prevented from recording for three years, due to management and legal problems, he spent the time developing his highly acclaimed live shows. Later albums included *Darkness On The Edge Of Town* (1978), *The River* (1980), *Born In The USA* (1985) and *Tunnel Of Love* (1987). By the mid 1980s he had become the world's most popular white rock star, and in 1984 *Born In The USA* became the first rock album to be quoted from by both candidates in a US presidential election, when it was co-opted by both **Ronald Reagan** and **Walter Mondale**. Springsteen managed successfully to combine his celebrity status with a populist style dramatizing the lives of working-class Americans.

SPRUANCE, Raymond Ames (1885–1969) American naval officer, born in Baltimore. Educated at the US Naval Academy, Annapolis, he became a specialist in gunnery. He commanded the USS *Mississipi* in 1938. He led Task Force 16 at the decisive Battle of Midway (June 1942). He played an important part in the planning and execution of massive amphibious operations, supported by carrier-borne and shore-based aircraft (1942–45), and notably as Commander Fifth Fleet (1944–45). He was president of the US Naval War College (1946–48), and US ambassador to the Philippines (1952–55).

SPRUCE, Richard (1817–93) English botanist, born near Malton, plant collector and traveller. A schoolmaster at St Peter's School in York, he became a professional plant collector and travelled to the Pyrenees and to South America (1849–64) with Sir **Joseph Hooker** and **George Bentham**. He published several important works on liverworts and on the flora of South America.

SPURGEON, Charles Haddon (1834–92) English Baptist preacher, born in Kelvedon, Essex. In 1854 he became pastor of the New Park Street Chapel, London. The Metropolitan Tabernacle, seating 6000, was erected for him in 1859–61 and provided him with a pulpit until his death (it burnt down in 1898). In 1887 he withdrew from the Baptist Union because no action was taken against persons charged with fundamental errors. Apart from 50 volumes of sermons, he wrote collections of pithy sayings in *John Ploughman's Talk* (1869) and many other works.

SPURR, Josiah Edward (1870–1950) American geologist, born in Gloucester, Massachusetts. He was mining engineer to the sultan of Turkey (1901), geologist in the US geological survey (1902) and eventually professor of geology at Rollins College (1930–32). As a result of his work, the age of the Tertiary period has been estimated at 45 to 60 million years ago. His exploration in Alaska in 1896 and 1898 was commemorated by the naming of Mt Spurr. He did considerable research on lunar topography and geology, and among other works, he wrote *Geology Applied to Mining* (1904) and *Geology Applied to Selenology* (1944–49).

SPURZHEIM, Johann (Christoph) Caspar (1776–1832) German phrenologist, born near Trier. He studied medicine in Vienna and became the disciple of **Franz Joseph Gall** the phrenologist, and, lecturing in Britain, gained a powerful adherent in **George Combe**.

SQUARCIONE, Francesco (1394–1474) Italian painter, and founder of the Paduan school of painters. The teacher of **Mantegna**, he painted panels and frescoes for the church of S Francesco in Padua.

SQUIER, Ephraim George (1821–88) American archaeologist, born in Bethlehem, New Hampshire. While a newspaper editor in Ohio in the 1840s, he surveyed and analyzed, with the help of the physician Edwin Hamilton Davis, the native American burial mounds and earthworks of the Mississippi valley, publishing the results in the earliest classic of North American archaeology, *Ancient Monuments of the Mississippi Valley* (1848). Following a second survey, of the mounds of western New York state, which appeared the following year, Squier became a diplomat, first in Nicaragua (from 1849), then (from 1863) in Peru. His experiences of travel and exploration are recounted in two popular books, *Nicaragua* (1852) and *Peru* (1877).

SQUIRE, Sir John Collings (1884–1958) English author, born in Plymouth. He was educated at Blundell's and St John's College, Cambridge, and was literary editor of *The New Statesman*. and founder editor of *The London Mercury* (1919–34). His work is composed of light verse and parody, as in *Steps to Parnassus* (1913) and *Tricks of the Trade* (1917); in anthologies he favoured minor poets. His writings also include criticisms and short stories.

SSU-MA CH'IEN See **SI-MA QIA**

SSU-MA HSIANG-JU (d.117 BC) Chinese poet, born in Ch'engtu, Suzechuan province. He wrote the *Tzu Hse Fu*, a series of poems describing and denouncing the pleasures of the hunt, which hold an important place in Chinese literary history.

STAAL, Marguerite Jeanne, Baronne de (1684–1750) French writer of memoirs, born in Paris, the daughter of a poor Parisian painter, Cordier, whose name she dropped for that of her mother, Delaunay. Her devotion to the interests of her employer, the Duchess of Maine, brought her two years in the Bastille, where she had a love affair with the Chevalier de Menil. In 1735 she married the Baron Staal. Her *Mémoires* (1755; trans 1892) describe the world of the regency with intellect, observation and a subtle irony, and are written in a clear, firm and individual style. Her *Œuvres complètes* appeared in 1821.

STABLER, Harold (1872–1945) English designer/craftsman. Trained as a woodworker, he studied metalwork at Keswick School of Art, and taught there before moving to London in the early 1900s, joining the staff at the Sir John Cass Technical Institute. He was an instructor at the Royal College of Art from 1912 to 1926 and served on the first council of the Design and Industrial Association in 1915. With his wife, Phoebe Stabler, he designed and produced ceramic figures and groups, decorative and architectural details, enamels and jewellery. He became a partner in the Poole pottery firm of Carter & Co in 1921, changing the name to Carter, Stabler & Adams when he acted as the firm's artistic consultant.

STACPOOLE, Henry de Vere (1863–1951) Irish physician and writer, born in Kingstown (Dun Laoghaire), the son of a Presbyterian minister. Educated at Malvern College and St George's and St Mary's Hospitals, London, he made several voyages as a ship's doctor. He was the author of many popular novels, including *The Blue Lagoon* (1909), *The Pearl Fishers* (1915) and *Green Coral* (1935). He wrote his autobiography in *Men* and *Mice* (1942 and 1945).

STAËL, Anne Louise Germaine Necker, Madame de (Baronness of Staël-Holstein) (1766–1817) French writer, born in Paris, the only child of the financier and statesman, **Jacques Necker**. In her girlhood she wrote romantic comedies, tragedies, novels, essays and *Lettres sur Rousseau* (1789). She married in 1786 the Baron Eric Magnus of Staël-Holstein (1742–1802), the bankrupt Swedish ambassador in Paris. She bore him two sons (1790 and 1792) and a daughter (1797), but the marriage was unhappy and she had many affairs, especially with the writer Benjamin Constant. To protect her fortune, she separated formally from him in 1798. Her vast enthusiasms and the passionate intensity of her affections gave force and colour to her rich and versatile character, and combined to form a personality whose influence was irresistible. Her brilliant *salon* became the centre of political discussion, but with the Revolution and her father's fall she felt compelled to leave Paris for Coppet, by Lake Geneva in Switzerland in 1792. From Coppet she went to England, where at Mickleham in Surrey she was surrounded by **Talleyrand** and others of the French *émigrés*. She joined her husband at Coppet in May 1793, and published her *Réflexions sur le procès de la reine* in the vain hope of saving **Marie Antoinette**. In 1795 she returned to Paris, where her husband had re-established himself as ambassador. She prepared for a political role by her *Réflexions sur la paix intérieure* (1795), but was advised to return to Coppet. Her *Influence des passions* appeared in 1796. **Napoleon** allowed her to return to Paris in 1797, but received her friendly advances with such studied coldness that admiration soon turned to hatred. In 1800 she published her famous *Littérature et ses rapports avec les institutions sociales*. She was again back in Paris in 1802, when her *salon* was more brilliant than ever, and published *Delphine*, a novel. At length her friendship with disaffected men like **Moreau** and **Bernadotte**, and the appearance of Necker's *Dernières vues*, exhausted the patience of Napoleon, and in the autumn of 1803 she received orders to keep 40 leagues from Paris. Her husband had died, and in December 1803 she set out with her children for Weimar, where she dazzled the court, and met **Schiller** and **Goethe**. In Berlin she made the acquaintance of **August Schlegel**. She next went to Vienna, but learned of her father's death and returned to Coppet, writing the touching eulogy, *Du caractère de M. Necker*. Then she set out for Italy with Schlegel, **Wilhelm von Humboldt**, and Bonstetten, but in 1805 returned to Coppet, where once again a brilliant circle assembled, to write *Corinne* (1807), a romance which at once brought her European fame. She visited Germany at the end of 1807, and began to turn for consolation to religion—she was a Protestant. Her famous *De l'Allemagne* was finished in 1810, passed by the censor, and partly printed, when the whole impression was seized and destroyed, and she herself was ordered from Paris to Coppet. The work was published by **John Murray** in London in 1813. But her exile had now become a bitter reality; she found herself surrounded by spies. She escaped secretly to Berne, and from there made her way to St Petersburg, Stockholm and (1813) London. In England admiration reached its climax on the publication of *De l'Allemagne*, the most finished of all her works. It revealed Germany to the French and made Romanticism—she was the first to use the word—acceptable to the Latin peoples. **Louis XVIII** welcomed her to Paris in 1814, and the two million francs which Necker had left in the Treasury was honourably paid to her. The return of Napoleon drove her from Paris, and she spent the winter in Italy for the sake of the health of Albert de Rocca, an Italian officer in the French service, whom she had married secretly in 1811. She returned to Paris, where she died. Her surviving son and daughter published her unfinished *Considérations sur la Révolution française* (1818), considered her masterpiece by **Saint-Beauve**, the *Dix Années d'exil* (1821), and her complete works (1820–21).

STAËL, Nicolas de (1914–55) Russian-born French painter, born in St Petersburg. He studied in Brussels, travelled in Spain and Italy, and worked in Paris. His paintings were mainly abstract, and he made inspired use of rectangular patches of colour; his later pictures were more representational and in subdued colours.

STAFFORD, Jean (1915–79) American short-story writer and novelist, born in Covina, California. Her father had an unsuccessful career as a writer of westerns under the pseudonyms Jack Wonder and Ben Delight. Educated at Colorado University, she won a travelling scholarship to Heidelberg, Germany, in 1936. Returning to the USA she met literary establishment figures **Randall Jarrell**, and **Robert Lowell**, whom she married against his family's wishes in 1940. She worked on the *Southern Review* and taught at Flushing College. *Boston Adventure*, her first novel, was published in 1944 to great praise; *The Mountain Lion*, her second, appeared in 1947. But her stormy marriage to Lowell collapsed and she was admitted to psycho-alcoholic clinics. Divorced from Lowell in 1948, she married Oliver Jensen, an editor on *Life*, in 1950. In 1952 *The Catherine Wheel* was published. She was divorced for a second time in 1955 and later married the writer A J Liebling. She taught throughout the 1960s and published diverse books: short stories, children's books and interviews with the mother of **Lee Harvey Oswald**, *A Mother in History* (1966). One of America's most admired short-story writers, her *Collected Stories* appeared in 1969 and was awarded a Pulitzer prize.

STAFFORD, William Howard, 1st Viscount Stafford (1614–80) English Catholic nobleman, beheaded on Tower Hill as a victim of the perjuries of **Titus Oates**. His attainder was reversed in 1824.

STAFFORD-CLARK, Max (1941–) English stage director, born in Cambridge. He began his career as associate director of the Traverse Theatre, Edinburgh, in 1966, becoming artistic director there (1968–70). He then became director of the Traverse Theatre Workshop company, (1970–74), when he co-founded the Joint Stock Theatre Company. He became artistic director of the English Stage Company at the Royal Court Theatre, London, in 1981.

STAGNELIUS, Erik Johan (1793–1823) Swedish Romantic poet, son of the bishop of Kalmar. After graduating at Uppsala he became an unsalaried civil servant in Stockholm. He led a solitary life, was often indisposed, suffering from a heart disease, the effects of which he tried to mitigate with alcohol and perhaps opium. After his death, of unknown causes, his works were collected and published (1824–26). His considerable output, all written within a decade, comprises epics, like *Vladimir den store* (1817, Vladimir the Great), plays like *Martyrerna* (The Martyrs) and *Bacchanterna* (1822, The Bacchanalians), but it is above all his lyric poetry, much of it found in *Liljan i Saron* (1821), which captures the essence of his genius. He was constantly torn between idealism and erotic sensualism. The object of his desire often centred on Amanda—whether she was a factual character is uncertain and perhaps unimportant for in his poems she became a vision of all that is desirable in woman. Influenced by his reading of **Plato**, **Schelling**, theosophy, gnosticism and Romantic contemporaries, he gradually accepted the view of two warring factions in the universe: God versus the Devil, spiritual versus temporal; in the beginning the soul (Anima), Christ and the angels inhabited the perfect world but were tempted by an evil angel (Achamot) and plunged into an earthly existence under Demiurgen. Man's spirit is captive but can reach out to its divine origins in dreams, memories, poetry, beauty, nature and, above all, faith in Christ's redeeming sacrifice. Stagnelius contrasts dream and reality in a series of poems like *Endymion*, *Narcissus* and *Till Natten* (Ode to Night). His love for Amanda, expressed earlier by the disillusioned unrequited poet, can now become a noble denial of Amanda the beautiful symbol of earthly love (as in *Resa*, *Amanda jag skall*—Amanda I must depart—and *Uppoffringen*—Sacrifice). In other poems themes from nature symbolize the soul's longing for heaven, as in *Floden*—The River—and *Flyttfåglarna*—Migrant Birds. Stagnelius employs a variety of verse forms with consummate skill. His poetry has an in-built tension between eroticism and spiritualism and is imbued with nature symbolism and imagery couched in the most melodic language in Swedish literature. Little-known in his lifetime, he became posthumously the most influential of Swedish Romantics on succeeding generations.

STAHL, Georg Ernst (1660–1734) German chemist, born in Ansbach. He became professor of medicine (1694) at Halle, and personal physician (1714) to the king of Prussia and expounded the phlogiston theory and animism.

STÅHLBERG, Kaarlo Juho (1865–1952) Finnish lawyer, and politician. Professor of law at Helsinki (1908–18) and a member of the Finnish Diet (1908–17), he drafted the Finnish constitution of 1919. In that year he was elected the first president (1919–25) of the republic of Finland. Kidnapped in 1930, he was narrowly defeated in the presidential elections of 1931.

STAINER, Jakob (1621–83) Austrian violin maker, born in Absam near Hall in Tyrol. He made violins in Innsbruck, and died in a Benedictine monastery.

STAINER, Sir John (1840–1901) English composer, born in London. He became organist of Magdalen College, Oxford, in 1860, and of St Paul's (1872), and Oxford professor of music (1889). He wrote cantatas and church music, notably *The Crucifixion* (1887).

STAIR, James Dalrymple, 1st Viscount (1619–95) Scottish jurist. He studied at Glasgow University, served in the Covenanting army, as regent in philosophy taught at Glasgow, joined the bar (1648), and in 1659 was recommended by General **George Monk** to **Cromwell** for the office of a lord of session. He advised Monk to call a free parliament (1660). He was confirmed in office and created a Nova Scotia baronet in 1664. The luckless marriage in 1669 of his daughter Janet inspired Sir **Walter Scott**'s *The Bride of Lammermoor* (1819). In 1671 he was made president of the Court of Session and member of the privy council; but when the Duke of York (**James VII and II**) came to govern at Edinburgh in 1679 he retired to the country, and prepared his famous *Institutions of the Law of Scotland*, still the most authoritative work on Scots law. His wife and his tenants were devoted to the Covenant, and he was soon involved in a fierce dispute with **Dundee**. He fled in 1682 to Holland, returned with **William III,** and, restored to the presidency, was created in 1690 Viscount Stair. He also published reports of court decisions and works on physics and religion.

STAIR, Sir John Dalrymple, 1st Earl of (1648–1707) Scottish judge and politician, son of James Dalrymple Viscount **Stair**. He studied law, and was knighted in 1667. He came into violent collision with **Dundee**, and was flung into prison in Edinburgh and heavily fined, but early in 1686 became king's advocate, and in 1688 lord justice-clerk. Under **William III** he was lord advocate, and as secretary of state from 1691 had the chief management of Scottish affairs. He was held responsible for the infamous massacre of Glencoe (1692), and resigned in 1695. In 1703 he was created an earl. He took an active part in the debates and intrigues that led to the Treaty of Union.

STAIR, John Dalrymple, 2nd Earl (1673–1747) Scottish soldier, born in Edinburgh. At eight he shot his elder brother dead by accident, so was exiled by his parents to Holland, where he studied at Leiden, fought under **William III** at Steenkerk (1692), and by 1701 was lieutenant-colonel in the Scots Footguards, and in 1706 colonel of the Cameronians. He was aide-de-camp to **Marlborough** in 1703, commanded an infantry brigade at Ramillies (1706), was made colonel of the Scots Greys in 1706 and in 1708 secretly married Viscountess Primrose. He distinguished himself greatly at Oudenarde (1708) and Malplaquet. General in 1712, he retired to Edinburgh to intrigue for the Hanoverian succession. Under **George I** he was ambassador to Paris, and checkmated the Young Pretender (**James Stewart**) and **Alberoni**. Recalled in 1720, he devoted himself to agriculture, growing turnips and cabbages. Made field-marshal (1742), he was governor of Minorca and fought at Dettingen.

STAKHANOV, Aleksei Grigorievich (1906–77) Russian coalminer. He started an incentive scheme (1935) for exceptional output and efficiency by individual steel workers, coalminers, etc. Such prize workers were called Stakhanovites.

STALIN, Joseph, properly **Iosif Vissarionovich Dzhugashvili** (1879–1953) Soviet leader, born near Tiflis in Georgia, the son of a shoemaker. He was educated at the Tiflis Theological Seminary, from which he was expelled for 'propagating Marxism'. Joining the Bolshevik 'underground', he was arrested and transported to Siberia, whence he escaped in 1904. The ensuing years witnessed his closer identification with revolutionary Marxism, his many escapes from captivity, his growing intimacy with **Lenin** and Bukharin, his early disparagement of **Trotsky**, and his co-option, in 1912, to the illicit Bolshevik Central Committee. With the 1917 Revolution and the forcible replacement of the **Kerensky** government by Lenin and his supporters, Stalin was appointed commissar for nationalities and a member of the politburo, although his activities throughout the counter-revolution and the war with Poland were confined to organizing a Red 'terror' in Tsaritsin—subsequently renamed Stalingrad. With his appointment as general secretary to the Central Committee in 1922, Stalin began stealthily to build up the power that would ensure his control of the situation after Lenin's death. When this occurred in 1924, he took over the reins, putting his over-riding authority to successful test in 1928 by engineering Trotsky's degradation and banishment. Stalin's reorganization of the soviets' resources, with its successive Five Year Plans, suffered many industrial setbacks and encountered consistently stubborn resistance in the field of agriculture, where the *kulaks*, or peasant proprietors, steadfastly refused to accept the principle of 'collectivization'. The measures taken by the dictator to 'discipline' those who opposed his will involved the death by execution or famine of up to 10 million peasants (1932–33). The blood bath which eliminated the 'Old Bolsheviks' and the alleged right-wing 'intelligentsia', and the carefully staged 'engineers' trial', were followed by a drastic purge of some thousands of the officer corps, including Marshal Tuchachevsky, Stalin professing to believe them guilty of pro-German sympathies. Red Army forces and material went to the support of the Spanish Communist government in 1936, although Stalin was careful not to commit himself too deeply. After the Munich crisis Franco-British negotiations for Russian support in the event of war were guilefully protracted until they ended in the *volte face* of a non-aggression pact with **Hitler**, which gained Stalin the time to prepare for the German invasion he sensed to be inevitable. In 1941 the prosperity of the Nazis' initial thrust into Russia could be accounted for in part by the disposal of the Red Army on the frontiers, ready to invade rather than repel invasion. Thereafter, Stalin's strategy followed the traditional Muscovite pattern of plugging gaps in the defences with more and more bodies and trading space for time in which the attrition begotten of impossible climatic conditions could whittle away the opponents' strength. Sustained by many millions of pounds' worth of war material furnished by Britain and America, the Red Army obediently responded to Stalin's astutely phrased call to defend not the principles of Marx and Engels, but 'Mother Russia'; although the Red dictator lost no time in demanding a 'Second Front' in Europe to relieve the strain on his unnumbered forces. Quick to exploit the unwarranted Anglo-American fear that Russia might 'go out of the war', Stalin easily outwitted the allied leaders at the Teheran and Yalta conferences. Seeming to acquiesce in decisions he had no intention of implementing, he never deviated an inch from the path he had marked out for himself. With the Red Army's invasion of German soil, Soviet bayonets were encouraged to penetrate far beyond the point where they had last been employed. Thus Stalin's domination of the Potsdam conference, followed by the premature break-up of the Anglo-American forces, left the red dictator with actual possessions enlarged by 182480 square miles which, with 'satellites', increased the Soviet sphere of influence by 763940 square miles, bearing alien but submissive populations totalling 134188000. While Stalin consolidated his gains an 'iron curtain' was dropped to cut off Soviet Russia and her satellites from the outside world. At the same time the 'Hozyain' inaugurated a 'cold war' against all non-communist countries—which included the blockade of Berlin—prosecuting it with all the ruthlessness, resource and cunning at his command. Stalin consistently manipulated communist imperialism for the greater glory of Soviet Russia and the strengthening of his own autocratic sway as its satrap. He died in somewhat mysterious circumstances. Stalin's 'Cult of Personality' and brutal purges were denounced after his death by **Khrushchev**, but this criticism was halted by **Brezhnev**. However, with the accession to power, in 1985, of the new **Gorbachev** administration re-interpretation of the Stalin era has resumed. In November 1987, Gorbachev himself, while praising his wartime leadership and agreeing that the strategy of collectivization was substantially correct, asserted that Stalin had committed 'unforgivable crimes' and had seriously distorted the Soviet political system. In 1988, Stalin's official biographer, Dmitri Volkoganov, went further, castigating the September 1939 'friendship pact' with Nazi Germany, his resort to bloody purges and his reliance on incompetent advisers, and suggesting that the once revered leader may have been insane. Many of the opponents of Stalin who were found guilty in the 1930s show trials have since been posthumously rehabilitated.

STALKER, James (1848–1927) Scottish theologian, born in Crieff. A student at Edinburgh, Halle and Berlin, and a minster in Kirkcaldy and Glasgow, he was professor of church history at the United Free Church College, Aberdeen from 1902 to 1924. He wrote more than a dozen books, including lives of **Jesus** (1879) and **Paul** (1884), *Imago Christi: the Example of Jesus Christ* (1889), and *The Preacher and his Models* (1891).

STAMBOLOV, Stephan Nikolov (1854–95) Bulgarian statesman, born in Trnova. He took part in the rising of 1875–76. Chief of the Russophobe regency (1886) and premier (1887–94), he ruled with a strong hand. Forced then to retire, he was assassinated.

STAMITZ, Carl Philipp (1745–1801) German composer and violinist, son of **Johann Stamitz**. He studied under his father and became a travelling instrumentalist in Paris, London, St Petersburg, Prague and Nuremberg. He wrote 80 symphonies, one of which was for a double orchestra, and concertos for violin, viola, cello, flute, oboe, clarinet and harpsichord. His brother, Anton Johann Baptista (c.1754–1809), was also a musician.

STAMITZ, Johann (1717–57) Bohemian violinist and composer, founder of the Mannheim school, born in Havlickuv Brod. He first attracted attention at the coronation celebrations in Prague (1741) and was engaged by the Mannheim court, where he became a highly salaried court musician and concert master. He visited Paris (1754–55). His compositions include 74 symphonies, concertos for harpsichord, violin, oboe, flute and clarinet (the last possibly the first of its kind), chamber music and a mass. He developed the sonata form, introduced sharp contrasts into symphonic movements and wrote some of the finest concerto music of the 18th century.

STAMP, Josiah Charles, 1st Baron Stamp of Shortlands (1880–1941) English economist, born in London. He served on the **Dawes** Committee on German reparations, was chairman of the London, Midland and Scottish railway, director of Nobel Industries, and on the outbreak of World War II was made economic adviser to the government. An expert on taxation, he wrote on this and other financial subjects. He was killed in an air-raid.

STAMP, Sir Lawrence Dudley (1898–1966) English geographer, born in London. Educated at King's College, London (geology and botany, 1917 and geography, 1921), he did fieldwork in Burma and became professor of geology and geography at Rangoon in 1923. He became reader at the London School of Economics in 1926 and eventually professor of geography there (1945–58). He founded and worked on the British Land Utilisation Survey until after World War II, and both during and after the war he was adviser to the government on many land-related topics.

STANDISH, Myles (c.1584–1656) English soldier of fortune and colonist, born probably in Ormskirk, Lancashire. He served in the Netherlands, and in 1620 was hired by the Pilgrim Fathers to accompany them on the *Mayflower*. He was appointed military captain of the settlement at Plymouth, supervised the defences, and negotiated with the Indians. In 1625 he went to London to negotiate ownership of their land. He became treasurer of Massachusetts (1644–49). In 1631 he was one of the founders of Duxbury, Massachusetts. **Longfellow** and **Lowell** wrote about his exploits against the Indians.

STANFORD, Sir Charles Villiers (1852–1924) Irish composer, born in Dublin. He studied at Cambridge, Leipzig and Berlin, and became organist at Trinity College (1872–93), and professor at the Royal College of Music (1882); as Cambridge professor of music (1887), he taught generations of young British composers. Among his works are choral settings of **Tennyson**'s *Revenge* (1886) and *Voyage of Maeldune* (1889); the oratorios *The Three Holy Children* (1885) and *Eden* (1891); the operas *The Veiled Prophet of Khorassan* (1881), *Savonarola*, *The Canterbury Pilgrims* (1884), *Shamus O'Brien* (1896), *Much Ado About Nothing* (1901) and *The Critic* (1916); and he set a high standard in English church music.

STANFORD, (Amasa) Leland (1824–93) American railway magnate, born in Watervliet, New York. In 1856 he settled in San Francisco, became president of the Central Pacific Company, superintended the construction of the line, and was governor of California (1861–63), and US senator from 1885. In memory of their only son, he and his wife founded and endowed Leland Stanford Junior University (now Stanford University) at Palo Alto (1891).

STANHOPE, Charles, 3rd Earl Stanhope (1753–1816) English scientist and politician, grandson of James, 1st Earl **Stanhope**, born in London. Educated at Eton and Geneva, he married Lady Hester Pitt, sister of **William Pitt** the Younger, in 1774 and became an MP in 1780. He broke with Pitt over the French Revolution, and advocated peace with **Napoleon**, becoming a 'minority of one'. As a scientist he invented a microscope lens that bears his name, two calculating machines, the first hand-operated iron printing press, and a process of stereotyping adopted in 1805 by the Clarendon Press in Oxford. He also experimented with electricity, and wrote *Principles of Electricity* (1779).

STANHOPE, Edward Stanhope (1840–93) English politician. He became Conservative colonial secretary (1886), and as secretary for war (1887–92) reformed army administration, established the Army Service Corps and adopted the magazine rifle.

STANHOPE, Lady Hester Lucy (1776–1839) English traveller, eldest daughter of **Charles, 3rd Earl Stanhope**. She went in 1803 to reside with her uncle, **William Pitt**, and as mistress of his establishment and his most trusted confidante, had full scope for her queenly instincts. On Pitt's death (1806) the king gave her a pension of £1200. The change from the excitements of public life was irksome to her; in 1809 she was grieved by the death at La Coruña of her brother Major Stanhope, and of Sir **John Moore**, whom she had loved; and in 1810 she left England, wandered in the Levant, went to Jerusalem, camped with Bedouins in Palmyra, and in 1814 settled on Mount Lebanon. She adopted Eastern manners, interfered in Eastern politics, and obtained a wonderful ascendancy over the tribes around her, who regarded her as a sort of prophetess. Her last years were poverty-striken on account of her reckless liberality.

STANHOPE, James, 1st Earl (1673–1721) English soldier and statesman. After a distinguished career in the field under **Marlborough** in the War of the Spanish Succession, he became leader of the Whig opposition in 1711. He helped to suppress the Jacobite Rising of 1715, and became chief minister to **George I** in 1717.

STANHOPE, Philip Dormer See **CHESTERFIELD**

STANHOPE, Philip Henry, 5th Earl Stanhope (1805–75) English historian, born in Walmer. He studied at Oxford, entered parliament in 1830, was instrumental in passing the Copyright Act (1842), and was foreign under-secretary under Sir **Robert Peel** (1834–35), and secretary to the Indian Board of Control (1845–46). He was known as Lord Mahon until he succeeded to the earldom. His principal work was *A History of England 1713–83* (1836–54); and his other works include Lives of **Belisarius, Condé** and **Pitt**, *War of the Succession in Spain*, *History of Spain under Charles II*, *Essays* and *Miscellanies*. He helped to secure the appointment of the Historical MSS Commission and the foundation of the National Portrait Gallery.

STANIER, Sir William Arthur (1876–1965) English mechanical engineer, born in Swindon where his father was stores superintendent at the Great Western Railway's works. He began as an apprentice there in 1892 and ended his railway career as chief mechanical engineer of the London, Midland & Scottish Railway from 1932 to 1942. During that time he brought out many successful locomotive designs, including in 1937 the 4-6-2 'Coronation' class, at first streamlined and later in conventional form with distinctive tapered boilers.

STANISLAS LESZCZYŃSKI (1677–1766) king of Poland, born in Lemberg. He was elected king in 1704, but in 1709 was driven out by **Peter II, the Great** to make room for **Augustus II**. He formally abdicated in 1736, receiving the duchies of Lorraine and Bar; and he died of a burning accident in Lunéville. See also **Poniatowski**.

STANISLAVSKY, professional name of **Konstantin Sergeivitch Alexeyev** (1865–1938) Russian actor, producer and teacher, born in Moscow. His first notable production was in 1891, **Tolstoy**'s *Fruits of Enlightenment*, and when he joined the Moscow Arts Theatre in 1898 he was able to develop his theories to the full. These were to present an illusion of reality by means of a highly stylized combination of action, setting and production, based on an exhaustive examination of the background and psychology of the characters. His 'method' was most successful in **Chekhov**, **Gorky**, **Maeterlinck** and **Andreyev**. A superb actor, he gave up acting because of illness, but his influence on the theatre remains enormous.

STANLEY See **DERBY, Edward Geoffrey Smith Stanley**

STANLEY, Arthur Penrhyn (1815–81) English theologian, born in Alderley, Cheshire. Educated at Rugby under **Thomas Arnold**, whose Life he wrote (1844), and at Balliol College, Oxford, he won the Ireland and Newdigate prizes, and in 1838 was elected fellow of University College and took orders. He travelled in the East, accompanied the Prince of Wales to the Holy Land, in 1851 became a canon of Canterbury, in 1856 professor of ecclesiastical history at Oxford and in 1864 dean of Westminster. For all his large tolerance, charity and sympathy, High Church Anglicans could never forgive him for championing **Colenso** and for preaching in Scottish Presbyterian pulpits. He was pre-eminently representative of the broadest theology of the Church of England. He cared little for systematic theology and not at all for the pretensions of the priesthood; while he regarded as 'infinitely little' the controversies about postures, lights, vestments and the like. His works include *Memorials of Canterbury* (1854), *Sinai and Palestine* (1856), and *Christian Institutions* (1881).

STANLEY, Sir Henry Morton (1841–1904) Welsh explorer and journalist, born of unmarried parents in Denbigh, Wales, and at first called **John Rowlands**. In 1859 he went as cabin boy to New Orleans, where he was adopted by a merchant named Stanley. He served in the Confederate army and US navy, contributed to several journals, and in 1867 joined the *New York Herald*. As its special correspondent he accompanied Lord **Napier**'s Abyssinian expedition; and the first news of the fall of Magdala was conveyed to Britain by the *New York Herald*. Stanley next went to Spain for his paper, and in October 1869 received from **James Gordon Bennett** the laconic instruction, 'Find **Livingstone**'. But first he visited Egypt for the opening of the Suez Canal, and travelled through Palestine, Turkey, Persia and India. In March 1871, he left Zanzibar for Tanganyika and on 10 November he 'found' Livingstone at Ujiji. The two explored the north end of Lake Tanganyika, and settled that it had no connection with the Nile basin. In 1872, he returned alone and published *How I found Livingstone*. An expedition under Stanley, who had followed the Ashanti campaign for the *New York Herald*, was fitted out jointly by the *Herald* and the *Daily Telegraph* to complete Livingstone's work, and in August 1874 he left England for Bagamoyo. From there he made for the Victoria Nyanza, circumnavigated the lake, and formed a close friendship with King Mtesa of Uganda. He next determined the shape of Lake Tanganyika, passed down the Lualaba to Nyangwé, and traced the Congo to the sea. Having published *Through the Dark Continent* (1878), in 1879 he again went out to found, under the auspices of the king of the Belgians, the Congo Free State, having been refused help in England. He took part in the Congo Congress in Berlin in 1884–85. In March 1886 his expedition for the relief of **Emin Pasha** landed at the mouth of the Congo. In June he left a part of his 650 men under Major Barttelot on the Aruwimi, and with 388 men marched into the forest. Disaster overtook the rear column but Emin and Stanley met in April 1888 on the shores of Lake Albert. After relieving the rearguard he returned with Emin overland to the east coast, and Bagamoyo was reached in December 1889. He had discovered Lake Edward and Mount Ruwenzori. In 1890 he married the artist, Dorothy Tennant. He was naturalized as a British subject in 1892, and sat as a Unionist for Lambeth (1895–1900).

STANLEY, John (1713–86) English composer, born in London. He was blind from the age of two, having fallen on a stone hearth while holding a china bowl, but his musical talent was such that he became organist at All Hallows, Bread Street, at the age of eleven. Later he held posts at St Andrew's, Holborn, and at the Inner Temple. His compositions, which include oratorios (*Zimri* and *The Fall of Egypt*), cantatas, organ voluntaries, concerti grossi and instrumental sonatas, have won increasing recognition, and today he is regarded as one of the greatest of 18th-century English composers.

STANLEY, Thomas (1625–78) English author, born in Cumberlow, Hertfordshire. He studied at Pembroke Hall, Cambridge, practised law, and published translations from the Greek, Latin, French, Spanish and Italian poets. His great works were a *History of Philosophy* (1655–62) based on **Diogenes Laertius**, and an edition of **Aeschylus** (1663).

STANLEY, Venetia See **DIGBY, Sir Kenelm**

STANLEY, Wendell Meredith (1904–71) American biochemist, born in Ridgeville, Indiana. Educated at Earlham College and Illinois University, he joined the Rockefeller Insitute at Princeton in 1931, where he did important work on the chemical nature of viruses. He isolated and crystallized the tobacco mosaic virus and worked on sterols and stereo-isomerism. He shared the 1946 Nobel prize for chemistry with **John Northrop** and Howard Sumner. He was professor of molecular biology and of biochemistry at California from 1948.

STANLEY, William (1858–1916) American electrical engineer, born in Brooklyn, New York. After working for **Maxim**, he set up on his own and invented the transformer (1885). His work also included a long-range transmission system for alternating current.

STANSGATE, William Wedgwood Benn, 1st Viscount (1877–1960) English politician. He was a Liberal MP from 1906 until 1927, when he joined the Labour party and was next year elected for North Aberdeen. From 1929 to 1931 he was secretary for India and in 1945–46 secretary for air. He won the DSO and DFC in World War I, served in the RAF in World War II, and was created a viscount in 1941. He was the father of **Anthony Wedgwood Benn**.

STANTON, Edwin McMasters (1814–69) American lawyer and statesman, born in Steubenville. He rose to legal prominence when he successfully opposed the plan for bridging the Ohio at Wheeling on the grounds of interference with navigation. He was secretary of war under **Lincoln**, was suspended by **Andrew Johnson** (1867) and reinstated by the senate. When Johnson's impeachment failed, Stanton resigned (1868).

STANTON, Elizabeth, née **Cady** (1815–1902) American social reformer and women's suffrage leader, born in Johnstown, New York. At her wedding in 1840 to Henry B Stanton she insisted on dropping the word 'obey' from the marriage vows. In 1848, with **Lucretia Coffin Mott**, she organized the first women's rights convention at Seneca Falls, New York, which launched the women's suffrage movement. With **Susan Brownell Anthony** she founded the National Woman Suffrage Movement in 1869, and compiled the *History of Woman Suffrage* (1881–86). Her daughter, Harriet Eaton Blatch (1856–1940), was also a leading suffragette.

STANWYCK, Barbara, originally **Ruby Stevens** (1907–90) American actress, born in Brooklyn, New York. A working girl from the age of 13, she became a dancer, appearing in the *Ziegfeld Follies of 1923*, and made her dramatic stage début in *The Noose* (1926). Her first film was *Broadway Nights* (1927). Established as a major star in the 1930s, she is best remembered as gutsy, pioneering women in westerns like *Annie Oakley* (1935) and *Union Pacific* (1939), or as sultry femmes fatales in such films noirs as *Double Indemnity* (1944). A durable leading lady, she was frequently seen as strong-willed women, often struggling to escape from the wrong side of the tracks, although her range also extended to melodramas like *Stella Dallas* (1937) and deft comic performances as in *Lady Eve* (1941) and *Ball of Fire* (1941). Active in radio and television, she enjoyed a long-running series *The Big Valley* (1965–69). She received a special Academy Award in 1982.

STAPELDON, Walter de (1261–1326) English prelate, born in Annery, in Devon. Bishop of Exeter from 1308 to 1326, he was founder of Stapeldon Hall, later Exeter College, Oxford. He was the Treasurer of **Edward II**, and for this reason was killed by insurgent Londoners in Cheapside.

STAPLETON, Maureen (1925–) American actress, born in New York, and a major interpreter of the plays of **Tennessee Williams**. She made her New York début, however, in **Synge**'s *The Playboy of the Western World* in 1946. Her first Williams role, Serafina in *The Rose Tattoo* (1951), brought her great acclaim. She followed with Flora in *Twenty-Seven Wagons Full of Cotton* (1955), Lady Torrance in *Orpheus Descending* (1957), and the turbulent Amanda Wingfield in a revival of *The Glass Menagerie* in 1965. She has been acclaimed as one of the great American stage actresses, and has also appeared in a number of films.

STAPLETON, Ruth, née **Carter** (1929–83) American evangelist and faith healer, born in Plains, Georgia, younger sister of President **Jimmy Carter**, and said to have been influential in his conversion to Christianity. Unlike many of her fellow-Southern Baptists, she co-operated with other Christians, including Roman Catholics, and used her graduate training in psychology in a remarkable ministry which stressed the necessity for inner healing ('communicating love to the negative, repressed aspects in a human being'). In the 1976 Presidential campaign she addressed the National Press Club, Washington, DC largely on her brother's behalf—reportedly the first time that it had listened to a woman preacher.

STAPLETON, Thomas (1535–98) English theologian and controversialist, born in Henfield, Sussex. Educated at Winchester and New College, Oxford, he became prebendary of Chichester, but was deprived of his prebend in 1563, went in 1569 to Douai, became a professor there and in 1590 at Louvain. A learned Catholic controversialist in Latin, he is remembered for his fine Elizabethan English prose translations of **Bede** (1565), and his careful Latin Life of Sir **Thomas More** (1588).

STARK, Dame Freya Madeline (1893–) English writer and traveller, born in Paris. She spent her childhood in England and Italy, and attended Bedford College, London University, under the tutelage of **W P Ker**, professor of literature. She was a nurse on the Italian front during World War I, and afterwards studied Arabic at the School of Oriental and African Studies, London University, and was invited to Baghdad by the prime minister. There she worked on the *Baghdad Times*, followed the crusader routes and mapped the Valley of the Assassins in Luristan, described in *Valley of the Assassins* (1934). During World War II she worked for the ministry of information in Aden and Cairo, and was personal assistant to Lady Wavell, describing her experiences in *West is East* (1945). She has travelled extensively, financed by her writings, in Europe, the Middle East and Asia. She has more than 30 titles to her name, including *The Southern Gates of Arabia* (1938), *Traveller's Prelude* (1950), *Beyond Euphrates* (1951), *The Coast of Incense* (1953), *Dust in the Lion's Paw* (1961) and *The Journey's Echo* (1963).

STARK, Harold Raynsford (1880–1972) American naval officer, born in Wilkes-Barre, Pennsylvania. Educated at the US Naval Academy, Annapolis, he served in a destroyer flotilla (1914–15). He was chief of the Bureau of Ordnance (1934–37). Chief of Naval Operations from 1939 to 1942, he was relieved after Pearl Harbor (December, 1942) and became commander US Naval Forces Europe (1942–43) with headquarters in London, where he made a great contribution to the success of Allied Operations in the European theatre.

STARK, Johannes (1874–1957) German physicist. Educated at Munich, he became professor at Würzburg. He discovered the Stark effect concerning the splitting of spectrum lines by subjecting the light source to a strong electrostatic field, and also the Doppler effect in canal rays. He was awarded the Nobel prize for physics in 1919.

STARK, John (1728–1822) American Revolutionary soldier, born in Londonderry, New Hampshire. He saw service in the French and Indian War (1754–59). In the American War of Independence (1775–83) he served at Bunker Hill (1775), and won a victory at Bennington (1777). He was a member of the court martial which condemned **John André.**

STARKIE, Enid Mary (1897–1970) Irish critic of French literature, born in Killiney, County Dublin, daughter of the classicist W J M Starkie and sister of the Hispanicist and Gypsy-lover, Walter Starkie (author of *Raggle-Taggle*, *Spanish Raggle-Taggle*, and *Scholars and Gypsies*). She was educated at Alexandra College, Dublin, Somerville College, Oxford, and the Sorbonne, where she wrote a doctoral thesis on **Émile Verhaeren**. She taught modern languages at Exeter and Oxford, wrote perceptively on **Baudelaire** (1933) and **Gide** (1954), played a major part in establishing the poetic reputation of **Arthur Rimbaud** (1938), and crowned her work by two outstanding volumes on **Flaubert** (1967, 1971). In 1951 she campaigned successfully to have the quinquennially-elected professor of poetry at Oxford be a poet rather than a critic, whereby **C S Lewis** was defeated by **C Day Lewis**. She portrayed her early life in *A Lady's Child* (1941).

STARLEY, James (1831–81) English inventor, born in Albourne, Sussex. He worked in a factory in Coventry manufacturing sewing-machines and bicycles, and invented a new, improved sewing-machine and the 'Coventry' tricycle. He also invented the 'Ariel' geared bicycle in 1871, and set up as a manufacturer of these.

STARLING, Ernest Henry (1866–1927) English physiologist, born in London. He was lecturer in physiology at Guy's Hospital and later professor at University College (1899–1923). He introduced the term *hormones* for the internal secretions of the ductless glands and, with Sir **William Bayliss**, discovered the intestinal hormone *secretin* (1902). His studies of cardiovascular physiology did much to elucidate the physiology of the blood circulation. He wrote *Principles of Human Physiology* (1912).

STARR, Ringo See **BEATLES, The**

STAS, Jean Servais (1813–91) Belgian chemist, born in Louvain. Professor of chemistry at Brussels, he developed progressively more accurate methods for determination of atomic weights which appeared first to prove and then to disprove **William Prout**'s hypothesis.

STASSEN, Harold Edward (1907–) American politician, born in West St Paul, Minnesota. He studied law at the University of Minnesota, and became at 31 the youngest governor in Minnesota history. He served in the navy in World War II, failed in 1948 and 1952 to secure the Republican presidential nomination, and became administrator of foreign aid under **Eisenhower**. He represented the USA at the London disarmament conference in 1957. He resigned in 1958 following disagreements with **John Foster Dulles**. He wrote *Where I Stand* (1947).

STATHAM, (John) Brian (1930–) English cricketer, born in Denton. A Lancashire fast bowler, he formed a profound contrast to his rumbustious partner in the England attack, **Freddie Trueman**. A quiet, undemonstrative man, he took 252 Test wickets in 70 appearances, and 2260 in his first-class career. For almost 20 years he was a Lancashire stalwart and took 100 wickets in a season on 13 occasions.

STATIUS, Publius Papinius (c.45–96) Roman poet, born in Naples, the son of a school-teacher. He won a poetry prize in Naples, and went to Rome, where he flourished as a court poet and a brilliant improviser in the favour of **Domitianus** until 94, when he retired to Naples. His major work was the *Thebaïs*, an epic in twelve books on the struggle between the brothers Eteocles and Polynices of Thebes. Of another epic, the *Achilleïs*, only a fragment remains. His *Silvae*, or occasional verses, have freshness and vigour.

STAUDINGER, Hermann (1881–1965) German organic chemist, the founder of polymer chemistry, born in Worms. He was professor of organic chemistry at Freiburg (1926–51) and was awarded the Nobel prize for chemistry in 1953 for his research in macromolecular chemistry.

STAUFFENBERG, Count Berthold von (1907–44) German soldier, born in Bavaria. A colonel on the General Staff in 1944, he was one of the ringleaders in the unsuccessful attempt to assassinate **Hitler** at the headquarters at Rastenburg on 20 July 1944. He was shot next day.

STAUNFORD, Sir William (1509–58) English judge and text-writer, born in Hadley, Middlesex and educated at Oxford. Involved in the administration of property devolving on the Crown after the dissolution of the monasteries, he sat in several parliaments and became a judge in 1554. He wrote *An Exposition of the King's Prerogative* (1567) and *Les Plees del Coron* (1557), both in the form of commentaries on texts of relevant statutes or textbooks.

STAUNTON, Howard (1810–74) English Shakespearean scholar, actor and chess player. He studied at Oxford, and settled down to journalism in London. He was world chess champion 1843–51, and and wrote *The Chess-player's Handbook* (1847) and other books. His edition of **Shakespeare**'s works contained excellent textual emendations.

STAVISKY, Serge Alexandre (c.1886–1934) Russian-born French swindler, born in Kiev. He moved to Paris in 1900, and floated fraudulent companies, liquidating the debts of one by the profits of its successor until, in 1933, he was discovered to be handling bonds to the value of more than five hundred million francs on behalf of the municipal pawnshop in Bayonne. Stavisky fled to Chamonix and probably committed suicide; but in the meantime the affair had revealed widespread corruption in the government and ultimately caused the downfall of two ministries. Stavisky was found guilty during a trial that ended in 1936 with the conviction of nine others.

STEAD, Christina Ellen (1902–83) Australian novelist, born in Rockdale, Sydney, the daughter of English immigrants. She trained as a teacher, but in 1928 left Australia for Europe, where she lived in London and Paris, working as a secretary in a Paris bank (1930–35). She went to live in Spain but left at the outbreak of war and, with her husband, the novelist and political economist William Blake, she settled in the USA. From 1943 to 1944 she was an instructor at the Workshop in the Novel at New York University, and in 1943 became a senior writer for M-G-M in Hollywood. *The Salzburg Tales*, her first collection of stories, was published in 1934. In all she published eleven novels, including *The Beauties and Furies* (1936), *The Man Who Loved Children* (1940), *For Love Alone Letty Fox: Her Luck* (1946), *A Little Tea, A Little Chat* (1948), *The People with the Dogs* (1952), *Cotter's England* (1956), and *Miss Herbert* (*The Suburban Wife*) (1976). The author of several novellas and the contributor of many short stories to the *New Yorker*, she left the USA in 1947 and settled in England, but finally returned to her homeland in 1974. *I'm Dying Laughing*, a novel begun in the 1940s and ridiculing American Hollywood radicals, was published posthumously in 1986.

STEAD, William Thomas (1849–1912) English journalist and reformer, born in Embleton, Alnwick. He was editor of the Darlington *Northern Echo* (1871–80), and assistant editor of the *Pall Mall* (1880–83), and editor (1883–90). He drew attention to the practice of purchasing child prostitutes by openly committing the offence himself and writing an article about it (*The Maiden Tribute of Modern Babylon*), for which he was imprisoned for three months; it led to the Criminal Amendment Act of 1885. He founded the *Review of Reviews* (1890), and crusaded for peace and spiritualism. He wrote *If Christ Came to Chicago* (1893) and *The Americanization of the World* (1902). He drowned in the *Titanic* disaster.

STEBBINS, George Ledyard (1906–) American botanist, born in Lawrence, New York. He studied biology at Harvard and spent his career at the University of California at Davis (1950–73) where he established the department of genetics. He was the first to apply modern ideas of evolution to botany, as expounded in his *Variation and Evolution in Plants* (1950). From the 1940s he used artificially induced polyploidy (the condition of having more than twice the basic number of chromosomes) to create fertile hybrids, of value both in taxonomy and in economic plant breeding. His other books include *Processes of Organic Evolution* (1966) and *Flowering Plants: Evolution Above the Species Level* (1974).

STEDMAN, Charles (1753–1812) American-born British historian, born in Philadelphia. He served with the British in the American War of Independence and fought at Lexington and Bunker Hill. He settled in England in 1783, and wrote a standard history (with valuable maps) of the American War of Independence from the British point of view (1794).

STEDMAN, Edmund Clarence (1833–1908) American poet, critic and financier, born in Hartford, Connecticut. He studied at Yale, was war correspondent of the *New York World* (1861–63), and then became a New York stockbroker and banker. He published *Poems* (1860), *Victorian Poets* (1875), *Edgar Allan Poe* (1880), *Poets of America* (1886), *Nature of Poetry* (1892), *Victorian Anthology* (1896), and other works.

STEED, Henry Wickham (1871–1956) English journalist and author, born in Long Melford. He joined *The Times* as foreign correspondent in 1826, and was editor from 1919 until his resignation in 1922. He was proprietor and editor of the *Review of Reviews* from 1923 to 1930. He published a number of books on European history and affairs.

STEEL, Sir David (Martin Scott) (1938–) Scottish politician, last leader of the Liberal party. A journalist and broadcaster, he was the youngest MP when first elected in 1965. He sponsored a controversial Bill to reform the laws on abortion (1966–67) and was active in the Anti-Apartheid Movement before succeeding **Jeremy Thorpe** as leader of the Liberal party in 1976. He led his party into an electoral pact with Labour (1977–78) and subsequently an alliance with the Social Democratic party (SDP) (1981–88). Despite Steel's undoubted popularity and the polling of a quarter of the total vote by the Alliance at the 1983 General Election, they won only 23 seats. Steel is the author of several political publications. Immediately after the 1987 general election he called for a merger of the Liberals and SDP and announced that he did not intend to seek the leadership of the merged party.

STEELE, Sir Richard (1672–1729) Irish essayist, dramatist and politician, born in Dublin. He was educated at Charterhouse, where **Addison** was a contemporary, and Merton College, Oxford, after which he entered the army as a cadet in the Life Guards. Reacting against military life, he wrote *The Christian Hero* (1701), to show that the gentlemanly virtues can be practised only on a Christian basis. He next wrote three comedies, *The Funeral, or Grief à la mode* (1702), *The Tender Husband* (1703) and *The Lying Lover* (1704). In 1706 he became gentleman waiter to Prince George of Denmark, and in 1707 **Robert Harley** (Earl of Oxford) appointed him gazetteer. Steele's first venture in periodical literature, *The Tatler*, ran from 1709 to 1711 and was published on Tuesdays, Thursdays and Saturdays to suit the outgoing post-coaches. Its predecessor was **Defoe**'s *Review*, and like the *Review* included items of current news, but after No. 83 it concentrated on social and moral essays, with occasional articles on literature, usually written by Addison who had joined forces with Steele on issue No 18. The chief fare, however, was social comedy, which covered the affectations and vices of society. These were exposed by humorous satire, with the aim of putting the Christian at ease in society. Christianity was to become fashionable and to this end—for formal preaching was unpalatable—a wealth of concrete social situations and types was created, including coffee-house politicians, 'pretty fellows', pedants and bores at every level of society. The coffee houses and chocolate houses provided most of these types, but society women and the family were the theme of many of the articles, for Steele's plea in *The Christian Hero* for a more chivalrous attitude to women implied the correction of female frivolity in high places and the insistence on the family as the source of genuine happiness. Steele is perhaps at his best in scenes of domestic felicity (cf Nos 95, 104 and 150), and these contain the intrusion of bourgeois sentiment and morality which was to be the mark of the age, in contrast to the aristocratic ethos of the Restoration. The beginnings of the domestic novel are here, not only in the relations between the pseudonymous editor, Isaac Bickerstaff, and his half-sister Jennie, but in numerous conversation pieces and in the social context provided by the Trumpet Club, forerunner of the more famous Spectator Club which Steele first outlined in No. 2 of that periodical, though Addison wrote most of the articles. In 1713 Steele entered parliament, but was expelled the following year on account of a pamphlet, *The Crisis*, written in favour of the house of Hanover, a cause to which his periodical *The Englishman* was also devoted. He was rewarded on the succession of **George I** with the appointment of supervisor of Drury Lane theatre, and a knighthood followed. In 1718 a difference on constitutional procedure led to an estrangement from Addison, who was in the ministry, and loss of his office. In 1722 financial troubles made him retire to Wales, where he lived until his death. His letters to his wife ('dearest Prue'), whom he married in 1707, attest the sincerity of his sermons on married love.

STEELE, Tommy, originally **Thomas Hicks** (1936–) English actor, singer and director, born in London. During the 1950s and 1960s, he achieved considerable success as a pop singer, after making his stage début in variety at the Empire Theatre, Sunderland, in 1956, and his London variety début at the Dominion Theatre in 1957. He played Tony Lumpkin in **Goldsmith**'s *She Stoops to Conquer*, at the Old Vic in 1960. He continued to appear in musicals during the 1960s, most notably in *Half a Sixpence* (1963–64). He had his own one-man show in London in 1979, and in 1983 starred in and directed a stage adaptation of *Singin' In The Rain* at the London Palladium.

STEELL, Sir John (1804–91) Scottish sculptor, born in Aberdeen. Educated as an artist in Edinburgh and Rome, most of his chief works are in Edinburgh, including the equestrian statue of the Duke of **Wellington** (1852), *Alexander taming Bucephalus* at the City Chambers, Sir **Walter Scott** and Prince **Albert**. His brother Gourlay (1819–94) was an animal painter and curator of the National Gallery in Edinburgh.

STEEN, Jan (1626–79) Dutch painter, born in Leiden, the son of a brewer. A pupil of **Ostade** and Van Goyen, he joined the Leiden guild of painters in 1648 and next year went to The Hague until 1654, afterwards following his father's trade at Delft. He spent his last years as an innkeeper in Leiden. His best works were genre pictures of social and domestic scenes depicting the everyday life of ordinary folk with rare insight and subtle humour.

STEENSEN, Niels See **STENSEN**

STEENSTRUP, Johannes (1844–1935) Norwegian scholar, son of **Johannes Iapetus Steenstrup**. He was professor of northern antiquities at Copenhagen (1877) and wrote numerous works, including *Normannerne* (1876–82), a book about Viking times.

STEENSTRUP, Johannes Iapetus Smith (1813–97) Norwegian zoologist, born in Vang. He was professor of zoology at Copenhagen (1845–85). His books treat of hermaphroditism, alternation of generations, flounders' eyes, and cephalopods; and he identified the animal remains from Ertebølle settlements and shell mounds in 1851, thus making the earliest contribution to the discipline of archaeozoology.

STEENWIJK, Hendrik van (c.1550–1603) Dutch painter of architectural interiors. He settled in Frankfurt in 1579. His son Hendrik (1580–1649), also a painter, came to London on **Van Dyck**'s advice in 1629.

STEER, Philip Wilson (1860–1942) English painter, born in Birkenhead. He studied at Paris, and began as an exponent of Impressionism, to which he added a traditionally English touch. A founder of the New English Art Club, he taught at the Slade. He excelled, too, as a figure painter, as shown in the Pitti *Self-Portrait*, *The Music Room* (Tate), and the *Portrait of Mrs Hammersley*, painted in the style of **Gainsborough**.

STEEVENS, George (1736–1800) English Shakespearean commentator, born in Stepney, London. He was educated at Eton and King's College, Cambridge. His reprint from the original quartos of *Twenty Plays* *of Shakespeare* (1766) brought him employment as Dr **Edmund Johnson**'s collaborator in his edition (1773). Jealous of **Malone**, Steevens issued a doctored text using his own emendations (15 vols, 1793–1803), which held authority till **Boswell**'s publication of Malone's *Variorum Shakespeare* (1821).

STEFAN, Josef (1835–93) Austrian physicist, born near Klagenfurt to shopkeeper parents. He became professor at Vienna in 1863 after being a school teacher for seven years. He proposed Stefan's law (or the Stefan-Boltzmann law), that the amount of energy radiated per second from a black body is proportional to the fourth power of the absolute temperature. He used this law to make the first satisfactory estimation of the sun's surface temperature.

STEFÁNSSON, Davið (1895–1964) Icelandic poet, born in Fagriskógur, Eyjafjörður. Educated in Akureyri and Reykjavík, he worked as a librarian in Akureyri (1925–52). He became the most popular Romantic poet of his time with a series of volumes of lyrical poetry, starting with *Svartar fjaðrir* (Black Feathers, 1919) and including *Kveðjur* (Greetings, 1924), *Í byggðum* (In Human Habitations, 1933) and *Aðnorðran* (From the North, 1936). He also wrote a historical novel, *Sólon Islandus* (2 vols, 1940), and a successful play, *Gullna Hliðið* (The Golden Gate, 1941).

STEFÁNSSON, Jón (1881–1962) Icelandic landscape painter, born in Sauðárkrókur in the north of Iceland, and one of the three founders, with **Ásgrímur Jónsson** and **Jóhannes Kjarval**, of modern art in Iceland. He went to Copenhagen to study engineering in 1900, but in 1903 decided to devote himself to art. He went to Paris in 1908 and studied under **Matisse**. A man of strong temperament, he painted landscapes on a grand scale, exploiting colour with extraordinary luminosity.

STEFÁNSSON, Vilhjalmur (1879–1962) Canadian Arctic explorer, born of immigrant Icelandic parents in Arnes, Manitoba. He studied anthropology and archaeology before going to live among the Eskimo (1906–07). Between 1908 and 1912 he conducted further studies amongst the Mackenzie and Copper Eskimo. From 1913 to 1918 he led the Canadian Arctic Expedition to map the Beaufort Sea, the last such expedition to be unsupported by radio or aeroplanes. Later he became a consultant on the use of Arctic resources. He wrote several popular books, including *My Life with the Eskimo* (1913) and *The Friendly Arctic* (1921).

STEFFANI, Agostino (1654–1728) Italian priest, operatic composer and diplomatist, born in Castelfranco. In 1688 he settled at the Hanover court. He wrote a fine *Stabat Mater*, several operas and vocal duets, and was a friend of **Handel**.

STEFFENS, (Joseph) Lincoln (1866–1936) American journalist, born in San Francisco. He studied at French and German universities as well as graduating from the University of California. He began as a reporter on the New York *Evening Post* (1892–98), ultimately becoming assistant city editor, from where he graduated to city editor on the New York *Commercial Advertiser* (1898–1902). He was managing editor of *McClure's Magazine* (1902–06) where his revision of an article on city corruption in St Louis resulted in his outstandingly successful series later republished as *The Shame of the Cities* (1904), an epoch-making work in urban reform. Although identified with what would later be termed the 'muck-raking' movement, the articles were distinguished by careful research, outspoken courage and an insistence that the real villain was not boss corruption so much as public apathy. He followed it with an analysis of corruption and reform on state level (*The Struggle for Self-Government*, 1906), and became associate editor of the *American* and *Everybody's* magazines (1906–11). He visited post-Revolutionary Russia in 1919 and popularized his famous comment 'I have seen the future and it works'. His delightful *Autobiography* (2 vols, 1931) was ironic and somewhat disillusioned but exceedingly informative on his times, as well as on his own realism and innocence.

STEICHEN, Edward Jean (1879–1973) American photographer, born in Luxembourg but taken as a child to the USA, where he grew up in Michigan. He studied art in Milwaukee (1894–98) and practised both painting and photography in Europe until 1914; a member of The Linked Ring in England, he was noted for his studies of the nude. In 1902 he helped **Alfred Stieglitz** to found the American Photo-Secession Group, his later work having a marked Symbolist content. In World War I he served as commander of the photographic division of the US army, and in the 1920s moved with enthusiasm into New Realism, achieving success with his fashion photography which was elegant but human, and with some outstanding portraits. He was head of US Naval Film Services during World War II and director of photography at the New York Museum of Modern Art from 1945 to 1962, organizing the world-famous exhibition *The Family of Man* in 1955.

STEIN, Sir (Mark) Aurel (1862–1943) Hungarian-born British archaeologist and explorer, born in Budapest. He held educational and archaeological posts under the Indian government, from 1900 to 1930 conducting a series of expeditions in Chinese Turkestan and Central Asia tracing the ancient caravan routes between China and the West. His discoveries included the Cave of a Thousand Buddhas near Tan Huang, walled up since the 11th century. Later superintendent of the Indian Archaeological Survey (1910–29), he died at Kabul when about to begin an exploration of Afghanistan.

STEIN, Charlotte von, née **von Schardt** (1742–1827) German writer and the friend of **Goethe**. Lady-in-Waiting at the Weimar court, in 1764 she married Friedrich von Stein, the Duke of Saxe–Weimar's Master of the Horse. In 1775, she met Goethe, who fell in love with her. Their friendship was broken suddenly (1788), but renewed before her death. She was the inspiration for many of Goethe's love poems and plays; she herself wrote dramas such as *Rino* and *Dido*.

STEIN, Gertrude (1874–1946) American writer, born in Allegheny, Pennsylvania. She spent her early years in Vienna, Paris and San Francisco, and then studied psychology at Radcliffe College under **William James**, and medicine at Johns Hopkins University, but settled in Paris, where she was absorbed into the world of experimental art and letters. She sometimes attempted to apply the theories of abstract painting to her own writing, which led to a magnified reputation for obscurity and meaningless repetition. From 1907 she shared an apartment with a close friend from San Francisco, Alice B Toklas. Her first book, *Three Lives* (1908), reveals a sensitive ear for speech rhythms, and by far the larger part of her work is immediately comprehensible. Her influence on contemporary artists—particularly **Picasso**—is probably less than she imagined, though her collection of pictures was representative of the best of its era. Her main works include *Tender Buttons* (1914), *The Making of Americans* (1925), *The Autobiography of Alice B. Toklas* (1933), *Four Saints in Three Acts* (1934, an opera with music by **Virgil Thomson**), and *Everybody's Auto-*

biography (1937). She stayed in Germany in the village of Chloz during World War II, and afterwards wrote *Wars I Have Seen* (1945), and the novel, *Brewsie and Willie* (1946), about the liberation by American soldiers.

STEIN, Heinrich Friedrich Carl, Baron vom (1757–1831) Prussian Liberal statesman and German nationalist, born in Nassau. He entered the service of Prussia in 1780, and became president of the Westphalian chambers (1796). His tenure as secretary for trade (1804–07) was unfruitful and he resigned, only to be recalled after the treaty of Tilsit, when he abolished the last relics of serfdom, created peasant proprietors, extirpated monopolies and hindrances to free trade, promoted municipal government, and supported **Scharnhorst** in his schemes of army reform. **Napoleon** insisted upon his dismissal, and Stein withdrew (1808) to Austria, but not before issuing his *Political Testament*. In 1812 he went to St Petersburg and built up the coalition against Napoleon. From the battle of Leipzig to the Congress of Vienna he was the ruling spirit of the opposition to French imperialism. Stein liberalized the Prussian state, but at the same time fostered the dangerous myth of German destiny and aggressive nationalism, not least by founding the *Monumenta Germaniae Historica* in 1815.

STEIN, Jock (John) (1922–85) Scottish footballer and manager, born in Burnbank, Lanarkshire. A player of only average ability, he became the greatest Scottish football manager of all time. His managerial career began with the unfashionable Fife club Dunfermline Athletic, which under his management won the Scottish Cup and became briefly a force in Europe. A short though highly successful spell followed with Hibernian and he then returned to his last senior club as a player, Glasgow Celtic, in 1965. In the next 13 years Celtic won nine championships in a row, the League Cup on five consecutive occasions and several Scottish Cups. Celtic also won the European Cup in 1967 and were finalists in 1970. Stein left Celtic in 1978 for a brief period as manager of Leeds United, but returned to Scotland to become national manager. Under him the Scottish side qualified for the World Cup Finals in Spain in 1982. He died during an international against Wales at Cardiff as his side was about to qualify for a World Cup play-off.

STEIN, William Howard (1911–80) American biochemist, born in New York. He studied at Harvard and Columbia and spent his career at the Rockefeller Institute. There, with **Stanford Moore**, he developed a method for finding the number of amino acid residues in a protein molecule, and shared the 1972 Nobel prize for chemistry with him and **Christian Anfinsen**.

STEINARR, Steinn, pen-name of **Aðalsteinn Kristmundsson** (1908–58) Icelandic poet, born in the Westfjords. A pioneer of Modernist poetry in Iceland, he moved to Reykjavík and joined the Communist party as a young man. He wrote poetry of tremendous skill and sensibility which became progressively more abstract and metaphysical. His chief works were *Rauður loginn brann* (The Red Flame Burned, 1934), *Spor í sandi* (Tracks in the Sand, 1940), *Ferð án fyrirheits* (Journey without Promise, 1942), and his final masterpiece, *Tíminn og vatnið* (Time and Water, 1948).

STEINBECK, John Ernest (1902–68) American novelist, born in Salinas, California. *Tortilla Flat* (1935), his first novel of repute, is a faithful picture of the shifting *paisanos* of California, foreshadowing the solidarity which characterizes his major work, *The Grapes of Wrath* (1939), a study of the poor in the face of disaster and threatened disintegration. His journalistic grasp of significant detail and pictorial essence make this book a powerful plea for consideration of human values and common justice. It led to much-needed reform, and won for Steinbeck the 1940 Pulitzer prize. His other works include *Of Mice and Men* (1937), *The Moon is Down* (1942), *East of Eden* (1952) and *Winter of our Discontent* (1961), as well as the light-hearted and humorous *Cannery Row* (1945), *The Wayward Bus* (1942) and *The Short Reign of Pippin IV* (1957). He won the Nobel prize for literature in 1962.

STEINEM, Gloria (1934–) American feminist and writer, born in Toledo, Ohio. In the 1960s she emerged as a leading figure in the women's movement, protesting volubly against the Vietnam War and racism. A co-founder of Women's Action Alliance in 1970, she was likewise formative in setting up *Ms Magazine* which brought to the fore women's issues.

STEINER, Jakob (1796–1863) German-Swiss geometer, born in Utzendorf. From 1834 he was professor at Berlin, and pioneered 'synthetic' geometry, particularly the properties of geometrical constructions, ranges and curves.

STEINER, Max (Maximilian Raoul Walter) (1888–1971) Austrian-born American film composer, born in Vienna. A student at the Imperial Academy there, he was a child prodigy, his first operetta *The Beautiful Greek Girl* being performed in 1902. A conductor of musical comedies in London, Paris and Berlin, he was invited to New York in 1914 by **Florenz Ziegfeld** and worked for a number of impresarios in the Broadway theatre. Invited to Hollywood to conduct music for a film of *Rio Rita* (1929) he was subsequently offered a permanent position at RKO where he was able to establish the power of music to enhance the dramatic mood and emotions of a production, seen most notably in *King Kong* (1933). Resident at Warner Brothers from 1936, he contributed many vivid and full-blooded scores to some of the most enduring screen classics, among them *Gone With the Wind* (1939), *Casablanca* (1942) and *The Treasure of the Sierra Madre* (1948). Nominated on 26 occasions for the Academy Award, he won Oscars for *The Informer* (1935), *Now Voyager* (1942) and *Since You Went Away* (1945). Failing eyesight brought his retirement in 1965.

STEINER, Rudolph (1861–1925) Austrian social philosopher, born in Kraljevíc, the founder of anthroposophy, a spiritual doctrine still influential in Europe and America. He studied science and mathematics, and edited **Goethe**'s scientific papers in Weimar from 1889 to 1896. He was much influenced by **Annie Besant** and the Theosophists, but went on to found his own Anthroposophical Society in 1912 and established at Dornach near Basel his Goetheanum, a 'school of spiritual science'. He aimed to restore by training the innate human capacity for spiritual perception, which had become dulled by the material preoccupations of the modern world. His work helped inspire many other, still flourishing, educational and therapeutic enterprises, usually emphasizing the importance of activities centred on art, myth, drama and eurhythmy. He founded his first school for maladjusted children in 1919, the first of more than 70 Rudolf Steiner schools now operating. His main publications were *The Philosophy of Freedom* (1894), *The Philosophy of Spiritual Activity* (1894), *Occult Science: an Outline* (1913) and *Story of my Life* (1924).

STEINITZ, Wilhelm (1836–1900) Czechoslovakian chess player, the first official world chess champion. Born in Prague, then capital of Bohemia, he moved to Vienna to complete studies in mathematics which he funded by playing chess for stakes. From 1862 he settled in London for 20 years as a chess professional, supplementing his income as chess editor of *The Field*. After moving to New York he won decisively over **Zukertort** in the 1886 match organized to decide the first official championship of the world. He defended his title three times successfully before losing it in 1894 to **Lasker**. He died, impoverished, in a New York mental asylum following an unsuccessful attempt to challenge God to a chess match.

STEINLEN, Théophile Alexandre (1859–1923) Swiss painter and illustrator, born in Lausanne. He settled in Paris in 1878, and made his name as a poster-designer and by his work in French illustrated phapers.

STEINMETZ, Carl Friedrich von (1796–1877) Prussian general, born in Eisenach. He fought through the campaign of 1813–14, and in 1866 routed three Austrian corps at Náchod and Skalitz. In 1870 he commanded the right wing of the German advance; but he proved unequal to the task, and after Gravelotte was appointed governor-general of Posen and Silesia.

STEINMETZ, Charles Proteus, originally **Karl August Rudolf** (1865–1923) German-born American electrical engineer, born in Breslau. Educated at the Technical High School, Berlin, he was forced to leave Germany in 1888 for socialist activities and emigrated to the USA in 1889. He was consulting engineer to General Electric from 1893 and professor at Union College from 1902. He discovered magnetic hysteresis, a simple notation for calculating alternating current circuits, and lightning arresters for high-power transmission lines.

STEINTHAL, Heymann (1823–99) German philologist, born in Gröbzig in Anhalt. In 1850 he became lecturer in philology at Berlin, and in 1863 extraordinary professor. He wrote *The Origin of Language* (1851), and other works.

STEINWAY, originally **Steinweg, Heinrich Engelhard** (1797–1871) German-born American pianomaker, born in Wolfshagen. As a young man he fought in the Prussian army at the battle of Waterloo (1815) and in 1836 established a piano factory in Brunswick. In 1850 he moved with his family to the USA and established a business in New York, leaving one son, Theodor, to carry on the German branch.

STELLA, Frank Philip (1936–) American painter, born in Malden, Massachusetts. He studied at Phillips Academy and Princeton (1954–58) and his earliest Minimal paintings, symmetrical patterns of black stripes, date from 1959. Using house-painters' techniques to avoid any trace of 'artistic' brushwork, he creates a totally impersonal effect, which has made a significant impression on younger artists like **Donald Judd**.

STELLA, Joseph, originally **Giuseppe Stella** (1877–1946) Italian-born American painter, born in Muro Lucano, near Naples. He emigrated to New York in 1896, studied at the Art Students' League (1897), then at the New York School of Art, before going back to Europe in 1909. In Italy he painted in an Impressionist style, then visited Paris in 1911. He returned to New York in 1913 and painted the first American Futurist pictures, swirling compositions in the manner of **Gino Severini**, interpretations of New York scenery, eg *Brooklyn Bridge*, c.1919.

STELLER, originally **Stöhler, Georg Wilhelm** (1709–46) German naturalist and explorer, born in Windsheim, near Nuremberg. He studied theology at Wittenburg, but switched to medicine and botany there and joined the Academy of Sciences at St Petersburg. He was seconded to the second Kamchatka expedition led by **Vitus Bering** (1737–44); he travelled across Russia to the east, explored Siberia and Kamchatka, met Bering in Okhotsk, sailed on the *St Paster* and *St Paul* via the Aleutian Islands to Alaska and landed on Kayak Island, and returned via Bering Island where they were shipwrecked and where Bering died. There Steller wrote his most famous work, *De Bestiis Marinis* (published posthumously in 1751). He died on his way back to St Petersburg. Steller's sea-cow (now extinct), Steller's sea lion and Steller's eider are named after him.

STENDHAL, pseud of **Henri Marie Beyle** (1783–1842) French novelist, born in Grenoble where he was educated at the École Centrale. During a Bohemian youth he wrote for the theatre but his plays are poorly constructed and stiff. A cousin offered him a post in the ministry of war, and from 1800 he followed **Napoleon**'s campaigns in Italy, Germany, Russia and Austria. Between wars he spent his time in Paris drawing-rooms and theatres. When Napoleon fell he retired to Italy, adopted his pseudonym, and began to write books on Italian painting (*Histoire de la Peinture en Italie*, 1817), on **Haydn** and **Mozart**, and travels in Italy (*Rome, Naples et Florence en 1817*, 1817), as well as copious journalism. In 1821 the Austrian police expelled him from the country, and on his return to Paris he completed his book *De l'Amour* (1822). After the 1830 revolution he was appointed Consul at Trieste and Civitavecchia, but his health deteriorated and he returned to Paris where he started a Life of Napoleon. His recognized masterpieces, *Le Rouge et le Noir*, and *La Chartreuse de Parme*, were published in 1830 and 1839 respectively. The first follows the rise and decline of Julien Sorel, a provincial youth in the France of the Restoration who can be relied on to make a drama out a crisis. The second details the fortunes of Fabrice del Dongo at an insignificant Italian court during the same period. Though seminal French novels of the 19th century, neither received great understanding during his lifetime. Among his other novels are *Armance* (1822) and *L'Abesse de Castro* (1839). *Lucien Leuwen* (1894) and *Lamiel* (1889), both unfinished, were published posthumously. Autobiographical volumes include his *Journal* (1888), *La Vie de Henri Brulard* (1890) and *Souvenirs d'égotisme* (1892).

STENGEL, Casey (Charles Dillon) (1889–1975) American baseball player and manager, born in Kansas City, Missouri. As a player (1912–31), he was an outfielder with the Brooklyn Dodgers in the National League and also had spells with Pittsburgh, Philadelphia, Boston and New York. From 1932 as manager, he led the New York Yankees to seven World Series victories between 1949 and 1960, including five in a row (1949–53). He then moved across the city to manage the New York Mets (1962–65). He was elected to the Baseball Hall of Fame in 1966.

STENMARK, Ingemar (1956–) Swedish champion skier, born in Swedish Lapland. He began competing at the age of eight when he won a regional Donald Duck trophy. His international fame began in 1974–75 when he won the slalom and was second overall in the World Cup. He subsequently won the World Cup three years in succession (1976–78) and went on to become the most successful competitor in slalom and grand slalom ever recorded. He was World Master in 1978 and 1982 and won the Olympic Gold medal at Lake Placid in 1980. He was the first man to win three consecutive slalom titles (1980–82).

STENSEN, Niels, also known as **Nicolaus Steno** (1638–86) Danish physician, naturalist and theologian who did fundamental work in anatomy, geology, crystallography, palaeontology and mineralogy. He was born in Copenhagen and brought up a strict

Lutheran, but turned Catholic when he settled in Florence; he was appointed personal physician to the Grand Duke of Tuscany in 1666, royal anatomist at Copenhagen (1672), and vicar-apostolic to North Germany and Scandinavia in 1677. He was the first to point out the true origin of fossil animals (1669), explain the structure of the earth's crust and differentiate between stratified and volcanic rocks. As a physician he discovered Steno's duct of the parotid gland, and explained the function of the ovaries. He is buried in the crypt of the **Medici** in Florence.

STEPHANSSON, Stephan G, originally **Stefán Guðmundarson** (1853–1927) Icelandic-born Canadian poet, born in Kirkjuhóll in Skagafjörður. He emigrated with his family to North America in 1873, and worked as a railroad labourer and farmhand in Wisconsin before settling in Markerville, Alberta, as a farmer in 1889. There he raised a large family, took a prominent part in local affairs, and in the evenings composed several volumes of poetry in Icelandic, including *Úti á víðavangi* (Out in the Open, 1894), *Á ferð og flugi* (En route, 1900), and his major work, *Andvökur* (Wakeful Nights, 6 vols, 1909–38). A lifelong socialist, he expressed his horror of war in a controversial volume, *Vígslóði* (The War Trail, 1920). Recognized as one of the finest of Icelandic poets, his works also give a vivid picture of landscapes and conditions in western Canada.

STEPHEN, St one of the seven chosen to manage the finance and alms of the early church. Tried by the Sanhedrin for blasphemy, he was stoned to death—the first Christian martyr.

STEPHEN I (d.257) pope from 254 to 257. He maintained against **Cyprian** that heretics baptized by heretics need not be rebaptized.

STEPHEN I, Saint (c.977–1035) first king of Hungary, and her patron saint, baptized as a boy with his father Duke Géza by St **Adalbert** of Prague. Married to Gisela, the sister of the emperor Henry II, he succeeded to his father's dukedom in 997. He welded Pannonia and Dacia, inhabited by semi-independent Magyar chiefs, into a regular kingdom, and in 1000 was crowned king with the title of 'Apostolic King' bestowed by Pope **Sylvester II**. He suppressed paganism, organised the church and endowed abbeys, and laid the foundations of many institutions surviving to this day. He was canonized in 1083.

STEPHEN II (d.752) pope in 752. He died two days after his election, and so is often not reckoned as a pope.

STEPHEN II or **III** (d.757) pope from 752 to 757. When Rome was threatened by the Lombards, he turned to **Pepin the Short**, king of the Franks, who forced the Lombards to withdraw, and gave the pope the exarchate of Ravenna, the real foundation of the temporal power.

STEPHEN (c.1097–1154) king of England and grandson of **William I, the Conqueror**, the third son of Stephen, Count of Blois, by William's daughter Adela. In 1114 he was sent to the court of his uncle, **Henry I** of England; he received from him the countship of Mortain in Normandy, and acquired that of Boulogne by his marriage to Matilda, daughter of Eustace, Count of Boulogne. When Henry I resolved to settle the crown on his own daughter **Matilda** (or **Maud**), widow of the emperor **Henry V** and afterwards wife of Geoffrey Plantagenet of Anjou, Stephen and the English barons swore fealty to her. But on Henry's death on 1 December 1135, he hurried over from Normandy, was enthusiastically received, and was crowned on 22 December. He declared the empress Matilda illegitimate, attempted to strengthen his position with the help of Fleming mercenaries, and made more enemies than friends by the favours he heaped on some of the great lords. King **David I** of Scotland invaded the north on Matilda's behalf, was defeated near Northallerton (1138), but retained Cumberland. The first powerful enemy that the king made was Robert, Earl of Gloucester, an illegitimate son of Henry I; next he arrayed against himself the clergy, by his quarrel with the justiciar, Bishop Roger of Salisbury. The civil war now began in earnest although the extent of the anarchy has often been exaggerated. In 1139 Matilda landed at Arundel, in 1141 took Stephen prisoner at Lincoln, and was acknowledged queen, but her harshness and greed soon disgusted Englishmen. The men of London rose, and she fled to Winchester. In November 1141 Stephen regained his liberty and his crown, and in 1148 Matilda finally left England. In 1151, Stephen nominated his son Eustace as heir apparent to the throne, but this was not accepted by the church authorities. Eustace died in 1153, and Matilda's son Henry of Anjou (**Henry II**) crossed over to England, and forced Stephen to acknowledge him as his successor. Stephen died in Dover the following year.

STEPHEN, James (1758–1832) English lawyer, born in Poole. He was first a parliamentary reporter, then a colonial official at St Kitts in the West Indies, an experience which turned him into a slavery abolitionist. He married **Wilberforce**'s sister (1800), entered parliament (1808) and became colonial under-secretary. He was the author of *The Slavery of the British West Indies* (1824–30).

STEPHEN, Sir James Fitzjames, 1st Baronet (1829–94) English jurist, grandson of **James Stephen**, born in Kensington. He was a legal member of the Viceregal Council (1869–72) where he promoted codification. Professor of common law at the Inns of Court (1875–79) and a judge of the High Court (1879–91), he prepared various codes for England, none of which was enacted. Holding in the main a retributive theory of punishment, he wrote a standard *History of the Criminal Law* (1883) and was responsible for the Indian Evidence Act.

STEPHEN, Sir Leslie (1832–1904) English scholar and critic, born in London, brother of Sir **James Fitzjames Stephen** and grandson of the abolitionist **James Stephen**, and father of **Virginia Woolf** and **Vanessa Bell**. Brought up in a Christian circle known as the 'Clapham Sect', he was educated at Eton, King's College, London, and Trinity Hall, Cambridge. He was ordained, and became a fellow of Trinity Hall (1864), but he left the church in 1870 and became an agnostic. He published his reasons in *Essays on Free Thinking and Plain Speaking* (1873) and *An Agnostic's Apology* (1893). He helped to found the *Pall Mall Gazette*, and was editor of the *Cornhill Magazine* (1871–82). He launched the *English Men of Letters* series with a biography of **Samuel Johnson** (1878), followed by **Pope** (1880), **Swift** (1882), **George Eliot** (1902) and **Hobbes** (1904). In 1876 he published *The History of English Thought in the Eighteenth Century* (1876), which is generally regarded as his most important work. He also wrote *The Science of Ethics* (1882), and *The Utilitarians* (3 vols, 1900). He was the first editor of the *Dictionary of National Biography* (1882–91), from 1890 jointly with Sir **Sidney Lee**. A noted athlete and mountaineer, he published a collection of mountaineering sketches in *Playground of Europe* (1871).

STEPHEN BATHORY (1533–86) Hungarian king of Poland, elected prince of Transylvania in 1571. He succeeded to the Polish throne in 1575. An able administrator and fine soldier, he easily suppressed a revolt of dissident burghers in Danzig and went on to defeat an attempted Russian invasion of Livonia under **Ivan IV, the Terrible** and retake Polotsk. He was responsible for many administrative reforms and was notably successful in achieving a tolerant resolution of the religious divisions brought about by the Reformation in Poland.

STEPHEN DUSHAN (c.1308–1355) Serbia's greatest tsar (1336–55), the subjugator of Bulgaria, Macedonia and Albania.

STEPHENS, Alexander Hamilton (1812–83) American politician, born near Crawfordsville, Georgia. He was admitted to the bar in 1834, and sat in congress 1843–59. He advocated the annexation of Texas in 1838, in 1854 defended the Kansas-Nebraska Act, at first opposed secession, but in 1861 became Confederate vice-president. He sat in congress again (1874–83), in 1882 was elected governor of Georgia, and wrote *War between the States* (1867–70).

STEPHENS, Charles (1504–64) French printer, son of the founder, **Henri I Stephens**, and brother of **Robert Stephens**. He studied medicine, but later took charge in Paris as royal printer in 1552 when his brother retired to Geneva and started another branch of the firm. He wrote and printed an encyclopaedic work, *Dictionarium Historicum ac Poeticum* (1953), *Praedium Rusticum* (1554), and much else.

STEPHENS, Henri I (French **Étienne,** Latin **Stephanus)** (c.1460–1520) born in Provence, founder of the great firm of printers and publishers of that name. He had three sons: François, **Robert** and **Charles**.

STEPHENS, Henri II (1528–98) French printer, grandson of the firm's founder and son of **Robert Stephens**. A classical scholar, he travelled in Italy, England and the Netherlands, collating MSS. In 1556 he joined his father in the printing business in Geneva, and issued many Greek and Latin classics, including some 20 'first editions', and compiled a Greek dictionary (*Thesaurus graecae linguae*, 1572). He also wrote the semi-satirical *Apologie pour Hérodote* (1566). His son Paul (1566–1627) continued the family printing business in Paris.

STEPHENS, James (1825–1901) Irish nationalist and chief founder of the Fenians, born in Kilkenny. A civil engineer on the railways, he became an active agent of the Young Ireland party. Slightly wounded during the rising at Ballingarry (1848), he hid for three months in the mountains, and then escaped to France. In 1853 he journeyed round Ireland, and founded the Irish Republican Brotherhood (Fenians), of which he became the leader ('Head Centre'). He started the *Irish People* newspaper (1863) to urge armed rebellion, visited America on fund-raising missions, and was arrested in Dublin in November, 1865, but escaped within a fortnight. He found his way to New York, was deposed by the Fenians and with the decline in his political importance was allowed to return to Ireland in 1891.

STEPHENS, James (1882–1950) Irish poet, born in Dublin. Sent to an orphanage as a child, he found work as a solicitor's clerk. His first published work was a volume of poems, *Insurrections* (1909), followed by his first novel, *The Charwoman's Daughter* (1912). *The Crock of Gold* (1912), a prose fantasy, made him famous, and turned him into a full-time writer. His later volumes were *Songs from the Clay* (1914), *The Demi-Gods* (1914), *Reincarnation* (1917), and *Deirdre* (1923). He moved to London in 1924.

STEPHENS, John Lloyd (1805–52) American archaeologist and traveller, born in Shrewsbury, New Jersey. Trained as a lawyer, he travelled extensively in the Levant, the Balkans, and Central Europe before embarking with the architect and artist Frederick Catherwood (1799–1856) on an extended exploration of Mesoamerica in 1839–42. Their work founded the field of Mayan archaeology, and rediscovered the cities of Copan, Quirigua, Palenque, Uxmal and Chichen Itza, then unknown except to the local Indians. Published as *Incidents of Travel in Central America, Chiapas and Yucatan* (1841) and *Incidents of Travel in Yucatan* (1843), it established, with the contemporary surveys of **Squier** in the Mississippi valley, American archaeology as a discipline in its own right.

STEPHENS, Joseph Rayner (1805–79) Scottish social reformer, born in Edinburgh. In 1834 he was expelled from his Methodist ministry for supporting church disestablishment. He made himself a name as a factory reformer, opened three independent chapels at Ashton-under-Lyne, and took an active part in the anti-poor-law demonstrations (1836–37) and the Chartist movement, of which, however, he refused actual membership. He was imprisoned for his struggle for the Ten Hours Act (1847).

STEPHENS, Meic (1938–) Welsh poet and editor, born in Treforest, Glamorgan and educated at the universities of Aberystwyth and Rennes. He founded *Poetry Wales* in 1965, and compiled and edited *The Oxford Companion to the Literature of Wales* in both Welsh and English. He has been literature director of the Welsh Arts Council since 1967.

STEPHENS, Robert (1503–59) French printer, son of the firm's founder, **Henri I Stephens**, and elder brother of **Charles Stephens**. He succeeded his father in 1526, and in 1539 and 1540 was appointed printer to King **Francis I** in Latin, Greek and Hebrew. He early became a Protestant and got into difficulties with the University of Paris; in 1550 he retired to Geneva and founded a branch of the family printing firm, where he printed several of **Calvin**'s works. A scholar in his own right, he published a Latin dictionary (*Thesaurus Linguae Latinae*, 1532), as well as a Latin New Testament (1523), a Latin Bible (1528) and a Greek New Testament (1550).

STEPHENSON, George (1781–1848) English railway engineer, son of a colliery enginekeeper, born in Wylam near Newcastle. He rose to be fireman in a colliery, and contrived meanwhile to pay for a rudimentary education at night school. In 1815 he invented, contemporaneously with **Davy**, a colliery safety lamp, the 'Geordie', for which he received a public testimonial of £1000. In 1812 he had become enginewright at Killingworth Colliery, and there in 1814 he constructed his first locomotive. *Blucher* was slow and unreliable on the inadequate wooden colliery tram roads, and Stephenson's reputation stemmed from his success in improving both locomotives and rails. In 1821 he was appointed engineer for the construction of the Stockton and Darlington mineral railway (opened on 27 September 1825), and in 1826 for the Liverpool and Manchester Railway, which, after unprecedented difficulties, was opened on 15 September 1830. The previous October had seen the memorable contest of engines at Rainhill, resulting in the triumph of Stephenson's *Rocket* at 30 miles an hour. Thereafter he was engineer on the North Midland, Manchester and Leeds, Birmingham and Derby, and many other railways in England, and was consulted about proposed lines in Belgium and Spain.

STEPHENSON, Robert (1803–59) English mechanical and structural engineer, son of **George Stephenson**, born in Willington Quay. Apprenticed to a coalviewer at Killingworth, in 1822 his father sent him for six months to Edinburgh University. In 1823 he assisted his father in surveying the Stockton and Darlington Railway; and after three years in Colombia, he returned to become manager of his father's locomotive engine-works in Newcastle. He attained independent fame by his Britannia Tubular Bridge (1850), those at Conway (1848) and Montreal (1859), the High Level Bridge at Newcastle (1849), the Royal Border Bridge at Berwick (1850), etc. He was MP for many years from 1847 and was buried in Westminster Abbey.

STEPINAC, Aloysius (1898–1960) Yugoslav prelate and cardinal, primate of Hungary, born in Krasić near Zagreb. He was imprisoned by **Tito** (1946–51) for alleged wartime collaboration and with failing health, released, but lived the remainder of his life under house arrest.

STEPNYAK, 'Son of the Steppe', nom de guerre of **Sergius Mikhailovich** (1852–95) Russian revolutionary. He was an artillery officer, but becoming obnoxious to government as an apostle of freedom, he was arrested, and subsequently kept under such surveillance that he left Russia and settled (1876) in Geneva, and then (1885) in London. He was, however, held to be the assassin of General Mesentzieff, head of the St Petersburg police (1878). He was run over by a train in a London suburb. Among his works were *La Russia Sotteranea* (1881, trans *Underground Russia*, 1883), studies of the Nihilist movement; *Russia under the Tsars* (trans 1885); and the novel *The Career of a Nihilist* (1889)

STEPTOE, Patrick Christopher (1913–88) English gynaecologist and reproduction biologist, born in Witney and educated at King's College London and St George's Hospital Medical School. Following military service, he specialized in obstetrics and gynaecology, becoming senior obstetrician and gynaecologist in the Oldham Hospitals in 1951. In 1980 he became medical director of the Bourn Hall Clinic in Cambridgeshire. He had long been interested in laparoscopy (a technique of viewing the abdominal cavity through a small incision in the umbilicus) and in problems of fertility. In 1968, he met **Robert Edwards** and together they worked on the problem of *in vitro* fertilization of human embryos, which ten years later resulted in the birth of a baby after *in vitro* fertilization and implantation in her mother's uterus. The ethical issues are still controversial.

STERLING, John (1806–44) Scottish man of letters, born at Kames Castle on the island of Bute. Educated at Glasgow University and Trinity College, Cambridge, he turned to writing, and bought the literary magazine, *The Athenaeum*, which he edited. He published numerous essays and long poems, and a novel, *Arthur Coningsby* (1833). He is best known as the subject of **Carlyle**'s *Life of John Sterling* (1851).

STERN, Daniel See **AGOULT, Marie de Flavigny**

STERN, Isaac (1920–) Russian-born American violinist, born in Kreminiecz. He studied at the San Francisco Conservatory (1928–31) and made his début with the San Francisco Symphony Orchestra as guest artist (1934) and in New York (1937). He played subsequently as soloist and in chamber music throughout the world.

STERN, Otto (1888–1969) German-American physicist, the son of a grain-merchant, born in Sohrau. He was educated at Breslau and worked at Zürich, Frankfurt, Rostock and Hamburg, before becoming research professor of physics at the Carnegie Technical Institute (1933–45). He worked on the quantum theory and the kinetic theory of gases; and, for his work on the magnetic moment of the proton and for his development of the molecular-ray method of studying atomic particles, he was awarded the Nobel prize for physics in 1943.

STERNE, Laurence (1713–68) Irish novelist, born in Clonmel, County Tipperary, the son of an impoverished infantry ensign who died when the boy was two. His early youth was a struggle. In 1724 he was sent to Halifax Grammar School in Yorkshire and, seven years later, to Jesus College, Cambridge. In 1738 he was ordained, and appointed to the living of Sutton-on-the-Forest and made a prebendary of York, where his great-grandfather had been archbishop. In 1758 his marriage failed and his wife was committed to a lunatic asylum. In 1759 he wrote *The History of a Good Warm Watchcoat* (not published until after his death), and also the first two volumes of *The Life and Opinions of Tristram Shandy*, first published in York, but published anew in London in 1760. The public welcomed it; and in April **Robert Dodsley** brought out a second edition. This was followed by *Sermons* of the 'Rev. Mr Yorick'. In 1761, vols. III and IV of *Tristram* came out, Sterne having meanwhile moved to Coxwold, thenceforward his infrequent home. Between 1761 and 1767 the rest of *Tristram* appeared; Sterne, whose health was now failing, spending much of the time in France and Italy. *A Sentimental Journey through France and Italy* appeared in 1768; and the author died in London of pleurisy. Few writers have displayed such mastery over every form of humour both in situation and in character, a humour at times coming near to that of his acknowledged master **Cervantes**. Yet the wild eccentricity of his manner and arrangement—a deliberate and usually successful bid for laughter—was also the convenient cloak for what some, such as **Goldsmith**, might call a singularly slipshod literary style. His indecencies, less gross than those of **Swift** or **Rabelais**, are all too prurient. He was unscrupulous in his borrowings. His pathos too often takes the form of overstrained sentimentalism. Yet this very sentimentalism was also his strength. For Sterne's great contribution to the development of the novel was to widen its scope and loosen its structure; and in his hands it became the channel for the utterance of the writer's own sentiments. His *Letters from Yorick to Eliza* (1775–79) contained his correspondence with a young married woman to whom he was devoted.

STERNHOLD, Thomas (1500–49) English psalmist, joint-author with John Hopkins (d.1570) of the English version of psalms formerly attached to the Prayer Book. He was born near Blakeney in Gloucestershire, or in Hampshire. He was Groom of the Robes to **Henry VIII** and **Edward VI**. The first edition (undated) contains only 19 psalms; the second (1549), 37. A third edition, by Whitchurch (1551), contains seven more by J H (John Hopkins). The complete book of psalms, which appeared in 1562, formed for nearly two centuries almost the whole hymnody of the Church of England and was known as the 'Old Version' after the rival version of **Nathum Tate** and **Nicholas Brady** appeared in 1696. Forty psalms bore the name of Sternhold.

STEUBEN, Frederic William Augustus, Baron (1730–94) German soldier in the American Revolutionary army, born in Magdeburg. At 14 he served at the siege of Prague, and in 1762 was on the staff of **Frederick II, the Great**. While in Paris in 1777 he was induced by **Franklin** to go to America, and his services were joyfully accepted by congress and **Washington**. He was appointed inspector-general, prepared a manual of tactics for the army, remodelled its organization, and improved its discipline. In 1780 he received a command in Virginia, and took part in the siege of Yorktown. A naturalized American citizen in 1783, congress in 1790 voted him an annuity of 2400 dollars and land near Utica, New York. From 1778 to 1889 he published *Regulations for the Order and Discipline of the Troops of the United States*.

STEVENS, Alfred (1818–75) English painter and sculptor, born in Blandford, Dorset. He studied in Italy and became assistant to **Thorvaldsen** in Rome, and became teacher of architectural design at Somerset House, London (1845–47). During the next ten years he decorated and designed household furniture, fireplaces and porcelain. From 1856 he worked on the **Wellington** monument in St Paul's Cathedral (completed after his death by John Tweed) and the mosaics under the dome of St Paul's. He also designed the lions at the British Museum.

STEVENS, Bernard (1916–83) English composer, born in London. From 1948 to 1981 he was an influential teacher of composition at the Royal College of Music. His first work to achieve recognition was the *Symphony of Liberation* (*Daily Express* prize, 1946) and his subsequent output included a further symphony, an opera *The Shadow of the Glen* (1978–79), concertos for piano, violin and cello, two string quartets and other chamber, choral and instrumental pieces.

STEVENS, John (1749–1838) American engineer and inventor, born in New York City of a wealthy and influential family. He studied law at King's College (now Columbia University) but never practised. After some years' service in the Revolutionary Army, in 1787 he saw **John Fitch**'s steamboat on the Delaware river and resolved to improve on his design. In 1803 he patented a multi-tubular boiler and used it in his first steamboat, the *Little Juliana*, which was propelled by twin Archimedean screws driven through gears by a high-pressure steam engine. Inevitably the high pressure gave trouble and he had to revert to paddle wheels which could be driven by low-pressure engines, but this did not prevent him from building a number of other successful steamships, including the *Juliana* in 1811 which became the world's first steam ferry on the Connecticut river. In this and other enterprises he was assisted by his son **Robert Livingston Stevens**.

STEVENS, Richard John Samuel (1757–1837) English organist and composer, born in London. He composed harpsichord sonatas and glees, mostly to **Shakespeare**'s songs.

STEVENS, Robert Livingston (1787–1856) American engineer and inventor, born in Hoboken, New Jersey, second son of the inventor **John Stevens**. He began at an early age to assist his father in the design and construction of steamboats, experimenting with various improvements to the hulls and engines in pursuit of speed, strength and efficiency. In 1830 he became president and chief engineer of the Camden & Amboy Railroad and Transportation Company, invented the cow-catcher and the hook-headed railroad spike, and was the first to burn anthracite coal in a locomotive engine. He spent many years on the design of an armour-plated warship but it was still unfinished at the time of his death.

STEVENS, Siaka Probin (1905–88) Sierra Leone politician. His father, who was illiterate, served in the Royal West Africa Frontier Force, undertaking guard duty at the residence of the governor, Sir Leslie Probin, after whom he named his son. Although a Christian, his father had several wives, Siaka's mother being a Muslim, allowing him to bridge the gap between the two religions. He joined the Sierra Leone police force in 1923 but left seven years later for industry, soon becoming an active trade unionist and then a politician, founding the moderate, socialist All People's Congress (APC) in 1960. The APC won the 1967 general election but the result was disputed by the army and Stevens withdrew from the premiership; but in 1968 an army revolt brought him back and in 1971, under a revised constitution, he became Sierra Leone's first president. He created a one-party state and remained in power until his retirement at the age of 80.

STEVENS, Stanley Smith (1906–73) American experimental psychologist, born in Ogden, Utah. Educated at Harvard (PhD 1933), he taught there from 1932 until his death. He made important contributions to the science of psychophysics, an important strand in the history of psychology which began with the work of Ernst Heinrich and of **Gustav Fechner** (1801–77), later known as the 'Father of Experimental Psychology'. He made a number of contributions to our understanding of the sense of hearing in particular, but also devised general theories and experimental techniques for the study of the 'scaling' of sensory qualities (eg, loudness, brightness, pain). He also edited a major work of reference, *The Handbook of Experimental Psychology* (1951).

STEVENS, Thaddeus (1792–1868) American statesman, born in Danville, Vermont. In 1816 he settled as a lawyer at Gettysburg, Pennsylvania, was member of congress (1849–53), a Republican leader, and chairman at the trial of President **Andrew Johnson** (1868).

STEVENS, Wallace (1879–1955) American poet, born in Reading, Pennsylvania. His father, of Dutch descent, was a lawyer for the Reading Hardware Company and wrote poetry. His education began at private schools, then schools attached to Lutheran churches and later Reading Boys' High School. He enrolled at Harvard (1897–1900) and afterwards went to New York where he started out in journalism but was neither successful nor happy. He entered New York Law School in 1901 and at the age of 28 began working for various law firms, ultimately becoming a diligent executive with an insurance company in Hartford, Connecticut. Poetry was a spare-time activity, and his first collection, *Harmonium*, was not published until 1923. His poetic career falls into three phases: 1898–1900, 1907–24, and 1928–55. Most of his early work, both poems and short stories, was published in *The Harvard Advocate*. In 1907 he began composing poems for Elsie Moll, his future wife. It was from the late 1920s to the middle 1950s, however, that he published the work that has established him as one of the century's great poets: *Ideas of Order* (1936), *The Man With the Blue Guitar* (1937), *Parts of a World* (1942), *Transport to Summer* (1947) and *The Auroras of Autumn* (1950). The *Collected Poems* was published in 1954. Critics invariably point out the great influence of the French Symbolist movement, but he drew from many sources and his poems range over an extraordinary variety of subjects. His constant theme was the exploration of aesthetic experience as the key to fundamental reality.

STEVENSON, Adlai Ewing (1900–65) American Democrat politician and lawyer, the grandson of another A E Stevenson (1835–1914) who was vice-president under **Cleveland** (1893–97). He was born in Los Angeles, studied at Princeton, spent two years editing a family newspaper and then took up law practice in Chicago. From 1943 he took part in several European missions for the State Department and from 1945 served on the American delegations to the foundation conferences of the United Nations Organization. In 1948 he was elected governor of Illinois, where his administration was exceptional for efficiency and lack of corruption. He stood against **Eisenhower** as Democratic presidential candidate in 1952 and 1956, but each time his urbane 'egg-headed' campaign speeches, published under the titles *Call to Greatness* (1954) and *What I Think* (1956), had more appeal abroad than at home.

STEVENSON, Robert (1772–1850) Scottish engineer, born in Glasgow. He lost his father in infancy; and his mother in 1786 married Thomas Smith, first engineer of the Northern Lighthouse Board. Stevenson then took to engineering, and in 1796 succeeded his stepfather. During his 47 years' tenure of office he planned or constructed 23 Scottish lighthouses, most notably that on the Bell Rock off Arbroath, employing the catoptric system of illumination, and his own invention of 'intermittent' or 'flashing' lights. He also acted as a consulting engineer for roads, bridges, harbours, canals and railways. One of his sons, Alan (1807–65), built the Skerryvore Lighthouse (1844).

STEVENSON, Robert Louis Balfour (1850–94) Scottish author, born in Edinburgh, grandson of **Robert Stevenson** and son of Thomas Stevenson, engineer to the Board of Northern Lighthouses. A constant invalid in childhood, he was educated at the Edinburgh Academy (1861–63) before his ill health forced the family to travel abroad. He studied engineering at Edinburgh University for a session (1867) with a view to the family calling, but transferred to law, becoming an advocate in 1875. His true inclination, however, was for letters. He collaborated in four mediocre plays, but for the next few years he travelled chiefly in France. His *Inland Voyage* (1878) describes a canoe tour in Belgium and northern France, and his *Travels with a Donkey in the Cevennes* describe a tour undertaken in the same year. In 1876 he was at Fontainebleau (which he made the subject of travel sketches), and it was at the neighbouring Barbizon that he met the divorcée, Fanny Osbourne, née Vandegrift (1840–1914), whom he followed to America and married in 1880. His return to Europe with his wife and stepson **Lloyd Osbourne** marked the beginning of a struggle against tuberculosis which his natural gaiety as a writer conceals. His wife and stepson have described their makeshift homes—Davox, Pitlochry and elsewhere—but in those difficult circumstances he was 'making himself' as a writer not only of travel sketches but also of essays and short stories which found their way into the magazines. *Thrawn Janet*, a story in the vernacular, appeared in *Cornhill Magazine* (1881), although an earlier tale, *An Old Song*, appeared in 1877 and was then lost until it was located and republished in 1982. *The Merry Men* was published serially in 1882, in which year also appeared *The New Arabian Nights*. *Treasure Island*, the perfect romantic thriller, brought him fame in 1883 and his most successful adventure story, *Kidnapped*, appeared in 1886. *Catriona* (1893), introducing the love element, was also very popular. *The Master of Ballantrae* (1889) is a study in evil of a sort not uncommon in Scottish fiction, but here also are the wildest adventures. *The Strange Case of Dr Jekyll and Mr Hyde* (1886) is not a romance, but it further illustrates Stevenson's metaphysical interest in evil. *The Black Arrow* (1888) shows declining powers, but *Weir of Hermiston* (published posthumously in 1896), though unfinished, is acclaimed his masterpiece and it may be, for the canvas is larger, and the issues involved more serious. *St Ives*, which was also left unfinished, was completed by Sir **Arthur Quiller Couch** in 1897. Stevenson's work as an essayist is seen at its best in *Virginibus Puerisque* (1881) and *Familiar Studies of Men and Books* (1882). *A Child's Garden of Verses* (1885) is not poetry in the adult sense; but it is one of the best recollections of childhood in verse. *Underwoods* (1887) illustrates his predilection for preaching in prose or verse and is the poetry of the good talker rather than the singer, and the tone is usually nostalgic. Only occasionally, as in *The Woodman*, does he touch on metaphysical problems, but vernacular poems such as *A London Sabbath Morn* subtly describe the Calvinism he had renounced but which intrigued him to the end. In 1889 Stevenson settled in Samoa and there with his devoted wife and stepson he spent the last five years of his life on his estate of Valima, which gives its name to the incomparable series of letters which he wrote, chiefly to friends in Britain.

STEVENSON, Ronald (1928–) Scottish composer, pianist and writer on music, born in Blackburn, Lancashire. He studied at the Royal Manchester College of Music. He champions music as world-language, seeking in his works to embrace a vast spectrum of international culture: notably the 80-minute *Passacaglia on DSCH* for piano, Piano Concerto No. 2 *The Continents* (1972), Violin Concerto (1979), choral settings, many songs ranging from settings of Scots to Japanese Haiku, and his transcriptions from the broadest range of music. His concern is 'an ethnic aesthetic'; he has composed for mentally-handicapped children and played in geriatric homes. He is an eminent contrapuntist, a master of keyboard technique and a distinguished melodist. He has written *Western Music: An Introduction*, many articles on music, and is an authority on **Busoni**.

STEVENSON, William (d.1575) English scholar. He entered Christ's College, Cambridge, in 1546, and became a fellow; he is known to have staged plays there. He was probably the author of the earliest surviving English comedy, *Gammer Gurton's Needle* (1553), sometimes attributed to John Still or John Bridges.

STEVIN, Simon (1548–1620) Flemish mathematician and engineer, born in Bruges. He held offices under Prince **Maurice of Orange**, wrote on fortification, book-keeping and decimals, and invented a system of sluices and a carriage propelled by sails. He was responsible for introducing the use of decimals which were soon generally adopted.

STEWARD, Julian Haynes (1902–72) American cultural anthropologist, born in Washington DC. He studied at Cornell and the University of California, and subsequently taught at Michigan, Utah and California. In 1935 he joined the Bureau of American Ethnology, becoming director of the Institute of Social Anthropology at the Smithsonian Institution in 1943. In 1946 he was appointed professor at Columbia, and from 1956 to 1972 was research professor in anthropology at Illinois. He developed the method of cultural ecology which seeks regularities in the relationships between environment, technology, social organization and culture. He was concerned with cultures as adaptive systems geared to specific environments, and advocated a multilinear approach to cultural evolution. His views are set out in his *Theory of Culture Change* (1955) and *Evolution and Ecology* (1977). He also edited the encyclopaedic, seven-volume *Handbook of the South American Indians* (1946–59), the major reference work on the subject.

STEWART, House of a Scottish family, from whom came the royal line of the (Stuart) sovereigns of Scotland and, later, of Great Britain and Ireland, from **Robert II** of Scotland (1371) to Queen **Anne** (1714). The original family was descended from a Breton immigrant, Alan Fitzflaald (d.c.1114), who received the lands of Oswestry in Shropshire from **Henry I**. His elder son was William Fitzalan (c.1105-60).

STEWART, Alexander (1214–83) fourth hereditary Steward of Scotland. He was regent of Scotland in **Alexander III**'s minority and commanded at the battle of Largs (1263).

STEWART, Alexander, Earl of Buchan (c.1343–c.1405) son of King **Robert II**, the 'Wolf of Badenock', and overlord of Badenoch. He received the earldom on his marriage (1382). He earned his nickname from his continued attacks on the bishopric of Moray.

STEWART, Prince Charles Edward Louis Philip Casimir (1720–88) known variously as the 'Young Pretender', the 'Young Chevalier', and 'Bonnie Prince Charlie', elder son of **James Francis Stewart**. Born in Rome, and educated there, he became the centre of Jacobite hopes. He first saw service at the siege of Gaeta (1734); fought bravely at Dettingen (1743); and next year repaired to France, to head Marshal **Saxe**'s projected invasion of England. But the squadron which was to have convoyed the transports with 15000 troops to Kent fled before the British fleet; the transports themselves were scattered by a tempest; and for a year and a half Charles was kept hanging on in France, until at last, sailing from Nantes, he landed with seven followers at Eriskay in the Hebrides on 23 July 1745, and on 19 August raised his father's standard in Glenfinnan. The clansmen flocked in; on 17 September Edinburgh surrendered, though the castle held out; and Charles kept court at Holyrood, the palace of his ancestors. There followed the victory over Sir **John Cope** at Prestonpans (21 September), and on 1 November he left for London at the head of 6500 men. He took Carlisle and advanced as far as Derby. Londoners became alarmed, especially since the cream of the British army was engaged on the Continent. Eventually William, Duke of **Cumberland** was dispatched against the insurgents. Charles meanwhile had been unwillingly argued into a withdrawal by his commanders and the Highlanders turned back, winning one last victory against the government forces at Falkirk, 17 January 1746, before suffering a crushing defeat at the hands of Cumberland's troops at Culloden Moor on 16 April. The rising was ruthlessly suppressed by the duke, who earned the name 'Butcher Cumberland', and Charles was hunted in the highlands and islands for five months with a price of £30000 on his head, but no one betrayed him. He was helped by **Flora Macdonald** when he crossed from Benbecula to Portree in June 1746, disguised as 'Betty Burke', her maid. He landed in Brittany on 29 September, and was given hospitality at the French court until the peace of Aix-la-Chapelle (1748) caused his forcible expulsion from France, although he spent a while at Avignon until the English found out and protested, and afterwards lived secretly in Paris with his mistress, **Clementina Walkinshaw**. He made two or three secret visits to London between 1750 and 1760, even declaring himself a protestant. He assumed the title of Charles III of Great Britain and retired to Florence, where he married in 1772 Louisa, Countess of **Albany**, but the marriage was later dissolved. His natural daughter, Charlotte (1753–89) by his mistress Clementina Walkinshaw, he had created Duchess of Albany. He died in Rome and was buried at Frascati, later at St Peter's.

STEWART, Henry Benedict Maria Clement, Duke of York (1725–1807) Scottish cardinal, brother of Prince **Charles Edward Stewart** and the last of the Stuarts, born in Rome. After the failure of the 1745 rising he became in 1747 a cardinal and priest, and in 1761 bishop of Frascati. He enjoyed, through the favour of the French court, the revenues of two rich abbeys, as well as a Spanish pension. The French Revolution stripped him of his fortune, and he had to take refuge in Venice for three years. In 1800 **George III** granted him a pension of £4000. The crown jewels, carried off by **James VII and II**, were bequeathed by him to **George IV**, then Prince of Wales, who in 1819 gave 50 guineas towards **Canova**'s monument in St Peter's to 'James III, Charles III, and Henry IX'. Next to the exiled Stuarts came the descendants of Henrietta, **Charles I**'s youngest daughter, who in 1661 was married to the duke of Orléans. From this marriage sprang Anne Mary (1669–1728), who married **Victor Amadeus**, duke of Savoy and king of Sardinia; their son Charles Emmanuel III (1701–73), king of Sardinia; his son, Victor Amadeus III (1726–96), king of Sardinia; his son, **Victor Emmanuel I** (1759–1824), king of Sardinia; his daughter Mary (1792–1840), who married Francis, duke of Modena; their son, Ferdinand (1821–49), who married Elizabeth of Austria; and their daugher, Maria Teresa (1849–1919), who in 1868 married Prince (from 1913 to 1918 king) **Ludvig III** of Bavaria, and whom, as 'Mary III and IV', the 'Legitimist Jacobites' of 1891 put forward as the 'representative of the Royal House of these realms'. Rupert, her son, was ninth in descent from Charles I; he represented Bavaria at Queen **Victoria**'s Diamond Jubilee, 1897, and early in World War I took command of a German army group in France. The branch of the family which the Act of Settlement (1701) called to the throne on the death of Anne were the descendants of the electress Sophia of Hanover, granddaughter of **James VI and I** by her mother Princess **Elizabeth**, electress palatine and queen of Bohemia. By that act the above-mentioned descendants of Henrietta of Orléans were excluded, and also the Roman Catholic descendants of the Princess Elizabeth's sons. Queen **Elizabeth II** is 26th in descent from Walter Fitzalan, 20th from **Robert II** and 12th from James VI and I. Lady Arabella Stuart (1575–1615), was the daughter of the Earl of Lennox, Darnley's younger brother, and so a great-great-grandaugher of **Henry VII**, a third cousin to Queen **Elizabeth**, and a first cousin to James VI and I. At 27 she was suspected of having a lover in the boy **William Seymour**, who had Tudor blood in his veins; but on James's accession (1603) she was restored to favour, only, however, to contract a secret marriage in 1610 with him. Both were imprisoned, and both escaped—Seymour successfully to Ostend, but she was retaken, and died, insane, in the Tower. The cadets of the house of Stewart are: (1) descendants of **Robert II**; (2) descendants of natural sons of his descendants; (3) descendants of natural sons of Stewart kings; and (4) legitimate branches of the Stewarts before their accession to the throne. To the first belong the Stuarts of Castle-Stewart, descended from Robert, Duke of Albany, Robert II's third son, through the Lords Avondale and Ochiltree. They received the titles of Lord Stuart of Castle-Stewart in the peerage of Ireland (1619), Viscount Castle-Stewart (1793), and Earl (1809). To the second class belong the Stuart earls of Traquair (1633–1861), descended from a natural son of James Stewart, Earl of Buchan. To the third class belong the Regent **Moray**, the Marquis of Bute, and the Shaw-Stewarts; and to the fourth belong the Earls of Galloway (from a brother of the fifth High Steward), the Lords Blantyre, the Stewarts of Fort-Stewart, and the Stewarts of Grandtully (from the fourth High Steward; the last baronet died in 1890).

STEWART, James (1243–1309) fifth hereditary Steward of Scotland. He was one of the six regents of Scotland after the death of **Alexander III**.

STEWART, Prince James Francis Edward (1688–1766) Claimant to the throne of Great Britain, known as the

'Old Pretender', the only son of **James VII** and **II** and his second wife, **Mary of Modena**, born in St James's Palace, London. Six months later, he was conveyed by his fugitive mother to St Germain, where, on his father's death in 1701, he was proclaimed his successor as **James III**. On an attempt (1708) to make a descent upon Scotland, the young 'Chevalier de St George' was not allowed to land; after his return he served with the French in the Low Countries, distinguishing himself at Malplaquet. But in **Mar**'s ill-conducted rebellion, he landed at Peterhead (December 1715), only to sneak away six weeks afterwards from Montrose. France was then closed to him by the Treaty of Utrecht, and almost all the rest of his life was passed in Rome, where he died. In 1719 he had married Princess Clementina Sobieski (1702–1735), who bore him two sons.

STEWART, John (c.1381–1424) Scottish soldier, nephew of **Alexander Stewart**, Earl of Buchan. At the head of a Scottish force, he defeated the English at Baugé (1421). He became constable of France but fell fighting at Verneuil.

STEWART, Walter (d.1177) second son of William Fitzalan. He moved to Scotland and received from **David I** large possessions in Renfrewshire, Teviotdale, and Lauderdale, along with the hereditary dignity of Steward of Scotland, which gave his descendants the surname of Stewart, by some branches modified to 'Steuart' or the French form 'Stuart'.

STEWART, Walter (1293–1326) sixth hereditary Steward of Scotland. He fought in the Scottish victory over the English at Bannockburn (1314), and defended Berwick against **Edward II**. His marriage in 1315 with Marjory, **Robert the Bruce**'s daughter, brought the crown of Scotland to his family; their son Robert came to the throne as **Robert II** in 1371.

STEWART, Alexander Turney (1803–76) Irish-born American merchant, born near Belfast. He acquired great wealth in America in the retail store business. A noted philanthropist, he founded Garden City, Long Island as a model middle-class township. His body was stolen in 1878, and restored to his widow three years later on payment of $20000 through a lawyer.

STEWART, Balfour (1828–87) Scottish physicist, born in Edinburgh. He studied at St Andrews and Edinburgh, and became assistant to **Edward Forbes** at Edinburgh and afterwards director of Kew Observatory (1859), and professor of physics at Owens College, Manchester (1870). He made his reputation by his work on radiant heat (1858), was one of the founders of spectrum analysis and wrote papers on terrestrial magnetism and sunspots.

STEWART, Sir Charles See **CASTLEREAGH, Sir Robert Stewart**

STEWART, Douglas Alexander (1913–85) New Zealand-born Australian author, born in Eltham, Taranaki, and educated at the Victoria University College. For 40 years he was at the forefront of Australian writing, first as assistant and then, from 1940 to 1961, as editor of the 'Red Page' in the *Bulletin* magazine. Stewart then became literary editor for the old-established Australian publishing house of Angus & Robertson, a position which he held until his retirement in 1971. His early books of lyric verse were followed by *The Dosser in Springtime* (1946) which introduced his love of the ballad form, later used to dramatic effect in *Glencoe* (1947). His work includes short stories, biographies and literary criticism, and verse dramas for stage and radio, of which *Fire in the Snow* (1939) about **Scott**'s ill-fated Antarctic expedition, is recognized as a classic of radio drama. His major contributions to Australian literature include two collections of bush ballads (1955–57, edited with Nancy Keesing), and *Modern Australian Verse* (edited, 1964), and his biographies, *Norman Lindsay, a Personal Memoir* (1975) and *A Man of Sydney, an Appreciation of Kenneth Slessor* (1977).

STEWART, Dugald (1753–1828) Scottish philosopher, born and educated in Edinburgh, where his father was professor of mathematics; he also studied at Glasgow under **Thomas Reid**. He succeeded to his father's chair in 1775, then from 1785 to 1810 was professor of moral philosophy at Edinburgh in succession to **Adam Ferguson**. He was much influenced by Reid's 'Common Sense' philosophy and himself became the leader of the Scottish School. He was not a highly original thinker but a great teacher and lecturer, of whom a pupil said 'without derogation from his writings it may be said that his disciples were among his best works'. He was in fact a prolific author, his major work being *Elements of the Philosophy of the Human Mind* (3 vols 1792, 1814, 1827). He also wrote *Outlines of Moral Philosophy* (1793) and *Philosophical Essays* (1810). A remarkably large monument on Calton Hill, Edinburgh, attests to his fame at the time of his death.

STEWART, Frances Teresa, Duchess of Richmond and Lennox (1647–1702) Scottish noblewoman, the daughter of the 6th Duke of Lennox. A remarkable beauty and known as 'la belle Stewart', she was appointed maid of honour to **Charles II**'s queen, **Catherine of Braganza**. She is thought to have become one of Charles' mistresses, and posed as the effigy of Britannia on the coinage. In 1667 she married the 3rd Duke of Richmond, and fled the court. In later years she was restored to the king's favour.

STEWART, Jackie (John Young) (1939–) Scottish racing driver and world champion, born in Dunbartonshire. In 1968 he won the Dutch, German and US Grand Prix in a Tyrell. He had been third in the world championships in 1965, his first season of Grand Prix racing, and he won the world title in 1969, 1971 and 1973. He retired at the end of the 1973 season. Gifted with exceptional reflexes, his second sport was clay-pigeon shooting, in which he reached Olympic standard.

STEWART, James Maitland (1908–) American film actor, born in Indiana, Pennsylvania. An architecture student at Princeton University, his work with a summer stock company prompted him to pursue an acting career, initially on Broadway and later in Hollywood. Tall, gangly, and with a distinctive drawl, he was cast as naive, gauche, all-American idealists fighting corruption in films like *Mr. Smith Goes to Washington* (1939) and *Destry Rides Again* (1939). After distinguished war service in the air force, he returned as the quintessential small-town man in *It's A Wonderful Life* (1946), and starred in the title role of *The Glenn Miller Story* (1953), before developing a more mature image as tough westerners and resourceful heroes in thrillers like *Rear Window* (1954), *Vertigo* (1958) and *Anatomy of a Murder* (1959). Nominated five times for the Academy Award, he won an Oscar for *The Philadelphia Story* (1940), and received an honorary award in 1984.

STEWART, James Stuart (1896–) Scottish preacher and devotional writer, born in Dundee. A Church of Scotland parish minister before becoming professor of New Testament at New College, Edinburgh (1947–66), he was moderator of the General Assembly of the Church of Scotland (1963–64). He was joint-editor of the 1928 English translation of **Schleiermacher**'s *The Christian Faith*, wrote popular books on **Jesus**, **Paul**, and the art of preaching, lectured widely in Britain and overseas, and published several volumes of sermons, including *The Gates of New Life* (1937), *River of Life* (1972), and *King for Ever* (1974).

STEWART, Baron (Robert) Michael Maitland (1906–) English Labour politician, born in London. He was educated at Christ's Hospital and St John's College, Oxford. A schoolmaster before World War II, he stood unsuccessfully for parliament in 1931 and 1935. MP for Fulham from 1945, he had a varied ministerial career. Secretary of state for war (1947–51), then for education and science (1964–65), he came to the fore as foreign minister (1965–66), as minister for economic affairs (1966–67) and as first secretary of state from 1966. He replaced **George-Brown** on the latter's resignation in March 1968 and was foreign secretary (1968–70). He was the leader of the British Labour delegation to the European Parliament (1975–76), and remained an MP until 1979 when he was made a life peer.

STEYN, Martinus Theunis (1857–1916) South African statesman, born in Winburg, Orange Free State, of which he was president (from 1896), joining with the Transvaal in the war (1889–1902). He promoted the Union of 1910, but later encouraged Boer extremists and their rebellion of 1914. His son, Colin Fraser (1887–1959), mediated between Generals **Botha** and **de Wet**, and was minister of justice in the **Smuts** government (1939–45) and of labour (1945–48).

STICKLEY, Gustav (1857–1942) American designer and metalworker, born in Osceola, Pennsylvania. He began his career as a stonemason, but soon turned to chair-making in Pennsylvania as an apprentice to his uncle. In 1898 he met **Charles Frances Voysey** on a journey through Europe and on his return formed the Gustav Stickley Company in Eastwood, Syracuse, New York, where he produced interesting solid furniture with a hint of Art Nouveau and which he first exhibited at Grand Rapids in 1900. The same year he enlarged the company, which became the Craftsman Workshops, done to distinguish his products from those made by his two brothers. He was influenced by the Arts & Crafts Movement and, in particular, **William Morris** and **Ruskin** and, subsequently, his (often plagiarized) sturdy oak output became known as 'Mission Furniture'. He set up an office in New York in 1905 and in 1913 acquired larger premises with showrooms and offices. He went bankrupt in 1915.

STIEGLITZ, Alfred (1864–1946) American photographer. Born in Hoboken, New Jersey, he studied engineering and photography in Berlin and travelled extensively in Europe before returning to New York in 1890. With **Edward Steichen** he founded the Photo-Secession Group in 1902, the counterpart of Britain's Linked Ring, both groups devoted to photography as a means of artistic expression rather than barren pictorialism. He exerted great influence through his magazine *Camera Work* (1903–17) and his gallery of modern art at 291 Fifth Avenue, New York. From 1910 he was an advocate of 'straight' photography, seeking precision and clarity of image, especially in his studies of New York architecture (1910–16) and again in the 1930s, but he also created many outstanding portraits, and his studies of clouds, *Equivalents* (1922–31), are lyrical and evocative. A voluminous and polemical correspondent on behalf of photographic creativity, he was a major figure in establishing photography as an art form.

STIERNHIELM, Georg, originally **Olofsson** (1598–1672) Swedish poet and linguist, known as the 'father of Swedish poetry'. He was elevated to the peerage with the name of Stiernhielm in 1631, and held various government appointments, including councillor of war (1663) and director of the college of antiquities (1667). He was the first Swedish poet to write in hexameters, in *Hercules* (1658), an epic allegorical poem about a young man at the crossroads of life. He helped to reform and purify the Swedish language by studying Old Norse literature and incorporating the old vocabulary into modern Swedish.

STIFTER, Adalbert (1805–68) Austrian novelist and painter, born in Oberplan, Bohemia. He studied at Vienna, and as private tutor to various aristocratic families had several unhappy love affairs. Deeply disturbed by the Revolution of 1848, he settled in Linz and became an official in the ministry of education. Unhappiness and illness terminated in suicide. His humanism, his love of traditional values and his belief in the greatness of life pervade the *Bildungsroman*, *Der Nachsommer* (1857), *Witiko* (1865–67), a heroic tale set in 12th-century Bohemia, and the short stories *Der Condor* (1840). He was also a considerable painter of city views. He also wrote two collections of stories *Studien* (1844–50) and *Bunte Steine* (1853).

STIGAND (d.1072) English prelate. Chaplain to King **Knut** (Canute) and chief adviser to his widow **Emma**, he was appointed chaplain by **Edward the Confessor**, and then bishop of Elmham (1044) and bishop of Winchester (1047), and, uncanonically, archbishop of Canterbury (1052). On the death of Harold Godwinssone (whom, possibly, he had crowned), Stigand supported **Edgar Ætheling**. Hence he was deprived by **William I**, whom he had helped to crown, of Canterbury and Winchester (1070), and he died a prisoner at Winchester.

STIGLER, George Joseph (1911–) American economist, born in Renton. Educated at Chicago, he has held professorships at Minnesota (1944–46), Brown (1946–47), Columbia (1947–57) and Chicago (1958–) universities. His books include *Production and Distribution Theories* (1941), *The Theory of Price* (1946), *The Citizen and the State* (1975) and *The Economist as Preacher* (1983). He was awarded the Nobel prize for economics in 1982 for his work on market forces and regulatory legislation.

STILICHO, Flavius (c.365–408) Roman soldier, by blood a Vandal. He was sent as ambassador to Persia in 384, and rewarded with the hand of Serena, niece of the emperor **Theodosius I**. In 394 he left Constantinople for Rome in charge of the youthful **Flavius Honorius**, placed him on the throne of the Western empire, and administered in his name the affairs of state. On the death of Theodosius (394) Stilicho's rival, Rufinus, instigated **Alaric I** to invade Greece. Stilicho marched against Alaric, blocked him up in the Peloponnesus, but permitted him to escape with captives and booty. In 398 his daughter became the wife of Honorius. Alaric invaded Northern Italy, but was signally defeated by Stilicho at Pollentia (403) and Verona. When Radagaisus, at the head of 200000 to 400000 Goths, ravaged the country as far as Florence (406), Stilicho routed the invaders and saved the Western empire a second time. Next Vandals, Alans and Suevi invaded Gaul; Stilicho's proposed alliance with Alaric against them was interpreted as treachery and he was credited with aiming at the imperial dignity. A Roman army mutinied, and Stilicho fled to Ravenna, where he was murdered at the behest of Honorius. Three months later Alaric was at the gates of Rome.

STILL, Clyfford (1904–80) American painter and printmaker, born in Grandin, North Dakota. He studied art at Spokane University, graduating in 1933. By c.1940 he considered that he had arrived at his personal style, rejecting European ideas and employing the currently fasionable organic forms of Biomorphism. He taught at the California School of Fine Arts, San Francisco, from 1946 to 1950.

STILL, William Grant (1895–1978) black American composer, born in Woodville, Mississippi. He worked as an arranger of popular music and played in theatre and night-club orchestras while studying under Varèse. His music shows the influence of this work and of racial and European styles. It includes five operas, four symphonies, one of which is a study of the modern American black, three ballets, chamber and choral music and orchestral pieces.

STILLER, Mauritz (1883–1928) Swedish film director, born in Helsinki of Finnish-Russian extraction. He and **Victor Sjöström** were leading figures of the Swedish silent cinema. He grew up in Helsinki but settled in Sweden in 1909. In 1912 he began directing films for Svenska Bio and displayed an instinctive filmatic narrative technique. He learned to combine this with a dramatic force which proved just right for the new medium. Of the 45 films he made in Sweden, *Herr Arnes pengar* (1919, Sir Arne's Treasure), *Gunnar Hedes saga* (1922) and *Gösta Berlings saga* (1924) showed skill in producing cinematically the imaginative world of **Selma Lagerlöf**. His versatility is shown in *Erotikon* (1920), a sophisticated comedy about sexual rivalry which greatly influenced the comedies of **Ernst Lubitsch**. Stiller discovered **Greta Garbo** (some called him her Svengali) and took her to Hollywood in 1925. Being autocratic and demanding complete control as director, he encountered difficulty there and completed only two films, including *Hotel Imperial* (1926) with **Pola Negri**.

STILLINGFLEET, Benjamin (1702–71) English author and botanist, grandson of **Edward Stillingfleet**, born in Norfolk. He studied at Trinity College, Cambridge, and published essays on music and the art of conversation, but is best known for his preface 'Observation on Grasses' to his own translation (1759) from the Latin of six of **Linnaeus**'s botanical essays. The term 'blue stocking' originated from those he habitually wore at the fashionable, mixed 'evening assemblies without card playing' at Mrs Vesey's of Bath, to which he contributed erudite conversation.

STILLINGFLEET, Edward (1635–99) English theologian, born in Cranborne in Dorset. In 1653 he became fellow of St John's College, Cambridge, later vicar of Sutton, Bedfordshire. His *Irenicum* (1659) advocated union between the Episcopalians and the Presbyterians. His *Origines Sacrae* (1662) and *Rational Account of the Grounds of the Protestant Religion* (1664), defending the Church of England's breach of Rome, led to preferment. He became chaplain to **Charles II**, dean of St Paul's (1678) and after the deposition of **James VI and II**, bishop of Worcester. In three letters or pamphlets (1696–97) he defended the doctrine of the Trinity against the consequences of what he understood to be **Locke**'s denial of substance in the latter's *Essay Concerning Human Understanding*, but Locke merely denied that one can have a genuine idea of 'pure substance in general' and give it a significant content. His Collected Works were published in 1710.

STILWELL, Joseph, nicknamed **'Vinegar Joe'** (1883–1946) American soldier, born in Florida. He graduated at West Point in 1904, and rose to lieutenant-colonel in World War I. An authority on Chinese life and an expert Chinese speaker, he was military attaché to the US Embassy in Peking from 1932 to 1939. In 1941 he became US military representative in China and in 1942 commander of the 5th and 6th Chinese Armies in Burma. He planned the Ledo road (later known as the Stilwell road). In the Burma counter-offensive in 1943 he was commanding general of the US Forces in China, Burma and India, but was recalled to America following a dispute with **Chiang Kai-Shek**.

STIMSON, Henry Lewis (1867–1930) American politician, born in New York City. He studied law at Yale and Harvard, and joined the New York bar in 1891. He entered the law firm of **Elihu Root** in 1893 and became US attorney for the New York Southern district in 1906. He reflected President **Theodore Roosevelt**'s wishes in vigorously prosecuting large companies whose railroad rebate offences showed contempt for the presidency. Defeated as Republican candidate for New York governor (1910), he was made secretary of war under President **Taft** (1911–13). He served briefly in France as artillery colonel in World War I, and was governor general of the Philippines (1927–29) and became **Hoover**'s secretary of state (1929–33). He produced the 'Stimson Doctrine' denouncing Japanese aggression in Manchuria. Recalled by President **Franklin D Roosevelt** as secretary of war (1940–45), his experience made him a formidable influence on US wartime policy and his influence was decisive in leading the inexperienced President **Truman** to use the atomic bomb against Japan. He retired after six months of training Truman for what would become the Cold War. His books include his memoirs, *On Active Service in Peace and War* (1946).

STINFALICO See **MARCELLO, Benedetto**

STIRLING, James, known as **'the Venetian'** (1692–1770) Scottish mathematician, born in Garden, Stirlingshire. He studied at Glasgow and Oxford (1711–16), but left without graduating. His first book, on **Newton**'s classification of cubic curves, was published in Oxford in 1717. He visited Venice at about this time, returned to Scotland in 1724, and went to London, where he taught mathematics. From 1735 he was superintendent of the lead mines at Leadhills, Lanarkshire, and corresponded with **Colin Maclaurin**. For his survey of the Clyde in 1752 he was presented with a silver tea-kettle by Glasgow Town Council. His principal mathematical work was *Methodus differentialis* (1730), in which he made important advances in the theory of infinite series and finite differences, and gave an approximate formula for the factorial function, still in use and named after him.

STIRLING, James Hutchison (1820–1909) Scottish philosopher, born in Glasgow. He was trained as a physician, but became fascinated by **Hegel**'s philosophy, moved to the continent for some years to study his work, and was responsible for introducing it to an English readership in his exposition *The Secret of Hegel* (1865). This was an influential work but almost as difficult as the original, prompting the unkind remark from one critic that the secret had been well kept. He also wrote an introduction to **Kant** (1881), and critical studies of Sir **William Hamilton** (1865), **Thomas Huxley** (1869) and **Darwin** (1894), all of whom he regarded as misguided apostles of enlightenment.

STIRLING, Mary Ann, née **Kehl** (1816–95) English actress, born in Mayfair, London. She was educated in France, and made her début in 1833, continuing to perform until 1886. Her finest parts were 'Peg Woffington' and the Nurse in *Romeo and Juliet*. Her first husband was the Drury Lane stage manager, Edward Stirling, and in 1894 she married Sir Charles Hutton Gregory.

STIRLING, Patrick (1820–95) Scottish mechanical engineer, born in Kilmarnock, son of the Rev **Robert Stirling**. He became the most eminent of a remarkable family of locomotive engineers that included his brother James (1835–1917), his son Matthew (1856–1931) and his cousin Archibald Sturrock (1816–1909). He was apprenticed to his uncle James

(1800–76) who was manager of the Dundee Foundry which built steamers and locomotives, then gained experience in several engineering works before being appointed in 1853 the locomotive superintendent of the Glasgow & South Western Railway. He moved to the Great Northern Railway in Doncaster in 1866 and succeeded his cousin as chief locomotive superintendent. It was there in 1870 that his famous 8-ft diameter driving wheel 4-2-2 'Stirling Single' first appeared, becoming a legend for its speed and power; one is preserved in the National Railway Museum in York.

STIRLING, Robert (1790–1878) Scottish clergyman and inventor, born in Cloag, Perthshire. Educated for the ministry at the Universities of Glasgow and Edinburgh, he was ordained in the Church of Scotland in 1816, and was minister of Galston, Ayrshire, 1837–78. In the same year he patented a hot-air engine operating on what became known as the Stirling cycle, in which the working fluid (air) is heated at one end of the cylinder by an external source of heat. In drawing up the patent he was assisted by his brother James who was a mechanical engineer, and manager of a foundry in Dundee where in 1843 a steam engine was modified to work as a Stirling engine developing some 40 horsepower. It suffered, however, from the same problem as all the other hot-air engines built at that time: the hot end of the cylinder burnt out and had to be replaced after only one or two years' work. In spite of their greater efficiency, hot-air engines were superseded by the internal combustion engine and the electric motor, although some development work has been undertaken recently because of their non-polluting characteristics.

STIRLING, William Alexander, 1st Earl of (c.1567–1640) Scottish poet and courtier, born in Alva. A tutor of young noblemen, in 1613 he was attached to the household of Prince Charles **(Charles I)**. He had already published a collection of songs and madrigals in *Aurora* (1604); in 1614 he published part i of his huge poem *Doomesday*, (part ii, 1637). He received in 1621 the grant of 'Nova Scotia'—a vast tract in North America soon rendered valueless by French expansion. In 1631 he was made sole printer of King **James VI and I**'s version of the Psalms. From 1626 until his death he was the secretary of state for Scotland. He was created Viscount (1630) and Earl of Stirling (1633), also Earl of Dovan (1639), but he died insolvent in London. His tragedies include *Darius* (1603), *Croesus* (1604), *The Alexandrean Tragedy* (1605) and *Julius Caesar* (1607).

STIRLING-MAXWELL, Sir William (1818–78) Scottish historian and art critic, born in Kenmure, Stirlingshire. Educated at Trinity College, Cambridge, he travelled in Italy and Spain and became a connoisseur of Spanish art. He wrote *Annals of the Artists of Spain* (3 vols, 1848), *Cloister Life of Charles V* (1852) and *Velasquez* (1855). In 1866 he inherited property from his uncle and added the name Maxwell to his own. He was MP for Perthshire, from 1852. In 1877, just before his death, he married Mrs **Caroline Norton**.

STIRNER, Max, pseud of **Johann Kaspar Schmidt** (1806–56) German anarchistic writer, born in Bayreuth. He taught in a girls' school in Berlin, and wrote *Der Einziger und das Eigentum* (1845, trans 1912).

STOBAEUS, Johannes (fl.500 AD) Greek anthologist, born in Stobi in Macedonia. About AD 500 he compiled an anthology from 500 Greek poets and prose-writers. It has preserved fragments from many lost works.

STOCKHAUSEN, Karlheinz (1928–) German composer, born in Mödrath, near Cologne. Educated at Cologne and Bonn Universities, he studied under **Frank Martin** and **Olivier Messiaen**, employed the twelve-tone system, but advanced further. He joined the *Musique Concrète* group in Paris, experimenting with compositions based on electronic sounds. He has written orchestral, choral and instrumental works, including some which combine electronic and normal sonorities; also some piano pieces in an advanced idiom.

STOCKMAR, Christian Friedrich, Baron (1787–1863) German diplomat, born of Swedish descent at Coburg. He became physician and adviser to Prince **Leopold** of Coburg, the husband first of the Princess Charlotte and then king of the Belgians. He was made a baron in 1831. In 1836 he became the mentor of Prince **Albert**, and was the trusted friend of the young Queen **Victoria** of England.

STOCKTON, Francis Richard (1834–1902) American humorist and engraver, born in Philadelphia, became assistant editor of *St Nicholas*. He first attracted notice by his stories for children. He is best known as author of *Rudder Grange* (1879). Later works include *The Lady, or the Tiger?* (1884), *Mrs Cliff's Yacht* (1896), *The Great Stone of Sardis* (1897), and *The Girl at Cobhurst* (1898).

STODDARD, Richard Henry (1825–1903) American poet and critic, born in Hingham, Massachusetts. He wrote literary reviews for New York periodicals from 1860. His poems include *Songs in Summer* (1857), *The Book of the East* (1867) and *Lion's Cub* (1891). *Under the Evening Lamp* (1893) and *Recollections* (1903) contain literary studies. His wife, Elizabeth Drew, née Barstow (1823–1902), was a novelist and poet.

STODDARD, Solomon (1643–1729) American Congregational theologian and pastor, born in Boston, Massachusetts. He graduated from Harvard (where he was the first librarian, 1667–74) and ministered at nearby Northampton (1672–1729), where he was succeeded by his grandson, **Jonathan Edwards** (1703–58). He helped prepare the controversial Half-Way Covenant, and urged the admission to full church membership of those who, though without a conversion experience, showed signs of godliness. A significant figure in the development of American Protestantism, he wrote *The Safety of Appearing* (1687), *The Doctrine of Instituted Churches* (1700), *An Appeal to the Learned* (1709), and *A Guide to Christ* (1714).

STOKER, Bram, properly **Abraham** (1847–1912) Irish writer, born in Dublin. He was educated at Trinity College, Dublin, and studied law and science. He entered the civil service, but turned to literature, and partnered **Henry Irving** in running the Lyceum Theatre in London from 1878 to 1905. He wrote, among other books, the classic horror tale *Dracula* (1897) and *Personal Reminiscences of Henry Irving* (1906).

STOKES, Sir George Gabriel (1819–1903) Irish mathematician and physicist, born in Skreen, Sligo. He graduated in 1841 from Pembroke College, Cambridge, and in 1849 became Lucasian professor of mathematics. From 1887 to 1892 he was Conservative MP for Cambridge University. He first used spectroscopy as a means of determining the chemical compositions of the sun and stars, published a valuable paper on diffraction (1849), identified X-rays as electromagnetic waves produced by sudden obstruction of cathode rays and formulated Stokes' law for the force opposing a small sphere in its passage through a viscous fluid.

STOKES, Whitley (1830–1909) Irish jurist, son of William Stokes (Regius professor of medicine at Dublin). He studied law at Trinity College, Dublin, went to India in 1862, and was in 1879 president of the Indian law commission and draughtsman of the law and criminal codes. He wrote many legal works and edited Irish and other Celtic texts.

STOKESLEY, John (c.1475–1539) English clergyman, born in Collyweston, Northamptonshire, bishop of London. He was chaplain to **Henry VIII** and wrote in favour of the divorce (1531). He condemned **John Frith** and other Protestants, but opposed the translation of the bible into English and was in opposition to **Thomas Cromwell**.

STOKOWSKI, Leopold (1882–1977) American conductor of Polish origin, born in London. He studied at the Royal College of Music, London, and built up an international reputation as conductor of the Philadelphia Symphony Orchestra (1912–36), the New York Philharmonic (1946–50) and the Houston Symphony Orchestra (1955–60). He appeared with Deanna Durbin in the film *A Hundred Men and a Girl* (1937) and in **Walt Disney**'s *Fantasia* (1940). In 1962 he founded the American Symphony Orchestra in New York.

STOLBERG, Christian, Count of (1748–1821) German poet, born in Hamburg. He was one of the Göttingen poet band and was in the public service of Holstein (1777–1800). Besides writing poems, he translated **Sophocles**.

STOLBERG, Friedrich Leopold, Count of (1750–1819) German poet, brother of **Christian Stolberg**. He was also a member of the Göttingen school, and was in the Danish service (1789–1800). Then turning Catholic, he published a history of Christianity. He produced poems, dramas and translations from the Greek.

STONE, Harlan Fiske (1872–1946) American lawyer and judge, born in Chesterfield, New Hampshire. Educated at Amherst College and Columbia University, he practised law in New York and served as dean of the Columbia Law School (1910–23) before being appointed Federal attorney-general in 1924–25. He was appointed an associate justice of the US Supreme Court in 1925 and chief justice in 1941. He upheld the view that in matters of constitutionality, except where questions of individual liberty were involved, courts should defer to legislatures; he also developed the constitutional test for regulation of inter-state commerce. Many of his early minority opinions, supporting the New Deal, were later upheld by a majority of the court.

STONE, Irving, originally **Irving Tennenbaum** (1903–89) American popular novelist and playwright, born in San Francisco. He took his stepfather's name when his parents divorced and his mother remarried. He studied political science at the University of California at Berkeley, and worked as a saxophonist in a dance band. He wrote 25 books in all and is sometimes credited with having created the non-fiction novel. *Lust for Life* (1934), based on the life of **Van Gogh**, became a bestseller and did much to enhance the Dutch painter's reputation in the USA. *The Agony and the Ecstasy* (1961) fictionalizes the life of **Michelangelo**. He also wrote *Love Is Eternal* (1954), about **Abraham Lincoln**'s wife; *Passions of the Mind* (1971), about **Sigmund Freud**; *The Origin* (1980), about **Charles Darwin**; and *Depths of Glory* (1985), about **Camille Pissarro**.

STONE, Isidor Feinstein (1907–89) American radical journalist, born in Philadelphia into a Jewish family. He studied at Pennsylvania University while gaining journalistic experience on the local press, and then moved to New York City to join the liberal reformist *New York Post* (1933–38) and its weekly long-time ally, the *New York Nation* (1938–46), ultimately becoming its Washington editor. Stone was from the first hostile to the Cold War, and took highly unfashionable positions to the left of the **Truman** administration, expressed in *The Hidden History of the Korean War* (1952), after which he founded his own *I F Stone's Weekly* which he ran with his wife, Esther, bringing to it an amazing capacity to pin-point the salient but deliberately concealed features in official documents. An early supporter of Israel (*This is Israel*, 1948), he became increasingly critical of rising Israeli militarism in the Middle East while still stressing the anti-Jewish attitudes of many of Israel's enemies and supposed friends. He was the American 'New Left' before it began, denouncing USSR repression while exposing the hypocrisy of anti-communist reactionaries. He expressed educated American protest almost single-handedly on the covert support for tyranny in South Vietnam which gave credentials to the Viet Cong. The growing anti-war protest in the USA over Vietnam was a deepening realization that his lonely crusade had been justified. He broadened his analyses into longer essays in *The New York Review of Books*, and his anthologies of his *Weekly* (later *Bi-Weekly*) are invaluable revelations on the history of his times (*The Haunted Fifties*, *In a Time of Torment*, etc.). He ended the *Weekly* in 1971, wrote many more significant essays on geopolitical chicaneries, and finally devoted himself to studying the ancient classics, his last book being on the trial and death of **Socrates**.

STONE, Lucy (1818–93) American feminist, born in West Brookfield, Massachusetts. She studied at Oberlin College and soon started giving lectures on abolitionism and women's suffrage. She called the first national Women's Rights Convention at Worcester, Massachusetts, in 1850. In 1855 she married a fellow-radical, Henry Brown Blackwell, but with his agreement retained her maiden name as a symbol of equality ('doing a Lucy Stone' became a standard phrase). She helped to form the American *Women's Journal*, which she co-edited with her husband. It was later edited by their daughter, Alice Stone Blackwell (1857–1950).

STONE, Nicholas, the elder (1586–1647) English mason and architect. Master mason to **James VI and I** and **Charles I**, he carried out designs of **Inigo Jones** and completed the tombs of Sir **Thomas Bodley** in Oxford and **John Donne** in St Paul's Cathedral. His sons, Nicholas, John and Henry, were also sculptors.

STONE, Sir (John) Richard (Nicholas) (1913–) English economist, born in London. He studied economics at Cambridge under **J M Keynes**, and then spent three years in the City and the war years (1939–45) as a government economist. He became director of the Department of Applied Economics at Cambridge (1945–55) and was then appointed professor of economics (1955–80). He was awarded the 1984 Nobel prize for economics, for his development of the complex models on which worldwide standardized national income reports are based. His books include *Mathematical Models for the Economy* (1970).

STONEHOUSE, John Thompson (1925–88) English politician. Born in Southampton and educated there and at the London School of Economics, he worked in the probation service before joining the Royal Air Force (1944–47). He became active in the co-operative movement, working in Uganda and London (1952–57), and was then elected to the House of Commons, representing Wednesbury, Staffordshire, from 1957 and Walsall North, from 1974. He held junior ministerial posts under **Harold Wilson** before being appointed minister of technology (1967–68) and minister of posts and telecommunications (1968–70). In 1974 he disappeared in Miami, Florida, feared drowned, but suspicions of a faked death for financial gain grew. He reappeared in Australia, amid stories in the popular press of his estrangement from his wife, Barbara, and his association with his secretary, Sheila Buckley, and was extradited to Britain in 1975 to face charges of fraud and embezzlement. In 1976 he was found guilty and given a seven-year prison sentence, being released, for good behaviour, in 1979. He married Sheila Buckley in 1981 and became a not wholly welcome member of the Social Democratic party (SDP) in 1982.

STONEY, George Johnstone (1826–1911) Irish physicist. He became professor of natural philosophy at Queen's College (1852), and was elected FRS in 1861. He calculated an approximate value for the charge of an electron (1874), a term he himself introduced.

STOPES, Marie Charlotte Carmichael (1880–1958) English birth-control pioneer and palaeobotanist, born near Dorking, Surrey. She studied at University College, London, and took a PhD at Munich, and in 1904 became the first female science lecturer at Manchester, specializing in fossil plants and coal-mining. In 1907 she lectured at Tokyo, and with Professor Sakurai wrote a book on Japanese *No plays* (1913). In 1916 the annulment of her first marriage (to R R Gates) turned her attention to the marital unhappiness caused by ignorance and she began a crusade to disseminate information about contraception. In 1916 her book, *Married Love*, caused a storm and was banned in the USA. In 1918 she married the aircraft manufacturer **Humphrey Vernon Roe**, with whom she opened the first British birth control clinic, in North London. Her 70 books included *Wise Parenthood* (1918), *Contraception: Its Theory, History and Practice* (1923), *Sex and the Young* (1926), *Sex and Religion* (1929), and a play, *Our Ostriches* (1923).

STOPPARD, Tom, originally **Thomas Straussler** (1937–) British dramatist, born in Zlin, Czechoslovakia. He went to England in 1946 from India, his mother having married a British army officer after being widowed in Singapore during World War II. The family settled in Bristol, and after attending schools in Nottingham and Yorkshire, Stoppard became a journalist in Bristol. In 1960 after his first play, *A Walk on the Water*, he went to London as a freelance journalist and theatre critic and wrote radio plays including *Albert's Bridge* (1967), *The Dissolution of Dominic Boot* and *M is for Moon Among Other Things* (both 1964). He made his name in 1967 with *Rosencrantz and Guildenstern are Dead* at the Edinburgh Festival, which then transferred to the National Theatre, having won the Evening Standard Award. Built around the two 'attendant lords' in **Shakespeare**'s *Hamlet*, the play hilariously examines the meaninglessness of life and questions the possibility of free will. His aim is a 'perfect marriage between the play of ideas and farce': *Jumpers*, commissioned in 1972 by the National Theatre, is a farcical satire of logical positivism, and *Travesties* (1974), written for the Royal Shakespeare Company, has **James Joyce**, **Lenin** and the Dadaist painter Tristan Zara, who all happened to be living in Zürich during World War I, working together on an amateur production of **Wilde**'s *The Importance of Being Earnest*. His other plays include *The Real Inspector Hound* (1968), *Dirty Linen* (1976), *Professional Foul* (1977, written for television and inspired by Amnesty International's Prisoner of Conscience Year), *Night and Day* (1978), *On the Razzle* (1981) and *The Real Thing* (1982). In 1977 he collaborated with **André Previn** on a 'play for actors and orchestra', *Every Good Boy Deserves Favour*, performed with the London Symphony Orchestra. He has also written a novel, *Lord Malaquist and Mr Moon* (1966), short stories, screenplays and film scripts. His wife, Miriam Stoppard (b.1937) is a doctor and broadcaster specializing in child care and health.

STORACE, Anna Selina (1766–1817) English singer and actress of Italian descent, born in London, sister of **Stephen Storace**. She sang in Florence and at La Scala, Milan, and in London. She was the original Susanna in **Mozart**'s *Nozze di Figaro*, in Vienna (1786) and partnered **John Braham** on the continent.

STORACE, Stephen (1763–96) English composer, born in London, brother of **Anna Selina Storace**. He composed *The Haunted Tower* (1789) and other operas.

STOREY, David (1933–) English dramatist and novelist, born in Wakefield. An art student and professional Rugby League player, he made a hit with his novel, *This Sporting Life* (1960). His later novels include *Pasmore* (1972), *Saville* (1976) and *Present Times* (1984). His first play, *The Restoration of Arnold Middleton*, was staged at the Royal Court Theatre, London, in 1966. *In Celebration* (1969) was followed by *The Contractor* (1969), and *Home* (1970), a piece for four elderly characters who, it transpires, are the inmates of an asylum. *The Changing Room* (1971) deals with a rugby football team. Subsequent plays include *Cromwell* and *The Farm* (both 1973), and *Life Class* (1974), based on his experiences as an art student. *Mother's Day* (1976) and *Sisters* (1978) were premièred in Manchester, while *Early Days* (1980) and *The March on Russia* (1969) were put on at the National Theatre.

STORM, Theodor Woldsen (1817–88) German poet and storywriter, born in Husum in Schleswig-Holstein. He was a magistrate and judge (1864–80), wrote one volume of poems (1857) and a number of tales, characterized by a vivid, often eerie descriptive power.

STÖRMER, Carl Fredrik Mülertz (1874–1957) Norwegian mathematician and geophysicist. Educated at Oslo, he became professor there in 1903. He carried out research on cosmic rays and discovered the 'forbidden' directions lying within the Störmer cone. He gave his name to the unit of momentum at which a particle can circle around the equator.

STORNI, Alfonsina (1892–1938) Argentinian feminist and poet, born in Switzerland. Starting young as an actress with a travelling theatrical company, she later became a teacher and journalist. Her poetry is largely concerned with love and sexual passion. Her books include *La inquietud del rosal* (1916), *El dulce daño* (1918), *Ocre* (1925) and *Mascarillo y trébol* (1938). She committed suicide on discovering that she was suffering from cancer.

STORR, Paul (1771–1844) English goldsmith. He began his career in partnership with William Frisbee in 1792, establishing his firm in Dean Street, Soho, in 1807. He produced much domestic silver and monumental work from the designs of the sculptor **John Flaxman** for the royal collection at Windsor Castle.

STORRIER, Timothy Austin (1949–) Australian figurative and landscape artist, born in Sydney. He studied at the National Art School, Sydney, and made working trips to central Australia including Ayers Rock in 1973 and Lake Eyre in 1976, producing a series of vivid paintings. His delicate greys, pinks and blues unite the harsh desert environment with symbolic or domestic *trompe l'œil* objects in a blending of classic and romantic styles. He won the Sulman prize in 1968, and again in 1984 with *The Burn*. His travels to Egypt in that year resulted in his 'Ticket to Egypt' exhibitions at the State Art Galleries of New South Wales and Western Australia during 1986.His Sydney exhibition in 1989 included the powerful *Burning of the Gifts* which shows Storrier's continuing preoccupation with fire.

STORY, John (c.1510–1571) English jurist. The first Regius professor of civil law at Oxford (1544), he opposed the Act of Uniformity (1548) and went into exile at Louvain from where he returned during Queen **Mary I**'s reign to become a persecutor of Protestants and proctor at **Thomas Cranmer**'s trial (1555). Pardoned by Queen **Elizabeth**, he soon fell foul of the authorities again, fled to Spain but was kidnapped and executed at Tyburn.

STORY, Joseph (1779–1845) American jurist, born in Marblehead, Massachusetts. He graduated from Harvard in 1798, was admitted to the bar in 1801, elected to the state legislature in 1805, and became a leader of the Republican party. In 1808 he entered congress, from 1811 to 1845 was a justice of the Supreme Court, and also professor of law at Harvard from 1829. His numerous works include *Commentaries on the Constitution of the U.S.* (1833), *The Conflict of Laws* (1834), and *Equity Jurisprudence* (1835–36); all were of high authority and great value; they were great achievements and no man has done more to create American law.

STORY, William Wetmore (1819–95) American poet and sculptor, born in Salem, Massachusetts, son of **Joseph Story**. He practised law in Boston, but in 1856 settled in Rome and devoted himself to poetry and sculpture. His writings include *Poems* (1847–56–86), *Roba di Roma* (1862), *Castle of St Angelo* (1877), *He and She* (1883), *Fiametta* (1885), *Excursions* (1891) and *A Poet's Portfolio* (1894).

STOSS, or **Stozz, Veit** (1447–1553) German woodcarver and sculptor, born probably in Nürnberg. Except for a period in 1486 when he worked in the church of St Sebald in Nürnberg, he was from 1477 to 1496 in Cracow, where he carved the high altar of the Marienkirche. He returned to Nürnberg, and for the next 30 years worked in various churches there, including St Lorenz's, where his *Annunciation* can be seen. Despite the great size of many of his works, they all show great delicacy of sculpture.

STOTHARD, Thomas (1755–1834) English painter and engraver, born in London. A series of designs for the *Town and Country Magazine* was followed by illustrations for Bell's *Poets* and the *Novelist's Library*. His earliest pictures exhibited at the Academy were *The Holy Family* and *Ajax Defending the Body of Patroclus*. Some 3000 of his designs were engraved, including those to **Boydell**'s *Shakespeare* and *The Pilgrim's Progress*. His *Canterbury Pilgrims* and *Flitch of Bacon* are well known by engravings.

STOTT, John Robert Walmsley (1921–) English Anglican clergyman and writer, born in London. He graduated at Cambridge, and had a remarkable ministry at All Souls', Langham Place (in the heart of London's West End) as curate and then rector (1945–75). Widely acknowledged as a leading spokesman for Anglican Evangelicals, he has also had an effective ministry worldwide as conference speaker, especially among students, and has been a royal chaplain since 1959. He was director of the London Institute for Contemporary Christianity (1982–86) and is now its president. His many books include *Basic Christianity* (1958), *Fundamentalism and Evangelism* (1959), *Our Guilty Silence* (1967), *Christian Counter-Culture* (1978), *Issues facing Christians Today* (1984), and *The Cross of Christ* (1986).

STOUT, George Frederick (1860–1944) English philosopher and psychologist, born in South Shields, Durham. He studied at St John's College, Cambridge, and taught at Cambridge (**George Edward Moore** and **Bertrand Russell** were among his students), Aberdeen, and Oxford, and became professor of logic and metaphysics at St Andrews (1903–36). He was editor of the journal *Mind* from 1891 to 1920. He made important contributions to psychology and the philosophy of mind in his publications *Analytic Psychology* (1896), *Manual of Psychology* (1899) and *Mind and Matter* (1931), and his theories were later to receive some experimental development in the work of the Gestalt school of psychology.

STOUT, Rex Todhunter (1886–1975) American detective-story writer, born in Noblesville, Indiana. Before becoming a writer he invented a school banking system that was installed in 400 cities throughout the USA. His great creation is Nero Wolfe, the phenomenally fat private eye who with the help of his confidential assistant, Archie Godwin, got to the bottom of numerous mysteries, among them *A Question of Proof* (1935), *The Smiler with the Knife* (1939) and *Malice in Wonderland* (1940).

STOW, David (1793–1864) Scottish educationist and pioneer of coeducation, born in Paisley. He founded Glasgow Normal school, and advocated the mixing of the sexes and the abolition of prizes and corporal punishment in schools.

STOW, John (1525–1605) English chronicler. A tailor in Cornhill, he later devoted himself to antiquarian pursuits from about 1560. His principal works, which, for his time, are accurate and businesslike, are his *Summary of English Chronicles* (1565); *Annals, or a General Chronicle of England* (1580); and the noted *Survey of London and Westminster* (1598), an account of their history, antiquities, and government for six centuries. Stow also assisted in a second edition of **Holinshed**'s *Chronicle* (1585–87) and other editions of earlier writers.

STOWE, Harriet Elizabeth, née **Beecher** (1811–96) American novelist, daughter of **Lyman Beecher**, born in Litchfield, Connecticut. She was brought up with puritanical strictness and joined her sister **Catherine Beecher** at her Connecticut Female Seminary at Hartford in 1824. In 1836 she married the Rev Calvin Ellis Stowe, a theological professor at Lane Seminary, with whom she settled at Brunswick, Maine in 1850. She contributed sketches of southern life to *Western Monthly Magazine*, and won a short-story competition with *A New England Sketch* (1834). She became famous for her *Uncle Tom's Cabin* (1852), prompted by the passing of the Fugitive Slave Law, which immediately focused anti-slavery sentiment in the North. Her second anti-slavery novel, *Dred* (1856), had a record sale in England, but she lost her English popularity with *Lady Byron Vindicated* (1870), although the charges made against **Byron** in the book were later proven. She wrote a host of other books, fiction, biography and children's books. Her best books deal with New England life, such as *The Minister's Wooing* (1859) and *Old Town Folks* (1869).

STOWELL, William Scott, 1st Baron (1745–1836) English judge, eldest brother of Lord **Eldon**, born in Heworth. Educated at Corpus Christi College, Oxford, he became a college tutor (1765–77), and in 1780 was called to the bar. In 1788 he was made a judge and privy councillor. Both as an ecclesiastical and admiralty judge he won high distinction, and he was the highest English authority on the law of nations. To a large extent he created the law of prize during the Napoleonic wars. He sat for Oxford, 1801–21, when he was made Baron Stowell; in 1828 he retired.

STOZZ, Veit See **STOSS**

STRABO (c.60 BC–20 AD) Greek geographer and Stoic (his name means 'squint-eyed'), born in Amasia in Pontus, of Greek descent on his mother's side. He seems to have spent his life in travel and study, was at Corinth in 29 BC, explored the Nile in 24 BC, seems to have been settled at Rome after AD 14, and died sometime after AD 20. Of Strabo's great historical work in 47 books, *Historical Studies*, only a few fragments survive; but his *Geographica* in 17 books has come down almost complete and is of great value for the results of his own extensive observation. He makes copious use of his predecessors, **Eratosthenes**, **Polybius**, **Aristotle**, **Thucydides**, and many writers now lost to us, but he depreciates **Herodotus** and quotes few Roman writers.

STRACHAN, Douglas (1875–1950) Scottish artist, born in Aberdeen. After being political cartoonist for the *Manchester Chronicle* (1895–97) and a portrait painter in London, he found his true medium in stained-glass work. His first great opportunity was the window group which Britain contributed to the Palace of Peace at The Hague. He designed the windows for the shrine of the Scottish National War Memorial. Other examples of his work may be seen in King's College Chapel, Aberdeen, the University Chapel, Glasgow, and the church of St Thomas, Winchelsea. As an artist Strachan never wholly identified himself with any movement. His work glows with rich colour schemes and his subjects are treated with originality and imagination.

STRACHEY, (Evelyn) John St Loe (1901–63) English Labour politician. Educated at Eton and Magdalen College, Oxford, he was Labour MP from 1929 until 1931, when he resigned from the Labour party and gave his support to extremist political organizations. He served in the RAF during World War II and in 1945 became Labour under-secretary for air. His controversial period as minister of food (1946–50) included the food crisis (1947), the unpopular prolongation of rationing, and the abortive Tanganyika ground-nuts and Gambia egg schemes (1947–49). As secretary of state for war (1950–51) he had to contend with the Korean war and the communist insurrection in Malaya. His numerous books include *The Menace of Fascism* (1933), *The Theory and Practice of Socialism* (1936), *Contempory Capitalism* (1956) and *The Strangled Cry* (1962).

STRACHEY, (Giles) Lytton (1880–1932) English biographer, born in London, the son of an Indian civil engineer and soldier. Educated at Leamington College and Liverpool University, where he read history, and Trinity College, Cambridge, he was a book reviewer for the *Spectator* (1904–14). He began his writing career as a critic with *Landmarks in French Literature* (1912), which shows clearly his affinities with **Sainte-Beuve** and his francophile sympathies. He was a conscientious objector during World War I. *Eminent Victorians* (1918) was a literary bombshell, constituting, as it did, a vigorous, impertinent challenge to Victorian smug self-assurance. The irony, the mordant wit, the ruthless pinpointing of foible that was his method of evoking character, demolished stuffed legendary figures, and this book was a turning-point in the art of biography. After him, mere accumulation of facts (the product of conscientious hacks) could no longer be the accepted thing. Through Strachey, biography had become a literary genre. He followed up his success with *Queen Victoria* (1921), *Books and Characters, French and English* (1922), *Elizabeth and Essex: A Tragic History* (1928), *Portraits and Miniatures* (1931) and *Characters and Commentaries* (1933).

STRADELLA, Alessandro (1638/39–1682) Italian composer, born in Nepi, near Viterbo. His oratorio *San Giovanni Battista* influenced **Purcell** and **Scarlatti**. Legend has it that he eloped from Venice to Turin with the mistress of one of the Contarini, who sent assassins to murder him. He was wounded, but recovered. Others say that his would-be murderers found him conducting one of his oratorios, and, touched by the music, allowed him to escape. He was, however, eventually murdered in Genoa. His legend has furnished the story for operas and Marion Crawford used it for his novel *Stradella* (1909). As well as dramatic oratorios he wrote operas and instrumental works of the *concerto grosso* type.

STRADIVARI, or **Stradivarius, Antonio** (c.1644–1737) Italian violin maker of Cremona. A pupil of **Niccolo Amati** he experimented with the design of stringed instruments and perfected the Cremona type of violin. His two sons, of two marriages, Francesco (1671–1743) and Omobono (1679–1742), assisted him. Estimates suggest that he made over a thousand violins, violas and violoncellos in the years 1666–1737.

STRAFFORD, Thomas Wentworth, 1st Earl of (1593–1641) English statesman, born in London of a Yorkshire family with royal connections. He studied at Cambridge; in 1611 was knighted; and in 1614 became MP for Yorkshire. He was originally an opponent of **Charles I**, but in 1628 became a royalist. In 1632 he was appointed lord deputy of Ireland and governed the province despotically, his aim being to make Charles 'the most absolute prince in Christendom'. In 1639 he became the king's chief adviser, and in this capacity was made earl of Strafford and lord-lieutenant of Ireland (1640). When rebellion broke out in Scotland as a result of Charles' ill-judged policies, and began to spread to England, Strafford was seen as the only obstacle to **Pym** and his followers' triumph. He and Archbishop **Laud** were impeached by Pym, leader of the Puritans in parliament, and at a time when he might have expected backing from the king, Strafford was abandoned and later beheaded.

STRAND, Paul (1890–1976) American photographer, born in New York City where he studied under **Lewis W Hine**. He became a commercial photographer in 1912 and followed **Alfred Stieglitz** in his commitment to 'straight' photography of precision and clarity in both landscape and close-up detail. He collaborated with **Charles Sheeler** in the documentary film *Manhattan* (1921), and in 1933 was appointed chief of photography and cinematography in the government Secretariat of Education in Mexico. After visiting **Eisenstein** in the USSR in 1935 he returned to New York to produce socially significant documentary films, often with re-staged action, both independently and for the US government, until 1942. He subsequently concentrated on still photography for his records of life in many different parts of the world, and after 1953 lived mostly in France, where he died.

STRANGE, Sir Robert, originally **Strang** (1721–92) Scottish line-engraver, born in Kirkwall. He fought on the Jacobite side at Prestonpans, Falkirk and Culloden, and in 1747 married a Jacobite, Isabella Lumisden. He studied in Paris and settled in London (1750). He had a European reputation as a historical line-engraver, in opposition to the stippling of his rival, **Bartolozzi**.

STRANGFORD, George Augustus Frederick Percy Sydney Smythe, 7th Viscount (1818–57) English politician and one of **Disraeli**'s 'New England' party. He was MP for Canterbury (1841–52), but after 1846 abstained from debate. In 1852, he fought what is said to have been the last duel in England. He wrote articles for the press and *Historic Fancies* (1844).

STRANGFORD, Percy Clinton Sydney Smythe, 6th Viscount (1780–1855) English diplomat and man of letters. Educated at Trinity College, Dublin, he was secretary of legation at Lisbon, and ambassador to Portugal, Sweden, Turkey and Russia. In 1803 he published *Poems from the Portuguese of Camoëns*. His smooth translation of the *Rimas of Camoëns* was published in 1803.

STRANGFORD, Percy Ellen Frederick William Smythe, 8th Viscount (1826–69) English philologist, younger brother and successor of **George Augustus**, 7th Viscount. Born in St Petersburg and educated at Harrow and Merton College, Oxford, he entered the diplomatic service, early acquired an unexampled command of eastern languages, and was Oriental secretary during the Crimean war. In 1857 he succeeded as eighth and last viscount, thereafter living mostly in London, immersed in philological studies, but wrote little more than a few brilliant *Saturday*, *Pall Mall* and *Quarterly* articles. His *Selected Writings* (1869) and his *Letters and Papers* (1878) were published by his widow.

STRAPAROLA, Giovan Francesco (d.c.1557) Italian novelist, born in Caravaggio. Between 1550 and 1554 he published *Piacevoli notti*, a collection of 74 stories in the style of the *Decameron*.

STRASBERG, Lee, originally **Israel Strassberg** (1901–82) Austrian-born American actor, director and teacher, born in Budzanow, Galicia (now in the USSR). He emigrated to the USA in 1909 and became a professional actor in 1925. A founding member of Group Theatre in New York (1931–37), he quickly built up a reputation with the Theatre Guild company of New York. He began directing but his time was increasingly taken up by the training of actors; in 1947 he was a co-founder (with **Elia Kazan**) of the Actors Studio in New York, where the technique and discipline he evolved became known everywhere as 'the Method'. His teaching owed much to the Russian director **Stanislavsky** whose book *An Actor Prepares* dealt with the psychology of interpretation in acting. His pupils, among whom were **Marlon Brando**, **James Dean** and **Paul Newman**, were taught to make a close psychological study of the character they were about to play. In 1969 he established the Lee Strasberg Institute of Theatre.

STRASBURGER, Eduard Adolf (1844–1912) German botanist, born in Warsaw. He studied botany in Paris, Bonn and Jena and spent his career at Jena (1869–80) and Bonn (1880–1912). He studied the alternation of generations in plants; the embryo sac found in gymnosperms and angiosperms; and double fertilization in angiosperms. In his book *Cell Formation and Cell Division* (1875) and its later editions he laid down the basic principles of cytology, the study of cells, for which he made Bonn the world's leading centre. His work did much to show that mitosis (normal somatic cell division) in plants is a process essentially similar to that described for animal cells by **Eduard van Beneden** and others. *Strasburger's Textbook of Botany*, written with other botanists under his guidance, is a classic, much used in over 30 editions from 1894 onwards.

STRATFORD, John de (d.1348) English prelate and statesman. Appointed bishop of Winchester in 1323 by the pope against the wishes of **Edward II**, he was closely connected with the deposition of Edward in 1327, and was chancellor and principal adviser to **Edward III** for ten years. He was made archbishop of Canterbury in 1333.

STRATFORD DE REDCLIFFE, Stratford Canning, 1st Viscount (1786–1880) English diplomat, born in London, educated at Eton and King's College, Cambridge. In 1807 he became précis writer to his cousin, **George Canning**, at the Foreign Office; in 1808 first secretary to the Constantinople embassy; and in 1810 minister-plenipotentiary. His duty was to counteract French influence at the Porte, and he negotiated the treaty of Bucharest (1812) between Russia and Turkey. He was minister in Switzerland 1814–17, commissioner at the Vienna Congress of 1815 and minister to the United States 1819–23. In 1824 he was sent on a mission to Vienna and St Petersburg, and in 1825 went to Constantinople as ambassador, where he mediated on behalf of Greek independence, but his efforts were frustrated by the battle of Navarino (1827). He resigned in 1828, and was made GCB; in 1831 he was again sent to Constantinople to delimit Greece. When in 1833, after a mission to Portugal, he was gazetted ambassador to St Petersburg the tsar declined to receive him. During the intervals in his diplomatic career he sat in parliament. As ambassador at Constantinople 1842–58 he built up that extraordinary influence which gained him the name of the 'Great Elchi'. He induced the sultan to inaugurate reforms. His peace efforts failed owing to the obstinacy of **Nicholas I** and the weakness of Lord **Aberdeen**'s government. His alleged responsibility for the Crimean War rests on his known determination not to accept Russia's protectorate over the Orthodox Christians, and his clear realization that if this could be prevented in no other way, then it was necessary to prepare for war. He returned home in 1858.

STRATHCONA, Donald Alexander Smith, 1st Baron (1820–1914) Scots-born Canadian statesman, born in Forres. He emigrated to Canada and rose from clerk (1838) to governor (1889) of the Hudson's Bay Company. Chief promoter of the Canadian Pacific Railway (completed 1855), he became high commissioner for Canada in London in 1896, and a peer in 1897.

STRATHNAIRN, Hugh Rose, 1st Baron (1801–85) English soldier, born in Berlin, son of the diplomatist Sir George Rose. Military attaché to the Turkish army in 1840, he was consul-general for Syria (1841–48), secretary to Lord **Stratford de Redcliffe** and *chargé d'affaires* at Constantinople from 1852 to 1854. On the arrival of **Menshikoff** in 1853, he precipitated a crisis by sending for the British fleet. He was commissioner at French headquarters during the Crimean war. Sent to India in 1857, he virtually reconquered Central India. In 1860 he succeeded Lord Clyde (Sir **Colin Campbell**) as commander-in-chief in India, held the same post in Ireland (1865–70), and was made a peer in 1866, a field marshal in 1877.

STRATO, or **Straton, of Lampsacus** (d.c.269 BC) Greek philosopher, the successor to **Theophrastus** as the third head of the Peripatetic School (from about 287 to 269) which **Aristotle** founded. His writings are lost, but he seems to have worked mainly to revise Aristotle's physical doctrines. He had an original theory about the void, its distribution explaining differences in the weights of objects. He also denied any role to teleological, and hence theological, explanations in nature, which led naturally to the position **Hume** dubbed 'Stratonician atheism'—the universe is ultimate, self-sustaining and needs no further external or divine explanation to account for it.

STRATTON, Charles Sherwood known as **'General Tom Thumb'** (1838–83) American midget dwarf, 40 inches high, born in Bridgeport, Connecticut. He was put on show by the circus impresario, **Phineas Barnum**, and toured the USA and Europe. In 1863 he married another midget, Lavinia Warren (1841–1919).

STRATTON-PORTER See **PORTER, Gene**

STRAUS, Oskar (1870–1954) Austrian-born French composer, born in Vienna. From 1939 he was a naturalized French citizen. A pupil of **Max Bruch**, he is best known for his many operettas and comic operas, such as *Waltz Dream* (1907) and *The Chocolate Soldier*

(1908, from **George Bernard Shaw**'s *Arms and the Man*).

STRAUSS, David Friedrich (1808–74) German theologian, born in Ludwigsburg in Württemberg. He studied for the church at Tübingen, where in 1832 he became *repetent* in the theological seminary, lecturing also on philosophy in the university as a disciple of **Hegel**. In his *Leben Jesu* (1835; trans by **George Eliot**, 1846) he sought to prove the gospel history to be a collection of myths, and by an analytical dissection of each separate narrative to detect a nucleus of historical truth free from every trace of supernaturalism. The book marks an epoch in New Testament criticism and raised a storm of controversy. Strauss, dismissed from his post at Tübingen, in 1839 was called to be professor of dogmatics and church history at Zürich; but the appointment provoked such opposition that it had to be dropped. His second great work followed, *Die christliche Glaubenslehre*, a review of Christian dogma (1840–41). A new *Life of Jesus, composed for the German People* (1864; trans 1865), attempts to reconstruct a positive life of **Jesus**. In *Der alte und der neue Glaube* (1872) Strauss endeavoured to prove that Christianity as a system of religious belief is dead, and that a new faith must be built up out of art and the scientific knowledge of nature. He also wrote several biographies, notably that of **Ulrich von Hutten** (trans 1874), and lectures on **Voltaire** (1870). He separated from his wife, the opera singer Agnese Schebest (1813–70).

STRAUSS, Franz-Josef (1915–88) West German politician, born and educated in Munich, the son of a butcher. He served in the German army during World War II and in 1945 joined the rightist, Bavarian-based Christian Social Union (CSU), being elected to the Bundestag (federal parliament) in 1949. He became leader of the CSU in 1961 and was successively minister for nuclear energy (1955–56), defence (1956–62) and finance (1966–69). His career was seriously blighted when, for security purposes, he authorized a raid on the offices of *Der Spiegel* newspaper. This led to his sacking as defence minister in 1962. Throughout the 1970s he vigorously opposed the Ostpolitik initiative of the **Brandt** and **Schmidt** administrations. In 1980 he sought election as federal chancellor for the Christian Democratic Union (CDU) and CSU alliance, but was heavily defeated. Nevertheless, from 1978 he had success as state premier of Bavaria, using this base to wield significant influence within the Bundesrat (federal upper house) and, from 1982, in the coalition government headed by Chancellor **Kohl**.

STRAUSS, Johann, 'the elder' (1804–49) Austrian violinist and conductor, born in Vienna. With composer Joseph Lanner (in whose quartet he played for a while) he founded the Viennese Waltz tradition, a development from **Schubert**. He toured extensively in Europe with his own orchestra, played during Queen **Victoria**'s coronation festivities (1838) in London and composed the *Radetzky March* (1848) in honour of the general. He composed numerous waltzes including the *Lorelei* and the *Donaulieder*, but was eclipsed by his son, **Johann Strauss**, 'the younger'.

STRAUSS, Johann, 'the younger' (1825–99) Austrian violinist, conductor and composer, born in Vienna, son of **Johann Strauss**, 'the elder', who made him take up law. He began to flout his father's wishes from 1844 when he appeared as a young conductor and composer of promise. He toured with his own orchestra, performing in London in 1869 and visiting the USA in 1872. His waltzes, which number over 400, are more full-blooded, more melodious and tasteful than his father's, and although they often seem to be written purely for the violin, he showed in his introduction to *Wine, Women and Song* (1869) and in *Perpetuum Mobile* that the art of orchestration was not by any means beyond him. The best known include that symbol of romantic Vienna, *The Blue Danube*, *Artist's Life* (both 1867), *Tales from the Vienna Woods* (1868), *Voices of Spring* (1882) and *The Emperor* (1888). He also wrote a number of operettas, including *Die Fledermaus* (1874) and *A Night in Venice* (1833). His brothers Josef (1827–70) and Eduard (1835–1916) also composed waltzes and polkas.

STRAUSS, Richard (1864–1949) German composer, son of the first horn player in the court opera in Munich, where he was born. He began to compose at the age of six, and his first publications date from 1875. In 1882 he entered Munich University, but began musical studies in Berlin the following year, and shortly afterwards became assistant conductor to **von Bülow** at Meiningen. There he was converted from the school of **Brahms**, under whose influence his early compositions had been written, to that of **Wagner** and **Liszt**, composing his first symphonic poems and succeeding von Bülow in 1885. After a period (1886–89) as assistant conductor at the Munich opera he moved to Weimar, and was invited by Wagner's wife Cosima to conduct at Bayreuth in 1891. His symphonic poems include *Don Juan* (1889), *Till Eulenspiegel* (1894–95), *Also sprach Zarathustra*, (1895–96), *Tod und Verklärung*, *Don Quixote* and *Ein Heldenleben* (1898). Throughout his career he was a fine, prolific songwriter. The first of his operas, *Guntram*, was produced at Weimar in 1894 and in the same year he became conductor of the Berlin Philharmonic Orchestra. *Salome*, his opera upon a German translation of **Oscar Wilde**'s play, produced in 1905, led to his concentration upon opera, and *Elektra* (1909) began the collaboration with the dramatic poet **Hugo von Hofmannsthal** which produced much of his best work for the theatre, including the popular *Der Rosenkavalier* (1911) and *Ariadne auf Naxos* (1912, revised 1916). His work with **Stefan Zweig** on *Die schweigsame Frau* led him into difficulties with the Nazi government, which had previously appointed him president of the Reichsmusikkammer, a post which he resigned; his commanding position at the head of German musical life protected him from serious political persecution, and, active to the end of his life, he worked on two operas with Josef Gregor. After the completion of *Capriccio*, his final opera, he ended his career with a series of small-scale concerto and orchestral works and the *Four Last Songs*.

STRAVINSKY, Igor Fedorovich (1882–1971) Russian composer, born in Oranienbaum near St Petersburg. He studied law but soon turned to musical composition under **Rimsky-Korsakov**, whose influence pervades his first symphony in E flat (1907). It was with the **Diaghilev** ballet that he leapt to fame with the glittering and enchanting music for *The Firebird* (1910). A second ballet, *Petrushka* (1911), consolidated his international reputation, as did *The Rite of Spring* (1913), after its sensational première. The **Hans Andersen** opera, *The Nightingale* (1914), was followed by the wartime 'shoe-string' entertainments, *Renard* (1917) and *The Soldier's Tale* (1918), which aptly illustrate Stravinsky's adaptability. Essentially an experimenter, he then plunged headlong into neoclassicism. The ballets *Pulcinella* (1920) based on Pergolesi, *Apollo Musagetes* (1928), *The Card Game* (1937), *Orpheus* (1948) and the austere *Agon* (1957), using **Schoenberg**'s 12-tone system, exemplify this trend, no less than the opera-oratorio *Oedipus Rex*

(1927) based on a **Jean Cocteau** version but translated into Latin for greater dignity, and the magnificent choral *Symphony of Psalms* (1930) 'composed to the glory of God'. He settled in France in 1934 and finally in the USA (1945). Other characteristic and outstanding works include the *Symphonies of Wind Instruments*, dedicated to **Debussy** (1921), the *Symphony in C major* (1940), the opera *The Rake's Progress* (1951) for which **Auden** helped to write the libretto, and the serial-music *In Memoriam Dylan Thomas* (1954), for voice, string quartet and four trombones, *The Flood* (1962), a musical play, *Elegy for J.F.K.* (1964), for voice and clarinets, *Variations* (1965) for orchestra in memory of **Aldous Huxley**, and *Requiem Canticles* (1966), for voice and orchestra. In 1939, he was Charles Eliot Norton professor of poetry at Harvard and in 1954 was awarded the gold medal of the Royal Philharmonic Society. His son, Sviatoslav Soulima (1910–), is also a pianist, composer and teacher.

STRAWSON, Sir Peter Frederick (1919–) English philosopher, born in London. Educated at Christ's College, Finchley, and St John's College, Oxford. He taught at Oxford as a fellow of University College from 1948, and was Waynflete professor of metaphysical philosophy from 1968. His early work dealt particularly with the links between logic and language, in the general tradition of 'Oxford' linguistic or 'ordinary language' philosophy, as for example in his *Introduction to Logical Theory* (1952). He went on to extend and integrate this with metaphysical studies of the structure of human thought about the world, as in *Individuals: an Essay in Descriptive Metaphysics* (1959) and *The Bounds of Sense* (1966).

STREEP, Meryl (Mary Louise) (1949–) American actress, born in Summit, New Jersey. A graduate of Vassar College and a student at Yale Drama School, she made her New York stage début in *The Playboy of Seville* (1969). She appeared in summer stock, off-Broadway and in *Trelawney of the Wells* (1975) before her film début in *Julia* (1977), followed by *The Deerhunter* (1978) and winning her first Academy Award for *Kramer vs. Kramer* (1979). Established as a first-rank star she has consistently underlined her range, showing sensitivity and a facility with accents in a series of acclaimed characterizations in films like *The French Lieutenant's Woman* (1981), *Sophie's Choice* (1982), for which she won a second Academy Award, *Silkwood* (1983), *Out of Africa* (1985), *Ironweed* (1987) and *A Cry in the Dark* (1988).

STREET, George Edmund (1824–81) English architect, born in Woodford, Essex. He was assistant to Sir **George Gilbert Scott**, and started his own practice in 1849; from his practice, and influence, emerged major figures like **William Morris**, **Philip Webb** and **Richard Norman Shaw**. He restored Christ Church in Dublin, and designed neo-Gothic buildings, including the London Law Courts and scores of churches. His publications include *Brick and Marble in the Middle Ages* (1855), *The Architecture of North Italy* (1855), and *Some Account of Gothic Architecture in Spain* (1865).

STREET, Lady Jessie Mary Grey (1889–1970) Australian feminist and writer, born in Ranchi province of Chota Nagpur, north-east India, where her father was in the Indian civil service. She was educated at private schools in England and at Sydney University and soon developed a concern for social reform, becoming an early activist for the League of Nations, and in 1920 secretary to the National Council of Women, and later president of the Feminist Club. In 1929 she became founding president of the United Associations of Women, an umbrella group for the New South Wales feminist movement. She stood as Labor candidate in the federal election of 1943 and again in 1946. Meanwhile, in 1945, she was the only woman delegate to the formative San Francisco conference, from which evolved the United Nations Organization. Her husband, Sir Kenneth Whistler Street (1890–1972), was lieutenant-governor and chief justice of New South Wales. Their son, Laurence (1926–) became chief justice and lieutenant-governor in 1974.

STREETON, Sir Arthur Ernest (1867–1943) Australian landscape painter, born in Mount Duneed, Victoria. He studied at the National Gallery School in Melbourne and in 1886 joined **Frederick McCubbin** and **Tom Roberts** at their artists' camp at Box Hill, Victoria. In 1888 with Roberts and **Charles Conder** he helped establish the 'Heidelberg school' of painting named after their camp near there. The next year Streeton contributed 40 paintings to Australia's first impressionist exhibition, '9 x 5 Impressions' in Melbourne. Purchases by the Art Gallery of New South Wales in 1890 of his *Still Glides the Stream* and by the National Gallery of Victoria in 1896 of *The Purple Noon's Transparent Might* confirmed Streeton's national reputation. In 1898 he went to London and exhibited at the Royal Academy in 1900. He visited Europe and his Italian pictures evoked **Turner**'s use of light. Streeton also worked in France as an official war artist from 1914. He returned to Melbourne in 1924, where from 1929 he wrote art criticism for a local newspaper.

STREICHER, Julius (1885–1946) German journalist and politician, born in Bavaria. He was associated with **Hitler** in the early days of the National Socialist party, taking part in the 1923 putsch. A ruthless persecutor of the Jews, he incited anti-Semitism through the newspaper *Der Stürmer*, which he founded and edited, and of which copies were widely displayed in prominent red boxes throughout the Reich. He was hanged at Nuremberg as a war criminal.

STREISAND, Barbra Joan (1942–) American singer and actress, born in Brooklyn, New York. Her career began in amateur talent contests before a New York début in *Another Evening with Harry Stones* (1961) led to Broadway successes in *I Can Get It For You Wholesale* (1963) and *Funny Girl* (1964), whose success she repeated in the film version (1968), in which she made her film début, and earned herself an Academy Award. She followed this with *Hello Dolly* (1969), *The Way We Were* (1973), and *A Star Is Born* (1976), which she produced. A multi-talented entertainer, her 1965 television special, *My Name is Barbra*, won five Emmy Awards and she has been the recipient of numerous Grammy Awards, including three as best female vocalist (1964,1965,1978). She has maintained parallel careers as a top-selling recording artist and film actress, and diversified further in 1983 as the producer, director and co-writer of *Yentl*, in which she also acted and sang.

STRESEMANN, Gustav (1878–1929) German statesman, born in Berlin. Entering the Reichstag in 1907 as a National Liberal, he rose to become leader of that party, and after World War I founded and led its successor, the German People's party. He was chancellor of the new German (Weimar) Republic for a few months in 1923, when, and as minister of foreign affairs (1923–29), he pursued a policy of conciliation, and in 1925 negotiated the Locarno Pact of mutual security with **Aristide Briand** and **Austen Chamberlain**. He secured the entry of Germany into the League of

Nations in 1926, and shared with Briand the Nobel peace prize for that year.

STRESEMANN, Rewin (1889–1972) German ornithologist. He explored the East Indies, and in 1921 was appointed head of the bird department of the Berlin Museum. He was editor of the *Journal für Ornithologie* from 1922, and was the author of the magisterial *Aves* (1927–34), which dealt with every aspect of avian biology, and *Entwicklung der Ornithologie* (*Development of Ornithology*, trans 1975).

STREUVELS, Stijn, pen-name of **Frank Lateur** (1871–1969) Flemish writer. He was a master baker at Aragelm until 1905. His novels and short stories of peasant life in Flanders are masterpieces of Flemish literature.

STRICKLAND, Hugh Edwin (1811–53) English naturalist and geologist, grandson of **Edmund Cartwright** (inventor of the power loom). Educated at Oriel College, Oxford, he travelled in Asia Minor and Europe. In 1837 he toured northern Scotland. He drew up *Rules of Zoological Nomenclature* (1841), and co-authored *The Dodo and its Kindred* (1848). He was killed by a train in a railway cutting while studying the geological strata there. His *Ornithological Synonyms* was published posthumously (1855).

STRIJDOM, Johannes Gerhardus (1893–1958) South African statesman, born in Willowmore, Cape Province. He was educated at Stellenbosch and Pretoria, and after a start as a farmer, took up law practice in the Transvaal. Elected MP for Waterberg in 1929 he became leader of the extremists in the National party. His two main political ends were native apartheid and the setting up of an Afrikaner Republic outside the Commonwealth. He was prime minister of South Africa from 1954 until shortly before his death.

STRINDBERG, (Johan) August (1849–1912) Swedish dramatist and novelist, born in Stockholm, considered the greatest writer of modern Sweden. After uncompleted studies at Uppsala University, he returned to Stockholm and worked as a private tutor, actor, journalist and librarian while attempting to begin his career as an author. He had a turbulent personal life, including three unsuccessful marriages and periods of severe persecution mania. He had a propensity for involvement in cultural and personal feuds and lived abroad for long periods, mainly in France and Italy. His first major play was *Mäster Olof* (1872), a historical drama—a genre he was to return to prolifically in the years around 1900 with, for instance, *Gustav Vasa* and *Erik XIV* (both 1899). His breakthrough came with a satirical novel about the art circles of Stockholm, *Röda rummet* (The Red Room, 1879), which created an uproar, but is regarded as marking both the arrival of the modern realistic novel in Sweden and that of the naturalist movement. His later naturalist novel *Hemsöborna* (The People of Hemsö 1887), his sunniest work, has become a popular classic. Two collections of short stories, *Giftas I* and *II* (Married 1884–86), put forward his ideas on marriage, women and emancipation. A small incident in the first volume led to his trial on a charge of blasphemy, of which he was acquitted. He then published a bitter autobiography, *Tjänstekvinnans son* (The Son of a Servant, 1886) to be followed by *Le Plaidoyer d'un fou* (Confessions of a Fool, 1888). The battle between the sexes is at the centre of the three major plays that follow: *Fadren* (The Father 1887) and *Fröken Julie* (Miss Julie, 1888), and *Fordringsägare* (The Creditors, 1889). In the 1890s he turned for a time to experiments with the occult and pseudo-science, suffered a spiritual crisis verging on madness, and underwent a conversion with elements of Swedenborgian mysticism, all of which he described in his autobiographical *Inferno* (1897), and which is given dramatic expression in the trilogy *Till Damaskus* (To Damascus, 1898–1904). His efforts to find a dramatic means of expressing inner reality in those and later plays, like *Ett drömspel* (A Dream Play, 1902), make him a forerunner of expressionism and a major influence on modern theatre.

STRINGFELLOW, John (1799–1883) English inventor, born in Attercliffe, the son of a skilled mechanic. He was apprenticed to a lacemaker and some years later set up a workshop in Chard to serve the lace industry there. With the assistance of William Henson he built a steam-powered model aeroplane with a 20-foot wing span which they tested during the summer of 1847, but it proved incapable of sustained flight, and the disappointed Henson left for America. Stringfellow built a smaller model, tested it indoors in a disused lace factory, and in 1848 showed that it was capable of climbing flight under its own power; in subsequent tests in London it flew distances of up to 120 feet. Some twenty years later he built a model triplane which, however, was never flown; its engine was particularly remarkable, developing more than one horse-power with a combined weight of engine and boiler of only 13 lb.

STRODE, Ralph (fl.14th century) English scholastic logician and philosopher. He was a fellow of Merton College, Oxford (1359–60), a colleague of **John Wycliff**, and a friend of **Chaucer**, who dedicated *Troylus and Cryseyde* to him and to the poet **John Gower**. His main publications were the *Logica* (now largely lost), and the *Consequentiae* and *Obligationes* which were required texts at several European universities in the 15th century.

STRODE, William (1602–45) English poet and clergyman, born in Plympton. He was educated at Westminster School and Christ Church College, Oxford, where he became canon and public orator. He is best known for his elegies and lyric verse, which were rediscovered by **Bertram Dobell** in 1907, and for his tragi-comedy, *The Floating Island*, performed by the students of Christ Church before **Charles I** in 1636.

STROESSNER, Alfredo (1912–) Paraguayan soldier and politician. After military training at Asuncion he joined the army, was commissioned in 1932 and rose to become commander-in-chief in 1951. In conformity with Paraguay's long history of military governments, operating through the right-wing Colorado party, he became president in a coup d'état in 1954 and was re-elected on no fewer than seven occasions, despite his despotic record over civil rights. One faction within the Colorado party favoured his continuation in office while another wanted him to retire in 1988 but, although he chose to stay, in February 1989 he was ousted in a coup led by General Andres Rodriguez.

STROHEIM, Erich von, originally **Erich Oswald** (1886–1957) Austrian film director and actor, born in Vienna. An officer in the Austrian cavalry (1902–09), he emigrated to the USA and made his film début in small parts in the **D W Griffith**'s classics *Birth of a Nation* (1915) and *Intolerance* (1916), in which he was also an assistant to the director. His first success as a film director was with *Blind Husbands* (1919), followed by *The Devil's Passkey* (1920), *Foolish Wives* (1922) and *Greed* (1923). His career was punctuated with furious rows with producers about his extravagance and arrogance, but he had box-office hits with *The Merry Widow* (1925) and *The Wedding March* (1928). In the 1930s he moved to France and starred as a sadistic Prussian officer in **Jean Renoir**'s *La Grande*

Illusion (1937). After World War II he played **Rommel** in *Desert Fox* (1951).

STROMEYER, Friedrich (1776–1835) German chemist, born in Göttingen. Professor of chemistry there, he was the discoverer of cadmium (1817).

STRONG, Augustus Hopkins (1836–1921) American Baptist pastor and educator, born in Rochester, New York. He graduated from Yale, and after theological studies held pastorates in Massachusetts and Ohio. He was then appointed professor of systematic theology and president of Rochester Theological Seminary (1872–1912). Trying to find middle ground between his conservatism and 19th-century German theology, he still favoured the former, as seen in his works which included the still-used *Systematic Theology* (3 vols, 1886), *Philosophy and Religion* (1888), and *The Great Poets and Their Theology* (1897).

STRONG, Leonard Alfred George (1896–1958) English novelist and poet, born in Plymouth. He was educated at Brighton College and Wadham College, Oxford. He took up school teaching until he established a reputation as a lyric poet with *Dublin Days* (1921) and *The Lowery Road* (1923) and other volumes. He also wrote novels, including *Dewer Rides* (1929), a macabre novel set in Dartmoor, and *Deliverance* (1955). His collection of short stories, *Travellers*, won the James Tait Black memorial prize (1945).

STRONGBOW, name given to **Richard de Clare, 2nd Earl of Pembroke** (c.1130–1176) English soldier. He succeeded to estates in Normandy and Wales and in 1170 crossed to Ireland by permission of **Henry II** to give military help to Dermot, King of Leinster, whose daughter he married. He offered his Irish conquests to Henry to appease the latter's jealousy of his success.

STROUD, William (1860–1938) English physicist and inventor, born in Bristol. From 1885 to 1909 he was Cavendish professor of physics at Leeds, where began his long association with **Archibald Barr** with whom he invented range finders and founded Barr Stroud Ltd (1931), a firm of scientific instrument makers.

STROZZI, Filippo the Elder (1428–91) Florentine banker. Having been deprived by the **Medici**, he was exiled to Sicily but returned in 1466. He began building the famous Palazzo Strozzi in 1489.

STROZZI, Filippo the Younger (1489–1538) properly Giovanni Battista, son of **Filippo the Elder**, Florentine nobleman. He was prominent in the revolt which overthrew the **Medici** in 1527, but the republic then established lasted only three years. The restored Medici, Alessandro, having been assassinated in 1537, Filippo judged the time opportune to launch an attack on his successor, **Cosimo I, the Great**, but was captured and executed.

STROZZI, Piero (1510–58) Italian soldier, son of **Filippo the Younger**. He fought the **Medici**, escaped to France and was made a marshal of France by **Henri II** of France in 1556 after campaigns in Italy. He found out the weaknesses of the defences of Calais before its capture by Francis, 2nd Duke of **Guise** in 1558, and was killed at the siege of Thionville.

STRUBE, Sidney (1891–1956) English cartoonist, born in London. Apprenticed as a designer of overmantels, he learned cartooning from the **John Hassall** School, selling his first to *The Conservative and Unionist* (1909). After supplying a weekly cartoon to *Throne and Country* he joined the *Daily Express* as staff cartoonist in 1910, staying with the paper until he retired in 1946. Among Strube's many characters, the favourite was his 'Little Man', symbolic of the average *Express* reader.

STRUENSEE, Johann Friedrich, Count (1737–72) German-born Danish statesman, son of a Halle pastor. In 1768 he became physician to **Kristian VII** of Denmark. He soon gained the confidence of the young king and queen and, with their backing, sought to free Denmark from Russian influence and win Sweden as an ally. Court intrigue, however, thwarted his ambitions and he was found guilty of treason and beheaded.

STRUTHER, Jan, pseud of **Mrs Joyce Anstruther Piaczek** (1901–53) English writer, born in London. Her most successful creation was Mrs Miniver, whose activities, first narrated in articles to *The Times*, became the subject of one of the best films of World War II.

STRUTT, Joseph (1742–1802) English antiquary and engraver, born in Springfield, Essex. Apprenticed to an engraver at the age of 14, he studied at the Royal Academy, and from 1771 devoted himself to research at the British Museum. He published *Regal and Ecclesiastical Antiquities of England* (1773); *Chronicle of England, down to the Conquest* (1777–78); *Dictionary of Engravers* (1785–86); *Dresses of the People of England* (1796–99); and, his best-known work, *Sports and Pastimes of the People of England* (1801).

STRUVE, Friedrich Georg Wilhelm (1793–1864) German astronomer, born in Altona. He became director of the Dorpat observatory in 1817, and in 1839 of Pulkova near St Petersburg, which was constructed to his specifications through the patronage of Tsar **Nicholas**. He made important observations of double stars, carried out one of the first determinations of stellar distance and several geodetic surveys.

STRUVE, Otto Wilhelm (1819–1905) German astronomer, son of **Friedrich Struve**, born in Dorpat. He succeeded his father at Pulkova, discovered 500 double stars and a satellite of Uranus (1847), and studied the rings of Saturn. His son Hermann (1854–1920) was director of the Berlin observatory (1904) and superintended its transfer to Babelsberg. He made micrometric observations of the satellites of Mars, Neptune and Saturn. Another son, Ludwig (1858–1920), was professor of astronomy at Kharkov and investigated the proper motion of the solar system. Ludwig's son Otto (1897–1963) became an American citizen and director of the Yerkes and McDonald observatories (1932).

STRUVE, Peter Bergardovich (1870–1944) Russian political economist, grandson of **Friedrich Struve**, born in Perm. As a leading Marxist he wrote *Critical Observations on the Problem of Russia's Economic Development* (1894), which **Lenin** attacked for its 'revisionism'. He edited several political magazines with Liberal tendencies, was professor at the St Petersburg Polytechnic (1907–17) and was closely connected with the 'White' movement in South Russia after the Revolution. After 1925 he lived in exile in Belgrade and Paris, where he died during the Nazi occupation. His principal work is *Economy and Price* (1913–16).

STRYDOM, Jonannes Gerhardus See **STRIJDOM**

STRYPE, John (1643–1737) English ecclesiastical historian, born in London. Educated at St Paul's School and Cambridge, he became curate of Low Leyton, Essex. His prolix and reliable, if ill-arranged, works (19 vols, 1812–24) include *Memorials of Cranmer* (1694); Lives of Bishop **Aylmer** (1701), Sir **John Cheke** (1705), Archbishop **Grindal** (1710), Archbishop **Parker** (1711), and Archbishop **Whitgift** (1718); *Annals of the Reformation* (1709–31); *Ecclesiastical Memorials, 1513–58* (1721). He also completely re-edited and enlarged **Stow**'s *Survey of London* (1720).

STUART family See **STEWART** and **ALBANIE**

STUART, Gilbert Charles (1755–1828) American painter, born in North Kingstown, Rhode Island. He travelled to Edinburgh in 1772 but soon returned to the

USA and began to paint portraits at Newport. In 1775 he went to London, where he studied under **Benjamin West** and became a fashionable portrait painter in the manner of **Reynolds**. In 1792 he returned to America, and painted portraits of **Washington**, **Jefferson**, **Madison** and **John Adams**.

STUART, James (1713–88) English architect, born in London. He went to Rome (1741) and Athens (1751), and became known as the 'Athenian Stuart' for his drawings and measurements with Nicholas Revett of *The Antiquities of Athens* (1762–1814). He also rebuilt the interior of the chapel of Greenwich Hospital (1779).

STUART, John McDouall (1815–66) Scottish-born Australian explorer, born in Dysart, Fife. He accompanied Captain **Charles Sturt**'s expedition (1844–45), made six expeditions into the interior (1858–62), and in 1860 crossed Australia from south to north. Mount Stuart is named after him.

STUBBES, John (c.1541–1591) English Puritan pamphleteer. He was educated at Cambridge and Lincoln's Inn and wrote an answer to Cardinal **Allen**'s *Defence of the English Catholics*. He also wrote *The Discoverie of a Gaping Gulf* (1579), against the marriage of **Elizabeth** with the duke of Anjou, for which he and his printer had their right hands struck off. He died in France. His kinsman, Philip Stubbes (d.1593), was also a Puritan pamphleteer, and wrote *Anatomie of Abuses* (1583), a vehement denunciation of the luxury of the times.

STUBBS, George (1724–1806) English painter, born in Liverpool, the most famous animal painter of his time. He specialized in horses, of which he had a thorough anatomical knowledge (he published the *Anatomy of the Horse* in 1766), but also painted portraits, conversation pieces and rural scenes. His pictures of racehorses are distinguished from other run-of-the-mill animal painting by masterly composition and a feeling for atmosphere.

STUBBS, William (1825–1901) English churchman and historian, born in Knaresborough. He studied at Ripon and Christ Church College, Oxford, and became a fellow of Trinity, vicar of Navestock, Essex (1850), diocesan inspector of schools (1860), regius professor of modern history at Oxford (1866), rector of Cholderton, Wiltshire (1875), a canon of St Paul's (1879), and Bishop of Chester (1884), and then of Oxford (1889). His chief works are *Registrum Sacrum Anglicanum*, on the Episcopal succession in England (1858); Mosheim's *Institutes* (revised 1863); *Select Charters*, from the earliest period to the reign of **Edward I** (1870); the monumental three-volume *Constitutional History of England*, down to 1485 (1874–78), which put the study of English constitutional origins on a firm basis; *The Early Plantagenets* (1876); and he edited a number of volumes for the 'Rolls Series'. He also began a collection of *British Councils and Ecclesiastical Documents* (1869–78).

STUCKENBERG, Viggo (1863–1905) Danish poet, born in Copenhagen. He was an important figure in the lyrical revival of the 1890s. His works include *Fagre Ord* (1895) and *Flyvende Sommer* (1898).

STUDDY, George Edward (1878–1948) English cartoonist, born in Devon, the creator of Bonzo the dog. After trying both engineering and stockbroking he created the comic strips *Professor Helpemon* and *Bob the Navvy* for *Big Budget* (1903). Graduating to the glossy weekly, *Sketch*, he executed several semi-animated cartoon films for Gaumont, *Studdy's War Studies* (1915). After World War I he began specializing in dog cartoons, from which the Bonzo character emerged. In 1924 he produced the first fully-animated cartoon film series made in England (*Bonzo*: 26 films). He drew a *Bonzo* strip for *Titbits* (1926), and a daily and Sunday strip for USA syndication by King Features.

STUKELEY, William (1687–1765) British antiquarian, born in Holbeach, and known as the 'Arch-Druid'. Educated at Cambridge, he took orders in 1729, and in 1747 became a London rector. His 20 works (1720–26) include records of his valuable and objective fieldwork at Stonehenge and Avebury, but are marred by his later speculations relating them to the Druids. His account of his travels round Britain was published in *Itinerarium Curiosum* (1724).

STURDEE, Sir Frederick Charles Doveton, 1st Bart (1859–1925) English naval commander. He entered the navy in 1871. Rear admiral in 1908, he commanded the *Invincible* in the action which wiped out the German squadron under **von Spee** off the Falkland Islands in 1914. Thereafter he served with the Grand fleet, including the battle of Jutland (1916). In 1921 he was promoted Admiral of the Fleet (1921).

STURE name of a powerful Swedish family which during 1470–1520, when Sweden was nominally united with Denmark, gave it three wise and patriotic regents—**Sten Sture the Elder** (d.1503); his nephew, Svante Nilsson Sture (d.1512); and his son, **Sten Sture the Younger** (d.1520).

STURE, Sten, known as **the Elder** (c.1440–1503) Swedish regent, (*riksföreståndare*) from 1471 to 1497 and from 1501 to 1503. On the death of his uncle, King **Karl VIII Knutsson**, who had opposed the Kalmar Union and attempts to keep all the Scandinavian realms under one (Danish) monarch, he proclaimed himself ruler. He strengthened his position by defeating his opponents in the Swedish Council and the Danish king **Kristian I** at the Battle of Brunkeberg (1471), and ruled for the next 26 years. In 1497 King Hans of Denmark and Norway resumed the struggle successfully and Sten relinquished power, although he served as Hans's court master. In 1501 the Swedes rebelled against the Danes and Sten became regent again until his death. Older Swedish histories depicted him as a selfless patriot fighting for Sweden's independence, but more recent studies present him as a ruthless opportunist with a driving personal ambition.

STURE, Sten, known as **the Younger** (1493–1520) Swedish regent from 1512 to 1520, son of Svante Nilsson, Swedish regent (1504–12) and a distant relative of **Sten Sture the Elder**. An able but ambitious, and ruthless ruler, he attempted to turn the regency into a hereditary monarchy, which brought him into sharp conflict with several influential members of the Swedish Council, including Archbishop Gustav Trolle. **Kristian II** of Denmark meanwhile attempted to bring Sweden back into the Kalmar Union by force. Sten repulsed his attacks at Vädla (1517) and Brännkyrka (1518) but was mortally wounded at Åsunden (1520) and died on the journey back to Stockholm, a scene depicted with pathos by Swedish national romantic artists over three centuries later. His death left the way open for **Gustav I Vasa**'s successful bid for the Swedish crown.

STURGE, Joseph (1794–1859) English Quaker philanthropist and reformer, born in Elberton. A prosperous grain merchant in Birmingham, he became a prominent campaigner against slavery in the British West Indies, which he helped to abolish in 1837. In 1841 he toured the American slave states with **John Greenleaf Whittier**, and later campaigned for the repeal of the Corn Laws, the extension of adult suffrage, and Chartism.

STURGEON, William (1783–1850) English scientist, born in Whittington, North Lancashire. He became a shoemaker's apprentice and in 1825 constructed the first practical electromagnet, the first moving-coil galvanometer (1836) and various electromagnetic machines. His *Annals of Electricity* (1836) was the first journal of its kind in Britain.

STURGES, Preston, originally **Edmund Preston Biden** (1898–1959) American filmmaker and inventor, born in Chicago. Educated in America and Europe, he enlisted in the Air Corps in 1917 and later worked in the cosmetics industry, inventing a 'kiss-proof' lipstick. A dramatist from 1927, he later moved to Hollywood and wrote screenplays including *The Power and the Glory* (1933) and *The Good Fairy* (1935). A director from 1940, he enjoyed a brief run of successes with inventive, freewheeling comedies that combined wit, slapstick and social concerns. His enduring hits include *The Lady Eve* (1941), *Sullivan's Travels* (1942) and *Hail, the Conquering Hero* (1944). Commercial success eluded him thereafter and he spent his last ten years in Paris, directing one final film *Les Carnets du Major Thompson* (1957). He received an Academy Award for the script of *The Great McGinty* (1940) and a posthumous Laurel Award for achievement in 1974 from the Writer's Guild of America.

STURLUSON, Snorri (1179–1241) Icelandic historian, poet and chieftain, the outstanding man of letters of medieval Scandinavia. He was born at Hvammur in western Iceland and fostered at Oddi, the home of the powerful chieftain, Jón Loptsson. He amassed wealth and property, including the estate of Borg (former home of his ancestor, the saga hero **Egill Skallagrimsson**) and Reykholt, where he lived much of his life, and rapidly rose to prominence in national life, becoming law-speaker (president) of the Althing (parliament) for the first time in 1215. It was a time of great civil unrest in Iceland (the so-called Sturlung Age), with warring factions in the Icelandic republic jockeying for power, aided and abetted by King **Haakon IV Haakonsson** ('the Old') of Norway. Eventually, Snorri was assassinated at the king's behest at his home at Reykholt. As an author, Snorri Sturluson towers over his contemporaries. He wrote *Heimskringla*, a monumental prose history of the kings of Norway down to the year 1177, and compiled a prose account of Norse mythology in his *Prose* (or *Younger*) *Edda*, which is also a handbook of poesy illustrated with his own poetry. He is also believed to have written *Egils saga*, a prose biographical history of his ancestor, Egill Skallagrimsson.

STURM, Jacques Charles François (1803–55) French mathematician, born in Geneva. He discovered the theorem named after him concerning the location of the roots of a polynomial equation. He also did important work on linear differential equations. In 1826 he measured the velocity of sound in water by means of a bell submerged in Lake Geneva.

STURM, Johannes (1507–89) German educationist, born in Schleiden near Aix-la-Chapelle. Educated at the Liège school of the Brethren of the Common Life and at Louvain University, he went to Paris in 1530 and lectured on **Cicero**. He favoured the Reformation, and in 1536 was invited by Strasbourg to reorganize the education of the town. He took a prominent part both in religion and politics, siding with **Zwingli** against **Luther**; and he was sent on missions to France, England and Denmark. Through his efforts, Strasbourg became a great educational centre. In 1538 a gymnasium was established, with Sturm as its rector, and in 1564 an academy, the two together supplying a complete course of instruction. In 1581 he was driven from Strasbourg by Lutheran intolerance, but was eventually permitted to return.

STURT, Charles (1795–1869) English explorer. He went as an army captain to Australia, and during 1828–45 headed three important expeditions, discovering the Darling (1828), the lower Murray (1830). Blinded by hardship and exposure, he received in 1851 a pension from the first South Australian parliament. He wrote two narratives of his explorations (1833–48), and died in Cheltenham, England.

STURTEVANT, Alfred Henry (1891–1970) American geneticist born in Jacksonville, Illinois. He developed an enthusiasm for heredity through devising pedigrees for his father's farm horses, and later became a student of genetics under **Thomas Hunt Morgan** at Columbia. There, working as an undergraduate on fruit fly genetics, he had the idea of chromosome mapping; his pioneer paper on this, showing how genes can be mapped on chromosomes, appeared in 1913. He went on to develop a range of related ideas, fundamental to modern genetic analysis. From 1928 his career was spent at the California Institute of Technology; his main concern remained in animal genetics, but he was also a knowledgeable naturalist with a special interest in social insects.

STUYVESANT, Peter (1592–1672) Dutch administrator, born in Holland. He became governor of Curaçao and lost a leg in the attack on St Martin in 1644. As director from 1646 of New Netherland colony (later New York), he proved a vigorous but arbitrary ruler, a rigid sabbatarian, and an opponent of political and religious freedom. Yet he did much for the commercial prosperity of New Amsterdam (later New York City) until his reluctant surrender to the English in 1664.

STYLITES See **SIMEON STYLITES**

STYRON, William (1925–) American novelist, born in Newport News, Virginia. His first novel, *Lie Down in Darkness*, appeared in 1951. Concerned with oppression in its myriad forms he has tackled the black-white question in *The Confessions of Nat Turner* (1967) and the Holocaust and how it affects its survivors in *Sophie's Choice* (1979).

SU SUNG (1020–1101) Chinese astronomer and inventor, born in Fukien Province. He was a typical member of the administrative ruling class but possessed of unusually wide interests in science and technology. The dependence of the Chinese imperial court on astrological predictions demanded accurate time-keeping and knowledge of celestial positions, and he was ordered by the emperor in 1086 to construct an armillary clock far more elaborate than that of

SUÁREZ, Francisco de (1548–1617) Spanish philosopher and theologian, born in Granada. He entered the Society of Jesus in 1564, was ordained in 1572, taught theology at Segovia, Valladolid, Rome, Alcalá, Salamanca and Coimbra, and is often rated as the greatest of scholastic philosophers after **Aquinas**. His *Disputationes Metaphysicae* was a very influential text in Catholic, and some Protestant, universities in the 17th and 18th centuries, and both **Descartes** and **Leibniz** studied it closely. He also wrote important studies in political theory, the *Tractatus de Legibus ac Deo Legislatore* (1612) which foreshadows the modern doctrine of international law, and the *Defensio Fidei Catholicae et Apostolicae adversus Anglicanae Sectae Errores* (1613) condeming the divine-right theories of kingship of **James VI and I**.

SUCHET, Louis Gabriel, Duc d'Albufera (1770–1826) French Napoleonic soldier, born in Lyon. He fought in Italy and Egypt and was made a general. He checked an Austrian invasion of the south of France (1800), took part in the campaigns against Austria (1805) and Prussia (1806), and as generalissimo of the French army in Aragon reduced the province to submission, defeating Admiral **Robert Blake** outside Saragossa and again at Belchite, and securing a marshal's baton. He captured Tortosa in 1811, in 1812 he destroyed Blake's army at Sagunto, and by his capture of Valencia earned the title of Duc d'Albufera. He was created a peer of France by **Louis XVIII**, but joined **Napoleon** on his return from Elba. Deprived of his peerage after Waterloo, he did not return to court till 1819.

SUCKSDORFF, Arne E (1917–) Swedish film director, and acknowledged master of Swedish nature cinematography in the 1940s. He has made a series of prominent nature films which although poetic—even magical—at times, emphasize the cruel and dramatic aspects of animal life. Among his best documentaries are *Människor i stad* (1947, Rhythm of a City) about Stockholm, *En kluven värld* (1948, A Divided World) and *Indisk by* (1951, Indian Village). His feature films include stories with exotic settings, for instance *En djungelsaga* (1957, A Jungle Story) and *Mitt hem är Copacabana* (1965, Home in Copacabana, filmed in Rio de Janeiro's slum district), but the best of them remains *Det stora äventyret* (1953, The Great Adventure), a touching story of two Swedish boys learning by experience that animals (here a baby otter) must remain in their natural habitat.

SUCRE, Antonio José de (1793–1830) South American soldier and revolutionary, born in Cumana, Venezuela. He was **Bolivar**'s lieutenant and first president (1826) of Bolívia, which he freed from Spanish rule by the victory of Aya Cucho (1824). He resigned after a rebellion in 1828. He took service with Colombia, winning the battle of Giron (1829) and was assassinated on his way home from the Colombian Congress at Bogotá, of which he had been president. Sucre, the capital of Bolivia, is named after him.

SUDERMANN, Hermann (1857–1928) German dramatist and novelist, born in Matzicken, East Prussia. He wrote a succession of skilful, if superficial, realist plays, *Die Ehre* (1889), *Sodoms Ende* (1891), *Heimat* (1893; English version, *Magda*), and others, and equally successful novels, including *Frau Sorge* (1887), *Der Katzensteg* (1890) and *Es war* (1894).

SUE, (Marie Joseph) Eugène (1804–57) French novelist, born in Paris. He served as a surgeon in Spain (1823) and at Navarino Bay (1827) and wrote a vast number of Byronic novels, many of which were dramatized, idealizing the poor to the point of melodramatic absurdity, but nevertheless highly successful at the time. They had a profound influence on **Victor Hugo**, whose *Les Misérables* has much in common with Sue's *Les Mystères de Paris* (1843). Other novels include *Le Juif errant* (1845), *Les Sept Péchés capitaux* (1849) and *Les Mystères du peuple* (1849), the last condemned as immoral and seditious. A republican deputy, he was driven into exile in 1851.

SUESS, Eduard (1831–1914) Austrian geologist, born in London, founder of the 'new geology'. He became professor of geology at Vienna (1857–1901). Of his works, *Das Antlitz der Erde* (1885–1909; translated as *The Face of the Earth*, 1904–10) was the most important. His theory that there had once been a great supercontinent made up of the present southern continents has led to modern theories of continental drift. A man of varied interests and enthusiasms, he was a Radical politician, an economist, an educationist, a geographer, and sat in the Austrian Lower House.

SUETONIUS, Gaius Suetonius Tranquillus (75–160) Roman biographer and antiquarian. He was for a time a member of the Imperial service (117–22) and secretary to the Emperior **Hadrian**. His best-known work is *The Lives of the First Twelve Caesars*, remarkable for terseness, elegance and impartiality. Other works were *De Illustribus Grammaticis*, *De Claris Rhetoribus*, and *De viribus illustris*.

SUETONIUS PAULINUS See **BOUDICCA**

SUFFOLK See **BRANDON, Charles** and **POLE, de la**

SUFFREN DE SAINT TROPEZ, Pierre André de (1729–88) French naval commander, a younger son of a Provençal noble. He fought in the action with the English off Toulon (1744) and in the vain attempt to retake Cape Breton (1746), was captured by **Hawke** next year, and served six years in Malta amongst the Knights Hospitallers. He was again captured in **Boscawen**'s destruction of the Toulon fleet (1759), took part in the bombardment of Sallee (1765), was again four years in Malta, and returned to France as captain in 1772. In 1777 he sailed to America, and fought at Grenada in 1779. In 1781 he was placed in command of a French squadron for service in the Indian Ocean. On passage he attacked a British squadron at anchor off the Cape Verde Islands, thus preventing action against the Cape of Good Hope. He commanded the French fleet against the British off the Indian coast and Ceylon with great skill and captured Trincomalee. Returning to Paris in 1784 he was received with great honours as one of France's greatest admirals.

SUGDEN, Samuel (1892–1950) English chemist, born in Leeds. Professor at Birkbeck College (1932) and University College London (1937), he did original work on molecular volumes and surface tension and introduced the word *parachor*.

SUGER (c.1081–1151) French prelate, abbot of St Denis from 1122. He carried out substantial reforms and rebuilt its church in the Gothic style, the first building to be so done. **Louis VI** and **Louis VII** employed him on a number of missions, and during the latter's absence on the second crusade, Suger was one of the regents. His *Life of Louis VI* is valuable for the view it affords of the time.

SUGGIA, Guilhermina (1888–1950) Portuguese cellist, born in Oporto. She became a member of the Oporto City Orchestra at the age of twelve and, aided by a royal grant, she subsequently studied at Leipzig and under **Pablo Casals**, whom she married in 1906. After extensive concert tours she settled in England in 1914, last appearing in public at the 1949 Edinburgh Festival.

SUHARTO, or **SOEHARTO, Thojib N J** (1921–) Indonesian soldier and statesman, born in Kemuju, Jogjakarta, Java, and educated for service in the Dutch colonial army. In 1943 he was given command of the Japanese-sponsored Indonesian army and in 1965 he became Indonesia's chief of the army staff. The extravagant policies of President **Sukarno** led to a threat of civil war in 1965 and 1966. After three weeks of unrest General Suharto assumed executive power in 1967, ordering the mass arrest and internment of alleged communists. He became titular president in 1968, thereafter being re-elected to office every five years. Although ten political parties contested the parliamentary elections of 1971, all criticism of the government was banned. Suharto's virtual dictatorship saw an improvement in Indonesia's relations with her neighbours in south-east Asia and the republic's return to membership of the UNO. By 1970 he had succeeded in stabilizing the currency and increasing both the agricultural yield and the output of oil.

SUHRAWARDY, Husein Shaheed (1893–1963) Pakistani politician, born in East Bengal and educated at Oxford. In 1921 he became a member of the Bengal

Assembly. He was Pakistan's minister of law (1954–55) and prime minister (1956–57).

SUK, Joseph (1875–1935) Czech composer and violinist, born in Křechaovice. He studied in Prague under **Dvořák**, whose daughter he married, and carried on the master's romantic tradition by his violin *Fantaisie* (1903), the symphonic poem *Prague* and particularly by his deeply-felt second symphony, *Asrael* (1905), in which he mourned the deaths of his master and of his wife. He was for 40 years a member of the Czech Quartet and in 1922 became professor of composition in the Prague Conservatory.

SUKARNO, Achmad (1902–70) Indonesian statesman, born in Surabaya, Eastern Java. He was early identified with the movement for independence, forming the Partai National Indonesia in 1927. He was freed by the Japanese and became the first president of the Indonesian Republic in 1945. The tremendous popularity of 'Bung Karno' with the people was gradually eroded as Indonesia suffered increasing internal chaos and poverty, while Sukarno and his government laid themselves open to charges of corruption. His protestations of political 'neutralism' were offset by his increasingly virulent anti-Western foreign policy. The abortive Communist coup of 1965 led to student riots and Congress criticism of Sukarno's alleged part in it, and the army eventually took over. Sukarno's absolute powers were gradually weakened until finally in 1967 General **Suharto** took complete control, Sukarno remaining president in name only.

SÜLEYMAN, the Magnificent (1494–1566) Ottoman emperor, son of **Selim I**, the greatest of the Ottoman sultans. He succeeded his father in 1520 at a time when the empire was militarily strong both on land and at sea, while he himself was an experienced soldier and administrator. Known in the West as 'the Magnificent', he was known to his own people as *Kanuni*, the 'Law Giver'. He instituted a programme of internal reforms, aimed at securing higher standards of justice and administration and ensuring freedom of religion throughout the empire. He extended the bounds of the empire, both to the east and west; he captured Belgrade in 1521 and Rhodes in 1522. In 1529 he unsuccessfully besieged Vienna. He conquered Mesopotamia from the Persians and annexed much of Hungary to the empire. Under **Barbarossa** the Ottoman fleet was able to establish Ottoman naval supremacy in the eastern Mediterranean and Aegean while also challenging the Portuguese in the East. The constant campaigning led Süleyman to withdraw increasingly from the active direction of government at home, a tendency which, continued by his successors, fatally weakened the empire in the long term. Nevertheless during his reign Ottoman power abroad and Ottoman institutions and culture at home reached the peak of their achievement.

SÜLEYMAN (1838–92) Turkish soldier. He entered the army in 1854, fought in Montenegro, Crete and Yemen, and in peace taught at the military academy in Constantinople, of which he became director. He distinguished himself against the Serbians in 1876. When the Russians declared war (1877) Süleyman checked them at Eski Zagra, but destroyed his army in heroic attempts to force them from the Shipka Pass. In October he became commander-in-chief of the army of the Danube, but suffered defeat near Philippopolis (January 1878). Court-martialled, he was condemned to 15 years' imprisonment, but the sultan pardoned him.

SÜLEYMAN II (1641–91) Ottoman emperor, son of Ibrahim I. He succeeded his brother **Mehmed IV** when he was deposed in 1687. He was defeated by the Austrians in 1688, but from 1689 his grand vizier, Mustafa Kiuprili, drove the Austrians out of Bulgaria, Serbia and Transylvania and retook Belgrade; Kiuprili also introduced numerous liberal reforms, but was killed in battle in 1691.

SULLA, Lucius Cornelius, by himself surnamed **Felix the Fortunate** (138–78 BC) Roman general and statesman, born in the patrician family of the Cornelii. He first came to the fore as quaestor in 107 under **Marius** in Africa when he induced the Mauretanian king Bocchus to surrender **Jugurtha** (106), thus bringing the war to an end. He served again under Marius in the wars against the Cimbri and Teutones (104–101). He was praetor (97 or 93) and subsequently propraetor in Cilicia when he restored Ariobarzanes to the throne of Cappadocia. In the Social War (91–89) Sulla fought successfully and developed his popularity with the troops. Consul in 88, he sought to resist the coalition of the tribune Sulpicius Rufus and Marius, and marched on Rome rather than be dispossessed by Marius of the command against **Mithradates VI** which the Senate had granted to him. By the beginning of 87 Sulla was able to sail to the East. During his four years there he won the victories of Chaeronea (86) and Orchomenus. Next he crossed the Hellespont, disposed of the general sent out by the Marian faction (which had again seized power in Rome during his absence, though Marius himself died early in 86), arranged a peace with Mithradates at Dardanus (85), then returned to Italy in 83 to deal with his opponents. The victory over the Samnites and Lucanians at the Colline Gate ended the conflict (82) and left Sulla master of Italy. He had himself appointed dictator with full powers, instituted the proscriptions, and forcibly settled his veterans on land confiscated from hostile Italian communities. He carried through a systematic programme of legislation designed mainly to restore control of government to the Senate, and reformed the criminal courts. Within a decade, the principal aim of his constitutional laws was seriously undermined with the restoration in 70 of the legislating powers of the tribunes. His work completed, Sulla retired into private life and dissipation in 79 and died the following year. The cold-blooded ruthlessness of his dictatorship and the proscriptions were long remembered by later generations of Romans.

SULLIVAN, Sir Arthur Seymour (1842–1900) English composer, born in London, best known for his partnership with the librettist, Sir **William Schwenck Gilbert** in the 'Gilbert and Sullivan' light operas. He studied music under **Sterndale Bennett** and at the Leipzig Gewandhaus. Together with his friend Sir **George Grove** he discovered the lost *Rosamunde* music by **Schubert**. He was organist and choirmaster of St Michael's, London, from 1861 to 1872. His association with the theatre, begun with his music to **John Morton**'s *Box and Cox*, was consolidated by his eighteen-year partnership with Gilbert, starting with *Thespis* (1871), which produced 14 comic operas from 1871, including *Trial by Jury* (1875), *The Sorcerer* (1877), *H.M.S. Pinafore* (1878), *The Pirates of Penzance* (1880), *Patience* (1881), *Iolanthe* (1882), *Princess Ida* (1884), *The Mikado* (1885), *Ruddigore* (1887), *The Yeoman of the Guard* (1888), *The Gondoliers* (1889), *Utopia Limited* (1893) and *The Grand Duke* (1896). Sullivan also composed an opera, *Ivanhoe* (1891), cantatas, ballads, a *Te Deum* (1872), and hymn-tunes, and became first principal of the National Training College (1871), later the Royal College of Music. His best-known songs include 'Orpheus with his Lute', 'The Lost Chord', and the tune for the hymn 'Onward Christian Soldiers'. He was buried in St Paul's Cathedral.

SULLIVAN, Ed (Edward Vincent) (1902–74) American newspaper columnist and broadcaster, born in New York City. A reporter with the Port Chester *Daily Item* (1918–19), he worked as a sports writer and columnist for a variety of publications before becoming a syndicated Broadway gossip columnist based at the New York *Daily News* (1932–74). He was master of ceremonies for such theatrical events as the *Harvest Moon Ball* (1936–52) before moving into radio with *Ed Sullivan Entertains* (1942). Nationwide popularity followed as the host of the television variety show *Toast of the Town*, which was later renamed *The Ed Sullivan Show* and ran from 1948 to 1971. He also wrote books and screenplays, including the film *Big Town Czar* (1938).

SULLIVAN, John (1740–95) American revolutionary soldier and statesman, born in Somersworth, New Hampshire. A lawyer by profession, he was a member of the Continental Congress in the 1770s. In the American War of Independence (1775–83) he served as a major general in the siege of Boston (1775–76) and Staten Island (1777). He failed at the siege of Newport (1778), and in 1779 fought against the Six Nations and won the battle of Elmira, New York. He resigned his commission in 1779 and became attorney general of New Hampshire (1782–86), and later president of the state.

SULLIVAN, John Lawrence (1858–1918) American pugilist, born in Roxbury, Massachusetts. He won the world heavyweight boxing championship as a bare-knuckle fighter by defeating Paddy Ryan in 1882, but lost it under the Queensberry rules in 1892 to **'Gentleman Jim' Corbett**.

SULLIVAN, Louis Henri (1856–1924) American architect, born in Boston. He studied in Paris and won the New Exposition building contract (1886) with Dankmar Adler (1844–1900). He was one of the first to design skyscrapers, such as the Wainwright building in St Louis (1890–91) and the Carson store in Chicago (1899–1904). His experimental, functional skeleton constructions of skyscrapers and office blocks, particularly the Gage building and stock exchange, Chicago, earned him the title 'Father of Modernism' and greatly influenced **Frank Lloyd Wright** and others.

SULLY, Maximilien de Béthune, Duc de (1560–1641) French financier, **Henri IV**'s great minister, the second son of the Huguenot Baron de Rosny, born in the château of Rosny near Mantes. He accompanied Henri of Navarre in his flight from the French court (1576), took an active part in the war, and helped materially to decide the victory of Coutras (1587). At Ivry he captured the standard of Mayenne. He approved of the king's politic conversion to Roman Catholicism in 1572, but refused himself to become a Roman Catholic, and throughout the reign remained a trusted counsellor. His first task was the restoration of the economy after 30 years of civil war. Before his time the whole administration was an organized system of pillage; but Rosny made a tour through the provinces, examined the accounts, reduced exemptions from taxation and amassed 110 million livres revenue in the Bastille. The arsenals and fleet were put into good order. In 1606 he was created Duc de Sully. After Henri's assassination (1610) he had to resign the superintendence of finance, but was presented by **Marie de' Médici** with 300 000 livres. He retired to his estates, Rosny and Villebon, where he died.

SULLY-PRUDHOMME, René François Armand (1839–1907) French poet, born in Paris. He studied science and developed an interest in philosophy which underlies most of his poetical works. His early *Stances et poèmes* (1865) was praised by **Sainte-Beuve**. Later volumes, *Les Épreuves*, *Croquis italiens*, *Les Solitudes*, *Impressions de la guerre*, *Les Destins*, *Les Vaines Tendresses*, *La France*, and *La Révolte des fleurs*, confirmed his fame as a poet. His didactic poems *La Justice* (1878) and *Le Bonheur* (1888) are masterpieces of subtlety. Other works are a metrical translation of book one of **Lucretius** (new ed 1886); in prose, *L'Expression dans les beaux arts*, *Réflexions sur l'art des vers* (1892), *Testament poétique* (1901), and *La Vraie Religion selon Pascal* (1905). His *Oeuvres complètes* appeared between 1883 and 1908. He was awarded the first Nobel prize for literature in 1901.

SULPICIUS SEVERUS (c.365–425) French monk and historian, born in Aquitania. He wrote a *Chronica*, from the Creation to AD 403, and a Life of **St Martin of Tours**.

SUMMERS, (Alphonsus Joseph-Mary Augustus) Montague (1880–1948) English priest and man of letters. He wrote brilliantly on the theatre and drama of the Restoration and on other literary subjects, but his most important works are two major reference books on witchcraft, *the History of Witchcraft and Demonology* (1926) and *The Geography of Witchcraft* (1927).

SUMMERSKILL, Baroness Edith (1901–80) English doctor and politician, born in London. Educated at King's College, London, she shared a practice with her husband in London. She worked with the Socialist Medical Association, and became a member of Middlesex County Council (1934). From 1938 to 1955 she was Labour MP for Fulham West, continuing an unremitting fight for women's welfare on all issues, and often provoking great hostility. She became undersecretary to the ministry of food (1949), and was chairman of the Labour party (1954–55). She was created a life peeress in 1961.

SUMNER, Charles (1811–74) American statesman, born in Boston. He graduated at Harvard in 1830, and in 1834 was admitted to the bar and also studied jurisprudence in Europe (1837–40). He took little interest in politics until the threatened extensions of Negro slavery over newly-acquired territory. In 1848 he joined with others to form the Free Soil party. Nominated for congress, he was defeated by the Whig candidate but in 1851 was elected to the national senate by the combined Free Soil and Democratic votes of the Massachusetts legislature. This post he held for life. At the outset, through abiding by the terms of the Constitution, he stood alone in the senate as the uncompromising opponent of slavery; in 1856, in the senate chamber, he was struck on the head by Preston S Brooks, a South Carolina member of congress, and incapacitated for public life for nearly four years. In 1860 he delivered a speech on the admission of Kansas as a free state, published as *The Barbarism of Slavery*. The secession of the southern states left the republican party in full control of both houses of congress, and in 1861 Sumner was elected chairman of the senate committee on foreign affairs. He supported the impeachment of President **Andrew Johnson**, and opposed President **Ulysses Grant**'s project for the acquisition of San Domingo. His continuous and acrimonious censures on Grant's administration brought about a rupture with the leading Republican politicians, which was rendered complete by his support of **Horace Greeley** as candidate for the presidency in 1872.

SUMNER, James Batcheller (1887–1955) American biochemist, born in Canton, Massachusetts. Educated at Harvard, he became professor of biochemistry at Cornell in 1929. He was the first man to crystallize an enzyme (urease), in 1926, proving it to be a protein. He shared the 1946 Nobel prize for chemistry with **John Northrop** and **Wendell Meredith Stanley**.

SUMNER, John Andrew Hamilton, Viscount (1859–1934) English judge, born in Manchester, educated at Manchester Grammar School and Balliol College, Oxford. After a slow start at the bar he built up an extensive commercial practice, frequently appearing in opposition to Sir **Thomas Scrutton**. He became a judge in 1909, a lord justice of appeal in 1912 and a lord of appeal in ordinary in 1913. A master of legal principles, exceptionally eloquent in expressing his judgments, he was very highly regarded. He wrote many entries, particularly of lawyers, for the *Dictionary of National Biography*.

SUMNER, John Bird (1780–1862) English prelate, born in Kenilworth. Educated at Eton and King's College, Cambridge, he became rector of Mapledurham, Oxon (1818), bishop of Chester (1828), and archbishop of Canterbury (1848). An Evangelical, but conciliatory and moderate, he wrote *Apostolical Preaching* (1815) and *Evidences of Christianity* (1824).

SUMTER, Thomas (1734–1832) American revolutionary soldier, born near Charlottesville, Virginia. In the War of Independence (1775–83) he opposed the British under **Tarleton** in South Carolina. He was defeated at Fishing Creek but gained a victory at Blackstock Hill (1780). He became a member of the US House of Representatives, and the US Senate from 1801 to 1810. Fort Sumter was named after him.

SUNDERLAND (11th century–17th century) name of an earldom, granted with that of Spencer and the dukedom of Marlborough to members of the English family of Spencer, originating from Robert Despenser, steward to **William I the Conqueror**, and from the Hugh Despensers, favourites of **Edward II**. Henry Spencer, 3rd Baron **Spencer** (1620-43), was created 1st Earl of Sunderland (1643) and fell in the Civil War at the first battle of Newbury, fighting for the king.

SUNDERLAND, Charles Spencer, 3rd Earl of (1675–1722) English statesman. He became secretary of state in 1706 and under **George I** rose to be all-powerful, but was forced to resign in 1721 through public indignation at his part in the South Sea Bubble. His grandson, John (1734–83), was created 1st Earl **Spencer** in 1765.

SUNDERLAND, Charles Spencer, 3rd Duke of Marlborough, 5th Earl of Sunderland (1706–58) English soldier, second son of **Robert Spencer, 2nd Earl of Sunderland**. He succeeded his brother to the earldom (1729) and in 1733 to the honours of his maternal grandfather, John Churchill, the dukedom of **Marlborough**. He fought at Dettingen (1743) and in the expedition against St Malo (1758).

SUNDERLAND, Robert Spencer, 2nd Earl of (1641–1702) English statesman, son of Henry Spencer, 3rd Baron **Spencer**, father of Charles Spencer, 3rd Earl of **Sunderland**, born in Paris. He was made secretary of state to **Charles II** in 1679 and in that capacity negotiated a secret treaty whereby England would become subservient to France and, in return, Charles would receive an annual pension. The treaty was annulled and Sunderland thereupon diverted the king's attention to a possible union with Spain. After being out of office for some years, he returned as a principal adviser to **James II**. While professing to the king his Catholic beliefs, he was secretly negotiating with William of Orange (**William III**) and, when William came to power, was made his lord chamberlain.

SUNG, Quingling See SUN YAT-SEN

SUN YAT-SEN, or **Sun Wen** or **Sun Zhong Shan** (1866–1925) Chinese revolutionary, born in Tsuiheng near Canton (Guangzhou), the son of a Christian farmer. He was brought up by his elder brother in Hawaii, and graduated in medicine at Hong Kong in 1892, practising at Macao and Canton. He visited Honolulu in 1894 and founded his first political organization there, the *Hsin Chung Hui* (New China party). After his first abortive uprising against the Manchus in Canton in 1895, he lived abroad in Japan, America and Britain, studying Western politics and canvassing the support of the Chinese in these countries for his cause. While in London in 1896, he was kidnapped and imprisoned in the Chinese legation and was saved from certain death by the intervention of **Sir Edward Cantlie**, the surgeon, his former tutor, to whom he smuggled out a letter and who enlisted the help of the British foreign office to get him released. After ten unsuccessful uprisings, engineered by Sun from abroad, he was at last victorious in the revolution of 1911. In February 1912 China was proclaimed a republic with Sun as its provisional president. Sun, however, made way for the Northern general, **Yüan Shih kai**, who had forced the emperor's abdication, but as president (1913–16) sought to make himself dictator. Sun, opposing him from the South, was defeated and found himself again in exile. In 1923 he was back in Canton and elected president of the southern republic. With expert help from the Russians, Sun reorganized the Kuomintang and established the Whampoa Military Academy under **Chiang Kai-Shek**, who three years after Sun's death achieved the unification of China under a government inspired by Sun's *San Min Chu I* (1927) or *The Three Principles of the People*, in short nationalism, democracy and social reform. While at a conciliatory conference with other Chinese political leaders he died of cancer in Peking. Acknowledged by all political factions as the father of the Chinese Republic, he was re-interred in a mausoleum built in his honour in Nanking in 1928. Sun was essentially empirical in his political teachings and rejected the communist dogma of the class war. Sung Quingling (1890–1981), daughter of **Charles Jones Soong** was educated in the USA, became Sun's secretary and in 1916 married him. After his death she lived in Moscow (1927–31) and became a bitter left-wing opponent of her brother-in-law, Chiang Kai-shek, returning to China from Hong Kong during the Japanese war in 1937. In 1950 she was one of the three non-communist vice-chairmen of the new Chinese Communist Republic, and between 1976 and 1978 served as acting head of state.

SUPERVIELLE, Jules (1884–1960) Uruguayan-born French writer, born in Montevideo. He wrote many volumes of poems (including the notable *Poèmes de la France malheureuse*, 1939–41), novels, tales (*L'Enfant de la haute mer*, 1931; *L'Arche de Noè*, 1938), plays (*La Belle au bois*, 1932; *Shéhérazade*, 1949), and the libretto for *Bolivar*, an opera with music by **Milhaud** (1950).

SUPPÉ, Franz von (1820–95) Austrian composer, born in Spalato of Germano-Belgo-Italian origin. Originally intended for a medical career, after his father's death he moved to Vienna and took up music. He conducted for the Josephstadt and Leopoldstadt theatres, and began to compose. His works include operettas, songs and masses, and his *Light Cavalry* and *Poet and Peasant* overtures are still firm favourites.

SURAJA DOWLAH, Siraj-ud-Dowla, (d.1757) nawab of Bengal. Having captured Fort William, the fort of the English factory at Calcutta (1756), he confined his 146 prisoners in the military prison, the 'Black Hole' (300 sq ft). In the morning there were 23 survivors. In June 1757 **Clive** at Plassey (*Palási*) inflicted a crushing defeat on Suraja Dowlah, who fled and was slain.

SURCOUF, Robert (1773–1827) French privateer, born in St Malo. He preyed on the English shipping in the Indian seas during the Revolutionary and Napoleonic wars, his greatest exploits being the capture of the *Triton* (1795) and *Kent* (1800).

SURREY, Henry Howard, Earl of (c.1517–1547) English courtier and poet, eldest son of **Thomas Howard** (who in 1524 succeeded as third Duke of Norfolk). He commanded troops in France but is now better remembered as a poet than a soldier, having helped to introduce the sonnet to England and being a pioneer of blank verse. He made a number of enemies in high places, however, and in 1547 was charged with high treason, on very flimsy evidence, found guilty and executed.

SURTEES, Robert (1779–1834) English antiquary and topographer, born in Durham. He studied at Christ Church College, Oxford, and the Middle Temple, and in 1802 inherited Mainsforth near Bishop Auckland. Here he compiled his *History of the County of Durham* (1816–23). To Sir **Walter Scott**'s *Minstrelsy of the Scottish Border* he contributed two 'ancient' ballads he himself had made—*Barthram's Dirge* and *The Death of Featherstonhaugh*. The Surtees Society was founded in 1834 in his honour to publish unedited MSS relating chiefly to the northern counties.

SURTEES, Robert Smith (1803–64) English journalist and novelist, born in Durham, where he was educated. He practised as a lawyer and later became a Justice of the Peace and High Sheriff of Durham County. He started the *New Sporting Magazine* in 1831 where he introduced John Jorrocks, a sporting Cockney, in whom there is an appealing blend of the vulgar and the absurd. Later Jorrocks's adventures were contained in the highly popular *Jorrock's Jaunts and Jollities* (1838) and in *Hillingdon Hall* (1845). Their influence on **Dickens**' *Pickwick Papers* is conspicuous. His other great character, Mr Soapy Sponge, appears in *Mr Sponge's Sporting Tour* (1853), by which time he was combining his passion for sport with his literary work.

SUSANN, Jacqueline (?1926–1974) American popular novelist, born in Philadelphia. After a moderately successful career as an actress she turned to writing, her first novel, *Valley of the Dolls* (1968) becoming an immediate best-seller. *The Love Machine*, published the following year, enjoyed the same success. She made no literary claims for her work but admitted to writing to provide her readers with an escape from their daily lives into the more sensational world of show business, where ruthless ambition leads to frustration and unhappiness.

SUSLOV, Mikhail Andreyevich (1902–82) Soviet politician. He joined the Communist party of the Soviet Union in 1921, and was member of the Central Committee from 1941 till his death. Throughout his long political career he showed himself to be an ideologist very much of the Stalinist school. A graduate of the Moscow Institute of Economics and the Plekhanov Economic Institute (1928), he became a ruthless and strongly doctrinaire administrator. Among other posts, he was the editor of *Pravda* (1949–50); he was first appointed to the Praesidium (the most important party organ) in 1952, then permanently from 1955. Suslov differed greatly from **Krushchev** both in temperament (Suslov was introverted and aloof) and in political outlook (he disagreed with Khruschev's 'de-Stalinization', liberalizing measures in literature and the arts, economic reforms and foreign policy), and was instrumental in unseating Krushchev in 1964.

SUSO, or **Seuse, Heinrich** (c.1295–1366) German mystic, born probably in Swabia, Baden. A Dominican monk and a disciple of **Eckhart**, his *Das Büchlein der ewigen Weisheit* (1328) achieved great popularity.

SU SUNG (1020–1101) Chinese astronomer and inventor, born in Fukien Province. He was a typical member of the administrative ruling class but possessed of unusually wide interests in sciences **I-Hsing** almost four centuries previously. The task was of such complexity that he enlisted a team of ten advisers, and built a full-scale working model in wood which was carefully tested before the metal parts were cast. In 1094 he completed a detailed monograph describing the construction and operation of the clock, from which it is known that it was housed in a tower some ten metres in height, was driven by a water-wheel 3.3 m in diameter, and was probably accurate to within 100 seconds a day, a much better performance than contemporary European clocks.

SUTCLIFFE, Bert (1923–) New Zealand cricketer, born in Auckland. One of New Zealand's greatest batsmen, he played 42 Tests and made 2727 runs, scoring five centuries. He took part in four New Zealand record partnerships and showed great courage in repeatedly coming back to top-class cricket after sustaining serious injury.

SUTCLIFFE, Frank Meadow (1853–1941) English photographer, born near Whitby, Yorkshire, where he was a successful portraitist until his retirement in 1923. His outstanding creative work was achieved from 1880 in genre studies of the vanishing world of English farmhands and fisher-folk in the local country and seacoast, which brought him numerous awards from international exhibitions between 1881 and 1905. From the late 1890s he made extensive use of the new lightweight Kodak cameras to obtain intimate natural snapshots rather than formal poses. Reviving interest in Victoriana led to the publication of a fully illustrated account of his work in 1974.

SUTCLIFFE, Peter, known as 'the Yorkshire Ripper' (1946–) convicted English murderer, born in Bingley, near Bradford. He murdered 13 women over five years in northern England and the Midlands until his capture in January 1981. While his identity was unknown, he was dubbed 'the Yorkshire Ripper'. His first victim was a prostitute, Wilma McCann, whose body was found on 30 October 1975. Several of his other victims were also prostitutes. Most were killed in the same way—their heads were beaten with a hammer and multiple stab wounds from a screw-driver pierced their bodies. Sutcliffe, who was married to a schoolteacher, was a lorry-driver. He was interviewed by the police several times during the Ripper inquiry, but was released on each occasion. He was finally caught as police conducted a routine check on a prostitute and her client (Sutcliffe). He was found guilty of 13 murders and 7 attempted murders on 22 May 1981 and was given a life sentence on each account.

SUTHERLAND, Graham Vivian (1903–80) English artist, born in London. He studied at Goldsmiths' College of Art, and worked mainly as an etcher till 1930. During the next ten years he made his reputation as a painter of romantic, mainly abstract landscapes, with superb, if arbitrary, colouring. From 1941 to 1945 he was an official war artist. In 1946 he was commissioned to paint a *Crucifixion* for St Matthew's Church, Northampton, and after that he produced several memorable portraits, including **Somerset Maugham** (1949) and a controversial portrait of Sir **Winston Churchill** (1955) which was destroyed on the instructions of Lady Churchill. He also designed ceramics, posters and textiles: his large tapestry, *Christ in*

Majesty, was hung in the new Coventry Cathedral in 1962.

SUTHERLAND, Dame Joan (1926–) Australian soprano, born in Sydney. Educated in Sydney, she made her début there as Dido in **Purcell**'s *Dido and Aeneas* in 1947. She came to London in 1951 to continue her training, and joined the Royal Opera in 1952, making her début at Covent Garden as the First Lady in *The Magic Flute* and remained resident soprano for seven years. She gained international fame in 1959 with her roles in **Donizetti**'s *Lucia di Lammermoor* and **Handel**'s *Samson*. She has sung regularly in opera houses and concert halls all over the world and in 1965 returned to Australia for a triumphant tour with her own company. In 1954 she married Richard Bonyng (b.1930), who became her principal conductor. He has been musical director of the Australian Opera Company since 1976.

SUTHERLAND, Margaret Ada (1897–1984) Australian composer, born in Adelaide, South Australia. She studied at the Melbourne Conservatorium of Music and at the age of 19 appeared as piano soloist with the New South Wales State Orchestra under Henri Verbrugghen. She went in 1923 to study in Vienna and London, returning to Australia in 1925, where for many years she was active in music administration and promotional work. Recognition came late, but her violin concerto (1954) was warmly received and her opera, *The Young Kabbarli*, based on the life of **Daisy Bates**, was performed in 1965. She has written much chamber music, and has set a number of song cycles including one by Australian poet **Judith Wright**.

SUTRO, Alfred (1863–1933) English dramatist, born in London. He gave up a successful business, translated **Maeterlinck**, and from 1900 wrote a series of successful plays—*The Foolish Virgins* (1904), *The Walls of Jericho* (1906), *John Glayde's Honour* (1907), *The Perplexed Husband* (1913), *Freedom*, and others.

SUTTNER, Bertha Félice Bertha von, née **Kinsky** (1843–1914) Austrian writer and pacifist, born in Prague. She married a fellow novelist, Baron Arthur von Suttner (1850–1902) in 1876, and founded in 1891 an Austrian Society of Friends of Peace. She edited a pacifist journal, *Die Waffen nieder* (Lay Down your Arms, 1892–99), which was published in book form (1889), and translated into many European languages. She wrote many other books on pacifism, and was awarded the Nobel peace prize in 1905.

SUTTON, Thomas (1552–1611) English merchant in London, and founder of Charterhouse School in 1611. A surveyor of ordnance in the north, he obtained a lease of rich coal lands in Durham, and made an enormous fortune.

SU TUNG-P'O, pen-name of **SU SHIH** (1036–1101) Chinese painter, calligrapher, poet, philosopher and politician from Meishan, Sichuan province. Of peasant origins, his family had only recently moved into the mandarinate. Su Tung-p'o's father as well as his own son were literati, collectively known as 'the three Su'. Su Tung-p'o is almost unanimously referred to as one of the most prominent men of his time, a 'universal genius'. Excelling in all the fields of a literati, he epitomized the cultural ideal of 11th-century Chinese humanism. In addition, his checkered political career ranged from prime ministership to exile. A great part of Chinese aesthetics, now being taken for granted, derives from his writings and his formulation of wen jen hua (literati painting). According to him, the spiritual process of pictorial creation had to be the fruit of the identification of the painter with the object of his painting: 'To paint the bamboo, it is necessary to have it entirely within yourself'. Thus, he also saw the forms born out of the brush as revealing the state of mind of the painter, another concept which only appeared in the West during the latter half of the 19th century.

SUVOROV, Count Aleksandr Vasilyevich (1729–1800) Russian soldier, born in Moscow. He won fame in the Seven Years' War (1756–63), the Russo-Polish War (1768–72) and against the Turks (1787–92) and in 1799 was sent to Italy to assist the Austrians against the French. He defeated **Moreau** on the Adda, **Macdonald** at Trebbia, and **Joubert** at Novi. Then he was directed to join Korsakov to sweep the French out of Switzerland. After a terrible march over the Alps he found that **Masséna** had defeated Korsakov, and, too weak to attack, he barely escaped over the mountains into Austria. He died in St Petersburg.

SUZMAN, Helen née **Gavronsky** (1917–) South African liberal politician, born in Germiston, in the Transvaal, the daughter of a Lithuanian immigrant. After graduating in economics and statistics from Witwatersrand University, she married Dr Moses Suzman at 20 and then lectured part time at Witwatersrand (1944–52). Deeply concerned about the apartheid system erected by the National party under **Daniel Malan**, she joined the opposition United party, later the Progressive and then the Democratic party, and was elected to parliament in 1953. She gradually gained the respect of the black community, including the ANC leader **Nelson Mandela**, and, as a member of the South African Institute of Race Relations, was a fierce opponent of apartheid. In 1978 she received the UN Human Rights Award and retired from parliament, after 36 uninterrupted years, in 1989.

SUZUKI, Zenko (1911–) Japanese politician, born in Yamada, Honshu island. He trained at the Japanese agriculture ministry's Academy of Fisheries during the 1930s and in 1947 was elected to the lower house of the Diet as a Socialist party deputy, but moved to the Liberal party in 1949 and then, on its formation in 1955, to the conservative Liberal Democratic party (LDP). During the 1960s and 1970s he held a succession of ministerial and party posts, including post and telecommunications (1960–64), chief cabinet secretary (1964–65), health and welfare (1965–68) and agriculture, forestry and fisheries (1976–80). Following the death of his patron, Masayoshi Ohira, he succeeded to the dual positions of LDP president and prime minister in 1980. His premiership was marred by factional strife within the LDP, deteriorating relations with the USA and opposition to his defence policy. He stepped down in 1982, but remained an influential LDP faction leader.

SVEDBERG, Theodor (1884–1971) Swedish physical chemist, born in Valbo, Gävleborg. He invented the ultracentrifuge for the study of colloidal particles and won the Nobel prize for chemistry in 1926.

SVEIN I HARALDSSON, 'Fork-Beard' (d.1014) king of Denmark from 985 and, for five winter weeks, of England in 1014. He was the son of **Harald Gormsson, 'Blue-Tooth'**, but rebelled against his father and deposed him in 985. His reign was notable for a series of military campaigns against England from 994 onwards. On each occasion, King **Æthelred 'the Unready'** paid escalating amounts of *Danegeld* to buy off the Danish invaders; but each time they returned for more. In 1013 Svein Fork-Beard launched another expedition with imperial intent, taking with him his son **Knut Sveinsson** (Canute). By the end of the year, King Ethelred had fled to safety in Normandy, leaving Svein to take up the crown; but five weeks later, on 3 February 1014, Svein died, and Knut Sveinsson returned for a time to Denmark.

SVEIN II ULFSSON, sometimes known as **Estridsson** (d.1074) king of Denmark from 1047. The son of a regent of Denmark, Earl Ulf, and nephew of **Knut Sveinsson** (Canute the Great)—his mother was Knut's sister, Estrid—he was appointed regent of Denmark in 1045 by king **Magnus I Olafsson** of Norway (and Denmark), and acclaimed king himself when Magnus died in 1047. **Harald III Sigurdsson ('Hardraade')**, who became sole king of Norway, laid claim to Denmark as well, and now began a long and unrelenting war of attrition against Svein. Svein lost every battle, but never lost the war, and in 1064 peace was made and Harald accepted Svein's right to the throne of Denmark. In 1069, after the conquest of England by **William I, the Conqueror**, Svein's army descended on the north of England and captured York, but Svein made peace with William the following year and withdrew. Svein was a major informant for the historian **Adam of Bremen**, and died in 1074; he was succeeded by five of his sons in turn.

SVEINSSON, Ásmundur (1893–1982) Icelandic sculptor, born on the farm of Kolsstaðir in the west of Iceland. An artist of immense versatility, he studied for many years in Stockholm and Paris, visited Greece and Italy, and returned to Iceland in 1930. His work was monumental, both figurative and abstract, and drew for inspiration on traditional Icelandic Saga material and folk-tales, but becoming more and more abstract and Expressionist. He worked with equal ease in stone, cement, metal and wood. Many of his works stand in public places around Reykjavíck, and a collection of his sculptures is on display in the spherical workshop he built for himself in Reykjavíck, now a museum devoted to his work.

SVEINSSON, Brynjóolfur (1605–74) Icelandic prelate and scholar, born in Holt in Önundarfjörður. He studied theology, philosophy and grammar in Copenhagen under **Caspar Bartholin** the elder, and became exceptionally well versed in Greek, Latin and Disputation, as well as the classical literature of Iceland. He taught at the cathedral school in Roskilde in Denmark (1632–38), but in 1638 he was elected bishop of Skálholt in Iceland. He was a sonorous preacher of imposing presence and an excellent administrator, and built a fine new timber cathedral at Skálholt. An enthusiastic collector of manuscripts of Old Icelandic literature, he sent to King **Frederik III** of Denmark for publication two priceless manuscripts books, *Flateyjarbók* (The Book of Flatey) and the Codex Regius MS of the *Edda*, which became part of the Royal Library in Copenhagen. His latter years were darkened with personal tragedy, when his beloved daughter, Ragnheiður, bore a child out of wedlock and died soon after childbirth.

SVENDSEN, Johan Severin (1840–1911) Norwegian composer, born in Christiania (Oslo), the son of a bandmaster. After travelling extensively, he became court kapellmeister at Copenhagen (1883). He wrote two symphonies and a violin concerto. His best-known work is his *Carnival at Paris*.

SVENSSON, Jon Stefán (1857–1944) Icelandic writer and churchman, born at Möðruvellir. Educated in France, he became a Jesuit scholar and taught at a Catholic school in Denmark. During convalescence in Holland from a severe illness (1911–12) he began to write a series of children's books about a boy called Nonni growing up in the north of Iceland, which made him a bestselling author. The *Nonni* books, originally written in German, have been translated into many languages.

SVERRIR SIGURDSSON (c.1150–1202) king of Norway from 1184, often called the 'the Usurper'. Brought up in the Faroes, he claimed to be the illegitimate son of a king of Norway (Sigurd Haraldsson, 'the Mouth', d.1155). He emerged from obscurity in 1179 to lay claim to the throne from **Magnus V Erlingsson**, whom he finally defeated and killed in 1184. He turned out to be one of Norway's greatest kings, strengthening the crown against both church and nobles with the support of the freeholding farmers. He commissioned one of the first Icelandic Sagas — a biography of himself, *Sverris saga*, written during his lifetime by his contemporary and friend, Karl Jónsson, abbot of the monastery of Thingeyrar in Iceland.

SVEVO, Italo, pseud of **Ettore Schmitz** (1861–1928) Italian novelist of German-Jewish descent, born in Trieste. Educated primarily in Bavaria, he wrote in Italian, but had to work as a French and German correspondence clerk in a Trieste bank. In 1892 he wrote and published privately his first novel, *Una Vita* (A Life, 1963), whose autobiographical hero felt ill at ease in the commercial world. It was followed in 1898 by *Senilità* (As a Man Grows Older, 1932). Both fell flat largely through Svevo's ineptitude as a publisher, and in dejection he gave up writing and resolved to concentrate on business. His luck changed in 1906 when he went to a teacher of English then living in Trieste, **James Joyce**, who bolstered his confidence and promoted *La coscienza di Zeno* (Confessions of Zeno, 1923). Through Joyce a translation was published in Paris and Svevo soon won recognition in France and the rest of Europe, but he died soon afterwards in a car accident. He wrote a fourth novel, *La novella del buon vecchio e della bella fanciulla* (The Nice Old Man and the Pretty Girl, 1929), and a fifth, *Il vecchione* (The Grand Old Man, 1967), was incomplete on his death. Critic Renato Poggioli wrote that 'For a cultivated Italian it is very easy to understand, but almost impossible to appreciate, the Italian of Svevo, perhaps the least literary and even the least literate, certainly the least polished Italian ever used by a man of letters in our time.' To **V S Pritchett** he was 'the first of the psychological novelists to be beatified by a spirit of humility'.

SVOBODA, Ludwik (1895–1979) Czechoslovak soldier and politician, born near Bratislava. He fought with the Czechoslovak Legion in Russia in 1917 before becoming a professional soldier. After escaping from Czechoslovakia in 1939 he became commanding general of the Czechoslovak army corps attached to the Red Army in 1943, and helped to liberate Kosiče, Brno and Prague in 1944 to 1945. In 1948 he joined the Communist party and was minister of defence until 1950. From 1952 to 1963 he lived in obscurity, mistrusted by the Stalinists; but, with **Kruschev**'s backing, he was subsequently brought forward as a 'safe' patriotic father-figure and, in 1968, he succeeded the discredited **Antonin Novotný** as president. He gave loyal support to the abortive reforms of **Dubček** and, after the hostile Soviet intervention in 1968, he travelled to Moscow to seek relaxation of the repressive measures imposed on the Czechoslovaks. He remained in office until 1975, when failing health forced his retirement.

SWAINSON, William (1789–1855) English naturalist and bird illustrator, born in Hoylake, Cheshire. He worked as a junior clerk in the Liverpool Customs office, then obtained a post in the army commissariat in Malta and Sicily (1807–15), where he amassed a large collection of zoological specimens. He travelled in Brazil (1817–18), and in London learned the new technique of lithography, with which he produced *Zoological Illustration* (3 vols, 1820–23), *Naturalist's*

Guide (1822) and *Exotic Conchology* (1822). In 1825 he moved to Tittenhagner Green in Hampshire as a full-time artist and author. He contributed 11 volumes to **Lardner**'s *Cabinet Cyclopaedia* (1830–44) and three volumes to Jardine's *Naturalist's Library* (1833–45). He emigrated to New Zealand in 1840. Swainson's Thrush is named after him.

SWAMI VIVEKANANDA, originally **Narendranath Dutt** (1863–1902) Hindu missionary and chief disciple of **Rāmakrishna Paramahansa**, born in Calcutta. A highly-educated representative of Vedanta as the universal religion at the Chicago Parliament of Religions (1893), he was a persuasive exponent of Hinduism in the West and proclaimed a reformed Hinduism with a social conscience in India. His organization of the now worldwide Ramakrishna Mission owed much to the methods of Christian missionaries. His *Collected Works* were published in 1931.

SWAMMERDAM, Jan (1637–80) Dutch naturalist, born in Amsterdam, the son of an apothecary. He studied medicine at Leiden, but never practised. Instead, his system for classifying insects laid the foundations of entomology. His *Biblia Naturae* (published posthumously, 1737–38) is the finest one-man collection of microscopical observations. He first observed red blood corpuscles (1658) and discovered the valves in the lymph vessels, and the glands in Amphibia named after him. He published *Historia insectorum generalis* (1669). He finally succumbed to the fanatical mystic influences of **Bourignon** and abandoned science.

SWAN, Annie S (Shepherd) (1859–1943) Scottish novelist, born near Coldingham, Berwickshire, and brought up in Edinburgh and at Gorebridge, Midlothian. She married a schoolmaster (later doctor), James Burnett Smith, in 1883, and from 1896 they lived in England; she returned to Scotland in 1927 after her husband's death. She published her first novel, *Ups and Downs*, in 1878, and made her name with a Border romance *Aldersyde* (1883), followed by *Carlowie* (1884), *A Divided House* (1885) and *The Gates of Eden* (1887). From then on she published a large number of light romantic novels, and stories for women's magazines like *The Woman at Home*. She published her autobiography, *My Life*, in 1934.

SWAN, Sir Joseph Wilson (1828–1914) English physicist and chemist, born in Sunderland. He became a manufacturing chemist, patented the carbon process for photographic printing in 1864, and invented the dry plate (1871) and bromide paper (1879). In 1860 he invented an electric lamp which anticipated **Edison**'s by 20 years, and in 1897 demonstrated a lamp which considerably improved on Edison's patent model. He was the first to produce practicable artificial silk.

SWANN, Donald (1923–) Welsh composer and lyricist, born in Llanelli. He began his writing career by contributing music to revues such as *Penny Plain* (1951), *Airs on a Shoestring* (1953), and *Pay the Piper* (1954). His long collaboration with **Michael Flanders** began in 1956, when he wrote the music, and Flanders the words and dialogue, for *At the Drop of a Hat*, followed by *At the Drop of Another Hat* in 1965. Since the 1970s he has become a frequent broadcaster on musical and other matters, and has written a musical fable for Christmas, and three books of new carols.

SWANSON, Gloria, originally **Gloria May Josephine Svensson** (1897–1983) American actress, born in Chicago. After studying as a singer she entered the nascent film industry as an extra and bit part player in 1915. She became one of **Mack Sennett**'s bathing beauties before an association with director **Cecil B de Mille** brought her leading roles as chic sophisticates in the front line of the battle of the sexes. Her many silent features include *Male and Female* (1919), *The Affairs of Anatol* (1921) and *Manhandled* (1924). Despite the extravagances of the unfinished *Queen Kelly* (1928) she survived the arrival of sound, receiving Academy Award nominations for *Sadie Thompson* (1928) and *The Trespasser* (1929). However, her film career gradually dwindled away despite a sensational comeback in *Sunset Boulevard* (1950). Never relinquishing her glamorous star status she continued to appear on stage and television. Married six times, she published her autobiography, *Swanson on Swanson*, in 1980.

SWEDENBORG, Emanuel (1688–1772) Swedish mystic, theologian and scientist, born in Stockholm. The family name was Svedberg, but was changed to Swedenborg when they were ennobled in 1719. He studied at Uppsala, travelled widely in Europe, interesting himself particularly in technology and engineering, and returned to Sweden to be assessor at the Royal Board of Mines (1716). He wrote prolifically on all manner of technical and mathematical topics—the differential calculus, astronomy, docks, sluices and navigation, followed by a mighty treatise, *Opera Philosophica et Mineralia* (1734), a remarkable mixture of metaphysics and metallurgy, and huge works on anatomy and physiology entitled *Oeconomia Regni Animalis* (1740–41) and *Regnum Animale* (1744–45). In 1743–44 he had a religious crisis, recorded in his *Journal of Dreams*, which he interpreted as a direct vision of the spiritual world and which led him to resign his scientific post (1747) to expound his experiences and the mystical doctrines he based on them. He continued to write with prodigious energy and produced some 30 volumes of religious revelations in Latin, the best-known being *Arcana Coelestia* (8 volumes, 1749–56), *De Coelo et eius Mirabilibus et de Inferno* (1758) and *Vera Christiana Religio* (1771). He made no attempt to found a sect himself, but his followers organized a society in London known as the Church of the New Jerusalem (1787), which proliferated many further branches throughout the world (Swedenborgianism).

SWEELINCK, Jan Pieterszoon (1562–1621) Dutch composer, organist and harpsichordist, born in Deventer or Amsterdam. He studied in Venice and composed mainly church music and organ works, and developed the fugue. He founded the distinctive North German school which later included **Diderik Buxtehude** and **J S Bach**.

SWEET, Henry (1845–1912) English philologist, pioneer of Anglo-Saxon philological studies, born in London. As reader in phonetics at Oxford, his works include Old and Middle English texts, primers, and dictionaries, a historical English grammar, *A History of English Sounds* (1874), an *Anglo-Saxon Reader* (1867), *A New English Grammar* (1892) and *A History of Language* (1900). He constructed a 'Romaic' phonetic alphabet, and *The Practical Study of Languages* (1899) advocated 'the living philology', ie teaching the spoken language utililizing the new science of phonetics. Professor Higgins of **Bernard Shaw**'s *Pygmalion* was based on him.

SWETTENHAM, Sir Frank Athelstane (1850–1946) English colonial administrator. He was British resident in Selangor (1882) and Perak (1889–95), and later resident-general in the Federated Malay States (1896–1901). He was governor and commander-in-chief of the Straits Settlement from 1901 to 1904 and became an authority on Malay language and history, writing a number of books on the subject. Port Swettenham, Selangor, is named after him.

SWIFT, Jonathan (1667–1745) Anglo-Irish poet, satirist and clergyman, born in Dublin, the son of English parents. He was educated at Kilkenny Grammar School and Trinity College, Dublin, where he obtained his degree only by 'special grace' in 1685. Family connections helped him to embark on a career as secretary to the renowned diplomat, Sir **William Temple**, then resident at Moor Park, Farnham. He supported his patron on the side of the Ancients in the 'Querelle des Anciens et des Modernes' which had spread to Britain from France. Swift's contribution was the mock-epic *Battle of the Books* which was published along with the much more powerful satire on religious dissension, *A Tale of a Tub*, in 1704. At Moor Park he first met Esther Johnson (1681–1728), then a child of eight, who from then on as pupil and lover or friend was to play an important role in his life and to survive for posterity in Swift's verse tributes and the *Journal to Stella* (1710–13), but it is uncertain if he ever married her. When Swift was presented to the living of Laracor near Dublin, 'Stella' accompanied him. In 1708, during one of his numerous visits to London, he met Esther Vanhomrigh (1690–1723), who insisted on being near him in Ireland with unhappy consequences to herself. She is the Vanessa of Swift's too clever poem *Cadenus and Vanessa*, a tribute to the lady but also a manoeuvre of disengagement. His visits to London were largely political, but he also visited the great in the literary and aristocratic circles. For the first time the literary world met on equal terms with statesmen. Having been introduced to the political world by Temple, he supported the Whigs, but, his first care being the English Church, he gradually veered to the Tory party. The friendship of **Harley**, later Earl of Oxford, assisted the change which was decisively made in 1710 when Harley returned to power. His *Four Last Years of the Queen Anne* described the ferment of intrigue and pamphleteering during that period. The chief aims of the Tory party were to make the Establishment secure and to bring the war with France to a close. The latter object was powerfully aided by his *On the Conduct of the Allies* (1713), one of the greatest pieces of pamphleteering. The death of Queen Anne in 1714 disappointed all the hopes of Swift and his friends of the Scriblerus Club, founded in 1713. Swift accepted his 'exile' to the Deanery of St Patrick's Cathedral, Dublin, and from then on, except for two visits in 1726 and 1727, correspondence alone kept him in touch with London. Despite his loathing for Ireland he threw himself into a strenuous campaign for Irish liberties, denied by the Whig government. The *Drapier's Letters* is the most famous of these activities, which were concerned with England's restrictions on Irish trade, particularly the exclusion of Irish wool and cattle. This campaign, and his charitable efforts for Dublin's poor, greatly enhanced his reputation. On his first visit to London after the Tory debacle of 1714 he published the world-famous satire *Gulliver's Travels* (1726). In 1729 he published his ironical *A Modest Proposal*. His poems in light verse now range from the diverting *The Grand Question Debated* (1729) to the *Verses on His Own Death* (1731), which, with its mixture of pathos and humour, ranks with the great satirical poems in the lighter manner. He himself considered his *On Poetry; a Rhapsody* (1733), his best verse satire. The ironical *Directions to Servants* and *A Complete Collection of Genteel and Ingenious Conversation* followed in 1731. The satire in the first part of *Gulliver's Travels* is directed at political parties and religious dissension. The second part can be equally enjoyed for the ingenious adventures and the detailed verisimilitude which is part of the manner. But there is deepening misanthropy culminating in the king's description of mankind as 'the most pernicious race of little odious vermin that Nature ever suffered to crawl upon the surface of the earth'. The third part, a satire on inventors, is good fun though less plausible. The last part, in the country of the Houyhnhnms, a race of horses governed only by reason, is a savage attack on man which points to the author's final mental collapse. Politics apart, Swift's influence, like that of the 'Scriblerus Club' generally and **Pope** in particular, was directed powerfully against the vogue of deistic science and modern invention and in favour of orthodoxy and good manners.

SWINBURNE, Algernon Charles (1837–1909) English poet and critic, born in London, the eldest son of Admiral Charles Swinburne and Lady Jane Ashburnham. He was educated partly in France and at Eton (where he was savagely beaten and bullied) and Balliol College, Oxford, but left without taking a degree. He travelled on the Continent, where he came under the spell of **Victor Hugo**. He visited **Landor** in Florence (1864), and on his return became associated with **D G Rossetti** and **William Morris**. After a breakdown due to intemperate living, he submitted to the care of his friend **Theodore Watts-Dunton**, in whose house, No. 2, The Pines, he continued to live in semi-seclusion for the rest of his life. His first publication, the two plays *The Queen Mother* and *Rosamond* (1860), attracted little attention, but *Atalanta in Calydon* (1865), a drama in the Greek form but modern in its spirit of revolt against religious acquiescence in the will of Heaven, proved a success. He returned to Greek myth with his noble lyric drama *Erectheus* (1876). It was, however, the first of the series of *Poems and Ballads* (1866) which took the public by storm. The exciting rhythms of 'Hesperia', 'Itylus', 'The Garden of Proserpine', and 'The Triumph of Time' were intoxicating to English ears, but the uninhibited tone of certain passages affronted English puritanism. The second series of *Poems and Ballads* (1878) found it hard to maintain the excitement and the third series (1889) witnessed his waning vogue in this kind. Meanwhile he found scope for his detestation of kings and priests in the struggle for Italian liberty. *Songs before Sunrise* (1871) best expresses his fervent republicanism. He had been working on a trilogy of **Mary, Queen of Scots**, since before 1865 when his *Chastelard* appeared. The second play of the series, *Bothwell, a Tragedy*, appeared in 1874 and *Mary Stuart* completed the trilogy in 1881. The year following, *Tristram of Lyonesse*, an Arthurian romance in rhymed couplets, achieved a real success and must be considered among the best of Victorian dealings with the medieval cycle. He had resented **Tennyson**'s moralistic treatment of the theme in *The Idylls of the King*. *Tristram* is intense and passionate and has some great descriptive passages. When he returned to medieval romance in *A Tale of Balen* (1896), there was obvious lack of power. Swinburne represented the last phase of the Romantic movement. His absorption in romantic themes which he treated with a wealth of rhetoric and an excess of neologisms and archaisms has caused his reputation to diminish, but he made a genuine and lasting contribution to the poetic scene. His novel, *Love's Cross Currents* (1877), published under the pseudonym Mrs H Manners, is a curiosity, but his critical works, above all his work on **Shakespeare** and his contemporaries, are stimulating. His *Essays and Studies* (1875) and *Studies in Prose and Poetry* (1894) are his chief contribution to criticism.

SWINBURNE, Sir James, 9th Baronet (1858–1958) British scientist, 'the father of British plastics'. He was a pioneer in that industry and the founder of Bakelite,

Ltd. His research on phenolic resins resulted in a process for producing synthetic resin, but his patent for this was anticipated by one day, by the Belgian chemist **Leo Baekeland**.

SWINHOE, Robert (1836–77) English naturalist and consular official, born in Calcutta. He went to Hong Kong in 1854, and was posted to Amoy in 1855. He was on the naval expedition that captured Peking and negotiated the Treaty of Tiensin (1860). He was British consul in Formosa (1861–66) Amoy (1866–69) and Ningpo (1871–75). He compiled the first checklist of Chinese birds (1871). Swinhoe's Pheasant, Swinhoe's Petrel and Swinhoe's Snipe are named after him.

SWINTON, Alan Archibald Campbell (1863–1930) Scottish electrical engineer and inventor, born in Edinburgh. He was interested in all things mechanical and electrical from an early age, linking two houses some distance apart by telephone at the age of 15, only two years after its invention by **Alexander Graham Bell**. In 1882 he began an engineering apprenticeship in the Newcastle works of **William George Armstrong**, for whom he devised a new method of insulating electric cables on board ship by sheathing them in lead. While practising as a consulting engineer in London he was one of the first to explore the medical applications of radiography (1896), and in a letter to *Nature* in 1908 he outlined the principles of an electronic system of television.

SWINTON, Sir Ernest Dunlop (1868–1951) British soldier, writer and inventor, born in Bangalore, India. One of the originators of the tank, he was responsible for the use of the word 'tank' to describe armoured fighting vehicles. Under his pseudonym **Ole Luk-Oie** he wrote *The Green Curve* (1909), *A Year Ago* (1916), and translations. He became professor of Military History at Oxford (1925–39).

SWITHIN, St (d.862) Anglo Saxon ecclesiastic. He was adviser to **Egbert** and was made bishop of Winchester (852) by Ethelwulf. When in 971 the monks exhumed his body to bury it in the rebuilt cathedral, the removal, which was to have taken place on 15 July, is said to have been delayed by violent rain. Hence the current belief that if it rains on 15 July it will rain for 40 days more.

SWYNFORD, Katharine See **JOHN OF GAUNT**

SYBEL, Heinrich von (1817–95) German historian, born in Düsseldorf. He studied at Berlin under **Leopold von Ranke**, became professor of history at Bonn (1844), Marburg (1845), Munich (1856) and Bonn again (1861), and in 1875 was made director of the state archives at Berlin. He published the political correspondence of **Frederick II, the Great**, shared in issuing the *Monumenta Germaniae Historica*, and founded and edited the *Historische Zeitschrift*. His history of the First Crusade (1841) often ran counter to the accepted opinions of centuries; his next work was on the title 'German king' (1844). Then came his masterpiece, *Geschichte der Revolutionszeit, 1789–95* (1853–58), a history of the French Revolution based upon official documentary evidence. He also wrote a history of the founding of the German empire (1889–94; trans 1891–92), marred by its Prussian bias. He was a member of the Prussian Diet.

SYDENHAM, Floyer (1710–87) English scholar. Educated at Wadham College, Oxford, he became a barrister at Lincoln's Inn. He published an excellent translation of **Plato**'s *Dialogues* (1759–80), which failed to make money, as did his dissertation on **Heraclitus** (1775) and his *Onomasticon Theologicum* (1784). Arrested for unpaid meals, he died in prison. The Literary Fund was founded as a consequence of his death, to help deserving authors.

SYDENHAM, Thomas (1624–89) English physician, 'the English **Hippocrates**', born in Wynford Eagle, Dorset. He served as captain of horse for the Parliamentarian army in the Civil War. In 1647 he went to Oxford and studied medicine at Wadham College, and was elected fellow of All Souls College. In 1651 he was severely wounded at Worcester. From 1655 he practised in London. A great friend of such empiricists as **Robert Boyle** and **John Locke**, he stressed the importance of observation rather than theory in clinical medicine. He wrote *Observationes Medicae* (1667) and a treatise on gout (1683), a disease from which he himself suffered, distinguished the symptoms of venereal disease (1675), recognized hysteria as a distinct disease and gave his name to the mild convulsions of children, 'Sydenham's chorea' (St Vitus's dance), and to the medicinal use of liquid opium, 'Sydenham's laudanum'. He remained in London except when the plague was at its peak (1665). Some of his epidemiological theories on the fevers of London are supported today, although he failed to stress the roles of contagion and infection. One of his quainter 'remedies' for senile decrepitude was to put the patient to bed with a vital young person. In England he suffered professional opposition, but on the Continent his fame was immediate; **Hermann Boerhaave** is said never to have referred to him without raising his hat.

SYDNEY, Algernon See **SIDNEY**

SYKES, Eric (1923–) English comedy writer and performer, born in Oldham. Wartime service in the RAF allowed him to perform in service shows and, after his discharge, he became a gag writer. Progressing to full scripts, he wrote for such radio shows as *Variety Bandbox* (1947) and *Educating Archie* (1950–54), rising to become Britain's highest-paid scriptwriter. The creator of his own BBC series, which ran from 1959 to 1965 and 1972 to 1980, he offered simple, innocent humour devoid of malice or offence and with a propensity towards physical jokes and slapstick antics. His stage performances include *Large As Life* (1960), *Hatful of Sykes* (1979) and *Cinderella* (1981–82). His film appearances include *One Way Pendulum* (1964), *Shalako* (1968) and *Theatre of Blood* (1973). Almost totally deaf, he has written, directed and acted in short, silent comedies like *The Plank* (1967) and *Rhubarb* (1970). Other television series include *Curry and Chips* (1969) and *The Nineteenth Hole* (1989–).

SYLVESTER I (d.335) pope from 314 to 335. He is falsely claimed to have baptized and cured of leprosy **Constantine the Great**, and to have received from him the famous Donation, now considered apocryphal. Under him the Council of Nicaea (325) defined the articles of the Christian faith. He was canonized.

SYLVESTER II (c.940–1003) pope from 999. He was born Gerbert in Aurillac in Auvergne. From his erudition in chemistry, mathematics and philosophy he acquired the reputation of being in league with the Devil. He made a large collection of classical manuscripts and is said to have introduced Arabic numerals and to have invented clocks. He became abbot of Bobbio (982) and Archbishop of Rheims (991) and Ravenna (998). He upheld the primacy of Rome against the separatist tendencies of the French church.

SYLVESTER III (?d.1046) antipope from 1044 to 1046 to **Benedict IX**, but recognized his claims and resigned. He and was bishop of Sabina.

SYLVESTER, James Joseph (1814–97) English mathematician, born in London. He studied at St John's College, Cambridge, became second wrangler in 1837 but, as a Jew, was disqualified from graduating. He became professor at University College, London

(1837), and the University of Virginia (1841–45). Returning to London he left academic life, worked as an actuary, and was called to the Bar in 1850. He was professor of mathematics at Woolwich (1855–70), and at Johns Hopkins University, Baltimore (1877–83). Finally he became Savilian professor at Oxford (1883–94). Making important contributions to the theory of invariants and to number theory, his mathematical style was flamboyant, and he wrote in haste, continually coining new technical terms, most of which have not survived.

SYLVIUS, Franciscus, or **Franz de la Boë** (1614–72) German physician, born in Hanau, Prussia. He became professor of medicine at Leiden (1658). The first to treat the pancreatic, saliva and other body juices chemically, he also described the relationship between the tubercle and phthisis, and founded the iatro-chemical school.

SYLVIUS, properly **Jacques Dubois** (1478–1555) French physician, born in Amiens. He became professor of medicine at the Collège de France. He discovered the fissure in the brain, described many anatomical structures and systematized anatomical terms. He wrote commentaries on **Galen** and **Hippocrates**.

SYME, James (1799–1870) Scottish surgeon, born in Edinburgh. He studied under **Robert Liston** at Edinburgh University and at Paris and in Germany. In 1818 he announced a method of waterproofing, afterwards patented by **Charles Macintosh**. From 1823 to 1933 he lectured on clinical surgery. In 1831 he published his treatise on *The Excision of Diseased Joints*, and in 1832 his *Principles of Surgery*. In 1833 he became professor of clinical surgery. He also wrote on pathology, stricture, fistula, and incised wounds.

SYME, Sir Ronald (1903–89) New Zealand historian. He studied classics at Oriel College, Oxford, and was fellow of Trinity College, Oxford, from 1929 to 1949, when he became Oxford's Camden professor of ancient history. He had served in British Embassies in Belgrade and Ankara during the war and was made professor of classical philology at Istanbul University from 1942 to 1945. He wrote a masterly account of *The Roman Revolution* (1939), in which he ruthlessly subjected politics in Rome after **Caesar**'s murder to objective analysis, deflating such figures as **Cicero** and **Augustus** and making an effective case for **Marcus Antonius**, whose alliance with **Cleopatra** he saw as more pragmatic than erotic. It broke absolutely from traditional British cults of Roman virtue. In 1958 he produced a magisterial work on *Tacitus*; and in 1964 published his *Sallust*.

SYMEON OF DURHAM See **SIMEON OF DURHAM**

SYMINGTON, William (1763–1831) Scottish engineer and inventor, born in Leadhills. He became a mechanic at the Wanlockhead mines. In 1787 he patented an engine for road locomotion and, in 1788, he constructed for **Patrick Miller** a similar engine on a boat 25 feet long, having twin hulls with paddle-wheels between, which was launched on Dalswinton Loch. In 1802 he completed at Grangemouth the *Charlotte Dundas*, one of the first practical steamboats ever built. It was intended as a tug, but vested interests prevented its use, asserting that the wash would injure the sides of the Forth and Clyde Canal. Symington died in London, in poverty.

SYMMACHUS, Coelius (d.514) pope from 498 to 514, born in Sardinia. Strongly orthodox, he expelled the Manichaeans from Rome.

SYMMACUS, Quintus Aurelius (c.340–c.402) Roman orator. He became prefect of Rome in 384 and consul in 391 under the emperor **Theodosius I**. He was devoted to the old religion, and showed the highest nobility of character. His extant writings consist of letters, three panegyrics on **Valentinian I** and **Gratian**, and a *Relatio* (Report) addressed to **Valentinian II** in 384, urging the restoration of the Altar of Victory.

SYMONDS, Henry Herbert (1885–1958), British educationist and classical scholar, a leading figure in the establishment of the Youth Hostel movement and the National Parks. After a distinguished career at Oxford, as a teacher at Rugby School, and as headmaster of Liverpool Institute, he retired early to devote his formidable energies and clear-sightedness to the service of the countryside and its protection from vandalism. He was instrumental in opening the first Youth Hostels in Britain (in North Wales 1931) and served as treasurer, later vice-president of the Friends of the Lake District, and as drafting secretary of the standing committee on National Parks. His book *Walking in the Lakes District* (1933) became one of the classic guides. He also wrote *Afforestation in the Lake District* (1937).

SYMONDS, John Addington (1840–93) English author, born in Bristol. He was educated at Harrow School and Balliol College, Oxford, where he won the Newdigate prize for poetry, and was elected a fellow of Magdalen College in 1862. His *Introduction to the Study of Dante* (1872) was followed by *Studies of the Greek Poets* (1873–76), his great *Renaissance in Italy* (6 vols, 1875–86), and *Shakespeare's Predecessors in the English Drama* (1884). He also wrote sketches of travel in Italy and elsewhere and monographs on **Shelley**, **Sidney**, and **Ben Jonson**. He translated the *Sonnets of Michelangelo and Campanella* (1878), **Benvenuto Cellini**'s autobiography, and 12th-century students' Latin songs (1884). He wrote a *Life of Michelangelo* (1892), some verse, and an account of his residence (for health reasons) in Davos (1892).

SYMONS, Alphonse James Albert (1900–41) English bibliophile and biographer, born in London. His greatest success was *The Quest for Corvo* (1934), an extraordinary biography of the writer and novelist **Frederick Rolfe**, Baron Corvo. He was active in founding the First Edition Club and the Wine and Food Society, and worked for years on a bibliography of the 1890s writers. He published brief lives of the explorers **H M Stanley** and **Emin Pasha** and also wrote some brilliant impressionistic chapters of a biography of **Oscar Wilde** which, like many other projects, he left uncompleted. His brother, Julian Symons (1912–), is a novelist and popular historian.

SYMONS, Arthur (1865–1945) Welsh critic and poet, born of Cornish stock in Wales. He did much to familiarize the British with the literature of France and Italy. He translated **d'Annunzio** (1902) and **Baudelaire** (1925). He wrote a number of volumes of lyrics, and critical works on *The Symbolist Movement in Literature* (1899) and *The Romantic Movement in English Poetry* (1909).

SYMONS, George James (1838–1900) English meteorologist, born in London. He served as clerk in the meteorological department of the board of trade, and founded the British Rainfall Organization for collecting rainfall data with the co-operation of the general public. Through his efforts the number of rainfall reporting stations in Britain was increased from 168 to over 3500. The Royal Society appointed him to investigate the Krakatoa eruption in 1883. He was twice president of the Royal Meteorological Society, the highest award of which, the Symons Memorial Gold Medal, bears his name.

SYNESIUS (c.370–413) Greek neoplatonist philosopher and poet, born in Cyrene. He studied at

Alexandria under **Hypatia** and at Athens. He became a Christian in about 401 and was bishop of Ptolemais in about 410. He wrote a number of neoplatonic *Hymns*, treatises *Concerning Providence* and *Concerning Dreams*, and a burlesque essay *The Praise of Baldness*.

SYNGE, John Millington (1871–1909) Irish dramatist, born near Dublin. He studied at Trinity College, Dublin, and then studied music in Germany before spending several years in Paris on literary pursuits until, on the advice of **Yeats**, he settled among the people of the Aran Islands (1899–1902) who provided the material for his plays, *In the Shadow of the Glen* (1903), *Riders to the Sea* (1904), *The Well of the Saints* (1905), and his humorous masterpiece *The Playboy of the Western World* (1907) followed by *The Tinker's Wedding* (1909). He had a profound influence on the next generation of Irish playwrights and was a director of the Abbey Theatre from 1904.

SYNGE, Richard Laurence Millington (1914–) English biochemist, born in Chester, the son of a stockbroker. He studied at Winchester and Trinity College, Cambridge, and spent much of his career at the Rowett Research Institute in Aberdeen (1948–67) and the Food Research Institute at Norwich (1967–76). At the Wool Industry Research Association in Leeds (1941–43) he worked with **Archer Martin** in devising the chromatographic methods which revolutionized analytical chemistry from 1941 onwards; they shared the Nobel prize for chemistry in 1952 for this work.

SZASZ, Thomas Stephen (1920–) Hungarian-born American psychiatrist, born in Budapest. He went to the USA in 1938 and received his MD from Cincinatti University in 1944. Since 1956 he has been professor of psychiatry at Syracuse University, New York. He has written many books, most of which argue that all disease must by physical, that consequently the idea of 'mental disease' is a myth and that contemporary psychiatrists are often the agents of repression. His brand of individualism interprets all behaviour as purposeful and intentional, and he argues that people should be allowed to do what they wish as long as they do not break the law, and that all psychiatric therapy should be contractual.

SZELL, George (1897–1970) Hungarian-born American conductor and pianist, born in Budapest. He was educated at the Vienna State Academy, and made his début as a conductor in Berlin (1914); he later conducted many of the world's major orchestras. He settled in the USA in 1939 and in 1946 began his long tenure of office as musical director and conductor of the Cleveland Symphony Orchestra.

SZENT-GYÖRGYI, Albert von Nagyrapolt (1893–1986) Hungarian-born American biochemist, born in Budapest. He lectured at Groningen and Cambridge, was professor at Szeged (1931–45) and at Budapest (1945–47), then emigrated to the USA and was director of the Institute of Muscle Research at Woods Hole, Massachusetts (1947–75), becoming scientific director of the National Foundation for Cancer Research, Massachusetts, in 1975. He discovered actin, isolated Vitamin C and was awarded the Nobel prize for physiology or medicine in 1937. He made important studies of biological combustion, muscular contraction and cellular oxidation.

SZERING, Henryk (1918–88) Polish-born Mexican violinist, born in Warsaw. He was educated at Warsaw, Berlin and Paris, where he studied composition with **Nadia Boulanger** (1934–39). During World War II he worked as an interpreter for the Polish government in exile while giving concerts for the Allied troops. He took Mexican citizenship in 1946, and was Mexican cultural ambassador from 1960. He wrote several violin and chamber music works, and taught internationally.

SZEWINSKA, Irena (1946–) Polish athlete, born in Leningrad, Russia. The greatest female athlete of her generation, her career spanned five Olympiads from 1964 to 1980. In the first of these she won a gold medal in the sprint relay. Four years later, at Mexico, she won the 200 metres gold medal. Her greatest triumph came at the Montreal Games of 1976, when she won the 400 metres in a world record time of 49.28 seconds.

SZILARD, Leo (1898–1964) Hungarian-born American physicist, born in Budapest. He studied electrical engineering there, and physics in Berlin, working with **Max von Laue**. In 1933 he fled from Nazi Germany to England, and in 1938 emigrated to the USA, where he began work on nuclear physics at Columbia. In 1934 he had taken a patent on nuclear fission as an energy source, and on hearing of **Otto Hahn** and **Lise Meitner**'s fission of uranium (1938), he immediately approached **Einstein** in order to write together to President **Roosevelt** warning him of the possibility of atomic bombs. Together with **Enrico Fermi**, Szilard organized work on the first fission reactor, which operated in Chicago in 1942. He was a central figure in the Manhattan Project leading to the atomic bomb: eccentric and highly politically aware, he was a source of both inspiration and exasperation to his colleagues.

SZYMANOWSKI, Karol (1883–1937) Polish composer, born in Tymoszowska, in the Ukraine. He became director of the State Conservatory in Warsaw and is reckoned by many to be the greatest Polish composer since **Chopin**. His works include operas, incidental music, symphonies, concertos, chamber music, piano music and many songs.

T

TAAFFE, Eduard Franz Josef, Graf von (1833–95) 11th Viscount Taaffe and Baron of Ballymote in the Irish peerage, Austrian statesman, born in Vienna. He became minister of the interior (1867) and chief minister (1869–70, 1879–93). He showed great tact in an attempt to unite the various nationalities of the Empire into a consolidated whole.

TABARI, Abu Jafar Mohammed Ben Jariral- (839–923) Arab historian, born in Persia. He travelled in the Middle East, and wrote in Arabic invaluable Muslim annals, and died in Baghdad.

TACITUS, Publius or **Gaius Cornelius** (c.55–120) Roman historian, born perhaps in Narbonese Gaul. He studied rhetoric in Rome, rose to eminence as a pleader at the Roman bar, and in 77 married the daughter of **Agricola**, the conqueror of Britain. By 88 he was already praetor and a member of one of the priestly colleges. Next year he left Rome for Germany, and did not return till 93. He was an eye witness to **Domitianus**'s reign of terror, and we have his own testimony as to the relief wrought by the accession of **Nerva** and **Trajan**. Under Nerva he became consul suffrectus, succeeding Virginius Rufus. We may assume that he saw the close of Trajan's reign, if not the opening of **Hadrian**'s. The high reputation he enjoyed is attested by the eulogistic mention of him in **Pliny**'s letters of which there are eleven addressed to him. The earliest work generally attributed to him, the *Dialogus de Oratoribus*, treats of the decline of eloquence under the empire. It is doubtful whether the *Agricola* is a funeral *éloge* or a panegyric for political ends. As biography it has grave defects, partly due to his admiration for his father-in-law; but it will always be read for its elevation of style, its dramatic force, invective and pathos. The third work, the *Germania*, is a monograph of great value on the ethnography of Germany. Fourth in order comes the *Historiae*, or the history of the empire from the accession of **Galba** in AD 68 to the assassination of Domitian in 96. Of the twelve books originally composing it, only the first four and a fragment of the fifth are extant. Tacitus is at his strongest here, and his material was drawn from contemporary experience. His last work, the so-called *Annales*, is a history of the Julian line from **Tiberius** to **Nero** (AD 14 to 68); of probably 18 books only eight have come down to us entire, four are fragmentary, and the others lost. His statuesque style is often obscure from condensation. He copied much from earlier historians and was biased in his republican ideals and hatreds.

TACZANOWSKI, Ladislas (1819–90) Polish ornithologist. Trained at the Paris Museum, he was conservator of the Zoological Museum of Warsaw from 1855. He wrote *Birds of Poland* (1882) and *The Ornithology of Peru* (1884–86).

TADDEO DI BARTOLI (c.1362–c.1422) Italian painter of the Sienese school. Most of his early work was executed in Pisa, where he was responsible for the frescoes of Paradise and Hell in the Cathedral and paintings in the Palazzo Publico. He was also active in Siena, San Gimignano, Perugia and Volterra. His conservative, but agreeable style was dependent upon **Simone Martini** and **Lorenzetti**. *A Descent of the Holy Ghost* in the church of San Agostino at Perugia is his masterpiece but he was usually more successful in his smaller pictures.

TADEMA See **ALMA-TADEMA**

TAFT, Robert Alfonso (1889–1953) American lawyer, Republican senator, son of President **William Howard Taft**, born in Cincinnati, Ohio. He studied law at Yale and Harvard and in 1917 became counsellor to the American Food Administration in Europe under **Hoover**. Elected senator in 1938, he co-sponsored the Taft-Hartley act (1947) directed against the power of the trade unions and the 'closed shop'. A prominent isolationist, he failed three times (1940, 1948, 1952) to secure Republican nomination for the presidency.

TAFT, William Howard (1857–1930) 27th president of the USA (1909–13), born in Cincinnati, the son of President **Grant**'s secretary of war and attorney-general. Having studied at Yale and qualified as a lawyer in Cincinnati, he held numerous appointments in Ohio, and in 1890 became solicitor-general for the USA. In 1900 he was made president of the Philippine Commission, and in 1901 first civil governor of the islands. From 1904 to 1908 he was secretary of war for the USA, and in 1906 provisional governor of Cuba. From 1909 to 1913 he was Republican president of the USA, but was defeated by **Woodrow Wilson** for a second term. He secured an agreement with Canada that meant relatively free trade. From 1913 he was professor of law at Yale and from 1921 chief justice of the USA. As such he improved the judicial machinery and proved himself a sound judge.

TAGLIACOZZI, or **Talicotius, Gasparo** (1546–99) Italian surgeon, born in Bologna. As professor there of surgery and of anatomy, he developed a technique for repairing injured noses by transplanting skin from the arm.

TAGLIONI, Maria (1804–84) Italian dancer, born in Stockholm, daughter of Italian ballet master Filippo Taglioni and a Swedish mother. Badly formed and plain, she danced with astonishing grace and individuality, and after some initial setbacks triumphed with her creation of *La Sylphide* in 1832 which marked the great romantic era in ballet. She married Count de Voisins in 1832, and ended her career teaching deportment to the British royal children. Her brother Paul (1808–84) and his daughter Marie Paul (1833–91) were also famous dancers.

TAGORE, Sir Rabindranath (1861–1941) Indian poet and philosopher, born in Calcutta, the son of a wealthy Hindu religious reformer, Debendranath Tagore (1817–1905). He studied law in England (1878–80) and for 17 years managed his family estates at Shileida, where he collected the legends and tales he later used in his work. His first book was a volume of poetry, *A Poets' Tale*, when he was 17 (1878), followed by a novel, *Karuna*, and a drama, *The Tragedy of Rudachandra*. In 1901 he founded near Bolpur the Santiniketan, a communal school to blend Eastern and Western philosophical and educational systems, which developed into Visva-Bharati University. He received the Nobel prize for literature in 1913, the first Asiatic to do so, and was knighted in 1915—an honour which he resigned in 1919 as a protest against British policy in the Punjab. He was openly critical of **Mahatma Gandhi**'s nonco-operation as well as of the Government attitude in Bengal. His major works include *Binodini* (1902, the first truly modern novel by an Indian writer), *The Crescent Moon* (1913, poems about childhood), *Gitanjali* (1912, a volume of spiritual verse), *Chitra* (1914, his first and finest play), *The Religion of Man* (1931) and *Farewell My Friend* (1940). He also wrote *My Reminiscences* (1917), and *My Boyhood Days*.

TAILLEFER (d.1066) Norman minstrel. He sang war songs at the battle of Hastings, in which he was killed. He is shown in the Bayeux tapestry.

TAILLEFERRE, Germaine (1892–1983) French pianist and composer, born in Park-St-Maur, one of 'les Six'. Her works include chamber music, a ballet, *Le Marchand d'oiseaux*, a piano concerto and songs.

TAINE, Hippolyte Adolphe (1828–93) French critic, historian and philosopher, born in Vouziers in Ardennes. He studied for a year at Paris before turning author. He made a reputation by his critical analysis of **La Fontaine**'s *Fables* (1853), followed by the *Voyage aux eaux des Pyrénées* (1855). His positivism was forcefully expressed in his critical *Les Philosophes français du dix-neuvième siècle* (1857) and also coloured his *Philosophie de l'art* (1881) and *De l'intelligence* (1870), in which moral qualities and artistic excellence are explained in purely descriptive, quasi-scientific terms. Taine's greatest work, *Les Origines de la France contemporaine* (1875-94), constitutes the strongest attack yet made on the men and the motives of the Revolution. *Derniers Essais* appeared in 1895, and *Carnets de voyage* in 1897. His *Notes sur l'Angleterre* (1871) are too ambitious in scope on the basis of only ten weeks' stay in England.

TAIT, Archibald Campbell (1811–82) Scottish Anglican prelate, and archbishop of Canterbury, born in Edinburgh, the son of solicitor from Clackmannan. Reared as a presbyterian, he was educated at the newly-founded Edinburgh Academy (where he was *dux* in two successive years), Glasgow University and Balliol College, Oxford, and became a fellow there. He entered the church of England in 1836, and became an opponent of the Oxford Movement, protesting in 1841 against **John Newman**'s *Tract* 90. He succeeded Dr **Thomas Arnold** as headmaster of Rugby (1842), became dean of Carlisle in 1849, and in 1856 bishop of London. He showed firmness and broadmindedness, as well as tact, in dealing with controversies over church ritual; he condemned bishop **Colenso**'s critical views on the accuracy of the Bible, but intervened on his side against attempts to have him deposed. In 1869 he was appointed archbishop of Canterbury (the first Scotsman to hold the post), and helped to lull the strife caused by Irish disestablishment, but was less successful in dealing with resentments over the Public Worship and Regulation Act (1874) and the Burials Act (1880). He did much to extend and improve the organization of the church in the colonies, and presided over the 1878 Lambeth Conference. His books included *The Dangers and Safeguards of Modern Theology* (1861) and *Harmony of Revelation and the Sciences* (1864). His biography was published in 1891 by his son-in-law, the future archbishop of Canterbury, **Randall Thomas Davidson**.

TAIT, Peter Guthrie (1831–1901) Scottish mathematician and golf enthusiast, born in Dalkeith. He was educated at the universities of Edinburgh and Cambridge, where he graduated as senior wrangler in 1852. He became professor of mathematics at Belfast (1854) and of natural philosophy at Edinburgh (1860–1901). He wrote on quaternions, thermodynamics and the kinetic theory of gases, and collaborated with Lord **Kelvin** on a *Treatise on natural philosophy* (1867). His study of vortices and smoke rings led to early work on the topology of knots. He studied the dynamics of the flight of a golf-ball and discovered the importance of 'underspin'.

TAIT, Thomas Smith (1882–1952) Scottish architect, the most prominent Scots architect of the inter-war period. He designed Adelaide House (1921–24), the *Daily Telegraph* office in London (1927) and St Andrew's House, Edinburgh (1934), and won the competition for the Hawkhead Infectious Diseases Hospital in Paisley (1932). He was controlling designer of the Glasgow Empire Exhibition of 1938.

TAIT, William (1792–1864) Scottish publisher. He was the founder of *Tait's Edinburgh Magazine* (1832–64), a literary and radical political monthly, to which **De Quincey**, **John Stuart Mill**, **Cobden** and **Bright** contributed.

TAKAMINE, Jokichi (1854–1922) Japanese-born American chemist, born in Takaoka. He studied chemical engineering in Tokyo and Glasgow, and in 1887 opened his own factory, the first to make superphosphate fertilizer in Japan. Then in 1890, having married an American, he moved to the USA and set up an industrial biochemical laboratory there; and in 1891 he isolated crystalline adrenalin from adrenal glands. After 1905, when **Ernest Henry Starling** first used the word hormone to describe the animal body's 'chemical messengers', it was realized that adrenalin was the first hormone to be isolated in pure form from a natural source.

TAKEI, Kei (1939–) Japanese post-modern dancer and choreographer, born in Tokyo. She studied in Tokyo and then travelled on a scholarship to the Juilliard School of Music, where **Anna Sokolow** taught dance. In 1969 she formed her own company, Moving Earth, and began her major work, *Light*, which has so far twenty-five parts lasting at least an hour each. Fifteen sections of this harsh depiction of survival, which starts with the Vietnam War and includes both primitive and contemporary images, were shown in a single performance in 1981.

TAKESHITA, Noboru (1924–) Japanese politician, born in Kakeyamachi, in western Japan, the son of an affluent sake brewer. He trained as a kamikaze pilot during World War II. After university and a brief career as a schoolteacher, he was elected to the House of Representatives as a Liberal Democratic party (LDP) deputy in 1958, rising to become chief cabinet secretary (1971–72) to prime minister Sato and minister of finance (1982–86) under prime minister **Nakasone**. Formerly a member of the powerful 'Tanaka faction', he founded his own faction, the largest within the party, in 1987, and three months later was elected LDP president and prime minister. Although regarded as a cautious, consensual politician, he pushed through important tax reforms. His administration was undermined by the uncovering of the Recruit-Cosmos insider share dealing scandal, which, though dating back to 1986, forced the resignation of senior government ministers, including, eventually, Takeshita himself, in June 1989.

TAL, Mikhail Nekhemyevich (1936–) Russian chess player, born in Riga, and world champion (1960–61). In 1960 he defeated **Mikhail Botvinnik** to become the youngest grandmaster to hold the world title until then. His withering stares over the board were held by opponents as attempts at hypnotism, but it is more likely that they succumbed to his unusually inventive style of attack. Major kidney problems terminated his reign at the top, but he has remained an active tournament player and chess journalist.

TALBERT, Bruce James (1838–81) Scottish designer. Educated at Dundee High School, he became a prolific and influential designer specializing in Gothic-style furniture. Originally apprenticed to a wood-carver, he was later trained as an architect. He moved from Glasgow to Manchester and Coventry, working for various firms before settling in London where he published his *Gothic Forms Applied to Furniture and Decoration for Domestic Purposes* in 1867. By 1873 he was working for Villons. Apart from furniture, he designed metalwork, wallpapers, tapestries and carpets.

TALBOT name of an English family, descended from Richard de Talbot, named in the *Domesday* book, and from Gilbert (d.1346), the first baron. The Earl of Shrewsbury and Talbot is the premier earl on the Rolls of England and Ireland and hereditary lord high steward of Ireland. The Lords Talbot de Malahide represent a family in Ireland which settled there in 1167.

TALBOT, Charles,12th Earl and only **Duke of Shrewsbury** (1660–1718) English statesman. He served under **Charles II** and **James II**, but gave money to William of Orange (**William III**) and did much to bring about the revolution of 1688. Twice secretary of state (1689 and 1694), he withdrew from public affairs in 1700, and went to Rome. In 1710 he helped to bring about the fall of the Whigs and was made lord chamberlain.. In 1712 he was ambassador to France, and then lord-lieutenant of Ireland. At the crisis on the death of Queen **Anne** (1714), as treasurer and lord justice, he acted with courage and decision and did much to secure the peaceful succession of the Hanoverians. He was created Duke of Shrewsbury in 1694, but the dukedom died with him.

TALBOT, George, 6th Earl of Shrewsbury (c.1528–1590) English soldier. He took part in the 'Rough Wooing' of Scotland by **Edward Seymour**, 1st Duke of Somerset (1543–44). From 1569 to 1584 he was entrusted by Queen **Elizabeth** with the custody of **Mary, Queen of Scots** at Tutbury, Chatsworth and Sheffield Castle. He was the fourth husband of Elizabeth Hardwick (1518–1608), familiarly known as 'Bess of Hardwick', widow of Sir William **Cavendish** of Chatsworth.

TALBOT, Sir John, 4th Baron, and 1st Earl of Shrewsbury (c.1390–1453) English soldier and statesman, the famous champion of English arms in France in **Henry VI**'s reign. Successful in many engagements, he was finally checked at Orléans by **Joan of Arc** (1429), and taken prisoner at Patay (1429), remaining a captive till 1431. He returned to France for further heroic exploits, and was made Marshall of France. He was lord lieutenant of Ireland twice (1414–19, and 1445). Created Earl of Salop (1422), Earl of Shrewsbury (1442) and Earl of Waterford (1455), he fell at Castillon, after taking Bordeaux.

TALBOT, Mary Anne (1778–1808) English woman soldier, known as the 'British Amazon'. She served as a drummer boy in Flanders (1792–93) and as a cabin boy in the navy (1793–96). She later became a maidservant in London, and her story was published in *The Life and Surprising Adventures of Mary Anne Talbot* (1809).

TALBOT, William Henry Fox (1800–77) English physicist and pioneer of photography, born in Melbury House, Evershot, and educated at Harrow and Trinity College, Cambridge. In 1839 he announced his invention of photography ('photogenic drawing'), a system of making photographic prints on silver chloride paper, in the same year as the invention of the daguerrotype by **Louis Daguerre**. In 1841 he patented the calotype, the first process for photographic negatives from which prints could be made, and was awarded the Rumford Medal of the Royal Society in 1842. He also discovered a method of making instantaneous photographs, using electric spark illumination (the first use of 'flash photography'), in 1851. His *Pencil of Nature* (1844) was the first photographically illustrated book to be published. He also published works on astronomy and mathematics, and helped to decipher the cuneiform inscriptions at Ninevah. A 16th century converted barn at the gates of Lacock Abbey in Wiltshire, where Fox Talbot lived from 1833 onwards, is now a museum of his work and equipment run by the National Trust.

TALESE, Gay (1932–) American journalist, born in Ocean City, New Jersey. **Tom Wolfe**, generally regarded as the pioneer of 'new journalism' has recognized Talese as its true inventor. A reporter for the *New York Times* (1955–65), he wrote his first non-fiction 'short stories' for *Esquire* magazine, beginning in 1963. His new style reached maturity in his bestselling nonfiction 'novels', *The Kingdom and the Power* (1969), about the *New York Times*, and *Honor Thy Father* (1971), about the Mafia. He has been described as 'a reporter who can write and a writer who can report'.

TALFOURD, Sir Thomas Noon (1795–1854) English lawyer and author, born in Reading, which he represented in parliament. He wrote a tragedy *Ion* (1835) produced at Covent Garden, and wrote on **Charles Lamb**, but is best known for his Copyright Act (1842).

TALIACOTIUS See **TAGLIACOZZI**

TALIESIN (fl.c.550) Welsh bard and prophet from north Britain, considered (with the mythical Merlin) one of the two great founders of the Welsh poetic tradition. He is named in the *Saxon Genealogies* appended to the *Historia Britonum* of **Nennius**, but later mythical material accreted to his legend. A mass of poetry, much of it of later date, has been ascribed to him, but some 12 heroic poems in the 13th-century *Book of Taliesin* are thought to be from his hand.

TALLEMANT DES RÉAUX, Gédéon (c.1619–1700) French man of letters, born in La Rochelle. He married his cousin Élisabeth Rambouillet, whose fortune enabled him to devote himself to letters and society. His famous *Historiettes* (written 1657–59; published 1834–40), 376 in number, are illustrative anecdotes rather than biographies.

TALLEYRAND-PÉRIGORD, Charles Maurice de, prince of Benevento (1754–1838) French statesman, born in Paris, son of the Comte Talleyrand de Périgord (1734–88) who fought in the Seven Years' War. He was educated for the church, made himself a fair scholar, and cultivated the character of a rake and a cynical wit. Abbot of St Denis (1775) and *agent-général* to the French clergy (1780), he was nominated bishop of Autun by **Louis XVI** in 1788. Next year the clergy of his diocese elected him to the States General, and he was one of the members of the Assembly selected to draw up the Declaration of Rights. He took a cynical delight in attacking the calling to which he still nominally belonged, and proposed the measure confiscating the landed property of the church. In February 1790 he was elected president of the Assembly. In 1791 he consecrated two new bishops, declaring at the same time his attachment to the Holy See, but, excommunicated by the pope, he gave up his clerical career. Early in 1792 Talleyrand was sent to London, but failed to conciliate **Pitt**; in December he was placed on the list of *émigrés*. He was again in London, an exile, until January 1794, when the Alien Act drove him to the United States. After the fall of **Robespierre** he returned to Paris (1796), attached himself to **Barras,** and in 1797 was made foreign minister under the Directory; he was for a time the first man in France. He had already recognized the genius of **Napoleon Bonaparte** and established intimate relations with him. For a time he was in disgrace for his willingness to sell his services towards a treaty between Great Britain and the United States. But under the Consulate he was restored to his post, and was privy to the kidnapping and murder (March 1804) of the **Duc d'Enghien**. He was greatly instrumental in consolidating the power of Napoleon as consul for life (1802) and as emperor (1804). When in 1805 Great Britain formed a European coalition against France, it was partially broken up by Talleyrand. To him as much as to Napoleon was owed the organization (1806) of the Confederation of the Rhine. After being created Prince de Bénévent, he withdrew from the ministry. His voice was on the whole for a policy of wisdom during the later years of the first empire. He was opposed to the invasion of Russia; and this gives some justification for his desertion of Napoleon in 1814. As far back as Tilsit (1807) he seems to have been in communication with Britain; at Erfurt (1808), he had revealed state secrets to Russia; and he had mortally offended Napoleon, after the disasters in Spain, by making, with **Fouché**, tentative arrangements for the succession. Now he became the leader of the anti-Napoleonic faction; and through him communications were opened with the allies and the **Bourbons.** He dictated to the Senate the terms of Napoleon's deposition, and he became minister of foreign affairs under **Louis XVIII**. He negotiated the treaties by which the allies left France in possession of the boundaries of 1792, and at the Congress of Vienna he established her right to be heard. He had not calculated on the Hundred Days, and offered no help to Louis; being taken back after the second restoration, he became, through pressure of the allies, prime minister for a short time, but he was not *persona grata* with the king, and was disliked by all parties in France. Under Louis XVIII and **Charles X** he was little better than a discontented senator; but he was **Louis-Philippe**'s chief adviser at the July revolution, for which he was partly responsible, went to London as ambassador and reconciled the British ministry and court to France. He retired into private life in 1834.

TALLIEN, Jean Lambert (1769–1820) French revolutionary, born in Paris. During the revolution he made himself famous in 1791 by his Jacobin broadsheets, *L'Ami des citoyens*. He was conspicuous in the attack on the Tuileries and in the September massacres, was elected to the Convention (1792), voted for the death of the king, was elected to the committee of general safety, and played a part in the downfall of the Girondins. On his mission to Bordeaux (1793) during the Terror he quenched all opposition with the guillotine. Comtesse Thérèse de Fontenay, born Jeanne Marie Ignace Thérèsa Cabarrus (1773–1835), whom he married in 1794 after saving her from death on the guillotine, also became famous for her harsh and dissolute conduct. He was recalled to Paris, and in March 1794 was chosen president of the Convention. But **Robespierre** hated him, and Tallien, recognizing his danger, led the successful attack of 9th Thermidor which brought about his downfall. He helped to suppress the Revolutionary Tribunal and the Jacobin Club, and drew up the accusations against **Carrier**, Le Bon and other Terrorists; but his importance ended with the Convention, though he was a member of the Council of Five Hundred under the Directory and accompanied **Napoleon** to Egypt and edited the *Décade Égyptienne* at Cairo. On the voyage home he was captured by an English cruiser, and in England was made a hero by the Whigs (1801). Consul at Alicante (1805), he lost an eye there by yellow fever, and died in Paris in poverty.

TALLIS, Thomas (c.1505–1585) English musician, born in London, 'the father of English cathedral music'. He was organist of Waltham Abbey at the dissolution in 1540, when it is conjectured he became 'a gentleman of the Chapel Royal'. Queen **Elizabeth** gave him, with **Byrd**, a monopoly of music printing. In **John Day**'s Psalter (1560) there are eight tunes by him, one of which, known as Tallis's Canon, is now used for **Thomas Ken**'s Evening Hymn. The *Cantiones* (1575) contained 18 motets by Byrd and 16 by Tallis. He was one of the greatest contrapuntists of the English School; an adaptation of his plainsong responses, and his setting of the Canticles in D Minor, are still in use. He wrote much church music, among it a motet in 40 parts.

TALMA, François Joseph (1763–1826) French tragedian, born in Paris. He made his début in 1787. Before him actors had worn the garb of their own time and country; Talma made a point of accuracy in costume. He achieved his greatest success in 1789 as **Charles IX** in **Chénier**'s play.

TAMAYO, Rufino (1899–) Mexican artist. He studied at the Academy of San Carlos (1917–21) and became engrosed in tribal sculpture as a curator at the National Museum of Anthropology. His own style combines pre-Columbian art with the art of modern Europe. Among his works are the miracle *Birth of Nationality* and *Mexico Today* for the Palace of Fine Arts, and murals in the UNESCO building in Paris.

TAMBO, Oliver (1917–) South African politician, born in Bizana, Transkei, the son of a peasant farmer. At 16 he travelled to Johannesburg to attend a school set up by the Community for the Resurrection, where he came under the influence of Father **Trevor Huddleston**. After graduating at Fort Hare University he began a teacher's diploma course but was expelled for organizing a student protest and in 1944 joined the African National Congress (ANC), being appointed vice-president of its youth league. As his thoughts turned to the church, he asked Trevor Huddleston to help him join the priesthood, but before he was accepted as a candidate, in 1956, he was imprisoned, but released the following year. Now ANC secretary-general, when it was banned in 1960 he left South Africa to set up an external wing. With the continued imprisonment, until 1990, of **Nelson Mandela**, he became acting ANC president in 1967 and president in 1977 and travelled extensively promoting its cause.

TAMERLANE, anglicized form of **Timur-i-Lang, 'lame Timur'** (1336–1404) Turkic conqueror, born in Kash near Samarkand. In a series of devastating wars (in which he sustained the wounds which gave him his nickname) he made himself master of Transoxiana (1360–70). From there he led his army of nomadic Turks and Mongols to the conquest of Persia (1392–96), northern India (1398), and the defeat of the Ottomans and the Mamluks (1402), and died leading a campaign against China. His capital, Samarkand, profited greatly from his conquests.

TAMM, Igor Yevgenyevich (1895–1971) Soviet physicist, born in Vladivostock, the son of an engineer. He was educated at the universities of Edinburgh and Moscow: he taught at Moscow State University (1924–34) and then moved to the Physics Institute of the Academy. He shared the 1958 Nobel prize for physics with **Pavel Cherenkov** and **Ilya Frank** for their work in explaining the 'Cherenkov effect'. The Cherenkov effect is used in highly sensitive atomic particle detectors.

TAM'SI, Tchicaya U (1931–88), Congolese poet, novelist and playwright, born at Npili in what was then the French colony of Moyen Congo and is now the Congolese Republic. He was educated in French Lycées in Orléans and Paris from the age of 15, after his father was elected a deputy to the French National Assembly, and lived in Paris for most of the rest of his life. He published several volumes of Surrealist poetry, notably *Le Mauvais Sang* (1955), *Le Ventre* (1964) and *Feu de Brousse* (1964); his best-known poems are in *Epitomé* (1962), which records the events surrounding the imprisonment and murder of **Patrice Lumumba.** The best of his poems were translated into English by Gerald Moore in *Selected Poems* (1970).

TANAKA, Kakuei (1918–) Japanese politician, born into a bankrupted rural family in Futuda village, in western Japan. After training as a civil engineer and establishing a successful building contracting business, he was elected to Japan's House of Representatives in 1947. He rose swiftly within the dominant Liberal Democratic party (LDP), becoming minister of finance (1962–65), party secretary-general (1965–67) and minister of international trade and industry (1971–72), before serving as LDP president and prime minister (1972–74). He was arrested in 1976 on charges of accepting bribes from the Lockheed Corporation while he was prime minister, and eventually in 1983 was found guilty and sentenced to four years imprisonment. He had resigned from the LDP in 1976, becoming an independent deputy, but remained an influential, behind-the-scenes, faction leader. His appeal against the 1983 verdict was rejected by the High Court in 1987, but a further appeal was lodged.

TANCRED (1078–1112) Norman crusader, a son of Odo 'the Good Marquis' and Emma, daughter of **Robert Guiscard**. He went on the First Crusade (1096–99) with his uncle **Bohemond I**, and distinguished himself in many sieges. He established the great principality of Galilee, but after a short tenure went to Antioch where he ruled as regent. He is the hero of *Gerusalemme liberata* by **Tasso** (1593).

TANDY, (James) Napper (1740–1803) Irish nationalist, born in Dublin. He worked as an ironmonger, and became a prosperous merchant and land agent there. A Presbyterian, he took an active part in corporation politics, and was the first secretary to the Dublin United Irishmen. In 1792 he challenged the solicitor-general for his abusive language, and was arrested. In 1793 he was to have stood trial on the minor charge of distributing a 'seditious' pamphlet against the Beresfords, when the government learned that he had taken the oath of the Defenders' Society, a treasonable offence. He fled to America, crossed to France in 1798, shared in the ill-fated invasion of Ireland by landing on Rutland Island, sailed away for Norway but was eventually apprehended in Hamburg and handed over to the English government. In February 1800 he was acquitted in Dublin. Again put on trial (April 1801) at Lifford for the treasonable landing on Rutland Island, he was sentenced to death, but permitted to escape to France, and died in Bordeaux.

TANEY, Roger Brooke (1777–1864) American judge, born in Calvert County, Maryland. Admitted to the bar in 1799, he was elected to the Maryland senate in 1816. In 1824 he passed from the Federal to the Democratic party, and supported **Andrew Jackson**, who in 1831 made him attorney-general, and in 1833 secretary of the Treasury. The senate, after rejecting his appointment as chief justice in 1835, confirmed it in 1836. His early decisions were strongly in favour of state sovereignty, but his most famous decision was in the **Dred Scott** case, when he ruled that the Missouri compromise over the colour question was unconstitutional and that no negro could claim state citizenship for legal purposes. This precipitated the Civil War. Although an early opponent of slavery, he wished to put an end to anti-slavery agitation.

TANEYEV, Sergei Ivanovich (1856–1915) Russian composer and pianist, born in Vladimir. He studied at Moscow Conservatory and became professor there. A pupil of **Tchaikovsky**, he wrote music of all kinds, including two cantatas, *John of Damascus*, *After the Reading of a Psalm*, and six symphonies. Well known as a teacher, his pupils included **Scriabin** and **Rachmaninov**.

TANFUCIO, Neri See **FUCINI, Renato**

TANGE, Kenzo (1913–) Japanese architect, born in Toyko. Trained in Tokyo, his early buildings such as the Hiroshima Peace Centre (1949–55) owe a debt to tradition and **Le Corbusier**. His later works, such as the Shizoka Press and Broadcasting Centre (1966–67), provide incompleteness, flexibility and ability for change. He also designed the dramatic National Gymnasium for the 1964 Olympic Games, and the theme pavilion for the 1970 Osaka Exposition. Professor of architecture at Tokyo University (1946–74), he has published several highly influential works, including *A Plan for Tokyo* (1960). *Toward a Structural Reorganization* (1960) expresses his later structuralist or metabolist approach.

TANGUY, Yves (1900–55) French-born American artist, born in Paris. He was mainly self-taught, and began to paint in 1922, joining the Surrealists in 1926. In 1930 he travelled to Africa, and went to the USA in 1939, becoming an American citizen in 1948. All his pictures are at the same time Surrealist and non-figurative, being peopled with numerous small objects or organisms, whose meaning and identity, as in the landscape of another planet, are unknown.

T'ANG YIN, (T'ang Liu-jiu) (1470–1523) Chinese painter and poet, born in the Su-chou region, and counted among the Four Great Masters of the **Ming** dynasty. Of modest means, but considered a young genius, he passed the exams for the local government with excellence and found many benefactors, among them various masters of the Wu school of painting. At 28 he went to Peking, passing the State's Exam which would have opened the gates to a great career in government. But a scandal involving cheating forced him to return home. Rejected by his wife and friends he turned to drinking. In order to survive, he started painting in a popular and decorative style for the burghers of Souchou: portraits, pretty women, erotica. Although his work tends to be uneven in terms of quality, at his best he presents a refinement of expression which is rare amongst the professionals and a technical know-how seldom achieved by the amateurs.

TANNAHILL, Robert (1774–1810) Scottish poet and songwriter, born in Paisley, the son of a handloom weaver. He composed many of his best songs to the music of his shuttle. He helped to found a Burns Club in 1803 for which he composed songs set on traditional airs. His *Poems and Songs* (1807) proved popular, the best-known being 'Gloomy Winter's noo awa', 'Jessie the Flower o' Dunblane', 'The Braes o' Gleniffer', 'Loudon's Bonnie Woods and Braes' and 'The Wood o' Craigielea'. But after a publisher declined a revised edition he drowned himself in a canal near Paisley.

TANSLEY, Sir Arthur George (1871–1955) English botanist, born in London. Sherardian professor at

Oxford (1927–37), he founded the precursor (1904) of the Ecological Society (1914), and was founder-editor of the *New Phytologist* (1902). A pioneer British ecologist, he published *Practical Plant Ecology* (1923) and *The British Isles and their Vegetation* (1939), and contributed to anatomical and morphological botany and to psychology.

TANTIA TOPEE, properly **Ramchandra Pandurangez** (d.1859) Indian Brahman soldier and rebel from Gwalior. He was **Nana Sahib**'s lieutenant in the Indian Mutiny (1857–58). He took part in the massacre of the British at Cawnpore (July 1857). With the Rani of Jhansi he occupied Gwalior and then held the field after his chief had fled. He was captured in April 1859, and executed.

TAPIÈS, Antoni (1923–) Spanish painter, born in Barcelona where he studied law from 1943 to 1946. Taking up painting, he was a founder member of the *Dau al Set* ('Die with the Seven') group of avant-garde artists and writers. Inspired by Surrealism, he makes collages from everyday rubbish—rags, bits of string, torn canvas—splashed with paint. His first one-man show in America, at the Martha Jackson Gallery in 1953, was followed by numerous exhibitions and international prizes, eg the Venice Biennale, 1958. In 1957 he was a founder of the El Paso group, which championed informalism.

TARBELL, Ida Minerva (1857–1944) American reform journalist, born in Erie County, Pennsylvania. Educated at Allegheny college, she was associate editor of *The Chautauquan* (1883–91). She then studied in Paris at the Sorbonne (1891–94) and joined the *McClure's Magazine* on the editorial staff (1894–1906). Her explosive denunciation of **John D Rockefeller**'s fortune-building methods, *History of the Standard Oil Company* (published in book form in 1904), established the place of women in the new 'muckraking' journalism. Her previous books had been conventional lives of **Napoleon**, Madame Roland and **Lincoln**. She joined **Lincoln Steffens** and other *McClure's* writers in running the *American* magazine (1906–15), campaigning against corruption and big business interests. Her feminist writing included *The Business of Being a Woman* (1912) and *The Ways of Women* (1915). Her history, *The Nationalizing of Business* (1936), was a standard work on American post-Civil War economic growth for 20 years. Her last book was an autobiography, *All in the Day's Work* (1939).

TARKINGTON, (Newton) Booth (1869–1946) American author, born in Indianapolis. Many of his novels have an Indiana setting, but he is best known as the author of *Monsieur Beaucaire* (1900) and his 'Penrod' books—*Penrod* (1914) and *Seventeen* (1916). His other works include a trilogy, *Growth* (1927), including *The Magnificent Ambersons* (1918), which won the Pulitzer prize, *Alice Adams* (1921, Pulitzer prize), which was made into a successful film by **Orson Welles**, and a book of reminiscences, *The World does Move* (1928).

TARKOVSKY, Andrei (1932–86) Soviet filmmaker, born in Moscow. A student of Oriental languages, he worked as a geological prospector in Siberia before studying at the State Film School and directing the short film *Segodnya Otpuska Nye Budyet* (There Will Be No Leave Today, 1959). His modest body of work gained him critical recognition as one of the cinema's true poets with a distinctive, slow-moving style that incorporated elliptical imagery and lengthy, enigmatic and often impenetrable subject material. He examined youth in *Ivanovo Detstvo* (Ivan's Childhood, 1962) and *Zerkalo* (Mirror, 1974) whilst offering bleak visions of the future in *Solaris* (1972) and *Stalker* (1979). Latterly a Soviet exile in Paris, his final film *Offret* (The Sacrifice, 1986) featured a man willing to relinquish his own life and possessions to prevent a forthcoming apocalypse, and was characteristic of his concern for the future and his advocacy of peace.

TARLETON, Sir Banastre (1754–1833) English soldier, born in Liverpool. Educated at Oxford, he served under **Clinton** and **Cornwallis** in the American War of Independence (1775–83). He defeated Buford at Waxham Creek (1780) and **Gates** at Camden, but was beaten by Morgan at Cowpens. He held Gloucester till it capitulated (1782), and then returned to England. He was MP for Liverpool (1790–1806 and 1807–12).

TARLETON, Richard (d.1588) English comedian. He was introduced to Queen **Elizabeth** through the **Earl of Leicester** and became one of the Queen's Players (1583). *Tarleton's Jests* (?1592–?1611), in three parts have been ascribed to him. He died in poverty.

TARQUINIUS an Etruscan family, named after the city of Tarquinii, to which two of the kings of Rome belonged.

TARQUINIUS, Lucius Tarquinius Priscus according to tradition the fifth king of Rome. Of Etruscan origin he is said to have reigned 616–578 BC, to have modified the constitution, and to have begun the Servian agger and the Circus Maximus.

TARQUINIUS, Lucius Tarquinius Superbus traditionally the seventh and last king of Rome (534–510 BC). According to Roman tradition, his cruelty and the rape of **Lucretia** by his son Sextus provoked an uprising of the Roman people under **Lucius Junius Brutus**, his expulsion from Rome, and the establishment of the Republic. He is then said to have tried to re-establish himself in Rome with the help of Lars Porsena of Clusium, but died in exile.

TARSKI, Alfred (1902–83) Polish-born American logician and mathematician, born in Warsaw. Educated in Warsaw, he taught there until 1939, when he moved to the USA and taught at the University of California at Berkeley (1942–68). He made contributions to many branches of pure mathematics and mathematical logic, but is most remembered for his definition of 'truth' in formal logical languages, as presented in his monograph *Der Wahrheitsbefriff in den Formalisierten Sprachen* (1933, The Concept of Truth in Formalized Languages).

TARTINI, Giuseppe (1692–1770) Italian composer, born in Pirano in Istria. Originally intended for the church and the law, he abandoned these for music and fencing. Having secretly married the niece of the Archbishop of Padua, he fled to Assisi, but, after living in Venice, Ancona and Prague, returned before 1728 to Padua. Described as 'one of the greatest violinists of all time, an eminent composer, and a scientific writer on musical physics', his best-known work is the *Trillo del Diavolo*.

TASMAN, Abel Janszoon (1603–c.1659) Dutch navigator, born in Lutjegast near Groningen. In 1642 he discovered Tasmania—named Van Diemen's Land—and New Zealand, and in 1643 Tonga and Fiji, having been dispatched in quest of the 'Great South Land' by Antony Van Diemen (1593—1645), governor-general of Batavia. He made a second voyage (1644) to the Gulf of Carpentaria and the north-west coast of Australia.

TASSIE, James (1735–99) Scottish modeller and engraver, born in Pollokshaws, Glasgow. Apprenticed to a stone mason, he studied art at Foulis Academy in Glasgow. In 1763 he went to Dublin, where he developed a special 'white enamel composition' for making portrait medallions. In 1766 he moved to London where he used his paste to make reproductions of the most famous gems. He also executed many cameo portraits of his contemporaries, and the plaster reproductions of the Portland Vase.

TASSO, Bernardo (1493–1569) Italian poet, born in Venice of an illustrious family of Bergamo. After suffering poverty and exile owing to the outlawry by **Charles V** (1547) of his patron, the Duke of Salerno, he took service with the Duke of Mantua. His romantic epic *Amadigi di Gaula* (1560), an epic on the Amadis of Gaul, is a melodious imitation of **Ariosto**'s manner, but exaggerated in sentiment. He began another epic, *Iloridante*, which was finished by his son **Torquato Tasso** (1587), and wrote numerous lyrics (1560).

TASSO, Torquato (1544–95) Italian poet, son of **Barnardo Tasso**, born in Sorrento. He shared his exiled father's wandering life, but in 1560 he was sent to study law and philosophy at Padua, where he published his first work, a romantic poem, *Rinaldo*. In the service of Cardinal Luigi d'Este he was introduced to the court of the Duke of Ferrara; and there, encouraged by the sisters of the duke, he began his great epic poem and masterpiece, *Gerusalemme Liberata*, an idealized story of the First Crusade. In 1571 he accompanied Cardinal d'Este to France, and on his return to Italy in 1572 became attached to the service of Duke Alfonso at Ferrara. For the court theatre he wrote his beautiful pastoral play, *Aminta* (1581). Tasso completed his great epic in 1575, and submitted it before publication to the critics of the day. Their fault-finding and Tasso's replies are recorded in his correspondence and in his *Apologia*. In 1576 he showed the first signs of mental disorder; he became suspicious and melancholy, and obsessed with fears of assassination. He was confined at Ferrara, but escaped, and eventually made his way to Naples, Rome and Turin, where he was welcomed by the Duke of Savoy. Returning to Ferrara in 1579 he met with a cold reception, and, wounded by some real or imagined slight, broke into furious invectives against the duke, his courtiers, and all the world. He was confined at Ferrara by order of the duke as insane, not, as is often alleged, for his love for the Princess Leonora, a story on which **Byron** based his *Lament of Tasso*. In his seven years' confinement he wrote many noble verses and philosophical dialogues and a vigorous defence of his *Gerusalemme Liberata*, published without his leave and with many errors. The cruel contrast between his fate and the growing fame of his great poem had excited popular interest, and in July 1586 he was freed on the intercession of Prince Vincenzo Gonzaga. He followed his new patron to Mantua, where he wrote his only tragedy, *Torrismondo*. Broken in health and spirits, he began again his restless wanderings, spending, however, most of these later years in Rome and Naples, helped and protected by many kind friends and patrons. He busied himself in rewriting his great epic, according to the modifications proposed by his numerous critics. The result, a poor semblance of his masterpiece, was published as *Gerusalemme Conquistata* (1593). Summoned to Rome by Pope **Clement VIII** to be crowned on the Capitol as poet laureate, he took ill on arrival and died in the monastery of Sant' Onofrio on the Janiculum.

TATA, Jamsetji Nasarwanji (1839–1904) Indian industrialist, born in Gujerat. He built cotton mills at Nagpur (1877) and at Cooria near Bombay. He did much to promote scientific education in Indian schools. His son, Sir Dorabji (1859–1932), developed the Indian iron-ore industry, applied hydro-electricity to the Cooria cotton mills and founded a commercial airline.

TATE, (John Orley) Allen (1899–1979) American poet, born in Winchester. He made an abortive start in a business career before entering academe, and became a professor first at Princeton and later at Minnesota University. He was editor of the influential *Sewanee Review*. A metaphysical poet in thrall of **T S Eliot**, his writing career was diverse and encompassed many books including biographies of **Thomas Stonewall Jackson** (1928) and Jefferson Davies (1929). Collections of verse include *Mr Pope and Other Poems* (1928), *Poems* 1928–31 (1932), *The Mediterranean and Other Poems* (1936) and *Winter Sea* (1945). His marriage to the novelist Caroline Gordon ended in divorce.

TATE, Sir Henry (1819–99) English sugar magnate, art patron and philanthopist, born in Chorley, Lancashire. He patented a method for cutting sugar cubes in 1872 and attained great wealth as a Liverpool sugar refiner. He founded the University Library at Liverpool and gave the nation the Tate Gallery, Millbank, London, which was opened in 1897, and contained his own valuable private collection.

TATE, Nathum (1652–1715) Irish poet and dramatist, born in Dublin. He studied at Trinity College there and saw his first play staged in London in 1678. With Dr **Johnson**'s approval, he wrote a number of 'improved' versions of **Shakespeare**'s tragedies, substituting happy endings to suit the popular taste. With **Dryden**'s help he wrote a second part to the poet's *Absalom and Achitophel* (1682) and with **Nicholas Brady** compiled a metrical version of the psalms. 'While Shepherds watched their Flocks by Night' is attributed to him, and he wrote the libretto of **Purcell**'s *Dido and Aeneas* (1689). He succeeded **Shadwell** as poet laureate in 1692. His best-known work is *Panacea or a Poem on Tea* (1700).

TATI, Jacques, pseud of **Jacques Tatischeff** (1908–82) French actor, author and film producer, born in Le Pecq, Paris. A skilled rugby player in his youth, he began his career with a wordless cabaret act in which he mimicked various sporting activities, an entertainment he continued in short films like *Oscar, champion de tennis* (1934). His first feature film as a director and performer was *Jour de Fête* (1949). With *Monsieur Hulot's Holiday* (1951) and *Mon Oncle* (1958) he perfected his best-known character of the pipe-smoking, lugubrious Hulot, forever beset by physical mishaps and confrontations with modern technology. Although a graceful pantomimist, inventive visual humourist and exacting perfectionist, his later films (*Playtime* in 1968, *Traffic* in 1981) were less successful.

TATIAN (2nd century) Syrian Christian thinker. He became a pupil of the martyr **Justin** at Rome and was converted to Christianity by him. After Justin's death in c.165 he was estranged from the Catholic Church and returned to Syria c.172 where he established, or was at least closely associated with, an ascetic religious community of Encratites, which fostered a heretical combination of Christianity and Stoicism. Only two of his many writings survive: the *Oratio ad Graecos* ('Speech to the Greeks') is a denunciation of the intellectualism of Greek culture and the corruption of its moral and religious values, which he compares unfavourably with the 'barbarian philosophy' of Christianity; the *Diatessaron* (literally 'Out of Four') is a patchwork version of the four gospels arranged as a continuous narrative, which in its Syriac version was used as a text in the Syrian Church for centuries.

TATIUS, Achilles (fl.2nd century) Greek writer. A rhetorician at Alexandria, he wrote the romance *Leucippe and Cleitophon*.

TATLIN, Vladimir (1885–1953) Russian painter and designer, born in Moscow. He studied in Moscow in 1910, and exhibited with such avant-garde artists as **Goncharova** and **Larionov**, before visiting Berlin and Paris (where he met **Picasso** in 1913). He founded

Russian Constructivism, a movement at first approved by the Soviet authorities, and he was commissioned to design the gigantic *Monument to the Third International* (model exhibited 1920, monument itself never built).

TATTERSALL, Richard (1724–95) English auctioneer, born in Hurstwood, Lancashire. In London he entered the Duke of Kingston's service, became an auctioneer, and in 1776 set up auction rooms at Hyde Park Corner, which became a celebrated mart of thoroughbred horses and a great racing centre. They were transferred to Knightsbridge in 1867.

TATUM, Art (Arthur) (1909–56) American jazz pianist, born in Toledo, Ohio. Largely self-taught, he became the music's first supreme keyboard virtuoso. Although near-blind from birth, he was a professional musician from his teens. Moving to New York in 1932, he made solo recordings and club appearances which have hardly been equalled for technique, drive and improvisational powers. The most influential of the swing-style pianists, Tatum continued to work in the idiom until his death, most effective as a soloist or leading a piano-bass-guitar trio.

TATUM, Edward Lawrie (1909–75) American biochemist, born in Boulder, Colorado, joint winner of the 1958 Nobel prize for physiology or medicine. Educated at Wisconsin, he taught at Stanford (1937–45, 1948–57), Yale (1945–48) and Rockefeller University (1957–75). With **George Beadle** he demonstrated the role of genes in biochemical processes, and with **Joshua Lederberg** he showed that bacteria reproduce by a sexual process, thus founding the science of bacterial genetics. All three shared the 1958 Nobel prize.

TAUBE, Henry (1915–) Canadian-born American inorganic chemist, born in Saskatchewan. He studied at Saskatchewan University, and gained his PhD at Berkeley. He became a naturalized American in 1942 and worked at Cornell University; he was appointed professor of chemistry at Chicago in 1952 and ten years later was appointed to Stanford. He devised new methods for the study of electron transfer reactions in inorganic chemistry. He was awarded the 1983 Nobel prize for chemistry.

TAUBER, Richard (1892–1948) Austrian-born British tenor, born in Linz. He established himself as one of Germany's leading tenors, particularly in Mozartian opera, until 1925 when he increasingly appeared in light opera, notably Lehár's *Land of Smiles*, which he brought to London in 1931. This won him great popularity, repeated by his part in his own *Old Chelsea* (1943), and appearances in several films. He appeared at Covent Garden in 1938, and later became a British citizen.

TAUCHNITZ, Karl Christoph Traugott (1761–1836) German publisher, born near Grimma. In 1796 he set up a small printing business in Leipzig, to which he added publishing and typefounding. In 1809 he began to issue his cheap editions of the classics. He introduced stereotyping into Germany (1816). His nephew, Christian Bernhard, Baron von Tauchnitz (1816–95), also founded in 1837 a printing and publishing house in Leipzig famous for its collection of 'British and American Authors', begun in 1841.

TAUFA'AHAU, (Tupouto Tungi) Tupou IV (1918–) King of Tonga. The eldest son of Queen **Salote Tupou III**, he was educated at Newington College and Sydney University. He served successively as minister for education (1943) and health (1944–49), before becoming prime minister under his mother in 1949. On succeeding to the throne on his mother's death in 1965 he assumed the designation King Taufa'ahau Tupou IV, sharing power with his brother, Prince Fatafehi Tu'ipelehake, who became prime minister. King Taufa'ahau, while negotiating the country's independence within the Commonwealth in 1970, remains the strongest supporter of the Western powers in the Pacific region.

TAULER, Johann (c.1300–1361) German mystic and preacher, born in Strasbourg. He became a Dominican c.1318. Driven from Strasbourg by a feud between the city and his order, he settled at 24 in Basel and associated with the devout 'Friends of God', having before then been a disciple of Meister **Eckhart**. His fame as a preacher spread far and wide, and he became the centre of the quickened religious life in the middle Rhine valley.

TAUNTON, Henry Labouchere, Baron (1798–1869) English politician, born in Hylands, Essex. Educated at Winchester, Christ Church College, Oxford, and Lincoln's Inn, he was never called to the bar. MP for Michael Borough (1826) and Taunton (1830–59) he was a member of Whig governments from 1832 to 1859. He presided over the Schools Inquiry Commission (1864) to deal with schools not included in the *Newcastle Report* (1861) on elementary education or the *Clarendon Report* (1864) on the great public schools. The enormous Report showed that 100 towns of 5000 or more population had no endowed grammar schools, and called for a reform of educational charities which was effected under the Endowed Schools Act of 1869. The Report's wider proposals for a national system of secondary schools, graded according to whether parents would keep children at school until the age of 14, 16 or 18, were not adopted.

TAUSSIG, Helen Brooke (1898–1986) American paediatrician, born in Cambridge, Massachusetts. She received her MD from Johns Hopkins University in 1927 and later became the first woman to become a full professor there. Her work on the pathophysiology of congenital heart disease was done partly in association with the cardiac surgeon **Alfred Blalock**, and between them they pioneered the 'blue baby' operations which heralded the beginnings of modern cardiac surgery. Taussig was actively involved in the diagnosis and after-care of the patients on whom Blalock operated.

TAVERNER, John (c.1490–1545) English musician, born in Boston. He was organist at Boston and Christ Church, Oxford, and composed notable motets and masses. Accused of heresy, he was imprisoned by **Wolsey**, but released, 'being but a musitian'.

TAVERNER, Richard (c.1505–1575) English author. He was patronized by **Wolsey** and **Thomas Cromwell**, for whom he compiled Taverner's Bible (1539), a revision of *Matthew's Bible* by **John Rogers** (1537). On Cromwell's fall he was sent to the Tower but soon released, and found favour with **Henry VIII**.

TAVERNIER, Jean Baptiste, Baron d'Aubonne (1605–89) French traveller, born in Paris, the son of a Protestant engraver from Antwerp. His first journey to the East (1631–33) was by way of Constantinople to Persia, and from there by Aleppo and Malta to Italy. The second journey (1638–43) was across Syria to Ispaham, Agra and Golconda; the third (1643–49), through Ispahan, much of Hindustan, Batavia and Bantam, then to Holland by the Cape; and the fourth (1651–55), fifth (1657–62) and sixth (1663–68) to many districts of Persia and India. Tavernier travelled as a dealer in precious stones. **Louis XIV** gave him 'letters of nobility' in 1669, and the following year he bought the barony of Aubonne near Geneva. In 1684 he started for Berlin to advise **Frederick William**, the Elector of Brandenburg, on his projects for eastern trade. In 1689 he went to Russia, and died in Moscow. His famous *Six Voyages* was published in 1676; the complementary *Recueil* in 1679.

TAWNEY, Richard Henry (1880–1962) English economic historian, born in Calcutta. He was educated at Rugby School and Balliol College, Oxford, of which he was elected fellow in 1918. After a spell of social work at Toynbee Hall in the East End of London, he became tutor, executive (1905–47) and president (1928–44) of the Workers' Educational Association. During World War I, a sergeant in the Manchester Regiment, he was severely wounded during the battle of the Somme (1916). A socialist and a Christian, he wrote a number of studies in English economic history, particularly of the Tudor and Stuart periods, of which the best known are *The Acquisitive Society* (1926), *Religion and the Rise of Capitalism* (1926), *Equality* (1931), and *Business and Politics under James I* (1958). He was professor of economic history at London (1931-49). In 1909 he married a sister, Annette Jeanie (d.1958), of Lord **Beveridge**.

TAYFIELD, Hugh Joseph (1929–) South African Test cricketer, born in Durban. One of the most famous of South African spin bowlers, his foot-tapping action at the crease earned him the nickname of 'Toey'. In 37 Tests he amassed 170 Test wickets, taking 13 wickets in a match against both Australia and England; against England at Johannesburg in 1956–57 he had 9–113 in the English second innings.

TAYLOR, Alan John Percivale (1906–) English historian, born in Lancashire. He attended Bootham School, York, and studied at Oriel College, Oxford. He was lecturer in modern history at Manchester University, and then fellow of Magdalen College, Oxford (1938–76) and lecturer in international history at Oxford (1953–63). A brilliant diplomatic historian, he established his authority in modern European history by studies of the **Habsburg** monarchy, and of **Bismarck**, and in the first lectures ever given in British TV (on the Russian Revolution). His major work was *The Struggle for Mastery in Europe* 1848–1918 (1954). He aroused passionate hostility with his revisionist *The Origins of the Second World War* (1961), arguing for accident and miscalculation rather than grand design as the cause of the conflict that broke out, whatever **Hitler** had planned. British history also fascinated him, and his *English History* 1914–1945 (1965) is a masterpiece of interpretation, weaving expertly together all facets of history. His own favourite was his *The Trouble Makers* (1957), examining critics of British foreign policy 1792–1939. He inspired many brilliant students, was a devoted friend and biographer of **Beaverbrook**, wrote many stimulating essays and an autobiography, *A Personal History* (1983).

TAYLOR, Alfred Edward (1869–1945) English scholar and philosopher, born in Oundle, Northamptonshire. He became professor of logic at McGill University (1903–08) and of moral philosophy at St Andrews (1908–24) and Edinburgh (1924–41). An authority on **Plato**, he wrote *Plato, The Man and his Work* (1926), *A Commentary on Plato's Timaeus* (1928), and translated his *Laws* (1934). Other notable works are *The Problem of Conduct* (1901), *Elements of Metaphysics* (1903), the Gifford lectures which he gave at St Andrews on *The Faith of a Moralist*, and studies of St **Thomas Aquinas** (1924) and **Socrates** (1932).

TAYLOR, (James) Bayard (1825–78) American travel-writer and poet, born in Chester county, Pennsylvania. Apprenticed to a printer, he wrote a volume of poems (1844), visited Europe, published *Views Afoot* (1846), and obtained a post on the *New York Tribune*. As its correspondent he made extensive travels in California and Mexico, up the Nile, in Asia Minor and Syria, across Asia to India, China and Japan, which he recorded in a great number of travel books which he later published. In 1862–63 he was secretary of legation at St Petersburg and in 1878 became ambassador at Berlin, where he died.

TAYLOR, Brook (1685–1731) English mathematician, born in Edmonton. He studied at St John's College, Cambridge, and in 1715 published his *Methodus incrementorum*, containing his theorem on power series expansions.

TAYLOR, Cecil Percival (1933–) American avant garde pianist and composer, born in New York to a musical family. Given piano lessons from the age of five he went on to study at the New York College of Music and the New England Conservatory, Boston. His interest in jazz and black culture was awakened in his early twenties, and in 1956 he made his first important quartet recordings which displayed startling divergencies from the established approach to jazz language and harmony. Taylor's refusal to compromise his artistic direction led to a difficult decade in which he was given little paid work. During the 1970s the avant garde gained recogniton (particularly in Europe) and Taylor began to make records and tour, often as a soloist, working in a controversial style of powerful extended free improvisation.

TAYLOR, Elizabeth, born **Elizabeth Coles** (1912–75) English novelist, born in Reading, Berkshire. The daughter of an insurance inspector, she was educated locally at the Abbey School and worked as a governess and librarian. She married John Taylor, the director of a sweet factory, when she was 24, and wrote her first novel, *At Mrs Lippincote's* (1945), while her husband was in the Royal Air Force. This was followed by such novels as *Palladian* (1946), *A Wreath of Roses* (1949), *A Game of Hide-and-Seek* (1951), *Angel* (1957), *The Wedding Group* (1968), *Mrs Palfrey at the Claremont* (1971) and *Blaming*, published posthumously in 1976. Her hallmark is quiet, shrewd observation of middle-class life in the south-east of England, reminiscent of **Jane Austen** with whom she is quite often compared. Like her, her life was more domestic than literary. Her stories, collected in four volumes (1954–72), are no less admired than her novels.

TAYLOR, Elizabeth (1932–) American film actress, born in London of American parents. In 1939 she moved with her family to Los Angeles, where her beauty took the eye of the Hollywood film world, and she made her screen début in 1942 at the age of ten, in *There's One Born Every Minute*. As a child star she made a number of films including two 'Lassie' stories (1943 and 1946), *National Velvet* (1944) and *Little Women* (1949). She was first seen as an adult in *The Father of the Bride* (1950) at the time of her first marriage, to Nick Hilton of the hotelier family. Her career continued through the 1950s with films including *Raintree County* (1957), *Cat on a Hot Tin Roof* (1958) and *Suddenly Last Summer* (1959), for all of which she received Oscar nominations. She married first Nick Hilton, 1950, then the actor Michael Wilding in 1952, then the producer **Mike Todd** in 1957, who was killed in an air-crash the following year. In 1959 she married Eddie Fisher, divorcing him in 1964. In 1960 she won her first Academy Award for *Butterfield* 8, and the making of the spectacular *Cleopatra* (1962) provided the background to her well-publicized romance with her co-star **Richard Burton** whom she married for the first time in 1964. She made several films with Burton, including *Who's Afraid of Virginia Woolf?* in 1966, for which she won her second Academy award. Divorced from and remarried to Richard Burton, she was divorced from him again in 1976, and married the US Senator John Warner in 1978, from whom she separated in 1981. Her other films include *Reflections in* *a Golden Eye* (1967), *A Little Night Music* (1976) and *The Mirror Crack'd* (1981). She made her stage debut in New York in 1981 with *The Little Foxes*. After treatment for alcohol addiction, she resumed her acting career, mostly in television with *Malice in Wonderland* (1985), *Poker Alice* (1986), and other films.

TAYLOR, Ernest Archibald (1874–1951) Scottish furniture and stained glass designer and painter, born in Greenock, the 15th of 17 children. He trained as a draughtsman in a shipyard before studying at Glasgow School of Art in the 1890s. Influenced by **Mackintosh** he joined the firm of Wylie and Lochhead, the Glasgow cabinet makers, in 1900. He designed a drawing-room for their Pavilion at the 1901 Glasgow International Exhibition. He also exhibited at Turin in 1902 alongside his fellow Glasgow School artists where he won a diploma and medal. He married the artist **Jessie Marion King** and moved to Manchester in 1908 after completing two important architectural commissions. He was very involved in stained glass design. From 1911 to 1914 he taught, along with his wife, at the Shealing Atelier of Fine Art in Paris. He retired to Kirkcudbright after the outbreak of World War I and spent the remainder of his life there.

TAYLOR, Frederick Winslow (1856–1915) American engineer, born in Germantown, Pennsylvania. While employed in the Midvale steelworks in Philadelphia (1878-90) he studied at night and obtained a degree in engineering from the Stevens Institute of Technology in 1883. He became chief engineer in 1889, having invented several devices and modified processes to increase efficiency; he then turned his attention to the part played by the workers themselves, and introduced time-and-motion study as an aid to efficient management. From 1893 he worked as an independent consultant in what he called 'scientific management', and applied its principles successfully to both small and large-scale businesses. He published in 1911 *The Principles of Scientific Management* and *Shop Management*.

TAYLOR, Sir Geoffrey Ingram (1886–1975) English physicist and applied mathematician, born in London. He was educated at Cambridge, where he stayed for the rest of his career; he was appointed reader in dynamic meteorology in 1911, and became Yarrow research professor in physics in 1923–52. He was an original researcher in a wide range of studies, particularly on turbulent motion in fluids which he applied to meteorology and oceanography, in aerodynamics and even to Jupiter's Great Red Spot. He proposed in 1934 the important idea of 'dislocation' in crystals, a form of atomic misarrangement which enables the crystal to deform at a stress less than that of a perfect crystal.

TAYLOR, Sir Henry (1800–86) English poet, born in Bishop-Middleton in Durham, the son of a gentleman farmer. He was an administrator in the colonial office (1824–72). He wrote four tragedies, *Isaac Comnenus* (1827), a remarkable study in character, *Philip van Artefelde* (1834), *Edwin the Fair* (1842) and *St Clement's Eve* (1862). A romantic comedy, *The Virgin Widow* (1850), was afterwards entitled *A Sicilian Summer*. In 1845 he published a volume of lyrical poetry, and in 1847 *The Eve of the Conquest*. His prose included *The Statesman* (1836) and an *Autobiography* (1885).

TAYLOR, Isaac (1829–1901) English philologist, born in Stanford Rivers. He studied at Trinity College, Cambridge, and became rector of Settrington (1875) and canon of York (1885). His *Words and Places* (1864) made him known, while *The Alphabet* (1883) brought him a wide reputation. Other publications include *Etruscan Researches* (1874), *The Origin of the Aryans* (1890) and *Names and their Histories* (1896).

TAYLOR, Jeremy (1613–67) English theologian, the third son of a Cambridge barber. He entered Caius College, Cambridge and became a fellow of All Souls College, Oxford (1636), chaplain to Archbishop **Laud**, and in 1638 rector of Uppingham. *The Sacred Order and Offices of Episcopacy* (1642) gained him his DD. During the Civil War he is said to have accompanied the royal army as chaplain, and was taken prisoner at Cardigan Castle (1645). After the downfall of the cause he sought shelter in Wales, kept a school, and found a patron in the Earl of Carbery, then living at Golden Grove, Llandilo, immortalized in the title of Taylor's still popular manual of devotion (1655). During the last 13 years (1647–60) of Taylor's enforced seclusion appeared all his great works, some of them the most enduring monuments of sacred eloquence in the English language. The first was *The Liberty of Prophesying* (1646), a noble and comprehensive plea for toleration and freedom of opinion. *The Life of Christ, or the Great Exemplar* (1649) is an arrangement of the facts in historical order, interspersed with prayers and discourses. *The Rule and Exercises of Holy Living* (1650) and *The Rule and Exercises of Holy Dying* (1651) together form the choicest classic of English devotion. The *52 Sermons* (1651–53), with the discourses in the *Life of Christ* and many passages in the *Holy Living and Dying*, contain the richest examples of their author's characteristically gorgeous eloquence. The more formal treatises were *An Apology for Authorised and Set Forms of Liturgy* (1646); *Clerus Dominio* (on the ministerial office, 1651); *The Real Presence in the Blessed Sacrament* (1654); *Unum Necessarium* (on repentance, 1655, which brought on him the charge of Pelagianism); *The Worthy Communicant* (1660); *The Rite of Confirmation* (1663); *The Dissuasive from Popery* (1664); and the famous *Ductor Dubitantium* (1660), the most learned and subtle of all his works, intended as a handbook of Christian casuistry and ethics. During the Civil War Taylor was thrice imprisoned, once for the preface to the *Golden Grove*; the last time in the Tower for an 'idolatrous' print of **Christ** in the attitude of prayer in his *Collection of Offices* (1658). In 1658 he got a lectureship at Lisburn, at the Restoration the bishopric of Down and Connor, with next year the administration of Dromore; he also became vice-chancellor of Dublin University and a member of the Irish privy council. In his first visitation (in spite of his *Liberty of Prophesying*) he ejected 36 Presbyterian ministers, but neither severity nor gentleness could prevail to force a form of religion upon an unwilling people. His works were published in 1820–22 (rev 1847–54).

TAYLOR, John (1580–1653) English poet and pamphleteer, known as the 'Water-poet', born in Gloucester. He became a Thames waterman, but, pressed into the navy, served at the siege of Cadiz (1625). At the outbreak of the Civil War (1642) he kept a public house in Oxford, but gave it up for another in London, and there wrote his own doggerel poems, full of natural humour and low wit. The chief event of his life was his journey on foot from London to Edinburgh (1618), described in his *Penniless Pilgrimage* (1618); similar books were his *Travels in Germanie* (1617) and *The Praise of Hempseed*, a story of a voyage in a brown paper boat from London to Queensborough (1618).

TAYLOR, John Edward (1791–1844) English journalist, born in Ilminster, the son of a Unitarian minister. He was the founder in 1821 of the liberal newspaper, the *Manchester Guardian*.

TAYLOR, John Henry (1871–1963) English golfer, born in Northam, Devon, the first Englishman to win the British Open championship (1894, 1895, 1900, 1909 and 1913). He also won the French Open twice, and the German Open once. He was a founder and first president of the PGA (British Professional Golfer's Association).

TAYLOR, Nathaniel William (1786–1858) American theologian, born in New Milford, Connecticut. He was ordained as a Congregational minister in 1812, and in 1822 he became professor of theology at Yale. His 'New Haven theology', long assailed as heretical, was a softening of the traditional Calvinism of New England, maintained the doctrine of natural ability, and denied total depravity; sin is a voluntary action of the sinner, but there is, derived from Adam, a bias to sin, which is not itself sinful.

TAYLOR, Sir Patrick Gordon (1896–1966) Australian pioneer aviator, born in Mosman, New South Wales. He served with the Royal Flying Corps during World War I, and received the MC. He worked on developing aviation instruments after the war, and was associated with Sir **Charles Kingsford Smith** and **Charles Ulm** in many of their pioneering flights, including a single-engined flight from Australia to the USA in 1934. In 1935, over the Tasman Sea with Kingsford Smith in his *Southern Cross*, one engine cut out and oil pressure was lost on another. Taylor spent the rest of the flight clambering across the wings every half-hour, transferring oil from the dead engine into the ailing one; for this he was awarded the George Cross. He created a number of aviation 'firsts' and worked with RAF Transport Command during World War II.

TAYLOR, Paul (1930–) American modern-dance choreographer, born in Pittsburgh, Pennsylvania. At college he studied painting and trained as a swimmer. His first dancing steps were taken with **Merce Cunningham** (1953/54) and **Martha Graham** (1958–62). He began choreographing as early as 1956 and from then has developed a highly original, ebullient, lyrical style. Often using classical music to contemporary effect, he creates movement which, whether plumbing depths or reaching to the heavens, is one of earthly life. While not an experimentalist, his dances nevertheless have a creativity and wit which put him among the top American choreographers. Work includes *Three Epitaphs* (1956), *Aureole* (1962), *Big Bertha* (1971), *Esplanade* (1975), *Cloven Kingdom* (1976), *Le Sacre du printemps* (1980) and *Arden Court* (1981). His autobiography, *Private Domain*, was published in 1987.

TAYLOR, Peter Hillsman (1917–) American short story writer, novelist, and playwright, born in Trenton, Tennessee and educated in Nashville, Memphis, and Kenyon College, Ohio. Concerned with the smaller crises and collisions of urban middle-class life in the southern states of America, primarily Tennessee, his vision is an alloy of sentiment and irony. He writes about what he knows and the areas he grew up in Memphis, St Louis, and Nashville. Representative stories are 'The Scoutmaster', 'The Old Forest', 'The Death of a Kinsman' and 'A Long Fourth'. *The Collected Stories of Peter Taylor* was published in 1969; *A Summons to Memphis*, his sole novel, in 1987.

TAYLOR, Rowland (d.1555) English Protestant martyr, born in Rothbury. A chaplain to **Cranmer** in 1540, he became rector of Hadleigh (1544), archdeacon of Exeter (1551), and a canon of Rochester. He spoke in favour of Lady **Jane Grey**, and under **Mary I** he was imprisoned as a heretic, then burned near Hadleigh.

TAYLOR, Thomas (1758–1835) English scholar, known as 'the Platonist', born in London. Educated at St Paul's School, he entered Lubbock's bank as a clerk. His 50 works include translations of the Orphic Hymns, parts of **Plotinus**, **Proclus**, **Pausanias**, **Apuleius**, Iamblichus, **Porphyry**, **Plato** (nine of the Dialogues by Floyer Sydenham, 1804), and **Aristotle** (1806-12). *The Spirit of All Religions* (1790) expressed his strange polytheistic creed.

TAYLOR, Tom (1817–80) Scottish dramatist and editor, born in Sunderland. He studied at Glasgow and Trinity College, Cambridge, and was elected a fellow. Professor of English for two years at University College, London, and called to the bar in 1845, he was secretary to the Board of Health (1850–72), and then to the Local Government Act Office. From 1846 he wrote or adapted over 100 pieces for the stage, among them *Still Waters Run Deep* (1855), *Our American Cousin*, (1858), *The Ticket of Leave Man* (1863), and *'Twixt Axe and Crown*. He edited the autobiographies of **Benjamin Haydon** and **Charles Robert Leslie**, completed the latter's *Life and Times of Reynolds*, translated *Ballads and Songs of Brittany* (1865), and in 1874 became editor of *Punch*. He was *The Times* art critic, and appeared as a witness for **Ruskin** in the libel action brought against him by **Whistler** in 1878.

TAYLOR, William (1765–1836) English author, 'of Norwich', son of a Unitarian merchant. He entered his father's counting-house in 1779 and, travelling extensively on the Continent, introduced the works of **Lessing**, and **Goethe**, to English readers, mainly through criticisms and translations, collected in his *Historic Survey of German Poetry* (1828–30).

TAYLOR, William Howson (1876–1935) English potter. He studied at Birmingham School of Art where his father was principal. In 1898 he established the Ruskin Pottery in West Smethwick in an old malthouse. Normally using local clay, he developed a white body containing china clay and calcined flint. Two great influences moulded Taylor's outlook—a deep appreciation of the Sung and Ming periods in Chinese pottery and an intense admiration of **John Ruskin**, who gave permission for his name to be used at the pottery. His particular interest in glazes developed into the production of soufflé ware, lustre ware and, the most notable, high-fired ware which he produced at a loss and had to subsidize. He carefully guarded the secret of his glazes and destroyed all his notes and materials shortly before he died. Production continued until 1935, only months before his death.

TAYLOR, Zachary (1784–1850) 12th president of the USA, born in Orange County, Virginia. He entered the army in 1808. In 1812 he held Fort Harrison on the Wabash against Indians, and in 1832 fought with Black Hawk. In 1836, now colonel, he was ordered to Florida, and in 1837 defeated the Seminoles at Okeechobee Swamp, and won the brevet of brigadier-general. In 1840 he was placed in command of the army in the southwest. When Texas was annexed in 1845 he gathered 4000 regulars at Corpus Christi in March 1846, marched to the Rio Grande, and erected Fort Brown opposite Matamoros. The Mexicans crossed the Rio Grande to drive him out. But the battles of Palo Alto and Resaca de la Palma on 8 and 9 May repulsed them, and Taylor seized Matamoros. In September he captured Monterey. After seven weeks' vain waiting for reinforcements the march was resumed. Victoria was occupied, but the line of communication was too long for the meagre force, while President **Polk**'s Democratic administration, fearing the rising fame of Taylor, who was a Whig, crippled him by witholding reinforcements. Taylor was falling back to Monterey when his regulars were taken from him to form part of a new expedition under General

Winfield Scott. **Santa Anna**, the Mexican general, overtook his 5000 volunteers near the pass of Buenta Vista; but Taylor, on 22 February 1847, repulsed the 21 000 Mexicans with a loss thrice as great as his own. In 1848 the Whigs selected Taylor as their candidate for the presidency. He was elected in November and inaugurated next March. The struggle over the extension of slavery had begun. The Democratic congress opposed the admission of California as a free state, while the president favoured it. To avert the threatened danger to the Union **Henry Clay** introduced his famous compromise. Taylor remained firm and impartial though his son-in-law, **Jefferson Davis**, headed the extreme proslavery faction. Before a decision was reached, President Taylor died.

TAZIEFF, Haroun (1914–) Polish-born French volcanologist and mountaineer, born in Warsaw. He studied in Russia, France and Belgium, first agricultural engineering and then geology. A keen boxer, rugby player and mountaineer, he has investigated many of the world's volcanoes, both active and inactive. From 1958 to 1974 he made 26 expeditions to Nyiragongo, Zaire. As adviser to the **Mitterrand** government in 1982, he became the first French secretary of state for the prevention of natural and technological disasters in 1984.

TCHAIKOVSKY, Piotr Ilyich (1840–93) Russian composer, born in Kamsko-Votinsk, where his father was inspector of government mines. His early musical talents were encouraged, but when the family moved to St Petersburg he entered the school of jurisprudence and started his life as a minor civil servant. In 1862 he enrolled at the recently opened conservatory, but after three years he was engaged by his previous orchestration teacher, Nicholas Rubinstein, to teach harmony at his conservatory in Moscow. His operas and 2nd symphony brought him into the public eye, and in 1875 his piano concerto in B flat minor had its première in Moscow. Unsuited to marriage, he left his bride Antonina Ivanovna Miliukova a month after the wedding (1877) in a state of nervous collapse. After recuperation abroad he resigned from the conservatory and retired to the country to devote himself entirely to composition. He made occasional trips abroad and in 1893 was made an honorary MusD of Cambridge University. Soon after his return to Russia from England, and after the first performance of his 6th ('Pathétique') symphony, he died in St Petersburg. He was said to have died of cholera but it is more plausibly thought to have been suicide through swallowing poison, at the behest of a 'court of honour', following his alleged relationship with a young male aristocrat. Three years earlier his correspondence, dating back to 1876, with Nadezhda von Meck, widow of a wealthy engineer, had come to a stop. Though they never met, her artistic, moral and financial support played a very important part in his career. Though acquainted with **Balakirev**, **Rimsky-Korsakov** and other members of the group of late 19th-century composers known as the 'Five', he was not in sympathy with their avowedly nationalistic aspirations and their use of folk material, and was himself regarded by them as something of a renegade cosmopolitan. The melodiousness, colourful orchestration, and deeply expressive content of his music brought him then and now an enthusiastic following exceeding that of any other Russian composer. His introspective and melancholy nature is reflected in some of his symphonies and orchestral pieces, but not in his ballet music—*Swan Lake*, *The Sleeping Beauty* and *Nutcracker*—which are by common consent masterpieces of their kind. In such cases his weakness in large-scale structural organization was concealed. His works include six symphonies, of which the last three are best known, two piano concertos (a third was left uncompleted), a violin concerto, a number of tone poems including *Romeo and Juliet* and *Italian Capriccio*, songs and piano pieces. Of his eleven operas, *Eugene Onegin* and *The Queen of Spades* have successfully survived.

TCHEREPNIN, Nikolai Nikolaievich (1873–1945) Russian composer, born in St Petersburg. He was trained as a lawyer, but abandoned this profession to study under **Rimsky-Korsakov**, and first appeared as a pianist. In 1901 he became conductor of the Belaiev Concerts and took charge of opera at the Maryinsky Theatre. From 1908 to 1914 he worked with **Diaghilev**, conducting ballet and opera throughout Europe. In 1914 he went to Petrograd (later Leningrad), leaving there four years later to become director of the Tiflis Conservatory. He settled in Paris in 1921. His works include operas, ballets, symphonies, and other orchestral music, and piano pieces. His son, Alexander Nikolaievich (1899–1977), was a conductor, pianist and composer of four symphonies, concertos, sonatas, and other works.

TEAGUE, Walter Dorwin (1883–1960) American designer and writer on design, born in Decatus, Indiana. He moved to New York in 1903 and trained at the Art Students' League, and after varied experience in design established his own industrial design consultancy in 1926. Among the most important clients were Kodak, Ford, National Cash Register and Texaco, for which he created a 'corporate identity', designing petrol stations, equipment and graphics. From the mid 1940s his office became closely associated with the design, especially of the interiors, of Boeing airliners. He was a first president of the American Society of Industrial Designers which he, **Dreyfuss** and **Loewy** founded in 1944. His book *Design This Day* (1940), a comprehensive vindication of modern design in the context of universal aesthetic criteria, was an important contribution to the literature on the subject.

TEBALDI, Renata (1922–) Italian operatic soprano, born in Pesaro. She studied at Parma Conservatory, made her début at Rovigo in 1944, and was invited by **Toscanini** to appear at the re-opening of La Scala, Milan, in 1946. She has appeared in England, France, Spain, South America and at the Metropolitan, New York, and San Francisco.

TEBBIT, Norman Beresford (1931–) English Conservative politician, born in Enfield, the son of a shop manager. He left grammar school at 16 and began his career as a journalist. After national service in the RAF he became an airline pilot and was later to head the British Airline Pilots' Association (BALPA). He was elected to parliament in 1970, representing Epping, and later Chingford, and became noted for his radical, 'New Right', convictions. Already an influential backroom strategist and junior minister, he was brought into the cabinet of **Margaret Thatcher** as employment secretary in 1981 and trade and industry secretary in 1983. Noted for his robust invective and anti-union stance, he came to personify a new type of 'Thatcherite' conservativism. His career, however, was partially checked by the injuries he and, in particular, his wife Margaret sustained as victims of the 1984 IRA bombing of the Grand Hotel, Brighton. He was appointed Conservative party chairman in 1985 and helped mastermind the 1987 general election victory. However, soon afterwards, his relations with Mrs Thatcher cooled and he retired to the backbenches.

TECUMSEH (c.1768–1813) American Indian chief of the Shawnees. He joined his brother, 'The Prophet', in a rising against the whites, suppressed at Tippecanoe by **William Harrison** in 1811. Passing into the English service, he commanded the Indian allies in the war of 1812–13 as brigadier-general. He fell fighting at the Thames in Canada (1813).

TEDDER, Arthur William, 1st Baron Tedder of Glenguin (1890–1967) Scottish marshal of the RAF, born at Glenguin, Stirlingshire. He was in the Colonial Service when war broke out in 1914. By 1916 he had transferred to the RFC. (Royal Flying Corps). Remaining in the service, at the outbreak of World War II he was director-general of research and development, air ministry. From 1940 he organized the Middle East Air Force with great success, moving on to the Mediterranean theatre and later becoming deputy supreme commander under **Eisenhower**. His services were recognized in his appointment as marshal of the RAF (1945). Created a baron in 1946, in 1950 he became chancellor of the University of Cambridge and also a governor of the BBC. He wrote *Air Power in the War* (1948) and an autobiography, *With Prejudice* (1966).

TEGETTHOFF, Baron Wilhelm von (1827–71) Austrian naval commander, born in Marburg. He defeated the Danes off Heligoland (1864) and an Italian fleet near Lissa (1866), the first battle between ironclads.

TEGNÉR, Elaias (1782–1846) Swedish poet and churchman, born in Kyrkerud in Värmland, the son of a pastor. Educated at Lund, he was appointed lecturer there in 1802. His stirring *Krigssång för Landtvärnet* (War-song for the Militia of Scania, 1808) made his name as a poet, and *Svea* (1811) made him famous. He was appointed professor of Greek at Lund (1812–26), and bishop of Växjö (1824). His best-known works include *Sång till Solen* (Song to the Sun, 1817), *Epilog vid magisterpromotionen i Lund 1820* (Degree Day at Lund, 1820), his religious idyll *Nattvardsbarn* (The Communion Children, 1820), *Axel*, a narrative romance of the days of King **Karl XII** (1822), and his masterpiece, *Frithjof's Saga* (1825). He also had a keen interest in education.

TEILHARD DE CHARDIN, Pierre (1881–1955) French Jesuit theologian, palaeontologist, and philosopher, the son of an Auvergne landowner. He was educated at a Jesuit school, lectured in pure science at the Jesuit College in Cairo, was ordained a priest in 1911, and in 1918 became professor of geology at the Institut Catholique in Paris. Between 1923 and 1946 he undertook palaeontological expeditions in China, (where he helped to discover Peking Man in 1929) and later in central Asia, but increasingly his researches did not conform to Jesuit orthodoxy and he was forbidden by his religious superiors to teach and publish, and in 1948 was not allowed to stand for a professorship at the Sorbonne in succession to the Abbé **Breuil**. Nevertheless, his work in Cenozoic geology and palaeontology became known and he was awarded academic distinctions, including the Legion of Honour (1946). From 1951 he lived in the USA and worked at the Wenner-Gren Foundation for Anthropological Research in New York. Posthumously published, his philosophical speculations, based on his scientific work, trace the evolution of animate matter to two basic principles: nonfinality and complexification. By the concept of *involution* he explains why *homo sapiens* is the only species which, in spreading over the globe, has resisted intense division into further species. This leads on to transcendental speculations, which allow him original, if theologically unorthodox, proofs for the existence of God. This work, *The Phenomenon of Man* (1955), is complementary to *Le Milieu divin* (1957).

TEISSERENCE DE BORT, Léon Philippe (1855–1913) French meteorologist, born in Paris. He became chief meteorologist at the Bureau Central Météorologique in Paris, and using instrumented balloons discovered and named the stratosphere as distinct from the troposphere, in the upper atmosphere. He was awarded the Symons Gold Medal by the Royal Meteorological Society in 1908.

TEIXEIRA, Pedro (c.1575–1640) Portuguese soldier. In 1614 he fought against the French in Brazil. He helped to found Pará in 1615, of which he was governor (1620 and 1640). He led an important expedition up the Amazon (1637–39) and across the mountains to Quito, returning by the same route.

TE KANAWA, Dame Kiri (1944–) New Zealand operatic soprano, born in Gisborne, Auckland. After winning many prizes and awards in New Zealand and Australia she came to the London Opera Centre, and made her début with the Royal Opera Company in 1970. Her first major role was **Mozart**'s Countess, which has been followed by a brilliant international career of soprano roles, including those of Donna Elvira, Desdemona, Mimi and Micaela. She was made a DBE in 1982.

TELEKI, Count Paul (1879–1941) Hungarian statesman, born in Budapest, where he became professor of geography at the university in 1919. Combining politics with an academic career, he was also in that year appointed foreign minister and, from 1920 to 1921, premier. Founder of the Christian National League and chief of Hungary's boy scouts, he was minister of education in 1938 and again premier in 1939. He was fully aware of the German threat to his country, but all measures to avert it, including a pact with Yugoslavia, were unavailing through lack of support. When Germany marched against Yugoslavia through Hungary, he took his own life.

TELEMANN, George Philipp (1681–1767) German composer, born in Magdeburg, the son of a clergyman. Largely self-taught, he gained his musical knowledge by learning to play a host of instruments (including the violin, recorder and zither, and later the shawm, oboe, flute and bass trombone) and studying the scores of the masters. In 1700 he was a student of languages and science at Leipzig University, and in 1704 was appointed organist of the New Church and kapellmeister to Prince Promnitz at Sorau. In 1709 he was kapellmeister at Eisenach, from 1712 to 1721 kepellmeister to the Prince of Bayreuth. In 1721 he was appointed music director of the Johanneum at Hamburg, holding this post until his death. One of the most prolific composers, his works include church music, 44 passions, 40 operas, oratorios (including *Der Tag de Gerichts* and *Die Tageszeiten*), countless songs and a large body of instrumental music. Ranked in his lifetime above his friend **J S Bach** and admired by **Handel**, who borrowed from his music, he lost popularity after his death and his musical gifts were not rediscovered until the 1930s. Though his masterly grasp of the techniques of all forms of musical composition was always recognized, especially his skill as a contrapuntist, critics regarded him as unoriginal and condemned his easily turned out works as lacking in depth and sincerity. But through his study of and admiration for the French composers, notably **Giovanni Lully**, a new grace and richness was introduced into German music. Much of the liveliness and gaiety in his work sprang from his sense of humour and from an interest in folk music. He wrote three autobiographies, the last of which was published in 1739.

TELFORD, Thomas (1757–1834) Scottish civil engineer, born in Westerkirk, Langholm, a shepherd's son. At the age of 14 he was apprenticed to a stonemason, in 1780 went to Edinburgh, and in 1782 to London. In 1784 he got work at Portsmouth dockyard; in 1787 he became surveyor of public works for Shropshire, and his reputation was enhanced by his masonry arch bridge over the Severn at Montford (1790–92) and even more by the spectacular Pont Cysylte aqueduct and other works on the Ellesmere Canal (1793–1805). In 1801 he was commissioned by the government to report on the public works required for Scotland; and he constructed the Caledonian Canal (1803–23), more than 1000 miles of road, and 1200 bridges, besides churches, manses, harbours, etc. Other works by him included the road from London to Holyhead, with the remarkable 579-ft span wrought-iron Menai Suspension Bridge (1819–26), and the St Katherine's Docks (1824–28) in London; he was also responsible for draining large tracts of the Fen country.

TELL, William legendary Swiss patriot of Bürglen in Uri, reputedly the saviour of his native district from the tyranny of Austria. The Swiss historian **Johannes von Müller** tells at length, in his *History of Switzerland* (1786), how Albert II of Austria strove to annex the Forest Cantons; how in 1307 his tyrannical steward Gessler compelled the Swiss to do reverence to the ducal hat erected on a pole in Altorf; how Tell, a famous marksman, was for noncompliance condemned to shoot an apple off his own son's head; and how afterwards Tell slew the tyrant, and so initiated the movement which secured the independence of Switzerland. The story is possibly pure legend and Tell's very existence is disputed.

TELLER, Edward (1908–) Hungarian-American physicist, a major figure in the development of nuclear energy, born in Budapest. He graduated in chemical engineering at Karlsruhe, studied theoretical physics at Munich, Göttingen and under **Niels Bohr** at Copenhagen. He left Germany in 1933, lectured in London and Washington (1935) and contributed profoundly to the modern explanation of solar energy, anticipating the theory behind thermonuclear explosions. He worked on the atomic bomb project (1941–46), and joined **Oppenheimer**'s theoretical study group at Buckley, California, where he was director of the new nuclear laboratories at Livermore (1958–60). From 1963 he was professor of physics at California University. He repudiated, as a scientist, any moral implications of his work, stating that, but for Oppenheimer's moral qualms, the US might have had hydrogen bombs in 1947. After Russia's first atomic test (1949) he was one of the architects of President **Harry S Truman**'s crash programme to build and test (1952) the world's first hydrogen bomb. He wrote *Our Nuclear Future* (1958, with a letter).

TÉLLEZ See **TIRSO DE MOLINA**

TEMIN, Howard Martin (1934–) American virologist, and joint winner of the 1975 Nobel prize for physiology or medicine. He did graduate work at the California Institute of Technology (1955–59) and taught at Wisconsin from 1960. For his work on the way viruses can make normal cells malignant, he shared the Nobel prize with **Renato Dulbecco** and **David Baltimore**.

TEMMINCK, Coenraad Jacob (1778–1858) Dutch ornithologist, born in Amsterdam, the son of the treasurer of the Dutch East India Company. At the age of 17 he became an auctioneer with the company, and amassed a collection of bird specimens. He published *Histoire naturelle générale des Pigeons et des Gallinacées* (3 vols, 1813–15), followed by his famous *Manuel d'Ornithologie* (1815 onwards). He was also co-author of *Nouveau Receuil de Planches coloriées d'Oiseaux* (1820–39). He was the first director of the new natural history museum at Leiden, from 1820. Temminck's Stint and Temminck's Horned Lark are named after him.

TEMPLE, Frederick (1821–1902) English prelate, and archbishop of Canterbury, born in Santa Maura in the Ionian islands. Educated at Blundell's School and Balliol College, Oxford, of which he became a mathematics lecturer and fellow, he was principal of Kneller Hall Training College (1858–69), inspector of schools and headmaster of Rugby (1857–69). He wrote the first of the allegedly heterodox *Essays and Reviews* (1860) which almost prevented his appointment to the bishopric of Exeter in 1869, and supported the disestablishment of the Irish Church. In 1885 he became bishop of London and in 1897 archbishop of Canterbury. He was responsible, with Archbishop Maclagen of York, for the 'Lambeth Opinions' (1889) which attempted to solve some ritual controversies.

TEMPLE, Richard Grenville, 1st Earl (1711–79) English statesman, elder brother of **George Grenville**. In 1756–61 he held office as First Lord of the Admiralty and lord privy seal under the elder Pitt (**Chatham**), who had married his sister. He bitterly opposed **Bute** and broke with Pitt on the Stamp Act in 1766.

TEMPLE, Shirley (1928–) American child entertainer, born in Santa Monica, California. Precociously talented, she appeared in a series of short films from the age of three and a half, and graduated to full stardom with a leading role in *Little Miss Marker* (1934). An unspoilt personality who sang, danced and did impressions, she captivated Depression-era audiences, becoming the world's favourite golden-haired moppet in films like *Curly Top* (1935) and *Dimples* (1936). Her appeal faded, however, and when attempts at an adult comeback floundered, she retired from the screen. Involved with Republican party politics as Mrs Shirley Temple Black, she was appointed America's representative to the United Nations General Assembly in 1969 and served as Ambassador to Ghana (1974–76) and White House chief of protocol (1976–1977). She received an honorary Academy Award in 1934.

TEMPLE, Sir William (1628–99) English diplomatist and essay writer, born in London. He studied at Emmanuel College, Cambridge. After a successful diplomatic career, during which he helped to cement the Triple Alliance between England, Holland and Sweden against France, and suggested the scheme of a reformed privy council of 30, he decided to concentrate on a literary life and established a considerable reputation as an essayist. His works include *Miscellanea* (1679, 1692) and the famous essay 'Upon the Ancient and Modern Learning'.

TEMPLE, William (1881–1944) English prelate, and archbishop of Canterbury, born in Exeter, son of **Frederick Temple**. He was educated at Rugby and Oxford, where he became a fellow of Queen's College (1904–10). He took orders in 1908, was headmaster of Repton School (1910–14) and became a canon of Westminster in 1919. In 1921 he became bishop of Manchester, in 1929 archbishop of York and in 1942 archbishop of Canterbury. With interests as broad as his humanity, he united solid learning and great administrative ability. As primate, he was one of the greatest moral forces of his time. An outspoken advocate of social reform, he made as his main task the application to current problems of his conception of the Christian philosophy of life, crusading against usury, slums, dishonesty, and the aberrations of the profit motive. Temple's leadership was also seen in his chairmanship of the Doctrinal Commission of the Church of England and in his work for the Ecumenical

Movement of Christian Union. His publications include *Church and Nation* (1915), *Christianity and the State* (1928) and *Christianity and the Social Order* (1942).

TEMPLER, Sir Gerald (1898–1979) English soldier. Educated at Wellington College and the Royal Military College, Sandhurst, he was commissioned in the Royal Irish Fusiliers and served with them in World War I. In World War II he became commander of the 6th Armoured Division. He was vice-chief of the Imperial General Staff (1948–50), and CIGS (1955–58). As high commissioner and commander-in-chief Malaya (1952–54) he frustrated the Communist guerrillas' offensive. In 1965 he succeeded Field-Marshal Lord **Alexander of Tunis** as constable of the Tower of London.

TEMPLEWOOD, Sir Samuel John Gurney Hoare, 1st Viscount (1880–1959) British Conservative politician, educated at Harrow and Oxford. He entered politics in 1905 as assistant private secretary to the colonial secretary and in 1910 became MP for Chelsea, a seat he held till he received a peerage in 1944. He was secretary of state for air (1922–29), and as secretary of state for India (1931–35) he piloted the India Act through the Commons against the opposition of **Winston Churchill**. In 1935, as foreign secretary, he was criticized for his part in the discussions which led to the abortive Hoare-**Laval** pact over the Italian invasion of Ethiopia. He resigned, and in 1936 was appointed First Lord of the Admiralty. Home secretary (1937–39), he was a strong advocate of penal reform. His Criminal Justice Bill (1938) never became law because of the outbreak of war, but much of it was embodied in the Act of 1948. From 1940 to 1944 he was ambassador on special mission to Madrid. In his later years he continued as an apologist for the National Government, whose 'appeasement' policy towards the dictators he helped to direct, and as a determined opponent of capital punishment. His publications include *The Shadow of the Gallows* (1951) and *Nine Troubled Years* (1954).

TEN BRINK See **BRINK**

TENCIN, Claudine Alexandrine Guérin de (1681–1749) French writer and courtesan, born in Grenoble. She entered the religious life, but in 1714 came to Paris, where her wit and beauty attracted a crowd of lovers, among them the regent and Cardinal **Dubois**. She had much political influence, enriched herself, and helped the fortunes of her brother, Cardinal Pierre Guérin de Tencin (1680–1758). But her importance died with the regent and the cardinal in 1723. In 1726 she was imprisoned for a short time in the Bastille, after one of her lovers had shot himself in her house. Her later life was more decorous, and her *salon* one of the most popular in Paris. **Fontenelle** was one of her oldest lovers; **D'Alembert** one of her children. Her romances include *Mémoires du Comte de Comminges* (1735), *Le Siège de Calais* (1739) and *Les Malheurs de l'amour* (1747).

TENIERS, David, the elder (1582–1649) Flemish genre painter, born in Antwerp. His subjects are generally homely tavern scenes, rustic games, weddings, and so on. His *Temptation of St Anthony* is well known.

TENIERS, David, the younger (1610–90) Flemish genre painter, son of **David Teniers** the elder. He quickly gained distinction, enjoying the favour and friendship of the Austrian archduke, **William the Silent** the Prince of Orange, and the bishop of Ghent. In 1647 he moved to his abode in Brussels. His 700 pictures possess, in superlative degree, the qualities that mark his father's work.

TENISON, Thomas (1636–1715) English theologian, born in Cottenham, Cambridgeshire. He studied at Corpus Christi, Cambridge, and was made bishop of Lincoln by **William III** in 1691, and archbishop of Canterbury in 1694. He was a favourite at court, crowned Queen **Anne** and **George I**, and strongly supported the Hanoverian succession. His works comprise antipapal tracts, sermons, and a criticism of **Hobbes**.

TENNANT, Charles (1768–1838) Scottish chemical industrialist, born in Ochiltree. Educated at the parish school there, he was apprenticed as a weaver; he studied bleaching and set up his own bleachfields near Paisley. He became one of the first to make a fortune out of a heavy chemical industry. In 1799 he took out a patent for the manufacture of a dry bleaching powder made from chlorine and slaked lime (probably the invention of one of his partners, **Charles Macintosh**). Being easily transportable to the expanding textile industry (where chlorine could be regenerated by mixing with acid), demand for the bleaching powder grew until the factory at St Rollox near Glasgow became the largest chemical works in the world at that time.

TENNANT, Smithson (1761–1815) English chemist, born in Selby. He was educated at Edinburgh and Cambridge. He discovered osmium and iridium (1804) and proved that diamond is pure carbon. Professor of chemistry at Cambridge (1814), he was killed the following year in a riding accident.

TENNANT, William (1784–1848) Scottish poet and scholar, born in Anstruther, Fife. He studied at St Andrews, and in 1812 published a mock-heroic poem *Anster Fair*, which was the first attempt to naturalize the Italian *ottavo rima*. He was a teacher from 1816 at Lasswade, from 1819 at Dollar Academy, and from 1835 professor of oriental languages at St Andrews. Other poems were the *Thane of Fife* (1822) and *Papistry Stormed* (1827); dramas were *Cardinal Beaton* (1823) and *John Baliol* (1825).

TENNIEL, Sir John (1820–1914) English cartoonist and illustrator, born in London, the son of a dancing-master. A self-trained artist, he was selected in 1845 to paint one of the frescoes (**Dryden**'s 'St Cecilia') in the Houses of Parliament. He was on the staff of *Punch* for 50 years (1851–1901), succeeding **John Leech** as chief cartoonist in 1864. His most celebrated cartoon was 'Dropping the Pilot' (1890), referring to **Bismarck**'s resignation. His main claim to fame, however, are his delicate illustrations for **Lewis Carroll**'s *Alice's Adventures in Wonderland* (1865) and *Through the Looking Glass* (1872). He also illustrated *Aesop's Fables*, **Thomas Moore**'s *Lalla Rookh*, and **Barham**'s *Ingoldsby's Legends*, amongst others.

TENNYSON, Alfred, 1st Baron Tennyson (1809–92) English poet, born in Somersby rectory, Lincolnshire, the fourth son of the rector. His elder brothers, Frederick and Charles, also wrote poetry. He was educated at Louth Grammar School, and in 1827 went to Trinity College, Cambridge, where he became a member of an ardent group of young men, including **Arthur Hallam**, whose early death was to be mourned in that great elegiac poem *In Memoriam* (1850). His early ventures in verse, *Poems Chiefly Lyrical* (1830) and *Poems* (1833), were understandably slighted by the critics as being too sentimental. But the critics ought to have detected the great poet in the first version of 'The Lady of Shallott', 'Oenone', 'The Lotus-eaters' and other poems in the 1833 volume. Nine years of revising these poems and adding fresh material resulted in the volume of *Poems* of 1842, which established his fame. He had been engaged since 1833 in writing the series of loosely connected lyrics or elegies which as *In Mem-*

oriam crowned his fame in 1850, the year he succeeded **Wordsworth** as poet laureate and the year of his marriage to Emily Sarah Sellwood. He moved to Farringford in the Isle of Wight and Aldworth in Sussex, and was flattered by the homage of the entire nation from Queen **Victoria** downwards, such was his popularity. With his wife he made short tours but rarely left his Victorian England. The volume of 1842 and *In Memoriam* contain some of the most finished artistry in English poetry, in which the mood of the poem is perfectly reflected in rhythm and language. After 1850 he devoted himself to the fashionable verse novelette—*Maud; a Monodrama* (1855), *Enoch Arden* (1864), and *Locksley Hall Sixty Years After* (1886). The public, however, was waiting for what was to be the crowning triumph. The first instalment of *Idylls of the King* (1859) seemed to the Victorians to be just that, but in *Geraint and Enid* and *Lancelot and Elaine* and throughout the whole series (completed in 1885) Victorian morality imposed on the old chivalric matter stifles the poetry except in the descriptive passages. In the 1870s he attempted drama. **Irving** gave *Becket* a considerable run, but *Harold*, *Queen Mary* and others were not successful. He had a late flowering in his seventies when he wrote the perfect poem *To Virgil*, *Tiresias*, and the powerful *Rizpah*, but the conflict between science and the Faith, discussed optimistically in *In Memoriam*, now becomes an obsession. *The Princess* (1847) gave him a chance to make a social comment, but the subject of woman's education is treated in serio-comic fashion, which is trying, and the image of John Bull he projects in the poem is offensive to modern taste. His last poem was a 16-line lyric written in 1889 while crossing from Lymington to the Isle of Wight, *Crossing the Bar*.

TENTERDEN, Charles Abbott, 1st Baron (1762–1832) English lawyer, born a barber's son in Canterbury. He became a fellow and tutor of Corpus Christi College, Oxford, was called to the bar and in 1801 became recorder of Oxford. Lacking in eloquence, he made his reputation by the *Law relating to Merchant Ships and Seamen* (1802), a work based on principles rather than merely precedents. In 1816 he became puisne judge in the court of common pleas, in 1818 he was knighted and became chief justice of the King's Bench, and, raised to the peerage in 1827, strongly opposed the Catholic Relief and Reform Bills. Though hardly a great judge, he was a master of legal principles and a sound judge.

TENZING NORGAY, known as Sherpa Tenzing (1914–86) Nepalese mountaineer, born in Tsa-chu near Makalu. He made his first climb as a porter with a British expedition to Everest in 1935. In the years following he climbed many of the Himalayan peaks and on two later attempts on the ascent of Everest he reached 23 000 ft. in 1938 and 28 215 ft. in 1952. In 1953 on Colonel John Hunt's expedition, he, with **Edmund Hillary**, succeeded in reaching the summit of Everest, and for this triumph he was awarded the George Medal. In 1954 he studied at a mountaineering school in Switzerland, and on his return to Darjeeling, was appointed head of the Institute of Mountaineering. He also became president of the Sherpa Association.

TERBORCH, or **Terburg, Gerard** (c.1617–1681) Dutch painter, born in Zwolle. He studied at Haarlem and visited England (1635), Italy (1640), and Germany, where he painted the conference of 'The Peace Congress of Münster' (1648; National Gallery, London). He also visited **Velasquez** in Spain. From 1654 to his death he lived at Deventer, where he became burgomaster. He worked mostly on a small scale, producing genre pictures and fashionable portraits.

TERBRUGGHEN, Hendrik (1588–1629) Dutch painter, born in Deventer. He studied under **Bloemaert**, and went to Italy from 1604–16 where he came under the influence of **Caravaggio**. Like the latter he excelled in chiaroscuro effects and in the faithful representation of physiognomical details and drapery. His *Jacob and Laban* (1627) is in the National Gallery, London.

TERBURG, Gerard See **TERBORCH**

TERENCE, Publius Terentius Afer (c.190–159 BC) Roman comedy writer, born in Carthage. He became the slave of the Roman senator P Terentius Lucanus, who brought him to Rome, educated him, and set him free. His first play was the *Andria* (166 BC); its success introduced Terence to the most refined society of Rome. His chief patrons were Laclius and **Scipio Æmilianus,** the younger. After spending some years in Rome he went to Greece. Six of his comedies are still extant: *Andria*, *Eunuchus*, *Heauton Timoroumenos*, *Phormio*, *Hecyra* and *Adelphi*. His plays, Greek in origin and Greek in scene, were mostly based on **Menander**. His excellence lies in the fact that he wrote in singularly pure and perfect Latin. Many of his conventions and plot constructions were later used by **Sheridan**, **Molière**, and others.

TERESA, of Ávila, St (1515–82) Spanish mystic and saint, born of a noble family in Ávila in Old Castile. In 1533 she entered a Carmelite convent there. About 1555 her religious exercises reached an extraordinary height of asceticism; she was favoured with ecstasies, and the fame of her sanctity spread far and wide. She obtained permission from the Holy See in 1562 to remove to a humble house in Ávila, where she founded the Convent of St Joseph to re-establish the ancient Carmelite rule, with additional observances. In 1567 the general of the Carmelite order urged on her the duty of extending her reforms; in 1579 the Carmelites of the stricter observance were united into a distinct association; and within her own lifetime 17 convents of women and 16 of men accepted her reforms. She was canonized in 1622. The most famous of her many works are her autobiography; *The Way of Perfection*, *The Book of the Foundations*, which describes the journeys she made and the convents she founded or reformed; and *The Interior Castle* (trans 1852).

TERESHKOVA, Valentina Vladimirovna (1937–) Russian astronaut, born in Maslennikovo, Yaroslavl, the first woman in space and the tenth human being in orbit. A farmer's daughter, she was a cotton mill worker and amateur parachutist with 126 jumps to her credit before joining the cosmonaut corps in 1962. As a 2nd Lt in the Soviet air force she was the solo pilot in the space capsule Vostock 6 which was launched from the Tyuratam Space Station in the USSR on 16 June 1963. She remained in orbit for three days, returning after 48 orbits and travelling a distance of 1 242 800 miles.

TERKEL, Studs (Louis) (1912–) American writer and oral historian, born in New York City. He grew up and went to Law School in Chicago. He has acted in radio soap operas, been a disc jockey, a radio commentator and a television host, and has travelled worldwide conducting interviews with the famous and the anonymous. Described by **J K Galbraith** as 'a national resource', his publications include *Giants of Jazz* (1957), *Division Street: America* (1967), *Hard Times* (1970), *Working* (1974), about the Depression, *American Dreams: Lost and Found* (1980), and *The Good War: An Oral History of World War Two* (1984) for which he was awarded the Pulitzer prize . He also published an autobiography, *Talking to Myself* (1977).

TERMAN, Lewis Madison (1877–1956) American psychologist and pioneer of intelligence tests, born in Johnson County, Indiana. At Stanford University he developed an English version of the Binet-Simon intelligence test and introduced Terman Group Intelligence Tests into the US army in 1920. He pioneered the use of the term IQ (Intelligence Quotient) in his *The Measurement of Intelligence* (1916) and launched the five volume *Genetic Studies of Genius* (1926–59).

TERRY, Daniel (c.1780–1829) English actor and playwright, born in Bath. After an architectural apprenticeship he joined a theatrical company under the elder **Macready** at Sheffield, probably in 1805, making his London début in 1812. He played in many dramatizations of Sir **Walter Scott**'s novels, and they became intimate friends, with Terry copying Scott in many ways, down to imitating his handwriting. He also played the major Shakespearean roles, and in **Sheridan**, etc at Covent Garden and Drury Lane, London.

TERRY, Edward O'Connor (1844–1912) English comedian, born in London. He made his début at Christchurch in 1863, and, after four years in the provinces, played in London in 1867. He opened Terry's Theatre in 1887.

TERRY, Dame Ellen Alice (1848–1928) English actress, sister of **Fred Terry**, born in Coventry, the daughter of a provincial actor. She was apprenticed to the stage from infancy, and at eight appeared as Mammilius in *The Winter's Tale* at the Prince's Theatre, London. From 1862 she played in Bristol and after a brief marriage to the painter, **George Frederick Watts** in 1864, and a second retirement from the stage (1868–74) during which her two children, Edith and **Edward Gordon Craig**, were born, she established herself as the leading Shakespearean actress in London and from 1878 to 1902 dominated the English and American theatre in partnership with **Henry Irving** Her natural gentleness and vivacity made her excel, particularly as Portia and Ophelia, and she would have made an ideal Rosalind, but Irving's professional jealousy withheld such an opportunity at the Lyceum. In 1903 she went into theatre management without Irving and engaged her son to produce **Ibsen**'s *Vikings*. **Barrie** and **Shaw** wrote parts especially for her, eg Lady Cicely Waynflete in the latter's *Captain Brassbound's Conversion* (1905). She married Charles Kelly (Wardell) in 1876 and in 1907 the American actor, James Carew. She received the DBE in 1925.

TERRY, Fred (1863–1933) English actor, brother of **Ellen Terry**, born in London. He played in the companies of **Herbert Beerbohm Tree**, **Forbes-Robertson** and **Irving Henry** and established a reputation as a romantic actor as Sir Percy Blakeney in *The Scarlet Pimpernel* (1905). His sisters, Kate (1844–1924), Marion and Florence were also actresses, as was his wife **Julia Neilson**.

TERTULLIAN, properly **Quintus Septimius Florens Tertullianus** (c.160–c.220) Carthaginian theologian, one of the fathers of the Latin church, born in Carthage, and known as the 'Father of Latin theology'. He was brought up in Carthage as a pagan, then lived for some time in Rome, where he was converted to Christianity (c.196) and then returned to Carthage. That he was married is shown by his two books *Ad Uxorem*, in which he argues against second marriages. His opposition to worldliness in the church culminated in his becoming a leader of the Montanist sect about 207. He had the heart of a Christian with the intellect of an advocate. His style is vivid, vigorous and concise, abounding in harsh and obscure expressions, abrupt turns and impetuous transitions, with here and there bursts of glowing eloquence. He was the creator of ecclesiastical Latinity, and many of his sentences have become proverbial, eg, 'The blood of the martyrs is the seed of the church' and 'The unity of heretics is schism'. His works are divided into three classes: (1) controversial writings against heathens and Jews, as in *Apologeticum*, *Ad Nationes* and *Adversus Judaeos*; (2) against heretics, as in *De Praescriptione Haereticorum*, *Adversus Valentinianos*, *De Anima*, *De Carne Christi* (against Docetism), *De Resurrectione Carnis*, *Adversus Marcionem* and *Adversus Praxean*; (3) practical and ascetic treatises, in which can be traced his increasing hostility to the church and his adoption of Montanist views. Hence the division of these treatises into Pre-Montanist and Montanist, of which *De Virginibus Velandis* marks the transitional stage. Tertullian had a greater influence on the Latin Church than any theologian between **Paul** and **Augustine**. His Montanism, indeed, prevented its direct exercise, but **Cyprian** was the interpreter who gave currency to his views.

TERZAGHI, Karl (1883–1963) Czechoslovakian-born American civil engineer, born in Prague. Educated at the Technische Hochschule in Graz, he held professorships at Istanbul, Massachusetts Institute of Technology, Vienna and Harvard, becoming a naturalized US citizen in 1943. Through his teaching and research he established the subject of soil mechanics, the behaviour of soil under stress, as an independent scientific discipline, enabling engineers to design foundations, cuttings and earth dams, for example, on an analytical rather than an empirical basis.

TESLA, Nikola (1856–1943) Yugoslav-born American physicist and electrical engineer, born in Smiljan, Croatia. He studied at Graz, Prague and Paris, emigrating to the USA in 1884. He left the Edison Works at Menlo Park after quarrelling with **Edison** and concentrated on his own inventions, which included improved dynamos, transformers and electric bulbs and the high-frequency coil which bears his name.

TESSIN, Carl-Gustaf (1695–1770) Swedish statesman, writer and court official, son of **Nicodemus Tessin 'the Younger'.** He was educated in France and Italy, and on his return to Sweden became active in politics, assuming a leading position in the anti-Russian Hat party which hoped to regain territory lost to Russia during **Karl XII**'s reign. He was elected leader of the Nobility Estate when the Hats gained a majority in 1738, and bore heavy responsibility for the unsuccessful war against Russia in 1741. He gained the favour of King **Adolf Fredrik** and Queen Louisa Ulrika and in 1746 was appointed head of chancellory and governor to the future king **Gustav III**, but fell from grace for disapproving of their attempts to increase royal power. He left the court, spending most of his life on his Åkerö estate, where he wrote his memoirs (31 volumes, mostly in French), fables and didactic letters in the style of **Fénélon** to the Crown Prince. He had immense influence on Swedish culture of his period. His interior decoration of the Royal Palace introduced French rococo style into Sweden. He founded the Academy of Art and on his European journeys he acquired works by **Boucher** and Dutch and Flemish 17th-century masters. He sold his collection to the royal family and it forms the basis of the present National Museum and Royal Library.

TESSIN, Nicodemus, known as **the Elder** (1615–81) Swedish architect, born in Stralsund. In 1636 he moved to Stockholm where he became the most eminent architect during a period of affluence and expansion. Entering first the service of the Lord Chancellor, **Axel Oxenstierna**, whose handsome castle Tidö, Västerås, he completed in 1645, he was then appointed royal architect in 1646 and was city architect in Stockholm from 1661. He drew up plans in the Renaissance style for several Norrland towns in the late 1640s. Then, supported by Queen **Kristina**, he studied in Italy, France and Holland (1651–53), after which his structures show clear Italian (mainly Roman) influence, the furnishings reflect French styles and the gardens reveal the spirit of **Lenôtre**. Among his many commissions on returning to Sweden were Admiral **Ferdinand Wrangel**'s Skokloster on Lake Mälaren and *Wrangelska palatset* (1652–64), which now houses the Supreme Court in Stockholm; Kalmar Cathedral (started 1660); the Caroline Mausoleum in Riddarholm Church (1671) and the Bank of Sweden in Stockholm (1676). Most notable of all is the charming palace of Drottningholm on Mälaren, residence of the present monarch, commissioned by Queen Hedvig Eleonara in 1662 and completed by Tessin's son, **Nicodemus** the Younger, some 20 years later.

TESSIN, Nicodemus, known as **the Younger** (1654–1728) Swedish architect, son of **Nicodemus 'the Elder'.** He rounded off his education with long periods in Rome (1673–78) and Paris (1678–80). Under the protection of Queen **Kristina**, living in Rome since her abdication, he studied ancient and baroque culture and was highly appreciative of **Bernini** and **Carlo Fontana**. His genius lay in his ability to borrow from baroque and French models and create a harmonious, uniquely Northern, edifice. He was appointed royal architect in 1676 and succeeded his father as Stockholm city architect in 1682. He completed Drottningholm Palace and added the royal church (1690–99). Other notable structures include Steninge Castle (1694–98) and his own beautifully proportioned Tessin palace (1696–1700), situated near the Royal Palace, and now the Governor's palace. He planned gardens for royal palaces, including Ulriksdal and Karlberg in the manner of **Lenôtre**; he designed ecclesiastical buildings such as Trinity Church, Karlskrona (1697–1747) and Fredrik's Church, Karlshamm (1720–58) and renovated others, notably Västerås Cathedral spire. He also did important work on Amelienborg Castle, Copenhagen (1697), the Louvre (1704–06) and the Apollo Temple, Versailles. His greatest achievement was the Royal Palace, Stockholm. When fire destroyed the old *Tre kronor* castle in 1697 he had designs ready for a royal stately home with an Italian type façade and French interior design. Building was in abeyance for many years because of severe shortage of money and manpower caused by **Karl XII**'s disastrous wars, but was started again shortly before Tessin's death and completed by his son, **Carl-Gustaf Tessin**.

TETLEY, Glen (1926–) American contemporary ballet dancer and choreographer, born in Cleveland, Ohio. He gave up medical studies to become a dancer and trained with **Hanya Holm**. After a period performing on Broadway and with **Martha Graham** (1957–59), he shifted towards ballet, dancing with both American Ballet Theatre and as an original member of the Joffrey Ballet (1956). Working with Netherlands Dance Theatre during the 1960s, guest choreographing for Ballet Rambert, and a two-year contract with Stuttgart Ballet from 1973 to 1975 after **John Cranko**'s sudden death, have given him a stronger hold and reputation in Europe than he enjoys in the USA. In 1986 he was commissioned by the National Ballet of Canada to choreograph *Alice*, a popular version of the Lewis Carroll (**Charles Dodgson**) tale. He subsequently became artistic director there. Work includes *Pierrot lunaire* (1962), *Voluntaries* (1973), and *The Tempest* for Ballet Rambert (1979), his only full length ballet to date.

TETRAZZINI, Luisa (1871–1940) Italian coloratura soprano, born in Florence. She made her début in 1895 in **Meyerbeer**'s *L'Africaine*. Appearing mostly in Italian opera of the older school, one of her most notable successes was in *Lucia di Lammermoor*. She sang in London and in America and in 1913–14 was a member of the Chicago Opera Company. In 1921 she published *My Life of Song*.

TETZEL, Johann (c.1465–1519) German monk, born in Leipzig. He entered the Dominican order in 1489. A famous preacher, he was appointed in 1516 to sell indulgences in return for contributions to the building fund of St Peter's in Rome. This he did with great ostentation, thereby provoking the 95 Wittenberg Theses of **Martin Luther**. In reply he published 122 counter-theses (written for him by Conrad Wimpina), but was rebuked by the papal delegate for his literary extravagance.

TEWFIK PASHA, Mohammed (1852–92) khedive of Egypt. Eldest son of **Ismail Pasha**, he succeeded on his abdication in 1879. The chief events of his reign were Arabi's insurrection (1882), the British intervention, the war with the Mahdi **Mohammed Ahmed** (1884–85), the pacification of the Sudan frontiers, and the improvement of Egypt under British administration. He was succeeded by his son **Abbas Hilmi**.

TEY, Josephine See **MACKINTOSH, Elizabeth**

THACKERAY, William Makepeace (1811–63) English novelist, born in Calcutta, where his father was in the service of the East India Company. The father died in 1816 and his mother remarried, so the boy was sent home. He went to Charterhouse (1822) and Trinity College, Cambridge (1829), but left without taking a degree. His first venture in print was a parody of **Tennyson**'s prize poem *Timbuctoo*. After dissipating much of his patrimony in travelling abroad, he decided to improve his fortune by journalism, though art equally attracted him. A four-year stay in Paris as an art student came to a close through lack of funds in 1836. He had now married Isabella Shawe (1836), but financial worry, due to the bankruptcy of his stepfather, finally made him decide to earn a living in journalism, and he returned to London. He contributed regularly to *The Times*, the *New Monthly* and *Fraser's Magazine*. Domestic trouble now engulfed him. The birth of his third daughter affected Mrs Thackeray's mind, the home was broken up and the children sent to their grandmother in Paris. His first publications, starting with *The Paris Sketchbook* (1840), and written under various pseudonyms (Wagstaff, Titmarsh, Fitz-Boodle, Yellowplush, Snob, etc) were a comparative failure although they included *The Yellowplush Papers*, *The Great Hoggarty Diamond* and *The Luck of Barry Lyndon*, all contributed to *Fraser's Magazine* (1841–44). It was his work on *Punch* from 1842 onwards which attracted attention by exploiting the view of society as seen by the butler ('Jeames' Diary') and the great theme of English snobbery. The great novels that were to follow—*Vanity Fair* (1847–48), *Pendennis* (1848), *Henry Esmond* (1852) and *The Newcomes* (1853–55), all monthly serials, established his fame. *Vanity Fair* is the first novel to give a view of London society with its mingling of rich parvenus and decadent upper class, through both of which the social climber, Becky Sharp, threads her way. The great historical novel, *Henry Esmond*, shows Thackeray's consuming love of the 18th century. Its sequel, *The Virginians* (1857–59), is not considered a success. *The Newcomes* shows a young love at the mercy of scheming relatives and mean-spirited rival suitors. Thackeray retired from *Punch* in 1854 and became the editor of the *Cornhill Magazine*, where much of his later work appeared—ballads, novels, and so on, now largely unreadable. He also undertook lecturing tours at home and in America, the fruit of which, apart from *The Virginians*, was *The English Humorists of the 18th century* (1853) and *The Four Georges* (1860).

THAIS (4th century BC) Athenian courtesan, famous for her wit and beauty. She was, according to a doubtful legend, the mistress of **Alexander the Great**, whom she induced to burn down Persepolis. She had several children by Ptolemy Lagos. She was the subject of an opera by Massenet.

THALBEN-BALL, Sir George Thomas (1896–1987) Australian-born British organist and composer, born in Sydney. Educated privately, he then became an exhibitioner and Grove scholar at the Royal Academy of Music, London. He became assistant organist at the Temple Church, London, in 1919 and was appointed organist in 1923, which position he held for 58 years until his retirement in 1981. From the early 1920s Thalben-Ball was synonymous with the Temple Church both in radio broadcasts and on HMV records. He also made regular appearances in the Henry Wood promenade concerts for the BBC, as music adviser and consultant from 1941. He was organ professor and examiner at the RCM, and curator-organist at the Royal Albert Hall, London, in addition to his many other professional positions. He toured abroad, and visited Australia in 1951 as guest of the Commonwealth jubilee celebrations. As a composer Thalben-Ball studied under **Frank Bridge**, Sir **Charles Stanford**, Charles Wood and Sir **Charles Parry**, and wrote much organ and choral music.

THALBERG, Sigismond (1812–71) Swiss-German pianist, born in Geneva. He studied music at Vienna under **Johann Hummel**, and from 1830 made extensive tours in Europe and North America, settling near Naples in 1858. His compositions comprise fantasias and variations, a piano concerto and operas.

THALES (c.624–c.545 BC) Greek natural philosopher, astronomer and geometer, traditionally the founder of Greek, and therefore European, philosophy. He came from Miletus on mainland Ionia (Asia Minor), as did his intellectual successors **Anaximander** and **Anaximines**, and his importance is to have proposed the first natural cosmology, identifying water as the original substance and (literally) the basis of the universe. He seems to have had wide-ranging practical and intellectual interests, with a reputation as a statesman, engineer, geometer and astronomer. He is supposed to have visited Egypt and developed his interest in land-surveying and astronomical techniques there, to have predicted accurately a solar eclipse in 585 BC, and to have proposed a federation of the Ionian cities of the Aegean. He was included in the traditional canon of 'Seven Wise Men', and attracted various apocryphal anecdotes, for example as the original absent-minded professor who would fall into a well while watching the stars. He left no writings, except possibly a nautical star-guide.

THANT, U (1909–74) Burmese diplomat, born in Pantanaw. He became a schoolmaster under Thakin Nu, the future prime minister, whom he later succeeded as headmaster of Pantanaw National High School. When Burma became independent in 1948 he took up government work and after holding several appointments he became permanent UN representative for Burma in 1957. In 1961 he was elected acting secretary-general of the UN after the death of **Dag Hammarskjöld**, and became permanent secretary-general in 1962. He played a major diplomatic role during the Cuban crisis and headed a mission to the Cuban leader (1962). He formulated a plan for the ending of the Congolese civil war (1962) which ended the Katanga secession (1963) and mobilized a UN peace-keeping force containing British troops for Cyprus in 1964. He resigned in 1971.

THARP, Twyla (1941–) American dancer and choreographer, born in Portland, Indiana. An accomplished musician and dancer as a child (ballet, jazz, baton-twirling, viola and acrobatics), she danced with the *Paul Taylor* Dance Company (1963–65), and founded her own small troupe in 1965. A choreographer and performer famed for her ability to create modern dance with a popular appeal without losing either integrity or depth, her work was at first structural and sombre. But from *Eight Jelly Rolls*, (1971, set to the jazz piano of **Jelly Roll Morton**), she struck a note which delighted audiences. *Coupe*, a piece made to music by the Beach Boys for the Joffrey Ballet in 1973, was a sensation, as was *Push Comes to Shove* (1976), the first dance made by an American choreographer for the Russian star **Mikhail Baryshnikov**, then at the American Ballet Theatre. Her work includes *The Bix Pieces* (1971), *Sue's Leg* (1976), *Baker's Dozen* (1979), *Nine Sinatra Songs* (1982), *Bach Partita*, for American Ballet Theatre (1984), two Broadway works (*When We Were Very Young*, 1980, and *The Catherine Wheel*, with music by David Byrne, 1983), and dance for the films *Hair* (1979) and *White Nights* (1985).

THATCHER, Margaret Hilda, née **Roberts** (1925–) English Conservative statesman, born in Grantham, the daughter of Alderman Alfred Roberts, a grocer with a small, but expanding, business in the High Street. Margaret Roberts lived over the premises with her parents and sister and assisted in the shop. From Grantham High School she went to Somerville College, Oxford, to read chemistry. She stood unsuccessfully as a Conservative candidate for Dartford in 1950 and 1951, in which year she married Denis Thatcher. She studied law, specializing in tax law, and was called to the bar in 1953. She was elected MP for Finchley (1959), and was appointed joint parliamentary secretary to the ministry of pensions and national insurance (1961–64). She joined the shadow cabinet in 1967. She was secretary of state for education and science (1970–74) and joint shadow chancellor (1974–75). In 1975 she was elected leader of the Conservative party, the first woman party leader in British politics. The Conservative party was elected to government in May 1979 and re-elected with a large majority in June 1983 despite the worst unemployment figures for fifty years. She was greatly assisted by the tide of popular feeling generated by the Falklands War and by the disarray in the opposition parties. Under her leadership, the Conservative party has moved towards a more right-wing position, placing considerable emphasis on the market economy and the shedding of public sector commitments through an extensive privatization programme. Despite the persistence of high unemployment she maintained her parliamentary majority in the 1987 general election, again greatly helped by a fragmented opposition. After ten years in office she has established a personal political philosophy popularly spoken of as 'Thatcherism' and based on a mixture of values gained during her formative years and the resolution to persevere with policies despite objections from her critics and doubts among her supporters.

THAYER, James Bradley (1831–1902) American jurist, born in Haverhill, Massachusetts. Educated at Harvard, where he became a distinguished teacher of law, he wrote an important *Preliminary Treatise on*

Evidence at the Common Law (1898) and numerous other texts.

THEAETETUS (c.414–c.369 BC) Greek mathematician. He was an associate of **Plato** at the Academy, whose work was later used by **Euclid** in Books X and XIII of the *Elements*. Plato named after him the dialogue *Theaetetus*, which was devoted to the nature of knowledge.

THEBAW (1858–1916) last king of Burma. He reigned from 1878; in 1885 he was deposed by the British, and sent as a prisoner to India.

THEED, William (1804–91) English sculptor, born in Trentham, the son of the sculptor William Theed (1764–1817). He studied under **Thorvaldsen** in Rome and executed the Africa group on the Albert Memorial.

THEILER, Max (1899–1972) South African-born American bacteriologist, born in Pretoria. He settled in the USA in 1922, and worked at the Harvard Medical School (1922–30) and the Rockefeller Institute, New York (1930–64), and was later professor at Yale Medical School (1964–67). He was awarded the 1951 Nobel prize for physiology or medicine for his work in connection with yellow fever, for which he discovered the vaccine 17D in 1939.

THELWALL, John (1764–1834) English reformer and lecturer on elocution, born in London. He started as a tailor's apprentice and then studied law, but abandoned his studies for journalism. He supported **Horne Tooke**, with whom he was arrested (1794) for his revolutionary views and sent to the Tower of London, but was acquitted of high treason. Later he took up elocution, and wrote *Treatment of Cases of Defective Utterance* (1814).

THEMISTOCLES (c.523–c.458 BC) Athenian soldier and statesman. As archon in 493 he convinced his countrymen that a powerful fleet was necessary for their welfare. During the second Persian invasion under **Xerxes** he commanded the Athenian squadron, and through his strategy the Greeks won the battle of Salamis (480). The rebuilding of the walls of Athens by his advice on a vastly larger scale aroused uneasiness in Sparta, but Themistocles cajoled the ephors until the walls were high. So the Spartan faction in Athens plotted his ruin, and in 470 he was ostracized. Argos was his first retreat, but the Spartans secured his expulsion (467) and he fled to Corcyra and thence to Asia; **Artaxerxes** of Persia received him with great favour in 484, and listened to his schemes for the subjugation of Greece, and made him governor of Magnesia on the Maeander. His patriotism seems at times to have been merely a larger kind of selfishness, but he was convinced that only he could realize the dream of a great Athenian empire.

THÉNARD, Louis Jacques (1777–1857) French chemist, born in Louptière, a peasant's son. He studied pharmacy at Paris, became professor at the Collège de France and was made a baron in 1825 and chancellor of the University of Paris. He discovered sodium and potassium peroxides, Thénard's blue, which is used for colouring porcelain, and proved that caustic soda and potash contain hydrogen. He was closely associated with **Gay-Lussac** and wrote a once-standard work on chemistry.

THEOBALD, or **Tebaldus** (d.1161) English ecclesiastic. He was a monk at Bec, abbot (1137) and in 1138 became Archbishop of Canterbury. He crowned King **Stephen** in Canterbury, and after the latter's death refused to regard Stephen's son as his successor and eventually crowned **Henry II** (1154). He advanced his archdeacon, **Thomas á Becket**, to the chancellorship in 1155, introduced the study of civil law into England and resisted all attempts by the monasteries to throw off episcopal jurisdiction.

THEOBALD, Lewis (1688–1744) English Shakespearean critic, born in Sittingbourne. He studied law but turned to literature. He published translations of the Greek classics, thirty papers in *Mist's Journal* (1715), and started the *Censor*, a tri-weekly paper. His pamphlet *Shakespeare Restored* (1726) was directed against **Pope**'s edition, and Pope took revenge by making him, unfairly, the hero of the *Dunciad*, though he incorporated many of his corrections in the second edition. Theobald's edition of **Shakespeare** (1734), however, surpassed that of his rival.

THEOCRITUS (c.310–250 BC) Greek pastoral poet, born probably in Syracuse, Sicily. He was brought up on the island of Cos, but lived for a time at the court of **Ptolemy III, Philadelphus** in Alexandria, returning later to Cos. The authenticity of some of his 30 extant bucolic poems has been disputed. They fall into three classes—half-epic, mimic and idyllic. Probably the half-epic poems were the earliest. He wrote a series of poems dealing with heroic legend, especially that of Heracles. His famous 15th Idyll, *The Ladies of Syracuse*, said to be copied from Sophron, describes delightfully the visit of a Syracusan lady and her friend, both living in Alexandria, to the festival of Adonis. Theocritus raised the rude pastoral poetry of the Doric race in Sicily into a new and perfect form of literature. His short poems dealing with pastoral subjects, and representing a single scene, came to be called Idylls (*eidullia*). He combined realism with romanticism, and every touch is natural. **Virgil** imitates him closely in his *Eclogues*; **Tennyson** was deeply influenced by him, as were the pastoral poets of the Renaissance.

THEODERIC See **THEODORIC**

THEODORA (c.500–548) Byzantine empress, wife of **Justinian I**, and the daughter of a circus bear-tamer. An actress and noted beauty, she married Justinian in 525. As his most trusted counsellor she wielded enormous influence in the work of government, and saved the throne by her courage at the crisis of the Nika riots (532). She lavished her bounty on the poor, especially the unfortunate of her own sex.

THEODORAKIS, Mikis (1925–) Greek composer, born in Khios. He studied at the Paris Conservatoire, and in 1959 his ballet *Antigone* was produced at Covent Garden. On his return to Greece he became intensely critical of the Greek musical establishment, and during the 1960s his attacks broadened to embrace most of the artistic world. When the right-wing government took power in 1967 he was imprisoned and his music was officially banned—one of his songs became an 'anthem' of opposition to the military régime. In 1970, after world-wide appeals, he was released, and resigned from the Communist party in 1972, standing as a United Left parliamentary candidate two years later. His prolific musical output includes oratorios, ballets, song-cycles, and music for film scores, including *Zorba the Greek* (1965). His work is inspired by the history and traditions of Greece, and influenced by Byzantine music and Cretan folk tunes.

THEODORE, Kassai (1816–68) king of Abyssinia, nephew of the governor of Kuara. In 1853 he crushed the vice-regent Ras Ali, and, overthrowing the prince of Tigré in 1855, had himself crowned negus of Abyssinia as Theodore II. At first he was guided by two Englishmen, Plowden and Bell; but after they were killed in a rebellion (1860) his rule became tyrannical. He had made several vain attempts to procure the alliance of England and France against his Muhammadan neighbours, and he now began to hate Europeans. A letter sent to Queeen **Victoria** in 1862 went somehow unnoticed, and a fancied slight was also received from **Napoleon III**. Theodore imprisoned the consuls along with other Europeans. Negotiations failed, and a British military expedition under General **Napier** landed in Abyssinia in the spring of 1868, and reached Magdala in April. An Abyssinian attack was repulsed. Theodore sued for peace and released the prisoners, but, as he declined to surrender, the fort was stormed and Theodore shot himself.

THEODORE, 'King of Corsica', otherwise **Baron von Neuhoff** (1686–1756) German adventurer, son of a Westphalian noble. He was born in Metz, served in the French army and the Swedish diplomatic service, became chargé d'affaires to the emperor **Charles VI** and, in 1736, led a Corsican rising against the Genoese, supported by the Turks and the Bey of Tunis. He was elected king, solemnly crowned and raised money by selling knighthoods. He left after seven months to procure foreign aid, but his attempts to return in 1738 and in 1743 were frustrated. He settled in London in 1749, was imprisoned for debt but was set free by a subscription raised by **Horace Walpole**. In Spain he had married an Irish lady, daughter of the Earl of Kilmallock. His only son by her, known as Colonel Frederick (c.1725–97), wrote a book on Corsica, and shot himself in the porch of Westminster Abbey.

THEODORE OF MOPSUESTIA (c.350–428) Greek theologian, born in Antioch. He studied with St **John Chrysostom** under the Greek Sophist Libarines, then became first a monk, then a deacon there, and in 392 bishop of Mopsuestia in Cilicia. The teacher of **Nestorius**, he was, perhaps, the real founder of Nestorianism. He wrote commentaries on almost all the books of Scripture, of which remain, in the Greek, only that on the Minor Prophets; in Latin translations, those on the Epistles of Paul besides many fragments. As an exegete he eschews the allegorical method, adopts the literal meaning, considers the historical and literary circumstances, and assumes varying degrees of inspiration. Already suspected of leaning towards the 'Pelagians', as he was, when the Nestorian controversy broke out, he was attacked over his polemical writings, which were condemned by **Justinian** (544). The fifth ecumenical council (553) confirmed the condemnation.

THEODORE OF TARSUS, St (c.602–690) Greek prelate, born in Tarsus in Cilicia, and consecrated archbishop of Canterbury by Pope Vitalian in 668. In Canterbury he established a Greek school, and organized the administrative system of the English Church.

THEODORET (c.393–458) Greek theologian and Church historian, born in Antioch. He entered a monastery, and in 423 became bishop of Cyrrhus, a city of Syria. As a foremost representative of the school of Antioch he became deeply involved in the Nestorian and Eutychian controversies, and was deposed, in his absence, by the 'Robber Council' of Ephesus in 449. He was restored by the general Council of Chalcedon in 451. His works consist of commentaries on Canticles, the Prophets, Psalms and St Paul's Epistles; a *History of the Church*, from 325 to 429; a *Religious History*, being the lives of the so-called Fathers of the Desert; the *Eranistes*, a dialogue against Eutychianism; and *A Concise History of Heresies*, together with orations and nearly 200 letters.

THEODORIC, or **Theoderic,** surnamed **the Great** (455–526) king of the Ostrogoths and founder of the Ostrogothic monarch. Shortly before he became king (475) the Ostrogoths had overrun Macedonia. After 14 years of petty warfare, sometimes as the ally, sometimes as the enemy, of the Romans, Theodoric obtained from the emperor **Zeno** permission to wrest Italy from **Odoacer.** With 250000 Ostrogoths he completed the conquest after a five years' war, and Odoacer was soon after murdered by Theodoric's own hand. His reign secured for Italy tranquility and prosperity. The Goths and the Romans continued distinct nations, each with its own tribunals and laws. Catholics and Jews enjoyed full liberty of worship, and protection from all encroachment on their civil rights (Theodoric was an Arian). His official letters show his unwearied energy and enlightened zeal for his subjects' welfare. His last three years are tarnished by the judicial murders of **Boethius** and **Symmachus**, and by acts of oppression against the Catholic church. To the Germans he is Dietrich von Bern, and one of the great heroes of legend, figuring in the *Nibelungenlied*.

THEODORIC I (d.451) king of the Visigoths, the son of **Alaric I**, elected king in 418. Alternately an ally and an enemy of Rome, in 421 (or 422) he treacherously joined the Vandals and attacked the Roman troops from behind. In 435 he attacked the Romans in Gaul and besieged Narbonne. Forced to retreat to Toulouse, he there defeated a Roman army (439). On the invasion of **Attila** in 451, he joined the Romans, under **Aëtius**, and at Troyes commanded the right wing. He drove back the Huns under Attila but was killed.

THEODORIC II (d.466) king of the Visigoths, son of **Theodoric I**. He rebelled against his brother and predecessor Thorismund, had him assassinated and ascended the throne in 453. His policy at first was to spread Gothic dominion in Spain and Gaul through the Roman alliance. On the murder of the Emperor Petronius Maximus in 455, he supported Eparchius Avitus in his bid for the Empire, and marched with him into Italy, where he was proclaimed emperor. On his abdication in 456, Theodoric broke the friendship with Rome and besieged Arles, but was forced by the emperor Majorian to make peace. In 462 he made another attempt in Gaul, but was defeated near Orléans (464). He was murdered in 466 by his brother Euric, who succeeded him.

THEODORUS OF SAMOS (6th century BC) Greek sculptor. He is said to have developed sculptural hollow-casting for large figures in bronze, and invented several kinds of tools for use in casting.

THEODOSIUS, the Elder (d.376) Roman soldier, father of **Theodosius I the Great**. By birth a Spaniard, he campaigned in Britain (368–70) against the Caledonians, naming a reconquered district *Valentia* after the emperors. After a victorious campaign on the Upper Danube he quelled a revolt in Africa, but was executed at Carthage on some trumped-up charge.

THEODOSIUS I, the Great (c.346–395) Roman Emperor, son of **Theodosius the Elder**. He was born in Cauca in northwest Spain. He served with distinction until his father's execution induced him to retire (376), but was recalled by **Gratianus** to become his colleague and emperor in the East (379). He campaigned against the Goths, first from Thessalonica, then from Constantinople, but had to allow them to settle within the Roman empire (382). He secured peace with the Persian Sassanids by partitioning Armenia with them (c.386). When the usurper Magnus Maximus killed Gratianus in 383, Theodosius at first recognized him, but when in 387 Maximus expelled **Valentinian II** from Italy, he marched west and defeated and killed Maximus at Aquileia (388). For some years Theodosius lived at Milan in friendship with St **Ambrose** who had great influence over him. In 390, when the governor of Thessalonica was lynched by a circus mob, Theodosius invited the citizens into the circus, and had 7000 of them massacred. Ambrose excommunicated Theodosius for eight months until he had done public penance. In 392 Valentinian II was murdered, and in 394 Theodosius marched against the Franks and their puppet emperor Eugenius. He defeated Eugenius, and for the remaining four months of his life ruled as sole Roman emperor. A pious and intolerant Christian, he summoned in 381 a council at Constantinople to affirm the Nicene Creed, pursued heretics and pagans, and eventually in 391 ordered the closing of all temples and banned all forms of pagan cult.

THEODOSIUS II (401–50), Eastern Roman Emperor from 408, grandson of **Theodosius I, the Great.** He succeeded his father, Arcadius, but allowed the affairs of empire to be managed by his sister, Pulcheria, and his empress, **Eudoxia**.

THEOGNIS (fl.544–541 BC) Greek elegiac poet, a Dorian noble of Megara on the Isthmus of Corinth. During the confusion which followed the overthrow of the tyrant Theagenes, he was driven from Megara, and visited Euboea and Sicily. Under his name survive 1389 elegiac verses, social, political and gnomic, but perhaps only some of them are his.

THEON See **HYPATIA**

THEOPHILUS (d.180), Syrian prelate, and one of the Fathers of the Church. Bishop of Antioch (169–177), he wrote an important Apology of Christianity (c.180).

THEOPHILUS (d.412) patriarch of Alexandria from 385 till his death. He destroyed the pagan temple of Serapis, drove out the Originist monks of Nitria and defended his actions before a synod at Constantinople called by the Emperor **Arcadius** and **St John Chrysostom**. He made peace with the monks but used his influence with the empress **Eudoxia** to have St John banished to Armenia.

THEOPHRASTUS (c.372–c.287 BC) Greek philosopher, born in Eresus on Lesbos. He studied at Athens under **Aristotle**, succeeded him as head of the Peripatetic School (Lyceum) from 322, and shared his encyclopaedic conception of philosophy. Most of his prolific output is lost, but there are still extant important treatises on plants (representative of his interest in natural science), reconstructed fragments of his history of earlier philosophers, and the more literary volume of *Characters*, containing 30 deft sketches of different moral types, which has been widely translated and imitated.

THEOPHYLACT (c.1078–c.1107) Greek ecclesiastic, born in Euripus in Euboea. He became archbishop of Achrida in Bulgaria in 1078. He wrote Bible commentaries, printed in Venice (1754–58), and *The Education of a Prince* for the son of the emperor Michael VII, to whom he had been tutor.

THEOPOMPUS OF CHIOS (c.378–c.300 BC) Greek historian and rhetorician. He studied under **Isocrates**, and was a friend of **Philip II** and **Alexander the Great** of Macedon. He was twice exiled from Chios for Spartan sympathies and wrote *Hellenica*, a history of Greece (411–394), and *Philippica*, a history of the world based on Philip's life, of both of which only fragments remain.

THEORELL, (Axel) Hugo Theodor (1903–82) Swedish biochemist, born in Linköping. Educated at the Karolinska Institute in Stockholm, he was professor at Uppsala (1932) and then director of the Nobel Institute of Biochemistry at Stockholm (1937–70). He worked on myoglobin and was awarded the 1955 Nobel prize for physiology or medicine for his work on oxidation enzymes.

THEOTOCOPOULI See **GRECO, EL**

THERAMENES (fl.411–403 BC) Athenian statesman. He made himself unpopular by a policy of compromise between oligarchy and democracy, and while a member of the government of the Thirty Tyrants incurred the hatred of the most notorious of them all, **Critias**, whose health he drank in the hemlock cup.

THERESA, St See **TERESA**

THERESA OF CALCUTTA, Mother (Agnes Gonxha Bojaxhiu) (1910–) Roman Catholic nun and missionary to India, born in Yugoslavia of Albanian parents. She lived in Skopje as a child. She went to India in 1928, where she joined the Sisters of Loretto (an Irish order in India) and taught at a convent school in Calcutta, taking her final vows in 1937. She became principal of the school, but in 1948 left the convent to work alone in the slums. She went to Paris for some medical training before opening her first school for destitute children in Calcutta. She was gradually joined by other nuns and her House for the Dying was opened in 1952. Her sisterhood, the Order of the Missionaries of Charity (started in 1950), became a pontifical congregation in 1956. In 1957 she started work with lepers. The congregation now has 2000 sisters in 200 branch houses in several countries. In 1971 she was awarded the Pope John XXIII peace prize. She was awarded the Nobel prize for peace in 1979.

THERÈSE OF LISIEUX, St, originally **Thérèse Martin** (1873–97) born in Alençon, France, the youngest daughter of a watchmaker. An intensely religious child, she entered the Carmelite convent of Lisieux in Normandy at the age of 15, where she remained until her death from tuberculosis nine years later. During her last years she wrote an account of her childhood and later life which was edited and published posthumously as the *Histoire d'une âme*. Showing how the most ordinary and insignificant person can attain sainthood by following her 'little way' of simple, childlike, trusting Christianity, the book immediately gained great popularity. She was canonized in 1925, and in 1947 associated with **Joan of Arc** as patron saint of France. Her feast day is 3 October.

THEROUX, Paul Edward (1941–) American writer, born in Medford, Massachusetts. His literary output reflects his footloose life. *Waldo* (1969), his first novel, was followed by fictions that drew on his experience of three years in Africa. He subsequently taught at Singapore University, a sojourn that produced a collection of short stories, *Sinning with Annie* (1976), and a novel, *Saint Jack* (1973). Others, for example *The Family Arsenal* (1976), *Doctor Slaughter* (1984), which made an unfortunate transition to celluloid, and *The London Embassy* (1982), have been based in London where he lives part of the year. His novels are urbane and paradoxical, sometimes bleak and frequently funny. The same can be said of his extended rail journeys, recounted in *The Great Railway Bazaar: By Train Through Asia* (1975), and *The Old Patagonian Express: By Train Through the Americas* (1979), in which Theroux emerges as a crusty loner, an intelligent observer with the tolerance of a misanthrope.

THESEUS legendary hero of Athens, the son of Aegeus, king of Athens, by Aethra, daughter of Pittheus, king of Troezen, at whose court he grew up. His perilous journey back to Athens to succeed his father, according to legend, was a succession of Herculean feats against powerful adversaries, including Procrustes, who fitted everyone he caught into his bed, either by stretching the victim or cutting him down to size; the grey sow of Crommyon and the rebellious Pallantidae, his uncles, at Athens. He was then sent as part of the annual human tribute of six youths and six maidens exacted by **Minos** of Crete, who had defeated the Athenians, to the Minotaur's labyrinth on Crete. Here he was saved by the help of Minos's daughter,

Ariadne, who provided him with a sword to slay the Minotaur and a thread to find his way out of the labyrinth. He forgot to change the black sails of his boat to white ones, signalizing success, on his return to Athens, and Aegeus, expecting the worst, drowned himself. Theseus as ruler continued his legendary exploits, such as his defeat of the Amazons, and is alleged to have united the various communities of Attica into one state. His supposed remains were later brought back by **Cimon** from Scyros to Athens.

THESIGER See **CHELMSFORD**

THESIGER, Wilfred Patrick (1910–) British explorer of Arabia, born in Addis Ababa. Educated at Eton and Oxford, where he got a blue for boxing, he attended the coronation of **Haile Selassie** in 1930, and in 1933 returned to Ethiopia to hunt with the Danakil tribes, exploring the Sultanate of Aussa. In 1935 he joined the Sudan Political Service and while on leave travelled by camel across the Sahara to the Tibesti Mountains. He was seconded to the Sudan Defence Force at the outbreak of World War II, and later served in Abyssinia, Syria and with the SAS in the Western Desert. From 1945 to 1950 he explored the Empty Quarter of southern Arabia and the borderlands of Oman with Bedu companions, which he described in *Arabian Sands* (1959); from 1951 to 1958 he lived with the Marsh Arabs of Iraq. He first travelled in East Africa in 1961, and returned to live with tribal peoples there from 1968 onwards, occasionally returning to London. His travels elsewhere include the Zagros Mountains of Iran, the Hindu Kush and Karakoram mountains, Pakistan, Afghanistan and Northern India, the Atlas Mountains of Morocco, and Yemen. His autobiography, *The Life of My Choice*, was published in 1987.

THESPIS (6th century BC) Greek poet from Icaria, the reputed founder of Greek drama. He is said to have won the first prize for tragedy at a festival in Athens in c.534 BC. According to **Aristotle**, he used single actors to deliver speeches, in addition to the traditional chorus.

THEURIET, André (1833–1907) French poet and novelist, born in Marly-le-Roi, Seine-et-Oise. In 1857 he received a post under the finance minister. His collections of verse include *Le Chemin des bois* (1867), the so-called epic *Les Paysans de l'Argonne*, 1792 (1871) and *Le Bleu et le Noir* (1872). He is best known for his novels *Le Mariage de Gérard* (1875), *Raymonde* (1877) and *Sauvageonne* (1880).

THIARD, Pontus de See **TYARD**

THIBAUD, Jacques (1880–1953) French violinist, born in Bordeaux. He studied at the Paris Conservatoire and, as well as his solo performances, played with **Alfred Cortot** and **Pablo Casals**. He was particularly renowned for his interpretations of **Mozart**, **Beethoven** and **Debussy**. He died in an air crash.

THIBAULT, Jacques See **FRANCE, Anatole**

THIELICKE, Helmut (1908–86) German Lutheran theologian and preacher, born in Barmen. He was dismissed from his post at Heidelburg for criticizing the Nazis, and in 1944 contributed to a draft declaration on church-state relations for a revolutionary government to follow a successful plot against **Hitler**. He was appointed professor of theology at Hamburg after World War II, becoming dean of theology (1954) and university rector (1960), retiring in 1974. A prolific author, best-known perhaps for *The Waiting Father* (1960) and other volumes of sermons, he published substantial studies in theology and ethics, including *The Evangelical Faith* (1974–82), *Theological Ethics* (1951–64, abridged trans 1966–69), *The Ethics of Sex* (1964) and *Living with Death* (1983), though these appeared in Engish much later than his devotional works.

THIERRY, Augustin (1795–1856) French historian, born in Blois. He joined the Paris Liberals in 1814, and published *De la réorganisation de la société européenne*, inspired by **Saint-Simon**, whose secretary he became. In 1817, however, they disagreed, and Thierry attached himself to **Comte**. In 1825 he published his masterpiece, the *Norman Conquest of England*, followed in 1827 by *Lettres sur l'histoire de France*. In 1835 he became librarian at the Palais Royal, and published his *Dix Ans d'études historiques*. His last work was on the *Tiers État* (1853).

THIERS, Louis Adolphe (1797–1877) French statesman and historian, born in Marseilles, and the first president of the Third Republic in 1870. He studied law at Aix, where he made the acquaintance of **Mignet** and cultivated literature rather than the law. In Paris from 1821 he became associated with the Opposition, and wrote his massive *Histoire de la révolution française* (10 vols, 1823–27). In January 1830, along with **Armand Carrel** and Mignet, he started the *National*, and waged relentless war on the Polignac administration. Its attempted suppression brought about the July Revolution; and Thiers entered on an active career as a politician. He was elected deputy for Aix, was appointed secretary-general to the minister of finance, and became one of the most formidable of parliamentary speakers. In 1832 he became minister of the interior, and of commerce and public affairs, and then foreign minister. In 1836 he was appointed president of the council, but in August he resigned, and led the Opposition. Again president of the council and foreign minister (1840), he refused **Palmerston**'s invitation to enter into an alliance with Britain, Austria and Prussia for the preservation of the integrity of the Ottoman Empire, aiming like **Napoleon** at French supremacy in the Levant. Irritation at the isolation of France led to his resignation. He published *L'Histoire du consulat et de l'empire* (20 vols, 1845–62), the most ambitious of all his literary enterprises. Thiers would have hindered the revolution of 1848, and, though he accepted the Republic, was arrested and banished at the *coup d'état* of 1851, being allowed, however, to return the next year. He re-entered the Chamber in 1863, and his speeches were filled with taunts at **Napoleon III** and the second Empire on account of its loss of prestige. After the collapse of the Empire during the Franco-Prussian War, he became head of the provisional government and was elected president of the Republic in August 1870. He negotiated peace with Prussia, and did much to ensure France's economic recovery. He suppressed the Commune in Paris in 1871. He resigned in 1873 and became leader of the opposition.

THIRKELL, Angela Margaret, née **Mackail** (1891–1961) English novelist, daughter of **John William Mackail**, grand-daughter of Sir **Edward Burne-Jones**, and cousin of **Rudyard Kipling**. She wrote more than 30 novels set in 'Barsetshire', dealing with the descendants of characters from **Trollope**'s Barsetshire novels, including *Coronation Summer* (1937) and *Growing Up* (1943).

THIRLWALL, Connop (1797–1875) English prelate and historian, born in Stepney, London. Educated at Charterhouse and Trinity College, Cambridge, he was called to the bar in 1825, but in 1827 took orders. In 1828 he published (with **Julius Charles Hare**) a translation of **Niebuhr**'s *Roman History* (1828); and their Philological Museum (1831–33) contained Thirlwall's 'On the Irony of Sophocles'. He petitioned and wrote (1834) in favour of the admission of Dissenters to degrees and was forced to resign his university appointments, but was given the Yorkshire living of Kirby-Underdale. Here he wrote for *Lardner's Cyclopaedia* his *History of Greece* (1835–44). In 1840 he was made bishop of St David's, Cardiff. He supported the admission of Jews to parliament, and, alone amongst the bishops, the disestablishment of the Irish Church. He was buried in Westminster Abbey, in the same grave as **George Grote**.

THISTLEWOOD, Arthur (1770–1820) English conspirator, born near Lincoln. He served in the army, but, full of revolutionary ideas from his time in America and France, organized a mutiny at Spa Fields (1816) and in 1820 the Cato Street Conspiracy to murder **Castlereagh** and other ministers at Lord Harrowby's. The conspirators were arrested in a stable in Cato (Homer) Street, Edgware Road, and Thistlewood, with four others, was convicted of high treason and hanged.

THOM, Alexander (1894–1985) Scottish engineer and archaeo-astronomer. Educated at Glasgow University, he worked in various engineering firms then returned to Glasgow as lecturer from 1922 to 1939. He was professor of engineering science at Oxford University from 1945 to 1961. From 1934 he was engaged on a detailed study of all the stone circles in the British isles and Brittany, and after his retirement published two major works, *Megalithic Sites in Britain* (1967) and *Megalithic Lunar Observatories* (1971). He brought his engineering skills of mathematics and surveying to bear on the analysis of the data he had collected, and he claimed to have discovered two basic units, the 'megalithic yard' and the 'megalithic inch', which had been used in the setting out of most if not all of the circles. His conclusions have not been universally accepted, but his meticulous surveys are of lasting value in themselves.

THOM, René Frédéric (1923–) French mathematician, born in Montbéliard. He studied at the École Normale Supérieure, and worked at Grenoble and Strasbourg, where he became professor. Since 1964 he has been at the Institut des Hautes Études Scientifiques. In 1958 he was awarded the Fields Medal (the mathematical equivalent of the Nobel prize). His work has been in singularity theory of differentiable manifolds, but he is best known for his book *Stabilité structurelle et morphoqenèse* (1972) which introduced 'catastrophe theory', with applications to widely differing situations such as the development of the embryo, social interactions between human beings or animals, and physical phenomena such as breaking waves. This has had much publicity and aroused some controversy.

THOMA, Hans (1839–1924) German painter and lithographer, born in Bernau in the Black Forest. He is known especially for his landscapes, genre scenes and religious and allegorical works. His early style was influenced by **Courbet**. His paintings include *At Lake of Garda*, *Solitude* and *Scenes from the Life of Christ*.

THOMAS, St, called **Didymus** (1st century) one of the Twelve Apostles. According to John xx, 24–29, he doubted until he had seen proof of **Jesus**' resurrection. One tradition has it that he founded the church in Parthia and was buried in Edessa; another, that he preached in India. The Christians of St Thomas claim him as their founder. He is patron saint of Portugal and his feast day is 21 December.

THOMAS (fl.12th century) Anglo-Norman poet. He was author of the earliest extant text (c.1155–1170) of the legend of Tristan and Iseult, a fragment of 3144 lines covering the final episodes including the death of the lovers. Though he has greater pretensions to a literary style, Thomas lacks the impressive primitive simplicity of Béroul, author of the slightly later and fuller of the two early versions, both of which appear to be based on an earlier poem now lost. He is sometimes confused with **Thomas the Rhymer**.

THOMAS, Albert (1878–1932) French politician, born in Champigny-sur Marne. He was a Socialist member of the Chamber from 1910 to 1921, when he became director of the International Labour Office of the League of Nations.

THOMAS, (Charles Louis) Ambroise (1811–96) French composer, born in Metz. He studied at the Paris Conservatoire (1828–32).He wrote many light operas, of which *Mignon* (1866) is the best known, for the Opéra Comique and the Grand Opéra, and innumerable cantatas, part-songs and choral pieces. He became a member of the Institute (1851), professor of composition (1852) and director of the Conservatoire (1871).

THOMAS, Brandon (1849–1914) English actor and playwright, born in Liverpool. He first appeared as a comedy actor in 1879, and wrote a number of successful light plays, one of which, *Charley's Aunt* (1892), has retained enormous popularity.

THOMAS, Dylan Marlais (1914–53) Welsh poet, born in Swansea, the son of a schoolmaster. He worked for a time as a reporter on the *South Wales Evening Post* and established himself with the publication of *Eighteen Poems* in 1934. He married Caitlin Macnamara in 1936 and published *Twenty-Five Poems* the same year. His other works include *The Map of Love* (1939), *Portrait of the Artist as a Young Dog* (1940), *The World I Breathe* (1940), *Deaths and Entrances* (1946) and a scenario, *The Doctor and the Devils*. His *Collected Poems, 1934–52*, were published in 1952 and he then turned to larger dramatic works. From 1944 he worked intermittently on a radio script about a Welsh seaside village and in its first form it was called *Quite Early One Morning*. Thomas expanded it into *Under Milk Wood* (published 1954). Until then his work had been praised by critics, among them **Edith Sitwell**, for his striking rhythms, his original imagery and his technical ingenuities, but he could in no sense be called a popular writer. *Under Milk Wood* was immediately comprehensible, Rabelaisianly funny, with moments of lyric tenderness, fresh yet recognizable similes, and it presented most of the non-intellectual English concepts of Welsh thought and behaviour. It had a second success as a stage play. In 1955 *Adventures in the Skin Trade* was published, an unfinished novel. He died of alcoholic abuse on a lecture tour of the USA.

THOMAS, Sir Daniel Lleufer (1863–1940) Welsh lawyer, born near Llandeilo, Carmarthenshire. Educated at Jesus College, Oxford, and at Lincoln's Inn, he served as secretary to the Welsh Land Commission before he returned to Wales to serve for 30 years as stipendary magistrate for Pontypridd and Rhondda. He was influential in the establishment of the National Library of Wales and took a keen interest in the University of Wales and in other Welsh educational and cultural bodies.

THOMAS, (Philip) Edward (1878–1917) English poet and nature writer, born in London of Welsh parents. He was educated at St Paul's School and Lincoln College, Oxford, where he got married. He became a hack writer of reviews, critical studies and topographical works. Not until 1914, encouraged by **Robert Frost**, did he realize his potential as a poet, writing most of his poetry during active service in World War I. *Six Poems* was published in 1916. He died in action at Arras (April 1917) before the publication of *Poems* (1917), under the pseudonym 'Edward Eastaway'. His impressive poetry, though rooted in the English tradition of nature poetry, broke with the

Georgian tradition in its lack of rhetoric and formality and in its emphasis on the austerity of Nature and solitariness of man. He also wrote a novel, *The Happy-Go-Lucky Morgans* (1913), and several books about the English countryside

THOMAS, Freeman Freeman- See **WILLINGDON**

THOMAS, George Henry (1816–70) American soldier, born in Southampton County, Virginia. He graduated at West Point, entered the artillery in 1840, and gained three brevets for gallantry. In the Civil War (1861–65) he joined the Federal army in 1861, was appointed brigadier-general of volunteers, and in January 1862 won the battle of Mill Springs. Major-general in command of the centre of Rosencrans's army, he saved the battle of Stones River; and at Chickamauga again rendered the victory a barren one for the Confederates (September 1863). In October 1863 he was given the command of the Army of the Cumberland, and in November captured Mission Ridge. In 1864 he commanded the centre in **Sherman**'s advance on Atlanta, was sent to oppose **Hood** in Tennessee in December and won the battle of Nashville. He afterwards commanded the military division of the Pacific.

THOMAS, Hugh Owen (1833–91) Welsh orthopaedic surgeon, born in Anglesey. He studied medicine at University College, London, Edinburgh University and in Paris, and practised surgery in Liverpool. He pioneered orthopaedic surgery, constructing many appliances which are still used, especially Thomas's splints for the hip and the knee.

THOMAS, James Henry (1874–1949) Welsh Labour politician, born in Newport, Monmouthshire; an enthusiastic trade unionist, he was elected MP for Derby in 1910. As assistant secretary of the Amalgamated Society of Railway Servants he helped to organize the strike of 1911 and the merger of smaller unions in 1913 which formed the National Union of Railwaymen, of which he ultimately became general secretary (1917). He led the successful railway strike of 1919. When Labour came to power in 1924 he was appointed colonial secretary, and in **Ramsay MacDonald**'s 1929 Cabinet he was lord privy seal, subsequently becoming dominions secretary (1930–35). His adherence to the 1931 National Government aroused the hostility of his former Labour colleagues; and the ensuing bitterness clouded the last few years of his political career, which came to an untimely end when, as colonial secretary (1935–36), he was found guilty by a judicial tribunal of divulging budget secrets. He wrote *My Story* (1937).

THOMAS, Margaret Haig, Viscountess Rhondda (1883–1958) Welsh feminist and owner-editor of *Time and Tide*, born in London, the daughter of David Alfred Thomas (1st Viscount **Rhondda**). She studied, briefly, at Somerville College, Oxford (before women were allowed to take degrees at Oxford), became a suffragette, was arrested for trying to chemical-bomb letters inside a postbox, but was released after hunger-striking. She worked in her father's business during his wartime goverment service as Food Controller; she had previously been lucky to escape from the *Lusitania* (1915). On her father's death in 1918 she attempted to take her seat in the House of Lords as Viscountess Rhondda, but was kept out after extensive legal proceedings. She founded *Time and Tide*, a weekly journal of politics and literature, in 1920, and personally ran it from 1926. It was largely liberal Right-wing, with a warm welcome for refugees and outcasts whose work was boycotted elsewhere. **Orwell** published his *exposé* of Stalinist repression in Republican Spain in it after they were rejected by the *New Statesman* and he later became its film critic with visible effects in *1984*. It probably tapped a more fruitful and more independent cross-section of British intellectual life than most journals, but it was in deep financial trouble when she died.

THOMAS, Martha Carey (1857–1935) American feminist and educationist, born in Baltimore. Educated privately and at Cornell University, she took a PhD at Zürich (1882), and became dean and professor of English at Bryan Mawr College for Women, which she had helped to organize (president 1894–1922). She established summer schools for women working in industry (1921) and campaigned for women's right to vote. She was author of *The Higher Education of Women* (1900).

THOMAS, Norman Mattoon (1884–1968) American socialist leader, born in Marion, Ohio. Educated at Bucknell University and Princeton, he worked in social settlements, studied theology and was ordained a Presbyterian minister, becoming pastor of East Harlem Church in New York City (1911–31). Horrified by the poverty he encountered, he became imbued with the Social Gospel, and became a pacifist and socialist. He founded and edited *The World Tomorrow* (1918–21), helped found the American Civil Liberties Union in 1920, worked as associate editor on the *Nation* weekly (1921–22), and was co-director of the League for Industrial Democracy (1922–37). He was unsuccessful socialist candidate for governor of New York (1924) and for the US presidency in 1928, 1932, 1936, 1940, 1944 and 1948, his best showing being in 1932. He became leader of the Socialist Party of America on the death of **Eugene V Debs** in 1926. His many books included *Is Conscience a Crime?* (1927), *As I See It* (1932), *A Socialist's Faith* (1951) and *The Prerequisites for Peace* (1959).

THOMAS, R S (Ronald Stuart) (1913–) Welsh poet and priest, born in Cardiff. Educated at the University College of North Wales, Bangor, he trained for the church at St Michael's College, Llandaff. He was ordained deacon in 1936 and priest in 1937. He was rector of Manafon (1942–54), vicar of Eglwysach (1954–67), and vicar of St Hywyn, Aberdaron (1967–78). He published his first, deceptively simple volume of poetry, *The Stones of the Field* in 1946, followed by *An Acre of Land* (1952) and *The Minister* (1953). He only came to attention outside Wales with the publication of *Song at the Year's Turning* (1955). His later volumes, such as *Poetry for Supper* (1958), *The Bread of Truth* (1963), *Laboratories of the Spirit* (1976), and *Between Here and Now* (1981), deal with pastoral themes and the nature of God, coupled with an intense love of Wales and its people, evoked by his use of nature imagery. His recent works include *Later Poems, 1972–1982* (1983) and *Experimenting with an Amen* (1986).

THOMAS, Sidney Gilchrist (1850–85) English metallurgist, born in London. A police-court clerk, he studied at Birkbeck College and discovered a method of separating the phosphorus impurities from iron in the Bessemer converter.

THOMAS À BECKET See **BECKET**

THOMAS À KEMPIS See **KEMPIS**

THOMAS AQUINAS See **AQUINAS**

THOMASIUS, Christian (1655–1728) German philosopher and jurist, born in Leipzig. He lectured on law there and at Berlin, and became professor of jurisprudence at the newly founded University of Halle. He helped establish Halle as a leading, progressive centre, departing from the medieval, scholastic curriculum and separating philosophy from theology. In this spirit he was the first to lecture not in Latin but in vernacular German. His works include *Institutiones Jurisprudentiae divinae* (1688) and *Fundamenta iuris naturae et gentium* (1705).

THOMAS OF CELANO See **CELANO**

THOMAS OF HEREFORD, St See **CANTELUPE**

THOMAS OF WOODSTOCK (1355–97) youngest son of **Edward III**, born at Woodstock. He was created Duke of Gloucester in 1385. He led the opposition of the lords appellant to **Richard II**, was arrested in 1397 and imprisoned at Calais, where he died.

THOMASON, George (d.1666) English bookseller and publisher. He made a complete and valuable collection of tracts and pamphlets printed in England during the years of the Civil War and the Restoration. These were given to the British Museum by **George III** in 1762.

THOMAS THE RHYMER, or **Thomas Rymour of Erceldoune** (c.1220–c.1297) Scottish seer and poet. He lived at Erceldoune (now Earlston, Berwickshire), and in 1286 is said to have predicted the death of **Alexander III** and the battle of Bannockburn, thus becoming known as 'True Thomas'. **Boece** calls him Thomas Learmont. Legend relates that he was carried off to Elfland, and after three years allowed to revisit the earth, but ultimately returned to his mistress, the fairy queen. In a charter of Petrus de Haga of Bemersyde c.1260–70 the Rhymer appears as a witness; and in another of 1294 Thomas of Erceldoune, 'son and heir of Thomas Rymour of Erceldoune', conveys lands to the hospice of Soutra. The Rhymer's 'prophecies' were collected and published in 1603. Sir **Walter Scott** believed him to be the author of the poem of *Sir Tristrem*, which was founded on a 12th-century French poem by another Thomas, a poet of genius, almost certainly an Englishman.

THOMPSON, Benjamin See **RUMFORD**

THOMPSON, Daley (1958–) English athlete, born in London. A specialist in the decathlon, he won the gold medal at the Olympic Games of 1980 and 1984. He was victorious in the 1983 World Championships, but at Seoul in 1988 was affected by injury and came fourth.

THOMPSON, Sir D'Arcy Wentworth (1860–1948) Scottish zoologist and classical scholar, born in Edinburgh and educated at The Edinburgh Academy and Trinity College, Cambridge. He was professor of biology at Dundee (1884–1917) and St Andrews (from 1917). His study *On Growth and Form* (1917) has literary as well as scientific merit. Other works include papers on fisheries and oceanography, a *Glossary of Greek Birds* (1895) and a *Glossary of Greek Fishes* (1945).

THOMPSON, David (1770–1857) English-born Canadian fur trader and explorer. Educated at the Grey Coat School, Westminster, and apprenticed to the Hudson Bay Company he spent 13 years working as a fur trader, before becoming surveyor under Philip Turner mapping the Saskatchewan, Hayes, Nelson and Churchill Rivers and a route to Lake Athabasca. In 1797 he joined the North West Company travelling 4000 miles from Lake Superior to Lake Winnipeg and across the Rockies to settle on the Columbia River (1907), subsequently surveying its entire course and opening many trading posts. He settled in Montreal in 1812 after travelling 50000 miles and drew his outstanding map of western Canada. He took part in the US-Canada Boundary Commission of 1816. He was married to a half-Indian woman, had 16 children and campaigned against alcohol abuse among the Indians.

THOMPSON, Edith (d.1923) English murderess. With her accomplice Frederick Bywaters she was tried in 1922 for stabbing her husband on the way home from a London theatre. The trial at the Old Bailey caused a sensation; the couple were found guilty, and in spite of many petitions for reprieve were executed.

THOMPSON, Elizabeth Southerden See **BUTLER, Sir William Francis**

THOMPSON, Flora (June), née **Timms** (1876–1947) English social historian, born in Juniper Hill, Oxfordshire. She left school at 14 to work in the local post office. She married young and with her postmaster husband settled in Bournemouth, writing mass-market fiction to help support her increasing family. In her sixties she published the semi-autobiographical trilogy combined as *Lark Rise to Candleford* (1945), its three parts, *Lark Rise*, *Over to Candleford* and *Candleford Green* having appeared separately. It is an oustanding feat of observation and memory, showing the erosion of rural society before modern industrialism.

THOMPSON, Francis (1859–1907) English poet, born in Preston, Lancashire. He was brought up in the Catholic faith and studied for the priesthood at Ushaw College. By temperament unsuited for this, he turned to medicine at Owens College, Manchester, but failed to graduate. He moved to London, where extreme poverty and ill-health drove him to become an opium addict. From this he was rescued by Wilfrid and **Alice Meynell**, to whom he had sent some poems for the magazine *Merry England*. His health was restored at the monastery of Storrington Priory in Sussex, where he wrote several poems, including the well-known *Hound of Heaven*. From then on the Meynells looked after him until his death from tuberculosis. His works include *Poems* (1893), *Sister Songs* (1895, written for the Meynell girls) and *New Poems* (1897). His notable *Essay on Shelley* (1909) appeared posthumously, as did his *Life of St Ignatius Loyola* (1909). His poems, mainly religious in theme, are rich in imagery and poetic vision.

THOMPSON, Hunter Stockton (1939–) American journalist, author, editor and small game hunter, born in Louisville, Kentucky. An adherent of the 'new journalism', he eshews objectivity, his search for a story taking him into 'the middle of whatever I'm writing about'. This has led to bizarre incidents and idiosyncratic reportage, marked by intemperate language and behaviour. He was the first reporter to infiltrate the Hell's Angels and rode with them for a year, an experience which led to his being savagely beaten up and a book, *Hell's Angels: A Strange and Terrible Saga* (1966). The acme of the anti-establishment, he styled his unique brand of journalism 'Gonzo', awarded himself a doctorate and produced a stream of books as outspoken as they were outrageous, including *Fear and Loathing in Las Vegas* (1972), *Fear and Loathing on the Campaign Trail* (1972), *The Great Shark Hunt* (1972), *The Curse of Lono* (1977) and *Generation of Swine* (1988). Much of his work appeared originally in magazines, particularly *Scanlan's*, *Rolling Stone* and the *National Observer*, and at the end of the 1980s he contributed a weekly column to the *San Francisco Examiner*.

THOMPSON, Sir John Sparrow David (1844–94) Canadian statesman, born in Halifax. He entered the Nova Scotia Legislature in 1877, became premier of Nova Scotia (1881) and of Canada in 1892. He was knighted in 1888 and died at Windsor, on a visit to England.

THOMPSON, John Taliaferro (1860–1940) American soldier and inventor, born in Newport, Kentucky. He graduated in 1882 at the Military Academy. In 1920 he invented the Thompson submachine gun known as the 'Tommy' gun, which was a .45 calibre gun weighing

10 lb. It was first used for military purposes by the US Marines in Nicaragua in 1925.

THOMPSON, John Vaughan (1779–1847) English zoologist and army surgeon. He studied marine zoology, distinguishing himself by his discoveries, especially that crustaceans passed through a series of metamorphoses when young, and that barnacles were crustaceans and not molluscs.

THOMPSON, Randall (1899–1984) American composer, born in New York. He studied under **Ernest Bloch**, and from 1922–25 was a fellow of the American Academy at Rome, subsequently teaching at Harvard, Princeton and California. His music assimilates romantic and popular American idioms, and includes symphonies, an oratorio (*The Peaceable Kingdom*), *The Testament of Freedom*, (a setting of passages from the writings of **Thomas Jefferson**), and chamber, piano, orchestral and theatre music, including two operas. In the 1960s and 70s he concentrated mainly on sacred vocal music.

THOMPSON, Silvanus Phillips (1851–1916) English physicist, born in York. Professor of physics and principal of the City and Guilds Technical College, Finsbury, he wrote on electricity, light and magnetism as well as a witty, effective little book called *Calculus made Easy* (1910).

THOMPSON, William (1785–1833) Irish economic theorist and feminist, born in Rosscarbery, County Cork. He inherited extensive landed wealth, which led him to study economic problems. He adopted the co-operatist ideas of **Robert Owen**, and his awareness of wealth as the product of labour later influenced **Karl Marx** and **James Connolly**. His *An Enquiry into the Principles of the Distribution of Wealth Most Conducive to Human Happiness* (1824) demanded the reapportionment of wealth and denounced unearned income and private property. He followed it with a manifesto calling for sexual equality in *Appeal of One Half of the Human Race, Women, against the Pretentions of the Other Half, Men, to Retain them in Political, and thence in Civil and Domestic, Slavery* (1825). On his death he left most of his estate to aid the poor, but his will was set aside after years of litigation.

THOMS, William John (1803–85) English antiquary and bibliographer, born in Westminster. After 20 years as a clerk in Chelsea Hospital, he became a clerk to the House of Lords, and its deputy librarian (1863–82). He founded (1849) and edited (till 1872) *Notes and Queries*, devised the word 'folklore', and edited *Early Prose Romances* (1828).

THOMSEN, Christian Jörgensen (1788–1865) Danish archaeologist and numismatist, whose Three Age System introduced the idea of time and sequence to prehistoric studies. Born in Copenhagen, the son of a wealthy businessman, he collected coins, antiquities and paintings from an early age, but continued to work part time for the family firm until his 50s. In 1816 he was appointed secretary of the Royal Commission for the Preservation of Antiquities, charged with organizing its pre-Roman collections for display in the new National Museum in Copenhagen. On the basis of the material used in making weapons and tools, he classified the specimens into three groups representing chronologically successive ages of Stone, Bronze and Iron, expounding this scheme vigorously to the public when the museum opened in 1819 and eventually describing it in print in 1836 in his *Ledetraad til Nordisk Oldkyndighed* (*A Guide to Northern Antiquities*, 1848). Its message reinforced in his pupil **Jens Jacob Worsaae**'s *Danmarks Oldtid* (*The Primeval Antiquities of Denmark*, 1849), the book became widely influential, establishing the basis for the subsequent development of Old World prehistory.

THOMSEN, Vilhelm (1842–1927) Danish philologist, born in Copenhagen. He was professor there from 1875, wrote *The Relations between Ancient Russia and Scandinavia* (1878) and deciphered the Orkhon inscriptions (1893).

THOMSON, Sir Charles Wyville (1830–82) Scottish marine biologist and oceanographer, born in Bonsyde, Linlithgow. He studied at Edinburgh and held professorships in natural history at Cork, Belfast (1854–68) and Edinburgh (1870–82). He was famous for his deep-sea researches, described in *The Depths of the Oceans* (1872), and in 1872 was appointed scientific head of the *Challenger* round-the-word expedition (1872–76), and wrote *The Voyage of the Challenger* (1877).

THOMSON, David Couper (1861–1954) Scottish newspaper proprietor, born in Dundee. At the age of 23 he left the family shipping firm to take charge of the newly-acquired Dundee newspaper concern, which he owned and managed until his death. Its principal publications were the *Dundee Courier and Advertiser*, the *Sunday Post*, the *Scots Magazine* (founded in 1739) and *The People's Friend*, but it was known outside Scotland particularly for its many popular children's comics, such as the *Beano* and *Dandy*. Well-known for his concern for local interests, he was a deputy lieutenant for the City of Dundee for 54 years, and a governor of the university college of Dundee for 62 years. He always resisted unionization in his company.

THOMSON, Elihu (1853–1937) English-born American inventor, born in Manchester. He emigrated to the USA and was educated in Philadelphia, becoming a chemistry teacher. He co-operated in his 700 patented electrical inventions, which include the three-phase alternating-current generator and arc lighting, with **Edwin James Houston**, founding the Thomson-Houston Electric Company (1883), which merged with **Thomas Edison**'s in 1892 to form the General Electric Company.

THOMSON, George (1757–1851) Scottish folksong collector and music publisher, born in Limekilns, Fife. He was chief clerk to the Board of Trustees for the Encouragement of Art and Manufacture in Scotland for 60 years. He collected melodies of folksongs and engaged **Robert Burns** and others to contribute works and settings. He published *A Select Collection of Original Scottish Airs* (6 vols, 1793–1841).

THOMSON, Sir George Paget (1892–1975) English physicist, son of Sir **Joseph Thomson**. He was born and educated in Cambridge, where he became a fellow of Trinity College. He served in the Royal Flying Corps in World War I, was professor of physics at Aberdeen (1922) and Imperial College, London (1930), and master of Corpus Christi (1952–62). In 1937 he shared the Nobel prize for physics with **Clinton Davisson** for their discovery, separately and by different methods, of electron diffraction by crystals. He was scientific adviser to the UN Security Council (1946–47) and for his contributions to electrical science he was awarded the Faraday medal by the Institution of Electrical Engineers (1960). His works include *The Atom* (1937) and *Theory and Practice of Electron Diffraction* (1939).

THOMSON, James (1700–48) Scottish poet, born in Kelso. He was educated at Jedburgh School and studied at Edinburgh University for the ministry, but he abandoned his studies and went to seek his fortune as a writer in London. He published *Winter* (1726), a short poem in blank verse, *Summer* (1727), *Spring*, (1728), and *Autumn* which appeared with the other three under the collective title *The Seasons* (1730). It was substantially revised in 1744, and became a source-book for much later bird poetry. In 1729 his *Sophonisba* was produced. His other tragedies were *Agamemnon* (1738), *Edward and Eleonora* (1739), *Tancred and Sigismunda* (1745) and *Coriolanus* (1748). The poem *Liberty* (1735–1736) was inspired by the Grand Tour which he undertook as tutor to **Charles Talbot**'s son in 1731, and was dedicated to the Prince of Wales, who awarded him a pension. 'A Poem sacred to the Memory of Isaac Newton' (1727) and 'Britannia' (1729), which criticized **Walpole**'s foreign policy, secured him further patronage and the sinecure of surveyor-general of the Leeward Isles (1744). *Alfred, a Masque* (1740) contains the song 'Rule Britannia', also claimed by **Mallet**. The Spenserian *The Castle of Indolence* (1748) is considered his masterpiece.

THOMSON, James (1822–92) Scottish engineer, elder brother of Lord **Kelvin**, born in Belfast. He was professor of engineering at Belfast (1851) and Glasgow (1873–89). An authority on hydraulics, he invented a turbine, discovered the effect of pressure upon the freezing-point of water, and wrote papers on elastic fatigue, under-currents and trade winds.

THOMSON, James, occasional pseud **'B V'** (1834–82) Scottish poet, born in Port Glasgow, the son of a merchant seaman. He was educated in the Royal Caledonian Asylum orphanage and trained as an army schoolmaster at the Royal Military Asylum, Chelsea, but was dismissed from army service for alcoholism in 1862. Through his friend **Charles Bradlaugh** he contributed (1862–75) to the *National Reformer*, in which appeared many of his sombre, sonorous poems, including *The City of Dreadful Night* (1874), his greatest work. He became a lawyer's clerk in 1862, went into business (1864–69), went to the USA as a mining agent (1872–73), was war correspondent in Spain with the Carlists (1873), and from 1875 onwards depended largely on contributions to a tobacconists' trade monthly. Ill-health and melancholia drove him to narcotics and stimulants. *The City of Dreadful Night and other Poems* (1880) was followed by *Vane's Story* (1881), *Essays and Phantasies* (1881), *A Voice from the Nile* (1884), *Shelley, a Poem* (1885), and *Biographical and Critical Studies* (1896). His pseudonym B V, Bysshe Vanolis, was partly from **Shelley**'s second name, partly from an anagram of **Novalis**.

THOMSON, John (1778–1840) Scottish clergyman and painter, born in Dailly manse, Ayrshire. He was minister of Dailly in succession to his father from 1800, and from 1805 of Duddingston. He studed painting under **Alexander Nasmyth** and became one of the first and most successful landscape painters of Scotland.

THOMSON, Joseph (1858–95) Scottish explorer, born near Thornhill, Dumfriesshire. He studied geology at Edinburgh University and joined the Royal Geographical Society east-central African Expedition (1878–79), taking charge on the death of the leader. He was the first European to reach Lake Nyasa (Malawi) from the north and went on to Lake Tanganyika which he described in *To the Central African Lakes and Back* (1881). An unsuccessful attempt to search for coal in the Rovuma River valley for the sultan of Zanzibar was followed in 1882 by an invitation from the Royal Geographical Society to find a route through hostile Masai country from the coast via Mount Kilimanjaro to Lake Victoria; this took him across the Nijiri Desert through the Great Rift Valley and led to his discovery of Lake Baringo and Mount Elgon. His careful notes throughout greatly added to the geographical knowledge of East Africa. For the British National African (later Royal Niger) Company he explored Sokoto in north-western Nigeria (1885), and for a South African company the Upper Congo (1890). He also travelled in the Atlas mountains of Morocco.

THOMSON, Sir Joseph John (1856–1940) English physicist, discoverer of the electron, one of the outstanding pioneers of nuclear physics, born in Cheetham Hill near Manchester, the son of a Scottish bookseller. He entered Owen's College, Manchester, at 14 with the intention of becoming a railway engineer, but a scholarship took him to Trinity College, Cambridge, where he graduated second wrangler. In 1884 at the age of 27 he succeeded Lord **Rayleigh** as Cavendish professor of experimental physics, and in 1919 was himself succeeded by his brilliant student, **Ernest Rutherford**. Thomson's early theoretical work was concerned with the extension of **James Clerk Maxwell**'s electromagnetic theories. This led to the study of gaseous conductors of electricity and in particular the nature of cathode rays. Using **Wilhelm Röntgen**'s discovery of X-rays (1895), he showed that cathode rays were rapidly-moving particles, and by measuring their speed and specific charge, the latter by two independent methods, he deduced that these 'corpuscles' (electrons) must be nearly two thousand times smaller in mass than the lightest known atomic particle, the hydrogen ion. This, the greatest revolution in physics since **Newton**, was inaugurated by his lecture to the Royal Institution, in 1897, and published in the *Philosophical Magazine*. Before the outbreak of World War I, Thomson had successfully studied the nature of positive rays (1911), and this work was crowned by the discovery of the isotope. During the war he was engaged in admiralty research and helped to found the department of scientific and industrial research. 'J J' made the Cavendish Laboratory the greatest research institution in the world. Although simplicity of apparatus was carried to 'string and sealing wax' extremes, seven of his research assistants subsequently won the Nobel prize. He was the first man of science to become master of Trinity College (1918–40). Thomson himself was awarded the Nobel prize for physics (1906). He was buried near Newton in the nave of Westminster Abbey. In 1936 he published *Recollections and Reflections*.

THOMSON, Peter (1929–) Australian golfer, born in Melbourne. The first outstanding golfer to emerge from Australia after World War II, he won the British Open three times in succession (1954–56) and on two later occasions. He also played in Australia's winning World Cup teams of 1954 and 1959.

THOMSON, Robert William (1822–73) Scottish engineer and inventor, born in Stonehaven. He was intended for the pulpit but, rebelling against classical studies, spent some time as a workshop apprentice while educating himself in mathematics and other practical subjects. He devised a method of detonating explosive charges by electricity, and for some time was employed as a civil engineer on the construction of railways. In 1845 he patented a vulcanized rubber pneumatic tyre which was successfully tested in London but was thought to be too expensive for general use; it had been quite forgotten by the time **John Boyd Dunlop** re-invented the pneumatic tyre in 1888. Thomson patented the principle of the fountain pen in 1849, and while working as a sugar plantation engineer in Java he designed greatly improved production machinery and the first mobile steam crane. He patented in 1867 a steam traction engine with hinged segmental driving wheels supporting the weight of the vehicle on rubber pads; it was very successful in moving the heaviest loads over poor or even non-existent roads.

THOMSON, Roy Herbert, 1st Baron Thomson of Fleet (1894–1976) Canadian-born British newspaper and television magnate, born in Toronto, son of a Scottish barber. Successively clerk, salesman, farmer, stenographer and book-keeper, he gained a commission in the Canadian militia during World War I. He became prosperous when, as a radio salesman, he set up his own commercial transmitter at North Bay (1931) in an area of poor reception, thus boosting sales and founding what later became the NBC network. He started more radio stations and acquired 28 Canadian and 6 American newspapers, which he turned over to his son in 1953. In that year he settled in Edinburgh on acquiring his first British paper, *The Scotsman*, and associated publications. In 1957 he obtained a licence for commercial television in Scotland and in 1959 he became one of Britain's leading newspaper proprietors with the acquisition of the Kemsley newspapers, which included the *Sunday Times*. In 1966 he acquired *The Times*. His son, Kenneth Roy, 2nd Baron Thomson (1923–), succeeded him as Chairman of the Thomson Organization.

THOMSON, Thomas (1768–1852) Scottish antiquary, educated at Dailly parish school and Glasgow University. A friend of Sir **Walter Scott**, he became deputy clerk register and collaborated in founding the Bannatyne Club to publish historical records. He edited many vital Scottish historical records, particularly the great *Acts of the Parliaments of Scotland (1424–1707)*, and instituted systems for the orderly preservation of the public records of Scotland, work which is still continuing.

THOMSON, Virgil (1896–1989) American composer and critic, born in Kansas City. Educated at Harvard and Paris, he set some of the writings of **Gertrude Stein** to music, and wrote operas, *Four Saints in Three Acts* (1934), first performed by a black cast, and *The Mother of Us All* (1947), besides symphonies, ballets, choral, chamber and film music. His work was notable for its simplicity of style. He was music critic of the *New York Herald Tribune* from 1940 to 1954.

THOMSON, Sir William See **KELVIN, Lord**

THONET, Michael (1796–1871) German furniture manufacturer, born in Boppard-am-Rhein. Trained as a cabinet-maker, he established a workshop in Boppard (1819) and first gained prominence for his techniques, developed in the 1830s, of laminating wood veneers with glue to construct a form of bentwood furniture. Having moved to Vienna in 1842 he developed the method of steaming and bending solid beech components for making a wide range of furniture, some of which was mass-produced on an enormous scale. The company passed to his sons as Gebrüder Thonet in 1853, while he retained effective control until his death. The firm built several factories in areas of beech forest in various parts of what are now Czechoslovakia and Hungary, and developed into possibly the largest-ever furniture-making enterprise. It has adapted readily to technological and design developments, and having been a leader in the use of tubular steel and plastics while maintaining its use of laminated veneers, it remains today a major manufacturer.

THORARENSEN, Bjarni Vigfússon (1786–1841) Icelandic romantic poet and jurist, born at Brautarholt and brought up at Hlíðarendi. A precociously brilliant student, he went to Copenhagen University at the age of 15 to study law. After government service in Denmark, he was appointed a deputy justice in Reykjavík (1811), and justice of the supreme court (1817). In 1833 he was appointed governor of North and East Iceland. As a lyric poet he celebrated Icelandic nature and nationalism, using the metres of classical heroic poetry; one of his poems, *Eldgamla Ísafold* ('Ancient Iceland') was regarded as an unofficial national anthem, set to the music of *God Save the Queen*.

THORBURN, Archibald (1860–1935) Scottish bird artist, born in Lasswade, near Edinburgh, the son of a painter. He studied at St John's Wood School of Art in London, and his first paintings were hung in the Royal Academy when he was only 20. He painted the majority of the plates of the monumental *Coloured Figures of the Birds of the British Isles* (1885–97). He also published *British Birds* (4 vols, 1915–16) and *British Mammals* (1920), and his paintings were used for T A Coward's *The Birds of the British Isles and their Eggs* (1920) and the immensely popular *Observer's Book of British Birds* (1937). More than 100 of his paintings have been reproduced as prints.

THOREAU, Henry David (1817–62) American essayist and poet, the 'hermit of Walden', born of Jersey stock in Concord, Massachusetts. He graduated from Harvard in 1837, became a teacher in Concord, and lectured. He soon gave up teaching, and joined his father in making lead pencils, but about 1839 began his walks and studies of nature as the serious occupation of his life. In 1839 he made the voyage described in his *Week on the Concord and Merrimack Rivers* (1849). Thoreau made the acquaintance of **Emerson**, and between 1841 and 1843 and in 1847 was a member of his household. In 1845 he built himself a shanty in the woods by Walden Pond, where he lived from 1845 to 1847 and wrote much of the *Week*, his essay on **Carlyle**, and the American classic, *Walden, or Life in the Woods* (1854). After the Walden episode he supported himself by whitewashing, gardening, fence building and land surveying. He also lectured now and then, and wrote for magazines. He made three trips to the Maine woods in 1846, 1853 and 1857, described in papers collected after his death (1864). In 1850 he made a trip to Canada, which produced *A Yankee in Canada* (1866). In 1835 he began to keep a daily journal of his walks and observations, from whose 30 volumes were published *Early Spring in Massachusetts* (1881), *Summer* (1884), and *Winter* (1887). Other publications are *Excursions in Field and Forest*, with memoir by Emerson (1863), *Cape Cod* (1865), *Letters to Various Persons*, with nine poems (1865), *Familiar Letters* (1894) and *Poems of Nature* (1896), and a celebrated essay, *Civil Disobedience* (1849), provoked by his opposition to the Mexican War.

THORFINN, properly **Thorfinnur Karlsefni** (fl.1000) Icelandic explorer, and colonizer of 'Vínland' (Wineland, North America). Around 1000 AD he led an expedition of would-be colonists from Greenland, which sailed along the north-eastern coasts of North America, which had previously been discovered and explored by **Leif the Lucky**. He attempted to found a Norse colony in an area called *Vínland*, somewhere to the south of Newfoundland. The venture was abandoned after three years because of hostility from the native Indians. The story is told in two Icelandic sagas, *Eiriks saga* and *Grænlendinga saga*.

THORGILSSON, Ari (1068–1148) known as 'Ari the Learned', Icelandic churchman and historian, the first to write a prose history of Iceland in the vernacular. He wrote *Íslandingabók* (Book of Icelanders, c.1120), a brief account of the Settlement of Iceland and the Conversion to Christianity in the year 1000 AD. He is also believed to have been the author of the seminal work on Iceland's origins, *Landnámabók* (Book of Settlements), which gives an account of 430 of the principal Norse settlers and their families and descendants.

THORKELIN, real name **Grímur Jónsson** (1752–1829) Icelandic scholar and antiquary, the first editor of the Anglo-Saxon epic, *Beowulf*. Educated at the university in Copenhagen, he was professor there, and in 1791 was appointed keeper of the secret Danish archives. He found the manuscript of *Beowulf* in the British Museum in London and made two transcripts of it; his original edition was destroyed during the British bombardment of Copenhagen in 1807, but he set to work again and published it in 1815 as *De danorum rebus gestis . . . poema Danicum, dialecto Anglo-saxonia*. He also encouraged **John Jamieson** in the production of his *Etymological Dictionary of the Scottish Language*.

THORLÁKSSON, Guðbrandur (1542–1627) Icelandic prelate and scholar, born at Staðarbakki, Miðfjörður, the son of a Catholic priest and his mistress. He studied theology at Copenhagen University, and became a versatile humanist scholar. Appointed bishop of Hólar, in north Iceland, in 1570, he was responsible for the translation and production of the first complete Bible in Icelandic (*Guðbrandarbiblía*, 1584) at the printing press there. This Bible completed the process of the Reformation in Iceland, and stabilized the classical Icelandic language as effectively as the *Authorized Version* of the English Bible (1611). He wrote and published a host of other works, including a hymnbook (1589), an anthology of poetry (1612), and the best map of Iceland hitherto produced.

THORLÁKSSON, Jón (1744–1819) Icelandic poet and scholar, born in Selárdalur, the son of a parson. He himself became a parson, but was twice defrocked for illegal carnal intercourse. He was eventually rehabilitated and lived in penury in a country parish at Bægisá. He was a prolific writer of poetry and occasional verse, but his most important work was as a translator into Icelandic of **Pope**'s *Essay on Man* (1798), **Milton**'s *Paradise Lost* (1828), and **Klopstock**'s *Messiah* (published 1834–38).

THORLÁKSSON, Thórarinn B (1867–1924) Icelandic landscape painter, born on the farm of Undirfell, the founder of modern art in Iceland. The son of the pastor at Undirfell, he worked as a bookbinder in Reykjavík and became the first Icelander to receive a state grant for studies abroad. He spent nine years in Copenhagen, where he turned to painting at the late age of 30. He held a one-man show of his landscape paintings in Reykjavík in 1900 (the first private one-man exhibition in Iceland), where he displayed his most famous painting, *Thingvellir*. In 1902 he returned to Iceland permanently, but remained an amateur all his life, only painting in his spare time.

THORNDIKE, Edward Lee (1874–1949) American psychologist, born in Williamsburg, Massachusetts. He studied at Wesleyan University and afterwards, under **William James**, at Harvard. As professor at Teachers College, Columbia (1904–40), he formulated important theories of educational psychology and in the psychology of animal learning. He devised intelligence tests and stressed the effect of chance associations in educational processes. His works include *The Principles of Teaching* (1905), *Psychology of Learning* (1914), and *The Measurement of Intelligence* (1926).

THORNDIKE, Dame Sybil (1882–1976) English actress, born in Gainsborough. She trained as a pianist but turned, despite considerable discouragement, to the stage. She made her first stage appearance with Greet's Pastoral Players in *The Merry Wives of Windsor* in 1904. After four years spent touring the USA in Shakespearean repertory, she became a prominent member of Miss Horniman's Repertory Company in Manchester, and worked from 1914 to 1919 at the Old Vic, subsequently collaborating with her husband, Sir **Lewis Casson**, whom she married in 1908, in a biography of **Lilian Baylis**. In 1924 she played the title role in the first English performance of **George Bernard Shaw**'s *Saint Joan*, and, during World War II, was a notable member of the Old Vic Company, playing at the New Theatre, London. She was created DBE in 1931.

THORNEYCROFT, (George Edward) Peter, Baron (1909–) English politician. He was educated at Eton and the RMA Woolwich, served as a regular artillery officer (1930–33), left the army to become a barrister, and entered parliament in 1938. President of the board of trade from 1951 to 1957, he was appointed Chancellor of the Exchequer in 1957, but, disagreeing with government financial policy, resigned after a year in office. Minister of aviation (1960–62), of defence (1962–64), and secretary of state for defence (1964), he lost his parliamentary seat in the 1966 election. In 1967 he was created a life peer. He was chairman of the Conservative party, 1975–81.

THORNHILL, Sir James (1675–1734) English painter, born in Melcombe Regis, Dorset. He executed Baroque paintings for the dome of St Paul's (1707), the hall at Blemheim Palace, Hampton Court and the Painted Hall at Greenwich Hospital. He painted some portraits, including those of Sir **Isaac Newton**, **Steele**, **Codrington**, the robber **Jack Sheppard** and a self-portrait. He founded a drawing school, and **Hogarth**, who became his son-in-law, was one of his pupils. He was knighted by George I in 1720 and was appointed serjeant-painter, becoming in 1728 history painter to the king. From 1722 he was MP for Melcombe Regis.

THORNTON, Henry (1760–1815) English banker and economist, born in London. An MP in 1782, he was a strong abolitionist supporter of **William Wilberforce**. He wrote *An Enquiry into the Nature and Effects of the Paper Credit of Great Britain* (1802), and was a member of the bullion committee (1810), and a director and governor of the Bank of England. He gave a great part of his personal fortune to charitable causes.

THORNYCROFT, Sir (William) Hamo (1850–1925) English sculptor, born in London. He made his name with *Warrior Beasino: a Wounded Youth* (1876), followed by *Artemis* (1880), *The Mower* (1884), and statues of General **Gordon** in Trafalgar Square (1885), **John Bright** in Rochdale (1892), and **Cromwell** in Westminster (1899). His grandfather, John Francis (1780–1861); his mother, Mary (1814–95); and his father, Thomas (1815–85), were all sculptors. His brother, Sir John Isaac (1843–1928), was a naval architect and engineer.

THORODDSEN, Jón, originally **Thórðarson** (1818–68) Icelandic novelist and poet, born in Reykhólar. Regarded as the father of the modern Icelandic novel, he studied law at Copenhagen and wrote drinking songs in the style of **Bellmann**. He was an avid reader of Sir **Walter Scott**, and used him as a model for his first book, *Piltur og stúlka* (Boy and Girl, 1850), the earliest proper novel produced in Iceland. In 1850 he returned to Iceland and was appointed a district magistrate on the island of Flatey. In addition to a sheaf of lyrics, he also wrote an unfinished sequel to his first novel, *Maður og kona* (Man and Woman, published posthumously in 1876).

THORPE, Benjamin (1782–1870) English philologist, a pioneer in studies of the Anglo-Saxon period. He edited numerous Old English texts, including *Anglo-Saxon Poems of Beowulf* (1855) and *The Anglo-Saxon Chronicle* (1861), and wrote *Northern Mythology* (1852).

THORPE, Sir (Thomas) Edward (1845–1925) English chemist, physicist and historian of science, born near Manchester, the son of a cotton merchant. Educated at Owens College in Manchester, and at the universities of Heidelberg and Bonn, he was appointed to chairs of chemistry at Anderson's College, Glasgow, the Yorkshire College of Science at Leeds, and the Royal College of Science, London (1885). He was also the first government chemist at the British government laboratories, concerned with analytical investigations for revenue purposes and control over chemical hazards. His early work was on the chemistry of vanadium with Sir **Henry Roscoe** and on phosphorus compounds; later he worked in inorganic and analytical chemistry. He wrote on the history of chemistry, including a biography of **Joseph Priestley**; his *Dictionary of Applied Chemistry* (1893) was a long-used standard work.

THORPE, Jim (James Francis) (1888–1953) American all-round athlete of Indian extraction, born in Prague, Oklahoma. His first sport was American football although he was also a baseball player of exceptional ability. In the 1912 Olympic Games at Stockholm he came first in both pentathlon and decathlon but was subsequently disqualified on a charge of having played semi-professional baseball. His name was expunged from the records and he played professional baseball (1913–19) with New York Giants, Cincinnati Reds and Boston Braves, and professional football (1919–26). He later became the first president of the National Football League, but lacked administrative ability and his period in office was brief (1920–21). After his death the American Athletics Union reinstated him as an amateur for the years 1909–12, and his Olympic titles were restored.

THORPE, John Jeremy (1929–) English Liberal politician. Educated at Eton and Trinity College Oxford (where he was president of the Union), he was called to the bar in 1954. Thorpe, whose father and grandfather were both Conservative MPs, was the Liberal member for North Devon from 1959 to 1979. He was elected leader of the Liberal party in 1967 but resigned the leadership in 1976 following allegations that some years previously he had had a homosexual relationship with a Mr Norman Scott. In 1979, shortly after losing his seat in the general election, he was acquitted at the Central Criminal Court on charges of conspiracy and incitement to murder Mr Scott.

THORPE DAVIE, Cedric (1913–83) Scottish composer, born in London. He studied in Glasgow at the Royal Scottish Academy, the Royal Academy, the Royal College, and with **Kodaly**; he became professor of composition at the Scottish National Academy of Music in 1936. His early compositions include a string quartet, a sonatina for cello and piano and the *Dirge for Cuthullin* for chorus and orchestra in 1935. His *Symphony in C* appeared in 1945, and he wrote the music for **Tyrone Guthries**'s acclaimed production of **David Lyndsay**'s *Satyre of the Thrie Estaitis* at the 1948 Edinburgh Festival; he also wrote many film scores and music for theatre productions and schools. In 1945 he became master of music at St Andrews University.

THORSTEINSSON, Steingrímur (Bjarnason) (1831–1913) Icelandic poet and scholar, born in Arnarstapi on Snæfellsnes. He studied classical philology and modern European literature at Copenhagen (1851–63), and worked in Copenhagen (1863–72), where he wrote patriotic poetry in support of **Jón Sigurðsson**'s independence movement. He returned to Iceland as teacher, later headmaster, at the Latin School in Reykjavík (1872–1913). His major importance was to enrich Icelandic native culture through his fine translations of all the modern European poets, as well as *King Lear*, *The Arabian Nights*, *Robinson Crusoe*, and **Hans Andersen**.

THORVALDSEN, Bertel (1770–1844) Danish sculptor, born probably in Copenhagen, the son of an Icelandic woodcarver. He studied in Copenhagen, and from 1797 lived for the most part in Rome. He revived ancient classical sculpture with statues of Jason, Venus, Psyche and others. Among his most celebrated works are *Triumphal Entry of Alexander into Babylon*, *Christ and the Twelve Apostles*, the reliefs *Night and Morning*, the *Dying Lion* at Lucerne and the Cambridge statue of **Byron**. He left all the works in his possession, with the bulk of his fortune, to Denmark.

THOTHMES See **TUTHMOSIS**

THOTHMES, I and **II** See **HATSHEPSUT**

THOU, Jacques Auguste de, (Latinized **Thuanus)** (1553–1617) French historian and statesman, born in Paris of a great legal family. He was intended for the church, but turned to law, became president of the *parlement* of Paris, and was a distinguished diplomat under **Henri III** and **Henri IV**. His great Latin history of his own time (5 vols, 1604–20) was placed on the Index. At his death, he left also commentaries on his own life and some Latin verse.

THRALE, Mrs See **PIOZZI**

THRASYBULUS (d.388 BC) Athenian naval commander. A strenuous supporter of the democracy, in 411 BC he helped to overthrow the Four Hundred, and was responsible for the recall of **Alcibiades**. In that year he defeated the Spartans in naval battles at Cynossema, and at Cyzicus in 410. In 404 he was banished by the Thirty Tyrants, but restored the democracy in 403 by seizing Piraeus. He conquered Lesbos and defended Rhodes, but was slain in 388 at Aspendus. **Cornelius Nepos** wrote a Life of him.

THRING, Edward (1821–87) English educationist, born in Alford House, Somerset. From Eton he passed to King's College, Cambridge, where he was elected a fellow. He was curate at Gloucester and elsewhere, but in 1853 became headmaster of Uppingham, which he made one of the best public schools of England, raising its numbers from 25 to 330 and rethinking the whole curriculum. His works include volumes of school songs, an English grammar, *Theory and Practice of Teaching* (1883), and *Uppingham Sermons* (1886).

THRING, Henry, Lord (1818–1907) English parliamentary draftsman, born in Alford, Somerset. He was educated at Shrewsbury and Magdalene College, Cambridge. As a young barrister he was employed by the Board of Trade to draft the Merchant Shipping Bill (1854) and the Companies Bill (1862). He became Home Office Counsel in 1860 and in 1868, as first parliamentary counsel to the Treasury, was the first official parliamentary draftsman, an office he held until 1886, though he continued to serve on the Statute Law Committee until his death. He published the continuation volumes of the *State Trials* (1820–58) and *Practical Legislation* (1902).

THROCKMORTON, Francis (1554–84) English conspirator, son of **John Throckmorton**. He was apprehended in the act of writing in cipher to **Mary Queen of Scots**, confessed under torture and was executed at Tyburn.

THROCKMORTON, Sir John (d.1445) English courtier. He was a clerk in the treasury who became chamberlain of the exchequer and under-treasurer to **Henry VI**.

THROCKMORTON, Sir Nicholas (1515–71) English diplomatist. He fought bravely at Pinkie (1547), was ambassador to France, where he was imprisoned for siding with the Huguenots, and was repeatedly ambassador to Scotland from 1561 to 1567. In 1569 he was sent to the Tower for promoting the scheme for marrying **Mary, Queen of Scots**, to the Duke of Norfolk. His daughter, Elizabeth, married Sir **Walter Raleigh**.

THUANUS See **THOU, Jacques Auguste de**

THUCYDIDES (c.460–c.400 BC) Greek historian of the Peloponnesian war, born near Athens. He suffered in the Athenian plague (430) but recovered. He commanded an Athenian squadron of seven ships at Thasos (424), when he failed to relieve Amphipolis; and, condemned therefore to death as a traitor, took refuge in exile, and retired to his Thracian estates. He lived in exile for 20 years (possibly visiting Sicily), and wrote his eight volume *History of the Peloponnesian War*, and probably returned to Athens in 404. He did not live long enough to revise book viii or to bring his history down to the end of the war. Thucydides wrote in a difficult style, his matter often based on speeches made by prominent politicians and analyzed according to his own rationalist principles of historical criticism, which aimed at impartiality. He admired **Pericles** and clearly understood the causes of Greece's future decline.

THUMB, Tom See **STRATTON, Charles Sherwood**

THUNBERG, Carl Per (1743–1828) Swedish botanical explorer, born in Jönköping. As a medical student at Uppsala he was taught botany by **Linnaeus** and collected plants for him; after graduation in 1770 he travelled as a ship's surgeon to South Africa, Java and Japan, collecting many plant species new to Europe and later publishing floras for the Cape and Japan. From 1778 he taught botany at Uppsala, and in 1784 succeeded Linnaeus's son as professor.

THÜNEN, Johann Heinrich von (1783–1850) German economist, born in Jever, West Germany, and educated at the Agricultural College, Gröss-Flöttbeck, and at Göttingen. A farm upbringing and a flair for mathematics drew him to question fundamental aspects of farm economics. Research done on his own estate of Tellow (1810–19) provided data for an abstract model of a space economy based upon fact, and the results, which appeared in his major work, *The Isolated State* (1826), completed his key contribution to location theory. His later research into wage theory was not published until 1850.

THURBER, James Grover (1894–1961) American humorist and cartoonist, born in Columbus, Ohio. When he was six years old, one of his brothers shot him with an arrow and he lost the sight of his left eye; towards the end of his life, he gradually lost the sight in his good eye. He attended schools in Columbus and went to Ohio State University where, as he stated modestly in his fragmentary autobiography, *My Life and Hard Times* (1933), he passed all his courses save botany. He served as a code clerk in the United States State Department in Washington DC at the end of World War I and at the American embassy in Paris before embarking on a career in journalism. In the early 1920s he reported for various papers in America and Europe but in February 1927 **E B White** introduced him to **Harold Ross**, editor of the *New Yorker*, and he was instantly appointed its managing editor after being told, for no apparent reason, that 'sex is an incident'. It was not a job to which he was suited and he drifted into writing, despite injunctions from Ross, before leaving the staff altogether. But he contributed regularly, humorous essays at first, then the inimitable sketches of dogs, barking seals and marital discord. His drawings first appeared in *Is Sex Necessary?* (1929) which he co-authored with White. A plethora of books followed, often combining humorous essays with characteristic doodles, including *The Owl in the Attic and Other Perplexities* (1931), *The Seal in the Bedroom and Other Predicaments* (1932), *The Middle-Aged Man on the Flying Trapeze* (1935), *Men Women and Dogs* (1943) and *The Wonderful O* (1957). He was also a dramatist and appeared as himself in a brief run of *A Thurber Carnival* in 1960, and wrote a number of notable short stories, of which *The Secret Life of Walter Mitty*, filmed with **Danny Kaye** (1946), is best known. *The Years With Ross* (1959) is an anecdotal memoir recounting his experience of the unpredictable *New Yorker* editor.

THURLOE, John (1616–68) English parliamentarian politician. He was secretary of the council of state (1652), a member of **Oliver Cromwell**'s second council (1657) and supported **Richard Cromwell**. He was accused of high treason at the Restoration, but was eventually set free. His correspondence (1742) is an important source for the history of the Protectorate.

THURLOW, Edward, 1st Baron (1731–1806) English politician, born in Bracon-Ash, Norfolk. He was as insolent and insubordinate at Caius College, Cambridge, as he had been at King's School, Canterbury, and was sent down. He was called to the bar in 1754 and as King's Counsel in the Douglas peerage case (1769) made his reputation, entered parliament as a loyal supporter of Lord **North**, became solicitor-general (1770) and attorney-general (1771) and won **George III**'s favour by upholding the latter's American policy. In 1778 he became Lord Chancellor and while retaining office under the **Rockingham** administration, opposed all its measures. Under **Fox** and North he was compelled to retire (1783), but was restored by **Pitt** and presided at the trial of **Warren Hastings** (1788). He was finally removed by Pitt in 1792 with the king's approval. He was vulgar, arrogant, profane and immoral, but 'no Man' said Fox, 'was so wise as Thurlow looked'.

THUROT, François (1726–60) French privateer, born in Nuits in Côte-d'Or. He served first on a privateer. Captured and imprisoned for a year at Dover, he escaped by seizing a small boat and crossing the Channel. By 1748 he was able to fit out a merchant ship. He spent a few years in England, dividing his time between music, mathematics and dissipation, varied by smuggling and possibly piracy. At the outbreak of war (1755) he was given the command of a squadron with which he scoured the east coast of Britain, and engaged two frigates off the Forth. In 1759 he sailed for Lough Foyle with a squadron carrying 1200 soldiers. High gales made it impossible to enter; and three British frigates appearing, Thurot fought until he was killed.

THURSTAN (d.1140) Anglo-Norman prelate, a native of Bayeux. Secretary to **Henry I**, he was made Archbishop of York in 1114. As archbishop, he struggled for primacy with Canterbury. On the invasion of King **David I** of Scotland (1137), he first persuaded him to accept a truce, and then collected forces at York and beat him at the Battle of the Standard (1138). He did much to help the growth of monasticism in the North and was concerned in the foundation of Fountains Abbey (1132). He entered the Cluniac order and died at Pontefract Priory.

THURSTONE, Louis Leon (1887–1955) American psychologist, born in Chicago. After studies at Cornell University, he gained his PhD in engineering at Chicago University in 1917, by which time he was teaching at the Carnegie Institute of Technology (1915–23). He was the author of the trade tests used by the US Army for the occupational classification of conscripts during World War I. He was later professor of psychology at Chicago University (1927–52) and research professor and director of the Psychometric Laboratory at North Carolina University from 1952 to 1955. His academic work was devoted to the theory and practice of intelligence testing and to the development of statistical techniques (especially multiple-factor analysis) to analyze the results. His battery of tests designed to measure the 'Primary Mental Abilities' have enjoyed wide application, especially in the USA. His books included *The Vectors of Mind* (1935) and *Multiple-Factor Analysis* (1947).

TIBERIUS, Tiberius Claudius Nero (42 BC–37 AD) second emperor of Rome, son of Tiberius Claudius **Nero** and of **Livia**, born three years before her complaisant husband yielded Livia to the triumvir Octavianus **Augustus**. He was 9 when his father's death transferred him to the tutelage of his stepfather. Almost the whole of his first 20 years of adulthood were spent in the field—in Spain, Armenia, Gaul, Pannonia and Germany. Tiberius was compelled (12 BC) to divorce his wife, Vipsania Agrippina, daughter of **Agrippa** by his former wife Pomponia, in order to marry Agrippa's widow **Julia**, the profligate daughter of **Augustus**. He was then sent to crush a revolt in Dalmatia and Pannonia; and for his wars in Germany received a full triumph (9 BC). But he retired to Rhodes (6 BC) where he devoted himself to study and astrology. Before his return (AD 2) Julia was banished to Pandataria (2 BC), and the deaths of the young princes Lucius and Gaius led Augustus to adopt Tiberius (AD 4) as heir to the imperial dignity. He spent the next seven years in active service in north Germany, suppressing insurrections in Pannonia and Dalmatia, and taking vengeance upon the Germans who had annihilated the army of **Varus** in AD 9. Along with **Germanicus Caesar** he made two marches into the heart of Germany (9–10), returning to enjoy a triumph (12). Tiberius succeeded Augustus in 14. Tiberius' tragedy was that despite his eminent qualities and many services, his loyalty to Augustus and his devotion to the public good, he was not suited to the role that was thrust on him. His rule began well, but was gradually eroded by suspicion and insecurity, which resulted in a growing number of treason trials and executions. Tiberius came to rely increasingly on the services of his friend the praetorian prefect Sejanus. In 26 he left Rome for Campania, and then took up residence in the island of Capreae. Sejanus in the meantime assumed effective control in Rome until at last Tiberius became suspicious of his intentions and struck him down (31). Tiberius' reign was darkened by conflicts within the ruling dynasty: the murder of Agrippa Postumus (14), the mysterious death in the East of the popular Germanicus Caesar (19), the alleged poisoning of Tiberius' own son Drusus by Sejanus (23), the banishment of Agrippina and the death of her young sons Nero and Drusus (31 and 33). The oppressive gloom of Tiberius' last years all but obliterated the memory of much good government earlier in his reign.

TIBULLUS, Albius (c.54–19 BC) Roman elegiac poet, born, it is believed, in Gabii. He acquired the friendship of the poet-statesman, M Valerius Messala, and joined his staff, when **Augustus** commissioned him (30 BC) to crush a revolt in Aquitania. While he distinguished himself in the campaign, he disliked a soldier's life as much as he enjoyed Roman society. When he started with Messala on a mission to Asia, he became ill on the voyage, and turned back at Corcyra. His sentimental elegiac love poems to his mistresses persuaded **Quintilian** to place Tibullus at the head of Roman elegiac poets.

TICHBORNE See **ORTON, Arthur**

TICKELL, Thomas (1686–1740) English poet, born at Bridekirk, Carlisle. He was a fellow of Queen's College, Oxford (1710–26). His complimentary verses on *Rosamond* (1709) gained him the favour, and his own virtues the friendship, of **Joseph Addison**, who, on becoming in 1717 secretary of state, made him his under-secretary; from 1725 he was secretary to the lords justices of Ireland. He was skilful in occasional poetry, and was favourably reviewed in the *Spectator*. His translation of book i of the *Iliad* appeared in 1715, about the same time as **Pope**'s. Pope professed to believe it the work of Addison himself, designed to eclipse his own version, and wrote the famous satire on Atticus. But though Addison corrected it, the translation was doubtless by Tickell. His longest poem is *Kensington Gardens*; his most popular, *Colin and Lucy*; his finest, the exquisite elegy prefixed to his edition of Addison's Works (1721).

TICKNOR, George (1791–1871) American author, born in Boston, Massachusetts. He gave up his legal practice in order to study and travel in Europe, recounted in his interesting *Letters and Journals* (1876). He was professor of French and Spanish and belles lettres at Harvard (1819–35) and then spent three more years in Europe, collecting materials for his great *History of Spanish Literature* (1849).

TICKNOR, William Davis (1810–64) American publisher, born in Lebanon, New Hampshire, a cousin of **George Ticknor**. He became a publisher in Boston in 1832, at first with John Allen, and then with **James T Fields**. As Ticknor & Fields they published the *Atlantic Monthly* and the *North American Review*, and their office was frequented by **Emerson**, **Longfellow**, **Hawthorne**, **Holmes**, **Lowell** and **Whittier**. Ticknor was one of the first Americans to remunerate foreign authors.

TIECK, Johann Ludwig (1773–1853) German critic and poet of the Romantic school, born in Berlin. He lived the life of a man of letters, in Berlin, Dresden and near Frankfurt an der Oder. After two or three immature romances, he produced a new line in clever dramatized versions of 'Puss in Boots', 'Blue Beard', and others. He followed up this first success (1797) by a tragedy, a comedy (1804) and *Phantasus* (1812–17), a collection of traditional lore in story and drama. Besides supervising the completion of **A W Schlegel**'s translation of **Shakespeare**, he edited the doubtful plays and wrote a series of essays (*Shakespeares Vorschule*, 1823–29). He translated *Don Quixote* in 1799–1804. He holds an honourable place among Germany's dramatic and literary critics, because of his *Dramaturgische Blätter* (2nd ed 1852) and *Kritische Schriften* (1848).

TIEPOLO, Giovanni Battista, real name **Giambattizta Chiepoletto** (1696–1770) Italian decorative painter, born in Venice, the greatest and most quintessentially Rococco figure of his age. His work is to be found in palaces and churches throughout Europe. In 1750 he began his most important decorative scheme, in the Archbishop's Palace at Würzburg. In 1761 **Charles III** of Spain called him to Madrid to work in the new Royal Palace; the work was still incomplete at his death. Tiepolo's compositions are full of movement and energy, and a sense of awe is created by the use of dramatically exaggerated foreshortening and subtle chiaroscuro. Ethereal scenes are treated with a light touch and a sense of real atmosphere. He was a superb draughtsman; his influence on all subsequent decorative painting was enormous.

TIFFANY, Charles Lewis (1812–1902) American goldsmith and jeweller, born in Killingly, Connecticut, and founder of Tiffany & Co. He began dealing in fancy goods in New York in 1837, and by 1883 had become so successful that he was one of the largest manufacturers of silverware in America. His work reflected current tastes with an accent on the traditional and historical. His finest works were the rich presentation pieces. He held official appointments to 23 royal patrons, including the tsar of Russia, Queen **Victoria** and the shah of Persia. He maintained a consistently high standard of workmanship throughout his entire output, whether household wares or special commissions. Latterly, he marketed some of the Art Nouveau lamps made by his son, **Louis Comfort Tiffany**.

TIFFANY, Louis Comfort (1848–1933) American glassmaker and interior decorator, born in New York, the son of **Charles Lewis Tiffany**. He began studying painting and became interested in the decorative arts in 1878. He established a firm of interior decorators which became one of the most popular firms in New York by the early 1880s and he decorated some rooms in the White House in 1882, along with various commissions in New York. He became better known, however, for his work in glass. He acquired glass furnaces at Cirona, New York, in 1892, where the first year's production went to museums. The following year the first lamps were made available to the public, and by 1896 the first 'Favrile Glass' (hand made) was offered for sale. Apart from stained glass, furniture, fabrics, wallpaper and lamps, he produced goblets and glasses in the Art Nouveau manner, suggesting flowing patterns: leaves and organic forms utilizing the fluidity of glass to a great degree of craftsmanship.

TIGLATH-PILESER I (c.1115–1093 BC), king of Assyria. He extended his dominions to the upper Euphrates, and defeated the king of Babylonia.

TIGLATH-PILESER III, known also as **Pulu** (750–720 BC) king of Assyria from 745 to 727 BC. A great empire-builder, he conquered the cities of north Syria and Phoenicia, including Damascus and Babylon.

TIGRANES I, the Great (d. after 56 BC) king of Armenia. He was set on the throne by Parthian troops c.94 BC. In alliance with **Mithridates VI**, he posed a threat to Rome, and **Sulla** was sent East to quell them (92). Left undisturbed owing to a Roman agreement with the Parthians, he made many conquests and founded Tigranocerta. In 69, **Lucullus** was sent out from Rome, and captured the new capital; and eventually Tigranes surrendered to **Pompey** (66), from this time ruling over Armenia only.

TIKHONOV, Nikolay Aleksandrovich (1905–) Soviet politician. He began his career as an assistant locomotive driver, before training in the late 1920s at the Dnepropetrovsk Metallurgical Institute, where he met **Leonid Brezhnev**, then a Communist party (CPSU) organizer. Tikhonov worked for two decades in the ferrous metallurgy industry, before being appointed deputy minister for the iron and steel industry (1955–57), deputy chairman of Gosplan (1963–65) and deputy chairman of the Council of Ministers (1965–80). He was inducted into the CPSU politburo as a full member by party leader Brezhnev in 1979 and appointed prime minister in 1980, a post which he held until 1985. A cautious, centralist Brezhnevite, his period as state premier was characterized by progressive economic stagnation.

TILDEN, 'Bill' (William Tatem II) (1893–1953) American tennis player, born in Philadelphia, one of the greatest players of his time. Renowned for the ferocity of his serve, he was Wimbledon singles champion three times (1920, 1921, 1930), and doubles champion in 1927; he was also six times American singles champion, and four times doubles champion in the 1920s. In 1931 he turned professional, and went on circuit for 20 years—one of the first players to do so. He was publisher and editor of Racquet Magazine and wrote several books on tennis, including *The Art of Lawn Tennis* (1920) and *The Phantom Drive* (1924), as well as a novel, *Glory's Net*.

TILDEN, Samuel Jones (1814–86) American statesman, born, a farmer's son, in New Lebanon, New York. He was admitted to the bar, and secured a large railway practice. By 1868 he had become leader of the Democrats in the state, and he attacked and destroyed **William Marcy Tweed** and the Tammany Society. In 1874 he became governor of New York; in 1876 he was the unsuccessful Democratic candidate for the presidency, after a special tribunal controlled by his opponents had vetted the votes cast. He left much of his fortune to found a free library in New York City.

TILDEN, Sir William Augustus (1842–1926) English chemist, born in St Pancras, London. Professor at the Royal College of Science, London, he made possible the manufacture of artificial rubber by his synthetic preparation of isoprene.

TILLEMONT, Louis Sébastien le Nain de (1637–98) French ecclesiastical historian, born in Paris, and educated by the Port Royalists. He entered the priesthood in 1676, and after the dispersion of the Solitaires in 1679 lived mostly on his estate at Tillemont near Paris. His chief works are the laborious and solid *Histoire ecclésiastique des six premiers siècles* (1693–1712) and *Histoire des empereurs* (1691–1738).

TILLETT, Benjamin (1860–1943) English trade-union leader, born in Bristol. He worked as brickmaker, bootmaker, sailor and Labour MP (1917–24, 1929–31). He was notable as organizer of the Dockers' Union in London and leader of the great dockers' strike in 1889, and of the London transport workers' strike (1911). He was expelled from Hamburg and from Antwerp (1896) for supporting dock strikes.

TILLEY, Vesta, professional name of **Lady de Frece,** née **Matilda Alice Powles** (1864–1952) English comedienne, born in Worcester. She first appeared as The Great Little Tilley, aged four, in Nottingham, and did her first male impersonation the following year. She adopted the name of Vesta Tilley and became, through her charm, vivacity and attention to sartorial detail, the most celebrated of all male impersonators. Of the many popular songs sung by her, *Burlington Bertie*, *Following in Father's Footsteps*, *Sweetheart May* and *Jolly Good Luck to the Girl who loves a Soldier* are the best known. She wrote *Recollections of Vesta Tilley* (1934).

TILLICH, Paul Johannes (1886–1965) German-born American Protestant theologian and philosopher, born in Starzeddel, Brandenburg. He became a Lutheran pastor (1912) and served as military chaplain in the German army in World War I, a traumatic experience which led him to take an active political interest in social reconstruction. He taught at Berlin (1919–24), and held professorships in theology at Marburg (1924–25), Dresden (1925–28), Leipzig (1928–29) and in philosophy at Frankfurt (1929–33). He was an early critic of **Hitler** and the Nazis and in 1933 was barred from German universities, the first non-Jewish academic 'to be so honoured', as he put it. He emigrated to the USA, and taught at the Union Theological Seminary in New York (1933–55), Harvard Divinity School (1955–62) and Chicago Divinity School (1962–65), becoming a naturalized US citizen in 1940. His influence on the development of theology in this century has been very substantial and is characterized by an attempt to mediate between traditional Christian culture and beliefs and the secular orientation of modern society. His main work is *Systematic Theology* (3 vols, 1951–63), which combines elements from existentialism and depth-psychology, as well as from the ontological tradition in Christian thought. He explains faith as a matter of 'ultimate concern' with a reality transcending finite existence rather than a belief in a personal God, and this has led to oversimplified accusations of atheism or crypto-atheism. His popular works like *The Courage to Be* (1952) and *Dynamics of Faith* (1957) have reached very large general readerships.

TILLOTSON, John (1630–94) English prelate, and archbishop of Canterbury, born in Sowerby, Yorkshire. He studied at Clare Hall, Cambridge, becoming a fellow in 1651. Although siding with the Presbyterians at the Savoy conference, he submitted to the Act of Uniformity (1662) and thenceforth received preferment, becoming dean of Canterbury in 1672 and archbishop, in place of the deposed nonjuror **Sancroft**, in 1691. He advocated the Zwinglian doctrine of the eucharist. According to **Gilbert Burnet** 'he was not only the best preacher of the age, but seemed to have brought preaching to perfection'. In 1664 he married a niece of **Oliver Cromwell**.

TILLY, Jan Tserklaes, Count of (1559–1632) Flemish soldier, born at the castle of Tilly in Brabant. Brought up by the Jesuits, he learned the art of war under Parma, fought in Hungary against the Turks, and was appointed in 1610 by Duke Maximilian of Bavaria to reorganize his army. He was given the command of the Catholic army at the outbreak of the Thirty Years' War, and by his decisive victories at Weisser Berg and Prague (both 1620) dissipated the dreams of the Elector Palatine. He separated the armies of Mansfeld and of the Margrave of Baden, beat the latter at Wimpfen (1622), and expelled Christian of Brunswick from the Palatinate, defeating him in two battles. Created a count of the empire, he defeated King **Kristian IV** of Denmark at Lutter (1626), and with **Wallenstein** compelled him to sign the Treaty of Lübeck (1629). Next year he succeeded Wallenstein as commander-in-chief of the imperial forces, and stormed Magdeburg (20 May 1631), when the atrocities he allowed his Croats and Walloons to perpetrate cast a foul stain upon his reputation. **Gustav II Adolph** at Breitenfeld (17 September) drove him to retreat behind the Lech, and forced the passage of the river (5 April 1632), after a desperate conflict in which Tilly received his death-wound.

TILMAN, Harold William (1898–1978) English mountaineer, explorer and sailor, born in Wallasey, Cheshire. Commissioned into the Royal Artillery, he served on the Western Front in World War I. After the war he went as a planter to Kenya and started climbing with **Eric Shipton**, first in East Africa and then in the Himalayas and Karakoram. He made the first ascents of Midget Peak, Mount Kenya (1930), and Nanda Devi (1936), was a member of the 1935 Everest expedition and led the 1938 attempt. During World War II he served in France, the Western Desert, behind enemy lines in Albania, and with the Italian resistance. In 1947 he joined the Swiss expedition to Rakaposhi, before joining Shipton in Kashgar and attempting to climb Muztagh Ata. In 1948 he travelled through Central Asia from China to Chitral with Shipton, filling in many blanks of the map, and then went to Nepal, attempting Annapurna IV. He became consul at Maymyo, Burma, in 1952. He returned to England in 1953 and took up long-distance sailing. He purchased *Mischief*, sailed to Patagonia and crossed the ice-cap, and then completed the circumnavigation of South America. In 1957 to 1958 he circumnavigated Africa. From 1959 to 1972 he sailed in both Arctic and Antarctic waters and was shipwrecked twice. In 1977 he sailed with Simon Richardson aboard *En Avant* from Southampton to the South Shetland Islands, but was never seen again after leaving Rio on 1 November.

TILPINUS See **TURPIN**

TIMBS, John (1801–75) English antiquarian and miscellanist, born in London. He wrote over 150 volumes on interesting facts gathered on a varied number of subjects and places, often antiquarian, such as *Curiosities of London* (1855), *Romance of London* (1865) and *Abbeys, Castles, and Ancient Halls of England and Wales* (1869).

TIMOLEON (d.c.337 BC) Greek statesman and general of Corinth. He overthrew the tyranny of his brother Timophanes, and retired from public life. But when **Dionysius II the Younger** and others tried to establish themselves in Syracuse, he was prevailed upon to return to public life. He manoeuvred Dionysius II into abdication and fought the Carthaginians, who were supporting the other tyrants, defeating them at the Crimessus in 341. He then promptly retured again, having taken measures to stabilize the economy of Greek Sicily.

TIMON, the Misanthrope of Athens (5th century BC) Athenian nobleman, a contemporary of **Socrates**. According to the comic writers who attacked him, he was disgusted with mankind on account of the ingratitude of his early friends, and lived a life of almost total seclusion. **Lucian** made him the subject of a dialogue. **Shakespeare**'s play *Timon of Athens* is based on the story, as told in **Painter**'s *Palace of Pleasure*.

TIMON OF PHLIUS (c.325–c.235 BC) Greek philosopher and poet from the Northern Peloponnese. He was **Pyrrho**'s leading disciple and his biographer, and an enthusiastic exponent of the theories of scepticism. After a period as an itinerant lecturer he retired to Athens where he was a leading member of the local intelligentia and a versatile author. He wrote satyr-plays, comedies, tragedies, epic poems and a famous series of *Silloi*, satirical mock-heroic poems which parody and insult most earlier Greek philosophers, who are seen as doctrinaire, pretentious and generally aberrant predecessors of the Pyrrhonian enlightenment.

TIMOSHENKO, Semyon Konstantinovich (1895–1970) Russian soldier, born in Bessarabia of peasant stock. In 1915 he was conscripted into the tsarist army, but in the Revolution (1917) he took part in the defence of Tsaritsin. In World War II he led part of the invasion of Finland (1940), with 27 divisions to smash the resistance of $3\frac{1}{2}$ Finnish divisions. With the German invasion of 1941 he took command in the Ukraine, 'Russia's breadbasket'; but his attempt to stem the 1942 Nazi drive on the Crimea resulted in no more than a Pyrrhic victory. From 1940 to 1941 he served as People's Commissar of Defence, and commanded the Byelo-Russian district from 1956 to his retiral in 1960.

TIMOSHENKO, Stepan (Stephen) Prokofyevich (1878–1972) Russian-born American civil engineer. Educated at the two technical institutes in St Petersburg (now Leningrad), he worked for a time as a railway engineer, then in 1906 began lecturing at Kiev University. Dismissed for his pro-Jewish views in 1911, he nevertheless remained in Russia until 1920 when he fled to Yugoslavia and thence to the USA in 1922. In 1936 he joined the staff of Stanford University in California where he taught engineering mechanics and strength of materials until he was 76 years of age. His many books and technical papers on these subjects continue to inspire students and practising engineers alike.

TIMUR See **TAMERLANE**

TINBERGEN, Jan (1903–) Dutch economist, and brother of Nobel prize-winning zoologist **Nikolaas Tinbergen**. Educated at Leiden, he taught economics at the Erasmus University in Rotterdam (1933–73). He analyzed the American Depression in *Business Cycles in the USA 1919–32* (1939), and was economic adviser to the League of Nations (1936–38). After World War II he directed the Netherlands Central Planning Bureau (1945–55). His works include *Econometrics* (1941), *Economic Policy: Principles and Design* (1956), and *Shaping the World Economy* (1962). He shared the first Nobel prize for economics in 1969, with **Ragnar Frisch**.

TINBERGEN, Nikolaas (1907–88) Dutch ethologist, born in The Hague, brother of the Nobel prize-winning economist **Jan Tinbergen**. The co-founder with **Konrad Lorenz** of the science of ethology (the study of animal behaviour in natural surroundings), he studied zoology at Leiden. After World War II he taught at Oxford (1949–74), and analyzed the social behaviour of certain animals and insects as an evolutionary process with considerable relevance to human behaviour, especially courtship and aggression. His works include his classic, *The Study of Instinct* (1951), *The Herring Gull's World* (1953), *Social Behaviour in Animals* (1953), *Animal Behaviour* (1965), and *The Animal in its World* (2 vols, 1972–73), and (with his wife Lies) his controversial *Autistic Children* (1973). He shared the 1973 Nobel prize for physiology or medicine with Lorenz and **Karl von Frisch**.

TINDAL, Matthew (1655–1733) English Deist, born in Beer-Ferris rectory, in south Devon. He was elected a fellow of All Souls College, Oxford. A Roman Catholic under **James VII and II**, he reverted to Protestantism of a somewhat freethinking type, and wrote *An Essay of Obedience to the Supreme Powers* (1693), and *Rights of the Christian Church asserted against the Romish and all other Priests* (1706). The latter raised a storm of opposition; but even a prosecution failed to prevent a fourth edition in 1709. In 1730 Tindal published his *Christianity as Old as the Creation*, which was soon known as 'the Deist's Bible'; its aim was to eliminate the supernatural element from religion, and to prove that its morality is its only claim to the reverence of mankind. Answers were issued by **Waterland**, **Conybeare** and others.

TINDALE, William See **TYNDALE**

TING, Samuel Chao Chung (1936–) American physicist, born in Ann Arbor, Michigan, where his father was a student at the time. He was raised in China and educated there and on Taiwan, and at Michigan University (1956–62). He worked in elementary-particle physics at the European Organisation for Nuclear Research at Geneva (CERN) and at Columbia University, then led a research group at DESY, the German synchrotron project in Hamburg, and from 1967 worked at the Massachusetts Institute of Technology. He conducted an experiment in which protons were directed onto a beryllium target, and a long-lived product particle was observed in 1974 and named the J particle. At the same time, and independently, **Burton Richter** did similar work and named the particle the psi particle. It is now named the J/psi particle and Ting and Richter shared the 1976 Nobel prize for physics. Other related particles of the J/psi family have been detected.

TINGUELY, Jean (1925–) Swiss sculptor, born in Fribourg. He studied at the Basle Kunstgewerbeschule from 1941 to 1945. A pioneer of Kinetic Art, he worked in Paris from 1953 onwards, exhibiting his 'meta-mechanical' works moving metal constructions, sometimes powered by small motors. Some of these clatter and ping, striking bottles or metal pans (*musique concrète*) and even make abstract drawings, but about 1960 he began programming them to destroy themselves ('auto-destructive art').

TINO, di Camaino (c.1285–1337) Italian sculptor, born in Siena. He probably trained in Pisa under **Giovanni Pisano**, and was certainly working there in 1311. In 1315 he succeeded Giovanni as master of works at Pisa Cathedral, and was commissioned to make the tomb of Emperor Henry VII. He then held an equivalent position at Siena cathedral, and later worked in Florence, where his sepulchral monuments included that of Bishop Orso in Florence Cathedral. Around 1324 he entered the service of the Angevin rulers in Naples, and worked there on architectural projects as well as sculpture. His dignified, monumental style was influential in both the north and south of Italy.

TINSLEY, Pauline (1928–) English dramatic soprano, born in Wigan. She studied singing in Manchester, at the Opera School, London, and with Eva Turner. She excels as a singing actress in roles as diverse as Elektra, Turandot, the Dyer's Wife, Lady Macbeth, Kostelnička (*Jenufa*), Brünnhilde (*Die Walküre*), Santuzza, and Lady Billows (*Albert Herring*). In additon to Britain she has sung at houses throughout the USA, at La Scala Milan, Hamburg, Amsterdam and elsewhere in Europe.

TINTORETTO, properly **Jacopo Robusti** (1518–94) Venetian painter, born probably in Venice, the son of a silk dyer or *tintore* (hence his nickname of 'Little Dyer'). Little is known of his life. He is supposed to have studied under **Titian**, but only for a short time. He claims to have set up independently, practically untaught, by 1539, but it is likely that he had some supervision. Except for visits to Mantua (1580, 1590–93), he lived all his life in Venice. Tintoretto pioneered the way from the Classical to the Baroque. In his early work, such as *The Miracle of the Slave* (1548), in which he consciously set out to combine Titian's colours with **Michelangelo**'s sculptural draughtsmanship. After 1556 he began to develop his mature style. *The Last Judgment*, *The Golden Calf* (both c.1560) and *The Marriage of Cana* (1561) were followed by two masterpieces of perspective and lighting effects, both c.1562, *The Finding* and *The Removal of the Body of St Mark*. From 1564 he was employed in decorating the Albergo, and the Halls of the Scuola of San Rocco and its church. The Scuola contains probably the largest collection of works by one artist in a single building, prearranged in a vast iconographical scheme from the Old and New Testaments. Other notable late works are *The Origin of the Milky Way* (after 1570), the *Paradiso* (1588), famous for its colossal size, *Entombment*, and his last version of *The Last Supper* (1592–94), no longer an exclusive gathering but set among maids and attendants and fully expressing the religious fervour of the Counter-Reformation. The 'painter of dark turbulence' left an unrivalled number of paintings. Three of his seven children also became painters, including Marietta (1560–90), known as La Tintoretta.

TINWORTH, George (1843–1913) English artist in Terracotta, born in London, the son of a poor wheelwright. He entered the Royal Academy schools in 1864, and in 1867 obtained an appointment in the Doulton art pottery. The works which made him famous were mainly terracotta panels with groups of figures in high relief illustrating scenes from sacred history.

TIPPETT, Sir Michael (1905–) English composer, born in London. He studied at the Royal College of Music and became conductor of educational organizations under the London County Council and from 1940 to 1951 director of music at Morley College. He first attracted attention with his chamber music and Concerto for Double String Orchestra (1939), but his oratorio, *A Child of our Time* (1941), reflecting the political and spiritual problems of the 1930s and 1940s, won him wide recognition. A convinced pacifist, he went to prison for three months as a conscientious objector during World War II. He scored a considerable success with the operas, *The Midsummer Marriage* (1952) and *King Priam* (1961). His other works include symphonies, a piano concerto (1957), the operas *The Knot Garden* (1970) and *The Ice Break* (1977), piano sonatas and an oratorio *The Vision of St Augustine* (1963–65). He was created CBE in 1959, and was knighted in 1966. He wrote *Moving into Aquarius* (collected writings, revised edition, 1974).

TIPPOO SAHIB, or **Tipú Sultán** (1749–99) sultan of Mysore, son of **Haidar Ali**. During his father's wars with the British he completely routed Bailey (1780 and 1782) and Braithwaite (1782). In 1782 he succeeded his father as Sultan of Mysore. In 1783 he captured and put to death most of the garrison of Bednur, but after the conclusion of peace between France and Britain he agreed to a treaty (1784) stipulating for the *status quo* before the war. He sent ambassadors in 1787 to France to stir up a war with Britain, and, failing in this, invaded (1789) the protected state of Travancore. In the ensuing war (1790–92) the British, under Stuart and **Cornwallis**, were aided by the Mahrattas and the Nizam, and Tippoo was compelled (1792) to resign half of his dominions, pay an indemnity of 3030 lakhs of rupees, restore all prisoners, and give his two sons as hostages. Resuming his intrigues, he sent another embassy to the French. Hostilities began in 1799, and Tippoo was driven from the open field, attacked in Seringapatam, and after a month's siege slain at the storming, by General **Harris**.

TIRABOSCHI, Girolamo (1731–94) Italian scholar, born in Bergamo. He became professor of rhetoric at Milan, and in 1770 librarian to the Duke of Modena. His *Storia della Letteratura Italiana* (1772–1781) is an accurate survey down to 1700.

TIREL or **TYRELL, Sir Walter** See **WILLIAM II**

TIRO, Marcus Tullius (1st century) Roman freedman who invented the 'Tironian' system of shorthand. He was a friend and amanuensis of **Cicero**, and devised the system to take down dictation and record speeches. He was the author of a lost *Life of Cicero* and editor of some of Cicero's letters. His shorthand system was taught in Roman schools, and was in widespread use for several centuries.

TIRPITZ, Alfred P Friedrich von (1849–1930) German naval commander, born in Küstrin, in Brandenburg. He entered the Prussian navy in 1865. He later distinguished himself in torpedo craft and received accelerated promotion to commander. He commanded the Asiatic squadron (1896–97), and in 1897 was appointed state secretary of the Imperial German navy. He was responsible for its material development, and raised a fleet to challenge British supremacy of the seas. Ennobled in 1900, he rose to be Grand Admiral (1911). An upholder of unrestricted submarine warfare, he commanded the German navy from August 1914 to March 1916, when he resigned over naval policy. He later became a right-wing member of the Reichstag (1924–28).

TIRSO DE MOLINA, pseud. of **Gabriel Téllez** (c.1571–1648) Spanish playwright, born in Madrid. He was prior of the monastery of Soria. Lacking his great contemporary **Vega Carpio**'s lyrical gifts, he wrote *Comedias*, partly Interludes, and *Autos Sacramentales* (originally about 300), excelling in the portrayal of character, particularly of spirited women, and in his treatment of the Don Juan legend in his masterpiece, *El Burlador de Sevilla* (1634).

TISCHENDORF, (Lobegott Friedrich) Konstantin von (1815–74) German biblical scholar, born in Lengenfeld in Saxony. In 1839 he became a lecturer, in 1845 a professor, at Leipzig. His search for MSS of the New Testament resulted in the discovery of the 4th-century Sinaitic Codex at the monastery of St Catherine on Mount Sinai; he described his journeys in *Reise in den Orient* (1846) and *Aus dem Heiligen Lande* (1862). Among his works are the editions of the Sinaitic (1862) and many other MSS, the *Editio VIII* of the New Testament (1864–72), an edition of the Septuagint, and the *Monumenta Sacra Inedita* (1846–71). *When were our Gospels Written?* was translated in 1866.

TISELIUS, Arne Wilhelm Kaurin (1902–71) Swedish chemist, born in Stockholm. He became professor of biochemistry at Uppsala (1938), investigated serum proteins by electrophoretic analysis, and in chromatography evolved new methods for the analysis of colourless substances. He won the Nobel prize for chemistry in 1948, and was president of the Nobel Foundation (1960–64).

TISSANDIER, Gaston (1835–99) French aviation pioneer. In 1883, with his brother Albert, he invented a navigable balloon, propelled by electricity.

TISSAPHERNES (d.395 BC) Persian satrap in Asia Minor from 413, notorious for his duplicity in the conflicts between Athens and Sparta. Deprived of a province in favour of **Cyrus the Younger**, brother of **Artaxerxes II**, he denounced him to Artaxerxes, for whom he fought and won the battle of Cunaxa (401 BC). He then murdered the leaders of the Greeks, including Cyrus, and harassed **Xenophon** and the ten thousand Greek mercenaries who had fought in the battle. But he was himself defeated by **Agesilaus** in the war with Sparta, and murdered for the murder of Cyrus on the orders of Artaxerxes.

TISSOT, James, originally **Jacques Joseph** (1836–1902) French painter, born in Nantes. He studied in Paris, where he was influenced by **Degas**, and settled in London in the 1890s. He travelled to Palestine in 1886 and as a result produced his best-known work, a series of 300 watercolours of the life of Christ. He was also known for his paintings of life in Victorian times.

TISZA, Kalman (1830–1902) Hungarian statesman, father of **Stephen Tisza**. He was premier and virtually dictator from 1875 to 1890.

TISZA, Count Stephen (1861–1918) son of **Kalman Tisza**, Hungarian Liberal leader. a patriotic Magyar, he was premier of Hungary (1903–05, 1913–17), supported Germany, and was assassinated on 31 October, the first day of the Hungarian Revolution.

TITCHENER, Edward Bradford (1867–1927) English-born American psychologist, born in Chichester. He studied at Oxford and Leipzig before going to America in 1892 to Cornell University. A follower of **Wilhelm Wundt**, under whose influence he had come in Leipzig, he became the great exponent of experimental psychology in America, founding the Society of Experimental Psychologists in 1904. He wrote many scholarly works on the subject, including the 4-volume *Experimental Pscyhology* (1901–05), *Psychology of Feeling and Attention* (1908) and *Experimental Psychology of the Thought Processes* (1909).

TITIAN, properly **Tiziano Vecellio** (c.1488–1576) the greatest of the Venetian painters, born in Pieve di Cadore in the Friulian Alps. He lived from the age of ten with an uncle in Venice and studied under Zuccato, a mosaicist, **Gentile** and **Giovanni Bellini** and assisted **Giorgione**. Bellini's influence is apparent in such early works as *Bishop Pesaro before St Peter* (c.1505). Titian assisted Giorgione with the paintings for the Fondaco dei Tedeschi (1508) and completed many of the latter's works, eg, *Noli me tangere* (c.1510) and the *Sleeping Venus* (c.1510), which was to serve as a model for Titian's more naturalistic *Venus of Urbino* (1538). The first works definitely attributable to Titian alone are the three frescoes of scenes in the life of St Anthony at Padua (1511), but Giorgione's influence predominates in these, the pastoral setting of *The Three Ages of Man* (c.1515) and the masterly fusion of romantic realism and classical idealism achieved in the *poesa, Sacred and Profane Love* (c.1515), a masterpiece of Renaissance art. After 1516 restrained postures and colouring give way to dynamic compositions in which bright colours are contrasted and the classical intellectual approach gives way to sensuous, full-blooded treatment. *Assumption of the Virgin* (1516–18), *Madonna of the Pesaro Family* (1519–26), both in the Frari, Venice, and *St Peter Martyr* (destroyed 1867) exemplify the beginnings of Titian's own revolutionary style. For the Duke of Ferrara he painted three great mythological subjects, *Feast of Venus* (c.1515–18), *Bacchanal* (c.1518) and the richly coloured exuberant masterpiece *Bacchus and Ariadne* (1523). In sharp contrast is the finely-modelled historical picture, *Presentation of the Virgin* (1534–38). In 1530 he met the Emperor **Charles V**, of whom he painted many portraits, including the striking equestrian *Charles V at the Battle of Mühlberg* (1548), also the portraits of many notables assembled for the Augsburg peace conference, and was ennobled. To this period also belongs *Ecce Homo* (1543), and portraits of the Farnese family including Pope **Paul III** and his nephews (1545–46), painted on Titian's first visit to Rome. The impact of the art collections there is reflected in a new sculptural treatment of the *Danae* (1545). For **Philip II** of Spain he executed a remarkable series of *poesies* on mythological scenes, to which belong *Diana and Actaeon* (1559) and *Diana and Callisto* (1559) and *Perseus and Andromeda* (c.1556). To the poignant religious and mythological subjects of his last years belong *The Fall of Man* (c.1570), *The Entombment* (1565), *Christ Crowned with Thorns* (c.1570), *Madonna Suckling the Child* (1570–76), *Lucrezia and Tarquinius* (c.1570) and the unfinished *Pietà* (1573–76). He was fortunate in his patrons, despite his negligence and delays and a polished courtier's love of pensions, privileges and sinecures. He was ceremoniously buried in the church of S Maria dei Frari, Venice. Titian revolutionized the oil techniques and has been described as the founder of modern painting. His influence on later artists, including **Tintoretto**, **Rubens**, **Velazquez**, **Poussin**, **Van Dyck** and **Watteau**, was profound.

TITMUS, Fred (Frederick John) (1932–) English cricketer, born in Kentish Town. Although primarily an off-spin bowler who took 153 wickets in 53 Tests, he also scored 1449 Test runs. In a long career which spanned five decades, he first played for Middlesex in 1949. His last appearance was in 1981. He took 2830 wickets all in first-class matches, taking 100 wickets in a season on no fewer than 16 occasions.

TITO, the name adopted by **Josip Broz** (1892–1980) Yugoslav leader, born near Klanjec, in Croatia. In World War I he served with the Austro-Hungarian Army, and, taken prisoner by the Russians, he adopted Communism and took part in the 1917 Revolution. In 1928 he was imprisoned in Yugoslavia for conspiring against the régime. In mid-1941 he organized partisan forces to harry the Axis conquerors of his country and his efforts were sufficiently effective to pin down about 30 enemy divisions, and to have the price of 100000 gold marks set on his head. With exceptional guile he contrived to discredit utterly the rival partisan leader, **Mihailovich**, in Anglo-American eyes and win support, in arms and material, solely for himself. In November 1943 Tito established a provisional government at liberated Jajce in Bosnia, and following the expulsion of the remaining Axis forces, a new Yugoslav Federal Republic was declared in November 1945. Effectively one-party elections followed, establishing the dominance of the Communist party, with Tito serving as prime minister and, from 1953, as president. In 1948 the new Federal Republic broke with the Cominform as a result of growing policy differences: **Stalin** viewing the successful system of decentralized profit-sharing workers' councils introduced by Tito as dangerously 'revisionist'. Thereafter, Tito became a leader of the non-aligned movement, pursuing a policy of 'positive neutralism'. He was made president-for-life in 1974 and proceeded to establish a unique system of collective, rotating leadership within the country during his later years.

TITTERTON, Sir Ernest William (1916–90) English atomic physicist, born in Tamworth, Staffordshire. Educated at Birmingham University, he was a research officer for the Admiralty during World War II, before becoming in 1943 a member of the British mission to USA for the development of the atomic bomb (the 'Manhattan Project'). He was senior member of the timing team at the first atomic test in 1945, and advisor on instrumentation at the Bikini Atoll tests in 1946, before returning to Los Alamos, New Mexico, as head of the electronics division until 1947. Titterton then worked at the Atomic Energy Research Establishment at Harwell, Berkshire until 1950 when he became professor of nuclear physics at the Australian National University, Canberra. He was involved in the British nuclear tests at Maralinga, South Australia until 1957 and subsequently held various research and advisory appointments in the field of nuclear energy.

TITUS (1st century) early Christian churchman a companion of the apostle **Paul**. He was a Greek, and remained uncircumcized, an important factor in the Church's acceptance of Gentiles. Ecclesiastical tradition makes Titus 'bishop' of Crete.

TITUS, Flavius Sabinus Vespasianus (39–81) Roman emperor, eldest son of **Vespasian**. From an early age he served with credit in Germany and Britain, and in Judaea under his father. On Vespasian's elevation to the throne Titus brought the Jewish war to a close by the capture of Jerusalem (70). For a time he gave himself up to pleasure, conducting a liaison with Berenice, sister of **Herod Agrippa**; but when he assumed undivided power (79) his character changed, he put a stop to treason trials, and decreed heavy punishments againt informers. He completed the Colosseum, built the baths which bear his name, and lavished his generosity upon the sufferers from the eruption of Vesuvius (79), the three days' fire at Rome, and the pestilence. He was now the idol of his subjects, but he died suddenly. The suspicion that he had been poisoned by his brother and successor, **Domitianus** was probably unfounded.

TIZARD, Sir Henry Thomas (1885–1959) English scientific administrator. Educated at Westminster School and Magdalen College, Oxford, of which he was elected president in 1942, he was the first scientist to hold such an office in an Oxford College. He served in the RAF. during World War I and was assistant comptroller of aeronautical research (1918–19). He was secretary to the DSIR (1927–29), chairman of the

Aeronautical Research Committee (1933–43), from 1947 chairman of the Defence Research Policy Committee and president of the British Association in 1948.

TOBIAS, Phillip Vallentine (1925–) South African anatomist and physical anthropologist, born in Durban. He studied at Witwatersrand and Cambridge universities, and has taught since 1951 at Witwatersrand, becoming professor of anatomy in 1959. He is a leading authority on human biological evolution, with over 700 publications including *The Brain in Hominid Evolution* (1971), *The Meaning of Race* (1972) and *Hominid Evolution: past, present and future* (1985).

TOBIN, James (1918–) American economist, born in Champaign. He was educated at Harvard and, following wartime service in the US navy, went on to teach there. In 1955 he became a professor at Yale and in 1981 he won the Nobel prize for economics, primarily for his 'portfolio selection theory' of investment.

TOCQUEVILLE, Alexis Charles Henri Clérel de (1805–59) French historian, born in Verneuil of an aristocratic Norman family. He was called to the bar in 1825 and became assistant-magistrate at Versailles. Sent in 1831 to the USA to report on the prison system, he returned to publish a penetrating political study, *De la Démocratie en Amerique* (1835), which gave him a European reputation and in which he came to certain general conclusions, for example, that greater equality requires greater centralization and therefore diminishes liberty. Before publication, then still relatively unknown, he paid his first visit to England in 1833, married a Miss Mottley and kept an extensive diary of his *Journeys to England and Ireland*, in which his abiding impression of the English, confirmed by a later visit in 1857, was of underlying national solidarity, despite political dissensions. In 1839 he was returned to the Chamber of Deputies by the Norman farmers. After 1848 he was the most formidable opponent of the Socialists and extreme Republicans, and as strenuously opposed Louis Napoleon; but he became in 1849 vice-president of the Assembly, and from June to October was minister of foreign affairs. After the *coup d'état* he retired to his Norman estate, Tocqueville, and agricultural pursuits, and there wrote the first volume of *L'Ancien Régime et la Révolution* (1856), in which he argued with masterful objectivity that the Revolution did not constitute a break with, but merely accelerated a trend of, the past, namely centralization of government.

TODD, Alexander Robertus, Baron of Trumpington (1907–) Scottish chemist, born in Glasgow. He became professor at Manchester (1938) and Cambridge (1944), fellow and master (1963–78) of Christ's College, Cambridge, and, from 1978, first chancellor of the new University of Strathclyde. He was awarded the Nobel prize for chemistry in 1957 for his researches on vitamins B_1 and E. He was made a life peer in 1962.

TODD, Mike (Michael), originally **Avrom Hirsh Goldbogen,** (1909–58) American showman, born in Minneapolis. The son of a poor rabbi, he started life as a fairground attendant at nine, but was already making his first fortune at 14 in sales promotion. In 1927 he went to Hollywood as a soundproofing expert, staged a real 'Flame Dance' spectacle at the Chicago World Fair in 1933, which was later followed by plays, musical comedies and films, including a jazz version of **Gilbert** and **Sullivan**, *The Hot Mikado* (1939), and an up-to-date *Hamlet* (1945). He perfected with Lowell Thomas the three-dimensional film and sponsored the 'TODD-AO' wide-screen process, by which his greatest film, **Jules Verne**'s *Around the World in Eighty Days*, was made and presented, winning him The Academy Award (1956). He married his third wife, the film actress **Elizabeth Taylor**, in 1957 and was killed in an aircrash over New Mexico the following year.

TODD, Ron (Ronald) (1927–) English trade union leader, born in Walthamstow, the son of a market trader. After serving in the Far East with the Royal Marine commandos, he joined the Ford Motor Company in 1954 as a line-worker and became a member of the country's largest trade union, the Transport and General Workers' (TGWU). He rose steadily from shop steward to district officer, regional secretary and then national organizer, before becoming general-secretary in 1985. A hardworking, skilled and trusted negotiator with a direct oratorical style, Todd won the union's leadership with strong left-wing support. Although viewed as a staunch supporter of Labour party leader **Neil Kinnock**, on many economic and social issues, his union's, and his own personal, commitment to unilaterial nuclear disarmament have led to strains in the TGWU-Labour relationship.

TODD, Sweeney (fl.late 18th century) supposed murderer of late 18th-century London. Known as the 'Demon Barber of Fleet Street', he supposedly carried out his dark deeds in the 1780s. It has never been proved that he did in fact exist, although his story is well-known. Using a revolving floor which had a barber's chair on each side of it, he is supposed to have swung unsuspecting clients into his cellar via the trap and then cut their throats. Their bodies were carried through a series of underground passages to a nearby bakery. There, Mrs Lovett is said to have used human flesh in her meat pies. The name of Sweeney Todd, nicknamed 'Old Cut 'Em Up', first appeared in a story, *The String of Pearls*, which was serialized in 1846 in a penny newspaper, *The People's Periodical and Family Library*. This substantiates the notion that Todd was never more than fiction, but it has been argued that his character was based on real murderers. Sawney Bean, a Scottish cannibal, may have been the source of the London tale, as may a French murderer who operated in Paris in 1800.

TODI, Jacopone da (c.1230–1306) Italian religious poet, born in Todi in the duchy of Spoleto. He practised as an advocate, was converted to an ascetic life in 1268 and became a Franciscan lay brother in 1278. He was imprisoned (1298–1303) for satirizing Pope **Boniface VIII**. To him is ascribed the authorship of the *Stabat Mater* and other Latin hymns. He also wrote *Laude*, which became important in the development of Italian drama.

TODLEBEN, or **Totleben, Eduard Ivanovitch** (1818–84) Russian soldier and military engineer, born of German descent in Mitau in Courland. He served in the Caucasus, and in the Danubian principalities in 1853. He conducted with skill and energy the defence of Sebastopol until he was severely wounded (June 1855) ; thereafter he completed the fortification of Nikolaieff and Cronstadt. During the Turkish war of 1877–78 he was called to besiege Plevna, which he took after a brilliant defence.

TODT, Fritz (1891–1942) German engineer, born in Pforzheim. As **Hitler**'s inspector of German roads (1933) he was responsible for the construction of the *Reichsautobahnen*. The 'Todt Organization' was also responsible for the constuction of the Siegfried Line (1937). Nazi minister for armaments (1940), fuel and power (1941), he was killed in an aircrash.

TOGO, Count Heihachiro (1847–1934) Japanese naval commander, born in Kagoshima, which was bombarded by British warships in 1863. He was educated at the naval academy in Japan and in the nautical training ship HMS *Worcester* at Greenluthe in

England (1871). He saw active service against China (1894) and was commander-in-chief during the Russian war (1904-05). He bombarded Port Arthur, and defeated the Russian fleet at Tsushima in 1905. He was awarded the British Order of Merit (1906), and created count (1907).

TOJO, Hideki (1885–1948) Japanese soldier, born in Tokyo. He attended military college and in 1919 was appointed military attaché in Germany. He served with the Kwantung army in Manchuria as chief of the secret police and chief of staff from 1937 to 1940. He became minister of war (1940–41) and from 1941 he was premier and dictator of Japan, resigning in 1944. Arrested, he attempted and failed to commit suicide. He was sentenced to death in 1948.

TOKUGAWA the family name of 15 shoguns who were the effective rulers of Japan for two and a half centuries. **Ieyasu** (d.1616) was the eldest son of a warrior chieftain named Matsudaira. He became an ally of the warlord Nobunaga whose policy of unification he supported. Following the death of the regent Hideyoshi in 1598, there was a power struggle between Ieyasu and Ishida Mitsunari that resulted in civil war and Ieyasu's victory at the battle of Sekigahara in 1600. Ieyasu established his capital at Yedo and was appointed shogun by the emperor in 1603. Although he soon resigned the dignity (1605) to his son Hidetada, he remained in practice the national leader of Japan until his death. Under his grandson, Iemitsu (shogun 1623–51), the three Expulsion decrees were passed (1633–39). Aimed at the suppression of Christianity, they effectively closed Japan to foreign trade. During the shogunate of Yoshimune (1716–45), the Code of One Hundred Articles was drawn up embodying the legal reforms instituted by the Tokigawa shoguns. Thereafter the shogunate lost much of its vigour although it did not finally come to an end until 1867 with the resignation of Hitotsubaki Keiki, the 15th shogun.

TOLAND, John (1670–1722) Irish deist, born of Catholic parents in Inishowen, County Donegal. He turned Protestant at the age of 16 and entered Glasgow University in 1687, took his MA at Edinburgh in 1690, and studied theology at Leiden and Oxford. In *Christianity not Mysterious* (1696) he adopted a rationalistic attitude, and his work was burnt by the hangman in Dublin by order of the House of Commons, as being 'atheistical and subversive'. In *Amyntor* (1699) and other works he debated the comparative evidence for the canonical and apocryphal scriptures. He took refuge in England and his pro-Hanoverian pamphlet *Anglia Libera* secured him the favour of the Electress **Sophia** when he accompanied the ambassador to Hanover in 1701. Thereafter he made a meagre living as a literary adventurer and political agent. He also wrote a life of **Milton** (1698) and a *History of the Druids* (1726).

TOLKIEN, John Ronald Reuel (1892–1973) South African-born philologist and author, born in Bloemfontein. Educated at King Edward VI School, Birmingham, and Merton College, Oxford, he became professor of Anglo-Saxon there (1925–45), and of English language and literature (1945–59). His scholarly publications include an edition of *Sir Gawain and the Green Knight* (1925), and studies on **Chaucer** (1934) and *Beowulf* (1937). His interest in language and saga and his fascination for the land of Faerie prompted him to write tales of a world of his own invention peopled by strange beings with their own carefully constructed language and mythology. These include *The Hobbit* (1937), a fascinating tale of the perilous journey of Bilbo Baggins and the dwarfs to recover treasure from Smaug, the dragon, and the more complex sequel, *The Lord of the Rings* (3 vols, 1954–55) in which Bilbo's nephew, Frodo, sets out to destroy a powerful but dangerous ring in Mordor, the land of darkness and evil. Later works include *The Adventure of Tom Bombadil* (1962), *Smith of Wootton Major* (1967) and *The Silmarillion* (1977).

TOLLENS, Hendrik (1780–1856) Dutch poet, born in Rotterdam. He was the author of the Dutch national hymn, *Wien Neerlandsch Bloed*. He also wrote comedies and a tragedy, romances and ballads.

TOLLER, Ernst (1893–1939) German-Jewish poet and playwright, born in Samotschin. A political activist, he was imprisoned in Germany as a socialist revolutionary (1919–24). He was elected to the Bavarian diet in 1924, was banished by the Nazis in 1933 and went to the USA, where he committed suicide in New York in 1939. His expressionist plays include *Masse Mensch* (trans 1923), *Die Maschinenstürmer* (trans 1923), and others. He also wrote poetry and the autobiographical *Eine Jugend in Deutschland* (1933).

TOLMAN, Edward Chace (1886–1959) American psychologist, born in West Newton, Massachusetts. He was educated at MIT, Harvard and Yale. After a short spell of teaching at Northwestern University, he taught at the University of California in Berkeley (1918–54). With his first book, *Purposive Behaviour in Animals and Men* (1932), he broke with the prevailing behaviourist tradition, and attempted to introduce explanatory ideas into animal psychology which were widely dismissed as 'mentalistic'. He argued the need to postulate purpose (goals), as well as spatial representations ('cognitive maps') in the minds of animals in order fully to explain their behaviour. It was not sufficient, he believed, to rely entirely on passive associations as the basis for all learning. His ideas are now more acceptable in academic psychology, largely as a result of the realization that machines (eg guided missiles) can behave as if they have goals, and also because there is clear evidence that brain damage can cause selective disorders in such capacities as planning and spatial orientation, without affecting simple learning abilities.

TOLSTOY, or **Tolstoi,** name of a family of Russian nobles. Count Peter (1645–1729) was a trusted agent of **Peter I, the Great**. Count Peter Alexandrovich (1761–1844) was one of **Suvorov**'s generals and under **Nicholas I** head of a government department. Count Dmitri Andreievich (1823–89) was a reactionary minister of Education, champion of Russian orthodoxy and a 'russifier' of the Poles.

TOLSTOY, Count Alexey Konstantinovich (1817–75) Russian dramatist, lyrical poet and novelist, born in St Petersburg. He wrote a historical trilogy in verse, *The Death of Ivan The Terrible* (1867), *Tsar Fyodor Ioannovich* (1868) and *Tsar Boris* (1870), nonsense verse and the historical novel, *Prince Serebrenni* (trans 1874).

TOLSTOY, Count Alexey Nikolayevich (1882–1945) Russian writer. He joined the White Army after the 1917 Revolution which he portrayed vividly in *The Road to Calvary* (trans 1945), was an émigré in Paris (1919–23) but returned to Russia as an honoured man of letters. Other novels include *The Lame Squire*.

TOLSTOY, Count Leo Nikolayevich (1828–1910) Russian writer, aesthetic philosopher, moralist and mystic, born on the family estate of Yasnaya Polyana in Tula province. He was educated privately and at Kazan University, where he read law and oriental languages but did not graduate. He led a dissolute life in town, played the gentleman farmer, and finally, in 1851, accompanied his elder brother Nicholay to the

Caucasus, where he joined an artillery regiment and there began his literary career. *An Account of Yesterday* (1851) was followed by the autobiographical trilogy, *Childhood* (1852), *Boyhood* (1854) and *Youth* (1856). Commissioned at the outbreak of the Crimean War (1854), he commanded a battery during the defence of Sebastopol (1854–55). After the war, the horrors of which inspired *Tales of Army Life* and the *Sketches of Sevastopol*, he left the army, was fêted by the literary circle in St Petersburg (1856), travelled abroad, visiting Britain, and in 1862 married Sophie Andreyevna Behrs who bore him 13 children. He settled on his Volga estate and combined the duties of a progressive landlord with the six years' literary toil which produced *War and Peace* (1863–69), by many considered the greatest novel ever written. This is at the same time a domestic tale, depicting the fortunes of two notable families, the Rostovs and the Bolkonskis, and a national epic of Russia's struggle, defeat and victory over **Napoleon**. The proud, shy, duty-conscious Prince Andrew and the direct, friendly, pleasure-loving but introspective, morally questing Pierre reflect the dualism in Tolstoy's own character. On his vivid description of military life Tolstoy mounts his conception of history, which demotes 'great men' to mere creatures of circumstance and ascribes victory in battle to the confused chance events which make up the unpredictable fortunes of war. In Pierre's association with freemasonry, Tolstoy expressed his criticism of the established autocratic order. His second great work, *Anna Karenina* (1874–76), carries with it the seeds of Tolstoy's personal crisis between the claims of the creative novelist and the moralizing, 'committed' propagator of his own ethical code, which culminated in *A Confession* (1879–82) and the dialectical pamphlets and stories such as *The Death of Ivan Ilyitch* (1886), *The Kreutzer Sonata* (1889) and *What I Believe*. Christianity is purged of its mysticism and transformed into a severe asceticism based on the doctrine of nonresistance to evil. *The Kingdom of God is within You* (1893), *Master and Man* (1894), the play *The Fruits of Enlightenment* (1891) and *Resurrection* (1899–1900) strayed so far from orthodoxy that the Holy Synod excommunicated him (1901), and he denounced the worship of Jesus as blasphemy. In *What is Art?* he argued that only simple works, such as the parables of the Bible, constitute great art. Everything sophisticated, stylized and detailed, such as his own great novels, he condemned as worthless. He handed over his fortune to his wife and lived poorly as a peasant under her roof. Domestic quarrels made him leave home clandestinely one October night, accompanied only by a daughter and his personal physician. He caught a chill and died in a siding of Astapovo railway station, refusing to see his waiting wife to the last. His doctrines founded a sect and Yasnaya Polyana became a place of pilgrimage. **Mahatma Gandhi**, who had corresponded with him, adopted the doctrine of nonresistance. But he is best known as the consummate master of the 'psychological' novel. **Boris Pasternak**'s father, Leonid, illustrated Tolstoy's works.

TOMBAUGH, Clyde William (1906–) American astronomer, born in Streator, Illinois. Too poor to attend college, he built his own 9-inch telescope, and in 1929 became an assistant at the Lowell Observatory, Arizona State College; he then went to California University as professor. He is the discoverer (1930) of Pluto, the existence of which had been predicted by **Percival Lowell**, and of galactic star clusters. In 1946 he became astronomer at the Aberdeen Ballistics Laboratories in New Mexico, and was astronomer (1955–59), associate professor (1961–65) and professor from 1965, at New Mexico State University.

TOMKINS, Thomas (1572–1656) English composer and organist, born in St David's where his father was organist, one of five brothers who were all accomplished musicians. He studied under **William Byrd**, and in his early twenties became organist of Worcester Cathedral, where he spent most of his life. In 1621 he became one of the organists of the Chapel Royal, and composed music for the coronation of **Charles I** five years later. His compositions include a vast amount of church music, madrigals, part songs and instrumental works.

TOMLINSON, Henry Major (1873–1958) English author, born in London. He wrote *The Sea and the Jungle* (1912), *Tidemarks* (1924) and other travel books as well as novels such as *Gallions Reach* (1927) and a Life of **Norman Douglas** (1931).

TOMONAGA, Sin-Itiro (1906–79) Japanese scientist, born and educated in Kyoto. Professor of physics at Tokyo University, he was awarded the Nobel prize for physics in 1965 together with **Richard Feynman** and **Julian Schwinger** for work in quantum electrodynamics.

TOMPION, Thomas (1639–1713) English clockmaker, known as 'the father of English watchmaking', possibly born in Northhill, Bedfordshire. He reputedly began his career as a furrier, but in 1664 was apprenticed to a London clockmaker and by 1704 was a master clockmaker. In 1675, under the supervision of **Robert Hooke**, he made one of the first English watches equipped with a balance spring; this was subsequently gifted to **Charles II**. By this time he had gained a great reputation, and in 1676 he was appointed clockmaker for the newly-opened Royal Observatory. Continuing to develop watch and clockmaking techniques, he patented the cylinder escapement in 1695 (with Edward Barlow), and branched out into barometers and sundials. From 1690 until his death his workshop was established at No. 67 Fleet Street. He was buried in Westminster Abbey.

TONE, (Theobald) Wolfe (1763–98) Irish nationalist, born in Dublin, the son of a coachmaker. He studied at Trinity College, and was called to the bar in 1789, but soon turned to politics. In 1791 he published a pamphlet, *An Argument on Behalf of the Catholics of Ireland*, and helped to found the Society of United Irishmen. In 1792 he became secretary of the Catholic Committee, which worked for the United Catholic Relief Act of 1793. In 1795 he was forced to leave Ireland to avoid a charge of treason, and made his way via America to Paris (February 1796). He worked hard to induce the Republican government to invade Ireland, and held a command in the small expedition despatched under General **Hoche** that never reached Ireland. After Hoche's death (1797) he tried again. In September 1798 he embarked in a small French squadron, which after a fierce fight in Lough Swilly was captured. Tone was taken to Dublin, tried, and condemned to be hanged as a traitor, but cut his throat in prison.

TONKS, Henry (1862–1937) English artist, born in Solihull. After becoming a fellow of the Royal College of Surgeons he gave up medicine for art, joined the New English Art Club, and was associated with **Sickert** and **Steer**. From 1917 to 1930 he was Slade professor of fine art at the University of London.

TONSON, Jacob (1656–1736) English publisher and bookseller. He published for **Otway**, **Dryden** and **Pope**, **Addison** and **Steele**. He was one of the founders of the Kit Cat club.

TONTI, Lorenzo (1620–90) French banker, born in Naples. He proposed the tontine or latest-survivor system of life insurance.

TOOKE, John, originally **John Horne** (1736–1812) English politician, born in Westminster, a poulterer's son. Educated at Eton and Cambridge, he entered the Middle Temple, but, to please his father, left to take the living of New Brentford. Travelling as a tutor, he met **John Wilkes** in Paris, becoming great friends with him; but when they later fell out, a rasping epistolary controversy followed (1771). While unsuccessfully trying to obtain a Commons seat, he founded the Constitutional Society for parliamentary reform (1771). In 1773 he went back to study law, and during this time came under the favour of the rich William Tooke of Purley who greatly admired his spirited opposition to an enclosure bill. As a result of this encounter Tooke adopted his surname (1782). He was eventually elected to represent Old Sarum in 1801, but was soon excluded by a special Act.

TOOLE, John Lawrence (1832–1906) English comedian, born in London. He went to the City of London School, and in 1853 gave up his desk in a wine merchant's to become an actor. He first played at Ipswich and in London at the St James's Theatre in 1854. In 1874–75 he played in the USA, and in 1890 in Australia. In 1879 he became lessee of the Folly Theatre, which he enlarged, changing the name to 'Toole's Theatre'.

TOPELIUS, Zacharias Sakari (1818–98) Finnish novelist and scholar, born in Unsikaarlepyy. He studied at Helsinki, and became editor of the *Helsingfors Tidningar* newspaper (1842–78). He was appointed professor of Finnish history at Helsinki (1854–78) and rector (1875–78). Writing in Swedish, he is regarded as the father of the Finnish historical novel, with stories of life in the 17th and 18th centuries, published as *Fältskärns berättelten* (The Surgeon's Stories, 1851–60). He also published five volumes of lyrical poetry, and wrote several plays.

TÖPFFER, Rodolphe (1799–1846) Swiss cartoonist and writer, born in Geneva. In 1825 he founded a boarding-school (which he ran for the rest of his life), and in 1832 became professor of rhetoric at Geneva Academy. He was the author of the humorous short story 'La Bibliothèque de mon oncle' (1832), published in *Nouvelles genevoises* (1841), and *Rosa et Gertrude* (1846), amongst others. His drawings were equally felicitous, especially in his *Voyages en zig-zag* (1843–53).

TOPLADY, Augustus Montague (1740–78) English clergyman and hymnist, born in Farnham. Educated at Westminster and Trinity College, Dublin, in 1768 he became vicar of Broad Hembury, Devon, and in 1775 preacher in a chapel near Leicester Fields, London. A strenuous defender of Calvinism, he was a bitter controversialist. His *Church of England vindicated from Arminianism* (1769) is forgotten; but no hymn is better known than 'Rock of Ages' (1775). In 1759 he published *Poems on Sacred Subjects*; his *Psalms and Hymns* (1776) was a collection with only a few of his own.

TOPOLSKI, Feliks (1907–89) Polish-born British painter, draughtsman and illustrator. He studied at Warsaw, and in Italy and Paris, and went to England in 1935. From 1940 to 1945 he was an official war artist, and he was naturalized in 1947. Lively and sensitive drawings by him, depicting everyday life, appeared in many books and periodicals, and he also designed for the theatre. His publications included *Britain in Peace and War* (1941), *88 Pictures* (1951), *Topolski's Chronicle* (1953–79 and 1982–89), *Face to Face* (1964), *Shem, Ham and Japheth Inc.* (1971) and *Topolski's Panoramas* (1981).

TORQUEMADA, Tomas de (1420–98) Spanish Dominican monk, and first inquisitor-general of Spain, born in Valladolid, the nephew of a cardinal. He entered the Dominican order and became prior at Segovia. Chaplain to **Ferdinand** and **Isabella** from 1474, he persuaded them to ask the pope to sanction the institution of the 'Holy Office' of the inquisition, with himself as inquisitor-general from 1483. In this office he displayed pitiless cruelty. He was responsible for the expulsion of the Jews from Spain in 1492.

TORRANCE, Thomas Forsyth (1913–) Scottish theologian, born of missionary parents in Chengtu, Szechwan, western China. He was professor of dogmatics at New College, Edinburgh (1952–79), moderator of the Church of Scotland General Assembly (1976–77), and winner of the Templeton prize (1978). Drawing on the Greek Fathers and **Karl Barth**, he holds that while much recent theology mirrors an outdated model of detached and objective scientific investigation, post-Einsteinian science is open-ended, reponding to the reality it encounters. Theology, therefore, should abandon its preconceptions and do the same, both in relation to science and in the quest for an acceptable ecumenical theology. His views have been expounded in many books including *Theological Science* (1969), *Theology in Reconciliation* (1975), *Divine and Contingent Order* (1981), and *The Trinitarian Faith* (1988).

TORRENS, Sir Robert Richard (1814–86) Australian legal reformer. Collector of customs (1841) and colonial treasurer and registrar general of South Australia (1852), he became an official member of the Legislative Council. Leading a movement for reform of titles to land he sponsored the Real Property Act of 1857 which introduced the Torrens system, whereby title to land was secured by registration. He became first registrar general under the new system, which was widely adopted in Australia, New Zealand and in some states of the USA.

TORREY, John (1796–1873) American botanist, born in New York City. He qualified in medicine and taught physical sciences at the West Point Military Academy and at Cornell, before becoming chief assayer at the US Assay Office in New York from 1854–73. However, throughout his life his main interest was botany, and he prepared several floras for North America and also collected over 40000 plant species; his collection formed the basis for the herbarium of the New York Botanical Gardens. The genus *Torreya* in the yew family is named after him, as well as the Torrey Botanical Club. His publications include *A Flora of the Northern and Middle Sections of the United States* (1824), *A Flora of North America* (1838–43) and *Flora of the State of New York* (1843).

TORRICELLI, Evangelista (1608–47) Italian physicist and mathematician, born probably in Faenza. In 1627 he went to Rome, where he devoted himself to mathematical studies. His *Trattato del Moto* (1641) led **Galilei** to invite him to become his amanuensis; on Galileo's death he was appointed mathematician to the grand-duke and professor to the Florentine Academy. He discovered that, because of atmospheric pressure, water will not rise above 33 feet in a suction pump. To him are owed the fundamental principles of hydromechanics, and in a letter to Ricci (1644) the first description of a barometer or 'torricellian tube'. He greatly improved both telescopes and microscopes, and made several mathematical discoveries.

TORRIGIANO, Pietro (c.1472–1522) Florentine sculptor, born in Florence. He was forced to leave his native city after he had broken the nose of his fellow-pupil **Michelangelo** in a quarrel. After working in Bologna, Siena, Rome and in the Netherlands, he went to England, where he introduced Italian Renaissance art. He executed the tombs of **Margaret Beaufort** in Westminster Abbey, and of her son **Henry VII** and his queen. He settled in Spain and died in the prisons of the Inquisition.

TORRINGTON, Viscount See **BYNG, George**

TORSTENSSON, Lennard, Count of Ortala (1603–51) Swedish soldier, born in Torstena. He served under **Gustav II Adolf** in Germany from 1630 to 1632, and in 1641 was appointed to the command of the Swedish army in Germany. He invaded Silesia, and, when driven back by the imperialists, turned and defeated them at Breitenfeld (November, 1641). Next winter he swept the Danes out of Holstein, and then drove the Austrians back into Bohemia. In 1645 he advanced to the walls of Vienna; in 1646 he returned in ill-health to Sweden.

TORTELIER, Paul (1914–) French cellist, conductor and composer, born in Paris and trained at the conservatoire there. His solo career began with the Concertgebouw, Amsterdam (1946) and with **Beecham** in London (1947); he subsequently toured worldwide. A distinguished teacher, his memorable masterclasses have been televized. He has composed and edited music for his own instrument, and an international anthem, *The Great Flag*, for the UNO.

TORVILL, Jayne (1957–) English ice-skater, born in Nottingham, the partner of **Christopher Dean**. She started skating at the age of ten, and met Dean in 1975. The pair were six times British champions, and won the World, Olympic and European ice-dance titles in 1984. At the height of their success, Torvill and Dean's personal relationship became the fascination of tabloid newspapers. With her partner she received a record 136 perfect 'sixes' (the highest award a judge can give in ice-skating). After retiring from amateur competition in 1985 she continued performing professionally with her partner in their own ice-show.

TOSCANINI, Arturo (1867–1957) Italian conductor, born in Parma, the son of a tailor. He won a scholarship to the Parma conservatory at the age of nine and studied the cello and composition. While on tour with an Italian opera company, presenting *Aïda* in Rio de Janeiro in 1886, the audience hooted at the conductor and in the crisis the orchestra prevailed upon him to take the rostrum. His impeccable musical memory made it a triumphant performance. In 1891 he opened the season at the Carlo Felice in Genoa and by 1898 he had reached La Scala, Milan, where he remained until 1908, returning in 1920–29. He conducted at the Metropolitan Opera House, New York (1908–15), the New York Philharmonic (1926–36), at Bayreuth (1930–31) and Salzburg (1934–37) festivals, and created the National Broadcasting Orchestra of America (1937–53). As late as 1952 he conducted at the Festival Hall, London. Scornful of any need for 'interpreting' a work, his fanatical concern for musical values caused his dislike of exhibitionism. Unremittingly faithful to every detail of the musical score, he was possibly the most tyrannical, yet self-effacing, conductor of his time.

TOSTI, Sir Francesco Paolo (1846–1916) Italian-born British composer, born in Ortona (Abruzzi). He became a naturalized British subject, taught the British royal family and was knighted in 1908. He was the composer of many popular drawing-room songs, including *Good-bye* and *Mattinata*.

TOSTIG See **HAROLD II**

TOTLEBEN See **TODLEBEN**

TOTNES, Earl of See **CAREW, George**

TOTTEL, Richard (d.1594) English printer, working in London, publisher of *Tottel's Miscellany*. From his shop at the 'Star in Hand' inn at Temple Bar, Fleet Street, he published **Thomas More**'s *Dialogue of Comfort against Tribulacion* (1553), **John Lydgate**'s *The Falls of Princes* (1554), and the **Earl of Surrey**'s translations of parts of the *Aeneid*. He also compiled an anthology of contemporary Elizabethan poetry, *Songes and Sonettes* (1557), containing the chief works of Surrey and Sir **Thomas Wyatt**, which came to be known as *Tottel's Miscellany*. He was an original member of the Stationer's Company, founded in 1557.

TOULOUSE-LAUTREC (-MONFA), Henri (Marie Raymond) de (1864–1901) French painter and lithographer, born into a wealthy aristocratic family in Albi. Physically frail, he was encouraged to engage in the traditional field sports, but at the age of fourteen broke both his legs, which then ceased to grow. From 1882 he studied under **Bonnat** in Paris and in 1884 settled in Montmartre, the area which his paintings and posters were to make famous. **Degas** was the decisive influence upon him, but whereas Degas painted the world of ballet from a ballet-lover's theatrical point of view, Lautrec's studies of the cabaret stars, the prostitutes, the barmaids, the clowns and actors of Montmartre betrayed an unfailing if detached interest in the individuality of the human being behind the purely professional function. Hence his dislike of models, and his concentration on the human form caught in a characteristic posture which his superb draughtsmanship facilitated to the neglect of chiaroscuro and background effects. His revolutionary poster designs influenced by Japanese woodcuts which flatten and simplify the subject matter also served to sharpen his gifts for caricature, as in the posters of the music-hall star Aristide Bruant (1892) and Yvette Guilbert (1894). No one has portrayed so effectively the clientèle of these establishments as Lautrec in *Monsieur Boileau at the Café* (1892), *The Bar* (1898) and the *Moulin Rouge* paintings (1894). In 1895 he visited London, in 1896 Spain and in 1897 Holland. His alcoholism brought on a complete breakdown, forcing him to go into a sanatorium; he recovered to resume his hectic life until his death, 1901, from a paralytic stroke brought on by venereal disease. His works also depict fashionable society, as in *At the Races* (1899), and he executed remarkable portraits of his mother (1887), of Van Gogh in pastel (1887; Amsterdam) and of Oscar Wilde, a drawing (1899). Over 600 of his works are in the Musée Lautrec in Albi.

TOURGUENIEFF, Ivan Sergeevich See **TURGENEV**

TOURNEFORT, Joseph Pitton de (1656–1708) French botanist, born in Aix. He travelled in Greece and Turkey with the artist **Claude Aubriet**, and became professor at the Jardin des Plantes in Paris (1688–1708). His definitions of the genera of plants were of fundamental importance to **Linnaeus**, who rejected his general classification in favour of one based on the number of the sexual parts of the flower.

TOURNEUR, Cyril (c.1575–1626) Engish dramatist. In 1600 he published his *Transformed Metamorphosis* (discovered in 1872), a satirical poem; and in 1609 a *Funeral Poem* on Sir **Francis Vere**. In 1613 he wrote an *Elegy* on Prince Henry. His fame rests on two plays, *The Revenger's Tragedy* (printed in 1607), which some critics believed was written by **Thomas Middleton** or **John Webster**, and the inferior *The Atheist's Tragedy*, printed in 1611.

TOURNIER, Paul (1898–1986) Swiss physician and writer on the integration of psychology and

Christianity, born in Geneva, the son of a pastor, Louis Tournier. He spent his whole professional life as a general practitioner in private practice in Geneva. Discovering religious faith through contact with the Oxford Group in 1932, he realized the need to treat his patients as whole human beings. *A Doctor's Casebook in the Light of the Bible* (1954) and *The Meaning of Persons* (1957) were followed by more than a dozen other best-selling books, including *The Strong and the Weak* (1963) and *Learning to Grow Old* (1972). *A Listening Ear: Fifty Years as a Doctor of the Whole Person* (1986) collects his occasional autobiographical reflections.

TOURVILLE, Anne Hilarion de Cotentin, Comte de (1642–1701) French naval commander, born in the Château Tourville, near Coutances. In the year 1690 he inflicted a disastrous defeat on the English and Dutch off Beachy Head, and cast anchor in Torbay. In 1692, **Louis XIV** having resolved to invade England on behalf of **James II**, Tourville sailed from Brest with 42 ships of the line. The English and Dutch, 82 ships strong, under Admiral **Russell**, completely defeated him off Cape La Hogue. In 1693 he defeated an Anglo-Dutch fleet off Cape St Vincent, and a month later, he defeated **Rooke** in the Bay of Lagos, capturing or destroying a large part of the Smyrna fleet. Tourville, made a marshal of France (1693), inflicted enormous damage on English shipping (1694).

TOUSSAINT L'OUVERTURE, Pierre Dominique (1746–1803) Haitian black revolutionary leader (the surname derives from his bravery in once making a breach in the ranks of the enemy). Born of African slave parents in Haiti, he was freed in 1777. In 1791 he joined the black insurgents and in 1797 was made commander-in-chief in the island by the French Convention. He drove out British and Spaniards, restored order and prosperity, and about 1800 began to aim at independence. **Napoleon** proclaimed the re-establishment of slavery, but Toussaint declined to obey. He was eventually overpowered and taken prisoner, and died in a prison in France.

TOUT, Thomas Frederick (1855–1929) English historian, born in London. Educated at St Olave's School, Southwark, and Balliol College, Oxford, he became professor at Manchester (1890–1925). He wrote *Chapters in the Administrative History of Mediaeval England* (1920–33), in which he first used household and wardrobe accounts in the public record office, so becoming the leading authority on English mediaeval history.

TOVEY, Sir Donald Francis (1873–1940) English pianist, composer and writer on music, born in Eton College. He studied under Walter Parratt at Windsor and **Charles Parry** at Balliol College, Oxford, and was influenced by **Joseph Joachim** and by a schoolmistress to whom he owed his musical education until he was 19. He made his professional début as a pianist in 1900, but his reputation stood higher on the Continent than in England, where his musical erudition annoyed the critics. In 1914 he became professor of music at Edinburgh, where he built up the Reid Symphony Orchestra. He composed an opera, *The Bride of Dionysus*, in 1907–8, a symphony, a piano concerto (1903), a cello concerto (for **Pablo Casals**; 1937), and chamber music. But his fame rests largely on his writings, remarkable for great musical perception and learning: *Companion to the Art of Fugue* (1931), *Essays on Musical Analysis* (1935–39), and his articles on music in the *Encyclopaedia Britannica*. He edited **Beethoven**'s sonatas and edited and completed **J S Bach**'s *Art of Fugue*.

TOVEY, John Cronyn, 1st Baron Tovey (1885–1971) English naval commander. He distinguished himself as a destroyer captain in World War I, notably at the battle of Jutland (1916). As commander-in-chief of the Home fleet (1941–43) he was responsible for the operations leading to the sinking of the German battleship *Bismarck*. He became admiral of the fleet in 1943.

TOWER, John (1925–) American politician, born in Houston, Texas, the son of an itinerant Methodist minister. He served with the navy during World War II and afterwards undertook political science research at Georgetown University, Texas and the London School of Economics. Originally a Democrat, he switched parties during the later 1950s and became, in 1961, the first Republican to be elected senator for Texas. Specializing in defence matters, he established himself as an influential figure in the senate, becoming chairman of the Armed Services Committee in 1981. He retired from the senate in 1983 and became a paid consultant to influential arms industry contractors, and also chaired the 1986–87 'Tower Commission' which investigated the role of the National Security Council in the 'Irangate scandal'. In 1989 he was chosen by President **Bush** as defence secretary, but his nomination was rejected by the senate after voiced concern about his defence industry connections and previous alcohol problems.

TOWNE, Francis (c.1739–1816) English painter, born probably in London. As a landscapist he was little known until the 20th century, when his gift for painting simple but graphic watercolours was recognized. Works done in Italy, which he visited in 1780, are now in the British Museum.

TOWNES, Charles Hard (1915–) American physicist. Professor of physics at Massachusetts Institute of Technology (1961–67), he then became professor-at-large at California University. He was joint winner of the Nobel prize for physics with **Nikolai Basov** and **Alexander Prokhorov** in 1964 'for fundamental work in the field of quantum electronics', which had led to the construction of oscillators and amplifiers based on the maser-laser principle.

TOWNSEND, Sir John Sealy Edward (1868–1957) Irish physicist, born in Galway. He became a demonstrator at the Cavendish Laboratory, Cambridge, under Sir **J J Thomson** before becoming professor of physics at Oxford (1900). He contributed to the theory of ionization of gases by collision, and calculated in 1897 the charge on a single gaseous ion.

TOWNSHEND, Charles, 2nd Viscount Townshend (1674–1738) English statesman, born in Raynham Hall, Norfolk. He was educated at Eton and King's College, Cambridge. In 1687 he succeeded his father, Sir Horatio, who, though a Presbyterian, had zealously supported the Restoration and been made baron (1661) and viscount (1682). Charles entered public life as a Tory, but soon, as a disciple of Lord **Somers**, co-operated with the Whigs. He was one of the commissioners for the Union with Scotland (1707), was joint-plenipotentiary with **Marlborough** at The Hague, and negotiated the Barrier Treaty with the States-General. Dismissed in 1712 on the formation of the **Harley** ministry, Townshend obtained the confidence of the Elector of Hanover, who, on his succession as **George I**, made him secretary of state. With **Stanhope**, he formed a Whig ministry, which had **Walpole**, his brother-in-law, for Chancellor of the Exchequer and which passed the Septennial Act (1716). He was lord-lieutenant of Ireland (1717) and became president of the Council and secretary for the Northern Department. His reputation unsullied by the South Sea scandal, he became secretary of state in 1721, but retired in 1730 to Raynham, to grow turnips and improve the rotation of crops.

TOWNSHEND, Charles (1725–67) English statesman, grandson of **Charles, 2nd Viscount Townshend**. He entered the House of Commons in 1747. He was a Lord of the Admiralty and secretary at war (1761–62), and became first lord of trade and the plantations in 1763. In the **Chatham** ministry of 1766 he became Chancellor of the Exchequer, and Chatham's failing health allowed Townshend to assert British authority over the American colonies by imposing swingeing taxes, especially on tea, that ultimately provoked the American War of Independence (1775–83). He was about to form a ministry when he died. A brilliant speaker, by his witty irrelevancies he was able to intoxicate the House of Commons, as in his famous 'champagne speech' (1767).

TOWNSHEND, Sir Charles Vere Ferrers (1861–1924) English soldier, great-grandson of **George, 4th Viscount Townsend**, whose *Military Life* (1901) he wrote. He joined the Indian army and held Chitral Fort for 46 days (1895). In World War I, as major-general in 1915, in conjunction with naval forces up the Tigris, he took Amara. Defeated at Ctesiphon, he fell back upon Kut, where he held out for a month before surrendering (1916). He was MP from 1920.

TOWNSHEND, George, 4th Viscount and 1st Marquess (1724–1807) English soldier, brother of **Charles Townsend** (1725–67). He was educated at St John's College, Cambridge, and fought at Culloden (1746), but retired owing to a difference with William, Duke of **Cumberland**. He was brigadier-general under **Wolfe** at Quebec (1759), and, after Wolfe's death, assumed the command. As lord-lieutenant of Ireland (1767–72), he tried to break down the government by the introduction of settlers as 'undertakers', but his habits became dissipated and he was recalled. He was created marquess in 1786.

TOYNBEE, Arnold (1852–83) English economic historian and social reformer, born in London. He lectured in economic history at Balliol College, Oxford, and to numerous workers' adult education classes, and undertook social work in the East End of London with **Samuel Barnett**. He is best known as the coiner of the phrase and author of *The Industial Revolution in England* (1884). Toynbee Hall, a university settlement in Whitechapel, London, was founded in his memory in 1885. His brother, Paget (1855–1932), was a biographer and authority on the works of **Dante**.

TOYNBEE, Arnold Joseph (1889–1975) English historian, born in London, nephew of **Arnold Toynbee**. Educated at Winchester and Balliol College, Oxford, he became a fellow there. In 1913 he married a daughter of **Gilbert Murray** (divorced 1946), served in the Foreign Office in both World Wars and attended the Paris peace conferences (1919 and 1946). He was Koraes professor of modern Greek and Byzantine history at London (1919–24) and director and research professor of the Royal Institute of International Affairs, London (1925–55). Profound scholarship in the histories of world civilizations, combined with the wide sweep of a near metaphysical turn of mind, produced the brilliant, if later unfashionable, historical writing and synthesis on the grand scale, the monumental ten-volume *History of the World* (1934–54), echoes of which reverberated through his stimulating and controversial BBC Reith Lectures, *The World and the West* (1952). His numerous works include *Greek Historical Thought* (1924) and, *War and Civilization* (1951). One of his sons, (Theodore) Philip (1916–81), was a well-known novelist and journalist (with *The Observer* from 1950); his works include *The Savage Days* (1937), *Comparing Notes* (with his father, 1963), and *Two Brothers* (1964).

TRACEY, Stanley William (1926–) British jazz pianist, bandleader and composer, born in London and largely self-taught. After working with dance orchestras such as the Roy Fox and Ted Heath Bands as well as with modern jazz groups in the 1950s, he was 'house pianist' from 1960 to 1967 at Ronnie Scott's Club, Soho, accompanying many leading contemporary touring musicians. He developed a distinctive, percussive keyboard style. Since the mid 1960s he has led a succession of bands from quartets to 16-piece orchestras, has toured abroad and has written jazz suites such as *Under Milk Wood* (1965) and *Genesis* (1987).

TRACY, David (1939–) American theologian, born in Yonkers, New York. A professor of theology at Chicago University Divinity School, he has explored questions of hermeneutics: the problems of theological communication in modern pluralistic society where addressing the Church, the academic world and society in general is a difficult task requiring imagination, sensitivity and learning from the arts of conversation. Drawing on the thought of **Tillich**, **Lonergan**, **Gadamer** and others, he develops these themes in *Blessed Rage for Order* (1975), *The Analogical Imagination* (1980), and *Plurality and Ambiguity* (1986).

TRACY, Spencer (1900–67) American film actor, born in Milwaukee, Wisconsin. Trained at the American Academy of Dramatic Arts, he made his Broadway début in *A Royal Fandango* (1923) and his feature film début in *Up the River* (1930). Initially typecast as a tough guy and gangster, his simple technique and reliability eventually earned him the calibre of role that contributed to his reputation as one of the screen's finest actors. Nominated nine times for the Academy Award, he won it for his performances in *Captains Courageous* (1937) and *Boy's Town* (1938). A long personal and professional association wth **Katharine Hepburn** resulted in a series of 'battle of the sexes' comedies, from *Woman of the Year* (1942) to his final, poignant performance in *Guess Who's Coming to Dinner* (1967).

TRADESCANT, John (the Elder) (1570–c.1638) English naturalist, gardener and traveller, probably born in Suffolk. He became head gardener to the Earls of Salisbury and later to King **Charles I**. He travelled to Arctic Russia in 1618, and later established the first museum open to the public, the Musaeum Tradescantianum, in Lambeth, London. He and his son, **John Tradescant** (the Younger), introduced many plants into English gardens.

TRADESCANT, John (the Younger) (1608–62) English gardener, born in Meopham, Kent, son of **John Tradescant** (the Elder). He went out to Virginia to collect plants and shells (1637) and succeeded his father as head gardener to King **Charles I** in 1638. He was tricked when drunk into bequeathing the celebrated Musaeum Tradescantianum in Lambeth to **Elias Ashmole**, and it became the basis for the Ashmolean Museum in Oxford.

TRAHERNE, Thomas (c.1636–1674) English poet, born in Hereford, the son of a shoemaker. He studied at Brasenose College, Oxford, became rector of Credenhill (1657) and in 1667 became chaplain to the lord keeper of the great seal, Sir Orlando Bridgeman. He wrote the anti-Catholic *Roman Forgeries* (1673), and *Christian Ethicks*, published after his death in 1675. His major work, *Centuries of Religious Meditations* in prose, was first published in 1908. He also wrote poetry, which was not published until 1903. A late discovery, *Poems of Felicity*, was published in

1910. His work is full of the strikingly original imagery of the mystic, yet a mystic who as a 'Christian Epicurean' was prepared to give *Thanksgiving for the Body*.

TRAILL, Henry Duff (1842–1900) English journalist and man of letters, born in Blackheath, London. He was editor of *The Observer* (1889–91) and of *Social England* (1893–97).

TRAJAN, Marcus Ulpius Trajanus (c.53–117) Roman emperor, born near Seville. Gaining distinction in the Parthian and German campaigns, he was made consul (91), was adopted by Nerva as his colleague and successor (97), and became sole ruler in 98. Militarily ambitious, Trajan set out in 101 on his campaign against the Dacians. The struggle was long and fierce; but the Romans at last gained a decisive superiority, and Dacia was made a Roman province (106). In 113 the emperor left Italy for his great expedition in the East, directed mainly against the Parthians. He made Armenia and Mesopotamia into Roman provinces, but met with some defeats, despite the capture of Ctesiphon (115). Meanwhile the Jews rose in Cyprus and Cyrene; other enemies took advantage of the emperor's absence; and Trajan, already in failing health, set sail for Italy, but died at Selinus in Cilicia. Though most of Trajan's reign was spent in the field, the internal administration was excellent. Informers were severely punished and peculating governors of provinces prosecuted. The empire was covered in all directions by new military routes; canals, bridges, and harbours were constructed, new towns built, the Pontine Marshes partially drained, and the magnificent 'Forum Trajani' erected. Few Roman emperors enjoyed such a favourable reputation in their lifetime and after death.

TRANSTRÖMER, Tomas (1931–) Swedish poet and psychologist, born in Stockholm. He graduated there in 1956, since when he has worked as a psychologist, including a spell at Roxtuna institution for young offenders. His first collection of poems, *17 dikter* (1954, 17 Poems), characterized by a visionary reality couched in precise pictures, aroused attention and he has since become a leading poet of the post-war era. Refusing to be hustled by his activist colleagues demanding political 'commitment' he chose to ponder 'the great mystery of existence'. His poems consider the contrast between man's spiritual and mental existence, his need for solitude and yet social contact; and how history lives on in the present. These tensions are reflected in his poetic style which skilfully juxtaposes movement and stasis, muted language and striking images. His metaphors are often inspired by music, travel and nature. His ten collections of poems have been translated into English either in part or *in toto* by Robin Fulton in *Three Swedish Poets* (1970), *Selected Poems* (1974) and *Collected Poems* (1987).

TRAPASSI, Pietro See **METASTASIO**

TRAUBE, Ludwig (1818–76) German pathologist, brother of **Moritz Traube**, born in Ratibor. He became professor at the Berlin Friedrich-Wilhelm Institute (1853) and at Berlin University (1872). He pioneered the study of experimental pathology in Germany, using animal experimentation.

TRAUBE, Moritz (1826–94) German wine merchant and chemist, brother of **Ludwig Traube**, born in Ratibor. At Breslau he made artificial semipermeable membranes and so made possible the determination of osmotic pressures.

TRAUBEL, Helen (1899–1972) American soprano, born in St Louis, where she made her début in 1923. She first sang at the New York Metropolitan in 1937, then as Sieglinde (1939), and was the leading Wagnerian soprano there after **Kirstin Flagstad**'s departure (1941), resigning after a dispute over her nightclub appearances (1953). She also worked in film and television, and wrote detective novels.

TRAVEN, B, pseud of **Berick Traven Torsvan,** originally **Albert Otto Max Feige,** also known as **Ret Marut** (1890–1969) Polish-born German novelist of working-class stock, born in Swiebodzin, a Polish town since subsumed into Germany. His first stories emerged in Germany in 1925 (as *Die Baumwollpflücker—The Cottonpickers*) and it is thought he was active as a Communist there at the end of World War I. *The Death Ship*, an anti-capitalist tale of a seaman cought up in a plan by shipowners to sink the Yorikke and cash in on the insurance, was highly popular. In the mid-1920s, he went to Mexico and from there, in German, came twelve novels and short stories, the most famous being *The Treasure of the Sierre Madre* (1934), filmed by **John Huston** in 1947.

TRAVERS, Ben (Benjamin) (1886–1980) English dramatist and novelist, born in Hendon. He was educated at Charterhouse, served in the RAF in both World Wars and was awarded the Air Force Cross (1920). A master of light farce, he wrote to suit the highly individual comic talents of Ralph Lynn, **Robertson Hare** and Tom Walls in such pieces as *A Cuckoo in the Nest* (1925), *Rookery Nook* (1926), *Thark* (1927) and *Plunder* (1928), which played in the Aldwych Theatre, London, for many years. His last work was a comedy, *The Bed Before Yesterday* (1976).

TRAVERS, Morris William (1872–1961) English chemist, born in London. Educated at Blundells, London, and Nancy, he was an authority on glass technology. Professor at Bristol from 1903 to 1937, he was technical consultant to the ministry of supply (1940–45). He discovered, with **Ramsay**, the inert gases krypton, xenon and neon (1894–1908), and investigated the phenomena of low temperatures. He wrote *The Discovery of the Rare Gases* (1928).

TREDGOLD, Thomas (1788–1829) English engineer and cabinet-maker, born in Brandon, Durham. He became a carpenter and studied building construction and science in London. His *Elementary Principles of Carpentry* (1820) was the first serious manual on the subject. He also wrote manuals on cast iron (1821), *The Steam Engine* (1827), and other works.

TREE, Sir Herbert Beerbohm (1853–1917) English actor-manager, half-brother of Sir **Max Beerbohm**, born in London. After a commercial education in Germany, he took to the stage and scored his first success as Spalding in *The Private Secretary*. In 1887 he took over the Haymarket Theatre until in 1897, with the box-office success of *Trilby*, he built His Majesty's Theatre, where he rivalled, by his mastery of stagecraft, the Shakespearean productions of **Irving** at the Lyceum. A great character actor, he excelled in roles such as Svengali, Falstaff, Hamlet, Fagin, Shylock, Malvolio, and Micawber. He scored a tremendous success when he first produced Shaw's *Pygmalion* in 1914. His wife, Helen Maud (1864–1937), whom he married in 1883, was also an accomplished actress, and directed His Majesty's Theatre from 1902; she made her last professional appearance in the film *The Private Life of Henry VIII* (1936).

TREITSCHKE, Heinrich von (1834–96) German historian, born in Dresden. He studied at Bonn, Leipzig, Tübingen and Heidelberg, and became a professor at Freiburg-im-Breisgau (1863), Kiel (1866), Heidelberg (1867) and Berlin (1874). He succeeded **Ranke** in 1886 as Prussian historiographer. He was member of the Reichstag from 1871–88. His chief work, *History of Germany in the Nineteenth Century* (1879–94; trans 1915–18), though written from the dogmatic Prussian viewpoint, is of great literary and historical value, and his method, scope and treatment of the subject have been compared to those of **Macaulay** in his *History of England*. An ardent believer in a powerful Germany with a powerful empire, and in the necessity of war to achieve and maintain this, his writings had a strong influence before World War I.

TRELAWNY, Edward John (1792–1881) English author and adventurer, born of a famous Cornish family. He entered the navy at eleven but deserted, and lived a life of adventure in the East. He was the author of the autobiographical *Adventures of a Younger Son* (1831) and of *Records of Shelley, Byron and the Author* (1858). In 1821 he made the acquaintance of **Shelley** at Pisa, and helped to burn the drowned poet's body.

TRELAWNY, Sir Jonathan (1650–1721) English prelate. He became bishop in turn of Bristol (1685), Exeter (1688) and Winchester (1707). Though intensely loyal to the crown, he was one of the Seven Bishops who petitioned against **James II**'s Declaration of Indulgence (1688) and were tried for libel. He is the hero of **R S Hawker**'s ballad, 'And shall Trelawny die?'

TRENCH, Frederick Herbert (1865–1923) Irish poet, dramatist and producer, born in Avoncore, County Cork. He was educated at Haileybury and Keble College, Oxford, wrote volumes of verse such as *Deirdre Wed* (1900) and *New Poems* (1907), and was artistic director of the Haymarket Theatre (1909–11).

TRENCH, Richard Chenevix (1807–86) Irish prelate, philologist and poet, born in Dublin. Educated at Harrow and Trinity College, Cambridge, he became curate in 1841 to **Samuel Wilberforce**, and during 1835–46 published six volumes of poetry. In 1845 he became rector of Itchenstoke; in 1847 professor of theology in King's College, London; in 1856 dean of Westminster; and from 1864 to 1884 he was archbishop of Dublin. He was buried in Westminster Abbey. In philology he popularized the scientific study of words, and the *New English Dictionary*, later the *Oxford English Dictionary*, was begun at his suggestion. His principal works were *Notes on the Parables of our Lord* (1841), *Notes on the Miracles of our Lord* (1846), and *The Study of Words* (1851).

TRENCHARD, Hugh Montague, 1st Viscount Trenchard (1873–1956) English service chief, marshal of the RAF. He entered the Forces in 1893, serving on the North West Frontier, in South Africa, and with the West African Frontier Force. His early interest in aviation led to his appointment as assistant commandant, Central Flying School (1913–14), and to his posting as the first general officer commanding the RFC in the field. Chief of the Air Staff between 1919 and 1929, his subsequent work as commissioner of the metropolitan police did nothing to obscure his fame as the 'Father of the RAF', though he carried out a number of far-reaching reforms, including the establishment of the Police College at Hendon. He was raised to the peerage in 1930.

TRENCK, Franz, Baron, or **Freiherr von der** (1711–49) Austrian adventurer, born in Reggio in Calabria, where his father was an Austrian general. At 16 he entered the army, but soon had to leave it. In the Austrian War of Succession (1740–48) he raised (1741) at his own cost a body of Pandours, who were even more distinguished for cruelty than for daring. In September 1742, he attacked and destroyed Cham, in the Palatinate, and in 1745 he offered to capture **Frederick II, the Great**, and managed to seize the king's tent and much booty. He was suspected, however, of treachery, and imprisoned; he escaped, but was recaptured and condemned to lifelong imprisonment on the Spielberg at Brünn, where he poisoned himself.

TRENT See **BOOT, Sir Jesse**

TRÉSAGUET, Pierre Marie Jerome (1716–96) French civil engineer, born in Nevers into a family of engineers. He made his career in the Corps des Ponts et Chaussées, becoming inspector-general of the Corps in 1775. He is best known for the improved method of road construction he introduced, involving the use of carefully placed stones in the base layer with progressively smaller sizes towards the surface. He also emphasized the importance of good drainage and regular maintenance. His system was generally adopted in France and elsewhere in Europe; in Britain it was followed by **Thomas Telford** and developed by **John Loudon McAdam**.

TREURNICHT, Andries Petrus (1921–) South African politician, born in Piketberg. He studied theology at the universities of Cape Town and Stellenbosch and practised as a minister in the Dutch Reformed Church from 1946, before being elected to South Africa's parliament in 1971 under the National party banner, representing the Waterberg constituency. He became Transvaal provincial party leader in 1978 and held a succession of posts in the cabinets of **P W Botha** from 1979, where he gained a reputation as a hardliner ('verkrampte'). Staunchly opposed to Botha's programme of constitutional reform, which involved a degree of power-sharing with coloureds and Asians, he resigned from the party with 15 colleagues in 1982 to form the new, right-wing Conservative party (CP). The CP, which has pressed for a return to traditional apartheid values and effective partitioning of the country, has secured the support of more than a quarter of the white electorate.

TREVELYAN, Sir Charles Edward, 1st Baronet (1807–86) English administrator, father of Sir **George Otto Trevelyan**. Educated at Charterhouse and Haileybury, he became a writer in the Bengal civil service, assistant-secretary to the Treasury (1840–59), governor of Madras (1859–60) and Indian finance minister (1862–65), when he carried out great social reforms and a public works programme. He had married Hannah Moore, **Macaulay**'s sister, in 1834. He was created a baronet in 1874 and wrote on Indian education (1838), etc.

TREVELYAN, Sir Charles Philips, 3rd Baronet (1870–1958) English politician, son of Sir **George Otto Trevelyan**. He was educated at Harrow and Trinity College, Cambridge, entered parliament in 1899 and in 1908 became Liberal parliamentary secretary to the board of education. He resigned in 1914, disapproving of war with Germany. From 1922 he sat as a Labour MP and became president of the Board of Education (1924, 1929–31), but resigned when his School Attendance bill was rejected. He was lord lieutenant of Northumberland (1930–49).

TREVELYAN, George Macaulay (1876–1962) English historian, born in Stratford-on-Avon, son of Sir **George Otto Trevelyan**. He was educated at Harrow and Trinity College, Cambridge, of which he was elected master (1940–51). He served in World War I and was regius professor of modern history at Cambridge (1927–40). He is best known for his *English Social History* (1944), in which his considerable literary gifts find full expression; it is a companion volume to his *History of England* (1926). Other works include studies of **Garibaldi** (1907, 1909, 1911), Lives of **John Bright** (1913) and of his father (1932), *British History in the Nineteenth Century* (1922), and several volumes of lectures and essays, including an autobiography (1949).

TREVELYAN, Sir George Otto, 2nd Baronet (1838–1928) English statesman, son of Sir **Charles Edward Trevelyan**, born in Rothley Temple, Leicestershire. Educated at Harrow and Trinity College, Cambridge, he entered parliament in 1865 as a Liberal and became a Lord of the Admiralty (1868–70), parliamentary secretary to the same (1880–82), chief secretary for Ireland (1882–84) and secretary for Scotland (1886, 1892–95). He wrote a number of historical works, among them a Life of his uncle, **Macaulay** (1876–1908), a Life of **Fox** (1880), and the *American Revolution* (1909).

TREVES, Sir Frederick (1853–1923) English surgeon, born in Dorchester. Educated in London, he became professor at the Royal College of Surgeons. He was a founder of the British Red Cross Society and made improvements in operations for appendicitis. The 'Elephant Man' was one of his patients.

TREVET, Nicholas See **TRIVET**

TREVINO, Lee Buck (1939–) American golfer, born in Dallas, Texas, of Mexican extraction. Known as 'Supermex', he won his first US Open in 1968. In 1971 he established a golfing record by winning three Open championships (the US, Canadian and British) in the same year, retaining his British title the following year. In 1975, while playing in the Western Open, he had a remarkable escape from death after being struck by lightning. He won the PGA Open at the age of 44. A shrewd match commentator, he continues to earn a living from professional golf.

TREVIRANUS, Gottfried Reinhold (1776–1837) German biologist and anatomist, born in Bremen, brother of **Ludolf Christian Treviranus**. He wrote an important work on biology (1802–22) and made histological and anatomical studies of vertebrates.

TREVIRANUS, Ludolf Christian (1779–1864) German naturalist, born in Bremen, brother of **Gottfried Treviranus**. He was professor at Bremen, Rostock, Breslau and Bonn, and is known for his discovery of intercellular spaces.

TREVISA See **JOHN OF TREVISA**

TREVITHICK, Richard (1771–1833) English engineer and inventor, born in Illogan, Redruth. He became a mining engineer, and devoted his life to the improvement of the steam engine. Unlike **James Watt**, he favoured higher steam pressures which gave greater power from smaller cylinders; from 1800 to 1815 he built several steam road carriages, the first steam railway locomotives and a large number of stationary steam engines. Nothing he did was commercially successful, however, and he died in debt.

TREVOR, Sir John (c.1637–1717) English politician. He was elected speaker in 1685, and made master of the rolls. Though a minion of Judge **Jeffreys**, he was again speaker (1690–95). For accepting a bribe as first commissioner of the court of Chancery, he was expelled from parliament in 1695; he still, however, retained the mastership of the rolls and is deemed an able judge.

TREVOR, William (William Trevor Cox) (1928–) Irish short-story writer, novelist and playwright, born in Mitchelstown, County Cork. Educated at St Columba's College and Trinity College, Dublin, he taught history and art, sculpted and wrote advertising copy before devoting himself to literature. His first book was a novel, *A Standard of Behaviour* (1958), but though he has published ten subsequently, including *Mrs Eckdorff in O'Neill's Hotel* (1969) and *The Children of Dynmouth* (1976), he is by inclination a short story writer. He has lived in England for much of his life but Ireland is the source of his inspiraton. A superlative storyteller, his collections include *The Day We Got Drunk on Cake* (1967), *The Ballroom of Romance* (1972), *Angels at the Ritz* (1975) and *The News from Ireland* (1986). *The Stories of William Trevor* appeared in 1983.

TREVOR-ROPER, Hugh Redwald, Baron Dacre of Glanton (1914–) English historian and controversialist, the son of a Northumberland doctor. He was educated at Charterhouse and Christ Church College, Oxford, and, having written a somewhat derisive biography of **William Laud**, won international fame for a vivid reconstruction based on research on behalf of British forces in occupied Germany, *The Last Days of Hitler* (1947). He was Regius professor of modern history at Oxford (1957–80), and was an amusing if patronizing and abrasive lecturer and essayist, engaging enthusiastically on such questions as medieval Christendom, European witch-hunting, the **Kennedy** assassination, the **Kim Philby** affair, the Scottish Enlightenment, British devolution, and, in an exceptionally ill-judged moment, the so-called **Hitler** diaries whose authenticity he championed until their fraudulence was revealed. He was master of Peterhouse College, Cambridge, from 1980 to 1987.

TRIBONIANUS (c.470–c.544) Byzantine jurist, born, probably, in Pamphylia. He held various offices under the emperor **Justinian**, and directed the compilation of Justinian's *Pandecta* and the revised Codex, and participated in the preparation of the Institutes. As minister of justice thereafter he was probably responsible for some of Justinian's *Novellae*.

TRIDUANA, St (4th century) Christian religious. She is said to have come to Scotland with St **Regulus** and lived at Rescobie in Angus. Legend relates that, troubled by the attentions of the local king and learning of his admiration for her eyes, she plucked them out and sent them to him. She retired to Restalrig, where there is a well once famous as a cure for eye diseases.

TRIKOUPIS, Spyridon (1788–1873) Greek statesman and writer, born in Missolonghi. He was private secretary to Lord Guilford in the Ionian Isles, studied in Rome, Paris and London, and joined the patriots on the outbreak of the War of Independence (1821). He was thrice envoy-extraordinary to London, was minister of foreign affairs and of public instruction (1843), vice-president of the Senate (1844–49), and envoy-extraordinary to Paris (1850). His *Speeches* appeared in 1836; his *History of the Greek Revolution* from 1853 to 1857. His son, Kharilaos (1832–96), was foreign minister (1866) and premier repeatedly from 1875 to 1895.

TRILLING, Lionel (1905–75) American literary critic, born in New York and educated at Columbia University, where he became professor of English in 1948. A trenchant and influential writer, he held that culture was central to the human experience, and that art and literature cannot exist in a vacuum. In the tradition of **Matthew Arnold**, on whom he wrote a standard book (1939), his interests were wide-ranging and his voluminous oeuvre includes *The Liberal Imagination* (1950), *The Opposing Self* (1955), *Beyond Culture* (1965) and *Sincerity and Authenticity* (1972). His only novel, *The Middle of the Journey*, was published in 1947.

TRINDER, Tommy (Thomas Edward) (1909–89) English comedian and actor, born in Streatham, London, the son of a tram driver. He first went on stage at the age of 12 and went on to gain experience in small-town variety shows. With cockney sparrow jauntiness, a perennial trilby, and an ear-to-ear grin, he was a master of ad lib and the quick retort, and happily performed without a script. His first big break came in 1939 when he was invited to join the Band Waggon show at the London Palladium, and went on to become a national name, both as a stand-up comic in such revues as *Happy and Glorious* and *Best Bib and Tucker*, and as a leading man in films like *Sailors Three* (1940),

The Bells Go Down (1943) and *Champagne Charlie* (1944). The self-confessed 'Mr Woolworth of show-business' whose famous catchphrase was 'You lucky people', he worked tirelessly during World War II, travelling to Italy, the Middle East and the Far East to entertain the troops. After the war he successfully compered the ITV show *Sunday Night at the London Palladium* (1954–58). A football enthusiast, he was chairman of Fulham Football Club from 1955 to 1976. He continued to perform until his late seventies.

TRINTIGNANT, Jean-Louis (1930–) French actor, born in Port-St Esprit. He abandoned his legal studies to become an actor, making his Paris stage début in *A Chacun Selon Sa Faim* (1951). His first major role in *Responsabilité Limité* (1954) led to his film début in the short *Peachinef* (1955), and his subsequent appearance in *Et Dieu Créa La Femme* (And God Created Woman, 1956) brought him popular attention. His pale-skinned impassivity and sensitive eyes have lent themselves to the portrayal of romantic vulnerability and the illumination of the interior life of the psychologically disturbed. His career includes the comedy *Le Cœur Battant* (The French Game, 1960), the internationally successful romance *Un Homme et Une Femme* (A Man and a Woman, 1966) and a variety of work for Europe's most distinguished directors including *Les Biches* (The Does, 1968), *Z* (1968), *Ma Nuit Chez Maud* (My Night at Maude's, 1969) and *Il Conformista* (The Conformist, 1970). *Under Fire* (1983) marked a rare venture into English-language productions. He has also directed *Une Journée Bien Remplie* (A Well-Filled Day, 1972) and *Le Maître Nageur* (1979).

TRIPP, John (1927–86) Welsh poet, born in Bargoed, Glamorgan, and brought up, a farrier's son, in Whitchurch, Cardiff. After working as a journalist in London, he returned to Wales in 1969 and worked as a free-lance writer for the rest of his life. He published six volumes of poetry, his principal subjects being the history of Wales and the present condition of its people.

TRIPPE, Juan Terry (1899–1981) American airline founder, born in Seabright, New Jersey. The son of an investment banker, he graduated from Yale in 1922, interrupting his studies to fly with the navy as a night bomber pilot. The following year he organized Long Island Airways, then Colonial Air Transport and founded Pan American Airways in 1927. Other airlines were absorbed into the company, including Compania Mexicana de Aviacion and Grace Airways, from which a subsidiary, PANAGRA, existed until 1965. The company offered the first scheduled round-the-world air service in 1947. In 1955 Trippe placed the first US order for jet transports. He was an indomitable fighter for his airline and the power of US civil aviation.

TRISTRAM, Henry Baker (1822–1906) English clergyman, naturalist and traveller, born in Eglingham, near Alnwick, Northumbria. Educated at Durham School and Lincoln College, Oxford, he became an Anglican clergyman. Tuberculosis forced him to go abroad to Algeria, of which he wrote *The Great Sahara* (1860), but his main interest was in the flora and fauna of Palestine, where he made several long journeys and was the author of the first ornithological surveys of the region, including *The Land of Israel* (1865), *Natural History of the Bible* (1867), *The Flora and Fauna of Palestine* (1884), and *The Land of Moab* (1873). Tristram's Warbler and Tristram's Serin are named after him.

TRIVET or **Trevet, Nicholas** (fl.1300) English chronicler. A Dominican friar, he wrote *Annales Sex Regum Angliae*, covering the period 1136–1307.

TROCHU, Louis Jules (1815–96) French soldier, born in Palais (Morbihan). After a distinguished military career in the Crimea and elsewhere, he entered the ministry of war. But the unpalatable truths contained in his *L'Armée française en 1867* set the court against him. In 1870 he received a command at Toulouse, on 17 August was made governor of Paris, and under the republic became chief of the national defence. Regarded as overcautious and timid, he resigned the governorship in January 1871, but remained president of the national defence until 1872. Works by him in his own defence are *Pour la vérité et pour la justice* (1873) and *La Politique et le siège de Paris* (1874).

TROG, Walter originally **Ernest Fawkes** (1924–) Canadian-born British cartoonist and musician, born in Ontario. He came to England in 1931 and studied art at Camberwell, then did camouflage work during World War II and joined the *Daily Mail* as staff cartoonist in 1945, creating *Rufus* (later *Flook*), a daily strip for children (1949). Beginning as whimsy, this strip developed into satirical comment under many scriptwriters, including Sir **Compton Mackenzie** and eventually Trog himself. Trog (the pen-name comes from the Troglodytes, his jazzband for which he plays clarinet) expanded into political cartooning in the *Spectator* (1959), then the *Daily Mail* (1968), and colour covers for *Punch* (1971).

TROLLOPE, Anthony (1815–82) English novelist, born in London. His father was an unsuccessful lawyer and barrister and consequently his school days at Harrow and Winchester were miserable. Later, when the family's financial circumstances were at their lowest, they moved to Belgium where his father died. His mother, **Frances Trollope**, a woman of enviable energy, maintained the family by her prolific writing. In 1834, Trollope became a junior clerk in the General Post Office in London where he marked time, professionally speaking, until he was transferred to Ireland in 1841. He left the Civil Service in 1867, an important but idiosyncratic official whose achievements included the introduction in Great Britain of the pillar-box for letters. A year later he stood unsuccessfully for parliament, and from 1867 to 1870 he edited the *St Paul's Magazine*, in which several of his books were serialized. His first novel, *The Macdermots of Ballycloran*, did not appear until 1847, and his second, *The Kellys and the O'Kellys* (1848), shared its lack of success. With *The Warden* (1855), the first of the Barchester novels, came an inkling of Trollope's genius. It is the story of the struggle over Harding's Hospital, and introduced into English fiction some of its most durable and memorable characters—Mr Harding, who recurs constantly throughout the Barchester series, Archdeacon Grantly, and Bishop Proudie who with his redoubtable wife dominates *Barchester Towers* (1857). The rest of the series are: *Doctor Thorne* (1858), *Framley Parsonage* (1861), *The Small House at Allington* (1864), and *The Last Chronicle of Barset* (1867). Interconnected by character and unified by their West Country setting in the imaginary town of Barset, the novels are distinguished by their quiet comedy, slow pace and piquant detail. The series format appealed to Trollope's industry and he embarked on a second, more ambitious sequence—known collectively as the 'Palliser' novels, after Plantagenet Palliser, who features in each—with the publication in 1864 of *Can You Forgive Her?*. Its sequel was *Phineas Finn* (1869), and others in the series are *The Eustace Diamonds* (1873), *Phineas Redux* (1876), *The Prime Minister* (1876), and *The Duke's Children* (1880). Regarding himself more of a craftsman than an artist, Trollope began work every morning at 5.30 and generally completed his literary work before he dressed for breakfast. His output was consequently prodigious and comprises 47 novels, travel books, biographies of **Thackeray**, **Cicero** and Lord **Palmerston**, plays, short stories and literary sketches. His two renowned series apart, other novels worthy of note include *The Three Clerks* (1857), *The Bertrams* (1859), *Orley Farm* (1862), *The Vicar of Bullhampton* (1870), *The Way We Live Now* (1875) and *Doctor Wortle's School* (1881). Periodically he falls from fashion but is currently enjoying a resurgence. His *Autobiography* (1833) is an antidote to more romantic accounts of the literary life.

TROLLOPE, Frances, née **Milton** (1780–1863) English novelist, born in Stapleton near Bristol, the mother of **Anthony Trollope**. In 1809 she married Thomas Anthony Trollope (1774–1835), a failed barrister and fellow of New College, Oxford. In 1827 he fell into dire financial difficulties, which were not relieved by moving to Cincinnati, Ohio, in 1827. During her three years in the USA, Mrs Trollope amassed the material for her *Domestic Manners of the Americans* (1832), a critical and witty book much resented in America. Left a widow in 1835, she travelled widely on the Continent, writing articles and fiction for her livelihood, and eventually settled in Florence (1843), where she lived until her death. Of her novels, the most successful were *The Vicar of Wrexhill* (1837), and *The Widow Barnaby* (1839), with its sequel, *The Widow Married* (1840). In all she wrote 115 volumes, now mostly forgotten.

TROMP, Cornelis (1629–91) Dutch naval commander, the son of **Maarten Tromp**. He shared the glory of de **Ruyter**'s Four Days' battle (1666) off Dunkirk, and won fame in the battles against the combined English and French fleets, 7 and 14 June 1673. On a visit to England in 1675 he was created baron by **Charles II** and was appointed lieutenant-governor of the United Provinces (1676).

TROMP, Maarten Harpertszoon (1597–1653) Dutch naval commander, born in Briel. He went to sea as a child with his father, and was captured by an English pirate and compelled to serve two years as a cabin boy. In 1624 he was in command of a frigate; lieutenant-admiral, he defeated a superior Spanish fleet off Gravelines in 1639. The same year he defeated a combined Spanish-Portuguese fleet off the Downs, and captured 13 richly-laden galleons. In the first Dutch War (1652–53) he fought several engagements with **Blake**, winning some and losing some. He was killed in an engagement with **Monk** off the coast of Holland.

TROTSKY, Leon, alias of **Lev Davidovich Bronstein** (1879–1940) Russian Jewish revolutionary, born in Yanovka in the Ukraine and educated in Odessa. At the age of 19 he was arrested as a member of a Marxist group and was sent to Siberia. He escaped in 1902, joined **Lenin** in London, and in the abortive 1905 revolution became president of the first Soviet in St Petersburg. Escaping from a further exile period in Siberia, he became a revolutionary journalist among Russian émigrés in the West. After the March 1917 revolution he returned to Russia, joined the Bolshevik party and with Lenin was mainly responsible for organizing the November Revolution. As commissar for foreign affairs he conducted negotiations with the Germans for the peace treaty of Brest-Litovsk. In the civil war Trotsky, as commissar for war, brought the Red Army of 5000000 men into being from a nucleus of 7000 men. On Lenin's death in 1924 Trotsky's influence began to decline. Within two years **Stalin** had ousted him from the politburo and in 1927 he was exiled to Central Asia. His repetition of Lenin's warnings against Stalin, and his condemnation of Stalin's autocratic ambition, led to Trotsky's expulsion from Russia in 1929. He continued to agitate and intrigue as an exile in several countries. In 1937, having been sentenced to death in his absence by a Soviet court, he found asylum in Mexico City. There he was assassinated with an ice pick in 1940 by Ramon del Rio (alias Jacques Mornard). Ruthless, energetic, a superb orator and messianic visionary, Trotsky inspired as much confidence in Lenin as he awakened mistrust in the still wilier Stalin. In his later years he was the focus of those Communists, Russian and otherwise, who opposed the endless opportunism of Stalin. He was the revolutionary 'pur sang'—and a writer of power, wit and venom. He was an advocate of permanent revolution and, in contrast to Stalin's 'socialism in one country', world revolution. His publications include *History of the Russian Revolution* (1932) *The Revolution Betrayed* (1937), *Stalin* (1948) and *Diary in Exile* (trans 1959), and remain influential in Western Marxist circles. Although not yet formally rehabilitated, Trotsky left the ranks of Soviet 'non-persons' in 1987 and his ideas and contributions to Soviet Communism are now, during the new 'glasnost' era, being discussed in Soviet media and academic circles. His son, Sergei Sedov, who was shot dead in Moscow in 1937, was rehabilitated by the Soviet Supreme Court in 1988.

TROTZENDORF See **FRIEDLAND, Valentin**

TROUGHTON, Edward (1753–1835) English instrument-maker, born in Corney, Cumberland. He was apprenticed to his eldest brother, John, and set up in business with him in London as makers of measuring and surveying instruments. In 1778 John made a copy of **Ramsden**'s dividing engine and they began to produce precisely graduated sextants and a variety of other navigational and astronomical instruments. One of Edward's most important innovations was his equatorial mounting for astronomical telescopes, which rapidly became the standard mounting for all large instruments; he also devised the compensated mercurial pendulum whose period is not affected by changes of temperature.

TROYON, Constant (1810–65) French painter of landscapes and particularly of animals, born in Sèvres. A member of the Barbizon Group, many of his paintings are in the Louvre and two are in the Wallace Collection, London.

TRÜBNER, Nicholas (1817–88) German publisher, born in Heidelberg. He came to London in 1843, started up his business in 1852 and developed a business connection in the USA. An oriental scholar, he published a series of oriental texts as well as works for the Early English Text society. The business was merged in 1889 to become Kegan Paul, Trench, Trübner & Co.

TRUDEAU, Pierre Elliott (1919–) Canadian politician, born in Montreal. He was called to the Quebec bar in 1943. One of the founders in 1950 of *Cité Libre*, a magazine opposed to the policies of Maurice Duplessis, then premier of Quebec, he began to practise law in Montreal in 1951. He urged the reform of the educational and electoral systems and the separation of church and state in Quebec and in 1956 was active in the short-lived *Rassemblement*, a group of left-wing opponents of Duplessis. From 1961 to 1965 he was associate professor of law at the University of Montreal and in 1965, having rejected the New Democratic party for the Liberal party, was elected to the House of Commons. In 1966 he was appointed parliamentary secretary to the prime minister and in 1967, as minister of justice and attorney-general, he opposed the separation of Quebec from the rest of Canada. In April 1968 he succeeded **Lester Pearson** as federal leader of the Liberal party and prime minister. He then called a general election at which his party secured an overall majority. His government was defeated the following year, but returned to power in 1981. He retired from active politics in 1984.

TRUEBLOOD, (David) Elton (1900–) American Quaker scholar, born in Pleasantville, Iowa. He had a comprehensive education, including a Harvard PhD, before teaching philosophy at various institutions, notably at Earlham College (1946–54). He retained his link there as professor-at-large after his appointment in 1954 as chief of religious information at the United States Information Agency. His books include *The Yoke of Christ* (1958), *The Company of the Committed* (1961), *The People Called Quakers* (1966), and *The Validity of the Christian Mission* (1972).

TRUEMAN, Freddy (Frederick Sewards) (1931–) English cricketer, born in Stainton. Educated at Maltby Secondary School, he became an apprentice brick-layer before developing into the first genuinely fast bowler in post-war English cricket. A Yorkshire player for 19 years (1949–68), he played in 67 Tests between 1952 and 1965 and took a record number of 307 wickets in a match. In his first-class career he took 2304 wickets, 3 times taking 10 wickets, and made 3 centuries. A bluff and downright Yorkshireman, he has worked as a cricket writer and commentator since he retired.

TRUFFAUT, François (1932–84) French filmmaker, born in Paris. His early life as an unhappy child, reform school pupil and army deserter later formed elements of his more autobiographical works. He began writing criticism for *Cahiers du Cinéma* in 1953 and made his directorial début on the short *Une Visite* (1955). A founding father of the French New Wave, he made his feature début with *Les Quatre Cents Coups* (The Four Hundred Blows, 1959), a haunting study of deprived childhood that gained him an international reputation. Compassionately dealing in human emotions, his diverse œuvre included work in most of the popular genres with films like *Jules et Jim* (1961), *La Mariée était en Noir* (The Bride Wore Black, 1967), *La Nuit Américaine* (Day for Night, 1973) and *Le Dernier Métro* (The Last Metro, 1980). He acted in his own films and in *Close Encounters of the Third Kind* (1977). His many writings included an autobiography, *Les Films de Ma Vie* (1975).

TRUMAN, Harry S (1884–1972) 33rd president of the USA, born in Lamar, Missouri, and educated at Independence, Missouri. After World War I, in which he served as an artillery captain on the Western Front, he returned to his farm and later went into partnership in a men's clothing store in Kansas City which failed. In 1922 he became judge for the Eastern District of Jackson County, Missouri, and in 1926 presiding judge, a post he held until 1934 when Missouri elected him to the US senate. He was re-elected in 1940 and was chairman of the special committee investigating defence which was said to have saved the US more than $1 000 000 000. He was elected vice-president in 1944 and became president in April 1945 on the death of President **Franklin D Roosevelt**. He was re-elected in November 1948 in a surprise victory over **Thomas E Dewey**, which made nonsense of Dr **Gallup**'s forecasts. As the 'everyday American' who became president, Truman astonished his earlier critics. Few presidents have had to take so many historically important decisions—dropping the first atom bombs on Japan; pushing through congress a huge postwar loan to Britain; making a major change in US policy towards Russia, signalized by the 'Truman doctrine' of Communist containment and support for free peoples resisting subjugation; organizing the Berlin Airlift (1948–49); establishing NATO (1949), sending US troops on behalf of the UN to withstand the Communist invasion of South Korea in 1950; dismissing General **Douglas MacArthur** from all his commands in 1951. For seven crucial years President Truman, who called himself 'the hired man of 150 000 000 people', held the American people together while new alignments were taking shape. He did not stand for re-election in 1952 and retired to Independence. Later he became a strong critic of the **Eisenhower** Republican administration.

TRUMBULL, John (1750–1831) American lawyer and poet, born in Watertown, Connecticut, first cousin of **Jonathan Trumbull**. He practised law in Boston, New Haven and Hartford, and became a judge of the Connecticut supreme court (1809–13). He wrote a satire on educational methods, *The Progress of Dullness* (1772–73), and a satire on British blunders in the American War of Independence, *McFingal* (1775–82), in imitation of **Samuel Butler's** *Hudibras*.

TRUMBULL, John (1756–1843) American historical painter, born in Lebanon, Connecticut, son of **Jonathan Trumbull**. After service as a colonel and deputy adjutant-general in the American War of Independence, between 1780 and 1785 he made three visits to London to study art under **Benjamin West**, and began a series of celebrated war paintings such as *The Battle of Bunker's Hill*, and a number of portraits of **George Washington**. He was ambassador to London from 1794–1804, and in 1817 painted four large historical pictures for the Rotunda of the Capitol in Washington DC. The Trumbull Gallery at Yale was built to accommodate his collection of paintings (1832).

TRUMBULL, Jonathan (1710–85) American patriot, father of **John Trumbull**, born in Lebanon, Connecticut. He was judge, deputy-governor, and governor of Connecticut, and took a prominent part in the War of Independence. 'Brother Jonathan', the personification of the United States, was once thought, but erroneously, to refer to him.

TRUMPLER, Robert Julius (1886–1956) Swiss-born American astronomer, born in Zürich. He went to university there and at Göttingen. He moved to America in 1915 and remained for most of his career at the Lick Observatory in California. In 1930, measuring the distance and size of star clusters, he explained the apparent larger size of the more distant clusters as a result of the interstellar absorption of light by dust grains, giving an approximately 20% decrease in brightness for every thousand light-years travelled by starlight. This had an important effect on ideas about the scale of the universe.

TRUTH, Sojourner, originally **Isabella Van Wagener** (1777–1883) American abolitionist, born a slave in Ulster County, New York. After working for several years for a variety of owners, she eventually gained her freedom and settled in New York, taking her surname from her previous master, and becoming an ardent evangelist. In 1843 she felt called by God to change her name to Sojourner Truth, and to fight against slavery and for woman suffrage. Preaching widely across the USA, her infectious style of speaking drew large crowds. In 1850 she produced a biography, *The Narrative of Sojourner Truth*, written by Olive Gilbert. She was appointed counsellor to the freedmen of Washington by **Abraham Lincoln**, and continued to promote Negro rights until her retirement in 1875.

TRYON, Sir George (1832–93) English naval commander, born in Bulwick Park, Northamptonshire. He saw service as a midshipman in the Crimean War (1854–55). He was second-in-command of HMS *Warrior*, the first British ironclad (1861), and director of transports to the British expedition against emperor Theodore of Abyssinia (1867). He became commander-in-chief in the Mediterranean in 1891. He died when his flagship, the ironclad *Victoria*, sank in collision with the *Camperdown* off Tripoli during exercises, the result of an inexplicable error on his part. Most of the crew perished with him.

TSAI LUN (?50–118) Chinese inventor (105) of paper made from tree bark and rags. According to Han history, he was the eunuch at the Han court.

TSCHAIKOWSKY, Piotr Ilyich See **TCHAIKOVSKY**.

TSCHUDI, Aegidius, or **Gilg** (1505–72) Swiss historian, born in Glarus. He was active on the Catholic side during the Reformation in the Swiss canton of Glarus. His *Schweizerchronik* (1734–36) was long the standard Swiss history.

TSO CH'IU MING (c.6th century BC) Chinese author, mentioned by **Confucius** in his *Analects*. He wrote the *Tso Chuan*, a commentary on the *Ch'un Ch'iu*, one of the five classics. Scholars also ascribe to him the *Kuo Yü* and these two works comprise the most important historical sources of the period. The simplicity of his style served as a model to later writers.

TSWETT, or **Tsvett, Mikhail Semenovich** (1872–1919) Russian botanist, reared and educated in Switzerland. He went to Kazan university, then taught in Warsaw and Tarto. He devised a percolation method of separating plant pigments in 1906, thus making the first chromatographic analysis.

TUCKER, Josiah (1712–99) English economist and clergyman. Dean of Gloucester from 1758, he wrote on economics, as well as on politics and religion, and anticipated some of **Adam Smith**'s arguments against monopolies.

TUCKWELL, Barry Emmanuel (1931–) Australian conductor and instrumentalist, born in Melbourne, Victoria. He studied at the Conservatorium of Music, Sydney, and played French horn with the Sydney Symphony Orchestra from 1947 to 1950, before going to Britain and playing with the Hallé and other British orchestras. In 1955 he became principal horn with the London Symphony Orchestra, a position he was to hold for 13 years. As principal and as soloist, he featured on most of the LSO's recordings in this period. Since then he has appeared as a horn soloist and also with his own wind quintet. Turning to conducting, Tuckwell has worked with many international orchestras and was from 1979 conductor of the Tasmanian Symphony Orchestra, and is now its principal guest conductor. He was professor of horn at the Royal Academy of Music in London from 1963 to 1974, and has written two books on the subject.

TUDOR, Antony originally **William Cook** (1908–87) English dancer, choreographer and teacher, born in London. He worked at Smithfield meat market in London while first studying dance with **Marie Rambert**. In 1930 she gave him the job of stage manager/secretary of her Ballet Club, which gave him the financial security to perform and train with the Rambert company. There, he made several key pieces, his first, *Cross Garter'd*, in 1931, the celebrated *Lilac Garden* in 1936 and the moody *Dark Elegies* in 1937. That same year he and a number of other Rambert members formed their own group, Dance Theatre, known from 1938 to 1940 as London Ballet. **Agnes de Mille** then stepped in and persuaded Tudor and his friend Harold Laing to move to New York City, where he was position staff choreographer with Ballet Theatre (now American Ballet Theatre) for ten years. *Pillar of Fire* and a one-act Romeo and Juliet were among his ABT triumphs. The years following were spent primarily in teaching, as director of the Metropolitan Opera Ballet School and tutoring at the Juilliard School of Music, though he was a seasonal guest choreograher with both ABT and the Royal Swedish Ballet. In the early 1960s his considerable talent for choreography was again showcased in *Echoing of Trumpets* (1963) and *Shadowplay*. In 1974 he returned to ABT to create *The Leaves are Fading* (1975) and *The Tiller in the Fields* (1978). Though his output of major work was comparatively small, he is considered one of the great contemporary choreographers.

TUDOR, Owen See **HENRY VII**

TUKE, Samuel (1784–1857) English psychiatric reformer, grandson of **William Tuke**. Born in York, he acquired in his childhood an intense interest in the York Retreat, the psychiatric hospital founded by his family. He wanted to study medicine but the family wished him to enter the family business. This he did, but the Retreat, and psychiatric matters more generally, remained his primary concern. His *Description of the Retreat* (1813) contains a classic account of the principles of 'moral therapy' which was the basis of the therapeutic milieu there. Tuke's son, Daniel Hack Tuke (1827–95), became a leading psychiatrist.

TUKE, William (1732–1822) English Quaker philanthropist. A tea and coffee merchant in York, he founded a home for the mentally sick (the York Retreat) in 1796, the first of its kind in England, and contemporaneously with **Philippe Pinel** in France pioneered new methods of treatment and care of the insane.

TUKHACHEVSKY, Mikhail Nikolayevich (1893–1937) Russian soldier and politician. He served as an officer in the Tsarist Army in World War I (1914–17), but became a member of the Communist party in 1918. He commanded Bolshevik forces against Poles under **Wladyslaw Sikorski** and **Józef Pilsudski** in the Russo-Polish War (1920), against the White Russians (1919–20) and the Kulak uprising of 1921. He served on the commission on military invention (1922), and was chief of armaments (1931). He is renowned for his work on tactical doctrine, notably on tank warfare. Appointed to the Military Soviet in 1934, he was created marshal of the Soviet Union in 1935. He was later executed for treason.

TULASNE, Louis René (1815–85) and his brother **Charles** (1816–1884), French mycologists. They made important researches in the structure and development of fungi, and wrote *Selecta Fungorum Carpologia* (3 vols, 1861–65).

TULL, Jethro (1674–1741) English agriculturist, born in Basildon in Berkshire. Educated at St John's College, Oxford, he invented a seed drill, and introduced new farming methods in his native county, his chief innovation being the planting of seeds in rows. He wrote *The Horse-Hoing Husbandry* (1733).

TULLOCH, John (1823–86) Scottish theologian, born in Bridge of Earn. He was a minister in Dundee (1844) and at Kettins (1849), and in 1854 was appointed principal and professor of divinity at St Mary's College, St Andrews. He was a founder of the Scottish liberal church party (1878) and wrote many religious and philosophical works and an address to young men, *Beginning Life* (1862).

TULLY See **CICERO**

TULSĪDĀS (1532–1623) Indian Hindi devotional poet, born in Eastern India. Traditionally believed to have lived for 120 years, the time allotted to a sinless human being, he wrote more than a dozen works. His best-known is *Rāmacaritamānas* ('The Holy Lake of Rāma's Deeds'), an immensely popular Eastern Hindi version of the *Rāmyana* epic, which he began in 1574.

His *bhakti* or devotional approach, concern for moral conduct, and idea of salvation through Rāma incarnated as absolute knowledge and love, suggests a Nestorian Christian influence on his work.

TUNNEY, Gene (James Joseph) (1897–1978) American boxer and world heavyweight champion, born in New York City. A high-school drop-out, he joined the US marines at the age of 19. He won the world light-heavyweight championship by defeating Georges Charpentier, then took the world heavyweight crown from **Jack Dempsey** in 1926, and retained it in a controversial re-match in 1927 when he was given a 'long count' which saved him after a knock-down. He retired undefeated in 1928, with a remarkable career record of 76 wins, one loss. In World War II he was director of athletics and physical fitness for the US Navy.

TUNNICLIFFE, Charles Frederick (1901–79) English bird artist, born in Langley, Macclesfield, the son of a shoemaker turned farmer. He studied at Macclesfield School of Art and won a scholarship to the Royal College of Art. He illustrated **Henry Williamson**'s *Tarka the Otter* (1927) and *Salar the Salmon* (1935) with his own wood-engravings, provided innumerable illustrations for the Royal Society for the Protection of Birds, and published six books of his own, including *Shorelands Summer Diary* (1952), *My Country Book* (1945) and *Bird Portraiture* (1945).

TUNSTALL, Cuthbert (1474–1559) English prelate, born in Hackforth, Yorkshire, brother of Sir Brian Tunstall who fell at Flodden. He became rector of Stanhope, archdeacon of Chester, rector of Harrow-on-the-Hill, master of the Rolls, dean of Salisbury (1519), bishop of London (1522), and in 1530 succeeded **Wolsey** as bishop of Durham. From 1516 to 1530 he was repeatedly sent by **Henry VIII** on embassies to the emperor (making friends with **Erasmus**) and to France. He accepted the royal supremacy, but took alarm at the sweeping reforms under **Edward VI**, and in 1552 was deprived. The accession of **Mary I** restored him. Under his mild rule not a single victim died for heresy thoughout the diocese. On **Elizabeth**'s accession he refused to take the oath of supremacy and was again deprived.

TUNSTRÖM, Göron (1937–) Swedish author, born in Sunne, Värmland. His first work, *Inringing* (Encircling), appeared in 1958, since when he has published poems, plays, travel books (he and his wife, the painter Lena Cronquist, are intrepid travellers) and several long novels. His novels have an inventive plot borne by a rich tapestry of vivid, eccentric characters, but the underlying message is that we need more human love and kindness in our lives. Recurring themes are a search for identity, lost childhood and, inter-connected, father-and-son relationships. His own father, a clergyman whom he dearly loved, died when he was twelve and his world fell apart. In his fiction he recaptures his childhood and tries to come to terms with his loss. He also looks at human responsibility and betrayal in both provincial and international settings. His most popular novels to date are the prize-winning *Juloratoriet* (1982, The Christmas Oratorio) and *Tjuven* (1986, The Thief).

TUPOLEV, Andrei Nikolaevich (1888–1972) Russian aeronautical engineer, born in Moscow. A founder of the Central Institute of Aerodynamics and Hydrodynamics (originally the Aerodynamic Aircraft Design Bureau) in Moscow, he became its first assistant director (1918–35). In the 1930s he produced the ANT-6 four-engined bomber and the gigantic ANT-20, 'Maxim Gorky', with eight engines and a span of 260 ft. Arrested during the purges, he was sent to the Gulag in 1939, but was released during World War II, and rehabilitated in the 1960s. His twin-engined bombers, designed during World War II, were followed by jet-propelled aircraft: the Tu 104 twin-jet 100-seat airliner (1955); the Tu 114 four-turboprop which, at 180 metric tons, was the largest transport of its day; and the ill-fated Tu 144 supersonic passenger plane (1955) which, although flying before Concorde, was a failure.

TUPPER, Martin Farquhar (1810–89) English writer, born in Marylebone. He studied at Charterhouse and at Christ Church College, Oxford. He was called to the bar (1835), but soon turned to writing. Of his 40 works, only *Proverbial Philosophy* (1838–67), a series of moralizing commonplaces in free verse, achieved huge worldwide popularity. He also published some novels.

TURA, Cosima (c.1430–1495) Italian artist, born in Ferrara. The leader, with **Cossa**, of the Ferrarese school, he studied under **Squarcione** at Padua, and his metallic, tortured forms and unusual colours give a strange power to his pictures, such as the *Pietà* in the Louvre and the *S. Jerome* in the National Gallery, London.

TURBERVILE, George (c.1540–c.1610) English poet, and secretary to Sir **Thomas Randolph**, born in Whitchurch, Dorset. He was educated at Winchester and New College, Oxford. He wrote epigrams, songs, sonnets, *The Booke of Falconrie* (1575), *The Noble Art of Venerie* (1576), and translated **Ovid**, the Italian poets and others. He was a pioneer in the use of blank verse.

TURENNE, Henri de la Tour d'Auvergne, Vicomte de (1611–75) French soldier, born in Sedan, the second son of the Duke of Bouillon and Elizabeth of Nassau, **William the Silent**'s daughter. Brought up in the Reformed faith, he learned the art of war in the Dutch War of Independence (1625–30) under his uncle, Prince **Maurice of Nassau**, and in 1630 received a commission from **Richelieu**. During the alliance of France with the Protestants in the Thirty Years' War (1618–48) he fought with distinction, and in 1641 was entrusted with the supreme command. For the conquest of Roussillon from the Spaniards in 1642 he was made a marshal of France (1644), and received the chief command on the Rhine. For a time he was superseded by **Condé**; and his restoration to supreme command was followed by his rout by the Imperialists at Marienthal (May 1645). But in August his disgrace was avenged by Condé at Nördlingen; and Turenne concluded France's share in the war by the conquest of Trèves electorate and of Bavaria (with the Swedes, 1646–47), and by a successful campaign in Flanders. In the civil wars of the Fronde, Turenne joined the *frondeurs*, and after being defeated at Rethel (1650) he withdrew to Flanders. On **Mazarin**'s return Turenne joined his party, while Condé deserted to the *frondeurs*. Turenne twice triumphed over his former chief (1652), and forced him to retire from France; afterwards he subdued the disaffected cities, conquered much of the Spanish Netherlands, and defeated Condé at the Dunes (1658). In 1660 he was created marshal-general of France, and in 1668 turned Catholic. His next campaign in Holland was triumphant (1672), and in 1673 he held his ground against both the Imperialist **Montecucculi** and the Elector of Brandenburg. In 1674 he crossed the Rhine, mercilessly ravaged the Palatinate, crushed Brandenburg at Colmar, laid waste Alsace, and then advanced into Germany again to meet Montecucculi, but he was killed reconnoitring at Sasbach.

TURGENEV, Ivan Sergeevich (1818–83) Russian novelist, born in the province of Orel. The child of landed gentry, he had an unsatisfactory childhood through the cruelty of his mother, whose great inherited wealth made her a petty tyrant in the home. After graduating from St Petersburg University he broke away by going to study philosophy in Berlin and there mingled with the radical thinkers of the day. He became firm friends with **Alexander Herzen**. He returned to Russia in 1841 to enter the civil service, but in 1843 abandoned this to take up literature. His mother strongly disapproved and his infatuation for a singer, **Paulina Garcia** (Mme Viardot), also displeased her. She stopped his allowance and until her death in 1850, when he came into his inheritance, he had to support himself by his writings. He began with verse, *Parasha* (1843) showing the influence of **Pushkin**, but soon recognized prose as his medium and in 1847 produced *Khor and Khalynich*, his first sketch of peasant life, which appeared again in *Sportsman's Sketches* (1852). This book, sympathetic studies of the peasantry, made his reputation, but earned governmental displeasure, as it was interpreted as an attack on serfdom. A notice praising **Gogol** on his death in 1852 exacerbated the ill-feeling and resulted in a two years' banishment to his country estates. After his exile he spent much time in Europe, writing nostalgically of life in Russia. *Rudkin* appeared in 1856, *The Nest of Gentlefolk* in 1859, *On the Eve* in 1860, all faithful descriptions of Russian liberalism, with its attendant weaknesses and limitations. In his greatest novel, *Fathers and Children* (1862), he portrayed the new generation with its reliance on the practical and materialistic, its faith in science and lack of respect for tradition and authority, in short the Nihilists. But the hero, Bazarov, pleased neither the revolutionaries who thought the portrait a libel nor the reactionaries who thought it a glorification of iconoclasm. Turgenev's popularity slumped in Russia but rose abroad, particularly in Britain, where the book was recognized as a major contribution to literature. Successive novels were *Smoke* (1867) and *Virgin Soil* (1877). He returned to the short story, producing powerful pieces like *A Lear of the Steppes*, and tales of the supernatural to which his increasing melancholy of spirit drew him.

TURGOT (d.1115) a Saxon monk of Durham, where he became an archdeacon, and helped to found the new cathedral. He was bishop of St Andrews (1109–15), and confessor to St **Margaret**, of whose *Life* he was the probable author.

TURGOT, Anne Robert Jacques (1727–81) French economist and statesman, born of Norman stock in Paris. Destined for the church, he became a lawyer. Appointed intendant of Limoges in 1761, he found the people poor, degraded, immoral and superstitious. He introduced better administration of imposts and abolished compulsory labour on roads and bridges. He was supported in this by central government and the rural priests. Soon after the accession of **Louis XVI** (1774) he was appointed comptroller-general of finance. At once he began to introduce wide reforms. He reduced expenditure and increased public revenue without imposing new taxes. He established free trade in grain within France and removed the fiscal barriers between the provinces. He abolished the exclusive privileges of trade corporations and sought to break down the immunity from taxation enjoyed by the privileged classes—who, threatened by these moves towards a more efficient, economical and equitable administration, pressed for his dismissal. Louis was too weak to resist and Turgot was removed from office after only 20 months. France drifted rapidly towards the revolution of 1789. Turgot occupied himself with literature and science until his death, in Paris. His chief work, *Reflexions sur la formation et la distribution des richesses* (1766), was the best outcome of the Physiocratic school (founded by **Quesnay**) and largely anticipated **Adam Smith**.

TURINA, Joaquín (1882–1949) Spanish composer and pianist, born in Seville. His early promise was fostered by the organist of Seville Cathedral, and at 15 he made his first appearance as a pianist. By the time he went to Madrid, in 1902, and came under the influence of **Manuel de Falla** and the Spanish Nationalist composers, he had a large number of compositions to his credit, including his first opera. In 1905 he went to Paris to study at the Schola Cantorum, and became an important figure in French musical life. Returning to Madrid in 1914, he was immensely active as composer, pianist and critic until the Spanish Civil War, in which he was an ardent supporter of General **Franco**, curtailed his activities. When peace was restored, he found himself regarded as the leader of Spanish music. He wrote four operas, orchestral and chamber works and piano pieces, the best of which combine strong Andalusian colour and idiom with traditional forms.

TURING, Alan Mathison (1912–54) English mathematician, born in London. He studied at Cambridge and worked at Princeton and the National Physical Laboratory before becoming reader in mathematics at Manchester University. His main contribution was in what was then the very new field of computers: he gave a precise mathematical characterization of the intuitive concept of computability. Through his development of an idealized computer—the *Turing machine*—he was able to show that a number of important mathematical problems could have no effective decision procedure. He put his theoretical work on computability into practice, supervising the building of the ACE computer at the National Physical Laboratory. He committed suicide after a prosecution for alleged indecency.

TURNBULL, Colin (1924–) English-born American anthropologist, born in Harrow. He studied at Oxford, then carried out fieldwork first in India (1949–51) and later among the Mbuti pygmies of the Ituri Forest, Zaire. He worked at the American Museum of Natural History in New York City (1959–69), and was appointed professor at George Washington University in 1976. He has written many books on social change and relationships in Africa, including *The Forest People* (1961), *Wayward Servants* (1964), *Tradition and Change in African Tribal Life* (1966) and *The Human Cycle* (1983).

TURNBULL, William (1922–) Scottish artist, born in Dundee. He studied at the Slade School of Art (1946–48) and lived in Paris from 1948 to 1950. He held his first one-man show at the Hanover Gallery, London, in 1950, and taught at the Central School of Arts & Crafts in London from 1952 to 1972. He is married to the sculptor and printmaker Kim Lim. His sculptures are typically upright forms of roughly human height, standing directly on the floor; in the 1950s he liked organic forms and titles like 'Totemic Figure', but since the 1960s he has preferred purely abstract, geometrical shapes.

TURNER, Charles, originally **Tennyson** (1808–79) English poet, born in Somersby, an elder brother of **Alfred Tennyson**. He graduated from Trinity College, Cambridge, in 1832, and was for many years vicar of Grasby, Lincolnshire. He took the name Turner under the will of a great-uncle. As well as collaborating with his brother in *Poems by Two Brothers* (1827), he wrote 341 sonnets (collected, with introductory essay by **Spedding**, 1880).

TURNER, Ethel Sibyl (1872–1958) English-born Australian novelist and children's author, born in Doncaster. She moved to Australia at the age of nine.

With her sister, Lilian, she started a magazine, and wrote the children's page, later doing the same for two other Sydney periodicals. Her first book, *Seven Little Australians*, published in 1894, was an immediate success and is now a classic of Australian literature. A sequel came out in the following year and there followed a steady stream of juvenile books, short stories and verse. *Seven Little Australians* has been in print ever since publication. She was the mother of Sir **Adrian Curlewis**, and her daughter Jean wrote a number of children's books, collaborated with her mother on others, and edited a newspaper column for children.

TURNER, Frederick Jackson (1861–1932) American historian, born in Portage, Wisconsin. He studied at Johns Hopkins and returned to Wisconsin University in 1885, rising rapidly (1892) to full professorial status. His chance came in 1893 when the American Historical Association met at Chicago World's Fair, where he delivered his paper on 'The Significance of the Frontier in American History', boldly asserting that American democracy derived from its frontier experience and not its European inheritance. He expanded this theme in *Rise of the New West* (1906) and *The Frontier in American History* (1920). He also stressed, in *The Significance of Sections in American History* (1932, Pulitzer prize) that the history of 'sections' of the USA was best considered in terms of North-west, South-west, North-east and South-east, allowing for their differing interests, in place of its limitation to North *versus* South. His views were extremely vulnerable to comparative analysis with frontiers in other lands, and his frontier was a white one, showing almost no interest in Amerindians. He was professor at Harvard from 1910 to 1924.

TURNER, Glenn (1947–) New Zealand cricketer, born in Dunedin. A fluent, free-scoring batsman, he scored almost 3000 runs and in Test cricket made seven Test centuries. In English county cricket he made 311 not out in a day against Warwickshire, scored 1000 runs before the end of May in 1973, 6144 runs in Sunday League cricket and had an average of 90.07 runs in the season of 1982.

TURNER, John Napier (1929–) Canadian politician. After studying at the University of British Columbia he won a Rhodes Scholarship and read political science and jurisprudence at Oxford. He then practised law in Britain and was called to the English bar, and later the bars of Quebec and Ontario, being made a QC in 1968. He entered the Canadian House of Commons in 1962 and was a junior minister in **Lester Pearson**'s government and later attorney-general and finance minister under **Pierre Trudeau**. When Trudeau retired in 1984, Turner succeeded him as leader of the Liberal party and prime minister. He lost the general election later the same year and became leader of the opposition. He resigned the leadership of his party in 1989.

TURNER, Joseph Mallord William (1775–1851) English painter, born in London, one of the great masters of landscape art and of watercolour. At 14 he entered the Royal Academy and in the following year was already exhibiting. At 18 he began wandering about England and Wales in search of material and made architectural drawings in the cathedral cities. For three years in the mid-nineties he joined forces with **Thomas Girtin**, the latter drawing the outlines and Turner washing in the colour; between them they raised the art of watercolour to new heights of delicacy and charm. From 1796 he gradually abandoned his niche as a topographical watercolourist, and, strongly influenced by **Wilson** and **Claude**, took to oils. In 1802 he visited the Louvre collections, swollen with **Napoleon**'s loot, and was greatly attracted by **Titian** and **Poussin**. More and more he became preoccupied with the delicate rendering of shifting gradations of light on such diverse forms as waves, shipwrecks, fantastic architecture and towering mountain ranges, conveying a generalized mood or impression of a scene, sometimes accentuated by a theatrically arbitrary choice of vivid colour. *Frosty Morning* (1813), *The Shipwreck* and *Crossing the Brook* (1815) embody Turner's trend. For one who defined painting as 'a rum thing', he found it easier to defend himself against the critics by producing a collection of engravings, *Liber Studiorum* (1807–19), which remained uncompleted and failed because he underpaid the engravers. In 1819 he paid his first visit to Italy; his second visit to Italy (1829) marked his last great artistic period, which included the famous pictures of Venice, *The Fighting Téméraire* (1839) and *Rain, Steam and Speed* (1844). Turner led a secretive private life, he never married and when not staying with his patron Lord Egremont at Petworth, he lived in London taverns such as the 'Ship and Bladebone' at Limehouse Reach. He died in a temporary lodging at Chelsea under the assumed name of Booth. He bequeathed 300 of his paintings and 20000 water-colours and drawings to the nation. Turner's revolution in art foreshadowed Impressionism and found a timely champion in **John Ruskin**, whose *Modern Painters* (Vol I, 1843) helped to turn the critical tide in Turner's favour.

TURNER, Sir Tomkyns Hilgrove (c.1766–1843) English soldier. He fought at Aboukir Bay and Alexandria, and brought to Britain from French custody the Rosetta stone (1801–02).

TURNER, Victor Witter (1920–83) Scottish social anthropologist, born in Glasgow. He studied literature at London University, but after war service he studied anthropology under **Max Gluckman** at Manchester. He taught at Manchester (1949–63) before moving to the USA where he was professor of anthropology at Cornell (1963–68), professor of social thought at Chicago from 1968 to 1977 and at Virginia from 1977 to 1983. He carried out fieldwork among the Ndembu of Zambia (northern Rhodesia) from 1950 to 1954, which resulted in the classic monograph *Schism and Continuity in an African Society* (1957). In his later work he moved to the analysis of symbolism, as in *The Forest of Symbols* (1967), *The Drums of Affliction* (1968), *The Ritual Process* (1969) and *Dramas, Fields and Metaphors* (1972).

TURNER, Walter James Redfern (1889–1946) Australian poet, novelist and critic, born in Melbourne. He was educated there and at Munich and Vienna. He published *The Dark Fire* (1918), *The Landscape of Cytherea* (1923) and other volumes of poetry. His other writings include studies of **Beethoven**, **Mozart** and **Wagner**, a play *The Man Who Ate the Popomack* (1922), and novels such as *The Aesthetes* (1927) and *The Duchess of Popocatepetl* (1939).

TURNER, William (c.1510–1568) English clergyman, physician and naturalist, known as the 'father of British botany', born in Morpeth, Northumberland. A fellow of Pembroke Hall, Cambridge, he became a Protestant and to escape religious persecution in England travelled extensively abroad, studying medicine and botany in Italy. He formed a close friendship with **Conrad Gessner** in Zürich, and became the author of the first original English works on plants, including *Names of Herbes* (1548) and *A new Herball* (1551–62). He was Dean of Wells (1550–53), left England during the reign of **Mary I**, but was restored to Wells in 1560. He named many plants, including goatsbeard and hawkweed. The basis he laid for 'a system of nature' was developed by **John Ray** in the next century.

TURPIN, or **Tilpinus** (d.c.794) French ecclesiastic. He became archbishop of Reims (c.753), and was the suppositious author of the *Historia Karoli Magni et Rotholande*, really written after 1131 by a French monk of Compestela, and continued about 1220.

TURPIN, Dick (1705–39) English robber, born in Hempstead, Essex. He was, successively or simultaneously, butcher's apprentice, cattle-lifter, smuggler, housebreaker, highwayman and horse-thief. He entered into partnership with Tom King and, going north, was hanged at York, for the murder of an Epping keeper. His ride to York belongs, if to any one, to 'Swift John Nevison', who in 1676 is said to have robbed a sailor at Gadshill at 4am, and to have established an 'alibi' by reaching York at 7.45pm.

TURPIN, Randolph (1925–) English middleweight boxer, born in Leamington Spa, and one of a well-known boxing family which included his brother Dick. British middleweight champion (1950–54) and European champion (1951–54), he defeated **Sugar Ray Robinson** in the summer of 1951 and for a few months was world champion before losing the title to Robinson in New York in the autumn of that year. He later moved up to light heavyweight but without much success.

TURRETIN, Jean Alphonse (1671–1737) Swiss theologian, born in Geneva. He became pastor of the Italian congregation in Geneva, in 1697 professor of church history, in 1705 of theology. He laboured to promote a union of the Reformed and Lutheran churches, and succeeded in abolishing the Helvetic Consensus in 1725. His famous *Discourse concerning the Fundamental Articles in Religion* was translated in 1720. His *Cogitationes et Dissertationes Theoligicae* appeared in 1737.

TURVILLE-PETRE, Gabriel (1908–78) English scholar and pioneer in Old Icelandic studies. He was the first **Vigfússon** reader in ancient Icelandic literature and antiquities at Oxford University from 1941 (professor, 1953–75). A man of immense erudition and wide scholarly interests, he published many seminal books in his field, including an edition of *Víga-Glúms Saga* (1940), *The Heroic Age of Scandinavia* (1951), *Origins of Icelandic Literature* (1953), *Myth and Religion of the North* (1964), and *Scaldic Poetry* (1976).

TUSSAUD, Marie, née **Grosholtz** (1761–1850) Swiss modeller in wax, known as 'Madame Tussaud', born in Strasbourg. She was early apprenticed to her uncle, Dr Philippe Curtius, in Paris and inherited his wax museums after his death in 1794. After the Revolution, she attended the guillotine to take death masks from the severed heads. After a short imprisonment, she married a French soldier, François Tussaud, but separated from him in 1800 and went to England with her two children. She toured Britain with her life-size portrait waxworks, a gallery of heroes and rogues, and in 1835 set up a permanent exhibition in Baker Street, London, which was burnt down in 1925 and re-opened in Marylebone Road in 1928. The exhibition still contains her own handiwork, notably of **Marie Antoinette**, **Napoleon**, Sir **Walter Scott**, and **Burke and Hare** in the Chamber of Horrors, the last two having been joined by a succession of notable murderers, including **John Christie** and his kitchen sink.

TUSSER, Thomas (c.1520–c.1580) English writer on agriculture, born in Rivenhall, Essex. For a time a chorister at St Paul's, he was educated at Eton and Trinity Hall, Cambridge. After a residence at court as musician to Lord Paget he married and settled as a farmer at Cattawade in Suffolk, where he compiled his famous work, *A Hundreth Good Pointes of Husbandrie* (1557). **Tottel** published (1573) an enlarged edition, *Five Hundreth Pointes of Good Husbandrie*.

TUT'ANKHAMUN (d.c.1340 BC) Egyptian Pharaoh of the 18th Dynasty, the son-in-law of **Akhenaton.** He became king at the age of twelve and died at eighteen in c.1340 BC. His magnificent tomb at Thebes was discovered in 1922 by Lord **Carnarvon** and **Howard Carter**.

TUTHMOSIS III (15th century BC) Egyptian pharaoh of the 18th Dynasty from 1479 to 1447 BC, one of the greatest of Egyptian rulers. Son of Tuthmosis I and father of **Amenhotep II**, he reigned jointly at first with his aunt and stepmother, Queen **Hatshepsut** from c.1501. He invaded Syria, extended his territories to Carchemish on the Euphrates and made several invasions into Asia. He built the great temple of Amen at Karnak, restored those at Memphis, Heliopolis and Abydos, and erected obelisks, including 'Cleopatra's Needle', brought back to London in 1878 by Sir **Erasmus Wilson**.

TUTHMOSIS IV (1470–1400 BC) Egyptian pharaoh of the 18th Dynasty from c.1420 to 1411 BC, son of **Amenhotep II** and father of **Amenhotep III**. He fought campaigns in Syria and Nubia.

TUTU, Desmond Mpilo (1931–) Black South African Anglican prelate, born in Klerksdorp, the son of a primary school headmaster. He studied theology at the University of South Africa and London University. After briefly working as a schoolteacher he became an Anglican parish priest (1960) and rapidly rose to become bishop of Lesotho (1977), secretary-general of the South African Council of Churches (1979), the first black bishop of Johannesburg (1984) and archbishop of Cape Town (1986). A fierce critic of the apartheid system, he has repeatedly risked imprisonment for his advocacy of the imposition of punitive sanctions against South Africa by the international community. He has also, however, condemned the use of violence by opponents of apartheid, seeking instead a peaceful, negotiated reconciliation between the black and white communities. He was awarded the Nobel prize for peace in 1984.

TUTUOLA, Amos (1920–) Nigerian novelist, born in Abookuta. He was educated at a Salvation Army school and later taught at Lagos High School. *The Palm-Wine Drinkard* (1952), his most popular book, written in a musical pidgin, deals with its hero's adventures among the 'Deads'—the spirits of the departed.

TWAIN, Mark, pseud of **Samuel Langhorne Clemens** (1835–1910) American writer, born in Florida, Missouri. A printer first (1847–55), and later a Mississippi river-boat pilot (1857–61), he adopted his pen-name from a well-known call of the man sounding the river in shallow places ('mark twain' meaning 'by the mark two fathoms'). In 1861 he went to Carson City, Nevada, as secretary to his brother, who was in the service of the governor, and while there tried gold-mining without success. He next edited for two years the Virginia City *Territorial Enterprise* and in 1864 moved to San Francisco as a reporter. His first success was *The Celebrated Jumping Frog of Calaveras County* (1865), published as a book with other sketches in 1867. In 1867 he visited France, Italy and Palestine, gathering material for his *Innocents Abroad* (1869), which established his reputation as a humorist. Later he was editor of a newspaper in Buffalo, where he married the wealthy Olivia Landon. Later he moved to Hartford, Connecticut, and joined a publishing firm which failed, but largely recouped his losses by lecturing and writing. *Roughing It* (1872) is a humorous account of his Nevada experiences, while *The Gilded*

Age (1873), written with **Charles Dudley Warner**, a novel which was later dramatized, exposes the re-adjustment period after the Civil War. His two greatest masterpieces, *Tom Sawyer* (1876) and *Huckleberry Finn* (1884), drawn from his own boyhood experiences, are firmly established among the world's classics; other favourites are *A Tramp Abroad* (1880) and *A Connecticut Yankee in King Arthur's Court* (1889). Mark Twain pokes fun at entrenched institutions and traditions, but his 'debunking' is mostly without malice and his satire is free from bitterness, except in his later work, when fate had been unkind to him. In places his subject-matter is inclined to date, but his best work is not only classic humorous writing but a graphic picture of the 19th-century American scene.

TWEED, William Marcy (1823–78) American criminal and politician, one of the most notorious 'bosses' of the Tammany Society. Born in New York, he trained as a chairmaker. He became an alderman (1852–53), sat in congress (1853–55), and was repeatedly in the state senate. In 1870 he was made commissioner of public works for the city; and, as head of the 'Tweed Ring', he controlled its finances. His gigantic frauds exposed in 1871, he was convicted, and, after escaping to Cuba and Spain (1875–76), died in New York jail while suits were pending against him for recovery of $6 000 000.

TWEEDMOUTH, Edward Marjoribanks, 2nd Baron (1849–1909) English Liberal politician. As First Lord of the Admiralty, he speeded up British naval construction to keep pace with rival German increases, but was censured for an alleged disclosure of British naval estimates (1908) and resigned.

TWEEDSMUIR See **BUCHAN, John**

TWISS, Sir Travers (1809–97) English jurist, born in Westminster, London. He became professor of international law at King's College, London (1852–55), and then of civil law at Oxford. In 1867 he became queen's advocate-general and was knighted. He resigned all his offices in 1872. In 1884 he drew up a constitution for the Congo Free State and in 1885 was legal adviser to the African Conference at Berlin. His *Law of Nations* (1861–63) was long a standard work but his editions of The Black Book of the Admiralty and, particularly, of **Bracton** were unsatisfactory.

TWOMBLY, Cy (1928–) American painter, born in Lexington, Virginia. He studied at the Boston Museum of Fine Arts School (1948–49), at the Art Students' League (1950–51) and at Black Mountain College (1951–52), going on to settle in Rome in 1957. His gestural or 'doodle' technique derives from Surrealist belief in the expressive power of automatic writing to tap the unconscious. Since 1951 he has had numerous exhibitions.

TWORT, Frederick William (1877–1950) English bacteriologist, born in Camberley, Surrey. He studied medicine in London, and became professor of bacteriology there in 1919. He studied Jöhne's disease and methods of the culture of acid-fast organisms; and in 1915 he discovered the bacteriophage, a virus for attacking certain bacteria.

TWYSDEN, Sir Roger (1597–1672) English antiquary and politician. He represented Kent in the Short Parliament but was imprisoned (1643–50) as a royalist, though, having refused to pay ship money, he was not *persona grata* with the court. He wrote many important historical works, including the pioneering *Historia Anglicanae Scriptores Decem* (1652).

TYANA See **APOLLONIUS OF TYANA**

TYARD, or **Thiard, Pontus de** (1521–1605) French poet, born in Bissy-sur-Fleys (Saône-et-Loire). He belonged to the group of Lyons poets who took **Petrarch** for their master. Influenced, however, by the work of **Ronsard**, his verse bridges the gap between the Petrarchan style and that of the Pléiade poets. Volumes of poetry include *Erreurs amoureuses* (1549–55), *Le Livre des vers lyriques* (1555) and *Œuvres poétiques* (1573). He was bishop of Chaolon-sur-Saône (1578–94) and wrote also theological and philosophical works, including *Discours philosophiques* (1587).

TYCHO See **BRAHE**

TYE, Christopher (c.1505–c.1572) English musician, born in Westminster, London. He was musical instructor to **Edward VI**. In 1545–48 he received his MusD from Cambridge and Oxford. Under **Queen Elizabeth** he was organist to the Chapel Royal, and wrote some notable church music.

TYLER, Anne (1941–) American novelist and short story writer, born in Minneapolis, Minnesota, and raised in Raleigh, North Carolina. She graduated from Duke University at 19, where she twice won the Anne Flexner award for creative writing, and has been a Russian bibliographer and assistant to the librarian, McGill University Law Library. Writing mainly of life in Baltimore or in Southern small towns, and concerned with the themes of loneliness, isolation and human interactions, she has had a productive career since her début in 1964 with *If Morning Ever Comes*. Significant subsequent titles include *Morgan's Passing* (1980), *Dinner at the Homesick Restaurant* (1982) and *The Accidental Tourist* (1985).

TYLER, John (1790–1862) tenth president of the USA, born in Charles City County, Virginia. In 1809 he was admitted to the bar, and having sat in the state legislature (1811–16), he entered congress. In 1825 he was elected governor of Virginia, and in December 1826 US senator. In the case of the United States Bank he resented the despotic methods by which **Jackson** overthrew it, supported **Clay**'s motion to censure the president, and, declining to vote for expunging this motion from the minutes, in 1836 resigned his seat. In 1840 he was elected vice-president. President **Harrison** died in 1841, a month after his inauguration, and Tyler became president. The Whig majority, headed by Clay, regarded his election as a victory for them and for the project of a re-established national bank, but the president's firmness destroyed the project. The Ashburton Treaty and the annexation of Texas in 1845 marked his administration. Adhering to the Confederate cause, he was a member of the Confederate congress until his death.

TYLER, Wat (Walter) (d.1381) English rebel and leader of the Peasants' Revolt of 1381. He was probably a tiler from Essex, chosen by a mob of peasants to be their spokesman after taking Rochester Castle. Under him they moved to Canterbury, Blackheath and London. At a conference with **Richard II** at Smithfield, London, demanding an end of serfdom and greater freedom of labour, blows were exchanged; William Walworth, mayor of London, wounded Wat, and finding he had been removed to St Bartholomew's Hospital, had him dragged out and beheaded.

TYLOR, Sir Edward Burnet (1832–1917) English anthropologist, born in Camberwell, London. He travelled with **Henry Christy** to Mexico and published *Ahahuac*, an account of his journey, in 1861. His first major anthropological study, *Researches into the Early History of Mankind*, appeared in 1865, and in 1871 he published his monumental *Primitive Culture* (2 vols). In this work he sought to show that human culture, above all in its religious aspect, is governed by definite laws of evolutionary development, such that the beliefs and practices of primitive nations may be taken to represent earlier stages in the progress of mankind.

After the appearance of **Darwin's** *The Descent of Man* (1871). he veered towards the view that cultural variation may be due to racial differences in mental endowment, a view reflected in his general introductory work *Anthropology* (1881). Tylor is widely regarded as the founder of the systematic study of human culture, and his definition of culture is still current today. Though he never obtained a university degree, he became one of the leading professional anthropologists of his time. He was Keeper of the University Museum at Oxford and from 1896 to 1909 the first professor of anthropology at Oxford University.

TYNAN, Katharine (1861–1931) Irish poet and novelist, born in Clondalkin, County Dublin. She was a friend of **Parnell**, the **Meynells** and the **Rossettis** and a leading author of the Celtic literary revival. She married in 1893 H A Hinkson, who was a resident magistrate in County Mayo from 1914 to 1919. She wrote volumes of tender, gentle verse, over 100 (novels including *Oh! What a Plague is Love*, 1896), *She Walks in Beauty*, 1899, and *The House in the Forest*, 1928, novels and five autobiographical works, the last of which was *Memoires* (1924).

TYNAN, Kenneth (1927–80) English theatre critic, born in Birmingham. While reading English at Magdalen College, Oxford, where he was regarded as something of a juvenile prodigy, Tynan became deeply involved in the theatre, and his first book, *He that plays the King* (1950) was a brilliant and provocative personal view of the current theatre scene. He became drama critic for several publications, notably *The Observer* (1954–63), where he was one of the first to champion **John Osborne** and the other new playwrights of the time. Tynan abandoned drama criticism to become Literary Manager of the National Theatre (1963–69) under Sir **Laurence Olivier**, and he was an important influence on the image and direction of that company. Tynan also worked for a while as an editor in films and television, and later achieved further fame and notoriety with his revue *Oh, Calcutta!* (1969) which featured much nudity, and the first use of a four-letter word on British television. He was a powerful force in British theatre, and his collected reviews were published as *Curtains* (1961) and *Tynan Right and Left* (1967).

TYNDALE, Tindale, or **Hutchins, William** (c.1494–1536) English translator of the Bible, born probably in Slymbridge in Gloucestershire. He was educated at Magdalen Hall, Oxford (1510–15). After a spell at Cambridge he became chaplain and tutor in a household at Little Sodbury. His sympathy with the New Learning aroused suspicion and, already a competent Greek scholar, in 1523 he went to London. Bishop **Tunstall** having refused support for his translation of the Bible, he went in 1524 to Hamburg, to Wittenberg, where he visited **Luther**, and in 1525 to Cologne, where he began that year the printing of his English New Testament. This had not proceeded beyond the gospels of Matthew and Mark when the intrigues of **Cochlaeus** forced Tyndale to flee to Worms, where **Peter Schoeffer** printed for him 3000 New Testaments in small octavo. The translation owed much to Luther and **Erasmus**, much to his own scholarship and literary skill. Tunstall and **Warham** denounced the book; hundreds of copies were burned; but it made its way. In 1527 he moved to Marburg to the protection of Philip the Magnanimous; in 1529 he was shipwrecked on the way to Hamburg, where he met **Coverdale**; in 1531 he went to Antwerp. There probably (ostensibly at Marburg) was published his *Pentateuch* (1530–31) where the marginal glosses, almost all original, contain violent attacks on the pope and the bishops. Here he leans heavily on Luther. In 1531 appeared his version of *Jonah*, with a prologue. An unauthorized revision of Tyndale's New Testament was made at Antwerp in August 1534, and in November Tyndale himself issued there a revised version. One copy of his works was struck off on vellum for presentation to **Anne Boleyn**, under whose favour, apparently, a reprint of Tyndale's revised New Testament was printed in 1536 by T Godfray, the first volume of Holy Scripture printed in England. Tyndale revised his Testament in 1535, this time without the marginal notes. The emissaries of **Henry VIII** had often tried to get hold of him; at last in 1535 he was arrested in Antwerp through the treachery of Henry Philips, a Roman Catholic zealot, imprisoned in the Castle of Vilvorde, tried there (1536), and on 6 October strangled and burned. His other original works were *The Parable of the Wicked Mammon* (1528); *The Obedience of a Christian Man*, his most elaborate book (1528); and *Practyse of Prelates* (1530), a pungent polemic. His *Works* were published in 1573.

TYNDALL, John (1820–93) Irish physicist, born in Leighlin-Bridge, County Carlow. Largely self-educated, he was employed on the ordnance survey and as a railway engineer, before studying physics in England and at Marburg in Germany under **Robert Bunsen**. He became professor at the Royal Institution in 1854. In 1856 he and **T H Huxley** visited the Alps and collaborated in *The Glaciers of the Alps* (1860), when he made the first ascent of the Weisshorn. In 1859 he began his researches on heat radiation, followed by the acoustic properties of the atmosphere and the blue colour of the sky, which he suggested was due to the scattering of light by small particles of water. A prolific writer on scientific subjects, his presidential address to the British Association in 1874 in Belfast was denounced as materialistic. He died from accidental poisoning with chloral.

TYRCONNEL, Richard Talbot, 1st Earl of (1630–91) Irish Jacobite leader. He went to London at the Restoration, and soon gained the favour of the royal family by a readiness for dirty work. **James II** created him Earl of Tyrconnel, with command of the troops in Ireland, and in 1687 appointed him lord-deputy of Ireland. He strove to undo the Protestant ascendency, but the Revolution brought his schemes to nothing; and he tried in vain to intrigue with **William III**. After the Battle of the Boyne Tyrconnel retired to France until 1691, when he returned as lord-lieutenant, dying of apoplexy soon after the Battle of Aughim. He was created earl (1685) and made titular duke (1689) by the deposed James II.

TYRONE See **O'NEILL, Hugh**

TYRRELL, George (1861–1909) Irish theologian, born in Dublin. He became a Roman Catholic in 1879, and a Jesuit in 1880. His 'modernism' led to his expulsion from the society (1906) and the minor excommunication. His works include *Christianity at the Crossroads* (1909) and *Essays on Faith and Immortality* (1914).

TYRTAEUS (fl.c.685–668 BC) Greek elegiac poet, probably born in Sparta. His warsongs inspired the Spartans during the second Messenian War (669 BC).

TYRWHITT, Thomas (1730–86) English classical commentator, born in London. He was educated at Eton and Queen's College, Oxford, and in 1762 became clerk of the House of Commons, resigning in 1768. He published a classic edition of the *Canterbury Tales* (2 vols, 1775–78) and commentaries on classical texts, notably **Aristotle**'s *Poetics* (1794).

TYSON, Edward (1651–1708) English physician, born in Bristol. He studied at Magdalen Hall, Oxford, and set up practice in London, lectured in anatomy and was a physician to Bridewell and Bethlehem Hospitals. His papers on comparative anatomy (comparing man with the orang-utan), on the porpoise (which he classified as both fish and mammal), on the respiratory and genital organs of the rattlesnake and (with **William Cowper**) on the female and male opossum, as well as his work on the classification of the male pygmy (1699), marked important advances.

TYSON, Frank Holmes (1930–) English cricketer, born in Farnworth. A fast bowler, his nickname 'Typhoon' was apt, as he swept opposing batsmen aside but blew himself out in a comparatively brief Test career. Of his 17 Tests only four were played in England and he is best remembered for his performance in the Australian tour of 1954–55 under **Len Hutton**. In that series he bowled at tremendous pace, having almost halved his run-up, but he found the dead pitches at Northampton unresponsive and left county cricket to become a coach and commentator in Australia.

TYTLER, Alexander Fraser (1747–1813) Scottish jurist and historian, son of **William Tytler**. In 1780 he became professor of universal history at Edinburgh. He was judge advocate of Scotland (1790) and a judge of the Court of Session (1802) as Lord Woodhouselee. He published a memoir of Lord **Kames** (1807) and various legal works.

TYTLER, James 'Balloon' (1745–1804) Scottish journalist, scientist and balloonist, born in Fearn in Angus, the son of a minister. He was a surgeon's apprentice in Forfar, a student at Edinburgh University and sailed to Greenland on a whaling ship, before embarking on the first of many ill-fated literary ventures, *The Gentleman and Lady's Magazine*, which lasted 13 issues. Always ready to accept hack work to keep his creditors at bay, he took on the editorship of the second edition of the *Encyclopaedia Britannica* which he laboured on for six or seven years for a modest wage of sixteen shillings a week. In 1783 he constructed a balloon, and like others of his ventures it threatened never to take off. But it did, with him aboard, on 27 August 1784, and reached a height of 350 feet, thus earning him a footnote in aviation history as, according to the *Edinburgh Advertiser*, 'the first person in Great Britain to have navigated the air'. Following this he fell into debt, was divorced, arrested, outlawed, and fled to Ireland before journeying to America, where, in Salem, Massachusetts, he drowned while intoxicated.

TYTLER, Patrick Fraser (1791–1849) Scottish historian, son of **Alexander Fraser Tytler**. He published a critical *History of Scotland 1249–1603* (1828–43), which is still valuable.

TYTLER, William, of Woodhouselee (1711–92) Scottish historian. An Edinburgh lawyer, he published an exculpatory *Inquiry into the Evidence against Mary, Queen of Scots* (1759), and edited the *Poetical Remains of James I of Scotland* (1783).

TYUTCHEV, Fyodor Ivanvich (1803–73) Russian lyric poet, of a noble landowning family. He spent 20 years abroad in the diplomatic service and then worked in the censorship department. His first collection of poems appeared in 1854 and was hailed with enthusiasm. A metaphysical romantic, he reached full recognition with the advent of symbolism. The tragic love poems of his later period are outstanding in Russian literature.

TZETZES, Johannes (c.1120–1183) Byzantine author. He wrote commentaries and treatises on grammar, and *Iliaca;* and *Biblos Istorike*, or *Chiliades*, a review of Greek literature and learning, a collection (in worthless verse) of over 600 stories.

TZU-HSI See **CI-XI**

U

UBALDINI, Petruccio (c.1524–1588) Florentine illuminator on vellum. He went to England in 1549, and wrote an Italian version of **Boece**'s *Description of Scotland* (1588), *Lives of English and Scottish Ladies* (1591), and other works.

UCCELLO, Paolo (c.1396–1475) Florentine painter, of the Early Renaissance period, primarily concerned with developing the new science of perspective in painting. He was originally apprenticed to **Ghiberti** but is more closely associated with the circle of **Donatello**. During his lifetime he became unfashionable with patrons and was forgotten until the 20th century when Abstract artists found their own concerns anticipated in his richly patterned compositions. Uccello's style is seen developed to its furthest in the three large-scale panel decorations he executed as decorations for the Palazzo Medici, *The Rout of San Romano* (1454–57). The panel in the London National Gallery is a highly decorative arrangement of diagonal lances—receding ranks of cavalry depicted in clearly defined space.

UDALL, or **Uvedale, John** (1560–92) English Puritan clergyman. Educated at Cambridge, he was one of the authors of the underground, anti-clerical *Martin Marprelate* tracts (1588–89), was arrested in 1590 and sentenced to death, but pardoned. He was author of a Hebrew grammar (1593) and several volumes of sermons.

UDALL, Nicholas (1504–56) English dramatist, born in Hampshire. He was educated at Winchester and Corpus Christi College, Oxford, and became headmaster of Eton c.1534. He published a selection from **Terence**, *Flowers of Latin Speaking*, for his pupils, who soon learnt of his predilection for corporal punishment. His dismissal in 1541 for indecent offences did not affect his standing at the court. **Edward VI** appointed him prebendary of Windsor, and despite his great enthusiasm for the Reformation, he survived the reign of Queen **Mary I** without disfavour. He translated **Erasmus**, selections from the Great Bible and Latin commentaries on the later, but is chiefly remembered as the author of the comedy, *Ralph Roister Doister*, written c.1553 but not published until 1567, which, inspired by his favourite classical writers, **Plautus** and Terence, was to influence later English writers of comedies.

UDET, Ernst (1896–1941) German airman, born at Frankfurt-am-Main. He was a leading German air ace in World War I, and from 1935 worked in the German air ministry. A *Luftwaffe* quartermaster-general in World War II, he committed suicide by an air crash, having fallen foul of the Gestapo. The authorities described his death as an accident while testing a new air weapon. **Zuckmayer**'s play, *The Devil's General*, is based on his life.

UDINE, Giovanni da (1487–1564) Italian painter, decorative artist and architect, born in Udine. He entered the workshop of **Raphael** in Rome and became a specialist in a style of decoration called 'grotesque' which was influenced by the graceful ornamental schemes, employing fantastic animals, medallions, foliage and similar elements, which were being discovered in the excavations of ancient Rome. He later moved back to Udine and, by 1552, was in charge of all public building there. His decorative style rapidly spread throughout Europe and was especially popular during the Neoclassical period of the 18th century.

UEMURA, Naomi (1942–84) Japanese explorer and mountaineer, born in Tajima region. He studied agriculture at Meiji University, Tokyo, where he started climbing. After solo ascents of Mount Blanc, Kilimanjaro, Aconcagua and Mt McKinley, he reached the summit of Everest with Teruo Matsura in 1970, and so became the first person to reach the highest peak on five continents. He was a member of the ill-fated 1971 International Everest Expedition, and made two attempts to climb Everest in winter. From 1977 to 1978 he spent a year living with Inuit (Eskimos) in the Canadian Arctic, travelling by dog sled 2000 miles up the coast of Greenland, and 7500 miles from Greenland to Alaska. He made a solo dog-sled journey from Ellesmere Island to the North Pole, arriving on 1 May 1978 after 450 miles, and was then airlifted to his base to undertake a north-south traverse of Greenland using 16 dogs. He left Kap Morris on 12 May 1978 and arrived after 1600 miles at Narssarssuaq on 22 August 1978. He led the Japanese attempt to climb Mt Everest in the winter of 1981. His attempt to do a solo crossing of Antarctica with an ascent of Mt Vinson was foiled by the outbreak of the Falklands War (1982). In February 1984 he completed the first winter ascent of the West Buttress Route of Mt McKinley and is presumed to have died during the descent, probably above 14300 ft. Although a team from his old university searched for him, his body has not been found.

UGOLINO DELLA GHERARDESCA, Count (d.1289) Ghibelline Count of Donoratico. With Giovanni Visconti, head of the **Guelfic** party, he laid a plot to secure arbitrary power in Pisa. The plot was discovered, and they were banished; but Ugolino, allying himself with the Florentines and Lucchese, forced the Pisans in 1276 to restore to him his territories. During the war with the Genoese, in the battle at Malora (1284), Ugolino, by treacherously abandoning the Pisans, occasioned the annihilation of their fleet, with a loss of 11000 prisoners; but when Florentines and other enemies of the republic gathered together to destroy it, the Pisans had no resource but to throw themselves into his arms. Ugolino now gave free scope to his despotic nature, persecuting and banishing all who were obnoxious to him, till at length a conspiracy was formed against him in 1288. Dragged from his palace, he was starved to death in the Tower of Gualandi, with his two sons and two grandsons.

UHLAND, Johannn Ludwig (1787–1862) German lyric poet, the leader of the 'Swabian School', born in Tübingen, where he studied law. He published poems from an early age and gradually added to his *Gedichte* (1815), which contain such popular songs as 'Der gute Kamerad'. He also wrote a number of admirable literary essays. He was a Liberal deputy for Tübingen at the assemblies of Württemberg (1819) and Frankfurt (1848).

UHLE, Max (1856–1944) German archaeologist, whose pioneering work in Peru and Bolivia between 1892 and 1912 revolutionized the archaeology of South

America. Trained as a philologist, he later transferred his allegiance to archaeology, becoming interested in Peru while a curator at Dresden Museum. From 1892 he undertook field research for the universities of Pennsylvania and California, excavating on the Peruvian coast at Pachacamac and on Mochica and Chimu sites. He later extended his work into the highlands and to Bolivia, Ecuador, and Chile, making also a notable contribution to North American archaeology with his excavations of the Emeryville shell-mound in San Franciso Bay. The rigour of his approach, influenced by the work of **Flinders Petrie** in Egypt, emphasized stratigraphic excavation and the ordering of finds in their correct evolutionary sequence as a means of establishing chronology. The basic framework he established for South America has only recently been superseded.

ULANOVA, Galina (1910–) Russian ballerina. She studied at the Petrograd State Ballet and made her début in *Les Sylphides* at the Kirov Ballet in Leningrad in 1928. She joined the Bolshoi Ballet in 1944 and became the leading ballerina of the Soviet Union and was four times a Stalin prizewinner. She visited London in 1956 with the Bolshoi ballet, when she gave a memorable perfomance in *Giselle*, perhaps her most famous role. She has appeared in several films made by the Moscow State Ballet Company and in 1957 was awarded the Lenin prize. She retired in 1962, but continued to teach at the Bolshoi.

ULBRICHT, Walter (1893–1973) East German communist politician, born in Leipzig. In 1928, after some years in Russia, he became communist deputy for Potsdam. He left Germany on **Hitler**'s advent in 1933. He went first to Paris and was in Spain during the civil war, but spent the greater part of his exile in Russia. As Marshal **Zhukov**'s political adviser and head of the German Communist party, he came back in 1945, and by 1950 had become deputy premier of the German Democratic Republic. The same year he was made secretary-general of the Party, and was largely responsible for the 'sovietization' of East Germany. He survived a workers' uprising in 1953 and went on to establish his position. He will be remembered chiefly for building the Berlin wall in 1961. He retired in 1971.

ULFILAS, or **Wulfila** (c.311–383) Cappadocian prelate, and translator of the Bible, born among the Goths north of the Danube. Consecrated a missionary bishop to the Visigoths by **Eusebius** of Nicomedia in 341, after seven years' labour he was forced to migrate with his converts across the Danube. For over 30 years he worked in Lower Moesia. He attended the Council of Constantinople in 360 in the interest of the Arian party, and again in 383, only to die a few days after his arrival. He translated the Bible into Gothic from Greek, using an alphabet based on Latin and Greek.

ULIANOV See **LENIN, Vladimir Ilyich**

ULLMANN, Liv Johanne (1939–) Norwegian actress, born in Tokyo. She studied acting at the Webber-Douglas School in London before beginning her career with a repertory company in Stavanger. She made her film début in *Fjols til Fjells* (1957) but her screen image was largely defined through a long professional and personal association with the Swedish director **Ingmar Bergman** in which she laid bare the inner turmoil of women experiencing various emotional and sexual crises. Their films together include *Persona* (1966). *Visknigar och Rop* (Cries and Whispers, 1972), *Ansikte mot Ansikte* (Face to Face, 1975) and *Herbstsonate* (Autumn Sonata, 1978). Her work for other filmmakers has been less challenging, particularly in English-language productions like *Lost Horizon* (1973). She made her Broadway début in *A Doll's House* (1975), and regular theatre appearances include *I Remember Mama* (1979) and *Old Times* (1985, London). She has worked extensively for the charity UNICEF and written two autobiographical works: *Changing* (1977) and *Choices* (1984).

ULM, Charles Thomas Philippe (1898–1934) Australian pioneer aviator, born in Melbourne, Victoria. He fought with the Australian Imperial Forces at Gallipoli in 1915 and later qualified as a pilot. In 1921 he first met **Charles Kingsford Smith** and in 1927 joined him in a record-breaking round-Australia flight. In 1928 Ulm was copilot with Kingsford Smith in the first flight across the Pacific and, later in that year, in the first trans-Tasman flight (from Richmond, New South Wales to Christchurch, New Zealand and back). In 1929 he partnered Kingsford Smith again, in a new record 13-day flight from Australia to England, a record which he lowered to seven days in 1933 in his own Avro Ten *Faith in Australia*. With Kingsford Smith he formed the first Australian National Airways in 1929, and was managing director until the company ceased in 1931. In 1934, in *Faith in Australia*, Ulm carried the first airmail deliveries between Australia and New Zealand and, later, New Guinea. In December the same year, investigating the possibilities of regular airmail flights across the Pacific, he set out from California with two companions in his new twin-engine *Stella Australis*; the plane vanished without trace somewhere over the Hawaiian islands.

ULPIANUS, Domitius (c.170–228) Roman jurist, born in Tyre. He held judicial offices under **Septimius Severus** and **Caracalla** and, on the accession of **Alexander Severus** (222), became his principal adviser and *praefectus praetorio*. He was murdered by his own soldiery. He was the last of the great classical jurists and a voluminous writer; in **Justinian**'s *Digest* there are 2462 excerpts from Ulpian; the originals are almost wholly lost.

ULRIKA ELEONORA (1688–1741) Queen of Sweden (1719–20), younger sister of **Karl XII**. Married to Prince Frederick of Hesse in 1715, she was elected queen after her brother's death. A new constitution, however, inaugurated the so-called 'Era of Liberty' (1718–71), and saw the abolition of royal absolutism, giving power to the Riksdag (parliament). Ulrika was so displeased that she abdicated in 1720 in favour of her husband, who ascended the throne as **Frederik I**.

ULUGH-BEG (fl.c.1430) ruler of Turkestan from 1447. A grandson of **Tamerlane**, he made his name particularly as an astronomer; he founded an observatory at Samarkand and compiled astronomical tables and wrote poetry and history. After a brief reign, he was defeated and slain by a rebellious son in 1449.

ULYANOV See **LENIN, Vladimir Ilyich**

'UMAR See **OMAR**

'UMAR KHAYYÁM See **OMAR KHAYYÁM**

UMAYYADS an Arab dynasty belonging to the Quraysh tribe of Mecca, caliphs from 661 to 750. The founder of the dynasty was Mu'āwiya I, born Abi Sufyān (c.605–680), governor of Syria, who led opposition to the caliph **'Ali** in demanding vengeance for his kinsman **'Uthmān** and was accepted as caliph by the majority of the Muslim community on 'Ali's death. He established his capital at Damascus (661). The caliphate, previously elective, became a hereditary monarchy with the succession of his son Yazīd (683), who defeated the first of several Shi'ite revolts at the battle of Karbala in which 'Ali's son al-Husayn was killed (680). On the death of Yazīd's son Mu'āwiya II in 683, the caliphate passed to a collateral branch of the family in the person of Marwān I, born al-Hakam (c. 623–685). 'Abd al-Malik (c.646–705) carried out lasting reforms, substituting Arabic for the pre-Conquest languages as the medium of administration and introducing a Muslim coinage. The reign of al-Walīd I (c. 670–715), caliph from 705, saw the conquest of Transoxania, North Africa, and the overthrow of the Visigothic kingdom in Spain by the general Tāriq, an advance not halted by the Christian West until 732. 'Abd al-Malik and his sons were also great patrons of architecture, responsible for the Dome of the Rock in Jerusalem and the Great Mosque of Damascus as well as numerous palaces and hunting-lodges. After the reign of Hishām (691–743), the tenth caliph, Umayyad rule was progressively weakened by struggles over the succession, exacerbated by tribal rivalries among the Arabs, provincial resentment at the dominance of Syria and discontent among many of the non-Arabic converts to Islam. In 750 Marwān II al-Himār (c. 692–750) was overthrown by a revolution led by the **'Abbasids** and later killed. One of the few Umayyads to escape the ensuing massacre of the entire family was a grandson of Hishām, **'Abd er-Rahmān I**, who in 756 established himself as emir of Muslim Spain (*al-Andalus*) with his capital at Cordoba, where the Umayyads continued to rule until 1031.

UMBERTO I (1844–1900) king of Italy, born in Turin. In 1868 he married his cousin Margherita of Savoy and in 1878 succeeded his father, **Victor Emmanuel II**. He was assassinated in Monza.

UMBERTO II (1904–83) king of Italy in 1946 on the abdication of his father, **Victor Emmanuel III**, but himself abdicated a month later, after a national referendum had declared for a republic. He left Italy and settled in Portugal, at Cascais. Some of his descendants, notably his daughter, have been allowed back.

UNAMUNO, Miguel de (1864–1936) Spanish philosopher and author, born in Bilbao, of Basque parentage. He was professor of Greek at Salamanca from 1892. He wrote mystic philosophy, historical studies, brilliant essays, books on travel, and austere poetry. Among his most important works are *Vida de Don Quijote y Sancho* (1905), his novel *Niebla* (1914), *Del sentimiento trágico de la vida* (1913) and a volume of religious poetry, *El Cristo de Velázquez* (1920). From 1924 to 1930 he was exiled as a republican to the island of Fuerteventura, and reinstated at Salamanca on the founding of the republic in 1931. Always a rebel and an individualist though with the deepest faith in and interest of his country at heart, he was soon at variance with the socialist régime. The Civil War for him was a nationalist struggle and he denounced foreign interference.

UNDERHILL, Evelyn (1875–1941) English poet and mystic, born in Wolverhampton. She was educated at King's College, London. In 1907 she married Herbert Stuart Moore, a barrister, and in 1921 became lecturer on the philosophy of religion at Manchester College, Oxford. A friend and disciple of **Hügel**, she found her way intellectually from agnosticism to Christianity, wrote numerous books on mysticism, including *The Life of the Spirit* (1922), volumes of verse and four novels. Her *Mysticism* (1911) became a standard work.

UNDERWOOD, Derek Leslie (1945–) English cricketer, born in Bromley. A slow left-arm bowler, he took 296 wickets in 86 Tests, and this total would have been much larger had he not suffered two bans, first for defecting to World Series cricket in 1977 and later for playing unauthorized matches in South Africa. Forty-seven times in his career he took ten wickets in a match, and very late on he made his only first-class century, for Kent against Sussex at Hastings in 1984.

UNDI the dynastic title of chiefs of the Chewa kingdom who replaced the kalonga as the dominant political authority in central southern Africa during the eighteenth century.

UNDSET, Sigrid (1882–1949) Norwegian novelist, born in Kalundborg, in Denmark. The daughter of a noted Norwegian archaeologist, she inherited an interest in medieval Norway. From 1899 she worked in an office, and the problems facing young contemporary women formed the basis of her early novels, including *Jenny* (1911). Her masterpiece, *Kristin Lavransdatter* (3 vols, 1920–22), which tells a graphic story of love and religion in 14th-century Norway was followed by *Olav Audunssön* (4 vols, 1925–27), *Gymadenia* (1929) and *Den trofaste hustru* (The Faithful Spouse, 1936). She became a Roman Catholic in 1924, after which her work deepened in religous intensity. She was awarded the Nobel prize for literature in 1928.

UNGARETTI, Giuseppe (1888–1970) Italian poet, born in Alexandria. He first visited Italy when he was 26; soon afterwards he joined the army and fought on the Austrian front. From 1912 to 1914 he lived in Paris where he met **Apollinaire**. His first collection, *Il porto sepolto* (The Buried Harbour), was published in 1916) with a preface by **Mussolini**, and immediately gained him admission to the ranks of the great Italian poets of the 20th century. Largely defying translation, he is less well known than **Montale** or **Quasimodo**, but among his distinguished collections are *Vita d'un uomo* (1966, Life of a Man) and *Il dolore* (1947, Grief). He studied in Paris, and was professor of Italian literature at São Paulo, Brazil (1936–42) and at Rome (1942–58). He is the author of 'hermetic' poems characterized by their symbolism, compressed imagery and modern verse structure.

UNGARO, Emanuel Maffeolti (1933–) French fashion designer, born in Aix-en-Provence, of Italian parents. Originally he trained to join the family tailoring business, but went instead to Paris in 1955, worked for a small tailoring firm, and later joined **Balenciaga**. In 1965 he opened his own house, with Sonia Knapp designing his fabrics. Initially featuring rigid lines, his styles later softened. In 1968 he produced his first ready-to-wear lines.

UNITAS, Johnny Constantine (1933–) American footballer, born in Pittsburgh, Pennsylvania, one of the game's first television heroes. A quarter-back, he signed for the Baltimore Colts in 1956. Two years later he led them to a championship victory against the New York Giants in overtime. The game was broadcast live in the USA and helped American football to its big television breakthrough. In 1973, at 40 years of age, he joined the San Diego Chargers but was injured after only three games and retired. He then set up his own restaurant back in Baltimore.

UNRUH, Fritz von (1885–1970) German playwright and novelist, born in Koblenz. He served in World War I as a cavalry officer. An ardent pacifist, the ideal of a new humanity underlies all his Expressionist works, particularly the novel *Opfergang* (1916), and the two parts of an unfinished dramatic trilogy, *Ein Geschlecth* (1916) and *Platz* (1920). He left Germany in 1932 and went to the USA, where he wrote *The End is not Yet* (1947) and *The Saint* (1950). He returned to Germany in 1952.

UNVERDORBEN, Otto (1806–73) German chemist, born in Dahme. He prepared aniline by the distillation of indigo (1826).

UNWIN, Mary See **COWPER, William**

UNWIN, Sir Stanley (1884–1968) English publisher, chairman of the firm of George Allen and Unwin, founded in 1914. He studied the book-trade in

Germany. An international figure in publishing, he was president of the Publishers Association of Great Britain (1933–35) and president of the International Publishers Association (1936–38, 1946–54). His books include *The Truth about Publishing* (1926; revised 1960), *Publishing in Peace and War* (1944) and *The Truth about a Publisher* (autobiography; 1960).

UPDIKE, John Hoyer (1932–) American novelist, poet and critic, born in Shillington, Pennsylvania. He studied at Harvard and the Ruskin School of Drawing and Fine Art in Oxford (1954–55), then returned to New York and served for two years on the staff of *The New Yorker* (1955–57), the beginning of a long and fruitful relationship with the magazine to which he has contributed short stories, poems and book reviews. His first book was a collection of verse, *The Carpentered Hen and Other Tame Creatures* (1958). But his status as one of the world's major writers is due largely to his fiction. Beginning with *The Poorhouse Fair* (1959), he has published 13 novels and many collections of short stories. Sophisticated, linguistically supple, fluent and inventive, his beat is middle-class America, his concerns those that have dominated the 20th century: sex, marriage, adultery, divorce, religion, materialism. Among his best known books are, *The Centaur* (1963), the Rabbit trilogy—*Rabbit, Run* (1960), *Rabbit Redux* (1971) and *Rabbit is Rich* (1981)—spanning 30 years in the life of a car salesman, *Couples* (1968), *The Coup* (1978), *The Witches of Eastwick* (1984), *Roger's Version* (1986), and *S* (1988). *Self-Consciousness*, a memoir consisting of six chapters concerning his hometown, his suffering from psoriasis, his stuttering, his thoughts on the Vietnam War, his paternal ancestors, and his attitude towards his religion, was published in 1989.

URBAIN, Georges (1872–1938) French chemist, born in Paris. He became professor of inorganic chemistry at the Sorbonne (1908), discovered the rare earth lutecium (1907) and the law of optimum phosphorescence of binary systems, and showed that several elements which were hitherto considered pure were in fact mixtures.

URBAN I (d.230) bishop of Rome (222–230). He is said to have been a martyr.

URBAN II (c.1035–1099) pope from 1088, born in Châtillon-sur-Marne, France. He became cardinal-bishop of Ostia (1078), and was elected pope during the schismatical pontificate of Guibert the antipope Clement III. He laid **Henry IV** of Germany under ban and drove him out of Italy, and triumphed by the same means over **Philip I** of France. He inspired the first Crusade (1095–99) by his eloquence at the council he held at Piacenza and Clermont (1095).

URBAN IV (c.1200–1264) pope from 1261, born Jacques Pantaléon, the son of a cobbler of Troyes. He was bishop of Verdun (1253) and patriarch of Jerusalem (1255). He instituted the feast of Corpus Christi (1264).

URBAN V (c.1310–1370) pope from 1362, born Guillaume de Grimoard in Grisac, France. He was abbot of St Victor at Marseilles, and was elected pope at Avignon. He made a determined attempt to move the papacy to Rome (1367–70), but had to return to Avignon a few months before his death.

URBAN VI (1318–89) pope from 1378, born Bartolomeo Prignano in Naples. He became archbishop of Bari (1377). The French cardinals set up against him the bishop of Cambray as the antipope **Clement VII**, beginning the Great Schism in the West.

URBAN VIII (1568–1644) pope from 1623, born Maffeo Barberini, in Florence. He supported **Richelieu**'s policy against the Habsburgs in the Thirty Years' War, condemned **Galilei** and **Jansen**, canonized **Ignatius Loyola** and **Philip Neri**, and wrote sacred poetry. He carried out much ecclesiastical reform and established his own family in the Roman aristocracy, and built Castel Gandelfo.

URE, Andrew (1778–1857) Scottish chemist, born in Glasgow. He studied at Glasgow University, became professor of chemistry and natural philosophy in Anderson's College, astronomer in the city observatory, and in 1834 analytical chemist to the board of customs in London. He produced a *Dictionary of Chemistry* (1821), and other works.

URE SMITH, Sydney George (1887–1949) English-born Australian artist, editor and publisher, born in Stoke Newington, London. He arrived in Australia as an infant in 1888, was educated in Melbourne and, later, at Sydney Grammar School. He attended **Julian Ashton**'s Art School in Sydney, and his etchings appeared in a number of volumes including *The Charm of Sydney* (1918) and *Old Colonial Byways* (1928). He organized the Australian art exhibition held at Burlington House, London, in 1923, published the seminal journal *Art in Australia* from 1916 to 1939, and edited books on Hilder, **Streeton**, Blamire Young and others. He founded his own publishing house in 1939 and was active in promoting the contemporary arts in Australia through a variety of periodicals and books.

UREY, Harold Clayton (1893–1981) American physical chemist, born in Walkerton, Indiana. Educated at Montana, California, and Copenhagen, he became professor of chemistry at Columbia (1934) and at Chicago (1945–52). He was director of war research, atomic bomb project, Columbia (1940–45). In 1932 he isolated heavy water and discovered the heavy hydrogen isotope, deuterium, which was of great importance in the development of nuclear fission. He also investigated entropy of gases, absorption spectra and isotopes. He was awarded the Nobel prize for chemistry in 1934 and the Davy medal of the Royal Society (1940), of which he was elected foreign member (1947).

URFÉ, Honoré d' (1568–1625) French writer, born in Marseilles. He fought in the religious wars of France and later settled in Savoy. He was the author of the pastoral romance, *Astrée* (1610–27), which is regarded as the first French novel. He was killed at Villefranche-sur-Mer during the war between Savoy and Genoa.

URIS, Leon Marcus (1924–) American popular author, born in Baltimore. He dropped out of high school and joined the Marine Corps, taking part in battles in the Pacific. *Battle Cry* (1956) uses the experience to telling effect. *Exodus* (1958) remains the book by which he is best known. Depicting the early years of the state of Israel, it was made into a highly successful film though it was not commended by the critics. *The Haj* was published in 1984.

URQUHART, David (1805–77) Scottish diplomatist, born in Cromarty. He served in the Greek navy during the Greek War of Independence and received his first diplomatic appointment in 1831, when he went to Constantinople with Sir **Stratford de Canning**. His anti-Russian policy caused his recall from Turkey in 1837 and he was member of parliament for Stafford from 1847 to 1852. A strong opponent of **Palmerston**'s policy, he believed Turkey was capable of dealing with Russia without European intervention. He founded the *Free Press*, afterwards called the *Diplomatic Review*, in which these views were expressed. He retired in 1864. Among his many writings were *The Pillars of Hercules* (1850), in which he suggested the introduction of Turkish baths into Britain, and *The Lebanon* (1960).

URQUHART, Fred (1912–) Scottish short-story writer and novelist, born in Edinburgh, the son of a chauffeur. He grew up in Fife, Perth and Wigtown, leaving school at 15 and then working as bookseller's assistant and labourer. He published his first novel, *Time Will Knit*, in 1938. He has published eleven collections of his short stories, many initially broadcast by the BBC, and has edited nine anthologies of short stories. His other novels to date are *The Ferret Was Abraham's Daughter* (1949), *Jezebel's Dust* (1951) and *Palace of Green Days* (1979, the first of a projected series). He has been publisher's reader, and literary editor of *Tribune*. His outstanding achievement is his quite exceptional ability to convey narrative plots through the eyes of female characters, initially in the Scotland of his childhood and adolescence and more recently using ghost stories, historical fiction and other forms.

URQUHART, Sir Thomas (c.1611–1660) Scottish author, born in Cromarty, the son of a land-owner. He studied at King's College, Aberdeen, and travelled in France, Spain and Italy. On his return he took up arms against the Covenanting party in the north but was defeated and forced to flee to England. Becoming attached to the court, he was knighted in 1641. The same year he published his *Epigrams: Divine and Moral*. On succeeding his father in 1642 he returned north. In Cromarty, though much troubled by his creditors, he produced his *Trissotetras; or a most exquisite Table for Resolving Triangles, etc* (1645), a study of trigonometry based on **Napier**'s invention of logarithms. In 1649 his library was seized and sold. He again took up arms in the royal cause, and was present at the battle at Worcester (1651), where he lost most of his MSS. In London, through **Cromwell**'s influence, he was allowed considerable liberty, and in 1652 he published his *Pantochronochanon* (1652), an exact account of the Urquhart family, in which they are traced back to Adam. He also published *Ekskubalauron*, better known as *The Discoverie of a most Exquisite Jewel*, an attack on the Scottish clergy which contains a ribald account of **James Crichton** (the 'Admirable Crichton'), but is chiefly a work praising the Scots nation. In 1653 he issued his *Introduction to the Universal Language* and the first two books of that English classic, his brilliant translation of *Rabelais*. The third was not issued till after his death. He is said to have died abroad, in a fit of mirth on hearing of the Restoration. His learning was vast, his scholarship defective.

URSULA, St legendary saint and martyr. She is especially honoured in Cologne, where she is said to have been slain with her 11000 virgins by a horde of Huns on her journey home from a pilgrimage to Rome. She became the patron saint of many educational institutes, particularly the teaching order of the Ursulines. Her feast day is 21 October.

USHER, James See **USSHER**

USPENSKI, Gleb Ivanovich (c.1840–1902) Russian author. He wrote novels of peasant life, such as *Power of the Soil* (1882), notable for their realism in contrast to the prevalent romantic conception of the agricultural worker. He died insane.

USSHER, James (1581–1656) Irish prelate, and archbishop of Armagh, born in Dublin, the son of a gentleman of good estate, and nephew of the preceding archbishop of Armagh, Henry Ussher (c.1550–1631). He was a scholar (1594) and fellow (1599–1605) of Trinity College, Dublin. About 1606 he became chancellor of St Patrick's, in 1607 professor of divinity, in 1620 bishop of Meath, in 1623 privy councillor for Ireland, and in 1625 archbishop of Armagh. He left Ireland for England in 1640, continued to live in England, declined to sit in the Westminster Assembly, and for about eight years was preacher at Lincoln's Inn. He was constant in his loyalty to the throne, yet was treated with favour by **Cromwell**, and was buried in Westminster Abbey. He was distinguished not only by his learning but also by his charity and good temper. He was calvinistic in theology and moderate in his ideas of church government. Of his numerous writings, the best known is the *Annales Veteris et Novi Testamenti* (1650–54), which propounded a long-accepted chronology of Scripture which fixed the Creation precisely at 4004 BC Amongst his other works, the *De Graeca Septuaginta Interpretum Verisone Syntagma* (1655) was the first attempt at a real examination of the Septuagint.

USTINOV, Peter Alexander (1921–) British actor and dramatist, born in London. The son of White Russian parents, Ustinov first appeared on the stage in 1938, and had established himself as an accomplished artist both in revues and legitimate drama by 1942, when four years' army service interrupted his career. His subsequent work for films as actor, writer and producer, and in broadcasting as a satirical comedian, has enhanced his reputation. A prolific playwright, his works— most successful amongst which are *The Love of Four Colonels* (1951) and *Romanoff and Juliet* (1956)—are marked by a serious approach to human problems often presented with an acute sense of comedy and a mastery of unconventional stagecraft. Among his other plays are *Photo Finish* (1962), *The Unknown Soldier and his Wife* (1967) and *Overheard* (1981). He has published an autobiography, *Dear Me* (1977).

USUMAN DAN FODIO (1754–1817) ruler of Hausaland, born in Maratta, in the Hausa kingdom of Gobir, of a scholarly Muslim family. An influential itinerant preacher throughout the kingdoms of Hausaland, he was known to his followers as the *shehu* (chief). His repeated calls for reform in line with strict Islamic doctrine were resisted by successive Hausa rulers. An attempt by Yunfa, king of Gobir, to have him assassinated led to a full-blown *jihad* or holy war throughout Hausaland in the early years of the 19th century. The *shehu* and his allies had succeeded by 1812 in establishing a new Muslim empire in the region, divided between Gwandu in the west and Sokoto in the east, with Usuman dan Fodio himself as spiritual leader of both halves. During the last five years of his life, he devoted himself increasingly to scholarship and left the practical administration of the empire to his lieutenants.

UTAMARO, Kitigawa (1753–1806) Japanese painter and engraver. Born and trained in Edo (modern Tokyo), he came to specialize in portraits of court ladies, in which the gracefulness of face, figure and flowing robes was depicted with a precise detail and personally-developed use of close-up which brought him great contemporary success. He also painted flowers, birds and fish, and carried the technique of the *Ukiyo-e* or 'popular school' to its highest artistic level.

'UTHMĀN (d.656) fourth caliph. He was elected in succession to **Umar**, in preference to **Alī** (644). He established a commission of scholars who collected the revelations of **Muhammad** to produce the definitive version of the Qur'an. However, Uthmān's administration was badly organized, and disagreements concerning the division of the gains made in the Muslim conquests gave rise to increasing social tensions, culminating in a revolt in which he was killed.

UTRILLO, Maurice (1883–1955) French painter, born in Montmartre, Paris, the illegitimate son of the painter **Suzanne Valadon**. Adopted by the Spanish writer Miguel Utrillo, he began to paint at Montmagny in 1902, but it was the streets of Paris, particularly old Montmartre, and village scenes which were to provide him with most of his subjects. Despite acute alcoholism and drug addiction, and consequent sojourns in various nursing-homes, his productivity was astonishing, and by 1925 he was famous. His 'White Period' paintings of about 1908–14 are much sought after, for their subtle colouring and sensitive feeling for atmosphere. He signed his work 'Maurice Utrillo V', incorporating the initial of his mother's family name.

UTTLEY, Alison (1884–1976) English author of children's stories, born on a farm in Derbyshire. She was widowed in 1930 and turned to writing to support herself and her young son. *The Country Child* (1931) was followed by a flood of books, mainly for children, which revealed her great love for and knowledge of the countryside and country lore. Many of her books were in the **Beatrix Potter** tradition, featuring much-loved characters such as Grey Rabbit and Sam Pig.

UTZON, Jørn (1918–) Danish architect. Educated at the Royal Danish Academy, his buildings include the Sydney Opera House, Bank Melhi (Teheran), the Kuwait House of Parliament, Bagsvæ Church (Copenhagen) and Paustian's House of Furniture (Copenhagen). In 1966 he won the competition for the design of the Zürich Schausspielhaus. He was awarded the Bund Deutscher Architektens Ehrenplachette (1965), the gold medal of the Royal Institute of British Architects (1978), the Alvar Aalto medal (1982), and the Fritz Schumacher prize (1988).

UVEDALE See **UDALL**

V

VACARIUS (c.1115–1198) Italian jurist. A law teacher at Bologna, he came to England and lectured at Oxford in 1149, where he was the first to teach the rediscovered Roman law. His book, *Liber Pauperum*, was a popular medieval text.

VACHEROT, Étienne (1809–97) French philosopher, born in Langres. He became professor of philosophy at the Sorbonne in 1839 but was dismissed in 1852 when he refused to sign the oath of allegiance to the empire. His book *La Démocratie* (1859) led to his imprisonment. His other writings include *La Métaphysique et la Science* (1858) and *La Religion* (1868).

VAIHINGER, Hans (1852–1933) German philosopher, born in Württemberg. He was professor at the University of Halle (1884–1906), founded the **Kant** Society in 1904 and wrote a famous commentary on Kant's *Critique of Pure Reason* (1881–92). He developed his own brand of idealism and pragmatism through his theory of 'fictions' in *Die Philosophie des Als Ob* (1911), translated as *The Philosophy of 'As If'* (1924).

VALADON, Suzanne (1869–1938) French painter, the mother of **Utrillo**. She became an artist's model after an accident ended her career as an acrobat, modelling for **Renoir** and others. With the encouragement of **Toulouse-Lautrec**, **Degas** and **Cézanne**, she took up painting herself and excelled in her realistic treatment of nudes, portraits and figure studies, her work having some affinity with that of Degas.

VALBERT, G See **CHERBULIEZ, Charles Victor**

VALDEMAR I, 'the Great' (1131–82) king of Denmark from 1157. The son of King Knut Lavard, he emerged victorious from 30 years of civil strife to give Denmark an unparalleled period of prosperity and expansion. In 1169 he destroyed the power of the Wends by capturing the island of Rügen. He strengthened the defences of the Danevirke and increased the size and effectiveness of the Danish army. He was succeeded by his eldest son, Knut VI (1163–1202).

VALDÉS, Armando Palacio (1853–1938) Spanish novelist, born in Entralgo in Asturias. Some of his psychological and naturalistic novels were translated as *The Marquis of Peñalba*, *Maximina*, *Sister Saint Sulpice*, *Froth* and *The Grandee*.

VALDÉS, Juan de (1500–41) Spanish humanist and religious reformer, born in Cuenca. He became an object of suspicion to the Inquisition, and lived in Naples from 1534, but he sought the regeneration of the church from within, and never inclined to Lutheranism. Among his works are *The Christian Alphabet* (1536) and Commentaries, some of them translated into English (1865–83). His twin brother, Alphonso (1500–32), was also a humanist theologian.

VALDIVIA, Pedro de (c.1510–1559) Spanish soldier, born near La Serena, Estremadura. He went to Venezuela (c.1534) and then to Peru, where he became **Pizarro**'s lieutenant. He won renown at Las Salinas (1538), and was in real command of the expedition to Chile. He founded Santiago (1541) and other cities, including Concepción (1550) and Valdivia (1552). In 1559, attempting, with a small force, to relieve Tucapel, which was besieged by the Araucanians, he was captured and killed by the Indians.

VALENTINE, Saint (d.c.269) Roman priest and Christian martyr, said to have been executed during the persecution inaugurated under Claudius II, the Goth; but claims have been made for another St Valentine, supposedly bishop of Turni, taken 60 miles to Rome for martyrdom. Neither Valentine is associated with writing love-letters, hardly surprisingly; the custom originated in the later middle ages, having been linked with the day in the belief that it opened the mating season for the birds.

VALENTINE, Alfred Lewis (1930–) West Indian cricketer, born in Kingston, Jamaica. A spin bowler of genius, especially in partnership with **Sonny Ramadhin**, he posed unanswerable problems of spin for the England batsmen during the 1950 tour of England. Both men had been selected for Test cricket after a mere handful of first-class matches. In 36 Tests he took 139 wickets, twice taking ten or more in a match, without any previous experience of the English county game. The achievements of the two spinners are immortalized in the famous calypso by Lord Beginner, 'Cricket, lovely cricket'.

VALENTINIAN I (321–75) Roman emperor from 364, born in Cibalis in Pannonia. He rose rapidly in rank under **Constantius** and **Julian**, and on the death of the emperor Jovian (331–64) was chosen as his successor (364). He resigned the East to his brother Valens, and himself governed the West with watchful care until his death.

VALENTINIAN II (371–92) second son of **Valentinian I**, Roman emperor from 375 with his half-brother **Gratian**. He received from Gratian the provinces of Italy, Illyricum and Africa. During his minority the empress Justina administered the government; about three years after her death Valentinian was murdered, probably by Arbogastes, commander-in-chief of his army.

VALENTINIAN III (c.419–455) Roman emperor, grand-nephew of **Valentinian II**, the son of **Constantius III**, was given the western empire by Theodosius II, emperor of the east, in 425. A weak prince, he never really ruled during his thirty years' reign. At first his mother Placidia was the dominant influence, then after 433 the commander-in-chief **Aetius**. He lost control of Africa to the Vandal **Gaiseric** in 442. He stabbed Aetius to death in 454, but next year was himself slain by two of Aetius' bodyguards.

VALENTINO See **GARAVANI, Valentino**

VALENTINO, Rudolph, originally **Rodolpho Alphonso Guglielmi di Valentina d'Antonguolla** (1895–1926) Italian-born American film actor, born in Castellaneta. He studied agriculture but emigrated to the USA in 1913 and first appeared on the stage as a dancer. In 1919 he made his screen début, but his first starring role was as Julio in *The Four Horsemen of the Apocalypse* (1921), and his subsequent performances in *The Sheikh* (1921), *Blood and Sand* (1922), *The Young Rajah* (1922), *Monsieur Beaucaire* (1924), *The Eagle* (1925) and *The Son of the Sheikh* (1926) established him as the leading 'screen lover' of the 1920s. He died suddenly in New York of peritonitus at the height of his fame, and his funeral resembled that of a popular ruler. Besides good looks and athletic bearing, he had considerable dramatic gifts. He also wrote *Daydreams* (1923), a book of poems.

VALERA See **DE VALERA, Eamon**

VALERA, Don Juan (1824–1905) Spanish novelist and critic, born in Cabra in Córdoba. He held diplomatic posts in Europe and the USA, and was a deputy, minister of commerce, minister of public instruction and councillor of state senator. His literary studies (1864) and essays (1882) made his reputation but his fame depends on his romances, *Pepita Jiméne* (1874, trans 1891), *Las ilusiones del Doctor Faustino* (1876), *El comendador Mendoza* (1877, trans 1893), *Doña Luz* (1878, trans 1892) and *La buena fama* (1895). He was also a noted translator of **Goethe**'s *Faust* and other classics.

VALERIAN, Publius Licinius (c.193–260) Roman emperor. He was proclaimed emperor by the legions in Rhaetia after the murder of Gallus (253), and assumed as colleague his eldest son, **Gallienus**. Throughout his reign trouble hovered on every frontier of the empire; and marching against the Persians, he was completely defeated at Edessa (260). He was seized by King Sapor, and died in captivity.

VALERIUS MAXIMUS (20 BC–50 AD) Roman historian. He wrote (c.29 AD) nine books of *Facta et dicta memorabilia*, historical anecdotes, biased in favour of the emperor **Tiberius**.

VALÉRY, Paul Ambroise (1871–1945) French poet and writer, born in Cette. He settled in Paris in 1892, and after publishing some remarkable verse in the style of **Mallarmé**, he relapsed into a 20 years' silence, taken up with mathematics and philosophical speculations. He emerged in 1917 with a new poetic outlook and technique in *La Jeune Parque* (1917), a poem full of difficult symbolism. This was followed by a significant collection, *Charmes* (1922), containing 'Le Cimetière marin,' 'L'Ébauche d'un serpent,' 'Au platane,' and others, noted for the poetic shorthand, the compression and conciseness of his imagery and ideas. His prose works include *Soirèe avec M Teste* (1895), and several aesthetic studies, such as the dialogue *Eupalinos* (1924), in which architecture and music are compared, and *L'Âme et la danse* (1924). A late, short play, *Le Solitaire*, foreshadows **Samuel Beckett**.

VALETTE, Jean Parisot de la (1494–1568) French knight of St John, nobly born in Toulouse. He became grand master in 1557. His exploits against the Turks culminated in his successful defence of Malta, from 18 May–8 September, 1565. He founded the city of Valetta.

VALLA, Laurentius (c.1405–1457) Italian humanist, born in Rome. He taught classics at Pavia, Milan and Naples. He was expelled from Rome for attacking the temporal power in his *De Donatione Constantini Magni*, was prosecuted by the Inquisition in Naples, but in 1448 was again in Rome as apostolic secretary to Pope **Nicholas V**. His Latin versions of **Xenophon**, **Herodotus** and **Thucydides** were admirable; and he greatly advanced New Testament criticism by his comparison of the Vulgate with the Greek original. His *De Elegantia Latinae Linguae* was long a textbook.

VALLE-INCLÁN, Ramón María del (1869–1936) Spanish novelist, dramatist and poet, born in Puebla de Caramiñal. Among his works are four *Sonatas* on the seasons (1902–07), written in fine prose in the form of novels, a graphic but erroneous history *La guerra carlista*, and the masterly *Águila de blasón* (1907) and *Romance de Lobos* (1908), set in a vivid medieval background. Many of his novels and plays are collected in *Esperpentos*, and among several volumes of fine verse is his *Cara de Plata* (1923).

VALLIÈRE, Louise Françoise de Labaume Leblanc See **LA VALLIÈRE**

VALLISNIERI, Antonio (1661–1730) Italian naturalist, born in Modena. He became professor of medicine at Padua, made important studies of the reproductive systems of insects, and wrote treatises on the ostrich (1712) and the chameleon (1715). The waterweed *Vallisneria spiralis* is named after him.

VALLOTTON, Felix (1865–1925) Swiss-born French painter, born in Lausanne. He studied at the Academy Julian with **Toulouse-Lautrec** and Charles Maurin. Early in his career he assiduously copied the old masters in the Louvre and made engravings in the manner of **Millet**, **Rembrandt** and others. He was a member of the 'Nabis' symbolist movement, and one of the principal collaborators in *Le Revue Blanche* between 1894 and 1901. His most notable works were wood engravings which were immensely popular and brought him immediate success. He is regarded as a forerunner of the generation of artist engravers, which included such names as **Kandinsky**, **Munch** and **Beardsley**. His main themes of portraits, landscapes and scenes of modern life were much admired throughout his life and his striking images were later transferred to his oil painting.

VALOIS, Dame Ninette de, stage-name of **Edris Stannus** (1898–) Irish ballerina, born in Baltiboys, Blessington, County Wicklow. She studied under **Cecchetti** and first appeared, in 1914, in the pantomime at the Lyceum Theatre. She subsequently appeared with the Beecham Opera Company and at Covent Garden. After a European tour with **Diaghilev** (1923–25), she partnered **Anton Dolin** in England, and became director of ballet at the Abbey Theatre, Dublin. She was a founding member of the Camargo Society and the Vic-Wells Ballet (which became Sadler's Wells Ballet and the Royal Ballet). She was artistic director of the Royal Ballet until 1963. In 1935 she married Dr A B Connell. She organized the National Ballet School of Turkey (1947) and was created DBE in 1951. She wrote *Invitation to the Ballet* (1937) and her autobiography, *Come Dance with Me*, was published in 1957. Her rarely performed choreographic works include *The Rakes's Progress*, *Checkmate* and *Don Quixote*.

VÁMBÉRY, Arminius, properly **Ármín** (1832–1913) Hungarian traveller and philologist, born in Duna-Szerdahely. Apprenticed at the age of twelve to a ladies' dressmaker, he later took to teaching. He travelled to Constantinople, where he taught French in the house of a minister, and in 1858 issued a German-Turkish dictionary. Having travelled between 1862 and 1864 in the disguise of a dervish through the deserts of the Oxus to Khiva and Samarkand, he wrote *Travels and Adventures in Central Asia* (1864). Professor of oriental languages in Budapest till 1905, he published works on Turkish and other Altaic languages, the ethnography of the Turks, the origin of the Magyars, and on many other oriental subjects.

VAN those not listed below may be found under their respective surnames.

VAN AKEN See **BOSCH, Hieronymus**

VAN ALLEN, James Alfred (1914–) American physicist, he discovered the magnetosphere (the Van Allen radiation belts). During World War II he developed the radio proximity fuse (a device that guided explosive weapons close to their targets and then detonated them), and gained expertise in the miniaturization of electronics and rocket controls, later to be of use in the scientific exploration of the earth's upper atmosphere; he studied cosmic rays, and was involved in the launching (1958) of America's first satellite, Explorer I. Satellite observations showed that the earth's magnetic field traps high-speed charged particles in two zones; these were later named the Van Allen belts. Van Allen, who has produced a large number of scientific papers and received numerous scientific awards, has been a member of several US governmental committees concerned with space exploration.

VANBRUGH, Dame Irene (1872–1949) English actress, sister of **Violet Augusta Mary Vanbrugh**, born in Exeter. She was trained by Sarah Thorne and made her first appearance at Margate as Phoebe in *As You Like It* (1888). She married **Dion Boucicault** the younger, in 1901, and acted with **Beerbohm Tree**, **George Alexander**, **Robertson Hare** and Frohman (1860–1915), winning a reputation as an interpreter of **Pinero** and **Barrie** heroines. She was created DBE in 1941.

VANBRUGH, Sir John (1664–1726) English playwright and baroque architect, born in London, the son of a tradesman and grandson of a Protestant refugee merchant from Ghent. He was educated in France, commissioned into Lord Huntingdon's regiment and suffered imprisonment in the Bastille as a suspected spy (1690–92). A staunch Whig, he became a leading spirit in society life and scored a success with his first comedy, *The Relapse* (1696), followed, again with success, by *The Provok'd Wife* (1697). *The Confederacy* (1705) was put on in the Haymarket, where **Congreve** and Vanbrugh joined together as theatre managers. His *The Provok'd Husband* was left unfinished, and was completed by **Colley Cibber** (1728). A natural playwright of the uninhibited Restoration comedy of manners period, he also achieved success as architect of Castle Howard (1702) and in 1705 was commissioned to design Blenheim Palace at Woodstock. The immense baroque structure aroused the ridicule of **Swift** and **Pope**, and the Duchess of **Marlborough** disliked the plans and was so appalled at its enormous cost that she long refused to pay Vanbrugh. He was made comptroller of royal works in 1714, and was Clarencieux king-of-arms (1705–25).

VANBRUGH, Violet Augusta Mary (1867–1942) English actress, sister of **Irene Vanbrugh**, born in Exeter. She first appeared in burlesque in 1886 and two years later played Ophelia at Margate, where she had been trained by Sarah Thorne. She joined the **Kendals** for their American tour and on her return played Ann Boleyn in **Irving**'s production of *Henry VIII*, also understudying **Ellen Terry**. She married Arthur Bourchier in 1894 and enhanced many of his successes with her elegance and ability.

VAN BUREN, Martin (1782–1862) 8th president of the USA, born in Kinderhook, New York. Called to the bar in 1803, in 1812 and 1816 he was elected to the state senate, and from 1816 to 1819 was state attorney-general. In 1821 he entered the US senate as a Democrat and was elected governor of New York in 1828. He supported **Andrew Jackson** for the presidency, and in 1829 became secretary of state. In 1832 he was elected vice-president, and in 1836 president, but by a popular majority of less than 25 000, largely owing to his opposition to the 'slightest interference' with slavery. His four years of office were darkened by financial panic; but he did what he could to lighten it by forcing a measure for a treasury independent of private banks. He was strictly neutral during the Canadian rebellion of 1837. In 1840 he and his party were overwhelmingly defeated by the Whigs.

VANCOUVER, George (1757–98) English navigator and explorer. He sailed with **James Cook** on his second and third voyages and, promoted captain (1794), did survey work in Australia, New Zealand and extensive detailed charting along the west coast of North America, sailing round Vancouver Island in 1795.

VANDAMME, Dominique Joseph (1770–1830) French Napoleonic soldier, born in Cassel in Nord. In 1799 he fought at Austerlitz, in 1806–07 reduced Silesia, but was defeated and taken prisoner at Kulm in 1813. He held a command during the Hundred Days 1816, but, after the second Restoration was exiled. He returned from America in 1824.

VAN DE GRAAFF, Robert Jemison (1901–67) American physicist, born in Tuscaloosa, Alabama. An engineering graduate, he was inspired to study physics by **Marie Curie**'s lectures at the Sorbonne in 1924. During research at Oxford he conceived of an improved type of electrostatic generator, in which electric charge could be built up on a hollow metal sphere. He constructed the first model (later to be known as the *Van de Graaff generator*) in which the charge was carried to the sphere by means of an insulated fabric belt; in this way, potentials of over a million volts could be achieved. At the Massachusetts Institute of Technology, Van de Graaff developed his generator for use as a particle accelerator, and this *Van de Graaff accelerator* became a major tool of atomic and nuclear physicists. The generator was also adapted to produce high-energy X-rays, useful in the treatment of cancer and the examination of the interior structure of heavy ordnance.

VAN DE HULST, Hendrik Christofell (1918–) Dutch astronomer, born in Utrecht, where he was educated. In 1944 he suggested that intersteller hydrogen might be detectable at radio wave-lengths, due to the 21-centimetre radiation emitted when the orbiting electron of a hydrogen atom flips between its two possible spin states. Due to World War II it was not until 1951 that such emissions were first detected, by **Edward Purcell** and H Ewen. The technique has since proved invaluable in detecting neutral hydrogen in both our own and other galaxies, as well as in interstellar space. In 1970 he became director of the Leiden Observatory.

VAN DE KAMP, Peter (1901–) Dutch-born American astronomer, born in Kampen in the Netherlands. He studied at Utrecht University and in 1923 emigrated to the USA, where he worked at the Lick Observatory in California and Virginia University. He became director of the Sproul Observatory in 1937 and professor of astronomy at Swarthmore College, Pennsylvania, and research professor after his retirement in 1972. His best-known work began in the 1960s with his deduction that some stars, other than the Sun, possess planets; by 1988 further evidence led many astronomers to believe that van de Kamp's view is correct.

VANDENBERG, Arthur Hendrick (1884–1951) United States Republican senator, born in Grand Rapids, Michigan. He studied at the university there and was elected to the senate (1928). An isolationist before World War II, he strongly supported the formation of UNO, and was delegate to the San Francisco conference and to the UN Assembly from 1946.

VANDERBILT, Cornelius (1794–1877) American financier, born on Staten Island, New York. At the age of 16 he bought a boat and ferried passengers and goods between Staten Island and New York City. By 40 he had become the owner of steamers running to Boston and up the Hudson. In 1849, during the Gold Rush, he established a route by Lake Nicaragua to California, and during the Crimean War a line of steamships to Havre. In 1862 he sold his ships and entered on a great career of railroad financing, gradually obtaining a controlling interest in a large number of railways. He gave $1 000 000 to found Vanderbilt University at Nashville, Tennessee. William Henry Vanderbilt (1821–85), his eldest son, greatly extended the Vanderbilt system of railways. Another son, Cornelius Vanderbilt (1843–99), left some $25 000 000.

VAN DER GOES, Hugo (c.1440–1482) Flemish painter, born probably in Ghent. Dean of the painters' guild at Ghent (1473–75), he painted the magnificent Portineri Altarpiece containing *The Adoration of the Shepherds* (now in the Uffizi Gallery) for the S Maria Nuova Hospital in Florence, and many other notable works. He spent the last years of his life in the monastery of Soignies, near Brussels.

VAN DER MEER, Simon (1925–) Dutch physicist and engineer, born in The Hague. Educated at the Technical University, Delft, he worked at the Philips research laboratories in Eindhoven (1952–55) before becoming senior engineer for CERN (the European Organization for Nuclear Research) at Geneva. He shared the Nobel prize for physics in 1984 with **Carlo Rubbia** for their work on the CERN project which led to the discovery of the field particles W and Z, which transfer the weak nuclear interaction.

VAN DER POST, Sir Laurens (Jan) (1906–) South African soldier, explorer, writer and philosopher. He served with distinction in World War II in Ethiopia, the Western Desert, Syria and the far east, where he was captured by the Japanese. On his release he joined **Mountbatten**'s staff in Java. He has since worked for the British government on a variety of missions in Africa, and with the Kalahari Bushmen of southern Africa. His books include *The Lost World of the Kalahari* (1958), *The Heart of the Hunter* (1961), *The Seed and the Sower* (1963, filmed as *Merry Christmas, Mr Lawrence*, 1983), *The Hunter and the Whale* (1967), *A Story Like the Wind* (1972), *A Far Off Place* (1974), *A Mantis Carol* (1975), *Jung and the Story of Our Time* (1976), and *Yet Being Someone Other* (1982).

VAN DER WAALS, Johannes Diderik (1837–1923) Dutch physicist. Professor at Amsterdam University (1877–1908), he is famed for the discovery (1873) of van der Waals' equation, defining the physical state of a gas or liquid, and as the investigator of the weak attractive forces (van der Waals' forces) between molecules. He was awarded the Nobel prize for physics in 1910.

VAN DIEMEN See **TASMAN, Abel Janszoon**

VAN DOREN, Carl Clinton (1885–1950) American critic and biographer, brother of **Mark Albert Van Doren**, born in Hope, Illinois. He studied at the state university and at Columbia, where he lectured in English literature (1911–30). He was literary editor of the *Nation* (1919–22), of the *Century Magazine* (1922–25) and of the *Cambridge History of American Literature* (1917–21). He was also a distinguished biographer of **Thomas Love Peacock** (1911), **James Branch Cabell** (1925), **Swift** (1930), **Sinclair Lewis** (1933) and **Benjamin Franklin** (1938, Pulitzer prize, 1939). He edited Franklin's *Letters and Papers* (1947); his critical studies include *The American Novel* (1921) and, with his brother, *American and British Literature since 1890* (1925). He also wrote *The Ninth Wave* (1926), a novel, and his autobiography, *Three Worlds* (1936).

VAN DOREN, Mark Albert (1894–1972) American poet and critic, brother of **Carl Clinton van Doren**, born in Hope, Illinois. He studied at the state university and at Columbia, where he taught from 1920 and became professor of English in 1942. He served in the army during World War I, followed his brother to the editorship of the *Nation* (1924–28) and was awarded the Pulitzer prize (1940) for his *Collected Poems* (1939), chosen from such volumes of verse as *Spring Thunder* (1924) and *Now the Sky* (1928). Later volumes include *The Mayfield Deer* (1941), *The Country Year* (1946), *New Poems* (1948) and *Spring Birth* (1953). He collaborated with Carl in *American and British Literature since 1890* (1925), edited the *Oxford Book of American Prose*, wrote critical studies of **Thoreau** (1916), **Dryden** (1920), **Shakespeare** (1939) and **Hawthorne** (1949), and the novels *Transients* (1935) and *Windless Cabins* (1940). Further collections of poetry were published in 1963, 1964 and 1967.

VAN DYCK, or **Vandyke, Sir Anthony** (1599–1641) Flemish painter, one of the great masters of portraiture of the 17th century, born in Antwerp, the son of a cloth manufacturer. He studied painting under Hendrick van Balen (1575–1632) and **Rubens**. In 1618 he was admitted a master of the guild of St Luke at Antwerp and in 1620 was commissioned to paint the Lady Arundel, wife of **Thomas Howard**, 2nd Earl of Arundel. On this visit to England (1620–21) records show that he also executed a full-length portrait of **James VI and I** at Windsor. From 1621 he was in Italy. At Genoa he painted a number of portraits and some religious subjects for the pope, but in this field he did not rival his Italian contemporaries. By 1627 he was back in Antwerp. His fine draughtsmanship is apparent in the heads he etched for his *Iconographia* (1641). At The Hague he painted the Prince of Orange (later **William III**) and his family. In 1632 he returned to London, and was knighted by **Charles I**, who made him a painter-in-ordinary. Back in Holland on leave (1634–35), he painted Ferdinand of Austria and *The Deposition*. His flair for, and psychological accuracy in, rendering the character of his sitters, always with a hint of flattery and in the most favourable settings, greatly influenced the great British school of portraiture in the next century and imparted to posterity a thoroughly romantic glimpse of the Stuart monarchy. Among the best of these portraits are the large group of Charles I, Queen **Henrietta Maria** and the two royal children, the equestrian portrait of the king, the three aspects of the king (1637) to serve as a model for **Bernini**'s sculpture (all at Windsor) and the magnificent *Le Roi à la chasse*. In 1639 he married Mary Ruthven, a grand-daughter of the Earl of Gowrie. His scheme for decorating the banqueting hall in Whitehall with scenes from the history of the Order of the Garter was turned down and he failed to obtain the commission for the decoration of the gallery of the Louvre, which went to **Poussin**.

VAN DYKE, Dick (1925–) American popular entertainer, born in West Plains, Missouri. After performing in school plays and amateur dramatics, he became a radio announcer in the US air force during World War II. He later toured as part of the nightclub act *The Merry Mutes* and as half of 'Eric and Van'. Moving into television, he acted as master of ceremonies on such programmes as *The Morning Show* (1955), *The Cartoon Show* (1956) and *Flair* (1960). His Broadway début in *The Boys Against the Girls* (1959) was followed by *Bye, Bye Birdie* (1960–61) a role which won him a Tony Award and which he repeated on film in 1963. A gangling, breezy fellow with a ready smile, strong sense of visual humour and a talent for clowning, singing and dancing, his television series *The Dick Van Dyke Show* (1961–66) was one of the most popular in the history of the medium and won him Emmys in 1962, 1964 and 1965. A subsequent film career includes *Mary Poppins* (1964) and *Chitty, Chitty, Bang, Bang* (1968). After conquering alcoholism, he displayed his dramatic worth on film in *The Morning After* (1974) and *The Runner Stumbles* (1979). Active in television specials, films and touring theatre, he published *Faith, Hope and Hilarity* in 1970.

VAN DYKE, Henry (1852–1933) American clergyman and writer, born in Germantown, Pennsylvania. He studied theology at Princeton and Berlin and was a prominent pastor of the Brick Presbyterian Church, New York (1883–99). He was professor of English literature at Princeton (1899–1923), and, under **Woodrow Wilson**, American minister to the Netherlands (1913–16). He was awarded the Legion of Honour for his services as naval chaplain in World War I. His many writings include poems, essays and short stories, mostly on religious themes, such as the Christmas tale *The Story of the other Wise Man* (1896), *The Ruling Passion* (1901), *The Blue Flower* (1902), *The Unknown Quantity* (1912) and *Collected Poems* (1911). His brother Paul (1859–1933) was professor of history at Princeton (1898–1928).

VANE, Sir Henry (1613–62) English statesman, born in Hadlow, Kent. Educated at Westminster School and Magdalen Hall, Oxford, he became a staunch Republican. In 1635 he sailed for New England. As governor of Massachusetts his inclination towards Antinomianism made him unpopular, and in 1637 he returned to England. In 1640 he entered the House of Commons, representing Hull. He played a major part in securing the execution of **Strafford** and between 1643 and 1653 was, in effect, the civilian head of the parliamentary government. He was himself executed after the Restoration.

VANE, Sir John Robert (1927–) English biochemist, joint winner of the 1982 Nobel prize for physiology or medicine. He studied chemistry and pharmacology at Birmingham and St Catherine's College, Oxford, and taught at Yale (1953–55) and the Institute of Basic Medical Services in London (1955–61). He taught pharmacology at London, and then joined the Wellcome Research Laboratories in Beckenham (1973–85). He researched the chemistry of prostaglandins and discovered a type that inhibits blood clots, as well as illuminating the operation of aspirin in treating pain. He shared the Nobel prize with **Sune Bergström** and Bengt Samuelsson.

VAN GOGH, Vincent (Willem) (1853–90) Dutch Post-Impressionist painter, born in Groot-Zundert, the son of a Lutheran pastor. At 16 he became an assistant (1869–76) with an international firm of art dealers in their shops in The Hague, London and Paris. An unrequited love affair with an English schoolmistress accentuated his inferiority complex and religious passion. He became an assistant master at Ramsgate and Isleworth (1876) and there trained unsuccessfully to become a Methodist preacher. In 1878 he became an evangelist for a religious society at the Belgian coalmining centre of Le Borinage (1878–80), where, first as a resident, later as an itinerant preacher, he practised the Christian virtues with great zeal, sleeping on the floor of a derelict hut and giving away his possessions. In April 1881 he at last set off for Brussels to study art, but another unfortunate love affair, this time with a cousin, threw him off balance and he eventually settled in The Hague, where he lived with his model Christien or 'Sien', a prostitute. She appears in the drawing *Sorrow* (1882) and *Sien Posing* (1883). In his father's new parish at Nuenen he painted that dark, haunting, domestic scene of peasant poverty, *The Potato Eaters* (1885), his first masterpiece, and *Boots*. His devoted brother, Théo, now an art dealer, made it possible for him to continue his studies in Paris (1886–88) under Cormon, and there he met **Gauguin**, **Toulouse-Lautrec**, **Seurat** and the art-collector Tanguy, who is the subject, surrounded by Japanese woodcuts, of one of Van Gogh's remarkable portraits (1887–88). These new influences brightened his palette and on Lautrec's advice he left Paris to seek the intense colours of the Provençal landscape at Arles, the subject of many of his best works. There also he painted *Sunflowers* (1888), *The Bridge* (1888) and *The Chair and the Pipe* (1888) and invited Gauguin to found a community of artists. Gauguin's stay ended in a tragic quarrel in which Van Gogh in remorse for having threatened the other with a razor, cut off part of his own ear and was placed in an asylum at St Rémy (1889–90). There he painted the grounds, the *Ravine* (1889, with increasingly frantic brushstrokes), the keeper and the physician. In 1890 he went to live at Auvers-sur-Oise near Paris, under the supervision of a physician, Dr Paul Gachet, himself an amateur painter and engraver, whom he painted. That year an exhaustive article appeared by A Aurier which at last brought Van Gogh some recognition. But on 27 July 1890, Van Gogh shot himself at the scene of his last painting, the foreboding *Cornfields with Flight of Birds*, and died two days later. Théo, deeply shocked at the news, followed his brother to the grave within six months. Van Gogh was one of the pioneers of Expressionism. He used colour primarily for its emotive appeal and profoundly influenced the Fauves and other experimenters of 20th-century art.

VAN GOYEN, Jan Josephszoon (1596–1656) Dutch painter, born in Leiden. He produced many sea and river pieces in soft browns and greys, and, unusually for his time, omitted small details and developed a broad atmospheric effect. **Jan Steen**, who became his son-in -law, was one of his pupils. His *River Scene* (c. 1645) is in the National Gallery, London.

VANHOMRIGH, Esther See **SWIFT, Jonathan**

VANINI, Lucilio (1584–1619) Italian philosopher, born in Taurisano. He studied at Naples and Padua, and took orders. But his enthusiasm for the new learning and science of the Renaissance, and perhaps his personality too, soon brought him into conflict with the Church. He moved around, teaching in France, the Low Countries and Switzerland, then fleeing in 1614 to England where he was imprisoned. Finally he was arrested again in Toulouse, had his tongue cut out, and was strangled and burned as a heretic. His books *Amphytheatrum aeternae providentiae* (1615) and *De admirandis naturae reginae deaegue mortalium arcanis* (1616) expound a form of extreme, materialistic pantheism, if not technically atheism.

VANLOO, Charles André (1705–65) French painter, born in Nice, the brother of **Jean Baptiste Vanloo**. He studied in Rome and settled as a portrait painter in Paris but executed also some sculpture. He became chief painter to **Louis XV** and director of the Academy (1763). His vigorous, colourful majestic style gave rise to a new French verb 'vanlooter'. He painted portraits of many of his notable contemporaries, and also some large genre paintings.

VANLOO, Jean Baptiste (1684–1745) French painter, born in Aix-en-Provence of Flemish parentage, brother of **Charles André Vanloo**. He studied in Rome and became a fashionable portrait painter in Paris, and was appointed professor of painting (1735). In 1737 he visited England, where he painted the actor **Colley Cibber**, the Prince and Princess of Wales and Sir **Robert Walpole**.

VAN LOON, Hendrik Willem (1882–1944) Dutch-born American popular historian, born in Rotterdam.

He emigrated to the United States in 1903 as a journalist and history teacher and in 1922 published the best selling, illustrated *Story of Mankind*, and from then onwards produced a number of popular histories.

VAN MEEGEREN, Han, or **Henricus van** (1889–1947) Dutch artist and forger, born in Deventer. In 1945 he was accused of selling art treasures to the Germans. To clear himself, he confessed to having forged the pictures, and also the famous *Supper at Emmaus*, 'discovered' in 1937, and accepted by the majority of experts as by **Vermeer**. His fakes were subjected to a detailed scientific examination, and in 1947 their maker was sentenced to twelve months' imprisonment for forgery. He died a few weeks later, a popular hero.

VANNUCCI, Pietro See **PERUGINO**

VAN PRAAGH, Dame Margaret (Peggy) (1910–) English ballet dancer, teacher and producer, born in London. She trained with Margaret Craske, joined the Ballet Rambert in 1933 and created many roles with that company. In 1941 she joined the Sadler's Wells Ballet as dancer and teacher, and worked as producer and assistant director with **Ninette de Valois** at the Sadler's Wells Theatre Ballet until 1956. She produced many ballets for BBC television and for international companies, and in 1960 became artistic director for the Borovansky Ballet in Australia. She was founding artistic director for the Australian Ballet between 1962 and 1979, and a member of the council and guest teacher until 1982. She became a DBE in 1970.

VAN RENSSELAER, Stephen (1765–1839) American soldier and politician, eighth 'patroon' of the vast estate near Albany, born in New York City. He was a leader of the Federalists in his state, and served in congress (1823–29). In the war of 1812 he held command on the northern frontier, and captured Queenston Heights; but the refusal of his militia to cross the Niagara enabled the British to recover the place, and he resigned. He was a member of the US House of Representatives (1822–29). He promoted the construction of the Erie and Champlain canals and founded the Rensselaer Technical Institute (1826).

VANSITTART, Nicholas, 1st Baron Bexley (1766–1851) English statesman, son of Henry Vansittart (1732–70), a governor of Bengal of Dutch extraction. He became a Tory Chancellor of the Exchequer (1812–23), and in 1823 was raised to the peerage.

VANSITTART, Robert Gilbert, 1st Baron Vansittart of Denham (1881–1957) English diplomat. Educated at Eton, he joined the diplomatic service in 1902 and served successively in Paris, Teheran, Cairo and Stockholm with intervals at the Foreign Office. From 1920 to 1924 he was private secretary to Lord **Curzon** and in 1930 became permanent under-secretary for foreign affairs. He visited Germany in 1936, talked with **Hitler** and his henchmen and became the uncompromizing opponent of Nazi Germany. His warnings of coming catastrophe unless Britain armed to meet the German menace—warnings expressed with undiplomatic pungency—put him at variance in 1937 with **Neville Chamberlain**. On 1 January 1938, he was steered into a backwater as 'chief diplomatic adviser to the Government'. He retired in 1941, and was raised to the peerage. He threw himself into parliamentary work, authorship and journalism, fiercely denouncing Nazism and ridiculing the 'myth' of the 'two Germanys' (good and bad). After the war he was no less active in exposing communist methods, lashing out at injustice and illuminating the shortcomings of statesmen. He wrote *The Singing Caravan* (poems, 1933); *Black Record* (1941); *Lessons of My Life* (1943); and his autobiography, *The Mist Procession* (1958).

VAN'T HOFF See **HOFF, Jacobus Henricus van't**

VAN TIEGHEM, Phillipe (1839–1914) French botanist and biologist. He is well known for his studies of myxomycetes, bacteria, etc, and a new classification of plants.

VAN VEEN, Otto van (c.1556–1634) Dutch painter, born in Leiden. He settled first in Brussels, and later in Antwerp, where **Rubens** was his pupil. The name Van Veen is also sometimes given to the Haarlem painter, Martin van Heemskerk (1498–1574), whose *Ecce Homo* and *Holy Family* are at Haarlem.

VAN VLECK, John Hasbrouck (1899–1980) American physicist, born in Middletown, Connecticut, the son of a professor of mathematics. He largely founded the modern theory of magnetism, taking **Paul Dirac**'s quantum mechanics and working out the implications for the magnetic properties of atoms. Unusually in that field, his training had been in the USA; and after study at Wisconsin and Harvard, he took up posts at Minnesota, Wisconsin and finally Harvard (1934–69). His book, *The Theory of Electric and Magnetic Susceptibilities* (1932), is a classic text. He also elucidated chemical bonding in crystals and the usefulness of the crystal field and ligand field theories, which allow description of some features of atomic or ionic behaviour in a crystal. In 1977 his pioneering research was recognized with a joint award of the Nobel prize for physics, with **Philip Anderson** and Sir **Nevill Mott**.

VANZETTI, Bartolomeo See **SACCO, Nicola**

VARDON, Harry (1870–1937) British golfer, born in Grouville in Jersey. He won the British Open championship six times: 1896, 1898, 1899, 1903, 1911 and 1914. He also won the US Open in 1900, the German Open in 1911, and the *News of the World* Tournament in 1912. He turned professional in 1903, and is remembered for the fluency of his swing, and his overlapping grip which is still known as the 'Vardon grip'.

VARÈSE, Edgar (1885–1965) American composer of Italo-French parentage, born in Paris. He studied under **Albert Roussel**, **Vincent D'Indy** and **Charles Widor** in Paris, and later under **Ferruccio Busoni**. Until World War I, he was active in movements to bring music to the French people. After two years' service in the French army, he settled in New York, where in 1919 he founded the New Symphony Orchestra to further the cause of modern music, and in 1921 organized the international Composers' Guild, which has become the leading organ of progressive musicians. His work is almost entirely orchestral. Often using unconventional percussion instruments, its abstract nature is demonstrated by such titles as *Metal*, *Ionisation* and *Hyperprism*.

VARGAS, Getulio Dornelles (1883–1954) Brazilian rancher, lawyer and politician, and president of Brazil, born in Sao Boria. He was elected federal deputy for his native province of Rio Grande del Sul from 1923 to 1926, and governor from 1928 to 1930. In 1930, following his narrow defeat in the presidential elections and the murder of his running mate, he seized power with the help of the military. Promising election within two years, he began reforms to lift Brazil from the depression, including public works, school-building, attempts to raise the price of coffee by burning surpluses, and social measures such as establishing a 48-hour work week and a minimum wage. He peacefully ended a regional rebellion in São Paulo in 1932, and then in 1934 held elections which he won, following the creation of a new constitution giving women the vote. His harassment of the communists produced a revolt led by Carlos Prestes and a bloody repression, which he used as an excuse to continue in office at the end of his term in 1937. Except for a coup, ironically by Brazil's Fascists, Vargas' corporatist dictatorship, which he called *O estado novo* after that of **Antonio Salazar** in Portugal, met little opposition. Repressive measures such as censorship, political repression and prohibition of strikes and unions, were combined with paternalistic social legislation, and he had remarkable success in modernizing Brazil through a combination of private and state capitalism. He expanded trade with Germany and the Fascist powers, and although he used these relations to gain economic concessions from the USA, Brazil joined the Allied Powers during World War II. A coup by democratic military officers retired Vargas in 1945 to ensure free elections, yet in 1950 he was returned to power in a landslide election. In 1954, falsely charged with ordering the murder of an opposition newspaper editor, Vargas shot himself rather than resign, as demanded by the military.

VARLEY, John (1778–1842) English watercolourist, born in Hackney, London. He was a highly successful teacher, and was a founder member of the Watercolour Society. A friend of **William Blake**, he was also interested in astrology and wrote on perspective. His brothers Cornelius (1781–1873) and William Fleetwood (1785–1856), were also watercolourists.

VARNHAGEN, Francisco Adolpho de, Viscount de Porto Seguro (1816–78) Brazilian historian, born in São João de Ypanema, São Paulo. He spent his youth in Portugal but took Brazilian nationality in 1841, afterwards holding several diplomatic posts. Amongst his works are a *History of Brazil* (1854–57) and monographs on **Amerigo Vespucci**.

VARNHAGEN VON ENSE, Karl August (1785–1858) German writer and diplomat, born in Düsseldorf. In 1809 he joined the Austrian army and was wounded at the battle of Wagram. In 1813 he went over to the Russian service, and was sent to Paris as an adjutant. Here he was called to the Prussian diplomatic service, and accompanied **Hardenberg** to the Congress of Vienna (1814) and to Paris, becoming next resident minister at Karlsruhe (till 1819). In 1814 he married Rahel Levin, who presided over a glittering literary salon in Berlin. He wrote lives of **Goethe** (1823), Marshal **Keith** (1844), General **von Bülow** (1853), and others; *Biographische Denkmäler* (1824–30), and *Denkwürdigkeiten* (1843–59). His Correspondence and Diaries fill 22 volumes (1860–70).

VARRO, Marcus Terentius (116–27 BC) Roman scholar and author, born in Reate. He studied at Athens, saw service under **Pompey**, and in the Civil War was legate in Spain. He awaited the result of Pharsalia with **Cicero** and **Cato** at Dyrrachium, and was kindly treated by the conqueror, who appointed him librarian. Under the second triumvirate **Marcus Aurelius** plundered his villa, burned his books, and placed his name on the list of the proscribed. But he was soon exempted, and **Augustus** restored his property. His prose writings embraced oratory, history, jurisprudence, grammar, philosophy, geography and husbandry. The chief were *Saturae Menippeae*, *Antiquitates Rerum Humanarum et Divinarum*, *De Lingua Latina*, and *Rerum Rusticarum*. His *Disciplinarum Libri IX* was an encyclopaedia of the liberal arts; his *Imagines*, or *Hebdomades*, a series of 700 Greek and Roman biographies.

VARRO, Publius Terentius (c.82–37 BC) Roman poet, called Atacinus from his birth in the valley of the Atax in Narbonensian Gaul. He wrote satires and an epic poem on **Caesar**'s Gallic wars, called *Bellum Sequanicum*. His *Argonautica* was an adaptation of **Apollonius Rhodius** and his erotic elegies pleased **Propertius**.

VARTHEMA, Ludovico de (c.1465–c.1510) Italian traveller and writer, born in Bologna. He was the first European and Christian recorded to have entered, and left alive, the Islamic City of Mecca. He made a six-year journey through Arabia, Persia, India and on across the Pacific to the Spice Islands (1502–07). He published an account of his travels in *Itinerario de Lodovico de Varthema Bolognese* (1510).

VARUS, Publius Quintilius (d.9) Roman official, consul in 13 BC. As governor of Syria he suppressed the revolt of Judaea, and in 9 AD was sent by **Augustus** to command in Germany. Utterly routed by **Arminius**, he killed himself.

VASA See **GUSTAV I, VASA**

VASARELY, Viktor (1908–) Hungarian-born French painter, born in Pecs. He began as a medical student in Budapest before studying art from 1928 to 1929 at the Mühely Academy (the 'Budapest Bauhaus') under **Moholy-Nagy**. He moved to Paris in 1930. From c.1947 he painted abstract pictures using repeated geometrical shapes ('cinétisme') which looked forward to the Op Art of the 1960s. He has also experimented with Kinetic Art. He exhibited widely from the late 1940s and won many prizes including the Guggenheim prize, New York (1964) and the Tokyo Biennale (1967).

VASARI, Giorgio (1511–74) Italian artist and art historian, born in Arezzo. He studied under **Michelangelo**, and lived mostly in Florence and Rome. He was a greater architect than painter; but today his fame rests on his *Vite de' più eccellenti Pittori, Scultori, e Architettori* (1550). In spite of inaccuracies in the earlier biographies, it remains a model of art criticism and biography.

VASCO DA GAMA See **GAMA**

VASCONCELOS, Caroline Michaelis De (1851–1925) Portuguese scholar and writer, born in Berlin. She studied and wrote on romance, philology and literature. An honorary professor of Hamburg University, she lived, after her marriage in 1876, in Oporto, where she did much scholarly research on the Portuguese language, its literature, and especially its folk literature. Most noteworthy is her edition of the late 13th or early 14th century *Cancioneiro da Ajuda*. Other writings include *Notas Vicentinas* (1912), an edition of the poetry of Francisco Sá de Miranda, (1485–1558) and essays, studies and correspondence with other Portuguese scholars.

VASSILOU, Georgios Vassos (1931–) Cypriot politician and businessman, born in Famagusta. Educated at the universities of Geneva, Vienna and Budapest, he embarked upon a highly successful business career, initially with the Reed Paper Company, eventually becoming a self-made millionaire. Despite a lively interest in politics, he did not align himself with any of the established parties and in 1988, believing that a fresh approach to the divisions in Cyprus was needed, stood as an independent candidate for the presidency and, with Communist party support, won it. As president, Vassilou has worked consistently towards the reunification of the island.

VATTELL, Emmerich de (1714–67) Swiss jurist, born in Couret in Neuchâtel. He entered the diplomatic service of Saxony, and was Saxon representative at Bern (1746–64). His *Droits des gens* (1758) systematized the doctrines of **Grotius**, **Puffendorf** and **Wolff**. and modernized the whole law of nations, becoming recognized as a classic work.

VAUBAN, Sébastien le Prestre de (1633–1707) French military engineer who revolutionized siege warfare, born in Saint Léger near Avallon. He enlisted under **Condé**, and followed him into the service of Spain. Taken prisoner in 1653, he was persuaded by **Mazarin** to enter the French king's service; by 1658 he was chief engineer under **Turenne**. In 1667 he helped to reduce Lille; from 1672 to 1678 in the Netherlands he took part in 17 sieges and one defence. He introduced the method of approach by parallels at the siege of Maestricht (1673) with great effect; notable also were his defence of Oudenarde and the sieges of Valenciennes and Cambrai. During 1678–88 he surrounded the kingdom with a cordon of fortresses; and he planned the magnificent aqueduct of Maintenon. He invented the socket bayonet (1687) and at the siege of Philippsburg (1688) he introduced his invention of ricochet-batteries. In 1703 he became marshal of France. After the peace of Ryswick in 1697 he had applied himself to study the faults in the government of France. His *Dîme royale* (1707), in which he discussed the problem of taxation, was condemned and prohibited, and within a few weeks the disappointed Vauban was dead.

VAUCANSON, Jacques de (1709–82) French engineer and inventor, born in Grenoble. He went to Paris to study mechanics and became adept at constructing automata such as a duck which swam, quacked, flapped its wings and swallowed its food; for this delicate work he designed special lathes, drills and other tools. Appointed an inspector of silk factories in 1741 he devised various improvements to the machines for weaving and dressing the silk, and in 1745 succeeded in making the first fully automatic loom, controlled through a system of perforated cards. It was cumbersome and not wholly reliable, however, and it was not until the turn of the century when it was further improved by **Jacquard**, that it came into widespread use.

VAUGELAS, Claude Favre de (1585–1650) French grammarian. A member of the literary circle of the Marquise de **Rambouillet**, he was the author of *Remarques sur la langue française* (1647), which helped to standardize the language. He was a founder of the French Academy.

VAUGHAN, Charles John (1816–97) English clergyman and educationist, born in Leicester. Elected fellow of Trinity College, Cambridge, he was vicar of St Martin's, Leicester (1841–44); headmaster of Harrow (1844–59); vicar of Doncaster (1860–69); master of the Temple (1869–94); and dean of Llandaff from 1879. An eloquent preacher of the Liberal evangelical school, he prepared in his home a large number of men for ordination, popularly known as 'Vaughan's Doves'.

VAUGHAN, Henry (1622–95) Welsh religious poet, born in Newton-by-Usk, Llansantfraed, Powys, twin brother of the alchemist Thomas Vaughan (1622–66). He was called the self-styled 'Silurist' as a native of south Wales, the land of the ancient tribe of Silures. He entered Jesus College, Oxford, in 1638, and in 1646 published *Poems, with the tenth Satyre of Juvenal Englished*. He took his MD, and practised as a physician first in Brecon and then in Newton-by-Usk. The collection of poems entitled *Olor Iscanus* was published by his twin brother, without authority, in 1651. In 1650 he printed his *Silex Scintillans* (Sparkling Flint), a notable volume of mystical and religious poems, enlarged in 1655. In 1652 he published *The Mount of Olives*, devotions in prose, and the *Flores Solitudinis*, also in prose. *Thalia Rediviva: the Pastimes and Diversions of a Country Muse*, a collection of elegies, translations and religious pieces, was also published without authority (1678) by a friend.

VAUGHAN, Herbert (Alfred) (1832–1903) English Roman Catholic prelate and cardinal, born in Gloucester. He was educated at Stonyhurst and at Rome, entered the priesthood in 1854, and in 1872 was consecrated bishop of Salford. In 1892 he succeeded **Manning** as archbishop of Westminster, and the following year was raised to the cardinalate. He was founder of St Joseph's College for foreign missions at Mill Hill, and proprietor of the *Tablet* and the *Dublin Review*. He was responsible for the building of Westminster Cathedral.

VAUGHAN, Sir John (1603–74) Welsh lawyer and politician, born in Trawscoed, near Aberystwyth, Cardiganshire. Educated at Christ Church College, Oxford, and the Inner Temple, he sat in parliament from 1640 but withdrew into private life after the execution of **Charles I**. A royalist, he was elected to parliament again in April 1661. Promotion to Chief Justice of the Court of Common Pleas in 1668 was accompanied by a knighthood. Vaughan's ruling that juries could return verdicts against the judge's direction without being fined was an important legal decision.

VAUGHAN, Keith (1912–77) English artist, born in Selsey Bill. He was associated with the younger romantic artists influenced by **Graham Sutherland**. In 1951 he executed a large mural in the Festival of Britain Dome of Discovery, and he illustrated several books.

VAUGHAN, Robert (1795–1868) Welsh clergyman and historian. He was Independent minister at Worcester and Kensington, professor of history at London University (1830–43), and president of the Independent College at Manchester (1843–57). He founded the *British Quarterly* in 1845, and edited it till 1867. Among his books are *Life of Wycliffe* (1828), *History of England under the Stuarts* (1840) and *Revolutions in History* (1859–63).

VAUGHAN, Sarah Lois, known as '**Sassy**' (1924–90) American jazz singer and pianist, born in Newark, New Jersey. As a child she sang gospels in church and spent ten years studying the organ. Winning a talent competition in 1942 at the Apollo Theatre, Harlem, she came to the attention of singer BIlly Eckstine, and through him of **Earl Hines**, who promptly hired her as a singer and pianist. In 1944 she made her first recording with 'I'll Wait and Pray', the following year launching out on a solo career. By the early 1950s she was internationally acclaimed. A master of vibrato, range and expression, whose abilities could inspire envy in opera singers, her singing was once described as 'instrumental stunt flying'. Her most notable hits include 'It's Magic', 'Send in the Clowns', and 'I cried for you'.

VAUGHAN, William (1577–1641) Welsh poet and colonizer, born in south Wales. He graduated at Jesus College, Oxford (1597), and bought an interest in Newfoundland, where he sent out settlers in 1617. He wrote an allegory *The Golden Fleece* (1626) and other works.

VAUGHAN WILLIAMS, Ralph (1872–1958) English composer, born in Down Ampney, Gloucestershire. His early aptitude for music was encouraged by his parents and by the teaching he received at Charterhouse School. He subsequently worked under **Stanford** at the Royal College of Music, under **Bruch** in Berlin and under **Ravel** in Paris. The essentially English character of all his music, unaffected by the European influence which still clung to the work of Stanford and **Parry**, makes him the first fundamentally national composer since the 16th century. In touch from the start with the English choral tradition, his first success was the choral *Sea Symphony* (1910), set to words by **Walt Whitman**, in which traditional choral styles were married to a vigorously contempory outlook. Under the influence of **Gustav Holst** he became an enthusiastic leader in the English folksong movement, adding this tradition to the number of influences —Tudor church music, the choral and orchestral styles of Parry and the refinement gained from Ravel's teaching—that were assimilated in his own work. Of his early orchestral music his *Fantasia on a Theme of Tallis* (1909) for strings is noteworthy and is the work performed most regularly by orchestras outside Britain. Between the *London Symphony* (1914) and the *Pastoral Symphony* (1922) came a large number of works in all forms, including the ballad opera *Hugh the Drover* (1911–14). The ballet *Job* (1930) opened a new chapter in his career, notable for its obvious concern with the moral issues of contemporary life, and it was followed by seven further symphonies, the opera *The Pilgrim's Progress* (1948–49) and numerous choral works. The wide range, exploratory vigour and innate honesty of his works was illustrated by his ability to provide music of equal excellence for hymns, for the stage (as for **Aristophanes**' *The Wasps*, 1909), and for films such as *49th Parallel* and *Scott of the Antarctic*. During World War I he served with the RAMC and with the Artillery; from 1905 he was director of the Leith Hill Festival and in 1935 he was awarded the OM. His artistic credo is contained in his books *National Music* (1934) and *Beethoven's Choral Symphony and Other Papers*.

VAUQUELIN, Louis Nicolas (1763–1829) French analytical chemist, born in St André d'Hébertot. He rose from being an apothecary's assistant to be professor of chemistry at Paris (1809). In 1798 he discovered chromium and its compounds, later beryllium compounds, and was the first to isolate an amino acid, asparagine, which he obtained from asparagus.

VAUVENARGUES, Luc de Clapiers, Marquis de (1715–47) French moralist and soldier, born in Aix. He entered the army in 1733, and fought at Dettingen (1743), but retired in poor health in 1744 to settle in Paris and write. He is remembered mainly for his *Introduction à la connaissance de l'esprit humain* with *Réflexions et maximes* appended (1746), in which he esteemed particularly the heroic virtues of courage, energy and ambition, tempered by human sympathies.

VAVILOV, Nikolai Ivanovich (1887–c.1943) Russian botanist and plant geneticist, brother of the physicist Sergei Vavilov (1891–1951). He trained in Moscow and at the John Innes Horticultural Institute at Merton, Surrey. He was appointed director of the All Union Institute of Plant Industry in 1920. He established 400 research institutes and built up a collection of 26000 species and varieties of wheat. This enabled him to formulate the principle of diversity, which postulates that, geographically, the centre of greatest diversity represents the origin of a cultivated plant. His international reputation was challenged by the politico-scientific 'theories' of **Lysenko**, who denounced him at a genetics conference (1937) and gradually usurped his position. He was arrested in 1940 and died of starvation in a Siberian labour camp.

VAZOV, Ivan (1850–1921) Bulgarian national poet, born in Sopot. He wrote a collection of poems and songs under the title *Sorrows of Bulgaria* and *Under the Yoke* and other novels. He was twice exiled from his native land for his nationalist sympathies, but became minister of education in 1897.

VECELLIO, Tiziano See **TITIAN**

VEDDER, Elihu (1836–1923) American painter and illustrator, born in New York. He studied in Paris and in Italy, settling in Rome in 1866. He executed *Minerva* and other murals in the Library of Congress, Washington, and illustrated the *Rubáiyát of Omar Khayyám*.

VEEN See **VAN VEEN, Otto**

VEGA See **GARCILASO DE LA VEGA**

VEGA CARPIO, Lope Félix de (1562–1635) Spanish dramatist and poet, born in Madrid. Orphaned at an early age, he was a student and graduate of Alcalá. He served in the Portuguese campaign of 1580, and in the Spanish Armada (1588). He became secretary to the Duke of Alva, Marquis of Malpica, and Marquis of Sarria. A favourite with the ladies, he had many love affairs, was twice married, and fathered at least six children, three of them illegitimate, was banished from Madrid because of a quarrel, and lived two years in Valencia. He took orders in 1614, and became an officer of the Inquisition. He died poor, for his large income from his dramas and other sources was all but wholly devoted to charity and church. The mere list of Lope's works presents a picture of unparalleled intellectual activity. His first work of any length was a poem, the *Angelica*, written at sea in 1588, but not printed till 1602. The *Arcadia*, the story, in a pompous, pastoral setting, of the prenuptial vagaries of the Duke of Alva, was written before the duke's marriage, July 1590, but it was kept back till 1598. The *Dragoneta*, celebrating the death of **Drake**, appeared the same year, and was Lope's first publication under his name. But it was as a ballad-writer that he made his mark. The more notable of his miscellaneous works are the *Rimas* (1602); *Peregrino en su Patria* (1604), a romance; *Jerusalén Conquistada* (1609), an epic; *Pastores de Belén* (1612), a religious pastoral; *Filomena* and *Circe* (1621–24), miscellanies in the style of **Cervantes**; *Corona Trágica* (1627), an epic on **Mary, Queen of Scots**; *Laurel de Apolo* (1630); *Rimas de Tomé de Burguillos* (1634), a collection of lighter verse, with the *Gatomaquia*, a mock-heroic. *Dorotea* (1632), in form a prose drama, is obviously the story of his own early love adventures. Lope was a master of easy, flowing, musical, graceful verse. Though he had written plays, he did not become a writer for the stage until after 1588. He gave the public what it wanted—excitement pure and simple. Lope's plays may be roughly divided into the historical or quasi-historical and those that deal with everyday life. Of the latter the most characteristic are the 'cloak and sword plays'. The *Noche de San Juan*, one of his very last plays; the *Maestro de Danzar*, one of his first; and the *Azero de Madrid*, the source clearly of **Molière's** *Médecin malgré lui*, are excellent examples. Other plays include *Perro del hortelano*, *Desprecio agradecido*, *Esclava de su Galán*, *Premio del bien hablar*; and *Alcalde de Zalamea*, a bold vigorous outline which **Calderón** improved upon. The number of Lope's plays seems to have been 1500, exclusive of 400 *autos*. Of these the very names of all but between 600 and 700 have been lost, and often nothing but the name survives. There are about 440 plays and 40 *autos* in print or MS.

VEGETIUS, (Flavius Vegetius Renatus) (4th century) Roman military writer under the emperor **Theodosius I the Great**. After AD 375 he produced the *Epitome Institutionum Rei Militaris* on classic legionary operations, mainly extracted from other authors, which during the middle ages was a supreme authority on warfare.

VEIT, Philipp (1793–1877) German painter, born in Berlin, the son of Dorothea **Schlegel** and grandson of **Moses Mendelssohn**. A Catholic convert, he settled in Rome in 1815 and became conspicuous among the young German painters who sought to infuse into modern art the earnestness of medieval times. In 1830 he became director of the Art Institute at Frankfurt-am-Main.

VEITCH, John (1829–94) Scottish poet and scholar, born in Peebles, the son of a Peninsular War veteran. He studied at Edinburgh and, after the Disruption of the Church of Scotland, studied theology at New College, Edinburgh. In 1856 he was appointed assistant to Sir **William Hamilton**, professor of logic and metaphysics at Edinburgh, and in 1860 was appointed professor of logic at St Andrews. He wrote biographies of **Dugald Stewart** (1857) and Hamilton (1869), and as a poet wrote of the Border country. His critical works included *History and Poetry of the Scottish Border* (1877) and *The Feeling for Nature in Scottish Poetry* (1877).

VEITCH, William (1794–1885) Scottish classical scholar, born in Spittal near Jedburgh. He qualified for the Scottish ministry, but devoted himself to a life of scholarship at Edinburgh. His chief work was the invaluable *Greek Verbs Irregular and Defective* (1848). He revised **Liddell** and **Scott**'s *Greek Lexicon*, and Smith's *Latin Dictionary*.

VELASQUEZ, or **Velazquez, Diego de Silva y** (1599–1660) Spanish painter born in Seville, and considered the greatest master of them all. He may have studied under **Francisco Herrera** the Elder, but in 1613 he did become the pupil of **Francisco Pacheco**, an indifferent painter but considerable art historian, whose daughter he married in 1618 and who (1639), in his *Art of Painting*, provides an account of the young Valasquez. In 1618 Velasquez set up his own studio. His early works were *bodegónes*, characteristically Spanish domestic genre pieces, of which *Old Woman Cooking Eggs* (1618) is a typical example. In 1622 he tried his luck at court in Madrid and persuaded **Góngora y Argote**, the poet, to sit for him. The following year he achieved lifelong court patronage with his equestrian portrait, since lost, of **Philip IV**, who had all other portraits of himself withdrawn. The other court artists accused Velasquez of being incapable of painting anything but heads. The king ordered a competition on an historical subject, which Velasquez won with his *Expulsion of the Moriscos by Philip III*, now lost. In 1628 **Rubens** visited Madrid and befriended him. His advice and the palace collection of Italian art encouraged Velasquez's visit to Italy (1629–31). His sombre, austere, naturalistic style was transformed into the lightly modelled, more colourful styles of **Titian** and **Tintoretto**, as is apparent in his *Forge of Vulcan* (c.1630) and *Joseph's Coat* (1630) and in the new type of portrait which Velasquez improvised, of the king (c.1634) or his brother, or son, in hunting costume with dog and landscape. One of the most striking of his many portraits of his royal master is full length (c.1632; National Gallery, London). The only surviving historical painting is his Baroque *Surrender of Breda* (c.1634). There are also many portraits of the royal children, particularly *Infante Baltasar Carlos on Horseback* (1635–36), the *Infanta Margarita* (1653–54, 1656, 1659) and the *Infanta Maria Theresa* (1652–53), and of the court dwarfs (1644,1655) and jester, nicknamed *Don Juan de Austria* (1652–59). In 1650 he was again in Rome to obtain art treasures for the king and there painted the portrait of Pope **Innocent X** and the two impressionistic *Views from Villa Medici*. On his return he captured the pathetic facial expression of the new queen, the young Maria Anne of Austria, in his best feminine full-length portrait (1552). But he is best remembered for his three late masterpieces, *Las Meniñas*, 'Maids of Honour' (1656), in which the Infanta Margarita, her dwarf and attendants and the artist himself with easel are grouped around a canvas in a large palace room, hung with paintings, *Las Hilanderas*, 'The Tapestry Weavers' (c.1657), and the famous *Venus and Cupid*, known as the 'Rokeby Venus' (c.1658), one of the few nudes in Spanish painting. Velasquez was apppointed usher to the king's chamber (1627), superintendent of works (1643), palace chamberlain (1652) and was made a knight of the order of Santiago (1658), the highest court award. His painting is distinguished for its unflattering realism, in which nothing is imaginatively embellished or otherwise falsified, a remarkable achievement for a court painter. **Goya** carried on his tradition a century later and **Whistler**, **Manet** and the French Impressionists acknowledged his influence.

VELAZQUEZ DE CUELLAR, Diego (1465–1524) Spanish conquistador and colonialist. He accompanied **Columbus** to Hispaniola in 1494, and in 1511 conquered Cuba, of which he became governor (1511–24) and founded Havana. He sent out various expeditions of conquest, including the Mexican expedition of **Hernando Cortés** in 1519.

VELDE, Henri Clemens van de (1863–1957) Belgian architect, designer and teacher, born in Antwerp. One of the originators of the Art Nouveau style, he started as a painter before pioneering the modern functional style of architecture. A disciple of **William Morris** and **John Ruskin** in the Arts and Crafts movement, he founded (with his pupil **Walter Gropius**) the Deutscher Werkbund movement in Germany in 1906, and was a director of the Weimar School of Arts and Crafts from which the Bauhaus sprang. His designs ranged beyond architecture to graphics, furniture, ceramics, metalwork and textiles. His works included the Werkbund Theatre in Cologne, the Museum Kröller-Muller in Otterloo, the university library in Ghent, and the Belgian pavilions at the international exhibitions in Paris (1937), and New York (1939). His publications include *Vom neuen Stil* (1907), *Les Formules d'une esthétique moderne* (1925), and *Le nouveau style* (1929).

VELDE, Willem van de, the Elder (c.1611–1693) Dutch marine painter, born in Leiden. In 1657 he went to England and painted large pictures of sea battles in indian ink and black paint for **Charles II** and **James II**.

VELDE, Willem van de, the Younger (1633–1707) Dutch painter, born in Leiden, son of **Willem van de Velde**, the Elder. Like his father he was almost exclusively a marine painter. With him he worked in England for **Charles II**, which accounts for the large number of his works in English collections. He specialized in depicting naval encounters.

VELLEIUS PATERCULUS (c.19 BC–c.30 AD) Roman historian. He served for many years in the army in Germany under **Tiberius**, was alive in AD 30, and may have perished next year as a friend of **Sejanus**. He was the author of *Historiae Romanae*, a compendium of universal, but more particularly of Roman, history, which is not complete, and is somewhat superficial and rhetorical.

VENDÔME, Louis Joseph, Duc de (1654–1712) French soldier, born in Paris. He saw his first service in the Dutch campaign of 1672. He next served with distinction under **Turenne** in Germany and Alsace, again in the Low Countries at Steenkirke (1692) under **Luxembourg**, and in Italy under **Catinat**; in 1695 he received the command of the army in Catalonia. He crowned a series of brilliant successes by the capture of Barcelona (1697). After five years of sloth and sensuality he superseded **Villeroi** in Italy in the War of the Spanish Succession (1701–14). He fought an undecided battle with Prince **Eugene** at Luzzara (1702), then burst into Tirol, returning to Italy to check the united Savoyards and Austrians. In August 1705, he fought a second indecisive battle with Prince Eugene at Cassano, and at Calcinato he crushed the Austrians (April 1706). That summer he was recalled to supersede Villeroi in the Low Countries. The defeat at Oudenarde by **Marlborough** (July 1708) cost him his command, but in 1710 he was sent to Spain to aid **Philip V**. His appearance turned the tide of disaster; he brought the king back to Madrid, and defeated the English at Brihuega, and next day the Austrians at Villaviciosa. After a month of gluttony beyond even his wont, he died at Vinaroz in Castellón de la Plana.

VENING MEINESZ, Felix Andries (1887–1966) Dutch geophysicist, born in The Hague, a pioneer of submarine gravity measurements. After graduating in civil engineering from the Technical University of Delft in 1910, he worked on a gravity survey of the Netherlands. In 1927 he was appointed professor extraordinary of geodesy, cartography and geophysics at Utrecht, and also professor of geophysics at Delft. Very accurate measurements are necessary since the variation in gravity is small. However, as the majority of the earth's surface is covered by oceans, the lack of a stable platform makes the measurements by the conventional pendulum technique impossible. Vening Meinesz used a submarine to provide a sufficiently stable base and made the first marine gravity determinations in the Pacific in 1923. His later voyages led him to deduce the presence of subduction zones, where compressive down-buckling of oceanic crust occurs.

VENIZELOS, Eleutherios (1864–1936) Greek statesman, born near Canea, Crete. He studied law in Athens, led the Liberal party in the Cretan chamber of deputies and took a prominent part in the Cretan rising against the Turks in 1896. When Prince George (**George I** of Greece) became governor of Crete, Venizelos first served under him as minister of justice, then opposed him from the mountains at Therisso with guerrilla warfare. In 1909 he was invited to Athens, became prime minister (1910–15), restored law and order but excluded the Cretan deputies from the new parliament and promoted the Balkan League against Turkey (1912) and Bulgaria (1913) and so extended the Greek kingdom. His sympathies with France and Britain at the outbreak of World War I clashed with those of King **Constantine I** and caused Venizelos to establish a provisional rival government at Salonika and in 1917 forced the king's abdication. He secured further territories from Turkey at the Versailles Peace Conference, but his prestige began to wane with his failure to colonize Turkish Asia Minor and he was heavily defeated in the general elections (1920) which brought the royalists and King Constantine back to power. He was prime minister again (1924, 1928–32 and 1933). In 1935 he came out of retirement to support another Cretan revolt staged by his sympathizers, but it failed and he fled eventually to Paris, where he died.

VENN, Henry (1725–97) English clergyman, born in Barnes, father of **John Venn**. As vicar of Huddersfield (1759) he took a prominent part with Lady **Huntingdon** and **George Whitefield** in the Evangelical revival. He wrote *The Compleat Duty of Man* (1763) and other sermons.

VENN, John (1759–1813) English clergyman son of **Henry Venn**, born in Clapham. In 1792 he became vicar there and a prominent member of the wealthy group of families with their distinctive religious and social ideals, known as the Clapham sect. In 1799 he founded the Church Missionary Society, of which his son, Henry (1796–1873), was secretary from 1841.

VENN, John (1834–1923) English logician, born in Drypool, Hull. A fellow of Caius College, Cambridge (1857), he developed **George Boole**'s symbolic logic and in his *Logic of chance* (1866) the frequency theory of probability. He is best known for 'Venn diagrams', pictorially representing the relations between sets, though similar diagrams had been used by **Gottfried Leibniz** and **Leonhard Euler**.

VENTRIS, Michael George Francis (1922–56) English linguist (though by profession an architect), born in Wheathampstead. As a teenager he became interested in the undeciphered Minoan scripts found on tablets excavated, under Sir **Arthur Evans**, at palace sites in Crete. These were apparently palace records and inventories. The earlier Linear A tablets had been found exclusively in Crete; Linear B tablets, of the late Minoan period, had appeared only at Knossos, but were beginning to turn up at Mycenaean sites in mainland Greece. His analysis proved that the language of Linear B was an early form of Greek. He was killed in a road accident shortly before the publication of his joint work with John Chadwick, *Documents in Mycenaean Greek*.

VENTURI, Giovanni Battista (1746–1822) Italian physicist, born near Reggio. Ordained a priest at the age of 23, he was appointed professor of geometry and philosophy at the University of Modena at 27, and later became professor of physics. His research concentrated on the flow of fluids, and he kept in close touch with the work of **Daniel Bernoulli** and **Leonhard Euler** in fluid mechanics. He is remembered for his discovery of the 'Venturi effect', the decrease in the pressure of a fluid in a pipe where the diameter has been reduced by a gradual taper. In 1898 the hydraulic engineer Clemens Herschel (1842–1930) invented the Venturi flow-meter based on the Venturi effect discovered more than a century earlier.

VERDAGUER, Mosen Jacinto (1845–1902) Catalan poet, born in Folgarolas. He became a priest with a vast popular following. He wrote *L'Atlántida*, and *Lo Canigó*, two epic poems of great beauty, and on the first of these **Manuel de Falla** based his choral work *Atlántida*. His *Idilis y Cants Místichs* (1870), also set to music, have become part of the music of the Catalan church.

VERDI, Giuseppe Fortunino Francesco (1813–1901) Italian composer, born in Roncole. Of humble rural origin—his father kept an inn and grocer's store—much of his early musical education came from Provesi, organist of Busseto Cathedral. Subsidized by locals who admired his talent, he was sent to Milan, but was rejected by the conservatory as over age. Instead he studied profitably under Lavigna, *maestro al cembalo* at La Scala. On returning home he failed in his ambition of succeeding Provesi as cathedral organist, but was given a grant by the Philharmonic Society. Three years later he married the daughter of his friend and patron Barezzi, but both she and their two children died (1839–40). By this time his first opera, *Oberto*, had already been produced at La Scala, but it was with *Nabucco* (1842) that he achieved his first major success. Thereafter his career was one of almost continuous triumph. Although few of his pre-1850 operas, apart from *Macbeth* and *Luisa Miller*, remain in the normal repertory, *Rigoletto* (1851), *Il Trovatore* (1853) and *La Traviata* (1853) established unshakably his position as the leading Italian operatic composer of the day. These three works and their successors like *Un Ballo in Maschera* (1859) and *La Forza del Destino* (1862) were products of his maturity. This phase came to an end with the spectacular *Aïda*, commissioned for the new opera house in Cairo, built in celebration of the Suez Canal. Its première was in fact delayed until 1871 because of the Franco-Prussian war. Apart from the *Requiem* (1873), written in commemoration of **Manzoni,** there was then a lull in output until, in his old age, goaded and inspired by his brilliant literary collaborator **Boito,** he produced two masterpieces, *Otello* (1887) and *Falstaff* (1893). Both had their premières at La Scala, so ending nearly 20 years of feud with that theatre. Apart from some sacred choral pieces Verdi wrote no more before his death. Though his reputation was worldwide he stayed at heart a country-man, preferring above all to cultivate his property at Busseto in the intervals of composition. His long association with the former operatic soprano Giuseppina Strepponi, who became his wife in 1859, ensured a happy domestic context for his work. In his young days he had been an enthusiastic nationalist; some of his choruses were freely construed by patriots as being anti-Austrian, and were liable to lead to demonstrations. However, active participation in politics was not to his taste, and he soon resigned his deputyship in the first Italian parliament (1860). Later in life he became a senator. Though rich and greatly esteemed, Verdi led a simple life, and took almost as much pride in his estate management and in the founding of a home for aged musicians in Milan as in his creative work. Verdi dominated Italian opera between the **Bellini-Donizetti** era and that of **Puccini.** Over the years his methods changed from the robust melodramatic effectiveness of his youthful production to the extraordinary subtlety and sophistication of the last two operas. But at the root of his genius was his superb sense of theatre and his reservoir of unforgettable tunes.

VERDROSS, Alfred (1890–1980) Austrian jurist. A member of the Permanent Court of Arbitration at The Hague and the International Law Commission, he was a judge of the European Court of Human Rights (1958–77), and president of the Institute of International Law. He wrote *Die Verfassung des Volkerrechtsgemeinschaft* (1926), *Volkerrecht* (1937), and other works in international law.

VERDY, Violette, originally **Nelly Guillerm** (1933–) French dancer and ballet director, born in Pont-L'Abbé-Lambour. She made her début with Ballets des Champs-Élysées in 1945, and subsequently appeared in films and theatre as an actress and dancer. She joined **Roland Petit**'s Ballets de Paris in 1950, later freelancing with a string of companies including London Festival Ballet (1954), American Ballet Theatre (1957) and New York City Ballet (1958–77). She has won a following on both sides of the Atlantic with her charming, effervescent stage personality. She was artistic director of Paris Opéra Ballet (1977–80) and an associate of Boston Ballet.

VERE, Aubrey Thomas de See **DE VERE**

VERE, Edward de, 17th Earl of Oxford (1550–1604) English court poet, a cousin of Sir **Francis Vere** and Sir **Horace Vere**. He was an Italianate Englishman, violent and a spendthrift, but one of the best of the Elizabethan courtier-poets. Of his lyrics, published in various collections, 'What cunning can expresse' is perhaps the best.

VERE, Sir Francis (c.1560–1609) English soldier, grandson of the 15th Earl of Oxford, and brother of Sir **Horace Vere.** He obtained a company in the Bergen-op-Zoom garrison in 1586, and won his first laurels in the defence of Sluys; in 1589 he took over the chief command in the Netherlands. He shared the glory of the Cadiz expedition (1596), and next year the failure of the Island Voyage. Again in Holland, he governed Brill, and helped **Maurice of Nassau** to victory at Turnhout (1597) and Nieuwpoort (1600), as well as in the heroic defence of Ostend (1601–02). He wrote commentaries on his campaigns (1657).

VERE, Sir Horace, 1st Baron Vere of Tilbury (1565–1635) English soldier, brother of Sir **Francis Vere**. He took a hero's share in all his brother's battles. Knighted for his courage at Cadiz (1596), he succeeded his brother as governor of Brill, and, sent in the Thirty Years' War to defend the Palatinate, was shut in at Mannheim and forced to surrender to **Tilly** (1623). He was created baron in 1625.

VERENDRYE, Pierre Gaultier de Varennes, Sieur de la (1685–1749) French explorer, born in Three Rivers, Quebec. He served with the French army, and after being wounded at Malplaquet, returned to Canada to become a trader, making his base at Nipigon on Lake Superior. Fired by Indian tales, he and his three sons travelled over much of unexplored Canada, discovering Rainy Lake, the Lake of the Woods, and Lake Winnipeg. On later expeditions he and his remaining two sons (the eldest having been killed by the Sioux) reached the Mandan country south of the Assiniboine river, upper Missouri, Manitoba and Dakota. Finally, before his death, one of his sons traced the Saskatchewan river to its junction.

VERESHCHAGIN, Vasili (1842–1904) Russian painter of battles and executions, born in Tcherepovets in Novgorod. He entered the navy in 1859, but studied art under **Gérôme** in Paris. He travelled widely as a war correspondent and portrayed what he saw in gruesomely realistic pictures of plunder, mutilated corpses and executions, with **Tolstoy**'s aim of fostering revulsion against war. He was blown up off Port Arthur in the Russian-Japanese War (1904–05).

VERGA, Giovanni (1840–1922) Italian novelist, born in Catania in Sicily. He wrote numerous violent short stories describing the hopeless, miserable life of Sicilian peasantry, including *La vita de' campi* (1880) and *Cavalleria rusticana* (1884), which was made into an opera by **Mascagni**. The same Zolaesque theme prevails in his novels, *I Malavoglia* (1881), *Mastro Don Gesualdo* (1888), and others. **D H Lawrence** translated some of his works.

VERGENNES, Charles Gravier (1717–87) French statesman, **Louis XVI**'s foreign minister. He sought to humble England by promoting the independence of the United States. He negotiated the Peace of Paris (1783) and **Pitt**'s commercial treaty (1786).

VERGIL See **VIRGIL**

VERGIL, Polydore, otherwise named **De Castello** (c.1470–c.1555) Italian-born English historian, born in Urbino. Educated at Bologna and Padua, his first work was *Proverbiorum Libellus* (1498); his second, *De Inventoribus Rerum* (1499), also the earliest book of its kind, was translated into English, Spanish and Italian. He was sent by Pope **Alexander VI** to England in 1501 as deputy-collector of Peter's pence, and was presented to the Leicestershire living of Church Langton in 1503. In 1507 he became a prebendary of Lincoln, in 1508 archdeacon of Wells, and in 1513 a prebendary of St Paul's, having been naturalized in 1510. In 1515 he published the first genuine edition of **Gildas**, in 1526 the treatise *De Prodigiis*. His great *Historiae Anglicae Libri XXVI* appeared at Basel in 1534; a 27th book (to 1538) was added in the third edition (1555). About 1550 he returned to Italy.

VERGNIAUD, Pierre Victurnien (1753–93) French politician, born in Limoges. He settled as an advocate at Bordeaux in 1781, and was sent to the National Assembly in 1791. His eloquence made him the leader of the Girondists. In the Convention he voted for the king's death, and as president announced the result. When the Girondists clashed with the rival revolutionary faction, known as the Mountain, composed mainly of Parisians who had borne the brunt of the revolution and wanted to retain power by dictatorial means, Vergniaud and his party were arrested and guillotined on 31 October.

VERHAEREN, Emile (1855–1916) Belgian poet, born in St Armand near Termonde. He studied law, but turned to literature, writing in French. His poetry hovers between powerful sensuality, as in *Les Flamandes* (1883) and the harrowing despair of *Les Débâcles* (1888), the affirmation of the life force and the revulsion against modern industrial conditions. His best work is possibly *La Multiple Splendeur* (1906). He died in a train accident.

VERHEIDEN, Jakob (16th–17th century) Dutch publisher in The Hague. In 1602 he published the *Effigies et Elogia* of the leading Reformers, the portraits (including the well-known one of **John Knox** based on that in **Beza**'s *Icones*) being engraved by **Jodocus Hondius**.

VERLAINE, Paul (1844–96) French poet, born in Metz. He was educated at the Lycée Condorcet and entered the civil service. Already an aspiring poet, he mixed with the leading Parnassian poets and writers in the cafés and salons. Under their battle cry 'Art for art's sake', against the formless sentimentalizing of the Romantic school, he gained recognition by contributing articles and poems to their avant garde literary magazines, especially the short-lived *Le Parnasse contemporain*. The youthful morbidity of his first volume of poems, *Poèmes saturniens* (1867), was criticized by **Saint-Beuve** as trying vainly to outdo **Baudelaire**. The evocation of a past age, the 18th century, provided the theme of his second work, *Fêtes galantes* (1869), by many considered his finest poetical achievement. His love for the 16-year-old Mathilde Mauté during an engagement prolonged by the doubts of the girl's father was expressed in *La Bonne Chanson* (1870). During the Franco-Prussian war Verlaine did guard duty in Paris and then served as press-officer for the Communards. The birth of a son did nothing to heal the incompatibilities of his married life, from which he escaped (1872) on travels in Flanders, Belgium and England in a homosexual affair with the fledgling poet **Rimbaud**, ten years his junior. Their friendship ended in Brussels in 1873, when Verlaine, drunk and desolate at Rimbaud's intention to leave him, shot him in the wrist. Verlaine's overpowering remorse made it psychologically impossible for Rimbaud to leave, so he staged an incident in the street and had Verlaine arrested. He did not foresee that the police, searching for a motive, would suspect immorality. Verlaine was convicted and sentenced to two years' hard labour, and his past associations with the Communards disqualified him from any intercession by the French ambassador. *Romances sans paroles* (1874) were written in Mons prison, where he studied **Shakespeare** in the original, and after his wife had left him, he turned Catholic (1874). He unsuccessfully attempted to enter a monastery on release, taught French at Stickney, Lincolnshire, and St Aloysius' College, Bournemouth (1875), where he completed his second masterpiece *Sagesse* (1881), full of the spirit of penitence and self-confession that appeared again in *Parallèlement* (1889). In 1877 he returned to France to teach English at the Collège of Notre Dame at Rethel. There he adopted a favourite pupil, Lucien Létinois, for whom he acquired a farm at Coulommes and whose death of typhus (1883) occasioned *Amour* (1888). *Poètes maudits* (1884), comprising critical studies, were followed by the short stories *Louis Leclerc* and *Le Poteau* (1886), sacred and profane verse *Liturgies intimes* (1892) and *Élégies* (1893). Verlaine is the consummate master of a poetry which sacrificed all for sound, in which the commonplace expressions take on a magic freshness. He lived during his last years in Parisian garret poverty, relieved by frequent spells in hospitals and finally by a grand lecture tour in Belgium, Holland and England (1893), the last sponsored in part by **William Rothenstein**, who drew several portraits of him.

VERMEER, Jan (1632–75) Dutch painter, born in Delft, the son of an art dealer. He inherited his father's business and painted purely for pleasure. His life was obscure, possibly because he was a Catholic in a Protestant country. He may have studied under **Carel Fabritius**. His work shows some Neapolitan influence as well as that of the genre painting of **Pieter de Hooch**. In 1653 he married Caterina Bolones, who was to bear him eleven children, and in the same year he was admitted master painter to the guild of St Luke, which he served as headman (1662–63; 1670–71). He gained some recognition in his lifetime in Holland and his work was sought by collectors, but he made little effort to sell. After his death his baker held two pictures for outstanding bills, and Vermeer's wife, declared a bankrupt, could not retrieve them. His importance was only established in the 19th century. Apart from a few portraits, *The Allegory of Faith*, *The Procuress* (1656; Dresden), *Christ in the House of Martha and Mary* and two views of Delft, he confined himself to the domestic interiors of his own house, spiced with an art dealer's furnishings and trappings, every scene perfectly arranged so that everything, material or human, should obtain equal prominence and meticulous attention. Fewer than 40 of his paintings are known. These include three music-making scenes, the *Allegory of Painting*, two *Woman reading a Letter* and other domestic scenes. During World War II, forged Vermeers were produced by **Van Meegeren**, who for some time deceived the experts.

VERMEER, Jan, of Haarlem (1628–91) a notable Dutch landscape painter. His son, Jan the Younger (1656–1705), was also a painter.

VERMIGLI, Pietro Martire See **PETER MARTYR**

VERMUYDEN, Sir Cornelius (c.1595–c.1683) Dutch-born British drainage engineer, born on the island of Tholen, Zeeland. In 1621 he went to Britain commissioned to repair the breach of the Thames at Dagenham, and thereafter succeeded in draining the 122 000 hectares of the Bedford Level (1634–52).

VERNE, Jules (1828–1905) French novelist, born in Nantes. He studied law, and from 1848 wrote opera libretti until in 1863, with the publication of *Cinq Semaines en ballon*, he struck a new vein in fiction—exaggerating and often anticipating the possibilities of science and describing adventures carried out by means of scientific inventions in exotic places, like submarines and space travel. He greatly influenced the early science fiction of **H G Wells**. His best-known books, all of which have been translated, are *Voyage au centre de la terre* (Journey to the Centre of the Earth, 1864), *De la Terre á la Lune* (From the Earth to the Moon, 1865), *Vingt mille lieues sous les mers* (Twenty Thousand Leagues Under the Sea, 1870) and *Le Tour du monde en quatre-vingts jours* (Around the World in Eighty Days, 1873). Film versions of the last two achieved an astonishing popularity.

VERNET, Antoine Charles Horace, known as **Carle** (1758–1835) French historical and animal painter, born in Bordeaux, the son of **Claude Joseph Vernet**. He showed early promise and went to Italy, where he decided to become a monk. Back in Paris, however, he took to painting horses again and the vast battle pieces of Marengo and Austerlitz (now at Versailles) for which **Napoleon** awarded him the Légion d'honneur, and *The Race* (Louvre), which earned him the Order of St Michael from **Louis XVIII**.

VERNET, Claude Joseph (1714–89) French landscape and marine painter, born in Avignon, the father of **Antoine Charles Vernet.** A voyage to Rome gave him a fascination for the sea and he became primarily known for his seascapes and the paintings in the Louvre of France's 16 chief seaports, commissioned by the king.

VERNET, (Emile Jean) Horace (1789–1863) French battle painter, born in Paris, the son of **Antoine Vernet**. He became one of the great French military and sporting painters. He decorated the vast Constantine room at Versailles with battle scenes from Valmy, Wagram, Bouvines and *Napoleon at Friedland*. His *Painter's Studio* depicts him as he loved to be, surrounded by groups of people, boxing, playing instruments and leading horses.

VERNIER, Pierre (1584–1638) French scientific instrument-maker, born in Ornans near Besançon. He spent most of his life serving the king of Spain in the Low Countries and in 1631 invented the famous auxiliary scale to facilitate an accurate reading of a subdivision of an ordinary scale.

VERNON, Edward (1684–1757) English naval commander, known as 'Old Grog'. He entered the royal navy in 1700. He was present at the capture of Gibraltar in 1704, and fought in the great battle off Málaga. A captain at 21 and a rear admiral at 24, he sat in parliament as MP for Penhryn and then Portsmouth (1727–41). In 1739, at the outbreak of the War of Jenkins' Ear, he was sent to harry the Spaniards in the Antilles, and his capture of Portobello made him a national hero. He continued to be a thorn in the administration's side until his death in 1757. He was nicknamed 'Old Grog', from his grogram coat; and when in 1740 he ordered the dilution of navy rum with water, the mixture was thenceforward known as 'grog'.

VERNON, Robert (1774–1849) English breeder of horses, known as the 'father of the Turf'. A member of Parliament (1754–90), he was a founder of the Jockey Club, and established horse-training at Newmarket. In 1847 he gave to the nation the Vernon Gallery.

VERONESE, real name **Paolo Caliari** (c.1528–1588) Venetian painter, born in Verona from where he took his name. He was, along with **Titian** and **Tintoretto**, one of the greatest decorative artists of the 16th-century Venetian School. He trained as a stone cutter, but under the influence of Titian he settled in Venice in 1553. All his works are bravura displays of technical virtuosity which concentrate on rich costumes set off against sumptuous architectural frameworks. His first frescoes in the Doge's Palace and the Library of Saint Mark's in Venice were admired by the older Titian. In 1573, however, he was called upon by the authorities to explain his rendering of the *Marriage at Cana* as an opulent party in which dwarves, among other unlikely participators, are introduced into the scene. The religious foundations of Venice provided Veronese with most of his commissions.

VERONICA, St (1st century) according to legend, she met **Jesus Christ** and offered him her veil to wipe sweat from his brow, when the divine features were miraculously imprinted upon the cloth. The veil is said to have been preserved in Rome from about 700, and was exhibited in St Peter's in 1933. Possibly *Veronica* is merely a corruption of *vera icon*, 'the true image' (ie, of Christ).

VERRES, Gaius (d.43 BC) Roman official, was quaestor in 84, and then attached himself to **Sulla**. He went to Cilicia in 80 under **Dolabella**, and after helping to plunder the provincials, gave evidence against his chief in 78. He was praetor in 74, owing to bribery, and governor of Sicily (73–70), where he trampled on the rights of Roman and provincial alike. On his return he was summoned before a senatorial court, and **Cicero**, for the prosecution, amassed such strong evidence that Verres fled before the trial. He seemed to have lived at Massilia, but perished under **Marcus Antonius**' proscription.

VERRIO, Antonio (c.1640–1707) Italian decorative painter, born in Lecce. He was brought to London by **Charles II** and decorated Windsor Castle, and by **William III** to decorate Hampton Court and elsewhere.He also executed an equestrian portrait of **Charles II**, now in Chelsea Hospital.

VERROCCHIO, Andrea del (c.1435–c.1488) Florentine artist, best known as the master of **Leonardo da Vinci** but an important and innovatory figure of the Early Renaissance period in his own right. Although much of his work as goldsmith and sculptor has not survived, his *David* of 1476 is a milestone in the treatment of the standing male figure by Renaissance artists. With that of **Donatello** it is one of a trio which culminates in the virtuosity of **Michelangelo**'s nude version. The equestrian monument to **Colleoni** in Venice shows Verrochio to be as capable of monumental public work of this kind as Donatello. Very little of his painting remains, but his *Baptism* is a good indicator of his naturalism, ability to create the illusion of space and superb draughtmanship. According to **Vasari**, the head of one of the angels is by Leonardo da Vinci.

VERTUE, George (1684–1756) English engraver and antiquary, born in London. He made his name with a fine line-engraving of Lord **Somers**. **Horace Walpole** bought his notes for a history of art and used them as his *Anecdotes of Painting in England* (1761–71).

VERULAM See **BACON, Francis**

VERWOERD, Hendrik Freusch (1901–66) South African politician, born in Amsterdam. He was a professor at Stellenbosch (1927–37). He edited the nationalist *Die Transvaler* (1938–48) and opposed South Africa's entry into World War II. Exponent of the strict racial segregation policy of apartheid, Verwoerd became vice-chairman of the National Party of the Transvaal in 1946, was elected senator in 1948 and minister of native affairs in 1950. In 1958 he was elected national leader by the Nationalist party parliamentary caucus and as 6th prime minister of South Africa he dedicated himself to the founding of a South African republic. After strong opposition to his policy of apartheid and an attempt on his life in 1960, South Africa broke from the commonwealth on becoming a republic in 1962, after which Verwoerd pursued a strict apartheid policy. He was assassinated in 1966.

VERY, Edward Wilson (1847–1910) American ordnance expert and inventor. He served in the American Navy from 1867 to 1885, became an admiral, and in 1877 invented chemical flares ('Very Lights') for signalling at night.

VERY, Jones (1813–80) American mystic and poet, born in Salem in Massachusetts. He wrote sonnets and prose pieces of intense religious inspiration, published in *Essays and Poems* (1839).

VESAAS, Tarjei (1897–1970) Norwegian novelist and lyric poet, from Telemark. A writer of symbolic and allegorical works, he was the most important novelist using *Landsmål* ('national language', renamed *Nynorsk*, New Norwegian) after World War II. His first novel was *Die svarte hestane* (The Black Horses,

1928). His best-known books are *Fuglane* (The Birds, 1957) and *Is-slottet* (The Ice Castle, 1963). He published his autobiography, *Båten om kvelden* (Boat in the Evening) in 1968.

VESALIUS, Andreas (1514–64) Belgian anatomist, one of the first dissectors of human cadavers, born in Brussels. He became professor at Padua, Bologna and Basle, and was court physician to emperor **Charles V** and **Philip II** of Spain (1559). In 1538 he published his six anatomical tables, still largely Galenian, and in 1541 edited **Galen**'s works. His great work, however, *De Humani Corporis Fabrica* (1543), greatly advanced the science of biology with its excellent descriptions and drawings of bones and the nervous system, and repudiated Galenism. It was condemned by the Galenists and he was sentenced to death by the Inquisition for 'body snatching' and for dissecting the human body. The sentence was commuted to a pilgrimage to Jerusalem, which he undertook, but died on the return journey on the island of Zante.

VESPASIAN, Titus Flavius Vespasianus (9–79) Roman emperor, founder of the Flavian dynasty, born near Reate. He served as tribune in Thrace, and as quaestor in Crete and Cyrene. In the reign of **Claudius** he commanded a legion in Germany and in Britain; was consul in 51, and next proconsul of Africa; and in 67 was sent by **Nero** to reduce the Jews to subjection. When the struggle began between **Otho** and **Vitellius** he was proclaimed imperator by the legions in the East and on the death of Vitellius was appointed emperor. Leaving the war in Judaea to his son **Titus**, he reached Rome in 70, and soon restored the government and finances to order, besides setting a personal example in the simplicity of his life. He embarked on an ambitious building programme in Rome, began the Colosseum, and extended and consolidated Roman conquests in Britain and Germany.

VESPUCCI, Amerigo (1451–1512) Italian-born Spanish explorer after whom the continent of America was named, born in Florence. As a contractor in Seville from 1495 to 1498 he provisioned one (or two) of the expeditions of **Christopher Columbus**. Although not a navigator or pilot himself, in 1499 he promoted an expedition to the New World commanded by Alonso de Hojeda and sailed there in his own ship, in which he explored the coast of Venezuela. In 1505 he was naturalized in Spain, and in 1508 was appointed pilot-major of Spain. His name (Latinized as 'Americus') was somewhat fortuitously given to the American continents by the young German cartographer **Martin Waldseemüller** after the publication at St Diè in Lorraine of a distorted account of his travels, based on forged versions of his letters (*Four Voyages*, 1507).

VESTRIS, Auguste, (Marie Jean Augustin) (1760–1842) French dancer and teacher, born in Paris, the illegitimate son of Gaetano Vestris (1729–1808). He made his début at the age of twelve, going on to join the Paris Opéra. Physically not typical of dancers of the time, his brilliant technique and energy led him to become the most celebrated dancer in Europe. The French Revolution drove him to London for five years, but he returned in 1793 to continue dancing in Paris until 1816. He then became renowned as a teacher, his pupils including **Auguste Bournonville**, Marie Taglioni and Didepot. He is recorded as having danced in his father's ballet *Endymion* (1773), **Noverre**'s *Les petits riens* (1778) and Gardel's ballets.

VESTRIS, Lucia Elizabeth (1797–1856) English actress, née **Bartolozzi**, a grand-daughter of the engraver, born in London. At 16 she married the dancer Armand Vestris (1787–1825), member of an originally Florentine family that gave to France a series of distinguished chefs, actors and ballet-dancers. In 1815 they separated and she went on the stage in Paris. She appeared at Drury Lane in 1820, became famous in *The Haunted Tower*, was even more popular as Phoebe in *Paul Pry*, and in light comedy and burlesque was equally successful. She had been nine years lessee of the Olympic when in 1838 she married **Charles James Mathews**. She afterwards undertook the management of Covent Garden and the Lyceum.

VEZIN, Hermann (1829–1910) American actor, born in Philadelphia. He made his début at York in 1850 and acted in London from 1852. Among his leading roles were Hamlet, Jacques and Ford.

VIAN, Boris (1920–59) French playwright, novelist and poet, born in Ville d'Avray. A Bohemian with a bad heart, he dabbled in many things—acting, jazz, engineering, anarchism, pornography—and excelled in fiction. A tragi-comic writer, he won a cult following for such novels as *L'Écume des jours* (1947, trans *Froth on the Daydream*, 1967) and *L'Arrache-coeur* (1953, trans *Heartsnatcher*, 1968).

VIAN, Sir Philip (1894–1968) English naval commander, educated at the Royal Naval College, Dartmouth. In 1940, as captain of a destroyer flotilla in HMS *Cossack*, he penetrated Norwegian territorial waters to rescue 300 British seamen held on board the German supply ship *Altmark*. His flotilla later played a leading role in his final destruction of the German battleship *Bismarck* (1941). As commander of the 15th Cruiser Squadron in the Mediterranean fleet he distinguished himself with his skilful handling of escort forces in the hazardous convoy operations for the relief of Malta (1941–42). He took part in the assault landings in Sicily and Italy (1943), and Normandy (1944), and later commanded an aircraft carrier group in the Far East. He was fifth sea lord (1946), and later admiral of the fleet.

VAIRDOT-GARCÍA See **GARCÍA, Paulina**

VIAU, Théophile de (1590–1626) French poet, born in Clairac. He wrote the tragedy *Pyramé et Thisbé* (1621) and love poetry distinguished by its naturalness. He was condemned to the stake (1623) for the impiety and obscenity of the poems he contributed to *Le Parnasse satyrique*, but his sentence was commuted to exile for life.

VIAUD, Louis Marie Julien, pseud **Pierre Loti** (1850–1923) French naval officer and novelist, born in Rochefort. He entered the navy in 1869 and served in the east, retiring as captain in 1910, but was recalled to service in World War I. His voyages as a sailor and as a traveller provide the scenes for most of his writings, and from the native women of the South Sea Islands he gained his pseudonym Loti, 'Flower of the Pacific'. *Aziyadé* (1879), his first novel, was a series of pictures of life on the Bosphorus and it was followed by the very successful *Rarahu* (1880), published in 1882 as *Le Mariage de Loti*. Semi-autobiographical, and set among the coral seas, this story of the love of an Englishman for a Tahitian girl immediately captured the imagination. Of his novels, the best known is *Pêcheur d'Islande* (1886), a descriptive study of Breton fisher life in Icelandic waters. Other works include *Le Roman d'un Spahi* (1881), *Mon Frère Yves* (1883), *Madame Chrysanthème* (1887), and *Vers Ispahan* (1904).

VICAT, Louis Joseph (1786–1861) French civil engineer, born in Nevers. He studied at the École des Ponts et Chaussées, and worked on various road and canal projects until 1812 when he was sent to build a bridge at Souillac on the Dordogne river, notorious for its severe floods. Searching for a way to build a stronger bridge, after many trials he succeeded in producing a hydraulic lime that would set hard even under water, as **John Smeaton** had done equally fortuitously some 60 years earlier. For 20 years he pursued his research into the manufacture and properties of mortar, hydraulic lime and concrete, publishing his results in a series of papers. With **Aspdin**, who invented Portland cement in England at about the same time, he gave architects and engineers an extremely useful and versatile new building material, concrete.

VICENTE, Gil (c.1470–c.1537) Portugese dramatist, considered the father of Portuguese drama. His *Belém monstrance* is in the Lisbon museum. He wrote 44 plays, 16 in Portuguese, 11 in Spanish and 17 using both languages. His early plays were religious, but gradually social criticism was added. His farces *Inês Pereira*, *Juiz da Beira* and the three *autos das barcas* (*Inferno, Purgatório and Glória*) are his best. He displays great psychological insight, superb lyricism and a predominantly comical spirit.

VICKY, pseud of **Victor Weisz** (1913–66) German-born British political cartoonist, born in Berlin, of Hungarian-Jewish extraction. He emigrated to Britain in 1935, worked with the *News Chronicle*, the *Daily Mirror*, the *New Statesman* and the *Evening Standard*, and established himself as the outstanding left-wing political cartoonist of the period. He published collections of his work, including *Vicky's World* (1959), and *Home and Abroad* (1964).

VICO, Giovanni Battista (Giambattista) (1668–1744) Italian philosopher and historian, born in Naples. He lived there for most of his life, apart from a period from 1686 to 1695 when he was tutor to the Rocca family at the castle of Vatolla, south of Salerno. He read prodigiously, if erratically, among classical and Renaissance writers and was appointed to the chair of rhetoric at the University of Naples in 1699, which was also the year of his marriage. The chair carried a poor stipend and as Vico subsequently had eight children he had to augment his income with commissions to compose ceremonial orations, official histories, biographies and the like. His own published work was extremely wide-ranging, extending into social and political theory, jurisprudence, philology, anthropology, history and rhetoric; but his major work is undoubtedly the *Scienza Nuova* (*The New Science*) which went through three major editions (1725, 1730 and 1744). He presents an original, and often strikingly modern, view of the methods and presuppositions of historical enquiry; he explains the fundamental distinctions between scientific and historical explanation, rejects the idea of single, fixed, human nature invariant over time, and argues that the recurring cyclical developments of history can only be understood through a study of the changing expressions of human nature through language, myth and culture. His other works include the *Autobiography* (not published until 1818), *De nostri temporis studiorum ratione* (On method in contemporary fields of study, 1709), *De antiquissima Italorum sapientia* (On the ancient wisdom of the Italians, 1710), and two volumes jointly titled *On Universal Law* (1720–22).

VICTOR, Claude Perrin, Duc de Belluno (1764–1841) French soldier, born in La Marche. **Napoleon** made him a marshal on the field of Friedland (1807), and later Duke of Belluno. From 1808 to 1812 he commanded in Spain, and, after initial successes, lost the battles of Talavera and Barrosa; in the Russian campaign he covered the crossing of the Berezina. He fought at Dresden and Leipzig, lost the emperor's favour by neglecting to occupy the bridge of Montereau-sur-Yonne, and was wounded at Craonne. **Louis XVIII** gave him high command and the presidency of the commission trying his old companions who had deserted to Napoleon during the 'Hundred Days'. He was minister of war (1821–23).

VICTOR AMADEUS II (1666–1732) succeeded his father as Duke of Savoy in 1675, and was saved from the clutches of France by the military genius of Prince **Eugene**, a distant cousin, who routed the French before Turin in 1706. By the Treaty of Utrecht (1713) he gained the principality of Montferrat and the kingdom of Sicily. Seven years later the emperor of Austria forced him to exchange the crown of Sicily for that of Sardinia. He abdicated in 1730.

VICTOR EMMANUEL I (1759–1824) king of Sardinia from 1802 to 1821. His oppression of liberalism led to a rising in 1821, when he abdicated in favour of his brother Charles Felix.

VICTOR EMMANUEL II (1820–78) first king of Italy, son of **Charles Albert** of Sardinia. In 1848–49 he displayed great gallantry at Goito and Novara. Charles Albert abdicating in his favour, he ascended the throne of Sardinia in 1849; and in August peace was concluded between Sardinia and Austria. Perhaps the most important act of his rule was the appointment (1852) of **Cavour** as his chief minister. In January 1855 Sardinia joined the allies against Russia and a contingent of 10 000 men landed in the Crimea. At the Congress of Paris (1856) the Sardinian envoys urged upon the attention of France and England the opressive government of the states of Italy. In 1857 diplomatic relations were broken off with Austria. In 1859 Austria demanded the disarmament of Sardinia; this was refused, and next day the Austrians crossed the Ticino. A French army advanced to aid the Sardinians, and the Austrians were defeated at Montebello (May 20), Magenta (June 4) and Solferino (June 24). By the Treaty of Villafranca, Lombardy was ceded to Sardinia. In 1860 Modena, Parma, the Romagna and Tuscany were peacefully annexed to Sardinia. Sicily and Naples were added by **Garibaldi**, while Savoy and Nice were ceded to France. The papal territories were saved from annexation only by the presence of a French force of occupation. In February 1861 Victor Emmanuel was proclaimed king of Italy at Turin, whence the capital of Italy was transferred to Florence. In 1866 the Austro-Prussian war, in which Italy took part as the ally of Prussia, added Venetia to the Italian kingdom. In the same year the French withdrew from Rome, but owing to an incursion by Garibaldi they returned. After the fall of the Empire in 1870 the French occupation of Rome was at an end, the king entered Rome, and the province was added to his kingdom. The 'honest king' reigned as a strictly constitutional monarch. He was succeeded by his eldest son, **Umberto I**.

VICTOR EMMANUEL III (1869–1947) king of Italy (1900–46), son of **Umberto I**, born in Naples. He generally ruled as a constitutional monarch with **Giolitti** as premier, but defied parliamentary majorities in bringing Italy into World War I on the side of the Allies in 1915, and in 1922 when he offered **Mussolini** the premiership. The latter reduced the king to a constitutional façade, conferring on him in May 1936 the title of emperor of Abyssinia. The king, however, supported the dictator until the latter's fall in June 1944. Victor Emmanuel then retired from public life, leaving his son **Umberto II** as lieutenant-general of the realm, and abdicated in May 1946.

VICTORIA, in full **Alexandrina Victoria** (1819–1901) queen of the United Kingdom of Great Britain and Ireland, and (in 1876) empress of India, only child of George **III**'s fourth son, Edward, Duke of Kent, and

Victoria Maria Louisa of Saxe-Coburg, sister of **Leopold**, king of the Belgians. She was born in Kensington Palace, London. Called to the British throne on the death of her uncle, **William IV**, in 1837, the provisions of Salic Law excluded her from dominion over Hanover, which passed to another uncle, **Ernest Augustus**, Duke of Cumberland. Crowned at Westminster on 28 June 1838, she speedily demonstrated that clear grasp of constitutional principles and the scope of her own prerogative in which she had been so paintstakingly instructed in the many tutelary letters from her uncle, **Leopold I** of Belgium, who remained her constant correspondent. Companioned in girlhood almost exclusively by older folk, her precocious maturity and surprising firmness of will were speedily demonstrated. With the fall of **Melbourne**'s government in 1839 she resolutely exercised her prerogative by setting aside the precedent which decreed dismissal of the current ladies of the bedchamber. **Peel** thereupon resigned, and the Melbourne administration, which she personally preferred, was prolonged till 1841. Throughout the early formative years of her reign, Melbourne was both her prime minister and her trusted friend and mentor. His experience and thoroughly English outlook served as a useful counter-balance to that more 'Continental' line of policy of which 'Uncle Leopold' was the untiring and far from unprejudiced advocate. On reaching marriageable age the queen became deeply enamoured of Prince **Albert** of Saxe-Coborg and Goth, to whom she was married in 1840. Four sons and five daughters were born: Victoria, the Princess Royal, who married **Frederick III** of Germany; Albert Edward, afterwards **Edward VII**; Alice, who married the Duke of Hesse; Alfred, Duke of Edinburgh and of Saxe-Coburg-Gotha; Helena, who married Prince **Kristian** of Schleswig-Holstein; Louise, who married the Marquis of Lorne (see **Argyll**); Arthur, Duke of Connaught; Leopold, Duke of Albany; and Beatrice, who married Prince Henry of Battenberg. Strongly influenced by her husband, with whom she worked in closest harmony, after his death the stricken queen went into lengthy seclusion, which brought her temporary unpopularity. But with the adventurous **Disraeli** administration vindicated by the queen's recognition as empress of India, Victoria rose high in her subjects' favour. Her experience, shrewdness and innate political flair brought powerful influence to bear on the conduct of foreign affairs, as did the response to the country's policy made by her innumerable relatives amongst the European royal houses. Unswerving in her preference for ministers of conservative principles, such as Melbourne and Disraeli, rather than for counsellors of more radical persuasion, such as **Palmerston** and **Gladstone**, in the long run the queen's judgment of men and events was rarely to be faulted; although her partiality for all things German had the effect of throwing her heir almost too eagerly into the arms of France. Her *Letters*, although prolix and pedestrian in style, bear witness to her unwearying industry, her remarkable practicality, and her high sense of mission. She published *Leaves from the Journal of our Life in the Highlands* (1869), and *More Leaves* (1884).

VICTORIA, Tomás Luis De, or **Vittoria, Tommaso Ludovico da** (1548–1611) Spanish composer, born in Avila. He was sent as a priest to Rome by **Philip II** to study music. At Loyola's Collegium Germanicum he was appointed chaplain in 1566 and in 1571 choirmaster. In 1576 he became chaplain to the widowed Empress Maria, sister of Philip, returning with her to Madrid in 1583 to the convent of the Descalzas Reales, where he remained as choirmaster until his death. Deeply devout, he wrote only religious music and all of equal excellence. Often compared with his contemporary **Palestrina**, his music, though similar, is more individualistic. Often flavoured with Spanish melody, it is exalted but serene. Among his 180 works are the *Officium Hebdonadae Sanctae* (1585), books of motets and masses and his last work, the masterly *Requiem Mass*, composed at the death of the Empress Maria in 1603 and published in 1605.

VIDA, Marco Girolamo, the 'Christian Virgil' (c.1480–1566) Italian Latin poet, born in Cremona. He was made bishop of Alba in 1532. He wrote Latin orations and dialogues, a religious epic, *Christias* (1535), *De Arte Poetica* (1537), and poems on silk-culture and chess (1527).

VIDAL, Gore (Eugene Luther Vidal, Jr) (1925–) American novelist, essayist and polemicist, born at the United States Military Academy in West Point, New York, where his father, an aviation expert and later director of air commerce, was an aeronautics instructor. Much of his childhood was spent in Washington under the influence of his scholarly, witty and blind grandfather, Senator Thomas Gore. He was educated at Phillips Exeter Academy, where he began to write an (unfinished) novel about **Mussolini.** But he was a mediocre student and in 1943, instead of going to Harvard, joined the United States Army Reserve Corps, which gave him the material for his first novel, *Williwaw* (1946), published when he was just 19. Favourable reviews encouraged him to move to Guatemala to devote himself to writing. However his second novel, *In a Yellow Wood* (1947), was slated and his third, *The City and the Pillar* (1948), a clinical and unsentimental account of a young man coming to terms with his homosexuality, precipitated a decline in his career. His next five novels, among them *Dark Green, Bright Red* (1950), *A Search for the King* (1950) and *The Judgment of Paris* (1952), had a lukewarm reception and he looked towards other outlets to make a living. After a period as a TV commentator he returned to the novel in 1964 with *Julian*, his first major book, which purports to be the emperor **Julian**'s autobiographical memoir and journal, followed by a trilogy of books dealing with affairs of state—*Washington, DC* (1967), *Burr* (1973) and *1876* (1976). His taste for camp extravagance reached its apotheosis in the 'apocalyptic' *Myra Breckenridge* (1968) and *Myron* (1974), 'Myra's comeback'. Since then his historical fiction has been dominant. Even his *tour de force*, *Creation* (1981), was overshadowed by *Lincoln* (1984), an engrossing, meticulously-researched, insightful portrait of America's 16th president. In *Empire* (1987), set at the beginning of the American Empire, his fascination with power (he ran for congress in 1960) was again to the fore, and, that same year he published *Armageddon*: *Essays 1983–1987*, 'random pieces' that reflect his ambivalent obsession with what he has called, with characteristic hauteur, 'the land of the dull and the home of the literal'.

VIDAL DE LA BLACHE, Paul (1845–1918) French geographer, born in Pézenas, Hérault. Educated at the École Normale Supérieure in Paris, he taught at the University of Nancy (1872–77) and the École Normale Supérieure, then became the first geographer appointed to the chair of geography at the Sorbonne (1898–1918) and is regarded as the founder of modern French geography. Reacting to environmental determinism, he advocated a regional geography based on the intensive study of small physically-defined regions such as the 'pays' of France. He formulated the concept of possibilism. His expanding influence on French academic geography became known as 'la tradition vidalienne'. He was founder-editor of the journal *Annales de Géographie* (1891–1918).

VÍDALÍN, Jón Thorkelsson (1666–1720) Icelandic Lutheran prelate, born in Garðar, near Reykjavík, the grandson of **Arngrímur Jónsson, the Learned**. A precocious student of theology at Copenhagen University, he enlisted in the Danish army, but soon returned to Iceland and achieved rapid promotion within the bishopric of Skálholt, where he became bishop himself in 1697. A preacher of great fire and vigour, his simple but vivid sermons were published in a collection, *Húspostilla* (Household Sermons, 1718–20), which remained the most widely-read book in Iceland until well into the 19th century.

VIDOCQ, Eugène François (1775–1857) French criminal, known as 'the detective', the son of an Arras baker, whose till he often robbed. After a spell in prison he worked as an acrobat, then served in the army till disabled by a wound, and in 1796 was sentenced for forgery to eight years in the galleys. Escaping, he joined a band of highwaymen, whom he betrayed to the authorities. In 1808 he offered his services as a spy on the criminal classes. In 1812 a 'Brigade de Sûreté' was organized, with Vidocq as chief; its efficiency was marvellous, but suspicions grew that Vidocq himself originated many of the burglaries that he showed such skill in detecting, and in 1825 he was superseded. His *Mémoires* (1828) are untrustworthy.

VIDOR, King Wallis (1894–1982) American film director, born in Galveston, Texas. A cinema projectionist and freelance newsreel cameraman, he made his début as the director of the documentary *Hurricane in Galveston* (1913). In Hollywood from 1915, he worked as a writer and extra before directing a series of short films on juvenile crime, and a feature, *The Turn of the Road* (1919). A successful mounting of *Peg o' My Heart* (1922) brought him a long-term contract with MGM. Interested in social issues and the everyday struggles of the average American, his many films included *The Big Parade* (1925), *The Crowd* (1928) and *Our Daily Bread* (1934). His range of work also included westerns, melodramas and historical epics like his final feature *Solomon and Sheba* (1959). His autobiography, *A Tree is a Tree*, was published in 1953. He also acted in *Love and Money* (1982). Nominated five times for an Academy Award, he received an honorary one in 1979.

VIEBIG, Clara (1860–1952) German novelist, born in Trier. She wrote Zolaesque novels and short stories, including *Kinder der Eifel* (1897), *Das Weiberdorf* (1900) and *Das schlafende Heer* (1904).

VIEIRA, Antonio (1608–97) Portuguese ecclesiastic and Jesuit missionary, born in Lisbon. He went to Brazil in 1614, where he joined the Jesuit order in 1623 and preached amongst the Indians and Negro slaves. He was chaplain to John IV in Portugal from 1641 to 1652 and from 1653 to 1661 was back in Brazil as director of missions, and converted and emancipated the Indians. Unpopular with the colonists, who forced him to return to Portugal, he was imprisoned for two years (1665–67) by the Inquisition. In 1681, with the support of Pope Clement X, he returned to Brazil and became superior in Bahia, where he remained until his death. Of his writings, his *Sermons* are noteworthy and his *Letters* give a clear picture of his time.

VIEIRA, Joao Bernardo (1939–) Guinea-Bissau politician, born in Bissau. He joined the African Party for the Independence of Portuguese Guinea and Cape Verde (PAIGC) in 1960, and in 1964 became a member of the political bureau during the war for independence from Portugal. After independence had been achieved in 1974 he served in the government of Luiz Cabral, but in 1980 led the coup which deposed him, becoming chairman of the Council of Revolution and head of state. In 1984 constitutional changes combined the roles of head of state and head of goverment, making Vieira executive president.

VIELÉ-GRIFFIN, Francis (1864–1937) American-born French symbolist poet, the son of the American general Egbert Louis Vielé (1825–1902), born in Norfolk, Virginia. He made his home in Touraine, France, and became a leading exponent of *vers libre*. His poems collected under the titles *Cueille d'avril* (1886), *Poèmes et Poésies* (1895), *Sapho* (1911), and *La Sagesse d'Ulysse* (1925), are of high lyrical quality, tending towards musical impressionism, and embody a serene outlook on life. His brother, Herman Knickerbocker Vielé (1856–1908), was a painter and novelist.

VIETA, Franciscus or **François Viète** (1540–1603) French mathematician, born in Fontenay-le-Comte. He became a privy councillor to **Henri IV** of France and decoded an important Spanish cypher. His *In Artem Analyticam Isagoge* (1591) is probably the earliest work on symbolic algebra, and he devised methods for solving algebraic equations up to the fourth degree. He also wrote on trigonometry and geometry and obtained the value of π as an infinite product.

VIEUXTEMPS, Henri (1820–81) Belgian violinist and composer, born in Verviers. He made his début at the age of eight, and became solo violinist to the tsar He composed six violin concertos, and taught at the St Petersburg and Brussels conservatories.

VIGÉE LEBRUN, (Marie) Élisabeth Louise, née **Vigée** (1755–1842) French painter, born in Paris, daughter of a painter. In 1776 she married J B P Le Brun, picture dealer and grandnephew of **Charles le Brun**. Her great beauty and the charm of her painting speedily made her work fashionable. Her portrait of **Marie Antoinette** (1779) led to a lasting friendship with the queen and she painted numerous portraits of the royal family. She left Paris for Italy at the outbreak of the Revolution, and after a triumphal progress through Europe, arrived in London in 1802. There she painted portraits of the Prince of Wales, Lord Byron, etc. In 1805 she returned to Paris.

VIGFÚSSON, Guðbrandur (1827–89) Icelandic scholar and philologist, born in western Iceland. He studied and lived in Copenhagen (1849–64), and thereafter in London and Oxford. He completed and edited the monumental *Icelandic-English Dictionary* (1874) originally undertaken by Richard Cleasby, and edited and translated (with **Frederick York Powell**) almost the entire body of Old Icelandic poetry (*Corpus poeticum boreale*, 2 vols, 1883), and a major anthology of early prose (*Origines Islandicae*, 2 vols, 1905). He was appointed reader in Scandinavian language and literature at Oxford University in 1884.

VIGNEAUD, Vincent du (1901–) American biochemist, born in Chicago. Professor at Cornell from 1938, he synthesized penicillin and oxytocin, discovered the structure of biotin, and won the 1955 Nobel prize for chemistry for his work on hormone synthesis.

VIGNOLA, Giacomo Barozzi da (1507–73) Italian architect, born in Vignola. He studied in Bologna and became the leading mannerist architect of his day in Rome. He designed the Villa di Papa Giulio for Pope **Julius III** and the church of the Il Gesu in Rome, which with its cruciform plan and side chapels had a great influence on French and Italian church architecture. His other works included the Palazzo Farnese in Piacenza.

VIGNOLES, Charles Blacker (1793–1875) Irish civil engineer, born in Woodbrook, County Wexford. He served in the British Army before starting work for **John Rennie** (1794–1874) as a railway civil engineer. He was involved with **George Stephenson** on the Liverpool–Manchester Railway, built the first railway in Ireland in 1832, and surveyed or built many others at home and abroad over the next 30 years. In 1841 he was appointed the first professor of civil engineering at University College, London. From 1848 to 1855 he was engaged on his greatest work, the construction of the four-span Nicholas suspension bridge over the Dnieper river at Kiev, at the time the longest in the world.

VIGNY, Alfred Victor, Comte de (1797–1863) French romantic writer, born in Loches, Indre-et-Loire. He served in the Royal Guards (1814–28), retiring with a captaincy. His experiences provided the material for *Servitude et grandeur militaires* (1835), a candid commentary on the boredom and irresponsibility, yet desire for devotion and self-sacrifice, induced by peacetime soldiering. He married an Englishwoman, Lydia Bunbury (1828). He had already published anonymously a volume of verse (1822) followed by *Eloa* (1824), the fallen angel condemned for self-pity, and *Poèmes antiques et modernes* (1826; expanded 1829), which includes his grand poetic conception of Moses as the hopelessly overburdened servant of God. His life, marred by domestic unhappiness and his failure to enter parliament (1848–49), was that of a congenital misfit who bears his loneliness with dignity. This is reflected in his work, especially in that masterpiece of romantic drama, *Chatterton* (1835), written for his love, the actress Marie Dorval, as well as in *Stello*, which describes the tragic fates of the young poets, **Chatterton**, Gilbert and Chénier, and is concluded in the posthumously published sequel *Daphné* (1912). These exemplify Vigny's pessimism, his exaltation of the poet as a godlike outsider whose knowledge is yet necessary for society. Other notable works include the historical novel *Cinq Mars* (1826), the plays *Othello* (1829) and *La Maréchale d'Ancre* (1831), the philosophical poems glorifying social order and discipline, *Les Destinées* (posthumous, 1864), and the biographical notes, *Journal* (1867).

VILLA-LOBOS, Heitor (1887–1959) Brazilian composer and conductor, born in Rio de Janeiro. His first published composition was *Salon Waltz* (1908), and a set of *Country Songs* (1910) show his interest in Brazilian folk music and folklore. After taking part in a scientific expedition up the Amazon studying folk music in 1915, he composed 12 symphonies, 16 string quartets, five operas and a number of large-scale symphonic poems on Brazilian subjects. He was also responsible for several ballets. A meeting with **Darius Milhaud** in 1918 aroused his interest in modern music and led him to spend several years in Paris, where his music was first heard in 1923. He composed several *Chôros*, in popular Brazilian styles, following these with the series of suites *Bachianas Brasileiras*, in which he treats Brazilian-style melodies in the manner of **Bach**. In 1932 he became director of musical education for Brazil and in 1945 founded the Brazilian Academy of Music.

VILLANI, Giovanni (c.1275–1348) Florentine historian. He wrote the *Cronica Universale* (1559), valuable for its vivid portrayal of Florence at the beginning of its prosperity. The chronicle was continued by his brother Matteo and his nephew Filippo.

VILLARD DE HONNECOURT (fl.1225–35) French master-mason and craftsman, working in north-west France. He is best known for his sketchbook of plans, drawings, details and texts held in the Bibliothèque Nationale, Paris, which served to disseminate the Gothic style and illustrate the operation of a masonic lodge. It is probable that he was the master mason of Cambrai Cathedral (no longer extant). He travelled widely and was evidently familiar with the cathedrals of Reims, Chartres and Laon.

VILLARI, Pasquale (1827–1917) Italian historian, born in Naples. He took part in the Neapolitan revolution of 1848 and was professor of history at Florence (1866–1909). He was made a senator in 1884 and was minister of education (1891–92). His works, of which *Machiavelli* (1877–82; trans 1888) was the best, were all translated by his English wife, Linda White.

VILLARS, Claude Louis Hector, Duc de (1653–1734) French soldier, born in Moulins. He distinguished himself in the wars of the Low Countries, on the Rhine, and in Hungary, fighting against the Turks. From 1699 to 1701 he represented France at Vienna. As commander in the War of the Spanish Succession (1701–14) he was sent to help the Elector of Bavaria in 1701. He crossed the Rhine, defeated the Markgraf of Baden at Friedlingen, and was made a marshal of France; next year he again crossed the Rhine, but his scheme for advancing upon Vienna was defeated by the obstinacy of the Elector. He was next commissioned to put down the Camisards (1704). He defended the north-eastern frontier against **Marlborough**; in 1708 he defeated the attempts of Prince **Eugene** to penetrate into France. In 1709 he was sent to oppose Marlborough in the north, but at Malplaquet was severely wounded. In 1711 he headed the last army France could raise, and with it fell upon the British and Dutch under **Albemarle**, who were entrenched at Denain (July 1712). He carried their entrenchments, and turning upon Prince Eugene, drove him under the walls of Brussels; then as plenipotentiary he signed the peace of Rastatt (1714). He became the principal adviser on military affairs and on foreign policy, was a strong opponent of **John Law**'s financial measures, and for a time lost favour at court. But the war of 1732–34 in Italy showed that the weight of years had left his military genius untouched. He died in Turin.

VILLEHARDOUIN, Geoffroi de (c.1160–1213) French nobleman and historian, born in the castle of Villehardouin in Aube. He took part in the Fourth Crusade (1199–1207), and became marshal of 'Romania'. His *Conqueste de Constantinople*—he was present at the capture—describing the events from 1198 to 1207, is one of the first examples of French prose.

VILLELLA, Edward (1936–) American dancer, born in Bayside, New York. An atheletic child, he studied at the School of American Ballet and the High School of Performing Arts before securing a degree from New York Maritime College, where he was a welter-weight boxing champion. Immediately upon graduation in 1957 he joined New York City Ballet, where **George Balanchine** gave him roles in *A Midsummer Night's Dream* (1962) and *Tarantella* (1964), which showed off his bravura speed and high jumps, while a piece like **Jerome Robbins**' *Watermill* (1972) underscored his contemplative control. He also scored hits in Balanchine's *The Prodigal Son* and Robbins' *Afternoon of a Faun*. He was artistic director of the Eglevsky Ballet Company from 1979 to 1984.

VILLEMAIN, Abel François (1790–1870) French author and politician, born in Paris. He became professor of rhetoric at the Lycée Charlemagne, the École Normale, and the Sorbonne (1816-26), and was minister of Public Instruction under **Guizot**. He wrote on the history of French literature, studies of Pindar and **Chateaubriand**, *Histoire de Cromwell* (1819),

Lascaris, ou les Grecs du XVe siècle (1825), and other works.

VILLEMIN, Jean-Antoine (1827–92) French physician and experimentalist, born in Prey (Vosges). He studied medicine in Strasbourg and Paris, where he received his MD in 1853. A modest man, he continued medical practice in Paris, but in addition operated a private laboratory where he worked assiduously in his spare time. Among his most fundamental observations was the discovery, in the 1860s, that material taken from the lung of a person with tuberculosis would, when inoculated into an animal, produce tuberculosis in the animal. This work pointed towards a specific infective agent, which **Robert Koch** discovered in 1882.

VILLENEUVE, Pierre Charles Jean Baptiste Sylvestre de (1763–1806) French naval commander, born in Valensoles (Basses Alpes). As rear-admiral, he commanded the rear division of the French navy at the battle of the Nile (1798), and saved his vessel and four others. In 1805 he took command of the fleet designed to invade England, but was brought to battle by **Nelson** off Cape Trafalgar and defeated. He was taken prisoner but released in 1806. On his way to report to **Napoleon** in Paris, he committed suicide.

VILLERMÉ, Louis-René (1782–1863) French physician, statistician and public health reformer, born in Paris. He studied medicine there before seeing medical military duty in the Napoleonic Wars. From the 1820s he turned his attention to preventive medicine, to the state of the prison system and to the causes of premature death in human beings. His works, especially *Tableau de l'état physique et moral* (2 vols, 1840), brought home the value of vital statistics to reformist-minded individuals in early industrial France.

VILLEROI, François de Neuville, Duc de (1644–1730) French soldier. He was educated with **Louis XIV** at court, where he was the glass of fashion, but was banished on account of a love affair. In 1680 he returned to court, and in 1693 became a marshal, having distinguished himself at Neerwinden. As commander in the Netherlands (1695–96) he showed great incapacity; and in Italy in 1701 he was defeated and taken prisoner by Prince **Eugene** at Cremona (1702). Again in command in the Netherlands, he was defeated by **Marlborough** at Ramillies (1706). Madame **de Maintenon** had him made guardian to **Louis XV**. **Philippe, Duke of Orléans**, sent him to live on his estate in 1722 because of his intrigues; but he was subsequently governor of Lyon.

VILLIERS See **BUCKINGHAM** and **CLARENDON, 4th Earl of**

VILLIERS, Barbara (1640–1709) Countess of Castlemaine and Duchess of Cleveland, mistress of King **Charles II**. The daughter of the 2nd Viscount Grandison, she was a noted society hostess. In 1659 she married Roger Palmer, who was created Earl of Castlemaine as a consolation when she became the king's mistress. Notorious for her amours, she became a Roman Catholic in 1663 and trafficked in the sale of offices, and in 1670 was created Duchess of Cleveland. Supplanted in the king's favours by the Duchess of Portland in 1673, she moved to Paris, where in 1705 she bigamously married Robert 'Beau' Fielding (the marriage was annulled in 1707). She had seven children, five of whom were acknowledged by King Charles as his: Anne, Countess of Suffolk (b.1661); Charles Fitzroy, Duke of Southampton (b.1662); Henry Fitzroy, Duke of Grafton (b.1663); Charlotte, Countess of Lochfield (b.1664); and George Fitzroy, Duke of Northumberland (b.1665).

VILLIERS, Charles Pelham (1802–98) English statesman and corn-law reformer, a younger brother of George, 4th Earl of **Clarendon**. He was educated at Haileybury and St John's College, Cambridge, and was called to the bar in 1827. He was returned for Wolverhampton as a Free Trader in 1835, and continued as its member for upwards of 60 years, latterly as a Liberal Unionist, becoming the 'Father of the House of Commons'. He made his first motion in favour of Free Trade in 1838, moving a resolution against the corn laws each year till they were repealed in 1846. From 1859 to 1866 he sat with cabinet rank as president of the poor-law board.

VILLIERS DE L'ISLE ADAM, Auguste, Comte de (1838–89) French writer, pioneer of the Symbolist movement, born in St Brieuc. He was a Breton count who claimed descent from the Knights of Malta. He dedicated his *Premières Poésies* (1856–58) to **de Vigny**, but developed into a considerable stylist in prose. His famous short stories, *Contes cruels* (1883) and *Nouveaux Contes cruels* (1888), are after the manner of **Poe**. Hegelian idealism and Wagnerian Romanticism inspire his highly didactic novels and plays. The former include *Isis* (1862) on the Ideal and *L'Ève future* (1886), a satire on the materialism of modern science. The latter include his masterpiece, *Axel* (1885). A pronounced Catholic aristocrat, he lived for a while with the monks of Solesmes.

VILLON, François, originally **François de Montcorbier** or **de Logos** (1431–after 1463) French poet, born in Paris. He took the surname of his guardian, Guillaume de Villon, a priest and a close relative, who enabled François to study at university, to graduate (1449) and to become MA (1452). While a student he fell into bad company and in 1455 had to flee from Paris after fatally wounding a priest in a street brawl. He joined a criminal organization, the 'Brotherhood of the Coquille', which had its own secret jargon in which Villon was to write some of his ballades. Pardoned in 1456, he returned to Paris and there wrote the *Petit Testament*. He took part in the organized robbery of the funds of the Collège of Navarre, and fled to the court of the Duke of Orléans at Blois. There he was sentenced to death for another unknown crime, but released as an act of grace on a public holiday. The same happened again at Meung-sur-Loire (1461), the year of the *Grand Testament*. In 1462–63 he was in trouble again for theft and brawling. Sentence of death was commuted to banishment in January 1463. He left Paris and nothing further is known of him. The first printed edition of his works was published in 1489. The *Petit Testament* comprises 40 octosyllabic octaves, the *Grand Testament* comprises 172, bridged by 16 ballades and other verse forms. Six of the Coquille jargon ballades have been definitely attributed to him.

VILLON, Jacques, real name **Gaston Duchamp** (1875–1963) French painter, born in Damville, half-brother of **Marcel Duchamp** and **Raymond Duchamp-Villon**. He began as a law student but went to Paris in 1894 to study art, met **Toulouse-Lautrec**, and exhibited at the Salon d'Automne from 1904. He took up Cubism c.1911 and exhibited with **Léger** and others working in that new style. He was represented in the Armory Show in New York in 1913, but did not win international fame until after World War II.

VINCENT, St (d.304) Spanish protomartyr, born in Saragossa. According to St **Augustine** he became a deacon. Under **Diocletian**'s persecutions, he was imprisoned and tortured at Valencia, where he died. His feast is on 22 January.

VINCENT, Sir Charles Edward Howard (1849–1908) English politician, born in Slinfold, in Sussex. He was the first director of CID, Scotland Yard. He wrote on criminal law and police code (1882), the law of extradition (1881), and was knighted (1896).

VINCENT DE BEAUVAIS (Latin **Vincentius Bellovacensius**) (c.1190–1264) French Dominican and encyclopaedist. He gathered together, under the patronage of **Louis IX**, the entire knowledge of the middle ages in his *Speculum Majus*, in three parts; *Naturale* and *Doctrinale et Historiale* (1473), to which *Speculum Morale* was added anonymously.

VINCENT DE PAUL, St (c.1581–1660) French priest and philanthropist, born in Pouy in Gascony. He was admitted to priest's orders in 1600. On a voyage from Marseilles to Narbonne in 1605 he was captured by corsairs and was sold into slavery in Tunis. His master, a renegade Savoyard, was persuaded by Vincent to return to the Christian faith; so, escaping, they landed in France in 1607. Having gone to Rome, he was entrusted with a mission to the French court in 1608, and became almoner of **Henri IV**'s queen. He formed associations for helping the sick, and in 1619 was appointed almoner-general of the galleys. Meanwhile he had laid the foundation of the Congregation of Priests of the Missions, sanctioned by **Urban VIII** in 1632, and called Lazarists from their priory of St Lazare in Paris. The Paris Foundling Hospital, the Sisterhood of Charity (1634), and associated lay nursing organizations were of his founding. He was canonized in 1737. His feast day is 19 July.

VINCENT OF LÉRINS, St (d.c.450) French religious, a monk of the island of Lerna (Lérins). He defined the three marks of Catholicity—'Quod ubique, quod semper, quod ab omnibus'. His *Commonitoria*, a treatise against heresies, was published in 1895.

VINCI See **LEONARDO DA VINCI**

VINER, Charles (1678–1756) English legal scholar, born in Salisbury. He studied law at Oxford but never qualified and never practised, yet he produced a massive *Abridgment* of the law of England in 23 volumes (1741–56). He left most of his considerable estate to Oxford University to enable it to found the Vinerian Scholarships and the Vinerian chair of English law, first held by Sir **William Blackstone**.

VINET, Alexandre Rodolphe (1797–1847) Swiss Protestant theologian and critic, born in Ouchy near Lausanne. He was ordained in 1819, became in 1835 professor of French language and literature at Basel and in 1837 of practical theology at Lausanne. He was forced to resign when he led a secession from the Swiss church in 1845. He published studies of French literature of the 16th–19th centuries, defended freedom of conscience and the disestablishment of the church.

VINJE, Aasmund, originally **Olavson** (1816–70) Norwegian poet and critic, born in Vinje. He was a leader of the movement to establish the 'national language' called *Landsmål* (later known as *Nynorsk*, New Norwegian), and produced a weekly journal, *Dølen*, from 1858 to 1866. He wrote a book of travel reminiscences on Norway (1861), and visited England in 1862 and published a critical *Norseman's View of Britain and the British* in English in 1863. His poetic works include *En Ballade om Kongen* (1853), his epic cycle *Storegut* (1866) and *Blandkorn* (1867).

VINNIUS, Arnoldus (Arnold Vinnen) (1588–1657) Dutch jurist. Professor of law at Leiden from 1633, he wrote a *Commentarius* on **Justinian**'s *Institutes* (1642) which, for at least a century, was the leading textbook on Roman law in European universities. It gives the text of each section, a commentary on the topic of each section and notes drawn from the best of the earlier text writers, with an observation on how the section was applied in contemporary Holland. *Selectarum juris quaestionum* (1653) is mainly devoted to Roman law but deals also with the law of his own time.

VINOGRADOFF, Sir Paul (1854–1925) Russian-born British social historian, born in Kostroma. He studied at Moscow and became professor of history there. He settled in England and in 1903 he was appointed professor of jurisprudence at Oxford. Knighted in 1917, he was an authority on medieval England, and among his writings are *Villeinage in England* (1892), *Growth of the Manor* (1905) and *English Society in the Eleventh Century* (1908).

VIOLLET-LE-DUC, Eugène Emmanuel (1814–79) French architect and archaeologist, born in Paris. In 1840 he became director of the restoration of the Sainte Chapelle in Paris, and from then on was the great restorer of ancient buildings in France, including the cathedrals of Notre Dame in Paris, Amiens, Laon, and the Château de Pierrefonds. He served as engineer in the defence of Paris, and was an advanced republican politician. His best-known work was his great *Dictionnaire raisonné de l'architecture française du XIe au XVe siècle* (1854–86).

VIOTTI, Giovanni Battista (1753–1824) Italian violinist and composer, born in Fontanetto. He lived mostly in Paris, where he was director of the Italian Opera and from 1792 was a wine merchant in London. He was one of the leading violinists of his day; his works include many violin concertos, and compositions for piano and for strings.

VIRCHOW, Rudolf (1821–1902) German pathologist and politician, and founder of cellular pathology, born in Schivelbein, Pomerania. He became professor of pathological anatomy at Würzburg (1849) and at Berlin (1856). His *Cellularpathologie* (1858) established that every morbid structure contained cells derived from previous cells. He contributed to the study of tumours, leukaemia, hygiene and sanitation. As a Liberal member of the Reichstag (1880–93) he strenuously opposed **Bismarck**.

VIRET, Pierre (1511–71) Swiss Protestant reformer, born in Orbe in Vaud. An associate of **Farel**, he converted Lausanne to the Protestant faith (1536).

VIRGIL, Polydore See **VERGIL**

VIRGIL (Publius Vergilius Maro) (70–19 BC) Roman poet, born in Andes, near Mantua in Cisalpine Gaul, where his father owned a small property. The boy was sent to school at Cremona and Milan, and at 16 went to Rome and studied rhetoric and philosophy. In 41 BC the victorious triumvirs were settling disbanded soldiers on confiscated lands throughout Italy. Virgil's farm was part of the confiscated territory; but by advice of the governor of the district, Asinius Pollio, he went to Rome, with special recommendations to Octavian (**Augustus**); and though his own property was not restored to him, he obtained ample compensation from the government, and became one of the endowed court poets who gathered round the statesman **Maecenas**. In 37 BC his *Eclogues*, ten pastorals modelled on those of **Theocritus**, were received with great enthusiasm. Soon afterwards he left Rome and moved to Campania. The generosity of Maecenas had placed him in affluent circumstances. He had a villa at Naples and a country-house near Nola. The *Georgics*, or *Art of Husbandry*, in four books, dealing with tillage and pasturage, the vine and olive, horses, cattle, and bees, appeared in 30 BC, and confirmed his position as the foremost poet of the age. The remaining eleven years of his life were devoted to a larger task, undertaken at the urgent request of the emperor, the composition of a great national epic based on the story of Aeneas the Trojan, legendary founder of the Roman nation and of the Julian family. This covered the hero's life from the fall of Troy to his arrival in Italy, his wars and alliances with the native Italian races, and his final establishment in his new kingdom. By 19 BC the *Aeneid* was practically completed, and in that year Virgil left Italy to travel in Greece and Asia; but in Athens he fell ill, and returned only to die. At his own wish he was buried in Naples, on the road to Pozzuoli; his tomb, for many hundreds of years after, was worshipped as a sacred place. A few juvenile pieces of more or less probable authenticity are extant under his name. These are the *Culex* and the *Moretum*, both in hexameter verse; the *Copa*, a short elegiac piece; and fourteen little poems in various metres, some serious, others trivial. The *Ciris* is now agreed to be by a contemporary imitator. The supremacy of Virgil in Latin poetry was immediate and almost unquestioned; his works were established classics even in his lifetime, and soon after his death they had become the textbooks of western Europe. By the 3rd century his poems ranked as sacred books, and were regularly used for purposes of divination. In the dark ages his fabled powers as a magician almost eclipsed his real fame as a poet; but with the revival of learning he resumed his old place.

VIRGINIA See **CLAUDIUS, Appius**

VIRIATHUS (d.139 BC) Lusitanian rebel. A herdsman, he headed a rising against the Romans, and from 151 to 141 BC repeatedly defeated Roman armies. He was murdered by the Romans.

VIRTANEN, Artturi Ilmari (1895–1973) Finnish biochemist, born in Helsinki. He became professor of biochemistry in 1939 at Helsinki, elucidating the processes by which plants obtain nitrogen and complex organic substances from the soil. He showed that silage can be preserved by dilute hydrochloric acid, and studied nutrition and the development of food resources, for which he was awarded the Nobel prize for chemistry (1945).

VISCHER, Peter (1455–1529) German sculptor in bronze, born in Nuremberg. He was responsible for the *King Arthur* statue at Innsbruck, the tomb of Archbishop Ernst at Magdeburg and the basic structure of that of St Sebald in Nuremberg. His sons Hans (1489–1550), Hermann (1486–1517) and Peter, the younger (1487–1528), were also distinguished sculptors.

VISCONTI the name, taken from the hereditary office of viscount, of a Milanese family of Ghibelline nobility which rose to prominence when Ottone Visconti (d. 1295) became archbishop of Milan in 1262 and his nephew Matteo (1250–1322) captain of the people.

VISCONTI, Ennio Quirino (1751–1818) Italianarchaeologist, son of **Giovanni Battista Antonio Visconti**. He was keeper of the Capitoline Museum from 1787. During the Roman Republic of 1798 he was one of the five consuls, then fled to Paris, where he became curator at the Louvre and professor of archaeology. In 1817 he went to England to examine the Elgin marbles. He wrote *Iconographie grecque* (1801) and *romaine* (1817).

VISCONTI, Filippo Maria (1392–1447) Milanese statesman, son of **Gian Galeazzo Visconti**, restored the unity of his father's dominions, but died without issue. The duchy passed to the **Sforza** family.

VISCONTI, Gian Galeazzo (1351–1402) Milanese statesman. He succeeded his father, Galeazzo II, as joint ruler (1378–85) with his uncle Bernabo, whom he put to death (1385). As duke (1385) he made himself master of the northern half of Italy bringing many independent cities into one state, arranged marriage alliances with England, France, Austria and Bavaria, and was a great patron of the arts.

VISCONTI, Giovanni (1290–1354) Italian prelate, archbishop and lord of Milan from 1349. He brought Genoa and Bologna under his jurisdiction.

VISCONTI, Giovanni Battista Antonio (1722–84) Italian archaeologist, father of **Ennio Visconti**. He succeeded **Winckelmann** as prefect of antiquities at Rome (1768), reorganized the Museo Pio-Clementino in the Vatican and with his son edited the catalogue of the museum's engravings. He supervised the excavations which led to the discovery of **Scipio**'s tomb.

VISCONTI, Lodovico Tullio Gioacchino (1791–1853) Italian architect, son of **Ennio Quirino Visconti**. From 1799 he worked in Paris; he built **Napoleon**'s mausoleum and was responsible for the scheme joining the Louvre and the Tuileries. His nephew, Pietro Ercole (1802–80), was commissioner of antiquities at Rome and curator of the Vatican art collections.

VISCONTI, Count Luchino (1906–76) Italian stage and film director, born in Milan. An early interest in music and the theatre led him to stage designing and the production of opera (notably his stagings at La Scala for **Maria Callas**), and ballet. A short spell as assistant to **Jean Renoir** turned his attention to the cinema. His first film as director, *Ossessione* (1942), took Italy by storm, in spite of trouble from the Fascist censors. In that film, and in *La Terra Trema* (1947) and *Rocco e i sui Fratelli* (1960), he showed the strict realism, formal beauty and the concern with social problems which are the hallmarks of all his films. These include *Il Gattopardo* (The Leopard, 1963), *The Damned* (1969) and *Death in Venice* (1971).

VISSER 'T HOOFT, Willem Adolf (1900–85) Dutch ecumenist, born in Haarlem. He graduated in theology at Leiden and served young people's organizations until his appointment in 1938 as general secretary of what was to become the World Council of Churches, a post he held until retirement in 1966. In that role he proved himself the foremost ecumenical statesman of his generation. He insisted that the younger churches be regarded as equal partners in the common Christian task. A versatile scholar who spoke several languages fluently, he wrote many books, among which were *None Other Gods* (1937), *The Struggle of the Dutch Church* (1946), and his *Memoirs* (1973).

VIT, Vincenzo de (1811–91) Italian scholar, born in Padua. He was editor of **Faccioloti** and Forcellini's *Lexicon Totius Latinitatis* (1858-79). A canon of Rovigo and town librarian, in 1850 he joined the brotherhood of **Rosmini**. His unfinished *Onomasticon* was to contain all proper names down to the 5th century.

VITELLIUS, Aulus (15–69) Roman emperor, a favourite of **Tiberius**, **Caligula**, **Claudius** and **Nero**. Appointed by **Galba** to the command of the legions on the Lower Rhine, he was proclaimed emperor at Colonia Agrippinensis (Cologne) at the beginning of 69; and his generals put an end to the reign of **Otho** by the victory of Bedriacum. Vitellius, during his brief reign, gave himself up to pleasure and debauchery. Many of his soldiers deserted when **Vespasian** was proclaimed emperor in Alexandria. Vitellius was defeated in two battles by his rival, dragged through the streets of Rome and murdered.

VITORIA See **ESPARTERO, Baldomero**

VITRUVIUS POLLIO, Marcus (1st century) Roman architect and military engineer. A north Italian in the service of **Augustus**, he wrote *De Architectura* (before AD 27), which is the only Roman treatise on architecture still extant.

VITRY, Jacques de (d.1240) French prelate and historian. Bishop of Acre (1216) and cardinal bishop of

Tusculum (1228), he is known by his *Historia Orientalis et Occidentalis*, a valuable source book.

VITTORIA See **VICTORIA, Tomás Luis de**

VITTORINI, Elio (1908–66) Sicilian novelist, critic and translator, born in Syracuse. He educated himself despite great obstacles, and he became Italy's most influential writer, helping younger writers. He was founder editor of *Il Politecnico* (1945–47) and *Il Menabò* (1959–66), and translated modern American writers like **Poe**, **Steinbeck** and **Faulkner**. *Conversazione in Sicilia* (1941, trans *Conversations in Sicily*, 1948) is his metaphorical masterpiece.

VITTORINO DA FELTRE (c.1378–1446) Italian educationist. In 1423 he was summoned to Mantua as tutor to the children of the Marchese Gonzaga and founded a school for both rich and poor children there (La Giacosa), in which he applied his own methods of instruction.

VITUS, St (early 4th century) Christian martyr, said to have been the son of a Sicilian pagan. He was converted by his nurse Crescentia and her husband Modestus, with whom he suffered martyrdom under **Diocletian**. He was invoked against sudden death, hydrophobia and chorea or St Vitus' Dance, and is sometimes regarded as the patron of comedians and actors. His feast day is 15 June.

VIVALDI, Antonio (1678–1741) Venetian violinist and composer, born in Venice, known as 'the Red Priest' because of his red hair. He took orders (1703), but gave up officiating and was attached to the hospital of the Pietà at Venice (1703–40). The twelve concertos of *L'Estro Armonico* (1712) gave him a European reputation; *The Four Seasons* (1725), an early example of programme music, proved highly popular; and he wrote many operas and some sacred music. Though he really consolidated and developed the solo concerto, he was forgotten after his death. **J S Bach** transcribed many of his concertos for the keyboard and from the 19th century they were increasingly played.

VIVARINI, Antonio (15th century) Venetian painter. He first worked in partnership with his brother-in-law Giovanni d'Alemagna and later with his brother **Bartolommeo Vivarini**. His paintings, often of Madonnas and saints, are modelled first on **Gentile da Fabriano** and then on **Mantegna** and **Giovanni Bellini**.

VIVARINI, Bartolommeo (15th century) Venetian painter, brother of **Antonio Vivarini**. He worked under the same influences, but his painting shows a step forward towards the Renaissance style.

VIVARINI, Luigi or **Alvise** (c.1446–c.1505) Venetian painter, son of **Antonio Vivarni**. He was possibly a pupil of both his father and uncle. Influenced by Antonello da Messina and **Bellini**, his works include portrait busts and altarpieces, especially a *Madonna and six Saints* (1480) in the Academy, Venice.

VIVES, Juan Luis, also known as **Ludovicus** (1492–1540) Spanish philosopher and humanist, born in Valencia. He studied at Paris and went on to become professor of humanities at Louvain in 1519. He dedicated his edition of **Augustine**'s *De Civitate Dei* to **Henry VIII**, who summoned him to England in 1523 as tutor to Princess Mary (**Mary I**). But he was imprisoned in 1527 for opposing Henry's divorce from **Catherine of Aragon** and after 1528 lived mostly in Bruges. His other writings include a treatise on education, *De Disciplinis* (1531) and a major three-volume work on psychology and scientific method, *De anima et Vita* (1538).

VIVIANI, René (1862–1925) French statesman, born in Sidi-bel-Abbés, Algeria. He was prime minister at the outbreak of World War I and in order to demonstrate France's peaceful intentions withdrew French forces from the German frontier. He was minister of justice (1915) and French representative at the League of Nations (1920).

VIVIN, Louis (1861–1936) French Primitive painter, born in Hadol. He was a post office employee until he retired in 1922. He painted mainly still-lifes and views of Paris and its parks. His naïve and charmingly coloured pictures are meticulous in every detail.

VIZETELLY, Henry Richard (1820–94) English journalist and publisher of Italian descent, born in London. As an engraver he soon contributed to the newly founded *Illustrated London News* and in 1843 set up in competition his own *Pictorial Times*. He became a foreign correspondent to the *Illustrated London News* in Paris (1865-72) and in Berlin (1872). He witnessed the siege of Paris and with his son, Ernest, wrote *Paris in Peril* (1867). As a publisher in later life, he produced inexpensive translations of French and Russian authors (later called the Mermaid series), notably of the works of **Zola**, which involved him in two legal actions for obscene libel. In 1893 his memoirs were published as *Glances Back Through Seventy Years*. His brother, Frank (1830–83), also a foreign correspondent for the *Illustrated London News*, was killed in the Sudan.

VLADIMIR I, Saint, known at **'the Great'** (c.956–1015) first Christian sovereign of Russia from 980. The son of Svyatoslav, Grand Prince of Kiev (d. 972), he became Prince of Novgorod in 970, and in 980 seized Kiev from his brother after his father's death. He consolidated the Russian realm from the Baltic to the Ukraine, extending its dominions into Lithuania, Galicia and Livonia, with Kiev as his capital. He made a pact with the Byzantine emperor **Basil II** (c.987), accepting Christianity and marrying his sister. He encouraged education and reformed legal institutions.

VLADIMIR II, Monomachus (1053–1125) ruler of Russia, great grandson of **Vladimir I**. He became by popular demand Grand Prince of Kiev in 1113 instead of the prior claimants of the Sviatoslav and Iziaslav families, thus founding the Monomakhovichi dynasty. A popular, powerful, enlightened and peaceful ruler, he colonized, built new towns, dethroned unruly princes and introduced laws against usury. He left careful instructions to his son and cousin in the manuals *Puchenie* and *Poslanie*.

VLAMINCK, Maurice de (1876–1958) French artist, born in Paris. He was largely self-taught, and for a time was a racing cyclist. About 1900 he began to work with **Derain**. At this time he was much influenced by **Van Gogh**, and by 1905 he was one of the leaders of the Fauves, using typically brilliant colour. From 1908 to 1914, however, he painted more realist landscapes under the influence of **Cézanne**. After 1915 his palette was more sombre, and his style more romantic than Cézannesque, though still with an Expressionist zest. He mainly lived in the country as a farmer, and this may have given him his consistent sensitivity to the nuances of landscape and atmosphere. Also a talented violinist, he wrote several books, including *Communications* (1921).

VODNIK, Valentin (1758–1819) Slovene poet and teacher, born in Zgornja Šiška, near Ljubljana. By his writings he helped to revive Slovene nationalism. He wrote poetry, educational and school books in the language of the peasantry, and this became established as the literary language of Yugoslavia.

VOELCKER, Augustus (1822–84) German agricultural chemist and writer, born in Frankfurt-am-Main. After studying at Göttingen and Utrecht, he worked in Edinburgh for the Highland and Agricultural Society of Scotland, was appointed professor of agriculture at the Royal Agricultural College, Cirencester (1849), and in 1857 was consulting chemist to the Royal Agricultural Society of England. His work on farm feeding stuffs, on soil research and on artificial manures greatly advanced agricultural chemistry.

VOET, Johannes (1647–1713) Dutch jurist, son of **Paulus Voet**. Professor at Utrecht and then at Leiden, he was the leading text-writer on the Roman-Dutch law. He compiled a great *Commentarius ad Pandectas* (1698–1704), a detailed exposition of **Justinian**'s *Digest* as adapted to conditions in the Netherlands, which is still a high authority in South African courts. He also wrote *Compendium Juris* (1683) widely used as a students' text, and *Elementa Juris* (1700).

VOET, Paulus (1619–77) Dutch jurist, father of **Johannes Voet**. Professor at Utrecht, he was a great scholar, and his two books, *De statutis eorum concursu* (1661), relevant in conflict of laws, and *De mobilium et immobilium natura* (1666), are both still referred to in South Africa.

VOGEL, Hans-Jochen (1926–) West German politician. He was successor to **Helmut Schmidt** as leader of the Social Democratic party (SPD) and the party's unsuccessful nominee for the chancellorship in 1983. Born in Göttingen into a Catholic family and educated as a lawyer at Munich University, he became SPD Land (state) chairman in Bavaria in 1972 and was elected, in the same year, mayor of Munich. Between 1972 and 1974 he was minister of housing and town planning, and between 1975 and 1981 he served in the Schmidt cabinet as justice minister, before being sent to West Berlin to serve as mayor and to 'clean up' and overhaul the unpopular local party machine. An efficient, if somewhat colourless, party centrist, Vogel has been SPD Bundestag leader since October 1982. Following his party's convincing defeat in the March 1983 federal election, he did not put himself forward as chancellor-candidate in January 1987. In June 1987, however, he replaced **Willy Brandt** as SPD chairman and has set about restoring the party's fortunes. His younger brother, Bernhard, has been Christian Democrat minister-president of Rhineland-Palatinate since 1976.

VOGEL, Hermann Carl (1841–1907) German astronomer, born in Leipzig. He became assistant and later director of the observatory at Potsdam (1882); known for spectroscopic studies of planets and stars, in 1889 he discovered spectroscopic binaries.

VOGEL, Hermann Wilhelm (1834–98) German chemist, born in Dobrilugk, Brandenburg. He taught at Berlin, and invented the orthochromatic photographic plate (1873), studied spectroscopic photography and designed a photometer.

VOGEL, Sir Julius (1835–99) New Zealand statesman, born in London. He edited and founded newspapers in Australia and New Zealand, where he was elected colonial treasurer in 1869. He established a government public trust office (1872), improved immigration facilities and planned the introduction of trunk railways, borrowing £10000000 for his public works programme. He formed a government in 1872 and was premier (1873–75). His resolution (1874) foreshadowed the abolition of the provinces. He resigned in 1875 to devote himself to business, but was again treasurer during the economic crisis in 1884.

VOGEL, Vladimir (1896–1984) Russian composer, born in Moscow. He studied in Moscow and under **Busoni** in Berlin. He composed orchestral works, chamber music and secular oratorios, including *Wagadu Destroyed* (1935) with saxophone accompaniment.

VOGLER, Abt (Georg Joseph) (1749–1814) German composer, born in Würzburg, the son of a violin maker. He was ordained priest at Rome in 1773, and made Knight of the Golden Spur and chamberlain to the pope. At Mannheim he established his first school of music; his second was in Stockholm. After years of wandering and brilliant successes in London and Europe as a player on his 'orchestrion' (a modified organ), he settled as kapellmeister at Darmstadt, and opened his third school, his pupils including **Weber** and **Meyerbeer**. His compositions and his theories of music are now forgotten; but his name survives in **Robert Browning**'s poem.

VOGÜÉ, Charles Jean Melchior, Marquis de (1829–1916) French archaeologist and diplomatist, born in Paris. He travelled in Syria (1853–54 and 1861), and was ambassador at Constantinople (1871-75) and at Vienna (1875–79). Elected to the Académie (1901), he wrote on the churches of Palestine (1860 and 1865).

VOGÜÉ, Eugéne Marie Melchior, Vicomte de (1848–1910) French historian, born in Nice, a cousin of Charles, Marquis de **Vogüé.** He was secretary at St Petersburg (1876–82) and was admitted to the Académie (1888). He wrote *Le Roman russe* (1886), a valuable study of the Russian novels of **Tolstoy** and **Dostoevsky**, *Les Morts qui parlent* (1899) and works on Syria and Egypt.

VOITURE, Vincent (1598–1648) French poet and letter-writer, born in Amiens. He was an original member of the Académie, and enjoyed the favour of **Gaston d'Orléans**, **Richelieu**, **Mazarin** and **Louis XIII**. His brilliant sonnets and *vers de société* were the delight of the Hôtel Rambouillet, but were not published till 1650.

VOLNEY, Constantin François Chasseb œuf, Comte de (1757–1820) French scholar and author, born in Craon in Mayenne. He studied medicine, history and oriental languages at Paris, adopted the name of Volney, and travelled in Egypt and Syria (1783–87) before publishing his valuable *Voyage* (1787). A zealous reformer, he was elected to the Constituent Assembly in 1789, but later was thrown into prison until the downfall of **Robespierre** (1794). His reputation chiefly rests on his famous work *Les Ruines, ou Méditations sur les révolutions des empires* (1791).

VOLSTEAD, Andrew J (1860–1947) American politician, born in Goodhue County, Minnesota. He practised law and entered congress as a Republican in 1903. He was the author of the Farmers' Co-operative Marketing Act, but is best known for the Prohibition Act of 1919, named after him, which forbade the manufacture and sale of intoxicant liquors. This Act, passed over President Woodrow **Wilson**'s veto, was in force until 1933.

VOLTA, Alessandro Giuseppe Anastasio, Count (1745–1827) Italian physicist, inventor of the electric battery, born in Como. From 1774 to 1804 he was professor of natural philosophy at Pavia. He retired to Como, but was summoned to show his discoveries to **Napoleon**, and received medals and titles at home and abroad. He developed the theory of current electricity, discovered the electric decomposition of water, invented an electric battery, the electrophorus, an electroscope and made investigations on heat and gases. His name is given to the unit of electrical potential difference, the volt.

VOLTAIRE, François Marie Arouet de (1694–1778) French author, the embodiment of the 18th-century 'enlightenment', born in Paris. His father, François Arouet, held a post in the chambre des comptes in Paris. He was educated at Collège Louis-le-Grand, the chief French seminary of the Jesuits. Leaving college at the age of 17, he was destined for the bar, but law disgusted him. Alarmed by the dissipated life which he was leading, his father gladly saw him admitted into the service of his godfather's brother, the Marquis de Châteauneuf, the French ambassador to Holland; but in consequence of an undiplomatic love affair with a French Protestant *émigrée* in The Hague, he was sent home. He again entered an attorney's office, but his stay there was short, and he soon obtained notoriety as the author of a satire on his successful rival in the poetic competition for an Academy prize. In 1716, on suspicion of satirizing the regent, the Duc d'**Orléans**, he was banished for several months from Paris; and in 1717–18, a savage attack accusing the regent of all manner of crimes resulted in eleven months' imprisonment in the Bastille, where he rewrote his tragedy *Œdipe*, began a poem on **Henri IV** and assumed the name Voltaire. *Œdipe* was performed in 1718, and was triumphantly successful. His next dramatic attempts were almost failures, and he devoted himself to his poem on Henri IV. But the authorities refused to sanction its publication on account of its championship of Protestantism and of religious toleration, so Voltaire had the epic poem surreptitiously printed in Rouen (1723) and smuggled into Paris, as *La Ligue ou Henri le Grand*. Now famous and a favourite at court, he was denounced by the Chevalier de Rohan-Chabot as a parvenu. Voltaire retorted with spirit, and circulated caustic epigrams on the Chevalier, whose revenge was to have Voltaire beaten up. Voltaire challenged the Chevalier and was once more thrown into the Bastille, and freed only on the condition that he would go at once to England, where he landed in May 1726. Here **Bolingbroke** introduced him to **Pope** and his circle. He made the acquaintance of **Peterborough**, **Chesterfield**, the Herveys and the Duchess of **Marlborough**, and became friendly with **Edward Young**, **James Thomson**, the Scottish poet, and **Gay**. He acquired some knowledge of **Shakespeare** and **Milton**, **Dryden** and **Butler**, **Addison**'s *Cato*, and the Restoration dramatists. He was strongly attracted to **Locke**'s philosophy, and he mastered the elements of **Newton**'s astronomical physics. Queen **Caroline of Brunswick** accepted his dedication to her of the *Henriade*, the new form of *La Ligue*; and when permitted to return to France in 1729 he took with him his *History of Charles XII* and the materials for his *Letters on the English*. He laid the foundation of his great wealth by purchasing shares in a government lottery and by speculating in the corn trade, ultimately increased by the profits from large army contracts. He formed an intimacy with Madame **du Châtelet-Lomont**, and went to live with her at her husband's château of Cirey in Champagne (1734). Here he wrote dramas (*Mahomet* (1741) and *Mérope* (1743) among them), poetry, his *Treatise on Metaphysics*, much of his *Siècle de Louis Quatorze* (1751) and *Les Mœurs et l'esprit des nations*, with his *Elements of the Philosophy of Newton* (1738). As well as from Madame du Châtelet, his correspondence (1740–50) testifies to a love affair with his niece, the widowed Madame Denis. Since the appearance of his *Letters on the English* he had been out of favour at the French court. But his *Princesse de Navarre*, performed on the occasion of the Dauphin's marriage (February 1745), pleased **Louis XV** by its clever adulation. This and the patronage of Madame **de Pompadour** procured him the appointments of official royal historian and of gentleman-in-ordinary to the king. In 1747 an imprudent speech at a court card-party drove him to take refuge with the Duchess de Maine, for whose amusement he now wrote *Zadig* and other oriental tales. When he was allowed to reappear at court, some injudicious flattery of Madame de Pompadour excited the indignation of the queen, and Voltaire had again to migrate. The death (1749) of Madame du Châtelet allowed him at last to accept the repeated invitation of **Frederick II, the Great**. In July 1750 Voltaire found himself in Berlin as king's chamberlain, with a pension of 20000 francs and board in one of the royal palaces. But he entered into questionable financial transactions with a Berlin Jew and Frederick was still more gravely offended by his satirical criticisms on **Maupertuis** in *Micronégas*, and in March 1753 Frederick and Voltaire parted, never to meet again. In Prussia Voltaire had published his *Siècle de Louis Quatorze* (1751). On his way home he was arrested at Frankfurt, through Frederick's representative there, instructed to recover from Voltaire a volume of the king's poems. Voltaire avenged himself by writing a malicious sketch of Frederick's character and account of his habits, first printed after Voltaire's death. He settled in 1755 near Geneva and after 1758 at Ferney, four miles from Geneva. In 1756–59 appeared his *Mœurs et l'Esprit des nations*, his pessimistic poem on the earthquake of Lisbon and that satirical masterpiece, the short story *Candide* which attacked what Voltaire understood by the Leibnizian optimistic theology that 'all is for the best in this best of all possible worlds'. The suspension of the *Encyclopédie* by the French government, and the condemnation by the parliament of Paris of a harmless poem of his own on natural religion, impelled him to declare war by word and deed against the bigoted, 'L'Infâme'. In 1762 appeared the first of his anti-religious writings which were to include didactic tragedies, biased histories, pamphlets and the *Dictionnaire philosophique* (1764). The judicial murder (1762) of **Jean Calas**, falsely accused of having, from Protestant zeal, killed one of his sons to keep him from turning a Catholic, aroused Voltaire to exert himself successfully to get his innocence established and to rescue members of the Calas family from punishment. This and similar efforts on behalf of victims of French fanaticism, for whom he provided a refuge at Ferney, won widespread admiration. The Genevan government prevented Voltaire from staging plays and from establishing a theatre in Geneva. **Rousseau**'s support for the Swiss government terminated Voltaire's friendship with the philosopher (1758). In 1778, in his eighty-fourth year, he was given a 'royal' welcome in Paris, when he arrived to put on his last tragedy, *Irène*. The excitement brought on illness and his death. After the revolution, which his works and ideas helped to foster, his remains were reinterred in the Panthéon, Paris.

VOLTERRA, Daniele da (c.1509–1566) Italian artist, born in Volterra. He was **Michelangelo**'s assistant, and painted the *Descent from the Cross* in the Trinità dei Monti in Rome.

VOLTERRA, Vito (1860–1940) Italian mathematician, born in Ancona. He was professor at Pisa, Turin and Rome. In 1931 he was dismissed from his chair at Rome for refusing to sign an oath of allegiance to the Fascist government, and he spent most of the rest of his life abroad. He worked on integral equations, mathematical physics and the mathematics of population change in biology.

VONDEL, Joost van den (1587–1679) Dutch poet and dramatist, born in Cologne of Dutch immigrant parents. He became a prosperous hosier in Amsterdam and devoted his leisure to writing satirical verse, himself turning from Anabaptism through Armenianism to Roman Catholicism. Having acquired a wide knowledge of the classics, he turned to Sophoclean drama and produced *Jephtha* (1659) and *Lucifer* (1654), a masterpiece of lyrical religious drama. He greatly influenced the German poetical revival after the Thirty Years' War (1618–48).

VON DER DECKEN See **DECKEN, Karl Klaus von der**

VON GUERARD, Eugene (Eugen John Joseph) (1811–1901) Austrian-born Australian landscape artist, born in Vienna, where his father was court painter to King **Francis I** of Austria. He studied in Düsseldorf and Naples before arriving in Geelong, Victoria, in 1852 to join the gold rush. He painted and worked in the goldfields around Ballarat, Victoria, before going to Melbourne in 1854. In 1855 he travelled extensively in Tasmania and South Australia and was a member of two expeditions to north Victoria and the Australian alps, which resulted in a number of mature landscapes. A painting from a later visit to New South Wales was accepted by the Royal Academy in 1865, and an album of Von Guerard's lithographs, *Australian Landscapes* was published in 1867. He was an influential teacher at the National Gallery of Victoria's School of Art from 1870 until 1882 when he left for Europe and London.

VON KLITZING, Klaus (1943–) German physicist, born in Schroda/Posen. He discovered the quantum Hall effect. He studied at Brunswick and Würzburg and became professor at Munich in 1980, and in 1985 director of the Max Planck Institute, Stuttgart. In 1977 he presented a paper on two-dimensional electronic behaviour in which the quantum Hall effect was clearly seen, but few realized its significance and von Klitzing only appreciated what had occurred in 1980. He was awarded the 1985 Nobel prize for physics.

VONNEGUT, Bernard (1914–) American physicist, born in Indianapolis. Educated at Massachusetts Institute of Technology, he spent his career with the A D Little Company, and from 1967 as professor of atmospheric science at New York State University. In 1947 he improved a method for artificially inducing rainfall, by using silver iodide as a cloud-seeding agent.

VONNEGUT, Kurt, Jr (1922–) American novelist, born in Indianapolis, Indiana. Educated at Cornell University, Chicago University and the Carnegie Institute, Pittsburgh, he served in the US army infantry (1942–45) and was given the Purple Heart. During the 1960s he emerged as one of America's most influential, potent and provocative writers, a ribald commentator of the horrors of the century: holocaustic wars, the desperate state of the environment, and the dehumanization of the individual in a society dominated by science and technology. *Player Piano* (1952) was his first novel and there were another three before *Slaughterhouse-Five* (1969), in which its two main characters—the author himself and the protagonist, Billy Pilgrim—see beneath the tragic realities of human history but make no attempt to effect change. The central event of the novel is the destruction of Dresden during World War II which the author witnessed as a prisoner-of-war. Later novels continued to satirize human folly in its various manifestations: *Breakfast of Champions* (1973), *Slapstick* (1973), *Jailbird* (1979) and *Deadeye Dick* (1982).

VON NIDA, Norman George (1914–) Australian golfer, born in New South Wales. He has some claim to be regarded as the pioneering Australian professional golfer in terms of competition: he was Australian Professional champion five times and Australian Open champion three times, winning both titles in 1950. Abroad his achievements were comparatively modest. He came third in the British Open in 1948 and won the Vardon Trophy for consistent overall performance in 1947 but his real importance was as a trailblazer for such as **Peter Thomson** and **Kelvin Nagle**. A peppery little man, he demanded high standards of conduct from spectators and was not slow to complain if these standards were infringed.

VON REZZORI, Gregor (1914–) Austrian novelist, born in the Bukovina, the remote eastward tip of the old Austrian empire. He was a descendant of an impoverished Sicilian noble family who moved to Vienna in the 18th century. He studied at Vienna University and for a time lived in Bucharest. In Germany after the war he was a filmmaker, broadcaster and writer. His most significant books are *Memorien eines Antisemiten* (1979; trans *Memories of an Anti-Semite*, 1984) and *Der Tod Meines Bruders Abel* (1976; trans *The Death of My Brother Abel*, 1986).

VON SYDOW, Max Carl Adolf (1929–) Swedish actor, born in Lund. A student at the Royal Academy in Stockholm, he made his film début in *Bara en Mor* (1949). A member of various theatrical companies, he began a long association with director **Ingmar Bergman** at the Municipal Theatre of Malmö. On film their many collaborations include *The Seventh Seal* (1957), *Through A Glass Darkly* (1961) and *The Shame* (1968). He made his American film début as **Jesus Christ** in *The Greatest Story Ever Told* (1965) and has spent many years as a character actor of international standing in films like *Hawaii* (1966), *The Exorcist* (1973), *Hannah and Her Sisters* (1986) and *Pelle, the Conqueror* (1988). He has also continued to appear on stage, making his Broadway début in *The Night of the Tribades* (1977) and performing at the Old Vic in *The Tempest* (1988). In 1988 he made his début as a film director with *Katinka*.

VON WRIGHT, Georg Henrik (1916–) Finnish philosopher and logician, born in Helsinki. He associated with the Vienna Circle of logical positivists and worked closely with **Wittgenstein** in Cambridge (1948–51). He was professor of philosophy at Helsinki from 1946 to 1961 and held many visiting positions in American universities. He has made particular contributions to philosophical logic and to ethics in works such as *The Logical Problem of Induction* (1941, 2nd edition 1957), *Form and Content in Logic* (1941), *The Varieties of Goodness* (1971), *Norm and Action* (1971) and *Freedom and Determination* (1980).

VORAGINE, Jacobus de (1230–98) Italian prelate and hagiologist, a Dominican, born in Viareggio near Genoa. He became archbishop of Genoa in 1292. He wrote the *Golden Legend*, a famous collection of lives of the saints, translated by **Caxton** in 1483, and he is also said to have produced the first Italian translation of the Bible.

VORONOFF, Serge (1866–1951) Russian physiologist, born in Voronezh. Educated in Paris, he became director of experimental surgery at the Collège de France. He specialized in grafting animal glands into the human body and wrote on his theory connecting gland secretions with senility.

VOROSHILOV, Klimenti Efremovich (1881–1969) Soviet politician, born near Dnepropetrovsk in the Ukraine. He was president of the Soviet Union from **Stalin's** death (1953) to 1960. He joined the Communist party in 1903 and political agitation soon brought about his exile to Siberia. He remained a fugitive right up to 1914, and took a military rather than a political role in the 1917 Revolution. From 1925 to 1940 he was commissar for defence and so mainly responsible for the modernization of the Red Army and its success in defeating **Hitler**'s invasion of 1941. His long friendship with Stalin, dating from 1906, possibly excused some of his later mistakes.

VÖRÖSMARTY, Michael (1800–55) Hungarian poet and dramatist, born in Szekesfehervar. He was an advocate and, after **Kossuth**'s revolution, a member of the National Assembly in 1848. He wrote the national song, *Szozat* (1840), lyric and epic poetry and eleven plays, of which the fairy drama *Csongor es Tünde* (1831) is his masterpiece. He also translated Shakespearean tragedies.

VORSTER, Balthazar Johannes (1915–83) South African politician, born in Jamestown. He graduated in law at Stellenbosch University in 1938. He had developed an interest in politics as a student and joined an extreme Afrikaner nationalist movement. He contested the Brakpan seat for the Afrikaner party in 1948, being narrowly defeated, but was later accepted in the National party, becoming MP for Nigel in 1953. In Dr **Verwoerd**'s government he was from 1961 minister of justice, being responsible for several controversial measures. After the assassination of Dr Verwoerd in September 1966 he was elected prime minister. Under him apartheid remained the official policy. In 1978, after the 'information scandal' involving large-scale misappropriation of government funds, he resigned for health reasons and was elected state president; the following year he resigned this position after the Erasmus commission found him jointly responsible.

VORTIGERN (5th century) British ruler, reported by **Gildas, Bede** and **Nennius** to have invited the Saxons, led by **Hengist** and Horsa, into Britain to help him against the Picts, and to have married Hengist's daughter, Rowena.

VOS, Cornelis de (1585–1651) Flemish painter in Antwerp, chiefly of portraits and religious and mythological pieces. He worked occasionally for **Rubens**. His brother, Paul (1590–1678), painted animals and hunting scenes.

VOSS, Johann Heinrich (1751–1826) German poet and philologist, born in Sommersdorf in Mecklenburg. He studied at Göttingen, and in 1778 went from editing the *Musenalmanach* at Wandsbeck to be schoolmaster at Otterndorf. Here he translated the *Odyssey*. In 1782 he became rector of a school at Eutin, and in 1789 he issued his translation of **Virgil**'s *Georgics*. In 1802 he settled in Jena, and in 1805 was appointed professor at Heidelberg, where he translated **Horace**, **Hesiod**, **Theocritus**, Bion, Moschus, **Tibullus** and **Propertius**; other translations were of **Aristophanes** and (with the aid of his two sons) **Shakespeare**. *Luise* (1795), an idyll, is his best original poem.

VOSSIUS, Gerard Jan (1577–1649) Dutch scholar, born near Heidelberg. He studied at Leiden, and became in 1600 rector of the school at Dort and in 1615 of the theological college of Leiden. His *Historia Pelagiana* (1618), with its Arminian leanings, brought down upon him the wrath of the orthodox. **Laud** made him a prebend in Canterbury. In his *De Historicis Latinis* (1627) he made a prudent recantation. In 1632 he became professor of history in the Athenaeum in Amsterdam. His chief works are *Commentaria Rhetorica* (1606), *De Historicis Graecis* (1624) and *Aristarchus* (1635).

VOSSIUS, Isaak (1618–88) Dutch scholar, son of **Gerard Jan Vossius**, born in Leiden. He travelled in England, France and Italy, collecting many valuable manuscripts, and was at the court of Queen **Kristina** of Sweden, but returned to Holland in 1658. In 1670 he settled in England, and, although a libertine, was appointed by **Charles II** a canon of Windsor. He edited the epistles of **Ignatius** (1646), **Justin**, **Pomponius Mela** and **Catullus**, and wrote on chronology.

VOUET, Simon (1590–1649) French painter, born in Paris. After 14 years in Italy, he returned to France, where his religious and allegorical paintings and decorations in the Baroque style became very popular. A contemporary of **Poussin**, who criticized him but was not a serious rival during his lifetime, his pupils included **Lebrun** and **Le Sueur**.

VOWELL, John See **HOOKER, Richard**

VOYNICH, E L See **BOOLE, George**

VOYSEY, Charles (1828–1912) English theistic theologran, born in London, father of **Charles Francis Annesley Voysey**. He studied at St Edmund's Hall, Oxford, was transferred from his curacy at St Mark's, Whitechapel, in 1863, to the living of Healaugh near Tadcaster, for preaching against the doctrine of perpetual punishment. His sermons and writings on inspiration led to the deprivation of his living in 1871. He then became founder and pastor of a Theistic church in London, and wrote on *The Mystery of Pain, Death and Sin* and on *Theism*.

VOYSEY, Charles Francis Annesley (1857–1941) English architect and designer, born in London, son of the theologian **Charles Voysey**. A disciple of **John Ruskin** and **William Morris**, he designed traditional country houses influenced by the Arts and Crafts Movement, with accentuated gables, chimney stacks, buttresses and long sloping roofs. He was also an important designer of wallpaper, textiles, furniture, and metalwork.

VRANITZKY, Franz (1937–) Austrian politician. Educated at what is now the University of Commerce, Vienna, he embarked on a career in banking and in 1970 became adviser on economic and financial policy to the minister of finance. After holding senior appointments in the banking world he became minister of finance himself in 1984 and two years later succeeded Fred Sinowatz as federal chancellor.

VRCHLICKY, Jaroslav pseud of **Emil Frída** (1853–1912) copy mertv.txt a: Czech poet and translator of the classics of European poetry, born in Laun. He was a pupil of **Victor Hugo** who inspired the *Fragments of the Epic of Humanity*. His best ballads, *Legend of St Procopius* (1879) and *Peasant Ballads* (1886), are on nationalistic and patriotic themes. His early lyric poetry on love and the pleasures of life gave way to reflections upon suffering and misfortune. In 1893 he was appointed professor of European literature at Prague.

VRIENDT, Cornelis de See **FLORIS, Cornelis**

VRIES See **DE VRIES, Hugo**

VUILLARD, (Jean) Édouard (1868–1940) French artist, born in Cuiseaux. He shared a studio with **Bonnard**, and was strongly influenced by **Gauguin** and by the vogue for Japanese painting. Although his outlook was limited and mainly devoted to flower pieces and to simple and intimate interiors, these are painted with an exquisite sense of light and colour. He also produced murals for public buildings, such as the Théâtre des Champs-Elysees and Palais de Chaillot.

VULPIUS, Christiane See **GOETHE**

VYGOTSKY, Lev Semyonovich (1896–1934) Russian psychologist, born in Orsha. He studied various social sciences at Moscow University, and turned to psychology when aged 28. This last decade of his life, when he was at the Institute of Psychology in Moscow (1924–34), was his productive period. His theories of cognitive development, especially his view of the relationship between language and thinking, have strongly influenced both Marxist and western psychology. His best-known work, *Thought and Language* (1934), was briefly suppressed as being against Stalinist-approved psychology. He was open to intuition, had an undogmatic approach to experimental methodology, and moved easily between the pure and applied fields. He always emphasized the role of the cultural and social factors in the development of cognition.

Thought and Language is now a classic text in university courses in psycholinguistics. He died from tuberculosis.

VYSE, Charles (1882–1971) English potter and sculptor, born in Staffordshire into a family of potters. He trained as a modeller at the Hanley School of Art, obtaining a sculpture scholarship to the Royal College of Art where he also worked from 1905 to 1910. After working in the Staffordshire Potteries, he established a workshop with his wife at their studio in Cheyne Row, Chelsea. From the beginning they made stylized figures and groups realistically modelled and coloured. He exhibited his work regularly and experimented with wood-ash glazes and early Chinese glaze effects. In the early 1930s he specialized in skilfully drawn brushwork decoration on more simple forms. The studio was damaged by air raids in 1940 and they moved from London. He became modelling and pottery instructor at the Farnham School of Art.

VYSHINSKY, Andrei (1883–1954) Soviet jurist and politician, born of Polish origin in Odessa. He studied law at Moscow University but was debarred from a lectureship on account of his Menshevik revolutionary activities until 1921, when he left the Red Army. He became professor of criminal law and simultaneously attorney-general (1923–25) and was rector of Moscow University (1925–28). He was notoriously the public prosecutor at the Metropolitan-Vickers trial (1933) and the subsequent state trials (1936–38) which removed **Stalin**'s rivals, Bukharin, **Radek**, **Zinoviev**, **Kamenev** and Sokolnikov. He was promoted deputy foreign minister under **Molotov** (1940) and was permanent Soviet delegate to the United Nations (1945–49, 1953–54), succeeding Molotov as foreign minister in 1949 until the death of Stalin (1953). He was the cynically brilliant advocate of the disruptive and negative Stalin-Molotov foreign policies, the author of many textbooks on Soviet Law and the recipient of the Order of Lenin and the Stalin prize in 1947.

W

WAAGE, Peter (1833–1900) Norwegian chemist. He became professor at Christiania (Oslo) in 1862, and established (1864) with **Cato Guldberg** the law of mass action.

WACE, Robert (c.1115–c.1183) Anglo-Norman poet, born in Jersey. He studied in Paris, and was a canon of Bayeux between 1160 and 1170. He wrote several verse lives of the saints, but his main work was *Roman de Brut* (1155), a free Norman-French version of **Geoffrey of Monmouth**'s *Historia Regum Britanniae*, used by **Layamon** and **Mannyng**. He also wrote the *Roman de Rou* (**Rollo**), an epic of the exploits of the Dukes of Normandy.

WACKENRODER, Wilhelm Heinrich (1773–98) German writer. He was an early exponent of Romanticism and a close friend of **Tieck**, with whom he collaborated in *Herzensergiessungen eines kunstliebenden Klosterbruders* (1797) and *Phantasien über die Kunst* (1799).

WADDELL, Helen (1889–1965) English medievalist and writer, born in Tokyo. She published *Lyrics from the Chinese* (1913), *Mediaeval Latin Lyrics* (1929), *The Wandering Scholars* (1927), *Peter Abelard* (1933), *The Desert Fathers* (1936), amongst others.

WADDING, Luke (1588–1657) Irish theologian and scholar, born in Waterford. He studied in Lisbon and Coimbra, and entered the Franciscan order in 1607. In 1617 he became president of the Irish college in Salamanca, and was a founder in 1625 of the Irish Franciscan College of Saint Isidore in Rome, and the Ludovisian College for Irish secular clergy in 1627. He was famed for his *Annales Ordinis Minorum* (8 vols, 1625–54; the history of the Franciscans), *Scriptores Ordinis Minorum* (1650), and a monumental edition (1639) of **Duns Scotus**.

WADDINGTON, Conrad Hal (1905–75) English embryologist and geneticist. He was professor of animal genetics at Edinburgh University 1947–70. He introduced important concepts into the discussion of evolutionary theory (including the proposal that Lamarckianism could be incorporated into orthodox Darwinian genetics) and wrote a standard textbook on embryology, *Pıincipals of Embryology* (1956). In addition to his important work in genetics and embryology, he also helped to popularize science through more general texts such as *The Ethical Animal* (1960) and *Biology for the Modern World* (1962).

WADDINGTON, David Charles (1929–) English politician. After Oxford University, where he was president of the Conservative Association, he qualified and practised as a barrister but soon sought election to the House of Commons. Following three unsuccessful attempts he became member for Nelson and Colne in 1968, subsequently representing the Clitheroe and Ribble Valley constituencies. After a number of junior posts under **Margaret Thatcher** he was made government chief whip in 1987 and in 1989, when **Douglas Hurd** became foreign secretary, succeeded him as home secretary. A right-winger within his party, Waddington became one of the very few home secretaries openly to have supported the return of capital punishment.

WADDINGTON, William Henry (1826–94) French statesman and archaeologist, born in Paris, the son of an Englishman who became a French subject. He was educated chiefly in England, devoted himself to study and travel in Asia Minor, Syria and Cyprus and wrote *Voyage archéologique en Grèce et en Asie Mineure* (1866–77). He became a member of the national assembly and the senate, and was ambassador at London from 1883 until 1892.

WADE, George (1673–1748) English soldier, born probably in Westmeath. He entered the army in 1690, and after the Jacobite rebellion of 1715 judiciously pacified and disarmed the clans in the Scottish highlands, where he constructed (1726–37) a system of metalled military roads, with forty stone ('Wade') bridges. He became a privy councillor and a lieutenant-general in 1742, and a field marshal in 1743. He was unsuccessful in engagements in the Netherlands in 1744. During the Jacobite Rising of 1745 he was commander-in-chief of **George II**'s forces in England, but failed to engage Prince **Charles Edward Stewart**'s army, both on its advance into England and on its retreat from Derby. He was replaced by the Duke of **Cumberland**.

WADE, Sir Thomas Francis (1818–95) English diplomat and scholar, born in London. After a short career as a soldier, including active service in China, he became a member of the diplomatic corps in China and was the British ambassador in Peking from 1871–83. In 1888 he was appointed the first professor of Chinese at Cambridge University, holding this post until 1895. Among his works is the *Peking Syllabary* (1859), in which the Wade system of romanization is employed; this transliteration system was later modified by Wade's successor at Cambridge, **Herbert Giles**.

WADE, (Sarah) Virginia (1945–) English tennis player, born in Bournemouth, but brought up in South Africa. She competed at Wimbledon for 20 years, and won the singles there in 1977 when she was ranked number two. In 1968 she took the American Open title, and she also won the Italian championship in 1971 and the French championship in 1972. She was a Wightman Cup player for 16 years, and towards the end of her career captained the side.

WADSWORTH, Edward (1889–1949) English artist, born in Yorkshire. He studied engineering in Munich, attended the Slade School in 1910, and was associated with **Wyndham Lewis**, **Roger Fry**, Unit One, and the London Group. He is known for his still-lifes and seascapes with marine objects, painted in tempera with dreamlike clarity and precision.

WAERDEN, van der, Bartel Leendert (1903–) Dutch mathematician, born in Amsterdam, where he obtained his doctorate in 1926. He was professor at Groningen (1928–31), Leipzig (1931–45), Johns Hopkins (1947–48), Amsterdam (1948–51), and Zürich (1951–62). He has worked in algebra, algebraic geometry, and mathematical physics, and more recently has published books on the history of science and mathematics in the ancient world such as *Science awakening* (1954). His classic textbook *Moderne Algebra* (1931) was influential in publicizing the new algebra developed by **David Hilbert**, Ernst Steinitz, **Emil Artin**, **Emmy Noether** and others, and his book on the application of group theory to quantum mechanics (1932) showed its relevance to physics.

WAGENFELD, Wilhelm (1900–) German designer, born in Bremen. He studied, and later taught, at the Bauhaus, and has remained faithful to the principles which it enshrined. His designs are simple, unadorned and functional. Best known are those for mass-produced glass, and for Rosenthal ceramics. He has taught during much of his career, thus extending his influence as a designer.

WAGNER, Adolph (1835–1917) German economist, born in Erlangen. He was professor at Vienna, Hamburg, Dorpat, Freiburg and Berlin. In his numerous works he represented the historical school and supported state socialism.

WAGNER, Otto (1841–1918) Austrian architect and teacher, considered the founder of the modern movement. Professor at the Vienna Academy (1894–1912), his pupils included **Josef Hoffmann** and **Joseph Olbrich**. His most influential work was produced at the end of his career, such as Karlsplatz Station (1898–99) and Am Steinhof Church (1905–07), both flourishes of Art Nouveau tempered by traditional construction. In the main hall of K K Portsparkasse (savings bank) in Vienna (1904–06) he created what is universally regarded as the first example of modern architecture in the 20th century. His aims were to create an architecture appropriate to the age, out of a synthesis of historical models, modern materials and technology able to function practically and symbolically.

WAGNER, Robert, originally **Robert John Wagner Jnr** (1930–) American actor, born in Detroit, Michigan. He attended Black-Foxe Military Institute and decided to become an actor, winning a long-term contract with Twentieth Century Fox. After a small role in *The Happy Years* (1950) he appeared as charming juvenile leads in a succession of war, western and adventure films like *The Silver Whip* (1953), *Prince Valiant* (1954) and *The True Story of Jesse James* (1957). He was cast against type as a killer in *A Kiss Before Dying* (1956) and also played comedy in *The Pink Panther* (1963). However, his greatest popularity has been on television where his boyish romantic appeal, suave manner and light humour were seen as a jewel thief in *It Takes A Thief* (1965–69), an ex-con man in *Switch* (1975–77) and a jet-set detective in *Hart to Hart* (1979–84). He was married to actress Natalie Wood from 1957 to 1962 and again from 1972 until her death in 1981.

WAGNER, (Wilhelm) Richard (1813–83) German composer, born in Leipzig. He was educated chiefly at Dresden. His musical training was perfunctory until he was accepted as a pupil by Weinlig of the Thomasschule in 1831. This came as the result of a formidable but abortive concert overture which Heinrich Dorn (1804–92), a friend of the family and conductor at the new Leipzig Court Theatre, had been cajoled into performing. Some immature efforts were followed by his first opera *Die Feen* (1834), adapted from **Gozzi**'s *Donna Serpente* and owing much to **Weber**'s *Oberon*. It was not, however, performed during the composer's lifetime. His next effort, *Das Liebesverbot* (1836), flopped deservedly after one performance at Magdeburg, where he had obtained the post of conductor at the opera house, and where he met Minna Planer, a member of the company, who became his wife in 1836. The Magdeburg opera soon went bankrupt, as did the theatre at Königsberg, where Wagner had found his next post. Riga, where Dorn was now teaching, seemed more promising, but he resolved to try his luck in Paris with his new partially-finished opera based on **Bulwer-Lytton**'s romance *Rienzi*. There, in spite of **Meyerbeer**'s help, he barely made a living by journalism and doing hack operatic arrangements. He left Paris in 1842 with *Rienzi*, which he had finished in a debtors' prison, still unperformed but now accepted for presentation at Dresden, where it scored a resounding success. *Der fliegende Holländer* (1843) was not so well received, but Wagner was shortly appointed kapellmeister at Dresden. *Tannhäuser* (1845) also failed through too stringent economies in production and poor interpretation by the cast; when restaged at a later date it succeeded. *Lohengrin* was finished in 1848, but by this time Wagner was deeply implicated in the revolutionary movement and barely escaped arrest by fleeing from Saxony. Aided financially by **Liszt** at Weimar, he went first to Paris and later to Zürich. *Lohengrin* was eventually produced at Weimar by Liszt in 1850. During his exile he again had to make a living by writing, among other things, *Art of the Future* (1849), the anti-Semitic *Judaism in Music* (1850), *Opera and Drama* (1851), and the autobiographical *Communication to my Friends* (1851–52). The poem of the *Ring* cycle was finished in 1852, and in 1853 he began the music of *Das Rheingold*, followed by *Die Walküre* (1856) and Acts 1 and 2 of *Siegfried* (1857). In 1857–59 he was at work on *Tristan und Isolde*, based on the old German version of the legend by Gottfried von Strassburg, and the opera is often claimed to have been inspired by his current love affair with Mathilde, wife of his friend and patron Otto Wesendonck. Once again he sought to gain favour in Paris, and eventually **Napoleon III** called for a command performance of *Tannhäuser*, but the opera failed. In 1861 he was allowed to return to Germany, but he still had a hard battle for recognition. *Tristan* was accepted at Vienna but abandoned as impracticable before it could be performed, and, now aged 50, pursued by creditors and vilified by critics, the composer was on the point of giving up in despair when the tide dramatically turned. The eccentric young king of Bavaria, **Ludwig II**, impressed by the pageantry of *Lohengrin*, read Wagner's *Ring* poem with its pessimistic preface. He summoned Wagner to his court, and lavished hospitality on him. *Tristan* was staged with brilliant success at Munich in 1865, but Wagner's extravagance, political meddling, and preferential treatment aroused so much hostility that he was obliged to withdraw temporarily to Switzerland. Cosima, wife of the musical director, **von Bülow**, and daughter of Liszt, left her husband and joined him, eventually marrying him in 1870 after being divorced, Minna having died in 1866. In Switzerland he finished *Die Meistersinger*, his only non-tragic piece, which scored a success in 1868. But his greatest ambition, a complete performance of the *Ring*, was as yet unfulfilled. Productions in Munich of *Das Rheingold* in 1869 and *Die Walküre* in 1870 were against Wagner's wishes, as he dreamed of an ideal theatre of his own. Determined to fulfil his wish, he set about raising funds himself, and on a fraction of the required total plus a large amount of credit he started the now famous theatre at Bayreuth, which opened in 1876 with a first complete programme of the *Ring* cycle. *Parsifal*, his last and perhaps greatest opera, was staged in 1882, a year before his sudden death from a heart attack. Wagner reformed the whole structure of opera. The one canon was to be dramatic fitness, and to this end he abandoned the classical tradition of recitative and aria, replacing it with an ever-changing dramatic line linked with the emotional colour of the story and accentuated skilfully by use of the *leitmotiv*, which he was the first to adopt with a definite purpose. His works show a progressive development. *Rienzi* is in the grand opera style of Meyerbeer and **Spontini**; *Der* *fliegende Holländer* strikes out in a new style, followed up in *Tannhäuser* and reaching perfection in *Lohengrin*. From this time dates the music drama, of which *Tristan* is the most uncompromising type. The *Ring* (*Walküre*, *Siegfried*, *Gotterdämmerung*, with the *Rheingold* as introduction) is full of his most characteristic writing and orchestration. It is loosely based on the old Teutonic legend of the Nibelungen, but the symbolism and the purport of the story is purely Wagnerian, while the ideology stems from **Schopenhauer**. *Parsifal*, from **Wolfram von Eschenbach**'s version of the Grail legend with its mysticism, stands by itself. Wagner's music, life and writings are apt to arouse either blind adulation or violent antipathy, but seldom indifference. Supremely egotistical and unable to sense when he was wrong, he was capable of somersaults of opinion and conduct which mystified and sometimes antagonized his friends, as with Meyerbeer, his erstwhile Good Samaritan, whom he mercilessly insulted in *Judaism in Music*, and his one-time admirer **Nietzsche**, for whom Siegfried had once appeared as the prototype of his Superman, but who later came to see in the composer the embodiment of decadence. In his own time Wagner was set up with Liszt as the deity of the Romantic faction in opposition to the followers of **Brahms** and **Schumann**, and for many years clashes between the rival partisans were the bane of concert-promoters and conductors all over Europe. Wagner was a prolific writer of letters and prose, and many editions and translations have appeared. He wrote an autobiography, *My Life* (new ed, 1983).

WAGNER, Siegfried (1869–1930) German musician, son of **Richard Wagner**, born near Lucerne. He was trained as an architect but later turned to music as a conductor and composer of operas and other music. He was director of the Bayreuth Festspielhaus from 1909. In 1915 he married Winifred Williams (1897–1980), who directed the Bayreuth Festivals until 1944.

WAGNER, Wieland (1917–66) son of **Siegfried Wagner**, born in Bayreuth. He took over the directorship of the Festspielhaus at his father's death and revolutionized the production of the operas, stressing their universality as opposed to their purely German significance. He died at Munich.

WAGNER-JAUREGG, or **Wagner von Jauregg, Julius** (1857–1940) Austrian neurologist and psychiatrist, born in Wels. He became professor at Graz (1889) and Vienna (1893). He won the 1927 Nobel prize for physiology or medicine for his discovery in 1917 of a treatment for general paralysis by infection with malaria, the forerunner of shock therapy.

WAGONER, Dan (1932–) American modern dancer and choreographer, born in Springfield, West Virginia. With a degree in pharmacy, he started dancing for fun, but by his mid twenties was dancing full time, studying dance at Connecticut College and then with **Martha Graham** in New York. From 1958 to 1962 he performed with her company and with the **Merce Cunningham** Dance Company. He joined **Paul Taylor**'s company in 1962, creating many roles there in pieces like *Aureole* and *Orbs*. In 1969 he formed the small group, Dan Wagoner and Dancers, and has been making work for them since. With the retirement of **Robert Cohan** he was appointed artistic director of London Contemporary Dance Company in 1988. Work includes *Taxi Dances* (1974), *Seven Tears* (1979), *Spiked Sonata* (1981), *An Occasion for Some Revolutionary Gestures* (for Ballet Rambert, 1985) and *Fleet as a Bird* (1985). *George's House* (1985), set in and outside the poet **George Montgomery**'s New Hampshire home, was made for video.

WAIN, John Barrington (1925–) English critic and novelist, born in Stoke-on-Trent. He studied at, and was elected fellow of, St John's College, Oxford, and lectured in English literature at Reading University (1947–55) before turning freelance author. His first four novels, *Hurry on Down* (1953), *Living in the Present* (1955), *The Contenders* (1958) and *Travelling Woman* (1959), tilt at post-war British, particularly London, social values as viewed by a provincial. His debunking vigour and humour has affinities with that of **Kingsley Amis**. He has also written poetry such as *Weep Before God* (1961) and *Feng* (1975), edited literary magazines and produced a notable collection of *Preliminary Essays* (1957) in literary criticism. Later publications include *The Young Visitors* (1965), *The Pardoner's Tale* (1978), and *Lizzie's Floating Shop* (1981); he was professor of poetry at Oxford (1973–78). He also wrote the autobiographical *Sprightly Running* (1962).

WAINEWRIGHT, Thomas Griffiths (1794–1847) English art critic, painter, forger and probably poisoner, born in Chiswick. He took to writing art criticisms and miscellaneous articles for the periodicals under various pseudonyms, including 'Janus Weathercock'. He married and, soon outrunning his means, committed forgery (1822, 1824), and almost certainly poisoned with strychnine his half-sister-in-law (1830), probably also his uncle (1828), mother-in-law (1830) and possibly others. The sister-in-law had been fraudulently insured for £16000, but two actions to enforce payment failed; and Wainewright, venturing back from France in 1837, was sentenced to life transportation for his old forgery. In Van Diemen's Land (Tasmania) he painted portraits, ate opium, and died in Hobart Hospital. He was the subject of several literary works, and was the 'Varney' of **Lytton**'s *Lucretia* (1846) and the 'Slinkton' of **Dickens**'s *Hunted Down* (1860). His *Essays and Criticisms* were edited, with a memoir, by William Carew Hazlitt (1880).

WAINWRIGHT, Jonathan Mayhew (1883–1953) American soldier, born in Walla-Walla, Washington. In World War II he commanded the epic retreat in the Bataan peninsula after **MacArthur**'s departure during the Philippines campaign in 1942. Taken prisoner by the Japanese he was released in 1945 and awarded the Congressional Medal of Honour.

WAISMANN, Friedrich (1896–1959) Austrian philosopher, born in Vienna. He became a prominent member of the Vienna Circle, along with **Carnap** and **Schlick**, but modified the doctrines of logical positivism in important ways. He later taught at Cambridge and at Oxford. He argued that most empirical concepts have an 'open texture', which means that we cannot completely foresee all the possible conditions in which they might properly be used, and that even empirical statements cannot therefore be strictly verified by observation. His main philosophical works include *The Principles of Linguistic Philosophy* (1965) and *How I See Philosophy* (1968).

WAITE, Terry (Terence Hardy) (1939–) English religious adviser, born in Cheshire. Educated at Wilmslow School, the Church Army College, London and, privately, in the USA, he was appointed lay training adviser to the bishop of Bristol (1964–68), the archbishop of Uganda, Rwanda and Burundi (1968–71), consultant with the Roman Catholic Church (1972–79) and adviser on Anglican Communion affairs to **Robert Runcie**, archbishop of Canterbury, in 1980. A man of great diplomatic skills, he undertook many overseas assignments and in 1987, while making inquiries in Beirut about European hostages, disappeared. Despite worldwide efforts to secure his release and that of his fellow hostages, no precise news of his whereabouts has been forthcoming.

WAITZ, Georg (1813–86) German historian, born in Flensburg. He was professor from 1849 till 1875 at Göttingen, where he formed the Göttingen historical school. Editor of (1875–86) and contributor to the *Monumenta Germaniae Historica*, he wrote the great *Deutsche Verfassungsgeschichte* (1844–78) and works on Schleswig-Holstein and Ulfilas.

WAITZ, Greta (1953–) Norwegian athlete, born in Oslo. Rising to prominence in 1975, when she set a world record at 3000 metres (9:34.2, and later, in 1977, 8:46.6), for more than a decade she rivalled Ingrid Kristiansen as the world's greatest female distance runner. She has set a unique four world best times for the marathon. In 1979, in the New York marathon—a race she won eight times—she became the first woman to run it in under two and a half hours. By 1983 she had brought her time down to 2:25.29. As winner of the marathon at the inaugural world championships in 1983, she became the first ever official world champion at any event.

WAITZ, Theodor (1821–64) German anthropological psychologist, born in Gotha. He was professor of philosophy at Marburg from 1848, and author of *Anthropologie der Naturvölker* (1859–71) and works on psychology and pedagogics.

WAJDA, Andrzej (1926–) Polish film director, born in Suwalki. A member of the Polish Resistance at the age of 16 in World War II, he later studied art at the Krakow Academy of Fine Arts, and in the Lodz film school. His first feature film, *A Generation* (1954), dealt with the effects of the war on disillusioned Polish youth. The results of war, the hollowness of the traditional idea of military heroism, and the predicament of individuals caught up in political events were themes to which he was continually to return in such films as *Kanal* (1956), *Ashes and Diamonds* (1957), *Lotna* (1959) and *Landscape after the Battle* (1970). In *Everything for Sale* (1968) he made a deeply personal tribute to the star of several of his films and his close friend, Zbigniew Cybulski, killed in a car accident in 1967. In this he used the making of a film as the framework of the story, and he was to use the film-making process as a setting in the two films for which he is now best known outside Poland, *Man of Marble*, (1977) and *Man of Iron* (1981). The former deals with the Stalinist era, and the latter uses film made during the events of 1981 in Gdansk and the rise of the Solidarity trade union. Wajda has made many other films, ranging from romantic comedy to epic, including literary adaptations such as *The Wedding* (1972) and *Shadow Line* (1976); he has also worked in television and the theatre. He is now resident and working in France. Andrzej Wajda has worked extensively with the Stary Theatre of Krakow, and has produced several adaptations from **Dostoyevsky**, including a section from *Crime and Punishment*, in a vivid, expressionistic style.

WAKE, William (1657–1737) English prelate, born in Blandford. He became bishop of Lincoln (1705) and archbishop of Canterbury (1716–37). His writings include *State of the Church and Clergy of England* (1703). He worked for union between the Anglican and Nonconformist churches.

WAKEFIELD, Edward Gibbon (1796–1862) English colonial statesman, born in London. Sentenced for abduction in 1827, he wrote in prison *A Letter from Sydney* (1829), which outlined his theory of colonization by the sale of smallholdings, not transportation. He expanded his theories in *England and America* (anon, 1833) and *A View of the Art of Colonization* (1849). He influenced the South Australian Association (which founded South Australia in 1836) and, as a secretary (1838) to Lord **Durham**, the Durham Report on Canada. He formed (1837) the New Zealand Association and sent a shipload of colonists there to force the British government to recognize it as a colony and forestall France. With George William, 4th Baron **Lyttleton**, he founded (1850) the Anglican colony of Canterbury, and emigrated there in 1853.

WAKEFIELD, Gilbert (1756–1801) English scholar and controversialist, born in Nottingham. He became a fellow of Jesus College, Cambridge, renounced his Anglican orders and became classical tutor in dissenting colleges at Warrington and Hackney. He was opposed to the slave trade, field sports, war and public worship, and was a critic of civil and ecclesiastical government and of **Pitt**. **Richard Watson**'s defence of the latter evoked Wakefield's libellous 'Reply', for which he was imprisoned for two years (1799–1801) in Dorchester. His works include editions of Greek and Roman poets, notably **Lucretius** (1796–99), Bion, Moschus and **Horace**'s *Georgics*. He also published *Silva Critica* (1789–95), illustrating the Scriptures from classical sources.

WAKELEY, Thomas (1795–1862) English surgeon, born in Membury, Devon, the founder and first editor of the *The Lancet* (1823). Through this weekly medical paper he denounced abuses in medical practice and made exposures which led to the Adulteration of Food and Drink Act (1860). He was MP for Finsbury (1835–52), and coroner from 1839, procuring reforms for coroners' courts.

WAKSMAN, Selman Abraham (1888–1973) Russian-born American biochemist, born in Priluka in the Ukraine. He took US nationality in 1915, graduating the same year at Rutgers University, where he ultimately became professor of microbiology in 1930. His researches into the breaking down of organic substances by micro-organisms and into antibiotics led to his discovery of streptomycin (1943), for which he was awarded the Nobel prize for physiology or medicine in 1952. He wrote *Enzymes* (1926), *Principles of Soil Microbiology* (1938), and the autobiographical *My Life with the Microbes* (1954).

WALBURGA, Walpurgis, or **Walpurga, St** (c.710–c.779) English religious, born in Wessex, sister of St **Willibald**. She joined St **Boniface** on his mission to Germany, and became abbess of Heidenheim, where she died. Her relics were transferred (c.870) to Eichstätt. Walpurgis night (April 30) arose from the confusion between the day of the transfer of her remains (the night of 1 May), and the popular superstitions regarding the flight of witches on that night. Her feast day is 25 February.

WALCOTT, Clyde (1926–) West Indian cricketer, born in Bridgetown, Barbados. With **Everton Weekes** and **Frank Worrall**, he formed the great trilogy of West Indian batsmen of the 1950s. Although very tall he started off as a Test wicket-keeper, but later concentrated on his batting. He played 44 times for West Indies, scoring 3798 runs, averaging 56.88, and 15 of his 40 centuries were obtained in Tests. Against Australia in 1954–55 he twice scored two centuries in the same Test match.

WALD, George (1906–) American biochemist, born in New York City. He studied zoology at New York University and at Colombia, and did research under **Otto Warburg** in Berlin, and spent his career thereafter at Harvard (1932–77), working mainly on the biochemistry of vision. His discovery in 1933 of vitamin A in the retina was a major step; later work showed that rhodopsin, the light-sensitive pigment of the eye, has a molecule composed of a protein fragment linked to a structure derived from vitamin A. For their discoveries concerning the primary physiological and chemical visual processes in the eye, he shared the 1967 Nobel prize for physiology or medicine with **Ragnar Granit** and **Haldan Hartline**

WALDEN, Paul (1863–1957) Russian chemist, born in Wenden, Latvia. He discovered, and gave his name to, a type of optical isomerism (Walden inversion).

WALDHEIM, Kurt (1918–) Austrian statesman, born near Vienna, educated at Vienna. He entered the Austrian foreign service in 1945, worked at the Paris embassy (1948–51) and was head of the personnel department at the foreign ministry (1951–55). He was minister and subsequently ambassador to Canada (1955–60) and director-general of political affairs at the ministry (1960–64). From that year he was permanent representative at the UN, with a break (1968–70) to take the post of foreign minister. In 1971 he fought unsuccessfully the Austrian presidential election, and in 1972 succeeded **U Thant** as secretary-general of the UN, a post he held until 1981. In 1986 he sought the Austrian presidency again and this time was successful but his victory was marred by allegations that, as a Nazi intelligence officer in World War II, he had some involvement in the transportation of Jews to death camps.

WALDO, or **Valdes, Peter** (fl.1175) French religious leader, born in Lyon. A merchant to trade, he became a preacher in Lyon (1170) and practised voluntary poverty. He was eventually excommunicated and banished from Lyon in 1184 with his followers, who because of their vow of poverty were known as 'The Holy Paupers'. They became known as the Waldenses.

WALDOCK, Sir Claud Humphrey Meredith (1904–81) English jurist, born in Colombo, Sri Lanka. Educated at Uppingham and Brasenose College, Oxford, he was professor of international law at Oxford (1947–72), member of the European Commission on Human Rights (1954–61) (president, 1955–61), and judge of the European Court of Human Rights (1966–74) (president 1971–74). A judge of the International Court of Justice (1973–81) (president 1979–81), he acted as consultant on many issues of international law, wrote *The Regulation of the Use of Force by Individual States* (1952) and edited Brierley's *Law of Nations* (1963).

WALDORF See **ASTOR**

WALDSEEMÜLLER, Martin (c.1480–c.1521) German cartographer, born in Radolfzell. At St Dié he made use of an account of the travels of **Vespucci** to publish (1507) the map and globe on which the new world was first said to have been called America.

WALDSTEIN See **WALLENSTEIN, Albrecht Wenzel Eusebius von**

WALDTEUFEL, Emile (1837–1915) French composer, born in Strasbourg. He studied at the Paris Conservatoire and joined a piano manufacturer's until he was appointed pianist to the Empress Eugénie, wife of **Napoleon III**. A prolific composer of dance music, several of his waltzes, notably *The Skaters* and *Estudiantina*, remain popular.

WAŁESA, Lech (1943–) Polish trade unionist, born in Popowo into a once affluent, but by then ruined, agricultural family. Following a technical education, he worked as an electrician at the Lenin Shipyard at Gdansk between 1966–76 and became a trade union organizer, chairing the shipyard's strike committee in 1970. He was sacked in 1976, after leading a major strike, and moved to the ZREMB concern, before being dismissed in 1979. In 1980 he was re-employed at the Lenin Shipyards at Gdansk and, after chairing an Inter-Institutional Strike Committee, founded the Solidarność (Solidarity) 'free trade union'. Solidarność organized a series of strikes which, led by Walesa, a charismatic and devout Catholic, drew widespread public support and forced substantial political and economic concessions from the Polish government during 1980–81. However, in December 1981 Solidarność was outlawed and Walesa arrested, following the imposition of martial law by General **Jaruzelski**. Walesa was released in November 1982 and was awarded the Nobel prize for peace in October 1983 and granted a personal audience with Pope **John Paul II** when he visited Poland during the same year. After leading a further series of crippling strikes during 1988, he negotiated an historic agreement with the Jaruzelski government in 1989, under whose terms Solidarność was re-legalized, and a new, semi-pluralist 'socialist democracy' established. Following parliamentary elections in 1989, a Solidarność-led coalition government was formed later that year.

WALEWSKA, Marie (1789–1817) Polish countess. Mistress of **Napoleon.** Their son became **Count Walewski**.

WALEWSKI, Alexandre Florian Joseph Colonna, Count (1810–68) French diplomat, illegitimate son of **Napoleon**. He held various appointments, including that of ambassador to Britain (1851), and was foreign minister (1855–60) and minister of state (1860–63).

WALKER, Sir Alan Edgar (1911–) Australian Methodist clergyman and social activist, born in Sydney. He graduated there and in 1935 was ordained. His ministry in a coal-mining area of New South Wales first prompted his Christian social views, further developed while superintendent of the Waverley Methodist Mission (1944–54), and in the influential Sydney Central Methodist Mission (1958–78). He began a telephone counselling ministry that soon spread throughout the world, and after official retirement became the World Methodist Council's director of evangelism. His publications include *The Whole Gospel for the Whole World* (1957), *God the Disturber* (1973), *Standing up to Preach* (1983), and *Life in the Holy Spirit* (1986).

WALKER, Alice Malsenior (1944–) American novelist and poet, born in Eatonville, Georgia, into a poor black family. Educated at Spelman College, Atlanta, and Sarah Lawrence College, she has been employed registering voters, as a social worker, and as a teacher and a lecturer. An accomplished poet, she is, however, better known for her novels, of which *The Color Purple* (1982) is her third and most popular. The winner of the 1983 Pulitzer prize for fiction and later made into a successful film, it tells in letters the story of two sisters in the cruel, segregated world of the Deep South between the wars. It was preceded by *The Third Life of Grange Copeland* (1970) and *Meridian* (1976).

WALKER, George (1618–90) Irish clergyman, and governor of Derry (Londonderry), born of English parents in County Tyrone. He studied at Glasgow University, and became rector of Lissan, County Derry (1669), and Donaghmore near Dungannon, in 1674. In 1688 he raised a regiment at Dungannon to help garrison Londonderry for its successful resistance to the 105-day siege in 1689 by **James II**'s forces, and became joint governor. He led sallies against the enemy and exhorted the citizens by rousing sermons. For this he received the thanks of **William III** and the House of Commons, degrees from Oxford and Cambridge, and was nominated bishop of Derry. He fell at the battle of the Boyne and is commemorated by the Walker

Monument (1828) in Londonderry. He wrote *A True Account of the Siege of Londonderry* (1689).

WALKER, Sir James (1863–1935) Scottish chemist, born in Dundee. Professor at Dundee (1894–1908) and at Edinburgh (1908–28), he is known for his work on hydrolysis, ionization, and amphoteric electrolytes.

WALKER, John (1674–1747) English ecclesiastical historian, born in Exeter. He is noted for his account (1714), called forth by the writings of **Calamy** on the ejected Nonconformists, of the sufferings of the clergy in the Revolution (1689).

WALKER, John (1732–1807) English dictionary-maker, born in Colney Hatch. He was by turns actor, schoolmaster and peripatetic teacher of elocution (from 1771). He compiled a *Rhyming Dictionary* (1775), still in print as the *Rhyming Dictionary of the English Language*, and a *Critical Pronouncing Dictionary* (1791).

WALKER, John (1770–1831) English antiquary, born in London. His works included *Curia Oxoniensis*, *Oxoniana*, *Curious Articles from the Gentleman's Magazine* (1809), and *Letters Written by Eminent Persons* (1813).

WALKER, John (c.1781–1859) English inventor, born in Stockton-on-Tees. There, in 1827, as a chemist, he made the first friction matches, called by him 'Congreves' (alluding to **William Congreve**'s rocket), but which were later named lucifers and matches by others.

WALKER, Kath (Kathleen Jean) (1920–) Australian poet and aboriginal rights activist, born in Brisbane, Queensland, and brought up with the Noonuccal tribe on Stradbroke Island, Queensland. Of part aboriginal ancestry, from the age of 13 she worked in domestic service in Brisbane, gaining her education mainly from the libraries of her employers. She became a member of the Australian Women's Army Service during World War II, and afterwards became involved in aboriginal activism. In 1964 she became the first aboriginal writer to be published in English, with her collection of poems *We are Going*, followed by *The Dawn is at Hand* (1966). These poems, with other writings, were republished in 1970 as *My People, a Kath Walker Collection*. In 1972 she published a book of stories in traditional aboriginal form, *Stradbroke Dreamtime*. She has won a number of awards including the Mary Gilmore Medal. She visited the USA on a Fulbright Scholarship from 1978 to 1979, lecturing on aboriginal rights, and has been active on many aboriginal interest committees including the Aboriginal Arts Board. In 1985 she published *Quandamooka, the art of Kath Walker*. She runs a Centre for Aboriginal Culture, for children of all races, on Stradbroke Island, and has adopted the tribal name of Oodgeroo Noonuccal.

WALKER, Peter Edward (1932–) English Conservative politician. As a young man he was sufficiently successful in the City of London to have the wealth to pursue a political career. He was chairman of the Young Conservatives (1958–60) and has represented Worcester, where he farms, in the House of Commons since 1961. He held ministerial posts under **Edward Heath** and in **Margaret Thatcher**'s governments was agriculture secretary (1979–83), energy secretary (1983–87) and secretary of state for Wales (1987–90). Regarded as a Conservative 'liberal', he is noted for his 'coded criticisms' of some of the extreme aspects of Mrs Thatcher's policies.

WALKER, Thomas (1784–1836) English author, born in Chorlton-cum-Hardy near Manchester. A fellow of Trinity College, Cambridge, he was called to the bar in 1812 and became a magistrate of Lambeth Police Court in 1829. From May until December 1835, he published the weekly periodical *The Original*, a general magazine containing well-known articles on gastronomy. This has since reappeared in editions and selections under other titles such as *The Art of Dining* (1928).

WALKER, William (1824–60) American buccaneer and adventurer, born in Nashville, Tennessee. He studied medicine at Edinburgh and Heidelberg, which he practised in the US, as well as law and journalism. He landed (1853) with a force in the Mexican state of Lower California, declaring (1854) it, with the neighbouring Sonora, an independent republic, but was soon forced to withdraw to US territory. He next invaded (1855) Nicaragua, took Granada, and was elected president; his government, recognized (1856) by the US, restored slavery. He published *The War in Nicaragua* (1860). Twice expelled (1857) from Nicaragua, he entered (1860) Honduras, taking Trujillo, but was apprehended by the captain of a British sloop-of-war and given up to the Honduran authorities, who had him shot.

WALKINSHAW, Clementina See **STEWART, Charles Edward**

WALL, Max (Maxwell George Lorimer) (1908–1990) English actor and comedian, born in London. He made his first stage appearance when he was 14, playing Jack in *Mother Goose* with a travelling pantomime company in the West Country. He made his first London appearance in 1925, as a speciality dancer in *The London Revue*. He subsequently appeared in variety, revue, pantomime and radio. Over the years he perfected a laconic comedy routine, and earned acclaim as one of the finest British comics of his time. In 1966 he appeared as Père Ubu in **Jarry**'s *Ubu Roi*. Subsequently, the plays of **Samuel Beckett** became his forte. He appeared in a notable one-man show, *Aspects of Max Wall*, in 1974.

WALLACE, Alfred Russel (1823–1913) Welsh naturalist, born in Usk, in Gwent. He worked as a surveyor and a teacher in Leicester, then travelled and collected (1848–52) in the Amazon basin, with **Henry Walter Bates**, and (1854–62) in the Malay Archipelago. His memoir, sent to **Darwin** in 1858 from the Moluccas, formed an important part of the Linnaean Society meeting which first promulgated the theory of evolution by means of natural selection, modifying the nature, and hastening the publication, of Darwin's *The Origin of Species*, a work amplified by Wallace's *Contributions to the Theory of Natural Selection* (1870) and *Darwinism* (1889). Excluding man from the unaided operation of natural selection, he wrote *On Miracles and Modern Spiritualism* (1881). In his great *Geographical Distribution of Animals* (1876), *Island Life* (1880), and earlier work, Wallace contributed much (including 'Wallace's Line' between faunas) to the scientific foundations of zoogeography. Other works include *Travels on the Amazon and Rio Negro* (1853), *Palm Trees of the Amazon* (1853), *The Malay Archipelago* (1869), *Tropical Nature* (1878), *Australasia* (1879), *Land Nationalization* (an advocation, 1882), *Vaccination, a Delusion* (1898), *The Wonderful Century* (1898), *Man's Place in the Universe* (1903), *My Life, an Autobiography* (1905), and *The World of Life* (1910).

WALLACE, DeWitt (1889–1981) American publisher and founder of *The Reader's Digest* magazine, born in St Paul, Minnesota, the son of the dean (later president) of Macalester Presbyterian College. A student drop-out from the University of California, he took various odd jobs while building up a collection of articles he had condensed in order to improve his mind. In 1921 he married a Canadian-born social worker, Lila Bell Acheson (1889–1984), and in 1922 they launched *The Reader's Digest* as a pocket-sized mail-order magazine with 1500 subscribers. It became the largest-circulation magazine in the world, with its headquarters at Pleasantville, near New York. In 1938 a British editon was launched, followed by several foreign-language editions. In 1972 both he and his wife were awarded a Presidential Medal of Freedom, and in 1973, at the age of 83, they both officially retired.

WALLACE, Edgar (1875–1932) English writer. He was found abandoned in Greenwich when nine days old and brought up by a Billingsgate fish-porter. He served in the army in South Africa, where he later became a journalist (1899), and in 1905 he published his first success, the adventure story *The Four Just Men*. Another early series in a different vein was set in West Africa and included *Sanders of the River* (1911) and *Bones* (1915). From then on he wrote prolifically—his output numbering over 170 novels and plays—being best remembered for his crime novels, such as *The Clue of the Twisted Candle* and *The Ringer* and *The Squeaker*. He became a scriptwriter in Hollywood, where he died. He published his autobiography, *People*, in 1926.

WALLACE, Henry (1836–1916) American agriculturist and writer, born near West Newton, Pennsylvania. He trained for the church but turned to farming and agricultural journalism, founding in 1895 the successful periodical *Wallace's Farmer*.

WALLACE, Henry Agard (1888–1965) American agriculturist and statesman, son of **Henry Cantwell Wallace**, born in Adair County, Iowa. He edited *Wallace's Farmer* from 1933 until 1940, when he was nominated vice-president to **Franklin D Roosevelt**, whose 'new deal' policy he supported. He was chairman of the Board of Economic Warfare (1941–45) and secretary of commerce (1945–46). He failed to obtain renomination as vice-president in 1944, and unsuccessfully stood for president in 1948.

WALLACE, Henry Cantwell (1866–1924) American agriculturist, born in Rock Island, Illinois, son of **Henry Wallace**. He helped his father to found *Wallace's Farmer*, which he edited from 1916. For a long time secretary of the Corn Belt Meat Producers' Association, he was appointed US secretary of agriculture in 1921.

WALLACE, Lew (Lewis) (1827–1905) American author and soldier, born in Brookville, Indiana. He served in the Mexican War (1846–48) and with distinction as a major-general in the Federal army in the American Civil War (1861–65). Governor of Utah (1878–81) and minister to Turkey (1881–85), he was author of several novels, including the remarkably successful religious novel *Ben Hur* (1880), which has twice formed the subject of a spectacular film.

WALLACE, Sir Richard (1818–90) English art collector and philanthropist, born in London, illegitimate son of the 3rd Marquis of Hertford. He was MP from 1873 to 1885. In 1842 he inherited from his father a large collection of paintings and objets d'art later bequeathed (1897) by his widow to the nation. These now comprise the Wallace Collection, housed in Hertford House, London, once his residence. During the siege of Paris (1870–71) he equipped ambulances and founded a British hospital there.

WALLACE, (William) Vincent (1813–65) Irish operatic composer, born in Waterford. He emigrated to Australia and is well-known for the first of his operas, *Maritana* (1845), and for *Lurine* (1860).

WALLACE, also **Walays** or **Wallensis ('Welshman') Sir William** (c.1274–1305) Scottish patriot, chief champion of Scotland's independence, reputedly the second son of Sir Malcolm Wallace of Elderslie, near Paisley. Blind **Harry** associates his early years with Dundee and Ayrshire; but it is uncertain whether he was present at the burning of the English garrison in Ayr, or if this marked the start of the War of Independence. In 1297, leading a small band of men, Wallace burnt Lanark and killed the English sheriff, Hazelrig. Later that year he met **Edward I**'s army and won a decisive victory at Stirling Bridge, routing the English. Following this, the English were expelled from Scotland and a devastating raid was inflicted on the north of England. In retaliation Edward invaded Scotland in 1298, meeting Wallace at Falkirk, where the Scots were this time crushed. Wallace continued briefly to wage a guerrilla war before escaping to France in 1299 where he tried to enlist support for the Scottish cause. He returned in 1303, but in 1305 was arrested near Glasgow by Sir **John Menteith**, sheriff of Dumbarton. Taken to London he was condemned and hanged, drawn and quartered. His quarters were sent to Newcastle, Berwick, Stirling and Perth.

WALLACE, William (1860–1940) Scottish composer, born in Greenock. He trained in medicine, but from 1889 devoted himself to music. He was the first British composer to experiment with symphonic poems, of which he wrote six. His other works include a symphony and songs.

WALLACH, Otto (1847–1931) German organic chemist, born in Königsberg. He won the Nobel prize for chemistry in 1910 for his work on the essential oils and terpenes.

WALLAS, Graham (1858–1932) English political psychologist, born in Monkwearmouth, Sunderland. Educated at Shrewsbury and Corpus Christi College, Oxford, he became a lecturer at the London School of Economics, and an early member of the Fabian Society (1886–1904). He became professor of political science at the University of London (1914–23). He was also involved in local authority politics as a Socialist councillor on London County Council (1904–07). His influential teaching and writings in social psychology, including *Human Nature in Politics* (1908) and *The Great Society* (1914), emphasized the role of irrational forces which determine public opinion and political attitudes.

WALLENBERG, André Oscar (1816–86) Swedish financier and politician, founder of a Swedish banking dynasty. After serving as a naval officer (1837–51) and captaining (1846–47) the *Linköping*, Sweden's first propeller-driven ship, he was a businessman in Sundsvall (1851–55) and in 1856 founded Stockholm's Enskilda Bank which pioneered modern Swedish banking methods.

WALLENBERG, Knut Agathon (1853–1938) Swedish financier and politician, son of **André Oscar Wallenberg**, whom he succeeded as managing director of Stockholm's Enskilda Bank. Under his direction the bank took a leading part in Sweden's finance. He was active in founding the Banque du Pays du Nord in Paris (1911), the British Bank of Northern Countries in London in 1912 and was largely instrumental in founding Stockholm's Chamber of Commerce in 1912. In 1906–19 he was the conservative leader of the upper House of Parliament and served in **Hammarskjöld**'s wartime ministry as foreign secretary (1914–17). One of Sweden's richest men, he was also one of her greatest benefactors, setting up in 1917 the Wallenberg Foundation which gives donations for the furtherance of science, culture and education.

WALLENBERG, Marcus (1899–1982) Swedish financier, son of **Marcus Laurentius Wallenberg**. He was managing director of Stockholm's Enskilda Bank (1946–58) and of Skandinaviska Enskilda Banken

(1972–76). He was active in the reconstruction of several large companies after the **Kreuger** crash in 1932, and in World War II he helped Swedish trade links with the West. He played an important part in setting up Scandinavian Airline Systems, and until his death held prominent positions in large Swedish and international concerns. He was an excellent yachtsman and tennis player, and was the first Swedish tennis player on the centre court at Wimbledon.

WALLENBERG, Marcus Laurentius (1864–1943) Swedish financier, son of **André Oscar Wallenberg** and half brother of **Knut Agathon Wallenberg**. He was managing director of Stockholm's Enskilda Bank (1911–20) and was active in founding or restructuring several concerns, including AB papyrus and AB Diesels Motorer (later Atlas Copco), and ASEA. With Sam Eyde he also founded Norsk Hydro in 1905.

WALLENBERG, Raoul (1912–?) Swedish diplomat, nephew of **Marcus Laurentius Wallenberg**. He took a science degree at Ann Arbor in 1935 and then worked at a bank in Haifa, Palestine, where he met Jewish refugees from Nazi Germany. In 1936 he entered partnership with a Hungarian Jew, running an import and export firm, which after 1939 involved business trips to Germany, Hungary and Nazi-occupied France. **Hitler**'s occupation of Hungary in 1944 put its 700000 Jewish population at immediate risk and the American War Refugee Board and the Swedish government sent Wallenberg to Budapest to initiate a rescue plan. He designed a Swedish protection passport (Schutz-pass) and arranged 'Swedish houses' offering Jews refuge. Through bribery, threats, blackmail or sheer strength of conviction and at great personal risk he saved up to 100000 Jews. When Soviet troops occupied Hungary in 1945 he was taken to Soviet Headquarters and never returned. Eye witnesses say he was imprisoned by the KGB at Ljubyanka prison. On insistent Swedish requests Soviet authorities produced a document signed by Smoltsov, head of Ljubyanka prison hospital, stating that Wallenberg died of a heart attack in July 1947, but testimony of ex-prisoners suggested that he was still alive in the 1950s, and persistent rumours imply he was still in prison in the 1970s. Wallenberg was made an honorary citizen of the USA in 1981, of Canada in 1985 and of Israel in 1986. A tree in the Avenue of the Righteous in Jerusalem was planted to honour his memory.

WALLENSTEIN, or **Waldstein, Albrecht Wenzel Eusebius von** (1583–1634) Austrian soldier, Duke of Friedland and of Mecklenburg, prince of Sagan, born in Heřmanice in Bohemia. When his father, a Czech Protestant noble, died, a Catholic uncle entrusted the boy's education to the Jesuits. He married a Bohemian widow, whose vast estates he inherited in 1614. In 1617 he personally commanded a force, chiefly of cavalry, which he supplied to Archduke Ferdinand (later **Ferdinand II**) for use against Venice. At the outset of the Thirty Years' War (1618–48) he assisted in the crushing of the Bohemian revolt (1618–20) under **Frederick V**, thereafter acquiring numerous confiscated estates, and consolidating them into Friedland, of which he became (1623) duke. In 1625, for raising an army for Ferdinand II, he was appointed commander-in-chief of all the imperial forces, and at Dessau Bridge defeated the army of **Mansfeld**. Establishing the peace in Hungary by a truce imposed on the combined forces of Mansfeld and **Bethlen Gabor**, he subdued (1627) Silesia, acquiring the dukedom of Sagan, joined **Tilly** against **Kristian IV**, was invested (1628) with the duchies of Mecklenburg, which he had overrun, but encountered resistance in garrisoning the Hanse towns, notably at his unsuccessful siege (1628) of Stralsund, consequently failing to remove the threat of Protestant invasion by sea. This materialized in 1630, following Ferdinand II's Edict of Restitution, when **Gustav II Adolf** of Sweden and his forces invaded northern Germany. Enmity of the Catholic princes, aroused by Wallenstein's ambition, forced Ferdinand to dismiss him (1630) and appoint Tilly commander-in-chief. After Tilly's defeat at Breitenfeld and death on the Lech, Wallenstein was reinstated. His new army, in repulsing the attempt by the Swedish forces to storm his entrenched camp near Nuremberg, prevented the Swedish king from advancing on Ferdinand in Vienna. Wallenstein was defeated (1632) by Gustav Adolf at Lützen, where, however, the king fell. In the interests of a united Germany with himself as its supreme authority, Wallenstein now intrigued with Protestants and Catholics. At length his enemies persuaded the emperor to depose him again and denounce him. Threatened in Pilsen by **Piccolomini** and others, he went to Eger, hoping for support from **Bernhard, Duke of Weimar**; there he was assassinated by Irish and Scottish officers in his retinue. The Wallenstein trilogy by **Schiller** is based on Wallenstein's career.

WALLER, Augustus Volney (1816–70) English physiologist, born near Faversham. He discovered the Wallerian degeneration of, and the related Wallerian method of tracing, nerve fibres.

WALLER, Edmund (1606–87) English poet and politician, born in Coleshill near Amersham, Hertfordshire (now Buckinghamshire), a cousin of **John Hampden.** He was educated at Eton and King's College, Cambridge. Thought to have represented Amersham in 1621, he was returned for Ilchester in 1624, Chipping Wycombe in 1625 and Amersham in 1627. In 1631 he married a London heiress, who died in 1634, and from about 1635 to 1638 he unsuccessfully courted Lady Dorothy Sidney, eldest daughter of the Earl of Leicester, whom he commemorated in verse as 'Sacharissa'. Returned to the Long Parliament in 1640, he opened the proceedings in 1641 against the judge, Sir Francis Crawley, impeached for his judgments in the king's favour. In 1643 Waller plunged into a conspiracy ('Waller's plot') against Parliament on behalf of Charles I, was arrested, and expelled from the House. He avoided execution, unlike his fellow conspirators, by abject confession and the payment of a £10000 fine, and was banished from the realm. He lived mostly in France, entertaining impoverished exiles in Paris, his own banishment being revoked in 1651, after which he returned to England. His collected poems, reviving the heroic couplet and including 'Go, lovely Rose', had been published in 1645 and were followed by *A Panegyric to my Lord Protector* (1655) and *To the King upon his Majesty's Happy Return* (1660) addressed to **Cromwell** and **Charles II** respectively.

WALLER, Fats (Thomas Wright) (1904–43) American jazz pianist, composer and entertainer, born in New York, the son of a Baptist preacher who encouraged him to play the organ for services as a child. A professional musician at 15, he gained experience as a theatre organist, movie-house pianist and in clubs. Influenced by 'stride' pianist **James P Johnson**, who coached him, Waller began his recording career in 1922 and the first records by 'Fats Waller and his Rhythm', featuring his novelty singing, were made in 1934. Waller wrote many jazz standards, such as 'Ain't Misbehavin' and 'Honeysuckle Rose'.

WALLER, Sir William (c.1597–1688) English parliamentary soldier. A member of the Long Parliament, he fought in 1643 in the West Country, at Oxford and Newbury in 1644, and at Taunton in February 1645.

He suggested reforms on which the New Model Army was to be based, but in April 1645 was removed from command by the Self-denying Ordinance. By June 1647 he was levying troops against the army, from 1648 to 1651 he was imprisoned for Royalist sympathies, and in 1659 he plotted for a royalist rising and was again imprisoned. In 1660 he became a member of the Convention Parliament, but was unrewarded at the Restoration.

WALLIS, Sir Barnes (Neville) (1887–1979) English aeronautical engineer and inventor. After winning a scholarship to Christ's Hospital and training as a marine engineer at Cowes, he was appointed a designer in the airship department of Vickers Ltd, where he designed the R100 which made its maiden flight in 1929 and successfully crossed the Atlantic. He was subsequently appointed chief designer of structures at Vickers Aviation, Weybridge, and among his many successes were the design of the Wellington bomber, the bombs which destroyed the German warship *Tirpitz* and V-rocket sites, and the 'bouncing bombs' which destroyed the Mohne and Eder dams in World War II (1943). From 1945 to 1971 he was chief of aeronautical research and development at Weybridge. In the 1950s he was also responsible for the design of the first swing wing aircraft, used in the Tornado fighter.

WALLIS, John (1616–1703) English mathematician, born in Ashford, Kent. He graduated at Cambridge, and took holy orders, but in 1649 became Savilian professor of geometry at Oxford. In the Civil War he sided with the parliament, was secretary in 1644 to the Westminster Assembly, but favoured the Restoration. Besides the *Arithmetica Infinitorum* (1656), in which he presaged the calculus and the binomial theorem and gave an infinite product for π, he wrote on proportion, mechanics, the quadrature of the circle (against **Thomas Hobbes**), grammar, logic, theology, and the teaching of the deaf and dumb. He was also an expert on deciphering, and edited some of the Greek mathematicians. He was a founder of the Royal Society.

WALLIS, Samuel (1728–95) English explorer and naval officer. From 1766 to 1768 he made a circumnavigation of the globe, and discovered Tahiti and the Wallis Islands.

WALPOLE, Horace, 4th Earl of Orford (1717–97) English man of letters, youngest son of Sir **Robert Walpole**, born in London. At Eton and at King's College, Cambridge, he had the poet **Thomas Gray** as a friend, and while still at the university was appointed by his father to lucrative government sinecures. Gray and he started on the Grand Tour, but quarrelled and separated at Reggio, where Walpole fell ill. He returned to England (1741) to take his seat for Callington in Cornwall. Although he interested himself in cases like the **John Byng** trial of 1757, his function in politics was that of the chronicling spectator rather than the earnest actor. He exchanged his Cornish seat in 1754 for the family borough of Castle Rising, which he vacated in 1757 for the other family borough of King's Lynn. In 1745 his father died, leaving him with ample means. In 1747 he purchased, near Twickenham, the former coachman's cottage which he gradually 'gothicized' (1753–76) into the stuccoed and battlemented pseudo-castle of Strawberry Hill, which helped in its way to reverse the fashion for classical and Italianate design. He spent all his time on this transformation, on his correspondence and writings, visits to Paris, and the establishment of a private press on which some of his own works as well as **Lucan**'s *Pharsalia* with **Richard Bentley**'s notes, and Gray's *Progress of Poesy* and *The Bard*, were printed. He inherited his brother's title in 1791. His essays in **Edward Moore**'s *World* exhibit a light hand, and he had gifts as a verse-writer. In such satires as the *Letter from Xo Ho to his friend Lien Chi at Pekin* (1757) he is at his best. His *Castle of Otranto* (1764) set the fashion for supernatural romance. His tragedy of *The Mysterious Mother* (1768) is strong but gruesome. Other works are *Catalogue of Royal and Noble Authors* (1758), *Fugitive Pieces in Verse and Prose* (1758), *Anecdotes of Painting in England* (1761–71), *Catalogue of Engravers* (1763), *Historic Doubts on Richard III* (1768) and *Essay on Modern Gardening* (1785). His literary reputation rests chiefly upon his letters, which deal, in the most vivacious way, with party politics, foreign affairs, literature, art and gossip. His firsthand accounts in them of such events as the Jacobite trials after the 1745 Rising and the **Gordon** Riots are invaluable. Two of his chief correspondents were Sir **Horace Mann** and Madame **du Deffand**; with the latter he exchanged more than 1600 letters.

WALPOLE, Sir Hugh Seymour (1884–1941) English novelist, born in Auckland, New Zealand, son of the Reverend G H S Walpole who subsequently became bishop of Edinburgh. He was educated in England at King's School, Canterbury, and graduated from Emmanuel College, Cambridge, in 1906. He was intended for the church but turned schoolmaster at a boys' prep school and then author. Widely read in English literature, he wrote prolifically. His books, which were enormously popular during his lifetime, display a straightforward, easy-flowing style, great descriptive power, and a genius for evoking atmosphere which he unfortunately overworked at times, and which sometimes made his work open to parody. His many novels include *Mr Perrin and Mr Traill* (1911), based on his experience as a school teacher, *Fortitude* (1913), *The Dark Forest* (1916), *The Secret City* (1919, Tait Black Memorial Prize), *The Cathedral* (1922), which owes much to **Trollope**, one of Walpole's favourite authors, and *The Herries Chronicle* (1930–33).

WALPOLE, Sir Robert, Earl of Orford (1676–1745) English statesman, born in Houghton in Norfolk. Educated at Eton and King's College, Cambridge, and destined for the church, he entered politics largely by accident when his two elder brothers died, leaving him the family estate and sufficient wealth to follow a political career. He entered the House of Commons in 1701 as the Whig member for Castle Rising, Norfolk, and in 1702 for King's Lynn, and, being a formidable speaker, quickly rose in the ranks of his party becoming, by 1715, first lord of the Treasury and Chancellor of the Exchequer. The new king, **George I**, could not speak English and, quickly bored by the proceedings of parliament, ceased to attend, leaving Walpole considerable freedom and discretion as leader of the government. Gradually Walpole established his supremacy, chairing, on the king's behalf, a small group of ministers which was the forerunner of the present-day cabinet. Walpole thereby came to be seen as England's first prime minister. He was also the longest serving holder of that office, being in control from 1721 to 1742. He was rewarded by being created Earl of Orford. His relationship with the prince of Wales, who became **George II**, and with his wife, Queen **Caroline**, was excellent and, in addition to his earldom, he was presented with No 10 Downing Street, which was to become the permanent London home of all future prime ministers.

WALPOLE, Sir Spencer (1839–1907) English historian, born in London. Educated at Eton, he joined the civil service, and became (1882–93) lieutenant-governor of the Isle of Man. His principal work is the *History of England from 1815* (1878–86), continued in his *History of Twenty-Five Years* (1904–08). He wrote Lives of **Spencer Perceval** (1874; his grandfather) and Lord **John Russell** (1889).

WALPURGA, St See **WALBURGA**

WALSCHAERTS, Égide (1820–1901) Belgian mechanical engineer, born in Malines. He studied at Liège and in 1842 entered the state railway workshops. He invented the famous Walschaerts valve gear in 1844 but could not patent it under his own name in Belgium because of the rules of the state railways. He did, however, patent it in other countries, and it was quickly recognized as a considerable advance on **Stephenson**'s valve gear and became very widely adopted on railway locomotives throughout the world. He invented several other improvements to steam engines, and was awarded a gold medal at the Paris Exposition of 1878.

WALSH, Donald See **PICCARD, Auguste**

WALSINGHAM, Sir Francis (c.1530–1590) English statesman, born in Chislehurst, Kent. He studied at King's College, Cambridge. **William Cecil**, Lord Burghley, sent him on an embassy to France in 1570–73; and having discharged his diplomatic duties with consummate skill, he was appointed one of the principal secretaries of state to **Elizabeth**, sworn onto the privy council, and knighted. In 1578 he was sent on an embassy to the Netherlands, in 1581 to France, and in 1583 to Scotland. He contrived a most effective system of espionage at home and abroad, enabling him to reveal the **Babington** plot, which implicated **Mary Queen of Scots** in treason, and to obtain in 1587 details of some of the plans for the Spanish Armada. He was one of the commissioners to try Mary at Fotheringhay. His personal integrity and disinterested patriotism are undoubted. He favoured the Puritan party, and in his later days gave himself up to religious meditation. Elizabeth acknowledged his genius and important services, yet she kept him poor and without honours; and he died in poverty and debt.

WALSINGHAM, Thomas (d.c.1422) English chronicler and monk. He was associated chiefly with St Albans abbey but for a time was prior of Wymondham. An authority for English history from 1377 until 1422, he compiled *Historia Anglicana, 1272–1422* (1863–64) and other works.

WALTARI, Mika (Toami) (1908–79) Finnish novelist. Writing in Finnish, he was the best-known of the pre-war 'Torch-bearers' circle of writers on urban themes, including his novel *Suuri illusioni* (The Great Illusion, 1928). After the war he turned to historical novels, as in *Sinuhe, egyptiläinen* (Sinuhe, the Egyptian, 1945), *Mikael Hakim* (The Wanderer, 1949) and *Turms, kuolematen* (The Etruscan, 1955). He also wrote detective stories and plays.

WALTER, properly **Schlesigner, Bruno** (1876–1962) German-born American conductor, born in Berlin. He first conducted at Cologne while still in his teens, and following this worked with **Mahler** in Hamburg and Vienna, an experience which profoundly influenced his musical outlook. He was in charge of Munich Opera 1913–22, and from 1919 was chief conductor of the Berlin Philharmonic. International tours won him a great British and American reputation, and driven from both Germany and Austria by the Nazis, he settled in the USA, where he became chief conductor of the New York Philharmonic in 1951. Perhaps the last great exponent of the German romantic tradition, he was most famous for his performances of **Haydn**, **Mozart** and **Mahler**.

WALTER, Hubert (d.1205) English statesman and prelate. He became a judge in 1185, Dean of York in 1189 and Bishop of Salisbury in the same year. He went crusading with **Richard I**, after whose capture by the Saracens he negotiated the ransom, and on whose recommendation he was made Archbishop of Canterbury (1193). As chief justiciar he played a major part in the suppression of **John's** rebellion, and during Richard's absence was virtual ruler of England until the pope made him resign political office. On the accession of King John (1199) he became chancellor, and was instrumental in avoiding war with France.

WALTER, John (1739–1812) English printer and newspaper publisher, born in London. He started as a coal merchant (1755–81), and went bankrupt as an underwriter at Lloyds. Having bought the patent for printing from logotypes (1782), in 1784 he acquired a printing office in Blackfriars, London. In 1785 he founded a scandal sheet, *The Daily Universal Register* which in 1788 was renamed *The Times*.

WALTER, John (1776–1847) English newspaperman, son of **John Walter** (1739–1812). He became manager and editor of *The Times* in 1803 and under him the newspaper attained its great status. He obtained news, especially from abroad, often more rapidly transmitted than official reports and from sources independent of them. In 1814 he adopted for the printing of *The Times* the double-cylinder steam-driven press invented by **Friedrich König**.

WALTER, John (1819–94) English newspaper proprietor, son of **John Walter** (1776–1847). A barrister by profession, he became proprietor of *The Times* in 1847. In 1866 he introduced the important cylindrical Walter press, in which, for the first time, curved stereotyped plates and reels of newsprint were used. His son Arthur Fraser (1846–1910), was proprietor until 1908, but the fortunes of *The Times* were impaired by the publication (1887) of articles on **C S Parnell** by **R Pigott**, and the controlling interest was acquired by **Alfred Harmsworth** (Northcliffe) in 1908.

WALTER, Lucy, also known as **'Mrs Barlow'** (1630–58) English gentlewoman, born probably in Dyfed, mistress of the future **Charles II**. They met in the Channel Islands when he was fleeing England in 1644 during the Civil War, and she bore him a son, James, duke of **Monmouth**.

WALTHER VON DER VOGELWEIDE (c.1170–1230) greatest of the German minnesinger, born probably in Tirol. From 1180–98 he was in high favour at the court of Austria; later he was at Mainz and Magdeburg; in 1204 he outshone his rivals in the great contest at the Wartburg. He first sided with the **Guelphs**, but made friends with the victorious Hohenstaufen, **Frederick II**, who gave him a small estate.

WALTON, Brian (c.1600–1661) English clergyman, and editor of the *London Polyglott Bible*, born in Seymour, Yorkshire. He studied at Cambridge, and held cures in London and Essex. Sequestered in 1641, he found refuge in Oxford, and then in London devoted himself to his great bible (6 vols, 1653–57), aided by **Ussher**, **John Lightfoot**, **Pococke** and other scholars. He was consecrated bishop of Chester in 1660. Nine languages are used in the *Polyglott*—Hebrew, Chaldee, Samaritan, Syriac, Arabic, Persian, Ethiopic, Greek and Latin. Other works were an *Introductio* to Oriental languages (1654) and *Considerator Considered* (1659), a defence of the *Polyglott*.

WALTON, Ernest Thomas Sinton (1903–) Irish physicist, born in Dungarvan, Waterford. He was professor of natural and experimental philosophy at Trinity College, Dublin (1947–74). With **John Cnockcroft** in 1932 he disintegrated lithium by proton bombardment, for which work they were jointly awarded the 1951 Nobel prize for physics.

WALTON, George (1867–1933) Scottish designer, mainly of interiors, born in Glasgow. After studying at Glasgow School of Art, he set up in practice, obtaining the first of a number of commissions to design for the Cranston tea-rooms in conjunction with **Charles Rennie Mackintosh**. Their styles were similar, though later work by Walton was clearly influenced by **C F A Voysey**, who was a close friend. His work extended to architecture, furniture, glass and textiles.

WALTON, Izaak (1593–1683) English writer, born in Stafford, the son of an alehouse-keeper. In 1621 he was settled in London as an ironmonger or a linen-draper in Fleet Street, where he became friends with **John Donne**, and about 1644 he retired. In 1626 he married a great-grandniece of **Cranmer**, and in 1647 Ann Kenn, a half-sister of **Thomas Ken**. He spent most of his time 'in the families of the eminent clergymen of England'. His later years were spent in Winchester. His most celebrated work is his *The Compleat Angler, or the Contemplative Man's Recreation*, which first appeared in 1653; the fifth edition, expanded from 13 chapters to 21 in 1676, also contained a treatise by **Charles Cotton**. The description of fishes, of English rivers, of fishponds, and of rods and lines is interspersed with scraps of dialogue, moral reflections, quaint old verses, songs and sayings, and idyllic glimpses of country life. The anonymous *Arte of Angling* (1577), discovered in 1957, has been found to be one of his chief sources. Not less exquisite are his Lives—of **Donne** (1640), **Wotton** (1651), **Hooker** (1665), **Richard Herbert** (1670) and **George Sanderson** (1678).

WALTON, Sir William Turner (1902–83) English composer, born in Oldham. He received his earliest musical training as a cathedral chorister at Christ Church College, Oxford, before going to university in 1918, the year in which he wrote his first major work, a piano quartet, which was performed at the Salzburg festival of contemporary music in 1923. His *Façade* (1923), originally an extravaganza accompanying declamatory verses by **Edith Sitwell**, created quite a sensation and subsequently reappeared *sans* orator as a pair of suites and as ballet music. Scored for an unusual instrumental glockenspiel and varied percussion, it vivaciously caricatures conventional song and dance forms. The *Sinfonia Concertante* (1927) for piano and orchestra, and the viola concerto (1929) are more serious; *Belshazzar's Feast* (1931), a biblical cantata with libretto by **Osbert Sitwell**, is a powerful and vital work in which exciting instrumentation for an augmented orchestra is contrasted with moving unaccompanied choral passages. The *Symphony* (1932–35) is characterized by use of the pedal-point bass to preserve orientation in the midst of advanced harmonies and cross-rhythms. Some of his subsequent compositions make more concessions to melody, and his ballet music for *The Wise Virgins* (1940), based on pieces by **J S Bach**, contains a concert favourite in his orchestral arrangement of the aria *Sheep May Safely Graze*. During World War II he began composing incidental music for films and emerged as the supreme exponent of this art, with a masterly flair for building up tension and atmosphere, as in **Shakespeare**'s *Henry V*, *Hamlet* and *Richard III*. Later works include the opera *Troilus and Cressida* (1954), a cello concerto (1956), a second symphony and a song-cycle, *Anon in Love* (1960), *A Song for the Lord Mayor's Table* (1962), and a comic opera, *The Bear* (1967).

WANAMAKER, Sam (1919–) American actor and director, born in Chicago. He worked with summer stock companies in Chicago as an actor and director from 1936 to 1939, and made his début in 1942. After serving in World War II he returned to the New York stage in 1946, and in 1952 he made his London début in **Odet**'s *Winter Journey*, which he also directed. He remained based in England, directing and acting in several plays. In 1957, he was appointed director of the New Shakespeare Theatre, Liverpool, and in 1959 he joined the Shakespeare Memorial Theatre company at Stratford-upon-Avon. He has continued to direct on both sides of the Atlantic, but has concentrated increasingly upon his ambition to build a replica of **Shakespeare**'s Globe Theatre near its original site on London's Bankside. In 1970, he founded the Globe Theatre Trust, and opened a temporary tent theatre in 1972. The Bear Garden Museum, founded by Wanamaker and displaying exhibits from Shakespeare's era, is nearby.

WAND, John William Charles (1885–1977) English Anglican churchman and scholar, born in Grantham, Lincolnshire. Appointed dean of Oriel College, Oxford, in 1925, he went to Australia as archbishop of Brisbane in 1934. Returning to Britain in 1943 to be bishop of Bath and Wells, he was bishop of London from 1945 to 1955. Remembered by students for his many books on church history, he became an even more prolific author in his long retirement, writing numerous popular books commending Christian faith, editing the *Church Quarterly Review*, writing a weekly devotional column for the *Church Times*, and publishing a brief autobiography, *Changeful Page* (1965).

WANG, AN (1920–) Chinese-born American physicist and business executive, born in Shanghai, the son of a schoolteacher. He graduated in science from Jiao Tong University in Shanghai (1940), and in 1945 emigrated to the USA, where he studied applied physics at Harvard. A computer specialist, he invented the magnetic core memory, and founded Wang Laboratories in Boston, Massachusetts, in 1951, now one of the world's largest automation systems firms. He introduced a desktop computer named LOCI in 1956, the forerunner of Wang electronic desk calculators. A leading philanthropist in Boston, he was inducted into the National Inventors Hall of Fame in 1988.

WANG CHING (d.83) Chinese civil engineer, descended from a family that had gained engineering distinction in Korea. In the service of the emperor Ming Ti he was ordered to reconstruct the 500-mile Pien Canal which had been extensively damaged by floods on the Yellow River. He erected large dykes at the junction of the canal and the Yellow River, restored the canal's existing flash locks and increased their number to a total of about 200. The work on the Pien Canal was completed in 70 AD, and eight years later he began to rebuild the Peony Dam, a project that was still incomplete at the time of his death.

WANG MENG (1934–) Chinese novelist, born in Beijing, the son of a professor of philosophy. He joined the Communist youth league in 1949 as a schoolboy, and published two novels, *Long Live Youth* (1953) and *The Young New-comer in the Organization Department* (1956). He was denounced as a rightist in the 'Anti-Rightist Campaign' of 1958, and forced to work as a manual labourer for 20 years in the remote provinces. He was then allowed to return to Beijing, and re-emerged with *Young Forever* (1979). Since then he has held various party posts, and published collections of short stories like *A Night in the City* (1980) and *Andante Cantabile* (1981). After the fall of the Gang of Four he was rehabilitated and became minister of culture.

WANG WEI (699–759) Chinese poet and painter of the T'ang dynasty. An ardent Buddhist, he founded a monochrome school of painting.

WANKEL, Felix (1902–) German mechanical engineer, born in Luhran. He was employed in various engineering works before opening his own research establishment in 1930. While carrying out work for several German motor manufacturers he devoted himself to the development of an alternative configuration to the conventional piston-and-cylinder internal combustion engine. After many trials he produced a successful prototype engine in 1956, with a curved equilateral triangular rotor in a fat figure-of-eight shaped chamber. A few types of motor car have used the Wankel engine, but continuing problems with the sealing of the rotor have prevented its large-scale adoption.

WARBECK, Perkin (c.1474–1499) Flemish impostor, pretender to the English throne, born in Touranai. He appeared in 1490 at the court of the Duchess of Burgundy, sister of **Edward IV** of England, and professed to be Richard, Duke of York, younger of the two sons of **Edward IV** murdered in the Tower. In 1491 he was welcomed at Cork, in 1492 at the court of **Charles VIII** of France; and from Burgundy he made an ineffectual landing in Kent (July 1495). In Scotland, **James IV** gave him his kinswoman, Catherine Gordon, a daughter of the Earl of **Huntly**, in marriage. In 1498 he attempted to besiege Exeter, then went off to Taunton, but ran away to the sanctuary at Beaulieu in Hampshire, surrendered on promise of pardon, and was imprisoned. On a charge of endeavouring to escape, he was thrown into the Tower, and executed.

WARBURG, Otto Heinrich (1883–1970) German biochemist, born in Freiburg Baden. Educated at Berlin and Heidelburg, he won the *Pour le Mérité* (the German VC) in World War I. He worked in the Kaiser Wilhelm (later Max Plack) Institute from 1913, and became director in 1953. Engaged on cancer research, he was awarded the 1931 Nobel prize for physiology or medicine, but as a Jew was prevented from accepting it by **Hitler**.

WARBURTON, Eliot, in full **Bartholomew Elliott George** (1810–52) Irish novelist, born in Tullamore, County Offaly. Educated at Cambridge, he was called to the bar in 1837, but soon devoted himself to literature. His eight works include *The Crescent and the Cross* (1844, a collection of travel articles for the *Dublin University Magazine*), *Memoirs of Prince Rupert* (1849), Memoirs of Horace Walpole (1852), and *Darien* (1851), describing the horrors of a ship on fire. Sailing to Panama, he was lost in a fire on board the *Amazon* off Land's End on its maiden voyage to Darien.

WARBURTON, Peter Egerton (1813–89) English-born Australian soldier and explorer, born in Cheshire. He served in the Indian Army for 24 years and then settled in Australia in 1853, where he became police commissioner until 1867. After earlier journeys to explore the South Australian Salt Lakes, he became in 1873 the first to cross Australia from the south coast to central Australia via Alice Springs and across the worst of the desert country to the De Grey River on the west coast.

WARBURTON, William (1698–1779) English churchman and controversialist,, born in Newark, the town clerk's son. He practised as attorney until he took deacon's orders in 1723. He was ordained priest in 1727 and became rector of Brant Broughton in Lincolnshire in 1728, and for 18 years immersed himself in study. His *Alliance between Church and State* (1736) first called attention to his abilities, but *The Divine Legation of Moses* (1737–41) formed the foundation of his fame. The work displays no profundity of thought, but vigour in verbal logic, much (if inaccurate) reading, dogmatism, and extreme arrogance. In 1739 he defended the orthodoxy of **Pope**'s *Essay on Man*, became his friend and literary executor, and secured influential patrons. Successively preacher of Lincoln's Inn (1746), prebendary of Gloucester (1753), king's chaplain (1754), prebendary of Durham (1755), dean of Bristol (1757) and bishop of Gloucester (1759), he spent his time in endless warfare with **Hume**, Jortin, the Deists, **Voltaire**, **Lowth** and **Wesley**. In his early years he had aided **Lewis Theobald** in his *Shakespeare*, and in 1747 he himself issued an edition which brought him no credit. Other works were *Julian* (1750), *The Principles of Natural and Revealed Religion* (1753–67), and *Doctrine of Grace* (1762).

WARD, Artemus See **BROWNE, Charles Farrer**

WARD, Arthur Sarsfield See **ROHMER, Sax**

WARD, Dame Barbara Mary, Baroness Jackson of Lodsworth (1914–81) English economist, journalist and conservationist, born in Sussex. Educated in Paris, Germany, and Somerville College, Oxford, she became foreign editor of *The Economist* in 1939. After World War II she lectured in the USA, including Harvard (1957–68) and Columbia (1968–73). She was president of the International Institute for Environment and Development from 1973 to 1980. Married to a UN official, Robert Jackson, she was made a life peer in 1976. She was a prolific and popular writer on politics, economics and ecology. Her books included *The International Share Out* (1936), *The Rich Nations and the Poor Nations* (1962), *Spaceship Earth* (1966) and *Only One Earth—the Care and Maintenance of a Small Planet* (1972).

WARD, Edward, called **Ned** (1667–1731) English 'Grubstreet' writer, born in Oxfordshire. He became a London innkeeper, wrote coarse satirical and humorous verse, and was sentenced to the pillory for attacking the Whigs in his *Hudibras Redivivus* (1705). His chief work was the *London Spy* (1703), published in monthly parts from 1698.

WARD, Frank Kingdon- See **KINGDON-WARD**

WARD, Dame Geneviève (1838–1922) American prima donna and actress, born in New York. In her youth she was a great singer and she became a great tragedienne. She was still acting at 83. She was created DBE in 1921. She wrote *Both Sides of the Curtain* (1918) with Richard Whiteing.

WARD, Harry Marshall See **KINGDON-WARD**

WARD, James (1843–1925) English psychologist and philosopher, born in Hull. He studied for the Congregationalist ministry at Spring Hill College, Birmingham, but abandoned his religious beliefs and studied moral sciences at Trinity College, Cambridge, where he became a fellow in 1875. He published articles on psychology in the ninth and subsequent editions of the *Encyclopaedia Britannica* (from 1886) which were influential in establishing that subject as a proper science in England, and was appointed professor of mental philosophy and logic at Cambridge from 1897–1925. He published in book form two volumes of Gifford Lectures: *Naturalism and Agnosticism* (1899) and *The Realm of Ends* (1911), *Psychological Principles* (1918) and *A Study of Kant* (1922).

WARD, Sir Joseph George (1856–1930) New Zealand statesman, born in Melbourne. He entered parliament in 1887 and was Liberal prime minister from 1906 to 1912 and 1928 to 1930.

WARD, Sir Leslie (1851–1922) English caricaturist and portrait painter. He earned fame as the caricaturist 'Spy' in *Vanity Fair* (1873–1909) and also signed some of his work 'Drawl' (L Ward backwards). He was knighted in 1918, and wrote *Forty Years of 'Spy'* (1915).

WARD, Mary (1585–1645) English religious reformer, the founder in 1609 of a Catholic society for women, modelled on the Society of Jesus. She and her devotees founded schools and taught in them, gave up the cloistered existence and the habit of nuns. Although their work was not questioned, these innovations were, and Pope **Urban VIII** at last called her to Rome and suppressed her society in 1630. She was allowed to return to England in 1639. Her institute was fully restored, with papal permission, in 1877 and became the model for modern Catholic women's institutes.

WARD, Mary Augusta, Mrs Humphry, née **Arnold** (1851–1920) English novelist, born in Hobart, Tasmania, a grand-daughter of Dr **Thomas Arnold** of Rugby, and niece of **Matthew Arnold**. The family returned to Britain in 1856 and, after attending private boarding schools, she joined them in Oxford in 1867. In 1872 she married Thomas Humphry Ward (1845–1926), a fellow and tutor of Brasenose College, Oxford, member of the staff of *The Times*, and editor of *The English Poets* (5 vols, 1880–1918). Mrs Ward contributed to *Macmillan's* and, a student of Spanish literature, Lives of early Spanish ecclesiastics to Sir **William Smith**'s *Dictionary of Christian Biography*. In 1879 she became secretary to Somerville College, Oxford, before moving to London in 1881, where she wrote for various periodicals. A children's story, *Milly and Olly* (1881), *Miss Bretherton* (1884), a slight novel, and a translation (1885) of **Amiel**'s *Journal intime* preceded her greatest success, the best-selling spiritual romance *Robert Elsmere* (1888) which inspired the philanthropist Passmore Edwards to found a settlement for the London poor in 1897 in Tavistock Square. Her later novels, all on social or religious issues, include *Marcella* (1894), *Sir George Tressady* (1896) and *The Case of Richard Meynell* (1911). She was an enthusiastic social worker and anti-suffragette, and became first president of the Anti-Suffrage League in 1908. She published *A Writer's Recollections* in 1918.

WARD, Nathaniel (1579–1652) English lawyer and clergyman, born in Haverhill, Suffolk. He studied law at Emmanuel College, Cambridge, and entered the ministry in 1619, but was dismissed for nonconformity in 1633. In 1634 he emigrated to Massachusetts Bay, where he was pastor of Agawam (now Ipswich) for a brief period. In 1638 he was appointed to help to frame the first legal code in New England (enacted 1641). He returned to England in 1645, and wrote a satirical book of political and religious reflections, *The Simple Cobler of Aggawam in America* (1647).

WARD, Nathaniel Bagshaw (1791–1868) English physician and botanist, born in London. He published *On the Growth of Plants in closely glazed Cases* (1842), and invented the Wardian Case which enabled live plants to be transported successfully on long voyages, and also their cultivation in Victorian drawing rooms.

WARD, Seth (1617–89) English astronomer and clergyman, born in Hertfordshire. He was educated at Cambridge, was Savilian professor of astronomy at Oxford from 1649 to 1660, propounded (1653) a theory of planetary motion, and took part with **John Wallis** in the latter's controversy with **Thomas Hobbes**. He was bishop of Exeter from 1662 to 1667, when he became bishop of Salisbury.

WARD, William George (1812–82) English theologian, born in London. He was educated at Winchester and Christ Church College, Oxford, and became fellow and tutor of Balliol College, Oxford. A strong Tractarian and member of the Oxford Movement, he published in 1844 *The Ideal of a Christian Church*, for which he was deprived of his degree and had to leave the university. He joined the Roman Catholic church and became editor of the *Dublin Review*.

WARDLAW, Henry (d.1440) Scottish prelate. He studied and lived for some years in France, and later became tutor to King **James I** of Scotland. In 1403 he became bishop of St Andrews, and played a prominent part in the foundation (1411) of St Andrews University, the first university in Scotland, of which he was the first chancellor. He also restored St Andrew's Cathedral.

WARHAM, William (c.1450–1532) Engish prelate, born near Basingstoke. He took orders, but practised law, and became advocate in the Court of Arches. His diplomatic services to **Henry VII** obtained for him rapid preferment—master of the Rolls (1494), lord chancellor (1501), bishop of London (1503) and archbishop of Canterbury (1503). In 1515 he had to resign the great seal to **Wolsey**. He was a close friend of the New Learning and its apostles, but had no stomach for fundamental reform though he agreed to recognize the king's supremacy.

WARHOL, Andy (1926–87) American pop artist and filmmaker, born in Pittsburgh of Czech parents. He studied at the Carnegie Institute of Technology and from 1961 became the pioneer of 'pop art', with colourful reproductions of familiar everyday objects, such as the famous Campbell soup-can label, and magazine illustrations directly reproduced by silk-screen. His first films endeavoured to eliminate the individuality of the filmmaker by use of a fixed camera viewpoint without sound, like his three-hour *Sleep* (1963). In later sound production from his Greenwich Village 'film factory' his avant-garde style employed continual violent changes of visual and aural perspective within long single scenes, typically *Chelsea Girls* (1966). After 1968, when he was shot and wounded by one of his starlets, his films were controlled by his former assistant and cameraman, Paul Morrissey, with much more commercial exploitation of Warhol's cult reputation—*Flesh* (1968), *Trash* (1969), *Frankenstein* (1973) and *Dracula* (1974). In the 1970s Warhol turned to portrait painting, still attempting to suppress artistic individuality by painting in series, such as the ten Mao portraits of 1972.

WARLOCK, Peter, pseud of **Philip Arnold Heseltine** (1894–1930) English musicologist and composer, born in London. In 1910 he met **Delius** and in 1916 **Bernard van Dieren**, both of whom had a profound musical influence on him; his friendship with **D H Lawrence** is also reflected in his music. In 1920 he founded *The Sackbut*, a spirited musical periodical, and his works include the song cycle *The Curlew* (1920–22), *Serenade* (1923) to Delius, the orchestral suite *Capriol* (1926), many songs, often in the Elizabethean manner, and choral works. He edited much Elizabethean and Jacobean music, wrote *Frederick Delius* (1923, under his own name) and *The English Ayre* (1926).

WARMERDAM, Cornelius ('Dutch') (1915–) American pole-vaulter, born in Long Beach, California, the first man to break the 15-foot (4.57m) landmark (1941). Seven times the world record holder, he set a new standard in the sport. Using a bamboo pole, he set records during World War II that were not bettered until the next decade. His career-best indoor vault of 4.78 metres, set in 1943, was not beaten for more than 14 years. The development of more flexible glass-fibre poles since the 1950s have led to dramatic improvements in vaulting records, but in his own time his achievements were exceptional.

WARMING, Johannes Eugenius Bülow (1841–1924) Danish botanist, born in the North Frisian island of Manö. Professor at Stockholm (1882–85) and Copenhagen (1885–1911), he wrote important works on systematic botany (1879) and plant ecology (1895), being regarded as a founder of the latter.

WARNER, Charles Dudley (1829–1900) American writer, born in Plainfield, Massachusetts. He practised law in Chicago until 1869, then settled as an editor in Hartford. In 1884 he became co-editor of *Harper's Magazine*, in which his papers on the South, Mexico and the Great West appeared. He published several books of essays, and in 1873 he wrote with **Mark Twain** *The Gilded Age*.

WARNER, Jack Leonard, originally **Jack Leonard Eichelbaum** (1892–1978) American film mogul, born in London, Ontario, youngest son of a large and impoverished immigrant family. A boy soprano and inveterate performer, he embarked upon a show-business career, later joining his brothers Harry (1881–1958), Albert (1884–1967) and Samuel (1887–1927) in the exhibition and distribution of motion pictures in Pennsylvania. Building a nationwide company, they moved into production with *Perils of the Plains* (1910) and built a studio of their own in Los Angeles in 1919. Pioneering work on the synchronization of sound and picture led to *Don Juan* (1926) and *The Jazz Singer* (1927). The sensational popularity of the latter made Warner Brothers into a major studio, specializing in gangster films, musicals and historical biographies, and home to such stars as **Bette Davis**, **James Cagney** and **Humphrey Bogart**. As a tough head of production, Warner oversaw such films as *Yankee Doodle Dandy* (1942), *Auntie Mame* (1958), *My Fair Lady* (1964) and *Camelot* (1967). His autobiography, *My First Hundred Years in Hollywood*, was published in 1965.

WARNER, Sir Pelham (Plum) (1873–1963) English cricketer, born in Trinidad. Educated at Rugby and Oriel College, Oxford, he won his cricket blue, played for Middlesex, and captained the victorious England team in the Australian tour of 1903. He also led the team in South Africa in 1905 and again in Australia in 1911. He was secretary of the MCC (1939–45), president in 1950, and was knighted in 1937. Editor of the periodical *Cricket*, his many books on the game include *The Fight for the Ashes* and *Lord's 1787–1945*.

WARNER, Rex (1905–86) English author, born in Birmingham. A specialist in classical literature, he was a teacher before turning to writing. Pre-eminently a novelist of ideas, his distinction lies in the original, imaginative handling of conflicting ideologies. *The Wild Goose Chase* (1937), *The Professor* (1938) and *The Aerodrome* (1941) established his reputation as a writer concerned with the problems of the individual involved with authority. *Men of Stones* (1949) explores the nature of totalitarianism, but it and *Why was I Killed?* (1944), are less successful than his other works. He was perhaps best known for his later historical novels such as *The Young Caesar* (1958), *Imperial Caesar* (1960) and *Pericles the Athenian* (1963). He was a poet of sensuous quality (*Poems*, 1931, and *Poems and Contradictions*, 1945), and also a translator of Greek classics.

WARNER, Susan Bogert, pseud **Elizabeth Wetherell** (1819–85) American novelist, born in New York. She had a huge success with *The Wide, Wide World* (1851), followed by *Queechy* (1852) and other sentimental and emotional tales. She collaborated in many books with her sister Anna Bartlett (1827–1915) who, as Amy Lothrop, wrote popular stories such as *Stories of Vinegar Hill* (6 vols, 1892) and was the author of popular children's hymns like 'Jesus Loves Me, This I Know' and 'Jesus bids us Shine'.

WARNER, Sylvia Townsend (1893–1978) English novelist, born in Harrow. A student of music, she researched music in the 15th and 16th centuries and was one of the four editors of the ten-volume *Tudor Church Music* (1923–29). A communist and a lesbian, she lived most of her life with the extraordinary Valentine Ackland, an alcoholic amazon. A writer of great gifts whose novels defy strait-jacketing, Warner published seven novels, four volumes of poetry, essays and eight volumes of short stories, many of which had previously appeared in the *New Yorker*. Ranging widely in theme, locale and period, significant titles are *Lolly Willowes* (1926), *Mr Fortune's Maggot* (1927), *Summer Will Show* (1936), *Afer the Death of Don Juan* (1938) and *The Corner That Held Them* (1948).

WARNER, William (c.1558–1609) English poet, born in London. Educated at Oxford, he practised as an attorney, wrote *Pan his Syrinx Pipe* (1585), translated **Plautus** (*Menaechmi*, 1595), and gained a high contemporary reputation with his *Albion's England* (1586–1606), a long metrical history in fourteen-syllable verse.

WARNER, William Lloyd (1898–1970) American anthropologist, born in Redlands, California. He studied at the University of California, and became professor of anthropology, sociology and human development at the University of Chicago in 1935. From 1959 until his death he was professor of social research at the University of Michigan. He is noted for his studies of Australian Aboriginal social and kinship organization, and for pioneering the field of urban anthropology. His major works include *A Black Civilization* (1937) and *Social Class in America* (1960).

WARREN, Sir Charles (1840–1927) Welsh soldier and archaeologist, born in Bangor. He entered the Royal Engineers in 1857. He played a conspicuous part during the late 19th century as a commander of British forces in South Africa, where he helped to delimit Griqualand West, and served also elsewhere. He is, however, chiefly remembered for his work in connection with the archaeological exploration of Palestine, especially Jerusalem, and for his writings arising from it: *Underground Jerusalem* (1876), *Temple and Tomb* (1880) and *Jerusalem* (with Condor, 1884). He also wrote on ancient weights and measures.

WARREN, Earl (1891–1974) American politician and judge, born in Los Angeles. Educated at the University of California, he practised law in California and served successively as state attorney-general and governor (1943–53). He was then appointed chief justice of the US Supreme Court (1953–69). A dynamic leader of the court, he led it to a number of notably liberal decisions particularly in civil rights and individual liberties, such as ending segregation in schools, guaranteeing the right to counsel in criminal cases, and protecting accused persons from police abuses. He headed the Commission which in 1963–64 investigated the assassination of President **John F Kennedy** and found that the killing was not part of a domestic or foreign conspiracy.

WARREN, Robert Penn (1905–89) American novelist and poet, born in Guthrie, Kentucky. He was educated at Vanderbilt, Berkeley and Yale universities, and was a Rhodes scholar at Oxford. Professor of English at Louisiana (1934–42) and Minnesota (1942–50), he was professor of drama (1951–56) and of English at Yale (1962–73). Recipient of two Pulitzer prizes (Fiction, 1947; Poetry, 1958), he established an international reputation by his political novel about the governor of a Southern state, *All the King's Men* (1943; filmed 1949), in which the demagogue Willie Stark closely resembles Governor **Huey Long**. Other works include *John Brown, the Making of a Martyr* (1929); *Night Rider* (1939); *The Cave* (1959); *Wilderness* (1961), the story of a Jew in the Civil War; and *Meet Me in the Green Glen* (1971). He also published some volumes of short stories, and verse including *Selected Poems, Old and New, 1923–66* (1966), *Or Else* (1974) and *Rumour Verified* (1981).

WARTON, Joseph (1722–1800) English critic, born in Dunsfold, Surrey, brother of **Thomas Warton** and son of the Reverend Thomas Warton (1688–1745), vicar of Basingstoke and later Oxford professor of poetry. Educated at Winchester and Oriel College, Oxford, he became rector of Winslade from 1748, returned to Winchester as a schoolmaster in 1755, and became its head (1766–93). His *Odes* (1746) marked a reaction away from **Pope**. An edition of **Virgil** (1753), with a translation of the *Eclogues* and *Georgics*, gained him a high reputation. He and his brother Thomas Warton joined with **Dr Johnson** in the Literary Club. In 1757 appeared volume i of his *Essay on Pope* (volume ii in 1782), with its distinction between the poetry of reason and the poetry of fancy. Later works were editions of Pope (1797) and **Dryden** (completed by his son, 1811).

WARTON, Thomas (1728–90) English critic, born in Basingstoke, brother of **Joseph Warton**. Educated at Winchester and Trinity College, Oxford, in 1751 he became a fellow of Trinity, and in 1757 professor of poetry. His *Observations on Spencer's Faerie Queene* (1754) established his reputation; but he is best remembered for his *History of English Poetry* (1774–81). In 1785 he became poet laureate and Camden professor of history. His miscellaneous writings included burlesque poetry and prose, genial satires on Oxford, an edition of **Theocritus** (1770), and *Inquiry into the Authenticity of the Rowley Poems*.

WARWICK, John Dudley, Earl of, and **Duke of Northumberland** (1502–53) English soldier and statesman, son of **Edmund Dudley**. He was deputy governor of Calais, and served under **Edward Seymour**, Duke of Somerset, in his Scottish campaigns. Created Earl of Warwick in 1546, he was appointed joint regent for **Edward VI** and high chamberlain of England in 1547. As virtual ruler of England he was created Duke of Northumberland in 1551 and brought about the downfall and eventual execution of Somerset (1550–52). He married his fourth son, Lord **Guildford**, to Lady **Jane Grey**, and proclaimed her queen on the death of Edward VI in 1553, but was executed on the accession of **Mary I**.

WARWICK, John Rich, 2nd Earl of (1587–1658) English colonial administrator, son of Robert Rich, 1st Earl of Warwick. He played a large role in the early history of the American colonies, and managed New England, Bermudas and Providence companies. In 1628 he got the patent of the Massachusetts Bay colony, and in 1635 founded the settlement of Saybrook, Connecticut. A Puritan, he fought for the Parliamentary side as admiral of the fleet (1642–49) during the English Civil War. Later he was instrumental in the incorporation of Providence Plantations (now Rhode Island) in 1644. Warwick on Rhode Island was named after him by **Samuel Gorton**.

WARWICK, Richard Neville, Earl of (1428–71) 'the Kingmaker', English soldier and statesman, eldest son of Richard, Earl of Salisbury. He married as a boy the daughter of the Earl of Warwick, and so at 21 obtained the earldom. He acquired the earldom of Salisbury in his own right when his father died in 1460. In consequence he had so much land and wealth that during the Wars of the Roses he was able to hold the balance between the Yorkist and Lancastrian factions. He first supported the Yorkists and established the son of Richard, Duke of York, as **Edward IV**, supplanting **Henry VI**. But Edward resented Warwick as the 'power behind the throne' and forced him into exile in France. He returned to England in 1460, now supporting the Lancastrian cause, and compelled Edward to leave the country so that he could reinstate Henry VI. Edward soon returned, however, and routed Warwick's forces at Barnet in March 1471. The 'kingmaker' was killed in the battle.

WASHBURN, Sherwood Larned (1911–) American biological anthropologist, born in Cambridge, Massachusetts. Educated at Harvard, he later taught at Columbia (1939–47), Chicago (1947–58) and the University of California at Berkeley (1958–79). He is a leading authority on primate and human evolution, and has stressed the importance of field studies of primate behaviour for modelling the behaviour of extinct hominid forms. He was editor of *Social Life of Early Man* (1962) and numerous other publications.

WASHINGTON, Booker Taliaferro (1856–1915) black American educationist, born a Mulatto slave in Franklin Country, Virginia. Educated at Hampton Institute, he became a teacher, writer and speaker on negro problems. In 1881 he was appointed principal of the Tuskegee Institute for coloured persons, Alabama, to train black people in trades and professions. A moderate in the negro movement, he wrote *Up from Slavery* in 1901.

WASHINGTON, George (1732–99) 1st president of the United States of America, born in Bridges Creek, Westmoreland County, Virginia, of English stock from Northamptonshire. In 1658 his great-grandfather, John Washington, appeared in Virginia, and soon acquired wealth and position. His grandson, Augustine, died while his son George was still a boy, leaving a large family and inadequate means. George seems to have been a good, healthy boy, with a sober-mindedness beyond his years, although the incident of the cherry tree and hatchet is probably the invention of his biographer, Mason Weems. In 1747 he went to Mount Vernon, the residence of his eldest half-brother, Lawrence, who had received the better part of the Washington property. Here the boy had access to books, and came to know the Fairfaxes, the family of his brother's wife; in 1748 Lord Fairfax employed him to survey his property. Surveying alternated for a while with hunting; he learned, too, the use of arms, and studied the art of war. In 1751 he accompanied his half-brother, who was dying of consumption, to Barbados, and on his death the next year was left guardian of his only daughter and heir to his estates in the event of her death without issue. The French were at this time connecting their settlements on the Great Lakes with those on the Mississippi by a chain of posts on the Ohio, within the sphere of English influence. Governor **Dinwiddie** of Virginia determined to warn the intruders off, and his second messenger was Washington. The French, however, paid no attention to these warnings, and an expedition was sent against them of which Washington was (by the death of his superior early in the campaign) in command. Washington was driven back, shut up in a little fort, and forced to surrender. He served on the personal staff of **Braddock**, and saved the remnant of the van of Braddock's army in 1755. He was then placed at the head of the Virginia forces (1756). In 1759 he married a rich young widow, Martha Custis (1732–1802). His niece was now dead, and the conjoint estates of Mount Vernon and of the widow Custis made him one of the richest men in the land. He kept open house, entertained liberally, led the hunting, and farmed successfully. He represented his county in the House of Burgesses. On the quarrel with the mother country (1765–70) he favoured peaceful measures first, and was thus one of the leaders in the anti-importation movements; but he soon became convinced that nothing save force would secure to his countrymen their rights. He represented Virginia in the first (1774) and second (1775) Continental Congresses, and at once took a leading part. He was neither orator nor writer, but in plain common sense and in the management of affairs he excelled. He was the one American soldier of national reputation, and was the inevitable commander-in-chief. He had remarkable powers as a strategist and tactician, but was pre-eminent as a leader of men. It was this dignified, well-dressed gentleman who took command of the New England farmers and mechanics assembled at Cambridge in the summer of 1775. It seems scarcely credible that these half-disciplined, half-armed men should have held cooped up in Boston a thoroughly-disciplined and well-equipped British army and forced their evacuation (1776); the retreat from Concord and the slaughter at Bunker Hill were largely due to the incompetence of the English commander. The only really able English commander was **Cornwallis**, and he was hampered by the stupidity of his superior. Following reverses in the New York area, Washington made a remarkable retreat through New Jersey, inflicting notable defeats on the enemy at Trenton and Princeton (1777). He suffered defeats at Brandywine and Germantown but held his army together through the winter of 1777–78 at Valley Forge. After the alliance with France (1778), and with the assistance of **Rochambeau**, Washington forced the defeat and surrender of Cornwallis, at Yorktown in 1781, which virtually ended the War of Independence. Washington retired to Mount Vernon, and sought to secure a strong government by constitutional means. In 1787 he presided over the convention of delegates from twelve states at Philadelphia which formulated the constitution; and the government under this constitution began in 1789 with Washington as first chief-magistrate or president. Unlike the old, the new administration was a strong consolidated government. Parties were formed, led by Washington's two most trusted advisers, **Jefferson** and **Hamilton**. At the outset Washington sought to enlist on the side of the new government the ablest men in the country, whether they had approved or disapproved that precise form of the constitution. As time went on however, it became evident that those desiring greater liberty for the individual would no longer be content with passive opposition. A strong party sprang into life, and began a campaign which has never been surpassed for personal abuse and virulence. Stung by their taunts, Washington lost his faith in American institutions, went over heart and soul to the Federalist party, and even doubted whether Republicans should be admitted into the army. He retired from the presidency in 1797 and died (childless) at Mount Vernon on the Potomac, 14 December 1799. The federal capital of the USA, in the planning of which he associated, bears his name.

WASSERMAN, August Paul von (1866–1925) German bacteriologist, born in Bamberg. He studied medicine at Erlangen, Vienna, Munich and Strasbourg, and worked at bacteriology and chemotherapy at the Robert Koch Institute in Berlin from 1890. He discovered in 1906, and gave his name to, a blood-serum test for syphilis.

WASSERMAN, Jakob (1873–1933) German novelist, born in Fürth in Bavaria. He lived in Vienna and in Syria. His impressive novel *Die Juden Von Zirndorf* (1897) was followed by a succession culminating in the trilogy completed just before his death: *Der Fall Maurizius* (1928), *Etzel Andergast* (1931) and *Joseph Kerkhovens dritte Existenz* (1934). He wrote also short stories, lives of **Columbus** and **H M Stanley**, and an autobiography (1921).

WATERHOUSE, Alfred (1830–1905) English architect, born in Liverpool. A leader of the Gothic revival, he designed Manchester town hall and assize courts. He made designs for several Cambridge colleges and Owens College, Manchester. He was the designer of the Natural History Museum in London's South Kensington (1873–81). His use of terracotta and brick for scholastic institutions gave rise to the term 'redbrick' for new universities and colleges.

WATERHOUSE, John William (1847–1917) English painter, born in Rome. Among his pictures are *Ulysses and the Sirens* (1892) and *The Lady of Shalott* (1894).

WATERLAND, Daniel (1683–1740) English theologian, born in Walesby, Lincolnshire. A fellow of Magdalene College, Cambridge (1704), he became canon of Windsor (1727), archdeacon of Middlesex and vicar of Twickenham (1730). He controversially opposed the views of **Samuel Clarke** and **Daniel Whitby**.

WATERS, Muddy, real name **McKinley Morganfield** (1915–83) American blues singer, composer and guitarist, born in Rolling Fork, Mississippi. He learnt to play the harmonica and the guitar in his teens and was first recorded in 1941 by Alan Lomax, the folk music researcher for the American Library of Congress. He moved to Chicago in 1943, where he recorded his first solo single 'I Can't Be Satisfied' in 1948 and gained his first national success with 'Rollin' Stone' (1950). In that same year he put together a band consisting of Little Walter, Otis Spann and Jimmy Rogers which was to have a profound influence not only on other blues musicians but also on the white rhythm-and-blues artists of the mid 1960s. The band's best-known singles include 'I've Got My Mojo Working' (1957), 'Hoochie Coochie Man' (1954) and 'She's 19 Years Old' (1957).

WATERSTON, John James (1811–83) Scottish physicist, born in Edinburgh. He studied science and medicine at Edinburgh, and practised as an engineer in London and Bombay, before returning home. He did some work in chemistry and then turned to physics, attracted by **Joule**'s work on heat and gases. By 1845 he had developed the basis of the kinetic theory of gases and submitted a paper on it to the Royal Society, but their referee dismissed it. Lord **Rayleigh** found it in the Society's archives in 1892, saw its worth and had it printed. It was then clear that Waterston had anticipated key ideas in kinetic theory and thermodynamics published by **Clausius** and others in the 1850s. Waterston himself turned to studies in medicine, and particularly the physiology of mental processes.

WATKINS, Dudley Dexter (1907–69) English strip cartoonist and illustrator, born in Manchester, the creator of *Desperate Dan*, *Oor Wullie*, and many favourite comic characters. Acclaimed as a schoolboy genius for his painting of the Nottingham Historical Pageant at the age of ten, he studied at Nottingham School of Art, and joined the window display department of Boots the Chemist, contributing his first cartoon to the staff magazine in 1923. Joining Dundee publisher **D C Thomson**'s art department, he created *Oor Wullie* and *The Broons* strips for the *Sunday Post* (1936), then *Desperate Dan* for the *Dandy* (1937), *Lord Snooty* for the *Beano* (1938), and many more. He created classic picture serials, such as *Treasure Island*, later reprinted as books (1948). Highly religious, he contributed strips to *Young Warrior* (1960) without charge. He was the first D C Thomson artist allowed to sign his name.

WATKINS, Vernon Phillips (1906–67) Welsh poet, born in Maesteg, Glamorgan, and educated at Magdalene College, Cambridge. For much of his life he lived at Pennard, Gower, and used the shoreline as illustrative material for his poetry. He published eight collections of verse during his lifetime, including *Ballad of Mari Lwyd* (1941), *Death Bell* (1954) and *Affinities* (1962). Regarded as one of the greatest Welsh poets in English, as well as one of the most unusual, he was long overshadowed by his friend **Dylan Thomas**.

WATSON, Foster (1860–1929) English historian of education, born in Lincoln. Educated at Lincoln Grammar School and Owens College, Manchester, he became professor of education at University College, Aberystwyth (1895–1913) and professor of rhetoric at Gresham College, London (1915–29). His works included a classic, *The Beginnings of the Teaching of Modern Subjects in England* (1909). An authority on **Juan Luis Vives**, he was engaged in a theory of education based on the success of great teachers at the time of his death.

WATSON, James Dewey (1928–) American biologist, born in Chicago. He studied under geneticist **Hermann Joseph Muller** at Indiana University, and in 1951 joined the Cavendish Laboratory in Cambridge, where he worked with **Francis Crick** on the structure of DNA; with **Maurice Wilkins** they were awarded the 1962 Nobel prize for physiology or medicine. He taught at Harvard from 1955, and became director of the Cold Spring Biological Laboratories in New York (1968). He wrote a personal account of the discovery of the DNA structure in *The Double Helix* (1968).

WATSON, John See **MACLAREN, Ian**

WATSON, John Broadus (1878–1958) American psychologist, born in Greenville, South Carolina. As professor at Johns Hopkins University (1908–20) he was a leading exponent of behaviourism, holding that a scientific psychology could only study what was directly observable, ie behaviour. His most important work is *Behavior—An Introduction to Comparative Psychology* (1914). He later resigned from Johns Hopkins and became an advertising executive.

WATSON, Richard (1737–1816) English theologian and scientist, born in Heversham. He was educated at Trinity College, Cambridge, where he later became professor of chemistry (1764) and regius professor of divinity (1771). He later became bishop of Llandaff (1782). He published a famous *Apology for Christianity* (1796) in reply to **Thomas Paine**. He gave much time to agriculture at his estate on Windermere, and introduced the larch to that district.

WATSON, Thomas (c.1557–1592) English lyric poet, born in London. He was educated at Oxford, and studied law in London. Coming to **Marlowe**'s help in a street fight, he killed a man in 1589. He excelled in English 'sonnets' in *Hecatompathia or Passionate Century of Love* (1582) and *The Tears of Fancie* (1593) and his sonnets were very probably studied by **Shakespeare**. He also translated classics into Latin and English, including **Sophocles**, **Tasso**, and Italian madrigals.

WATSON, Thomas Edward (1856–1922) American Populist politician and racialist demagogue, born in Columbia County, Georgia. He was admitted to the bar and became a member of the Georgia House of Representatives (1882–83). He left the Democrats, entrenched in Georgia as the party of rising capitalism, and won election as US Congressman for the Populists, serving from 1891 to 1893. As Congressman he won the first appropriation for free rural delivery of mails. With other Southern fellow-Populists he bitterly opposed Populist 'fusion' with the Democrats, their hated enemy in the South, but was forced to accept the Vice-Presidential nomination on the Populist ticket with **William Jennings Bryan**, who was also the Democratic nominee. He was Populist candidate for president in 1904, but the party had been shattered by Bryan's defeats and Watson, formerly an advocate of working co-operation with black voters, now became a ferocious supporter of segregation, increasingly employing the rhetoric of racial hatred. He also became obsessively anti-Catholic and anti-Semitic, edited various magazines, and exercised strong influence on Georgia politics by use of former Populist Democrats with which to pressurize the democratic establishment. He ultimately won election to the US Senate (1921) and died in office, having violently opposed US involvement in World War I, for which his magazines were banned from the US mail.

WATSON, Thomas John (1914–) American businessman, the son of the head of IBM (International Business Machines). He joined the company in 1937, served with the USAF from 1940 to 1945 as a lieutenant colonel, and rejoined IBM in 1946. He succeeded his father as president in 1952, became chairman in 1961 and chief executive officer from 1972 to 1979. He served as US Ambassador to USSR from 1979 to 1981.

WATSON, Tom (Thomas Sturges) (1949–) American golfer, born in Kansas City, Missouri. Through the mid 1970s and early 1980s Watson, with **Jack Nicklaus**, dominated world golf, winning the US Open, two Masters tournaments and five British Opens, and was the US Player of the Year on no fewer than six occasions.

WATSON, Sir William (1715–87) English scientist, born in London. He was one of the earliest experimenters on electricity, being the first to investigate the passage of electricity through a rarefied gas, and did much to introduce the Linnaean system to Britain.

WATSON, Sir (John) William (1858–1935) English poet, born in Burley-in-Wharfedale, Yorkshire. He first attracted notice with *Wordsworth's Grave* (1890). *Odes and Other Poems* followed in 1894, *The Father of the Forest* in 1895, *For England* (1903), *Sable and Purple* (1910), *Heralds of the Dawn* (1912), *The Man who Saw* (1917), *The Superhuman Antagonists* (1919), and *Poems, Brief and New* (1925). His poem 'April, April, Laugh thy girlish daughter' appears in many anthologies.

WATSON, William, Lord (1827–99) Scottish judge, born in Covington, Lanarkshire. Educated at Glasgow and Edinburgh Universities, Watson initially had little legal practice but by 1874 he was solicitor-general for Scotland. He became dean of the Faculty of Advocates (1875–76) and lord advocate and MP (1876–80). At this point he was promoted direct from the bar to be a lord of appeal in ordinary (1880–99). As a judge he was greatly esteemed and the authority of his judgments is high, particularly in Scottish cases. His son William also became a lord of appeal, as Lord Thankerton (1929–48).

WATSON-WATT, Sir Robert Alexander (1892–1973) Scottish physicist, born in Brechin. Educated at Dundee and St Andrews, he worked in the meteorological office, the DSIR, and the National Physical Laboratory before becoming scientific adviser to the air ministry in 1940. He played a major role in the development and introduction of radar, for which he was knighted in 1942. In 1958 he published *Three Steps to Victory*. His wife, Katherine Jane (1899–1973), was director of the Women's Auxiliary Air Force from 1939–43.

WATT, James (1736–1819) Scottish engineer and inventor, born in Greenock, the son of a merchant and town councillor. He went to Glasgow in 1754 to learn the trade of a mathematical-instrument maker, and there, after a year in London, he set up in business. The Hammermen's guild put difficulties in his way, but the university made him its mathematical-instrument maker (1757–63). He was employed on surveys for the Forth and Clyde canal (1767), the Caledonian and other canals, and was engaged in the improvement of harbours and in the deepening of the Forth, Clyde and other rivers. As early as 1759 his attention had been directed to steam as a motive force. In 1763–64 a working model of the **Newcomen** engine was sent for repair. He easily put it into order, and, seeing the defects of the machine, hit upon the expedient of the separate condenser. Other progressive improvements included the air pump, steam jacket for cylinder, and double-acting engine. After an abortive enterprise funded by **John Roebuck**, he entered into a partnership with **Matthew Boulton** of Soho, near Birmingham, in 1774, when (under a patent of 1769) the manufacture of the new engine was commenced at the Soho Engineering Works. Watt's soon superseded Newcomen's machine as a pumping-engine; and between 1781 and 1785 he obtained patents for the sun and planet motion, the expansion principle, the double engine, the parallel motion, a smokeless furnace, and the governor. He described a steam locomotive in one of his patents (1784), but discouraged **Murdock** from further experiments with steam locomotion. The watt, a unit of power, is named after him, and the term horsepower, another unit, was first used by him. He retired in 1800, and died at Heathfield Hall, his seat near Birmingham. His son, James (1769–1848), a marine engineer, fitted the engine to the first English steamer to leave port in 1817, the *Caledonia*.

WATT, Robert (1774–1819) Scottish bibliographer and physician, born near Stewarton in Ayrshire. He began life as a ploughboy, went to university at Glasgow and Edinburgh, and became a schoolmaster in Symington, Ayrshire (1797). He turned to medicine and became a physician in Glasgow. He compiled a *Catalogue of Medical Books* (1812), and a monumental general catalogue of authors and subjects, *Bibliotheca Britannica*, published posthumously (1819–24).

WATTEAU, (Jean) Antoine (1684–1721) French painter, born in Valenciennes. He studied under a local artist, but in 1702 ran away to Paris and worked as a scenepainter at the Opera and as a copyist. After 1712 his early canvases were mostly military scenes, but it was the mythological *Embarquement pour Cythère* which won him membership of the Academy in 1717. While staying at the castle of Montmorency he painted his *Fêtes galantes*, quasi-pastoral idylls in court dress which became fashionable in high society. A lifelong sufferer from tuberculosis, he visited London in 1720 to consult the celebrated Dr **Richard Mead**, but his health was rapidly deteriorating, and on his return he painted his last great work, depicting the interior of the shop of his art-dealer friend Gersaint, drawn from nature and intended as a signboard, but in fact the most classical and most prefectly composed of his paintings. Essentially aristocratic in conception, Watteau's paintings fell into disfavour at the Revolution, and it was not until the end of the 19th century that they regained popularity. Watteau is now regarded as a forerunner of the Impressionists in his handling of colour and study of nature. He influenced and was imitated by many later artists, notably **Fragonard** and **Boucher**.

WATTS, Alaric Alexander (1797–1864) English journalist and poet, born in London. He founded the *United Services Gazette* (1833) and the annual *Literary Souvenir* (1823–37), and published two volumes of poetry, but is now remembered chiefly for his alliterative alphabetical *jeu d'esprit*, 'An Austrian army awfully arrayed'.

WATTS, George Frederick (1817–1904) English painter, born in London. He formed his style after the Venetian masters and first attracted notice by his cartoon of *Caractacus* (1843) in the competition for murals for the new Houses of Parliament. He became known for his penetrating portraits of notabilities, 150 of which he presented to the National Portrait Gallery in 1904, and in these his best work is to be seen; but in his lifetime his moral and allegorical pieces enjoyed enormous popularity, and monochrome reproductions of *Paolo and Francesca*, *Sir Galahad*, *Love Triumphant*, *Hope* and so on adorned the walls of countless late Victorian middle-class homes. He also executed some sculpture, including *Physical Energy* (Kensington Gardens). In 1864 he married **Ellen Terry**, but parted from her within a year.

WATTS, Isaac (1674–1748) English hymnwriter, born in Southampton. In 1702 he succeeded an Independent minister in Mark Lane, London, becoming eminent as a preacher. His hymns and psalms are contained in *Horae Lyricae* (1706), *Hymns and Spiritual Songs* (1707–09) and *Psalms of David Imitated* (1719), and include 'Jesus shall reign where'er the sun', 'When I survey the wondrous cross', and 'O God, our help in ages past'.

WATTS-DUNTON, Walter Theodore (1832–1914) English poet and critic, born in St Ives, Cambridgeshire, the son of a solicitor. He practised law for a time, but in London he became the centre of a remarkable literary and artistic company, and the intimate friend of **Dante Gabriel Rossetti**, **William Morris**, **Swinburne**, **Philip Marston** and afterwards **Tennyson**. He wrote enough to fill many volumes in the *Athenaeum* (1876–98) and elsewhere. In *The Coming of Love* (1897) he gave a selection of his poems. In 1898 appeared his novel of gypsy life, *Aylwin*. *Old Familiar Faces* (1915) contains recollections from the *Athenaeum*. At his home in Putney he looked after Swinburne for the last 30 years of the poet's life (1879–1909).

WAUGH, Alec (Alexander Raban) (1898–1981) English novelist and travel writer, born in London, brother of **Evelyn Waugh**. He was educated at Sherborne where he was involved in a homosexual scandal and left in 1915 to become a cadet in the Inns of Court Officers Training Corps. He spent two years in training before being posted to a machine-gun unit in France, just in time for Passchendaele. In seven and a half weeks he wrote his first book, the autobiographical *Loom of Youth* (1917), in which he expressed the bitterness and love he felt for his school. A good novel, it was an immediate success, but it was tainted with notoriety and has overshadowed worthy successors: *Wheels within Wheels* (1933), *Where the Clock Chimes Twice* (1952), and various travel books, the most popular being *Island in the Sun* (1975). He wrote several autobiographical volumes including *The Early Years of Alec Waugh* (1962) and *My Brother Evelyn and Other Portraits* (1976).

WAUGH, (Alexander) Auberon (1939–) English journalist and novelist, the eldest son of **Evelyn Waugh**, born in Pixton Park, Dulverton, Somerset. His school days were miserable and left him with a deep detestation of the public school system. He did his National Service in the Royal Horse Guards and was sent to Cyprus where he accidentally shot himself, losing a lung, his spleen, several ribs and a finger. He denied speculation that he had been fired on by his own troops. Completing his education at Oxford, he got a job on the *Daily Telegraph* in 1960, the same year he published his first novel, *The Foxglove Saga*. There followed four novels, each courteously received and, in varying degrees, funny, but he abandoned fiction for lack of financial reward and the government's prevarication over implementing a scheme for public lending right. There are few national papers to which he has not contributed, but his best work has appeared in the *New Statesman*, the *Spectator* and the defunct *Books and Bookmen*. He is currently editor of the *Literary Review*.

WAUGH, Evelyn Arthur St John (1903–66) English novelist, travel writer and biographer, born in Hampstead, London, younger brother of **Alec Waugh**. He was educated at Lancing and Hertford College, Oxford, where he read modern history but with little application. From 1925 to 1927 he was a schoolmaster, an unhappy period during which he attempted suicide, but the experience gave him the material for *Decline and Fall* (1928), his first and immoderately successful novel which had been preceded only by *PRB; an essay on the Pre-Raphaelite Brotherhood* (privately printed in 1926) and a life of **Dante Gabriel Rossetti** published earlier in 1928. The novel made him the talk of the town for, its comic genius apart, it was obviously a *roman à clef*. After a brief and unsuccessful marriage, he spent the next few years travelling restlessly. He contributed variously to newspapers, particularly the *Daily Mail*, published the social satire *Vile Bodies* (1930) and two travel books, *Labels* (1930) and *Remote People* (1931). In 1930 he became a Roman Catholic, an event which he regarded as the most important in his life. His itinerant existence continued and between 1932 and 1937 (when he re-married) he visited British Guiana, Brazil, Morocco and Abyssinia, and cruised in the Mediterranean. After he married Laura Herbert he settled at Piers Court, Stinchcombe, Gloucestershire, and in 1938 published *Scoop*, a hilarious newspaper farce in which the wrong correspondent is sent to cover the civil war in the African Republic of Ishmaelia. Further travels to Hungary and Mexico followed before the outbreak of the war, which Waugh spent in a variety of postings as a junior officer. He managed to publish in the war years four books, including *Put Out More Flags* (1942) and the enduring *Brideshead Revisited* (1945), a nostalgic, highly-wrought evocation of halcyon days at Oxford. From the war he also mined 'The Sword of Honour' trilogy—*Men at Arms* (1952), *Officers and Gentlemen* (1955) and *Unconditional Surrender* (1961)—in which he described, in parallel to his own experience, the significance to men and women of the ordeal of crisis of civilization which received its climax in World War II. Other books published during this period include *The Loved One* (1947), *Helena* (1950) and *The Ordeal of Gilbert Pinfold* (1957), a painfully personal but fictionalized account of a middle-aged writer's mental collapse. In 1964 he published *A Little Learning*, intended as the first of several volumes of an autobiography he never completed. He died suddenly in Combe Florey in Somerset, revered as a wit and a stylist and one of the 20th century's greatest comic novelists. *The Diaries of Evelyn Waugh* were published in 1976; his *Letters*, edited by Mark Amory, in 1980.

WAVELL, Archibald Percival Wavell, 1st Earl (1883–1950) English soldier, born in Winchester. Educated at Winchester and the Royal Military College, Sandhurst, he was commissioned in the Black Watch in 1901, and served in the 2nd Boer War (1899–1902) and the Indian frontier (1908). Wounded in 1916, he lost the sight of one eye. Posted to the General Staff, he became chief of staff to **Allenby** in Palestine. From 1938 to 1941 he was commander in chief of British forces in the Middle East. With dangerously slender resources he speedily found himself fighting eight separate campaigns, five of them simultaneously. He defeated a numerically superior Italian army, with the capture of 130 000 prisoners, and conquered Abyssinia, but was defeated by **Rommel** in North Africa. He became commander-in-chief in 1941 and supreme commander of Allied forces in Southwest Pacific (1942). From 1943 to 1947, during the difficult years which preceded the transfer of power, he was viceroy in India. He became field-marshal and viscount (1943), earl (1947), constable of the Tower (1948) and lord-lieutenant of London (1949). He published an anthology of poetry, *Other Men's Flowers* (1944), and wrote a book on *Generals and Generalship* (1941).

WAVERLEY, John Anderson, 1st Viscount (1882–1958) Scottish administrator and politician, born in Eskbank, Midlothian. Educated at Edinburgh and Leipzig, he entered the colonial office in 1905, was chairman of the board of inland revenue (1919–22), and permanent under-secretary at the home office from 1922 until his appointment as governor of Bengal in 1932. He was home secretary and minister of home security from 1939 to 1940 (the Anderson air-raid shelter being named after him), became in 1940 lord president of the council, and Chancellor of the Exchequer in 1943, when he introduced the pay-as-you-earn system of income-tax collection devised by his predecessor Sir **Kinglsey Wood**. He was created viscount in 1952.

WAYNE, Anthony, known as **'mad Anthony'** (1745–96) American Revolutionary soldier, born in Easttown (now Waynesboro), Pennsylvania. In 1776 he raised a volunteer regiment, and in Canada covered the retreat of the provincial forces at Three Rivers. He commanded at Ticonderoga until 1777, when he joined **Washington** in New Jersey. He fought bravely at Brandywine (1777); led the attack at Germantown; captured supplies for the army at Valley Forge; carried Stony Point; and saved **Lafayette** in Virginia (1781). In 1793 he led an expedition against the Indians.

WAYNE, John, originally **Marion Michael Morrison** (1907–79) American film actor, born in Winterset, Iowa. After a long succession of small parts in low-budget films and serials he first achieved stardom as the Ringo Kid in *Stagecoach* (1939). Known as 'Duke', he went on to make over 80 films in the next 40 years, typically starring as a tough but warm-hearted gunfighter or lawman. He specialized in Westerns such as *Red River* (1948), *The Searchers* (1956), and *True Grit* (1969, Academy Award) and *The Shootist* (1976), his final film and one of his best.

WAYNFLETE See **WILLIAM OF WAYNFLETE**

WEBB, Sir Aston (1849–1930) English architect, born in London. He designed the eastern façade of Buckingham Palace, the Admiralty Arch, Imperial College of Science, and many other London buildings.

WEBB, Beatrice See **WEBB, Sidney James**

WEBB, Harri (1920–) Welsh poet, born in Swansea and educated at Magdalen College, Oxford. He has published two collections of verse (*The Green Desert*, 1969, and *A Crown for Branwen*, 1974) and two collections of Welsh songs and ballads (*Rampage and Revel*, 1967, and *Poems and Points*, 1983), and has written numerous scripts for television. His work is ingrained with a strong nationalism and a biting wit. A prolific journalist, public speaker and pamphleteer, he has been active since 1959 on behalf of *Plaid Cymru*, the Welsh Nationalist party, mainly in the industrial valleys of south-east Wales.

WEBB, Mary Gladys, née **Meredith** (1881–1927) English writer, born in Keighton, near the Wrekin. In 1912 she married Henry B L Webb and lived mostly in Shropshire, market gardening and novel-writing. *Precious Bane* (1924) won her belated fame as a writer of English and a novelist of the soil, the dialect, and superstition, of Shropshire, expressing 'the continuity of country life'. Her other works include the novels *The Golden Arrow* (1916), *Gone to Earth* (1917), *The House in Dormer Forest* (1920), *Seven for a Secret* (1922) and the unfinished *Armour Wherein He Trusted* (1929); nature essays, *The Spring of Joy* (1917); and poems.

WEBB, Matthew (1848–83) English swimmer, born in Dawley, Shropshire, the first man to swim the English Channel. He trained as a seaman and became a master mariner, before becoming a professional swimmer in 1875. On 24–25 August, 1875, he swam from Dover to Calais in $21\frac{3}{4}$ hours. He was drowned attempting to swim the Niagara rapids.

WEBB, Philip (1831–1915) English architect and designer. After his training, he joined the practice of **G E Street** (1852) where he met **William Morris**, who joined Street briefly in 1856. Thus began a long association, Webb becoming a central figure in the Arts and Crafts movement and its offshoots. He designed furniture, metalwork and stained glass for Morris' firm, as well as animals and birds for textiles, at which Morris himself was not proficient. In architectural practice on his own from 1858, he designed several important houses such as the 'Red House', Bexley, for William and Jane Morris (1859), 'Clouds' in Wiltshire (1881–86) and 'Standen', East Grinstead (1891).

WEBB, Sidney James, Baron Passfield (1859–1947) and **(Martha) Beatrice**, née **Potter** (1858–1943), English social reformers, social historians and economists. They married in 1892. Sidney was born in London, the son of an accountant, and in 1885 graduated LLB at London University. He was largely instrumental in establishing the London School of Economics and Political Science (1895), where he was a professor of public administration (1912–27). An active member of the Labour party, he entered parliament in 1922 and held several administerial posts between 1924–31. He was also a founder of the Fabian Society (1884).

WEBBER, Dr William Lloyd See **LLOYD WEBBER, Andrew**

WEBER, Carl Maria Friedrich Ernst von (1786–1826) German composer and pianist, born of a noble but impoverished Austrian family, in Eutin near Lübeck. Soon after, his father took his wife (a singer) from town to town at the head of a small dramatic company. As soon as he could sit at the piano Weber was plied with music lessons; but his serious training began in 1796. His second opera, *Das Waldmädchen* (1800), was produced at Freiberg before he was 14, and was afterwards remodelled in *Silvana*. At Vienna in 1803 he was warmly welcomed as a pupil by Abt Vogler, who obtained for him the conductorship of the opera at Breslau, where he gave evidence of rare talent for organization. In 1806 he became secretary to a brother of the king of Württemberg, ran into debt and dissipation, was through his thriftless old father's fault charged with embezzlement, and with his father ordered to leave the country (1810). He spent the next twelve months at Mannheim and Darstadt, composing the operetta *Abu Hassan*; at Munich in 1811 he was writing concertos. In 1813 he settled in Prague as opera kapellmeister, and about this time composed ten patriotic songs and the cantata *Kampf and Sieg*. In 1816 he was invited by the king of Saxony to direct the German opera at Dresden, superseding Italian opera. In 1817 he married Carolina Brandt, the famous singer. In 1818 he wrote his Mass in E flat and the Jubel cantata and overture, in 1819 the Mass in G for the royal golden wedding. *Der Freischütz* was completed in May 1820, and produced with great success at Berlin (1821). His next opera, *Euryanthe*, was produced at Vienna in 1823. His final masterpiece, *Oberon*, was undertaken at the request of **Charles Kemble** for Covent Garden Theatre. In March 1826 Weber was in London, and the first performance of *Oberon* was the crowning triumph of his life. During the next few weeks he conducted frequently at the theatre and played at many concerts but he died shortly after this, and was buried at St Mary's Moorfields; in 1844 his remains were removed to Dresden. As founder of German romantic opera, he was the forerunner of **Wagner**. Other works include the music to *Preciosa*, the Overture, *Der Beherrscher der Geister*, two symphonies, three concertos, sonatas, as well as scenas, cantatas and songs.

WEBER, Ernst Heinrich (1795–1878) German physiologist, born in Wittenberg, brother of **Wilhelm Weber**. As professor of anatomy (1818), and of physiology (1840) at Leipzig, he devised a method of determining the sensitivity of the skin, enunciated in 1834, and gave his name to the Weber-**Fechner** Law of the increase of stimuli.

WEBER, Max (1864–1920) German sociologist. Born in Erfurt, he was educated at the universities of Heidelberg, Berlin and Göttingen. He taught law at Berlin from 1892, political economy at Freiburg from 1894, and economics at Heidelberg from 1897. Not until the end of his life did he consider himself a sociologist. In 1897, following the death of his father, he suffered a serious nervous breakdown, and was given leave to recover. Until 1918, when he accepted a chair of sociology in Vienna, he lived largely as a private scholar. In 1919 he took over the chair of sociology at Munich. Weber is regarded as one of the founders of sociology. His work is extremely wide-ranging, with perhaps his greatest achievements being his comparative and historical studies of large-scale social institutions. He was also an advocate of the interpretive approach to social science.

WEBER, Max (1881–1961) Russian-born American painter, born in Bailystok. He emigrated to the USA with his family in 1891, and studied art in New York (1898–1900) and then under **Matisse** in Paris, and became one of the pioneer Abstractionist painters in New York. He later abandoned this extreme form for a distorted naturalism. His works include *Chinese Restaurant* (1915) *The Two Musicians* (1917), *Tranquillity* (1928), *Latest News* (c.1940) and *Three Literary Gentlemen* (1945). His writings include *Cubist Poems* (1914), *Essays on Art* (1916) and *Primitives* (1926).

WEBER, Wilhelm Eduard (1804–91) German scientist, brother of **Ernst Weber**. From 1831 to 1837 he was professor of physics at Göttingen, from 1843 professor at Leipzig, associated with Johann Gauss in his researches on electricity and magnetism. He was the inventor of the electrodynamometer, the first to apply the mirror and scale method of reading deflections, and author, with his brother, of a notable treatise on waves.

WEBERN, Anton von (1883–1945) Austrian composer, born in Vienna. He studied under **Schoenberg** and became one of his first musical disciples, even surpassing his master in the extreme application of the latter's twelve-tone techniques. His fragmentation of melody to achieve feeling, and impressionistic effects (*Klangfarbenmelodien*) make the maximum demands on the listener, and performances of his works at first always invited hostile demonstrations. For a while he conducted the Vienna Workers' Symphony Orchestra, founded a choir called the *Kunstelle*, but lived most of his life in retirement at Mödling. The Nazis banned his music and he worked as a proofreader during World War II. He was accidentally shot dead by a US soldier near Salzburg. His works include a symphony, three cantatas, *Four Pieces for Violin and Pianoforte* (1910), *Five Pieces for Orchestra* (1911–13), a concerto for nine instruments and songs, including several settings of **Stefan George**'s poems (1908–1909).

WEBSTER, Daniel (1782–1852) American orator, lawyer and statesman, born in Salisbury, New Hampshire. He studied at Dartmouth, Salisbury and Boston, was admitted to the bar in 1805, and was sent to congress in 1813. Settling in Boston as an advocate in 1816, he distinguished himself in the Dartmouth College case, and as an orator became famous by his oration on the bicentenary of the landing of the Pilgrim Fathers. Returning to congress in December 1823 as a Massachusetts representative he found new rivals there; in 1827 he was transferred to the senate. He had favoured free trade, but in 1828 defended the new protective tariff. His whole career was marked by a deep reverence for established institutions and accomplished facts, and for the principle of nationality. His 'Bunker Hill' oration was made in 1825 and another, on the supremacy of the Union, in 1830. The Whig party triumphed in 1840, and Webster was called into **Benjamin Harrison**'s Cabinet as secretary of state. Under President **John Tyler** he negotiated the Ashburton treaty with Great Britain, but resigned in May 1843. In 1844 he refused his party's nomination for president and supported **Henry Clay**. He opposed the war with Mexico. In 1850 he said that he abhorred slavery, but was unwilling to break up the Union to abolish it. Under President **Millard Fillmore** he was called to his former post as secretary of state to settle differences with England. Unquestionably the greatest of American orators, his speeches were published in 1851.

WEBSTER, John (c.1580–c.1625) English dramatist, supposed to have been at one time clerk of St Andrews, Holborn. In *Lady Jane* and *The Two Harpies* (both lost) he was the collaborator of **Dekker**, **Drayton**, **Chettle** and others. In 1604 he made some additions to *The Malcontent* of **Marston**. In 1607 were printed the *Famous History of Sir Thomas Wyat*, a tragedy, and two comedies, *Westward Hoe* and *Northward Hoe*, all three the joint work of Webster and Dekker. *The White Divel* (1612) first revealed his powers. *The Duchess of Malfi* (1623) is a yet greater achievement. *Appius and Virginia* (first published 1654) may be **Heywood**'s (or partly); *The Devil's Law Case* (1623) is largely disagreeable and sordid. A poem of the death of Prince Henry, and other fragments of verse, survive, with some doubtful works. The tragedy, *A Late Murder of the Son upon the Mother* (1624), unpublished and lost, although licensed, was written by **Ford** and Webster. Not popular in his own day, Webster was first recognized by **Charles Lamb**.

WEBSTER, Noah (1758–1843) American lexicographer, born in West Hartford, Connecticut. He graduated at Yale in 1778, and, after a spell as a teacher, was admitted to the bar in 1781. But he soon resumed teaching, and made a great hit with the first part of *A Grammatical Institute of the English Language* (1783; later known as 'Webster's Spelling Book'). Political articles and pamphlets (including *Sketches of American Policy*, 1785), lecturing, and a few years of law practice and journalism occupied him until 1798, when he retired to a life of literary labour at New Haven. He published *A Compendious Dictionary of the English Language* (1806), an English grammar (1807) and the great *American Dictionary of the English Language* (2 vols, 1828), now *Webster's New International Dictionary of the English Language*.

WEBSTER, Tom (Gilbert Thomas) (1890–1962) English sports cartoonist and animator, born in Bilston and considered the greatest sports cartoonist of all time. While working as a railway booking clerk in 1904 he won a newspaper cartoon contest. His first sports cartoon was published in *Athletic News*, prompting him to join the art staff of the *Birmingham Sports Argus* where he evolved a unique style of cartoons in a free-ranging strip format with commentary. In 1919 he joined the *Daily Mail* drawing animated cartoons of several sporting characters, like *Tishy the Racehorse*, and painted the *Calvalcade of Sport* mural on the *Queen Mary* liner (1936).

WEDDELL, James (1787–1834) English navigator, born in Ostend. In his principal voyage (1822–23) he penetrated to the point 74° 15′ S by 34° 17′ W in that part of Antarctica which later took his name (Weddell Sea; Weddell Quadrant), as did a type of seal taken by him in the area.

WEDDERBURN, Alexander, 1st Baron (1780) Loughborough, 1st Earl (1801) of Rosslyn (1733–1805) Lord Chancellor, born in Edinburgh, son of a Scottish judge. In 1757 he abruptly left the Scottish bar for the English, entered parliament in 1752, and distinguished himself in the Douglas cause (1771).

WEDDERBURN, Joseph Henry Maclagan (1882–1948) Scottish-born American mathematician, born in Forfar. He graduated in mathematics at Edinburgh in 1903, visited Leipzig, Berlin and Chicago, and returned to Edinburgh as a lecturer (1905–09). In 1909 he went to Princeton but returned to fight in the British Army during World War I. After the war he settled at Princeton until his retiral in 1945. His work on algebra includes two fundamental theorems known by his name, one on the classification of semisimple algebras, and the other on finite division rings.

WEDEKIND, Frank (1864–1918) German dramatist, born in Hanover. He won fame with *Erdgeist* (1895), *Frühlings Erwachen* (1891; first performed 1906), *Die Büchse der Pandora* (1903; first performed 1918), and other unconventional tragedies.

WEDGWOOD, Dame Cicely Veronica (1910–) English historian, born in Stocksfield, Northumberland. She studied at Lady Margaret Hall, Oxford. A specialist in 17th-century history, her publications include biographies of *Strafford* (1935), *Oliver Cromwell* (1939), *William the Silent* (James Tait Black prize, 1944) and *Montrose* (1955), *The Thirty Years' War* (1938); also *The King's Peace* (1955), *The King's War* (1958) and *The Trial of Charles I* (1964). She was created DBE in 1968.

WEDGWOOD, Josiah (1730–95) English potter, born in Burslem of a family notable in the industry. In 1763 he patented a beautiful cream-coloured ware (Queen's Ware). He emulated antique models, producing the unglazed blue Jasper ware with its raised designs in white, the black basalt ware, and, in 1769, gave the name 'Etruria' to his new works near Hanley. His products, and their imitation, were named after him (Wedgwood ware). From 1775 he employed **John Flaxman** to furnish designs.

WEED, Thurlow (1797–1882) American journalist, born in Cairo, New York. In 1830 he founded the Albany *Evening Journal*, which he controlled for 35 years, and in 1867–68 he edited the New York *Commercial Advertiser*. He wrote *Autobiography* (1884).

WEEKES, Everton Decourcey (1925–) West Indian cricketer, born in Bridgetown, Barbados. Although comparatively small in stature, he was a batsman of immense power. Almost half his first-class centuries (15 of 36) were made in Test cricket, and in 48 Tests he scored 4455 runs at an average of 58.61. Against India at Calcutta in 1949 he scored two centuries in the same Test and he holds the record for two West Indian partnerships and two fifth wicket partnerships.

WEELKES, Thomas (c.1575–1623) English madrigal composer. One of the three greatest, he was organist at Winchester College (1597) and Chichester Cathedral (1602) and graduated BMus at New College, Oxford, in 1602. A friend of **Thomas Morley**, he contributed to the *Triumphes of Oriana*.

WEENIX, Jan (1640–1719) Dutch painter, born in Amsterdam, the son of **Jan Baptist Weenix**. He was known for hunting scenes, animal subjects and still-life paintings featuring dead gamebirds, hares, and other creatures.

WEENIX, Jan Baptist (1621–60) Dutch painter. He specialized in landscapes and seaport subjects.

WEGENER, Alfred Lothar (1880–1930) German meteorologist and geophysicist, born in Berlin. He proposed the theory of continental drift and was professor of meteorology at Hamburg (1919), and of geophysics and meteorology at Graz (1924). His theory of continental drift is named after him (Wegener Hypothesis), and is the subject of his chief work (1915; translated 1924 as *Origin of Continents and Oceans*). His ideas initially met with great hostility, but by the 1960s plate tectonics was established as one of the major tenets of modern geophysics. He died in Greenland on his fourth expedition there.

WEIDENREICH, Franz (1873–1948) German anatomist and anthropologist, born in Edenkoben. He studied medicine at Munich, Kiel, Berlin and Strasbourg. He taught anatomy at Strasbourg (1903–18) and Heidelberg (1919–24), and was professor of anthropology at Frankfurt from 1928 to 1933. In 1934 he left Nazi Germany and worked for seven years in China (1935–41) at the Peking Union Medical College, collaborating with **Pierre Teilhard de Chardin** on fossil remains of Peking Man. From 1941 to 1948 he worked at the American Museum of Natural History in New York City. His early work was concerned with blood, bone, teeth and connective tissue. Later studies of hominid fossil remains led him to espouse an orthogenetic view of human evolution, which he summarized in *Apes, Giants and Man* (1946).

WEIDMAN, Charles (1901–75) American dancer, choreographer and teacher, born in Lincoln, Nebraska. He was trained at the Denishawn school, later joining the company and remaining there for eight years. In partnership with **Doris Humphrey**, he formed a company in 1928, developing his work as a choreographer. After the company was dismantled in 1945, he founded a school and his own eponymous company. His choreography at this time included *A Home Divided* (1945), *The War Between Men and Women* (1954) and *Is Sex Necessary?* (1959). He moved to New York City Opera and continued teaching, numbering amongst his pupils **José Limón** and **Bob Fosse**.

WEIERSTRASS, Karl Theoodor Wilhelm (1815–97) German mathematician, born in Ostenfelde. Educated at the universities of Bonn and Münster, he became professor at Berlin in 1856. He published relatively little but became famous for his lectures, in which he gave a systematic account of analysis with previously unknown rigour, basing complex function theory on power series in contrast to the approach of **Augustin-Louis Cauchy** and **Georg Riemann**. He made important advances in the theory of elliptic and abelian functions, constructed the first example of a continuous but nowhere-differentiable function, and showed that every continuous function could be uniformly approximated by polynomials.

WEIGEL, Helene (1900–72) Austrian-born actress and manager. She began her acting career in Frankfurt but went to Berlin in 1923 and met **Bertolt Brecht**, whom she married in 1929. She appeared in the title role of his adaptation of **Gorky**'s *The Mother* in 1932. From 1933 to 1948, she accompanied him in his exile from Germany. On their return to East Berlin in 1948, she and Brecht co-founded and ran the Berliner Ensemble, regarded as one of the great world theatre companies. She found her greatest role as Mother Courage in *Mother Courage and her Children* (1949). After Brecht's death in 1956 she managed the Ensemble on her own.

WEIL, André (1906–) French mathematician, brother of **Simone Weil**, born in Paris. He studied at the University of Paris, spent two years in India, Strasbourg (1933–40), USA (1941–42), Brazil (1945–47) and Chicago (1947–58), before settling at Princeton in 1958. One of the most brilliant mathematicians of the century, he has worked in number theory, algebraic geometry and group theory. He was one of the founders of the **Bourbaki** group, and has also written on the history of mathematics.

WEIL, Simone (1909–43) French philosopher and religious writer, born in Paris. She came from a Jewish intellectual family and had a brilliant academic career at school and university in Paris. Throughout her short life she combined the most sophisticated scholarly and philosophical interests with an extreme moral intensity and a dedicated identification with the interests of the oppressed and exploited. She taught philosophy in schools from 1931–38, interspersing this with periods of hard manual labour on farms and at the Renault works in order to experience directly working-class life. Her political commitment was intensified in 1936 when she served in a non-military capacity with the Republican side in the Spanish Civil War. In 1941 she settled briefly in Marseille where, under the influence of the Dominican Father Perrin and Gustave Thibon, she developed a deep mystical feeling for the Catholic faith, yet a profound temperamental reluctance to join any organized religion or institutional framework. She left France in 1942, first for the USA, then Britain, where she worked for the French resistance in London. She finally starved herself to death, refusing to eat while the victims of World War II still suffered. Her posthumously-published writings are highly individual, often combining severe argumentation with impassioned spiritualism, and they have reached a large popular readership. They include: *La Pesanteur et la Grâce* (1947, translated as *Gravity and Grace*, 1952), *L'Enracinement* (1949, translated as *The Need for Roots*, 1952), *Attente de Dieu* (1950, translated as *Waiting for God*, 1951), *Oppression et Liberté* (1955, translated as *Oppression and Liberty*, 1958), and *Leçons de Philosophie* (1933–34, translated as *Lectures on Philosophy*, 1978).

WEILL, Kurt (1900–50) German composer, born in Dessau. He studied under **Humperdinck** and **Busoni** and early works included chamber music, two symphonies (1921, 1933) and stage works. He achieved fame with *Die Dreigroschenoper*, **Brecht**'s modernization of **Gay**'s *Beggar's Opera*, in 1928. Other works of that time included *Happy End* (1929), *Aufstieg und Fall der Stadt Mahagonny* (1930), *Die sieben Todsünden* (1933) (all with Brecht), *Die Bürgschaft* (1932) and *Der Silbersee* (1933). A refugee from the Nazis, he settled in the USA in 1934. In all his works Weill was influenced by jazz idioms; his later songs, operas and musical comedies, many of which contain elements of social criticism, rank among the finest musical products written for the American stage. They include *Lady in the Dark* (1940), *Street Scene* (1946) and *Lost in the Stars* (1949).

WEIMAR, Marguerite Josephine See **GEORGE, Mlle**

WEINBERG, Steven (1933–) American physicist, born in New York City, the son of a New York court stenographer. He was educated at Cornell and Princeton universities and held appointments at Columbia, Berkeley, the Massachusetts Institute of Technology and Harvard before becoming professor of physics at Texas in 1986. In 1967 he produced a gauge theory (ie, one involving changes of reference frame) that correctly predicted both electromagnetic and weak nuclear forces (such as are involved in nuclear decay) despite the two differing in strength by a factor of about 10^{10}. The theory also predicted a new interaction due to 'neutral currents', whereby a chargeless particle is exchanged giving rise to a force between particles. This was duly observed in 1973, giving strong support to the theory (now called the Weinberg-Salam theory). As the work was independently developed by Weinberg and **Abdus Salam**, and subsequently extended by **Sheldon Glashow**, all three shared the 1979 Nobel prize for physics.

WEINBERGER, Caspar Willard (1917–) American politician, born in San Francisco. After military service (1941–45) he trained and worked as a lawyer, before entering politics as a member of the California state legislature in 1952. He served as finance director (1968–69) in the California administration of **Ronald Reagan** and then moved to Washington, to work first as director of the office of management and budget (1972–73) and then as secretary of health, education and welfare (1973–75) in the **Nixon** and **Ford** administrations. Following a period in private industry, working for the Bechtel Corporation (1975–80), he was appointed defence secretary by President Reagan with the brief to oversee a major military build up. This he successfully did, developing such high-profile projects as the strategic defence initiative, though there was congressional criticism of the budgetary consequences and of Pentagon inefficiency. A 'hawk' with respect to East-West issues, Weinberger opposed the rapprochement with Soviet Union during the final years of the Reagan administration and resigned in November 1987. He was later, in 1988, awarded an honorary knighthood (KBE) by the British monarch for 'service to British interests', most notably during the Falklands War (May–June 1982).

WEINBERGER, Jaromir (1896–1967) Czech composer, born in Prague. He studied under **Max Reger**, was professor of composition at Ithaca Conservatory, New York (1922–26) and settled in the USA in 1939. He wrote theatre music, orchestral works, and four operas, the most famous of which is *Schwanda the Bagpiper* (1927).

WEINGARTNER, (Paul) Felix (1863–1942) Austrian conductor and composer, born in Zara, Dalmatia. He studied under **Liszt**, succeeded **Mahler** (1908) as conductor of the Vienna Court Opera, and later toured extensively in Britain and America. His works include operas, symphonies, and *Über das Dirigieren* (1895). He wrote an autobiographical work, *Lebenserinnerungen* (trans 1937 as 'Buffets and Rewards').

WEINSTOCK, Arnold, Baron Weinstock of Bowden (1924–) English industrial executive, born in London. He worked at the Admiralty from 1939 to 1945, was engaged in finance and property development (1947–54) and then entered the radio and allied industries. He joined GEC in 1961, becoming managing director in 1963. Since then he has developed greatly the power and influence of the company through a series of 'take-overs'.

WEIR, Peter (1944–) Australian film director, born in Sydney. Educated at Sydney University, he joined a local television station in 1967 and began directing short films with *Count Vim's Last Exercise* (1967). His imaginative flair, thoughtful camerawork and sense of the macabre were soon evident in *Michael* (1970) and *Homesdale* (1971), both winners of the Australian Film Institute Grand Prix. His feature length début, *The Cars That Ate Paris* (1974), and the languid ghost story *Picnic at Hanging Rock* (1975), established him at the forefront of the indigenous film industry. *The Last Wave* (1977) illustrated his fascination with the clash between ancient and modern cultures. Since then he has looked increasingly to international projects, bringing sensitivity, skill and an atmosphere of mystery to such films as *The Year of Living Dangerously* (1982), *Witness* (1985) and *The Dead Poets Society* (1989).

WEISMANN, August Friedrich Leopold (1834–1914) German biologist, born in Frankfurt-am-Main. In 1867 he became professor of zoology at Freiburg. One of his first works was on the development of the Diptera. In 1868–76 appeared a series of papers, translated in 1882 as *Studies in the Theory of Descent*. His theory of germ-plasm (Weismannism—a form of neo-Darwinism), expressed in a series of essays (trans as *Essays upon Heredity and Kindred Biological Problems*, 1889–92), raised opposition in Britain. He wrote other works on evolution.

WEISS, Peter Ulrich (1916–82) German dramatist, painter, filmmaker and novelist, born in Berlin. Known initially as a graphic artist and novelist, he fled Nazi Germany and settled in Sweden in 1939. He became famous with his first play, *The Persecution and Assassination of Marat as Performed by the Inmates of the Asylum of Charenton under the direction of the Marquis de Sade* (1964), known more simply as *Marat/Sade*. His next play, *The Investigation* (1965), was a documentary based on transcripts of the Auschwitz trials. *The Song of the Lusitanian Bogey* (1967) was a more cogent attack on the capitalist system. Among his other works are *Vietnam Discourse* (1968), *Trotsky in Exile* (1970), and *Hölderlin* (1971). He also wrote the autobiographical novels *Leave Taking* (1961) and *Vanishing Point* (1962).

WEISSMULLER, Johnny (Peter John) (1903–84) American swimmer and actor, born in Windber, Pennsylvania, the son of Austrian immigrants. He was the first man to swim 100 metres in under a minute, and 440 yards in less than five minutes. Undefeated from 1921 to 1928, he won a total of five Olympic gold medals. His physique, swimming prowess and popularity won him the film role of Tarzan. From 1932 to 1948 he made 19 Tarzan films, and is credited with inventing the King of the Jungle's celebrated yodelling signature tune.

WEISZ, Victor See **VICKY**

WEIZMANN, Chaim (1874–1952) Russian-born chemist and Israeli statesman, born near Pinsk. He studied in Germany and lectured on chemistry at Geneva and Manchester. His complete and articulate faith in Zionism played a large part in securing the Balfour Declaration of 1917, by which the Jews were promised a national home in Palestine. He was president of the Zionist Organization (1920–30, 1935–46), and of the Jewish Agency (from 1929). When the state of Israel came into being in 1948, he became its first president.

WEIZSÄCKER, Karl Heinrich (1822–99) German Protestant theologian, born in Oehringen. He became professor at Tübingen. His most notable work was translated as *The Apostolic Age* (1894–95).

WEIZSACKER, Richard Freiherr, Baron von (1920–) West German politician, born in Stuttgart, the son of a baron-diplomat who was tried at Nuremberg. He was educated at Berlin, Oxford, Grenoble and Göttingen universities, studying history and law. During World War II he served in the Wehrmacht. After the war he worked as a professional lawyer and was active in the German Protestant Church, becoming president of its congress (1964–70). A member of the conservative Christian Democratic Union (CDU) since 1954, he served as a deputy in the Bundestag from 1969, as CDU deputy chairman (1972–79) and, from 1981, as a successful mayor of West Berlin, before being elected federal president in May 1984. A cultured, centrist Christian Democrat, he has been a popular president, making his mark with a well received speech to the Bundestag in May 1985, on the 40th anniversary of the end of World War II, in which he urged Germans never to forget the lessons of the Nazi era. He was re-elected in May 1989.

WELCH, John See **WELSH**

WELCH, Raquel, originally **Raquel Tejada** (1940–) American actress, born in Chicago, Illinois. As a child she studied ballet and began entering beauty contests as a teenager. A model, waitress and television weather-girl before she made her film début in *A House is Not a Home* (1964), she was launched as a curvaceous sex symbol after her scantily-clad appearance in *One Million Years B.C.* (1966). Rarely challenged by later roles, she did evince some comic ability in *The Three Musketeers* (1973), for which she received a Best Actress Golden Globe Award. Absent from the cinema since 1979, she continues to be regarded as one of the world's great beauties and her professional career has included nightclub entertaining, the Broadway musical *Woman of the Year* (1982) and the publication of a *Total Beauty and Fitness Programme* (1984).

WELCH, Robert (1929–) English silversmith and product designer, born in Hereford. He trained at Birmingham School of Art and afterwards at the Royal College of Art, London. In 1955 he began his long association with the stainless-steel manufacturer J and J Wiggin, for which he designed cutlery, tea sets etc under the name 'Old Hall'. In the same year he established a workshop in Chipping Campden. His work has included jewellery, ceramics, glass, lighting and ironmongery. He has bridged successfully the gap between the making of single pieces of fine craftsmanship and industrial production, while maintaining a high degree of elegance and quality in the products for which he is reponsible. He was made a royal designer for industry in 1965.

WELCKER, Friedrich Gottlieb (1784–1868) German philologist and archaeologist, born in Grünberg (Hessen). He was professor at Giessen, Göttingen and Bonn, and was notable for his works on Greek history and literature.

WELENSKY, Sir Roy (1907–) Rhodesian politician, born in Salisbury, Southern Rhodesia, the son of a Lithuanian Jew. He was a notable railway trade union member who was elected to the Legislative Council of Northern Rhodesia in 1938, in 1940 became a member of the Executive Council, was knighted in 1953, and from 1956 to its break-up in 1963 was prime minister of the Federation of Rhodesia and Nyasaland, of which he was a most energetic advocate and architect.

WELLER, Thomas Huckle (1915–) American physiologist, educated at Harvard. After war service as an army medical researcher into tropical diseases, he joined **John Enders** and **Frederick Robbins** in devising techniques for cultivating the poliomyelitus virus (thus making possible the development of a polio vaccine), for which they shared the 1954 Nobel prize for physiology or medicine. He also isolated the causative agents of chicken pox, german measles and shingles.

WELLES, (George) Orson (1915–85) American director and actor, born in Kenosha, Wisconsin. He appeared at the Gate Theatre, Dublin, in 1931, returned to America, became a radio producer in 1934, and founded the Mercury Theatre in 1937. In 1938 his radio production of **HG Wells**'s *War of the Worlds* was so realistic that it caused panic in the USA. In 1941 he wrote, produced, directed and acted in the film *Citizen Kane*, a revolutionary landmark in cinema technique, and in 1942 produced and directed a screen version of **Booth Tarkington**'s *The Magnificent Ambersons*, a masterly evocation of a vanished way of American life. His later work, giving ample rein to his varied and unpredictable talents, although never equalling his two masterpieces, includes his individual film versions of *Macbeth* (1948), *Othello* (1951), **Kafka**'s *The Trial* (1962) and *Chimes at Midnight* (based on **Shakespeare**'s Falstaff character, 1965); and a variety of memorable stage and film roles, the most celebrated being that of Harry Lime in *The Third Man* (1949).

WELLESLEY, Arthur See **WELLINGTON**

WELLESLEY, Richard Colley Wellesley, 1st Marquis (1760–1842) Irish administrator, brother of the 1st Duke of **Wellington**, born in County Meath. He became (1781) 2nd Earl of Mornington on the death of his father, and was returned to Westminster in 1784. He supported **Pitt**'s foreign policy and **Wilberforce**'s efforts to abolish the slave trade, and in 1786 became a lord of the Treasury. In 1797 he was raised to the English peerage as Baron Wellesley and made governor-general of India. Under his outstanding administration (1797–1805) British rule became supreme in India; the influence of France there was extinguished with the disarming of its forces in Hyderabad, the power of the princes much reduced by the crushing (1799) of **Tippoo Sahib** at Seringapatam by General **George Harris**, and (1803) of the Marathas, with the help of his brother, and the revenue of the East India Company was more than doubled. In 1799 he was given the rank of marquis in the Irish peerage, in 1805 he returned to England and in 1809 went as ambassador to Madrid. On his return he was made foreign minister (1809–12), and later (in 1821 and 1833) lord-lieutenant of Ireland.

WELLESZ, Egon Joseph (1885–1974) Austrian composer and musicologist, born in Vienna. He studied under **Schoenberg** and subsequently became professor of musical history at Vienna, specializing in Byzantine, Renaissance and modern music. Exiled from Austria by the Nazis, he became a research fellow at Oxford in 1938, and was lecturer in music there from 1944–48. His works include five operas, nine symphonies and a quantity of choral and chamber music.

WELLHAUSEN, Julius (1844–1918) German biblical scholar, born in Hameln. He was professor at Greifswald (1872), Halle (1882), Marburg (1885) and Göttingen (1892), best known for his investigations into Old Testament history and source criticism of the Pentateuch. He published several works, notably the *Prolegomena zur Geschichte Israels* (1883; translated as *History of Israel* 1885).

WELLINGTON, Arthur Wellesley, 1st Duke of, known as the **'Iron Duke'** (1769–1852) Irish soldier and statesman, brother of **Richard Wellesley**, born in

Dublin, son of the 1st Earl of Mornington. Desultory study at Chelsea, Eton, Brussels and a military school at Angers led, in 1787, to an ensign's commission in the 73rd Foot. Something of a dilettante, he transferred to the 76th Foot, thence to the 41st, 12th Light Dragoons and then to the 58th Foot, which brought him to captain's rank. As aide-de-camp to two lord-lieutenants of Ireland and member for Trim in the Irish Parliament (1790–95), his lack of means forbade immediate marriage with Lady Katherine Pakenham. His brother now bought him command of the 33rd Foot, and he campaigned with it on the Ems in 1794. In 1797 his regiment was sent to India, where his brother arrived as governor-general within a year. With **Napoleon** gaining victories in Egypt, Wellesley was dispatched to deal with **Tippoo Sahib** of Mysore. As brigade commander under General **George Harris** he did admirable work throughout the Seringapatam expedition and as subsequent administrator of the conquered territory. His campaigns against Holkar and Scindia saw the enemy capital of Poona subjected in 1803, Mahratta power broken at Ahmednagar and hard-fought Assaye, and final victory achieved at Argaum. Returning home in 1805, in 1806 he married 'Kitty' Pakenham—who bore him three sons and three daughters—and was returned MP for Rye, becoming Irish Secretary in 1807. The same year he accompanied the Copenhagen expedition, defeating the Danes at Sjaelland. In 1808 he was sent to the aid of the Portuguese against the French, defeating **Junot** at Roliça, and winning a victory at Vimeiro. He resumed his parliamentary post; but **Moore**'s retreat on Coruña sent him back, in 1809, to assume chief command in the Peninsula. Talavera (July 1809) was nearly a blunder, but it was quickly retrieved. Salamanca (July 1812) was a good victory; and although there were minor setbacks, ultimately the French were driven out of Spain and brought to submission at Toulouse in 1814. Wellesley was created Duke of Wellington and heaped with honours. With **Napoleon**'s escape from Elba Wellington hastened from the Congress of Vienna to take command of the scratch force—'an infamous army', he termed it—mustered to oppose the Corsican. **Blücher**'s supporting forces having been defeated at Ligny, Wellington took up opposition on the well-reconnoitred field of Waterloo, where the French were routed on 18 June 1815. Rewarded with the Hampshire estate of Strathfieldsaye, in 1818 the Duke joined the **Liverpool** administration as master-general of the Ordnance. In 1826 he was made constable of the Tower, and in 1827 commander-in-chief, an office in which he was confirmed for life in 1842. In 1829 he materially assisted in **Peel**'s reorganization of the Metropolitan Police. In general, Wellington's political policy was to refrain from weakening established authority and to avoid foreign entanglements, since Britain never possessed a sufficient army to enforce her will. When **Canning** intervened to bind Britain, France and Russia to impose recognition of Greek autonomy on Turkey, he resigned; but with Canning's death in 1827 and the collapse of the nebulous Goderich (**Ripon**) administration, the Duke became prime minister. His reluctance to oppose the Test and Corporation Acts cost him the allegiance of **Huskinsson** and the Liberals; while his support of Catholic emancipation culminated in a bloodless duel with the Earl of Winchilsea. His non-intervention in the East after Navarino offended the majority of his party; while his opposition to the indiscriminate enlargement of the franchise brought widespread unpopularity—and broken windows at Apsley House (London) on the anniversary of Waterloo. In the political crisis of 1834 Wellington again formed a government; in Peel's temporary absence abroad he acted for all the secretaries of state. Chosen chancellor of the University of Oxford in 1834, with Peel's return to power in 1841 Wellington joined his cabinet, but without portfolio. He retired from public life in 1846. Made lord high constable of England, in 1848 he organized the military in London against the Chartists. He was buried in St Paul's Cathedral. His London home at Apsley House, Piccadilly, is now the Wellington Museum.

WELLS, Charles Jeremiah (c.1800–1879) English poet, born in London. He was educated at Edmonton, where he met **John Keats**. He practised as a solicitor in London (1820–30) and taught English in France. He died in Marseilles. His *Stories after Nature* (1822) were followed in 1824 by the biblical drama, *Joseph and his Brethren*, which remained unknown until **Swinburne** praised it in the *Fortnightly* (1875).

WELLS, H G (Herbert George) (1866–1946) English novelist, short story writer and popular historian, born in Bromley, Kent, the third son of an unsuccessful shopkeeper. At 18 he left his job as a draper's apprentice and became a pupil teacher at the Midhurst Grammar School, from where he won a scholarship to the Normal School of Science, South Kensington, and studied biology under **T H Huxley**. Although distracted by politics, writing and teaching he obtained a BSc in 1890 and then lectured for the Universal Tutorial College until the success of his short stories allowed him to concentrate full-time on writing. Idealistic, impatient and dynamic, he threw himself into contemporary issues—free love, Fabianism, progressive education, scientific theory, 'world government' (he was an early agitator for a League of Nations) and human rights. His private life was no less restless than his public. His first marriage was to his cousin Isabel in 1890, but ended in divorce. His second, to Amy Catherine ('Jane') Robbins, in 1895, suited him domestically but he sought physical solace elsewhere and had numerous affairs, notably with 'new' women including Amber Reeves, Elizabeth von Arnim, **Rebecca West**, Odette Keun and Moura Budberg, **Gorky**'s mistress. He wrote over a hundred books and countless articles, achieving unparalleled fame in his lifetime, but by the time of his death his popularity had waned. *The Time Machine* (1895), an allegory set in the year 802701 describing a two-tier society, pioneered English science fiction and was followed by significant contributions to the genre: *The Wonderful Visit* (1895), *The Island of Doctor Moreau* (1896), *The Invisible Man* (1897), *The War of the Worlds* (1898), *When the Sleeper Awakes* (1899), *The First Men in the Moon* (1901), and *Men Like Gods* (1923). A satirical visionary, he was disputatious and fought with Fabian colleagues—**George Bernard Shaw** and the **Webbs**, for instance—as well as with his fellow novelist **Henry James**, who sprinkled condescension on Wells' novels. Wells responded with sarcasm and continued to produce a spate of social satires, drawing heavily on his own varied experience. He wrote some of the best known English comic novels—*Love and Mr Lewisham* (1900), *Kipps* (1905) and *The History of Mr Polly* (1910)—and books that concentrated on specific contemporary issues: *Ann Veronica* (1909), an early feminist novel, *Tono Bungay* (1909), which charts the decline of the upper classes, and *The New Machiavelli* (1911), about a politician embroiled in a sex scandal. *Mr Britling Sees It Through* (1916) and *The World of William Clissold* (1926) are lesser books but autobiographically illuminating. *The Country of the Blind, and other stories* (1911) is the best of his several collections. In 1920 he published *The Outline of History*, which enjoyed a vast circulation, and among his many other works is *The Shape of Things to Come* (1933), a plea to confront Fascism before it was too late. *Experiment in Autobiography* (1934) includes a striking self-portrait and studies of friends and contempories.

WELLS, Horace (1815–48) American dentist, born in Hartford, Vermont. He foresaw the value of nitrous oxide as an anaesthetic but his attempt to demonstrate it at Harvard in 1845 was a failure, and he later committed suicide.

WELLS, John (1936–) English actor, dramatist, humorist and director. He read French and German at Oxford, and taught both languages at Eton (1961–63), while contributing material for revues at the Edinburgh Festival. He was a co-editor of the satirical magazine, *Private Eye* (1964–67), and has written for the magazine ever since, notably the supposed diary of Mrs Wilson, **Harold Wilson**'s wife and the Dear Bill letters, the supposed correspondence of Denis Thatcher, husband of **Margaret Thatcher**. He has written a number of plays for the theatre, starting with *Listen to the Knocking Bird* in 1965. *Mrs Wilson's Diary* (1968) was followed by *Anyone for Denis* (1981), in which he played the title role. He is also highly regarded as a translator of plays and opera from the French and German. He directed a revival of *The Mikado* in 1989. As an actor he made his London début in the farce *An Italian Straw Hat*, in 1961.

WELLS, Sir Thomas Spencer (1818–97) English surgeon, born in St Albans. He was the first to practise ovariotomy successfully. He was the author of *Diseases of the Ovaries* (1865).

WELSH, John (c.1568–1622) Scottish Presbyterian clergyman, born in Colliston, Dumfriesshire. An ancestor of **Jane Carlyle** he was imprisoned and banished by **James VI**.

WELTE, Benedikt See **WETZER, Heinrich Josef**

WELTY, Eudora (1909–) American novelist and short-story writer, born in Jackson, Mississippi. She was educated at the Mississippi State College for Women, the University of Wisconsin and the Columbia University School of Advertizing in New York. After leaving college she was a publicity agent with the Works Progress Administration in Mississippi which involved extensive travel through the state. She took numerous photographs which were published as *One Time, One Place: Mississippi in the Depression: A Snapshot Album*, in 1971. During World War II she was on the staff of the *New York Review of Books*. She started by writing short stories, with 'Death of a Travelling Salesman', and published several collections from 1941 to 1954. She has also written five novels, mostly drawn from Mississippi life: *The Robber Bridegroom* (1942), *Delta Wedding* (1946), *The Ponder Heart* (1954), *Losing Battles* (1970) and *The Optimist's Daughter* (1972). *The Collected Stories of Eudora Welty* was published in 1980. Among her many accolades, she has received two Guggenheim fellowships, three O Henry awards, the Pultizer prize and the National Medal for Literature. Her autobiography, *One Writer's Beginnings*, was published in 1984.

WENCESLAS, Saint (c.907–929) prince-duke of Bohemia and patron saint of Czechoslovakia, the 'Good King Wenceslas' of the Christmas carol. He was raised as a Christian by his grandmother, St **Ludmilla**, who was murdered by his pagan mother in 921, who then became regent until he came of age in 924. He encouraged German missionaries to come to Bohemia, and put his duchy under the protection of King **Henry the Fowler** of Germany. In 929 he was murdered by his pagan brother, Boleslav. His remains were interred in St Vitus Cathedral in Prague.

WENCESLAS IV (1361–1419) Holy Roman Emperor. The son of the emperor **Charles V** and elder brother of the emperor **Sigismund**, he was crowned king of Bohemia in 1378 and emperor in the same year. An ineffective ruler, he allowed Germany to slide into anarchy, and was deposed as emperor in 1400.

WENDERS, Wim (1945–) German film director, born in Düsseldorf. Originally a student of medicine and philosophy, he attended Munich's Cinema and Television College from 1967 to 1970, where he made his first short film, *Schauplatze* (1967). A writer for *Filmkritik* and *Die Süddeutsche Zeitung* between 1968 and 1972, he made his feature début with *Summer in the City* (1970). Concerned with the influence of American culture on post-war German society, his work deals with isolation and alienation, often involving journeys in search of enlightenment. These themes are especially evident in *Alice in the Cities* (1974) and *The State of Things* (1982). He has been frequently honoured by the Cannes Film Festival, winning the International Critics Award for *Kings of the Road* (1976), the Golden Palm for *Paris, Texas* (1984) and Best Director for *Wings of Desire* (1987).

WENG T'UNG, or **WEN TONG** (d.1079) Chinese painter, born in Hu-Chou, in Che Kiang Province, where he became a magistrate. Known under the name Wen Huzhou, he was the first great master of bamboo painting. A representative of the last of the five categories of Sung painting, the Spontaneous Style (characterized by an intuitive response to nature in combination with brush discipline and mastery of pictorial composition), he owes his place in Chinese art largely to the fact that he was the teacher and close friend of **Su Tung-p'o**.

WENNER-GREN, Axel Leonard (1881–1961) Swedish financier and industrialist. To exploit an improved vacuum cleaner he founded AB Electrolux in 1919, which he owned until 1956. Through Electrolux he also launched the Platen-Munter refrigerator. He owned Svenska Cellulosa AB from 1934 to 1941 and had interests in AB Bofors, but from 1930 onwards spent most of his time abroad, where his large-scale projects included a holiday resort in the Bahamas, a telephone company in Mexico and, in 1956, a huge development complex in British Columbia comprising electrical plants, mining and forestry. His Swedish interests were united in Fulcrum AB, which went into liquidation in 1975. During his lifetime and in his will he donated vast sums to institutions for scientific research, best known of which are the Wenner-Gren Institut for experimental biology (1937, part of Stockholm University), the Wenner-Gren Foundation for anthropological research, established in New York in 1941, and above all the Wenner-Gren Center, an international scientific research centre set up in Stockholm in 1962.

WENTWORTH, Charles Watson See **ROCKINGHAM, Charles**

WENTWORTH, Thomas See **STRAFFORD**

WENTWORTH, William Charles (1793–1872) Australian statesman, born on Norfolk Island. He took part in the expedition which explored the Blue Mountains in 1813 before he went to England to study at Cambridge. When called to the bar in 1822 he had already published his classic *Statistical Account of the British Settlements in Australasia* (1819). A staunch protagonist of self-government, which he made the policy of his newspaper *The Australian* (established 1824), he founded Sydney University in 1852.

WERFEL, Franz (1890–1945) Austrian author, born in Prague. He lived in Vienna until 1938, when he moved to France, from where he fled from the Nazi occupation in 1940 to the USA. His early poems and plays were expressionistic but he is best known for his novels, including *The Song of Bernadette* (1941).

WERGELAND, Hendrik Arnold (1808–45) Norwegian poet and patriot, known as 'Norway's Lord Byron', and brother of the novelist **Camilla Collett**. He championed the cause of Norwegian nationalism in literature. A prolific lyrical poet and playwright, his chief work was a philosophical verse drama, *Skabelsen, mennesket og messias* (Creation, Man and Messiah, 1830). His last work, *Den engelske Lods* (The English Pilot, 1844), celebrated the liberation of the human mind.

WERNER, Abraham Gottlob (1749–1817) German geologist, born in Wehrau, Silesia. A teacher at Freiburg in Saxony from 1775, he was one of the first to frame a classification of rocks, and gave his name to the Wernerian or Neptunian theory of deposition, which he advocated in controversy with **James Hutton**.

WERNER, Alfred (1866–1919) German-born Swiss inorganic chemist, born in Mülhausen, Alsace. Professor in Zürich from 1893, he was notable for his researches on isomerism and the complex salts, which rejuvenated inorganic chemistry, and was awarded the Nobel prize for chemistry in 1913.

WERNER, (Friedrich Ludwig) Zacharias (1768–1823) German romantic dramatist, born in Königsberg. His chief works are *Die Söhne des Thals* (1803), *Das Kreuz an der Ostsee* (1804) and *Martin Luther* (1806). A convert to Catholicism, he died a priest in Vienna.

WERNICKE, Carl (1848–1905) German neurologist. Professor at Breslau (1885–1904), he studied brain damage leading to aphasia or dysphasia (the loss of certain kinds of language ability). 'Wernicke's area' in the brain is named after him.

WERTHEIMER, Max (1880–1943) German psychologist and philosopher. After studying in Prague, Berlin and Würzburg, in 1912 he conducted experiments in perception with **Kurt Koffka** and **Wolfgang Köhler** which led to the founding of the Gestalt school of psychology. He was professor at Berlin and Frankfurt, but left Germany for the USA in 1933 at the Nazi assumption of power, and taught at the New School for Social Research in New York City (1933–43).

WESKER, Arnold (1932–) English dramatist, born in London's East End, of Russian-Jewish parentage. He left school at 14. His ultimate Jewish family background and his varied attempts at earning a living are important ingredients of his plays. The Kahn family trilogy, *Chicken Soup with Barley*, *Roots* and *I'm talking about Jerusalem* (1959–60), echo the march of events, pre- and post-World War II, in the aspirations and disappointments of the members of a left-wing family. *Roots* is an eloquent manifesto of Wesker's socialism: an aesthetic recipe for all which he attempted to put into practice by taking art to the workers through his Centre-42 (1961–70). Other plays are *The Kitchen* (1959), *Chips with Everything* (1962), *The Four Seasons* and *Their Very Own and Golden City* (1966), *The Old Ones* (1972) and *The Merchant* (1978). He also wrote *Words—as Definitions of Experience* (1976). No major new Wesker play has been produced in Britain for some time, although a one-woman play, *Annie Wobbler* (1984), was well received. At the end of the 1980s, however, his reputation still rests firmly on his earliest plays.

WESLEY, Charles (1707–88) English hymnwriter and evangelist, brother of **John Wesley**, born in Epworth, Lincolnshire. He studied at Christ Church College, Oxford, where he formed (1729) a small group of fellow students, nicknamed the 'Oxford Methodists', or the 'Holy Club', later joined by his brother. Ordained in 1735, he accompanied John to Georgia as secretary to governor **James Oglethorpe**, returning to England in 1736. He was the indefatigable lieutenant of his more famous brother; after an evangelical conversion in 1738, he wrote over 5500 hymns, including such well-loved favourites as 'Jesu, Lover of my soul', 'Hark, the Herald Angels sing', and 'Love divine, all loves excelling'.

WESLEY, John (1703–91) English evangelist and founder of Methodism, brother of **Charles Wesley**, and son of the rector of Epworth. In 1720 he passed from the Charterhouse to Christ Church College, Oxford. He was ordained deacon in 1725, priest in 1728, and in 1726 became a fellow of Lincoln and Greek lecturer. In 1727 he left Oxford to assist his father, but returned as tutor in 1729. At this time he was much influenced by the spiritual writings of **William Law**. He became leader of a small dedicated group which had gathered round his brother Charles, nicknamed the 'Holy Club' or the 'Oxford Methodists', a name later adopted by John for the adherents of the great evangelical movement which was its outgrowth. The members of the club, who in 1730 were joined by James Hervey and **George Whitefield**, practised their religion with a then extraordinary degree of devotion, in strict accordance with the rubrics. On his father's death (1735), accompanied by Charles, he went as a missionary to Georgia, where his lack of experience led him to make many mistakes and aroused the hostility of the colonists. After an unfortunate love-affair he returned to England (1738). He had been influenced by Moravians on the voyage out, and now he met Peter Böhler, and attended society meetings. At one of these, held in Aldersgate Street, during the reading of **Luther**'s preface to the epistle to the Romans, he experienced an assurance of salvation which convinced him that he must bring the same assurance to others. But his unwonted zeal alarmed and angered most of the parish clergy, who closed their pulpits against him; this intolerance, Whitefield's example, and the needs of the masses drove him into the open air at Bristol (1739). There he founded the first Methodist chapel. He preached in, and bought, the ruinous Foundry in Moorfields, London, Methodist anniversaries sometimes being reckoned from this event; the Foundry was for long the headquarters of Methodism in the capital. During his itinerary of half a century, 10000 to 30000 people would wait patiently for hours to hear him. He gave his strength to working-class neighbourhoods; hence the mass of his converts were colliers, miners, foundrymen, weavers, and day-labourers in towns. His life was frequently in danger, but he outlived all persecution, and the itineraries of his old age were triumphal processions from one end of the country to the other. During his unparalleled apostolate he travelled 250000 miles and preached 40000 sermons. Yet he managed to do a prodigious amount of literary work, and produced grammars, extracts from the classics, histories, abridged biographies, collections of psalms, hymns and tunes, his own sermons and journals, and founded the *Methodist Magazine* (1778). His works were so popular that he made £30000, which he distributed in charity during his life. He founded charitable institutions at Newcastle and London, and Kingswood School in Bristol. Wesley broke with the Moravians in 1745, and his acceptance of what was then known as an Arminian theology led to divergences with Whitefield in 1741, a separate organization of Calvinistic Methodists under the Countess of **Huntingdon**, and to an acute controversy (1769–78) with **Toplady**. Wesley was determined to remain loyal to the

Church of England and urged his followers to do the same; but increasing pressures were brought to bear on him and in 1784 he himself ordained one of his assistants (**Francis Asbury**) for work in the USA (much to his brother's distress), a practice which he later extended. However, he always regarded Methodism as a movement within the Church and it remained so during his lifetime. In 1751 he married the widow Mary Vazeille, who deserted him in 1776. His journeys and spiritual odyssey were recorded in his *Journal*.

WESLEY, Samuel (1766–1837) English organist and composer, born in Bristol, son of **Charles Wesley**. One of the most famous organists of his day, he was an early and ardent enthusiast of **J S Bach**. Though a Roman Catholic (to the displeasure of his father and uncle), he wrote also for the Anglican liturgy, leaving a number of fine motets and anthems, including *In Exitu Israel*. His illegitimate son, Samuel Sebastian (1810–76), born in London, was a brilliant cathedral organist.

WESSEL, Horst (1907–30) German national socialist, born in Bielefeld. He was the composer of the Nazi anthem 'Die Fahne Hoch', known as the Horst Wessel song.

WESSELMANN, Tom (1931–) American painter, born in Cincinnati, Ohio. He studied psychology at Cincinnati University before taking art courses. In 1961 he moved to New York, abandoning the Abstract Expressionist style and turning instead to Pop Art. Most of his paintings depict overtly erotic female nudes in contemporary all-American environments; these works form the series known as 'The Great American Nude'.

WESSON, Daniel Baird (1825–1906) American gunsmith, born in Worcester, Massachusetts. With Horace Smith (1808–93) he devised a new type of repeating mechanism for small-arms in 1854 and founded the firm of Smith and Wesson at Springfield, Massachusetts, in 1857.

WEST, Benjamin (1738–1820) American-born British painter, born in Springfield, Pennsylvania. He showed early promise as a portraitist and was sent on a sponsored visit to Italy, and on his return journey was induced to settle in London (1763). **George III** was his patron for 40 years. The representation of modern instead of classical costume in his best-known picture, *The Death of General Wolfe*, was an innovation in English historical painting.

WEST, Jerry Alan (1938–) American professional basketball player, born in Cabin Creek, West Virginia. He was an All-American guard at West Virginia University (1956–60), and then played for the Los Angeles Lakers from 1960 to 1974. He then went on to coach and manage the club, remaining in the sport as an executive. He was captain of the USA Olympic basketball side in 1960.

WEST, Mae (1893–1980) American vaudeville and film actress, born in Brooklyn, New York. She made her début on Broadway in 1911, specializing in roles of sultry sexual innuendo. She wrote many of the plays she starred in, like *Sex* (1926) and *Diamond Lil* (1928, later filmed as *She Done Him Wrong* with **Cary Grant**, 1933). Her other films included *I'm No Angel* (1933), *Klondyke Annie* (1934) and *My Little Chickadee* (1940). She returned to the screen in 1970 in *Myra Breckenridge*. The 'Mae West', an inflatable life-jacket, is affectionately named after her.

WEST, Morris Langlo (1916–) Australian novelist, born in St Kilda, Victoria. He attended a Christian Brothers College in St Kilda before going to Melbourne University. He joined the Christian Brothers, a Catholic teaching order, but resigned in 1940 before taking vows, and served in the Australian Imperial Forces during World War II. In 1955 West moved to Italy and his first major work *Children of the Sun*, about the homeless children of Naples, was published in that year. Many successful novels followed, including *The Devil's Advocate* (1959) which won the James Tate Black memorial prize, *The Shoes of the Fisherman* (1963), *The Tower of Babel* (1968), and *The Clowns of God* (1981).

WEST, Nathanael, pseud of **Nathan Wallenstein Weinstein** (1903–40) American novelist, born in New York City. After attending Brown University, Rhode Island, he lived in Paris for a few years, where he wrote *The Dream Life of Balso Snell* (1931), self-consciously avant garde but illuminating in his preoccupation with the hollowness of contemporary life. On his return to New York he mismanaged a hotel and was associate editor with William Carlos William of the magazine *Contact*. *Miss Lonelyhearts*, the story of a newspaper agony columnist who becomes more involved with his correspondents than is good for him, appeared in 1933. There are parallels in West's own life but he renounced journalism and went to Hollywood in 1935 to write scripts for a minor studio, plundering this experience for *The Day of the Locust* (1939), his neurotic masterpiece. His only other novel, *A Cool Million*, was published in 1934. A black humorist and biting satirist, he was killed, along with his wife, when he ignored a traffic signal.

WEST, Dame Rebecca, the adopted name of **Cecily Isabel Fairfield** (1892–1983) Irish novelist, biographer, journalist and critic, born in County Kerry. Her father, a journalist, left her mother and the family moved to Edinburgh where they lived in straitened circumstances. She was educated at George Watson's Ladies College, and trained for the stage in London, where in 1912 she adopted the nom de plume Rebecca West, the heroine of **Ibsen**'s *Rosmersholm* which she had once played, and who is characterized by a passionate will. From a formative age she was involved with the suffragettes and in 1911 joined the staff of the *Freewoman*, the following year becoming a political writer on the *Clarion*, a socialist newspaper. Her love affair with **H G Wells** began in 1913 and lasted for ten turbulent years during which time she bore him a son and laid the foundations for her career as a writer. Her first published book was a critical study of **Henry James** (1916); her second, a novel, *The Return of the Soldier* (1918), describes the homecoming of a shell-shocked soldier. After the final break with Wells she went to the USA where she lectured and formed a long association with the *New York Herald-Tribune*. In 1930 she married Henry Maxwell Andrews, a banker, and they lived in Buckinghamshire until his death in 1968. She published eight novels including *The Judge* (1922), *Harriet Hume* (1929), *The Thinking Reed* (1936) and the largely autobiographical *The Fountain Overflows* (1957). Her last (unfinished) novel was *Cousin Rosamund* (1988). In the mid-1930s she made several trips to the Balkans to gather material for a travel book, but her interest deepened and resulted in her masterful analysis of the origins of World War II, *Black Lamb and Grey Falcon*, published in two volumes in 1941. It is generally considered her magnum opus. During the war she superintended BBC broadcasts to Yugoslavia and in its aftermath she attended the Nuremberg War Crimes Trials. From this and other cases came *The Meaning of Treason* (1949) and *A Train of Powder* (1955). Witty, incisive and combative, she was described by **George Bernard Shaw** as handling a pen 'as brilliantly as ever I could and much more savagely'.

WESTBROOK, Mike (Michael John David) (1936–) English jazz composer, bandleader and pianist, born in High Wycombe, Buckinghamshire. He turned to music after studying painting. He concentrated on writing extended pieces specifically for his own ensembles, ranging from trios to big bands, often in partnership with his wife Kate Westbrook (tenor horn, piccolo, voice). His major suites have included *The Cortege* (1982) and *On Duke's Birthday* (1984).

WESTBURY, Richard Bethell, Baron (1800–73) English judge, born in Bradford-on-Avon. Called to the bar in 1823, he became solicitor-general in 1852, attorney-general in 1856, and in 1861 lord chancellor, with the title of Baron Westbury. He promoted measures of law reform, and persuaded the Inns of Court to improve the training of barristers but failed to carry his schemes for codifying the statutes and for combining law and equity. Noted for his sarcastic wit, he was an unpopular judge.

WESTCOTT, Brooke Foss (1825–1901) English scholar and prelate, born in Birmingham. Educated at King Edward VI School, Birmingham, and Trinity College, Cambridge, he was possessed of exceptional intellectual curiosity and energy from early childhood. He took both the mathematical and the classical triposes and became a fellow of Trinity in 1849. Ordained in 1851, he went to Harrow as assistant master (1852). Though he became a housemaster, he was not effective as a class teacher. He wrote a number of books while at Harrow. Appointed examining chaplain to the bishop of Peterborough (1868), and a canon of the cathedral (1869), he became also regius professor of divinity at Cambridge (1870). He reformed the teaching and regulations for theology degrees and exerted much influence on members of the university. Canon of Westminster (1883), after resigning from Peterborough, he was heavily involved in the preparation of the Revised Version of the Bible, published in 1881 and became bishop of Durham (1890). He held conferences at Auckland Castle, of employers, trade unionists and others and played a unique conciliatory role in the coal strike of 1892. He won the respect of Durham miners and Greek scholars alike.

WESTERMARCK, Edvard Alexander (1862–1939) Finnish social philosopher, born and educated in Helsinki. He was lecturer of sociology there, and from 1907–30 was professor of sociology in London. His *History of Human Marriage* (3 vols, 1922) was an attack on the theory of primitive promiscuity. He also wrote on the evolution of ethics, in *The Origin and Development of Moral Ideas* (1906–08) and *Christianity and Morals* (1939). He travelled widely in Morocco, and published several accounts of its peoples, including *Ritual and Belief in Morocco* (2 vols, 1926) and *Marriage Ceremonies in Morocco* (1914).

WESTINGHOUSE, George (1846–1914) American engineer, born in Central Bridge, New York. In 1863 he gave his name to an air-brake for railways, which he invented, and a company (now a corporation), which he founded for the manufacture of this and other appliances. He was a pioneer in the use of alternating current for distributing electric power, and founded the Westinghouse Electrical Co in 1886.

WESTLAKE, John (1828–1913) English international lawyer, born in Lostwithiel, Cornwall. Educated at Trinity College, Cambridge, he wrote a treatise on *Private International Law* (1858) which was a valuable pioneering work, though now superseded. From 1888–1908 he held the Whewell chair of international law at Cambridge and published a text on *International Law* (1904–07). He became president of the Institute of International Law in 1895.

WESTON, Edward (1886–1958) American photographer, born in Highland Park, Illinois. He established his own studio in Glendale in c.1910, but moved to Mexico in 1923. He rebelled against the prevalent 'soft-focus' style and became recognized as a modernist, emphasizing sharp images and precise definition in landscapes, portraits and still-life. In 1932 he joined **Ansel Adams** and others in forming the 'straight photography' purists Group f/64 in California. His close-up studies of inanimate objects such as shells and vegetables exemplified his vision of detailed form and the richness of his control of tone. He produced notable landscapes of the Mohave Desert and in 1937, with the first-ever award of a Guggenheim Fellowship to a photographer, travelled widely throughout the American West, followed by a long tour of the South and Eastern States to illustrate an edition of **Walt Whitman**'s *Leaves of Grass*. In later years he was incapacitated by ill-health.

WESTON, Frank (1871–1924) English Anglican bishop of Zanzibar, born in South London. He graduated from Oxford, and after ordination in 1894 served London curacies before going to East Africa under the Anglo-Catholic Universities' Mission to Central Africa in 1898. Ten years later he was made bishop of Zanzibar. A man of great dedication and not a few prejudices, he spoke out against a scheme to unite East Africa's Protestant denominations (though not against reunion in principle), and he disliked theological liberalism. He is said to have understood Africans as few Englishmen have done. He wrote several books, notably *The One Christ* (1907).

WETHERELL, Elizabeth See **WARNER, Susan Bogert**

WETSTEIN, or **Wettstein, Johann Jakob** (1693–1754) Swiss scholar, born in Basel. Charged with heresy in the preparation of his famous text, *Novum Testamentum Graecum* (1751–52), and his *Prolegomena* (1730) he left Basel, and was appointed (1733) to the chair of church history in the Remonstrants' College at Amsterdam.

WETTACH, Adrien See **GROCK**

WETTE See **DE WETTE, Wilhelm Martin Lebrecht**

WETTSTEIN See **WETSTEIN, Johann Jakob**

WETZER, Heinrich Josef (1801–53) German scholar, born in Anzefahr, Hesse. He was editor with Benedikt Welte of the great Roman Catholic theological encyclopaedia (12 vols, 1846–60). He became professor of Oriental Philology at Tübingen in 1830.

WEYDEN, Rogier van der, real name **Rogier de la Pasture** (1400–64) Flemish painter. After the death of **Jan van Eyck** in 1441, he was the most important Early Netherlandish painter. Very little is known of his life and even his identity has been disputed. Between 1435–49 he was in Brussels where he was appointed painter to the city. It is likely that he visited Italy since there are distinct Italian influences evident in his work. Patronized by the Burgundian court, his famous *Last Judgment* was painted for Chancellor Rolin. Akin to other members of the Early Netherlandish school in his meticulous attention to detail and technical expertise in describing texture, Weyden's work is distinguished by his ability to convey drama and emotion.

WEYER See **WIER, Johann**

WEYGAND, Maxime (1867–1965) French soldier, born in Brussels. He trained at St Cyr and became a cavalry officer and instructor. As chief of staff to **Foch** (1914–23), he rendered admirable service, but as chief of staff of the army (1931–35) he was handicapped by his lack of experience as a field commander. In 1940 his employment of an outmoded linear defence to hold a penetration in depth completed the rout of the French army. A prisoner of the Germans, and later of the French provisional government, he was allowed to retire into obscurity.

WEYL, Hermann (1885–1955) German mathematician, born in Elmshorn. He studied at Göttingen under **David Hilbert**, became professor at Zürich (1913), and Göttingen (1930). Refusing to stay in Nazi Germany, he went to Princeton in 1933. He made important contributions to the theory of **Riemann** surfaces, the representation theory of **Lie** groups, the mathematical foundations of relativity and quantum mechanics, and the philosophy of mathematics. His book *Symmetry* (1952) is a largely non-technical account for the general reader of the relation between group theory and symmetry in pattern and design.

WEYMAN, Stanley John (1855–1928) English novelist, born in Ludlow. He became popular with *A Gentleman of France* (1893), *Under the Red Robe* (1894) and other historical romances.

WHALLEY, Edward (d.c.1675) English regicide. He fought at Marston Moor and Naseby, was a member of the court which tried **Charles I**, and was a signatory of the death warrant. In 1660 he fled to New England with his son-in-law **William Goffe** and remained in hiding until his death.

WHARTON, Edith Newbold, née **Jones** (c.1861–1937) American novelist and short story writer, born in New York. Her family was wealthy and aristocratic and she was educated at home and in Europe. In 1885 she married Edward Wharton, a friend of the family, and they travelled widely, before settling in Paris in 1907. Her husband, however, was mentally unbalanced and they were divorced in 1913. Socially gregarious, she formed a durable friendship with **Henry James** who did much to encourage and influence her work, and a voluminous correspondence with, among others, **Bernhard Berenson**. *The Greater Inclination* (1899), her first collection of short stories, was followed by a novella, *The Touchstone* (1900), but it was *The House of Mirth* (1905), a tragedy about a beautiful and sensitive girl who is destroyed by the very society her upbringing has designed her precisely to meet, that established her as a major novelist. Many other works followed, almost 50 in all, including travel books and volumes of verse, but she is known principally as a novelist of manners, a keen observer of society, witty and satirical. Her most uncharacteristic novel is *Ethan Frome* (1911), which deals partly with her unhappy marriage, partly with primitive people in rural America. Important later works are *The Age of Innocence* (1920), *The Mother's Recompense* (1925), *The Children* (1928), and *Hudson River Bracketed* (1929). Her approach to her work is discussed in *The Writing of Fiction* (1925). *A Backwards Glance* (1934) is her revealing autobiography.

WHARTON, Philip, Duke of Wharton (1698–1731) Irish politician, son of **Thomas Wharton**. He was given an Irish dukedom in 1718 for his support of the government in the Irish House of Peers, but in England set up an opposition political paper, the *True Briton* (1723–24). While travelling in Europe he accepted the Garter from the Old Pretender, **James Francis Stewart**, in Rome, assumed the title of Duke of Northumberland, and fought for Spain, for which he was convicted of high treason in his absence and deprived of his estates.

WHARTON, Thomas, 1st Marquis of Wharton (1648–1714) Whig statesman. Lord-lieutenant of Ireland (1708–10), he was created earl in 1706 and marquis in 1714. He is remembered as author of the satirical anti-Catholic ballad *Lilliburlero*.

WHATELY, Richard (1787–1863), English scholar and prelate, born in London. Educated at Oriel College, Oxford, he was elected a fellow there in 1811. He became a college tutor and rector of Halesworth, and for the *Encyclopaedia Metropolitana* wrote what he afterwards expanded into treatises on logic (1826) and rhetoric (1828). In 1825 he was appointed principal of St Alban Hall, in 1829 professor of political economy at Oxford and in 1831 archbishop of Dublin. A founder of the Broad Church party, he opposed the Tractarian movement, supported Catholic emancipation, and worked for unsectarian religious instruction. His caustic wit and outspokenness made him unpopular.

WHEATLEY, Denis Yates (1897–1977) English novelist, born in London. He inherited the family wine business but sold up in 1931 to concentrate on novel writing. His métier was an alloy of satanism and historical fiction, highly coloured and frequently burdened with undigested research, but enormously popular. Indicative titles in a lurid œuvre are *The Devil Rides Out* (1935), *The Scarlet Impostor* (1942) and *The Sultan's Daughter* (1963). His three-volume autobiography was published posthumously (1978–80).

WHEATLEY, Phillis (c.1753–1785) American Negro poet, born in Africa, possibly Senegal. As a child she was shipped to the slave-market in Boston, Massachusetts (1761), and sold as a maidservant to the family of a Boston tailor, John Wheatley, who educated her with the rest of his family. She studied Latin and Greek, and started writing poetry in English at the age of 13. She published *Poems on Various Subjects, Religious and Moral* (1783), and visited England in that year, to huge popular interest, although some cast doubt on their authenticity. In 1778 she married John Peters, a free negro of Boston.

WHEATON, Henry (1785–1848) American jurist, born in Providence, Rhode Island. From 1812 to 1815 he edited the *National Advocate* in New York, where for four years he was a justice of the Marine Court, and from 1816 to 1827 reporter for the Supreme Court. From 1827 to 1835 he was *chargé d'affaires* at Copenhagen, and from 1835 to 1846 minister at Berlin. His most important work was *Elements of International Law* (1836, with many later editions).

WHEATSTONE, Sir Charles (1802–75) English physicist, born in Gloucester. He first became known as a result of experiments on sound. He invented the concertina (1829), and became professor of experimental philosophy at King's College, London (1834). In 1837 he and Sir **William Cooke** took out a patent for an electric telegraph. In 1838, in a paper to the Royal Society, he explained the principle of the stereoscope (see **Brewster**). He invented a sound magnifier for which he introduced the term *microphone*. Wheatstone's Bridge, a device for the comparison of electrical resistances, was brought to notice (though not invented) by him.

WHEELER, Sir Charles (1892–1974) English sculptor, born in Codsall, Staffordshire. He studied at the Wolverhampton Art School and the Royal College of Art, and is noted for his portrait sculpture and his decorative sculptures on monuments and buildings.

WHEELER, John Archibald (1911–) American theoretical physicist, born in Jacksonville, Florida. Educated at Johns Hopkins and in Copenhagen he spent his career at Princeton (1938–76) and finally in Texas. He worked with **Niels Bohr** on the theory of nuclear fission, and on the hydrogen bomb project; and he worked on the search for a unified field theory, and (with **Richard Feynman**) on the concept of action at a distance.

WHEELER, Sir (Robert Eric) Mortimer (1890–1976) English archaeologist, born in Glasgow. Educated at Bradford and London, he became director of the National Museum of Wales (1920), and keeper of the London Museum (1926–44). He carried out notable excavations in Britain at Verulamium (St Albans) and Maiden Castle, and from 1944–47 was director-general of archaeology in India, working to particular effect at Mohenjo-daro and Harappa. He then became professor of the archaeology of the Roman provinces at the newly founded Institute of Archaeology in London (1948–55). Knighted in 1952, he was well known for spirited popular accounts of his subject, in books and on television. His works include *Archaeology from the Earth* (1954), and the autobiographical *Still Digging* (1955).

WHELDON, Sir Huw (1916–86) Welsh broadcaster, the son of Sir Wyn Wheldon, permanent secretary for education. Partly educated in Germany, he joined the army in 1939 and was awarded the MC in 1944. He joined the BBC in 1952 and was responsible for the seminal arts programme *Monitor* (1957–64) where the cultural life of the land was reviewed and illuminated with a rare passion and enthusiasm. He became head of documentaries and music programmes in 1963, controller of programmes for BBC Television in 1965, and the Corporation's managing director (1968–75). Afterwards he returned to active programme-making as the co-writer and presenter of *Royal Heritage* (1977) before serving as the president of the Royal Television Society (1979–85).

WHEWELL, William (1794–1866) English scholar, born in Lancaster, the son of a joiner. He became a fellow and tutor of Trinity College, Cambridge. He was professor of mineralogy at Cambridge (1828–38), and of moral theology (1838–55). In 1841 he became master of Trinity, and in 1855 vice-chancellor of the university. His works include *History of the Inductive Sciences* (1837), *Elements of Morality* (1855), and other writings on the tides, electricity and magnetism, besides translations of **Goethe**'s *Hermann and Dorothea*, **Grotius**'s *Rights of Peace and War* and **Plato**.

WHICHCOTE, Benjamin (1609–83) English philosopher and theologian, born in Stoke in Shropshire. He was a student at Cambridge, became a fellow of Emmanuel College in 1633, was ordained and appointed Sunday Afternoon Lecturer in Trinity Church (1636–56) where he lectured to large audiences each week. He became Provost of King's College in 1644 but lost the post at the Restoration in 1660 by order of **Charles II**. He published nothing in his lifetime but is regarded as the spiritual founder of the 'Cambridge Platonists'. The posthumous selections from his sermons (1698) and aphorisms (1703) emphasize the moral rather than the doctrinal certainties in religion, and express the general belief that religion must harmonize with reason since God himself endowed human beings with reason and reveals himself principally through the mind.

WHICKER, Alan Donald (1925–) English broadcaster and journalist, born in Cairo. Commissioned in the Devonshire Regiment during World War II, he rose to the rank of major and served with the Army Film and Photo Unit. Thereafter, he was a war correspondent, reporting on the Inchon landings in Korea before joining the BBC (1957–68) where he worked on the 'Tonight' (1957–65) programme and began his *Whicker's World* documentary series in 1958. Television's most travelled man, he has allowed viewers a privileged eavesdrop on the lives of the rich and famous as well as discovering the exotic and extraordinary aspects of everyday lives in all parts of the world. Among his many specific series over the past three decades are *Whicker Down Under* (1961), *Whicker Within a Woman's World* (1972), *Whicker's World Aboard the Orient Express* (1982) and *Living With Waltzing Matilda* (1987–88). Consistently in the top-ten ratings, he has received numerous awards including the Royal Television Society Silver Medal (1968) and the **Richard Dimbleby** Award (1977). Among his books are *Some Rise By Sin* (1949) and the autobiography *Within Whicker's World* (1982).

WHIPPLE, Fred Lawrence (1906–) American astronomer, born in Red Oak, Iowa. He studied at California University, and became professor of astronomy at Harvard in 1945. An expert on the solar system (his *Earth, Moon and Planets* (1941) is a standard work), he is known especially for his work on comets. In 1950 he suggested that they are composed of ice and dust and that many aspects of their behaviour could be interpreted on this basis; later work, and especially the study of **Halley**'s comet in 1986 by space probes, has confirmed this 'dirty snowball' model.

WHIPPLE, George Hoyt (1878–1976) American pathologist, born in Ashland, New Hampshire. A graduate of Yale and Johns Hopkins, in 1921 he became professor of pathology at Rochester. In 1934 he shared with **George Minot** and **William Murphy** the Nobel prize for physiology or medicine, as a result of their researches on the liver treatment of anaemia.

WHISTLER, James Abbott McNeill (1834–1903) American artist, born in Lowell, Massachusetts. He spent five years of his boyhood in St Petersburg (Leningrad), where his father, an engineer, was engaged on a railway project for the tsar. Returning home, he studied first for the army at West Point but failed his exams, and after a fruitless year with the Coast Survey he left America, never to return, and went to study art in Paris. His teacher, **Charles Gleyre**, had little influence on his subsequent work, but he was deeply impressed by **Courbet** and later by the newly-discovered **Hokusai**, and he exhibited at the *Salon des réfusés*. He began spending more and more time in London; when his mother came over from the USA in 1863 it became the centre of his activities, and he became celebrated as a portraitist. **Ruskin**'s vitriolic criticism of his contributions to the Grosvenor Gallery exhibition of 1877, accusing him of 'flinging a pot of paint in the public's face', provoked the famous lawsuit in which Whistler was awarded a farthing damages. His feelings on the subject are embodied in his *Gentle Art of Making Enemies* (1890). A recalcitrant rebel at a time when the sentimental Victorian subject picture was still *de rigueur*, Whistler conceived his paintings, even the portraits, as experiments in colour harmony and tonal effect; the famous portrait of his mother, now in the Louvre, was originally exhibited at the Royal Academy as *An Arrangement in Grey and Black*, and evening scenes such as the well-known impression of Battersea Bridge (Tate Gallery) were called 'nocturnes'. If there was little emphasis on draughtsmanship in his painting technique, the reverse is true of his etchings, especially his 'Thames' set, which succeed in imparting beauty to some unpromising parts of the London riverside. Witty, argumentative, quick to take offence, and theatrical in his manner, he often dressed like the cartoonist's stock artist-type.

WHISTLER, Rex John (1905–44) English artist. He studied at the Slade School, and excelled in the rendering of 18th century life, ornament and architecture, particulary in book illustration (eg, a fine edition of *Gulliver's Travels* in 1930), murals (eg, in the Tate Gallery) and designs for the theatre and ballet.

WHISTON, William (1667–1752) English clergyman and mathematician, born in Norton rectory in Leicestershire. In 1693 he became a fellow of Clare College, Cambridge, chaplain to the bishop of Norwich in 1696, and in 1698 rector of Lowestoft. His *Theory of the Earth* (1696) attracted attention, and in 1703 he became Lucasian professor at Cambridge, in succession to **Newton**. He was expelled from the university in 1710 for Arianism, and then wrote *Primitive Christianity revived* (1711–12). He spent the remainder of his life in London, engaged in one controversy after another, and joined the Baptists in 1747. His translation of **Josephus** was his best-known work. He also published his whimisical memoirs (1749–50).

WHITAKER, Joseph (1820–95) English bookseller and publisher, born in London, the son of a silversmith. He started the *Educational Register*, *Whitaker's Clergyman's Diary*, *The Bookseller* in 1858, and in 1868 *Whitaker's Almanac*.

WHITBREAD, Samuel (1758–1815) English politician, son of Samuel Whitbread (1720–1796), founder of the famous brewing firm. From Eton he passed to Oxford, and in 1790 entered parliament. The intimate friend of **Fox**, under **Pitt** he was leader of the Opposition, and in 1805 headed the attack on **Henry Dundas** (Viscount Melville).

WHITBY, Daniel (1638–1726) English theologian, born in Rushden near Higham Ferrers. In 1664 he became a fellow of Trinity College, Oxford, prebendary of Salisbury in 1668, and rector of St Edmund's there in 1669. After attacking 'popery' he tried from 1682 to find a basis of union with the Dissenters; his *Protestant Reconciler* (1682) was publicly burned at Oxford. His *Last Thoughts* appeared in 1727.

WHITE, Canvass (1790–1834) American civil engineer, born in Whitesboro, New York. In 1816 he became an assistant to **Benjamin Wright**, chief engineer of New York's Erie Canal. He was later one of the project's leading engineers, working on it until 1824. He was sent to England in 1817–18 to study the latest methods of canal and lock construction, and on his return surveyed an improved route for the canal in several places. He also made a type of cement equal in quality to the much more expensive imported cements, patenting his discovery in 1820. Later he worked on other canals, and reported on the best way of meeting the future water supply needs of New York City.

WHITE, Ellen Gould, neé **Harmon** (1827–1915) American Seventh-day Adventist leader, born in Gorham, Maine. She was converted to Adventism in 1842 through the preaching of **William Miller** (1781–1849). In 1846 she married an Adventist minister, James White. She was said to have experienced during her lifetime 'two thousand visions and prophetic dreams'. With the official establishment of the Seventh-day Adventist Church in 1863, she became leader and her pronouncements regarded as the 'spirit of prophecy'. Through more than 60 works she still dominates the denomination. One of her books, *Steps to Christ*, has gone through numerous editions and sold more than 20 million copies.

WHITE, Elwyn Brooks (1899–1985) American essayist, children's novelist, poet and parodist, born in Mount Vernon, New York, in Westchester County. Long associated with the *New Yorker* from 1925, he did as much to make its name as it did his. His reputation rests on his three best-selling novels for children (*Stuart Little*, 1945; *Charlotte's Web*, 1952; and *The Trumpet of the Swan*, 1970), the essays he wrote in the column 'One Man's Meat', his collaboration with **James Thurber** on *Is Sex Necessary? Or Why You Feel The Way You Do* (1929), *The Elements of Style* (1959), a long article entitled 'Here Is New York', and a peerless parody of **Hemingway**, 'Across the Street and into the Grill'. Succinct, graceful and witty, his writing prompted Thurber to declare that 'Many of the things he writes seem to me as lovely as a tree'. Inclined towardes rusticity, he spent much time in Maine fretting over livestock, retiring to a boathouse to sculpt his pieces. He was married to Katharine Angell, the first fiction editor of the *New Yorker*.

WHITE, Sir George Stuart (1835–1912) English soldier. Entering the army in 1855, he served in the 2nd Afghan war of 1878–80, where he won the Victoria Cross. He was commander-in-chief in India (1893–98), and in the 2nd Boer War through a 119-day siege (1899–1900). He became governor of Gibraltar (1900–04).

WHITE, Gilbert (1720–93) English clergyman and naturalist, born at 'The Wakes' in Selborne, Hampshire. Educated at Oriel College, Oxford, he took orders in 1747, in 1752 became junior proctor, and in 1758 obtained the sinecure college living of Moreton Pinkney, Northants. From 1755 he lived uneventfully at Selborne as curate of Farringdon in Hampshire, and latterly curate of Selborne (from 1784). His charming *Natural History and Antiquities of Selborne* (1789) based on letters written over a 20-year period, has become an English classic. White's Thrush is named after him.

WHITE, Henry Kirke (1785–1806) English poet, born in Nottingham, the son of a butcher. Articled to a solicitor, in 1803 he published his verse sketch *Clifton Grove*, which brought him the friendship of **Southey** and the Rev **Charles Simeon**, through whom he became a sizar of St John's College, Cambridge. After his tragically early death, Southey edited his *Remains* (1807).

WHITE, Joseph, originally **José Maria Blanco** (1775–1841) Spanish-born British theological writer, born in Seville of an Irish Catholic father and an Andalusian mother. Ordained a priest in 1800, he lost his faith in 1810 and went to London, where he edited a monthly Spanish patriotic paper (1810–14). He then received an English pension of £250, was tutor to Lord **Holland**'s son (1815–16), and was admitted to Anglican orders. He was tutor in Archbishop **Whately**'s family in Dublin (1832–35), but fled to Liverpool on adopting unitarian views. He contributed to the *Quarterly* and *Westminster*, edited the short-lived *London Review*, wrote *Letters from Spain* (1822), *Evidence against Catholicism* (1825), and one notable sonnet, 'Night and Death'.

WHITE, Leslie Alvin (1900–75) American cultural anthropologist, born in Salida, Colorado. He studied at Columbia University, the New School for Social Research and the University of Chicago, and taught at Michigan from 1932 to 1975 (professor from 1943). He carried out many field trips among the Pueblo Indians between 1926 and 1957. He is principally known for his theory of cultural evolution, propounded in *The Science of Culture* (1949) and *The Evolution of Culture* (1959) and several other works, in which he argued that culture in general tends to advance as technological efficiency in harnessing and using environmental energy sources increases.

WHITE, Minor (1908–76) American photographer and editor, born in Minneapolis. From 1937 he originally worked for the US government Works Progress Administration but from 1945 he was greatly influenced by **Edward Weston** and **Alfred Stieglitz** developing both the realism of the photographic sequence and the abstraction of the 'equivalent', the visual metaphor in which he continued Stieglitz's symbolism of natural formations. In 1946 he moved to San Francisco and worked with **Ansel Adams** whom he followed as director of the photographic department in the California School of Fine Art (1947–52). He was a prolific and influential writer, founding and editing the periodicals *Aperture* (1952) and *Image* (1953–57; he was subsequently appointed professor of creative photography at the Massachussets Institute of Technology (1965–76).

WHITE, Patrick (1912–) Australian author, born in London of Australian parents. He was educated at Cheltenham College and then worked in Australia for two years before going to King's College, Cambridge. After war service in the RAF he wrote *Happy Valley* (1939), *The Living and the Dead* (1941) and *The Aunt's Story* (1946), and then bought a farm near Sydney and settled in Australia. He achieved international success with *The Tree of Man* (1954). In this symbolic novel about a small community in the Australian bush, he attempts to portray every aspect of human life and to find the secret that makes it bearable. In 1957 appeared *Voss*, an allegorical account, in religious terms, of a gruelling attempt to cross the Australian continent. This was followed by *Riders in the Chariot* (1961), *The Solid Mandala* (1966), *The Eye of the Storm* (1973) and *The Twyborn Affair* (1979). He has also published short stories—*The Burnt Ones* (1964) and *The Cockatoos* (1974), and plays, including *Four Plays* (1965) and *Signal Driver* (1981). His own 'self-portrait', *Flaws in the Glass* (1981), describes the background to his supposedly 'ungracious' receipt of the Nobel prize for literature in 1973.

WHITE, Paul Dudley (1886–1973) American cardiologist, the son of a physician who practised in Roxburg, Massachusetts. White was an undergraduate and medical student at Harvard, and for many years on the staff of its famous affiliated hospital, the Massachusetts General Hospital. He studied in 1913–14 with Sir **Thomas Lewis** in London and returned to the USA fired with enthusiasm over the value of the electrocardiogram in the diagnosis of heart disease. He acquired an international reputation with the publication of his textbook, *Heart disease* (1931), which went through several editions. He treated President **Eisenhower** when he had a heart attack, and Eisenhower's recovery did much to foster public awareness that heart disease need not be crippling. White preached the value of diet, exercise and weight control in the prevention of cardiovascular disease.

WHITE, Pearl Fay (1892–1938) American cinema actress, born in Green Ridge, Missouri. She began her film career in 1910, and as the heroine of *The Perils of Pauline* (1914), *The Exploits of Elaine* (1914–15), and others, made an enormous reputation as the exponent *par excellence* of the type of serial film popularly called 'cliff-hanger'. She retired in 1924, and went to live in France.

WHITE, Richard Grant (1821–85) American Shakespearean scholar, born in New York. After studying medicine and law, he became a journalist. His Shakespearean studies included criticisms on **John Payne Collier**'s folio MS emendations (*Shakespeare's Scholar*, 1854) and two editions (1857–65, 1883) of the *Works*. His other publications included *Words and their Uses* (1870), *Everyday English* (1881), and *England Without and Within* (1881). His son, Stanford White (1853–1906), was an eminent architect who designed a number of public buildings in New York.

WHITE, Terence Hanbury (1906–64) English novelist, born in Bombay, India. He was educated at Cheltenham College and Queens' College, Cambridge. Until 1936 he was a master at Stowe and later lived in a gamekeeper's cottage near the school. Always a keen sportsman, he was an ardent falconer and fisherman, and his knowledge and love of nature are imbued in his work. He wrote more than 25 books but he is best known for his interpretation of the Arthurian legend, a tetralogy known collectively as *The Once and Future King* (1958), the first part of which, *The Sword in the Stone* (1937), is a children's classic. *The Goshawk* (1951), set at the onset of World War II, is a chronicle of the taming and training of one of Germany's noblest birds of prey.

WHITE, William Allen (1868–1944) American editor and writer, known as the 'Sage of Emporia', born in Emporia, Kansas. He was proprietor and editor of the Emporia *Daily* and *Weekly Gazette* in 1895. He gained national fame in the presidential election of 1896 by his ferocious anti-Populist editorial 'What's the Matter with Kansas?', much used by the Republican (**McKinley**) campaign, but subsequently he became alarmed at conservative control of the party and lent support to the growing Progressive movement, placing his hopes in New York governor and then president **Theodore Roosevelt**. In addition to 'muckraking' articles he published a book of short stories of mordant social criticism, *Stratagems and Spoils* (1901), and a novel in the same vein, *A Certain Rich Man* (1909). He later wrote shrewd appraisals of national politicians of his time in *Masks in a Pageant* (1928), and an ironic life of **Calvin Coolidge**, *A Puritan in Babylon* (1933). He maintained that he laughed the Ku Klux Klan out of Kansas in his anti-Klan campaign for governor in the 1920s. He remained a Republican, although President **Franklin D Roosevelt** publicly thanked him for supporting his New Deal. He won a Pulitzer prize for his editorials in 1923.

WHITE, William Hale, pseud **Mark Rutherford** (1831–1913) English writer, born in Bedford. He was the son of William White (1797–1882), bookseller, and doorkeeper (1850–80) to the House of Commons who wrote *Inner Life of the House of Commons*, published in 1897. From 1848 to 1851 he qualified at Cheshunt and New College for the congregational ministry, but, expelled for his views on inspiration, became a civil servant in 1854 and journalist and writer. His translations of **Spinoza**'s *Ethica* (1883) and *Tractatus* (1885) were published under his own name but he owed his literary eminence to the series of novels, *The Autobiography of Mark Rutherford* (1881), *Mark Rutherford's Deliverance* (1885), and *The Revolution in Tanner's Lane* (1887).

WHITEFIELD, George (1714–70) English evangelist, one of the founders of Methodism, born in the Bell Inn, Gloucester. At 18 he entered Pembroke College, Oxford, as a servitor. The **Wesley**s had already laid the foundations of Methodism at Oxford, and Whitefield became an enthusiastic evangelist. He took deacon's orders in 1736, and preached his first sermon in the Crypt Church, Gloucester. In 1738 he followed John Wesley to Georgia and was appointed minister at Savannah. He returned to England in 1739 to be admitted to priest's orders, and to collect funds for an orphanage. The religious level of the age was low, and Whitefield was actively opposed by his fellow churchmen, but when the parish pulpits were denied him he preached in the open air, the first time with great effect, on Kingswood Hill near Bristol. He quickly returned to Georgia and made extensive preaching tours. About 1741, differences on predestination led to his separation as a rigid Calvinist from John Wesley as an Arminian. His supporters now built him a chapel in Bristol and the Moorfields 'Tabernacle' in London. He reached immense audiences, but founded no distinct sect, and many of his adherents followed the Countess of **Huntingdon** in Wales and ultimately helped to form the Calvinistic methodists. The Countess appointed him her chaplain, and built and endowed many chapels for him. He made seven evangelistic visits to America, and spent the rest of his life in preaching tours through England, Scotland (1741) and Wales. He compiled a hymn book in 1753. He set out for America for the last time in 1769, and died near Boston.

WHITEHEAD, Alfred North (1861–1947) English mathematician and Idealist philosopher, born in London. He was educated at Sherborne and Trinity College, Cambridge, where he was senior lecturer in mathematics until 1911. He became professor of applied mathematics at Imperial College, London (1914–24), and of philosophy at Harvard (1924–37). Extending the Booleian symbolic logic in a highly original *Treatise on Universal Algebra* (1898), he contributed a remarkable memoir to the Royal Society, 'Mathematical Concepts of the Material World' (1905). Profoundly influenced by **Giuseppe Peano**, he collaborated with his former pupil at Trinity, **Bertrand Russell**, in the *Principia Mathematica* (1910–13), the greatest single contribution to logic since **Aristotle**. In his Edinburgh Gifford Lectures, *Process and Reality* (1929), he attempted a metaphysics comprising psychological as well as physical experience, with events as the ultimate components of reality. Other more popular works include *Adventures of Ideas* (1933) and *Modes of Thought* (1938). He was awarded the first James Scott prize (1922) of the Royal Society of Edinburgh.

WHITEHEAD, Charles (1804–62) English poet and novelist, born in London, the son of a wine merchant. He devoted himself to letters after publishing *The Solitary* (1831), a poem of reflection. His *Autobiography of Jack Ketch* (1834) showed humour, but when Chapman & Hall asked him for a popular book in instalments he declined, recommending young **Dickens**, who thus began the *Pickwick Papers*. His novel, *Richard Savage* (1842), earned the praises of Dickens and **Dante Gabriel Rossetti**. Whitehead went out to Melbourne in 1857, but died miserably, leaving unfinished the *Spanish Marriage*, a drama.

WHITEHEAD, Paul (1710–74) English satirist and minor poet, born in Holborn, a tailor's son. He was apprenticed to a mercer, and later married a short-lived imbecile with a fortune of £10000. He spent some years in Fleet prison for the nonpayment of a sum for which he had stood security. He became active in politics, was one of the infamous 'monks' of Medmenham Abbey, and became deputy treasurer of the Chamber. Among his satires are *State Dunces* (1733), inscribed to **Pope**, and *Manners* (1739), for which **Dodsley** the publisher was brought before the House of Lords. His *Collected Works* appeared in 1777.

WHITEHEAD, Robert (1823–1905) English inventor, born in Bolton-le-Moors. He trained as an engineer in Manchester and settled (1856) in Fiume, where he invented the first self-propelling torpedo (1866).

WHITEHEAD, William (1715–85) English poet and dramatist, born in Cambridge, the son of a baker. He was educated at Winchester and Clare Hall, Cambridge, and became a fellow in 1742. He travelled as tutor to Lord Jersey's son, became in 1755 secretary of the Order of the Bath, and in 1757 was appointed poet laureate. He wrote tragedies (*The Roman Father*, in imitation of **Corneille**'s *Horace*, 1750; *Creusa*, 1754), and a comedy, *School for Lovers* (1762).

WHITELAW, Billie (1932–) English actress, born in Coventry, noted as an interpreter of the plays of **Samuel Beckett**. She made her London début in **Feydeau**'s *Hotel Paradiso* in 1956, and joined the National Theatre in 1964, appearing in Beckett's one-act *Play*. She joined the Royal Shakespeare Company in 1971 and returned to Beckett in 1973 to play Mouth in *Not I*. She played in Beckett's *Footfalls* at the Royal Court in 1976, and in a revival of Beckett's *Happy Days* at the Royal Court in 1979. She has played many other modern roles on stage, and appeared in several films.

WHITELAW, Viscount William (Stephen Ian) (1918–) English politician, farmer and land-owner. He was educated at Winchester and Cambridge, served in the Scots Guards during and after the war, and first became a Conservative MP in 1955. A former secretary of state for Northern Ireland (1972–73) and for employment (1973–74), he was home secretary for four years before being made a viscount in 1983. He was made a Companion of Honour in 1974. During the Conservative leadership contest of 1975 his loyalty to **Edward Heath**, which persuaded him not to stand directly against him in the first ballot, is thought to have allowed **Margaret Thatcher** to win in the second ballot. As her deputy, however, he displayed the same loyalty and was one of her firmest, although sometimes privately critical, allies.

WHITELEY, Brett (1939–) Australian artist, born in Paddington, Sydney. He studied in Sydney but a scholarship enabled him to study in France. He was represented in the 1961 Whitechapel Gallery exhibition and won the international prize at the second Paris biennale of the same year. He worked in New York from 1967 to 1969, and continued to travel and exhibit abroad regularly. He won the prestigious Archibald prize in 1976 and again in 1978, the Sulman prize (1976 and 1978) and the Wynne prize (1977 and 1978).

WHITELEY, William (1831–1907) English merchant, born in Wakefield. In 1863 he opened what became London's first department store, off Bayswater Road. He applied to himself the name of 'Universal Provider'.

WHITELOCKE, Bulstrode (1605–76) English lawyer and statesman, born in London, the son of a judge. He studied law, sat in the Long Parliament for Great Marlow, and took a half-hearted part on the Parliamentary side in the Civil War. He was appointed a commissioner of the Great Seal (1648), but would not act in the king's trial, and was sent as ambassador to Sweden (1653). Although nominated by **Richard Cromwell** keeper of the Great Seal, he was later included in the Act of Oblivion. Whitelock's *Memorials* was first published in 1682 in a falsified form; better in 1732. His *Journal of the Embassy to Sweden* was edited by Reeve (1855).

WHITEMAN, Paul (1891–1967) American bandleader, born in Denver, Colorado. He became famous in the 1920s as a pioneer of 'sweet style', as opposed to the traditional 'classical' style jazz. His band employed such brilliant exponents of true jazz as **Bix Beiderbecke**, the trumpeter, and Whiteman became popularly regarded as the 'inventor' of jazz itself rather than of a deviation from true jazz style. He was responsible for **Gershwin**'s experiments in 'symphonic' jazz, commissioning the *Rhapsody in Blue* for a concert in New York in 1924.

WHITFIELD, June Rosemary (1925–) English comic actress, born in Streatham, London. A graduate of the Royal Academy of Dramatic Art, she worked in revues, musicals and pantomimes as a foil to some of the top comedians in showbusiness before enjoying her own success as Eth Glum in the long-running radio series *Take It From Here* (1953–60). She has been an indispensable part of television light entertainment in such series as *Fast and Loose* (1954), *Faces of Jim* (1962–63) and *Beggar My Neighbour* (1966–67). A long professional association with Terry Scott has resulted in the series *Scott on . . .* (1969–73), *Happy Ever After* (1974) and *Terry and June* (1979–87). Her film appearances include *Carry on Nurse* (1959), *The Spy With the Cold Nose* (1965) and *Bless This House* (1973).

WHITGIFT, John (c.1530–1604) English prelate, and archbishop of Canterbury, born in Grimsby. In 1555 he was elected fellow of Peterhouse, Cambridge, took orders in 1560, and rose to be regius professor of divinity at Cambridge (1567), dean of Lincoln (1571), bishop of Worcester (1577), archbishop of Canterbury (1583), and privy councillor (1586). He was a great pluralist. He attended Queen **Elizabeth** in her last moments, and crowned **James VI and I**. Although personally biassed towards Calvinism, he vindicated the Anglican position against the Puritans and enforced the policy of uniformity in the Church of England. He was the founder of Whitgift School in Croydon, Surrey.

WHITING, John (1917–63) English playwright. Educated at Taunton School, he studied at the Royal Academy of Dramatic Art (1935–37). After serving in the Royal Artillery in World War II he resumed his acting career before emerging as a dramatist. *Saint's Day* (1951), depicting the sense of hopelessness, failure and self-destruction of the Southman ménage, gained recognition for his talent although it was not a popular success. It was followed by *A Penny for a Song* (1951), a comedy, and *Marching Song* (1954), a play of ideas with little action or dramatic situation whose plot deals with the decision facing General Rupert Forster: to stand trial as a scapegoat for his country's failure or to commit suicide. After *Gates of Summer* (1956) he was commissioned by the Royal Shakespeare Company to dramatize **Huxley**'s *The Devils of Loudon*, as *The Devils* (1961), which achieved great success, despite harrowing scenes such as the torture of Grandier.

WHITLAM, (Edward) Gough (1916–) Australian politician, educated at the University of Sydney. After war service in the RAAF he became a barrister, and MP for Werriwa, NSW, in 1952. Made leader of the Australian Labor party in 1967, he became prime minister (1972–75), the first year of this term also serving as minister of foreign affairs. He resigned as MP in 1978 to take up a visiting appointment at the Australian National University in Canberra. His many publications, chiefly political and constitutional, also include *The Italian Inspiration in English Literature* (1980).

WHITLEY, John Henry (1866–1935) English politician, born in Halifax. Educated at Clifton and London University, he was Liberal MP for Halifax (1900–28), speaker (1921–28) during the difficult period which culminated in the general strike, and presided over the committee that proposed (1917) Whitley Councils for joint consultation between employers and employees.

WHITMAN, Walt (1819–91) American poet, born in West Hills, Long Island, New York, the son of a radical, free-thinking carpenter. He was brought up in Brooklyn from the age of four. He served first in a lawyer's and then in a doctor's office, and finally in a printer's. He next became an itinerant teacher in country schools. He returned shortly to printing, and in 1846 became editor of the *Brooklyn Eagle*. This and his other numerous press engagements were only of short duration. In 1848 he travelled with his brothers to New Orleans in search of work on the New Orleans *Crescent*, but came back to Brooklyn as a journalist (1848–54). He seemed unable to find free expression for his emotions until he hit upon the curious, irregular, recitative measures of *Leaves of Grass* (1855), originally a small folio of 95 pages, which grew in the eight succeeding editions to nearly 440 pages. This, with his prose book, *Specimen Days and Collect* (1882), constitutes his main life-work as a writer. Summoned to tend his brother, wounded in the Civil War, he became a volunteer nurse in the hospitals of the Northern army. The exertion, exposure, and strain of those few years left Whitman a shattered and prematurely aged man. In 1865 he received a government clerkship, but was dismissed by Secretary Harlan as the author of 'an indecent book' (*Leaves of Grass*). Almost immediately he obtained a similar post. In 1873 he was stricken with paralysis and left Washington for Camden, New Jersey, where he spent the remainder of his life. He would have fallen into absolute poverty but for the help of trans-Atlantic admirers. Later on, several wealthy American citizens liberally provided for his simple wants. Whitman set himself the task of uplifting into the sphere of poetry the whole of modern life and man. Thus the inclusion of subjects at that time which were tabooed. Many of his poems for *Leaves of Grass* are now considered American classics, such as 'Drum Taps', 'When Lilacs Last in the Courtyard Bloom'd' and 'O Captain! My Captain!'.

WHITNEY, Eli (1765–1825) American inventor, born in Westborough, Massachusetts. Educated at Yale, he went to Georgia as a teacher, but finding a patron in Mrs Nathaniel Greene, widow of a general, he stayed on her plantation, read law and set to work to invent a cotton-gin for separating cotton fibre from the seeds. His machine was stolen, and lawsuits in defence of his rights took up all his profits and the $50 000 voted him by the state of South Carolina. In 1798 he got a government contract for the manufacture of firearms, and made a fortune in this business.

WHITNEY, Josiah Dwight (1819–96) American geologist, brother of **William Dwight Whitney**, born in Northampton, Massachusetts. He graduated at Yale, and in 1840 joined the New Hampshire survey. In 1855 he was made professor at Iowa University, in 1860 state geologist of California, and in 1865 professor at Harvard. Mount Whitney, South California, the highest mountain in the USA, is named after him.

WHITNEY, William Dwight (1827–94) American philologist, brother of **Josiah Dwight Whitney**. He studied at Williams and Yale, and in Germany prepared an edition of the *Atharva Veda Sanhita* (1856). In 1854 he became professor of Sanskrit at Yale, in 1870 also of comparative philology. He was an office-bearer of the American Oriental Society, edited numerous Sanskrit texts, and contributed to the great Sanskrit dictionary of **Böhtlingk** and Roth (1855–75). He waged war with **Max Müller** on fundamental questions of the science of language. Among his works were *Language and the Study of Language* (1867) *Material and Form in Language* (1872), *Life and Growth of Language* (1876), *Essentials of English Grammar* (1877) and *Mixture in Language* (1881). He was editor of the 1864 edition of *Webster's Dictionary* and editor-in-chief of the *Century Dictionary and Cyclopedia* (1889–91).

WHITTIER, John Greenleaf (1807–92) American Quaker poet and abolitionist, born near Haverhill, Massachusetts, the son of a poor farmer. Largely self-educated, in 1829 he entered journalism, and in 1831 published *Legends of New England*, a collection of poems and stories. In 1840 he settled at Amesbury, a village near his birthplace, and devoted himself to the cause of emancipation. His collection *In War Time* (1864) contains the well-known ballad 'Barbara

Frietchie'. *At Sundown* was published in 1892. In his day he was considered second only to **Longfellow**.

WHITTINGTON, Richard ('Dick') (c.1358–1423) English merchant and philanthropist, the youngest son of Sir William Whittington of Pauntley in Gloucestershire. As a young man he was apprenticed to a prosperous London mercer, and by 1392 he was a member of the Mercers' Company, and in 1393 an alderman and sheriff. In 1397 he took over as mayor of London at the previous incumbent's death, and was mayor again three times in 1398, 1406, and 1419. He became a member of parliament in 1416. He traded with and loaned money to **Henry IV** and **Henry V**. A generous benefactor, he built a library at Greyfriars, and left his fortune to a trust which provided for the building of a library at Guildhall, the rebuilding of Newgate Gaol, and the foundation of a college and almshouse (now at East Grinstead). The legend of his cat is an accepted part of English folklore, dating from the early 17th century.

WHITTLE, Sir Frank (1907–) English aeronautical engineer and inventor. He joined the RAF as apprentice (1923), and studied at Cranwell and Cambridge (1934–37). He began research into jet propulsion before 1930, while still a student, and after a long fight against official inertia his engine was flown successfully in a Gloster aircraft in 1941, leading to world-wide use of jet engines in high-speed high-altitude aircraft.

WHITWORTH, Sir Joseph (1803–87) English engineer and inventor, born in Stockport. At the Great Exhibition of 1851 he exhibited many tools and machines. In 1859 he invented a gun of compressed steel, with spiral polygonal bore. He founded Whitworth scholarships for encouraging engineering science. He was responsible for the standard screw-thread named after him.

WHORF, Benjamin Lee (1897–1941) American linguist, born in Winthrop, Massachusetts. A chemical engineer and fire prevention officer by profession, he studied linguistics and American Indian languages in his spare time. Influenced by the teaching of **Edward Sapir** at Yale University (1931–32), he developed Sapir's insights into the influence of language on people's perception of the world into what became known as the Sapir-Whorf hypothesis. He illustrated his theory in particular with comparisons between the grammar and vocabulary of what he called 'standard average European' on the one hand and the language of the Hopi Indians on the other.

WHYMPER, Edward (1840–1911) English wood-engraver and mountaineer, born in London. He was trained as an artist on wood, but became more famous for his mountaineering. In 1860–69 he conquered several hitherto unscaled peaks of the Alps, including the Matterhorn. In 1867 and 1872 he made many geological discoveries in North Greenland. His travels in the Andes (including ascents of Chimborazo) took place in 1879–80. He illustrated his books *Scrambles amongst the Alps* (1871, 1893) and *Travels Amongst the Great Andes* (1892).

WHYTE-MELVILLE, George John (1821–78) Scottish novelist and authority on field sports, born in Mount-Melville, St Andrews. Educated at Eton, he became a captain in the Coldstream Guards and served in the Crimean War, commanding a regiment of Turkish cavalry irregulars. For the rest of his life he devoted himself to field-sports, and wrote numerous novels involving fox-hunting and steeplechasing, including *Digby Dand* (1853) and *Tilbury Nego* (1861). He also wrote serious historical novels, including *The Gladiators* (1863) and *The Queen's Maries* (1862), on **Mary, Queen of Scots**.

WICLIFFE See **WYCLIFFE, John**

WIDGERY, John Passmore, Lord (1911–81) English judge, born in South Molton, Devon. Educated at Queen's College, Taunton, he qualified as a solicitor but was called to the bar in 1947. He became a judge in 1961, a lord justice of appeal in 1968 and lord chief justice of England (1971–80). He was responsible for overseeing a restructuring of the English courts recommended by a Royal commission; he was also chairman of an enquiry into a clash between the army and demonstrators in Londonderry in 1972.

WIDOR, Charles Marie (1845–1937) French composer, born in Lyon. Organist of St Sulpice, Paris, he became professor of organ and composition at the Paris Conservatoire (1891) and secretary of the Académie de Beaux-Arts from 1914 until his death. He composed ten symphonies for the organ, as well as a ballet, chamber music and other orchestral works. He wrote *La Technique de l'orchestre moderne* (1904).

WIECHERT, Ernst (1887–1950) German writer, born in Kleinort in East Prussia. He published novels dealing with psychological problems such as post-war readjustment, among them *Der Wald* (1922), *Der Totenwolf* (1924), *Der silberne Wagen* (1928), *Die Majorin* (1934) and *Das einfache Leben* (1939), the last-named probably his masterpiece. *Wälder und Menschen* (1936) is autobiographical, as is *Der Totenwald* (1946), which describes his six months confinement in Buchenwald concentration camp.

WIECK, Clara See **SCHUMANN, Clara Josephine**

WIELAND, Christoph Martin (1733–1813) German writer, born near Biberach, the son of a pietist pastor. In 1752 **Bodmer** invited him to Zürich, and inspired him to write *Der geprüfte Abraham* and other books full of sentimentality and religious mysticism. But Wieland turned away from that particular style of writing, and from 1760 to 1770, as well as making the first German translation of **Shakespeare** (1762–66), he wrote the romances *Agathon* and *Don Silvio von Rosalva*, *Die Grazien* and other tales, and the didactic poem *Musarion*. Their elegance, grace and lightness made Wieland popular with fashionable society. After holding for three years a professorship at Erfurt, he was called to Weimar to train the grand-duchess's sons, and there he spent most of the rest of his life, the friend of **Goethe** and **Herder**. The Weimar period produced his heroic poem *Oberon*, by which he is best remembered, and various other works; he also edited several magazines.

WIELAND, Heinrich Otto (1877–1957) German organic chemist, born in Pforzheim. He did important work on the structure of cholesterol and other steroids, and studied at Munich, Berlin and Stuttgart before returning to Munich as professor of organic chemistry at the Technische Hochschule (1917). In 1921 he went to Freiburg and in 1925 again became a professor at Munich. Two years later he was awarded the 1927 Nobel prize for chemistry, in recognition of his research on the bile acids, organic radicals, nitrogen compounds, etc.

WIEN, Wilhelm (1864–1928) German physicist, born in Gaffken in East Prussia. He became professor at Aachen, Giessen, Würzburg and finally Munich (1920). In 1911 he was awarded the Nobel prize for physics for his work on the radiation of energy from black bodies. His researches also covered X-rays and hydrodynamics.

WIENER, Norbert (1894–1964) American mathematician, born in Columbia. He studied zoology at Harvard and philosophy at Cornell; in Europe he studied with **Bertrand Russell** at Cambridge and at Göttingen. He was professor of mathematics at the

Massachusetts Institute of Technology (1932–60). He worked on stochastic processes and harmonic analysis until World War II, when he studied mathematical communication theory applied to predictors and guided missiles. His study of the significance of feedback in the handling of information by electronic devices led him to compare this with analogous mental processes in animals in *Cybernetics, or control and communication in the animal and the machine* (1948) and other works. His frankly egocentric autobiography *I am a mathematician—the later life of a prodigy* was published in 1956.

WIENIAWSKI, Henri (1835–80) Polish composer of music for the violin, born in Lublin. For twelve years he was solo violinist to the tsar, and taught at the Brussels Conservatoire. His brother, Joseph (1837–1912), a pianist, taught in the Moscow Conservatory, and was a conductor at Warsaw (1871–77).

WIER, or **Weyer, Johann** (1516–88) Belgian physician, one of the first opponents of the witchcraft superstition, born in Grave in North Brabant. He studied medicine at Paris and Orléans, and became physician to the Duke of Jülich in Dusseldorf, to whom he dedicated his *De Praestigiis Daemonum et Incantationibus ac Veneficiis* (1563), a plea against the folly and cruelty of the witchcraft trials. The book roused the fury of the clergy, but the duke protected Wier until his death.

WIERTZ, Anton Joseph (1806–65) Belgian painter, born in Dinant. In 1836 he settled in Liège, and in 1848 in Brussels. His original aim was to combine the excellences of **Michelangelo** and **Rubens**; but about 1848–50 he began to paint speculative and mystical pieces, dreams, visions, and the products of a morbid imagination. In 1850 the state built him a studio which became the Musée Wiertz.

WIESEL, Torsten Nils (1924–) Swedish neurobiologist, joint winner of the 1981 Nobel prize for physiology and medicine. He studied medicine at the Karolinska Institute in Stockholm, and neurology at Johns Hopkins Medical School with **David Hubel**. At Harvard Medical school they worked together on the way the brains of cats and monkeys process visual information, for which they shared the Nobel prize with **Roger Sperry**.

WIGGIN, Kate Douglas, née **Smith** (1856–1953) American novelist, born in Philadelphia. She wrote novels for both adults and children, but was more successful with the latter. *Rebecca of Sunnybrook Farm* (1903) is probably her best-known book, although the *Penelope* exploits, *The Birds' Christmas Carol* (1888) and *Mother Carey's Chickens* (1911), were all firm favourites.

WIGGLESWORTH, Michael (1631–1705) English-born American poet and clergyman, born in Yorkshire. He was taken to Massachusetts Bay colony at the age of seven. Educated at Harvard, he was married to Mary Reyner (1655), to Martha Mudge (1679), and to Sybil Sparhawk Avery (1691) and eight children resulted. Fellow and tutor at Harvard from 1652 to 1654, and again from 1697 to 1705, he was ordained to the ministry of the Puritan Church in Malden, c.1656. His epic poem, the first American epic, 'Day of Doom' (1662), takes a lengthy and somewhat pessimistic view of the Day of Judgment. He wrote a shorter poem intended for edification in 1669: 'Meat out of the Eater or Meditations Concerning the Necessity, End and Usefulness of Afflictions Unto God's Children'.

WIGMAN, Mary, originally **Marie Wiegmann** (1886–1973) German dancer, choreographer and teacher, born in Hanover. The most famous German dancer of her era, she exerted a great influence on European modern dance. She studied eurhythmics with **Émile Jaques-Dalcroze** and assisted **Rudolf von Laban** during World War I. She subsequently made her name as a soloist, but her ensemble dances were landmarks in the German Expressionist style. She opened a school in Dresden in 1920, branches of which grew thoughout Germany and, through her star pupil **Hanya Holm**, in the USA; the Nazis later closed the German schools. She retired from the stage in 1942, but continued to choreograph and opened another school in West Berlin in 1949.

WIGMORE, John Henry (1863–1943) American jurist, born in San Francisco. Educated at Harvard, he taught law in Tokyo from 1889 to 1893 and at Northwestern University (1893–1943) where he proved an innovative teacher. He wrote extensively, his major work being *Treatise on Evidence* (1909, 3rd edition, 10 vols, 1940), a work of great scholarship; other important works include *The Principles* (in the last edition *The Science of Judicial Proof*) and various series which he edited, such as the Modern Legal Philosophy series (1911–22), the Modern Criminal Science series (1911–17), the Continental Legal History series (1912–28) and the Evolution of Law series (1915–18).

WIGNER, Eugene Paul (1902–) Hungarian-born American physicist, a native of Budapest. Educated at Berlin Technische Hochschule, and professor of mathematical physics at Princeton (1938–71), he is known for his many contributions to the theory of nuclear physics, especially the Breit-Wigner formula for resonant nuclear reactions and the Wigner theorem concerning the conservation of the angular momentum of electron spin. His name is also given to the most important class of mirror nuclides (Wigner nuclides), and to a number of other physical phenomena. His calculations were used by **Fermi** in building the first reactor in Chicago. He received the Fermi award in 1958, the Atom for Peace award in 1959, and the Nobel prize for physics in 1963.

WILAMOWITZ-MOELLENDORFF, Ulrich von (1848–1931) German classical scholar, born in Markowitz, Posen. He studied at Bonn and Berlin, and became professor at Greifswald (1876), Göttingen (1883), and Berlin (1897–1922). He was **Mommsen**'s son-in-law. He published several works on Greek history and literature, and editions of Greek classics.

WILBERFORCE, Samuel (1805–73) English prelate, third son of **William Wilberforce**, born in Clapham, London. In 1826 he graduated from Oriel College, Oxford, and was ordained in 1828. In 1830 he became rector of Brightstone, Isle of Wight, in 1840 rector of Alverstoke, canon of Winchester and chaplain to **Albert**, the Prince Consort, in 1845 dean of Westminster and bishop of Oxford. He took part in the controversies of the **Hampden**, **Gorham**, *Essay and Reviews*, and **Colenso** cases. Instrumental in reviving Convocation (1852), he instituted Cuddesdon theological college (1854). The charm of his many-sided personality and his social and oratorical gifts earned him the nick-name of 'Soapy Sam'. He edited *Letters and Journals of Henry Martyn* (1837), wrote along with his brother, Robert, the life of his father (1838), and himself wrote *Agathos* (1839), *Rocky Island* (1840) and *History of the Protestant Episcopal Church in America* (1844). Bishop of Winchester from 1869, he was killed by a fall from his horse. Of his two younger sons, Ernest Roland (1840–1908) became first bishop of Newcastle (1882) and bishop of Chichester (1895); Albert Basil Orme (1841–1916) became archdeacon of Westminster (1900), chaplain to the Speaker, and an eloquent advocate of temperance.

WILBERFORCE, William (1759–1833) English philanthropist, born in Hull, the son of a wealthy merchant. Educated at St John's College, Cambridge, in 1780 he was elected MP for Hull, in 1784 for Yorkshire, and became a close friend of **William Pitt** the Younger, though he remained independent of party. In 1784–85, during a tour on the continent, he was converted to evangelical Christianity, and in 1787 he founded an association for the reformation of manners. In 1788, suported by **Thomas Clarkson** and the Quakers, he entered on a 19-year struggle for the abolition of the slave trade, which ended in success in 1807. He next sought to secure the abolition of the slave trade abroad and the total abolition of slavery itself; but declining health compelled him in 1825 to retire from parliament. He was for long a central figure in the 'Clapham sect' of Evangelicals. He was buried in Westminster Abbey. He wrote *A Practical View of Christianity* (1797), helped to found the *Christian Observer* (1801), and promoted many schemes for the welfare of the community.

WILBYE, John (1574–1638) English madrigal composer, born in Diss in Norfolk. He was a household musician at Hengrave Hall, 1593–1628, and after that at Colchester. His madrigals are marked by sensitive beauty and excellent workmanship.

WILCKE, Johan Carl (1732–96) German-born Swedish physicist, born in Wismar. He was educated at Uppsala and taught in Stockholm. He did useful early work on electricity, but is best known for his studies of heat: independently of **Joseph Black** and **Henry Cavendish**, he recognized the distinctions between latent and specific heat capacity, and unlike them he published his measurements on this, in 1781.

WILCOX, Ella, née **Wheeler** (1850–1919) American journalist and prolific producer of verse, born in Johnstown Center, Wisconsin. In 1884 she married Robert M Wilson (d.1916). She had completed a novel before she was ten, and later wrote at least two poems a day. The first of her many volumes of verse was *Drops of Water* (1872); the most successful was *Poems of Passion* (1883). She also wrote a great deal of fiction, and contributed essays to many periodicals. Her *Story of a Literary Career* (1905), and *The World and I* (1918) were autobiographical.

WILDE, Lady Jane Francesca, known as **'Speranza'** (1826–96) Irish poet and hostess, born in Dublin. An ardent nationalist, she contributed poetry and prose to the *Nation* from 1845 under the pen-name of 'Speranza'. In 1851 she married Sir **William Wilde**; their son was **Oscar Wilde**. Her salon was the most famous in Dublin. After her husband's death she moved to London, and published several works on folklore, including *Ancient Legends of Ireland* (1887) and *Ancient Cures* (1891).

WILDE, Oscar Fingall O'Flahertie Wills (1854–1900) Irish playwright, novelist, essayist, poet and wit, born in Dublin. His father was Sir William Wilde; his mother Lady **Jane Francesca Wilde**. From the age of nine to sixteen he went to Portora Royal School in Enniskillen, which **Samuel Beckett** later attended. He went on to Trinity College, Dublin, and to Magdalen College, Oxford, where he was dandified, sexually ambiguous, sympathetic towards the Pre-Raphaelites, and contemptuous of conventional morality. He was also an accomplished classicist, and won the Newdigate prize in 1878 for the poem 'Ravenna', which his biographer, **Richard Ellmann**, described as 'a clever hodgepodge of personal reminiscence, topographical description, political and literary history'. In 1881 his first volume of poetry was published, *Patience*, and the next year he embarked on a lecture tour of the USA where, apparently, when asked if he had anything to declare he replied, 'Only my genius'. The tour, wrote Ellmann, 'was an advertisement of courage and grace, along with ineptitude and self-advertisement'. Wilde boasted to **Whistler**, 'I have already civilized America'. He married, in 1884, Constance Lloyd, and had two sons for whom he wrote the classic children's fairy stories, *The Happy Prince and Other Tales* (1888). Two years later came *The Picture of Dorian Gray*, modelled on his presumed lover, the poet John Gray. More fairy stories appeared in 1891, *A House of Pomegranates* and *Lord Savile's Crime and Other Stories*. It was also the year of his second play, *The Duchess of Padua*, an uninspired verse tragedy. But over the next five years he built his dramatic reputation, first with *Lady Windermere's Fan* (1892), followed by *A Woman of No Importance* (1893), *An Ideal Husband* (1895) and, the *pièce de resistance*, *The Importance of Being Earnest* (1895). *Salome*, originally written in French, appeared in 1894 in a translation by Lord **Alfred Douglas**. By now his homosexuality was commonly known, and the Marquis of Queensberry, father of Lord Alfred, left a card at Wilde's club addressed 'To Oscar Wilde posing as a Sodomite' (*sic*). Wilde took it that he meant 'ponce and Sodomite' and sued for libel. He lost the case, and was himself prosecuted and imprisoned for homosexuality. In 1905 his bitter reproach to Lord Alfred was published as *De Profundis*. He was released in 1897 and went to France under the alias Sebastian Melmoth, the name of his favourite martyr from *Melmoth the Wanderer*, the novel written by his great-uncle, **Charles Maturin**. *The Ballad of Reading Gaol* was published in 1898. His last years were spent wandering and idling on the continent.

WILDE, Sir William Robert Wills (1815–76) Irish oculist, aurist and topographer, born in Castlerea, County Roscommon, into an Irish Protestant family. He studied at London, Berlin and Vienna, and on his return to Dublin became the leader of his medical specialization. He served as medical commissioner on the Irish Census (1841 and 1851), publishing a major medical report, *The Epidemics of Ireland* (1851). He wrote on ocular and aural surgery and made a valuable medical study, *The Closing Years of Dean Swift's Life* (1849), with important evidence against the common belief that **Swift** had died insane. He pioneered the operation for mastoiditis, invented an ophthalmoscope and founded St Mark's Ophthalmic Hospital. His *The Beauties of the Boyne and the Blackwater* (1849) established him as the leading authority on the Boyne valley, where he took the appreciative **T B Macaulay** as background for the latter's *History*. *Lough Corrib, with Notes on Lough Mask* (1867) did comparable service in Galway, where he had bought an estate at Illaunroe. He was an antiquarian of significance, publishing a major catalogue of the holdings of the Royal Irish Academy, and was apparently fluent in Gaelic, He married (1851) Jane Francesca Elgee (**Wilde**), famous as the Young Ireland poet 'Speranza' of the Dublin *Nation*, but his own politics seem to have been Tory Home Rule. He was named Queen **Victoria**'s Irish oculist in ordinary and also attended King **Oskar I** of Sweden.

WILDENBRUCH, Ernst von (1845–1909) German romantic novelist, poet and dramatist, born in Beirut. He served in the army and Foreign Office. His strongly-expressed patriotism made him the national dramatist of Prussia during the empire of the **Hohenzollern**, to whom he was related.

WILDER, Billy (Samuel) (1906–) Austrian-born American filmmaker, born in Sucha. A law student at Vienna University, he worked as a journalist and crime reporter, making his film début in Germany as the co-writer of *Menschen am Sonntag* (1929). In Paris he co-directed *Mauvaise Graine* (1933) before moving to Hollywood and embarking on a fruitful collaboration with writer Charles Brackett. Their scripts include *Ninotchka* (1939) and *Ball of Fire* (1941). An American citizen from 1934, he made his American directorial début with *The Major and the Minor* in 1942, then distinguished himself as the creator of incisive dramas, acerbic comedies and bittersweet romances, winning multiple Academy Awards for *The Lost Weekend* (1945), *Sunset Boulevard* (1950) and *The Apartment* (1960). His many popular successes include *Double Indemnity* (1944), *The Seven Year Itch* (1955) and *Some Like It Hot* (1959). He made seven films with actor **Jack Lemmon** and worked with writer I A L Diamond from 1957.

WILDER, Laura, née **Ingalls** (1867–1957) American children's author, born in Pepin, Wisconsin. A farm woman all her life, it was not until she was in her 60s, when her daughter suggested that she write down her childhood memories, that her evocative 'Little House' series began to appear. *Little House in the Big Woods* (1932) caught on instantly in the USA and was followed by several sequels: *Little House on the Prairie* (1935), *By the Shores of Lake Silver* (1939), *Little Town on the Prairie* (1941), *Farmer Boy* (1933), and *Those Happy Golden Years* (1943). A television series in the 1950s assured their success in Britain.

WILDER, Thornton Niven (1897–1976) American author and playwright, born in Madison, Wisconsin. He was educated at Yale and served in both wars, becoming a lieutenant-colonel in 1944. He started his career as a teacher of English at Lawrenceville Academy (1921–28) and the University of Chicago (1930–37). His first novel, *The Cabala*, appeared in 1926. Set in contemporary Rome, it established the cool atmosphere of sophistication and detached irony that was to permeate all his books. These include *The Bridge of San Luis Rey* (1927), a bestseller and winner of the Pulitzer prize, *The Woman of Andros* (1930), *Heaven's My Destination* (1935) and *The Ides of March* (1948). His first plays—*The Trumpet Shall Sound* (1926), *The Angel That Troubled the Waters* (1928) and *The Long Christmas Dinner* (1931)—were literary rather than dramatic; but in 1938 he produced *Our Town*, a successful play that evokes without scenery or costumes a universal flavour of provincial life. This was followed in 1942 by *The Skin of Our Teeth*, an amusing yet profound fable of humanity's struggle to survive. Both these plays were awarded the Pulitzer prize. His later plays include *The Matchmaker* (1954), *A Life in the Sun* (1955), *The Eighth Day* (1967), *Theophilus North* (1974), and, in 1964, the musical *Hello Dolly*, based on *The Matchmaker*.

WILDGANS, Anton (1881–1932) Austrian poet and dramatist, born in Vienna. His plays include *Dies Irae* (1918) and the biblical tragedy *Kain* (1920). The epic poem *Kirbisch* appeared in 1927. From 1921 to 1923 he was director of the Vienna Burgtheater.

WILENSKI, Reginald Howard (1887–1975) Engish art critic and art historian, born in London. His analysis of the aims and achievements of modern artists, *The Modern Movement in Art* (1927), has had considerable influence.

WILEY, Harvey Washington (1844–1930) American food chemist, born near Kent, Indiana. He served in the civil war and qualified in medicine at Indiana Medical College in 1871. He was professor of chemistry at Purdue (1874–83), when he became chief of the chemical division of the US department of agriculture, where he did major work on the analysis of foods. However, his main interest was in improving purity and reducing food adulteration, and despite many obstacles his efforts led to the Pure Food and Drug Act of 1906. Conflicts over its enforcement led to his resignation in 1912, but he continued as an active propagandist on food purity until his death. His works include *Not by Bread Alone* (1915).

WILFRID, or **Wilfrith St** (634–709) English prelate born in Northumbria. Trained at Lindisfarne, he was bishop of York from c.665. He upheld the Roman views on Easter, and the tonsure, which triumphed at the Synod of Whitby (664), and was made bishop of Ripon and bishop of York. He improved the minster of York, built a spendid church at Hexham, and raised a new minster at Ripon. When Archbishop **Theodore** divided Northumbria into four sees in 678, Wilfrid appealed to Rome. On the journey he was driven by a storm to the coast of Friesland, where he baptized thousands of pagans. Pope Agatho decided in his favour, but King Ecgfrid flung him into prison. He escaped to Sussex, was allowed to return by the new king Aldfrith in 686, and was finally allowed to keep the sees of Ripon and Hexham, but not York.

WILHELM I (1797–1888) seventh king of Prussia and first German emperor, second son of **Frederick-William III**, born in Berlin. In 1814 he received his 'baptism of fire' on French territory at Bar-sur-Aube, and entered Paris with the allies. During the king's absence in Russia he directed Prussian military affairs. In 1829 he married Princess Augusta of Saxe-Weimar (1811–90), on the accession of his brother, **Frederick-William IV**, in 1840, he became heir-presumptive. In 1844 he visited England and formed a friendship with Queen **Victoria** and **Albert**, the Prince Consort. During the revolution of 1848 his attitude towards the people made him very unpopular. He was obliged to quit Prussia, and took up his quarters at the Prussian Legation in London. Within two months, however, he received his recall. In 1849 he subdued the disaffection in Baden. He was appointed regent (1858) in consequence of the prolonged ill-health of the king, on whose death, in 1861, he succeeded as Wilhelm I. He soon made plain his intention of consolidating the throne and strengthening the army. A few months after his accession he narrowly escaped assassination. Prince **Bismarck** was placed at the head of the ministry, with Albrecht von Roon (1803–79), the author of the new army system, as war minister. The scheme was very unpalatable to the parliament, but the minister-president forced it upon the nation, with the necessary increased expenditure, by overriding the constitution. In 1864 the Schleswig-Holstein difficulty led to a war with Denmark, in which the Prussian and Austrian troops were victorious; but in 1866 the allies quarrelled over the spoils, and struggled for the supremacy over the German states. Austria was crushed at Sadowa, and Prussia gained in territory and prestige. The affair of the Duchy of Luxemburg nearly led to a war between France and Prussia in 1867, but the difficulty was adjusted by the treaty of London. In 1870 the inevitable struggle between France and Prussia was precipitated. The Spanish throne having become vacant, Prince Leopold, son of the Prince of Hohenzollern-Sigmaringen, was put forward as a candidate. As King Wilhelm was the head of the House of Hohenzollern, this gave great umbrage to France. Although the candidature was withdrawn, **Napoleon III** forced a quarrel on Prussia, by making impossible demands. Wilhelm took the field on 31 July, and in the deadly struggle which ensued the French forces were defeated almost everywhere; Napoleon capitulated at Sedan; and by the end of September Paris was invested.

At Versailles on 18 January 1871, William was proclaimed German emperor. Peace was signed on 26 February. An Austro-German alliance of 1871 was strengthened in 1873 by the adhesion of the tsar. The rapid rise of socialism in Germany led to severe repressive measures, and in 1878 the emperor's life was twice attempted by socialists, as again in 1883. Wilhelm I, though holding tenaciously to the prerogatives of his kingly office, was of a simple and unassuming personal character.

WILHELM II (1859–1941) third German emperor 1888–1918, and ninth king of Prussia, born in Berlin, the eldest son of Prince Frederick, later **Frederick II** and of Victoria, the daughter of Britain's Queen **Victoria**. He received a strict military and academic education at the Kassel gymnasium and the University of Bonn, taking part in military exercises despite a deformed left arm. Wilhelm had a passion for military splendour, a deep conviction of the divine right of the **Hohenzollerns**, and a quick intelligence although his temper was uneven. He quarrelled with and dismissed (1890) the elder statesman **Bismarck**, who disapproved of Wilhelm's projected overtures to capture working-class support and who had forbidden any minister to see the emperor except in his presence. A long spell of personal rule followed, but in the closing months of 1908 he suffered a nervous breakdown and had less influence on the making of policy in the last ten years of his reign than world opinion believed. Wilhelm's speeches had as their constant theme German imperialism. In 1896 he sent a telegram to President **Kruger** of South Africa congratulating him on the suppression of the **Jameson** raid. He adopted an anti-British attitude at the start of the Boer War, but after several visits to England was for a while seriously, if clumsily, concerned with Anglo-German reconciliation. But despite such temporary goodwill, he backed **von Tirpitz**'s plans for a large German navy to match the British, and as an ally of Turkey, he encouraged German economic penetration of the middle east. He supported immoderate demands on Serbia after the assassination of the archduke **Franz Ferdinand** at Sarajevo (1914), but made strenuous efforts to preserve the peace once he realized that a world war was imminent. Political power passed from him to the generals, and during the war he became a mere figurehead far removed from the great warlord of popular imagination. With the collapse of the German armies and a revolution in progress, Wilhelm was forced to abdicate on 9 November 1918 and flee the country. He and his family settled first at Amerongen, then at Doorn near Arnheim, where he wrote his *Memoirs 1878–1918* (trans 1922), and ignored the Nazi 'Liberation' (1940) of Holland. He married Princess Augusta Victoria of Schleswig-Holstein in 1881, by whom he had six sons and one daughter, and after her death in 1921, Princess Hermine of Reuss. He wrote *My Early Life* (1926).

WILHELMINA, Helena Pauline Maria of Orange-Nassau (1880–1962) queen of the Netherlands from 1890 to 1948. She succeeded her father William III at a very early age; until 1898 her mother, Queen Emma, acted as regent. Queen Wilhelmina fully upheld the principles of constitutional monarchy, especially winning the admiration of her people during World War II. Though compelled to seek refuge in Britain, she steadfastly encouraged Dutch resistance to the German occupation. In 1948, in view of the length of her reign, she abdicated in favour of her daughter **Juliana** and assumed the title of Princess of the Netherlands. She wrote *Lonely but not Alone* (1960).

WILKES, Charles (1798–1877) American naval officer, born in New York. He joined the US navy in 1818 and studied hydrography. He explored the South Pacific islands and the Antarctic continent, including the stretch that bears his name (1839–40). During the Civil War he intercepted the British mail-steamer *Trent* off Cuba, and took off two Confederate commissioners accredited to France, thereby creating a risk of war with Britain (1861). As acting rear admiral he commanded a squadron against commerce raiders in the West Indies. He was court-martialled for disobedience in 1866, and retired.

WILKES, John (1727–97) English politician, born in Clerkenwell, the son of a distiller. He studied at Leiden, and became a man of fashion and profligate. He became prominent as a member of the Hell-fire Club which indulged in orgies at Medmenham Abbey, the home of **Sir Francis Dashwood**. He entered parliament in 1757 as member for Aylesbury and became fiercely critical of **George III**'s chief minister, Lord **Bute**. As a vehicle for his criticism, he established a weekly newspaper *The New Briton*, in issue No 45 of which he alleged that the speech from the throne had resulted in ministers putting lies into the king's mouth. He was charged with libel but acquitted on the ground of parliamentary privilege. The government then obtained a copy of his privately distributed *Essay on Women*, which they claimed was obscene. Readings from it in the House of Lords led to a duel, after which Wilkes took refuge in France. When he returned to England in 1768 he was imprisoned for 22 months and not allowed to resume his seat in parliament. He returned to active politics, however, being elected sheriff of Middlesex (1771), lord mayor of London (1774) and returning to parliament in the same year. Despite his apparently outrageous private behaviour, he became a symbol of free speech and earned the epitaph, which he composed himself, 'a friend of liberty'.

WILKES, Maurice Vincent (1913–) English computer scientist, born in Dudley. Educated at King Edward's School, Stourbridge, and St John's College, Cambridge, he directed the Mathematical (later Computer) Laboratory at Cambridge (1946–80) and became known for his pioneering work with the EDSAC (Electronic Delay Storage Automatic Calculator). Around this machine, operational after 1949, Wilkes built the world's first computing service. He published his *Memoirs* in 1985.

WILKIE, Sir David (1785–1841) Scottish painter, born in Cults manse in Fife. In 1799 he was sent to study at the Trustees' Academy in Edinburgh, and returning home in 1804, painted his *Pitlessie Fair*. The great success of *The Village Politicians* (1806) caused him to settle in London. In 1817 he visited Sir **Walter Scott** at Abbotsford, and painted the family group now in the Scottish National Gallery. His fame mainly rests on his genre pictures in the Dutch style, such as the *Card Players*, *Village Festival*, *Reading the Will*, *The Penny Wedding* and others. Later he changed his style, sought to emulate the depth and richness of colouring of the old masters, and chose more elevated historical subjects, like *John Knox preaching before the Lords of Congregation*. He also painted portraits, and was successful as an etcher. In 1823 he was appointed king's limner in Scotland, and in 1830 painter-in-ordinary to King **William IV**. In 1840, for his health, he visited Syria, Palestine and Egypt, but died on his voyage home.

WILKINS, Sir George Hubert (1888–1958) Australian polar explorer, born in Mt Bryan East. He first went to the Arctic in 1913; in 1919 he flew from England to Australia, the years 1920–22 he spent in the Antarctic, and after that collected material in Central

Australia on behalf of the British Museum. In 1926 he returned to the Arctic, and in 1928 was knighted for a pioneer flight from Alaska to Spitsbergen, over polar ice. In 1931 he was again exploring in the Arctic, this time with the submarine *Nautilus*, but an attempt to reach the North Pole under the ice was unsuccessful. After his death his ashes were conveyed to the pole, where they were scattered into the wind. He wrote *Flying the Arctic* (1928), *Undiscovered Australia* (1928), and *Under the North Pole* (1931).

WILKINS, John (1614–72) English churchman and scientist, born near Daventry. A graduate of Magdalen Hall, Oxford, he became a domestic chaplain but studied mathematics and mechanics, and was one of the founders of the Royal Society. In the Civil War he sided with parliament, and was appointed warden of Wadham. In 1656 he married a widowed sister of **Oliver Cromwell**, and in 1659 was appointed by **Richard Cromwell** master of Trinity College, Cambridge. Dispossessed at the Restoration, he soon recovered court favour, and became preacher at Gray's Inn, rector of St Lawrence Jewry, dean of Ripon and bishop of Chester (1668). In his *Discovery of a World in the Moon* (1628) he discusses the possibility of communication by a flying-machine with the moon and its supposed inhabitants; the *Discourse concerning a New Planet* (1640) argues that the earth is one of the planets; *Mercury, or the Secret and Swift Messenger*, shows how a man may communicate with a friend at any distance; *Mathematical Magic* dates from 1648; the *Essay towards a Real Character and a Philosophical Language* (1668) is founded on **Dalgarno**'s treatise.

WILKINS, Maurice Hugh Frederick (1916–) British physicist, born in New Zealand. Educated at King Edward's School, Birmingham, and St John's College, Cambridge, he did research on uranium isotope separation at the University of California in 1944. He joined the Medical Research Council's Biophysics Research Unit at King's College, London, in 1946, becoming director 1970–72. With **Francis Crick** and **James Watson** he was awarded the Nobel prize for physiology or medicine in 1962 for work on the structure of DNA.

WILKINSON, Ellen Cicely (1891–1947) English feminist and Labour politician, born in Manchester. She was an early member of the Independent Labour party and an active campaigner for women's suffrage. In 1920 she joined the Communist party, but had left it by 1924, when she became MP for Middlesborough East. Losing this seat in 1931, she re-entered parliament in 1935 as member for Jarrow. In 1940 she became parliamentary secretary to the ministry of home security, and in 1945 minister of education, the first woman to hold such an appointment.

WILKINSON, Sir Geoffrey (1921–) English inorganic chemist, born in Todmorden, Yorkshire. He studied at Imperial College, London, and returned there as professor in 1956 after teaching at the Massachusetts Institute of Technology and Harvard. He worked on inorganic complexes and their use as catalysts and especially on the 'sandwich compounds' having a metal atom between two rings of carbon atoms. He shared the Nobel prize for chemistry in 1973 with **Ersnt Otto Fischer**.

WILKINSON, John (1728–1808) English iron-master and inventor, born in Clifton in Cumberland. He was the son of a farmer who by 1750 had become an iron-master near Wrexham. He followed his father into iron-founding and by 1770 was master of three furnaces making grenades, shells and cannon as well as a wide variety of castings for domestic and industrial use. His most important achievement was the invention in 1774 of a cannon-boring machine considerably more accurate than any in use up to that time, and he was not slow to see that it could be used also to bore more accurate cylinders for steam engines such as those of **Boulton** and **Watt**, to whom he supplied several hundred cylinders over the next two decades. Wilkinson in turn installed a Watt engine in 1776 as a blowing engine at one of his furnaces, the first Watt engine to be used other than for pumping. He designed and built the first iron bridge in England (1779) and the first iron barge (1787).

WILKINSON, Sir John Gardner (1797–1875) English Egyptologist, born in Hardendale in Westmorland. He was educated at Harrow and Exeter College, Oxford. Between 1821–33 he made a detailed survey of Egypt, publishing his famous three-volume *Manners and Customs of the Ancient Egyptians* (1837–41). Knighted in 1839, he visited Egypt again several times. He presented his antiquities to Harrow.

WILLAERT, Adrian (c.1490–1562) Flemish composer, born probably in Bruges. He is thought to have studied in Paris, changing from the law to music, and to have first gone to Italy, into the service of the D'Este family, in 1515. He was appointed *maestro di capella* of St Mark's, Venice, in 1527, and during his 35 years in the post Venice became the centre of Italian and, indeed, western European music. He gained a great reputation as a composer and teacher, and among his pupils were Zarlino, Ciprian de Rore (who briefly succeeded him at St Mark's), and **Andrea Gabrieli**. He composed works in most of the many contemporary genres of sacred music, as well as secular chansons and madrigals.

WILLARD, Emma, née **Hart** (1787–1870) American educationist, a pioneer of higher education for women, born in Berlin, Connecticut. Educated at Berlin Academy (1802–03), she married Dr John Willard (d.1825) in 1809. From her husband's nephew, who was studying at Middlebury College, she learned about the subjects studied there, such as geometry and philosophy, which were never taught to women. In 1814 she opened Middlebury Female Seminary, offering an unprecedented range of subjects, in order to prepare women for college. Unsuccessful in gaining funding for her school, she moved to Troy, New York, where she received financial help. The school developed fast, and she wrote several highly-regarded history text-books. Her campaign for equal educational opportunities for women paved the way for coeducation.

WILLARD, Frances Elizabeth Caroline (1839–98) American temperance campaigner, born in Churchville, New York. She studied at the Northwestern Female College, Evanston, Illinois, and became professor of aesthetics there. In 1874 she became secretary of the Women's Christian Temperance Union, and edited the Chicago *Daily Post*. She helped to found the international Council of Women.

WILLETT, William (1856–1915) English builder, born in Farnham. He is chiefly remembered for his campaign of 'daylight saving'. A Bill was promoted in parliament in 1908, but opposition was strong and the measure was not adopted until a year after his death.

WILLIAM I, 'the Conqueror' (1027–87) king of England from 1066, born in Falaise, the bastard son of Robert, Duke of Normandy, by Arlette, a tanner's daughter. On his father's death in 1035 the nobles accepted him as duke; but his youth was passed in difficulty and danger. In 1047 the lords of the western part of the duchy rebelled, but **Henri I** of France came to his help, and the rebels were defeated at Val-ès-dunes. In 1051 he visited his cousin, **Edward the Confessor**, king of England, and may well have received the promise of the English succession. He married Matilda, daughter of Baldwin V, Count of Flanders, in 1053. In the next ten years William repulsed two French invasions, and in 1063 conquered Maine. Probably in 1064 **Harold Godwinsson** was at his court, and swore to help him to gain the English crown on Edward's death. When, however, Edward died in 1066, Harold became king. William laid his claim before the pope and western Christendom. The pope approved his claim, and William invaded England that autumn. At the battle of Hastings (or Senlac) on 14 October 1066 Harold was defeated and killed, and William was crowned king of England on 25 December. The west and north of England were subdued in 1068; but next year the north revolted, and William devastated the country between York and Durham. English government under William assumed a more feudal aspect, the old national assembly becoming a council of the king's tenants-in-chief, and all title to land was derived from his grant. In 1086 he ordered the compilation of the Domesday Book, which contains details of the land settlement. The church was also reformed and feudalized. The Conqueror's rule was successful despite several revolts which occurred even after 1069. In 1070 there was a rebellion in the Fen Country, and under the leadership of **Hereward the Wake** the rebels for some time held out in the Isle of Ely. English exiles were sheltered by the Scottish king, **Malcolm III Canmore**, who occasionally plundered the northern shires; but William in 1072 compelled Malcolm to do him homage at Abernethy. In 1073 he was forced to reconquer Maine. He made a successful expedition into South Wales. In 1079 his eldest son, Robert, rebelled against him in Normandy; and, having entered on a war with **Philip I** of France in 1087, William burned Mantes. As he rode through the burning town his horse stumbled, and he received an injury, of which he died at Rouen on 9 September; he was buried in the abbey he had founded at Caen. He left Normandy to his son Robert, and England to his other surviving son, **William II**.

WILLIAM II 'Rufus' (the Red) (c.1056–1100) king of England from 1087, was the second surviving son of **William I, the Conqueror**, and succeeded to the throne on his father's death. The next year many of the Norman nobles in England rebelled against him in favour of his eldest brother Robert, Duke of Normandy. Rufus appealed to the English people for help, promising them good government and a relaxation of the forest laws and of fiscal burdens. The rebellion was suppressed, but he did not keep his promises. Treating ecclesiastical benefices as royal possessions, Rufus sold them, and kept them vacant for long periods, seizing their revenues during vacancy. The see of Canterbury had been vacant for four years, when, in 1093, he fell sick, repented, and appointed **Anselm** as archbishop. When he recovered he quarrelled with Anselm for maintaining the liberties of the church. Rufus warred with Robert in Normandy, but peace was made in 1091; and in 1096 the duchy was mortgaged to him. In 1098 he conquered Maine, but failed to hold the whole of it. **Malcolm III, Canmore**, king of Scotland, invaded Northumberland in 1093, and was killed at Alnwick. Rufus thrice invaded Wales, twice with little success. As he was hunting in the New Forest he was killed by an arrow, probably shot by a Norman knight called Walter Tirel, although this was never established. He was buried in Winchester Cathedral. It was he, rather than his father, who was largely responsible for the Norman Conquest of the north of England.

WILLIAM III (1650–1702) king of Great Britain and Ireland from 1689, with **Mary II**. Born in the Hague, he was the posthumous son of **William II** of Orange (1626–50) and Mary (1631–60), eldest daughter of **Charles I** of Great Britain. As Prince of Orange he played an undistinguished role in republican Holland until 1672 when, following the French invasion of the United Provinces and the assassination of the Grand Pensionary, **De Witt**, he was chosen stadholder of Holland and appointed to command the army. An inexperienced soldier, he showed courage and determination in the face of seemingly hopeless odds and, by opening the dykes to flood the countryside, was able to halt the advance of the French army and negotiate favourable peace terms at Nijmegen in 1678. All his energies thereafter were devoted to the defeat of French ambitions in Europe. Britain, who had been an ally of the French, was forced out of the war following a highly successful propaganda campaign linking the French alliance with British fears of Catholicism and arbitrary government. In 1677, in an attempt to retrieve the situation, **Charles II** agreed to a marriage between William and Mary, eldest daughter of James, Duke of York (**James II**). When James became king of Scotland and England in 1685, his policy of Catholicization soon alienated the affections of his subjects and provided William with a favourable opportunity for invading his father-in-law's kingdoms in the name of his wife. Although he landed at Torbay on 5 November 1688, following an invitation from seven British notables (the Immortal Seven), ostensibly to protect the protestant religion and traditional parliamentary liberties, he was more concerned to mobilize British resources in money and manpower for the continental war-effort. On James' flight to France, the throne was declared vacant and William and Mary were proclaimed king and queen jointly in February 1689. With French aid, James' adherents held out in Scotland and Ireland, but their defeat at Killicrankie (July 1689) and on the Boyne (1690) and the surrender of Limerick (1691) effectively ended Jacobite resistance. Leaving Mary as regent, William was able to turn his attention to the continental war, which was ended indecisively at the Peace of Ryswick (1697). In Britain, William was never popular and his position was materially weakened by the death of Mary in 1694. His reign nevertheless brought stability at home after a period of considerable political unrest, and the financing of the war led directly to the establishment of a system of National Debt and to the founding in 1694 of the Bank of England. By the settlement of 1698, control of the standing army was vested in parliament and, with the lapsing of control of the press in 1695, a wider freedom of the press was secured. He died after a fall when his horse stumbled over a molehill, and was succeeded by Mary's sister, Queen **Anne**.

WILLIAM IV (1765–1837) king of Great Britain, known as the 'sailor king', third son of **George III**, born in Buckingham Palace. He entered the navy in 1779, and saw some service in America and the West Indies. In 1789 he was created Duke of Clarence and St Andrews and Earl of Munster, with an allowance of £12000 a year. He was formally promoted through the successive ranks to that of admiral of the fleet (1811), and in 1827–28 he held the revived office of lord high admiral. From 1790 to 1811 he lived with the actress **Dorothy Jordan**, who bore him ten children; but in 1818 he married Adelaide (1792–1849), eldest daughter of the Duke of Saxe-Meiningen. The two daughters born of this marriage (1819 and 1820) died in infancy. By the Duke of York's death in 1827 the Duke of Clarence became heir-presumptive to the throne, to which he succeeded at the death of his eldest brother, **George IV**, in 1830. A Whig up to his accession, he then turned Tory, and did much to obstruct the passing of the first Reform Act (1832) but then accepted a succession of liberal reforms. William was succeeded by his niece, **Victoria**.

WILLIAM I and **WILLIAM II of Prussia** See **WILHELM I** and **WILHELM II**

WILLIAM I (1143–1214) king of Scotland from 1165, the grandson of **David I**, and brother of **Malcolm IV**, whom he succeeded in 1165. His epithet, 'the Lion', was not used by contemporaries. His reign demonstrated both the continuing consolidation of Scotland as a feudal kingdom and increasing efforts to defend its integrity against the threats of Angevin kings of England. The homage paid by him to **Henry II** 'for Scotland and his other lands' after his capture at Alnwick in 1174, was more explicit than that paid by previous Scottish kings. This treaty (The Treaty of Falaise) was revoked by **Richard I** in 1189 with the Quitclaim of Canterbury in return for payment of 10000 marks. He enjoyed a reputation for personal piety and after he died he was buried in the abbey church at Arbroath, which he had founded in 1178.

WILLIAM II (1626–50) stadholder and captain-general of the Netherlands, born in The Hague, son of the Stadholder Frederick Henry who had succeeded his brother **Maurice** of Nassau in 1625. Anglo-Dutch diplomacy established what would prove a fateful marital linkage of the houses of Orange and Stuart by William's marriage in 1641 to Mary, daughter of **Charles I**, and William was elected to follow his father in office, which he duly did in 1647. Dutch independence was recognized at the end of the Thirty Years' War in the Peace of Westphalia (1648), but William wished to support the French in their continued war with Spain in the hope of conquering the remaining Spanish Netherlands. He arrested his leading opponents in Holland, laid siege to Amsterdam and won an advantageous compromise, but died of smallpox before he could make much use of its results. His posthumous son, the future **William III** of Britain and Ireland, would spend his life in opposition to France, for whose alliance William II had laboured in vain.

WILLIAM IV, originally **Charles Henry Friso** (1711–51) stadholder and captain-general of the Netherlands, born of a cadet branch of the House of Orange (Nassau-Dietz). In 1711 he was named Friesland stadholder in succession to his father, John William Friso. He was chosen as stadholder to the other provinces at various intervals, all these posts having been untenanted since the death of **William III** in 1702. His appointments were not completed until 1747 when Holland, Zeeland and Utrecht bowed to popular pressure in the riots after the French invasion. His offices were then declared hereditary in male and female lines, all of which were a simple tribute to the historical reputation of the House of Orange.

WILLIAM V (1748–1806) hereditary stadholder and captain-general of the Netherlands, son of **William IV**. He succeeded his father in 1751 but did not rule until 1766. He abandoned the old alliance of Orange and Britain, leaning instead towards alliance with Prussia, itself hostile to Britain after its loss of British support towards the end of the Seven Years' War. During the American Revolution (1775–83), Britain declared war on the Netherlands because of its financial and moral support for the American rebels, but it was the pro-French 'Patriots' who pressed for reforms and led William to leave The Hague in order to live outside what was now the hostile Province of Holland. Prussian armed intervention restored him in 1787. French revolutionary armies invaded the Netherlands in 1794 and in 1795 William fled to England, whose occupation of the Dutch provinces he supported, including the abortive Anglo-Russian invasion of 1799. After that he lost heart, and allowed his followers to accept office in the Batavian Republic, the French client state which had been formed in his absence.

WILLIAM OF AUVERGNE, also known as **William of Paris** and **Guillaume d'Auvergne** (c.1180–1249) French philosopher and theologian, born in Aurillac, Aquitaine. He became professor of theology in the University of Paris in 1225, and was bishop of Paris from 1228 to 1249, in which role he defended the mendicant orders and introduced various clerical reforms. His most important work is the monumental *Magisterium divinale* (*The Divine Teaching*, 1223–40) and his main achievement was the attempted integration of classical Greek and Arabic philosophy with Christian theology.

WILLIAM OF AUXERRE (c.1140–1231) French theologian and philosopher, born in Auxerre. He became a master of theology and was for many years an administrator at the University of Paris. In 1230 he was sent as French envoy to Pope **Gregory IX** to advise on dissension in the university and he pleaded the cause of the students against King **Louis IX**. Gregory appointed him in 1231 to a council which was to censor the works of **Aristotle** in the university curriculum to ensure their conformity with the Christian faith, but William was opposed to suppression and died before the council's work had far advanced. His main publication is the *Summa aurea in quattuor libros sententiarum* (Golden Compendium on the Four Books of Sentences), a commentary on early and medieval Christian thought, tending to emphasize the value of philosophy and rational analysis as a tool for Christian theology.

WILLIAM OF CHAMPEAUX (c.1070–1171) French theologian and philosopher, born in Champeaux near Melun. He taught at the Cathedral School of Notre Dame in Paris, where **Abelard** was a pupil, later to become a bitter opponent in the scholastic controversies of the day. In 1110 he moved on to the nearby abbey of Saint-Victor in Paris, established a school with **Anselm**'s help, and taught rhetoric, logic and philosophy there. In 1113 he was elected bishop of Châlons-sur-Marne, where he ordained St **Bernard of Clairvaux**. Some of his theological texts survive in anthologies, but his logical works are lost and his views are known only indirectly, particularly through Abelard who vehemently attacked his extreme realism in the dispute about universal terms.

WILLIAM OF CONCHES (c.1080–c.1154) French philosopher, born in Conches in Normandy. He was a pupil of Bernard of Chartres and taught at Chartres and Paris, and was tutor to the future **Henry II** of England. He wrote commentaries on **Plato** and **Boethius** and two original works, *Philosophia Mundi* and *Pragmaticon Philosophiae*. He may also be the author of *Summa Moralium Philosophorum*, an early medieval ethical treatise. He espoused some original cosmological ideas of a pantheistic tendency.

WILLIAM OF JUMIÈGES (d.c.1090) Norman Benedictine monk. He compiled a history of the Dukes of Normandy from **Rollo** to 1071, of value for the story of the Conquest.

WILLIAM OF MALMESBURY (c.1090–c.1143) English chronicler, born probably near Malmesbury, Wiltshire. He became a monk in the monastery at Malmesbury, and in due time librarian and precentor. He took part in the council at Winchester against King **Stephen** in 1141. His *Gesta Regum Anglorum* provides a lively history of the kings of England from the Saxon invasion to 1126; the *Historia Novella* brings down the narrative to 1142. The *Gesta Pontificum* is an ecclesiastical history of the bishops and chief monasteries of England to 1123. Other works are an account of the church at Glastonbury and *Lives* of St **Dunstan** and St **Wulfstan**.

WILLIAM OF NEWBURGH (c.1135–c.1200) English chronicler, perhaps a native of Bridlington. A monk of Newburgh Priory (Coxwold), his *Historia Rerum Anglicarum*, is one of the chief authorities for the reign of **Henry II**.

WILLIAM OF NORWICH, St (?1132–1144) English martyr, apparently the first of the Christian boys alleged to have been ritually crucified by Jews (see **Hugh of Lincoln**). *The Life and Miracles of St William of Norwich* is a story from a 12th-century manuscript of a boy whose mutilated body was found in a wood outside Norwich in 1144, and (much later) was rumoured to have been murdered by Jews. His feast day is 26 March.

WILLIAM OF TYRE (c.1130–1185) Syrian churchman and historian, probably of Italian birth. He became archdeacon of Tyre in 1167, and archbishop in 1175. He was tutor in 1170 to Baldwin I, son of King Amalric of Jerusalem, and in 1179 was one of the six bishops representing the Latin Church of the East at the Lateran Council. His *Historia Rerum in Partibus Transmarinis Gestarum* deals with the affairs of the East from 1095 to 1184.

WILLIAM OF WAYNFLETE (1395–1486) English prelate. Educated probably at New College, Oxford, he became provost of Eton in 1443, Bishop of Winchester in 1447, and in 1448 founded Magdalen College, Oxford. He was involved in the negotiations which ended **Jack Cade**'s rebellion in 1450, and as a Lancastrian played an important role as adviser to **Henry VI** in the Wars of the Roses. He was Lord Chancellor (1456–60).

WILLIAM OF WYKEHAM (1324–1404) English churchman and statesman, born in Wickham, near Fareham. Educated at a school in Winchester, he was appointed surveyor of Windsor and other royal castles by **Edward III** in 1356–59. He built Queensborough Castle in 1361, was keeper of the privy seal and secretary to the king in 1364, became Bishop of Winchester (1367) and chancellor of England (1367–71 and 1389–91). In 1379 he founded New College, Oxford, and in 1382 Winchester School. In 1394 he undertook the transformation of the nave of Winchester Cathedral, and personally supervised the work. In 1404 he endowed a magnificent chantry at Winchester and, dying the same year, was buried in it. Wykeham was not an ardent theologian; he founded his colleges 'first for the glory of God and the promotion of divine service, and secondarily for scholarship'. He has been called the 'father of the public school system', and he established (though he did not invent) the perpendicular architecture.

WILLIAM THE SILENT (1533–84) Count of Nassau and Prince of Orange, the eldest son of William, Count of Nassau-Dillenburg. At the age of 11 he inherited the princedom of Orange and became one of the wealthiest noblemen in Europe, and at the age of 22 he became stadholder of Holland, Zeeland and Utrecht. A Roman Catholic, but a man of moderate and tolerant views, he was appalled by **Philip II**'s programme for the extirpation of heresy throughout his dominions and took a leading part in the confederation of nobles who promulgated the *Compromis*, which called for a relaxation of the heresy laws and the suspension of the Inquisition. The confederates also asked that the states general should be called. Philip responded by sending the hard-line Duke of **Alva** as military commander in the Netherlands and in 1567 Alva replaced Philip's half-sister, **Margaret** of Parma, as Regent. William resigned his offices and withdrew to his lands in Germany. During his exile, he converted to Protestantism and set about organizing an army to liberate the Netherlands from Alva's repressive régime. He invaded the Netherlands in 1572, making himself master of the northern provinces, which by the Pacification of Ghent (1576) and the Union of Utrecht (1579) were formed into the independent United Provinces. Spanish attempts to regain the North were unsuccessful and in 1584 the United Provinces formally renounced their allegiance. In the same year, William was assassinated at Delft by Balthasar Gérards.

WILLIAMS, Bernard Arthur Owen (1929–) English philosopher. Educated at Chigwell School, Essex, and Balliol College, Oxford, he taught in London and Oxford, before being appointed professor of philosophy at Bedford College, London (1964–67). He became professor of philosophy at Cambridge in 1967, and provost of King's College, Cambridge, in 1979. He has held many visiting positions at universities in the USA, Australia and Africa, and in 1987 emigrated to become professor of philosophy in the University of California at Berkeley as a much-publicized addition to the 'brain-drain'. He returned to the UK to become professor of philosophy at Oxford in 1990. His philosophical work has been wide-ranging, but there have been particularly influential contributions to moral philosophy, in works such as *Morality: an introduction to Ethics* (1972), *Utilitarianism* (with J J C Smart, 1973), *Moral Luck* (1981) and *Ethics and the Limits of Philosophy* (1985). He chaired the Committee on Obscenity and Film Censorship which produced the Williams Report in 1979. He was married (1955–74) to the politician **Shirley Williams**.

WILLIAMS, Edward ('Iolo Morganwg') (1747–1826) Welsh poet, antiquary and cultural inventor, born in Llancarfan, Glamorgan. He worked there as a stonemason, and became a poet in Welsh and English. He had links with 18th-century Radicalism, mingling its ideas with Romantic exaltation of the Welsh past and established neo-Druidic cults and celebrations in Wales from 1792. He published collected poems purportedly by the 14th-century poet Dafydd ap Gwilym, which in fact were his own work. He co-edited *The Myvyrian Archaeology* (3 vols, 1801–07), and produced posthumously a vast corpus of cultural material from the Welsh past in varying degrees of authenticity. A brilliant forger whose deceptions far outlived his own time, his work prolonged, revived and reinvigorated ancient and modern Welsh culture.

WILLIAMS, Emlyn (1905–) Welsh playwright and actor, born in Clwyd, the son of an ironmonger. He won a scholarship to Oxford, where he entered Christ Church College. In 1927, attracted by the stage, he joined J B Fagan's repertory company. His first real success as a dramatist was with *A Murder has been Arranged* (1930). He then adapted a French play by René Fauchois—*The Late Christopher Bean* (1933)—and continued his success with the terrifying psychological thriller *Night Must Fall* (1935). He was not limited to light entertainment, and a seriousness of purpose characterizes most of his other work. Other successes have been *The Corn is Green* (1938), *The Light of Heart* (1940), *The Wind of Heaven* (1945), *Trespass* (1947), *Accolade* (1951). He has generally played the lead in his own and has acted in other dramatists' plays, as well as appearing at the Old Vic and at Stratford, and featuring in films. His solo performance as **Charles Dickens** giving his celebrated readings from his works was greeted with acclaim but a similar endeavour as **Dylan Thomas** did not meet with such success. He wrote the autobiographical *George* (1961), and *Emlyn* (1973), as well as *Beyond Belief* (1967), and a novel, *Headlong* (1980).

WILLIAMS, Fred (Frederick Ronald) (1927–82) Australian landscape painter and etcher, born in Richmond, Victoria. He enrolled at the age of 16 at the National Gallery School, and studied under Sir William Dargie. In the early 1950s he studied in London, at the Chelsea and Central Schools of Art. Although a painter of distinguished portraits, his considerable reputation lies in his landscapes, where his personal vision, use of colour and sense of scale brought him recognition as the most significant painter of the Australian landscape since Sir **Arthur Streeton**. This was acknowledged when their work was shown together at an exhibition held at the National Gallery of Victoria in 1970. An international reputation was secured by his 1977 exhibition *Landscapes of a Continent* at the Museum of Modern Art, New York. He won the Wynne prize in 1966, and again in 1976.

WILLIAMS, Sir Frederic Calland (1911–77) English electrical engineer, born in Manchester. He became professor of electrical engineering there in 1946 after study at Oxford University and war experience in radar. He is chiefly known for his development of the Williams tube, the first successful electrostatic random access memory for the digital computer. This enabled him, together with his collaborator **Tom Kilburn**, to operate the world's first stored-program computer in June 1948.

WILLIAMS, Sir George (1821–1905) English social reformer and founder of the YMCA, born in Dulverton. A wealthy draper, he made a hobby of temperance work, lay preaching, and teaching in ragged schools. In 1844 he founded the Young Men's Christian Assocation.

WILLIAMS, Harold (1893–1976) Australian baritone, born in Woollahra, New South Wales. He served with the Australian Imperial Forces in France during World War I, after which he studied at the Royal Academy of Music. In 1919 he made his recital début at Wigmore Hall, London, and made his name the following year at a concert under Sir **Henry Wood**. In the same year he began his long recording career, and soon became a regular member of the English National Opera. In 1929 he returned to Australia, touring in a series of recitals. He was in great demand for oratorios, especially in works by **Handel**, **Mendelssohn** and **Elgar**, and was one of the original 16 distinguished soloists for whom **Vaughan Williams** composed his *Serenade to Music* (1938). In 1938 he toured for the ABC, but returned to London in 1946. In 1952, he became professor of singing at the New South Wales Conservatorium of Music, and made occasional appearances with the National Opera.

WILLIAMS, Isaac (1802–65) Welsh clergyman and tractarian, born near Aberystwyth. He was ordained in 1831, and wrote religious poetry, but is best remembered as the author of Tract 80, on 'Reserve in Religious Teaching'.

WILLIAMS, John (1796–1839) English missionary, the martyr of Erromango, born in Tottenham, London. In 1817 he was sent by the London Missionary Society to the Society Islands, where he worked in Raïatéa with marvellous success. Going in 1823 to Raratonga, he christianized the whole Hervey group, and during the next four years visited many of the South Sea islands, including Samoa. In 1834 he returned to England, superintended the printing of his Raratongan New Testament, and raised £4000 to equip a missionary-ship. In 1838 he visited many of his stations, and sailed for the New Hebrides, where he was killed and eaten by the natives of Erromango. He published his *Narrative of Missionary Enterprises* in 1837.

WILLIAMS, John (1949–) Welsh Rugby Union footballer, born in Ogmore-by-Sea. An excellent all-round athlete who was good enough to win the Wimbledon Junior tennis championships, he became a medical student and embarked on a distinguished rugby career with London Welsh. Almost suicidally courageous, he won 52 caps and was a star of the highly successful Lions tour to New Zealand in 1971 and to South Africa in 1974. He subsequently became a surgical registrar at the University Hospital of Wales.

WILLIAMS, John Christopher (1941–) Australian classical and jazz guitarist, born in Melbourne, Victoria. He received his training at the Accademia Musicale Chigiana di Siena, Italy, and at the Royal College of Music, London. He has toured widely and his extensive repertoire is well represented on records. As well as solo recitals he has also performed in chamber groups and as soloist with most international orchestras. Williams also formed the group *Sky* which has played at jazz and popular concerts.

WILLIAMS, Kenneth (1926–87) English actor and comedian, born in London. He made his London début as Slightly in *Peter Pan* in 1952, and two years later played the Dauphin in a revival of **Shaw**'s *St Joan* in the West End. He later starred in comedies and in such revues as *Share My Lettuce* (1957), *Pieces of Eight* (1959), and *One Over the Eight* (1961). He became well-known in such radio series as *Round the Horne*, and *Stop Messing About*, in which his affected style of speech and rich, punctilious enunciation, made him instantly recognizable. He make several films. appearing regularly in the *Carry On* series of comedies.

WILLIAMS, Mary Lou (1910–81) American jazz pianist, arranger and composer, born in Atlanta, Georgia, and brought up in Pittsburgh. She interrupted her high school studies to become a touring show pianist; her first important period as a performer and arranger was during the 1930s with the Kansas City-based Andy Kirk and his Clouds of Joy. Her outstanding qualities as an arranger brought her work from **Duke Ellington** (for whom she arranged the well-known *Trumpets No End*), **Earl Hines** and **Benny Goodman**, among others. She later embraced the bebop style as well as writing several sacred works, such as 'Mary Lou's Mass' (1970). Her *Waltz Boogie* (1946) was one of the first jazz pieces in 3/4 time.

WILLIAMS, Sir Monier Monier- (1819–99) English Sanskrit scholar, born in Bombay. Educated at King's College School, London, and Balliol College, Oxford, he became professor of Sanskrit at Haileybury (1844–58), master at Cheltenham (1858–60), and then Boden professor of Sanskrit at Oxford (1860). He was knighted in 1886 at the opening of the Indian Institute, established mainly through his energy, and completed in 1896. His books include Sanskrit grammars (1846 and 1860) and dictionaries (1854 and 1872), editions of the *Sákuntalá* (1853) and other Sanskrit texts, books on India, and *Reminiscences of Old Haileybury* (1894).

WILLIAMS, Raymond (1921–88) Welsh critic and novelist, born in Pandy, Gwent, the son of a railway signalman. Educated at King Henry VIII Grammar School, Abergavenny and Cambridge, he wrote *Culture and Society* (1958) which required socialists to seek inspiration in such figures as **Burke**, **Southey**, and **Carlyle**. He opened up questions of mass readership and cultural and ethical values in *The Long Revolution* (1966). He was made a fellow of Jesus College,

Cambridge, in 1961, and was professor of drama there from 1974 to 1983. He was active in New Left intellectual movements, producing the *May Day Manifesto* (1968), but his novels *Border Country* (1960), *Second Generation* (1964), *The Volunteers* (1978), *The Fight for Manod* (1979), and *Loyalties* (1985) underline the significance of Welsh consciousness for him, and he was later identified with Welsh nationalism. Of his many major works in socio-literary criticism, *The Country and the City* (1973) was perhaps the most inspirational.

WILLIAMS, Robley Cook (1908–) American biophysicist, born in Santa Rosa, California. He studied physics at Cornell and from 1950 taught at the University of California at Berkeley. His early research was in astronomy, but from the 1940s he was concerned with electron microscopy, and with R Wyckoff he devised a metal-shadowing technique which could be used for sensitive biological materials. From this basis he became concerned with viruses, and made major contributions to knowledge of their structure in the 1950s.

WILLIAMS, Roger (c.1604–1683) English-born American clergyman, born in London, the founder of Rhode Island. Educated at the Charterhouse and Pembroke College, Cambridge, he took Anglican orders, became an extreme Puritan, and emigrated to New England in 1630. He refused to join the congregation at Boston because it would not make public repentance for having been in communion with the Church of England; he therefore went to Salem, but was soon in trouble for denying the right of magistrates to punish Sabbath-breaking. For his opposition to the New England theocracy he was driven from Salem, and took refuge in Plymouth. Two years later he returned to Salem, only to meet renewed persecution and banishment (1635). He escaped to the shores of Narragansett Bay on Rhode Island, where he purchased lands of the Indians, founded the city of Providence (1636), and established a pure democracy. Having adopted the tenet of adult baptism, he established (1639) the first Baptist church in America. In 1643 and 1651 he came to England to procure a charter for his colony, and published a *Key into the Language of America* (1643), *The Bloudy Tenent of Persecution for Cause of Conscience* (1644), *The Bloudy Tenent yet more bloudy by Mr Cotton's Endeavour to wash it White in the Blood of the Lamb* (1652), etc. He returned to Rhode Island in 1654, and was president of the colony till 1658. Renowned as an apostle of religious toleration, he refused to persecute the Quakers, but had a famous controversy with them—recorded in *George Fox digged out of his Burrowes* (1676).

WILLIAMS, Shirley Vivien Teresa Brittain (1930–) English politician, daughter of **Vera Brittain**. A former journalist, she first became a Labour MP in 1964, holding ministerial posts in education and science (1967–69) and the home office (1969–70) before being appointed secretary of state for prices and consumer protection (1974–76), then for education and science (1976–79). She was a co-founder of the Social Democratic party in 1981 and became the party's first elected MP later that year. She became president of the SDP the following year, but lost her seat in the 1983 General Election. In 1988 she joined the new, merged Social and Liberal Democratic party (SLDP). In the same year she married, for the second time. Her first husband (1955–74) was **Bernard Williams**, professor of moral philosophy at Oxford University and her second husband, Richard Neustadt, professor of politics at Harvard. After her marriage she moved to the USA but remains involved in British politics.

WILLIAMS, Ted (Theodore Samuels) (1918–) American baseball player, born in San Diego, California. Known as the 'Splendid Splinter', he was an outstanding hitter, playing with the Boston Red Sox for 19 seasons (1939–60) despite war service in World War II and the Korean War. He was twice named Most Valuable Player (MVP), and won the last of his six league batting championships in 1958 at the age of 40. In 1966 he was elected by an overwhelming majority to the National Baseball Hall of Fame.

WILLIAMS, Tennessee, originally **Thomas Lanier** (1911–83) American playwright, born in Columbus, Mississippi, the son of a travelling salesman. Prone to illness as a child, he found writing to be a tonic. He had an itinerant college education, first at Washington University in St Louis, then at the University of Missouri, finally receiving a degree from the University of Iowa in 1938. He worked at various menial jobs, among them as a poet-waiter at a Greenwich Village restaurant and as a cinema usher. Recognition of his literary skill came in 1940, when he received a Rockefeller Fellowship for his first play, *Battle of Angels*. In 1943 he signed a six-month contract with M-G-M, later cancelled when he submitted a script that became *The Glass Menagerie*. This play, which in 1945 earned him the New York Drama Critics' Circle Award, introduced him as an important American playwright. He then wrote *Summer and Smoke* (1948), and in 1948 was awarded the Pulitzer prize for *A Streetcar Named Desire*. After *The Rose Tattoo* (1951) and *Camino Red* (1953), he won the Pulitzer prize again in 1955 for *Cat on a Hot Tin Roof*. He continued with *Suddenly Last Summer* (1958), *Sweet Bird of Youth* (1959) and *The Night of the Iguana* (1961). He won the Gold Medal for Literature in 1969 from both the American Academy of Arts & Letters and the National Institute of Arts and Letters. In addition to his plays, he published collections of poetry—*The Summer Belvedere* (1944), *Winter of Cities* (1956); and short stories—*Hard Candy* (1954), *Eight Mortal Ladies Possessed* (1974) and *It Happened the Day the Sun Rose* (1982). He wrote one novel, *The Roman Spring of Mrs Stone* (1950), and wrote the scripts for several films, including *Baby Doll* (1956). *Where I Live: Selected Essays* (1978) is autobiographical.

WILLIAMS, Waldo (1904–71) Welsh poet, born in Haverfordwest. He was educated at Narberth Grammar School and University College, Aberystwyth. Considered by many to be the most astonishingly original poet in the Welsh language, his work, deeply influenced by the Romantic poets, is concerned with universal brotherhood and mankind's relationship with the natural world. A committed pacifist, he supported civil disobediance as advocated by **Henry Thoreau** and **Mahatma Gandhi**. In 1950 he withheld his income tax in response to the Korean War. He spent six weeks in prison for non-payment of tax in 1960, and served a second sentence in 1961.

WILLIAMS, Sir William Fenwick (1800–83) British soldier, born in Halifax, Nova Scotia. A colonel of engineers, he was engaged in defining the Turko-Persian boundary when the Crimean War broke out (1834–36). In 1854 he was appointed British military commissioner with the Turkish army in Asia. He reached Kars in September, and reformed and reinvigorated the Turkish garrison. From June to November he held Kars against the Russians in a heroic defence before having to surrender. On his release he was given a baronetcy and an annuity of £1000.

WILLIAMSON, Alexander William (1824–1904) English chemist, born in London. He studied medicine at Heidelberg and chemistry at Giessen. From 1849 to 1887 he was professor of chemistry at University College, London. His researches on etherification, in which he demonstrated the chemical relationship between alcohol and ethers, were of great importance.

WILLIAMSON, David Keith (1942–) Australian playwright, born in Melbourne, Victoria. He graduated in mechanical engineering from Monash University, Melbourne, but turned to writing plays and scripts for films and television. His first works to receive recognition were *The Removalists* and *Don's Party* in 1971, and other successes included *The Club* (1977) and *The Perfectionist* (1982). Some of his stage works have subsequently been filmed, and Williamson has also written other film scripts including those for *Gallipoli* (1981) and *Phar Lap* (1983).

WILLIAMSON, Henry (1895–1977) English author, born in Bedfordshire. After service in World War I he became a journalist, but turned to farming in Norfolk and eventually settled in a cottage on Exmoor. He wrote several semi-autobiographical novels, including his long series *A Chronicle of Ancient Sunlight* on the life story of the hero, Phillip Maddison. He is best known, however, for his classic nature stories, starting with *The Peregrine's Saga* (1923) and *The Old Stag* (1926). He achieved enduring fame with *Tarka the Otter* (1927, Hawthornden prize), and *Salar the Salmon* (1935). He wrote two autobiographical works, *The Wet Flanders Plain* (1929), and *A Clear Water Stream* (1958).

WILLIAMSON, James Cassius (1845–1913) American-born Australian theatrical producer, born in Mercer, Pennsylvania. He made his stage début at the age of 16, and was an established actor in New York by 1870. He toured Australia in 1874 at the invitation of actor-manager George Coppin, and later visited Europe and London. Williamson returned to Australia with his actress wife in 1879, playing Sir Joseph Porter and Buttercup in *HMS Pinafore*. He then leased the Melbourne Theatre Royal and with two partners, went into management, establishing the theatrical organization popularly known as 'The Firm', which was to dominate Australasian theatre for four decades. He supported tours by overseas artists, but concentrated on established, long-running successes such as the Savoy operas, for which he held the Australian rights, rather than the contemporary theatre of the day.

WILLIAMSON, Malcolm Benjamin Graham Christoper (1931–) Australian-born British composer, born in Sydney. He studied under **Eugene Goossens** and **Elizabeth Lutyens**, coming to England in 1953. He began his career as a soloist with many orchestras, in London, Vienna, Haifa, Sydney and Melbourne, and now lives in England, performing as a pianist and organist, lecturing and composing. His operas include *Our Man in Havana* (1963), *The Violins of Saint-Jacques* (1966) and *The Red Sea* (1972). He has written for television and films, including *The Happy Prince* (1965), and *Julius Caesar Jones* (1966), and composed ballets, orchestral works, vocal, choral and piano music, and 'cassations', often involving the audience. He was made Master of the Queen's Music in 1975, and was president of the Royal Philharmonic Orchestra (1977–82).

WILLIAMSON, William Crawford (1816–95) English botanist, zoologist and palaeontologist, born in Scarborough. He trained in medicine and became the first professor of natural history and geology (later of botany) at Owens College, Manchester (1851–92). He was the first to investigate thoroughly the plant remains (coal balls) in coal. At the time, however, the full significance of his work in fossil botany was not appreciated, and after 41 years of teaching at Owens College (later Manchester University) he was refused a pension.

WILLIBALD (700–86) Anglo-Saxon churchman and missionary from Wessex, and brother of St **Walburga**. He made a pilgrimage to Palestine, settled as a monk in Monte Cassino (730–40). He was sent by Pope **Gregory III** to Germany to help his kinsman St **Boniface**, who made him the first bishop of Eichstätt. His *Hodoeporicon* is an account of his pilgrimage to Palestine. His feast day is 11 July.

WILLIBROD, St (c.658–739) Anglo-Saxon missionary, born in Northumbria. He became a Benedictine monk at Ripon under St **Wilfrid**, and about 690 was sent as missionary to Friesland, was made bishop of Utrecht and later archbishop of the Frisians (695). In 700 he founded the monastery of Echternach in Luxembourg. His feast day is 7 November.

WILLINGDON, Freeman Freeman-Thomas, 1st Marquis of (1866–1941) English administrator. Educated at Eton and Cambridge, he was Liberal MP for Hastings (1900–06) and for Bodmin (1906–10), governor of Bombay (1913–19) and of Madras (1919–24). From 1926 to 1931 he was governor-general of Canada. As viceroy of India (1931–36) he persuaded **Mahatma Gandhi** to come to London to the second Round Table Conference, helped to shape the Government of India Bill, and started the new machine of government in India. An administrator of great tact and brilliance, he was one of the few commoners to be rewarded with a marquisate (1936).

WILLIS, Nathaniel Parker (1806–67) American editor and writer, born in Portland, Maine. He published several volumes of poetry, founded the *American Monthly Magazine* in Boston (1829) and in 1831 visited Europe, and contributed to the *New York Mirror* his *Pencillings by the Way*. Appointed *attaché* to the American legation at Paris, he visited Greece and Turkey, and returned to England in 1837. He contributed to the London *New Monthly* his *Inklings of Adventure* (collected 1836), and published *Letters from under a Bridge* (1840). In 1844 he engaged in editing the *Daily Mirror*, revisited Europe, and published *Dashes at Life with a Free Pencil* (1845). He returned to New York in 1846, and established the *Home Journal*, in which much of his work first appeared. His sister, Sara Payson Willis, 'Fanny Fern' (1811–72), married to James Parton, was a popular writer.

WILLIS, Norman David (1933–) English trade union leader. Educated at Ashford County Grammar School and Ruskin and Oriel colleges, Oxford, he worked for two years for the Transport and General Workers' Union (TGWU) before national service (1951–53). He returned to the TGWU as personal assistant to the general-secretary (1959–70) and national secretary for research and education (1970–74), before being appointed assistant general-secretary of the Trades Union Congress (TUC) in 1974. He succeeded **Len Murray** as general-secretary in 1984.

WILLIS, Thomas (1621–73) English physician, one of the founders of the Royal Society (1662). He was Sedleian professor of natural philosophy at Oxford (1660–75), but became famous as a physician in Westminster. He was a pioneer in the study of the anatomy of the brain, and of diseases of the nervous system and muscles. He discovered the 'circle of Willis' in the brain, and wrote *Cerebri anatomi* (1664).

WILLISTON, Samuel (1861–1963) American jurist, born in Cambridge, Massachusetts. Educated at Harvard, he taught there from 1890 to 1938, then became professor emeritus till 1963. His major work was *Treatise on Contracts* (1920), and he was regarded as the outstanding American scholar of his time on contract law. Mainly responsible for the American Law Institute's *Restatement of Contracts*, he was draftsman of uniform legislation on sales, bills of lading and stock certificates which led up to the Uniform Commercial Code.

WILLKIE, Wendell (1892–1944) American politician, born in Elwood, Indiana. He became first a lawyer, later an industrialist. Having removed his support from the Democrat to the Republican cause in 1940, he was nominated as presidential candidate by the party and narrowly defeated in the election of that year. In 1941–42 he travelled the world representing the president. An opponent of Isolationism, he was leader of the left-wing element in his party.

WILLOUGHBY, Sir Hugh (d.c.1554) English explorer, of whom little is known save his unfortunate fate. In 1553 an expedition was fitted out by the merchants of London 'for the discovery of regions, dominions, islands, and places unknown', and Willoughby was appointed its commander. On 10 May he sailed from Deptford with three vessels, one commanded by **Richard Chancellor**. They crossed the North Sea in company, and sighted the coast of Norway. In September Chancellor's ship parted company in a storm with the two others, which reached Russian Lapland. Here Sir Hugh determined to pass the winter but here with his 62 companions he perished of scurvy. Next year Russian fishermen found the ships with the dead bodies and the commander's journal (published by Hakluyt Society, 1903).

WILLS, William Gorman (1828–91) Irish playwright and poet, born in Kilkenny County. He studied at Trinity College, Dublin, and started as an artist. His *Man o'Airlie* (1866) was a huge success on the stage, followed by *Charles I* (1872), *Jane Shore* (1876), *Olivia* and *Claudian* (1885). He also wrote novels. His ballads include 'I'll sing thee Songs of Araby'.

WILLS, William John (1834–61) English-born Australian explorer, born in Devonshire. He studied medicine, became a surveyor of crown lands in Victoria and became second-in-command of **Robert O'Hara Burke**'s ill-fated expedition to the north, on which he died of starvation.

WILLS (MOODY), Helen Newington, née **Wills** (1905–) American tennis player, born in Centreville, California. From the retirement of **Suzanne Lenglen** in 1926 until the outbreak of World War II she dominated women's tennis, winning eight singles finals at Wimbledon and seven US championships. While she was married (1929–37) she added her husband's name to her own. Her great rivalry with Helen Jacobs drove her to continue to play during the 1938 Wimbledon final, despite being severely handicapped by injury. She retired in 1939.

WILLSTÄTTER, Richard (1872–1942) German organic chemist, born in Karlsruhe. His interest in chemistry was sparked by his uncle's factory where carbon for batteries was produced. He studied at Munich and became professor at Zürich, Berlin, and finally Munich in 1917. His researches included alkaloids and their derivatives, and the work on plant pigments for which in 1915 he was awarded the Nobel prize for chemistry. In 1925 he resigned his professorship at Munich, and in 1939 left Germany for Switzerland, where he died.

WILLUGHBY, Francis (1635–72) English naturalist, born in Middleton, Warwickshire. He studied at Cambridge and Oxford, and then started on a Continental tour (1663–64) with **John Ray**, collecting zoological specimens. Ray edited and translated his *Ornithologia* (3 vols, 1676–78) and edited his *Historia Piscium* (1686).

WILLUMSEN, Jens Ferdinand (1863–1958) Danish painter and sculptor, born in Copenhagen. His best-known painting, *After the Storm* (1905), is in the Oslo National Gallery. As a sculptor his masterpiece is the *Great Relief*, in coloured marbles and bronze. He bequeathed his works and his art collection to form a Willumsen museum in Frederikssund.

WILMOT See **ROCHESTER, Earl of**

WILSON, Alexander (1766–1813) Scottish-born American ornithologist, born in Paisley, the son of a prosperous weaver, and regarded as the 'father of American ornithology'. He worked as a weaver from the age of 13, and as a travelling pedlar. He also wrote nature poetry and verses about life in the weaving sheds, and published *Poems* (1790) and *Watty and Meg* (1792). He was prosecuted for a libellous poem against the mill-owners, which he denied writing, but was jailed for 18 months. In 1794 he emigrated to the USA, and became a schoolteacher in rural schools in New Jersey and Philadelphia. Encouraged by a neighbour, the naturalist William Bartram (son of **John Bartram**), he decided to devote himself to ornithology. He made several journeys across America, collecting species and drawing them, and wrote a poetic account of his first journey, an excursion on foot to Niagara Falls, in *The Foresters, A Poem* (1805). In 1806 he was employed on the American edition of *Rees's Cyclopaedia*, and prevailed on the publisher to undertake an illustrated *American Ornithology* (7 vols, 1808–14); the 8th and 9th volumes were completed after his death. Wilson's Storm-Petrel and Wilson's Phalarope were named in his honour.

WILSON, Sir Angus Frank Johnstone (1913–) English writer, born in Bexhill, Sussex, the son of an English father and a South African mother. He was educated at Westminster School and Merton College, Oxford. He joined the staff of the British Museum library in 1937. He began writing in 1946 and rapidly established a reputation with his brilliant collection of short stories, *The Wrong Set* (1949), satirizing the more aimless sections of pre-war middle-class society. *Such Darling Dodos* (1950), *For Whom the Cloche Tolls* (1953) and *A Bit off the Map* (1957) added to his prestige, and in 1955 he gave up his office of deputy-superintendent of the British Museum reading room to devote himself solely to writing. The novels *Hemlock and After* (1952) and *Anglo-Saxon Attitudes* (1956) were both best-sellers, and his later novels, including *The Old Men in the Zoo* (1961), *Late Call* (1965) and *No Laughing Matter* (1967), an ambitious family chronicle of the egocentric Matthews family spanning the 20th century, also received critical acclaim. His recent novels include *As If By Magic* (1973) and *Setting the World on Fire* (1980). He has also written one play, *The Mulberry Bush* (1955). He was professor of English literature at the University of East Anglia from 1966 to 1978.

WILSON, Sir Arthur Knyvet (1842–1921) English naval commander. He saw active service in the Crimea (1854), China (1865), Egypt (1882), and Sudan (1884), where he won the Victoria Cross at the battle of El Teb as a captain with naval brigade. He was commander-in-chief of the Home and Channel fleets 1903–07, admiral of the fleet 1907, and First Sea Lord 1909–12. He was nicknamed 'Old Art Eart'.

WILSON, Betty (1943–) Irish peace activist, born in Belfast. A Roman Catholic housewife in Belfast, she founded with **Mairead Corrigan** the Northern Ireland

Peace Movement in 1976 (the 'Peace People'). They shared the 1977 Nobel peace prize.

WILSON, Charles Thomson Rees (1869–1959) Scottish pioneer of atomic and nuclear physics, born in Glencorse near Edinburgh. Educated at Manchester and at Cambridge, where later he became professor of natural philosophy (1925–34), he was noted for his study of atmospheric electricity, one by-product of which was the successful protection from lightning of Britain's wartime barrage balloons. His greatest achievement was to devise the cloud chamber method of marking the track of alpha-particles and electrons. The movement and interaction of atoms could thus be followed and photographed. In 1927 he shared with **Arthur Compton** the Nobel prize for physics, and in 1937 received the Copley medal.

WILSON, Sir Daniel (1816–92) Scottish archaeologist, born in Edinburgh. Educated at the university there, he had been secretary to the Scottish Society of Antiquaries when in 1853 he became professor of history and English literature at Toronto. President of the university from 1881, he was knighted in 1888. One of the first writers to popularize the use of the term 'prehistory' for the pre-literate past, his numerous works include *Edinburgh in the Olden Time* (1847; new ed 1892), *The Archaeology and Prehistoric Annals of Scotland* (1851; 2nd ed 1863), and *The Lost Atlantis* (1892).

WILSON, Edmund (1895–1972) American literary critic, social commentator and novelist, born in Red Bank, New Jersey. He was educated at Princeton, became a journalist with *Vanity Fair* and editor of the *New Republic* (1926–31), and was chief book reviewer for the *New Yorker*. A lively, waspish critic of other writers, his own fiction, of which *Memoirs of Hecate Country* (1946) is the most notable example, is largely forgotten. But few critics have caused such a stir as he, and he was more listened to than most. *Axel's Castle* (1931), a study of Symbolist literature, is a landmark, but *To a Finland Station* (1940) and *The Wound and the Bow* (1941) are no less significant. In *Patriotic Gore: Studies in the Literature of the Civil War* (1962) he surveyed in detail the writers of the period. Over a wide-ranging oeuvre and argumentative life he published on many subjects and in a variety of forms, encompassing plays, articles, correspondence (see his correspondence with **Vladimir Nabokov**) and, in *The Scrolls from the Dead Sea* (1955), for which he learned Hebrew, a contentious but illuminating guide to a complex subject. Various memoirs detailing his life have appeared; he married four times, the third marriage being to the novelist **Mary McCarthy**, whose own turbulent career he defended even after their relationship had foundered.

WILSON, Edmund Beecher (1856–1939) American zoologist, born in Geneva, Illinois. He studied at Yale and Johns Hopkins universities, and after several teaching posts became Da Costa professor of zoology at Columbia University, New York. He contributed greatly to cytology and embryology and wrote *The Cell in Development and Inheritance* (1925).

WILSON, Edward Adrian (1872–1912) English physician, naturalist and explorer with **Scott** of the Antarctic. Born in Cheltenham, he first went to the Antarctic with Scott in the *Discovery* (1900–04). On his return to England he did research on grouse diseases and made illustrations for books on birds and mammals. In 1910 he returned to the Antarctic on the *Terra Nova* as chief of the expedition's scientific staff. One of the party of five that reached the South Pole just after **Roald Amundsen**, he died with the others on the return journey.

WILSON, Edward Osborne (1929–) American biologist, born in Birmingham, Alabama. He studied there and at Harvard, and taught at Harvard from 1956. His entomological interests led to his book *The Insect Societies* (1971); and he went on to consider a range of biological and genetic controls affecting social behaviour and organization in a variety of animal species in his book *Sociobiology: the New Synthesi* (1975). This virtually created a new subject, dealing with ideas on the behaviour of species from termites to man, and both stimulated valuable research and provoked vigorous discussion. He also wrote *On Human Nature* (1978, Pulitzer prize).

WILSON, Sir Erasmus (1809–84) English surgeon and antiquarian, born in London. He is best known as a specialist on skin diseases. He published *Anatomist's Vademecum*, *Book of Diseases of the Skin*, *Report on Leprosy*, and *Egypt of the Past*. A generous patron of Egyptian research, he brought Cleopatra's Needle to London in 1878 at a cost of £10000.

WILSON, Ernest Henry known as **'Chinese Wilson'** (1876–1930) English-born American botanist, plant collector and traveller, born in Chipping Campden, Gloucestershire. He was sent to China as a plant collector by Veitch and Sons of Chelsea (1899–1902, 1903–05) and then by the Arnold Arboretum of Massachusetts (1906–09, 1910–11) and to Japan (1914, 1917–19). He became assistant director, later keeper, of Arnold Arboretum, was supremely successful in the introduction of hardy Chinese plants into the gardens of Western Europe and North America. He published many books on plants, including *Lilies of Eastern Asia* (1925), *The Cherries of Japan* (1916), *Aristocrats of the Trees* (1930), *Plantae Wilsonianae* (1913–17), and on his travels, including *A Naturalist in Western China* (1913) and *Plant Hunting* (1927).

WILSON, Sir (James) Harold, Baron Wilson (1916–) English Labour politician, born in Huddersfield. He was educated there, in Cheshire and at Oxford, where he became a lecturer in economics in 1937. From 1943 to 1944 he was director of economics and statistics at the ministry of fuel and power. Becoming MP for Ormskirk in 1945, he was appointed parliamentary secretary to the ministry of works. In 1947 he became successively secretary for overseas trade and president of the board of trade till his resignation on the tide of Bevanism in April 1951. In 1951 and 1955 he was re-elected MP for Huyton, the division he had represented since 1950. The youngest cabinet minister since **Pitt**, after 1956, when he headed the voting for the Labour 'shadow' cabinet, he became the principal opposition spokesman on economic affairs. An able and hard-hitting debater, in 1963 he succeeded **Gaitskell** as leader of the Labour party, becoming prime minister in October 1964 with a precariously small majority and being re-elected in April 1966 with comfortably large support. His government's economic plans were badly affected by the balance of payments crisis, leading to severe restrictive measures; while abroad he was faced with the Rhodesian problem (increasingly severe economic sanctions being applied), continued intransigence from **de Gaulle** over Britain's proposed entry into the Common Market, and the important question of Britain's new status in world politics as a lesser power. His party lost power in the 1970 general election and he became leader of the opposition, then led them back into government in 1974, resigning as Labour leader two years later; he was made a life peer in 1983.

WILSON, Harriette, née **Dubochet** (1786–1855) English courtesan, born in Mayfair, London, of French descent. Her long career as a genteel courtesan began at the age of 15 with the Earl of Craven; subsequent paramours included the Duke of Argyll, the Duke of **Wellington**, the Marquis of Worcester and a host of others. All these figured in her lively but libellous *Memoirs*, brought out in parts from 1825 to the accompaniment of a barrage of suggestive advance publicity aimed at blackmail of the victims, most of whom echoed the celebrated outburst of Wellington on the occasion—'Publish and be damned!'

WILSON, Henry, originally **Jeremiah** (1812–73) American politician, born James Colbath, the son of a farm-labourer at Farmington, New Hampshire. He changed his name when he came of age, worked as a shoemaker, became prominent as an Abolitionist in the 'thirties, and was elected to the Massachusetts legislature and state senate. He was an active leader of the Free-soilers, assisted in forming the new Republican party, sat in the US Senate 1855–73, and then became vice-president of the United States (1873–75). In the civil war he was chairman of the military committee. He wrote *Rise and Fall of the Slave Power in America* (1872–75).

WILSON, Sir Henry Hughes (1864–1922) Irish soldier, born in Edgeworthstown, County Longford. He served in Burma and the Boer War, and won fame in World War I, starting (1914) as director of military operations, and ending (1918) as chief of the Imperial General Staff (1918–22). He left the army in 1922 and became MP for North Down. He was shot dead by two Irish ex-servicemen on the doorstep of his house in London.

WILSON, Henry Maitland, 1st Baron Wilson (1881–1964) English soldier. Educated at Eton, he was commissioned in the 'Greenjackets' in 1900. He fought in South Africa and in World War I, and by 1937 was GOC 2nd Division, Aldershot. On the outbreak of World War II he was appointed General Officer Commanding-in-Chief, Egypt, and after leading successfully the initial British advance in Libya and capturing Bardia, Tobruk and Benghazi, he was given command of the short and ill-fated Greek campaign. In 1943 he was appointed commander in chief Middle East, and in 1944 he became Supreme Allied Commander in what had become the relatively subordinate Mediterranean theatre. He headed the British Joint Staff Mission in Washington (1945–47) and in 1955 became constable of the Tower.

WILSON, Horace Hayman (1786–1860) English Orientalist, born in London. In 1808 he went to India as assistant surgeon, and became assistant to **John Leyden** in Calcutta. He was Boden professor of Sanskrit at Oxford (1832–60), and librarian at East India House (1836–60). His *Sanskrit-English Dictionary* (1819) and Sanskrit grammar (1841), together with his other works, helped to lay the foundations of Indian philology in Europe.

WILSON, James (1742–89) Scots-born American political ideologist and parent of the US Constitution, born in Carskerdo. He studied successively at St Andrews, Glasgow and Edinburgh (1757–65), subsequently moving to Philadelphia where he became an active philosophico-legal publicist in the cause of American devolution. Elected to the Continental Congress in 1775 (serving 1775–76, 1782–83, 1785–86), he supported independence, advocated stronger US central government, and supported individual colonies' cession of their western land claims in common cause to result in the creation of new states. As delegate to the Constitutional Congress of 1787, he played such a major part in using Scottish precedents that modern scholars acknowledge his co-paternity of the final document with **James Madison**. His influence was outstanding in gaining almost immediate ratification of the constitution of Pennsylvania in 1790, the first major state to do so. He was associate justice of the US Supreme Court (1789–98), and was the first professor of law at Pennsylvania University from 1790.

WILSON, James (1805–60) Scottish economist, born in Hawick. He settled in business in London, and became an authority on the corn-laws and the currency, founded the *Economist*, entered parliament as a Liberal in 1847, and was financial secretary to the Treasury, vice-president of the board of trade, and member of the council of India.

WILSON, John, pseud **Christopher North** (1785–1854) Scottish critic and essayist, born in Paisley. He studied at Glasgow and Magdalen College, Oxford, where he won the Newdigate poetry prize and gained a reputation as an outstanding athlete. In 1807 he bought an estate at Elleray, Westmorland, and became acquainted with the Lake District circle of poets (**Wordsworth**, **Coleridge**, **De Quincey**, **Southey**). Here he wrote three long poems, *The Isle of Palms* (1812), *The Magic Mirror* (1812, addressed to **Sir Walter Scott**), and *The City of the Plague* (1816). Having lost his estate through an uncle's mismanagement, he settled in Edinburgh as an advocate in 1815. In 1817 he joined **John Gibson Lockhart** and **James Hogg** in launching *Blackwood's Magazine*. Despite lacking any qualification for the post, he was appointed professor of moral philosophy at Edinburgh (1820–51) in succession to **Thomas Brown**. As contributing editor of *Blackwood's* he wrote several notable series under the pseudonym 'John North', such as *Noctes Ambrosianae* (1822–35), and a series of rural short stories, *Lights and Shadows of Scottish Life* (1822). He also published two novels, *The Trials of Margaret Lyndsay* (1823) and *The Foresters* (1825). His *Works* (1855–58) were edited by his son-in-law, **James Frederick Ferrier**.

WILSON, John (1804–75) Scottish missionary, born, a farmer's son, near Lauder. Educated at Edinburgh University, he became a missionary with the Scottish Missionary Society and went to Bombay in 1829. He was much consulted by government, especially during the crisis of 1857. He founded the *Oriental Christian Spectator*, and was twice president of the Bombay branch of the Asiatic Society, and was vice-chancellor of Bombay University. He founded the English School (later Wilson College) in Bombay in 1832. His chief writings were *The Parsi Religion* (1843) and *Lands of the Bible* (1847). His son, Andrew (1830–81), edited the *China Mail* and later the *Bombay Gazette*, but is best known for his account of **Gordon**'s *Ever-Victorious Army* (1868) and his book on the Himalayas, *The Abode of Snow* (1875).

WILSON, John Dover (1881–1969) English Shakespearean scholar, born in London. Educated at Cambridge, he spent some years as teacher, lecturer and HM inspector of adult education, then became professor first of education at King's College, London (1924–35), and of rhetoric and English literature at Edinburgh (1935–45). He is best known for his Shakespearean studies, particularly on the problems in *Hamlet*. From 1921 till 1966 he was editor of the New Shakespeare series. His works include *Life in Shakespeare's England* (1911), *The Essential Shakespeare* (1932), *The Fortunes of Falstaff* (1943), *What Happens in Hamlet* (1935) and *Shakespeare's Sonnets—An Introduction for Historians and Others* (1963).

WILSON, John Mackay (1804–35) Scottish writer and editor, born in Tweedmouth. He is known for his *Tales of the Borders* (6 vols, 1834–40), originally issued in weekly numbers, and continued after his death for his widow with Alexander Leighton (1800–74) as editor.

WILSON, Kenneth Geddes (1936–) American theoretical physicist, the son of a chemistry professor of Harvard. He studied at the California Institute of Technology, and taught at Cornell from 1971. He applied ingenious mathematical methods to the understanding of the magnetic properties of atoms, and later used similar methods in the study of phase transitions between liquids and gases, and in alloys. He was awarded the Nobel prize for physics in 1982.

WILSON, Richard (1714–82) Welsh landscape painter, born in Penegoes rectory, Powys. After a visit to Italy (1749–56), he gave up portrait painting for landscape and anticipated **Gainsborough** and **Constable** in forsaking straitlaced Classicism for a lyrical freedom of style. In London in 1760 he exhibited his *Niobe*, and became one of the leading painters of his time. Famous also was his *View of Rome from the Villa Madama*. In 1776 he became librarian to the Royal Academy.

WILSON, Robert (1941–) American epic theatre-maker, director and designer, born in Waco, Texas. America's most flamboyant post-modern creator of theatrical spectacle, his concentration on visual impact goes back to his early training as a painter, first in Texas, then Paris and finally New York. In contrast with the traditional language of theatre, he mixes a combination of movement, contemporary music by composers like **Philip Glass** and David Byrne, and exciting imagery, often in very long performances (some have reached twelve hours). His work includes *The Life and Times of Sigmund Freud* (1969), *The Life and Times of Joseph Stalin* (1973), *A Letter for Queen Victoria* (1974), *Death, Destruction and Detroit* (1979), *Great Day in the Morning* (1983), and *The CIVIL WarS* (conceived 1984), one of the most ambitious theatrical events ever proposed and still to be mounted in full.

WILSON, Sir Robert Thomas (1777–1849) English soldier, born in London. Having served in Belgium, and against the Irish rebels (1798), and in the campaign of the Helder, he commanded **Abercromby**'s cavalry in Egypt, helped to conquer the Cape of Good Hope in 1806, and went with a mission to Prussia. In the Peninsular War he helped to train the Portuguese army, and commanded a Spanish brigade at Talavera (1809). He was attached in 1812 to the Russian army, in Germany and France was in the camp of the allies, and at Lützen commanded the Prussian reserve. Involved in Queen **Caroline**'s affairs, he was dismissed from the army, but reinstated. From 1818 to 1831 he sat as a Liberal for Southwark; in 1841 he became general, from 1842 to 1849 was governor of Gibraltar. He wrote several works on military history.

WILSON, Robert Woodrow (1936–) American physicist, born in Houston, Texas. He graduated from Rice University, and the California Institute of Technology. He then joined Bell Laboratories in New Jersey and became head of the radiophysics research department in 1976. There he collaborated with **Arno Penzias** in using a large radio telescope designed for communication with satellites; they detected in 1964 a radio noise background coming from all directions with an energy distribution corresponding to a black body at 3.5K. **Robert Dicke** and P J E Peebles suggested that this radiation is the residual radiation from the big bang at the universe's creation, which has cooled to 3.5K by the expansion of the universe. This cosmic background radiation had been predicted to exist by **George Gamow**, **Ralph Alpher** and R C Hermann in 1948. Wilson and Penzias shared the 1978 Nobel prize for physics for their work, which can reasonably be claimed to be the most important contribution to cosmology in this century.

WILSON, Roy (Royston Warner) (1900–65) English strip cartoonist, born in Kettering, acclaimed as 'the king of comic artists' in the Golden Age of British Comics. He studied at Nottingham School of Art and was then apprenticed as a furniture designer (1915). In 1920 he started working on strips for Amalgamated Press children's comics. From 1930 he went solo on *Steve and Stumpy* (*Butterfly*) and many more, notably *George the Jolly Gee-Gee* (*Radio Fun*, 1938) and *Chimpo's Circus* (*Happy Days*, 1938), which was a vari-designed front page in full colour. He designed many painted annual covers and frontispieces and, from 1955, many personality strips; eg *Jerry Lewis*, *Harry Secombe*, *Morecambe and Wise*.

WILSON, Teddy (Theodore Shaw) (1912–86) American pianist, bandleader and arranger, one of the most influential stylists of the swing era of the late 1930s. Born in Austin, Texas, he studied music briefly at Talladega College, Alabama, and while still in his teens was working in Chicago with such major artists as **Louis Armstrong** and clarinettist Jimmy Noone. With his move to New York in 1933 to join the Benny Carter Orchestra his career as a pianist and arranger was firmly established. When he joined the Benny Goodman Trio in 1935 he was one of the first black musicians to appear with whites. He led many studio groups accompanying the singer **Billie Holiday**, and these recordings show his elegant, graceful style at its best.

WILSON, Thomas (1663–1755) English churchman, born in Burton in Cheshire. He became bishop of Sodor and Man in 1698. His *Principles of Christianity*, or 'the Manx Catechism' (1707), and *Instruction for the Indians* were combined to form *The Knowledge of Christianity made Easy* (1755). Better known are *Short Instructions for the Lord's Supper* (1733) and *Sacra Privata* (1781).

WILSON, Thomas Woodrow (1856–1924) 28th president of the USA, born in Staunton, Virginia. He studied at Princeton and Johns Hopkins, practised law at Atlanta, lectured at Bryn Mawr and Princeton, became president of Princeton in 1902, and governor of New Jersey in 1911, and in 1912 and 1916, as Democratic candidate, was elected president of the United States. Wilson's administration, ending in tragic failure and physical breakdown, is memorable for the prohibition and women's suffrage amendments of the constitution, trouble with Mexico, America's participation in World War I, his part in the peace conference, his 'fourteen points' and championship of the League of Nations, and the senate's rejection of the Treaty of Versailles. He wrote a *History of the American People* (1902) and other works.

WILTON, Marie See **BANCROFT, Sir Squire**

WINCHILSEA, Anne Finch, Countess of, née **Kingsmith** (1661–1720) English poet, born in Sidmonton, near Southampton. She was daughter of Sir William Kingsmill, and in 1684 she married Heneage Finch, Earl of Winchilsea (from 1712). Her longest poem, a Pindaric ode called *The Spleen*, was printed in 1701; her *Miscellany Poems* in 1713. She was a friend of **Pope**.

WINCKELMANN, Johann Joachim (1717–68) German archaeologist, born in Stendal in Prussian Saxony. He studied the history of art, published a treatise on the imitation of the antique (1754), and was librarian to a cardinal at Rome (1755). In 1758 he examined the remains of Herculaneum, Pompeii, and Paestum, and went to Florence. He wrote a treatise on ancient architecture (1762), the epoch-making

Geschichte der Kunst des Alterhums (1764), and *Monumenti Antichi Inediti* (1766). In 1763 he was made superintendent of Roman antiquities. He was murdered in Trieste.

WINDAUS, Adolf Otto Reinhold (1876–1959) German chemist, educated at Freiburg and Berlin, he was professor of applied medical chemistry at Innsbruck and Göttingen. In 1928 he was awarded the Nobel prize for chemistry for his work on sterols, in particular for his discovery that ultraviolet light activates ergosterol and gives vitamin D_2. He was also an authority on cardiac poisons.

WINDELBAND, Wilhelm (1848–1915) German philosopher, born in Potsdam. Educated at Jena, Berlin and Göttingen, he was professor at Zurich, Freiburg, Strasbourg and Heidelberg. He was the leading figure in the Baden school of neo-Kantianism, and tried to relate the historical sciences to the natural and mathematical sciences, which had always been taken to represent the archetypes of knowledge, and to show how philosophy stood in a quite separate relationship to all the different sciences and disciplines. His publications include *Praëludien: Aufsätze und Reden zur Einführung in die Philosophie* (2 vols, 1884) and *Lehrbuch der Geschichte der Philosophie* (1892, translated as *History of Philosophy*, 1893).

WINDHAM, William (1750–1810) English statesman, born in London, studied at Eton, Glasgow and Oxford. In 1784 he was elected to parliament as a Whig to represent Norwich. He was a strong supporter of **Pitt** and held a number of offices under him. Among his friends and colleagues he counted **William Cobbett** and Dr **Samuel Johnson**. Although a highly talented man, his abilities were never truly demonstrated.

WINDISCHGRÄTZ, Prince Alfred (1787–1862) Austrian solder. As commander in Bohemia from 1840, he suppressed the revolution of 1848–49 in Prague, and another in Vienna. In 1848 he helped to bring **Franz Joseph** to the throne. He defeated the Hungarians repeatedly, but was superseded after his defeat by them at Gödöllö.

WINDSOR, Duke of See **EDWARD VIII**

WINDSOR, Wallis Warfield, Duchess of (1896–1986) wife of **Edward VIII**, born in Blue Ridge Summit, Pennsylvania. An extrovert socialite, in 1916 she married Lieutenant Earl Winfield Spencer of the US navy, but in 1927 the marriage was dissolved. The following year she married, in London, Ernest Simpson, an American-born Briton. Well known in London society, she met Edward, the Prince of Wales, at a country house party in 1931. In 1936, the year of his accession, she obtained a divorce in England, and the king subsequently made clear to **Stanley Baldwin** and his government his determination to marry her, even if it meant giving up the throne. They married in 1937 in France, but Wallis was not accepted by the British royal family until the late 1960s. She and Edward lived in France and the Bahamas; after Edward's death she lived virtually as a recluse in Paris. In 1956 she published her memoirs, *The Heart has its Reasons*.

WINDTHORST, Ludwig (1812–91) German Catholic politician, born near Osnabrück. He became distinguished as an advocate and politician in Hanover. After the absorption of Hanover by Prussia, he became leader of the Ultramontanes in the German parliament and chief opponent of **Bismarck** during the Kulturkampf.

WINER, Johann Georg Benedikt (1789–1858) German New Testament scholar, born in Leipzig. He became professor of theology there, at Erlangen in 1823, and at Leipzig again in 1832. The most important of his many works is his *Grammar of New Testament Greek* (1882).

WINFIELD, Sir Percy Henry (1878–1953) English jurist, born in Stoke Ferry, Norfolk. Educated at King's Lynn Grammar School and St John's College, Cambridge, he became Rouse Ball professor of English law at Cambridge (1928–43). He is principally remembered as a scholar in the law of torts, notably for his perceptive *Province of the Law of Tort* (1931) and *Textbook of the Law of Tort* (1937) which has maintained a place as a leading textbook. Among his other works is *Chief Sources of English Legal History* (1925), which reveals keen scholarship in that field also.

WINGATE, Orde Charles (1903–44) English soldier, and leader of the Chindits. Educated at Charterhouse and the Royal Military Academy, he joined the Royal Artillery in 1922. With the Sudan Defence Force from 1928 to 1933, he later saw service in Palestine and Transjordan. In the Burma theatre in 1942, realizing that the only answer to penetration is counter-penetration, he obtained sanction to organize the Chindits—specially trained jungle-fighters. Supplied by air, they thrust far behind the enemy lines, gravely disrupting the entire supply system. He was killed in a plane crash in Burma.

WINGATE, Sir Reginald (1861–1953) English soldier. He entered the Royal Artillery in 1880, and served in India and Aden and with the Egyptian Army. He was governor-general of the Sudan from 1899–1916 in succession to **Kitchener**. He retired in 1922 after service as high commissioner of Egypt.

WINGTI, Paias (1951–) Papua New Guinea politician. Educated at Port Moresby University, he joined the Pangu Pati (Papua New Guinea party) and served as minister of transport and then planning under prime minister **Michael Somare** during the later 1970s and early 1980s. He eventually became deputy prime minister, but resigned in 1985 to form the breakaway People's Democratic Movement (PDM). In November 1985 he became prime minister at the head of a five-party coalition. He championed Melanesian interests in both the South Pacific Forum and the newly formed Spearhead Group, which also included Vanuatu and the Solomon Islands: but with opposition mounting to his economic strategy and leadership style, he was defeated on a 'no confidence' motion in July 1988.

WINIFRED, St (7th century) legendary Welsh saint, a noble British maiden, beheaded by Prince Caradog for repelling his unholy proposals. The legend relates that her head rolled down a hill, and where it stopped a spring gushed forth—famous still as a place of pilgrimage, Holywell in Clwyd. Her head was replaced by St Beuno.

WINKELRIED, Arnold von (d.1386) Swiss patriot, knight of Unterwalden. At the battle of Sempach (July 1386), when the Swiss failed to break the compact line of Austrian spears, he is said to have grasped as many pikes as he could reach, buried them in his bosom and borne them by his weight to the earth. His comrades rushed into the breach, slaughtered the Austrians like sheep, and gained a decisive victory.

WINKLER, Clemens Alexander (1838–1904) German chemist, born and educated in Freiberg, where he became professor of chemistry. In 1886 he discovered the element germanium. He also made important contributions to the study of the analysis of gases.

WINSLOW, Edward (1595–1655) American colonist, and one of the Pilgrim Fathers, born in Droitwich. He sailed in the *Mayflower* in 1620, and from 1624 was assistant governor or governor of the Plymouth colony, which he described and defended in *Good Newes from New England* (1624), *Hypocrisie Unmasked* (1646) and *New England's Salamander* (1647). Sent by **Cromwell** against the West Indies, he died at sea. His son, Josiah (1629–80), was assistant governor 1657–73, and then governor. In 1675 he was chosen general-in-chief of the United Colonies. His grandson, John (1702–74), carried out the removal of the Acadians; and John Ancrum Winslow (1811–73), descendant of one of Edward Winslow's brothers, commanded the *Kearsarge* in her action with the Confederate raider *Alabama* in 1864 during the American Civil War (1861–65).

WINSOR, Justin (1831–97) American librarian and historian, born in Boston, Massachusetts. He studied at Harvard and Heidelberg and was librarian at Boston (1868–77), and then at Harvard. He published bibliographical and other works, including *Memorial History of Boston* (1880–81), *Narrative History of America* (1884–90) and a Life of **Columbus** (1891).

WINT, Peter de (1784–1849) English watercolourist, born, of Dutch descent, in Stone, Staffordshire. His fame rests on his watercolour illustrations of English landscape, English architecture, and English country life. Among them are *The Cricketers*, *The Hay Harvest*, *Nottingham*, *Richmond Hill* and *Cows in Water*. Many of his works are in Lincoln Art Gallery. His watercolours are well represented in the Victoria and Albert Museum, which also owns the oils *A Cornfield* and *A Woody Landscape*.

WINTER, Jan Willem de (1750–1812) Dutch naval commander, born on the island of Texel. He was defeated by **Adam Duncan** at Camperdown in 1797. He was ambassador to France (1798–1802).

WINTERHALTER, Franz Xaver (1805–73) German painter and lithographer. He made a successful portrait of Grand Duke Leopold of Baden and was appointed his court painter. In 1834 he went to Paris, with Queen **Marie Amélie** as his patron. One of his many royal sitters was Queen **Victoria**, and Winterhalter became the fashionable artist of the day. Some of his works are at Versailles, and he is represented in the British royal collection.

WINTERS, (Arthur) Yvor (1900–68) American critic and poet, born in Chicago. He was educated at Chicago, Colorado, and Stanford universities, and in 1949 was appointed professor of English at Stanford. A versifier whose *Collected Poems* were published in 1960, winning the Bollingen Prize, he is remembered primarily as a quirky, irascible critic, anti the expressionists and with a sharp eye for detail. Significant books are *In Defence of Reason* (1947), *The Function of Criticism* (1957) and *Uncollected Essays and Reviews* (1976).

WINTHROP, John (1588–1649) English colonist, born in Groton in Suffolk. He was bred to the law, and in 1629 was appointed governor of Massachusetts colony. He was re-elected governor, with brief intervals, during his life, and had more influence probably than any other man in forming the political institutions of the northern states of America. The first part of his *Journal* was published in 1790, and the whole in 1825–26 (later ed with additions, 1853).

WINTHROP, John (1606–76) American colonist, born in Groton, son of **John Winthrop** (1588–1649). He went to America in 1631, landing in Boston, and became a magistrate in Massachusetts, in 1635 went to Connecticut, and founded New London in 1646. In 1657 he was elected governor of Connecticut, and, except for one year, held that post till his death. He obtained from **Charles II** a charter uniting the colonies of Connecticut and New Haven, and was named first governor under it; he was the father of paper currency in America.

WINTHROP, John, known as **Fitz-John** (1639–1707) Anglo-American soldier and colonial administrator, born in Ipswich, Massachusetts, son of **John Winthrop** (1606–76). He served under **Monk** in the parliamentary army (1660), and settled in Connecticut in 1663. He was a commander against the Dutch, the Indians and the French. He was agent in London for Connecticut (1693–97), and governor of the colony from 1698.

WINTHROP, John (1714–79) American physicist, descendant of **John Winthrop** (1588–1649), born in Boston. In 1738 he became professor of mathematics and natural philosophy at Harvard. In 1740 he observed the transit of Mercury. He published papers on earthquakes, comets, etc.

WINTHROP, Robert Charles (1809–94) American orator and politician, born in Boston. A descendant of the colonist **John Winthrop** (1588–1649), he was admitted to the bar in 1831, and was in the state legislature (1834–40), then in congress, and in 1847–49 its speaker. In 1850–51 he was senator from Massachusetts. He published *Addresses and Speeches* (1852–86); a Life of the first John Winthrop; and *Washington, Bowdoin, and Franklin* (1876).

WINTHROP, Theodore (1828–61) American, born in New Haven, Connecticut, a descendant of **John Winthrop** (1588–1649). He studied at Yale, was admitted to the bar (1855), but, volunteering in the Civil War, fell in battle at Great Bethel. His novels, all published postumously, include *Cecil Dreeme* (1861), *John Brent* (1861) and *Edwin Brothertoft* (1862).

WINZET, Ninian (1518–92) Scottish churchman, born in Renfrew. He was ordained priest in 1540, and about 1552 became schoolmaster in the grammar school at Linlithgow, and was later provost of the collegiate church there. At the Reformation (1561) he was deprived of his office, came to Edinburgh, and as a Catholic wrote *Certane Tractatis for Reformation of Doctryne and Maneris* (1562). Forced to leave Scotland in 1563, he published his *Buik of Four Scoir Thre Questiouns*. He held office in the University of Paris, and in 1574 moved to the English College of Douai, and in 1577 became abbot at Ratisbon.

WIRÉN, Dag I (1905–86) Swedish composer. Influenced by **Stravinsky** and **Prokofiev**, he was at first a neo-classicist, but in his Third Symphony (1943–44) he adopted a 'metamorphosis technique' by which whole works were created from small units. His large output includes five symphonies, five string quartets, a variety of large-scale orchestral works, film and theatre music and even *Annorstädes vals* (Waltz for Elsewhere), the (unsuccessful) Swedish entry for the 1965 Eurovision Song Contest. His most popular work remains the *Serenade for Strings* (1937), the last movement of which formed the title music music for the BBC2 television series *Monitor*.

WIRTH, Philip Peter Jacob (1864–1937) Australian circus proprietor of German descent, born in Victoria. His family moved to Queensland where his father joined a travelling circus. In 1878 his father, Peter, and his three brothers formed their own troupe, touring New South Wales and Queensland in a second-hand stagecoach. Within four years the circus had grown so popular that a special train had to be chartered for its tours, and in 1890 it visited New Zealand. A world tour later took in South Africa, South America and England, and the circus returned through Asia to establish permanent bases in Sydney and Melbourne. An Australian tradition, Wirth's circus continued to tour the country in special trains and frequently returned to New Zealand. Philip Wirth was renowned for his ability to break in and school wild animals, and his sons and daughters continued the family tradition until the 1960s.

WISDOM, Arthur John Terence Dibben (1904–) English philosopher. Educated at Aldeburgh Lodge School and Fitzwilliam College, Cambridge, he became professor at Cambridge (1952–68) and at the University of Oregon (1968–72). He was profoundly influenced by **Wittgenstein**, but developed a distinctive mode and style of philosophizing which represented philosophical paradoxes as revealing partial truths rather than linguistic confusions. His most important works are *Other Minds* (1952), *Philosophy and Psychoanalysis* (1953) and *Paradox and Discovery* (1965).

WISDOM, Norman (1918–) English comedian, born in London. He made his stage début in 1946, and in 1948 appeared in variety at the London Casino, and in concert parties and summer seasons throughout Britain. He appeared regularly at the London Palladium, and continued to work on stage in revue, pantomime and comedies. He made his film début as a slapstick comedian in *Trouble in Store* (1953), followed by a string of successes including *Man of the Moment* (1955); *Just My Luck* (1958); *There was a Crooked Man* (1960); *On the Beat* (1962); *A Stitch in Time* (1963); *Sandwich Man* (1966), and *What's Good for The Goose* (1969). He also made a film in America, *The Night They Raided Minsky's*, in 1968.

WISE, Thomas James (1859–1937) English bibliophile and literary forger, born in Gravesend. He began collecting books in his youth and built up a library of rare editions of the English poets and other works, including a collection of pamphlets and MSS, especially of the 19th-century romantics and the literary wing of the pre-Raphaelite movement. In 1934 certain pamphlets which he had sold to dealers and others for high prices were alleged to be faked and a sensational literary scandal ensued which was only checked by his death. His collection (the Ashley Library) was sold to the British Museum.

WISEMAN, Nicholas Patrick Stephen (1802–65) English prelate and cardinal, born in Seville, of an Irish family settled in Spain. He was brought up at Waterford and Ushaw, entered the English College at Rome, received holy orders in 1825, and became rector of the college (1828–40). He established the *Dublin Review* (1836), and in 1840 was named Coadjutor Vicar-apostolic and president of St Mary's College at Oscott. In 1847 he was transferred to the London district. In 1850 he was appointed the first Roman Catholic Archbishop of Westminster, and Cardinal, arousing a storm of indignation which led to the passing of the Ecclesiastical Titles Assumption Act; in response he published his conciliatory *Appeal to the Reason and Good Feeling of the English People* (1850). One of his best known works was a novel *Fabiola* (1854).

WISHART, George (c.1513–1546) Scottish reformer and martyr, born in Angus; his eldest brother was a lawyer (king's advocate). In 1538 he was a schoolmaster at the grammar school in Montrose, where he incurred a charge of heresy for teaching the Greek New Testament. In 1539 he was in Bristol, and had to abjure heresy again. The next few years he spent on the continent, and translated the Swiss *Confession of Faith*. In 1543 he accompanied a commission sent to Scotland by **Henry VIII** to negotiate a marriage contract between his infant son, Prince Edward (the future **Edward VI**) and **Mary, Queen of Scots**; and he preached the Lutheran doctrine of justification by faith at Dundee and Montrose, in Ayrshire and East Lothian. At Cardinal **David Beaton**'s insistence he was arrested in 1546, and burned at St Andrews on 1 March. **John Knox** was first inspired by Wishart.

WISLICENUS, Johannes Adolf (1835–1902) German chemist, born near Querfurt in Prussian Saxony. He went to America as a young man, taught chemistry at Cambridge (USA), New York, Zürich and Würzburg, and in 1885 became professor at Leipzig. He did important work, particularly on the lactic acids, and edited a handbook of chemistry (1874–77).

WISTER, Owen (1860–1938) American author, born in Philadelphia. He took a music degree at Harvard and intended to be a composer, but won fame with his novel of cowboy life in Wyoming, *The Virginian* (1902), and other books.

WITHER, George (1588–1667) English poet and pamphleteer, born in Bentworth, Hampshire. He studied at Magdalen College, Oxford (1604–06), and entered Lincoln's Inn in 1615. For his *Abuses Stript and Whipt* (1613) he was imprisoned. In prison he wrote a book of five pastorals, *The Shepherd's Hunting* (1615), followed by a love elegy, *Fidelia* (1617). It is supposed that his satire addressed to the king (1614), together with the Earl of Pembroke's intercession, procured his release. In 1621 appeared the satirical *Wither's Motto*, a curious piece of self-confession, which landed him in jail again. His finest poem is *Fair Virtue, or the Mistress of Philarete* (1622). There followed his *Hymns and Songs of the Church* (1623), *Psalms of David translated* (1631), *Emblems* (1634), and *Hallelujah* (1641). Now a fiery Puritan, in 1642 he sold his estate to raise a troop of horse for parliament, but was taken prisoner. Later **Cromwell** made him major-general in Surrey and master of the Statute Office. At the Restoration (1660) he lost his position and property, and, on suspicion of having written the *Vox Vulgi*, a satire on the parliament of 1661, was imprisoned. He was released in 1663. His poetry fell into almost complete oblivion, but the praises of **Southey**, Sir Egerton Brydges, **Hallam**, and **Charles Lamb** in particular revived interest in his work.

WITHERING, William (1741–99) English physician, born in Wellington in Shropshire and educated at Edinburgh. He wrote a *British Flora* and *An Account of the Foxglove* (1785), introducing digitalis as a drug for cardiac disease. He was the first to see the connection between dropsy and heart disease.

WITHERSPOON, John (1723–94) Scots-born American clergyman and theologian, born in Gifford. He was minister at Beith and then Paisley, and in 1768 emigrated to America to become president of the College of New Jersey (now Princeton University) from 1768 to 1794. He taught many future leaders in American public life, including president **James Madison**,whose co-authorship of *The Federalist* papers bore the influence of his teacher's calvinist social and political thought. He was a representative of New Jersey to the Continental Congress (1776–82), and helped to frame the American Declaration of Independence (1776). His writings include *Ecclesiastic Characteristics* (1753), against the Moderates; *Serious Enquiry into the Nature and Effects of the Stage* (1757); and two on *Justification* (1756) and *Regeneration* (1764).

WITSIUS, Hermann (1636–1708) Dutch Calvinist theologian. In 1675 he became a professor at Francker, in 1680 at Utrecht, and in 1698 at Leiden. His great work is *De Oeconomia Foederum Dei cum hominibus* (trans 1763). Other writings translated are *Antinomians and Neonomians* (1807), *The Creed* (1823), and *The Lord's Prayer* (1839).

WITTGENSTEIN, Ludwig Josef Johann (1889–1951) Austrian-born British philosopher who became one of the most influential and charismatic figures in British philosophy this century. He was born in Vienna into a wealthy and cultivated family, the son of an industrialist. He was educated at home until the age of 14, then at an Austrian school for three years; he went on to study mechanical engineering at Berlin (1906–08) and at Manchester (1908–11), where he did research on aeronautics and designed a reaction jet propeller. He became seriously interested in mathematics, and then in the foundations of mathematics, and in 1911 abandoned his engineering research and moved to Cambridge to study mathematical logic under **Bertrand Russell** (1912–13). He studied with enormous intensity and Russell said admiringly that he 'soon knew all that I had to teach'. Wittgenstein served in World War I in the Austrian army as an artillery officer and was taken prisoner on the Italian front in 1918. Throughout the war he had continued to work on problems in logic, carrying his notebooks round with him in his rucksack, and in the POW camp near Monte Cassino he completed his first work, the only one published in his lifetime, and sent it to Russell in England. It was eventually published in 1921 under the title *Logisch-philosophische Abhandlung* (and then in 1922, with a parallel German-English text and an introduction from Russell, as *Tractatus Logico-Philosophicus*). This was a novel, rather startling work, consisting of a series of numbered, aphoristic remarks centred on the nature and limits of language. Meaningful language, he conceived, must consist in propositions (or combinations of propositions) that are 'pictures' of the facts of which the world is composed. On this criterion we must discard as literally meaningless a lot of our conventional discourse, including judgments of value, and many of the claims of speculative philosophy. And since the limits of language are also the limits of thought he reaches the rather portentous conclusion 'whereof one cannot speak, thereof one must be silent'. This scheme for a logically foolproof language, a perfect instrument for meaningful assertion, seemed to represent a kind of terminus and Wittgenstein now turned away from philosophy to find another vocation. He gave away the money he had inherited and lived a simple ascetic life, working as an elementary schoolteacher in Austrian country districts (1920–26), a gardener's assistant in a monastery, and an amateur architect and builder commissioned by one of his sisters. In the late '20s he was sought out by various philosophers who had found inspiration in the *Tractatus*, particularly **Schlick** and the logical positivists of the Vienna Circle, and he revived his philosophical interests and returned to Cambridge in 1929, first as research fellow of Trinity College and then as professor of philosophy (1939–47), interrupted only by a period of war service as a porter at Guy's Hospital, London, and a lab assistant at the Royal Victoria Infirmary in Manchester. He became a naturalized British subject in 1938. At Cambridge his philosophy began to take a quite new direction; he attracted a group of devoted pupils and through his lectures and the circulation of his students' notes he came to exert a powerful influence on philosophy throughout the English-speaking world. The work of this second period of his philosophical career is best summarized in the posthumous *Philosophical Investigations* (1953), a discursive and often enigmatic work which rejects most of the assumptions and conclusions of the *Tractatus*. In the *Investigations* Wittgenstein no longer tries to reduce language to a perfect logical model, but rather points to the variety, open-endedness and subtlety of everyday language and explores the actual communicative and social functions of different modes of speech or 'language games'. Language is seen as a toolkit not a calculus. Philosophy then becomes a therapeutic technique of 'assembling reminders' of usage, which reveal the source of many philosophical paradoxes in the misunderstanding of ordinary language and the obsessive search for unity or simplicity where none exists. Instead of expecting each concept to have a single, defining essence we should rather look for a range of overlapping 'family resemblances'. Wittgenstein died of cancer in Cambridge, and there has been a continuous stream of posthumously edited publications from his prolific notebooks and manuscripts, including *Remarks on the Foundations of Mathematics* (1956), *The Blue and Brown Books* (1958), *Philosophische Bemerkungen* (1964) and *On Certainty* (1969).

WITTIG, Georg (1897–) German organic chemist, born in Berlin. Educated in Marburg, he held professorships at Freiburg (1937–44), and Tübingen (1944–65) and Heidelberg (1956–67). He worked especially on novel reactive intermediates, including carbanions, ylides, and benzyne. The Wittig reaction using ylides is a valuable general method and has been used in syntheses of vitamins and prostaglandins. At the age of 82 he shared the Nobel prize for chemistry in 1979 with **Herbert Brown**, for work he had done 30 years earlier.

WITZ, Konrad (c.1400–1444/47) German painter, born in Rottweil, Swabia. He joined the Basle guild of painters in 1434 and spent most of his life in what is now Switzerland. His extremely realistic style suggests that he was aware of the work of his contemporary **Jan van Eyck**. The only signed and dated painting of his which survives is a late work, *Christ Walking on the Water* (1444). This particular work is remarkable not only for its quality and attention to detail but also because it is set on Lake Geneva—the earliest known recognizable landscape in European art.

WODEHOUSE, Sir Pelham Grenville (1881–1975) English novelist, born in Guildford. He was educated at Dulwich College, and worked for the Hong Kong and Shanghai Bank for two years before beginning to earn a living as a journalist and story writer, writing the 'By the Way' column on the *Globe*. He also contributed to a series of school stories in a magazine for boys, the *Captain*, in which 'Psmith' first made an appearance. Going to America before World War I, he sold a serial to the *Saturday Evening Post* and for a quarter of a century almost all his books appeared first in that magazine. He was co-author and writer of the lyrics to 18 musical comedies, including *Kissing Time*. He married in 1914. World War II blighted his otherwise stainless reputation. Captured by the Germans at Le Touquet, he was interned then released but not allowed to leave Germany. Foolishly he agreed to make broadcasts for the Germans and though they were harmless he was branded as a traitor. Writing in his defence **Orwell** observed that 'The general upshot of the talks ... was that he had not been ill-treated and bore no malice'. Eventually his name was cleared but he made America his home where the climate allowed him to indulge his passion for golf. He became an American citizen in 1955. His copious oeuvre—he wrote over 100 books—falls into three well-marked periods; the school stories which include *The Pothunters* (1902), *The Gold Bat* (1904); the American period, during which he wrote *Psmith, Journalist* (1915), *The Indiscretions of Archie* (1921) and *Piccadilly Jim* (1917); and what might be called the country house period in which can be included a plethora of titles set in country mansions, bachelor pads in the metropolis and exclusive golf clubs. It is to this group that characters like Lord Emsworth, Gussie Fink-Nottle, Bertie Wooster and his legendary valet, Jeeves, belong. Of his many felicitous titles, *Right Ho, Jeeves* (1934), *Quick Service* (1940) and *The Mating Season* (1949) stand out. Wodehouse summed up his attitude to writing thus: 'I believe there are two ways of writing novels. One is mine, making a sort of musical comedy without music and ignoring real life altogether; the other is going deep down into life and not caring a damn ...'. There is a wax effigy of him in Madame **Tussaud**'s.

WODROW, Robert (1679–1734) Scottish church historian, born in Glasgow. He studied theology under his father, who was professor of divinity there. He was university librarian at Glasgow from 1697–1701, and in 1703 became minister of Eastwood. His *History of the Sufferings of the Church of Scotland 1660–88* (1721–22) was dedicated to **George I**. Posthumous works include *Lives of the Scottish Reformers* (1834–45), and *Analecta, or a History of Remarkable Providences* (1842–43).

WOFFINGTON, Peg (Margaret) (1720–60) Irish actress, born in Dublin, the daughter of a bricklayer and a laundress. From 17 to 20 she played on the Dublin stage. In 1740 she made her London debut at Covent Garden as Sylvia in *The Recruiting Officer*. Her beauty and vivacity carried all hearts by storm. **David Garrick** was one of her many lovers. She was famous for her 'breeches' parts, particularly as Sir Harry Wildair in *The Constant Couple*. She played at Drury Lane until 1746, then Covent Garden, with a triumphant return to Dublin (1750–54). In 1756 she stabbed another actress, **George Anne Bellamy**, and in 1757 was taken ill on stage, never to return. Her last days were given to charity and good works, endowing alms houses in Teddington. She was the subject of **Charles Reade**'s first novel, *Peg Woffington* (1853).

WOGAN, Terry (Michael Terence) (1938–) Irish broadcaster and writer, born in Limerick. He joined Radio Telefis Eireann in 1963 as an announcer and hosted various BBC radio programmes from 1965, including *Late Night Extra* (1967–69) and *The Terry Wogan Show* (1969–72). Resident in Britain from 1969, he endeared himself to millions of listeners with a mixture of merry badinage, whimsy and music when he presented Radio Two's *Breakfast Show* (1972–84). Active on television in many capacities, he presented the cheerily banal game show *Blankety Blank* (1977–81), *You Must Be Joking* (1981) and the annual charity telethon *Children in Need*. He began a regular chat show in 1982 and in 1985 it became a thrice-weekly fixture, reliant on his charm, nimble wit and relaxed professionalism. In 1977 he enjoyed success in the pop charts with *The Floral Dance* and has written several books including *Banjaxed* (1979), *The Day Job* (1981) and *Wogan on Wogan* (1987).

WÖHLER, Friedrich (1800–82) German chemist, born near Frankfurt. Educated at Heidelberg, he became professor at Göttingen in 1836. He isolated aluminium (1827) and beryllium (1828), and discovered calcium carbide, from which he obtained acetylene. His synthesis of urea from ammonium cyanate in 1828 revolutionized organic chemistry.

WOHLGEMUTH See **WOLGEMUT, Michael**

WOLCOT, John, pseud **Peter Pindar** (1738–1819) English satirist, born in Dodbrooke, Devon. He studied medicine for seven years in London, took his MD at Aberdeen (1767), and, going to Jamaica, became physician-general of the island. He returned to England to take holy orders, but soon started medical practice at Truro. Here he discovered the talents of the young painter **John Opie**, and went with him in 1780 to London, to devote himself to writing audacious satires in verse. His 60 or 70 poetical pamphlets (1778–1818) include *The Lousiad, The Apple-dumplings and a King, Whitbread's Brewery visited by their Majesties, Bozzy and Piozzi*, and *Lyrical Odes* on the Royal Academy Exhibitions. Although witty and fluent, his works were coarse and ephemeral.

WOLF, Friedrich August (1759–1824) German classical scholar, born in Hagewrode. In 1779 he established his fame by an edition of **Plato**'s *Symposium*, and in 1783 he became professor at Halle. He edited **Demosthenes**'s *Oratio adversus Leptinem* (1789), and in his *Prolegomena ad Homerum* (1795) he argued that the *Odyssey* and *Iliad* were composed of ballads by different minstrels, strung together by later editors—a view defended in his sprited *Briefe an Heyne* (1797). His *Darstellung der Alterhumswissenschaft* (1807) championed the cause of classical studies.

WOLF, Hugo (1860–1903) Austrian composer, chiefly of songs, born in Windischgraz in Styria. He was destined for the family leather business, but early turned to music. For a time he studied without satisfaction at the Vienna Conservatory, then earned a meagre living by teaching and conducting. From 1884–88 he was music critic of the *Wiener Salonblatt*, violently attacking **Brahms** and extolling **Wagner**. All this time he was composing, but his best work came after 1888 and includes the Mörike set of 53 songs (1888), settings of poems by **Goethe** (1888–89), the *Italienisches Leiderbuch* of Heyse and **Emanuel von Geibel** (1889–90), and three sonnets of Michelangelo (1897). He also wrote an opera, *Der Corregidor* (1895), and other works. He was at his best in his treatment of short lyrical poems, giving many of them a new significance by the sensitive commentary of his settings. For the most part he lived in poverty. In 1897 he became insane. After a brief period of recovery he was confined from 1898 onwards in the asylum at Steinhof near Vienna, where he died.

WOLF, Maximilian Franz Joseph Cornelius (1863–1932) German astronomer, born in Heidelberg. Educated at Heidelberg and Stockholm, he became professor of astronomy at Heidelberg (1896) and director of the Königstuhl astrophysical observatory there. He invented the photographic method of discovering asteroids, and with **Edward Barnard** was the first to appreciate 'dark' nebulae in the sky.

WOLFE, Charles (1791–1823) Irish poet and clergyman, born in Blackhall, County Kildare. He was educated at Winchester, and Trinity College, Dublin. He took holy orders in 1817 and became curate of Ballyclog, County Tyrone, and Donoughmore, County Down (1818). He is remembered for his poem *The Burial of Sir John Moore* after Corunna, which appeared anonymously in 1817 and at once caught the admiration of the public.

WOLFE, Humbert (1885–1940) English poet and critic, born in Milan, Italy. In 1908 he entered the Civil Service, becoming in 1938 deputy secretary to the ministry of labour. He published *London Sonnets* (1919), *Lampoons* (1925), *Requiem* (1927), and several other collections of verse, all marked by deep feeling and meticulous craftsmanship. His critical writings included *Notes on English Verse Satire* (1929) and studies of **Tennyson**, **Herrick**, **Shelley** and **George Moore**.

WOLFE, James (1727–59) English soldier, born in Westerham vicarage, Kent, the eldest son of General Edward Wolfe (1685–1759). In 1742 he received an ensign's commission, in 1743 fought at Dettingen, in 1745–46 served against the Scottish Jacobites at

Falkirk and Culloden, and in 1747 was wounded at Lawfeldt. From 1749 to 1757 he was engaged in garrison duty in Scotland and England. In the mismanaged expedition against Rochefort (1757) he was quartermaster-general; in 1758, with the rank of colonel, he received from **Pitt** the command of a brigade in the expedition against Cape Breton under General **Jeffrey Amherst**; and to him was mainly due the capture of Louisburg (1758). Pitt was now organizing his grand scheme for expelling the French from Canada, and the expedition for the capture of Quebec he entrusted to Wolfe's command. As major-general, and commanding 9000 men, Wolfe sailed from England in February 1759, and in June landed below Quebec. The attack on **Montcalm**'s strong position proved one of stupendous difficulty, and Wolfe was completely foiled. But at last, scaling the cliffs at a point insufficiently guarded, at dawn on 13 September he found himself on the plains of Abraham. After a short struggle the French were routed; Montcalm was killed; Quebec capitulated; and its fall decided the fate of Canada. Wolfe died in the hour of victory. His body was buried in Greenwich church.

WOLFE, Thomas Clayton (1900–38) American novelist, born at Asheville, North Carolina, into a large family in an overcrowed house. His father, an alcoholic, was a skilled stone-cutter who sculpted tombstones for a living. In 1904 his mother decided to open a boarding-house in St Louis during the World's Fair, but her attempt at independence ended with the death of one of her sons. But in 1906 she opened 'The Old Kentucky Home', taking with her her youngest son, leaving the other children with their father. Thomas was educated at the University of North Carolina and at Harvard. His writing career began abortively as a playwright, and in 1925 he embarked on a turbulent affair with Mrs Aline Bernstein, a maternal figure who did much to encourage his writing, particularly his first novel *Look Homeward, Angel* (1929), which was patently autobiographical. *Of Time and the River* (1935), its sequel, was honed into shape by Max Perkins, his editor at Scribner's. Both these novels feature Eugene Gant, Wolfe's alter ego. He later changed publishers and *The Web and the Rock* (1939) and *You Can't Go Home Again* (1940) were published posthumously. Prolix, careless, bombastic and over-ambitious, he wrote nevertheless vividly of people and places. Some assert that his best work is to be found in the stories in *From Death to Morning* (1935). His *Letters* were published in 1956.

WOLFE, Tom (Thomas Kennerley) (1931–) American journalist, pop-critic and novelist, born in Richmond, Virginia. Graduating from Washington and Lee University, he received his doctorate in American Studies from Yale University. Later he worked as a reporter for the *Springfield Union*, *The Washington Post* and the New York *Herald Tribune*. A proponent of the New Journalism, his style is distinctive, hyper-clever and narcissistic. A fashion-leader and follower, he has written a number of books with eye-catching titles: *The Electric Kool-Aid Acid Test* (1968), about **Ken Kesey** and the Merry Pranksters, *Radical Chic & Mau-Mauing the Flak Catchers* (1970), and *The Kandy-Kolored Tangerine-Flake Streamline Baby* (1965). Much of his work previously appeared in periodicals like *The Rolling Stone*, as did his only novel, *The Bonfire of the Vanities* (1988), which was a bestseller.

WOLF-FERRARI, Ermanno (1876–1948) Italian composer, born in Venice. Sent to Rome to study painting, he turned to music and became a pupil of **Joseph Rheinberger** in Munich. In 1899 he returned to Venice, where his first opera was unsuccessfully produced the following year. His later operas, however, were equally successful in both Italy and Germany. From 1902–12 he was director of the Liceo Benedetto Marcello, in Venice. He composed choral and chamber works, and music for organ and piano as well as the operas, notably *Susanna's Secret* (1909), *The Jewels of the Madonna* (1911) and *School for Fathers* (1906).

WOLFENDEN, John Frederick, Baron (1906–85) English educationist and governmental adviser on social questions, born in Halifax and was fellow and tutor in philosophy at Magdalen College, Oxford (1929–34), headmaster of Uppingham School (1934–44) and Shrewsbury (1944–50), and vice-chancellor of Reading University from 1950. He is best known as the chairman of the royal commission on homosexuality and prostitution, the report of which (1957) is known by his name. He was also chairman of another royal commission (1960) on sport. He was made a life peer in 1974.

WOLFF, or **Wolf, Christian von** (1679–1754) German philosopher, mathematician and scientist, born in Breslau, Silesia. He studied at the universities of Breslau, Jena and Leipzig and was a pupil of the philosopher **Leibniz**, on whose recommendation he was appointed professor of mathematics at the University of Halle in 1707. He was banished in 1723, following a theological dispute with the Pietists, became professor at Marburg (1723–40), was recalled by **Frederick II, the Great** to Halle in 1740 to become professor of the law of nations, and became chancellor of the university in 1743. He was made Baron of the Empire by the Elector of Bavaria. Wolff published widely in philosophy, theology, mathematics and the natural sciences, but his main intellectual achievement was to systematize and popularize the philosophy of Leibniz, in works such as *Philosophia prima sive ontologia* (1729). His work gave rationalism a further great impulse in the German tradition, and he is usually regarded as the German spokesman of the Enlightenment in the 18th century.

WOLFF, Gustav William See **HARLAND, Sir Edward James**

WOLFIT, Sir Donald (1902–68) English actor-manager, born in Newark-on-Trent. He began his stage career in 1920, and made his first London appearance in 1924 in *The Wandering Jew*. With his own company, formed in 1937, he played **Shakespeare** in the provinces, and during World War II he instituted the first London season of 'lunchtime Shakespeare' during the Battle of Britain. Known especially for his portrayal of Shakespearean heroes and of **Jonson**'s Volpone, he was knighted in 1957. He also appeared in several films and on television. His autobiography, *First Interval*, appeared in 1954.

WOLFRAM VON ESCHENBACH (fl. beginning of 13th century) German poet, born near Anspach in Bavaria. He lived some time in the Warburg near Eisenach, at the court of the Count of Thuringia. As well as *Parzival* he left seven *Love Songs*, a short epic, *Willehalm*, and two fragments called *Titurel*. The *Parzival* is an epic, having for its main theme the history of the Grail, and is one of the most notable poems of the Middle Ages. From it **Wagner** derived the libretto of his *Parsifal*.

WOLFSON, Sir Issac (1897–) Scottish businessman and philanthropist, born in Glasgow. Educated at Queen's Park School in Glasgow, he left school early and became a travelling salesman. He joined Great Universal Stores in 1932 and became managing director in 1934, and is now honorary life president. In 1955 he set up the Wolfson Foundation, for the advancement of health, education and youth activities in the UK and the Commonwealth. He also founded Wolfson College, Oxford, in 1966. In 1973, University College, Cambridge, was renamed Wolfson College after a grant from the foundation. He is active in Jewish causes. His son, Leonard (1927–), is now a life peer.

WOLGEMUT, Michael (1435–1519) German painter and engraver, born in Nuremberg, the son of Valentin Wolgemut, also an engraver. He was the teacher of **Albrecht Dürer**, who did a portrait of him. His altarpieces show some Flemish influence.

WOLLASTON, William (1659–1724) English philosopher and moralist, born in Coton near Stafford. He studied at Sidney Sussex College, Cambridge, became a schoolteacher in Birmingham in 1682 and was ordained a priest. But in 1688 he inherited a large fortune and retired to London to devote himself to study. He destroyed much of what he wrote through fastidiousness, the major work surviving being *The Religion of Nature Delineated* (1722). A best-seller in its day, it presents an extreme intellectualist theory of ethics, whereby wrong acts are regarded as simply the assertion in conduct of false propositions.

WOLLASTON, William Hyde (1766–1828) English chemist born in East Dereham, Norfolk, into a family of scientists and physicians. He went to Caius College, Cambridge, took his MD in 1793, and gained a fellowship. Starting practice as a physician at Bury St Edmunds in 1789, he soon removed to London; but being beaten in a competition for the post of physician to St George's Hospital in 1800, he vowed to devote himself to scientific research. His researches were extremely fruitful both in chemistry and in optics. He discovered new compounds connected with the production of gouty and urinary concretions; and in the ore of platinum distinguished two new metals, palladium (1804) and rhodium (1805). By his method of rendering platinum ductile he made £30000; other practical discoveries were also highly lucrative. Among his contributions to optics were the reflecting goniometer, the camera lucida, the discovery of the dark lines in the solar spectrum and of the invisible rays beyond the violet. He did much to establish the theory of definite proportions, and demonstrated the identity of galvanism and electricity.

WOLLSTONECRAFT, Mary (Mrs Godwin) (1759–97) Anglo-Irish feminist and writer, born in London. After a number of jobs she obtained work with a publisher (1888) as a translator and became acquainted with a group of political writers and reformers known as the English Jacobins, including her future husband **William Godwin**. In 1790 she wrote *Vindication of the Rights of Man* (a response to **Thomas Paine**'s *Reflections on the French Revolution*), and in 1792 produced her controversial *Vindication of the Rights of Woman*, which advocated equality of the sexes and equal opportunities in education. In Paris in 1792 to witness the Terror and collect material for her *View of the French Revolution* (vol 1, 1794), she met an American timber-merchant, Captain Gilbert Imlay, by whom she had a daughter, Fanny Imlay (1794, committed suicide 1816). Deserted by him, she tried to commit suicide. In 1797 she married William Godwin, and gave birth to a daughter, Mary (the future **Mary Wollstonecraft Shelley**), but died soon afterwards.

WOLSELEY, Garnet Joseph, Viscount (1833–1913) English soldier, born of an old Staffordshire line in Golden Bridge House, County Dublin, Entering the army in 1852, he served in the Burmese war of 1852–53, and was dangerously wounded; in the Crimea he lost the use of one eye, and received the cross of the *Légion d'honneur*. He was in India during the Mutiny (1857–59), and in the Chinese war of 1860. Next year he went to Canada, and in 1870 put down the Red River rebellion under **Louis Riel** without losing a man. On the outbreak of the Ashanti war (1873–74) he was appointed to the command, and on his return received the thanks of parliament and a grant of £25000. In 1875, now a major-general, he was dispatched to Natal; in 1876 he was nominated a member of the Indian Council. In 1878 he was made high commissioner in Cyprus, and in 1879 held supreme civil and miitary command in Natal and the Transvaal. He was commander-in-chief of the expedition to Egypt in 1882, and was made general in the same year. He commanded the Sudan expedition in 1884 that arrived too late to save **Gordon** at Khartoum. From 1890 to 1895 he was commander-in-chief of the entire army. Besides his *Story of a Soldier's Life* (1903–04), he wrote *Narrative of the War with China in 1860* (1862), the *Soldier's Pocket Book*, *Field Manoeuvres* (1872), a novel (*Marley Castle*, 1877), a Life of **Marlborough** (2 vols, 1894), *The Decline and Fall of Napoleon* (1895), and several essays.

WOLSEY, Thomas (c.1475–1530) English prelate and statesman, born in Ipswich, the son of a prosperous butcher and grazier. He studied at Magdalen College, Oxford, succeeding to a fellowship and obtaining a post as master in the seminary attached to the foundation. After 19 years at Oxford, the powerful Dorset interest secured him the living at Lymington in Somerset. Influence also brought him the post of secretary and domestic chaplain to the archbishop of Canterbury. With the primate's death in 1502 Wolsey was endowed with the chaplaincy of Calais, where his ability brought him to the notice of **Henry VII**. Appointed a chaplain to the king (1507), he was careful to cultivate the favour of Bishop Fox, the lord privy seal, and that of the treasurer of the royal household, Sir Thomas Lovel. Entrusted with the transaction of much of the sovereign's private business, the skill in negotiation he exhibited in his embassies to Scotland and the Low Countries brought him the lucrative deanery of Lincoln. With the accession of **Henry VIII**, Wolsey strove to render himself indispensable. From almoner to royal councillor, from the registrarship of the Order of the Garter to a Windsor canonry, his progress to the deanery of York was steady and encouraging for a pluralist whose growing need for money was only matched by his increasing arrogance. In 1513 Wolsey accompanied the king to France; and with the English monarch ready to come to terms with **Francis I**, Wolsey's conduct of the negotiations brought him the bishopric of Lincoln, the archbishopric of York (1514) and a cardinalate (1515), and the promise of Gallic support for further claims to preferment. In the same year, he was made lord chancellor and his very considerable estates were augmented by Henry's award of the administration of the see of Bath and Wells and the temporalities of the wealthy abbey of St Alban's. Wolsey even hazarded a breach of the Statute of Praemunire by accepting the appointment of papal legate from **Leo X**. Deep in the king's confidence, the cardinal had attained a position more powerful than that enjoyed by any minister of the Crown since **Thomas à Becket**. As the controller of England's foreign policy he lent support to France and Germany alternately, entering into a secret alliance with the emperor **Charles V** against Francis I, always seeking to improve England's position. His aim in England was absolute monarchy with himself behind the throne. He established Cardinal's College (later Christ Church College) at Oxford and a grammar school at Ipswich.

Wolsey's downfall originated in his prevarication and evasiveness over the question of Henry's divorce from **Catherine of Aragon**. This not only provoked the king's angry impatience but aroused the bitter enmity of the **Anne Boleyn** faction and of many other enemies, outraged by the Cardinal's haughtiness, his parvenu display, and his punishing fiscal exactions. In effect, Wolsey's outmoded assertion of the ecclesiastical right to dominate secular policy had proved entirely unacceptable to the upstart but powerful aristocracy of the counting-house bred by the new spirit of mercantilism. Prosecuted under the Statute of Praemunire in 1529, the cardinal had to surrender the Great Seal and retire to Winchester. Impeachment by the House of Lords was followed by the forfeiture of all his property to the Crown. Arrested again on a charge of high treason, he died while journeying from his York diocese to London.

WONDER, Stevie, real name **Steveland Judkins** (1950–) American pop/rock singer and instrumentalist, born in Saginaw, Michigan. A premature baby, he was blinded permanently by receiving too much oxygen in the incubator. He played the harmonica from an early age and was signed to Motown Records in 1961. His first album *Little Stevie Wonder: The 12-Year-Old Genius* (released when he was actually 13) was an immediate success. Most of his early recordings followed the orthodox Motown sound, but 'Where I'm Coming From' (1971) moved towards progressive rock. In 1971 he also renegotiated his recording contract to gain full artistic control over his work—the first Motown artist to do so. During the 1970s he became one of the most proficient users of synthesizer technology and developed musically to the point where he was widely regarded as one of the most important popular composers of the era. His music ranged from the up-tempo rock of 'Superstition' and the social commentary of 'Living In The City' to the simple balladry of 'I Just Called To Say I Love You'. One of America's best-loved entertainers, he also led the campaign to make **Martin Luther King**'s birthday a national holiday. His most important albums have included *Songs In The Key Of Life* (1976), *Talking Book* (1972), *Innervisions* (1973) and *Hotter Than July* (1980).

WOOD, Sir Andrew (c.1455–1539) Scottish naval commander, a native of Largo, Fife. He was associated with **James IV** in his efforts to build up a Scottish navy. He was specially successful against English vessels raiding in the Firth of Forth.

WOOD, or **À Wood, Anthony** (1632–95) English antiquary, born in Oxford. He studied at Merton College, Oxford (1647–52), and devoted himself to heraldry and antiquarian studies. He wrote a *History of Oxford*, translated into Latin as *Historia et Antiquitates Universitiatis Oxoniensis* (1674). He also wrote the monumental *Athenae Oxonienses* (1691–92), a biographical compendium of notable Oxford graduates from 1500–1690. Other works were *The Ancient and Present State of the City of Oxford* (1773) and the ill-natured *Modius Salium, a Collection of Pieces of Humour* (1751).

WOOD, Sir Charles See **HALIFAX, 1st Viscount**

WOOD, Christopher (1901–30) English artist, born in Knowsley. Between 1920 and 1924 he wandered over most of Europe, and painted in various styles, but it was in his landscapes of Cornwall and Brittany that he found himself as an artist. They are simple and apparently childlike in conception, but they show a fine sensitivity to colour, light, and atmosphere.

WOOD, Edward Frederick Lindley See **HALIFAX, 1st Earl of**

WOOD, Haydn (1882–1959) English composer and violinist, born in Slaithwaite, Yorkshire. He studied at the Royal College of Music and worked for a time in music halls with his wife, Dorothy Court, for whom he wrote a large number of ballads, but withdrew from these activities as his serious compositions attracted attention. He wrote prolifically for orchestra, brass band, chamber music groups and voices. Of his ballads, the best known is 'Roses of Picardy'.

WOOD, Mrs Henry, née **Ellen Price** (1814–87) English novelist, born in Worcester, the daughter of a manufacturer. A spinal disease confined her to bed or a sofa for most of her life. She married Henry Wood, a ship agent living in France, but returned to England with him in 1860 and settled in Norwood. After his death in 1866 she settled in London, and wrote for magazines. Her second published novel, *East Lynne* (1861), had an almost unparalleled success. She never rose above the commonplace in her many novels, but showed some power in the analysis of character in her anonymous *Johnny Ludlow* stories (1874–80). In 1867 she bought the monthly *Argosy*, which she edited, and her novels went on appearing in it long after her death.

WOOD, Sir Henry Evelyn (1838–1919) English soldier, born in Braintree, Essex. He entered the navy in 1852, and served in the Crimea in the Naval Brigade. As cavalry officer and brigade-major he fought in the Indian mutiny (1857–59), winning the Victoria Cross. As lieutenant-colonel he was with **Wolseley** during the Ashanti war (1873–74). He was called to the bar in 1874, but commanded a column through the Zulu War. He had a share in the Transvaal war (1880–81). He served in Egypt in 1882, and in the same year became commander-in-chief of the Egyptian army. From 1886 onwards he held home appointments. In 1897 he was made adjutant-general of the army, in 1903 field marshal. He wrote *From Midshipman to Field-marshal* (1906), and *Winnowed Memories* (1917).

WOOD, Sir Henry Joseph (1869–1944) English conductor, born in London. With **Robert Newman** he founded the Promenade Concerts which he conducted annually from 1895 until his death. As 'Paul Klenovsky' he arranged **Bach's** Organ Toccata and Fugue in D minor as an orchestral work. He composed operettas and an oratorio, *Saint Dorothea* (1889), but his international reputation was gained as conductor of the Queen's Hall symphony and promenade concerts. He was knighted in 1911. In 1938 he published *My Life of Music*.

WOOD, John (1930–) English actor, born in Derby. He studied at Jesus College, Oxford, and joined the Old Vic in 1954. He made his west end début in **Tennessee Williams**'s *Camino Real* in 1957. During the following decade, he worked extensively in good quality television drama. On stage in New York, he played Guildenstern in **Stoppard**'s *Rosencrantz and Guilderstern Are Dead* in 1967. Back in Britain, he won great acclaim for his performance as Richard Rowan in **James Joyce**'s *Exiles* at the Mermaid Theatre in London in 1970. He joined the Royal Shakespeare Company at Stratford-upon-Avon in 1971, where he established himself as a classical actor of the front rank. He emerged as one of the leading interpreters of Stoppard's work with a stunning performance in the central role in *Travesties* (1974). For the National Theatre in 1979 he played the title role in *Richard III* and at the RSC in 1988 he gave a towering performance as Prospero in *The Tempest*.

WOOD, John, the elder (c.1705–1754) English architect, known as 'Wood of Bath'. He was responsible for many of the best-known streets and buildings of Bath, such as the North and South Parades, Queen

Square, the Circus, Prior Park and other houses. His son John the younger (d.1782) designed the Royal Crescent and the Assembly Rooms.

WOOD, Sir Kingsley (1881–1943) English statesman, born in London. He was trained as a solicitor, entered parliament in 1918 as Conservative member for Woolwich West, was knighted in 1919, and after holding several junior ministerial offices became postmaster-general (1931–35), minister of health (1935–38), secretary of state for air (1938–40), and Chancellor of the Exchequer (1940–43), in which capacity he devised the pay-as-you-earn income-tax system.

WOOD, Robert Williams (1868–1955) American physicist, born in Concord, Massachusetts. Educated at Harvard, Chicago and Berlin, he was professor of experimental physics at the Johns Hopkins University (1901–38). He carried out researches on optics, atomic and molecular radiation and sound waves; wrote *Physical Optics* (1905), some fiction, and illustrated nonsense verse, in *How to Tell the Birds from the Flowers* (1907).

WOOD, Victoria (1953–) English comedienne, born in Prestwich, Lancashire. She studied drama at Birmingham University and began singing her own comic songs on local radio and television while still a student. In 1976 she secured a regular slot on national television in *That's Life*. Her first play, *Talent* (1978), was adapted for television and won her the Pye Award for Most Promising New Writer. The creator of all her own sketches, songs and stand-up routines, her bubbly, outsize personality has offered witty observations on everyday life, sexual relations and inexpert soap-operas. Her television series include *Wood and Walters* (1981–82), *Victoria Wood As Seen on Television* (1984–87) and *An Audience With Victoria Wood* (1988, British Academy Award). Her frequent stage tours include *Funny Turns* (1982), *Lucky Bag* (1984) and *Victoria Wood* (1987). She has also published several books, including *Up To You, Porky* (1985) and *Barmy* (1987).

WOOD, William (1671–1744) English iron-founder in London. In 1772 he was granted a royal license to coin halfpennies and farthings for circulation in Ireland ('Wood's Halfpence'), sharing the profits with one of King **George I**'s mistresses. He was also granted the license to strike coins for the American colonies ('Wood's Metal'). The scandal was denounced by **Jonathan Swift** in his *Drapier's Letters* (1724), and the patent was withdrawn; Wood was compensated with a pension.

WOODCOCK, George (1904–79) English trade union leader, born in Bamber Bridge, Lancashire. Educated at the local elementary school and, under trade union auspices, Ruskin College and New College, Oxford, where he obtained first class honours in philosophy and politics, he was a civil servant (1934–36) before joining the research and economic department of the Trades Union Congress (TUC). He became assistant general secretary (1947–60) and general secretary (1960–69). A man of great intelligence, he was sometimes seen as vain and arrogant, but did much to enhance the reputation of the TUC. He sat on several royal commissions, including the Donovan Commission on Trade Unions and Employers' Associations (1965–68). After retiring from the TUC he was chairman of the Commission on Industrial Relations (1969–71).

WOODEN, John Robert (1910–) American basketball coach, born in Martinsville, Indiana. He enjoyed unprecedented success in the college game and was head basketball coach at the University of California, Los Angeles, from 1948 to 1975. As a student he had earned a reputation as College Player of the Year (1932), but it was as coach that his reputation grew. He was named Coach of the Year by the US Writers Association six times between 1964 and 1973. His books include *They Call Me Coach* (1972).

WOODFALL, Henry Sampson (1739–1805) English printer and journalist. He published the anonymous vituperous letters against public figures of 'Junius' in the *Public Advertiser* (1769–71) and in book form (1772).

WOODHULL, Victoria, née **Claflin** (1838–1927) American reformer, born in Homer, Ohio. One of a large family which earned a living by giving fortune-telling and medicine shows, she performed a spiritualist act with her sister, Tennessee (1846–1923). From 1853 to 1864 she was married to Dr Canning Woodhull, but on her divorce returned to the family business. In 1868 she went with Tennessee to New York where they persuaded the rich **Cornelius Vanderbilt** to set them up as stockbrokers. At this time they became involved with a socialist group called Pantarchy, and began to advocate its principles of free love, and equal rights and legal prostitution. In 1870 they established the magazine *Woodhull and Claflin's Weekly* (1870–76), outlining these views. A vigorous speaker, Victoria won support from the leaders of the woman suffrage movement, and became the first woman nominated for the presidency. In 1877 she moved to London, with Tennessee, where she continued to lecture and write. Her publications include *Stirpiculture, or the Scientific Propagation of the Human Race* (1888) and *The Human Body the Temple of God* (1890, with Tennessee).

WOODSWORTH, James Shaver (1874–1942) Canadian reformer and political leader, born in Islington, Ontario, to a Methodist home mission family. After education in Canada and England, he was ordained a Methodist minister in 1900. He wrote *The Stranger Within Our Gates* (1909) and other works about problems of recent European immigrants in the most recently settled Canadian Western prairie lands. At this stage he reflected little more than advanced progressive views, but his pacifist stand throughout World War I led to his break with his church in 1918, after which he worked as a longshoreman and became a labour agitator, being drawn into the Winnipeg General Strike of 1919 as bulletin editor, which caused his arrest for seditious libel. He was elected as a Labor member of parliament for Winnipeg North Centre, serving from 1921 until his death. He manoeuvred skilfully in parliament, using government majority vulnerability in 1926 to force old age pension legislation. He was founder and first chairman of the Commonwealth Co-operative Federation in 1932 but once again was driven into isolation as a pacifist on the outbreak of World War II.

WOODVILLE, Elizabeth (c.1437–1492) queen consort of **Edward IV** of England. The eldest daughter of Sir Richard Woodville, 1st Earl **Rivers**, she married first, in 1461, Sir John Grey, who was killed at St Albans (1461), and in 1464 she was married privately to Edward IV, and was crowned in 1465. When Edward fled to Flanders in 1470, she sought sanctuary in Westminster. In 1483 her sons, **Edward V** and Richard, Duke of York, were murdered (the 'Princes in the Tower'). After the accession of **Henry VII** in 1485 her rights as dowager queen were restored, but soon she was forced to retire to the abbey of Bermondsey, where she died. Her eldest daughter, Elizabeth of York (1465–1503), married Henry in 1486

WOODVILLE, Richard See **RIVERS**

WOODWARD, Sir Arthur Smith (1864–1944) English geologist, born in Macclesfield. He was keeper of geology at the British Museum (1901–24). He did notable work on fossil fishes, but is chiefly remembered for his part in the controversy over the Piltdown Man. He was the one to whom **Charles Dawson** gave the skull for identification, and his firm conviction that the remains were human was the main reason for the success of the hoax. In 1898 he published *Outlines of Vertebrate Palaeontology*.

WOODWARD, Comer Vann (1908–) American historian, born in Vanndale, Arkansas. He graduated from Emory University, Georgia, and studied at Columbia University and at the University of North Carolina. He taught at Johns Hopkins (1946–61) and Yale (1961–77). He reflected the agrarian philosophy prominent among inter-war white Southern intellectuals, notably that of his life-long friend **Robert Penn Warren**. His first work, *Tom Watson, Agrarian Rebel* (1938), his major masterpiece *Origins of the New South 1877–1913* (1951), its spin-off *Reunion and Reaction: The Compromise of 1877 and the End of Reconstruction* (1951), and several essays later collected in *The Burden of Southern History* (1961), all argued that the prevailing white Southern myth of patriotic 'Redeemers' rescuing the White South from greedy Northern capitalist exploiters masked a reality in which the 'Redeemers' were the real instruments of capitalist destruction of Southern agrarianism. *The Strange Career of Jim Crow* (1955, 1957 and later revisions) taught that Southern segregation was a largely artificial growth, prompted as the race issue was fomented by interested political groups. His later work, after his final transfer to Yale, produced its highest acclaim with his edition of the full diary of Mary Boykin Chesnut, *Mary Chesnut's Civil War* (1982).

WOODWARD, Robert Burns (1917–79) American organic chemist, probably the greatest deviser of organic syntheses, born in Boston, Massachusetts. Professor of science at Harvard University from 1950 and director of the Woodward Research Institute at Basel from 1963, he was awarded the Nobel prize for chemistry in 1965 for work on organic synthesis, including his synthesis of chlorophyll in 1961.

WOODWARD, Roger Robert (1944–) Australian concert pianist, born in Sydney. He studied at the New South Wales State Conservatorium, and afterwards at the Warsaw Academy of Music, Poland, making his début there in 1967 with the Warsaw Philharmonic Orchestra. He is particularly known for his playing of **Chopin**, and of **Beethoven**, whose complete piano sonatas he has performed many times. Woodward appeared for four successive seasons at the London promenade concerts, and has appeared with most international orchestras and conductors. He is keenly involved in contemporary music through *London Music Digest* and the Australian *Music Rostrum* which he founded in 1973.

WOOLDRIDGE, Sydney William (1900–63) English geographer, born in Hornsey, North London. He was educated at Kings College, London. After various teaching appointments at London University, he became professor of geography at Birkbeck College there (1944–63). His original research was in geology but he played a leading role in the establishment of geomorphology within British geography. He was an adviser on Greater London, new towns, and on the use of sands and gravel, to post-war governments.

WOOLF, Arthur (1766–1837) English mechanical engineer, born in Camborne. After an apprenticeship as a carpenter he turned to engineering, and in 1786 helped **Jonathan Hornblower** to repair a compound steam engine he had installed in a London brewery. After the expiry of **James Watt**'s patent in 1800 Woolf patented a compound engine and boiler in 1803, but it was several years before he evolved a satisfactory design and eventually he abandoned the principle of compounding and concentrated on perfecting the high-pressure Cornish engines of **Richard Trevithick**, in which he was particularly successful.

WOOLF, Leonard Sidney (1880–1969) English publisher and writer, born in London. He was educated at St Paul's School and Trinity College, Cambridge. He worked in the Ceylon Civil Service (1904–11), and his early novels, such as *The Village and the Jungle* (1913), have Ceylon as a background. In 1912 he married **Virginia Woolf**. In 1916 he joined the Fabian Society and in 1917 along with his wife he founded the Hogarth Press, and they became the centre of the so-called 'Bloomsbury Group'. His works include *Socialism and Co-operation* (1921), *After the Deluge* (1931, 1939) and *Principia Politica* (1953). He published his autobiography in five volumes, *Sowing* (1960), *Growing* (1961), *Beginning Again* (1964), *Downhill all the Way* (1967), and *The Journey to the Arrival Matters* (1969).

WOOLF, (Adeline), Virginia, née **Stephen** (1882–1941) English novelist, critic and essayist, born in London, daughter of Sir **Leslie Stephen**. She was close to her sister, **Vanessa Bell**, and was from an early age the family story-teller. She was taught at home, by her parents and governesses, and received an uneven education. In 1891 she started the *Hyde Park Gate News* which was read by grown-ups and appeared weekly until 1895. In it appeared her first efforts at fiction. Her father died in 1904 and the family moved to Bloomsbury where the family formed the nucleus of the Bloomsbury Group, comprising—among others—**Keynes**, **E M Forster**, **Roger Fry**, **Duncan Grant** and **Lytton Strachey**: philosophers, writers and artists. A year later she began her long association with the *Times Literary Supplement*. She married **Leonard Woolf** in 1912 and her first novel, *The Voyage Out* was published in 1915. It was greeted cordially and though realistic there were hints of the lyricism which would later become her hallmark. But already her health was poor and she suffered recurring depressions and had attempted suicide in 1913. In 1917, she and Leonard formed the Hogarth Press, partly for therapeutic reasons. Its first publication was *Two Stories*, one by each of the founders. Her second novel, *Night and Day*, appeared in 1919. Again its mode is realistic, centring on Katherine Hilberry, whose activities in a literary milieu are counterpointed with those of her friend Mary who is involved in the women's movement. Some critics still think it her best work. *Jacob's Room* followed in 1922 and marked a turning point in her fiction, and shows her experimenting with narrative and language. Well-received, it made her a celebrity. In 1924 she went to Cambridge to speak on 'Character in Modern Fiction'; the result was *Mr Bennett and Mrs Brown*, an attack on the 'Georgian novelists' **Bennett**, **Galsworthy** and **Wells**, and can be read as her own aesthetic manifesto. Regarded now as an archetypal Modernist, she published in six years the three novels that have made her one of the century's great writers; *Mrs Dalloway* (1925), *To the Lighthouse* (1927), and *The Waves* (1931). But her work took its toll on her health and though she wrote prolifically she was beset by deep depressions and debilitating headaches. Throughout the 1930s she worked on *The Years*, which was published in 1937. A year later appeared *Three Guineas*, provisionally titled, 'Professions for Women', intended as a sequel to *A Room of One's Own* (1929), regarded as epochal by feminists. In this she stated that

'A woman must have money and a room of her own if she is to write fiction.' *Between the Acts*, an experimental novel, was published posthumously in 1941, after she had forced a large stone into her pocket and drowned herself in the River Ouse, near her home at Rodmell in Sussex. There are several volumes of essays, letters and diaries, indispensable to literary historians and gossips, as well as offering a remarkable entrée to the creative mind. She is, with **James Joyce** (whose novel, *Ulysses*, the Hogarth Press declined to publish), regarded as one of the great modern innovators of the novel in English.

WOOLLETT, William (1735–85) English line-engraver, born in Maidstone, Kent. An outstanding practitioner of the art, his first important plate, from **Richard Wilson**'s *Niobe*, was published by **John Boydell** in 1761. In 1775 he was appointed engraver to **George III**.

WOOLLEY, Frank (1887–1978) English cricketer, born in Tonbridge. His Test career spanned a quarter of a century (1909–34), and although best remembered as a batsman he was a skilled all-rounder. He played 64 Test matches for England, scoring 3283 Test runs and recording five centuries. Against Australia at The Oval in 1912 he took 10 wickets for 49 runs in the match, and no-one in first-class cricket has equalled his tally of 1018 catches.

WOOLLEY, Sir (Charles) Leonard (1880–1960) English archaeologist, born in London. He was educated at St John's School, Leatherhead, and New College, Oxford, and was assistant keeper of the Ashmolean Museum, Oxford, from 1905–07. He carried out excavations at Carchemish (1912–14) and in Sinai, and directed the important excavations (1922–34) at Ur in Mesopotamia, which included the royal cemetery discoveries. He was knighted in 1935, and from 1943–46 was archaeological adviser to the war office. His publications include *Digging up the Past* (1930), *Ur Excavations* (1934), and works on Carchemish, and *Alalakh* (1955).

WOOLMAN, John (1720–72) American Quaker preacher and reformer, born in Rancocas, New Jersey, a farmer's son. A tailor by trade, he became a Quaker in 1843 and campaigned against slavery, and published several religious works. His *Journal* (1774) was a favourite book of **Charles Lamb**. He died in York on a visit to England.

WOOLNER, Thomas (1826–92) English poet and sculptor, born in Hadleigh. He studied at the Royal Academy from 1842. In 1843 his first major work, *Eleanor sucking the Poison from Prince Edward's Wound*, attracted much attention. As a conspicuous member of the Pre-Raphaelite Brotherhood he contributed poems to *The Germ*, which with others were published in a volume as *My Beautiful Lady* (1863). From 1852 to 1854 he was in Australia. He produced statues or portrait busts of most of his famous contemporaries (his bust of **Tennyson** is in Westminster Abbey). He was professor of sculpture at the Academy (1877–79).

WOOLSEY, Sarah Chauncey See **COOLIDGE, Susan**

WOOLSEY, Theodore Dwight (1801–89) American scholar, born in New York. He was professor of Greek at Yale (1831–46), and then its president till 1871. He was chairman of the American committee for the revision of the New Testament (1871–81). Besides editions of Greek classics, he wrote an *Introduction to International Law* (1860), *Divorce Legislation* (1869) and *Political Science* (1877).

WOOLSTON, Thomas (1670–1731) English Deist, born in Northampton. He became a fellow of Sidney Sussex College, Cambridge, and took orders. In 1705 he published *The Old Apology for the Truth of the Christian Religion Revived*, affirming that the Old Testament was allegorical only. In 1721 his college deprived him of his fellowship. He joined the Deist controversy with *The Moderator between an Infidel and an Apostate* (1725). In his famous six *Discourses on the Miracles of Our Saviours* (1727–29, with two *Defences*) he maintained that the gospel narratives, taken literally, were a tissue of absurdities. Sixty answers were made to the *Discourses*; and an indictment for blasphemy was brought against him. Fined and sent to prison, he died there.

WOOLTON, Frederick James Marquis, 1st Baron (1883–1964) English politician and businessman, born in Liverpool. He attended Manchester Grammar School and Manchester University, and then taught mathematics at Burnley Grammar School. During a spell as warden of Liverpool University Settlement, in the dock area, he ran the David Lewis Club and this brought him to the attention of Lewis, the managing director of the Manchester store, who took him into the business. He rose rapidly in Lewis's, where he revolutionized the merchandizing side, and became chairman in 1935. He was made a baron in 1939. At the beginning of the war, he went to the ministry of supply, but made his name at the ministry of food, where from 1940 he had the responsibility of seeing that the entire nation was well-nourished. In 1946 he became chairman of the Conservative party, and is credited with much of the success in rebuilding the party's reorganization which led it to victory in 1951. Woolton became lord president of the Council, but ill-health later led him to take on the less onerous office of chancellor of the duchy of Lancaster. He published his Memoirs in 1959.

WOOLWORTH, Frank Winfield (1852–1919) American businessman, born in Rodman, Jefferson County, New York. In 1873, after several years as a farm worker, he became a shop-assistant. His employers backed his scheme to open in 1879 in Utica a store for five-cent goods only; this failed, but later the same year a second store, in Lancaster, Pennsylvania, selling also ten-cent goods, was successful. In partnership with his employers, his brother, and cousin, from 1905 he began building a large chain of similar stores, and at the time of his death the F W Woolworth company controlled over a thousand stores from their headquarters in the Woolworth building in New York. Woolworth's stores came to Britain in 1910, but their main development outside America was after the death of the founder.

WOOTTON, Barbara Frances, Baroness Wootton of Abinger (1897–1988) English social scientist, born in Cambridge, the daughter of a don. She studied and lectured (1920–22) in economics at Girton College, Cambridge. She was a research worker of the Labour party (1922–25), principal of Morley College, London (1926–27), director of studies (1927–44) and professor in social studies (1948–52) at London. A frequent royal commissioner and London magistrate, she is best known for her work, *Testament for Social Science* (1950), in which she attempted to assimilate social to the natural sciences. Another work was *Social Science and Pathology* (1959). She was created a life peeress in 1958.

WORCESTER, Edward Somerset, 2nd Marquis of (c.1601–1667) English aristocrat and inventor of a steam water-pump, probably born in London. In the Civil War he sided with the king, in 1642 was made General of South Wales, in 1644 was created Earl of Glamorgan, and in 1645 was sent to Ireland to raise troops for the king. His mission failed, King **Charles**

disowned him, and he was imprisoned for a short time. In 1646 he succeeded his father, and in 1648 went into exile in France. In 1652, venturing back to England, he was sent to the Tower, but in 1654 was let out on bail and at the Restoration recovered a portion of his vast estates—he claimed to have disbursed £918000 'for king and country'. His *Century of Inventions* (written 1655; printed 1663) gives a brief account of a hundred inventions—ciphers, signals, automata, mechanical appliances, and so on. No. 68 is a steam apparatus which could raise a column of water 40 feet, and which seems to have been at work at Vauxhall in London (1663–70).

WORCESTER, Joseph Emerson (1784–1865) American lexicographer, born in Bedford, New Hampshire. He taught at Salem, Massachusetts, and then turned author. He compiled a number of gazetteers, manuals of geography and history. He edited *Johnson's English Dictionary, with Walker's Pronouncing Dictionary* (1828). He abridged **Webster** (1829) without permission, and printed his own *Comprehensive English Dictionary* (1830), a *Critical Dictionary* (1846), and the great illustrated quarto *Dictionary of the English Language* (1860).

WORCESTER, Sir Thomas Percy, Earl of (1344–1403) English soldier, son of Sir Henry, 3rd Baron **Percy**. He fought in France, accompanied **Geoffrey Chaucer** on a diplomatic mission to Flanders in 1377, was made an admiral by **Richard II** and commanded in several expeditions, notably those of **John of Gaunt** to Spain (1386) and of the Earl of Arundel to La Rochelle (1388). He was created an earl in 1397. Having joined the rebellion of Northumberland (Henry Hotspur Percy) in 1403, he was captured at Shrewsbury and executed.

WORDE, Wynkyn de (?d.1535) English printer, born in Holland or in Alsace. A pupil of **William Caxton**, in 1491 he succeeded to his stock-in-trade in Westminster. In 1500 he moved to Fleet Street. He made great improvements in printing and typecutting, including the use of italic, and printed hundreds of books.

WORDSWORTH, Charles (1806–92) English Episcopal clergyman in Scotland, second son of **Christopher Wordsworth**. Educated at Christ Church College, Oxford, he became a tutor, with **Manning** and **Gladstone** among his pupils. After being a master of Winchester he became the first Warden of Trinity College, Glenalmond (later Glenalmond School) in Perthshire (1846) and thereafter bishop of St Andrews (1853). He was an ardent champion of reunion of the Churches of Scotland and England. His *Annals of my Life* (1891–93) is curious reading on that and similar contemporary topics. A noted cricketer and scholar, he also published *Shakespeare's Knowledge and Use of the Bible* (1864).

WORDSWORTH, Christopher (1774–1846) English clergyman, youngest brother of **William Wordsworth**. He was elected a fellow of Trinity College, Cambridge, in 1798 and after occupying various livings became master of Trinity (1820–21). His *Ecclesiastical Biography* (6 vols, 1909–10) is a good selection of the lives, and his *Christian Institutes* (1836) of the writings, of the great English divines. His book, *Who Wrote Eikon Baslike?* attempted to ascribe the authorship to **Charles I**.

WORDSWORTH, Christopher (1807–85) English clergyman and educationist, youngest son of **Christopher Wordsworth** (1774–1846). He had an unsuccessful career as headmaster of Harrow School (1836–44), and became bishop of Lincoln (1869). In 1851 he produced a memoir of his uncle the poet, to whom he was literary executor. He also wrote *Athens and Attica* (1836) and a commentary on the Bible (1856–70). His daughter Elizabeth (1840–1932), became first principal of Lady Margaret Hall, Oxford (1868–1908).

WORDSWORTH, Dorothy (1771–1855) English writer, only sister of **William Wordsworth**, born in Cockermouth, Cumberland. She was his constant companion through life, both before and after his marriage, and on tours to Scotland, the Isle of Man and abroad, the records of which are to be found in her *Journals*. The *Journals* show that Dorothy's keen observation and sensibility provided a good deal of poetic imagery for both her brother and his friend **Coleridge**—more than that, they regarded her as the embodiment of that joy in Nature which it was their object to depict. In 1829 she suffered a breakdown from which she never fully recovered. Her *Recollections of a Tour made in Scotland AD 1803* (1874) is a classic.

WORDSWORTH, William (1770–1850) English poet, born in Cockermouth, the son of an attorney. Orphaned at an early age, he was sent to Hawkshead in the Lake District for board and education and this was one of the formative periods of his life. His guardian sent him to Cambridge (1787–91), where he was exposed to agnostic and revolutionary ideas. A walking tour through France and Switzerland in 1790 showed him France under the influence of the earlier stage of the revolution before disillusionment had set in. Two immature poems belong to this period—*An Evening Walk* and *Descriptive Sketches*, both published in 1793. Leaving Cambridge without a profession, he stayed for a little over a year at Blois, and there he had an affair with Annette Vallon, the result of which was an illegitimate daughter, Ann Caroline. The incident is reflected in *Vaudracour and Julia*. The declaration of war with France (January 1793) drove the poet back to England, but the depressing poem *Guilt and Sorrow*, which dates from this period, shows that he was not yet cured of his passion for social justice. For a time he fell under the spell of **William Godwin**'s philosophic anarchism, but the unreadable *Borderers* shows that by 1795 he was turning his back both on the revolution and on Godwinism. With the help of his sister **Dorothy**, with whom he set up house at Racedown in Dorset, and of **Coleridge**, who had renounced his revolutionary ardour somewhat earlier, he discovered his true vocation, that of the poet exploring the lives of humble folk living in contact with Divine nature and untouched by the rebellious spirit of the times. When the Wordsworths settled at Alfoxden in Somerset with Coleridge three miles away at Nether Stowey (1797), there began a close association which resulted in *Lyrical Ballads* (1798), the first manifesto of the new poetry, which opened with Coleridge's *Ancient Mariner* and concluded with Wordsworth's *Tintern Abbey*. The removal of the Wordsworths to Grasmere after a visit to Germany with Coleridge, and the marriage of the poet to Mary Hutchinson (1802), closes this first stormy period, with Wordsworth set on his proper task and modestly provided for by a legacy of £900. Now followed a long spell of routine work and relative happiness broken only by family misfortunes—the death of his sailor brother John (1805), which may have inspired the *Ode to Duty*, and Dorothy's mental breakdown. Meanwhile **Napoleon**'s ambitions had completely discouraged the poet from revolutionary sympathies, as the patriotic sonnets sent to the *Morning Post* at about the time of the Peace of Amiens (1802–03) and after show. Apart from the sonnets, this was his most inspired period. The additions to the third edition of *Lyrical Ballads* (1801) contained the grave pastoral *Michael*, *Ruth* and four of the exquisite *Lucy* poems. The first of his tours in Scotland (1803), of which Dorothy wrote the perfect tour journal, yielded some fine poems, including *The Solitary Reaper*. The great poem he was now contemplating—*The Recluse*—was never finished, but *The Prelude*, the record of the poet's mind, was read to Coleridge in 1805. It remained unpublished till after his death, when it appeared with all the tamperings of a lifetime but substantially in its form of 1805, which fortunately has survived. Two volumes of poems appeared in 1807, the product of five years of intense activity. The ode *Intimations of Immortality* is only the loftiest of a number of masterpieces, including the patriotic sonnets, the *Affliction of Margaret*, the *Memorials of a Tour in Scotland*, the *Ode to Duty*, and many others. He had now reached the peak of his poetic form and the remainder of his work, including *The Excursion* (1814), the *Ecclesiastical Sonnets* and the *Memorials* of his various tours, do not reflect his genius. He succeeded **Southey** as poet laureate in 1843.

WORDSWORTH, William Brocklesby (1908–88) English composer, a descendant of **Christopher Wordsworth** (1774–1846), born in London. He studied under Sir **Donald Tovey**, and achieved prominence when his second symphony won the first award in the Edinburgh International Festival Competition in 1950. He has composed symphonies, a piano concerto, songs and a quantity of chamber music.

WORM, Ole (1588–1654) Danish scholar and antiquary. A physician by training, he became a pioneer of Old Icelandic studies in Denmark through his interest in runes. He published *Runir seu danica literature antiquissima* (1636) and *Monumenta danica* (1643), but also promoted the publication of Icelandic sagas, such as *Heimskringla* (1633). He corresponded voluminously with **Arngrímur Jónsson** and other Icelandic scholars.

WORNER, Manfred (1934–) West German politician, born in Stuttgart, the son of an affluent textile retailer. He studied law at the universities of Heidelberg, Paris and Munich, then joined the conservative Christian Democratic Union (CDU) and was elected to the Bundestag (federal parliament) in 1965. Establishing himself as a specialist in strategic issues, he was appointed defence minister in 1982 by Chancellor **Kohl** and then oversaw the controversial deployment of American Cruise and Pershing-II nuclear missiles in West Germany, an extension of military service from 15 to 18 months to compensate for a declining birthrate, and, in 1984, the dismissal of General Gunter Kiessling, for alleged, though subsequently disproven, homosexual contacts. Worner succeeded Lord **Carrington** as secretary-general of NATO in 1988.

WORRALL, Denis John (1935–) South African politician, born in Benoni. Educated at Cape Town and Cornell universities, where he subsequently taught political science, he held a succession of academic posts during the 1960s and 1970s and also worked as a journalist before being elected a National party (NP) senator in 1974 and MP in 1977. He was appointed to the key post of ambassador to the United Kingdom in 1984 by President **P W Botha**, but on his return to South Africa in 1987 resigned from the NP and unsuccessfully contested the general election of that year as an independent. In 1988 he established the Independent party (IP), and in 1989 the IP merged with other white opposition parties to form the reformist Democratic party (DP), which advocated dismantlement of the apartheid system and universal adult suffrage. A co-leader of the DP, he was elected to parliament in 1989.

WORRELL, Sir Frank Mortimer Magilinne (1924–67) West Indian cricketer and the first black West Indian Test captain, born in Bridgetown, Barbados. In 51 Test matches he made 9 centuries, and was a useful pace bowler. He captained West Indies in Australia in 1960–61 in one of the greatest Test series ever, and matches between these countries today are played for the Worrell Trophy which commemorates him. He was vice-chancellor of the University of the West Indies, a senator in the Jamaican parliament, and was knighted for services to cricket.

WORSAAE, Jens Jacob Asmussen (1821–85) Danish antiquary and archaelogist. He was assistant to **Christian Jörgensen Thomsen** at the Museum of Northern Antiquities in Copenhagen (1838–43), inspector of monuments (1847), and director from 1865. In 1842–54 he made repeated visits to Europe and the rest of Scandinavia on archaeological expeditions, and pioneered palaeobotany with his study of vegetation changes in peat-bogs. His major published work was *Danmarks Oldtid* (1843), but others of his works were translated into English, such as *Primeval Antiquities of England and Denmark* (1849) and *The Danes and Norwegians in England* (1852). He was appointed minister of education (1874–75).

WORTH, Charles Frederick (1825–95) Anglo-French costumier, born in Bourn in Lincolnshire. He went to Paris in 1846, and achieved such success as a fashion designer that he gained the patronage of the Empress **Eugénie**. His establishment in the Rue de la Paix became the centre of the fashion world.

WORTH, Irene (1916–) American actress, born in Nebraska, equally at home on both sides of the Atlantic. Originally a teacher, she made her professional début with an American touring company in 1942, and appeared on Broadway a year later. In 1944 she moved to London, where she spent many of the next 30 years. She created the role of Celia Copplestone in **T S Eliot**'s *The Cocktail Party* at the 1949 Edinburgh Festival. She joined the Old Vic in 1951 and in 1953 appeared in the inaugural season at Stratford, Ontario. She played the title role in **Schiller**'s *Mary Stuart* in New York in 1957. She joined the Royal Shakespeare Company at Stratford-upon-Avon in 1960. Since then she has given memorable performances in most of the major leading roles available.

WOTTON, Sir Henry (1568–1639) English traveller, diplomatist, scholar and poet, born of ancient family at Boughton Malherbe in Kent. He was educated at Winchester and Oxford, then set out for a seven years' sojourn in Bavaria, Austria, Italy, Switzerland and France. On his return he became the confidant of Robert Devereux, 2nd Earl of **Essex**. On his friend's downfall (1601) he went to France, then to Italy, and was sent by Ferdinand, Duke of Florence, on a secret mission to **James VI** of Scotland. James on his succession to the throne of England as James I knighted him and sent him as ambassador to Venice (1604), where he was intermittently employed for nearly 20 years, being next sent to the German princes and the emperor **Ferdinand II, the Great**, returning to England a poor man in 1624. He was made provost of Eton, and took orders. His tracts, letters etc, were collected as *Reliquiae Wottonianae* (1651). One of his few poems is 'The Character of a Happy Life'. It was Wotton who described an ambassador as an honest man sent abroad to lie for the good of his country.

WOUK, Herman (1915–) American novelist, born in New York City, the son of Jewish immigrants. He attended Columbia University, wrote radio scripts and served in the US navy in the South Pacific in World War II, the experience of which he drew on for his classic war novel, *The Caine Mutiny* (1951). It won the Pulitzer prize and became a successful play and film. Later books—*Marjorie Morningstar* (1955) and *Youngblood Hawke* (1962)—sold well but did not critically eclipse his earlier success. Other books include *The Winds of War* (1971) and *War and Remembrance* (1975), which became popular television serials.

WOUTERS, Rik (1882–1916) Belgian painter, born in Mechlin. He came under the influence of **Cézanne** and was the leading exponent of Fauvism in Belgium.

WOUWERMAN, Philips (1619–68) Dutch painter of battle and hunting pieces, born in Haarlem. His pictures are mostly small landscapes, with plenty of figures in energetic action. His cavalry skirmishes, with a white horse generally in the foreground, were specially characteristic and popular. He had two brothers, also painters, Peter (1623–82) and Jan (1629–66), who chose similar subjects.

WRANGEL, Ferdinand Petrovitch, Baron von (1794–1870) Russian vice-admiral and explorer, born in Livonia. He made extensive explorations in Arctic waters and on Siberian coasts, and made valuable surveys and observations. The island he nearly reached in 1821 was sighted by Sir Henry Kellett in 1849, and named after Wrangel by an American whaler, Long, in 1867. He published *Polar Expedition* (trans 1840).

WRANGEL, Friedrich Heinrich Ernst (1784–1877) Prussian solder, born in Stettin. He distinguished himself in the campaigns of 1807, 1813, and 1814, and in 1848 commanded the Federal troops in Schleswig-Holstein. He crushed the insurrection in Berlin (1848); in 1856 became field-marshal; in 1864 had supreme command over Prussian and Austrian troops in the Danish war; and, ennobled in 1866, served that year against the Austrians.

WRAXALL, Sir Nathanael William (1751–1831) English writer of memoirs, born in Bristol. He was in the East India Company's service, travelled over Europe (1772–79), and had a confidential mission from Queen Caroline-Matilda of Denmark to her brother **George III**. He published his *Cursory Remarks made in a Tour* in 1775, his *Memoirs of the Valois Kings* in 1777, entered parliament in 1780 as a follower of Lord **North**, but went over to **Pitt**. His next books were the *History of France from Henry III to Louis XIV* (1795); *Memoirs of the Courts of Berlin, Dresden, Warsaw, and Vienna* (1799); and the famous *Historical Memoirs of my own Time, 1772–84* (1815). For a libel on Count Woronzov, Russian envoy to England, he was fined £500 and sentenced to six months' imprisonment. Violent attacks on his veracity were made by the reviews, but Wraxall's *Answers* were accounted on the whole satisfactory. A continuation of *Memoirs* (1784–90) was published in 1836.

WREDE, Karl Philipp (1767–1838) Bavarian soldier, born in Heidelberg. He shared in the campaigns of 1799 and 1800, and as commander of the Bavarians invaded Tyrol in 1805. He fought at Wagram (1809) along with the French, and was made a count by **Napoleon**. He led the Bavarians under Napoleon to Russia in 1812. In 1813 he negotiated an alliance with Austria, and commanded a united Bavarian and Austrian army against the French, by whom he was defeated at Hanau. He was, however, victorious in several battles in France in 1814, and was made field-marshal and prince. He represented Bavaria at the Vienna Congress (1814).

WREN, Sir Christopher (1632–1723) English architect, born in East Knoyle in Wiltshire. He was the son of Dr Christopher Wren, dean of Windsor, and the nephew of Dr Matthew Wren (1585–1667), the High Church bishop successively of Hereford, Norwich and Ely. Educated at Westminster and Wadham College, Oxford, he became a fellow of All Souls, distinguished himself in mathematics and physics, and helped to perfect the barometer. In 1657 he became professor of astronomy at Gresham College in London, but in 1661 returned to Oxford as Savilian professor of astronomy. Before leaving London, Wren had, with **Boyle**, **John Wilkins** and others, laid the foundation of the Royal Society. In 1663 he was engaged by the dean and chapter of St Paul's to make a survey of the cathedral with a view to repairs. The first work built from a design by Wren was the chapel at Pembroke College, Cambridge, in 1663; and from 1663–66 he designed the Sheldonian Theatre at Oxford and the library, etc, of Trinity College, Cambridge. In 1665 he visited Paris. The Great Fire of London (1666) opened a wide field for his genius. He drew designs for the rebuilding of the whole city, embracing wide streets and magnificent quays, but, thwarted by vested interests, the scheme was never implemented. In 1669 he was appointed surveyor-general and was chosen architect for the new St Paul's (1675–1710) and for more than 50 other churches in place of those destroyed by the Great Fire. Other works by him were the Royal Exchange, Custom House, Temple Bar, the College of Physicians, Greenwich Observatory, Chelsea Hospital, the Ashmolean Museum at Oxford, Hampton Court, Greenwich Hospital, Buckingham House, Marlborough House, and the western towers and north transept of Westminster Abbey. In 1684 he was appointed comptroller of the works at Windsor Castle, and in 1698 surveyor-general of Westminster Abbey. He was buried in St Paul's, where his monument reads *Si monumentum requiris, circumspice* (if you seek a monument, look around you).

WRIGHT, Sir Almroth Edward (1861–1947) English bacteriologist, born in Yorkshire. Educated at Dublin, Leipzig, Strasbourg and Marburg, he became professor of experimental pathology in the University of London. He was known specially for his work on the parasitic diseases, and for his research on the protective power of blood against bacteria. He introduced a system of antityphoid inoculation.

WRIGHT, Benjamin (1770–1842) American civil engineer, born in Wethersfield, Connecticut. He was trained as a lawyer and surveyor by his uncle, and became chief engineer on the construction between 1817 and 1825 of the Erie Canal, the first major engineering project in America with a total length of 363 miles. He went on to build the original St Lawrence Ship Canal and the Chesapeake and Ohio Canal between 1825 and 1831, then turned to railway engineering and was appointed chief engineer of the New York and Erie Railroad. His son Benjamin Hall Wright also became a civil engineer, and after his father's death completed several of the schemes on which he had been working.

WRIGHT, Billy (William Ambrose) (1924–) English footballer, born in Wolverhampton. An industrious wing-half, latterly a central defender, he was the first player to win more than 100 caps for England (105, 90 as captain). His only senior club was Wolverhampton Wanderers, with whom he won one FA Cup medal and three League championships. A model of deportment and sportsmanship, he went into football managership with Arsenal, and later became a television sports executive.

WRIGHT, Frances, or **Fanny,** also known as **Frances Darusmont** (1795–1852) Scottish-born American reformer and abolitionist, born in Dundee, the heiress to a large fortune. She emigrated to the USA in 1818 and toured widely, publishing *Views of Society and Manners* *in America* in 1821. In the company of **Lafayette**, she founded a short-lived community for freed slaves at Nashoba in Western Tenessee. Settling in New York in 1829, she published with **Robert Dale Owen** a socialist journal, *Free Enquirer*. One of the early suffragettes, she campaigned vigorously against religion and for the emanicipation of women. In 1838 she contracted an unhappy marriage with a Frenchman.

WRIGHT, Frank Lloyd (1867–1959) American architect, born in Richland Center, Wisconsin. He studied civil engineering at Wisconsin University, but the collapse of a newly-built wing of the Wisconsin State Capitol turned him to architecture with a determination to apply engineering principles to architecture. After setting up in practice in Chicago, he became known for low-built prairie-style bungalows like Chicago's Robie House, but soon launched into more daring and controversial designs that exploited modern technology and cubist spatial concepts, and is considered one of the outstanding architects of the 20th century. He designed his own home, Taliesin, at Spring Green, Wisconsin (1911), and another home and school, Taliesin West, near Phoenix in Arizona (1938). His best-known public buildings include the earthquake-proof Imperial Hotel in Tokyo (1916–20), the 'Falling Water' weekend retreat at Mill Run near Pittsburgh in Pennsylvania (1936), the Johnson Wax office block in Racine, Wisconsin (1936), Florida Southern College (1940), and the Guggenheim Museum of Art in New York (1959), in which the exhibits line the walls of a continuous spiral ramp. He was an innovator in the field of open planning, and also designed furniture and textiles. He wrote an *Autobiography* (1932) and numerous other works.

WRIGHT, Georg von See **VON WRIGHT**

WRIGHT, Joseph (1734–97) English genre and portrait painter, called 'Wright of Derby'. He passed his whole life in his native town, save a few years spent in London, in Italy and at Bath. His fireside portrait groups often show odd light effects. He also painted industrial scenes.

WRIGHT, Joseph (1855–1930) English philologist, born in Bradford. He worked in a wool mill as a boy, but became professor of comparative philology at Oxford, editor of the *Dialect Dictionary*, and author of many philological works.

WRIGHT, Judith (1915–) Australian poet, born in Armidale, New South Wales. Her upbringing was on the family sheep farm, Wallamumbi, in pastoral New South Wales. She was educated at Sydney University and travelled in Britain and Europe before returning to Sydney (1938–39) to concentrate on her writing. The war disrupted her plans and lack of work led her back to her rural roots in the Queensland mountains and the source of her inspiration. *The Moving Image* (1946) was her first collection, since when she has been an industrious poet, critic, anthologist, editor, and short story writer. Her main volumes of poetry are *Woman to Man* (1949), *The Gateway* (1953), *The Two Fires* (1955), *Birds* (1962), *City Sunrise* (1964), *The Other Half* (1966), *Alive* (1973), and *Fourth Quarter and Other Poems* (1976). Her *Collected Poems* 1942–1970 and *The Double Tree: Selected Poems: 1942–1976* were published in 1971 and 1978 respectively. Her literary criticism was published in *Preoccupations in Australian Poetry* (1965). *The Cry for the Dead* (1981) is an account of the impact of European immigration on the aboriginal inhabitants of New South Wales and Queensland.

WRIGHT, Mark Robinson (1854–1944) English educationist. He taught at High Grade School, Gateshead, before becoming principal of the Day Training College, Newcastle-upon-Tyne (1890). In 1894 he was appointed professor of normal education at Durham University—the first appointment to a university chair of education in England—and professor of education from 1899 to 1920. He was founder editor of the *Training College Record*, later the *British Journal of Educational Psychology*, and instituted school journeys for teachers in training.

WRIGHT, Orville (1871–1948) born in Dayton, Ohio, and his brother **Wilbur** (1867–1912), born near Millville, Indiana. They were self-taught American airplane pioneers, the first to fly in a heavier-than-air machine (17 December 1903), at Kitty Hawk, North Carolina. Encouraged by this, they abandoned their cycle business and, patenting their flying machine, formed an aircraft production company (1909). In 1915 Orville sold his interests in the business in order to devote himself to research.

WRIGHT, Peter (1916–) English intelligence officer, born in Chesterfield, the son of a Marconi electronics engineer who served with MI6 during World War I. He initially entered farming before joining the Admiralty's Research Laboratory during World War II as a scientific officer. He remained in government service after the war, transferring to MI5 (counter-intelligence) in 1955. Here he specialized in the invention of espionage devices and the detection of Soviet 'moles'. He retired from MI5 in 1976 and bought a sheep ranch in Tasmania and, to supplement his pension, wrote his autobiography, *Spy Catcher* (1987), in which he alleged that Sir Roger Hollis, the former director-general of MI5, had been a Soviet double-agent, the so-called 'Fifth Man', and that elements within MI5 had tried to overthrow the **Wilson** government during the mid 1960s. Attempts by the **Thatcher** government to suppress the book's publication and distribution for 'security reasons' were eventually unsuccessful.

WRIGHT, (Philip) Quincy (1890–1970) American international lawyer, born in Medford, Massachusetts. Educated at Lombard College and the University of Illinois, he was professor at Chicago, adviser to the US State Department and the Nuremburg Tribunal. He wrote *The Enforcement of International Law through Municipal Law in the U.S.* (1916), *The Causes of War and the Conditions of Peace* (1935), *A Study of War* (1942), *Problems of Stability and Progress in International Relations* (1954), *The Study of International Relations* (1955) and *The Role of International Law in the Prevention of War* (1961).

WRIGHT, Richard (1908–60) American novelist, short story writer and critic, born on a plantation in Mississippi. His father abandoned his family when he was five. His mother having had a stroke, he was ill-treated by relatives, received a poor education and was exposed to religious fanaticism. A pessimistic humanist, a naturalist and later in Paris an existentialist who knew **Sartre**, he is best known for *Black Boy* (1945), a harrowing autobiographical novel, the short story, 'The Man Who Lived Underground' (1942), and *Native Son* (1940), a novel about a Negro youth who murders a white woman and is sent to the electric chair.

WRIGHT, Robert Alderson, Lord, of Durley (1869–1964) English judge born in South Shields, Tyne and Wear. He was educated at Trinity College, Cambridge. A pupil of **Scrutton**, he developed a large practice in commercial cases and was appointed a judge in 1925. In 1932 he was promoted direct to be a lord of appeal, and sat as such till 1947, except during 1935–37 when he served as master of the rolls. He delivered notable judgments in many important cases and has been highly regarded as a thoughtful and forward-looking judge. In several cases he helped to develop the concept of the duty on an employer to provide a safe system of working for his employees. He was also willing to allow the House of Lords to overrule its own previous judgments, a development not achieved until 1966, and showed a liberal approach in constitutional cases.

WRIGHT, Thomas (1810–87) English antiquary, born near Ludlow, of Quaker parentage. Educated at Trinity College, Cambridge, he helped to found the Camden Society, the Archaeological Association, and the Percy and Shakespeare Societies. He edited *Piers Plowman* and *The Canterbury Tales*, and wrote many books, including *Biographia Britannica Literaria* (1842–46); *England in the Middle Ages* (1846); *Dictionary of Obsolete and Provincial English* (1857); *Political Poems, 1327–1485* (1859–61); *History of Domestic Manners and Sentiments in England during the Middle Ages* (1862); and *Anglo-Latin Twelfth Century Satirical Poets* (1877).

WRIGHT, William Aldis (1836–1914) English scholar and critic, born in Beccles. He became librarian, and in 1888 vice-master, of Trinity College, Cambridge. He edited the Cambridge and Globe Shakespeares (with William George Clark), *Generydes*, **Robert of Gloucester**, and **Edward FitzGerald**'s *Letters*, and was well known for his *Bible Word-Book* (1866).

WRIOTHESLEY See **SOUTHAMPTON**

WRÓBLEWSKI, Zygmunt Florenty von (1845–88) Polish physicist, born in Grodno. Professor of physics at Cracow University, he was noted for his work on the liquefaction of gases. He was the first to liquefy air on a large scale. Working with Olszewski at Krakow he liquefied oxygen, nitrogen and carbon monoxide.

WU, Chien-Shiung (1912–) Chinese-born American physicist, born in Shanghai. She studied at the National Centre University in China, and from 1936 in the USA, at the University of California at Berkeley. From 1946 she was on the staff of Columbia University, New York (professor from 1957). Her work has included notable experimental proofs of particle theories; for instance, in 1957 she showed that parity is not conserved in beta emission, and in 1963 that a vector current is conserved in this change. Both of these remarkable results had been predicted previously by other workers.

WU CHENG-EN (fl.16th century) Chinese author of the novel *Monkey* (1593, trans 1942), based on the pilgrimage of **Hsuang Tsang**.

WULFILA See **ULFILAS**

WULFSTAN, St (c.1009–1095) Anglo-Saxon prelate and saint. Educated at the abbey of Peterborough, he became a monk, subsequently prior, at Worcester, and was appointed bishop of Worcester in 1062. At the Norman Conquest of 1066 he made submission to **William I**, and was the only Englishman left in his see. Later he supported **William II Rufus**. By his preaching at Bristol against the slave-trade practised by merchants there, he put an end to it. He helped to compile the *Domesday Book*, and may have written part of the *Anglo-Saxon Chronicle*. He was canonized in 1203. His feast day is 19 January.

WULFSTAN (fl.c.1000) a monk of Winchester. He was author of a Life of Bishop Ethelwold and a poem on St **Swithin**'s Miracles.

WULFSTAN (d.1023) Anglo-Saxon prelate and writer. He was bishop of London (996–1002) and archbishop of York from 1002, and also bishop of Worcester (1003–16). He was the author of homilies in the vernacular, including a celebrated address to the English, *Sermo Lupi ad Anglos*.

WUNDERLICH, Carl August (1815–77) German physician, born in Sulz-on-Neckar. Professor of medicine at Leipzig, he was the first to introduce temperature charts into hospitals, contending that fever is a symptom and not a disease. His clinical thermometer was a foot long and took 20 minutes to register the temperature.

WUNDT, Wilhelm Max (1832–1920) German physiologist and psychologist, founder of experimental psychology, born in Neckarau, Baden. In 1875 he became professor of physiology at Leipzig. He made studies of the nervous system and the senses, the relations of physiology and psychology, logic and other subjects. He wrote *Human and Animal Psychology* (1863) and *Outlines of Psychology* (1873), *Ethics* (1886) and *Folk Psychology* (1900–20).

WURTZ, Charles Adolphe (1817–84) French organic chemist, born in Strasbourg, pioneer of organic synthesis. He wrote numerous works, of which *The Atomic Theory* (1880) and *Modern Chemistry* (4th ed 1885), among others, have been translated. From 1875 he was professor of chemistry at the Sorbonne. He was the discoverer of glycol (1856).

WYATT, James (1746–1813) English architect, born in Staffordshire. A contemporary of the **Adam** brothers, he made his name with his Neoclassical design for the London Pantheon (1772). In 1796 he succeeded Sir **William Chambers** as surveyor to the Board of Works, and carried out restorations at the medieval cathedrals of Durham, Hereford, Lichfield and Salisbury. His uncritical enthusiasm for rebuilding earned him the nickname of 'Wyatt the Destroyer'. He is best known for the extravagant Gothic Revival country house he built for **William Thomas Beckford** at Fonthill Abbey in Wiltshire. One son, Matthew Cotes Wyatt (1777–1862), was a sculptor. Another son, Benjamin Dean Wyatt (1775–1850), designed the Drury Lane Theatre (1811).

WYATT, Sir Matthew Digby (1820–77) English architect, born in Rowde, near Devizes. He was secretary to the royal commissioners for the Great Exhibition of 1851, and in 1869 was appointed the first Slade professor of fine arts at Cambridge. He published numerous books on art, including *Geometric Mosaics of the Middle Ages* (1848), *Metal Works and its Artistic Design* (1852), *Industrial Arts of the Nineteenth Century* (1853), *Art Treasures of the United Kingdom* (1857), *Fine Art* (1870), and *Architect's Handbook in Spain* (1872).

WYATT, Sir Thomas, the Elder (1503–42) English courtier and poet, born at Allington Castle, Kent. He studied at St John's College, Cambridge.

WYATT, Sir Thomas, the Younger (?1520–1554) English soldier son of the poet Sir **Thomas Wyatt** (1503–42). He fought bravely at the siege of Landrecies (1544), and continued in service on the Continent till 1550. In 1554, with Lady **Jane Grey**'s father, he led the Kentish men to Southwark; and failing to capture Ludgate, was taken prisoner and executed.

WYCHERLEY, William (c.1640–1716) English dramatist, born in Clive near Shrewsbury. In early youth he was sent to France, left Queen's College, Oxford, without a degree, and entered the Middle Temple. For some years he lived as a man about town and a courtier, but took early to work as a dramatist. *Love in a Wood, or St James's Park*, a brisk comedy founded on **Sedley**'s *Mulberry Garden*, was acted with much applause in 1671. **Buckingham** gave him a commission in a regiment, and King **Charles II** made him a present of £500. He served for a short time in the fleet, and was present at a sea fight—probably one of the drawn battles fought between Prince **Rupert** and **De Ruyter** in 1673. *The Gentleman Dancing-master* (1672) was a clever farcical comedy of intrigue, *The Country Wife* (1675), Wycherley's coarsest but strongest play, partly founded on **Molière**'s *École des Femmes*, was followed in 1677 by *The Plain Dealer*, founded partly on Moliére's *Misanthrope*. A little after 1679 Wycherley married the young widowed Countess of Drogheda, with whom he lived unhappily. At her death a few years later she left him all her fortune, a bequest which involved him in a lawsuit whereby he was reduced to poverty and cast into the Fleet prison for some years. At last **James II**, having seen a representation of *The Plain Dealer*, paid his debts and gave him a pension of £200 a year. At 64 Wycherley made the acquaintance of **Pope**, then a youth of 16, to whom he entrusted the revision of a number of his verses, the result being a quarrel. Wycherley's money troubles continued to the end of his days. At the age of 75 he married a young woman in order to balk the hopes of his nephew; and he died eleven days after his marriage; according to Pope, in the Roman Catholic faith. In literary brilliance **Congreve** infinitely outshines him, but Wycherley is a far more dexterous playwright.

WYCKOFF, Ralph (Walter Greystone) (1897–) American biophysicist, born in Geneva, New York. He studied at Cornell and worked at the Rockefeller Institute in the 1930s, doing valuable work on viruses. In 1944 at Chicago with **R C Williams** he developed the metal shadowing method for imaging viruses in the electron microscope, which has since been widely used.

WYCLIFFE, John (c.1329–1384) English religious reformer, born near Richmond in Yorkshire, probably of a family which held the manor of Wycliffe on Tees. He distinguished himself at Oxford, where he was a popular teacher. In 1360 he was master of Balliol College, but resigned soon afterwards on taking the college living of Fillingham, which he exchanged in 1368 for Ludgershall, Buckinghamshire. He was possibly warden for a time of Canterbury Hall. He also held some office at court, where he was consulted by government and employed as a pamphleteer. In 1374 he became rector of Lutterworth, and the same year was sent (doubtless as a recognized opponent of papal intrusion) to Bruges to treat with ambassadors from the pope concerning ecclesiastical abuses. His strenuous activity gained him support among the nobles and the London citizenry. In 1376 he wrote *De Dominio Divino*, expounding the doctrine that all authority is founded in grace and that wicked rulers (whether secular or ecclesiastical) thereby forfeited their right to rule. His maintenance of a right in the secular power to control the clergy was offensive to the bishops, who summoned him before the archbishop in St Paul's in 1377; but the council was broken up by an unseemly quarrel between the bishop of London and Wycliffe's supporter, **John of Gaunt** (Duke of Lancaster). Pope **Gregory XI** now banned him, and addressed bulls to the king, bishops and University of Oxford, bidding them to imprison Wycliffe and make him answer before the archbishop and the pope. When at last proceedings were undertaken, at Lambeth in 1378, the prosecution had little effect upon Wycliffe's position. The whole fabric of the church was now (1378) shaken by the Great Schism and the election of an antipope. Hitherto Wycliffe had attacked the manifest abuses in the church, but now he began to strike at its constitution, and declared it would be better without pope or prelates. He denied the priestly power of absolution, and the whole system of enforced confession, of penances, and indulgence, and asserted the right of every man to examine the bible for himself. Up to this time his works had been written in Latin; he now appealed to the people in their own language, and by issuing popular tracts became a leading English prose writer. He organized a body of itinerant preachers, his 'poor priests', who spread his doctrines widely through the country, and began a translation of the bible, of which as yet there was no complete English version. The work was carried through rapidly, and widely circulated. He entered upon more dangerous ground when in 1380 he assailed the central dogma of transubstantiation. A convocation of doctors at Oxford condemned his theses; he appealed without success to the king. In 1382 Archbishop Courtenay convoked a council and condemned Wycliffite opinions. Wycliffe's followers were arrested, and all compelled to recant; but for some unknown reason he himself was not judged. He withdrew from Oxford to Lutterworth, where he continued his incessant literary activity. His work in the next two years, uncompromising in tone, is astonishing in quantity, and is consistently powerful. The characteristic of his teaching was its insistence on inward religion in opposition to the formalism of the time; as a rule he attacked the established practices of the church only so far as he thought they had degenerated into mere mechanical uses. The influence of his teaching was widespread in England, and, though persecution suppressed it, continued to work up to the Reformation. His supporters came to be derisively known as 'Lollards' (from a Dutch word meaning 'mumblers'); **Huss** was avowedly his disciple; and there were Lollards or Wycliffites in Ayrshire down to the Reformation. 30 years after Wycliffe's death, 45 articles extracted from his writings were condemned as heretical by the Council of Constance, which ordered his bones to be dug up and burned and cast into the Swift—a sentence executed in 1428.

WYETH, Andrew Newell (1917–) American painter, born in Chadds Ford, Pennsylvania. He studied under his father, a book illustrator. His soberly realistic pictures, usually executed with tempera and watercolour rather than oils, typically represent poor people or rustics in landscapes, using off-centre compositions to give a sense of haunting unease, as in *Christina's World* (1948), perhaps the most famous American picture of the century.

WYKEHAM, William of See **WILLIAM OF WYKEHAM**

WYLER, William (Willy) (1902–81) German-born American film director, born in Mulhausen, Alsace-Lorraine (now in France). Invited to America by his cousin Carl Laemmle, the head of Universal Pictures, he began in the publicity department there, graduated to assistant director and directed his first film, *Crook Buster*, in 1925. Over the next five years he made numerous westerns before moving on to more prestigious productions, usually involving star actors and noted literary sources. Renowned for his obsessively meticulous approach to composition, performance and narrative structure, his many films include *These Three* (1936), *Wuthering Heights* (1939), *The Little Foxes* (1941), *The Collector* (1965) and *Funny Girl* (1968). He served as a major in the US Army Air Corps (1942–45) and helped form the Committee to defend the First Amendment in 1947. He received Academy Awards for *Mrs. Miniver* (1942), *The Best Years of Our Lives* (1946) and *Ben Hur* (1959). He retired in 1972.

WYLIE, Elinor Hoyt (1885–1928) American author, born in Somerville, New Jersey. Her first volume of poetry, *Ness to Catch the Wind*, which won the Julia Elsworth Ford prize in 1921, was followed by several more collections and by four highly individual novels, *Jennifer Lorn* (1923), *The Venetian Glass Nephew* (1925), *The Orphan Angel* (1927) and *Mr Hodge and Mr Hazard* (1928).

WYNDHAM, Sir Charles (1837–1919) English actor-manager, born in Liverpool. He trained as a doctor, and first appeared on the stage in New York in 1861, making his début in London in 1866. Among the parts he played were those of Charles Surface and David Garrick. In 1899 he opened Wyndham's Theatre. He was knighted in 1902.

WYNDHAM, John, pseud of **John Wyndham Parkes Lucas Beynon Harris** (1903–69) English science-fiction writer, born in Knowle, Warwickshire. As a child he was fascinated by the stories of **H G Wells**, and in the late 1920s began to write science-fiction tales for popular magazines, showing a much greater regard for literary style and moral and philosophical values than was common in this field. In 1951 he published his first novel, *The Day of the Triffids*, which describes the fortunes of the blinded survivors of a thermo-nuclear explosion who are threatened by the triffids, intelligent vegetable beings hostile to man. Here, as in his later novels, he is less concerned with the inventive, imaginative aspect of the 'logical fantasies' than with what happens to man's behaviour and moral values when faced with unforeseen and uncontrollable situations. His other novels are: *The Kraken Wakes* (in the USA, *Out of the Deeps*: 1953), *The Chrysalids* (in the USA, *Rebirth*: 1955) *The Midwych Cuckoos* (1957), *The Trouble With Lichen* (1960) and *Chocky* (1968). *Consider Her Ways* (1961) and *Seeds of Time* (1969) are collections of short stories.

WYNKYN DE WORDE See **WORDE**

WYNTOUN, Andrew of (?1350–?1420) Scottish chronicler. He was a canon regular of St Andrews, and about 1395 became prior of the monastery of St Serf on Loch Leven. He wrote *The Orygynale Cronykil of Scotland*, written in rhyming couplets specially valuable as a specimen of old Scots. It is brought down to 1406, and of its nine books the first five give a fragmentary outline of the history and geography of the ancient world.

WYON, Benjamin (1802–58) English seal-engraver, elder son of **Thomas I Wyon**. He was chief engraver of seals to **William IV**, for whom he designed the great seal and a number of medals.

WYON, Joseph Shepherd (1836–73) English seal-engraver, son of **Benjamin Wyon**. He succeeded his father as chief engraver of seals, and designed many medals and the great seal of Canada.

WYON, Leonard Charles (1826–91) English seal-engraver eldest son of **William Wyon**. He designed contemporary coinage and military medals, including the South African, Indian, and Albert medals.

WYON, Thomas (I) (1767–1830) English seal-engraver, founder of a dynasty, father of **Benjamin Wyon** and **Thomas Wyon**. He was chief engraver of the seals from 1816.

WYON, Thomas (II) (1792–1817) English seal-engraver, younger son of the founder **Thomas I Wyon**. He became chief engraver at the mint at the age of 23. He designed the new silver coinage in 1816 and the Waterloo medal.

WYON, William (1795–1851) English seal-engraver, born in Birmingham. He became chief engraver to the mint in 1828. He designed much of the new British and colonial coinage of **George III** and **George IV**.

WYSPIANSKI, Stanislaw (1869–1907) Polish poet and painter, born in Krakow. A leader of the Polish Neo-Romantics, besides portraits and genre pictures he executed window designs for the cathedral and the Franciscan church at Krakow. The loss of an arm obliged him to abandon art for poetry and drama and he became the father of modern Polish theatre. His plays used themes from mythology and Polish history.

WYSS, Johann Rudolf (1781–1830) Swiss writer, born in Bern. Professor of philosophy at Bern from 1805, he was the author of the Swiss national anthem, 'Rufst du mein Vaterland' and collected Swiss folk-tales. He is best known for his connection with *The Swiss Family Robinson*; he completed and edited the novel originally written by his father, Johann David Wyss (1743–1818).

WYSZYNSKI, Stepan (1901–81) Polish prelate and cardinal, born in Zuzela, near Warsaw. He was educated at Wloclawek seminary and Lublin Catholic University. He was professor at the Higher Seminary, Woclawek (1930–39), and founded the Catholic Workers university there (1935). During World War II he was associated with the resistance movement during the German occupation of Poland. In 1945 he became rector of Wloclawek seminary, in 1946 bishop of Lublin and in 1949 archbishop of Warsaw and Gniezno and primate of Poland. He was made a cardinal in 1952. In 1953, following his indictment of the communist campaign against the church, he was suspended from his ecclesiastical functions and imprisoned. He was freed after the 'bloodless revolution' of 1956 and agreed to a reconciliation between church and state under the 'liberalizing' **Gomulka** régime, but relations became increasingly strained, culminating in the 1966 celebrations of 1000 years of Christianity in Poland. A further attempt at co-existence was made after widespread strikes in 1970, but uneasiness remained.

WYTHER, George See **WITHER**

X

XANTHIPPE See **SOCRATES**

XAVIER, Saint Francis See **FRANCIS, St**

XENOCRATES (c.395–314 BC) Greek philosopher and scientist, born in Chalcedon on the Bosphorus. He was a pupil of **Plato** and in 339 succeeded **Speusippus** as head of the Academy which Plato had founded. He is recorded as travelling with **Aristotle** after Plato's death in 348 to do research under the patronage of Hermeias, tyrant of Atarneus in NW Asia Minor, and as joining some Athenian embassies on foreign diplomatic missions. He wrote prolifically on natural science, astronomy and philosophy but only fragments of this output survive. He generally systematized and continued the Platonic tradition but seems to have had a particular devotion to threefold categories, perhaps reflecting a Pythagorean influence: philosophy is subdivided into logic, ethics and physics; reality is divided into the objects of sensation, belief and knowledge; he distinguished gods, men and demons; he also probably originated the classical distinction between mind, body and soul.

XENOPHANES (6th century BC) Greek philospher, poet and religious thinker, born in Colophon in Ionia (Asia Minor) where he probably lived until the Persian conquest of the region in 546. He seems then to have lived a wandering life round the Mediterranean, perhaps settling in Sicily for a while and visiting Elea in Southern Italy. He wrote poetry, fragments of which survive, and seems to have been an independent and original thinker, though later traditions tried to claim him as a member either of the Ionian or the Eleatic school. He attacked the anthropomorphism of popular religion and Homeric mythology (pointing out that each race credits the gods with their own physical characteristics, and that animals would do the same), posited by way of reaction a single deity who somehow energizes the world ('without toil he shakes all things by the thought of his mind'), and made some bold speculations about the successive inundations of the earth based on the observation of fossils.

XENOPHON (c.435–354 BC) Greek historian, essayist, and military commander, the son of Gryllus, an Athenian knight, and disciple of **Socrates**. In 401 he accepted the invitation of Proxenus of Boeotia, a commander of Greek mercenaries, to join him in Sardis and take service under the Persian prince, **Cyrus the Younger**, ostensibly against the Pisidians, but really against Cyrus's own brother, King **Artaxerxes II Mnemon**. After the failure of this bold scheme, and the death of the rebel prince at Cunaxa (401), Xenophon succeeded Proxenus in the command of the Ten Thousand Greeks. He became the life and soul of the army in its march of 1500 miles, as they fought their way against the ferocious mountain tribes through the highlands of Armenia and the ice and snow of an inclement winter; and with such skill did he lead them in their retreat through hostile Persian territory that in five months they reached Trapezus (Trebizond), a Greek colony on the Black Sea, and ultimately Chrysopolis (Scutari), opposite Byzantium (399). After serving a while under a Thracian chief, he got his soldiers permanent service in the Spartan army engaged to fight against the Persians. Sentence of banishment from Athens for thus taking service with Sparta was passed against him. Forming in 396 the closest friendship with the Spartan king, **Agesilaus**, he accompanied him in his eastern campaign; was in his suite when he returned to Greece to conduct the war against the anti-Spartan league of Athens, Corinth, and Thebes (394); and witnessed the battle of Coronea (394). He went back with the king to Sparta, where he resided on and off until the Spartans presented him with an estate at Scillus, near Olympia, a town taken from Elis. He went there in 391 with his wife Philesia and his two sons, Gryllus and Diodorus; and here he spent the next 20 years of his life, writing his books and indulging in the pursuits of a country gentleman. But the break-up of Spartan ascendency after the battle of Leuctra (371) drove him from his retreat, when Elis reclaimed Scyllus. The Athenians, who had now joined the Spartans against Thebes, repealed the sentence of banishment against him. But he settled and died in Corinth. His writings give us the idea of having been written with great singleness of purpose, modesty, and love of truth. They may be distributed into four groups: (1) historical—the *Hellenics* (the history of Greece for 49 years), *Anabasis* (the story of the expedition with Cyrus) and *Encomium of Agesilaus*; (2) technical and didactic—on *Horsemanship*, the *Hipparchicus* ('guide for a cavalry commander') and the *Cynegeticus* ('guide to hunting'); (3) politico-philosophical—*The Lacedaemonian Polity*, *The Cyropaedeia* ('the education of Cyrus', rather a historical romance) and *Athenian Finance*; (4) ethico-philosophical—*Memorials of Socrates* (sketches and dialogues illustrating the life and character of his master), *Symposion*, *Oeconomicus*, *Hieron* and *Apology of Socrates*. The *Polity of Athens* is probably an anonymous work written about 415 BC Xenophon's style and language are unaffected, simple and clear, without any attempt at ornamentation.

XERXES I king of Persia from 486 to 465 BC. He succeeded when his father, **Darius I**, died preparing for a second expedition against Greece. He first subdued the rebellious Egyptians, then started with a vast army drawn from all parts of the empire, and a fleet furnished by the Phoenicians. A bridge, consisting of a double line of boats, was built across the Hellespont, and a canal cut through Mount Athos. In the autumn of 481 BC, Xerxes arrived at Sardis. Next year the army began its march towards the Hellespont and from there into Greece. When this immense force reached Thermopylae, it was brought to a temporary stand by **Leonidas**. After he and his men had been slain Xerxes marched on to Athens (480), and, finding it deserted, destroyed it. Meantime the fleet had sailed round from Euboea. Xerxes witnessed the fight in the strait between Salamis and Attica. Defeated at sea, he withdrew to the Hellespont; and his hopes of conquest died with the fall of his general, Mardonius, on the field of Plataea (479 BC). Xerxes, possibly the Ahasuerus of Ezra iv. 6 and Esther i.-x., was later murdered by Artabanus.

XIA GUI, old style **Hsia Kuei** (fl.1180–1230) Chinese artist, a pupil of Li T'ang. He worked for the Song dynasty court, and executed delicate, almost impressionistic landscapes.

XIMENES, Cardinal, in full **Francisco Jimenez de Cisneros** (1436–1517) Spanish churchman and statesman, born of an ancient family in Torrelaguna in Castile. He was educated at Alcalá, Salamanca and Rome, where he obtained from the pope a nomination to the archpriestship of Uzeda in 1473. The archbishop, however, refused to admit him, and for six years imprisoned him. On his release in 1479 he was named vicar-general of Cardinal **Mendoza**, but gave this up to enter a Franciscan monastery at Toledo (1482). Queen **Isabella** chose him for her confessor in 1492, and in 1495 made him archbishop of Toledo. As archbishop he maintained the austerity of a monk and carried out extensive reforms in several monastic orders. As the queen's spiritual counsellor he was the guiding spirit of Spanish affairs; and on her death in 1504 he held the balance between the parties of **Ferdinand** and Philip of Burgundy, husband of Joanna, the mad heiress to the crown. Appointed regent in 1506, he conducted the affairs of the kingdom through a critical time with consummate skill. In 1507 he was created cardinal, and next year organized at his own expense, and commanded, the expedition for the conquest of Oran and extirpation of piracy. Ferdinand on his deathbed (1516) named Ximenes regent of Spain till the arrival of his grandson Charles (later **Charles V**); and the aged cardinal quickly overawed the hostile grandees into submission, and quelled a revolt in Navarre. He died, possibly of poison, at Roa, on his way to greet Charles, just arriving in Spain. Ximenes was fanatical in his hatred of heresy, and as grand inquisitor caused the death of 2500 'heretics'. The revolution he effected in breaking down the feudal power of the nobles has often been compared with the change wrought in France by **Richelieu**. He was a munificent patron of religion and learning and founded out of his private income the University of Alcalá de Henares. He also published the famous Complutensian Polyglot Bible.

XU BEIHONG (1895–1953) Chinese artist, born in Jiting Qiao, Yixing county, Jiangsu province, the son of a self-taught painter. Poverty and flooding caused father and son to take up the wandering life, painting and drawing. They returned to their own province when Xu was 17 and he became an art teacher. He later attended art lectures at Minzhi University, and in 1917 he went to Tokyo to study fine arts. On his return to Beijing (Peking) he began to be known for his own vigorous style of painting, and he was engaged as a tutor at the Peking University for the Society of Painting Technique. From 1919 to 1927 he studied abroad, in Paris, Belgium, Italy, and Switzerland, mastering the western style of drawing and oils, especially of figures, nudes, horses and portraits. He was professor of the art department of the Central University in Nanjing (1928–46), and president of the Art College of Beijing (1946–53). His home in Beijing has been turned into a museum of his works.

Y

YAHYA KHAN, Agha Muhammad (1917–80) Pakistani soldier, born in Chakwal town, in Jhelum district, the son of a Pathan police superintendent. Educated at Punjab University and the Indian Military Academy, Dehra Dun, he was commissioned in 1938, fought with the British 8th Army during World War II and afterwards rose to become chief of the army general staff (1957–62). He supported General **Ayub Khan**'s successful coup in 1958, became army commander-in-chief in 1966 and, in 1969, with popular unrest mounting, replaced Ayub Khan as military ruler. In 1980 he sanctioned the nation's first national elections based on universal suffrage, but his mishandling of the Bangladesh separatist issue led to civil war and the dismemberment of the republic in 1971. After defeat by India in the Bangladesh war, Yahya Khan resigned and was sentenced to five years' house arrest.

YALE, Elihu (1649–1721) English colonial administrator and benefactor, born in Boston, Massachusetts, of English parents. They returned to Britain in 1652, and he was educated in London; in 1672 he went out to India in the service of the East India Company, becoming governor of Madras in 1687. He was resident in England from 1699, and, through the sale in America of some of his effects, donated money to the collegiate school established (1701) at Saybrook, Connecticut, which afterwards moved to New Haven. There in 1718 it took the name of Yale College in honour of its benefactor, and in 1887 the much-expanded institution became Yale University, the third oldest in the United States.

YALE, Linus (1821–68) American inventor and manufacturer, born in Salisbury, New York. He set up business as a locksmith in Shelburne Falls, Massachusetts, and invented various types of locks, including the small cylinder locks by which his name is known.

YALOW, Rosalyn, née **Sussman** (1921–) American physiologist, born in New York. She studied physics at Hunter College, New York, and turned her attention to nuclear medicine with Solomon Berson at the Bronx Veterans Administration Hospital (1950–72). There she developed 'radioimmunoassay', an ultra-sensitive technique for measuring minute concentrations of active biological substances such as hormones and enzymes in the blood. She shared the 1977 Nobel prize for physiology or medicine with **Roger Guillemin** and **Andrew Schally**. She was senior medical investigator for the Veterans Administration from 1972.

YAMAGATA, Prince Aritomo (1838–1922) Japanese soldier and politician, born Hagi. He became adviser to the emperor, and was appointed war minister (1873) and chief of staff (1878), in which capacity his modernization of the military system led to the emergence of Japan as a significant force in world politics. He was twice prime minister (1889–93, 1898), chief of staff in the Russo-Japanese war (1904), and president of the privy council (1905).

YAMAMOTO, Isoroku, originally surnamed **Takano** (1884–1943) Japanese naval officer, the son of a schoolmaster. Educated at the Naval Academy, Etajima, he was wounded in the battle of Tsushima in the Russo-Japanese war of 1904–05. Adopted by the Yamamoto family, he studied at Harvard (1917–1919) and served thereafter as a language officer (1919–21). He was naval attaché at the Japanese embassy in the USA (1926–28). He became chief of the aviation department of the Japanese navy in 1935, and vice-navy minister from 1936 to 1939. He was opposed to the Japanese entry into World War II. Admiral (1940), and commander-in-chief Combined Fleet (1939–43), he planned and directed the attack on Pearl Harbor in December 1941. His forces were defeated at the battle of Midway (June 1942), and he was killed when his plane was shot down over the Solomon Islands.

YAMAMOTO, Yohji (1943–) Japanese fashion designer, born in Tokyo. He studied law at Kaio University, then helped his mother with her dress shop. He started his own company in 1972; his first collection was produced in 1976 in Tokyo. After some time in Paris he opened a new headquarters in London in 1987. He designs loose, functional clothes for men and women, which conceal rather than emphasize the body.

YAMANI, Sheikh Ahmed Zaki (1930–) Saudi Arabian politican. Educated at Cairo, New York and Harvard, he was a lawyer before entering politics. Yamani has been minister of petroleum and mineral resources since 1962, and an important and 'moderate' member of the Organization of Petroleum-Exporting Countries.

YAMASHITA, Tomoyuki (1885–1946) Japanese soldier. He commanded a division in China in 1939, and in 1942 commanded the forces which overran Singapore, and then took over the Philippines campaign, capturing Bataan and Corregidor. Still in charge when **MacArthur** turned the tables in 1944–45, he was captured and hanged in Manila for atrocities perpetrated by his troops.

YANG, Chen Ning (1922–) Chinese-born American physicist, born in Hofei, the son of a professor of mathematics. He gained a scholarship to Chicago in 1945, was professor at the Institute for Advanced Studies, Princeton (1955–65), and from 1965 was professor of science at New York State University Centre. With **Tsung-Dao Lee**, who had been his fellow student at Chicago, he disproved the established physical principle known as the parity law, and for this the two were awarded the Nobel prize for physics 1957.

YANG SHANGKUN (1907–) Chinese politician. The son of a wealthy Sichuan province landlord, he joined the Chinese Communist party (CCP) in 1926 and studied in Moscow (1927–30). He took part in the Long March (1934–35) and the liberation war (1937–49), and became an alternate member of the CCP's secretariat in 1956, but during the Cultural Revolution (1966–69) was purged for alleged 'revisionism'. He was subsequently rehabilitated in 1978 and in 1982 inducted into the CCP's politburo and military affairs commission. A year later he became a vice-chairman of the state central military commission and in 1988 was elected state president. Viewed as a trusted supporter of **Deng Xiaoping**, he has strong personal ties with senior military leaders and in June 1989 it was 27th Army troops, loyal to him, who carried out the brutal massacre of pro-democracy students in Tiananmen Square, Beijing (Peking).

YANOFSKY, Charles (1925–) American geneticist, born in New York City. He studied there and at Yale. Working at Stanford on gene mutations from 1961, he used ingenious microbiological methods to prove that the sequence of bases in the genetic material DNA acts by determining the order of the amino acids which make up proteins, including the enzymes which control biochemical processes.

YARMOUTH, Sophia von Walmoden, Countess of (d.1765) German noblewoman. Already known to King **George II** in Hanover, on Queen **Caroline**'s death (1737) she was brought to England as the king's mistress, and created a countess.

YARRELL, William (1784–1856) English naturalist, born in London. A newsagent by trade, he turned his attention to ornithology and studied zoology systematically. He wrote a *History of British Fishes* (1836), and a popular *History of British Birds* (1837–43) which was for long a standard text. There is a memorial to him in St James' Church, Piccadilly, London.

YASHIN, Lev (1929–) Russian footballer, born in Moscow. A tall, commanding goalkeeper, he did not begin to play football seriously until the age of 22. He then took over from the great Russian goalkeeper Khomich as goalkeeper for Moscow Dynamo, and for the next 17 years was his country's goalkeeper. Between 1958 and 1966 he took part in three World Cups, and was voted European Footballer of the Year in 1963.

YATES, Dornford, pseud of **Cecil William Mercer** (1885–1960) English novelist, born in London. He was educated at Harrow and Oxford, and achieved great popularity with an entertaining series of fanciful escapist adventure fiction, such as *Berry and Co* (1921) and *Jonah and Co* (1922).

YATES, Edmund (1831–94) Scottish journalist and novelist, born in Edinburgh, the son of the actor-manager Frederick Henry Yates (1797–1842). From 1854 he published over a score of novels and other works; was editor of *Temple Bar*, *Tinsley's* and other periodicals; and in 1874 founded, with Grenville Murray, a successful 'society' weekly, *The World*, which, for a libel on the 5th Earl of **Lonsdale**, involved him in 1884 in two months' imprisonment.

YEAGER, Charles Elwood (1923–) American test pilot, born in Myra, West Virginia, the first man to break the sound barrier. Enlisting in the air force in 1941, he graduated as a fighter pilot in 1943. During combat missions he gained 2 victories before being captured, but after escaping he went on to secure a further ten victories. On 14 October 1947 he flew the Bell X-1 rocket research aircraft to a level speed of more than 670 mph, thus 'breaking the sound barrier', and while in the Bell X-1A he flew at more than $2\frac{1}{2}$ times the speed of sound (1953). He was commander of the USAF Aerospace Research Pilot School and commanded the 4th Fighter Bomber Wing.

YEAMES, William Frederick (1835–1918) British historical and subject painter, born in Taganrog. He studied in London, Florence and Rome. His best-known work is *When did you last see your Father?*.

YEATS, Jack B (John Butler) (1870–1957) Irish strip cartoonist and impressionist painter, born in London, son of the artist John Butler Yeats (1839–1922) and brother of **William Butler Yeats**. Educated in County Sligo, his first drawing was published in 1888. He sketched horses for *Paddock Life* magazine (1891), then drew joke cartoons for *Cassell's Saturday Journal*, etc (1892). In 1894 he created the first cartoon strip version of Sherlock Holmes, *Chubblock Homes*, for *Comic Cuts*, then many strips featuring horses (*Signor McCoy*, 1897) and show business. He wrote and illustrated children's books beginning with *James Flaunty* (1901), and drew many further strips until 1918, when he concentrated on painting, playwriting and writing.

YEATS, William Butler (1865–1939) Irish poet, born in Sandymount, a Dublin suburb. His father was the artist John Butler Yeats (1839–1922). His mother came from Sligo, a wild and naturally beautiful county where Yeats spent much time as a child. When he was nine the family moved to London, where he attended the Godolphin School, Hammersmith, but the connection with Ireland was always potent, and in 1880 they moved back there and lived in Howth near Dublin where he went to the High School. In 1884 he entered art school but his early enthusiasm for poetry surfaced the following year when his first lyrics were published in *The Dublin University Review*. Preoccupied with mysticism and the occult, with a few friends he founded the Dublin Hermetic Society, and pursued his interest in Irish mythology, the source from which so much of his poetry springs. His first volume of verse was *Mosada: A Dramatic Poem* (1886) which had previously appeared in *The Dublin University Review*. Returning to London the following year with his family he contributed to anthologies of Irish poets and edited *Fairy and Folk Tales of the Irish Peasantry* (1888) to which he was also a contributor. Gradually poems were accepted by English magazines, and two American newspapers appointed him literary correspondent. His circle of friends widened and he knew **William Morris**, **George Bernard Shaw**, **Oscar Wilde** and others. In 1889 came *The Wanderings of Oisin and Other Poems*, which was charitably reviewed and established him as a literary figure; but the more accepted he became the more homesick he felt and he returned to Ireland in 1891. A year later he published *John Sherman* and *Dhoya* (1892), two stories on Celtic themes suggested by his father. He toyed with the idea of writing a novel but his meeting with Maud Gonne (see **Maud MacBride**), an ardent Irish nationalist who ultimately refused to marry him, led him down another road. Inspired by her he began *The Countess Kathleen* (1892), a Celtic drama rich in imagery, and founded the Irish Literary Society. In 1893 he published *The Celtic Twilight* (1893), a collection of stories and anecdotes, whose title haunted him until his death and stalks his reputation with its connotation of romantic vagueness. His best known drama, *The Land of Heart's Desire* (1894), is slight but potent, telling of a young woman spirited away by a fairy child. He met Olivia Shakespear and worked on *Poems* (1895) which elevated him to the ranks of the major poets. In 1896 came his fateful meeting with Lady **Gregory**, the mistress of an estate at Coole in Galway, where he set and composed many of his finest poems. He published a plethora of books and his life was a tangled skein of political and cultural involvement and personal upheaval. With the move in 1904 to the Abbey Theatre of the Irish Players, the Irish cultural renaissance had something tangible to show for its agitation and Yeats played an important part in propagandizing. Significant books during these years were *The Wind Among the Reeds* (1899), which concludes with 'The Fiddler of Dooney', *The Shadowy Waters* (1900) and *Cathleen ni Houlihan* (1902), a play with Maud Gonne in the title role, which it is thought may have sparked the Rising of Easter 1916. Yeats went to America in 1903 where he heard that Maud Gonne had married John MacBride, who was executed in the aftermath of the 1916 rising. Yeats remembered him and others in his famous poem, 'Easter 1916'. *The Collected Works in Prose and Verse* in eight volumes were published in 1906 and he wrote *The Player Queen* for the actress Mrs **Patrick Campbell**. His last attempt to write poetic drama using legends as a source appeared in *The Green Helmet and Other Poems* (1910) and in 1916 he published *Responsibilities*, aimed at philistines. It was highly effective. He was awarded a Civil List pension in 1910 on condition that he remained active in Irish political matters. He married Georgie Hyde-Lees in 1917, having had an earlier proposal turned down, when he was 52 and she 15. Together they shared an interest in psychical research which influenced later work. *A Vision* was published in 1924, and *The Wild Swans at Coole* the same year. *Michael Roberts and the Dancer* (1920) pre-empted the outbreak of the civil war a year later and it was eight years before he published his next collection of poems. But during the intervening years he was engaged in playwriting, politics (he became a member of the Irish senate in 1922), and in 1923 was awarded the Nobel prize for literature. In 1928 he moved to Rapallo in Italy and in that year published *The Tower*, a dark vision of the future exquisitely expressed. *The Winding Stair* (1933) is more optimistic. The controversial anthology, *The Oxford Book of Modern Verse 1892–1935*, appeared in 1936. He was very much a public figure and a grand man of letters but his reputation was tainted by his flirtation with Fascism. He moved to Cap Martin, Alpes Maritimes, in 1938, where he died. A titan of 20th-century literature, his various volumes of autobiography are collected in *Autobiographies* (1955).

YELTSIN, Boris Nikolayevich (1931–) Soviet politician, born in Sverdlovsk. Educated at the same Urals Polytechnic as **Nikolai Ryzhkov**, he began his career in the construction industry. He joined the Communist party of the Soviet Union (CPSU) in 1961 and was appointed first secretary of the Sverdlovsk region in 1976. He was inducted into the CPSU's central committee (CC) in April 1985 by **Mikhail Gorbachev** and briefly worked under the new secretary for the economy, Ryzhkov, before being appointed Moscow party chief in 1985, replacing the disgraced Viktor Grishin. Yeltsin, a blunt-talking, hands-on reformer, rapidly set about renovating the corrupt 'Moscow machine' and was elected a candidate member of the CPSU politburo in 1986, but in 1987, at a CC plenum, after he had bluntly criticized party conservatives for sabotaging political and economic reform (*perestroika*), he was downgraded to a lowly administrative post. No longer in the politburo, he returned to public attention in 1989 by being elected to the new Congress of USSR People's Deputies. In 1990 he was elected president of the Russian Federation.

YENDYS, Sydney See **DOBELL, Sydney Thompson**

YERKES, Charles Tyson (1837–1905) American railway financier, born in Philadelphia. He made and lost several fortunes, and in 1899 was forced to sell out in Chicago after allegations of political chicanery. In London in 1900 he headed the consortium that built the London Underground. In 1892 he had presented the Yerkes Observatory to the University of Chicago.

YERSIN, Alexandre Émile John (1863–1943) Swiss-born French bacteriologist, born in Rougemont and educated at Lausanne, Marburg and Paris. He did research at the Pasteur Institute in Paris, working along with **Pierre Roux** on diphtheria antitoxin. In Hong Kong in 1894 he discovered the plague bacillus at the same time as **Kitasato**. He developed a serum against it, and founded two Pasteur Institutes in China. He introduced the rubber tree into Indo-China.

YEVTUSHENKO, Yevegeny Aleksandrovich (1933–) Russian poet, born in Zima in Siberia. He moved permanently to Moscow with his mother in 1944. His work attracted no great attention until the publication of *The Third Snow* (1955), *Chaussé Eutuziastov* (1956) and *The Promise* (1957) made him a spokesman for the young post-**Stalin** generation, and he became a well-known and controversial figure. His long poem *Zima Junction*, considering issues raised by the death of Stalin, prompted criticism, as did *Babi Yar* (1962) which attacked anti-Semitism in Russia as well as Nazi Germany. In 1960 travel abroad inspired poems such as those published in *A Wave of the Hand* (1962). He has never been afraid to express his beliefs and opinions even at the risk of official disapproval and in 1974 he publicly supported **Solzhenitsyn** on his arrest. His hatred of hypocrisy has compelled him to speak out clearly for his ideal of a new, post-Stalinist spiritual revolution. His later work includes *Love Poems* (1977), *Heavy Soils* (1978), *Ivan the Terrible and Ivan the Fool* (1979) and a novel, *Berries* (1981). **Shostakovich** set five of his poems, including *Babi Yar*, as his Thirteenth Symphony. He published his *Precocious Autobiography* in 1963.

YONAI, Mitsumasa (1880–1948) Japanese naval officer and politician, born of Samurai descent. Educated at the Naval Academy, Etajima, he served in Russia (1915–17). He was commander of the Imperial Fleet from 1936 to 1937. Navy Minister from 1937 to 1939 and from 1944 to 1945, he was briefly prime minister in 1940.

YONGE, Charlotte Mary (1823–1901) English novelist, born in Otterbourne, Hampshire. She achieved great popular success with *The Heir of Redclyffe* (1853) and its successors, publishing some 120 volumes of fiction, high church in tone. Part of the profits of her *Heir of Redclyffe* was devoted to fitting out the missionary schooner *Southern Cross* for Bishop **George Selwyn**; and the profits of the *Daisy Chain* (£2000) she gave to build a missionary college in New Zealand. She also published historical works, a book on *Christian Names* (1863), a *Life of Bishop Patterson* (1873), and a sketch of *Hannah More* (1888). She edited the girls' magazine, *Monthly Packet*, from 1851 to 1890.

YORCK VON WARTENBURG, Hans David Ludwig (1759–1830) Prussian soldier, the son of a Pomeranian captain, Von Yorck, York or Jarck, claiming English descent. He entered the army in 1772, was cashiered for insubordination but reinstated in 1787, and served in the Dutch East Indies, but rejoining the Prussian service, gained glory in the wars of 1794, 1806, 1812 and 1813–14. Ennobled in 1814, he was made a field marshal in 1821.

YORK, Cardinal See **STEWART, Henry Benedict**

YORK, Duke of the title normally reserved for the second son of the reigning British monarch. **Edward III**'s son, Edmund of Langley, founded that House of York that fought the Wars of the Roses. **Charles II**'s brother **James** bore the title until his accession in 1685. **George I** conferred it on his brother Ernest Augustus, and **George III** on his second son, **Frederick Augustus**. **George V** bore the title until created Prince of Wales in 1901; as did **George VI** prior to his accession on the abdication of **Edward VIII**.

YORK, Richard, 3rd Duke of York, later **Plantagenet** (1411–60) English nobleman, and claimant to the English throne, and father of **Edward IV**, **Richard III**, and George, Duke of **Clarence**. He loyally served the weak-minded **Henry VI** in Ireland and France, and was appointed protector during his illnesses, but was always in conflict with the king's wife, **Margaret of Anjou** and her Lancastrian forces. In 1460 he marched on Westminster and claimed the crown, was promised the succession and appointed protector again, but was killed in a rising by Lancastrian forces at Wakefield.

YORKE, Philip, 1st Earl of Hardwicke See **HARDWICKE, Philip Yorke**

YORKSHIRE RIPPER, The See **SUTCLIFFE, Peter**

YOSHIDA, Shigeru (1878–1967) Japanese politician, born in Tokyo. Educated at Tokyo Imperial University, he entered diplomacy in 1906 and after service in several capitals was vice-minister for foreign affairs. From 1930 to 1932 he was ambassador to Italy and from 1936 to 1938 ambassador in London. In October 1945 he became foreign minister and in May 1946, as first chairman of the Liberal party, he formed the government which inaugurated the new constitution. He was re-elected in 1950 and resigned in 1954.

YOSHIHITO (1879–1926) emperor of Japan, born in Tokyo, the only son of emperor **Mutsuhito**. He was proclaimed crown prince in 1889 and succeeded his father on the imperial throne in 1912. His 14-year reign saw the emergence of Japan as a world great power. Unlike his father, however, he took little part in active politics, for his mental health gave way in 1921. In the last five years of his life, Crown Prince **Hirohito** was regent. Japanese custom accorded Yoshihito the posthumous courtesy title, **Taisho Tenno**.

YOUNG, Andrew John (1855–1971) Scottish poet and clergyman, born in Elgin. Educated at the Royal High School, Edinburgh, and at New College, Edinburgh, he became a United Free Church minister in Temple, Midlothian, in 1912. During World War I he was attached to the YMCA in France. After the war he left Scotland and took charge of the English Presbyterian Church at Hove in Sussex (1941–59). Later he joined the Anglican church and became vicar of Stoneygate, Sussex (1941–59). His early verse—*Songs of Night* (1910), which was paid for by his father, *Boaz and Ruth* (1920) and *Thirty-One Poems* (1922)—revealed an almost mystical belief in the sanctity of nature and the part it plays in Christian belief, later confirmed by *Winter Harvest* (1933), and his *Collected Poems* (1936). He also wrote an account of the poetry, folklore and natural history of the British Isles in *The Poets and the Landscape* (4 vols, 1962).

YOUNG, Arthur (1741–1820) English agriculturist and writer, born in London. He spent his boyhood at Bradfield near Bury St Edmunds, his father being rector and a prebendary of Canterbury. In 1763 he rented a small farm of his mother's, on which he made 3000 unsuccessful experiments. During 1766–71 he failed with a farm in Essex; from 1776 to 1778 was in Ireland; resumed farming at Bradfield; and in 1793 was appointed the first secretary to the board of agriculture. He was one of the first to elevate agriculture to a science. His writings include *A Tour through the Southern Counties* (1768), *A Tour through the North of England* (1771), *The Farmer's Tour through the East of England* (1770–71), *Tour in Ireland* (1780), *Travels in France*, *The Farmer's Kalendar*, and 'Agricultural Surveys' of eight English counties, besides many papers in *The Annals of Agriculture*, which he edited (1784–1809).

YOUNG, Brigham (1801–77) American Mormon leader, born in Whitingham, Vermont. He was a carpenter, painter, and glazier in Mendon, New York. He first saw the 'Book of Mormon' in 1830, and in 1832, converted by a brother of **Joseph Smith**, was baptized and began to preach near Mendon. Next he went to Kirtland, Ohio, was made an elder, and preached in Canada (1832–33). In 1835 he was appointed to the Quorum of the Twelve Apostles of the church and directed the Mormon settlement at Nauvoo, Illinois. In 1844 he succeeded Joseph Smith as president; and when the Mormons were driven from Nauvoo, he organized and led the trek to Utah in 1847. From 1839 to 1842 he visited England and made 2000 proselytes. In 1847 the great body of Mormons arrived at Utah, and founded Salt Lake City; and in 1850 President **Fillmore** appointed Brigham Young governor of Utah Territory. The Mormon practice of polygamy occasioned growing concern, and in 1857 a new governor was sent with a force of United States troops under **Albert Sidney Johnston** to suppress it; and the appointment in 1869 of another 'Gentile' governor further reduced Young's authority. Practical and far-seeing as an administrator, he encouraged agriculture and manufactures, made roads and bridges, and carried through a contract for 100 miles of the Union Pacific Railroad. He died leaving $2 500 000 to 17 wives and 56 children.

YOUNG, Charles Mayne (1777–1856) English tragedian, son of a rascally London surgeon. He was driven from home with his mother and two brothers, and had worked for a while as a clerk in a West India house, when in 1798 he made his début at Liverpool; in 1807 he appeared in London as Hamlet. He was a most original actor, second only to **Kean** himself. In 1832 he retired with a fortune of £60 000. In 1805 he had married a brilliant young actress, Julia Anne Grimani (1785–1806). Their son, Julian Charles Young (1806-73), was rector of Southwick in Sussex (1844–50), and then of Ilmington, Worcestershire; he published a most amusing *Memoir of Charles Mayne Young* (1871), four-fifths of it his own journal, and supplemented in 1875 by *Last Leaves* from that same journal.

YOUNG, Chic (Murat Bernard) (1901–73) American strip cartoonist, born in Chicago, the creator of the popular *Blondie*. Born to a painter mother, he studied art at the Chicago Institute and joined Newspaper Enterprise Association, creating his first strip, *Affairs of Jane*, in 1920. Pretty girls were to dominate his career: *Beautiful Bab* (1922), *Dumb Dora* (1925), and finally *Blondie* (1930) which became King Features most widely syndicated strip, with the millionaire's daughter, Blondie Boopadoop, developing into a suburban housewife and mother of two. Twenty-eight films were based on the strip, as well as radio and television series.

YOUNG, Cy (Denton True) (1867–1955) American baseball pitcher, born in Gilmore, Ohio. Between 1890 and 1911 he recorded a total of 511 victories, a record that remains unequalled. He is commemorated by the annual Cy Young award to the most successful pitcher in the American major leagues. In 1904 he pitched the first 'perfect game' in baseball, ie one in which no opposing batter reached first base either on a hit or on a walk.

YOUNG, David Ivor, Baron Young of Graffham (1932–) English Conservative politician and businessman. Educated at Christ's College, Finchley and University College, London, where he took a law degree, he qualified as a solicitor and became an executive with the large clothing and household goods company, Great Universal Stores (GUS), from 1956 to 1961. He continued to pursue a successful industrial career until his talents were recognized by Sir **Keith Joseph** and **Margaret Thatcher**, who persuaded him to become director of the Centre for Policy Studies, a right-wing 'think tank' (1979–82). He was chairman of the Manpower Services Commission (MSC) (1981–84), then made a life peer and brought into the Thatcher cabinet, initially as minister without portfolio, and then, from 1985, as employment secretary. In 1989 he moved out of the political centre and returned to commerce. He is chairman of the International Council of Jewish Social and Welfare Services.

YOUNG, Douglas (1913–73) Scottish poet, scholar and dramatist, born in Tayport, Fife. He spent his early childhood in India, and was educated at Merchiston Castle School, Edinburgh, and St Andrews University, where he read classics, and New College, Oxford. He was a lecturer in Greek at Aberdeen until 1941. He joined the Scottish National party, and was jailed for refusing war service except in an independent Scotland's army; his attitude split the Scottish National party, of which he was controversially elected chairman (1942). After the war he became a Labour parliamentary candidate. After teaching at University College, Dundee and St Andrews University, he was appointed professor of classics at McMaster University in Canada, and professor of Greek at the University of North Carolina in 1970. His three collections of verse were *Auntran Blads* (1943), *A Braird o'Thristles* (1947), and *Sellected Poems* (1950). He is best known for *The Puddocks* (1957) and *The Burdies* (1959), translations into Lallans of **Aristophanes**' plays.

YOUNG, Edward (1683–1765) English poet, born in Upham rectory near Winchester, the son of a future dean of Salisbury. Educated at Winchester and New College and Corpus Christi College, Oxford, in 1708 he received a law fellowship of All Souls, Oxford. His first poetic work was in 1712, an *Epistle* to George Granville on being created Lord Lansdowne. In 1719 he produced a tragedy, *Busiris*, at Drury Lane. His second tragedy, *The Revenge*, was produced in 1721; his third and last, *The Brothers*, in 1753. His satires, *The Love of Fame, the Universal Passion* (1725–28), brought financial reward as well as fame. For *The Instalment* (1726), a poem addressed to Sir **Robert Walpole**, he got a pension of £200. In 1724 Young took orders and in 1727 he was appointed a royal chaplain. In 1730 he became rector of Welwyn. The following year he married Lady Elizabeth Lee, widowed daughter of the 2nd Earl of Lichfield. *The Complaint, or Night Thoughts on Life, Death and Immortality* (1742–45), usually known as *Night Thoughts*, occasioned by her death and other sorrows, is a remarkable piece of work, and many of its lines have passed into proverbial use.

YOUNG, Francis Brett (1884–1954) English novelist, born in Halesowen, Worcestershire. Established first as a physician, with a period as ship's doctor, he achieved celebrity as a writer with *Portrait of Clare* (1927), which won the Tait Black Memorial prize. From then on he wrote a succession of novels of leisurely charm, characterized by a deep love of his native country. Noteworthy titles are *My Brother Jonathan* (1928), *Far Forest* (1936), *Dr. Bradley Remembers* (1935), *A Man about the House* (1942) and *Portrait of a Village* (1951).

YOUNG, George Malcolm (1882–1959) English historical essayist, born in Greenhithe, the son of a waterman. He won scholarships to St Paul's School and Balliol College, Oxford, winning a brief fellowship at All Souls College and tutorship at St John's College, after which he joined the board of education in 1908, becoming secretary of the future University Grants Committee. He was joint secretary of the new ministry of reconstruction (1917), and accompanied **Arthur Henderson** of the war cabinet on his journey to post-revolutionary Russia. Leaving the civil service in disillusionment, he published his first book, an admiring brief life of **Gibbon** (1932), and then edited the comprehensive and stimulating *Early Victorian England* (2 vols, 1934), afterwards enlarging his own final essay into *Victorian England: Portrait of an Age* (1936). His engaging *Charles I and Cromwell* (1935) was followed by a volume of essays and reviews entitled *Daylight and Champaign* (1937), which with its sequels *Today and Yesterday* (1948) and *Last Essays* (1950) are models of their kind. *Stanley Baldwin* (1952) disappointed both him and his readers as a subject.

YOUNG, James (1811–83) Scottish industrial chemist, born in Glasgow. He started as a joiner, studied chemistry at Anderson's College and became Thomas Graham's assistant there (1832) and (1837) in University College, London. As manager of chemical works near Liverpool (1839) and near Manchester (1843), he discovered cheaper methods of producing sodium stannate and potassium chlorate; and it was his experiments (1847–50) that led to the manufacture of paraffin oil and solid paraffin on a large scale from the shales of central Scotland.

YOUNG, Lester Willis ('Prez') (1909–59) American tenor saxophonist and (occasionally) clarinettist, born in Woodville, Mississippi. He first played alto saxophone in a family band, but changed to tenor saxophone in 1927 and worked with a succession of bands in the mid-west, including Walter Page's Blue Devils and Eddie Barefield's Band. He joined the newly-formed **Count Basie** Orchestra in 1934 for a spell, rejoining it in 1936. The band's rise to national prominence in the late 1930s brought Young recognition as an innovative soloist, whose light tone and easy articulation marked a break from the baroque swing-style saxophone and inspired such modernists as **Charlie Parker** and Dexter Gordon. Around this time, Young accompanied singer **Billie Holiday** on several important recording sessions. After 1940, Young led small bands and freelanced, rejoining **Basie** in 1943 for a year. During the 1950s, his dependence on alcohol became marked, and his later performances diminished in creative power.

YOUNG, Michael, Baron Young of Dartington (1915–) British educationalsit, a pioneer in the field of consumer protection. Trained as a sociologist and barrister, he was chairman and later president of the Consumers' Association (1965–), whose journal *Which?* introduced a new openness in the expression of consumer opinion. He also played a leading role in the development of 'distance learning' in the third world and, via the National Extension College, within Britain. His publications include *The Rise of the Meritocracy* (1958); *Distance Teaching for the Third World* (1980), and *Revolution from within: cooperatives and cooperation in British industry* (1983). He was created a life peer in 1978.

YOUNG, Thomas (1587–1655) Scottish Puritan theologian, born in Perthshire. He studied at St Andrews, was **Milton**'s tutor until 1622, and afterwards held charges at Hamburg and in Essex. He was the chief author in 1641 of an anti-espiscopal pamphlet, *Answer* to Bishop **Joseph Hall** by 'Smectymnuus', a name compounded of the initials of Stephen Marshall, **Edmund Calamy**, **Thomas Young**, Matthew, Newcomen and William Spurstow.

YOUNG, Thomas (1773–1829) English physicist, physician and Egyptologist, born in Milverton, Somerset. He studied medicine at London, Edinburgh, Göttingen and Cambridge, and started as doctor in London in 1800, but devoted himself to scientific research, and in 1801–03 was professor of natural philosophy to the Royal Institution; his *Lectures* (1807) expounded the doctrine of interference, which established the undulatory theory of light. He did valuable work in insurance, haemodynamics and Egyptology, and made a fundamental contribution to the deciphering of the inscriptions on the Rosetta Stone.

YOUNGHUSBAND, Sir Francis Edward (1863–1942) British explorer, born in Murree in India. He explored Manchuria in 1886 and on the way back discovered the route from Kashgar into India via the Mustagh Pass. In 1902 he went on the expedition which opened up Tibet to the western world. British resident in Kashmir (1906–09), he wrote much on India and Central Asia. Deeply religious, he founded the World Congress of Faiths in 1936.

YOURCENAR, Marguerite, pseud of **Marguerite de Crayencour** (1903–87) Belgian-born French novelist and poet, born in Brussels. Educated at home in a wealthy and cultured household, she read Greek authors at the age of eight, and her first poems were privately printed in her teens. She travelled widely, and wrote a series of distinguished novels, plays, poems and essays. Her novels, many of them historical reconstructions, include *La Nouvelle Eurydice* (1931), *Le Coup de Grâce* (1939, translated in a revised edition in 1957), *Les Mémoires d'Hadrien* (1941, trans 1954), and *L'oeuvre au Noir* (1968). She has also written on her religious experiences in *Préface à Gita-Gavinda* (1958), an anthology of American spirituals (*Fleuve profonde, sombre rivière*, 1964), a long prose poem (*Feux*, 1939), and an autobiography, *Souvenirs pieux* (1977). She emigrated to the USA in 1939, but was later given French citizenship by presidential decree, and in 1980 became the first woman writer to be elected to the Académie Française.

YOURIEFFSKAIA, Princess See **DOLGORUKOVA, Katharina**

YOUSEF, Sidi Mohammed ben See **SIDI MOHAMMED**

YPRES, Earl of See **FRENCH, John**

YPSILANTI, Alexander (1725–1805) Greek administrator. He became Ottoman hospodar (governor) of Wallachia, but was put to death on suspicion of fostering Greek ambitions.

YPSILANTI, Alexander (1783–1828) Greek soldier, eldest son of **Constantine Ypsilanti**. He served with distinction in the Russian army from 1812 to 1813, and was chosen by the Greek 'Hetairists' as their chief in 1820. He headed a Rouman movement, but, defeated by the Turks, took refuge in Austria, where he died.

YPSILANTI, Constantine (d.1816) Greek administrator, son of **Alexander Ypsilanti** (1725–1805). He became Ottoman hospodar (governor) of Moldavia and Wallachia. Deposed in 1805, he came back with some thousands of Russian soldiers and he stirred the Serbs to rebellion; he made another plan for restoring Greece, but had to flee to Russia.

YPSILANTI, Demetrius (1793–1832) Greek soldier, younger son of **Constantine Ypsilanti**. He served in the Russian army, and aided the schemes of his brother **Alexander Ypsilanti** (1783–1828), for emancipating the Christian population of Turkey. In Greece he took part in the capture of Tripolita (October 1820). His gallant defence of Argos stopped the victorious march of the Turks, and from 1828 to 1830 he was Greek commander-in-chief. He died in Vienna.

YRIARTE, Charles (1832–98) French man of letters, born in Paris, of Spanish ancestry. He studied architecture but from 1861 devoted himself to literature. He was editor-in-chief of *Le Monde Illustré*. Specially interested in the Italian Renaissance period, he wrote histories of Venice (1877) and Florence (1880), as well as biographies of **Francesca da Rimini** (1882) and **Cesare Borgia** (1889).

YSAYE, Eugène (1858–1931) Belgian violinist, born in Brussels. One of the greatest violinists of his time, he toured extensively in Europe and America. First teacher of the violin at the Brussels Conservatory (1886–98), he composed violin concertos, sonatas, and chamber music.

YUAN SHIKAI old style **SHIH-KAI** (1859–1916) Chinese dictator, born in Henan province. He served in the army and became imperial adviser, minister in Korea (1885–94), governor of Shantung (1900), but was banished after the death of Emperor Kuang Hsü (1908). He participated in the revolution of 1911 and became first president of China (1912–16), **Sun Yat-Sen** standing down for him, but was opposed by the latter from the south when he tried to make himself emperor. His manner of death is unknown.

YUKAWA, Hideki (1907–81) Japanese physicist. He predicted (1935) the existence of the meson, a particle hundreds of times heavier than the electron. He developed his theory of strong nuclear forces, and for his work on quantum theory and nuclear physics was awarded the Nobel prize for physics in 1949, the first Japanese to be so honoured. Professor of physics at Kyoto University (1939–50) and director of Kyoto Research Institute (1953–70), he was visiting professor at Princeton and Columbia Universities (1948–53).

YUSUF BIN HASSAN (JERONIMO CHINGULIA) (ruled 1526–1531) last sheik of the Malindi dynasty of Mombasa (Kenya). As a youth he studied under Portuguese tutelage in Goa and was baptized a Christian as Dom Jeronimo Chingulia. Following his succession in 1526 he took up arms in 1531 against Portuguese domination. He was driven out of Mombasa and direct Portuguese rule was established.

Z

ZACCARIA, Antonio Maria, St (1502–39) Italian religious. Ordained a priest in 1528, he founded the Barnabite preaching order (1530), and the Angelicals of St Paul order for women (1535). He was canonized in 1897.

ZACHARIAS, St (d.752) Greek prelate, born in Calabria. He was pope from 741 to 752, and recognized **Pepin the Short** as king of the Franks (752).

ZADKIEL, pseud of **Richard James Morrison** (1794–1874) English astrologer. After service in the Royal Navy (1806–29) he started a best selling astrological almanac in 1831, *Zadkiel's Almanac*.

ZADKINE, Ossip (1890–1967) Russian-born French sculptor, born in Sindensk. He settled in Paris in 1909, and developed an individual style, making effective use of the play of light on concave surfaces, as in *The Three Musicians* (1926), *Orpheus* (1940), and the war memorial in Amsterdam, entitled *The Destroyed City* (1952).

ZAHARIAS, Babe (Mildred Ella), née **Didrikson** (1914–56) American golfer and athlete, born in Port Arthur, Texas. One of the greatest all-round athletes ever, she was in the All-American basketball team (1930–32), then turned to athletics and won two gold medals (javelin and 80 metres sprint) at the 1932 Olympics in Los Angeles; she also broke the world record in the high jump, but was disqualified for using the new Western Roll technique. Excelling also in swimming, tennis and rifle-shooting, in 1934 she turned to golf, and after being briefly banned as an amateur for an unauthorized endorsement, she won the US National Women's Amateur Championship in 1946 and the British Ladies' Amateur Championship in 1947. In 1948 she turned professional and won the US Women's Open three times (1948, 1950, 1954). In 1938 she married George Zaharias.

ZAHAROFF, Sir Basil, originally **Basileios Zacharias** (1850–1936) Turkish-born French armaments magnate and financier, born in Anatolia, of Greek parents. He entered the munitions industry in the 1880s and became a shadowy but immensely influential figure in international politics and finance, amassing a huge fortune in arms deals, oil, shipping and banking. He became a French citizen in 1913, and was knighted by the British in 1918 for his services to the allies in World War I. He donated large sums of money to universities and other institutions.

ZAHIR SHAH, King Mohammed (1914–) king of Afghanistan from 1933 to 1973. Educated in Kabul and Paris, he was assistant minister for national defence and education minister before succeeding to the throne in 1933 after the assassination of his father Nadir Shah. His reign was characterized by a concern to preserve neutrality and promote gradual modernization. He became a constitutional monarch in 1964, but, in 1973, while in Italy receiving medical treatment, was overthrown in a republican coup led by his cousin, General Daud Khan, in the wake of a three-year famine. Since then he has lived in exile in Rome and remains a popular symbol of national unity for moderate Afghan opposition groups.

ZAKHAROV, Rostislav (1907–84) Soviet dancer, choreographer, ballet director and teacher, born in Astrakhan. After his graduation from ballet school in the mid 1920s, he joined both the Kharkov and Kirov Ballets as soloist and choreographer while continuing to study (until 1932) at the Leningrad Theatre Institute. He was accepted into the Kirov Theatre, where he choreographed *The Fountain of Bakhchisaray*, a milestone in Soviet ballet because of the depth with which its characters were delineated. He was associated with the Bolshoi Ballet from 1936 until the mid 1950s, variously as artistic director, choreographer and tutor.

ZAMENHOF, Lazarus Ludwig (1859–1917) Polish oculist and philologist, born in Bialystok. An advocate of an international language to promote world peace, he invented Esperanto ('One who hopes').

ZAMYATIN, Yevgeny Ivanovich (1884–1937) Russian writer, born in Lebedyan, Tambov Province. His first published work was *A Provincial Tale*, which appeared in 1913. In 1914 he wrote a novella, *At the World's End*, satirizing the life of army officers in a remote garrison town, and was tried but ultimately acquitted of 'maligning the officer corps'. A naval architect by training, he spent 18 months in Glasgow and the north of England during World War I, designing and supervising the building of ice-breakers for Russia. He returned to Russia and St Petersburg in 1917 and wrote stories, plays and criticism, lectured on literature and participated in various co-operative literary projects. But while supportive of the revolution, he was also an outspoken critic and he was among the first writers to be hounded by the party *apparatchiks*. **Trotsky** branded him 'an internal émigré' and he was repeatedly attacked as 'a bourgeois intellectual', but he was a man of incorruptible and uncompromising courage who refused to tailor his art to political dogma. *We*, a fantasy set in the 26th-century AD and written in 1920, prophesied Stalinism and the failure of the revolution to be revolutionary. Its influence on **Aldous Huxley**'s *Brave New World* is striking and it was read by **George Orwell** before he wrote *Nineteen Eighty-four*. His best stories are contained in *The Dragon*, first published in English in 1966. With **Gorky**'s help he was allowed to leave Russia in 1931 and he settled for exile in Paris, where he died.

ZANGĪ (1084–1146) in full 'Imād al-Dīn Zangī, the son of Aksundur (d.1094), a Turk in the service of the **Seljuks**. Appointed governor of Mosul by the sultan Mahmūd II in 1126, he proceeded to create an independent principality for himself in northern Syria, away from the centre of Seljuk power, incorporating Aleppo, Hamāh, and Hims. The capture of Edessa from the Franks (1144) earned him the title *al-malik al-mansūr* ('victorious king') from the '**Abbāsid** caliph and was the direct cause of the Second Crusade. He was murdered by some of his own retinue before he could fulfil his greatest goal, the capture of Damascus, and was succeeded by his son, **Nūr al-Dīn**.

ZANGWILL, Israel (1864–1926) English writer, born in London. He went to school in Plymouth and Bristol, but was mainly self-taught, and graduated with honours at London University, and, after teaching, became a journalist, as editor of the comic journal *Ariel*, in which he published witty tales collected as *The*

Bachelors' Club (1891) and *The Old Maids' Club* (1892). A leading Zionist, he wrote poems, plays, and essays, and became widely known for his novels on Jewish themes including *Children of the Ghetto* (1892) and *Ghetto Tragedies* (1894). Other works are *The Master*, *Without Prejudice* (essays) and *A Revolted Daughter*, and the plays *The Melting Pot* (1908) and *We Moderns* (1925).

ZANUCK, Darryl Francis (1902–79) American film producer, born in Wahoo, Nebraska. He worked with Warner Brothers and Twentieth-Century Pictures, becoming vice-president of that company and, after its merger with Fox Films in 1935, of Twentieth-Century Fox Films Corporation. Among his many successful films are *The Jazz Singer* (1927, the first 'talkie'), *Little Caesar* (1930), *The Grapes of Wrath* (1940), *How Green was my Valley*? (1941), *The Robe* (1953), *The Longest Day* (1962), *Those Magnificent Men and Their Flying Machines* (1965), and *The Sound of Music* (1965). He retired in 1971.

ZAPOLYA, John (1487–1540) king of Hungary from 1526. A prince of Transylvania, he was proclaimed king despite the superior Habsburg claim of the emperor **Ferdinand I**, who drove him out in 1527; but John was supported by **Süleyman II, the Magnificent**, who reinstated him as a puppet ruler.

ZAPOLYA, John Sigismund (1540–71) king of Hungary, son of John Zapalya (1487–1540). He succeeded his father, but, **Süleyman II, the Magnificent** having made Hungary a Turkish province, he had to content himself with the voivodship of Transylvania.

ZAPOLYA, Stephen (d.1499) Hungarian soldier. He gained renown as a military leader under **Matthias Cordvinus** by his defeat of the Turks and his conquest of Austria, of which he was made governor (1485). He was the father of **John Zapolya**, king of Hungary.

ZARATHUSTRA See **ZOROASTER**

ZASLAVSKAYA, Tatyana Ivanova (1927–) Soviet economist and sociologist, born in Kiev. Educated at Moscow University, she wrote the 'Novosibirsk Memorandum' (1983), a criticism of the Soviet economic system which was one of the factors behind the change of policies in Russia in the late 1980s. She joined the Communist party in 1954, and has been a full member of the Soviet Academy of Sciences since 1981. She is president of the Soviet Sociological Association, personal adviser to President **Gorbachev** on economic and social matters and, as an academic, is developing the new discipline, economic sociology.

ZATOPEK, Emil (1922–) Czech athlete and middle-distance runner, born in Moravia. After many successes in Czechoslovak track events, he won the gold medal for the 10000 metres at the 1948 Olympics in London. For the next six years, despite an astonishingly laboured style, he proved himself to be the greatest long-distance runner of his time, breaking 13 world records. In the 1952 Olympics in Helsinki he achieved a remarkable golden treble: he retained his gold medal in the 10 000 metres, and also won the 5000 metres and the marathon. His wife, fellow athlete Dana Zatopkova, also won a gold medal (for the javelin) in 1952.

ZEEMAN, Pieter (1865–1943) Dutch physicist, born in Zonnemaire, Zeeland. Lecturer at Leiden (1897), and professor at Amsterdam (1900), he was an authority on magneto-optics. While at Leiden he discovered the *Zeeman effect*, ie, when a ray of light from a source placed in a magnetic field is examined spectroscopically the spectral line is widened or occasionally doubled. In 1902 he shared with **Hendrik Lorentz** the Nobel prize for physics. In 1922 he was awarded the Rumford medal of the Royal Society.

ZEFFIRELLI, Franco (1923–) Italian stage, opera and film director, born and educated in Florence. He began his career as actor and theatre-set and costume designer (1945–51). His first opera production, *La Cenerentola* (1953) at La Scala, was followed by a brilliant series of productions in Italy and abroad, culminating in *Lucia di Lammermoor*, *Cavelleria Rusticana* and *I Pagliacci* at Covent Garden in 1959 and an outstanding *Falstaff* at the New York Metropolitan Opera House in 1964. His stage productions include *Romeo and Juliet* at the Old Vic (1960), universally acclaimed for its originality, modern relevance and realistic setting in a recognizable Verona, and *Who's Afraid of Virginia Woolf?* (Paris 1964, Milan 1965). He has also filmed lively and spectacular versions of *The Taming of the Shrew* (1966) and *Romeo and Juliet* (1968), and, in 1977, *Jesus of Nazareth* for television.

ZEISS, Carl (1816–88) German optician and industrialist. In 1846 he established at Jena the factory which became noted for the production of lenses, microscopes, field glasses etc. His business was organized on a system whereby the workers had a share in the profits.

ZEMLINSKY, Alexander von (1871–1942) Austrian composer and conductor, born in Vienna of Jewish Polish parents. In Vienna he became the friend, mentor and brother-in-law of **Schoenberg**. He was Kapellmeister in Vienna (1906–11), opera conductor of the Deutsches Landestheater in Prague (1911–27), and conductor of the Kroll Opera in Berlin (1927–32). His works, in post-Romantic style, include seven complete and six incomplete operas, orchestral works including a *Lyric Symphony* (settings of **Rabindranath Tagore**), chamber music including four string quartets, choral works and songs. In 1938 he emigrated to America, where he died.

ZENO (c.440–491) Byzantine emperor from 474. An Isaurian noble, he married Ariadne, daughter of Leo I (466) and became sole ruler on the death of their son, Leo II. He tried to achieve a reconciliation between the orthodox church and the monophysite churches of the east, but his doctrinal compromise, the *Henoticon*, merely antagonized both parties and caused a schism with the Roman church.

ZENOBIA (3rd century) queen of Palmyra, born there probably of Arab descent. She became the wife of the Bedouin Odenathus, lord of the city, who in AD 264 was recognized by **Gallienus** as governor of the East. On her husband's murder (c.267) she embarked on a war of expansion, conquered Egypt in 269 and in 270 overran nearly the whole of the eastern provinces in Asia Minor, and declared her son the eastern emperor. When **Aurelian** became emperor he marched against her, defeated her in several battles, besieged her in Palmyra, and ultimately captured her as she was attempting flight (272). She saved her life by imputing the blame of the war to her secretary, **Longinus**; he was beheaded and Palmyra destroyed. Zenobia, decked with jewels, was led in triumphal procession at Rome, and presented by her conqueror with large possessions near Tivoli, where, with her two sons, she passed the rest of her life in comfort and even splendour. Strikingly beautiful and of high spirit, she governed with prudence, justice, and liberality.

ZENO OF CITIUM (334–262 BC) Greek philosopher, the founder of Stoicism. He was born in Citium in Cyprus, went to Athens as a young man and did the rounds of the various philosophy schools there. In about 300 he set up his own school in the *Stoa Poikile* (Painted Colonnade), which gave the Stoics their name, and had a formative role in the development of Stoicism as a distinctive and coherent philosophy. None of his many treatises survive, but his main contribution seems to have been in the area of ethics, which was in any case always central to the Stoic system. He supposedly committed suicide, after a long life.

ZENO OF ELEA (c.430–c.490 BC) Greek philosopher and mathematician. Little is known of his life: he was a native of Elea, a Greek colony in southern Italy, where he lived all or most his life. He was a disciple of **Parmenides**, and in defence of his monistic philosophy against the Pythagoreans he devised his famous paradoxes which purported to show the impossibility of motion and of spatial division. The paradoxes are: 'Achilles and the Tortoise', 'The Flying Arrow', 'The Stadium' and 'The Moving Rows'. **Aristotle** attempted a refutation but they were revived as raising serious philosophical issues by Lewis Carroll (**Charles Dodgson**) and by **Bertrand Russell**.

ZENO OF SIDON (1st century BC) Greek philosopher, born in Sidon in Phoenicia. He was head of the Epicurean School at Athens and a contemporary of **Cicero**.

ZENO OF TARSUS (3rd century BC) Greek philosopher. He succeeded **Chrysippus** as head of the Stoic School in about 206 BC and seems to have had views about the division of philosophy as a subject in the curriculum.

ZEPHANIAH (7th century BC) Old Testament prophet of the time of King Josiah of Judah. His account of a coming Day of Wrath inspired the medieval Latin hymn *Dies Irae*.

ZEPPELIN, Count Ferdinand von (1838–1917) German army officer, born in Constance, Baden. He served in the American Civil War (1861–65) in the Union Army, and in the Franco-German War (1870–71), and from 1897 to 1900 constructed his first airship or dirigible balloon of rigid type, named a *zeppelin*, which first flew on 2 July 1900. Zeppelin set up a works for their construction at Freidrichshafen.

ZERMELO, Ernst Friedrich Ferdinand (1871–1953) German mathematician, born in Berlin. He studied mathematics, physics and philosophy at Berlin, Halle and Freiburg, and was professor at Göttingen (1905–10) and Zürich (1910–16). From 1926 to 1935 he was an honorary professor at Freiburg im Breisgau. Although he worked in physics and the calculus of variations among other subjects, he is now remembered for his work in set theory. After **Georg Cantor**'s pioneering work, Zermelo gave the first axiomatic description of set theory in 1908; though later modified to avoid the paradoxes discovered by **Bertrand Russell** and others, it remains one of the standard methods of axiomatizing the theory. He also first revealed the importance of the axiom of choice, when he proved in 1904 that any set could be well-ordered, a key result in many mathematical applications of set theory.

ZERNIKE, Frits (1888–1966) Dutch physicist, born in Amsterdam. Professor of physics at Groningen (1910–58), he developed the phase-contrast principle used in microscopy. He was awarded the Nobel prize for physics in 1953.

ZEROMSKI, Stefan (1864–1925) Polish novelist, born in Strawczyn. He wrote *The Homeless* (1900), *The Ashes* (1904, trans 1928), an epic of life during the Napoleonic Wars, *The Faithful River* (1912, trans 1943), about the 1883 national uprising, *The Fight with Satan* (trilogy, 1916–18), and other books, pessimistic, patriotic, and lyrical in tone.

ZETKIN, Clara, née **Eissner** (1857–1933) German communist leader, born in Wiederau. While studying at Leipzig Teacher's College for women she became a socialist and staunch feminist, and from 1881 to 1917 was a member of the Social Democratic party. In 1917 she was one of the founders of the radical Independent Social Democratic party (the Spartacus League), and was a founder of the German Communist party (1919). A strong supporter of the Russian Revolution, and a friend of **Lenin**, she spent several years in the USSR, where she died.

ZEUSS, Johann Kaspar (1806–56) German philologist, born in Vogtendorf in Bavaria. He became a professor of history, and was the founder of Celtic philology. His *Grammatica Celtica* (1853; 2nd ed by Ebel 1868–71) has been called one of the great philological achievements of the century. He also wrote a number of historical works.

ZEUXIS (5th century BC) Greek painter, born in Heraclea, in Italy. He excelled in the representation of natural objects. According to legend, his painting of a bunch of grapes was so realistic that birds tried to eat the fruit.

ZHAO ZIYANG (1918–) Chinese politician, the son of a wealthy Henan province landlord. He joined the Communist Youth League in 1932 and worked underground as a Chinese Communist party (CCP) official during the liberation war (1937–49). He rose to prominence implementing land reform in Guangdong (1951–62), becoming the province's CCP first secretary in 1964. As a supporter of the reforms of **Liu Shaoqi**, he was dismissed during the 1966–69 Cultural Revolution, paraded through Canton in a dunce's cap and sent to Nei Monggol. However, enjoying the support of **Zhou Enlai**, he was rehabilitated in 1973 and appointed party first secretary of China's largest province, Sichuan, in 1975. Here he introduced radical and successful market-orientated rural reforms, which attracted the eye of **Deng Xiaoping**, leading to his induction into the CCP Politburo as a full member in 1979 and his appointment as prime minister a year later. As premier he oversaw the implementation of a radical new 'market socialist' and 'open door' economic programme, and in 1987 replaced the disgraced **Hu Yaobang** as CCP general-secretary, relinquishing his position as premier. However, in June 1989, like his predecessor, he was controversially dismissed for his allegedly overly liberal handling of student prodemocracy demonstrations in Beijing.

ZHIVKOV, Todor (1911–) Bulgarian statesman, born and educated in Sofia. A printer by trade, he joined the (illegal) Communist party in 1932. He fought with the Bulgarian resistance in 1943 and took part in the Sofia coup d'état that overthrew the pro-German régime in 1944. He became first secretary of the Bulgarian Communist party in 1954, prime minister in 1962 and, as chairman of the Council of State in 1971, became effectively the president of the People's Republic. His period in office was characterized by unquestioned loyalty to the Soviet Union, and caution and conservatism in policy-making, which led to mounting economic problems in the 1980s. He was eventually ousted in 1989 by the reformist Petar Mladenov in a committee-room coup and, with his health failing, was subsequently expelled from the BCP and placed under house arrest, pending trial on charges of nepotism, corruption, and the dictatorial abuse of power.

ZHOU ENLAI, (Chou Enlai) (1898–1976) Chinese politician, born into a declining mandarin gentry family in Jaingsu province near Shanghai. He was educated at an American missionary college in Tientsin and studied up to degree level in Japan (1917–18) and Paris (1920–24), where he became a founder member of the overseas branch of the Chinese Communist party (CCP). He married Deng Yingchao (1903–) in 1924 and was an adherent to the Moscow line of urban-based revolution in China, organizing communist cells in Shanghai and an abortive uprising in Nanchang in 1927, and served as head of the political department of the Whampoa Military Academy in Canton. In 1935, at the Zunyi conference, Zhou supported the election of **Mao Zedong** as CCP leader and remained a loyal ally during the next 40 years. Between 1937 and 1946 he served as a liaison officer between the CCP and **Chiang Kai-shek**'s Nationalist government. In 1949 he became prime minister, an office he held until his death, and also served as foreign minister between 1949 and 1958. Zhou, standing intermediate between the opposing camps of **Liu Shaoqi** and Mao Zedong, served as a moderating influence, restoring orderly progress after the Great Leap Forward (1958–60) and the Cultural Revolution (1966–69). He was the architect of the 'Four Modernizations' programme in 1975 and played a key role in foreign affairs. He sought to foster Third World unity at the Bandung Conference of 1955, averted an outright border confrontation with the Soviet Union by negotiation with **Kosygin** in 1969 and was the principal advocate of detente with the USA during the early 1970s.

ZHU DE, old style **Chu Teh** (1886–1976) Chinese soldier and statesman, the son of a wealthy Sichuan province landlord. Educated at the Yunnan Military Academy, he graduated in 1911 and joined the **Sun Yat-sen** Revolution (1911) and was a brigadier-general in 1916, but succumbed to opium. Cured in 1922, he left China to study political science at Göttingen, but was expelled from Germany in 1926 for communist activities. As commandant of the Nanchang Military Training School, he took part in the Nanchang Army Revolt (1927), from which there emerged a nucleus of the Chinese Red Army. He was elected commander-in-chief of the Fourth Army and led it in the famous Long March (1934–36). Working closely with **Mao Zedong**, Zhu devised the successful tactic of mobile guerrilla warfare, commanding the Eighteenth Route Army during the 'liberation war' of 1937–49. He was made a marshal in 1955 and served as head of state and chairman of the standing committee of the National People's Congress between 1975 and 1976.

ZHUKOV, Georgi Konstantinovich (1896–1974) Russian soldier, born of peasant parents in Strelkovka, Kaluga region. He worked in Moscow as an apprentice furrier, and was conscripted into the Tsarist army. In 1918 he joined the Red Army. An expert in armoured warfare, in 1939 he commanded the Soviet tanks in Outer Mongolia, and in 1941, as general, became army chief of staff. In December 1941 he lifted the siege of Moscow, and in February 1943 his counter-offensive was successful at Stalingrad. In command of the First Byelo-Russian Army in 1944–45, he captured Warsaw and conquered Berlin. On 8 May 1945, on behalf of the Soviet high command, he accepted the German surrender. After the war he became commander-in-chief of the Russian zone of Germany, in 1955 becoming minister of defence, and in 1957 supported **Khrushchev** against the **Malenkov-Molotov** faction. He was dismissed by Khrushchev in 1957, and in 1958 was attacked for his 'revisionist' policy and for his alleged 'political mistakes' in the administration of the forces.

ZIA UL-HAQ, Mohammed (1924–88) Pakistani soldier and politician, born in Jalandhar, into a strict, middle class Punjabi-Muslim family. He was educated at Stephen's College, Delhi and the Royal Indian Military Academy at Dehra Dun (India). He fought in Burma, Malaya and Indonesia during World War II, before becoming an officer in the Pakistan army in 1947. After further training at Quetta and Fort Leavenworth (USA) staff colleges, he served in a variety of staff and command posts before becoming a general and being made army chief-of-staff in 1976. He led the military coup against **Zulfikar Ali Bhutto** in July 1977 and became chief martial law administrator and, in September 1978, president. He proceeded to introduce a new policy of Islamization and a freer-market economic programme. Zia's opposition to the Soviet invasion of Afghanistan in December 1979 drew support from the USA but his refusal to commute the death sentence imposed on Zulfiqar Ali Bhutto, who was hanged in April 1979, was widely condemned. From 1981, Zia began to engineer a gradual return to civilian government, lifting martial law in December 1985, but was killed when a military transport aircraft mysteriously crashed near Bahawalpur in south eastern Punjab.

ZIAUR RAHMAN (1935–81) Bangladeshi soldier and politician, president of Bangladesh from 1977 until his death. He followed a military career and was a major when the insurrection against Pakistan broke out in 1971. He played an important part in the civil war and the eventual emergence of the state of Bangladesh. Rahman was appointed chief of the army staff after the assassination of the ruling Sheikh Mujibur Rahman in 1975 and became the dominant figure among the military rulers. His government was of a military character, even after the presidential election of 1978 which confirmed his popularity, and he survived several attempted coups. He was eventually assassinated.

ZIEGFELD, Florenz (1869–1932) American theatre manager, born in Chicago, the son of the president of Chicago Musical College. He devised and perfected the American revue spectacle, based on the *Folies Bergères*, and his *Follies of 1907* was the first of an annual series that continued until 1931 and made his name synonymous with extravagant theatrical production. The *Follies* featured a chorus line of some of America's most beautiful women, all personally chosen by Ziegfeld, whose aim was to 'glorify the American girl'. He also personally supervized the choice of music (frequently by eminent composers such as **Berlin** and **Kern**), costumes and stage effects, and he directed the production of each number. The result was a popularization of revue, and new standards of artistry and production. The *Follies* also helped the careers of such stars as Eddie Cantor, Fannie Brice and **W C Fields**. He produced other musical shows, such as *The Red Feather*, *Kid Boots*, *Sally*, *Show Boat*, and the American production of *Bitter Sweet*.

ZIEGLER, Karl (1898–1973) German chemist, born in Helsa (Oberhessen). He taught at Marburg from 1920, at Heidelberg from 1936, and in 1943 was appointed director of the Max Planck Carbon Research Institute at Mulheim. With **Giulio Natta** he was awarded the Nobel prize for chemistry in 1963 for researches on long-chain polymers leading to new developments in industrial materials.

ZIETEN, or **Ziethen, Hans Joachim von** (1699–1786) Prussian cavalry officer, born in Wustrau (Brandenburg). He was dismissed from the Prussian cavalry for insubordination in 1727, but reinstated in 1730. As colonel of Hussars (1741) he increased the efficiency of the Prussian light cavalry. In 1744 he burst into Bohemia, then executed a dexterous retreat; in the Seven Years' War (1756–63) he covered himself with glory at Prague, Collin, Leuthen, Liegnitz and Torgau. 'Old Father Zieten' thereafter lived in retirement at Berlin, in high favour with **Frederick II, the Great**.

ZIMBALIST, Efrem (1889–1985) Russian-born American violinist and composer, born in Rostov. He became director of the Curtis Institute of Music in Philadelphia (1941–68) and composed for both violin and orchestra.

ZIMISCES, John (c.924–976) Byzantine emperor. He was a successful general who intrigued with the empress Theodora to murder her husband Nicephorus II Phocas (956), but after seizing the throne was forced by the church to repudiate her. He won a major victory over the Bulgars (971) and went on to reconquer much of Syria and Palestine from the Muslims.

ZIMMERMANN, Arthur (1864–1940) German politician, born in East Prussia. After diplomatic service in China he directed from 1904 the eastern division of the German foreign office and was foreign secretary (November 1916–August 1917). In January 1917 he sent the famous 'Zimmermann telegram' to the German minister in Mexico with the terms of an alliance between Mexico and Germany, by which Mexico was to attack the United States with German and Japanese assistance in return for the American states of New Mexico, Texas and Arizona. This telegram finally brought the hesitant US government into the war against Germany.

ZIMMERMANN, Johann Georg, Ritter von (1728–95) Swiss physician and writer, born in Brugg. He studied medicine at Göttingen, and became town physician at Brugg, where he published his sentimental book *On Solitude* (1755; rewritten 1785). He also wrote on 'national pride' and on medical subjects. In 1768 he went to Hanover with the title of physician to **George III** (then also Elector of Hanover), and in 1786 was summoned to Berlin to the last illness of **Frederick II, the Great** of Prussia.

ZINDER, Norton David (1928–) American geneticist, born in New York. He studied at Columbia and with **Joshua Lederberg** at Wisconsin and became professor of genetics at Rockefeller University in 1964. Studies with mutants of the bacterium *Salmonella* led him to discover bacterial transduction; this is the transfer, by a phage particle, of genetic material between bacteria, and has led to new knowledge of the location and behaviour of bacterial genes.

ZINOVIEV, Grigori (1883–1936) Russian politician, born in Elisavetgrad, Ukraine. He was from 1917 to 1926 a leading member of the Soviet government. A letter allegedly written by him to the British Communist Party in 1924 was used in the election campaign to defeat Ramsay MacDonald's first Labour government. In 1927 Zinoviev suffered expulsion, and in 1936 death, having been charged with conspiring with **Trotsky** and **Kamenev** to murder Sergei Kirov and **Stalin**. In 1988 he was posthumously rehabilitated, his 1936 'show trial' sentence having been annulled by the Soviet Supreme Court.

ZINSSER, Hans (1878–1940) American bacteriologist and immunologist, born in New York City, the son of a prosperous German immigrant. He was educated at Columbia University and its College of Physicians and Surgeons (MD, 1903). His predeliction for science led him to bacteriology and immunology, which he taught at Columbia and Stanford universities before going to Harvard in 1923. He worked on many scientific problems, including allergy, the measurement of virus size and the cause of rheumatic fever. Above all, however, he clarified the rickettsial disease typhus, differentiating epidemic and endemic forms (the endemic form is still called Brill-Zinsser's disease), researches which he brilliantly described in his popular book, *Rats, Lice and History* (1935). His *Textbook of Bacteriology* (1910) and *Infection and Resistance* (1914) became classics. A highly cultured man, he wrote poetry and essays, and left an evocative autobiography, *As I Remember Him* (1940), written in the third person while he was dying from leukemia.

ZINZENDORF, Nicolaus Ludwig, Graf von (1700–60) German religious leader, refounder of the Moravian Brethren, born in Dresden. He studied at Wittenburg, and held a government post at Dresden. He invited the persecuted Hussite refugees from Moravia to his Lusatin estates in Saxony, and there founded for them the colony of Herrnhut ('the Lord's keeping'). His zeal led to troubles with the government, and from 1736 to 1748 he was exiled. He visited England, and in 1741 went to America. During his exile from Saxony he was ordained at Tübingen, and became bishop of the Moravian Brethren. He died at Herrnhut, having written over 100 books. His emphasis on feeling in religion influenced German theology.

ZIOLKOVSKY, Konstantin Eduardovitch (1857–1935) Russian engineer, known as the 'Father of Astronautics', born in Ijevsk in the district of Ryasan. Scarlet fever at the age of ten led to permanent deafness and limited his schooling and subsequent career. In 1892 he became a teacher in Kaluga, a position he retained until 1920. He built the first wind tunnel in Russia in 1891, designed large airships, and in 1903 published his first scientific paper on spaceflight. He continued to research designs of rocket propelled aircraft and spacecraft, and, in 1924, presented conceptual studies for manned orbital craft capable of reentry. His outstanding work on the fundamental physics and engineering of space vehicles was recognized by the Soviet authorities, and all his works were translated into English by NASA in 1965.

ZISKA, or **Žižka, John** (c.1370–1424) Bohemian Hussite leader, nobly born in Trocznov. He was brought up as page to King **Wenceslas**. He fought for the Teutonic knights against the Poles, for the Austrians against the Turks, and for the English at Agincourt (1415). In Bohemia soon after the murder of **Huss** he became chamberlain to King Wenceslas, joined the extremist party of hatred against Rome and lost an eye in the civil wars. After the outbreak at Prague (30 July 1419), Ziska was chosen leader of the popular party; with 4000 men he defeated the emperor **Sigismund**'s 40000, captured Prague (1421), and erected the fortress of Tabor, from which his party, the Taborites, took its name. In 1421 he lost his remaining eye at the siege of Raby, but continued to lead his troops to a succession of twelve unexampled victories, with but one defeat, compelling Sigismund to offer the Hussites religious liberty. He died of plague at the siege of Przibislav before the war was over, and was buried ultimately at Caslav.

ZITTEL, Karl Alfred von (1839–1904) German geologist and palaeontologist, born in Bahlingen, Baden. A distinguished authority on his subjects and their history, he taught at Vienna, Karlsruhe and Munich, and was president of the Bavarian Academy. His *Textbook of Palaeontology* appeared in English translation 1900–02 (ed Eastman). It was later revised by Woodward (1925).

ZOË (980–1050) empress of the eastern Roman empire, daughter of the Byzantine emperor Constantine VIII. In 1028 she married Romanus III, but had him murdered in 1034 and made her paramour emperor as Michael IV. When his successor Michael V was deposed in 1042 she became joint empress with her sister Theodora, and married her third husband, Constantine IX.

ZOFFANY, John (1733–1810) British portrait painter, of German origin. After studying art in Rome, in 1758 he settled in London. Securing royal patronage, he painted many portraits and conversation pieces. He was a founder member of the Royal Academy in 1768. He travelled in Italy (1772–79), and later was a portraitist in India (1783–90).

ZOG I, originally **Ahmed Bey Zogu** (1895–1961) king of the Albanians, born in central Albania. The son of a highland tribal chieftain, he was educated in Constantinople. He became head of the clan at the age of twelve, growing up in an atmosphere of tribal feuds, and in 1912, when Albania declared her independence, Zog took a blood oath to defend it. As the outstanding nationalist leader, in 1922 he formed a republican government and was its premier president and commander-in-chief; in 1928 he proclaimed himself king. When, at Easter 1939, Albania was annexed by the Italians, Zog came to Britain, and in 1946 took up residence in Egypt, moving to France in 1955 and dying in Paris. In 1938 he married Geraldine Apponyi (b.1915); their son, Leka (b.1939), was proclaimed king in exile on his father's death.

ZOILUS (4th century BC) Greek rhetorician and Cynic philosopher, born in Amphilpolis. He became known as *Homeromastix* (scourge of Homer), from the bitterness with which he attacked **Homer**. His name became proverbial for a malignant critic.

ZOLA, Émile (1840–1902) French novelist, born in Paris, the son of an Italian engineer. He entered the publishing house of **Hachette** as a clerk, but soon became an active journalist. His work in criticism, politics and drama was almost uniformly unfortunate. His true forte for short stories showed itself in the charming *Contes à Ninon* (1864), *Nouveaux Contes à Ninon* (1874), the collections entitled *Le Capitaine Burle* and *Naïs Micoulin*, and the splendid *Attaque de Moulin* (1880). In the later years of the Empire he had formed with **Flaubert**, **Daudet**, the **Goncourts**, and **Turgenev** a sort of informal society, out of which grew the 'Naturalist school'. In this direction *Thérèse Raquin* (1867) is a very powerful picture of remorse. But it was not until after the war that he began the great series of novels with a purpose called *Les Rougon-Macquart*; it comprises a score of volumes, all connected by the appearance of the same or different members of the family. The two 'mother ideas' of Zola's naturalism were heredity and a certain cerebral infirmity; and in order to apply his theory to the study of *le document humain*, he mastered the technical details of most professions, occupations and crafts, as well as the history of recent events in France. He began with a sort of general sketch called *La Fortune des Rougon*. *La Curée* and *Son Excellence Eugène Rougon* deal with the society of the later days of the Second Empire. *La Faute de l'Abbé Mouret* is an attack upon celibacy, and is, like *La Conquête de Plassans*, a vivid study of provincial life. *Le Ventre de Paris* deals with the lowest strata of the Parisian population, *L'Assommoir* depicts drunkenness; *Pot-Bouille* the lower *bourgeoisie* and their servants; *Au Bonheur des Dames* 'universal providers'. *Une Page d'amour* and *La Joie de vivre* are more generally human. *Nana* is devoted to the cult of the goddess Lubricity. *L'Oeuvre* deals with art and literature, *La Terre* is an appallingly repulsive study of the French peasant, and *Germinal* of the miner; *La Bête Humaine* contains minute information as to the working of railways; *Le Rêve* displays a remarkable acquaintance with the details of church ritual; *L'Argent* exploits financial crashes, and *La Débâcle* recounts the great disaster of 1870. *Dr Pascal* (1893) is a sort of feeble summing-up. *Lourdes* (1894), dealing with faith-healing, is hardly a novel, any more than is *Rome* (1896), a critical study of the Papal Curia, or *Paris* (1898). *Fécondité* (1899), *Travail* (1901), and *Vérité* (1903) form part of 'Les Quatre Évangelis'. Zola espoused the cause of **Dreyfus**, impeached the military authorities, and was sentenced to imprisonment (1898), escaped for a year to England, but was welcomed back as a hero. He died in Paris, accidentally suffocated by charcoal fumes.

ZONCA, Vittorio (1568–1603) Italian architect and mechanical engineer, born in Padua. His one extant work, *New Theatre of Machines and Buildings*, was published posthumously in 1607. As in the similar works by **Besson** and **Ramelli**, he illustrated a wide variety of machines and other devices in use at the time.

ZORN, Anders Leonhard (1860–1920) Swedish etcher, sculptor and painter, born in Utmeland, near Mora. His bronze statue of **Gustav II Vasa** is in his native town of Mora. His paintings deal mainly with Swedish peasant life. He achieved European fame as an etcher, with studies of **Verlaine**, **Proust**, **Rodin** and others, and a series of nudes executed with unique skill.

ZOROASTER, Grecized form of **Zarathustra,** mod **Zaradusht** (c.630–c.553 BC) Iranian religious leader and prophet, the founder or reformer of the ancient Parsee religion as Zoroastrianism. He appears as an historical person only in the earliest portion of the Avesta, the sacred book of Zoroastrianism. His family name was Spitama. As the centre of a group of chieftains, one of whom was king Vîshtâspa, he carried on a political, military, and theological struggle for the defence or wider establishment of a holy agricultural state against Turanian and Vedic aggressors. The keynote of his system is that the world and history exhibit the struggle between Ormuzd and Ahriman (the creator or good spirit, and the evil principle, the devil), in which at the end evil will be banished and the good reign supreme.

ZORRILLA Y MORAL, José (1817–93) Spanish poet and dramatist, born in Valladolid. He wrote many plays based on national legends. His play *Don Juan Tenorio* (1844) is performed annually on All Saints' Day in Spanish-speaking countries.

ZOSIMUS, St (d.418) pope from 417. He was involved in the Pelagian controversy. See **Pelagius**.

ZOSIMUS (5th century) Greek historian, who held office at Constantinople under **Theodosius II**. A pagan, he wrote a four volume history of the Roman empire *Historia Nova*, which deals with the Roman emperors from **Augustus** to the sack of Rome by the Visigoths in 410.

ZOUCHE, Richard (1590–1662) English legal scholar, educated at Winchester and New College, Oxford. Learned in Roman law he became professor of civil law at Oxford (1620–61), and judge of the High Court of Admiralty (1641–49 and 1661). Active in the courts, he was also a prolific writer, his most notable works being *Elementa Jurisprudentiae* (1629), an attempt to establish a framework of a scheme of legal science generally applicable; and *Juris et Judicii Fecialis sive Juris inter Gentes Explicatio* (1650), the first text covering the whole field of international law, in which he placed more reliance than his predecessors on the practice of states and contemporary precedents.

ZSCHOKKE, Johann Heinrich Daniel (1771–1848) Swiss writer, born in Magdeburg. A strolling playwright, then a student at Frankfurt, he lectured there and adapted plays, and finally opened a boarding-school at Reichenau in the Grisons. In 1799 he settled in Aarau, where he became a member of the Great Council. His books include histories of Bavaria and Switzerland, and a long series of tales—*Der Creole*, *Jonathan Frock*, *Clementine*, *Oswald*, *Meister Jordan*, and others. The most popular of all was the *Stunden der Andacht* (1809–16, trans as *Hours of Meditation*, 1843), a Sunday periodical, expounding rationalism with eloquence and zeal. His collected writings fill 35 volumes (1851–54).

ZSIGMONDY, Richard Adolf (1865–1929) Austrian chemist, born in Vienna. From 1907 a professor at Göttingen, he was a pioneer of colloid chemistry, gaining the Nobel prize for chemistry in 1925. In 1903 he introduced the ultramicroscope.

ZUCCARO, Taddeo (1529–66) Italian painter, born in S Angelo in Vado, near Urbino. He did much work for the Farnese family and examples may be seen in the Palazzo Farnese, Rome and Caparola. His brother, Federigo (1543–1609), during his travels painted portraits (Queen **Elizabeth**, **Mary Queen of Scots**, and others), but devoted most of his time to decorating frescoes in Florence, Venice, the Escorial, and elsewhere. He founded in Rome the Academy of St Luke (1595).

ZUCCHI, Antonio Pietro (1726–95) Italian painter. He was taken to England in about 1766 by the **Adam** brothers, for whom he executed decorative work (Kenwood, Harewood House, Osterley Park and elsewhere). Also working for the brothers was **Angelica Kauffmann**, whom he married in 1781.

ZUCKERMAN, Solly, Baron (1904–83) South African-born British zoologist and educationist, born in Cape Town. He joined the faculty of Oxford University in 1934 and during the war investigated the biological effects of bomb blasts. He became professor of anatomy at Birmingham (1946–68) and secretary of the Zoological Society of London in 1955. He was chief scientific adviser to the British government from 1964 to 1971. He did extensive research work on primates, publishing such classic works as *The Social Life of Monkeys and Apes* (1932) and *Functional Affinities of Man, Monkeys and Apes* (1933). In his collection of essays *Man and Aggression* (1968) he criticized the **Lorenz**-Ardey view that man's aggressiveness is instinctive. He published his autobiography, *From Apes to Warlords*, in 1978.

ZUCKMAYER, Carl (1896–1977) German dramatist, born in Nackenheim, Rhineland. He lived in Austria, but after that annexation he emigrated to the USA. He lived in Switzerland from 1946. His best-known plays are *Der Hauptmann von Köpenick* (1931) and *Des Teufels General* (1942–45), both filmed. His work also includes the plays *Das Kalte Licht* (1955) and *Die Uhr schägst Eins* (1961), a novel and some poetry. He wrote his autobiography *Als wärs ein Stück von mir* in 1966.

ZUKOFSKY, Louis (1904–78) American poet, born in New York City. Associated with the 'Objectivist' school, his poetry was first published in *An 'Objectivists' Anthology* (1932), edited by himself. *First Half of 'A'* appeared in 1940 and for the next 38 years he continued to work on it; it was finally completed in the year of his death. Labyrinthine in its explorations, its main themes are the inter-relationship of literature and music, aesthetics, history and philosophy.

ZULOAGA, Ignacio (1870–1945) Spanish painter, born in Eibar. He studied painting in Rome and Paris, and won recognition abroad and then at home as a reviver of the national tradition in Spanish painting. He painted bullfighters, gipsies, beggars and other themes of Spanish life.

ZUMALACÁRREGUY, Tomás (1788–1835) Spanish Carlist soldier, born in Ormáiztegui in the Basque province of Guipúzcoa. He fought against **Napoleon**, on the re-establishment of absolutism was made governor of Ferrol, but in 1832, with other Carlists, was dismissed from the army. Head of the Basque Carlist insurrection (1833), he kept his opponents at bay, and gained a series of victories over the Cristino generals. This turned the head of **Don Carlos**, and led him to interfere with the plans of his general, who was anxious to strike for Madrid, but who, ordered to lay siege to Bilbao, was mortally wounded by a musketball.

ZÚÑIGA See **ERCILLA Y ZÚÑIGA**

ZURBARÁN, Francisco (1598–1662) Spanish religious painter, born in Fuente de Cantos in Andalusia, the son of a labourer. He spent most of his life in Seville, where he was appointed city painter, and court painter to **Philip IV** in 1538. He also specialized in religious themes, particularly saints' lives. In Madrid he painted mythological and historical subjects. He came to be called the 'Spanish **Caravaggio**'.

ZUSE, Konrad (1910–) German computer pioneer, born in Berlin. He was educated at the Berlin Institute of Technology before joining the Henschel Aircraft Company in 1935. In the following year he began building a calculating machine in his spare time, a task which occupied him until 1945. He built a number of prototypes, the most historic of which was the Z3, the first operational general-purpose program-controlled calculator. Until 1964 he built up his own firm Zuse KG, becoming honorary professor of Gottingen University in 1966.

ZWEIG, Arnold (1887–1968) German writer, born in Glogua. His writing is socialistic in outlook and is also coloured by the interest in Zionism which led him to seek refuge in Palestine when exiled by the Nazis in 1934. He lived in East Germany from 1948. His works include the novels *Claudia* (1912), *Der Streit um den Sergeanten Grischa* (The Case of Sergeant Grischa, 1928), *Junge Frau von 1914* (1931) and *De Vriendt kehrt heim* (1932), all of which have appeared in English translation; also the play *Die Umkehr* (1927), and some penetrating essays.

ZWEIG, Stefan (1881–1942) Austrian writer, born in Vienna of Jewish parentage. He studied in Austria, France and Germany, and settled in Salzburg in 1913. He was first known as poet and translator of **Ben Jonson**, then as biographer of **Balzac**, **Dickens**, and **Marie Antoinette**. He also wrote short stories such as *Kaleidoscope* (1934) and novels, including *The Tide of Fortune* (1927) and *Beware of Pity* (1939). A feature of all his work is its deep psychological insight. From 1934 to 1940 he lived in London, and acquired British nationality. He later went to the USA and Brazil. He died by his own hand. His autobiographical *The World of Yesterday* was published posthumously (1943).

ZWEMER, Samuel Marinus (1867–1952) American missionary to Islam, born in Vriesland, Michigan. Going out initially (1890) under the auspices of the independent Arabian Mission which he had founded (with two colleagues), his work in Basrah, Bahrain and Muscat was adopted by the mission board of the (Dutch) Reformed Church in the USA in 1894. As a scholar, preacher and evangelist he worked tirelessly to spread Christianity in Islamic countries and to arouse interest in missions in the USA and Europe, writing numerous popular books and founding and editing *The Moslem World* (1911–). He was professor of Christian missions at Princeton (1929–37). His early missionary career is recalled in *The Golden Milestone* (1938).

ZWICKY, Fritz (1898–1974) American physicist, born in Bulgaria. Educated at Zürich, he joined the staff of the California Institute of Technology in 1927, being professor of astrophysics there (1942–68). He is known for his research on novae, cosmic rays and slow electrons.

ZWINGLI, Huldreich, Latin **Ulricus Zuinglius** (1484–1531) Swiss reformer, born in Wildhaus in St Gall. He studied at Bern, Vienna and Basel, and became priest at Glarus in 1506. Here he taught himself Greek, and twice went as field-chaplain with the Glarus mercenaries to war in Italy, and took part in the battles of Novara (1513) and Marignano (1515). Transferred in 1516 to Einsiedeln, whose Black Virgin was a great resort of pilgrims, he made no secret of his contempt for such superstition. In 1518 he was elected preacher at the Grossmünster in Zürich, and roused the council not to admit within the city gates Bernhardin Samson, a seller of indulgences. He preached the gospel boldly, and in 1521 succeeded in keeping Zürich from joining the other cantons in their alliance with France. The bishop of Constance sent his vicar-general, who was quickly silenced in debate with Zwingli (1523), in presence of the council and six hundred; whereupon the city adopted the Reformed doctrines as set forth in Zwingli's 67 theses. A second disputation followed (1523), with the result that images and the mass were swept away. On Easter Sunday 1525 he dispensed the sacrament in both kinds; and the Reformation spread widely over Switzerland. Zwingli first made public his views on the Lord's Supper in 1524. At Marburg in 1529 he conferred with other Protestant leaders, and there disagreed with **Martin Luther** over the Eucharist, a dispute which was destined to rend the Protestant Church, He rejected every form of local or corporeal presence, whether by transubstantiation or consubstantiation. Meantime the progress of the Reformation had aroused bitter hatred in the Forest Cantons. Five of them formed in 1528 an alliance, to which the Archduke Ferdinand of Austria was admitted. Zürich declared war in 1529 on account of the burning alive of a Protestant pastor seized on neutral territory, but bloodshed was averted for a time by the first treaty of Cappel (1529), but in October 1531, the Forest Cantons made a sudden dash on Zürich with 8000 men, and were met at Cappel by 2000, including Zwingli. The men of Zürich made a desperate resistance, but were completely defeated, and Zwingli was among the dead. Zwingli preached substantially the Reformed doctrines as early as 1516, the year before the appearance of **Luther**'s theses. Original sin he regarded as a moral disease rather than as punishable sin or guilt. He maintained the salvation of unbaptized infants, and he believed in the salvation of such virtuous heathens as **Socrates**, **Plato**, **Pindar**, **Scipio** and **Seneca**. On predestination he was as calvinistic as **Calvin** or **Augustine**. With less of fire and power than Luther, he was the most open-minded and liberal of the Reformers. Zwinglis's *Opera* fill four folios (1545). The chief is the *Commentarius de vera et falsa religione* (1525); the rest are mainly occupied with the exposition of scripture and controversies on the Eucharist, and other subjects.

ZWORYKIN, Vladimir Kosma (1889–1982) Russian-born American physicist. He was educated at Petrograd Technical Institute and the University of Pittsburgh, took US nationality in 1924, joined the Radio Corporation of America in 1929, in 1934 was appointed director of electronic research, and in 1947 vice-president and technical consultant. Known for his work in the fields of photoelectricity and television, he invented the iconoscope (an early type of television camera) in 1938, and was a pioneer in the development of the electron microscope (1939).